Real Estate Review's

WHO'S WHO IN REAL ESTATE

THE DIRECTORY OF THE REAL ESTATE PROFESSIONS

1983

WG&L
WARREN, GORHAM & LAMONT, INC.
Boston and New York

REALTOR® and REALTOR-ASSOCIATE® are registered names of the National Association of REALTORS® and apply only to those real estate professionals who are members of the Association.

ISBN: 0-88262-876-3

Contents

Introduction to Who's Who in Real Estate: The Directory of the Real Estate Professions

REAL ESTATE REVIEW is pleased to offer to the real estate community the premier edition of WHO'S WHO IN REAL ESTATE: THE DIRECTORY OF THE REAL ESTATE PROFESSIONS. This directory fills a long-existing need for in-depth background information on the leading professionals in the real estate industry.

Approximately twelve thousand individuals are profiled here, covering the full range of industry activities. Among the professional categories represented are top real estate executives from the *Fortune 1000* firms, leading developers and syndicators, officials from state and federal governmental agencies, attorneys and bankers specializing in real estate, and mortgage and real estate brokers and consultants.

Some of the people listed are famous for their accomplishments in the real estate professions, while others are well known primarily among those actively involved in the field. Still others are in positions of great influence and leadership, though their names may be familiar to relatively few of their colleagues.

Individuals were selected for inclusion based on their demonstration of superior professional achievement in the real estate field. The editors appreciate that evidence of this level of achievement takes a variety of forms and evaluated each applicant on his or her own merits. Chief among the qualifying criteria are professional honors and awards, noteworthy and unique accomplishments, publication credits, and a record of influential positions in the industry.

The information presented about these leaders in the field is oriented strongly toward professional background and includes current position, firm, business address and telephone; primary real estate activity; relevant previous employment; professional affiliations and honors; services offered; representative clients (when applicable); and education. Useful personal information such as date of birth, nonprofessional affiliations and honors, military service, and home address also is provided in most cases.

Reflecting the publisher's intent that this be a useful professional reference, the information included here also is indexed by both geographic area and primary professional activity.

All candidates for inclusion in this first edition of WHO'S WHO IN REAL ESTATE were requested to submit the biographical information outlined above for subsequent review by the editors of *Real Estate Review.* Biographical sketches were drawn up from these submissions for those individuals who met the criteria for inclusion, and proofs of these sketches were returned to the biographees for their signed approval. Any changes indicated by the biographees were then incorporated during the final editing in preparation for printing.

For those candidates who satisfied the selection criteria but did not submit biographical information, our researchers compiled biographical sketches based on information obtained from a wide variety of industry sources. We have marked these biographies with an asterisk (*) to indicate that the information has not been verified by the individuals themselves.

The material in this directory has undergone complete editorial review no fewer than three times; even so, some errors are to be expected in a book of this scope. The editors apologize for this eventuality and encourage users of the directory to make known to us any errors they discover, so that corrections can be made in future editions.

WHO'S WHO IN REAL ESTATE will be updated annually to assure that the information included is as current and comprehensive as possible. All sketches will be reviewed and amended by the biographees themselves whenever possible, and the editors will be doing continuous research in the field to add and delete biographies as necessary. It is our hope that readers will assist us in this task by suggesting the names of individuals who merit consideration for inclusion in subsequent editions. We welcome also any suggestions for improving the style and format of the book.

Guide to Using This Directory

THIS DIRECTORY comprises two sections: individual biographical sketches and an index of individual names arranged by geographic region and primary professional activity.

Individual biographies are listed in alphabetical order by last name and are presented in the standardized format explained below.

The index lists individual names alphabetically by both geographic region and by primary professional activity. The index is arranged first by state, then by city within each state. (City names were determined by the first three digits of each individual's business address zip code.) Under each city, individual names appear alphabetically within primary professional activity categories, which are as follows:

- Appraiser
- Architect
- Assessor
- Attorney
- Banker
- Broker
- Builder
- Consultant
- Developer
- Engineer
- Instructor
- Insuror
- Lender
- Owner/Investor
- Property Manager
- Real Estate Publisher
- Regulator
- Syndicator

In most cases, biographees were responsible for indicating their primary areas of activity, and an individual's name appears under as many of these categories as he or she noted on the application form.

The editors designated primary activity categories for those biographees who did not submit their own information. (These biographical sketches are marked by an asterisk (*) to indicate that the information presented has not been verified by the individuals themselves.)

A sample biography is shown below with an explanation of the standardized format and abbreviated labels used for the various categories of information covered. Readers are advised that not all biographies contain every one of these categories of information.

① **SMITH, John Downing, Jr.** — ② **B:** Dec. 4, 1940, Philadelphia, PA, ③ *Vice Pres.*–Site Acquisition,④ Liebermann Development Corp.;⑤ **PRIM RE ACT:** Developer, Investor, Property Manager, Syndicator; ⑥ **OTHER RE ACT:** Consultant; ⑦ **SERVICES:** Investment counseling, valuation, development and syndication of commercial properties, property management; ⑧ **REP CLIENTS:** Lenders and individual or institutional investors in commercial properties; ⑨ **PREV EMPLOY:** Dept. of Housing and Urban Development, 1966-70; ⑩ **PROFL AFFIL & HONORS:** NYC Planning Commission, RESSI, Consultant to the Society for the Preservation of NYC Landmarks, Recipient of the Donnelly Investment Award, 1977; ⑪ **EDUC:** BA, Urban Planning, NY Univ., 1962; ⑫ **GRAD EDUC:** MBA, Harvard Bus. School, 1966; ⑬ **EDUC HONORS:** President's List, Magna Cum Laude; ⑭ **MIL SERV:** US Army, Sgt., 1962-64; ⑮ **OTHER ACT & HONORS:** Board of Advisers of the NYC Boys Clubs, Inc.; ⑯ **HOME ADD:** 240 W. 57 St., New York, NY 10019, (212) 543-5686; ⑰ **BUS ADD:** 203 Broadway, New York, NY 10007, (212) 337-5794;⑱ *

① Name
② Date and place of birth
③ Current title and division
④ Current firm affiliation
⑤ Primary real estate activities
⑥ Other real estate activities
⑦ Services offered
⑧ Representative clients
⑨ Previous employment
⑩ Professional affiliations and honors
⑪ Undergraduate education
⑫ Graduate education
⑬ Educational honors
⑭ Military service
⑮ Other activities and honors
⑯ Home address and phone
⑰ Business address and phone
⑱ Biography not verified by individual

Table of Abbreviations

A

AA Associate in Arts
AAAE American Association of Airport Executives
AAAS American Association for the Advancement of Science
AABB American Association of Business Brokers
AACA American Association of Certified Appraisers
AACE American Association of Cost Engineers
AAI American Appraisal Institute
AB Alberta; Bachelor of Arts
ABA American Bar Association
ABC Associated Builders and Contractors
ABCA American Business Communications Association
Acad. Academic; Academy
Acctg. Accounting
ACM Army Commendation Medal
ACREA American College of Real Estate Attorneys
AD Doctor of Arts
Adj. Gen. Adjutant General
Adm. Admiral
Admin. Administration; administrative
AEDC American Economic Development Council
AFA Air Force Association; Association of Federal Appraisers
Affil. Affiliate,-d
AFP Associate Financial Planner
AIA American Institute of Architects
AIB American Institute of Banking
AIBA American Industrial Bankers Association
AIC American Institute of Constructors
AICPA American Institute of Certified Public Accountants
AIIE American Institute of Industrial Engineers
AIP American Institute of Planners
AIREA American Institute of Real Estate Appraisers
AJS American Judicature Society
AK Alaska
AL Alabama
ALI American Law Institute
A&M Agriculture and Mining
AM Master of Arts
AMA American Management Association; American Marketing Association; American Medical Association
Amer. America,-n
AMS Administrative Management Society
AOMA Apartment Owners & Managers Association
AOPA Aircraft Owners and Pilots Association
APO Army Post Office
Apr. April
Apt. Apartment
AR Arkansas
ARA American Rental Association
Arch. Architectural; architecture
ARM Accredited Resident Manager
AR/WA American Right of Way Association
AS Associate in Science
ASA American Society of Appraisers
ASME American Society of Mechanical Engineers
ASSE American Society of Sanitary Engineers
Assn. Association
Assoc. Associate,-d,-s
Asst. Assistant
Atl. Atlantic
ATLA Association of Trial Lawyers of America
Atty. Attorney
AUA Association of University Architects
Aug. August
Auth. Authority
Ave. Avenue
AZ Arizona

B

BA Bachelor of Arts
BArch. Bachelor of Architecture
BBA Bachelor of Business Administration
BBB Better Business Bureau
BC British Columbia
BCE Bachelor of Civil Engineering
Bd. Board
BE Bachelor of Education
BEE Bachelor of Electrical Engineering
BFA Bachelor of Fine Arts
BGS Bachelor of General Studies
BIA Building Industry Association
BIE Bachelor of Industrial Engineering
BL Bachelor of Letters
Bldg. Building
Blvd. Boulevard
BOCA Intl. Building Officials & Code Administrators International
BOMA Building Owners and Managers Association
BOMI Building Owners and Managers International
B/PAA Business Professional Advertising Association
BPOE Benevolent and Protective Order of Elks
Brig. Gen. Brigadier General
Brit. British
Bros. Brothers
BS Bachelor of Science; Bronze Star
B&T Bank & Trust
Bus. Business

C

C. of C. Chamber of Commerce
CA California
CAE Certified Assessment Evaluator
CAI Community Association Institute
CAM Certified Apartment Manager
Can. Canada; Canadian
Capt. Captain
CBSE Certified Building Service Executive
CCIM Certified Commercial Investment Member
CCNY City College of New York
CDP Certified Data Processor
CEO Chief Executive Officer
Cert. Certified
CFA Chartered Financial Analyst
Chap. Chapter
Chmn. Chairman
CID Certified Industrial Developer
CIF Certified International Financier
Cir. Circle
CLU Chartered Life Underwriter
CMB Certified Mortgage Banker
CMC Construction Management Council
CO Colorado
Co. Company
COB Chairman of the Board
Col. Colonel
Coll. College
Cmdr. Commander
Comdt. Commandant
Comm. Committee
Comml. Commercial
Commn. Commission
Commnr. Commissioner
Condo. Condominium
Conf. Conference
Cong. Congress
Congrl. Congressional
Consol. Consolidated
Const. Construction
COO Chief Operating Officer
Corp. Corporation
CPA Certified Public Accountant
CPCU Chartered Property and Casualty Underwriter
Cpl. Corporal
CPM Certified Property Manager
CPO Chief Petty Officer
CRA Certified Review Appraiser
CRB Certified Real Estate Brokerage Manager
CRE Counselor of Real Estate
CREA Canadian Real Estate Association; Certified Real Estate Appraiser
CRS Certified Residential Specialist
CSI Credit Systems, Inc.
CSM Certified Shopping Center Manager
CT Connecticut
Ct. Court
Ctr. Center
Ctry. Country
Cty. County
CUNY City University of New York
CWO Chief Warrant Officer
CZ Canal Zone

D

DBA Doctor of Business Administration; doing business as...
DC District of Columbia
DE Delaware
Dec. December
Dep. Deputy
Dept. Department
Devel. Develop,-ed,-er,-ing,-ment
DFC Distinguished Flying Cross
Dir. Director
Dist. District
Div. Division
Dr. Doctor; Drive
DSC Distinguished Service Cross
DSM Distinguished Service Medal

E

E. East
Econ. Economic,-s
ED Doctor of Engineering
EdB Bachelor of Education
EdD Doctor of Education
EdM Master of Education
Educ. Education
EE Electrical Engineering
Eng. English
Engr. Engineer
Engrg. Engineering
Ens. Ensign
Esq. Esquire
Eval. Evaluation
Exec. Executive
Exper. Experience,-d
Ext. Extension

F

Feb. February
Fed. Federal
FHA Federal Housing Administration
FHLB Federal Home Loan Bank
FHLBB Federal Home Loan Bank Board
FHLMC Federal Home Loan Mortgage Corporation
FIABCI International Real Estate Federation (French acronym)
Fin. Financial
FL Florida
FLI Farm and Land Institute
FMCA Family Motor Home Association
FNMA Federal National Mortgage Association
For. Foreign
Found. Foundation
FPO Fleet Post Office
Frat. Fraternity
FRI Fellow Realtors Institute
Frwy. Freeway
Ft. Fort

G

GA Georgia
Gen. General
GNMA Government National Mortgage Association
Gov. Governor
Govt. Government
Grad. Graduate,-d
GRI Graduate Realtors Institute
Grp. Group
Gt. Great
GU Guam

H

HBA Home Builders Association
HI Hawaii
Hist. Historical; history
Histn. Historian
Ho. of Del. House of Delegates
Ho. of Rep. House of Representatives
Hon. Honorable; honorary
HUD Department of Housing and Urban Development
Hwy. Highway

I

IA Iowa
IAAO International Association of Assessing Officers
IBA International Business Association
IBM International Business Machines Corporation
ICA International Certified Appraiser
ICSC International Council of Shopping Centers
ID Idaho
IDC Industrial Development Council
IDRC Industrial Development Research Council
IEEE Institute of Electrical and Electronics Engineers
IFA Independent Fee Appraisers
IFAC Independent Fee Appraiser Counselor
IFAS Independent Fee Appraiser, Senior
IIV International Institute of Valuers
IL Illinois
IN Indiana
Inc. Incorporated
Indep. Independent
Indiv. Individual
Indus. Industrial; industries
Ins. Insurance
Insp. Gen. Inspector General
Inst. Institute
Instn. Institution
Instnl. Institutional
Instr. Instructor
INTEREX International Exchangors Association
Intl. International
IREA International Organization of Real Estate Appraisers
IREBA Industrial Real Estate Brokers Association
IREF International Real Estate Federation (see FIABCI)
IREM Institute of Real Estate Management
IRS Internal Revenue Service
Is. Island

J

Jan. January
JB Jurum Baccolaureus
Jct. Junction
JD Juris Doctor
Jr. Junior
Judge Adv. Gen. Judge Advocate General

K

KS Kansas
KY Kentucky

L

LA Louisiana
LB Labrador
LCDR Lieutenant Commander
L/Cpl. Lance Corporal
Lic. Licensed
LLB Bachelor of Laws
LLM Master of Laws
LOM Legion of Merit
Lt. Lieutenant
Ltd. Limited
Lt.j.g. Lieutenant Junior Grade

M

MA Massachusetts; Master of Arts
MAI Member Appraisal Institute
Maj. Major
Mar. March
MArch Master of Architecture
MB Manitoba
MBA Master of Business Administration
MBAA Mortgage Bankers Association of America
MCE Master of Civil Engineering
MCP Master of City Planning
Mcpl. Municipal
MD Doctor of Medicine; Maryland
MDiv. Master of Divinity
ME Maine; Mechanical Engineering
Mech. Mechanical
MEd Master of Education
MEE Master of Electrical Engineering
Mex. Mexican; Mexico
MFA Master of Fine Arts
Mfg. Manufacturing
Mfr. Manufacturer
Mgmt. Management
Mgr. Manager
MI Michigan
MIB Master of Industrial Brokerage
Mil. Military
MIT Massachusetts Institute of Technology
Mkt. Market
Mktg. Marketing
MLL Master of Laws
MLS Multiple Listing Service
MME Master of Mechanical Engineering
MN Minnesota
MO Missouri
Mort. Mortgage
MPA Master of Public Administration
MRP Master of Regional Planning
MS Master of Science; Mississippi
M/Sgt. Master Sergeant
MT Montana
Mt. Mount
MUP Master of Urban Planning
MUS Master of Urban Studies

N

N. North
NAA National Apartment Association; National Association of Accountants
NACORE National Association of Corporate Real Estate Executives
NAHB National Association of Home Builders
NAHRO National Association of Housing and Redevelopment Officials
NAIFA National Association of Independent Fee Appraisers
NAIOP National Association of Industrial and Office Parks
NAR National Association of Realtors
NARA National Association of Review Appraisers
NAREA National Association of Real Estate Appraisers
NAREB National Association of Real Estate Brokers
NASD National Association of Securities Dealers
Nat. National
NB New Brunswick
NC North Carolina
NCARB National Council of Architectural Registration Boards
ND North Dakota
NE Nebraska
N.E. Northeast,-ern
NF Newfoundland
NFA National Fee Appraiser
NH New Hampshire
NIREB National Institute of Real Estate Brokers
NJ New Jersey
NM New Mexico
No. Northern
Nov. November
NS Nova Scotia
NSIA National Security Industrial Association
NSPE National Society of Professional Engineers
NT Northwest Territories
NV Nevada
NW Northwest,-ern
NY New York
NYC New York City

O

Oct. October
Ofcl. Official
OH Ohio
OK Oklahoma
ON Ontario
OR Oregon
Org. Organization

P

PA Pennsylvania
Pac. Pacific
Part. Partner
PC Professional Corporation
PE Professional Engineer
PEI Prince Edward Island
Pfc. Private First Class
PhB Bachelor of Philosophy
PhD Doctor of Philosophy
Pkwy. Parkway
Pl. Place
PMAA Property Management Association of America
PO Petty Officer; Post Office
POA Property Owners Association
Poli. Political
Poly. Polytechnic,-al
PR Puerto Rico
P.R. Public Relations
Pres. President
Prin. Principal
Prof. Professor
Profl. Professional
Prop. Property
PRSA Public Relations Society of America
Psych. Psychology
Pvt. Private

Q

Que. Quebec
QM Quartermaster
QMC Quartermaster Corps

R

RAdm. Rear Admiral
RAM Registered Apartment Manager
RCAF Royal Canadian Air Force
RD Rural Delivery
Rd. Road
RE Real Estate
RECI Real Estate Certificate Institute
Rehab. Rehabilitation
REI Real Estate Investor
REIT Real Estate Investment Trust
Rep. Representative
RES Residential Evaluation Specialist
Res. Reserve
Resid. Residential
RESSI Real Estate Securities and Syndication Institute
Retd. Retired
RFD Rural Free Delivery
Rgn. Region
Rgnl. Regional
RI Rhode Island
RM Residential Member
RNMI Realtors National Marketing Institute
ROTC Reserve Officers Training Corps
RPA Real Property Appraiser
RPI Rensselaer Polytechnic Institute
Rte. Route

S

S. South
SAFE Society of Associated Financial Executors
SB Bachelor of Science
SBA Small Business Administration
SC South Carolina
ScD Doctor of Science
Sci. Science
SCUP Society for College & University Planning
SCV Senior Certified Valuer
SD South Dakota
SE Southeast,-ern
Sec. Secretary
Sect. Section
Sen. Senate; Senator
Sept. September
Serv. Service
Sgt. Sergeant

SIR Society of Industrial Realtors
SK Saskatchewan
S&L Savings & Loan
SLU Senior Loan Underwriter
SM Master of Science
SMU Southern Methodist University
SNAME Society of Naval Architects & Marine Engineers
So. Southern
Soc. Social; Society
Sor. Sorority
SP Specialist
Spec. Specialist
Sq. Square
Sr. Senior
SRA Senior Residential Appraiser
SREA Senior Real Estate Analyst; Society of Real Estate Appraisers
SRPA Senior Real Property Appraiser
S/Sgt. Staff Sergeant
St. Saint; Street
Subs. Subsidiary
SUNY State University of New York
Supr. Supervisor
Supt. Superintendent
SW Southwest,-ern
Synd. Syndicate; syndication

T

Tech. Technical
Technol. Technological; technology
Ter. Territory
Terr. Terrace
TN Tennessee
Tpk. Turnpike
Tr. Trustee
Treas. Treasurer
TX Texas

U

UCLA University of California at Los Angeles
ULI Urban Land Institute
Univ. University
UPC Urban Planning Council
US United States
US Army United States Army
USAAF United States Army Air Force
USAF United States Air Force
USAFR United States Air Force Reserve
USANG United States Army National Guard
USAR United States Army Reserve
USC University of Southern California
USCG United States Coast Guard
USCGR United States Coast Guard Reserve
USMC United States Marine Corps
USN United States Navy
USNR United States Naval Reserve
UT Utah

V

VA Virginia
VAdm. Vice Admiral
VChmn. Vice Chairman
Vet. Veterans
VFW Veterans of Foreign Wars
VI Virgin Islands
Voc. Vocational
VP Vice President
VT Vermont

W

W. West
WA Washington
WAC Women's Army Corps
WAVES Women's Reserve, USN
WCR Women's Council of Realtors
WI Wisconsin
WO Warrant Officer
WV West Virginia
WY Wyoming

Y

YK Yukon
YMBA Young Mortgage Bankers Association
YMCA Young Men's Christian Association
YMHA Young Men's Hebrew Association
Yr. Year
YWCA Young Women's Christian Association
YWHA Young Women's Hebrew Association

Biographies

AARON, Donald F., Sr.——B: Nov. 21, 1928, Leavenworth, KS, *Owner/Broker*, Don Aaron Realty Co.; **PRIM RE ACT:** Broker, Consultant, Appraiser, Developer, Builder, Owner/Investor, Property Manager; **OTHER RE ACT:** Specialist in Dist. Ct. Appraisals; **SERVICES:** VA-FHA - inspector and appraiser; **REP CLIENTS:** Comml. Banks and thrift instit. as well as City of Leavenworth, Leavenworth Cty., KS; State of KS and Fed. Govt. also appraise and consult with indiv. Prop. owners; **PREV EMPLOY:** Leavenworth Cty. Commnr. 1967-71; Bd. of Equalization; Member and Chmn. Leavenworth Cty. Post Auth. 1971-72; **PROFL AFFIL & HONORS:** GRI; **EDUC:** USAF Air Univ., Lowry AFB, Denver, CO; **MIL SERV:** USAF, PFC 1948-49; **OTHER ACT & HONORS:** 1st Dist., Leavenworth Cty. Commnr.; Eagles Arie 55, BPOE 661; St. Joseph Soc.; Central Comm. Leavenworth Cty. Democrat Club; **HOME ADD:** RR 4, Box 178, Leavenworth, KS, (913)682-7167; **BUS ADD:** RR 4, Box 178, Leavenworth, KS 66048, (913)682-7167.

ABAYA, Carol——B: Feb. 23, 1937, Englewood, NJ, *Partner*, Abaya Assocs.; **PRIM RE ACT:** Broker, Consultant, Property Manager, Insuror, Syndicator; **SERVICES:** RE sales; investment counseling; devel. representatives; prop. mgmt.; devel. fin. brokerage; **PREV EMPLOY:** Editor, RE Investment Dept. Quarterly magazine for Prudential Ins. Co.; **PROFL AFFIL & HONORS:** NJ Assn. of Realtors; **EDUC:** BA, 1959, Major, Intl. Relations, Univ. of WI; **GRAD EDUC:** MA, 1963, Govt., NY Univ.; **OTHER ACT & HONORS:** Marlboro Township Zoning Bd. of Adjustment, V. Chmn., Current; Marlboro Township Econ. & Indus. Mayoral Advisory Comm., V Chmn. Current; **HOME ADD:** 46 St. Lawrence Way, Marlboro, NJ, (201)536-6215; **BUS ADD:** 46 St. Lawrence Way, Marlboro, NJ 07746, (201)536-6215.

ABBEY, Alfred E.——B: Feb. 28, 1929, Bryn Mawr, PA, *Partner*, Trabue, Sturdivant & DeWitt; **PRIM RE ACT:** Attorney; **REP CLIENTS:** Life & Casualty Ins. Co. of TN, State Mutual Life Assn. Co. of Amer., Commonwealth Life Ins. Co., GMR Props.; **PREV EMPLOY:** Assoc. Gen. Counsel, Life & Casualty Ins. Co. of TN; Gen. Counsel, Wiggins and Co., Inc.; **PROFL AFFIL & HONORS:** Amer. (Tax Section), TN and Nashville Bar Assns.; **EDUC:** BS, 1951, Acctg., Univ. of Notre Dame; **GRAD EDUC:** JD, 1957, Law, Vanderbilt Univ.; **EDUC HONORS:** Cum Laude, Order of the Coif, Mgn. Ed. - Vanderbilt Law Review, Pres. - Vanderbilt Bar Assn.; **MIL SERV:** USNR, Commdr.; **HOME ADD:** 104 Steeplechase Ln., Nashville, TN 37221, (615)373-8063; **BUS ADD:** 26th Floor, Life & Casualty Tower, Nashville, TN 37219, (615)244-9270.

ABBEY, Douglas D.——B: July 18, 1949, Brockton, MA, *Associate*, John McMahan Associates; **OTHER RE ACT:** Investment adviser; **SERVICES:** Fin. advisory and devel. mgmt.; **REP CLIENTS:** Corp., inst., and indiv. with subst. RE holdings; **PREV EMPLOY:** Gladstone Assoc., 1975-1977; **PROFL AFFIL & HONORS:** ULI; NAIOP; ICSC; **EDUC:** BA, 1971, Eng., Amherst Coll.; **GRAD EDUC:** Masters in City Planning, 1979, RE, Univ. of CA at Berkeley; **HOME ADD:** 24 Randwick Ave., Oakland, CA 94611, (415)653-5895; **BUS ADD:** 201 California St., San Francisco, CA 94111, (415)433-7770.

ABBOTT, C. Webster——B: Mar. 3, 1922, Baltimore MD, *Pres.*, Abbott Assoc., Inc.; **PRIM RE ACT:** Broker, Consultant, Appraiser, Developer, Owner/Investor, Insuror; **OTHER RE ACT:** Bus. Broker; **PREV EMPLOY:** Sigler & Co., Baltimore, Comml. & Indus. RE, 3 yrs.; Palermo Co., Lanham, Comml. & Indus. RE, 1 yr.; Univ. of MD Law Sch., 1 1/2 yrs.; Francis Co., Louisville, Mgr. Francis Bldg. & Gar; Chm. & Mgr. 2 yrs., Asst. VP Citizens Fidelity B&T Co., Louisville, 5 yrs; **PROFL AFFIL & HONORS:** Gr. Baltimore Bd. of Realtors, MD Assn. of Realtors, NAR, NAIFA; **EDUC:** BS, 1944, Econ., Haverford Coll.; **MIL SERV:** USNR, Ens., Theater Ribbons (Atlantic & Pacific); **OTHER ACT & HONORS:** Rotary, Bd. Member of Historic Hampden, Past Pres. Mason-Dixon Exchange Clubs; **BUS ADD:** 2530 N. Calvert St., Ste. 203, Baltimore, MD 21218, (301)366-7077.

ABBOTT, Edward L.——B: Dec. 18, 1930, Dayton, OH, *Exec. VP & Treas.*, Acacia Mutual Life Ins. Co.; **PRIM RE ACT:** Lender, Owner/Investor; **PREV EMPLOY:** NW Mutual Life Ins. Co. 1956-1973; **PROFL AFFIL & HONORS:** Metro Wash. Bd. of Trade, Mort. Bankers Assn. of Amer.; **EDUC:** AB, 1952, Bus. Admin. & Econ., Wittenberg Univ., Springfield, OH; **GRAD EDUC:** work, 1952-1953, Econ., OH State Univ. Grad School, Columbus; **MIL SERV:** USA; **HOME ADD:** 6605 Goldsboro Rd., Falls Church, VA 22042, (703)237-8454; **BUS ADD:** 51 Louisana Ave., NW, Wash., DC 20001, (202)628-4506.

ABBOTT, Robert P.——B: Sept. 16, 1951, Nashville, TN, *Regional Appraiser*, Doane-Western, Inc.; **PRIM RE ACT:** Consultant, Appraiser; **SERVICES:** Comml., indus. & agricultural appraising; **PREV EMPLOY:** Chief Appraiser with SFS Serv. Corp. of Sec. Fed. S&L, Sikeston, MO 1976-1980; **PROFL AFFIL & HONORS:** AIREA, Intl. Soc. of RE Appraisers, Nat. Assn. of Indep. Fee Appraisers, MAI, SRPA, IFAS, MGA; **EDUC:** BS, 1975, RE and Ins., AK State Univ.; **GRAD EDUC:** Mgmt., SE MO State Univ.; **MIL SERV:** US Army, E-5, Army Commendation Medal, Joint Service Commendation Medal; **OTHER ACT & HONORS:** Contributing author to *Appraisal Review* and *Appraisal Digest*; **HOME ADD:** 7750 Burntwood Cove, Southhaven, MS 38671, (601)393-2377; **BUS ADD:** 813 Ridge Lake Blvd. Ste 440, Memphis, TN 38119, (901)761-3276.

ABDO, Mark J——B: Jan. 16, 1954, Detroit, MI, *Dir. of Legal Review Section for Condos.*, Michigan Dept. of Commerce, Corp. and Securities Bureau, Condo. and Living Care Div.; **PRIM RE ACT:** Regulator; **PREV EMPLOY:** Atty. at Law, Lic. RE Salesperson; **PROFL AFFIL & HONORS:** MI Bar Assn.; **EDUC:** BA, 1976, Bus. Law, Psycho., Hist., MI State Univ.; **GRAD EDUC:** JD, 1979, RE and Prop., Thomas M. Cooley Law School; **EDUC HONORS:** Grad. "with honor"; **HOME ADD:** 900 Long Blvd.,Apt.786, Lansing, MI 48910, (517)694-1776; **BUS ADD:** 6546 Mercantile Way, Lansing, MI 48909, (517)373-8026.

ABEL, Charles W., Sr.——B: Nov. 15, 1924, Williamsport, PA, *Realtor-Appraiser*, Abel, Inc., Realtors; **PRIM RE ACT:** Broker, Appraiser; **SERVICES:** Gen. RE brokerage & appraising; **REP CLIENTS:** VA, Gloucester Cty. Fed. S&L Assn., attys., banks, indivs.; **PREV EMPLOY:** RE broker & appraiser, 25 yrs.; **PROFL AFFIL & HONORS:** Intl. Inst. of Valuers, Amer. Appraisal Co., part. Gol. Cty. Bd. of Realtors, Pres. 1963, AACA, Better Bus. Bureau of S.J., Dir. 12 yrs. Williamstown Rotary Club, Pres., 1963-64; **MIL SERV:** USMC, Pacific theatre 1943-1946; **OTHER ACT & HONORS:** Williamstown Planning Bd, 2 yrs., Williamstown Rotary Club "Man of the Year" 1977; **HOME ADD:** PO Box 1, Williamstown, NJ 08094, (609)629-7735; **BUS ADD:** Black Horse Pike & Berlin Road, PO Box 1, Williamstown, NJ 08094.

ABELL, Ronald R.——B: Nov. 8, 1942, Harrisburg, IL, *Owner*, Abell Agency; **PRIM RE ACT:** Broker, Appraiser, Builder, Owner/Investor, Property Manager, Assessor; **SERVICES:** Brokerage, narrative appraisals, resid. prop. mgmt., farm and multi-township assessments; **REP CLIENTS:** Attys., indivs., prop. owners and prospective RE owners; **PREV EMPLOY:** Farm owner and operator (900 acres), builder of single and multi-family units; **PROFL AFFIL & HONORS:** Nat. Assn. of Indep. Fee Appraisers and Nat. Assn. of Review Appraisers, IFA, CRA; **EDUC:** Cert. in RE, 1980, Southeastern IL Coll.; **OTHER ACT & HONORS:** Member of North Gallatin Comm. Unit School Bd. of Educ. Sec. 1979-80, Pres. 1980-81 Ridgway C of C and Ridgway Lions Club; **HOME ADD:** RR 1 Box 2, Ridgway, IL 62979, (618)272-8303; **BUS ADD:** Main St., Ridgway, IL 62979, (618)272-7500.

ABELMANN, William W.——B: Feb. 11, 1915, Elgin, IL, William W. Abelmann Assoc.; **PRIM RE ACT:** Broker, Consultant, Appraiser, Owner/Investor, Instructor, Property Manager; **REP CLIENTS:** State of CA; major oil cos. (Exxon, Gulf, Mobil, Phillips 66, Shell etc.); automotive dealerships (Chrysler, Ford, GM, Mazda, VW); comml. firms. (Gen. Foods, Dow Chem., Union Carbide, United Airlines); **PREV EMPLOY:** 40 yrs. as appraiser; **PROFL AFFIL & HONORS:** ASRE; AIREA; Sr. Cert. Valuer; SREA; Lamba Alpha; Hon Land Econ. Frat.; IREM, CRE; SREA; CPM; MAI; SCV; CRA; SCV; **EDUC:** BS, 1938, Speech & Econ., Northwestern Univ., Evanston, IL; **GRAD EDUC:** Grad. study, UCLA, Univ. of Chicago and Columbia Univ., NY; **EDUC HONORS:** Elected to Delta Sigma Rho, Hon Speech Frat., Pres. Award; **OTHER ACT & HONORS:** 25 yr. member of Kiwanis; Member of Civic Advisory Bd.; Bd. of Trustees, Gelndale Adventist Med. Ctr.; **HOME ADD:** 902 Chehalem Rd., La Canada, CA 91011, (213)790-0880; **BUS ADD:** 902 Chehalem Rd., PO Box 1035, La Canada, CA 91011, (213)681-3549.

ABEND, William M.——B: Jan. 11, 1931, San Francisco, CA, *Principal*, Wm. M. Abend, AIA, Arch.; **PRIM RE ACT:** Architect; **SERVICES:** Arch., RE Consultant; **REP CLIENTS:** McDonalds, Chartered Bank, Mrs. Fields; **EDUC:** BA, 1954, Arch., Univ. of CA, Berk., CA; **MIL SERV:** USA, 1st Lt., NSDR.; **BUS ADD:** 1300 Monterey Blvd., San Francisco, CA 94127, (415)333-5595.

ABERCROMBIE, Jerry T.——B: Sept. 13, 1930, Beloit, KS, *Asst. VP*, CA First Bank, Trust RE; **PRIM RE ACT:** Broker, Consultant, Appraiser, Property Manager; **OTHER RE ACT:** Mgr., Trust RE Div.; **SERVICES:** Prop. mgmt., RE mktg., RE investment counseling & analysis, valuation & appraisals; **REP CLIENTS:** Brokers, mort. loan brokers, lenders; **PREV EMPLOY:** RE broker - comml./indus. props., Naval officer - aviation facilities mgmt.; **PROFL AFFIL & HONORS:** IREM (CPM candidate), BOMA, San Diego Apt. Assoc., San Diego Bd. of Realtors, RE Certificate (CA Dept. of RE/Community Coll.), Lic. RE Broker; **EDUC:** BS, 1965, Engrg., Naval Sci., Univ. of KS (1948-50), US Naval Postgrad. School (1964-65); **GRAD EDUC:** MBA, 1979, RE Mgmt., Nat. Univ. - San Diego; DBA (Candidate) 1981 Int. Bus. Admin., U.S. International University; **MIL SERV:** USN, Comdr. (0-5), Bronze Star, Navy Commendation (2); **OTHER ACT & HONORS:** Prof. of RE, adjunct faculty, Nat. Univ., CA Community Coll. Lifetime Teaching Credentials in RE, Bus. and Indus. mgmt.; **HOME ADD:** 4325 Vista Way, La Mesa, CA 92041; **BUS ADD:** 530 'B' St., POB 109, San Diego, CA 92101, (714)294-4467.

ABERNATHY, David D.——B: Aug. 24, 1936, Gulfport, MS, *Pres.*, Briarwood Devel. Corp.; **PRIM RE ACT:** Developer, Builder; **PROFL AFFIL & HONORS:** Member of the Inst. of Resid. Mktg.; Serve on Educ. Comm. of VA Assn. of Home Builders; Past Dir. of Fredericksburg Home Builders; Inst. Speaker on Topic of Const. Mgmt.; **EDUC:** BS, 1958, Physics, MS Coll.; **HOME ADD:** 112 Wildwood Ln., Fredericksburg, VA 22401, (703)373-0831; **BUS ADD:** 2 Heritage Rd., Fredericksburg, VA 22401, (703)371-6644.

ABLAN, Michael C.——B: Mar. 11, 1949, LaCrosse, WI, *Atty.*, Joanis Davis Ablan & Joanis; **PRIM RE ACT:** Attorney; **OTHER RE ACT:** General-all phases; **EDUC:** BA, 1971, Bus., Gustavus Adolphus Coll., St. Peter WI; **GRAD EDUC:** JD, 1974, Law School, Marquette Univ.; **BUS ADD:** 405 Allen Bldg., LaCrosse, WI 54601, (608)782-1433.

ABLE, Robert L.——B: Jan. 20, 1926, Louisville, KY, Able & Co.; **PRIM RE ACT:** Broker, Consultant, Developer, Owner/Investor, Engineer, Instructor; **PROFL AFFIL & HONORS:** CCIM; **EDUC:** BS, 1949, Bus. Admin., Univ. of Louisville; **GRAD EDUC:** MBA, 1955, Econ., Univ. of KY; PhD, 1962, Fin., Univ. of KY; **EDUC HONORS:** Beta Gamma Sigma; **MIL SERV:** USAF, Lt. Col., DFC; **OTHER ACT & HONORS:** Distinguished Prof. Univ. CO; **HOME ADD:** 1 Par Cir., Littleton, CO 80123, (303)794-2070; **BUS ADD:** 5524 S. Prince, Littleton, CO 80120, (303)798-7653.

ABLON, Arnold N.——B: July 12, 1921, Ft. Worth, TX, Arnold N. Ablon & Co., CPAs; **PRIM RE ACT:** Broker, Consultant, Developer, Owner/Investor, Property Manager; **OTHER RE ACT:** CPA; **SERVICES:** Tax and fin. planning; **PREV EMPLOY:** Accountant, Peat, Marwick, Mitchell & Co., CPAs; **PROFL AFFIL & HONORS:** AICPA; Nat. Assn. of Accountants; Dallas Homebuilders Assn.; Dallas Apt. Assn.; **EDUC:** 1941, Bus. Admin., LA State Univ.; **GRAD EDUC:** 1942, Bus., Northwestern Univ. Grad. School of Bus.; **EDUC HONORS:** Valedictorian; Phi Kappa Phi; Omicron Delta Kappa; Varsity Debate; Beta Gamma Sigma; Phi Eta Sigma, Beta Gamma Sigma; **MIL SERV:** Field Artillery, Capt., Italian Campaign; **OTHER ACT & HONORS:** Bd. of Trs., St. Mark's School of TX, Greenhill School, June Shelton School, Temple Emanuel; Bd. of Dirs., Hunsaker Truck Lease Inc. and First Continental Enterprises, Inc.; **HOME ADD:** 9129 Clearlake, Dallas, TX 75201; **BUS ADD:** 1620 Republic Nat. Bank Bldg., Dallas, TX 75201, (214)741-4577.

ABRAHAM, David J.——B: Sept. 27, 1961, Toledo, OH, *Associate*, Abraham Realty Co., Investment Counseling; **PRIM RE ACT:** Consultant, Owner/Investor; **OTHER RE ACT:** Exchangor; **SERVICES:** Prop. Analysis, Relocation, Fee Appraisals, Investment Counseling; **REP CLIENTS:** Corp. Investors, Indiv. Investors, Appraisals for MGIC, GM Realty, Exec. Relocation, Attys. & Indiv.; **PREV EMPLOY:** First Federal S&L Assn.; **PROFL AFFIL & HONORS:** NAR, FLI AIREA, MI Assn. Realtors Exchange Div., CRA, RM Candidate; **EDUC:** Siena Heights Coll. 2 yrs., 1978, 79, Bus. Admin.; **HOME ADD:** 426 S. Winter St., Adrian, MI 49221, (517)263-2712; **BUS ADD:** 4210 W. Maple Ave., Adrian, MI 49221, (517)263-2712.

ABRAHAM, Jack H., Jr.——B: Aug. 1, 1924, Montgomery, AL, *Owner*, Abraham Bros.; **PRIM RE ACT:** Broker, Developer, Builder, Owner/Investor, Property Manager, Insuror; **SERVICES:** Mgmt., devel. & owner/investor in real properties; own gen. insurance agency; **REP CLIENTS:** Medicine Shoppes Inc.; **PROFL AFFIL & HONORS:** Member, Montgomery,AL & Nat. Assn. of Realtors; **EDUC:** 1948, Personnel Mgmt./Fin., Univ. of AL; **MIL SERV:** US Army, Col., Meritorious Service, Army Res. Achievement Medal, EAME Campaign w/2 Battle Stars; **OTHER ACT & HONORS:** Past Deputy Dist., Gov., Lions Clubs; Zeta Beta Tau Fraternity; **HOME ADD:** 3318 Stratford Ln., Montgomery, AL 36111, (205)264-3053; **BUS ADD:** 559 S. Court St., Montgomery, AL 36104, (205)262-4411.

ABRAHAM, John——B: Jan. 1, 1923, Detroit, MI, *Pres.*, Abraham Realty Co.; **PRIM RE ACT:** Broker, Consultant, Appraiser, Developer, Builder, Property Manager; **REP CLIENTS:** Merrill-Lynch Reloc., Realty Reloc. Servs., Home Equity Exec. Reloc., Executrans; **PREV EMPLOY:** Resid. Builder-1950-1970; Land Devel., 1954-1978; Realtor 1958-1981, RE Appraisals, 1977-1981; **PROFL AFFIL & HONORS:** NAR, AACA, RAM, GRI, CRB, Realtor of the Yr. 1971; **EDUC HONORS:** Completed all Univ. of MI RE Classes; **OTHER ACT & HONORS:** Rotary Club of Adrian United Methodist Church; **HOME ADD:** 360 Alexander Dr., Adrian, MI 49221, (517)265-8261; **BUS ADD:** 4210 Maple Ave., Adrian, MI 49221, (517)263-2148.

ABRAHAM, Richard S.——B: July 18, 1951, Chicago, IL, *VP*, Romanek Golub & Co., Prop. Mgmt.; **PRIM RE ACT:** Broker, Consultant, Property Manager; **SERVICES:** Prop. Mgmt.; comml. brokerage, operations consultant; **REP CLIENTS:** Prudential, NY Life, Northwestern Mutual, Xerox; **PREV EMPLOY:** Gen. Mgr., Prop. Mgmt. Div., Bank of Amer.; **PROFL AFFIL & HONORS:** BOMA; Greater N. Michigan Ave. Assn. - Dir.; IREM; **EDUC:** BS, 1973, Bus., So. IL Univ.; **HOME ADD:** 65236 Sutton Pl., Hinsdale, IL 60521; **BUS ADD:** 625 N. Michigan, Chicago, IL 60611, (312)440-8725.

ABRAMOWITZ, Roy A.——B: Jan. 29, 1948, New York NY, *Tax Mgr.*, Peat, Marwick, Mitchell & Co, Intl. Tax Div.; **PRIM RE ACT:** Consultant, Regulator; **OTHER RE ACT:** Expertise in taxation of foreign investment in US RE, tax consulting to structure of RE operations; **REP CLIENTS:** Jones Lang Wootten, Cushman & Wakefield, Gestam Group, Pivko Group, Irish Life Assurance Co.; **PROFL AFFIL & HONORS:** AICPA, NY State Soc. of CPA's; **EDUC:** BS, 1971, Acctg. & Econ., Brooklyn Coll. of the City - Univ. of NY; **GRAD EDUC:** MBA, 1974, Taxation, New York Univ. Grad. School of Bus.; **EDUC HONORS:** Cum Laude, Dept. Honors in Econ. & 2 years Dean's Honor List; **OTHER ACT & HONORS:** Bd. of Trustees - Nat. Found. for Ileitis & Colitis; **HOME ADD:** 345 E 80th St., New York, NY 10021, (212)794-2475; **BUS ADD:** 345 Park Ave., New York, NY 10054, (212)872-5890.

ABRAMS, Lloyd R.——B: Dec. 23, 1953, St. Louis, MO, *VP*, Lipton Realty, Inc.; **PRIM RE ACT:** Broker, Attorney, Developer, Owner/Investor, Property Manager, Syndicator; **SERVICES:** Devel., synd., investment, prop. mgmt.; **REP CLIENTS:** Instnl. lenders, Pvt. investors; **PREV EMPLOY:** A.A. Ranger, P.E.; Nooney Co.; **EDUC:** BSCE, 1976, CE, Univ. of CO; **GRAD EDUC:** JD, 1980, Law, WA Univ.; **EDUC HONORS:** Tau Beta Pi, Chi Epsilon; **HOME ADD:** 703 Fairways Cir., St. Louis, MO 63141, (314)569-1659; **BUS ADD:** 800 Chestnut St., St. Louis, MO 63101, (314)421-6666.

ABRAMS, Philip——B: Nov. 13, 1939, Boston, MA, *Gen. Deputy Asst. Sec. - Deputy Fed. Housing Commnr.*, US Dept. of HUD, Office of Housing; **PRIM RE ACT:** Regulator; **SERVICES:** Assists in direction of housing programs and functions of Dept. including production, fin., ins. & mgmt. of govt.-assisted housing and preservation and rehab. of housing stock. In addition oversees the Govt.-backed housing mort. ins. program of FHA; **PREV EMPLOY:** Superintendent & Project Mgr. - Poley-Abrams Corp (1965-1966); Treas. Abreen Corp. (1966-1981); **EDUC:** BA, 1961, Hist., Williams Coll.; **MIL SERV:** USN, 1961-1965, Lt., US Naval Res. 1961-1969; **OTHER ACT & HONORS:** Dir., Found. for Brookline Housing; Selective Serv., Local Bd. Brookline, 1970-1974; Past Dir., Shawmut Credit Union; Past. Sec., B'nai B'rith,

Architects-Engrs. Lodge; Gov. Sargent's Advisory Comm. on the Const. Indus. 1971-1972; Brookline Redevel. Authority, 1971-1974 (Gov's. Appointee); Nat. Defense Exec. Res., US Dept. of Commerce 1978-Present; Governor King's Transition Team, Exec. Office of Community Devel., 1978; Member, Newton, MA Republican City Comm. since 1978, Exec. Comm. since 1980; Chmn. Newton, MA Ward 5 Republican Comm. 1980-1981; Pres., Assoc. Builders and Contractors, 1975; Chmn., Nat. Const. Indus. Council, 1976-1977; **BUS ADD:** HUD Bldg., 451 7th St., SW, Washington, DC 20401.

ABRAMS, Stanton V.——B: Mar. 20, 1943, Providence, RI, *Pres.*, Condo. Realty Co., Inc.; **PRIM RE ACT:** Broker, Attorney, Developer; **SERVICES:** Resid. & comml. condo. devel. mktg., sales; **PREV EMPLOY:** VP Devel., The Druker Co., 50 Federal St., Boxton, MA 02110; **PROFL AFFIL & HONORS:** MA Bar Assn., RI Bar Assn., ABA, Harvard Club of Boston, Harvard Faculty Club; **EDUC:** BA, 1964, Eng., Harvard Univ.; **GRAD EDUC:** LLB, 1976, RE, Univ of PA Law Sch.; **EDUC HONORS:** Cum Laude, RE Book Award; **OTHER ACT & HONORS:** Also associated with Condo. Conversion Consultants, Inc. (Pres.); **HOME ADD:** 85 E India Row, Boston, MA 02110, (617)367-1940; **BUS ADD:** 131 Clarendon St., Boston, MA 02116, (617)262-5433.

ABRAMS, Stephen A.——B: Oct. 21, 1956, NYC, NY, *Pres.*, Abrams & Associates, Inc.; **PRIM RE ACT:** Broker, Consultant, Owner/Investor, Property Manager, Syndicator; **SERVICES:** Investment analysis, prop. mgmt., comml. leasing, comml. sales; **REP CLIENTS:** Indiv. investors in comml. properties; **PREV EMPLOY:** Arlen Realty Mgmt., Inc., 1977-1978; Monumental Props. Trust, 1978-1979; Terry Martin Realty, 1977-1979; Amprop. Inc., 1979-1980; **PROFL AFFIL & HONORS:** Apt. Owners & Mgrs. Assn.; Building Owners & Mgrs. Assn., GA RE Broker; **EDUC:** BBA, 1978, Fin., Emory Univ.; **EDUC HONORS:** Pres. of Bus. School; Named to Who's Who in Amer. Colleges; **HOME ADD:** 2733 Old Mill Tr., Marietta, GA 30062; **BUS ADD:** One Park Pl., Suite 200, 1900 Emery St., NW, Atlanta, GA 30318, (404)352-0922.

ABRAMSON, C. E.——B: Aug. 24, 1943, Cincinnati, OH, *Part.*, Abramson & Deschamps, Realtors, RE Brokers; **PRIM RE ACT:** Broker, Consultant, Developer, Builder, Instructor; **OTHER RE ACT:** VP, Missoula Valley Bldg. & Devel. Co., Inc.; **SERVICES:** Guidance & rep. in buying, selling, leasing and devel. of interests in real prop.; **REP CLIENTS:** Indiv. investors, devels. and bldrs., lenders, trustees, and public agencies; **PREV EMPLOY:** Assoc. RE salesperson & Assoc. RE broker with Security Agency, Inc., Realtors, Missoula, MT (1975-79); USAF Officer; **PROFL AFFIL & HONORS:** Nat., MT & Missoula Co. Bd. of Realtors; RESSI; RNMI; FLI; NAHB; MI-CRA; MEC; REEA; MAREX; IREF (FIABCI), GRI, Gov. Citation, State of MT (1980); **EDUC:** BA, 1963, Hist., Univ. of FL; **MIL SERV:** MTANG; Maj.; (still active); **OTHER ACT & HONORS:** Public Member, MT Bd. of Prof. Engrs. and Land Surveyors (1980-83); MT Club; Lic. as RE Broker in MT, ID, ND; Visiting Lecturer in RE, Sch. of Bus. Admin., Univ. of MT (1981); Chmn., Bd. of Trustees, Missoula City-Cty. Library; Bd. Member, Missoula Museum of the Arts; Bd. Member, Missoula Civic Symphony Assn.; **HOME ADD:** 7302 Hellgate Sta., Missoula, MT 58807, (406)549-0774; **BUS ADD:** 310 N Higgins Ave., PO Box 8807, Missoula, MT 59807, (406)721-3585.

ABRAMSON, Keith V.——B: Aug. 8, 1953, Norwalk, CT, *Dir. of Advanced Sales/Atty. Private Practice*, Cal Western Life; **PRIM RE ACT:** Consultant, Attorney, Instructor, Syndicator, Owner/Investor, Insuror, Real Estate Publisher; **SERVICES:** All legal aspects of real prop. investment and ownership; **PREV EMPLOY:** CT Gen. Life, CT Bank and Trust Co.; **PROFL AFFIL & HONORS:** CT Bar Assn. Amer. Bar Assn., Fed. Bar Assn., Sacramento Estate Planning Council, Sacramento Assn. of Life Underwirters, Admitted to CT, Fed. and Tax Courts, Nat. Assn. of Securities Dealers, Lic. registered rep., Who's Who in Amer. Law; **EDUC:** BA, 1975; Hist., Mass communications, Tulane Univ.; **GRAD EDUC:** JD, 1978, Bus., tax and estate planning, Univ. of CT; **EDUC HONORS:** Dean's List, Dean's List; **HOME ADD:** 1176 Spruce Tree Cir., Sacramento, CA 95831, (916)427-0224; **BUS ADD:** 2020 L St., Sacramento, CA 95831, (916)444-7100.

ABSTEIN, J. Bart——B: Dec. 6, 1941, Tallahassee, FL, *Pres.*, The Abstein Co.; **PRIM RE ACT:** Consultant, Developer, Owner/Investor; **SERVICES:** Primarily involved in devel. of comml. prop. for own account; perform devel. services for others for a fee; **PREV EMPLOY:** Pres. & CEO Regency Sq. Props., Inc. 1978-81; Exec. VP & COO Barnett Winston Investment Trust 1972-78; **PROFL AFFIL & HONORS:** Reg. RE Broker; **EDUC:** BS, 1964, Acctg., FL State Univ.; **MIL SERV:** US Army, Sp. 5; **OTHER ACT & HONORS:** VP Jacksonville Univ. Council; Tr. FL State Univ. Alumni Assn.; Comm. of 100-Jacksonville C of C; **HOME ADD:** 2100 S Ocean Dr., Jacksonville Beach, FL 32250, (904)249-0732; **BUS ADD:** 2100 S Ocean Dr., Jacksonville Beach, FL 32250, (904)246-0044.

ACETO, Frank R.——B: Jan. 16, 1927, Milano, Italy, *Chief Appraiser*, Allstate Appraisal Assc.; **PRIM RE ACT:** Consultant, Appraiser; **PREV EMPLOY:** Chief appraiser/Devel. Amer. Co.; **PROFL AFFIL & HONORS:** SRA/ Sr., CRPA/Sr., CRA/Sr.; **EDUC:** BA, 1949, Econ., San Gabrial Coll.,Santa Ana, CA; **EDUC HONORS:** Cum Laude; **MIL SERV:** USN, S/P/X 3rd class, American & European; **HOME ADD:** 16614 N. 33rd Dr., Phoenix, AZ 85023, (602)993-8450; **BUS ADD:** 16614 N. 33rd. Dr., Phoenix, AZ 85023, (602)993-8450.

ACKERMAN, Charles C.——*Pres.*, Ackerman & Co.; **PRIM RE ACT:** Developer; **BUS ADD:** 100 Tower Pl., 3340 Peachtree Rd. NE, Atlanta, GA 30326, (404)262-7171.*

ACKERMAN, Sol——B: Feb. 6, 1923, Buffalo, NY, *Pres.*, The Forest City - Meridian Mort. Corp.; **OTHER RE ACT:** Mort. Banker; **PREV EMPLOY:** State Planning Coor., Dept. of Resource Dev., State of WI; Dir. for Econ. Analysis, Dept. of HUD, Washington, DC; **PROFL AFFIL & HONORS:** Nat. Housing Conf.; MBA - Insured Project Comm.; Cleveland MBA; **EDUC:** BA, 1944, Econ., OH State Univ.; **GRAD EDUC:** 1945-46, Amer. Univ.; 1957-59, Univ. of WI (Milwaukee); **HOME ADD:** 24465 Greenwich Lane, Beachwood, OH 44122, (216)464-8671; **BUS ADD:** 10800 Brookpark Rd., Cleveland, OH 44130, (216)267-1200.

ACKMAN, Kenneth A.——B: Sep. 25, 1942, Lawrence, MA, *Assoc. Prof.*, Miami-Dade Comm. Coll., Bus. Admin. Dept.; **PRIM RE ACT:** Broker, Attorney, Instructor; **OTHER RE ACT:** Teaching RE Principles & Practices; **PREV EMPLOY:** Staff Atty, MOD Foundation, San Francisco, CA, 1972-73; **PROFL AFFIL & HONORS:** State Bar of CA, State Bar of FL; **EDUC:** BS, 1965, Mktg., Bus. Admin, Univ. of Bridgeport, CT; **GRAD EDUC:** JD, 1970, Suffolk Law School, Boston, MA; **EDUC HONORS:** Top 10%; **OTHER ACT & HONORS:** Parliamentarian of G.A.P. Club, Miami, FL; **HOME ADD:** 6125 W. 20 Ave, Hialeah, FL 33176, (305)558-9207; **BUS ADD:** 11011 SW 104th St., Miami, FL 33176, (305)596-1375.

ACKMAN, Lawrence D.——B: Apr. 29, 1939, NY, *Chairman & President*, Ackman Brothers & Singer Inc.; **PRIM RE ACT:** Broker; **OTHER RE ACT:** RE Financing Specialist; **REP CLIENTS:** The Durst Organization, Larry A. Silverstein, Harry B. Helmsley, The William Kaufman Organization; **PROFL AFFIL & HONORS:** Community Serv. Award, Realty Found. of NY 1974; Chmn., Mort. Committee, Real Estate Bd. of NY 1978; **EDUC:** AB, 1960, Econ., Brown Univ.; **GRAD EDUC:** MBA, 1963, Fin., Harvard Grad. School of Bus. Admin.; **HOME ADD:** Chappaqua, NY 10514; **BUS ADD:** 110 East 42nd St., New York, NY 10017, (212)697-7242.

ACOLIA, George R.——B: May 28, 1924, Trenton, NJ, *Prop. Tax Mgr.*, Sears, Roebuck and Co., Eastern Territory; **PRIM RE ACT:** Consultant, Appraiser, Instructor, Property Manager; **OTHER RE ACT:** Tax Analyst; **PREV EMPLOY:** Assessor-City of Trenton NJ - 1951-1955; Chief Appraiser - Assessment Evaluator - NJ State Div. of Taxation Local Prop. Tax Bureau - 1955-1969; **PROFL AFFIL & HONORS:** ASA, SREA, IAAO, Instit. of Prop. Taxation, NY State Assessors Assn., CT Assn. of Assessing Officers, NE Rgnl. Assn. of Assessing Officers, Assn. of Municipal Assessors of NJ, VA Assn. of Assessing Officers, Assessor Assn. of PA, SRA, CAE, CPE (Cert. PA Assessor); CTA (Cert. NJ Tax Assessor); **EDUC:** 1941-1943;1946-1947, Rutgers Univ.; **EDUC HONORS:** Cert. of Profl. Accomplishment-I.A.A.O. - 1975 and 1980. Liberty Bell Award - N.R.A.A.O. - 1981; **MIL SERV:** USA, S Sgt., 4 Battle Stars, 1943-1946; **HOME ADD:** 267 Chickagami Trail, Medford Lakes, NJ 08055, (609)654-4539; **BUS ADD:** Dept. 568E, 555 E. Lancaster Ave., St. Davids, PA 19087, (215)293-2249.

ACTON, William——*Exec. VP*, Phoenix Steel Corp.; **PRIM RE ACT:** Property Manager; **BUS ADD:** 4001 Philadelphia Pike, Claymont, DE 19703, (302)798-1411.*

ACUFF, J. Patrick——B: Mar. 20, 1945, Coeur d'Alene, ID, *Pres.*, Acuff Realty, Inc.; **PRIM RE ACT:** Broker, Owner/Investor; **OTHER RE ACT:** Comml. - Investment Broker; **SERVICES:** Sales, leasing, consulting; **PROFL AFFIL & HONORS:** NAR, RNMI, CCIM-ID Chap.-City Long Range Planning Comm., VP ID Assn. Realtors; Past Pres. Coeur d'Alene Bd. of Realtors; Past Chmn. Coeur d'Alene; MLS Realtor of the Year; **EDUC:** BS Bus. Admin., 1967, RE and Mktg., Univ. of ID; **OTHER ACT & HONORS:** Past Pres. & Founder, Little League Football; Past Pres. Jaycees; Dir. Coeur d'Alene C of C; **HOME ADD:** 112 Hazelwood Dr., Coeur d'Alene, ID 83814, (208)667-8000; **BUS ADD:** 1103 Sherman, Coeur d'Alene, ID 83814, (208)667-8406.

ACUFF, John E., Jr.——B: Dec. 14, 1918, Nashville, TN, *Consulting Engr.*, John E. Acuff, Jr., P.E.; **PRIM RE ACT:** Engineer; **SERVICES:** Draw inspections (construction loans); **REP CLIENTS:** Banks, mort. cos., etc.; **PREV EMPLOY:** Metro. Devel. & Housing Agency, 30 yrs., last position, Exec. Dir., 1949-1979; **PROFL AFFIL & HONORS:** Amer. Soc. of Civil Engrs.; Nashville Engineers Assn.; Natl. Assn. of Housing & Redevel. Officials, Reg. Profl. Engr.; **EDUC:** BCE, 1946, Civil Engrg., Vanderbilt Univ.; **EDUC HONORS:** Tau Beta Pi, Hon. Engrg. Soc.; **OTHER ACT & HONORS:** Chmn., Wilson Co. Tn. Planning Commn.; Nashville Rotary;Cedar Creek Club; Nashville Yacht Club; Nat. Dir., Nat. Assn. of Housing and Redev. Officials; Previously Served as State and Rgnl. Pres. now Serve as Sec. Treas. for TN; Previous Dir. of Amer. Right-of-Way Assn.; **HOME ADD:** Route 1, Sanford Dr., Mt. Juliet, TN 37122, (615)754-5872; **BUS ADD:** Route 1, Sanford Dr., Mt. Juliet, TN 37122, (615)754-5872.

ACUÑA, Richard M.——B: Aug. 7, 1948, Los Angeles, CA, *Lawyer*, Security Pacific National Bank, Legal Dept.; **PRIM RE ACT:** Banker; **PREV EMPLOY:** Nat. Broadcasting Co.; **PROFL AFFIL & HONORS:** ABA; **EDUC:** 1971, Bus. Admin., St. Mary's College, CA; **GRAD EDUC:** Hastings Coll. of Law, 1974, Law, Golden Gate Univ. - San Francisco; MBA, 1982; RE Banking; **BUS ADD:** 333 S Hope St., Los Angeles, CA 90071, (213)613-5685.

ADAMO, Vincent E.——B: Aug. 29, 1915, Staten Island, NY, Raymond A. Vomero Associates, Inc, RE Appraisers and Consultants; **PRIM RE ACT:** Consultant, Appraiser; **SERVICES:** Valuation and counseling in the acquisition, sale, leasing, and fin. of investment RE. Corp., inst. and indiv. owners, purchasers, sellers and investors in RE; **PREV EMPLOY:** 1974-1981 VP and Appraisal Div. Exec., The Chase Manhattan Bank; **PROFL AFFIL & HONORS:** AIREA, SREA, RE Bd. of NY; Pres. of Greater NY Chap. of RE Appraisers in 1967, MAI, SRA; **EDUC:** 1940, Banking and RE, Amer. Inst.; **MIL SERV:** USN, CPO 1942-1945, Pacific Ribbon; **OTHER ACT & HONORS:** Received the Crusade Citation from the Amer. Cancer Soc. for outstanding serv. and dedication as Chmn. of the NY City Div. of the Cancer Crusade; **HOME ADD:** 16 Meisner Ave., Staten Island - New York, NY 10306, (212)987-9675; **BUS ADD:** 183 New Dorp Lane, Staten Island - New York City, NY 10306, (212)351-3957.

ADAMS, Alfred Gray——B: Feb. 28, 1946, Winston-Salem, NC, *RE Partner*, Van Winkle, Buck, Wall, Starnes & Davis, PA, Attorneys at Law; **PRIM RE ACT:** Attorney; **SERVICES:** Counsel and representation of RE clients; **REP CLIENTS:** Indivs., lenders, and investors in resid. and comml. props., including condos. and leases; **PROFL AFFIL & HONORS:** ABA, NC Bar Assn., Sect. Council RE Sect. of NC Bar Assn., author and lecturer RE and Future Interests, NC Bar Assn. Bar Review Course; **EDUC:** BA, 1968, Hist. and Educ., Wake Forest Univ.; **GRAD EDUC:** JD, 1973, Bus. and RE, Wake Forest Univ.; **EDUC HONORS:** Assoc. Editor, Wake Forest Law Review; **OTHER ACT & HONORS:** Sigma Chi Frat.; **HOME ADD:** 72 Brookwood Rd., Asheville, NC 28804, (704)255-0071; **BUS ADD:** PO Box 7376, Asheville, NC 28807, (704)258-2991.

ADAMS, Arsia Ahulia——B: Temple, Bell County, TX, *Broker*, AAA Real Estate; **PRIM RE ACT:** Broker; **OTHER RE ACT:** Mkt. RE; **SERVICES:** Mkt. Comml.- Investment, Resid. RE; **PREV EMPLOY:** RE since 1975; **PROFL AFFIL & HONORS:** CCIM Candidate; **EDUC:** Brigham Young Univ., UT; Tarrant Cty. Jr. Coll., TX; Univ of TX at Arl., TX; **GRAD EDUC:** RE, Bus. Mgmt., Music, Voice; **EDUC HONORS:** Nat. Hon. Soc.; **HOME ADD:** Dallas/Fort Worth Texas Metroplex, Arlington, TX 76014, (817)467-3292; **BUS ADD:** Dallas/Fort Worth Texas Metroplex, Arlington, TX 76014, (817)467-3292.

ADAMS, Daniel L.——B: Oct. 3, 1936, Beaver, OH, *Partner*, English, McCaughan & O'Bryan; **PRIM RE ACT:** Attorney; **REP CLIENTS:** 1st Fed. Savings & Loan Assn. of Broward Cty.; Landmark Banking Corp.; Outlook Devel. Corp.; **PREV EMPLOY:** Lawyers Title Guaranty Fund; **EDUC:** 1958, Poli. Sci., OH State Univ.; **GRAD EDUC:** LLB-JD, 1960, OH State Univ.; **HOME ADD:** 600 Petunia Dr., Fort Lauderdale, FL 33317, (305)587-3914; **BUS ADD:** PO Box 14098, Ft. Lauderdale, FL 33302, (305)462-3301.

ADAMS, Gregg——B: Apr. 24, 1945, Dayton, OH, *Mgr.*, Nyman Realty, Inc.; **PRIM RE ACT:** Broker, Property Manager; **SERVICES:** Comml. sales, leasing, prop. mgmt.; **PREV EMPLOY:** Nyman Realty, Inc. 1967; **PROFL AFFIL & HONORS:** IREM, RNMI, CPM, CCIM; **EDUC:** 1968, RE, The Amer. Univ.; **MIL SERV:** USN, Submarines; **OTHER ACT & HONORS:** VP, Prince George's Cty. Bd. of Trade; Sec., Prince George's Cty. Travel and Promotion Council; **HOME ADD:** 1069 B Chapel Point Rd., Port Tobacco, MD 20677, (301)932-6828; **BUS ADD:** 5823 Allentown Way, Camp Springs, MD 20748, (301)449-3780.

ADAMS, James R.——B: May 8, 1942, Springfield, VT, *Pres.*, Northwoods Corp.; **PRIM RE ACT:** Developer, Builder, Lender, Owner/Investor; **SERVICES:** Lend within owned projects, build single family homes; **PROFL AFFIL & HONORS:** No. Worcester Bd. of Realtors, NAHB of Lowell; **EDUC:** BBS, Bus., NH Coll.; **EDUC HONORS:** Cum Laude; **OTHER ACT & HONORS:** Lyons Club; **HOME ADD:** Pearl Brook Rd., Townsend, MA 01469, (617)597-6940; **BUS ADD:** 540 Main St., Townsend, MA 01469, (617)597-2737.

ADAMS, John F., Jr.——B: Nov. 10, 1936, Hartford, CT, *Owner*, John F. Adams Assoc.; **PRIM RE ACT:** Broker, Consultant, Appraiser, Instructor; **SERVICES:** Real prop. valuation & analysis; **REP CLIENTS:** Equity investors & lenders in comml., indus. & resid. RE; **PROFL AFFIL & HONORS:** AIREA; Soc. of RE Appraisers; Nat. & Local Assns. of Realtors, MAI, Sr. RE Analyst, Realtor of the Year 1976 (Greater New Britain Bd. of Realtors), Profl. Recognition Award AIREA, 1980-1982; **EDUC:** BA, 1959, Fine Arts & Econ., Trinity Coll., Hartford, CT; **MIL SERV:** USA Reserve Nat. Guard, Lt., Assn. of US Army Leadership Award 1964; **OTHER ACT & HONORS:** Berlin Republic Town Comm. 1964-1968; Pres. Berlin Strollers Rugby Club 1977-1978; Chmn. Comm. for MLS (New Britain) 1964; 1st Pres. MLS of Greater New Britain 1965; Pres. Greater New Britain Bd. of Realtors 1969; Pres. CT Chapter Soc. of RE Appraisers 1973-1974; Vice Governor New England Soc. of RE Appraisers 1975; Pres. CT Chapter AIREA 1981; **HOME ADD:** 125 Crater Lane, Kensington, CT 06037, (203)828-3691; **BUS ADD:** 19 Bassett St., New Britain, CT 06051, (203)225-8454.

ADAMS, John W., Jr.——B: Apr. 5, 1925, Atlanta, GA, *Atty.*, John W. Adams Jr., Atty.; **PRIM RE ACT:** Attorney; **SERVICES:** Titles, closings and other; **REP CLIENTS:** IL Central Gulf Railroad Co., MS; Export RR Co., Local investors; **PROFL AFFIL & HONORS:** Mobile Cty., AL & ABA; **EDUC:** BA, 1947, Hist., Poli. Sci., Vanderbilt Univ., Univ. of AL; **GRAD EDUC:** LLB, JD, 1949, Real Prop., Univ. of AL; **EDUC HONORS:** Pres. of Social Frat. (SAE); Omicron Delta Kappa; **OTHER ACT & HONORS:** Mobile Ctry. Club, Athelstan Club, Univ. Club of Chicago; **HOME ADD:** 4050 Cty. Club Rd., Mobile, AL 36608; **BUS ADD:** 4050 Country Club Rd. Box 8271, Mobile, AL 36608, (205)432-7282.

ADAMS, Joseph A.——B: May 11, 1937, Westfield, NJ, *Atty. at Law*, Adams, Kouba & Dickson; **PRIM RE ACT:** Attorney; **OTHER RE ACT:** Conversions, resid. & comml.; **SERVICES:** Legal, tax shelters, etc.; **EDUC:** BA, 1959, Eng., Pomona Coll.; **GRAD EDUC:** JD, 1964, Boalt Hall, Univ. of CA, Berkeley; **HOME ADD:** 430 Arlington Ave., Berkeley, CA 94707, (415)524-6508; **BUS ADD:** 660 Market St. 300, San Francisco, CA 94104, (415)392-2800.

ADAMS, Michael Timothy——B: July 30, 1948, Augusta, GA, *VP*, Lynes Realty Co.; **PRIM RE ACT:** Broker, Instructor, Consultant; **SERVICES:** Residential and comml. brokerage, investment counseling; **PROFL AFFIL & HONORS:** RNMI, CRB; **EDUC:** BBA, 1975, Mgmt., Armstrong State Coll., Savannah, GA; **MIL SERV:** USN, CTR2; **OTHER ACT & HONORS:** Optimist Club-Past Pres.; **HOME ADD:** 743-A Morningside Dr., Savannah, GA 31410, (912)897-6457; **BUS ADD:** 120 E St. Julian St., PO Box 10107, Savannah, GA 31412, (912)236-6381.

ADAMS, Nicholas——B: Jan. 15, 1952, Seattle, WA, *VP and Legal Counsel*, Grays Harbor Enterprises, Inc. and James W. Hodges, Inc. Realtors, Legal/Land Development; **PRIM RE ACT:** Attorney, Developer; **SERVICES:** RE and Land use Law, Subdivision Project Mgmt.; **REP CLIENTS:** Buyers and sellers of RE, RE Brokers, Land Devels.; **PROFL AFFIL & HONORS:** ABA, WA Bar Assn., Environmental and Land Use Section, WA Bar Assn., Natl. Assn. of Realtors, WA Assn. of Realtors, Pres. of Thurston Regional Land Use Federation; **EDUC:** BA in Bus. Admin., 1974, Acctg., Univ. of WA; **GRAD EDUC:** JD/MBA, 1974, RE/Personnel, Univ. of WA; **EDUC HONORS:** Cum Laude; **HOME ADD:** 4108 Candlewood Ct. SE, Lacey, WA 98503, (206)491-9281; **BUS ADD:** 2312 Pacific Ave., Olympia, WA 98501, (206)943-7839.

ADAMS, Norman J.——B: May 17, 1933, Norwich, CT, *Pres. & CEO*, North American Industries, Inc.; **PRIM RE ACT:** Syndicator, Consultant, Appraiser, Developer, Property Manager, Banker, Lender, Owner/Investor; **OTHER RE ACT:** Inv. Banker; **SERVICES:** Indus. Park Dev., Indus. Bldg.; **REP CLIENTS:** L.I.G. London, England; **PREV EMPLOY:** Asst. Chief - RE Dev. Council, 1967-1973, Mgr. Area Dev. - Hartford Natl. Bk. & Tr. Co.; **PROFL AFFIL & HONORS:** A.I.D.C./F.M., NIDA Past Dir., AMA, Who's Who in Fin. and Indus., Who's Who in the East; **EDUC:** BS, 1958, Acctg. and Fin., Bryant Coll.; **GRAD EDUC:** MMA, 1971, 1973, Indus. Dev., U.R.I., Univ. of OK; **MIL SERV:** USN, Yn3 (ss), Good Conduct Medal; **OTHER ACT & HONORS:** Gov. N.E. Econ. Prop. - RI, 1972-1973, Indus. RE Brokers Assn.; **HOME ADD:** 14 Laurel La., Barrington, RI 02806, (401)245-2713; **BUS ADD:** PO Box 348, Pawtucket, RI 02862, (401)725-6788.

ADAMS, Paul A.——*Dept. Inspector Gen.*, Department of Housing and Urban Development, Ofc. of Insp. Gen.; **PRIM RE ACT:** Lender; **BUS ADD:** 451 Seventh St., S.W., Washington, DC 20410, (202)755-6430.*

ADAMS, Robert Miller——**B:** Mar. 5, 1931, Indianapolis, IN, *VP*, Indiana Mortgage Corp. (a sub. of IN Nat. Corp.); **PRIM RE ACT:** Broker, Consultant, Appraiser, Instructor; **OTHER RE ACT:** Mtg. banker; **SERVICES:** Investment counseling, valuation, mort. lending, constr. loans; **REP CLIENTS:** Lenders & indiv. instl. investors in income props., equities, loans; **PREV EMPLOY:** Shell Oil Co., 1956-61; **PROFL AFFIL & HONORS:** Metro. Indianapolis Bd. of Realtors, SBA, IN Sort. Bankers Assn. (Past Pres. 1974), Sr. Member NARA (CRA); **EDUC:** BS, Bus. Admin., IN Univ., Bloomington, IN; **OTHER ACT & HONORS:** Precinct Comm., 16 yrs., Lions Intl. (Past Chapt. Pres.); **HOME ADD:** 222 W OH St., Fortville, IN 46040, (317)485-7374; **BUS ADD:** 151 N DE St., Indianapolis, IN 46266, (317)266-5033.

ADAMS, William M.——**B:** Mar. 25, 1949, Spokane, WA, *VP*, Keith Adams and Associates, Inc.; **PRIM RE ACT:** Broker, Consultant, Property Manager, Syndicator; **SERVICES:** Site acquisition, feasibility analysis, investment sales; **PROFL AFFIL & HONORS:** Natl. Assn. of Realtors, CCIM; **EDUC:** BA, 1971, Mktg., Eastern WA Univ.; **HOME ADD:** 4216 W. Klamath, Kennewick, WA 99336, (509)783-7528; **BUS ADD:** 3400 W. Clearwater, Suite #1, Kennewick, WA 99336, (509)783-4147.

ADAMSON, James R.——**B:** Nov. 12, 1925, Birmingham, AL, *Owner*, James R. Adamson, Realtor-Appraiser; **PRIM RE ACT:** Broker, Appraiser; **SERVICES:** RE appraising and prop. mgmt., sales; **PROFL AFFIL & HONORS:** Nat. and Laurel Bds. of Realtors, Nat. Assn. of Review Appraisers; Nat. Assn. of Real Estate Appraisers; **EDUC:** Auburn Univ. 2 yrs.; **MIL SERV:** US Army, WO, Engrg. RE; **HOME ADD:** 1433 Amy Rd., Laurel, MS 39440; **BUS ADD:** 1134 Hwy 15 N., Laurel, MS 39440, (601)649-1771.

ADAMSON, Jeanne A.——**B:** Mar. 12, 1950, Phoenix, AZ, *Admin. VP*, David R. Johns Real Estate Grp.; **PRIM RE ACT:** Broker, Developer, Builder, Owner/Investor, Property Manager, Syndicator; **PROFL AFFIL & HONORS:** Phoenix Bd. of Realtors; AZ Assn. of Realtors; NAR; RESSI; AZ Network of Profl. Women; Profl. Exchange; Nat. Assn. for Female Exec., Inc., Realtor; **OTHER ACT & HONORS:** Phoenix Art Museum League; **HOME ADD:** 2925 N Casa Tomas, Phoenix, AZ 85016, (602)264-1761; **BUS ADD:** 1414 E Indian School Rd., Phoenix, AZ 85014, (602)265-9951.

ADDISON, David D.——**B:** Aug. 23, 1941, Richmond, VA, *Atty.*, Browder, Russell, Morris & Butcher; **PRIM RE ACT:** Attorney; **SERVICES:** Legal; **PROFL AFFIL & HONORS:** Amer., VA & Richmond Bar Assns., Fellow of Amer. College of Probate Counsel; **EDUC:** BA, 1964, Eng., Hampden-Sydney Coll.; **GRAD EDUC:** LLB, 1967, Univ. of VA Law School; **EDUC HONORS:** Cum Laude, ODK, Who's Who; **HOME ADD:** 113 Tempsford Lane, Richmond, VA 23219, (804)285-2816; **BUS ADD:** 1200 Ross Building, Richmond, VA 23219, (804)771-9310.

ADKINS, Winston L.——**B:** June 24, 1932, Amarillo, TX, *Corporate Counsel*, Redman Industries, Inc.; **PRIM RE ACT:** Attorney; **SERVICES:** Legal; **PREV EMPLOY:** Century Devel. Corp., Houston; **PROFL AFFIL & HONORS:** TX Bar Assn., ABA, Dallas Bar Assn.; **EDUC:** BA, 1953, Govt., Univ. of TX; **GRAD EDUC:** JD, 1955, Univ. TX; **EDUC HONORS:** Order of the Coif, Case Note Editor, TX Law Review; **MIL SERV:** US Army; Specialist CIC; **OTHER ACT & HONORS:** Rotary Club; **HOME ADD:** 4641 Irvin Simmons, Dallas, TX 75229, (214)363-3823; **BUS ADD:** 2550 Walnut Hill Ln., Dallas, TX 75229, (214)353-3600.

ADKISSON, Charles Ralph——**B:** Apr. 15, 1939, Glasgow, MT, *Pres.*, Golden West Real Estate, Inc.; **PRIM RE ACT:** Broker, Consultant, Owner/Investor, Instructor, Property Manager, Syndicator; **SERVICES:** Profl. brokerage & mgmt. of investment RE, and investment counseling; **PREV EMPLOY:** Deloitte, Haskins & Sells, CPAs; **PROFL AFFIL & HONORS:** Nat. Assn. of Realtors, NV Apt. Owners Assn., C of C; **EDUC:** B.S., 1969, Acctg., econ., Univ.of NV; **GRAD EDUC:** JD, 1973, RE, Fed. Tax, corp. & bus. law, Univ. of AZ; **MIL SERV:** US Army, 1962-64; **HOME ADD:** PO Box 19762, Las Vegas, NV 89119, (702)736-6776; **BUS ADD:** 919 E. Tropicana Ave., Las Vegas, NV 89119, (702)732-1919.

ADLER, David G.——**B:** Mar. 22, 1944, Chicago, IL, *Partner-in-Charge*, Laventhol & Horwath, Dallas Office; **OTHER RE ACT:** CPA, Consulting; **SERVICES:** Acctg., auditing, tax structuring, fin. planning; **REP CLIENTS:** Devels., synds., contractors, etc.; **PROFL AFFIL & HONORS:** AICPA; ABA; TX Soc. of CPAs; Dallas Chap. of TX Soc. of Public Accountants; ABA Sect. on Taxation, Comm. on Real Prop.; Dallas Estate Planning Council; Dallas Petroleum Accountants Soc., Past Chmn. of Taxation Comm. and 1980 Chmn. of N. Amer. Petroleum Acctg. Conf.; Intl. Lawyers Assn. of Dallas; Advisory Comm., So. Methodist Univ. School of Law, Annual Symposium on Fed. Taxation; **EDUC:** BSBA, 1965, Acctg., Northwestern Univ.; **GRAD EDUC:** JD, 1969, Law, DePaul Univ. School of Law; **EDUC HONORS:** Beta Alpha PSI; **HOME ADD:** 6822 Ledyard, Dallas, TX 75248; **BUS ADD:** 2550 Bryan Tower, Dallas, TX 75201, (214)741-1600.

ADLER, Thomas W.——**B:** Dec. 21, 1940, Rochester, NY, *Principal*, Adler, Galvin, Rogers, Inc.; **PRIM RE ACT:** Broker, Consultant, Developer, Owner/Investor, Instructor; **SERVICES:** Investment RE Counseling & Brokerage on Nat. Basis; **REP CLIENTS:** All major institu. investors; **PREV EMPLOY:** Chmn. Exec. Comm., Cragin Lang Free & Smythe until 4/79, Pres. Clevetrust Advisors 1970-73 & VP & Trustee Clevetrust Realty (REIT); **PROFL AFFIL & HONORS:** ASREC, SIR, Pres. Soc. Indus. Realtors Educ. Trust Fund; **EDUC:** BS, 1962, Hist., Univ. Wisconsin; **OTHER ACT & HONORS:** Bd. Dir./Exec. Comm.-Gr. Cleveland Growth Assn.; Pres. Cleveland Area Devel. Finance Corp.; Truatee Frields Shaker Square; Member Mayor's Play House Square Task Force; Bd. Dir.-Cleveland Area Devel. Corp. (CADC); **HOME ADD:** 2851 Winthrop Rd., Shaker Hts., OH 44120, (216)921-2663; **BUS ADD:** 1801 E Ninth St., Cleveland, OH 44114, (216)861-3040.

ADOMATIS, Richard——**B:** Aug. 16, 1931, Indianapolis, IN, *Appraiser*, Richard Adomatis & Assoc.; **PRIM RE ACT:** Instructor, Appraiser; **SERVICES:** Appraising, counseling, site or prop. locating; **REP CLIENTS:** S&Ls, Comml. Banks, Mort. Bankers, Attys., Gov. Agencies, major indus.; **PROFL AFFIL & HONORS:** MAI, (NAR), Cert. RE instr. (IREI); **EDUC:** BS, 1954, Bus. Admin & RE, Greenville Coll. in Greenville, IL; **EDUC HONORS:** Cum Laude; **MIL SERV:** USA, PFC, Good Conduct; **HOME ADD:** 301 E. Jefferson, Valparaiso, IN 46383, (219)462-2251; **BUS ADD:** 301 E. Jefferson, Valparaiso, IN 46383, (219)464-8517.

ADORNO, Robert A.——**B:** Nov. 22, 1938, Torrington, CT, *Prin. Broker/Owner*, Adorno RE; **PRIM RE ACT:** Broker, Developer, Builder, Property Manager; **SERVICES:** For single family or multi-family development / comml. & indus.: site selection, demographics, merchandise, mktg.; **PROFL AFFIL & HONORS:** Member Columbus Bd. of Realtors & State & Nat. Assn. of Realtors; RE Securities and Synd. Inst. member; **EDUC:** BS, BA, 1964, Mgmt./Mech. Engr., Univ. of Denver; **MIL SERV:** US Air Nat. Guard Res., Reserve 1962-1966; **HOME ADD:** 1248 Creekside Place, Reynoldsbury, OH 43068, (614)864-1807; **BUS ADD:** 5150 E. Main St., Columbus, OH 43213, (614)866-2333.

ADREON, Leonard J.——**B:** Sept 12, 1926, St. Louis, MO, *Exec. VP*, The Siteman Organization, Inc., Leasing; **PRIM RE ACT:** Consultant, Developer, Owner/Investor; **PROFL AFFIL & HONORS:** Immediate past pres., BOMA; **EDUC:** BS, 1950, Wash. Univ., St. Louis, MO; **EDUC HONORS:** Grad. with Final Honors, Beta Gamma Sigma; **MIL SERV:** USNR 1944-1946/1950-1951, in Korean War, 1st Marine Div.; **HOME ADD:** 2 Creekwood Ln., St. Louis, MO 63124, (314)993-5789; **BUS ADD:** 7751 Carondelet Ave., Clayton, MO 63105, (314)725-6200.

ADREON, Roy M.——**B:** Mar. 20, 1924, St. Louis, MO, *Sr. VP*, Comml. Sec. Bank, Mort. Loan Admin.; **PRIM RE ACT:** Lender; **PREV EMPLOY:** Mercantile Mort. Co., 1960-1975; **PROFL AFFIL & HONORS:** Mort. Bankers Assn. of Amer., Amer. Bankers Assn.; **EDUC:** BSBA, 1949, Bus., Washington Univ.; **MIL SERV:** Army Air Corp., Lt.; **HOME ADD:** 505 Perry Hollow Rd., Salt Lake, UT 84103, (801)532-6159; **BUS ADD:** 50 South Main Suite 2000, Salt Lake City, UT 94144, (801)535-1000.

ADRIAN, James J.——**B:** Apr. 1, 1944, LaSalle, IL, *Pres.*, Adrian & Associates; Also Prof. of Const., Bradley Univ.; **PRIM RE ACT:** Broker, Consultant; **OTHER RE ACT:** CPA; **SERVICES:** RE Taxation, Appraising, Feasibility Studies; **REP CLIENTS:** Numerous; **PREV EMPLOY:** Prof.; **PROFL AFFIL & HONORS:** Engineer of the Year, 1977, IL; Lic. RE Broker; Lic. CPA; Ph.D. Lic. P.E.; Profl. Excellence Award, 1979, Bradley Univ.; **EDUC:** BS, 1977, Const., Acctg., Univ. of IL, Champaign; **GRAD EDUC:** MS, 1968, Construction and RE, Univ. of IL; PhD, 1972, Civil Engrg., Univ. of IL; **EDUC HONORS:** James Scholar Student, Honor Student, Nat. Fellow; **OTHER ACT & HONORS:** Various; **HOME ADD:** 5317 N. Woodview Ave., Peoria, IL 61614, (309)692-2370; **BUS ADD:** 5317 N. Woodview Ave., Peoria, IL 61614, (309)692-2370.

AEGERTER, Bob——B: July 15, 1935, Mitchell, SD, *Asst. VP*, Seattle FNB, Props. Div. Design Section; **PRIM RE ACT:** Architect; **OTHER RE ACT:** Facilities planner; **SERVICES:** Strategic branch bank planning; **REP CLIENTS:** For banks owned / leased banking premises; **PREV EMPLOY:** City of Bellingham; Univ., Arch. W. WA Univ.; **PROFL AFFIL & HONORS:** Corp. Member, AIA; **EDUC:** BArch., 1958, Arch., IA State Univ.; **EDUC HONORS:** Tau Sigma Delta; **OTHER ACT & HONORS:** Pres., Assn. Univ. Arch.; **BUS ADD:** Exchange Bldg. 15th Floor, 821 2nd Ave., Seattle, WA 98104, (206)583-5562.

AERENSON, Norman N.——B: July 12, 1930, Wilmington, DE, *Atty.*, Aerenson & Balick; **PRIM RE ACT:** Consultant, Attorney, Owner/Investor; **REP CLIENTS:** Builders, devel. & purchasers of RE; **EDUC:** BS, 1952, Econ., Dickinson Coll.; **GRAD EDUC:** LLB, 1955, Dickinson Law School; **OTHER ACT & HONORS:** Atty. for NewCastle Co., 1960-1966; **HOME ADD:** 110 Hackney Cir., Wilmington, DE 19803, (302)478-3533; **BUS ADD:** 604 Farmers Bank Bldg., Wilmington, DE 19801, (302)658-4265.

AGEE, Phillip Michael——B: Jan. 12, 1947, Kansas City, MO, *Atty. and Gen. Counsel*, Modern Realty of Missouri, Inc.; **PRIM RE ACT:** Consultant, Attorney, Developer, Owner/Investor; **OTHER RE ACT:** Corp. manages & markets recreational projects; **SERVICES:** Gen. RE law; state & HUD OILSR filings; direct mail advertisements; sweepstakes & other on-site & off-site market; **REP CLIENTS:** Recreational vehicle, time-share and other recreational RE land devels. in midwest, southeast & southwest US; **PREV EMPLOY:** Gen. Counsel for SC corp. in 1977 on Hilton Head Island, SC which was a pioneer in time-sharing; **EDUC:** BA, 1969, Hist., Univ. of KS; **GRAD EDUC:** JD, 1973, Urban Affairs, Univ. of MO - Kansas City; **EDUC HONORS:** Dean's List (2 semesters); publications; **OTHER ACT & HONORS:** Univ. of MO - KC Communiversity Convener; **HOME ADD:** 4700 Booth, Westwood, KS 66205, (913)432-7884; **BUS ADD:** 555 Westport Rd., Kansas City, MO 64111, (816)531-5730.

AGGARWAL, Dr. R.——B: June 27, 1947, *Pres.*, AB Associates; **PRIM RE ACT:** Consultant, Lender, Instructor; **SERVICES:** Preperation Evaluation and fin. of RE investment proposals; **REP CLIENTS:** Fortune 500 cos. and indep. indiv. investors; **PREV EMPLOY:** Prof. at the Univ. of MI, IN, and Toledo. Consultant to major banks and multinational cos.; **PROFL AFFIL & HONORS:** Fin. Mgmt. Assn., Academy for Intl. Bus., Amer. Fin. Assn., Amer. Acctg. Assn., etc.; **EDUC:** BS, 1968; **GRAD EDUC:** MBA, DBA, 1970, 1975, Fin., Kent State Univ., The Univ. of Chicago; **EDUC HONORS:** Research Fellowship; **OTHER ACT & HONORS:** Published 5 books and over 50 articles in bus. journals; **BUS ADD:** 2667 Cheltenham Rd., Toledo, OH 43606, (419)475-8528.

AGIN, Herbert S.——B: Mar. 4, 1948, Brooklyn, NY, *VP Resident Manager*, Coldwell Bnaker Commercial Real Estate Services; **PRIM RE ACT:** Broker; **SERVICES:** Indus., comml., office, investment, consulting; **PROFL AFFIL & HONORS:** Long Is. Assn., NY Bd. of Realtors; **EDUC:** BA, 1970, Pol. Sci., Hunter Coll.; **HOME ADD:** 5 W. Terrace Rd., Great Neck, NY 11021, (516)487-4472; **BUS ADD:** 2001 Marcus Ave., Lake Success, NY 11042, (516)437-7100.

AGLIO, Frank Alfred, Jr.——B: Sept. 14, 1951, Burlington, VT, *RE Devel., Broker, Gen. Contractor, Synd.*, Industrial West; **PRIM RE ACT:** Broker, Consultant, Developer, Builder, Owner/Investor, Instructor, Property Manager, Syndicator; **OTHER RE ACT:** Gen'l Contractor; **SERVICES:** Investment counseling, valuation, devel., and synd. of comml. props., prop. mgmt., contractor builder; **REP CLIENTS:** Lenders and private investors in comml. props.; **PREV EMPLOY:** Century 21, Nova; Owner, Pacific West; Aglio Construction Co.; **PROFL AFFIL & HONORS:** RE Securities & Synd.; Candidate for Cert. Comml. Investment; Member of Cert. Prop. Mgmt.; Lifetime Teaching Credentials; Cert. in RE; Sadleback Coll. Nat. Exchange Councilor, Million Dollar Sales Club; **EDUC:** Teaching Credentials (RE), 1980, Saddleback Coll.; **GRAD EDUC:** Saddleback Coll., UCLA Extention; **EDUC HONORS:** Dean's Honor List; **OTHER ACT & HONORS:** Aventura Sailing Club; Dana Point Athletic Club; AMA Racing; Newport Beach Magic Island Club; **HOME ADD:** 110 Via Zapata, San Clemente, CA 92672, (714)498-4576; **BUS ADD:** 110 Via Zapata, San Clemente, CA 92672, (714)492-1234.

AGNEW, Patrick J.——B: May 9, 1942, Chicago, IL, *Gen. Counsel*, St. Paul Fed. S&L Assn. of Chicago; **PRIM RE ACT:** Attorney; **PREV EMPLOY:** Partner-Righeimer, Righeimer & Martin-law firm-Chicago, IL; **PROFL AFFIL & HONORS:** ABA, IL and Chicago Bar Assns.; **GRAD EDUC:** JD, 1966, DePaul Univ. Law School; **HOME ADD:** 239 S. Scoville, Oak Park, IL 60302; **BUS ADD:** 6700 W. N Ave., Chicago, IL 60635, (312)622-5000.

AGRESTI, Gerald R.——B: Apr. 16, 1943, Medford, MA, *Pres.*, Dev. Three Realty Inc.; **PRIM RE ACT:** Broker, Developer, Builder; **OTHER RE ACT:** 2-5mill. annual constr. vol.; **SERVICES:** Constr. and Dev. for single and multi-family joint ventures; **PROFL AFFIL & HONORS:** NAHB, RESSI, NAR, St. Cert. Bldg. Contr.; **EDUC:** Mech. Design/Constr. Tech., 1964-1980, Constr., Wentworth Inst., Univ. of N. FL; **EDUC HONORS:** Dean's List; **MIL SERV:** USN, Lt. 64-73, Jet Pilot, DFC & Air Medals (4); **OTHER ACT & HONORS:** Kiwanis, Mission Bd. St. Margarets, Bd. of Dirs. HOW Corp.; **HOME ADD:** 7417 Fleming Isl. Rd., Green Cove Springs, FL 32043, (904)284-7231; **BUS ADD:** 2017 Doctors Lake Dr., Orange Park, FL 32073, (904)264-3514.

AGUILAR, Rodolfo J.——B: Sept. 28, 1936, San Jose, Costa Rica, *Pres.*, Aguilar & Associates, Inc.; **PRIM RE ACT:** Broker, Consultant, Engineer, Appraiser, Architect, Developer, Builder, Owner/Investor, Instructor; **SERVICES:** Planners, arch., engrs., RE appraisers; **REP CLIENTS:** LA Dept. of Transportation and Devel.; State of LA Div. of Admin.; pvt. clients; **PREV EMPLOY:** Prof. of Arch. & Fin., LA State Univ., Baton Rouge, LA; **PROFL AFFIL & HONORS:** AIA; ASCE; LA Engrg. Soc., Profl. Engr., Registered Arch., Profl. Land Surveyor; RE Broker; **EDUC:** BS Arch., Engrg., 1958, Arch., Engrg., LA State Univ.; **GRAD EDUC:** BArch, 1960, Arch., LA State Univ.; MS, 1961, CE, LA State University/IL Inst. of Technol.; PhD, 1964, Structures; Math., NC State Univ.; **EDUC HONORS:** Phi Kappa Phi; Tau Beta Pi; Chi Epsilon; L.S.U. Scholarships, Sigma Xi, N.S.F. Fellowship; **OTHER ACT & HONORS:** LA Bd. of Commerce and Indus., 1977-1980; Baton Rouge Mental Helath Asc's. Bd.; Chmn., LA Arch. Selection Bd., 1976-78; **HOME ADD:** 4866 Whitehave St., Baton Rouge, LA 70808, (504)766-8056; **BUS ADD:** 4626 Jamestown Ave., Baton Rouge, LA 70808, (504)927-6885.

AGUILERA, Guido A.——B: Sept. 24, 1932, Havana, Cuba, *Atty. at Law*, Guido A. Aguilera PA; **PRIM RE ACT:** Attorney, Banker, Lender; **REP CLIENTS:** Ponce de Leon Fed. S&L Assn.; **PROFL AFFIL & HONORS:** Coral Gables Bar Assn., FL Bar Assn., ABA, Inter-Amer. Bar Assn., Hon. Bd. Member & Founder of Latin RE Assn.; Chmn. of Bd. Ponce de Leon Fed.; **EDUC:** BA, 1950, LaSalle; **GRAD EDUC:** JD, 1971, Stetson Univ. Coll. of Law; JD, 1955, Havana Univ. Coll. of Law; **HOME ADD:** 815 Ponce de Leon Blvd., Coral Gables, FL 33134, (305)444-4979; **BUS ADD:** 815 Ponce de Leon Blvd., Coral Gables, FL 33134, (305)445-8748.

AHERN, Francis——*VP Corp. Plng.*, Dorsey Corp.; **PRIM RE ACT:** Property Manager; **BUS ADD:** 400 West 45th St., Chattanooga, TN 37410, (615)821-6551.*

AHERN, George I., Jr.——B: Mar. 20, 1945, Salt Lake City, UT, *Comml. Sales*, Iliff Thorn & Co.; **PRIM RE ACT:** Broker, Consultant, Appraiser, Owner/Investor; **SERVICES:** Brokerage & devel. consultation for office bldgs.; **REP CLIENTS:** Users, devels & indiv. & instnl. investors; **PREV EMPLOY:** Coldwell Banker Comml. Brokerage (1976-81), Hammer Siler George Assoc. (1973-76), RE Consulting; **EDUC:** 1967, Econ., Univ. of CO; **GRAD EDUC:** MBA, 1971, Fin., Bus.; **EDUC HONORS:** Sr. Class Pres., Dean's List, Outstanding Sr. Man; **MIL SERV:** USNR, Lt.; **OTHER ACT & HONORS:** Denver Athletic Club, Crestmoor Comm. Assn.; **HOME ADD:** 1133 Monaco Prkwy, Denver, CO 80220, (303)399-5007; **BUS ADD:** 1777 S. Harrison, Suite 1200, Denver, CO 80201, (303)753-9300.

AHERN, William J., Jr.——B: Nov. 26, 1927, Elmira, NY, *Atty.*; **PRIM RE ACT:** Attorney, Appraiser, Banker, Developer, Builder, Property Manager; **SERVICES:** All aspects of RE, specializing in RE tax assessment law; **REP CLIENTS:** Many natl. tenants; **PREV EMPLOY:** Former counsel for PhiliP J. Levin for over 20 yrs.; devel. of 10 million sq. feet of shopping ctr. store space; **PROFL AFFIL & HONORS:** NJ Bar Assn., ABA; **EDUC:** BA, 1949, Psych. & Lang., Seton Hall Univ.; **GRAD EDUC:** LLB(JD), 1957, Seton Hall Univ.; **EDUC HONORS:** Award in trusts; **MIL SERV:** USA, Cpt.; **OTHER ACT & HONORS:** Mayor Kenilworth, NJ, 1961-69; Freeholder (cty. comm.) Union Cty., NJ., 1965-67; **HOME ADD:** RR 3, Box 81, Califon, NJ 07830; **BUS ADD:** RR 3, Box 81, White Oak Dr., Califon, NJ 07830, (201)832-5443; **BUS TEL:** (201)832-7065.

AHLBERG, Henry B.——*Indust. Location Consultant*, Henry B. Ahlberg, PE; **PRIM RE ACT:** Consultant; **SERVICES:** Site Search, Evaluate Sites; **REP CLIENTS:** many; **PREV EMPLOY:** Lockwood Greene Eng. Inc.; **EDUC:** BS, MIT; **BUS ADD:** 133 Grant St., Needham, MA 02192, (617)444-6856.

AHRENS, Valerie J.——B: Sept. 20, 1951, St. Louis, MO, *Account Exec.*, D'Arcy MacManus & Masius, Inc.; **PRIM RE ACT:** Consultant; **OTHER RE ACT:** Adv. account exec. for Gallery of Homes Inc.; **PREV EMPLOY:** Present Sales Counselor, David H. Pope, Gallery of Homes, Past Agent for Century 21 Gaing W. (all in St.

Louis); **PROFL AFFIL & HONORS:** NAR, MO Assn. of Realtors & RE Bd. Metropolitan St. Louis, Sales Counselor; **EDUC:** AA, 1977, Liberal Arts, Meramec Community Coll.; also attended Univ. of MO, Columbia 1970-72; **HOME ADD:** 7269 Emerald Forest Dr., St. Louis, MO 63129, (314)846-6089; **BUS ADD:** 1 Memorial Dr., St. Louis, MO 63102.

AIKEN, Jeffrey P.——B: Dec. 19, 1946, Milwaukee, WI, *Atty.*, Frisch, Dudek and Slattery, Ltd.; **PRIM RE ACT:** Attorney; **SERVICES:** Counseling regarding RE sales, acquisitions, devel., synd., mort. lending and fin., const. contract prop. and negotiation, const. and RE litigation; **REP CLIENTS:** First Fin. Savings & L Assn., Combustion Systems, Inc., RME Assoc., Republic Devel., Inc., National Devel. and Investment; **PROFL AFFIL & HONORS:** State Chmn. and Bd. of Gov. of Amer. Coll. of Mort. Attys. 1980-present, WI and ABA 1972-present, Reporter for WI Bar RE 1981; **EDUC:** BA, 1969, Engrg, liberal arts, philosophy, psych., Marquette Univ.; **GRAD EDUC:** JD, 1972, comml. law and trial, Marquette Univ. Law School; **EDUC HONORS:** Deans List 1968, cum laude grad., cum laude; **HOME ADD:** 1614 E Cumberland Blvd., Whitefish Bay, WI 53210, (414)962-0829; **BUS ADD:** 825 N. Jefferson, Milwaukee, WI 53202, (414)273-4000.

AILEEN, Porter——B: Jan. 3, 1929, Oxnard, CA, *Owner, Broker*, Aileen Porter Realty; **PRIM RE ACT:** Broker, Appraiser, Developer; **SERVICES:** Appraising, Sale, Developing, Building, Package Loans; **PREV EMPLOY:** Sales Associate, Cosmotologist; **PROFL AFFIL & HONORS:** Glenn Cty. Bd. of Realtors; CA Assn. Realtors, Nat. Assn. Realtors, Grad. Realtor Inst.; Certified RE Specialist; Nat. Assn. RE Appraisers, Womens' Council of RE, GRI, CRS, CREA; **EDUC:** 1972, Butte Community Coll.; **OTHER ACT & HONORS:** Certified Loan Packager Farmers Home Admin.; Glenn Co. Planning Commission, 1975-Present; Glenn Co. Chamber of Commerce; Orland Chamber of Commerce Director; Christian Church; **HOME ADD:** 10 E. Walker St., Orland, CA 95963, (916)865-9709; **BUS ADD:** 10 E. Walker St., Orland, CA 95963, (916)865-3585.

AINBINDER, Seymour——B: July 10, 1928, *Pres.*, Ainbinder Bramalea Shopping Centers; **PRIM RE ACT:** Developer; **PREV EMPLOY:** VP Allied Stores 1961-72; VP Arlen Shopping Ctrs. 1972-77; **PROFL AFFIL & HONORS:** Intl. Council of Shopping Ctrs.; **EDUC:** Attended Rutgers & Upsala, 1952-54, Bus.; **OTHER ACT & HONORS:** Westwood Ctry. Club, Houston, TX; Senatorial Advisory Comm., Steering Comm.; **HOME ADD:** 11919 Longleaf Ln., Houston, TX 77024, (713)977-3357; **BUS ADD:** 5850 San Felipe, Suite 500, Houston, TX 77057, (713)978-7800.

AIRING, Richard E., CPA——B: Sept. 4, 1942, Hanover, PA, *VP/Controller*, S.L. Nusbaum & Co., Inc.; **OTHER RE ACT:** Fin. reporting - cash mgmt.; **PROFL AFFIL & HONORS:** AICPA - VA Soc. of CPA's - MD Assn. of CPA's - Lions Club of Norfolk - Tidewater Bd. of Realtors, C.P.A.; **EDUC:** BS Acctg., 1968, Acctg./Econ., Univ. of Baltimore; **EDUC HONORS:** Magna Cum Laude; **MIL SERV:** USN, 2nd Class Petty Officer; **HOME ADD:** 3005 Watergate Ln., Virginia Beach, VA 23452, (804)340-0183; **BUS ADD:** 922 Maritime Tower, P O Drawer 2491, Norfolk, VA 23501, (804)627-8611.

AKERLOW, Charles W.——B: June 24, 1940, Janesville, WI, *Pres.*, Akerlow Thomas Dyer, Inc.; **PRIM RE ACT:** Broker, Syndicator, Developer, Property Manager, Owner/Investor; **SERVICES:** land acquist., design, dev. invest., prop mgmt.; **REP CLIENTS:** invest. lenders, tenants of comml. r.e. prop.; **PREV EMPLOY:** Dir. Model Cities Program, Salt Lake City; **PROFL AFFIL & HONORS:** Salt Lake City Bd. of Realtors, Grad. Realtors Inst., Million Dollar Club, Salt Lake City Bd. of Realtors; **EDUC:** BS, 1962, Poli Sci, Univ. of UT; **GRAD EDUC:** MS, 1970, Poli Sci and Bus. Admin., U of UT; **EDUC HONORS:** Phio T. Sherman Prize and Elbert D. Thomas Award; **MIL SERV:** USA, Mjr., Bronze Star, Army Commendation Medal; **OTHER ACT & HONORS:** Chmn. UT Rep. Party, 1981; **BUS ADD:** 68 S. Main St., Salt Lake City, UT 84101, (801)521-0107.

AKERSON, Charles B.——B: Nov. 8, 1922, Minneapolis, MN, *Pres.*, Akerson Valuation Co.; **PRIM RE ACT:** Consultant, Appraiser; **PROFL AFFIL & HONORS:** ASREC, AIREA, Lifetime Member, Past Pres., AIREA, George L. Schmutz Award 1972; **EDUC:** AB, 1947, Tufts Univ.; **MIL SERV:** USNR, Lt.; **HOME ADD:** 63 Atlantic Ave., Boston, MA 02110; **BUS ADD:** 50 Congress St., P.O. Box 52, Boston, MA 02101, (617)742-2300.

AKIN, Paul R.——B: July 31, 1912, Wachula, FL, *Pres.*, Paul R. Akin & Assoc., Inc.; **PRIM RE ACT:** Broker, Consultant, Appraiser; **SERVICES:** Appraisals; **REP CLIENTS:** Trust Dept., Atlantic Nat. Bank; Employee Transfer Corp.; **PREV EMPLOY:** Norton Realty Co., 1939 to 1964; RE Sales, Mgmt. Ins. Dept.; **PROFL AFFIL & HONORS:** SREA; Nat. Assoc. of RE Bds.; Pres. of Jacksonville Bd. of Realtors; Dist. VP of FL RE Bd.; Pres. of Jacksonville Chapt., Amer. Soc. of Appraisers; **EDUC:** AB, 1936, Eng. Lit., Univ. of FL; **EDUC HONORS:** Grad. with honors; Pres., Farr Literary Soc.; **MIL SERV:** USA, Pvt.; **OTHER ACT & HONORS:** Duval Cty. Housing Finance Comm., 5/1981 to date; Civil Service Bd, Duval Co., FL, 1949 to 1968; Seminole Club, Member Bd. of Dir., Jay Day Corp. Ctr.; **HOME ADD:** 6923 Almohrs Dr., Jacksonville, FL, (904)733-9913; **BUS ADD:** 1649 Atlantic Blvd., Suite 201, Jacksonville, FL 32207, (904)398-1114.

AKKERMAN, Wayne E.——B: June 1, 1925, Ellsworth, MN, *Owner*, Century 21 Akkerman All Areas RE; **PRIM RE ACT:** Broker, Property Manager, Owner/Investor; **OTHER RE ACT:** List & Sell, Sell & List; **PROFL AFFIL & HONORS:** CRB, CRS; **EDUC:** AA, 1947, Lib. Arts., Worthington, MN Jr. Coll.; **MIL SERV:** USA, 1st Lt., Expert Infantry Badge; **HOME ADD:** 3209 SW 35th, Des Moines, IA 50315, (515)285-2112; **BUS ADD:** 2720 SW 9th, Des Moines, IA 50315, (515)282-2121.

AKUFFO, Boafo——B: Mar. 29, 1940, New Orleans, LA, *Pres.*, Secaucus Grp. (USA) Ltd; **PRIM RE ACT:** Banker, Lender, Property Manager, Syndicator, Insuror; **SERVICES:** Funding for comml. props., mgmt., synd.; **REP CLIENTS:** Devels. for comml. props., bldg. owners, provision of ins. for owners; **PREV EMPLOY:** Chase, Tarifero & Morgan, NV Grp. VP; **EDUC:** BS, 1963, Acctg., Univ. of IL; **GRAD EDUC:** MBA, 1969, Urban Planning & Fin., Univ. of PA; **MIL SERV:** USA, Lt.; **OTHER ACT & HONORS:** Bd. of Trs. Amer. Land Found.; **BUS ADD:** PO Box 11680, Chicago, IL 60611.

ALALA, George William——B: Aug. 26, 1945, Greensboro, NC, *Sr. VP*, Stockton, White & Co., Home Equity Div.; **OTHER RE ACT:** Mort. banker; **SERVICES:** First and second mort. resid. loans; **PREV EMPLOY:** Cameron-Brown Co.; Mort. Bankers, 1967-1975; **PROFL AFFIL & HONORS:** Wake County Assn. of Mort. Lenders; Wake County Home Builders Assn.; Raleigh Bd. of Realtors; **EDUC:** Guilford Coll., Greensboro, NC; **MIL SERV:** US Army Res.; E-4; **OTHER ACT & HONORS:** St. Michaels Catholic Church; **HOME ADD:** 1210 Larkhall Court, Cary, NC 27511, (919)467-7536; **BUS ADD:** POB 30300, 4509 Creedmoor Rd., Raleigh, NC 27622, (919)782-8900.

ALALA, Joseph B., Jr.——B: Apr. 29, 1933, Aleppo, Syria, *Pres.*, Garland & Alala, P.A.; **PRIM RE ACT:** Consultant, Attorney, Owner/Investor, Syndicator; **REP CLIENTS:** Branch Banking & Trust Company, Fiber Controls Corp. and Belmont Abbey Coll., and others; **PREV EMPLOY:** Arthur Andersen & Co.; **PROFL AFFIL & HONORS:** ABA, AAA-CPA, NC Bar Assn., AICPA, NC Assn. CPA's, NAA, Atty., CPA; **EDUC:** BS, 1957, Acctg., Univ. of NC at Chapel Hill; **GRAD EDUC:** JD, 1959, Tax & Corp. Law, Univ. of NC Law Sch.; **EDUC HONORS:** Beta Gamma Sigma Hon. Soc., Grad. Cum Laude Member Bd. of Law Review; **MIL SERV:** USA; **OTHER ACT & HONORS:** Gaston Ctry. Club, Dir. YMCA, Member C of C; **HOME ADD:** 1216 South St., Gastonia, NC 28052, (704)865-4610; **BUS ADD:** 192 South St., Gastonia, NC 28052, (704)864-2634.

ALAND, Richard——B: Dec. 7, 1946, Los Angeles, CA, *Prin.*, Richard Aland Assoc.; **PRIM RE ACT:** Architect, Developer, Builder, Owner/Investor; **OTHER RE ACT:** Planning, Solar Energy Systems; **SERVICES:** Architecture, Construction; **REP CLIENTS:** Developers, Investors, Private Individuals; **PREV EMPLOY:** Restoration Project Architect, Santa Barbara Public Library, Santa Barbara, CA; **PROFL AFFIL & HONORS:** Corporate Member, AIA, Professional Member, CSI, Nat. Trust for Hist. Preserv.; **EDUC:** BArch, 1972, Arch. Design, CA Poly. State Univ., San Luis Obispo, CA; **MIL SERV:** US Army; PFC, 1969-1971; **HOME ADD:** 360 Treichal Lane, Watsonville, CA 95076, (408)722-9905; **BUS ADD:** Box 1359, Aptos, CA 95003, (408)722-5998.

ALANIS, Paul R.——B: July 17, 1948, Denver, CO, Riordan, Caps, Carbone & McKinzie; **PRIM RE ACT:** Broker, Attorney; **EDUC:** BA, 1970, Govt., Georgetown Univ.; **GRAD EDUC:** JD, 1973, Harvard Law Sch.; **EDUC HONORS:** Phi Beta Kappa, Cum Laude; **HOME ADD:** 6218 Hamilton Ln., La Crescenta, CA 91214, (213)249-8310; **BUS ADD:** 523 W 6th St., Suite 1234, Los Angeles, CA 90014, (213)629-4824.

ALARUPI, Edward A.——B: Aug. 22, 1930, Milwaukee, WI, *Proj. Dir.*, Dept. of City Devel., City of Milwaukee; **OTHER RE ACT:** Proj. dir.; **SERVICES:** Urban renewal, city RE acquisition; **REP CLIENTS:** Disposition, appraisals; **PREV EMPLOY:** Henry W. Mary Co., RE; **PROFL AFFIL & HONORS:** Soc. of Real Prop. Admin., Natl. Assn. Review Appraisers, Intl. Org. of RE Appraisers, ICA, RPA, CPA; **EDUC:** BS, 1955, Fin. & RE, Marquette Univ.; **MIL SERV:** USA, Lt., Army Commendation Medal; **OTHER ACT & HONORS:** Dir. Commonwealth Savings Bank, Pres. Calvary Presbyterian Church Corp.; **HOME ADD:** 747 N. 26th St., Milwaukee, WI, (414)933-5638;

BUS ADD: 734 N 9th St., Milwaukee, WI, (414)278-2107.

ALBAN, Robert——*Fac. Supv.*, California Computer Products, Inc.; **PRIM RE ACT:** Property Manager; **OTHER RE ACT:** Property Manager; **BUS ADD:** 2411 W. LaPalma Ave., Anaheim, CA 92801, (714)821-2011.*

ALBAN, William R.——**B:** Aug. 27, 1936, Steubenville, OH, *Pres.*, Northern Appraisal Co.; **PRIM RE ACT:** Attorney; **PROFL AFFIL & HONORS:** ABA, IL Bar Assn., Chicago Bar Assn.; **EDUC:** BA, 1958, Pol. Sci., Hist. & Eng., OH State Univ.; **GRAD EDUC:** JD, 1960; **EDUC HONORS:** Pi Sigma Alpha Honorary Frat.; **HOME ADD:** 1126 S. 13th St., St. Charles, IL 60174, (312)584-9563; **BUS ADD:** 39 S. LaSalle St., Chicago, IL 60603, (312)372-6528.

ALBANY, Tony——**B:** May 17, 1938, Inglewood, CA, *Pres.*, Western System Fin. Corp.; **PRIM RE ACT:** Broker, Consultant, Developer, Owner/Investor, Property Manager, Syndicator; **SERVICES:** Devel. of co-ml., indus. props.; **REP CLIENTS:** Indiv. & Inst. Investors; **PREV EMPLOY:** Jefferson Standard Life Ins. Co., 1965-69, First Int. Bank (UCB) 1963-65; **PROFL AFFIL & HONORS:** Airventurer's Inc., CA Broker's Lic. 1965; Comml. Pilot Lic 1976; **EDUC:** BA, 1961, Econ., RE, Univ. of CA, Los Angeles; **GRAD EDUC:** MBA, 1966, Fin., Univ. Northwestern; **MIL SERV:** USA, Quartermaster Corps., 1st Lt., Commander General's Highest Prof. Award, 1962; **BUS ADD:** 10960 Wilshire Blvd., 1504, Los Angeles, CA 90024, (213)477-6775.

ALBERT, Burton L.——**B:** Sept. 25, 1941, Sioux City, IA, *Part.*, Lutins, Shapiro and Albert; **PRIM RE ACT:** Attorney; **SERVICES:** Full range of RE legal services; **REP CLIENTS:** Loeb Const. Co., Builders Investment Grp., Inc., STB Assoc., Physicians Realty Co. and F & B Dev.; **PREV EMPLOY:** Lawyers Title Ins. Co. 1967 to 1968; **PROFL AFFIL & HONORS:** ABA, Roanoke Bar Assn., VA Trial Lawyers; **EDUC:** AB, 1963, Hist. and Eng., Dartmouth; **GRAD EDUC:** JD, 1966, Duke; **MIL SERV:** USAR, 1st Lt.; **OTHER ACT & HONORS:** Torch Intl., VA Home Builders, Mensa; **HOME ADD:** 2622 Stephenson Ave., SW, Roanoke, VA 24014, (703)342-9420; **BUS ADD:** 347 Highland Ave. SW, PO Box 180, Roanoke, VA 24002.

ALBERT, Eugene——**B:** June 28, 1924, New York, NY, *Pres.*, The Albert Appraisal Co., Inc.; **PRIM RE ACT:** Consultant, Appraiser, Instructor; **SERVICES:** Investment and tax counseling, valuation, ct. testimony; **REP CLIENTS:** Fortune 500 cos., govt. agencies, attys., estates, banks, ins. cos., pension funds, investors; **PREV EMPLOY:** Est. in present enterprise since 1950; **PROFL AFFIL & HONORS:** AIREA, SREA, ASA, Columbia Soc. of RE Appraisers, Westchester Cty. Soc. of RE Appraisers (Past Pres.), RE Bd. of NY, Amer. Arbitration Assn., NY State Assn. of Realtors, Bronx Bd. of Realtors, Westchester Cty. Bd. of Realtors, Rockland Cty. Bd. of Realtors, Dutchess Cty. Bd. of Realtors, Intl. Right of Way Assn., ULI, Rgnl. Plan Assn., Inst. of Prop. Taxation, Amer. Planning Assn., Advisor Nat. Forensic Ctr., MAI, Sr. RE Analyst, Amer. Inst. Profl. Recognition Award; **EDUC:** BS, 1950, Soc., Columbia Univ.; **EDUC HONORS:** Cum Laude; **MIL SERV:** USAF, 2nd Lt.; **OTHER ACT & HONORS:** Village of Croton-on-Hudson Planning Bd., 1980-81, Adjunct Assoc. Prof. of RE, Pace Univ.; **HOME ADD:** 220 Cleveland Dr., Croton-on-Hudson, NY 10520, (914)271-9584; **BUS ADD:** 60 E 42nd St., NY, NY 10065, (212)986-5445.

ALBERT, Roy I.——**B:** Aug. 16, 1924, Norway, MI, *Arch.*, Roy I. Albert/Archs.; **PRIM RE ACT:** Architect; **SERVICES:** Arch.-Constr. Mgmt.; **PROFL AFFIL & HONORS:** AIA, MSA, MAP; **EDUC:** BA, 1953, Arch., Univ. of MI; **MIL SERV:** 4 Yrs. WW II; **BUS ADD:** 28400 Southfield Rd., Lathrup Village, MI 48076, (313)557-8140.

ALBERT, Timothy D.——**B:** Mar. 9, 1957, Tiffin, OH, *Prop. Appraiser*, Maricopa County Assessor's Office, Comml. Props.; **PRIM RE ACT:** Appraiser, Assessor; **SERVICES:** Assessing for cty.; **PREV EMPLOY:** Appraiser, A-1 Appraisal Serv., Phoenix, AZ; **PROFL AFFIL & HONORS:** IFA, Candidate Member, IFA; **EDUC:** BA, 1980, RE, OH State Univ.; **EDUC HONORS:** 2 Scholarships awarded by OH Bd. of Realtors; **HOME ADD:** 2002 W Glendale Ave. Apt. 7H, Phoenix, AZ 85021, (602)864-1010; **BUS ADD:** 111 S Third Ave., Phoenix, AZ 85003, (602)262-3797.

ALBERT, Yvan——**B:** Mar. 30, 1931, Rumford, ME, *Pres.*, Albert - Noble Co.; **PRIM RE ACT:** Broker, Attorney, Developer, Property Manager; **PREV EMPLOY:** VP Devel., Will C. Hass Co., VP Pro Publishing; **PROFL AFFIL & HONORS:** ICSC, RE Broker; **EDUC:** BS in Bus. Admin., 1954, Mktg., Boston Univ. Sch. of Mgmt.; **EDUC HONORS:** Who's Who, Scarlet Key, Distinguished Mil. Grad.; **MIL SERV:** US Army, 1st Lt., Expert Inf. Badge; **OTHER ACT & HONORS:** V. Chmn, Pleasanton Housing Auth.; **HOME ADD:** 7926 Hillsboro Ct., Pleasanton, CA 94566, (415)846-1971; **BUS ADD:** 39111 Paseo Padre Pkwy, Ste. 301, Fremont, CA 94538, (415)794-3555.

ALBIN, Mac——**B:** May 18, 1915, USA, *Owner*, M. Albin Real Estate; **PRIM RE ACT:** Broker, Owner/Investor, Property Manager; **SERVICES:** Rehabs.; **EDUC:** RE, City Coll; **BUS ADD:** 20618 N.E. 6 Ct., N. Miami Beach, FL 33179, (305)651-0870.

ALBION, Donald L.——**B:** July 19, 1923, New York, NY, *Tr.*, J.E.M. Realty Trust; **PRIM RE ACT:** Attorney, Developer, Owner/Investor; **SERVICES:** Investment, devel., tax-wise synd.; **GRAD EDUC:** LLB, 1947, Law, Univ. of VA, Dept. of Law; **MIL SERV:** US Army Air Force; **HOME ADD:** 1028 Bayamo Ave., Coral Gables, FL 33146, (305)666-8676; **BUS ADD:** 1028 Bayamo Ave., Miami, FL 33146.

ALBRECHT, H. Karl——**B:** Feb. 21, 1925, Aalen, Germany, *Appraiser*, Albrecht Appairsals; **PRIM RE ACT:** Consultant, Appraiser; **SERVICES:** Appraisals and counseling; **REP CLIENTS:** Home Equity, Relocation Realty, Equitable Relocation, Executrans; **PREV EMPLOY:** Barnett & Follevaag Inc.; **PROFL AFFIL & HONORS:** SREA, SRA; **EDUC:** BS, 1950, EE, CO State Univ.; **GRAD EDUC:** MS, 1958, EE, Univ. of IL; MA, 1971, Hist., Univ. of OR; **MIL SERV:** USAF, Lt. Col., Joint Servs. Commendation Medal; **HOME ADD:** E 10809 35th Ave., Spokane, WA 99206, (509)928-4889; **BUS ADD:** E 10809 35th Ave., Spokane, WA 99206, (509)928-4889.

ALBRECHT, Robert H.——**B:** Feb. 8, 1932, Russell Cty. KS, *Asst. Broker*, Marvin Mayers RE & Auctions; **PRIM RE ACT:** Broker, Appraiser, Insuror; **SERVICES:** All lines of ins., resid., farm & comml.; appraising-sales of RE; **REP CLIENTS:** Indivs. and lenders or instnl. investors in farm & urban areas; **PREV EMPLOY:** US Postal Serv.; **PROFL AFFIL & HONORS:** NAR; KS Assn. of Realtors; Russell Cty. Bd. of Realtors; Natl. Assn. of Indep. Fee Appraisers; KS Soc. of Farm Mgmt. and Rural Appraisers; Amer. Soc. of Farm Mgrs. & Appraisers; Central KS Assn. of Home Builders; **MIL SERV:** USN; First Class; **HOME ADD:** 408 W. 17th, Russell, KS 67665, (913)483-4400; **BUS ADD:** 262 South 281 Highway, Box 388, Russell, KS 67665, (913)483-4400.

ALBRECHT, Vance E.——**B:** Aug. 12, 1933, Seattle, WA, *Sales Mgr.*, Century 21, Tom Liedtke Realty; **PRIM RE ACT:** Broker, Appraiser, Instructor, Property Manager; **SERVICES:** Brokerage of homes, acreage, farms & investments; **PROFL AFFIL & HONORS:** Wood Cty. Bd. of Realtors; TX Assn. of Realtors; NAR, GRI; CRS; CRB; Eddy Award from WA RE Esvc. Found.; **OTHER ACT & HONORS:** C of C; **HOME ADD:** 132 Meadow Brook Dr., Mineola, TX 75773, (214)569-2002; **BUS ADD:** 1235 N. Pacific, PO Box 321, Mineola, TX 75773, (206)569-5405.

ALBRIGHT, Allen J.——**B:** Mar. 6, 1923, Ontario, NY, *Ret. Sr. VP, Pt. time Appraiser & Consultant*, Security Trust Co., RE; **PRIM RE ACT:** Owner/Investor, Broker, Consultant, Appraiser; **OTHER RE ACT:** Have NYS RE Salesman License under Knox B Phagon, Realtor; **REP CLIENTS:** Trust Depts.; Law Firms; **PREV EMPLOY:** Mgr. Lending Div. of Security Trust Co.; **PROFL AFFIL & HONORS:** Society of RE Appraisers, SRA; **EDUC:** BS, 1947, Agric. Econ., Cornell Univ.; **MIL SERV:** US Army, Capt.; **OTHER ACT & HONORS:** Chmn. Assessment Review Bd., Ontario 8 yrs.; Dir., Better Bus. Bureau; Dir., Assn. for the Blind; Trustee, Furnaceville Cemetary Assn.; **HOME ADD:** 7020 Knickerbocker Rd., Ontario, NY 14519, (315)524-8308; **BUS ADD:** 7020 Knickerbocker Rd., Ontario, NY 14519, (315)524-8308.

ALBRIGHT, Norman——*Pres. and Asst. Sec.*, Albright Investment Co.; **PRIM RE ACT:** Broker, Instructor, Appraiser, Property Manager, Owner/Investor; **OTHER RE ACT:** Mort. Banker; **BUS ADD:** 116 E Ninth Ave., Winfield, KS 67156.

ALBRIGHT, Richard A.——**B:** Nov. 28, 1948, Erie, PA, *Pres.*, Sibley Real Estate Services, Inc.; **PRIM RE ACT:** Property Manager; **SERVICES:** All prop. mgmt. service, investment counseling; **REP CLIENTS:** Indivs., gen. partnerships, limited partnerships, lenders, instnl. investors; **PROFL AFFIL & HONORS:** IREM (Pres. of Chap. 58); RE Bd. of Rochester NY, CPM; 1980 "Mgr. of the Year" of Chap. 58 of IREM; **EDUC:** BS, 1971, Bus. Admin. & Mktg., Cornell Univ.; **EDUC HONORS:** Dean's List; **OTHER ACT & HONORS:** Treas. of Cornell Chap. of Lambda Chi Alpha Frat., Alumni Assn. since 1980; **HOME ADD:** 1183 Northrup Rd., Penfield, NY 14526, (716)872-2716; **BUS ADD:** 100 White Spruce Blvd., Rochester, NY 14623, (716)424-6950.

ALBRIGHT, Stephen J.——**B:** Dec. 9, 1947, Houston, TX, *Pres.*, Albright & Associates of Ocala, Inc.; **PRIM RE ACT:** Appraiser; **SERVICES:** Investment counseling; **REP CLIENTS:** Seaboard Coast Line RR, Seminole Electric Cooperative, City of Ocala, Mid State Federal S&L Assn. etc.; **PREV EMPLOY:** Numerous condemnation assignments for transmission rights of way, road widenings; various comml. appraisals of many, many types of prop.; **PROFL AFFIL &**

HONORS: Amer. Inst. of RE Appraisers; Soc. of RE Appraisers; Ocala Bd. of Realtors, FAR & NAR, MAI, SRPA, SRA; **EDUC:** BA, Presbyterian Coll., 1969, Hist. & Pol. Sci., Presbyterian Coll.; **MIL SERV:** US Army, Lt., 90 day serv. medal; **OTHER ACT & HONORS:** Ocala-Silver Springs Rotary Club, Elks Club of Ocala, First Presbyterian Church of Ocala (ruling elder); **HOME ADD:** 2145 SE 27th Terrace, Ocala, FL 32671, (904)732-5139; **BUS ADD:** 2137 SE Fort King St., Ocala, FL 32671, (904)622-9191.

ALBRITTAIN, James Sydney——B: Nov. 21, 1948, Chicago, IL, *CEO/Dir.*, The Albrittain Co., J.S. Albrittain & Associates; **PRIM RE ACT:** Broker, Developer, Builder, Owner/Investor; **SERVICES:** Land valuation analysis, devel. & construction partnership; **REP CLIENTS:** Investors & owners of resid. prop.; **PROFL AFFIL & HONORS:** NAR, RNMI, VAR, NVBR, VCCIM, Cert. Comml. Investment Member (CCIM); **EDUC:** BS, BA, 1978, Fin., Amer. Univ., Wash., DC; **GRAD EDUC:** MBA, 1981, Amer. Univ., Wash., DC; **OTHER ACT & HONORS:** FXCO Metro Task Force; WFC Metro Task Force; Dir., VESTA Corp.; Gen. Bldg. Corp.; AB Inc.; Bond Builders, Inc., Mgmt. Dittmar Co.; **HOME ADD:** 4004 No. Richmond St., Arlington, VA 22207, (703)527-1373; **BUS ADD:** 410 Pine St., Vienna, VA 22180, (703)938-5477.

ALBRITTON, Harold D.——B: Dec. 8, 1939, Ellaville, GA, *Pres.*, Albritton, Schultz & Assoc.; **PRIM RE ACT:** Consultant, Appraiser; **SERVICES:** RE valuation and analysis; **PROFL AFFIL & HONORS:** AIREA, MAI, Recipient Profl. Recognition Award (1976 & 1978 of AIREA); **EDUC:** BBA, 1965, RE, GA State Univ.; **MIL SERV:** Army Pvt.; **HOME ADD:** 265 Pine Brook Way, Roswell, GA 30076, (404)992-6376; **BUS ADD:** 390 Courtland St. NE, Atlanta, GA 30308, (404)875-0003.

ALBUSCHE, Leo J.——B: Aug. 3, 1928, Oakland, CA, *Pres.*, Leo J. Albusche Enterprises; **PRIM RE ACT:** Developer, Builder, Owner/Investor, Property Manager; **PROFL AFFIL & HONORS:** El Dorado Cty. Econ. Devel. Award, 1979; **OTHER ACT & HONORS:** Chmn., El Dorado Cty. Bldg. Comm.; **BUS ADD:** 1291 Broadway, Placerville, CA 95667.

AL CHALABI, Margery——B: Oct. 20, 1939, Tarentum, PA, *Dir., RE & Urban Affairs Consulting Grp.*, Laventhol & Horwath, Chicago Office; **PRIM RE ACT:** Consultant; **SERVICES:** A variety of consulting servs. including: mkt. studies, econ. feasibility studies, fin. projections, design servs., land mgmt., Downtown Devel., Adaptive Reuse, Mixed Use Devel.; **REP CLIENTS:** Private & public clients; **PREV EMPLOY:** Formerly VP, RE Research Corp. (Chicago) 7 yrs.; Work with HUD (Chicago), City of Chicago; Work with Architect/Engrg. Firms in Chicago, Pittsburgh, Athens; **PROFL AFFIL & HONORS:** Amer. Planning Assn.; ULI; World Soc. for Ekistics; Intl. Federation of Housing & Planning, Lambda Alpha Intl. Frat.; Author of numerous articles for profl. journals; **EDUC:** BArch, 1961, Arch., Carnegie-Mellon Univ.; **GRAD EDUC:** MS, 1965, Rgnl. Planning & Econ., Athens Technol. Inst.; **EDUC HONORS:** various scholarships; **OTHER ACT & HONORS:** Arts Club of Chicago; Advisory Bds. of Corlands; Friends of Downtown Chicago; **HOME ADD:** 330 W. Diversey Parkway, Chicago, IL 60657, (312)248-9515; **BUS ADD:** 111 East Wacker Dr., Chicago, IL 60601, (312)644-4570.

ALCOCK, Gerald V.——B: June 23, 1929, Chicago, IL, *Owner*, Gerald Alcock Co.; **PRIM RE ACT:** Consultant, Appraiser, Developer; **SERVICES:** RE consulting & appraising; **PREV EMPLOY:** Harris Trust & Savings Bank, Chicago; **PROFL AFFIL & HONORS:** MAI; **EDUC:** BA, 1951, Econ., De Pauw Univ.; **GRAD EDUC:** MBA, 1956, Fin., Univ. of Chicago; Stonier Grad. School of Banking, 1968, Bank, U. Rutgers; **HOME ADD:** 2691 Byington, Ann Arbor, MI 48103, (313)662-7331; **BUS ADD:** Suite 507, First Natl. Bldg, 201 S. Main St., Ann Arbor, MI 48104, (313)994-0554.

ALCORN, John G.——B: June 27, 1941, Franklin, NH, *Pres./Treas.*, Alcorn, Inc.; **PRIM RE ACT:** Builder; **SERVICES:** RE devel. and mgmt. of resid. prop.; **REP CLIENTS:** Pvt. prop. owners in the Falmouth-Mashpee area of Cape Cod; **PREV EMPLOY:** Builder & realtor in W. Springfield, MA prior to relocating on Cape Cod in 1976; **PROFL AFFIL & HONORS:** Nat. Assn. of Home Builders; HOW warranty Cape Cod Contractors & Builders Assn.; Falmouth C of C; Cape Cod Bd. of Realtors, Inc.; Better Bus. Bureau of E. MA, Realtor; RE Broker; Notary Public; **HOME ADD:** POB AA, Teaticket, MA 02536, (617)548-9470; **BUS ADD:** 19 Capricorn Cir., POB AA, Teaticket, MA 02536, (617)548-2000.

ALCOULOUMRE, Hank——*Dir. Publ. Rel.*, CCI Corp.; **PRIM RE ACT:** Property Manager; **BUS ADD:** PO Box 51500, Tulsa, OK 74151, (918)836-0151.*

ALDER, Gary D.——B: Jan. 14, 1939, Washington, D.C., *RE Appraiser*, Alder Appraisal Serv.; **PRIM RE ACT:** Appraiser; **SERVICES:** RE Appraising; **REP CLIENTS:** Most banks, S&L & mort. cos. in the Salt Lake area, plus Merrill Lynch Relocation and many other relocation firms; **PREV EMPLOY:** UT State Tax Commn.; UT State Dept. of Hwys.; Zions S&L; **PROFL AFFIL & HONORS:** Soc. of RE Appraisers & Salt Lake Bd. of Realtors, SRA; **OTHER ACT & HONORS:** Gov., Dist. 6, SREA; CO., UT & WY '81-'83; **HOME ADD:** 10966 S 2000 E, Sandy, UT 84092, (801)571-5092; **BUS ADD:** 10966 S 2000 E, Sandy, UT 84092, (801)571-5622.

ALDER, William E.——B: Oct. 11, 1953, Kansas City, MO, *RE Appraiser/Owner*, Alder Real Estate Appraisals; **PRIM RE ACT:** Appraiser, Insuror; **SERVICES:** RE sales, mgmt., appr. & ins. sales; **PROFL AFFIL & HONORS:** MO Assn. Realtors, NAR, IIAM, IIAA, GRI; **EDUC:** Public Admin., 1976, Poli. Sci., Univ. of MO - Columbia; **OTHER ACT & HONORS:** Kiwanis Club, Jaycees, US Ski Assn., Recipient C. William Brownfield Award (Jaycees) - Selected as one of the Outstanding Young Men of Amer. (1981); **HOME ADD:** 218 Morningside Terr., Richmond, MO 64085; **BUS ADD:** 126 E. N. Main, Richmond, MO 64085, (816)776-2208.

ALDIERI, Michael J.——B: May 8, 1933, Bristol, CT, *Pres.*, Aldieri Assoc. Inc.; **PRIM RE ACT:** Broker, Consultant, Appraiser; **SERVICES:** RE appraisals & consultation; **REP CLIENTS:** lenders, attys., US Govt., State of CT; **PREV EMPLOY:** US Dept. of HUD, FHA; **PROFL AFFIL & HONORS:** Nat. Bd. of Realtors; Amer. Inst. of RE Appraisers; Soc. of RE Appraisers, MAI, AIREA; SRPA; **MIL SERV:** US Army, Sgt.; **HOME ADD:** 22 Glenview Dr., Bristol, CT 06010, (203)583-3448; **BUS ADD:** PO Box 796, Bristol, CT 06010, (203)589-3355.

ALDRICH, C. Elbert——B: Sept. 12, 1923, Rosebud, TX, *Pres.*, Elbert Aldrich Realtor, Inc.; **PRIM RE ACT:** Broker, Developer, Owner/Investor; **SERVICES:** Land Sales & Dev. - Comml., Indus. and investment prop. Also, indus. site locator; **REP CLIENTS:** Individual, instnl., and corp. investors in comml., indus. and investment prop.; **PROFL AFFIL & HONORS:** AFLM; SIR; NAR; TX Assn. of Realtors; Temple-Belton Bd. of Realtors; RNMI, FLI; MIR, Realtor of the Year Temple-Belton Bd. of Realtors '71 '73 '77; TX Farm & Land Broker of the Yr. 1977; St. Award for Best Ex. over $250,000, '75, '77; Pres. TX Farm & Land: Pres. TX Prop. Exchangors, 1977; Reg. VP FLI, 76-77; Omega Tau Rho, '78; CCIM; **EDUC:** 1946-47, Bus. Admin., Temple Jr. Coll.; **MIL SERV:** USNAC, 1942-46, Av. Mach. Mate 1st Cl., Air Medal, 2 Oak Leaf Clusters, Dist. Flying Cross; **OTHER ACT & HONORS:** Temple Rotary Club; Karem Shrine; Temple C of C - Dir. and VP; **HOME ADD:** 2410 Bird Creek Dr., Temple, TX 76501, (817)773-5537; **BUS ADD:** 18 N 3rd, Temale, TX 76501, (817)773-4901.

ALDRIDGE, John W.——*VP Mfg. & Engr.*, Union Special Corp.; **PRIM RE ACT:** Property Manager; **BUS ADD:** 400 N. Franklin St., Chicago, IL 60610, (312)266-4000.*

ALDRIDGE, L. Rollins, Jr.——B: July 19, 1920, Columbus, GA, *VP*, W.C. Bradley Co., RE; **PRIM RE ACT:** Engineer, Developer, Owner/Investor, Property Manager; **PREV EMPLOY:** Private consulting Civil Engr., 1941-1966; **PROFL AFFIL & HONORS:** Assoc., Soc. of RE Appraisers, Reg. Civil Engr., GA & AL; **EDUC:** BS, 1940, Civil Engr., Auburn Univ.; **GRAD EDUC:** 1940, Public Health Engrg., Univ. of NC; **EDUC HONORS:** Phi Kappa Phi, Tau Beta Pi, Chi Epsilon, Omicron Delta Kappa; **MIL SERV:** US Army, Corps of Engrs., Maj.; **OTHER ACT & HONORS:** Sigma Chi; **HOME ADD:** 6145 Cape Cod Ct., Columbus, GA 31904, (404)322-2039; **BUS ADD:** 1017 Front Ave., Columbus, GA 31993, (404)322-7348.

ALESCHUS, Justine——*Pres.*, Justine Aleschus Realty; **PRIM RE ACT:** Broker; **SERVICES:** Specializing in land sales; **REP CLIENTS:** Exclusive broker for estate Kenneth H. Leeds. (Mr. Leeds was a major land dealer in Suffolk Cty.) (He owned millions of dollars worth of land at his death), and rep. other prop. owners and investors; **PREV EMPLOY:** Sales Mgr. new home subdivs.; **PROFL AFFIL & HONORS:** Suffolk Co. RE Bd., L.I. Mid-Suffolk Businessmen's Assn., Smithtown Profl. & Businesswomen's Network, 110 Center Bus. & Profl. Women, Listed in Nassau-Suffolk RE Guide "Who's Who in Real Estate"; **EDUC:** Attended: Rutgers Univ. Coll., New Brunswick, NJ; **OTHER ACT & HONORS:** Currently Pres.: Nassau-Suffolk Council of Hospital Auxiliaries, Past Pres. and Hon. Member, St. John Episcopal Hospital, Smithtown Auxiliary (since 1977), Member: Comm. on Hospital Auxiliaries of the Hospital Assn. of NY State; **HOME ADD:** 26 Tanglewood Dr., Smithtown, NY 11787, (516)265-2205; **BUS ADD:** P O Box 267, Smithtown, NY 11787, (516)265-2205.

ALESSANDRO, Michael——**B:** Sept. 5, 1946, NY, *Owner*, Pasco Homes & Land, Realtors; **PRIM RE ACT:** Broker, Consultant, Appraiser, Owner/Investor, Instructor, Property Manager; **OTHER RE ACT:** Mort. Broker; **SERVICES:** Buyer's Broker/Exchangor; **PREV EMPLOY:** Dir. of Law & Records, Pasco Cty. Clerk of Circuit Ct.; **PROFL AFFIL & HONORS:** Dade City Bd. of Realtors; FL Assn. of Realtors; FL Assn. of Mort. Bankers; FL RE Exchangors; Amer. Mort. Brokers Assn.; NAR, Dir., Law and Records, Clerk Circuit Court, Pasco Cty., FL May 1974-July 1977; Lic. RE Broker, State of FL; Lic. Mort. Broker, State of FL; Lic. Ins. Salesman, State of NY; Lic. Ins. Salesman, State of FL; Lic. RE Salesman, State of CA; Lic. RE Broker, State of NY; FL Dept. of Educ., Teaching Certification; Pasco Hernanco Community College, Dade City, FL, Instr.; Saint Leo College, Saint Leo, FL, Instr.; Licensed RE Instr., State of FL; Admin./Owner Michael Schools of RE, Pasco Cty., FL; Past/Veterans Admin. Mgmt. Broker, Pasco, Hernando Citrus Counties; Past Pres. Dade City Bd. of Realtors, Dade City, FL 1979-1980; Century 21 Academy of RE, Tampa, FL, Staff Instr.; **EDUC:** BA, 1974, Pre-Law, St. Leo Coll., FL; AS, 1975, RE, Pasco Hernando C.C.; **EDUC HONORS:** Magna Cum Laude, AA, Social Science, 1971, Laney CC, Cum Laude; **MIL SERV:** USAF, A1c, Nat. Defense; **OTHER ACT & HONORS:** Civil Air Patrol; Bicentennial Comm.; Jaycees; Yesterday's Air Force; **HOME ADD:** 204 S. Elm St., San Antonio, FL 33576, (904)588-2006; **BUS ADD:** 305 Pennsylvania Ave., P.O. Box 637, San Antonio, FL 33576, (904)588-2006.

ALEVIZOS, Peter——**B:** Feb. 27, 1955, Boston, MA, *Associate*, Goldman, Sachs Realty Corp.; **OTHER RE ACT:** RE financing, sales and advisory services; **PREV EMPLOY:** Equity Trust Associates - Developers, Norwood, MA; **PROFL AFFIL & HONORS:** MA Lic., RE Broker; **EDUC:** AB, 1977, Psych., Harvard; **GRAD EDUC:** MBA, 1981, RE Fin./Devel., Wharton School of Fin.; **OTHER ACT & HONORS:** Pres., RE Club; Teaching Fellow in RE; **HOME ADD:** 45 E. End Ave., Apt. 2B, NY, NY 10028, (212)472-3068; **BUS ADD:** 55 Broad St., NY, NY 10004, (212)676-5025.

ALEXANDER, Bill——*VP Personnel & Adm.*, Mesa Petroleum Co.; **PRIM RE ACT:** Property Manager; **BUS ADD:** 1 Mesa Sq. Box 2009 Vaughn Bldg., Amarillo, TX 79189, (806)378-1000.*

ALEXANDER, Doris M.——**B:** Aug. 22, 1914, Dryad, WA, *Owner - Broker*, Palisades West; **PRIM RE ACT:** Broker, Consultant, Appraiser, Developer, Owner/Investor, Instructor, Property Manager, Insuror, Syndicator; **SERVICES:** Sales-res.-comml.-bus. brokerage estate planning and invest.; **PREV EMPLOY:** ITT Fin. Services - Dist. Mgr. 1968-1972; **PROFL AFFIL & HONORS:** State - Local & Natl. Bd. of Realtors - Multiple Listing Olympia, Amer. Bus. Women's Assn. - Past Pres. Farm & Land Inst., GRI, AIC; **EDUC:** Major Bus. Admin & Bookeeping, Grays Harbor Bus. Coll. - 1 yr. Self educated (WA State Security Lic.) also N.A.S.P. Ins. & Agent Lic. Taught RE Invest. - Olympia Voc. Coll. Yakima Valley Coll. - 1 yr. Million Dollar Club - I.T.T. Hamilton Life Ins.; **OTHER ACT & HONORS:** Precinct Comm. Person 1972-1981, Past Pres. ABWA (Olympia C of C Ex. Bd.) - Pres. - Thurston Cty. Women's Republican Club; Olympia C of C Bd. of Dirs., Exec. Bd.-1979-1981; Nat. C of C-Top Twenty Sales Award in Memberships 1977; Marquis Who's Who American Women 1979-1981; **HOME ADD:** 621 S. Plymouth, Olympia, WA 98502, (206)352-1590; **BUS ADD:** 621 S. Capitol Way, Governor House Lobby and 704-706, Olympia, WA 98501, (206)357-8200.

ALEXANDER, Kyle——*VP*, Iroquois Brands, Ltd.; **PRIM RE ACT:** Property Manager; **BUS ADD:** 41 W. Putnam Ave., Greenwich, CT 06830, (203)622-9000.*

ALEXANDER, R.C.——**B:** Oct. 20, 1940, Philadephia, PA, The Towle RE Co.; **PRIM RE ACT:** Property Manager; **OTHER RE ACT:** Office Leasing Broker; **SERVICES:** Mgt. & leasing of office bldgs.; **REP CLIENTS:** Marquette Assoc.; Bor - Son Bldg. Corp.; **EDUC:** BS, 1963, Ind. Mgt., Chem. Engrg., Purdue Univ.; **MIL SERV:** USN, Cdr.; **HOME ADD:** 7333 Gallagher Dr., Edina, MN 55435, (612)831-7498; **BUS ADD:** 600 2nd Ave. S., Minneapolis, MN 55402, (612)341-4444.

ALEXANDER, Robert B.——**B:** Aug. 20, 1930, Waco, TX, *Pres.*, The Alexander Grp., Inc.; **PRIM RE ACT:** Attorney, Developer, Owner/Investor, Syndicator; **OTHER RE ACT:** RE Tax Law Planning; **SERVICES:** Devel., synd., investment, tax law planning; **PREV EMPLOY:** Trial Atty. (Tax), Office of Chief Counsel, Ct. of Appeals Branch, Tax Ct. Litigation Div., IRS, Wash. DC (4 yrs); Tax counsel for devels. and mort. trusts.; **PROFL AFFIL & HONORS:** Membership in State Bar of TX, The FL Bar; **EDUC:** BS, 1952, Hotel Admin., Cornell Univ., Rice (2 1/2 yrs.); **GRAD EDUC:** LLB, 1959, Law, Baylor Univ. Law School; **MIL SERV:** US Army, Third Infantry Div., 1st Lt.; **OTHER ACT & HONORS:** Houston Racquet Club; Capt. of Cornell tennis team; TX high school tennis doubles winner; Houston Racquet Club winner of club championship A doubles; Publications: "US Taxation of US RE Owned by Nonresident Aliens and Foreign Corps." and "RE Synd," Univ. of Miami Law Review lead articles (republished in The Monthly Digest of Tax Articles); TX Bar Journal articles, TX CPA articles, law review case notes; favorable tax rulings published nationally by RE trade assns.; outlines presented at speaking engagements, including "Short-term Trusts Funded with Oil & Gas Props." for the Houston Chapt. of TX Soc. of CPAs in 1980; **HOME ADD:** 1523 Bering Dr., Houston, TX 77057, (713)977-9519; **BUS ADD:** 4801 Woodway, Ste. 340 W, Houston, TX 77056, (713)965-0818.

ALEXANDER, Robert G.——**B:** May 19, 1949, Madison, WI, *Atty.*, McLario Law Offices; **PRIM RE ACT:** Consultant, Attorney; **SERVICES:** Legal and investment counseling, Tax Counsel; **REP CLIENTS:** Apple Valley Development Corp., Menomonee Falls, WI; Harris Business Group; Steve G. Walker, VP Sales, Blunt, Ellis & Loewi, Milw., WI (Investors, Builders, Devel., Brokers, Synd. in comml. and resid. props.; **PROFL AFFIL & HONORS:** ABA, Sect. Real Prop, Probate & Trust, Tax; WI Bar Assn.; Milwaukee Bar Assn.; **EDUC:** 1971, Eng., Univ. of WI; **GRAD EDUC:** JD, 1976, Corporate and Bus. Law; **EDUC HONORS:** Cum Laude, Phi Kappa Phi, Henry Austin Scholarship winner; **OTHER ACT & HONORS:** Graduate work in taxation; Univ. of WI, Milwaukee; LLM - Taxation Candidate DePaul Univ., Chicago, IL; **HOME ADD:** W158 N8314 Apple Valley Dr., Menomonee Falls, WI 53051, (414)255-6173; **BUS ADD:** N88 W16783 Main St., Menomonee Falls, WI 53051, (414)251-4210.

ALEXANDER, Ross A.——**B:** Jan. 1, 1913, Detroit, MI, *Appraiser, Consultant*, Ross Alexander & Co.; **PRIM RE ACT:** Broker, Consultant, Appraiser; **SERVICES:** All types RE appraisals & RE consulting; **REP CLIENTS:** Nat. firms, banks, attys., municipalities, estates, investors & devel.; **PREV EMPLOY:** Self employed; **PROFL AFFIL & HONORS:** AIREA; Soc. of RE Appraisers; Amer. Soc. of RE Consultants, MAI; SRPA; CRE; **EDUC:** Univ. of MI, Univ. of Chicago, Univ. of FL, Univ. of Tampa, St. Pete Jr. Coll.; **MIL SERV:** US Army; **OTHER ACT & HONORS:** 4 yr. special master tax hearings for Pinellas Cty. FL; RE Instr. St. Pete Jr. Coll.; Realtor of year 1969; Clearwater-Largo-Dunedin Bd. of Realtors; **HOME ADD:** 1512 S. Betty Lane Ct., Clearwater, FL 33516, (813)442-9973; **BUS ADD:** 901 Chestnut St., Suite "E", Clearwater, FL 33516, (813)461-4057.

ALEXANDER, Sandra Jeane——**B:** Dec. 5, 1950, Tulsa, OK, *Sr. Assoc. for Legal Serv., Policy Devel. & Research*, Pragmatics, Inc.; **PRIM RE ACT:** Consultant, Attorney; **OTHER RE ACT:** Urban planning, computer programming; **SERVICES:** Rgnl. and city planning, legal servs., data processing and regulatory analysis; **PREV EMPLOY:** U.S. Dept. of HUD, 1978-1981; Atty., Jan. 1980 - May 1981; **PROFL AFFIL & HONORS:** ABA; OK Bar Assn.; DC Bar (licensed to practice law in OK and DC); **EDUC:** BA, 1974, Pol. Sci., Swarthmore Coll.; **GRAD EDUC:** JD, 1976, Local Govt. Law/Admin. Law/Land Use Planning, Univ. of Tulsa Coll. of Law; **EDUC HONORS:** Dean's Honor Roll; **HOME ADD:** 3624 N. Harvard, Tulsa, OK 74115, (918)425-2908; **BUS ADD:** 1629 K St., N.W., Suite 520, Washington, DC 20006, (202)296-6097.

ALEXANDER, Willis W.——*Exec. VP*, American Bankers Assn.; **PRIM RE ACT:** Banker; **BUS ADD:** 1120 Connecticut Ave. NW, Washington, DC 20036, (202)467-4000.*

ALEXANDRA, Victoria Soto——**B:** Dec. 31, 1950, Chicago, IL, *Consultant*, TransAmerican Invest. and Exch. Corp.; **PRIM RE ACT:** Consultant, Developer, Property Manager; **OTHER RE ACT:** buyers agent for invst. R.E. and bus. also dev.; **REP CLIENTS:** indiv. in the med. field; **PREV EMPLOY:** instr. in primary grades, instr. in R.E. law and fin.; **PROFL AFFIL & HONORS:** IL chptr. of CCIM, NAR, RNMI, RESSI, N.W. Suburb. Bd. of Realtors, Interex Academy of R.E., Intl. Mktg. Clearing House; **EDUC:** BA, 1973, Educ., psych., Gov. St. IL; **GRAD EDUC:** 1974, Psych., N.W.U., IL; **BUS ADD:** 999 Plaza Dr., Schaumburg, IL 60195, (312)885-1031.

ALFONSO, Raymond H.——**B:** Sept. 4, 1945, NY, NY, *Pres.*, Intl. Comml. Brokerage Co.; **PRIM RE ACT:** Broker, Attorney, Developer, Owner/Investor, Syndicator; **OTHER RE ACT:** Investment advisor and consultant; **REP CLIENTS:** CA Realty Investments, Los Angeles; The Jacuzzi Found. Trust, San Francisco; **PREV EMPLOY:** Urban Planner, Rouse Corp., Columbia, MD; **EDUC:** BS, 1968, Transportation Planning, Univ. of TX; **GRAD EDUC:** MA, 1970, Urban Planning, Northwestern Univ.; **HOME ADD:** 14 Greenway Plaza, Suite 170, Houston, TX 77046, (713)629-1483; **BUS ADD:** 11 Greenway Plaza, Ste. 2127, Houston, TX 77046, (713)629-9100.

ALJOE, Daniel W.——B: July 16, 1946, Kane, PA, *VP & Mgr.*, The Bank of CA, Bank Prop. Mgmt. (99-05); **PRIM RE ACT:** Consultant, Builder, Property Manager, Banker; **OTHER RE ACT:** Corp. RE and Bank Premises; **SERVICES:** Prop., Asset, and Fin. Mgmt., Acquisition & Disposition, Facilities Planning, Design and Const.; **PROFL AFFIL & HONORS:** IREM, BOMA, Western Bank Prop. Mgmt. Grp., CA RE Assn., Scholarship Award - 1973; **EDUC:** BS, 1968, Econ./Fin./Ins., Univ. of PA - Wharton; **GRAD EDUC:** MBA, 1974, Fin./RE/Taxation, Univ. of CA - Berkeley; **EDUC HONORS:** Deans List Jr. & Sr. Yrs., 3.7 GPA Out of 4.0; **MIL SERV:** USM, Lt.; **OTHER ACT & HONORS:** B.P.O. Elks; Toastmasters Intl.; USNR; **HOME ADD:** 1729 Santa Clara Ave., Alameda, CA 94501, (415)521-2723; **BUS ADD:** PO Box 45000, San Francisco, CA 94145, (415)765-2236.

ALLAIS, Richard C.——B: Jan. 18, 1925, Terre Haute, IN, *Owner*, R.C. Allais Investments; **PRIM RE ACT:** Broker, Consultant, Developer, Lender, Builder, Owner/Investor; **SERVICES:** Ch. of Bd. & CEO - Delta Western Mtg. Co.; **REP CLIENTS:** FHA Approved Multi-Family Lender; Chmn. of Bd., Pres. & CEO - Delta Western Systems, Inc., OTC, Real Estate Dev. Co.; **EDUC:** BA, 1948, Univ. of IN; **GRAD EDUC:** JD, 1953, Univ. of Miami, FL; **MIL SERV:** USAF, Lt. Col., Several Decorations; **OTHER ACT & HONORS:** U. Club; Warwick Club; **HOME ADD:** 1434 So. Gessner, Houston, TX 77042, (713)972-1207; **BUS ADD:** 7001 Corporate Dr., Suite 245, Houston, TX 77036, (713)776-1413.

ALLAN, Victor——B: Nov. 4, 1915, Budapest, Hungary, *Pres.*, 'Allandia'; **PRIM RE ACT:** Consultant; **SERVICES:** Community resource analyses; **REP CLIENTS:** Municipalities, C of C, Corps., indiv. investors & devels.; **PREV EMPLOY:** 22 yrs. CBS NY, 12 yrs. CT Dept. of Econ. Devel.; **PROFL AFFIL & HONORS:** AEDC, NIDA, CAMDC, IAAO, CT/IABC; **EDUC:** PhD, 1940, Liberal Arts, Univ. of WI; Purdue; Univ. of Chicago; Univ. of VA; **GRAD EDUC:** MBA, 1956, Columbia Grad. Sch. of Bus.; **MIL SERV:** USAF, Maj., many service ribbons; **OTHER ACT & HONORS:** Chmn. Town Planning Comm.; Chmn. King's Mark RC&D, Inc.; Chmn. CNVRPA; 1st Pres. Old Bethlehem Hist. Soc.; founder World Future Soc.; **HOME ADD:** Wood Creek Rd., Bethlehem, CT 06751, (203)266-7943; **BUS ADD:** Wood Creek Rd., Bethlehem, CT 06751, (203)266-7943.

ALLARD, Warren J.——B: Aug. 27, 1947, Burlington, VT, *Sr. Appraiser*, Bank of America N.T. & S.A., Appraisal Dept. (San Diego Region); **PRIM RE ACT:** Consultant, Appraiser, Owner/Investor; **SERVICES:** Comml. Indus. and Resid. Appraisals; **REP CLIENTS:** Banking and investment clients as well as investors who deal with devel. and synd.; **PROFL AFFIL & HONORS:** Sr. member: IREA, ICA Designation (IREA); Certified Appraiser FNMA; **EDUC:** BA, 1970, Econ. Geography/Bus., Univ. of Miami, Coral Gables, FL; **GRAD EDUC:** MBA, 1976, Econ. and Organizational Behavior, Pepperdine Univ., Orange, CA; **MIL SERV:** USAF (1969-1973); **HOME ADD:** 5083 Brooklawn Pl., Riverside, CA 92504, (714)359-0468; **BUS ADD:** 303 N. D St., San Bernardino, CA 92401, (714)383-6261.

ALLEMAN, Bruce E.——B: Oct. 23, 1946, Bartlesville, OK, *Mgr. - Comml. RE*, Oklahoma Mortgage Co., Inc.; **PRIM RE ACT:** Broker, Consultant, Appraiser, Lender, Owner/Investor, Property Manager; **OTHER RE ACT:** Oil and gas investment and mineral mgmt.; **SERVICES:** Investment consulting, joint ventures, equity purchase; **REP CLIENTS:** Insurance cos., synd., and indiv. investors; **PREV EMPLOY:** Ten years in RE; analysis, devel., mgmt., sales, appraisal, fin. and construction; **PROFL AFFIL & HONORS:** MBA Realtors, CCIM Candidate; **EDUC:** BS, 1969, Acctg. & Econ., East Central Univ., Ada, OK; **MIL SERV:** USAR; 2nd Lt.; **OTHER ACT & HONORS:** Young Exec. Tip Club; **HOME ADD:** 4233 NW 58th St., Oklahoma City, OK, (405)947-2942; **BUS ADD:** 5100 N. Brookline, Suite 900, Oklahoma City, OK 73112, (405)947-5761.

ALLEN, Albert N.——B: Aug. 8, 1946, San Antonio, TX, *Owner*, Albert Allen Associates, Inc.; **PRIM RE ACT:** Consultant, Appraiser, Instructor; **SERVICES:** RE appraisal for litigation purposes; **REP CLIENTS:** Attys., Oil Co's., Governmental Agencies, Lenders, Accountants, Corps.; **PREV EMPLOY:** Real Prop. Analyst, Inc., 1972-1977; **PROFL AFFIL & HONORS:** Intl. Right of Way Assn.; Soc. of RE Appraisers; AIREA, MAI; SRPA; CRA; Key Man Award, Soc. of RE Appraisers; **EDUC:** BS, 1968, Agric. Econ., TX A&M Univ.; **EDUC HONORS:** Ross Volunteers; **MIL SERV:** U.S. Army, Lt., Bronze Star; **OTHER ACT & HONORS:** Listed in Outstanding Young Men of Amer. Directory, 1975; **HOME ADD:** 2306 Lazybrook, Houston, TX 77008, (713)862-6503; **BUS ADD:** 10120 Northwest Freeway, Suite 107, Houston, TX 77092, (713)686-8134.

ALLEN, B.E.——*Corp. Land Agent*, Union Camp Corp.; **PRIM RE ACT:** Property Manager; **BUS ADD:** 1600 Valley Rd., Wayne, NJ 07470, (201)628-9000.*

ALLEN, B.K.——B: Nov. 25, 1945, Louisville, KY, *Pres.*, Allen/Fredlock Properties; **PRIM RE ACT:** Broker, Consultant, Instructor, Syndicator; **OTHER RE ACT:** Minerals & timber sales & acquisition; **SERVICES:** Investment consulting, sales comml. investment props., minerals sales; **REP CLIENTS:** Indiv. investors in comml. props. and minerals; **PROFL AFFIL & HONORS:** NAR, RNMI, WCR, Metropolitan Washington Exchangers, Nat. Federation of Indep. Bus. Persons, Appointed to the grading team for RNMI Comml. Investment Div. Feb. 1981; GRI; CCIM; **EDUC:** Attended KY Wesleyan Coll., Univ. of VA Realtors Inst.; **OTHER ACT & HONORS:** Morgantown C of C; **HOME ADD:** 25 Cedarwood Dr., Morgantown, WV 26505, (304)599-4143; **BUS ADD:** Suite 7, 453 Oakland St., Morgantown, WV 26505, (304)599-0597.

ALLEN, Bob——B: Aug. 9, 1938, Bangor, ME, *VP - 1976*, IMCAL, Inc.; **PRIM RE ACT:** Broker, Consultant, Developer, Property Manager; **SERVICES:** Prop. mgmt., investment counseling, comml. devel., agricultural devel.; **REP CLIENTS:** Indiv. comml. and agricultural invest.; **PREV EMPLOY:** Also VP of Canyon Realty Co., Inc.; Half Moon Bay, CA, Resid. & Agricula, Agricultural RE Bus.; Multiple RE Offices in Ct; **EDUC:** RE Bus. & investment, appraisal, USC & CSM; **MIL SERV:** USAF; 1956-1962, A1c; **OTHER ACT & HONORS:** Rotary Club, Amer. Horse Shows Assn., Inc.; **HOME ADD:** 5 Isabelle Terr., Newington, CT 06111, (203)666-8535; **BUS ADD:** 5 Isabelle Terr., Newington, CT 06111, (203)666-8535.

ALLEN, Charles H., III——B: July 23, 1953, New Haven, CT, *Exec. Dir.*, Heritage Hall Development Corp.; **PRIM RE ACT:** Consultant, Developer; **SERVICES:** Housing devel. packaging, fin., etc.; **REP CLIENTS:** City of New Haven, New Haven Housing Authority, Turner Construction Corp.; **PREV EMPLOY:** Dir. of neighborhood based multi-service corp. having housing provision as one of its programs; **PROFL AFFIL & HONORS:** Member, Council of Urban Econ. Devel., ULI, CT Community Devel. Assn.; **EDUC:** BS, 1975, Acctg.; **GRAD EDUC:** MPA, 1977, Public Admin., Urban Econ.; **OTHER ACT & HONORS:** Alderman, City of New Haven, 20th Ward 4 1/2 years (since 1976); Scoutmaster, Boy Scouts of Amer., Man of the Year, OIC's of CT 1978; **HOME ADD:** 200 Shelton Ave. Apt. 31, New Haven, CT 06511, (203)624-0393; **BUS ADD:** PO Box 8147, New Haven, CT 06530, (203)777-4417.

ALLEN, Chester W.——B: July 6, 1931, Long Beach, CA, *Pres.*, Chet Allen, Inc.; **PRIM RE ACT:** Broker, Instructor, Consultant, Developer, Owner/Investor, Real Estate Publisher; **PROFL AFFIL & HONORS:** CCIM, VP and Gov. of Natl. Soc. of Exchange Counselors, Snyder trophy, best exchange in US 1973, Assn. of Realtors Best Exchange over -500,000 or most outstanding exchange, 1975, 1976, 1977, 1979; **EDUC:** BA, 1953, Econ., Stanford; **MIL SERV:** USMC, 1st Lt.; **HOME ADD:** Route 1, Box 692, Sutter Creek, CA 95685, (209)267-0405; **BUS ADD:** P.O. Box 610, Jackson, CA 95642, (209)223-3554.

ALLEN, Frank W.——*Pres.*, Allen Properties, Inc.; **PRIM RE ACT:** Developer; **BUS ADD:** 2710 Stemmons Freeway, Ste 100, Dallas, TX 75207, (214)634-0666.*

ALLEN, G. Keith——B: Dec. 28, 1936, Lower Jemseg, Queens Co. NB, *Atty.*, Mockler, Allen & Dixon; **PRIM RE ACT:** Attorney; **SERVICES:** Gen. legal and all RE related serv.; **REP CLIENTS:** Bank of Nova Scotia, Bank of Montreal, Mutual Life Assurance Co. of Can., Crown Life, Imperial Life; **PROFL AFFIL & HONORS:** New Brunswick Barristers Soc., Can. Bar Assn., Fredericton RE Bd., Fredericton Barristers Soc.; **EDUC:** BA, 1958, Poli. Sci., Univ. of NB; **GRAD EDUC:** Bach. of Civil Law, 1960, Gen. Law, Univ. of NB Law School; Master of Law, 1970, Municipal Law and Community Planning, York Univ. Osgood Hall, Law School; **EDUC HONORS:** Canada Law Book prize; **OTHER ACT & HONORS:** Provincial Court Judge (1960-1970), Fredericton Planning Comm., Lecturer, UNB Law School; **HOME ADD:** 85 Canterbury Dr., Fredericton, E3B4L7, NB, (506)455-7304; **BUS ADD:** 836 Churchill Row, PO Box 1362, Fredericton, E3B5E3, NB, Canada, (506)455-5515.

ALLEN, Gary——*Dir. Ind. Rel.*, Titantium Metals Corp. of America; **PRIM RE ACT:** Property Manager; **BUS ADD:** 400 Rouser Rd., PO Box 2824, Pittsburgh, PA 15230, (412)262-4200.*

ALLEN, George F., Jr.——B: June 1, 1945, Bridgeton, NJ, *Pres.*, GFA Management; **PRIM RE ACT:** Broker, Appraiser, Property Manager; **OTHER RE ACT:** Corp. purchasing; **SERVICES:** Prop. mgmt.; **PREV EMPLOY:** VP, Turtle Creek Management, Inc.; **PROFL AFFIL & HONORS:** IREM, Apt. Assn. of IN, IMHA, Cert. Apt. Mgr., CPM, (Candidate), Cert. Purchasing Mgr., Lic. RE broker; **EDUC:** BA, 1967, Anth., Soc., Eastern Coll.; **MIL SERV:** USMC, Maj., Navy Commendation Combat Action Ribbon; **OTHER ACT & HONORS:** Little League coach of wrestling and football; **HOME**

ADD: 271 Restin Rd., Greenwood, IN 46142; **BUS ADD:** 271 Restin, Greenwood, IN 46142, (317)881-3815.

ALLEN, Gerald Frank——B: Aug. 27, 1944, Lincoln, IL, *Atty.*, Klamen & Danna; **PRIM RE ACT:** Attorney; **SERVICES:** Legal; **REP CLIENTS:** Inst. lenders, devels, owner/investor & synds.; **PREV EMPLOY:** Chicago Title Ins. Co.; Bank Bldg. Corp.; **PROFL AFFIL & HONORS:** Metro St. Louis Bar Assn.; MO & IL Bar Assns.; **EDUC:** BA, 1966, Hist. & Pol. Sci., Millinin Univ., Decatur, IL; **GRAD EDUC:** JD, 1970, IL Inst. of Tech., Chicago Kent Coll. of Law; **EDUC HONORS:** Law degree with honors; **HOME ADD:** 15610 Cedarmill Dr., Chesterfield, MO 63017, (314)532-4149; **BUS ADD:** 7820 Maryland Ave., St. Louis, MO 63105, (314)726-1000.

ALLEN, Grant——*Mgr. Fac. & Const.*, Scientific-Atlantic, Inc.; **PRIM RE ACT:** Property Manager; **BUS ADD:** 3845 Pleasantdale Rd., Atlanta, GA 30340, (404)449-2000.*

ALLEN, H. Rollin——B: June 15, 1927, Decatur, IL, *Partner*, Kiefer, Allen, Cavanagh & Toohey; **OTHER RE ACT:** Legal; Investment; **REP CLIENTS:** Rattle Run RE Co.; White Pine Land Co., Inc.; Chicago Title Ins. Co.; Lawyers Title Ins. Co.; Ramada Inns., Inc.; Stewart Title Guaranty Co.; Meehan Props. Inc.; **PROFL AFFIL & HONORS:** Detroit Bar Assn.; MI State Bar Assn.; Delta Theta Phi Legal Frat.; Fiduciary & Estate Planning Council, City of Detroit; **EDUC:** BS, 1950, Speech/Hist., Univ. of IL; **GRAD EDUC:** JD, 1951, Wayne State Univ.; Master of Law, 1971, Taxation, Wayne State Univ.; **MIL SERV:** USN; **OTHER ACT & HONORS:** Memberships: Engrg. Soc. of City of Detroit; Grosse Pointe Hunte Club; Rattle Run Golf & Country Club; **HOME ADD:** 85 Lakeshore Ln., Grosse Pointe Shores, MI 48236, (313)884-0800; **BUS ADD:** 1565 City Nat. Bank Bldg., Detroit, MI 48226, (313)961-8080.

ALLEN, Harold A., Jr.——B: Dec. 29, 1926, Tacoma, WA, *Pres.*, Harold A. Allen Co.; **PRIM RE ACT:** Broker; **PROFL AFFIL & HONORS:** Tacoma Pierce Cty. Bd. of Realtors, WA Assn. of Realtors; NAR; RNMI; WAR, MAI, SRPA, CCIM, GRS, GRI; **EDUC:** Stanford Univ.; **MIL SERV:** USN, SKD 3; **OTHER ACT & HONORS:** Tacoma C of C, Assn. United US Army, Past Pres. Taluma - Pierce County Chap. Amer. Red Cross, Past Pres. Sales & Mktg. Execs.; **HOME ADD:** 5 Forest Glen Lane SW, Tacoma, WA 98498, (206)588-5978; **BUS ADD:** 9805 Gravelly Lake Dr. SW, P.O. Box 99580, Tacoma, WA 98499, (206)582-6111.

ALLEN, Peter T.——B: June 4, 1945, St. Charles, IL, *Pres.*, Peter T. Allen & Assoc.; **PRIM RE ACT:** Developer, Builder, Owner/Investor, Instructor, Property Manager; **SERVICES:** Investments: counseling, sales & prop. mgmt., hist. rehab., new const. of office & retail space; 6 office & rental props. including 250,000 plus 500,000 resl. condo. convers.; **REP CLIENTS:** Indiv. & inst. investors all MI residents; **PREV EMPLOY:** Project Mgr., Mathews Philips, Inc. creator/developer 5 P.U.D.'s in SE MI (1972-75); **PROFL AFFIL & HONORS:** ULI, NAHB, NAR, Faculty Univ. of MI (Adjunct Prof. of RE); **EDUC:** BA History, 1967, DePauw Univ.; **GRAD EDUC:** MBA, 1973, RE & Acctg., Univ. of MI; **EDUC HONORS:** With Distinction (top 6%); **MIL SERV:** USNR, 1967-1971, Lt., usual decorations; **OTHER ACT & HONORS:** Pres., Newport W. Condo. Assn., Dir. (Member of Bd.) Huron Resid. Serv. for Youth; **HOME ADD:** 2224 Applewood Ct., Ann Arbor, MI 48103, (313)769-2700; **BUS ADD:** 202 E. Washington, Ann Arbor, MI 48104, (313)995-5221.

ALLEN, Randall Gray——B: Aug. 28, 1953, Jefferson City, MO, *Arch.*, The Architects Alliance, Inc.; **PRIM RE ACT:** Architect; **SERVICES:** Arch. design serv.; **REP CLIENTS:** Devels., const. cos., and indivs. in comml., retail, indus. & resid. projects; **PROFL AFFIL & HONORS:** AIA; **EDUC:** BArch., 1976, Arch. Design, KS State Univ.; **EDUC HONORS:** Cum Laude, Blue Key, Tau Sigma Delta, Phi Kappa Phi; **OTHER ACT & HONORS:** Jefferson City Jaycees (Pres. 1981), Jefferson City Area C of C Bd. of Dirs., Cole Cty. Parks and Recreation Commn. - Member; **HOME ADD:** 114 W. Atchison St., Jefferson City, MO 65101, (314)636-7286; **BUS ADD:** 1431 Southwest Blvd., Jefferson City, MO 65101, (314)636-2041.

ALLEN, Richard——B: Feb. 22, 1928, Milwaukee, WI, *Chmn.*, Murdock Mgmt. Co., Inc.; **PRIM RE ACT:** Broker, Consultant, Developer, Owner/Investor, Property Manager; **SERVICES:** Consulting, Mgmt., Leasing, Brokerage; **REP CLIENTS:** Banks, Trusts, Partnerships, Indiv. Pension Funds; **PROFL AFFIL & HONORS:** BOMA, IREM, SOPRA, Phoenix C of C, Phoenix Indus. Devel. Authority, CPM, RPA; **EDUC:** BSME, 1950, Engrg., Univ. of MI; **EDUC HONORS:** Engrg. Honor Soc.; **MIL SERV:** US Army; Lt.; **OTHER ACT & HONORS:** AZ Club, Boy Scouts, YMCA, United Fund, etc.; **HOME ADD:** 322 W Montebello, Phoenix, AZ 85013, (602)274-2150; **BUS ADD:** 3550 N. Central Ave., Phoenix, AZ 85012, (602)279-6261.

ALLEN, Robert H.——B: July 20, 1948, Mobile, AL, *Atty.*, Allen & Fernandez, Attorneys at Law; **PRIM RE ACT:** Attorney; **SERVICES:** Hist. preservation and devel.; **REP CLIENTS:** Mobile Hist. Devel. Commn.; Mobile Hist. Devel. Found.; **PREV EMPLOY:** Merchants Nat. Bank of Mobile, 1970-1972; **PROFL AFFIL & HONORS:** ABA (Comm. on Historic Preservation and Easements), AL and Mobile Cty. Bar Assns.; **EDUC:** BS, 1966, Fin./Acctg., Auburn Univ.; **GRAD EDUC:** JD, 1975, Univ. of AL School of Law; **EDUC HONORS:** Omicron Delta Kappa; **OTHER ACT & HONORS:** Pres., Mobile Historic Devel. Commn; Dir., Mobile Hist. Devel. Found.; Pres., Mobile Auburn Alumni Assn.; **HOME ADD:** 959 Charleston St., Mobile, AL 36604, (205)432-7148; **BUS ADD:** POB 1945, Mobile, AL 36633, (205)432-1303.

ALLEN, Roger H.——B: Mar. 8, 1938, Boise, ID, *Professor of RE*, Boise State Univ.; **PRIM RE ACT:** Broker, Instructor, Syndicator, Consultant, Developer, Real Estate Publisher; **PREV EMPLOY:** RE Dev. - Mobile Home Parks, Rental Storage and Subdivision; **PROFL AFFIL & HONORS:** NAR & Mort. Banker Assoc., CCIM & MBA (Graduate of School of Mort. Banking); **EDUC:** BA, 1961, Acctg., Univ. of NV; **GRAD EDUC:** MBA, 1962, Fin., Northwestern Univ., Chicago; **EDUC HONORS:** Top 5%; **MIL SERV:** Nat. Guard, E-5; **HOME ADD:** 6904 Randolph Dr., Boise, ID 83709, (208)376-1862; **BUS ADD:** 6904 Randolph Dr., Boise, ID 83709, (208)376-1862.

ALLEN, William——*RE & Risk Mgr.*, Leggett & Platt, Inc.; **PRIM RE ACT:** Property Manager; **BUS ADD:** 18th Rd., Carthage, MO 64836, (417)358-8131.*

ALLENDORF, Richard——*Dir. Mktg.*, Ravenhorst Corp.; **PRIM RE ACT:** Developer; **BUS ADD:** 2200 Northwestern Financial Ctr., 7900 Xerxes Ave S., Minneapolis, MN 55431, (612)830-4444.*

ALLEY, Susan J.——B: Sept. 11, 1954, St. Louis, MO, *Research/Marketing Coordinator*, Russo Properites, Inc.; **OTHER RE ACT:** Market Research;Leasing; **SERVICES:** Market and locational analysis, office devel. profiles, investor relations, comml. leasing; **PREV EMPLOY:** Rice Center of Community Design and Research 1979-80; Los Angeles Cty. Dept. of Community Devel. 1977-79; **PROFL AFFIL & HONORS:** Neighborhood Devel. Subcomm. of the Houston C of C, Amer. Planning Assn., Downtown Houston Assn.; **EDUC:** Urban Planning, 1977, Urban and regional planning/recreational land use, Univ. of OK; **GRAD EDUC:** MPL, 1979, Community-Neighborhood devel., Univ. of S CA; **OTHER ACT & HONORS:** Jr. League of Houston; The Museum of Fine Arts, The Arts Symposium; PEO; Houston Symphony;Downtown Houston Assn. Membership Comm.; Chmn. of the Parks Task Force of the Neighborhood Devel. Subcomm.; **HOME ADD:** 1360 Winrock Blvd., Houston, TX 77057, (713)974-7226; **BUS ADD:** 7500 San Felipe, Houston, TX 77063, (713)780-2000.

ALLGEIER, E.M.——B: June 25, 1918, Mt. Grove, MO, *Pres.-Alpha Const. Co., Pres.-Alpha Mgmt., Inc., Gen. Ptr.-Housing Assoc.*, Assoc., VP - Allgeier, Martin & Assoc. of TX; **PRIM RE ACT:** Architect, Developer, Engineer, Builder, Owner/Investor, Property Manager, Syndicator; **SERVICES:** Design, Devel., Const., Synd. & Mgmt. of Apt. Complexes; **REP CLIENTS:** Gen. & Ltd. Partnerships; **PROFL AFFIL & HONORS:** AIA, NSPE, PEEP - Registered as Arch. and Eng. is Several States.; **EDUC:** BArch, 1941, Arch., McKinley-Roosevelt Coll.; **GRAD EDUC:** MS Civil Engrg., 1946, Structural Engrg., IN Inst. of Tech.; **EDUC HONORS:** I.T.K.; **MIL SERV:** USA, C.E., Lt. Col., Army Comd. Medal; **HOME ADD:** 4040 Boxque Dr., Plano, TX 75074, (214)424-4347; **BUS ADD:** 3727 Dilido Rd. Suite 152, Dallas, TX 75226.

ALLISON, Frank E.——B: Nov. 7, 1929, San Saba, TX, *Own. and Princ.*, Allison Associates AIA; Pres. Allison/Walker Interests, Inc.; **PRIM RE ACT:** Broker, Consultant, Appraiser, Architect, Developer, Builder, Owner/Investor, Property Manager; **SERVICES:** Master planning, urban renewal and invest. analysis, arch., engineering, consulting, RE devel., marketing, interior design, leasing, building mgmt., constr., land use studies, investment building, etc.; **REP CLIENTS:** Comml./retail prop. investors; **PREV EMPLOY:** Project Arch., PittsMebane & Phelps, Beaumont, TX 1954-59; Dir. of Plan. & Project Arch., Welton Becket Assoc., Houston 1961-63, NY 1963-66. Arch. in 11 states; **PROFL AFFIL & HONORS:** Corp. Member AIA, TX Soc. of Arch., Houston Chapter AIA. Member Amer. Plann. Assn., Construction Specifications Institute, Amer. Craft Council, Natl. Fire Prevention Assn., The Real Estate Soc. for Industry Members, Nat. Council of Arch. Bds., Lic. RE Broker, TX, Featherlite Competition TX Region-1950, Houston Lighting & Power Design Awards NW Plaza One-1970, NW Plaza Three-1971; **GRAD EDUC:** BArch-Design, 1953, TX A&M Univ., College Station, TX; **EDUC HONORS:** Distinguished Student; **MIL SERV:** USN, airman; **OTHER ACT & HONORS:** Dir., TX Gulf Coast Chap. Cystic

Fibrosis Foundation; Dir., Soc. for the Prevention of Blindness; Member, The 100 Club, Houston, Sheriff's Assn. of TX; Patron, Museum of Fine Arts, Houston; Sustaining Member, Smithsonian Nat. Assn.; 32nd Degree Mason; Shriner, Member Exec. Club, Presidential Inaugural Fin. Comm. 1981; Member Pres. Reagan's Coalition Comm. 1981; **BUS ADD:** 9898 Bissonnet, Sixth Floor, Houston, TX 77036, (713)988-9000.

ALLORA, Anthony J.——**B:** Aug. 14, 1947, Newark, NJ, *VP*, New Jersey Bank, N.A., Mort. Loan Dept.; **PRIM RE ACT:** Appraiser, Banker, Lender; **SERVICES:** Const. Loans, comml. indus., resid.; **PROFL AFFIL & HONORS:** Mort. Bankers Assn.; **EDUC:** BA, 1970, Econ., Fairleigh Dickinson Univ.; **GRAD EDUC:** MBA, 1980, Fin., FDU; **MIL SERV:** US Army National Guard, 1st Lt., 1968-1974; **HOME ADD:** 69 Irving Terrace, Bloomfield, NJ 07003; **BUS ADD:** One Garret Mountain Plaza, West Paterson, NJ 07509, (201)881-5543.

ALLUM, Jerry——**B:** Nov. 23, 1950, Minneapolis, MN; **PRIM RE ACT:** Consultant, Owner/Investor, Property Manager; **OTHER RE ACT:** Current RE Sales License, Creative Fin. Counsellor, RE Investor; **PREV EMPLOY:** Technical Engr. - Trans Alaska Pipeline 3 yrs.; **GRAD EDUC:** BA, Speech Communications, 1973, TV & Radio Broadcasting, Jounalism, Public Speaking, Univ. of MN; **HOME ADD:** PO Box 10-383, Anchorage, AK 99511; **BUS ADD:** PO Box 10-383, Anchorage, AK 99511, (907)345-5327.

ALMEIDA, Irene M.——**B:** Aug. 20, 1929, San Pedro, CA, *Associate*, Landmark Realty Center; **PRIM RE ACT:** Consultant, Owner/Investor; **SERVICES:** Property valuations & appraisals; **PROFL AFFIL & HONORS:** San Pedro-Wilmington Bd. of Realtors; **EDUC:** BS, 1977, Bus. Mgmt., CA State Univ., Dominguez Hills; **EDUC HONORS:** Distinction, Magna cum laude; **OTHER ACT & HONORS:** Grand juror for Los Angeles County 1979-80; San Pedro Bay Hist. Soc.; 30 yr. club; Grand Jurors Assn.; Las Angelenas; Olympic Commn.; Friends of CSUDH; **HOME ADD:** 1159 Amar St., San Pedro, CA 90732, (213)833-2872; **BUS ADD:** 134 S. Gaffey St., San Pedro, CA 90731, (213)833-2411.

ALMY, Earle V. "Buddy", Jr.——**B:** July 29, 1931, Ft. Worth, TX, *Owner & Mgr.*, Almy & Co. - Realtors; **PRIM RE ACT:** Broker, Consultant, Appraiser, Developer, Owner/Investor, Instructor, Property Manager, Insuror, Syndicator; **SERVICES:** Primarily selling shopping ctrs., office bldgs., apts., ranches and farms; **PREV EMPLOY:** Worked at one of the larges banks in Ft. Worth, TX for approximately 5 yrs. and one of the largest feed mfrs. for about 5 yrs.; held NASD license selling stocks, bond and mutual funds at one time; **PROFL AFFIL & HONORS:** NAR; TX Assn. of Realtors; Hood-Somervell Bd. of Realtors; Soc. of RE Appraisers; FLI; RNMI, Accredited Farm & Land Member; CRB; GRI; **EDUC:** BS, 1952, Animal Husbandry/Agric. Econ., TX Tech Univ.; **EDUC HONORS:** Sears Roebuck Scholarship; **MIL SERV:** USAF; Airman 1st Class; 1952-1956; **OTHER ACT & HONORS:** Grad. Cert. in Comml. Banking from Amer. Inst. of Banking in Ft. Worth; Past Pres., Ft. Worth Toastmaster Club; Past VP, TX Tech. Ex-Students Assn.; Member of the Ft. Worth Farm & Ranch Club; The Steeplechase Club; Lake Granbury C of C; **HOME ADD:** Rte. 2 Box 65-1, POB 129, Granbury, TX 76048, (817)326-2132; **BUS ADD:** Rt. 1 Box 65-1, POB 129, Granbury, TX 76048, (817)572-0531.

ALMY, Richard, Jr.——**B:** July 15, 1932, Boston, MA, *Pres.*, Alcore Inc.; **PRIM RE ACT:** Broker, Consultant; **OTHER RE ACT:** Comml. indus.; **SERVICES:** Brokerage, Mktg. & consulting; **PREV EMPLOY:** Pierson & Smith, Inc., Stamford Realtech. Corp.; **PROFL AFFIL & HONORS:** Stamford Bd. of Realtors, CAR, NAREB, CID of CT, CCIM; **EDUC:** AB, 1954, Amer. Hist., Harvard Coll.; **GRAD EDUC:** MBA, 1966, Bus. (Fin. & Mktg.), Northeastern Univ.; **MIL SERV:** USA; **OTHER ACT & HONORS:** Riverside Yacht Club; **HOME ADD:** 22 Oval Ave., Riverside, CT 06878, (203)637-5013; **BUS ADD:** 5 Landmark Sq., Stamford, CT 06901, (203)348-2710.

ALONZO, Richard——*VP Engrg.*, Guardian Industries Corp.; **PRIM RE ACT:** Property Manager; **BUS ADD:** 43043 W. Nine Mile Rd., Northville, MI 48167, (313)349-6700.*

ALPER, Eliot A.——**B:** Jan. 1, 1946, Brooklyn, NY, *Pres.*, Spacefinders Realty, Inc.; **PRIM RE ACT:** Broker, Builder, Syndicator; **SERVICES:** Synd. of unimproved prop.; **PROFL AFFIL & HONORS:** FLI; RESSI, CRS; GRI; **GRAD EDUC:** 1971, Aircraft Tech., Northrup Univ. (CA); **MIL SERV:** US Army, Sp-4, 1965-1968, Vietnam Service Medals; **OTHER ACT & HONORS:** Aircraft Owners & Pilots Assn.; **HOME ADD:** 3175 Vicki Ave., Las Vegas, NV 89118, (702)361-1502; **BUS ADD:** 3955 Blue Diamond Rd., Las Vegas, NV 89118, (702)361-2100.

ALPERN, Andrew——**B:** Nov. 1, 1938, New York, NY, *Mgr. of RE and Facilities Planning*, Coopers & Lybrand; **PRIM RE ACT:** Architect, Property Manager, Owner/Investor; **OTHER RE ACT:** Leasing and Planning Domestic Offices of Major Intl. Acctg. Firm; **PREV EMPLOY:** Resgistered Architect; **PROFL AFFIL & HONORS:** AIA; RE Bd. of NY; Soc. of Arch. Hist., Const. Indus. Arbit. for the Amer. Arbit. Assn.; **EDUC:** BArch, 1964, Columbia Univ. Grad. School of Arch. and Planning; **OTHER ACT & HONORS:** Author of "Apartments for the Affluent" (McGraw-Hill 1975); "Alpern's Architectural Aphorisms" (McGraw-Hill 1979); "Handbook of Specialty Elements in Architecture" (McGraw-Hill 1981); "Holdouts" (McGraw-Hill, 1982); "Time-Saver Standards for Interior Architecture" (McGraw-Hill 1982); Also Editor of Semi-Monthly "Legal Briefs for the Construction Industry" published by McGraw-Hill; Publisher of "F.M.R.A." by Edward Gorey; **BUS ADD:** 315 Eighth Ave., NY, NY 10001, (212)536-3228.

ALPERT, Janet A.——**B:** Dec. 6, 1946, Peoria, IL, *VP, Dir. Natl. Div.*, Lawyers Title Insurance Corp.; **PRIM RE ACT:** Insuror; **SERVICES:** Coordinate title ins. for multi-state customers; **PROFL AFFIL & HONORS:** Assoc. Member IDRC, NACORE; **EDUC:** BA, 1968, Pol. Sci., Univ. of CA, Santa Barbara; **GRAD EDUC:** MBA, 1978, Univ. of CT; **EDUC HONORS:** Beta Gamma Sigma; **HOME ADD:** 13209 Court Ridge Rd., Midlothian, VA 23113; **BUS ADD:** PO Box 27567, 6630 W. Broad St., Richmond, VA 23261, (804)281-6868.

ALPERT, Maurice D.——**B:** Mar. 16, 1929, Dover-Foxcroft, ME, *Pres.*, Alpert Southeast, Inc.; **PRIM RE ACT:** Broker, Consultant, Attorney, Developer; **SERVICES:** RE devel., brokerage, consultation; **PREV EMPLOY:** Devel., Omni Intl. Hotels, Norfolk, Miami; Pres., Comml. Realty, Jacksonville; VP Housing Investment Corp., San Juan, P.R.; **PROFL AFFIL & HONORS:** Phi Delta Phi, Legal Frat. Sigma Phi Epsilon, Downtown Auth., Jacksonville, FL; **EDUC:** B of Marine Sci., ME Maritime Acad.; **GRAD EDUC:** LLB, NYU School of Law; **EDUC HONORS:** With Honors; **OTHER ACT & HONORS:** Dir., S. FL S&L, Miami, Big Orange "Man of the Year" award, 1977-78; **BUS ADD:** 350 N.E. 15th St., Miami, FL 33132, (305)358-4020.

ALSOP, S. Reid——**B:** Aug. 31, 1940, Providence, RI, *Atty./Advisor*, Chief Counsel's Office, Federal Highway Admin., US DOT, Right of Way and Environmental Law Div.; **PRIM RE ACT:** Attorney; **SERVICES:** Legal assistance relating to land use and acquisition, relocation assistance, and environmental matters; **REP CLIENTS:** Employees of the Fed. Hwy. Admin. and US Dept. of Transportation; **PROFL AFFIL & HONORS:** ABA, Section of Local Govt. Law; Transportation Research Bd., Administrator's Superior Achievement Award, 1978; **EDUC:** BA, 1962, Hist., Brown Univ.; **GRAD EDUC:** JD, 1968, Law, Boston Univ. Law School; **MIL SERV:** USN, Lt.j.g., 1962-1965; **HOME ADD:** 225 Sixth St., S.E., Washington, DC 20003, (202)547-1663; **BUS ADD:** 400 Seventh St., S.W., Washington, DC 20590, (202)426-0800.

ALSTON, Thaddas Lee——**B:** Apr. 7, 1945, Cairo, IL, Bogle & Gates, RE Dept.; **PRIM RE ACT:** Attorney; **OTHER RE ACT:** Lender Representation; **REP CLIENTS:** Nat. and Intl. Clients - for rep. list of clients of the firm, please see Martindale lenders, devel., forest products mfrs., farming in Seattle, King Cty. Bar Assn.; WA State Bar Assn.; ABA; Nat. Bar Assn.; Loren Miller Bar Assn.; **EDUC:** BA, 1967, Psych., Harvard Coll.; **GRAD EDUC:** 1970, Harvard Law School; **EDUC HONORS:** Cum Laude; **HOME ADD:** 3616 NE 169th, Seattle, WA 98155, (206)367-6593; **BUS ADD:** 900 4th Ave., Seattle, WA 98164, (206)682-5151.

ALSTROM, John——**B:** March 29, 1942, Fresno, CA, *VP*, John D. Lusk & Son, Indus.; **PRIM RE ACT:** Developer, Builder, Owner/Investor, Property Manager; **OTHER RE ACT:** Industrial Park Devel., Marketing; **SERVICES:** Buy, sale, lease, manage, devel. indus. parks; **PREV EMPLOY:** The Irvine Co., Coldwell Banker Brokerage Co.; **PROFL AFFIL & HONORS:** Nat. Assn. of Industrial and Office Parks (NAIOP); **EDUC:** BS, 1966, Bus. Admin., Brigham Young Univ.; **OTHER ACT & HONORS:** Member of 1968, US Olympic Mens Volleyball Team; **HOME ADD:** 6 Rimrock, Irvine, CA 92715, (714)851-2290; **BUS ADD:** 17550 Gillette Ave., Irvine, CA 92713, (714)557-8220.

ALTERSON, Marvin——**B:** Sept. 21, 1937, St. Louis, MO, *Owner*, Alterson Realty, Ltd.; **PRIM RE ACT:** Broker, Consultant, Developer, Owner/Investor, Property Manager, Syndicator; **SERVICES:** Devel., sales & synd. of comml. props.; **REP CLIENTS:** Indus. & inst. interests; **PREV EMPLOY:** Exec. VP, Creative Fin. Corp. of AZ and CA; **PROFL AFFIL & HONORS:** Phoenix Bd. of Realtors; Intl. Assn. of Realtors; IREF; **HOME ADD:** 5110 N. 42nd Pl., Phoenix, AZ 85018, (602)956-1000; **BUS ADD:** 2231 N. 24th St., Phoenix, AZ 85008, (602)267-1111.

ALTMAN, Leo S.——Preston, Altman, Parlapiano, Keilbach & Lytle; **PRIM RE ACT:** Attorney; **SERVICES:** RE, probate, corp. ins., water rights law; **PROFL AFFIL & HONORS:** Pueblo Cty., State of CO and ABA; Amer. Judic. Soc.; **EDUC:** Univ. of CO; **GRAD EDUC:** JD, Law, Univ. of CO; **BUS ADD:** POB 333, 501 Thatcher Bldg., Pueblo, CO 81002, (303)545-7325.

ALTMAN, Richard S.——**B:** Oct. 19, 1939, Erie, PA, *Pres.*, RSA Assoc.; **PRIM RE ACT:** Consultant, Architect, Developer, Owner/Investor; **SERVICES:** Devel. planning; **REP CLIENTS:** The Rouse Co., Forest City Enterprises, Nationwide Ins.; **PREV EMPLOY:** The Rouse Co., Design Mgr.; **PROFL AFFIL & HONORS:** AIA, APA, ULI, Nat. Trust; **EDUC:** BArch, 1962, Arch., Rensselaer, Troy, NY; **GRAD EDUC:** MArch, 1966, Urban Design, Washington Univ., St. Louis MO; **EDUC HONORS:** AIA Medal, NY Soc. of Arch. Award; **HOME ADD:** 5820 Pimlico Rd., Baltimore, MD 21209, (301)664-0488; **BUS ADD:** 5820 Pimlico Rd., Baltimore, MD 21209, (301)664-2926.

ALTMAYER, Jay P., II——**B:** Feb. 13, 1950, Chicago, IL; **PRIM RE ACT:** Developer, Owner/Investor; **PREV EMPLOY:** RE Appraiser, Prudential Ins. Co. 1976-77; **PROFL AFFIL & HONORS:** ULI; ABA; AL Bar Assn.; Intl. Council of Shopping Ctrs.; **EDUC:** BA, 1972, Hist., Tufts Univ.; **GRAD EDUC:** JD, 1975, RE, Tulane Univ.; MBA, 1976, RE, So. Methodist Univ.; **OTHER ACT & HONORS:** Pres., Kidney Found. of So. AL; Mbr., Bd. of Dir., Jr. Achievement of Mobile; Mobile Cty. Urban League; **HOME ADD:** 4904 Carmel Dr. N., AL, Mobile 36608, (205)343-1364; **BUS ADD:** 75 St. Michael St., P.O. Box 2782, Mobile, AL 36652, (205)438-2526.

ALTOBELL, Ernest J.——**B:** June 28, 1921, Detroit, MI, *V. Chmn.*, United Jersey Mortgage Co., Comml. Lending; **PRIM RE ACT:** Broker, Appraiser, Lender; **SERVICES:** Mort. banking, appraisal and consulting; **REP CLIENTS:** Builders, devels. and instit. lenders; **PREV EMPLOY:** Prudential Ins. Co., Mort. Loan Dept. 1948-69; United Jersey Bank 1969-72; **PROFL AFFIL & HONORS:** MBA, Builders Assn. of N. NJ, Dir.; **EDUC:** BS, 1954, Fin., Rutgers Univ., Newark, NJ; **MIL SERV:** US Army, Pvt.; **OTHER ACT & HONORS:** Condemnation Commr., Superior Ct., State of NJ; Lecturer and Speaker at Various Seminars and RE Courses.; **HOME ADD:** 721 Orchard Ln., Franklin Lakes, NJ 07417, (201)891-0608; **BUS ADD:** 25 E. Salem St., Hackensack, NJ 07602, (201)646-5900.

ALTOBELLI, Frank R.——**B:** Sept. 1, 1933, Dudley, PA, *Rgnl. Dir.*, RE/MAX of Mid Atlantic Sales, Inc.; **PRIM RE ACT:** Broker, Developer, Builder, Owner/Investor, Property Manager, Insuror; **OTHER RE ACT:** Rgnl. Dir. for RE/MAX franchise; **SERVICES:** Listings and sales, valuation, devel. of comml. & investment props., prop. mgmt., ins.; **REP CLIENTS:** Indiv. investors in comml. & investment props.; **PROFL AFFIL & HONORS:** NAR, MD Assn. of Realtors, RNMI, Prince George's Cty. Bd. of Realtors, Montgomery Cty. Bd. of Realtors, GRI, CRB; **EDUC:** BA, 1956, Rutgers Univ.; **MIL SERV:** USA; **OTHER ACT & HONORS:** Coll. Park City Councilman, 1969-71; Knights of Columbus, Coll. Park Bd. of Trade; **HOME ADD:** 800 Cliftonbrook Ln., Silver Spring, MD 20904, (301)384-1492; **BUS ADD:** 10013 Rhode Island Ave., College Park, MD 20740, (301)474-2400.

ALZOFON, Ethel Veedell——**B:** Aug. 6, 1921, Laconia, NH, *House Counsel*, Couch Mortgage Co.; **PRIM RE ACT:** Attorney; **SERVICES:** Atty. spec. in mort. loan law; **PREV EMPLOY:** Lecturer in Bus. Law (2 courses per semester, 1975-78) at Univ. of Houston, Central Campus, while working as house counsel for Couch Mort. Co.; **PROFL AFFIL & HONORS:** ABA; TX State Bar Assn.; Houston Bar Assn.; South Texas Coll. of Law Alumni Assn.; Assn. of Women Attys.; Iota Tau Tau (Prof. sorority of women attorneys) Treasurer '67-'68; **EDUC:** BA, 1940, Rice Univ.; **GRAD EDUC:** JD, 1967, S. TX Coll. of Law; **EDUC HONORS:** Lady Geddes Writing Award, 1937 (at Rice), E. E. Townes Scholastic Award, 1967 (at S. TX Coll. of Law); **OTHER ACT & HONORS:** Sharpstown Civic Club; Life Member Brandeis Univ. Women's Comm.; Hadassah; & Z.O.A.; Who's Who in TX, 1973-74, Who's Who Houston '80; **HOME ADD:** 6629 Sandstone, Houston, TX 77074, (713)776-0004; **BUS ADD:** 6401 Southwest Freeway, Houston, TX 77074, (713)771-4681.

AMARANTOS, Peter Thomas——**B:** Sept. 12, 1952, Chicago, IL, *RE Sales Assoc.*, Koenig & Strey, Inc.; **PRIM RE ACT:** Broker; **SERVICES:** All facets of listing and selling resid., comml. and indus. props.; **PROFL AFFIL & HONORS:** V Chmn. RPAC comm., V Chmn. Sprots Comm. for N. Shore Bd. of Realtors; **OTHER ACT & HONORS:** Northfield Township Tr. (1 yr., Northbrook, Glenview, Northfield and Unincorp., Cook Co.), Northfield Twp./ Regular Republican Org. Chicago Council on For. Affairs, Township officials of Cook Cty., Township Officials of IL; **HOME ADD:** 2144 Ash Ln., Northbrook, IL 60062, (312)564-5982; **BUS ADD:** 819 Waukegan Rd., Northbrook, IL 60062, (312)272-0330.

AMAYA, Al, Jr.——**B:** Feb. 23, 1954, Los Angeles, CA, *Pres.*, Limousines - West; **PRIM RE ACT:** Broker, Owner/Investor; **PROFL AFFIL & HONORS:** Better Bus. Bureau; Assn. of Bus. Mgmt.; **EDUC:** BA, 1978, Mktg. Mgmt., CA State, Los Angeles; **GRAD EDUC:** MBA, 1980, Bus. Mgmt., UCLA; **HOME ADD:** 18922 Gold Hill Dr., Walnut, CA 91789, (213)964-6795; **BUS ADD:** 1704 South 5th St., Suite 1, Alhambra, CA 91803, (213)289-5029.

AMBERG, Robert S., Jr.——**B:** Apr. 11, 1948, Detroit, MI, *Prop. Mgr.*, Oxford Group, Oxford Mgmt. Co. Inc.; **PRIM RE ACT:** Property Manager; **SERVICES:** Prop. Mgmt.; **REP CLIENTS:** Gen. partners; **PREV EMPLOY:** RE Sales; **PROFL AFFIL & HONORS:** Lansing Bd. of Realtors; W. MI Chapt., IREM, CPM; **EDUC:** BBA, 1970, Mktg., Western MI Univ.; **HOME ADD:** 3638 E. Meadows, Okemos, MI 48864, (517)349-9288; **BUS ADD:** 4295 Okemos Rd., Okemos, MI 48864, (517)349-2281.

AMBROSI, Robert J.——**B:** Apr. 2, 1950, Newark, NJ, *Exec. VP*, The Pivko Group, Inc.; **PRIM RE ACT:** Consultant, Owner/Investor, Syndicator; **EDUC:** BS Engrg., 1972, Engrg. Sci., NJ Inst. of Technology; **GRAD EDUC:** M Fin., 1974, Fin., Rutgers Univ.; **HOME ADD:** 5 Ronald Dr., Clifton, NJ 07013; **BUS ADD:** 10 E. 53rd St., NY, NY 10022, (212)355-4460.

AMBROSIO, Louis——*Dir. Fac. Engr.*, Everest & Jennings Intl.; **PRIM RE ACT:** Property Manager; **BUS ADD:** 2310 S. Sepulveda, Los Angeles, CA 90065, (213)879-1131.*

AMDUR, Ted——**B:** May 17, 1933, Chicago, IL, *Pres.*, Amdur Assoc., Inc., AMO; **PRIM RE ACT:** Property Manager; **SERVICES:** Devel. mktg. & mgmt. of multi-family housing devels. & comml. devels.; **REP CLIENTS:** HUD, IL Housing Devel. Auth., synds., lenders, investment grps.; **PROFL AFFIL & HONORS:** NAR, IAR, Chicago RE Bd., IREM, NAHB, Multi-Family Housing Assn. of IL, CPM, RAM; **EDUC:** BBA, 1955, Econ. & Fin., Univ. of MI; **MIL SERV:** USA, 1956-57, Cpl.; **OTHER ACT & HONORS:** 1981 VP IREM Chicago Chap.; Dir. Multi-family Housing Assn., of IL; Chmn. Shelter II; Chmn. Prop. Mgmt. Council of Chicago RE Bd.; Chmn. Legislative Affairs Comm. & Subsidized Housing Liaison Comm. of IREM, Chicago Chapt.; Author of numerous articles in profl. journals on prop. mgmt., lecturer & teacher before nat. confs. seminars & local RE indus. grps; **HOME ADD:** Deerfield, IL; **BUS ADD:** 666 Dundee Rd., Suite 305, Northbrook, IL 60062, (312)291-0010.

AMENTA, Michael J.——**B:** Apr. 21, 1933, NY, *Nat. RE Partner*, Laventhol & Horwath; **PRIM RE ACT:** Consultant; **OTHER RE ACT:** CPA, Tax Consultant; **SERVICES:** Acctg., Tax, Auditing & Consulting (RE Consulting div. is the largest in the world); **PREV EMPLOY:** CPA; **PROFL AFFIL & HONORS:** NAHB, RESSI, ICSC, Nat. Synd. Forum, NACREE, ULI, NACORE, NAR, MBA; **EDUC:** BBA, 1955, Public Acctg., City Univ. of NY; **EDUC HONORS:** Beta Alpha Psi (Acctg. Hon. Frat.); **MIL SERV:** USA, Spec.; **OTHER ACT & HONORS:** Pres., NYS Chapter of RESSI (1982); Bd. of Appeals & Zoning, Inc., Village of Port Washington N, 1966-81, Pres. Nassau Cty. Chapt. Catholic League, Assoc. Tr. Fin. Comm. of N. Shore Univ. Hosp., St. Francis Hosp., Dinner Comm., Treas. & Dir. Plandome Prop. Assoc., Inc., Co-Chmn. Plandome Imitation Tournament; **HOME ADD:** 102 Boulder Rd., Manhasset, NY 11030; **BUS ADD:** 919 Third Ave., NY, NY 10022, (212)980-3100.

AMES, Gil——**B:** Nov. 15, 1943, Chelsea, MA, *Asst. VP*, CT Savings Bank; **PRIM RE ACT:** Broker, Appraiser, Banker, Lender, Property Manager; **SERVICES:** Investment counseling,evaluation, const. & permanent fin., prop. mgmt.; **PROFL AFFIL & HONORS:** Assoc. Member, Soc. of RE Appraisers, Nat. Assn. of Review Appraisers, Assoc. Member, Nat. Assn. of Home Builders, CRA; **HOME ADD:** 92 Briarcliff Rd., Hamden, CT 06518, (203)288-0593; **BUS ADD:** 55 Church St., New Haven, CT 06510, (203)773-4226.

AMES, Ronald——**B:** Jan. 23, 1939, Bronx, NY, *Pres.*, Ames Mortgage Associates, Inc.; **PRIM RE ACT:** Appraiser, Lender; **PREV EMPLOY:** Central Savings Bank of NY 1964; Fin. S & L Assn. 1964-1967; Transcontinental Mort. Co. 1967-1972; Ames Mort. Assocs. 1973-Present; **PROFL AFFIL & HONORS:** Appraisal Instit. of RE Appraisers with MAI Designation; Soc. of RE Appraisers w/SREA Designation; Miami Bd. of Realtors; Builders Assn.of S. FL; Mort. Bankers Assn. of Greater Miami; Builders Assn. of S. FL; Econ. Soc. of S. FL; Intl. Council of Shopping Centers; Nat. Assn. of Indus. and Office Parks; FL Indus. Devel. Council; So. Indus. Devel. Council, Mort. Broker of the Year - 1970; Past Pres., FL Assn. of Mort. Brokers and twice Past Pres. of Miami Chap. of FL Assn. of Mort. Brokers; Designated S.M.C. Sr. Mort. Consultant - Nat. Assn. of Mort. Brokers; Introduced the Code of Ethics and Standards of Profl. Practices to the

FL Assn. of Mort. Brokers; Recipient of "Mort. Broker of the Year" award for the State of FL 1970 from the FL Assn. of Mort. Brokers; Past Pres. of the Soc. of RE Appraisers, Greater Ft. Lauderdale; SREA designated member of the Soc. of RE Appraisers; Soc. of RE Appraisers offices held: Program Chmn., Admissions Chmn., Research Comm. Chmn., Employment Chmn., Sec., Second VP, First VP, Chmn. - Merit Award Program Licensed RE Broker since 196l; Licensed Mort. Broker since 1967; **EDUC:** BA, 1961, Econ., Rutgers Univ.; **EDUC HONORS:** Dean's List; **OTHER ACT & HONORS:** Econ. Soc. of So. FL; **HOME ADD:** 4301 Monroe St., Hollywood, FL 33021, (305)989-2254; **BUS ADD:** 1825 N.W. 167th St./Ste. 108, Miami, FL 33056, (305)621-1500.

AMICK, Steven Hammond——B: May 13, 1947, Ithaca, NY, *Staff Atty.*, E.I. Dupont De Nemours & Co., Legal Dept. Corp. Law Div.; **PRIM RE ACT:** Attorney; **SERVICES:** Legal counsel (relocation and other RE); **REP CLIENTS:** Corp. house counsel representing Dupont's RE Div.; **PREV EMPLOY:** Private legal practice, Daley & Lewis, Attys., Wilmington, DE; **PROFL AFFIL & HONORS:** ABA, DE Bar Assn. (Comm. on Real and Personal Prop.); **EDUC:** BA, 1969, Pol. Sci., Washington Coll., Chestertown, MD; **GRAD EDUC:** JD, 1972, Law, Dickinson Sch. of Law; **OTHER ACT & HONORS:** Pres. Comm. of 39, Inc.; Pres. Breezewood Civic Assn.; Bd. of Dirs. Civic League for New Castle Cty.; **HOME ADD:** 449 W Chestnut Hill Rd., Newark, DE 19713, (302)738-0215; **BUS ADD:** Wilmington, DE 19898, (302)774-5667.

AMIEL, Victor——B: Apr. 28, 1934, Hilo, HI; **PRIM RE ACT:** Instructor, Property Manager; **SERVICES:** Comml. and Condo. Mgmt.; **REP CLIENTS:** (Type) Shopping Ctrs., Office Bldg., Condo's-Resid. & Office; **PROFL AFFIL & HONORS:** Honolulu Bd. of Realtors, IREM, CPM; **BUS ADD:** PO Box 8284, Honolulu, HI 96815, (808)923-0845.

AMIN, Purander Ambalal——B: Oct. 28, 1940, India, *Pres.*, Purander International, Inc.; **PRIM RE ACT:** Broker, Developer, Owner/Investor, Syndicator; **SERVICES:** Synd. Prop. Mgmt., Devel.; **REP CLIENTS:** Indiv., partnerships; **PROFL AFFIL & HONORS:** Bd. of Realtors; **GRAD EDUC:** BA (Econ.) B.Com. LL.B.ACA, Acctg. & Law, Gujarat Univ., India; **EDUC HONORS:** honors in Econ.; **HOME ADD:** 1442 N. Fairfax Ave., Los Angeles, CA 90046, (213)874-8421; **BUS ADD:** 7060 Hollywood Blvd #912, Los Angeles, CA 90028, (213)467-2206.

AMINOFF, Gary A.——B: Feb. 12, 1937, Los Angeles, CA, *Pres.*, Aminoff & Co.; **PRIM RE ACT:** Broker, Consultant, Developer, Owner/Investor, Property Manager, Syndicator, Real Estate Publisher; **OTHER RE ACT:** Instit. RE investment advisor; **SERVICES:** Investment counseling, devel. and synd. of comml. prop., prop. mgmt., rehab. of older comml. prop.; **REP CLIENTS:** Confidential, but available at personal interview; **PROFL AFFIL & HONORS:** National Assn. of Realtors; CA Assn. of Realtors; (NACORE); (FIABCI); (ICSC); National Apartment Assn.; (NAHB); Building Industry Assn. of So. CA; (AICPA); CA Syndication Forum; Ca Soc. of Public Accts.; Los Angeles Bd. of Realtors; Beverly Hills Bd. of Realtors (Pres. 1982); Beverly Hills C of C, CPA; **EDUC:** BS, 1959, Acctg., UCLA; **HOME ADD:** 478 Daniels Dr., Beverly Hills, CA 90210, (213)552-2556; **BUS ADD:** 9601 Wilshire Blvd., Suite 220, Beverly Hills, CA 90210, (213)858-6700.

AMIRKHAN, Michael——*Dir. Fac.*, Dataproducts Corp.; **PRIM RE ACT:** Property Manager; **BUS ADD:** 6200 Canoga Ave., Woodland Hills, CA 91365, (213)887-8000.*

AMIS, James J.——B: Nov. 25, 1939, Greenville, TX, *Pres.*, Urban Associates, Inc.; **PRIM RE ACT:** Consultant, Architect, Developer, Owner/Investor; **OTHER RE ACT:** Land planning, asset mgmt.; **SERVICES:** Devel. consulting, design, and asset mgmt.; **REP CLIENTS:** Northcross Assocs., Ltd.; Oryx Realty, Inc., D.F. Coker Investments; **PREV EMPLOY:** Pres., BOMA, San Francisco; **PROFL AFFIL & HONORS:** ULI; AIA; **EDUC:** BArch, 1962, Arch., TX A & M Univ.; **GRAD EDUC:** MBA, 1978, RE; Fin., Grad. School of Bus. Harvard Univ.; **EDUC HONORS:** Distinguished Student; AIA Medal; **HOME ADD:** 2803 Wooldridge Dr., Austin, TX 78703, (512)474-7166; **BUS ADD:** 708 West Tenth St., Austin, TX 78701, (512)474 6008.

AMMANN, Michael S.——B: May 27, 1947, Jackson, MI, *VP*, Grand Rapids Area C of C, Economic Devel.; **OTHER RE ACT:** Chamber Devel. Program; **SERVICES:** All available indus. bldg. & sites; **REP CLIENTS:** Deal with local firms interested in expanding plus new firm locations; **PREV EMPLOY:** Exec. Dir., Kalamazoo Cty. Econ. Expansion Corp. 1978-80; G.R. Chamber 1972-78 and 1980 to present; **PROFL AFFIL & HONORS:** Amer. Econ. Devel. Council; Great Lakes Devel. Council; VP, MI-IN Devel. Assn.; **EDUC:** BS, 1974, Bus., Grand Valley State Coll; **GRAD EDUC:** MBA, 1980, Seidman Grad. School; **MIL SERV:** USAF, S/Sgt.; **HOME ADD:** Apt. 6, 2734 Woodlake Rd., Wyoming, MI 49509; **BUS ADD:** 17 Fountain NW, Grand Rapids, MI 49509, (616)459-7221.

AMMAR, N.A., Jr.——B: Oct. 15, 1946, Beckley, WV, *VP-RE*, Ammar's Inc.; **PRIM RE ACT:** Attorney, Developer, Owner/Investor; **EDUC:** BA, 1968, WV Univ.; **GRAD EDUC:** JD, 1971, Harvard Law School; **EDUC HONORS:** Phi Beta Kappa, Magna Cum Laude, Fulbright Scholarship Recipient; **MIL SERV:** US Army, Capt.; **HOME ADD:** 520 Oakhurst Ave., Bluefield, WV, (304)325-3557; **BUS ADD:** S. College Ave., Bluefield, VA 24605, (703)322-4686.

AMMERMAN, Don——Major Realty Corp.; **PRIM RE ACT:** Developer; **BUS ADD:** Ste. 500, 5750 Mayer Blvd., Orlando, FL 32805, (305)351-1111.*

AMOS, John——*Ed.*, Farm & Land Inst. of the Nat'l. Assn of Realtors, Farm & Land Realtor; **PRIM RE ACT:** Real Estate Publisher; **BUS ADD:** 401 N. Michigan Ave., Chicago, IL 60611, (312)440-8040.*

AMSTADTER, Laurence——B: Apr. 9, 1922, Chicago, IL, *Pres.*, A. Epstein & Sons, Inc.; **PRIM RE ACT:** Architect; **PROFL AFFIL & HONORS:** Corp. Member AIA; Corp. Member Soc. of Amer. Registered Archs.; **EDUC:** Northwestern Univ.; **MIL SERV:** USAAF, Sgt., 4 Bronze Stars; **OTHER ACT & HONORS:** Standard Club, Chicago; **HOME ADD:** 1633 Cambridge Ave., Flossmoor, IL 60422, (312)798-1196; **BUS ADD:** 2011 Pershing Rd., Chicago, IL 60609, (312)847-6000.

ANASTASIA, Gary W.——B: Feb. 17, 1942, Newark, NJ, *Dir. of Devel.*, New Jersey Housing Finance Agency, Devel.; **PRIM RE ACT:** Lender; **SERVICES:** Review, evaluation, and recommendation of applications for fin. of multi-unit housing devels.; **REP CLIENTS:** Ltd. dividend and nonprofit sponsors of proposed housing devel. for families and the elderly; **PROFL AFFIL & HONORS:** Nat. Assn. of Housing and Redevelopment Officials; **EDUC:** BA, 1964, Govt., Seton Hall Univ.; **HOME ADD:** 32 York St., Lambertville, NJ 08530, (609)397-1065; **BUS ADD:** 3625 Quakerbridge Rd., Hamilton Twp., NJ 08619, (609)890-8900.

ANAYA, Toney——B: Apr. 29, 1941, Moriarty, NM, *Broker*, The Toney Anaya Agency; **PRIM RE ACT:** Attorney; **SERVICES:** Full; **PREV EMPLOY:** Seven years private law practice; NM Atty. General 1975-1978; Admin. Asst. Gov. Bruce King; 1970-1972; **PROFL AFFIL & HONORS:** Santa Fe Bd. of Realtors, NM Bar Assn.; Delta Theta Phi, New Mexico Jaycees Three Outstanding Young Men Award; New Mexico Press Award, 1976; Honorary Member Congregation B'Nai Israel; **EDUC:** 1964, Georgetown Univ., School of Foreign Service; **GRAD EDUC:** JD, 1968, Amer. Univ.; **OTHER ACT & HONORS:** State of NM, Atty. Gen. 75-78; **HOME ADD:** 826 Gonzales Rd., Santa Fe, NM 87501, (505)982-1638; **BUS ADD:** 915 Cerrillos St., Santa Fe, NM 87501, (505)983-3881.

ANDERFUREN, John A.——B: Jan. 8, 1949, Waukegan, *Pres.*, Anderfuren & Co.; **PRIM RE ACT:** Consultant, Developer, Builder, Syndicator; **SERVICES:** Mkt. research, mktg. packaging, investment counsel; **REP CLIENTS:** Comml. RE firms, owners, devels.; **PREV EMPLOY:** Govtl. Planning Exper., 5 yrs.; VP, Res. Const. Firm, 2 yrs.; **EDUC:** BS, 1973, Geography, Bradley Univ.; **GRAD EDUC:** MBA, 1977, RE/Mktg., Univ. of GA; **HOME ADD:** 1605 Cornus Ct., Suffolk, VA 23433, (804)238-2672; **BUS ADD:** Box 6065, Suffolk, VA 23433, (804)461-1311.

ANDERSON, Allan S.——B: Aug. 6, 1934, NY, NY, *Arch.*, Allan Anderson & Assoc., Arch. & Planners; **PRIM RE ACT:** Architect; **SERVICES:** Design, Const. Documents, Programming, Feasibility Studies.; **REP CLIENTS:** City of Rye, White Plains City School Dist., IBM, Allied Intl., Mamaroneck Schools.; **PREV EMPLOY:** 1960-72 Ulrich Franzen & Assoc, NY, 1958-59 Lawrence & Anthony Wolf, Archs., Pittsburgh, PA; **PROFL AFFIL & HONORS:** AIA, BOD., CEFP, NY Assn. Archs, Honor Award for excellence, 1977, etc.; **EDUC:** B. Arch., 1957, Carnegie-Mellon Univ.; **GRAD EDUC:** M. Arch., 1960, MIT; **EDUC HONORS:** AIA medal for gen. excellence in Arch., PA Soc. of Archs award, Overly prize, Thesis Prize, **MIL SERV:** USA Corps. of Engrs., 1st Lt., Post Engr. Commendation; **OTHER ACT & HONORS:** City of Rye Planning Comm. Chmn., Bd. of Advisors, Arts in Gen. Educ., Comm. Tr., Rye Presbyterian Church; **HOME ADD:** Mead Pond Lane, Rye, NY 10580, (914)967-2059; **BUS ADD:** Purchase St., Rye, NY 10580, (914)967-3494.

ANDERSON, Charles H.——B: Mar. 16, 1927, Brooklyn, NY, *Broker-Pres.*, Realty World Abide; **PRIM RE ACT:** Broker, Consultant, Developer, Property Manager; **SERVICES:** Res. sales new & existing, comml, ind., devel.; **PREV EMPLOY:** LTC (ret.) US Army; **PROFL**

AFFIL & HONORS: NAR, UAR, CRB; **EDUC:** Bus. Admin., 1950, Univ. of OR; **MIL SERV:** US Army, Lt. Col., Bronze Star-V, Legion Merit; **OTHER ACT & HONORS:** Mason, Shriner; **HOME ADD:** 1739 Apache Way, Ogden, UT 84403, (801)479-6237; **BUS ADD:** 3080 Wash. Blvd., Ogden, UT 84401, (801)394-6685.

ANDERSON, Connie K.——B: Oct. 8, 1941, Wymore, NE, *RE Comm. State Exec.*, WY RE Comm.; **PRIM RE ACT:** Broker; **SERVICES:** Lic. RE brokers and salesmen; **HOME ADD:** PO Box 2342, Cheyenne, WY 82001, (307)634-2026; **BUS ADD:** Supreme Ct. Bldg., Cheyenne, WY 82002, (307)777-6141.

ANDERSON, Daniel G.——B: July 26, 1939, Chicago, IL, *Sr. VP*, Strobeck Reiss & Co., Mgmt.; **PRIM RE ACT:** Broker, Consultant, Appraiser, Owner/Investor; **PROFL AFFIL & HONORS:** IREM - Chicago Board, CPM; **EDUC:** W. MI Univ.; **HOME ADD:** 118 Lewis Lane, Wheaton, IL 60181, (312)682-9729; **BUS ADD:** 134 S. LaSalle St., Chicago, IL 60603, (312)644-4800.

ANDERSON, David C.——B: Dec. 29, 1931, Honolulu, HI, *Pres.*, Resort Development Corp.; **PRIM RE ACT:** Developer, Builder; **PREV EMPLOY:** Pres., Inter-Is. Builders & Devels., Ltd., Pres., Grove Investment Grp., Inc., VP Papillon Helicopters, VP, Pooku Stables, Gen. Partner, Ke Nani Kai Resport, Gen. Partner, Ski Crest Lodge (CO); **EDUC:** BA, 1954, Bus. Admin., Claremont Men's Coll.; **MIL SERV:** US Army, Capt.; **OTHER ACT & HONORS:** Member, Young Presidents Organ., Member, AOPA; **HOME ADD:** Discovery Bay #3104, 1778 Ala Moana, Honolulu, HI 96817, (808)941-1402; **BUS ADD:** 1750 Kalakaua Ave., Suite 3704, Honolulu, HI 96826, (808)955-3727.

ANDERSON, David T.——*Chrmn/HUD Brd of Contract Appeals*, Department of Housing and Urban Development, Ofc. of Secy./Under Secy.; **PRIM RE ACT:** Lender; **BUS ADD:** 451 Seventh St., S.W., Washington, DC 20410, (202)673-6130.*

ANDERSON, Dennis——*Fin. Serv. Adm.*, Land O'Lakes Creameries, Inc.; **PRIM RE ACT:** Property Manager; **BUS ADD:** PO Box 116, Minneapolis, MN 55440, (612)481-2222.*

ANDERSON, Dennis C.——B: Mar. 13, 1948, Chicago, IL, *Pres.*, MBC Capital Corp.; **PRIM RE ACT:** Broker, Syndicator, Consultant, Owner/Investor; **SERVICES:** consulting, inv., synd., sec. brokerage; **REP CLIENTS:** Phys. & dentists; **PREV EMPLOY:** Gen Mgr. Coller RE, a small synd. and dev. co. in IN and FL; **PROFL AFFIL & HONORS:** RESSI; **EDUC:** BS, 1970, Fin., Univ. of IL; **GRAD EDUC:** JD, 1973, Law, IN Univ.; **OTHER ACT & HONORS:** Instructor at Northwestern Univ. Dental Sch.; **HOME ADD:** 600 Thames Pkwy., Park Ridge, IL 60068, (312)825-7345; **BUS ADD:** 460 S. NW Hwy, Park Ridge, IL 60068, (312)696-0220.

ANDERSON, Fenton——B: Chicago, IL, *Appraiser*, Fenton Anderson Agency; **PRIM RE ACT:** Broker, Consultant, Appraiser; **REP CLIENTS:** City of Phoenix, GM, Transamerica Employee Transfer, Employee Transfer Co.; **PROFL AFFIL & HONORS:** SREA, SRA; **OTHER ACT & HONORS:** Pres. Flint SREA Chap. 30, 1974-75; Accepted Nat. Award for Flint MI Chap. 30 as the Outstnading Chap. 1974-75; **HOME ADD:** PO Box 1961, Glendale, AZ 85311, (602)979-6065; **BUS ADD:** PO Box 1961, Glendale, AZ 85311, (602)979-6065.

ANDERSON, Fred M.——*Pres. R.E. Div.*, Union Oil of California; **PRIM RE ACT:** Property Manager; **BUS ADD:** PO Box 7600, Los Angeles, CA 90051, (213)977-7600.*

ANDERSON, Gene——B: Aug. 6, 1945, Charleston, SC, *Partner*, Industrial Property Group; **PRIM RE ACT:** Broker, Consultant; **SERVICES:** Indus. & Investment RE; **PREV EMPLOY:** VP, J.H. Ewing & Sons Atlanta; **PROFL AFFIL & HONORS:** SIR; Atlanta Indus. Network; Nat. Assn. of Indus. and Office Parks; GIDA and SIDC, Realtor Assoc. of the Year; Past Editor of the Atlanta RE Journal, Life Member Atlanta Million Dollar Club; **EDUC:** BA, 1967, Econ., Univ. of GA; **MIL SERV:** US Army, Capt., Commendation Medal; **HOME ADD:** 745 Heards Ferry Rd. NW, Atlanta, GA 30339; **BUS ADD:** Suite 360, 6520 Powers Ferry Rd. NW, Atlanta, GA 30339, (404)952-6100.

ANDERSON, Gerald E.——B: Apr. 22, 1934, Morris, IL, *Pres.*, Gerald E. Anderson & Assoc. Inc.; **PRIM RE ACT:** Broker, Syndicator, Consultant, Appraiser, Developer, Builder, Property Manager, Banker, Owner/Investor, Insuror; **SERVICES:** All the Above; **HOME ADD:** 251 Montgomery Rd., Montgomery, IL 60538, (312)897-7902; **BUS ADD:** 617 Montgomery Rd., Aurora, IL 60538, (312)898-7010.

ANDERSON, Harry——*VP Engr.*, Echlin Manufacturing Co.; **PRIM RE ACT:** Property Manager; **BUS ADD:** 175 N. Branford Rd., Branford, CT 06405, (203)481-5771.*

ANDERSON, Henry B.——B: May 30, 1918, Wilkinsburg, PA, *Atty.*, Cramer and Anderson; **PRIM RE ACT:** Attorney, Owner/Investor, Instructor; **SERVICES:** RE closing; lectures on resid. RE; **REP CLIENTS:** New Milford Savings Bank; CT Attys. Title Guaranty Fund; **PROFL AFFIL & HONORS:** Amer., CT., Litchfield Cty. Bar Assns.; **EDUC:** BA, 1940, Math/Classics, Wesleyan Univ.; **GRAD EDUC:** MA, 1948, Hist., Wesleyan Univ.; LLB, 1948, Law, UConn School of Law; **MIL SERV:** USN; Lt. Cdr.; Bronze Star, Silver Star; **HOME ADD:** Tower Hill Rd., Warren, CT 06754, (203)868-0757; **BUS ADD:** 51 Main St., New Milford, CT 06776, (203)355-2631.

ANDERSON, James K.——B: Aug. 3, 1935, San Rafael, CA, *Pres.*, MJM Inc.; **PRIM RE ACT:** Broker, Consultant, Developer; **OTHER RE ACT:** Mort. broker; **SERVICES:** Mgmt., Consulting brokerage (r.e. & mort.), devel.; **REP CLIENTS:** Urban cos., Various Fin. institutions & devel.; **PREV EMPLOY:** Prin. broker Cushman & Wakefield; Broker, Grubb & Ellis Comml. Brokerage Co.; **PROFL AFFIL & HONORS:** RNMI; NAR, CCIM; **EDUC:** BSEE, Egnrg & Mathematics, San Jose State Univ.; **MIL SERV:** USA, Enlisted man, Honorable discharge; **OTHER ACT & HONORS:** Bd. Dir. Exchange Club of Honolulu, Republican Party, Member of State Central Comm.; **HOME ADD:** 3176 E. Monoa Rd., Honolulu, HI 96822, (808)988-7788; **BUS ADD:** 900 Fort St. Mall, Suite 1410, Honolulu, HI 96813, (808)521-4791.

ANDERSON, Jerry D.——B: May 13, 1948, Canton, OH, *VP*, T.K. Harris/Realtors, Comml/Investment Div.; **PRIM RE ACT:** Broker, Instructor, Consultant, Owner/Investor, Real Estate Publisher; **SERVICES:** Faculty of RNMI of NAR Investment RE courses, Spec. in Mktg. of RE projects on the open brokerage mkt.; **PREV EMPLOY:** Developed racquetball clubs during 1977 and 1978; **PROFL AFFIL & HONORS:** Active nat. in RNMI, CCIM given by RNMI of NAR; **EDUC:** BS, 1970, Eng. and Educ., Univ. of Akron; **OTHER ACT & HONORS:** Articles published by NAR. Contractural agreement for investment text for RNMI; **HOME ADD:** 2970 Demington NW, Canton, OH 44718, (216)453-2637; **BUS ADD:** 3930 Fulton Drive NW, Canton, OH 44718, (216)492-8660.

ANDERSON, Joel H.——B: Nov. 4, 1942, Shreveport, LA, *Pres.*, Select Props., Realtor; **PRIM RE ACT:** Broker, Consultant, Developer, Builder, Property Manager, Syndicator; **PROFL AFFIL & HONORS:** Shreveport-Bossier Bd. of Realtors, Shreveport and Nat. Assn. of Home Builders; **EDUC:** BS, 1966, Bus. Admin. and RE, Centenary Coll. of LA; **OTHER ACT & HONORS:** St. Marks Episcopal Church, Petroleum Club of Shreveport, Univ. Club of Shreveport, Ambassodores Club of Shreveport; **HOME ADD:** 1022 Erie St., Shreveport, LA 71106; **BUS ADD:** 900 Pierremont, Suite 111, Shreveport, LA 71106, (318)865-0252.

ANDERSON, John A.——B: Dec. 23, 1951, Kenosha, WI, *Partner*, The Naiman Co.; **PRIM RE ACT:** Developer; **SERVICES:** Devel. comml. props.; prop. mgmt.; **PREV EMPLOY:** Chemical Bank 1975-78; **EDUC:** BSBA, 1974, Fin., Denver Univ.; **GRAD EDUC:** MBA, 1978, Fin., Mktg., NYU; **HOME ADD:** 1982 Azure Way, Encinitas, CA, (212)832-8298; **BUS ADD:** 45 W. 81st St., Ste. 1108, NYC, NY 10024, (212)362-9200.

ANDERSON, John H.——B: Sept. 27, 1947, Cherry Point, NC, *Sec./Treas.*, Rahn Properties, Inc.; **PRIM RE ACT:** Developer; **PREV EMPLOY:** VP in charge of Pittsburgh office of Galbreath Mort. Co.; **PROFL AFFIL & HONORS:** ULI; **OTHER ACT & HONORS:** Pittsburgh Athletic Assn.; **HOME ADD:** 1416 Ponce de Leon Dr., Fort Lauderdale, FL 33316, (305)463-3927; **BUS ADD:** 1702 Cordova Rd., Fort Lauderdale, FL 33316, (305)524-5336.

ANDERSON, John H.——B: Sept. 1, 1943, Brooklyn, NY, *Pres.*, John H. Anderson Development Corp.; **PRIM RE ACT:** Consultant, Developer, Builder, Owner/Investor, Property Manager; **REP CLIENTS:** Comml. prop. devel. and ownership for indiv., corp. and inst. investors; **PREV EMPLOY:** The Prudential Ins. Co. of Amer., RE Investment Dept., 1971-1980; **PROFL AFFIL & HONORS:** Houston C of C; The Forum Club of Houston; **EDUC:** BA, 1969, Bus. Mgmt., Fairleigh Dickinson Univ.; **GRAD EDUC:** MBA, 1971, Fin., Fairleigh Dickinson Univ.; **EDUC HONORS:** Cum Laude; **MIL SERV:** U.S. Army, Sp. 4, 1963-1965; **OTHER ACT & HONORS:** Boy Scouts of Amer.; **HOME ADD:** 10611 Riverview, Houston, TX 77042, (713)782-0409; **BUS ADD:** 1801 Main, Suite 1030, Houston, TX 77002, (713)650-1800.

ANDERSON, John Mackenzie——B: Dec. 1, 1938, Newark, OH, Peck, Shaffer & Williams; **PRIM RE ACT:** Attorney; **SERVICES:** Bond Counsel, FHA Counsel; Indus. Devel. and Fin.; **PROFL AFFIL & HONORS:** Assn. of the Bar of the City of NY; Cincinnati, OH State Bar Assns.; ABA; Nat. Assn. of Bond Lawyer; Amer. Judicature Soc.; VChmn. Amer. Found. for Temple Bar; Nat. Assn. of Coll. & Univ. Attys. & Local Govt. Law Comm. of ABA; **EDUC:** AB, 1960, Kenyon Coll.; **GRAD EDUC:** LLB, 1963, Yale Univ.; **BUS ADD:** 2000 First National Bank Center, 425 Walnut St., Cincinnati, OH 45202, (513)621-3394.

ANDERSON, John R.——B: May 11, 1931, Norfolk, VA, *Pres.*, Anderson Belanger Realty; **PRIM RE ACT:** Broker, Appraiser, Developer, Builder, Owner/Investor, Instructor, Property Manager; **SERVICES:** RE sales, servicing, appraising, mgmt., bldg. devel., ins. serv. & valuation; **REP CLIENTS:** Lenders first & second morts., instnl. investors in both resid. & comml. props.; **PREV EMPLOY:** Comml. trans pvt. indus., 1950-65; VA State Ports Auth., 1965-70; Dir. of Planning, 1970 to pres RE brokerage; **PROFL AFFIL & HONORS:** NAR, VA Assn. of Realtors, Tidewater Bd. of Realtors, Ind. Ins. Agents of Amer., Indep. Ins. Agents of VA, Ind. Ins. of Tidewater, Profl. Ins. Agents of VA, Metro. MLS, GRI, Univ. of VA, CRS; **EDUC:** 1948-51, Coll. of William & Mary; **MIL SERV:** USN, 2nd class Petty Officer, 1951-52; **OTHER ACT & HONORS:** Past Pres. & Bd. of Dirs. MLS of Tidewater, 1973-76; Bd. of Dirs. & VP VA Bch., Bd. of Realtors; **HOME ADD:** 4316 Delray Dr., Virginia Bch., VA 23455; **BUS ADD:** 3213 Virginia Bch. Blvd., Virginia Bch., VA 23452, (804)486-2262.

ANDERSON, Keith——B: June 21, 1917, Phoenix, AZ, *Partner*, Baker & Hostetler; **PRIM RE ACT:** Attorney; **SERVICES:** Representation in comml. RE transactions; shopping centers, office bgs., synds.; **PROFL AFFIL & HONORS:** Member, ABA, CO and Denver Bar Assns.; **EDUC:** AB, 1939, Dartmouth Coll.; **GRAD EDUC:** LLB, 1942, Harvard Law School; **OTHER ACT & HONORS:** Denver Planning Bd., 1968-1970; **BUS ADD:** 1600 Sherman St., #500, Denver, CO 80203, (303)861-0600.

ANDERSON, L.E.——*Director Corp Plng. & Dev.*, Pittsburgh-Des Moines Steel Co.; **PRIM RE ACT:** Property Manager; **BUS ADD:** Neville Island, Pittsburgh, PA 15225, (412)331-3000.*

ANDERSON, R. Bruce——B: Aug. 16, 1946, Cincinnati, OH, *Pres.*, Sterling-Mead, Inc.; **PRIM RE ACT:** Developer, Owner/Investor, Property Manager, Syndicator; **SERVICES:** Devel. of multi-family, single family & comml. props.; **PREV EMPLOY:** Hague Realtors - 1972 thru 1980; **PROFL AFFIL & HONORS:** Cincinnati Bd. of Realtors, Million Dollar Sales Status - 1979; **EDUC:** BBA, 1969, Acctg., Univ. of Cincinnati; **GRAD EDUC:** MBA, 1970, Fin., Univ. of Cincinnati; **MIL SERV:** US Army Res., Sgt.; **HOME ADD:** 9494 Raven Lane, Cincinnati, OH 45442, (513)984-1899; **BUS ADD:** 614 Provident Bank Bldg., Seventh & Vine St., Cincinnati, OH 45202, (513)381-5263.

ANDERSON, Richard C.——B: May 18, 1947, Long Beach, CA, *Mgr.-Comml. Props.*, Fairfield Communities, Inc., Fairfield Green Valley, Inc.; **PRIM RE ACT:** Syndicator, Developer, Builder, Property Manager; **SERVICES:** Acquisition, Devel. Const., Synd. & Mgmt. of Comml. Props.; **REP CLIENTS:** Safeway, Thrifty Drugs, Coast-to-Coast Stores, AZ Bank, Valley Natl. Bank, Pima Savings, First Natl. Bank, Home Fed. Savings, W. Savings, A.G. Edwards & Sons, Inc., Radio Shack; **PREV EMPLOY:** Del E. Webb Corp. 1974-1977; **PROFL AFFIL & HONORS:** ICSC, UNI, BOMA; **EDUC:** BS, 1969, Mktg., OR State Univ.; **GRAD EDUC:** MBA, 1970, Fin. Mktg., So. OR State; **EDUC HONORS:** Phi Kappa Theta Scholastic Frat.; **MIL SERV:** USA, E-5; **OTHER ACT & HONORS:** Exchange Club of Green Valley, Past Pres., T.E.A.M., No. Men's Golf Club; **HOME ADD:** 6710 Camino Padre Isidoro, Tucson, AZ 88718, (602)297-9579; **BUS ADD:** 999 S, LaCanada Dr., Green Valley, AZ 85614, (602)625-4441.

ANDERSON, Richard L.——B: Mar. 3, 1949, Omaha, NE, *Partner*, McGill, Koley, Parsonage & Lanphier P.C.; **PRIM RE ACT:** Attorney; **SERVICES:** Gen. legal serv.; **REP CLIENTS:** Lenders, indiv. and corp. investors, builders, suppliers; **PREV EMPLOY:** Planner,Omaha City Planning Dept. 1971-74; **PROFL AFFIL & HONORS:** ABA, NE Bar Assn., Omaha Bar Assn.; **EDUC:** BA, 1971, Econ., Univ. of PA; **GRAD EDUC:** JD, 1976, Creighton Univ.; **EDUC HONORS:** Cum Laude, Rock Mountain Mineral Law Found. Scholar., Articles Editor, Creighton Law Review; **HOME ADD:** 687 N. 59th St., Omaha, NE 68132, (402)551-0367; **BUS ADD:** 10010 Regency Cir. Ste. #300, Omaha, NE 68114, (402)397-9988.

ANDERSON, Robert——*VP*, David Cronheim Co.; **PRIM RE ACT:** Developer; **BUS ADD:** 205 Main St., Chatham, NJ 07928, (201)635-2180.*

ANDERSON, Robert Barber——B: Apr. 17, 1944, NJ (Summit), *Principal*, Kerns Group Arch.; **PRIM RE ACT:** Architect; **SERVICES:** Full range of arch. serv. and office space planning; **REP CLIENTS:** Fed. and Local Gov., and Private Corp., Dev. and Indiv.; **PROFL AFFIL & HONORS:** AIA, Progressive Arch. Nat. Design Citation 1981; **OTHER ACT & HONORS:** Falls Church City Arch. Adv. Bd.; **BUS ADD:** 1101 17th St., N.W., Suite 900, Washington, DC 20036, (202)466-4876.

ANDERSON, Robert H.——B: Oct. 13, 1944, Dayton, OH, *Assoc. Reg. Counsel Atty.*, Chicago Title Ins. Co.; **PRIM RE ACT:** Attorney; **OTHER RE ACT:** Title Ins. Counsel; **SERVICES:** Counseling in RE legal issues & all settlement servs.; **REP CLIENTS:** Lenders & devels. in all phases of resid. & comml. devel.; **PREV EMPLOY:** Counsel to Mort. Dept. of CT Hon. Fin. Auth.; **PROFL AFFIL & HONORS:** ABA; Officer of Real Prop. Exec Comm. of CT Bar Assn., Legislative Comm. & Said Comm.; **EDUC:** BA, 1966, Pol. Sci., Hist., So. CT State Coll.; **GRAD EDUC:** JD, 1974, Law, U Conn.; **EDUC HONORS:** Dean's List, Jr. & Sr. yrs., Jurisprud. award, torts; **MIL SERV:** USMC; Cpl.; Distinguished Meritorious Medal; **OTHER ACT & HONORS:** Republican Town Comm. & Congressional Delegate, Vernon Permanent Municipal Bldg. Comm.; **HOME ADD:** 139 Jonathan Dr., Vernon, CT 06066, (203)875-5220; **BUS ADD:** 60 Washington St., Hartford, CT 06106, (203)249-1661.

ANDERSON, Roger O.——B: July 27, 1955, Elmhurst, IL, *Mgr.*, Filbey Summers & Co.; **PRIM RE ACT:** Consultant; **OTHER RE ACT:** CPA; **SERVICES:** Investment analysis, tax planning, projections, audits, lectures; **REP CLIENTS:** Investors, brokers, devel., prop. mgrs.; **PROFL AFFIL & HONORS:** IL Soc. of CPA's; DuPage Cty. Estate Planning Council; **EDUC:** BS, 1977, Acctg., Univ. of IL (Urbana); **GRAD EDUC:** MAS, 1978, Acctg., Tax, Univ. of IL (Urbana); **EDUC HONORS:** Bronze Tablet, Highest Honors; **OTHER ACT & HONORS:** Instr. of Taxation - Aurora Coll.; CPA; **BUS ADD:** 2121 W. Galena Blvd., Aurora, IL 60506, (312)859-7400.

ANDERSON, William H.——B: July 28, 1933, Conroe, TX, *Arch*, Anderson Assoc. Architects/Planners; **PRIM RE ACT:** Architect; **SERVICES:** Arch./Planning; **PROFL AFFIL & HONORS:** AIA, SCAIA Hon. & Merit Award; **EDUC:** BArch, 1956, TX AM; **MIL SERV:** USAF 1956-59, Capt.; **OTHER ACT & HONORS:** SC Building Code Council; **HOME ADD:** 1518 Richland St., Columbia, SC 29201, (803)254-8788; **BUS ADD:** 1518 Richland St., Columbia, SC 29201, (803)254-8788.

ANDERSON, William V.——B: Cincinnati, OH, *Consultant, Project Mgr.*, Self Employed; **PRIM RE ACT:** Syndicator, Consultant, Developer, Owner/Investor; **SERVICES:** Fin. and Dev.; **EDUC:** AB, 1972, Hist., Eng., Dartmouth Coll.; **GRAD EDUC:** MBA, 1974, Fin. & Planning, Amos Tuck; **EDUC HONORS:** Cum Laude; **HOME ADD:** 38 Elm St., Marblehead, MA 01945, (617)639-0322; **BUS ADD:** 38 Elm St., Marblehead, MA 01945, (617)523-8678.

ANDRADE, Eugene J.——B: March 6, 1937, Hanford, CA, *Pres.*, Andrade Devel. Co./ Andrade Realty, Inc.; **PRIM RE ACT:** Broker, Developer, Builder, Property Manager, Owner/Investor; **PROFL AFFIL & HONORS:** BIA, Fresno Bd. of Realtors; **EDUC:** BS, 1960, Bus., Fresno State Coll.; **HOME ADD:** 1511 W. Dovewood, Fresno, CA 93711, (209)439-9580; **BUS ADD:** 1620 W. Fairmont, Fresno, CA 93711, (209)225-4400.

ANDRESS, Nina J.——B: Nov. 3, 1942, TX, *Dir. of Acquisitions, Equities, & Loan Placement*, Joe Feagin Investments; **PRIM RE ACT:** Broker, Syndicator, Consultant; **OTHER RE ACT:** Loan Placements; **PREV EMPLOY:** 6 yrs. in comml. mort. banking; **PROFL AFFIL & HONORS:** Member of the RE Securities & Synd. Inst., NAR, NASD; **EDUC:** Econ. and Mktg., TX Tech. Univ.; **HOME ADD:** 9201 Fair Oaks, #309, Dallas, TX 75231, (214)348-5682; **BUS ADD:** 4835 L.B.J. Freeway, #640, Dallas, TX 75234, (214)386-4336.

ANDREWS, Al E., Jr.——B: Aug. 31, 1945, McComb, MS, *Part.*, Trammell Crow - Farnsworth Co.; **PRIM RE ACT:** Broker, Developer, Property Manager, Owner/Investor; **SERVICES:** Office Space Dev., Mktg., Managing; **PREV EMPLOY:** Admin. Asst. - US Congressman; **PROFL AFFIL & HONORS:** BOMA; **EDUC:** BS, 1967, Bus. & Mktg., Univ. of S MS; **EDUC HONORS:** Outstanding Male Grad. O.D.K., Distinguished Mil. Grad.; **MIL SERV:** USA, 1st Lt., Bronze Star, Army Commendation Medal W/"V" Device, Vietnam 1968; **HOME ADD:** 6656 Corsica, Memphis, TN 38101, (901)685-1015; **BUS ADD:** #266 1255 Lynnfield Rd., Memphis, TN 38119, (901)761-1700.

ANDREWS, Frank L.——B: June 8, 1950, Rhinebeck, NY, *Atty.*, Miller Canfield Paddock and Stone; **PRIM RE ACT:** Consultant, Attorney; **SERVICES:** Counseling & closing service in RE fin.

transactions, land acquisition and devel., construction contracts, prop. leasing; **REP CLIENTS:** Construction and permanent lenders and devel. of comml. prop.; public urban devel. authorities; **PREV EMPLOY:** MI State Housing Devel. Authority, 1972-1973; **PROFL AFFIL & HONORS:** ABA; MI Bar Assn., Real Prop. Law Sect., Seminar Speaker, MI Bar Assn., topic 'Aids to Devel., 1981'; **EDUC:** BS, 1972, Math./Econ., MI State Univ.; **GRAD EDUC:** JD, 1976, Harvard Law School; **EDUC HONORS:** Magna Cum Laude, Phi Beta Kappa, Cum Laude, CRCL Law Review; **HOME ADD:** 2880 W. Huron St., Pontiac, MI 48054, (313)683-2416; **BUS ADD:** Wabeek Bldg., Birmingham, MI 48012, (313)645-5000.

ANDREWS, LeRoy M.——B: May 20, 1921, Hughesville, PA, *Pres.*, LeRoy Andrews Architects, Inc.; **PRIM RE ACT:** Architect, Syndicator, Consultant, Developer; **SERVICES:** Arch.; Energy Consultant; prop. devel.; **REP CLIENTS:** Govt. and Private Clients; **PREV EMPLOY:** Aeronautical Engr. 1943-1952; **PROFL AFFIL & HONORS:** Amer. Inst. of Arch. - Past Pres. - Ventura Chapter, Designer of First Solar Fire Station in World; Masonry Inst. Arch. Award; So. CA Edison Co. Arch. Award; **EDUC:** 1940, Engrg., Williamsport Tech. Inst.; **EDUC HONORS:** Grad third in class; **MIL SERV:** US Army, Pvt.; **OTHER ACT & HONORS:** Chmn., Bldg. Code Appeals Bd., City of Ventura; Mason; Rotary; Advisory Bd., Ventura Coll. District; Advisory Bd., Ventura School for Girls; Pres., Ventura Cty. Vocational Resources Comm.; Indus. Education Council; **HOME ADD:** 344 Lynnbrook Ave., Ventura, CA 93003, (805)642-3382; **BUS ADD:** 2284 South Victoria Ave., Suite 2A, Ventura, CA 93003, (805)642-3288.

ANDREWS, William J., Jr.——B: Oct. 21, 1931, Tappahannock, VA, *VP*, F. & M. Mortgage Corp., Resid.; **PRIM RE ACT:** Banker, Lender; **SERVICES:** Acquisition, devel., constr., and permanent fin. on resid. props.; **REP CLIENTS:** Devel. & builders of resid. props.; **PREV EMPLOY:** Phillips-Hall, Inc., Realtors, Richmond, VA, 1956-64; **PROFL AFFIL & HONORS:** AIB, MBA; **EDUC:** BA, 1952, Bus. Admin., Univ. of Richmond; **MIL SERV:** USA, 1952-54, 1st Lt.; **HOME ADD:** 5700 Mechanicsville Pike, Mechanicsville, VA 23111, (804)746-5144; **BUS ADD:** 1512 Willow Lawn Dr., PO Box 27571, Richmond, VA 23261, (804)289-3637.

ANDÚJAR, Edwin Andújar——B: Oct. 18, 1927, Utuado, PR, *Pres.*, Lcdo. Edwin Andújar & Assoc.; **PRIM RE ACT:** Attorney, Consultant, Appraiser; **SERVICES:** RE Consultants & Appraisers, City and Regional Planning Consultants; **PREV EMPLOY:** Atty. for the Land Div. of the Dept. of Justice of the Commonwealth of PR and Atty. for the Planning Bd. of PR; Chief of the RE Dept. of the Municipality of San Juan, PR; **PROFL AFFIL & HONORS:** Who's Who's Among Students in Amer. Univ. & Coll. (1951); **EDUC:** Baccalaurei, 1951, Econ., Univ. of PR; **GRAD EDUC:** JD, 1954, Civil Law, Univ. of PR; **EDUC HONORS:** Cum Laude, Ad Gradum; **OTHER ACT & HONORS:** Atty. for the Commonwealth in the Land Div., Planning Db. and Municipality of San Juan, PR; Disciples of Christ Christian Church; **HOME ADD:** #108 Rubicón, Paradise Hills, Río Piedras, PR 00926, (809)767-5104; **BUS ADD:** Urb. Baldrich, Calle Presidente Uamírez 173-A, Hato Rey, PR 00919, (809)764-6222.

ANGEL, Joseph W.——B: Feb. 23, 1944, Kansas City, MO, *Pres*, Restaurant Management Northwest, Inc.; **PRIM RE ACT:** Developer, Property Manager, Owner/Investor, Builder, Syndicator; **SERVICES:** Devel. of restaurant & retail props.; **PROFL AFFIL & HONORS:** Restauranteur of the Yr., 1981; Pres. Restaurants of OR Assn., 1978-79; **EDUC:** BS, 1967, Bus. Adm., KS Univ.; **MIL SERV:** USCG, E-4; **HOME ADD:** 5100 NW Skyline Blvd., Portland, OR 97229; **BUS ADD:** 1523 NE 6th Ave., Portland, OR 97232, (503)249-6931.

ANGEL, Robert S.——B: Aug. 8, 1925, Oakland, CA, *Pres.*, Angel Investment & Ins.; **PRIM RE ACT:** Broker, Syndicator, Consultant, Developer, Property Manager, Owner/Investor, Insuror; **SERVICES:** Synd. of Apt. Bldgs./Investment Consultation; **REP CLIENTS:** Prop. Mgmt.; **PREV EMPLOY:** John Hancock Life Ins.; **PROFL AFFIL & HONORS:** RESSI, Realtor Contra Costa Bd.; **EDUC:** BS, 1948, Econ., Univ. CA - Berkeley; **MIL SERV:** USA Air Corps., Lt.; **OTHER ACT & HONORS:** Past Pres. Mt. Diablo Life Underwriters Commonwealth Club; **HOME ADD:** 61 St. Thomas Ln., Pleasant Hill, CA 94523, (415)671-9234; **BUS ADD:** 1791 Detroit Ave., Concord, CA 94523, (415)676-3210.

ANGELUS, Loukas M.——B: May 16, 1929, Minneaplis, MN, *Supr.*, City of Minneapolis, Assessors Dept.; **PRIM RE ACT:** Assessor; **REP CLIENTS:** not applicable; **PROFL AFFIL & HONORS:** SREA, Sr. Resid. Appraiser (SRA), Accredited MN Assessor (A.M.A.); **EDUC:** BS, BA, 1954, Bus. Admin., Macalester Coll., St. Paul, MN.; **MIL SERV:** USNR, LCDR; **OTHER ACT & HONORS:** Amer. Legion, Shrine; **HOME ADD:** 6424 Josephine Ave. So., Edina, MN 55435, (612)941-1847; **BUS ADD:** A2106 Hennepin Govt. Ctr. 55487, (612)348-2397.

ANNEKAN, William——*Exec. VP Fin.*, Palm Beach Co.; **PRIM RE ACT:** Property Manager; **BUS ADD:** 400 Pike St., Cincinnati, OH 45202, (513)241-4260.*

ANNELIN, James S.——B: Jan. 18, 1947, Ishpeming, MI, *Dir. Contract Admin.*, Resort Condominiums Intl. Inc.; **PRIM RE ACT:** Attorney; **SERVICES:** Timeshare Exchange; Legal; **PREV EMPLOY:** General Counsel, Non-Profit S&L Corp. 1976-1981; **PROFL AFFIL & HONORS:** PA, IN, & Amer. Bar Assn.; **EDUC:** BA, 1969, Hist., Univ. of MI; **GRAD EDUC:** JD, 1976, Univ. of Pittsburgh; **EDUC HONORS:** Dean's List; **HOME ADD:** 4502 Washington Blvd, Indianapolis, IN 46205, (317)283-7106; **BUS ADD:** PO Box 80229, Indianapolis, IN 46280, (317)846-4724.

ANSTIS, James H.——B: Feb. 4, 1941, Hobe Sound, FL, *Arch.*, Anstis Vass Ornstein Arch. & Planners, Inc.; **PRIM RE ACT:** Architect; **SERVICES:** Arch. & Planners; **REP CLIENTS:** STP Corp., IBM Corp., State of FL, Palm Beach Cty., FL Nat. Serv. Ind., Lennar Corp.; **PROFL AFFIL & HONORS:** AIA, Sec. of FL Assn. of the AIA; **EDUC:** BArch, 1967, Univ. of FL; **EDUC HONORS:** Gargoyle Arch. & Fine Arts Hon.; **MIL SERV:** USN, SM2; **OTHER ACT & HONORS:** Chmn.-Palm Beach Cty. Citizen's Task Force on Zone & Land Dev. Codes 16 yrs.; **HOME ADD:** 204 Rutland Blvd., W Palm Beach, FL 33405, (305)588-2794; **BUS ADD:** 333 S Blvd., West Palm Beach, FL 33405, (305)655-2540.

ANTHONY, Alvin H.——*Vice President*, Anthony Industries; **PRIM RE ACT:** Property Manager; **BUS ADD:** 4900 Triggs Street, Lawrence, CA 90022, (213)268-4877.*

ANTHONY, Clifford E.——B: GA, *Pres.*, Florida American Corp.; **PRIM RE ACT:** Developer, Owner/Investor; **EDUC:** AB, Fremont Univ.; **GRAD EDUC:** MA, Fremont Univ.; PhD, London Coll. of Applied Sci.; **HOME ADD:** P O Box 160, Ft. Walton Beach, FL 32549; **BUS ADD:** Fort Walton Beach, FL 32549P O Drawer 160, (602)867-4500.

ANTINOZZI, D.P., Jr.——B: Feb. 2, 1920, Derby, CT, *Pres. & Principal of Firm / All Phase Supr.*, Antinozzi Assoc., P.C., Arch.; **PRIM RE ACT:** Architect; **OTHER RE ACT:** Registered Arch./Lic. in NY (1951) CT (1953) NJ (1952) FL (1955) and NC (1977); **PROFL AFFIL & HONORS:** AIA; Nat. Council of Arch. Registration Boards, AIA / Medal of Excellence in Arch./1943; Who's Who in the East /1942 & 1943; **EDUC:** BArch, 1943, Catholic Univ. of Amer., Wash.,DC; **EDUC HONORS:** AIA Award for Excellence in Arch./ 1943; **MIL SERV:** USN, Lt./Sr. 1943/1947; **OTHER ACT & HONORS:** Gov.'s Task Force on Housing / 1972; Gov.'s Commn. on Feasibility Study for Bridge from Bridgeport Area to Long Island/ 1970; Dinan Ctr. Commn., Bridgeport/ 1972; **HOME ADD:** 3392 Huntington Rd., Stratford, CT 06497, (203)378-4531; **BUS ADD:** 4021 Main St., Stratford, CT 06497, (203)377-1300.

ANTONICH, M. Betty——B: Sept. 20, 1937, Charlotte, NC, *Pres. (Broker/Owner)*, RE/MAX Realty, Inc.; **PRIM RE ACT:** Broker, Syndicator, Consultant, Developer, Property Manager, Owner/Investor; **SERVICES:** Full Service RE Co.; **PREV EMPLOY:** 15 yrs. exper. RE broker; **PROFL AFFIL & HONORS:** FL Assn. of Realtors; NAR; FL RE Exchangors; Delta, Delta, Delta, GRI; CRS; CCIM; **EDUC:** 1958, Eng./Chem./Educ., Brenau Coll., Gainsville, GA; **HOME ADD:** 437 N. Halifax #11, Daytona Beach, FL 32018, (904)253-4983; **BUS ADD:** 444 Seabreeze Blvd., Suite 325, Daytona Beach, FL 32018, (904)253-1115.

ANTONUCCI, Francis J.——B: Nov. 7, 1949, Cleveland, OH, *Atty.*, Berkowitz, Balbirer & McLachlan, PC; **PRIM RE ACT:** Attorney; **SERVICES:** Condo., co-operative conversions; RE tax planning; synds.; **REP CLIENTS:** Several Banks and RE Devels. and Builders; **PREV EMPLOY:** Numerous condo. and co-operative conversions; sale and leaseback transactions; synds.; **PROFL AFFIL & HONORS:** ABA; CT Bar Assn., MA Bar Assn.; **EDUC:** 1969, Fin. and Acctg., Boston Coll.; **GRAD EDUC:** 1974, Univ. of Toledo; JD, 1975, Boston Univ.; **EDUC HONORS:** LLM taxation; **MIL SERV:** US Army 1970-72, Spec. 4; **HOME ADD:** 105 Katona Dr., Fairfield, CT 06430, (203)334-4441; **BUS ADD:** 64 Post Rd., W., Westport, CT 06880, (203)226-1001.

APICELLI, Anthony J., Jr.——B: Oct. 5, 1947, Neptune,NJ, *Part.*, Kelsey, Kelsey, Radick, Apicelli and Kline, Esq.; **PRIM RE ACT:** Attorney; **SERVICES:** Legal services and investment counseling in residential, comml. and indus. R.E.; **REP CLIENTS:** The Natl. State Bank, Elizabeth, NJ, Purchasers and sellers of residential, comml. and indus. props. including lending instns.; **PROFL AFFIL & HONORS:** ABA, NJ Bar Assn., Mercer Cty. Bar Assn.(Bd. of Tr.)Assn. of R.E.

Attys.(Sec.); **EDUC:** BA, 1969, Pol. Sci., LaSalle Coll., Phila. PA; **GRAD EDUC:** JD, 1972, Tax and Comml. Law, Rutgers Univ. School of Law, Camden; **OTHER ACT & HONORS:** Lawrence Fed. Credit Union, Pres., DE Valley United Way (Chmn. Lawyers Div.); Rotary Club of Trenton, Bd. of Tr. DE Valley Council Girl Scouts of Amer.; Delegate to the General Council NJ State Bar Assn. (1982); **HOME ADD:** One Tina Dr., Titusville, NJ 08560, (609)883-6955; **BUS ADD:** 28 W. State St., Trenton, NJ 08608, (609)396-9135.

APPEL, Allan F.——B: Feb. 23, 1946, Brooklyn, NY, *Tax Partner*, Fiske & Company, CPA's; **OTHER RE ACT:** CPA; **SERVICES:** Consultations & Project Org.; **PROFL AFFIL & HONORS:** AICPA; FL Inst. of CPA's; FL Bar; ABA; Greater Miami Tax Inst.; Amer. Assn. of Atty CPA's, CPA; Atty.; **EDUC:** BA, 1967, Labor Relations/Acctg., PA State Univ.; **GRAD EDUC:** MPA; MSM; JD, 1971/1980/1973, Public Admin.; Acctg. (Tax); Law, Golden Gate Univ.; FL Intl. Univ.; Univ. of Miami Law School; **MIL SERV:** USAF, 1st LT (1969-1972), USAF Commendation Medal; **OTHER ACT & HONORS:** Author of Various Published Tax Articles/Seminars/ Books, etc.; **HOME ADD:** 12410 SW 106 Terr., Miami, FL 33186; **BUS ADD:** 18441 NW 2nd Ave., Suite 218, Miami, FL 33169, (305)653-4200.

APPEL, James R.——B: July 3, 1920, St. Louis, MO, *Pres.*, Real Estate Analysts Ltd.; **PRIM RE ACT:** Consultant, Appraiser; **SERVICES:** RE appraisals, market analyses; **PREV EMPLOY:** Pres., RE Research Corp., Chicago, IL; **PROFL AFFIL & HONORS:** MAI, SRPA, AIREA; **EDUC:** AB, 1942, Poli. Sci., Municipal Govt., Econ., Univ. of IL; **MIL SERV:** US Army, T/Sgt.; **HOME ADD:** 40 Springfield Ct., Glendale, MO 63122, (314)962-5072; **BUS ADD:** 9818 Clayton Rd., St. Louis, MO 63124, (314)997-7325.

APPEL, Stanley S.——B: Nov. 16, 1922, NY, NY, *Chmn. of The Bd.*, First Hospitality Corporation of America/First Companies of America; **PRIM RE ACT:** Broker, Consultant, Appraiser, Developer, Builder, Owner/Investor, Property Manager, Syndicator, Real Estate Publisher; **SERVICES:** Devel. of hotels, motels & inns, feasibility studies, hotel mgmt. office parks & bldgs.; **PREV EMPLOY:** RE appraiser FHA, HUD 1955-64; Prime Equities 1965-75; **PROFL AFFIL & HONORS:** NAREE; RE War Veterans Assn.; Rights of Way Soc.; Young Bankers Assn.; Pres. Fin. Comm., Republican Party CT, Licensed RE Broker NJ, NY, CT; Bd. of Dir. , Interchange State Bank; Man of Yr.-Young Fin. of Amer., 1972; **EDUC:** BA, 1942, Econ., Bus. Admin., NYU; **GRAD EDUC:** MA, 1948, Econ., banking, W TX State; **EDUC HONORS:** Nat. Honor Soc.; **MIL SERV:** USAF; Maj.; Varied awards, CT State Guard, Res.; Lt. Col.; **OTHER ACT & HONORS:** Justice of the Peace, Danbury, CT 12 yrs.; Danbury Club; Tau Alpha Omega Frat. Delta Chap.; Archaelogical Inst. of Amer.; Nat. Archeology Inst. (trustee); also assoc'd with First Realty Advisors; First Union Mort.; Huntly Mgmt. Grp., Ltd.; **HOME ADD:** 5 Horizon Dr., Ft. Lee, NJ 07024, (201)368-1400; **BUS ADD:** 395 W. Passaic St., Rochelle Park, NJ 07662, (201)368-1400.

APPINO, Robert J.——B: Jan. 3, 1947, Frontenaz, KS, *VP*, Southboro Development Co., Inc. - Southboro Estates, Inc.; **PRIM RE ACT:** Consultant, Developer, Builder, Owner/Investor; **SERVICES:** Land Devel. and/or Consultant, Right of Way Land Purchasing; **PREV EMPLOY:** RE Agent 1975-Present, Mgt. Analyst KS Dept. of Transportation, Counselor - HUD; **PROFL AFFIL & HONORS:** Topeka Homebuilders Assoc., Nat. Home Builders Assoc., Topeka Board of Realtors, KA Board of Realtors, NAR, International Right of Way Assoc.; **EDUC:** BS, 1970, Bus. Psych., Pittsburgh State Univ.; **HOME ADD:** PO Box 5435, Topeka,, KS 66605, (913)267-5708; **BUS ADD:** 701 Jackson, Topeka, KS 66603, (913)233-1208.

APPLEBAUM, Jerome M.——B: Apr. 7, 1930, Chicago, IL, *Atty. at Law*; **PRIM RE ACT:** Attorney, Instructor, Consultant, Developer; **SERVICES:** Legal serv. related to real prop. investment, mgmt., synd., etc.; **REP CLIENTS:** San Gabriel Valley Bank, various independent and franchise RE brokerage groups; **PREV EMPLOY:** Govt. contract Admin. and mgmt. systems consultant, 1968-73; **PROFL AFFIL & HONORS:** Foothill Bar Assoc., Lawyers Club of Los Angeles Cty., Voluntary (pro bono) judge pro tem program, Santa Anita Judicial district, Alhambra judicial district, Rio Hondo judicial district; **EDUC:** BS, Bus. Admin., Engrg., UCLA; **GRAD EDUC:** JD, 1970, UCLA School of Law; **EDUC HONORS:** Assoc. Editor Law Review; **MIL SERV:** USA, Major, Field art.; **OTHER ACT & HONORS:** Bd. of Tr., Temple Sharei Tikvah; Pres., Men's Club, Temple Sharei Tikvah, Arcadia; **HOME ADD:** 5210 N. Ansdeil Pl., Arcadia, CA 91006, (213)442-3103; **BUS ADD:** 11706 Ramona Blvd. Suite 210, El Monte, CA 91732, (213)579-0877.

APPLEFIELD, Lawrence——B: Oct. 4, 1930, NY, *VP*, Ctry Manor Homes, Inc., Ctry Manor Const.; **PRIM RE ACT:** Broker, Developer, Builder; **PROFL AFFIL & HONORS:** FL Home Builders, Pasco Builders Assn., NAHB., Past Pres. Pasco Builders Assn.; **EDUC:** BA, Educ. Hist., C.W. Post Coll., Brooksville, NY; **GRAD EDUC:** LLB, 1968, Portia Law School, Boston, MA; **EDUC HONORS:** Law Review; **MIL SERV:** USA, PFC, 1951-53; **HOME ADD:** 772 Harbor Dr. N., Port Richey, FL 33568, (813)848-8846; **BUS ADD:** 1648 U.S. 19 N., Port Richey, FL 33568, (813)848-3844.

APPLEWHITE, John C.——B: Apr. 6, 1946, Tulsa, OK, *Sr. VP, Mktg.*, Vantage Companies, Dallas; **PRIM RE ACT:** Broker, Developer, Property Manager; **SERVICES:** Land and Building Sales, leasing, custom bldg., prop. mgmt., mkt. analysis; **PROFL AFFIL & HONORS:** TX RE Commn., Dallas Area Indus. Devel. Assn., Comml. Investment Div., Greater Dallas Bd. of Realtors; **EDUC:** BBA, 1969, Mktg. & Econ., N. TX State Univ.; **MIL SERV:** US Army, E-5, Sgt.; **HOME ADD:** 4648 Twinpost St., Dallas, TX 75234, (214)386-4568; **BUS ADD:** 2525 Stemmons 1000, Dallas, TX 75207, (214)631-0600.

ARADO, Joseph E.——B: June 20, 1929, Chicago, IL, *Dir., Indus. Devel. & RE*, Elgin, Joliet & Eastern Railway Co.; **PRIM RE ACT:** Developer, Property Manager; **SERVICES:** Indus. site selection services, RE acquisition, conveyance, and leasing; **PROFL AFFIL & HONORS:** SIR; NARA; Intl. Coll. of RE Consulting Profls.; Indus. Devel. Research Council; Amer. Econ. Devel. Council; Assn. of Amer. Geographers; Great Lakes Area Devel. Council; Amer. Railway Devel. Assn.; Nat. Assn. of Corp. RE Execs., Cert. Indus. Devel. (AEDC); CRA (NARA); RE Consulting Profl. (ICRECP); **EDUC:** BS, 1951, Geog., Northwestern Univ.; **GRAD EDUC:** MS, 1952, Geog., Northwestern Univ.; **EDUC HONORS:** Departmental Honors, C.S. Hammond Scholarship; **MIL SERV:** USN/USNR, Capt., 1952-1977; **OTHER ACT & HONORS:** Dir., Grundy Cty. Ind. Dev. Corp., IL; Member, Will Cty., IL, Econ. Affairs Commn.; Morris, IL Planning Commn.; Union League Club of Chicago; Naval Reserve Assn.; **HOME ADD:** 701 Briar Ln., Morris, IL 60450, (815)942-4849; **BUS ADD:** POB 880, Joliet, IL 60434, (815)740-6640.

ARAGONA, Frank J.——B: Brooklyn, NY, *Pres.*, F. J. Aragona Realty, Inc.; **PRIM RE ACT:** Broker, Appraiser, Builder; **SERVICES:** RE appraisal service; **REP CLIENTS:** Brookhaven Township, Suffolk Cty.; Relocation Companies; **PREV EMPLOY:** Self-employed (since 1968); **PROFL AFFIL & HONORS:** Nat. Assn. of Independent Fee Appraisers; **EDUC:** RE Appraisal; **MIL SERV:** USCG; Seaman; **HOME ADD:** 47 Bieselin Rd., Bellport, NY, (516)286-9108; **BUS ADD:** 670 South Country Rd., East Patchogue, NY 11772, (516)475-7577.

ARANT, William J.——B: Oct. 10, 1943, Birmingham, AL, *Pres.*, Southeastern Investment Props., Inc.; **PRIM RE ACT:** Broker, Consultant, Owner/Investor, Property Manager; **SERVICES:** RE sales, mgmt. & renovation; **PREV EMPLOY:** Loan Officer Natl. Bank of GA; **EDUC:** BA, 1966, Poli. Sci., Washington & Lee Univ.; **MIL SERV:** USMC Res., Capt., Navy Commendation Medal; **OTHER ACT & HONORS:** Mountain Brook Club, The Reley House; **HOME ADD:** 3500 Cliff Rd., Birmingham, AL 35205, (205)254-3235; **BUS ADD:** 666 Bank For Savings Bldg., Birmingham, AL 35203, (205)251-3233.

ARBUCKLE, C. Steve——B: Jan. 28, 1941, Wichita, KS, *Owner & Pres.*, ERA Valley Metro Realty; **SERVICES:** Resid. & comml. RE and investment; **PREV EMPLOY:** 8 yrs. in the resid. & comml. RE sales in Phoenix; **PROFL AFFIL & HONORS:** RESSI; **EDUC:** Abilene Christian Univ.; **HOME ADD:** 302 W. Sweetwater Ave., Phoenix, AZ 85029, (602)866-8432; **BUS ADD:** 2860 W. Peoria, Phoenix, AZ 85029, (602)993-6500.

ARCHAMBAULT, Reynold J., Jr.——B: Nov. 16, 1928, Waterbury, CT, R. J. Archambault Jr.-R.E. Appr. and Consultant; **PRIM RE ACT:** Consultant, Appraiser, Property Manager, Banker, Lender; **SERVICES:** R.E. appraising or analysis, mort. pkg. consulting, all types of R.E.; **REP CLIENTS:** Corp. and indiv. R.E. clients or investors, lending inst.; **PREV EMPLOY:** Bristol Savings Bank, 150 Main St., Bristol Ct.; Sr. V.P. Lending, Union Trust Co., Church and Elm St., New Haven, CT., V.P. Reg. Mort. Off.; **PROFL AFFIL & HONORS:** CT. Chapt. 38 Soc. of R.E. Appraisers; Past Pres. CT Devel. Auth.; Credit Screening Comm. since 1964, **EDUC:** BS, 1952, Bus. Mgmt., Providence Coll.; **GRAD EDUC:** Amer. Inst. of Banking, 1967, Banking, OH St. Univ., ABA Nat. Mort. School; **EDUC HONORS:** Jr. Yr.; **MIL SERV:** US Army, PFC; **OTHER ACT & HONORS:** Knights of Columbus, Providence Coll. Alumni Assn.; Charter Member, North Haven, CT Housing Authority; Instructor - University of New Haven, Principles of Real Estate Appraisal 1967-1977; **HOME ADD:** 285 Glendale Dr., Bristol, CT 06010, (203)589-5978; **BUS ADD:** P.O. Box 675, Bristol, CT 06010, (203)583-9290.

ARCHER, Guy P.D.——**B:** Jan. 18, 1943, New York City, NY, *Deputy Corp. Counsel*, Cty. of Maui, State of Hawaii; **PRIM RE ACT:** Attorney; **SERVICES:** Legal Counsel to Maui Cty. Council, Maui Planning Dept., Maui Planning Comm., Bd. of Ethics; **REP CLIENTS:** Pvt. practice 1974 to 1981: S&L Cons. Maui. Inc. (condo devel.); Pac. Land Co., Inc. (brokerage); Whalers Realty Inc., etc.; **PREV EMPLOY:** Assoc. with Marshall, Bratter, Greene, Allison & Tucker, New York City; branch mgr. of HI Escrow & Title Inc., Kihei, Maui, HI, lic. RE broker in HI; **PROFL AFFIL & HONORS:** Member of ABA, HI State Bar Assn., Maui Cty. Bar Assn., Who's Who of the West 1981; **EDUC:** BA, 1965, Govt., Wesleyan Univ., Middletown, CT; **GRAD EDUC:** JD, 1968, Corporate and securities, Columbia Univ. School of Law; **EDUC HONORS:** Honors in Govt.; **HOME ADD:** 1109 Kau St., Kula, Maui, HI 96790, (808)878-6216; **BUS ADD:** 200 South High St., Cty. Bldg., Wailuku, HI 96793, (808)244-7740.

ARCHER, Heber——**B:** May 24, 1933, Wagoner, OK, *RE Consultant*, Heber Archer; **PRIM RE ACT:** Consultant; **SERVICES:** Mkt. studies, econ. analysis, investment prop. analysis; **REP CLIENTS:** Devels., prop. owners & mgrs. investors; **PREV EMPLOY:** VP, Dorchester Cos.; **PROFL AFFIL & HONORS:** ULI, BOMA, NAR, NAIOOP, SRA, TULSA Metro Bd. of Realtors; **EDUC:** BA, 1958, Personnel Admin., Econ., OK State Univ.; **MIL SERV:** USA, Cpl.; **HOME ADD:** 5903 S. 72 E Ave., Tulsa, OK 74145, (918)494-3089; **BUS ADD:** 1505 Philtower Bldg., Tulsa, OK 74103, (918)583-6333.

ARCHIBALD, Norman L.——**B:** Mar. 9, 1947, Mexia, TX, *VP*, Bill C. Dotson & Assoc. Inc.; **PRIM RE ACT:** Broker, Consultant, Appraiser; **SERVICES:** Appraisal valuation & counseling, comml. brokerage; **REP CLIENTS:** Lenders, indivs., instnl. investors in income producing props.; **PREV EMPLOY:** Crosson-Dannis Inc., First TX Fin. Corp.; **PROFL AFFIL & HONORS:** AIREA, SREA, MAI, SRPA; **EDUC:** BA, 1969, Speech, N TX State Univ., Denton, TX; **EDUC HONORS:** Honor Grad.; **MIL SERV:** USA Nat. Guard, Sgt.; **HOME ADD:** 327 Robin Hill, Duncanville, TX 75137, (214)296-1324; **BUS ADD:** 13789 Noel Rd., Dallas, TX 75240, (214)387-4970.

ARCHILLA, Carlos A.——**B:** Dec. 31, 1943, San Juan, PR, *Prin.*, Yanez & Archilla Assoc.; **PRIM RE ACT:** Architect, Engineer; **OTHER RE ACT:** Const. and Project Mgrs.; **PREV EMPLOY:** The Office of Jaime Torres Gaztambide; **PROFL AFFIL & HONORS:** AIA; Coll. of Arch. of PR; **EDUC:** BArch, 1968, Tulane Univ. of LA; **OTHER ACT & HONORS:** Phi Eta Mu Frat.; Amer. Radio Relay League; **HOME ADD:** E-19, 14th St., Quintas de Cupey, Rio Piedras, PR 00926, (809)790-1949; **BUS ADD:** Box 10596, San Juan, PR 00922, (809)783-5935.

ARDEN, Bruce——**B:** May 2, 1934, Minneapolis, MN, *Salesman*, Coldwell Banker, Comml.; **PRIM RE ACT:** Broker; **PREV EMPLOY:** IBM OP Sales; **PROFL AFFIL & HONORS:** Rotary; NAR, CCIM; **MIL SERV:** USMC; Sgt.; **HOME ADD:** 226 SW Kingston, (503)223-6907; **BUS ADD:** 1300 SW 5th, Portland, OR 97201, (503)221-4808.

ARDEN, John Real——**B:** Aug. 17, 1944, Louisville, KY, *Atty.*, John R. Arden:Attorney at Law; **PRIM RE ACT:** Attorney; **SERVICES:** Investment counseling, devel. fin. package, prop. mgmt., prop. devel.; **PREV EMPLOY:** Donald P. Conway, Atty. at Law, 1972-73, Dr. Ronald A. Anderson, The Research Group Inc. 1974; **PROFL AFFIL & HONORS:** ABA, Boston Bar Assn., Hampshire Cty. Bar, Tau Beta Pi, Eta Kappa Nu; **EDUC:** BEE, 1967, engrg., MI State Univ.; **GRAD EDUC:** JD, 1972, Univ. of Notre Dame; **EDUC HONORS:** Tau Beta Pi, Eta Kappa Nu, Moot Court; **OTHER ACT & HONORS:** Former Chmn., Fin. Comm. Town of Southampton, MA, 21st & 22nd Edition Marquis Who's Who in Fin. & Indus.; **HOME ADD:** 23 Sandra Rd., Easthampton, MA 01027, (413)527-5912; **BUS ADD:** 181 Main St. 2, Northampton, MA 01060, (413)586-5757.

ARDIS, Ronald E.——**B:** July 31, 1942, Salisbury, MD, *Arch., Part.*, Ciancitto & Assoc.; **PRIM RE ACT:** Architect, Consultant; **SERVICES:** Design, Inspection, Constr. Mgmt, Planning; **REP CLIENTS:** State of MD, Dept. of Health & Hygiene, Natural Resources, Var. City Agents, FMHA; **PROFL AFFIL & HONORS:** AIAM MD. Soc. of Arch.; **GRAD EDUC:** Certs, 1970-71, Struc. Design, Arch. Hist., Johns Hopkins Univ., Baltimore, MD; **OTHER ACT & HONORS:** Jaycees, Elks 817; **HOME ADD:** 701 Regency Dr., Salisbury, MD 21801, (301)546-4683; **BUS ADD:** 100 N. Division St., Salisbury, MO 21801, (301)749-8001.

ARESTY, Joel M.——**B:** July 23, 1949, Chicago, IL, *Atty.*, Blackwell, Walker, Gray, Powers, Flick & Hoehl, RE Transactions & Litigation, including Bankruptcy; **PRIM RE ACT:** Broker, Attorney, Owner/Investor, Syndicator; **OTHER RE ACT:** Bankruptcy, Foreclosure, Workouts; **REP CLIENTS:** AmeriFirst Fed. S&L Assn., Miami, FL; **EDUC:** 1972, Univ. of Miami; **GRAD EDUC:** JD, 1975, Univ. of Miami, School of Law; **HOME ADD:** 916 N.E. 90th St., Miami, FL 33138, (305)754-8137; **BUS ADD:** 2400 AmeriFirst Bldg., 1 S.E. 3rd Ave., Miami, FL 33131, (305)358-8880.

ARFA, Harvey Z.——**B:** Apr. 28, 1945, New York City, NY, *Atty. at Law*; **PRIM RE ACT:** Attorney, Owner/Investor, Syndicator; **PROFL AFFIL & HONORS:** Assn. of Bar of City of NY; Comm. on Partnerships, Sec of Bus. Corp. and Comm'l Law and Comm. on Energy Law, Sec. of Real Property, Probate and Trust Law, ABA; Member, Comm. on Public Policy, Citizens Housing and Planning Council; **GRAD EDUC:** MBA, 1970, Fin., Columbia Univ. Graduate School of Bus.; JD, 1970, Columbia Univ. Law School; **OTHER ACT & HONORS:** Dir., Camp Ella Fohs, Inc. (Federation of Jewish Philanthropies); Exec. Bd., National Jewish Resource Center; **HOME ADD:** 301 E. 69th St., New York, NY 10021, (212)861-7488; **BUS ADD:** 1133 Ave. of the Americas, New York, NY 10036, (212)869-2600.

ARIAS, Capt. Antonio——**B:** Mar. 17, 1911, Havana, Cuba, *Pres.*, International Tower Developer Corp.; **PRIM RE ACT:** Consultant, Developer, Builder, Owner/Investor, Property Manager; **SERVICES:** Bldg. and devel.; **REP CLIENTS:** Republic Nat. Bank (Pres. Aristias Sastre), LeJenne & Flagler St., Miami, FL; **PREV EMPLOY:** Same bus. for 35 years in Havana Cuba; Miami, FL; San Juan, Puerto Rico; Tampa, FL; Fort Lauderdale, FL; **EDUC:** 4 years Military Academy in Cuba; **MIL SERV:** Cuban AF, Capt.; Lt.; 1931; WWII; **OTHER ACT & HONORS:** Amer. Club; Camara Comercio Latina; Big Five Club; **HOME ADD:** 900 Andalusia, Coral GabLes, FL 33134, (305)443-3073; **BUS ADD:** 1015 Anastasia Ave., Coral Gables, FL 33134, (305)443-1119.

ARIES, Peter L.——**B:** May 28, 1937, Yonkers, NY, *Chmn. of the Bd.*, Aries Brandenberg Co., Inc.; **PRIM RE ACT:** Broker, Developer, Property Manager, Owner/Investor; **SERVICES:** Devel., and prop. mgmt. and investments of comml. prop. specializing in shopping ctrs. & office bldgs.; **REP CLIENTS:** Caldor, Shop Rite Supermarkets, Grand Union, A & P, Shopwell, Bradlee's, Jamesway; **PROFL AFFIL & HONORS:** Intl. Council of Shopping Ctrs., Young Men's RE Assn. of NY, NY & Westchester RE Bds. Intl. RE Federation, & Amer. Coll. of RE Consultants, ICSC, Certificate of Appreciation; **EDUC:** 1959, Hobart Coll., Geneva NY; **GRAD EDUC:** RE-Law, NY Univ. Grad. School of Bus. Admin.; **OTHER ACT & HONORS:** Founding member of East Yonkers Lions Club, Lecturer for NY Univ. Mgmt. Ctr. (RE Acquisition & Site Locations); **HOME ADD:** 75 Donnybrook Rd., Scarsdale, NY 10583, (914)235-7642; **BUS ADD:** 80 Bus. Park Dr., Armonk, NY 10504, (914)273-6300.

ARIKO, John G., Jr.——**B:** May 30, 1943, Wash., DC, *Pres.*, Epoch Mgmt., Inc.; **PRIM RE ACT:** Broker, Consultant, Builder, Property Manager, Owner/Investor, Insuror, Syndicator; **SERVICES:** Prop. Mgmt., Const., Consultation, Synd.; **REP CLIENTS:** Major Banks, Ins. Cos., Partnerships; **PREV EMPLOY:** USN CE Corps. 1965-1973; **PROFL AFFIL & HONORS:** IREM, CPM; **EDUC:** BS, 1965, Engrg. Mgmt., US Naval Acad.; **GRAD EDUC:** MS, 1968, Elec. Eng. and Bus. Admin., Univ. of MI; **EDUC HONORS:** Grad. with merit, Eta Kappa Nu, Hon. Elec Eng. Frat.; **MIL SERV:** USN, Lt., Vietnam Service, Expert Rifle and Pistol; **HOME ADD:** 271 Prescott Dr., Orlando, FL 32809, (305)859-8927; **BUS ADD:** 199 Whooping Loop, Altamonte Springs, FL 32701, (305)830-5499.

ARMAN, Henry A.——**B:** July 16, 1930, New Haven, CT, *VP*, Pyms-Suchman RE Co.; **PRIM RE ACT:** Broker, Appraiser, Developer, Owner/Investor, Syndicator, Property Manager; **SERVICES:** Prop. mgmt., farm leasing, valuation, devel., synd. of comml. & acreage props., appraisals, review appraisal, RE tax appeals, investment counseling; **REP CLIENTS:** Indivs., lenders & instnl. investors; **PREV EMPLOY:** Dade Cty. Realty; 20 yrs. with Pyms-Suchman RE Co.; **PROFL AFFIL & HONORS:** RESSSI; Nat. Soc. of Fee Appraisers; Nat. Assn. of Review Appraisers; So. FL Planning & Zoning Assn.; NAR; FL Assn. Realtors; Kendall-Perrine Bd. of Realtors; RE Assn. of Profls.; Assoc. Member, Amer. Soc. of Farm Mgrs. & Rural Appraisers, NFA, CRA; **EDUC:** AB, 1959, Univ. of Miami; **MIL SERV:** US Army; **OTHER ACT & HONORS:** Tiger Bay Club, Inc.; Asst. Scoutmaster Troop 300, Miami; Optimist International, Life Member; **HOME ADD:** 5000 SW 89th Pl., Miami, FL 33165, (305)274-0463; **BUS ADD:** 9205 So. Dixie Hwy, Miami, FL 33156, (305)667-6461.

ARMFIELD, Peter D.——**B:** Aug. 16, 1948, Kansas City, MO, *VP*, Armfield-Houck Appraisal & Research, Inc.; **PRIM RE ACT:** Instructor, Consultant, Appraiser; **PROFL AFFIL & HONORS:** SRPA, RM, SREA, AIREA; **EDUC:** BS/BA, 1970, Mktg., Univ. of FL; **GRAD EDUC:** MBA, 1972, Mktg., U of FL; **OTHER ACT & HONORS:** Exchange Club; **HOME ADD:** 2626 Tropical Ave., Vero

Beach, FL, (305)567-7478; **BUS ADD:** 2001 9th Ave. Suite 206, PO Box 791, Vero Beach, FL 32960, (305)562-0532.

ARMIGER, Milton W.——B: July 30, 1944, Wash., DC, *Pres.*, Armiger Assoc.: Indus. RE; **PRIM RE ACT:** Broker, Syndicator, Consultant, Property Manager; **SERVICES:** Fin. Feasibility and Mkt. Feasibility Analysis; **REP CLIENTS:** Specializing in Indus. RE; **PREV EMPLOY:** US Senate Anti-Trust and Monopoly Subcomm. - Economist; **PROFL AFFIL & HONORS:** AIREA; **EDUC:** BS, 1975, Bus. Fin. & Econ., Univ. of MD; **GRAD EDUC:** MS, 1976, Mgmt., Univ. of MD; **MIL SERV:** USA, E-5, AFEM 82nd Airborne Div.; **OTHER ACT & HONORS:** Bd. of Dir., Armiger Transportation Systems; **HOME ADD:** Box 2717, Laurel, MD 20811, (301)953-3792; **BUS ADD:** 5811 Baltimore Ave., Riverdale, MD 20840, (301)927-3403.

ARMKNECHT, Richard F., Jr.——*Sr. VP Fin.*, Carter, William, Co.; **PRIM RE ACT:** Property Manager; **BUS ADD:** 963 Highland Ave., Needham Heights, MA 02194, (617)444-7500.*

ARMS, Charles P.——B: Feb. 20, 1932, Worcester, MA, *VP, RE*, Adams Drug Co.; **PRIM RE ACT:** Consultant, Owner/Investor, Property Manager; **OTHER RE ACT:** RE, Retail; **PREV EMPLOY:** Sears, Roebuck and Co., 8 yrs.; W.T. Grant Co., 8 yrs.; **PROFL AFFIL & HONORS:** ICSC; NACORE, Past Officer; **OTHER ACT & HONORS:** Vestry Member, Emmanuel Episcopal Church, Cumberland, RI; **HOME ADD:** 18 Lonesome Pine Rd., Cumberland, RI 02864, (401)333-1131; **BUS ADD:** 75 Sabin St., Pawtucket, RI 02860, (401)724-9500.

ARMSTRONG, Bret Alan——B: Nov. 12, 1959, Monterey Park, CA, *Pres.*, Diamond West Development of Arizona, Inc.; **PRIM RE ACT:** Consultant, Developer, Builder, Owner/Investor, Property Manager; **SERVICES:** Land devel. & bldg., prop. mgmt., land & comml. investment, CA, AZ & HI; **REP CLIENTS:** Consultant to to corp., partnerships, & indiv.; RE mgmt.; **PREV EMPLOY:** Armstrong Devel. Corp.; Westlake Village, CA, VP, 1978-1980; **PROFL AFFIL & HONORS:** Amer. Mktg. Assn.; AZ Thoroughbred Breeders Assn.; CA Thoroughbred Breeders Assn.; **EDUC:** Letters & Sci., pres. enrolled, Econ./Pre-Law, Univ. of CA at Los Angeles; **HOME ADD:** PO Box 11364, Beverly Hills, CA 90213; **BUS ADD:** 4653 S. Lakeshore Dr., Tempe, AZ 85282, (602)839-7502.

ARMSTRONG, G. William——B: Sep. 4, 1939, Chatham, Ont. Can., *Pres.*, Armstrong & Co.; **PRIM RE ACT:** Broker, Consultant, Developer, Owner/Investor; **SERVICES:** Consulting & brokerage services for comml. dev.; **REP CLIENTS:** Corp. Clients; **PREV EMPLOY:** Sales mgr., Procter & Gamble Distributing Co.; **PROFL AFFIL & HONORS:** RNMI; Metro. Indianapolis Bd. of Realtors, CCIM, RNMI; **EDUC:** BA, 1961, Mgmt., Clarkson Coll. of Tech.; **GRAD EDUC:** MBA, 1965, Mktg., IN Univ.; **EDUC HONORS:** With distinction, Beta Gamma Sigma; **OTHER ACT & HONORS:** Bd. of Dir., Exec. Comm. Ice/Mgmt.; Dir. Christian Bus. Mens Comm. of Indianapolis; **HOME ADD:** 12220 Brookshire Pkwy, Carmel, IN 46032, (317)846-8175; **BUS ADD:** PO Box 50904, Indianapolis, IN 46250, (317)849-5599.

ARMSTRONG, J.——B: Sept. 30, 1938, New York, NY, *VP, Land Planning*, FPA Corp.; **PRIM RE ACT:** Consultant, Developer, Regulator, Builder; **OTHER RE ACT:** Feasibility Studies; **SERVICES:** Land Planning, Project Coordination, Project Administration, Land Devel. Supervision; **PREV EMPLOY:** Raymond, Parish, Pine & Weiner, NYC 1966-1970; State of Israel Settlement Dept. 1970-1973; **PROFL AFFIL & HONORS:** Urban Land Instit., Nat. Assn. of Home Builders; **EDUC:** 1962, Dept. of Arch., School of Fine Arts, Univ. of PA; **GRAD EDUC:** MA, 1966, School of Arch., Columbia Univ., NYC; MBA, 1981, Admin. & Fin., Nova Univ., Ft. Lauderdale, FL; **HOME ADD:** 700 Orchid Dr., Plantation, FL 33317, (305)581-4622; **BUS ADD:** 2501 Palm Aire Dr., N. Pompano Beach, FL 33060, (305)972-3300.

ARMSTRONG, Richard A.——B: June 20, 1941, Spfld., IL, *Exec. VP*, Rock Island Cty. Bd. of Realtors; **PRIM RE ACT:** Real Estate Publisher; **OTHER RE ACT:** Trade Assoc., Admin.; **SERVICES:** P.R., M.L.S., Professional STDS, Training etc.; **PREV EMPLOY:** Exec. Boy Scouts of Amers.; **EDUC:** MacMurray Coll.; **HOME ADD:** 47 Manor Dr., Eldridge, IA 52748, (319)285-4860; **BUS ADD:** PO Box 718, Moline, IL 61265, (309)797-4158.

ARMSTRONG, Richard C.——B: Apr. 11, 1930, NYC, *VP & Mgr., Commercial Mortgage Department*, Citizens Fidelity Mortgage Co., Mort. Banking Div.; **OTHER RE ACT:** Mort. banker; **SERVICES:** Fin. for comml. RE; **REP CLIENTS:** RE devel.; **PREV EMPLOY:** Western Mort. Corp. (1976-78, Atlanta), Chase Manhattan Realty Capital Corp. (1973-76, Atlanta); **PROFL AFFIL & HONORS:** Member Editorial Advisory Bd., SE RE News, Dir. Louisville Apt. Assn., Member Intl. Council of Shopping Ctrs., Amer. Hotel/Motel Assn.; **EDUC:** Mktg., Univ. of NC; **MIL SERV:** USA, 1951-53, Cpl.; **OTHER ACT & HONORS:** Lt. Gov. Optimist Clubs, KY, WV, Dist. Past Pres., Sales & Mktg. Execs. Club., Pres. Univ. of NC Alumni Assoc., Louisville, KY; **HOME ADD:** 710 Danes Hall Dr., Louisville, KY 40206, (502)896-9770; **BUS ADD:** 437 W Jefferson St., Louisville, KY 40202, (502)581-3112.

ARMSTRONG, William J., Jr.——*Broker*, Carl Storey Co.; **PRIM RE ACT:** Broker; **SERVICES:** Sales & Leasing of Comml., Indus. and income props.; **REP CLIENTS:** Corporations, Indiv. and Instnl. Investors; **PROFL AFFIL & HONORS:** Soc. of Indus. Realtors; NAR, Salesman Affiliate SIR; CCIM; **EDUC:** BA, 1964, Vanderbilt Univ.; **BUS ADD:** 13th Floor Third Nat. Bank Bldg., Nashville, TN 37220, (615)244-7560.

ARMY, Lawrence F.——B: Oct. 25, 1944, Worcester, MA, Army & Capone; **PRIM RE ACT:** Attorney; **SERVICES:** Loan Closing Atty., RE Conveyancer, Title Ins. Agent and Authorized Title Ins. Atty.; **REP CLIENTS:** First Amer. Title, Amer. Title Ins., Nelson & O'Connell Title Co., Millbury Nat. Bank, Farmers Home Adm., Dept. of Agric., Gardner Savings Bank; Employee Transfer Corp. of New Jersey; **PROFL AFFIL & HONORS:** Member of Municipal City Solicitors and Town Counsel Assn., MA Conveyancers Assn., MA Bar Assn., ABA, Worcester County Bar Assn., Member of the Fed. Bar; **EDUC:** BA, 1970, Hist. and Gov., Minor in secondary educ., Univ. of MA, Amherst; **GRAD EDUC:** JD, 1973, Law, Suffolk Univ. Law School; **EDUC HONORS:** Cum Laude, Selected for Law Review, Moot Court Award; **MIL SERV:** USA, SP/5; **OTHER ACT & HONORS:** Member of Grafton School Comm., Member of Grafton Bd. of Appeals, Town Counsel Spencer, K of C, 200 Sportsmens Club, Treas. & Bd. of Dirs. Legal Aid Soc. of Worcester, Inc.; **HOME ADD:** 49 Countryside Rd., Grafton, MA, (617)839-5094; **BUS ADD:** 390 Main St., Suite 500, Worcester, MA 01608, (617)756-8571.

ARNASON, Albert F.——B: Oct. 24, 1927, Hensel, ND, *Owner*, A.F. Arnason, Attorney; **PRIM RE ACT:** Attorney, Owner/Investor; **REP CLIENTS:** Grand Forks Fed. S&L, 1st Fed. S&L of Grand Forks and Grafton, Trust Dept. of First Nat. Bank; **PROFL AFFIL & HONORS:** ABA; ND Bar Assn.; **EDUC:** Bus., Univ. of ND; **GRAD EDUC:** LLB, 1952, Univ. of ND School of Law; **MIL SERV:** US Army, Sgt.; **OTHER ACT & HONORS:** Boy Scouts of Amer.; **HOME ADD:** 2304 Chestnut St., Grand Forks, ND 58201, (701)772-7419; **BUS ADD:** Rm. 250, 13 S. 4th St., Grand Forks, ND 58201, (701)775-0654.

ARNDTS, Jerome Theodore——B: Mar. 5, 1956, Dayton, OH, *Pres.*, JARA Construction and Software Co.; **PRIM RE ACT:** Engineer, Builder; **OTHER RE ACT:** Computer System Devel.; **SERVICES:** Investment Analysis, Construction, Prop. Mgmt. Computer Systems RE Appraisers, Devel., Prop. Mgrs.; **PREV EMPLOY:** RJ Software; **PROFL AFFIL & HONORS:** Amer. Soc. of Civil Engrs., OH RE Salesman, Profl. Engr.; **EDUC:** BS, 1974, Computers, Structural & Soil Engrg., Univ. of Dayton; **GRAD EDUC:** RE Appraisal & Land Econom., 1980, RE Feasibility & Investment Analysis (Uncompleted), Univ. of WI at Madison; **OTHER ACT & HONORS:** Pilot; **HOME ADD:** 1197 S Main St., W Milton, OH 45383; **BUS ADD:** 8430 N Dixie Dr., Dayton, OH 45414, (513)890-1830; **BUS TEL:** (513)698-6025.

ARNESON, H.R.——B: 1914, Fargo, ND, *Pres.*, Arneson & Assoc.; **PRIM RE ACT:** Broker, Consultant, Appraiser, Instructor, Property Manager, Insuror; **REP CLIENTS:** US Govt., City of Fargo, City of Bismarck, Cass Cty. Bank & accts., ins. cos., RR, Radio & TV, oil cos., nat. corps.; **PREV EMPLOY:** Coll. lecturer; **PROFL AFFIL & HONORS:** AIREA, AIREM; **EDUC:** BS, Pre Med, ND State Univ.; **HOME ADD:** 1100 S 8th, Fargo, ND 58108, (701)235-4770; **BUS ADD:** 19 N 10th St., Box 2742, Fargo, ND 58108.

ARNESON, Thomas G., II——B: Sept. 2, 1942, Minneapolis, MN, *Land Surveyor*, Bennett, Ringrose, Wolsfield, Jarvis, Gardner, Inc.; **OTHER RE ACT:** Land Surveyor; **SERVICES:** Boundary surveys, land title surveys, mort. surveys; **REP CLIENTS:** Dayton Hudson; The Preserve; Raunhorst; **PROFL AFFIL & HONORS:** Amer. Congress on Surveying & Mapping (ACSM); MN Land Surveyors Assn.; Hennegin Cty. Surveyors Assn.; **EDUC:** BS, 1979, Surveying and Computer Sci., Univ. of MN; **MIL SERV:** US Army; Staff Sgt.; Bronze Star; **HOME ADD:** 6825 Abbott Ave. No., Brooklyn Ctr, MN 55429, (612)566-7327; **BUS ADD:** 2829 Univ. Ave. SE, Minneapolis, MN 55414, (612)379-7878.

ARNHEIM, Stanley W.——B: Sept. 25, 1913, Pittsburgh, PA, *Chmn.*, Arnheim & Neely, Inc.; **PRIM RE ACT:** Broker, Consultant, Appraiser, Property Manager; **REP CLIENTS:** Pittsburgh Nat. Bank, Aluminum Co. of Amer., Mercy Hospital, Pittsburgh Press, Eickenhoff

Corp., PA Railroad; **PROFL AFFIL & HONORS:** Amer. Soc. of RE Counselors, IREM, Soc. of RE Appraisers, Amer. Soc. of Appraisers, BOMA, CRE, CPM, Nat. Pres. of IREM 1953, Pres. of Greater Pittsburgh Bd. of Realtors 1976, Realtor of the Year 1967, Mgr. of the Year 1970; **EDUC:** 1934, Journalism, Univ. of MI; **HOME ADD:** 334 S Lexington, Pittsburgh, PA 15208, (412)371-1700; **BUS ADD:** 820 Grant Bldg., Pittsburgh, PA 15219, (412)391-1900.

ARNOLD, Alvin L.——B: Feb. 12, 1929, NY, NY, *VP*, Warren, Gorham & Lamont, Inc.; **PRIM RE ACT:** Attorney, Instructor, Real Estate Publisher; **SERVICES:** Author and editor of RE books and periodicals; **PROFL AFFIL & HONORS:** Adjunct Prof. of RE, NY Univ.; Nat. Assn. of RE Editors; **EDUC:** AB, 1949, Pol. Sci., Cornell Univ.; **GRAD EDUC:** JD, 1952, Law, Harvard Law School; **EDUC HONORS:** Phi Beta Kappa; AB with Gen. Honors, Cum Laude; **MIL SERV:** USAF, Capt.; **OTHER ACT & HONORS:** Acting Justice, Village of Saddle Rock, 1979 to date; VP, Nassau Lyric Opera Co.; **HOME ADD:** 25 Longfellow Rd., Great Neck, NY 11023, (516)487-6674; **BUS ADD:** 390 Plandome Rd., Manhasset, NY 11030, (516)627-4810.

ARNOLD, John E.——B: Feb. 1, 1928, Philadelphia, *Pres.*, Eastman-Arnold Co.; **PRIM RE ACT:** Broker, Attorney, Consultant, Appraiser, Property Manager, Engineer; **SERVICES:** Primarily leasing and mgmt. of office bldgs.; **REP CLIENTS:** Prudential Ins. Co., Inco Electric Energy, Colonial Penn Grp., Cent. Penn Nat. Bank; **PROFL AFFIL & HONORS:** NAR, BOMA, RESSI; **EDUC:** BS in Civil Engineering, 1949, Structures, Univ. of PA; **GRAD EDUC:** B of Laws, 1953, Temple Univ.; **EDUC HONORS:** Penn's List; **OTHER ACT & HONORS:** Bd. of Dir. Camp Fire Girls; **HOME ADD:** 207 Heacock Ln., Wyncote, PA 19095, (215)887-5703; **BUS ADD:** 2022 Two Penn Ctr. Plaza, Philadelphia, PA 19102, (215)568-8090.

ARNOLD, John H.——B: Mar. 1, 1938, Los Angeles, CA, *Pres.*, Arnold & Assoc. Realty, Inc.; **PRIM RE ACT:** Broker, Syndicator, Consultant, Appraiser, Property Manager, Owner/Investor, Insuror; **SERVICES:** Consultant/appraiser-30 person R.E. office; **PREV EMPLOY:** Retail mgmt. 5 yrs., US Dept. of State/foreign service 5 yrs.; **PROFL AFFIL & HONORS:** NAR, SREA, AIREA, Soc. Las Vegas Exchangers, FLI, Profl. Ins. Agents; **EDUC:** BBA, 1967, CA State Univ. Fullerton; **OTHER ACT & HONORS:** Republican Silver Club; **HOME ADD:** 1254 Vista Dr., Las Vegas, NV 89102; **BUS ADD:** 5300 W. Charleston, Las Vegas, NV 89102, (702)870-3068.

ARNOLD, Michael Neal——B: June 6, 1947, Madera, CA, *Partner*, Hammock, Arnold & Co.; **PRIM RE ACT:** Consultant, Appraiser, Instructor; **REP CLIENTS:** Fin. inst., govt. agencies, indus. corp., private investors, trust dept's., attys., etc.; **PREV EMPLOY:** Pickthorn Appraisal; Madera Cty. Assessors Office; Robert Raymond MAI; **PROFL AFFIL & HONORS:** Soc. of RE Appraisers; Amer. Right of Way Assn.; S. Santa Barbara Cty. Bd. of Realtors; CA Assn. of Realtors; NAR; **EDUC:** BA, Geography, Univ. of CA; **OTHER ACT & HONORS:** Instructor, "RE Appraiser"; **HOME ADD:** 211 East Victoria St., Santa Barbara, CA 93101, (805)687-4073; **BUS ADD:** 211 East Victoria St., Santa Barbara, CA 93101, (805)966-0869.

ARNOLD, Peter J.——B: July 20, 1942, Milwaukee, WI, *Pres.*, U.S. Investors Resources, Inc.; **PRIM RE ACT:** Broker, Consultant, Engineer, Attorney, Developer, Lender, Owner/Investor, Instructor, Syndicator, Real Estate Publisher; **SERVICES:** Consulting on condo. conversions, fin. analysis; **REP CLIENTS:** Arthur Tonsmeire, Chmn. of Bd., 1st S. Fed. S&L, Mobile, AL; Stephen Nichols, Pres., Premier Props. Corp., Chicago, IL; **PREV EMPLOY:** Loan Officer, Percy Wilson Mort. Corp., Chicago, IL; Asst. VP, Amer. Fletcher Mort., Chicago, IL; VP Fin., Amer. Invsco Corp., Chicago, IL; **PROFL AFFIL & HONORS:** ABA; RE Securities and Synd. Instit. (an affiliate of the Nat. Assn. of Realtors); **EDUC:** BS, 1964, Engrg., Univ. of WI; **GRAD EDUC:** MS, 1965, Engrg., Univ. of DE; JD, 1969, NYU; **OTHER ACT & HONORS:** Author, Condo. Conversion Guidelines; **HOME ADD:** 701 W Diversey, Chicago, IL 60614, (312)528-8977; **BUS TEL:** (312)935-4000.

ARNOLD, R. Jeffery——B: Nov. 1, 1946, Cleveland, OH, *VP*, American Trading Real Estate Co.; **PRIM RE ACT:** Broker, Developer, Property Manager, Owner/Investor; **SERVICES:** Develop & manage/operate large comml. props. for own Acct.; **PREV EMPLOY:** Baltimore Realty (Pres.); BTR Realty, Inc. (Project Dir.) 1973-1977; **PROFL AFFIL & HONORS:** BOMA (Dir.), ICSC, NAIOP, NACORE, RPA Candidate; **EDUC:** BA, 1968, Poli. Sci./Econ., Wesleyan Univ.; Middletown, CT; **GRAD EDUC:** MBA, 1971, Fin. & RE, Wharton Grad. School at Univ. of PA; **EDUC HONORS:** Deans List, Directors List; **MIL SERV:** USAR, E-5 (Sgt.), 1969-1975; **HOME ADD:** 740 Bridgeman Terrace, Towson, MD 21204, (301)825-3289; **BUS ADD:** Blaustein Bldg., PO Box 238, Baltimore, MD 21203, (301)685-4230.

ARNOLD, Robert B.——B: May 22, 1923, Philadelphia, PA, *VP*, Republic Appraisal Co.; **PRIM RE ACT:** Consultant, Appraiser; **REP CLIENTS:** Industrial Valley Bank, Germantown Savings Bank, Beneficial Savings Bank, Boulevard Mortgage Co., Lomas & Nettleton VNB Mort. Co., Thriftway Foods, F.H.A., F.N.M.A.; **PROFL AFFIL & HONORS:** SRA, AACA, AGA, CRA; **HOME ADD:** 118 Dewey Rd., Cheltenham, PA 19012, (215)635-1070; **BUS ADD:** G.S.B. Bldg., Balacynwyd, PA 19004, (215)839-6368.

ARNOLD, Robert L.——B: Oct. 13, 1944, Salt Lake City, UT, *VP*, Morter Fisher Arnold, AIA, Prof. Corp.; **PRIM RE ACT:** Architect; **SERVICES:** Arch. & Planning for Comml. & Condo. Projects; **REP CLIENTS:** Dev. of Comml. and Residential Projects; **PROFL AFFIL & HONORS:** AIA, AIA Western Mtn. Region Honor Award - 1980, for Coldstream Condo.; **EDUC:** BA, 1967, Art Hist./Design, Dartmouth Coll.; **GRAD EDUC:** MArch., 1972, Univ. of PA, Grad. School of Fine Arts; **EDUC HONORS:** Rufus Choate Scholar 1966-1967; Degree with Distinction in Art; Ames Fine Arts Prize; **MIL SERV:** USA, 1st Lt.; **OTHER ACT & HONORS:** Bd. of Dir., Lake Creek Meadows Homeowners Assn.; **HOME ADD:** PO Box 3262, Vail, CO 81658, (303)926-3469; **BUS ADD:** 143 E. Meadow Dr., Vail, CO 81657, (303)476-5105.

ARNOLD, Robert Marvin——B: Aug. 9, 1930, Baltimore, MD, *Pres.*, Parker Frames & Co., Inc.; **PRIM RE ACT:** Broker, Consultant, Appraiser, Property Manager; **PROFL AFFIL & HONORS:** Soc. of Indus. Realtors, Nat. Assn. of Realtors, Nat. Assn. of Indus. and Office Parks, SIR; **EDUC:** BS, 1952, Bus. & Public Admin., Univ. of MD; **GRAD EDUC:** JD, 1958, Law, Univ. of MD School of Law; **MIL SERV:** US Air Force, Capt., Korean Serv. Medal, United Nation Serv., Nat. Defense Serv.; **OTHER ACT & HONORS:** Greater Baltimore Comm., Dir. - N. Arundel Hospital - Member - MD Bar-Admitted to Practice Before Ct. of Appeals of MD; **HOME ADD:** 622 Gayle Dr., Linthicum Heights, MD 21090, (301)859-8252; **BUS ADD:** Sun Life Bldg., 20 S. Charles St., Baltimore, MD 21201, (301)727-2284.

ARNOLD, Robert S.——B: Feb. 26, 1919, Colorado Springs, CO, *CEO*, The Arnold Co's.; **PRIM RE ACT:** Developer, Builder, Owner/Investor; **SERVICES:** Devel. and build both single family homes and condos.; **PREV EMPLOY:** In RE in Denver since 1939; Previously broker, devel., builder, appraiser, investor, instr. (Univ. of Denver); **PROFL AFFIL & HONORS:** Retired member, AIREA; MAI, Pres., CO Chap. AIREA - 1971; **EDUC:** BSBA, 1961, RE, Univ. of Denver; **OTHER ACT & HONORS:** Land Officer, City & Cty. of Denver (1957 - 1963); **HOME ADD:** 3335 S. Pontiac St, Denver, CO 80224, (303)756-2413; **BUS ADD:** 1190 S Colorado Blvd., Denver, CO 80222, (303)758-5525.

ARNOLD, William L.——B: Oct. 7, 1952, Cleveland, OH, *Leasing Atty.*, Jacobs, Visconsi & Jacobs Co.; **PRIM RE ACT:** Attorney; **SERVICES:** Drafting and negotiation of tenant mall leases and ground leases; **PREV EMPLOY:** Devel. Diversified, Ltd. 1977-79; **PROFL AFFIL & HONORS:** ICSC; ABA; OH and Greater Cleveland Bar Assns.; **EDUC:** BA Pol. Sci., 1974, Bowling Green State Univ., Bowling Green, OH; **GRAD EDUC:** JD, 1977, Law, Cleveland State Univ.; **EDUC HONORS:** Academic-Leadership Scholarship; Student Body Pres.; **HOME ADD:** 621 Dade Ln., Richmond Htg., OH 44143, (216)481-6751; **BUS ADD:** 25425 Center Ridge Rd., Cleveland, OH 44145, (216)871-4800.

ARNOUTS, Robert A.——B: July 29, 1943, Antwerp, Belgium, *Principal*, Robert A. Arnouts, Arch.; **PRIM RE ACT:** Architect; **SERVICES:** Comprehensive arch. servs. for comml., indus. & residential; **REP CLIENTS:** Banks, Stores, Multipal Housing & Residential; **PREV EMPLOY:** Berger & Hennesy Arch., NYC; Louis Battoglia Assoc. Arch., Fishkill, NY; **PROFL AFFIL & HONORS:** AIA, Appointed to curriculum advisory committee for Arch. Tech. Program at Dutchess Comm. Coll.; **EDUC:** Assoc. Applied Sci., 1968, Arch. Design & Tec., Dutchess Comm. Coll.; **OTHER ACT & HONORS:** Prof. status Licensed in NY & CT; Cert. by the Natl. Council of Arch. Registration Bds.; Poughkeepsie South Rotary; Chelsea Yacht Club; St. Johns Lutheran Church; **HOME ADD:** 7 Pye Lane, Poughkeepsie, NY 12603, (914)462-3488; **BUS ADD:** 7 Pye Lane, Poughkeepsie, NY 12603, (914)462-3117.

ARNOVITZ, Eliot M.——B: Feb. 19, 1948, Atlanta, GA, *Pres.*, M&P Shopping Ctrs., Inc.; **PRIM RE ACT:** Broker, Developer, Builder, Owner/Investor, Property Manager; **SERVICES:** Owner/Operators of Shopping Ctrs.; **PROFL AFFIL & HONORS:** Intl. Council of Shopping Ctrs.; **EDUC:** BA, 1970, Sociology, Tulane Univ.; **MIL SERV:** USA, 2nd Lt.; **HOME ADD:** 665 Idlewood Dr. NW, Atlanta, GA 30349; **BUS ADD:** 2645 N. Decatur Rd., Decatur, GA 30033, (404)373-0191.

AROGETI, James——B: Aug. 17, 1925, Atlanta, GA, *CPA, Atty.*, Habif, Arogati & Wynne, P.C.; **PRIM RE ACT:** Consultant, Instructor, Lender, Owner/Investor; **PROFL AFFIL & HONORS:** AICPA, GA Soc. of CPA's, GA Bar Assn., CPA, Atty.; **EDUC:** BBA, 1946, Acctg., Woodrow Wilson Law Sch.; **EDUC HONORS:** LLB; **MIL SERV:** USAF, 2nd Lt.; **HOME ADD:** 1198 Arborvista Dr. NE, Atlanta, GA 30329, (404)636-1747; **BUS ADD:** 1073 W. Peachtree St. NE, Atlanta, GA 30367, (404)892-9651.

ARON, Ruthann——B: Oct. 24, 1942, Brooklyn, NY, *Pres.*, Professional Equity Group; **PRIM RE ACT:** Consultant, Attorney, Developer, Owner/Investor, Syndicator; **SERVICES:** Devel. and investment in comml. & resid. prop. consultation, zoning and land use law and analysis, prop. mgmt.; **PREV EMPLOY:** Practice of RE law, zoning, land use and devel.; **PROFL AFFIL & HONORS:** ABA; MD Bar Assn.; Montgomery Cty. Bar Assn.; ULI; **EDUC:** BS, 1964, Microbiology/Psych., Cornell Univ.; **GRAD EDUC:** MA, 1967, Psych., NY Univ.; JD, 1980, Catholic Univ. Law School; **OTHER ACT & HONORS:** Rep. Central Comm. Issues Chairperson; Cornell Club of Wash.; Bd. of Wash. Hebrew Congregation; **HOME ADD:** 9205 Falls Bridge La., Potomac, MD 20854, (301)299-2094; **BUS ADD:** Suite 2, 10220 River Rd., Potomac, MD 20854, (301)299-4804.

ARONSON, Frank D.——B: July 26, 1947, Malden, MA, *Partner in Law Firm*, Lane & Altman; **PRIM RE ACT:** Attorney; **SERVICES:** Legal services with respect to all aspects of RE transactions; **REP CLIENTS:** Chainstores, RE devel., banks, insurance companies; **PROFL AFFIL & HONORS:** MA Bar Assn., ABA, Sect. on Corp. Banking and Bus. Law; Sect. on Real Prop., Probate and Trust Law; **EDUC:** 1969, Amer. Studies, Yale Coll.; **GRAD EDUC:** JD, 1972, Columbia Univ.; **EDUC HONORS:** Harlan Fiske Stone Scholar; **OTHER ACT & HONORS:** Yale Club of Boston, various synagogue comm. and officerships, profl. organist, United Way and United Jewish Appeal solicitor; **HOME ADD:** 18 Lantern Ln., Newton Centre, MA 02159, (617)244-2457; **BUS ADD:** 201 Devonshire St., Boston, MA 02110, (617)357-5200.

ARTHUR, James William——B: Jan. 29, 1940, Akron, OH, *Pres.*, Trans. Ohio Building Co.; **PRIM RE ACT:** Developer, Builder, Owner/Investor, Property Manager; **SERVICES:** Office rentals; **REP CLIENTS:** Self; **PREV EMPLOY:** RE Sales, Security Sales; **EDUC:** 1963, Bus. Mgmt./RE/Econ., Kent State Univ.; **MIL SERV:** US Army; E-5; **HOME ADD:** 1515 Lake Martin Dr., Kent, OH 44240, (216)626-3560; **BUS ADD:** 1640 Franklin Ave., Kent, OH 44240, (216)626-3560.

ASCHENBREMER, F.A.——*VP Research, Development*, Ball Corporation; **PRIM RE ACT:** Property Manager; **BUS ADD:** 345 South High Street, Munroe, IN 47302, (317)747-6100.*

ASH, C. Neil——*Secy.*, Signal Companies, Inc.; **PRIM RE ACT:** Property Manager; **BUS ADD:** PO Box 2820, LaJolla, CA 92038, (213)278-7400.*

ASH, James H.——B: Oct. 21, 1947, Camden, NJ, *VP*, Builders Investment Group; **PRIM RE ACT:** Property Manager; **PROFL AFFIL & HONORS:** IREM, BOMA, PA Assn. of Realtors, CPM; **EDUC:** BA, 1972, Bus. & Econ., Rutgers Univ.; **GRAD EDUC:** MBA, 1974, Fin., Drexel Univ.; **EDUC HONORS:** High Honors; **MIL SERV:** US Army, Officer, Army Commendation, Vietnam; **HOME ADD:** 314 S. Balderston Dr., Exton, PA 19341, (215)363-1769; **BUS ADD:** Valley Forge Park Place, 1018 West Ninth Ave. Suite 204, King of Prussia, PA 19406, (215)337-1030.

ASH, Willis L.——B: Mar 4, 1934, Philadelphia, PA, *Partner*, Cholette, Perkins & Buchanan; **PRIM RE ACT:** Attorney, Banker, Lender; **SERVICES:** Legal advice to banks & lenders in consumer and comml. RE loans; **REP CLIENTS:** MI Nat. Bank, Bank of Rockford, Western State Bank, First Security Bank, J.T. Barnes & Co.; **PREV EMPLOY:** Chief Counsel, MI Nat. Bank; **PROFL AFFIL & HONORS:** State Bar of MI; ABA; Comml. Law League; Grand Rapids Bar Assn.; **EDUC:** BA, 1956, Hist./Econ., Albian Coll.; **GRAD EDUC:** LLB, 1975, Gen., Detroit Coll. of Law; **EDUC HONORS:** Columbo Award; **OTHER ACT & HONORS:** Peninsula Club; Macatawa Bay Y.C., YMCA; **HOME ADD:** 4481 Fruit Ridge Ave. NW, Grand Rapids, MI 49504, (616)784-2031; **BUS ADD:** 755 Old Kent Bldg., Grand Rapids, MI 49503, (616)774-2131.

ASHEIM, Erling——B: Jan. 26, 1936, NY, NY, *VP*, Morgan Guaranty Trust Co., RE Investment; **PRIM RE ACT:** Owner/Investor, Property Manager; **SERVICES:** Responsible for mgmt. of all assets acquired for investing clients; **PREV EMPLOY:** IBM; Irving Trust Co.; **PROFL AFFIL & HONORS:** NY State Soc. of Prof. Engrs.; NY RE Bd., Lic. Prof. Engr., NY; **EDUC:** BCE, 1961, Civil Engrg., City Coll. of NY; **GRAD EDUC:** ME, 1966, CUNY; **MIL SERV:** USMC; Sgt.; 1953-1956; **HOME ADD:** 15 Gregory St., New City, NY 10956, (914)634-9630; **BUS ADD:** 9 W. 57th St., NY, NY 10019.

ASHER, Richard W.——B: July 22, 1916, Perry Cty., KY, *Atty. at Law*, Self-employed; **PRIM RE ACT:** Broker, Consultant, Attorney, Appraiser, Property Manager, Syndicator; **OTHER RE ACT:** RE fin. and investment counseling; **REP CLIENTS:** Comml. and indus. prop. devels.; **PREV EMPLOY:** RE Investment Dept., The Prudential Insurance Co.; **PROFL AFFIL & HONORS:** KY Bar Assn.; **EDUC:** BA, 1939, Eng./Hist., Union Coll., Barbourville, KY; **GRAD EDUC:** JD, 1948, Law, College of Law, Univ. of KY; **MIL SERV:** USAF; Col. (ret.); 1941-45, DFC Air Medal and others; **HOME ADD:** 1263 Bordeaux Drive, Lexington, KY 40504, (606)233-1357; **BUS ADD:** 1263 Bordeaux Dr., Lexington, KY 40504, (606)233-1357.

ASHLEY, Lawrence D.——B: Aug. 15, 1948, Kansas City, MO, *VP/CFO*, Weber & Company Real Estate Investments; **PRIM RE ACT:** Developer, Builder, Owner/Investor, Property Manager, Syndicator; **SERVICES:** Devel. and synd./prop. mgmt.; **PREV EMPLOY:** Partner, Fox & Co, CPA's; **PROFL AFFIL & HONORS:** ABA; MO Bar Assn., Amer. Inst. of CPA's; ABA - Tax Sect: Partnership Taxation; **EDUC:** BSBA, 1971, Corp. Fin., Univ. of MO; **GRAD EDUC:** JD, 1974, Law, Univ. of MO; **EDUC HONORS:** Law Review; **HOME ADD:** 10203 Lowell, Overland Park, KS 66212, (913)381-1827; **BUS ADD:** 1102 Grand Ste. 2300, Kansas City, MO 64106, (816)421-5300.

ASHLINE, Karl C.——B: July 10, 1934, Alburg, VT, *Pres.*, Ashline Const., Inc.; **PRIM RE ACT:** Developer, Builder, Property Manager; **PROFL AFFIL & HONORS:** NAHB; **EDUC:** BA, 1960, Pol. Sci., Hist. & Econ., Univ. of VT, Burlington, VT; **HOME ADD:** 20 Sebring Rd., So. Burlington, VT 05401, (802)868-7347; **BUS ADD:** 1908 Airport Pkwy, S. Burlington, VT 05401, (802)864-9170.

ASHTON, Fred L., Jr.——B: Mar. 7, 1931, Easton, PA, *VP*, Ashton Assoc.; **PRIM RE ACT:** Consultant; **PREV EMPLOY:** Exec Dir., Dover Indus. Comm., 1976-79; Mayor & Chief Exec Officer City of Easton, PA, 1968-76; **PROFL AFFIL & HONORS:** IREBA, CID; **EDUC:** BA, 1952, Econ., Lafayette Coll.; **GRAD EDUC:** MS, 1959, Educ., Temple Univ.; **MIL SERV:** US Army, 1st Lt.; **OTHER ACT & HONORS:** City Council, Easton, PA, 1965-69; **HOME ADD:** 509 Reeder St., Easton, PA 18042, (205)258-1117; **BUS TEL:** (201)830-3800.

ASHTON, George T.——B: Dec. 7, 1920, Piqua, OH, *Dir. Indus. & Comm. Devel.*, Buckeye Power, Inc.; **PRIM RE ACT:** Developer; **SERVICES:** Develop & provide site information to prospects; **REP CLIENTS:** Honda, Airco Corp., Air Products, Owen Corning; **PROFL AFFIL & HONORS:** AEDC, Glad OH Devel. Assn., OH Devel. Council; **MIL SERV:** Army, 1940-45, 1st Sgt., Purple Heart, Bronze Star; **HOME ADD:** 6449 Baffin Dr., Dublin, OH 43017, (614)889-0521; **BUS ADD:** 6677 Busch Blvd., Columbus, OH 43229, (614)846-5757.

ASHTON, R.S.——B: May 9, 1957, Vernal, UT, *Pres. & CEO*, Ashton-Utah Corp./Para Devel. Corp./Para Mgmt. Corp.; **PRIM RE ACT:** Developer, Builder, Owner/Investor, Property Manager; **OTHER RE ACT:** Project coordination, planning, acquisitions, corp. coordination; **SERVICES:** Specializing in energy-related comml. and indus. projects, data processing, marketing; **HOME ADD:** 245 N. Vine 801, Salt Lake City, UT; **BUS ADD:** 10 Exchange Pl., POB 1925, Salt Lake City, UT 84110, (801)363-2263.

ASHWORTH, Dell S.——B: July 20, 1923, Salt Lake City, UT, *Arch.*, Dell S. Ashworth & Assn., Arch.; **PRIM RE ACT:** Architect, Developer; **OTHER RE ACT:** Licensed RE salesman; **REP CLIENTS:** City & Cty. Ctrs., Schools, condos, churches, stores, office bldgs., indus. plants, resid. devels.; **PREV EMPLOY:** Dell S. Ashworth & Assn., practicing prof. of arch. since 1949; **PROFL AFFIL & HONORS:** Pres. TAG 1971-pres.; Part. TAG RE; **EDUC:** BArch, 1949, Arch., UC, Berkeley; **MIL SERV:** USA, CM2/C, Amer. Theater Ribbon, Victory Medal, Asiatic Pacific Theater Ribbon with 3 stars; Philippine Liberation, 1 Star; **OTHER ACT & HONORS:** Pres. Provo C of C, 1969; State Pres. Sons of Amer. Rev.; O&F Dist. Comm Boy Scouts, 1960-66; Who's Who in World; Who's Who in Commerce & Industry; Intrl. Who's Who in Community Serv.; Who's Who in Fin. & Indus.; Intrl. Who's Who in Arts & Antiques; **HOME ADD:** 1965 N 1400 E, Provo, UT 84601, (801)373-2552; **BUS ADD:** 36E 400 N (PO Box 479), Provo, UT 84601, (801)374-8025.

ASKEY, William Hartman——B: June 21, 1919, Williamsport, PA, *Atty & Counselor at Law*; **PRIM RE ACT:** Regulator; **SERVICES:** Title examinations, legal draftsmanship, title ins., rep. clients who are buying, selling, leasing & financing; **REP CLIENTS:** Commonwealth

Land Title Ins. Co., N. Central Motor Club of PA; **PROFL AFFIL & HONORS:** PA Bar Assn., ABA, Lycoming Law Assn.; **EDUC:** BA, 1941, Poli. Sci., Bucknell Univ.; **GRAD EDUC:** JD, 1951, Law, Univ. of Pittsburgh; **EDUC HONORS:** Phi Eta Sigma; **MIL SERV:** USAF, Capt.; **OTHER ACT & HONORS:** Comm. & US Magistrate for Middle Dist. of PA, 1964 to date; **HOME ADD:** 345 Lundy Dr., Williamsport, PA 17701, (717)322-0798; **BUS ADD:** 35 West Third St., Williamsport, PA 17701, (717)323-9881.

ASKIN, Phyllis——B: Oct. 31, 1945, Baker, MT, *Owner-Broker*, X.Sell Realty; **PRIM RE ACT:** Broker; **SERVICES:** Listing & sale of resid., comml., and small tracts; **PROFL AFFIL & HONORS:** MT Realtors Assn., FLI; **HOME ADD:** Pine Hills Stage, Miles City, MT 59301, (406)232-2398; **BUS ADD:** 4 N. Ninth, Miles City, MT 59301, (406)232-5452.

ASMAR, Mark A.——B: May 23, 1945, Danbury, CT, *Partner*, Hyman, Asbel, Channin & Harding, PC; **PRIM RE ACT:** Attorney; **SERVICES:** All legal for devel. of RE; **REP CLIENTS:** The Bronson Hutensky Cos., Martin, Belair & Co., Aetna Life Ins. Co., City Place Venture, The Richard Roberts Group, Inc.; **PROFL AFFIL & HONORS:** Amer., CT and Hartford Cty. Bar Assns., Intl. Council of Shopping Cts. (State Action Chmn.); **EDUC:** AB, 1967, Govt., econ., IN Univ.; **GRAD EDUC:** JD, 1970, Univ. of CT Sch. of Law; **EDUC HONORS:** Deans list, Law Review; **MIL SERV:** US Army, E-6; **HOME ADD:** 29 Old Village Rd., Bloomfield, CT 06002, (203)243-9207; **BUS ADD:** 100 Constitution Plaza, Hartford, CT 06103, (203)549-6070.

ASPER, Merle——*VP & Secy.*, Purex Corp.; **PRIM RE ACT:** Property Manager; **BUS ADD:** 5101 Clark Ave., Lakewood, CA 90712, (213)634-3300.*

ASTARABADI, Zaid A.——B: Sept. 20, 1942, Baghdad, Iraq, *Pres.*, Z. Astarabadi Associates; **PRIM RE ACT:** Broker, Consultant, Developer, Owner/Investor, Syndicator; **OTHER RE ACT:** Portfolio investment consultant; **SERVICES:** RE investment; **REP CLIENTS:** Intl.; **PREV EMPLOY:** Mktg. and sales mgmt., Borg-Warner Corp.; Honeywell Inc.; VP Finance, 4J Corp.; **EDUC:** BS, 1966, Organic Chem., Univ. of CA, Berkeley; **GRAD EDUC:** BA, 1971, Gen. Mgmt., Amer. Grad. School of Intl. Mgmt.; MBA, 1970, Quant. Analysis, CA State Univ., Fresno; **EDUC HONORS:** Dean's List; **OTHER ACT & HONORS:** Sigma Pi Social Frat.; Alpha Kappa Psi, Prof. Frat.; Who's Who in the West; **HOME ADD:** 21 Whitewood Way, Irvine, CA 92715, (714)559-1513; **BUS ADD:** 3 Corporate Plaza, Suite 102, Newport Beach, CA 92660, (714)720-1330.

ASTHEIMER, Kenneth——B: Nov. 27, 1948, Pottstown, PA, *Natl. Div. Mgr. (Richmond)*, Lawyers Title Insurance Corporation, National Div.; **OTHER RE ACT:** Title Insurance; **SERVICES:** Land title ins. servs.; **PREV EMPLOY:** F&M Savings Bank, Minneapolis, MN; **PROFL AFFIL & HONORS:** Natl. Assn. Corp. RE Execs.; **EDUC:** BS, 1970, Econ., Westmar Coll., Lemars, IA; **GRAD EDUC:** VA Commonwealth Univ., Richmond, VA; **HOME ADD:** 2406 Manlyn Rd., Richmond, VA 23229, (804)270-3946; **BUS ADD:** PO Box 754, Richmond, VA 23206, (804)643-1691.

ATKINS, A. Anthony——B: Mar. 5, 1938, Augusta, GA, *VP and Sec.*, Athins and Simkins Realty Co.; **PRIM RE ACT:** Broker, Syndicator, Consultant, Appraiser, Developer, Property Manager; **PREV EMPLOY:** Sales Mgr. Atlantic Bottling Co.; **PROFL AFFIL & HONORS:** Won H. Gould Barrett Award twice; Comml. salesman in Augusta; Board GRI; CCIM; **EDUC:** BBA, 1961, Personnel Admin., Univ. of GA; **MIL SERV:** GA AirNG; **HOME ADD:** 519 Winchester Ave., Augusta, GA 30909, (404)736-6966; **BUS ADD:** 2534 Central Ave., Augusta, GA 30904, (404)736-6631.

ATKINS, Cleve L.——*VP (Partner)*, Atkins, Green, Stauffer, Clark & Co.; **PRIM RE ACT:** Broker, Appraiser, Developer, Owner/Investor, Syndicator; **PROFL AFFIL & HONORS:** OWP; BOR; FAR; NAR; RESSI, CRA; SOSFA; **OTHER ACT & HONORS:** Bd. of Tr., Lucerne Gen. Hospital, Orlando; **BUS ADD:** 211 E Colonial, Orlando, FL 32801, (305)841-6060.

ATKINS, Merle E.——B: Dec. 2, 1946, Fairbury, IL, *Area VP & Appraiser Mgr.*, Marshall & Stevens, Inc.; **PRIM RE ACT:** Appraiser; **SERVICES:** Valuation, counseling & tax guidance; **PROFL AFFIL & HONORS:** Amer. Soc. of Appraisers; Assoc. Member of Soc. of RE Appraisers; NY RE Bd., Sr. Member ASA; **EDUC:** BS, 1968, Agric., Fin. & RE, Univ. of IL; **HOME ADD:** 204 Carmen Cir., Oaks, PA 19456, (215)666-0881; **BUS ADD:** 1845 Walnut St., Philadelphia, PA 19103, (215)299-5700.

ATKINSON, Herbert Emerson, Jr.——B: Feb. 27, 1943, Raleigh, NC, *Pres., Emerson Atkinson & Co.; Managing Partner, Atkinson-Van Horn Assoc.*, Atkinson-Van Horn Associates; **PRIM RE ACT:** Developer; **SERVICES:** Devel. of medical & professional office condos., full serv. custom-built medical and professional offices, prop. mgmt.; **REP CLIENTS:** Professional users, investors; **PREV EMPLOY:** Exec. VP, A.G. Spanos Development, Inc. 1976-1980; Bus. Econ., Federal Reserve Bank of Atlanta, 1969-1972; **EDUC:** BA, 1965, Econ., NC State Univ.; **GRAD EDUC:** MS, 1967, Econ., NC State Univ.; **MIL SERV:** USNR, Ensign 1967-68; **OTHER ACT & HONORS:** Alumnus, Leadership Pinellas, Clearwater, FL; **HOME ADD:** 429 Magnolia Dr., Clearwater, FL 33516, (813)461-4089; **BUS ADD:** 2280 U.S. 19 N., Suite 155, Clearwater, FL 33515, (813)796-3903.

AUBLE, David C.——B: May 24, 1931, Elgin, IL, *VP & Mgr., Appraisal Dept.*, James S. Black & Co.; **PRIM RE ACT:** Appraiser; **SERVICES:** Appraisals of all types of real prop.; **REP CLIENTS:** Real prop. investors & owners, governmental agencies, lenders, relocation mgmt. firms; **PROFL AFFIL & HONORS:** AIREA;SREA; Intl. Right-of-Way Assn.; **MIL SERV:** Signal Corp., Cpl.; **HOME ADD:** S. 5704 Mohawk Dr., Spokane, WA 99206, (509)928-4914; **BUS ADD:** 500 Columbia Bldg., Spokane, WA 99204, (509)838-2511.

AUCUTT, Charles Henry——B: July 23, 1934, MO, *Pres.*, Charles H. Aucutt, Realtor; **PRIM RE ACT:** Broker, Developer, Owner/Investor; **SERVICES:** Locating, analyzing and purchasing investment prop. for clients; **PREV EMPLOY:** Comptroller of the Currency, National Bank Examiners; **PROFL AFFIL & HONORS:** RNMI; RE Securities and Synd. Inst.; FLI; IREF, CCIM; CRS; GRI; **EDUC:** BS, Bus. Admin., 1966, Fin., Univ. of San Francisco; **MIL SERV:** USAF; **OTHER ACT & HONORS:** Honorary Dir. of Planned Parenthood of Monterey Cty.; Member of Commonwealth Club; Pres. of Pacific Grove Rotary Club; Governors Rep., Area 10, Dist. 522; **HOME ADD:** P.O. Box 532, Pebble Beach, CA 93953, (408)625-0743; **BUS ADD:** 1011 Cass St., Monterey, CA 93940, (408)373-2691.

AUDLEMAN, Don——B: July 16, 1943, Oklahoma City, OK, *Pres.*, Bus. Facilities Development; **PRIM RE ACT:** Broker, Consultant, Architect, Developer, Owner/Investor, Property Manager, Syndicator; **PROFL AFFIL & HONORS:** Amer. Inst. of Arch., Dir., Empire Savings Assn.; **EDUC:** BArch, 1966, OK State Univ., So. Methodist Univ. Pres. Honor Roll, OK State Univ.; **OTHER ACT & HONORS:** Chandlers Landing Yacht Club (commodore, Past), Chmn. of ANPH, Inc. Architects; **HOME ADD:** 3240 Rankin, Dallas, TX 75205, (214)692-1862; **BUS ADD:** 5499 Glen Lakes, Dallas, TX 75231, (214)369-3120.

AUFRECHT, Michael D.——B: Oct. 4, 1940, Chicago, IL, *Atty.*, Taylor, Miller, Magner, Sprowl & Hutchings; **PRIM RE ACT:** Attorney, Owner/Investor; **PROFL AFFIL & HONORS:** Chicago Bar Assn. RE Sect.; **EDUC:** BS, 1962, Bus. Sch., Univ. IL; **GRAD EDUC:** 1965, Law, Northwestern Univ.; **HOME ADD:** 6612 N. Le Mai, Lincolnwood, IL 60646, (312)679-8551; **BUS ADD:** 120 S. LaSalle St., Chicago, IL 60603, (312)782-6070.

AUGUSTIN, Drew——B: Mar. 16, 1954, Indpls., IN, *Leasing Salesman*, Klein & Kuhn, F.C. Tucker Co.; **PRIM RE ACT:** Broker, Property Manager; **PREV EMPLOY:** Landau & Heyman, Melvin Simon Assoc.; **EDUC:** 1976, Fin., Econ., Acct., IN Univ.; **EDUC HONORS:** BS; **HOME ADD:** 110 Round Up Trail, Noblesville, IN 46060, (317)842-7867; **BUS ADD:** One American Square, Indianapolis, IN 46204, (317)634-6363.

AUGUSTINE, Jon W.——B: Sept. 28, 1935, Chicago, IL, *RE Counselor*, Golden Rule; **PRIM RE ACT:** Consultant, Builder, Property Manager, Owner/Investor; **OTHER RE ACT:** Exchange & Investment Counselor; **SERVICES:** Spec. in creative RE problem solving; **PREV EMPLOY:** 14 yrs. in Gen. Motors Mgmt.; Indust. Engineering, Accounting, & EDP Problem Solving; **PROFL AFFIL & HONORS:** Member: Nat. Council of Exchangors, Interex, Hold "Gold Card" Designation; **EDUC:** BS Ind. Engrg. & Bus. Admin., 1958, Fin., Mktg., Iowa State Univ. - Ames; **OTHER ACT & HONORS:** Mensa, Past V Chrmn. Los Angeles Area, Henry Knox-Westlake 392 F&AM; **HOME ADD:** 23542 Ladrillo St., Woodland Hills, CA 91367, (213)887-1539; **BUS ADD:** 23542 Ladrillo St., Woodland Hills, CA 91367, (213)887-1539.

AULD, John W., Jr.——B: Nov. 22, 1953, Kansas City, MO, *Pres.*, Auld Brothers Realty & Development Corp.; **PRIM RE ACT:** Broker, Developer, Builder; **SERVICES:** Complete devel. & mktg. resid. props.; **PROFL AFFIL & HONORS:** Local, state & nat. Bd. of Realtors; Urban Planning League (KC); Local zoning comm., ULI; **EDUC:** BA, 1976, Bus. & Fin., West Point & KS Univ.; **GRAD EDUC:** MBA, RE & Const., Univ. of MO in Kansas City; **MIL SERV:** US Army, West Point; **OTHER ACT & HONORS:**

Republican Party-delegate 1976 & 80; **HOME ADD:** 9126 Lee Blvd., Leawood, KS 66206, (913)649-9297; **BUS ADD:** 9126 Lee Blvd., Leawood, KS 66206, (913)649-9297.

AULD, John William——B: Aug. 21, 1928, Kansas City, MO, *Pres.*, Auld Realty & Devel. Corp.; **PRIM RE ACT:** Broker, Consultant, Developer, Builder, Property Manager, Insuror, Syndicator; **SERVICES:** Acquisition, planning, zoning, devel., const., mktg., prop. mgmt.; **PROFL AFFIL & HONORS:** NARB, KARB, MREB, KCMBR, JCBR, Nat. Assn. of Home Builders, Home Builders Assn.; **EDUC:** BS, 1951, Sci., Kansas Univ.; **HOME ADD:** 9135 Manor Rd., Leawood, KS 66206, (913)649-8338; **BUS ADD:** Box 36, Stillwell, KS 66085, (913)649-8478.

AUST, Jurgen——B: Dec. 3, 1938, Tarnewitz, Germany, *Prin.,Tr.*, HKS Associates; **PRIM RE ACT:** Consultant; **OTHER RE ACT:** Planner; **SERVICES:** Environmental analysis, land use programming & planning; **REP CLIENTS:** Public & pvt., land devel.; **PROFL AFFIL & HONORS:** Amer. Planning Assn., Profl. Serv. Mgmt. Assn.; **EDUC:** 1965, Engrg., Tech. Univ., Graz, Austria; **GRAD EDUC:** MArch. & Urban Design, 1971, WA Univ., St. Louis MO; **HOME ADD:** 2416 Hillside Ave., Berkeley, CA 94704, (415)548-6525; **BUS ADD:** 731 Market St., San Francisco, CA 94103, (415)777-2666.

AUSTIN, Brock J.——B: Oct. 14, 1950, Cleveland, OH, Schine Julianelle Karp & Bozelko PC; **PRIM RE ACT:** Attorney; **PROFL AFFIL & HONORS:** Exec. Comm., Real Prop. Sect. CT Bar Assn.; ABA; **EDUC:** BA, 1972, Hist., Univ. of NH; **GRAD EDUC:** MA, 1973, Hist., Univ. of NH; JD, 1976, Cornell Law School; **EDUC HONORS:** Phi Beta Kappa, 1971, Magna Cum Laude; **HOME ADD:** 226 Papurah Rd., Fairfield, CT 06430, (203)255-5202; **BUS ADD:** 830 Post Rd. E. Suite 100, Westport, CT 06881, (203)226-6861.

AUSTIN, Charles E.——B: May 29, 1936, Flint, MI, *Owner*, Austin & Assoc.; **PRIM RE ACT:** Appraiser; **PROFL AFFIL & HONORS:** SREA, SRA Designation; Gov. Dist. 4, SREA; **EDUC:** MI State Univ.; **HOME ADD:** 4036 Verde Vista Dr., Thousand Oaks, CA 91360, (805)492-3028; **BUS ADD:** POB 1102, Thousand Oaks, CA 91360, (805)496-4397.

AUSTIN, Janet T.——B: June 8, 1937, Burlington VT, *Gen. Mgr.*, Lang Assoc. Inc./Hometrend; **PRIM RE ACT:** Broker; **OTHER RE ACT:** Mgmt. consultant in RE; **PROFL AFFIL & HONORS:** NAR; VT Assn. of Realtors; VT CRS, GRI, CRS; **EDUC:** BS, 1956, Nursing, Univ. of VT; **OTHER ACT & HONORS:** Civic organizations; **HOME ADD:** 301 Swift St., South Burlington, VT 05401; **BUS ADD:** 360 Main St., Burlington, VT 05401, (802)864-0541.

AUSTIN, Larry D.——B: Dec. 2, 1944, Memphis, TN, *Atty.*, Lowrance and Austin, P.C.; **PRIM RE ACT:** Attorney; **SERVICES:** RE closings, single and multi-family, HUD programs closings, counselling and appeals; synds.; RE trouble shooting; **PREV EMPLOY:** Atty. for US Dept. of HUD 1968-1971; **PROFL AFFIL & HONORS:** ABA; TN Bar Assn.; Memphis Shelby Cty. Bar Assn., HUD Outstanding Performance Award 1971; **EDUC:** BA, 1965, Poli. Sci., Vanderbilt Univ.; **GRAD EDUC:** LLB, 1968, Harvard Law School; **EDUC HONORS:** Cum Laude; **OTHER ACT & HONORS:** TN State Soccer Assn. - Youth Commnr.; **HOME ADD:** 1817 Greensprings Ln., Germantown, TN 38138, (901)754-2473; **BUS ADD:** 6263 Poplar Ave., Suite 300, Memphis, TN 38119, (901)761-1212.

AUSTIN, Leslie J.——B: Feb. 4, 1941, Worthington, MN, *Pres.*, Austin Construction & Development Co., Inc.; **PRIM RE ACT:** Broker, Architect, Developer, Builder, Owner/Investor, Syndicator; **PREV EMPLOY:** Sea Pines Co.: VP - Devel., 1972-1974; Ryan Homes: VP, Div. Mgr., 1974-1977; **PROFL AFFIL & HONORS:** ULI, Nat. Assn. of Home Builders, Amer. Inst. of Planners, Realtor, Nat. Bd. of Dir., NAHB; Pres., Local Chap. of NAHB; **EDUC:** B of Arch., 1969, Arch. & Planning, Univ. of KS; **GRAD EDUC:** M in Planning, 1970, Planning, Univ. of KS; MBA, 1972, Harvard Grad. Sch. of Bus.; **EDUC HONORS:** Tau Sigma Delta, Degree with Distinction, 1st in Class; **HOME ADD:** 20 Donax Rd., Port Royal Plantation, Hilton Head Is., SC 29928, (803)785-5373; **BUS ADD:** 14 Pope Ave., Hilton Head Is., SC 29928, (803)785-6876.

AUSTIN, Margaret S.——B: June 5, 1950, Buffalo, NY, *Atty.*, Dobson, Griffin & Westerman, P.C.; **PRIM RE ACT:** Attorney; **SERVICES:** Legal Counseling and document prep. for all aspects of RE transactions from single family homes to condo. devel.; **PROFL AFFIL & HONORS:** State Bar of MI, MI Trial Lawyers Assn.; Women Lawyers of MI; ABA; **EDUC:** AB, 1972, Hist., Univ. of MI; **GRAD EDUC:** MA, JD, 1973, 1979, Hist. of Early Mod. Europe, Northwestern Univ., Univ. MI; **EDUC HONORS:** With Honor and With Distinction; **HOME ADD:** 2997 S. Fletcher Rd., Chelsea, MI 48118, (313)475-2908; **BUS ADD:** 500 City Center Bldg., Ann Arbor, MI 48104, (313)761-3780.

AUSTIN, Thomas G.——B: Dec. 18, 1946, Houston, TX, *Broker Assoc.*, Merrill Lynch Realty; **PRIM RE ACT:** Broker, Developer; **SERVICES:** Hotel Brokerage; **PREV EMPLOY:** Holiday Inns, Inc.-Dir. of Franchise devel.; Fox & Carskadon Fin. Corp.-Portfolio Mgr.; **EDUC:** BA, 1970, Econ., Hist., SMU; **GRAD EDUC:** M of Intl. Mgmt., 1972, Thunderbird Grad. Sch. of Int. Mgmt.; **HOME ADD:** Box 736, Ross, CA 94957, (415)454-9682; **BUS ADD:** 919 Sir Francis Drake Blvd., Kentfield, CA 94904, (415)459-0850.

AUSTIN, Wayne B.——B: July 1, 1927, Stamford, TX, *Owner*, Wayne Austin and Assoc.; **PRIM RE ACT:** Broker, Appraiser; **SERVICES:** Realtor, Appraiser Consultant; **REP CLIENTS:** Lender and indiv. involved in comml. and form and ranch props.; **PROFL AFFIL & HONORS:** AIREA; Soc. of RE Appraisers, MAI, SRPA; **EDUC:** Hardin-Simmons Univ., Abilene, TX; **MIL SERV:** USN, Fireman - 2nd Class; **OTHER ACT & HONORS:** Flood Study Comm., City of Abilene, Housing Comm. (W Tx.) Council of Govts.; **HOME ADD:** Route 5 Box 932, Abilene, TX 79605, (915)692-2299; **BUS ADD:** Suite 213, 1st State Bank Bldg., Abilene, TX 79602, (915)673-2578.

AUSTIN, William W.——B: June 18, 1945, Effingham, IL, *Atty.*, *Partner*, Parker, Brummer, Siemer, Austin & Resch; **PRIM RE ACT:** Attorney; **SERVICES:** Legal; **REP CLIENTS:** Lenders, indiv. and instnl. devels. and investors; **PROFL AFFIL & HONORS:** ABA, real prop. sect., comm. on recent devels., IL Bar Assn.; **EDUC:** BS, 1967, Fin., Univ. of IL; **GRAD EDUC:** JD, 1970, Univ. of IL; **MIL SERV:** IL ARNG, Maj., JAGC, 1970-date; **OTHER ACT & HONORS:** Special Asst. Atty. Gen., IL 1971-date; **HOME ADD:** 900 S First St., Effingham, IL 62401, (217)347-7324; **BUS ADD:** 307 N Third St. Box 607, Effingham, IL 62401, (217)342-9291.

AUSTRIAN, James A.——B: June 24, 1934, NY, *Partner*, Jones Lang Wootton; **PRIM RE ACT:** Consultant; **SERVICES:** Full Serv. Profl. Firm with Worldwide Facilities; **REP CLIENTS:** UK, European, US Investors, Devels., Owners, etc.; **PREV EMPLOY:** 8 yrs.-VP Landauer Assoc.; **PROFL AFFIL & HONORS:** Amer. Soc. of RE Counselors, FIABCI, NY State Soc. of RE Appraisals, CRE; **EDUC:** BA, 1956, Soc. Sci., Harvard Univ.; **MIL SERV:** USMC, Lt.; **HOME ADD:** 517 E 87 St., NY, NY 10028, (212)988-3991; **BUS ADD:** 499 Park Ave., NY, NY 10022, (212)688-8181.

AUTEN, David C., Esq.——B: Apr. 4, 1938, Philadelphia, PA, *Partner*, Reed Smith Townsend & Munson; **PRIM RE ACT:** Attorney, Instructor; **SERVICES:** Legal; **PROFL AFFIL & HONORS:** ABA; PA Bar Assn.; Chmn. RE Fin. Comm. and Treasurer, Real Property, Probate Trust Law Section, Philadelphia Bar Assn.; **EDUC:** BA, 1960, Univ. of PA; **GRAD EDUC:** JD, 1963, Univ. of PA Law School; **EDUC HONORS:** Phi Beta Kappa, Editor, Law Review; **HOME ADD:** 120 Delancy St., Philadelphia, PA 19106, (215)627-2535; **BUS ADD:** 1600 Western Savings Bank Bldg., Philadelphia, PA 19107, (215)875-4362.

AUTENRIETH, Glenn E.——B: Oct. 27, 1940, Chicago, IL, *Sr. VP & Tr. Officer*, The First National Bank of Batavia; **PRIM RE ACT:** Banker; **SERVICES:** Gen. banking; **PROFL AFFIL & HONORS:** IL Bankers Assn., Land Trust Council of IL, Bank Admin. Inst., Nat. Assn. of Review Appraisers; **EDUC:** BS, 1961, Fin., Northwestern Univ.; **GRAD EDUC:** Grad. Sch. of Banking, 1980, Univ. of WI; **MIL SERV:** US Army, Sgt.; **BUS ADD:** 155 W. Wilson St., Batavia, IL 60501, (312)879-2600.

AVANT, Walter W.——B: Feb. 26, 1933, Darling, MS, *Pres.*, Phoenix Realty Co.; **PRIM RE ACT:** Broker, Appraiser, Developer, Builder, Owner/Investor; **OTHER RE ACT:** Construction mgmt.; **SERVICES:** Valuation, devel., const. mgmt.; **REP CLIENTS:** Prop. mgmt. , govt. agencies and investment groups; **PREV EMPLOY:** Indust. devel. rep. for the city of E. St. Louis; **PROFL AFFIL & HONORS:** Realtors, NAHB; **EDUC:** BS, 1966, fin. and mgmt., So. IL Univ.; **MIL SERV:** US Army, Pvt.; **OTHER ACT & HONORS:** United Black Contractors of Metro. E. St. Louis; **HOME ADD:** 499 N. 33rd St., E. St. Louis, IL 62205, (618)274-9280; **BUS ADD:** 495 N. 33rd. St., E. St. Louis, IL 62205, (618)271-9677.

AVEDON, Peter M.——*Pres.*, Sherwood Development Corp. & Century 21 Eastward Realty; **PRIM RE ACT:** Broker, Developer, Builder; **SERVICES:** Resid. & comml. brokage & devel. builder custom houses; **BUS ADD:** 167 Glen Head Rd., Glen Head, WY 11545, (516)674-3882.

AVERY, Cyrus Stevens, II——B: Oct. 19, 1932, Tulsa, OK, *Pres. & Dir.*, Westfinance Corp.; **PRIM RE ACT:** Broker, Consultant, Syndicator; **SERVICES:** Investment counseling, valuation, brokerage & synd. of comml. prop.; supervision & admin. of devel. projects for foreign clients; **REP CLIENTS:** Foreign indiv. and instnl. investors and devel. of comml. and resid. prop.; **PREV EMPLOY:** Pres. of RE Affil. of Intl. Bank; **PROFL AFFIL & HONORS:** Member: Wash. Bd. of Realtors; Wash. Bd. of Trade; Wash. Soc. of Investment Analysts, Licensed RE Broker - DC and VA; **EDUC:** BS, 1954, Civil Engrg., US Mil. Acad.; **GRAD EDUC:** MBA, 1962, Fin., Harvard Grad. School of Bus. Admin.; **MIL SERV:** Artillery, Capt.; **OTHER ACT & HONORS:** Chmn. of the Bd., DC Devel. Corp. & DC Investment Corp.; 1976-1979, appointed by the Mayor; West Point Soc. of DC; Harvard Bus. School Club of DC; Dir. of Transemantics, Inc.; **HOME ADD:** 8016 Georgetown Pike, McLean, VA 22102, (703)893-5464; **BUS ADD:** 4801 Massachusetts Ave., NW, Suite 400, Washington, DC 20016, (202)364-8890.

AVERY, Hartford R.——B: Sept. 18, 1928, RE, *Mgr.*, Merrill-Lynch Realty - Tom Fannin, Phoenix N; **PRIM RE ACT:** Broker; **SERVICES:** Residential RE Specialist; **PROFL AFFIL & HONORS:** RNMI, GRI, Cert. RE Brokerage Mgr.; **MIL SERV:** USN, 1948-1952, ME/2; **OTHER ACT & HONORS:** Shrine, Masons, Phoenix W Rotary, Moon Valley Soccer Club - Coach; **HOME ADD:** 4332 W Monte Cristo, Glendale, AZ 85306, (602)978-4614; **BUS ADD:** 7150 N 7th St., Phoenix, AZ 85020, (602)997-7471.

AVERY, Jonathan H.——B: Mar. 11, 1948, Boston, MA, *Principal*, Avery Assoc.; **PRIM RE ACT:** Instructor, Consultant, Appraiser; **SERVICES:** Member AIREA; Member, Intl. Soc. of RE Appraisers; **PREV EMPLOY:** 6 yrs. mort. banking exp. in various capacities within the S&L Indus.; **PROFL AFFIL & HONORS:** AIREA, Intl. Soc. of RE Appraisers, MA Bd. of RE Appraisers, Prof. Designations: MAI, RM, SRA, SRPA, MRA; **EDUC:** BA, Bus. Admin., 1970, Fin., RE, Univ. of MA, Amherst; **OTHER ACT & HONORS:** Instr. Bentley Coll (RE Valuation); 1980 Pres. MA Bd. of RE Appraisers; 1978 Pres. Trustee, MA Bd. of RE Appraisers; **HOME ADD:** 2 Paul Revere Rd., Acton, MA 01720, (617)263-8185; **BUS ADD:** 556 Mass. Ave., PO Box 834, Acton, MA 01720, (617)263-5002.

AVIRETT, Abner——*Cont. & Treas.*, Oxford Industries, Inc.; **PRIM RE ACT:** Property Manager; **BUS ADD:** 222 Piedmond Ave. NE, Atlanta, GA 30312, (404)659-2424.*

AXEL, Marc——B: Sept. 8, 1945, Richmond, VA, *Assoc. Broker*, Joyner & Co., Realtors, Comml. & Investment; **PRIM RE ACT:** Broker, Consultant, Owner/Investor; **SERVICES:** Investment counseling, leasing & improved & unimproved sales of comml. & investment prop. & apt. land; **REP CLIENTS:** Indiv. investors, indiv. & corporate comml. prop. users, prop. devel.; **PROFL AFFIL & HONORS:** Richmond Bd. of Realtors; Richmond Comml. MLS; VA Assn. of Realtors; VA Cert. Comml. Investment Member Chap.; NAR; RNMI, CCIM; **EDUC:** BA, 1972, Pol. Sci., Univ. of Richmond; **MIL SERV:** US Army, Sgt.; **HOME ADD:** 9105 Avalon Dr., Richmond, VA 23229, (804)741-1356; **BUS ADD:** 2727 Enterprise Pkwy., Richmond, VA 23229, (804)270-9440.

AXELRAD, Thomas L.——B: Oct. 23, 1945, Freeport, TX, *Comml./Indus. VP*, Stan Weber & Assoc., Inc., Realtors; **PRIM RE ACT:** Broker, Instructor, Consultant, Owner/Investor; **SERVICES:** Comml., Indus. & Investment RE Brokerage; **REP CLIENTS:** Indiv. Investors, Corp. Users, Fin. Instns.; **PROFL AFFIL & HONORS:** NAR; RNMI; Jefferson Bd. of Realtors; LA CCIM Chap. (Pres.); LA Realtors Assn., CCIM of RNMI; Million Dollar Club (Jefferson Bd. of Realtors); **EDUC:** BA, 1968, Econ., Univ. of TX; **OTHER ACT & HONORS:** Greater N.O. Tourist Commn., Dir; N.O. Jaycees, Past Pres.; St. Martin's School, Alumni Bd. Pres.; C of C; Econ. Devel. Council; **HOME ADD:** 822 Burdette St., New Orleans, LA 70118, (504)866-5893; **BUS ADD:** 3841 Veterans Blvd., Metairie, LA 70002, (504)888-1777.

AXELROD, Alan L.——B: Feb. 23, 1946, Detroit, MI, *Pres.*, The Axelrod Co.; **PRIM RE ACT:** Consultant, Attorney, Developer, Owner/Investor, Syndicator; **OTHER RE ACT:** Securities Broker-Dealer; **PREV EMPLOY:** VP/Corp. Counsel, Commonwealth Pacific, Inc., Seattle, WA 1979-1980; Law Practice 1974-1979; Corporate Counsel, Security Pacific, Inc., 1972-1974; **PROFL AFFIL & HONORS:** ABA, WA State Bar Assn., Seattle-King Cty. Bar Assn., Ressi-WA Chapt., JD; **EDUC:** AB, 1968, Hist./Econ., Univ. of MI; **GRAD EDUC:** JD, 1971, Law, Univ. of MI Law Sch.; **HOME ADD:** 3926 N.E. Surber Dr., Seattle, WA 98105, (206)525-6199; **BUS ADD:** 405 Columbia, Suite 508, Seattle, WA 98104, (206)623-7700.

AXSON, G. Michael——B: Dec. 13, 1941, Ft. Wayne, IN, *Pres.*, Rousseau Realty House Inc.; **PRIM RE ACT:** Broker, Builder, Owner/Investor; **SERVICES:** RE Sales; **PREV EMPLOY:** Waterfield Mfg. Co. Inc.; **PROFL AFFIL & HONORS:** GRI, CRS, CRB; **HOME ADD:** 8223 Ravinia Dr., Ft. Wayne, IN 46815, (219)489-3691; **BUS ADD:** 5720 St. Joe Rd., Ft. Wayne, IN 46815, (219)486-2471.

AXT, James Robert——B: Apr. 14, 1952, Milwaukee, WI, *Atty.*, Axt Law Office; **PRIM RE ACT:** Attorney; **SERVICES:** Title Opinions, complete RE closing asst., RE investment consultation for agri-bus.; **REP CLIENTS:** Farmers Community Cooperative of Rockwell, Community State Bank of Rockwell, Partners Four Investment of Rockwell, Screenprint Ltd. of Mason City; **PROFL AFFIL & HONORS:** ABA; Cerro Gordo Cty. Bar Assn.; Dist. 2A Bar Assn., J.D., M.P.A.; **EDUC:** BA, 1974, Hist./Educ., St. Olaf Coll., Northfield, MN; **GRAD EDUC:** MPA, 1979, Drake Univ., Des Moines, IA; JD, 1978, Drake Univ., Des Moines, IA; **EDUC HONORS:** Magna Cum Laude; **OTHER ACT & HONORS:** Part-time judicial magistrate, Cerro Gordo Cty., 1979; Member Bd. of Dir. North IA Voc. Ctr., Inc.; **HOME ADD:** Box 370, Rockwell, IA 50469, (515)822-3209; **BUS ADD:** Box 370, Rockwell, IA 50469, (515)822-3208.

AYALA, Aurelio——B: Mar. 11, 1941, Comal County, *Assoc.*, National Associates of Latino Elected & Appointed Officials, Area of Legislation; **OTHER RE ACT:** Legal Asst.; **SERVICES:** Deals with representation of educ.; **REP CLIENTS:** Assoc. & Representative of the Assn.; **PREV EMPLOY:** Southwest TX State Univ., San Marcos, TX 70666; **PROFL AFFIL & HONORS:** Nat. Legal Aid & Defenders Assn. (Wash., DC), Nat. Joint Ctr. for Poli. Studies (Wash., DC); **EDUC:** 1982 (graduate), Poli. Sci. (major) Legal Studies (area) Philosophy (minor), Southwest TX State Univ., San Marcos, TX 78666; **OTHER ACT & HONORS:** Legal Aid & Assoc. (80-81), Amer. G.I. Forum, Church Council Member; Pre-Law Soc.-Bilingual Educ. Student Org.; HALT-Org. of Americans for Legal Reform-(Wash. DC); Law Student Civil Rights Research Council (NY); **HOME ADD:** 794 Mulberry Ave., New Braunfels, TX 78130, (512)625-1201; **BUS ADD:** 776 Mulberry Ave., New Braunfels, TX 78130, (512)625-7127.

AYELLA, Albert J.——B: May 21, 1945, Philadelphia, PA, *CPA*, Albert J. Ayella, CPA; **OTHER RE ACT:** CPA, Gen. practise w/concentration in RE; **SERVICES:** Tax planning consultation concerning RE transactions; **REP CLIENTS:** J. David Diaco, RE DeveL.; Cape Devel. Co., Const. Co.; Tom Robbins, RE Consultant & Investor; Century 21 - Spruce/Center City Realty, Realtor; and many other clients concerning RE transactions; **PREV EMPLOY:** Partner in Century 21 - Spruce/Center City Realty; gen. partner & ltd. partner in several RE partnerships; **PROFL AFFIL & HONORS:** AICPA; PICPA; Nat. Soc. of CPA's, CPA; RE Salesman's Lic. in PA; **EDUC:** BA, 1973, Acctg., Philadelphia Textile & Scis.; **GRAD EDUC:** Masters of Taxation, 1981, Taxation, Widener Univ.; **EDUC HONORS:** Grad. with highest grade point avg. of evening div., Straight 'A' avg.; **OTHER ACT & HONORS:** UNICO & Knights of Columbus; **HOME ADD:** 2219 S. Hemberger St., Philadelphia, PA 19145, (215)389-8711; **BUS ADD:** 1027 Chews Landing Rd., Laurel Springs, NJ 08021, (609)435-7737.

AYER, Gordon C.——B: Dec. 9, 1946, Portland, ME, *Atty. at Law*, Ayer, Hodsdon & Austin; **PRIM RE ACT:** Attorney; **SERVICES:** Land devel. counsel, title specialist with emphasis on condo. projects; **PROFL AFFIL & HONORS:** RE and Title Sects. ME State Bar Assn.; **EDUC:** BA, 1969, Eng. Govt., Nasson Coll.; **GRAD EDUC:** JD, 1972, Univ. of ME Sch. of Law; **HOME ADD:** S. Maine St., Kennebunkport, ME 04046, (207)967-4046; **BUS ADD:** 25 Main St. Box 1001, Kennebunk, ME 04043, (207)985-7152.

AYERS, Charles K.——B: Dec. 28, 1944, Rockport, IN, *Atty.*, Snell & Wilmer, Attorneys; **PRIM RE ACT:** Attorney; **SERVICES:** Zoning, RE Subdivision, Condem., Broker's Liability, General RE and Complex Comml. Litigation; **PROFL AFFIL & HONORS:** ABA; Maricopa Cty. Bar Assn.; AZ Bar Assn.; **EDUC:** BA, 1966, Germanic Languages/Fine Arts, Wabash Coll., Crawfordsville, IN; **GRAD EDUC:** MA, 1971, Germanic Languages/Literature, Yale Univ.; JD, 1974, Law, Univ. of Iowa; **EDUC HONORS:** Phi Beta Kappa; Cum Laude, JD with Highest Distinction; **HOME ADD:** 5116 E Orchid Ln., Paradise Valley, AZ 85253, (602)991-0683; **BUS ADD:** 3100 Valley Ctr., Phoenix, AZ 85073, (602)257-7326.

AYERS, Raymond H.——B: June 9, 1945, Sussex, NJ, *VP RE*, The Grand Union Co.; **OTHER RE ACT:** Corp. RE; **EDUC:** BS, 1968, Rutgers Univ.; **BUS ADD:** 100 Broadway, Elmwood Park, NJ 07407, (201)794-2237.

AYLWARD, J. Patrick——B: Aug. 20, 1951, Walla Walla, WA, *Atty.*, Jeffers, Danielson, Sonn & Aylward, P.S.; **PRIM RE ACT:** Attorney; **SERVICES:** Negotiation, documentation, closing and litigation relative to resid., comml. and agricultural RE transactions; **REP CLIENTS:** Pvt. clients, realtors, ins. carriers; **PROFL AFFIL & HONORS:** ABA, WA State Bar Assn., Real Prop. Sect. of WA Bar Assn.; **EDUC:** BA, 1973, Psych., Stanford; **GRAD EDUC:** JD, 1976, Law, Univ. of WA; **EDUC HONORS:** Dean's List; **HOME ADD:** 10 S. Cove, Wenatchee, WA 98801, (509)662-6022; **BUS ADD:** P.O. Box 1688, 317 N. Mission, Wenatchee, WA 98801, (509)662-3685.

AYLWARD, James F.——**B:** Feb. 3, 1929, Walla Walla, WA, *Pres. and CEO*, Sherwood & Roberts, Inc., Corporate; **PRIM RE ACT:** Broker, Appraiser, Banker, Lender, Insuror; **SERVICES:** Mort. loans, income prop. and comml. loans; ins.; RE brokerage; investments; **PROFL AFFIL & HONORS:** Pres., MBAA (Wash., DC), Cert. Mort. Banker; MBAA; SRPA; Soc. of RE Appraisers; MAI; AIREA; RE Broker, WA & OR; **EDUC:** BA, 1950, Bus. Admin./Econ., WA State Univ.; **GRAD EDUC:** Grad., School of Mort. Banking and Advanced Case Study Seminar on Income Property Fin.; **MIL SERV:** USAF, Capt.; **OTHER ACT & HONORS:** Bd. of Trs., Gonzaga Univ., Spokane, WA; Bd. of Dirs., United Way of King Cty., WA; **HOME ADD:** 9357 Hilltop Rd., Bellevue, WA 98004, (206)455-3047; **BUS ADD:** 1417 Fourth Ave., Seattle, WA 98101, (206)682-5400.

AZAR, Edward J.——**B:** Oct. 23, 1923, Montgomery, AL, *Atty. at Law*, Azar, Campbell & Azar - Attys.; **PRIM RE ACT:** Attorney, Instructor; **SERVICES:** Any and all legal serv. of every kind pertaining to RE transactions of every kind and nature; **REP CLIENTS:** Molton, Allen & Williams, Inc.; AmSouth Fin. Corp.; Colonial Fin. Serv., Inc.; (Mort. Brokers) Fed. Land Bank of New Orleans; So. Title Ins. Co. of Knoxville, TN; Commonwealth Land Title Ins. Co.; State Abstract & Title Co.; **PROFL AFFIL & HONORS:** ABA; AL State Bar Assn.; Montgomery Cty., AL Bar Assn.; Phi Alpha Delta Legal Frat., Lecturer on RE Law and Transactions, Univ. of AL (Montgomery Extension Ctr.) and Auburn Univ. at Montgomery; **EDUC:** Univ. of Notre Dame; **GRAD EDUC:** JD, 1947, Univ. of AL; **OTHER ACT & HONORS:** State Admin. - AL Alcoholic Beverage Control Bd. 1959-1963; **HOME ADD:** 116 Brantwood Dr., Montgomery, AL 36109, (205)272-4165; **BUS ADD:** 260 Washington Ave., Montgomery, AL 36104, (205)265-8551.

AZRACK, Joseph——**B:** Apr. 8, 1947, NJ, *VP*, John McMahan Associates, Inc.; **OTHER RE ACT:** Asset/investment mgmt.; **SERVICES:** Portfolio mgmt., devel. mgmt., prop. disposition, fin. advisory; **REP CLIENTS:** Corp., pension funds, fin. insts., for. investors; **PREV EMPLOY:** Prop. Grp. Controller, Dillingham Corp., 1976-1978; Asst. VP, RE Research Corp., 1972-1976; **PROFL AFFIL & HONORS:** ULI; ICSC; BOMA; NAIOP; **EDUC:** BS, 1969, Econ., Villanova Univ.; **GRAD EDUC:** MBA, 1972, Fin./RE, Columbia Univ.; **EDUC HONORS:** Dean's List; **BUS ADD:** 201 California St., Suite 400, San Francisco, CA 94111, (415)433-7770.

AZZOLINA, Ronald——**B:** May 11, 1943, Cleveland, OH, *Sr. VP - RE Mgmt.*, Security Pacific National Bank; **PRIM RE ACT:** Broker, Consultant, Engineer, Appraiser, Architect, Developer, Regulator, Builder, Owner/Investor, Property Manager, Syndicator, Assessor; **REP CLIENTS:** Security Pacific Bank & Subs.; **PROFL AFFIL & HONORS:** ULI, CA Bus. Prop. Assn., Intl. Council of Shopping Ctrs., Fin. Exec. Inst.; **EDUC:** BA, 1965, Letters, Arts & Sci., USC; **GRAD EDUC:** MBA, 1968, Fin., Univ. of So. CA; **OTHER ACT & HONORS:** Harvard Bus. School, Advanced Mgmt. Program 1981; **BUS ADD:** 333 S. Hope St., Los Angeles, CA 90071.

BAACK, John E.——*VP*, Houghton Mifflin Co.; **PRIM RE ACT:** Property Manager; **BUS ADD:** One Beacon St., Boston, MA 02107, (617)725-5000.*

BABB, Janice——*Ed.*, Gale Research Co., Real Estate Information Sources; **PRIM RE ACT:** Real Estate Publisher; **BUS ADD:** 1400 Book Tower, Detroit, MI 48226, (313)961-2242.*

BABB, Kenneth P.——**B:** Mar. 20, 1919, Saugus, MA, *VP*, R.M. Bradley & Co., Inc., Mgmt.; **PRIM RE ACT:** Property Manager; **PROFL AFFIL & HONORS:** IREM, RHA, BREB, CPM; **MIL SERV:** USAF, Sgt.; **OTHER ACT & HONORS:** Library Trustee, Town of Saugus; St. Vincent DePaul Soc.; Box 25 Club; **HOME ADD:** 171 Essex St., Saugus, MA 01906, (617)233-5059; **BUS ADD:** 250 Boylston St., Boston, MA 02116, (617)421-0746.

BABCOCK, A. Judson——**B:** Aug. 20, 1941, Richmond, VA, *Pres.*, T.H.A. Inc.; **PRIM RE ACT:** Developer, Builder, Property Manager; **SERVICES:** Devel. and project mgrs. of luxury resort condo. projects; services include prop. mgmt. and const. mgmt., fin. forecast; **PROFL AFFIL & HONORS:** Nat. Assn. of Home Builders; Urban Land Inst.; ALDA; **EDUC:** BS, 1963, Fin., Washington & Lee Univ.; **GRAD EDUC:** MBA, 1971, Harvard Bus. School; **EDUC HONORS:** Pres. of RE Club; **MIL SERV:** USMC Reserve; **OTHER ACT & HONORS:** Pres., Valley C of C; Dir., Valley Steering Comm., Pres. Mad River Yacht Club; **HOME ADD:** Rt. 100, Moretown, VT 05673; **BUS ADD:** Rt. 100, Waitsfield, VT 05673, (802)496-3121.

BABER, William S.——**B:** Feb. 25, 1942, Wheeling, WV, *Buyers Broker*, William S. Baber, Chartered; **PRIM RE ACT:** Broker, Instructor, Insuror; **SERVICES:** Exclusively representing buyers of single family houses and duplexes as buyers broker and prop. mgr.; **PREV EMPLOY:** Insurance broker; **PROFL AFFIL & HONORS:** NAR, Founder: Amer. Buyers Broker Inst., GRI; **EDUC:** Middle TN State Univ.; **MIL SERV:** US Air Force, E-5, Good Conduct, Vietnam Veteran; **HOME ADD:** 3633 Beneva Oaks Blvd., Sarasota, FL 33583, (813)924-1032; **BUS ADD:** 3800 S. Tamiami Trail, Sarasota, FL 33579, (813)365-3244.

BABIARZ, Stan T.——**B:** May 10, 1942, Hartford, CT, *RE Officer, Investments*, Phoenix Mutual Life Ins. Co., Investment RE; **PRIM RE ACT:** Appraiser, Property Manager, Lender, Owner/Investor; **OTHER RE ACT:** Responsible for the Mgmt., Leasing and Sales of Co. RE Portfolio as well as Const. of Co. Regional Office Facilities; **PREV EMPLOY:** Brokerage Underwriter, 4 yrs. Phoenix Mutual, 9 yrs. RE Phoenix M.; **PROFL AFFIL & HONORS:** Toastmasters Intl., Phi Kappa Phi; **EDUC:** BA, 1968, Univ. CT; **GRAD EDUC:** MBA Western New England Coll., 1973, Fin. Mgmt./Accounting, Bus.; **EDUC HONORS:** Magna Cum Laude; **MIL SERV:** USN, 1960-1964; **OTHER ACT & HONORS:** Hartford Gun Club & NRA; **HOME ADD:** Wedemeyer St., Windsor Locks, CT 06096, (203)623-9151; **BUS ADD:** One American Row, Hartford, CT 06115, (203)278-1212.

BACH, Clarence——*Supr. of RE*, Porter, H.K., Co., Inc.; **PRIM RE ACT:** Property Manager; **BUS ADD:** Porter Bldg., 601 Grant St., Pittsburgh, PA 15219, (412)391-1800.*

BACH, Harold J., Jr.——**B:** Sept. 27, 1942, Hartford, CT, *Owner*, Harold J. Bach, Jr., CPA; **PRIM RE ACT:** Consultant, Owner/Investor, Syndicator; **SERVICES:** Tax consultant, advisor and acct.; **PROFL AFFIL & HONORS:** MN Bd. of Realtors, Amer. Inst. of Acctg., Amer. Acctg. Assn., Acctg. Research Assoc. & MN Soc. of CPA's, CPA License: MN, IA, VA, LA, NC, MD; RE License: MN; **EDUC:** AA, 1965, RE Acctg. and Tax, Univ. of VA and John Hopkins Univ.; **MIL SERV:** US Army, Army Security and Defense Agencies, Intelligence Agencies, 1962 to 1965; **OTHER ACT & HONORS:** Wayzata and NW C of C; **HOME ADD:** 17830 24th Ave. N, Plymouth, MN 55447, (612)473-9678; **BUS ADD:** 1421 E. Wayzata Blvd., Wayzata, MN 55391, (612)473-0181.

BACHAND, Oscar J.——**B:** Sept. 8, 1928, Sanford, ME, *Pres.*, Bryant Realty Inc.; **PRIM RE ACT:** Broker, Consultant, Appraiser, Developer, Owner/Investor, Instructor, Property Manager, Syndicator; **PREV EMPLOY:** USAF Recruit 1947-68, ret. as maj.; 1966-69 salesman, Merced Rental Agency; 1969-70 salesman Boise Cascade Pine Mtn. Lake Props.; 1970-71 sales mgr. Bryant Realty; 1971-81, Owner Broker, Managed Bryant Realty Inc.; **PROFL AFFIL & HONORS:** NAR, RNMI, CA Assn. of RE Teachers, Merced Cty. Bd. of Realtors CA Assn. of Realtors, GRI, RECI, CRS, CRB, Realtor of the Year, Merced Cty. Bd. of Realtors; **MIL SERV:** USAF, Maj., Air Medal, Korea; **OTHER ACT & HONORS:** BPOE 25 yrs., North Merced Rotary Club 7 yrs., Comm. Chmn. Boy Scouts of Amer. Troop 102, since 1976; **HOME ADD:** 519 Lelsie Ct., Merced, CA 95340, (209)383-4757; **BUS ADD:** 805 W 18th St., Merced, CA 95340, (209)384-1000.

BACHRACH, Jonathan David——**B:** June 20, 1946, Ann Arbor, MI, *Partner*, Jonathan David Bachrach, P.C.; **PRIM RE ACT:** Consultant, Attorney, Owner/Investor; **PREV EMPLOY:** Olympia & York; **PROFL AFFIL & HONORS:** NY Bar; CA Bar; **EDUC:** BA, 1969, Psych./Languages, Univ. of CA, Berkeley; **GRAD EDUC:** JD, 1974, Tax, Univ. of CA, Berkeley School of Law; **HOME ADD:** 10 Overlook Terr., NY, NY 10033; **BUS ADD:** 11 E. 44th St., NY, NY 10017, (212)687-3344.

BACHTIGER, Joseph H.——**B:** Jan. 21, 1937, Philadelphia, PA, *VP*, The Bryn Mawr Trust Co., Trust; **PRIM RE ACT:** Consultant, Banker, Property Manager; **SERVICES:** Mgmt. of RE for trusts and estates; **PROFL AFFIL & HONORS:** Amer. Inst. of Banking, Philadelphia Chap.; Philadelphia Estate Planning Council, Montgomery Cty. Estate Planning Council; Bank Mktg. Assn.;PA Licensed salesperson; **EDUC:** BA, 1960, Liberal Arts - Philosophy, St. Charles Coll. - Wynnewood, PA; **HOME ADD:** 1420 Locust St., Philadelphia, PA; **BUS ADD:** 801 W Lancaster Ave., Bryn Mawr, PA 19010, (215)525-1700.

BACKMAN, Garett A.——**B:** Mar. 19, 1953, Lynn, MA, *Partner*, Garett A. Backman; **PRIM RE ACT:** Attorney, Owner/Investor, Syndicator; **SERVICES:** Act as closing atty.; put together pvt.

placement memoranda; gen. devel. activity; **PREV EMPLOY:** Assoc. with Troutman, Sanders, Lockerman & Ashmore; **PROFL AFFIL & HONORS:** Atlanta Bar Assn., GA Bar Assn., ABA, Atlanta C of C; **EDUC:** BA, 1975, Econ., Dartmouth Coll.; **GRAD EDUC:** JD, 1977, Boston Univ. School of Law; **HOME ADD:** 30 Collier Rd., N.W., No. 11, Atlanta, GA 30309, (404)351-3123; **BUS ADD:** 4137 Roswell Rd., N.E., Atlanta, GA 30342, (404)256-5475.

BACKMAN, Jean A.——B: Mar. 3, 1931, NYC, *V.P. - Mktg. & Sales*, Panorama RE, Inc.; **PRIM RE ACT:** Broker; **OTHER RE ACT:** V.P. Mktg. and Sales, Mgmt. Dev.; **PREV EMPLOY:** Lic. Broker in MD, VA, Wash., DC and DE, RE Educ. Assn.; **PROFL AFFIL & HONORS:** Member of Bd. of Realtors in MD, DC, Harford Cty., PGC and Central MD. Amer. Mgmt. Assn., GRI, CRB; **EDUC:** BA, 1953, Journalism, Hunter College; **HOME ADD:** 11611 Karen Dr., Potomac, MD 20854, (301)983-1066; **BUS ADD:** 10220 River Rd., Potomac, MD 20854, (301)299-6700.

BACKSTROM, Lathrop G., Jr.——B: Dec. 22, 1931, Kansas City, KS, *VP - Div. Mgr.*, Eugene D. Brown Co. Realtors, Comml. - Investment & Land Div.; **PRIM RE ACT:** Broker, Consultant; **SERVICES:** Comml. investment & farm land brokerage; **PREV EMPLOY:** Rgnl. Mktg. Operations Mgr. - Champlin Petroleum Co. 1959-1971; **PROFL AFFIL & HONORS:** MO Assn. of Realtors; KS Assn. of ReaLtors; RE Bd. of KC, MO; Realtors Nat. Mktg. Inst.; FLI; Intl. RE Fed., CCIM; Accredited FLI (AFLM); Dir. RE Bd. of KC, MO; Dir., Johnson City Bank Shares, Dir., Johnson City Bank; Bd. of Gov. of KC Oil Men's Club; Sales & Mktg. Execs. of KC; **EDUC:** BS, 1954, Agric. Econ., Univ. of MO, Columbia, MO; **MIL SERV:** USAF; 1954-1957; Capt; **HOME ADD:** 3316 West 68th St., Mission Hills, KS 66208, (913)384-0690; **BUS ADD:** Suite 100, 8301 State Line Rd., Kansas City, MO 64114, (816)444-6600.

BACKUS, Paul B.——B: Oct. 22, 1933, Oak Hill, WV, *Region Dir. of Devel.*, Howard Johnson Co.; **PRIM RE ACT:** Consultant, Appraiser, Developer, Builder, Owner/Investor, Property Manager, Syndicator; **PREV EMPLOY:** McDonalds Corp.; Kennilworth Assn.; **PROFL AFFIL & HONORS:** NACORE; NARA, Sr. Member, CRA; **EDUC:** BS, 1959, Bus. Admin., Concorde Coll.; **MIL SERV:** USMC, S/Sgt.; **HOME ADD:** 699 Lincoln Dr., Mt. Laurel, NJ 08054; **BUS ADD:** 1101 Kings Highway No., Suite 307, Cherry Hill, NJ 08034, (609)482-1800.

BACON, Elmore C.——B: July 6, 1945, Cleveland, OH, *VP-Sales*, Real Corp.; **PRIM RE ACT:** Broker, Property Manager; **SERVICES:** Comml. Broker, Land, Shopping Ctr. Office Leasing and Mgmt.; **PREV EMPLOY:** Price Devel. Co.-Salt Lake City; Devels. Diversified Cleveland OH; **PROFL AFFIL & HONORS:** Intl. Council of Shopping Ctrs.; **EDUC:** BS in Bus. Admin., 1968, Mktg. Mgmt., Southeast Missouri State Univ.; **MIL SERV:** USA, E-4; **HOME ADD:** 1324 Elizabeeth 3, Las Vegas, NV 89109, (702)737-1258; **BUS ADD:** 1830 E. Sahara, Suite 100, Las Vegas, NV 89104, (702)733-9600.

BADEN, Gerald M.——B: Aug. 5, 1932, Hamilton OH, *Regional RE VP*, Lloyds Bank CA, RE Indus. Div.; **PRIM RE ACT:** Consultant, Banker, Lender; **SERVICES:** RE Const. Loans; **REP CLIENTS:** Numerous in S. CA; **PREV EMPLOY:** Owner, First Western Mort. Corp.; **PROFL AFFIL & HONORS:** MBA, CA & S. CA; **EDUC:** BS, 1956, Fin., Bus. Admin., Univ. of CO; **GRAD EDUC:** MBA, 1961, Fin. & RE, Bus. Admin., USC; **MIL SERV:** USA, Cpl; **OTHER ACT & HONORS:** Balboa Bay Club, Newport Beach; Back Bay Club, Newport Beach; **HOME ADD:** 1808 Vista del Oro, Fullerton, CA 92631, (714)526-2404; **BUS ADD:** 1622 N. Main St., Ste. 500, Santa Ana, CA 92701, (714)835-3161.

BAEHREL, Peter——*Mgr. of Adm. Serv.*, Carter-Wallace, Inc.; **PRIM RE ACT:** Property Manager; **BUS ADD:** 767 Fifth Ave., NY, NY 10022, (212)758-4500.*

BAER, Dan W——B: Aug. 9, 1942, Scranton, PA, *Owner*, Dan Baer & Assoc.; **PRIM RE ACT:** Developer, Owner/Investor, Syndicator, Real Estate Publisher; **OTHER RE ACT:** Profl. Fin. Lecturer (Worldwide); Publisher of "Baer Facts"; Resid., Comml., & Indus. RE; **SERVICES:** Ltd. partnership synd., investment counseling, devel. of resid. & comml. props.; **REP CLIENTS:** Investors, builders; **PREV EMPLOY:** Dean Witter & Co., Hornblower & Weeks, NY Life Ins. Co.; **PROFL AFFIL & HONORS:** Intl. Assn. of Fin. Planners, Life Underwriters Assn., Past Member NY Stock Exchange and NASD, Pres., So. Calif. Sunbelt Dev., Inc.; **EDUC:** 1964, Bus. Admin., Rider Coll.; **GRAD EDUC:** RE & Ins., Bryn Mawr Coll., Saddleback Coll., Santa Ana Coll.; **MIL SERV:** USA, Security, Classified; **OTHER ACT & HONORS:** Yorba Linda Ctry. Club; **HOME ADD:** 19369 Easy St., Yorba Linda, CA 92686; **BUS ADD:** 1823 E 17th St., 312, Santa Ana, CA 92701, (714)558-2664.

BAGBY, Joseph R.——B: Sept. 23, 1924, Banner Elk, NC, *Pres.*, Property Resources Co, Inc., Investors & Owners of Real Estate/Wesley, Lambert, Inc., Corp. Fin.; **PRIM RE ACT:** Owner/Investor, Syndicator; **OTHER RE ACT:** Buyer of net lease props.; **SERVICES:** Private placement of corporate debt and other diversified types of corp. fin.; **REP CLIENTS:** NW Life Ins. Co.; Pizza Hut, Inc.; Shell Oil Co.; Sun Life; CT General; First Nat. Bank of Chicago; Chase Manhattan Bank; **PREV EMPLOY:** Pillsbury's Burger King Corp.; **PROFL AFFIL & HONORS:** Founder, Pres., Chmn. of the Bd. of Trus., NACORE; **EDUC:** BBA, 1959, Econ., Univ. of Miami; **EDUC HONORS:** Iron Arrow, Highest Honor Attained by Men; Pres., Sigma Chi; Pres. Intra-Frat. Council; Editor, Coll. Newspaper; **MIL SERV:** US Army, PFC, Cert. of Achievement, 82nd Airborne; **OTHER ACT & HONORS:** Dist. Sec. Treas. Young Democrats; Founding Member, Progress Club of Miami; Founding Member, Downtown Optimists Club; **HOME ADD:** 125 Brazillian Ave., Palm Beach, FL 33480, (305)655-9467; **BUS ADD:** #3471 Spencer Dr. S., W Palm Beach, FL 33409, (305)684-7335.

BAGG, Carter Davis——B: May 12, 1945, Evanston, IL, *Project Planner*, GSAS Architects-Planners, Planning; **PRIM RE ACT:** Architect, Consultant; **OTHER RE ACT:** Land Use Planning; **SERVICES:** Architecture, Land & Space Planning; **REP CLIENTS:** State of AZ, Cities of Mesa & Glendale, AZ, Rey West, Chillingsworth, Martens Development Corp.; **PREV EMPLOY:** Kenneth S. Allison & Assoc., 1978-1981, VP Petera Lendrum & Assoc., 1976-1978, Proj. Arch.; **PROFL AFFIL & HONORS:** AIA; **EDUC:** BArch, 1969, Univ. of CA-Berkeley; **MIL SERV:** USAR, SFC, ARCOM; **OTHER ACT & HONORS:** Neighborhood Housing Serv., Inc. Corp. Bd. and Planning Comm.; **HOME ADD:** 2506 n 8th St., Phoenix, AZ 85006, (602)258-7316; **BUS ADD:** 3122 N. 3d Ave., Phoenix, AZ 85013, (602)462-0217.

BAGGA, Roshan——B: July 13, 1935, INDIA(Dist. Sargodha, Pak), *Devel. Coordinator*, Harrisburg Housing Auth.; **PRIM RE ACT:** Architect; **SERVICES:** Devel. Rehab. and Modernization Consultant; **PROFL AFFIL & HONORS:** Registered Arch. in PA; AIA, RE Sales License , PA 1977 (Held in escrow); **EDUC:** BArch, 1960, Sch. of Planning & Arch. Univ. of Delhi, India; **GRAD EDUC:** Grad. Diploma in City Planning, 1963, City and Town Planning, Sch. of Planning & Arch. Univ. of Delhi, India; **HOME ADD:** 7310 Hiola Rd., Philadelphia, PA 19128, (215)483-4673; **BUS ADD:** 351 Chestnut St., Harrisburg,, PA 17101, (717)232-6781.

BAGLEY, James J., II——B: Nov. 23, 1948, Chicago, IL, *Atty. at Law*; **PRIM RE ACT:** Attorney; **REP CLIENTS:** Corporate and indiv. investors in comml. prop.; **PREV EMPLOY:** Counsel, IL Ho of Rep, 1976-1979; **PROFL AFFIL & HONORS:** ABA, IL State Bar Assn., Chicago Bar Assn.; **EDUC:** BA, 1970, North Park Coll., Chicago, IL; **GRAD EDUC:** JD, 1976, John Marshall Law School, Chicago, IL; **HOME ADD:** 7 East Goethe St., Chicago, IL 60610, (312)266-1511; **BUS ADD:** Suite 2024, 134 North LaSalle St., Chicago, IL 60602, (312)782-4992.

BAHARY, Kamel S.——B: Jan. 3, 1932, Iran, *VP*, Williams Real Estate Co., Inc.; **PRIM RE ACT:** Broker, Appraiser, Owner/Investor, Instructor; **PROFL AFFIL & HONORS:** Soc. of Indus. Brokers, Lambda Alpha Frat.; Indus. RE Brokers Assn.; Young Men's RE Assoc.; **EDUC:** BA, 1954, Bus., Columbia Coll.; **GRAD EDUC:** MBA, 1956, RE, NY Univ. Grad. School of Bus.; **HOME ADD:** 322 Central Park West, New York, NY 10025, (212)662-0533; **BUS ADD:** 1700 Broadway, New York, NY 10019, (212)582-8000.

BAHAT, Ari——B: May 4, 1941, Jerusalem, Israel, *Pres.*, Ari Bahat Incorporated and Ari Bahat A.I.A.; **PRIM RE ACT:** Architect, Developer; **OTHER RE ACT:** Space planner & interior designer; **SERVICES:** Arch., devel. & interior design; **PROFL AFFIL & HONORS:** Amer. Inst. of Archs.; **EDUC:** BArch, 1967, Technion, Israel Inst. of Tech.; **EDUC HONORS:** Cum Laude; **MIL SERV:** Israeli Army, Paratroopers; **BUS ADD:** Plaza Hotel, Suite 1705, 768 Fifth Ave., NY, NY 10019, (212)832-6750.

BAHR, Wilbur——*Mgr. Corp. Services*, Keystone Consolidated Industries, Inc.; **PRIM RE ACT:** Property Manager; **BUS ADD:** 7000 South Adams, Peoria, IL 61641, (309)697-7020.*

BAIER, Roger——*Fin. Analyst*, Dr. Pepper; **PRIM RE ACT:** Property Manager; **BUS ADD:** PO Box 225086, Dallas, TX 75265, (214)824-0331.*

BAILEY, Arthur E.——B: Oct. 4, 1932, Springfield, MA, *Partner*, Debenham Tewson & Chinnocks Assoc.; **PRIM RE ACT:** Consultant; **SERVICES:** Prop. acquisition, sale, consultation, etc.; **REP CLIENTS:** Brit. Petroleum Pension Trust; **PREV EMPLOY:** Brooks Harvey & Co., New York, NY; **PROFL AFFIL & HONORS:** RE Bd. NYC, Intl. Council Shopping Ctr., ULI; **EDUC:** BA, 1954, Econ.,

Philosophy, Poli. Sci., Miami Univ., Oxford, OH; **EDUC HONORS:** Hon. in Econ.; **MIL SERV:** USAF, Capt., Commendation Medal; **HOME ADD:** Meeting Grove Ln., West Norwalk, CT 06850, (203)853-3092; **BUS ADD:** 450 Park Ave., New York, NY 10022, (212)758-8218.

BAILEY, Charles D.——B: Feb. 23, 1941, Morgantown, WV, *Pres.*, Charles D. Bailey & Assoc.; **PRIM RE ACT:** Broker, Consultant, Appraiser, Property Manager; **SERVICES:** Appraising, Feasibility Studies, Comml. Brokerage; **REP CLIENTS:** Lenders, Corps, Attys., Govt. Agencies; **PREV EMPLOY:** Sea First Mort. Co., Ralph Arendt Realty; **PROFL AFFIL & HONORS:** AIREA, NAR, RNMI, MAI; **EDUC:** BS, 1971, R.E., CA State Univ.; **MIL SERV:** USAF, E-4, 1960-1964; **OTHER ACT & HONORS:** Ski Patrol; **HOME ADD:** 12375 Mt. Jefferson Terr. 8F, Lake Oswego, OR 97034, (503)636-6758; **BUS ADD:** The Carriage House,, 1331 SW Broadway, Suite 300, Portland, OR 97201, (503)222-2505.

BAILEY, Charles Williams——B: July 26, 1925, Spartanburg, SC, *Pres.*, Bailey & Casey, Inc.; **PRIM RE ACT:** Broker, Appraiser, Property Manager, Owner/Investor; **SERVICES:** RE brokerage, Prop. mgmt.; **PREV EMPLOY:** Arvida Corp., 13 yrs., 1957-70; **PROFL AFFIL & HONORS:** CPM, IREM, NLI, NAR, IREF, NARA, Amer. Soc. of Appraisers, Past Pres. ASA of FL, CPM, AFLM; **EDUC:** BS, 1947, Elect. Engrg., Clemson Univ.; **GRAD EDUC:** MS, 1950, Elect. Engrg., NC State Univ.; **MIL SERV:** USA; **HOME ADD:** 701 S Mashta Dr., Key Biscayne, FL 33149, (305)361-2210; **BUS ADD:** 1200 AmeriFirst Bldg., 1 SE 3rd Ave., Miami, FL 33131, (305)374-0600.

BAILEY, E. Norman——B: Oct. 20, 1934, Peru, IN, *Assoc. Prof. of Fin.*, Univ. of IA, College of Business Administration; **PRIM RE ACT:** Consultant, Appraiser, Developer, Builder, Owner/Investor, Property Manager; **PREV EMPLOY:** Fin. Dept., Coll. of Bus., Univ. of TX; **PROFL AFFIL & HONORS:** Amer. RE & Urban Econ. Assn.; ULI; Soc. of RE Appraisers, SRPA; **EDUC:** BS, 1960, Acctg., IN Univ.; **GRAD EDUC:** Doctor of Bus. Admin., 1964, MBA, 1961, RE and Fin., IN Univ.; **MIL SERV:** USAF; 1954-58, 1st Lt.; Pilot; **OTHER ACT & HONORS:** Nat. Assn. of Home Builders; Pres., North Bay Const., Inc.; **HOME ADD:** 919 Talwrn Ct., Iowa City, IA 52240, (319)338-5421; **BUS ADD:** College of Business Administration, Phillips Hall, Univ. of IA, Ames, IA 50010, (319)353-5970.

BAILEY, John B.——B: June 4, 1926, Auburn, IN, *Exec. VP*, Landauer Assoc., Inc.; **PRIM RE ACT:** Consultant, Appraiser; **SERVICES:** RE investment counseling & valuation of urban props. throughout the US; **REP CLIENTS:** Indiv. & instl. prop. investors; **PREV EMPLOY:** Equitable Life (Mort. Dept.), 1951-61; Brooks, Harvey & Co., 1961-69; **PROFL AFFIL & HONORS:** ASREC (CRE), AIREA (MAI), SIR, RE Bd. of NY; **EDUC:** BS, 1951, Bus. Admin, RE, OH State Univ.; **EDUC HONORS:** OH Assn. of RE Bds. Scholarship; **MIL SERV:** USAAF, Av. Cadet/Cpl., 1944-45; **OTHER ACT & HONORS:** Beta Theta Pi, Dir., Davis Park Medical Assn.; Past Pres. Mort. Bankers Assn. of NY; Dir. HMG Prop. Investors, Inc.; **HOME ADD:** 401 E. 65th St., NY, NY 10021, (212)535-0988; **BUS ADD:** 200 Park Ave., NY, NY 10021, (212)687-2323.

BAILEY, L. William——B: June 25, 1925, Winona, MN, *Owner/Broker*, Bill Bailey, Realtor-Exchangor; **PRIM RE ACT:** Broker, Instructor, Syndicator, Owner/Investor; **OTHER RE ACT:** Specialist in RE Tax Deferred Exchanges (1031); **SERVICES:** Brokerage, Counseling, Exchanging; **PROFL AFFIL & HONORS:** NAR; RNMI; MAR; Rochester Bd. of Realtors; RESSI, Designated 'Cert. Comm'l./Invest. Member' of RNMI of NAR; **HOME ADD:** 604 Second Ave., N.W., Byron, MN 55920, (507)775-6343; **BUS ADD:** 1500 1st Ave., NE, Rochester, MN 55901, (507)289-8000.

BAILEY, Robert C.——B: Dec. 3, 1954, Hanover, NH, *Sole Prop.*, Bayley Assoc.; **PRIM RE ACT:** Broker, Consultant, Developer, Owner/Investor, Property Manager, Syndicator; **OTHER RE ACT:** Exchangor, 1031; **SERVICES:** Almost all employment-type income; **PREV EMPLOY:** Resid. RE Sales; **PROFL AFFIL & HONORS:** Past Bd. of Dir. NHCID - Realtors-VP-Treas.-Dir.-RESSI, Outstanding Young Men in Amer. - 2 yrs.; **EDUC:** BA, 1977, Hist. and Soc. Sci., Plymouth State Coll.; **GRAD EDUC:** Grad. Credits in Bus. and RE, Plymouth State Coll.; **EDUC HONORS:** with Honors-Who's Who in Coll. and Univ.; **OTHER ACT & HONORS:** Lions Club Bd. of Dir. - Credit Union, VP - Fire Dept. - Hanover - Etna, - Volunteer; **HOME ADD:** Wolfeboro Rd., Etna, NH 03750, (603)643-2493; **BUS ADD:** Wolfeboro Rd., Etna, NH 03750, (603)643-6380.

BAILEY, Sherwood R., Jr.——B: Dec. 31, 1952, Gulfport, MS, *Pres.*, Bailey Homes and Insurance, Inc.; **PRIM RE ACT:** Broker, Attorney, Developer, Builder, Insuror; **SERVICES:** Resid. and comml. brokerage, resid. & comml. bldg. and devel.; **PREV EMPLOY:** Law practice specializing in RE; **PROFL AFFIL & HONORS:** MS State Bar Assn.; Amer. Bar Assn.; **EDUC:** BA, 1974, Univ. of AL; **GRAD EDUC:** JD, 1977, Univ. of MS; **EDUC HONORS:** Omicron Delta Kappa, Jason's, Moot Court Bd., Phi Delta Phi; **HOME ADD:** 1012 E. Beach Blvd., Gulfport, MS 39501, (601)863-7085; **BUS ADD:** POB 4557, 4646 W. Beach Blvd., Biloxi, MS 39531, (601)388-4430.

BAILLY, Barbara A.——*Mgr., RE*, Stauffer Chem. Co., RE; **PRIM RE ACT:** Consultant, Owner/Investor, Property Manager; **OTHER RE ACT:** Negotiating leases, subleases & contracts; **PREV EMPLOY:** Project mgr. for condo devel.; Mktg. research for condo devel.; **BUS ADD:** Nyala Farm Rd., Westport, CT 06881, (203)222-4009.

BAILOWITZ, Stanley A.——B: Nov. 22, 1938, NY, *Sr. VP*, Drexel Burnham Lambert Realty, Inc.; **PRIM RE ACT:** Consultant, Developer, Owner/Investor, Property Manager, Syndicator; **SERVICES:** Synd. of investment props., condo. conversion; **REP CLIENTS:** For. clients, indiv. int. investors; **PREV EMPLOY:** Donaldson Lufkin Jenrette-pres. of prop. mgmt. div. & numerous gen. partners; **PROFL AFFIL & HONORS:** AICPA, NY State Soc. of CPAs Community assns. inst., Nat. Apt. Assn., NASD Princ., CPA; **EDUC:** BS, 1962, Acctg., Brooklyn Coll.; NY Univ. School of fin. & taxation; **OTHER ACT & HONORS:** Tr. Shores condo. assn., Legislature coordinator-Orangetown PTA, guest lecturer Paul Smith Hotel Coll., Listed Who's Who in Finance, East; **BUS ADD:** 405 Lexington Ave., NY, NY 10173, (212)986-2800.

BAIN, James S.——B: Aug. 10, 1928, Minneapolis, MN, *Pres.*, Bain Devel. Corp., Bain Investment Co., J.B. Indus.; **PRIM RE ACT:** Broker, Consultant, Developer, Owner/Investor; **SERVICES:** Feasibility, Site Location, Fin., Engrg., Legal Survey, Const.; **REP CLIENTS:** Construction; Light Indus. Owner Occupied. Under 25,000 S.F., Less than 25 Employee Firms; **PREV EMPLOY:** Fin. and Construction; **PROFL AFFIL & HONORS:** CCIM, SCV, Intl. RE Fed.; State Small Bus. Council; GRI; **EDUC:** BS, BBA, 1949, 1956, Econ., Acctg., Fin., Univ. of MN; **MIL SERV:** US Army; **HOME ADD:** 4708 Tuxedo Blvd., Mound, MN 55364, (612)472-4716; **BUS ADD:** 1100 Lewis Ave. S., Watertown, MN 55388, (612)955-2900.

BAIN, William J., Jr.——B: June 26, 1930, Seattle, WA, *Partner*, Naramore, Bain, Brady and Johanson; The NBBJ Group; **PRIM RE ACT:** Architect, Consultant; **SERVICES:** Arch., Interiors, Planning, Econ., Cost Mgmt., Graphics, Landscape Arch.; **REP CLIENTS:** Devels. and Major Intsns.; **PROFL AFFIL & HONORS:** AIA, NAIOP, NACORE (Natl. Assn. of Corp. RE Execs.), ULI (Urban Land Inst.), FAIA, Lambda Alpha; **EDUC:** BArch, 1953, Cornell Univ.; **EDUC HONORS:** First York Prize, 1949, Charles Goodwin Sands Memorial Medal, 1953; **MIL SERV:** USA Army, Corps of Engineers, 1st Lt.; **OTHER ACT & HONORS:** Seattle Symphony Orchestra, Past Pres., BOD Seattle C of C, BOD Downtown Seattle Development Assn., Amer. Arbit. Assn., Comml. Panel, University of Washington - Juror & Lecturer; **HOME ADD:** 1631 Rambling Lane, Bellevue, WA 98004, (206)454-0735; **BUS ADD:** 904 Seventh Ave., Seattle, WA 98104, (206)223-5555.

BAIRD, David——*Corp. Mgr. Fin. Serv.*, Tracor, Inc.; **PRIM RE ACT:** Property Manager; **BUS ADD:** 6500 Tracor Lane, Austin, TX 78721, (512)926-2800.*

BAIRD, John——*Corp. Secy.*, Liquid Air Corp. of North America; **PRIM RE ACT:** Property Manager; **BUS ADD:** One Embarcadero Center, San Francisco, CA 94111, (415)765-4500.*

BAIRD, Morton W., II——B: Jan. 22, 1949, Selma, AL, *Atty.*, Law Offices of Morton W. Baird II; **PRIM RE ACT:** Attorney, Owner/Investor; **SERVICES:** Synd., RE litigation, RE document; **REP CLIENTS:** Represent numerous RE brokers in San Antonio area, Legal rep. for several large RE lenders in San Antonio area; **PROFL AFFIL & HONORS:** San Antonio & TX Bar Assns., San Antonio Bd. of Realtors, RE Securities and synd. Inst. (RESSI), BA, JD; **EDUC:** BA Plan II with Special Honors, 1971, Econ., German, Univ. of TX at Austin; **GRAD EDUC:** JD, 1974, Univ. of TX Sch. of Law; **EDUC HONORS:** 2 undergrad. Excellence Award Grants, Academic Scholar., Order of Barristers, Nat. Moot Ct. Team 1974, State Moot Ct. Team 1974; **OTHER ACT & HONORS:** Dist. Dir. Univ. of TX Law Sch. Assn., Dir., Central Branch YMCA; **HOME ADD:** 345 Garraty, San Antonio, TX 78218, (512)822-7816; **BUS ADD:** 5205 Fredericksburg Rd., San Antonio, TX 78229, (512)342-9836.

BAIRD, Robert E.——*Mgr. Corp RE*, Masonite Corp.; **PRIM RE ACT:** Property Manager; **BUS ADD:** 29 North Wacker Dr., Chicago, IL 60606, (312)372-5642.*

BAKER, B. Richard——**B:** Sept. 30, 1942, Charlotte, NC, *Mgr., Bank RE*, NC Nat. Bank; **PRIM RE ACT:** Broker, Consultant, Developer, Property Manager; **PROFL AFFIL & HONORS:** IREM, CPM; **EDUC:** BS, 1964, Indus. Mgmt., GA Tech.; **MIL SERV:** USA, 1st Lt., 1965-66; **OTHER ACT & HONORS:** Paw Creek Presbyterian Church, Bd. Dir. The Presbyterian Home at Charlotte; **HOME ADD:** 515 Belmorrow Dr., Charlotte, NC 28214, (704)394-2798; **BUS ADD:** Bank RE Dept., Charlotte, NC 28255, (704)374-5276.

BAKER, Bruce H.——**B:** Mar. 3, 1936, Salina, KS, *Gen. Mgr.*, Southeast Venturers; **PRIM RE ACT:** Consultant, Engineer, Developer, Builder, Owner/Investor, Property Manager; **PROFL AFFIL & HONORS:** ULI, Broker, Profl. Engr.; **EDUC:** BSCE, 1958, Civil Engrg., VA Mil. Inst.; **MIL SERV:** USAF, Capt.; **HOME ADD:** 5830 Happy Canyon Dr., Englewood, CO 80111, (303)756-5928; **BUS ADD:** 317 Inverness Way S., Englewood, CO 80112, (303)771-4130.

BAKER, Carl G.——**B:** Feb. 7, 1942, Beaver, PA, *Pres.*, Carl. G. Baker Corp.; **PRIM RE ACT:** Consultant, Engineer, Architect, Developer, Owner/Investor, Syndicator; **SERVICES:** Planning, feasibiltiy studies, arch. and engrg., devel capabilities; **PROFL AFFIL & HONORS:** AIA; PA Soc. of Arch.; Natl. Council of Arch. Registration Bds.; Amer. Land Devel. Assn.; Soc. for Mktg. Profl. Services; **EDUC:** 1959, Profl.; **GRAD EDUC:** BArch, 1965, Arch., Carnegie Mellon Univ.; **EDUC HONORS:** Natl. Honor Soc.; **HOME ADD:** 333 Fourth St., Beaver, PA 15009, (412)728-7269; **BUS ADD:** 971 Third St., PO Box 520, Beaver, PA 15009, (412)774-8054.

BAKER, David Guy——**B:** Feb. 4, 1947, Columbus, OH, *Partner*, Bricker & Eckler Law Firm; **PRIM RE ACT:** Attorney; **SERVICES:** Legal work for RE acquisition, devel., leasing and fin.; **REP CLIENTS:** RE investors, devels. and lenders, including RE investment trusts; **PREV EMPLOY:** Schottenstein, Garel, Swedlow & Zox, 1972-74; **PROFL AFFIL & HONORS:** ABA, OH Bar Assn. and Columbus Bar Assn. and all real prop. comms. thereof; **EDUC:** BS, 1969, Econ. and bus. Admin., Wittenberg Univ, Springfield, OH; **GRAD EDUC:** JD, 1972, Univ. of MI, Ann Arbor, MI; **EDUC HONORS:** Blue Key Men's Hon., Tau Pi Phi (Econ. Hon.); **OTHER ACT & HONORS:** The OH State Univ. Pres. Club; **HOME ADD:** 2454 Kensington Dr., Columbus, OH 43221, (614)488-6948; **BUS ADD:** 100 E. Broad St., Colombus, OH 43215, (614)227-2364.

BAKER, Donald——**B:** May 28, 1929, Chicago, IL, *Partner*, Baker & McKenzie, Tax Dept.; **PRIM RE ACT:** Consultant, Attorney, Owner/Investor; **SERVICES:** Legal servs., tax, intl.; **REP CLIENTS:** Kuwait RE Investment Consortium; **PROFL AFFIL & HONORS:** ABA, IL State Bar, Chicago Bar, Intl. Bus. Council; **EDUC:** 1951, Univ. of Chicago; **GRAD EDUC:** JD, 1954, Law, Univ. of Chicago Law School; **HOME ADD:** 544 Earlston Rd., Kenilworth, IL 60043, (312)251-0761; **BUS ADD:** 2800 Prudential Plaza, Chicago, IL 60601, (312)861-2960.

BAKER, Donald W.——**B:** Mar. 19, 1926, St. Paul, MN, *Pres.*, Baker Co., Inc.; **PRIM RE ACT:** Broker, Developer, Owner/Investor; **EDUC:** 1947, Education, Univ. of MN; **MIL SERV:** USA, Sgt., Bronze Star, Purple Heart; **OTHER ACT & HONORS:** City Councilman (4 yrs.) 1969-1973, Mason (32d); DeMolay Legion of Honor, Member-City Study Commission 1974-76; Member Inter-local Study Commission 1981; **BUS ADD:** 1005 Central Ave., Billings, MT 59102.

BAKER, Dorothy——*Ed.*, Real Estate Data, Inc., Real Estate Record & Builders Guide, Real Estate Directory of Manhattan; **PRIM RE ACT:** Real Estate Publisher; **BUS ADD:** 12 E. 41st St., New York, NY 10017, (212)532-2705.*

BAKER, Gary L.——**B:** Mar. 14, 1942, San Jose, CA, *Pres.*, Baker & Cramer, Inc.; **PRIM RE ACT:** Broker, Consultant, Developer, Owner/Investor; **SERVICES:** Brokerage, investment counseling, lease arbitration and site location; **REP CLIENTS:** Indiv. investors, chain and regional retailers; **PREV EMPLOY:** Norris, Beggs & Simpson, San Francisco, CA 1966-69; Safeway Stores, Inc. - Div. RE Mgr. 1969-79; **PROFL AFFIL & HONORS:** San Mateo-Burlingame Bd. of Realtors; **EDUC:** BA, 1964, Hist., Bus. minor, Univ. of CA, Berkeley; **MIL SERV:** USAF, Cang, S. Sgt.; **OTHER ACT & HONORS:** Ducks Unlimited, CA Waterfowl Assn., U.C. Alumni Assn.; Coordination Comm., The Menlo Fund, Menlo Coll. 1972-74; **HOME ADD:** 71 Mission Dr., San Mateo, CA 94402, (415)343-3967; **BUS ADD:** 1499 Bayshore Hwy, Suite 120, Burlingame, CA 94010, (415)697-5761.

BAKER, Harold D.——**B:** Feb. 12, 1942, Rome, NY, *Pres.*, Harold D. Baker & Co., Inc.; **PRIM RE ACT:** Broker, Consultant; **OTHER RE ACT:** RE fin. (primary activity); **SERVICES:** Arrangement of debt & equity fin.; **REP CLIENTS:** RE devel., public corps., and domestic and foreign instl. and private investors; **PREV EMPLOY:** VP, Brooks, Harvey & Co., Inc., NY, 1969-1974; **PROFL AFFIL & HONORS:** Mort. Bankers Assn. of NY, Inc.; Young Mort. Bankers Assn.; Young Men's RE Assn.; RE Bd. of NY, Inc.; Nat. Assn. of Realtors; **EDUC:** BS, 1964, RE, Wharton School of Univ. of PA; **GRAD EDUC:** MBA, 1966, Banking, Columbia Univ.; **MIL SERV:** U.S. Army, 1st Lt.; **HOME ADD:** 35 Springdale Rd., Scarsdale, NY 10583, (914)472-9584; **BUS ADD:** 60 East 42nd St., NY, NY 10165, (212)687-8856.

BAKER, J. William——*Sr. VP*, First Chicago Realty Services Corp.; **PRIM RE ACT:** Banker, Lender; **SERVICES:** Mort. & equity fin. of comml. props.; **REP CLIENTS:** Maj. inst. investors, including domestic and offshore pension funds; **PREV EMPLOY:** Advance Mort. Corp. (1970/1976); **PROFL AFFIL & HONORS:** Lake Cty. (IL) Econ. Devel., Commission; IL MBA; Mort. Bankers Assn. of Amer., Governor's Task Force on Homeownership; **EDUC:** AB, 1964, Econ., Wash. Univ., St. Louis, MO; **GRAD EDUC:** JD, 1967, Law, Wash. Univ.; **BUS ADD:** Two-First Natl. Plaza, Suite 2200, Chicago, IL 60670, (312)732-2630.

BAKER, James——*President*, Arvin Industries; **PRIM RE ACT:** Property Manager; **BUS ADD:** 1531E 13th St., Columbus, IN 47201, (812)372-7271.*

BAKER, James B.——**B:** Oct. 12, 1924, Tacoma, WA, *Pres.*, Jim Baker Realty Co.; **PRIM RE ACT:** Broker, Consultant, Developer; **SERVICES:** Investment counseling, devel. of land & comml. prop., invest. brokerage; **REP CLIENTS:** Investors, owners of comml. prop.; **PROFL AFFIL & HONORS:** NAR & RNMI, CCIM - Realtor of the Year, OR; **EDUC:** BA, 1949, Speech, Washington St. Univ.; **MIL SERV:** US Army, 1st Lt., Bronze Star with "V"; Purple Heart; **HOME ADD:** 621 S.W. Burlingame Terrace, Portland, OR 97201, (503)244-5793; **BUS ADD:** 1750 S.W. Skyline Blvd. No. 120, Portland, OR 97221, (503)292-0761.

BAKER, James Barnes——**B:** Feb. 18, 1933, New York, NY, *Pres.*, Tower Development; **PRIM RE ACT:** Architect, Developer, Owner/Investor; **SERVICES:** Arch., devel. mgmt., consultant; **PREV EMPLOY:** Consultant Llewelyn Davies Assocs. Private Practice Baker & Blake, Arch.; **PROFL AFFIL & HONORS:** AIA, Amer. Arbitration Assn., Fellow Amer. Inst. of Arch.; **EDUC:** AB, 1954, Arch., Princeton Univ.; **GRAD EDUC:** MArch., 1960, Yale Univ.; **EDUC HONORS:** Alpha Rho Chi Medal; **MIL SERV:** US Army, Capt.; **OTHER ACT & HONORS:** Prof. of Arch., Adjunct Faculty, City Coll., City Univ. Trustee, Darrow School, New Lebanon, NY; **HOME ADD:** 105 East 63rd St., New York, NY 10021, (212)826-6518; **BUS ADD:** 15 East 26th St., New York, NY 10010, (212)696-2300.

BAKER, James D., Jr.——**B:** Dec. 21, 1924, Jacksonville, FL, *Pres.*, Jim Baker, Corp.; **PRIM RE ACT:** Broker, Property Manager; **SERVICES:** RE sales, prop. mgmt., mort. brokerage; **REP CLIENTS:** Investors, indivs. & corp. clients; **PROFL AFFIL & HONORS:** Jacksonville Bd. of Realtors, IREM, Past Pres. Realty Bd., 1974, MLS, 1973, Realtor of Yr., 1976, Dir. FL Assn. of Realtors; **EDUC:** BSBA, 1950, RE, Univ. of FL; **MIL SERV:** USN, EM 3/C; **OTHER ACT & HONORS:** Comm. of 100 Jacksonville C of C, Elder in Riverside Presbyterian Church; **HOME ADD:** 3571 Hedrick St., Jacksonville, FL 32205, (904)388-3275; **BUS ADD:** 1919 Atlantic Blvd., Jacksonville, FL 32207, (904)396-4033.

BAKER, James H., III——**B:** Oct. 11, 1943, Baltimore, MD, *Dir., Bldgs. and Grounds*, Mecklenburg Cty., Public Works and Environmental Serv.; **PRIM RE ACT:** Consultant, Engineer, Builder, Property Manager; **SERVICES:** Mgmt. of all cty. facilities; **REP CLIENTS:** Mecklenburg Cty.; **PREV EMPLOY:** Spaulding and Slye Mgmt. Corp., Gen. Serv. Admin.; **PROFL AFFIL & HONORS:** BOMA, IREM; **GRAD EDUC:** AAS, 1965, Air Conditioning Engrg. Tech., Old Dominion Univ.; **HOME ADD:** 7324 Cedarbrook Dr., Charlotte, NC 28215, (704)545-6999; **BUS ADD:** 720 East 4th St., Charlotte, NC 28202, (704)374-2058.

BAKER, Jeffrey A.——**B:** Nov. 6, 1953, Charleston, IL, *Sec., Treas. and Chief Exec. Officer*, Columbian Savings and Loan Assn.; **PRIM RE ACT:** Lender; **SERVICES:** Home and comml. mort. lending, investment counseling, appraisals; **REP CLIENTS:** Indiv. & instit. investors; **PROFL AFFIL & HONORS:** US League of Savings Assns.; IL Savings & Loan League Legislative Initiative Comm.; Coles Cty. Home Builders Assn., Sec., IL Savings & Loan League, Career Devel. School, 1980 Grad.; **EDUC:** BS in Bus., 1976, Personnel Mgmt., Eastern IL Univ.; **OTHER ACT & HONORS:** Carnegie Public Library of Charleston, Pres., 1981; Lincoln Tr. Libraries System, Pres., 1981; United Way of Eastern Coles Cty., Past Pres.; Charleston Area C of C, Legislative Comm. Member; Charleston Jaycees, Past Dir.; Central Christian Church, Sunday School Supt.; **HOME ADD:** 1515 11th St., Charleston, IL 61920, (217)345-7181; **BUS ADD:** 511 Jackson St., Charleston, IL 61920, (217)345-4824.

BAKER, John R.——**B:** July 25, 1949, Walton Cty., GA, *Gen. Mgr.*, Bessemer Props. Inc., Bessemer Securities Corp.; **PRIM RE ACT:** Developer, Owner/Investor; **OTHER RE ACT:** Cirtus Groups; **PROFL AFFIL & HONORS:** Home Builders contractors Assn.; Bd. of Realtors; **EDUC:** BBA, 1971, RE, Univ. of GA; **HOME ADD:** 112 Lakeshore Dr., N. Palm Beach, FL 33408, (305)627-2333; **BUS ADD:** 1001 N. US Hwy. 1, Jupiter, FL 33458, (305)747-7272.

BAKER, John S.——**B:** Jan. 15, 1941, Milwaukee, WI; **PRIM RE ACT:** Owner/Investor, Syndicator; **EDUC:** BS, 1962, US Naval Academy; **MIL SERV:** USN, Comdr.; **BUS ADD:** PO Box 1121, Ft. Myer, VA 22211, (703)486-0125.

BAKER, Judith E.——**B:** Jan. 1, 1946, Cleveland, OH, *Atty. at Law*, Judith E. Baker, P.A.; **PRIM RE ACT:** Attorney; **SERVICES:** All aspects of RE law, including RE settlement; **PREV EMPLOY:** Formerly RE sales agent; **PROFL AFFIL & HONORS:** ABA, MD St. Bar Assn.; Montgomery Cty. Bar Assn., Mont. Cty. Bd. of Realtors; Phi Alpha Delta Law Frat.; Women's Bar Assns. of DC and MD; **EDUC:** BA, 1963, Poli. Sci., OH State Univ.; **GRAD EDUC:** JD, 1974, Amer. Univ., Wash. D.C.; **OTHER ACT & HONORS:** Dist. Ct. Commr., Montgomery Cty.; LWV, PTA, NAWBO, BPW, Gaithersburg; C of C; YMCA Volunteer; **HOME ADD:** 9411 Warfield Rd., Gaithersburg, MD 20879, (301)869-0963; **BUS ADD:** 702 Russell Ave., Suite 407, Gaithersburg, MD 20877, (301)258-9636.

BAKER, Philip G.——**B:** May 4, 1933, Framingham, MA, *Pres.*, Business Investment Advisory Corp.; **PRIM RE ACT:** Owner/Investor; **OTHER RE ACT:** Fin.; **SERVICES:** Debt & equity fin. for RE & corp. projects, indus. comml., resort; **PREV EMPLOY:** First Mgmt. & Mktg. Corp., Portsmouth, NH; **PROFL AFFIL & HONORS:** Nat. Assn. of Small Bus. Investment Cos.; **EDUC:** 1955, Pub. Rels., Bus., School of Public Comm., Boston Univ.; **EDUC HONORS:** Scarlet Key Honor Soc.; **MIL SERV:** USAF, 1955-57, Capt.; **OTHER ACT & HONORS:** Chmn. Republican Town Comm., Dir. Nat. Employee Benefits Corp., 1973-78; Investment Advisor, Hampshire Capital Corp., 1980-81; Consultant, DASA Corp., Employee Benefits Serv. Corp., & Grp. Legal Plans, Inc.; **HOME ADD:** Wild Rose Lane, New Castle, NH 03854, (603)436-7578; **BUS ADD:** One Middle St., Portsmouth, NH 03801, (603)431-1415.

BAKER, Robert L.——**B:** May 17, 1942, *Sr. Partner*, Law Offices of Robert L. Baker; **PRIM RE ACT:** Attorney; **SERVICES:** All aspects of RE law including litigation and planning; **REP CLIENTS:** RE agents and brokers; escrow cos., S&L assn., indivs. purchasing, selling, transfering or exchanging real prop.; **PROFL AFFIL & HONORS:** Past Pres., San Gabriel Valley Bar Assn., Member of Los Angeles Cty. Bar Assn., Member of State Bar of CA; **EDUC:** AB, 1964, Legal, CA Univ.; **GRAD EDUC:** JD, 1967, RE Law and Bus., CA Western Univ.; **EDUC HONORS:** Dean's List, Scholarship; **OTHER ACT & HONORS:** Past Pres. of Kiwanis, Past Bd. Member for C of C; **BUS ADD:** 111 S. Hudson Ave., Suite A, Pasadena, CA 91101, (213)795-1488.

BAKER, Scott R.——**B:** Apr. 9, 1952, Cleveland, OH, *Asst. VP & Counsel*, Fidelity Union Life Insurance Co. (FULICO), Legal Staff; **PRIM RE ACT:** Attorney; **SERVICES:** Legal counsel; **REP CLIENTS:** FULICO; Allianz Realty, Allianz Invest.; **PREV EMPLOY:** Coffee & Coffee, Attys. at Law, Dallas, TX; **PROFL AFFIL & HONORS:** ABA; ABA Sect. on Real Prop.; TX State Bar; Dallas Bar Assn., FLMI; USPTA; **EDUC:** BA, 1975, Govt./Pre-Law, Univ. of TX; **GRAD EDUC:** JD, 1980, Corp./Tax, Southern Methodist Univ., School of Law; **EDUC HONORS:** Dean's List; **OTHER ACT & HONORS:** TM, Inc.; NW Bible Church; **HOME ADD:** 646 N. Buckner, Dallas, TX 75218, (214)321-9542; **BUS ADD:** PO Box 500, Dallas, TX 75221, (214)653-4265.

BAKER, Thomas F., IV——**B:** Dec. 17, 1946, Memphis, TN, *Sr. Counsel*, First Tennessee National Corp.; **PRIM RE ACT:** Attorney; **SERVICES:** Advising divs. of bank holding co. including RE div. and props. mgmt. div.; **PREV EMPLOY:** Martin, Tate, Morrow & Marston, PC (Assoc.) 1971-1973; **PROFL AFFIL & HONORS:** ABA (Sec. of Real Prop., Probate & Trust Law Sect. of Corporate, Banking & Bus. Law); TN Bar Assn.; Memphis & Shelby Cty. Bar Assns.; **EDUC:** BA, 1968, Eng., Univ. of VA; **GRAD EDUC:** JD, 1971, Law, Washington & Lee Univ., School of Law; **EDUC HONORS:** Dean's List; Distinction on Eng. Comprehensive Examinations, Law Review; **OTHER ACT & HONORS:** Univ. of VA Alumni Assn. (Exec. Comm.); Washington & Lee Alumni Assn. (Treas.); Stratton YMCA (Bd. of Dir.); Univ. Club; Delta Club; **HOME ADD:** 2137 Rolling Valley Dr., Germantown, TN 38138, (901)754-8492; **BUS ADD:** 165 Madison Ave., Memphis, TN 38101, (901)523-5597.

BALAGUR, Perry——**B:** Jan. 9, 1943, NY, NY, Graubard, Moskovitz, McGoldrick, Dannett & Horowitz; **PRIM RE ACT:** Attorney; **SERVICES:** Legal counsel and representation on condos., coops., zoning and RE devel.; **REP CLIENTS:** Amer. Invesco; The DeMatteis Org.; Charles H. Shaw Co. of Chicago; Helmsely-Spear, Inc.; and Waldbaums, Inc.; **PREV EMPLOY:** Lipsig, Sullivan, Mollen & Liapakis, P.C., 1978-1980; Gen. Counsel, Community Technology, Inc., 1974-1978; **PROFL AFFIL & HONORS:** Condo. Sect., Real Prop. Comm., NY State Bar Assn.; Housing Comm., NY City Lawyers Assn., Lecturer for NY State Bar Assn.; Assn. of the Bar of the City of NY and Brooklyn Bar Assn., Condos., Cooperatives and Conversions; **EDUC:** 1963, Liberal Arts, Univ. of Pittsburgh; **GRAD EDUC:** 1966, Law, St. John's Univ. School of Law; **MIL SERV:** US Army, MSM; **OTHER ACT & HONORS:** Pres., Onondaga Cty. Title Assn., 1977; **HOME ADD:** 60 Woodmere Blvd., Woodmere, NY 11598; **BUS ADD:** 345 Park Ave., NY, NY 10154, (212)593-3000.

BALAS, Francis P.——**B:** June 19, 1940, Lowell, MA, *Atty./Part.*, Hall, Balas, & Finnegan, PC; **PRIM RE ACT:** Attorney; **SERVICES:** Title Examinations/Closings/ Represent Clients before various Local Bd. Agcy. and Land Court, Consultations RE Purchase, Sale and Devel. of Resid. and Comml. RE Devel., Bldrs., Inst. Lenders, Indiv. Buyers and Sellers; **PROFL AFFIL & HONORS:** ABA, MA Conveyancers Assn., MA Bar Assn., Merrimack Valley Conveyancers Assoc., Lowell Bar Assoc.; **EDUC:** BS, 1962, Educ., State Coll. at Lowell; **GRAD EDUC:** MEd. , JD, 1965, 1969, Law, MEd. Coll. at Salem, JD Suffolk Univ. Law School; **OTHER ACT & HONORS:** Pres., Greater Lowell YMCA Pres., Wehahmet Bluff Improvement Assn.; **HOME ADD:** 120 Holyrood Ave., Lowell, MA 01856, (617)485-0310; **BUS ADD:** 187 Littleton Rd., Westford, MA 01886, (617)692-3107.

BALBACH, Stanley B.——**B:** Dec. 26, 1919, Normal, IL, Balbach & Fehr; **PRIM RE ACT:** Attorney, Owner/Investor; **PROFL AFFIL & HONORS:** IL State Bar Assn.; ABA; FL Bar Assn., Atty.; **EDUC:** BS, 1940, Univ. of IL; **GRAD EDUC:** JD, 1942, Univ. of IL; **MIL SERV:** USAF, Capt.; **OTHER ACT & HONORS:** First Methodist Church; Masons; Urbana C of C; The Champaign Ctry. Club; The Union League; **BUS ADD:** POB 217, Urbana, IL 61801.

BALDAUF, Dayle——**B:** Aug. 12, 1934, Indianapolis, IN, *V.P.*, Baldauf-Echols Co., Realtors, Comml.; **PRIM RE ACT:** Broker, Syndicator, Appraiser; **SERVICES:** Comml. and Indus. brokerage; **PREV EMPLOY:** Exploration geologist, Shell Oil; **PROFL AFFIL & HONORS:** Indiv. Mbr. Soc. of Indus. Realtors, Realtor of the Yr.,1976; CCIM; **EDUC:** BS, 1956, Geology, Principa Coll, Elsah, IL; **GRAD EDUC:** MS, 1960, Geology, George Washington Un.,Washington, DC; **MIL SERV:** USA, SP5; **OTHER ACT & HONORS:** Past Pres. Comm. Concerts, Exec. V.P. Channel 23, NY NBC TV Stat. which I helped to syndicate and build; **HOME ADD:** 65 Lakeshore Dr., Brownsville, TX 78521, (512)546-9864; **BUS ADD:** 2035 Price Rd., Suite C, P.O. Box 4034, Brownsville, TX 78520, (512)542-5635.

BALDINGER, Joseph A.——*Secretary*, American Conference of Real Estate Investment Trusts; **OTHER RE ACT:** Profl. Assn. Admin.; **BUS ADD:** 608 13th St. NW, Washington, DC 20005, (202)347-9464.*

BALDUS, Donald L.——**B:** Aug. 19, 1930, Chicago, IL, *Owner-Broker*, Realty World-Settlers Realty, Inc.; **PRIM RE ACT:** Broker; **SERVICES:** Resid., rental, appraisal, prop. mgmt.; **PREV EMPLOY:** 25 yrs. in indus., 15 of which were in plant mgmt.; **PROFL AFFIL & HONORS:** Sr. Member Amer. Inst. of Indus. Engrs., CRB; **EDUC:** BS, 1950, Fin., Intl. Coll., Purdue Univ.; **MIL SERV:** USN, Ct 1, Nat. Serv., China Serv., Good Conduct, Korean Medal; **OTHER ACT & HONORS:** Rotary; **HOME ADD:** Appalachain Trace Crockett Ridge, Morristown, TN 37814, (615)586-8322; **BUS ADD:** 1125 W. First N. St., Morristown, TN 37814.

BALDWIN, Brad——**B:** Aug. 9, 1953, St. Petersburg, FL, *Partner-Owner*, Parsley-Baldwin Realty, Development & Comml.; **PRIM RE ACT:** Developer, Owner/Investor, Syndicator; **REP CLIENTS:** Local S&L serv. corps. & indiv. investors; **PROFL AFFIL & HONORS:** St. Petersburg Bd. of Realtors, Nat. Bd. of Realtors; **EDUC:** BSBA, 1975, Fin. and RE, Univ. of FL; **GRAD EDUC:** Various RE School, CCIM Courses (all completed); **HOME ADD:** 1 Beach Dr. SE #1305, St. Petersburg, FL 33701, (813)823-4171; **BUS ADD:** 1 Plaza Place, Suite 809, St. Petersburg, FL 33701, (813)823-2500.

BALDWIN, C. Jackson——**B:** Dec. 15, 1921, Miami, FL, *Chmn.*, Baldwin Caldwell Co.; **OTHER RE ACT:** Mort. banker, mort. broker, gen. ins.; **SERVICES:** Creative fin. for income producing RE; **REP CLIENTS:** Devels., lenders, banks; **PREV EMPLOY:** Baldwin Mort. Co.; **PROFL AFFIL & HONORS:** MBAA, CRA; **EDUC:** BSBA, 1943, Acctg., Univ., of FL; **MIL SERV:** US Army, 1st LT, Bronze Star, Purple Heart, Combat Infantryman's Badge; **OTHER ACT & HONORS:** Chief Execs. Forum, Orange Bowl Comm.; **HOME ADD:**

1340 Mendavia Ave., Coral Gables, FL 33146, (305)661-1176; **BUS ADD:** 840 Biscayne Blvd., Miami, FL 33132, (305)374-8181.

BALDWIN, Jeffry B.——B: Feb. 11, 1939, PA, *Partner*, Touche Ross & Co.; **PRIM RE ACT:** Consultant; **SERVICES:** Mgmt. consulting, fin., feasibility analysis; **REP CLIENTS:** Builders, devels., inst. investors; **PROFL AFFIL & HONORS:** Urban Land Inst., Nat. Assn. of Home Builders; **EDUC:** BS, 1960, Mechanical Engrg., PA State; **GRAD EDUC:** MBA, 1964, Bus., Harvard Bus. School; **HOME ADD:** 9817 Clydesdale St., Potomac, MD 20854, (301)299-5971; **BUS ADD:** 1900 M Street N.W., Washington, DC 20036, (202)452-1200.

BALDWIN, John R.——B: Aug. 22, 1919, Long Branch, NJ, *Realtor*, John R. Baldwin Agency; **PRIM RE ACT:** Broker, Appraiser; **PREV EMPLOY:** Zone Mgr., Texaco, Inc., Div. Mgr., Household Research Inst., subsid. of American Home Products Corp.; **PROFL AFFIL & HONORS:** GRI, IFA, RNMI, Realtor of the Year, 1976, Pascack Valley Bd. of Realtors, Pres. Pascack Valley M.L.S., Inc., 1974-1975, Pres., Pascack Valley Bd. of Realtors, 1976; **EDUC:** BA, 1941, Journ., Bus. Admin., Univ. of IA; **MIL SERV:** USA, Sgt., Pacific Theatre Ribbon; **HOME ADD:** 300 Lafayette Rd., Harrington Pk., NJ 07640; **BUS ADD:** 300 Lafayette Rd., Harrington Pk., NJ 07640, (201)768-7117.

BALDWIN, Robert——*Adm. Assistant to Pres. & Gen. Mgr.*, Allegheny Beverage Corp.; **PRIM RE ACT:** Property Manager; **BUS ADD:** N. Charles St., Baltimore, MD 21218, (301)467-7300.*

BALDWIN, William E.——B: Nov. 5, 1941, Evergreen Park, IL, *Pres.*, William Baldwin and Assoc., Ltd./Future Environment Co., Inc.; **PRIM RE ACT:** Architect, Developer, Builder; **SERVICES:** Full turn key services or arch./const.; **PROFL AFFIL & HONORS:** AIA, ARA, CSI, 2 service awards ARA; Past Pres., IL Council ARA; Currently Regent ARA and Nat. convention chmn.; Nat. Executive Bd.; **EDUC:** 1965, Arch. Engrg., Univ. of IL; **OTHER ACT & HONORS:** Ad-Hoc Committee on gasoline service stations, Village of Downers Grove; Chmn., Arch. Commn. of Downers Grove, IL, 1976; Who's Who of Midwest, 1980-1981; Reg. Arch., IL, IN, FL; Holds N.C.A.R.B. certificate; Appointed to Du Page County (IL) Zoning Bd. of Appeals 1981; **HOME ADD:** 1908 Elmore Ave., Downers Grove, IL 60515, (312)964-9347; **BUS ADD:** 1319 Butterfield Rd., Downers Grove, IL 60515, (312)963-3430.

BALEY, Robert Z.——B: Aug. 6, 1934, Chicago, IL, *Pres.*, Bo-Nita Productions, Inc.; **PRIM RE ACT:** Broker, Consultant, Appraiser, Developer, Instructor; **SERVICES:** Appraising-resid. comml., condemnations; **PROFL AFFIL & HONORS:** RNMI, NAR, NAIFA, NAREA, ARA, AR investment soc., NFIB, CREA-Pres. Ozark Clarksville-Paris Bd. of Realtors 1979-80, Realtor of the Yr. 1980, OCP Bd. of Realtors; **MIL SERV:** USAF, E-6, GC Joint Commendation; Nat. Defense-European Theatre-Korean Serv.; **OTHER ACT & HONORS:** Knights of Columbus, Past Grand Knight; **HOME ADD:** Route 2, Box 49 A, Clarksville, AR 72830, (501)754-8909; **BUS ADD:** Route 2, Box 49 A, Clarksville, AR 72830, (501)754-8909.

BALISTRERI, Steve——B: Oct. 14, 1944, Milwaukee, WI, *Coordinator*, Chillicothe Devel. Co.; **PRIM RE ACT:** Consultant, Developer, Property Manager; **OTHER RE ACT:** Coordinator/Sales Rep.; **SERVICES:** Indus. Devel. bond money available for light indus. & retail; **REP CLIENTS:** Kroger's Foods, Mr. Donut, Economy Insurance Co.; **PREV EMPLOY:** M&S Devel. Corp.; **PROFL AFFIL & HONORS:** Amer. Land Devel. Assn.; IL Devel. Council; **EDUC:** Assoc. Applied Scis., 1967, Bus. Admin., Milwaukee Inst. of Technol.; **MIL SERV:** USA, Sgt. E5; **OTHER ACT & HONORS:** Past Pres. of Tau Theta Epsilon; Bd. of Dirs. Valley Community YMCA & Chillicothe Lions Club; Co-Chmn. 1981 United Way Chillicothe, IL; **HOME ADD:** 1223 N. 6th St., Chillicothe, IL 61523, (309)274-2041; **BUS ADD:** 1st Natl. Bank Bldg., 2nd & Pine St., PO Box 339, Chillicothe, IL 61523, (309)274-6353.

BALKE, Garrett A.——B: June 9, 1937, Racine, WI, *Pres.*, Garrett A. Balke, Inc.; **PRIM RE ACT:** Consultant, Developer, Builder, Owner/Investor; **OTHER RE ACT:** Fin.; **SERVICES:** Devel. of a consulting for most types of comml. and Indus. Props.; **REP CLIENTS:** Major Corps. and investors in Comml. and Indus. props.; **PREV EMPLOY:** VP Linclay Corp., St. Louis, MO 1970-1979; **PROFL AFFIL & HONORS:** RE Broker; NAIOP; Indust. Devel. Research Council; **EDUC:** BA, 1959, Arch., Univ. of MN; **GRAD EDUC:** Grad. Studies, 1959-1960; **EDUC HONORS:** Deans List 2 yrs.; **MIL SERV:** US Army, Counter Intelligence Corp (C.C.); **HOME ADD:** 40 Frederick Ln., Glendale, MO 63122, (314)962-4522; **BUS ADD:** 8850 Ladue Rd., St. Louis, MO 63124, (314)862-7290.

BALL, Elliott B.——B: June 4, 1919, San Francisco, CA, *Pres.*, Elliott B. Ball Assoc. Inc., a CA Corp., Head Office; **PRIM RE ACT:** Appraiser; **SERVICES:** Appraisal and eval. of all types of RE & bus.; **REP CLIENTS:** Banks, mort lenders, attys., govt. entities, devel., superior ct.; **PREV EMPLOY:** Wells Fargo Bank; **PROFL AFFIL & HONORS:** NARA, Intl. Inst. of Valuers, Amer. Assn. of Cert. Appraisers, Nat. Assn. of RE Appraisers, CRA, CREA, CAS, CBA, SCV; **EDUC:** BA, 1941, Econ., Stanford Univ.; **GRAD EDUC:** LLB, 1973, Law, LaSalle Ext. Univ.; **MIL SERV:** USAF, S/Sgt., Pres. Unit Citation; **OTHER ACT & HONORS:** Realtor Member So. Alameda Cty. Bd. of Realtors, Right of Way Assn.; **HOME ADD:** 25983 Abbington Pl., Hayward, CA 94542, (415)582-2768; **BUS ADD:** 1312 'B' St., Hayward, CA 94541, (415)582-7716.

BALL, Thomas A.——B: Dec. 21, 1929, Morris, IL, *Owner*, Thomas A. Ball & Assoc.; **PRIM RE ACT:** Consultant, Appraiser; **PREV EMPLOY:** Self employed since 1951; **PROFL AFFIL & HONORS:** SREA, MAI, CRA; **EDUC:** BS, 1951, RE, Univ. of Denver; **EDUC HONORS:** Outstanding Jr. in RE School, 1 full yr. Scholarship awarded by Denver Realtors; **HOME ADD:** 539 E. Fairmont Dr., Temla, AZ 85282, (602)966-1334; **BUS ADD:** 5470 S. Lake Shore Dr., Ste A2, Tempe, AZ 85283, (602)897-1818.

BALLARD, John W., Jr.——B: Mar. 8, 1922, Kingston, Ont., Can., *Pres. and Chmn. of the Bd.*, Safety Fed. Savings and Loan Assn.; **PRIM RE ACT:** Banker, Lender, Insuror; **PROFL AFFIL & HONORS:** Pres., Safety Ins. Agency 1966-70; Tr., Savings & Loan Found.; Dir., RE Bd., 1964-1965, 1971-1974; Pres., MO Savings & Loan League, 1964-1965; K.C. Savings & Loan League, 1966-1967, Listed in Who's Who in KS; Who's Who in Amer.; Who's Who in World Commerce & Indus.; Member of Garden of the Gods Club, Colorado Springs, CO; **EDUC:** BS, 1947, Bus., Univ. of KS; **EDUC HONORS:** Sigma Alpha Epsilon; **MIL SERV:** AUS, 1942-1945, Bronze Star, 1945; **OTHER ACT & HONORS:** K.C. Blue Cross, Tr., Treas., Chmn. of Bd. (1960 - present); Dir., Mission Hills Ctry. Club, Shawnee Mission, KS; Dir., KS City Club, KS City, MO; Dir., Armour Home, KS City, MO; **HOME ADD:** 9311 Buena Vista, Prairie Village, KS 66207, (913)649-7528; **BUS ADD:** 910 Grand Ave., Kansas City, MO 64106, (816)421-3535.

BALLIN, Arthur L.——B: May 13, 1906, Lwow, Austria, *Atty. at Law*, Arthur L. Ballin, Law Offices; **PRIM RE ACT:** Attorney; **SERVICES:** Legal serv. in the field of RE law; **REP CLIENTS:** RE Bd. of New Orleans, Inc.; **PROFL AFFIL & HONORS:** New Orleans, LA & Amer. Bar Assns.; **GRAD EDUC:** JD, Loyola Univ. of the South; Dr. of Law, 1930, Univ. of Vienna, Austria; **MIL SERV:** USA, Mil. Gov., 1943-46, 1st Lt., Bronze Star; **OTHER ACT & HONORS:** Legal counsel to consulate Gen. of Switzerland & Fed. Republic of Germany, Lakewood Ctry. Club, Intl. House, Recipient of Medal of Honor from Fed. Republic of Germany; **HOME ADD:** 6925 Canal Blvd., New Orleans, LA 70124, (504)288-1075; **BUS ADD:** 1121 Carondelet Bldg., 226 Carondelet St., New Orleans, LA 70130, (504)523-2155.

BALLUFF, Douglas Paul——B: Nov, 8, 1941, Chicago, IL, *Pres.*, The San Francisco Group; **PRIM RE ACT:** Consultant, Developer, Owner/Investor; **OTHER RE ACT:** Venture Capital; **SERVICES:** Domestic and Intl. investment/devel.; **REP CLIENTS:** Inst. Inventors, pvt. indiv., corporate; **PREV EMPLOY:** Ford Motor Co. Intl., Motorola Communications Intl., FMC Corp., Douglas Bolluff & Assoc.; **EDUC:** AB, 1965, Econ./Latin Amer. Area Studies, The George Washington Univ.; **GRAD EDUC:** MBA, 1967, Intl. Bus. & Fin., UCLA Grad. Sch. of Mgmt.; **OTHER ACT & HONORS:** Rotary Intl., Big Brothers of Amer., Japan Soc. of San Francisco; **BUS ADD:** 44 Montgomerty St., Suite 500, San Francisco, CA 94104, (415)955-2610.

BALSAM, Arthur——B: Jan. 11, 1916, Philadelphia, PA, *Pres.*, Lanard & Axilbund, Inc.; **PRIM RE ACT:** Broker, Consultant, Appraiser, Developer, Builder, Lender, Owner/Investor; **SERVICES:** Active in all phases of comml./indus. RE only; **REP CLIENTS:** We have represented many of the nation's largest corps. as well as the entire spectrum of small cos.; **PREV EMPLOY:** Have been affiliated with the present firm for 46 yrs.; **PROFL AFFIL & HONORS:** SIR, ASREC, Assoc. Member of Amer. Soc. of Appraisers, Phila. Bd. of Realtors, PA Assoc. of Realtors, NAR, CCIM; **MIL SERV:** USA, T/4, 3 Combat Stars - World War II - ETO; **OTHER ACT & HONORS:** Member of the Bd. of Deborah Heart & Lung Ctr. & Deborah Hospital Foundation, Browns Mills, NJ, Member/Bd. of Exec. Member of Explorers Club, Various other Comm. Grps.; **HOME ADD:** 1911 Fawn Dr., Philadelphia, PA 19118, (215)887-2138; **BUS ADD:** 21 S 12th St., Philadelphia, PA 19107, (215)563-1252.

BALTES, Terry——B: Aug. 21, 1950, Greenville, OH, *Pres.*, Baltes Commercial Realty, Inc., Comml. Investment; **PRIM RE ACT:** Broker, Developer, Owner/Investor; **PREV EMPLOY:** McAfee

Schiller & Ryan, Inc. Realtors, Comml. Mgr., Mills Wright Realtors Comml.; **PROFL AFFIL & HONORS:** Dayton Area Bd. of Realtors, State of OH Realtors, NAR; **EDUC:** BS, 1973, RE, OH State Univ.; **HOME ADD:** 6290 Millbank Dr., Centerville, OH 45459, (513)435-5190; **BUS ADD:** 871 E. Congress Park Dr., Dayton, OH 45459, (513)435-6900.

BALTIS, Russell V, Jr.——B: July 26, 1928, Kan. City, MO, *Dir. of Prop.*, Leo Eisenberg & Co., Prop. Mgmt.; **PRIM RE ACT:** Broker, Architect, Syndicator, Developer, Property Manager, Owner/Investor; **REP CLIENTS:** TG & Y, Walmart, K-Mart, Ravco Clients (Prop. Mgmt.), NY Life, Equitable, Amer. Natl.; **PREV EMPLOY:** Gen. Mgr., N KS City Dev. Co. 1971 & 1979; **PROFL AFFIL & HONORS:** BOMA, RPA; **EDUC:** BA, Arch, Univ. of KS; **EDUC HONORS:** Scarab Society; **MIL SERV:** Corp. of Eng., Lt.; **HOME ADD:** 1209 W 57th Terr, Kansas City, MO 64113, (816)363-1656; **BUS ADD:** 1101 Walnut, Kansas City, MO 64106, (816)221-8000.

BANAS, C. Leslie——B: Oct. 29, 1951, Swindon, England, *Partner*, Hyman, Gurwin, Nachman, Friedman & Winkelman; **PRIM RE ACT:** Attorney; **SERVICES:** Negotiation and drafting of documents relating to acquisition, sales and synd. of RE projects; **REP CLIENTS:** Purchasers and sellers of comml. or multi-family resid. RE; synd. sponsors; **PROFL AFFIL & HONORS:** ABA; State Bar of MI; Detroit Bar Assn.; RESSI; **EDUC:** BA, 1973, Econ., Univ. of Detroit; **GRAD EDUC:** JD, 1975, Wayne State Univ. Law School; **EDUC HONORS:** Dean's Key, Magna Cum Laude, Cum Laude; **HOME ADD:** 6574 Cathedral, Birmingham, MI 48010, (313)851-3612; **BUS ADD:** Suite 1600, 17117 W. Nine Mile Rd., Southfield, MI 48075, (313)559-7500.

BANDER, E.J.——B: Aug. 10, 1923, *Law Librarian*, Suffolk Univ., Library; **OTHER RE ACT:** Librarian; **SERVICES:** Books; **REP CLIENTS:** Law students and bar; **PROFL AFFIL & HONORS:** Assn. Amer. Law Libraries; **EDUC:** AB, 1949, Literature, Boston Univ.; **GRAD EDUC:** LLB, LS in BS, Law, Simmons Coll.; **MIL SERV:** US Navy, Rm 2/c; **HOME ADD:** 50 Church St., Boston, MA 02114; **BUS ADD:** 41 Temple St., Boston, MA 02114, (617)723-4700.

BANE, Jim——B: July 8, 1932, Kalamazoo, MI, *Prop. Mgr.*, Frederick Ross Co.; **PRIM RE ACT:** Broker, Property Manager; **SERVICES:** Mgmt. of comml. RE including retail; **PREV EMPLOY:** Broker, Arrowhead Realty, Denver; **PROFL AFFIL & HONORS:** BOMA, IREM; **EDUC:** BS, 1956, Voc. Educ. Bus., Construction, KS State at Pittsburg, KS; **GRAD EDUC:** MS, 1956, Admin., Educ., Voc. Educ. Construction, KS State at Pittsburg, KS - Two additional yrs., CO Univ.; **MIL SERV:** USNR; **OTHER ACT & HONORS:** Model T Ford Club; **HOME ADD:** 5124 W 26th Ave., Denver, CO 80212, (303)477-6607; **BUS ADD:** 717 17th St., Su. 1400, Denver, CO 80202, (303)696-6670.

BANIS, Andrew P.——*Ed.-Mng. Ed.*, American Inst. of Real Estate Appraisers, Appraisal Journal; **PRIM RE ACT:** Real Estate Publisher; **BUS ADD:** 430 N. Michigan Ave., Chicago, IL 60611, (312)440-8174.*

BANK, Herbert——*Dir. RE*, Maryland Cop Corp.; **PRIM RE ACT:** Property Manager; **BUS ADD:** Owings Mills, MD 21117, (301)363-1111.*

BANKER, Joel I.——B: July 7, 1927, New York City, NY, *Sr. VP and Shareholder*, Landauer Associates, Devel. Mgmt. Services; **PRIM RE ACT:** Consultant, Developer, Owner/Investor; **SERVICES:** Consultant in Devel. Mgmt. Services; **REP CLIENTS:** Major Corps., Inst. and Investors; **PREV EMPLOY:** VP, Tishman Realty & Construction Co. Inc.; Owner/Devel., Joel I. Banker Realty, Inc.; **PROFL AFFIL & HONORS:** ASREC; Trustee, Produce Exchange Realty Trust; Dir., Citizens Housing & Planning Council of NY; Dir. of Natl. Realty Club; Past Dir. of the Realty Bd. of NY, CRE; **EDUC:** AB, 1949, Public Admin., Maxwell School, Syracuse Univ.; **MIL SERV:** US Navy, P.O. 3/C; **OTHER ACT & HONORS:** Realty Advisory Comm., Bd. of Educ. in Mamaroneck, NY; Past Dir., Orienta Pt. Assn.; Gov., Beach Point Club; **HOME ADD:** 726 Forest Ave., Mamaroneck, NY 10543, (914)698-9236; **BUS ADD:** 200 Park Ave., New York, NY 10166, (212)687-2323.

BANKS, Douglas T.——B: Feb. 13, 1931, Hobart, OK, *Pres.*, Barbara Bancroft Realty, Inc.; **PRIM RE ACT:** Broker; **OTHER RE ACT:** Resid. specialist in ocean and river prop.; **PROFL AFFIL & HONORS:** NAR; FL Assn. of Realtors; Womens Council of Realtors, GRI; **EDUC:** BS, 1953, Univ. of OK, Norman, OK; **GRAD EDUC:** MA, 1973, Counseling, Ball State Univ.; **MIL SERV:** US Army, Lt. Col., Legion of Merit, Meritorious Service Medal, Commendation Medal, 9 Air Medals; **OTHER ACT & HONORS:** Rotary Club of Indialantic, Advisor, Indialantic Police Explorers (BSA); **HOME ADD:** 325 Miami Ave., Indialantic, FL 32903, (305)724-2918; **BUS ADD:** 600 S. Miramar, Indialantic, FL 32903, (305)723-0934.

BANKS, Lawrence K.——B: Mar. 12, 1943, Greensboro, NC, *Partner*, Greenbaum Doll & McDonald; **PRIM RE ACT:** Attorney; **SERVICES:** Legal servs. in synd., acquisitions and fin.; **REP CLIENTS:** Lenders, devels. in comml. props. and multi-family projects; **PROFL AFFIL & HONORS:** KY State Bar, NC State Bar, CA State Bar, ABA Sect. on Taxation; **EDUC:** BA, 1965, Hist. & Pol. Sci., Duke Univ.; **GRAD EDUC:** LLB, 1967, Duke Univ. Law School; LLM, 1971, Taxation, Georgetown Law Center; **EDUC HONORS:** Cum Laude; Order of the Coif; Law Journal; **HOME ADD:** 783 Harbor Point, Lexington, KY 40502, (606)269-6864; **BUS ADD:** 600 Merrill Lynch Plaza, Lexington, KY 40507, (606)231-8500.

BANNER, Knox——B: Apr. 9, 1914, Ft. Worth, TX, *Chmn.*, Banner Associates, Ltd.; **PRIM RE ACT:** Consultant; **SERVICES:** Econ. devel. and urban affairs consultants; **REP CLIENTS:** Devels., other businessmen and local govts.; **PREV EMPLOY:** Exec. Dir., National Capital Downtown Comm., Inc. (Downtown Progress); Exec. Dir., Mayor's Office of Bus. and Econ. Devel., Washington, DC; **PROFL AFFIL & HONORS:** Tr., ULI; Tr., Found. for Cooperative Housing; Past Pres., NAHRO; APA; IPA; Nat. Housing Conf., Phi Beta Kappa; Intl. Hon. Soc. of Lambda Alpha for the Study of Land Econ.; Hon. Life Member, IDEA; **EDUC:** BA, 1935, Rice Univ.; **EDUC HONORS:** Grad. with Distinction; Phi Beta Kappa; **MIL SERV:** USMC; Lt. (USNR); **OTHER ACT & HONORS:** Rice University, President's Gold Club; Nat. Cathedral Assn., Washington Cathedral; **HOME ADD:** 2501 Calvert St., NW Apt. 403, Wash., DC 20008, (202)265-4301; **BUS ADD:** PO Box 4981, Cleveland Park Station, Wash., DC 20008, (202)483-4363.

BANTA, W. Clifton——B: Oct. 13, 1910, Moselle, MS, *Pres.*, MS Cty. Savings & Loan Assn.; **PRIM RE ACT:** Broker, Attorney, Appraiser, Lender; **PREV EMPLOY:** Ret'd. Atty.; Banta, Banta & Hopkins, Attys.; **PROFL AFFIL & HONORS:** MS Bar Assn.; **GRAD EDUC:** LLB/JD, 1969, Univ. of MO School of Law; **EDUC HONORS:** Order of the Coif; **OTHER ACT & HONORS:** Probate Judge, MS Cty., MO, 1977-1980; **HOME ADD:** 701 E. Cypress, Charleston, MS 63834, (314)683-4815; **BUS ADD:** PO Box 469, Charleston, MS 63834.

BANWART, Gerald H.——B: Oct. 7, 1947, LaPorte, IN, *CPA*, Heinold-Banwart; **PRIM RE ACT:** Consultant; **OTHER RE ACT:** CPA; **SERVICES:** HUD Audits; tax advice, synd., consulting; **REP CLIENTS:** Monge Realty; Investments, Inc.; Noah Herman Sons Realtors; Century 21 Gold Key; **PROFL AFFIL & HONORS:** AICPA, IL Soc. of CPA's; **EDUC:** BS, 1969, Acctg., IN Univ.; **EDUC HONORS:** Grad. with High Distinction; **OTHER ACT & HONORS:** Nat. Silver Medal Winner in May 1969 CPA exam; **HOME ADD:** Box 132, Congerville, IL 61729, (309)448-2416; **BUS ADD:** 2400 N. Main, E. Peoria, IL 61611, (309)694-4251.

BARALT, Carlos M.——B: Aug. 4, 1936, Havana, Cuba, *Rgnl. VP*, Marshall and Stevens, Inc.; **PRIM RE ACT:** Consultant, Engineer, Owner/Investor; **OTHER RE ACT:** Intl.; **SERVICES:** Valuation, consultation, investment advice & mgmt.; **PREV EMPLOY:** VP, Fin., Lyons Container Servs.; Systems Mgr., Intl. Telegraph & Telephone; Systems Mgr., Baxter Labs.; **PROFL AFFIL & HONORS:** Nat. Assn. of Accountants; Assn. for Corporate Growth; Nat. Assn. of Indiv. Investors; **EDUC:** BS, Indus. Engrg., Lehigh Univ.; **EDUC HONORS:** Indus. Engrg. Honor Soc.; **OTHER ACT & HONORS:** Biography in Marquis "Who's Who in Finance" & "Who's Who in the World"; **HOME ADD:** 24 Yeger Rd., Cranbury, NJ 08512, (609)799-4707; **BUS ADD:** 71 Broadway, NY, NY 10006, (212)425-4300.

BARASCH, Clarence S.——B: May 20, 1912, NY, NY, Clarence S. Barasch, Esq.; **PRIM RE ACT:** Attorney; **SERVICES:** Consultation & litigation of RE brokerage & other real prop. actions.; **REP CLIENTS:** Wm. A. White & Sons., Edward S. Gordon Realty Co., Inc., Helmsley Spear, Inc., Cross & Brown Realty Co., Coldwell-Banker, Sutton & Towne, Inc., Charles H. Greenthal Co., Inc., Herbert Charles Co., James Felt Realty Serv., Inc., Kenneth D. Laub Co., Lansco Corp., Gronich & Karr Co., Inc.; **PREV EMPLOY:** Member Pfeiffer & Crames Esqs; **PROFL AFFIL & HONORS:** RE Bd. of NY (Legislation Comm.), NY Cty. Lawyers Assn., NY State & Amer. Bar Assns.; **EDUC:** AB, 1933, Phil., Columbia Coll.; **GRAD EDUC:** JD, 1935, Law, Columbia Univ. Sch. of Law; **MIL SERV:** USA, 1942-46, Capt.; **OTHER ACT & HONORS:** Pres. Jewish Campus Life Fund of Columbia Univ., Co-Author 'The Law of RE Brokers' (Clark Boardman, 1969), and bi-annual supplements (1971-1981), Author Brokerage Articles in the RE Law Journal, NY Law Journal & Intl. Real Prop. Law Journal (1981), Citation of Appreciation, Columbia Univ. (1981); **HOME ADD:** 1016 Fifth Ave., NY, NY 10028, (212)988-3466; **BUS ADD:** 540 Madison Ave., NY, NY 10022, (212)838-0286.

BARASCH, Stephen B.——B: May 9, 1949, Los Angeles, CA, *Pres.*, Barasch Arch. & Associates, Inc.; **PRIM RE ACT:** Architect, Developer, Builder; **SERVICES:** Arch./RE, Devel/Const., Mgmt./Interior Design; **PROFL AFFIL & HONORS:** AIA; BIA, Various Arch. Design Awards; **EDUC:** BArch, 1970, Univ. of AZ; **GRAD EDUC:** MArch, 1972, Urban Design, Rice Univ.; **EDUC HONORS:** Cum Laude, Grad. Student Schol.; Post Grad. Studies at the Architectural Assn., London, Eng.; **OTHER ACT & HONORS:** San Marino Tennis Foundation, Pasadena C of C, Econ. Devel. Comm.; **HOME ADD:** 6820 N La Presa, San Gabriel, CA 91175, (213)285-1594; **BUS ADD:** 25 N. Mentor St., Pasadena, CA 91106, (213)449-7214.

BARATTA, Philip J.——B: Nov. 24, 1935, Chicago, IL, *VP; Head of RE Div.*, Sears B&T Co., RE Lending; **PRIM RE ACT:** Lender; **SERVICES:** Comml. & indus. loans; **REP CLIENTS:** Major builders, devel. & RE brokers; **PREV EMPLOY:** Continental IL Nat. Bank, RE Div., Staff Appraiser and Consultant; Harris trust & saving Bank, VP Lending; **PROFL AFFIL & HONORS:** Sr. Member, Amer. Soc. of Appraisers; Intl. Council of Valuers; Member, Comml. Panel of the Amer. Arbitration Assn.; Past Officer, Chicago Chap., Past Chmn., Publicity and Programming Comm. of the Chicago Chap., Amer. Soc. of Appraisers; Past Member, Intl. Bd. of Examiners, Past Chmn., Legislative Comm. of the Chicago Chap., Amer. Soc. of Appraisers; Past Member, Intl. Conf. Location Comm. of the Amer. Soc. of Appraisers; Past Member, Intl. Legislative Comm. for the Licensing/Cert. of Appraisers; Former Member, Intl. Council of Shopping Ctrs.; **EDUC:** Wright Jr. Coll.; **MIL SERV:** US Army, Pfc.; **OTHER ACT & HONORS:** Publications: The Appraiser's Role in Mobile Home Park Devel. and Investment, 1972 Jan.-Feb. issue, The Real Estate Appraiser; **HOME ADD:** 152 Jefferson Ln., Bloomingdale, IL 60108; **BUS ADD:** Sears Tower, Chicago, IL 60606, (312)876-4137.

BARBATO, John R.——B: Sep. 26, 1946, Boston, MA, *Asst. VP, RE*, Ames Dept. Stores, Inc.; **PRIM RE ACT:** Developer, Builder, Property Manager; **OTHER RE ACT:** Direct the Selection & Devel. of New Stores; **PREV EMPLOY:** First Hartford Realty Corp., Manchester, CT-Greenville, SC; **PROFL AFFIL & HONORS:** ICSC; **EDUC:** BBA, 1970, Gen. Bus. & Fin., Univ. of MA, Amherst; **MIL SERV:** USANG, SP-4, 70-76; **OTHER ACT & HONORS:** RE Broker, Comm. of MA; **HOME ADD:** 53 Seminary Rd., Simsbury, CT 06070; **BUS ADD:** 2418 Main St., Rocky Hill, CT 06067, (203)563-8234.

BARBEE, Cliff——B: May 25, 1929, Graham, TX, *Pres., 1972-Present*, Barbee Company, Realtors; Hall Real Estate Inst.; **PRIM RE ACT:** Broker, Instructor, Consultant, Real Estate Publisher; **OTHER RE ACT:** Brokerage, RE Education; **SERVICES:** Relocation of indiv./families, or cos.; **REP CLIENTS:** TX Instruments; IBM; Merrill Lynch; **PREV EMPLOY:** Fellowship, Amer. Univ., 1970-72; Exec. Office, The White House, 1968-70; USAF 1950-68; **PROFL AFFIL & HONORS:** Temple-Belton Bd. of Realtors, TAR, NAR, RNMI, TX GRI; CRB; Lead RE Instructor, TX RE Research Ctr., TX A & M Univ.; **EDUC:** BS, 1950, Bus., Geology & Land, Econ., ND State Univ.; **GRAD EDUC:** MS, 1965, Bus. Mgmt., FL State Univ.; PhD, 1972, Bus./Mgmt., Amer. Univ.; **EDUC HONORS:** Distinguished Military Grad, USAF ROTC, Fellowship; **MIL SERV:** USAF; Lt. Col.; DFC, MSM/OLC, OAFU; **OTHER ACT & HONORS:** RELO-Inter City Relocation Serv.; TX RE, Teachers Assn.; RE Educators Assn.; Assn. of US Army; AFA; Retd. Officers Assn.; Sierra Club; **HOME ADD:** 2002 Azalea, Killeen, TX 76541, (817)634-3714; **BUS ADD:** Old Church Pl., Box 737, Salado, TX 76571, (817)947-5200.

BARBER, Kenneth H.——B: Nashville, TN, *Pres./Broker*, The Rawhide Co., Realtors; **PRIM RE ACT:** Broker, Syndicator, Consultant, Developer, Owner/Investor; **OTHER RE ACT:** Collection & Closing Serv.; **SERVICES:** Gen. RE, Land Dev., Recreat. Land Dev., Sund., Comml.; **PROFL AFFIL & HONORS:** CRB, GRI, CCIM Candidate; **EDUC:** BS, 1948, Engineering, USMA, West Point, NY; **MIL SERV:** USAF; **OTHER ACT & HONORS:** Dir., Colo. Spgs. Bd. Realtors & Dir. Symphony; **HOME ADD:** 39 Maryland Rd., Colo. Springs, CO, (303)630-3464; **BUS ADD:** 15160 N Union Blvd., Colo. Springs, CO 80918, (303)598-3198.

BARBER, Peter K.——B: Dec. 8, 1947, Denver, CO, *VP*, Northland Investment Corp. (since 1971); **PRIM RE ACT:** Developer, Appraiser; **SERVICES:** Investment Analysis and valuation, devel. & synd., prop. mgmt.; **REP CLIENTS:** Indiv. & instnl. investors in comml. RE; **PROFL AFFIL & HONORS:** MA RE Broker, NH RE Broker, Member Intl. Council of Shopping Centers; **EDUC:** BA, 1970, Soc. Relations, Harvard Coll.; **OTHER ACT & HONORS:** Dir., Newton Needham C of C; Dir. W. Suburban YMCA; Treas., Newton Community Development Found.; **HOME ADD:** 63 Windsor Rd., Waban, MA O2168; **BUS ADD:** 20 Walnut St., Wellesley Hills, MA 02160, (617)235-2900.

BARBER, Stephen R.——B: Dec. 9, 1946, Pendleton, OR, *C.P.M., (owner/broker)*, Invest West Mgmt.; **PRIM RE ACT:** Broker, Syndicator, Consultant, Property Manager, Owner/Investor; **SERVICES:** Income Prop. Mgmt. Serv. - Dev. Consultant; **PREV EMPLOY:** Prop. Mgmt. Services, Inc., 1973-1976 managed over 5,000 multiple residential units; **PROFL AFFIL & HONORS:** IREM; Sec.- IREM Chap. 29 - 1981-82; RNMI; **EDUC:** BS, 1969, Recreation Mgmt. & Admin., OR State Univ.; **HOME ADD:** 12402 SE 13th St., Vancouver, WA 98660, (206)696-0214; **BUS ADD:** 1001 1/2 Main St., Suite 4, Vancouver, WA 98660, (206)699-4850.

BARBER, William T., Jr.——B: Sept. 4, 1951, Wilmington, NC, *Owner*, W.T. Barber & Co.; **PRIM RE ACT:** Consultant, Appraiser; **OTHER RE ACT:** Realtor; **SERVICES:** RE appraising and consulting; **PROFL AFFIL & HONORS:** AIREA; Soc. of RE Appraisers; Member, Richmond. of Realtors; VA Assn. of Realtors; NAR, MAI; SRPA; **EDUC:** BSBA, 1973, Mktg., Univ. of Richmond, School of Bus.; **OTHER ACT & HONORS:** Alumnus, Sigma Alpha Epsilon Frat.; Univ. of Richmond Spider Club; Derbyshire Baptist Church; Pres., Richmond Chap. 102, Soc. of RE Appraisers; **HOME ADD:** 8403 Kalb Rd., Richmond, VA 23229, (804)270-1176; **BUS ADD:** POB 86, Richmond, VA 23201, (804)329-0615.

BARBERG, W. Warren——B: Oct. 12, 1928, Minneapolis, MN, *Owner*, Barberg Associates; **PRIM RE ACT:** Developer, Owner/Investor, Property Manager, Syndicator; **OTHER RE ACT:** Tax, fin. planning; **SERVICES:** RE Devel., Mgmt.; **PROFL AFFIL & HONORS:** ULI; **EDUC:** Univ. of WI, 1951, Indus. Arts.; **EDUC HONORS:** Grad. with distinction; **HOME ADD:** 3717 State St., Eau Claire, WI 54201, (715)835-3618; **BUS ADD:** 307 S. Farwell, Eau Claire, WI 54201, (715)835-5161.

BARCLAY, John A.——B: Feb. 14, 1951, Los Angeles,CA, *Partner*, Barclay & Moskatel, a Profl. Corp.; **PRIM RE ACT:** Attorney; **SERVICES:** Legal, tax and security counseling RE all aspects of RE bus. including devel. and public and pvt. offerings; **REP CLIENTS:** Devel., synd., and lenders and brokers; **PREV EMPLOY:** Lic. RE broker; **PROFL AFFIL & HONORS:** CA State Bar - Tax and Real Prop. Sections; Real Prop. Trust and Probate Section of ABA; **EDUC:** BA, 1972, Speech Communication, USC; **GRAD EDUC:** JD, 1975, Law, USC; **EDUC HONORS:** Adv. Bd. - Moot Court Honors Program; **BUS ADD:** 9595 Wilshire Blvd., Beverly Hills, CA 90212, (213)273-7080.

BARD, Stanley——*RE Director*, American Brands, Inc.; **PRIM RE ACT:** Property Manager; **BUS ADD:** 245 Panc Avz, New York, NY 10067, (212)557-7000.*

BARDWELL, Princeton M.——B: Mar. 18, 1948, Baton Rouge, LA, RE Invest. Servs.; **PRIM RE ACT:** Broker; **SERVICES:** Mkt. research, invest. evaluations, prop. acquisitions, consulting.; **REP CLIENTS:** RE investors, devels., users, brokers, lenders; **PROFL AFFIL & HONORS:** NAR, ULI, CCIM; **EDUC:** BS BA, 1971, RE & Urban Land Studies, Univ. of FL; **HOME ADD:** 12441 Sheebrook Dr., Baton Rouge, LA 70815, (504)275-1678; **BUS ADD:** 353 Napoleon St., Baton Rouge, LA 70802, (504)344-3269.

BARE, Donald R.——B: Sep. 27, 1931, WV, *Pres.*, Big Bear Co.; **PRIM RE ACT:** Broker, Appraiser, Developer, Builder, Owner/Investor, Property Manager, Insuror; **SERVICES:** Brokerage, counseling, appraisals, relocation, devel.; **REP CLIENTS:** Lending instns. (local); Homequity, Merrill Lynch Relocation; **PREV EMPLOY:** Pres., Ins. Plans Inc.; **PROFL AFFIL & HONORS:** Bd. of Dir., WV Assn. of Realtors; Exec. Comm. & Bd. of Dir., WV Homebuilders Assn.; **MIL SERV:** US Navy, EM 3; **OTHER ACT & HONORS:** Chmn., Raleigh Co. Housing Authority; V. Chmn., Raleigh Cty. Indus. Devel. Authority; Bd. Dir., Beckley C of C; **HOME ADD:** Rt. 9, Box 91-D, Beaver, WV 25813, (304)763-2701; **BUS ADD:** 809 S. Kanawha St., Beckley, WV 25801, (304)252-0795.

BARELS, Larry——B: Sept. 7, 1948, Los Angeles, CA, *Pres.*, Sun Pacific Props.; **PRIM RE ACT:** Broker, Consultant, Developer, Builder, Owner/Investor, Syndicator; **SERVICES:** computer forecasting; **REP CLIENTS:** IMS Fin. Corp., Bamod Co.; **PREV EMPLOY:** VP Invest West Financial; **EDUC:** BA, 1970, Communications, Brigham Young Univ.; **GRAD EDUC:** MBA, 1974, Fin., Amer. Inst. of the West; **HOME ADD:** 2407 Foothill Ln., Santa Barbara, CA 93101; **BUS ADD:** 21 B.E. Canon Perdido, Santa Barbara, CA 93101, (805)965-8464.

BARENSCHEER, James Patrick——B: July 29, 1945, Grand Forks, ND, *Housing Devel. Dir./Multifamily Prop. Mgr.*, Ryan Construction Co. of MN, Inc., Multifamily; **PRIM RE ACT:** Developer, Property Manager; **SERVICES:** Devel., designers, bldrs., prop. mgmt.; **REP CLIENTS:** Numerous local and nat. retail and indus. clients/HRAs,

HUD, MN Housing Fin. Agency; **PREV EMPLOY:** MN Housing Fin. Agency, Dir. of Multifamily Mgmt. Div., 1975-1977; **PROFL AFFIL & HONORS:** MN Multi Housing Assn.; IREM, CPM; **EDUC:** BA, 1968, Mankato State Univ.; **HOME ADD:** 9490 Risewood Cir., Eden Prairie, MN 55344, (612)944-3088; **BUS ADD:** One Corp. Ctr., 7401 Metro Blvd., Suite 500, Edina, MN 55435, (612)835-7990.

BAREWIN, Lee B.——B: May 14, 1936, Kansas City, MO, *Owner*, The Barewin Co.; **PRIM RE ACT:** Broker, Property Manager; **SERVICES:** Leasing, Sales, Mgmt.; **PROFL AFFIL & HONORS:** NAR, RNMI, IREM, CPM, CCIM, Bd. of Kansas City, MO; Johnson Cty., KS Bd. of Realtors; **EDUC:** BS, 1958, Bus. Admin., Washington Univ., St. Louis, MO; **MIL SERV:** USA, Capt.; **BUS ADD:** 5501 W 97 St., Overland Park, KS 66207, (913)649-0555.

BARHYTE, Donald J.——*Treas.*, Multimedia, Inc.; **PRIM RE ACT:** Property Manager; **BUS ADD:** PO Box 1688, Greenville, SC 29602, (803)298-4373.*

BARIBEAU, Michael H.——B: Feb. 4, 1953, Brunswick, ME, *Mgr.*, The Baribeau Agency, Inc.; **PRIM RE ACT:** Broker, Consultant, Appraiser, Developer, Builder, Property Manager; **SERVICES:** RE sales, prop. mgmt., appraisals, consultation; **REP CLIENTS:** Indivs.; **PROFL AFFIL & HONORS:** Merrymeeting Bd. of Realtors, Brunswick Area C of C; **EDUC:** BA, 1975, Anthroplogy, Fine Arts, Beloit Coll., Beloit, WI 53511; **OTHER ACT & HONORS:** Pejebscot Jaycees; Who's Who in Bus. & Fin. 1981; Century 21, Million Dallar Club 1981; **HOME ADD:** RFD 1, Box 101, Richmond, ME 04357; **BUS ADD:** 51 Pleasant St., Brunswick, ME 04011, (207)729-3333.

BARKAN, Abram——B: Feb. 22, 1919, Brooklyn, NY, *Pres.; Princ.*, James Felt Realty Services; Joint Venture James Felt/Grubb & Ellis; **PRIM RE ACT:** Consultant, Appraiser; **SERVICES:** Counseling on valuation, devel. & mktg.; **REP CLIENTS:** Major corp., banks, insurance companies, pension & trust funds; **PROFL AFFIL & HONORS:** ASREC; AIREA, CRE; MAI; Pres.-1978 American Society of Real Estate Counselors; Pres.-1971 New York Chapter American Institute of Real Estate Appraisers; Member-Real Estate Valuation Council, American Arbitration Association; **MIL SERV:** US Army, PFC 82nd Airborne Division, Purple Heart w/OLC, 1942-1945; **OTHER ACT & HONORS:** Bd., Settlement Housing Fund; Bd., Advisory Services for Better Housing; Lecturer, New School, Ctr. For NYC Affairs; **HOME ADD:** 11 Briar Ct., S. Orange, NJ 07079, (201)763-0219; **BUS ADD:** 488 Madison Ave., NY, NY 10022, (212)421-2100.

BARKER, Ann S.——B: Feb. 25, 1934, Lincoln, NE, *Atty.*, Ann S. Barker, Atty. at Law; **PRIM RE ACT:** Broker, Attorney; **SERVICES:** Legal counsel in all areas concerning RE; **REP CLIENTS:** Closely held corp., partnerships, indiv. transacting RE Bus., prop. mgmt.; **PREV EMPLOY:** Barker Mgmt. Inc., a prop. mgmt. Co., Geyser & Marlin, law firm; **PROFL AFFIL & HONORS:** ABA, State Bar of CA, Orange Cty. Bar Assn., Orange Cty. Women Lawyers, CA Brokers License, Article: " The High Cost of Property Insurance in HUD Urban Core Housing Developments", The Insurance Law Journal, December, 1978; **EDUC:** Liberal Arts, 1955, Poli. Sci., Univ. of NE; **GRAD EDUC:** 1978, Law, Pepperdine Univ. Sch. of Law; **EDUC HONORS:** Phi Beta Kappa; **OTHER ACT & HONORS:** Vol.: Chairperson, Housing Element of the Gen. Plan, Laguna Beach, CA, Member, Advisory Comm., Orange Cty. Housing Authority; **HOME ADD:** 811 Wendt Terrace, Laguna Beach, CA 92651, (714)497-1378; **BUS ADD:** 1720 W. Ball Rd., Suite 3, Anaheim, CA 92804, (714)533-1932.

BARKER, James H.——B: Jan. 31, 1942, Seattle, WA, *Arch.*, The Barker Collaborative Archs. AIA; **PRIM RE ACT:** Architect; **OTHER RE ACT:** Unit Devel. & Re-zones; **SERVICES:** Arch., Planning & Programing; **REP CLIENTS:** Comml. & Resid. Land Devel. & Mgrs.; **PROFL AFFIL & HONORS:** Seattle & Nat. AIA, Home of the Month Award; **EDUC:** BArch., 1967, Arch. & Planning, Univ. of WA; **GRAD EDUC:** BS Bldg. technology & admin., 1967, Programing, Systems, Univ. of WA; **OTHER ACT & HONORS:** Seattle Art Museum; **HOME ADD:** 11230 75th Ave., NE, Kirkland, WA 98033, (206)823-1485; **BUS ADD:** 12951 Bel Red Rd., Bellevue, WA 98005, (206)454-9471.

BARKER, Jock——B: Dec. 16, 1937, Hollywood, CA, *Gen. Sales Mgr.*, Moore and Company Realtor; **PRIM RE ACT:** Broker, Consultant, Instructor; **PROFL AFFIL & HONORS:** RNMI VP 1981 R.S. Div., GRS, CRB; **OTHER ACT & HONORS:** RE Speaker for conventions and Sr. inst. RNMI; Dillon Yacht Club; **HOME ADD:** 12345 W. 17 Ave., Lakewood, CO, (303)238-5681; **BUS ADD:** 390 Grant St., Denver, CO 80203, (303)778-6600.

BARKER, John R.——B: Mar. 9, 1947, St. Joseph, MO, *Atty.*, Gable, Gotwals, Rubin, Fox, Johnson & Baker; **PRIM RE ACT:** Attorney; **OTHER RE ACT:** Comml.; **SERVICES:** Investment Counseling, Title Opinions, Comml. RE Loans, Indiv. RE Loans, Contracts and Closings, Synd. and Parternships; **REP CLIENTS:** Lenders or Instit. investors in comml. props. and indiv. purchasers and sellers of RE; **PROFL AFFIL & HONORS:** Young Lawyers' Div. of ABA and OK Bar Assn.; Title Lawyers' Assn.; Tulsa Cty. Bar Assn., ABA, OBA & TCBA Outstanding Young Lawyer of 1978; Chmn. of Young Lawyers' Div. of OK Bar Assn. for 1978; Dist. Rep. for Young Lawyers' Div. of ABA; **EDUC:** AB, 1969, Hist./Bus., Univ. of MO at Columbia; **GRAD EDUC:** JD, 1974, Law, Univ. of MI; **EDUC HONORS:** Sigma Rho Sigma; Dean's List, Senior Judge of Carpenter Case Club; **MIL SERV:** U.S. Army, Sgt., Distinguished Serv. Medal, Rep. of S. Vietnam Comm. Medal; **OTHER ACT & HONORS:** Vestry St. Dunstan's Episcopal Church; **HOME ADD:** 3006 E 75th St., Tulsa, OK 74136, (918)494-3691; **BUS ADD:** 20th Flr., Fourth National Bank Bldg., Tulsa, OK 74119, (918)582-9201.

BARKER, Robert E.——B: June 22, 1942, Bangor, ME, *VP*, Dutch Institutional Holding Corporation, Inc.; **PRIM RE ACT:** Lender, Owner/Investor; **SERVICES:** Lender/investor in SE for projects over $30 million; **REP CLIENTS:** Major RE devels.; **PREV EMPLOY:** Cousins Properties - VP; **EDUC:** BS, 1965, Fin., Univ. of ME; **MIL SERV:** US Army, 1Lt., 1965-1967; **HOME TEL:** (404)394-4558; **BUS ADD:** 5500 Interstate N. Pkwy., Suite 410, Atlanta, GA 30328, (404)952-3940.

BARKLEY, Paul H.——B: Sept. 24, 1937, Washington, DC, *Partner*, Barkley Pierce O'Malley, Arch. & Planners; **PRIM RE ACT:** Architect, Developer, Owner/Investor; **SERVICES:** Arch. Engrg. Design, devel. & fin., feasibility studies, constr. admin., promotional packages; **REP CLIENTS:** Comml., indus. & housing devels., owners; **PROFL AFFIL & HONORS:** AIA (Treas. VA Soc. AIA, 1980-81, V.P., 1982); **EDUC:** B Arch., 1960, Arch., Univ. of VA; **GRAD EDUC:** Ecoles D'Art Americaines, Fontainebleau, France, 1959; **MIL SERV:** USAF, Airman 1st Cl., Berlin Crisis; **OTHER ACT & HONORS:** Gr. Falls Church C of C, Pres. 1976; Pillar of Community Award, 1977; Cty. Branch Member Bd. of Mgmt., Fairfax, YMCA, 1976-81; Member Falls Church Bus. & Profl. Devel. Commn. (Chmn., 1978-81); **HOME ADD:** 311 Chestnut St., Falls Church, VA 22046, (703)534-1424; **BUS ADD:** 111 Park Pl., Falls Church, VA 22046, (703)532-5757.

BARNARD, John——B: June 10, 1947, Buffalo, NY, *Partner*, Davis, Young & Mendelson; **PRIM RE ACT:** Attorney; **SERVICES:** Gen. Real Prop. Law emphasizing devel.; **REP CLIENTS:** Lenders, devels., condo. converters, resort time-sharing projects; **EDUC:** AB, 1969, Hist., Princeton Univ.; **GRAD EDUC:** JD, 1975, Law, Boalt Hall (Univ. of CA, Berkeley); **EDUC HONORS:** Magna Cum Laude; **MIL SERV:** US Naval Reserves, Lt. J.G.; **HOME ADD:** 189 Canyon Vista Pl, Danville, CA 94526, (415)838-0443; **BUS ADD:** 1134 Ballena Blvd., PO Box 2426, Alameda, CA 94501, (415)521-1211.

BARNES, John R.——B: July 20, 1945, Spartanburg, SC, *VP*, Coldwell Banker Realtors; **PRIM RE ACT:** Broker, Consultant, Instructor; **SERVICES:** Resid. sales, valuation, resid. rental mgmt.; **REP CLIENTS:** Indivs., and 3rd party corp., out of town relocation servs.; **PROFL AFFIL & HONORS:** NAR; GA Assn. of Realtors; Cobb Cty. Bd. of Realtors; Cobb Cty. C of C; R-Pac Chmn. Atl. Bd. of Realtors, GRI, Young Realtor of the Year, Atlanta Bd. of Realtors; **EDUC:** 1968, Bus. Admin., Univ. of TN; **GRAD EDUC:** 1968, Bus. Admin., Univ. of TN; **OTHER ACT & HONORS:** Dist. Assistant & Staff to U.S. Congressman Larry McDonald, 1974-76; First Baptist Church of Atlanta; **HOME ADD:** 2425 Oldfield Rd. N.W., Atlanta, GA 30327, (404)352-1444; **BUS ADD:** 547 Roswell St., Marietta, GA 30060.

BARNES, Orville L.——B: May 27, 1927, McCall, ID, *Pres.*, McCarthy Management & Development Co.; **PRIM RE ACT:** Broker, Developer, Property Manager; **SERVICES:** Comml. prop. mgmt., devel., leasing & sales; **PREV EMPLOY:** Worked for McCarthy Mgmt. Corp. 23 yrs before purchasing same; **PROFL AFFIL & HONORS:** ICSC, BOMA, Spokane Bd. of Realtors, IREM, CPM, CSM, CPA; **EDUC:** BS, 1950, Acctg., Univ. of ID; **MIL SERV:** USN; **OTHER ACT & HONORS:** Spokane Sch. Dist. Sch. Bd. 1968-73; State Bd. of Educ. 1974-79; Pres. of Spokane Taxpayers Assn. 1975-present; Member of Rotary Club; **HOME ADD:** S. 2324 Magnolia Ct., Spokane, WA 99203, (509)534-1494; **BUS ADD:** 217 Northtown Office Bldg., N. 4407 Div., Spokane, WA 99207, (509)489-4332.

BARNES, Paul T.——B: July 30, 1942, Yonkers, NY, *Owner*, Paul T. Barnes Real Estate; **PRIM RE ACT:** Broker, Instructor, Consultant, Property Manager, Owner/Investor; **SERVICES:** Investment Analysis; **PREV EMPLOY:** Systems Engineer at IBM; Gen. Sales Mgr. for Lusk Devel. Co. 12/68 to 4/74; **PROFL AFFIL & HONORS:** RNMI, CCIM since 11/79; **EDUC:** BS, 1967, Indus. Mgmt., Fairfield Univ., CT; **GRAD EDUC:** MA, 1970, Computer Assisted Instr., Fairfield Univ.; **EDUC HONORS:** Named to Who's Who Among Students in Amer. Univs. - yrs. '66 & '67; **MIL SERV:** USA, SP-4, Good Conduct Medal; **HOME ADD:** 103 Southport Woods Dr., Southport, CT 06490, (203)255-3285; **BUS ADD:** 40 Reef Rd., Fairfield, CT 06430, (203)255-6195.

BARNES, W.P.——*Office Adm.*, Dennison Manufacturing Co.; **PRIM RE ACT:** Property Manager; **BUS ADD:** 300 Howard St., Framingham, MA 01701.*

BARNETT, Herman H.——*Chmn. Bus. Div.*, Texarkana College; **PRIM RE ACT:** Broker, Consultant, Owner/Investor, Instructor; **BUS ADD:** 2500 N. Robinson Rd., Texarkana, TX 75501, (214)838-4541.

BARNETT, Robert Spencer——**B:** Sept. 10, 1944, NYC, NY, Gruen Assoc.; **PRIM RE ACT:** Architect; **SERVICES:** Arch., Engrg., Planning; **PROFL AFFIL & HONORS:** Amer. Inst. of Arch., LA Chap., Reg. Architect, CA & NY; **EDUC:** BA, 1967, Arch., Univ. of PA; **GRAD EDUC:** MArch, 1975, Arch., Arch. & Urban Planning - Columbia Univ.; **EDUC HONORS:** William Kinne Fellows Traveling Fellowship; **OTHER ACT & HONORS:** Bd. of Dirs., Family Serv. of Santa Monica; Vestry, St. Augustine's Episcopal Church; **HOME ADD:** 2611 Euclid St., Santa Monica, CA 90405; **BUS ADD:** 6330 San Vicende Blvd., Los Angeles, CA 90048, (213)937-4270.

BARNHILL, Charles William——**B:** March 21, 1943, Fairhope, AL, *VP*, Omega Prop. Inc.; **PRIM RE ACT:** Broker, Syndicator, Consultant, Owner/Investor; **SERVICES:** Gen. RE Brokerage and Investment Consulting; **REP CLIENTS:** Indiv. Investors in Comml. Props.; **PROFL AFFIL & HONORS:** Reissi, AL CCIM Chap., Mobile RE Exchange, Who's Who in Commercial and Investment RE, CCIM, FLI, NAIOP, Mobile Cty. Bd. of Realtors; **EDUC:** BS Biology Univ. AL, 1965, Biology Chemistry, Univ. of AL in Tusca Loosa; **GRAD EDUC:** MS Phd, 1968, 1974, Biochemistry, Univ. of AL (Birmingham); **MIL SERV:** USA, Capt.; **OTHER ACT & HONORS:** Bd. of Dir., AL Systic Fibrosis Foundation, Toastmasters Internatl., Mobile C of C; **HOME ADD:** 5 Signal Hill Rd., Spanish Fort, AL 36527, (205)626-3524; **BUS ADD:** 3961 Springhill Ave., Mobile, AL 36608, (205)343-5230.

BARNHORN, C. Barry——**B:** Dec. 25, 1935, Cin., OH, *Pres.*, Barnhorn, Inc. DBA Barnhorn Realtors Better Homes and Gardens; **PRIM RE ACT:** Broker, Consultant, Appraiser, Developer, Builder, Owner/Investor, Insuror, Syndicator; **SERVICES:** Sales, Sales Mgmt. Resid. & Comml. Indus.; **REP CLIENTS:** Northside Bank, Proctor and Gamble; Mutual of Omaha Ins., Worthington Indus., Franklin Mint.; **PROFL AFFIL & HONORS:** NAR, Home Builders, Better Homes and Gardens Advisory Bd.; **EDUC:** BBA, 1958, Mktg., Mgmt., Econ., Univ. of Cincinnati; **EDUC HONORS:** All; **OTHER ACT & HONORS:** St. Joseph Orphanage (Pres.); **HOME ADD:** 351 Circlewood Ln., Cincinnati, OH 45215, (513)931-6931; **BUS ADD:** 11180 Reed Hartman Hwy., Cincinnati, OH 45242, (513)791-5522.

BAROFSKY, Frederick J.——**B:** May 16, 1945, Chicago, IL, *Partner*, Gahlberg & Barofsky Interests, Inc.; **PRIM RE ACT:** Broker, Developer, Owner/Investor; **SERVICES:** Full service RE devel., leasing and mgmt. co.; **PREV EMPLOY:** Trammell Crow Co.; **EDUC:** BS, 1967, Civil Engrg./Military Scis., US Military Academy - West Point, NY; **GRAD EDUC:** MBA, 1974, Econ. and Fin., Univ. of Chicago; **EDUC HONORS:** Pres. of Class for 3 years; **MIL SERV:** US Army, Capt., Silver Star & Purple Heart; **HOME ADD:** 5216 Harvey Ave., Western Springs, IL 60558, (312)246-7757; **BUS ADD:** 2211 York Road, Oak Brook, IL 60521, (312)654-0600.

BARON, Hal——**B:** Apr. 12, 1923, NY, NY, *Gen. Partner*, H.B. Development; **PRIM RE ACT:** Attorney, Developer, Syndicator; **PROFL AFFIL & HONORS:** State Bar of CA; L.A. Cty. Bar Assn.; BIA; **EDUC:** BS, 1959, Acctg., Univ. of CA; **GRAD EDUC:** LLB/JD, 1965, Univ. of S. CA, Sch. of Law; **EDUC HONORS:** Honors Program Selectee, Moot Court; **OTHER ACT & HONORS:** Mayor's Comm.; Shriners; UJA; Bnai Brith; **BUS ADD:** 5900 Sepulveda Blvd., N Sherman Oaks, CA 91411, (213)994-9500.

BARON, Louis C.T.——**B:** May 10, 1947, Ft. Worth, TX, *Admin.*, State Capitol Investments; **PRIM RE ACT:** Broker, Consultant, Lender, Owner/Investor; **SERVICES:** Broker 1st & 2nd. T.D. loans, serv. loans for clients; **REP CLIENTS:** Pvt. investors and small pension funds; **PROFL AFFIL & HONORS:** Fin. Planners; **EDUC:** BS, 1975, Chem. & Psych., CA State Univ., Fullerton; **HOME ADD:** 3109 Kadema Dr., Sacramento, CA 95825; **BUS ADD:** 720 Howe Ave., Suite 104, Sacramento, CA 95825, (916)929-8900.

BARON, Mitchell Neal——**B:** Nov. 8, 1947, New York City, NY, *Attorney - Partner*, Gelberg & Abrams; **PRIM RE ACT:** Attorney; **SERVICES:** Legal; **PROFL AFFIL & HONORS:** Assn. of the Bar of the City of NY; Member of the NY Bar; **EDUC:** BS, 1969, Acctg., Boston Univ. Coll. of Bus. Admin.; **GRAD EDUC:** JD, 1973, Law, Columbia Univ. School of Law; **EDUC HONORS:** Admin. Editor - Journal of Law and Social Problems; **BUS ADD:** 711 Third Ave., New York, NY 10017, (212)599-3200.

BARON, Richard E.——**B:** Nov. 19, 1940, Sioux City, IA, *Pres.*, Greater AZ Devel. Corp.; **PRIM RE ACT:** Broker, Instructor, Syndicator, Consultant, Appraiser, Developer, Builder, Property Manager; **OTHER RE ACT:** Other related Cos.; **SERVICES:** Sales, leasing, bldg., synd., mgt. consultant valuation; **REP CLIENTS:** Various local and national; **PREV EMPLOY:** Realty Consultants Inc., 1967 - 1969; **PROFL AFFIL & HONORS:** GRI; IFA; CRA; **EDUC:** BS, 1967, Bus./Acctg./Econ., Univ. of AZ; **OTHER ACT & HONORS:** Various local and civic; various articles published; Guest lecturer, Phoenix Coll.; **HOME ADD:** 5107 N. 86th Pl., Scottsdale, AZ 85251, (602)947-6111; **BUS ADD:** 1035 E. Camelback Rd., Phoenix, AZ 85014, (602)994-9000.

BARONE, Don S.——**B:** June 30, 1931, Buffalo, NY, *Prop. Serv. Supervisor (1979-present)*, The City of San Diego, Prop. Mgmt. Serv.; **OTHER RE ACT:** Lease and sale of public R.E./Facilities; **SERVICES:** Negotiations, mktg. contract compliance, admin.; **PREV EMPLOY:** Various positions with the City of San Diego in Prop. Dept. and Engng. Dept. Title Insurance; **PROFL AFFIL & HONORS:** San Diego Bd. of Realtors (Affiliate 5770); IREM; Intl. Right-of-Way Assoc., San Diego, CPM; So. CA Marina Auth.; **EDUC:** BA, 1957, Liberal Arts (Eng. Lit.), San Diego State Univ.; **GRAD EDUC:** Cert. in RE, 1965, RE, Univ. of CA, Extension, San Diego; **MIL SERV:** USA, CADRE-CPL (1950-52); **OTHER ACT & HONORS:** Admin. VP, Courthouse Toastmasters, San Diego (Toastmasters Intl.) 1981; **HOME ADD:** 3447 Copley Ave., San Diego, CA 92116, (714)281-4316; **BUS ADD:** 1222 First Ave., M.S. 503, San Diego, CA 92101, (714)236-6722.

BARR, H. Dennis——**B:** Oct. 26, 1942, Los Angeles, CA, *Pres.*, Jay Prop. Systems, Inc., A Member of the Jacobs Engin. Grp.; **PRIM RE ACT:** Broker, Attorney, Architect, Developer, Builder, Property Manager, Engineer, Owner/Investor; **REP CLIENTS:** Major Ind. Corps.; **PREV EMPLOY:** VP-Law, Jacobs Eng. Grp. Inc.; **PROFL AFFIL & HONORS:** State Bar of CA, ABA; **EDUC:** AB, 1964, Econ. and Poli. Sci., USC; **GRAD EDUC:** LLB and MBA, 1967 & 1969, Corp., Taxation and Fin., Acctg., Stanford Law Sch., Grad. Sch. of Bus., USC; **EDUC HONORS:** Magna Cum Laude, Phi Beta Kappa, Phi Kappa Phi, Order of Palm, Law Forum, Outstanding Grad. Bus. Stdt. 1969; **HOME ADD:** 2239 Moreno Dr., Los Angeles, CA 90039, (213)664-2833; **BUS ADD:** 251 S. Lake Ave., Pasadena, CA 91101, (213)449-2151.

BARR, H. Robert——**B:** Apr. 22, 1928, Albany, OR, *Pres.*, Center Investments, Inc.; **PRIM RE ACT:** Broker, Consultant, Developer, Owner/Investor, Property Manager, Syndicator; **PREV EMPLOY:** Safeway Stores, Seattle Times Newspeper, Baker-Stimpson Advertising, Associated Grocers, Inc.; **PROFL AFFIL & HONORS:** Intl. Council of Shopping Ctr., Inc., LUI; **EDUC:** BA, 1953, Mktg. Research, U. of WA (Seattle); **MIL SERV:** USMC, Sgt.; **HOME ADD:** 5553 So. Sunset Dr., Freeland, WA 98249, (206)221-7822; **BUS ADD:** P O Box 820, Freeland, WA 98249, (206)321-6283.

BARR, Lawrence M.——**B:** Oct. 20, 1939, San Francisco, CA, *Mgr.-Mktg. RE*, Union Oil Co. of CA, 76 Div., W Region; **OTHER RE ACT:** Asset Mgmt.; **PROFL AFFIL & HONORS:** NACORE; **EDUC:** BA, 1961, Bus. Admin., San Fran. State Coll.; **OTHER ACT & HONORS:** Tournament of Roses Comm., S CA Golf Assn.; **HOME ADD:** 1303 Descanso Dr., La Canada-Flintridge, CA 90100, (213)790-4578; **BUS ADD:** 911 Wilshire Blvd., Room 1316, Los Angeles, CA 90017, (213)977-6710.

BARR, T.H., Jr.——**B:** Sept. 25, 1948, Temple, TX, *Pres.*, T.H. Barr Investments, Inc.; **PRIM RE ACT:** Owner/Investor, Syndicator; **OTHER RE ACT:** TX Broker/dealing in securities, spec. in private placements in oil & gas, cattle, RE; **REP CLIENTS:** Profls. business owners. Also active synd. in oil & gas, RE; **PREV EMPLOY:** Estate & Fin. Planning for 6 yrs. prior to entering securities work; **PROFL AFFIL & HONORS:** Nat. Synd. Forum & Affiliate Member of RESSI, LUTC Grad., Past Pres. of Greater Killeen Assn. of Life Underwriters; **EDUC:** BS, 1973, Computer Sci., Univ. of MD, Hardin-Baylor, Belton, TX; **GRAD EDUC:** Admin. Course, Grad. RESSI's Part. & Pvt. Placement Broker/Dealer; **OTHER ACT & HONORS:** Member Bd. of Advancement, Univ. of Mary Hardin-Baylor; Past. Pres. Killeen Centexan Kiwanis Club; Past Comm. Chmn. Ambassador & Current member, Greater Killeen C of C;

Sunday Sch teacher, 1st Baptist Church; Member Temple C of C; Member Greater Killeen Assn. of Life Underwriters; Corp. Member Assn. of US Army Ft. Hood Chapt.; **HOME ADD:** 106 Suzanne, Harker Hts., TX 76543, (817)698-3608; **BUS ADD:** 1020 Bluebird, PO. Box 2395, Harker Hts., TX 76543, (817)699-5051.

BARRAGAR, Harvey C.——**B:** Feb. 20, 1934, Seattle, WA, Miller, Nash, Yerke, Wiener & Hager; **PRIM RE ACT:** Attorney; **SERVICES:** Documentation of trans., govnt. relations & formation of joint ventures & synds.; **REP CLIENTS:** Lenders, brokers, investors & developers involved in comml. & resid. RE; **PROFL AFFIL & HONORS:** ABA, Sect. of Real Prop., Probate & Tr. Law, Comm. on New Devels. in RE Law & Practice, OR State Bar Bd. of Editors for OR State Bar Assn. RE Handbook; **EDUC:** AB, 1956, Poli. Sci., Univ. of WA; **GRAD EDUC:** JD, 1962, Univ. of OR; **EDUC HONORS:** Cum Laude, Student Editor of OR Law Review, Paul Patterson Memorial Fellow; **MIL SERV:** USN, Lt.; **HOME ADD:** 7730 SW Fairmoor St., Portland, OR 97225, (503)292-5147; **BUS ADD:** 900 SW Fifth Ave., Portland, OR 97204, (503)224-5858.

BARRE, Loren D.——*President*, RTE Corp.; **PRIM RE ACT:** Property Manager; **BUS ADD:** 1900 E. North St., Waukesha, WI 53187, (414)547-1251.*

BARRETT, Christopher J.——**B:** Feb. 24, 1932, Wakefield, MA, *Owner*, Christopher J. Barrett, Realtors; **PRIM RE ACT:** Broker, Appraiser, Owner/Investor; **SERVICES:** Gen. Brokerage, Appraising; **PROFL AFFIL & HONORS:** Dir. Eastern Middlesex Bd. of Realtors, Million Dollar Club; **EDUC:** 1959, Eng. Lit., Boston Coll.; **MIL SERV:** USN, AO/3, Pres. Unit Cits.; **OTHER ACT & HONORS:** NAREA, Tr. Wake. Sav. Nat. Assn. of RE Bd., VP Wakefield C of C; **HOME ADD:** 38 Plymouth Rd., Wakefield, MA, (617)245-9021; **BUS ADD:** 25 Tuttle St., Wakefield, MA 01880, (617)245-9021.

BARRETT, Frederick R.——**B:** Jan. 17, 1915, Montpelier, VT, *VP*, McCaughan Mort. Co. Inc.; **PRIM RE ACT:** Appraiser; **SERVICES:** First mort. loans; **REP CLIENTS:** Instnl. investors; **PREV EMPLOY:** With McCaughan Mort. Co. Inc. since 1955; Investors Diversified Servs., 1946-55; **PROFL AFFIL & HONORS:** The NARA, CRA; **EDUC:** BA, 1937, Humanities, St. Michael's, Winooski Park, VT; **MIL SERV:** USA, 1942-46, 1st Lt.; **OTHER ACT & HONORS:** Saturday Speakers Club; St. Vincent de Paul Soc.; **HOME ADD:** 480 NE 114 St., Miami, FL 33161, (305)895-2016; **BUS ADD:** 1320 S Dixie Hwy., Coral Gables, FL 33146, (305)665-9100.

BARRETT, P. Lauren——**B:** Nov. 11, 1945, Atlanta, GA, *Pres.*, P. Lauren Barrett Arch., Inc.; **PRIM RE ACT:** Architect, Consultant; **OTHER RE ACT:** Arbitrator, Amer. Arbitration Assn.; **SERVICES:** Full Arch. & Consultation; **REP CLIENTS:** Private and Public; **PREV EMPLOY:** H.G. Elliott, Arch., Birmingham, AL; **PROFL AFFIL & HONORS:** AIA; **EDUC:** BArch, 1971, Design, GA Inst. of Tech.; **MIL SERV:** USAR, SP E-5; **OTHER ACT & HONORS:** Chmn. Exec. Comm., Birmingham Rgnl. Planning Commn; **HOME ADD:** 5498 Broken Bow Dr., Birmingham, AL 35243, (205)969-0123; **BUS ADD:** 12 Office Park Cir., Suite 211, Birmingham, AL 35223, (205)871-8711.

BARRETT, Phillip H.——**B:** May 7, 1943, Detroit, MI, *Part.*, Porter, Wright, Morris & Arthur; **PRIM RE ACT:** Attorney; **SERVICES:** Legal; **REP CLIENTS:** The Klingbeil Co.; Drever, McIntosh & Co. Inc.; The Anden Group; R.W. Foster & Assoc. Inc.; **PROFL AFFIL & HONORS:** ABA, OH State Bar Assn., Columbus Bar Assn.; **EDUC:** BS, 1965, Fin., OH State Univ; **GRAD EDUC:** JD, 1968, OH State Univ; **EDUC HONORS:** Phi Eta Sigma; **MIL SERV:** USA, Capt., Bronze Medal with oak leaf cluster, Air Medal; **HOME ADD:** 1809 Upper Chelsea, Columbus, OH, (614)488-7220; **BUS ADD:** 37 W Broad St., Columbus, OH 43215, (614)227-2000.

BARRINGTON, Claude O.——**B:** Jul. 30, 1940, Trinidad, W. Indies, *Asst. Cashier*, Industrial Bank of Washington, Main Office; **PRIM RE ACT:** Banker, Lender, Instructor; **SERVICES:** Mort. to purchase prop. or re-fin.; **PROFL AFFIL & HONORS:** Amer. Bankers Assn., Wash. RE Brokers Assn; **EDUC:** BA, 1971, Econ., Bus. Admin., Howard Univ., School of Liberal Arts; **GRAD EDUC:** JD & LLM, 1974 & 1978, Comml. Law & Labor Law, Intl. Comm. Trans., Howard Univ. & Georgetown Law Ctr.; **HOME ADD:** 1685 Crescent Pl., NW 23, Wash., DC 20009, (202)332-6266; **BUS ADD:** 4812 Georgia Ave., NW, Wash., DC 20011, (202)722-2018.

BARROW, Richard E.——**B:** Feb. 3, 1940, Birmingham, AL, *Part.*, Arnold & Barrow Architects; **PRIM RE ACT:** Architect, Consultant; **SERVICES:** Full arch. services-contract admin. & observation; **REP CLIENTS:** The Mutual Life Ins. Co. of NY, The Philadelphia Saving Fund Soc. Mutual Benefit, Robinson-Humphrey, Omnia Props., Metropolitan Props.; **PREV EMPLOY:** Marcellus Wright, Cox & Cilimberg Architects, Richmond, VA; Cobb/Adams/Benton Architects, Birmingham, AL; Dean L. Gustauson FAIA, Salt Lake City, UT; **PROFL AFFIL & HONORS:** AIA, Student Honors/NIH Fellowship/Chap. Awards AIA; **EDUC:** B.Arch., 1963, Auburn Univ.; **GRAD EDUC:** 1967-70, Arch. Psych., Univ. of Utah; **EDUC HONORS:** AIA Scholarship- Henry Adams Book Award, Natl. Inst. of Health Fellowship; **MIL SERV:** USAF, Capt., 1963-67; **HOME ADD:** 2464 Jannebo Rd., Birmingham, AL 35216, (205)979-0433; **BUS ADD:** 2104 Fourteenth Ave. S., Birmingham, AL 35205, (205)326-8982.

BARROWS, Ronald Thomas——**B:** Jan. 19, 1954, Detroit, MI, *Atty., Counsel, Broker*, Ronald T. Barrows & Assoc., P.C.; Ronald T. Barrows, Assoc., Inc.; **PRIM RE ACT:** Broker, Consultant, Owner/Investor, Instructor, Attorney; **SERVICES:** Full service RE investment and devel.; private legal and consulting work; **REP CLIENTS:** Manor Mort. Co., Urban Homes Assocs.; First Equity assocs. REIT; Dart Const. Co.; **PREV EMPLOY:** Atty. for tax, corporate and RE specialty law firm; Evelyn Wood Reading Dynamics Reading Instr.; Securities Agent Lic.; **PROFL AFFIL & HONORS:** ABA, MI, Detroit Bar Assn.; NAR; Detroit Bd. of Realtors; MI RE Broker, Real Prop., Corp. Fin., Bus. Law, Sect. of ABA, MIBA, Nat. Order of the Barristers; CCIM Candidate; **EDUC:** BA, 1976, Pre-Law, Eng. and Pol. Sci., Oakland Univ., Rochester, MI; **GRAD EDUC:** JD, 1979, Taxation and Comml. Law, Wayne State Univ., Detroit MI; Seeking LLM, Taxation, Wayne State Univ. Law School; **EDUC HONORS:** Magna Cum Laude; Univ. Honors-Eng.; Univ. Scholar & Student of Great Distinction; Student Life & Academic Achievement Scholarships, Oralist for Nat. Moot Ct. Team; 1978 Goldman Scholarship; 1978 Macomb County Lawyer Wives Scholarship; Winner 1978 Marshall D. Goldberg Law Day Competition; **OTHER ACT & HONORS:** Elite For. Car Assn. of Amer.; **HOME ADD:** 5730 Somerset, Detroit, MI 48224, (313)886-3268; **BUS ADD:** 19925 Vernier Harper Woods, MI 48225, (313)885-1200.

BARRY, Donald D.——**B:** Apr. 25, 1937, Kane, IL, *Atty.*; **PRIM RE ACT:** Attorney, Developer, Owner/Investor, Property Manager; **PROFL AFFIL & HONORS:** KS Bar Assn., ABA; **EDUC:** BS, 1959, S. IL Univ.; **GRAD EDUC:** JD, 1965, Washburn Law School; **EDUC HONORS:** Law Journal - Comments Editor; Moot Court; **MIL SERV:** US Army, Cpl.; **OTHER ACT & HONORS:** Spec. Asst. to Atty. Gen.; Comm., KS RE Commn.; Dir. Columbian Trust Co.; Dir. of YMCA; **HOME ADD:** 1836 Arrowhead, Topeka, KS 66604; **BUS ADD:** 5020SW 28th, PO Box 4816, Topeka, KS 66604, (913)273-3153.

BARRY, Gerald W.——**B:** Sep. 29, 1923, Chicago, IL, *Pres.*, Barry & Key, Arch., Inc.; **PRIM RE ACT:** Architect; **MIL SERV:** USA, 2nd Lt., Air Medal; **OTHER ACT & HONORS:** Member IL Bldg. Authority 5 yrs., Rotary, APX; **HOME ADD:** 1311 Pine St., Glenview, IL 60025, (312)729-9852; **BUS ADD:** 1311 Pine St., Glenview, IL 60025, (312)724-8117.

BARRY, James T., Jr.——**B:** Aug. 21, 1933, Milwaukee, WI, *Pres.*, James T. Barry Co., Inc.; **PRIM RE ACT:** Broker, Consultant, Appraiser, Developer, Owner/Investor, Syndicator; **SERVICES:** Brokerage and attendant services in Comml./Indust. RE; **REP CLIENTS:** Most of Fortune 1000 plus municipal corp. and other govt. entities; Instit. such as Milwaukee Catholic Archdiosese; **PROFL AFFIL & HONORS:** SIR, CRE, State Bar Assn., NAR, FIABCI; **EDUC:** BE, 1955, Bus.; **GRAD EDUC:** JD, 1958, Law, Univ. WI Law School; **HOME ADD:** 6001 N. Shore Dr., Milwaukee, WI 53217, (414)332-7255; **BUS ADD:** 735 N. Water St., Milwaukee, WI 53202, (414)271-1870.

BARRY, Mark D.——**B:** Feb. 11, 1947, Palo Alto, CA, *Asst. VP - Comml. RE Loans*, Equitable S&L, Mort. Loan Dept.; **PRIM RE ACT:** Lender; **SERVICES:** I am responsible for all comml. loans in the RE lending field; **REP CLIENTS:** Builders, investors, devels, etc.; **PREV EMPLOY:** Consultant 1973-5 Marlett & Assocs.; **PROFL AFFIL & HONORS:** AIREA, Member - MBA, MAI; **EDUC:** BA, 1969, Econ., Univ. of CA Berkeley; **GRAD EDUC:** MBA, 1972, RE, Amer. Univ. - Wash., DC; **OTHER ACT & HONORS:** Instr. in RE Appraisal - Mt. Hood Community Coll.; **HOME ADD:** 3044 NW Thurman, Portland, OR 97210, (503)223-7650; **BUS ADD:** 1300 SW Sixth Ave., Portland, OR 97201, (503)243-1668.

BARRY, Robert C.——**B:** Nov. 30, 1926, Albany, NY, *VP Mktg. & Sales*, R.A. Homes, Inc.; **PRIM RE ACT:** Broker, Consultant; **SERVICES:** Home builder sales & mktg. research; **PREV EMPLOY:** Solot Realty; Red Carpet; Barry & Assocs., Inc.; **PROFL AFFIL & HONORS:** Tucson Bd. of Realtors; AZ Assn. of Realtors; Nat. Assn. of Realtors; So. AZ Home Builders Assn.; Nat. Assn. of Home Builders, GRI; CRS; Cert. RE Mgmt. Broker (CRB); Member Inst. of Resid. Mktg (MITM); Realtor of Yr., 1978; Boss of the Yr., 1979; **EDUC:** BS, 1950, Bus. Admin., Bryant Coll.; **MIL SERV:** USN; PHM 2/C;

HOME ADD: 4251 E. Placita Baja, Tucson, AZ 85718, (602)299-3854; **BUS ADD:** 2127 E Speedway Blvd., Tucson, AZ 85719, (602)326-4383.

BARRY, Stanley L.——**B:** July 7, 1936, New York, NY, *Pres.*, Century Operating Corp.; **PRIM RE ACT:** Syndicator, Developer, Property Manager, Owner/Investor; **PROFL AFFIL & HONORS:** Bd. - Rent Stabilization Assoc., Realty Advisory Bd.; **EDUC:** BBA, 1958, Mgmt., Econ., Fin., Hofstra Univ., Hampstead, NY; **HOME ADD:** 15 Kenwood Ct., Rockville Center, NY 11570, (516)536-4222; **BUS ADD:** 370 Seventh Ave., NY, NY 10001, (212)279-7600.

BARTELL, Paul——**B:** Mar. 28, 1922, Milwaukee, WI, *Sales Dir.*, Wauwatosa Realty Co.; **PRIM RE ACT:** Broker, Consultant, Appraiser; **OTHER RE ACT:** Transferee Specialist, Management & Marketing; **SERVICES:** Investment counseling & evaluation; residental transferee specialist; marketing; **PROFL AFFIL & HONORS:** RNMI; NAR; WI Realtors Assn.; Milwaukee Bd. of Realtors, CRB; CRS; GRI; Honor Society, WI Realtors Assn.; **EDUC:** Marquette Univ.; **OTHER ACT & HONORS:** Citations for Meritorious Public Serv. from: The Heart Assn., United Cerebral Palsy, Muscular Dystrophy, The Nat. Found., Boys Clubs of Amer.; **HOME ADD:** 8966 N. Navajo Rd., Bayside, WI 53217, (414)352-9440; **BUS ADD:** 5261 N. Pt. Washington Rd., Milwaukee, WI 53217, (414)963-1717.

BARTELS, Dwayne A.——**B:** Nov. 9, 1941, Colorado Springs, CO, *Realtor*, Bartels-Realtors; **PRIM RE ACT:** Broker, Owner/Investor; **PROFL AFFIL & HONORS:** NAR; CAR; RNMI, CRB; CRS; GRI; **EDUC:** BA, 1963, Pol. Sci., Univ. of CO; RE Cert., 1977, RE, Contra Costa Coll.; **MIL SERV:** US Army; Capt.; Bronze Star, Commendation Medal, Vietnam, 1963-1969; **HOME ADD:** 2516 Heide Ct., El Sobrante, CA 94803, (415)222-3042; **BUS ADD:** 12996 San Pablo Ave., Richmond, CA 94805, (415)232-1462.

BARTH, R. Gary——**B:** Nov. 10, 1944, NY, *Partner*, Jones Lang Wootton; **PRIM RE ACT:** Consultant; **SERVICES:** Investment counseling, valuation; **REP CLIENTS:** Inst. investors in comml. props.; **PREV EMPLOY:** Landauer Assoc. Inc., VP; **EDUC:** BSc, 1966, Engrg., Rensselaer Polytech. Inst.; **GRAD EDUC:** MBA, 1968, Fin., Harvard Bus. Sch.; **EDUC HONORS:** Tau Beta Pi, Eta Kappa Nu; **OTHER ACT & HONORS:** Harvard Club of NYC; **HOME ADD:** 6 Sherwood Gate W, Oyster Bay, NY 11771; **BUS ADD:** 499 Park Ave., NY, NY 10022, (212)688-8181.

BARTHOLOMEW, Richard W.——**B:** Sep. 28, 1941, Bristol, PA, *Sr. Assoc. Part., Arch. and Urban Designer*, Wallace, Roberts, and Todd; **PRIM RE ACT:** Architect, Instructor, Consultant; **SERVICES:** Site Planning, Urban Design, Arch.; **REP CLIENTS:** Developers, cities, corps.; **PROFL AFFIL & HONORS:** AIA, APA, Inst. for Urban Design; **EDUC:** BA, 1963, Arch., Univ. of PA; **GRAD EDUC:** M Arch., 1965, Arch., Univ. of PA; **EDUC HONORS:** Major Honors, Major Honors, Alpha Rho Chi Medal, Charles Merrick Gay Prize, Thouron British-American Fellowship, Fulbright Scholarship (declined); **OTHER ACT & HONORS:** Fellow of the Amer. Academy in Rome, Lecturer in Urban Design, Grad. School of Fine Arts, Univ. of PA, 1974 to pres.; **HOME ADD:** 6813 McCallum St., Philadelphia, PA 19119, (215)843-6516; **BUS ADD:** 1737 Chestnut St., Philadelphia, PA 19103, (215)564-2611.

BARTHROP, John A.——**B:** June 5, 1942, Seattle, WA, *Owner*, John A. Barthrop; **PRIM RE ACT:** Broker, Consultant, Attorney, Developer, Builder, Owner/Investor; **SERVICES:** Devel. and synd. of comml. and resid. props.; advice and negotiation regarding RE devels., investments, sales, fin. and comml. leasing; **REP CLIENTS:** Vassallo Corp., World RE, BEC Devel. Co., L & L Builders, Dave Dray Builders, Inc., Richard Hansen Architects, indiv. and corporate devels. of resid. and comml. prop.; **PREV EMPLOY:** Gen. Counsel, Newman Props., Hahn-Newman Investments; Associate Counsel, Beneficial Standard Props.; Consultant, Continental-IL Props.; **PROFL AFFIL & HONORS:** ABA; Orange Cty. Bar Assn.; RE Research Council of So. CA, Alpha Kappa Psi, Acctg. Hon. Soc.; **EDUC:** BA, 1965, Pol. Sci., Univ. of WA; **GRAD EDUC:** JD, 1968, Univ. of CA, Hastings Coll. of Law; **EDUC HONORS:** Dean's List, David E. Snodgrass Appellate Advocacy Award; **HOME ADD:** 18021 Santa Clara Ave., Santa Ana, CA 92705, (714)953-5888; **BUS ADD:** 1020 North Ross St., Santa Ana, CA 92701, (714)972-9999.

BARTLETT, Art——*Chmn. of the Bd.*, Century 21 Real Estate Corp.; **OTHER RE ACT:** Franchising; **SERVICES:** Various services through 7500 indep. owned offices; training and other programs through 33 rgnl. offices; **BUS ADD:** 18872 MacArthur Blvd., Irvine, CA 92715, (714)752-7521.

BARTLETT, James M.——**B:** Mar. 20, 1945, Virginia, MN, *Pres.*, Development Assoc. of Minnesota, Inc.; **PRIM RE ACT:** Broker, Consultant, Developer, Owner/Investor; **SERVICES:** Devel. & synd. of rehab. projects; **PREV EMPLOY:** Thorpe Bros. RE, Commerce RE; **PROFL AFFIL & HONORS:** Nat. Assn. of Indep. RE Appraisers; Nat. Trust for Hist. Preservation; Smithsonian Inst.; **EDUC:** 1963-1967, Bus./RE, Univ. of MN/Univ. of CO; **MIL SERV:** USA, Sgt. E-5; **HOME ADD:** 435 Portland Ave., St. Paul, MN 55102, (612)227-9809; **BUS ADD:** 310 Grovelawn Ave., Minneapolis, MN 55403, (612)339-5753.

BARTLETT, L.R., Sr.——*Corporate RE Manager*, Anchor Hocking Corp.; **PRIM RE ACT:** Property Manager; **BUS ADD:** 109 N. Broad St., Lancaster, OH 43130, (614)687-2330.*

BARTLETT, Theodore D.——**B:** Sept. 25, 1922, Pasadena, CA, *Realtor, CPM*, Ted Bartlett Co.; **PRIM RE ACT:** Broker, Instructor, Syndicator, Property Manager; **SERVICES:** Manage apts. & condos, teach at local city coll.; **REP CLIENTS:** Small ind. investors; **PROFL AFFIL & HONORS:** NAR, CAR, IREM; **EDUC:** Prop. Mgmt.; **GRAD EDUC:** RE, 1962, Genl. Brokerage, UCLA Ext.; **MIL SERV:** USA, S/Sgt., 1942-46, Honarable Discharge, Meritorious Serv. Med., Asian Pacific Theatre; **HOME ADD:** 1305 Solita Rd., Pasadena, CA 91103, (213)681-4339; **BUS ADD:** 1554 N. Lake Ave., Pasadena, CA 91104, (213)798-6791.

BARTLETT, William W.——**B:** Mar. 14, 1936, New York, NY, *VP*, Thomson McKinnon Securities, Inc.; **OTHER RE ACT:** RE Investment Banking; **SERVICES:** Packaging, Underwriting and Placement of Mort. pools; equity synd.; **REP CLIENTS:** Major pension funds, ins. cols., and banks; **PREV EMPLOY:** The First Boston Corp. 1970-1976; **PROFL AFFIL & HONORS:** Publisher & Editor, "Executive Mortgage Reports"; Mort. Bankers Assn., Consultant to Dept. of HUD, Advisor to The VA Plan; **EDUC:** BA, 1958, European Hist., Columbia Coll.; **GRAD EDUC:** MBA, Mktg., Columbia Bus. Sch.; **EDUC HONORS:** Gold Crown, John Jay Assoc.; **OTHER ACT & HONORS:** Officer and/or Tr. of several sport & recreation affiliated clubs, Frequent speaker for Mort. Bankers Assn., US League; published in Barron's, Wall Street Journal, Bus. Week; **HOME ADD:** 42 Annandale Dr., Chappaqua, NY 10514, (914)241-0575; **BUS ADD:** One New York Plaza, New York, NY 10004, (212)482-7300.

BARTLEY, Theodore T., Jr.——**B:** Nov. 23, 1938, Philadelphia, PA, *Arch.*, Bartley, Long, Mirenda; **PRIM RE ACT:** Architect; **SERVICES:** Feasibility studies, design, const. documents; **REP CLIENTS:** Delancey Corp.; **PROFL AFFIL & HONORS:** AIA; PSA; **EDUC:** BArch, 1961, Univ. of PA; **EDUC HONORS:** Honors; numerous prizes incldg. Woodman Fellowship; **OTHER ACT & HONORS:** Arch. Comm. to Philadelphia Historical Commn. (1975-present); YM/YW Community Services Review Comm. of United Way, Chmn. (1981-1982); AIA Nat'l. Comm. on Historic Resources, Chmn. (1979); Philadelphia AIA, Sec./Treas. (1980-1981); **HOME ADD:** 268 St. Joseph's Way, Philadelphia, PA 19106, (215)627-3813; **BUS ADD:** 1104 Architects Bldg., 117 S. 17th St., Philadelphia, PA 19103, (215)567-6980.

BARTON, Bruce——**B:** Sept. 4, 1930, Valentine, NE, *Pres.*, Conservative Savings & Loan; **PRIM RE ACT:** Lender; **SERVICES:** Savings & loan; **EDUC:** BS, 1956, Law, Univ. of NE; **GRAD EDUC:** JD, 1958, Law, Univ. of NE; **OTHER ACT & HONORS:** Dir., US League of Savings Assn.; Legislative Chmn., NE League of Savings Assn.; **HOME ADD:** 2928 S 99th Ave., Omaha, NE 68123; **BUS ADD:** 11207 W Dodge Rd., Omaha, NE 68154, (402)334-8475.

BARTON, David A.——**B:** June 11, 1939, Omaha, NE, *VP*, Mutual of Omaha & United of Omaha, Life Ins. Grp.; **PRIM RE ACT:** Attorney, Lender, Instructor; **SERVICES:** RE investment atty.; RE investment instr.; **REP CLIENTS:** United Benefit Life Ins. Co.; Mutual of Omaha; Univ. of NE at Omaha; indiv. and instnl. investors; **PREV EMPLOY:** Broker; consultant and synd.; **PROFL AFFIL & HONORS:** ABA, Atty.; **EDUC:** AA, 1959, Theology, St. John's Coll.; BA, 1962, Hist., Univ. of NE; **GRAD EDUC:** JD, Law, Northwestern Univ.; **HOME ADD:** 3523 Howard St., Omaha, NE 68105, (402)978-2959; **BUS ADD:** Mutual of Omaha Plaza, Omaha, NE 68131, (402)978-2550.

BARTON, James M.——**B:** Apr. 13, 1942, White Plains, NY, *Partner*, Cummings & Lockwood; **PRIM RE ACT:** Attorney; **SERVICES:** Representation of synd. and RE fin. clients of all types; **PROFL AFFIL & HONORS:** Amer., CT and Greenwich Bar Assns.; **EDUC:** 1964, English, Yale Coll.; **GRAD EDUC:** LLB, 1967, Univ. of VA; **OTHER ACT & HONORS:** Lecturer on RE tax law and the application of the securities laws to RE transactions; author of articles, etc.; **BUS ADD:** Two Greenwich Plaza, Greenwich, CT 06830, (203)327-1700.

BARTON, W.C.——*Dir., RE Planning*, Raytheon Corp.; **PRIM RE ACT:** Property Manager; **BUS ADD:** 141 Spring St., Lexington, MA 02173, (617)862-6600.*

BARTRAM, Maynard C.——**B:** Sept. 9, 1926, Sharon, CT, *Pres./Treas./Managing Trustee*, Connecticut General Mortgage and Realty Investments; **PRIM RE ACT:** Owner/Investor; **OTHER RE ACT:** Pres. of publicly-held RE investment trust; **PREV EMPLOY:** CT Gen. Life Ins. Co., 1950-1970, Sec., Mort. & RE; Congen Realty Advisory Co., 1970-1981, Pres.; **PROFL AFFIL & HONORS:** Bd. of Gov., Nat. Assn. of RE; Assoc. Member, Soc. of Indus. Realtors; Chmn., Yale RE Comm.; **EDUC:** BS, 1950, Econ., Yale Univ.; **GRAD EDUC:** HBS, 1980, Harvard Univ.; **MIL SERV:** USN; QM; **OTHER ACT & HONORS:** Interfaith Homes, Inc.; Church Homes; **HOME ADD:** 56 Gun Mill Rd., Bloomfield, CT 06002, (203)242-5757; **BUS ADD:** 950 Cottage Grove Rd., Bloomfield, CT 06002, (203)726-5005.

BASCIANI, George R.——**B:** June 5, 1947, *VP, Operations*, The Albert Appraisal Co., Inc.; **PRIM RE ACT:** Consultant, Appraiser; **SERVICES:** RE valuation and counseling; **REP CLIENTS:** Lenders, attys., pvt. and inst. investors in comml. props.; **PROFL AFFIL & HONORS:** AIREA; The Nat. Assn. of RE Bds., MAI designation; **EDUC:** BS, 1969, Bus. Admin., NY Inst. of Tech.; **GRAD EDUC:** Grad. Studies, Econ., St. John's Univ.; **HOME ADD:** RD #2, McKrown Dr., Hopewell Junction, NY 12533, (914)896-8222; **BUS ADD:** 383 S. Riverside Ave., Croton-on-Hudson, NY 10520, (914)271-4777.

BASHAW, John M., Jr.——**B:** Dec. 31, 1933, Providence, RI, *Owner/Broker*, John Manning RE; **PRIM RE ACT:** Broker, Syndicator, Consultant, Appraiser, Developer, Builder; **PREV EMPLOY:** Gen. Mgr., Polar Realtor, Anchorage, AK; **PROFL AFFIL & HONORS:** AIREA, NAR, SREA, RESSI; **EDUC:** BGE, 1965, Mil. Sci., Univ. of NE; **GRAD EDUC:** MBA, 1975, Bus., Univ. of AK; **MIL SERV:** USAF, Ltc, Rated; **OTHER ACT & HONORS:** C of C, Rotary; **HOME ADD:** SRA 1698J, Anchorage, AK 99501, (907)345-3212; **BUS ADD:** 1577 C St., Suite 101, Anchorage, AK 99501, (907)276-1614.

BASILE, Frank——**B:** Oct. 6, 1939, New Orleans, LA, *VP*, Gene Glick Management Corp. (Reponsible for mgmt. of 20,000 apts. in 13 states); **PRIM RE ACT:** Consultant, Property Manager, Real Estate Publisher; **OTHER RE ACT:** Speaker/Trainer; **SERVICES:** Mgmt. of multifamily housing; **PROFL AFFIL & HONORS:** IREM, Nat. Apt. Assn., NAHB, CPM, Cert. Speaking Profl. (CSP); **EDUC:** BBA, 1961, Econ./Acctg., Tulane Univ. in New Orleans; **EDUC HONORS:** Grad. first in class and Student body pres. Who's Who in Amer. Colleges and Univ., Tulane Hall of Fame; **OTHER ACT & HONORS:** Former Nat. VP of the Nat. Apt. Assn.; Former Pres. of Apt. Assn. of IN; Pres.of Sales & Marketing Exec. of Indpls.; Member of IREM Nat. Faculty and Pres. of In Chpt. of Nat. Speakers Assn.; Author of 6 books; including 4 on Property Management; Member of IREM Academy of Authors; Author of Professional Multihousing Management - Official Textbook for the NAHB RAM Training Program; VP of Indianapolis Free Univ.; Contributing Editor for Indiana Realtor and Indianapolis Business Journal; Listed in Who's Who in the Midwest; Member of the NAHB RAM Bd. of Govs.; **HOME ADD:** 49 Horseshoe Ln., Carmel, IN 46032, (317)844-6067; **BUS ADD:** 9102 N Meridian, Indianapolis, IN 46260, (317)844-0719.

BASILE, Robert——**B:** Jul. 13, 1940, Springfield, MA, *Pres.*, The Basile Corp.; **PRIM RE ACT:** Broker, Banker, Developer, Builder, Property Manager; **OTHER RE ACT:** Mortgage Banker; **SERVICES:** All phases large scale resid. RE devel.; planning, const., mktg. fin. mgmt.; **PREV EMPLOY:** Gulf-Reston Inc. 1968-1969; **PROFL AFFIL & HONORS:** Community Association Inst., AIA, Nat. Assn. of Home Builders, Officer, Local, State Nat. Homebuilders Assn.; Dir./Officer, Mid Atlantic Chapter Community Association Inst.; Reg. Arch. CA, PA, NJ; RE Sales Lic. PA; **EDUC:** BArch, 1963, RPI; **GRAD EDUC:** MBA, 1968, Fin., Stanford Univ.; **OTHER ACT & HONORS:** Dir., School Bd. 1975-1976; Lecturer, Community Association Inst. Seminars on Condo. and Homeowner Assn. Resid. Devels.; **HOME ADD:** 90 Black Mat Rd., Douglassville, PA 19518, (215)326-9380; **BUS ADD:** 90 Black Mat Rd., Douglassville, PA 19518, (215)326-9090.

BASNEY, Dana A.——**B:** June 3, 1948, Cambridge, MA, *CPA/VP*, Leuitz, Zacks & Ciceric, Inc.; **PRIM RE ACT:** Consultant, Owner/Investor, Property Manager; **OTHER RE ACT:** Certified Public Accountant/Tax Advisor; **SERVICES:** Tax Consultation; **PROFL AFFIL & HONORS:** Amer. Inst. of CPA's; CA Society of CPA's, Nat. Assn. of Accountants; **EDUC:** BA, 1970, Liberal Arts, Bates Coll.; **GRAD EDUC:** MBA, 1975, Acctg./Fin., San Diego State Univ.; **EDUC HONORS:** Phi Kappa Phi; **HOME ADD:** 6205 Estrella Ave., San Diego, CA 92120, (714)287-7212; **BUS ADD:** 620 "C" Street, San Diego, CA 92101, (714)238-1077.

BASS, Irwin J.——**B:** Dec. 31, 1934, Philadelphia, PA, *Part.*, Bass & Elias Arch.; **PRIM RE ACT:** Architect, Developer, Owner/Investor; **REP CLIENTS:** Smithkline, Barness, John Hancock; **PROFL AFFIL & HONORS:** AIA; **EDUC:** B.Arch., 1957, Design & Const., PA State Univ.; **OTHER ACT & HONORS:** Past Bd. Member N/E Mental Health Ctr., Member MSTA-Pres. Logan Tennis Club; **HOME ADD:** 1409 Stephen Rd., Meadowbrook, PA 19046, (215)884-1095; **BUS ADD:** 704 Oak Lane Ave., Philadelphia, PA 19126, (215)927-2400.

BASSE, Arthur——*Mgr. Prop. Mgmt.*, Ford Motor Co.; **PRIM RE ACT:** Property Manager; **BUS ADD:** The American Rd., Darborn, MI 48121, (313)323-0880.*

BASSETT, Peter J.——**B:** Jan. 14, 1947, Boston, MA, *Pres.*, Shelter Mgmt. Assoc., Inc.; **PRIM RE ACT:** Consultant, Owner/Investor, Property Manager; **SERVICES:** Total Hotel investment and mgmt. servs., including new devel. & fin.; **REP CLIENTS:** Banks; Ins. Cos.; private investors; **PROFL AFFIL & HONORS:** MA Hotel Motel Assn., CT Hotel Motel Assn., FL Hotel Motel Assn., Amer. Hotel Motel Assn., IAHI, Var. C of C's and Convention & Visitor's Burs., Bristol Cty. Devel. Council; **EDUC:** ME/BA, 1970, Devel. Econ., Colby Coll., Waterville, ME; **GRAD EDUC:** MBA, 1972, RE Corp. Fin., Wharton Sch. of Fin. & Commerce, Univ. of PA; **EDUC HONORS:** Dean's List; **MIL SERV:** USAR, Sgt., Hon. Disch.; **BUS ADD:** 545 Boylston St., Suite 1103, Boston, MA 02116, (617)424-1010.

BASSIN, Phillip——**B:** May 20, 1939, St. Louis, MO, *VP*, Centerco Properties, Inc.; **PRIM RE ACT:** Developer, Owner/Investor, Property Manager, Syndicator; **PROFL AFFIL & HONORS:** BOMA; **EDUC:** BSIE, 1961, Washington Univ., St. Louis, MO; **GRAD EDUC:** MEA, 1966, Washington Univ., St. Louis, MO; **HOME ADD:** 12969 Lampadaire Dr., St. Louis, MO 63141, (314)576-4342; **BUS ADD:** 7710 Carondelet Ave., Clayton, MO 63105, (314)721-3000.

BASSO, Robert——**B:** Apr. 22, 1943, Stockton, CA, *Pres.*, Century 21 Exchange Realtors, Inc.; **PRIM RE ACT:** Broker, Owner/Investor, Property Manager; **SERVICES:** Investment counseling, prop. mgmt.; **PROFL AFFIL & HONORS:** Stockton Bd. of Realtors; CA Assn. of Realtors; NAR, 1979 Pres., Stockton Bd.; 1979, Realtor of Yr.; 1981 Rgnl. VP, CA Assn. of Realtors; **EDUC:** AA, 1969, Bus., Delta Coll.; **HOME ADD:** 4273 Boulder Creek Cir., Stockton, CA 95207, (209)477-8736; **BUS ADD:** 6011 N. El Dorado St., Stockton, CA 95207, (209)951-2115.

BASSUK, Bertram L.——**B:** Jan. 26, 1918, Brooklyn, NY, *Architect*, Bertram L. Bassuk, AIA; **PRIM RE ACT:** Architect; **OTHER RE ACT:** Lecturer on: Home Bldg./ Design & Const. of Dwellings, at R.E. Inst. N.Y. Univ. School of Continuing Educ.; **SERVICES:** Arch. Design, Environmental Cons.; **REP CLIENTS:** Individuals and Inst. Corp.; **PROFL AFFIL & HONORS:** Member, N.Y. Chap. AIA; Member, Interfaith Forum for Religion, Art & Arch., Prizewinner: Gas-Range Design competition, 1946 - Amer. Stove, Co.; Prizewinner: Housing for the Elderly, St. Joseph's Village for Sr. Citizens, Brookhaven, NY 1976; **EDUC:** BS, 1938, Chem. & Physics, N.Y. Univ.; **GRAD EDUC:** BARCH, 1947, N. Y. Univ. School of Arch. and Allied Arts., Ecole Des Beaux - Arts Americaine, Fontainebleau, France; **MIL SERV:** USAAF; T. Sgt.; **OTHER ACT & HONORS:** Designer with Henry Wright of Prototype Composite (Passive & Active) Solar-Orientated Energy-Conscious Houses for Chrysler Airtemp Corp. 1958; Article, "The Necessity of Arch." Published in First Issue of Real Estate Review (of R.E. Inst. of N.Y. Univ.) Volume 1, No. 1, Spring 1971; **HOME ADD:** 241 Sixth Ave, NY, NY 10014, (212)243-4021; **BUS ADD:** 137 E. 25th St., N.Y., NY 10010, (212)679-4564.

BATEMAN, Earl, Jr.——**B:** Sept. 23, 1926, Dallas, TX, *Sr. VP*, Southland RE Resources, Inc., Prop. Mgmt.; **PRIM RE ACT:** Property Manager; **PROFL AFFIL & HONORS:** Pres. in 1978, Dallas BOMA, CPM, SRA; **EDUC:** BBA, 1950, Mktg., Southern Methodist Univ. - Dallas; **MIL SERV:** USN, Air Cadet; **OTHER ACT & HONORS:** Elder - Presbyterian Church, Dallas Bd. Member - Amer. Cancer Soc.; **HOME ADD:** 7421 Caruth Blvd., (214)739-3371; **BUS ADD:** 201 East John W. Carpenter Freeway, Irving, TX 75062, (214)556-3756.

BATES, G. Del——**B:** Oct. 9, 1926, Lakewood, OH, *Mgng. Part.*, Parks, Eisele, Bates & Wilsman; **PRIM RE ACT:** Attorney, Lender, Owner/Investor; **REP CLIENTS:** Cardinal Fed. Savings & Loan Assn.; **EDUC:** BS, 1949, Bus. Admin., Pre-law, OH State Univ.; **GRAD EDUC:** LLD, 1951, OH State Univ.; **OTHER ACT & HONORS:** Law Dir. City of Avon Lake, 1950-60, Cleveland, OH Amer. ABA, Lorain Cty. Bar Assn.; **HOME ADD:** 32290 Lake Rd., Avon Lake, OH 44012, (216)933-5306; **BUS ADD:** 1100 Illuminating Bldg., Cleveland, OH 44113, (216)241-2840.

BATES, Joseph E.——**B:** Nov. 5, 1909, Cobb Co., GA, *Trustee*, Bates Realty Trust; **PRIM RE ACT:** Developer, Owner/Investor; **SERVICES:** Buy and develop RE; **PROFL AFFIL & HONORS:** Quincy So. Shore C of C; **OTHER ACT & HONORS:** AF & AM; Quincy Hist. Soc.; Ward Two Civic Assn.; **HOME ADD:** 2 Apex St., Quincy, MA 02169, (617)479-2569; **BUS ADD:** 275 Quincy Ave., Quincy, MA 02169, (617)773-6658.

BATESOLE, Jon E.——**B:** July 14, 1939, Marshalltown, IA, *Pres.*, General Growth Companies; **PRIM RE ACT:** Developer; **OTHER RE ACT:** Shopping Ctr. Devel./Mgr.; **PREV EMPLOY:** Dayton's Dept. Store, Buyer; Downing Hardware, Inc., Pres./Owner; **PROFL AFFIL & HONORS:** Intl. Council of Shopping Ctrs., Cert. Shopping Ctr. Mgr.; **EDUC:** BS, 1961, Bus. Admin., Drake Univ.; **HOME ADD:** 1115 16th St., W Des Moines, IA 50265, (515)223-0555; **BUS ADD:** 215 Keo, POB 1536, Des Moines, IA 50306, (515)281-9115.

BATTARD, Frank Paul——**B:** Oct. 24, 1950, Sherman, TX, *Part.*, Voelker and Jeffers; **PRIM RE ACT:** Attorney; **SERVICES:** Legal rep.; **REP CLIENTS:** Commwlth Savings Assn.; **PROFL AFFIL & HONORS:** ABA, RE Div., LA Bar Assn., New Orleans Bar Assn., LA Notaries Assn.; **EDUC:** BS, 1972, Biology, Tulane Univ.; **GRAD EDUC:** JD, 1976, Law, Loyola Univ. of New Orleans; **HOME ADD:** 7109 Crowder Blvd., New Orleans, LA 70127, (504)242-4398; **BUS ADD:** 140 Carondelet, Ste. 300, New Orleans, LA 70130, (504)566-1667.

BATTY, E. Jerome——**B:** Sept. 2, 1945, Providence, RI, *Atty.*, Hinckley Allen.; **PRIM RE ACT:** Attorney; **SERVICES:** Legal services; **REP CLIENTS:** RE devel. cos., gen. contractors, fin. lending inst.; **PROFL AFFIL & HONORS:** Boston Univ. Law Review, 1971-1972; RI and ABA; **EDUC:** AB, 1968, Brown Univ.; **GRAD EDUC:** JD, 1972, Boston Univ.; **EDUC HONORS:** Cum Laude; **OTHER ACT & HONORS:** Brown Club of RI, Bd. of Dir.; **HOME ADD:** Tower Hill Rd., Cumberland, RI 02864, (401)333-5619; **BUS ADD:** 2200 Industrial Bank Bldg., Providence, RI 02903, (401)274-2000.

BATZER, Jon P.——**B:** Nov. 1, 1942, Warren, OH, *Pres.*, Investment One Inc.; **PRIM RE ACT:** Broker, Property Manager, Owner/Investor, Syndicator; **OTHER RE ACT:** Advisor to RE and Investment Trust; **SERVICES:** Broker, Mgmt. and Investment, Counseling of Income Prop.; **REP CLIENTS:** Physicians, Attys., Bankers, and Other Profls.; **PROFL AFFIL & HONORS:** Nat. Bd. of Realtors; IREM, Realtor; CPM (Candidate); **EDUC:** BS, 1964, Indus. Engrg., Eastern MI Univ. and Univ. of MI; **GRAD EDUC:** 30 hrs. toward MA, Civil Engrg., Univ. of MI; **MIL SERV:** Army, 1st Lt.; **HOME ADD:** 1210 Northfield NE, Grand Rapids, MI 49505, (616)774-2177; **BUS ADD:** 825 Leonard St. NE, Suite 201, Grand Rapids, MI 49503, (616)451-8162.

BAUCHNER, Eugene Richard——**B:** July 24, 1946, Elizabeth, NJ, *Mgr. Corporate RE Planning and Devel.*, The Perkin-Elmer Corp., Corp.; **OTHER RE ACT:** Planning and devel. facilities and offices, leasing, purchasing, dispositions for corp. needs; **SERVICES:** Asset mgmt., space planning; **PREV EMPLOY:** Prop. mgmt., leasing, const.; **PROFL AFFIL & HONORS:** NACORE Lic. RE Broker, CT; **EDUC:** BS, 1970, Business Econ., Univ. of Bridgeport; **GRAD EDUC:** MBA, 1980, gen. RE, Univ. of New Haven; **MIL SERV:** US Army Res., 1969-75, E5; **HOME ADD:** 26 Alexander Dr., W. Haven, CT 06516; **BUS ADD:** 185 Main Ave., Norwalk, CT 06856, (203)762-4041.

BAUER, Henry L.——**B:** June 7, 1928, Portland, OR, *Atty.*, Bauer, Winfree & Schaub, P.C.; **PRIM RE ACT:** Attorney; **SERVICES:** Legal: negotiations, drafting, closing, foreclosing; **REP CLIENTS:** Far West Federal Savings and Loan Assn.; Stevens-Ness Law Publishing Co.; fin. insts. and private investors; **PROFL AFFIL & HONORS:** OR State Bar Assn.; ABA; Delta Theta Phi; **EDUC:** Bus. & Technol., BS, 1950, Engrg., OR State Univ.; **GRAD EDUC:** JD, 1953, Univ. of OR; **MIL SERV:** USAF; 1st Lt.; **OTHER ACT & HONORS:** Arlington Club; Multnomah Athletic Club; Kappa Sigma Frat. (Nat. Pres. 1977-79); A.F.&A.M. Bd. of Dir., St. Vincent Hosp. (Vice Chmn., 1980); **HOME ADD:** 1130 S.W. Myrtle Dr., Portland, OR 97201, (503)222-7034; **BUS ADD:** 1105 Commonwealth Bldg., 421 S.W. Sixth Ave., Portland, OR 97204, (503)223-6113.

BAUERSFELD, Lynn W.——**B:** Dec. 19, 1937, Pasadena, CA, *Mgr.*, Sunset Co. Realtors, Montecito; **PRIM RE ACT:** Broker, Consultant, Appraiser, Developer, Property Manager; **SERVICES:** Sales, leasing, prop. mgmt., synd., relocation assistance, devel.; **REP CLIENTS:** Delco, Raytheon, Santa Barbara Clinic, Santa Barbara Research, Gen. Research Corp., Effects Tech., Rancho Matiliha; **PROFL AFFIL & HONORS:** Bd. of Realtors, Santa Barbara WCR, Santa Barbara C of C; **EDUC:** Bus & Psych., Univ. of AZ; **OTHER ACT & HONORS:** Soroptimist Intl.; **HOME ADD:** 214 Selrose Ln., Santa Barbara, CA 93109, (805)962-9848; **BUS ADD:** 140 Hot Springs Rd., Santa Barbara, CA 93108.

BAUGH, James E.——*Dpty Asst. Secy.*, Department of Housing and Urban Development, Public & Indian Housing; **PRIM RE ACT:** Lender; **BUS ADD:** 451 Seventh St., S.W., Washington, DC 20410, (202)755-0950.*

BAUGH, Marrin——*Asst. Mgr. RE Dept.*, Burlington Industries, Inc.; **PRIM RE ACT:** Property Manager; **BUS ADD:** 3330 W. Friendly Ave., PO Box 21207, Greensboro, NC 27420, (919)379-2000.*

BAUGHMAN, W.C.——*Dir.*, Camden County Economic Development; **PRIM RE ACT:** Developer; **BUS ADD:** 600 Market St., Camden, NJ 08101, (609)757-8289.*

BAUM, Charles C.——**B:** Jan. 29, 1942, Montgomery, AL, *Dir. of RE*, Sollers Point Co., Affiliate of United Iron & Metal Co., Inc.; **PRIM RE ACT:** Attorney, Consultant, Owner/Investor; **PREV EMPLOY:** Loeb, Rhondes & Co., VP 1966-73; **EDUC:** 1964, Princeton Univ.; **GRAD EDUC:** 1966 & 1979, Harvard Bus. School & Univ. of MD Law School; **EDUC HONORS:** Phi Beta Kappa; **HOME ADD:** 6724 Westbrook Rd., Baltimore, MD; **BUS ADD:** 2545 Wickins Ave., Baltimore, MD 21223, (301)947-8000.

BAUM, Raymond N.——**B:** Mar. 5, 1944, Pittsburgh, PA, *Partner*, Baskin & Sears; **PRIM RE ACT:** Attorney; **REP CLIENTS:** RE devels., synds., investors, prop. mgrs., const. and permanent lenders in connection with resid. and comml. props., HUD, FNHA, HFA & IDA Fin., and UDAG projects; **PREV EMPLOY:** Dept. of HUD, 1970 through 1972; **PROFL AFFIL & HONORS:** ABA, PA Bar Assn., Alleheny Cty. Bar Assn., Nat. Assn. of Housing & Redevel. Officials; **EDUC:** BA, 1965, Econ., Univ. of Pittsburgh; **GRAD EDUC:** JD, 1968, Univ. of Pittsburgh; **OTHER ACT & HONORS:** Atty. US Dept. of HUD, 1970-73, Asst. Prof. of Pol. Sci. Point Park Coll., 1968-70; **HOME ADD:** 7511 Tuscarora St., Pittsburgh, PA 15208; **BUS ADD:** 10th Fl., Frick Bldg., Pittsburgh, PA 15319, (412)562-8656.

BAUMANN, Phillip A.——**B:** Feb. 17, 1949, Milwaukee, WI, *Atty.*, Shackleford, Farrior, Stallings & Evans, P.A.; **PRIM RE ACT:** Attorney; **SERVICES:** Legal services, RE bus. and decedents' estates; **PROFL AFFIL & HONORS:** Member, Probate Law Comm., FL Bar; Member, ABA; Member, FL Bar Assn.; Member, Hillsborough Cty. Bar Assn.; Real Prop. and Probate and Trust Law Section of ABA and FL Bar; **EDUC:** 1974, Univ. of WI, Milwaukee; **GRAD EDUC:** JD, 1978, Geo. Washington Univ.; **EDUC HONORS:** Honors Degree, Honors in Major, Summa Cum Laude, Phi Kappa Phi Honor Soc., Degree awarded with honors; **MIL SERV:** USAF, Staff Sgt., 1968-1972; **OTHER ACT & HONORS:** VP, The Sertoma Club of Tampa; Dir., Judeo-Christian Coalition Clinic; **HOME ADD:** 502 Columbia Dr., Tampa, FL 33606; **BUS ADD:** POB 3324, Tampa, FL 33601, (813)273-5000.

BAUMGARDNER, Rick——**B:** June 13, 1957, Louisville, KY, *Broker, Owner*, Baumgardner Valuation Serv., Appraisal; **PRIM RE ACT:** Broker, Instructor, Consultant, Appraiser, Insuror; **SERVICES:** RE Appraisal; **REP CLIENTS:** Employee Transfer Corp.; Homequity; Merrill Lynch Relocation Mgmt.; **PROFL AFFIL & HONORS:** AACA; NAR; Amer. Right of Way Assn.; AIREA, Realtor of Yr. - 1980; Hold Designation of CA-R; Cert. Appraiser - Residential; **EDUC:** Assoc. RE, 1976, Univ. of KY; **OTHER ACT & HONORS:** Knights of Colombus, St. James Church; **HOME ADD:** 305 Deepwood Dr., Elizabethtown, KY 42701, (502)737-4631; **BUS ADD:** PO Box 721, Elizabethtown, KY 42701, (502)765-6072.

BAUMGARTEN, H.J.——*VP & Couns.*, National Starch & Chemical Corp.; **PRIM RE ACT:** Property Manager; **BUS ADD:** 10 Finderne Ave., Bridgewater, NJ 08807, (201)685-5000.*

BAUMRIND, Vernon——**B:** May 10, 1944, Mullins, SC, *Owner, Broker in Charge*, The Baumrind Co., Bldg. & Devel.; **PRIM RE ACT:** Broker, Developer, Builder; **SERVICES:** Bldg., Devel., Comml. Investment Analysis, Counseling; **PREV EMPLOY:** Coll. Instr. Francis Marion College, Florence, SC; **PROFL AFFIL & HONORS:** NAR, FLI, NAHB, GRI; **EDUC:** BA, 1967, Hist. Geogr., Jacksonville Univ, FL; **MIL SERV:** USN, E-5; **OTHER ACT & HONORS:** Sec. Bd. of Realtors, Bd. of Dirs. of Florence Bd. of Realtors; **HOME ADD:** 405 Harmon Pk, Marion, SC 29571, (803)423-7411; **BUS ADD:** Exec. Park, 300 Rainbow Dr., Florence, SC 29501, (803)665-6666.

BAUR, Edward O.——**B:** Dec. 27, 1940, Terre Haute, IN, *VP*, Metroplex, Inc. Realtors, Comm. ad investment div.; **PRIM RE ACT:** Broker, Syndicator, Owner/Investor; **SERVICES:** Comml. brokerage, site assemblage, improved prop. synd.; **REP CLIENTS:** Fin. inst.;

PROFL AFFIL & HONORS: NAR, RESSI, RNMI; **EDUC:** BA, 1963, Hist., Northwestern Univ.; **GRAD EDUC:** MS, 1965, Hist., Univ. of FL; **HOME ADD:** 10416 NW 18th Ave., Gainesville, FL 32601, (904)372-1989; **BUS ADD:** 5200 W. Newberry Rd., Gainsville, FL 32607, (904)373-3583.

BAVAR, David I.——**B:** Sept. 30, 1935, Jamestown, NY, *VP*, Kayne/Levin/Neilson/Bavar Realtors; **PRIM RE ACT:** Broker, Developer, Owner/Investor; **SERVICES:** Brokerage of comml. and indus. props.; **PROFL AFFIL & HONORS:** SIR; RE Bd. of Greater Baltimore; SIR Budget & Finance Comm., Pres, MD-Wash. DC Chap. of SIR, 1976-76; Nat. Bd. of SIR 1978-80; **EDUC:** BS, 1957, Bus. Admin., PA State Univ.; **GRAD EDUC:** MBA, 1959, Acctg. and Fin., Univ. of PA - Wharton School; **MIL SERV:** USAR, Sgt.; **OTHER ACT & HONORS:** Pres., Comprehensive Housing for the Aged Inc.; Bd. of Dir., Assoc. Jewish Charities; **HOME ADD:** 4 Windsong Ct., Baltimore, MD 21208, (301)653-0220.

BAXTER, B. Hunt, Jr.——**B:** Feb. 21, 1943, New Bern, NC, *Atty., Sec., Treas.*, Henderson & Baxter, P.A.; **PRIM RE ACT:** Attorney, Regulator; **SERVICES:** all legal servs. relating to RE; **REP CLIENTS:** NCNB; Wachovia B & T Co. NA, various RE firms; **PREV EMPLOY:** Special Asst. Atty. Gen., NC Dept. of Justice; **PROFL AFFIL & HONORS:** Claven Cty.; NC & Amer. BAR Assns.; NC Academy of Trail Lawyers; NARELLO, Public Admin., Craven Cty.; Member, NC RE Lic. Bd.; **EDUC:** BSBA, 1966, Bus. Admin., Univ. of NC; **GRAD EDUC:** MBA, 1969, Bus., ECU; JD, 1971, Univ. of NC Law School; **MIL SERV:** NC Nat. Guard, E-5; **HOME ADD:** 4717 Trent Woods Dr., New Bern, NC 28560, (919)633-3826; **BUS ADD:** PO Drawer U, New Bern, NC 28560, (919)638-5792.

BAXTER, Oscar F., V——**B:** Apr. 6, 1945, Norfolk, VA, *VP*, Baxter Realty Corp.; **PRIM RE ACT:** Broker, Consultant, Appraiser, Developer, Builder, Instructor, Property Manager, Insuror, Syndicator; **SERVICES:** Prop. mgt., devel. & synd. of multi-family projects, bldg. of multi-family projects, comml. brokerage & investment counseling; **PREV EMPLOY:** Sam Miriello & Assoc. Realtors; Dunn, North Carolina, 1970-72; **PROFL AFFIL & HONORS:** NAR, Inst. of RE Mgt. Tidewater Bd. of Realtors, Dartnell Inst. of Bus. Research, NAHB, Tidewater Builders Assn., CPM, GRI, State Reg. Contr. 16825; **EDUC:** BBA, 1972, Bus. Admin. & Econ., Campbell Univ.; GRI, Univ. of VA; CPM, Inst. of RE Mgmt.; **MIL SERV:** USN, 1965-1969, Vietnam Medal, Good Conduct, Nat. Defense Medal; **OTHER ACT & HONORS:** Kiwanis Club; **HOME ADD:** 3004 Milford Ln., Virginia Bch., VA 23452, (804)463-1917; **BUS ADD:** 6040 Virginia Bch. Blvd., Norfolk, VA 23502, (804)461-3212.

BAXTER, Robert J., Jr.——**B:** Sept. 21, 1951, New Orleans, LA, *Attorney-at-Law*, Baxter, Syracuse & Traverse; **PRIM RE ACT:** Attorney; **OTHER RE ACT:** Title Insurance; **SERVICES:** Legal services oriented towards RE acquisition and devel. including title ins. services through First Amer. Title; **PREV EMPLOY:** Kehl & Pickering, Attys. at Law Servicing Dixie Federal S&L; **PROFL AFFIL & HONORS:** LA State Bar Assn., ABA, Jefferson Bar Assn., RE Sec. and Synd. Inst., Fed. Bar Assn., Juris Doctor, Notary Public; **EDUC:** BA, 1973, Poli. Sci., Psych., LA State Univ.; **GRAD EDUC:** JD, 1976, Loyola Univ.; **HOME TEL:** (504)833-1633; **BUS ADD:** 3456 Clearly Ave., Suite 410, Metairie, LA 70002, (504)887-2810.

BAXTER, Sharon Davis——**B:** Oct. 1, 1953, Durango, CO, *Office Mgr.*, Brooks-Lomax & Assoc., Santa Fe Branch; **PRIM RE ACT:** Broker, Consultant, Appraiser, Owner/Investor; **SERVICES:** RE Appraisal; Consultation & Analysis; **REP CLIENTS:** Instit. & Mort. Lenders, Employment Relocation Cos., Investor, Devels., etc.; **PREV EMPLOY:** Lomax & Assoc. (1976-1979); **PROFL AFFIL & HONORS:** Soc. of RE Appraisers; NAR, Santa Fe Bd. of Realtors, Womens Council of Realtors, NM RE Comm., SRA; GRI (NAR); **EDUC:** 1971-present, Arch. & English, Univ. of NM & Coll of Santa Fe; **HOME ADD:** Star Route, Box 263, Placitas, NM 87043; **BUS ADD:** 200 W. DeVargas, Suite #8, Santa Fe, NM 87501, (505)982-1262.

BAYDALA, Troy G.——**B:** Apr. 21, 1946, Mineola, NY, *Pres.*, Maritime Realty Corp., RE Mgmt. and Investments; **PRIM RE ACT:** Broker, Consultant, Appraiser, Instructor, Property Manager; **OTHER RE ACT:** Asset Mgr.; **SERVICES:** Valuation, prop. mgmt., mortg. brokerage, investment counseling; **REP CLIENTS:** Indiv. investors; **PROFL AFFIL & HONORS:** Soc. of RE Appraisers, AIREA, Lic. RE Broker - NY, Company's Representative Intl. Council of Shopping Centers, SRPA, MAI, CPM; **EDUC:** BS, 1968, Fin., Seton Hall Univ., South Orange, NJ; **EDUC HONORS:** Member of Who's Who in Amer. Colls. & Univs. 1968; **MIL SERV:** AGC, Capt. (1968-1971), Bronze Star, Army Commendation Medal, Air Medal; **HOME ADD:** 116 Vorrhis Ave., Rockville Centre, NY 11570; **BUS ADD:** 170 Broadway Suite 1506, New York, NY 10038, (212)962-2116.

BAYER, Jeffrey A.——**B:** Feb. 18, 1949, Birmingham, AL, *VP*, Metropolitan Properties, Inc., Devel.; **PRIM RE ACT:** Developer; **SERVICES:** Fully integrated comml. devel. and construction firm; **REP CLIENTS:** IBM, Xerox, S. Central Bell, Aetna Life Insurance; **PREV EMPLOY:** Hyatt Corp.; **PROFL AFFIL & HONORS:** NAR; Birmingham Area, Bd. of Realtors, Realtors Nat. Mktg. Instit.; Member $2,000,000 Club Birmingham Area Bd. of Realtors; Intl. Council of Shopping Ctrs.; NACORE, CCIM; **EDUC:** BS, 1972, Fin. & Mktg., Univ. of AL, School of Commerce and Bus. Admin; **GRAD EDUC:** MUS, Urban Econ., Univ. of AL in Birmingham; **OTHER ACT & HONORS:** Jefferson Cty. Commn. of Pardon & Paroles Pres. Comm., Birmingham C of C, VP B'Nai B'rith District Seven; Member Commerce Exec. Comm.; Univ. of AL; United Way Comm.; Bd. of Dir., Birmingham Jewish Community Ctr.; **HOME ADD:** 4284 Old Brook Trail, Birmingham, AL 35243, (205)967-1354; **BUS ADD:** #2 Metroplex Dr., Suite 500, Birmingham, AL 35209, (205)870-9960.

BAYER, Theodore F.——**B:** Sept. 14, 1948, Huntingdon, PA, *Atty.*, Gwire & Bayer; **PRIM RE ACT:** Broker, Attorney, Owner/Investor; **SERVICES:** RE loan brokerage, legal rep. of devels., investors and owners; **REP CLIENTS:** Subdivs., pension plan investors, RE brokers, synds., condo. converters; **PROFL AFFIL & HONORS:** CA State Bar, Real Prop. Law Sect.; Member San Francisco Coalition for Better Housing; CA Dept. of RE Subdiv. Sect. Member; **EDUC:** BS, 1970, Econ., Mktg., Lehigh Univ.; **GRAD EDUC:** JD, 1976, Real Prop. Law, Golden Gate Univ.; **EDUC HONORS:** Amer. Jur. Award, Comm. Prop.; **MIL SERV:** USAF; 1st Lt.; 1970-72; **OTHER ACT & HONORS:** San Francisco Bar Assn, Speakers' Comm.; **HOME ADD:** 1115 Green St., San Francisco, CA 94109, (415)776-2521; **BUS ADD:** 332 Pine St., San Francisco, CA 94104, (415)433-4500.

BAYLESS, Craig W.——**B:** May 5, 1947, Portland, OR, *Sr. VP, Branch Mgr.*, Cushman & Wakefield of TX, Inc.; **PRIM RE ACT:** Broker, Consultant, Appraiser, Property Manager; **PREV EMPLOY:** Exec. VP, The Gilley Co., Portland, OR & Seattle, WA; **EDUC:** 1969, RE, Univ. of OR; **MIL SERV:** USMC, PFC, 1969; **HOME ADD:** 9333 Memorial Dr., Houston, TX 77024, (713)683-9946; **BUS ADD:** 1001 Fannin St., Houston, TX 77092, (713)658-1800.

BAYLIFF, Clarence W.——*Pres.*, 20th Century Investment Co., RE Sales and Devel.; **PRIM RE ACT:** Broker, Consultant, Developer; **SERVICES:** Consultation and participation in comml. and resid. devels.; **BUS ADD:** 43648 Acacia Ave., Hemet, CA 92343, (714)927-1813.

BAYNE, James M.——*Architect; Chief, Real Estate Management*, James M. Bayne, AIA; **PRIM RE ACT:** Architect; **OTHER RE ACT:** Govt. Official; RE Mgmt. & Physical Plant Operations & Maintenance; **SERVICES:** Overall mgmt. of 33 million sq. ft. of bldgs. & 133,000 acres of land worldwide; **BUS ADD:** 600 Independence Ave., SW, Washington, DC 20546.

BAYUK, Carl D.——**B:** Mar. 27, 1938, Plainfield, NJ, *Pres.*, Carl D. Bayuk, Realtors; **PRIM RE ACT:** Broker, Consultant, Appraiser; **SERVICES:** RE Brokerage, consulting, appraising, testimony; **REP CLIENTS:** Banks (appraising), local municipalities, expert testimony, planning boards; **PROFL AFFIL & HONORS:** SREA, NAR, NJ Assoc. of Realtors; **EDUC:** Syracuse Univ., Rutgers Univ., Somerset Cty Coll.; **OTHER ACT & HONORS:** F & AM, Exchange, Bd. of Dir, YMCA, Bd. of Dirs. Huitt Hist. Museum Village; **HOME ADD:** RD 1, Box 204, Lebanon, NJ 08833, (201)236-6177; **BUS ADD:** Rte. 31 S, Box 5167, Clinton, NJ 08809, (201)735-4888.

BAZEMORE, Walton L., Jr.——**B:** Dec. 25, 1938, Savannah, GA, *VP*, Maddox & Assoc. PC; **PRIM RE ACT:** Architect; **PROFL AFFIL & HONORS:** AIA; **EDUC:** AS, 1963, Building Const., So. Technical Inst.; **MIL SERV:** USNR, GM-3; **OTHER ACT & HONORS:** City of Sav., Building & Housing Code Bd. of Adjustments and Appeals.; **HOME ADD:** 3 Marsh Point Dr., Savannah, GA 31406, (912)354-8384; **BUS ADD:** P.O. Box 9962, Savannah, GA 31412, (912)233-4751.

BEACH, Eugene H.——**B:** Nov. 17, 1919, MI, *Pres.*, Eugene H. Beach, Architects Inc.; **PRIM RE ACT:** Architect; **SERVICES:** Architectural Serv. to Devels.; **PROFL AFFIL & HONORS:** AIA; **EDUC:** BIE, 1947, Univ. of FL, **MIL SERV:** USAF, Capt.; **HOME ADD:** 19102 Lutz Lake Fern Rd., Lutz, FL 33549; **BUS ADD:** 11809 N. Dale Mabry, Tampa, FL 33618.

BEACH, Robert T.——**B:** July 28, 1943, Ossining, NY, *Architect & Prin.*, Beach Assocs., Architects & Engineers; **PRIM RE ACT:** Architect, Consultant; **OTHER RE ACT:** Interior Designer, Landscape Designer, RE Prop. Inspector, Cert. Energy Auditor; **SERVICES:** Architecture, Engineering, Const. & RE Inspection and Related Serv.; **REP CLIENTS:** E TN School Depts., Continental Tel. Co., New York Life Ins. Co., Ins. Investigations for Local Adjustors, Local

Medical, Comml. & Resid. Prop. Owners; **PREV EMPLOY:** Milton P. Robelot, Architect, Kingsport TN, Goodyear Tire & Rubber Co., Staff Architect, Arch. Div., RE Dept., Akron, OH; **PROFL AFFIL & HONORS:** CSI, AIA, TN Energy Auditor, TN Soc. of Architects, Upper E TN Solar Energy Assoc., Reg. Arch in 6 states, Past Sec./Tr. for the Wataugia Chapt. of the Amer. Inst. of Arch.; **EDUC:** Assoc. in Const. Tech., BArch, 1964, 1971, Const. Technology, Pre-Architecture, Architecture, Const. Mgmt., Const. Admin., Const. Law, SUNY, Delhi, Kent State Univ.; **GRAD EDUC:** Grad. Courses in RE, 1972, 1973, RE Devel., City Planning, Urban Redev., Kent State Univ., Kent, OH; Broward Comm. Coll., Ft. Lauderdale, FL; **EDUC HONORS:** Honor Roll 1966, 1967, 1969; **OTHER ACT & HONORS:** Member Bd. of Ed. St. Dominic's School-1979, 4th Degree Knights of Columbus, Loyal Order of Moose, Elected "Knight of the Year" for 1980 by the Knights of Columbus-Kingsport, TN; **HOME ADD:** 2101 Beechnut Dr., Kingsport, TN 37660, (615)288-7073; **BUS ADD:** 135 E New Street, Suite 204, Kingsport, TN 37660, (615)247-9221.

BEAL, Alexander S.——**B:** July 22, 1908, Boston, MA, *Consultant, Owner*, The Beal Cos.; **PRIM RE ACT:** Consultant, Appraiser; **SERVICES:** Investment and appraisal consulting; **REP CLIENTS:** Investors and owners in comml. props.; **PREV EMPLOY:** Chmn. of the Bd., Beal & Co., Inc.; **PROFL AFFIL & HONORS:** Nat. Assn. RE Bds., MA Bd. of RE Appraisers, Gr. Boston RE Bds., Inst. RE Mgmt., ULI, RE BOMA; **EDUC:** BS, 1931, Harvard Coll.; **MIL SERV:** USNR Lt.; **OTHER ACT & HONORS:** Dir. Boston Municipal Research Bur.; **HOME ADD:** 130 Sunrise Ave., Palm Bch., FL 33480, (305)833-8886; **BUS ADD:** 15 Broad St., Boston, MA 02109.

BEAL, Bruce A.——**B:** June 28, 1936, Boston, MA, *Pres.*, The Beal Companies, Beal & Co., Inc.; **PRIM RE ACT:** Consultant, Appraiser, Developer, Owner/Investor, Property Manager, Syndicator; **SERVICES:** Investment counseling, valuation,devel., synd., prop. mgmt., brokerage; **REP CLIENTS:** Ltd. partnerships, instns., instnl. families, publicly held nat. corp. municipalities and indiv. involvind comml. and indus. props.; **PROFL AFFIL & HONORS:** NAR, MA Assn. of Realtors, Greater Boston RE Bd., Amer. Soc. of RE Counselors, BOMA, Institute of Property Taxation (IPT), International Assn. of Assessing Officers (IAAO), Various Arch. & landscaping awards for devel.; **EDUC:** BA, 1960, eng., Rollins Coll; **GRAD EDUC:** 2yrs., Boston Univ.; **EDUC HONORS:** High Honors, cum laude; **OTHER ACT & HONORS:** Tr., MA Eye and Ear Infirmary, Boston Public Library, Overseer, Boston Symphony Orch., Member, Lincoln Conservation Commn.; **HOME ADD:** Old Winter St., Lincoln, MA 01773, (617)259-0408; **BUS ADD:** 15 Broad St., Boston, MA 02109, (617)742-1500.

BEAL, Charlotte——*Ed.*, Hawaii Assoc. of Realtors, Hawaiian Realtor; **PRIM RE ACT:** Real Estate Publisher; **BUS ADD:** 700 Bishop St., Honolulu, HI 96813, (808)538-3641.*

BEAL, Fred B.——**B:** Jan. 9, 1912, Muskogee, OK, *Commissioner*, South Carolina Real Estate Commission; **PRIM RE ACT:** Regulator; **REP CLIENTS:** Southern Life Ins. Co., Coastal Fed. S & L Assn.; **PREV EMPLOY:** Commerce Clearing House, Inc., IL 1935-49; Fred Beall Agency, Inc., SC 1950-75; **PROFL AFFIL & HONORS:** SC RE Com., 1960, 1975; SC Assn. of Realtors, Dir. 1963-68; Oasis Temple, NC 1946 - present; **EDUC:** St. Johns Military Acad., 1930; **GRAD EDUC:** BS, 1934, Univ. of AR, Fayetteville; **OTHER ACT & HONORS:** Commissioner of the SC Real Estate Com., 1976 - present; **HOME ADD:** 101 Huntsman Ln., Lexington, SC 29072, (803)359-7219; **BUS ADD:** 2221 Devine St., Columbia, SC 29205, (803)758-3981.

BEAL, Robert L.——**B:** Sept. 10, 1941, Boston, MA, *Gen. Partner and Exec. VP*, The Beal Cos.; **PRIM RE ACT:** Broker, Consultant, Appraiser, Developer, Owner/Investor, Instructor, Property Manager; **OTHER RE ACT:** Guest Lecturer at Harvard, MIT and Bentley Coll.; **SERVICES:** Consulting, investment counseling, appraisal and RE tax valuation, devel., prop. mgmt. in all types of RE; **REP CLIENTS:** Fin. insts.; corp. clients; pvt. indiv.; also own, develop and manage extensive RE holdings for own account including office, resid., comml. and indus. props.; **PREV EMPLOY:** The Beacon Cos., Partner and VP, 1965-1976; **PROFL AFFIL & HONORS:** Greater Boston RE Bd., Pres., 1978, 1979, Dir., 1970-1972, 1976 -; Bldg. Owners & Mgrs. Assn., Dir., 1970-1972; MA Assn. of Realtors, Dir., 1979-; MA Taxpayers Found., Inc., Dir., 1980-; Amer. Soc. of RE Counselors, Member (by invitation), 1980; Nat. Realty Comm., Dir. & Member Exec. Comm., 1974-, Sec., 1981; **EDUC:** BA, 1963, Harvard Coll.; **GRAD EDUC:** MBA, 1965, Bus. Admin., Harvard Bus. School; **EDUC HONORS:** Cum Laude; **OTHER ACT & HONORS:** Belmont Hill School, Member of the Corp., 1974-; Harvard Coll., Reunion Gift Chmn., 1973, Capital Fund Drive, Class 1963, 1979-; Harvard Coll. Council, Dir., 1972-1973; NE Univ., Instr. and Lecturer, 1969-1975; Ripon Soc., Co-Founder, Nat. Treas. and Nat. Exec. Bd., 1968-1972, Dir., 1979-; Boston Zoological Soc., VP, Treas. and Dir., 1972-1980, Pres., 1980-; The School of the Museum of Fine Arts, Visiting Comm.; The Boys' Club of Boston, Overseer, 1975-; MA Indus. Fin. Agency, Dir. & VChmn., 1976-; The Boston Comm., Inc., Tr., 1981-; Beacon Hill Civic Assn., Dir., 1975-1978; **HOME ADD:** One Spruce St., Boston, MA 02108, (617)523-7313; **BUS ADD:** 15 Broad St., Boston, MA 02109, (617)742-1500.

BEALE, Joseph S.——**B:** Dec. 21, 1937, Hinsdale, IL, *Chmn. of the Bd.*, Hawthorne Realty Grp.; **PRIM RE ACT:** Consultant, Developer, Property Manager, Owner/Investor; **SERVICES:** A full range of dev. and mgmt. services for comml. prop.; **REP CLIENTS:** Indiv. and instl. investors; Corp. clients with indus., office or retail space needs (i.e., IBM, Nalco Chem., Gen. Motors, Prentice-Hall, Warner Commu., Dominick's Finer Foods, Walgreen's, etc.); **PREV EMPLOY:** Gottlieb/Beale & Co., Inc. - VP & Partner - 1969-1972; Harrington, Tideman, O'Leary & Co. - VP & Partner - 1962-1969; **PROFL AFFIL & HONORS:** NAREB, NACORE; ULI Assn. of Indus. RE Brokers, Chicago RE Bd., The Realty Club of Chicago, IL; **EDUC:** BA, 1959, Econ., Brown Univ.; **GRAD EDUC:** MBA, 1962, Fin., Univ. of Chicago Grad. School of Bus.; **HOME ADD:** 318 W Willow St., Chicago, IL 60614; **BUS ADD:** 8 E Huron St., Chicago, IL 60611, (312)266-8100.

BEALE, Sam T.——*Atty.*, Beale, Eichner, Wright, Denton & Shields P.C.; **PRIM RE ACT:** Attorney, Owner/Investor, Instructor, Syndicator; **BUS ADD:** 1 North 5th St., Richmond, VA 23219, (804)788-1500.

BEALL, Alan Cory——**B:** Apr. 11, 1938, Seattle, WA, *Pres./Owner*, The Beall Cos.; **PRIM RE ACT:** Broker, Consultant, Developer, Owner/Investor, Instructor, Property Manager; **PREV EMPLOY:** Blackfield HI Corp. (Pres), a wholly owned sub. of Pacific Lighting (NYSE); **PROFL AFFIL & HONORS:** ICSC, (Past State Dir.), Lic. RE Broker, State of HI, RE Bd. of HI (Past Dir.), Retail Merchants of HI (Past Dir.), Downtown Improvement Assn. (Dir.), HI Visitors Bur. (Past Dir.), HI Employers Council (Past Dir.), CSM; **EDUC:** BA, 1961, Math. & Econ., Univ. of HI; **EDUC HONORS:** Dean's List; **OTHER ACT & HONORS:** HI Visitors Bur., HI Hist. Found., Dir. Bank of Honolulu, Big Bros. of HI, Aloha United Way, Honolulu Theatre for Youth & HI Humane Soc.; **HOME ADD:** 4821 Kaimoku Way, Honolulu, HI 96821, (808)373-1363; **BUS ADD:** 2201 Kalakaua Ave., Ste A-403, Honolulu, HI 96815, (808)926-3606.

BEALLE, Thomas B., III——**B:** Sept. 27, 1952, Opp, AL, *Pres.*, Bealle & Hanes, Inc.; **PRIM RE ACT:** Broker, Consultant, Appraiser, Developer, Owner/Investor, Instructor, Property Manager, Insuror, Syndicator; **SERVICES:** Investment counseling, prop. mgmt., synd. of investment props.; **REP CLIENTS:** Indiv. & instnl. investors; **PROFL AFFIL & HONORS:** NAR, RNMI, GRI; **EDUC:** BA, 1975, Psych., Unv. of S AL; **HOME ADD:** 5221 Azalea Cir., Mobile, AL 36608, (205)343-9110; **BUS ADD:** 3729 Cottage Hill Rd., Mobile, AL 36609, (205)666-0002.

BEAN, Terry R.——**B:** Oct. 17, 1942, E. St. Louis, IL, *RE Broker*, Bean Inv. Realty; **PRIM RE ACT:** Broker, Syndicator, Consultant, Developer, Property Manager, Owner/Investor; **OTHER RE ACT:** Loan Prep.; **SERVICES:** Inv. Counseling, valuation, synd., prop. mgmt.; **EDUC:** BSIE, 1965, Indus. Engrg., Univ. of AR; **GRAD EDUC:** MBA, 1967, Mgmt., Univ. of AR; **MIL SERV:** USA, 1st Lt.; **HOME ADD:** 1607 Lenore, Benton, AR 72015, (501)778-1772; **BUS ADD:** 204 Woodland St., Benton, AR 72015, (501)778-4477.

BEAN, William H.——**B:** June 10, 1943, Newton, MA, *Exec. VP*, Warren, Gorham & Lamont, Inc.; **PRIM RE ACT:** Real Estate Publisher; **SERVICES:** Publishers of 30 RE publications; **EDUC:** BA, 1965, Harvard Univ.; **GRAD EDUC:** MBA, 1967, MIT; **HOME ADD:** Glen Rd., Weston, MA 02193, (617)237-3692; **BUS ADD:** 210 South St., Boston, MA 02111, (617)423-2020.

BEARCE, David W.——**B:** Feb. 18, 1935, Foxboro, MA, *Chief Appraiser*, Dept. of HUD, Hartford,CT; **PRIM RE ACT:** Appraiser; **SERVICES:** HUD Mort. Insurance; **REP CLIENTS:** CT Banks and Mort. Cos.; **PREV EMPLOY:** Better Homes for Springfield, Exec. Dir.; **EDUC:** BSBA, 1960, Mktg., Suffolk Univ.; **MIL SERV:** USMC, Sgt., 1953-56; **HOME ADD:** 193 Franklin Rd., Longmeadow, MA 01106; **BUS ADD:** One Hartford Square W., Hartford, CT 06106.

BEARD, John R.——**B:** June 22, 1942, Cleveland, OH, *Partner*, Beard & Lawer; **PRIM RE ACT:** Attorney; **SERVICES:** Legal serv.: all aspects of banking, fin., real prop. transactions; **REP CLIENTS:** The First Nat. Bank of Anchorage; Other lenders & instnl. mort. loan investors; real prop. vendors & purchasers; **PREV EMPLOY:** Office of the Gov., State of AK, 1969-1970; Roger Cremo (Law Office) 1971-1976; John R. Beard (Law Office) 1977-1980; **PROFL AFFIL &**

HONORS: AK Bar Assn.; ABA (Sect. of Corp., Banking & Bus. Law); **EDUC:** AB, 1964, Econ., Princeton Univ.; **GRAD EDUC:** JD, 1967, Law, Univ. of Chicago Law School; **EDUC HONORS:** Cum Laude; **OTHER ACT & HONORS:** Dir., Local Affairs Agency, State of AK, 1969; Legislative Asst. to Gov., AK, 1970; AK Children's Services, Dir., 1972-1979, 1981-present ; Anchorage Community Mental Health Center, Dir., 1975-1979, Pres., 1979; **HOME ADD:** 7014 Madelynne Way, Anchorage, AK 99504, (907)333-1440; **BUS ADD:** 425 G St., Suite 630, Anchorage, AK 99501, (907)277-2119.

BEARD, Linda Vance——B: Apr. 5, 1949, Tahlequah, OK, *Owner*, Cherokee Capitol Abstract and Title Co.; **OTHER RE ACT:** Abstracting, title ins. and escrow serv.; **SERVICES:** Same as primary RE activities; **PROFL AFFIL & HONORS:** OK Land and Title Assn., Amer. Land & Title Assn.; **EDUC:** 1973, Bus., Northeastern OK State Univ.; **HOME ADD:** 281 Redbud Lane, Tahlequah, OK 74464, (918)456-5430; **BUS ADD:** 107 E. Delaware, Tahlequah, OK 74464, (918)456-8851.

BEASLEY, Oscar H.——B: Sept. 30, 1925, Denver, CO, *VP, Counsel*, First American Title Insurance Co.; **PRIM RE ACT:** Attorney; **OTHER RE ACT:** Underwriting; **PREV EMPLOY:** Practiced Law in Albuquerque, NM; Prof. at Western State Univ. Coll. of Law in Fullerton, CA (present); **PROFL AFFIL & HONORS:** Lecturer for Practicing Law Instit. and CA Continuing Educ. of the Bar; ABA; Amer. Land Title Assn.; ABA's Committee on Title Insurance; Chmn. of ALTA's Wetlands Committee; ALTA's Title Forms, Indian Claims and ABA Liaison Committee; **EDUC:** BA, 1949, Pol. Sci., Univ. of Omaha; **GRAD EDUC:** JD, 1950, State Univ. of IA; **MIL SERV:** USN, Seaman; **OTHER ACT & HONORS:** NM House of Representatives, 1959-1963; **HOME ADD:** 13432 Eton Pl., Santa Ana, CA 92705, (714)558-8093; **BUS ADD:** 114 E Fifth St., Santa Ana, CA 92701, (714)558-3211.

BEASLEY, Robert Scott——B: Mar. 17, 1949, Baltimore, MD, *VP*, Mercantile-Safe Deposit & Trust Co., Asset Mgmt.; **PRIM RE ACT:** Broker, Consultant, Attorney; **OTHER RE ACT:** Offeree repres.; **SERVICES:** Eval., structuring, and placement of RE equity; **REP CLIENTS:** Indiv. and trust accts. of Mercantile Safe Deposit; **PROFL AFFIL & HONORS:** ABA, CPA, Member of Maryland Bar; **EDUC:** BS, 1971, Acctg. & Econ., Lehigh Univ.; **GRAD EDUC:** JD, 1976, Univ. of MD School of Law; **OTHER ACT & HONORS:** Biography in Who's Who in the East; **HOME ADD:** 107 St. Dunstans Rd., Baltimore, MD 21212, (301)323-1676; **BUS ADD:** 2 Hopkins Plaza, Baltimore, MD 21201, (301)237-5543.

BEATH, Andrew B.——B: July 20, 1917, Antioch, IL, *Realtor Assoc.*, Norm House Realty; **PRIM RE ACT:** Syndicator, Consultant, Owner/Investor; **OTHER RE ACT:** Exchanging; Ranch Sales; **SERVICES:** Represent buyer; **PREV EMPLOY:** Retd. Fed. Admin. Law Judge; WI Attny.; **PROFL AFFIL & HONORS:** Sierra Vista & AZ Exchangers; **EDUC:** BA, 1938, Intnl. Law, U of WI; **MIL SERV:** USA, 1st. Lt.; **OTHER ACT & HONORS:** Trail Atty., US Dept. of Justice 1957-1960; Fed. Bar Assn.; Soc Philatelic Amer.; Author: Intelligence Subjects; **HOME ADD:** 5040 Equestrian Ave., Sierra Vista, AZ 85635, (602)378-6090; **BUS ADD:** 2700 E. Fry Blvd., Sierra Vista, AZ 85635, (602)458-8440.

BEATTIE, Donald M.——B: Nov. 11, 1928, Ryderwood, WA, *RE Broker*, Beattie RE; **PRIM RE ACT:** Broker, Consultant, Appraiser, Lender, Owner/Investor, Instructor; **SERVICES:** Gen. brokerage & tax consultant; **PROFL AFFIL & HONORS:** Soc. of Exchange Counselors; Puget Sound Exchanger; Comm. Investment of OR; CCIM; Sec./Treas. of the Soc. of Exchange Counselors; Bd. of Gov., Soc. of Exchange Counselors, 1978 REaltor of Year Local Bd.; **EDUC:** BA, 1957, Acctg., Univ. of WA; **MIL SERV:** USN; RM2; **OTHER ACT & HONORS:** Masonic; Shriner; Eastern Star; Rotarian; Elk; Moose; **HOME ADD:** 2010 Cascade Longview, WA 98632, (206)423-8878; **BUS ADD:** 856 15th PO Box 1117, Longview, WA 98632.

BEATY, James A., Jr.——B: June 28, 1949, Whitmire, SC, *Bd. Member*, NC RE Licensing Bd.; **PRIM RE ACT:** Attorney, Regulator; **OTHER RE ACT:** Member of NC RE Licensing Bd.; **PREV EMPLOY:** Partner, Beaty & Friende Attys. at Law; **EDUC:** BA, 1971, Pol. Sci. & Hist., Western Carolina Univ.; **GRAD EDUC:** JD, 1974, Law, Univ. of NC, Chapel Hill; **EDUC HONORS:** Cum Laude; **HOME ADD:** 325 Mayfair Dr., Winston Salem, NC 27105, (919)748-1245; **BUS ADD:** 548 N Main St., Winston Salem, NC 27101, (919)723-5572.

BEATY, Richard E.——B: June 26, 1931, Huntington, IN, *Pres.*, Century 21 Beaty Realtors & Auctioneers; **PRIM RE ACT:** Broker, Consultant, Appraiser, Owner/Investor; **SERVICES:** Resid., comml. R.E. sales, farm and intl., investment counseling, appraising; **PROFL AFFIL & HONORS:** AFLM, 2nd V.P. Nat. Farm & Land Inst. of NAR 1981, 1980 IN. Farm & Land Broker of the Year, 1976 Pres. IN Chpt. 24 Farm & Land Inst., CRB, CRS, GRI; **EDUC:** BS, Agriculture, Purdue Univ., W. Lafayette, IN; **EDUC HONORS:** Scabbard and Blade and Purdue Order of Military Merit; **MIL SERV:** USA, 1st Lt.; **OTHER ACT & HONORS:** Kiwanis, C of C (past Dir.); **HOME ADD:** 1309 Iitzfield Rd., Huntington, IN 46750, (219)356-4411; **BUS ADD:** 617 Cherry St., Huntington, IN 46750, (219)356-2922.

BEAUBIEN, C. Gordon——B: Oct. 11, 1920, Detroit, MI, *Asst. Sec.*, Lambrecht Realty Co., Brokerage; **PRIM RE ACT:** Broker, Appraiser; **PREV EMPLOY:** Silloway & Co., 850 Buhl Bldg., Detroit, MI 48226, 1970-1976; **EDUC:** Univ. of Detroit; **MIL SERV:** USMC, Sgt.; **OTHER ACT & HONORS:** Bd. of Advisors, Salvation Army; **HOME ADD:** 1490 Larkmoor Blvd., Berkley, MI 48072, (313)547-6195; **BUS ADD:** 3300 City National Bank Bldg., Detroit, MI 48226, (313)964-4522.

BEAUCHAMP, Randolph L.——B: Feb. 2, 1949, Salisbury, MD, *Pres.*, Beauchamp Const. Co., Inc.; **PRIM RE ACT:** Builder; **SERVICES:** Design & Const.; **EDUC:** BS Engrg., 1971, Physics, Loyola Coll.; **HOME ADD:** 512 Market St., Pocomoke, MD 21851, (301)957-2872; **BUS ADD:** Rte. 1 Box 37, Pocomoke, MD 21851, (301)957-0589.

BEAUPRE, Armand G.——*Engr. Dept.*, Norton Co.; **PRIM RE ACT:** Property Manager; **BUS ADD:** One New Bond St., Worcester, MA 01606, (617)853-1000.*

BEAVEN, Clinton——*Director Fac.*, Analog Devices; **PRIM RE ACT:** Property Manager; **BUS ADD:** PO Box 280, Norwood, MA 02062, (617)329-4700.*

BECHARD, Jerold J.——B: Mar. 4, 1938, Outagamie Cty., WI, *Pres.*, Bechard Investments Inc.; **PRIM RE ACT:** Broker, Syndicator, Consultant, Developer, Property Manager, Owner/Investor; **SERVICES:** Invest. and tax shelter counseling, dev. and syndication of comml. prop. mktg. and prop. mgmt.; **PREV EMPLOY:** Commerce Clrg. House-Law Book Publ.; **PROFL AFFIL & HONORS:** Invest. R.E. Inst., WI Realtors Assn., CCIM; **EDUC:** BBA, 1971, Mktg. and R.E., GA State Univ.; **MIL SERV:** USN, PO-2nd Class; **OTHER ACT & HONORS:** Butte Des Morts Golf Club; **HOME ADD:** 3915 W. Broadway, Appleton, WI 54911, (414)739-8968; **BUS ADD:** 1216 W. Wisconsin Ave., Appleton, WI 54911, (414)731-0251.

BECHHOEFER, Ina S.——B: Feb. 22, 1935, Providence, RI, Self-employed consultant; **PRIM RE ACT:** Consultant, Owner/Investor, Instructor; **SERVICES:** Investment counseling; market analysis; feasibility studies; teaching; research; writing; valuation studies; primary specialization; housing; **REP CLIENTS:** Investors; developers; lenders; bldrs.; govt. agencies; assns.; **PREV EMPLOY:** Instructor, The Amer. Univ. (full time 1973-77; part-time until present); **PROFL AFFIL & HONORS:** Amer. RE & Urban Econ. Assn.; Assn. of Amer. Geographers; Amer. Planning Assn.; NAHRO (Washington Chap.); Lambda Alpha (By Invitation); Washington Women's Network; **EDUC:** BS, 1956, Bus. Admin., Simmons Coll.; **GRAD EDUC:** MS, 1973, RE & Urban Devel. Studies, Amer. Univ.; PhD Cand., 1977, Urgan Geography and Land Use Planning, Univ. of MD; **EDUC HONORS:** Luchs Memorial Scholarship; NAHB Found. Award; SREA Fellowship; Lambda Alpha Student Award, Phi Kappa Phi; **HOME ADD:** 6600 Elgin Lane, Bethesda, MD 20817, (301)229-4692; **BUS ADD:** 2609 Klingle Rd., NW, Washington, DC 20008, (301)229-4692.

BECHTEL, Clarence R.——*Exec. Dir.*, Building Officials and Code Administrators International; **PRIM RE ACT:** Regulator; **BUS ADD:** 17926 S. Halsted St., Homewood, IL 60430, (312)799-2300.*

BECK, Chester——B: Sept. 12, 1929, New York, NY, *Pres.*, Chester Beck Associates, Inc.; **PRIM RE ACT:** Broker; **SERVICES:** Mort. brokerage, sales, owner/investor; **REP CLIENTS:** Investors, major devel. and inst. in comml. prop.; **PROFL AFFIL & HONORS:** RE Bd. of NY; Mort. Bankers Assn.; **EDUC:** BBA, 1951, Acctg., CCNY; **HOME ADD:** 400 E 54th St., New York, NY 10022, (212)753-3354; **BUS ADD:** 615 Fifth Ave., New York, NY 10022, (212)688-4790.

BECK, David——B: Jan. 29, 1954, Louisville, KY, *CPA*, Potter & Co.; **PRIM RE ACT:** Consultant; **OTHER RE ACT:** CPA; **SERVICES:** Audits, cash flows, initial co. formation, tax, computer systems servs.; **REP CLIENTS:** Condo devels., Hilton Head Is. & FL; **PROFL AFFIL & HONORS:** AICPA, KY Soc. of CPA's; **EDUC:** BA, 1976, Acctg., Univ. of KY; **HOME ADD:** 150 St. Phillip Dr., Lexington, KY 40502, (606)266-4374; **BUS ADD:** First Fed. Plaza, 110 W Vine St., Lexington, KY 40507, (606)253-1100.

BECK, Edward L.——**B:** Apr. 8, 1938, Cincinnati, OH, *Appraiser*, Beck Appraisal Service; **PRIM RE ACT:** Appraiser; **SERVICES:** RE Appraisals; **REP CLIENTS:** Banks, Reloc. Co.; etc.; **PREV EMPLOY:** FHA, VA, Transamer.; **PROFL AFFIL & HONORS:** SREA, SRA; **EDUC:** BS, 1960, Agric., OH State; **MIL SERV:** USA, SP4; **HOME ADD:** Rt. 2, Cynthiana, KY 41031, (606)234-3670; **BUS ADD:** PO Box 17005, Ft. Mitchell, KY 41017, (606)341-4475.

BECK, Howard Fred——**B:** Oct. 28, 1928, Yonkers, NY, *Pres.*, Lake Forest, Inc.; **PRIM RE ACT:** Broker, Developer, Builder, Property Manager, Owner/Investor; **SERVICES:** Devel. and sale of resid/ and comml. props.; prop. mgmt.; **REP CLIENTS:** resid. and comml. builders/devel.; **PREV EMPLOY:** devel. in NY State; **PROFL AFFIL & HONORS:** The Chamber, New Orleans Home Loan Authority, Almonaster Michoud Indus. Commn., NAIOP, NAHB, New Orleans E. Bus. Ass. Econ. Devel. Council of the Chamber.; **GRAD EDUC:** LLB, 1955, NY Law School; **OTHER ACT & HONORS:** Rotary Club of E. New Orleans; **HOME ADD:** 20737 Old Spanish Trail, New Orleans, LA 70129, (504)254-3234; **BUS ADD:** 7300 Downman Rd., New Orleans,, LA 70126, (504)241-4400.

BECK, Roger——*Space Mgr.*, Dow Corning Corp.; **PRIM RE ACT:** Property Manager; **BUS ADD:** PO Box 1767, Midland, MI 48640, (517)496-4211.*

BECK, Samuel H., Jr.——**B:** Aug. 25, 1919, Wash., DC, *Arch.*, Booker Assoc., Inc.; **PRIM RE ACT:** Architect, Consultant, Appraiser, Engineer; **SERVICES:** Design, space planning, const., mgmt., cost consultant, appraising, consultant engineer; **REP CLIENTS:** Owners, Investors & Lenders; **PREV EMPLOY:** Savage/Fogarty Mgmt. & Leasing Co., Inc.; **PROFL AFFIL & HONORS:** AIA, Const. Specifications Inst., Soc. of Amer. Mil. Engineers; **EDUC:** Arch., Univ. of VA; **MIL SERV:** USA Air Corps., Sgt., Victory Medal Amer. Theater; **HOME ADD:** 9939 Good Luck Rd., Seabrook, MD 20801, (301)794-6189; **BUS ADD:** 10905 Ft. Washington Rd., Ft. Washington, MD 20022, (301)292-9440.

BECKER, Fred P.——**B:** Sept. 2, 1926, KS, *Merrill Lynch Realty, Investment Comml.*; **PRIM RE ACT:** Broker, Consultant, Instructor; **SERVICES:** Investment counseling, valuation, sales and leasing comml., indus. prop.; **REP CLIENTS:** Attys., investors, owners; **PROFL AFFIL & HONORS:** Nat. Assn. of Realtors; CA Assn. of Realtors, CCIM; GRI; Hon. Dir. for Life, CA Assn. of Realtors; **EDUC:** 1960, Cert. in RE, UCLA; **MIL SERV:** USAF; **OTHER ACT & HONORS:** Rotary Club of Burbank; **HOME ADD:** 912 Scenic Way, Ventura, CA 93003, (805)644-2562; **BUS ADD:** 1501 W. Magnolia Blvd., Burbank, CA 93003, (213)848-6671.

BECKER, Kenneth H.——**B:** Mar. 11, 1950, Washington DC, *Pres.*, The Kenneth Becker Co.; **PRIM RE ACT:** Developer, Broker; **OTHER RE ACT:** Packaging; **SERVICES:** Packaging, devel. & synd. of fed. assisted housing & conv. RE; **REP CLIENTS:** Nat. Corp. for Housing Partnerships, Wash. DC; **PREV EMPLOY:** Srl Project Mgr. Nat. Corp. for Housing Partnerships; **EDUC:** BBA, 1972, Bus. RE, George Washington Univ.; **HOME ADD:** 9408 Reach Rd., Potomac, MD 20854; **BUS ADD:** 9408 Reach Rd., Potomac, MD 20854, (301)251-1814.

BECKER, Michael A.——**B:** Oct. 29, 1938, New York, NY, *VP, RE Acquisitions and Mgmt.*, Kenrich Corp., Kennbee Mgmt. Inc.; **PRIM RE ACT:** Consultant, Owner/Investor, Property Manager, Syndicator; **SERVICES:** Evaluates props. for acquisition while directing mgmt. dept. which oversees our considerable portfolio of Shopping Ctrs., Indus. and Office Ctrs. throughout the Eastern Seaboard and Mid-West; **PREV EMPLOY:** C.E.O. Allstate Aluminum Corp. (Construction & R.E. Operations) Pres., Michael Becker RE, Inc., Acquisitions Mgr. for own Acct. & Brokerage; **PROFL AFFIL & HONORS:** The RE Bd. of NY, Inc.; RE Investment; Member Nat. Assoc. of Indus. and Office Parks; **EDUC:** BBA, 1961, Money and Banking, Sch. of Bus. Admin., Long Is. Univ.; **MIL SERV:** USA, E-1, Unit Citation; Commendation by Sec. of the Army Cyrus Vance for Special Service; **OTHER ACT & HONORS:** Guest Lecturer: Long Island Univ.; **BUS ADD:** 777 Third Ave., NYC, NY 19917, (212)421-6400.

BECKER, Richard N.——**B:** Apr. 6, 1920, Jackson, MN, *Corp. RE Mgr.*, Consumers Petroleum Inc., RE; **PRIM RE ACT:** Broker, Consultant, Appraiser, Property Manager; **SERVICES:** Sale, lease, devel. of comml. and indus. prop., valuation, consultation, prop. mgmt., sale/leaseback, site search; **REP CLIENTS:** Indiv. and corporate investors in comml. and indus. props.; **PREV EMPLOY:** Kerr-McGee Inc., Rgnl. Mgr., Petroleum mktg. & RE D.H. Overmeyer Co., Inc., VP Corp. Devel.; **PROFL AFFIL & HONORS:** Licensed RE broker, CT & NY; **EDUC:** BS, 1946, Pol. Sci., Parsons Coll.; Cert., 1948 & 1962, RE and Mktg., Univ. of MI & MN School of Bus.; **MIL SERV:** USN, FC1/c; **HOME ADD:** 73 Range Rd., Wilton, CT 06897, (203)762-5426; **BUS ADD:** 808 Post Rd., Fairfield, CT 06430, (203)259-5211.

BECKER, Ronald H.——**B:** Dec. 16, 1934, Chicago, IL, *VP*, Witkowsky, Becker Assoc. Inc.; **PRIM RE ACT:** Consultant, Appraiser; **SERVICES:** RE Counseling & Valuation; **REP CLIENTS:** Attys. Investors, Fin. Instns. Govt. Agencies; **PREV EMPLOY:** Pres. George Becker & Co.; **PROFL AFFIL & HONORS:** AIREA, SREA, Lambda Alpha, 1980 Pres. IL Chap. AIREA, 1971 Chmn. Appraisers Council, Chicago RE Bd.; **EDUC:** BS, 1956, Mktg., Roosevelt Univ., Chicago; **HOME ADD:** 1672 Cavell, Highland Park, IL 60035, (312)831-2737; **BUS ADD:** 79 W. Monroe St., Rm 714, Chicago, IL 60603, (312)346-3810.

BECKER, Walter D., Jr.——**B:** Sept. 9, 1944, Los Angeles, CA, *Pres.*, The Becker & Bridges Co.; **PRIM RE ACT:** Broker, Consultant, Developer; **SERVICES:** Comml. RE serv.; **PREV EMPLOY:** Fin. Div. with Shell Oil Co.; **PROFL AFFIL & HONORS:** Bd. of Realtors; CCIM Chap. #38 (Sec.-Treas.) Jackson Comml. Exchange; A.C.I.; MS Econ. Council; C of C; RNMI; MS Org. Realty Exchangors, CCIM Candidate; **EDUC:** BS, 1966, Bus., MS State Univ.; **GRAD EDUC:** MBA, 1967, Bus., Univ. of S. MS; **EDUC HONORS:** Dean's List; **OTHER ACT & HONORS:** Bd. of Dir. & VP of Hinds (MSU) Cty. Alumni Assn.; Past Pres. Men's Y Club; The Jackson Club; Jackson Touchdown Club; **HOME ADD:** 4698 Londonderry Drive, Jackson, MS 39206, (601)362-7370; **BUS ADD:** 5305 Executive Place, Jackson, MS 39206, (601)982-5325.

BECKER, William E.——**B:** Jan. 25, 1927, Somerville, MA, *Pres. & Chmn. of the Bd.*, The William E. Becker Org.; **PRIM RE ACT:** Instructor, Consultant, Appraiser, Owner/Investor; **SERVICES:** Mkt. Research/Feasibility, Mkt. Planning of Projects, Mkt. Consulting of Residential & Comml. Projects, Review Appraising; **PREV EMPLOY:** VP Mktg., Leisure Tech. Corp.; Mktg. Positions with various Fortune 500 Cos.; **PROFL AFFIL & HONORS:** Sr. Member, NARA, Memver, Inst. of Residential Mktg., NAHB, ULI, Multi-Family Leadership Award, NAHB Mktg. Award Honors, Prof. Builder Mkt. Award; **EDUC:** BS, 1950, Mktg., School of Commerce, NYU; **GRAD EDUC:** MBA, 1952, Mgmt. & Fin., Grad. School of Bus., NYU; **MIL SERV:** USN, PHM 3/c; **OTHER ACT & HONORS:** Who's Who in Indus. & Fin., Instr. & Lecturer, The RE Inst. of NYU; **HOME ADD:** 894 Barbara Dr., Teaneck, NJ, (201)833-2342; **BUS ADD:** 894 Barbara Dr., Teaneck, NJ 07666, (201)833-2608.

BECKET, Thomas L.——**B:** Aug. 14, 1951, Los Angeles, CA, *Atty.*, Memel, Jacobs, Pierno & Gersh; **PRIM RE ACT:** Broker, Attorney; **SERVICES:** Legal advice, analysis and documentation; **REP CLIENTS:** Devel., lenders, arch., brokers, landlords, tenants, indiv. & corp. investors; **PROFL AFFIL & HONORS:** ABA, State Bar of CA, Los Angeles Cty. Bar Assn., Century City Bar Assn., Beverly Hills Bar Assn., Assoc. of RE Attys. of Los Angeles, Amer. Land Devel. Assn., Nat. Assn. of Realtors, CA Assn. of Realtors, Nat. Assn. of Corp. RE Execs.; **EDUC:** BS, 1973, Public Admin., Univ. of SC; **GRAD EDUC:** JD, 1976, Univ. of CA, Hastings Coll. of Law; **EDUC HONORS:** Cum Laude; **BUS ADD:** 1801 Century Park E, 25th Fl, Los Angeles, CA 90067, (213)556-2000.

BECKLEY, John W.——**B:** Sept. 18, 1944, Baltimore, MD, *Partner*, Fowley, Beckley, Stevens & Davis, P.A.; **PRIM RE ACT:** Attorney, Owner/Investor; **REP CLIENTS:** Mkt. Place Assoc. Ltd. Partnership, Baltimore, MD; **PROFL AFFIL & HONORS:** Baltimore City Bar Assn.; MD Bar Assn.; ABA, Member, Baltimore City Ethics Comm.; Member - MD Atty's. Grievance Commn.; **EDUC:** BS, 1967, Fin., Univ. of MD; **GRAD EDUC:** JD, 1974, Law, Univ. of Baltimore; **OTHER ACT & HONORS:** Pres., Stevenson Brooklandville Improvement Assn.; Member of Bd. of Tr., Park School; **HOME ADD:** Wiltonwood Rd., Stevenson, MD 21153, (301)484-7299; **BUS ADD:** 11 E. Lexington St., 4th Floor, Baltimore, MD 21202, (301)547-1919.

BECKMAN, William Roger——**B:** May 25, 1948, Brainard, MN, *VP/Investment Mgr.*, Genstar Pacific Investments, Genstar, Ltd.; **PRIM RE ACT:** Owner/Investor; **OTHER RE ACT:** Joint venture partnerships; **SERVICES:** Equity Part. for all types of devel. in W. U.S.; **REP CLIENTS:** Devels. with a well established track record; **PREV EMPLOY:** Don Wudtke & Assoc. (S.F.)- Project Arch. 1972-74; City & Cty. of S.F. Project Arch. 1975; Citibank(NY), Corp. fin. dept. 1977-79; **PROFL AFFIL & HONORS:** AIA, ICSC, Registered Arch.(CA) since 1976; **EDUC:** BArch, 1972, Design, IA State Univ., Ames IA; **GRAD EDUC:** MBA, 1977, Fin. and R.E., Stanford Univ.; **EDUC HONORS:** Knights of St. Patrick(Engrg. Honorary), student senate exec. comm.; **OTHER ACT & HONORS:** BOD of Stanford Bus. School Alumni Assn. 1981-83; member of the foundation for S.F. Arch. heritage; **HOME ADD:** 1740 Bay Laurel Dr., Menlo Pk., CA 94025; **BUS ADD:** 1000 Cherry Ave., San Bruno, CA 94066,

(415)583-7730.

BECKMEYER, H. Edward——*Treas.*, Watkins-Johnson Co.; **PRIM RE ACT:** Property Manager; **BUS ADD:** 3333 Hillview Ave., Palo Alto, CA 94304, (415)493-4141.*

BECKSTROM, R.L.——*Land Mgr.*, Pauley Petroleum; **PRIM RE ACT:** Property Manager; **BUS ADD:** 1000 Santa Monica Blvd., Los Angeles, CA 90067, (213)879-5000.*

BEDELL, Frank A.——**B:** Oct. 10, 1928, Cedar Rapids, IA, *VP*, West Shell Inc., Comml. Ind. Div.; **PRIM RE ACT:** Broker, Banker, Property Manager; **EDUC:** 1951, Univ. of IA; **MIL SERV:** US Army, Cpl., Several Decorations; **HOME ADD:** 7118 Windwood Dr., Cincinnati, OH 45242, (513)777-7172; **BUS ADD:** 3 E 4th St., Cincinnati, OH 45202.

BEDELL, Reginald H.——**B:** Feb. 8, 1948, Richmond, VA, *Broker-Associate*, Lakeside Sales Co.; **PRIM RE ACT:** Broker, Consultant, Instructor, Syndicator; **SERVICES:** Brokerage, consultant & synd.; **PROFL AFFIL & HONORS:** RESSI, RNMI, NV Chap. of Cert. Comml. Investment Group, Sierra Reno Exchangors, NV & CA RE Broker; **EDUC:** BA, 1971, Pol. Sci., Coll. of William & Mary; **HOME ADD:** Box 7546, Incline Vill., NV 89450, (702)831-1730; **BUS ADD:** PO Box 5296, Incline Village, NV 89450, (702)831-0752.

BEDICS, Joseph S.——**B:** May 20, 1957, Bethlehem, PA, *Supr. Energy Mgmt.*, Consolidated Rail Corp., RE Dept.; **PRIM RE ACT:** Engineer, Property Manager, Owner/Investor; **PROFL AFFIL & HONORS:** Amer. Inst. of Indus. Engrs.; **EDUC:** BS, 1979, Indus. Engrg., Ops. Research, Lehigh Univ.; **HOME ADD:** 450 Forrest Ave., Apt. R-203, Norristown, PA 19401; **BUS ADD:** 1528 Walnut St., Rm. 1205, Philadelphia, PA 19102, (215)893-6354.

BEDINGER, Kenneth L.——**B:** June 3, 1943, Portales, NM, *Owner*, Master Realty; **PRIM RE ACT:** Broker, Consultant, Appraiser, Developer, Owner/Investor, Instructor, Property Manager, Syndicator; **SERVICES:** Brokerage, appraisal, prop. mgmt., consulting, land devel. & appraisal; **PREV EMPLOY:** J.C. Penney Co., 1963-1970 (Mgmt.); **PROFL AFFIL & HONORS:** Nat. Assn. of RE Appraisers; NAR, Cert. RE Appraiser; GRI; **EDUC:** BA, 1970, Mktg., Eastern NM Univ.; **GRAD EDUC:** MBA, 1971, RE, Eastern NM Univ.; DBA, In Process, Fin./RE, TX Tech. Univ.; **MIL SERV:** US Army Nat. Guard, Sp. 5; **OTHER ACT & HONORS:** Vice-chmn. of Bd., Mental Health Resources, Inc.; **HOME ADD:** 1416 S. Globe, POB 26, Portales, NM 88130, (505)350-1583; **BUS ADD:** 712 W. 1st St., POB 817, Portales, NM 88130, (505)356-6607.

BEDSOLE, Ken——**B:** Apr. 21, 1942, Dothan, AL, *Pres.*, First Federal S & L Assn. of Henry Cty.; **PRIM RE ACT:** Broker, Appraiser, Banker, Lender, Builder, Owner/Investor, Insuror; **SERVICES:** Investment counseling, appraising, lending, building, insuring; **EDUC:** BBA, 1968, Fin., RE, Univ. of AL; **MIL SERV:** USMC; Cpl.; **OTHER ACT & HONORS:** Past Pres. Jaycees; **HOME ADD:** 101 Oak Dr., Abbeville, AL 36310, (205)585-5329; **BUS ADD:** 519 Kirkland St., Abbeville, AL 36310, (205)585-2237.

BEEBE, Edmund C., Jr.——**B:** June 7, 1938, Newton, MA, *Pres.*, Beebe Real Estate, Inc.; **PRIM RE ACT:** Broker, Developer, Builder, Owner/Investor; **OTHER RE ACT:** Contractor; **PROFL AFFIL & HONORS:** Dir., Nashua Bd. of Realtors; Dir., NH Bd. of Realtors; Dir., Nashua Home Builders; Member, FLI; **EDUC:** BA, 1961, Hist./Econ., Hobart Coll.; **MIL SERV:** USAF, 2nd Lt.; **OTHER ACT & HONORS:** Dir., Boys Club of Nashua; Tr., Hollis Congregatinal Church; **HOME ADD:** Box 578, Hollis, NH 03049, (603)465-2070; **BUS ADD:** 23 Ash St., Hollis, NH 03049, (603)465-2070.

BEEDERMAN, Asher J.——**B:** Oct. 29, 1949, Chicago, IL, *Atty.*; **PRIM RE ACT:** Attorney; **SERVICES:** Legal rep.; **PROFL AFFIL & HONORS:** ABA, IL State Bar Assn., Chicago Bar Assn., IL Trial Lawyers Assn.; **EDUC:** BA, 1971, Pol. Sci., Univ. of IL, Chicago, Circle; **GRAD EDUC:** JD, 1974, Law, DePaul Univ., Chicago, IL; **EDUC HONORS:** Hons. in Lib. Arts, Admitted Supreme Court of IL, 1974; **HOME ADD:** 8746 Kedrale Ave., Skokie, IL 60076, (312)677-6996; **BUS ADD:** 188 W Randolph St., Suite 827, Chicago, IL 60601, (312)372-3822.

BEELER, Joel I.——**B:** June 7, 1943, NJ, *Pres.*, Equidyne Props., Inc.; **PRIM RE ACT:** Broker, Attorney, Property Manager, Syndicator; **OTHER RE ACT:** Equidyne Securities, Inc.; **SERVICES:** Gen. Partner in Comml. and Resid. Synd.; **PREV EMPLOY:** Atty.; Marshall, Bratter, Greene, Allison and Tucker, NYC, 1969-1971; Loeb and Loeb, Los Angeles, 1971-1972; Finley, Kumble, Heine, Underberg and Grutman, NYC, 1972-1974; Asst. Gen. Counsel and Asst. Sec., Internatl. Playtex Co., Stamford, CT, 1974-1976; Pvt. Practice Law, NYC, 1976-; Pres., Dir., Eastland Industries, Inc., NYC, 1976-; Sec., Treas., Dir., Equidyne Corp., 1977-; Eastern Mining Systems, 1979-; Pres., Dir., Equidyne Props., Inc. subs. Equidyne Corp., 1978-; **PROFL AFFIL & HONORS:** NY State Bar Assn.; US Dist. Ct. for So. & Eastern Dist.; NY Assn. of Bar of NYC; **EDUC:** AB, 1965, Univ. of Pittsburgh; **GRAD EDUC:** MA, 1967, Pol. Sci., Rutgers Univ.; JD, 1969, Law, Rutgers Univ.; **EDUC HONORS:** Phi Delta Phi; **OTHER ACT & HONORS:** Friends of Israel Mus. (Assoc. Co-Chmn. Comm. 1979-); Jose Limon Dance Foundation, Inc. 38 E. 19th St., New York, NY 10003 (533-8560), VP; **HOME ADD:** 351 E. 84th St., Apt. 25B, NY, NY 10028, (212)734-6444; **BUS ADD:** 950 Third Ave., NY, NY 10022, (212)832-1600.

BEELER, Thomas T.——**B:** Aug. 13, 1946, Buffalo, NY, *Owner*, Chateau Mgmt.; **PRIM RE ACT:** Syndicator, Consultant, Property Manager, Owner/Investor; **SERVICES:** Consultant, prop. mgmt., synd.; **EDUC:** BME, 1968, Mech. Eng., Grove City Coll.; **GRAD EDUC:** MBA, 1973, Mktg, Wayne State Univ.; **EDUC HONORS:** Grad. with hon.; **OTHER ACT & HONORS:** Registered PE, State of MI; **HOME ADD:** 3563 Ravinewood Ct., Milford, MI 48042, (313)685-2759; **BUS ADD:** P.O. Box 107, Milfort, MI 48042, (313)685-2759.

BEEMAN, Gordon L.——**B:** Mar. 3, 1947, Anderson, IN, *Atty.*, DeVine, DeVine & Serr; **PRIM RE ACT:** Attorney; **SERVICES:** Counseling as to mort. lending, estate & prop. admin., litigation, oil & gas interests; **REP CLIENTS:** Mort. lenders, arch. & const. firms, RE purchasers, sellers; **PREV EMPLOY:** Assoc. Counsel, IN Mort. Corp., 1977-78; IN Nat. Bank; Dir. Anderson Motel Devel., Inc.; Holiday Inn of Columbus, Inc.; **PROFL AFFIL & HONORS:** Member Real Prop. Law Sect. of State Bar of MI, Member Real Prop. Probate & Trust Law Sect. of ABA; **EDUC:** 1970, Econ., IN Univ.; **GRAD EDUC:** JD, 1974, IN Univ.; **EDUC HONORS:** Omicron Delta Epsilon (Econ. Hon. Frat.), Magna Cum Laude; **OTHER ACT & HONORS:** Member of the Bar in MI, IN; **HOME ADD:** 2130 Agincourt, Ann Arbor, MI 48103, (313)995-1788; **BUS ADD:** 101 E Wash. St., Ann Arbor, MI 48104, (313)663-2445.

BEENEY, Robert W.——**B:** Oct. 11, 1940, Pembury, England, *Partner*, Jones Lang Wootton; **PRIM RE ACT:** Broker, Consultant, Appraiser; **SERVICES:** Investment counseling Corp. RE Serv.; **PREV EMPLOY:** Robert Beeney & Co., 1970-1978; **PROFL AFFIL & HONORS:** ULI; FIABCI; FRICS, Harriott Prize 1963; **EDUC:** Frics, 1963, Univ. of London Coll. of Estate Mgmt.; **HOME ADD:** 4387 Chevy Chase Dr., Flintridge, CA 91011, (213)790-5526; **BUS ADD:** 523 W. Sixth St., Los Angeles, CA 90014, (213)624-2800.

BEER, Murray L.——**B:** May 15, 1928, NJ, *Pres.*, Globe Mortgage Co.; **PRIM RE ACT:** Consultant, Appraiser, Banker, Developer, Lender, Builder, Owner/Investor; **SERVICES:** Mort. banking; **REP CLIENTS:** Serv. loans for major instnl. investors; **PROFL AFFIL & HONORS:** MBAA, SRA; **EDUC:** 1947, Bus. Admin., Bergen Coll.; **MIL SERV:** USA, M/Sgt.; **HOME ADD:** 35 Essex Dr., Tenafly, NJ 07670, (201)569-1886; **BUS ADD:** 110 Main St., Hackensack, NJ 07602, (201)489-6120.

BEER, Robert A.——**B:** Apr. 8, 1918, NY, NY, *Chmn.*, Beer-Litwin and Co., Inc., Realtors; **PRIM RE ACT:** Broker, Instructor, Syndicator, Consultant, Appraiser, Property Manager, Banker, Owner/Investor; **REP CLIENTS:** Retail chains, Oil cos., Banks, Users Invest.; **PROFL AFFIL & HONORS:** Greater Dallas R.E. Bd., Instructor SMU, CCIM, SIR, REB, Former CCIM Chptr. organizer and pres.; **EDUC:** BS in Econ., 1939, Mktg., Wharton School, Univ. of PA; **MIL SERV:** USN, Seabees, Cf. Storekeeper, Several medals; **OTHER ACT & HONORS:** City Tax Panels, many community officer, directorships; **HOME ADD:** 6573 Ridgeview Cir., Dallas, TX 75240, (214)661-9505; **BUS ADD:** 12800 Hillcrest Rd., Dallas, TX 75230.

BEESE, Dennis D.——**B:** April 7, 1942, Cedar Rapids, IA, *VP*, Columbia Communities Inc.; **PRIM RE ACT:** Architect, Consultant, Developer, Builder; **SERVICES:** Design, package, dev., build & mkt. condominiums; **PREV EMPLOY:** Nonprofit Housing Center of Urban Amer. Inc. 1968-74, Exec. VP 1973-1974; **PROFL AFFIL & HONORS:** AIA, Nat. Hsg. Conf., Comm. Assoc. Inst., Chmn. AIA National Housing Comm. 1979, 1st VP Houston Chapt. CAI 1981; **EDUC:** BArch, 1966, Univ. of OK; **OTHER ACT & HONORS:** Past

Bd. Mem. & VP of Seabrook Sharks Football Booster Club; **HOME ADD:** Watergate Yachting Ctr, Kemah, TX 77565, (713)334-3934; **BUS ADD:** 6009 Richmond Ave, Houston, TX 77057, (713)783-5930.

BEESLEY, H. Brent——*Dir.*, Department of Housing and Urban Development 2d Fed.Home Loan Bank Board; **PRIM RE ACT:** Lender; **BUS ADD:** 451 Seventh St., S.W., Washington, DC 20410, (202)377-6610.*

BEESLEY, H.E.——*Ed.*, American Industrial Real Estate Assn., American Industrial Real Estate Association Journal; **PRIM RE ACT:** Real Estate Publisher; **BUS ADD:** 5670 Wilshire Blvd., Los Angeles, CA 90036, (213)933-5740.*

BEESON, Brant R.——**B:** Dec. 28, 1951, Breckenridge, MN, *Atty.*; **PRIM RE ACT:** Attorney; **SERVICES:** All aspects of gen. practice of law; **REP CLIENTS:** Stauss, Inc., Northern Tier Plumbing & Heating, Inc., Builders Supply, Inc., Ind. Sch. Dist. 595; **PROFL AFFIL & HONORS:** Amer. & MN & ND Bar Assns., Agent for Chicago Title Ins. Co., JD, Cum Lause, Hamline Univ. Sch. of Law; **EDUC:** BA, 1973, Pol. Sci., Pre-law, Univ. of MN, Minneapolis; **GRAD EDUC:** JD, 1976, RE & Corp. Law, Hamline Univ., Sch. of Law, St. Paul, MN; **EDUC HONORS:** Cum Laude, Silver Gard Hon. Soc.; **OTHER ACT & HONORS:** Dir. E Grand Forks C of C, Charter Pres. EGF Optimist Club; **HOME ADD:** 1114 River Dr. SE, E Grand Forks, MN 56721, (218)773-9183; **BUS ADD:** 208 3rd Ave. NW, PO Box 498, E Grand Forks, MN 56721, (218)773-9888.

BEGELFER, David I.——**B:** Apr. 8, 1948, Cambridge, MA, *Exec. VP*, Endevor Devel. Corp.; **PRIM RE ACT:** Consultant, Developer, Owner/Investor; **SERVICES:** Devel. of office prop. and res. condos.; **PROFL AFFIL & HONORS:** Building Owners and Mgr. Assoc., NAR; **EDUC:** AB, 1969, Clark Univ.; **GRAD EDUC:** MS, 1971, Univ. of MA; **HOME ADD:** 209 St. Paul St., Brookline, MA 02146, (617)566-1170; **BUS ADD:** 77 N. Washington St., Boston, MA 02114, (617)523-7040.

BEGG, Charles F.H.——*VP*, The Spaly Group, Inc., Realtors; **PRIM RE ACT:** Broker, Consultant, Appraiser, Owner/Investor; **SERVICES:** RE Investment consulting; valuation, mktg.; sale or exchange of residential; income producing; comml. and/or indus. prop. sellers and investors; **BUS ADD:** 726 Packard, Ann Arbor, MI 48103, (313)769-7000.

BEHAR, Elazar——**B:** July 23, 1923, Seattle, WA, *Pres.*, Investors Preferred Realty, Inc.; **PRIM RE ACT:** Broker, Developer; **OTHER RE ACT:** Comml. & indus. investments & consultant; **SERVICES:** Develop, lease or sell unimproved props. for clients; **PROFL AFFIL & HONORS:** GRI; **MIL SERV:** US Navy, 1942-46, AMM 2/c; **HOME ADD:** 6010 S. Eddy St., Seattle, WA 98118, (206)725-4625; **BUS ADD:** 935 Securities Bldg., Seattle, WA 98101, (206)623-0523.

BEHAR, Larry J.——**B:** May 16, 1952, Cairo, Egypt, *Atty.*, Law Offices of Larry J. Behar; **PRIM RE ACT:** Consultant; **SERVICES:** RE law, immigration, bus. law; **PROFL AFFIL & HONORS:** FL Bar; **EDUC:** BA, 1974, N. Amer. Studies, McGill Univ.; **GRAD EDUC:** LLL Quebec Civil Law, JD Amer. Common Law, 1977, 1979, Univ. of Montreal, Nova Univ.; **OTHER ACT & HONORS:** Pres. - Club Richelieu, Hollywood, FL; **HOME ADD:** 1077 N.E. 202 Ln., North Miami Beach, FL 33179 33179, (305)651-7071; **BUS ADD:** 700 S.E. Third Ave., Suite 200, Fort Lauderdale, FL 33316, (305)763-2122.

BEHLING, Ralph T.——**B:** Buffalo, NY, *Pres.*, Ralph T. Behling Inc.; **PRIM RE ACT:** Owner/Investor; **EDUC:** BS, 1940, Pharmacy, Univ. of Buffalo; **GRAD EDUC:** MD, 1943, Univ. of Buffalo; **MIL SERV:** USPHS, Maj.; **OTHER ACT & HONORS:** Bd. of W. Coast Fed. S & L, Bd. of San Mateo C of C, Bd. of Kiwanis Club; **BUS ADD:** 145 No. San Mateo, San Mateo, CA 94401.

BEHLING, R.H.——*Exec. VP Mfg.*, Simpson Industries, Inc.; **PRIM RE ACT:** Property Manager; **BUS ADD:** 917 Anderson Rd., Litchfield, MI 49252, (517)542-2951.*

BEHN, G.E.——*Mgr. RE Dept.*, B.F. Goodrich; **PRIM RE ACT:** Property Manager; **BUS ADD:** 500 S. Main St., Akron, OH 44318.*

BEHR, Dick A.J.——**B:** Apr. 3, 1925, Detroit, MI, *Pres.*, Behr Appraisal Co., Inc.; **PRIM RE ACT:** Consultant, Appraiser; **REP CLIENTS:** Lenders, indivs., instnl., corp. investors, mfrs., legal; **PROFL AFFIL & HONORS:** AIREA, SREA, Amer. Soc. of Appraisers, Amer. Right of Way Assn., MAI, SREA, ASA, ARWA; **EDUC:** 1950, Bus. Admin., Wayne Univ., Univ. of MI; **MIL SERV:** USAF, S/Sgt., Purple Heart; **OTHER ACT & HONORS:** Advisory Bd. of Salvation Army, Antique Automobile Club of Amer.; **HOME ADD:** 2044 Belmont, Dearborn, MI 48128; **BUS ADD:** 727 Park Lane Towers, W Dearborn, MI 48126, (313)271-7900.

BEHR, Richard H.——**B:** Apr. 23, 1942, Albert Lea, MN, *Pres./Partner*, Landmark Devel. Corp. of Amer./Maitland/Strauss/Behr Arch.; **PRIM RE ACT:** Architect, Instructor, Consultant, Developer, Owner/Investor; **SERVICES:** Investment Counseling, Arch. & Engrg., RE Devel.; **REP CLIENTS:** Cities, Prvt. Devel., Investors in Comml. & Resid. Props.; **PREV EMPLOY:** Prof. Grad. School of Arch.-Yale; Chief Architect, NYS Urban Devel. Corp. (UDC) 1970-74; **PROFL AFFIL & HONORS:** AIA, NY Soc. of Architects, AIA Design, Award, Urban Design Award for Housing, Design for Better Living Award/ Sensible Growth Grand Award; **EDUC:** BArch, 1965, Univ. of MN; **GRAD EDUC:** MBA, 1979, Fin., NYU; **EDUC HONORS:** Cum Laude; **OTHER ACT & HONORS:** Additional studies at Cornell, Harvard, Columbia & University of Illinois; **HOME ADD:** 1023 Post Rd., Scarsdale, NY 10583, (914)472-3157; **BUS ADD:** 80 Mason St., Greenwich, CT 06830, (203)661-0898.

BEHRENS, Alfred H.——**B:** Mar. 27, 1926, Germany, *VP & Gen. Mgr.*, Vorelco, Inc.; **PRIM RE ACT:** Developer, Owner/Investor; **OTHER RE ACT:** RE and const. subs. of Volkswagen of Amer.; **PROFL AFFIL & HONORS:** NACORE; Indus. Devel. Research Council; Fin. Exec. Inst.; **HOME ADD:** 23 Shaw Rd., Woodcliff Lake, NJ 07675, (201)391-3685; **BUS ADD:** 600 Sylvan Ave., Englewood Cliffs, NJ 07632, (201)894-6380.

BEIM, Robert B.——**B:** Aug., 1943, Minneapolis, MN, *Gen. Partner*, Beim & James; **PRIM RE ACT:** Developer, Owner/Investor; **PREV EMPLOY:** Grubb & Ellis Co.; Arthur Andersen & Co.; **PROFL AFFIL & HONORS:** Brokers Lic. - CA; CPA in CA; **EDUC:** AB, 1965, Biological Sci., Univ. of CA, Berkeley; **GRAD EDUC:** MBA, 1970, Fin., Stanford Grad School of Bus.; **MIL SERV:** Army Field Artillery, 1st Lt.; **HOME ADD:** Atherton, CA 94025; **BUS ADD:** 3000 Sand Hill Rd., Menlo Park, CA 94025.

BEITELSHEES, Everett D.——**B:** June 12, 1927, Montgomery, MI, *Pres.*, Now RE Co., Inc.; **PRIM RE ACT:** Broker, Consultant, Owner/Investor; **OTHER RE ACT:** RE Investment Counseling; **SERVICES:** Gen. RE Office with 23 Assoc. & Brokers; **PREV EMPLOY:** Leasing Agent & Sales Rep. for Burger Chef Systems, State of MI; **PROFL AFFIL & HONORS:** NAR, FL Assoc. Realtors, FL RE Exchangers, CCIM, CRB, CRS, GRI; Past Pres. of Sarasota Bd. of Realtors in 1979; **EDUC:** Huntington Coll., Huntington, IN; **MIL SERV:** USNAC, CAC trainee 1945; **OTHER ACT & HONORS:** Moslem Temple Shrine, Detroit, MI, 320 Mason, Valley of Tamps, FL, Masonic Lodge Dir. & Life Member, Sertoma Club Aircraft Owner & Pilot Assoc.; **HOME ADD:** 5547 Merrimac Dr., Sarasota, FL 33581, (813)922-1773; **BUS ADD:** 2120 Bee Ridge, Sarasota, FL 33579, (813)921-5702.

BEKASSY, Virginia——*VP Admin.*, Grolier, Inc.; **PRIM RE ACT:** Property Manager; **BUS ADD:** Sherman Turnpike, Danbury, CT 06816, (203)797-3500.*

BEKKENHUIS, Alan J.——**B:** Sept. 9, 1936, Watertown, MA, *RE Mktg.*, Exxon Corp., Exxon Co., USA; **PRIM RE ACT:** Broker, Developer, Owner/Investor; **EDUC:** BBA, 1961, Econ., Univ. of Miami; **HOME ADD:** PO Box 262, Great River, NY 11739, (516)581-2337; **BUS ADD:** 1900 Hempstead Tpk., E. Meadow, NY 11554, (516)794-5449.

BELDEN, Thomas G.——**B:** June 15, 1944, Cincinnati, OH, *Atty.*, Cavitch, Familo & Durkin; **PRIM RE ACT:** Attorney; **PROFL AFFIL & HONORS:** Cleveland Bar Assn.-Member of RE Sect., Order of Coif; **EDUC:** BBA, 1966, Acctg., Univ. of Notre Dame; **GRAD EDUC:** MBA; JD, 1967; 1971, Acctg. and Fin.; Law, Univ. of MI (MBA); Case Western Res. Univ. (JD); **EDUC HONORS:** Law School - Law Review; Order of Coif; **HOME ADD:** 2368 Lalemant, University Heights, OH 44118, (216)381-7451; **BUS ADD:** 1401 East Ohio Bldg., Cleveland, OH 44114, (216)621-7860.

BELES, Florian L.——*Pres.*, Berrien RE Service, Inc.; **PRIM RE ACT:** Broker, Consultant, Owner/Investor, Property Manager, Syndicator; **PROFL AFFIL & HONORS:** Bd. of MI Realtors, past Dir., VP and Past Pres., GRI; CRS; RAM; **EDUC:** 1968, RE Inst., Univ. MI, Univ. ND; **BUS ADD:** 1014 Main St., St. Joseph, MI 49085, (616)983-1584.

BELFER, Andrew B.——**B:** Nov. 11, 1953, NY, NY, *Counsel, Exec*, Belfer Realty & Devel. Co.; **PRIM RE ACT:** Broker, Attorney, Developer, Builder, Owner/Investor, Property Manager; **PROFL AFFIL & HONORS:** ABA Member, NY, NJ, FL Bars; **EDUC:** BA, 1975, Hist., Arts & Scis., Cornell Univ.; **GRAD EDUC:** 1979, Boston Univ. School of Law; **EDUC HONORS:** With distinction in all subjects; **HOME ADD:** 20 Canterbury Rd., Great Neck, NY 11021,

(516)466-9813; **BUS ADD:** 17 Barstwo Rd., Great Neck, NY 11021, (516)829-5720.

BELIAVSKY, Leonid——B: May 25, 1938, Russia, *M.A.I./Instr. of RE*, Los Angeles City Coll., Los Angeles, CA, Sch. of Bus. Admin.; **PRIM RE ACT:** Broker, Instructor, Consultant, Appraiser, Developer; **SERVICES:** Appraising, Mkt. analysis/consultation, packaging; **REP CLIENTS:** Comml. banks, devel., lenders, pvt. investors; **PREV EMPLOY:** State of CA, Dept. of Transportation Right-of-Way Agent, 1964; **PROFL AFFIL & HONORS:** A.I.R.E.A., RE Broker/State of CA Instr. in RE, M.A.I.; **EDUC:** AA, AB, 1959, 1964, Econ., Bus. Admin., Monterey Peninsula Coll., San Francisco State Coll.; **GRAD EDUC:** MS, 1970, Fin., RE, Mgmt., Long Beach State; **EDUC HONORS:** Who's Who in CA, 3.7 G.P.A., Jr. Coll. Teaching Credentials; **MIL SERV:** US Army, Sp./4, Airborne Wings (82nd Airborne Div.) 1953-1961; **OTHER ACT & HONORS:** Cert. in RE, U.C.L.A. Ext. 1970; **HOME ADD:** 30051 Knoll View Dr., Rancho Palos Verdes, CA 90274, (213)831-4411; **BUS ADD:** 18411 S Crenshaw Blvd., Suite 350, Torrance, CA 90504, (213)327-7852.

BELKNAP, Michael——B: Oct. 27, 1940, South Bend, IN, *Pres.*, The Belknap Co., Ltd.; **PRIM RE ACT:** Consultant, Developer, Owner/Investor; **SERVICES:** Land devel. and planning for own account and as a joint venture; **REP CLIENTS:** Hartford Ins. Grp.; Lazard Freres & Co.; Mitchell, Hutchins; Levitt Corp.; **PREV EMPLOY:** Levitt & Sons, Inc.; Corporate Prop. Investors; Sullivan & Cromwell; **PROFL AFFIL & HONORS:** ULI; Amer. Planning Assn.; **EDUC:** 1963, Eng., Harvard Coll.; **GRAD EDUC:** LLB, 1965, Cambridge Univ.; JD, 1967, Harvard Law School; **EDUC HONORS:** Cum Laude; **OTHER ACT & HONORS:** Bd. of Tr., Mountain Rd. Children's School; Bd. of Advisors, Wave Hill Environmental Center; **HOME ADD:** Warner Crossing Rd., Canaan, NY 12029, (518)781-4292; **BUS ADD:** Warner Crossing Road, Canaan, NY 12029, (518)781-4646.

BELL, Allen——B: Mar. 31, 1957, Tyler, TX, *Bldg. Mgr.*, CFNB/Beck Joint Venture - First Place; **PRIM RE ACT:** Property Manager; **OTHER RE ACT:** Resid. & comml. sales & leasing; **SERVICES:** Prop. mgmt.; **REP CLIENTS:** Citizens First Nat. Bank; **PROFL AFFIL & HONORS:** BOMA, Tyler Bd. of Realtors, TX Assn., Nat. Assn.; **EDUC:** Bus. Admin., Univ. of TX; **HOME ADD:** Rt 8 Box 1184, Tyler, TX 75703, (214)581-1589; **BUS ADD:** 908 First Place, Tyler, TX 75702, (214)595-1941.

BELL, Calvin E.——B: July 29, 1926, NY, NY, *Pres.*, Calina S. Co., Ltd. 1976-; **PRIM RE ACT:** Developer, Builder, Owner/Investor; **SERVICES:** R.E. Devel. & ownership of shopping ctr. and other income prop.; **PREV EMPLOY:** Bristol Devel. Corp., Pres. NY, NY - 1970-76; **PROFL AFFIL & HONORS:** ICSC; **EDUC:** BA, 1947, Sci., Princeton Univ.; **EDUC HONORS:** Cum Laude; **MIL SERV:** USNR, 1944-46, Lt.(jg), 1950-52; **HOME ADD:** 2001 Brightwaters Blvd., St. Petersburg, FL 33704, (813)823-6074; **BUS ADD:** Suite 100, 9450 Koger Blvd., St. Petersburg, FL 33702, (813)577-2994.

BELL, Daryl——*Dir.*, N.J., New Jersey Real Estate Commission; **PRIM RE ACT:** Property Manager; **BUS ADD:** 207 E. State St., Trenton, NJ 08625, (609)292-7055.*

BELL, Edward C.——B: Apr. 27, 1952, Cleveland, OH, *Asst. Corporate Controller*, The Robert A. McNeil Corp.; **PRIM RE ACT:** Property Manager, Syndicator; **PROFL AFFIL & HONORS:** CA Inst. of CPAs, AICPA, Beta Alpha Psi, CPA, BS; **EDUC:** 1970-1974, Acctg., UC Berkeley; **GRAD EDUC:** MBA, 1974-75, UC Berkeley; **EDUC HONORS:** UC Honor Soc.; **OTHER ACT & HONORS:** VP Bd. of Dir. Bayview Homeowner Assoc., 1980-1981; **HOME ADD:** 1550 Frontera #111, Millbrae, CA 94030, (415)697-6898; **BUS ADD:** 2855 Campus Dr., San Mateo, CA 94403, (415)572-0660.

BELL, Howard F.——*Exec. Dir.*, Independent Bankers Assn. of Amer.; **PRIM RE ACT:** Banker; **BUS ADD:** PO Box 267, Sauk Center, MN 56378, (612)352-6545.*

BELL, James F., Jr.——B: Sept. 15, 1939, Atlanta, GA, *Pres.*, The Allen Morris Co. of GA; **PRIM RE ACT:** Broker, Developer, Property Manager, Owner/Investor; **SERVICES:** Acquisition of office space/sites for clients; devel., leasing & mgmt. of office props.; **REP CLIENTS:** S. Bell, Burroughs Corp., Intl. Harvester Corp.; **PROFL AFFIL & HONORS:** Gov.(exec. comm.), RNMI, CCIM; CPM; Past Pres. BOMA; Atlanta; Dir. Atlanta Bd. of Realtors; Life Member Million Dollar Club; **EDUC:** BE, 1961, Mechanical Engrg., Vanderbilt Univ.; **GRAD EDUC:** MBA, 1968, Fin. & Mktg., Harvard Univ.; **MIL SERV:** USN, Lt. Cdr.; **OTHER ACT & HONORS:** Dir., Psych. Studies Inst. Atlanta, GA, Tr. King Coll. Bristol, TN; Member Alumni Advisory Council, Vanderbilt Univ., Eng. School; Elder N. Ave. Presbyterian Church; **BUS ADD:** 2301-100 Colony Sq., Atlanta, GA 30361, (404)892-1100.

BELL, Larry J.——B: July 5, 1949, Clovis, NM, *Pres.*, HBF Corp; **PRIM RE ACT:** Syndicator, Consultant, Developer, Builder, Property Manager, Owner/Investor; **SERVICES:** Prop. acquisition, dev. and synd. of comml. RE prop., prop. mgmt., gen. construction and construction mgmt.; **REP CLIENTS:** Individual and instnl. investors in comml. prop.; **PREV EMPLOY:** Main Lafrentz & Co., CPA; **PROFL AFFIL & HONORS:** ULI; AICPA; Nat. Assn. of Accountants; **EDUC:** BBA, 1971, Accounting, E NM Univ.; **EDUC HONORS:** Who's Who in Amer. Univ. and Coll., 1971, Nat. Student Register-1970; **OTHER ACT & HONORS:** Midland C of C Bd.; Midland Indus. Foundation Bd.; Midland United Way Bd.; Midland Jaycees; Salvation Army Bd.; Boys Club of Midland Bd.; Outstanding Young Men of Amer. (1975, 1978, 1979); Five Outstanding Young Texans (1979); Outstanding Young Man of Midland (1978); US Jaycees "Clint Dunagan Memorial Award" (1979); **HOME ADD:** 2503 Seaboard, Midland, TX 79701, (915)684-5844; **BUS ADD:** 216 HBF Bldg., Midland, TX 79701, (915)684-5844.

BELL, Martin M.——B: Nov. 24, 1918, PA, *Atty. at Law*, Martin M. Bell, P.A.; **PRIM RE ACT:** Attorney, Syndicator, Builder, Owner/Investor; **PREV EMPLOY:** IRS, 1959-1966, Tax Law Specialist; RE Broker 1952-58, AC NJ; Capt. USA Engr. Corps., 1941-45; **PROFL AFFIL & HONORS:** ABA, DC Bar Assn., MD Bar Assn.; **EDUC:** BS, 1942, Econ.; Acctg., Mkt, Wharton, Univ. of PA; **GRAD EDUC:** LLB, LLM, 1964, Law & Tax, Univ. of Georgetown Law School (DC); **MIL SERV:** Engr., Capt.; **HOME ADD:** 2408 Lillian Dr., Silver Spring, MD 20910, (301)933-2982; **BUS ADD:** 8720 Georgia Ave., Ste. 600, Silver Spring, MD 20910, (301)588-0200.

BELL, Robert——B: June 4, 1939, NY, NY, *Sr. Partner*, Bell, Kalnick, Beckman Klee & Green; **PRIM RE ACT:** Attorney; **OTHER RE ACT:** Teacher; **SERVICES:** Practice of law; **PREV EMPLOY:** Coopers & Lybrand; Simpson, Thacher & Bartlett; **PROFL AFFIL & HONORS:** NY State Bar Assn., Prof. of RE, NY Univ.; **EDUC:** BS, 1961, Micro Econ., NY Univ.; **GRAD EDUC:** JD, 1964, Taxation, Univ. of CA at Berkeley; **OTHER ACT & HONORS:** Who's Who in Amer. Law; **BUS ADD:** 501 Madison Ave., NY, NY 10022, (212)421-3311.

BELL, Robert C.——Bell Development Corp.; **PRIM RE ACT:** Developer; **BUS ADD:** 211 Commercial Ave., Pittsburgh, PA 15215, (412)782-5855.*

BELL, Robert L., Jr.——B: Aug 16, 1946, Everett, MA, *Part.*, Cook & Bell; **PRIM RE ACT:** Attorney; **SERVICES:** Full range of devel. & fin. legal services including public sector participation; **REP CLIENTS:** Melrose Savings Bank, Malden Bank, Malden Trust Co., Melrose Housing Authority, Melrose Redevl. Authority, Malden Redevl. Authority; **PROFL AFFIL & HONORS:** ABA, Mass. Bar Assn., Mass. Conveyancer's Assn.; **EDUC:** AB, 1968, Hist., Bowdoin Coll., Brunswick, ME; **GRAD EDUC:** JD, 1971, Law, Boston Univ.; **EDUC HONORS:** VP Student Gov., Athletic Awards, Best Brief/Best Speaker Moot Court Competition; **MIL SERV:** USA, Capt.; **OTHER ACT & HONORS:** Chmn Melrose Red Cross, Clerk Greater Boston Red Cross, Governing Bd., Dir. YMCA, Corp. Melrose Savings Bank; **HOME ADD:** 173 Ashland St., Melrose, MA 02176, (617)662-5847; **BUS ADD:** 70 W. Foster St., Melrose, MA 02176, (617)665-3360.

BELLA, Frank A., Jr.——B: Apr. 13, 1931, Blue Island, IL, *Broker Assoc.*, Coldwell Banker; **PRIM RE ACT:** Broker, Instructor, Consultant, Owner/Investor; **OTHER RE ACT:** Sr. Instr. for RNMI, Comm. Investment Section; Community Instr., Gov., State Univ., Park Forest South, IL; **SERVICES:** RE brokerage, investment analysis, site location assist., lecturing and seminars on RE topics; **PREV EMPLOY:** Asst. Dist. Dir. 1960 US Decennial Census; **PROFL AFFIL & HONORS:** NAR, State & Local Bds., CCIM; **EDUC:** BS, 1964, Poli. Sci., Loyola Univ., Chicago; **GRAD EDUC:** MA, 1967, Urban Studies, Loyola Univ., Chicago; **MIL SERV:** USA, Cpl.; **OTHER ACT & HONORS:** Chmn. IL Advisory Comm. to SBA 1980 Founding Bd. Member Moraine Valley Coll. 1967-1970; **HOME ADD:** 1338 Brassie Rd., Flossmoor, IL 60422, (312)799-1703; **BUS ADD:** 133 East Ogden Ave., Hinsdale, IL 60521, (312)887-5990.

BELLACH, Robin——B: Aug. 15, 1944, Canton, SD, *Pres.*, R.B. Enterprises; **PRIM RE ACT:** Consultant, Developer, Builder, Owner/Investor, Insuror; **OTHER RE ACT:** Constr. product dist., passive solar energy bldg.; **SERVICES:** Land devel. & synd.; **REP CLIENTS:** Indivs., RE brokers, contractors, bldg. suppliers; **PROFL AFFIL & HONORS:** RE securities & Synd. Inst.; **EDUC:** BS, 1966, Bus. Admin. & Econ., Univ. of SD; **OTHER ACT & HONORS:** Soaring Soc. of Amer., Aircraft Owners & Pilots Assn.; **HOME ADD:** Rt 2, Jasper, AR 72641; **BUS ADD:** Rt. 2, Jasper, AR 72641.

BELLAMY, Kenneth V.——**B:** March 28,1947, Edmonton, Alta, *Sr. V.P.- Pacific N.W.*, Daon Corp.; **PRIM RE ACT:** Developer; **SERVICES:** Devel. of Comml., Indust., Retail, and Land for Own Account.; **PREV EMPLOY:** Royal Bank of Canada 1971-1973, Trizec 1973-1975; **EDUC:** B. of Commerce, Fin. & Mktg., Univ. of Alberta; **OTHER ACT & HONORS:** Bds. of Trustees of :Downtown Seattle Dev. Assn.; Downtown Bellevue Dev. Assn.; Poncho; **BUS ADD:** 1000 10800-NE 8th, Bellevue, WA 98004, (206)453-3266.

BELLARD, Gary——*Pres.*, Bellard Realty Co.; **PRIM RE ACT:** Developer; **BUS ADD:** 64 Andrew La., Orange, CT 06477, (203)877-5997.*

BELLUCCI, Robert——**B:** July 27, 1922, Forest Hills, L.I., NY, *Pres.*, Robert Bellucci, Inc.; **PRIM RE ACT:** Broker, Consultant, Syndicator; **SERVICES:** RE Investment Counseling; Prop. Mgmt. Supervision; Joint Ventures; Synd. & Brokerage; **REP CLIENTS:** Indiv., Corp., Instnl. Investors; **EDUC:** 1947, Econ. & Poli. Sci., Amherst Coll.; **MIL SERV:** USN, Lt.; **HOME ADD:** 9195 Old Indian Hill, Cincinnati, OH 45243; **BUS ADD:** 2030 Central Trust Center, 201 E. 5th St., Cincinnati, OH 45202, (513)421-4100.

BELLUSH, John R., Jr.——**B:** Dec. 4, 1946, Morristown, NJ, *Atty. at Law*, Law; **PRIM RE ACT:** Attorney; **SERVICES:** Legal; **REP CLIENTS:** Countryside Estates, Wm. Getzoff, Denis Goddard, Norlin Corp.; **PREV EMPLOY:** Norlin Industries Inc.; **PROFL AFFIL & HONORS:** ABA, NJ Bar Assn.; **EDUC:** BA, 1968, Pol. Sci., Fairleigh Dickinson Univ./George Washington Univ.; **GRAD EDUC:** JD, 1974, Law, Fordham Univ. Law School; **OTHER ACT & HONORS:** US Peace Corp., Chile & Columbia 1968-71; **HOME ADD:** Two Hilltop Cir., Whippany, NJ 07981; **BUS ADD:** 175 South St., Morristown, NJ 07960.

BELOFSKY, Jerald Alan——**B:** Sept. 18, 1951, NY, *VP*, Kidder-Peabody Realty Corp.; **PRIM RE ACT:** Banker, Lender, Syndicator; **SERVICES:** RE investment banking; **REP CLIENTS:** Maj. US and foreign entities; **PREV EMPLOY:** Merrill Lynch, Citicorp.; **PROFL AFFIL & HONORS:** ABA, NJ & FL Bars, Amer. Express, JD; **EDUC:** BS, 1973, Journalism, Boston Univ.; **GRAD EDUC:** JD, 1976, RE Law, George Wash. Univ.; **OTHER ACT & HONORS:** Fin. Editor, Journal of Intl. Law and Econ.; **HOME ADD:** 40 Stoner Ave., Great Neck, NY 11021, (516)487-3299; **BUS ADD:** 10 Hanover Square, NY, NY 10005, (212)747-2000.

BELSHER, Harold R.——**B:** Jan. 7, 1936, Phoenix, AZ, *VP, Comml. Devel.*, Del E. Webb Realty & Mgmt. Co., Brokerage; **PRIM RE ACT:** Broker; **OTHER RE ACT:** Mort. broker; **SERVICES:** Market analysis, feasibility studies; **PROFL AFFIL & HONORS:** Past Pres., IREM Greater Phoenix Chapt., Past Pres. BOMA AZ Chapt., Bd. of Dirs. AZ Assoc. of Realtors, CPM; **EDUC:** BS, 1960, RE, AZ State Univ.; **OTHER ACT & HONORS:** Benevolent Protective Order of Elks; **HOME ADD:** 4525 E Lakeside Ln., Scottsdale, AZ 85253, (602)948-1162; **BUS ADD:** 3800 N. Central Ave., Phoenix, AZ 85012, (602)264-8011.

BELSON, Gordon A.——**B:** Nov. 4, 1911, Battle Creek, MI, *Arch.*, Sarvis Assoc. Inc.; **PRIM RE ACT:** Architect, Property Manager, Owner/Investor; **SERVICES:** Archs./engrs.; **PREV EMPLOY:** 35 yrs./ Sarvis Assoc.; **PROFL AFFIL & HONORS:** AIA, MSA; **EDUC:** BSArch, 1934, Design, Univ. of MI; **MIL SERV:** USA, T/Sgt., Bronze Star; **OTHER ACT & HONORS:** Kiwanis; **HOME ADD:** 309 Jennings Landing, Battle Creek, MI 49015, (616)965-5045; **BUS ADD:** 140 W. Michigan Ave., Battle Creek, MI 49017, (616)962-6291.

BENAROYA, Jack A.——**B:** July 11, 1921, Montgomery, AL, *Pres.*, Jack A. Benaroya Co.; **PRIM RE ACT:** Developer, Property Manager, Owner/Investor; **OTHER RE ACT:** Have devel. 5 indus. parks in the Gtr. Seattle, WA area and one in Portland, OR; **REP CLIENTS:** 600 local, rgnl. and nat. cos.; **PROFL AFFIL & HONORS:** NAIOP; **MIL SERV:** USNR, CPO; **OTHER ACT & HONORS:** Who's Who in Fin. and Industry; **HOME ADD:** 6060 52nd Ave., S, Seattle, WA 98118, (206)762-4750; **BUS ADD:** 5950 Sixth Ave. S, Suite 200, Seattle, WA 98108, (206)762-4750.

BENASSI, J. Steven——**B:** May 16, 1947, Teaneck, NJ, *VP*, Cooper-Horowitz, Inc.; **OTHER RE ACT:** Arranging of debt & equity fin. & maj. sales brokerage; **REP CLIENTS:** Maj. prop. owners & devels.; **PROFL AFFIL & HONORS:** Young Mort. Bankers Assn. of NY; **EDUC:** BS, 1971, Econ./Fin., St. Peter's Coll.; **GRAD EDUC:** MBA, 1977, Fin., Fairleigh Dickinson Univ.; Post Grad. - Wharton School of Bus., Univ. of PA; **OTHER ACT & HONORS:** Adjunct Prof., Econ./Fin. at St. Peter's Coll., Jersey City, NJ; **HOME ADD:** 224 Columbia Ave., Cliffside Pk., NJ 07010, (201)943-5444; **BUS ADD:** 342 Madison Ave., New York, NY 10073, (212)986-8400.

BENE, Andrew G.——**B:** Nov. 20, 1947, New York, NY, *Asst. VP*, Jamaica Savings Bank, New Mort. Loan; **PRIM RE ACT:** Consultant, Appraiser, Banker, Lender, Insuror, Syndicator; **PREV EMPLOY:** Royal Globe Ins. Co.; **PROFL AFFIL & HONORS:** AIREA (Advanced Candidate); **EDUC:** BA, 1969, Bus. and Econ., Univ. of Pittsburgh; **GRAD EDUC:** Grad. School of Mort. Banking - Stanford Univ.; Grad. School of Savings Banking - Brown Univ.; RE Inst. - NYU; **HOME ADD:** 24 Dale Rd., Huntington Bay, NY 11743; **BUS ADD:** 303 Merrick Rd., Lynbrook, NY 11563, (516)887-7000.

BENEDETTI, John A.——**B:** Feb. 11, 1950, Walsenburg, CO, *Broker-Owner*, Centennial RE; **PRIM RE ACT:** Broker, Owner/Investor; **SERVICES:** RE synd., brokerage, investments; **REP CLIENTS:** Wilson/Savage Devel. Co., CRI, Inc., Full serv. RE cos.; **PREV EMPLOY:** Lawyers Title Ins., 1972-77; **PROFL AFFIL & HONORS:** NAR; **EDUC:** BS/BA, 1982, Bus. Admin., Regis Coll., Denver, CO; **HOME ADD:** 665 Manhattan, Boulder, CO 80303, (303)499-3330; **BUS ADD:** 3405 Pensose Place, Suite 206 Diagonal Commons, Boulder, CO 80301, (303)444-1459.

BENENSON, Charles B.——**B:** Jan. 30, 1913, NY, *Pres.*, Benenson Realty Co.; **PRIM RE ACT:** Developer, Builder, Owner/Investor; **PROFL AFFIL & HONORS:** Pres. Citizens Tax Council; VP Nat., Realty Comm.; **EDUC:** BA, 1933, History, Yale Univ.; **OTHER ACT & HONORS:** Dir., Loews Corp.; United Cerebral Palsy; Realty Foundation of NY - Bd. of Dir.; **HOME ADD:** 630 Park Ave., NY, NY 10021, (212)737-6080; **BUS ADD:** 380 Madison Ave., NY, NY 10017.

BENJAMIN, Richard E.——**B:** Nov. 28, 1927, Ridgefield, CT, *Realtor, Appraiser-Owner*, Colonial Realty & Appraisers; **PRIM RE ACT:** Broker, Instructor, Consultant, Appraiser; **SERVICES:** All RE Serv. Including Relocation & Investment & Appraisal Consulting.; **REP CLIENTS:** IBM, Union Carbide, Homequity, Exxon; **PROFL AFFIL & HONORS:** CA-S, AACA, IAAO CRS & GRI of NAR & CAR, Consumers Research Bureau, Excellence Award, Customer Relations.; **EDUC:** High School (Ridgefield,CT), 1945; **GRAD EDUC:** Major Certificate in RE, June 2, 1980, RE & Appraisal, Univ. of CT; **MIL SERV:** USNAC, AMM, EYO,PTO; **OTHER ACT & HONORS:** Ridgefield C of C; **HOME ADD:** West Redding,, CT 06896, (203)438-0421; **BUS ADD:** 249 Danbury Road, Ridgefield, CT 06877, (203)483-0421.

BENJAMIN, Roger E.——**B:** Mar. 30, 1925, NY, NY, *Pres.*, M.H. Hausman Co.; **PRIM RE ACT:** Broker, Developer, Property Manager; **OTHER RE ACT:** Prop. Mgr. of Shopping Centers; **SERVICES:** Mgmt., leasing, devel.; **PROFL AFFIL & HONORS:** ICSC, Former Tr. and State Dir.; **EDUC:** BA, 1946, Pol. Sci., Williams Coll.; **OTHER ACT & HONORS:** Oakwood Ctry. Club; **HOME ADD:** 2951 Drummond Rd., Shaker Hts., OH 44120, (216)751-9877; **BUS ADD:** 23200 Chagrin Blvd., Beachwood, OH 44122, (216)464-5900.

BENKE, Donald R.——**B:** Apr. 26, 1943, Drayton, ND, *Mgr. Prop. & Sales Taxes*, Northern Telecom Inc., Electronic Office Systems; **PRIM RE ACT:** Property Manager; **OTHER RE ACT:** Tax Mgr.; **PROFL AFFIL & HONORS:** Inst. of Prop. Taxation, Tax Exec. Inst., Natl. Assn. Accountants; **EDUC:** BS, 1968, Acctg. & Bus. Admin., Univ. of ND; **GRAD EDUC:** 1973, Tax, Univ. of MN; **MIL SERV:** USA, S-4, Soldier Month Award; **OTHER ACT & HONORS:** Dir. 1979-1980, 1980-1981 Nat. Assn. of Accountants; **HOME ADD:** 3015 Garland Ln., Plymouth, MN 55447, (612)473-9606; **BUS ADD:** PO Box 1222, Minneapolis, MN 55440, (612)932-8288.

BENKERT, Arthur C.——**B:** May 20, 1911, Monroe, WI, *Partner*, Benkert, Spielman, Asmus & Deininger; **PRIM RE ACT:** Attorney; **REP CLIENTS:** Farmers Home Admin. (Green Cty., WI); **PROFL AFFIL & HONORS:** Green Cty. (WI) Bar Assn., WI Bar Assn., ABA, Past Pres., Green Cty. Bar Assn.; **EDUC:** BA, 1934, Commerce, Univ. of WI; **GRAD EDUC:** LLB, 1936, Law, Univ. of WI; **EDUC HONORS:** Phi Kappa Phi, Iron Cross; **MIL SERV:** Army 1945-1946; **OTHER ACT & HONORS:** City Atty., Monroe, WI 1939-1959; Kiwanis Club, Monroe, WI, Monroe Ctry. Club, Mason; **HOME ADD:** 1403 17th Ave., Monroe, WI, 53566, (608)325-3598; **BUS ADD:** PO Box 89, Monroe, WI 53566, (608)325-7188.

BENKERT, Kyle G.——**B:** June 17, 1931, Chicago, IL, *Princ.*, Kyle Benkert Assoc.; **PRIM RE ACT:** Architect, Developer, Builder, Owner/Investor; **SERVICES:** Land & Bldg. programming; design and const.; **REP CLIENTS:** Joint Venture Partners, Synds.; **PREV EMPLOY:** City of Cbicago, Dept. of City Planning 1961-66; **PROFL AFFIL & HONORS:** NCARB; **EDUC:** AB, 1953, City Planning, Harvard; **GRAD EDUC:** BArch, MArch, MCP, 1960 & 1961, Arch., City Planning, Univ. of PA; **EDUC HONORS:** Cum Laude; **MIL SERV:** USCG, SM1; **OTHER ACT & HONORS:** Arts Club - Chicago; Red Fox C.C., Tryon, NC; Cover Story Proffessional Builder Feb. 1971; **HOME ADD:** PO Box 1, Columbus, NC 28722,

(704)894-3132; **BUS ADD:** PO Box 1, Columbus, NC 28722, (704)894-3132.

BENN, Bernard L.——B: Oct. 24, 1942, Plainfield, NJ, *Arch.*, Benn/Metz Architects; **PRIM RE ACT:** Architect, Developer; **OTHER RE ACT:** Urban Design & Planning; **SERVICES:** Arch., Site Planning, Urban Design, Rehab., Energy Design; **REP CLIENTS:** Inst., Comml., Indus. and Indiv. Owners; **PROFL AFFIL & HONORS:** AIA; **EDUC:** BArch, 1965, Arch., Pratt Inst.; **GRAD EDUC:** MArch., 1968, Urban Design, Harvard Univ. Grad. Schl. of Design; **EDUC HONORS:** Dean's Scholar; **HOME ADD:** Union Village, VT 05043, (802)649-1271; **BUS ADD:** 25 Lebanon St., Hanover, NH 03755, (603)643-5058.

BENNETT, Charles Kirby——B: Oct. 19, 1947, Marietta, OH, *Admin. Officer*, Fifth Third Bank, Trust Div.; **PRIM RE ACT:** Attorney, Banker; **OTHER RE ACT:** Trust services; **PROFL AFFIL & HONORS:** Admitted to OH Bar, 1973; Admitted to MI Bar, 1979, Nat. Merit Scholar; **EDUC:** BA, 1969, Hist., Coll. of Wooster; **GRAD EDUC:** JD, 1973, Law, OH State Univ.; **OTHER ACT & HONORS:** MENSA; **HOME ADD:** 2988 Wardall Ave., Cincinnati, OH 45211, (513)662-5936; **BUS ADD:** Dept. 00850, Cincinnati, OH 45263, (513)579-5237.

BENNETT, Douglas Marshall——B: Sept. 15, 1947, Schenectady, NY, *Mgr. Corp. Contracts/Mktg.*, Turner Constr. Co.; **OTHER RE ACT:** Construction; **SERVICES:** Gen. contracting, const. mgmt.; **REP CLIENTS:** Many nat. owners and devels.; **PREV EMPLOY:** 1974 Wallace Floyd Ellenzweig, Moore, Arch. & Planners; Cambridge, MA 1970-74; Active Duty U.S. Navy, Asst. Resident Officer in charge of Const. Boston Naval Shipyard 1971-75, Instrc. (Part time) Boston Arch. Ctr.; **PROFL AFFIL & HONORS:** Soc. for Mktg. Profl. Servs.; NACORE; **EDUC:** BArch., 1970, Arch., Sch. of Design, NC State Univ., Raleigh, NC; **GRAD EDUC:** MBA, 1976, Bus., Harvard Grad. Sch. of Bus.; **EDUC HONORS:** Alpha Chi Omega Arch. Award for Serv.; **MIL SERV:** USN Res., Lt. JG(CEC); **OTHER ACT & HONORS:** Harvard Bus. Sch. Club of NYC; Harvard Club of NYC; **HOME ADD:** 345 E 86th St., 20-B, NY, NY 10028, (212)289-5970; **BUS ADD:** 633 Third Ave., NY, NY 10017, (212)878-0806.

BENNETT, Harry——B: May 5, 1918, Greenwich, CT, *Pres.*, Harry Bennett & Assoc., Inc.; **PRIM RE ACT:** Broker, Consultant, Developer, Builder, Owner/Investor; **PROFL AFFIL & HONORS:** Nat., Stamford & CT Bds. of Realtors; **EDUC:** BBA, 1940, Bus., NY Univ.; **MIL SERV:** USAF, Capt.; **OTHER ACT & HONORS:** Pres. Stamford Bd. of Realtors, 1963; State Dir. CT Bd. of Realtors; **HOME ADD:** 43 Bentwood Dr., Stamford, CT 06903, (203)322-0000; **BUS ADD:** 828 High Ridge Rd., Stamford, CT 06905, (203)322-1684.

BENNETT, Mark E.——B: Dec. 21, 1953, Topeka, KS, *Pres.*, O.R. Bennett, Inc.; **PRIM RE ACT:** Attorney, Developer, Lender, Owner/Investor, Property Manager, Syndicator; **PREV EMPLOY:** Coopers & Lybrand, Arthur Young & Co.; **PROFL AFFIL & HONORS:** AICPA, TX Soc. of CPA's, ABA, State Bar of TX, Dallas Bar Assn., CPA, JD; **EDUC:** BS, 1975, Acctg., Univ of KS; **GRAD EDUC:** JD, 1980, Univ. of KS; **HOME ADD:** 11301 Ferndale, Dallas, TX 75238, (214)341-4316; **BUS ADD:** 11301 Ferndale, Dallas, TX 75238, (214)341-4316.

BENNETT, R.H.——*Area Mgr.*, ABKO Properties, Inc.; **PRIM RE ACT:** Broker, Property Manager; **OTHER RE ACT:** Negotiator; **BUS ADD:** 25 Viscount Rd., Longmeadow, MA 01106, (413)567-3015.

BENNETT, Robert——B: Dec. 30, 1943, Newgulf, TX, *Prin.*, Robert Bennett Solar Arch. & Engr.; **PRIM RE ACT:** Architect, Engineer; **SERVICES:** Cost-efficient solar arch. & engr.; **PREV EMPLOY:** Chief Engr. - Seltzer Org.; **PROFL AFFIL & HONORS:** AIA, NSPE, ASHRAE, ISES, AS/ISES, MASEA; **EDUC:** BS, 1966, ME, Columbia Univ./Drexel Univ.; BS, 1977, Arch., Drexel Univ.; **GRAD EDUC:** MS, 1968, Space Physics, Rice Univ.; **EDUC HONORS:** 4 yr. schol., 2 yr. Fellowship; **OTHER ACT & HONORS:** Founder & Chairperson of Mid-Atlantic Solar Energy Assn.; **HOME ADD:** 6 Snowden Rd., Bala Cynwyd, PA 19004, (215)667-7365; **BUS ADD:** 6 Snowden Rd., Bala Cynwyd, PA 19004, (215)667-7365.

BENNETT, Robert F.——B: Apr. 10, 1935, Austell, GA, *Pres./CEO*, Century 21 Bennett Realty; **PRIM RE ACT:** Broker, Consultant, Builder; **OTHER RE ACT:** Pharmacist; **SERVICES:** Resid. sales, listings, prop. mgmt.; **REP CLIENTS:** Comml. sales and listings; **PREV EMPLOY:** USAF, 23 years; **PROFL AFFIL & HONORS:** NAR, CAR, SBOR, APHA, GRI, CRB; **EDUC:** BS, 1962, Pharmacy, Mercer Univ.; **GRAD EDUC:** Ed.M, 1973, Educ., Wayne State Univ.; **MIL SERV:** USAF, Capt., retd.; **HOME ADD:** Route 2 Box 420, Richmond Hill, GA 31324, (912)233-0198; **BUS ADD:** 7373 Hodgson Memorial Dr., Savannah, GA 31406, (800)841-7010.

BENOVENGO, Edward A, Jr.——B: Nov. 26, 1950, Newark, NJ, *Architect*; **PRIM RE ACT:** Architect; **SERVICES:** Design services, energy analysis, expert witness testimony; **REP CLIENTS:** Govt. agencies, Comml. Dev., Corp. Grps.; **PREV EMPLOY:** Corp. & speculative comml. dev., Health care facilities, Energy consultant to DOE, Const. & Energy consultant to HUD; **PROFL AFFIL & HONORS:** AIA, ISES, NCARB; **EDUC:** BS, 1971, Arch. Tech, NY Inst. Tech.; **GRAD EDUC:** MArch, 1973, Arch, Univ. of OK; **HOME ADD:** 1270 Robinson Ter, Union Twsp, NJ, (201)687-6755; **BUS ADD:** 400 Park Ave., 9th Fl, NY, NY, (212)759-2121.

BENSON, Alfred M.——B: Jan. 21, 1941, NY, *Partner*, Burke, Hansen & Homan, Inc., Burke, Hansen, Homan & Klafter; **PRIM RE ACT:** Consultant, Appraiser; **SERVICES:** Appraisal & consultation: purchase, loan, litigation, merger, etc.; **REP CLIENTS:** Federal, state, & local govts.; major local attys. & devels.; major corps.; investors; lenders; **PREV EMPLOY:** Partner, Klafter & Benson; VP Seamen's Bank for Savings,, NY; **PROFL AFFIL & HONORS:** MAI (Sec., AZ Chap.); SRPA (VP Tucson Chap.); Tucson Bd. of Realtors, MAI; SRPA; Member Governing Council AIREA, 1973, certified in prof. ed. program AIREA; **EDUC:** BA, 1963, Econ., Brown Univ. & C.W. Post Coll.; **OTHER ACT & HONORS:** Qualified as expert witness in State & Fed. Cts.; **HOME ADD:** 3232 N. Placita Brazos, Tucson, AZ 85715, (602)886-6124; **BUS ADD:** 6245 E. Broadway, Suite 690, Tucson, AZ 85711, (602)790-8555.

BENSON, Andy——*RE Mgr.*, Pertec Computer; **PRIM RE ACT:** Property Manager; **BUS ADD:** 12910 Culver Blvd., Los Angeles, CA 90066, (213)642-4601.*

BENSON, John J.——*Exec. Dir. & Sec.*, Construction Industry Manufacturers Association; **OTHER RE ACT:** Professional Assn. Admin.; **BUS ADD:** Marine Plaza, Suite 1700, 111 E. Wisconsin Ave., Milwaukee, WI 53202, (414)272-0943.*

BENSON, Stuart A.——B: Mar. 12, 1954, NYC, *Pres.*, Consultant Prop. Mgmt. & Investors, Inc.; **PRIM RE ACT:** Broker, Consultant, Developer, Builder, Owner/Investor, Property Manager, Syndicator; **SERVICES:** Synd. of income RE, prop. mgmt.; **REP CLIENTS:** Indiv. & corp. investors; **PREV EMPLOY:** Asst. to the Chmn. LeFrak Org., 97-77 Queens Blvd., Rego Park, NY; **PROFL AFFIL & HONORS:** ICSC, RE Bd. of NY, Apt. Owners & Mgrs. of Atlanta, ICSC, NYU Delegate to SCUSA; **EDUC:** BA, 1974, Hist., NYU; **EDUC HONORS:** NYU Delegate to SCUSA; **OTHER ACT & HONORS:** Seawane Club, UJA; **HOME ADD:** 26 Dell Dr., E Rockaway, NY, (516)569-4809; **BUS ADD:** 555 Chestnut St., Cedarhurst, NY 11516, (516)569-6970.

BENSON, Ted——B: Apr. 29, 1931, Moorcroft, WY, *Assoc. Broker*, Hoffman & Assoc., Ranch & Comml.; **PRIM RE ACT:** Broker, Consultant, Appraiser; **SERVICES:** Seller or Buyers agent; Investment Counseling; Appraisal; **REP CLIENTS:** Indiv. & Inst. Ranch and Resort Comml. Investors; **PREV EMPLOY:** US Army 1953-1976; **PROFL AFFIL & HONORS:** FLI, NAR, Teton Cty. Bd. Realtors, GRI; **EDUC:** BS, 1953, Bus. Admin., Univ. of WY; **MIL SERV:** USA, Lt. Col.; **HOME ADD:** P.O. Box 1072, Jackson, WY 83001, (307)733-6773; **BUS ADD:** PO Box 3729, Jackson, WY 83001, (307)733-3436.

BENTEL, Dr. Frederick R.——B: Jan. 2, 1928, NY, *Part.*, Bentel and Bentel, Arch., AIA; **PRIM RE ACT:** Architect, Instructor, Consultant, Developer, Builder, Owner/Investor; **OTHER RE ACT:** Prof., Ass't. Dir. Center for Architecture, N.Y. Inst. of Tech.; **SERVICES:** Site selection, programming, design, const.; **REP CLIENTS:** Thompson Aircraft Tires, Inc., General Electric Supply, Tesstoria Realty Corp., Cobblestone Enterprises, Azzarone Realty Co.; **PROFL AFFIL & HONORS:** AIA, NYSAA, NY Soc. of Arch., Fellow AIA, Fulbright Fellow, Austria; **EDUC:** BArch, 1949, Pratt Inst.; **GRAD EDUC:** MArch, 1950, Urban Design, MIT; **EDUC HONORS:** AIA Gold Medal, Grad. Fellowship; Dr. of Arch. Technische Hochschule-Graz, Austria; **MIL SERV:** Signal Corps, Cpl.; **OTHER ACT & HONORS:** Planning Advisory Bd., Town of Oyster Bay, Long Island; Historic Landmarks, Town of Oyster Bay, Long Island; **BUS ADD:** 22 Buckram Rd., Locust Valley, NY 11560, (516)676-2880.

BENTELE, Raymond E.——B: Apr. 21, 1953, NY, NY, *Partner*, Nebyn Peterson Assoc.; **PRIM RE ACT:** Consultant; **OTHER RE ACT:** Mktg. research; planning spec.; **SERVICES:** Creating & implementing mktg. programs for RE; **REP CLIENTS:** Corps. and fin. insts.; **PROFL AFFIL & HONORS:** RE Bd. of NY; **EDUC:** BArch., 1975, Arch. Planning; **HOME ADD:** 2025 Continental Ave., Bronx, NY 10461, (212)822-2681; **BUS ADD:** 15 E. 40th St., NY, NY 19916, (212)684-0086.

BENTKOWSKI, John A.——**B:** Feb. 4, 1926, Buffalo, NY, *RE Analyst/Mgr., Investment and Non-Investment,* Cornell Univ., RE Dept.; **PRIM RE ACT:** Consultant, Appraiser, Property Manager; **SERVICES:** Consultant, analyst, appraiser, RE gift devel.; **REP CLIENTS:** Educ. inst. and other tax-exempt institutions (coll., univs., founds., medical facilities); **PREV EMPLOY:** Indus. plant engr.; rental agent and start up mgr.; retirement home; RE broker; **PROFL AFFIL & HONORS:** Nat. Assn. of Corp. RE Execs.; AIREA; NY State Land Title Assn.; **EDUC:** BS, 1955, Indus. Educ., Sci., SUNY at Buffalo; **GRAD EDUC:** MS, 1957, Econ., Physics, Cornell Univ.; **EDUC HONORS:** Nat. Sci. Found. Research Fellowship; **MIL SERV:** USN; Seaman; **OTHER ACT & HONORS:** Ithaca Bd. of Zoning Appeals - 1966-1969; **HOME ADD:** 108 Treva Ave., Ithaca, NY 14850, (607)273-0215; **BUS ADD:** P O Box 611, Ithaca, NY 14850, (607)256-5341.

BENTLEY, Robert Clyde——**B:** July 5, 1926, Livermore, CA, *Arch.,* Bentley Architect; **PRIM RE ACT:** Architect, Instructor, Builder, Property Manager, Owner/Investor; **OTHER RE ACT:** Realtor, planner, genl. contractor, solar contractor; **SERVICES:** Arch., planning, RE, rentals, condos, estimates mgmt., const.; **REP CLIENTS:** Tiki Apt.; Camino Cul-De-Sac, Vacavaille, CA; Geodesic Dome; Bay Area Rapid Transit Electrical Quantity Take-Off; **PREV EMPLOY:** Inst. in School of Arch. at Univ. of CA; **PROFL AFFIL & HONORS:** AIA; San Jose RE Bd., SF C of C Code Comm.; **EDUC:** BArch, 1950, Arch., School of Arch., Univ. of CA; **EDUC HONORS:** Arch. lic. C-2672, Co-author, 'Planning for Business'; **MIL SERV:** USN Res.; Sea Bees, Lt. j.g., Civ. Engr., South Pacific War Zone twice; **OTHER ACT & HONORS:** The Asst. City Planner of Yakima WA 1959; Mechanics Inst. of SF; Phi Delta Theta Frat.; Who's Who in CA; Co owner of 16 apts., house, houseboat in Sausalito & 3 lots; **HOME ADD:** 595 Jay St., Los Altos, CA 94022, (415)948-9593; **BUS ADD:** 745 Distel Dr., Los Altos, CA 94022, (415)967-3500.

BENTLEY, Upshaw C., Jr.——**B:** Oct. 16, 1924, Greenville, SC, *Partner,* Fortson, Bentley & Griffin; **PRIM RE ACT:** Attorney; **SERVICES:** Title exam; loan closing; comd. dec.; **REP CLIENTS:** Clarke Fed. S & L; 1st Investors Mort. Co.; Equitable Relocation; 1st Nat. Bank of Athens; **PROFL AFFIL & HONORS:** College of Mort. Attys.; **EDUC:** BBA, 1947, Univ. of GA; **GRAD EDUC:** LLB, 1949, Univ. of GA; **EDUC HONORS:** Phi Delta Phi; **MIL SERV:** USAAF; Capt.; **OTHER ACT & HONORS:** Mayor, City of Athens, GA (1976-79); **HOME ADD:** 525 Riverview Rd., Athens, GA; **BUS ADD:** P.O. Box 1744, Athens, GA 30613, (404)548-1151.

BENTON, Alvin O.——**B:** Nov. 24, 1939, Monticello, NY, *VP, Mgr. Appraisal Servs.,* Coldwell Banker; **PRIM RE ACT:** Consultant, Appraiser; **SERVICES:** Full range of RE consultation, counseling, appraising; **REP CLIENTS:** Instl., devels., attys., accts., indivs.; **PREV EMPLOY:** A.O. Benton Agency, Pomeroy Appraisal Agency, Diversified Advisors, Citizen & Southern Nat. Bank RE; **PROFL AFFIL & HONORS:** AIREA, SREA, Atlanta RE Bd., MAI, SRPA; **EDUC:** BS, 1970, RE, Syracuse Univ.; **MIL SERV:** USA, SP-4; **HOME ADD:** 227 Rockwood Ct., Marietta, GA 30067, (404)973-2449; **BUS ADD:** 229 Peachtree St., NE, Ste., 1401, Atlanta, GA 30303, (404)656-1410.

BENTON, Joseph C.——**B:** July 5, 1952, W Liberty, KY, *Corp. Atty.,* Ashland Oil, Inc., Corp. Law Dept.; **PRIM RE ACT:** Attorney; **SERVICES:** Legal; **PROFL AFFIL & HONORS:** ABA, KY Bar Assn., Boyd Cty. Bar Assn.; **EDUC:** BA, 1975, Pol. Sci., Pre Law, Morehead State Univ.; **GRAD EDUC:** JD, 1979, Law, Chase Coll. of Law; **OTHER ACT & HONORS:** Pres. Bd. of Dirs., Boys Home; **HOME ADD:** Rt. 2, Box 101, Catlettsburg, KY 41129, (606)739-6493; **BUS ADD:** PO Box 391, Ashland, KY 41101, (606)329-4235.

BENTON, Steven P.——**B:** Mar. 5, 1953, Salt Lake City, UT, *Pres.,* Benton Investment Co.; **PRIM RE ACT:** Broker, Owner/Investor, Property Manager; **SERVICES:** RE brokerage, prop. mgmt.; **REP CLIENTS:** Indiv. and instn. investors in comml. RE; **PROFL AFFIL & HONORS:** Salt Lake Bd. of Realtors; NAR; RNMI, CCIM Candidate; **EDUC:** BS, 1975, Fin. RE, Univ. of UT; **OTHER ACT & HONORS:** U.S. C of C; **HOME ADD:** POB 8307, Salt Lake City, UT 84108, (801)583-7849; **BUS ADD:** POB 8307, Salt Lake City, UT 84108, (801)485-0666.

BENZ, Gregory P.——**B:** Mar. 7, 1946, NYC, *Part.,* HSR Assoc., Inc., Madison Div.; **PRIM RE ACT:** Architect; **PREV EMPLOY:** Gregory P. Benz, Arch. 1975-1977; **PROFL AFFIL & HONORS:** AIA; SMPS; **EDUC:** BArch, 1969, Design, Clemson Univ.; **HOME ADD:** Sun Prairie, WI 53704; **BUS ADD:** 2424 American Lane, Madison, WI 53704, (608)244-1341.

BERARDO, William J.——**B:** Dec. 21, 1944, Bay City MI, *Atty.;* **PRIM RE ACT:** Attorney; **SERVICES:** Research, counseling, litigation; **PROFL AFFIL & HONORS:** Real prop. law sect., State Bar of MI; ABA; Detroit Bar Assn.; Oakland Co. Bar Assn.; **EDUC:** BA, 1971, Soc. Sci., MI State Univ.; **GRAD EDUC:** JD, 1979, Univ. of Detroit, School of Law; **EDUC HONORS:** Cum Laude; **MIL SERV:** US Army; SP4; **OTHER ACT & HONORS:** Wayne Cty. Civic League; Huntington Woods Men's Club; **HOME ADD:** 13129 W Eleven Mile, Huntington Woods, MI 48070, (313)399-0757; **BUS ADD:** 2828 David Stott Bldg., Detroit, MI 48226, (313)961-5529.

BERENSON, David M., Esq.——**B:** Apr. 5, 1910, New York, NY, David M. Berenson, Esq.; **PRIM RE ACT:** Attorney; **SERVICES:** Legal; **PREV EMPLOY:** One of the attorneys of record for Marine Midland Bank, N.A. for 40 yrs.; **PROFL AFFIL & HONORS:** Nat. Panel of Arbitrators, Amer. Arbitration Assn.; ABA, Nassau Cty., NY State, and Intl. Bar Assns.; NY Cty. Lawyers Assn.; (Member, Civil Rights Comm. 1955-60); Amer. Judicature Soc.; Fed. Bar Council; Assn. of Trial Lawyers of Amer.; **EDUC:** PhB, 1932, Econ. and Philosophy, Brown Univ.; JD, 1935, Law, Harvard Univ.; **MIL SERV:** USAF; First Lt.; **OTHER ACT & HONORS:** B'nai B'rith, AF&AM; **HOME ADD:** 20 Whitby Ct., Rockville Centre, NY 11570, (516)678-5192; **BUS ADD:** 265 Sunrise Hwy., Rockville Centre, NY 11570, (516)678-5192.

BERENTSON, David——**B:** Jan. 5, 1944, Portland, OR, *Partner,* Berentson & Mead, Attys. at Law; **PRIM RE ACT:** Attorney; **SERVICES:** Negotiating and drafting conveyances, contracts & trades; **PROFL AFFIL & HONORS:** OR State Bar and ABA Real Prop., Probate and Trust Div. (Comm. member since 1979); **EDUC:** BA, 1966, Chem./Hist., St. Olaf Coll.; **GRAD EDUC:** JD, 1973, Northwestern School of Law at Lewis & Clark Coll.; **MIL SERV:** USMC, Capt., Decorations; **OTHER ACT & HONORS:** Rotary Club of Lake Oswego (past Pres.); **HOME ADD:** 816 Fifth, Lake Oswego, OR 97034, (503)636-1384; **BUS ADD:** 10175 SW Barbur Blvd., Suite 208, Portland, OR 97219, (503)246-8881.

BERG, James M.——**B:** June 8, 1943, Seattle, WA, *Part., Atty. at Law,* Dooley, Anderson, Berg & Pardini; **PRIM RE ACT:** Attorney; **SERVICES:** Consultation RE zoning, land use, eminent domain, synd., litigation, constr., devel., exchanges, transactions & investments.; **REP CLIENTS:** The Innisfree Cos., TRI Realtors, Amfac, RE Charles Schwab & Co., Inc., Dome Constr. Co., Realty Empire Corp.; **PROFL AFFIL & HONORS:** CA State Bar, RE Comm., San Francisco State Bar, RE Comm.; **EDUC:** BA, 1965, Econ., Univ. of WA; **GRAD EDUC:** JD, 1970, Law, Univ. of CA, Hastings Coll. of Law; **EDUC HONORS:** Granted Membership in *Fir Tree* for bringing nat. recognition to Univ. of WA, Purple Shield, Oval Club & scholastic activities Hons., Pres. Inter-Frat. Council, Juris Doctor, Ford Foundation Research Scholarship, Grad. School. of Poli. Sci., Univ. of WA; **MIL SERV:** Judge Adv., Army, Cen.; **OTHER ACT & HONORS:** Olympic Club, Commonwealth Club, WA State Legislature, Admin. Asst., Trans. Comm., Olympia; **HOME ADD:** 16 Cliff Rd., Belvedere, CA 94920; **BUS ADD:** 600 Montgomery St., 33rd Fl., Transamer. Pyramid, San Francisco, CA 94111, (415)986-8000.

BERG, Julius H.——**B:** June 19, 1925, St. Louis, MO, *Atty. at Law, Pres.,* Julius H. Berg, P.C.; **PRIM RE ACT:** Attorney; **SERVICES:** Legal servs.; **REP CLIENTS:** Mort. banker, RE Devel.; **PROFL AFFIL & HONORS:** ABA,(real prop sect.), Metropolitan Bar Assn. of St. Louis; **EDUC:** BS, 1947, Acctg., bus. admin., St. Louis Univ.; **GRAD EDUC:** LLB, 1950, Harvard Law School; **EDUC HONORS:** Summa Cum Laude; **MIL SERV:** US Army, Sgt.; **HOME ADD:** 83 Stoneyside Ln., Olivette, MO 63132, (314)993-5565; **BUS ADD:** 7777 Bonhomme, Clayton, MO 63105, (314)721-2222.

BERGE, Gail B.——**B:** Jan. 14, 1919, Niobrara, NE, *Co-Owner/Sec./Treas.,* Gail B. Berge Realty, Inc.; **PRIM RE ACT:** Broker; **SERVICES:** Listing and sales of resid. prop.; **PREV EMPLOY:** Mobile Home Indus. (Sales and Mfrg.), 1946-1968; **PROFL AFFIL & HONORS:** Member, Profl. RE Brokers Assn.; Member, NAR and CA Assn. of Realtors, GRI; CRS; **EDUC:** 130 hrs., Univ. of NE/LaSalle Ext. Univ.; **MIL SERV:** USAF, 1st Lt., DFC, 3 Air Medals; **OTHER ACT & HONORS:** BPOE, 33 yrs.; **HOME ADD:** 5555 Canyon Crest Dr. 2-C, Riverside, CA 92507, (714)684-6787; **BUS ADD:** 4141 Central Ave., Riverside, CA 92506, (714)684-6611.

BERGE, Palmer——**B:** July 29, 1918, Hoquiam, WA, *Pres.,* Palmer Berge Co.; **PRIM RE ACT:** Broker, Instructor, Consultant; **OTHER RE ACT:** RE & RE Fin. Computer Software; **SERVICES:** Brokerage Large Comml.-Investment, Industrial Prop.; **REP CLIENTS:** Lenders & Indiv. or Instnl. Investors; **PROFL AFFIL & HONORS:** NAR; RNMI, CCIM Snider Trophy (Exchange of the Year) 1976, Chmn., C.I. Div. RNMI 1977; **HOME ADD:** 7802 89th Pl. SE, Mercer Island, WA 98040, (206)232-8126; **BUS ADD:** 1200 Westlake Ave. N, Seattle, WA 98109, (206)284-7610.

BERGEN, Bruce Westbrook——**B:** Jan 2, 1942, NY, NY, *Part.*, Verrill & Dana, York Cty. Office; **PRIM RE ACT:** Attorney; **SERVICES:** Title searches, document prep., negotiations, purchase & sale agreements, title ins.; **REP CLIENTS:** ME Savings Bank, Casco B&T Co., Canal Nat. Bank, Robert P. Levesque, Sr., builder, Dame & Reaside, builders; **PROFL AFFIL & HONORS:** York Cty., Cumberland Cty., State of ME & Amer. Bar Assns. Member RE & Probate Sect., ABA; **EDUC:** Cornell Univ., 1964, Gen. agric., Agriculture; **GRAD EDUC:** JD, 1970, Law, Boston Univ.; **OTHER ACT & HONORS:** Sch. Bd., Kennebunk, ME, 2 yrs.; Dir. Brick Store Museum; Tr. S. Congregational Church; Sec. Treas. NE Belted Galloway Assn.; Dir. Native Resource Devel. Inc.; Chmn. York Cty. Bar Assn.; Registry of Deeds Comm.; Pres. Mousam River Protection Assn.; **HOME ADD:** Winnow Hill Farm, RFD 1, Kennebunk, ME 04043, (207)985-3958; **BUS ADD:** Depot Rd., Alfred, ME 04002, (207)324-7700.

BERGENSEN, Harry J.——*Exec. VP/COO*, Plaza Financial Corp.; **PRIM RE ACT:** Consultant, Developer, Builder, Owner/Investor, Property Manager; **SERVICES:** Land planning, land devel., RE fin. servs.; **BUS ADD:** 4950 Capital Bank Plaza, Houston, TX 77002, (713)654-4950.

BERGER, Albert I.——**B:** Oct. 18, 1937, NY, *Sr. VP*, Helmsley-Spear, Inc.; **PRIM RE ACT:** Broker, Consultant, Developer; **SERVICES:** Consulting, Devel., Brokerage; **REP CLIENTS:** Instns, MAS Intl. Corps.; **PROFL AFFIL & HONORS:** NACORE, IREBA; **EDUC:** BS, 1959, Econ. and Fin., NY Univ.; **EDUC HONORS:** Econ. Hon. Soc.; **MIL SERV:** USA, Med. Corp.; **OTHER ACT & HONORS:** Wrote articles on leasing, lectured on RE; **HOME ADD:** 141-22 68th Dr., Kew Garden Hills, NY 11367, (212)261-5116; **BUS ADD:** 150 Meadowlands Pkwy., Secaucus, NJ 07094, (201)864-4200.

BERGER, Bruce——**B:** June 10, 1939, Omaha, NE, *Pres.*, United States Land Resources, Inc.; **PRIM RE ACT:** Attorney, Developer, Owner/Investor, Syndicator; **PROFL AFFIL & HONORS:** ABA, Atty. at Law; CPA; **EDUC:** BSE, 1961, Acctg., Univ. of PA, Wharton School of Fin. & Commerce; **GRAD EDUC:** JD, 1964, Tax Law, Harvard Law School; **HOME ADD:** 4490 Upton St., Wash., DC 20016, (202)363-7664; **BUS ADD:** 1709 N St., MW, Washington, DC 20036, (202)293-1848.

BERGER, Donald E.——**B:** May 15, 1935, Baltimore, MD, *VP*, Planned Devel. Corp.; **PRIM RE ACT:** Attorney, Developer; **PREV EMPLOY:** Leonard L. Farber Co.; **PROFL AFFIL & HONORS:** MD Bar, State Comm. Chmn. FL State Action Comm., ICSC; Task Force Leader, Ft. Lauderdale C of C; **EDUC:** BA, 1957, Pol. Sci., Hist., Univ. of MD; **GRAD EDUC:** LLB, 1961, Univ. of MD; **OTHER ACT & HONORS:** Board of Trustees, Temple Beth EL of Boca Raton, Treasurer, South County Jewish Federation.; **HOME ADD:** 650 SW Elm Tree Ln., Boca Raton, FL 33432, (305)395-8988; **BUS ADD:** 3000 NE 30th Pl., Suite 500, Ft. Lauderdale, FL 33306, (305)562-2002.

BERGER, Herman M.——*VP and Treas.*, Planned Development Corp.; **PRIM RE ACT:** Developer, Builder, Owner/Investor, Property Manager; **EDUC:** BBA, 1957, Factory Mgmt., Baruch Sch. of Bus. Admin., City College of NY; **GRAD EDUC:** MBA, 1960, Columbia Univ.; **EDUC HONORS:** Mgmt. and Acctg. Honor Soc.; **BUS ADD:** 1440 Brickell Ave., Miami, FL 33131, (305)358-4100.

BERGER, Martin S.——**B:** June 19, 1930, NYC, NY, *Pres.*, Robert Martin Co.; **PRIM RE ACT:** Developer, Builder; **SERVICES:** RE devel. & constr.; **PROFL AFFIL & HONORS:** Past Pres. Builders Inst. of Westchester & Putnam Ctys. and Putnam Cty. Homebuilders Assn, Past Chmn. of Bd., Builders Inst. of Westchester & Putnam Ctys. and Joint Indus. Council of Labor and Mgmt.; Pres., Constr. Indus. Council; Chmn. of the Bd., Tremont S&L Assn., –130,000,000 Mutual Inst.; Chmn. Chemical Bank Westchester/Rockland Adv. Bd.; Member Westchester Cty. Parkway Commn.; Member Nat. Panel of the Amer. Arbitration Assn.; **EDUC:** BS, 1952, NY Univ.; **MIL SERV:** USAF, S/Sgt.; **OTHER ACT & HONORS:** Commnr., Westchester Cty. Pkwy Commn., 1980 to present; Past Pres., Local Civic Assn.; Past Dir. Fairview-Greenburgh Comm. Ctr.; Past Gov. Brae Burn Ctry. Club; Past Dir. Solomon Schechter Sch.; Past Tr., Hackley Sch.; Sponsor Young Men's Div. of Albert Einstein Coll. of Med.; Member Hebrew Inst. of White Plains; Member Westchester Cabinet & Gr. NY Bd. of Govs., State of Israel Bonds; Dir. Westchester Jewish Conference; Dir. Westchester Rgn. of Nat. Conf. of Christians and Jews; Chmn. Westchester Cty. Holocaust Comm.; **HOME ADD:** 27 Hawthorne Way, Hartsdale, NY 10530; **BUS ADD:** 101 Exec. Blvd., Elmsford, NY 10523, (914)592-4800.

BERGER, Randall Craig——**B:** May 18, 1955, Oakland, CA, *Gen. Mgr.*, Blackfield Enterprises; **PRIM RE ACT:** Broker, Consultant, Developer, Lender, Owner/Investor, Property Manager, Syndicator; **OTHER RE ACT:** Gen. Partner United Investors Fund; **PREV EMPLOY:** Public Acctg., comml. RE brokerage - Marcus & Millichap, Inc., S.F. CA; **PROFL AFFIL & HONORS:** CA RE Broker; **EDUC:** BA Econ., 1977, Acctg., UCLA; **EDUC HONORS:** Dean's List, Honors Program; **OTHER ACT & HONORS:** Oakland Resid. Rent Arbitration Bd. 9/80-9/81; 1980 member-Outstanding Young Men of Amer.; **HOME ADD:** 5610 Snake Road, Oakland, CA 94611, (415)482-5610; **BUS ADD:** 612 Howard St., San Francisco, CA 94105.

BERGER, Richard W.——*Broker/Mgr.*, Rocky Mountain Realtors; **PRIM RE ACT:** Broker, Developer, Owner/Investor, Instructor; **PREV EMPLOY:** Concepts Unlimited, 1973, 1980; Perry & Butler, Inc., 1965-73; Reder Realty 1961-65; **PROFL AFFIL & HONORS:** NAR, RNMI, Co-Assn. of Realtors, FLI, Denver Bd. of Realtors, Montrose Bd. of Realtors, CRB, CRS, GRI, Co-author & instr. for CO Assn. of Realtors, Montrose Bd. Dir., Denver Bd. Corp. Sec., 2nd VP, 1st VP, Member of Exec. Comm., Dir. in Charge of Consumer & Public Servs. Comm., Dir. serving two 3-yr. terms, Chmn. Grievance Comm., Chmn. Arbitration Comm., CO Assn. of Realtors Dir., Rocky Mountain Chapt. CRB Treas.; Author and Instr. for Univ. of CO's Cont. educ. 'RE Contract' course; Co-author and instr. for CO Assn. of Realtors 'The Code of Ethics and Profl. Practices' course; Guest speaker for Univ. of WY, CO Assn. of Realtors and numerous local Bds. of Realtors; **BUS ADD:** 802 Main, Montrose, CO 81401, (303)249-1100.

BERGER, Robert M.——**B:** Jan. 29, 1942, Chicago, IL, *Partner*, Mayer, Brown & Platt; **PRIM RE ACT:** Attorney; **PROFL AFFIL & HONORS:** Amer. Law Inst.; Amer. Bar Assn.; Chicago Bar Assn.; Chicago Council of Lawyers; **EDUC:** AB, 1963, Econ., Univ. of MI; **GRAD EDUC:** JD, 1966, Law, Univ. of Chicago Law School; **EDUC HONORS:** Phi Beta Kappa, Phi Kappa Phi, degree with high honors and high distinction, Order of the Coif, Comments Editor, Univ. Chicago Law Review; **OTHER ACT & HONORS:** Member, IL Supreme Ct. Atty. Disciplinary Hearing Bd., 1973-1979; Member, Special Tax Advisory Comm. to IL Dept. of Ins., 1972; Legal Assistance Found. of Chicago, Bd. of Dir. and Chmn. of Program Comm., 1975-1978; Consumer Federation of IL, Bd. of Dir. and Gen. Counsel (pro bono publico basis), 1967-1971; **HOME ADD:** 1506 Sheridan Rd., Highland Park, IL 60035, (312)432-9317; **BUS ADD:** 231 S. LaSalle St., Suite 1955, Chicago, IL 60604, (312)782-0600.

BERGER, Ronald——**B:** June 30, 1933, Chicago, IL, *Pres.*, Berger Realty Grp.; **PRIM RE ACT:** Broker, Consultant, Appraiser, Developer, Property Manager, Owner/Investor; **REP CLIENTS:** Evans, Inc., Chicago, Chase Manhattan, Nr, Crocker Bank, CA, Amer. Nat., & First Nat. Banks, Chicago, Bayswater Realty & Investment Tr., NY; **PREV EMPLOY:** Dir. of Econ. Research, Mid-Amer. Appraisal & Research, Gen. Foreman, Foremost Blders.; **PROFL AFFIL & HONORS:** Soc. of Resid. Appraisers, ULI, Nat. Assn. of Corp. RE Execs.; **EDUC:** BBA, 1955, Bus. Admin., Univ. of Miami; **OTHER ACT & HONORS:** Dir. Columbia Nat. Bank; **HOME ADD:** 1501 N. St. Pkwy, Chicago, IL 60610, (312)266-8446; **BUS ADD:** 180 N. LaSalle St., 2800, Chicago, IL 60601, (312)558-3000.

BERGER, Saul——**B:** Mar. 12, 1907, Passaic, NJ, *Owner*, Saul Berger; **PRIM RE ACT:** Broker, Attorney; **EDUC:** BA, 1927, CCNY; **GRAD EDUC:** LLB/JD, 1930, Fordham Univ. Law School; **HOME ADD:** 70 E 10th St., New York, NY 10003, (212)673-4041; **BUS ADD:** 799 Broadway, NY, NY 10003, (212)673-4040.

BERGERON, Norman A.——**B:** June 17, 1937, New Bedford, MA, *Director of Economic Development*, New Bedford Industrial Development Commission; **PRIM RE ACT:** Broker; **OTHER RE ACT:** Govt. economic developer; **SERVICES:** RE advising, financing; **PROFL AFFIL & HONORS:** NIDA, MEDC, C of C; **EDUC:** BA, 1963, Econ., Poli. Sci., Roger Williams, Univ. of MA; **MIL SERV:** USNR, PO-2; **OTHER ACT & HONORS:** Knights of Columbus, Kiwanis, YMCA; **HOME ADD:** 45 Jonathan St., New Bedford, MA 02740, (617)996-5344; **BUS ADD:** 1213 Purchase Street, New Bedford, MA 02740, (617)997-6501.

BERGERON, Raymond——**B:** Apr. 14, 1941, New Orleans, *Prin.*, Raymond C. Bergeron & Assoc.; **PRIM RE ACT:** Architect, Developer, Owner/Investor, Consultant; **SERVICES:** Architecture, Energy Consultant, Space Planning & Design; **PROFL AFFIL & HONORS:** V.P. N. Chap. AIA; **GRAD EDUC:** BArch, 1963, Tulane Univ.; **OTHER ACT & HONORS:** Pres. Kiwanis Club.; Bd. of Dir. Veterans Blvd. Bus. Assoc. & Metairie CBD; Bd. of Directors, E.B. C of C; Member, E.J. Hospital Citizens Advisory Comm.; **HOME ADD:** 4908 York St., Metairie, LA 70002; **BUS ADD:** 3636 N. Causeway Blvd. Suite #106, Metairie, LA 70002, (504)837-8890.

BERGGREN, Alan R.——**B:** Dec. 31, 1937, IL, *Pres.*, The Berggren Realty Corp.; **PRIM RE ACT:** Broker, Engineer, Developer, Banker, Owner/Investor, Property Manager; **SERVICES:** Brokerage, Devel. &

Mgmt. of Non-Residential Props.; **REP CLIENTS:** Developed 5 Major Indus. Parks in Chicago Area & Have Represented Many Cos. in location of New Facilities; **PREV EMPLOY:** Mgr. Indus. Devel.-New York Central RR Consultant, Civil Engrg.-1958-62; **PROFL AFFIL & HONORS:** Indus. Devel. Res. Council-Assoc. Member Assn. of Indus. RE Brokers-Pres. 1981, Chicago RE Bd., SIR-Active Member; **EDUC:** BS, 1958, Civil Engrg., Univ. of IL; **OTHER ACT & HONORS:** Past Pres.-Kiwanis Club of Oak Park; Dir., Heritage Bank of Oakwood; **BUS ADD:** 2625 Butterfield Rd., Oak Brook, IL 60521, (312)887-9600.

BERGHEL, Victoria Smouse——B: Nov. 20, 1952, Oakland, MD, Weinberg and Green; **PRIM RE ACT:** Attorney; **SERVICES:** Legal representation - comml. RE; **REP CLIENTS:** Regional devels. and investors, surety bond co., shopping centers, tenants, instit. lenders; **PROFL AFFIL & HONORS:** ABA, MD Bar Assn., Baltimore City Bar Assn.; **EDUC:** BA, 1974, English Language & Literature, Univ. of MD; **GRAD EDUC:** JD, 1977, Univ. of MD School of Law; **EDUC HONORS:** High Honors, Phi Beta Kappa, Notes & Comments Editor, MD Law Review; **HOME ADD:** 1034 Olive St., Baltimore, MD, (301)837-7292; **BUS ADD:** 100 S. Charles St., Baltimore, MD 21201, (301)332-8669.

BERGMAN, Edward, Jr.——B: Nov. 5, 1930, Fort Sam Houston, TX, *Pres.*, Bergman Assoc., Inc.; **PRIM RE ACT:** Broker, Consultant, Owner/Investor; **OTHER RE ACT:** Land Packager; **SERVICES:** Comml./Inv. RE Sales as Sellers or Buyers Agent; Inv. Counseling, Land Assembly; **REP CLIENTS:** Nat. Chains, Comml./Indus. Users & Dev., Indiv. Investors, Citrus Growers; **PROFL AFFIL & HONORS:** RNMI, RESSI, FLI, CCIM; GRI; Pres. FL CCIM Chap; Pres. Local Bd.; twice Realtor of the Yr.; Dir. FL Assn. of Realtors; **EDUC:** BA, 1952, Econ., Univ. of FL; **EDUC HONORS:** Distinguished Mil. Grad.; **MIL SERV:** USA/Armor, 1st Lt.; **HOME ADD:** 1210 Glenridge Dr., Leesburg, FL 32748, (904)787-3818; **BUS ADD:** Suite 403 First Family Oaks, 1330 W. Citizens Blvd., Leesburg, FL 32748, (904)787-8300.

BERGMILLER, Edgar A.——B: Jan. 14, 1928, Newark, NJ, *Registered Rep.*, Investors Diversified Serv., Inc.; **PRIM RE ACT:** Broker, Builder, Insuror; **SERVICES:** Money Mgmt., Fin. Planning, Investments, Tax Shelters, Ins.; **REP CLIENTS:** Indivs. & Industry Businessmen; **PREV EMPLOY:** Glenn J&G, Southbury, CT 06488, Resid. Const. Firm - Sec. & Treas.; **EDUC:** BS, 1952, Fin. Acct., Lehigh Univ., Bethlehem, PA; **MIL SERV:** USN; **HOME ADD:** 100 Sunburst Dr., Southbury, CT 06488, (203)263-0555; **BUS ADD:** 951 Chase Pkwy., Waterbury, CT 06708, (203)756-8933.

BERGNER, Richard——B: Jan. 5, 1930, Buffalo, NY, *Pres.*, Urban Research Corp.; **PRIM RE ACT:** Consultant; **OTHER RE ACT:** RE Mkt. Analyst & Urban Econ.; **SERVICES:** Downtown Rejuvenation Consultant, Investment Counseling, Bonding Analyses, Mkt. Analyses, Devel. Feasibility Evaluations, Branching Strategies; **REP CLIENTS:** RE Devels., Investors, Retail & Banking Chains, City Planning Commns. Redevel. Agencies, Downtown Improvement Grps.; **PREV EMPLOY:** VP, Larry Smith & Co., Inc. 1958-70, VP, RE Research Corp. 1976-80; **EDUC:** AB, American Studies, 1951, Amer. Econ., Hist. & Sociology, Yale Univ.; **GRAD EDUC:** MBA, 1958, Fin., Mktg., Harvard Bus. School; **MIL SERV:** USN 1952-1956, Lt., Commendations-Tachen Evacuation & Deployment Procedures-Regulus Missile; **HOME ADD:** 5229 Richwood Dr., Edina, MN 55436, (612)929-6309; **BUS ADD:** 5229 Richwood Dr., Minneapolis, MN 55436, (612)929-6309.

BERGSETH, Thomas——B: Mar. 1, 1944, Minneapolis, MN, *Arch.*, Dayton Hudson Corp., RE Grp.; **PRIM RE ACT:** Architect; **SERVICES:** Internal RE Function; **REP CLIENTS:** All Dayton Hudson Operating Co's.; **PROFL AFFIL & HONORS:** MN Soc., AIA, Const. Specifications Inst., Amer. Arbitration Assn.; **EDUC:** Arch., 1966, Univ. of MN; **MIL SERV:** USA, SFC; **OTHER ACT & HONORS:** NCARB Certificate: State Registrations in Arch. in MN & AZ; **HOME ADD:** 4370 Vernon Ave. S., Edina, MN 55436, (612)922-1229; **BUS ADD:** 777 Nicollet Mall, Minneapolis, MN 55402, (612)370-5564.

BERGSMA, Ralph——B: June 3, 1931, Detroit, MI, *CEO & Pres.*, Property Development Group, Inc.; **PRIM RE ACT:** Consultant, Architect, Developer, Owner/Investor; **SERVICES:** Turn-key RE devel.; **REP CLIENTS:** Corporate Hdqtrs. Complex, Public Stock Cos., Medical School State of IL, private investors; **PREV EMPLOY:** Project Designer and Dir., Smith Hinchman & Grylls; Arch. Engr., Detroit MI; Partner, Johnson Johnson & Roy Landscape Arch. & Planners; **PROFL AFFIL & HONORS:** AIA, MI Soc. of Arch.; **EDUC:** BS, 1953, Landscape Arch., MI State Univ.; **GRAD EDUC:** BArch, 1959, Arch., Univ. of MI; **MIL SERV:** USAF, 1st Lt., 1953-1955; **OTHER ACT & HONORS:** Econ. Club of Detroit; C of C; Traverse City Indus. Fund; **HOME ADD:** 622 Washington St., Traverse City, MI 49684, (616)941-1973; **BUS ADD:** P.O. Box 1266, Traverse City, MI 49684, (616)941-1250.

BERGSTROM, Robert L.——*Atty.*, Robert L. Bergstrom, Atty. at Law; **PRIM RE ACT:** Attorney, Owner/Investor; **SERVICES:** RE & land use legal advice and representation; **REP CLIENTS:** Daon Corp., Keating Homes, Inc., Springer Dev. (WA), Inc.; **PREV EMPLOY:** Weyerhaeuser Co., Law Dept., RE Council for subsidiaries; **PROFL AFFIL & HONORS:** Washington State Bar Assn.; **EDUC:** BA, 1966, Local Govt., Univ. of WA; **GRAD EDUC:** JD, 1969, RE and Bus. Law, Univ. of Washington Law School; **EDUC HONORS:** Dean's Honor Roll, Bogle-Gates Scholarship; **OTHER ACT & HONORS:** Lambda Chi Alpha; **BUS ADD:** 10909 NE Fourth St., Bellevue, WA 98004, (206)451-1837.

BERING, Donald R.——B: Feb. 16, 1925, TX, *Owner*, Donald R. Bering, RE Investments; **PRIM RE ACT:** Broker; **SERVICES:** Investment consultant, sales, valuation and devel.; **REP CLIENTS:** Indiv. and instnl. investors in investment RE; **PROFL AFFIL & HONORS:** SCV, IIV; **EDUC:** BS, 1948, Bus. Admin., TX A&M; **MIL SERV:** USAF; **HOME ADD:** 6027 Park Circle, Houston, TX 77057, (713)780-0445; **BUS ADD:** 2323 S. Voss Rd., Suite 550, Houston, TX 77057, (713)977-3975.

BERKE, Daniel E.——B: Oct. 20, 1948, Staten Isl., *Pres.*, Daniel Berke Inc.; **PRIM RE ACT:** Broker, Consultant, Appraiser, Property Manager; **OTHER RE ACT:** Apt. leasing; **SERVICES:** Conversion feasibility conversion sales agents; mortgage brokerage; **PREV EMPLOY:** Ownership of Prop.; Mgmt. Experience; Comml. Leasing and Sales Experience; Mautner-Glick Corp.; Williams RE; Sulzberger Rolfe Inc.; General Contracting and Rehabilitations; **PROFL AFFIL & HONORS:** Assoc. Member Soc. of RE Appraisers; **EDUC:** BA, 1971, Phil. and Drama, Univ. of WI, Madison; **GRAD EDUC:** BA, 1977, RE appr. & analysis, NY Univ.; **HOME ADD:** 530 E. 90th St., NY, NY 10028, (212)289-4202; **BUS ADD:** 1656 3rd. Ave., NY, NY 10028, (212)534-6000.

BERKMAN, Andrew S.——B: Apr. 7, 1944, New York, NY, *Part.*, Tufo & Zuccotti; **PRIM RE ACT:** Attorney; **PROFL AFFIL & HONORS:** Member, Bd. of Dir., Nat. Housing Rehab. Assn., Member, Law Comm., RE Bd. of NY, Sec. HUD, Assn. of the Bar of The City of NY; **EDUC:** BA, 1966, Yale Univ.; **GRAD EDUC:** JD, 1971, NY Univ. School of Law; **HOME ADD:** 27 W 96th St., NY, NY 10025, (212)865-2061; **BUS ADD:** 645 Madison Ave., NY, NY 10022, (212)752-8668.

BERKMAN, Bernard G.——B: Aug. 6, 1931, Boston, MA, *Pres.*, Pilgrim Capital Corp.; **PRIM RE ACT:** Broker, Consultant, Owner/Investor, Property Manager; **EDUC:** BSBA, 1952, Bus. Mgmt., Babson Coll.; **EDUC HONORS:** Blue Key; **HOME ADD:** 179 Bristol Rd., Wellesley, MA 02181, (617)235-5086; **BUS ADD:** 842A Beacon St., Boston, MA 02215, (617)566-5212.

BERKNER, Roger C.——B: Aug. 3, 1936, Sleepy Eye, MN, *Pres.*, Berkner Agency, Inc.; **PRIM RE ACT:** Broker, Syndicator, Owner/Investor; **SERVICES:** RE Sales and investment counseling; **REP CLIENTS:** Specializing in agricultural land; **PROFL AFFIL & HONORS:** FLI, AFLM Farm and Land Broker of the Yr. 1976 for state of MN; **EDUC:** BA, 1960, Univ. of MN; **HOME ADD:** 38 Woodland Dr., New Ulm, MN 56073, (507)359-2475; **BUS ADD:** 108 N. Minn. St., New Ulm, MN 56073, (507)359-9521.

BERKOWITZ, Abraham——B: Aug. 13, 1914, USA, *Prin. Atty.*, Attorney General's Office, NY State, RE Fin. and Investors Protection; **PRIM RE ACT:** Consultant, Attorney; **SERVICES:** Condo., cooperatives, home owners assns., subdivided land, securities, franchises, syndications; **PREV EMPLOY:** Hearing Officer, RE Licensing, Special Agent U.S.; **PROFL AFFIL & HONORS:** Soc. Profl. Investigators; **EDUC:** BS, 1933, Law/Psych./Sociology, NYU; **GRAD EDUC:** JD, 1935, Law, NYU Law School; CUNY; Acctng.; **MIL SERV:** US Coast Guard, (R) Seaman 1st; **OTHER ACT & HONORS:** Masons; Knights of Pythias; Shriner; ZOA; JNF; B'nai B'rith, Synagogues; **HOME ADD:** 1035 E. 43rd St., Brooklyn, NY 11210, (212)258-6999; **BUS ADD:** 2 World Trade Ctr., NY, NY 10047, (212)488-3310.

BERKOWITZ, Barry——B: Jan. 13, 1956, Detroit, MI, *Investment Analyst-Asst. to Pres.*, Vector Real Estate Corp.; **PRIM RE ACT:** Developer, Builder, Owner/Investor, Syndicator; **OTHER RE ACT:** Condo. conversions, joint venture financing, equity financing, prop. mgmt.; **PREV EMPLOY:** Asst. VP Marriott Corp. (R.E. Div.); **PROFL AFFIL & HONORS:** AMA, NACORE; **EDUC:** BS, 1978, Fin., R.E., Cornell Univ.; **GRAD EDUC:** MBA, 1980, Fin., R.E., Syracuse Univ.; **EDUC HONORS:** Magna Cum Laude; **HOME**

ADD: 170 West End Ave., NY, NY 10023, (212)873-1213; **BUS ADD:** 666 5th Ave., 28th Floor, NYC, NY 10023, (212)581-2400.

BERKOWITZ, Edward C.——B: Apr. 9, 1935, Perth Amboy, NJ, *VP*, Lane & Edson, P.C.; **PRIM RE ACT:** Attorney; **REP CLIENTS:** First Nat. Bank of MD, United VA Bank, Madison Nat. Bank (DC), Other lenders and devel. of comml. and resid. prop.; **PREV EMPLOY:** Gen. Atty. communications satellite corp.; **PROFL AFFIL & HONORS:** DC Bar, NJ Bar, ABA, DC Bar Div., (RE), Steering Comm. 1977-79; **EDUC:** BA, 1956, Govt., Cornell Univ.; **GRAD EDUC:** LLB, 1959, Harvard Law School; **MIL SERV:** US Army, Capt.; **OTHER ACT & HONORS:** Cornell Univ. Council, Cornell Club of Wash., Potomac Appalachian Trail Club; **HOME ADD:** 3339 Legation St. NW, Washington, DC 20015, (202)363-5534; **BUS ADD:** 1800 M St., NW, Suite 400 S., Washington, DC 20036, (202)457-6800.

BERLAND, Abel E.——B: Aug. 27, 1915, Cincinnati, OH, *VChmn.*, Arthur Rubloff & Co.; **PRIM RE ACT:** Broker, Consultant, Attorney; **SERVICES:** Specializes in counseling on the sale, purchase, lease and operation of office and store bldgs., loft-type props., shopping ctrs., downtown land assemblies and redevel.; **REP CLIENTS:** Banks, ins. cos., pension funds, corp. orgs., law and acctg. firms and Amer. and foreign investment groups; **PROFL AFFIL & HONORS:** NAR; Amer. Soc. of RE Counselors, Past Pres., 1970; RNMI; Retirement Planning Funds of Amer., Inc., Dir.; FIABCI, Counseling Comm.; Amer. Arbitration Assn., Nat. Panel of Arbitrators, CRE; CCIM; Omega Tau Rau Frat.; Ely Chap. of Lambda Alpha Intl. Frat.; **EDUC:** Law, DePaul Univ.; **GRAD EDUC:** LLB, 1938, Law; JD, 1970, Law; **EDUC HONORS:** Hon. Doctorate, 1975 (Dr. of Humane Letters); **OTHER ACT & HONORS:** IL State C of C, Dir.; Civic Federation of Chicago, Dir.; Chicago Crime Commn., Dir.; DePaul Univ., Tr., Member Exec. Comm.; Brandeis Univ., Fellow; **HOME ADD:** 251 Sylvan Rd., Glencoe, IL 60022; **BUS ADD:** 69 W. Washington St., Chicago, IL 60602, (312)368-5400.

BERLEY, David R.——B: Apr. 9, 1942, NY, NY, *Pres.*, David R. Berley, PA; **PRIM RE ACT:** Attorney; **SERVICES:** Legal; **REP CLIENTS:** Bank of Boston Intl.; Bank of FL, Banco de Amer. Central; **PROFL AFFIL & HONORS:** ABA; FL Bar Assn., MA BME; **EDUC:** BS, BA, 1963, Econ. & Fin., Boston Univ.; **GRAD EDUC:** JD, 1966, Boston Coll.; **EDUC HONORS:** Deans List, Moot Court; **HOME ADD:** 4181 Battersea Rd., Coconut Grove, FL 33133, (305)667-7780; **BUS ADD:** 151 SE 14 Terr., Miami, FL 33131, (305)371-5000.

BERLEY, Peter——B: July 13, 1951, NYC, *VP*, R. B. Schlesinger & Co., Inc.; **PRIM RE ACT:** Broker, Attorney, Owner/Investor; **SERVICES:** RE Brokerage; **PREV EMPLOY:** Asst. VP, Olympia & York Properties, 245 Park Ave., NY, NY; **PROFL AFFIL & HONORS:** ABA; NY State Bar Assn.; RE Bd. of NY; **EDUC:** BA, 1973, Philosophy, NYU, Washington Square Coll.; **GRAD EDUC:** MBA, 1976, Fin., Grad. School of Business, NYU; JD, 1980, Law, Brooklyn Law School; **HOME ADD:** 969 Park Ave., New York, NY 10028, (212)861-3277; **BUS ADD:** 230 Park Ave., NY, NY 10017, (212)661-7676.

BERLIN, Norman B.——B: Mar. 11, 1954, Wilmington, DE, *Atty.*, Conteut, Stewart, Tatusko & Patterson, Tax; **PRIM RE ACT:** Attorney; **SERVICES:** Legal advice regardings RE; **REP CLIENTS:** Acquisition, finance, taxation; **PREV EMPLOY:** Atty. with Weinberg & Green, Baltimore, MD; **PROFL AFFIL & HONORS:** ABA, MD State Bar Assn., DC Bar Assn.; **EDUC:** BA, 1976, Econ., Univ. of VA; **GRAD EDUC:** JD, 1979, Law, Harvard Law School; **EDUC HONORS:** Honors-Econ., Phi Beta Kappa; **HOME ADD:** 3003 Van Ness St. N.W. 818, Wash., DC 20008, (301)585-7866; **BUS ADD:** Suite 600, 1225 19th St. N.W., Wash., DC 20036, (202)887-1000.

BERMAN, Arnold——*Fac. Engineer*, Barry Corp.; **PRIM RE ACT:** Property Manager; **BUS ADD:** Box 129, Columbus, OH 43216, (614)864-6400.*

BERMAN, Daniel S.——B: Dec. 1, 1921, NY, NY, *Atty.*, Frank, Weinberger, Fredman, Berman & Lowell PC; **PRIM RE ACT:** Attorney; **PROFL AFFIL & HONORS:** Member, The Assn. of the Bar of the City of NY; NY Cty. Lawyers Assn., Member, RE Law Comm., 1965-1968; Member, Bankruptcy Law Comm., 1962-1965, Fed. Bar Assn., Tax Comm., 1966-1970, Author: RE Synd., 1961; Going Public, 1962; How to Org. RE Condo., 1966; Urban Renewal and FHA, 1967; Tax Aspects of RE, 1969; Distress RE Workouts, 1977; Contributor, Fin. Income Producing RE, 1978; Co-op and Condo Conversions in NY, 197; Foreign Investments in US RE, 1980; Joint Ventures and Equity Participation in RE, 1980; **EDUC:** BBA, 1942, CCNY; **GRAD EDUC:** JD, 1947, Law, NYU; **BUS ADD:** Rm. 1600, 551 5th Ave., NY, NY 10017, (212)682-0546.

BERMAN, Martin S.——B: May 30, 1933, Boston, MA, *Pres.*, Berman and Sons, Inc.; **PRIM RE ACT:** Broker, Attorney, Instructor, Property Manager, Owner/Investor; **SERVICES:** Prop. mgmt.; **PROFL AFFIL & HONORS:** IREM, CPM; **EDUC:** 1956, Bus., Boston Univ.; **GRAD EDUC:** Lawyer, 1965, New England School of Law; **EDUC HONORS:** Passed MA Bar, Nov., 1965; **OTHER ACT & HONORS:** Admitted to practice U.S. Supreme Court, 1979, Past. Pres. Rental Housing Assn., Past. Pres. N.E. Chptr. IREM, Trustee N.E. School of Law, Dir. Boston Chptr. Amer. Red Cross, Trustee, Beth Israel Hospital, Boston; **BUS ADD:** 52 North St., Stoneham, MA 02180, (617)322-4024.

BERMAN, Miles J.——B: Feb. 24, 1933, Bronx, NY, *Dir. RE Mgmt.*, First Republic Corp. of Amer.; **PRIM RE ACT:** Broker, Consultant, Property Manager; **PREV EMPLOY:** Owned own Co. for 8 yrs.-Brokerage & Mgmt. Consulting - Prior Firm VP Sales & Mgmt.; **PROFL AFFIL & HONORS:** CPM candidate; **EDUC:** BS, 1955-1958, RE, School of Commerce, Accts. & Finance, New York Univ.; **MIL SERV:** USA, 1953-55, Cpl.; **BUS ADD:** 302 Fifth Ave., NY, NY 10001, (212)279-6100.

BERMAN, Paul A.——B: July 25, 1935, Brooklyn, NJ, *Pres.*, Paul A. Berman Realties, Inc.; **PRIM RE ACT:** Broker, Banker; **SERVICES:** Devel. of office bldgs. for investors; **REP CLIENTS:** Fairleigh Dickinson Univ.; **PREV EMPLOY:** VP Joseph P. Day Inc. 1957-67; **PROFL AFFIL & HONORS:** Soc. of Indus. Realtors, NAIOP; **EDUC:** BS, 1957, NY Univ., Econ., RE; **MIL SERV:** US Army, SP-5; **OTHER ACT & HONORS:** B'nai B'rith Pascack Valley Lodge, Trustee; Assn. for Retarded Citizens, Bergen Passaic Unit-VP; Commerce and Indus. Assn. of No. NJ-Dir.; **BUS ADD:** 2 Univ. Plaza, Hackensack, NJ 07601, (201)488-1818.

BERMAN, W.I.——B: Oct. 12, 1911, Pittsburgh, PA, *Pres.*, Berman & Co., Inc.; **PRIM RE ACT:** Broker, Consultant, Appraiser, Property Manager; **SERVICES:** Appraisal, Mgmt., Sales of RE; **PROFL AFFIL & HONORS:** AIREA; SREA; IREM; **EDUC:** AB, 1933, Journ., Univ. of Pittsburgh; **GRAD EDUC:** LLB, 1939, Duquesne Univ.; **MIL SERV:** Cavalry, 1st. Lt.; **HOME ADD:** 1134 Arrowood Dr., Pittsburgh, PA 15219, (412)923-1312; **BUS ADD:** 901 Manor Bldg., Pittsburgh, PA 15219, (412)281-8400.

BERMANT, Robert A.——B: May 12, 1940, Chicago, IL, *VP*, The Robert A. McNeil Corp., Sr. VP, McNeil Securities Corp.; **PRIM RE ACT:** Syndicator; **OTHER RE ACT:** Mktg. of private placements; **SERVICES:** Structuring, packaging & mktg.; **REP CLIENTS:** Major and regional securities firms; **PREV EMPLOY:** 10 years specializing in RE and other tax sheltered investments, 7 years investments; **PROFL AFFIL & HONORS:** NASD Financial Principal, RESSI; **EDUC:** BSBA, 1961, Econ., Fin., Roosevelt Univ.; **MIL SERV:** US Army; PFC, 1961-1962; **HOME ADD:** 55 Dior Terr., Los Altos, CA 94022, (415)948-4334; **BUS ADD:** 2855 Campus Dr., San Mateo, CA 94403, (415)572-0660.

BERMINGHAM, Thomas V.——B: July 20, 1951, NY, NY, *VP & Branch Mgr.*, Cushman & Wakefield; **PRIM RE ACT:** Broker, Consultant; **SERVICES:** Comml. leasing & sales, investment counseling & valuation; **REP CLIENTS:** IBM, Ebasco Servs., Nestles, Dun & Bradstreet, Wagner Electric., Baker Ind., Prudential Ins.; **PROFL AFFIL & HONORS:** IREBA, NAR; **EDUC:** BA, 1973, Eng. & Hist., Boston Coll.; **EDUC HONORS:** Cum Laude, Dean's List; **HOME ADD:** 555 North Ave., Ft. Lee, NJ 07024, (201)592-6012; **BUS ADD:** 1099 Wall St. W, Lyndhurst, NJ 07071, (201)935-4000.

BERNARD, Bossom——B: Sept. 23, 1932, NYC, NY, *Pres.*, The Daisy Equity & Devel. Corp. Quad Holding Co., Inc.; **PRIM RE ACT:** Broker, Consultant, Developer, Owner/Investor, Syndicator; **SERVICES:** Project devel., feasibility studies and programs; **PROFL AFFIL & HONORS:** RE Bd. of NY Inc.; **EDUC:** BA, 1954, Brandeis Univ.; **GRAD EDUC:** MA, 1959, Wharton School, Univ. of PA; **BUS ADD:** 3 West 57th St., NYC, NY 10019, (212)758-4747.

BERNARD, J. Thomas——B: June 26, 1943, Denver, CO, *VP & Gen. Mgr.*, Cabot, Cabot & Forbes; **PRIM RE ACT:** Developer; **SERVICES:** Indus. bus. park and office devel.; **REP CLIENTS:** Ingersoll Rand, Boeing, Metro. Life, UPS; **PREV EMPLOY:** Bechtel Corp., 1966-67; US Army (Gen. Headquarters), 1967-69; **PROFL AFFIL & HONORS:** Bd. of Dirs. Bellevue Comm. Coll. Found., 1981- ; Nat. Assn. of Office & Indus. Parks (Pres. Seattle Chapt., 1980); Bellevue Downtown Assn. (VP, Dir. 1979-82); Bellevue C of C (Dir. 1980-83); Seattle C of C (Comm. Chmn. 1979-80); Soc. of Indus. Realtors (Assoc.); Tukwila C of C, Seattle Municipal League, Lambda Alpha (Scribe, 1981-82); **EDUC:** Engr. of Mines, 1966, Mining Engr., CO Sch. of Mines; **GRAD EDUC:** MBA, 1970, Gen. Mgmt., Boston Univ.; **MIL SERV:** USA Chem. Corps., Lt., 1967-69; **OTHER ACT & HONORS:** Republican Exec. Forum 1978- ; Bellevue Athletic Club,

WA Athletic Club, Seattle Tennis Club; **HOME ADD:** 1421 Shenandoah Dr. E, Seattle, WA 98112, (206)329-2671; **BUS ADD:** 1003 Andover Park E, Seattle, WA 98188, (206)585-0311.

BERNARD, Stephen Zouck——B: Jan. 28, 1947, Summit, NJ, *Pres.*, DB & M Ltd., RE; **PRIM RE ACT:** Broker, Consultant, Developer, Builder, Owner/Investor; **PREV EMPLOY:** 1963-1965 - Laborer for Bernard & Co., Builders; 1970-1970 - Field Engr. with Wm. Lyon Devel. Co.; 1970-1977 - VP of Bernard & Co. 1977-Present - Sec. of DB & M Ltd.; **PROFL AFFIL & HONORS:** Nat., AZ, and Phoenix Bd. of Realtors; RESSI; RNMI; AZ Mort. Bankers Assn.; Nat. Assn. of Indep. Fee Appraisers International Institute of Valuers, AZ State Lic. RE Broker; AZ State Lic. RE Mort. Broker; GRI; SCV; **EDUC:** BS, 1970, Const. Engrg., AZ State Univ. - Bus. & RE; **MIL SERV:** USN, E-3; **OTHER ACT & HONORS:** Theta Delta Frat., Amer. Soc of Profl. Estimators (Certified General Construction Estimator), Licensed General Contractor in State of AZ; **HOME ADD:** 5120 N. 22nd St., Phoenix, AZ 85016, (602)955-0699; **BUS ADD:** 4423 N. 24th St., Phoenix, AZ 85016, (602)954-9004.

BERNARD, William N.——B: Nov. 18, 1928, Hastings, MN, *Pres.*, Property Management, Inc.; **PRIM RE ACT:** Engineer, Attorney, Developer, Builder, Owner/Investor, Property Manager, Syndicator; **SERVICES:** Legal, develop, build & Manage; **REP CLIENTS:** Multiplex Properties; Mobile Estates, Inc.; Kandi Warehouse, Inc.; Planned Community Living; Hegstrom Properties; **PROFL AFFIL & HONORS:** MN Manufactured Housing Assn.; Local, State & ABA; **EDUC:** BAE, 1955, Engrg./Bus. Admin., Univ. of MN; **GRAD EDUC:** JD, 1963, Law, William Mitchell Coll. of Law; **MIL SERV:** USN, Comdr. (Retired) and Naval Aviator, Korean War; **HOME ADD:** 1415 Willmar Ave., Willmar, MN 56201, (612)235-1157; **BUS ADD:** 520 W. Litchfield Ave., Willmar, MN 56201, (612)235-2563.

BERND, Robert——*Dir. Corp. Rel. & Admin. Services*, Hobart Corp.; **PRIM RE ACT:** Property Manager; **BUS ADD:** World Headquarters, Troy, OH 45374, (513)335-7171.*

BERNELL, Ronald L.——B: Apr. 17, 1952, Houston, TX, *VP*, M.L. Bernell & Assoc., Inc.; **PRIM RE ACT:** Broker, Consultant, Attorney, Developer, Builder, Owner/Investor, Property Manager, Syndicator; **PROFL AFFIL & HONORS:** State Bar of TX, TX Real Estate Broker; **EDUC:** BA, 1974, English/Bus., Univ. of TX; **GRAD EDUC:** JD, 1977, Univ. of Houston; Bates Coll. of Law; **EDUC HONORS:** Cum Laude; **HOME ADD:** 5621 St. Paul, Bellaire, TX 77401, (713)668-6831; **BUS ADD:** 1527 West Alabama St., Houston, TX 77006, (713)526-1094.

BERNER, Robert M.——B: June 15, 1922, Dayton, OH, *Dir., RE Div.*, NCR Corp., Corporate; **PRIM RE ACT:** Developer, Builder, Owner/Investor; **OTHER RE ACT:** Site Selection; **REP CLIENTS:** Corporate RE, engineering and const., energy mgmt. for NCR Corp.; **PREV EMPLOY:** Pres., NCR Employees Benefit Assn. 1964-78; Dir., Adm. Services, NCR Corporation, 1964-73; **PROFL AFFIL & HONORS:** SIR; IDC; Nat. Assn. of Corp. RE Execs.; **EDUC:** BS, 1947, Econ., Bus. Mgmt., Univ. of Dayton, OH; **OTHER ACT & HONORS:** Jr. C of C - VP; C of C; United Appeal, Cty. Div. Chmn.; **HOME ADD:** 5749 Waterloo Rd., Dayton, OH 45459, (513)434-3028; **BUS ADD:** 1700 So. Patterson Blvd., Dayton, OH 45479, (513)445-2110.

BERNFELD, Herbert——B: June 17, 1919, Herbert Berfield Assoc.; **PRIM RE ACT:** Broker, Consultant, Appraiser, Lender; **SERVICES:** Lendg. inst., pension funds, banks, priv. investors, corps.; **PREV EMPLOY:** Major brokerage & consulting for natl. brokerage concerns; **PROFL AFFIL & HONORS:** CCIM, GRI, MEI, CTA, Omega Tau Rho, Only multiple winner of Natl. Trade of Yr., Award Div., of NAR; **EDUC:** BA, 1940, Lib. Arts, Union Coll., NY; **GRAD EDUC:** MBA, 1940, RE, Columbia Univ. Grad. School of Bus.; **OTHER ACT & HONORS:** Who's Who; **BUS ADD:** 21 S. Park Dr., Tenafly, NJ 07670, (201)569-4171.

BERNHARDT, Richard Charles——B: July 18, 1949, Atlanta, GA, *Planning Mgr.*, City of Gainesville, Dept. of Community Dev.; **PRIM RE ACT:** Regulator; **OTHER RE ACT:** Planner; **SERVICES:** Guide Growth and Dev.; **REP CLIENTS:** Public; **PREV EMPLOY:** Hopkinsville-Christian County, KY Planning Comm., Metropolitan Nashville, TN Planning Comm.; **PROFL AFFIL & HONORS:** APA; **EDUC:** BS, Econ., Auburn Univ.; **GRAD EDUC:** M. of City Planning, 1974, Housing and Urban Structure, OH State Univ.; **EDUC HONORS:** Omicron Delta Epsilon, Pi Sigma Alpha, AIP Student Award, First and Second Yr. Faculty Prize; **HOME ADD:** 3713 NW 46th Pl., Gainesville, FL 32605, (904)375-4825; **BUS ADD:** PO Box 490, Gainesville, FL 32602, (904)374-2031.

BERNHARDT, Roger——B: May 27, 1934, Cleveland, OH, *Prof. of Law*, Golden Gate Univ.; **PRIM RE ACT:** Attorney, Instructor; **OTHER RE ACT:** Author; **EDUC:** BA, 1955, Liberal Arts, Univ. of Chicago; **GRAD EDUC:** MA, JD, 1957, 1960, Law, Univ. of Chicago; **EDUC HONORS:** Phi Beta Kappa, Order of the Coif, Law Review; **HOME ADD:** 662 9th Ave., San Francisco, CA, (415)221-0262; **BUS ADD:** 536 Mission, San Francisco, CA 94105, (415)442-7281.

BERNHOLZ, Peter M.——B: May 27, 1934, New York, NY, *Pres./Prin.*, Bernholz Assoc.; **PRIM RE ACT:** Architect, Developer, Owner/Investor; **SERVICES:** Arch., RE Devels., Urban Planning; **REP CLIENTS:** RE Investors & Devels.; **PROFL AFFIL & HONORS:** AIA, NY Assn. of Archs.; NY Soc. of Archs.; **EDUC:** BArch, 1956, MIT; **MIL SERV:** USA, Maj.; **HOME ADD:** Lloyd Neck, Huntington, NY 11743, (516)271-9442; **BUS ADD:** 306 E. 61st St., NY, NY 10021, (212)838-6743.

BERNING, Paul E.——B: April 30, 1934, Cincinnati, OH, *Cert. Public Accountant*; **PRIM RE ACT:** Consultant, Owner/Investor; **SERVICES:** Investment Analysis, Tax & Financial Planning; **REP CLIENTS:** Investors & Devel.; **PROFL AFFIL & HONORS:** AICPA, OH Soc. of CPA's, RE Investors Assoc. of Cincinnati; **EDUC:** Certificate in Acctg., 1958, Acctg. & Econ. Majors, Xavier Univ. Cincinnati, OH; **OTHER ACT & HONORS:** Boy Scouts of Amer., St. George Award-O.A.Vigil Honor 4 Scouters Keys for Cubmaster, Scoutmaster, Explorer Advisor & Commissioner; **HOME ADD:** 9639 Leebrook DR., Cincinnati, OH 45231; **BUS ADD:** 9639 Leebrook Dr., Cincinnati,, OH 45231, (513)521-8000.

BERNS, H. Jerome——B: Feb. 25, 1907, New York, NY, *VP & Sec. 21 Club*, 21 Club, Inc.; **PRIM RE ACT:** Property Manager; **EDUC:** BS, 1929, Eng., Univ. of Cincinnati; **GRAD EDUC:** DCS, Comml. Law, Univ. of Cincinnati; **HOME ADD:** 14 E 75th St., New York, NY 10021, (212)582-7200; **BUS ADD:** 21 W 52nd St., New York, NY 10019, (212)582-7200.

BERNS, Martin A.——B: Dec. 8, 1936, Chicago, Il, *Pres.*, Univ. Props. Investment Corp.; **PRIM RE ACT:** Syndicator, Developer, Builder; **OTHER RE ACT:** Builder/devel.; **SERVICES:** Land devel.; single family and multi family const. and rental indications; **PROFL AFFIL & HONORS:** NAHB, Home Builders assn. of S. FL; Home Builders Assn. of Tampa; Home Builders Assn. of Marion Cty., UPIC, listed under NASDAQ, over the counter stocks of FL(public co.); **EDUC:** BS/BA, 1958, Mktg, Roosevelt Univ., Chicago, IL; **HOME ADD:** 4927 Bay Way Dr., Tampa, FL 33609, (813)876-3875; **BUS ADD:** 1011 S. Hwy. 301, Tampa, FL 33619, (813)621-8088.

BERNSTEIN, Asher——B: March 26, 1943, New York, NY, *VP*, Sidney J. Bernstein, Inc.; **PRIM RE ACT:** Broker, Property Manager, Owner/Investor; **SERVICES:** Owner mgmt., mgmt. of client props.; brokerage & leasing of comml. props. in Manhattan; **PROFL AFFIL & HONORS:** Young Mens RE Assn. of NY; RE Bd. of NY; NAR; Dir., Midtown Realty Owners Assn.; Tr. Building Employee 32B-J Health & Pension Fund, Chmn., Young Mens RE Assn. of NY-1980; **EDUC:** BA, 1964, Psych., Univ. Coll., NY Univ.; **GRAD EDUC:** MBA, 1966, Mktg., Grad. School of Bus. Admin., Columbia Univ.; **HOME ADD:** 25 W. Rd., Short Hills, NJ 07078, (201)379-6855; **BUS ADD:** 855 Ave. of Amer., NY, NY 10001, (212)594-1414.

BERNSTEIN, Edward M.——B: Sep. 9, 1949, Phila., PA, *Part.*, Bernstein & Piazza; **PRIM RE ACT:** Broker, Attorney, Syndicator, Owner/Investor; **SERVICES:** Law, brokerage; **PREV EMPLOY:** Edward M. Bernstein, chtd. law firm; **PROFL AFFIL & HONORS:** ABA, NV State Bar, NJ State Bar, PA State Bar, Am. Trial Laywers Assn., NV RE Broker; **EDUC:** BA, Pol., Psych, Long Island Univ.; **GRAD EDUC:** JD, DE Law School; **EDUC HONORS:** Dean's List, 5 times; **OTHER ACT & HONORS:** Varsity Club, Boy Scouts of Amer., Outstanding Young Men of Amer.; **HOME ADD:** 2479 Domingo Rd., Las Vegas, NV 89121; **BUS ADD:** 500 S 4th St., Las Vegas, NV 89101, (702)384-9971.

BERNSTEIN, Jack W.——B: Nov. 24, 1941, Columbus, OH, *Owner*, Olde Columbus Towne Realty; **PRIM RE ACT:** Broker, Property Manager, Owner/Investor; **SERVICES:** Pro. Mgmt. & Gen. Contracting; **PROFL AFFIL & HONORS:** IREM, Cols. & OH Bds. of Realtors; **EDUC:** BS, 1963, Mgmt., OH State Univ.; **GRAD EDUC:** MBA, 1969, Mgmt., Xavier Univ.; **HOME ADD:** 5926 Whitman Rd., Columbus, OH 43213, (614)861-5377; **BUS ADD:** 40 E. Fifth Ave., Columbus, OH 43201, (614)291-0791.

BERNSTEIN, Joel H.——B: Aug. 30, 1941, Elizabeth, NJ, *VP, Mktg.*, Equity Programs Investment Corp.; **PRIM RE ACT:** Property Manager, Owner/Investor, Syndicator; **SERVICES:** Buys model homes and lease them back to builders; synd. through investment partnerships; **REP CLIENTS:** Most major US homebuilders; **PREV**

EMPLOY: Keystone Co. of Boston; First Home Investment Co.; Vitt Assocs.; Realty-Vest, Inc.; **PROFL AFFIL & HONORS:** Bd. Member and Nat. Chap. Committeeman, RESSI; Intl. Assn. of Financial Planners; Advisor, Amer. Assn. of Ltd. Partners; **EDUC:** BS, 1963, Biology, Heidelberg College, Tiffin, OH; **HOME ADD:** 5130 Woodmire Lane, Alexandria, VA 22311, (703)379-9241; **BUS ADD:** 5201 Leesburg Pike, Suite 1600, Falls Church, VA 22041, (703)931-7600.

BERNSTEIN, Martin M.——B: Nov. 3, 1925, Greensboro, NC, *Exec. VP, RE*, Carlyle & Co. Jewelers; **OTHER RE ACT:** Leasing-Chain Stores; **PROFL AFFIL & HONORS:** Nat. Assn. of Corporate RE Execs., Intl. (past treas., presently member Bd. of Dir. and Chmn. of Audit Comm.); **EDUC:** Harvard Business School; **MIL SERV:** USAAC, Pilot; **OTHER ACT & HONORS:** Rotary Club; **HOME ADD:** 315 Meadowbrook Terr., Greensboro, NC 27408, (919)275-6063; **BUS ADD:** Wachovia Bank Bldg., PO Box 21768, Greensboro, NC 27420, (919)379-9437.

BERNSTEIN, Stanley——*VP Corp. Plng. & Dev.*, American Bakeries Co.; **PRIM RE ACT:** Property Manager; **BUS ADD:** 10S Riverside Plaza, Chicago, IL 60608, (312)454-7400.*

BERNSTEIN, Stephen M.——B: Feb. 10, 1941, Brooklyn, NY, *Esq.*; **PRIM RE ACT:** Attorney, Developer, Property Manager, Syndicator; **SERVICES:** Full range of legal & consultation servs. for RE clients; **REP CLIENTS:** Harlem Urban Devel. Corp., NY State Urban Devel. Corp., Richard Sherrill Assoc., MTS Assoc., East River Management Corp.; **PREV EMPLOY:** NY State Urban Devel. Corp., Assoc. Dir., Housing Devel.; **PROFL AFFIL & HONORS:** Member of Bar, State of NY; **EDUC:** BA, 1962, Hist., Brooklyn Coll.; **GRAD EDUC:** LLB, 1965, Columbia Univ. Law Sch.; JD, 1969, Columbia Univ. Law Sch.; **OTHER ACT & HONORS:** Member of Bd. Amer. Cancer Soc., NY City Div., Member of Bd. of Dir. Florence Ct. Coop.; **HOME ADD:** 187 Hicks St., Brooklyn, NY 11201, (212)625-2225; **BUS ADD:** 242 W 27th St., NY, NY 10001, (212)243-7913.

BERNTHAL, David G.——B: Apr. 18, 1950, Danville, IL, *Part.*, Meeker & Bernthal; **PRIM RE ACT:** Attorney; **SERVICES:** Legal representation of buyers, sellers & lenders in RE trans.; **REP CLIENTS:** Amer. S&L Assn. of Danville, IL; **PROFL AFFIL & HONORS:** IL State Bar Assn., Vermilion Cty. Bar Assn.; **EDUC:** BA, 1972, Pol. Sci., Univ. of IL; **GRAD EDUC:** JD, 1976, Univ. of IL; **EDUC HONORS:** High Honors; **MIL SERV:** US Army Nat. Guard, 1st Lt. (JAC); **OTHER ACT & HONORS:** Pres. of Rotary Club, Danville C of C, Salvation Army, United Fund; **HOME ADD:** 1418 Golf Terr., Danville, IL 61832; **BUS ADD:** 712 W Fairchild, Danville, IL 61832, (217)446-0600.

BERON, Gail L.——B: Nov. 13, 1943, Detroit, MI, *Pres.*, The Beron Co.; **PRIM RE ACT:** Consultant, Appraiser; **SERVICES:** Investment counseling, valuation, income props.; **REP CLIENTS:** Lenders, indiv. or instnl. investors, attys., govt. agencies; **PREV EMPLOY:** RE Appraisal & related work since 1971; **PROFL AFFIL & HONORS:** AIREA; Soc. of RE Appraisers, MAI; SRPA; Recipient of M. William Donnelly Award 1975; YMBC; MBAA; **OTHER ACT & HONORS:** Treas., Women's Comml.-Indus. Brokers Assn.; **HOME ADD:** 7008 Bridge Way, West Bloomfield, MI 48033, (616)851-1032; **BUS ADD:** 17228 Westhampton Rd., Southfield, MI 48075, (313)626-9539.

BERRY, Gregory A.——*Sales*, Cushman & Wakefield, Office Leasing, Seattle; **PRIM RE ACT:** Broker, Consultant; **SERVICES:** Office leasing, consultation & project planning; **PREV EMPLOY:** 6 yrs., Development of Office Bldgs. in suburban locations; **PROFL AFFIL & HONORS:** NAOIP; NAR; **BUS ADD:** 720 Olive Way, Suite 500, Seattle, WA 98101, (206)682-0666.

BERRY, Harry W.——B: Sept. 23, 1924, Bituman, PA, *Pres.*, The Berry & Berry Assocs.; **PRIM RE ACT:** Engineer, Architect; **PREV EMPLOY:** Assoc. Prof., WA State Univ.; **PROFL AFFIL & HONORS:** AIA, Past Chmn., WA State Licensing Bd., Commn., WA State Environ. Ed. Bd., Pres. WA State Council Arch.; **EDUC:** BArch., 1947, Design, Univ. of WA; **GRAD EDUC:** MArch., 1948, Design, Univ. of MI; **MIL SERV:** US Naval Reserves, Lt. jg.; **OTHER ACT & HONORS:** Kiwanis Club, C of C, Tacoma Yacht Club, Tacoma Bus. Club; **HOME ADD:** 3023 64th Ave. W., Tacoma, WA 98466, (206)564-4907; **BUS ADD:** One Washington Plaza, Tacoma, WA 98402, (206)383-5411.

BERRY, Joseph L.——B: July 26, 1948, Binghamton, NY, *Pres.*, Eastern Slope Inn and Attitash Mt. Village; **PRIM RE ACT:** Broker, Developer; **SERVICES:** Full Spectrum of RE Activity; **PREV EMPLOY:** Devel. and Realtor - Marblehead, MA - Glover Props. and Glover RE; **PROFL AFFIL & HONORS:** Amer. Land Develop. Assn.; **EDUC:** BS, 1971, Econ. and Bus., Univ. of VT; **GRAD EDUC:** JD, 1975, Environ. and Tax Law, New England School of Law; **HOME ADD:** Attitash Mt., Bartlett, NH 03812, (603)374-6622; **BUS ADD:** Main St., N. Conway, NH 03812, (603)356-6321.

BERRY, Keith C.——B: Dec. 24, 1939, Santa Barbara, CA, *Chief Exec. Officer. & Pres.*, Merrill Lynch Realty; **PRIM RE ACT:** Broker, Instructor; **PREV EMPLOY:** Security Title; **PROFL AFFIL & HONORS:** CA Assn of Realtors, Nat. Assn. of Realtors Grad. Realtors Inst., RECI, GRI, CRS, CRB; **EDUC:** Certificate of RE, Santa Barbara City Coll.; **MIL SERV:** USN, 3rd Cl. PO; **OTHER ACT & HONORS:** Santa Barbara Personnel Assn., Cbannel Cities Club; **HOME ADD:** 1160 Estrella Dr., Santa Barbara, CA 93110, (805)687-8373; **BUS ADD:** 3938 State St., Santa Barbara, CA 93105, (805)687-7531.

BERRY, Kenneth R.——B: July 7, 1923, St. Genevieve, MO, *Pres.*, Kenneth R. Berry Builder-Developer; **PRIM RE ACT:** Broker, Developer, Builder, Owner/Investor, Property Manager, Insuror, Syndicator; **SERVICES:** Home builder, apt. builder, land devel.; **EDUC:** 2 yrs. Coll.; **MIL SERV:** USMC; S/Sgt.; **HOME ADD:** 410 Oakwood, Webster Groves, MO 63119, (314)961-6669; **BUS ADD:** #25 East Frisco, Webster Groves, MO 63119, (314)968-5490.

BERRY, Richard B.——B: Feb. 2, 1919, Holly, CO, *Trust RE Officer & Bldg. Mgr.*, Union Bank & Trust Co., Tr. Dept.; **PRIM RE ACT:** Consultant, Banker, Property Manager; **SERVICES:** Mgmt. of B&T props.; **PREV EMPLOY:** First Nat. Bank of Englewood, Englewood, CO; **PROFL AFFIL & HONORS:** Montgomery Bd. of Realtors, BOMA, IREM, CPM, RPA; **MIL SERV:** USA, S/Sgt.; **OTHER ACT & HONORS:** AF&AM, LaJunta, CO; **HOME ADD:** 1930 Cottingham Dr., Montgomery, AL 36106, (205)272-6557; **BUS ADD:** 60 Commerce St., Montgomery, AL 36103, (205)265-8201.

BERRY, Richard S——B: June 20, 1945, NY, NY, *Pres*, Zuberry Development Corp.; **PRIM RE ACT:** Broker, Consultant, Attorney, Developer, Builder, Owner/Investor, Property Manager, Syndicator; **REP CLIENTS:** All aspects of RE devel.; **PREV EMPLOY:** Atty., Lord, Day & Lord; **PROFL AFFIL & HONORS:** Assoc. of Bar of City of NY, RE Bd. of NY; **EDUC:** BA, 1967, Univ. of PA; **GRAD EDUC:** JD, 1970, NY Univ. School of Law; **HOME ADD:** 123 E 75th St., NY, NY 10021, (212)249-7276; **BUS ADD:** 305 E 47th St., NY, NY 10017, (212)838-5020.

BERRYMAN, Dennis M.——B: Oct. 23, 1939, Los Angeles, CA, *Partner*, Pacific Development Group; **PRIM RE ACT:** Developer; **SERVICES:** Shopping ctr. devel.; **PREV EMPLOY:** Santa Anita Devel. Corp., Pres. 1970-1980; Coopers & Lybrand 1961-1970; **PROFL AFFIL & HONORS:** Amer. Inst. of CPA's; ICSC, CPA; **EDUC:** BS Bus. Admin., 1961, Acctg., CA State Univ., Long Beach; **HOME ADD:** 11 N LaSenda, Three Arch Bay, South Laguna, CA 92677, (714)499-2428; **BUS ADD:** 15 Corporate Plaza, Suite 250, PO Box 3060, Newport Beach, CA 92660, (714)760-8591.

BERTHIAUME, Normand——B: Nov. 19, 1936, Montreal, *Dir. Physical Plant Serv.*, Univ. of Ottawa, Admin.; **PRIM RE ACT:** Engineer; **SERVICES:** Phy. plant service; **PREV EMPLOY:** Nat. Bank of Canada; **PROFL AFFIL & HONORS:** APPA, BOMA; **EDUC:** BS, 1961, Civil Eng, Univ. of Montreal; **EDUC HONORS:** Prof. Eng.; **OTHER ACT & HONORS:** Alderman, Town of Aylmer, 1973-1975; **HOME ADD:** 10 Des Pommiers, Alymer, J9H SE1, Prov of Quebec, Canada, (819)776-3497; **BUS ADD:** 160 Nicholas, Ottawa, K1N 6N5, Ontario, Canada, (613)231-2296.

BERTOLINA, Richard R.——B: Jan. 4, 1939, San Francisco, CA, *VP*, Lee Saylor Inc., Project Analysis; **PRIM RE ACT:** Consultant, Appraiser, Architect, Developer, Lender, Builder, Owner/Investor, Syndicator, Real Estate Publisher; **OTHER RE ACT:** Cost Engrg.; **SERVICES:** Cost estimating, const. analysis, inspections, const./proj. mgmt., scheduling, claims; **REP CLIENTS:** lenders, developers, architects, appraiser, Attys.; **PREV EMPLOY:** Chief const. analyst for Bank of Amer., Appraisal Dept., Const. Analysis Project Mgmt. (San Francisco Office) for 11 1/2 years; Various Architectural offices; **PROFL AFFIL & HONORS:** AIA; Amer. Soc. of Prof. Estimators; **EDUC:** BS, 1964, Arch., Heald Engineering Coll. School of Architecture; AA San Francisco CC; **OTHER ACT & HONORS:** Amer. Entrepreneurs Assn., Amer. Investors Assn., CA Inventors Council; Lic. Architecture, CA; also Pres. of the Carnelian Group, RE Devel., loan packaging, lender liason; **HOME ADD:** PO Box 1706, Sausalito, CA 94966, (415)332-9100; **BUS ADD:** 1717 Union St., San Francisco, CA 94123, (415)474-5335.

BERTOT, Cathey H.——*Pres.*, GSG Fin.; **PRIM RE ACT:** Broker, Owner/Investor, Syndicator; **OTHER RE ACT:** Fin. & Tax Planning; **PROFL AFFIL & HONORS:** Pres., Sacramento Chap. Intl. Assn. of Fin. Planners, Cert. Fin. Planner; **EDUC:** BA, 1972, Poli. Sci.,

CSU Fullerton; **GRAD EDUC:** MBA, 1981, Taxation, Golden Gate Univ.; **BUS ADD:** 8801 Folsom Blvd., Sacramento, CA 95826, (916)381-9024.

BERTRAM, Dennis——*Chief Plant Engr.*, Dayton Malleable Inc.; **PRIM RE ACT:** Property Manager; **BUS ADD:** PO Box 98, Dayton, OH 45401, (513)298-5251.*

BERTRAND, Gilles——**B:** Sept. 4, 1923, Quebec City, Can., *Pres.*, Gilles Bertrand Property Management, Inc.; **PRIM RE ACT:** Broker, Owner/Investor, Property Manager; **SERVICES:** Investment Counsel.; Prop. Mgmt.; **REP CLIENTS:** Lenders, Banks, Indivs., Govt. Investors (for.); **PROFL AFFIL & HONORS:** IREM, BOMA, FIABCI, CPM; SCV; **EDUC:** Bus. Adm., 1947; **MIL SERV:** AF, S/Sgt.; **HOME ADD:** 2740 Bridgewater, Ste Foy, P.Q., Can., (418)651-0397; **BUS ADD:** 350 E Charest Blvd. Suite 508, Quebec City, GIK 3H5, P.Q., Canada, (418)529-8461.

BESSER, Bruce R.——**B:** Nov. 22, 1936, Milwaukee, WI, *Owner*, The Besser Group; **PRIM RE ACT:** Broker, Consultant, Developer, Builder, Owner/Investor, Property Manager, Syndicator; **EDUC:** BS, 1958, Corp. Fin. & Econ., Wharton School & Fin., Univ. of PA; **HOME ADD:** 1111 Forest, Evanston, IL 60201, (312)864-8647; **BUS ADD:** 1111 Forest, Evanston, IL 60202, (312)864-8647.

BEST, Minor L.——**B:** Dec. 23, 1944, Charleston, IL, *Pres.*, Country Mortgage Corporation; **PRIM RE ACT:** Broker, Consultant, Developer, Lender, Owner/Investor; **SERVICES:** Consulting and lending of single family and multifamily resid. props.; **REP CLIENTS:** Single and multifamily devels. and builders experienced in govt.-assisted programs; **PREV EMPLOY:** Amer. Fletcher Mortgage Co. - VP, The Hart Cos. - VP; **PROFL AFFIL & HONORS:** AICPA's, IN RE Commn. Broker Lic.; **EDUC:** BS, 1966, Bus. Educ., Eastern IL Univ., Charleston, IL; **GRAD EDUC:** Masters of Sci., 1969, Acctg., Eastern IL Univ., Charleston, IL; **EDUC HONORS:** Pi Omega Pi, Delta Pi Epsilon, Honorary Bus. Soc., Graduate Asst.; **HOME ADD:** 1731 Birch Ct., Plainfield, IN 46168, (317)839-9850; **BUS ADD:** 1134 S. Mickley Ave., Indianapolis, IN 46241, (317)244-2492.

BEST, Paul A.——**B:** Apr. 19, 1950, Conydon, IN, *VP*, First Nat. Bank of Louisville, Mort. Div.; **PRIM RE ACT:** Attorney, Banker, Lender; **PREV EMPLOY:** Prudential Ins. Co., RE Inv. Dept., 5 yrs.; **PROFL AFFIL & HONORS:** KBA, IN Bar Assn., ABA; **EDUC:** BS, 1972, Fin., Bus.; **GRAD EDUC:** JD, 1976, Univ. of Louisville, Sch. of Law; **HOME ADD:** 10600 Helmsdale Ln., Louisville, KY 40243, (502)245-9861; **BUS ADD:** 101 S Fifth St., Louisville, KY 40232, (502)581-6792.

BEST, Robert T.——**B:** Mar. 30, 1947, Santa Monica, CA, *Pres.*, Westar Assoc.; **PRIM RE ACT:** Developer, Owner/Investor, Property Manager; **PROFL AFFIL & HONORS:** Intl. Council of Shopping Ctrs.; Member CA R.E. Broker; **EDUC:** BS, 1969, Mktg./Mgmt., USC; **GRAD EDUC:** MBA, 1970, Mktg./ Mgmt., USC; **OTHER ACT & HONORS:** CA Community Coll. teaching credential (bus.); **HOME ADD:** 2 Jade Cove, Corona Del Mar, CA 92625, (714)640-6459; **BUS ADD:** 4425 Jamboree Rd. 130, Newport Beach, CA 92660, (714)975-0299.

BESTE, James D.——**B:** Nov. 5, 1944, Evanston, IL, *VP & Counsel*, Federated Stores Realty, Inc.; **PRIM RE ACT:** Attorney, Developer; **SERVICES:** Reg. shopping ctr. devel.; **PREV EMPLOY:** Gen. Counsel Bellante, Miller, Clauss & Nolan, Arch. Engrgs., Planners; **PROFL AFFIL & HONORS:** ABA, PA Bar Assn., Amer. Inst. of Planners, ULI, ICSC; **EDUC:** BA, 1967, Hist., Econ., Middlebury Coll.; **GRAD EDUC:** JD, 1971, Law, Univ. of PA, Sch. of Law; MCP, 1971, City Planning, Univ. of Pa, Sch. of Fine Arts; **EDUC HONORS:** Cum Laude; **HOME ADD:** 6925 Royalgreen Dr., Cincinnati, OH 45244, (513)231-2247; **BUS ADD:** 7 W 7th St., Cincinnati, OH 45202, (513)579-7905.

BETHEA, Basil L., Jr.——**B:** Jan. 20, 1940, Brewton, AL, *Pres.*, Realty House, Inc.; **PRIM RE ACT:** Broker, Owner/Investor; **SERVICES:** Realtor, comml. brokerage; **PROFL AFFIL & HONORS:** NAR; **EDUC:** Univ. of AL; **OTHER ACT & HONORS:** Dist. 9, VP, FL Assn. of Realtors; **HOME ADD:** 29 Bay Dr., N.E., Ft. Walton Beach, FL 32548, (904)243-3664; **BUS ADD:** 206 Hollywood Blvd. S.E., Ft. Walton Beach, FL 32548, (904)244-9117.

BETTENCOURT, Joe——Campanelli Enterprises; **PRIM RE ACT:** Developer; **BUS ADD:** 1 Campanelli Dr., Braintree, MA 02184, (617)843-8280.*

BETTS, Joan S.——**B:** Aug. 8, 1951, Atlanta, GA, *Asst. VP; Mgr. Southeast Regional Investment Division*, Fidelity Mutual Life Ins. Co., RE Investment; **PRIM RE ACT:** Lender, Owner/Investor, Syndicator; **OTHER RE ACT:** Mktg./Sales; **PREV EMPLOY:** RE Market Research & Appraisal; **EDUC:** BA, 1973, RE, Univ. of GA; **GRAD EDUC:** MBA, 1975, Fin., GA State Univ.; **EDUC HONORS:** Magna Cum Laude, Dean's List, Cameron Brown Scholarship, 1973; Beta Gamma Sigma, Phi Kappa Phi; **HOME ADD:** 3074 Vinings Ferry Dr., NW, Atlanta, GA 30339, (404)436-8289; **BUS ADD:** 380 Interstate N. Pkwy., Suite 150, Atlanta, GA 30339, (404)955-3880.

BETTS, Richard M.——**B:** Mar. 1, 1935, Baltimore, MD, *Pres.*, Richard M. Betts Prop. Analysis; **PRIM RE ACT:** Appraiser; **SERVICES:** Valuation, counseling, expert testimony; **REP CLIENTS:** Indiv. investors, lenders,litigation attys.; **PROFL AFFIL & HONORS:** AAA Panel of Arbitrators; Nat. Editorial Bd.; *The Appraisal Journal*, MAI; SRPA; ASA (RE); **EDUC:** BS, 1962, RE & Urban Econ., Univ. of CA, Berkeley, Sch. of Bus.; **GRAD EDUC:** MBA, 1963, RE & Urban Econ., Univ. of CA, Berkeley, Grad. Sch. of Bus.; **EDUC HONORS:** Cum Laude; **MIL SERV:** USN; 1953-57, 1st Class PO; **OTHER ACT & HONORS:** Berkeley Rotary Club, Pres. Elect. 1981-82; Co-Author, *The Essentials of RE Econ.*, 2nd., Wiley, NY, 1980; Co-Author, *Basic RE Appraisal*, Wiley, NY, 1982; Co-Author, RE Appraisal Instructors Guide, CADRE, Sacramento, 1979; Pres., East Bay Chapter No. 54, SREA, 1976-77; Sec-Treas., Northern CA Chapter 11, AIREA, 1982; **BUS ADD:** 2150 Shattuck Ave., Suite 405, Berkeley, CA 94704, (415)845-6988.

BEUC, Rudolph, Jr.——**B:** Nov. 7, 1931, St. Louis, MO, *Pres.*, R. Beuc, AIA, Archs.; **PRIM RE ACT:** Architect, Broker, Regulator, Consultant, Appraiser, Developer, Owner/Investor; **SERVICES:** Arch, planning, RE consulting & serv.; **PREV EMPLOY:** Architectural Draftsman & designer 1957 to 1960, R. Beuc, AIA Archs. 1960 to pres.; **PROFL AFFIL & HONORS:** AIA, Soc. of Amer. Archs., MO Assoc. of Bldg. Ofcls. & Inspectors, Soc. of Amer. Value. Engrgs., MARA; **EDUC:** BArch., 1955, Arch., Wash. Univ., St. Louis; **MIL SERV:** USA, Spec./2, Good Conduct; **OTHER ACT & HONORS:** Bldg. Commnr, Peerless Park, MO, Mason 32, Lions, Amer. Legion, High Twelve, Westborough Country Club; **HOME ADD:** 138 W. Glendale Rd., St. Louis, MO 63119, (314)962-8815; **BUS ADD:** 142 W. Glendale Rd., St. Louis, MO 63119, (314)962-8816.

BEURET, Jules W.——**B:** May 25, 1914, Jersey City, NJ, *VP*, Cummings Realty & Trust Co., Inc.; **PRIM RE ACT:** Broker, Consultant; **SERVICES:** RE brokerage, investment counseling; **REP CLIENTS:** Indiv., partnerships, corp.; **PREV EMPLOY:** Div. VP, ARA Services, Inc.; Dir. of Mktg., Pfizer Laboratories; **PROFL AFFIL & HONORS:** RNMI; AZ Chapter, CCIM (Pres.), CCIM; **EDUC:** BS, Bus., Columbia Univ.; **MIL SERV:** USAF; 1944-45, Cpl.; **OTHER ACT & HONORS:** Pres., Tucson Gen. Hosp. Found.; **HOME ADD:** 111 E. Florence Rd., Tucson, AZ 85704, (602)297-6986; **BUS ADD:** 1725 N. Swan Rd., Tucson, AZ 85712, (602)881-3210.

BEYEMIAN, Robert——*Pres.*, Instrument Systems Corp.; **PRIM RE ACT:** Property Manager; **BUS ADD:** 100 Jericho Quadrangle Ste. 224, Jericho, NY 11753, (516)938-5544.*

BEYERS, James L.——**B:** Mar. 30, 1945, Seattle, WA, *Managing Part.*, Misuraca, Beyers & Costin; **PRIM RE ACT:** Attorney; **SERVICES:** Land Use Planning, Dev., RE Fin. Gen. Bus. and RE Litigation, Synd., Admin. Agency Rep.; **PROFL AFFIL & HONORS:** CA Assn. of Realtors; ABA, RESSI, State Bar, Sonoma Ct. Bar Assn.; **EDUC:** BA, 1967, Econ., Univ. of WA; **GRAD EDUC:** JD, 1972, Boalt Hall, Univ. of CA at Berkeley; **EDUC HONORS:** Grad. with distinction, Order of the Coif; **MIL SERV:** USA, 1968-70, SP-5; **BUS ADD:** PO Box 878, Santa Rosa, CA 95402, (707)545-0142.

BEYNON, Robert L.——**B:** May 17, 1946, Pittsburgh, PA, *VP Sales & Mgmt.*, Beynon & Co. Inc.; **PRIM RE ACT:** Broker, Consultant, Appraiser, Owner/Investor, Property Manager, Insuror; **SERVICES:** Comml. investment analysis, prop. mgmt., ins., appraising, consulting; **REP CLIENTS:** Corps. or indivs. interested in comml. & indus. and investment props.; **PROFL AFFIL & HONORS:** Pittsburgh Athletic Assn., NIREB, Greater Pittsburgh Bd. of Realtors, PA Broker, CCIM Candidate; **EDUC:** BA Poli. Sci., 1968, Bus. & Poli. Sci., Gettysburg Coll.; **MIL SERV:** US Army Res., Sgt.; **HOME ADD:** 98 Morrison Dr., Pittsburgh, PA 15216; **BUS ADD:** 1000 Union Trust Bldg., Suite 1000, Pittsburgh, PA 15219, (412)261-3640.

BEZ, Charles G.——**B:** Dec. 13, 1939, Chicago, IL, *Managing Partner*, Narrows Plaza Development Company; **PRIM RE ACT:** Developer, Owner/Investor, Property Manager; **EDUC:** BS/BA, 1961, Mgmt./Purchasing, Roosevelt Univ.; **HOME ADD:** 541 Monterey Lane, Fircrest, WA 98466, (206)565-6266; **BUS ADD:** 6721 Regents Blvd., Tacoma, WA 98466, (206)565-1007.

BIAGI, Hazel——**B:** Sept. 27, 1918, KS, *Investment Div. Mgr.*, American Properties & Investments; **PRIM RE ACT:** Broker, Consultant, Appraiser, Owner/Investor, Property Manager, Syndicator; **OTHER**

RE ACT: Exchangor; **SERVICES:** Estate Planning-Counseling; **PREV EMPLOY:** RE; **PROFL AFFIL & HONORS:** San Jose RE Bd.; Central Valley Mktg. & Exchange; Assoc. Investment & Exchange Counselors; INTEREX; CCIM; & Santa Cruz Exchangors, BRI; **EDUC:** RE Law & Ethics, 1969, West Valley Coll.; **OTHER ACT & HONORS:** Ex Pres. of Alum Rock Bus. & Profl. Womens; Campbell C of C Ambassador; **HOME ADD:** 3965 Blue Gum Dr., San Jose, CA 95127, (408)227-5629; **BUS ADD:** 4608 Meridian Ave., San Jose, CA 95124, (408)448-5260.

BIAGI, R.C.——B: Aug. 29, 1925, Crockett, CA, *Corp. VP - RE*, Lucky Stores, Inc.; **PRIM RE ACT:** Instructor, Consultant, Property Manager, Owner/Investor; **SERVICES:** Direct co.-wide RE activities; **PREV EMPLOY:** Safeway Stores, Inc.; **PROFL AFFIL & HONORS:** ICSC; **EDUC:** BS, 1950, Mktg. and RE, Univ. of CA - Berkeley; **MIL SERV:** USN, ETM 2nd Class, Pacific Theater Okinawa campaign; **OTHER ACT & HONORS:** Past Tr. and Convention Chmn. of I.C.S.C.; Past Pres. UC Berkeley Bus. School Alumni Assn.; CA RE Certificate Inst.; CA Bus. Props. Bd. Member; **HOME ADD:** 1459 Montrose Dr., San Leandro, CA 94577, (415)351-9347; **BUS ADD:** 6300 Clark Ave., Dublin, CA 94566, (415)833-6000.

BIAGIOTTI, Stephen M.——B: July 16, 1945, Boston, MA, *Pres*, Victorio Mort. Co.; **PRIM RE ACT:** Broker, Developer; **OTHER RE ACT:** Mort. banker; **SERVICES:** RE Investment analysis, mort. banking; **REP CLIENTS:** Devel., lenders & inst. investors; **PREV EMPLOY:** Sr. VP, Mellon Natl. Morg. Co., VP Citi Corp Loan Officer, Ford Motor Credit Co., VP AMERCO Inc.; **PROFL AFFIL & HONORS:** RE Mort Bankers Assn. of CO, RE Broker; **EDUC:** BS, 1967, Fin., Univ. of CO; **GRAD EDUC:** MBA, 1971, Econ, RE, Univ. of OR; **HOME ADD:** 8531 E Dry Creek Pl., Englewood, CO 80112, (303)779-4735; **BUS ADD:** 3333 Quebec, Suite 3400, Denver, CO 80207, (303)399-5130.

BIANCA, Anthony T., Sr.——B: Feb. 8, 1920, New Britain, CT, *Gen. Partner*, Devcon Enterprises; **PRIM RE ACT:** Consultant, Developer, Builder, Owner/Investor, Property Manager, Syndicator; **OTHER RE ACT:** Synd., devel., bldg. & prop. mgmt. of multi-family, single family housing and comml. props.; **SERVICES:** Indiv. & inst. investors in housing and comml. props.; HUD/FHA/CT Housing Agency and FMHA; **PREV EMPLOY:** State of CT, Admin. Aide to Tax Commr. & Tax Marshal, 16 yrs.; **PROFL AFFIL & HONORS:** Nat. Leased Housing Assn., Hartford Cty. Home Builders; **EDUC:** Drafting, Hillyer Jr. Coll. (Evening School, 2 yrs.); RE Courses, Univ. of CT (Evening School, 2 yrs.); **MIL SERV:** US Army, S/Sgt., Purple Heart, Pres. Unit Citation, Combat Infantry Badge, ETO 3 battle stars; **OTHER ACT & HONORS:** Selectman; Parking Commr.; Charter Revision Commr.; WW II Memorial Chmn.; Justice of Peace; N.B. Lodge of Elks; K of C; 4th Degree; VFW; Amer. Legion; DAV, Corporator - Boys Club of New Britain, Inc., Corporator - New Britain General Hospital; **HOME ADD:** 223 Brittany Farms Rd., New Britain, CT 06053, (203)229-9866; **BUS ADD:** 740 N. Main St., W. Hartford, CT 06117, (203)233-2114.

BIANCHI, Philip A.——B: July 27, 1932, Newton, MA, *Pres.*, Bianchi Eng. Co., Inc.; **PRIM RE ACT:** Architect, Developer, Engineer; **SERVICES:** Land devel. subdivs.; **PROFL AFFIL & HONORS:** MSPE; MALSE; NSPE; **EDUC:** BBA, 1960, CE, Northeastern Univ.; **OTHER ACT & HONORS:** Alternate Bldg. Insp., Indust. Devel. Com.; **HOME ADD:** 10 Sherman Rd., Millis, MA 02054, (617)376-8817; **BUS ADD:** 37 Exchange St., Millis, MA 02054, (617)376-4144.

BIBLE, Douglas Spencer——B: Sept. 28, 1946, Wauseon, OH, *Asst. Prof.*, Old Dominion Univ., School of Bus.; **PRIM RE ACT:** Consultant, Owner/Investor, Instructor, Real Estate Publisher; **SERVICES:** Investment and valuation analysis, applied research; **PREV EMPLOY:** Asst. Prof., FL State Univ., 1976-1980; **PROFL AFFIL & HONORS:** Amer. RE and Urban Econ. Assn., Recipient of two SREA Research Awards to study fin. - appraising relationships; Recipient of ODU Research Award to study AMLs; Recipient of State of FL Severance Damage Research Award; **EDUC:** BS, 1968, Fin., Bowling Green State Univ.; **GRAD EDUC:** MBA, 1971, Fin., IN Univ.; PhD, RE/Urban Analysis, OH State Univ.; **EDUC HONORS:** Beta Gamma Sigma; **MIL SERV:** US Army Res., E-6, 1969-1976; **OTHER ACT & HONORS:** Published eight articles on RE Housing, Appraisal & Fin. in journals such as AREUEA Journal, Appraisal Journal & RE Appraiser; **HOME ADD:** 1140 Selwood Dr., VA Beach, VA 23464, (804)467-9430; **BUS ADD:** Norfolk, VA 23508, (804)440-3501.

BIBLE, Jim C., III——B: June 7, 1950, Augusta, GA, *Assoc. Broker*, Sherman and Hemstreet; **PRIM RE ACT:** Broker, Syndicator, Consultant, Builder, Property Manager; **SERVICES:** Prop. Mgmt., Synd. Resid. Prop. Mgmt. Consultant; **PREV EMPLOY:** US Shelter Corp. 1974-1977, Spaulding & Slye Corp. 1979; **PROFL AFFIL & HONORS:** IREM, RESSI, CPM; **EDUC:** 1968-1970, Engrg. & Econ., Univ. of SC; **MIL SERV:** USMCR; **OTHER ACT & HONORS:** Augusta Jaycees; **HOME ADD:** 4527 Dewey Dr., Martinez, GA 30907, (404)860-4056; **BUS ADD:** 3520 Walton Ext., Augusta, GA 30909, (404)738-6641.

BICK, J. Karl——B: Feb. 27, 1937, Chicago, IL, *VP, Dir. and Broker*, Elkhorn Realty & Devel. Co.; **PRIM RE ACT:** Broker, Developer, Builder, Owner/Investor, Syndicator; **SERVICES:** Planning, devel. and brokerage of resid. and comml. prop.; **REP CLIENTS:** Devels., investment synds.; **PREV EMPLOY:** VP, The Title Insurance Co. (now Safeco Title of ID); VP, Snowmas Corp., Aspen, CO; Audit Mgr., Arthur Andersen & Co.- CPAs; **PROFL AFFIL & HONORS:** NAR, ID RE Assn.; **EDUC:** AB, 1959, Econ., Univ. of Notre Dame; **GRAD EDUC:** MBA, 1961, Acctg., Northwestern Univ.; **MIL SERV:** US Army; **OTHER ACT & HONORS:** Member - Sun Valley City Council, Sun Valley, ID since 1977; Member - Blaine Cty ID Planning & Zoning since 1979; Dir. - Sun Valley ID Water & Sewer Dist.; Member - Blaine Cty. Airport Authority; Tr. & Chmn. of Exec. Comm., Sun Valley ID Ctr. for Arts and Humanities since 1978; **HOME ADD:** 214 Sunrise Dr., P O Box 2014, Sun Valley, ID 83353, (208)622-3634; **BUS ADD:** P O Box 7722, Sun Valley, ID 83353, (208)622-7722.

BICKSLER, Charles S.——B: Sept. 21, 1919, Lancaster, PA, *Sr. VP*, Sanders and Thomas, Inc.; **PRIM RE ACT:** Architect; **SERVICES:** Arch., Engrs., Plnrs., Constr. Mgmt.; **PROFL AFFIL & HONORS:** AIA, Parenteral Drug Assn., Intl. Soc. of Pharmaceutical Engrs.; **EDUC:** BArch, 1941, PA State Univ.; **OTHER ACT & HONORS:** BPOE; Found. Bd. Mbr., Sigma Pi Frat.; **HOME ADD:** 573 Mervine St., Pottstown, PA 19464, (215)323-3381; **BUS ADD:** 11 Robinson St., Pottstown, PA 19464, (215)326-4600.

BIDDLE, Eugene D., Jr.——*Dir. of Mktg.*, Princeton Forrestal Ctr.; **PRIM RE ACT:** Consultant, Developer, Owner/Investor; **SERVICES:** Land devel., build to suit, project fin.; **PREV EMPLOY:** Chemical Bank, Corp. Lending Office; **PROFL AFFIL & HONORS:** Nat. Assn. of Indus. & Office Parks, Indus. RE Brokers Assn.; **EDUC:** BFA, 1975, Arch., Cornell Univ.; **GRAD EDUC:** 1978, Fin., Stanford Univ.; **HOME ADD:** RD 4, Box 849, Princeton, NJ; **BUS ADD:** Princeton Forrestal Ctr., 105 Coll. Rd., E., 3rd Floor, Princeton, NJ 08540, (609)452-7720.

BIDDLE, J. Craig——*Ed.*, Cody Publications, Inc., Florida Realtor; **PRIM RE ACT:** Real Estate Publisher; **BUS ADD:** PO Box 1030, Kissimmee, FL 32741, (305)846-2800.*

BIEL, Howard Steven——B: June 16, 1947, Cleveland, OH, *VP, Mkt. Research and Land Devel.*, Edward J. DeBartolo Corp.; **PRIM RE ACT:** Developer, Builder, Owner/Investor, Property Manager; **SERVICES:** Comprehensive comml. RE devel.; **PREV EMPLOY:** Chmn./Urban & Environmental Studies Dept. Case Western Res. Univ. (1973-1977); Asst. Prof., Economic Geography & Planning Univ. of VT & Middlebury College (1977-1978); **EDUC:** BA, 1969, Econ./Geography, Miami Univ., Oxford, OH; **GRAD EDUC:** MA, PhD, 1971-1973, Geography/Econ. and Civil Engrg., OH State Univ.; **EDUC HONORS:** Cum Laude; **HOME ADD:** 82 Poland Manor, Poland, OH 44514, (216)757-4061; **BUS ADD:** 7620 Market St., Youngstown, OH 44512, (216)758-7292.

BIENIEK, Gary A.——B: June 1, 1957, Little Falls, MN, *Land Mktg. Spec.*, Minneapolis Comm. Devel. Agency, Land Mktg.; **PRIM RE ACT:** Consultant, Owner/Investor; **OTHER RE ACT:** RE sales agent; **SERVICES:** Sale of developable land, RE investment counseling; **REP CLIENTS:** Devels., builders, arch., prvt. investors; **PREV EMPLOY:** Minneapolis Housing and Redev. Auth., Apr. 1978-June, 1981; **EDUC:** BS, 1980, Environmental Design, Univ. of MN, Minneapolis, MN; **GRAD EDUC:** MBA, Coll. of St. Thomas, St. Paul, MN; **HOME ADD:** 5906 Oakland Ave., Minneapolis, MN 55417, (612)861-5537; **BUS ADD:** 1400 Park Ave., Minneapolis, MN 55404, (612)348-6362.

BIERBRIER, Leonard H.——B: June 14, 1944, Montreal, Can., *Pres.*, Leonard Bierbrier & Assoc. Inc.; **PRIM RE ACT:** Broker, Consultant, Developer; **PROFL AFFIL & HONORS:** ICSC, NACORE, GREEB; **GRAD EDUC:** 1968;, 1971, McGill Law School, Harvard Bus. School; **HOME ADD:** 8 Gracewood Park, Cambridge, MA 02138, (617)661-3274; **BUS ADD:** 51 Brattle, Suite 21, Cambridge, MA 02138, (617)661-2929.

BIERYLO, John I.——B: July 6, 1941, Cranbury, NJ, *Sr. VP*, Doric Devel., Inc.; **PRIM RE ACT:** Developer, Builder, Owner/Investor; **SERVICES:** Industrial, commercial and resid., devel., construction, prop. mgmt., brokerage; **PREV EMPLOY:** Digiorgio Devel. Corp., Chief Fin. Officer; **PROFL AFFIL & HONORS:** ULI; Soc. of Indus. Realtors; RE Research Council of N CA; AICPA; CA Soc. of CPA's,

CPA, CA; **EDUC:** AB, 1963, Econ., Rutgers Univ.; **MIL SERV:** USAF; Capt.; Commendation Medal; **HOME ADD:** 373 Lombard, San Francisco, CA 94133, (415)421-2571; **BUS ADD:** 936 Shorepoint Court, Alameda, CA 94501, (415)521-1771.

BIGELOW, Charles Glenford, III——B: Aug. 11, 1943, Pittsburgh, PA, *VP*, Warburg Paribas Becker Inc., Corporate Finance; **PRIM RE ACT:** Consultant, Banker, Owner/Investor, Syndicator; **OTHER RE ACT:** Investment Banker; **SERVICES:** Tax shelter, corp. fin., RE fin.; **REP CLIENTS:** U.S. Home, Dillingham Corp., MacArthur Found., Holiday Inns, Inc., various developers; **PREV EMPLOY:** Canal Randolph Corp., RE devel.; **PROFL AFFIL & HONORS:** RE broker; **EDUC:** BS, 1965, Chem. Engrg., Cornell Univ.; **GRAD EDUC:** MS; MBA, 1966; 1969, Chem. Engrg.; Fin., Cornell Univ.; Harvard Coll.; **EDUC HONORS:** Tau Beta Pi; **BUS ADD:** 55 Water St., New York, NY 10041, (212)747-4605.

BIGELOW, Ernest A.——B: June 29, 1926, NYC, NY, *Owner*, Ernest A. Bigelow Realty Investments and Pequot Properties; **PRIM RE ACT:** Broker, Owner/Investor, Syndicator; **PREV EMPLOY:** Talman Bigelow, Whittemore Ltd., NY; **PROFL AFFIL & HONORS:** Comml. investment div. of CT Assn. of Realtors (CID); **MIL SERV:** USAF, Cpl.; **OTHER ACT & HONORS:** Dir. C of C, Thames Sci. Ctr., CID; **HOME ADD:** Tangwonk Rd., Stonington, CT; **BUS ADD:** 58 Denison Ave., Mystic, CT 06355, (203)536-4906.

BIGELOW, George H.——B: Aug. 5, 1942, MA, *VP*, Property Capital Trust; **PRIM RE ACT:** Consultant, Owner/Investor; **OTHER RE ACT:** Asset Mgr. for Inst. Clients; **SERVICES:** Inv. Mgmt.; **REP CLIENTS:** Tax Exempts - Pension, Foundations, Endowments; **PREV EMPLOY:** CT General 1967-1972, Asst. Sec. RE Dept.; **PROFL AFFIL & HONORS:** MBA, ULI, NAR, NASD; **EDUC:** BA Classics, 1964, Classics - Archeology, Brown Univ.; **GRAD EDUC:** MBA, 1966, Fin., Suffolk Univ.; **EDUC HONORS:** Deans List; **OTHER ACT & HONORS:** Bd. of Dir.; Capital Life Ins. Co., NY, Capital for RE Inc. Property Capital Advisors Inc., PCA Financial Corp.; **HOME ADD:** Dover, MA 02030; **BUS ADD:** 200 Clarendon, Boston, MA 02116, (617)536-8600.

BIGGS, Dean——Builders Inc.; **PRIM RE ACT:** Developer; **BUS ADD:** 100 Parklane, Wichita, KS 67218, (316)522-4791.*

BIGGS, Harold——*VP*, Gifford-Hill & Co.; **PRIM RE ACT:** Property Manager; **BUS ADD:** PO Box 47127, Dallas, TX 75247, (214)637-3860.*

BIGGS, Hubbard K.——B: Jan. 31, 1920, Barberville, FL, *Appraiser*, Hubbard K. Biggs, SRA; **PRIM RE ACT:** Broker, Consultant, Appraiser; **PREV EMPLOY:** Self employed for over 30 years; **PROFL AFFIL & HONORS:** Soc. of RE Appraisers, NAR, FLI, Nat. Mktg. Inst., SRA, GRI, Accredited Farm & Land Member, CRG; **EDUC:** 1940, Econ., Univ. of FL; **MIL SERV:** US Army, 1941-46, Maj., 3 Battle Stars; **HOME ADD:** 241 Volusia Dr., Winter Haven, FL 33880, (813)324-4835; **BUS ADD:** 4820 Cypress Garden Rd., Winter Haven, FL 33880, (813)324-2202.

BILGREI, Michael Mark——B: May 2, 1942, Brooklyn, NY, *Pres*, MARC Air Conditioning & Refrigeration Corp.; **PRIM RE ACT:** Engineer; **OTHER RE ACT:** Contractor; **SERVICES:** Consulting engineering servs. & contracting; **REP CLIENTS:** Comml. & indus. clients, Cross & Brown, Chase Manhattan Bank, Precision Film Labs., Title Guarantee Co., '21' Club; **PREV EMPLOY:** Western Electroc Co., Inc., Plant Design & Constr., 1963-69; **PROFL AFFIL & HONORS:** ASME, ASHRAE, IEEE, NYSSPE, NY Bldg. Congress, Arch. Adv. Comm. of CUNY, Various ASME Citations; **EDUC:** BSEE/BSME, 1963, Polytechnic Inst. of NY; **GRAD EDUC:** MSIM, 1967, Mgmt., Poly. Inst. of NY; **OTHER ACT & HONORS:** Nat. Engrg. Cert., Bd. of Dir. YM-YWHA of Williamsburgh Inc., 1966-71; **HOME ADD:** 111-20 73rd Ave., Forest Hills, NY 11375, (212)793-4970; **BUS ADD:** 360 Broadway St., Brooklyn, NY 11211, (212)782-2244.

BILLER, Aaron——*Ed.-Mng. Ed.*, Hagedorn Publishing Co., Inc., Real Estate Weekly; **PRIM RE ACT:** Real Estate Publisher; **BUS ADD:** 235 Park Ave. S., NY, NY 10003, (212)677-3131.*

BILLINGS, Richard W.——B: Nov. 3, 1927, Rome, NY, *Part.*, Hinckley & Allen; **PRIM RE ACT:** Attorney; **SERVICES:** Atty. for major lenders and comml. RE; **REP CLIENTS:** Owners and users , Indus. Natl. Bank of RI Prudential Ins. Co. of Amer.; Sun Life Assurance of Can. (US); RI Port Authority and Econ. Devel. Co.; ITT Grinnell Corp.; **EDUC:** AB, 1949, Pol. Sci., Univ. of MI; **GRAD EDUC:** JD, 1952, Law, Univ. of MI; **EDUC HONORS:** JD with distinction; Editor, MI Law Review; Harry Helfman Legal Scholar; **HOME ADD:** Barrington, RI; **BUS ADD:** 2200 Indus. Bank Bldg., Providence, RI 02903, (401)274-2000.

BILLMEYER, C.J.——B: Nov. 28, 1901, Gr. Rapids, WI, *Arch.*, Billmer & Son; **PRIM RE ACT:** Architect; **PROFL AFFIL & HONORS:** AIA; **GRAD EDUC:** BS in Arch., 1923, Carnegie Mellon, Pittsburgh, PA; **MIL SERV:** ROTC; **OTHER ACT & HONORS:** Elks, K of C, Foresters, United Comm. Travelers, Amer. Assoc. Retired Persons, Rotary; **HOME ADD:** Wisconsin Rapids, 931 Wash. St., WI 55494, (715)423-5741; **BUS ADD:** 420 3rd St., Wisc. Rapids, WI 54494.

BILZERIAN, Paul A.——B: June 18, 1950, Miami, FL, *VP 1979-present*, Natl. Bus. Enterprises, Inc., Pres., S. Bus. Enterprises, Inc.; **PRIM RE ACT:** Developer, Property Manager, Owner/Investor; **PREV EMPLOY:** Crown Zellerbach Corp. 1977-1978; **EDUC:** BA, 1975, Pol. Sci., Stanford Univ.; **GRAD EDUC:** MBA, 1977, Gen. Mgmt., Harvard Univ.; **EDUC HONORS:** Grad. 'with distinction' and 'with honors' in Pol. Sci.; **MIL SERV:** USA, 1st Lt., Bronze Star, ACM, Vietnamese Gallantry Cross; **HOME ADD:** 1914 Carolina Ave. N.E., St. Petersburg, FL 33703, (813)522-9929; **BUS ADD:** One Plaza Place N.E.,Suite 1010, St. Petersburg, FL 33701, (813)821-7760.

BINDER, Hannan E.——B: Apr. 24, 1926, Chicago, IL, *Asst. VP & Reg. Prop. Mgmt. Officer*, Bank of America NT & SA, Trust RE; **PRIM RE ACT:** Banker, Property Manager; **SERVICES:** Total Prop. Mgmt. (buying, selling, etc.); **PROFL AFFIL & HONORS:** IREM; Los Angeles Bd. of Realtors, CPM; **EDUC:** BA, 1950, Indus. Arts and Physical Ed., N. TX State; **MIL SERV:** USN, SM 3/C; **OTHER ACT & HONORS:** Masons, Scottish Rite, Shriners, Soc. of Magical Arts; **HOME ADD:** 9356 Swinton Ave., Sepulveda, CA 91343, (213)894-4392; **BUS ADD:** 615 S. Flower St., Los Angeles, CA 90017, (213)683-4375.

BINGHAM, James "Jay"——B: May 1, 1940, San Francisco, CA, *Pres., Chmn. of the Bd.*, First National Financial Corp.; **PRIM RE ACT:** Banker, Developer, Lender, Owner/Investor, Syndicator; **SERVICES:** Synd. - owner - gen. partner; **REP CLIENTS:** Major fin. instns.; **EDUC:** BA, 1962, San Francisco State Univ.; **BUS ADD:** 256 South Robertson, Beverly Hills, CA 90211, (213)657-2968.

BINGS, William T.——*VP/Gen. Auditor*, Department of Housing and Urban Development, Fed. Home Loan Mortgage Corp.; **PRIM RE ACT:** Lender; **BUS ADD:** 451 Seventh St., S.W., Washington, DC 20410, (202)789-4765.*

BINKLEY, James L.——B: Mar. 12, 1942, Winston Salem, NC, *Sr. Arch.*, US Dept. of Energy, Bldgs. Div.; **PRIM RE ACT:** Architect, Regulator, Consultant; **OTHER RE ACT:** Mgr. of research programs on energy efficiency investment; **REP CLIENTS:** Fed. agencies, prof. soc. & assns., states and local govt. and consulting firms; **PREV EMPLOY:** Arch. US Gen. Services Admin, Wash. DC, Arch. Firm of Pietro Belluschi, FAIA, Boston, MA; **PROFL AFFIL & HONORS:** AIA; **EDUC:** BS, 1964, Eng., Davidson Coll.; **GRAD EDUC:** BA, 1969, Phil., NC State Univ.; BArch, 1969, Arch., NC State Univ.; **EDUC HONORS:** Hon.; **MIL SERV:** USA Engineers, Capt., USA Commendation Medal; **OTHER ACT & HONORS:** Reston Soccer Assn., Reston Swim Team, Assn. Boy Scouts of Amer., Who's Who in the S and SE, ASHRAE Roundtable 1981; **HOME ADD:** 10723 Midsummer Dr., Reston, VA 22091, (703)476-5438; **BUS ADD:** 1000 Independence Ave., SW, Wash. DC 20585, (202)252-9197.

BINNS, Donald A.——B: June 29, 1946, Salem, NH, *Exec. Dir.*, Westmass Area Development Corp.; **PRIM RE ACT:** Broker, Developer, Lender, Builder, Owner/Investor, Property Manager, Syndicator; **SERVICES:** Sales fin., turnkey, construction, consulting; **REP CLIENTS:** Prime Computer; **PREV EMPLOY:** Sr. Planner, City of Springfield, MA; **PROFL AFFIL & HONORS:** AEDC; MEDC; NIDA; ACCE; MACCE, CID; **EDUC:** BA, 1969, Urban Studies, Univ. of MA; **HOME ADD:** 3 Edson Dr., Wilbraham, MA 01095; **BUS ADD:** 1500 Main St., Suite 600, Springfield, MA 01115, (413)734-9060.

BIRD, Robert D.——B: Apr. 6, 1938, Ellensburg, WA, *VP*, Allen & O'Hara, Inc., Student Housing Mgmt. Branch; **PRIM RE ACT:** Property Manager; **SERVICES:** Resid. hall food serv. and housing contracts; **REP CLIENTS:** Creative Investments, Inc., Richmond, VA; Frank H. Kenan, Chapel Hill, NC; The Equitable, Pittsburgh, PA; Hartford, CT; The NW Mutual Life Ins. Co., Milwaukee, WI; Robert Louis Stevenson Sch., Pebble Beach, CA; **PREV EMPLOY:** Montgomery Ward; **PROFL AFFIL & HONORS:** IREM (past pres., VP, and Sec.), CPM; **EDUC:** BS, 1965, Educ., Hist.; **GRAD EDUC:** MS, 1967, Educ., guidance & counseling; **MIL SERV:** USMC, Cpl.; **BUS ADD:** 3385 Airways Blvd., Memphis, TN 38116, (901)345-7620.

BIRGE, R.D., Jr.——**B:** Sept. 15, 1916, N. Platte, NE, *Sr. VP*, Comml. Fed. Savings & Loan; **PRIM RE ACT:** Lender; **SERVICES:** All S&L Servs.; **EDUC:** BEE, 1938, Purdue Univ.; **HOME ADD:** PO Box 40, N. Platte, NE 69101, (308)532-4872; **BUS ADD:** 306 W Circle Dr., N. Platte, NE 69101, (308)534-9400.

BIRKEL, Richard L.——**B:** Sep. 5, 1926, Omaha, NE, *Owner*, Birkel Const. Co.; **PRIM RE ACT:** Broker, Appraiser, Builder, Property Manager, Owner/Investor; **PREV EMPLOY:** 30 yrs., 1951-81 Birkel Const. Co., Founder & Iwber; **PROFL AFFIL & HONORS:** 25 yrs Metro Omaha Bldrs. Assn., 25 yrs. NAHB, 25 yrs. Licensed NE Realtor; **EDUC:** 2 Yrs. Pre Eng., 1946, CE, Univ. NE at Omaha; **MIL SERV:** USN, Sgt, 3 Battle stars, 3 Major campaigns, 1944-46; **OTHER ACT & HONORS:** Pres. SLD, 100 NE, Church St. Bernards, Sen. Pres. School Bd. St. Bernards, Elect. Mem School Bd. St. James, 10 yrs. Boy Scouts of Amer, 1971-81; **HOME ADD:** 9824 Laurel St., Omaha, NE 68134, (402)571-0910; **BUS ADD:** 9824 Laurel St., Omaha, NE 68134, (402)571-0910.

BIRNBAUM, Mark D.——**B:** Sept. 8, 1952, Brooklyn, NY; **PRIM RE ACT:** Attorney, Owner/Investor, Syndicator; **PROFL AFFIL & HONORS:** ABA; Comm. on Real Prop., Pres., Hofstra Law School Alumni Assn., 1977-1979; Dir., 1979 - present; **EDUC:** BA, 1974, Law/Bus., Harpur Coll., SUNY; **GRAD EDUC:** JD, 1977, Law, Hofstra Univ. School of Law; **HOME ADD:** 71 Grace Ave., Great Neck, NY 11021, (516)482-0816; **BUS ADD:** 135 W. 41st St., NY, NY 10036, (212)944-2222.

BIRNBAUM, Robert J.——**B:** Oct. 15, 1930, New York City, NY, *Pres.*, Cohn and Birnbaum PC; **PRIM RE ACT:** Attorney; **REP CLIENTS:** Devels., lenders and tenants - shopping centers, office bldgs., office & indus. parks; **PROFL AFFIL & HONORS:** Exec. Comm., Real Prop. Section of CT Bar Assn., Intl. Council of Shopping Centers (Lecturer & panelist); **EDUC:** BA, 1952, Soc. Sci., Bucknell Univ.; **GRAD EDUC:** JD, 1955, Harvard Law School; **EDUC HONORS:** Phi Beta Kappa, Cum Laude; **MIL SERV:** USA, SP-4; **OTHER ACT & HONORS:** VP & Dir., Hartford Symphony; Dir., Hartford State Co.; **HOME ADD:** 15 Norwood Rd., West Hartford, CT 06117, (203)232-8935; **BUS ADD:** 37 Lewis St., Hartford, CT 06103, (203)549-7230.

BIRO, Dr. Michael V.——**B:** Aug. 12, 1935, CSR, *Realtor*, Earth Realty Inc.; **PRIM RE ACT:** Broker, Developer, Builder; **PROFL AFFIL & HONORS:** Daytona Beach Area Bd. of Realtors; **EDUC:** Dr. of Meraphycich. Sci., 1980, Divine Doctorate, Gaspal Ministry, Ukranien Free Univ., Munich, Germany; Univ. of NE; Univ. of Bridgeport; **EDUC HONORS:** Reg. psychologist(Genl.); **MIL SERV:** USA; **OTHER ACT & HONORS:** Chmn. Civil Service Bd.; Chmn. Citizens for Better Govt.; Genl. Contractor; Master Plumber; Master Electrician; Mechanical Contractor; Kiwanis; Elks; Eagles; **HOME ADD:** 760 Biro Dr., Port Orange, FL 32019, (904)767-1831; **BUS ADD:** 955 Herbert St., PO Box 127, Port Orange, FL 32019, (904)767-2189.

BISCHOF, Milton, Jr.——**B:** Aug. 17, 1929, St. Louis, MO, *Arch., Mktg. Dir., Dir. of S&L*, Jack D. Gillum & Assoc. - Home Fed. S&L Consulting Engineers; **PRIM RE ACT:** Architect, Consultant, Banker; **OTHER RE ACT:** Tr. - St. Louis Metropolitan Sewer Dist.; **PREV EMPLOY:** Hellmuth - Obata & & Kassabaum, Inc.; **PROFL AFFIL & HONORS:** AIA; SMPS, Who's Who; **EDUC:** BArch, 1952, Wash. Univ.; **MIL SERV:** USA, Sgt., Army Rifle Team; **OTHER ACT & HONORS:** Councilman - St. Louis Cty. 1968-1976; Advertising Club, MO Council of Arch.; Grand Jury Assn.; MO Athletic Club; **HOME ADD:** 6 Elmcrest Acres, St. Louis, MO 63138; **BUS ADD:** 100 N. Broadway, St. Louis, MO 63102, (314)421-5073.

BISCHOFF, Charles F.——**B:** Jan. 10, 1935, Newark, NJ, *Arch.*, Glazner - Bischoff and Assoc. Arch.; **PRIM RE ACT:** Architect; **SERVICES:** Planning, Design & Const. Details; **PROFL AFFIL & HONORS:** AIA; **EDUC:** BArch., 1963, Arch. Design, Clemson Univ.; **EDUC HONORS:** with Honors, AIA Advanced Student Award, SC Student Award; **MIL SERV:** USN, CPO, Nat. Defense; Good Conduct; Accom. w Star; **OTHER ACT & HONORS:** City of Mobile Arch. Review Board 1969-1978, Kiwanis Intl.; **HOME ADD:** 2250 Leroy Stevens Rd., Mobile, AL 36609, (205)633-7518; **BUS ADD:** 4859 Old Shell Rd., Mobile, AL 36608, (205)343-0464.

BISEDA, John F.——**B:** June 24, 1949, N. Charleroi, PA, *RE Assoc.*, Dravo Corp.; **PRIM RE ACT:** Architect, Consultant, Appraiser, Developer, Property Manager, Owner/Investor; **SERVICES:** Sale and Acquisition of Corp. RE; **REP CLIENTS:** Dravo Grps., Divs. & Cos.; Devel. of Surplus Prop.; Identification and Mgmt. of Expansion Plans; Valuation; Investment Analysis; **PREV EMPLOY:** Fin. Analyst, Dravo Corp., 1978 - 1980; Arch., Forrest Coile & Assoc., A & E, 1972 - 1976; **PROFL AFFIL & HONORS:** Reg. Arch., PA & VA; **EDUC:** BArch, 1972, Arch., Carnegie - Mellon Univ.; **GRAD EDUC:** MBA, 1978, Mgmt., Darden Grad. Bus. School, Univ. of VA; **EDUC HONORS:** C-M Univ. Scholarship, Darden Grad. Bus. School Scholarship; **OTHER ACT & HONORS:** Bd. Member, Delta Alpha Club; **HOME ADD:** 32 Iroquois Dr., Pittsburgh, PA 15228, (412)561-4563; **BUS ADD:** 1 Oliver Plaza, Pittsburgh, PA 15222, (412)566-3108.

BISHOP, Curtis L.——**B:** Feb. 22, 1931, Herndon, WV, *Regnl. Mgr.-Indus. RE*, Norfolk & Western Railway Co.; **PRIM RE ACT:** Property Manager; **SERVICES:** Sale or base indus. RE; **REP CLIENTS:** Most major rail using indus.; **EDUC:** BS, 1955, Gen. Bus., VA Polytechnic Inst. & State Univ.; **MIL SERV:** USA, 1st Lt.; **OTHER ACT & HONORS:** Interstate Commerce Commission Practitioner; **HOME ADD:** 17339 Chagrin Falls, OH 44022, (216)543-5719; **BUS ADD:** P.O. Box 6119, Cleveland, OH 44101, (216)621-9000.

BISHOP, Leonard L.——**B:** Aug. 6, 1900, Presque Isle, ME, *Owner*, Len Bishop-RE; **PRIM RE ACT:** Broker, Appraiser; **SERVICES:** Sales and Rentals; **PREV EMPLOY:** Len Bishop RE, Established 1948; **PROFL AFFIL & HONORS:** ME Realtors (Pres. Kennebec Valley Bd. 1967-Realtor of Yr. 1968); **EDUC:** 1921, Grad. Shaws Bus. Coll.; **EDUC HONORS:** Past Pres. & Chmn. ME State C of C (1960-1962); **OTHER ACT & HONORS:** Trial Justice-Sagadaboc Cty. (1954-1961); Cty. Comm. Sagadaboc Cty. 1974 & 1975; served two terms Chmn. Sagadaboc Cty. Repbulican Comm. and Two terms Republican State Comm.; Chmn. Town of Bowdoinham 200th Anniversary Celebration; Twelve yrs. Dir. Bourboinham Water Dist., 6 yrs. Chmn.; 32nd Degree Mason, Charter Member Maine's First 4-H Club; **HOME ADD:** 15 Ctr. St., Richmond, ME, (207)737-2236; **BUS ADD:** Corner Ctr. & Gardiner, Richmond, ME 04357, (207)737-2236.

BISSELL, George——**B:** Jan. 31, 1927, Los Angeles, CA, *Pres.*, Bissell Assoc.; **PRIM RE ACT:** Architect; **SERVICES:** Planning, design, engrg., feasibility; **REP CLIENTS:** Irvine Co., Arvida Corp., Kilroy Indus.; **PREV EMPLOY:** Bus. founded in 1957; **PROFL AFFIL & HONORS:** AIA, Fellow AIA, 1974, Nat. AIA Honor Award for design 1978; **EDUC:** BArch, 1953, USC; **EDUC HONORS:** Scarab, Hon. Prof. Soc., Trojan Knights; **MIL SERV:** US Maritime Serv., 3rd deck officer, Phillipines Liberation; **OTHER ACT & HONORS:** Newport Ctr. Assoc. (past VP), Bd. of Gov. USC, Balboa Bay Club; **HOME ADD:** 108 Via Havre, Newport Beach, CA 92663, (714)673-2079; **BUS ADD:** 190 Newport Cen., Newport Beach, CA 92660, (714)644-5670.

BISSETT, William P., Jr.——**B:** Sept. 15, 1940, Tampa, FL, *Pres.*, Bissett & Co., Inc.; **PRIM RE ACT:** Broker; **SERVICES:** Investment and devel. prop. brokerage; **REP CLIENTS:** Investors, devels. and synds. of comml., income producing and pvt. props.; **PROFL AFFIL & HONORS:** Member Urban Planning Council Comm. of 100; **EDUC:** BSBA, 1962, Bus. Econ., Univ. of FL; **HOME ADD:** 1904 Cape Bend Ave., Tampa, FL 33612, (813)961-5742; **BUS ADD:** Suite 3018, 1st FL Tower, Tampa, FL 33602, (813)229-2929.

BISSINGER, Paul A., Jr.——**B:** Apr. 3, 1934, San Francisco, CA, *Owner*, Self Employed; **PRIM RE ACT:** Broker, Consultant, Owner/Investor, Property Manager, Syndicator; **PREV EMPLOY:** Prop. Resources, Inc.; **PROFL AFFIL & HONORS:** Intl. Council of Shopping Centers, CA Lic. RE Broker; **EDUC:** BA, 1956, Hist., Stanford Univ.; **MIL SERV:** US Naval Res., Lt. j.g.; **BUS ADD:** 12 Geary St. 308, San Francisco, CA 94108, (415)981-8780.

BITETTO, Vincent J.——**B:** Aug. 9, 1929, NYC, *Sr. VP*, Williamsburgh Savings Bank, Mort. Originations; **PRIM RE ACT:** Banker, Lender; **OTHER RE ACT:** RE Joint Ventures; **PROFL AFFIL & HONORS:** Brooklyn Bd. of Realtors; Long Is. Builders Inst., Mort. Bankers Assn. of NY; **EDUC:** BBA, 1968, Mgmt., Adelphi Univ., Garden City, NY; **GRAD EDUC:** Amer. Inst. of Banking, 1959, Banking & Invest., Hofstra Univ.; **OTHER ACT & HONORS:** Pres., Republican Club; **HOME ADD:** 825 Forte Blvd., Franklin Sq., NY 11010, (516)486-2316; **BUS ADD:** 1 Hanson Pl., Brooklyn, NY 11243, (212)636-7221.

BITTEL, Jordan——**B:** Apr. 15, 1929, NYC, NY, *Prof.*, Univ. of Miami, Sch. of Law; **PRIM RE ACT:** Consultant, Attorney, Instructor; **SERVICES:** Counseling for. investors in US RE investments; **REP CLIENTS:** For. persons from most free nats.; **PREV EMPLOY:** Sr. Partner, Bittel, Langer & Blass, Miami, FL (1959-79); **PROFL AFFIL & HONORS:** ABA; AALST; **EDUC:** 1949, Pol. Sci., Univ. of FL; **GRAD EDUC:** LLB, 1952, Harvard Law Sch.; LLM, 1972, Miami Law Sch.; **EDUC HONORS:** Phi Beta Kappa; **MIL SERV:** US Army; Cpl.; **HOME ADD:** 11501 SW 72 Ct., Miami, FL 33156, (305)238-9940; **BUS ADD:** Coral Gables, FL 33134, (305)284-5535.

BITTING, Phyllis Diane——B: Oct. 11, 1935, Kosciusko Co., IN, *RE Broker/co-owner*, Center Realty, Inc.; **PRIM RE ACT:** Broker, Consultant, Appraiser, Owner/Investor; **SERVICES:** all types RE; **PROFL AFFIL & HONORS:** NAR; IN Assn. of Realtors, Kosciusko Bd. of Realtors, CRB Nat. & Indiana Chap., CRS Nat. & Ind., 1975 & 1976 Kosciusko Bd. Sec. & Treas. - 1977 Bd. VP, 1978 Kosciusko Bd. of Realtors Pres., 1980, 81, 82 IN State Dir. 1980 served on State MLS Comm., 1981 served on PR & Communication Comm. IAR; **EDUC:** 1953, Tippecanoe, IN; **OTHER ACT & HONORS:** Anthony Nigo Chap. DAR, Walnut Creek UM Church; **HOME ADD:** Rte. 2, Box 88, Warsaw, IN 46580, (219)267-5544; **BUS ADD:** 2304 E Center St., Warsaw, IN 46580, (219)267-5513.

BITTINGER, William A.——*Owner*, Georgetown Prop.; **PRIM RE ACT:** Developer, Owner/Investor, Syndicator; **SERVICES:** Specialize in the renovation and recycling of existing structures; **BUS ADD:** Box 690 RD #1, Princeton, NJ 08540, (609)921-2755.

BITZ, Brent W.——B: Feb. 9, 1947, Vancouver, Can, *VP*, Trizec Western Inc., Eastern U.S. Div.; **PRIM RE ACT:** Owner/Investor; **SERVICES:** Leasing; prop. mgmt.; **PROFL AFFIL & HONORS:** BOMA, Real Prop. Admin.; **EDUC:** Bachelor of Commerce, 1970, Mktg., RE, Univ. of BC; **GRAD EDUC:** MBA, 1972, Mktg., RE, Univ. of BC; **EDUC HONORS:** 1st Class Honours, Matthew Henderson Memorial Award, 1st Class Honours, Samuel Broneman Fellow; **HOME ADD:** 208-1645 Kirts Blvd., Troy, MI 48084, (313)643-6347; **BUS ADD:** Suite 450-3011 W. Grand Blvd., Detroit, MI 48202, (313)874-4444.

BJORNSON, Stella——B: Apr. 21, 1919, Kellogg, IA, *Owner*, Stella Bjornson Realty; **PRIM RE ACT:** Broker, Appraiser, Property Manager; **OTHER ACT & HONORS:** CA & Nat. Bd. of Realtors, Calaveras Co. Bd. of Realtors, Dir. C of C, Ebbetts Pass Wonderland Assn. & Loyal Order of Moose; **HOME ADD:** 3437 Moran Rd., Avery, CA 95224, (209)795-2070; **BUS ADD:** 3361 Highway "Four", Avery, CA 95224, (209)795-2070.

BLACK, Alexander——B: Nov. 19, 1914, Pittsburgh, PA, *Part., shareholder*, Buchanan, Ingersoll, Rodewald, Kyle, and Buerger, P.C.; **PRIM RE ACT:** Attorney; **SERVICES:** Legal counseling and rep.; **REP CLIENTS:** Sellers, purchasers, lenders, owners, tenants, and dev. of resdl., comml. and industl. prop.; **PREV EMPLOY:** Admitted to the Bar of Cty., state, and federal cts. in PA, U.S. Supreme Ct., Tax Ct. and Ct. of Claims; **PROFL AFFIL & HONORS:** Bar Assns., Allegheny Cty., Chmn. Real Prop Sect., 1975, PA Chmn. Real Prop. , Probate and Trust Law Sect. 1979-80, and Amer., Elected mbr. Amer. Law Inst., 1962, elected fellow Amer. Coll. of Trial Lawyers, 1968, chtr. fllw. Amer. Coll. of RE Lawyers; **EDUC:** AB, 1936, Mod. Hist., Woodrow Wilson Schl. of Public and Intl. Affairs, Princeton Univ.; **GRAD EDUC:** LLB, 1939, Law, Harvard Law School; **MIL SERV:** USNR, Lt., Pacific Theatre Ribbon with 14 battle stars; **HOME ADD:** 1309 Beaver Rd., Osborne, Sewickley, PA 15143, (412)741-6488; **BUS ADD:** 57th Floor, U.S. Steel Bldg.,, 600 Grant St., Pittsburgh, PA 15219, (412)562-8830.

BLACK, Edward P.——B: Aug. 18, 1943, Lincoln, NE, *Arch. AIA*, The BKLH Group, PC; **PRIM RE ACT:** Architect; **SERVICES:** Arch. planning, int. design; **PREV EMPLOY:** C.K.M., Denver, Intergroup Inc., Denver; **PROFL AFFIL & HONORS:** Denver Chap. AIA, CO Soc. of Archs.; **EDUC:** BArch, 1962-68, Design, Univ. of NE, Coll. of Arch.; **HOME ADD:** 3011 S. Franklin St., Englewood, CO 80110, (303)789-3056; **BUS ADD:** 1221 S. Clarkson, Suite 413, Denver, CO 80210, (303)777-2456.

BLACK, James F., Jr.——B: Mar. 24, 1945, W. Orange, NJ, *Pres.*, Black's Guide to the Office Space Market; **PRIM RE ACT:** Real Estate Publisher; **PREV EMPLOY:** Cushman & Wakefield, Allen Shopping Ctrs.; The Evans Partnership; **PROFL AFFIL & HONORS:** NAIOP, BOMA, IREBA, Rumson HHH; **EDUC:** BA, 1967, Psych., Colgate Univ.; **MIL SERV:** USN, Lt.; **HOME ADD:** 166 Brighton Ave., Rumson, NJ 07760, (201)741-0232; **BUS TEL:** (201)842-6060.

BLACK, James S.——B: Apr. 3, 1925, Great Falls, MT, *Pres.*, James S. Black & Co., Inc.; **PRIM RE ACT:** Broker, Syndicator, Consultant, Appraiser, Developer, Property Manager, Owner/Investor; **SERVICES:** Resid. brokerage, farm mktg., investment counseling, prop. mgmt., appraisal, land use planning, comml. and indus. dev., Resid., apt., shopping ctr. and indus. park dev.; **PROFL AFFIL & HONORS:** SIR, NIREB, Soc. of RE Counselors, IREM, WA Assoc. Realtors, Realtor of the Yr., 1969; Spokane Bd. of Realtors, Realtor of the Yr., 1969; **EDUC:** BS, 1946, Elec. Engrg., Univ. of WA; **GRAD EDUC:** MBA, 1948, Stanford Univ.; **MIL SERV:** USNR; **OTHER ACT & HONORS:** Pres.; Inland Empire Boy Scouts of Amer.; Spokane Kiwanis, Spokane C of C; Past Pres. Greater Spokane Devel. Council; Past Dir. Nat. Assoc. of RE Bds.; Member Building Owners and Mngrs. Assoc.; Past Pres. Intl. Traders Club; Past Member Advisory Comm. of Bus. Devel. WA State Univ.; Past Pres. WA RE Educ. Found.; **HOME ADD:** South 4119 Napa, Spokane, WA 99203, (509)448-1563; **BUS ADD:** 500 Columbia Bldg., Spokane, WA 99204, (509)838-2511.

BLACK, Kenneth W.——B: Dec. 10, 1912, Peoria, IL, *Partner*, Black & Black; Black, Black & Borden; **PRIM RE ACT:** Attorney, Owner/Investor; **PREV EMPLOY:** City Atty., Washington, 1941-53; 1957-77; **PROFL AFFIL & HONORS:** ABA, IL Bar Assn., Peoria and Tazewell Cty. Bar Assn.; **EDUC:** 1934, Bradley Univ.; **GRAD EDUC:** JD, 1937, Legal Educ., Univ. of Chicago; **HOME ADD:** 501 S. Main, Washington, IL 61571, (309)444-3746; **BUS ADD:** 115 Washington Sq., Washington, IL 61571, (309)444-3108.

BLACK, Marvin W.——B: July 3, 1940, Quanah, TX, *Dir. of Prop. Mgmt.*, Metropolitan Management; **PRIM RE ACT:** Property Manager; **SERVICES:** Specialty in mgmt. of smaller garden apts.; **REP CLIENTS:** Private investors; **PREV EMPLOY:** Joe Foster Co., Dir. of Prop. Mgmt. 1974-1977; **PROFL AFFIL & HONORS:** IREM; Nat. Apt. Assn., CPM; **EDUC:** BA, 1963, Govt., Hist., TX Christian Univ.; **MIL SERV:** USANG, E-4; **HOME ADD:** 6126 Highgate Lane, Dallas, TX 75214, (214)368-5391; **BUS ADD:** 6440 N. Central, Suite 102, Dallas, TX 75206, (214)521-6830.

BLACK, Nicholas J.——B: 1946, Denver, CO; **PRIM RE ACT:** Consultant, Attorney, Lender; **SERVICES:** Interim const., permanent financing, comml. acquisition; **PREV EMPLOY:** First Interstate Bank of CA; **PROFL AFFIL & HONORS:** State Bar of CA, Los Angeles Cty. Bar Assn., ABA; **EDUC:** BA, 1968, Poli. Sci., Univ. of WY; **GRAD EDUC:** JD, 1971, Natural Resources, Univ. of WY College of Law; **OTHER ACT & HONORS:** Law Clerk, USDC, Central Dist. of CA, Los Angeles, CA 1971-1973; **HOME ADD:** 308 N. Alabama, San Gabriel, CA 91775, (213)286-7309; **BUS ADD:** 308 N. Alabama., San Gabriel, CA 91775, (213)286-7309.

BLACK, Peter——*Ed.*, Black's Guide Inc., Black's Guide to Metro D.C. Office Space; **PRIM RE ACT:** Real Estate Publisher; **SERVICES:** Also assoc. w/Black's Guide to Metro D.C. & Metro. Phila. Office Space; **BUS ADD:** 332 Board St., Red Bank, NJ 07701, (201)842-6060.*

BLACK, Steve——B: Nov. 20, 1946, Hanover, PA, *Pres.*, Steve Black Inc.; **PRIM RE ACT:** Developer, Builder, Owner/Investor, Syndicator; **OTHER RE ACT:** Sale/Leaseback; **SERVICES:** Devel., Synd. of Comml. Indus.; **REP CLIENTS:** Devel. & synd. of comml., indus., institut. prop. for own investment, investors or corp. clients. Heavy involvement in packaged design, build, operators., & lease back of comml., indus. props.; **EDUC:** BS, 1968, RE, Amer. Univ.; **MIL SERV:** US Army & Air Force Reserves, E-5; **OTHER ACT & HONORS:** Advisory Bd.-Carlisle Branch-Commonwealth Natl. Bank Planning Commn.-South Middleton Tup; **BUS ADD:** RD#1 Box 40, Carlisle, PA 17013, (717)249-1550.

BLACKBURN, Betsy——*Executive Director*, American Industrial Real Estate Association; **OTHER RE ACT:** Profl. Assn. Admin.; **BUS ADD:** World Trade Center, 350 S. Figuero Ste. 275, Los Angeles, CA 90071, (213)687-8777.*

BLACKBURN, Cartier——B: June 8, 1919, Madison, WI, *Ret.*, Independent RE Appraiser; **PRIM RE ACT:** Appraiser, Instructor; **PREV EMPLOY:** VP & Chief Appraiser, First Interstate Bank of CA (Formerly United CA Bank); **PROFL AFFIL & HONORS:** SREA, Nat. Inst. of Valuers, CA Assn. of RE Teachers, SRA, SCV, CARET; **EDUC:** BS, 1941, Bus. Admin., Northwestern Univ.; **GRAD EDUC:** Cert., 1958, RE, Univ. of CA Ext. Berkeley; **MIL SERV:** USN, Capt., Navy Commendation Medal plus 9 decorations; **OTHER ACT & HONORS:** Commonwealth Club, San Francisco, Naval Res. Assn.; **HOME ADD:** 1521 Emerson St., Palo Alto, CA 94301, (415)327-8057; **BUS ADD:** 1521 Emerson St., Palo Alto, CA 94301, (415)327-8057.

BLACKBURN, Elizabeth Harris——B: Feb. 6, 1951, Americus, GA, *Architect*, Elizabeth Harris Blackburn AIA, Arch.; **PRIM RE ACT:** Architect; **SERVICES:** Full serv. planning, design, constr., documents, etc.; **REP CLIENTS:** Devel., investors, pvt. owners; **PREV EMPLOY:** Assoc. Winford Lindsay & Assoc., Archs, 1978-79; **PROFL AFFIL & HONORS:** AIA, Atlanta Women Architects; **EDUC:** B. Arch., 1974, GA Inst. of Tech., Atlanta, GA; **OTHER ACT & HONORS:** Walton Cty C of C; **HOME ADD:** Rt. 3, Box 211-D, Monroe, GA 30655, (404)267-8126; **BUS ADD:** Rt. 3, Box 211-D, Monroe, GA 30655, (404)267-8126.

BLACKBURN, James W.——B: Mar. 24, 1951, Ft. Lauderdale, FL, *RE Project Mgr.*, Wachovia Bank and Trust Co., N.A., Trust Investments - RE Section; **PRIM RE ACT:** Developer, Owner/Investor; **PREV EMPLOY:** Mid So. Engrg. Co. - Ft. Lauderdale, FL, Broward Cty.

Planning Council - Ft. Lauderdale, FL; **PROFL AFFIL & HONORS:** Amer. Inst. of Cert. Planners; **EDUC:** BA, 1973, Poli. Sci., Wake Forest Univ.; **GRAD EDUC:** MBA, 1981, Univ. of NC at Chapel Hill. MUP, FL State Univ., 1975; **HOME ADD:** 1418 Pinecroft Dr., Winston-Salem, NC 27104; **BUS ADD:** P O Box 3099, Winston-Salem, NC 27102, (919)748-5362.

BLACKBURN, Phyllis A.——B: Oct. 9, 1946, Madisonville, KY, *CPA*, Windes & McClaughry Accountancy Corp.; **OTHER RE ACT:** Accountant; **SERVICES:** Acctg., Tax preparation and tax planning; **REP CLIENTS:** RE Builders & devels., RE investors; **PROFL AFFIL & HONORS:** AICPA, CA Soc. of CPA's, RE Comm.; **EDUC:** BA, 1967, Math., So. IL Univ.; **EDUC HONORS:** Cum Laude; **HOME ADD:** 20242 Bancroft Circ., Huntington Beach, CA 92646, (714)968-7996; **BUS ADD:** 444 W. Ocean Blvd., Top Fl., Long Beach, CA 90802, (213)435-1191.

BLACKBURN, Robert Lee——B: March 10, 1942, Fort Smith, AR, *Atty. at Law*, Charles Dillingham, PC; **PRIM RE ACT:** Attorney, Instructor; **PROFL AFFIL & HONORS:** State Bar of TX; Houston Bar Assn.; ABA; Amer. Assn. of Univ. Prof.; Amer. Assn. of Trial Lawyers, Amer. Jurisprudence Award for Excellence in Torts; **EDUC:** BA, 1968, Hist. and Poli. Sci., Univ. of AR; **GRAD EDUC:** JD, 1974, S. TX Coll. of Law; **HOME ADD:** 1027 Omar, Houston, TX 77009; **BUS ADD:** Suite 1602, 1300 Main St., Houston, TX 77002, (713)651-9977.

BLACKERBY, William F.——B: June 24, 1925, Lexington, KY, *Owner*, Blackerby & Assoc.; **PRIM RE ACT:** Broker, Consultant, Appraiser, Builder; **SERVICES:** All above with staff; **REP CLIENTS:** Mort. Co's. - S&L Attys. investor; **PREV EMPLOY:** Realty Mort. Co., Lexington, KY, Exec. VP sold Co. to Kissell Co., Springfield Ohio; **PROFL AFFIL & HONORS:** NARS, SREA, Former VP Home Builder's Assoc., NARA; **GRAD EDUC:** BS, 1949, Acctg., Univ. of KY; **MIL SERV:** USMC, Cpl., Purple Heart; **BUS ADD:** 635 West Indian School Rd., Phoenix, AZ 85013, (602)264-9793.

BLACKFIELD, William——B: July 20, 1914, Stockton, CA, *Chmn. of Bd.*, Wm. Blackfield Org.; **PRIM RE ACT:** Consultant, Engineer, Attorney, Developer, Builder, Owner/Investor; **SERVICES:** Land Devel., Builder Consultant to Fin. Inst.; **REP CLIENTS:** Honolulu Fed. S&L; **PREV EMPLOY:** Dir. Housing, City of Honolulu; Adviser to City Govt.; **PROFL AFFIL & HONORS:** Nat. Assn. of Home Builders, US, Hall of Fame, Housing; **EDUC:** 1935, Engrg./Law, Hastings Coll., Univ. of CA; **GRAD EDUC:** LLD, 1938; **OTHER ACT & HONORS:** Dir., Dept. Housing Comm. Devel., 1974; Pres. of Nat. Assn. of Home Builders; Sr., Union of Hebrew Congregations; **HOME ADD:** 5900 Manchester Dr., Oakland, CA 94618, (415)658-3157; **BUS ADD:** Blackfield Bldg., 612 Howard St., San Francisco, CA 94105, (415)781-2103.

BLACKHAM, J. William, III——B: Nov. 10, 1953, Winchester, MA, *VP*, Tambone Corp.; **PRIM RE ACT:** Developer, Owner/Investor; **SERVICES:** Fully Integrated RE Devel. and Investment concern with all activities incidental thereto; **REP CLIENTS:** Maj. multinat. and domestic corps., as tenants or occupants of specification built structures; **PREV EMPLOY:** Account Officer, Citibank, N.A., NY, NY, Lending and Workout Functions; **EDUC:** BS, 1975, Bus. Admin. (Fin. & Mgmt.), Boston Coll.; **GRAD EDUC:** MBA, 1976, Fin., RE, The Wharton School; Univ. of PA; **EDUC HONORS:** Magna Cum Laude, Beta Gamma Sigma (Honorary Academic Soc.); **HOME ADD:** 72 Salisbury St., Winchester, MA 08190; **BUS ADD:** 2 Main St., Stoneham, MA 02180, (617)438-5900.

BLACKWELL, Ceylon B., Jr.——B: Oct. 2, 1943, Memphis, TN, *VP/Resid. Sales*, Boyle Investment Co.; **PRIM RE ACT:** Broker; **SERVICES:** Resid. counseling, valuation & mktg. of resid. prop.; **REP CLIENTS:** Buyers & sellers of resid. props., including transferees & 3rd party cos.; **PREV EMPLOY:** The Hobson Co., Realtors, 1972-74; **PROFL AFFIL & HONORS:** Memphis Bd. of Realtors, Realtors Nat. Mktg. Inst., Memphis Housing Auth. Bd. of Comm., CRB, GRI, Memphis Bd. of Realtors Salesman of the yr. 1973; **EDUC:** BS, 1966, Indus. Mgmt., GA Tech.; **EDUC HONORS:** Varsity Football & Wrestling; **OTHER ACT & HONORS:** Kiwanis, Mid South Foodball Officials Assn.; **HOME ADD:** 32 Shepherd Ln., Memphis, TN 38117, (901)767-1458; **BUS ADD:** 5900 Poplar Ave., Memphis, TN 38119, (901)767-0100.

BLACKWELL, Jean S.——B: Sept. 13, 1954, Dublin, GA, *Atty. at Law*, Bose McKinney & Evans; **PRIM RE ACT:** Attorney; **SERVICES:** All forms of legal work for builders, devels. , lenders, resid. purchases and sales; **REP CLIENTS:** P.R. Duke & Assoc., Duke Const. Corp, Duke Realty Corp., Keystone Crossing Devel. Co.; Park 100 Devel. Co. and Realty Investment Co.; **PROFL AFFIL & HONORS:** ABA, Young Lawyers, probate real prop. and trust sect., banking and bus. sect., comm. on real prop., IN State Bar Assn., Indpls. Bar Assn.; **EDUC:** BA, 1976, econ., William and Mary Coll.; **GRAD EDUC:** JD, 1979, Univ. of MI; **EDUC HONORS:** Omicron Delta Kappa, Omicron Delta Epsilon, Mortar Bd., Cum Laude, Sr. Judge, Writing and Advocacy; **HOME ADD:** 6008 Norwaldo, Indianapolis, IN 46220; **BUS ADD:** 8900 Keystone Crossing, Indianapolis, IN 46240, (317)637-5353.

BLACKWELL, Marion, Jr.——B: Sept. 4, 1931, Atlanta, GA, *Pres.*, Sharp-Boylston Co.; **PRIM RE ACT:** Broker, Consultant, Owner/Investor, Instructor, Property Manager, Syndicator; **SERVICES:** Negotiate sales, leases and exchanges of comml. and investment prop., synd.; **REP CLIENTS:** Banks, investors, devel.; **PROFL AFFIL & HONORS:** Atlanta Bd. of Realtors; GA Assn. of Realtors; RNMI; NAR, CCIM, Realtor of the Yr., Atlanta Bd. of Realtors, 1972; **EDUC:** BBA, 1953, RE, GA State Univ.; **EDUC HONORS:** Grad. in top 85% of class; **MIL SERV:** US Army, Cpl., Good Conduct; **OTHER ACT & HONORS:** Cherokee Town & Ctry. Club; **HOME ADD:** 3250 Farmington Dr., Atlanta, GA 30339, (404)432-9715; **BUS ADD:** 66 Luckie St., Atlanta, GA 30303, (404)522-2929.

BLAIR, Carl E.——B: June 17, 1934, Swarthmore, PA, *Mgr., RE & Administrative Serv.*, Sun Refining & Marketing Company, Inc.; **OTHER RE ACT:** Broad range of RE servs. for the corp.; **SERVICES:** Buy, sell, lease, manage, title records, lease admin., consulting; Admin. servs; **PROFL AFFIL & HONORS:** Natl. Assn. Corp. RE Execs.; Indus. Devel. Research Council; NARA; **EDUC:** BS, 1956, Econ., Bus., Franklin & Marshall Coll.; **MIL SERV:** US Army; SP-4; **HOME ADD:** 1051 Girard Ave., Swarthmore, PA 19081, (215)544-5256; **BUS ADD:** 10 Penn Ctr., 180 Market St., Philadelphia, PA 19103, (215)977-3000.

BLAIR, David M.——B: Sep 16, 1930, Springfield, MA, *VP Corp. Dev.*, Friendly Ice Cream Corp., Div. of Hershey Foods Corp.; **OTHER RE ACT:** Acquisition, disposition & mgmt. of corp. RE; **PREV EMPLOY:** Aetna Life Ins. Co., Mass Mutual Life Ins. Co., Mort. Dept.; **PROFL AFFIL & HONORS:** ICSC, Former Tr.; **EDUC:** BA, 1951, Econ., Trinity Coll., Hartford, CT; **MIL SERV:** USA, Sgt., 1951-53; **OTHER ACT & HONORS:** Springfield Bd. of License Commnrs., Tr. Comm. Savings Bank, Corp. Bay State Med. Ctr., Dir. Better Homes Inc. & Springfield Preservation Trust; **HOME ADD:** 432 Longhill St., Springfield, MA 01108, (413)734-7718; **BUS ADD:** Wilbraham, MA 010951855 Boston Rd., (413)543-2400.

BLAIR, Lee——B: Aug. 14, 1935, CT, *Sr. Resid. Appraiser*, Self-employed; **PRIM RE ACT:** Appraiser, Owner/Investor; **SERVICES:** RE appraiser for single family resid. units, comml., indus., land; **REP CLIENTS:** Appraising for mort. co., S&L, banks and indiv. RE owners; **PREV EMPLOY:** Sr. Appraiser, Allstate Savings, Orange S&L Assn., Quaker City Fed. S&L (Loan Officer, Head Appraiser), Santa Ana S&L Assn., Appraiser, Tract Inspector, Loan Servicing; **PROFL AFFIL & HONORS:** Member of Chapter 132 of the SREA, FNMA Level 3, Appraiser 04-2480; Sr. Resid. Appraiser; Treas. of the Whittier Host Lion's Club; Pres. of Futuro Del Oro, 1977-1978; **EDUC:** BA, 1957, Hist./Gen. Bus., Univ. of Redlands; **OTHER ACT & HONORS:** Member, Granada Hts. Friends Church, La Mirada, CA; **HOME ADD:** 355 S. Sequoia Ave., Brea, CA 92621, (714)990-4257; **BUS ADD:** 355 S. Sequoia Ave., Brea, CA 92621, (714)990-4257.

BLAIR, Vaniel Lee——B: Feb. 28, 1921, IN, *Pres.*, Vaniel L. Blair, Realtor; **PRIM RE ACT:** Broker, Appraiser, Property Manager; **SERVICES:** Complete resid. sales, custom home building, new/used brokerage; **PREV EMPLOY:** Electronic Realty Assn. Referral and Transfer; **PROFL AFFIL & HONORS:** State Nat. Assn. of Realtors; IN Assn. Realtors; RNMI; Calumet Multiple Listing Service; **MIL SERV:** USCG, Watertender 2/C; **OTHER ACT & HONORS:** Past Pres. Calumet Bd. of Realtor, 1979-80; Grad. Realtors Inst., 1975; Cert. RE Specialist, 1978; **HOME ADD:** 1627 Cardinal Drive, Munster, IN 46321, (219)924-0681; **BUS ADD:** 909 Ridge Rd., Munster, IN 46321, (219)836-2200.

BLAKE, Benjamin S.——B: Oct. 29, 1915, Weston, MA, *Prof.*, Wentworth Inst. of Tech., Arch. Engrg. Tech. Dept.; **PRIM RE ACT:** Broker, Consultant, Architect, Instructor; **SERVICES:** Teaching at present, contemplate RE sales; **PROFL AFFIL & HONORS:** AIA; Boston Soc. of Archs.; MA State Assn. of Archs.; **EDUC:** BS, 1939, Hist., Trinity Coll.; **MIL SERV:** A.V.S., Field Artillery, 5th Amphibious Force, Capt.; **OTHER ACT & HONORS:** Advisory Comm., Cohasset (past member) 5 yrs; Harvard Club, Boston, Cohasset Yacht Club; **HOME ADD:** 143 Atlantic Ave., Cohasset, MA 02025, (617)383-1309; **BUS ADD:** 550 Huntington Ave., Boston, MA 02115, (617)442-9010.

BLAKE, Brian P.T.——**B:** Apr. 8, 1940, Seattle, WA, *VP*, Dean Witter Reynolds, Inc., Tax Advantaged Investments, RE Dept.; **PRIM RE ACT:** Owner/Investor; **SERVICES:** Underwrite synd. limited partnership for sale to investors; **REP CLIENTS:** High net worth, high tax bracket indiv.; **PREV EMPLOY:** Mfrs. Hanover Trust Co., VP in charge of RE Advisory Grp. (Equity Investments); **PROFL AFFIL & HONORS:** NY Univ. cert. in RE Appraisal; **EDUC:** BA, 1962, Arch., Harvard Univ.; **EDUC HONORS:** Cum Laude; **MIL SERV:** USAF, Lt.; **OTHER ACT & HONORS:** New England Soc.; Saint Nicholas Society; Union Club (NY); St. Georges Church Fin. Comm.; **HOME ADD:** 31 Crest Rd., Chappaqua, NY 10514, (914)238-8973; **BUS ADD:** 2 World Trade Ctr., NY, NY 10048, (212)524-5277.

BLAKE, Donald N.——**B:** Aug. 2, 1945, Richmond, VA, *Pres.*, Blake Brothers, Inc.; **PRIM RE ACT:** Broker, Developer; **PROFL AFFIL & HONORS:** NAR, Natl. Home Builders Assn., G.R.I., C.R.S., C.R.B.; **EDUC:** BS, 1968, Mktg., VA Commonwealth Univ.; **MIL SERV:** USA, E-5, 1968-1970; **HOME ADD:** 1703 Winding Ridge Dr., Richmond, VA 23233, (804)740-0314; **BUS ADD:** P.O. Box 8570, Richmond, VA 23226, (804)285-1855.

BLAKE, D.S.——*VP Mfg. & Services*, Nalco Chemical Co.; **PRIM RE ACT:** Property Manager; **BUS ADD:** 2901 Butterfield Rd., Oakbrook, IL 60521, (312)887-7500.*

BLAKE, Edward W.——**B:** Mar. 30, 1929, Chattanooga, TN, *VP*, Commerce Union Bank, RE; **PRIM RE ACT:** Consultant, Appraiser, Banker, Lender, Owner/Investor; **SERVICES:** RE loans and appraisals; **PROFL AFFIL & HONORS:** Soc. of RE Appraisers, Mort. Bankers Assn., Chattanooga Bd. of Realtors, Home Builders, SRPA; **EDUC:** BBA, 1951, Econ. & Commerce, Univ. of Chattanooga, Now Univ. of TN, Chattanooga; **GRAD EDUC:** Fin., Univ. of TN; **MIL SERV:** USA, Cpl.; **OTHER ACT & HONORS:** Hamilton Cty. Tax Equalization Bd., Walden Club, Quarterback Club, Deacon 1st Presbyterian Church, Halt Century Club UTC Alumni Council; **HOME ADD:** 1516 Sunset Rd., Chattanooga, TN 37405, (615)267-4927; **BUS ADD:** 633 Chestnut St., Chattannooga, TN 37405, (615)756-6639.

BLAKE, Jack——*Director of Materials*, Philips Industry, Inc.; **PRIM RE ACT:** Property Manager; **BUS ADD:** 4801 Springfield St., Dayton, OH 45401, (513)253-7171.*

BLAKE, Peter L.——**B:** Nov. 18, 1936, Antwerp, Belgium, *Optometrist, Pres.*, Blake Enterprises, RE; **PRIM RE ACT:** Syndicator, Consultant, Developer, Builder, Property Manager, Owner/Investor; **PROFL AFFIL & HONORS:** AOA, COA, APH, Kiwanis, C of C; **EDUC:** BS, 1957, Optometry, LACO; **GRAD EDUC:** OD, 1960, Optometry, LACO; **MIL SERV:** USAF, Lt.; **HOME ADD:** 520 Walnut Ave., Vacaville, CA 95688, (707)448-2983; **BUS ADD:** PO Box 570, Vacaville, CA 95696, (707)446-2090.

BLAKE, Stephen H.——**B:** Oct. 12, 1943, Baltimore, MD, *Pres.*, Stephen H. Blake Co., Inc.; **PRIM RE ACT:** Consultant, Developer, Owner/Investor; **SERVICES:** Devel., devel. consulting, work outs; **REP CLIENTS:** Devels. investors, law firms, accountants, fin. insts.; **PREV EMPLOY:** Comml. RE Devel., Brokerage, Const., 1966 to present; 1969 to present, Stephen H. Blake Co., Inc., RE Devel.; **EDUC:** 1964, Arts and Sci., Univ. of MD; **GRAD EDUC:** 1965, Econ. Sci., Cornell Univ.; **EDUC HONORS:** Dean's Honor Roll; **MIL SERV:** USMCR, Cpl.; **HOME TEL:** (202)298-6999; **BUS ADD:** 3025 Orchard Ln., N.W., Washington, DC 20007, (202)298-6998.

BLAKE, Wayne C.——**B:** June 10, 1947, Richmond, VA, *Assoc. Broker*, James River Inc., Realtors; **PRIM RE ACT:** Broker, Developer, Owner/Investor; **PREV EMPLOY:** Blake Realty Co.; **PROFL AFFIL & HONORS:** Richmond Bd. of Realtors; NAR; Richmond Home Builders, Sales and Mktg. Council, CRB; CRS; GRI; **EDUC:** BS, 1972, Educ., VA Commonwealth Univ.; **MIL SERV:** US Army, E-5; **OTHER ACT & HONORS:** W. Central Richmond Optimist Club; **HOME ADD:** 1209 Hillside Ave., Richmond, VA 23229, (804)282-3663; **BUS ADD:** 8900 Three Chopt Rd., Richmond, VA 23229, (804)288-8351.

BLAKESLEY, Leonard E., Jr.——**B:** Mar. 12, 1941, Elgin, IL, *Chmn.*, Blakesley Comstock Development Co., Inc.; **PRIM RE ACT:** Broker, Consultant, Attorney, Developer, Owner/Investor, Property Manager; **REP CLIENTS:** Foreign clients from Europe, Far East, Southeast Asia, and Middle East; **PROFL AFFIL & HONORS:** CA Bar Assn., IL Bar Assn., Los Angeles Cty. Bar Assn.; **EDUC:** BA, 1963, Econs., Bus., Poli Sci., Univ. of IL, Coll. of Liberal Arts and Sci.; **GRAD EDUC:** JD, 1966, Intl. and RE Law, Univ. of IL, Coll. of Law; **EDUC HONORS:** Magna Cum Laude, Phi Beta Kappa; **HOME ADD:** 2912 Sanborn Ave., Marina del Rey, CA 90291; **BUS ADD:** 321 12th St., Manhattan Beach, CA 90266, (213)546-3324.

BLANCO, Fred C.——**B:** July 25, 1914, Alcala, Pangasinan, Philippines, *(Realtor) Princ. Broker/Proprietor*, Blanco Realty Co., Inc.; **PRIM RE ACT:** Broker, Owner/Investor, Insuror; **SERVICES:** Insurance Underwriter with Nat. Mortgage & Fin. Co., Ltd.; **PREV EMPLOY:** Used-Corps. of Engrs.-1942-1945; U. S. Army Trans. Corps.-1945-1947; **PROFL AFFIL & HONORS:** Honolulu Bd. of Realtors, HI Bd. of Realtors, Nat. Assn. of Realtors, Nat. Assn. of RE Appraisers, (IFA) Nat. Assn. of Indep. Fee Appraisers; **EDUC:** BS, 1948; **MIL SERV:** US Army, Pvt.; Army Transp. Corps - AARL-1st Lt.; **OTHER ACT & HONORS:** Member - Bd. of Taxation Review, 1st Div., State of HI; Member, Bd. of Dir., HI Fed. S&L; Immediate Past Pres., Lions Club of Hono.-1980-1981; Past Pres., Filipino C of C-1960-1962; **HOME ADD:** 1840 Vancouver Dr., Honolulu, HI 96822, (808)949-4546; **BUS ADD:** 925 Bethel St., Suite 202, Honolulu, HI 96813, (808)536-9314.

BLANCO, Joseph F.——**B:** Mar. 15, 1953, Honolulu, HI, *Pres.*, Blanco Realty Co., Inc.; **PRIM RE ACT:** Broker, Regulator, Owner/Investor; **SERVICES:** Comml. and indus. brokerage; **PROFL AFFIL & HONORS:** Realtors Nat. Mktg. Inst., HI and Honolulu Bd. of Realtors, HI Cert. Comml. investment member chap.; **EDUC:** BBA, 1976, RE, Univ. of HI; **OTHER ACT & HONORS:** Commnr., HI RE Commn.; VP, Filipino C of C; **HOME ADD:** 1840 Vancouver Dr., Honolulu, HI 96822, (808)949-4546; **BUS ADD:** 925 Bethel St. 202, Honolulu, HI 96813, (808)536-9314.

BLANCO, Rita M.——**B:** Oct. 16, 1934, Peekskill, NY, *Licensed RE Broker, Principal Owner*, Hillcrest Realty; **PRIM RE ACT:** Broker, Appraiser, Owner/Investor, Property Manager, Insuror; **SERVICES:** Profession above indicates services provided; **PREV EMPLOY:** Sec. - IBM;Sec. NY Telephone Co.; Sales Mgr. Grace China Co. Sales Mgr. Jewelry Co.; Welcome Wagon Hostess; **PROFL AFFIL & HONORS:** Natl. State Cty. Bd of Realtors, Westchester Multiple Listing Svc. (Member of Bd. of Dirs. on both). VP, Bronxville, Eastchester, Tuckahoe Chap., 1979-1980, Completed G.R.I.; **EDUC:** Bus. - taken courses, Westchester Community Coll.; **OTHER ACT & HONORS:** C of C - Sec. 1977-1978 VP 1979-1980-1981; Lake Isle Comm.; Cooper School Comm.; **HOME ADD:** 41 Fisher Ave., Tuckahoe, NY 10707; **BUS ADD:** 173 Fisher Ave., Eastchester, NY 10709.

BLANGA, Joseph——**B:** Jan. 21, 1943, Beirut, Lebanon, *Atty. in Fact*, Joeld Investors N.V.; **PRIM RE ACT:** Broker, Consultant, Owner/Investor, Syndicator; **SERVICES:** Brokerage - prop. investments - synd. and consultance RE; **REP CLIENTS:** Mostly for. investors from Europe - Middle East - Mex. and Latin Amer.; **GRAD EDUC:** Bus. Admin. and Econ., Lycee Francais De Beyrouth (Beirut); **HOME ADD:** 5639 San Felipe, Houston, TX 77056, (713)877-1769; **BUS ADD:** 1990 Post Oak Blvd., Suite 885, Houston, TX 77056, (713)877-1769.

BLANK, Harry D.——**B:** May 9, 1924, Pittsburgh, PA, *Exec. VP*, Recon Services, Inc.; **PRIM RE ACT:** Consultant, Appraiser; **SERVICES:** RE consulting and appraising, specialization in prop. tax (1961-1982); **REP CLIENTS:** Hilton Hotels Corp.; Rockefeller Realty Corp.; Prudential Life Ins. Co. of Amer.; Tishman West Mgmt. Corp.; Oxford Properties, Inc.; Olympia & York; Murdock Development Co.; (Major RE devels., operators and investors in prime comml. and indus. props. throughout the US); **PREV EMPLOY:** 6 1/2 yrs. employment in Los Angeles Cty. Assessor's Office as Deputy Assessor and Sr. RE Appraiser; **EDUC:** BA, 1950, Public Admin., UCLA; **MIL SERV:** US Army; S/Sgt., 1943-1946; **OTHER ACT & HONORS:** Pres., Carthay Circle Homeowners Assn.; Pres., Herzl School; Bd. Member, Temple Beth Am; Member, Town Hall; Member, Western LA Rgnl. C of C; **HOME ADD:** 6618 Moore Dr., Los Angeles, CA 90048, (213)939-3622; **BUS ADD:** 5670 Wilshire Blvd., Ste. 2260, Los Angeles, CA 90036, (213)937-1420.

BLANK, Peter Joseph——**B:** Aug. 18, 1933, NYC, NY, *Pres.*, Pinellas Service Corp., Subsidiary of Home Federal S&L Assn. of St. Petersburg, FL; **PRIM RE ACT:** Broker, Developer, Lender, Property Manager; **SERVICES:** Land devel., joint ventures, fin., RE sales; **PREV EMPLOY:** Employed at parent corp., Home Federal since 1959; currently hold position of Sr. VP, Mktg.; **PROFL AFFIL & HONORS:** Contractors and Builders Assn. of Pinellas Cty.; Nat. Assn. of Home Builders; St. Petersburg C of C; Comm. of 100 of Pinellas Cty.; **EDUC:** BS, 1959, Mktg., Univ. of FL; **GRAD EDUC:** Grad. Diploma, 1969, S&L Mgmt., Amer. S&L Inst.; **MIL SERV:** USAF; S/Sgt.; Korean Medal, Air Medal; **OTHER ACT & HONORS:** Commnr., Pinellas Cty. Public Employees Relations Commn.; St. Petersburg Lions Club; Commerce Club of St. Petersburg; **HOME ADD:** 6474 31st Ave. N., St. Petersburg, FL 33710, (813)345-6226; **BUS ADD:** 1901 Central Ave., POB 12288, St. Petersburg, FL 33733, (813)822-0690.

BLANK, Ruth——**B:** June 9,, PA, *Exec. VP*, Ben Blank Co.; **PRIM RE ACT:** Broker, Consultant, Appraiser, Owner/Investor, Property Manager; **OTHER RE ACT:** Writer (RE); Speaker; **SERVICES:** Sales, rentals, prop. mgmt., investments, counseling, appraisals, trades; **REP CLIENTS:** Indiv., Lenders, Civic Authorities; **PROFL AFFIL & HONORS:** IREM; CA Assn. of Realtors; Palm Springs Bd. of Realtors; NAR; RNMI; WCR, 1981, Realtor of Yr. of Palm Springs Bd. of Realtors; CPM; CRB; CRS; GRI; Dir., CA Assn. of Realtors; Panelist, Amer. Arbitration Assn.; **EDUC:** Bus., Swarthmore; **OTHER ACT & HONORS:** Tamarisk Ctry. Club; Desert Museum; Temple Isaiah; Advisory Comm., Coll. of the Desert; Amer. Aribtration Assn.; **BUS ADD:** 1478 N Palm Canyon Dr., Palm Springs, CA 92262, (714)320-5757.

BLANK, Stephen R.——**B:** July 26, 1945, NY, NY, *VP*, Kidder Peabody Realty Corp.; **PRIM RE ACT:** Consultant, Appraiser, Owner/Investor, Syndicator; **SERVICES:** RE investment banking (public offerings and pvt. placements), RE investment analysis, valuation and appraisal; **REP CLIENTS:** Indiv. and instnl. investors; **PREV EMPLOY:** Bache Halsey Stuart Shields 1971-79; **PROFL AFFIL & HONORS:** RE Securities and synd. inst., ULI; **EDUC:** BA, 1967, Hist., Syracuse Univ.; **GRAD EDUC:** MBA, 1971, Fin., Adelphi Univ.; **OTHER ACT & HONORS:** Faculty, practicing law inst., Tr., Nat. Found. for Ilietis & Colitis; **HOME ADD:** 49 Rutherford Rd., Berkeley Heights, NJ 07922, (201)464-4074; **BUS ADD:** 10 Hanover Sq., NY, NY 10005, (212)747-8840.

BLANKENSHIP, Bruce——**B:** Feb. 19, 1949, Lubbock, TX, *VP & Sec.*, Blankenship Developments, Inc.; **PRIM RE ACT:** Developer, Owner/Investor, Property Manager; **OTHER RE ACT:** Comml. prop. mgmt., reside & comml. devels. & investments; **PREV EMPLOY:** Amer. Express Intl. Banking Corp., 1972-78; **PROFL AFFIL & HONORS:** Intl. Council of Shopping Ctrs., Amer. Assn. of Indiv. Investors; **EDUC:** BA, 1971, Eng., Econ., TX Tech. Univ.; **GRAD EDUC:** M of Intl. Mgmt., 1972, Intl. Fin., Amer. Grad. Sch. of Intl. Mgmt.; **EDUC HONORS:** Grad. with honors; **OTHER ACT & HONORS:** Part-time instr. Dept. of Econ., TX Tech. Univ.; **HOME ADD:** 5401 17th Pl., Lubbock, TX 79416, (806)793-0742; **BUS ADD:** PO Box 5246, Lubbock, TX 79417, (806)762-5221.

BLANKMAN, Donald Warren——**B:** June 12, 1932, Niagara Falls, NY, *Comml. Mort. Officer and RE Mgr.*, The Banking Ctr., Mort. Div.; **PRIM RE ACT:** Appraiser, Developer, Builder, Property Manager, Banker, Lender; **SERVICES:** Prop. Mgmt., Comml. Mort. Orientation Servicing; **PREV EMPLOY:** Bishop Trust Co., Honolulu, HI; Rossmoor Corp., Laguna Hills CA; Title Ins. and Trust Co., Santa Ana, CA; **EDUC:** Econ., German, French, Attended Univ. of Innsbruck, Austria (2yrs.) Santa Ana Coll. CA (1 1/2 yrs.); **MIL SERV:** USN; HN; **OTHER ACT & HONORS:** VP, Bd. Member of CT Soc. of Genealogists, Kiwanis Intl.; **HOME TEL:** (203)274-2271; **BUS ADD:** 60 N. Main St., Waterbury, CT 06720, (203)573-7849.

BLANTON, John A.——**B:** Jan. 1, 1928, Houston, TX, *Arch.*, John Blanton, AIA, Arch.; **PRIM RE ACT:** Architect; **SERVICES:** Arch.; **PREV EMPLOY:** Collaborator w/ Richard J. Neutra until 1964; **PROFL AFFIL & HONORS:** Soc. of Arch. Hist., Amer. Inst. of Arch., Various Awards & publications work listed in a guide to the arch. of L.A. and S. CA by Gebhard & Winter; **EDUC:** BA, 1948, Arch., Rice; BS, 1949, Arch., Rice; **MIL SERV:** USA; **OTHER ACT & HONORS:** Rotary; **HOME ADD:** 712 The Strand, Manhattan Beach, CA 90266, (213)379-1046; **BUS ADD:** 2100 Sepulveda, Suite 14, Manhattan Beach, CA 90266, (213)546-1200.

BLASS, Noland, Jr.——**B:** May 28, 1920, Little Rock, AR, *Pres.*, Blass Chilcote Carter Lanford & Wilcox; **PRIM RE ACT:** Architect, Developer, Engineer, Owner/Investor; **SERVICES:** A/E Services - Feasibility Studies, Master Planning, Condo. Study - Off. & Residential; **REP CLIENTS:** AR Power & Light Co. - LR, Pleasant Valley, Inc. - LR, The Bailey Corp. - LR, Worthen B&T Co. N.A. - LR, Pulaslci B&T Co. - LR, Wengroup Cos. - LR; Murphy Oil Co. El Dorado, AR; **PROFL AFFIL & HONORS:** AIA, Winner of Many State & Regl. AIA Honor Awards, Who's Who - US and World; **EDUC:** BArch, 1941, Cornell Univ., Ithaca, NY; **EDUC HONORS:** Tau Beta Pi, Gargoyle, Quill & Dagger, L'Ogive Member - Advisory Council - Cornell Coll. of Arch., Treas. Cornell Alumni Council Coll of Arch.; **MIL SERV:** US Corp. of Engineers, Maj. 1941-1945; **OTHER ACT & HONORS:** Pres. - AIA AR Chap.; Pres. - AR Arts Ctr.; Pres. - AR Symphony Orchestra Soc.; Bd. - Mid-Amer. Arts Alliance; VP Leo N Levi Hosp., Hot Sprg.; AR; Pres. Metropolitan YMCA; **HOME ADD:** 217 Normandy Rd., Little Rock, AR 72207, (501)666-8137; **BUS ADD:** Little Rock, AR 72203PO Drawer 3019, 300 Fabco Bldg., (501)376-6671.

BLAVER, Leal B., Jr.——*Pres.*, Federal Home Loan Bank of Chicago; **PRIM RE ACT:** Banker; **BUS ADD:** 1111 East Wacker Dr., Chicago, IL 60601, (312)565-5700.*

BLAYER, Bernard——**B:** May 31, 1951, Chicago, IL, *Controller*, Intercorp, Inc.; **PRIM RE ACT:** Owner/Investor, Broker; **OTHER RE ACT:** Acquisitions, Fin. Analyst; **SERVICES:** Condo. Conversion, Comml. Devel.; **PREV EMPLOY:** The Acquest Grp. (U.S.A.), Inc., 1979-1980; **PROFL AFFIL & HONORS:** AICPA, CPA, Licensed RE Broker (IL); **EDUC:** BS, 1974, Acctg., DePaul Univ.; **HOME ADD:** 1132 W. George, Chicago, IL 60657, (312)327-9792; **BUS ADD:** 875 N. LaSalle St., Chicago, IL 60611, (312)943-6655.

BLAZAR, Sheldon M.——**B:** Mar. 30, 1931, Providence, RI, *VP Fin.*, Cadillac Fairview, Urban Development; **PRIM RE ACT:** Developer, Owner/Investor, Property Manager; **PREV EMPLOY:** Coopers & Lybrand 1974-1980; **PROFL AFFIL & HONORS:** FEI, AICPA; **EDUC:** BA, 1951, Econ., Brown Univ.; **GRAD EDUC:** MBA, LLB, 1955/1956, Acctg., Wharton Grad./NYU Law; **EDUC HONORS:** Alpha Beta Psi; **MIL SERV:** USN, YN 3; **HOME ADD:** 6554 Briarmeade Dr., Dallas, TX 75240, (214)934-2984; **BUS ADD:** 5252 First International Bldg., Dallas, TX 75270, (214)748-0441.

BLAZEJACK, John A.——**B:** Apr. 5, 1948, St. Augustine, FL, *VP*, Southeast Mort. Co.; **PRIM RE ACT:** Consultant, Appraiser, Lender; **SERVICES:** Apprsl. mkt. studies, feasibility rpts., cash flow studies and loans, Mort. Loans, Equity Placements, Pension Funds; **REP CLIENTS:** Life Ins. cos., devel., synd.; **PREV EMPLOY:** AVP RE Research Corp., 1976-1979; **PROFL AFFIL & HONORS:** MAI, SRPA, Young Advisory Council, SREA; **EDUC:** BA, 1970, Econ., Intl. Affrs., FL State Uni., Tallahassee, FL; **GRAD EDUC:** MSM, 1980, RE, FL Intl. Univ., Miami, FL.; **OTHER ACT & HONORS:** Pres. SREA No. 71, 1979-1980; Instr. AIREA and SREA; **HOME ADD:** 628 Mendoza Ave., Coral Gables, FL 33134, (305)445-6937; **BUS ADD:** 1390 Brickell Ave., Miami, FL 33131, (305)350-9421.

BLEEKER, James B.——**B:** July 17, 1949, St. Cloud, MN, *Pres. and Chmn.*, Bleeker & Zenner, Chartered; **PRIM RE ACT:** Attorney; **SERVICES:** Legal; **REP CLIENTS:** Buyers, sellers, some realty firms; **PROFL AFFIL & HONORS:** ABA, MSBA, 18th Dist. Bar Assn., Sect. Memberships; **EDUC:** BA, 1971, Math., Physics, & Econ., St. Cloud State Univ., Carleton Coll.; **GRAD EDUC:** JD, 1975, Northwestern Univ.; **EDUC HONORS:** Selected Outstanding Freshman Mathematician, Deans list for 2 quarters out of 5; **BUS ADD:** 1635 Coon Rapids Blvd., Coon Rapids, MN 55433, (612)755-1516.

BLEICH, Ronald L.——**B:** Jan. 29, 1943, NY, NY, *Tax Partner*, Laventhol & Horwath; **OTHER RE ACT:** Tax consultant; **SERVICES:** Tax advice & projections; **PROFL AFFIL & HONORS:** NYS & NJ Soc. of CPA's; ABA; NY & NJ Bar Assns., CPA; **EDUC:** BS, 1964, Acctg., NY Univ.; **GRAD EDUC:** JD, 1973, Brooklyn Law Sch.; LLM, 1976, NYU Grad. Law Sch.; **HOME ADD:** 39 Whitehall Rd., E. Brunswick, NJ 08816, (201)545-0427; **BUS ADD:** PO Box 11, E. Brunswick, NJ 08816, (201)257-6000.

BLEKRE, Charles P.——**B:** Nov. 1, 1944, Minneapolis, MN, *Owner*, The Blekre Company; **PRIM RE ACT:** Broker, Appraiser, Owner/Investor; **SERVICES:** Valuation, sales, investments income prop.; **REP CLIENTS:** Lenders, indiv., govt. agencies; **PREV EMPLOY:** S&L Assns., RE Appraisal firm; **PROFL AFFIL & HONORS:** Soc. of RE Appraisers (member), AIREA Cand., SRPA; **EDUC:** BS, 1972, Bus. Admin., Mankato State Univ.; **MIL SERV:** USN; 2nd Class PO, Navy Commendation Medal; **HOME ADD:** 625 7th Ave NE, Stewartville, MN 55976, (507)533-8749; **BUS ADD:** 302 SE 4th St., Rochester, MN 55901, (507)281-1093.

BLENKO, David B.——**B:** June 4, 1954, Philadelphia, PA, *RE Assoc.*, Continental Bank; **PRIM RE ACT:** Banker; **EDUC:** BA, 1976, Pol. Sci., Amherst Coll.; **GRAD EDUC:** MBA, 1980, RE/Fin., Stanford Univ.; **EDUC HONORS:** Cum Laude; **HOME ADD:** 2700 Hampden St., Chicago, IL 60614; **BUS ADD:** 231 S. LaSalle, Chicago, IL 60693, (312)828-7867.

BLESICH, Mirko——**B:** Mar. 17, 1946, Eboli, Italy, *RE Spec.*, Xerox Corp., Corporate RE Org./East; **OTHER RE ACT:** Site selections, lease negotiations, constr. and prop. mgmt. of corp. facilities; **PREV EMPLOY:** Romanek, Golub & Co., Chicago, M&J Wilkow, Ltd., Chicago; **EDUC:** BS, 1969, Fin. & Invest., USC; BS, 1973, RE, AZ State Univ., Tempe; **EDUC HONORS:** Dean's List; **MIL SERV:** USA, Sgt.; **OTHER ACT & HONORS:** Sigma Chi Frat., Serbian Nat. Fed., Amer. Numismatic Assn.; **BUS ADD:** 3000 Des Plaines Ave., Des Plaines, IL 60018, (312)297-3600.

BLEVINS, Gary Lynn——**B:** Feb. 17, 1941, St. Charles, AR, *Managing Arch./Broker*, Trammell Crow Co.; **PRIM RE ACT:** Broker, Architect, Consultant, Developer, Builder, Owner/Investor; **OTHER RE ACT:** Renovation/Restoration Serv.; **SERVICES:** Brokerage, Design, Build, Devel., Consulting; **PROFL AFFIL & HONORS:** AIA, TX Soc. of Arch., Dallas AIA; **EDUC:** BArch, BS Arch., 1964, 1969, Univ. of TX, Austin; **GRAD EDUC:** MBA, 1974, RE & Rgnl. Sci., S. Methodist Univ., Dallas; **MIL SERV:** USN; Lt., 5 decorations; **HOME ADD:** 1026 Tranquilla, Dallas, TX 75218, (214)327-0108; **BUS ADD:** 2001 Bryan Tower Suite 3200, Dallas, TX 75201, (214)742-2000.

BLEYER, Norman J.——**B:** Jan. 3, 1930, Toledo, OH, *Pres.*, Bleyer Services Ltd.; **PRIM RE ACT:** Broker, Consultant, Appraiser; **OTHER RE ACT:** MI Mkt. Data Service (Comml. Comp. Data Bank); **SERVICES:** RE Appraisals, counseling, const. inspections, field research, comparable data service; **REP CLIENTS:** Lenders, indivs., investors in RE, attys., trusts; **PREV EMPLOY:** City Nat. Bank of Detroit, 27 yrs., Chief Appraisal Officer; **PROFL AFFIL & HONORS:** Soc. of RE Appraisers; SRA; SRPA; AIREA, Candidate; Nat. Assn. of Review Appraisers; CRA; RE Broker, State of MI, SRA; SRPA; CRA; Past Pres., Soc. RE Appraisers Detroit Chap. 13; Past Pres., Const. Indus. Credit Grg.; **EDUC:** BBA, 1960, Mgmt., Univ. of Detroit; **MIL SERV:** USMC, Sgt.; **HOME ADD:** 273 S. Beech Daly, Dearborn Hts., MI 48125, (313)563-4072; **BUS ADD:** 273 S. Beech Daly, Dearborn Hts., MI 48125, (313)563-4072.

BLICKSILVER, Harvey——**B:** Nov. 15, 1939, Paterson, NJ, *VP & Corporate Counsel*, Berg Enterprises, Inc.; **PRIM RE ACT:** Attorney; **SERVICES:** RE Brokerage, Synds., Mort. Banking; **PREV EMPLOY:** Hovnanian Enterprises, Inc., Red Bank, NJ - VP, Gen. Counsel, Dir. 1969-73; **PROFL AFFIL & HONORS:** ABA, NJ & Middlesex Cty. Bar Assns.; NJ Assn. of Corporate Counsel; Community Assns. Inst., Member - NJ State Bar and United States Dist. Ct. for the Dist. of NJ; **EDUC:** BA, 1961, Econ., Rutgers Univ., New Brunswick, NJ; **GRAD EDUC:** JD, 1963, Law, Rutgers Univ. Law School - Newark, NJ; **EDUC HONORS:** Econ. Hon. Soc.; Scarlet Key; Exchange Student in Argentina, Articles Editor - Rutgers Law Review; **HOME ADD:** 575 Easton Ave., Somerset, NJ 08873, (201)249-3343; **BUS ADD:** 75 Rte. 27, Iselin, NJ 08830, (201)494-3200.

BLIGH, Robert A.——**B:** Dec. 7, 1946, Norfolk, NE, *Asst Prof. of Bus. Admin.*, Doane Coll., Bus.; **PRIM RE ACT:** Consultant, Attorney, Instructor, Real Estate Publisher; **OTHER RE ACT:** Profl.; **SERVICES:** Training in RE & Bus.; **REP CLIENTS:** Undergrad students desiring profl. training in bus. admin.; **PREV EMPLOY:** Legal counsel, NE Dept. of Educ., 1975-81; **PROFL AFFIL & HONORS:** ABA, RE, Probate & Estate Planning Sect.; NE State Bar Assn.; **EDUC:** BA, 1970, Zoology & Econ., Univ. of SD; **GRAD EDUC:** JD, 1975, Univ. of NE, Coll. of Law; **EDUC HONORS:** Dean's List, Am. Jr. Award in Labor Law (1974); **HOME ADD:** 4520 S 46th St., Lincoln, NE 68516, (402)488-0815; **BUS ADD:** Crete, NE 68333, (402)826-2161.

BLITZ, Stephen M.——**B:** July 29, 1941, New York City, *Partner*, Gibson, Dunn & Crutcher; **PRIM RE ACT:** Attorney; **SERVICES:** Legal Services; **PROFL AFFIL & HONORS:** ABA, Real Property Sect., CA State BAr Real Property Sect., Los Angeles Cty. Bar Assn. Real Prop. Sect.; **EDUC:** BS, 1963, EE, Columbia Univ.; BA, 1962, Columbia Univ.; **GRAD EDUC:** LLB, 1966, Stanford Law School; **EDUC HONORS:** Order of the Coif; **BUS ADD:** 2029 Century Park E, Los Angeles, CA 90067, (213)552-8543.

BLIWISE, Lester M.——**B:** Dec. 22, 1945, Philadelphia, PA, *Partner*, Trubin Sillcocks Edelman & Knapp; **PRIM RE ACT:** Attorney; **SERVICES:** Legal; **REP CLIENTS:** Lenders and instnl. or indiv. investors in comml. props.; **PROFL AFFIL & HONORS:** ABA, NY State Bar Assn. (Chmn., Comm. on RE Fin. and Liens, Real Prop. Sect.); Assn. of the Bar of the City of NY; **EDUC:** BA, 1967, Rutgers Univ.; **GRAD EDUC:** JD, 1970, Brooklyn Law School; **EDUC HONORS:** Notes Editor, Brooklyn Law Review; **HOME ADD:** Larchmont, NY 10538; **BUS ADD:** 375 Park Ave., NY, NY 10152, (212)759-5400.

BLOCH, Bruce——*RE Mgr.*, Ogden Corp.; **PRIM RE ACT:** Property Manager; **BUS ADD:** 277 Park Ave. 16th Flr., New York, NY 10017, (212)754-4000.*

BLOCH, Stuart Marshall——**B:** Nov. 5, 1942, Detroit, MI, *Partner*, Ingersoll and Bloch, Chartered, Law; **PRIM RE ACT:** Attorney; **OTHER RE ACT:** Fed. and State Regulation; **SERVICES:** Legal Serv.: Fed. and State Regulation; **REP CLIENTS:** Greyhound Leasing Corp.; Owens-IL Development Corp.; Mobil Land Devel. Corp.; ARVIBA; Branigar Org.; American Land Devel. Assn.; National Time Sharing Council; **PROFL AFFIL & HONORS:** ULI, ABA, AIA, Bar Member, MI and DC; **EDUC:** AB, 1964, Govt., Econ., Philosophy, Univ. of Miami, FL; **GRAD EDUC:** LLB, 1967, Law, Harvard; **EDUC HONORS:** Pres. Student Body; ZBT Man of the Year; Academic Honor Roll, Member, Civil Rights Law Review, Member Harvard Legal Common Taries; GOIF Team; **OTHER ACT & HONORS:** IVS; Vietnam Volunteer; Harvard Alumni Assn.; AIA Award for Adaptive Re-Use of Historic Mansion; **HOME ADD:** 1401 16th St. NW, Washington, DC 20036, (202)232-2144; **BUS ADD:** 1401 16th St., NW, Washington, DC 20036, (202)232-1015.

BLOCK, Burton——*Ed.-Mng. Ed.*, Division of Real Estate, Washington (State) Real Estate News; **PRIM RE ACT:** Real Estate Publisher; **BUS ADD:** PO Box 247, Olympia, WA 98504, (206)753-2700.*

BLOCK, Frederick——*SIR Mgr. RE*, Thiokol Corp.; **PRIM RE ACT:** Property Manager; **BUS ADD:** PO Box 1000, Newtown, PA 18940, (215)968-5911.*

BLOCK, Gene R.——*VP*, Conrock Co.; **PRIM RE ACT:** Property Manager; **BUS ADD:** 3200 San Fernando Rd., Los Angeles, CA 90065, (213)258-2777.*

BLOCK, Jon——**B:** Nov. 9, 1948, New York, *Rgnl. Mgr.*, General Electric Corp., Rec; **PRIM RE ACT:** Lender, Owner/Investor; **SERVICES:** Equity & Loan Funds for income prop.; **EDUC:** BBA, 1971, Fin., Univ. of Miami; **GRAD EDUC:** MBA, 1972, Gen. Bus./Mgmt., Univ. of Miami; **HOME ADD:** 2010 Oakwood Dr., Richardson, TX 75081, (214)690-4497; **BUS ADD:** 333 W. Campbell Rd., Richardson, TX 75880, (214)783-6600.

BLOCK, Kenneth George——**B:** Aug. 29, 1953, Kansas City, MO, *VP; Indus. Dept. Dir.*, Block & Company, Inc., Realtors; **PRIM RE ACT:** Broker, Consultant, Developer, Owner/Investor, Property Manager, Syndicator; **SERVICES:** Investment & devel. counseling valuation, devel. & synd. of comml. props., mgmt.; **REP CLIENTS:** Nat. as well as local indus. and office clients as well as local and nat. investors (My primary expertise is indus. while the co. is engaged in office, med., retail, franchising, etc.); **PROFL AFFIL & HONORS:** Membership in SIR, RE Bd. of Kansas City, NAIOP, Company Membership in ICSC, American Realty Services, NIREB, RESSI, NAR, IREM, Pres. of KC Chap. of NAIOP, Chmn. of Comml./Investment Branch of KC RE Bd., Selected for inclusion in 1981 Edition of Outstanding Young Men of Amer., Dir. of Kansas City RE Bd., Member of Million Dollar Club of KC RE Bd. 1977-80, Member of Multi-Million Dollar Club of MO Assn. of Realtors 1977-1980, Dir. of MO Assn. of Realtors 1982-1983; **EDUC:** BA, 1975, RE, Gen., MI State Univ.; **EDUC HONORS:** Grad. with Honors, Member of Honors Coll.; **HOME ADD:** 3220 West 82nd St., Leawood, KS 66206, (913)381-0856; **BUS ADD:** 605 West 47th St., Suite 100, Kansas City, MO 64112, (816)531-1400.

BLOCK, Norman E.——**B:** Feb. 5, 1949, Greensboro, NC, *Owner*, Heffner/Block Realtors; **PRIM RE ACT:** Broker, Instructor, Consultant, Developer; **REP CLIENTS:** Zephyr Const. Co.; Whaley Const. Co.; Orange Bldrs., Inc.; Bolin Forest Assoc.; Home Equity; HomeAmerica; **PROFL AFFIL & HONORS:** Chapel Hill Bd. of Realtors; Durham Bd. of Realtors, GRI; Durham - Chapel Hill Homebldrs. Assn.; Cert. RE Instr.; **EDUC:** BA, 1971, Eng., Univ. of NC at Chapel Hill; **GRAD EDUC:** JD/MBA, 1978, Univ. of NC at Chapel Hill; **EDUC HONORS:** Betta Gamma Sigma; Phi Eta Sigma, Grad. 1st in the MBA Class of 1978; **OTHER ACT & HONORS:** Bd. of Dirs. Chapel Hill C of C; Bd. of Dirs., The Village Bank; Bd. of Dirs. Chapel Hill Bd. of Realtors; Public Schools Supts. Advisory Bd.; **HOME ADD:** 1303 LeClair St., Chapel Hill, NC 27514, (919)929-6815; **BUS ADD:** 410 Airport Rd., Chapel Hill, NC 27514, (919)967-9234.

BLOCK, William K.——**B:** Oct. 23, 1950, New York, NY, *Asst. Comm. of Fin.*, NYC Dept. of Fin., Real Prop. Assessment Bur.; **PRIM RE ACT:** Attorney; **OTHER RE ACT:** Administrator in assessing dept.; **SERVICES:** Assessment of all real prop. in the city of NY; **PREV EMPLOY:** Gen. Counsel, NYC Tax Commission, June 1978-Apr. 1981; **PROFL AFFIL & HONORS:** Amer. Bar Assn., NY State Bar Assn., NY Cty. Bar Assn., Intl. Assn. of Assessing Officers; **EDUC:** BA, 1973, Phil. & Hist., Colgate Univ.; **GRAD EDUC:** JD, 1976, Law, Albany Law Sch. of Union Univ.; **EDUC HONORS:** Cum Laude, Hons. in Phil.; **HOME ADD:** 137-75 Geranium Ave., Flushing, NY 11355; **BUS ADD:** Rm 946, Municipal Bldg., NY, NY 10007, (212)566-3532.

BLOCKER, Henry C.——*Vice President, Purchasing*, Avondale Mills; **PRIM RE ACT:** Property Manager; **BUS ADD:** Sylacaugh, AL 35150, (205)245-5221.*

BLOM, Nicolas A.——B: Nov. 16, 1936, Holland, *Gen. Mgr.*, Grosvenor International Canada, Ltd.; **PRIM RE ACT:** Developer, Owner/Investor; **PREV EMPLOY:** Practiced law in RE field for 18 yrs.; **PROFL AFFIL & HONORS:** Can. Bar Assn., Law Soc. of BC; **EDUC:** BA, 1959, Math. & Econ., Univ. of BC; **GRAD EDUC:** LLB, 1962, Univ. of BC, Law School; **OTHER ACT & HONORS:** Rotary Club of Vancouver; **HOME ADD:** 1557 Nanton Ave., Vancouver, V6J2X3, BC, Can., (604)734-8037; **BUS ADD:** 1900-777 Mornby St., Vancouver, V6ZIA7, BC, Can., (604)683-1141.

BLOMSTRAND, Curt——B: Feb. 16, 1941, *VP*, The Desco Group, Inc.; **PRIM RE ACT:** Broker, Developer, Owner/Investor, Property Manager, Syndicator; **SERVICES:** Devel. & Synd. of comml. & resid. props., prop. mgmt., design constr. servs.; **REP CLIENTS:** Investors, pension funds, corp. clients; **PREV EMPLOY:** Bechtel Corp.; **PROFL AFFIL & HONORS:** Assn. Bldg. Indus.; Young Homebuilders of N CA, Nat. Assn. of Homebuilders; **EDUC:** BS, 1966, Fin., UCLA; **GRAD EDUC:** MBA, 1971, Univ. of CA at Northridge; **OTHER ACT & HONORS:** Lafayette Park & Recreation Commn; **HOME ADD:** 736 Glenside Cir., Lafayette, CA 94549, (415)284-5844; **BUS ADD:** 3685 Mt. Diablo Blvd., Suite 300, Lafayette, CA 94549, (415)283-8470.

BLOODWORTH, Edward R.——B: Nov. 14, 1932, Crosby County, TX, *Owner*, Valuation Services, RE, Appraisers/Consultants; **PRIM RE ACT:** Consultant, Appraiser; **SERVICES:** Comml. prop. appraisals, feasibility, consulting; **REP CLIENTS:** Natl. & local cos., lenders, gov. bodies, investors; **PREV EMPLOY:** Sr. VP, First Natl. Bank of Casper, 1975-1980; **PROFL AFFIL & HONORS:** MAI, Distinguished Member, Pres. Club, Van Schaack & Co., 1975; **EDUC:** BBA, 1960, Fin, TX Tech Univ.; **GRAD EDUC:** School of Mort. Banking, 1968, Mort. Lending, Northwestern Univ.; **MIL SERV:** USN; PO; Campaign Ribbons; **OTHER ACT & HONORS:** Rotary Intl.; **HOME ADD:** 1640 Kelly Dr., Casper, WY 82601, (307)235-5589; **BUS ADD:** 300 Ctry. Club Rd., Suite 215, Casper, WY 82601, (307)577-0601.

BLOODWORTH, Russell E.——B: July 1, 1945, Memphis, TN, *VP*, Boyce Investment Co.; **PRIM RE ACT:** Broker, Consultant, Appraiser, Developer, Owner/Investor; **OTHER RE ACT:** Zoning; **SERVICES:** Valuation and Devel. of Comml. and Resid. Properties, Zoning; **REP CLIENTS:** Lenders and Indiv. or Instnl. investors in comml. props.; **PROFL AFFIL & HONORS:** ULI; Bd. of Realtors, Lamda Alpha; **EDUC:** BArch, 1968, Arch, Univ. of VA; **GRAD EDUC:** Environmental Design, 1972, Market Analysis and Cash Flow Analysis, Yale Univ.; **EDUC HONORS:** 2st Prize VA Brick Competition, 1966; Honors program; Alpha Rho Chi Medal; Scarab., Amer.-Scandinavian Third-Gray Fellow, 1969; **MIL SERV:** USMC, 1st LT; **HOME ADD:** 2212 Kirby Rd., Memphis, TN 38119, (901)755-4733; **BUS ADD:** PO Box 17800, Memphis, TN 38119, (901)766-4204.

BLOOM, George F.——B: June 11, 1919, Columbia City, IN, *Prof. of RE Admin. and RE Dir.*, IN Univ., School of Bus.; **PRIM RE ACT:** Instructor, Appraiser, Developer, Owner/Investor; **OTHER RE ACT:** Author and Educ.; **SERVICES:** Consulting and appraising; **PROFL AFFIL & HONORS:** Lamba Alpha, AIREA, Beta Gamma Sigma; Appraisal Inst. Prof. Recognition Award; **EDUC:** BS, 1941, Mktg., IN Univ; **GRAD EDUC:** MBA, DBA, 1948, 1953, RE, IN Univ.; **EDUC HONORS:** Phi Eta Sigma; **MIL SERV:** USMCR, Major 1941-46, Unit Citation; **OTHER ACT & HONORS:** Bloomington Redev. Commn. 1959-72, IN Soc. to Prevent Blindness, Dir.; **HOME ADD:** 1608 Covenanter Dr, Bloomington, IN 47401, (812)336-3288; **BUS ADD:** 521 E 4th St, Bloomington, IN 47401, (812)337-3054.

BLOOM, Jack D.——B: Mar. 27, 1923, St. Louis, MO, *VP*, Diversified Realty Co., Inc./The Shirlou Corp.; **PRIM RE ACT:** Broker, Developer, Builder, Property Manager; **OTHER RE ACT:** Land devel., sales mgr., entrepreneur; **SERVICES:** Brokerage, devel., sales mgmt., leasing, prop. mgmt.; **REP CLIENTS:** Comml. office users, retailers, mfrs., land owners profl. office users and ind; **PREV EMPLOY:** VP, National Homes Construction Corp., VP, Inland Steel Development Corp. 27 years Self Employed Broker; **PROFL AFFIL & HONORS:** Past Member, St. Louis RE Bd., Past Member Nat. Assn. of Home Bldrs.; **EDUC:** BA, 1947, Journalism, WA Univ., St. Louis, MO; **MIL SERV:** US Army, Tech. Sgt., Bronze Star, Purple Heart; **HOME ADD:** 1255 Charter Oak Pkwy, St. Louis, MO 63141, (314)432-4234; **BUS ADD:** 9378 Olivd Blvd., St. Louis, MO 63132, (314)991-3344.

BLOOM, Jay B.——B: Sept. 20, 1932, Newark, NJ; **PRIM RE ACT:** Attorney; **SERVICES:** Gen. counseling and litigation practice with particular emphasis on RE, corp. and bus. law, substantial municipal, zoning and educ. law; **PROFL AFFIL & HONORS:** Union Lawyers Club, NJ State Bar Assn., Union Cty. Bar Assn.; **EDUC:** BA, 1954, Hist., Lafayette Coll.; **GRAD EDUC:** JD, 1959, Columbia Univ.; **MIL SERV:** USA, Army of Occupation of Germany; **OTHER ACT & HONORS:** Member of Town Council, Township of Springfield; Member Bd. of Adjustment, Planning Bd.; Solid Waste Disposal Comm., Bd. of Health; Union Cty. Chairman's Club; Atty, to the Union Cty. Vocational Tech. Bd. of Educ.; Township Atty. of the Township of Springfield; **HOME ADD:** 26 Irwin St., Springfield, NJ, (201)379-6233; **BUS ADD:** 8 Mountain Ave., Springfield, NJ 07081, (201)379-2444.

BLOOM, William R.——B: Mar 18, 1949, Brooklyn, NY, *Atty.*, Bloom & Schwartz; **PRIM RE ACT:** Attorney, Owner/Investor; **SERVICES:** Legal Advice & Representation, Gen. Part. RE Invest. Corps.; **REP CLIENTS:** Builders, Shopping Ctr. Devs., Sellers & Purchasers of comml. & Resid. RE; **PROFL AFFIL & HONORS:** MA Bar Assn., ABA, Worcester Cty. and S. Middlesex Bar Assn.; **EDUC:** BA, 1971, Poli. Sci., Boston Univ.; **GRAD EDUC:** JD, 1975, Law, Northeastern Univ. School of Law; **OTHER ACT & HONORS:** Town of Westborough By-Law Revision Comm.; Member, Various Local Soc. & Relig. Orgs., Bd. of Dir.; **HOME ADD:** 42 Adams St., Westborough, MA 01581, (617)366-0931; **BUS ADD:** PO Box 422, 18 Lyman St., Westborough, MA 01581, (617)366-1771.

BLOOMBERG, Burton——*Assoc. Gen. Counsel*, Department of Housing and Urban Development, Ofc. of Equal Opportunity & Administrative Law; **PRIM RE ACT:** Lender; **BUS ADD:** 451 Seventh St., S.W., Washington, DC 20410, (202)755-7203.*

BLOSSER, Dale A.——B: Oct. 3, 1927, Brussels, Belgium, *Princ.*, Dale Blosser & Assoc., Construction Admin.; **PRIM RE ACT:** Architect, Consultant; **OTHER RE ACT:** Construction Admin.; **SERVICES:** Feasibility Studies; Cost Surveys & Estimates; Design & Bldg. Inspection; **REP CLIENTS:** Metropolitan Life Ins.; New York Life Ins.; Stockton-White Co., First Congregational Church; N Plaza S/C; Aetna Life Ins. Co.; **PREV EMPLOY:** Synergetics, Inc., Raleigh, NC 1962-65; John D. Latimer & Assoc., Durham, NC 1960-62; Geodesics, Inc., Raleigh 1957-60; **PROFL AFFIL & HONORS:** AIA, ACI, AISC, AITC, ASTM, CSI, NCAP, Who's Who in S & SW, Fin. & Industry, in the World - 1960-present; **EDUC:** BArch, 1956, NC State Univ., Raleigh, NC; **EDUC HONORS:** Logo design, winning entry - 1955 (Still in use); **MIL SERV:** USA 1945-47, T/5; **OTHER ACT & HONORS:** Raleigh Bd. of Adjustment, 1974-80; Raleigh-Wake Land Use, NCSU Faculty Club; Capital City Club, Lecturer, School of Design, NCSU; Book reviewer - Prentice-Hall 1972-Present; **HOME ADD:** 3008 Ruffin St., Raleigh, NC 27607, (919)828-4914; **BUS ADD:** 2008 Hillsborough St., (Mail: Box 10547, Raleigh 27605), Raleigh, NC 27607, (919)833-6439.

BLOTNER, Norman D.——B: Dec. 6, 1918, Boston, MA, *Sr. VP, Sec., Dir.*, Lane Bryant, Inc., Corporate; **PRIM RE ACT:** Attorney; **OTHER RE ACT:** Oversee chain store & m/o RE; **PREV EMPLOY:** Spiro, Felstiner, Prager & Treeger, Law Firm; **PROFL AFFIL & HONORS:** Bar Assn., City of NY; **EDUC:** AB, 1940, Govt., Harvard Coll.; **GRAD EDUC:** JD, 1947, Law, Harvard Law School; **EDUC HONORS:** Cum Laude; **MIL SERV:** USNR, Lt. Comdr.; **OTHER ACT & HONORS:** BBB, Dir., Metro. NY; Harvard Varsity Club; Harvard Club, Westchester; **HOME ADD:** 140 Overlook Rd., New Rochelle, NY 10804, (914)235-2515; **BUS ADD:** 469 Fifth Ave., NY, NY 10017, (212)684-3863.

BLUE, Sheldon A.——B: June 10, 1933, Lafayette, LA, *Dir. of Mktg./Designated Broker*, Nu-West, Inc., Pac. NW; **PRIM RE ACT:** Broker, Consultant, Developer, Builder; **SERVICES:** Land Dev., Home Bldg., Joint-Venture, RE Brokerage, Mktg. Housing Studies & Consultation; **REP CLIENTS:** Builders-Dev.-Packagers; **PREV EMPLOY:** Private Architectural Practice, 1962-1970; Gen. Mgr. (Regional)/VP, Levitt & Sons, Inc., 1972-1975; Mktg. VP-Ewd. R. Carr & Assoc., 1975-1977; Gen. Mgr.-/Jack L. McIntosh RE Brokerage, 1977-1980; **PROFL AFFIL & HONORS:** AIA, NAHB; **EDUC:** Completed 4-yr curric., 1956, Arch. Engineering LA State Univ.; **MIL SERV:** USA, 1956-58, S/Sgt.; **OTHER ACT & HONORS:** Bellevue C of C, Kappa Sigma Frat. Alumni Assoc.; **HOME ADD:** 14318 SE 49th, Bellevue, WA 98006, (206)641-3397; **BUS ADD:** 1220 S 356th, Fed. Way, Seattle, WA 98003, (206)927-2700.

BLUESTEIN, Ronald W.——*Asst. VP - Construction, Engrg. & Tech. Serv.*, Aetna Life & Casualty, RE Investment Dept.; **PRIM RE ACT:** Lender; **SERVICES:** Construction lending; **REP CLIENTS:** Major RE Devel.; **PREV EMPLOY:** Buffalo Savings Bank 1961-1971; Mfrs. Hanover Mort. Co. 1974-1978; **PROFL AFFIL & HONORS:** Soc. of RE Appraisers; MBA; **BUS ADD:** One Civic Ctr. Plaza, Hartford, CT 06143, (203)273-7232.

BLUM, Gerald W.——**B:** Oct. 31, 1952, NY, NY, *Pres., Broker*, Management Professionals, Inc.; **PRIM RE ACT:** Broker, Consultant, Appraiser, Developer, Builder, Owner/Investor, Property Manager, Syndicator; **SERVICES:** Prop. mgmt., sales, appraisals, etc.; **REP CLIENTS:** Blum Assocs., Inc., W.G. Blum Realty Corp. (NY & FL), Omnia Properties (NY); International Travel Services; **PREV EMPLOY:** Fed. Dept. Stores, 1971-1976; **PROFL AFFIL & HONORS:** US C of C; REPI; Nat. Multiple Listing Service; **EDUC:** Johns Hopkins, Univ. of FL; **OTHER ACT & HONORS:** Sports Car Club of Amer., Porsche Club of Amer., Gold Coast Region - Bd. of Dir., Scuderia Veloce Sports Car Club, Pres.; **HOME ADD:** 1527 S. Flagler Dr., W. Palm Beach, FL 33401, (305)659-3230; **BUS ADD:** 226 S. Dixie Hwy., W. Palm Beach, FL 33401, (305)659-1156.

BLUM, Michael S.——**B:** Aug. 30, 1939, NYC, NY, *VP & Gen. Mgr. Residential Fin. Dept.*, Gen. Electric Credit Corp.; **PRIM RE ACT:** Lender, Owner/Investor; **SERVICES:** Residential RE fin. incl. mfd. Housing and all related serv.; **PROFL AFFIL & HONORS:** ULI, MBA; **EDUC:** BCE, 1960, CCNY; **GRAD EDUC:** MBA, 1965, Fin., Rutgers Univ.; **EDUC HONORS:** Beta Gamma Sigma; **HOME ADD:** 39 Ridgewood Rd., Ridgefield, CT 06877; **BUS ADD:** PO Box 8300, Stamford, CT 06904, (203)357-4881.

BLUM, Robert A.——**B:** Feb. 10, 1933, Newark, NJ, *Pres.*, R.A. Blum, Bus. Interests; **PRIM RE ACT:** Broker, Syndicator, Consultant, Owner/Investor; **PREV EMPLOY:** Pres., Fed. Automatic Co.; **EDUC:** BA, 1955, Bus., Lehigh Univ.; **MIL SERV:** USAF, Capt.; **OTHER ACT & HONORS:** Past Pres. NACLEO; **HOME ADD:** 765 Valley St., Orange, NJ 07050, (201)675-1364; **BUS ADD:** 12 S. Orange Ave., S. Orange, NJ 07079, (201)761-1204.

BLUMBERG, David——**B:** Jan. 19, 1925, Dothan, AL, *Chmn. of the Bd. & CEO*, First Mortgage Fin. Corp.; **PRIM RE ACT:** Owner/Investor; **PREV EMPLOY:** Pres. Planned Devel. Corp., (1953-), Chmn. Exec Comm. Prestressed Systems, Inc., (1957-73); **PROFL AFFIL & HONORS:** Exec Comm. So. FL Coordinating Council, Bd. of Dirs. FL Power & Light, Bd. of Dir. SE First Nat. Bank of Miami, 1973 Miami News Businesman of the Yr.; **EDUC:** 1940-42, Univ. of AL; 1942-43, Univ. of NC; **GRAD EDUC:** MBA, 1947, Harvard Grad. Sch. of Bus.; **MIL SERV:** USNR, Lt. JG; **OTHER ACT & HONORS:** Bd. of Govs. Miami C of C, Bd. of Dir. FL State C of C, Bd. of Tr. Univ. of Miami, Member of Orange Bowl Comm., Member of FL Council of 100, Bd. of Tr. The Two Hundred Club; **HOME ADD:** 1 Arvida Pkwy, Coral Gables, FL 33156, (305)666-2808; **BUS ADD:** 801 41st St., Miami, FL 33140, (305)532-7361.

BLUMBERG, Frederick——**B:** Dec. 24, 1927, New York, NY, *Partner*, Fox, Rothschild, O'Brien & Frankel, RE; **PRIM RE ACT:** Attorney; **PROFL AFFIL & HONORS:** Philadelphia, PA Bar Assns., ABA; **EDUC:** BS, 1950, Econ. & Philosophy, Cornell Univ.; **GRAD EDUC:** JD, 1953, Law, Harvard Univ.; **HOME ADD:** 646 Lindley Rd., Glenside, PA 19038, (215)886-3521; **BUS ADD:** 2000 Market St., 10th Floor, Philadelphia, PA 19103, (215)299-2030.

BLUMBERG, James Reich——**B:** Dec. 15, 1943, Knoxville, TN, *RE Mgr., Eastern Region*, Service Merchandise Co., Inc., Real Estate Dept.; **OTHER RE ACT:** Site selection & market research; **PREV EMPLOY:** Zayre Corp., Framingham, MA 01701 (1978-1982); **PROFL AFFIL & HONORS:** NACORE, ICSC, Pres. NACORE Intnl. Retail Indus. Council (1980-82); **OTHER ACT & HONORS:** Member B'nai B'rith Intnl., Young Leadership Cabinet (1977-81), Member New England Reg. Bd. ADL of B'nai B'rith; **HOME ADD:** 3601-A Hobbs Rd., Nashville, TN 37215, (615)292-7025; **BUS ADD:** P.O. Box 24600, Nashville, TN 37202, (615)366-3925.

BLUMBERG, Richard E.——**B:** June 22, 1944, Bronx, NY, *Associate Director, VP Sec./Partner*, National Housing Law Project/Madway Blumberg Bishop & Smith; **PRIM RE ACT:** Attorney, Owner/Investor, Instructor; **OTHER RE ACT:** Legislation, Litigation; **SERVICES:** Legal services in real estate transactions; **REP CLIENTS:** Corporate RE location, lease negotiations, development & syndication, all federal housing programs; **PREV EMPLOY:** Counsel to NJ Tenants Organization; **PROFL AFFIL & HONORS:** CA & NJ Bar Assn., Chmn. Private Landlord/Tenant Committee; CA Bar; Real Prop. Section; CA Assembly Housing Advisory Committee, Prof. of Law, John F. Kennedy Univ.; **EDUC:** BA, BS, 1966, Business/Import-Export, American Univ., Wash. DC; **GRAD EDUC:** LLB-JD, 1969, Law, Rutgers—The State Univ.; **EDUC HONORS:** Deans List, Moot Court Speakers Award; Bar Scholarship; **OTHER ACT & HONORS:** Bd. of Dirs., Piedmont Swim Team; Founder, Park Day School; **HOME ADD:** 894 Paramount Rd., Oakland, CA 94610, (415)451-5554; **BUS ADD:** 2150 Shattuck Ave., Suite 300, Berkeley, CA 94704, (415)548-9400.

BLUME, William M., Jr.——**B:** Mar. 6, 1948, Charleston, SC, *Tax Mgr.*, Ernst & Whinney, Tax; **OTHER RE ACT:** Accountant; **SERVICES:** Tax and fin. consulting; **REP CLIENTS:** Tax shelter mgrs. - brokers - devels., builders - arch.; **PREV EMPLOY:** Tax Shelter Analysis and Packaging; **PROFL AFFIL & HONORS:** State Tax Comm. - CO; Denver International Tax Group; Adjunct Prof. Taxation - Univ. of Denver LLM program; **EDUC:** BA, 1970, Econ., Presbyterian Coll.; **GRAD EDUC:** MA, 1974 and Master of Taxation, 1980, Acctg. & Taxation, Univ. of SC 1974 & Univ. of Denver 1980; **MIL SERV:** US Army, E-5; **OTHER ACT & HONORS:** The Denver Club; Denver Athletic Club; **HOME ADD:** 14317 B, East Montana Circle, Aurora, CO 80012, (303)755-6213; **BUS ADD:** 613 17th St., Suite 2400, Denver, CO 80202, (303)623-5211.

BLUMENFELD, Samuel G.——**B:** NYC, NY, *Controller & Managing Partner*, Bergen Cty. Assocs.; **PRIM RE ACT:** Developer, Owner/Investor; **PREV EMPLOY:** CPA own practice even today; **PROFL AFFIL & HONORS:** NJ Soc. of CPA's; **EDUC:** BCS, 1924, Acctg., NY Univ.; **OTHER ACT & HONORS:** Past Pres., Newark Zionist Org.; **HOME ADD:** 19 Kean Rd., Short Hills, NJ 07078, (201)379-3420; **BUS ADD:** 200 Murray Hill Parkway, E Rutherford, NJ 07073, (201)939-5533.

BLUMENTHAL, Morton J.——**B:** Oct. 14, 1931, Putnam, CT, *Exec. Dir.*, New England Non Profit Housing Devel. Corp.; **PRIM RE ACT:** Consultant, Attorney, Instructor; **OTHER RE ACT:** Rgnl. tech. assistance and loan funds to non profit housing grps.; **REP CLIENTS:** New Samaritian corp., CT, Joseph P. Kennedy Jr. Foundation; **PREV EMPLOY:** Exec. Dir. NE CT Community devel. corp. 1973-76; **PROFL AFFIL & HONORS:** NAHRO, Nat. leased Housing, CT Bar Assn., Assoc. Trainer Nat. Ctr. for Housing Mgmt.; **EDUC:** BS, 1953, Mktg., Univ. of CT; **GRAD EDUC:** JD, 1969, R.E. and Poverty Law, Univ. of CT Sch. of Law; **MIL SERV:** USAFR, Capt. 1954- 61; **OTHER ACT & HONORS:** State Rep. CT 1970-73; **HOME ADD:** 138 Lancelot Ave., Manchester, NH 03104, (603)668-6388; **BUS ADD:** 28 S. Main St., Concord, NH 03301, (603)224-3363.

BLY, Herbert——*VP Worldwide Engr. & Const.*, Squibb Corp.; **PRIM RE ACT:** Property Manager; **BUS ADD:** PO Box 4000, Route 206, Province Rd., Princeton, NJ 08540, (212)621-7000.*

BLY, Thomas K.——**B:** Jan. 21, 1939, St. Paul, MN, *Pres./Treas.*, Bly Lowe Inc.; **PRIM RE ACT:** Syndicator, Consultant, Developer, Builder, Property Manager, Owner/Investor; **OTHER RE ACT:** Reg. as RE Securities Agent; Lic. to sell RE; **SERVICES:** Work with comml. and indus. props. only; **REP CLIENTS:** Indiv. & Instnl. Investors in Comml. & Indus. Props., or anything that can be synd.; **PREV EMPLOY:** Self Employed in RE; **PROFL AFFIL & HONORS:** RESSI; Union of Profl. Airmen; Member of various apt. owner orgs. and bldrs. org.; **MIL SERV:** USA, Paratroopers, SP4; **OTHER ACT & HONORS:** Past - Kiwanis; Big Brothers; Big Sisters; Various Investment Grps., Various Pilot Organizations - Held Mgmt. Offices in all; **HOME ADD:** 1076 Riverside Dr., Battle Creek, MI 49015, (616)964-4404; **BUS ADD:** 572 W. Columbia, POB 549, Battle Creek, MI 49016.

BOBANIC, B.A.——*VP Mktg.*, Mathews Corp., A & E Design, Inc.; **PRIM RE ACT:** Broker, Engineer, Developer, Architect, Builder; **SERVICES:** Arch. and engrg. design servs., all const. and contracting servs.; **PROFL AFFIL & HONORS:** Assn. Gov. Contractors, Assoc. Builders and Contracters, AIA, SIDC, FIDC, Nat. Assn. of Indus. & Office Parks; **BUS ADD:** 5644 N Dale Mabry, Tampa, FL 33614, (813)885-1451.

BOBB, Robert J.——**B:** Dec. 16, 1947, Blue Island, IL, *Chmn. of the Bd.*, The Bellaman Group; **PRIM RE ACT:** Attorney, Developer, Builder, Owner/Investor, Property Manager; **EDUC:** 1969, Bus., Western MI Univ.; **GRAD EDUC:** JD, 1972, Law, Notre Dame Law School; **EDUC HONORS:** Honors College, Law Review; **HOME ADD:** 502 Burr Ridge Club Dr., Burr Ridge, IL, (312)655-0532; **BUS ADD:** 6121 Indian School Rd., Albuquerque, NM, (505)883-3000.

BOBLAK, Frank J.——**B:** Aug. 11, 1920, Chicago, IL, *Pres.*, Frank Boblak & Associates, Inc., Realtors; **PRIM RE ACT:** Broker, Consultant, Appraiser, Instructor, Property Manager, Insuror; **SERVICES:** Resid., Comml., Indus., Investment Prop. Sales, Appraisals, Employee Relocation; **PROFL AFFIL & HONORS:** SW Suburban, IL Assn. of Realtors, NAR - Pres. SW Bd. 1971, GRI, CRB, Realtor of the Yr., 1971; **EDUC:** BS, 1950, Poli. Sci., Econ., Bradley Univ., Peoria, IL; **GRAD EDUC:** Cert. in RE, 1964, RE Instit., GRI, IL Assn. of Realtors, CRB, NAR; **EDUC HONORS:** Dept. Honors Poli. Sci., Pi Kappa Delta, Pi Sigma Alpha; **MIL SERV:** USA, Inf., 1st Lt., Silver Battle Star; **OTHER ACT & HONORS:** Bi-Centennial Comm.; Pres. 1980-1981, Oak Lawn Rotary; Oak Lawn C of C Pres. 1974; **HOME ADD:** 4608 W. 98th St., Oak Lawn, IL 60453, (312)636-1932;

BUS ADD: Oak Lawn Postal Square 9241 S. Cicero Ave., Oak Lawn, IL 60453, (312)636-3033.

BOBOWICK, Morton——B: Oct. 8, 1942, Brooklyn, NY, *Atty.-Partner*, Eastman & Smith; **PRIM RE ACT:** Attorney; **PROFL AFFIL & HONORS:** ABA; OH Bar Assn.; Toledo Bar Assn.; **EDUC:** BA, 1962, Eng., Brooklyn Coll.; **GRAD EDUC:** JD, 1965, Harvard Law School; **EDUC HONORS:** Phi Beta Kappa, Honors in Eng., Magna Cum Laude, Cum Laude; **HOME ADD:** 4601 Beaconsfield Ct., Toledo, OH 43623, (419)882-8844; **BUS ADD:** 800 United Savings Bldg., Toledo, OH 43604, (419)241-6000.

BOCHMANN, W. Brad——B: Mar. 7, 1931, Casper, WY, *Pres.*, Bochmann Realty, Inc.; **PRIM RE ACT:** Broker; **OTHER RE ACT:** Dist. Mgr. for Red Carpet Inc., WY and MT; **PROFL AFFIL & HONORS:** NAR; FLI; Nat. Assn. of RE Brokers, Past Pres., Casper Bd. of Realtors; Past Pres., Casper Multi-list Exchange; **EDUC:** 1962, Bus. Law; **MIL SERV:** USMC, S/Sgt., Good Conduct Medal, UN Medal, Korean Service, Bronze Star; **OTHER ACT & HONORS:** Casper Elks Lodge 1353, Past Exalted Ruler 66-67; DDGER Grand Lodge, 1977-1978; Currently 3rd VP WY Elks State Assn.; Taught in the WY RE Inst.; **HOME ADD:** 3560 Big Horn, Casper, WY 82601, (307)265-1323; **BUS ADD:** 2501 E. 3rd, Casper, WY 82601, (307)237-3743.

BODDEN, Thomas A.——B: Dec. 18, 1945, *Pres.*, Thomas A. Bodden, Law Corp.; **PRIM RE ACT:** Broker, Consultant, Attorney, Owner/Investor, Instructor, Syndicator, Real Estate Publisher; **OTHER RE ACT:** Author; **SERVICES:** Atty., Realtor, teacher, author; **PREV EMPLOY:** Author-Taxation of RE in HI; **PROFL AFFIL & HONORS:** RESSI, State Chap. Pres., Nat. Instr., ABA, Comm. on Real Prop.; **EDUC:** AB, 1968, Hist., Cornell Univ.; **GRAD EDUC:** JD, 1974, Univ. Miami, FL; **EDUC HONORS:** Cum Laude, Law Review, Editorial Bd.; **MIL SERV:** USN, Lt., Navy Comm., Navy Univ., Vietnam Serv.; **OTHER ACT & HONORS:** Chmn., Instr., HI Assn. of Realtors, Teachers Inst. Comm.; **BUS ADD:** 1993-200 S. Kihei Rd., Kihei, HI 96753, (808)879-7755.

BODDICKER, Joe L.——B: Sept. 13, 1939, Independence, IA, *Atty. at Law*; **PRIM RE ACT:** Attorney; **SERVICES:** Legal representation; **PROFL AFFIL & HONORS:** Crawford Cty., IA State & Amer. Bar Assns.; **EDUC:** BA, 1961, Bus. Admin., Loras Coll., Dubuque, IA; **GRAD EDUC:** JD, 1964, Coll. of Law, Univ. of IA, IA City, IA; **OTHER ACT & HONORS:** Crawford Cty IA Atty., 1967-69 & Judicial Magistrate, Crawford Cty. IA, 1975-present; **BUS ADD:** 39 Pleasant St., Denison, IA 51442, (712)263-2209.

BODDIE, Joseph——*VP Admin.*, Crystal Oil Co.; **PRIM RE ACT:** Property Manager; **BUS ADD:** 229 Milan St., Shreveport, LA 71120, (318)222-7791.*

BODDY, G.G.——*Asst. Treas.*, Seaboard Allied Milling Corp.; **PRIM RE ACT:** Property Manager; **BUS ADD:** 200 Boylston St., Chestnut Hill, MA 02167, (617)332-8492.*

BODEL, Donald H.——B: Jan. 25, 1938, Kingston, Ontario, Can., *Pres.*, Richard Ellis, Inc.; **PRIM RE ACT:** Consultant, Appraiser, Property Manager; **OTHER RE ACT:** RE investment adviser, portfolio mgr.; **SERVICES:** Acquisition & sale of investment props., portfolio mgr., prop. mgmt., devel. supr., valuation; **REP CLIENTS:** Instnl. investors, foreign and domestic; **PROFL AFFIL & HONORS:** Amer. Soc. of RE counselors; Intl. Council of Shopping Ctrs.; Chicago RE Bd.; Real Estate Inst. of Can., Can. Inst. of Chartered Accts., CA, FRI, CRE; **EDUC:** Bachelor of Commerce, 1961, Acctg., Univ. of BC; **HOME ADD:** 840 Sheridan Rd., Winnetka, IL 60093, (312)446-8776; **BUS ADD:** 200 East Randolph Dr., Suite 6545, Chicago, IL 60601, (312)861-1105.

BODILY, Kerry D.——B: Apr. 10, 1940, SLC, UT, *Gen. Part.*, Bodily & Associates; **PRIM RE ACT:** Syndicator, Consultant, Property Manager, Owner/Investor; **SERVICES:** Tax counsel, investment counsel, fin. planning; **PROFL AFFIL & HONORS:** RESSI, GRI; **EDUC:** 1962, Bus. & Educ., Univ. of UT; **OTHER ACT & HONORS:** UT Apt. Assoc., SL Credit Bureau; **HOME TEL:** (801)262-6500; **BUS ADD:** 5130 S. State, Suite A, Murray, UT 84107, (801)262-6500.

BODLEY, Donald E.——B: Feb. 3, 1929, MI, *Prof./Chairholder for RE Studies*, Eastern Kentucky Univ., Coll. of Bus.; **PRIM RE ACT:** Consultant, Instructor; **SERVICES:** BBA degree, RE major; MBA RE concentration; **PREV EMPLOY:** Profl. consultant to RE builders/devels.; **PROFL AFFIL & HONORS:** NAHB, NAA, NACORE, REEA, NARA, CRA, CAM, Excellence in Teaching Award - 1976 EKU Coll. of Bus.; **EDUC:** BA, 1953, Communication Arts, Eastern MI Univ.; **GRAD EDUC:** MA, PhD, 1960-65, Educ., Beh. Psych., E. MI Univ., St. Andrew's Seminary, London, England; **EDUC HONORS:** Pi Kappa Delta, Stoic Society; **OTHER ACT & HONORS:** Rotary Club; Photographic Soc. of Amer.; Chmn., Natl. Apt. Mgmt. Accreditation Bd., Regional VP Natl. Apt. Assn.; **HOME ADD:** 153 Patchen Dr., Suite 30, Lexington, KY 40502, (606)266-9958; **BUS ADD:** Ellendale 2, Richmond, KY 40475, (606)622-1220.

BODY, Thomas D., III——B: May 16, 1938, Atlanta, GA, *Pres.*, Thomas D. Body & Company (1972); **PRIM RE ACT:** Broker, Consultant; **SERVICES:** Investment counseling valuation and brokerage of income producing prop. and conversion of multi-family rental prop., to Condo.; **REP CLIENTS:** Investors, synd., instnl. investors and converter/developers; **PREV EMPLOY:** Atlanta RE brokerage firm - six years as leading sales assoc.; **EDUC:** BBA, 1961, RE, Univ. of GA; **MIL SERV:** US Coast Guard, Presidential Ceremonial Guard; **HOME ADD:** 3188 Argonne Dr., NW, Atlanta, GA 30305, (404)237-9547; **BUS ADD:** Suite 106, 100 Northcreek, Atlanta, GA 30327, (404)231-0468.

BOE, Larry K.——B: Feb. 22, 1940, Iola, WI, *Exec. VP*, Security Spring & Boe Assoc., Inc.; **PRIM RE ACT:** Broker, Owner/Investor, Property Manager, Syndicator; **SERVICES:** Synd. of comml. & res. props., prop. mgmt. & brokerage of similar props.; **PREV EMPLOY:** VP Loewi Realty Corp., 1974-79; **EDUC:** Non-Credit Grad, 1971-73, Devel. Course, Securities Indus. Assn., Wharton Sch. of Fin., Univ. of PA; **MIL SERV:** USA, S/Sgt., E-6; **OTHER ACT & HONORS:** Chmn. of Exec. Comm., SE WI Chap. March of Dimes, Dir. Consul Corp.; **HOME ADD:** 17890 Wessex Dr., Brookfield, WI 53005, (414)781-6434; **BUS ADD:** 16655 W. Bluemound Rd., Brookdfield, WI 53005.

BOERSTLER, Herbert W.——B: Oct. 16, 1928, Johnstown, PA, *Mgr., RE*, Cooper Industries, Inc.; **PRIM RE ACT:** Attorney; **PREV EMPLOY:** Law Practice 1964-1979; **PROFL AFFIL & HONORS:** Houston Bar Assn., TX Bar Assn., ABA; **EDUC:** BA, 1952, Pre-Law, Univ. of Pittsburgh; **GRAD EDUC:** JD, 1957, Law, So. TX Coll. of Law; **MIL SERV:** US Navy, RM3SS 1946-1948; **HOME ADD:** 7203 Lacy Hill, Houston, TX 77036, (713)774-3437; **BUS ADD:** PO Box 4446, Houston, TX 77210, (713)654-8431.

BOGARD, Ward——B: Jan. 3, 1940, Ft. Worth, TX, *Princ.*, Ward Bogard & Assoc.; **PRIM RE ACT:** Architect; **SERVICES:** Architecture & Interiors; **PREV EMPLOY:** Part.; Wooten & Bogaro Architects, 1968-1978; **PROFL AFFIL & HONORS:** AIA, Pres. Ft. Worth Chap. AIA, Licensed Architect TX, AL, KS, FL, KY, MI, PA, MO, IL, WI, MN, NY, MD, SC, MS, TN; Dir. North Worth Business Assn.; **EDUC:** BArch, 1963, Design Option, TX Tech. Univ.; **HOME ADD:** 624 Little Horse Trail, Ft. Worth, TX 76108, (817)246-3527; **BUS ADD:** 131 E Exchange Ave. 235, Ft. Worth, TX 76107, (817)625-5504.

BOGATIN, Irvin——B: Aug. 4, 1915, Atlantic City, NJ, *Partner*, Bogatin, Lawson, Chiapella & Thomas; **PRIM RE ACT:** Attorney; **SERVICES:** Legal; **PROFL AFFIL & HONORS:** Memphis and Shelby Cty., TN Bar Assn., ABA, Member of Real Property; **EDUC:** BS, 1937, Poli. Sci., Temple Univ.; **GRAD EDUC:** JD, 1940, Law, Temple Univ. Law School; **EDUC HONORS:** Member, Beta Gamma Sigma; **MIL SERV:** US M.I., Lt. Colonel, Bronze Star; **OTHER ACT & HONORS:** Kiwanis; **HOME ADD:** 5169 Shady Grove Rd., Memphis, TN 38117, (901)682-6789; **BUS ADD:** 2675 One Commerce Sq., Memphis, TN 38103, (901)522-1234.

BOGDAN, Livius S.——*Pres.*, First Regency Devel. Corp.; **PRIM RE ACT:** Broker, Architect, Developer, Owner/Investor; **OTHER RE ACT:** RE Advertising; **SERVICES:** Mktg., arch., RE brokerage and advertising and devel.; **REP CLIENTS:** Finagest, Tsakos Shipping Co.; **BUS ADD:** 1343 Main St., Penthouse, Sarasota, FL 33577, (813)365-4500.

BOGOSIAN, Paul J.——B: Mar. 1, 1924, Providence, RI, *Partner*, Richard Alan, Realtors; **PRIM RE ACT:** Broker, Consultant, Appraiser, Owner/Investor, Property Manager; **SERVICES:** Principle bus. is RE Brokerage; **PROFL AFFIL & HONORS:** NAR; RI Assn. of Realtors; Kent Cty. Bd. of Realtors; RI Builders Assn., GRI; RE Cert. from the Univ. of RI; "RI Realtor of the Year" 1980, RI Assn. of Realtors, **EDUC:** RE Cert., 1964, Univ. of RI, **MIL SERV:** US Army, Sgt., European Combat & Good Conduct Medal; **OTHER ACT & HONORS:** Realtor of the Year, Kent Cty. Bd. Operations 1974 & 1981; Past Pres. Kent Cty. Bd. of Realtors 1972-73; Past Pres. RI Assn. of Realtors, 1977; Past Pres. of the Commercial Investment Div. CID of RI Assn. of Realtors 1975; Natl. Dir. in the NAR 1976-83; former Pres. of State-Wide MLS 1976; CID Member of the Year 1976; 32nd Degree Mason; **HOME ADD:** 2 Spinney Ln., North Kingstown, RI 02881, (401)884-1913; **BUS ADD:** 3604 Post Rd., Warwick, RI 02886, (401)739-6400.

BOHAN, L. Stewart——**B:** Mar. 26, 1929, Memphis, TN, *Pres.*, CT Attys. Title Guaranty Fund, Inc.; **OTHER RE ACT:** Title Insurance Law; **PROFL AFFIL & HONORS:** ABA, Co-Chmn. Nat. Conference of Attys., Title Insurers and Abstractors, 1979-81; Chmn., Comm. on the Role of the Lawyer in Res. RE Transactions (Real Property, Probate & Trust Law Sect.); ABA Real Prop., Probate and Trust Law Sect. Council, 1973-79; Amer. Coll. of RE Attys.; **EDUC:** BA, 1951, Yale Univ.; **GRAD EDUC:** JD, 1954, NY Univ. School of Law; **EDUC HONORS:** Phi Beta Kappa; **BUS ADD:** 711 Cottage Grove Rd., Bloomfield, CT 06002, (203)247-1745.

BOHANNAN, Robert C., Jr.——**B:** Jan. 21, 1919, Columbus, OH, *Pres.*, AZ Mort. & Investment Co.; **PRIM RE ACT:** Banker, Lender, Insuror; **SERVICES:** Mort. Banking, Resid.; **PROFL AFFIL & HONORS:** Charter Dir. Phoenix Soc. of Fin. Analysts, CMU (Cert. Mort. Underwriter), CRA (Cert. Review Appraiser), CMB Cert. Mort. Banker); **EDUC:** BS, 1941, Acctg., OH State Univ.; **MIL SERV:** USAF, 1941-46, Lt. Col., USAFR, Retired; **OTHER ACT & HONORS:** State Welfare Commr., AZ, 1951-52; State Legislator, AZ, 1949-50; Lions, Bd. Member, High Ctry. Hounds, Ltd.; **HOME ADD:** 7000 Berneil Dr., Paradise Valley, AZ 85253 85253, (602)948-2424; **BUS ADD:** PO Box 29038, Phoenix, AZ 85038, (602)264-6774.

BOHANNON, Charles L.——**B:** May 20, 1927, La Jolla, CA, *Pres.*, Charles Bohannon, Inc. Realtors; **PRIM RE ACT:** Broker, Instructor, Consultant, Property Manager, Owner/Investor; **SERVICES:** Gen. Brokerage; **PREV EMPLOY:** USAF Retd.; Realtor, Velva Bergevin Ltd., Honolulu, HI; **PROFL AFFIL & HONORS:** Treas. Maui Bd. of Realtors - 1980; Sec., Maui Bd. - 1981, GRI; **EDUC:** BA, 1950, Bus. Admin., Econ., San Diego State Coll.; **GRAD EDUC:** Masters, 1968, Educ. - Admin., Univ. of IL; **MIL SERV:** USAF, 1952-1973, Lt/Col.; **OTHER ACT & HONORS:** Rotary Intl.; **HOME ADD:** Island Sands Apt. 612, Maalaea, HI 96793, (808)244-5601; **BUS ADD:** PO Box 1750, Lahaina, Maui, HI 96761, (808)661-4848.

BOHLINGER, Thomas P.——**B:** Feb. 22, 1951, Long Beach, CA, *VP Comml. Devel.*, Howard Development Co.; **PRIM RE ACT:** Developer; **SERVICES:** Income prop. devel. & mgmt.; **PREV EMPLOY:** VP, Ross Campbell Co. Los Angeles, CA. Mort. Banking; **EDUC:** BS, 1974, Bus. Admin., USC; **GRAD EDUC:** MBA, 1975, Bus., USC; **EDUC HONORS:** Pacific 8 Honor Roll, Outstanding Sr. Student Athlete; **HOME ADD:** 435 E. Mtn., Glendale, CA 91207, (213)246-0536; **BUS ADD:** 800 W. Doran St., Glendale, CA 91203, (213)240-0400.

BOHRER, Nancy King——**B:** May 24, 1950, Evanston, IL, *Atty.*, Sole Practitioner; **PRIM RE ACT:** Attorney; **SERVICES:** Gen. practice of law; **PROFL AFFIL & HONORS:** Amer. Bar Assns.; IL Bar Assn.; Chicago Bar Assn.; N. Suburban Bar Assn.; **EDUC:** BS, 1972, Communications (Advtg.), Univ. of IL; **GRAD EDUC:** JD, 1979, John Marshall Law School; **BUS ADD:** 214 Hibbard Rd., Wilmette, IL 60091, (312)251-2192.

BOIRE, Richard L.——**B:** Nov, 9, 1952, Rochester, NH, *Atty.*, Cullimore & Boire Prof. Assn.; **PRIM RE ACT:** Attorney; **SERVICES:** Title Abstracts, Closing Agent, Subdiv., Zoning Condo. Consulting; **REP CLIENTS:** Sun Mort. Co., Inland Acres Assoc., Employee Transfer Corp., Daigle RE; **PROFL AFFIL & HONORS:** Amer., NH & Strafford Cty. Bar Assns.; **EDUC:** BS, Admin., 1974, Univ. of NH; **GRAD EDUC:** Law, JD, 1977, Suffolk Univ. Law School; **EDUC HONORS:** Cum Laude, Psi Epsilon Award, Sr. Key Award, Cum Laude; **OTHER ACT & HONORS:** Amer. Can. Cultural Exchange Commn., Rotary, Club Richelieu; **HOME ADD:** 13 Drury Dr., Rochester, NH 03867, (603)332-3061; **BUS ADD:** 17 Farmington Rd., Rochester, NH 03867, (603)332-7333.

BOISVERT, Hubert A.——**B:** Apr. 16, 1903, Syracuse, NY, *Owner*, Hubert Boisvert Co.; **PRIM RE ACT:** Broker, Owner/Investor; **PREV EMPLOY:** Title Bank Loan Officer, Escrow Officer; **PROFL AFFIL & HONORS:** SIR; Hdqtrs. City Devel. Assn. Los Angeles; Hollywood C of C; Los Angeles Bd. of Realtors; CA Assn. of Realtors, Pres. and Comm. Chmn. of above organizations; **OTHER ACT & HONORS:** Member, Los Angeles Planning Commn., 1953-1956; Masonic and Shrine Organizations; Kiwanis; YMCA; **HOME ADD:** 2450 Creston Way, Hollywood, CA 90068, (213)463-2161; **BUS ADD:** 2450 Creston Way, Hollywood, CA 90068, (213)463-2161.

BOKHARI, Ghazi——**B:** July 24, 1936, Pakistan, *Owner*, Ghazi Bokhari; **PRIM RE ACT:** Engineer, Owner/Investor; **PREV EMPLOY:** NYC Housing Authority; **PROFL AFFIL & HONORS:** ASME; **EDUC:** BS, 1961, Mech. Engrg., Punjab Engrg. Coll., Lahore Pakistan; **MIL SERV:** EME, Capt.; **HOME ADD:** 85-28 Homelawn St., Jamaica Estates, NY 11432, (212)523-1378; **BUS ADD:** 85-28 Homelawn St., Jamaica Estates, NY 11432.

BOLAN, Lewis——**B:** May 30, 1940, Boston, MA, *VP & Dir. of Investment Advisory Servs.*, RE Research Corp.; **PRIM RE ACT:** Consultant; **SERVICES:** Investment counseling, devel. planning, Mkt. & fin. analysis; **REP CLIENTS:** Lenders, devels., instnl. investors, govt. agencies, corps.; **PREV EMPLOY:** Victor Gruen Assoc., 1967-71; **PROFL AFFIL & HONORS:** Amer. Planning Assoc., ULI; **EDUC:** AB, 1982, Soc., Econ., Columbia Univ.; **GRAD EDUC:** MCP, 1967, Urban Planning, Univ. of IL; **HOME ADD:** 726112 11 St., SE, Wash. DC 20003, (202)543-9095; **BUS ADD:** 1101 17 St., NW, Wash. DC 20036, 02)223-4500.

BOLAND, Thomas F.——**B:** Oct. 11, 1932, Philadelphia, PA, *Sr. VP*, Beneficial Mutual Savings Bank; **PRIM RE ACT:** Consultant, Appraiser, Banker, Lender, Regulator, Instructor; **PROFL AFFIL & HONORS:** Mort. Bankers Assn. of Amer., CMU, Assn. of Mort. Underwriters; **EDUC:** 1953, Liberal Arts, Army Language School, Niagara Univ.; **MIL SERV:** USA Security Agency, E5, NormaL; **OTHER ACT & HONORS:** Bd. of Trustees, Immaculate Mary Nursing Home and Manor Jr. Coll. RE Advisory Bd.; Bd. of Governors Philadelphia Mort. Bankers Assn.; Fin. Comm. of Philadelphia Bd. of Realtors; Treas., Philadelphia Bd. of Realtors; **BUS ADD:** 1200 Chestnut St., Philadelphia, PA 19107, (215)864-6127.

BOLAS, Norman T.——**B:** July 15, 1927, Omaha, NE, *Regional Appraiser*, Fed. Natl. Mort. Assoc., W Div.; **PRIM RE ACT:** Appraiser; **SERVICES:** Appraisal review, loan underwriting; **PREV EMPLOY:** Chief appraiser, State Mutual (now Far West) S&L Assn., 1966-75; **PROFL AFFIL & HONORS:** AIREA, SREA, Winner, best manuscript submitted in 1979, NAIFA; MAI; **BUS ADD:** 3435 Wilshire Blvd., Los Angeles, CA 90010, (213)480-6240.

BOLDIZAR, Frank J.——**B:** Sept. 12, 1940, Cleveland, OH, *RE renovator of apt. bldgs., synd.*, Self employed; **PRIM RE ACT:** Broker, Syndicator, Property Manager, Owner/Investor; **OTHER RE ACT:** Renovator of Apt. Bldgs. is speciality; **PREV EMPLOY:** Life Ins. sales 17 yrs. (CLU plus Life Member Million Dollar Round Table); **PROFL AFFIL & HONORS:** RESSI; **EDUC:** BS, 1963, Miami Univ.; **GRAD EDUC:** CLU, 1971, Bryn Mawr; **HOME ADD:** 857 Pine Cone Oval, Sagamore Hills, OH 44067; **BUS ADD:** 857 Pine Cone Oval, Sagamore Hills, OH 44067, (216)467-1499.

BOLEN, Hal H., II——**B:** Oct. 10, 1949, Winchester, VA, *Atty.*, Baker, Manock & Jensen; **PRIM RE ACT:** Attorney; **SERVICES:** Legal; **REP CLIENTS:** Safeco Title Insurance Co., The London Co.; **PROFL AFFIL & HONORS:** Member State Bar Continuing Education Advisory Comm., Real Prop. Subcomm.; Pres. Fresno Cty. Young Lawyers Assn., Lecturer in Law, CA State Univ., Fresno; **EDUC:** BS Acctg./BA Econ., 1971, CA State Univ.; **GRAD EDUC:** MBA, 1973, Mgmt., CA State Univ.; JD, 1976, Univ. of CA, Davis; **EDUC HONORS:** Beta Gama Sigma, Bus. Advisory Council Award, Managing Editor Law Review, Moot Court Bd.; **HOME ADD:** 5280 E. McKenzie, Fresno, CA 93727, (209)252-6074; **BUS ADD:** 6th Floor, Security Bank Bldg., Fresno, CA 93721, (209)442-0550.

BOLER, James F.——**B:** Sept. 2, 1933, Sacramento, CA, *Partner*, Muncy, McPherson, McCune & Dieckman; **PRIM RE ACT:** Consultant; **SERVICES:** Fed. Income taxation and acctg. consultant; **REP CLIENTS:** leading US RE Synds. & investors; **PROFL AFFIL & HONORS:** Acctg. Comm. BOMA, AICPA, CPA; **EDUC:** BA, 1958, Acctg., San Francisco State Coll.; **GRAD EDUC:** MBA, 1976, Fed. Income Taxation, Golden Gate Univ.; **OTHER ACT & HONORS:** Pub. RE related articles in such nat. journals as Journal of Taxation, Taxation for Lawyers, Taxes - The Tax Magazine etc.; **HOME ADD:** 575 Craig Rd., Hillsborough, CA 94010, (415)347-2559; **BUS ADD:** 44 Montgomery St., San Francisco, CA 94101, (415)391-2330.

BOLEY, Robert E.——*Executive Vice President*, Society of Industrial Realtors; **OTHER RE ACT:** Profl. Assn. Admin.; **BUS ADD:** 925 15th Street NW, Washington, DC 20005, (202)637-6880.*

BOLLINGER, Stephen J.——**B:** 1948, Louisville, KY, *HUD Asst. Sec. for Community Planning & Devel.*, US Dept. of HUD, HUD Dept. Community Planning; **PRIM RE ACT:** Regulator; **SERVICES:** Mgmt. & admin. of community devel. Block grant and other programs of assistance to cities & urban areas; **PREV EMPLOY:** Exec. Dir. Columbus OH - Metropolitan Housing Authority 1977-1981; Laws Ins. Co. of Cincinnati - VP (1976-1977); **PROFL AFFIL & HONORS:** Co-founder & VP Public Housing Auth. Dirs. Assn.; Nat. Assn. of Housing & Redevel. Officials; Dir. and PR Comm. Chmn of OH Housing Auth. Conf.; **EDUC:** BA, 1970, Amer. 20th Century Urban Hist., Harvard Coll.; **HOME ADD:** Columbus, OH; **BUS ADD:** 451 7th St. SW, Washington, DC 20410.

BOLOTIN, Jeffrey W.——B: Dec. 31, 1946, NY, NY, *General Counsel*, Rozansky & Kay Construction Co.; **PRIM RE ACT:** Attorney; **PREV EMPLOY:** Partner - Alston, Miller & Gaines; **PROFL AFFIL & HONORS:** ABA; MD and DC Bar Assns.; **EDUC:** 1967, Univ. of MD; **GRAD EDUC:** JD, 1970, Univ. of MD; **EDUC HONORS:** Law Review; **OTHER ACT & HONORS:** Law Clerk, Hon. Roszel C. Thomsen, Chief Judge, U.S. Dist. Ct. for State of MD; **HOME ADD:** 5200 27th St., N.W., Washington, DC 20015, (202)362-5969; **BUS ADD:** 4520 East-West Hwy., Bethesda, MD 20814, (301)652-4288.

BOMHARD, Richard O.——B: Nov. 4, 1920, Springfield, OH, *Chmn., RE Dept.*, Columbus Technical Institute, Bus. & Public Admin.; **PRIM RE ACT:** Instructor; **OTHER RE ACT:** Sales Assoc.; **SERVICES:** Prof. of RE house style & design, appraisal & math.; **REP CLIENTS:** Coll. level students (Assoc. Degree Program), RE profls. - sales, brokers, appraisers & investors; **PREV EMPLOY:** Lic. Sales Assoc. 17 years; **PROFL AFFIL & HONORS:** OH Assn. of Realtors Educ. Comm., Scholarship Comm., GRI Comm. Advisory Council to RE Academy of Instrs.; **EDUC:** AB, 1942, Mathematics, Chemistry & Physics, Miami Univ., Oxford, OH; **GRAD EDUC:** MEd, 1972, Educ. Admin., Xavier Univ., Cincinnati, OH; **MIL SERV:** USAF, 1942-1964, Lt. Col. (Retd.), AF Commendation Medal, Army Commendation Medal, Outstanding Unit Award; **OTHER ACT & HONORS:** Lions Intl., Model A Restorers Club; Model A Ford Club of Amer.; Nat. Trust for Preservation; Amer. Hist. Soc.; Classic Thunderbird Intl. Clubs; **HOME ADD:** 1897 Stanford Rd., Columbus, OH 43212, (614)488-9995; **BUS ADD:** 550E Spring St., Columbus, OH 43215, (614)227-2447.

BONASTIA, Peter J.——B: Mar. 18, 1938, Glen Ridge, NJ, *Pres.*, North American Multicapital Corp.; **PRIM RE ACT:** Owner/Investor; **PROFL AFFIL & HONORS:** Amer. Mgmt. Assn., Young Pres., Intl. Council of Shopping Ctrs.; **EDUC:** 1960, Communication Arts, Univ. of Notre Dame; **EDUC HONORS:** Cum Laude; **MIL SERV:** US Army, Lt., Distinguished Military Grad.; **OTHER ACT & HONORS:** Tr. N. Caldwell Jr. Basketball Assn.; **HOME ADD:** 42 Brookside Terr., N. Caldwell, NJ 07006, (201)226-0340; **BUS ADD:** 409 Minnisink Rd., Totowa, NJ 07512, (201)256-8182.

BONAVOLONTA, Anthony A.——B: Dec. 31, 1935, Melrose Park, IL, *Architect-Partner*, Schaffer-Bonavolonta Architects, Inc.; **PRIM RE ACT:** Broker, Consultant, Architect, Developer, Builder, Property Manager, Owner/Investor; **SERVICES:** Archl. Devel. & Const. Mgmt.; **REP CLIENTS:** Devel., private investors, major corp.; **PROFL AFFIL & HONORS:** NCARB, APA, ISA; **EDUC:** BA Arch. Engrg., 1959, Structures, Univ. of IL; **OTHER ACT & HONORS:** Tr., Village of Roselle, 1961-1965; Plan Commn., Town Center Devel. Comm.; **HOME ADD:** 845 Butternut Ct., Roselle, IL 60172, (312)529-4516; **BUS ADD:** 24 West Erie St., Chicago, IL 60610, (312)943-2020.

BOND, Robert W.——Bellemead of Michigan, Inc.; **PRIM RE ACT:** Developer; **BUS ADD:** 900 Tower Dr., Troy, MI 48098, (313)879-5511.*

BOND, Sharon A.——B: July 1, 1947, Belleville, IL, *VP*, Continental IL Nat. Bank and Trust Co., Trust and Investment Serv.; **PRIM RE ACT:** Consultant, Banker, Lender, Owner/Investor, Property Manager; **SERVICES:** Asset mgmt.; **REP CLIENTS:** Pension funds, indiv. investors; **PREV EMPLOY:** Gen. Mgr., RE Operations, The Prudential Ins. Co. of Amer.; **PROFL AFFIL & HONORS:** CPM, IREM; **EDUC:** BS, 1969, Housing and Design, Cornell Univ.; **GRAD EDUC:** MUP, 1972, Urban Planning, MI State Univ.; **HOME ADD:** 9437 Hamlin Ave., Evanston, IL 60203; **BUS ADD:** 30 N. LaSalle St., Chicago, IL 60693, (312)828-3977.

BOND, William M.——B: Apr. 1, 1939, Wheeling, WV, *VP*, Baldwin-Harris Co.; **OTHER RE ACT:** VP - Leasing; **PREV EMPLOY:** VP, Western Mgmt. Corp.; VP, Vantage Cos.; **PROFL AFFIL & HONORS:** IREM, BOMA, Greater Dallas Bd. of Realtors, CPM; **EDUC:** AB, 1962, Bus., Duke Univ.; **MIL SERV:** USN, Lt.; **OTHER ACT & HONORS:** Farmers Branch C of C; **HOME ADD:** 8272 Club Meadows Dr., Dallas, TX 75243, (214)349-3027; **BUS ADD:** 12000 Ford Rd., Suite 100, Dallas, TX 75234, (214)243-1371.

BONDURANT, Kenneth K.——B: June 28, 1949, Radford, VA, *VP*, Bondurant Realty Corp.; **PRIM RE ACT:** Broker, Appraiser, Owner/Investor; **SERVICES:** Resid. sales, comml. sales & investment; **REP CLIENTS:** Individual investors; **PROFL AFFIL & HONORS:** NAR, VA Assn. of Realtors, Pres., VA Chap. 1980, Rgnl. VP, VA Assn. of Realtors 1981; **EDUC:** BA, 1971, Sociological Theory, Emory & Henry College; **OTHER ACT & HONORS:** 1980 Pres. Radford C of C, Dir. 78-80; **HOME ADD:** 208 Fairway Drive, Radford, VA 24141, (703)639-0069; **BUS ADD:** 1302 Norwood St., PO Box 1207, Radford, VA 24141, (703)639-9672.

BONEPARTH, Harvey Mitchel——B: Dec. 30, 1944, NY, NY, *Assoc. Atty.*, Parker, Chapin, Flattau & Klimpl; **PRIM RE ACT:** Consultant, Attorney; **SERVICES:** Legal rep. and counseling; **REP CLIENTS:** Indivs., partnerships, corps. and insts. in all aspects of comml., retail and resid. RE transactions; **PROFL AFFIL & HONORS:** NY State Bar; US Dist. Court, So. Dist. of NY (admitted 1970); **EDUC:** BA, 1966, Econ., Lafayette Coll.; **GRAD EDUC:** JD, 1969, RE and Contracts, Columbia Univ.; **EDUC HONORS:** Dean's List, Harlan Fiske Stone Scholar, Moot Court Judge, Cum Laude; **HOME ADD:** 37 Oak Hill Rd., Chappaqua, NY 10514, (914)238-9055; **BUS ADD:** 530 Fifth Ave., NY, NY 10036, (212)840-6200.

BONESTEEL, Richard D.——B: May 26, 1931, Seattle, WA, *VP & Counsel, Sec. Treas.*, Seafirst Mort. Corp., A subsidiary of Seattle-First Nat. Bank; **PRIM RE ACT:** Attorney; **OTHER RE ACT:** Mort. Banker; **PREV EMPLOY:** Evans, McLaren, Lane, Powell & Beeks (Assoc. 1956-61); **PROFL AFFIL & HONORS:** ABA; WA Bar Assn., (Pres. 1973-74); Seattle-King Cty. Bar Assn., (Pres. 1979-80); Mort. Bankers Assn.; Amer. Land Title Assn. (Founder & First Chmn.); Lender Counsel Grp., 1976, Amer. Coll. of RE Lawyers (Charter Member 1979-), Amer. Coll of Mort. Attys. (Fellow 1980-); **EDUC:** BA, 1953, Banking & Fin., Univ. of WA; **GRAD EDUC:** JD, 1956, Law, Univ. of WA; **EDUC HONORS:** Washington Law Review (Revisions Editor, 1955-56); **MIL SERV:** USAF, 1951-52, Amn. First Class; **OTHER ACT & HONORS:** Phi Delta Phi, Alpha Delta Phi, WA State Badminton Assn. (Pres. 1961-62), Seattle Tennis Club, WA Athletic Club; **HOME ADD:** 2203 W Viewmont Way W, Seattle, WA 98199, (206)283-1032; **BUS ADD:** 4th & Blanchard Bldg., Seattle, WA 98121, (206)583-7078.

BONFANTI, George M.——B: June 21, 1945, Baton Rouge, LA, Bonfanti Fackrell Co.; **PRIM RE ACT:** Consultant, Appraiser, Developer, Builder, Property Manager, Lender; **SERVICES:** Full Service RE & Dev. Firm with Fin., Planning, Dev., Bldg., Leasing, and Sales Functions; **REP CLIENTS:** Drs. Attys., Other RE Agents, CPA's; **PREV EMPLOY:** Indep. Mort. Corp., a subs. of Bonfanti Fackrell Co.; **PROFL AFFIL & HONORS:** MBA, Apart. Ass. of LA; Bd. of Realtors, Assoc. Builders and Contractors, N/A; **EDUC:** 1967, Chem., LA State Univ.; **GRAD EDUC:** MBA, 1973, Fin., LA State Univ.; **EDUC HONORS:** N/A, N/A; **MIL SERV:** USAF, S/Sgt.; **OTHER ACT & HONORS:** Baton Rouge Round Table, C of C; **HOME ADD:** 726 Woodstone DR., Baton Rouge, LA 70808; **BUS ADD:** 7414 Perkins Rd.,P.O. Box 14565, Baton Rouge, LA 70898, (504)769-3700.

BONGIORNO, Benedetto——B: May 19, 1938, NY, *Partner*, Touche Ross & Co.; **OTHER RE ACT:** CPA; **SERVICES:** Acctg.; **REP CLIENTS:** RE clients; **PROFL AFFIL & HONORS:** AICPA & State Socs.; **EDUC:** BS, 1960, Bus., Fordham Univ.; **BUS ADD:** 1633 Broadway, New York, NY 10019, (212)489-1600.

BONIN, Paul J.——B: Mar. 6, 1929, Malden, MA, *VP*, Citibank, N.A., RE Investment & Mgmt. Dept.; **PRIM RE ACT:** Broker, Syndicator, Property Manager, Owner/Investor; **OTHER RE ACT:** Head of Asset Mgmt. Staff; **SERVICES:** Supervisory Prop. Mgmt.; **REP CLIENTS:** US pension funds; foreign govts. & instns.; high net worth indiv. around the world; **PREV EMPLOY:** Portfolio (Asset) Mgr. for foreign and domestic instns. at Landauer Assn., Inc., 200 Park Ave., NY, NY (as VP); **PROFL AFFIL & HONORS:** BOMA; IREM; ICSC, CPM; **EDUC:** AA, 1950 and 1954, Acctg. & Fin., Bentley Coll. of Accounting & Fin. & NYU; **MIL SERV:** USN; HN 1st class; **HOME ADD:** 3 Nursey Lane, Westport, CT 06880, (203)226-1940; **BUS ADD:** 153 East 53rd St., 15th Floor, NY, NY 10043, (212)559-1951.

BONSALL, Edward H., III——B: Aug. 14, 1930, Philadelphia, PA, *Pres. and Chief Exec. Officer*, Jackson-Cross of DE, Inc.; **PRIM RE ACT:** Broker, Consultant, Property Manager; **SERVICES:** RE counseling, sales, leasing and mgmt. - comml., indus. retail; **REP CLIENTS:** E.I. duPont deNemours & Co.; Hercules Inc.; ICI Americas, Inc.; **PROFL AFFIL & HONORS:** Member, BOMA; Dir., Bldg. Owners Labor Relations; Charter Member, of Soc. of Real Property Admin.; Member, Assn. of MBA Exec.; Member, New Castle Cty. Bd. of Realtors; **EDUC:** BS, 1971, Bus. Admin., Univ. of PA/Benedictine; **GRAD EDUC:** MBA, Attending, Wharton Grad. School.; **MIL SERV:** US Army; Lt. Col.; (retired), Over 20 incl. Legion of Merit, Meritorious Service Medal, Bronze Star, Air Medal and Purple Heart; **OTHER ACT & HONORS:** Bd. of Dir., Chestnut Hill Academy; **HOME ADD:** 7711 St. Martins Ln., Philadelphia, PA 19118, (215)247-1185; **BUS ADD:** 300 Delaware Trust Bldg, Wilmington, DE 19801, (302)575-1900.

BONZ, Richard——B: Aug. 18, 1938, Boston, MA, *VP/Principal*, Minot, DeBlois & Maddison, Inc.; **PRIM RE ACT:** Consultant, Appraiser, Developer, Property Manager; **SERVICES:** Mkt., fin. &

devel. counseling, valuation of comml. props.; **PREV EMPLOY:** VP/Principal Gladstone Assoc., Washington, DC, 1969-1973; RE Dept., John Hancock, Boston, 1964-1967; **EDUC:** BA, 1969, Econ., Dartmouth; **GRAD EDUC:** MCP, 1969, Urban Planning, Univ. of PA; **MIL SERV:** USN; LT.; **HOME ADD:** 491 River St., Norwell, MA 02061; **BUS ADD:** 294 Washington St., Boston, MA 02108, (617)542-5910.

BOOHER, Henry——*Dir. RE*, Ideal Basic Industries; **PRIM RE ACT:** Property Manager; **BUS ADD:** PO Box 8789, Denver, CO 80201, (303)623-5661.*

BOOKHARDT, Fred B., Jr.——**B:** May 14, 1934, New Orleans, LA, *Owner*, Fred. B. Brookhardt, Jr. Arch.; **PRIM RE ACT:** Architect, Consultant, Property Manager; **OTHER RE ACT:** Museum consultant & exhibit designs; **SERVICES:** Arch. & Interior Design, Master Planning, Space Survey, Prop. Mgmt.; **REP CLIENTS:** Priv. co's & investment Mgmt. & govt. agencies; **PREV EMPLOY:** Part. VP, Wm. F. Pedersen & Assoc. Arch.; **PROFL AFFIL & HONORS:** AIA, NY State Assn. of Archs., NY Soc. of Archs., IES Lumen Award; **EDUC:** B. Arch., 1959, Art & Phil., Tulane Univ.; **MIL SERV:** USA, SP3, 1954-56; **OTHER ACT & HONORS:** Amer. Assn. of Museums, Northeast Museum Conference, Key West Bus. Guild; **HOME ADD:** 28 E 4th St., NY, NY 10003, (212)475-7671; **BUS ADD:** 28 E 4th St., NY, NY 10003, (212)475-7671.

BOOKHOUT, Leland T.——**B:** Apr. 22, 1939, Bath, NY, *Pres.*, L.T. Bookhout, Inc.; **PRIM RE ACT:** Consultant, Appraiser, Instructor; **SERVICES:** RE consultation, problem solving, valuations, teaching; **REP CLIENTS:** Lenders; attys.; state, fed., local govt. agencies; devel.; utility cos.; **PREV EMPLOY:** Poughkeepsie Savings Bank, Chief Comml. Appraiser, 1977; **PROFL AFFIL & HONORS:** AIREA; Soc. of RE Appraisers; NAR; NYS Assn. of Realtors; Dutchess Cty. Bd. of Realtors; Amer. Soc. of Farm Mgrs. & Rural Appraisers; Intl. ROW Assn., SREA; MAI; Young Men's Council, 1972, 1973; NY Soc. of RE Appraisers; **EDUC:** BS, 1961, Agriculture Econ., Cornell Univ.; **MIL SERV:** US Army, 1st Lt., 1961-1963; **OTHER ACT & HONORS:** Mid Hudson Valley Cornell Club; Hyde Park Baptist Church, Deacon; Sunday School Teacher; Youth Leader; 1974, Outstanding Young Men of Amer.; 1979-1980 Who's Who in the E.; Marquis Who's Who Pub. Bd.; Published article: 'Indoor Tennis Clubs: A New Problem'; **HOME ADD:** 3 Long Meadow Dr., Staatsburg, NY, (914)229-5539; **BUS ADD:** 42 Albany Post Rd., POB 278, Hyde Park, NY 12538, (914)229-5367.

BOONE, J. Sidney, Jr.——**B:** Feb. 1, 1944, Greensboro, NC, *Partner*, Morris, Duffy & Boone, RE Atty.; **PRIM RE ACT:** Attorney; **PROFL AFFIL & HONORS:** ABA, SC Bar Assn., & Community Assns. Inst.; **EDUC:** B.S. - Bus. Admin., 1966, Acctg., The Citadel, Charleston, SC; **GRAD EDUC:** JD - Duke Univ., 1969, Duke Univ. School of Law; **EDUC HONORS:** Palmetto Award; **MIL SERV:** C.E., Capt.; **OTHER ACT & HONORS:** Exchange Club of Charleston, past Pres.; **HOME ADD:** 1223 Long Point Rd., Mount Pleasant, SC 29464, (803)884-2274; **BUS ADD:** 141 E. Bay St., Charleston, SC 29401, (803)723-7831.

BOOTH, John N.——**B:** Oct. 28, 1912, Pine Bluff, AR, *Exec. VP*, OK Mort. Co., Inc.; **PRIM RE ACT:** Owner/Investor; **SERVICES:** Mort. loans; **PREV EMPLOY:** FHA, 14 yrs.; **PROFL AFFIL & HONORS:** MBAA, Rgnl. Gov., MBA; **EDUC:** LLB, 1937, Law, Univ. of MO; **GRAD EDUC:** JD, Law, Univ. of MO; **MIL SERV:** USA, Off. Cand.; **OTHER ACT & HONORS:** Pres. OK City Bd. of Realtors, Pres. Univ. of MO Nat. Alumni Assn.; **HOME ADD:** 3223 N.W. 18th St., Oklahoma City, OK 73107, (405)943-0359; **BUS ADD:** 5100 N. Brookline, Oklahoma City, OK 73112, (405)947-5761.

BOOTH, John S., III——**B:** Feb. 18, 1944, Baltimore, MD, *Pres.*, J. Booth and Co., J. Booth Securities, Inc.; **PRIM RE ACT:** Broker, Consultant, Syndicator; **SERVICES:** Comml. & resid. brokerage; prop. acquisition; synd.; sale of limited partnership interests; **REP CLIENTS:** 1st Nat. Bank of Venice; SW FL Banks, Inc.; Gulfstream Land & Devel.; **PREV EMPLOY:** Pres., Casa del Sol, Inc. (Condo. devel.); **PROFL AFFIL & HONORS:** Venice and Sarasota (FL) Bds. of Realtors; SECO Broker/Dealer, Venice Realtor of the Year 1975; **EDUC:** BJ, 1965, Journalism, Princeton Univ.; Univ. of MO; **EDUC HONORS:** Sigma Delta Chi Honorary Journalism Frat.; **OTHER ACT & HONORS:** Pres., South Cty. United Way; Treas. - Venice Area C of C; **HOME ADD:** 951 Pinto Cr., Nokomis, FL 33555, (813)485-3618; **BUS ADD:** 589 U.S. 41 ByPass, Venice, FL 33595, (813)485-3355.

BORAIKO, Carl G.——**B:** June 3, 1926, Ruskin, FL, *Pres.*, First IL Capital Corp.; **PRIM RE ACT:** Broker, Syndicator, Consultant, Developer, Property Manager, Owner/Investor; **OTHER RE ACT:** Indiv. and affiliated corp. are members of NASD; **SERVICES:** Invest. consultants and dev., synd. of comml. and apt. prop., prop. mgmt., investment banking; **REP CLIENTS:** Indiv. or inst. investors in comml. and apt. prop., govt. housing and Section 8 housing; **PROFL AFFIL & HONORS:** CCIM; **HOME ADD:** 19 Johns Woods Dr, Rockford, IL 61103, (815)877-2677; **BUS ADD:** Plaza 7, 424 Seventh St, Rockford, IL 61104, (815)962-2664.

BORAK, Carl H.——*Pres.*, Standard Securities & Mgmt. Corp.; **PRIM RE ACT:** Broker, Syndicator, Developer, Property Manager, Insuror; **BUS ADD:** 180 W. Washington St., Suite 1002, Chicago, IL 60602, (312)236-4877.

BORDEN, Bradford P.——*Dir. Corp. Dev.*, Textron Co.; **PRIM RE ACT:** Property Manager; **BUS ADD:** 40 Westminister St., Providence, RI 02903, (401)421-2800.*

BORDEN, William S.——**B:** Sep. 28, 1922, Trenton, NJ, *RE Broker*, W.S. Borden Real Estate; **PRIM RE ACT:** Broker, Consultant, Appraiser, Developer, Syndicator; **PROFL AFFIL & HONORS:** Realtor RESSI; SREA, CPCO; **EDUC:** AB, 1945, Econ., Princeton Univ.; **EDUC HONORS:** Cum Laude; **MIL SERV:** US Army, Capt., Bronze Star; **HOME ADD:** 865 L. Ferry Rd., Trenton, NJ 08628, (609)883-1900; **BUS ADD:** 865 L. Ferry Rd., Trenton, NJ 08628, (609)883-1900.

BORDWIN, Milton——**B:** Nov. 10, 1931, New York, NY, *Partner*, Guterman, Horvitz, Rubin & Rudman (law firm); **PRIM RE ACT:** Attorney; **REP CLIENTS:** Builders, devels., landlords, retail & comml. tenants; **PREV EMPLOY:** Faculty Harvard Law School 1957-1959; **PROFL AFFIL & HONORS:** ABA, Boston Bar Assn., MBA; **EDUC:** BA, 1952, Acctg., City Coll. of NY; **GRAD EDUC:** JD, 1957, Harvard Law School; LLM, 1959, Harvard Law School; **MIL SERV:** USA, Transp. Corps, PFC; **HOME ADD:** 87 Hillside Rd., Newton Highlands, MA 02161, (617)244-0019; **BUS ADD:** Three Ctr. Plaza, Boston, MA 02108, (617)227-8010.

BORG, Solomon J.——*Atty.*, Stroock & Stroock & Lavan; **PRIM RE ACT:** Attorney; **SERVICES:** Gen. representation in all aspects of RE law; **BUS ADD:** 61 Broadway, NY, NY 10006, (212)425-5200.

BORGES, Richard C.——**B:** Dec. 5, 1944, Fall River, MA, *Partner*, Prescott, Mullard & McLeod; **PRIM RE ACT:** Attorney; **REP CLIENTS:** New Bedford Inst. for Savings; New Bedford Five Cents Savings Bank; Fairhaven Savings Bank; **PROFL AFFIL & HONORS:** ABA; MBA; Bristol Cty. Bar Assn.; New Bedford Bar Assn.; **EDUC:** BA, 1966, Bus. Admin., Southeastern MS Univ.; **GRAD EDUC:** JD, 1969, New England School of Bus.; **EDUC HONORS:** Cum Laude; **BUS ADD:** 13 N. Sixth St., New Bedford, MA 02741, (617)999-2381.

BORKON, Benjamin M.——**B:** Mar. 29, 1930, Joliet, IL, *Owner*, Timber Lane Estates; **PRIM RE ACT:** Consultant, Architect, Developer, Owner/Investor; **SERVICES:** Land planning, project design, arch. serv., fin. feasibility analysis; **REP CLIENTS:** Maj. corp. clients, and pension funds; **PREV EMPLOY:** Owner devel., Jackson Heights, Meadow Wood Hills, Timber Land Estates, number of maj. office & comml. devels.; **PROFL AFFIL & HONORS:** NCARB, CACI, Soc. of Amer. Reg. Arch., NCARB; **EDUC:** BSAE, 1954, Arch., Engr., Univ. of IL; **GRAD EDUC:** 1954, Bldg. devel. & mgmt., Univ. of IL; **MIL SERV:** USAF, 1st Lt.; **OTHER ACT & HONORS:** Land Clearance Commnr., Mayor's Comm., Urban Renewal, M&M Club, N.B. Yacht Club, Chmn., Arch. Comm., Timber Lane Estates, Chmn., Arch. Comm., Meadow Wood Hills, Nat. Advisor Arch. Comm., McGraw-Edison Co.; **HOME ADD:** RR#1, 7 W. Middlefork Rd., Barrington, IL 60606, (312)381-6576; **BUS ADD:** 230 W. Monroe St., Chicago, IL 60606, (312)782-0808.

BORLENGHI, Giorgio——**B:** Mar. 8, 1952, Torino, Italy, *Pres.*, Interfin Corp.; **PRIM RE ACT:** Developer; **OTHER RE ACT:** Constr. Mgmt.; **SERVICES:** RE resid. and comml. devel., constr. budgeting and mgmt., design consulting; **REP CLIENTS:** European investors, lending inst.; **PREV EMPLOY:** RESDECO - RE Devel. Corp., Beverly Hills, CA; **PROFL AFFIL & HONORS:** Italian Assn. of Structural Engrs.; **GRAD EDUC:** Master's, 1975, Struc. Engrg., Polytechnic Univ. of Milan, Italy; **MIL SERV:** Italian Air Force, Lt.; **OTHER ACT & HONORS:** Dir., Allied Bank W. Loop NA, Houston, TX; Member, Aviation Comm. Houston C of C; Member, Exec. Comm., Houston Grand Opera; Member, Houston Lyric Theater Found. Bd. of Tr.; **HOME ADD:** 405 W. Friar Tuck Ln., Houston, TX 77024; **BUS ADD:** 1980 Post Oak Blvd. #1370, Houston, TX 77056, (713)840-8474.

BORMEL, Joseph——**B:** Nov. 8, 1927, Baltimore, MD, *Owner*, Bormel Realty Co.; **PRIM RE ACT:** Broker, Consultant, Appraiser, Insuror; **PROFL AFFIL & HONORS:** Nat. Assn. of RE Appraisers; NAR; MD Assn. of Realtors; Greater Baltimore Bd. of Realtors; **EDUC:**

Attended McCoy Coll. 1956-71, RE; **MIL SERV:** USN, Radarman 3/c; **OTHER ACT & HONORS:** Chmn., Comptroller's Harbor Comm. 1956-Present; MD Boat Act Advisory Chmn. 1972-1979; Hart-Miller Environmental Grp. 1974-Present; Patapsco River Power Squadron 1962 to present; MD Wildlife Federation 1974-Present; **BUS ADD:** Fairmount and Linwood Aves., Baltimore, MD 21224, (301)342-2000.

BORNSTEIN, Harold A.——B: July 8, 1942, New York, NY, *Pres.*, Harold A. Bornstein RE; **PRIM RE ACT:** Broker; **SERVICES:** Rental of retail locations in Manhattan; **REP CLIENTS:** Exclusive Boutiques, Restaurants & Salons; **EDUC:** BBA, 1965, Mgmt., Univ. of Miami, NYU, Suffolk Law School, Adelphi Univ.; **HOME ADD:** 152 E 94th St., New York, NY 10028, (212)722-6121; **BUS ADD:** 152 East 94th St., NY, NY 10028, (212)722-6121.

BORNSTEIN, William S.——B: Jan 12, 1941, Louisville, KY, *Part.*, Bornstein & Oppenheimer; **PRIM RE ACT:** Broker, Attorney, Developer, Owner/Investor, Syndicator; **SERVICES:** synd., repres. buyers during negotiations & closings; **REP CLIENTS:** Bull & Weisberg Realtors, Final prop.; **PROFL AFFIL & HONORS:** KY Bar Assn., Louisville Bar Assn., KY RE Comm., Atty JD, 1966, KY RE Broker; **EDUC:** BS, 1963, Bus., IN Univ.; **GRAD EDUC:** JD, 1966, Univ. of Louisville, Coll. of Law; **HOME ADD:** 5004 Dunweegan Rd., Louisville, KY 40222, (502)425-3901; **BUS ADD:** 808 Marion E Taylor Bldg., Louisville, KY 40404, (502)589-6612.

BORSARI, William E.——B: Feb. 23, 1939, South Bridge, MA, *Exec. VP*, William Walters Co.; **PRIM RE ACT:** Broker, Consultant, Owner/Investor, Property Manager, Syndicator; **SERVICES:** Acquisition, mgmt., renovation, sales; **REP CLIENTS:** Indiv., lenders, pension funds, REIT's or instnl. investors in comml. prop.; **PROFL AFFIL & HONORS:** IREM, Rgnl. VP; **EDUC:** BS, 1963, Hotel & restaurant admin., Cornell Univ.; **HOME ADD:** 6066 Cozzens St., San Diego, CA 92122, (714)453-5149; **BUS ADD:** 2251 San Diego Ave. A-250, San Diego, CA 92110, (714)296-6225.

BORSUK, Harvey——B: Oct. 19, 1936, NY, NY, *Chmn.*, Turner Properties, Inc.; **PRIM RE ACT:** Owner/Investor, Syndicator; **PREV EMPLOY:** Merrill Lynch & Co., Lehman Brothers Kuhn Loeb, Inc.; **PROFL AFFIL & HONORS:** ICSC; **EDUC:** 1957, Civil engrg., Renseller Polytechnic Inst.; **HOME ADD:** 8 Winker Ln., Westport, CT 06880, (203)226-3243; **BUS ADD:** 950 Third Ave., NY, NY 10022, (212)753-0200.

BORTMAN, David——B: Sept. 17, 1938, Detroit, MI, *Partner*, Bortman, Retson & Lipschultz; **PRIM RE ACT:** Attorney; **SERVICES:** Legal; **REP CLIENTS:** Linn Corp., Hobbit Intl., Sittler & Co.; **PREV EMPLOY:** Asst. Prosecuting Atty., Wayne Cty. Staff Atty., Securities and Exchange Commn.; **PROFL AFFIL & HONORS:** Amer., IL, Chicago & Fed Bar Assns., Chicago RE Bd., Chicago Assn. of Commerce & Indus.; **EDUC:** BA, 1961, Eng., Univ. of MI; **GRAD EDUC:** JD, 1965, Law, Univ. of MI; **OTHER ACT & HONORS:** Asst. Prosecuting Atty., Wayne Cty., 1965-70, Union League Club of Chicago; **HOME ADD:** 1340 N Astor, Apt. 1903, Chicago, IL 60610; **BUS ADD:** 140 S. Dearborn, Suite 810, Chicago, IL 60603, (312)346-0202.

BORTON, Lee G.——B: Feb. 29, 1944, Santa Anna, CA, *Owner*, Financial Advisory Services; **PRIM RE ACT:** Consultant, Owner/Investor, Property Manager, Insuror, Syndicator; **OTHER RE ACT:** Tax accountant, salesman RE; **SERVICES:** Tax preparation & research, RE investment exchanges and counseling; **REP CLIENTS:** RE investors and brokers, RE corps., ltd. partnerships, foreign investors; **PROFL AFFIL & HONORS:** Nat. Assn. Exchange Counselors; Nat. Assn. of Enrolled Agents; CA Soc. of Enrolled Agents; Nat. Soc. of Tax Consultants; **EDUC:** AS, 1971, Acctg., Long Beach Community Coll.; BS, 1973, Acctg., Univ. of CA at Long Beach; **MIL SERV:** US Army, E-4; **OTHER ACT & HONORS:** C of C, Optimists; **BUS ADD:** 4119 E. Ocean Blvd., Ste. 3, Long Beach, CA 90803, (213)438-6591.

BORTZ, Neil K.——B: Oct. 2, 1932, Cincinnati, OH, *Partner*, Towne Properties, Ltd.; **PRIM RE ACT:** Developer, Builder, Owner/Investor, Property Manager, Syndicator; **OTHER RE ACT:** Redevel., land devel.; **SERVICES:** Full devel. support for sale & investment prop.; **PROFL AFFIL & HONORS:** NAHB, Cincinnati Apt. Council, ULI; **EDUC:** AB, 1954, Hist., Harvard Coll.; **GRAD EDUC:** MBA, 1960, Mktg., Harvard Bus. School; **MIL SERV:** US Navy Air 1954-1958, LT(SG); **OTHER ACT & HONORS:** Committees: Cincinnati 2000 Plan, Cincinnati Downtown Council, Comm. Devel. Advisory Comm.; **HOME ADD:** 7175 Given Rd., Cincinnati, OH 45243, (513)561-5001; **BUS ADD:** 2261 Francis Ln., Cincinnati, OH 45206, (513)861-3375.

BOSCO, Louis C., Jr.——B: March 28, 1936, Detroit, MI, *Managing Partner*, Bosco Development Co.; **PRIM RE ACT:** Broker, Attorney, Developer, Owner/Investor; **PROFL AFFIL & HONORS:** Detroit Bar Assn.; Oakland Cty. Bar Assn.; MI Bar Assn.; **EDUC:** Ph.B., 1958, Fin., Univ. of Notre Dame; **GRAD EDUC:** JD, 1961, Law, Univ. of Detroit; **OTHER ACT & HONORS:** Notre Dame Club of Detroit; **HOME ADD:** 29733 Spring Hill Dr., Southfield, MI 48076, (313)559-2485; **BUS ADD:** 27830 Orchard Lake Rd., Farmington Hills, MI 48018, (313)626-6906.

BOSICH, Robert W.——B: July 11, 1940, Greensburg, PA, *Pres.*, Ameri-cand Prop. Mgrs.; **OTHER RE ACT:** Investment Counseling; RE Mgmt.; **SERVICES:** Prop. Mgmt, Counseling and Rehabilitation; **REP CLIENTS:** 100 different owners; **PROFL AFFIL & HONORS:** IREM, CA R.E. Broker, CPM; **EDUC:** BS, 1962, Traffic Mgmt., PA State; **GRAD EDUC:** MBA, 1971, Admin. Mgmt., USC; **EDUC HONORS:** Pres. of Kappa Delta RHO Social Frat.; **MIL SERV:** USN, Lt.j.g. (1962-66); **OTHER ACT & HONORS:** Instr.- R.E. Mgmt.- Santa ana Coll., Cypress Coll., CA Lecturer R.E. at CA Poly. Pomora; **HOME ADD:** 5014 E. Hillside Ave., Orange, CA 92669, (714)637-1022; **BUS ADD:** 135 N.Yorba St., Tustin, CA 92680, (714)730-6577.

BOSLEY, William L.——B: Nov. 24, 1950, Toronto, Can., *VP & Dir. Prop. Mgmt. Div.*, W.H. Bosley & Co., Ltd., Prop. Mgmt.; **PRIM RE ACT:** Consultant, Property Manager, Syndicator; **PREV EMPLOY:** William Walters Co., Los Angeles, CA; **PROFL AFFIL & HONORS:** IREM, BOMA, CPM; **GRAD EDUC:** BA, 1973, Psych., Univ. of W. ON; **HOME ADD:** 61 Carmichael Ave., Toronto, Canada; **BUS ADD:** 188 Eglinton Ave. E., M4P2E4, Toronto, Canada, (416)486-5770.

BOSLOUGH, Gary C.——B: Oct. 20, 1954, Detroit, MI, *Const. Mgr.*, Joe Hollman & Co.; **PRIM RE ACT:** Developer; **OTHER RE ACT:** Athleh's Club Devel.; **SERVICES:** Devel. and Const.; **EDUC:** BS, 1976, Const. Mgmt., MI State Univ.; **HOME ADD:** 8651 Brightfield Cir., Tigard, OR 97223, (503)643-6886; **BUS ADD:** 11200 SW Allen Blvd., Beaverton, OR 97223, (502)641-7766.

BOSSART, David T.——B: Oct. 9, 1949, Jersey City, NJ, *Pres.*, Providence Dev. Corp.; **PRIM RE ACT:** Broker, Appraiser, Developer, Property Manager; **SERVICES:** Comml./Indus. Appraisers, Multi-Family Mgmt.; Resid. Devel. Mort.; **REP CLIENTS:** United Jersey Bank, Midlantic, Equitable, Lenders Attys., Investors; **PREV EMPLOY:** United Jersey Mort. Co.; **PROFL AFFIL & HONORS:** NJ Realtors, NJ Homebuilders, Society of Real Estate Appraisers-Assoc. Morris Co. Bd. Realtors, SOM/Morris Homebuilders, CTA-Cert.-NJ Tax Assessor, Licensed NJ RE Broker; **EDUC:** Rutgers-BA, 1972, Engrg.; **OTHER ACT & HONORS:** Chmn. Trustees of Valley View Chapel, Prior Trustee of Mendham Area Sr. Housing Corp.; **HOME ADD:** Box 187E, Laurel Ln., Chester, NJ 07930, (201)879-7064; **BUS ADD:** 402 Rt. 24, Chester, NJ 07930, (201)879-7883.

BOSSUNG, Charles F.——B: Feb. 9, 1932, Queens, NY, *Staff VP-RE*, ARA Services Inc.; **PRIM RE ACT:** Architect, Property Manager; **OTHER RE ACT:** Corp. RE Exec.; **SERVICES:** Manage corp. RE function; **PREV EMPLOY:** Bus. devel. const. mgmt., RE devel., RE sales, Arch. practice; **PROFL AFFIL & HONORS:** NACORE, IDRC, Registered Arch.; **EDUC:** BArch., Pratt Inst. School of Arch.; **MIL SERV:** US Army Engrs., 1st Lt.; **OTHER ACT & HONORS:** Bd. of Dir.-Phila. Ctr. for Older People; **HOME TEL:** (215)647-3771; **BUS ADD:** Independence Square W., Philadelphia, PA 19106, (215)574-5666.

BOSTON, O.E.——B: Jan. 9, 1926, New Haven, WV, *Broker*, Keith Adams & Assoc.; **PRIM RE ACT:** Broker, Property Manager, Owner/Investor; **SERVICES:** Residential sales (new & resale); comml. & investment sales; corp. transfer/relocation serv., comml. leasing, prop. mgmt.; **REP CLIENTS:** Residential Purchasers and Sellers; Investors, Comml. users, comml. prop. owners, investment prop. owners; **PREV EMPLOY:** Personnel & Public Relations Mgmt., Battelle Memorial Inst. and Gen. Electric Co.; **PROFL AFFIL & HONORS:** RNMI; State License Law Comm. Chmn., Wash. Assn. of Realtors, 1979-1981, Amer. Arbitration Assn.; **EDUC:** BA, 1949, Econ. and Psych., OH Univ.; **GRAD EDUC:** MBA, 1950, Personnel Mgmt. and Labor Econ., OH State Univ.; **MIL SERV:** USN, PhM 3/C; **OTHER ACT & HONORS:** Franklin Cty. Boundary Review Bd., 1977-1979, Rotary Intl., Elks; **HOME ADD:** 420 Rd. 39, Pasco, WA 99301, (509)547-9844; **BUS ADD:** 677 George Washington Way, Richland, WA 99352, (509)946-4136.

BOTHEN, Thomas Charles——B: Dec. 27, 1947, Chicago, IL, *Sec./Treas.*, Westchester Square Bldg. Corp.; **PRIM RE ACT:** Consultant, Property Manager, Owner/Investor; **OTHER RE ACT:** Investment feasibility and mktg.; **SERVICES:** Investment review, budgeting, policy review and implementation; **PREV EMPLOY:** Tax consultant and fin. mgr. for individuals and fin. instns.; **PROFL AFFIL & HONORS:** BOMA; **EDUC:** BBA, 1974, Fin. and Public Accounting, Loyola Univ., Chicago, IL; **OTHER ACT & HONORS:** Trustee-Woodridge Police Pension Fund 1975-1976, Pres. - Lake Hinsdale Village Homeowners Assn.; **HOME ADD:** 20 Kent Court, Willowbrook, IL 60514, (312)887-1657; **BUS ADD:** 9865 W Roosevelt Rd., Westchester, IL 60153, (312)343-7075.

BOTKIN, Kermit M.——B: Mar. 20, 1950, Marion, IN, *Asst. VP*, Associates of Triangle, Inc. & Triangle Associates, Inc.; **PRIM RE ACT:** Property Manager; **SERVICES:** Prop. Mgr., consultant; **REP CLIENTS:** Corp. and owners of multi-family rental and comml. prop.; **PREV EMPLOY:** FCH Services, Inc. 1973-1978; **PROFL AFFIL & HONORS:** IREM, Metropolitan Indianapolis Bd. of Realtors, Broker, CPM; **OTHER ACT & HONORS:** Masonic Lodge, Scottish Rite, Fraternal Order of Police, Police Athletic League, Church, "Outstanding Young Man of Amer." 1980; **HOME ADD:** 8750 Royal Meadow Dr., Indianapolis, IN 46240, (317)881-7833; **BUS ADD:** 921 E. 86th St., Suite 111, Indianapolis, IN 46240, (317)257-5137.

BOTTELLI, Richard——B: Apr. 20, 1937, Orange, NJ, *Owner*, Bottelli Assoc., Arch./Planners; **PRIM RE ACT:** Architect, Regulator, Consultant, Owner/Investor; **SERVICES:** Arch., Planning, Feasibility Studies, Interior Design, Dev., Consulting & Processing; **PREV EMPLOY:** Prin. Becker & Becker Assoc., 1968-73; **PROFL AFFIL & HONORS:** Past Pres. NJ Soc. of Arch, Dir. since 1973 Editorial Bd. Chmn. *Architecture New Jersey* 1974-76, Member NJ Soc. of Prof. Planners, Dir. NJ Housing Forum since 1975, Member AIA; **EDUC:** Bach. of Arch., 1962, Arch., Univ. of VA; **OTHER ACT & HONORS:** Summit NJ Plan. Bd Chmn since 1974, Beacon Hill Club, Summit, NJ, Tr. Architects Community Design Center, 1972-76, Member, State of NJ Citizens Comm. on Permit Coordination; **HOME ADD:** 6 Primrose Pl., Summit, NJ 07901, (201)277-6883; **BUS ADD:** 26 Columbia Turnpike, Florham Park, NJ 07932, (201)822-3800.

BOTTHOF, C.L., Jr.——*VP*, Curto Reynolds Oelrich Inc.; **PRIM RE ACT:** Developer; **BUS ADD:** 1400 E. Touhy Ave., 230, Des Plaines, IL 60603, (312)635-2030.*

BOTTOM, Dale C.——*Exec. VP*, The Institute of Financial Education; **PRIM RE ACT:** Instructor, Banker; **BUS ADD:** 111 E. Wacker Dr., Chicago, IL 60601, (312)644-3100.*

BOUCHER, Craig——B: July 13, 1946, Bremerton, WA, *VP & Sec. & Legal Counsel*, Signal Landmark, Inc.; **PRIM RE ACT:** Developer; **OTHER RE ACT:** Gen. Counsel; **SERVICES:** In house legal counsel handling all aspects of resid. and comml. devel. and const.; **PREV EMPLOY:** Private practice; gen. law; **PROFL AFFIL & HONORS:** Orange Cty. Bar Assoc. & ABA; **EDUC:** BA, 1969, Cultural Anthropology & Zoology, Univ. of CA at Santa Barbara; **GRAD EDUC:** JD, 1976, Western State Univ., Coll. of Law; **HOME ADD:** 16891 Marina Bay Dr., Huntington Beach, CA 92649, (213)592-5071; **BUS ADD:** 17890 Skypark Cir., Irvine, CA 92714, (714)979-6900.

BOUCHER, Harold E.——B: May 24, 1936, Boston, MA, *Dir. of Mktg. & Project Mgr.*, Weymouth Port Sales & Sagamore Place Condos; **PRIM RE ACT:** Broker, Consultant, Developer; **OTHER RE ACT:** Condo Conversion; **SERVICES:** Sales, Mkt. Planning, Conversions, Project Mgmt.; **REP CLIENTS:** Boston Props.; Howard, Howard, & Barnard, Newport Beach, CA; 1st Amer. Bank for Savings; Natl. Bank of N. Amer., NY; Greenwich Savings Bank, NY; **PREV EMPLOY:** Successful work out of Weymouthport Condos; **PROFL AFFIL & HONORS:** Commonwealth of MA, RE Broker; Ins. Broker; Notary Public; **EDUC:** Univ. Coll., Northeastern Univ.; **GRAD EDUC:** Bus. - RE Law; **MIL SERV:** USMC; Enlisted; **HOME ADD:** 40 Oak St., Westwood, MA 02090, (617)762-9060; **BUS ADD:** 115 W. Squantum St., Quincy, MA 02171, (617)328-4992.

BOUD, John W., III——B: Feb. 5, 1950, Salt Lake City, UT, *Dir. of RE Devel.*, Grand Central, Inc., RE; **PRIM RE ACT:** Consultant, Attorney; **SERVICES:** Research and analysis of legal, RE & econ. issues; **REP CLIENTS:** Grand Central, Inc.; **PROFL AFFIL & HONORS:** ABA, Delta Theta Phi, Phi Kappa Phi, UT State Bar, Beta Gamma Sigma; **EDUC:** BS, 1975, Acctg., Brigham Young Univ.; **GRAD EDUC:** JD, 1978, J. Reuben Clark Law Sch., Brigham Young Univ.; **EDUC HONORS:** Cum Laude; **HOME ADD:** 4800 S Saxony Cir., Salt Lake City, UT 84117, (801)278-6191; **BUS ADD:** 2233 S 300 E, Salt Lake City, UT 84115, (801)486-7611.

BOUDREAU, Edward H.——B: Dec. 4, 1945, Monett, MO, *Pres.*, Capital Consultants Management Corp.; **PRIM RE ACT:** Broker, Owner/Investor, Property Manager, Syndicator; **SERVICES:** Client Comm. Brokerage, Prop. Mgmt., RE Synd.; **REP CLIENTS:** Lending Instns., Intl. Clients, Indiv. Owners; **PROFL AFFIL & HONORS:** IREM, Dallas Bd. of Realtors, TX Nat., Dallas Apt. Assn., Community Assn. Inst., CPM, *AMO*, Broker, Officer, Dir., Dallas Apt. Assn., Dir. TX Apt. Assn.; **EDUC:** BA, 1969, Econ. and Bus. Admin., IAU; **GRAD EDUC:** MBA, 1971, Mktg., IAU; **EDUC HONORS:** Cum Laude; **MIL SERV:** USAF, E-5, DSM; **HOME ADD:** 8712 Mediterranean, Dallas, TX 75238, (214)341-4388; **BUS ADD:** 4155 Buena Vista, Dallas, TX 75204, (214)528-4970.

BOUILLY, Roger Charles——B: June 7, 1945, Fargo, ND, Bouilly, Inc.; **PRIM RE ACT:** Broker, Consultant, Developer, Owner/Investor, Property Manager, Syndicator; **OTHER RE ACT:** Specializing in large projects with cash flow in areas such as AK, KS, & other states; **SERVICES:** Synd. of comml. prop., prop. mgmt. of same; **REP CLIENTS:** Portfolio clients who are interested in immediate return first & depreciation second; **PREV EMPLOY:** Always been in RE; **PROFL AFFIL & HONORS:** NAR; CAR; NAISV; SSSA; **EDUC:** BA, 1968, Mass Comm., Hamline Univ.; **MIL SERV:** USN, E-5, Vietnam Serv., and other decorations; **HOME ADD:** 1896 Alameda Diablo, Diablo, CA 94529, (415)837-7258; **BUS ADD:** Suite C, 3182 Old Tunnel Rd., Lafayette, CA 94549, (415)945-6678.

BOULAND, John T.——B: Nov. 6, 1946, Washington, DC, *VP and Gen. Counsel*, Florida Title & Abstract Co.; **PRIM RE ACT:** Attorney; **PREV EMPLOY:** Self-Employed; **PROFL AFFIL & HONORS:** ABA; FL Bar Assn.; FL Land Title Assn., Designated Real Prop. Law under FL Bar Designation Plan; Certified Land Title Searcher; **EDUC:** BA, 1968, Pol. Sci., Univ. of FL; **GRAD EDUC:** JD, 1971, Real Prop. Law and Taxation, Univ. of FL; **MIL SERV:** U.S. Army, Capt.; **HOME ADD:** POB 482, Ocala, FL 32678, (904)236-3557; **BUS ADD:** POB 2016, Ocala, FL 32678, (904)732-7910.

BOULTINGHOUSE, Richard F.——B: June 4, 1940, Evansville, IN, *VP*, Arvida Corp., S CA; **PRIM RE ACT:** Consultant, Developer, Builder, Property Manager; **PREV EMPLOY:** Kaiser Aetna; **PROFL AFFIL & HONORS:** ULI, Nat. Assn. of Home Builders, Bldg. Inst. of Amer.; **EDUC:** BS, 1963, Bus., IN Univ.; **MIL SERV:** USA, NC; **OTHER ACT & HONORS:** Dir. Santa Margarita Water Dist., S. Coast. Repertory Theatre, CHOC Patrines; **HOME ADD:** 26972 Highwood Cir., Laguna Hills, CA 92655, (714)831-6718; **BUS ADD:** PO Box 438, Trabuco Canyon, CA 92678, (714)586-0761.

BOUMIL, S. James——B: Nov. 15, 1947, Lowell, MA, *Atty. at Law*; **PRIM RE ACT:** Attorney, Developer, Owner/Investor; **SERVICES:** Acquisition, devel., fin., law; **PROFL AFFIL & HONORS:** MA Bar Assn., Boston Bar Assn.; **EDUC:** BS, 1969, Nuclear Physics, Lowell Technol. Inst.; **GRAD EDUC:** JD, 1972, Taxation/RE, Boston Coll. Law School; **EDUC HONORS:** Cum Laude; **OTHER ACT & HONORS:** Chairman, Univ. of Lowell Bldg. Authority; **HOME ADD:** 120 Fairmount St., Lowell, MA 01852; **BUS ADD:** 100 Summit St., Lowell, MA 01852, (617)458-0507.

BOURNE, Mary E.——B: Aug. 1, 1938, Dodge City, KS, *Pres.*, Bourne, Inc. Realtors; **PRIM RE ACT:** Broker, Instructor, Consultant, Appraiser, Property Manager, Lender, Owner/Investor, Insuror; **SERVICES:** Alternative Fin., Consultants, Investment Counseling, R.E. Sales & Exchanges; **REP CLIENTS:** Indiv. Investors, Borrowers; **PREV EMPLOY:** 5 yrs. Banking experience, 5 yrs. Prop. and Casualty Ins.; **PROFL AFFIL & HONORS:** NAR; KAR; RNMI; IIAA; IIAK; PIA; CRB; CRS; GRI; **HOME ADD:** 616 Magnolia, Garden City, KS 67846, (316)276-8666; **BUS ADD:** Box 1568, Garden City, KS 67846, (316)276-3258.

BOURNE, Thomas E.——B: Dec. 22, 1929, Cleveland, OH, *RE Mgr.*, Koppers Co., Inc., Law Dept.; **OTHER RE ACT:** Corporate RE Mgr.; **SERVICES:** Provide overall RE servs. for a multi-div. major mfg. corp.; **PREV EMPLOY:** Have been with Koppers RE Dept., since 1954; **EDUC:** BS, 1951, Econ., Bus. Admin., Law & Acctg., OH Univ., Athens, OH; **GRAD EDUC:** Post Grad. Work, 1955-57, RE Law, Constr. & Land Econ., Univ. of Pittsburgh; **MIL SERV:** USCG, LT (JG), Korean Serv. & Good Conduct; **HOME ADD:** 5314 Highgrove Rd., Pittsburgh, PA 15236, (412)884-3211; **BUS ADD:** Koppers Bldg., Pittsburgh, PA 15219, (412)227-2622.

BOURNE, William C.——B: June 30, 1938, Richmond, VA, *Assoc. Dir. of Interiors Grp.*, Hellmuth, Obata and Kassabaum, Inc.; **PRIM RE ACT:** Architect; **SERVICES:** Tenant Lease Servs. for Office Bldgs.; **REP CLIENTS:** Bldg. Owners, Devels. & Leasing Agents; **PREV EMPLOY:** Whisler Patri (Arch.) 1975-78; Skidmore, Owings & Merrill (Archs.) 1978-80; **PROFL AFFIL & HONORS:** AIA; **EDUC:** BArch, 1962, Arch. & City Planning, VA Polytechnic Inst.; **GRAD EDUC:** MArch, Master of City Planning, 1964, Arch. & Civic Design, Univ. of PA; **EDUC HONORS:** AIA School Medal, Henry Adams Fund Award; **OTHER ACT & HONORS:** Soc. for the Encouragement of Contemporary Art; **HOME ADD:** 210 Hillside Ave., Piedmont, CA 94611, (415)654-6979; **BUS ADD:** 1 Lombard St., San

Francisco, CA 94111, (415)986-4276.

BOUSCAREN, Pierre, Jr.——B: Jan. 17, 1935, Evanston, IL, *VP*, Latshaw Commercial Properties; **PRIM RE ACT:** Consultant, Property Manager; **OTHER RE ACT:** Leasing agent, Tenant representative; **SERVICES:** Merchandising plans, rent rolls, nat. & local leasing; **PREV EMPLOY:** The Rouse Co.; **PROFL AFFIL & HONORS:** Intl. Council of Shopping Ctrs.; **EDUC:** BA, 1957, Human Culture & Behavior, Yale Univ.; **MIL SERV:** US Army; E-4; **HOME ADD:** 4412 Norwood Rd., Baltimore, MD 21218, (301)243-6232; **BUS ADD:** 600E Joppa Rd., Baltimore, MD 21204, (301)243-6230.

BOUSFIELD, Michael C.——B: June 3, 1947, England, *VP*, Cabot, Cabot & Forbes, Indus. & West Coast Comml.; **PRIM RE ACT:** Developer; **EDUC:** BA, 1968, Oxford Univ., England; **GRAD EDUC:** MBA, 1973, Fin., Univ. of WA; **EDUC HONORS:** Honors; **BUS ADD:** 911 Wilshire Blvd. 1010, Los Angeles, CA 90017, (213)626-8171.

BOUTON, Kenneth T.H.——B: June 5, 1948, Laramie, WY, *Sr. Assoc.*, Economics Research Assoc.; **PRIM RE ACT:** Consultant, Appraiser; **SERVICES:** Market, feasibility, fin. and appraisal analysis; **REP CLIENTS:** Devels., lenders, corporate/instnl. investors, legal reps., indiv. investors/prop. owners; **PROFL AFFIL & HONORS:** Greater N. MI Ave. Assoc.; Chicago Assn. Commerce & Indus.; IL Conf. Outdoor Recreation, Historic Pres.; AREUA; Travel and Tourism Research Assn.; **EDUC:** BA, 1972, Poli. Sci., Urban Studies, Elmhurst Coll.; **OTHER ACT & HONORS:** Khyble Yacht Club, Pres.; Phi Kappa Tau frat.; **HOME ADD:** 602 Hillside Dr., Hinsdale, IL 60521, (312)325-6039; **BUS ADD:** 205 W. Wacker Dr., Chicago, IL 60606, (312)332-0110.

BOUWKAMP, Gerald R.——*Sr. Exec. VP*, Stanadyne, Inc.; **PRIM RE ACT:** Property Manager; **BUS ADD:** PO Box 2079, Hartford, CT 06145, (203)525-0821.*

BOVAIS, Frederic A.——B: Oct. 29, 1910, NJ, *Training Dir.*, Gribin Von Dyl, Realtors, Training; **PRIM RE ACT:** Consultant, Owner/Investor, Instructor, Property Manager; **OTHER RE ACT:** Prop. mgmt. consultant; **SERVICES:** Guidance, advice, etc.; **REP CLIENTS:** Owners of multiple income prop.; condo. and cooperative Bds. of Dirs.; **PREV EMPLOY:** Retd. from Active Prop. Mgmt.; **PROFL AFFIL & HONORS:** NAR; CA Assn. of Realtors; San Fernando Valley Bd. of Realtors; IREM, CPM; Nat. IREM Instr.; **EDUC:** AB, 1930, Acctg., Rider Coll.; BS, 1932, Educ., Rider Coll.; **MIL SERV:** USN; Chief Bandmaster; **HOME ADD:** 14155 Magnolia Blvd., Sherman Oaks, CA 91423; **BUS ADD:** 4645 Van Nuys Blvd., Sherman Oaks, CA 91403, (213)986-4663.

BOVEE, Michael C.——B: July 15, 1943, Los Angeles, CA, *CEO*, MCB Associates, Inc.; **PRIM RE ACT:** Broker, Owner/Investor, Syndicator; **SERVICES:** RE Mgmt., brokerage, synd., consulting; **REP CLIENTS:** Indiv. & instnl. owners/investors; **PREV EMPLOY:** Grubb & Ellis Prop. Servs., Inc.; **PROFL AFFIL & HONORS:** Inst. of RE Mgmt.; IREF; Intl. Inst. of Valuers; Contra Costa Bd. of Realtors; Austin Apt. Assn., CPM; **EDUC:** AA, 1965, Bus. Admin., Orange Coast Coll.; **OTHER ACT & HONORS:** Anciens Roseens; Native Sons Golden West; **HOME ADD:** 2205 Kenton Ct., Walnut Creek, CA 94596, (415)944-1443; **BUS ADD:** Suite 211, 620 Contra Costa Bldg., Pleasant Hill, CA 94523, (415)680-0296.

BOVEN, Thomas M.——B: Oct. 21, 1943, Kalamazoo, MI, Scholten and Fant, PC; **PRIM RE ACT:** Attorney; **SERVICES:** RE devel., consultation and servs.; **PROFL AFFIL & HONORS:** ABA, State Bar of MI, Real Prop. Law Sect. and Bus. Law Sect., Ottawa Cty. Bar Assn.; **EDUC:** 1965, Poli. and Social Scis., MI State Univ.; **GRAD EDUC:** JD, 1968, Wayne Law School; **OTHER ACT & HONORS:** Council Exec. Bd., Boy Scouts of Amer.; Spring Lake Ctry. Club, Spring Lake Yacht Club, Rotary; **HOME ADD:** 16212 Woodcrest Dr., Spring Lake, MI 49456, (616)846-2224; **BUS ADD:** Pacesetter Bank Bldg., P O Box 454, Grand Haven, MI 49417, (616)842-3030.

BOWDEN, Dwight R.——B: Nov. 25, 1931, Hope, AR, *Pres.*, ERA-Bowden, Inc.; **PRIM RE ACT:** Broker, Consultant, Developer, Builder, Owner/Investor, Property Manager, Syndicator; **PREV EMPLOY:** First Fed. S&L Assn. Loan Officer, Appraiser, Branch Mgr. (1962-68); **PROFL AFFIL & HONORS:** RMNI, RESSI, Pres. Anchorage Bd. of Realtors (1971); Pres.-Alaska Assn. of Realtors (1974); Nat. Dir.-NAR (1974); GRI; **MIL SERV:** USMC, Sgt. (1950-52); **OTHER ACT & HONORS:** Chmn. of the Bd.-Home Federal S&L of Anchorage (1974-1976); Dir. of Home Fed. S&L (1973-pres.); **HOME ADD:** 2101 Loussac Dr., Anchorage, AL 99503, (907)248-4569; **BUS ADD:** 2602 Seward Hwy., Anchorage, AL 99503, (907)276-4663.

BOWEN, Arthur F.——B: Nov. 15, 1943, LaPlata, MD, *Pres.*, Bowen Agency, Inc.; **PRIM RE ACT:** Broker, Appraiser, Owner/Investor, Instructor, Property Manager; **SERVICES:** Consultation, investment analysis; **REP CLIENTS:** Lenders, transfer companies, indiv. clients; **PROFL AFFIL & HONORS:** Central Susquehanna Valley C of C, GRI CCIM Candidate; **EDUC:** BS, 1965, Psych., Susquehanna Univ.; **EDUC HONORS:** Alumni Award for Sr. Man Most Typifying Ideals of SU; **MIL SERV:** USN, Submarines, LT; **HOME ADD:** 20 Meadowbrook Dr., Selinsgrove, PA 17870, (717)743-7556; **BUS ADD:** 22 No. Market St., Selinsgrove, PA 17870, (717)374-2165.

BOWEN, Lyall——B: Apr. 30, 1905, Hinsdale, NY, *Broker*, Five Star Realty; **PRIM RE ACT:** Broker, Owner/Investor; **SERVICES:** We list and sell RE of all kinds; **PREV EMPLOY:** Radio, TV, Motion Picture Recording Musician; **PROFL AFFIL & HONORS:** Las Vegas, NV State and NAR, Realtor of the month May 1975, Recipient of the 1st annual Gene Nebeker Award for professionalism in RE 1980, GRI, CRS; **EDUC:** BS in Econ., 1927, Wharton School of the Univ. of PA; **OTHER ACT & HONORS:** Dir.; Las Vegas Bd. of Realtors Dir.; NV Assn. of Realtors 1982 Pres. NV Chap of CRS; **HOME ADD:** 6209 W. Oakey, Las Vegas, NV 89102, (702)871-7339; **BUS ADD:** 1230 S. MD Parkway,, Las Vegas, NV 89104, (702)385-5567.

BOWEN, Peter Geoffrey——B: July 10, 1939, Iowa City, IA, *CEO*, The Investment Management Group, Ltd.; **PRIM RE ACT:** Broker, Consultant, Instructor, Property Manager, Syndicator; **OTHER RE ACT:** Author; Investor; **SERVICES:** RE analysis, acquisition and admin.; **REP CLIENTS:** RE investment trusts, ltd. partnerships and selected indiv. investors; **PREV EMPLOY:** Denver based RE investment cos.; **PROFL AFFIL & HONORS:** Denver Bd. of Realtors, Denver Council for Econ. Devel., 1965-69; AOPA; PSIA; **EDUC:** BA, 1960, Public Admin. & Econ., Lawrence Univ., Appleton, WI; **GRAD EDUC:** Law, Univ. of WI; **OTHER ACT & HONORS:** Bd. Member CO Plan for Apportionment, 1965-66; Listed, 1971 Edition, "Outstanding Young Men of America"; Bd. Member, Lawrence Univ. Alumni Assn.; **HOME ADD:** 4950 S Beeler, Greenwood Vill, Englewood, CO 80111; **BUS ADD:** 1562 S Parker Rd., Suite 208, Denver, CO 80231, (303)750-8833.

BOWER, Jay R.——B: July 8, 1936, Quincy, IL, *Broker/Realtor*, Bower Gallery of Homes; **PRIM RE ACT:** Broker, Appraiser; **OTHER RE ACT:** Resid., Agric., Comml.; **SERVICES:** Sales, appraisal, exchange; **PREV EMPLOY:** RE since 1958; **PROFL AFFIL & HONORS:** Nat. Mktg. Inst.; Farm & Land Inst., GRI; AFLM; CRB; CRS; AACA; **EDUC:** BS, 1957, Econ./Bus., Culver-Stockton Coll., Canton, MO; **MIL SERV:** US Army; Cpl.; **HOME ADD:** 2828 S Field Rd., Quincy, IL 62301, (217)222-2232; **BUS ADD:** 5th & Main, Quincy, IL 62301, (217)224-1598.

BOWER, Paul O.——B: Jan. 12, 1943, Pittsburgh, PA, *Sr. VP*, Allen & O'Hara, Inc., Mgmt. Services Dept.; **OTHER RE ACT:** Property Management; **SERVICES:** Mgmt. of Hotels, Office Bldgs., Apts., including leasing and complete accounting services; **REP CLIENTS:** The Northwestern Mutual Life Ins. Co., The Equitable, 1st Nat. Bank of Chicago and others; **PROFL AFFIL & HONORS:** Inst. of RE Mgmt., NAR, CPM; **EDUC:** BS, 1966, Hotel Admin., Cornell Univ.; **HOME ADD:** 8511 Sherman Oaks Dr., Germantown, TN 38138, (901)754-4931; **BUS ADD:** 3385 Airways Blvd., Memphis, TN 38116, (901)345-7620.

BOWER, William R.——B: Aug. 8, 1930, Marion, IN, *Pres.*, LNC Development Corp.; **OTHER RE ACT:** RE Investments; **PREV EMPLOY:** Lincoln Nat. Life Ins. Co., Asst. Mgr., RE Dept.; Rgnl. Mgr., Production, Mort. Loan Dept.; Mgr., SE Mort. Loan Office, Atlanta, GA; VP, LNC Devel. Corp.; **EDUC:** BA, 1952, Bus. Admin., MI State Univ.; **MIL SERV:** USAF, 2nd Lt.; **HOME ADD:** 2536 Fairfax Ave., Ft. Wayne, IN 46806, (219)447-2778; **BUS ADD:** 1300 S. Clinton St., Ft. Wayne, IN 46801, (219)427-3593.

BOWERING, C. Richard——B: Nov. 14, 1930, St. Joseph, MO, *Pres.*, Bowering Homes, Inc.; **PRIM RE ACT:** Developer, Builder; **PROFL AFFIL & HONORS:** Rochester Home Builders Assn.; **EDUC:** BS, 1958, Bus. & Econ., Univ. of Rochester; **MIL SERV:** USAF, S/Sgt.; **HOME ADD:** 10 Kurt Rd., Pittsford, NY 14534, (716)248-2643; **BUS ADD:** 304 Thornell Rd., Pittsford, NY 14534, (716)381-3376.

BOWERS, G.H.——*Dpty Asst. Secy.*, Department of Housing and Urban Development, Single Family Housing & Mortgage Activities; **PRIM RE ACT:** Lender; **BUS ADD:** 451 Seventh St., S.W., Washington, DC 20410, (202)755-6675.*

BOWLES, Sheila——*Dir.*, Arkansas, Arkansas Real Estate Commission; **PRIM RE ACT:** Property Manager; **BUS ADD:** State Capital, 5th & Woodlane, Little Rock, AR 72201, (501)371-3000.*

BOWLES, Walter F., Jr.——B: Apr. 29, 1938, Indianapolis, IN, *VP*, Greenfield Banking Co.; **PRIM RE ACT:** Appraiser, Banker, Lender; **SERVICES:** RE Mort. Loan, Const. Loans; **PROFL AFFIL & HONORS:** Natl. Assn. of Indep. Fee Apprasier, Natl. Assn. of Review Appraisers, IFA, CRA; **GRAD EDUC:** Amer. Inst. of Banking, 1969, Fin. & Banking, IN Univ. Extension; Natl. Mort. School, 1969, Fin. & Banking, OH State Univ.; Bank Admin. Inst., 1978, Fin. & Banking, Univ. of WI; **MIL SERV:** USA, Spec. 5th Cl., Good Conduct; **OTHER ACT & HONORS:** IN Heart Assn., Hancock Cty. Bd. of Realtors, Builders Assn. of Greater Indpls.; **HOME ADD:** RR 4, Box 39, Greenfield, IN 46140; **BUS ADD:** 10 E. Main St., PO Box 587, Greenfield, IN 46140, (317)462-1431.

BOWMAN, James S.——B: May 17, 1929, Cincinnati, OH, *Pres.*, Fourth Realty Corp.; **PRIM RE ACT:** Attorney, Property Manager, Owner/Investor; **PROFL AFFIL & HONORS:** BOMA (Cincinnati); KY Bar Assn., Past Pres. Cincinnati BOMA; **EDUC:** BS, 1952, Health, Univ. of Cincinnati; **GRAD EDUC:** JD, 1964, Chase Coll. of Law; **EDUC HONORS:** Soc. of Wing and Torch; **OTHER ACT & HONORS:** Member Cincinnati Rotary Club, Elder and Clerk of Session, First Presby. Church, Ft. Thomas; **HOME ADD:** 25 South Shaw Lane, Ft. Thomas, KY 41075, (606)441-3852; **BUS ADD:** 18 E. Fourth St., Cincinnati, OH 45202, (513)621-4556.

BOWMAN, Robert F.——B: Apr. 21, 1933, Camden, NJ, *Exec. VP*, Jackson Cross Co.; **PRIM RE ACT:** Broker, Consultant; **SERVICES:** Sales/Lease Negotiations, Relocation, Investments; **REP CLIENTS:** INA, Hercules Inc.; Price-Waterhouse, USF&G Smith-Kline Corp.; **PREV EMPLOY:** Armstrong Cork Co.; **PROFL AFFIL & HONORS:** SIR, BOMA, NACORE, ULI, The Office Network, Inc.; **EDUC:** BA, 1955, Econ., Wesleyan Univ., CT; **MIL SERV:** USA, Sgt. 1956-58; **HOME ADD:** 324 Bellevue Ave., Haddonfield, NJ 08033, (609)428-7658; **BUS ADD:** 2000 Market St., Philadelphia, PA 19103, (215)561-8930.

BOXER, Leonard——B: Feb. 11, 1939, New York, NY, *Sr. Partner*, Olnick, Boxer, Blumberg, Lane & Troy; **PRIM RE ACT:** Broker, Attorney, Developer; **EDUC:** BS, 1960, Acctg., NYU; **GRAD EDUC:** LLB, 1963, NY Univ., School of Law; **EDUC HONORS:** Beta Alpha Psi Honorary Soc, Gary, US Steel Scholarship, Founders Day Award; **MIL SERV:** US Army Reserve, First Sgt.; **OTHER ACT & HONORS:** Tr.-Nat. Jewish Hospital & Research Center of Denver, Advisory Bd. - Chicago Title Insurance Co.; **HOME ADD:** 187 Beach 136 St., Belle Harbor, NY 11694, (212)945-5461; **BUS ADD:** 909 Third Ave., NY, NY 10022, (212)755-7804.

BOYARSKY, Samuel G.——B: Dec. 23, 1927, Wallingford, CT, *Senior RE Analyst, Air Rights, Land Development*, Amtrak, Natl. Railroad Passenger Corp., RE; **PRIM RE ACT:** Broker, Consultant, Appraiser, Developer, Owner/Investor, Syndicator; **SERVICES:** Leasing, consulting, synd.; **REP CLIENTS:** Banks, ins. co., private investors, foreign corp., private synd.; **PREV EMPLOY:** US Railway Assn.; Indep. Appraiser Consultant; Rep. Cli.; lenders, indiv., inst. investors, devel. & comml. indus. prop.; **PROFL AFFIL & HONORS:** Amer. Soc. of Appraisers; Int. Coll. of RE Consulting Profl.; Nat. Assn.of Review Appraisers; Int. Right of Way Assn.; Assn. of Govt. Appraisers; Amer. Assn. of Cert. Appraisers; Int. Assoc. of Asses. Officers, ASA; IAAO; NARA; AACA; IRWA; **EDUC:** BA, 1950, Pol. Sci., Public Admin., Syracuse U., U. of Bridgeport, U. of CT; **EDUC HONORS:** Phi Theta Kappa; **MIL SERV:** US Army; SSgt.; **HOME ADD:** 200 Autumn Ridge Rd., Fairfield, CT 06432; **BUS ADD:** 250 W. 34 St., New York, NY 10119, (212)560-7338.

BOYCE, David M.——B: Sept. 7, 1940, Danbury, CT, *Devel.*, The Boyce Org., RE Investments and Land Mgmt.; **PRIM RE ACT:** Developer; **SERVICES:** Develop and manage comml. and resid. props.; **REP CLIENTS:** Lenders and indiv. or instit. investors in comml. props.; **PREV EMPLOY:** Chmn., Latimer & Buck Advisors, Inc.; Advisor and Mgr. of the assets of Fidelco Growth Investors, Phil, PA (1977-79); VP, Chase Manhattan Bank RE Fin. Dept. (1964-77); **PROFL AFFIL & HONORS:** Young Men's RE (NYC); **EDUC:** BS, 1962, Investments, Babson Coll.; **HOME ADD:** 27 Hawthorne Place, Summit, NJ 07901, (201)277-2650; **BUS ADD:** 83 Floral Ave, Murray Hill, NJ 07974, (201)464-2001.

BOYCE, Everette——B: Sept. 21, 1928, Utopia, TX, *Owner of Boyce Realtors*, Boyce Realtors, Farms, Ranches, Recreational; **PRIM RE ACT:** Broker, Appraiser, Owner/Investor; **PREV EMPLOY:** Moore RE; **PROFL AFFIL & HONORS:** NAR, TX State Bd. of Realtors, Uvalde Cty. Bd. of Realtors; **EDUC:** RE Law & Appraisal, San Antonio Coll., TX; **OTHER ACT & HONORS:** Member of Tax equalization Comm., Utopia School Dist., Lions Club Pres.; **HOME ADD:** Po Box 126, Utopia, TX 78884, (512)966-3349; **BUS ADD:** PO Box 126, Utopia, TX 78884, (512)966-3344.

BOYCE, Katherine——B: July 23, 1930, Dallas, TX, *Owner of Boyce Realtors*, Boyce Realtors, Farms, Ranches, Recreational; **PRIM RE ACT:** Broker, Appraiser, Owner/Investor; **PREV EMPLOY:** Moore RE; **PROFL AFFIL & HONORS:** NAR, TX State Bd. of Realtors, Uvalde Cty. Bd. of Realtors; **EDUC:** RE Law & Appraisal, San Antonio Coll., TX; **HOME ADD:** PO Box 126, Utopia, TX 78884, (512)966-3349; **BUS ADD:** PO Box 126, Utopia, TX 78884, (512)966-3344.

BOYCE, Shirley——*Ed.*, Stamats Publishing Co., Roster of Realtors; **PRIM RE ACT:** Real Estate Publisher; **BUS ADD:** 427 6th Ave., S.E., Cedar Rapids, IA 52406.*

BOYD, Bruce Michael——B: Jan. 12, 1947, Santa Monica, CA, *Atty.*, Bruce Michael Boyd, PC; **PRIM RE ACT:** Broker, Attorney, Owner/Investor, Instructor, Syndicator; **SERVICES:** Legal and RE consultation; **REP CLIENTS:** Triton Fin. corp., JMB Realty, Domus Devel. Corp, Highsmith Fin. Corp.; **PREV EMPLOY:** RE Fin. Dept., Metropolitan Life Ins. Co., Hession, Creedon, Hamlin, Kelly, Hanson & Williams, Tobin & Tobin; **PROFL AFFIL & HONORS:** ABA, CA Bar Assn.; **EDUC:** BA, 1969, Govt., Univ. of CA; **GRAD EDUC:** JD, 1973, Univ. of CA, Berkeley; **EDUC HONORS:** Summa cum laude, phi beta kappa, Editor, Ecology, Law Quarterly, Profl. Study in India; **OTHER ACT & HONORS:** Inst., Dept. of RE, Coll. of San Mateo, San Mateo, CA; **HOME ADD:** 161 Laurie Meadows Dr., San Mateo, CA 94403; **BUS ADD:** 1701 Franklin St., San Francisco, CA 94109, (415)441-0282.

BOYD, Jack N.——B: Dec. 29, 1930, Wichita Falls, TX, *Broker*, Allied Realty Group; **PRIM RE ACT:** Broker, Consultant, Owner/Investor, Property Manager, Syndicator; **PREV EMPLOY:** Govt. sub-contractor; **PROFL AFFIL & HONORS:** NAR, RNMI, CRB, TAR, ARA, Rotary Intl., GRI, CRB; **MIL SERV:** USMC, Cpl.; **OTHER ACT & HONORS:** Methodist, Mason, Shriner, Rotarian; **HOME ADD:** Rt. 3 Box 249K, Texarkana, TX 75503, (214)838-6016; **BUS ADD:** 1018 College Dr., Texarkana, TX 75501.

BOYD, Laurence A.——B: Nov. 16, 1954, Rochester, MN, *Leasing Mgr.*, Trizec/Pershing Square Redevelopment; **PRIM RE ACT:** Broker, Developer; **OTHER RE ACT:** Leasing Specialist; **PREV EMPLOY:** Moseley & Co., Brokers; **PROFL AFFIL & HONORS:** Kansas City and MO RE Bds., State Dir. for MO Assn. of Realtors; **EDUC:** Bus. Admin., 1977, RE & Rgnl. Sci., So. Methodist Univ.; **OTHER ACT & HONORS:** Phi Delta Theta Alumni Assn.; **HOME ADD:** 416 E. 74th, Kansas City, MO 64131, (816)361-5933; **BUS ADD:** 2301 Main St. 670, Kansas City, MO 64108, (816)474-4575.

BOYD, William D.——B: Oct. 4, 1929, Cisco, TX, *Arch, Owner*, Boyd & Assoc., Archs.; **PRIM RE ACT:** Architect, Consultant, Developer, Builder; **SERVICES:** Arch., Site Planning, Estimations; **REP CLIENTS:** Private Owners, Religions Instns., Public Schools, State & Local Govts.; **PROFL AFFIL & HONORS:** AIA, IFRAA; **EDUC:** BArch, 1953, Design, Univ. of OK; **EDUC HONORS:** Member Sigma Tau, Tau Beta Pi, Hon. frats.; **MIL SERV:** USA, 1st Lt.; **OTHER ACT & HONORS:** Lions Intl., United Methodist Church; **HOME ADD:** 508 Regency Dr., El Paso, TX 79912, (915)581-9147; **BUS ADD:** 300 E. Main, Suite 1238, El Paso, TX 79901, (915)545-1970.

BOYKIN, James H.——B: Nov. 28, 1936, Colonial Beach, VA, *Alfred L. Blake Prof. of RE*, VA Commonwealth Univ., RE and Urban Land Devel. Program; **OTHER RE ACT:** Educator; **SERVICES:** Appraisal, Feasibility Studies, Appraisal Reviews; **REP CLIENTS:** Municipalities, Devel., Mort. Lenders; **PREV EMPLOY:** Fed. Housing Admin. (1961-1963), Rountrey & Assoc. (1963-1967), ULI (1967-1969); **PROFL AFFIL & HONORS:** AIREA (Governing Council); Amer. Inst. of Corp. Asset Mgmt. (Bd. of Governors, Natl. Assn. of Certi. Mort. Bankers); AREUEA, MAI, SRPA, Lambda Alpha Honorary; **EDUC:** BS, 1961, Bus. Admin., VA Polytechnic Inst.; **GRAD EDUC:** MC, 1967, Univ. of Richmond; PhD, 1971, Bus., Specializing in RE and Land Devel., Amer. Univ.; **EDUC HONORS:** Natl. Sci. Found. Fellowship, J.C. Nichols Found. Research Grant; **OTHER ACT & HONORS:** Author of numerous articles, reports and books on RE topics; **HOME ADD:** 2431 Devenwood Rd., Richmond, VA 23235; **BUS ADD:** Box 17, School of Bus., VA Commonwealth Univ., Richmond, VA 23284, (804)257-1721.

BOYLAN, Arthur J.——B: Dec. 18, 1948, Chicago, IL, *Atty. at Law*, Hulstrand, Anderson, Larson & Boylan; **PRIM RE ACT:** Attorney; **SERVICES:** Document prep., title options, closings, RE litigation; **REP CLIENTS:** Citizens Nat. Bank; Bank of Willmar & Trust Co.; First Fed. S&L Assn.; Farmers Home Admin; Century 21-Action RE; Century 21-Kandi RE; **PROFL AFFIL & HONORS:** Member; RE Section, MN State Bar Assn.; Member; Real Prop. Probate and Trust Law Sect., ABA; **EDUC:** BA, 1971, Pre-Law, St. Mary's College, Winona, MN; **GRAD EDUC:** JD, 1976, Law, IL Inst. of Tech./Chicago-Kent College of Law; **HOME ADD:** 916 SW 14th Ave., Willmar, MN 56201, (612)235-3393; **BUS ADD:** Willmar Bldg., 201 SW 4th St., PO Box 130, Willmar, MN 56201, (612)235-4313.

BOYLAND, Nancy——*Ed.*, Audit Investment Research Inc., Realty Trust Review; **PRIM RE ACT:** Real Estate Publisher; **BUS ADD:** 230 Park Ave., Suite 954, NY, NY 10017, (212)661-1710.*

BOYLE, Andrew P.——B: July 16, 1946, Boston, MA, *VP, Resid. Mgr.*, Coldwell Banker & Co., Coldwell Banker Comm. RE Serv.; **PRIM RE ACT:** Broker, Consultant, Appraiser; **SERVICES:** Comml. RE, RE consultation, brokerage, RE mgmt., appraisal; **REP CLIENTS:** All major lenders, nat. devel. & fortune 100 companies; **PREV EMPLOY:** Garibaldi Realty Corp. 6 1/2 yrs.; **PROFL AFFIL & HONORS:** NAIOP, NACORE, IREBA, Amer. mgmt., Cert. Review Appraisers, NJ Alliance for Action, Dir. Central Bergen Bd. of Realtors, Cert. Review Appraisers, Co-chmn. of Gubernatorial Platform Comm.; **EDUC:** BS, 1968, Econ., Rutgers Univ.; **MIL SERV:** US Army, E-5; **OTHER ACT & HONORS:** Moonraker Assn.; **HOME ADD:** 14 Valley Point Rd., Holmdel, NJ, (201)671-2108; **BUS ADD:** 225 Old New Brunswick Rd., Piscataway, NJ 08854, (201)981-1555.

BOYLE, C. Edward——B: Feb. 5, 1943, Spokane, WA, *Pres.*, Westlake Associates, Inc.; **PRIM RE ACT:** Broker, Consultant, Owner/Investor, Syndicator; **SERVICES:** Sales of comml. and invest. props.; **REP CLIENTS:** Sellers and purchasers; **PROFL AFFIL & HONORS:** NAR; WA Assn. of Realtors; Seattle-King Cty. Bd. of Realtors, CCIM; **EDUC:** Engrg., Univ. of WA, College of Engrg.; **OTHER ACT & HONORS:** Rgn. 1, VP, WA Assn. of Realtors; Pres. Elect, Seattle King Cty. Bd. of Realtors; **HOME ADD:** 12005 8th N.E., Seattle, WA 98125, (206)363-3340; **BUS ADD:** 1627 Eastlake Ave. E., Suite 300, Seattle, WA 98102, (206)323-8090.

BOYLE, John O.——B: Mar. 18, 1952, Los Angeles, CA, *Owner*, John O. Boyle, Realtor; **PRIM RE ACT:** Broker, Owner/Investor, Instructor, Property Manager, Syndicator; **SERVICES:** Acquisition, mgmt. & exchange of apts. & comml. prop.; **REP CLIENTS:** Limited partnerships & indiv. investors; **PROFL AFFIL & HONORS:** IREM; RNMI; RESSI (NAR Inst.), CCIM (certified comml./investment member of RNMI); SRS (specialist in RE securities RESSI); **EDUC:** BA, 1975, Econ., Fin. & RE; **GRAD EDUC:** 1 yr. Law School, Univ. of San Diego; **EDUC HONORS:** Grad. with honors; with distinction in econ.; **HOME ADD:** 9860-B Apple Tree Dr., San Diego, CA 92124; **BUS ADD:** 3960 Park Blvd., Suite E., San Diego, CA 92103, (714)296-3166.

BOYLE, M. Ross——B: May 6, 1935, Spokane, WA, *Sr. VP*, McManis Associates, Inc.; **PRIM RE ACT:** Consultant, Syndicator; **SERVICES:** Feasibility analysis, synd., loan packaging; **REP CLIENTS:** Entrepreneurs, devel., econ. devel. corps., local govt. agencies; **PREV EMPLOY:** Dept. of HUD 1968-72, Eastman Kodak Co. 1960-68; **PROFL AFFIL & HONORS:** ULI, Council for Urban Econ. Devel.; **EDUC:** BS, 1957, Math Econ., Allegheny Coll.; **GRAD EDUC:** MS, 1958, MIT; **EDUC HONORS:** Phi Beta Kappa, Cum Laude; **MIL SERV:** USAF, 1st Lt.; **OTHER ACT & HONORS:** Pres. Rochester, NY Jaycees 1965-66, Rochester C of C Bd. of Tr.; **HOME ADD:** 1702 Putter Ln., Reston, VA 22090, (703)437-0368; **BUS ADD:** 1201 Connecticut Ave., Washington, DC 20036, (202)466-7680.

BOYLE, Marsilia A.——B: Sept. 18, 1948, Brooklyn, NY, *Dir. RE*, State of NY Metro. Trans. Auth., RE Dept.; **PRIM RE ACT:** Consultant, Engineer, Attorney, Appraiser, Architect, Developer, Regulator, Owner/Investor, Property Manager; **OTHER RE ACT:** mgmt. of all RE activities of MTA & its agencies including activities checked above; **PREV EMPLOY:** Dep. Commr. for Devel. NYC Dept. of Ports & Terminals; **EDUC:** BA, 1969, Soc. Sci., St. Joseph's Coll.; **GRAD EDUC:** M. of Public Admin., 1970, SUNY at Albany; **HOME ADD:** 114 Withers St., Brooklyn, NY 11211; **BUS ADD:** 347 Madison Ave., 10th Fl., NY, NY 10017, (212)878-7368.

BOYLE, Mary Ellen T., Esq.——B: Nov. 9, 1952, Paterson, NJ, Massachusetts Bay Transportation Authority, Dept. of RE Mgmt.; **PRIM RE ACT:** Broker, Attorney; **SERVICES:** Eminent Domain Acquisitions; **PREV EMPLOY:** Stavisky & Greeley (Authors of Volumes 33 and 34 MA Practice Series, Landlord and Tenant Law); **PROFL AFFIL & HONORS:** ABA, MA Bar Assn., Women's Bar Assn., Bar of US Ct. of Appeals for the First Circuit; Bar of US District Ct. for the Dist. of MA; **EDUC:** BA, 1973, Hist./Spanish, Seton Hall Univ.; **GRAD EDUC:** JD, 1978, New England School of Law; **EDUC HONORS:** Dean's List; Phi Alpha Theta Intl. Hist. Honor Soc., Phi Alpha Delta Law Frat.; **OTHER ACT & HONORS:** Notary Public for the Commonwealth of MA; Publication: Comment, US v. DiRusso: A Lack of Uniform Perception in the Imposition and Execution of a Sentence, 3 New England J. Prison Law, 589 (1977); Acknowledgment: 15, 15A, 16 MA Practice Series, Legal Bus. Forms (1979 Pocket Part); **HOME ADD:** 85 Grand View Ave., Quincy, MA 02170, (617)479-1581; **BUS ADD:** 50 High St., Room 501, Boston, MA 02110, (617)722-3428.

BOYLE, Richard J.——B: Dec. 4, 1943, New York, NY, *Sr. VP*, Chase Manhattan Bank NA; **PRIM RE ACT:** Banker; **EDUC:** BA, 1965, Sociology, Holy Cross Coll.; **GRAD EDUC:** MBA, 1969, Fin., NY Univ.; **MIL SERV:** US Army, Sgt., 1975; **HOME ADD:** 83 Druid Hill Rd., Summit, NJ 07901, (201)273-6897; **BUS ADD:** 1 Chase Manhattan Plaza, New York, NY 10081, (212)552-2502.

BOYLE, William H.——*VP for Corporate Planning & Devel.*, Department of Housing and Urban Development, Fed. Home Loan Mortgage Corp.; **PRIM RE ACT:** Lender; **BUS ADD:** 451 Seventh St., S.W., Washington, DC 20410, (202)789-4523.*

BOYLEN, Daniel B.——B: Dec. 12, 1941, Pittsburgh, PA, *Arch.*, Daniel B. Boylen, AIA; **PRIM RE ACT:** Architect; **SERVICES:** Arch., Planning; **REP CLIENTS:** State and local govts., corps. and gen. public; **PROFL AFFIL & HONORS:** AIA; Central Richmond Assn.; Rgnl. Purchasing Council of VA; Minority Imput Committe; **HOME ADD:** 60 Underwood Pl., NW, Washington, DC 20012, (202)882-4823; **BUS ADD:** 3805 Jefferson Davis Highway, Richmond, VA 23234, (804)743-7773.

BOYLES, Clarence A.——B: Nov. 11, 1927, Louisville, KY, *Owner*, Boyles Realty Co.; **PRIM RE ACT:** Broker, Consultant, Appraiser, Developer, Property Manager, Owner/Investor; **OTHER RE ACT:** Ct. approved receiver; **SERVICES:** Investment Sales, Prop. mgmt.; devel. Hud projects consultant-Eight million dollar estate; **REP CLIENTS:** Over 150 mgmt. contracts; **PREV EMPLOY:** Operated present bus. since 1953; **PROFL AFFIL & HONORS:** Louisville Bd. of Realtors, Natl. Assn. of Realtors, Past Pres. of IREM of Lou. Bd. of Realtors and IREM Chapt. No. 59, Named Realtor & Mgr. of the Yr. by respective organizations, Seventeen yrs. dir. Lou. Bd. of Realtors; **EDUC:** BS, 1950, Grp. work educ., George Williams Coll.; Chicago, IL; **MIL SERV:** USA, Cpl. 1946-47; **OTHER ACT & HONORS:** Member Louisville & Jeff Cty. Human Relations Commn., Member Manor's Advisory Commn. on Housing, Member of Cty. Judge's Task Force on Condo Conversion Legislation; **HOME ADD:** 410 Mockingbird Valley Rd., Louisville, KY 40207, (502)459-8146; **BUS ADD:** 1256 E. 3rd St. (MIA PO Box 3019), Louisville, KY 40201, (502)583-8896.

BOYLES, Lee E.——B: Apr. 5, 1939, Norristown, PA, *Pres.*, Wm. A. Emmerick, Inc.; **PRIM RE ACT:** Broker, Appraiser; **SERVICES:** Gen. RE brokerage and appraising; **PROFL AFFIL & HONORS:** Nat. Assn. Realtors; PA Realtors Assn.; N. PA Bd. of Realtors; Amer. Assn. of Cert. Appraisers, Realtor; **HOME ADD:** 135 Forty Foot Rd., Hatfield, PA 19440, (215)368-1318; **BUS ADD:** 30 E. Main St., Lansdale, PA 19446, (215)855-9950.

BOYLL, Guy Lee, II——B: Sept. 21, 1948, Meridian, MS, *Mgr.*, Highland Village Shopping Ctr. & Office Complex; **PRIM RE ACT:** Property Manager; **SERVICES:** Devel., prop. mgmt.; **PREV EMPLOY:** H.C. Bailey Co., Prop. Mgmt. 1971-1972; **PROFL AFFIL & HONORS:** ICSC; **EDUC:** BBA, 1971, Gen. Bus., Univ. of MS; **OTHER ACT & HONORS:** Jackson C of C, MS Econ. Council, Rotarian; **HOME ADD:** 301 Whipporwill Dr., Brandon, MS 39042, (601)992-9922; **BUS ADD:** Suite 281, 4500 I-55 No., Jackson, MS 39211, (601)982-5861.

BOYNS, Charles F., C.R.S., C.R.A.——B: June 29, 1917, Santa Cruz, CA, *Pres.*, Select Homes, Inc., Resid.; **PRIM RE ACT:** Broker, Appraiser, Instructor; **SERVICES:** Listing, mktg., appraising, managing, and counselling (residential); **REP CLIENTS:** Profl. - semi-profl. - executive; **PREV EMPLOY:** Investor - prop. restoration; **PROFL AFFIL & HONORS:** Natl. Assn. of Realtors - RENMI - Intl. Inst. of Valuers - NARA. Nat. Assn. of RE Educators, CRS - CRA - SIV - GRI - Cert. Rev. Appraiser; **EDUC:** A.S., 1937, Forestry, Modesto Jr. Coll.; **GRAD EDUC:** B.S., 1941, Forestry - Botany - Entomology, Univ. of CA - Berkeley, Cal. (also) French Natl. Forestry School - Nancy, France 1945-46; **EDUC HONORS:** Natl. School of Forests and Waters; **MIL SERV:** US Army, Capt., 8 decorations; **OTHER ACT & HONORS:** Kiwanis - Elks - Masons - Political Action Committees; **HOME ADD:** 7702 33rd Ave. N.E., Seattle, WA 98115, (206)525-6774; **BUS ADD:** 7509 35th Ave. N.E., Seattle, WA 98115, (206)524-1060.

BOYNTON, Robert A.——B: Oct. 3, 1944, Richmond, VA, *Project Mgr./Project Arch.*, Wiley & Wilson, Archs., Engrs. and Planners, Arch.; **PRIM RE ACT:** Architect, Consultant; **OTHER RE ACT:** Designer; **SERVICES:** Arch., Planning, Feasibility Studies; **REP CLIENTS:** Commonwealth Realty Dev. Corp., The Covington Co., Sea Pines; **PREV EMPLOY:** Self Employed 1973-1979 as Practicing Arch.;

PROFL AFFIL & HONORS: AIA (Nat., State Chap.); VA Assn. of Professions, Nat. Design Award for Housing Project given by NAHB; State AIA Award for same Housing Project; Distinctive Service Award from VAP; **EDUC:** BArch., 1969, VA Polytech. Inst.; **EDUC HONORS:** Dean's List & Dean's Student Council; **OTHER ACT & HONORS:** Bd. of Trustees for St. Michael's School; Pres.-Elect of Local Recreation Assn.; Past Pres. of Central VA Chapter, VA Assn. of Professions; James River Chapter AIA; Sec., VA Assn. of Professions; **HOME ADD:** 8905 Old Holly Rd., Richmond, VA 23235, (804)320-1911; **BUS ADD:** 6620 W. Broad St., Richmond, VA 23230, (804)282-5417.

BOYNTON, Wyman P.——B: Oct. 8, 1908, Portsmouth, NH, *Counsel*, Boynton, Waldron, Doleac & Woodman; **PRIM RE ACT:** Attorney; **SERVICES:** R.E. transfer and devel.; **REP CLIENTS:** All Portsmouth banks many title ins. cos.; **PREV EMPLOY:** Granite State Ins. Co.; **PROFL AFFIL & HONORS:** Rockingham Cty., NH Bar Assoc.; ABA, Soc. of Amer. Military Engrs.; NH & Natl. Assoc of Prof Engrs., Pres., Rockingham Cty. Bar Assn. 1967; PE; **EDUC:** SB, Engrg. Admin.;Civil Engrg., MIT; **GRAD EDUC:** LIB, Univ of MI; **MIL SERV:** USACE; Col.; Bronze Star; **OTHER ACT & HONORS:** NH House of Rep. 1933-34; Portsmouth City Council 1937-38; Rockingham Cty. Atty. 1948-51; VP Portsmouth Hist. Soc.; Soc. for Preserv. of N.E. Antiquities; Portsmouth Athenaeum, Pres., 1978-80; Rotary: Portsmouth C of C; **HOME ADD:** 668 Middle St., Portsmouth, NH 03801, (603)436-1309; **BUS ADD:** 70 Court St., Portsmouth, NH 03801, (603)436-4010.

BOYSON, Don E.——B: July 1, 1935, England, *VP, Appraisal*, Columbia S&L Assn.; **PRIM RE ACT:** Appraiser, Instructor; **SERVICES:** RE Appraisal; **PREV EMPLOY:** Pres Laramy Assoc. Inc., RE valuation and consultant co. (1968 to currently active); **PROFL AFFIL & HONORS:** SREA, AIREA, Nat. Assn. of Review Appraisers, SRA, SRPA, MAI, CRA, Lic. RE broker state of CO since 1968; **MIL SERV:** British Airborne, NCO; **OTHER ACT & HONORS:** Approved instr. SREA, Univ. of CO RE Ext. Course; Gov. Dist. 6, SREA, 1973-80; Intl. VP SREA, 1981; **HOME ADD:** 3450 E Geddes Dr., Littleton, CO 80122, (303)771-5913; **BUS ADD:** 2323 E Arapahoe Rd., Littleton, CO 80122, (303)795-3072.

BRACH, William L.——B: Dec. 21, 1924, E Orange, NJ, *Part.*, Brach, Eichler, Rosenberg, Silver, Bernstein & Hammer; **PRIM RE ACT:** Attorney; **SERVICES:** Land and prop. dev., residential, commercial, industrial, including legal, fin. and planning aspect; **REP CLIENTS:** James Felt & Co., Cali Assoc., Alan Sagner, Midtown S & L, Gebrow Hammer, Essex Cty. St. Bank, NJ Realty; **PREV EMPLOY:** Reg. Counsel HUD; **PROFL AFFIL & HONORS:** Essex Cty Bar, St. Bar Assn.; **EDUC:** BS, Chem. Eng, Cornell Univ.; **GRAD EDUC:** LOB, 1949, Cornell Law Sch.; **MIL SERV:** USN, ETM 2nd; **OTHER ACT & HONORS:** E Orange Governing Body, Exec. Dir. St. of NJ, Council of Urb. Affairs, Rotary Club, United Way, Newark Boys Club; **HOME ADD:** 191 S Mtn. Ave, Montclair, NJ 07042, (201)746-4585; **BUS ADD:** 101 Eisenhower Parkway, Roseland, NJ 07068, (201)228-5700.

BRACHFELD, Daniel——B: Mar. 24, 1929, NY, *Exec. VP*, Bellemead Development Corp.; **PRIM RE ACT:** Developer, Builder, Owner/Investor, Property Manager; **SERVICES:** Locate, purchase, plan, subdiv., const., mkt., manage surburban office & resid. props.; **PREV EMPLOY:** Simon Ent., Devel. of New Town, Reston, VA 1963-70; **PROFL AFFIL & HONORS:** Nat. Assn. of Indust./Office Parks; Indus. RE Brokers of NY; **EDUC:** AB, 1950, Liberal Arts, Columbia Coll., Columbia Univ.; **GRAD EDUC:** MBA, 1955, Harvard Grad. Bus. Sch.; **MIL SERV:** US Army, Lt., 1951-53; **HOME ADD:** 1411 Flagler Dr., Mamaroneck, NY 10543, (914)698-5522; **BUS ADD:** 210 Clay Acw., Lyndhurst, NJ 07071, (201)438-6880.

BRACKEN, Thomas R.J.——B: Jan. 1, 1950, Spokane, WA, *Pres.*, Fenix, Inc.; **PRIM RE ACT:** Consultant, Developer, Owner/Investor; **SERVICES:** Develop comml. RE for own acct. and for land-owner clients; annual volume - -12,000,000; **REP CLIENTS:** William Vieser, First City Investments, misc. others; **PREV EMPLOY:** VP, First City Investments (Comml. RE Devel.), 1978-1980; Various Titles, Prudential Ins. RE Inv. Dept., 1972-1978; **PROFL AFFIL & HONORS:** NAIOP, Chap. Officer; ICSC; **EDUC:** BS, 1971, Admin. Sciences, Yale Univ.; **GRAD EDUC:** MBA, 1972, Mktg./Corp. Relations, Columbia Univ.; **EDUC HONORS:** Departmental Honors; **OTHER ACT & HONORS:** Guest Lecturer at NYU, Wharton; **HOME ADD:** 4548 144th Ave. SE, Bellevue, WA 98006, (206)746-7897; **BUS ADD:** PO Box 2363, Kirkland, WA 98033, (206)881-9388.

BRADBURY, John E.——B: Mar. 16, 1940, Neillsville, WI, *Sr. VP RE*, B. Dalton Bookseller, Dayton Hudson Corp.; **OTHER RE ACT:** Retail leasing; **SERVICES:** Mkt. analysis and lease negotiation; **PROFL AFFIL & HONORS:** NRMA, NACORE, ICSC, ICSC Speakers Grp.; **EDUC:** BS, 1964, Bus., Univ. of MN; **MIL SERV:** USA; **HOME ADD:** 16272 S Temple Dr., Minnetonka, MN 55343, (612)933-0679; **BUS ADD:** 7505 Metro Blvd., Edina, MN 55435, (612)893-7207.

BRADFIELD, Gerald C.——B: Sept. 18, 1945, Tucson, AZ, *VP, Gen. Sales Mgr.*, Chester-Kappelman Group, Inc.; **PRIM RE ACT:** Broker, Appraiser, Instructor; **SERVICES:** Full Serv. RE Brokerage; **PREV EMPLOY:** 12 yrs. in Banking and S & L Indus.; **PROFL AFFIL & HONORS:** NAR, Wichita Area Bd. of Realtors, Wichita Area Builder's Assn., Pres. 1981 Indep. Brokers Assn.; **EDUC:** BS, 1967, Bus., Psych., Wichita State Univ.; **MIL SERV:** US Army, Sgt., Good Conduct; Meritorious Serv.; Nat. Defense Medal; **OTHER ACT & HONORS:** City Councilman, Andover, KS 1980-83; Chief Financial Officer, Andover, KS; Outstanding Young Man of Amer. 1976; Who's Who of Wichita 1980; **HOME ADD:** 226 Aaron Dr., Andover, KS 67002, (316)733-2965; **BUS ADD:** 144 N. Oliver, Wichita, KS 67208, (316)682-5581.

BRADFORD, Dalles H.——B: Jan. 19, 1941, Spanish Fork, UT, *Tax Partner*, Arthur Andersen & Co.; **OTHER RE ACT:** CPA; **SERVICES:** Tax and acctg.; **PROFL AFFIL & HONORS:** UT Assn. of CPAs, AICPA, Pres. UACPA, Bd. of Advisors, Inst. of Profl. Acctg., Brigham Young Univ., Nat. Advisory Council, Brigham Young Univ.; **EDUC:** BS, 1963, Acctg., Brigham Young Univ.; **EDUC HONORS:** Outstanding Sr. Acctg. Student; Haskins & Sells Foundation Award; **HOME ADD:** 889 South Davis Blvd., Bountiful, UT 84010, (801)292-8097; **BUS ADD:** 36 South State, Suite 1600, Salt Lake City, UT 84111, (801)533-0820.

BRADLEY, David M.——B: Dec. 13, 1935, NY, NY, *Pres.*, Robert J. Bradley Assoc.; **PRIM RE ACT:** Consultant, Appraiser; **PROFL AFFIL & HONORS:** Member AIREA, SREA, MAI, SRPA; **EDUC:** BS, 1958, Engrg., MIT, Cambridge, MA; **GRAD EDUC:** MBA, 1967, Fin., Adelphi Univ., Garden City, NY; **HOME ADD:** 30 Dickerson Ave., Bayville, NY 11709, (516)628-1673; **BUS ADD:** 85 Forest Ave., Locust Valley, NY 11560, (516)671-1424.

BRADLEY, Jeffrey——*Exec. VP Fin. & Adm.*, Scott & Fetzer Co.; **PRIM RE ACT:** Property Manager; **BUS ADD:** 14600 Detroit Ave., Lakewood, OH 44107, (216)228-6200.*

BRADLEY, Penny——B: Feb. 18, 1940, L.A., CA, *Pres.*, Bradley-McCarter, Ltd.; **PRIM RE ACT:** Broker; **PREV EMPLOY:** Associated with Earl Thacker, Realty for 4 yrs.; **PROFL AFFIL & HONORS:** Member, CCIM; Pres. of Bradley-McCarter, Ltd., GRI Instr., Dir. of Repac; Dir. Honolulu Bd. of Realtors; Member of Honolulu Bd. of Realtors Audit Comm. and Treas., Honolulu Bd. of Realtors, CCIM; **HOME ADD:** 4473 Aukai Ave., Honolulu, HI 96821, (808)735-3435; **BUS ADD:** 733 Bishop St. 1915, Honolulu, HI 96813, (808)523-0456.

BRADLEY, Robert D.——B: Mar. 16, 1935, Boston, MA, *Arch.*, Robert D. Bradley, Architect; **PRIM RE ACT:** Architect, Consultant, Developer; **SERVICES:** Arch., planning, engrg.; **PREV EMPLOY:** DRA East Inc., 40 William St., Wellesley, MA; **PROFL AFFIL & HONORS:** NCARB; **EDUC:** BA, 1958, Arch., William & Mary; **GRAD EDUC:** B/Arch, M/Arch, 1966, Arch., Harvard Univ.; **MIL SERV:** USA, Capt.; **HOME ADD:** 15 Rockville Ave., Lexington, MA 02173, (617)862-4630; **BUS ADD:** 15 Rockville Ave., Lexington, MA 02173, (617)862-4630.

BRADSHAW, Eugene B.——*Secy. & Gen. Counsel*, Goulds Pumps, Inc.; **PRIM RE ACT:** Attorney, Property Manager; **BUS ADD:** 250 Fall St., Seneca Falls, NY 13148, (315)568-2811.*

BRADSHAW, Jerry——B: Feb. 1, 1935, Curry Cty., Clovis, NM, *Pres./VP*, Investors Exchange, Realtors/Tara Land Co.; **PRIM RE ACT:** Broker, Instructor, Consultant, Developer; **PROFL AFFIL & HONORS:** TX Assn. of Realtors; FLI, CCIM; Exchanger of Yr./TX - 1977; Exchanger of Yr - 1979; VP & Pres., TX Prop. Exchangers; Regional VP FLI; GRI; CRS; **EDUC:** 1963, Farwell, TX; **HOME ADD:** 213 Zoar Ave., Lubbock, TX 79407, (806)795-7012; **BUS ADD:** 308 York Ave., Lubbock, TX 79407, (806)797-3314.

BRADSHAW, Thomas W., Jr.——B: Oct. 22, 1938, Alamanac Cty., NC, *Pres.*, Tom Bradshaw & Associates; **PRIM RE ACT:** Broker, Consultant, Developer, Builder, Property Manager; **SERVICES:** Comml. & indus. RE sales, consultants; **PREV EMPLOY:** Cameron Brown Co., Mort. Banking, 5yrs., North Hills Inc. RE Devel., Shopping Ctr. Devel. 12 yrs.; **PROFL AFFIL & HONORS:** Hon. Member Raleigh Bd. of Realtors; **EDUC:** Realtors Inst., Univ. of NC; **GRAD EDUC:** Exec. Prog., 1978, Bus., Econ., Univ. of NC; **MIL SERV:** US Army, Capt.; **OTHER ACT & HONORS:** Mayor, Councilman, City of Raleigh, 1969-73; Secy N.C. Department of Transportation 77-81; **HOME ADD:** 7416 Grist Mill Rd., Raleigh, NC 27609, (919)847-1459;

BUS ADD: PO Box 19112, Raleigh, NC 27619, (919)467-0200.

BRADSHAW, William——*Secy.*, Westmoreland Coal Co.; **PRIM RE ACT:** Property Manager; **BUS ADD:** 2500 Fidelity Bldg., Philadelphia, PA 19109, (215)545-2500.*

BRADSHAW, William D.——**B:** May 24, 1933, Baltimore, MD, *Sr. VP & Dir.*, R.M. Bradley & Co., Inc., Indus. Div.; **PRIM RE ACT:** Broker, Consultant; **OTHER RE ACT:** Principal; **PROFL AFFIL & HONORS:** Nat. Assn. of Indus. & Office Parks, Greater Boston RE Bd. & Exec. Club of the Greater Boston C of C; **EDUC:** BA, 1955, Yale Univ.; **HOME ADD:** 780 Boylston St., Boston, MA 02199, (617)267-1499; **BUS ADD:** 250 Boylston St., Boston, MA 02116, (617)421-0711.

BRADTKE, Philip J.——**B:** Aug. 13, 1934, Chicago, IL, *VP*, Charles Kober Assoc.; **PRIM RE ACT:** Architect; **SERVICES:** Full Arch. Serv.; **PREV EMPLOY:** VP, A.M. Kinney Assoc., Inc., 1964 - 1979; Project Arch., Belli and Belli, Arch. and Engrs., 1957 - 1964; **PROFL AFFIL & HONORS:** Corp. Member AIA; Chmn., Hon. Awards Comm., Chicago Chapt., AIA, 1973; Treas., Chicago Chapt., AIA, 1976, 1973 Distinguished Bldg. Award, Chicago Chapt., AIA; 1968 Distinguished Bldg. Award, Chicago Chapt., AIA; **EDUC:** BArch., 1956, Coll. of Engrg., Univ. of Notre Dame; **EDUC HONORS:** Cum Laude, 1st Prize - 1956 Church Prop. & Admin. Arch. Comp.; Hon. Mention - 1955 Beaux Arts Inst. of Design, Design Comp.; **OTHER ACT & HONORS:** Bldg. Commnr. - Village of Glenview (1981); Pres. - Glenview Tennis Club, 1980; Lecturer - Univ. of Notre Dame, 1975; 'Who's Who in Midwest' (1975 -); Design Awards - 1956 and 1959 Indianapolis Home Show; **HOME ADD:** 1040 Queens Lane, Glenview, IL 60025, (312)724-0317; **BUS ADD:** 230 W. Monroe St., Chicago, IL 60606, (312)236-6751.

BRADY, Gary——*Sec.*, Lincoln Developers, Inc.; **PRIM RE ACT:** Developer, Builder, Owner/Investor, Property Manager; **BUS ADD:** 280 SW 12 Ave., Deerfield Beach, FL 33441, (305)426-1700.

BRADY, George M., Jr.——**B:** Aug. 6, 1922, Baltimore, MD, *Pres. and Chief Exec. Officer*, Nat. Corp. for Housing Partnerships; **PRIM RE ACT:** Developer, Builder, Property Manager, Syndicator; **PREV EMPLOY:** Sr. VP, The Rouse Co., Chmn. of the Bd., Rouse-Wates; **PROFL AFFIL & HONORS:** Dir., The Rouse Co., Mort. Bankers Assn., ULI, Lambda Alpha, Nat. Assn. of Home Builders; **EDUC:** BA, 1947, Liberal Arts, Johns Hopkins Univ.; **GRAD EDUC:** JD, 1949, Law, Univ. of MD; **OTHER ACT & HONORS:** Chevy Chase Club, Metropolitan Club, Knights of Malta; Member, State Planning Comm., State of MD; **HOME ADD:** 29 Quincy St., Chevy Chase, MD 20015, (301)656-0528; **BUS ADD:** 1133 Fifteenth St., NW, Washington, DC 20005, (202)857-5700.

BRADY, Paul M.——**B:** May 12, 1924, Randolph, MA, *Sr. VP, Dir. of RE Investments*, First TX Savings Assn. of Dallas, RE; **PRIM RE ACT:** Consultant, Banker, Developer, Lender, Owner/Investor, Instructor, Property Manager, Real Estate Publisher; **SERVICES:** Fin. feasibility, income type props.; **PREV EMPLOY:** RE Consultant; Pres., Gananda Dev. Corp.; VP, MGIC Financial Corp.; Asst. Dir., RE, Nat. Life Insurance Co. of VT; **PROFL AFFIL & HONORS:** Contributor, RE Review; **EDUC:** 1950, For. Serv., Georgetown Univ., School of For. Serv.; **GRAD EDUC:** MBA, 1951, Bus. Admin./Fin., Univ. of MD; **MIL SERV:** USAF, Capt., Air Medal w/5 OLC, Pres. Unit Citation; **HOME ADD:** 7801 Kilbride Ln., Dallas, TX 75248, (214)387-2567; **BUS ADD:** 14951 Dallas N. Pkwy., Dallas, TX 75240, (214)960-4675.

BRADY, Philip H., Jr.——**B:** Dec. 17, 1938, New York, NY, *Sr. VP, RE*, Home Owners Fed. S&L Assn.; **PRIM RE ACT:** Banker, Developer, Lender, Owner/Investor; **OTHER RE ACT:** Condo. conversions; **SERVICES:** Equity financing & joint ventures, RE venture capital; **REP CLIENTS:** Builder, Developers, Investors; **PREV EMPLOY:** VP, FL Gulf Realty Trust; VP Morts. Loeb, Rhoades & Co., Inc.; VP & Dir. F.S. Smithers & Co., Inc. Investment Bankers; **PROFL AFFIL & HONORS:** Formers Trustee Dime Savings Bank Of Williamsburgh, SRA; **EDUC:** Mathematics; **MIL SERV:** USMC Res.; **OTHER ACT & HONORS:** Dir., RE Metro., Trans, Authority of the State of NY 1977-1980; **HOME ADD:** 365 King Caesar Rd., Duxbury, MA; **BUS ADD:** 21 Milk St., Boston, MA 02109, (617)482-0630.

BRAINERD, Bud——**B:** May 7, 1954, St. Louis, MO, *Pres.*, ReVest International Inc. of Belleville; **PRIM RE ACT:** Broker, Consultant, Owner/Investor, Instructor, Syndicator; **SERVICES:** Investment counseling, leasing, exchanges, sales, management; **REP CLIENTS:** Indiv. and instit. investors in Comm. and Investment RE; **PREV EMPLOY:** Acctg. with tax and cost accounting emphasis; **PROFL AFFIL & HONORS:** NAR, IL Assn. of Realtors, ReVist Intl., RESSI, Reg. Dir. - ReVest Intl.; **EDUC:** Acctg., So. IL Univ. - Edwardsville; **MIL SERV:** USN, E-3; **HOME ADD:** 7418 Foley Dr., Belleville, IL 62223, (618)397-5879; **BUS ADD:** 8205 West Main St., Belleville, IL 62223, (618)397-8104.

BRAITHWAITE, James C.——**B:** Apr. 16, 1940, Westport, CT, *Pres.*, Kan Am Realty, Inc.; **PRIM RE ACT:** Developer, Property Manager; **SERVICES:** Our group participates in joint ventures/devel. of comml. (office bldgs., shopping ctrs. and hotels) in major metropolitan cities; **REP CLIENTS:** We are affiliates with Kan Am Grundbesitz, GmbH of Munich, West Germany; **PREV EMPLOY:** Exec. VP, Glasmacher & Co., VP, Aetna Diversified Props.; **PROFL AFFIL & HONORS:** ULI, Intl. Council of Shopping Ctrs.; **EDUC:** BS in Econ., 1962, Mktg., Villanova Univ., Villanova, PA; **GRAD EDUC:** MBA, 1964, Mktg., NY Univ.; **EDUC HONORS:** Dean's List, Who's Who in Amer. Coll. and Univ.; **HOME ADD:** 437 Valley Rd., Atlanta, GA 30305, (404)233-8070; **BUS ADD:** Suite 290, 1810 Water Place, Atlanta, GA 30339, (404)955-6756.

BRAKE, R.F.——*Dir. Land Acquisition*, Chesapeake Corp. of Virginia; **PRIM RE ACT:** Property Manager; **BUS ADD:** PO Box 31, West Point, VA 23181, (804)843-5000.*

BRAMAN, Edwin C.——**B:** Mar. 12, 1922, Minneapolis, MN, *VP*, Resource Mgmt. Corp.; **PRIM RE ACT:** Broker, Consultant, Property Manager; **SERVICES:** Corp. RE advisory; **PREV EMPLOY:** VP, Dain Bosworth Inc., 1961-1980; Pres., Lease Consultant Div., Dain Bosworth Inc., 1975-1980; Pres., Dain Realty, 1973-1975; Territorial RE, Sears Roebuck & Co., 1948-1961; **PROFL AFFIL & HONORS:** BOMA; **EDUC:** BA, 1943, Bus./Advtg., Univ. of MN; **GRAD EDUC:** MA, 1951, Bus./Journalism, Univ. of MN; 1965, Investment Bankers Assoc., Wharton School of Fin.; **EDUC HONORS:** Cum Laude; **MIL SERV:** USN; Lt.; **OTHER ACT & HONORS:** Dir., MN Press Club; **HOME ADD:** 2218 Sargent Ave., St. Paul, MN 55105, (612)699-1633; **BUS ADD:** 1300 First Bank Pl. W., MinneapoLis, MN 55402, (612)338-7881.

BRAMBERG, R. William, Jr.——**B:** Aug. 28, 1935, IL, *Pres.*, The Bramberg Management Organization, Inc.; **PRIM RE ACT:** Broker, Consultant, Developer, Property Manager, Owner/Investor, Instructor, Syndicator; **SERVICES:** Brokerage (realty & mort.), consultants, prop. analysis & mgmt.; **REP CLIENTS:** 1st WI Mort. Trust, Barnett Winston REIT, Chase Manhattan, US Home, Urban Investment & Devel. etc.; **PREV EMPLOY:** US Home Corp., Urban Investment, Draper & Kramer, Inc., RE Research Corp., R.W. Bramberg & Co.; **PROFL AFFIL & HONORS:** NAR, IREM, Member IREM Found., Governing Councilor of IREM; **EDUC:** BA, 1957, psych., soc., Trinity Coll., Duke Univ.; **EDUC HONORS:** Univ. Marshal; **MIL SERV:** US Army, MSgt.; **OTHER ACT & HONORS:** Dir., Nat. Inst. of Bldg. Sciences (appointed by the Pres., approved by the US Senate reappointed 1983), Member, Pres. Roundtable Eckerd Coll.; **HOME ADD:** 2772 Westchester Dr. N., Clearwater, FL 33519, (813)796-3073; **BUS ADD:** 3590 US Hwy. 19 Box 3371, Holiday, FL 33590, (813)938-5555.

BRAME, Frank A., III——**B:** July 17, 1932, Greenville, TX, *Officer, Dir., Shareholder, Sr. Atty.*, Cohen Brame & Smith P.C.; **PRIM RE ACT:** Attorney; **SERVICES:** Tax advise for RE transactions; **PROFL AFFIL & HONORS:** CO & Amer. Bar Assns., Past Chmn., taxation sec., CO Bar Assn., Past Pres. Greater Denver Tax Counsels Assn., Past Chmn. Tax Lawyers, IRS Liaison Comm. SW Rgn.; **EDUC:** BS, 1954, US Naval Acad.; **GRAD EDUC:** JD, 1967, Univ. of CO; LLM, 1970, Tax, NYU; MBA, 1976, Univ. of CO; **EDUC HONORS:** with distinction, Bd. of Editors, Law Review; **MIL SERV:** USNR-R, Capt.; **HOME ADD:** 5329 Morning Glory Ln., Littleton, CO 80123, (303)795-2230; **BUS ADD:** 1660 Lincoln St. 1518, Denver, CO 80264, (303)837-8800.

BRAMLAGE, Paul S.——**B:** Oct. 2, 1952, Kansas City, KS, *VP*, B & M Sales; **PRIM RE ACT:** Appraiser; **OTHER RE ACT:** Sales, Investor, Beer Wholesaler; **SERVICES:** Investment counseling, investor; **PROFL AFFIL & HONORS:** KS Beer Wholesalers Assn.; KS Alumni Boy Scout Commnrs.; Assn. of the U.S. Army; Amer. Legion; Kiwanis; **EDUC:** BA, 1976, Bus., KS Univ.; **MIL SERV:** US Army, E-5, Sgt., 1970-1972; **OTHER ACT & HONORS:** Bd. of Dir., Turner State Bank, KCK's; **HOME ADD:** 408 N. 6th, Leavenworth, KS 66048; **BUS ADD:** 1119 Osage, Leavenworth, KS 66048, (913)682-7144.

BRAMMER, William——*Treasurer*, Bassett Furniture Industries, Inc.; **PRIM RE ACT:** Property Manager; **BUS ADD:** Box 626, Bassett, VA 24055, (703)629-7511.*

BRAMOS, Daniel D.——**B:** Dec. 28, 1947, Detroit, MI, *VP*, Amurcon Corp. of VA; **PRIM RE ACT:** Developer, Builder, Property Manager; **OTHER RE ACT:** Mgmt.; **PROFL AFFIL & HONORS:** IREM, CPM; **EDUC:** BA, 1970, Educ. - Pol. Sci., Univ. of MI; **OTHER ACT**

& HONORS: Also associated with Blakeway Management Co.; **HOME ADD:** 1816 Wren's Nest Rd., Richmond, VA 23232, (804)320-2166; **BUS ADD:** 11 S 12th St., Richmond, VA 23219, (804)644-1086.

BRAMWELL, H. Rich——**B:** Aug. 10, 1927, Ogden, UT, *Pres.*, H. Rich Bramwell Co., Inc.; **PRIM RE ACT:** Consultant, Appraiser; **SERVICES:** Investment and Development Consultation, Comml., Indus. & Devel. Appraisals; **PROFL AFFIL & HONORS:** Amer. Inst. of RE Appraisers, MAI; **EDUC:** BS, 1949, Bus. Admin., Uviv. of CA, Berkeley; **GRAD EDUC:** Cert. of RE, 1959, Univ. of CA; **OTHER ACT & HONORS:** Chmn., Bd. of Zoning Adjustment, San Joaquin Cty.; **HOME ADD:** 2238 Sheridan Way, Stockton, CA 95207, (209)957-9135; **BUS ADD:** 1350 W. Robinhood Dr., Suite 7, Stockton, CA 95207, (209)478-5422.

BRANAN, Brock H.——**B:** July 29, 1937, Evanston, IL, *VP*, Branan & Bailey, Inc.; **PRIM RE ACT:** Consultant, Appraiser; **SERVICES:** RE appraisers, Consultants, Feasibility Analysis; **REP CLIENTS:** Builders and Devels., Lending Instns., Govt. Agencies, Attys.; **PREV EMPLOY:** Appraisal and Comml. Loan Dept. Mgr., Amfac Mort., First Bank Mort. (OR Div.); **PROFL AFFIL & HONORS:** Member of the AIREA; MAI; Valuation Network; C of C, Outstanding Chamber Member of Year 1981, Beaverton Area; **EDUC:** BS, 1964, RE, San Jose State Univ.; **MIL SERV:** US Army Airborne; **OTHER ACT & HONORS:** Former Scoutmaster, Homeowner Assn. Pres.; Chmn. Mayors Citizen's Comm.; **BUS ADD:** The Carriage House, #100; 1331 SW Broadway, Portland, OR 97201, (503)222-2505.

BRANCO, James——**B:** Mar 14, 1951, Santa Maria, AZ, *Pres.*, Professional Condo Conversions; **PRIM RE ACT:** Appraiser, Lender, Owner/Investor; **SERVICES:** Synd. of comml. prop., consultant, ins.; **REP CLIENTS:** Indiv. & public investors; **PREV EMPLOY:** Investor; Realtor; Insuror; **PROFL AFFIL & HONORS:** NJ Realtors, Ind. Ins. Agents Assn.; **EDUC:** BA, 1977, Bus., Brandywine Coll.; **HOME ADD:** 607 Boston Blvd., Sea Girt, NJ 08750; **BUS ADD:** PO Box 396, 800 Rt. 71, Sea Girt, NJ 08750, (201)449-6520.

BRAND, Leon——**B:** Sept. 14, 1933, NY, *VP; Asn. Mgr.*, Perkins & Will Architects, Engrs., Planners, Eastern Region, NY Office; **PRIM RE ACT:** Architect, Consultant, Developer, Builder; **SERVICES:** Feasibility studies, econ. evaluation, master planning, Arch. & Engr.; **REP CLIENTS:** Devels., Banks, Ins. Cos., Hospitals, Hotels, Schools, Univ., Mfg. Cos.; **PREV EMPLOY:** Frost Assoc. Brand & Moore Assoc. Rentar Dev. Corp. Con Edison; **PROFL AFFIL & HONORS:** AIA, NYSAIA, Bard Award, Brooklyn Chap. AIA Award; **EDUC:** BArch, 1955, Pratt Inst.; 1956-57 Scuola Superiore Dell Architettura, Rome IT; **EDUC HONORS:** Cum Laude, Fulbright Scholar in Arch. to Italy; **OTHER ACT & HONORS:** Chmn. Comm. Bd. Forest Hills - Rego Park, NY; City Club of NY; **BUS ADD:** 800 2nd Ave., New York, NY 10017, (212)286-9750.

BRAND, W. Calvert——*Dpty Asst. Secy.*, Department of Housing and Urban Development, Policy & Budget; **PRIM RE ACT:** Lender; **BUS ADD:** 451 Seventh St., S.W., Washington, DC 20410, (202)755-6504.*

BRANDELL, David A.——**B:** Feb. 11, 1950, Minneapolis, MN, *Atty. at Law*; **PRIM RE ACT:** Broker; **SERVICES:** Legal representation in resid. trans., condo conversions; **REP CLIENTS:** Homeowners, small investors & large comml. investors, limited parts., and conversion project; **PREV EMPLOY:** RE Salesman; **PROFL AFFIL & HONORS:** MN Bar Assoc., RE Sect.; ABA, RE Sect., Qualified atty. for FHA submissions; **EDUC:** BA, 1972, Pre-Law, St. Olaf Coll.; **GRAD EDUC:** JD, 1976, RE & Estate Planning, William Mitchell Coll. of Law; **HOME ADD:** 1752 Hickory Hill, Eagan, MN 55122, (612)452-2918; **BUS ADD:** 10901 Red Cir. Dr., Suite 357, Minnetonka, MN 55343, (612)933-2406.

BRANDT, Raymond A.——**B:** Mar. 15, 1930, Chicago, IL, *Sr. Staff Appraiser*, Bell Fed. S&L Assn.; **PRIM RE ACT:** Appraiser; **SERVICES:** Resid. Appraisal Chicago Metr. Area; **PROFL AFFIL & HONORS:** Soc. of RE Appraisers, SRA; **EDUC:** Univ. of IL, 2 yrs.; **MIL SERV:** USAF, 1st. Lt., 1953-1956; **OTHER ACT & HONORS:** Zoning Bd. of Appeals, Elk Grove 8 yrs., K of C; **HOME ADD:** 1368 Cumberland Circle W, Elk Grove, IL 60007, (312)437-0152; **BUS ADD:** 79 W. Monroe St., Chicago, IL 60603, (312)346-1000.

BRANDZEL, Gene B.——**B:** Mar. 30, 1937, Chicago, IL, *Pres.*, Jones Grey & Bayley, P.S.; **PRIM RE ACT:** Attorney; **PROFL AFFIL & HONORS:** Wash. State Bar Assn., Amer. Land Devel. Assn.; **EDUC:** BBA, 1958, Bus., School of Bus. Admin. Univ. of MI; **GRAD EDUC:** JD, 1961, Univ. of Chicago; **HOME ADD:** 4416 50th NE, Seattle, WA 98105, (206)524-2115; **BUS ADD:** 36th Floor, 1 Union Sq., 6th & Univ., Seattle, WA 98101, (206)624-0900.

BRANNAN, Hugh——*Dir. RE Operations*, Dana Corp.; **PRIM RE ACT:** Property Manager; **BUS ADD:** 4500 Dorr St., PO Box 1000, Toledo, OH 43697, (419)535-4500.*

BRANNEN, Sam L.——**B:** Jan. 18, 1941, Bulloch Cty., GA, *Partner*, Johnston & Brannen; **PRIM RE ACT:** Attorney; **SERVICES:** Full RE, purchaser, borrower, lender, devel.; **REP CLIENTS:** 1st Bulloch Bank & Trust, 1st Fed. S&L Assn., Statesboro; **PREV EMPLOY:** Hansell, Post, Brandon & Dorsey, Attys. - Atlanta, GA, to 1966; Johnston & Brannen, Attys., 1966 to present; **PROFL AFFIL & HONORS:** GA Bar Assn.; ABA; **EDUC:** 1963, Pol. Sci., Emory Univ.; **GRAD EDUC:** LLD, 1966, Emory Univ. Lamar School of Law; **MIL SERV:** US Army, Capt., 1966-1971; **OTHER ACT & HONORS:** Solicitor of State Ct., 1968-1976; **HOME ADD:** Rt. #5, Statesboro, GA 30458, (912)764-4850; **BUS ADD:** Box 905, 23 Courtland St., Statesboro, GA 30458, (412)489-8621.

BRANSON, James E., Jr.——**B:** June 17, 1941, Marfa,TX, *Pres.*, Branson & Co., Inc.; **PRIM RE ACT:** Broker, Syndicator, Developer, Owner/Investor; **OTHER RE ACT:** Condo Conversions; **PROFL AFFIL & HONORS:** RESSI, CCIM, SRS; **EDUC:** BBA, 1964, Econ., Univ. of TX, at El Paso; **MIL SERV:** USA, SD-4; **HOME ADD:** 5100 Yucca Pl., El Paso, TX 79932, (915)584-4600; **BUS ADD:** 6006 N. Mesa, El Paso, TX 79912, (915)581-5499.

BRANSON, Robert E.——**B:** Aug. 12, 1919, Wichita, KS, *Pres. & Gen. Mgr.*, Branson & Associates, Inc.; **PRIM RE ACT:** Broker, Consultant, Builder, Property Manager; **SERVICES:** Comml. sales & leasing; prop. mgmt.; const. & remodeling (apts., offices, strip centers, warehouses, mini-storage); **PREV EMPLOY:** Gen. Contractor since 1953; **PROFL AFFIL & HONORS:** NAR, IREM, CPM; **EDUC:** BBA, 1941, Acctg., Univ. of Wichita (Now Wichita State Univ.); **EDUC HONORS:** Magna Cum Laude; **MIL SERV:** Anti-Aircraft, 1943-46, M/Sgt.; **HOME ADD:** 2040 Garland, Wichita, KS 67203, (316)264-8884; **BUS ADD:** 435 N. Broadway, Wichita, KS 67202, (316)267-4357.

BRANT, Debarah Staaey——**B:** Sept. 20, 1954, Wash., DC, *VP*, Grant Dev. Co., Inc.; **PRIM RE ACT:** Developer, Builder, Property Manager, Owner/Investor; **OTHER RE ACT:** Gen. Contractor; **PROFL AFFIL & HONORS:** Nat. Assn. of Women in Const., NAHB, Multi-Housing Assn.; **EDUC:** BA, 1976, Bus. Admin., Univ. of AL - Tuscaloosa; **OTHER ACT & HONORS:** MENSA; **HOME ADD:** 1929 East Avalon Dr., Phoenix, AZ 85016, (602)266-2581; **BUS ADD:** 4131 N 24th St., Suite 223, Phoenix, AZ 85016.

BRANTNER, Edward S., Jr.——**B:** Nov. 26, 1912, Indianapolis, IN, *Owner*, Brantner Agency; **PRIM RE ACT:** Broker, Consultant, Appraiser, Developer, Property Manager; **SERVICES:** Full line RE and ins.; **REP CLIENTS:** Comml. and indus. investors; **PREV EMPLOY:** Mgr., Nat. Life and Accident Ins. co. 1934-39; **PROFL AFFIL & HONORS:** NAR; SIR; RNMI, SIR First Named VP NAR, 1965-66 State President, NAR 1963 Realtor of Year State 1965 Intl. Dir. 64-84 Intnl. RE Fed.; **OTHER ACT & HONORS:** BPOE, Webb Lodge-Masons, Scottish Rite, Murat Shrine, Tarum Shrine Club-Past Pres. St. Paul Episcopal Past Vestryman, Noon Optimist Club Charter Member; **HOME ADD:** 125 Garwood Rd., Richmond, IN 47374, (317)962-5784; **BUS ADD:** 4511 East Main St., P.O. Box 37, Richmond, IN 47374, (317)962-5576.

BRASLER, Robert M.——**B:** Aug. 19, 1936, Philadelphia, PA, *Sr. VP - Partner*, Binswanger Co.; **PRIM RE ACT:** Broker, Consultant, Appraiser; **SERVICES:** Natl. Brokerage Comml. - Indust. - Investment Prop.; **REP CLIENTS:** Alco Standard; Campbell Soup; Hooker Chem. G. M. Midland Ross; Firestone; Goodyear; Pennwalt; Exide; Zurn Budd; **PROFL AFFIL & HONORS:** Soc. of Indust. Realtos NAR; NCUED, SIR; Past Pres., Comml. & Indus. Div., Philadelphia Bd. of Realtors; Past Pres., Philadelphia Chap., Soc. of Indus. Realtors; Former Chmn., Bd. of Dirs. & Past Pres., Mantua Indus. Devel. Corp.; Former Member Bd. of Dir., Exec. Comm., Philadephia Housing Devel. Corp.; **EDUC:** BA, 1958, Econ., Dickinson Coll.; **MIL SERV:** USMC; Air Res.; **OTHER ACT & HONORS:** Philadeplhia Sch. Dist.-nominating Panel 1976-1980; Dickinson Coll. Trustee/Chmn. Bd. of Advisors; **HOME ADD:** 4122 Apalogen Rd., Philadelphia, PA 19144, (215)848-4468; **BUS ADD:** 1845 Walnut St., Philadelphia, PA 19103, (215)448-6000.

BRATEMAN, Ron (Rocco)——*Pres.*, The Brateman Corp.; **PRIM RE ACT:** Consultant; **SERVICES:** Market Analysis, Site Selection, Lease/Purchase Negotiations; **REP CLIENTS:** Retail; **PREV EMPLOY:** Regional RE Mgr., The Gap Stores, Inc.; **EDUC:** BS, 1964, Social Studies/Bus.; **HOME ADD:** 111 Buena Vista Ave. E, San Francisco, CA 94117, (415)821-6221; **BUS ADD:** 1632 Union St., San Francisco, CA 94123, (415)928-1500.

BRAUER, Carl A., Jr.——B: Dec. 3, 1923, Ann Arbor, MI, *Owner*, Carl A. Brauer, Jr., Realtor; **PRIM RE ACT:** Broker, Developer, Owner/Investor, Property Manager; **PREV EMPLOY:** Engr. Lt., USNR; **PROFL AFFIL & HONORS:** Ann Arbor Bd. of Realtors, MI Assn. Realtors, NAR, SIR, SIR; **EDUC:** BEE, 1945, Univ. of MI; **MIL SERV:** USNR, Lt.; **OTHER ACT & HONORS:** Ann Arbor City Council, 1956-57; **HOME ADD:** 2686 Salisbury Ln., Ann Arbor, MI 48103, (313)761-1928; **BUS ADD:** 240 City Ctr. Bldg., Ann Arbor, MI 48104, (313)769-6407.

BRAUN, Franz R.——B: Oct. 14, 1926, Olewig, Germany, *Pres.; Exec. Dir. & Fin. Planner*, Hemisphere Mtge. Co.; Hemisphere Equity Realty; **PRIM RE ACT:** Broker, Consultant, Appraiser, Developer, Lender; **SERVICES:** All above for owner/devel. & synd. investors appraisals; **REP CLIENTS:** Key Largo Investors Inc. - Tamarind Bay Ltd.; **PREV EMPLOY:** Continental Mort. Investors, First WI Nat. Bank, First WI Mort. Co., Mort. Assoc., Skogman Construction Co., Midwest Investment Co.; **PROFL AFFIL & HONORS:** Intl. Org. REA, Fee Appraiser, SRA, CAS, CRA, CMU, SCV, RECP, ICA; **MIL SERV:** USN, WWII MM3, European & Pacific Theatres; **OTHER ACT & HONORS:** Commnr. City of Waterloo, IA 1950-1953, Jr. C of C Pres. Waterloo, IA 1950; **HOME ADD:** 177 Ocean Ln. Dr., Key Biscayne, FL 33149, (305)361-7570; **BUS ADD:** 10450 N. Overseas Hwy., Key Largo, FL 33037, (305)245-6253.

BRAUN, Gregory L.——B: Dec. 30, 1947, Charles City, IA, *VP RE*, Greeley National Bank; **PRIM RE ACT:** Banker, Lender; **SERVICES:** Const. loans, VA, FHA, Conventional homeloans; **PREV EMPLOY:** Piedmont Mort., Loveland, CO; **PROFL AFFIL & HONORS:** Northern CO Homebuilder, MBA; **EDUC:** BA, 1972, Bus. Mgmt., None listed; **GRAD EDUC:** Mort. Bankers Course, 1972, Univ. of MD; **OTHER ACT & HONORS:** Bd. of Jr. Achiev., Bd. of Optimists, Elks, Moose Lodge; **HOME ADD:** 2328 20th Rd., Greeley, CO 80631, (303)330-6461; **BUS ADD:** PO Box 1098, Greeley, CO 80632, (303)356-1234.

BRAUN, Steven A.——B: July 7, 1941, Philadelphia, PA, *Partner, CPA*, Alexander Grant & Co.; **OTHER RE ACT:** CPA, Tax Specialist; **SERVICES:** tax advice; acctg. services; forecasts; **REP CLIENTS:** Devel., Synds.; **PROFL AFFIL & HONORS:** AICPA, PICPA, CPA; **EDUC:** BS, 1963, Fin./Econ., PA State Univ.; **HOME ADD:** 1569 Hagys Ford Rd., Narberth, PA 19072, (215)667-2146; **BUS ADD:** 2000 Market St., Philadelphia, PA 19103, (215)561-4200.

BRAVERMAN, Merrill A.——B: Apr. 23, 1929, Bayonne, NJ, *Pres.*, Braverman Realty Interests; **PRIM RE ACT:** Syndicator, Developer, Builder, Owner/Investor; **EDUC:** BA, 1951, Bus. Admin., Syracuse Univ.; **GRAD EDUC:** MBA, 1955, Wharton School; **MIL SERV:** USA, Ft. Lt.; **OTHER ACT & HONORS:** Asbury Park Housing Authority; **HOME ADD:** 5 Pleasant Dr., W. Long Branch, NJ 07764; **BUS ADD:** 1200 Memorial Dr., Asbury Park, NJ 07712, (201)988-3100.

BRAVO, M. B., III——B: Oct. 18, 1956, San Antonio, TX, *Broker*, Bravo Realty; **PRIM RE ACT:** Broker, Consultant, Property Manager, Insuror; **OTHER RE ACT:** Ranch Investments; **SERVICES:** In-depth property analysis, investment counseling; **REP CLIENTS:** Mexican investors, groups interested in comm. prop.; **PROFL AFFIL & HONORS:** Laredo Bd. of Realtors, TX Bd. of Realtors, NAR; **EDUC:** BBA, 1978, RE, Univ. of TX at Austin; **OTHER ACT & HONORS:** Member, Small Bus. Comm. Laredo C of C; **HOME ADD:** 17 15-B Urbahn, Laredo, TX 78040, (512)727-4276; **BUS ADD:** 3512 Santa Ursula P O Box 1840, Laredo, TX 78041, (512)723-1228.

BRAZIER, Geoffrey L.——B: Nov. 8, 1929, Helena, MT, *Gen. Mgr.*, Guaranty Title Co. of Helena; **PRIM RE ACT:** Insuror; **SERVICES:** Title insurance, mineral reports, inc.; **REP CLIENTS:** Lenders, devels., builders, brokers and agents, mineral exploration cos.; **PREV EMPLOY:** Self-employed atty., govt. positions; **PROFL AFFIL & HONORS:** MT Bar Assn., MT Assn. of Realtors, MT Home Builders Assn., Member, Title Standards Comm., MT Bar Assn.; **EDUC:** BS, 1951, Mining Engrg., MT School of Mines; **GRAD EDUC:** LLB, 1957, Law, Univ. of MT; **MIL SERV:** US Army, Cpl.; **OTHER ACT & HONORS:** School Bd. Trustee, Delegate to Constitutional Convention, MT's First Consumer Counsel, Elks, Shrine, U.C.T., Exchange; **HOME ADD:** 516 Harrison, Helena, MT 59601, (406)442-8733; **BUS ADD:** 40 West 6th Ave., Helena, MT 59601, (406)443-7066.

BRAZO, Bruce Allen——B: May 26, 1930, Stamford, CT, *Pres./Owner*, Brazo Assocs.; **PRIM RE ACT:** Broker, Consultant, Appraiser, Developer, Regulator, Owner/Investor, Property Manager; **SERVICES:** Investment consulting, land & light comml., zoning; **REP CLIENTS:** Indivs. and small grps., plus resid. of estates, etc.; **PREV EMPLOY:** Owned own firm since 1956. Prior employment: Gateway RE, 1951-56; **PROFL AFFIL & HONORS:** CT Assn. of Realtors, NAR, GRI, CRA, CFAA, CREA; **EDUC:** 1953, Eng. & Psych., Univ. of Bridgeport; **GRAD EDUC:** Litt. D., World Acad. of Arts & Culture; **MIL SERV:** USA Airborne, Sgt.; **OTHER ACT & HONORS:** 3 yrs. V Chmn. Conservation Comm.; 3 yrs. chmn Bd. on Tax Review; Awards: 1st class grad. Commn. Realtors Inst.; Realtor of Yr. Town of Wilton (1973); Distinguished Serv. Award CT Heart Assn. (1967); Salvation Army (1973); Var. others. Member NAR, Wilton Bd. of Realtors, pres. (1961-69); CT Assn. Realtors Dir. (8 terms); Kiwanis Pres.; CT Heart Assn. Chmn.; NIREB CT chmn.; NAREA, NARA, Amer. Soc. Fine Art Appraisers, Chmn. Academy Poets of the Intl. Platform, Assn. (1978-), Rec. Collect and lecture on Ear Amer. Lighting & Fireplace Implements; **HOME ADD:** 87 Belden Hill Rd., Wilton, CT 06897, (203)762-9256; **BUS ADD:** PO Box 118, Piersall Bldg., Wilton, CT 06897, (203)762-8311.

BRECKENRIDGE, Hugh——B: Dec. 2, 1946, Santa Monica, CA, Breckenridge & McHolm, Lawyers; **PRIM RE ACT:** Attorney; **SERVICES:** Rep. atty. in negotiation and litigation; **REP CLIENTS:** Comml. RE devels. and RE brokerage firms; **PROFL AFFIL & HONORS:** ABA, Real Prop. Sect. and Environmental Law Sect.; Orange Cty. Bar Assn., RE Section, Bus. Litigation Sect.; **EDUC:** BA, 1968, Econ., Hist., Math, Stanford Univ.; **GRAD EDUC:** JD, 1975, Environmental Law, Pepperdine Univ.; **EDUC HONORS:** Law Review, Published comment, zoning and the vested right to use prop.; **MIL SERV:** USN, Lt.; **OTHER ACT & HONORS:** Chmn. of Bd., Member of Bd. of Dir. Terr. Community Assn. 1977-79, 1981-83; **HOME ADD:** 17303 Rosewood, Irvine, CA 92715, (714)551-1673; **BUS ADD:** 4650 Von Karman Ave., Newport Beach, CA 92660, (714)955-0031.

BREDEMEIR, Melvin W.——B: June 24, 1950, Ft. Wayne, IN, *Asst. VP & Legal Counsel*, Lincoln National Bank & Trust Co., Legal Dept.; **PRIM RE ACT:** Attorney; **SERVICES:** RE Law Journal; **PROFL AFFIL & HONORS:** ABA, IN State Bar Assn.; **EDUC:** AB, 1972, Econ., Govt., IN Univ. Bloomington, IN; **GRAD EDUC:** MBA/JD, 1976, Fin. & Law, IN Univ., Bloomington, IN; **EDUC HONORS:** MBA with honors; **HOME ADD:** 6130 Seabree Lane, Ft. Wayne, IN 46815, (219)486-2925; **BUS ADD:** 116 E. Berry St., Ft. Wayne, IN 46802, (219)423-6495.

BREDICE, Frank E.——B: Jan. 27, 1936, Torrington, CT, *Owner*, Bredice Appraisal Assocs.; **PRIM RE ACT:** Consultant, Appraiser; **SERVICES:** Specializes in RE counseling and appraising for lenders, governmental agencies, investors and corps. for acquisition, disposition, litigation, mort. fin., and tax equalization for all types of RE; **PREV EMPLOY:** Nat. Life Ins. Co.; Stockton, Whatley, Davin Mort. Co.; John Hancock Mutual Life Ins. Co.; **PROFL AFFIL & HONORS:** AIREA; Soc. of RE Appraisers; NAR; VT Assn. of Realtors; Central VT Bd. of Realtors; VT CID; Amer. Soc. of RE Counselors, MAI; CRE; SRPA; **EDUC:** BA, 1958, Hist., The King's Coll., Briarcliff Manor, NY; **OTHER ACT & HONORS:** Member of State of VT Valuation Appeals Bd.; 1982 Pres. Elect, New England Chap., AIREA; Past Pres., VT Chap. of Soc. of RE Appraisers; **HOME ADD:** 11 Greenfield Terr., Box 516, Montpelier, VT 05602, (802)223-5177; **BUS ADD:** 50 Bridge St., Box 268, Manchester, NH 03105, (603)668-1419.

BREGAR, Robert J.——B: Dec. 17, 1927, Cleveland, OH, *Pres.*, Robert J. Bregar Assoc. Inc., Architects; **PRIM RE ACT:** Architect; **PROFL AFFIL & HONORS:** AIA; ASO; NCARB; Amer. Arbitration Assn., City of Cleveland Neighborhood Improvement; **EDUC:** BSAE, 1950, Arch., Ohio Univ.; **EDUC HONORS:** Tau Beta Pi, Hon. Frat.; **MIL SERV:** USA, T-5; **OTHER ACT & HONORS:** Max S. Hayes High School, Cuy. Com. Coll., Catholic Social Serv. of Cuy. Co., Boy Scouts of Amer., Villa Angela High School; **HOME ADD:** 104 E 119, Euclid, OH 44119, (216)531-0135; **BUS ADD:** 22700 Shore Center Dr., Suite 303, Cleveland, OH 44123, (216)731-7011.

BREGMAN, Mark A.——B: Jan. 18, 1951, Philadelphia, PA, Mark A. Bregman, Ltd.; **PRIM RE ACT:** Attorney; **REP CLIENTS:** RE brokers, devels.; investors.; **PROFL AFFIL & HONORS:** ABA; **EDUC:** BA, 1973, Poli. Sci., VA Tech.; **GRAD EDUC:** 1979, Law, AZ State Univ.; **BUS ADD:** Box 5343, Scottsdale, AZ 85261, (602)947-4333.

BREGMAN, Petty——*Pres.*, The Piedmont Devel. Cos., **PRIM RE ACT:** Developer; **BUS ADD:** 1706 Northeast Expressway NE, Atlanta, GA 30329, (404)634-6692.*

BREHMER, Ralph E.——B: Dec. 24, 1930, Wyandotte, MI, *Mgr., Dealership Facilities*, Amer. Motors Sales Corp., Amer. Motors Realty Corp.; **OTHER RE ACT:** Corp. RE dept. mgr.; **SERVICES:** Acquisition, constr. mgmt. of AMC dealer facilities; **PREV EMPLOY:** RE Rep., The Detroit Edison Co.; **PROFL AFFIL & HONORS:** RE Alumnus of MI (Univ. of MI), Former Dir. NACORE, RAM (Univ. of

MI); **EDUC:** BA, 1953, Geog., Wayne State Univ.; **GRAD EDUC:** MA, 1973, Geog., Wayne State Univ.; **MIL SERV:** USA, SP-3; **HOME ADD:** 18147 Snow Rd., Dearborn, MI 48124, (313)336-7909; **BUS ADD:** 27777 Franklin Rd., Southfield, MI 48034, (313)827-3900.

BREHRENS, Alfred H.——*VP & Gen. Mgr.*, Voreleo, Inc.; **PRIM RE ACT:** Developer; **BUS ADD:** PO Box 9836, Englewood Cliffs, NJ 07632, (201)894-6390.*

BREITMAN, Bruce M.——**B:** Oct. 26. 1943, MN, *Prin.*, Green & Co.; **PRIM RE ACT:** Broker, Consultant, Attorney, Appraiser, Developer; **REP CLIENTS:** Grosoover Props., I Magnin, Macys, Pac. Telephone, IBM; **PREV EMPLOY:** CPA, Atty.; **EDUC:** BSBA, 1987, Acctg., Univ. of Denver; **GRAD EDUC:** JD, 1971, Loyola, Chicago; **EDUC HONORS:** Honors; **OTHER ACT & HONORS:** Atty., Securities & Exchange Commission Washington, DC, 1972 to 1978; ABA; **HOME ADD:** 3839 Divisadero, San Francisco, CA 94123, (415)929-9393; **BUS ADD:** 601 Brannan, San Francisco, CA 94107, (415)546-8799.

BRELAND, Kenneth R.——**B:** Oct. 16, 1952, Birmingham,AL, *Pres.*, Ken Breland Co.; **PRIM RE ACT:** Developer, Builder; **SERVICES:** Indus. and Comml.Const. and Devel.; **PROFL AFFIL & HONORS:** NAHB Home Builders Assn. of Greater Tampa, 1979 Award Recipient NAHB Research Found.; **EDUC:** BS, 1979, RE Fin., Univ. of AL; **EDUC HONORS:** Delta Sigma Pi Hon. Bus. Frat.; **OTHER ACT & HONORS:** Greater Tampa C of C; **BUS ADD:** 5511 N. 50M St., Tampa,, FL 33610, (813)623-1522.

BRENDEMUHL, Ruth Anne——**B:** Sept. 2, 1952, Chicago, IL, *Atty.*, Lusthoff & Brendemuhl; **PRIM RE ACT:** Attorney; **SERVICES:** Preparation of contracts; representation at RE closing; **PROFL AFFIL & HONORS:** Chicago Bar Assn.; ABA; **EDUC:** BS, 1974, Chem. and Psych., Valparaiso Univ.; **GRAD EDUC:** UD, 1977, School of Law; Valparaiso Univ., Valparaiso, IN; **BUS ADD:** Box L, 2914 Harlem Ave., Riverside, IL 60546, (312)447-5694.

BRENER, Harry——**B:** May 19, 1943, New York, NY, *Atty. at Law*, Brener, Wallack & Hill, Attys. at Law; **PRIM RE ACT:** Consultant, Attorney, Developer, Builder, Owner/Investor, Syndicator; **SERVICES:** Legal, fin., devel.; **REP CLIENTS:** John's Manville; Olympia & York; Kaufman and Broad; Ernest W. Hahn; Bellmead Devel.; **PROFL AFFIL & HONORS:** ABA, NJ Bar Assn., etc.; **EDUC:** BA, 1965, Hist., bus., Rutgers Univ., New Brunswick, NJ; **GRAD EDUC:** JD, 1968, Real Prop.; Corporate; Fin., Rutgers Univ. School of Law, Newark, NJ; **BUS ADD:** 2-4 Chambers St., Princeton, NJ 08540, (609)924-0808.

BRENER, Stephen W.——**B:** Apr. 20, 1926, NY, NY, *Exec. VP*, Helmsley - Spear Hospitality Serv., Inc.; **PRIM RE ACT:** Broker, Consultant, Appraiser, Property Manager; **SERVICES:** Specializes Solely in Hotels and Motels; **PREV EMPLOY:** Brener & Lewis, Inc., NYC (RE), 1947 - 1952 (Elected Pres. in 1949); **PROFL AFFIL & HONORS:** Amer. Hotel & Motel Assoc.; ASA; ASREC; IREM; NIREB; CCIM; CPM, Young Man of the Yr. Award, 1966; Young Men's RE Assoc. of NY; **EDUC:** GA School of Tech., Atlanta, GA; **MIL SERV:** USA, Priv., Purple Heart, Combat Infantry Badge; **OTHER ACT & HONORS:** Honorary Faculty Member, Mich. State, 1964; Outstanding Serv. Award, 1969, Daytona Beach Jr. Coll., Hospitality Magazine Silver Plate Award, 1965; Hon. Member of RE School, 1958, Bernard M. Baruch School of Bus. and P.A., CCNY; **HOME ADD:** 249 E. 48th St., New York, NY 10017; **BUS ADD:** 420 Lexington Ave., Rm. 205, New York, NY 10170, (212)689-6800.

BRENNAN, John B.——**B:** Sept. 24, 1944, Akron, OH, *Partner*, Brennan & Brennan, Realtors; **PRIM RE ACT:** Broker, Consultant, Appraiser; **SERVICES:** Consultant, sales, acquisitions and appraisals; **PROFL AFFIL & HONORS:** NAR; FLI; FL Assn. of Realtors; Lakeland Bd. of Realtors; Intl. Inst. of Valuers, Accredited Farm and Land Member, IFAS, GRI, SCV, Realtor of Year - FL Chap. of FLI, 1980; **MIL SERV:** US Army Res., E-4; **OTHER ACT & HONORS:** Lion's Club; **HOME ADD:** 415 Oak Trail, Lakeland, FL, (813)646-2246; **BUS ADD:** 124 W. Main St., P.O. Drawer 1809, Lakeland, FL 33802, (813)686-4103.

BRENNAN, John M.——**B:** Sept. 8, 1939, Washington DC, *Pres., Sr. Part.*, Brennan Yewell & Brooks, PA; **PRIM RE ACT:** Broker, Attorney, Syndicator; **REP CLIENTS:** Merrill Lynch Relocation Servs., Lomas & Nettleton Mort. Nat. Homes, Acceptance Corp., Exec. Relation, Coldwell Banker, MD, Nat. Bank, La Page Corp, Pioneer Title Corp.; **PROFL AFFIL & HONORS:** ABA, MD & Prince George Cty. Bar Assn., Amer. Trial Lawyers Assn., Nat. Bd. of Realtors; **EDUC:** BS, 1961, Phil., Spring Hill Coll.; **GRAD EDUC:** LLB/JD, 1967, Law, George Washington Univ.; **MIL SERV:** USA, 1st Lt.; **OTHER ACT & HONORS:** C of C, Anne Arundel Cty., JC's Waldorf, Council of Legal Advisors Nat. Republican Party; **HOME ADD:** 3463 Constellation Dr., Davidsonville, MD 21035, (301)798-6237; **BUS ADD:** 4710 Auth. Pl., Camp Springs, MD 20023, (301)423-4747.

BRENNAN, Robert——*VP Operations*, C.H. Masland and Sons; **PRIM RE ACT:** Property Manager; **BUS ADD:** PO Box 40, Carlisle, PA 17013, (717)249-1866.*

BRENNAN, Robert F.——*Ed.*, Nat'l. Assn. of Real Estate Editors, NAREE Membership Roster; **PRIM RE ACT:** Real Estate Publisher; **BUS ADD:** 901 Lakeside Ave., NE, Cleveland, OH 44114, (216)623-5721.*

BRENNAN, William G.——**B:** Nov. 3, 1942, Philadelphia, PA, *Pres.*, William G. Brennan, Inc.; **OTHER RE ACT:** Tax shelter newsletter publisher & advisor; **SERVICES:** Investment consultation; **PREV EMPLOY:** CPA, Investment Advisor; **PROFL AFFIL & HONORS:** Var. CPA orgs., CPA; **EDUC:** BS, 1968, Acctg., LaSalle Coll.; **EDUC HONORS:** Cum Laude; **MIL SERV:** Army, SP-4; **HOME ADD:** 1357 Nathan Hall Dr., Phoenixville, PA 19460, (215)933-6114; **BUS ADD:** Valley Forge Office Colony, PO Box 882, Valley Forge, PA 19482, (215)783-0647.

BRENNEINAN, Howard L.——*Pres.*, Hesston Corp.; **PRIM RE ACT:** Property Manager; **BUS ADD:** Box 788, Hesston, KS 67062, (316)327-4000.*

BRENNEMAN, Bruce M.——**B:** Dec. 1, 1952, Wash., DC, *VP*, Brenneman Assoc., Inc., Residential Brokerage, Dev.; **PRIM RE ACT:** Broker, Developer; **SERVICES:** Spec. in condo. and coop. Resales, cond. and coop. conversion; **PROFL AFFIL & HONORS:** NAR, RESSI; **EDUC:** BA, 1976, RE, Fin., Amer. Univ., Wash. D.C.; **HOME ADD:** 6732 Hillandale Rd., Chevy Chase, MD 20815, (301)986-1002; **BUS ADD:** 4590 Mac Arthur Blvd. NW, Wash., DC 20007, (202)966-2442.

BRENNEMAN, Cloyd E.——**B:** April 15, 1934, Clarion Co., PA, *VP & RE Officer*, McDowell Nat. Bank, Mort. Loans; **PRIM RE ACT:** Broker, Appraiser, Banker, Owner/Investor, Instructor; **PREV EMPLOY:** Private RE brokerage, specialized in eminent domain & comml. appraisers; **PROFL AFFIL & HONORS:** State & nat. assn. of realtors; American Right of Way Assn. of Realtors, RE Broker, PA & OH; **EDUC:** AB, 1963, Bus. Admin., Penn State Univ.; **GRAD EDUC:** RE Appraisal Courses, U of VA; U of CT; U of GA; AIREA, Bank Courses; Amer. Instit. of Banking; **HOME ADD:** 107 Parklane Dr., Greenville, PA 16125, (412)646-1493; **BUS ADD:** 62-66 E State St., Sharon, PA 16146, (412)981-1411.

BRENNEMAN, Peter T.——**B:** Aug. 17, 1949, Ontario, Can., *VP*, Haico Enterprises Ltd.; **PRIM RE ACT:** Consultant, Developer, Owner/Investor, Syndicator; **PREV EMPLOY:** Westmoreland Capital Ltd., VP; **PROFL AFFIL & HONORS:** APEGGA, PE; **EDUC:** BA, 1973, Mech. Engrg., Univ. of Waterloo; **GRAD EDUC:** MBA, 1975, Univ. of W Ontario; **HOME ADD:** 67 Coach Manor Terr., N.W., Calgary, Alb., Canada; **BUS ADD:** 202-A-5809 MacLeod Trail S., Calgary, Alb., Canada, (403)259-4084.

BRESLER, Charles S.——**B:** July 11, 1927, Philadelphia, PA, *Chmn.*, Bresler & Reiner, Inc.; **PRIM RE ACT:** Broker, Appraiser, Banker, Developer, Builder, Property Manager, Syndicator; **EDUC:** BS, 1949, Bus., Univ. of MD; **GRAD EDUC:** MA, 1972, Urban Affairs, Univ. of MD; MBA, 1975, Bus. Admin., SE Univ.; **OTHER ACT & HONORS:** MD State Representative 1962-1965; MD State Senator 1965-1966; Bd. of Dir. Security Nat. Bank; **HOME ADD:** 3217 Farmington Dr., Chevy Chase, MD 20015, (301)652-3333; **BUS ADD:** 401 M St. SW, Washington, DC 20024, (202)488-8800.

BRESLER, Stanley——**B:** Mar. 23, 1935, Chicago, IL, *Pres.*, Bresler Realty Co.; **PRIM RE ACT:** Developer, Builder, Owner/Investor, Syndicator; **REP CLIENTS:** Strip shopping ctrs.; manage for outside accts. as well as our own; **EDUC:** 1956, Bus., Roosevelt Univ.; **GRAD EDUC:** Agric., PA State; **OTHER ACT & HONORS:** Dir., Intl. Franchise Assn.; **BUS ADD:** 4000 W. Belden Ave., Chicago, IL 60639, (312)227-6700.

BRESLIN, Wilbur F.——*Pres.*, Breslin Realty Devel. Corp.; **PRIM RE ACT:** Broker, Consultant, Developer; **SERVICES:** Resid. & comml. devel. & mgmt.; **REP CLIENTS:** Diana Stores Corp., NY Stock Exchange, Korvettes, Southland Corp., Midland Resources, US Rubber Corp., Finast, Hamburg Savings Bank, A&P, Sears Roebuck Co., Supermarkets, McDonalds Corp., Burger King, Morse Shoe, US Post Office, K-Mart, Dime Savings Bank, Waldbaums, Long Island Lighting Co., Foodtown, Rickel, Pathmark, King Kullen, Flushing National Bank; **PROFL AFFIL & HONORS:** LI Bd. of Realtors, Nat. Assn. of RE Bds., IREA, ICSC, NAHB, F&LI, NAREC, NAPA; **BUS**

ADD: 500 Old Country Rd., Garden City, NY 11530, (516)741-7400.

BRESNAHAN, C.A.——B: Nov. 2, 1899, Greeley, CO, *Owner*, Western Realty Co.; **PRIM RE ACT:** Broker, Appraiser; **PROFL AFFIL & HONORS:** NAR; CO Assn. of Realtors; Amer. Soc. Farm Mgrs.; Rural Appraisers, ARA; **EDUC:** BS, 1921, Soils/Farm Mgt., CO State Univ.; **EDUC HONORS:** Student Body Pres., 12 athletic letters; **HOME ADD:** 160 S. Monaco Pkwy., Denver, CO 80224, (303)355-7966; **BUS ADD:** 102 Livestock Exc. Bldg., Denver, CO 80216.

BRETON, Richard Albert——B: Jan. 7, 1948, New York City, NY, *Pres.*, Breton Properties, Inc./Vintage Bldgs. of HI; **PRIM RE ACT:** Broker, Developer; **OTHER RE ACT:** Renovator, Comml. Props.; **SERVICES:** Comml. Prop. Devel., Adaptive Re-Use, leasing and brokerage; **REP CLIENTS:** Indiv. investors; **PROFL AFFIL & HONORS:** Nat. Assn. of Realtors, Amer. Instit. of CPA's, CPA, GRI; **EDUC:** BS, 1969, Acctg., Georgetown Univ.; **EDUC HONORS:** Academic Scholarship Recipient; **HOME TEL:** (808)261-4100; **BUS ADD:** 900 Fort St. Mall Suite 1030, Honolulu, HI 96813, (808)538-3355.

BRETT, Carl N.——B: Nov. 15, 1933, Decatur, IL, *VP*, National Bank of FL, RE; **PRIM RE ACT:** Banker, Lender; **EDUC:** BS, 1955, Journalism, FL State Univ.; **MIL SERV:** US Army, SP-4; **HOME ADD:** 6504 S.W. 33rd St., Miramar, FL 33023, (305)989-4483; **BUS ADD:** 265 S.E. 1st St., Miami, FL 33131, (305)576-4200.

BREVIK, Richard W.——B: Mar. 21, 1943, Fargo, ND, *Pres.*, Continental Mgmt. Co.; **PRIM RE ACT:** Broker, Consultant, Developer, Builder, Property Manager; **PREV EMPLOY:** VP, Kassuba Devel. Corp.; **PROFL AFFIL & HONORS:** IREM, CPM; **EDUC:** BBA, 1970, Bus., Augustana Coll., Rock Island, IL; **EDUC HONORS:** Cum Laude; **HOME ADD:** 2552 E. Geo. Wash. Blvd., Davenport, IA 52803, (319)355-0003; **BUS ADD:** 4323 N. Division, Davenport, IA 52806, (319)386-6424.

BREWER, Dana——B: Jan 25, 1952, Concordia, KS, *Atty.*, Baldwin, Paulsen & Buechel, Chartered; **PRIM RE ACT:** Attorney; **OTHER RE ACT:** RE law and farm and gen. estate planning including utilization of 'use valuation' of RE for death tax purposes; **PREV EMPLOY:** KS Revisor of Statutes - law clerk; KS Supreme Court - law clerk to Judicial Admin.; **PROFL AFFIL & HONORS:** KS Bar Assn., ABA, Past Sec. - Cloud Cty. Bar Assn.; **EDUC:** BS, 1974, Soc. - Pre Law, Arts and Sci. - KS State Univ.; **GRAD EDUC:** JD, 1976, Estate Planning, Washburn Univ.; **EDUC HONORS:** Cum Laude, Blue Key (Senior Men's Honorary), Putnam Scholar, Dean's Hon. Roll, Kline Scholar, Dean's Hon. Roll; **HOME ADD:** Rt.2, Concordia, KS 66901, (913)335-2535; **BUS ADD:** Box 327, 613 Washington St., Concordia, KS 66901, (913)243-3790.

BREWER, Dean M.——B: Aug. 27, 1953, *Pres.*, Irvine Financial Consultants, Inc.; **PRIM RE ACT:** Broker, Consultant, Owner/Investor, Syndicator; **OTHER RE ACT:** CPA; **SERVICES:** Tax and fin. planning, synd. and investment counseling; **PREV EMPLOY:** Peat, Marwick, Mitchell & Co.; **PROFL AFFIL & HONORS:** AICPA; CSCPA; NAA, CPA; **EDUC:** BA, 1977, Acctg., CA State Univ., Fullerton; **EDUC HONORS:** Man of Distinction; **MIL SERV:** US Army; Sgt.; Army Commendation; **OTHER ACT & HONORS:** AOPA; **HOME ADD:** 22705 Woodlake Ln., El Toro, CA 92630, (714)855-0419; **BUS ADD:** 610 Newport Center Dr. #950, Newport Beach, CA 92660, (714)833-1474.

BREWER, James M. (Jim), AFLM——B: Dec. 5, 1944, Memphis, TN, *Partner*, Brewer Realty; **PRIM RE ACT:** Broker, Syndicator, Consultant, Developer, Builder, Owner/Investor; **SERVICES:** Sales of investment prop. and devel. of subdivisions plus devel. of Skilled Care Nursing Homes; **PROFL AFFIL & HONORS:** NAR; FLI, Accredited Farm and Land Member of the FLI, youngest person to receive this designation; **EDUC:** BS Bus. Admin., Mktg. and Ins., 1967, MS State Univ.; **OTHER ACT & HONORS:** Rotary Club, Jaycees, First Baptist Church/Deacon; Elected Realtor of the Yr. for the State of MS in 1977; **HOME ADD:** Rt. 3, Box 4, Senatobia, MS 38668, (601)562-8702; **BUS ADD:** Main at Scott St., Senatobia, MS 38668, (601)562-4442.

BREWER, Robert H.——B: May 9, 1942, *Partner*, Brewer & Coombs; **PRIM RE ACT:** Attorney; **SERVICES:** Synd. of public and private partnerships; tax planning; **REP CLIENTS:** Systech Financial Corp., Consolidated Funding Corp., Leastec Corp.; **PREV EMPLOY:** Formerly VP & Corp. Counsel for Dillingham Systech; **PROFL AFFIL & HONORS:** RESSI, ABA Bus. & Tax Sect.; **EDUC:** AB, 1964, Washington & Lee Univ.; **GRAD EDUC:** LLB, 1967, Univ. of VA; **EDUC HONORS:** Cum Laude; **BUS ADD:** 177 Front St., Danville, CA 94526, (415)837-4600.

BREWSTER, George B.——B: Aug. 7, 1948, USA, *VP*, Calmark Asset Mgmt. Inc.; **PRIM RE ACT:** Syndicator, Developer, Property Manager, Owner/Investor; **SERVICES:** Identification, Analysis, Structuring, Investment Mgmt.; **REP CLIENTS:** Chase Manhattan Bank, Bank of Amer., Shearson, Loeb, Rhodes Indiv. Investors; **PREV EMPLOY:** VP Bankers Mort. Corp., VP Heritage Inc.; **PROFL AFFIL & HONORS:** RE Securities & Synd. Inst.; Nat. Synd. Forum; **EDUC:** BA, 1970, Lit. & Hist., Bard Coll.; **GRAD EDUC:** JD, 1973, RE (joint JD/MBA Program) & Fin., Columbia Univ.; **EDUC HONORS:** Editor-in-chief of the Bard Observer; Joint long-range planning comm.; **OTHER ACT & HONORS:** Lic. contractor (NC) & RE Broker (NC); writings published in Bus. Week; **HOME ADD:** 3023 Corral Canyon, Malibu, CA 90265, (213)456-2213; **BUS ADD:** 2121 Cloverfield Blvd., PO Box 2128, Santa Monica, CA 90406, (213)453-1721.

BREY, David M.——B: June 9, 1918, Uniontown, PA, *Architect*, David M. Brey, Architects & Assocs.; **PRIM RE ACT:** Architect; **PROFL AFFIL & HONORS:** Amer. Inst. of Architects, Fellow Amer. Inst. of Architects; MO Council of Architects; 1975 Architect of the Yr. Award; **EDUC:** BArch., 1940, Arch., Miami Univ.; **EDUC HONORS:** Heistand Prize Arch. Design; **MIL SERV:** USN, Lt., Pres. Unit Citation; **HOME ADD:** 214 E. 73 St., Kansas City, MO 64114, (816)444-4025; **BUS ADD:** 306 E. 12th St., Kansas City, MO 64106, (816)842-6762.

BREZNAI, Theodore A.——B: Nov. 9, 1948, Rochester, PA, *VP, Title counsel*, Midland Title Security, Inc.; **PRIM RE ACT:** Consultant, Attorney, Instructor, Insuror; **SERVICES:** Issuer of title evidence for RE, escrow servs., consultant for RE trans.; **PREV EMPLOY:** The Bissell Mort. Co. (formerly Howard S. Bissel, Inc.) mort. banking firm; **PROFL AFFIL & HONORS:** ABA., Cleveland Bar Assn., Mort. Bankers Assn. of Cleveland, Cleveland Title Assn., Pres. of Cleveland Title Assn.; **EDUC:** AB, 1970, Lib. Arts., Pre Law, John Carroll Univ.; **GRAD EDUC:** JD, 1975, Cleveland Marshall Coll. of Law; **HOME ADD:** 1282 Nicholson Ave., Lakewood, OH 44107, (216)228-1954; **BUS ADD:** 1404 E. 9th St., Cleveland, OH 44114, (216)241-6045.

BRICHLER, David D.——B: Feb. 4, 1934, Belleville, IL, *Rgnl. Dir.*, Pacific Mutual Life Ins. Co., Realty Fin. - So. Rgn.; **PRIM RE ACT:** Lender, Owner/Investor; **SERVICES:** Production of debt and equity realty investments; **PROFL AFFIL & HONORS:** Intl. Council of Shopping Centers; Natl. Assn. of Indus. Offices & Parks; TX Mort. Bankers Assn.; Houston Bd. of Realtors; AIREA; Soc. of RE Appraisers, MAI; SRPA; **EDUC:** BA, 1955, Econ., Westminster Coll.; **MIL SERV:** USN, Lt. j.g.; **HOME ADD:** 8310 Braesview, Houston, TX 77071, (713)771-6089; **BUS ADD:** 1980 Post Oak Blvd., Suite 2160, Houston, TX 77056, (713)871-8800.

BRICK, Steven R.——B: Oct. 6, 1945, Camden, NJ, *Pres.*, Brick RE; **PRIM RE ACT:** Broker, Developer, Owner/Investor; **PROFL AFFIL & HONORS:** NAR, NJ Assn. of Realtors, Burlington Cty. Bd. of Realtors, Certified RE Broker (CRB), NRI; **EDUC:** BA with Distinction, 1968, Econ., Univ. of VA; **GRAD EDUC:** MBA, 1976, Fin., Temple Univ.; **EDUC HONORS:** Member, Raven Soc.; **MIL SERV:** USAF, 1st Lt.; **OTHER ACT & HONORS:** Bd. of Dir., Cadbury-a Quaker related retirement community; Treas., DE Valley Council of Home for Living; Trustee, Soc. of Friends of Medford (Quakers); Island Heights Yacht Club; **HOME ADD:** 21 Maine Trail, PO Box 215, Medford, NJ 08055, (609)654-9086; **BUS ADD:** Taunton Rd., Medford, NJ 08055, (609)983-2888.

BRICKER, Richard——B: Nov. 27, 1946, Toronto, ON, Can., *Sr. VP, US Ops. & Asst. to Pres.*, Lakeview Props., Ltd.; **PRIM RE ACT:** Developer, Owner/Investor, Property Manager, Syndicator; **OTHER RE ACT:** Broad spectrum of devel. servs.; **PREV EMPLOY:** Atty. Aikins, MacAulay & Thorvaldson, Winnipeg, MB, 1969-79; **PROFL AFFIL & HONORS:** Law Soc. of Manitoba, Canadian Bar Assn.; **EDUC:** BA, 1967, Univ. of MB; **GRAD EDUC:** LLB, 1969, Univ. of MB; **OTHER ACT & HONORS:** Dir. and Officer Inland Tr. & Savings Corp., Ltd., Bd. of Govs. Winnipeg Art Gallery, Chmn. Can. Bar Grp. Ins. Comm.; **HOME ADD:** 129 Chataway Blvd., Winnipeg, MB, Canada, (204)489-2498; **BUS ADD:** 185 Carlton St., Winnipeg, R3C 3J1, MB, Canada, (204)947-1161.

BRICKLEY, David G.——B: Feb. 10, 1911, NY, *Pres.*, Dominion Mortgage & Investment Corp.; **PRIM RE ACT:** Broker, Syndicator, Lender, Owner/Investor; **SERVICES:** First and Second Morts., Investments, RE; **PREV EMPLOY:** Kennedy Mortgage & Investment Corp.; **PROFL AFFIL & HONORS:** Prince William C of C; **EDUC:** 1965, Bus. Mgmt., PA State Univ.; **MIL SERV:** USAF, Capt., USAF Bronze Star, Jt. Serv. Comm. Medal; **OTHER ACT & HONORS:** VA House of Delegates/State Legislature (1976 -); Dale City Civic Assn.; Amer. Heart Assn.; VFW; Sigma Chi; Amer. Legion; Jaycees; House Fin. Comm.; House Health, Welfare & Instits. Comm.; House Agric.

Comm.; State Cent. Comm.; House Dem. Caucus Chm., VA 8th Dist.; **HOME ADD:** 4804 Kellogg Dr., Woodbridge, VA 22193, (703)590-3569; **BUS ADD:** 4391 Davis Ford Rd., Suite H, Woodbridge, VA 22193, (703)590-2911.

BRIDDELL, Willis H.——**B:** March 19, 1919, Crisfield, MD, *Pres.*, Hartman, Briddell, Watkins Prop. Inc.; **PRIM RE ACT:** Broker, Developer, Property Manager; **PROFL AFFIL & HONORS:** NAR, IREM, CPM; **MIL SERV:** USAF, 1st Lt.; **HOME ADD:** 1794 Milboro Dr., Rockville, MD 20854, (301)762-6710; **BUS ADD:** 451 Hungerford Dr., Rockville, MD 20850, (301)424-2900.

BRIDGES, R.W.——*Treasurer*, Reliance Universal Inc.; **PRIM RE ACT:** Property Manager; **BUS ADD:** Ste. 1600, Watterson Tower, 1930 Bishop Lane, Louisville, KY 40218, (502)459-9110.*

BRIDWELL, Lowell W.——**B:** Feb. 8, 1931, Denver, CO, *Owner*, Bridwell & Co.; **PRIM RE ACT:** Consultant, Appraiser, Owner/Investor, Property Manager; **SERVICES:** Appraiser-consultant; **REP CLIENTS:** Instnl. lenders, mort. bankers, govt. agencies, corps., attys. and indiv.; **PREV EMPLOY:** Guaranty Federal S & L Assn.; Amer. Nat. Ins. Co.; Metropolitan Life Ins. Co.; Tenneco Oil Co., Comml. RE Loans & Acquisitions; **PROFL AFFIL & HONORS:** Member, Amer. Inst. of RE Appraisers, MAI Designation; **EDUC:** 1949-1952, Arch. Engrg., Univ. of CO; **HOME ADD:** 24285 Choke Cherry Lane, Golden, CO 80401, (303)526-9299; **BUS ADD:** 445 Union Blvd., Suite 121, Denver, CO 80228, (303)989-3912.

BRIGGS, Gary G.——**B:** Dec. 5, 1931, NJ, *Operating Mgr.*, Galbreath-Ruffin Corp., Operations; **PRIM RE ACT:** Developer, Property Manager; **SERVICES:** Mgmt. of large comml. props.; **PROFL AFFIL & HONORS:** Amer. Soc. Hospital Engrs.; **EDUC:** 1961, Physics, Drexel Univ., Philadelphia, PA; **HOME ADD:** 6195 Deer Path, Manassas, VA 22110, (703)369-2346; **BUS ADD:** 3225 Gallows Rd., Fairfax, VA 22037, (703)849-3017.

BRIGHT, Fletcher——**B:** June 27, 1931, Chattanooga, TN, *Pres.*, Fletcher Bright Co.; **PRIM RE ACT:** Broker, Owner/Investor, Property Manager; **OTHER RE ACT:** Mort. Banking; **PROFL AFFIL & HONORS:** MAI, CRE, ICSC; **EDUC:** BS, 1953, Bus., Econ., Davidson Coll.; **GRAD EDUC:** MBA, Univ. of TN at Chattanooga; LLB, McKenzie Coll. of Law; **HOME ADD:** 118 N Hermitage Ave., Lookout Mtn., TN 37350, (615)821-3561; **BUS ADD:** 1520 1st TN Bldg., Chattanooga, TN 37402, (615)756-4042.

BRIGNATI, David A.——**B:** Feb. 21, 1937, Brooklyn, NY, *Exec. VP*, Bonsignore Brignati & Mazzotta, P.C.; **PRIM RE ACT:** Consultant, Appraiser, Developer, Architect, Builder, Owner/Investor; **SERVICES:** Site evaluation, programming, design, budgeting, scheduling, const. mgmt.; **REP CLIENTS:** NY Stock Exchange, Commodities Exchange, AVIS, Newsweek, Chemical Bank, Irving Trust, Toronto Stock Exchange, Fiduciary Trust Co., AIA; **PROFL AFFIL & HONORS:** Design Awards: Amer. Registered Architects, Brooklyn Chapter AIA; **EDUC:** BArch, 1959, Arch., Pratt Inst.; **EDUC HONORS:** Cum Laude; **MIL SERV:** NY Nat. Guard; **HOME ADD:** 80 Wilmington Drive, Melville, NY 11791, (516)491-1786; **BUS ADD:** 370 Seventh Ave., New York, NY 10001, (212)868-9200.

BRILL, Mark Wm.——**B:** June 3, 1948, Austin, MN, *RE Broker*, Towle RE, Comml. Indus.; **PRIM RE ACT:** Broker; **PROFL AFFIL & HONORS:** NAR, GRI; **EDUC:** BS, 1972, Bus. Econ., Mankato State; **HOME ADD:** 15 Manitoba Rd., Hopkins, MN 55343, (612)938-5554; **BUS ADD:** 600 2nd Ave. S, Minneapolis, MN 55402, (612)341-4444.

BRILL, Ralph——**B:** Nov. 24, 1944, Cheltenham, England, *Pres.*, Ralph Brill Assocs.; **PRIM RE ACT:** Broker, Consultant, Architect, Developer, Owner/Investor; **SERVICES:** Land planning, arch. design, feasibility analysis, devel., investments, activies are intl.; **PREV EMPLOY:** Dir. of Devel., Townland Mktg. and Devel. Corp., 1970-1972, Partner BKW Architects, 1974-; **PROFL AFFIL & HONORS:** Soc. of Indus. Archaeology, Center for the Hudson River Valley, NY State Hist. Preservation Grantee, 1977; Lic. Architect, Lic. RE Broker; **EDUC:** Arch., 1966, Univ. of IL; **GRAD EDUC:** Masters, 1967, Urban Design, Kunstskolen, Copenhagen, Denmark; **OTHER ACT & HONORS:** Bd. of Dirs., Garrison Art Center 1976-81, Arch. Critic, Columbia Univ., 1969, Adjunct Asst. Professor of Urban Systems, Farleigh Dickinson Univ., 1974-1976; **HOME ADD:** Snake Hill Rd., Garrison, NY 10524, (914)265-3060; **BUS ADD:** P O Box 200, Garrison, NY 10524, (914)265-2326.

BRILL, Steven C.——**B:** Aug. 21, 1953, Miami, FL, *Atty.*, Steven C. Brill, Esq.; **PRIM RE ACT:** Broker, Attorney, Owner/Investor; **SERVICES:** Investment counseling, Legal Serv., Broker-Sales; **PROFL AFFIL & HONORS:** Nat. Assn. of Security Dealers, NY State Bar-Member, Notary Public, US District Court, US Tax Court - admitted, ABA, NY Cty. Lawyers Assn.; **EDUC:** AB, 1975, Philosophy/Psych., Boston Univ.; **GRAD EDUC:** JD, 1978, Taxes, W New England Coll. School of Law (Springfield, MA); **EDUC HONORS:** Deans List; **HOME ADD:** 215-03 17 Ave., Bayside, NY 11360, (212)423-9199; **BUS ADD:** 215-03 17 Ave., Bayside, NY 11360, (212)423-1001.

BRINCEFIELD, James C., Jr.——**B:** Mar. 6, 1941, Washington, DC, *Atty. at Law*, Of Counsel to Cohen and Annand, P.C., Alexandria, VA; **PRIM RE ACT:** Consultant, Attorney, Developer, Owner/Investor, Instructor, Syndicator; **SERVICES:** RE Counseling, synd. and devel. of real prop.; **REP CLIENTS:** Public and pvt. sector clients involved in RE law, fin., devel., mktg. and mgmt.; **PREV EMPLOY:** Broad legal and bus. mgmt. experience as an atty., devel., corp. officer and mgmt. consultant; **PROFL AFFIL & HONORS:** Approved atty. by all maj. title cos.; FNMA approved condo. atty., Amer., VA and DC Bar Assns.; N. VA Bd. of Realtors; C of C; Phi Kappa Phi Nat. Honor Soc.; Amer. Mensa Soc., Former Chmn, RE Comm. DC Bar; Current Chmn., Real Prop. Section, VA State Bar; Atty. (LLB/JD); **EDUC:** Eng., Phil., 1963, Georgetown Univ.; **GRAD EDUC:** LLB, JD/MBA, MS, 1966/1076, Law/RE, Georgetown Univ./Amer. Univ.; **EDUC HONORS:** Phi Kappa Phi Nat. Honor Soc.; **BUS ADD:** 320 King St., Suite 206, Alexandria, VA 22314, (703)836-2880.

BRINDELL, Charles R., Jr.——**B:** May 5, 1949, Jacksonville, NC, *Pres.*, Southwide Development Co., Inc., RE; **PRIM RE ACT:** Developer, Owner/Investor, Property Manager; **SERVICES:** Leasing, maintenance, prop. mgmt., devel., construction mgmt.; **PREV EMPLOY:** Cameron-Brown Co., Mort. Bankers, 1972-74; **PROFL AFFIL & HONORS:** ULI, NAIOP, Chapter Pres., Lambda Alpha Frat. (Profl. RE Frat.), ICSC; **EDUC:** AB, 1971, Hist., Univ. of NC; **OTHER ACT & HONORS:** Kiwanis Club, Phoenix Club (Boys Clubs service organization); **HOME ADD:** 83 Hollyoke Ln., Memphis, TN 38117, (901)685-0205; **BUS ADD:** P O Box 77, 165 Madison Ave., Memphis, TN 38101, (901)523-1211.

BRINDLE, William A.——**B:** Nov. 20, 1942, Chambersburg, PA, *Owner*, William A. Brindle Assoc., Land Surveying; **PRIM RE ACT:** Consultant, Developer, Owner/Investor; **OTHER RE ACT:** Devel. Consultant, Surveyor; **SERVICES:** Complete site planning, design & constr. mgmt. of projects; **REP CLIENTS:** Devels., Investors, Arch., bankers, attys., municipalities, realtors and accountants; **PREV EMPLOY:** Ctys Surveyors Office of Franklin Cty.; **PROFL AFFIL & HONORS:** Profl. Reg. in PA, MD, WV, Past Pres. PA Soc. of Profl. Engrgs. (Cty. Chapt), PA Soc. of Land Surveyors, Amer. Congress of Surveying & Mapping & Amer. Soc. of Photogrametry, Awards in Subdiv. contest for design and land use; **EDUC:** 1962, Civil Engrg., Land Surveying, Hagerstown Jr. Coll.; **OTHER ACT & HONORS:** Rotary Intl., C of C, Little League Bd. of Dir., Published Article in PA Township News (Aug. 81 issue), Dir. Continuing Educ. Work Sups. at PA State Univ., Published Articles in Soc. Newsletters; **HOME ADD:** 555 E King St., Chambersburg, PA 17201, (717)264-8157; **BUS ADD:** 220 Lincoln Way E, Chambersburg, PA 17201, (717)264-2790.

BRINKERHOFF, James J.——**B:** Sept. 8, 1950, Jersey City, NJ, *RE Investment Officer*, Phoenix Mutual Life Insurance Co., RE Investment Div.; **PRIM RE ACT:** Lender, Owner/Investor; **PREV EMPLOY:** MA Mutual Life Ins. Co.; **EDUC:** BS, 1972, Econ., Boston Univ.; **GRAD EDUC:** MBA, 1974, Wharton Grad. School, Univ. of PA; **HOME ADD:** 3 Hampton Village Dr., Granby, CT 06035, (203)653-3009; **BUS ADD:** One American Row, Hartford, CT 06115, (203)278-1212.

BRINKERHOFF, Philip R.——**B:** Apr. 2, 1943, Wilmington NC, *Pres. and CEO*, Federal Home Loan Mortgage Corp.; **OTHER RE ACT:** Secondary Mort. Mkt.; **SERVICES:** Purchase/sale of conventional resid. morts.; **PREV EMPLOY:** Streich, Lang, Weeks, Cardon & French, Phoenix, AZ; **PROFL AFFIL & HONORS:** Member of the State Bar of AZ, The Bar of the District of Columbia Ct. of Appeals; Member of the Young Pres. Org.; **EDUC:** BS, 1966, Acctg., Econ. & Bus. Mgmt., Brigham Young Univ.; **GRAD EDUC:** JD, 1969, Harvard Law School; **EDUC HONORS:** Beta Alpha Psi, Phi Kappa Phi, Deans List; **OTHER ACT & HONORS:** Church of Jesus Christ of Latter Day Saints; One of JC's Outstanding YOund Men of Yr. - 1976; Who's Who in Amer., 1980-81; **HOME ADD:** 9415 Macklin Ct., Alexandria, VA 22309, (703)780-7429; **BUS ADD:** 1776 G St., Wash., DC 20013, (202)789-4720.

BRINKMAN, Kenn——**B:** Apr. 28, 1941, Brooklyn, NY, *Pres.*, The Brinkman Interests, Inc.; **PRIM RE ACT:** Broker, Consultant, Developer, Owner/Investor; **SERVICES:** Office space mktg.; Sales & Purchases of Income Property and Land; **REP CLIENTS:** Amer. NV Corp. NW Mutual Life Ins. Co.; Bank of Amer.; ARCO; Union Oil Co.; **PREV EMPLOY:** VP of Cushman & Wakefield of CA; **PROFL AFFIL & HONORS:** NV Devel. Auth.; Downtown Progress Assn.;

EDUC: BS, 1964, Econ., Univ. of CA at Santa Barbara; **MIL SERV:** US Army Signal Corp, Capt.; **OTHER ACT & HONORS:** Las Vegas C of C; Bd. of Dir., Hebrew Acad.; Downtown Progress Assn.; MX Task Force Comm.; **HOME ADD:** 230 Dalmation Ln., Las Vegas, NV 89107, (702)870-0376; **BUS ADD:** 1001 S. Third St. Suite A, Las Vegas, NV 89101, (702)731-6700.

BRINKOETTER, Thomas——B: Nov. 6, 1927, Decatur, IL, *Pres.*, Tom Brinkoetter & Co. Realtors; **PRIM RE ACT:** Broker, Consultant, Developer, Builder, Property Manager; **SERVICES:** Prop. Mgmt. - Res. & Comml. Brokerage - Condo. Const. - Consulting with Investors; **REP CLIENTS:** Indiv. in Brokerage Bus. - Owners of Res. & Comml. Prop. via Prop. Mgmt.; **PROFL AFFIL & HONORS:** Decator Bd. of Realtors, IL Assn. of Realtors, NAA, RMNI, GRI, CR-S, CRB - Sec. IAR; **HOME ADD:** 4524 Baker Woods Place, Decatur, IL 62521, (217)422-2767; **BUS ADD:** 1968 E Pershing Rd., Decatur, IL 62526, (217)875-0555.

BRITT, Fredric A.——B: Feb. 1, 1949, Brooklyn, NY, *Dir. of Mktg. & Sales, Sec./Treas., Realtor-Pres.*, Islander Homes of FL, Inc., Islander Homes, I.H.C. Corp., Islander Realty; **PRIM RE ACT:** Broker, Syndicator, Consultant, Developer, Builder, Property Manager, Owner/Investor; **OTHER RE ACT:** Custom Homes, Comml. RE, Shopping Center; **SERVICES:** All; **PREV EMPLOY:** Rutenberg Homes, Div. of US Homes; **PROFL AFFIL & HONORS:** NAHB, Bd. of Realtors, Natl. & FL ICSC; **EDUC:** BS Econ., 1971, Econ. & Bus., Psychology & Pol. Sci., Univ. of Tampa; **OTHER ACT & HONORS:** Mason, Bd. of Dirs. Univ. of TPA; **HOME ADD:** 6603 Maybole Pl., Temple Terrace, FL 33617, (813)977-3996; **BUS ADD:** 12420 N. Dale Mabry Bldg. C-1, Tampa, FL 33618, (813)961-5063.

BRITT, George Gitton, Jr.——B: May 19, 1949, Brooklyn, NY, *Chmn.*, George Britt Jr. and Staff, Admin.; **PRIM RE ACT:** Consultant, Attorney, Owner/Investor, Instructor, Property Manager; **SERVICES:** Mgmt., consultant, legal, pol. consultant; **PREV EMPLOY:** Chmn., Community Devel. Program; **PROFL AFFIL & HONORS:** Amer. Mgmt. Assn.; Intl. City Mgmt. Assn.; Amer. Soc. for Public Admin.; **EDUC:** BA, 1972, Pol. Sci./Urban Studies, Cheyney State Coll.; **GRAD EDUC:** 1974, Georgetown Univ. Law School/USC; **OTHER ACT & HONORS:** Democratic State Nat. Comm.; Nat. Assn. of Puerto Rican Youth Inst. for Advancement; Puerto Rican Public Affairs; Co.-Pres., Council for Equal Job Opportunity; Hon. Citizen of MN, WV, TX, AL, AR, City of Minneapolis; Chmn. Inter-Racial Econ. Devel. Forum; Former Delegate to White House Conference on Small Bus. and on Families; **HOME ADD:** 906 S. 60th St., Philadelphia, PA 14143, (215)471-1263; **BUS ADD:** 436 W. Somerset St., Philadelphia, PA 19143, (215)474-5204.

BRITTON, Robert——*SIR, Asst. Secy. & Gen. Mgr. of Prop.*, TRW, Inc.; **PRIM RE ACT:** Property Manager; **BUS ADD:** 23555 Euclid Ave., Cleveland, OH 44117, (216)383-2121.*

BRITTON, Thomas B.——B: Feb. 11, 1944, New Rochelle, NY, *VP*, Landauer Assoc., Inc., Technical Services; **PRIM RE ACT:** Consultant, Appraiser; **OTHER RE ACT:** Appraiser/consultant/advisor; **SERVICES:** Investment counseling, evaluation reports for buyers, sellers/lenders; **REP CLIENTS:** Indivs., corps., synds., and lenders (comml. props.); **PREV EMPLOY:** Citibank N.A. 1970-73; Albert B. Ashforth 1973-78; William A. White & Sons 1978-80; **PROFL AFFIL & HONORS:** AIREA (MAI), SREA; **EDUC:** BS, 1969, Educ., Jacksonville Univ.; **EDUC HONORS:** Green Key Hon. Soc.; **HOME ADD:** 30 Club Rd., Rye, NY 10580, (914)967-7042; **BUS ADD:** 200 Park Ave., NY, NY 10017, (212)687-2323.

BRITTON, Willard B.——*Comptroller*, Knight-Ridder Newspapers, Inc.; **PRIM RE ACT:** Property Manager; **BUS ADD:** One Herald Plaza, Miami, FL 33101, (305)350-2921.*

BRITVAN, Max S.——B: Aug. 23, 1927, Brooklyn, NY, Britvan Realty Associates; **PRIM RE ACT:** Broker, Developer, Builder, Owner/Investor, Property Manager; **PROFL AFFIL & HONORS:** IREM, Officer & Dir. of Brooklyn Bd. of Realtors, AMO, CPM; **MIL SERV:** US Army, PFC; **HOME ADD:** 645 Barnard Ave., Woodmere, NY 11598, (516)295-2308; **BUS ADD:** 26 Court St., Brooklyn, NY 11242, (212)624-7700.

BRITZ, John——*Executive Vice President*, Bally Manufacturing Corp.; **PRIM RE ACT:** Property Manager; **BUS ADD:** 2640 Balmont Ave., Chicago, IL 60618, (312)267-6060.*

BROAD, Eli——B: June 6, 1933, NY, *Chmn. of the Bd.*, Kaufman & Broad, Inc.; **PRIM RE ACT:** Developer, Builder, Owner/Investor, Insuror; **PROFL AFFIL & HONORS:** CPA; Dir. Nat. Energy Found.; Dir., Citibank, NY; Bus. Comm. for the Arts; Member, Fed. Nat. Mort. Assn.; Member of Advisory Bd. of Exec. Comm., Council of Housing Producers, Co-Founder; CA State Univ. and Coll., Member of the Bd. of Trustees; The Claremont Coll., Claremont, CA; Member of the Exec. Comm. of the Bd. of Fellows; Inst. of Intl. Educ., Dir, Windward School, Santa Monica, CA; Founding Trustee, Pitzer Coll., Claremont, CA; Member of the Bd. of Trustees, Univ. of CA at Los Angeles; Grad. School of Mgmt.; Member of Visiting Comm.; Member of Chancellor's Associates; MI State Univ., Dir. of Devel. Bd., Member of Pres. Club, Beta Alpha Psi; Housing Man of the Yr., Nat. Housing Conference; Humanitarian Award, Nat. Conference Christians & Jews; Amer. Academy of Achievement; Distinguished Alumni Award, MI State Univ.; Builder of the Yr., Profl. Builder Magazine; Man of the Yr. Award, City of Hope; Listed in Who's Who in the World; in the US; in Bus. and Fin.; **EDUC:** BA, Acctg./Econ., MI State Univ.; **OTHER ACT & HONORS:** Museum of Contemporary Art, Los Angeles, Chmn., Bd. of Tr.; Los Angeles Area C of C, Bd. of Dir; YMCA, Los Angeles, Member of the 8d. of Dir.; Amer. Heart Assn., Los Angeles, Campaign Comm.; Maeght Found, St. Paul de Vence, France, Member; Los Angeles, Cty. Museum of Art, Member of Contemporary Arts Council; United Crusade, Los Angeles, Assoc. Chmn.; United Way, Los Angeles, Bd. of Dir., Chmn., Loaned Exec. Campaign; World Affairs Council, Member; Nat. Brotherhood of Christians & Jews, Bd. of Dir.; City of Hope, Bd. of Dir., Exec. Comm.; Eli and Edythe L. Broad Found.; Eli Broad Family Found; Music Ctr., Los Angeles, Founder; Supporter, Pitzer Coll., United Jewis, United Way; Hillcrest Ctry. Club, Los Angeles; The Regency Club, Los Angeles; **BUS ADD:** 10801 National Blvd., Los Angeles, CA 90064, (213)475-6711.

BROADBENT, William R.——B: Nov. 13, 1934, Los Angeles, CA, *Pres.*, Arnett & Broadbent Inc.; **PRIM RE ACT:** Broker, Consultant, Owner/Investor, Instructor, Syndicator, Real Estate Publisher; **PROFL AFFIL & HONORS:** Pres., Who's Who in Creative RE; NAR; Soc. of Exchange Counselors; Intl. Platform Assn.; SLO Cty. Exchangors; Intl. Assn. of Fin. Planners; CCIM, Award, 1973 CREA, Best Exchange Under –250,000; 1973 Counselor of the Yr., Nat. Soc. of Exchange Counselors; 1979 FLI Best Transaction over –250,000; **EDUC:** BS, 1956, CA Poly State Univ.; **GRAD EDUC:** MBA, 1958, Cornell Univ.; **OTHER ACT & HONORS:** Amer. Cancer Soc.; **HOME ADD:** 1237 Fredericks St., San Luis Obispo, CA 93401; **BUS ADD:** 1380 Broad St., San Luis Obispo, CA 93401, (805)543-9100.

BROADHURST, Rachel B.——B: May 11, 1941, NC, *Sec./Treas.*, Century 21 McAlpine Marsh Broadhurst, Inc.; **PRIM RE ACT:** Broker, Developer, Owner/Investor, Property Manager; **SERVICES:** Resid. sales and servicing, comml.-investment sales and serv. prop. mgmt.; **REP CLIENTS:** Indiv. and instnl. investors, gen. resid. Re purchasers and owners; **PROFL AFFIL & HONORS:** Myrtle Beach Bd. of Adjustments; NAR; Myrtle Beach, SC Assn. of Realtors; Past Pres., Sec., Treas. Myrtle Beach Bd. of Realtors; SC State Dir., C of C Past Dir., MLS Past Pres., GRI, CRS, and Candidate CCIM, SC Realtor of the Year (1974), Myrtle Beach Realtor of the Year (1974), Omega Tau Rho Medal of Serv. from NAR (1978), SC Honor Bd. of Pres. 1974 & 1975; **OTHER ACT & HONORS:** Dir. United Way, Pilot Club (Past Pres.), Cancer Soc. (Past Pres. & Chmn. of Bd. for Cty.), Bus. and Profl. Woman's Club (Past Pres.), Who's Who in Outstanding Young Women in Myrtle America 1976, Myrtle Beach Career Woman of the Year 1973, Who's Who in Sales & Mktg. 1974; **HOME ADD:** 4706 Camellia Dr., P O Box 2202, Myrtle Beach, SC 29577, (803)449-3211; **BUS ADD:** 3405 N. Kings Hwy., Myrtle Beach, SC 29577, (803)448-7169.

BROADMAN, Arthur R.——B: Jan. 2, 1915, NY, NY, *VP/Corp. RE*, Amerada Hess Corp.; **PRIM RE ACT:** Property Manager; **PREV EMPLOY:** Tenneco Inc., Houston, TX; **EDUC:** BS, 1936, Chemical Eng., Yale Univ.; **HOME ADD:** Crawford Rd., Harrison, NY 10528, (914)967-3892; **BUS ADD:** 1185 Ave. of America, NY, NY 10036, (212)536-8240.

BROCKMAN, Richard E.——B: May 2, 1929, Madison, WI, *Realtor*, Don Simon Realtors; **PRIM RE ACT:** Broker, Consultant, Appraiser, Property Manager, Lender; **OTHER RE ACT:** Exchanger; **PROFL AFFIL & HONORS:** Madison Bd. of Realtors, WI Realtors Assn., WI Exchange Club; **MIL SERV:** USMC, Cpl.; **OTHER ACT & HONORS:** K of C; Past Pres., Optimist Club; Sun Prairie Amer. Legion Post 333; Former Member, Sun Prairie Jaycees; **HOME ADD:** 6060 Town Hall Dr., Sun Prairie, WI 53590, (608)837-8000; **BUS ADD:** 1500 W Main St., Sun Prairie, WI 53590, (608)837-7345.

BROCKWAY, Dennis G.——B: Jan. 15, 1934, MI, *Pres.*, Brockway Financial Corp.; **PRIM RE ACT:** Broker, Syndicator, Consultant, Owner/Investor; **SERVICES:** Priv. Synds. on Props. in Wash. & Idaho; **PREV EMPLOY:** Gen. Investment RE Brokerage since 1967; **PROFL AFFIL & HONORS:** RESSI, CCIS, SRS Candidate; **EDUC:** BS Engrg., Math & Physics, Univ. of Toledo; **MIL SERV:** USA, Sgt.; **HOME ADD:** 1758 Valpico Dr., San Jose, CA 95124, (408)723-0189;

BUS ADD: 4010 Moorpark Ave., Suite 105, San Jose, CA 95117, (408)249-2100.

BRODERICK, Roger B.——**B:** Mar. 7, 1945, Clearwater, *Pres.*, Broderick Realty Co.; **PRIM RE ACT:** Broker, Attorney, Developer, Property Manager, Engineer, Owner/Investor; **OTHER RE ACT:** Class A Gen. Contractor; **SERVICES:** Site selection, devel., build & mkt.; **PREV EMPLOY:** 13 yrs. in RE, From resid. sales to synd.; **PROFL AFFIL & HONORS:** NAR, CBA, State of FL, Class A Gen. Cont., CCIM, CRB; CRS; GRI; Top Producer for St. Petersburg Bd. of Realtors, 1970-80; Member of Million Dollar Round Table; **EDUC:** BE, 1967, Univ. of FL; **EDUC HONORS:** Magna Cum Laude; **HOME ADD:** 446 18th Ave., St. Petersburg, FL 33706, (813)895-4797; **BUS ADD:** 5514 Park Blvd., Pinellas Park, FL 35565, (813)544-1403.

BRODIE, Douglas S.——**B:** Mar. 3, 1933, Tuxedo Park, NY, *Sr. VP and Mgr.*, Hunneman and Company, Inc., Comml., indus., investment div.; **PRIM RE ACT:** Broker, Consultant; **SERVICES:** Brokerage and consulting; **REP CLIENTS:** Comml. and indus. prop. owners and investors; **PROFL AFFIL & HONORS:** Greater Boston RE Bd., RNMI, C of C; **EDUC:** AB, 1956, eng., Williams Coll.; **MIL SERV:** US Army, Sgt., 1956-58; **HOME ADD:** 7 Curve St., Sherborn, MA 01770, (617)655-6232; **BUS ADD:** One Winthrop Sq., Boston, MA 02110, (617)426-4260.

BRODIE, M.J.——**B:** Sept. 25, 1936, Baltimore, MD, *Commnr.*, Dept. Housing/Community Dev., City of Baltimore; **PRIM RE ACT:** Architect; **OTHER RE ACT:** City Official; **SERVICES:** Planning, Devel., Managing; **PREV EMPLOY:** M.J. Brodie AIA/Architect; Cochran - Stephenson - Donkerjoet - Architect, Baltimore; **PROFL AFFIL & HONORS:** AIA; NAHRO; ULI; **EDUC:** B.Arch., Univ. of VA; **GRAD EDUC:** M.Arch., Rice Univ.; **HOME ADD:** 2217 Foxbane Sq., Baltimore, MD 21209, (301)542-2842; **BUS ADD:** 222 E. Saratoga St., Baltimore, MD 21202, (301)396-3232.

BRODSKY, Avrom D.——**B:** Dec. 2, 1933, Tulsa, OK, *VP*, United Properties, Inc.; **PRIM RE ACT:** Developer, Property Manager, Owner/Investor; **SERVICES:** Dev. of comml. prop.; **REP CLIENTS:** Indiv. investors; **PROFL AFFIL & HONORS:** AIA, ICSC; **EDUC:** BArch, 1957, Univ. of OK; **MIL SERV:** USAF, Lt.; **HOME ADD:** 2825 E. 56th Pl., Tulsa, OK 74105, (918)742-3047; **BUS ADD:** 6650 S. Lewis, Tulsa, OK 74136, (918)494-4034.

BRODSKY, Frederic L.——**B:** May 11, 1941, Rochester, NY, *Dir.*, Brodsky School of Real Estate; **PRIM RE ACT:** Consultant, Developer, Builder, Owner/Investor, Instructor, Property Manager; **OTHER RE ACT:** Dir. of school; **SERVICES:** RE sales and broker training; **EDUC:** BSME, 1964, Engrg., Rochester Inst. of Tech.; **GRAD EDUC:** MBA, 1967, Bus. & Law, Univ. of AZ; **OTHER ACT & HONORS:** Founding member and past pres. of AZ Assn. of RE Schools; Member, Bd. of Dirs. of Tuscon Youth Hockey Club; Member, RE Educators Assn.; Member, Associated Mortgage Brokers of AZ; **HOME ADD:** 7561 E. Lee Pl., Tucson, AZ 85715, (602)886-4501; **BUS ADD:** 720 S. Craycroft, Tucson, AZ 85711, (602)747-1485.

BRODTY, Charles——**B:** Nov. 8, 1940, Chicago, IL, *Owner*, Computer Realty; **PRIM RE ACT:** Banker, Owner/Investor, Real Estate Publisher; **OTHER RE ACT:** Attorney's consultant; **SERVICES:** Computer Simulations of Investment, Tax & Economic & Scenarios on Fee Basis for clients of –500,000+ net worth, and occasionally, agent for Realty Transactions; **REP CLIENTS:** Proprietary, But originally contacted via Pvt. Aircraft Brokerage Activity; **PREV EMPLOY:** Aircraft Sales and Computer Systems Analyst; **PROFL AFFIL & HONORS:** Data Processing Mgt. Assoc., Cert. Data Processing, former: S.F. Multiple Listing Assn., CPA Candidate; **EDUC:** Econ., 1963, Economic Hist., S.F. State Univ.; **GRAD EDUC:** MBA, Thesis incomplete, Quantitative Methods, G.G.U. - S.F. CA; **EDUC HONORS:** Woodrow Wilson Scholarship; **MIL SERV:** USA, Attache, Theatre Ribbon; **HOME TEL:** (415)332-9100; **BUS ADD:** POB 3503, San Francisco, CA 94119, (415)332-9100.

BROLL, William F., Esq.——**B:** Nov. 8, 1941, Atlantic City, NJ, *Atty. at Law (Partner)*, Lillick McHose & Charles, RE Grp.; **PRIM RE ACT:** Attorney; **SERVICES:** Advice regarding all RE matters with emphasis on lge. RE devels./acquisitions and for. investors; **PROFL AFFIL & HONORS:** ABA, CA Bar Assn., San Francisco Bar Assn.; **EDUC:** AB, 1963, Econ., Stanford Univ.; **GRAD EDUC:** JD, 1966, Law, Univ. of WI; **EDUC HONORS:** Grad. with honors in Econ., Order of Coif; **HOME ADD:** 3181-B Lucas Dr., Lafayette, CA 94549, (415)284-7256; **BUS ADD:** 2 Embarcadero Ctr., Suite 2600, San Francisco, CA 94111, (415)421-4600.

BROMS, Todd J.——**B:** Jan. 6, 1950, Queens, NY, *Pres.*, Broms Capital Group, Inc.; **OTHER RE ACT:** RE Investment Bankers; **SERVICES:** Debt and equity transactions; **EDUC:** BSBA, 1972, Fin., Denver Univ.; **HOME ADD:** 1660 N. LaSalle St., Chicago, IL 60601; **BUS ADD:** 180 N. LaSalle St., Chicago, IL 60601, (312)726-3663.

BRONNENKANT, Anna——**B:** Syracuse, NY, *Associate Counsel*, First Federal Savings of AZ; **PRIM RE ACT:** Attorney, Banker, Lender; **OTHER RE ACT:** Counsel for S & L, RE transactions, loan participations, secondary market activity, comml. law; **SERVICES:** Draft documents, advise clients in compliance w/fed. regulation; **REP CLIENTS:** Real estate transaction, loan participants and secondary market activity; **PREV EMPLOY:** Community Legal Services 2 1/2 years.; **PROFL AFFIL & HONORS:** AZ State Bar, Fed. Bar; Maricopa Cty. Bar, AZ Assn. Women Lawyers, Treasurer, AZ Assoc. Women Lawyers; **EDUC:** BA, 1971, Psych., Skidmore Coll.; **GRAD EDUC:** JD, 1975, Syracuse Univ. Coll. Law; **HOME ADD:** 4926 E. Dahlia Dr., Scottsdale, AZ 85254; **BUS ADD:** 3003 N. Central Ave., Phoenix, AZ 85012, (602)248-4582.

BROOKE, Barton E., Jr.——**B:** July 20, 1918, Youngstown, OH, *VP*, Interval Mktg. Grp., Inc. & Reap; **PRIM RE ACT:** Broker, Consultant, Appraiser, Developer, Owner/Investor, Syndicator; **SERVICES:** Project fin. and mktg.; RE investment counseling; valuation; comml. prop. synd.; **REP CLIENTS:** Comml., attys., investment counselors, indiv. and corp. RE investors; **PROFL AFFIL & HONORS:** NASD; RESSI; NACPA, GRI; CRPA; **EDUC:** BS, Engrg., Parks Air Coll., St. Louis Univ.; **MIL SERV:** US Army; T/Sgt.; Purple Heart; **OTHER ACT & HONORS:** Legislative & Taxation Comm., Appraisal Comm., Cleveland Area Bd. of Realtors; **HOME ADD:** 174 Willow Ln., Chagrin Falls, OH 44022, (216)247-6323; **BUS ADD:** 20515 Shaker Blvd., Cleveland, OH 44122, (216)991-8400.

BROOKE, Joseph A., Jr.——**B:** Dec. 15, 1928, Jenkintown, PA, *Pres.*, Treasure Lake Co., a subs. of Westinghouse Electric Corp.; **PRIM RE ACT:** Developer, Builder, Property Manager; **PROFL AFFIL & HONORS:** Exec. Group; Recreational Development Council of ULI; ALDA Assn.; **EDUC:** BBA, 1953, Fin., Acctg., Univ. of Miami, FL; **MIL SERV:** US Army; **HOME ADD:** 10132 Ramblewood Dr., Coral Springs, FL 33065, (305)752-4184; **BUS ADD:** 3300 Univ. Dr., Coral Springs, FL 33065, (305)752-1100.

BROOKS, Brenna C.——*VP*, Creative Financial Corp. II; **PRIM RE ACT:** Broker, Developer, Owner/Investor, Property Manager; **BUS ADD:** 1314 N 3rd St., Phoenix AZ 85004.

BROOKS, B.V.——**B:** Sept. 2, 1926, New York, NY, *Pres.*, Brooks, Torrey & Scott, Inc.; **PRIM RE ACT:** Broker, Consultant, Developer, Owner/Investor, Property Manager, Syndicator; **EDUC:** AB, 1947, Psych., Dartmouth Coll.; **GRAD EDUC:** MBA, 1949, Fin., Amos Tuck School of Bus. Admin.; **EDUC HONORS:** Magna Cum Laude, Phi Beta Kappa, MBA with Distinction; **MIL SERV:** US Naval Res., Midshipman; **OTHER ACT & HONORS:** Dir., R.C. Memhard & Co. (Investment Bankers); Dir., Warner Investing Corp., Dir., Member Exec. Comm., Cty. Fed. S&L Assn. Westport, CT, Trustee, King Indus. Props., Boston, MA; **HOME ADD:** Jones Park Dr., Riverside, CT 06878; **BUS ADD:** 136 Main St., Westport, CT 06880, (203)226-6363.

BROOKS, C. Donald——**B:** Oct. 25, 1932, Sudbury Ont., Can., *VP*, Markborough Props. Ltd., FL Region; **PRIM RE ACT:** Developer, Builder; **PREV EMPLOY:** Devel. interest in resid. comml. indust., & rec. land; **PROFL AFFIL & HONORS:** APEO; **EDUC:** RMC, 1956, Civil Engrg., Queens Univ. Kingston, Ont.; BS, 1957, Univ. Kingston Ontario; **MIL SERV:** RCN(ret.), Lt.; **OTHER ACT & HONORS:** Bd. of Gov. Peel Memorial Hospital 1975-79, RMC Ex. Cadet Club of Can.; **HOME ADD:** 1718 N. Goldeneye Lane, Homestead, FL 33035, (305)248-5860; **BUS ADD:** 311 NE 8th St., Homestead, FL 33030, (305)245-3030.

BROOKS, David Carl——**B:** June 26, 1942, Chicago, IL, *VP Corporate RE*, Majestic Savings & Loan Assn.; **PRIM RE ACT:** Banker, Developer, Lender, Builder, Owner/Investor, Property Manager; **OTHER RE ACT:** Leasing, consulting to other S&L owned by same holding co.; **SERVICES:** Acquisition, devel., mgmt. at companies RE; **PREV EMPLOY:** RE Analysis Columbia Corp.; Acquisition Assn. RE Investment Serv. Corp.; **PROFL AFFIL & HONORS:** CO RE Brokers Lic.; Nat. Assn. of Corporate RE Execs.; BOMA; **EDUC:** BA, 1965, Poli. Sci., Econ., Univ. of CO; **MIL SERV:** USAR, Sgt., 1965-1071; **HOME ADD:** 7221 E Hinsdale Ave., Englewood, CO 80112, (303)770-0807; **BUS ADD:** 2420 W 26th Ave., Denver, CO 80211, (303)455-1890.

BROOKS, Donald B.——**B:** Aug. 19, 1942, Chicago, IL, *Exec. VP & COO*, The Landmarks Group; **PRIM RE ACT:** Developer; **SERVICES:** RE devel., mktg. & mgmt.; **PROFL AFFIL & HONORS:** Nat. Assn. of Indus. & Office Parks; ULI; AICPA; ABA; **EDUC:** BA, 1965, Acctg., Duke Univ.; **GRAD EDUC:** JD, 1968, Duke Univ. School of

Law; **HOME ADD:** 1655 Huntingdon Trail, Atlanta, GA 30338, (404)396-0315; **BUS ADD:** Suite 100, 880 Johnson Ferry Rd., Atlanta, GA 30042, (404)252-6490.

BROOKS, Helen——B: July 27, 1930, Sioux City, IA, *Sales Representative*, Towle Real Estate Co.; **PRIM RE ACT:** Broker; **SERVICES:** Indus., comml. brokerage; **PREV EMPLOY:** Pres. Brokers Exchange Inc.; **PROFL AFFIL & HONORS:** Greater Minneapolis Bd. of Realtors; Nat. Assn. of Indus. & Office Parks, C-I/MLS; SIR (Soc. of Indus. Realtors; **EDUC:** BA, 1952, Univ. of MN; **HOME ADD:** 1044 Cedar View Dr., Minneapolis, MN 55405, (612)277-2580; **BUS ADD:** 600-2nd Ave. South, Minneapolis, MN 55402, (612)341-4444.

BROOKS, J. William——B: May 25, 1945, Lebanon, PA, *Part.*, Indus. Comml. Investments Co.; **PRIM RE ACT:** Broker, Instructor, Syndicator, Consultant, Appraiser, Developer, Owner/Investor; **OTHER RE ACT:** Mort. Broker; **SERVICES:** Acquisition of Investment RE, Counseling and Valuation of Comml. Investment RE; **PROFL AFFIL & HONORS:** RESSI; RNMI, CCIM; GRI; **EDUC:** BA, 1968, Eng., Colgate Univ.; **HOME ADD:** 268 Whitemarsh Pl., Macungie, PA 18062, (215)966-5646; **BUS ADD:** Hotel Traylor, Suite 501, Allentown, PA 18102, (215)776-0700.

BROOKS, Kenneth Donald——B: Sept. 26, 1931, Shelbyville, KY, *RE Devel. Officer*, The George Washington University; **PRIM RE ACT:** Architect, Appraiser, Developer, Builder, Owner/Investor; **PREV EMPLOY:** Deputy Comdr. for Acquisition, Asst. Comdr. for Const. & Contracts NAUFAC, USN; **PROFL AFFIL & HONORS:** Nat. Assn. of Corp. RE Execs., SAME, AIA (ASSO), ASPSB, Sec. & dir. 2000 PA Ave., Inc.; **EDUC:** BS, 1954, Arch. engrg., GA Tech.; **GRAD EDUC:** MS, 1966, Fin. mgmt., USN Post Grad. School Monterey; **MIL SERV:** USN, Capt., CEC, Bronze Star, Navy Commendation Medal; **OTHER ACT & HONORS:** Pres. Citizens Assn.; **HOME ADD:** 2701 Park Center Dr., Alexandria, VA 22302; **BUS ADD:** Rice Hall 7th fl., The George Washington Univ., Washington, DC 20052, (302)676-6600.

BROOKS, Peter S.——B: June 23, 1942, Newburgh, NY, *VP*, Chemical Bank, RE Div.; **PRIM RE ACT:** Banker, Lender; **OTHER RE ACT:** Mort. Officer; **REP CLIENTS:** Maj. New York City RE Owners, Devels. & Mgrs.; **PREV EMPLOY:** Assessor, City of Newburgh, NY, 1975-76; Self Employed RE Broker 1972-1975; **PROFL AFFIL & HONORS:** RE Bd. of NY; AIREA, MAI, Lic. RE Broker, NY State; **EDUC:** BA, 1963, Sociology, NYU; **HOME ADD:** 378 S. Little Tor Rd., New City, NY 10956; **BUS ADD:** 633 Third Ave., New York, NY 10017, (212)878-7792.

BROOKS, Robert H.——B: Feb. 25, 1936, Manchester, NH, *Pres.*, HABS/ERA Inc., Realtors; **PRIM RE ACT:** Broker, Consultant, Appraiser, Developer, Property Manager, Owner/Investor; **SERVICES:** Gen. RE brokerage, devel. & synd. appraising, consulting; **REP CLIENTS:** Indiv. & comml. investors; **PROFL AFFIL & HONORS:** RESSI, RNMI, NHCID, Nat. Assn. of Realtors, NH Homebuilders; **MIL SERV:** US Army, Sgt.; **OTHER ACT & HONORS:** Bd. of Selectmen, Town of Bedford, 12 years; Planning Bd., Town of Bedford, 4 years; S. NH Rgnl. Planning Commn., 2 years; Corporator Merchants Savings Bank; **HOME ADD:** Liberty Hill Road, Bedford, NH 03102, (603)472-3844; **BUS ADD:** 111 Route 101, Bedford, NH 03102, (603)669-7441.

BROOKS, Ron——B: Sept. 2, 1942, Jackson, MS, *VP - Gen. Mgr.*, Patterson RE Agency; **PRIM RE ACT:** Broker; **SERVICES:** Full Serv. RE; **REP CLIENTS:** Merrill Lynch; Van Relco; Equitable Relocation; Relocation Realty Serv.; **PREV EMPLOY:** LA Relations Assn.; **PROFL AFFIL & HONORS:** RNMI, CRB, GRI, IFA; **EDUC:** BS, 1965, Pharmacy, Univ. of MS; **MIL SERV:** USANG; T Sgt.; **OTHER ACT & HONORS:** Kiwanis Club; **HOME ADD:** 1612 Chantilly Dr., Houma, LA 70360; **BUS ADD:** PO Box 1867, Houma, LA 70360, (504)868-5230.

BROOKS, S.W.——B: Feb. 5, 1945, Bradley Cty., TN, *Training Dir.*, Phillips Real Estate; **PRIM RE ACT:** Broker, Appraiser, Owner/Investor, Instructor, Property Manager, Insuror; **SERVICES:** Resid. listing and sales and appraisal; **PROFL AFFIL & HONORS:** RNMI; TN Assn. of Realtors; NAR; Cleveland Bd. of Realtors, CRB; CRS; Realtor of Yr., 1979; Realtor/Assoc. of Yr., 1976; Pres., Cleveland Bd. of Realtors; Tr., TN RE Educ. Foundation; **EDUC:** BS, 1967, Mat./Nat. Sci., Univ. of TN; **GRAD EDUC:** Math, 1968, Math., Univ. of TN; **EDUC HONORS:** With Honors; **OTHER ACT & HONORS:** Jaycee Pres.; Senator; Child Shelter Bd.; **HOME ADD:** 533 Blueberry Hill Rd., NE, Cleveland, TN 37311, (615)479-2547; **BUS ADD:** 4021 Keith St., N.W., Cleveland, TN 37311, (615)472-7171.

BROOKS, Wendell F., Jr.——B: Feb. 10, 1935, Honolulu, HI, *Managing Dir.*, Chaney, Brooks & Co.; **PRIM RE ACT:** Broker, Consultant, Developer, Property Manager; **SERVICES:** Prop. Mgmt., brokerage & devel. mgmt. servs.; **REP CLIENTS:** Prop. owners, devels., leading insts.; **PREV EMPLOY:** Exec. VP Oceanic Props., Inc., Gen Mgr. Wailea Devel. Co.; **PROFL AFFIL & HONORS:** IREM, NAR, Home Builders Assn., CPM; **EDUC:** 1959, Bus. Admin./RE, Univ of CA; **OTHER ACT & HONORS:** Pacific Club, Outrigger Canoe Club, Maui Ctry. Club; **HOME ADD:** 1597 Kalaniuka Cir., Honolulu, HI 96821, (808)373-9554; **BUS ADD:** PO Box 212, Honolulu, HI 96810, (808)521-6971.

BROPHY, Jack——*Mgr. R.E. Adm.*, U.S. Gypsum; **PRIM RE ACT:** Property Manager; **OTHER RE ACT:** Property Manager; **BUS ADD:** 101 South Wacker Drive, Chicago, IL 60606, (312)321-4000.*

BROPHY, Mary Alice——*Commissioner of Securities & RE*, Minnesota, MN Real Estate Commission; **PRIM RE ACT:** Property Manager; **BUS ADD:** 500 Metro Sq., St. Paul, MN 55101, (612)296-9458.*

BROSHAR, Scott——B: Jan. 7, 1955, Ft. Belvoir, VA, *Assoc.*, O'Brien, Ehrick, Wolf, Deaner and Downing; **PRIM RE ACT:** Attorney; **SERVICES:** All legal serv. assoc. with purchase and sale of RE; **REP CLIENTS:** Buyers and sellers of RE, lending instns.; **PREV EMPLOY:** Amer. Title Ins. Co. of Wahtenaw 1978-80; **PROFL AFFIL & HONORS:** Olmsted Cty. Bar Assn. (real prop. comm.), MN State Bar Assn. (real prop. sect.), ABA (real prop., probate and trust law sect.), Forum Comm. on the Const. Indus.; **EDUC:** BA, 1977, Econ., Hist., Philosophy, Poli. Sci., Univ. of IA; **GRAD EDUC:** JD, 1980, Univ. of MI; **EDUC HONORS:** Pres. Local Chap. micron Delta Epsilon, Charles Leavitt Award, with Honors; **OTHER ACT & HONORS:** Rochester Bldg. Code Bd. of Appeals, 1981; **HOME ADD:** 948 8th Ave. SE, Rochester, MN 55901, (507)281-4905; **BUS ADD:** 611 Marquette Bank Bldg., Rochester, MN 55901, (507)289-4041.

BROSS, Joel L.——B: Dec. 31, 1933, Jersey City, NJ, *VP*, Republic Funding Corp.; **PRIM RE ACT:** Broker, Syndicator; **SERVICES:** Sales, Synd., Mort. broker; **REP CLIENTS:** Devel., Ins. Cos., Pension Fund Mgrs.; **PREV EMPLOY:** Webb & Knapp Inc. 1958-1962, Alcoa Props. Inc. 1962-1964; **EDUC:** BS, 1955, Bus. Admin., Lehigh Univ.; **MIL SERV:** USA, Sgt.; **HOME ADD:** 125 E. 84th St., NY, NY 10028, (212)861-5670; **BUS ADD:** 645 Madison Ave., New York, NY 10022, (212)688-3733.

BROUGHAM, Robert D.——B: Oct. 25, 1941, New Orleans, LA, *Pres.*, Broughan Real Estate Co.; **PRIM RE ACT:** Broker; **SERVICES:** Investment prop. exchanging; **PROFL AFFIL & HONORS:** CCIM, CO Exchange of the Year; **HOME ADD:** 23 Spyglass Dr., Littleton, CO 80123; **BUS ADD:** Suite 309, 1776 S. Jackson St., Denver, CO 80210, (303)753-0267.

BROUHARD, James A., Jr.——B: Mar. 28, 1943, Kansas City, MO, *VP*, Merrill Lynch Realty / Tom Fannin & Assoc.; **PRIM RE ACT:** Broker, Consultant; **SERVICES:** Complete Residential Dev. Services from Conception to Final Sale Including Fin. Mktg. and Sales Admin.; **REP CLIENTS:** Residential Dev., Lenders and Instnl. Investors; **PROFL AFFIL & HONORS:** NAR, RNMI, NAHB, RESSI, CRS, GRI; **EDUC:** Mktg., AZ State Univ.; **OTHER ACT & HONORS:** Commnr. Scottsdale Recreation & Parks Commn.; Bds. of Dirs.: Scottsdale Boys Club, Sales & Mktg. Execs. of Phoenix, Phoenix C of C InterCity Comm.; **HOME ADD:** 5225 N. Woodmere Fairway, Scottsdale, AZ 85253, (602)945-7333; **BUS ADD:** 3221 N. 24th St., Phoenix, AZ 85016, (602)956-5630.

BROUNSTEIN, Sam——B: Sept. 30, 1924, Brooklyn, NY, *Partner*, Advance Realty Assoc.; **PRIM RE ACT:** Broker, Consultant, Owner/Investor; **SERVICES:** Act as broker in large office bldg., shopping ctr. & apts.; **REP CLIENTS:** Indiv. & Synd.; **PREV EMPLOY:** Helmsley-Spear Inc.; **MIL SERV:** USA, T-5, Purple Heart; **HOME ADD:** 28 E 73rd St., New York, NY 10021, (212)734-5022; **BUS ADD:** 18 W 56 St., NY, NY 10021, (212)247-8148.

BROWDER, Olin L.——B: Dec. 19, 1913, Urbana IL, *James V. Campbell Prof of Law*, Univ. of MI, Law School; **PRIM RE ACT:** Instructor; **PROFL AFFIL & HONORS:** ABA, Phi Alpha Delta; **EDUC:** LLB, 1937, Univ. of IL; **GRAD EDUC:** SJD, 1941, Wills, Univ. of MI; **EDUC HONORS:** with Honors; **HOME ADD:** 1520 Edinborough, Ann Arbor, MI 48104, (313)971-7456; **BUS ADD:** Hutchins Hall, Ann Arbor, MI 48109, (313)764-0547.

BROWDY, Joseph E.——B: July 23, 1937, Brooklyn, NY, *Partner*, Paul, Weiss, Rifkind, Wharton & Garrison; **PRIM RE ACT:** Attorney; **PROFL AFFIL & HONORS:** ABA, NY State Bar Assn., Assn. of the Bar of the City of NY, Member of Bd. of Advisors, RE Bd. Report,

Member of Bd. of Advisors, Prime-PM Profl. Mgmt. Network; **EDUC:** BA, 1958, Hist., Oberlin Coll.; **GRAD EDUC:** LLB, 1961, NYU Law School; **EDUC HONORS:** Phi Beta Kappa, Order of the Coif; **MIL SERV:** USAR, sp5; **OTHER ACT & HONORS:** Pres. of Bd. of Trustees, Bronx House-Emanuel Camps, Inc.; Trustee, Lenox School; Trustee, Independence House, Inc.; **HOME ADD:** 1185 Park Ave., New York, NY 10028; **BUS ADD:** 345 Park Ave., New York, NY 10154, (212)644-8720.

BROWER, Barbara Brane——B: Nov. 13, 1936, Auburn, NY, *Atty.*, Own firm; **PRIM RE ACT:** Consultant, Attorney; **SERVICES:** Consultant on joint ventures, financing applications to HUD and state housing fin. agencies; Lawyer for HUD closings, private RE closings, coops and condos.; **REP CLIENTS:** City of Boston; City of Cambridge; Frankie O'Day Corp. (coop); Jasins & Sayles Associates, Inc.; Tenants' Development Corp.; Forest Hills Housing, Inc. (coop); **PREV EMPLOY:** Greater Boston Community Devel., Inc., Project Counsel, 1974-1976; Dir. of Housing Devel. for Boston Model Cities, 1972-1974; **PROFL AFFIL & HONORS:** MBA, Prop. Sect., Member of Urban Redevel. Comm. and Public Law Section; ABA, Prop. and Probate Sect., Citizens Housing & Planning Assn.; formerly on the Bd. of Dirs., New Communities Housing Mgmt. Corp.; Dir. and Treas., Women's Inst. for Housing & Econ. Devel., Inc.; **EDUC:** BA, 1958, Govt./Econ., Smith Coll.; **GRAD EDUC:** JD, 1972, Legal Studies, Boston Univ.; **EDUC HONORS:** Magna Cum Laude, Top fifth of class; Book Award (for highest grade) in Partnerships and Closed Corps.; **OTHER ACT & HONORS:** Cambridge Ward Seven Comm., Chairperson, 1974-1975, Sec., 1972-1973; Bd. of Dirs., Greater Boston Chap. of Amer. Red Cross; Bd. of Dirs. and Clerk, Neighborhood Development Corp. of Jamaica Plain; **HOME ADD:** 17 Union Ave., Jamaica Plain, MA 02130; **BUS ADD:** 54 Devonshire St., Boston, MA 02109, (617)227-1911.

BROWN, Albert E.——*Mgr. Admin. Services*, Marley Co.; **PRIM RE ACT:** Property Manager; **BUS ADD:** 1900 Johnson Dr., Mission Woods, KS 66205, (913)362-5440.*

BROWN, Alton R., III——B: Jan. 28, 1953, Columbus, GA, *Project Coordinator*, Herman Maisel & Co. Inc., Development; **PRIM RE ACT:** Broker, Developer, Property Manager; **SERVICES:** Full Service RE Brokerage, Devel., Mgmt. Firm; **PROFL AFFIL & HONORS:** NAR; RNMI; Mobile Cty. Bd. of Realtors; RE Exchange of Mobile; **EDUC:** BA, 1976, Hist./Poli. Sci., Univ. of S. AL; **GRAD EDUC:** MA, 1978, Hist./Econ. of US, Univ. of So. AL Grad. School; **EDUC HONORS:** Phi Alpha Theta Hist. Hon., Sigma Delta Tau Poli. Sci. Hon.; **OTHER ACT & HONORS:** Kiwanis Club of Mobile, Mobile Area C of C; **HOME ADD:** 2358 Taylor Ave., Mobile, AL 36606, (205)476-2155; **BUS ADD:** POB 160247, Mobile, AL 36616, (205)476-8000.

BROWN, Ayla S.——B: Jan. 10, 1939, Izmir, Turkey, *Mgr.*, Century 21, Armstrong Realty, Investment & Resid.; **PRIM RE ACT:** Broker, Consultant, Appraiser; **OTHER RE ACT:** Work with builder/devel. to put together subdivs.; **SERVICES:** Analyzing investment prop., clients counseling, mktg., working with City, Cty. & State Officials in putting together subdivs.; **REP CLIENTS:** Builders, devel., indiv. investors in resid. or comml. prop.; **PROFL AFFIL & HONORS:** NAR; CAR; RNMI; RESSI; Century 21 Investment Soc.; CCIM; **EDUC:** BA, 1957, Lib. Arts, Amer. Academy for Girls, Turkey/Alan Hancock Coll., Lompoc; **OTHER ACT & HONORS:** Boy Scouts of Amer., 1973-1975; Amer. Red Cross; **HOME ADD:** 4229 Centaur Ave., Lompoc, CA 93436, (805)733-1450; **BUS ADD:** 1700 N. H St., Lompoc, CA 93436, (805)736-5663.

BROWN, Benjamin L.——B: Nov. 22, 1929, Indianapolis, IN., *Pres.*, Brown Appraisals, Inc.; **PRIM RE ACT:** Appraiser; **PREV EMPLOY:** Phillip Pickens, MAI - Assoc., 1971-80; **PROFL AFFIL & HONORS:** W. Pasco-Tarpon Springs Bd. of Realtors., MAI, SRPA, ASA; **HOME ADD:** 515 Sandy Trail Ln., New Port Richey, FL 33553, (813)863-6819; **BUS ADD:** 1125 US Hwy. 19 S, Suite 305, New Port Richey, FL 33552, (813)847-6020.

BROWN, C. David, II——B: Nov. 29, 1951, W. Palm Beach, FL, *Atty.*, Broad and Cassel, RE; **PRIM RE ACT:** Attorney; **SERVICES:** All aspects of legal representation involving RE; **REP CLIENTS:** Amer. S&L Assn. of FL; MGIC-JANIS Props., Inc., Elmhurst Corp., Atl. So. Corp., Bel-Aire Homes, Inc., The RE Consortium and the Bank of Central FL; **PREV EMPLOY:** Rowland, Thomas, Bruggeman & Brown, P.A.; USAF; **PROFL AFFIL & HONORS:** ABA; FL Bar Assn.; ABA, Comm. on Real Prop.; FL Bar Assn., Comm. on RE & Condos.; **EDUC:** BS, 1973, Acctg., Univ. of FL; **GRAD EDUC:** JD, 1978, Real Prop./Tax/Comml. Law, Univ. of FL; **EDUC HONORS:** With Honors; **MIL SERV:** USAF, 1st Lt., Commendation Medal; **OTHER ACT & HONORS:** Rotary Club; Boys Club of Amer.; **HOME ADD:** 5018 Shelley Ct., Orlando, FL 32807; **BUS ADD:** 2699 Lee Rd., Suite 205, Winter Park, FL 32789, (305)645-1434.

BROWN, Campbell——B: Dec. 7, 1941, Nashville, TN, *VP*, Third Nat. Bank & Trust, RE; **PRIM RE ACT:** Broker, Attorney, Appraiser, Property Manager; **OTHER RE ACT:** Fund Mgr. - Third Natl. Bank in Nashville's Company Led RE Fund for Qualified Employee Benefit Plans; **PREV EMPLOY:** Self-employed - RE Devel. & Sales; **PROFL AFFIL & HONORS:** TN Bar Assn.; TN Bd. of Realtors; Amer. Inst. of Banking; Inst. of RE Mgrs., CPM; CRA (Natl. Assn. of Review Appraisers); SCV, (Intl. Inst. of Valuers); **EDUC:** BA, 1964, History/Poly Sci., Vanderbilt Univ.; **GRAD EDUC:** JD, 1967, Vanderbilt Law School; **EDUC HONORS:** Moot Court Justice; **OTHER ACT & HONORS:** Past Pres., Middle TN Chap. of The Inst. of RE Mgr.; Bd. of Dir. - Nashville Bd. of Realtors; **HOME ADD:** 4009 Harding Pl, Nashville, TN 37215, (615)383-8207; **BUS ADD:** 201 4th Ave. N., Nashville, TN 37215, (615)748-4610.

BROWN, Charles Earl——B: June 6, 1919, Columbus, OH, *Atty.*, Brown, Baker, Schlageter & Craig; **PRIM RE ACT:** Attorney; **PROFL AFFIL & HONORS:** Toledo Bar Assn.; Lucas Cty. Bar Assn.; OH State Bar Assn.; ABA; Toledo Estate Planning Council; OH Land Title Assn., Fellow, Amer. Coll. of Probate Counsel; Amer. Bar Found.; **EDUC:** AB, 1941, Hist./Educ., OH Wesleyan Univ.; **GRAD EDUC:** JD, 1949, Law, Univ. of MI; **EDUC HONORS:** Honors in Hist.; Cum Laude; **MIL SERV:** US Army, Col., FA, Bronze Star Medal; **HOME ADD:** 3758 Brookside Rd., Toledo, OH 43606, (419)535-3269; **BUS ADD:** First Federal Plaza, 711 Adams St., Toledo, OH 43624, (419)243-6281.

BROWN, Charles J.——B: May 29, 1930, Morrisville, PA, *Mgr.*, Tucson Realty & Trust Co., Casa Blanca Office; **PRIM RE ACT:** Broker, Owner/Investor; **PREV EMPLOY:** Roy H. Long Realty, Tucson, AZ 1979-1980 Mgr. Century 21, Charlie Brown Realtors, Hayward and Livermore, CA 1967-1978; **PROFL AFFIL & HONORS:** Tucson Bd. of Realtors, AZ Assn. of Realtors, Southern Alameda Cty. Bd. of Realtors, CA Assn. of Realtors, NAR, NIREB, CRB; **MIL SERV:** USMC, S/Sgt.; **OTHER ACT & HONORS:** Airport Advisory Commn., Livermore, CA - 3 years; AOPA, Tucson Multi-Housing Assn.; **HOME ADD:** 13000 Corsair Dr., Tucson, AZ 85704, (602)297-4191; **BUS ADD:** 5940 N. Oracle Rd., Tucson, AZ 85704, (602)887-1300.

BROWN, Dennis A.——B: Dec, 18, 1940, Sioux Falls, SD, *Chmn of the Bd. of Dir.*, Super 8 Motels, Inc.; **PRIM RE ACT:** Broker, Consultant, Attorney, Developer, Lender, Builder, Owner/Investor, Property Manager, Syndicator; **SERVICES:** Primarily engaged in devel. and franchising motels; **EDUC:** Univ. SD; **GRAD EDUC:** JD, 1964, Univ. SD; **OTHER ACT & HONORS:** Founder of Super 8 Motels, Inc., Chain of 112 Econ. motels located in 22 states; **BUS ADD:** 1700 S El Camino, Suite 505, San Mateo, CA 94402, (415)572-1868.

BROWN, Francis A.——B: Feb. 13, 1922, Baileyville, ME, *Atty. (Sr. Partner)*, Brown, Tibbetts, Churchill & Romei, Attys.; **PRIM RE ACT:** Attorney; **SERVICES:** Conveyancing, title examination for lenders and buyers, Title Insurance Certifications; **REP CLIENTS:** Georgia-Pacific Corp., The Merrill Trust Co., Machias Savings Bank, Calais Fed. Savings & Loan Assn.; **PROFL AFFIL & HONORS:** ABA, ME Bar Assn., Amer. Judicature Soc.; **EDUC:** BS, 1943, Chem. Engrg., Univ. of ME; **GRAD EDUC:** JD, 1950, Law, Boston Univ. Sch. of Law; **EDUC HONORS:** Tau Beta Pi (honorary engrg. soc.); **MIL SERV:** US Army, Maj.; **OTHER ACT & HONORS:** Cty. Atty., Washington Cty. 1962-66; Calais Rotary Club (Past Dist. Gov.); Trustee, Univ. of ME System; Past Bd. Chmn., ME Bd. of Bar Examiners, 1970-79; **HOME ADD:** 271 Main St., Calais, ME 04619, (207)454-3854; **BUS ADD:** 57 North St., Calais, ME 04619, (207)454-7543.

BROWN, Gordon V.——B: Jan. 22, 1929, Chicago, IL, *Architect*, Brown & Brown, Architects; **PRIM RE ACT:** Architect; **SERVICES:** Gen. architectural practice; **REP CLIENTS:** Owners, devels.; **PREV EMPLOY:** Arthur T. Brown, Architect 1960-1970; **PROFL AFFIL & HONORS:** AIA; Const. Specification Inst.; **GRAD EDUC:** BArch., 1960, Arch., OH State Univ.; **MIL SERV:** US Naval Res., Capt.; **OTHER ACT & HONORS:** Rotary, Navy League; **BUS ADD:** 726 N. Country Club Rd., Tucson, AZ 85716, (602)325-6431.

BROWN, Irving J. 'Sonny'——B: Oct. 19, 1934, Parral, Ch., Mexico, *Owner*, Sonny Brown Assoc.; **PRIM RE ACT:** Broker, Consultant, Developer, Owner/Investor, Syndicator; **SERVICES:** Leasing, site selection, investments, indus. devel.; **REP CLIENTS:** Assist local & nat. corps. in expansion and/or relocation; **PREV EMPLOY:** RE Consultant, La Salle Partners, Inc. (3 yrs.) El Paso, Dist. Sales Mgr., Gen. Cable Corp. (15 yrs.); **PROFL AFFIL & HONORS:** El Paso Bd. of Realtors, REMNI, NAR, TAR, RESSI, NAIOP; **EDUC:** BA, 1956, Econ., Pomona Coll.; **EDUC HONORS:** Dist. Mil. Grad.; **MIL SERV:** Army Med. Service Corp., 1st Lt.; **OTHER ACT & HONORS:** Pres. Rotary Club of El Paso (78-79), VP of El Paso C of C,

Bd. of Dr. Jr. Achievement, Bd. of Housing Auth. of El Paso; **HOME ADD:** 6501 La Cadena, El Paso, TX 79912, (915)584-9584; **BUS ADD:** 5862 Cromo Dr., El Paso, TX 79912, (915)584-5511.

BROWN, Jack W.——B: Oct. 17, 1922, MI, *Pres.*, Brown & Dayo & Assoc., Archs., Inc.; **PRIM RE ACT:** Architect; **SERVICES:** Complete arch. services; **PROFL AFFIL & HONORS:** AIA, MI Soc. of Arch.; **EDUC:** BS, 1945, Naval Arch. & Marine Engrg., Univ. of MI; **MIL SERV:** USNR, Lt.; **HOME ADD:** 5980 Braemoor, Birmingham, MI 48010, (313)851-4906; **BUS ADD:** 4190 Telegraph Rd., Suite 203, Bloomfield Hills, MI 48013, (313)646-8877.

BROWN, James M.——B: Sept. 17, 1938, Parksville, NJ, *Pres.*, James M. Brown Co., Realtors; **PRIM RE ACT:** Broker; **OTHER RE ACT:** Investor; **SERVICES:** RE sales & invests, comml. prop.; **PREV EMPLOY:** Resident Mgr. of Fairmont Hotel, Dallas, TX; **PROFL AFFIL & HONORS:** NAR, TX Assoc. of Realtors, Greater Dallas Bd. of Realtors, RNMI, FLI, RESSI, Home & Apt. Bldrs. Assoc., ULI; **EDUC:** BSIE, 1961, Indus. Engrg., So. Methodist Univ., Dallas, TX; **GRAD EDUC:** MSIE, 1966, MIE, So. Methodist Univ., Dallas, TX; **MIL SERV:** Texas NG, 1st Lt.; **HOME ADD:** 9906 Hathaway, Dallas, TX 75220, (214)750-8718; **BUS ADD:** 3128 Lemmon Av. E., Suite 200, Dallas, TX 75204, (214)528-3631.

BROWN, James P.——B: June 1, 1936, New York City, NY, *Pres.*, Ocean Trail Realty; **PRIM RE ACT:** Broker, Consultant, Developer, Syndicator; **SERVICES:** Site acquisition and feasibility for devels.; **REP CLIENTS:** Major for. devels.; **PROFL AFFIL & HONORS:** Applicable RE Center Membership; **EDUC:** BS, 1958, Indus. Admin., Yale Univ.; **MIL SERV:** USN Res.; Lt. j.g.; **HOME ADD:** 1000 Seminole Landing Blvd., North Palm Beach, FL 33403, (305)626-5419; **BUS ADD:** 2400 PGA Blvd., Suite 1, Palm Beach Gardens, FL 33410, (305)627-1910.

BROWN, John A.——B: Aug. 10, 1935, Concord, MA, *Pres.*, John Brown Assoc., Inc.; **PRIM RE ACT:** Consultant, Developer, Owner/Investor; **REP CLIENTS:** St. Joseph's Church, Belmont; St. Mary's Church, Charlestown; Various cities and towns, investment groups, investors; **PREV EMPLOY:** Pvt. Consultant for past 14 yrs., Prev. 10 yrs., with City Planning; **PROFL AFFIL & HONORS:** Amer. Planning Assn.; Nat. Assn. of Housing and Redevel. Officials, Former VP of N.E. Chapt., Amer. Inst. of Certified Planners, Registered landscape arch.; **EDUC:** BS, 1957, Landscape Arch., Univ. of MA; **GRAD EDUC:** M. of Pub. Admin., 1965, City Planning, NY Univ.; **MIL SERV:** USA, Sgt.; **OTHER ACT & HONORS:** Treasurer, Waterman Assn.; Past Pres., Sudbury Nonprofit Housing Corp.; **HOME ADD:** 31 Churchill St., Sudbury, MA 01776, (617)443-3386; **BUS ADD:** 131 State St., Boston, MA 02109, (617)742-1930.

BROWN, John Edgar, III——B: Apr. 2, 1936, Boone, NC, *Atty. at Law*, Bell, Painter, McMurray, Callaway, Brown & Headrick; **PRIM RE ACT:** Attorney, Owner/Investor, Instructor; **SERVICES:** Title examinations, title ins. policies; **REP CLIENTS:** Borrowers and lenders, buyers and sellers of RE; **PREV EMPLOY:** TN Valley Authority Prop. & Supply Div.; **PROFL AFFIL & HONORS:** ABA; TN Bar Assn.; Bradley Cty. Bar Assn., Pres., Bradley Cty. Bar Assn.; **EDUC:** BS, 1959, Bus., Univ. of NC; **GRAD EDUC:** LLB, 1962, Law, Univ. of NC; **HOME ADD:** POB 444, Cleveland, TN 37311; **BUS ADD:** POB 1169, Merchants Bank Bldg., Cleveland, TN 37311, (615)476-8541.

BROWN, John Thomas——B: Dec. 16, 1948, Ft. Dix, NJ, *Atty.*, Belzer & Jackl; **PRIM RE ACT:** Attorney, Instructor; **SERVICES:** Legal counseling; **REP CLIENTS:** RE brokers, mort. brokers, devel., synd., investors; **PROFL AFFIL & HONORS:** State Bar of CA, instr., Chabot Coll. legal aspects of RE, instr. Amer. Inst. of Cont. Educ.; **EDUC:** BA, 1975, Intl. Bus., CA State Univ.; **GRAD EDUC:** JD, 1978, Hastings Coll. of Law; **EDUC HONORS:** Grad. with Honors, distinction in special maj., Hastings Intl. & comparative law review-research editor; **HOME ADD:** 28 Baywood Ct., Fairfax, CA 94930; **BUS ADD:** 180 Grand Ave. 960, Oakland, CA 94612, (415)444-6400.

BROWN, Jonathan N.——B: Jan. 7, 1944, Manchester, NH, *Project Mgr.*, East Coast Properties, Inc.; **PRIM RE ACT:** Broker, Developer, Owner/Investor, Property Manager, Syndicator; **SERVICES:** Brokerage, Synd., Devel. of Comml./Indus. Props., Prop. Mgmt.; **PREV EMPLOY:** Lomas and Nettleton Co.; **PROFL AFFIL & HONORS:** NAR, IREM, CPM; **EDUC:** BA, 1972, Bus. Admin./Acctg., Parsons Coll.; **MIL SERV:** US Army Security Agency, 1968-71; **OTHER ACT & HONORS:** Hamden Dance and Figure Skating Club; **HOME ADD:** 241 Ridgewood Ave., Hamden, CT 06517, (203)281-1257; **BUS ADD:** 285 State St., North Haven, CT 06473, (203)281-7000.

BROWN, Joseph S.——B: July 2, 1941, Indianapolis, IN, *VP*, Landeco Inc.; **PRIM RE ACT:** Engineer, Architect, Developer, Builder, Owner/Investor; **SERVICES:** Bldg. design, construction & devel.; **REP CLIENTS:** 1st Union REIT, Harsh Investments; **PROFL AFFIL & HONORS:** AIA; **EDUC:** BA, 1963, Amer. Hist., Wesleyan Univ.; **GRAD EDUC:** BArch, 1966, Arch. Engrg., Univ. of IL; **EDUC HONORS:** Skull & Serpent; **HOME ADD:** 111 Harbour Trees Ln., Noblesville, IN 46060, (317)877-5047; **BUS ADD:** 5500 West Bradbury Ave., Indianapolis, IN 46241, (317)243-9331.

BROWN, Joshua——B: June 24, 1951, Houston, TX, *VP, Dir. of Investment Admin.*, Coldwell Banker & Co., Capital Mgmt. Servs.; **PRIM RE ACT:** Attorney, Developer, Owner/Investor, Property Manager, Syndicator; **SERVICES:** RE money mgr. for pension funds; **REP CLIENTS:** Hughes Aircraft, Burroughs Corp. AT&T, TWA; **PROFL AFFIL & HONORS:** State Bar of TX; ABA; **EDUC:** BA, 1973, Hist., Univ. of TX at Austin; **GRAD EDUC:** JD, 1976, Law, St. Mary's Univ., School of Law; **EDUC HONORS:** Student Body Pres.; **HOME ADD:** 751 Hartzell, Pacific Palisades, CA 90272, (213)454-2641; **BUS ADD:** 533 Fremont, Los Angeles, CA 90071, (213)613-3120.

BROWN, Karen A.——B: Apr. 25, 1941, McGregor, IA, *Realtor/Owner*, Karen A. Brown, Realtor; **PRIM RE ACT:** Broker, Consultant, Owner/Investor, Instructor, Property Manager; **OTHER RE ACT:** I act as a "Buyer's Broker" and have an exclusive listing contract with my buyers. I receive no fee from the seller when acting as a buyer's agent. Also, I work in joint ventures with investors in acquiring single family houses; **REP CLIENTS:** All referred to me-range is from first time home owners to investors who want to joint venture; **PREV EMPLOY:** Coldwell Banker (Thorsen) from 1971-1979, Downers Grove, IL; **PROFL AFFIL & HONORS:** NAR; DuPage & Will Cty. Bd. of Realtors; The Academy of RE Exchangers and CARE, GRI; CRS; **EDUC:** Wright Coll., Chicago, IL, 2 years; **OTHER ACT & HONORS:** Naper Racquet Club; **HOME ADD:** P O Box 1214, Bolingbrook, IL 60439-1214P, (312)420-0088; **BUS ADD:** 2332 Wehrli Rd., Naperville, IL 60565, (312)420-0088.

BROWN, Keith Thomas——B: July 5, 1947, Orange, CA, *Principal*, Brown & Weir; **PRIM RE ACT:** Consultant, Architect; **OTHER RE ACT:** Space planning, interior design; **SERVICES:** Comml. arch. and interior arch. including office bldgs., tenant spaces and restaurants; **REP CLIENTS:** Devel., office space tenants; **PROFL AFFIL & HONORS:** AIA; **EDUC:** BArch., 1970, Arch., Univ. of TN; **BUS ADD:** 724 Pine St., San Francisco, CA 94108, (415)362-2437.

BROWN, L. Cleue——B: Jan. 23, 1942, Montgomery, AL, *Dir. Project Fin.*, Beaver Greek Devel Co.; **OTHER RE ACT:** RE Devel. and Fin.; **SERVICES:** RE Fin., Joint ventures, land and RE devel.; **PREV EMPLOY:** RE Dept., NY Life Ins. Co., 1965-67 & 1972-78, Mort. Banking Dept., Van Schank & Co., 1978-80; **PROFL AFFIL & HONORS:** RE Broker; **EDUC:** BBA, 1964, Fin & Ins., Econ., Sanford Univ.; **EDUC HONORS:** 2nd in class; **HOME ADD:** 2572 Arosa Dr., Vail, CO 81657, (303)472-5029; **BUS ADD:** PO Box 7, Vail, CO 81658, (302)949-5750.

BROWN, Liston L.——B: Nov. 22, 1929, Charleston, SC, *Pres.*, Liston L. Brown Realty & Auctioneering Inc., LaPorte, Inc.; **PRIM RE ACT:** Broker, Appraiser, Owner/Investor, Property Manager; **OTHER RE ACT:** Auctioneering; **SERVICES:** Sales, Appraising, P.M., Investing, Auctioneering; **REP CLIENTS:** Resid., Comml., Sales, Leasing & Prop. Mgmt.; **PROFL AFFIL & HONORS:** NRA, IN State Realtors, Natl. Auctioneer & State G.R.I.-C.R.S., G.R.I., C.R.S., Realtor & Auctioneer; **EDUC:** Univ. of MD; **GRAD EDUC:** IN Univ., G.R.I. Graduate - 1979; **EDUC HONORS:** G.R.I.; **MIL SERV:** USAF, Sgt 1st CL, Good Conduct; **OTHER ACT & HONORS:** Moose, Elks, Amer. Legion; **HOME ADD:** 69 Keston Elm Dr, LaPorte, IN 46350, (219)362-5944; **BUS ADD:** 100 °J° St., LaPorte, IN 46350, (219)326-6066.

BROWN, Michael M.——B: July 19, 1949, New York, NY, *Field Engineer*, Michelin Tire Corp., Earthmover Dept.; **PRIM RE ACT:** Owner/Investor; **EDUC:** BS, 1971, Aerospace Engr., US Naval Acad.; **GRAD EDUC:** MS, 1976, Systems Mgmt., USC; **MIL SERV:** USMC, Capt.; **HOME ADD:** 1715D Lakecliffe Dr., Wheaton, IL 60187, (312)660-2370, **BUS ADD.** 750 N Expressway Dr., Itasca, IL 60143, (312)773-2190.

BROWN, Nancy Newman——B: Mar. 26, 1951, Wash., DC, *Claims Counsel*, Chicago Title Insurance Co., Capitol Region, Phila./S. Jersey Area; **PRIM RE ACT:** Attorney; **SERVICES:** Claims responsibility, S. Jersey, PA, DE; **PROFL AFFIL & HONORS:** ABA, NJ Bar Assn., Camden Cty. Bar Assn., PA Bar Assn., Philadelphia Bar Assn., Nat. Assn. of Female Execs., Assn. of Corp. Counsel of NJ; **EDUC:** BA, 1973, psych., Brandeis Univ.; **GRAD EDUC:** JD, 1976, Georgetown Univ. Law Center; **EDUC HONORS:** Magna Cum Laude, Deans

List; **HOME ADD:** 12 Beekman Pl., Cherry Hill, NJ 08034; **BUS ADD:** 1500 Chestnut St., Philadelphia, PA 19102, (215)665-1900.

BROWN, Paul R.——B: Feb. 9, 1915, Hariland, KS, *Pres.*, Paul R. Brown & Assoc., Inc.; **PRIM RE ACT:** Broker, Appraiser, Property Manager, Banker, Insuror; **SERVICES:** Sales, mgmt., appraisals, ins.; **PREV EMPLOY:** Been with same Co. since 38; Co. name originally "H. C. Brady Inc."; **PROFL AFFIL & HONORS:** Wichita Assn. of Realtors, Kansas Assn. of Realtors, NAR, AIREA, Pres. Wichita RE B. 1952, Member of Governing Council - AIREA (Current); **EDUC:** AB, 1938, Bus. Admin., Friends Univ., Wichita; **GRAD EDUC:** Hon. Dr. of Law Degree, 1978, Friends Univ.; **EDUC HONORS:** Distinguished Alumnus 1968; **MIL SERV:** USN Supply 1942-46, Lt.; **OTHER ACT & HONORS:** Wichita Club Univ. Friends Church; 33 years as Tr. of Friends U.; **HOME ADD:** 644 Brookfield, Wichita, KS 67206, (316)682-4698; **BUS ADD:** 102 Colorado-Derby Bldg., Wichita, KS 67202, (316)264-0394.

BROWN, Peter——B: Nov. 15, 1944, Highland Park, IL, *Pres.*, Four Season Shores Realty; **PRIM RE ACT:** Broker, Consultant, Appraiser, Developer, Builder; **REP CLIENTS:** Investors, devels., valuation, devel. & synd. resort props.; **PREV EMPLOY:** Instnl. investment mgr. NY Stock Exchange Firm Dempsey Tegelor 1968-1970; **PROFL AFFIL & HONORS:** NAR, NAIFA, Indep. Fee Appraiser; **EDUC:** BA, 1967, Fin., Univ. of Denver; **MIL SERV:** USMC, Cpl.; **HOME ADD:** 15 Country Club Dr., Lake Ozark, MO 65049, (314)365-2176; **BUS ADD:** Route 1, PO Box 11P, Lake Ozark, MO 65049, (314)365-5303.

BROWN, Richard D.——B: Feb. 19, 1947, Bangalore, India, *Devel. Officer & Econ.*, Bentall Investments; **PRIM RE ACT:** Consultant, Appraiser, Developer, Builder, Owner/Investor, Property Manager; **SERVICES:** Devel., constr., mgmt. & ownership; **PREV EMPLOY:** Cumberland Realty Grp., 1971-76; **PROFL AFFIL & HONORS:** RE Inst. of BC, RE Inst. of Can., Intl. Council of Shopping Ctrs., Nat. Assn. of Office & Indus. Parks, RI (BC), FRI's; **EDUC:** BA, Econ., Univ. of BC; **HOME ADD:** 2903 W. 42nd Ave., Vancouver, V6N 3G8, BC, Canada, (604)261-7040; **BUS ADD:** 3100 3 Bentall Ctr., PO Box 49001, Vancouver, V7X 1B1, BC, Can., (604)684-1131.

BROWN, Richard W.——B: Apr. 13, 1948, Sayre, PA, *VP*, Frederick Ross Co., Investment & Development Division; **PRIM RE ACT:** Developer, Owner/Investor; **SERVICES:** Sales, Leasing, Dev.; **REP CLIENTS:** Exxon, Amerada Hess Corp., Pan Handle Eastern Pipeline Co. subsidiaries, Metropolitan Life Ins. Co., World S&L Assoc.; **PREV EMPLOY:** Lee Tipton & Co.; **PROFL AFFIL & HONORS:** IREM, BOMA, MAI Cand., CPM CCIM (candidate); **EDUC:** BS, 1971, Bus., RE, Univ. of CO; **OTHER ACT & HONORS:** BOMA Treas. (Denver); **HOME ADD:** 7279 So. Ivy Ct., Englewood, CO 80112, (303)771-4571; **BUS ADD:** 717 17th St., Suite 1400, Denver, CO 80202, (303)892-1111.

BROWN, Robert Kevin——B: July 3, 1930, Teaneck, NJ, *Corp. Dir. RE*, Rockwell International Corp.; **OTHER RE ACT:** Corp. RE; **SERVICES:** Mgr. Corp. fixed asset portfolio; **PREV EMPLOY:** Prof. & RE Dept. Chmn., GA State Univ. & Univ. of SC, Assoc. Dean, GSB Univ. of Pittsburgh, Pres., Research, Inc., VP LBC&W; **PROFL AFFIL & HONORS:** NACORE, Bd. Member; IDRC Bd. Member; NARA Sr. Member, FCA, Amer. Inst. of Corp. Asset Mgmt., AICP, Amer. Inst. of Cert. Planners; **EDUC:** BS, 1952, Psych., The Johns Hopkins Univ.; **GRAD EDUC:** MA, 1954, Econ. & Fin., Univ. of Pittsburgh; PhD, 1958, Econ. and Fin., Univ. of Pittsburgh; **EDUC HONORS:** Omicron Delta Epsilon Frat. Honorary Econ., Lambda Alpha Hon. Land Econ. Frat.; **OTHER ACT & HONORS:** The Johns Hopkins Univ. Alumni Task Force, Author 8 books and numerous profl. articles on RE and related topics; **HOME ADD:** 2 Bayard Rd., Pittsburgh, PA 15213; **BUS ADD:** 600 Grant St., Pittsburgh, PA 15219.

BROWN, Rodney R.——B: Dec. 24, 1939, Bakersfield, CA, *Pres.*, Rodney R. Brown Inc.; **PRIM RE ACT:** Broker, Consultant, Developer, Builder, Owner/Investor; **SERVICES:** RE sales-land devel.- B-1 constr., investment counseling; **REP CLIENTS:** RE investments; **PROFL AFFIL & HONORS:** McGraw Hill Housing Advisory Panel, Kern Cty. Bldgs. Exchange, Bakersfield Bd. of Realtors, Nat. Assn. of Realtors, Better Bus. Bureau of Bakersfield; **EDUC:** AA, Bus. Admin., Bakersfield Coll.; **MIL SERV:** USN, Seaman 1st class; **OTHER ACT & HONORS:** Intl. Assn. Lions Club, Rotary Club of Bakersfield; **HOME ADD:** 215 Los Nietos Ct., Bakersfield, CA 93309, (805)834-4893; **BUS ADD:** 215 Los Nietos Ct., Bakersfield, CA 93309, (805)834-8889.

BROWN, Stephen D.——B: Jan. 21, 1948, Battle Creek, MI, *VP/Gen. Counsel*, Hillmark Corp.; **PRIM RE ACT:** Broker, Attorney, Owner/Investor, Instructor, Property Manager, Insuror; **SERVICES:** Invest. counseling; legal rep.; **REP CLIENTS:** Investors in resid./comml. RE; **PROFL AFFIL & HONORS:** ABA; **EDUC:** BA, 1970, Econ. & Poli. Sci., MI State Univ.; **GRAD EDUC:** JD, 1973, Law, Univ. of WI; **EDUC HONORS:** Dean's List, 1970 Club, Enzian and Blue Key Nat. Honors, Cum Laude, Dean's List; Pres. Student Body; **OTHER ACT & HONORS:** Bd. of Dir. WI MS Soc.; Bd. of Dir. Dane Cty. Housing Devel. Corp.; Instr., Bus. Law, Madison Area Tech Coll.; **HOME ADD:** 1922 Vilas Ave., Madison, WI 53711, (608)251-1922; **BUS ADD:** 6425 Odana Rd., Madison, WI 53719, (608)273-3900.

BROWN, Stewart J.——B: Oct. 11, 1947, St. Louis, MO, *VP, RE*, Citytrust; **PRIM RE ACT:** Banker, Lender, Owner/Investor; **SERVICES:** RE lending services, comml. bank; **PREV EMPLOY:** HNC Mort. & Realty Investors, Westport, CT; **PROFL AFFIL & HONORS:** MBA, Subcomm. Chmn., CRA; **EDUC:** BA, 1970, Econ./Pol. Sci., Univ. of CA; **GRAD EDUC:** MBA, 1980, Fin., NYU; **MIL SERV:** U.S. Army, Capt.; **OTHER ACT & HONORS:** Aircraft Owners & Pilots Assn.; **HOME ADD:** 49 1/2 Sherwood Pl., Greenwich, CT 06830, (203)869-0738; **BUS ADD:** 961 Main St., Bridgeport, CT 06602, (203)384-5116.

BROWN, T.A.——B: Sept. 1, 1942, New Orleans, LA, *VP*, Watergate Development Inc., Texas Region; **PRIM RE ACT:** Developer, Builder, Property Manager; **PREV EMPLOY:** Chief Fin. Officer, Western Div. Watergate Devel., Inc.; **PROFL AFFIL & HONORS:** BOMA; RE Fin. Execs.; **EDUC:** BS, 1965, Mktg. & Acctg., Univ. of New Orleans; **MIL SERV:** USN, Air Controller 3rd Class; **HOME ADD:** 10243 Sunridge Trail, Dallas, TX 75243, (214)690-6515; **BUS ADD:** 7616 L.B.J. Freeway, Ste. 616, Dallas, TX 75251, (214)980-1020.

BROWN, Thomas Howard——B: Dec. 30, 1944, Baltimore, MD, *Atty.*, Choate, Hall & Stewart; **PRIM RE ACT:** Attorney; **SERVICES:** Legal advice with respect to all types of RE devel., financing and leasing, both comml. and resid.; **PROFL AFFIL & HONORS:** ABA, Real Prop. and Probate Sect.; MA Conveyancers Assn.; Christian Legal Soc.; **EDUC:** BS, 1966, Math. & Pol. Sci., Loyola Coll.; **GRAD EDUC:** JD, 1969, Law, Boston Coll. Law Sch.; **EDUC HONORS:** Editor, Boston Coll. Indus. and Comml. Law Review; **HOME ADD:** 6 Marlborough St., Apt. 5D, Boston, MA 02116, (617)247-2240; **BUS ADD:** 60 State St., Boston, MA 02109, (617)227-5020.

BROWN, Timothy N.——B: Nov. 26, 1942, Tallahassee, FL, *Partner*, Chickering & Gregory; **PRIM RE ACT:** Attorney; **SERVICES:** Legal serv. in connection with comml. and indus. RE transactions; **PROFL AFFIL & HONORS:** ABA (Real Prop., Prob. & T. Law Sec.); State Bar of CA (Real Prop. Sec.); Bar Assn. of San Francisco; **EDUC:** AB, 1964, Econ., Harvard Coll.; **GRAD EDUC:** LLB, 1967, Law, Harvard Law School; **EDUC HONORS:** Cum Laude, Cum Laude; **MIL SERV:** US Army; 1968-70; **HOME ADD:** 3 Embareadero Ctr., Ste. 2300, San Francisco, CA 94111, (415)566-4189; **BUS ADD:** 3 Embarcadero Ctr.,, Ste. 2300, San Francisco, CA 94111, (415)393-9000.

BROWN, W. Randolph——B: Aug. 7, 1922, Spartanburg, NC, *VP*, Grier & Co., Inc., RE Div.; **PRIM RE ACT:** Broker, Consultant, Appraiser, Owner/Investor, Property Manager; **SERVICES:** Principally Resid. Sales, Appraisals & Prop. Mgmt.; **PREV EMPLOY:** US Army 1943-46; **PROFL AFFIL & HONORS:** RNMI, NAR SC Assn. Realtors, CRB, GRI; **EDUC:** AB, 1943, Wofford Coll.; **MIL SERV:** US Army, Capt., Purple Heart & Battle Stars E.T.O.; **OTHER ACT & HONORS:** S.M.E. (Former Civitan); **HOME ADD:** 1281 Brentwood Dr., Spartanburg, SC 29302, (803)583-4304; **BUS ADD:** 901 S Pine Str., Spartanburg, SC 29302, (803)585-8713.

BROWN, Willard A., Sr.——B: May 9, 1909, Madison, WI, *Sr. VP*, Arthur Rubloff & Co.; **PRIM RE ACT:** Consultant; **OTHER ACT & HONORS:** Tr., IL Jr. Coll. Bd.; Tr., Janitors Union Pension Fund; COB, Evergreen Plaza Bank; **HOME ADD:** 721 Old Barn Rd., Barrington, IL 60010, (312)382-1213; **BUS ADD:** 8600 S. Bryn Mawr, Chicago, IL 60631, (312)693-3000.

BROWN, William B.——B: June 19, 1939, Sioux Falls, SD, *Partner*, Deloitte Haskins & Sells, Tax; **PRIM RE ACT:** Attorney; **OTHER RE ACT:** CPA; **SERVICES:** Tax analysis; **PROFL AFFIL & HONORS:** AICPA, MSCPA, MN Bar Assn., ABA; Tax Roundtable; **EDUC:** BBA, 1961, Mgmt. & Acctg., Univ. of SD; **GRAD EDUC:** 1966, Law, Univ. of MN; LLM, NY Univ.; **MIL SERV:** USA, 1st Lt.; **OTHER ACT & HONORS:** Adjunct Prof., Univ. of MN Grad. School; Minneapolis Athletic Club; Interlachen Ctry. Club; Citizens League; **HOME ADD:** 2990 Tonkaha Dr., Wayzata, MN 55391, (612)475-0772; **BUS ADD:** 1950 IDS Tower, Minneapolis, MN 55402, (612)339-9744.

BROWN, William C.——B: May 26, 1934, Boston, MA, *Treas.*, Lufkin & Brown, Inc.; **PRIM RE ACT:** Broker, Consultant, Appraiser, Owner/Investor, Instructor, Property Manager; **SERVICES:** Res/

Comml. Brokerage Appraisals; **REP CLIENTS:** Banks-Attorneys Boston & North Shore; **PROFL AFFIL & HONORS:** MA Realtor Political Action Comm., Life Member 1980, RE Advisory Bd. North Shore Community Coll. 1978-1979, GRI (Charter Member - 1979 Certified Residential Specialist), Realtor of the Year 1972, 1976, Dir. NAR 1980, MA Assn. of Realtors Pres. 1980; **EDUC:** BA, 1958, Fine Arts; **MIL SERV:** US Army, SP-2, Several; **OTHER ACT & HONORS:** Governor's Advisory Comm. 1977-1979, Algonquin Club, 76 Club of Boston, Aleppo Temple, Manchester Club, Appalachian Mountain Club, US Golf Assn.; **HOME ADD:** Loading Place Rd., Manchester, MA 01944, (617)526-4987; **BUS ADD:** 222 Washington St., Gloucester, MA 01930, (617)281-0001.

BROWN, William H.——B: Apr. 18, 1940, Los Angeles, CA, *Atty.*, Self employed; **PRIM RE ACT:** Attorney, Owner/Investor; **OTHER RE ACT:** CPA Tax Planner; **SERVICES:** Tax Planning, Exchanges; **REP CLIENTS:** Investors & Dev.; **PROFL AFFIL & HONORS:** CA Bar Assoc., CA CPA Soc.; **EDUC:** BA, 1964, Bus., Brigham Young Univ.; **GRAD EDUC:** JD, 1967, U.C.L.A.; **EDUC HONORS:** Cum Laude; **HOME ADD:** 16465 Jackson Oaks Dr., Morgan Hill, CA 95037, (408)778-2021; **BUS ADD:** 16120 Monterey St., Morgan Hill, CA 95037, (408)779-3232.

BROWN, W.Z. Jefferson——B: Jan. 9. 1942, Baltimore, MD, *Partner*, Price, Burness, Price, Davis & Brown; **PRIM RE ACT:** Attorney; **SERVICES:** Legal; **REP CLIENTS:** Fin. S&L Assn., Oroville Title Co.; **PROFL AFFIL & HONORS:** ABA, State Bar of CA, Butte Cty. Bar Assn.; **EDUC:** BA, 1963, Econ., Pomona Coll.; **GRAD EDUC:** JD, 1966, Harvard Law School; **EDUC HONORS:** Cum Laude, Phi Beta Kappa, Cum Laude; **MIL SERV:** US Army, SP5; **HOME ADD:** 1438 Bidwell Ave., Chico, CA 95926, (916)895-8898; **BUS ADD:** 466 Vallombrosa Ave., Chico, CA 95926, (916)343-4412.

BROWNE, Aldis J., Jr.——B: Mar. 21, 1912, Chicago, IL, *Past VP & Dir.*, Browne & Storch, Inc.; **PRIM RE ACT:** Broker, Property Manager; **SERVICES:** Sales, leasing, all types of RE, bldg. mgmt.; **PREV EMPLOY:** USN Res. (30 yrs.); **PROFL AFFIL & HONORS:** Chicago RE Bd., IL RE Bd., Bldg. Mgrs. Assn., Apt. Bldg. Mgrs. (BOMA Intl); **EDUC:** BA, 1935, Eng., Yale Univ.; **MIL SERV:** USN, Capt., Navy Commendation Medal; **OTHER ACT & HONORS:** Past. Chmn. Bldg. Review Bd.; Lake Forest, IL; Civic Fed. (Dir.), Old People's Home, City of Chicago; Tr. & past. pres., Dir. English Speaking Union; VP Gov. Soc. of Colonial Wars, State of IL; **HOME ADD:** 165 W Onwentsia Rd., Lake Forest, IL 60045, (312)234-0819; **BUS ADD:** 100 E Ohio St., Chicago, IL 60611, (312)944-7373.

BROWNE, Donald K.——B: Nov. 23, 1946, Columbus, OH, *Pres.*, Browne & Co.; **PRIM RE ACT:** Developer, Owner/Investor, Property Manager, Real Estate Publisher; **SERVICES:** Devel. and mgmt. of resid. income props., newsletter publisher; **REP CLIENTS:** Indiv. investors in resid. props.; **EDUC:** BS, 1968, Educ., OH State Univ.; **OTHER ACT & HONORS:** Who's Who in Bus. & Fin.; **HOME ADD:** 6980 SW 83 Ct., Miami, FL 33143, (305)279-0062; **BUS ADD:** 6980 SW 83rd Ct., Miami, FL 33143, (305)279-0062.

BROWNE, Gary L.——B: Sept. 21, 1939, Lansing, MI, *Pres.*, Eden Assoc., Inc., EA, Inc. owns Eden Realty Co. of which I am V.P.; **PRIM RE ACT:** Instructor, Syndicator, Consultant, Developer, Builder, Property Manager, Real Estate Publisher; **SERVICES:** investment counseling, Dev. and planning, educ. prop. mgmt.; **REP CLIENTS:** indiv. and corp. co. clients; **PROFL AFFIL & HONORS:** Greater Baltimore Bd. of Realtors; Consultant to the MD Hist. Soc., Who's Who in the East (1982); **EDUC:** BA, 1962, Econ., Univ. of MI; **GRAD EDUC:** MA, 1965, Amer. Bus. Hist., Wayne State Univ.; Ph.D, 1973, Amer. Bus. Hist., Wayne State Univ.; **OTHER ACT & HONORS:** Prof. of Hist., Univ. of MD; Editor of the *Maryland Hist. Magazine*, author and lecturer; **HOME ADD:** 6 Woodlawn Ave., Catonsville, MD 21228, (301)744-5530; **BUS ADD:** 6120 Edmondson Ave., Catonsville, MD 21228, (301)744-4400.

BROWNE, Leslie M.——B: Jan. 6, 1948, Ithaca, NY, *Atty.*, Morrison & Foerster; **PRIM RE ACT:** Attorney; **OTHER RE ACT:** All aspects of RE devel. and fin.; **SERVICES:** RE legal advice; **EDUC:** BA, 1969, Barnard Coll.; **GRAD EDUC:** JD, 1975, Boalt Hall; **BUS ADD:** One Market Plaza, Spear St. Tower, San Francisco, CA 94105, (415)777-6001.

BROWNE, Robert W.——B: Oct. 17, 1948, Richland, WA, *Asst. VP*, Westlands Bank, RE Const. Loans; **PRIM RE ACT:** Banker, Lender; **SERVICES:** Provide RE const. loans (resid., comml., indus.); **PREV EMPLOY:** Lloyds Bank CA; CA 1st Bank; **PROFL AFFIL & HONORS:** Bldg. Indus. Assn.; Home Builders Council; Nat. Assn. Home Builders; American Inst. of Banking; **EDUC:** BA, 1970, Math., Lycoming Coll., PA; AA, 1979, Banking & Fin., Long Beach City Coll.; Basic and Standard Certificates, 1972 and 1974, American Inst. of Banking, California Chap., S.F.; **HOME ADD:** 9396 Wedgewood Ln., Westminster, CA 92683, (714)531-6604; **BUS ADD:** 2900 S. Harbor Blvd., Sanata Ana, CA 92704, (714)641-6145.

BROWNE, Roy E.——B: Mar. 10, 1947, Independence, MO, Browne & Assoc.; **PRIM RE ACT:** Architect, Consultant, Builder; **PREV EMPLOY:** Andes & Roberts Devels., Lund & Balderson Archs., Environmental Design for People; **PROFL AFFIL & HONORS:** AIA, Featured in RE Sect. of AC Star, Popular Sci.; **EDUC:** AA, 1967, Soc., Graceland Coll., Lamoni, IA; **GRAD EDUC:** B. Arch, 1971, Neighborhood Devel. & Bldg. Systems, Univ. of KS; **EDUC HONORS:** 2nd in Class, Outstanding Thesis award, School of Arch. & Urban Design; Tau Sigma Delta Natl. Hon. Soc.; **OTHER ACT & HONORS:** Rotary Intl.; Community Orchestra, RLDS Church, Elder; **HOME ADD:** 1128 W Waldo, Independence, MO 64050; **BUS ADD:** 413 S Liberty, Independence, MO 64051, (816)461-6400.

BROWNE, Thomas J.——B: Nov. 4, 1951, Wells, MN, *VP, Gen. Mge., Prop. Mgmt. Div.*, Midwest Realty & Mort. Co.; **PRIM RE ACT:** Broker, Consultant, Property Manager; **SERVICES:** Devel., brokerage, prop. mgmt., counseling; **PREV EMPLOY:** GRI; CRS; candidate for CPM designation; **PROFL AFFIL & HONORS:** Nat. Assn. of Realtors, Inst. of RE Mgmt. (Nat. MN 45), Realtor's Nat. Mktg. Inst. (CRS); **EDUC:** BA, 1976, Urban & Reg. Planning, Pol. Sci., minor in Hist., Mankato State Univ., Mankato, MN; **OTHER ACT & HONORS:** Exchange Club of Amer.; Benevolent & Protective Order of Elks; Ducks Unlimited; Nat. Rifle Assn.; **HOME ADD:** 221 Capital Dr., Mankato, MN 56001; **BUS ADD:** 505 Long St., Mankato, MN 56001, (507)387-1121.

BROWNING, Robert A.——B: Nov. 24, 1944, Forest Grove, OR, *Pres.*, Robert Andrew Browning - Attys. PC; Pres., Browning Enterprises, Ltd.; Broker, Robert Browning Realty; **PRIM RE ACT:** Attorney, Developer, Builder, Broker, Owner/Investor; **SERVICES:** RE consultation, devel. and construction; transaction negotiations; **REP CLIENTS:** Indiv. sellers and buyers, lending instns., and realty firms; **PREV EMPLOY:** City Planning Dir., City of Forest Grove, OR 1972-1975; Planning and Engrg. Consultation, 1969-1972; **PROFL AFFIL & HONORS:** ABA; OR State Bar; APA, AICP; Community Assn. Inst.; **EDUC:** BS, 1969, Gen. stud. in Phys.; Sci.;; BS, 1978, Philosophy; Post Baccalaureate Cert. in Urban Studies, 1978, Portland OR State Univ.; **GRAD EDUC:** JD, 1979, Lewis and Clark Coll. School of Law; **OTHER ACT & HONORS:** Trustee, Valley Art Assn.; **HOME ADD:** PO Box 657, Forest Grove, OR 97116; **BUS ADD:** 3012-B Pacific Ave., PO Box 928, Forest Grove, OR 97116, (503)640-6091.

BROXMEYER, Marc——B: Dec. 13, 1950, NY, NY, *Pres.*, Bellmarc Realty; **PRIM RE ACT:** Broker, Consultant, Owner/Investor, Property Manager; **SERVICES:** Brokerage comml./resid./investment counseling, prop. mgmt.; **REP CLIENTS:** Investors in comml. prop., purchasers of resid. RE; **PROFL AFFIL & HONORS:** RE Bd. of NY; **EDUC:** BA, 1972, Acctg., NYU; **HOME TEL:** (212)780-0232; **BUS ADD:** 770 Broadway, New York, NY 10003, (212)674-7700.

BRUCK, F. Frederick——B: Jan. 24, 1921, Breslau (Germany), *Assoc.*, The Architects Collaborative; **PRIM RE ACT:** Architect; **SERVICES:** Arch. Serv.; **REP CLIENTS:** Public and Pvt. Clients in US and Abroad; **PREV EMPLOY:** Pres.; F. Frederick Bruck, Architect & Assoc., Inc., Cambridge, MA 1966-; **PROFL AFFIL & HONORS:** AIA, BSA, Finalist, Boston City Hall Competition, AIA Merit Award 1964, Arch. Record Award for House Design, 1965; **EDUC:** BA, 1941, Harvard Coll.; **GRAD EDUC:** BArch, MArch, 1951, Harvard Grad. School of Design; **EDUC HONORS:** Cum Laude, Wheelwright Fellowship 1954-1955; **MIL SERV:** USA, T/Sgt., Served in ETO; **OTHER ACT & HONORS:** Dir. Cambridge Civic Assoc. 1979-80, Taught at Harvard Grad. School of Design 1953-1963; **HOME ADD:** 148 Coolidge Hill, Cambridge, MA 02138, (617)547-2124; **BUS ADD:** 46 Brattle St., Cambridge, MA 02138, (617)868-4200.

BRUCK, Paul Joseph——B: April 28, 1928, Oak Park, IL, *Pres.*, Sunbelt Bankers Investments, Inc., Div. Admin.; **PRIM RE ACT:** Broker, Syndicator, Insuror; **OTHER RE ACT:** Broker/Principal, Securities; **SERVICES:** Packager of RE for synd. and large investment grps.; **REP CLIENTS:** RE securities - sponsors; **PREV EMPLOY:** Econ. Devel. Corp., Pres.; Faculty of DePaul Univ. School of Bus.; Allstate Ins. Co., Sr. Mktg. Mgr.; **PROFL AFFIL & HONORS:** Chartered Life Underwriter, Chartered Prop. and Casualty Underwriter, CPA, licensed RE Broker, Soc. of RE Appraisers., Legislative and Taxation Comm. of the San Antonio Bd. of Realtors, the Budget Comm., the Educ. Comm. and the Bd. of Govs. of the RE Securities and Synd. Inst., Regional VP of RE Securities and Synd. Inst., Chmn. Intl. Assn. of Fin. Planners; **EDUC:** BBS, 1948, Bus. Admin., Georgetown Univ.; **GRAD EDUC:** MBA, 1951, Bus. Admin., Univ. of Chicago; **EDUC HONORS:** Cum Laude; **OTHER ACT & HONORS:** San

Antonio C of C; **HOME ADD:** 9386 Lamerton, San Antonio, TX 78250, (512)656-6420; **BUS ADD:** 7400 Louis Pasteur - Suite 110, San Antonio, TX 78229, (512)696-6666.

BRUCK, Sanford——**B:** Oct. 21, 1948, NY, NY, Isard-Greenberg Co.; **PRIM RE ACT:** Broker, Syndicator, Consultant, Appraiser, Developer, Builder, Property Manager, Owner/Investor; **SERVICES:** Investment Counselling, devel. and synd. of comml. & resid. props., prop. mgmt., appraisals, and gen. contracting; **REP CLIENTS:** Indiv. investors in comml. and resid. props.; **EDUC:** BBA, 1970, Fin., Univ. of Cincinnati; **HOME ADD:** 1342 Lindsay Ln., Meadowbrook, PA 19046, (215)887-0929; **BUS ADD:** 700 Land Title Bldg., Phila., PA 19110, (215)988-0500.

BRUCKNER, Daniel W.——**B:** Dec. 12, 1946, Milwaukee, WI; **PRIM RE ACT:** Broker, Attorney, Developer, Owner/Investor, Property Manager, Syndicator; **SERVICES:** Outright purchase of prop.; **PROFL AFFIL & HONORS:** ABA; WI Bar Assn.; **EDUC:** BS, 1969, Acctg., Marquette Univ.; **GRAD EDUC:** 1972, Law, Marquette Univ.; **EDUC HONORS:** 1st in Class, Amer. Jurisprudence Award; **BUS ADD:** 100 S. Second St., Milwaukee, WI 53204, (414)271-4005.

BRUGH, W. Patton——**B:** Jan. 2, 1946, Radford, VA, *VP*, First Union National Bank of N.C., Gen. Mort. Loans; **PRIM RE ACT:** Banker; **SERVICES:** Const. Loans; **PREV EMPLOY:** Nat./Intl. Div., First Union; **EDUC:** BS Bus., 1968, Mgmt., VA Tech.; **GRAD EDUC:** MBA, 1970, Fin., Emory Univ.; **HOME ADD:** 2160 Norton Rd., Charlotte, NC 28207; **BUS ADD:** First Union Plaza, Charlotte, NC 28288, (704)374-4238.

BRULATOUR, Peter E.——**B:** Oct. 17, 1917, Fort Lee, NJ, *Associate Broker Mgr. Comm. Investment Div.*, Wm. & Marion Higgins Agency, Inc.; **PRIM RE ACT:** Broker, Syndicator, Consultant, Appraiser, Developer, Builder, Property Manager, Lender, Owner/Investor; **SERVICES:** Investment Counseling, Valuation, Devel., Syno. Mgt.; **REP CLIENTS:** N/A; **PREV EMPLOY:** Pres. Microfilming Corp of Amer. (Div. of NY Times) Member Board of Directors (1967-1969) Pres. Video Presentations, Inc.; **PROFL AFFIL & HONORS:** Soc. Motion Picture & Television Engineers, also Internatl. Alliance Theatrical State employees; **EDUC:** 1947, Records Mgt., Archival Admin., REContractual, NY Univ. also Bergen Community Coll.; **MIL SERV:** USN, OPO; **OTHER ACT & HONORS:** Wakefield F & A.M. Salaam Temple (Shriners), Rotary Club; **HOME ADD:** 501 Weymouth Drive, Wyckoff, NJ 07481, (201)891-5240; **BUS ADD:** Werimus Rd. & Van Emburgh Ave., Hillsdale, NJ 07642, (201)664-2900.

BRUMALDS, George——*Asst. Treas.*, VSI Corp.; **PRIM RE ACT:** Property Manager; **BUS ADD:** 600 N. Rosemead Blvd., Pasadena, CA 91107, (213)681-4415.*

BRUMBAUGH, Robert R.——**B:** Nov. 6, 1942, Sioux City, IA, *Dir. Mgmt. Dept.*, Patterson, Schwartz, & Assoc. Inc.; **PRIM RE ACT:** Property Manager; **PROFL AFFIL & HONORS:** CPM; **EDUC:** BS, 1968, Bus. Admin., IL State Univ.; **GRAD EDUC:** MS, 1969, Bus. Admin., IL State Univ.; **HOME ADD:** RD 1 Box 412, Chadds Ford, PA 19317, (215)388-6916; **BUS ADD:** 913 Delaware Ave., Wilmington, DE 19806, (302)656-3141.

BRUMMAL, John V.——**B:** Apr. 28, 1947, Amarillo, TX, *Exec. VP*, El Paso Bd. of Realtors; **OTHER RE ACT:** Bd. Exec.; **SERVICES:** MLS, Educ.; **PREV EMPLOY:** Admin. Asst. Lubbock Bd. of Realtors; **PROFL AFFIL & HONORS:** The Amer. Soc. of Assn. Execs.; NAR; TX Assn of Realtors; **EDUC:** 1977, Acctg., TX Tech. Univ.; **MIL SERV:** USMC, S/Sgt., Vietnam; **HOME ADD:** 6823 Granero, El Paso, TX 79912, (915)584-3599; **BUS ADD:** 6400 Gateway East, El Paso, TX 79905, (915)779-3521.

BRUNE, Raymond L.——**B:** Oct. 12, 1932, Symerton, IL, *Owner*, Ray Brune & Co.; **PRIM RE ACT:** Broker, Instructor, Appraiser, Developer, Builder, Property Manager, Insuror; **SERVICES:** Full Scale (Serv.) Realtor; **REP CLIENTS:** Catipillar, Borg Warner, A.D.M. Staley's Muellar, Firestone; **PREV EMPLOY:** Worked in Factory Mgmt., Yrs. of Practical RE Exp.; **PROFL AFFIL & HONORS:** RNMI, Local, State & Natl. Bd. of Realtors, GRI, CRB; **MIL SERV:** USA, Cpl.; **OTHER ACT & HONORS:** C of C, Various State Realtors Comms., BOD Decatur Bd., Past Chmn. Decatur Multiple Listing Serv.; **HOME ADD:** 975 S Beal, Decatur, IL 62521, (217)963-2331; **BUS ADD:** 1610 Taylorville Rd., (217)428-4111.

BRUNE, W. Carl, Jr.——**B:** Oct. 24, 1923, Manila, Philippine Is., *Facility Location Consultant*, SRI International, RE Consulting Program; **PRIM RE ACT:** Consultant; **OTHER RE ACT:** Facility location consultation; **SERVICES:** Site analyses/plant location studies, socioeconomic impact analyses, comm. devel. programs, econ. devel. & revitalization programs, land use planning, environmental conflict resolution & strategy; **REP CLIENTS:** Hundreds of domestic & foreign manufacturers planning branch factories, warehouses, sales offices & headquarter relocations; **PREV EMPLOY:** Pacific Gas & Electric Co., San Francisco (1951-81); Indus. devel. site analyses/plant location studies, 1968-81; **PROFL AFFIL & HONORS:** Amer. Econ. Devel. Council, Indus. Devel. Research Council, CA Assn. for Local Econ. Devel.; **EDUC:** AB, 1947, Econ., Stanford Univ.; **GRAD EDUC:** MBA, 1949, Mktg., Stanford Grad. Sch. of Bus. Adm.; **MIL SERV:** USMC, Capt.; **OTHER ACT & HONORS:** San Francisco Bay Area Publicity Club, San Francisco Public Relations Round Table; **HOME ADD:** 50 Mt. Vernon Ln., Atherton, CA 94025, (415)322-7155; **BUS ADD:** 333 Ravenswood Ave., Menlo Pk, CA 94025, (415)859-6532.

BRUNEAU, Bill——**B:** May 29, 1948, Philadelphia, PA, *Prin.*, B.U.D.A. Assoc.; **PRIM RE ACT:** Architect, Consultant, Developer, Builder; **SERVICES:** Urban Design, Arch. and site planning; **REP CLIENTS:** Indiv. and Inst. investors, local and st. govt.; **PREV EMPLOY:** Nu-West Inc., CO Div.; **PROFL AFFIL & HONORS:** AIA, AICP, NCARM; **EDUC:** BArch, 1970, Arch, PA St. Univ.; **GRAD EDUC:** MArch, 1971, Urban Design, Univ. of CO; MArch, 1974, Urban Design, Harvard Univ; **EDUC HONORS:** Harvard Fellowship; **OTHER ACT & HONORS:** Outstanding Young Men of Amer. 1980; **HOME ADD:** 11100 E Dartmouth Ave. #300, Aurora, CO 80014, (303)695-4224; **BUS ADD:** 1399 S Havana St. Ste. 204, Aurora, CO 80012, (303)696-8808.

BRUNELLI, Richard J.——**B:** Jan. 20, 1947, Brooklyn, NY, *Pres.*, R.J. Brunelli & Co.; **PRIM RE ACT:** Broker, Consultant, Developer; **SERVICES:** Retail leasing spec. throughout NJ; **PREV EMPLOY:** Feist & Feist, Newark, NJ; **PROFL AFFIL & HONORS:** NAHB, NJ Homebuilders Assn.; **EDUC:** BS, 1969, Retail Mktg., Monmouth Coll.; **HOME ADD:** 49 Merritt Ave., South Amboy, NJ 08879; **BUS ADD:** 110 S. Broadway, South Amboy, NJ 08879, (201)721-5800.

BRUNGER, Mark A.——**B:** Nov. 3, 1952, Chicago, IL, *Atty.*, Hunt Props., Inc., Legal Dept.; **PRIM RE ACT:** Attorney; **SERVICES:** Legal aspects of comml. devels., including shopping ctrs.; office, hotels and indus. props. bldgs.; **PREV EMPLOY:** Southwestern Life Ins. Co. - Asst. Counsel - Comml. Mort. Loans and Joint Ventures; **PROFL AFFIL & HONORS:** RE Sec. of ABA, State Bar of TX and Dallas Bar Assn., Completed 2nd Annual Advanced RE Course of State Bar of TX; **EDUC:** BA, 1973, Pol. Sci., Calvin Coll.; **GRAD EDUC:** JD, 1976, So. Methodist Univ. School of Law; **EDUC HONORS:** Dean's List, Delta Theta Phi; **OTHER ACT & HONORS:** The 500, Inc.; **HOME ADD:** 711 Northill Dr., Richardson, TX 75080, (214)238-5516; **BUS ADD:** 5151 Belt Line Rd., Suite 1000, Dallas, TX 75240, (214)233-4800.

BRUNNER, Mark——**B:** Mar. 13, 1926, Vienna, Austria, *Pres.*, CENDEL; **PRIM RE ACT:** Developer; **SERVICES:** Office bldgs. and shopping ctr. devel.; **PROFL AFFIL & HONORS:** Intl. Council of Shopping Ctrs.; **HOME ADD:** 1614 Vallejo St. #101, San Francisco, CA 94123; **BUS ADD:** 210 Post St. #822, San Francisco, CA 94108, (415)986-3343.

BRUNNING, Geoffrey D.——*Pres.*, Hooker/Barnes Homes; **PRIM RE ACT:** Developer; **SERVICES:** Home Builder, FL, GA & TX; **PREV EMPLOY:** Bovis Homes (1966 through 1977), London, England; **PROFL AFFIL & HONORS:** NAHB; **BUS ADD:** 2175 Parklake Dr., NE, Suite 250, Atlanta, GA 30345, (404)939-8780.

BRUNO, Michael A.——**B:** June 22, 1932, New Orleans, LA, *Pres.*, Preferred Investment Corp.; **PRIM RE ACT:** Broker, Syndicator, Consultant, Appraiser, Developer, Property Manager, Lender, Owner/Investor; **OTHER RE ACT:** Synd. - Prop. Mgr.; **PROFL AFFIL & HONORS:** Realtor - RESSI Pres.; **OTHER ACT & HONORS:** Indep. Fee Appraisers; **HOME ADD:** 6032 Pontchartrain Train Blvd., New Orleans, LA 70124, (504)482-2786; **BUS ADD:** 1221 Amelia St., Gretna, LA 70053, (504)368-5626.

BRUNO, Victor S.——**B:** Sept. 24, 1950, Gary, IN, *Owner/Broker*, Vic Bruno Co.; **PRIM RE ACT:** Broker, Consultant, Property Manager; **SERVICES:** Mktg., site search, leasing, mgmt., consulting; **REP CLIENTS:** Corp. and indiv. users in indus. and office prop.; devel. of comml., indus. & office projects; **PREV EMPLOY:** Exclusively in comml., indus. & office brokerage since entering the field in 1973; **PROFL AFFIL & HONORS:** SIR; NAR; Exec. Assn. of Greater Albuquerque; **EDUC:** BUS, 1973, Bus./Econ., Univ. of NM; **HOME ADD:** 3208 Judy Pl., N.E., Albuquerque, NM 87111, (505)294-6487; **BUS ADD:** 2900 Louisiana Blvd., N.E. Suite G-1, N. Albuquerque, NM 87110, (505)884-4455.

BRUNS, David L.——**B:** Dec. 14, 1943, St. Louis, MO, *Pres.*, Bruns Realty & Development Co.; **PRIM RE ACT:** Broker, Consultant, Developer; **OTHER RE ACT:** Intl. RE Const. & Investment; **SERVICES:** Consultant; **PREV EMPLOY:** 17 yrs. in Houston, Brokerage & Const. Co.; **PROFL AFFIL & HONORS:** Assoc. Builders & Contractors, 17 yrs. in Houston Brokerage & Construction Co.; **EDUC:** Bus./RE, WA Univ./Univ. of Houston; **HOME ADD:** 12430 Plumbrook, Houston, TX 77099, (713)495-4149; **BUS ADD:** 9317 Ronda Ln., Houston, TX 77075, (713)271-2344.

BRUNSDON, William Richard Ian (Rick)——**B:** Oct. 9, 1946, Hardisty, Alberta, *VP*, Koyl Brunsdon Appraisals Ltd.; **PRIM RE ACT:** Consultant, Appraiser; **SERVICES:** All aspects of valuation and counseling of RE; **REP CLIENTS:** Indiv., provincial, nat. and multi-nat. firms; mcpl., province and fed. govts.; law and acctg. firms; **PREV EMPLOY:** Sales and Mktg. Mgr., Cairns Homes Ltd. 1972-1977; **PROFL AFFIL & HONORS:** RE Bd. of Saskatoon, Provincial and Nat. RE Assn., RE Inst., Nat. Assn. of Review Appraisers, Intl. Inst. of Valuers, FRI (RE Inst.), RRA (Sr. Member, Nat. Assn. of Review Appraisers), SCV (Sr. Member, Intl. Inst. of Valuers); **HOME ADD:** 518 Trent Crescent, Saskatoon, S7H 4T1, SK, Canada, (306)374-2996; **BUS ADD:** 116 - 103rd St., Saskatoon, S7N 1Y7, SK, Canada, (306)665-3171.

BRUNSKILL, James A.——**B:** Apr. 14, 1935, Toledo, OH, *Corp. VP RE*, Kobacker Stores, Inc.; **OTHER RE ACT:** Corp. RE Dev.; **PREV EMPLOY:** 14 yrs. RE exper. corp. and govt. (urban renewal); **PROFL AFFIL & HONORS:** Nat. Assn. of Corp. RE Execs.; **EDUC:** BBA, 1961, Econ. & Commerce, Univ. of Toledo; **MIL SERV:** USA, 1954-56, E-3, Good Conduct Medal, Hon. Discharge; **HOME ADD:** 1455 Candlewood Dr., Worthington, OH 43085; **BUS ADD:** 6606 Tussing Rd., Columbus, OH 43227, (614)863-7256.

BRUNST, William Todd——**B:** Dec. 8, 1949, Cincinnati, OH, *Senior VP*, Oxford Management Co., Inc., Asset Mgmt. & Acquisition; **PRIM RE ACT:** Developer, Owner/Investor, Property Manager; **SERVICES:** Asset Mgmt.; **PREV EMPLOY:** Wolverine Development Corp.; **PROFL AFFIL & HONORS:** NAR, IREM, Greater Lansing Bd. of Realtors; SE MI Builders Assn., MI Assn. of Realtors, CPM; **EDUC:** BA, 1971, Soc. Sci., WI State Univ.; **OTHER ACT & HONORS:** Dir., MI Assn. of Realtors (1982); Pres., W. MI Chap. 62 of IREM (1982); Lansing Rgnl. C of C; Meridian Township (Okemos) Bd. of Review; **HOME ADD:** 1940 Pawnee Trail, P.O. Box 248, Okemos, MI 48864, (517)349-2555; **BUS ADD:** 4295 Okemos Rd., Okemos, MI 48864, (517)349-2281.

BRUSH, Stephen A.——**B:** May 23, 1953, Atlanta, GA, *Rgnl. Marketing Rep.*, Homes For Living, Mktg.; **PRIM RE ACT:** Broker, Consultant, Instructor; **PREV EMPLOY:** Realty Masters of Charleston, Inc., VP; **PROFL AFFIL & HONORS:** NAR; Greater Charleston Bd. of Realtors; RNMI, CRB; GRI; **EDUC:** 1974, Bus., N. Greenville Coll.; **OTHER ACT & HONORS:** Ctry. Club of Charleston; Rosemont Golf Club of Orlando, FL; Northwood Sertoma Club; **HOME ADD:** 1811 Walsingham Way, Charleston, SC 29412, (803)795-6699; **BUS ADD:** 2423 Northline Industrial Dr., St. Louis, MO 63043, (800)325-4949.

BRUSMAN, William L.——**B:** Nov. 4, 1949, Elkhart, IN, *Asst. VP*, Northland Mortgage Co., Govt. Fin. Div.; **PRIM RE ACT:** Broker, Consultant, Lender; **OTHER RE ACT:** Mort. banking; **SERVICES:** RE consulting and lending regarding all types of govt. assisted or insured devel.; **REP CLIENTS:** For-profit and non-profit devel.; consultant to city and state agencies; **PREV EMPLOY:** MN Housing Fin. Agency, 1974-1977; Bor-Son Bldg. Corp., 1977-1979; **PROFL AFFIL & HONORS:** MBA of Amer.; Insured Projects Comm., MN Chapt. NAHRO, SREA Course 101 and 201 successfully completed; **EDUC:** BA, 1972, Sociology/Econ., IL Wesleyan Univ.; **GRAD EDUC:** MA, 1979, Urban Planning, Hubert H. Humphrey Inst. of Public Affairs, Univ. of MN; **EDUC HONORS:** Phi Kappa Phi, Magna Cum Laude; **HOME ADD:** 305 W. CO Rd. B2, Roseville, MN 55113, (612)483-6930; **BUS ADD:** 6600 France Ave. S., Minneapolis, MN 55435, (612)925-7721.

BRUSTAD, Orin D.——**B:** Nov. 11, 1941, Chicago, IL, *Partner*, Miller, Canfield, Paddock and Stona; **PRIM RE ACT:** Attorney; **SERVICES:** Legal: Counsel to comml. and condo. devels. and to lenders; **REP CLIENTS:** The Homestead (Glen Arbor, MI); Mitchell Creek Condos. (Traverse City); Mfrs. Hanover Mort. Corp.; **PROFL AFFIL & HONORS:** Real Prop. Sects. of ABA; MI State Bar Assn.; **EDUC:** BA, 1963, Hist., Yale Univ.; **GRAD EDUC:** MA, 1964, Yale Univ.; JD, 1968, Harvard Law School; **HOME ADD:** 1822 Huckleberry Ct., Traverse City, MI 49684, (616)946-5298; **BUS ADD:** 13999 W Bay Shore Dr., Traverse City, MI 49684, (616)946-1000.

BRUZZONE, Arthur A.——**B:** Nov. 14, 1945, San Francisco, CA, *Pres.*, Sorel Investments Corp.; **PRIM RE ACT:** Broker, Developer, Owner/Investor, Property Manager, Syndicator, Real Estate Publisher; **SERVICES:** Devel. & synd. of investment prop., prop. exchanges, prop. mgmt.; **REP CLIENTS:** Indiv. & instnl. investors; **PREV EMPLOY:** Bechtel Corp. 1973-1977; **PROFL AFFIL & HONORS:** Ritek Equities Group; NAR; CAR; **EDUC:** BA, 1963, Govt., St. Marys Coll., CA; **GRAD EDUC:** MA, 1972, Phil., Catholic Univ. of AMer.; **HOME ADD:** 1816 Scenic Dr., Modesto, CA; **BUS ADD:** 1230 13th Ste. C, Modesto, CA 95354, (209)524-9570.

BRYAN, Alonzo J., Jr.——**B:** Feb. 20, 1943, Washington, NJ, *Dir.*, National Association of Home Builders, Multi-Family; **PRIM RE ACT:** Consultant, Appraiser, Regulator, Builder, Property Manager, Assessor; **SERVICES:** Consulting, legislative review, appraisal, investment analysis; **REP CLIENTS:** Builders, devels., mgrs. and others involved in the devel. and mgmt. of multi-family housing; **PREV EMPLOY:** Office of L&T Affairs, RE Tax Assessment & Property Mgmt.; **PROFL AFFIL & HONORS:** RE & Urban Econ. Assn., GRI; **EDUC:** BS Fin., 1969, Univ. of TN; **GRAD EDUC:** Grad. Certificate in Housing & Urban Devel., 1977, RE Law, Appraisal, Urban Planning, Amer. Univ.; **MIL SERV:** USMC; 1966-1968, Cpl.; **HOME ADD:** 2059 Huntington Ave., Alexandria, VA 22303, (703)960-4920; **BUS ADD:** 15th & M Sts. N.W., Wash., DC 20005, (202)822-0218.

BRYAN, Joseph L., Jr.——**B:** Feb. 9, 1930, Richmond, VA, *Chief, RE*, Fed. Aviation Admin. Region; **PRIM RE ACT:** Regulator, Instructor, Consultant, Appraiser, Property Manager; **PROFL AFFIL & HONORS:** SRA, SREA; **EDUC:** Aurbun Univ.; **MIL SERV:** USA, SFC, Bronze Star; **HOME ADD:** 1912 Morris Dr., Riverdale, GA 30926, (404)996-2695; **BUS ADD:** 3400 Norman Berry Dr., East Point, GA 30344.

BRYAN, Mikel D.——**B:** April 9, 1948, Ft. Worth, TX, Clement, Fitzpatrick & Kenworthy Inc.; **PRIM RE ACT:** Attorney; **REP CLIENTS:** Brokers, devels, investors; **PROFL AFFIL & HONORS:** ABA, CA Bar Assn.; **EDUC:** BA, 1972, Hist., Math, Humboldt State Univ.; **GRAD EDUC:** JD, 1978, Univ.of the Pacific, McGeorge School of Law; **EDUC HONORS:** Cum Laude, Walker Scholarship, Life Member, Traynor Honor Soc.; **HOME ADD:** 622 Bishop Dr., Santa Rosa, CA 95405, (707)544-8950; **BUS ADD:** 3333 Mendocino Ave. Box 1494, Santa Rosa, CA 95402, (707)523-1181.

BRYAN, Robert L.——**B:** Nov. 23, 1951, Orlando, FL, *VP*, Grover Bryan Inc.; **PRIM RE ACT:** Broker, Consultant, Developer, Property Manager, Owner/Investor; **SERVICES:** Gen. brokerage and prop. mgmt.; **REP CLIENTS:** DisneyWorld, City of Orlando, William duPont III; **PROFL AFFIL & HONORS:** Orlando Winter Pk. Bd. of Realtors, FAR, NAR, CPM, Cert. RE Brokerage Mgr.; **EDUC:** BSBA, 1973, RE and Urban Land Studies, Univ. of FL; **GRAD EDUC:** MBA, 1981, Fin., Rollins Coll., Winter Pk., FL; **EDUC HONORS:** Phi Beta Gamma Sigma, High Honors, High Honors; **MIL SERV:** USAF, Cadet; **OTHER ACT & HONORS:** Boy Scouts, Big Brothers, Big Sisters, Episcopal Church; **HOME ADD:** 1214 Belleaire Cir., Orlando, FL 32804, (305)422-2924; **BUS ADD:** 200 E. Robinson St., Ste. 1250, Orlando, FL 32801, (305)425-3491.

BRYANT, Alan O.——**B:** June 2, 1942, Danville, KY, *VP & Rgnl. Counsel*, Commonwealth Land Title Ins., Co.; **PRIM RE ACT:** Attorney; **SERVICES:** Title ins. & legal consultant; **PROFL AFFIL & HONORS:** Louisville, KY and Amer. Bar Assn.; **EDUC:** AB, 1967, Govt. & Biology, Centre Coll.; **GRAD EDUC:** JD, 1970, Law, Univ. of KY; **EDUC HONORS:** Dean's List; **MIL SERV:** Peace Corps, Brazil 1964-1966; **OTHER ACT & HONORS:** Bd. of Dir., Louisville Audubon Soc.; **HOME ADD:** 1905 Lynn Way, Louisville, KY 40222, (502)425-3621; **BUS ADD:** 223 S Fifth St., Louisville, KY 40202, (502)584-0211.

BRYANT, Artis R.——**B:** Oct. 5, 1950, Leland, NC, *RE Officer*, City of Wilmington, Prop. Mgmt.; **PRIM RE ACT:** Broker, Appraiser, Regulator, Property Manager; **SERVICES:** Sales, negotiations, appraisals, regulatory compliance and mcpl. prop. mgmt.; **PREV EMPLOY:** Const. Loan Supervision and Prop. Mgmt. for RE Investment Trust; **EDUC:** BA, 1972, Bus. Admin., Morehouse Coll., Atlanta, GA, **EDUC HONORS:** Dean's List, **OTHER ACT & HONORS:** Kappa Alpha Psi Frat., Inc.; **HOME ADD:** 2069 Burnett Blvd., Wilmington, NC 28401, (919)763-2230; **BUS ADD:** P O Box 1810, Wilmington, NC 28402, (919)762-5442.

BRYANT, Carl H.——**B:** Jan. 11, 1918, Kansas City, MO, *Owner*, Carl H. Bryant, Real Estate; **PRIM RE ACT:** Broker, Consultant, Appraiser, Instructor, Property Manager, Syndicator; **SERVICES:** Investment counseling, valuation, mktg., prop. mgmt.; **PREV EMPLOY:** Wells Fargo Bank, Negotiator; **PROFL AFFIL & HONORS:** Inst. of Prop. Mgmt., State pres. 1960, of RE Certificate Inst., Contra

Costa Bd. of Realtors, CPM; **EDUC:** BS, 1979, Peninsula Univ. School of Law, Mt. View, CA; **GRAD EDUC:** JD, 1981, Peninsula Univ. School of Law; **EDUC HONORS:** Advanced Cert. in RE, Univ. CA Extension; **MIL SERV:** Air Corps, WWII, 1st Lt., DFC w/OLC, Air Medal w/4 OLC, Purple Heart; **HOME ADD:** 1929 Crisanto Ave. 632, Mt. View, CA 94040, (415)962-8834; **BUS ADD:** 1929 Crisanto Ave. 632, Mt. View, CA 94040, (415)962-8834.

BRYANT, Don——*Pres.*, Gallery of Homes; **PRIM RE ACT:** Syndicator; **BUS ADD:** 1001 International Blvd., Atlanta, GA 30354, (604)768-2460.*

BRYANT, Donnie L.——*Secy./Treas.*, Department of Housing and Urban Development, Neighborhood Reinvestment Corp.; **PRIM RE ACT:** Lender; **BUS ADD:** 451 Seventh St., S.W., Washington, DC 20410, (202)377-6480.*

BRYANT, James Elliott——**B:** Aug. 2, 1939, Auburn, NY, *Pres.*, The James Bryant Grp.; **PRIM RE ACT:** Architect, Developer, Builder; **SERVICES:** Dev. Arch., Gen. Contrs.; **REP CLIENTS:** Investors, Drs. & Dentists desiring Turnkey Projects; **PROFL AFFIL & HONORS:** AIA, Recipient of Grants, Thorne Ecological Found. 1970, Thorne Ecological/Rockefeller 1972; **EDUC:** BArch, 1964, Design & Const., USC; **OTHER ACT & HONORS:** Chmn. Bellevue Arts Commn. 1976; Dir. E. Side Chap. Full Gosper Bs. Men's Fellowship; **HOME ADD:** 6406 224th Ave. NE, Redmond, WA 98052, (206)882-0556; **BUS ADD:** 6406 224th Ave., NE, Redmond, WA 98052, (206)881-3397.

BRYANT, James Farnsworth——**B:** Dec. 26, 1945, Wash., DC, *Realty Specialist*, W. Div., Naval Facilities Engrg. Command, RE; **PRIM RE ACT:** Consultant, Regulator, Property Manager; **SERVICES:** Represent the Navy in all phases of RE activities; **PREV EMPLOY:** Atty.; Appraiser for Tax Purposes; **PROFL AFFIL & HONORS:** WA State Bar Assn.; Member, US Dist. Court, Western Div., WA - N. Dist. CA; **EDUC:** BS Bus. Admin., 1970, Bus./Acctg., Menlo Coll. School of Bus. Admin.; **GRAD EDUC:** JD, 1979, Law, Univ. of Puget Sound School of Law; **EDUC HONORS:** Dean's Scholar; **MIL SERV:** USN, YN3; **HOME ADD:** 460 Grove St., Half Moon Bay, CA 94019, (415)726-0457; **BUS ADD:** PO Box 727, San Bruno, CA 94066, (415)877-7617.

BRYANT, Jerry W.——**B:** July 31, 1941, Raleigh, NC, *Pres.-Dir.*, Integon Realty Corp.; **PRIM RE ACT:** Developer, Lender, Owner/Investor; **OTHER RE ACT:** Joint ventures; **SERVICES:** Const. lender; **PROFL AFFIL & HONORS:** IREM-Bd. of Realtors-NARA, CPM, CRA; **EDUC:** BS, 1964, Bus. Admin. Econ., Campbell Univ.; **GRAD EDUC:** MBA, 1965, Bus., Univ. NC Chapel Hill; **EDUC HONORS:** Cum Laude, Pres. Hon. Soc.; **OTHER ACT & HONORS:** W-Salem C of C Dir. of Jr. Achievement of W-Salem, Dir. Admore Youth Athletic Foundation, W-Salem Human Relations Commn.; **HOME ADD:** 610 Terrybrook Ct., Winston Salem, NC 27104, (919)768-5814; **BUS ADD:** 500 W. Fifth St., Winston Salem, NC 27104, (919)725-7261.

BRYANT, Norman F.——**B:** Jan. 26, 1925, Rushville, IN, *Pres.*, The Bryant Co. Inc.; **PRIM RE ACT:** Broker, Syndicator, Consultant, Developer, Property Manager, Owner/Investor; **SERVICES:** Prop. Mgmt., Dev. & Synd. of Comml. Prop., Investment Counseling; **REP CLIENTS:** Indiv. & Group Owners, Investors; **PREV EMPLOY:** VP, Banking; **PROFL AFFIL & HONORS:** Dir. Comml. Indus. Div.; Indiniapolis Bd. of Realtors; Inst. RE Mgmt; RNMI; RESSI, CPM, CCIM (Candidate); **EDUC:** BS, 1950, Econ. & Bus. Admin., Butler Univ.; **MIL SERV:** USAAF, Capt.; **OTHER ACT & HONORS:** Dir. Rgnl. Boy Scouts of Amer., Past Pres. of Several Civic Orgs., Dist. Service Award, U.S. Jr. C of C, Award for Exceptional Service, Amer. Heritage Found.; **HOME ADD:** 15018 Shoreway E., Carmel, IN 46032, (317)846-0377; **BUS ADD:** PO Box 40338, 3510 E. 96th St., Indianapolis, IN 46240, (317)848-7100.

BRYANT, Sherman R., Jr.——*Dir., Community Assn. Div.*, CEO Incorporated; **PRIM RE ACT:** Consultant, Property Manager; **SERVICES:** Consulting, community assn. devel; mgmt. comm. assns.; **PROFL AFFIL & HONORS:** Sustaining member - Comm. Assns. Inst., PCAM (candidate); **EDUC:** BA, 1977, Acctg., Amer. River Coll.; **BUS ADD:** 729 Sunrise Ave., 501, Roseville, CA 95678, (916)969-2700.

BRYANT, Virgil C.——**B:** May 1, 1919, Yuma, AZ, *VP*, Jay Prop. Syst. Inc., Member of Jacobs Engrg Grp. Inc.; **PRIM RE ACT:** Developer; **SERVICES:** RE Dev.; **REP CLIENTS:** Jacobs Engrg. Grp. Inc.; **PREV EMPLOY:** Pres. Design Science, Inc.; **PROFL AFFIL & HONORS:** Fellow ASCE; **EDUC:** BS, 1942, Civ. Engr., Univ. of CA at Berkeley; **MIL SERV:** USN, Const. battalion, Lt.; **HOME ADD:** 625 S. Orange Grove Blvd., Pasadena, CA 91105; **BUS ADD:** 251 So. Lake Ave., Pasadena, CA 91101, (213)578-6816.

BRYANT, William L.——**B:** Apr. 12, 1933, Richmond, VA, *Owner*, Bill Bryant RE; **SERVICES:** Indus. & comml. land sites of every nature, plus land for new subdiv. and investment acreage near Dulles Airport; **PREV EMPLOY:** 18 yrs. with own firm; **HOME ADD:** 1015 Basil Rd., McLean, VA 22101; **BUS ADD:** PO Box 17287, Dulles Airport, Wash., DC 20041, (703)430-3100.

BRYDON, Joe——**B:** Apr. 7, 1931, Kinghorn, Scotland, *Pres.*, Joe Brydon & Assoc.; **PRIM RE ACT:** Broker, Developer, Owner/Investor, Syndicator; **PROFL AFFIL & HONORS:** Realtor; Member of the Intl. Assn. of Fin. Planners; **EDUC:** BS, 1957, Engrg., Edinburgh Univ., Scotland; **EDUC HONORS:** Cum Laude; **HOME ADD:** 4138 Mesa St., Torrance, CA 90505, (213)373-2777; **BUS ADD:** 3812 Sepulveda Blvd., Suite 200, Torrance, CA 90505, (213)373-0787.

BRYSON, Hugh——**B:** Oct. 4, 1914, IL, *Pres.*, National Motel Brokers; **PRIM RE ACT:** Broker, Consultant, Appraiser; **OTHER RE ACT:** Editor and Publisher "Motel News"; **SERVICES:** Broker, Appraiser (CRA) Counselor for the hospitality indus. (hotels-motels); **PREV EMPLOY:** 27 years in developing, sales, leases, exchanges, and finances; **PROFL AFFIL & HONORS:** Motel Brokers Assn. of Amer., Amer. Hotel & Motel Assn., NARA, NAR, CA Hotel & Motel Assn.; **GRAD EDUC:** IL Bus. Coll., 1933; **MIL SERV:** Amer. Merchant Marine, 1936-1954; **OTHER ACT & HONORS:** San Mateo Horseman, Amer. Endurance Riders, Woodside Shack Riders, Los Viajeros; **HOME ADD:** 155 Prospect, Woodside, CA 94063, (415)851-8266; **BUS ADD:** 3-37th Ave., P O Box 5446, San Mateo, CA 94402, (415)349-1234.

BRYSON, Larry——*Director*, Century 21, Southwest; **PRIM RE ACT:** Syndicator; **BUS ADD:** 5201 N. 7th St., Phoenix, AZ 85011, (602)263-1222.*

BRYSON, Robert H.——**B:** Feb. 28, 1937, Tallahassee, FL, *Pres. and Chmn. of the Bd.*, Investors Companies of Florida, Inc.; **PRIM RE ACT:** Broker, Consultant, Developer, Owner/Investor, Property Manager, Insuror, Syndicator; **SERVICES:** RE brokerage, prop. mgmt., comml. & resid.; prop. devel., re synd., ins. agency, mort. brokerage; **PREV EMPLOY:** Officer of NYSE member firm. Dir. and exec. in major local devel. corp.; **PROFL AFFIL & HONORS:** Nat., FL and local Bd. of Realtors; Member, FL Assn. of Mort. Brokers; Dir., Bd. of Govs. of RESSI; Bd. of Gov. and State Sec. of RESSI; **EDUC:** BS, 1959, Bus. Mgmt./Fin. and Investments, FL State Univ., Sch. of Bus.; **OTHER ACT & HONORS:** Member Bd. of Tr., Southmark Props., Atlanta, GA; **HOME ADD:** 4514 Thomasville Rd., Tallahassee, FL 32308, (904)893-6675; **BUS ADD:** 1001 Thomasville Rd., Tallahassee, FL 32303, (904)224-6900.

BUBARIS, Gus J.——**B:** Feb. 3, 1952, NY, *Asst. Mgr. RE*, New Jersey Bell; **PRIM RE ACT:** Broker, Consultant, Owner/Investor, Property Manager; **SERVICES:** Tenant Representation, Lease Negotiations, Prop. Mgmt.; **PREV EMPLOY:** RE Officer-OPM Leasing, NYC, Kreisel Co. Inc., NYC; **EDUC:** BA, 1974, Econ., C.W. Post Coll.; **GRAD EDUC:** MA Economics, 1977, Urban Housing, SUNY Binghamton, NY; **EDUC HONORS:** Serv. Award 1973-1974; **OTHER ACT & HONORS:** Chmn.-Hellenic Univ. Club, NYC; **HOME ADD:** 25-19 30th Dr., Astoria, NY 11102, (212)278-5166; **BUS ADD:** 650 Park Ave., E Orange, NJ 07017, (201)675-8234.

BUBEL, Howard L.——**B:** April 19, 1938, San Diego, CA, Self employed; **PRIM RE ACT:** Consultant, Property Manager, Owner/Investor; **SERVICES:** Investment and Mgmt. Counseling, and Prop. Mgmt.; **REP CLIENTS:** Indiv. in Resid. Props.; **PREV EMPLOY:** USAF 1960-1976; Dept. of Defense 1976-1978; **PROFL AFFIL & HONORS:** CA Licensee; Apt. Builder/Owner Assn.; **EDUC:** BS, 1960, Acctg. and RE, San Diego State Univ.; **GRAD EDUC:** MS, 1969, Systems Mgmt., USC; **MIL SERV:** USAFR, Lt. Col., Joint Serv. Commendation Medal; Outstanding USAF Reserve Officer Mobilization Augmentee - 1980; **HOME ADD:** PO Box 2872, Fairfax, VA 22031, (703)280-5765; **BUS ADD:** Fairfax, VA 22031PO Box 2872, (703)280-5765.

BUCHALTER, William——**B:** Mar. 20, 1949, NY, *Pres.*, WEB Mgmt. Co. Inc.; **PRIM RE ACT:** Syndicator, Developer, Property Manager, Owner/Investor; **PROFL AFFIL & HONORS:** IREM, CRB, GRI; **EDUC:** BA, 1970, Soc. Sci., SUNY at Stonybrook; **BUS ADD:** 691 E Main St., Middletown, NY 10940, (914)343-7966.

BUCHANAN, L. Greggory——**B:** Sept. 23, 1946, Prescott, AR, *Part./Broker*, Robinson-Buchanan RE; **PRIM RE ACT:** Broker, Consultant, Appraiser, Property Manager, Assessor, Owner/Investor; **SERVICES:** Counseling, appraising, prop. mgmt.; **REP CLIENTS:** Indiv., lenders; **PROFL AFFIL & HONORS:** NAR, RNMI, AR Chapter of CRS, Pres. of Charter yr.(1980) AR Chap. Cert. Residential specialists, 4 time recipient of AR Realtors Assn. Pres. Award; **EDUC:** BBA, 1969,

Bus. Admin. & Econ., S. AR Univ.; **MIL SERV:** USAR, Sgt. 1968-74; **OTHER ACT & HONORS:** 1st Presbyterian Church, Civitan, Jaycees, SAU Alumni Assn. Past Pres.; **HOME ADD:** 2525 Calion Rd., El Dorado, AR 71730, (501)863-6722; **BUS ADD:** 123 W. Grove, El Dorado, AR 71730, (501)862-7957.

BUCHANON, John S.——*Exec. Staff Dir.*, Department of Housing and Urban Development, Federal Home Loan Bank Board; **PRIM RE ACT:** Lender; **BUS ADD:** 451 Seventh St., S.W., Washington, DC 20410, (202)377-6673.*

BUCHART, John R.——*Pres.*, H.G. Rotz Assocs., Inc.; **PRIM RE ACT:** Broker, Appraiser; **OTHER RE ACT:** Bus. brokerage; **SERVICES:** Indus. RE sales and leasing, bus. and bus. prop. brokerage; **REP CLIENTS:** Caterpillar Tractor; Allis Chalmers; Borg Warner; P.H. Glatfelter Co.; Fed. Paperboard; CampbellChain; Motter Printing Press; D&D Sewing; Danskin; Gulf & Western; **PROFL AFFIL & HONORS:** SIR; **BUS ADD:** 11 E. Market St., York, PA 17401, (717)843-8091.

BUCHBINDER, Norman M.——**B:** Mar. 29, 1917, NY, *Mgmt. Dir.*, Sulzberger-Rolfe Inc., Mgmt.; **PRIM RE ACT:** Broker, Property Manager; **PROFL AFFIL & HONORS:** IREM, RE Bd. of NY, VChmn., Mgmt. Div., CPM; **EDUC:** BSS, 1937, CCNY; **MIL SERV:** USAF; Maj. (Retd.); **BUS ADD:** 654 Madison Ave., NY, NY 10021, (212)593-7654.

BUCHER, William Ward——**B:** March 14, 1946, Summit, NJ, *Prin.*, Wm. Ward Bucher & Assoc.; **PRIM RE ACT:** Architect, Consultant; **OTHER RE ACT:** Zoning & City Planning Consultant; **SERVICES:** Design, Zoning Analysis, Econ. Feasibility Studies, Environmental Analysis, Interiors; **REP CLIENTS:** Non-Profit, profl. & bus. orgs., & devels.; **PREV EMPLOY:** DC Office of Planning & Devel. 1970-1974; **PROFL AFFIL & HONORS:** AIA, Const. Specifications Inst., D.C. Builders Assn.; **EDUC:** BS, 1968, Arch., RPI; **GRAD EDUC:** BArch, 1969, RPI; **HOME ADD:** 1744 Corcoran St. NW, Wash., DC 20009; **BUS ADD:** 1638 R St. NW, Washington, DC 20009, (202)387-0061.

BUCHHOLZER, Richard B.——**B:** Feb. 19, 1916, Alliance, OH, *Pres.*, Chapel Hill Management, Inc.; **PRIM RE ACT:** Consultant, Developer, Owner/Investor; **PREV EMPLOY:** Pres. - Howes Dept. Stores, Middlebury Manor Nursing Home; **PROFL AFFIL & HONORS:** LNHA; **EDUC:** BA, 1938, Akron Univ.; **OTHER ACT & HONORS:** ARDB; Beacon Journal Charity Fund; UF; Child Guidance; JrArc.; Litchfield Rehabilitiation Ctr.; **HOME ADD:** 255 N. Portaye Path, Akron, OH 44303, (216)867-7623; **BUS ADD:** 830 Chapel Hill Mall, Akron, OH 44310, (216)533-7100.

BUCHNER, James——*Pres.*, Economic Development Corp of Orange County; **PRIM RE ACT:** Developer; **BUS ADD:** 705 Bank of America Tower, One City Blvd. West, Orange, CA 92668, (714)834-2642.*

BUCK, Gordon Hall——**B:** Apr. 10, 1936, Hartford, CT, *Sr. Partner - RE*, Robinson, Robinson & Cole, RE Dept.; **PRIM RE ACT:** Attorney, Broker; **SERVICES:** Atty.-specializing in land use, condo., RE finance; **REP CLIENTS:** Condo. Devel. & Converters; Major Land Devels.; Realtors; Community Assns.; Bank; Municipalities; **PREV EMPLOY:** Shipman & Goodwin Attys. 1965-68; RF Broderick & Associates - Devels. VP &I Gen. Counsel 1968-70; Pelgrift, Byrne, Buck & Connolly; Byrne Buck & Steiner; **PROFL AFFIL & HONORS:** V Chmn. Condo. Comm., RE Sect., ABA; Nat. Trustee, Pres. CT Chapter Community Assns. Inst.; Pres., CAI Research Found.; Member, Gr. Hartford Bd. of Realtors; Licensed RE Broker; Member, CT, 2nd Circuit Bar; **EDUC:** BA, 1958, Eng., Coll. of Arts & Sci.; **GRAD EDUC:** JD, 1965, Land use, zoning, Univ. of PA; **EDUC HONORS:** Triangle Moot Court; **MIL SERV:** USCG; Lt.; **OTHER ACT & HONORS:** Chmn., Glastonbury Plan. & Zoning Commission, 1966-68; Region Chmn., Governors Task Force on Housing, 1975; Regional Chmn., Capitol Region Housing Council; **HOME ADD:** 20 Moseley Terrace, Glastonbury, CT 06033; **BUS ADD:** 799 Main St., Hartford, CT 06103, (203)278-0700.

BUCKELEW, E. Douglas——**B:** Mar. 31, 1932, TX, *Branch Mgr., Investments RE*, Gen. American Life Insurance Co., RE; **PRIM RE ACT:** Appraiser, Lender; **SERVICES:** Not active appraiser - Previously Investment Mgr. for Gen. Amer. Life; **PREV EMPLOY:** Jefferson Std. Life Ins. Co., Mort. Div.; Southern Trust & Mortgage, Dallas, TX; **PROFL AFFIL & HONORS:** Soc. of RE Appraisers, SRA; **EDUC:** BBA, 1959, Econ./Fin., Texas Tech.; **EDUC HONORS:** Brownfield Bk. & Trust Banking Scholarship, 1958; **MIL SERV:** Army, Eng., Sgt.; **HOME ADD:** 1500 Colony Rd., Metairie, LA 70003; **BUS ADD:** 3445 N. Causeway Blvd., Suite 912, Metairie, LA 70002, (504)834-3888.

BUCKELEW, Joseph E.——**B:** Aug. 16, 1929, New Brunswick, NJ, *Pres.*, Morales, Potter & Buckelew, Inc.; **PRIM RE ACT:** Broker, Appraiser, Banker, Builder, Owner/Investor, Insuror; **PROFL AFFIL & HONORS:** Ocean Cty. Bd. of Realtors - IFA; **MIL SERV:** US Army Military Police, Sgt.; **OTHER ACT & HONORS:** Mayor of Lakewood, NJ 1967; Dir. of the Ocean Cty. Bd. of Freeholders 1975; **HOME ADD:** 120 Adelaide Pl., Lakewood, NJ 08701, (201)363-7139; **BUS ADD:** 256 Route 37 W., Toms River, NJ 08753, (201)349-7400.

BUCKETT, Patrick W.——**B:** July 17, 1933, Milwaukee, WI, *Pres.*, WI Appraisal Co. & Pat Buckett Ltd., ReaLtor; **PRIM RE ACT:** Broker, Consultant, Appraiser, Developer, Owner/Investor, Instructor, Real Estate Publisher; **SERVICES:** RE valuation; Condemnation & Court Appraisals; Investment Counseling; Exchanging; Comml. & Investment Brokerage & Leasing; **REP CLIENTS:** SEMCO, General Motors, WI DVA, E.H. Boeckh Co., Lincoln Cty., City of Merrill, various lending insts. & law firms; **PREV EMPLOY:** Robedeaux Co., Realtors/Robedeaux Investment Co., Inc. Milwaukee, WI 1959-1969; **PROFL AFFIL & HONORS:** NAR, RNMI, WI Realtors Assn.; WI Exchange Club; Milwaukee Bd. of Realtors; SREA, CRA, CRS, GRI; **EDUC:** BS, 1956, Speech & Psych., Marquette Univ.; **GRAD EDUC:** SREA Course 101, Univ. of NM; 201 & 301, AZ State Univ.; **MIL SERV:** USA, SP-4, Far East Network, Radio Announcer, 1956-1959; **OTHER ACT & HONORS:** Past Pres.-WI Exchange Club & Wausau Chapter NAIFA; Past Gov. WI Realtors Inst.; State Membership, Commitee Chmn. WI Realtors Assn., Bd. of Dirs. Member (10 yrs.) WRA; Past VP Merrill Area Dev. Corp., Natl. Instr. various courses & seminars; **HOME ADD:** 1006 Elm St., Merrill, WI 54452, (715)536-2062; **BUS ADD:** Drawer 120, 1302 N. Center Ave., Merrill, WI 54452, (715)536-4572.

BUCKLE, Dr. F.T.——**B:** Nov. 17, 1949, Ghana, *Pres., CEO*, Chase, Tarifero & Morgan, N.V.; **PRIM RE ACT:** Consultant, Banker, Developer, Lender, Owner/Investor, Property Manager, Insuror; **SERVICES:** Mort. banking, prop. mgmt., fin. consultant; **REP CLIENTS:** Devels. & RE investors, profl. investors, bldg. owners, land owners; **PROFL AFFIL & HONORS:** Assn. of Intl. Financiers; Chicago Assn. of Commerce & Indus.; MBAA, Bd. of Dirs., Assn. of Intl. Financiers; **EDUC:** BBA, 1973, Fin. Mgmt./Org. Structure; **GRAD EDUC:** MBA/PhD, 1975, Fin. Mgmt./Intl. Trade & Relations; **HOME ADD:** 175 E. Delaware Pl., Chicago, IL 60611; **BUS ADD:** 201 E. Walton Pl., Chicago, IL 60611, (312)664-5056.

BUCKLES, Earl C.——**B:** Sept. 11, 1942, Omaha, NE, *Regn. Counsel*, Heiskell, Donelson, Bearman, Adams Williams & Kirsch; **PRIM RE ACT:** Attorney; **SERVICES:** Advice and Counsel on RE Legal questions; **REP CLIENTS:** Gen. Electric Credit Corp.; GMAC; International Harvester; **PREV EMPLOY:** Atty. - Smith Schwegler Swartzman & Winger Kansas City, MO - Comml. RE matters; General Electric Credit Corporation; **EDUC:** BA, 1967, Hist., Univ. of NE at Omaha; **GRAD EDUC:** JD, 1970, Law, Univ. of NE at Lincoln; **EDUC HONORS:** Phi Eta Sigma, Natl. Scholastic Hon. Deans Honor List; **BUS ADD:** 20th fl.-165 Madison, Memphis, TN 38103, (901)526-2000.

BUCKLEY, Charles E.——*VP Fin.*, Leesona Corp.; **PRIM RE ACT:** Property Manager; **BUS ADD:** 333 Strawberry Field Rd., Warwick, RI 02887, (401)739-7100.*

BUCKLEY, David F.——**B:** May 13, 1936, VT, *Atty.*, BSR Co., Inc. & Williams River Elec. Corp.; **PRIM RE ACT:** Attorney, Developer, Owner/Investor; **OTHER RE ACT:** Hydro elec. devel. and licensing; **EDUC:** AB, 1958, Univ. Notre Dame; **GRAD EDUC:** JD, 1965; **OTHER ACT & HONORS:** Town rep. State legislation and Moderator; **HOME TEL:** (802)463-4736; **BUS ADD:** 18 Bridge St., Bellows Falls, VT 05101, (802)463-3271.

BUCKLEY, Davis——**B:** May 5, 1942, Worcester, MA, *Pres.*, Davis Buckley, A Prof. Corp.; **PRIM RE ACT:** Architect, Developer; **SERVICES:** Consulting for Dev., Arch. and Dev. Mgmt., Mktg. Consultant; **REP CLIENTS:** Corps., trade assns., arch. firms; **PREV EMPLOY:** Principal, arch. firm of Hellmuth, Obata, Kassabaum; **PROFL AFFIL & HONORS:** AIA, NCARB Registration Member of the Soc. for Mktg. of Prof. Serv.; and the Amer. Arbitration Assn.; **GRAD EDUC:** MArch, 1970, Yale School of Arch.; **HOME ADD.** 3282 Worthington St., N.W., Washington, DC 20015, (202)966-7211; **BUS ADD:** 910 16th St., N.W., Washington, DC 20006, (202)223-1234.

BUCKO, Lee——**B:** Jan. 24, 1942, Dearborn, MI, *Broker/Owner*, Coast RE, Inc.; **PRIM RE ACT:** Broker, Developer, Property Manager, Owner/Investor; **OTHER RE ACT:** Bus. Opportunity Broker; **PROFL AFFIL & HONORS:** Cert. Bus. Counselors, BS, HBA, Realtors "Who's Who in Amer. Bus. 1980-81"; **EDUC:** BS, 1964, Mktg., UCLA; **GRAD EDUC:** MBA, 1965, Mktg., UCLA; **MIL SERV:** USCG, YN-2; **OTHER ACT & HONORS:** Chmn. - Dunes City

Planning Comm.; **HOME ADD:** 5400 Colorado Rd. 503, Dunes City, OR, (503)997-6565; **BUS ADD:** 100 Hwy. 101, Florence, OR 97439, (503)997-3473.

BUCUS, Uldis——B: Dec. 8, 1942, Latvia, *VP, RE,* The Fidelity Mutual Life Insurance Co., Investment Dept.; **PRIM RE ACT:** Attorney, Developer, Owner/Investor, Syndicator; **PREV EMPLOY:** Former Sr. Officer, Law Dept., The Fidelity Mutual Life Ins. Co.; **PROFL AFFIL & HONORS:** ABA; Amer. Land Title Assn., Assoc. Member; **EDUC:** BS, 1967, Hist./Sci.; **GRAD EDUC:** JD, 1970; **EDUC HONORS:** Woodrow Wilson Fellow, 1967; **HOME ADD:** 3 Kane Dr., Malvern, PA 19355; **BUS ADD:** The Fidelity Mutual Life Bldg., S. Penn Sq., Philadelphia, PA 19101, (215)977-8149.

BUDD, Val——*Commissioner,* Illinois, Illinois Real Estate Commission, Dept. of Registration & Education; **PRIM RE ACT:** Property Manager; **BUS ADD:** Charles A. Stevens Bldg., 17 N. State St., 17th Floor, Chicago, IL 60602, (217)785-0852.*

BUDNIK, Ronald J.——B: Mar. 15, 1943, Philadelphia, PA, *Sales Mgr.,* Norris, Beggs & Simpson; **PRIM RE ACT:** Broker, Developer, Lender, Property Manager; **SERVICES:** Comml. & indus. brokerage, investment counseling, mort. banking, & prop. mgmt; **REP CLIENTS:** Corp. RE clients, RE investment & trusts, and instit. lenders; **PREV EMPLOY:** RCA Corp.; **PROFL AFFIL & HONORS:** Amer. Indus. RE Assn.; Los Angeles Bd. of Realtors; CA MBA; **HOME ADD:** Los Angeles, CA; **BUS ADD:** 523 W. Sixth St., #219, Los Angeles, CA 90014, (213)624-5980.

BUEHRLE, Chip——B: Aug. 29, 1946, St. Louis, MO, *Sr. VP,* JBM Realty Investment Co.; **PRIM RE ACT:** Broker, Developer, Owner/Investor, Instructor, Property Manager, Syndicator; **SERVICES:** Investment Counseling, RE Exchanging, Conversions, Syndications, Rehabilitation Projects; **PREV EMPLOY:** Sr. VP, Indevco, Realtors; **PROFL AFFIL & HONORS:** Realtor, Exchangers; **EDUC:** BA, 1974, Communications Skills, Univ. of WI; **GRAD EDUC:** MFA, 1980, Communications, Univ. of AZ; **EDUC HONORS:** Grad. with Honors; **HOME ADD:** 12401 E Barbary Coast Rd., Tucson, AZ 85715, (602)749-9767; **BUS ADD:** 7977E Speedway Blvd., Suite 102, Tucson, AZ 85719, (602)886-3700.

BUERGER, Julius A.——B: Dec. 26, 1932, Denver,CO, *Broker, Comml. RE,* Prop. Brokers, Inc.; **PRIM RE ACT:** Broker, Consultant, Developer, Property Manager, Owner/Investor; **SERVICES:** Dev. Sales Counseling of Comml. RE & Prop. Mgmt.; **REP CLIENTS:** Investors & users of Comml. RE Dev. of Office Bldg., Apt. and Shopping Ctrs.; **PREV EMPLOY:** Moore & Co. 1975-1981; **PROFL AFFIL & HONORS:** Comml. Listing Service, Denver Exchangers, Denver Bd. of Realtors, NAR, CPM; IREM; Denver Roundtable Bd. Award (Sales over $1,000,000.00); Moore & Co. Gold Service Award; Earned commissions over $50,000.00; **EDUC:** BA/BA, 1955, Bus. Mgmt. & Acctg., Univ. of CO 1951-1953, Univ. of Denver 1953-1955; **OTHER ACT & HONORS:** Bd. Member Denver Mental Health Assn.; Bd. Member Denver Mental Health Ctr.; Timberline Toastmasters; Republican Men's Club; Denver Round Table; Columbine Ctry. Club; **HOME ADD:** 4351 W. Ponds Cir., Littleton, CO 80123, (303)794-3415; **BUS ADD:** 2755 S. Locust, Denver, CO 80222, (303)758-1070.

BUGHER, C. David——B: June 10, 1922, Ladysmith, WI, *Partner,* Bugher & Stewart; **PRIM RE ACT:** Broker, Appraiser, Developer, Builder, Owner/Investor, Property Manager; **PREV EMPLOY:** Realtor, Farmer Bugher; **PROFL AFFIL & HONORS:** Eau Claire - Chippewa Bd. of Realtors; WI Realtors; Nat. Assn. of Realtors, Past Pres., WI Assn.; Dir., Nat. Assn.; **EDUC:** BBA, 1947, Bus. Admin., Univ. of WI; **MIL SERV:** USAF, 1st Lt., Air Medal w/OLC, 40 combat missions; **OTHER ACT & HONORS:** YMCA, Pres. - 3 yrs., Bd. of Dir. - 12 yrs.; Eau Claire C of C, Pres. and Dir. 6 yrs.; **HOME ADD:** 611 E. Lowes Creek Rd., Eau Claire, WI 54701, (715)835-6509; **BUS ADD:** 826 So. Hastings Way, Eau Claire, WI 54701, (715)834-2691.

BUIGAS, Octavio D.——B: Dec. 15, 1935, Havana, Cuba, *Chmn. of the Bd., Chief Exec. Officer,* Southeast Enterprises, Inc. & Subsidiaries; **PRIM RE ACT:** Broker, Consultant, Engineer, Architect, Developer, Lender, Builder, Owner/Investor, Property Manager, Insuror; **OTHER RE ACT:** Mort. Broker, Land Planner; **SERVICES:** All related RE indus.; **REP CLIENTS:** Chase Enterprises, Inc.; Soc. for Savings both in Hartford, CT; Resnick/Dunaevsky, Miami, FL; The Sands, The Grove both in Ft. Pierce, FL; **PROFL AFFIL & HONORS:** Reg. Arch. in FL and Puerto Rico, Mort. Brokers Lic., RE Brokers Lic.; **EDUC:** BArch., Arch., Villanova Univ.; **HOME ADD:** 10361 S.W. 13th St., Miami, FL 33174, (305)553-6998; **BUS ADD:** 500 N.W. 165th St., Suite 102, Miami, FL 33169, (305)940-7781.

BUILTA, Howard C——B: Apr. 29, 1943, Lawton, OK, *Rgnl. Gen. Mgr.,* Marathon US Realties, Inc.; **PRIM RE ACT:** Developer; **SERVICES:** Office Bldg. Devel.; **PREV EMPLOY:** VP Gen. Mgr., The Whiston Grp., UP Rauch & Co.; **PROFL AFFIL & HONORS:** RPA, ULI, BOMA, IREM, Lic. RE & Ins. Broker, IL, CPM; **EDUC:** 1965, Econ., Univ. of IL; **GRAD EDUC:** MBA, 1967, Fin.; **MIL SERV:** USA, Quartermaster, 1st Lt., Bronze Star; **OTHER ACT & HONORS:** Palatine Township (IL) Tr. (1979-81); Dir. Chicago RE Bd.; Immediate Past Pres. BOMA of Suburban Chicago; Dir. Lutheran Comm. Servs. (NW); **HOME ADD:** 2316 Sunset Rd., Palatine, IL 60067, (312)358-5509; **BUS ADD:** Suite 2550, One First Nat. Plaza, Chicago, IL 60603, (312)782-5114.

BULL, V. Craig——B: Mar. 19, 1923, Oakland, CA, *Pres.,* Group Mgmt. and Investment Co., Inc.; **PRIM RE ACT:** Broker, Developer, Property Manager, Syndicator; **SERVICES:** Investment counseling, acquisition, devel. and synd.; **PREV EMPLOY:** Consolidated Capital Corp., Regional VP; **PROFL AFFIL & HONORS:** Soc. of former agents, FBI; **EDUC:** AB, 1948, Pol. Sci., Univ. of CA; **GRAD EDUC:** Law, Hastings Coll. of Law, Univ. of CA; **EDUC HONORS:** Distinguished Military Grad; **MIL SERV:** US Army, Lt., Bronze Star, Combat Infantry Badge; **OTHER ACT & HONORS:** Congrl. Candidate; Masonic Lodge; Scottish Rite; Shrine; Rotary; **HOME ADD:** 3 Donald Dr., Orinda, CA 94563, (415)254-5116; **BUS ADD:** 177 Front St., Suite F,, Danville, CA 94526, (415)838-8590.

BULLARD, Don——*Asst. Treas., Mgr. RE & Inc.,* Envirotech Corp.; **PRIM RE ACT:** Property Manager; **BUS ADD:** 3000 Sand Hill Rd., Menlo Park, CA 94025, (415)854-2000.*

BULLIER, Albert R., Sr.——B: Jan. 9, 1905, Portland, OR, *Chmn. of Bd.,* Bullier & Bullier, Inc.; **PRIM RE ACT:** Broker; **SERVICES:** Indus. and comml. prop. mgmt., sale, lease, devel.; **REP CLIENTS:** Industries, retailers, fin. instit., prop. owners; **PROFL AFFIL & HONORS:** SIR; Portland, OR Bd. of Realtors, Past Nat. Pres. SIR 1961; Past Pres. Portland Bd. of Realtors 1951; Past Pres. Portland BOMA 1953; **OTHER ACT & HONORS:** Chmn. Bd. of Educ. Portland, OR Public Schools 1950; Chmn. of Bd., E. Henry Wemme Endowment Fund; **HOME ADD:** 2211 SW 1st Ave., Apt. 1401, Portland, OR 97201, (503)243-2777; **BUS ADD:** 15th Fl., Bank of CA Tower, Portland, OR 97205, (503)223-3123.

BULLINGER, E. Eugene——B: Apr. 19, 1926, Wichita, KS, *Sec./Treas.,* Pettit & Bullinger, P.A. Arch; **PRIM RE ACT:** Architect, Instructor, Owner/Investor; **OTHER RE ACT:** Arch. instr. for GRI in KS; **SERVICES:** Arch. services & consulting; **PROFL AFFIL & HONORS:** KS Soc. of Arch., AIA, Past Pres. KS Soc. of Arch.; **EDUC:** BS, 1950, KS Univ.; **MIL SERV:** USN, Enlisted; **OTHER ACT & HONORS:** C of C, Constr. Specific. Inst.; **HOME ADD:** 1356 Iroquois, Wichita, KS 67203, (316)942-3826; **BUS ADD:** PO Box 2726, 1202 E. First, Wichita, KS 67214, (316)262-7435.

BULLOCK, Ellis W., Jr.——B: Sept. 11, 1928, Birmingham, AL, *Pres.,* The Bullock Assoc., Architects, Planners, Inc.; **PRIM RE ACT:** Architect, Regulator, Consultant; **SERVICES:** Zoning/Code compliance; site selection analysis; master planning; programming feasibility; A/E design; interior design; space planning; **REP CLIENTS:** Indiv., instl. & corp. investors in comml. props.; **PROFL AFFIL & HONORS:** AIA; Pensacola Zoning Bd. of Adjustments; Pensacola Bldg. Bd. of Appeals, Fellow, AIA, 1981; Profl. Bus. Leader of the Yr., Pensacola News Journal, 1977; State Community Serv. Award FA/AIA, 1970; **EDUC:** BArch, 1954, Auburn Univ.; **MIL SERV:** US Army, 1st Lt.; **OTHER ACT & HONORS:** Rotary, Pensacola Heritage Assn., Navy League; **HOME ADD:** 2 Hyde Park Rd., Pensacola, FL 32503, (904)438-9282; **BUS ADD:** 1823 N. Ninth Ave., Pensacola, FL 32503, (904)434-5444.

BULTHUIS, James H.——B: Oct. 16, 1939, Chicago, IL, *Asst. VP,* Harris Trust & Savings Bank; **PRIM RE ACT:** Consultant, Appraiser; **PREV EMPLOY:** Past Chmn. - Appraisers Council - Chicago RE Bd.; **PROFL AFFIL & HONORS:** AIREA, SREA, MAI - Sr. RE Analyst; **MIL SERV:** USA, SP-4; **HOME ADD:** 5628 Fairview, Downers Grove, IL 60516, (312)960-3470; **BUS ADD:** Chicago, IL 60690, (312)461-2210.

BUMBALEK, Marian E.——B: July 1, 1932, Chicago, IL; **PRIM RE ACT:** Broker, Consultant, Instructor; **OTHER RE ACT:** Trainer, time share spec., speaker; **SERVICES:** Consulting, training, time share mktg.; **REP CLIENTS:** Brokers, devels., investors; **PREV EMPLOY:** Sales Mgr., Trainer, Saffold Co. Realtors, Houston; **PROFL AFFIL & HONORS:** HBR, TAR Dir. NAR, RE Trainers Assn.; WCR, GRI, CRB; **EDUC:** Ball State Teachers Coll.; **OTHER ACT & HONORS:** Mensa, Pres. Bd. of Tr. TX REALTORS Found. (Tr. 80-83); **HOME ADD:** 8 Lakewood Ln., LYC, Seabrook, TX 77586, (713)474-4030; **BUS ADD:** 4801 Woodway-300 E, Houston, TX 77056, (713)771-1297.

BUMGARDNER, Albert O.——**B:** Jan. 3, 1923, Springfield, IL, *Sr. Prin.*, The Bumgardner Architects; **PRIM RE ACT:** Architect; **PROFL AFFIL & HONORS:** Member AIA, Fellow, AIA; **EDUC:** BSArch, 1949, Arch., Univ. of IL; **EDUC HONORS:** Summa Cum Laude; **MIL SERV:** USAF, S/Sgt.; **OTHER ACT & HONORS:** Member, Alpha Rho Chi; **HOME ADD:** 2017 Broadway E, Seattle, WA 98102, (206)325-5656; **BUS ADD:** 2021 Minor Ave. E, Seattle, WA 98102, (206)325-5200.

BUNDY, Willard L.——*Mgr. Corp. Ins.*, Mobasco Corp.; **PRIM RE ACT:** Property Manager, Insuror; **BUS ADD:** 57 Lyon St., Amsterdam, NY 12010, (518)841-2652.*

BUNESS, Everett W.——**B:** Oct. 11, 1923, Powers Lake, ND, *Owner*; **PRIM RE ACT:** Consultant, Developer, Owner/Investor; **PREV EMPLOY:** Lic. RE Broker, Public Accountant, and Gen. Ins. Agent. Partner in many partnerships and officer of several corporations.; **PROFL AFFIL & HONORS:** Nat. Assn. of Public Accountants, Member of Amer. Arbitration Assn.; **EDUC:** BBA, 1951, Acctg., Univ. of WA; **MIL SERV:** USA, 1st Lt.; **OTHER ACT & HONORS:** Former Commn. of the AK Dept. of Econ. Devel. 1969-1970; Former City Councilman; **HOME ADD:** 3550 Cottonwood St., Anchorage, AK 99504, (907)277-0954; **BUS ADD:** 3550 Cottonwood St., Anchorage, AK 99504, (907)276-1552.

BUNJE, Ralph B., Jr.——*Partner*, Bunje Dowse & Co.; **OTHER RE ACT:** CPA; Asset Mgmt.; **PREV EMPLOY:** Touche Ross & Co., San Francisco, CA; **PROFL AFFIL & HONORS:** CA Soc. of CPAs, AICPA, CPA; Profl. lecturer at Golden Gate Univ. Grad School of Acctg.; **EDUC:** BS, Mktg./Acctg., UCLA; **GRAD EDUC:** MBA, Taxation, Golden Gate Univ; MS, Acctg., Golden Gate Univ.; **MIL SERV:** US Naval Res., Comdr.; **BUS ADD:** 850 Montgomery St., Suite 400, San Francisco, CA 94133, (415)421-7503.

BUNKER, Kimberly Ann——**B:** Apr. 17, 1956, Lansing, MI, *Mort. Loan Officer*, Amer. Bank & Trust Co., Mort. Dept.; **PRIM RE ACT:** Banker, Lender; **SERVICES:** Comml. & Residential Mort. Loans; **PROFL AFFIL & HONORS:** Affiliate Member of Women's Council of Realtors, Member of Amer. Inst. of Banking; **EDUC:** BBA, 1978, Accounting, Western MI Univ.; **BUS ADD:** 1 Washington Sq., Lansing, MI 48902, (517)374-5372.

BUNTING, David F.——**B:** Mar. 25, 1941, Melrose, MA, *Pres.*, Capital Resources, Inc.; **PRIM RE ACT:** Consultant, Developer, Owner/Investor, Syndicator; **REP CLIENTS:** Indiv. and corporate investors in comml./indus. RE; **EDUC:** BA, 1963, Hist., Dartmouth Coll.; **GRAD EDUC:** MBA, 1979, Small Bus., Sloan School of Mgmt. (MIT); **MIL SERV:** USMC, Capt. 16 Air Medals; **HOME ADD:** 7 Gill St., Exeter, NH 03833, (603)772-2247; **BUS ADD:** Box 468, 1 Middle St., Portsmouth, NH 03833, (603)431-7755.

BUNTROCK, Tom——**B:** Oct. 24, 1946, Waukegan, IL, *Pres./owner*, Landmark Cos.; **PRIM RE ACT:** Developer, Builder, Owner/Investor; **EDUC:** BS, 1969, Bus.; **BUS ADD:** 224 Fox Fire Lane, Kingston, TN 37763, (615)376-6360.

BUR, William H.——**B:** July 22, 1926, Green Bay, WI, *Atty.*; **PRIM RE ACT:** Consultant, Attorney; **SERVICES:** Titles, title ins. (title ins. co. of MN); **REP CLIENTS:** Fed. Land Bank, Farmers Prod. Credit Assn., Mechanics Bldg. & Loan Corp., Safeco Title, Other Attys.; **PROFL AFFIL & HONORS:** ABA, OH State Bar Assn., OH Land Title Assn., Richland Cty. Bar Assn., LLB & JD (Univ. of Cincinnati); **EDUC:** 1948, RE, Probate, Univ. of Cincinnati; **GRAD EDUC:** LLB, 1948, Univ. of Cincinnati; JD, 1948, Univ. of Cincinnati; **MIL SERV:** USN, Appr. Seaman; **OTHER ACT & HONORS:** Kiwanis Club, Jaycees, Serra Club of Mansfield, Lay Minister of St. Peter's Cath. Church.; **HOME ADD:** 715 Clifton Blvd., Mansfield, OH 44906, (419)756-5432; **BUS ADD:** 404 Richland Trust Bldg., Mansfield, OH 44902, (419)524-1323.

BURCH, A. Lee——**B:** May 22, 1949, College Station, TX, *Part.*, Burch Assoc. Arch.; **PRIM RE ACT:** Architect; **OTHER RE ACT:** Sales license-TX; **SERVICES:** Full arch. services, R.E. sales, devel., planning; **REP CLIENTS:** Independent school dist., coll., city, cty., state, hospital dist.; **PROFL AFFIL & HONORS:** AIA, TX Soc. of Arch., Educ. liaison for N.E. TX Chap. of TSA; **EDUC:** B Arch., 1973, Univ. of TX, Austin; **GRAD EDUC:** MA, 1979, Pol. Sci., Univ. of TX, Tyler; **OTHER ACT & HONORS:** Historic Preservation Bd.; Eagle Scout Assn.; Advisor to Explorer Post; **BUS ADD:** 3025 S.E. Loop 323, Tyler, TX 75701, (214)593-5605.

BURCHETT, A.L., Jr.——**B:** Sept. 22, 1948, Memphis, TN, *Owner*, Burchett Enterprises; **PRIM RE ACT:** Broker, Developer, Owner/Investor, Property Manager; **SERVICES:** RE Mgmt. & Brokerage, Condo Devel.; **PROFL AFFIL & HONORS:** Sales & Mktg. Exec. Assn.; Jr. C of C; Gr. Little Rock Bd. of Realtors; **EDUC:** 1969, Eng. Lit., Univ. of AR; **MIL SERV:** USAF, SSgt.; **HOME ADD:** 901 N Pine St., Little Rock, AR 72205, (501)661-9290; **BUS ADD:** 2311 Biscayne Dr., Suite 310, Little Rock, AR 72207, (501)227-9925.

BURCHETT, Alan E.——**B:** May 18, 1943, Chico, CA, *Part., Atty.*, Stewart, Craig, Humphreys & Burchett; **PRIM RE ACT:** Attorney; **SERVICES:** Legal advice & asst. concerning real prop. matters; **PREV EMPLOY:** Deputy Butte Cty. Counsel; **PROFL AFFIL & HONORS:** ABA, Butte Cty. Bar Assn.; **EDUC:** BS, 1965, RE & Fin., Univ. of CA at Berkeley; **GRAD EDUC:** JD, 1968, Univ. of CA Hastings Coll. of Law; **OTHER ACT & HONORS:** Town Atty. Paradise, CA, 1979 to present; Bd. of Dir. Gr. Chico C of C; **HOME ADD:** 1388 Keri Ln, Chico, CA 95926, (916)891-0695; **BUS ADD:** 109 Parmac Rd., Suite 15, PO Box 658, Chico, CA 95927, (916)891-6111.

BURCHFIELD, James Ralph——**B:** Feb. 6, 1924, Vincennes, IN, *Partner*, Burchfield & Burchfield; **PRIM RE ACT:** Attorney, Owner/Investor, Insuror; **SERVICES:** Agent, OH Bar Title Ins. Co.; **PROFL AFFIL & HONORS:** OH Bar Assn., ABA, Columbus Bar Assn., OH Land & Title Assn., Amer. Judicature Soc., Nat. Consumers Fin. Assn., Arbitrator for Amer. Arbitrators Assn.; **EDUC:** BA, 1947, Hist./Pol. Sci., OH State Univ.; **GRAD EDUC:** JD, 1949, Law, OH State Univ. Law School; **EDUC HONORS:** Phi Alpha Theta, Scabbard & Blade, Student Senator from Coll. of Law; **MIL SERV:** US Air Corps, Cadet; **OTHER ACT & HONORS:** Spec. Counsel OH Atty. Gen., 1953-1956; Intl. Pres., Sertoma Intl., 1967-1968; Pres., OH Bar Liability Ins. Co., 1978 to present; **HOME ADD:** 42 Park Dr., Columbus, OH 43209, (614)252-8598; **BUS ADD:** 1313 E. Broad St., Columbus, OH 43205, (614)252-1131.

BURCHILL, Jack——*Secy./Treas.*, South Dakota Real Estate Bd.; **PRIM RE ACT:** Property Manager; **BUS ADD:** PO Box 490, Pierre, SD 57501, (605)773-3600.*

BURCHMAN, Leonard——*Asst. to Secy.*, Department of Housing and Urban Development, Ofc. of Public Affairs; **PRIM RE ACT:** Lender; **BUS ADD:** 451 Seventh St., S.W., Washington, DC 20410, (202)755-6980.*

BURD, Anthony M.——**B:** April 24, 1952, KY, *Pres.*, SW Land & Devel. Co., Inc.; **PRIM RE ACT:** Developer, Builder, Property Manager, Owner/Investor; **SERVICES:** Devel. Site Preparation Mktg. Mgmt.; **PROFL AFFIL & HONORS:** PEI, NABE, ASA; **EDUC:** Bus. BS, Econ. and Fin., AZ State Univ.; **GRAD EDUC:** MS, Econ., AZ State; **EDUC HONORS:** With Distinction; **BUS ADD:** PO Box 20128, Phoenix, AZ 85036, (602)241-4783.

BURD, Hal——**B:** Mar. 26, 1946, Philadelphia, PA, *VP and Controller*, Suburban Coastal Corp., Mid-Atlantic Rgnl. Office; **PRIM RE ACT:** Lender; **SERVICES:** Lending, conventional, FHA, VA of single family resid., condos, townhouses; **REP CLIENTS:** Builders, purchasers of housing; **PREV EMPLOY:** Federal Nat. Mort. Assn., 6 years as a Loan Acctg. Mgr.; **PROFL AFFIL & HONORS:** AICPA; MCPA; MBA; YMBA; DCMBA; **EDUC:** BBA, 1967, Bus. Admin., Philadelphia Coll. of Textiles & Sci.; **GRAD EDUC:** 1977, The School of Mort. Banking; **MIL SERV:** US Army; Spec. 5, Army Commendation Medal, Bronze Star For Achievement, Certificate of Achievement, Certificate of Appreciation; **OTHER ACT & HONORS:** Past Pres. of GCCA; **HOME ADD:** 12 Campbell Ct., Kensington, MD 20895, (301)585-3925; **BUS ADD:** 6001 Montrose Road, Rockville, MD 20852, (301)468-3990.

BURDEN, Christopher——**B:** June 14, 1941, NYC, NY, *Pres.*, New Seabury Corp.; **PRIM RE ACT:** Consultant, Developer, Builder, Property Manager; **SERVICES:** Resort devel. and operation; **REP CLIENTS:** Resid. devel. and resort devel., acct. firms; **PROFL AFFIL & HONORS:** ULI, Amer. Land Devel. Assn., MA Assn. of Homebuilders; **EDUC:** BS, 1964, Econ. Geography, Middlebury Coll., VT; **OTHER ACT & HONORS:** Bd. of Dir., Marineland of FL; Trustee, VT Wildland Found.; Member Recreational Devel. Council ULI; **HOME ADD:** Mall Way, New Seabury, MA 02649, (617)477-0469; **BUS ADD:** PO Box A, New Seabury, MA 02649, (617)477-9400.

BURDETTE, Forbes W.——**B:** Mar. 27, 1932, New Brighton, PA, *VP*, University Investment Management Co., RE Portfolio Mgmt.; **PRIM RE ACT:** Syndicator; **OTHER RE ACT:** Asset Mgr.; **SERVICES:** RE analysis to pub. partnership operations; **REP CLIENTS:** Affiliates include nine public ltd. partnerships and an equity RE investment trust; **PREV EMPLOY:** Challenge Devels., Inc. (land devel. and resid. housing), Aluminum Co. of Amer. (Alcoa) RE devel.; **PROFL AFFIL & HONORS:** Nat. Assn. of RE Investment Trusts (lic. CA contr.); **EDUC:** BBA, 1955, Mktg., Univ. of Pittsburgh; **GRAD EDUC:** MS (noncompleted), 1959, Mktg., Duquesne Univ.; **MIL SERV:** USAF, Capt. USAFR, 1955-59; **HOME ADD:** 15715 Castlewoods Dr., Los

Angeles, CA 91403, (213)990-4217; **BUS ADD:** 666 E. Ocean Blvd., Long Beach, CA 91802, (213)435-6344.

BURDETTE, William Charles——B: Apr. 7, 1930, Atlanta, GA, *Owner*, W.C. Burdette Agency; **PRIM RE ACT:** Broker, Consultant, Banker; **SERVICES:** Sales, Appraisals, Prop. Mgmt.; **PROFL AFFIL & HONORS:** Nat. Assn. of RE Appraisers (certified), Intl. Coll. of RE, Consulting Profls. (RECP); **EDUC:** Assoc. Sci., 1950, Bldg. Const. Tech., S. Technical Inst. , Marietta, GA; **GRAD EDUC:** BA of Laws, 1965, Woodrow Wilson Coll. of Law, Atlanta, GA; **EDUC HONORS:** Magna Cum Laude; **MIL SERV:** USMC, Sgt., Battle Star, Korean Campaign; **OTHER ACT & HONORS:** Mayor, City of Calhoun (8 yrs.) 1974-present; **HOME ADD:** 604 Pisgah Way, Calhoun, GA 3O701, (404)629-2827; **BUS ADD:** 121 W. Belmont Dr., Calhoun, GA 30701, (404)629-3008.

BURDICK, Daniel H., II——B: Dec. 27, 1935, Utica, NY, *Asst. Sec. Dir. Prop. Mgmt.*, Kmart Corp., R.E. Dept.; **PRIM RE ACT:** Consultant, Property Manager; **OTHER RE ACT:** Admin.; **PROFL AFFIL & HONORS:** NACORE; **EDUC:** BED, 1958, Hamilton Coll.; **MIL SERV:** USA, 1959-1961; **OTHER ACT & HONORS:** Who's Who in Finance and Industry; **HOME ADD:** 1011 N. Woodward Ave., Birmingham, MI 48009; **BUS ADD:** 3100 W. Big Beaver Rd., Troy, MI 48084, (313)643-1449.

BURDICK, Kenneth D.——B: May 24, 1943, Graham, TX, *Dir., Area Devel. Sect.*, Lone Star Gas Co., Energy Sales Div.; **PRIM RE ACT:** Consultant; **SERVICES:** Plant and office location assistance to indus.; **PROFL AFFIL & HONORS:** AIDC, S. Indus. Devel. Council, TX Indus. Devel. Council; **EDUC:** BBA, 1965, Univ. of TX at El Paso; **MIL SERV:** USAF, S-Sgt., Bronze Star, AF Commendation; **HOME ADD:** 4301 Three Oaks Dr., Arlington, TX 76016, (817)429-6130; **BUS ADD:** 301 S Harwood St., 705 North Bldg., Dallas, TX 75201, (214)670-2721.

BURDMAN, B. Richard——B: Sept. 6, 1933, Youngstown, OH, *Sr. Part.*, Burdman, Gillilaud, Fleck, Mostov & Kretzer; **PRIM RE ACT:** Attorney, Consultant, Developer, Owner/Investor; **SERVICES:** Rep. of Investors, Devels., Lenders & Synd.; **REP CLIENTS:** Numerous Devels. & Some 30 to 40 Lenders; **PROFL AFFIL & HONORS:** ABA, OH Bar, ICSC; **EDUC:** BA, 1954, Accts./Lib. Arts, Youngstown State; **GRAD EDUC:** JD, 1956, Bus. & Tax., Duke Univ.; **EDUC HONORS:** Deans List; **MIL SERV:** USA; **BUS ADD:** 1200 Wick Bldg., Youngstown, OH 44503, (216)747-8621.

BURFORD, Robert H.——B: Sept. 26, 1920, Indianapolis, IN, *Pres.*, Robert H. Burford Assoc.; **PRIM RE ACT:** Appraiser; **SERVICES:** Appraisals on comml. and resid. RE; **REP CLIENTS:** 1st Interstate Bank; Western Amer. Mtg. Co.; Mtg. Assn.; Percy Wilson Mtg.; Texaco; Gulf Oil; Shell Oil; Digital Equipment; **PREV EMPLOY:** Formerly Chief Appraiser, IN Nat. Bank; Formerly Asst. Dist. Mgr., Mtg. Loan Dept. (Indianapolis, IN); Pacific Mutual Life Ins.; **PROFL AFFIL & HONORS:** Soc. RE Appraisers; Nat. Assn. of Review Appraisers; Intl. Inst. of Valuers, SRA; CRV; CRV; **EDUC:** BM, 1942, Educ., Butler Univ.; **GRAD EDUC:** MM, 1951, Educ., IN Univ.; **EDUC HONORS:** Hon. Scholastic Frat.; **OTHER ACT & HONORS:** Pres., Hancock Cty. Council, Hancock Cty., IN; Murat Temple; Indianapolis AAONMS; Former Member, Kiwanis; **HOME ADD:** 4723 N. 34th Pl., Phoenix, AZ 85018, (602)955-1253; **BUS ADD:** 4723 N. 34th Pl., Phoenix, AZ 85018, (602)955-0191.

BURGE, H. Stewart——B: Sep. 12, 1936, Eugene, OR, *Broker/Owner*, Burge Realty Co.; **PRIM RE ACT:** Broker, Syndicator, Developer, Property Manager; **SERVICES:** Comml., indus. & invest. prop. sales, synd. & mgmt.; **REP CLIENTS:** Corp. & indiv. investors of comml., and indus. invest. prop.; **PROFL AFFIL & HONORS:** SREA; RESSI; Bd. of Realtors, Blders. Assn. Local; State, & Nat. Bd. of Dir., Blders. Assn.; Blder. of the month award; Carner Pubs.; Name in 10 top US Merchandisers (1965); **EDUC:** Bus. Mgmt., Linfield Coll.; **EDUC HONORS:** Theta Chi; **MIL SERV:** USAF; E-4 (1957-1961); **OTHER ACT & HONORS:** Elks; C of C; Jr. Achievement Officer/Bd. Member; **HOME ADD:** 2875 Riviera Ct., Springfield, OR 97401, (503)747-3360; **BUS ADD:** 224 East 11th Av., Eugene, OR 97401, (503)484-0057.

BURGER, Edward R.——B: July 24, 1938, Belleville, MI, *Partner*, Kauer & Burger Assoc.; **PRIM RE ACT:** Broker; **OTHER RE ACT:** S.I.R.; **SERVICES:** Indus./comml. brokerage; **REP CLIENTS:** devels., Ins. Cos., Corps., indivs.; **PREV EMPLOY:** 16 yrs. Byron W. Trerice Co. & Manhattan C.; **PROFL AFFIL & HONORS:** Realtor, S.I.R., S. Oakland Co. Bd. Realtors, Indiv. Member Soc. of Indus. Relators; **EDUC:** BS, 1961, Mktg., Eastern MI Univ.; **GRAD EDUC:** MBA, pending, RE, Univ. of MI; **MIL SERV:** Ordance, Capt.; **OTHER ACT & HONORS:** Boy Scouts, C of C; **HOME ADD:** 18541 San Jose, Lathrup Village, MI 48076, (313)559-3534; **BUS ADD:** Ste. 209, 26645 W. Twelve Mile Rd., Southfield, MI 48034, (313)358-2255.

BURGER, Eugene J.——B: Oct. 21, 1933, Chico, CA, *Pres.*, Eugene Burger Management Corp.; **PRIM RE ACT:** Property Manager; **SERVICES:** Full line prop. mgmt.; **REP CLIENTS:** CT General Life; US Dept. of Housing and Urban Devel.; Aetna Life Ins. Co.; Mid City Devel. Corp.; FP Lanthrop Constr. Co.; Various indiv. partnerships; Ford Found. Consulting; **PROFL AFFIL & HONORS:** 1981 Nat. Pres., IREM; BOMA; CAR; NAR, CPM; **EDUC:** AA, 1954, Bus., Napa Coll.; **HOME ADD:** 22 Underhill Rd., Mill Valley, CA 94941; **BUS ADD:** 180 Harbor Dr., Sausalito, CA 94965, (415)332-4730.

BURGESS, C. Geoffrey——B: Feb. 3, 1944, England, *Partner*, Burgess Austin & Assoc.; **PRIM RE ACT:** Broker, Consultant, Appraiser, Developer, Owner/Investor, Property Manager; **SERVICES:** Investment Analysis & Counseling, Valuation, Mgmt., Site Selection and Acquisition, Devel. Mgmt., Lease negotiation and arbitration; **PROFL AFFIL & HONORS:** AACI, ARICS, MAI; **EDUC:** Coll. of Estate Mgmt.; **OTHER ACT & HONORS:** RE Bd., Bd. of Trade; **HOME ADD:** 3127 W. King Edward, Vancouver, V6L7V4, BC, (604)738-0066; **BUS ADD:** 1160, 625 Howe St., Vancouver, V6C2T6, BC, (604)689-1233.

BURGESS, Elmo C.——B: Mar. 8, 1923, Louisville, KY, *Atty.*, Burgess and Rose, Attorneys; **PRIM RE ACT:** Broker, Attorney, Appraiser, Builder, Owner/Investor, Instructor, Insuror; **REP CLIENTS:** Banks, Mort. Cos., Builders, RE Brokers; **PREV EMPLOY:** Homebuilder, Apt. Builder; **PROFL AFFIL & HONORS:** Home Builders Assn.; Louisville Condo. Council; Louisville Apt. Assn. (Past Pres.); Louisville Bar Assn.; ABA, Rho Epsilon (RE Frat.); **EDUC:** BS, 1956, Bus. Admin., Univ. of Louisville; **GRAD EDUC:** LLB/JD, 1960, Law, Univ. of Louisville; **MIL SERV:** USAF, Lt. Col.; **OTHER ACT & HONORS:** Mason, Optimist Club; **HOME ADD:** 8216 Arnoldtown Rd., Louisville, KY 40214, (502)935-2120; **BUS ADD:** 116 S. Fifth St., Louisville, KY 40202, (502)585-5169.

BURGESS, Joe H.——B: Aug. 20, 1920, Noblesville, IN, *Asst. VP and Chief Title Officer*, Wainwright Abstract, Co., Inc.; **OTHER RE ACT:** Abstracter and licensed title insurance agent; **SERVICES:** Abstract of title or title ins. (title of RE); **PROFL AFFIL & HONORS:** IN Land Title Assn. (Past Pres.); Amer. Land Title Assn.; **MIL SERV:** US Army, 1941-45, T/Sgt., Amer. Defense Medal, European Theatre Medal with 5 Battle Stars, Good Conduct Medal; **OTHER ACT & HONORS:** City Councilman 1947-51; Deputy Clerk of Circuit Ct.; Amer. Legion; Eagles IN and Hamilton Cty. Hist. Soc.; Hamilton Cty. Historian by appointment of IN Hist. Bureau; **HOME ADD:** 384 No. 11th St., Noblesville, IN 46060, (317)773-3454; **BUS ADD:** 949 Conner St., Noblesville, IN 46060, (317)773-3177.

BURGIN, Wes——*Fac. Manager*, American Microsystems; **PRIM RE ACT:** Property Manager; **BUS ADD:** 3800 Homestead Rd., Santa Clara, CA 95051, (408)246-0330.*

BURGWEGER, Francis J., Jr.——B: July 5, 1942, Evanston, IL, *Partner*, O'Melveny & Meyers; **PRIM RE ACT:** Attorney; **SERVICES:** Legal counsel in the areas of sales, leases, RE secured financing, zoning, planning, devel., environmental law, mines & minerals; **REP CLIENTS:** Owners, landlords, tenants, lenders, devels. (office bldgs., shopping centers, indus. complexes), vendors, purchasers, miners, indus.; **PROFL AFFIL & HONORS:** State Bar of CA, Los Angeles Cty. Bar RE Section, ABA-RE, natural Resources & Local Government Sections; **EDUC:** BA, 1964, Eng., Yale Univ.; **GRAD EDUC:** JD, 1970, Univ. of PA School of Law; **EDUC HONORS:** Cum Laude; **MIL SERV:** US Army Intelligence, Capt., Bronze Star; **HOME ADD:** 5040 Don Pio Dr., Woodland Hills, CA 91364, (213)703-1953; **BUS ADD:** 611 West 6th St., Los Angeles, CA 90017, (213)620-1120.

BURK, John Rogers——B: May 6, 1945, Tuscon, AZ, *Atty.*, Burk, Lowe & Ruja, A Law Corp.; **PRIM RE ACT:** Attorney; **SERVICES:** Legal services regarding subdiv., homeowners assns., ltd. partnerships, sales practices; **REP CLIENTS:** Devel., fin. instns., RE brokers; **PREV EMPLOY:** ABA, Sect. of Real Prop. Probate and Trust Law; Comm. on Regulation of Land Sales; CA State Bar, Real Prop. Law Sect.; **EDUC:** BA, 1967, Arch. & CE, Univ. of CA, Berkeley; **GRAD EDUC:** JD, 1973, Real Prop. and Estate Planning, Univ. of CA, Hasting Coll. of the Law; **EDUC HONORS:** Fifth Place Moot Court Oral Agreement (400 participants); **OTHER ACT & HONORS:** Boy Scouts of Amer./Scoutmaster; Rotary Intl.; **HOME ADD:** 1001 Suffolk Way, Los Altos, CA 94022, (415)968-5077; **BUS ADD:** 167 South San Antonio Rd., Suite 16, Los Altos, CA 94022, (415)949-0110.

BURKE, Dorothy——*Senior Attorney*, Pfizer, Inc.; **PRIM RE ACT:** Property Manager, Attorney; **BUS ADD:** 235 E. 42nd St., New York, NY 10017, (212)573-2323.*

BURKE, Edmund——**B:** May 11, 1912, Nanticoke, PA, *Proprietor*, Edmund Burke (Appraisal); **PRIM RE ACT:** Broker, Consultant, Appraiser, Instructor; **SERVICES:** Teaching, appraising, consulting; **REP CLIENTS:** HUD, VA, SBA, Ins. Cos., Banks, S&L Assns., Major Oil Cos.; Instruct at PA State Univ. and at Elmira Coll.; **PREV EMPLOY:** School Bus. Admin., Assoc. In Educ. Fin. & Mgmt. Servs., NYS Educ. Dept.; **PROFL AFFIL & HONORS:** Nat. Assn. of Review Appraisers; Amer. Assn. of Cert. Appraisers; LocaL, State, Nat. Realtor; RE Educators Assn.; NYS Soc. of RE Appraisers; Intl. Assn. of School Bus. Officials; Amer. RE & Urban Econ. Assn., CRA, CA-C; **EDUC:** AB, 1934, Lib. Arts/Educ., Cornell Univ.; **GRAD EDUC:** MS, 1939, Admin./Supervision, Cornell Univ.; Pre-Doctoral, Cornell Univ.; **MIL SERV:** US Army, Lt. Col., Pre Pearl Harbor, EAME, Am. Theater, Occ. Germany, Army Commendation, Purple Heart, 1941-1946; **OTHER ACT & HONORS:** Ten O'Clock Club; Shepard Hills Ctry. Club; **HOME ADD:** 105 Tracy Rd., Waverly, NY 14892, (607)565-7394; **BUS ADD:** POB 122, Athens, PA 18810, (717)888-2415.

BURKE, Garrett C.——**B:** Nov. 17, 1952, Detroit, MI, *Counsel*, Federal Home Loan Mortgage Corp., Legal Dept.; **PRIM RE ACT:** Attorney; **PREV EMPLOY:** Private law practice 1977-1980; **PROFL AFFIL & HONORS:** ABA; **EDUC:** BA, 1974, Poli. Sci., Univ. of Mich.; **GRAD EDUC:** JD, 1977, 1980, George Wash. Univ.; LLM (Taxation), Georgetown Univ.; **HOME ADD:** 23 West Myrtle St., Alexandria, VA 22301, (703)549-2062; **BUS ADD:** 1776 "G" Street NW, P O Box 37248, Washington, DC 20013, (202)789-4542.

BURKE, Joseph T., II——**B:** Feb. 26, 1948, Harrisburg, PA, *VP*, Chas. H. Steffey, Inc., RE Fin. Div.; **PRIM RE ACT:** Consultant, Developer, Property Manager; **OTHER RE ACT:** Mort. Banker; **SERVICES:** Const., long-term and equity fin., appraising all in comml. RE prop.; **REP CLIENTS:** Lenders and indiv. and/or instnl. investors in comml. RE devel.; **PREV EMPLOY:** Sr. Devel. Dir., Dept. of HUD, Office of Urban Devel. Action Grants, 1978-1979; **PROFL AFFIL & HONORS:** Member of Bd. of Dir., MD Mort. Bankers Assn.; Past Comml. Loan Comm. Chmn.; **EDUC:** BS, 1971, Bus. Admin., Univ. of MD; **HOME ADD:** 917 Elmhurst Rd., Severn, MD 21144, (301)969-2335; **BUS ADD:** 2 E. Fayette St., Baltimore, MD 21202, (301)685-2412.

BURKE, Joyce M.——**B:** Aug. 30, 1939, LaCrosse, WI, *VP-Dir. of Sales*, First United, Realtors; **PRIM RE ACT:** Broker, Property Manager; **SERVICES:** Resid. RE; **PROFL AFFIL & HONORS:** GRI, CRS, CRB; **OTHER ACT & HONORS:** Dir. of DuPage Area Council for Boy Scouts of Amer.; **HOME ADD:** 300 S. Park Blvd., Glen Ellyn, IL 60137, (312)469-7656; **BUS ADD:** 1717 N. Naperville Rd., Naperville, IL 60566, (312)355-4350.

BURKE, Richard H.——**B:** Aug. 19, 1943, New York, NY, *Pres.*, The Branigar Organization, Inc./Branitek, Inc.; **OTHER RE ACT:** Large scale community devel., resort mgmt., interstate highway interchange devel., consumer land purchase fin., condo. construction and gen. contracting; **PREV EMPLOY:** Procter & Gamble, 1969-1974; Crown Zellerbach, 1974-1976; **EDUC:** BA, 1965, Eng. Lit., Univ. of PA; **GRAD EDUC:** MBA, 1967, Mktg., Univ. of PA, Wharton Sch. of Fin. and Commerce; **MIL SERV:** USA, 1st Lt., Bronze Star; **OTHER ACT & HONORS:** Rotary Club of Savannah; Marshwood Ctry. Club; **HOME ADD:** 20 Magnolia Csg., Savannah, GA 31411, (912)355-4821; **BUS ADD:** POB 14513, Savannah, GA 31405, (912)354-4885.

BURKE, Richard J.——**B:** Mar. 29, 1938, Medford, MA, *Owner*, Boston Brokers of Amer.; **PRIM RE ACT:** Broker, Property Manager; **OTHER RE ACT:** Owner and operator; **SERVICES:** Spec. in comm'l. office space and retail store leasing in downtown Boston; commercial real estate sales; **PREV EMPLOY:** Comm'l. RE Broker, Hunneman & Co., Boston (2 yrs.); Comm'l. Broker, Dolben Co., Boston (3 yrs.); RE Spec., Gen. Serv. Admin. (Fed Govt.) Boston (5 yrs.); **EDUC:** BA, 1960, Econ., Boston Coll.; **GRAD EDUC:** MEd, 1964, Boston State Coll.; **MIL SERV:** USMC; Lt. Col.; Reserve Officer, 1960 - Present; **OTHER ACT & HONORS:** USMC ROA; Winchester Little League; **HOME ADD:** 77 Middlesex St., Winchester, MA, (617)729-7745; **BUS ADD:** 153 Milk St., Boston, MA 02109, (617)426-1660.

BURKE, Richard S.——**B:** June 14, 1946, Phoenix, AZ, *VP and Mgr., San Francisco Real Estate Office*, The First National Bank of Chicago, San Francisco RE Office; **PRIM RE ACT:** Banker, Lender; **OTHER RE ACT:** Construction Lender; **SERVICES:** Admin., Supervisory and Credit; **REP CLIENTS:** RE Devels. - Interim Const.; **PROFL AFFIL & HONORS:** Mort. Bankers Assn., Bldg. Indus. Assn., Nat. Assn. of Home Builders; CA Mort. Bankers Assn, Bldg. Indus. Pol. Action Comm., Educ. Comm.; **EDUC:** BS/BA Fin./RE, 1969, RE, Univ. of AZ, Tucson, AZ; School of Mort. Banking, Northwestern Univ., Advanced Case Study on Income Prop. Fin., CA Polytech; **GRAD EDUC:** RE, Univ. of AZ; **OTHER ACT & HONORS:** Phi Delta Theta Alumni, Univ. Club, San Francisco; **HOME ADD:** 761 Old Creek Rd., Danville, CA, (415)820-5336; **BUS ADD:** 555 California St., Ste. 3800, San Francisco, CA 94104, (415)788-4311.

BURKE, Ronald G.——*Pres.*, Bank Administration Institute; **PRIM RE ACT:** Banker; **BUS ADD:** 303 S. Northwest Hwy., Park Ridge, IL 60068, (312)693-7300.*

BURKE, William J.——**B:** Aug. 30, 1927, NY, NY, *RE Counsel/Mgr.*, Wyatt Cafeterias, Inc.; **PRIM RE ACT:** Attorney, Developer, Property Manager; **OTHER RE ACT:** Site selection; **SERVICES:** Devel., evaluate & manage rental prop., prepare nec. documents, locate sites, negotiate leases and advise corp. staff; **PREV EMPLOY:** RE Counsel, J.J. Newberry & Co., 1969-71; Melvin Simon & Assoc., 1971-75; **PROFL AFFIL & HONORS:** Admitted NY State Bar; US Tax Court; **EDUC:** BS, 1951, Fordham Univ.; **GRAD EDUC:** 1959, Law, Fordham Univ. School of Law; **MIL SERV:** USAF; S/Sgt.; **BUS ADD:** 10726 Plano Rd., PO Box 38388, Dallas, TX 75238, (214)349-0060.

BURKEMPER, James J.——**B:** Sept. 25, 1931, St. Louis, MO, *Pres.*, Ira E. Berry, Inc.; **PRIM RE ACT:** Broker, Appraiser; **SERVICES:** Total RE Brokerage; **PROFL AFFIL & HONORS:** RE Bd. of Metro St. Louis; MO Assn. of Realtors; Home Builders Assn.; **EDUC:** BA, 1959, Soc., Washington Univ., St. Louis; **MIL SERV:** USN; 1st Class P.O., Various decorations; **OTHER ACT & HONORS:** The Repertory Theatre; **HOME ADD:** 26 Brentmoor Park, St. Louis, MO 63105, (314)721-1676; **BUS ADD:** 7711 Bonhomme, St. Louis, MO 63105, (314)725-9880.

BURKHARD, John W.——*Pres.*, Johnstown Area Econ. Devel. Corp., Johnstown Area Regional Indus., Inc.; **PRIM RE ACT:** Developer, Builder; **OTHER RE ACT:** Non-profit econ. devel. corp. in Cambria and Somerset Ctys. of SW PA; **PROFL AFFIL & HONORS:** Chmn. PA Dept. of Commerce Econ. Advisory Comm., Member Advisory Bd. S Alleghenies Planning and Devel. Commn., Past Chmn. Econ. Devel. Comm., Alleghenies Planning and Devel. Commn., Distinguished Serv. Award, Johnstown Jr. C of C, "Man of the Year" Johnstown; Phi Alpha Theta; **EDUC:** BS, 1949, Bus. Admin., Mt. St. Marys Coll.; **GRAD EDUC:** MA, 1951, Labor Econ., Univ. of MD; **EDUC HONORS:** Pres. Alumni Assn., Grad. Fellowship; **MIL SERV:** US Navy; **OTHER ACT & HONORS:** St. Columba Catholic Church, Johnstown - Member and Lay Commentator; Bachelors Club, BPO Elks, Knights of Columbus, Sunnehanna Ctry. Club; **HOME ADD:** 277 Fairfield Ave., Johnstown, PA 15906; **BUS ADD:** 607 Main St., Johnstown, PA 15901, (814)535-6553.

BURKHEIMER, Clark M.——**B:** July 16, 1949, Seattle, WA, *Pres., Designated Broker*, Burkheimer Consulting, Inc.; **PRIM RE ACT:** Broker, Consultant; **SERVICES:** Consulting RE; **EDUC:** BA, 1971, Mktg. and Poli. Sci., Univ. of Puget Sound; **HOME ADD:** 4915 NE Tolo Rd., Bainbridge, WA 98110, (206)842-5990; **BUS ADD:** 200 Madrone Ln. N., Bainbridge Isl., WA 98110, (206)842-8743.

BURMAN, Henry M.——**B:** Nov. 7, 1918, Phila., PA, *Self employed*; **PRIM RE ACT:** Appraiser; **REP CLIENTS:** Atlantic Refining Co., Gulf Oil Co., IBM Corp., Xerox Corp.; **EDUC:** 1941, Hist. and Spanish, Gettsyburg Coll.; **MIL SERV:** Army Air Corps, 1st Lt., B-17 Pilot; **OTHER ACT & HONORS:** PA Dept. of Trans., PA Dept. of Environ. Resources; **HOME ADD:** 578 Rock Rd., State College, PA 16801, (814)238-6959; **BUS ADD:** 578 Rock Forge Rd., State College, PA 16801, (814)238-6758.

BURMONT, Fred J.——**B:** Apr. 1, 1939, Denver, CO, *Pres.*, Development Concepts, Inc.; **PRIM RE ACT:** Developer; **SERVICES:** Resid. and comml. RE devel.; **PREV EMPLOY:** VP, Blue River Valley Corp.; VP, Chaparral Industries; VP, Daniels Prop.; **PROFL AFFIL & HONORS:** AICPA; CO Society of CPA's, CO Gov's. Advisory Comm.; **EDUC:** BS, 1961, Bus., Univ. of CO (School of Bus.); **EDUC HONORS:** Alpha Phi Omega (Honorary Frat.); Dean's Honor Roll; **OTHER ACT & HONORS:** Dir. of Fin., City of Boulder, CO (1963-68); **HOME ADD:** 5132 South Ironton Way, Englewood, CO 80111; **BUS ADD:** 730 17th St., Suite 320, Denver, CO 80202, (303)825-1025.

BURNETTE, Harvey D., Jr.——**B:** Dec. 14, 1929, Lamar Cty., GA, *Pres.*, Burnette Realty Inc.; **PRIM RE ACT:** Broker, Builder, Property Manager, Insuror; **PROFL AFFIL & HONORS:** Realtor Local State Nat. insuror-PIA, GRI, CIC; **MIL SERV:** GA Army Res. Nat. Guard, Maj.; **OTHER ACT & HONORS:** Kiwanis, Past Pres., PTA Past Pres.; **HOME ADD:** Rte. 1 Burnette Rd., Barnesville, GA 30204, (404)358-2495; **BUS ADD:** Westgate Plaza, Barnesville, GA 30204, (404)358-0162.

BURNS, Barry C.——B: Oct. 20, 1947, Tulsa, OK, *VP*, Bank of Commerce and Trust Co., Comml.; **PRIM RE ACT:** Banker, Lender; **SERVICES:** Const., devel., and interim RE loans; **REP CLIENTS:** Devels., builders, investors; **PREV EMPLOY:** Fin. Corp. (1973-1974); **EDUC:** BS Bus. Admin., 1971, Bus. Mgmt., Data Process., Phillips Univ.; **GRAD EDUC:** 1981, Comml. Banking, Nat. Commercial Lending School at Univ. of OK, Banking School of the South at LA State Univ.; **MIL SERV:** US Army Res., Capt.; **OTHER ACT & HONORS:** Amer. Bus. Clubs, OK Bankers Assn.; **HOME ADD:** 4829 West Seattle, Tulsa, OK 74133, (918)252-9461; **BUS ADD:** 120 West 7th St., P O Box 2269, Tulsa, OK 74101, (918)584-3321.

BURNS, Donald A.——B: Aug. 11, 1949, Dayton, OH, *VP*, The Robert Weiler Co., Appraisal & Counseling; **PRIM RE ACT:** Broker, Consultant, Appraiser; **SERVICES:** Investment advisory, valuation, portfolio mgmt., feasibility studies; **REP CLIENTS:** Corps., insts., govt., agencies, private investors; **PROFL AFFIL & HONORS:** Amer. Inst. of RE Appraisers, Soc. of RE Appraisers, MAI, SRPA; **EDUC:** BA, 1972, Pol. Sci., RE, The OH State Univ.; **HOME ADD:** 7827 Sable Ct., Dublin, OH 43017, (614)764-9649; **BUS ADD:** 21 E State St., Suite 908, Columbus, OH 43215, (614)221-4286.

BURNS, Franklin L.——B: Aug. 1, 1914, Denver, CO, *Pres.*, The D.C. Burns Realty & Trust Co.; **PRIM RE ACT:** Broker, Consultant, Developer, Property Manager, Owner/Investor; **PROFL AFFIL & HONORS:** Life Dir., past Sec. & Treas., NAHB; Tr. & Life Council Member, ULI; Member Denver & Co Realtor Bd., Dir. and Past Pres. of HBA of Metro Denver, CO Assn. of Housing & Bldg., NAR, MBA; Amer. Chap. IREF; Amer. Coll. of RE Consultants; Nat. Realty Comm., NAHB Housing Hall of Fame; Wisdom Hall of Fame; Industry Man of the Year, CAHB; Community Dev. Awards; **EDUC:** USC and Univ. of Denver; **MIL SERV:** USA; **OTHER ACT & HONORS:** Dir., United Bank of Denver; Tr. Emeritus, Mount Airy Psychiatric Ctr.; **BUS ADD:** 1636 Welton St., Denver, CO 80202, (303)629-1899.

BURNS, Harold J.——B: Oct. 26, 1917, Winsted, CT, *Pres.*, Harold J. Burns & Associates, Inc.; **PRIM RE ACT:** Broker, Appraiser; **PROFL AFFIL & HONORS:** SIR, AIREA, SREA, ARIWA, NAR, MAI, SRPA; **EDUC:** BS, 1941, Foreign Service, Georgetown Univ.; **MIL SERV:** USNR, LTDCR; **OTHER ACT & HONORS:** Assessor - City of Torrington 1949-1951; **HOME ADD:** Four Story Hill, Torrington, CT 06790, (203)489-3811; **BUS ADD:** 22 Migeon Ave., PO Box 719, Torrington, CT 06790, (203)482-4418.

BURNS, John A., Jr.——B: Sept. 23, 1939, Flushing, NY, *Pres.*, Munley, Meade, Burns & Nielsen, P.C.; **PRIM RE ACT:** Attorney; **SERVICES:** Legal representation and investment counseling; **REP CLIENTS:** Mfrs. Hanover Trust Co., Whitestone S & L Assn., and other indiv. and instit. clients dealing in resid. and comml. props.; **PREV EMPLOY:** Wall Street Law Firm of Simpson, Thacher & Bartlett; **PROFL AFFIL & HONORS:** Amer., Fed., NY State and Nassau Cty. Bar Assns.; Dir., Great Neck Lawyers Assn., Adv.Bd. of the First Amer. Title Insurance Co. of NY; **EDUC:** BBA, 1961, Acctg., Univ. of Notre Dame; **GRAD EDUC:** JD, 1964, Law, Fordham Univ. School of Law; **HOME ADD:** 216 Piping Rock Road, Matinecock, NY 11560, (516)671-8438; **BUS ADD:** 160 Middle Neck Rd., Great Neck, NY 11023, (516)487-6500.

BURNS, Paul L.——B: Aug 20, 1935, Roxboro, NC, *Exec. VP*, Love Mort. Co.; **OTHER RE ACT:** Mort. & Invest. Banker; **SERVICES:** Arrange debt and/or equity fin. for comml. RE; **REP CLIENTS:** Dev., Ins. Cos., Pension Funds & Foreign Investors; **PREV EMPLOY:** Sr. VP, Guardian Mort. Investors (1973-77); VP, Wachovia Mort. Co (1966-72); Sr. Appraiser, Prudential Ins. Co. of Am. (1960-65); **PROFL AFFIL & HONORS:** MBAA, Lic. RE Broker MD & IL, CRA; **EDUC:** Bus., 1957, Acctg., Wake Forest Univ.; **MIL SERV:** USA, 1st Lt., 1958-60; **OTHER ACT & HONORS:** Kappa Alpha Frat.; **HOME ADD:** Plaza Sq. Apts. (50-804), St. Louis, MO 63103; **BUS ADD:** 10 S. Broadway, Suite 1340, St. Louis, MO 63102, (314)621-1206.

BURNS, Richard F.——B: June 10, 1944, Albany, NY, *Exec. VP and COO*, Marsh & McLennan RE Advisors, Inc.; **PRIM RE ACT:** Consultant, Owner/Investor; **OTHER RE ACT:** RE Investment Fiduciary; **SERVICES:** RE investment mgmt.; **PREV EMPLOY:** John Hancock Mutual Life Ins. Co., Second VP, Equity RE Separate Account; **PROFL AFFIL & HONORS:** Intl. Council of Shopping Ctrs.; Nat. Assn. of Indus. and Office Parks; **EDUC:** BS, 1967, Boston Coll.; **GRAD EDUC:** MBA, 1971, Boston Univ.; **MIL SERV:** USAR, Sgt. E-5, 1968-1974; **HOME ADD:** 19 Princeton Rd., Wellesley, MA 02181, (617)237-6588; **BUS ADD:** 50 Milk St., 20th Floor, Boston, MA 02109, (617)423-4991.

BURNS, Robert L.——B: Jan. 6, 1922, Brunswick, MD, *Pres.*, Robert Burns & Assoc., Ltd.; **PRIM RE ACT:** Appraiser; **OTHER RE ACT:** RE; **SERVICES:** RE appraising; **PREV EMPLOY:** RE Sales Rep.; **PROFL AFFIL & HONORS:** NAIFA, Near future - IFA, Sigma Delta Kappa Law Frat. Sec./Treas. for 2 yrs.; **EDUC:** BA, 1960, Philosophy & Psych., San Francisco State Coll.; **GRAD EDUC:** No Degree (2 yrs. only), 1970 & 1971, Gen. Law, Univ. of Baltimore School of Law; **EDUC HONORS:** Award - Los Angeles City Coll. (Most Outstanding Man in Dept. of Psychology; **MIL SERV:** USMC, Sgt.; **OTHER ACT & HONORS:** Unsuccessful Candidate for US Congress 6th Dist. of MD - 1968, Republican, Unsuccessful Candidate for Cty. Commnr. Repub. 1974, Carroll Cty. MD, Masonic Lodge, VFW, ARRL - Amateur Radio League; **HOME TEL:** (813)932-0777; **BUS ADD:** PO Box 271141, Tampa, FL 33688, (813)932-0777.

BURR, David P.——B: Oct. 28, 1942, Columbus, OH, *Gen. Mgr.*, The Linpro Co., The Metro NY Partnership; **PRIM RE ACT:** Developer, Builder, Property Manager; **SERVICES:** Full Devel. and Prop. Mgmt.; **PREV EMPLOY:** Regl. Supr. - Nat. Investment Dev. Corp. 1978-1979, VP Patterson Merkie and Assoc. 1973-1978; **PROFL AFFIL & HONORS:** NAR, IREM, CPM; **EDUC:** BS, 1965, Bus. & Econ., Marietta Coll.; **GRAD EDUC:** MA, 1970, Bus. Admin., Central MO State Univ.; **MIL SERV:** USAF 1966-1970, Capt.; **HOME ADD:** Latchstring Ln., Gwynedd Valley, PA 19437, (215)699-5061; **BUS ADD:** The Office Ctr., Suite 2-C, Plainsboro, NJ 08536, (609)799-2880.

BURR, Stephen Ives——B: Aug. 13, 1947, Waterbury, CT, *Atty.*, Bingham, Dana & Gould; **PRIM RE ACT:** Attorney; **SERVICES:** Counseling clients on all aspects of acquiring, devel. and selling or leasing re; **REP CLIENTS:** Corporate and developer clients with respect to comml. and multi-unit resid. properties; constr. and permanent lenders; **PROFL AFFIL & HONORS:** Chmn. of the Arch. and Const. Comm. and member of the Property Law Section Council of the MA Bar Assn. Member of the RE Fin. Comm. of ABA, Fellow of the MA Bar Found.; **EDUC:** BA, 1969, Hist., Lawrence Univ.; **GRAD EDUC:** JD, 1976, Boston Coll. Law School; **EDUC HONORS:** Grad. with distinction in Major, Magna Cum Laude, Order of the Coif, Editor of Review, Environmental Affairs, Law Review; **MIL SERV:** USAF, Capt., Joint Serv. Commendation Medal; **HOME ADD:** 81 W. Main St., Georgetown, MA 01833, (617)352-8445; **BUS ADD:** 100 Federal St., Boston, MA 02110, (617)357-9300.

BURRELL, Randie——B: Nov. 20, 1947, San Diego, CA, *VP Fin.*, Black Mountain Corp.; **PRIM RE ACT:** Developer, Owner/Investor, Property Manager; **PREV EMPLOY:** Deloitte Haskins & Sells, CPA; **PROFL AFFIL & HONORS:** AICPA, CA Soc. of CPA's, CPA; **EDUC:** Acctg., 1972, Brigham Young Univ.; **HOME ADD:** 14018 Davenport Ave., San Diego, CA 92129, (714)578-1161; **BUS ADD:** 9393 Activity Rd., Suite I, San Diego, CA 92126, (714)578-1161.

BURRIS, William T.——B: June 19, 1924, Pueblo, CO, *Pres.*, William T. Burris and Company; **PRIM RE ACT:** Broker, Consultant, Engineer, Appraiser, Instructor, Property Manager; **SERVICES:** Appraisal; valuation engrg.; right-of-way acquisition & valuation; prop. mgmt. consulting; **REP CLIENTS:** Relocation cos.; governmental agencies; public utilities; prop. mgmt. cos.; condo. & homeowners assns.; **PREV EMPLOY:** Mountain Bell/CO, Engrg. and RE Depts., 1946-1979; Lt. Cmdr. USNR-RET, 1943-1966; **PROFL AFFIL & HONORS:** IREM, IRWA, NARA, Local, State & NAR; SREA Market Data Ctr.; CO R.E. Educa. Assn., Reg. Profl. Engr.; CPM-Certified Prop. Mgr. CRA; RPA; GRI; **EDUC:** USNR, 1945, Electrical Engr. & Naval Sci., USC; **MIL SERV:** USNR, LCDR-RET, (W.W.II & Korean); **OTHER ACT & HONORS:** Chmn., Dillon Planning & Zoning Commn., Amer. Mensa Soc., Amer. Radio Relay League, Past VP and Dir., Denver Bldg. Owners and Mgrs. Assn.; **HOME ADD:** 21677 Mountsfield Dr., Golden, CO 80401, (303)526-0727; **BUS ADD:** 167 Tenderfoot St., P O Drawer 449, Dillon, CO 80435(Dillion Office), (303)468-6850.

BURROUGHS, J. Michael——B: Oct. 26, 1942, Goldsboro, NC, *Pres.*, Southeastern Realty and Mortgage Co.; **PRIM RE ACT:** Broker, Consultant, Appraiser, Lender; **PREV EMPLOY:** 10 yrs. in mort. brokerage; 5 yrs. in appraising; **PROFL AFFIL & HONORS:** AIREA, SREA, Charlotte Bd. Realtors, MAI, SRA, SRPA; **EDUC:** BS, 1964, Bus. Admin., Fin., Univ. of NC - Chapel Hill; **MIL SERV:** USA, E-5; **HOME ADD:** 5800 Lancelot Dr., Matthews, NC 28105; **BUS ADD:** 5800 Lancelot Dr., Matthews, NC 28105, (704)847-2193.

BURROUGHS, Jonnie C.——B: Dec. 26, 1927, Miltonvale, KS, *VP*, Hovious Assoc., Inc., Gallery of Homes; **PRIM RE ACT:** Broker, Instructor, Consultant; **OTHER RE ACT:** Fin. Consultant/Advisor; **SERVICES:** Resid. Specialist - Resale/New/Reloc.; **PREV EMPLOY:** USA 1949-1970; **PROFL AFFIL & HONORS:** CRB, CRS; **EDUC:** BS, 1949, Bus. Admin., KS State Univ.; **MIL SERV:** USA, Lt. Col., Bronze Star, Meritorious Serv. Medal, Army Commendation

Medal; **HOME ADD:** 9213 McFall Dr., El Paso, TX 79925, (915)598-6565; **BUS ADD:** 800-810 E. Yandell, El Paso, TX 79902, (915)533-2635.

BURROUGHS, Richard R.——B: Aug. 13, 1946, Baytown, TX, *Owner*, Richard R. Burroughs; **PRIM RE ACT:** Attorney; **SERVICES:** Pres. of legal instruments, recording at Cty. Clerk; **PROFL AFFIL & HONORS:** ABA; State Bar of TX, Houston Bar Assn., Montgomery Cty. Bar Assn., Liberty Cty. Bar Assn., TX Trial Lawyers Assn., Cert. to practice before the Supreme Court of the US; **EDUC:** BA, 1968, Pol. Sci., Baylor Univ.; **GRAD EDUC:** JD, 1973, Baylor Univ., School of Law; **EDUC HONORS:** Delta Theta Phi; **MIL SERV:** USA, Sgt.; **OTHER ACT & HONORS:** Tr., Friendship United Methodist Church; **HOME ADD:** 306 Magnolia Bend, New Caney, TX 77357; **BUS ADD:** PO Box 1676, 112 S Bonham, Cleveland, TX 77327, (713)592-5234.

BURROW, Bruce——B: Jan. 11, 1943, *Pres.*, Realty Assoc.; **PRIM RE ACT:** Broker, Syndicator, Consultant, Developer, Owner/Investor; **SERVICES:** Site selection, acquisition, devel., build to suit, shopping ctrs, office bldgs., apt. devel., consulting; **PROFL AFFIL & HONORS:** Realtor, NACORE, ICSC, ULI, RE Million Dollar Club; **EDUC:** Harbor Jr. Coll., S & L Inst.; **OTHER ACT & HONORS:** Jonesboro C of C, Ctry. Club; **BUS ADD:** First Plaza Bank Bldg., Suite 1000, PO Box 974, Jonesboro, AR 72401, (501)932-1400.

BURROWS, James C.——B: Feb. 13, 1951, Boston, MA, *Chairman of the Bd.*, Sethco Corp.; **PRIM RE ACT:** Consultant, Appraiser, Developer, Owner/Investor; **SERVICES:** Mgmt. of clients portfolios; **PREV EMPLOY:** RE Broker; Contractor; **PROFL AFFIL & HONORS:** NAR; **EDUC:** BS, 1973, Poli. Sci., Northeastern Univ.; **GRAD EDUC:** MLS, 1977, Simmons Coll.; **OTHER ACT & HONORS:** ASIS; **HOME ADD:** 29 Milford St., Boston, MA 02118, (617)542-1636.

BURSTEIN, Frederick S.——B: July 28, 1946, NYC, NY, *VP-RE*, Channel Home Ctrs.; **OTHER RE ACT:** Retailer; **PROFL AFFIL & HONORS:** NACORE, ICSC; **EDUC:** BA, 1967, Econ., Univ. of MI; **GRAD EDUC:** JD, 1970, Northwestern Univ. Law School; **EDUC HONORS:** Law Review; **HOME ADD:** 5 Chaucer Ct., Livingston, NJ 07039, (201)992-2580; **BUS ADD:** 945 Route 10, Whippany, NJ 07881, (201)887-7000.

BURSTEIN, Melvin——B: May 19, 1927, NY, *CPA*, Melvin Burstein CPA PA; **PRIM RE ACT:** Consultant; **OTHER RE ACT:** Acctnt.; **SERVICES:** Tax & mgmt.; **PROFL AFFIL & HONORS:** NY State Soc., NJ State Soc., AICPA, Tax Comm. NJ Soc.; **EDUC:** BS, 1950, NY Univ.; **MIL SERV:** USN; **BUS ADD:** 9060 Palisade Ave., North Bergen, NJ 07047, (201)861-1887.

BURSTEIN, William Michael——B: Apr. 23, 1947, White Plains, NY, *VP*, Albany Title Co.; **PRIM RE ACT:** Attorney; **SERVICES:** Title insurance, abstracts of title; **REP CLIENTS:** Purchasers of real prop. and mort. lenders; **PROFL AFFIL & HONORS:** NY State Bar Assn., ABA; **EDUC:** BA, 1968, Psych., Yale Coll.; **GRAD EDUC:** JD, 1971, Columbia Univ. Sch. of Law; **OTHER ACT & HONORS:** Town Atty., Town of Petersburg, 1972-79; **HOME ADD:** R.D. 2 East Hollow Rd., Petersburg, NY 12138, (518)658-3567; **BUS ADD:** 75 State St., Albany, NY 12207, (518)434-3123.

BURTON, Edward Gould——B: July 20, 1940, Providence, RI, *Atty.-Shareholder-Sec.*, Burr, Pease & Kurtz, PC; **PRIM RE ACT:** Attorney, Instructor, Owner/Investor; **SERVICES:** RE and natural resources legal advise; **REP CLIENTS:** Maj. landholders, devel., resid. indus. and mineral props. acquisition & title work, zoning, land use planning, govt. regulation, & govt. serv. (Eklutna, Inc., Igiugig Native Corp., Knakanen Corp, Enserch Corp., Alyeska Pipeline Serv. Co., Louisiana-Pacific Corp., Gamel Homes, Inc. & others); **PROFL AFFIL & HONORS:** Anchorage & AK Bar Assns., Am. Judicature Soc., ABA (real prop. & probate sec., Natural res. sect., Rocky Mt. Mineral Law Found.; **EDUC:** AB, 1962, Woodrow Wilson Sch. of Public & Intl. Affairs, Princeton Univ.; **GRAD EDUC:** LLB, 1965, RE & Municipal Law, Harvard Law Sch.; **EDUC HONORS:** Cum Laude in Public Affairs; **MIL SERV:** AK ARNG, Pvt. E-1, 1st Lt., NDSM, Disaster Serv.; **OTHER ACT & HONORS:** Member & COB of Supervisors, Upper O'Malley Ltd. Rd. Serv. Area 1979-date; Tower Club, Hillside East Community Council, Inc. (Dir. 1978-date); Hillside Rd. Maintenance, Inc. (Dir. 1969-date); **HOME ADD:** 9200 Prospect Dr., Anchorage, AK 99504, (907)344-7982; **BUS ADD:** 810 "N" St., Anchorage, AK 99501, (907)276-6100.

BURTON, John P.——B: Feb. 26, 1943, New Orleans, LA, *Dir.*, Rodey, Dickason, Sloan, Akin & Robb, PA; **PRIM RE ACT:** Attorney; **SERVICES:** Legal problem solving, including analysis, negotiating, drafting, and litigation; **REP CLIENTS:** Instnl. and indiv. lenders, investors, devels. and landlords; **PROFL AFFIL & HONORS:** ABA; Real Prop. Litigation Comm. of Sect. of Real Prop., Probate and Trust Law; **EDUC:** BS, 1965, Bus. Admin., LA Polytechnic Inst.; **GRAD EDUC:** LLB, 1968, Harvard Law School; **EDUC HONORS:** Magna Cum Laude; **OTHER ACT & HONORS:** Vestry, Canterbury Chapel; **BUS ADD:** 20 First Plaza, P.O. Box 1888, Albuquerque, NM 87103, (505)765-5900.

BURTON, Robert Ellis——B: Jan. 14, 1922, Johnson City, NY, *Architect*, Robert Ellis Burton, AIA, Arch.; **PRIM RE ACT:** Architect, Consultant; **OTHER RE ACT:** Const. Dispute Arbitrator (AAA) (Home Owners and Comml.); **SERVICES:** Arch.-Interior Design: Arbitrator; **PROFL AFFIL & HONORS:** AIA, SMPS; **MIL SERV:** US Army (WWII); S/Sgt., Europe/etc.; **OTHER ACT & HONORS:** Soc. for Mktg. Prof. Serv., Newcomen Soc., Nat. Panel, Amer. Arbitration Assn.; NCARB certified #6731; Reg. Arch. PA, MD, NJ, NY, DE, KY, IL, IN, VA; **BUS ADD:** Four Boulder Creek Ln., Newtown Sq., PA 19073, (215)356-3215.

BURTSCHER, Art N.——B: Oct. 12, 1949, Hays, KS, *VP*, First Nat. B and T Co. of Lincoln; **PRIM RE ACT:** Consultant, Appraiser, Banker, Lender, Owner/Investor; **SERVICES:** Consultant on mort. bkg., invest. strategy, feasibilty studies, mort. loan placement, appraisal; **REP CLIENTS:** Merrill Lynch, North KS Savings Assn., Transamerica Corp., VA, FHA; **PREV EMPLOY:** Anchor Savings Assn., Kansas City, KS; **PROFL AFFIL & HONORS:** SRA Designation, SREA; **EDUC:** BS, 1972, Bus. Admin., Fort Hays KS State Univ.; **GRAD EDUC:** Grad. School of Mort. Banking, 1975, Mort. Banking, School of Mort. Banking, MBAA; **EDUC HONORS:** Dean's List, Athlete's Honor Roll; **OTHER ACT & HONORS:** Bd. mbr. NE Mort. Assn.; Chmn. Mayor's Reinvestment Task Force Admissions Comm. SREA; **HOME ADD:** 1709 Trelawney Cr., Lincoln, NE 68512, (402)423-7563; **BUS ADD:** PO 81008, Lincoln, NE 68501, (402)471-1137.

BURWELL, William O.——B: June 6, 1921, Seattle, WA, *Arch.*, Burwell & Bantel, Arch./Planners, AIA; **PRIM RE ACT:** Architect; **SERVICES:** Arch. design, site planning & feasibility, energy conserv. eval./consult., solar energy design (passive/active); **PROFL AFFIL & HONORS:** AIA, Former Pres. of Rochester Chapt., AIA Design Awards (local chapt.); **EDUC:** BA, 1942, Arch., Princeton Univ.; **GRAD EDUC:** MFA, 1949, Arch., Princeton School of Arch.; **EDUC HONORS:** Hon. in Arch., Honors; **MIL SERV:** USNR, Cdr., Bronze Star, Philippines liberation; Submarine Combat Insignia (w/5 stars); **OTHER ACT & HONORS:** Rotary Club of Rochester; **HOME ADD:** 198 Shoreham Dr., Rochester, NY 14618, (716)244-9037; **BUS ADD:** 311 Alexander St., Rochester, NY 14604, (716)232-7037.

BUSBY, Kenneth Michael——B: July 25, 1946, Edmonton, Alb., Can., *Pres.*, Manco West Development Co. Ltd.; **PRIM RE ACT:** Developer, Owner/Investor, Property Manager, Syndicator; **OTHER RE ACT:** Site selection & project conceptual analyst; **SERVICES:** Joint venture devel. mgmt. - office structures; **PREV EMPLOY:** Westform Devepment Corp. Ltd., 1974-1980; **PROFL AFFIL & HONORS:** BOMA; Calgary C of C; **EDUC:** 1973, B. Comm./Urban Econ., Univ. of Alberta (Edmonton); **HOME ADD:** 112 Canterbury Dr. SW, Calgary, Alb., Can., (403)281-0152; **BUS ADD:** PO Box 6104, Station A, Calgary, Alb., Can., (403)252-7852.

BUSCH, David A.——B: July 6, 1937, Rochester MN, *Partner-Gen. Mgr.*, Weis Management Co.; **PRIM RE ACT:** Consultant, Owner/Investor, Property Manager; **SERVICES:** Prop. Mgmt., resid., comml.; **REP CLIENTS:** Gen. partnerships Ltd. partnerships Govt. Assisted & conventional 2000 units; **PROFL AFFIL & HONORS:** IREM, NAR, NAHB, Nat. Assn. of Home Builders, Nat. Apt. Assn., MN Multi Housing Assn., CPM, RAM; **EDUC:** BA, 1959, Philosophy, secondary educ., St. Mary's Coll.; **GRAD EDUC:** MA, 1963, Secondary Educ. Admin., Catholic Univ.; **HOME ADD:** 412 18th St. SE, Rochester, MN 55901, (507)288-6185; **BUS ADD:** 2227 NW 7th St. Box 6757, Rochester, MN 55903, (507)288-7980.

BUSCH, Gary B.——B: Dec. 10, 1940, Orange, CA, *Assoc. Broker*, Sun Valley Realty; **PRIM RE ACT:** Broker; **SERVICES:** Sales, listing condos, homes, land, comml. farms & ranches; **REP CLIENTS:** Sun Valley Resort Area Investors; **PROFL AFFIL & HONORS:** Nat. Assn. of Realtors; ID Assn. of Realtors; Realtors Nat. Mktg. Inst.; RESSI, CRS; CRB; **EDUC:** BS, 1964, Agric. Econ., Univ. of NV, Reno; **MIL SERV:** US Army; Artillery, 1st Lt., Bronze Star, Air Medal; **HOME ADD:** PO Box 742, Sun Valley, ID 83353, (208)726-9215; **BUS ADD:** PO Box 43, Sun Valley, ID 83353, (208)622-3392.

BUSH, E. Clay——*Corp. Fac. Mgr.*, Fluke Manufacturing; **PRIM RE ACT:** Property Manager; **BUS ADD:** PO Box 43210, Terrace, WA 98043, (206)774-2211.*

BUSH, H. Ronald——**B:** Aug. 13, 1933, NY, NY, *Pres.*, Ronald Bush RE, Inc.; **PRIM RE ACT:** Owner/Investor; **OTHER RE ACT:** RE Brokerage; **PROFL AFFIL & HONORS:** E. Suffolk Bd. of Realtors; **EDUC:** BS, 1955, Agri., Cornell; **MIL SERV:** USN, Lt. j.g.; **OTHER ACT & HONORS:** Kiwanis, Past pres., C of C, Past VP, E. Suffolk Bd. of Realtors, Past VP; **HOME ADD:** 463 Middle Rd., Bayport, NY 11705, (516)472-0530; **BUS ADD:** 120 E. Main St., Patchogue, NY 11772.

BUSH, William C.——**B:** Dec. 7, 1939, Pittsburgh, PA, *VP*, Merrill Lynch Pierce Fenner & Smith, Merrill Lynch Leasing Inc.; **PRIM RE ACT:** Banker, Owner/Investor, Syndicator; **SERVICES:** Originate and structure bond type net lease financing of RE; **PREV EMPLOY:** Huntoon Paige & Co., Inc., 1974-1979; Pine Street Equity Corp., 1972-1974; Dewey Ballantine Bushby Palmer & Wood (1965-1972); **EDUC:** BA, 1961, English, Princeton Univ.; **GRAD EDUC:** LLB, 1964, Law, Yale Law School; **MIL SERV:** USMC; **HOME ADD:** 400 East 57th St., New York, NY 10022, (212)758-3912; **BUS ADD:** One Liberty Plaza, New York, NY 10080, (212)637-2734.

BUSHEE, Dean A.——**B:** June 9, 1946, Grand Forks, ND, *CPM*, Bushee Property Mgmt., Inc.; **PRIM RE ACT:** Property Manager; **SERVICES:** RE Mgmt.; **PROFL AFFIL & HONORS:** IREM, CPM; **EDUC:** BS, 1973, Bus. Admin.; **MIL SERV:** USN, E-5; **HOME ADD:** 504 S. 5th St., Grand Forks, ND 58201, (701)772-4678; **BUS ADD:** 117 N. Washington, Grand Forks, ND 58201, (701)746-4446.

BUSI, William L.——**B:** Jan. 18, 1946, Waltham, MA, *VP, Leasing*, American Prop. Corp.; **PRIM RE ACT:** Broker; **OTHER RE ACT:** Leasing of office space; **SERVICES:** Office space leasing, project leasing and/or tenant representative; **REP CLIENTS:** Energy cos., CPA firms, lawyers, ins.; **PREV EMPLOY:** Del E. Webb Corp.; **EDUC:** BSBA, 1969, Bus. & RE, Univ. of Denver; **HOME ADD:** 7043 E Warren Dr., Denver, CO 80224, (303)758-7395; **BUS ADD:** 999 18th St., Suite 300, Denver, CO 80202, (303)629-9393.

BUSKIRK, George A., Jr.——**B:** May 6, 1949, Indpls., IN, *VP & Trust Officer*, Indiana Nat. Bank & Trust; **PRIM RE ACT:** Attorney, Banker; **SERVICES:** Trust; **PROFL AFFIL & HONORS:** ABA, IN State Bar Assn.; **EDUC:** BS, 1971, Bus. Admin., Butler Univ.; **GRAD EDUC:** JD, 1973, IU Indpls.; **MIL SERV:** USA, Capt.; **BUS ADD:** 1 Indiana Sq. Dept. 621, Indianapolis, IN 46266, (317)266-6508.

BUSNY, Irving H.——**B:** Oct. 21, 1933, Boston, MA, *Partner*, The Slater Co.; **PRIM RE ACT:** Developer, Owner/Investor, Syndicator; **SERVICES:** Prop. mgmt., RE devel.; **PROFL AFFIL & HONORS:** BOMA, Dir. Boston Chapt. Gr. Boston RE Bd., Dir.; **EDUC:** BS, 1954, Bus. Admin., Boston Univ.; **MIL SERV:** USAF, 1st Lt., Pilot; **HOME ADD:** 17 Ferncroft Rd., Newton, MA 02168, (617)969-8516; **BUS ADD:** 33 Broad St., Boston, MA 02109, (617)367-0140.

BUSS, Richard Paul——**B:** May 29, 1946, Herington, KS, *Pres.*, Buss Silvers Hughes & Assocs.; **PRIM RE ACT:** Engineer, Architect; **SERVICES:** Arch. & engineering servs.; **REP CLIENTS:** Resid., comml. and office devels.; **PROFL AFFIL & HONORS:** AIA, Indiv. and firm design awards; **EDUC:** BArch., 1969, Arch., IA State Univ.; **GRAD EDUC:** MBA, 1977, Nat. Univ.; **EDUC HONORS:** Reynolds Aluminium Design Comp. Winner; **MIL SERV:** US Navy, Lt. (jg); **OTHER ACT & HONORS:** Pres., San Diego Chapter AIA; Chmn., Bd. of Mgrs., Copley YMCA; **BUS ADD:** 1875 Third Ave., San Diego, CA 92101, (714)239-2353.

BUSSE, David M.——**B:** June 24, 1936, Akron, OH, *Principal*, David M. Busse & Assocs.; **OTHER RE ACT:** RE Investment Counselor; **SERVICES:** Acquisition & exchange brokerage, investment & devel.; **EDUC:** AB, 1958, Chemistry, Harvard; **GRAD EDUC:** MBA, 1968, RE, Fin. & Control, Harvard Bus. School; **MIL SERV:** US Marine Corp, 1st Lt.; **HOME ADD:** 16 Stevens Place, Rocky Hill, CT 06067, (203)563-5580; **BUS ADD:** 18 Asylum St., Ste. 602, Hartford, CT 06103, (203)246-9777.

BUSSEY, Ronald J., CRE——**B:** Aug. 10, 1933, Lake Leelanau, MI, *VP*, Arthur Rubloff & Co., Dir., RE Counseling Group; **PRIM RE ACT:** Consultant; **SERVICES:** RE counseling, including market/fin. feasibility studies, best use evaluations, site location analyses, cost-benefit impact assessments; **REP CLIENTS:** Corp., devel., investors, instit., merchants, and govtl. bodies; **PREV EMPLOY:** Larry Smith & Co. 1961-1974; Urban Projects, Inc. 1974-1977; **PROFL AFFIL & HONORS:** Amer. Soc. of RE Counselors, ULI, Lambda Alpha, ICSC; **EDUC:** BS, 1957, Gen. Bus., Univ. of Detroit; **GRAD EDUC:** MR, 1959, Retailing-Store Location/Consumer Research, Univ. of Pittsburgh-Grad. School of Bus.; **HOME ADD:** 845 Greenwood Ave., Glencoe, IL 60022, (312)835-1915; **BUS ADD:** 69 W. Wash., Chicago, IL 60602, (312)368-5320.

BUSSEY, William Wallace, Jr.——**B:** Jan. 22, 1942, Atlanta, GA, *Sales Mgr.*, Eastbrook Companies; **PRIM RE ACT:** Broker, Consultant, Appraiser, Developer, Builder, Owner/Investor, Instructor, Property Manager, Syndicator; **OTHER RE ACT:** Realtor Assoc., Banking Advisor; **SERVICES:** RE dev., synd., investment consultation, prop. mgmt., appraisals; **REP CLIENTS:** Pvt. Investors, Corp. Clients Seeking Mergers, Inst. Investors; **PREV EMPLOY:** Part. Nasser & Assoc., Part. All Amer. Prop. Investors, Part. Grand Rapids Growth Props., Part. Park Assoc., Part. Bussey & Assoc.; **PROFL AFFIL & HONORS:** Rental Prop. Owners Assn., Listed in 'Who's Who in Indus. & Fin'; **EDUC:** BS, 1965, Indus. Engrg., Mktg., GA Inst. of Tech.; **OTHER ACT & HONORS:** C of C (Intl. Bus. Devel. Comm.), Grand Rapids Jaycees (VP, Bd. of Dir., Key Man Award), World Affairs Council (Bd. of Dir.), Advisor to Greater GR Charity Golf Classic, Jr. Achievement Advisor (Sales Advisor of the Yr.); **HOME ADD:** 1320 54th St. SE, Kentwood, MI 49508, (616)455-8909; **BUS ADD:** 2130 Enterprise SE, Kentwood, MI 49508, (616)455-0200.

BUSSIERE, Barry——**B:** Apr. 10, 1947, Santa Monica, CA, *Pres.*, Touchstone Realty, Inc.; **PRIM RE ACT:** Broker, Instructor; **SERVICES:** Resid. and investment counseling; **PREV EMPLOY:** Loan officer, Security Pacific Nat. Bank; Prop. mgr. for R & B Devel.; Office Mgr. Fredericks Develop.; **PROFL AFFIL & HONORS:** Huntington Beach Fountain Valley Bd. of Realtors; CA Assn. of Realtors, NAR, 1980 Realtor of the Year, HB/FV Bd. of Realtors 1979 & 80; Tres., HB/FV Bd. of Realtors; 1981 Realtor Dir.; HB/FV Bd. of Realtors, Pres. 1982; **EDUC:** BA, 1969, Zoology, UCLA; BS, 1973, Bus. Admin., RE, CA State Univ.; **EDUC HONORS:** Deans List, Grad. Magna Cum Laude; **OTHER ACT & HONORS:** Life time teaching credential, Coast Community Coll.; 1979 Cert. of Excellence from the Nat. Statistical Research Co.; 1980/81 Who's Who in the West; **HOME ADD:** 7703 Sagewood, Huntington Beach, CA 92648, (714)848-9415; **BUS ADD:** 18582 Beach Blvd. 8, Huntington Beach, CA 92647, (714)963-0867.

BUTCHER, Donald P.——**B:** Oct. 10, 1934, Ardmore, OK, *Prin. Owner*, Donald P. Butcher, AIA, Arch.; **PRIM RE ACT:** Architect, Builder; **SERVICES:** Arch., int. design, constr. mgmt, arch. engrg.; **PROFL AFFIL & HONORS:** Lic. in OK, KS, NM, Am. Inst. Arch., OK Solar Energy Assn.; Construction Arbitrator, Amer. Arbitration Assn, Cert. by Natl. Council of Arch. Registration Bds.; **EDUC:** B Arch., 1962, Univ. of OK; **EDUC HONORS:** Alpha Rho Chi Medal, Dean's Honor Roll, Pres. Student Chapt. AIA; **MIL SERV:** USA, E-5, Good Conduct Medal; **OTHER ACT & HONORS:** Past Pres. Kiwanis Club of Utica Sq., S. Tulsa Exec. Grp.; **HOME ADD:** 8417 S. Sandusky, Tulsa, OK 74136, (918)481-1110; **BUS ADD:** 4717 S. Yale, Tulsa, OK 74135, (918)663-1944.

BUTCHER, Douglas S.——**B:** Mar. 29, 1956, Parkersburg, WV, *Asst. Review Appraiser*, US Railway Assn., Law Dept.; **PRIM RE ACT:** Appraiser; **SERVICES:** Reviewing Right-of-Way Major Prop. Appraisal US Govt.; **PREV EMPLOY:** Larry M. McDaniel, Inc. Appraisers & Consultants, Parkersburg, WV; **PROFL AFFIL & HONORS:** NAR, WVA Assoc. Realtors; **OTHER ACT & HONORS:** Jaycees; **HOME ADD:** 516 N. Jordan St. 104, Alexandria, VA 22304, (703)370-3978; **BUS ADD:** 955 L'Enfant Plaza N. SW, Washington, DC 20595, (202)472-7484.

BUTLER, Edward Franklyn——**B:** July 1, 1937, Memphis, TN, *Atty. at Law*, Edward F. Butler, Atty.; **PRIM RE ACT:** Attorney, Owner/Investor; **SERVICES:** Negotiating contracts and leases; title work; RE closing; **REP CLIENTS:** Texaco, Inc.; Jefferson International Sales Corp.; Jefferson Chemical Co.; Litton Oil Corp.; Tentex Petroleum Corp.; **PROFL AFFIL & HONORS:** ABA (Sect. on RE and Probate Law); TN Bar; Memphis & Shelby Cty. Bar; TX Bar; Amer. State & Local Trial Lawyers Assoc., Who's Who in Amer. Law; Who's Who in the South and SW; Book of Honor; Notable Amer.; Men of Achievement; **EDUC:** BA, 1958, Pol. Sci./Eng. & Soc., Univ. of MS; **GRAD EDUC:** JD, 1961, Corporate Law, Vanderbilt Univ. School of Law; **EDUC HONORS:** Alpha Phi Omega; Regional Scholar, Phi Delta Phi; Ford Found. Scholar; Honors Award in Suretyship Legal Bibliography & Trial Practice; Law Day Moot Court Team, Nat. Moot Ct.; **MIL SERV:** US Navy Reserve, Cdr., Armed Force Reserve Medal with Hour Glass Device; **OTHER ACT & HONORS:** Special Judge State Probate & Gen. Sessions Cts. & City Juvenile Traffic & Municipal Cts.; Mensa Intertel; Comm. Chmn., Ship #1, Sea Scout Explorer Post, Memphis TN; Admin. Law Judge, TN Medical Malpractice Review Bd.; **HOME ADD:** 59 N. White Station Rd., Memphis, TN 38117, (901)685-6518; **BUS ADD:** Suite 3023, 100 North Main Bldg., Memphis, TN 38103, (901)526-1500.

BUTLER, Kent E.——**B:** July 15, 1946, Xenia, Ohio, *VP*, Merrill Lynch Realty/Chris Cole, Inc.; **PRIM RE ACT:** Broker; **OTHER RE ACT:** Assoc. Broker Mngr. 47 Assoc. office; **SERVICES:** All residential serv. except prop. mgmt.; **PROFL AFFIL & HONORS:**

NAR; RNMI; Anne Arundel Cty. (MD) Bd. of Realtors, GRI, CRB; **HOME ADD:** 1755 Meadow Hill Dr., Annapolis, MD 21401, (301)757-7073; **BUS ADD:** 501 Sixth St. at Chesapeake Ave., Annapolis, SD 21403, (301)263-8800.

BUTLER, Robert C.——**B:** Sept. 27, 1925, Lincoln, NE, *Pres.*, Gallup Insurance Agency, Inc., Ins. & RE; **PRIM RE ACT:** Broker, Appraiser, Owner/Investor, Property Manager, Insuror; **SERVICES:** Ins. & RE mktg., mgmt.; **PROFL AFFIL & HONORS:** NAR, RANM, IIAA, IIANM; **EDUC:** AB, 1950, Music - Instr. & Voice, Western St. Coll., Gunnison, CO; **GRAD EDUC:** M.M.Ed, 1951, Methods & Admin., Univ. of Notre Dame; **EDUC HONORS:** O'Hara Fellowship; **MIL SERV:** USAC, 1943-1945, Lt.; USAF, 1950-1955; **OTHER ACT & HONORS:** Sierra Intl., Knight of St. Gregory; **HOME ADD:** 1509 So. Grandview Dr., Gallup, NM 87301; **BUS ADD:** 105 West Aztec, Gallup, NM 87301P O Box 278, (505)863-4428.

BUTLER, Robert P.——**B:** July 18, 1933, Atlanta, GA, *Appraiser*, US Treasury - IRS, Field Examination; **PRIM RE ACT:** Engineer, Appraiser, Instructor; **SERVICES:** Appraisal service for Revenue Agents & Attys.; **PREV EMPLOY:** FHA, & Hunnicutt & Associates valuation Engrs.; **PROFL AFFIL & HONORS:** NARA, and Assn. of Govtl. Appraisers, SGA, SRA, CRA; **MIL SERV:** USA, Corp.; **OTHER ACT & HONORS:** Mayor, Town of Brocks, Senora Lodge 82 F&AM, Brooks Methodist Church, Fayette Cty. 6th Dist. Volunteer Fire Dept.; **HOME ADD:** 225 Butler Rd., Brecks, GA 30205, (404)599-3340; **BUS ADD:** 275 Peachtree St. NE, Atlanta, GA 30370, (404)221-6391.

BUTLER, Virgil——**B:** May 29, 1941, Chicago, IL, *Prop. Mgr.*, Wolin-Levin, Inc.; **PRIM RE ACT:** Instructor, Property Manager; **SERVICES:** Prop. mgmt., investment counseling; **REP CLIENTS:** Lenders, indiv. investors in rental prop., synd.; **PREV EMPLOY:** The Woodlawn Org., 1977; IL Housing Devel. Authority, 1973-1976; Draper & Kramer, Inc., 1969-1972; **PROFL AFFIL & HONORS:** IREM, CPM; **EDUC:** Bus. Admin., Hampton Inst.; **OTHER ACT & HONORS:** 1st Congrl. Dist. Housing Task Force; **HOME ADD:** 7000 S. Shore Dr., Chicago, IL 60649, (312)363-0724; **BUS ADD:** 1740 E. 55th St., Chicago, IL 60615, (312)684-6300.

BUTLER, William W.——**B:** June 25, 1944, Childress, TX, *Asst. VP*, Henry S. Miller Co., Comml., Regnl. Mall Leasing; **PRIM RE ACT:** Broker, Consultant, Developer, Property Manager; **SERVICES:** Leasing, merchandising, devel., managing; **PREV EMPLOY:** Gerald D. Hines Interests; **PROFL AFFIL & HONORS:** Intl. Council of Shopping Centers, CSM; **EDUC:** BBA, 1967, Mktg., N. TX State Univ.; **MIL SERV:** USN, Lt., 1967-70; **HOME ADD:** 7707 Del Glen Lane, Houston, TX 77072, (713)933-8271; **BUS ADD:** 3000 S. Post Oak, Suite 1750, Houston, TX 77056, (713)626-8880.

BUTTERFIELD, Harold L.——**B:** Mar. 19, 1918, Brookfield, MO, *Pres.*, Indian River Appraisers, Inc.; **PRIM RE ACT:** Appraiser; **SERVICES:** Appraising and counseling; **REP CLIENTS:** Lenders, govt. agencies, buyers, estates; **PROFL AFFIL & HONORS:** AIREA, Soc. of RE Appraisers, Intl. Inst. of Valuers, MAI, SRPA, SCV; **MIL SERV:** US Army, 1st Lt., 1941-1946; **OTHER ACT & HONORS:** Mayor, Sumner, MO 1952-1956, Amer. Legion, Masons, Scottish Rite, Shrine, FL Highway Patrol Auxiliary 40 & 8; **HOME ADD:** 5170 Burning Tree Cir., Stuart, FL 33494, (305)287-7477; **BUS ADD:** Ste 300, Waterside Place, 221 E. Osceola St., Stuart, FL 33494, (305)283-1103.

BUTTITTA, Joseph J.——**B:** Jan. 12, 1917, Chicago, IL, *Pres.*, 4-B Industrial Realty; **PRIM RE ACT:** Broker, Attorney, Developer, Owner/Investor, Insuror; **PROFL AFFIL & HONORS:** IL State Bar, LLB; JD; BA; **EDUC:** 1940, LLB - JD, John Marshall Law School, Chicago, IL; **MIL SERV:** USA, Sgt.; Military Intelligence; **OTHER ACT & HONORS:** Tr., Village of Elmwood Park, IL; Columbian Club, Knights of Columbus, 25 yrs with Selective Service System-Chmn.; **HOME ADD:** 950 Franklin St., River Forest, IL 60305, (312)366-0900; **BUS ADD:** 666 Barrington Rd., Streamwood, IL 60103.

BUTTS, Reginald F.——**B:** Mar. 16, 1951, Portland, ME, *Treas.*, Symonds Assoc., Inc.; **PRIM RE ACT:** Broker, Consultant, Developer, Owner/Investor, Property Manager; **OTHER RE ACT:** Acctg.; **SERVICES:** All aspects of comml., indus. & investment brokerage and devel.; **PREV EMPLOY:** Accountant; **PROFL AFFIL & HONORS:** Natl. Assn. of Acctg.; NAR, GRI; **EDUC:** BS, AB, 1975, Fin. & Investments, Univ. of ME; **GRAD EDUC:** BS, 1977, Acctg., Univ. of ME; **EDUC HONORS:** Deans List, Who's Who Among Students in Amer. Colls. & Univs. 1977; **MIL SERV:** USN; HM2, Presid. Citation; **OTHER ACT & HONORS:** Windham Jaycees; Pres. of Profl. Sales Club. of ME; United Way Chairperson; Corp. Dir. of Sigma Nu, Frat. House Corp.; Dir. of Windham C of C; **HOME ADD:** 4 White Rock Dr., Gorham, ME 04038, (207)892-2214; **BUS ADD:** Rte. 302, PO Box 769, Windham, ME 04062.

BUTZEN, Philip J.——*Atty. at Law*, Urban Economics, Ltd.; **PRIM RE ACT:** Broker, Consultant, Developer, Builder, Owner/Investor; **REP CLIENTS:** Freedom Fed. S & L, Berwyn, IL; **PROFL AFFIL & HONORS:** Big Bros., Kiwanis; **EDUC:** MA, 1969, Econs., Univ. of CA; **GRAD EDUC:** 1974, Law, Northwestern Univ.; **HOME ADD:** 13725 Acorn Patch Ln., Poway, CA 92064, (714)487-5250; **BUS ADD:** 2048 Aldergrove Ave., Ste F, Escondido, CA 92025, (714)489-8201.

BUXTON, Brian P.——**B:** Dec. 23, 1944, Detroit, MI, *VP*, Epoch Management, Inc.; **PRIM RE ACT:** Broker, Consultant, Owner/Investor, Property Manager; **PREV EMPLOY:** ITT Sheraton Corp. of Amer.; **PROFL AFFIL & HONORS:** Bd. of Dirs., Pinellas Apt. Assn.; RE Broker, FL, CPM Candidate; **EDUC:** BA, 1972, Hotel/Rest. Mgmt., MI State Univ.; **MIL SERV:** USAF; E-5; **OTHER ACT & HONORS:** Alpha Kappa Psi, Profl. Bus. Frat.; **HOME ADD:** 2068 Whitney Dr. N., Clearwater, FL 33520, (813)536-8135; **BUS ADD:** 199 Whooping Loop, Altamonte Springs, FL 32701, (305)830-5499.

BUZEK, Ken——*Asst. Corp. Plng.*, Oglebay Norton Co.; **PRIM RE ACT:** Property Manager; **BUS ADD:** 1100 Superior Ave., Cleveland, OH 44114, (216)861-3300.*

BYBEE, Dr. Barney C.——**B:** Aug. 29, 1915, Logan, UT, *Pres. & Broker of Record*, Bybee & Assoc., Inc.; **PRIM RE ACT:** Broker, Consultant; **SERVICES:** Investment Counseling; **EDUC:** BS, 1939, Psych., Educ., UT State Univ., Logan; **GRAD EDUC:** Dr. of Medical Dentistry, 1949, Dentistry, Univ. of OR Dental School; **EDUC HONORS:** Om. Kappa Upsilon Hon. Soc.; **HOME ADD:** 6162 SW Evelyn, Portland, OR 97219, (503)245-2048; **BUS ADD:** 6162 SW Evelyn, Portland, OR 97219, (503)245-1404.

BYE, Stephen P.——**B:** Feb. 8, 1951, LaCrosse, WI, *RE Fin. Officer*, Coldwell Banker, RE Fin. Servs.; **OTHER RE ACT:** Mort. Banker; **SERVICES:** Joint venture fin.; comml. mort. fin.; acquisitions; **REP CLIENTS:** Nationwide Life Ins. Co.; State Farm Life; Occidental Life; Mutual of NY; NY life; MA Mutual; Aetna Life; **PREV EMPLOY:** Mort. Officer, Northwestern Mutual Life; Mgr. of RE-Continental Mort. Ins. Co.; **PROFL AFFIL & HONORS:** Soc. of RE Appraisers; CO Mort. Bankers Assn.; Planning Commn. (Madison, Wis.) 1971-78, SRA; **EDUC:** BBA, 1973, Urvan Land Econ./RE, Univ. of WI; **GRAD EDUC:** MBA, 1974, RE Investment Analysis and Appraisal, Univ. of WI; **EDUC HONORS:** Grad. with Distinction; **HOME ADD:** 6424 S. Florence Way, Englewood, CO 80111, (303)741-0878; **BUS ADD:** 1050 17th St., Denver, CO 80265, (303)628-7400.

BYNOE, R.W. Bruce——**B:** Sept. 18, 1950, Toronto, ON, CAN, *Sr. Devel. Officer*, The Cadillac Fairview Corp., Ltd., Urban Devel. Group; **PRIM RE ACT:** Developer; **OTHER RE ACT:** Leasing of co. owned prop.; **PREV EMPLOY:** Cadillac Fairview, 1975 to present; **PROFL AFFIL & HONORS:** BOMA; **EDUC:** B. Commerce, 1973, Urban Land Econ., Fin., Univ. of BC, Vancouver; **GRAD EDUC:** MSBA, 1975, Urban Land Econ., Univ. of BC, Vancouver; **EDUC HONORS:** First Class Standing, First Class Standing; **HOME ADD:** 10732 Maplecrest Rd., SE, Calgary, T2J1X9, Alberta, CAN, (403)278-8963; **BUS ADD:** 1303-311 6th Ave., SW, Calgary, T2p3H2, Alberta, CAN, (403)261-2651.

BYNUM, David L.——**B:** Aug. 12, 1951, Martin, TN, *Principal*, Gresham, Smith and Partners, Dallas; **PRIM RE ACT:** Architect; **SERVICES:** Arch. design, Master Planning, Engr., Interior Design, Fin. feasibility analysis; **REP CLIENTS:** Devels., fin. instns., proprietary and non-profit health facilities; **PROFL AFFIL & HONORS:** TX Soc. of Arch., AIA; TX Hospital Assn.; **EDUC:** BArch., 1975, Arch., Univ. of TN School of Arch.; **EDUC HONORS:** with Honors; **OTHER ACT & HONORS:** Dallas C of C; **HOME ADD:** 609 Palomar Lane, Richardson, TX 75081, (214)235-6076; **BUS ADD:** Suite 1650, One Dallas Ctr., 350 N. St. Paul, Dallas, TX 75201, (214)749-0227.

BYRAN, Jack H.——*Ed.*, Dept. of Housing & Urban Development, Housing Statistics; **PRIM RE ACT:** Real Estate Publisher; **BUS ADD:** 451 7th St., S.W., Washington, DC 20410, (202)755-6442.*

BYRKIT, Larry W.——**B:** Jan. 19, 1943, Decatur, IL, *VP and Sr. Lending Officer*, Peoples Liberty Bank & Trust Co.; **PRIM RE ACT:** Appraiser, Banker, Lender, Instructor; **SERVICES:** Resid. & Comml. Mort. Lending with Secondary Market and Mort. Banking Activity; **PREV EMPLOY:** IL Nat. Bank-Springfield, IL 1971-79; **PROFL AFFIL & HONORS:** ABA; Amer. Inst. of Bankers; SREA; **EDUC:** BS, 1965, Bus. Admin.; **OTHER ACT & HONORS:** United Appeal Fund Chmn. for 1982; Past Pres. and Bd. Member of Jr. Achievement,

Inc.; **HOME ADD:** 121 Burdsall, Ft. Mitchell, KY 41017, (606)331-4845; **BUS ADD:** 6th and Madison Ave., Covington, KY 41011, (606)292-6101.

BYRNE, Bernard——*Asst. Secy., Treas.*, Chickasha Cotton Oil Co.; **PRIM RE ACT:** Property Manager; **BUS ADD:** PO Box 511, Fort Worth, TX 76101, (817)732-8595.*

BYRNE, Richard R.——**B:** Dec. 21, 1941, Orange, NJ, *VP*, Chase Manhattan Bank, RE Fin.; **PRIM RE ACT:** Lender; **EDUC:** BS, 1966, Bus., Fairleigh Dickinson Univ.; **GRAD EDUC:** 1974, Stonier Grad. School of Banking; **MIL SERV:** US Army, SP-4; **HOME ADD:** 1608 Grouse Ln., Mountainside, NJ 07092; **BUS ADD:** 1 Chase Pl., 22nd Fl., New York, NY 10015, (212)552-3611.

BYRNES, Randall W.——*VP*, Spaulding & Slye; **PRIM RE ACT:** Developer; **BUS ADD:** 6610 Rockledge Dr., Bethesda, MD 20817, (301)897-9550.*

BYRON, Herbert Mark——**B:** Feb. 17, 1951, Wichita, KS, *Staff Atty.*, U.S. Govt.-Soc. Security Admin./DHHS/Office of Hearings & Appeals; **PRIM RE ACT:** Attorney, Owner/Investor; **SERVICES:** Advice on investments-Income prop. & yields; **PROFL AFFIL & HONORS:** ABA, PA Bar, CA Bar; **EDUC:** BA, 1973, Hist. and Poli. Sci. (Double Major), Univ. of CA at Los Angeles; **GRAD EDUC:** JD, 1976, Law (Criminal and Real Prop.), Southwestern Univ. School of Law - L.A., CA; **EDUC HONORS:** Caldwell Scholarship (1973), Dean's List (1970), Delta Theta Phi Law Fraternity, Farmers Ins. Co. Legal Scholarship; **OTHER ACT & HONORS:** Eagle Scout-1968 (Boy Scouts of Amer., Sherman Oaks, CA); **HOME ADD:** 16367 McGill St., (PO Box 2252), Covina, CA 91722, (213)960-7941; **BUS ADD:** 624 S. Grand Ave., Ste. 2300, Los Angeles, CA 90017, (213)688-4286.

BYRON, Jules Russell——**B:** June 23, 1935, New York, NY, *Pres.*, Williams Realty of Long Island, Inc.; **PRIM RE ACT:** Broker; **SERVICES:** Sale & Leasing of comml. RE; **REP CLIENTS:** Nat. and local inst. users such as the Coca Cola Co., NY Life Ins. Co., Peat Marwick Mitchel Co.; **PROFL AFFIL & HONORS:** RE Bd. of NY, IREBA, Young Mens RE Assn.; **EDUC:** BS, 1957, Indus. Engrg., MIT; **MIL SERV:** US Army, Lt.; **HOME ADD:** 11 Seaview Lane, Port Washington, NY 11050, (516)883-8028; **BUS ADD:** 99 Powerhouse Rd., Roslyn Heights, NY 11577, (516)484-5000.

CABLE, Robert E.——**B:** Aug. 19, 1937, Chicago, IL, *VP, RE*, Elaine Powers Figure Salons, Inc.; **OTHER RE ACT:** Corp. RE Officer; **PREV EMPLOY:** Lee Wards Creative Crafts (Gen. Mills), Foodmaker, Inc. (Jack in the Box Drive through restaurants) (Ralston Purina); **PROFL AFFIL & HONORS:** NACORE, ICSC; **EDUC:** 1956-58, Univ. of IL; **MIL SERV:** US Army, S/Sgt., E-6, Mil. Police; **HOME ADD:** 19355 Benington Dr., Brookfield, WI 53005, (414)784-7889; **BUS ADD:** 105 W Michigan St., Milwaukee, WI 53203, (414)273-2200.

CABRERA, Roger A.——**B:** Aug. 17, 1944, Cuba, *Pres.*, Capital Investment & Management Corp.; **PRIM RE ACT:** Broker, Consultant, Appraiser, Developer, Builder, Property Manager; **SERVICES:** Complete RE and Construction Services; **PROFL AFFIL & HONORS:** NAR, NSFA, Hialeah Miami Spring Bd. of Realtors, FL Assn. of Realtors; **BUS ADD:** 1671 W. 38th Pl., Suite 1406, Hialeah, FL 33012, (305)822-6100.

CACCOMO, Anthony V.——**B:** Sept. 21, 1947, Poughkeepsie, NY, *VP*, Baird & Warner, Inc., Devel. Div.; **PRIM RE ACT:** Broker, Developer, Syndicator; **PROFL AFFIL & HONORS:** NAR; Chicago RE Bd.; RESSI; **EDUC:** BS, 1970, Transportation, Niagara Univ., NY; **HOME ADD:** 1010 St. James Place, Park Ridge, IL 60068, (312)823-2216; **BUS ADD:** 115 South LaSalle St., Chicago, IL 60603, (312)368-5751.

CADDIS, A. James——**B:** Aug. 25, 1927, Pittsburgh, PA, *Pres.*, Caddis & McFaddin, Inc.; **PRIM RE ACT:** Consultant, Appraiser; **SERVICES:** Real prop. appraising and consulting; **REP CLIENTS:** Indiv., attys., corp., lending inst., govt. agencies; **PREV EMPLOY:** U.S. Forest Service, 1956-1967; **PROFL AFFIL & HONORS:** AIREA; Soc. of RE Appraisers; Soc. of Amer. Foresters; Nat. Assn. of Realtors, MAI; SRPA; **EDUC:** BA, 1956, Forestry, Univ. of MI, Ann Arbor; **GRAD EDUC:** MA, 1962, Public Admin., Univ. of CA, Berkeley; **MIL SERV:** USMC, SSgt.; **OTHER ACT & HONORS:** Kiwanis Club; **HOME ADD:** S. 2509 Tekoa St., Spokane, WA 99203, (509)747-3201; **BUS ADD:** W. 418 Sprague Ave., Spokane, WA 99204, (509)624-2395.

CADY, William F.——**B:** Dec. 28, 1948, Lansing, MI, *Lic. Counselor of Ins.*, William F. Cady & Assoc., Fin. Planning; **PRIM RE ACT:** Consultant, Owner/Investor, Insuror; **SERVICES:** Fin. direction, leveraging, lending advice/assistance, tax planning; **PROFL AFFIL & HONORS:** Nat. Assn. of Life Underwriters; Fin. Planning Organization, Inc.; Organization of Fin. Planners, Inc., Licensed Counselor of Ins.; Reg. Rep., Nat. Assn. of Securities Dealers; **HOME ADD:** 106 Spicer St., Eaton Rapids, MI 48827, (517)663-2594; **BUS ADD:** Suite 304, 3721 W. Michigan Ave., Lansing, MI 48917, (517)323-2820.

CAFAGNA, Michael P.——**B:** July 26, 1943, Detroit, MI, *Pres.*, Square One, Inc.; **PRIM RE ACT:** Broker, Syndicator, Consultant, Developer, Property Manager, Owner/Investor; **SERVICES:** Investment counseling, devel., synd.; **REP CLIENTS:** Indiv. and Instnl. investors; **PREV EMPLOY:** T. L. Fin., Inc.; **PROFL AFFIL & HONORS:** BCA; ABC; S.D. Bd. of Realtors; CAR; NAR; **HOME ADD:** 14137 Los Nietos Ave., Poway, CA 92064, (714)486-3142; **BUS ADD:** 8950 Villa La Jolla Dr. 2172, La Jolla, CA 92037, (714)452-5710.

CAFFALL, Thomas A., Jr.——**B:** Dec. 25, 1941, Rio Hondo, TX, *Pres.*, The Last Design Shop Architects; **PRIM RE ACT:** Architect; **OTHER RE ACT:** Bldg. Const.; **SERVICES:** Architectural, Planning; **REP CLIENTS:** Sororities, Investors, etc.; **PREV EMPLOY:** Andres Caffall Architects, Dallas, TX; **PROFL AFFIL & HONORS:** AIA, Sec.-Brazos Chap.; **EDUC:** BArch, 1966, TX Tech. Univ.; **OTHER ACT & HONORS:** Optimist Intl.; March of Dimes Bd.; C of C; Brian Hist. Landmark Commn.; **HOME ADD:** 2509 Whispering Oaks, Bryan, TX, (213)779-5596; **BUS ADD:** 1735 Briarcrest #214, Bryan, TX 77801, (713)822-7818.

CAFFEY, H. Clayton——**B:** Apr. 13, 1926, Brownwood, TX, *Owner*, H. Clayton Caffey, RE Appraiser; **PRIM RE ACT:** Consultant, Appraiser; **SERVICES:** Evaluate Real Prop.; **REP CLIENTS:** Republic Natl. Bank of Dallas; Natl. Farm Life Ins. Co., Fort Worth; Southwestern Bell; **PREV EMPLOY:** Mutual S & L Assn. (now United Savings of TX), Fort Worth, TX; **PROFL AFFIL & HONORS:** Soc. of RE Appraisers, Intl. Inst. of Valuers, Intl. Org. of RE Appraisers, Natl. Assn. of Review Appraisers, Amer. Assn. of Certified Appraisers, Assn. of Governmental Appraisers, SRA, SCV, ICA, CRA, CA-S, SGA; **EDUC:** 1946-1949, Public School Admin. and Econs., Daniel Baker Coll., Brownwood, Tx.; **MIL SERV:** US Army, 1944-1946; 1950-1952, Sgt. 1st Class; **OTHER ACT & HONORS:** Bowie High School Dad's Club and the Band Booster Club; **HOME ADD:** 4405 Kingwick Dr., Arlington, TX 76016, (817)451-4959; **BUS ADD:** 2401 Garden Park Ct., Arlington, TX 76013, (817)461-9713.

CAFRITZ, James E.——**B:** Jan. 5, 1930, Wash., D.C., *Pres.*, James Cafritz, Inc.; **PRIM RE ACT:** Developer, Builder, Owner/Investor; **SERVICES:** Prov. Bldg. Single Family Homes & Townhouses and PUD's; **PROFL AFFIL & HONORS:** NAHB, SMHBA, ULI, Former Bd. of Dir. SMHBA; **EDUC:** BS, 1952, Econ., IN Univ.; **MIL SERV:** US Army PRC 1952-1955; **OTHER ACT & HONORS:** Former Bd. of Dir. Washington Hebrew Congregation; **HOME ADD:** 3225 Pooks Hill Rd., Bethesda, MD 20814, (301)530-6575; **BUS ADD:** 1010 Rockville Pike, Rockville, MD 20852, (301)424-3550.

CAGENELLO, Bruce H.——**B:** Nov. 15, 1937, Hartford, CT, *Exec. V.P.*, Westledge Assoc., Inc.; **PRIM RE ACT:** Broker, Instructor, Developer; **SERVICES:** Total relocation services; residential & comm'l. RE brokerage; **REP CLIENTS:** Relocation mgmt. (third party) companies; builders and dev.; indiv. & families; corp.; **PREV EMPLOY:** Phoenix Mutual Life Ins. Co., Mgr. 1961-1968; **PROFL AFFIL & HONORS:** Dir. & immediate past Pres., Greater Hartford Multiple List, svc; Dir. 1st V.P. & incoming Pres., Greater Hartford Bd. of Realtors; Dir., Conn. Assn. Realtors; Tr. Conn. Realtors Pol. Action Comm.; Member 3 other bds & NAR, CRS; GRI; Fortune Master Trainer; **EDUC:** BA, 1960, Gov./Econ., Univ. of CT; **OTHER ACT & HONORS:** J.P., State of CT, 1973 - pres.; Dir., Univ. of Htfd. Assoc.; Republican Town Comm.; Rotary Club; **HOME ADD:** West Simsbury, 14 Pondside La., CT 06070, (203)658-6038; **BUS ADD:** 700 Hopmeadow St., Simsbury, CT 06070, (203)651-3741.

CAGLE, J. Douglas——*Pres.*, Cagle's Inc.; **PRIM RE ACT:** Property Manager; **BUS ADD:** 1155 Hammond Dr., NE, Ste. 3000, Atlanta, GA 30328, (404)394-8223.*

CAGNEY, Joseph B.——**B:** Oct. 15, 1945, Chicago, IL, *Atty.*, Law offices of Nicholas Goschi; **PRIM RE ACT:** Attorney; **SERVICES:** Tax counseling, estate planning; **REP CLIENTS:** Indiv. and small bus. corps.; **PREV EMPLOY:** IRS; **PROFL AFFIL & HONORS:** ABA,

Member Section on Real Prop., Probate and Trust, Member Section on Taxation, Chicago Bar Assn., Member Comm. on Fed. Taxation: AICPA, CPA, IL, 1971; **EDUC:** BBA, 1967, Acctg., Univ. of WI; **GRAD EDUC:** JD - LLM, 1975-1981, Tax Law, Loyola Univ. - John Marshall Law Sch.; **MIL SERV:** US Army, 1968-1970, 1st Lt., Bronze Star, Vietnamese Service Ribbon, Vietnamese Campaign Ribbon, Combat Infantryman's Badge; **HOME ADD:** 28 S. Mitchell, Arlington Heights, IL 60005, (312)253-8415; **BUS ADD:** 135 S. LaSalle St., Suite 1616, Chicago, IL 60603, (312)641-3070.

CAHILL, Gerald——**B:** July 12, 1944, San Francisco, CA, *Treas.*, Cahill Construction Co., Inc.; **PRIM RE ACT:** Builder, Owner/Investor, Property Manager; **SERVICES:** Construction, devel., prop. mgmt.; **REP CLIENTS:** Hilton Hotels, CA Casualty, Tishman Realty, Bank of Amer., Wells Fargo Bank; **PREV EMPLOY:** Arthur Young & Co.; **PROFL AFFIL & HONORS:** AICPA; AGC, CPA, State of CA; **EDUC:** BA, 1966, Stanford; **GRAD EDUC:** MBA, 1968, Stanford; **BUS ADD:** 425 California St., San Francisco, CA 94104, (415)986-0600.

CAIN, George E.——**B:** Aug. 16, 1924, Woodland, CA, *Pres., CAINCO, Inc.*, Pres., Fairview Farms, Inc.; **PRIM RE ACT:** Developer, Owner/Investor; **OTHER RE ACT:** Farmer; **SERVICES:** Development of agricultural and commercial properties; **REP CLIENTS:** Myself on commercial and some agricultural. Non farmers who own agricultural land in other cases; **PREV EMPLOY:** Real property appraiser, CA State Bd. of Equalization (many years ago); **PROFL AFFIL & HONORS:** Profl. Farmers, Farm Bureau; **EDUC:** BS, 1950, Agricultural Econ., Univ. of CA, Berkeley, CA; **EDUC HONORS:** Alpha Zeta Honor Society; **MIL SERV:** USN, Y2c, Overseas Ribbon World War II; **OTHER ACT & HONORS:** Maxwell Unified School Trustee, USDA Rice Advisory Committee; Kiwanis; Elks; American Legion; **HOME ADD:** PO Box 278, Maxwell, CA 95955, (916)438-2494; **BUS ADD:** Box 298, Fairview Rd., Maxwell, CA 95955, (916)438-2577.

CAIRNES, William D.——**B:** May 16, 1914, Baltimore, MD, *VP*, Century 21, Chuck Willis & Associates, Inc., Chief Comml./Investment Div.; **PRIM RE ACT:** Broker, Instructor; **SERVICES:** Buying, selling, managing, counseling, exchanging; **PREV EMPLOY:** RE salesman & broker since 1962; **PROFL AFFIL & HONORS:** FL RE Exchangors; INTEREX; Brevard RE Exchange; NAR, GRI; **EDUC:** BS, 1936, Mil. Sci., U.S. Mil. Acad., West Point, NY; **GRAD EDUC:** MEd, 1969, Community Coll., Univ. of FL, Gainesville, FL; **MIL SERV:** USAF; Col.; **HOME ADD:** 432 St. George Court, Satellite Beach, FL 32937, (305)777-2819; **BUS ADD:** 1110 Highway A1A, Satellite Beach, FL 32937, (305)777-1177.

CALABRESE, Charles——**B:** Nov. 27, 1952, Springfield, MA, *Owner*, Calabrese Const. Co.; **PRIM RE ACT:** Developer, Builder; **PROFL AFFIL & HONORS:** Nat. Assoc. of Home Builders; **EDUC:** BS, 1977, Bus., Amer. Intl. Coll., Springfield, MA; **HOME ADD:** 10 Woodside Dr., Agawam, MA 01001, (413)786-4304; **BUS ADD:** 10 Woodside Dr., Agawam, MA 01001, (413)786-2412.

CALAMARI, Daniel L.——**B:** Apr. 25, 1948, New Orleans, LA, *Partner*, Henry A. Calamari's Sons Realtors; **PRIM RE ACT:** Broker, Appraiser, Owner/Investor; **PROFL AFFIL & HONORS:** NAR, LA Realtors Assn., RE Bd. of New Orleans, Nat. Assn. of RE Appraisers, Cert. RE Appraiser by the Nat. Assn. of RE Appraisers, RE Broker issued by the LA RE Commn.; **MIL SERV:** Air National Guard, E-5; **HOME ADD:** 3277 Arbor Dr., Slidell, LA 70458, (504)643-1741; **BUS ADD:** 4948 Chef Menteur Hwy., Suite 310, New Orleans, LA 70126, (504)944-5531.

CALANDRA, Fred M.——*Pres.*, F&S Enterprises; **PRIM RE ACT:** Developer, Builder, Owner/Investor, Property Manager; **PREV EMPLOY:** In Bus. 25+ years; **BUS ADD:** 80 Sugg Road, Buffalo, NY 14225, (716)632-4445.

CALARESE, Roger V.——**B:** Oct. 16, 1948, Milford, MA 01757, *Principal*, W. Central St. Dev., Rico's Supermarkets, Inc.; **PRIM RE ACT:** Broker, Developer, Owner/Investor; **PROFL AFFIL & HONORS:** ICSC; **EDUC:** BA, 1971, Acctg., Bentley Coll.; **HOME ADD:** 57 Blackstone St., Mendon, MA 01756, (617)478-0097, **BUS ADD:** 208 Main St., Milford, MA 01757, (617)478-3700.

CALDEIRA, J. Leonard——**B:** Sept. 7, 1944, Lowell, MA, *VP*, Lasalle Partners Inc., Acreage Group; **PRIM RE ACT:** Broker; **SERVICES:** Land sales, marketing and devel.; **REP CLIENTS:** US Gypsum Co., Zurich Insurance Co., 1C Indus., Rexnord Inc., Bankers Trust Co. of NY National Blvd. Bank, Indiv. and local devel.; **PREV EMPLOY:** Asst. VP, Cushman & Wakefield Inc., Chicago (1971-1976) and Wm. A. White & Sons, New York, NY (1969-1971); **PROFL AFFIL & HONORS:** Chicago RE Bd., National and IL Assn. of Realtors; **EDUC:** BA, 1966, Govt., Univ. of MA; **MIL SERV:** US Army, Capt., Bronze Star; **OTHER ACT & HONORS:** Bd. of Trustees, Village of W. Springs 1981-1984, Indianhead Racquet Club, Cubmaster Cub Scout Pack 65 in Western Springs, Officer Past and Present in Several Local Civic Groups; **HOME ADD:** 4333 Johnson Ave., Western Springs, IL 60558, (312)246-5829; **BUS ADD:** 208 S. Lasalle St., Chicago, IL 60604, (312)782-5800.

CALDWELL, Richard G.——**B:** Dec 20, 1946, Chicago, IL, *Partner*, Holland & Hart; **PRIM RE ACT:** Attorney; **SERVICES:** Conveyancing, leasing, lending, devel., condos, PUDs, zoning, subdiv.; **PREV EMPLOY:** US Army Engr. Command Europe, 1971-72, Tri-State Rgnl. Planning Commn. 1969, US Dept. HUD, 1967 and 1968; **PROFL AFFIL & HONORS:** Amer. Planning Assn., ABA (Denver, CO, and Nat.); adjunct prof., Univ. of Denver Coll. of Law; Faculty, CO Cont. Legal Educ.; ACLU; **EDUC:** BA, 1969, Phil., Arch., Cornell Univ.; **GRAD EDUC:** M. Rgnl. Planning/JD, 1970/1975, City & Regnl. Planning/Law, Cornell Univ./Harvard Law School; **EDUC HONORS:** Distinction in all subjects, Phi Beta Kappa, Cum Laude; **MIL SERV:** US Army, Spec/4, 1970-1972; **OTHER ACT & HONORS:** Dir. & Gen. Counsel (pro bono), Children's Museum of Denver; **HOME ADD:** 1925 Glencoe St., Denver, CO 80220, (303)388-8228; **BUS ADD:** PO Box 8749, Denver, CO 80201, (303)575-8113.

CALDWELL, Susan——*Mgr. Corp. RE*, Memorex Corp.; **PRIM RE ACT:** Property Manager; **BUS ADD:** San Tomas at Central Expressway, Santa Clara, CA 95052, (408)987-1000.*

CALDWELL, Ted——**B:** Mar. 1, 1945, Nashville, TN, *Pres.*, TCC Properties, Inc.; **PRIM RE ACT:** Owner/Investor, Syndicator; **OTHER RE ACT:** Redeveloper; **SERVICES:** To buy undervalued properties that need improvement; **PROFL AFFIL & HONORS:** Sacramento Apartment Assn.; **EDUC:** BS, 1969, Mktg., CA State Univ., Chico; **GRAD EDUC:** MBA, 1971, Mktg., CA State Univ., Chico; **MIL SERV:** US Army; **HOME ADD:** 1420 Gary Way, Sacramento, CA 95608, (916)485-7581; **BUS ADD:** 918 J Street, PO Box 13666, Sacramento, CA 95853, (916)443-6091.

CALECHMAN, Jeffrey Paul——**B:** Dec. 14, 1948, New Haven, CT, *Assoc. Broker*, Grubb and Ellis Co., Retail Mktg.; **PRIM RE ACT:** Broker; **PROFL AFFIL & HONORS:** NAR; **EDUC:** BA, 1970, Soc., Econ., Clark Univ.; **GRAD EDUC:** 1979, Fin., RE, Univ. of TX at Austin; **HOME ADD:** 1632 5th Ave. W., Seattle, WA 98119; **BUS ADD:** 2031 Third Ave., Seattle, WA 98119, (206)623-8901.

CALHOUN, Robert M.——**B:** Nov. 25, 1918, Bakersfield, CA, *Pres.*, Robert M. Calhoun & Associates, RE Investments; **PRIM RE ACT:** Broker, Consultant, Banker, Developer, Builder, Owner/Investor, Instructor, Property Manager, Syndicator, Real Estate Publisher; **PROFL AFFIL & HONORS:** Various realty bds., Arch. Comm., C of C, etc., Honorary Ph.D., Los Angeles Univ. of Arts & Scis.; Original Bd. of Govs., WAIF, Intl. Social Serv.; **EDUC:** Exten. Courses, 1936-1941, Bus. Admin./Psych., USC & UCLA; **MIL SERV:** USN; **OTHER ACT & HONORS:** Amer. Soc. of Profl. Consultants; Invited to be included in the next issues of Who's Who in the West and Who's Who in Training and Devel.; **HOME ADD:** 818 N. Doheny Dr., Penthouse Fl., Los Angeles, CA 90069, (213)273-3897; **BUS ADD:** 9701 Wilshire Blvd., Beverly Hills, CA 90212, (213)652-8527.

CALI, Angelo R.——**B:** June 16, 1915, Valdez, CO, *Partner*, Cali Associates; **PRIM RE ACT:** Consultant, Developer, Builder, Owner/Investor, Property Manager; **SERVICES:** Const., devel., mgmt. office bldgs and multi-family resid.; **PREV EMPLOY:** Const., 32 yrs.; **PROFL AFFIL & HONORS:** NJHB Assn.; Apt. House Council NJ; NJ & Nat. NAIOP; C of C, Union City. C of C, 6 times recipient of NJ 'New Good Neighbor' award; NAHB Nat. Merit Award for best comml. bldg.; **EDUC:** AB, 1936, Social Studies, Hist., Montclair State Coll.; **MIL SERV:** Mil. Int., 2nd Lt., 1942-45, Bronze Star & Battle Stars; **OTHER ACT & HONORS:** Dir., Adult Ed. Clifton NJ; Member, Adult Ed. Bd., S. Orange-Maplewood, NJ; Pres. Essex Cty. Mental Health Assn.; VP, NJ State Mental Health Assn.; Chmn. Bd. of Tr. Montclair State Coll. Devel. Bd.; Honorary Dr. of Laws - Montclair State Coll.; **HOME ADD:** 221 Montrose Ave., S. Orange, NJ 07097, (201)763-1521, **BUS ADD:** 11 Commerce Dr., Cranford, NJ 07016, (201)272-8000.

CALI, John J.——**B:** Aug. 8, 1918, CO, *Sr. Partner*, Cali Associates; **PRIM RE ACT:** Consultant, Developer, Builder, Owner/Investor, Property Manager; **OTHER RE ACT:** Prop. analysis and acquisition; devel. of more than 65 props. in more than 35 communities; **SERVICES:** Prop. mgmt., counseling prop., analysis & acquisition; **REP CLIENTS:** Indiv. and instnl. investors in comml. props.; **PREV EMPLOY:** Resid. Devel. 1948-70; Comml. & Resid. Investment Devel. 1960-present; **PROFL AFFIL & HONORS:** NJ Natl. NAIOP;

NAHB; NJ Home Builders Assn.; Assoc. US C of C; Union Cty. C of C; Apt. House Council NJ; NJ Office Builders Assn., 6 time recipient of NJ 'New Good Neighbor Award'; Recipient of NAHB Nat. Merit Award for best comml. bldg. in the Builders Choice Design & Planning awards program; Recipient Union Cty. Excellence Landscape/Arch. 1981; Recipient Graphic Design 1970; Outstanding Arch. Design and Site Devel. Union Cty. Planning Bd. 1970; **EDUC:** BA, 1941, Soc./Psych., IN Univ.; **GRAD EDUC:** MA, 1942, Soc./Bus. Psych., IN Univ.; **EDUC HONORS:** Alpha Kappa Delta (Honorary Soc. of Sociologists); **OTHER ACT & HONORS:** Lifetime member I.U. Alumni Assn.; Montclair Golf Club; Eagle Roc Court Club; Century Fitness Club; Bd. of Trs., Louis Braille Found. for Blind Musicians; Member NJ Meadowlands Cultural Ctr. Commn.; Active NJ Whole Theater Found.; Boys Town of Rome; Mental Health Assn. of NJ; **HOME ADD:** 61 Sutherland Rd., Montclair, NJ 07042, (201)746-3255; **BUS ADD:** 11 Commerce Dr., Cranford, NJ 07016, (201)272-8000.

CALKINS, Chet——B: Mar. 28, 1940, New Orleans, LA, *Pres.*, Homes by Calkins, Inc.; **PRIM RE ACT:** Builder, Owner/Investor, Property Manager; **SERVICES:** Construction of resid. and comml. condo., homes, and apts., owner and mgr. of apts.; **PROFL AFFIL & HONORS:** Homebuilders Assn. of Gr. Cincinnati, Cincinnati Apt. Assn., Bd. of Dirs. Cincinnati Homebuilders Assn.; **EDUC:** BS, 1963, Chemistry, LA State Univ.; **GRAD EDUC:** MBA, 1969, Mgmt., FL State Univ.; **EDUC HONORS:** Dean's List; **MIL SERV:** USMC, Capt., 19 Air Medals, Presidential Unit Citation, Vietnam Campaign; **OTHER ACT & HONORS:** VP, Fairchild Properties, Inc.; **HOME ADD:** 1982 Harrowgate, Fairfield, OH 45014, (513)829-5760; **BUS ADD:** 759 Wessel Dr., Fairfield, OH 45014, (513)868-9718.

CALKINS, Christopher——B: Feb. 25, 1946, Altadena, CA, *Partner*, Gray Cary Ames & Frye; **PRIM RE ACT:** Attorney; **SERVICES:** Comml. & resid. RE matters; **PROFL AFFIL & HONORS:** San Diego, CA and Amer. Bar Assns. and Real Prop. Sections; **EDUC:** BA, 1967, English Lit., Occidental Coll.; **GRAD EDUC:** JD, 1973, UC Berkeley (Boalt Hall); **EDUC HONORS:** Order of the Coif; Assoc. Editor, CA Law Review; **MIL SERV:** USN, Lt., Navy Achievement Medal; Vietnam Services; **OTHER ACT & HONORS:** Tr., LaJolla Museum of Contemporary Art; **HOME ADD:** 1435 Guizot, San Diego, CA 92107, (714)224-9214; **BUS ADD:** 1200 Prospect #575, La Jolla, CA 92037, (714)454-9101.

CALKINS, Glen S.——B: July 26, 1946, Bridgeport, CT, *Rgnl. Mgr.*, Southern Pacific Development Co.; **PRIM RE ACT:** Broker, Developer, Owner/Investor, Property Manager; **OTHER RE ACT:** Activities, large scale and mixed use devel. office; comml. resid., hotel & indus.; **REP CLIENTS:** Bank of Amer., Security Pac., Hilton; **PROFL AFFIL & HONORS:** Nat. Assn. of Indus. and Office Parks, ULI; **EDUC:** BBA, 1968, Fin.; **GRAD EDUC:** MBA, 1972, Fin.; **MIL SERV:** US Army Res.; **HOME ADD:** Mill Valley, CA 94941; **BUS ADD:** One Market Plaza, San Francisco, CA 94105, (415)541-2321.

CALLAHAN, Dennis William——B: Oct. 29, 1947, San Francisco, CA, *Atty. at Law*, Self-employed practice of Law, Atwater, CA since 1973; **PRIM RE ACT:** Attorney; **SERVICES:** Legal consultation and litigation; **PROFL AFFIL & HONORS:** ABA (Real Property, Probate and Trust Law Sect.); CA State Bar Assn.; Merced Cty. Bar Assn., Who's Who in American Law (1st and 2nd Editions)-current edition; **EDUC:** AA, 1967, Bus. and Fin., Merced Coll.; BS, 1969, Bus., Fresno State Coll.; **GRAD EDUC:** JD, 1972, Law, Univ. of the Pac.; **OTHER ACT & HONORS:** Who's Who in Finance and Industry (21st Edition) current edition; Who's Who in California (1981-1982); **HOME ADD:** 2792 Glen Avenue, Merced, CA 95340, (209)358-6481; **BUS ADD:** 800 Bellevue Rd., Atwater, CA 95301, (209)358-6481.

CALLAHAN, Gerald W.——*VP Legal Counsel*, Quaker State Oil Refining Corp.; **PRIM RE ACT:** Attorney; **BUS ADD:** Quaker State Bldg., 255 Elm St., Oil City, PA 16301, (814)676-0661.*

CALLAHAN, James J., III——B: Mar. 3, 1925, Worcester, MA, *Corp. Sec.*, 195 Broadway Corp, Subs. of AT&T; **PRIM RE ACT:** Engineer, Owner/Investor, Property Manager; **OTHER RE ACT:** RE Subs. for AT&T Corp. Depts.; Lesee; Owner; **SERVICES:** RE Ownership and mgmt.; **REP CLIENTS:** AT&T and Other Bell System Cos. Some Comml. Tenants in Office Bldgs.; **PREV EMPLOY:** Western Electric Co., Asst. Mgr. in Plant Design and Const. Div. 1957-1973; **PROFL AFFIL & HONORS:** NY RE Bd.; BOMA; Soc. of Real Prop. Administrators, Indus. Devel./Research Council, Profl. Engr. NY, NJ, GA, VA, WA, RPA; **EDUC:** BS, 1948, Engrg. Sci., Harvard Coll.; **EDUC HONORS:** Deans List; **MIL SERV:** USN, Lt., Campaign Ribbons, Atlantic Pacific Area, and Korea; **OTHER ACT & HONORS:** Bd. of Educationss Chatham, NJ 1965-1975+ Intl. Brotherhood of Magicians, Chatham Community Players Fairmount Ctry. Club, Chatham, NJ, Harvard Club, Knights of Columbus, Outstanding Leadership Award (Communication Sciences); Amer. Soc. Mechanical Engrs., May 1979; **HOME ADD:** 14 Parrott Mill Rd., Chatham, NJ 07928, (201)635-9748; **BUS ADD:** 195 Broadway Room 1720, New York, NY 10007, (212)393-4973.

CALLAHAN, John——B: Oct. 25, 1923, Independence, KS, *Atty.*; **PRIM RE ACT:** Attorney, Owner/Investor; **SERVICES:** All phases of RE law and brokerage for European investors; **PREV EMPLOY:** Owner Guarantee Title Co., Wichita, 1959-71; Asst. City Atty., Wichita, 1957-59; Law Clerk, KS Supreme Ct., 1949; **PROFL AFFIL & HONORS:** ABA; KS & Wichita Bars; **EDUC:** AB, 1948, KS Univ., Lawrence KS; **GRAD EDUC:** JD, 1949, KS Univ.; **MIL SERV:** US Army Infantry; DFC, Purple Heart; **OTHER ACT & HONORS:** Cty. Atty. Lakin, Kansas, 1950-54; Amer. Arbitration Assn.; Wichita Club; Rolling Hill Ctry. Club; **HOME ADD:** 330 S. Tyler, 618, Wichita, KS 67209, (316)722-5262; **BUS ADD:** 330 S. Tyler, 618, Wichita, KS 67209, (316)722-5262.

CALLAHAN, John H.——B: Oct 6, 1936, Beauty, KY, *VP, Sales Mgr.*, Gundaker Realtors, Better Homes & Gardens; **PRIM RE ACT:** Broker, Instructor, Consultant, Appraiser, Owner/Investor; **PROFL AFFIL & HONORS:** NAR; WCK, CRB; GRI; Candidate Member NAIFA; AACA; **MIL SERV:** USAF; A/1c; **HOME ADD:** 27 Crown Manor Dr., St. Louis, MO 63017, (314)227-7044; **BUS ADD:** 1284 Clayton Rd., St. Louis, MO 63011, (314)391-1122.

CALLANTINE, Douglas S.——B: Jan. 4, 1952, Hammond, IN, *Sr. Rep., 1976 to present*, The Northwestern Mutual Life Ins. Co., RE Investment Dept.; **PRIM RE ACT:** Lender; **PREV EMPLOY:** 1974-1976 Nat. Homes Acceptance Corp., Washington, DC, Asst. Mgr. Wash. Office, Resid. Mort. Banker; **EDUC:** BS, 1974, Fin. & Mktg. & Mgmt., Purdue Univ.; **GRAD EDUC:** MBA, 1078, Fin., Southern IL Univ.; **HOME ADD:** 2032 Horace Ave., Abington, PA 19001, (215)884-3460; **BUS ADD:** GSB Bldg., Ste. 501, One Belmont Ave., Bala Cynwyd, PA 19004, (215)667-2907.

CALLAWAY, Robert J.——B: Dec. 13, 1936, W Palm Beach, FL, *Pres.*, Callaway & Price, Inc.; **PRIM RE ACT:** Broker, Appraiser, Assessor, Property Manager; **PROFL AFFIL & HONORS:** AIREA, W. Palm Beach Bd. of Realtors, Soc. of RE Appraisers, MAI, SREA; **EDUC:** BS, 1957, Bus. Admin., Acctg., GA Coll.; **MIL SERV:** US Army, Capt.; **OTHER ACT & HONORS:** Advisory Bd., 1st Amer. Bank of Palm Beach Cty; **HOME ADD:** 301 Pine St., W Palm Beach, FL 33407, (305)832-3225; **BUS ADD:** 1639 Forum Pl., Suite 5, W. Palm Beach, FL 33401, (305)686-0333.

CALLENDER, Robert L.——B: Aug. 31, 1930, Scranton, PA, *VChmn./CFO*, Fairfield Communities, Inc.; **PRIM RE ACT:** Developer, Builder, Owner/Investor, Property Manager, Syndicator; **OTHER RE ACT:** Large timeshare devel.; **PROFL AFFIL & HONORS:** Fin. Exec. Inst.; **EDUC:** AB, 1953, Econ. & Hist., Dartmouth Coll.; **GRAD EDUC:** MBA, 1958, Fin., Amos Tuck School, Dartmouth Coll.; **MIL SERV:** USN, Lt.; **HOME ADD:** 2805 Foxcroft Sq., Little Rock, AR 72207, (501)225-8530; **BUS ADD:** P O Box 3375, Little Rock, AR 72203, (501)664-6000.

CALLISON, Anthony——B: May 21, 1932, Seattle, WA, *Pres.*, The Callison Partnership P.S.; **PRIM RE ACT:** Architect; **SERVICES:** arch., programming, interiors, space plang.; **PREV EMPLOY:** 1957-60 Lamont and Fey; **PROFL AFFIL & HONORS:** AIA Corp. Mbr.; ICSC, Assoc. Mbr.; ULI; Assoc. of Western Hosp.; **EDUC:** BArch, 1956, Arch, Univ. of Washington; **OTHER ACT & HONORS:** Seattle C of C, Seattle Econ. Dev. Council; Seattle Downtown Dev. Assoc.; Municipal League; United Way of Seattle; Seattle Rotary; **HOME ADD:** 4550 W. Laurel Dr., N.E., Seattle, WA 98105, (206)527-0955; **BUS ADD:** 1310 Ward St., Seattle, WA 98109, (206)623-4646.

CALLISON, James L.——B: May 12, 1949, Denver, CO, *Asst. VP*, VNB Mort. Corp., Resid. New Bus.; **PRIM RE ACT:** Lender; **SERVICES:** Originator, Underwriter, closing of resid. permanent mort. loans; **REP CLIENTS:** Devels., investors, builders, RE brokers; **PROFL AFFIL & HONORS:** Young Mort. Bankers Comm. of Washington, DC 1975-present, Chmn. 1980; **EDUC:** BA, 1971, Indus. Psych., Randolph-Macon Coll., Ashland, VA; **HOME ADD:** 2539 Oakhampton Place, Herndon, VA 22071, (703)860-4852; **BUS ADD:** 467 N. Washington St., Falls Church, VA 22046, (703)534-6600.

CALLNIN, William J.——B: Apr. 16, 1934, Buffalo, NY, *Sr. Principal*, Pannell Kerr Forster, Mgmt. Advisory Serv.; **OTHER RE ACT:** Mgmt. Consultant; **SERVICES:** Market Research, Fin. Planning, Investment & Operational Counseling; **REP CLIENTS:** Investors, Devel. & Operators of Hotel, Resort, Casino, Comml. & Res. Props.; **PREV EMPLOY:** 10 yrs. Consulting; 2 yrs. Casino - Hotel Operations, VP; **PROFL AFFIL & HONORS:** Amer. Hotel & Motel Assn.; Hotel - Casino Comm.; ULI, Pres., Cornell Soc. of Hotelmen; **EDUC:** BS,

Hotel Admin., 1956, Fin. Mgmt./Mktg., Sch. of Hotel Admin., Cornell Univ.; **EDUC HONORS:** Dean's List; **MIL SERV:** USN, Lt. Comdr.; **HOME ADD:** 1960 Liverpool Ave., Egg Harbor, NJ 08215, (609)965-0646; **BUS ADD:** 1325 Boardwalk, Atlantic City, NJ 08401, (609)348-9008.

CALNAN, Eugene M.——*Pres.*, Federal Home Loan Bank of Pittsburgh; **PRIM RE ACT:** Banker; **BUS ADD:** 11 Stanwix St., 4th Fl. Gateway Center, Pittsburgh, PA 15222, (412)288-3400.*

CALVIN, Roy E.——**B:** June 15, 1920, Smith Center, KS, *Pres.*, Calvin, Jelinek & Gegen Architects, PA; **PRIM RE ACT:** Consultant, Architect; **SERVICES:** Arch., Space planning, site studies, feasibility; **REP CLIENTS:** Comml., instnl., educational, indus. and multifamily resid. bldg. owners; **PROFL AFFIL & HONORS:** KS Soc. of Arch., AIA; Soc. of Arch. Historians, Past Pres., KS Soc. of Arch.; **EDUC:** BArch, 1942, Arch., Washington Univ. (St. Louis); **GRAD EDUC:** In process, Urban Affairs, Wichita State Univ.; **EDUC HONORS:** Frederic Joseph Widman Prize; **MIL SERV:** USN, AETM 3/C; **HOME ADD:** 7700 E. 13th, no. 29, Wichita, KS 67206, (316)681-3195; **BUS ADD:** Sutton Pl., 209 E. William, Wichita, KS 67202, (316)263-2221.

CALWIL, Warren W.——**B:** Aug. 16, 1930, Vienna, Austria, *Arch.*, Warren W. Calwil, Arch.; **PRIM RE ACT:** Architect; **PROFL AFFIL & HONORS:** AIA, NYS/AA; **EDUC:** BA, BArch., 1955, Arch., Columbia Coll., Columbia School of Arch.; **GRAD EDUC:** MArch., 1955, Arch., Col. Univ., School of Arch.; **BUS ADD:** 505 E. 79th St., NYC, NY 10021, (212)988-4636.

CAMBIANO, Mark S.——**B:** Aug. 1, 1955, Kansas City, MO, *Atty.*, Mark S. Cambiano, P.A.; **PRIM RE ACT:** Consultant, Attorney, Owner/Investor; **PROFL AFFIL & HONORS:** ABA; AR Bar Assn. of Trial Lawyers of Amer.; **EDUC:** BS, 1977, Law, Univ. of Central AR; **GRAD EDUC:** JD, 1979, General Law, Univ. of AR at Little Rock; **EDUC HONORS:** Dean's List; **HOME ADD:** 300 S. Div., Morrilton, AR 72110, (501)354-3747; **BUS ADD:** 108 S. Moose St., Morrilton, AR 72110, (501)354-0128.

CAMERON, Cindy Lou——**B:** Dec. 7, 1930, Wichita, KS, *Pres.*, Billion $$$ Enterprises, Inc.; **PRIM RE ACT:** Property Manager, Syndicator; **OTHER RE ACT:** Rehab. & Renovation, Tax Specialist, Financial Planners, Investments; **SERVICES:** Acquisitions & renovations in income props., and devel. of small group synd.; Financial Backers; **REP CLIENTS:** Indiv. & profl. investors in income prop.; Joint Ventures; **PREV EMPLOY:** Burreson Investment Co., Inc., Russ Vincent Realty Co., Allstate, & Owner of Cincy Cameron Insurance Service; **PROFL AFFIL & HONORS:** Beverly Hills C of C, Apt. Assn. of Los Angeles Cty., 1969 Charger Award for Leadership, Allstate Honor Ring, NASD License; **EDUC:** School of Life Coll., 1960; **EDUC HONORS:** Dean's List (top 10%); **OTHER ACT & HONORS:** Intl. Club Elite, Amer. Security Council, Other bus. address: PO Box 1803, Beverly Hills, CA 90213; **HOME ADD:** P O Box 1803, Beverly Hills, CA 90213; **BUS ADD:** 6318 Yucca St., Hollywood, CA 90028, (213)463-6500.

CAMERON, Donald D.——**B:** Sept. 16, 1919, Tulsa, OK, *Atty.*, Houston & Klein, Inc.; **PRIM RE ACT:** Attorney; **SERVICES:** RE Title Examination; **REP CLIENTS:** Sooner Federal Savings and Loan Assn.; **PREV EMPLOY:** Asst. Cty. Atty., Judge of the Court of Common Pleas; **PROFL AFFIL & HONORS:** ABA, OK Bar Assn., Tulsa Cty. Bar Assn., Amer. Judicature Soc.; **EDUC:** BS, Commerce, 1946, Gen. Bus., OK State Univ.; **GRAD EDUC:** MS, Econs., 1948, Econ. Theory, OK State Univ.; LLB, 1951, Law, Univ. of OK; **EDUC HONORS:** Phi Eta Sigma, Phi Kappa Phi; **MIL SERV:** US Army, Sgt.; **OTHER ACT & HONORS:** Sigma Phi Epsilon, Alpha Kappa Psi, Christian Church (Disciples of Christ); **HOME ADD:** 5849 S. Irvington, Tulsa, OK 74135, (918)494-9728; **BUS ADD:** Box 2967, Tulsa, OK 74103, (918)583-2131.

CAMERON, Donald R.——**B:** July 8, 1947, Jefferson City, TN, *Pres.*, Cameron, Downing & Co.; **PRIM RE ACT:** Broker, Consultant, Developer, Owner/Investor, Property Manager, Syndicator; **SERVICES:** Devel., acquisition and synd. of comml. prop., prop. mgmt., investment counseling, comml. RE brokerage; **REP CLIENTS:** Lenders, indivs. and instnl. investors in comml. RE props.; **PREV EMPLOY:** Pres. Southeastern Props. Inc.; VP Fin., Publix Oil Co., Inc.; present bus. affiliations: Pres. Cameron, Downing & Co., Pres. The Pegasus Corp., Partner Var RE partnerships; **PROFL AFFIL & HONORS:** TN Hotel Motol Assn., TN Soc. of Farm Mgrs. and Rural Appraisers, Amer. Soc. of Farm. Mgrs. and Rural Appraisers, Knoxville Apt. Council of Home Builders Assn. of Gr. Knoxville, Listed in Who's Who in the South and Southeast; **EDUC:** BS, 1975, Agric. Mech., Agric. Econ., Univ. of TN, Knoxville, TN; **GRAD EDUC:** MBA, 1976, RE & Urban Devel., Univ. of TN, Knoxville, TN; **EDUC HONORS:** Grad. with Honors; **MIL SERV:** USA, E-5, 1966-69; **HOME ADD:** Rt. 2, White Pine, TN 37890, (615)397-2467; **BUS ADD:** 2510 UAB Plaza, Knoxville, TN 37929, (615)525-5100.

CAMERON, Douglas H.——**B:** June 14, 1949, Chicago, IL, *VP*, JMB Realty Corp., Prop. Sales; **PRIM RE ACT:** Owner/Investor, Syndicator; **SERVICES:** Purchase & disposition of props. held by ltd. partnerships; **REP CLIENTS:** Instnl. investors and substantial indivs.; **PREV EMPLOY:** The Northern Trust Bank, 1974-77; **EDUC:** BA, 1971, Phil., Claremont Men's Coll.; **GRAD EDUC:** MBA, 1974, Fin., Univ. of S CA; **EDUC HONORS:** Cum Laude; **HOME ADD:** 1335 Astor St., Chicago, IL 60610; **BUS ADD:** 875 N. Michigan Ave., Chicago, IL 60611, (312)440-4800.

CAMERUCI, Victor H.——*Mgr.*, New England Business Center Assoc.; **PRIM RE ACT:** Developer; **BUS ADD:** 768 South St., Suffield, CT 06078, (203)668-7333.*

CAMMARATA, Jerry, PhD——**B:** Mar. 14, 1947, Staten Island, NY, *Pres. & CEO*, American Image Maker, RE Div.; **PRIM RE ACT:** Consultant, Developer, Instructor, Property Manager, Syndicator; **SERVICES:** Prop. mgmt. instr. including bldg. design, occupational safety & fire safety programs; planning and consultation on devel. & design for the handicapped & elderly; devel. oversea participation in comml. & resid. RE programs; provide public relations & image programs for RE props.; **REP CLIENTS:** Health related facilities and instns., lenders (overseas), indivls. and instl. investors in resid. & comml. props.; **PREV EMPLOY:** Lo Russo Realty, 1968-1979; Housing for the Disabled, UCP/NYS, 1979-1981; **EDUC:** BA, 1968, Communications, Hofstra Univ.; **GRAD EDUC:** MA, 1969, Communications, Hofstra Univ.; PhD, 1979, Communications, CA Western Univ.; **EDUC HONORS:** Dean's List, Sigma Pi; **OTHER ACT & HONORS:** Member, Community Bd., State Island; Member, Borough Pres., Council on Families; Member, White House Conf. on Families, Workplace Spec.; NY Press Club; Overseas Press Club; Health Systems Agency; Amer. Assn. of Univ. Professors; **BUS ADD:** Communication Towers, Suite PH, 185 Maryland Ave., Staten Island, NY 10305, (212)720-6400.

CAMMETT, Stuart H., Jr.——**B:** Jan. 27, 1931, Detroit, MI, *Sr. VP*, ABKO Prop. Inc.; **PRIM RE ACT:** Developer, Builder, Property Manager, Owner/Investor; **PROFL AFFIL & HONORS:** Past Chmn. of the Bd. (NACORE); **EDUC:** BA, 1952, Lib. Arts, Univ. of MI, Ann Arbor; **GRAD EDUC:** LLB, 1954, Law, Univ. of MI, Ann Arbor; **HOME ADD:** 8319 Overbrook, Wichita, KS 67206; **BUS ADD:** 4111 E 37th-N, PO Box 2236, Wichita, KS 67201, (316)832-5910.

CAMP, Ehney A., III——**B:** June 28, 1942, Birmingham, AL, *Pres.*, Camp & Co.; **PRIM RE ACT:** Broker, Developer, Property Manager; **OTHER RE ACT:** Mort. Banker; **SERVICES:** Mort. Banking; RE Sales, Mgmt., Dev.; **PREV EMPLOY:** The Rime Cos. (apt. Dev.); Cobbs, Allen and Hall Mort. Co., Inc., Birmingham, AL; **PROFL AFFIL & HONORS:** Birmingham Bd. of Realtors, MBAA and AL; **EDUC:** AB, 1964, Hist., Dartmouth Coll.; **GRAD EDUC:** Univ. of AL Law Sch.; **OTHER ACT & HONORS:** Bd. of Dir., United Way; Kiwanis Club of Birmingham - former Bd. Member.; **HOME ADD:** 3621 Rockhill Rd., Birmingham, AL 35223, (205)967-0140; **BUS ADD:** 3940 Montclair Rd., Ste. 502, Birmingham, AL 35213, (205)871-8146.

CAMP, R. Gounod, Sr.——**B:** Jan. 22, 1915, Northumberland, PA, *Pres., Atty. in Fact*, Bob Camp Agency Inc./AZ Growth Unltd. Assn., Inc.; **PRIM RE ACT:** Appraiser, Developer, Lender, Builder, Instructor, Property Manager; **OTHER RE ACT:** Exchangor; **SERVICES:** Appraising; **PREV EMPLOY:** Self, 41 yrs.; **PROFL AFFIL & HONORS:** Alumni, Univ. of MD, 1937; Past Nat. Dir. and State Pres., Profl. Ins. Agents; **EDUC:** AB, 1937, Acct./Fin., Univ. of MD; **GRAD EDUC:** Grad. Studies, 1952-1977, RE, Ins., Nat. Inst. of RE Brokers, Yavapai Coll.; **MIL SERV:** US Air Force, Flight Officer, Theatres-3; **OTHER ACT & HONORS:** Precinct Committeeman, 28 yrs.; Past Comdr., Amer. Legion, Prescott, AZ 6; Charter Member, Lions Club of Prescott, 1949; Charter Member, Optimist Club of Prescott, 1967; Comml. pilot MEL; **HOME ADD:** Rte. 3, Camp Bountiful, Prescott, AZ 86301, (602)445-5195; **BUS ADD:** RR 3, Camp Bountiful, Prescott, AZ 86301, (602)445-5195.

CAMPANELLA, Salvatore——*RE Mgr.*, Hoffmann-LaRoche Inc.; **PRIM RE ACT:** Property Manager; **BUS ADD:** 340 Kingsland, Nutley, NJ 07110, (201)235-5000.*

CAMPBELL, Arthur D.——**B:** Aug. 6, 1952, Philadelphia, PA, *Director Property Management and Commercial-Investment Divisions*, HH&B Realtors, Prop. Mgmt. and Comml.-Investment; **PRIM RE ACT:** Consultant, Appraiser, Owner/Investor, Instructor, Property Manager, Insuror; **OTHER RE ACT:** Founder and Partner of Prop. Services Co.;

SERVICES: Prop. mgmt., site selection, investment counseling, and condo. conversions; **REP CLIENTS:** Indiv. and inst. investors and owners; lessees of comml. space; comml. and resid. devels.; **PREV EMPLOY:** Prop. Mgmt., Inc., Federated Home & Mortgage Co.; **PROFL AFFIL & HONORS:** CCIM, IREM, Centre County Bd. of Realtors, State Coll. Area C of C, State Coll. Apt. Onwer & Mgrs.; **EDUC:** BS, 1975, Personnel Mgmt., PA State Univ.; **OTHER ACT & HONORS:** Hershey Country Club, Advanced Coursework encompassing appraisal, mgmt. of resid. prop., mgmt. of investments, CPM Candidate; **HOME ADD:** 430 N. 21st St., Camp Hill, PA 17011; **BUS ADD:** 5004 Lenker St., Mechanicsburg, PA 17055, (717)737-8080.

CAMPBELL, Caroline L.——**B:** Feb. 3, 1921, Richmond, VA, *Pres/Broker*, Caroline Campbell, Inc.; **PRIM RE ACT:** Broker, Consultant, Owner/Investor, Property Manager; **SERVICES:** Brokerage, mgmt., consultant (resid.); **PREV EMPLOY:** Broker-owner of firm since 1947; **PROFL AFFIL & HONORS:** N. VA Bd. of Realtors, Exec. Club of N. VA Bd., Old Dominion CRB Chap. (CP); VA Assn. of Realtors, NAR, Pioneer Club, CRB, CRS, GRI; **EDUC:** 1940, Lib. Arts, Averett Coll., Danville, VA; Attended Univ. of Richmond & TC Williams School of Law at Univ. of Richmond; **HOME ADD:** 1409 Whitley Dr., Vienna, VA 22180, (703)759-5891; **BUS ADD:** 10121 Colvin Run Rd., Great Falls, VA 22066, (703)759-3700.

CAMPBELL, Dee——**B:** Feb. 14, 1948, El Dorado, AR, *Primary Broker & Sales Agent*, Campbell Realty Co.; **PRIM RE ACT:** Broker, Consultant, Owner/Investor, Instructor, Property Manager; **SERVICES:** Investment counseling, mkt. analysis, sales instructions; **PREV EMPLOY:** Sec. for El Dorado RE and Ins. Co. 1966-67; Dept. of Fin. & Admin. of AR 1971-77; **PROFL AFFIL & HONORS:** LR/NLR Bd. of Realtors; Jacksonville RE Council, 1979 Million Dollar Club; **EDUC:** Broadway Sch. of RE 1978; **OTHER ACT & HONORS:** Chap. 520, Order or the Eastern Stars, Jacksonville; C of C; **HOME ADD:** 3207 T.P. White Dr., Jacksonville, AR 72076, (501)982-3645; **BUS ADD:** 215 Marshall Rd., Jacksonville, AR 72076, (501)982-7554.

CAMPBELL, Donald E.——**B:** Jan. 25, 1945, Long Beach, CA, *Pres.*, Goodman Props., The Goodman Co.; **PRIM RE ACT:** Consultant, Developer, Owner/Investor, Property Manager; **SERVICES:** Site selection, zoning, planning, devel., constr., leasing and mgmt.; **REP CLIENTS:** Lenders, private and comml. investors; **PREV EMPLOY:** VP & Dir. of Leasing, Gen. Growth Devel. Corp., Des Moines, IA; **PROFL AFFIL & HONORS:** BOMA, ICSC, NACORE, CSM (1973); **EDUC:** BS, 1967, Mktg., Drake Univ.; **MIL SERV:** USA, SFC; **HOME ADD:** 1135 Bellair Dr., Allentown, PA 18103, (215)820-9074; **BUS ADD:** 2030 Tilghman St., PO Box 2523, Allentown, PA 18001, (215)434-4444.

CAMPBELL, Donna Gene——**B:** June 5, 1952, New Castle, IN, *Controller*, Graves, Inc.; **PRIM RE ACT:** Developer, Builder, Property Manager; **SERVICES:** Devel. fin. and synd. of apt. props., major emphiasis HUD-ins. mort. props.; **REP CLIENTS:** Lenders and indiv. investors in tax shelter props.; **PREV EMPLOY:** Sr. Staff auditor, Geo. S. Olive & Co., CPA; **PROFL AFFIL & HONORS:** AICPA, IACPA; **EDUC:** BS, 1975, Acctg., Ball State Univ., Muncie, IN; **GRAD EDUC:** presently enrolled, Bus. Law, IN Univ. School of Law, Indianapolis; **EDUC HONORS:** Grad. Cum Laude; **HOME ADD:** RRI Box 21A, Charlottesivlle, IN 46117, (317)345-7136; **BUS ADD:** 3010 E 56th St., PO Box 20463, Indianapolis, IN 46220, (317)257-4103.

CAMPBELL, Gregory S.——**B:** May 5, 1948, *VP Portfolio Mgmt.*, Richard Ellis, Inc.; **PRIM RE ACT:** Consultant, Developer, Property Manager; **SERVICES:** RE investment counselors; **REP CLIENTS:** Instnl. investors in comml. props.; **PREV EMPLOY:** J. Emil Anderson; **PROFL AFFIL & HONORS:** ICSC, BOMA, IREM, CPM; **EDUC:** BS, 1970, Econ., Wheaton Coll., Wheaton, IL; **OTHER ACT & HONORS:** Chmn. of Honey Rock Camp, Wheaton Youth Outreach Bd.; **HOME ADD:** 407 Lorraine Rd, Wheaton, IL 60187, (312)653-4748; **BUS ADD:** 200 E Randolph Dr., Suite 6545, Chicago, IL 60601, (312)861-1105.

CAMPBELL, Homer D.——**B:** Jan. 11, 1918, Garden City, KS, *Pres.*, First Choice RE, Inc.; **PRIM RE ACT:** Broker, Appraiser; **SERVICES:** RE sales and appraisals; **REP CLIENTS:** Bank of St. Louis, Republic Nat. Bank of Dallas, MGIC, Merill-Lynch; **PROFL AFFIL & HONORS:** SREA, Candidate for MAI, AIREA, SRPA; **EDUC:** AB, 1939, Soc. Sci, Baker Univ, Baldwin, KS; **OTHER ACT & HONORS:** Optimist Club of Garden City, Past Pres. and Lt Gov.; **HOME ADD:** 806 Davis St, Garden City, KS 67846, (316)275-5569; **BUS ADD:** 202 W Pine St., PO Box 856, Garden City, KS 67846, (316)275-7340.

CAMPBELL, J. Thomas——**B:** Feb. 19, 1940, Michigan City, IN, *Dir PBC*, Gen. Devel. Corp., Homesite Devel.; **PRIM RE ACT:** Broker, Developer, Builder, Owner/Investor; **OTHER RE ACT:** Fin.; **SERVICES:** Consulting, cash flow analysis; **REP CLIENTS:** CBC Electronics, Trans Circuits; **PREV EMPLOY:** United Tech. Pratt & Whitney Div., 1965-71; **PROFL AFFIL & HONORS:** NARA; Sr. Member, Amer. RE & Urban Econ. Assn.; Nat. Assn. of Bus. Econ., Who's Who in the S & SW, 1979; **EDUC:** BS, 1962, Econ., Univ. of Bridgeport; **GRAD EDUC:** MBA, 1969, Fin. Analysis, Univ. of Hartford; **EDUC HONORS:** Regina C. Winter Prize for Econ, Research; **OTHER ACT & HONORS:** Treas. of Student Council; **HOME ADD:** 8415 SW 107th Ave., #268, Miami, FL 33173, (305)279-3470; **BUS ADD:** 1111 S Bayshore Dr., Miami, FL 33131, (305)350-1421.

CAMPBELL, John W.——**B:** Oct. 31, 1954, Shreveport, LA, Oscar Cloyd, Inc., Comml. Investment; **PRIM RE ACT:** Broker, Consultant, Property Manager, Syndicator; **SERVICES:** Synd. sponsor, investment consultant, prop. mgr.; **REP CLIENTS:** Indiv. and instnl. investors; **PREV EMPLOY:** Sales mgr., Maj. RE Brokerage Firm; **PROFL AFFIL & HONORS:** RESSI, GRI; **OTHER ACT & HONORS:** Sales and Mktg. Execs., Intl.; Rotary Intl.; **BUS ADD:** 2555 Flournoy-Lucas Rd., Shreveport, LA 71110, (318)687-2766.

CAMPBELL, Kenneth D.——**B:** Jan. 2, 1930, Grove City, PA, *Pres./Partner, Campbell & Dillmeier*, Audit Investments, Inc.; **PRIM RE ACT:** Real Estate Publisher; **OTHER RE ACT:** RE Investment banking, Publishing; **SERVICES:** Advisory and mgmt. servs. to RE investors; fin. advice on mergers, acquisitions and fin.; **REP CLIENTS:** Pac. Southern Mort. Trust; Westport Co.; Private clients; **PREV EMPLOY:** Standard & Poor's Corp.; **PROFL AFFIL & HONORS:** Member, NY Soc. of Security Analysts; RE Analysts Grp.; **EDUC:** BA, 1951, Eng. and Pol. Sci., Capital Univ., Columbus, OH; **GRAD EDUC:** MBA, 1970, Grad. School of Bus. Admin., NY Univ.; **EDUC HONORS:** Grad with honors, Degree with distinction; **HOME ADD:** 16 Glenwood Rd., Upper Saddle River, NJ 07458, (201)327-2214; **BUS ADD:** 230 Park Ave., New York, NY 10169, (212)661-1710.

CAMPBELL, Marie——*Exec. Secy.*, Missouri, MO Real Estate Commission; **PRIM RE ACT:** Property Manager; **BUS ADD:** PO Box 1339, Jefferson City, MO 65102, (314)751-2334.*

CAMPBELL, Nat——*VP*, Vermont American Corp.; **PRIM RE ACT:** Property Manager; **BUS ADD:** 100 E. Liberty St., Ste. 500, Louisville, KY 40202, (502)587-6851.*

CAMPBELL, Paul B.——**B:** Mar. 30, 1942, St. Louis, MO, *Pres.*, Greater MO Builders; **PRIM RE ACT:** Consultant, Developer, Instructor; **EDUC:** BS, 1964, Engrg., Univ. of IL; **GRAD EDUC:** MS, 1965, Physics, Univ. of IL; MBA, 1970, Fin., Univ. of Santa Clara; PhD, 1981, Econ.Fin., Univ. of CA - Berkeley; **HOME ADD:** 180 N. Forsyth, Clayton, MO, 63105; **BUS ADD:** 3651 N. Lindbergh, St. Ann, MO 63074, (314)291-2404.

CAMPBELL, Robert E.——**B:** July 30, 1922, Brooklyn, NY, *Dir. of Mgmt.*, Kenneth D. Laub & Co., Inc.; **PRIM RE ACT:** Consultant, Property Manager, Engineer, Insuror; **OTHER RE ACT:** Writer of RE Mgmt Articles; **SERVICES:** RE Mgmt., Consulting; **PREV EMPLOY:** Amer. Continental Props., James Felt & Co.; **PROFL AFFIL & HONORS:** IREM, CPM; **EDUC:** BS, 1944, Marine Engrg., USMMA (Kings Point); **EDUC HONORS:** 2nd in class; **MIL SERV:** USN, Lt. (j.g.); **HOME ADD:** 100 Henderson Rd., Kendall Pk., NJ 08824, (201)297-6733; **BUS ADD:** 1345 Ave of Amer., NY, NY 10020, (212)582-9282.

CAMPBELL, Robert E.——**B:** Sept. 20, 1935, Milwaukee, WI, *Pres.*, Land Investment & Development Corp.; **PRIM RE ACT:** Broker, Consultant, Developer, Builder, Owner/Investor, Property Manager; **PROFL AFFIL & HONORS:** MBA; WBA; NAHB, RE Broker, Devel. Consultant; **EDUC:** BS, 1959, Bus. Admin., Univ. of WI, Milwaukee; **MIL SERV:** USAF, A/2C; **BUS ADD:** 4810 So. 76th St., Suite 206, Greenfield, WI 53220, (414)421-7601.

CAMPBELL, Ronald D.——**B:** May 18, 1950, Ft. Collins, CO, *Pres.*, Campbell & Co, Investment RE, Inc.; **PRIM RE ACT:** Broker, Developer, Builder, Owner/Investor, Syndicator; **SERVICES:** Complete Devel. & const. (office bldgs); **PREV EMPLOY:** RE Investment Broker, RE Devel.; **PROFL AFFIL & HONORS:** BOMA, Assoc. Builders & Contractors; **EDUC:** BS, 1971, RE, Univ. of Co; **GRAD EDUC:** MBA, 1972, Fin., Univ. of CO; **HOME ADD:** 2634 Yorktown #465, Houston, TX 77056; **BUS ADD:** 441 Wadsworth, Suite 230, Lakewood, CO 80226, (303)232-5352.

CAMPBELL, Ronald E.——**B:** Apr. 9, 1949, NJ, *Sr. VP*, Margaretten & Co., Inc.; **PRIM RE ACT:** Lender; **PROFL AFFIL & HONORS:** MBAA, Young Mort. Bankers Assn., Southern NV Mort. Bankers Assn., 1977 First Place Award Nationally; 1978 Rgnl. Award First Place; 1978 First Place Award; 1979 Leading Rgnl. Producer; 1980

First Pl. Rgnl. Award; **EDUC:** BS, 1972, Fin. & Mktg., Northern AZ Univ.; **HOME ADD:** 1825 Lindell Rd., Las Vegas, NV 89102, (702)871-0087; **BUS ADD:** 3100 W. Sahara Ave. #110, Las Vegas, NV 89102, (702)873-2350.

CAMPBELL, Stanley W., Jr.——B: July 24, 1932, Cincinnati, OH, *Pres.*, Campbell Realty & Investment Co.; **PRIM RE ACT:** Broker, Consultant, Attorney, Developer, Owner/Investor; **SERVICES:** Comml. RE consultant involved in devel., brokerage & RE law, Condo. conversion services; **PREV EMPLOY:** Leasing Dir. of Metropolitan Structures for leasing of 1 IL Ctr., Chicago; **PROFL AFFIL & HONORS:** IL State Bar Assn.; IL State Court; IL Supreme Court; U.S. District Court, RE Broker; **EDUC:** Bus., Northwestern Univ.; **GRAD EDUC:** 1956, John Marshall Law Sch.; **MIL SERV:** USMC, Sgt.; **HOME ADD:** 619 S. Crescent, Park Ridge, IL 60068, (312)825-4783; **BUS ADD:** 233 E. Wacker Dr. #4411, Chicago, IL 60601, (312)938-0060.

CAMPBELL, Thomas W.——B: Aug. 1, 1932, Dayton, KY, *Pres.*, Campbell Homes Inc.; **PRIM RE ACT:** Developer, Builder; **SERVICES:** Custom builder/devel., -200,000 - -1,000,000 range; **PREV EMPLOY:** Raldon Homes, Pres.; Deal Devel., VP; Redman Homes, Pres.; Crest Communities, VP; Ryland Group, VP; Rossmoor Corp., VP/Gen. Mgr.; **PROFL AFFIL & HONORS:** NAHB; H & AB of Dallas; **EDUC:** BS, 1958, Commerce, Univ. of KY; **MIL SERV:** U.S. Army, Cpl., 1952-1954; **HOME ADD:** 16052 Chalfont Ct., Dallas, TX 75248, (214)661-3313; **BUS ADD:** 16052 Chalfont Ct., Dallas, TX 75248, (214)387-0642.

CAMPBELL, William Eugene——B: Sept. 27, 1935, Plainview, TX, *RE Coordinator*, TX Southmost Coll, RE; **PRIM RE ACT:** Broker, Consultant, Appraiser, Developer, Instructor, Property Manager; **OTHER RE ACT:** RE Dept. Coordinator; **SERVICES:** Developing degree programs, instr., selecting instrs., adoption of textbooks, counseling students; **REP CLIENTS:** Income prop. owners (consultation only); **PREV EMPLOY:** Self Employed Realtor (Hereford, TX); **PROFL AFFIL & HONORS:** NAR; TX Assn. of Realtors; RNMI; CO RE Broker, GRI; CRS; Realtor of the Yr., Hereford; Past Pres., Hereford Bd.; 2 TREPAC Membership Awards; **EDUC:** BBA, 1968, Mgmt., W. TX State Univ.; **OTHER ACT & HONORS:** Past Pres., Hereford Kiwanis; Twice Chmn., Key Club; Pres., Hereford Chamber Singers; Sponsor, Little Dribblers; **HOME ADD:** 710-2 Valley Inn Country Club, Brownsville, TX 78520, (512)541-7723; **BUS ADD:** 80 Ft. Brown, Brownsville, TX 78520, (512)544-8261.

CAMPBELL, William Glynn——B: Nov. 3, 1937, Muskogee, OK, *Exec. VP*, Diversified Financial Services, Synd. Dept.; **PRIM RE ACT:** Consultant, Developer, Owner/Investor, Property Manager, Syndicator; **PREV EMPLOY:** VP of Diversified Fin. Servs. from 1969 through 1979, Served as Exec. VP since 1980, Pathfinder Life Ins. Co. (1964-1967); Kane, Ferrill & Assoc. (1968-1969); **EDUC:** 1960, Univ. of AR; **OTHER ACT & HONORS:** Sigma Chi Frat.; **HOME ADD:** 7 Huntington Rd., Little Rock, AR, (501)225-5121; **BUS ADD:** PO Drawer 3197, Little Rock, AR 72203, (501)376-6451.

CAMPIGLIA, John E.——B: Jan. 16, 1951, Columbus, OH, *Realtor Assoc.*, Realty World - Cranbury Realtors, Resid. & Comml.; **PRIM RE ACT:** Broker, Property Manager, Owner/Investor; **SERVICES:** Sales & Mgmt.; **PREV EMPLOY:** RE Investments, Self- Employed; **EDUC:** GRI Grad., 1978, Bus., Econ., Univ. of CT; **MIL SERV:** USN, (PO2) E-5 1971-1975, Naval Achievement Sec. of Nav.; **OTHER ACT & HONORS:** Vol. Fireman; Norkwalk Jaycees; **HOME ADD:** 4 Thames St., Norwalk, CT 06851, (203)846-2649; **BUS ADD:** 34 West Ave., Norwalk, CT 06854, (203)838-1314.

CAMPISI, Dominic J.——B: Apr. 30, 1944, San Jose, CA, *Atty.*, Evans, Latham & Campisi; **PRIM RE ACT:** Attorney; **OTHER RE ACT:** Legal Advice; **SERVICES:** Litigation; **REP CLIENTS:** Bay View Federal S&L Assn.; BMA Properties, Inc.; **PROFL AFFIL & HONORS:** ABA Real Prop. Probate and Trust; V. Chmn., Litigation Procedures (Probate & Trust Div.); **EDUC:** BA, 1966, Pol. Sci., Univ. of Santa Clara; **GRAD EDUC:** MPA, 1978, Urban Affairs, Woodrow Wilson School, Princeton Univ.; JD, 1974, Law, Yale Law School; **EDUC HONORS:** Magna Cum Laude; Pol. Sci. Prize; Speaking Prize; **MIL SERV:** US Army, SP5, ArCom; **OTHER ACT & HONORS:** Law Clerk, Ninth Circuit Court of Appeals, 1974-1975; **BUS ADD:** 111 Sutter St., Suite 1800, San Francisco, CA 94104, (415)421-0288.

CAMPNEY, James T.——B: Sept. 3, 1943, Emmetsburg, IA, *Pres.*, Campney & Associates, Inc.; **PRIM RE ACT:** Broker, Consultant, Developer, Owner/Investor, Syndicator; **SERVICES:** investment counseling & formation of partnerships; **REP CLIENTS:** Private indiv. investors in comml. and office props.; **PREV EMPLOY:** Seven yrs. in fast food industry as dist. supervisor of site analysis and selection; **PROFL AFFIL & HONORS:** NAR, RNMI, CCIM; **EDUC:** BS, 1967, Bus. Admin., IA State Univ.; **OTHER ACT & HONORS:** Bd. of Dirs., W. DesMoines C of C; **HOME ADD:** 941-41st St., W. Des Moines, IA 50265, (515)225-0197; **BUS ADD:** 2400 86th St., Suite 24, Des Moines, IA 50322, (515)276-8282.

CAMPO, R.J.——B: Aug. 2, 1954, Carmel, CA, *Dir., Fin. Planning*, Century Devepment Corp.; **PRIM RE ACT:** Developer; **SERVICES:** Devel. of comml. prop.; **PREV EMPLOY:** Jemrico Inc., VP of Fin., 1973-1976; **PROFL AFFIL & HONORS:** NACORE; Urban Land Inst.; AICPA; TX Soc. of CPA's, CPA; TX RE Broker; **EDUC:** BMS, 1976, Acctg. and Fin., OR State Univ.; **HOME ADD:** 9603 Meadowglen, Houston, TX 77042; **BUS ADD:** 5 Greenway Plaza E., Suite 1700, Houston, TX 77046, (713)621-9500.

CANALE, Stephen F.——B: Aug. 22, 1954, Bronx, NY, *VP*, OTIC Management; **PRIM RE ACT:** Broker, Consultant, Property Manager; **SERVICES:** Comml. & resid. leasing, prop. mgmt., investment counseling; **PROFL AFFIL & HONORS:** Lic. RE Broker NY State IREM, Candidate for CPM, Lic. RE Broker, NY State and NJ, Notary Public; **EDUC:** BS, 1976, Bus. Mgmt., Niagara Univ.; **OTHER ACT & HONORS:** Notary Public, NY State; **HOME ADD:** 478 Sierra Vista Ln., Valley Cottage, NY 1O989; **BUS ADD:** 18 E. 41st, New York, NY 10017, (212)683-7510.

CANCRO, Anthony J.——B: May 30, 1927, Brooklyn, NY, *Pres.*, Abacus Management Corp., Div. of Abacus Group; **PRIM RE ACT:** Developer, Owner/Investor, Property Manager, Syndicator; **SERVICES:** Synd. of resid. and comml. props.; **REP CLIENTS:** Indiv. investors, builders; **EDUC:** Chemical Engrg., Polytechnic Inst. of NY; **GRAD EDUC:** Fordham Univ., City Coll.; **MIL SERV:** USAF, A1st Cl; **HOME ADD:** 101 Prospect Ave., Hackensack, NJ 07601, (201)343-6773; **BUS ADD:** 45 Essex St., Hackensack, NJ 07602, (201)342-6822.

CANDELL, Cass——B: June 20, 1936, Buffalo, NY, *Pres.*, Cass Candell, C.F.P., Inc.; **PRIM RE ACT:** Broker, Consultant, Owner/Investor, Insuror, Syndicator; **OTHER RE ACT:** Cert. Fin. Planner; **SERVICES:** Fin. planning; investment counseling with emphasis on RE & retirement plans; **PREV EMPLOY:** VP, Professional Health Research; **PROFL AFFIL & HONORS:** Intl. Assn. of Fin. Planners; Inst. Certified Fin. Planners, VP, East Bay Chapter, IAFP; **EDUC:** BS, 1957, Pharmacy, State Univ. of NY at Buffalo; **GRAD EDUC:** MBA, 1980, Golden Gate Univ., San Francisco, CA; **MIL SERV:** US Army, 1st Lt.; **OTHER ACT & HONORS:** Bd. of Dir., Family Service of the East Bay; **HOME ADD:** 4354 Edgewood Ave., Oakland, CA 94602, (415)530-4973; **BUS ADD:** 4354 Edgewood Ave., Oakland, CA 94602, (415)530-4967.

CANDELL, John T.——B: July 13, 1941, Eau Claire, WI, *Atty.*, Hagerty, Candell, Lindberg, Milota & Butler, PA; **PRIM RE ACT:** Attorney; **REP CLIENTS:** The Travelers Ins. Co. (RE Investment Dept.); The Prospect Co., Menard, Inc.; **PROFL AFFIL & HONORS:** ABA (Real Prop. Section); MN State Bar Assn.; Hennepin Cty. Bar Assn.; **EDUC:** BA, 1963, Notre Dame Univ.; **GRAD EDUC:** JD, 1966, Univ. of MN Law School; **HOME ADD:** 4721 W 60th St., Edina, MN 55424, (612)922-6696; **BUS ADD:** 1008 Soo Line Bldg., Minneapolis, MN 55402, (612)332-5344.

CANDEUB, Isadore——B: Mar 15, 1922, Rumania, *Pres.*, Candeub Fleissig & Assoc.; **OTHER RE ACT:** City planning/Econ. feasibility, etc.; **REP CLIENTS:** Prudential Ins. Co., Koppers Co., Helmsley-Spear; **PREV EMPLOY:** HUD, 1951-53; **PROFL AFFIL & HONORS:** AICP; **EDUC:** BSS, 1943, Soc. Studies, CCNY; **GRAD EDUC:** MCP, 1948, MIT; **EDUC HONORS:** Cum Laude, Phi Beta Kappa; **MIL SERV:** US Army, Cpl.; **OTHER ACT & HONORS:** Member Bd. of Dirs. Newark C of C, Member Bd. of Regents St. Peters Coll., Jersey City; **HOME ADD:** 19 Beacon Hill Dr., Metuchen, NJ 08840, (201)548-3660; **BUS ADD:** 744 Broad St., Newark, NJ 07102, (201)643-3919.

CANDLER, John S., II——B: Nov. 30, 1908, Atlanta, GA, *Part.*, Candler, Cox, Andrews & Hansen; **PRIM RE ACT:** Attorney, Owner/Investor; **EDUC:** AB, M.C.L., 1929, Mathematics; History and Pol. Sci., Univ. of GA; **GRAD EDUC:** JD, 1931, Emory Univ., **MIL SERV:** US Army, Col.; **HOME ADD:** 413 Manor Ridge Dr., NW, Atlanta, GA 30305, (404)355-3113; **BUS ADD:** 2400 Gas Light Tower, Atlanta, GA 30043, (404)577-9400.

CANEL, Richard L., Jr.——B: Jan. 17, 1954, Petersburg, VA, Blank, Rome, Comisky & McCauley; **PRIM RE ACT:** Attorney; **PREV EMPLOY:** Assoc. with Schwartz, Remsen, Shapiro & Kelm, Columbus, OH; **PROFL AFFIL & HONORS:** ABA (Real Prop., Probate & Trust Sect.); PA Bar Assn.; Philadelphia Bar Assn.; OH Bar Assn.; **EDUC:** BA, 1975, Pol., Fairfield Univ.; **GRAD EDUC:** JD, 1978,

Univ. of VA; **EDUC HONORS:** Magna Cum Laude; **HOME ADD:** Apt. 2207, 1500 Locust St., Philadelphia, PA 19102, (215)732-5967; **BUS ADD:** 4 Penn Ctr., Philadelphia, PA 19103, (215)569-3700.

CANESTARO, James C.——*Assoc. Prof. of Arch.*, VA Potech. Inst. & State Univ.; **OTHER RE ACT:** Prof. - Architectural & Development Econ., Feasibility & Cost Benefit Analysis, Architectural Programming; **PROFL AFFIL & HONORS:** AIA, AIA; **BUS ADD:** PO Box 194, Blacksburg, VA 24060, (208)552-3000.

CANEVARI, Thomas Joseph——**B:** March 19, 1947, San Francisco, CA, *Shareholder*, Berger, Lewis & Company, CPA's; **PRIM RE ACT:** Consultant; **OTHER RE ACT:** CPA, instr., grad. sch. of taxation, Golden Gate Univ.; **SERVICES:** Investment counseling, tax planning; **REP CLIENTS:** Devel., brokers and investors concerned with comml., agri. and resid. prop.; **PROFL AFFIL & HONORS:** CA Soc. of CPA's, Amer. Soc. of Traffic and Trans., Santa Clara Cty. Estate Planning council, CPA; **EDUC:** BA, 1969, Univ. of Santa Clara; **GRAD EDUC:** MBA, 1975, Bus., Univ. of HI; MBA, 1978, Taxation, Golden Gate Univ.; **EDUC HONORS:** Cum Laude; **MIL SERV:** US Army, Capt., Bronze Star, Army Commendation Medal (1OLC); **OTHER ACT & HONORS:** San Jose Civic Light Opera; **HOME ADD:** 6584 Northridge Dr., San Jose, CA 95120, (408)268-5219; **BUS ADD:** 84 W. Santa Clara St. #700, San Jose, CA 95113, (408)297-1964.

CANFIELD, Clinton M.——**B:** Mar. 17, 1934, El Centro, CA, *Owner*, Unique Prop. Investment; **PRIM RE ACT:** Syndicator, Consultant; **SERVICES:** Investment Consultant; **EDUC:** 1956, Bus., Univ. of MI; **MIL SERV:** US Army, 1958; **HOME ADD:** 9181 Gordon Ave., La Habra, CA 90631, (213)691-8750; **BUS ADD:** 2240 E. 7th St., Long Beach, CA 90804, (213)433-5176.

CANFIELD, Frederick W.——**B:** Feb. 1, 1930, Cambridge, MA, *Fin. VP (CFO)*, Southwide, Inc., Southwide Devel. Co., Inc.; Federal Compress & Warehouse Co.; Delta and Pine Land Co. L.D. Brown Co., Inc.; **PRIM RE ACT:** Developer, Owner/Investor, Property Manager; **OTHER RE ACT:** Chief Fin. Officer; **SERVICES:** RE devel., leasing, mgmt.; **REP CLIENTS:** The Prudential Insurance Co. of Amer., The Equitable Life Assurance Soc. of the US; **PROFL AFFIL & HONORS:** Financial Analysts Federation, Financial Executives Institute; **EDUC:** AB, 1952, Pol.Sci., Williams Coll.; **GRAD EDUC:** MBA, 1958, General, Harvard Bus. School; **MIL SERV:** USNR, Lt.; **HOME ADD:** 6572 Bramble Cove, Memphis, TN 38119, (901)754-6593; **BUS ADD:** 165 Madison Ave., Memphis, TN 38103, (901)523-1211.

CANIN, Brian C.——**B:** Jan. 13, 1941, Johannesburg, S. Africa, *Pres.*, Canin Associates, Inc.; **PRIM RE ACT:** Consultant; **SERVICES:** Urban and environmental planning; **REP CLIENTS:** FL Land Co., Intl. Community Corp. (William J. Levitt), FL Resid. Communities, Appalachian, Inc., Guaranty Props., Inc., Majestic Homes, Olin-Amer. Homes; I.E. Large Devel. Cos.; **PROFL AFFIL & HONORS:** AIA, Amer. Inst. of Certified Planners, Brian C. Canin, AIA, AICP; **EDUC:** BArch, 1966, Univ. of Witwatersrand, Johannesburg, S. Africa; **GRAD EDUC:** Master of Urban Design, 1968, Harvard Univ.; **HOME ADD:** 216 Sylvan Blvd., Winter Park, FL 32789, (305)628-4091; **BUS ADD:** 201 E. Pine St. #302, Orlando, FL 32801, (305)422-4040.

CANNON, Donald——**B:** Jan. 22, 1941, Front Royal, VA, *Co-owner*, LeRoy and Cannon; **PRIM RE ACT:** Broker, Syndicator, Consultant, Appraiser, Builder, Owner/Investor; **SERVICES:** RE brokerage, appraisal, expert witness; **REP CLIENTS:** Banks, S&Ls, Ins. Cos., Attys.; **PREV EMPLOY:** RE brokerage and appraisal since 1969; **PROFL AFFIL & HONORS:** VAR, NAR, CREA, NAREA; **EDUC:** BA, Biology, Poli. Sci., Amer. Univ., Univ. TN State, G.W. Univ, Univ. VA; **GRAD EDUC:** LLB, 1972, LaSalle Univ.; **OTHER ACT & HONORS:** Circuit Ct., Fairfax, VA, Architectural Review Bd., Fairfax, VA 1972 to 1977, AOPA, NHS; **HOME ADD:** Rte. 4 Box 122, Leesburg, VA 22075, (703)777-4399; **BUS ADD:** 7 E. Market St., Leesburg, VA 22075, (703)777-4411.

CANNON, George Q.——**B:** May 28, 1908, Salt Lake City, UT, *Chmn. of the Bd.*, Honolulu Fed. S&L; **PRIM RE ACT:** Lender, Banker; **SERVICES:** Full banking & lending; **PREV EMPLOY:** 32 yrs., Dir., Sec., Treas. & Chmn.; **EDUC:** Univ. of UT; Brigham Young Univ.; Harvard Univ. Bus. Admin.; **OTHER ACT & HONORS:** Pres., C of C, Honolulu; Pres., Aloha Council Boy Scouts; Chmn. Honolulu Police Comm.; Hon. Citizen of Korea; Past Pres. Navy League of US; Past Chmn. & Pres. of Meadow Gold Dairies, Hawaii; Past Managing Dir., Beatire Foods Co., Far East; Chmn. HA Manufactured Homes, Inc.; Pres. Far East Associated, Inc.; Member, Oahu Cty. Club; Pacific Club; Rotary Mason; Shriner; Jester & Red Cross of Constantine; Dir. of many Companies in US and Forgien Countries; **HOME ADD:** 1778 Ala Moana Blvd., Honolulu, HI 96815; **BUS ADD:** POB 518, Honolulu, HI 96809.

CANNON, Michael Y.——**B:** June 24, 1939, Brooklyn, NY, *Pres.*, Appraisal & RE Econ. Assoc., Inc. (A.R.E.E.A.); **PRIM RE ACT:** Broker, Consultant, Appraiser, Property Manager, Real Estate Publisher; **OTHER RE ACT:** RE Mkt. analyst; **SERVICES:** Mkt. research valuation, investment consulting Management; **REP CLIENTS:** Citibank NA, Chem. Bank, Cadillac Fairview, Nu-West Ltd., Chase Manhattan Bank NA, Coca Cola Arvida Corp. Genstar; **PREV EMPLOY:** VP, Chief Loan Officer, Citizens Fed. S&L of Miami, Metro Dade Tax Assessor; **PROFL AFFIL & HONORS:** SREA, ULI, AREEA, Soc. of Mort. Consultants, ARVEA, SRPA, SMC, Gov. Dist. 13, 1975-80 SREA; **EDUC:** BA, RE & Fin., Bus., Univ. of Miami; **OTHER ACT & HONORS:** Builders Assn. of S FL, MBA, Mort. Brokers Assn. of FL, Lic. RE Broker (FL), Lic. Mort. Broker (FL); **HOME ADD:** 9420 SW 25th St., Miami, FL 33156, (305)552-8573; **BUS ADD:** Ste. 225, 9200 S Dadeland Blvd., Miami, FL 33156, (305)661-1571.

CANTEY, William C., Jr.——**B:** Jan. 16, 1943, Columbia, SC, *Pres.*, Cantey & Co., Inc.; **PRIM RE ACT:** Consultant, Owner/Investor, Syndicator; **SERVICES:** Consulting only (no brokerage) for indiv. and inst. synd. of investment prop.; **REP CLIENTS:** Indiv. and inst. investors; **PROFL AFFIL & HONORS:** Amer. Soc. of RE Counselors; RE Securities & Synd. Inst.; Commnr. on City of Columbia Planning Commn., CRE, CCIM; **EDUC:** BA, 1964, Econ., Davidson Coll.; **GRAD EDUC:** MBA, 1966, Fin., Harvard Bus. School; **EDUC HONORS:** A.K. Phifer Scholar, Dean's List; **MIL SERV:** US Army, 1st Lt., 1966-1968; **OTHER ACT & HONORS:** Pres. of Keenan Securities, Inc., a SECO broker-dealer; **HOME ADD:** 1805 Glenwood Rd., Columbia, SC 29204, (803)782-0376; **BUS ADD:** Suite 205, 2712 Middleburg Dr., Columbia, SC 29204, (803)256-7150.

CANTOR, Philip S.——**B:** July 26, 1947, Passaic, NJ, *Managing Partner*, The Bruskin Agency; **PRIM RE ACT:** Broker, Consultant, Appraiser, Developer, Owner/Investor, Instructor, Property Manager; **SERVICES:** Acquisition, devel., mgmt. & appraisal of investment prop.; **REP CLIENTS:** Lenders, govt. agencies, indiv. and instnl. investors; **EDUC:** BA, 1968, Eng., Rutgers Univ.; **GRAD EDUC:** MBA, 1982, Fin., Rutgers Univ.; **OTHER ACT & HONORS:** VP, Bd. of Educ. (Milltown), Rutgers Univ. Devel. Comm., George St. Playhouse, Downtown Assn.; **HOME ADD:** 325 Clay St., Milltown, NJ 08850, (201)545-2408; **BUS ADD:** 24 Livingston Ave., New Brunswick, NJ 08901, (201)545-0095.

CANTRELL, W. Clyde——**B:** Jan. 26, 1944, San Angelo, TX, *Chief Appraiser*, San Angelo Savings Assn.; **PRIM RE ACT:** Consultant, Appraiser, Instructor; **SERVICES:** Appraisal of RE; RE analysis; **REP CLIENTS:** S&L, banks, attys, state govt., and indiv.; **PREV EMPLOY:** Right-of-Way Appraiser for TX State Dept. of Highways and Public Transportation; **PROFL AFFIL & HONORS:** Soc. of RE Appraisers; Nat. Assn. of Realtors; San Angelo Bd. of Realtors; TX Soc. of Farm Managers and Rural Appraisers, SRA, SREA, CRA, Nat. Assn. Review Appraisers; **EDUC:** BS, 1966, Agric. Econ., TX A&M Univ.; **HOME ADD:** Mereta Rte., San Angelo, TX 76901, (915)653-8257; **BUS ADD:** POB 5501, San Angelo, TX 76902, (915)655-4111.

CANTWELL, Stephen M.——**B:** Sep. 10, 1939, Indianapolis, IN, *Pres.*, Investors Research Associates, Inc.; **PRIM RE ACT:** Consultant, Appraiser; **SERVICES:** Econ. consultation, fin. analysis & valuation; **REP CLIENTS:** Banks, S & L, ins. cos., pension funds and devel.; **PREV EMPLOY:** Dept. of Transportation, Indianapolis, IN 1968-71; RE Research Corp. 1971-77; Southeast Mortgage Co. 1977-81; **PROFL AFFIL & HONORS:** MAI; SRPA Realtor; FL Broker; **EDUC:** BA, 1965, Econ., Marion Coll., Indianapolis; **MIL SERV:** USAF, A1c; **HOME ADD:** 10081 SW 98th Ave., Miami, FL 33176, (305)270-0111; **BUS ADD:** 7600 Red Rd., Miami, FL 33143, (305)665-3407.

CANULL, James, Jr.——**B:** Aug. 31, 1943, Mt. Vernon, IN, *Pres.*, A.M. Real Estate; **PRIM RE ACT:** Broker; **SERVICES:** Resid., Relocation, Rental Investments; **REP CLIENTS:** Transferred Personnel; **PROFL AFFIL & HONORS:** NAR, MIBDR, GRI, CRS, CRB; **EDUC:** AB, 1965, Poli. Sci., Univ. of NC; **OTHER ACT & HONORS:** ATO Alumni, UNC Alumni, Toastmasters; **HOME ADD:** 1001 E. Main St., Carmel, IN 40032, (317)844-0485; **BUS ADD:** 11588 Westfield Blvd., Carmel, IN 46032, (317)848-1588.

CAPAN, Robert G.——**B:** Jan. 1, 1943, Warren, OH, *VP*, First Interstate Mort. Co., A Div. of First Interstate Bank of CA; **PRIM RE ACT:** Broker, Consultant, Banker; **SERVICES:** Joint ventures and fin.; **REP CLIENTS:** Life cos., pension funds and pvt. investors; **PREV EMPLOY:** Ralph C. Sutro Co.; **PROFL AFFIL & HONORS:** CPA, RE Broker; **EDUC:** BS, 1969, Tulane Univ.; **GRAD EDUC:** MBA, 1972, Northwestern Univ.; **HOME ADD:** San Francisco, CA; **BUS ADD:** One Embarcadero Ctr., Suite 2401, San Francisco, CA 94111, (415)544-5929.

CAPEWELL, John——B: June 25, 1931, Trenton, NJ, *Pres. - Gen. Partner*, Capewell & Capewell, Inc. and John Capewell & Associates and Capewell Enterprises; **PRIM RE ACT:** Consultant, Appraiser; **OTHER RE ACT:** Mgmt. consultant; **SERVICES:** Large intl. funds, legal - comml. appraisals, corp./indivd. consulting; **REP CLIENTS:** Corp., ins. trusts, banks, indivs.; **PREV EMPLOY:** USN; **PROFL AFFIL & HONORS:** Amer. Mgmt. Assn.; ASA, NARA, ASA, CRA, MBA; **EDUC:** BSEE, 1972, Engrg., Naval Post Grad. School; **GRAD EDUC:** MBA, 1981, Mgmt./Intl. Fin., Golden Gate Univ.; **MIL SERV:** USN, Lcmdr., 2d FC & many; **OTHER ACT & HONORS:** Scottish Rite, 32 Mason, Boy Scouts, 26 years Eagle Scout w/3 Palms; **HOME ADD:** 245 Larkin St., Monterey, CA 93940, (408)375-1123.

CAPLAN, Bruce M.——B: Mar. 8, 1949, Boston, MA, *Exec. Officer*, Profl. Investment Assoc.; **PRIM RE ACT:** Broker, Consultant, Engineer, Appraiser, Owner/Investor, Instructor, Property Manager; **OTHER RE ACT:** Spec. in prop. improvement and rehab.; **SERVICES:** Investment counseling, landlord-tenant relationships, prop. mgmt., eval. of income resid. props.; **PROFL AFFIL & HONORS:** NE Investors, Boston area Income Group, Lowry Nickerson Alumni Fund, Recipient of Cert of Achievement by Lowry Nickerson & Educ. Advancement, Honored by John Philpott Enterprises; **EDUC:** 1968-70, Electronic Engrg., Wentworth Inst., Northeastern Univ.; **HOME ADD:** 22 Stevens St., Malden, MA 02148; **BUS ADD:** PO Box 20, Malden, MA 02148, (617)321-6634.

CAPONITRO, Ralph——*Sr. VP Fin. & Treas.*, Stroh Breweries; **PRIM RE ACT:** Property Manager; **BUS ADD:** 1 Stroh Drive, Detroit, MI 48226, (313)567-4000.*

CAPONNETTO, Joseph——B: Mar. 24, 1913, Catania, Italia, *Prin.*, Caponnetto & Assoc.; **PRIM RE ACT:** Consultant, Architect; **OTHER RE ACT:** Planner, interior & bldg. design; **SERVICES:** Feasibility studies, fin. analysis, prelim. studies, contract documents, constr. mgmt.; **REP CLIENTS:** RE brokers, devels., builders, engrs., owner/investors; **PREV EMPLOY:** Chief Arch., Francisco & Jacobus, A/E, Dir. of Arch., Frederic R. Harris, Inc. A/E; **PROFL AFFIL & HONORS:** AIA, NY Soc. of Arch. Nat. Inst. of Arch. Educ., Amer. Soc. of Planning Officials, Amer. Arbitration Assn., NY Univ. RE & Mort. Insts., 39th Paris Prize; Alternate, Fifth Ave. Assn. yrs. Award, 716-5th Ave.; Morse Prize for Graphics, 1941; **EDUC:** BA, 1939, Fine Arts, Arch., NY Univ.; **GRAD EDUC:** M.Arch., 1941, Arch. Planning, NY Univ.; **EDUC HONORS:** Delevie Prize in Arch., 5 first medals BAID, Sigma Kappa Tau Design Award, Sch. Art League Award; **MIL SERV:** US Army, Capt., ETO Campaign Ribbons; **OTHER ACT & HONORS:** Town of Greenburgh, Planning Bd., Commr. Environmental Quality Control Bd., 1973-76; Advisor Natl. Soc. of Mural Painter; Member Fine Arts Fed. of NY; Art Deco Soc. VP; Metro. Solar Energy Soc., Preservation League of NY; **HOME ADD:** 20 Jennifer Ln., Hartsdale, NY 10530, (914)693-2027; **BUS ADD:** 6 E 39th St., New York, NY 10016, (212)685-2265.

CAPORINA, Anthony J.——B: Apr. 11, 1938, Houston, TX, *Pres.*, Building Crafts, Inc.; **PRIM RE ACT:** Broker, Architect, Developer, Builder, Owner/Investor; **PREV EMPLOY:** Assoc. Prof. of Arch., TX A&M Univ. 1968-1976; **EDUC:** BArch., 1961, Arch., Univ. of Houston; **GRAD EDUC:** MArch., 1970, Arch., TX A&M Univ.; **EDUC HONORS:** Alpha Rho Chi; **OTHER ACT & HONORS:** Beyan Planning Commn.-1979; **HOME ADD:** 2801 Briarcheek, Bryon, TX 77801, (713)775-0263; **BUS ADD:** 505 Univ. Dr., Suite #401, Lollege Station, TX 77840, (713)846-4783.

CAPOZZA, Alfred A.——B: Mar. 21, 1919, New London, CT, *Asst. VP/Appraiser*, The Savings Bank of New London, Project Mgr.; Starr Street Rehabilitation; **PRIM RE ACT:** Broker, Appraiser, Instructor; **OTHER RE ACT:** Rehab. of older homes; **PREV EMPLOY:** Self employed 1958-72; **PROFL AFFIL & HONORS:** NAR, CT Assn., CT Realtor of the Yr., 1972; Pres. 1972 CT Assn. Realtors; **EDUC:** 1960-62, RE & Appraisals, Ext. courst, Univ. of CT; **GRAD EDUC:** 1969, CT Realtors Inst.; **MIL SERV:** USAF, 1944-46, Cpl., Pac.; **OTHER ACT & HONORS:** Pres. Bd. of Educ., 1962-68, Council City of New London, 1968-70; Past Pres. New London Lions Club; Past Comdr. Wtfd. VFW; Member Ocean Bch. Park Bd.; Corporator Lawrence Memorial Hosp., BPOE 360; **HOME ADD:** 36 Harris Rd., New London, CT 06320, (203)443-5874; **BUS ADD:** 63 Eugene O'Neill Dr., New London, CT 06320, (203)442-0301.

CAPP, Alvin——B: Feb. 23, 1939, St. Louis, MO, *Pres.*, Capp, Reinstein, Kopelowitz & Atlas, P.A.; **PRIM RE ACT:** Attorney, Instructor, Owner/Investor; **SERVICES:** Legal; **PROFL AFFIL & HONORS:** ABA; FL Bar; Broward Cty. Bar Assns.; US Supreme Court Bar, JD; **EDUC:** BA, 1961, Poli. Sci./Hist., George Washington Univ.; **GRAD EDUC:** JD, 1964, Law, The George Washington Univ.; **EDUC HONORS:** Book Review Editor, The George Washington Law Review, Grad. w/Honors; **MIL SERV:** US Army Res.; **OTHER ACT & HONORS:** Plantation, FL City Prosecutor, 1974-1976; Instructor RE law 1965-72; **BUS ADD:** 700 SE 3rd Ave., Ft. Lauderdale, FL 33316, (305)463-3173.

CAPPELLINI, Louis A., Jr.——B: Sept. 30, 1943, NY, NY, *Pres.*, Ely Cruikshank Co., Inc.; **PRIM RE ACT:** Broker, Consultant, Appraiser, Property Manager, Insuror; **SERVICES:** Prop. mgmt., sales, leasing, renting, appraising, consultant; **REP CLIENTS:** Metropolitan Life Ins. Co.; Bank of Montreal; Bank of NY; Georgeson; US Trust Co.; Atlantic Mutual Ins. Co.; etc.; **PREV EMPLOY:** Williamson, Picket, Gross RE, Asst. VP, 1971-1973; **PROFL AFFIL & HONORS:** RE Bd. of NY, Fin. Dist. Office Bldg. Comm., Ins. City Hall World Trade Ctr., BOMA; IREM; CPM; Young Men RE Assn.; **EDUC:** BA, 1970, Social Sci./RE, Pace Univ.; NYU; **OTHER ACT & HONORS:** Pace Univ. Alumni Bd. of Dir., 2nd VP, 1981-1982; Lenox Hill Dem. Club, Exec. Comm., Cty. Committeemen NY Cty., Dem. Party; **HOME ADD:** 340 E. 62nd St., New York, NY 10021, (212)838-6108; **BUS ADD:** 2 Wall St., New York, NY 10005, (212)233-7100.

CAPPUCCIO, Ronald Joseph——B: Mar. 3, 1954, Philadelphia, PA, *Counsellor at Law*; **PRIM RE ACT:** Attorney; **SERVICES:** Legal rep. and tax planning and opinions; **REP CLIENTS:** Solicitor for the Gloucester Township (NJ) Planning Bd.; **PROFL AFFIL & HONORS:** ABA, NJ State Bar Assn., Camden Cty. Bar Assn., DC Bar Assn., Atty. at Law in the State of NJ, DC, US Tax Court; **EDUC:** BS, 1974, Intl., Econ., Fin. Forn. Serv., Georgetown Univ., Edmund A. Walsh School of For. Serv.; **GRAD EDUC:** JD, 1976, Univ. of KS; LLM, 1977, Georgetown Univ. Law Center; **OTHER ACT & HONORS:** Adjunct Instr. Rutgers Univ. 'Practices and Procedures before Planning Bds. and Zoning Bds. of Adjustment' 1978-80; **HOME ADD:** 108 W Maple Ave., Merchantville, NJ 08109, (609)665-2121; **BUS ADD:** 212 Haddon Ave., Westmont, NJ 08108, (609)858-2121.

CARACI, Philip D.——B: Mar. 27, 1938, Brooklyn, NY, *Sr. VP*, B.F. Saul Advisory Co.; **PRIM RE ACT:** Consultant, Attorney, Developer, Lender, Property Manager, Owner/Investor; **SERVICES:** Legal, admin., mgmt. and devel. serv. for the ownership and devel. of income-providing props.; **REP CLIENTS:** B.F. Saul RE investment Trust, Franklin Prop. Co., B.F. Saul Co.; **PREV EMPLOY:** Teachers Ins. & Annuity Assn. of Amer. (Asst. Counsel); Atty. Dime Savings Bank; Coll. Retirement Equities Firm-Asst. Counsel; **PROFL AFFIL & HONORS:** Assn. of the Bar of the City of NY; MD State Bar Assn.; NY State Bar Assn.; Intl. Council of Shopping Ctrs.; WA Metropolitan Area Corp. Counsel Assn.; Sec. & Dir., NARIET; **EDUC:** BS, 1959, Bus. Admin., Univ. of AL; **GRAD EDUC:** LLB, 1963, Law, NY Law School; **HOME ADD:** 9816 Clydesdale St., Potomac, MD 20854, (301)299-8981; **BUS ADD:** 8401 Connecticut Ave., Chevy Chase, MD 20815, (301)986-6282.

CARAFELLO, John A.——B: Aug. 12, 1951, Paterson, NJ, *Mgr., Mktg.*, Vorelco, Inc., A Subsidiary of Volkswagen of America; **OTHER RE ACT:** Responsible for Diversified Corp. RE Holdings, Acquisitions, Feasibility Studies, Disposals; **SERVICES:** Value and feasibility determination, devel. and disposals; **PREV EMPLOY:** Dir. of RE, Bagel Nosh Restaurants, NJ RE Broker; **PROFL AFFIL & HONORS:** Nat. Assn. of Review Appraisers, Nat. Assn. of Corp. RE Execs., CRA, Senior member, Nat. Assn. of Review Appraisers; **EDUC:** BBA, 1973, Mktg., Econ., Upsala Coll.; **HOME ADD:** 606 Otterhole Rd., W. Milford, NJ 07480, (201)697-2090; **BUS ADD:** 600 Sylvan Ave., Englewood Cliffs, NJ 07632, (201)894-6394.

CARAHER, James C.——B: Feb. 16, 1946, Philadelphia, PA, *Pres.*, The Caraher Corp.; **PRIM RE ACT:** Developer, Owner/Investor; **PROFL AFFIL & HONORS:** ULI; Univ. Club of Chicago; Econ. Club of Chicago; **EDUC:** BA, 1967, Wheaton Coll., Wheaton, IL; **GRAD EDUC:** MBA, 1972, Univ. of Chicago, Grad. School of Bus.; **OTHER ACT & HONORS:** Univ. Club of Chicago; Econ. Club of Chicago; **HOME ADD:** 38 E. Elm St., Chicago, IL 60611, (312)266-1126; **BUS ADD:** 135 S. La Salle St., Chicago, IL 60603, (312)782-9100.

CARBONE, Josephine——*Secy.*, Triangle Pacific Corp.; **PRIM RE ACT:** Property Manager; **BUS ADD:** 9 Park Place, Great Neck, NY 11021, (516)482-2600.*

CARBONI, Joseph L.——B: Aug. 7, 1936, Philadelphia, PA, *Regnl. VP*, New England Merchants National Bank; **PRIM RE ACT:** Banker, Lender; **PROFL AFFIL & HONORS:** Robert Morris Assoc.; Philadelphia Mortgage Bankers Assn.; Homebuilders Assn; **EDUC:** BA, 1957, Liberal Arts, Hist., Eng., Univ. of Notre Dame; **EDUC HONORS:** Cum laude; **MIL SERV:** USMC, 1st. Lt.; **OTHER ACT & HONORS:** Trustee, PA Inst. of Technology; **HOME ADD:** 508 Graisbury Ave., Haddonfield, NJ 08033; **BUS ADD:** Philadelphia Stock Exchange Bldg., 1900 Market St., Ste. 512, Philadelphia, PA 19103, (215)568-7271.

CARDENAS, Al——**B:** Jan. 3, 1948, Cuba, *Atty.*, Barron, Lehman, Cardenas & Picken, P.A.; **PRIM RE ACT:** Attorney; **OTHER RE ACT:** RE & Zoning; **HOME ADD:** 5035 Orduna Dr., Coral Gables, FL 33146; **BUS ADD:** 888 Brickell Ave., Miami, FL 33131, (302)374-4747.

CARDILLO-LEE, James——**B:** Aug. 21, 1942, Indianapolis, IN, *CPA*, James Cardillo-Lee, CPA; **PRIM RE ACT:** Consultant; **SERVICES:** Tax consultation and fin. arrangements; **REP CLIENTS:** Devels.; **PROFL AFFIL & HONORS:** AICPA, CA Soc. of CPA's, CPA; **EDUC:** BS, 1970, Bus. Admin., Acctg., School of Bus. Admin., Univ. of CA, Berkeley; **EDUC HONORS:** Beta Alpha Psi, Nat. Hon. Acctg. Frat.; **MIL SERV:** USN (Res.), E-5; **OTHER ACT & HONORS:** Eagle Scout: Nat. Eagle Scout Assn.; **HOME ADD:** PO Box Z, Novato, CA 94948; **BUS ADD:** PO Box Z, Novato, CA 94948, (415)892-2122.

CARDWELL, John——*Dir. Capital Expenditures*, Northwest Industries, Inc.; **PRIM RE ACT:** Property Manager; **BUS ADD:** 6300 Sears Tower, Chicago, IL 60606, (312)876-7000.*

CAREY, Richard N.——**B:** Oct. 2, 1953, Wash., D.C., *Dir. of R.E. Acquisitions*, Manor Care, Inc.; Quality Inns, Inc.; **OTHER RE ACT:** Corp. R.E.; **SERVICES:** Acq., dev., sales, and mgmt.; **PREV EMPLOY:** Amer. Hospital Building Corp.; **EDUC:** BA, 1980, R.E., Univ. of MD; **HOME ADD:** 13120 Clifton Rd., Silver Spring, MD 20904, (301)384-3535; **BUS ADD:** 10750 Columbia Pike, Silver Spring, MD 20901, (301)593-5600.

CAREY, Robert Harrison——**B:** Aug. 18, 1927, Poy Sippi, WI, *Owner*, Robert H. Carey, R.E. Conslt.; **PRIM RE ACT:** Broker, Instructor, Consultant, Developer; **SERVICES:** Conslt. serv., primarily regarding development and land use zoning matters; **REP CLIENTS:** Attys., devel., apprais., owner-invest., bldrs., ldrs.; **PREV EMPLOY:** Thompson-Brown, Realtors, 1954-79, Pres.; **PROFL AFFIL & HONORS:** NAR, ULI, Omega Tau Rho, Realtors Honorary Frat.; Realtor of the Yr; CCIM; RNMI; **EDUC:** BS, 1953, Bus. Admin., Northwestern Univ.; **MIL SERV:** USNR; Y3,PNA3; **HOME ADD:** 5623 Raven Ct., Birmingham, MI 48010, (313)626-6758; **BUS ADD:** 4120 W. Maple Rd., Ste. 207, Foxcroft Bldg., Birmingham, MI 48010, (313)855-4140.

CAREY, Thomas——*Mgr. Land Resources*, General Refractories Co.; **PRIM RE ACT:** Property Manager; **BUS ADD:** 50 Monument Rd., Bala Cynwood, PA 19004, (215)667-7900.*

CAREY, William Polk——**B:** May 11, 1930, Baltimore, MD, *Pres.*, W.P. Carey & Co., Inc., NYC 1973; **PRIM RE ACT:** Banker, Owner/Investor; **SERVICES:** R.E. investment banking to maj. corps. and the synd. and mgmt. of ltd. partnerships for the purchase of corp. props.; **REP CLIENTS:** Maj. corps. such as G.D. Searle & Co., the Gap and Emerson Electric in Sale- Leasebacks; **PREV EMPLOY:** Chmn. Exec. Comm., dir. Hubbard, Westervelt & Mottelay, Inc. (now Merrill Lynch Hubbard, Inc.); Head of the R.E. & Equipment Fin. Dept. of Loeb Rhoades & Co. (now Shearson/Amer. Express, Inc.); **PROFL AFFIL & HONORS:** Former Tr., Member Exec. Comm. C.I. Realty Investors, Sponsor William Polk Carey Prize in Econ. Annually, Wharton School of Univ. of PA; Sponsor W.P. Carey & Co., Inc. prize in Applied Math., CA Inst. of Tech.; **EDUC:** BS, 1953, Pol. Sci., Fin., Princeton Univ., Wharton Sch., Univ. of PA; **MIL SERV:** USAF, 1st Lt., 1953-55; **OTHER ACT & HONORS:** Pres. Council CA Inst. of Tech.; Nat. Execs. Comm., Nat. Council on Crime and Deliquency; Tr., The Rensselaerville Inst.; VP and Dir., The Huyck Preserve; **HOME ADD:** 525 Park Ave., New York, NY 10021, (212)371-2738; **BUS ADD:** 689 Fifth Ave., New York, NY 10022, (212)888-7700.

CARL, Robert E.——**B:** Sept. 1, 1927, Independence, MO, *Sr. VP - Mktg. Services*, Vantage Companies, Corp.; **PRIM RE ACT:** Consultant, Engineer, Architect, Developer, Builder, Owner/Investor, Property Manager, Syndicator; **OTHER RE ACT:** Site selection, mktg. (sales & leasing); **SERVICES:** Centralized responsibility for all realty services; **REP CLIENTS:** Many of the "Fortune 500" cos. as well as smaller bus. enterprises from coast to coast; **PREV EMPLOY:** VP - Sales for Dunn Props. of TX, Inc. (1970-71); **PROFL AFFIL & HONORS:** Nat. Assn. of Corp. RE Execs.; Nat. Assn. of Review Appraisers; Southern Indus. Devel. Council; TX Industrial Devel. Council, Winner of 19 different "Literature of the Year" Awards (1978-80) presented by Natl. Assn. of Indus. and Office Parks; **EDUC:** BS, 1950, Journalism (Advertising), Univ. of KS; **GRAD EDUC:** NY Inst. of Fin. CRE, 1967, Investment Analysis, So. Methodist Univ.; **OTHER ACT & HONORS:** Member, Dallas Cable Television Bd.; Past Pres. of Big D Toastmasters Club; Sr. VP of Sales & Mktg. Execs. Intl. Assn.; Also recipient of "Silver Anvil Award" from the Public Relations Soc. of Amer.; Lgn. of Hon. degree from Intl. Order of DeMolay; **HOME ADD:** 4209 Gloster Rd., Dallas, TX 75220, (214)351-3392; **BUS ADD:** 2525 Stemmons Freeway, Dallas, TX 75207, (214)631-0600.

CARLBERG, Daniel J.——**B:** Oct. 2, 1945, Chicago, IL; **PRIM RE ACT:** Developer, Lender, Owner/Investor, Syndicator; **SERVICES:** Gen. Fin. Planning; **PREV EMPLOY:** CML; **PROFL AFFIL & HONORS:** LUTC; **EDUC:** BS, 1967, Acctg. & Tax Law, CA Poly. Univ.; **GRAD EDUC:** MBS, 1972, Acctg., Woodbury Univ.; **MIL SERV:** USN; **HOME ADD:** 637 E. Rainier, Orange, CA, (214)998-8194; **BUS ADD:** 21733 Norwalk Blvd., Hawaiian Gardens, CA 90716, (213)420-9320.

CARLETON, Buck G., III——**B:** May 27, 1940, NYC, NY, *Pres.*, Landtect Corp.; **PRIM RE ACT:** Broker, Consultant, Developer, Owner/Investor, Property Manager, Syndicator; **OTHER RE ACT:** Indus. parks, ski resorts, tennis facilities, comml. bldgs.; **SERVICES:** Synd., prop. mgmt., specializing in turning around defunct projects and indus. and recreation indus.; **REP CLIENTS:** Stanford Research Inst., WA Tech. Inst., Greenfield Realty, First Nat. Bank of Glens Falls; **PREV EMPLOY:** First Nat. City Bank, NYC; **PROFL AFFIL & HONORS:** SIR; Amer. Mgmt. Assn.; Nat. Tour Brokers Assn.; Amer. Bus. Assn.; Interval Intl. Time Share; Hanover-Lebanon Bd. of Realtors; VT and NH Broker; **EDUC:** BA, 1961, Gen. Studies, Harvard Coll.; **GRAD EDUC:** MBA, 1964, Fin., Stanford Grad. School of Bus.; **EDUC HONORS:** Cum Laude, Honors; **OTHER ACT & HONORS:** Merion Cricket Club; Racquet Club of Philadelphia; Norwich Racquet Club; **HOME ADD:** Bragg Hill Rd., Norwich, VT 05055; **BUS ADD:** Box A-247, 3 Lebanon St., Hanover, NH 03755, (603)643-2353.

CARLILE, Linda Lee——**B:** Apr. 14, 1940, Carnegie, OK, *Pres.*, Linda Carlile, Realtors; **PRIM RE ACT:** Broker, Owner/Investor; **SERVICES:** RE sales, resid. and ltd. comml.; **REP CLIENTS:** Builders and the public engaged in buying and selling new homes and existing homes; **PREV EMPLOY:** Fin. Analyst, Allied Chem. Corp., Internal Auditor, US Govt.; **PROFL AFFIL & HONORS:** NAR; OK Assn. of Realtors; Women's Council of Realtors; Realtors Nat. Mktg. Inst.; Oklahoma City Metropolitan Bd. of Realtors; Oklahoma City C of C; Sales & Mktg. Exec., Central Oklahoma Homebuilders Assn., CRS; Dir., Oklahoma City, Metro. Bd. of Realtors 1980-81; Sec-Treas, Okla. City Metro. Bd. of Realtors 1981; Pres. Elect Okla City, Metro. Bd. of Realtors, 1982; **EDUC:** BBA, 1966, Acctg., Univ. of OK, Norman, OK; **OTHER ACT & HONORS:** Phi Mu, Frat.; **HOME ADD:** 11717 Greenwick Dr., Oklahoma City, OK 73132, (405)722-6275; **BUS ADD:** 2945 West Hefner Rd., Oklahoma City, OK 73120, (405)751-9725.

CARLIN, Bruce L.——**B:** Mar. 26, 1941, Newark, NJ, *Pres.*, Carlin Appraisal Service; **PRIM RE ACT:** Broker, Consultant, Appraiser; **SERVICES:** R.E. Appraisal & Consulting, Resid. Comml., Qualified Expert Witness., Condemnation Commissioner; **REP CLIENTS:** Employee reloc. cos.; fin. instns.; attys.; local; cty; and state condemnation authorities; public utilities; private corps.; municipalities; **PREV EMPLOY:** Pres. Carlin Realtors, Basking Ridge, NJ., Sold bus. in 1980.; **PROFL AFFIL & HONORS:** NJ Assn. Realtors; NAR (Sr. Member); NARA; NAIFA; AACA (Sr. Member), NJ Realtor of the Yr., 1979; **EDUC:** BS, 1963, Bus. Admin., Albright Coll.; **OTHER ACT & HONORS:** Kiwanis, Dist. Past Pres. Award, 1978; **HOME ADD:** 86 Old Army Rd., Bernardsville, NJ 07924, (201)766-7688; **BUS ADD:** 1 Finley Ave., Basking Ridge, NJ 07920, (201)766-2600.

CARLIN, William L.——**B:** Dec. 22, 1926, Chicago, IL, *Dealership RE Mgr.*, Ford Motor Co., Sales Operations; **OTHER RE ACT:** Corporate; **SERVICES:** Secure Land Construct. Dealership, Lease and Manage; **PROFL AFFIL & HONORS:** Nat. Assn. of Corporate RE Exec.; **EDUC:** BA, 1948, Econ., Lake Forest Coll.; **HOME ADD:** 586 Neff Rd., Grosse Pointe, MI 48230, (813)882-6299; **BUS ADD:** 300 Renaissance Center, PO Box 43336, Detroit, MI 48243, (313)568-4665.

CARLISLE, Charles T., Jr.——**B:** July 27, 1946, Morristown, TN, *Pres.*, Sequoyah Equities, Inc.; **PRIM RE ACT:** Consultant, Owner/Investor, Syndicator; **SERVICES:** Acquisition & synd., valuation, tax planning; **PREV EMPLOY:** FIS Associates, Inc., RE Tax & Fin. Consultants, Pres., 1970-1981; **PROFL AFFIL & HONORS:** AICPA, TN Soc. of CPA's, RESSI, Fin. Mgmt. Assn., CPA (TN); **EDUC:** BS, 1968, Acctg., Univ. of TN; **GRAD EDUC:** MBA, 1970, Fin., Univ. of TN; **EDUC HONORS:** Cum Laude, Phi Beta Phi, Beta Alpha Psi; **HOME ADD:** Big Cove Rd., Louisville, TN, (615)982-1913; **BUS ADD:** 1919 United American Plaza, Knoxville, TN 37929, (615)521-8999.

CARLISLE, Dale L.——**B:** Apr. 24, 1935, Walla Walla, WA, *Atty./Partner*, Gordon, Thomas, Honeywell, Malanca, Peterson & O'Hern; **PRIM RE ACT:** Attorney, Developer, Owner/Investor, Syndicator; **OTHER RE ACT:** Adjunct Prof., Univ. of Puget Sound, School of Law, Modern RE Transactions and Secured Land Transactions; **SERVICES:** Atty. specializing in RE & securities, doing RE purchase & sale, loan & other transactions including condo., and doing synd. work on real prop. securities.; **REP CLIENTS:** Nu-West, Inc., L. B. Nelson Corp., Northwest; Standard Pacific Northwest Corp.; Washington Mort.; Rainier Mort.; SG Mort.; The Rainier Fund; LSI-United, Inc.; other misc. builders, lenders and devels.; **PREV EMPLOY:** West Coast Gen. Counsel, Levitt & Sons; **PROFL AFFIL & HONORS:** Member - Real Prop., Probate & Trust Sect., Washington Bar Assn., ABA; Lecturer & Writer - Wash. State Bar Assn., CLE Comm., various real prop. & security law topics; **EDUC:** BS, 1957, Acctg., Univ. of ID; **GRAD EDUC:** George Washington Univ. Law School, 1960, Bus. Law, Law School; **EDUC HONORS:** Top Ten Sr. Award, Grad. with High Honors, Outstanding Sr. Award; Law Review; Student Bar Assn. - Pres.; **MIL SERV:** USAF, Capt.; **OTHER ACT & HONORS:** Asst. U.S. Atty., Western Dist. of WA, 1963-65; **HOME ADD:** 1312 Sunset Place, NE, Tacoma, WA 98422, (206)927-3383; **BUS ADD:** 2200 First Interstate Plaza, Tacoma, WA 98401, (206)572-5050.

CARLISLE, Kurt——B: Apr. 11, 1938, Hammond, IN, *VP*, Northern Trust Co., RE Div.; **PRIM RE ACT:** Banker; **SERVICES:** Mgmt. and sale of trust RE; **PROFL AFFIL & HONORS:** IREM; Chicago RE Bd.; 40 Club; CPM; **EDUC:** BS, 1960, Bus. Admin., IN Univ.; **MIL SERV:** USAR, S/Sgt.; **OTHER ACT & HONORS:** VP - Lawrence Hall School for Boys; **HOME ADD:** 1101 E Mayfair, Arlington Heights, IL 60004, (312)392-7625; **BUS ADD:** 50 S LaSalle St., Chicago, IL 60673, (312)630-6000.

CARLSBERG, Richard Presten——B: March 2, 1937, Stockton, CA, *Pres.*, Carlsberg Corp.; **PRIM RE ACT:** Broker, Consultant, Developer, Builder, Property Manager, Syndicator; **REP CLIENTS:** Indiv. investors, synds., builders & devels; **PREV EMPLOY:** Officer/Dir. during past 20 yrs. of approx. 40 privately held corp. in RE, Fin., Devel., Research, Petroleum & Acquisition; **PROFL AFFIL & HONORS:** Y.P.O. Golden West Chap., CA State Legis. Resolution 1965-1971, Award of Merit Los. Angeles Cty. 1965, U.S. Dept. of Interior Commendation, 1971; **EDUC:** AA, 1956, City Coll. of San Francisco; BA, 1959, Geology, Univ. of CA at Los Angeles; **MIL SERV:** CA Nat. Guard, 1959-1965; **OTHER ACT & HONORS:** Member, Bd. of Trs., UCLA Found.; **BUS ADD:** 2800 28th St., Santa Monica, CA 90405, (213)450-6800.

CARLSEN, Paul R.——B: May 24, 1937, Detroit, MI, *Pres.*, Paul R. Carlsen, Inc.; **PRIM RE ACT:** Broker; **OTHER RE ACT:** CPA; **SERVICES:** Comml. and Investment Props., IRC, Sect. 1031 Exchanges; **REP CLIENTS:** Various; **PROFL AFFIL & HONORS:** AICPA, CA Soc. of CPA's, Sacramento RE Exchange Grp., CPA; **EDUC:** BBA, 1959, Acctg., Univ. of MI; **EDUC HONORS:** Beta Alpha Psi; **OTHER ACT & HONORS:** Rotary; **HOME ADD:** 3008 Boeing Rd., Cameron Park, CA 95682, (916)677-2440; **BUS ADD:** 3008 Boeing Rd., Cameron Park, CA 95682, (916)677-2440.

CARLSMITH, Curtis W.——B: Aug. 25, 1940, Hilo, HI, *Atty.*, Carlsmith & Dwyer; **PRIM RE ACT:** Consultant, Attorney, Developer, Builder, Owner/Investor; **SERVICES:** Legal; **REP CLIENTS:** Security Pacific Mort. Corp., Fidelity S & L Assn., First Nat. Bank of Chicago, Lone Star HI, Inc., Kraus-Anderson of St. Paul Devel. Corp., Gentry Homes; Anderson Systems Int'l., Inc.; **PROFL AFFIL & HONORS:** Who's Who in American Law; **EDUC:** BA, 1962, Poli. Sci., Stanford Univ.; **GRAD EDUC:** JD, 1965, Law education, Harvard Law Sch.; **OTHER ACT & HONORS:** Who's Who in HI; **HOME ADD:** PO Box 1020, Honolulu, HI 96808; **BUS ADD:** 1800 Pioneer Plaza 900 Fort St., Honolulu, HI 96808, (808)524-8000.

CARLSON, Dr. Jack——*Executive Vice President*, National Association of Realtors; **OTHER RE ACT:** Profl. Assn. Admin.; **BUS ADD:** 430 N. Michigan Ave., Chicago, IL 60611, (312)440-8000.*

CARLSON, LeRoy E.——B: Oct. 29, 1945, Los Angeles, CA, *Treas.*, Real Estate Investment Trust of CA; **OTHER RE ACT:** Advisor; **SERVICES:** Prop. admin. and acquisition, and acctg.; **PREV EMPLOY:** William Walters Co. (still employed); **PROFL AFFIL & HONORS:** AICPA, CPA; **EDUC:** BS, 1971, Bus., Univ. of Southern CA; **HOME ADD:** PO Box 353, Manhattan Beach, CA 90266, (213)379-6710; **BUS ADD:** 2444 Wilshire Blvd., Santa Monica, CA 90403, (213)829-6892.

CARLSON, Margaret C.——B: June 25, 1923, Atlantic City, NJ, *Pres.-Treas.*, Five Star Realty, Inc.; **PRIM RE ACT:** Broker; **SERVICES:** RE sales, prop. mgmt., appraising, time sharing sales; **REP CLIENTS:** Prime Computer, Digital, Data Gen., Honeywell, IBM; **PROFL AFFIL & HONORS:** Gr. Boston RE Bd., MA Assn. of Realtors, NAR, South Middlesex Area C of C, CRB, CRS, GRI, Realtor of the Year 1975; Business Woman of the Year 1981; **OTHER ACT & HONORS:** Assoc. Member Zoning Bd. of Appeals 1976-1982; 1980-1981 VP C of C - South Middlesex Area; Chairperson, Comm. on Admin. - West Suburban YWCA, Dir., YWCA, Corporator-Boston Five Cents Savings Banks; **HOME ADD:** 149 Summer St., Framingham, MA 01701, (617)872-5459; **BUS ADD:** 197 Worcester St., Natick, MA 01760, (617)655-0608.

CARLSON, Richard Wakefield——B: Apr. 25, 1939, Keene, NH, *Pres.*, R.W. Carlson Assoc. Inc., Carlson RE; **PRIM RE ACT:** Broker, Consultant, Appraiser, Property Manager; **SERVICES:** Consulting & mktg. servs. for resid., comml., investment and condo. props. located N. of Boston, feasibility studies, prop. mgmt., condo mgmt.; **REP CLIENTS:** Several public,pvt. investors, lenders, attys., and devel.; **PROFL AFFIL & HONORS:** NAR, MA Assn. of Realtors, Greater Salem Bd. of Realtors, Inter Community Relocation Serv., RNMI, GRI, CRS, CRB; **EDUC:** BS, 1962, Chem. Engrg., Univ. of Rochester, NY; **GRAD EDUC:** MBA, 1964, Bus. Admin., Harvard Bus. Sch.; **HOME ADD:** 83 Harbor Ave., Marblehead, MA 01945, (617)639-0636; **BUS ADD:** 148 Washington St., Salem, MA 01970, (617)741-0500.

CARLSON, Rudy——*Dir. of Bus. Dev.*, Electronics Memories & Magnetics Corp.; **PRIM RE ACT:** Property Manager; **BUS ADD:** 15760 Ventura Blvd., Ste. 1727, Encino, CA 91436, (213)995-1755.*

CARLSON, Russ——B: Apr. 4, 1938, Worcester, MA, *VP Sales*, F.I.P. Corp; **PRIM RE ACT:** Consultant, Developer, Builder, Owner/Investor, Property Manager; **SERVICES:** Design/build, sales/lease, sale/leaseback, prop. mgmt.; **REP CLIENTS:** Major intl. cos., Siemens, Warner Lambert, Royal Bus. Machine, Hewlett-Packard etc.; **PREV EMPLOY:** Northeast Utilities; **PROFL AFFIL & HONORS:** New Haven C of C, Wallingford C of C (on both Econ. Devel. Comm.) Greater New Haven Bd. of Realtors, SIR; **EDUC:** Bus. Admin./Econ., 1958-1962, RE, Univ. of NH; **MIL SERV:** US Army-Armor, 1st Lt.; **OTHER ACT & HONORS:** Dir., Cheshire Soccer Club; Member, Military Academy Selection Comm. Leader; Boy Scouts; **HOME ADD:** Bittersweet Lane, Cheshire, CT 06410, (203)272-6120; **BUS ADD:** P.O. Box 354, Farmington, CT 06032, (203)677-1361.

CARLSON, Tom——B: Nov. 28, 1932, Lodgepole, NE, *Owner*, Carlson Development; **PRIM RE ACT:** Developer, Builder, Owner/Investor, Property Manager, Syndicator; **PROFL AFFIL & HONORS:** Wharton Cty. Bd. of Realtors; **EDUC:** BS, 1957, Bus. Admin., Univ. of NE; **GRAD EDUC:** MPA/MA, 1963, Pub. Admin./Econ., George Washington Univ. & Amer. Univ.; **EDUC HONORS:** Omicron Delta Epsilon; **MIL SERV:** US Army, Cpl., Good Conduct, 1953-1955; **OTHER ACT & HONORS:** Republican Chmn., Wharton Co., 1975-present; Lions; Wharton C of C; K of C; Also affiliated w/Physical Therapy Assn., Inc., (Pres.); **HOME ADD:** Rt. 2, Box 148B, Wharton, TX 77488, (713)532-2233; **BUS ADD:** Rt. 2, Box 148B, Wharton, TX 77488, (713)532-4810.

CARLSTON, Michael R.——B: Mar. 5, 1945, Fairview, UT, *Atty.*, Snow Christensen and Martineau; **PRIM RE ACT:** Attorney; **REP CLIENTS:** Lenders and indiv. or instnl. investors in comml. prop.; **PROFL AFFIL & HONORS:** ABA; **EDUC:** BS, 1970, Poli. Sci., Univ. of UT; **GRAD EDUC:** JD, 1973, Univ. of UT; **EDUC HONORS:** Cum Laude, Order of the Coif; **OTHER ACT & HONORS:** ABA, Trusts and Real Property; **HOME ADD:** 855 Harwood Dr., Murray, UT 84107, (801)261-3877; **BUS ADD:** 10 Exchange Pl. 11th Floor, PO Box 3000, Salt Lake City, UT 84110, (801)521-9000.

CARLTON, Robert T.——*Sr. VP & Treas.*, MacAndrews & Forbes Co.; **PRIM RE ACT:** Property Manager; **BUS ADD:** 555 Fifth Ave., New York, NY 10017, (212)688-9000.*

CARMICHAEL, H. Elden——B: June 23, 1946, Washington, IN, *Managing Partner*, Barger and Carmichael, CPA's; **PRIM RE ACT:** Consultant, Developer, Owner/Investor; **PROFL AFFIL & HONORS:** Amer. Inst. of CPA's; GA Soc. of CPA's; Nat. Conference of CPA Practitioners; **EDUC:** BBA, 1968, Acctg., GA So. Coll., Statesboro, GA; **HOME ADD:** 111 Tolomato Trace, St. Simons Island, GA 31522, (912)638-4541; **BUS ADD:** PO Box 1572, 600 G St., Brunswick, GA 31521, (912)264-4737.

CARMICHAEL, Joseph R.——B: June 13, 1915, Eureka, UT, *VP*, Irving Trust Co., RE Services; **PRIM RE ACT:** Property Manager; **SERVICES:** Manages bank premises and fiduciary RE in US and abroad; **PREV EMPLOY:** Builder, Devel.; **PROFL AFFIL & HONORS:** MBAA, NY State Appraisal Soc., RE Bd. of NY; **EDUC:** BS, 1939, Engrg., Univ. of WA, Seattle, WA; **MIL SERV:** USN, Capt., Navy Cross; **HOME ADD:** 333 E. 30th St., New York, NY 10016, (212)686-0792; **BUS ADD:** One Wall St., New York, NY 10015, (212)487-3737.

CARNAHAN, John M., III——B: Mar. 9, 1949, Alton, IL, *Pres.*, Carnahan and Carnahan, P.C.; **PRIM RE ACT:** Attorney; **SERVICES:** Tax Atty.; **REP CLIENTS:** Midwest Aluminum Mfg. Co.; Nuclear Diagnosis, Inc.; Williamson Cattle Co.; **PROFL AFFIL & HONORS:** ABA - Sections of Taxation, Real Prop. and Trusts; MO Bar, Co-Chmn., MO Bar, Section of Taxation; Instr., MO Bar, Cont. Legal Educ. Programs; **EDUC:** BS, 1971, Econ., SMSU; **GRAD EDUC:** JD, 1974, Univ. of MO, Columbia; LLM, 1975, Taxation, Univ. of Miami, Miami, FL; **EDUC HONORS:** Cum Laude; Honors, Order of Coif; **HOME ADD:** Rte. 18, Springfield, MO 65804; **BUS ADD:** 1435 E. Sunshine, Springifeld, MO 65804, (417)887-8490.

CARNEGHI, Christopher C.——B: June 26, 1950, San Jose, CA, *Partner*, Mills-Carneghi Inc.; **PRIM RE ACT:** Consultant; **SERVICES:** RE/mkt. research & appraisals; **PREV EMPLOY:** Kaiser Aetna; **PROFL AFFIL & HONORS:** ULI; **EDUC:** BA, 1972, Urban Studies, Econ., Univ. of CA, Berkeley; **GRAD EDUC:** MBA, 1978, RE, San Jose State Univ.; **HOME ADD:** 2440 Cristorey Pl., Los Altos, CA 94022, (415)965-8771; **BUS ADD:** 235 Montgomery St. #1264, San Francisco, CA 94104, (415)398-2666.

CARNEY, Patrick——B: Aug. 16, 1948, New Bedford, MA, *Pres.*, The Claremont Co., Inc., Pres., Claremont Mgmt. Co., Inc.; Pres., Claremont Devel. Assocs., Inc.; **PRIM RE ACT:** Developer, Property Manager, Syndicator; **SERVICES:** RE devel., mgmt., synd., primarily in the resid. multi-family area; **PROFL AFFIL & HONORS:** NAHB; Nat. Leased Housing Assn.; NAR; **EDUC:** BA, 1970, Poli. Sci., Boston Coll.; **EDUC HONORS:** Grad. Magna Cum Laude; **HOME ADD:** Rockland Farm, Two Rockland St., S. Dartmouth, MA 02748; **BUS ADD:** 628 Pleasant St., PO Box 6001, New Bedford, MA 02742, (617)992-4200.

CARP, Mark B.——B: Dec. 20, 1946, Baltimore, MD, *Pres.*, Mark B. Carp and Co., Inc.; **PRIM RE ACT:** Broker, Developer; **SERVICES:** Full brokerage services; **REP CLIENTS:** Major chains in virtually all phases of comml. RE; **PREV EMPLOY:** Bd. of Realtors of Greater Baltimore; Erwin L. Greenberg and Associates, Developers; **EDUC:** BS, 1969, Journalism, Univ. of MD; **MIL SERV:** USAR, Sp 4; **HOME ADD:** 7121 Pheasant Cross Dr., (301)484-3153; **BUS ADD:** 2531 St. Paul St., Baltimore, MD 21218, (301)243-1333.

CARPE, Keith——*Ed.*, CA Assn. of Realtors, CA Real Estate Magazine; **PRIM RE ACT:** Real Estate Publisher; **BUS ADD:** 505 Shatto Place, Los Angeles, CA 90020, (214)380-7190.*

CARPENTER, Charlton H.——B: Jan 11, 1937, Pittsburgh, PA, *Partner*, Fairfield & Woods; **PRIM RE ACT:** Attorney; **SERVICES:** Legal assistance & counseling; **REP CLIENTS:** Aetna Life Ins. Co.; Bank of Amer.; John Hancock Mutual Life Ins. Co.; The Hartford Grp.; Midland Fed. S & L Assn.; Can. Comml. Bank; **PREV EMPLOY:** Law clerk to Chief Judge Alfred A. Arraj, US Dist. Ct., Dist. of CO, 1964-1965; **PROFL AFFIL & HONORS:** ABA, CO Bar Assn., Denver Bar Assn., Law Club of Denver, CO Bar Assn. RE Council (Chmn. 1981-82), Amer. Coll. of Mort. Attys.; Who's Who in Amer. Law; **EDUC:** BS, 1958, Econ., Univ. of PA (Wharton Sch. of Fin. & Commerce); **GRAD EDUC:** LLB, 1964, Univ. of CO; **EDUC HONORS:** Law Review; **MIL SERV:** USN, Lt.; **OTHER ACT & HONORS:** 26-Club, Valley Ctry. Club; **HOME ADD:** 9894 E. Ida Ave., Englewood, CO 80111, (303)770-4288; **BUS ADD:** 1600 Colorado Natl. Bldg., 950 17th St., Denver, CO 80202, (303)534-6135.

CARPENTER, Claude——B: Dec. 30, 1924, Little Rock, AR, *Atty.*; **PRIM RE ACT:** Attorney, Owner/Investor; **GRAD EDUC:** JD/MSE; **MIL SERV:** USN; (SOM); US Army Col. (Retd.); **BUS ADD:** 809 N. Palm St., Little Rock, AR 72205, (501)666-5544.

CARPENTER, J. Clifton——B: Sep. 3 1914, Taft, CA, *Pres.*, Carpenter Valuation Service, Inc.; **PRIM RE ACT:** Consultant, Appraiser; **SERVICES:** Valuation, consultant; **REP CLIENTS:** Attys., lenders, prop. owners; **PROFL AFFIL & HONORS:** SREA, ASA, SRPA, SRA, Bakersfield Bd. of Realtors, CA Assn. of Realtors, NAR, ASFMRA; **EDUC:** BS, Trans., Univ. of CA; **MIL SERV:** US Army, W.O.J.G.; **OTHER ACT & HONORS:** Kiwanis, Masons; **HOME ADD:** 2709 Primera Vista, Bakersfield, CA, (805)871-5446; **BUS ADD:** 1829 F St., Bakersfield, CA 93303, (805)325-5091.

CARPENTER, James L.——*Owner/Broker*, James L. Carpenter & Assoc., RE Brokerage; **PRIM RE ACT:** Broker; **SERVICES:** RE Brokerage, Shopping Ctrs., Office Bldgs., Apt. Complexes, Mobile Home Parks; **REP CLIENTS:** Synd., indiv. investors, pension funds, Investment Groups; **PREV EMPLOY:** RE 30 yrs., also sales rep. heavy machinery co.; **PROFL AFFIL & HONORS:** TX RE Assn.; **MIL SERV:** US Army; **HOME TEL:** (214)239-3687; **BUS ADD:** 5151 Placid Way, Dallas, TX 75234, (214)239-3687.

CARPENTER, Lyle——B: Aug. 3, 1941, Yuma, CO, *Pres.*, Mortgage Finance, Inc.; **OTHER RE ACT:** Mort. banker; **SERVICES:** RE morts.; **REP CLIENTS:** Comml. investors and devels.; **PROFL AFFIL & HONORS:** Nat. Assn. of Review Appraisers; Amer. Soc. of Farm and Mgrs.; **EDUC:** BS, 1964, Agricultural Bus., CO State Univ.; **EDUC HONORS:** Pacemaker, Student Body Pres., ODK; **OTHER ACT & HONORS:** Alpha Gamma RHO, Frat.; Nat. Pres., Future Farmer of Amer., Pres. Denver Agricult. & Livestock Club 1970; **HOME ADD:** 1250 Humboldt, Denver, CO 80218; **BUS ADD:** 1600 Broadway, 2120, Denver, CO 80202, (303)292-1133.

CARPENTER, Paul J.——B: Aug. 27, 1915, Kanab, UT, *Pres.*, Carpenter Realty, Inc.; **PRIM RE ACT:** Broker, Consultant, Owner/Investor; **SERVICES:** Sale, purchase, lease, exchange, fin.; **REP CLIENTS:** All major oil co's., Albertson, Independent Oil Co.'s. JB's Big Boy Restaurants, Discount fabrics, Taco Bell, Pic 'N' Save Stores, Safeway; **PREV EMPLOY:** 17 yrs. Std. Oil. of CA, 1 yr. United Oil, 1 year youngest postmaster in US; **PROFL AFFIL & HONORS:** SL Bd. Realtors, NAREB, SL C of C; **EDUC:** S. UT Coll., 1 yr.; **MIL SERV:** Infantry, Cpl., Victory Medal; **OTHER ACT & HONORS:** State delegate Republican CA, Chmn. Planning & Zoning Comm. - SL Bd. of Realtors; **HOME ADD:** 1653 Redondo Ave., Salt Lake City, UT 84105, (801)467-7960; **BUS ADD:** 444 S. State, Salt Lake City, UT 84111, (801)521-7391.

CARPENTER, R. Jay——B: Jan. 24, 1955, Mesa, AZ, *Partner*, Carpenter Investments; **PRIM RE ACT:** Consultant, Developer, Owner/Investor, Syndicator; **SERVICES:** Synd. of comml. props.; **REP CLIENTS:** Indiv. or instnl. investors in comml. props.; **PREV EMPLOY:** Mellon Nat. Mort. Constr. Loan Admin.; **EDUC:** BS, 1977, Gen. Bus. Admin., fin., RE, AZ State Univ.; **GRAD EDUC:** MBA, 1981, Fin., RE, Univ. of S. CA; **EDUC HONORS:** Cum Laude, Beta Gamma Sigma; **OTHER ACT & HONORS:** Delta Sigma Pi, Bus. Frat.; **BUS ADD:** 3300 N. Central, Suite 1300, Phoenix, AZ 85012, (612)241-9395.

CARPENTER, R.L., Jr.——B: Jan. 11, 1948, Batesville, AR, *Pres.*, Realty World-Carpenter & Assoc. Inc.; **PRIM RE ACT:** Broker, Appraiser, Property Manager, Insuror; **SERVICES:** Valuation, prop. mgmt.; **REP CLIENTS:** Work with sev. natl. relocation cos.; **PROFL AFFIL & HONORS:** Pres. of 1981 Batesville Bd. of Realtors, Member of both State and NAR, Member of Million Dollar Club, GRI; **EDUC:** BA, 1971, Bus. & Econ., AR Coll.; **HOME ADD:** 210 Jean St., Batesville, AR 72501, (501)793-5111; **BUS ADD:** PO Box 2891, 2035 Harrison St., Batesville, AR 72501, (501)793-8100.

CARPENTER, Tom——B: Jan. 25, 1944, San Antonio, TX, *Owner*, Tom Carpenter, Realtor; **PRIM RE ACT:** Broker; **SERVICES:** Resid., Comml. & Ranch Sales; **PROFL AFFIL & HONORS:** San Angelo Bd. of Realtors, Tar, NAR, San Angelo Bd. Pres. 1974-1975; **EDUC:** BS, 1967, Angelo State Univ.; **OTHER ACT & HONORS:** Dir., First City Natl. Bank of San Angelo; **HOME ADD:** 2725 Oak Mountain, San Angelo, TX 76901, (915)949-0035; **BUS ADD:** 2902 W. Beauregard, San Angelo, TX 76901, (915)949-0531.

CARPINO, Salvatore A.——B: Mar. 29, 1948, NY, NY, *Asst. Gen. Counsel*, Department of Professional Regulation; **PRIM RE ACT:** Attorney, Regulator, Owner/Investor; **SERVICES:** Regualation, prosecution & education of RE licensees; **REP CLIENTS:** State of FL; **PREV EMPLOY:** Chief Trial Counsel, Dept. Banking & Fin., Office of The Comptroller, St. of FL, Staff Atty. FL RE Commn.; **PROFL AFFIL & HONORS:** ABA, FL Bar, Middle, S. Dist. Fed. Ct.; **EDUC:** BA, 1971, Psych., Hofstra Univ.; **GRAD EDUC:** JD, 1976, Law, W. New England Law; **HOME ADD:** 2745 Hickory Ridge, Tallahassee, FL 32308, (904)386-4262; **BUS ADD:** 130 N. Monroe St., Tallahassee, FL 32308, (904)488-0062.

CARR, Edward J.——B: July 22, 1932, N.Y.C., NY, *Dir., Corp. Services Div.*, Amer. Hosp. Supply Corp.; **OTHER RE ACT:** Corp. user-owner; **SERVICES:** R.E., Arch. design, Constr., Prop. Mgmt.; **REP CLIENTS:** Div. of Amer. Hosp. Supply Corp.; **PROFL AFFIL & HONORS:** NACORE, IDRC, ULI; **EDUC:** BBA, 1970, Indus.Mgmt., Northwestern Univ.; **MIL SERV:** USN, RD1; **HOME ADD:** 1507 Appleby Rd., Palatine, IL 60067, (312)934-3907; **BUS ADD:** One American Plaza, Evanston, IL 60201, (312)866-4267.

CARR, Geo. Watts., Jr.——B: Dec. 6, 1918, Durham, NC, *Pres.*, Southland Assoc.; **PRIM RE ACT:** Broker, Developer, Insuror; **EDUC:** AB, 1940, Econ., Univ. of NC (Chapel Hill); **EDUC HONORS:** Phi Beta Kappa; **MIL SERV:** USMC, Col., 1940-45; **OTHER ACT & HONORS:** Durham City Council, 1949-57; **HOME ADD:** 15 Oak Dr., Durham, NC 27707, (919)489-2259; **BUS ADD:** 212 Corcoran St., Durham, NC 27702.

CARR, Howard——**B:** Mar. 17, 1949, Washington, DC, *Partner*, The Howard Companies, Comml-Investment; **PRIM RE ACT:** Broker, Consultant, Appraiser, Developer, Builder, Owner/Investor, Syndicator; **SERVICES:** Complete Appraisal, feasibility studies, purchase and synd.; **REP CLIENTS:** Chemical Bank, Bankers Trust, Ely Lilly Drug Co., G.D. Searle & Co., Chrysler Credit Corp., Dime Savings Bank of NY, (Mechanics Exchange Savings Bank, Albany, New York); **PROFL AFFIL & HONORS:** CCIM, NYSAR, NAR, SREA, NY State Appraisers Soc., RESSI; **EDUC:** BS, 1971, Mktg. & Mgmt., Long Island Univ.; **HOME ADD:** 17 Schalren Dr., Latham, NY 12110, (518)783-1200; **BUS ADD:** 50 State St., Albany, NY 12207, (518)434-8181.

CARR, James M.——**B:** July 13, 1921, Morgan Cty., KY, *Pres.*, Tenny Hill Inc.; **PRIM RE ACT:** Broker, Developer, Builder; **PREV EMPLOY:** 30 yrs. as builder, developer; **MIL SERV:** US Army, PFC; **HOME ADD:** 400 Kenawood Dr., Lexington, KY 40505, (606)299-6434; **BUS ADD:** 1035 N. Limestone St., Lexington, KY 40505, (606)255-7994.

CARR, James S.——**B:** Apr. 9, 1947, Norristown, PA, *Pres.*, Forge Builders, Inc.; **PRIM RE ACT:** Consultant, Engineer, Architect, Developer, Builder, Owner/Investor; **PROFL AFFIL & HONORS:** AIA, Chmn. E. Whiteland Township Municipal Authority, AIA, NCARB; **EDUC:** 1969, Arch., Bus., Drexel Univ.; **GRAD EDUC:** Masters, 1974, Arch., Bus., Drexel Univ.; **MIL SERV:** US Army, Capt.; **OTHER ACT & HONORS:** Chmn. E. Whiteland Township Municipal Authority; **HOME ADD:** 11 Dale Ln., Malvern, PA 19355, (215)644-3319; **BUS ADD:** 11 Dale Ln., Malvern, PA 19355, (215)647-8831.

CARRA, Lawrence——**B:** Sept. 16, 1953, Long Island, NY, Pascarella, Dehler, Illmensee & Carra; **PRIM RE ACT:** Attorney; **SERVICES:** Comml. & resid. RE counseling; **REP CLIENTS:** Indiv. and instnl. investors in comml. properties; **PROFL AFFIL & HONORS:** Nassau Cty. Bar; Federal Courts Comm.; NYS Bar Assn.; **EDUC:** BA, 1975, Hist./Pol. Sci., SUNY; Potsdam Coll.; **GRAD EDUC:** JD, 1978, Law, Univ. of Toledo; **EDUC HONORS:** Magna Cum Laude; **HOME ADD:** 43 Narcissus Dr., Syosset, NY 11791, (516)921-4655; **BUS ADD:** 1301 Franklin Ave., Garden City, NY 11530, (516)742-1134.

CARREL, Herbert L., CMB——**B:** Feb. 27, 1941, Bicknell, IN, *VP*, Allstate Enterprises Mortgage Corp., Subsidiary of Sears, Roebuck & Co.; **PRIM RE ACT:** Banker, Lender; **OTHER RE ACT:** Mort. banker; **SERVICES:** Originate and serv. mort. loans; **REP CLIENTS:** Banks, savings & loans, pension funds, FNMA & GNMA; **PROFL AFFIL & HONORS:** MBAA, Cert. Mort. Banker; **EDUC:** BS, 1966, RE, IN State Univ.; **MIL SERV:** US Army, E-5; **HOME ADD:** 23 Windsor Dr., Lincolnshire, IL 60015, (312)948-7146; **BUS ADD:** 104 Wilmot Rd., Suite 500, Deerfield, IL 60015, (312)291-6060.

CARRESE, John A.——**B:** Apr. 15, 1930, Brooklyn, NY, *Chief Appraiser*, Corp. Counsel, City of New York, Condemnation & Certiorar; **PRIM RE ACT:** Consultant, Appraiser; **PROFL AFFIL & HONORS:** Past Pres. Amer. Soc. of Appraisers; Past Pres. Soc. of Govt. Appraisers, SRA; ASA; CSA; CRA; **EDUC:** BA, 1953, Econ., Sociology, Philosophy, St. Francis Coll., Loretto, PA; **MIL SERV:** USA, Cpl.; **OTHER ACT & HONORS:** Past Comdr. Peter Minuit; RE Amer. Legion Post; **HOME ADD:** 9481 Ridge Blvd, Brooklyn, NY 11209, (212)238-6080; **BUS ADD:** 100 Church St., New York, NY 10007, (212)566-4588.

CARRIN, Marvin C.——*Dir. of Comml. RE & Planning*, D.H. 1 Enterprises, Inc.; **PRIM RE ACT:** Developer; **BUS ADD:** 984 North Breadway, Yonkers, NY 10107, (914)968-3700.*

CARRITHERS, Charles M.——*Pres.*, Carrithers Realty Co.; **PRIM RE ACT:** Broker, Consultant, Appraiser, Property Manager, Lender, Owner/Investor; **PROFL AFFIL & HONORS:** VP, VA RE Exchange; Dir. Tidewater RE Exchangors Assn., CRS, CRB; **OTHER ACT & HONORS:** Dir., Newport News Peninsula Kiwanis Club; **BUS ADD:** 12345 Warwick Blvd., Newport News, VA 23606, (804)599-5555.

CARROLL, Donald R.——**B:** May 31, 1950, Toledo, OH, *Asst. VP - Mgr. Probate Div.*, Ohio Citizens Bank; **PRIM RE ACT:** Attorney, Banker, Property Manager; **PROFL AFFIL & HONORS:** Amer., OH, Toledo Bar Assns., Admitted to OH Bar-1979; **EDUC:** BA, 1973, Hist., Philosophy, Psych., Univ. of Toledo; **GRAD EDUC:** JD, 1979, Law, Univ. of Toledo; **HOME ADD:** 1996 Rose Arbor Dr., Toledo, OH 43614; **BUS ADD:** PO Box 1688, Toledo, OH 43603, (419)259-6718.

CARROLL, James J.——**B:** Aug. 1, 1946, Cincinnati, OH, *Sec.-Treas.*, Sterling-Mead, Inc.; **PRIM RE ACT:** Developer, Syndicator; **SERVICES:** Devel. of multi-family, single family & comml. props.; **PREV EMPLOY:** Corp. Officer RE Devel./Public Practice as CPA; **PROFL AFFIL & HONORS:** ABA; OH Bar Assn.; Cincinnati Bar Assn.; Amer. Inst. of CPA; OH Soc. of CPA; RESSI; **EDUC:** BBA, 1969, Acctg., Univ. of Cincinnati; **GRAD EDUC:** JD, 1978, Chase Coll. of Law - NKU; **MIL SERV:** US Army Res., Sgt.; **HOME ADD:** 1343 Michigan Ave., Cincinnati, OH 45208, (513)321-8213; **BUS ADD:** 614 Provident Bank Bldg., Seventh & Vine St., Cincinnati, OH 45202, (513)381-5263.

CARROLL, James R.——**B:** Oct. 19, 1947, Little Rock, AR, *Pres.*, Block Mortgate Co., Inc.; **PRIM RE ACT:** Broker, Consultant, Attorney, Developer, Lender; **PROFL AFFIL & HONORS:** Mort. Bankers Assn. of Amer., Mort. Bankers Assn. of AR, 1981 Pres., ABA, AR Bar Assn., AR Realtors Assn., Home Builders Assn. of Greater Little Rock; **EDUC:** BA, 1973, Pol. Sci., OH State Univ., Columbus, OH; **GRAD EDUC:** JD, 1978, Univ. of AR at Little Rock School of Law; **EDUC HONORS:** Cum Laude, Cum Laude; **MIL SERV:** US Army, Sgt.; **HOME ADD:** #4 Silver Birch Ct., Little Rock, AR 72212, (501)227-4102; **BUS ADD:** PO Box 2060, Little Rock, AR 72203, (501)362-7700.

CARROLL, John C.——**B:** Feb. 26, 1942, Arlington, VA, *Pres.*, Housing Capital Corp.; **PRIM RE ACT:** Owner/Investor; **SERVICES:** Equity investment; subordinated loans, joint venture participants; **PREV EMPLOY:** Pres. of Nat. Mort. Corp., subsidiary of Fin. Gen. Bankshares; **EDUC:** BS, 1971, Pol. Sci., Brown Univ.; **HOME ADD:** 11625 Sourwood Ln., Reston, VA 22091, (703)860-2290; **BUS ADD:** 1133 15th St., N.W., Washington, DC 20005, (202)857-5753.

CARROLL, Stephen——**B:** Dec. 19, 1949, Darby, PA, *Atty.*, Kassab, Cherry & Archbold; **PRIM RE ACT:** Attorney, Banker, Lender; **PREV EMPLOY:** Continental Bank (PA); Community Fed. S&L; **PROFL AFFIL & HONORS:** Cty. Bar Assn., PA Bar Assn., ABA, PBA, Real Property, Probate & Trust Sec.; **EDUC:** BA, 1972, Liberal Arts, PA State Univ.; **GRAD EDUC:** JD, 1976, DE Law School; **EDUC HONORS:** Deans List, Delta Theta Phi Scholarship Key; **BUS ADD:** Lawyers Title Bldg., 214 N Jackson St, Media, PA 19063.

CARRUTH, Dennis——**B:** Feb. 26, 1943, Rawlins, WY, *Pres.*, Ken-Caryl Ranch Corp.; **PRIM RE ACT:** Broker, Developer, Builder, Owner/Investor; **OTHER RE ACT:** Manage 10,000 acre new town devel. including office, resid., recreational, municipal planning, devel., fin.; **REP CLIENTS:** Manville Corp., Columbia Savings & Loan Assn., Briarwood, NV; **PREV EMPLOY:** MCA Fin., 1970-73, RE Acquisition, Fin.; **PROFL AFFIL & HONORS:** ULI, CO Assn. of Housing and Building, Dir.; Denver Homebuilders Assn., Officer & Dir.; Water for CO officer & dir., CO Front Range Project; Denver C of C, 1978 Leadership Denver; **EDUC:** BS, 1966, Gen. Engrg., Bus. Admin.,, Univ. of WY; **GRAD EDUC:** MBA, 1968, Fin., Mgmt., Univ. of WY; **EDUC HONORS:** Deans list, Outstanding Gen. Engr., U of WY Ski team (capt.), Deans list, grad. assistantship, post grad. work, Univ. of Cincinnati; **MIL SERV:** US Public Serv. Lt., 03, 1968-70; **OTHER ACT & HONORS:** US Ski Assn., Metropolitan (Denver) Water Roundtable; Also Affiliated w/Recreations, Inc. - VP; **HOME ADD:** 7323 Silverhorn Dr., Evergreen, CO 80439, (303)674-1629; **BUS ADD:** 10579 Bradford Rd., Littleton, CO 80127, (303)979-1976.

CARSON, Christopher N.——**B:** Dec. 13, 1923, NY, NY, *Dir. of Mgmt.*, Abrams Benisch Riker, Inc.; **PRIM RE ACT:** Consultant, Property Manager, Engineer; **SERVICES:** Counseling indivs., instns. and corps. in prop. mgmt.; devel. and operations of high rise office bldgs. Supervise engineering, energy mgmt., budgeting, cost control. Negotiate both const. and serv. contracts. Perform problem prop. evaluations; **PROFL AFFIL & HONORS:** NAREB; ASREC; BOMA and IREM; **EDUC:** BEE, 1948, Manhattan Coll.; **MIL SERV:** USAF; 1st Lt.; **HOME ADD:** 12 Chelsea Ct, Hillsdale, NJ 07642, (201)664-4451; **BUS ADD:** 6 E. 43rd St, New York, NY 10017, (212)682-4900.

CARSON, J. Terrence——**B:** Apr. 2, 1938, Los Angeles, CA, *Pres.*, J.T. Carson & Co., Inc.; **PRIM RE ACT:** Broker, Consultant, Appraiser, Developer, Owner/Investor, Property Manager, Insuror, Syndicator; **OTHER RE ACT:** Converter; **SERVICES:** Prop. mgmt. brokerage, consulting synd.; **REP CLIENTS:** First Serv. Corp., Div. of First Fed. S&L; Prop. Mgr. Amer. Towers; South Hills Health System; **PROFL AFFIL & HONORS:** IREM, NAHB, RAM, CPM; **EDUC:** BA, 1961, Eng., Univ. of Pittsburgh; **GRAD EDUC:** MBA, 1970, Bus., Univ. of Pittsburgh; **MIL SERV:** USMC, Sgt.; **OTHER ACT & HONORS:** Pittsburgh Athletic Assn., Duquesne Club; **HOME ADD:** Box 32, Star Rte. 30, Ligonier, PA 15650, (412)539-2631; **BUS ADD:** 3 Bayard Rd., Pittsburgh, PA 15213, (412)682-0200.

CARSWELL, Robert S.——**B:** Aug. 21, 1939, Toronto, Ontario., *Lawyer*, Byers Casgrain; **PRIM RE ACT:** Attorney; **SERVICES:** Specialist in RE transactions; **REP CLIENTS:** The Cadillac Fairview Corp. Ltd.; Hudson's Bay Co., Ltd.; Credit Foncier; **EDUC:** BA, 1960, Math., McGill; **GRAD EDUC:** BCL, 1963, Law, McGill; **EDUC HONORS:** Honors, Math.; **HOME ADD:** 605 Roslyn Ave., Westmount, Que., Can., (514)481-5078; **BUS ADD:** 800 Victoria Sq., Suite 2401, Montreal, H4z1A6, Que., Can., (514)878-3711.

CARTER, Doris V.——**B:** Miami, FL, *Pres.*, Galaxy Intl. Realty, Inc.; **PRIM RE ACT:** Broker, Consultant, Property Manager; **OTHER RE ACT:** Decorator; **SERVICES:** We work mainly with the Intl. Investors (European, S & Central Amer.) who wish to own various types of prop. in FL; **BUS ADD:** 285 NW 27th Ave., Suite 26, Miami, FL 33125, (305)541-2000.

CARTER, Joe M., Jr.——**B:** Dec. 21, 1943, Nashville, TN, *VP & Mgr. Devel. Lending*, SC Nat. Bank, Mort. Loan; **PRIM RE ACT:** Banker; **SERVICES:** Income prop. & resort constr. loans and devel. loans; **REP CLIENTS:** RE devels.; **PREV EMPLOY:** Bankers Tr. of SC; **PROFL AFFIL & HONORS:** Mort. Bankers Assn.; Pi Sigma Epsilon; **EDUC:** BS, 1970, Bus. Admin., Mktg. Econ., Univ. of SC; **GRAD EDUC:** MBA, 1971, Fin., Univ. of SC; **MIL SERV:** USAF, 1962-66, Enlisted; **HOME ADD:** 1720 Terrace View Dr., W. Columbia, SC 29169, (803)791-0385; **BUS ADD:** 101 Greystone Blvd., Columbia, SC 29226.

CARTER, Lee——**B:** Sept. 8, 1917, Rock Island, IL, *Owner*, Lee Carter, Registered Professional Engr.; **PRIM RE ACT:** Consultant, Engineer; **OTHER RE ACT:** Project Analyst; **SERVICES:** Feasibility studies, site selection, advice to overseas investors; **REP CLIENTS:** US Econ. Dev. Admin., Mallinckrodt, Pakhoed, B.V.; **PREV EMPLOY:** Mgr. Engrg. Reports, Booker Assoc.; Mgr., Western Can., Stone & Webster; **PROFL AFFIL & HONORS:** Amer. Econ. Assn.; Amer. Con. Engrs. Council; Amer. Ind. Devel. Council, Reg. Profl. Engr., IL & MO; **EDUC:** BS, 1940, Chem. Engr., Purdue; **GRAD EDUC:** MS, 1945, Engr./Math., Cornell; **EDUC HONORS:** Phi Lambda Upsilon; **MIL SERV:** US Navy, Cmdr. (Ret.); **HOME ADD:** 622 Belson Ct., Kirkwood, MO 63122, (314)821-4091; **BUS ADD:** 622 Belson Ct., Kirkwood, MO 63122, (314)821-4091.

CARTER, Marcia H.——**B:** Apr. 25, 1947, Boston, MA, *VP Dir., Distinctive Prop.; Manager of 2 Offices (Branch)*, DeWolfe Realtors; **PRIM RE ACT:** Broker; **OTHER RE ACT:** Mgmt. of 2 Branch Offices; **SERVICES:** Dir. of the Distinctive Prop. Div.; **REP CLIENTS:** A program designed specifically to market unusual & unique residential prop.; **PREV EMPLOY:** Researcher in Investment Analysis; **PROFL AFFIL & HONORS:** Greater Boston RE Bd., RESSI; **EDUC:** AA, 1967, Psych., Chamberlayne Jr. Coll.; **EDUC HONORS:** Deans List-1966-1967; **OTHER ACT & HONORS:** Corporator Milton Savings Bank; **HOME ADD:** Milton, MA 021861 Green St., (617)333-0425; **BUS ADD:** 17 Canton Ave., Milton, MA 02186, (617)696-0075.

CARTER, Robert C.——**B:** June 4, 1917, Chicago, IL, *Of Counsel*, Carter, Mergens & Hardwick, P. A.; **PRIM RE ACT:** Attorney, Consultant, Owner/Investor; **PREV EMPLOY:** Active gen. practice of law since 1948; Member of Washington Bar and MN Bar; **PROFL AFFIL & HONORS:** Am. Trial Lawyers, MN Trial Lawyers Assn.; ABA, MN State Bar Assn.; Wash. Bar Assn.; **EDUC:** BS, 1946, Commerce and pre-law, Univ. of IL; **GRAD EDUC:** LLB, & JD, 1948-49, Gen. Law, Gonzaga Univ., Spokane, WA; **EDUC HONORS:** Dean's List; **MIL SERV:** USAF, 1st. Lt., 7 Air Medals; Pres. Unit Citation, Various theatre ribbons, ETO; **OTHER ACT & HONORS:** Roseau Co., MN, GOP Co., Chm., Sierra Club, Greenpeace Foundation. Nature Conservancy, American Legion, Vets. of Foreign Wars, Audubon Soc.; **HOME ADD:** Beaver Farms, Wannaska, MN 56761, (218)425-7490; **BUS ADD:** 101 Main Ave. No., Roseau, MN 56751, (218)463-2240.

CARTER, Steven Michael——**B:** Nov. 22, 1951, NY, NY, *Asst. to the President*, Mobil Land Development Corp., Western; **PRIM RE ACT:** Developer; **EDUC:** AB, 1976, Econ., Univ. of CA, Berkeley; **GRAD EDUC:** MBA, 1978, Harvard Bus. School; **EDUC HONORS:** First-Year; **HOME ADD:** 405 Davis Ct. #1001, San Francisco, CA 94111, (415)956-1498; **BUS ADD:** One Market Plaza, 1515 Spear St. Tower, San Francisco, CA 94105, (415)764-1527.

CARTER, William G.——**B:** Jan. 12, 1929, Bethany, MO, *Sales Assoc.*, Harrison Levy Co.; **OTHER RE ACT:** RE sales & development; **SERVICES:** Investment counseling; **PROFL AFFIL & HONORS:** OK City Metropolitan Bd. of Realtors; NAR, CCIM candidate; **EDUC:** BS, 1950, Agriculture/Journalism, Univ. of MO; **MIL SERV:** US Army, CIC, Special Agent; **OTHER ACT & HONORS:** Optimist Intl., Past Club Pres.; Past OK Dist. Lt. Gov.; Past Gov., OK Dist.; Current Member Intl. Activities Committee; **HOME ADD:** 11700 N. Victoria Dr., Oklahoma City, OK 73120, (405)751-0845; **BUS ADD:** 4801 Classen Blvd., Oklahoma City, OK 73118, (405)840-1505.

CARTON, Thomas W., Jr.——**B:** Sept. 25, 1948, Coshocton, OH, *Sr. RE Counsel*, Wendy's International, Inc.; **PRIM RE ACT:** Attorney; **PREV EMPLOY:** Jones, Day, Reavis & Pogue; **PROFL AFFIL & HONORS:** Columbus, OH and Amer. Bar Assns.; Intl. Council of Shopping Ctrs.; **EDUC:** BA, 1970, Amer. Studies, Bowling Green Univ., Bowling Green, OH; **GRAD EDUC:** JD, 1973, Law, OH State Univ.; **EDUC HONORS:** Omicron Delta Kappa; Student Commencement Speaker; Student Body VP; Alpha Tau Omega Frat VP, Summa Cum Laude; Order of the Coif; Managing Editor, Law Journal; **HOME ADD:** 39 W. Beaumont Rd., Columbus, OH 43214, (614)268-0382; **BUS ADD:** 4288 W. Dublin-Granville Rd., POB 256, Dublin, OH 43017, (614)764-3311.

CARTWRIGHT, Donald B.——**B:** July 9, 1950, Jacksonville, FL, *Dir. CDC Props.*, The Rouse Co., Community Devel.; **PRIM RE ACT:** Developer, Property Manager; **PROFL AFFIL & HONORS:** ICSC, BOMA, CSM; **EDUC:** BA, 1972, Hist., Washington and Lee Univ.; **HOME ADD:** 10943 Swansfield Rd., Columbia, MD 21044, (301)730-7479; **BUS ADD:** 10275 Little Patuxent Pkwy., Columbia, MD 21044, (301)992-6596.

CARTWRIGHT, Ed——**B:** Nov. 8, 1940, Evansville, IN, *Project Mgr.*, Calder Finance; **PRIM RE ACT:** Builder, Property Manager; **OTHER RE ACT:** Condo. conversions; **PREV EMPLOY:** Kasier/Athna; Azimuth Equities; Gramco; **EDUC:** BA, 1965, Advertising, Northwood Coll.; **MIL SERV:** USN; YN2; **HOME ADD:** 5842 E Sharon Dr., Scottsdale, AZ 85254, (612)996-6810; **BUS ADD:** 347E E Thomas Rd., Phoenix, AZ 85012, (602)277-4417.

CARUCCI, Samuel A.——**B:** Dec. 16, 1935, Bronx, NY, *Sec./Counsel*, Eutectic Corp.; **PRIM RE ACT:** Attorney, Builder, Owner/Investor, Property Manager; **PREV EMPLOY:** Olevetti Corp.; Litton Indus.; **PROFL AFFIL & HONORS:** ABA; NY State Bar Assn.; Bar Assn. of the City of NY; **EDUC:** BS, 1956, Fin., NYU; **GRAD EDUC:** LLB, 1959, Law, St. John's Univ.; **MIL SERV:** US Army; E-2; **HOME ADD:** 34 Country Club Dr., Manhasset, NY 11030, (516)627-1047; **BUS ADD:** 40-40 172nd St., Flushing, NY 11358, (212)358-4000.

CARUSO, Richard M.——**B:** Mar. 25, 1931, Chicago, IL, *Pres.*, Coldwell Banker Routh Robbins-Realtors; **OTHER RE ACT:** Residential Real Estate; **SERVICES:** Residential Sales, Property Management, Relocation Services; **PREV EMPLOY:** Past Pres., Rich Port, Realtor, La Grange, IL; Past Pres., Hometrend, Inc., Atlanta, GA; **PROFL AFFIL & HONORS:** Atlanta Bd. of Realtors; No. VA Bd. of Realtors, GRI; CRB; CRS; **EDUC:** 1953, Communications/Bus., IL Wesleyan Univ.; **OTHER ACT & HONORS:** Past Member, Exec. Club of Chicago; Past Member, Exec. Club of Oak Brook; Past VP, Oak Brook Kiwanis Club; Past Chmn., Income Devel., La Grange Unit, Amer. Cancer Soc.; Past VChmn., W. Suburban YMCA Century Club; Past Member, Hinsdale Rotary Club; **HOME ADD:** 6611 Madison McLean Dr., McLean, VA 22101, (703)821-1283; **BUS ADD:** 5205 Leesburg Pike, Suite 400, Falls Church, VA 22041, (703)998-3000.

CARVER, Enoch, IV——**B:** Mar. 3, 1955, Ripon, WI, *Fin. Analyst*, Fed. Land Bank of St. Paul; **PRIM RE ACT:** Attorney; **SERVICES:** Estate and fin. planning; **REP CLIENTS:** Farmers and ranchers; **PROFL AFFIL & HONORS:** ABA; Estate Planning Council of SE MI; **EDUC:** BA, 1977, Philosophy, Univ. of WI; **GRAD EDUC:** JD, 1979, Univ. of WI; **EDUC HONORS:** Grad. with Hon.; **HOME ADD:** 7611 Timbercreek Ct., #3, Portage, MI 49081, (616)329-0935; **BUS ADD:** 59252 US 131, Three Rivers, MI 49093, (616)279-5178.

CARVER, Eugene P.——**B:** Oct. 15, 1928, Bellingham, WA, *Pres.*, Hoffman Prop., Inc.; **PRIM RE ACT:** Consultant, Owner/Investor; **PREV EMPLOY:** Sr. VP, Western Mort. Corp., San Francisco, CA; **PROFL AFFIL & HONORS:** Amer. Soc. of RE Counselors, CRE; **EDUC:** AB, 1950, Econ., Dartmouth Coll.; **MIL SERV:** US Army, Lt., Bronze Star; **OTHER ACT & HONORS:** COB of Trs., BankAmerica Realty; Investors; **BUS ADD:** 626 Wilshire Blvd., Suite 1024, Los Angeles, CA 90017, (213)620-0621.

CARVER, Stuart——**B:** Oct. 15, 1933, Newark, NJ, *Stuart Carver, Inc.*; **PRIM RE ACT:** Consultant, Owner/Investor, Property Manager, Syndicator; **SERVICES:** Consultant in RE for Pension Accts; **EDUC:** BA, 1955, Soc. Sci. and Acctg., Montclair State Coll; **GRAD EDUC:** MA, 1958, Personnel, Montclair State Coll.; **OTHER ACT & HONORS:** Consultant, Bldg. Trades Council Morris County NJ (1965), NJ Gov's. Comm. to Hire Handicapped, Advisory Comm. (NJ) Assn. for Children with Learning Disabilities; **HOME ADD:** 13 Cambridge Rd., Freehold, NJ 07728, (201)431-5177; **BUS ADD:** 13 Cambridge Rd., Freehold, NJ 07728.

CARVIN, Philip J.——**B:** Westbury, LI, NY, *Sr. VP*, Gareath-Ruffin Corp., Corp. Mgmt.; **PRIM RE ACT:** Consultant, Engineer, Property Manager; **PREV EMPLOY:** VP, Mgmt. & Engrg., Ely-Cruikshank & Co., Inc.; **PROFL AFFIL & HONORS:** Amer. Soc. of Mech. Engrs.; Dir., Realty Advisory Bd. on Labor Relations, Inc.; Bldg. Owner's & Mgr.'s Assn.; **EDUC:** BS, Engrg., US Merchant Marine Acad., Kings Point, LI, NY; **GRAD EDUC:** Indus. Mgmt. Courses, Rutgers Univ.; Indus. Mgmt. Conferences, Harvard Univ.; **MIL SERV:** US Merchant Marine, Lt.j.g., Maritime Comm./USNR, Lt.; **HOME ADD:** 28 Spring Brook Ln., Wilton, CT 06897, (203)762-7055; **BUS ADD:** 150 E. 42nd St., New York, NY 10017, (212)922-1220.

CASAZZA, John——*Ed.*, ULI - The Urban Land Inst., Project Reference File; **PRIM RE ACT:** Real Estate Publisher; **BUS ADD:** 1200 18th St., NW, Washington, DC 20036, (202)331-8500.*

CASE, Charles——*Dir.*, Oklahoma, Oklahoma Real Estate Commission; **PRIM RE ACT:** Property Manager; **BUS ADD:** 4040 N. Lincoln Blvd., Ste. 100, Oklahoma City, OK 73105, (405)521-3387.*

CASE, Fred E.——**B:** Mar. 20, 1918, Logansport, IN, *Prof., RE & Mgmt.*, Grad. Sch. of Mgmt., Univ. of CA; **PRIM RE ACT:** Consultant, Appraiser, Instructor; **OTHER RE ACT:** Housing res. analyst, forecaster, author; **SERVICES:** Mkt. feasibility, value estimates, mkt. forecasts, mkt. trend analysis, mort. lending mkt. analysis & forecasts; **REP CLIENTS:** Basic lenders, builders, investors, indiv. corp., pension funds, private synds., fed., state, local govt. agencies; **PROFL AFFIL & HONORS:** AIREA; SREA; Amer. RE & Urban Econ Assn.; Western Rgnl. Sci. Assn.; Lambda Alpha, MAI; SRPA; **EDUC:** BS, 1942, Mgmt., IN Univ.; **GRAD EDUC:** MBA, 1948, Fin. RE, IN Univ.; DBA, 1951, Mgmt., fin., RE, IN Univ.; **EDUC HONORS:** Summa cum laude, Magna Cum Laude; **MIL SERV:** US Army; Col.; Bronze Star; Medal of War; (Brazil); Iron Crown; (Italy); 3 campaigns; **OTHER ACT & HONORS:** Los Angeles City bldg. and safety comm., 8 yrs.; Planning Comm. (pres.), 6 yrs, 1974-80; **HOME ADD:** PO Box 767, Pacific Palisades, CA 90272, (213)454-3160; **BUS ADD:** 405 Hilgard Ave., Los Angeles, CA 90024.

CASEY, C. L.——**B:** Apr. 25, 1935, Oklahoma City, OK, *Pres.*, The Monarch Group; **PRIM RE ACT:** Broker, Consultant, Developer, Builder, Owner/Investor, Property Manager, Syndicator; **OTHER RE ACT:** General Contractor, Lic. #371142; **SERVICES:** Investment consulting, RE sales and land devel.; **REP CLIENTS:** Investors; **PROFL AFFIL & HONORS:** San Jose/Sacramento Bd. of Realtors, CAR Synd. Div.,Amer. Bldg. Inst.; **EDUC:** (BS), 1972, Bus. Mgmt., LaVerne Coll.; **MIL SERV:** USAF, S/Sgt., usual decorations; **OTHER ACT & HONORS:** Pres., Los Paseos Homeowner Assn. 1974-1975; Pres., Casey and Jacquet Developers, Inc.; Pres., Western OMTEC Corp.; **HOME ADD:** 7121 Via Colina, San Jose, CA 95139, (408)629-0338; **BUS ADD:** 2542 So. Bascom Ave., Campbell, CA 95008, (408)371-7911.

CASEY, John——**B:** Dec. 11, 1930, Boston, MA, *Pres.*, Wellesley Const. Co.; **PRIM RE ACT:** Engineer, Developer, Builder, Owner/Investor, Syndicator; **SERVICES:** Owner-devel.-investor; **REP CLIENTS:** W. German & Nigerian Investors; **PREV EMPLOY:** Chrysler Realty - Investment Mgr. Eastern Area; **PROFL AFFIL & HONORS:** Top 400 Builder Devel. in the US 1975-80; SAE; Banker Institute; **EDUC:** BSEE, 1951-55, Elec. Engrg., Univ. of Detroit; **GRAD EDUC:** MBA, 1955-57, Synd., Fin., Harvard; **HOME ADD:** 4237 Rurik Dr., Howell, MI 48843, (313)538-3538; **BUS ADD:** 26040 Ivanhoe, Redford, MI 48239, (313)538-3538.

CASEY, Patrick Jon——**B:** July 5, 1943, OK, *Atty. & Partner*, McIntyre, McDivitt, Casey & Kivel; **PRIM RE ACT:** Consultant, Attorney, Owner/Investor; **OTHER RE ACT:** Seminar speaker; **SERVICES:** Bus. & tax planning; **REP CLIENTS:** Devel., builders, synd. & investors in over 30 states; **PROFL AFFIL & HONORS:** ABA & Nat. Assn. of Home Builders, Legal Cunsel OK St. HBA & COHBA; **EDUC:** BBA, 1967, Fin. & Mktg., O.U.; **GRAD EDUC:** JD, 1974, Law, O.C.U.; **EDUC HONORS:** Phi Delta Phi graduate of the year, Dean's Honor Roll; **OTHER ACT & HONORS:** Tax articles published and speaker at over 50 seminars throughout the US; **HOME ADD:** 1902 Joe Taylor Cir., Norman, OK 73069, (405)360-6732; **BUS ADD:** 1200 City National Bank Tower, Oklahoma City, OK 73102, (405)236-8405.

CASEY, Taylor J.——*Mgr.*, Landmark Land Co.; **PRIM RE ACT:** Developer; **BUS ADD:** PO Drawer "G", La Place, LA 70068, (504)652-6365.*

CASEY, Thomas——*Special Asst.*, Department of Housing and Urban Development, Ofc. of Secy/Undersecy.; **PRIM RE ACT:** Lender; **BUS ADD:** 451 Seventh St., S.W., Washington, DC 20410, (202)755-8663.*

CASHMAN, Rebecca M.——**B:** Apr. 6, 1944, *Sec./Treas./Broker*, Cashman Realty, Inc.; **PRIM RE ACT:** Broker, Consultant, Appraiser, Developer, Builder, Property Manager, Owner/Investor; **SERVICES:** Investment, const. home improvements, residential and comml. sales, synd. of comml. investment and also prop. mgmt.; **REP CLIENTS:** General Motors, Fieldcrest Mills, J.P. Stevens, So. Bell; **PREV EMPLOY:** Mgr. and exec. sec. of local mfg. co. 1969-72; operator of sporting goods bus. from 1962-69; **PROFL AFFIL & HONORS:** NCAE, NAR, Women's Council, Sullivan Award, Who's who in Amer. Bus., Past Pres. Local Bd. of Realtors, GRI, CRB, CRS, & Candidate - CCIM; **EDUC:** RE AND Bus., 1975, RE, Univ. of N.C., Chapel Hill; Univ. of Chicago; **OTHER ACT & HONORS:** Dir. of C of C, Dir. of Humane Soc., Past Pres. of Ladies Extension Club, Past Pres. LBG Bd. of Realtors, NC Dir. - Realtors; **HOME ADD:** Rt. 1 Box 21, Laurinburg, NC 28352, (919)276-3384; **BUS ADD:** 600 Atkinson St., P.O. Box 923, Laurinburg, NC 28352, (919)276-8680.

CASON, Mike——*Dir. RE*, General Portland Cement; **PRIM RE ACT:** Property Manager; **BUS ADD:** 12700 Park Central Place, PO Box 324, Dallas, TX 75221, (214)387-9000.*

CASPER, William T.——**B:** Sept. 12, 1949, Milwaukee, WI, *RE Rep.*, Rauenhorst Corp., RE Div.; **PRIM RE ACT:** Broker, Developer, Banker, Owner/Investor; **SERVICES:** Net lease ind., spec. office warehouse dev., sale/lease back, Mort. banking; **REP CLIENTS:** Honeywell, Philip Morris, ITT Fin., Hewlett-Packard, A.O. Smith; **PREV EMPLOY:** VP in Midwest Bank holding co., spec. in const. lending & mort. banking, Gen. part. Ctr Park Assoc., ARE Operating Co.; **PROFL AFFIL & HONORS:** WI MBA; **EDUC:** BS, 1971, Fin., Acctg., Marquette Univ.; **HOME ADD:** 5850 N. Shore Dr., Whitefish Bay, WI 53217, (414)332-8251; **BUS ADD:** 777 E. Wisconsin Ave., Suite 2980, Milwaukee, WI 53202, (414)873-5420.

CASSANO, Robert James——**B:** June 27, 1947, Santa Rosa, CA, *VP*, Robert C. Powell Devel.; **PRIM RE ACT:** Broker, Consultant, Developer, Builder, Property Manager; **SERVICES:** Gen. Brokerage, resid. devel., bldg. & prop. mgmt., consultant; **REP CLIENTS:** Indiv. investors, resid. RE; **PROFL AFFIL & HONORS:** Bldg. Indus. Assn., Superior CA (BIASC), Natl. Assn. of Home Builders, Sacramento Area Commerce & Trade Org., BIASC Sales & Mktg. Council; Sacramento Bd. of Realtors; CA Assn. of Realtors; Nat. Assn. of Realtors, BIASC Sales & Mktg. Council, Outstanding Realtor of the Yr. Award, 1975, 1976, 1977. 1980; **EDUC:** BS, 1970, Bus. Admin., Mgmt. & Fin., CA State Univ., Sacramento; **GRAD EDUC:** MBA, 1981, RE, Golden Gate Univ.; **OTHER ACT & HONORS:** Pres. BIASC Sales & Mktg. Council; **HOME ADD:** 361 Wyndgate Rd., Sacramento, CA 95825, (916)972-0899; **BUS ADD:** 3610 Amer. River Dr., Suite 150, Sacramento, CA 95825, (916)485-9121.

CASSARD, David, Sr.——**B:** Apr. 14, 1932, NYC, *Pres.*, Waters Bldg. Corp.; **PRIM RE ACT:** Consultant, Property Manager, Owner/Investor; **SERVICES:** Consultant Comml. RE Prop. Mgmt.; **PREV EMPLOY:** 305 W. 63rd St. Realty Corp., NYC, Asst. Bldg. Mgr.; **PROFL AFFIL & HONORS:** IREM, (CPM) Member of BOMA of Grand Rapids; **EDUC:** BA, 1954, Yale Univ.; **OTHER ACT & HONORS:** Member of Downtown Devel. Auth., (Mayor Appt.); Co-chair. Downtown Dist. Comm.. Mayor Appt.); Past Pres. Downtown, Inc.; Past Pres. BOMA, Bd. Member Heartside; Neighborhood Assoc.; CPM Member of IREM; **HOME ADD:** 2445 Oakwood Dr., SE, Grand Rapids, MI 49506, (616)949-4236; **BUS ADD:** 161 Ottawa Ave.NW, Grand Rapids, MI 49503, (616)459-4161.

CASSARD, David M., CPA——**B:** Oct. 6, 1953, NY, NY, *VP*, Waters Bldg. Corp.; **PRIM RE ACT:** Property Manager, Owner/Investor; **SERVICES:** Leasing and mgmt. of comml. office bldgs.; **PREV EMPLOY:** Touche Ross & Co., CPA's; **PROFL AFFIL & HONORS:** IREM, NAA, MACPA, AICPA, BOMA, CPA; **EDUC:** BBA, 1975, Bus. Admin., Univ. of MI; **GRAD EDUC:** MBA, 1976, Bus./ Fin., MI State Univ.; **EDUC HONORS:** Cum Laude; **OTHER ACT & HONORS:** Beta Gamma Sigma, BOMA G. Rapids; **HOME ADD:** 1132 Kenesaw S.E., E. Grand Rapids, MI 49503, (616)942-2996; **BUS ADD:** 161 Ottawa N.W. Suite 104, Grand Rapids, MI 49503, (616)459-4161.

CASSELL, Michael A.——**B:** Jan. 4, 1944, Baltimore, MD, *Broker/Owner/Pres.*, Cassell Assocs. Realty, Inc., Baltimore & Towson Offices; **PRIM RE ACT:** Broker, Consultant, Appraiser, Developer, Regulator, Builder, Owner/Investor, Instructor, Property Manager; **SERVICES:** Any servs. that involve RE; **PREV EMPLOY:** Exec. VP of RE Co., Sales Mgr. of RE Co., Trainer dir. of a RE Co., Mkt. dir. of a Health facility, Personnel Dir. of Health facility; **PROFL AFFIL & HONORS:** NAR, Nat. Assoc. of RE Brokers, MD Assn. of Realtors, RE Brokers of Baltimore, Inc., Greater Baltimore Bd. of Realtors, Realtor Mktg. Inst., Cert. RE brokerage mgr. (CRS), GRI; **EDUC:** BS,

1968, Bus. Admin., Morgan State Coll.; **BUS ADD:** 4525 Garrison Blvd., Baltimore, MD 21215, (301)664-2222.

CASSIDAY, Paul R.——**B:** Oct. 9, 1928, HI, *Pres.*, PR Cassiday, Inc.; **OTHER RE ACT:** Tr., large land holding estate (estate of James Campbell); **PREV EMPLOY:** Exec. VP, AMFAC Inc. 1975-78, Grp. Chmn. Asset Mgmt., AMFAC Inc. 1972-78; **PROFL AFFIL & HONORS:** MBAA, ULI; **EDUC:** BA, 1950, Econ., Stanford Univ.; **OTHER ACT & HONORS:** Chmn. HI Visitors Bureau; **HOME TEL:** (808)922-6827; **BUS ADD:** 900 Fort St. #1450, Honolulu, HI 96813, (808)536-1961.

CASTEIX, Barbara Treuting——**B:** May 29, 1953, New Orleans, LA, *Partner*, Carl W. Cleveland and Associates; **PRIM RE ACT:** Attorney, Owner/Investor; **REP CLIENTS:** Brokers, synd., devel., builders, indiv. investors in comml. and multi-family prop.; **PROFL AFFIL & HONORS:** ABA; ABA Real Prop. and Probate Section; LA Bar Assn.; New Orleans Bar Assn.; **EDUC:** BA, 1974, Hist., Univ. of New Orleans; **GRAD EDUC:** JD, 1977, Law, Loyola Univ.; **HOME ADD:** 48 Allard Blvd., New Orleans, LA 70119, (504)486-8210; **BUS ADD:** 600 Carondelet St., Suite 700, New Orleans, LA 70130, (504)522-7100.

CASTLEBERG, Robert Lee——**B:** July 15, 1930, Durand, WI, *Salesman, Realtor*, The Stark Co.; **PRIM RE ACT:** Syndicator, Property Manager, Owner/Investor; **OTHER RE ACT:** Realtor; **SERVICES:** Sales of single family home and Synd. of inv. RE; **REP CLIENTS:** Drs., Attys., and others with tax shelter needs; **PROFL AFFIL & HONORS:** CPM, CCIM Cand., CRS Realtor; **EDUC:** BS, 1953, Bus, Univ. of WI; **MIL SERV:** US Army, Sig. Corp, 1st Lt.; **OTHER ACT & HONORS:** City of Madison Tax Bd. of Appeals, WI Apt. Assoc., Former JCC, Trinity Lutheran Church, C of C, YMCA, Boy Scout Finance Comm., Red Cross Comm.; **HOME ADD:** 1321 Burning Wood Wy, Madison, WI 53704, (608)244-8480; **BUS ADD:** 117 Monona Ave, Madison, WI 53703, (608)256-9011.

CASTO, David Leroy——**B:** June 18, 1921, WV; **PRIM RE ACT:** Broker, Consultant; **OTHER RE ACT:** Office bldg. leasing and sales only; arbitration; **SERVICES:** Office space consulting, leasing, and evaluation in San Francisco Peninsula Area; **PREV EMPLOY:** Mgr. of RE, Stanford Univ. 1964-1966; Mgr. of RE, Newhall Land and Farming Co. 1974-1975; Mgr. of Mktg. Admin., Gas Turbine Dept., Gen. Electric Co. 1967-1973; **PROFL AFFIL & HONORS:** Panelist, Amer. Arbitration Assn.; **EDUC:** AB, 1947, Psych., Stanford Univ.; **GRAD EDUC:** MBA, 1950, Stanford Grad. School of Bus.; **MIL SERV:** US Army 1942-1946, 1951-1952; **HOME ADD:** 1472 Sierra, Redwood City, CA 94061, (415)366-2371; **BUS ADD:** 671 Oak Grove Ave., Menlo Park, CA 94025, (415)321-6980.

CASTRODALE, James L., Sr.——**B:** Nov. 17, 1934, Burlington, IA, *Pres.*, Colorado Development/Land Realty and Investment; **PRIM RE ACT:** Broker, Consultant; **SERVICES:** Land and water mktg. and devel.; **PREV EMPLOY:** Banker, 13 yrs.; Govt., 12 yrs.; **PROFL AFFIL & HONORS:** AWWA; City Mgrs. Assn.; **OTHER ACT & HONORS:** City Councilman; City Mgr.; C of C; Dir., YMCA; **HOME ADD:** 9835 Pennsylvania Dr., Thornton, CO 80229, (303)451-1522; **BUS ADD:** Suite 517, 1st Nat. Bank, Northglen, CO 80234, (303)451-0226.

CATALDO, Anthony M.——**B:** Jan. 27, 1937, NYC, NY, *Mgr.*, The Western Union Tel. Co., RE Operations; **PRIM RE ACT:** Instructor, Consultant, Property Manager, Owner/Investor; **PREV EMPLOY:** Cataldo Props., Inc. 1973-1978 (still active as owner (pres.)/investor); **EDUC:** BBA, 1960, Mgmt., Baruch Coll., CCNY; **GRAD EDUC:** MBA, 1977, Fin./RE, Fordham Univ.; **MIL SERV:** USA, Sp/3; **OTHER ACT & HONORS:** Instr., RE courses for Professional School of Bus.; **HOME ADD:** 5 Adams Rd., Saddle River, NJ 07458; **BUS ADD:** 1 Lake St., Upper Saddle River, NJ 07458, (201)825-5058.

CATANZANI, Charles J.——*Associate Chief Appraiser*, Equitable Life Assurance Society of US, RE Operations; **PRIM RE ACT:** Appraiser; **SERVICES:** Overall final appraisal responsibilities for all portfolios; **REP CLIENTS:** Territory, all of US and Canada; **PROFL AFFIL & HONORS:** Soc. of RE Appraisers, SRA; **EDUC:** BS, 1952, Econ., Amer. Int. Coll.; **EDUC HONORS:** Magna cum laude; **MIL SERV:** US Navy, MM 2/c, 1943-46; **HOME ADD:** 30 Waterside Plaza 3K, New York, NY 10010, (212)686-3637; **BUS ADD:** 1285 Ave. of the Americas, New York, NY 10010, (212)554-3005.

CATERINO, Michael A.——**B:** Oct. 8, 1941, Pittsburgh, PA, *Chief Financial Officer*, Centurion Community Corp.; **PRIM RE ACT:** Broker, Consultant, Developer, Builder, Property Manager, Syndicator; **SERVICES:** Investment analysis, creative fin. plans, fin. mgmt.; **PREV EMPLOY:** Pres. - Caterino & Chapman, Accts.; Treas. - Genge, Inc. (Amex); **PROFL AFFIL & HONORS:** AICPA, CPA, RE Broker (CA); **EDUC:** BS, 1968, Acctg., Sacramento State Univ.; **EDUC HONORS:** Cum Laude; **MIL SERV:** USAF, S/SGT; **OTHER ACT & HONORS:** Bd. of Dir., Stanford Children's Home; **HOME ADD:** 8212 Wachtel Way, Citrus Heights, CA 95610; **BUS ADD:** 6371 Auburn Blvd., Citrus Heights, CA 95610, (916)969-3700.

CATES, George E.——**B:** Sep. 25, 1937, Burlington, NC, *Pres.*, The Cates Co.; **PRIM RE ACT:** Developer, Property Manager, Owner/Investor; **OTHER RE ACT:** Public Warehousing; **SERVICES:** Offices, warehouses, neighborhood retail, apts., condos.; **REP CLIENTS:** Indiv. & Instnl. Investors, Income Props.; **PROFL AFFIL & HONORS:** BOMA, Apartment Council (NHBA), Lambda Alpha, Pres. Memphis Lambda Alpha, VP Memphis Apt. Council; **EDUC:** BS, 1959, IE, GA Inst. of Tech.; **EDUC HONORS:** AIIE, Who's Who, Koseme, Pres. Ramblin Reck Club. etc.; **OTHER ACT & HONORS:** Memphis & Shelby Cty. Airport Auth., Commnr. (1973-1981), Dir. Presbyterian Day School, Dir. Planned Parenthood of Memphis, Rotary, Memphis Ctry. Club; Commnr. of Memphis Light, Gas & Water Div. (1981-present); **HOME ADD:** 211 E Galloway, Memphis, TN 38111; **BUS ADD:** 6584 Poplar, Suite 210, Memphis, TN 38138, (901)682-6600.

CATHCART, David L.——**B:** Apr. 24, 1948, Monterey, CA, *RE Broker*, Real Estate Investment Counselors; **PRIM RE ACT:** Broker, Consultant, Appraiser; **OTHER RE ACT:** Notary Public; **SERVICES:** Brokerage, appraisals, investment counseling, exchanging; **REP CLIENTS:** Lenders, indivs. and instnl. investors in comml. and resid. props.; **PREV EMPLOY:** Century 21 RE, Pacific Grove, CA 1978-1980; **PROFL AFFIL & HONORS:** Monterey Cty. Exchange Counselors, RNMI, GRI; **EDUC:** Assoc. Sci., 1980, RE, Monterey Peninsula Coll.; **HOME ADD:** 210 11th St., Pacific Grove, CA 93950, (408)649-0154; **BUS ADD:** 157 15th St., Pacific Grove, CA 93950, (408)649-4833.

CATHCART, Faye——*Gen. Mgr.*, Bell Realty, Sales & Admin.; **PRIM RE ACT:** Broker, Instructor, Consultant, Owner/Investor, Insuror; **OTHER RE ACT:** Specialize in Residences; **PREV EMPLOY:** 18 yrs. with Bell Realty-4 1/2 yrs. escrow officer; **PROFL AFFIL & HONORS:** RNMI, WCR, CAR, NAR-4 Multiple Listing servs., TIC, ITC-C of C-RID, CRB, CRS, GRI Notarian; **EDUC:** BA, 1981, RE, Beverly Hills; **OTHER ACT & HONORS:** Sec./Treas. of SE Bd. of Realtors; **HOME ADD:** 1445 Graystone Ave., Norwalk, CA 90650, (213)863-7621; **BUS ADD:** 5200 E. Gage Ave., Bell, CA 90201, (213)583-0818.

CATTELL, David L.——**B:** Sept. 28, 1949, Kokomo, IN, *Dir. of RE*, Kentucky Fried Chicken Corp., Heublein Food Service & Franchising Group; **PRIM RE ACT:** Developer; **SERVICES:** Prop. admin.; facilities planning & devel.; **PREV EMPLOY:** Kroger Co., Columbus OH Div., Nat. Tea; **PROFL AFFIL & HONORS:** NACORE; **EDUC:** BS, 1977, RE Admin., Indiana Univ.; **OTHER ACT & HONORS:** NACORE, Retail Indus. Council 1981-82; Indiana Chapter NACORE, Pres. 1981-82; **HOME ADD:** 10207 Judith Ct., Louisville, KY 40223, (502)245-5539; **BUS ADD:** 1441 Gardiner Lane PO Box 3207, Louisville, KY 40232, (502)456-8454.

CAUBLE, Thomas V.——**B:** Oct. 21, 1919, Atlanta, GA, *Chmn.*, Cauble & Co.; **PRIM RE ACT:** Broker; **SERVICES:** Sales, leases, loans, retail devel.; **REP CLIENTS:** Instnl. investors, comml. props.; **PROFL AFFIL & HONORS:** ULI, MBAA, MAI; **EDUC:** Davidson BS, 1941, Pre-Law, Davidson Coll.; **GRAD EDUC:** LLB, 1948, Univ. of NC; **MIL SERV:** Infantry, Maj., Asiatic, Pacific, 2 stars; **OTHER ACT & HONORS:** Pres. Atlanta RE Bd., 1964; Assoc. Gov. MBA, 1967-68; Pres. GA Chapt. MAI, 1962; **HOME ADD:** 3230 Glen Arden Dr. NW, Atlanta, GA 30305, (404)237-2329; **BUS ADD:** 333 Peachtree Harris Bldg., Atlanta, GA 30303, (404)577-7332.

CAUDLE, Terry W.——**B:** Feb. 19, 1941, Forsyth Cty., NC, *Appraiser II*, North Carolina Dept. of Transportation, Div. of Hwys.; **PRIM RE ACT:** Appraiser; **SERVICES:** Appraiser of all types of real prop.; **REP CLIENTS:** NC Dept. of Transporation; **PREV EMPLOY:** Self-employed RE broker and resid. builder 1963-1970; **PROFL AFFIL & HONORS:** Soc. of RE Appraisers, SRA; **EDUC:** BBA, 1963, Econ., Wake Forest Univ.; **MIL SERV:** US Army Res., E-4; **HOME ADD:** 750 S. Peace Haven Rd., PO Box 304, Clemmons, NC 27012, (919)766-6183; **BUS ADD:** 619-G Peters Creek Pkwy., PO Box 5436, Winston-Salem, NC 27103, (919)761-2385.

CAULDWELL, R.L.——**B:** Jan. 11, 1939, Great Bend, KS, *Gen. Mgr.*, Control Data Corp., RE; **PRIM RE ACT:** Property Manager; **OTHER RE ACT:** Centralized RE serv. to multi-div., 60,000 employee org.; **SERVICES:** Purchase/sale/lease/sublease/admin. all prop. and bldgs. required by corp. org.; **PROFL AFFIL & HONORS:** NACORE; **EDUC:** BA, 1961, Econ., Ft. Hays KS State Coll.; **GRAD EDUC:** MS, 1965, Econ., AZ State Univ.; **EDUC HONORS:** Honors Seminar; **MIL SERV:** US Army; Sgt.; **OTHER ACT & HONORS:**

Charter Comm, 1975-present; Bloomington Art Center, Bd.; **HOME ADD:** 9127 Forest Hills Circle, Bloomington, MN 55431, (612)831-1061; **BUS ADD:** 8100 34th Ave. So., Bloomington, MN 55440, (612)853-5240.

CAULFIELD, Joycelyn Smith——B: Mar. 23, 1925, Kelly, LA, *Pres.*, Joycelyn Caulfield Agency & J.C. Assoc., Inc.; **PRIM RE ACT:** Broker, Appraiser, Developer, Property Manager, Owner/Investor; **SERVICES:** RE Sales, Prop. Mgmt., Devel., Appraising; **PROFL AFFIL & HONORS:** NH Assn. of Realtors; NAR; Seacoast Bd. of Realtors, Past Pres., Seacoast Bd. of Realtors; Past Chmn., SLMS; Realtor of the Yr.; GRI and CRB; Past Dir., NH Assn. of Realtors; **EDUC:** 1942, Bus. Coll.; **OTHER ACT & HONORS:** Member, Rye Beach Club; Past Pres., Abenaqui Ctry. Club Golf League; Jr. Master, Amer. Contract Bridge; **HOME ADD:** 734 Central Rd., Rye Beach, NH 03871, (603)964-8565; **BUS ADD:** 734 Central Rd., Rye Beach, NH 03871, (603)964-8565.

CAUNITZ, Richard W.——B: Feb. 21, 1940, New York City, NY, *Pres.*, Maurich Assocs.; **PRIM RE ACT:** Owner/Investor, Syndicator; **PROFL AFFIL & HONORS:** Rockland Cty. Historical Assn.; **EDUC:** BS, 1959, Acctg., Brooklyn Coll.; **MIL SERV:** US Army, Pfc.; **HOME ADD:** 45 Sturbridge Ct., Nanuet, NY 10954; **BUS ADD:** 45 Sturbridge Ct., Nanuet, NY 10954, (914)623-1927.

CAVANAGH, John B.——B: Apr. 21, 1947, NY, NY, *Pres.*, Cavanagh Fritz & Co.; **PRIM RE ACT:** Broker, Consultant, Property Manager; **PREV EMPLOY:** VP Cushman & Wakefield of N.E. Inc.; **EDUC:** BA, 1969, Econ., Boston Coll.; **GRAD EDUC:** RE, RE Law, NY Univ.; **MIL SERV:** US Army Reserve; **HOME ADD:** 3 Mountain Estates Dr., Avon, CT 06001; **BUS ADD:** 1 Corporate Ctr., Hartford, CT 06103, (203)549-6750.

CAVANAUGH, Gordon——B: Apr. 3, 1928, Philadelphia, PA, *Partner*, Roisman, Reno & Cavanaugh; **PRIM RE ACT:** Attorney; **REP CLIENTS:** Nat. Housing Law Project; Housing Assistance Council, Inc.; Council of Large Public Housing Authorities; **PREV EMPLOY:** Admin., Farmers Home Admin./USDA; Dir., Housing Assistance Council, Inc.; Housing Dir. for City of Philadelphia; **PROFL AFFIL & HONORS:** NAHRO, Honorary LLD. Delaware Valley Coll. of Sci. & Agriculture; **EDUC:** BA, 1950, Econ., Fordham Coll.; **GRAD EDUC:** LLB, 1953, Law, Univ. of PA; **EDUC HONORS:** Cum Laude, Law Review; **HOME ADD:** 10700 Shelley Ct., Garrett Park, MD 20896, (301)942-8757; **BUS ADD:** 1016 16th St., Suite 800, Washington, DC 20036, (202)659-0050.

CAVANAUGH, Ken C.——B: Apr. 30, 1916, Fremont, MI, *Indep. Housing Consultant*, Western Pacific Fin. Corp., Project Loan Div.; **PRIM RE ACT:** Consultant, Developer, Lender, Builder, Owner/Investor, Property Manager, Syndicator; **SERVICES:** Housing devel., synd., prop. mgmt., mort.; **REP CLIENTS:** Western Pacific Fin. Corp., Nat. Assn. of Housing and Redevel. Officials; **PREV EMPLOY:** US Dept. of HUD-30 yrs. (Asst. to Asst. Sec.; Dir. Office of Housing Mgmt.; Dir. of Fin. Mgmt. Dir., 202 Program Exec. Dir., Tax Exempt Fin.): Merrill, Lynch, Huntoon, Paige; Mort. Lending, DRG Fin. Corp.; Dir. of Housing Programs for US Dept. of HUD; **PROFL AFFIL & HONORS:** Bd. of Dir., Natl. Housing Conference; Life Member NAHRO; Council Member, NAA, Outstanding Achievement Awards, US Dept. of HUD; Superior Serv. Award; **EDUC:** BS, 1939, Bldg. Const., MI State Univ., E Lansing, MI; **EDUC HONORS:** Grad. Cum Laude-Elected to Honor Soc. Xi Sigma Chi; **MIL SERV:** USN; Capt. (ret.); Purple Heart and 7 service ribbons; **OTHER ACT & HONORS:** Honolulu Club; Honolulu Press Club; Mid Pacific Ctry. Club; **HOME ADD:** PO Box 1187, Kailua, HI 96734, (808)262-2298; **BUS ADD:** 733 Bishop St.-2540, Grosvenor Ctr. Pri Tower, Honolulu, HI 96813, (808)536-3795.

CAWLEY, John A., Jr.——B: July 14, 1943, Elkhart, IN, *Atty. at Law*; **PRIM RE ACT:** Attorney; **PREV EMPLOY:** Asst. City Attorney for Planning and Zoning; City of Elkhart, IN (1976-1980); **PROFL AFFIL & HONORS:** Elkhart City; IN State Bar Assn.; ABA; **EDUC:** AB, 1965, Poli. Sci., Duke Univ.; **GRAD EDUC:** JD, 1968, Law, IN Univ. School of Law; **HOME ADD:** 3115 Crabtree Lane, Elkhart, IN 46514, (219)264 0489; **BUS ADD:** 215 South Second St., P.O. Box 115, Elkhart, IN 46515, (219)294-2554.

CELANO, J.V., Jr.——B: June 29, 1931, Oak Park, IL, *Pres.*, Celano & Assoc.; **PRIM RE ACT:** Developer; **REP CLIENTS:** K-Mart, Natl. Tea, A&P; **PREV EMPLOY:** Arthur Rubloff & Co. 1965-1971; VP Devel.; **PROFL AFFIL & HONORS:** ICSC Urban Land Inst.; **EDUC:** BS, 1953, Fin., Univ. of Notre Dame; **OTHER ACT & HONORS:** Knollwood Club, Lake Forest, IL; **HOME ADD:** Shore Acres Rd., Lake Bluff, IL 60044, (312)234-9057; **BUS ADD:** 108 Wilmot Rd., Deerfield, IL 60015, (312)948-1020.

CELLI, Raymond C.——B: Dec. 2, 1949, Pittsburgh, PA, *Dir.*, Hellmuth, Obata & Kassabaum, Inc., Program Mgmt.; **OTHER RE ACT:** Mgmt. Consulting; **SERVICES:** Strategic planning; **REP CLIENTS:** Motorola, Exxon, AT&T; **EDUC:** AB, 1971, Arch., WA Univ.; **GRAD EDUC:** MBA, MArch, 1974, Mgmt., WA Univ.; **HOME ADD:** 7306 Princeton Ave., St. Louis, MO 63130, (314)727-8988; **BUS ADD:** 100 N. Broadway, St. Louis, MO 63102, (314)421-2000.

CENTOFANTE, Alfred V.——B: June 3, 1925, Chicago, IL, *VP*, Collins Devel. Corp.; **PRIM RE ACT:** Consultant, Developer, Builder, Owner/Investor, Property Manager; **SERVICES:** Land Devel. - Comml. - Indust. Resid.; **REP CLIENTS:** Builders - Investors - Indivs.; **PREV EMPLOY:** 1958 to 1968, Exec. Officer (Owner Private Corp.); 1968 to 1973 Del. E. Webb Corp. Chief of Oper. Oak Brook, IL; **PROFL AFFIL & HONORS:** Exchange Club Treas.; **EDUC:** 1943, Herzl Jr. Coll., USN Service Schools Basic Engrg.; **GRAD EDUC:** Allied School Mechanics, 1947; **MIL SERV:** USN, MMM 2nd; **OTHER ACT & HONORS:** Private Pilot - R.E. Sales Lic.; **HOME ADD:** 55 Whittington Course, St. Charles, IL 60174, (312)377-0693; **BUS ADD:** 303 E. Main St., St. Charles, IL 60174, (312)584-2500.

CERNE, Wence——*VP RE*, I.C. Industries; **PRIM RE ACT:** Property Manager; **BUS ADD:** 111 E. Wacker Dr., Chicago, IL 60601, (312)565-3000.*

CERNUDA, Carlos F.——B: Oct. 24, 1947, Mayaguez, PR, *Pres.*, C.F.C. Associates; **PRIM RE ACT:** Consultant, Appraiser; **SERVICES:** RE Appraisals; Investment Counseling; **REP CLIENTS:** Private lenders; S & L Assns.; Investors; Govt. (Federal, State and City) Depts. in resid., comml. and indus. props.; **PREV EMPLOY:** Cushman & Wakefield, Inc.; U.S. Dept. of H.U.D.; **PROFL AFFIL & HONORS:** PR Inst. of Appraisers (M.I.E.); Puerto Rico Coll. of Appraisers (M.C.E.); Govt. of Puerto Rico - Licensed Profl. RE Appraiser (EPA 175); International Institute of Valvers (R.I.M.); **EDUC:** BA, 1970, Pol. Econ., School of Soc. Sci., Univ. of PR; **HOME ADD:** 135 Oxford St., Manhattan Beach, Brooklyn, NY 11235, (212)934-8133; **BUS ADD:** 135 Oxford St., Manhattan Beach, Brooklyn, NY 11235, (212)934-3538.

CERSONSKY, H. Sol——B: June 17, 1922, Williston, ND, *M.D.*, Self or Solomon Enterprises; **PRIM RE ACT:** Developer, Owner/Investor; **OTHER RE ACT:** buy, sell, and/or develop 15-20 million in RE per year; **PROFL AFFIL & HONORS:** Sigma Xi (Scientific); **EDUC:** BA, 1943, Math, Univ., MN; BS, 1947, Psych., Univ. of MN; **GRAD EDUC:** MD, 1951, Pediatrics, Univ. of Rochester, NY; **MIL SERV:** USN; Lt.; Philippine Liberation; **HOME ADD:** 455 So. Colo. Blvd., (303)393-8097; **BUS ADD:** 455 So. Colo. Blvd., Denver, CO 80222, (303)388-5561.

CERTILMAN, Morton L.——B: Jan. 26, 1932, New York City, NY, *Sr. Partner*, Wofsey, Certilman, Haft & Lebow; **PRIM RE ACT:** Attorney; **SERVICES:** All RE legal work-specialists in Condos. Cooperatives and Home Owners Assns.; **REP CLIENTS:** Cenvill Communities, FPA Corp., H. Miller & Sons, Inc., Genstar Ltd., Leisure Techn. Corp., Lefrak Organization, Nat. Birchwood, etc.; **PROFL AFFIL & HONORS:** ABA, New York State Bar Assn, Nassau Cty. Bar Assn., Long Island Builders Institute, NY State Builders Assn., NAHB; **GRAD EDUC:** JD, LLB, 1956, Gen. Law, Brooklyn Law School; **EDUC HONORS:** Cum Laude; Law Review; **MIL SERV:** USNR; **OTHER ACT & HONORS:** New York State Asst. Atty. Gen. 56-59, Member of the faculty of Univ. of Miami Law School Condo. and Cluster Housing Instit.; New York Univ. RE Inst. Condo. and Cooperatives; Amer. Law Instit./ ABA; Past Chmn. Condo. Comm. of NYS Bar Assn.; **HOME ADD:** 71 S Central Ave., Valley Stream, NY 11580, (516)872-6222; **BUS ADD:** 55 Broad St., New York, NY 10004, (212)425-4321.

CERVIERI, John A., Jr.——B: Jan 28, 1931, NY, *Managing Trustee*, Property Capital Trust; **PRIM RE ACT:** Owner/Investor; **PROFL AFFIL & HONORS:** ASREC, NAREIT, Nat. Realty Comm., Greater Boston RE Bd., Boston Econ. Club; **EDUC:** BA, 1951, Columbia Coll.; **GRAD EDUC:** MBA, 1959, Grad. School of Bus. Admin., Harvard Univ.; **EDUC HONORS:** Baker Scholar; **MIL SERV:** USAF, 1st Lt.; **OTHER ACT & HONORS:** Harvard Club, Harvard Bus School Assn., The Hamilton Trust, Dedham Ctry. & Polo Club, The Dunes Club, The Algonquin Club, Member of the Bd., BayBanks Inc., Trustee New England Medical Ctr.; Member of the Corp. Sidney Farber Cancer Inst.; **HOME ADD:** 6 Miller Hill Rd., Dover, MA 02030, (617)785-1911; **BUS ADD:** 200 Clarendon St., Hancock Tower 47th fl., Boston, MA 02116, (617)536-8600.

CHADDERTON, Ed——B: Oct. 5, 1915, Sharon, PA, *Owner*, Chadderton Servs. Inc.; **PRIM RE ACT:** Developer, Owner/Investor; **SERVICES:** 450 acre devel.; **HOME ADD:** 100 Hazen Rd., Sharpsville, PA 16150; **BUS ADD:** PO Box 687, Sharon, PA 16146, (412)981-5050.

CHADDICK, Harry F.——B: Aug. 27, 1905, Chicago, IL, *Pres.*, First Amer. Realty Co., 8 Subsidiaries; **PRIM RE ACT:** Consultant, Appraiser, Developer, Builder, Property Manager; **SERVICES:** site selection and acquisition, architectural engineering, general contractor, planning, consulting, zoning, fin.; **REP CLIENTS:** Equitable Life Assurance Soc. of the U.S.; **PREV EMPLOY:** Owner and Chief Exec Officer of American Transporation Co./Standard Freight Lines, 1931 to 1947; **PROFL AFFIL & HONORS:** Chicago Assoc. Commerce and Indus., NARA, BBB, Chicago RE Bd., Golden Plate Award-1971, Horatio Alger Award-1970, City of Hope Award-1967, Chicago's Outstanding R.E. Devlr., 1965-Little Flower Soc.; **OTHER ACT & HONORS:** Chmn., Zoning Bd. of Appeals, Chmn. Mayor's Comm. on Rent Control; Co-Chairman, City of Chicago's Economic Development Commission; **BUS ADD:** 123 W. Madison St., Chicago, IL 60602, (312)782-2900.

CHAFFIN, R. Garry——B: June 10, 1951, Cookeville, TN, *Corp. Sec., House Counsel*, Security Federal Savings & Loan of Nashville; **PRIM RE ACT:** Attorney, Lender, Insuror; **PREV EMPLOY:** Staff Asst., TN State Senate 1973-1974; Exec. VP, Union Title Co., Inc., Nashville, TN; **PROFL AFFIL & HONORS:** ABA, TN Bar Assn., Young Mort. Bankers; **EDUC:** BS, 1972, Acctg., TN Technological Univ., Cookeville, TN; **GRAD EDUC:** JD, 1979, Law, YMCA Law School, Nashville, TN; **OTHER ACT & HONORS:** Former partner, Advice Associates Mgmt. Consultants of Nashville; United Way Citation for Community Service 1978.; Treas. Cumberland Valley Political Action Comm. Instr.-Middle TN Inst. of Fin. Educ.; **HOME ADD:** Route 8, Franklin, TN 37064; **BUS ADD:** 4235 Hillsboro Rd., Nashville, TN 37064, (615)383-6048.

CHAIBOONMA, Eaksith——B: Sept. 25, 1944, Thailand, *Asst. VP, RE*, Pac. Arch. & Engrgs. Inc., Pac. Props. Intl.; **PRIM RE ACT:** Broker, Developer, Property Manager, Syndicator; **SERVICES:** Investment counseling, devel. & synd. of resid. and comml. project, prop. mgmt.; **PREV EMPLOY:** Dept. of Air Force, Pac., 13th AF, 288th Combat Support Grp.; **PROFL AFFIL & HONORS:** NAR, CA Assn. of Realtors, Los Angeles Assn. of Realtors, Los Angeles Headquarter Assn.; **EDUC:** BSc, 1969, Acctg., Thammasat Univ., Thailand; **GRAD EDUC:** MSc, 1976, Fin. Mgmt., West Coast Univ., Los Angeles; **HOME ADD:** 2444 East Del Mar Blvd., No. 313, Pasadena, CA 91107, (213)793-8201; **BUS ADD:** 600 S. Harvard Blvd., Los Angeles, CA 90005, (213)384-2121.

CHAIKEN, Richard M.——B: Mar. 8, 1932, Newark, NJ, *Pres.*, Appraisal Consultants, Inc.; **PRIM RE ACT:** Consultant, Appraiser; **REP CLIENTS:** Owners, Investors, Lenders, Govt. Agencies; **PROFL AFFIL & HONORS:** SREA, AIREA, MAI; **EDUC:** BA, 1955, Rutgers Univ.; **MIL SERV:** US Army, Cpl, 1952-54; **HOME ADD:** 526 White Oak Ridge, Short Hills, NJ 07078, (201)379-6875; **BUS ADD:** 37 E. Willow St., Millburn, NJ 07041, (201)467-1580.

CHALFANT, William——B: Apr. 28, 1907, Westchester, PA, Self-employed; **PRIM RE ACT:** Appraiser; **SERVICES:** appraisal, farm dwellings; **REP CLIENTS:** Concord Natl. Bank, State St. Trust, Merril Lynch, Executrans; **PREV EMPLOY:** Appraiser, Concord Saving Bank, Riverhead (NY) Savings Bank; **PROFL AFFIL & HONORS:** SREA, designation, SRA; **EDUC:** 2 yrs., 1929, Univ. of PA; **MIL SERV:** USMC; LT. Col.; Commendation; **OTHER ACT & HONORS:** AAOMS; **HOME ADD:** Box 439 RE 1, Concord, NH 03301, (603)224-4379; **BUS ADD:** Box 439, RE 1, Concord, NH 03301, (603)224-4379.

CHALMERS, R. Scott——B: Mar. 27, 1947, Ross, CA, *Pres.*, C.D. Realty Inc.; **PRIM RE ACT:** Broker, Property Manager; **SERVICES:** Resid., comml. sales, prop. mgmt. of apt. complexes, shopping ctrs. and homeowner assns. of PUD & Condos.; **PREV EMPLOY:** VP of Admin & Controller of Devel. & Const. Co. 1979-81; **PROFL AFFIL & HONORS:** Amer. Mgmt. Assn.; **EDUC:** BS, 1972, Bus. Admin., CA State Univ., Chico; **GRAD EDUC:** MBA, 1974, Bus. Admin., CA State Univ., Chico; **MIL SERV:** US Army, E-4, Spec. 4, Vietnam Veteran; **OTHER ACT & HONORS:** Bd. Member Butte Cty. Special Olympics; **HOME ADD:** 1675 Hooker Oak Ave., Chico, CA 95926, (916)345-2889; **BUS ADD:** 585 Manzanita Ave., Suite 3, Chico, CA 95926, (916)893-8228.

CHAMBERLAIN, Scott D.——B: Sept. 15, 1952, Ogden, UT, *Fin. Mgr.*, The Kier Corp.; **PRIM RE ACT:** Builder; **REP CLIENTS:** Private investors in limited partnerships; **PREV EMPLOY:** Bowen and Dahlquist, CPA's; **PROFL AFFIL & HONORS:** Nat. Assn. Home Builders, Registered Cpt. Mgr. (RAM), CPA; **EDUC:** BS, 1975, Acctg.; **HOME ADD:** 1696 East 1300 South, Ogden, UT, (801)393-0453; **BUS ADD:** 3710 Quincy Ave., Ogden, UT 84403, (801)621-0330.

CHAMBERLIN, Thomas J.——B: June 4, 1947, Denver, CO, *Atty.*, Ratcliffe & Chamberlin; **PRIM RE ACT:** Attorney; **SERVICES:** Zoning, planning, subdiv. procedures, contract documents prep., closings, synds.; **REP CLIENTS:** Big Valley Ranch at Steamboat, Red Barn Ranch, Inc., The Pines, ERA, Big Country RE, Century 21 RE; **PREV EMPLOY:** CO Bar Assn., NW CO Bar Assn., Steamboat Springs Bar Assn., CO Trial Lawyers Assn.; **EDUC:** BA, 1969, Educ., Univ. of Denver; **GRAD EDUC:** JD, 1973, Litigation, land trans. & fin., Univ. of Denver; **EDUC HONORS:** Dean's List; **HOME ADD:** Box 2006, Steamboat Springs, CO 80477, (303)879-5472; **BUS ADD:** Box 772842, Steamboat Springs, CO 80477, (303)879-3440.

CHAMBERS, Charles——*Exec. Dir.*, MD, Maryland Real Estate Commission; **PRIM RE ACT:** Property Manager; **BUS ADD:** 1 So. Calvert St., Baltimore, MD 21202, (301)659-6230.*

CHAMBLES, Bert——*Corp. RE Mgr.*, Data General Corp.; **PRIM RE ACT:** Property Manager; **BUS ADD:** 4400 Computer Dr., Westborough, MA 01580, (617)366-8911.*

CHAMBLIN, W. Watson——B: Mar. 25, 1926, Dyersburg, TN, *Sr. VP*, Mid-South Mortgage Company, Inc.; **OTHER RE ACT:** Mortgage Banking; **SERVICES:** Developer; **PREV EMPLOY:** FHA, 1960-68; **PROFL AFFIL & HONORS:** Mort. Bankers, Soc. of Appraisers, SRA; **EDUC:** BA, 1950, Poli. Sci., Univ. of TN; **MIL SERV:** US Army, Col., Silver Star, Purple Heart; **HOME ADD:** 4711 Heath Hill Rd., Columbia, SC 29206, (803)787-2191; **BUS ADD:** 3710 Landmark Dr., Columbia, SC 29204, (803)738-9010.

CHAMNONGPHANIJ, Into B.——B: Feb. 27, 1957, Vientiane, Laos, *Sr. Staff Analyst*, H. Bruce Hanes, Inc.; **PRIM RE ACT:** Broker; **OTHER RE ACT:** RE Consultant; **SERVICES:** Investment properties sales & exchange, Condo conversion; **PROFL AFFIL & HONORS:** Member of (student) Amer. Bar Assn., RESSI; **EDUC:** BS, 1980, Decision Sci., Univ. of So. CA; **OTHER ACT & HONORS:** Advisor, Lao Mutual Assoc., Inc.; **HOME ADD:** 1250 Glenthorpe Dr., Walnut, CA 91789, (714)595-6109; **BUS ADD:** 2445 Huntington Dr., San Marino, CA 91108, (213)796-7000.

CHAMP, Frederick Winton——B: July 29, 1930, Logan, UT, *Pres. & CEO*, First Security State Bank & First Security Mort. Co.; **PRIM RE ACT:** Broker, Appraiser, Property Manager, Banker, Lender, Insuror; **OTHER RE ACT:** Mort. Banker; **SERVICES:** Complete banking services (Inc. mort. banking, prop. mgmt., ins., etc.); **PREV EMPLOY:** Exec. VP & Dir., UT Mort. Loan Corp.; **PROFL AFFIL & HONORS:** UT MBA; Amer. Inst. of Banking; MBAA; Bd. of Dir., Salt Lake Clearing House Assn.; Former member, Salt Lake Planning & Zoning Commn.; Downtown Planning Comm.; **EDUC:** AB, 1952, Econ., Stanford Univ.; **GRAD EDUC:** MBA, 1956, Bus., Harvard Univ.; **MIL SERV:** Fin. Corps., First Lt.; **OTHER ACT & HONORS:** Legislative Comm.; Bd. of Dir, YMCA; **HOME ADD:** 875 Donner Way, Apt. 1103, Salt Lake City, UT 84108, (801)582-7134; **BUS ADD:** 381 E. Broadway, Salt Lake City, UT 84111, (801)350-5420.

CHAMPAGNE, Philip M.——B: Oct. 2, 1942, Providence, RI, *Div. and State Counsel*, Commonwealth Land Title Ins., Co., Reliance Group; **PRIM RE ACT:** Consultant, Attorney, Banker, Lender, Insuror; **SERVICES:** Title and closing, RE structuring and fin. consultant; **PREV EMPLOY:** Counsel, Old Colony Co-operative Bank; **PROFL AFFIL & HONORS:** ABA; RI Bar Assn.; Amer. Judicature Soc.; Real Prop., Comm. ABA, Comm., East Providence Housing Authority; Military Order of Foreign Wars; **EDUC:** AB, 1964, Poli. Sci, Boston Univ.; **GRAD EDUC:** LLB, 1967, Law, Boston Univ.; **MIL SERV:** USN; 1967-1971; Lt.; **HOME ADD:** 252 Water St., Warren, RI 02885, (401)245-9281; **BUS ADD:** 66 South Main St., Providence, RI 02903, (401)331-5331.

CHAMPAGNE, Richard K.——B: Apr. 7, 1938, Marysville, KS, *Owner*, Champagne Appraisal Co.; **PRIM RE ACT:** Appraiser; **SERVICES:** RE Appraisals; **REP CLIENTS:** Mort. Cos., Investment Cos. S&L Assns.; **PREV EMPLOY:** Urban Renewal- Prop. Mgmt.; **PROFL AFFIL & HONORS:** SREA; **EDUC:** BS, 1961, Educ.-Law, KS State Univ.; **MIL SERV:** US Army, SP4; **OTHER ACT & HONORS:** Amer. Quarter Horse Assn.; **HOME ADD:** 9300 S. 7 Hwy., Olathe, KS 66061, (913)764-7811; **BUS ADD:** 9300 S. 7 Hwy., Olathe, KS 66061, (913)764-383

CHAMPION, Lee——B: Dec. 28, 1920, Denver, CO, *Dir.*, Institutional Consultants; **PRIM RE ACT:** Broker, Consultant, Developer; **SERVICES:** Sales, leasing, fin., devel., mgmt.; **REP CLIENTS:** Lenders & instnl. investors; **PREV EMPLOY:** Citibank (NY) VP 1969-1971; Federated Dept. Stores 1963-1968; **PROFL AFFIL & HONORS:** ABA; State Bar of CA and OH; **EDUC:** AB, 1942, Econ., Stanford Univ.; **GRAD EDUC:** JD, 1948, Law, Stanford Univ.; **MIL SERV:** USN, Res.; Lt.j.g.; **HOME ADD:** 1600 Ala Moana #2606, Honolulu, HI 96815, (808)947-2287; **BUS ADD:** 700 Richards St., #2303, Honolulu, HI 96813, (808)536-5973.

CHAN, Anthony——B: Feb. 3, 1953, Sydney, Australia, *Gen. Partner*, Worldco Company, Ltd.; **PRIM RE ACT:** Developer, Owner/Investor; **SERVICES:** Devel., investment comml. prop., prop. mgmt.; **PROFL AFFIL & HONORS:** IREM, NAR, ICSC, CPM; **EDUC:** BS, 1974, Bus. Admin., RE & Fin., Univ. of CA, Berkeley; **GRAD EDUC:** MBA, 1975, Bus., RE, Univ. of WI; **EDUC HONORS:** Honor Student; **HOME ADD:** 200 Bella Vista, Hillsborough, CA 94010, (415)348-7349; **BUS ADD:** 1378 Sutter St., San Francisco, CA 94109, (415)928-0368.

CHAN, Frederick M.——B: June 17, 1947, Hong Kong, *Pres.*, Nu West REI Corp.; **PRIM RE ACT:** Consultant, Architect, Developer, Owner/Investor, Property Manager, Syndicator; **OTHER RE ACT:** RE investment, devel. sale & mgmt.; **PROFL AFFIL & HONORS:** Intl. Council of Shopping Ctrs., Amer. Mgmt. Assn., Amer. Planning Assn.; **EDUC:** BA, 1969, Univ. of CA, Berkeley; **GRAD EDUC:** MArch., 1964, Urban Design, RE Devel., Harvard Univ.; **OTHER ACT & HONORS:** L.A. C of C, Marina City Club, L.A. Racquet Club, Intl. Club; **HOME ADD:** 4314 Marina City Dr., Marina Del Rey, CA 90291; **BUS ADD:** 350 S Figueroa, Suite 555, Los Angeles, CA 90071, (213)628-9378.

CHAN, Gayle——B: Nov. 5, 1949, Hong Kong, *Corporate Counsel*, Gen. Mills, Inc., Wallpapers to Go; **PRIM RE ACT:** Attorney; **SERVICES:** Legal Services in Leasing and Purchases; **REP CLIENTS:** Wallpapers to Go; Wild West; Good Earth; General Mills; **PREV EMPLOY:** The Gap Stores Inc. 1978-1980, Grubb & Ellis Intl. 1977-1978; **PROFL AFFIL & HONORS:** ABA, CA Bar Assn., San Francisco Bar Assn.; **EDUC:** BA, 1972, Eng./French, Simmons Coll.; **GRAD EDUC:** MA, 1973, Eng., Simmons Coll.; MS, 1974, Public Relations, Boston Univ.; MA, 1975, Educ., Stanford Univ.; JD, 1976, Law, Univ. of CA, Hastings Coll. of The Law; **HOME ADD:** 1205 Canterbury Rd., Hillsborough, CA 94010, (415)342-2665; **BUS ADD:** 3131 Corporate Place, Hayward, CA 94545, (415)785-7150.

CHANCE, Larry S.——B: May 24, 1949, Wichita, KS, *Fin. Analyst*, R.G. Billings Enterprises, Inc.; **PRIM RE ACT:** Consultant, Owner/Investor, Syndicator; **SERVICES:** Fin. & investment counseling, valuation, synd. of multifamily resid. & comm. props.; **REP CLIENTS:** Profl. and investors' in RE projects; **PREV EMPLOY:** Profl. Tax Service, Inc., IRS; **PROFL AFFIL & HONORS:** Enrolled to Practice before the IRS; **EDUC:** 1972, Bus. Admin., KS Univ., Bus. School; **MIL SERV:** US Army; **OTHER ACT & HONORS:** Cosmopolitan Intl.; **HOME ADD:** 2404 Yosemite Ct., Lawrence, KS 66044, (913)843-6519; **BUS ADD:** 1611 St. Andrews Dr., Lawrence, KS 66044, (913)843-1276.

CHANCELLOR, Max——*Corp. Facility Director*, Advanced Micro-Devices; **PRIM RE ACT:** Property Manager; **BUS ADD:** 901 Thompson Pl., Sunnyvale, CA 94086, (408)732-2400.*

CHANDLER, Dale O.——B: Jan. 20, 1948, Ellensburg, WA, *Co-Broker*, Walker-Ruth, Inc.; **PRIM RE ACT:** Broker, Consultant, Property Manager; **OTHER RE ACT:** Leasing Agent; **SERVICES:** Brokerage, Leasing and Consulting; **REP CLIENTS:** Comml. prop. owners as well as local profls. and public bodies; **PREV EMPLOY:** First Nat. Bank of OR, 1971-75; **PROFL AFFIL & HONORS:** NARA, BOMA; **EDUC:** BS, 1971, Fin.; **HOME ADD:** 2710 Garfield St., Eugene, OR 97405, (503)342-4787; **BUS ADD:** 700 Ctry. Club Rd., Eugene, OR 97401, (503)484-4422.

CHANDLER, Dean L.——*Dir., Area Dev.*, Iowa Power; **PRIM RE ACT:** Developer; **BUS ADD:** PO Box 657, 823 Walnut St., Des Moines, IA 50303, (515)281-2929.*

CHANDLER, Garth K.——B: Oct. 28, 1947, Rexburg, ID, *Assoc. Prof.*, Dept. of Law, US Military Academy; **PRIM RE ACT:** Attorney, Instructor, Owner/Investor; **PROFL AFFIL & HONORS:** ABA, (Real Prop. Sect.), UT State Bar, Court of Military Appeals, US Supreme Court, Phi Alpha Delta Law Frat.; **EDUC:** BA, 1973, Econ., Brigham Young Univ.; **GRAD EDUC:** JD, 1976, Law, J. Reuben Clark Law School, Brigham Young Univ.; **MIL SERV:** JAGC, Capt., NDSM, MSM, PARCHT BADGE; **OTHER ACT & HONORS:** Amateur Ski Instr. Assn.; **HOME ADD:** 4171 Sluga Dr., Newburgh, NY 12550, (914)564-2642; **BUS ADD:** Dept. of Law, US Military Academy, West Point, NY 10996, (914)938-3510.

CHANDLER, John——*Mgr. Corp. Fac.*, Texas Instruments, Inc.; **PRIM RE ACT:** Property Manager; **BUS ADD:** PO Box 225474, 13500 N. Central Expwy., Dallas, TX 75265, (214)995-2011.*

CHANDLER, William H.——B: May 5, 1948, Hemingway, SC, *Atty. at Law*, Chandler & Ruffin; **PRIM RE ACT:** Attorney; **SERVICES:** Title examinations, loan closings; **REP CLIENTS:** Canal Wood Corp. of Dillon; The Citizens and So. Nat. Bank of S.C.; **PREV EMPLOY:** Law Firm of Henry C. Nelson, Jr., Esq., Columbia, SC, 1970-1973; Judge Advocate with U.S. Air Force, 1974-1978; **PROFL AFFIL & HONORS:** ABA; SC Bar Assn.; Williamsburg Cty. Bar Assn.; **EDUC:** AB, 1970, Hist., Univ. of SC; **GRAD EDUC:** JD, 1973, Law, Univ. of SC School of Law; **EDUC HONORS:** Phi Eta Sigma, Student Senate, Distinguished mil. grad., Mens' Towers Council, Omicron Delta Kappa, Dean's Lists, Phi Delta Phi, Omicron Delta Kappa, contributor of articles to "Names of Places in SC"; **MIL SERV:** USAF, Capt, AF Commendation Medal w/OLC; **OTHER ACT & HONORS:** VChmn., Williamsburg Cty. School Bd.; SC Hist. Soc.; SC French Huguenot Soc.; Sons American Revolution; SC Soc.; Williamsburg Cty. Hist. Soc.; VP, Three Rivers Hist. Soc.; Elder of Indiantown Presbyterian Church; Chmn., Christian Educ. Comm. of Indiantown Presbyterian Church; SC Genealogical Soc.; Charleston Preservation Soc.; **HOME ADD:** Route 1, Box 189, Hemingway, SC 29554, (803)558-5889; **BUS ADD:** POB 218, Hemingway, SC 29554, (803)558-2588.

CHANG, William H.C.——B: May 9, 1956, Osaka, Japan, *Pres.*, Westlake Builders, Inc.; **PRIM RE ACT:** Developer, Builder; **SERVICES:** Construction, Land devel.; **PREV EMPLOY:** Westlake Devel. Co., Inc. VP Devel.; **PROFL AFFIL & HONORS:** CA licensed Gen. contractor, CA Licensed RE Broker; **EDUC:** BA, 1978, Econ., Harvard Coll.; **EDUC HONORS:** Cum Laude; **OTHER ACT & HONORS:** Asian Bus. League-Chmn., Chinese Amer. Assn. of Commerce, Dir.; **HOME ADD:** 43 Santiago Ave., Atherton, CA 94025, (415)328-5577; **BUS ADD:** 520 El Camino Real, Suite 840, San Mateo, CA 94402, (415)579-1010.

CHANIN, Ronald E.——B: June 13, 1952, Macon, GA, *Controller*, Wilma Southeast, Inc.; **PRIM RE ACT:** Developer, Owner/Investor, Property Manager; **PREV EMPLOY:** Staff Auditor-Arthur Anderson W-Atlanta, GA; **PROFL AFFIL & HONORS:** GA Soc. of CPA's, CPA, Beta Alpha Psi; **EDUC:** BS, 1974, Mgmt. Sci., GA Instit. of Technol.; **GRAD EDUC:** MBA, 1976, Acctg., Univ. of GA; **EDUC HONORS:** Beta Alpha Psi, Delta Gamma Sigma, Grad. Asst. Quantitatude Methods; **OTHER ACT & HONORS:** GA B'nai. B'rith Treas., Achim, Lodge B'nai B'rith Pres.; **HOME ADD:** 4530 Woodlawn Lake Dr., Marietta, GA 30303, (404)973-2123; **BUS ADD:** 233 Peachtree St., Suite 500, Atlanta, GA 30303, (404)524-2004.

CHANTENGCO, Rick D.——B: Sept. 30, 1928, Manila, Philippines, *Pres.*, ERA-Chantengco Realty, Inc.; **PRIM RE ACT:** Broker, Syndicator, Consultant, Property Manager, Engineer, Owner/Investor; **SERVICES:** Counseling, Exchanging & Synd. Investment; **REP CLIENTS:** Prop., valuation & Mktg. New Subdiv. & Trust Money, Indiv., Lenders, Builders & Investors; **PREV EMPLOY:** Electronic Engr. Shop 67, Olongapo, Philippines 1956; **PROFL AFFIL & HONORS:** RNMI of NAR, GRI ('73) CRS (Chartered Member '77) & CRB '79; **EDUC:** Aero Eng. & Pat (flying school), 1953 & 53A, Feati Inst. of Tech. (Manila) & Phil. Air Force Flying School; **MIL SERV:** USN 12 yrs.-US Submarine, EMC (SS), Vietnam Cold War; **OTHER ACT & HONORS:** CV Bd. of Ethics (77-79), Employment, Serv. Bd. Sacramento 80-present, Chartered Member FIL-AM Democratic Club of San Diego, Delegate to Central Democratic Party 40th Dist. (Senatorial); **HOME ADD:** 1213 Fallbrook Ct., Bonita, CA 92002, (714)421-5906; **BUS ADD:** 1952 Third Ave., Chula Vista, CA 92011, (714)426-9916.

CHAPEKIS, A. Frederick——B: Nov. 5, 1952, Chicago, IL, *Atty.*, Stamos & Chapekis; **PRIM RE ACT:** Broker, Attorney, Developer, Owner/Investor, Syndicator; **PROFL AFFIL & HONORS:** ABA; IL Bar Assn.; Chicago Bar Assn.; **EDUC:** BS, 1974, Econ., IN Univ.; **GRAD EDUC:** JD, 1977, Law, IL Inst. of Tech., Kent Coll. of Law; **HOME ADD:** 4116 Applewood Ln., Northbrook, IL 60062, (312)291-0774; **BUS ADD:** 69 Washington St., Suite 2247, Chicago, IL 60602, (312)236-3564.

CHAPIN, David F.——B: Apr. 26, 1926, Watertown, NY, *VP*, Equitable Life, Realty Operations; **PRIM RE ACT:** Owner/Investor; **SERVICES:** Investment and Prop. Mgmt.; **PROFL AFFIL & HONORS:** BOMA of NY, NACORE, RE Bd. of NY; **EDUC:** BBA, 1950, Mgmt. and Personnel, Clarkson Coll.; **MIL SERV:** USAAF, Cpl., 1944-46; **HOME ADD:** 180 Radcliff Dr., E. Norwich, NY 11732;

BUS ADD: 1285 Ave. of Americas, NY, NY 10019, (212)554-3187.

CHAPMAN, Carl A.——**B:** Aug. 29, 1946, Abington, PA, *Pres.*, Chapman Enterprises, Inc.; **PRIM RE ACT:** Developer, Builder, Owner/Investor, Syndicator; **PROFL AFFIL & HONORS:** Pres., Cape May Cty. Home Bldrs. Assn., NAHB; **EDUC:** BS, 1970, Structural, Civil Engrg., Lafayette Coll.; **MIL SERV:** USNR, PO6; **HOME ADD:** 294-47th St., Avalon, NJ 08202, (609)368-8496; **BUS ADD:** 4118 Landis Ave., Sea Isle City, NJ 08243, (609)263-1126.

CHAPMAN, George M.——**B:** Oct. 23, 1934, Cynthiana, KY, *Owner*, Chapman & Assoc.; **PRIM RE ACT:** Consultant, Engineer, Appraiser, Owner/Investor; **OTHER RE ACT:** Bus. Consultant; **SERVICES:** Valuations, land and bus. econ. studies and counseling; **REP CLIENTS:** Corp., lenders, indivs., instns., service in comml., indus. and multi-family props.; **PROFL AFFIL & HONORS:** AIREA, Soc. of RE Appraisers, MAI, SRPA, Past Pres. and Officer of State Org.; **EDUC:** BS, 1957, Sci., Eastern KY Univ.; **GRAD EDUC:** MS, 1960/1969, Sci./Bus., Univ. of KY/Univ. of Louisville; **EDUC HONORS:** Who's Who in Amer. Coll. and Univ.; **MIL SERV:** US Army, Capt.; **OTHER ACT & HONORS:** Chapman and company Branch Offices: 424 E. Court St. Jeffersonville, KY 47130; 2420 Frankfort Ave. Louisville, KY 40206; 400 W. Vine St. Lexington, KY 40107; **HOME ADD:** 6410 Glenwood Rd., Louisville, KY 40222, (502)425-7536; **BUS ADD:** 627 West Main St., Louisville, KY 40202, (502)583-6063.

CHAPMAN, Howard Stephen——**B:** Dec. 27, 1946, Cleveland, OH, *Gen. Counsel*, TransCon Builders, Inc.; **PRIM RE ACT:** Broker, Attorney, Developer; **SERVICES:** Legal services; **PREV EMPLOY:** Legal Counsel, Investors REIT One and Investors REIT Two, both OH Bus. Trusts, 1971-1975; Self Employed in General Practise of Law 1976-77; **PROFL AFFIL & HONORS:** ABA; OH Bar Assn.; Cuyahoga Cty. Bar Assn., JD degree; **EDUC:** BBA, 1968, Acctg., OH Univ., Athens, OH; **GRAD EDUC:** JD, 1971, Law, OH State Univ., Columbus; **EDUC HONORS:** Elected to Beta Alpha Psi, Accounting Honorary; Bus. Mgr. of 'The Post' School Newspaper for 2 Yrs.; **OTHER ACT & HONORS:** Fin. Sec., Cleveland Prof. Lodge B'nai B'rith; Univ. Hts. Lodge No. 738 F&AM; Ancient Accepted Scottish Rite; Aladdin Temple Shrine of Columbus, OH; **HOME ADD:** 5414 Kilbourne Dr., Lyndhurst, OH 44124, (216)461-9459; **BUS ADD:** 25250 Rockside Rd., Bedford Hts., OH 44146, (216)439-3400.

CHAPMAN, J. Winston, Jr.——**B:** Feb. 7, 1947, Houston, TX, *Senior Partner*, Weeks, Chapman & Buford; **PRIM RE ACT:** Attorney; **SERVICES:** Synds., Ltd. Partnerships, Closings; **REP CLIENTS:** Lenders, Devels., Contractors, Realtors, Investors; **PROFL AFFIL & HONORS:** State Bar of TX; Travis Cty. Bar Assn.; Bar RE Section; **EDUC:** BA, 1969, Liberal Arts, Psych., Univ. of TX; **GRAD EDUC:** JD, 1973, Bus.-law, Univ. of TX; **EDUC HONORS:** Phi Eta Sigma; Order of Alcalde; Dean's List, "Outstanding Student"; **MIL SERV:** TX Nat. Guard, S/Sgt.; **BUS ADD:** 807 Rio Grande, Austin, TX 78701, (512)476-6096.

CHAPMAN, John S.——**B:** July 6, 1936, Twin Falls, ID, *Lawyer*, Martin, Chapman, Martin & Hyde, Chartered; **PRIM RE ACT:** Attorney; **EDUC:** BA, 1958, Poli. Sci., Univ. of ID; **GRAD EDUC:** 1961, Law, ID Stanford Univ.; **MIL SERV:** USAR, Capt.; **OTHER ACT & HONORS:** Boise Rotary Club - Boise C of C; Democ. Natl. Comm.-ID; Exec. Comm.-Democratic Natl. Comm.; **HOME ADD:** 2423 Hillway Dr., Boise, ID 83702; **BUS ADD:** P.O. Box 2898, Boise, ID 83701, (208)343-6485.

CHAPMAN, L. Jerry——**B:** Mar. 21, 1934, Greenville, SC, *Sr. VP*, Liberty Life Ins. Co., Admin.; **PRIM RE ACT:** Broker, Property Manager, Owner/Investor; **PROFL AFFIL & HONORS:** Admin. Mgmt. Soc.; IREM; **EDUC:** BS Ind. Mgmt., 1961, Clemson Univ.; **MIL SERV:** US Army 1956-1962, Lt., Good Conduct Medal; **HOME ADD:** 14 Queensway, Greenville, SC 29615, (803)288-1866; **BUS ADD:** PO Box 789, Greenville, SC 29602, (803)268-8426.

CHAPMAN, Paul H.——*Pres.*, National Association of Business Brokers, Chapman Company, Inc.; **OTHER RE ACT:** Profl. Assn. Admin.; **BUS ADD:** 1835 Savoy Dr., Ste 206, Atlanta, GA 30341, (404)458-9226.*

CHAPMAN, Ronald J.——**B:** May 24, 1923, E. Moriches, NY, *Owner*, R.J. Chapman Co.; **PRIM RE ACT:** Consultant, Appraiser; **PROFL AFFIL & HONORS:** Eastern Suffolk Bd. of Realtors; NY State Soc. of RE Appraisers, GRI; **MIL SERV:** USCG, Petty Officer; **OTHER ACT & HONORS:** Deputy Registrar Brookhaven Town, 15 yrs.; L.I. Sunrise Chap. Nat. Railway Hist. Soc.; Amer. Legion; **BUS ADD:** 30 Osborne Ave., E. Moriches, NY 11940, (516)878-1081.

CHAPMAN, Toby G.——**B:** Apr. 19, 1946, Winnsboro, SC, *Prop. Mgr.*, Spaulding & Slye Copr.; **PRIM RE ACT:** Property Manager; **SERVICES:** Full line prop. mgmt. - releasing, acct., legal, operations, etc.; **REP CLIENTS:** Indiv. & inst. investors in comml. prop.; **PREV EMPLOY:** Prop. Mgr., Amer. Mutual Fire Ins. Co., Charleston, SC - 1974-1980; **PROFL AFFIL & HONORS:** BOMA, Soc. of Real Prop. Admin., RPA Candidate; **EDUC:** Indus. Mgmt., 1969, Fin., Clemson Univ.; **MIL SERV:** US Army Reserve, Spec. 5; **OTHER ACT & HONORS:** Diploma - Trident Technical Coll., Charleston, SC (1975) Air Conditioning & Refrigeration; **HOME ADD:** 417B W. Eighth St., Charlotte, NC 28202, (704)376-6111; **BUS ADD:** Wachovia Ctr., Suite 1907, 400 S. Tryon St., Charlotte, NC 28285, (704)333-6661.

CHARBONNEAU, Richard——**B:** Aug. 8, 1942, Mt. Clemens, MI, *Pres.*, D'Luge Real Estate Co.; **PRIM RE ACT:** Broker, Builder; **SERVICES:** RE, comml., bus. opportunities, exchanging prop. mgmt.; **PROFL AFFIL & HONORS:** NAR; Realtors Nat. Mktg. Network; Homes for Living Network, CRB, CRS, Realtor of Year 1978-Macomb Cty.; **OTHER ACT & HONORS:** Dir., Clinton Valley Kiwanis; **HOME ADD:** 37285 Vita Marie, Mt. Clemens, MI 48043, (313)469-6885; **BUS ADD:** 24416 Crocker Blvd., Mt. Clemens, MI 48043, (313)468-5936.

CHARLES, Walter J.——*Sr. VP*, Fort Howard Paper Co.; **PRIM RE ACT:** Property Manager; **BUS ADD:** 1919 S. Broadway, PO Box 130, Green Bay, WI 54305, (414)435-8821.*

CHARLSON, Richard H.——**B:** Oct. 13, 1943, Kittanning, PA, Pearce, Urstadt, Mayer & Greer, Inc., Finance/Sales Div.; **PRIM RE ACT:** Developer, Builder; **OTHER RE ACT:** RE Sales and Fin.; **SERVICES:** Investment Prop., Sales, Joint Venture Financing, and Condominium Dev.; **REP CLIENTS:** Office and Indus. Dev. and Pension Funds; **PREV EMPLOY:** 12 yrs. of RE brokerage - investment prop. and counseling; **EDUC:** BS, 1965, Engineering; **OTHER ACT & HONORS:** VP, Hot Line Cares, Inc.; **HOME ADD:** 201 W 77th St., NY, NY 10024, (212)799-5484; **BUS ADD:** 90 Park Ave., New York, NY 10016, (212)682-1400.

CHARLTON, Richard Edmund, III——**B:** Jan. 6, 1943, Akron, OH, *Atty. (Partner)*, Winchester, Huggins, Charlton, Leake, Brown & Slater; **PRIM RE ACT:** Attorney; **SERVICES:** Gen. RE legal counseling; synds., closings; zoning; fin. law; prop. mgmt. law; litigation; **REP CLIENTS:** Investors; devels.; const. contractors; realtors; bankers; **PROFL AFFIL & HONORS:** TN Bar Assn. (Member RE Sect.); AL Bar Assn.; ABA (Member RE, Probate and Trust Sect., Forum Comm. on Const. Law, Corp., Banking and Bus. Section); **EDUC:** BS, 1964, Bus. Admin., Auburn Univ.; **GRAD EDUC:** JD, 1969, Univ. of AL; **EDUC HONORS:** Bench and Bar Legal Honor Soc.; AL Law Reporter; **MIL SERV:** US Army; Capt.; **HOME ADD:** 166 Picardy Place, Memphis, TN 38111, (901)323-8873; **BUS ADD:** Suite 1900, First Tennessee Bank Bldg., 165 Madison Ave., Memphis, TN 38103, (901)526-7374.

CHARLTON, Steven L.——*Sr. President Real Estate Properties*, A-T-O, Inc.; **PRIM RE ACT:** Property Manager; **BUS ADD:** 4420 Sherwin Rd., Willoughby, OH 44094, (216)946-9000.*

CHASE, Blaine B.——**B:** Oct. 9, 1928, Denver, CO, *Pres.*, Chase and Co.; **PRIM RE ACT:** Appraiser, Owner/Investor; **OTHER RE ACT:** RE Counselor; **PREV EMPLOY:** Pres., Chase and Co. (1976-present); Sr. VP, Corp. Secy. (and part owner),, Frederick R. Ross Co. (1964-1976); Partner, A.F. Chase & Co. (1952-1964); **PROFL AFFIL & HONORS:** AIREA; Amer. Soc. of RE Counselors; Intl. ROW Assn.; NAR; Denver Bd. of Realtors, MAI, CRE; **EDUC:** BS, 1954, RE, Univ. of Denver; **EDUC HONORS:** Recipient Denver Bd. of Realtors Scholarship Award 1953-1954; **MIL SERV:** USAF, Capt.; **HOME ADD:** 7877 E. Mississippi Ave. No. 1404, Denver, CO 80231, (303)377-4750; **BUS ADD:** 817 17th St., Suite 1038, Denver, CO 80202, (303)629-7178.

CHASE, Jonathan D.——**B:** May 8, 1953, Hartford, CT, *Pres.*, Chase Realty Corp., Chase Indus.; **PRIM RE ACT:** Developer; **SERVICES:** Devel. Mgmt. & Consulting Apt. & Condo. Specialty; **PREV EMPLOY:** Chief Housing Planner State of VT - VP Chase Indus.; **PROFL AFFIL & HONORS:** Southeastern VT Bd. of Realtors, Inc.; **EDUC:** BS, 1976, Resource Econ./Environmental Sci., Univ. of VT, Deans List; **HOME ADD:** "Brookside", Brattleboro, VT 05301, (802)257-1090; **BUS ADD:** Brattleboro, VT 05301"Brookside", (802)257-1090.

CHASICK, Douglas D.——**B:** Mar. 11, 1950, Brooklyn, NY, *Asst. to the Pres.*, Diego Props.; **PRIM RE ACT:** Consultant, Instructor, Property Manager; **OTHER RE ACT:** Mgmt., leasing and synd. of comml RE; **REP CLIENTS:** The Traveler's Insurance Co.; Flagship Banks; Chase Manhattan Bank; and the Wachovia Bank and Trust Co. of North

Amer.; **PREV EMPLOY:** Gen. Mgr., Bailey & Casey Mgmt. Co.; VP Cheshire Mgmt. Co., Wallingford, CT; **PROFL AFFIL & HONORS:** BOMA; CAI; NAA; FL Assn. of Realtors; IREM; ICSC, CPM; Pres. Elect, FL East Coast Chap. of IREM; Instr., IREM; **HOME ADD:** 141 NE 30th St., Wilton Manors, FL 33334, (305)561-8213; **BUS ADD:** 221 NE 33rd Street, Ft. Lauderdale, FL 33311, (305)561-8900.

CHAZANKIN, Henry——B: Mar. 24, 1940, El Paso, TX, *Pres.*, Henry Chazankin, Inc.; **PRIM RE ACT:** Broker, Consultant, Owner/Investor; **SERVICES:** Investment counseling, brokerage, syndication, exchanges; **REP CLIENTS:** Indivs., partnerships & lenders; **PREV EMPLOY:** Personal investments; **PROFL AFFIL & HONORS:** Marin Investment Counselors, Bay Area Exchange Counselors, IREF; **EDUC:** BA, 1963, Speech, Univ. of MN; **GRAD EDUC:** MA, 1975, Psych., CA State Coll., Sonoma; **MIL SERV:** USMC; **OTHER ACT & HONORS:** MENSA, Alpha Epsilon Pi; **HOME ADD:** 58 Katrina Ln., San Anselmo, CA 94960, (415)457-2149; **BUS ADD:** 1100 Larkspur Landing Cir., Suite 305, Larkspur, CA 94939, (415)461-4994.

CHEATHAM, Harry H.——B: Jan. 2, 1946, Cape Girardeau, MO, *Asst. Mgr.*, The Travelers Insurance Co., RE Investment Dept.; **PRIM RE ACT:** Lender, Owner/Investor; **SERVICES:** Source of equity purchases and fin.; **PREV EMPLOY:** The Sheahan Investment Co., Mort. Bankers, 1976-1980; **PROFL AFFIL & HONORS:** Candidate for MAI; **EDUC:** BSBA, 1972, Fin./Banking/RE, Univ. of MO; **MIL SERV:** US Army, Sgt., 2 Bronze Stars; **HOME ADD:** 112 Portland Terr., Webster Groves, MO 63119, (314)961-9061; **BUS ADD:** 10 S. Brentwood Blvd., Clayton, MO 63105, (314)726-2100.

CHEATHAM, Robert W.——B: June 4, 1938, St. Paul, MN, *Atty.*, Brobeck, Phleger & Harrison; **PRIM RE ACT:** Attorney; **PREV EMPLOY:** Civil Engr. - Pvt. consulting co.; **PROFL AFFIL & HONORS:** Local, State and ABA, CEB speaker and author; arbitrator, American Arbitration Assn.; Adjunct Professor, 1972-76, U.C., Hastings College of Law; **EDUC:** BCE, 1961, Civil Engrg., Univ. of MN; **GRAD EDUC:** LLB, 1966, Law, Univ. of MN Law School; **EDUC HONORS:** Order of Coif, Law Review Editor; **HOME ADD:** 1217 Lorain Rd., San Morino, CA 91108, (213)284-7514; **BUS ADD:** 770 Wilshire Blvd., Suite 400, Los Angeles, CA 90017, (213)613-0900.

CHEKIJIAN, C.J.——B: Apr. 15, 1946, London, England, *Mgr., Corporate RE*, Warner Lambert Co.; **PRIM RE ACT:** Owner/Investor; **OTHER RE ACT:** Corporate RE; **SERVICES:** In-house corporate RE servs.; **PREV EMPLOY:** Tenneco, Inc., Houston, TX 1976-1980; Continental Grp., Boston MA 1970-1976; **PROFL AFFIL & HONORS:** Nat. Assn. of Corporate RE Execs.; IIV; NARA; Intl. Org. of RE Appraisers; ICSC; BOMA; MBA; AMA, CRA; SCV; **EDUC:** BS, 1970, Engrg., London Univ., London, England; **GRAD EDUC:** 1968, Econ./Fin., London School of Econ., London, England; **OTHER ACT & HONORS:** Chmn. Fin. Comm., Conservative Caucas, Mass.; **HOME ADD:** 7002 Blvd. East, 20C, Guttenberg, NJ 07093, (201)868-4216; **BUS ADD:** 201 Tabor Rd., Morris Plains, NJ 07950, (201)540-3303.

CHELLIS, Tom——B: Apr 14, 1917, Baltimore, MD, Tom Chellis, Ltd.; **PRIM RE ACT:** Broker, Consultant, Owner/Investor, Instructor; **SERVICES:** RE Counseling; **PROFL AFFIL & HONORS:** TIMS; NAR; CA Assn. of Realtors; CARET; Camarillo Bd. of Realtors, CA Broker, Realtor; **EDUC:** AA, 1959, Bus., Santa Anna Coll.; **GRAD EDUC:** BA, 1967, Econ., Chapman Coll.; MBA, 1973, Bus., Pepperdine Univ.; **MIL SERV:** USMC; Sgt. Maj./Capt.; 1936-1956; **HOME ADD:** 2358 N. Temple Ave., Camarillo, CA 93010, (805)484-1201; **BUS ADD:** 2358 N. Temple Ave., Camarillo, CA 93010, (805)484-1201.

CHENOWETH, Walter A.——B: Feb. 4, 1931, Los Angeles, CA, *VP*, Coldwell Banker, Comml. RE; **PRIM RE ACT:** Broker; **PREV EMPLOY:** IBM, 1959-1970; Computer Intelligence Corp. (Pres.) 1970-1972; **EDUC:** BA, 1953, Poli. Sci., UCLA; **GRAD EDUC:** MBA, 1959, Mktg., Harvard Bus. School; **EDUC HONORS:** Baker Scholar; **MIL SERV:** USN; Lt.; **HOME ADD:** El Secreto, Rancho Santa Fe, CA 92067, (714)756-4643; **BUS ADD:** 5130 Avenida Encina, Carlsbad, CA 92008, (714)721-1500.

CHERIKOF, Howard L.——B: Sept. 24, 1935, Baltimore, MD, *Pres.*, Howard L. Chertkof & Co.; **PRIM RE ACT:** Broker, Developer, Instructor, Property Manager, Syndicator; **PROFL AFFIL & HONORS:** NAR; SIR; Balt. Bd. of Realtors; MD Assn. Realtors; Indus. Devel. Research Council, SIR; **EDUC:** BS, 1957, Indus. Engrg., Johns Hopkins Univ.; **MIL SERV:** US Army; **OTHER ACT & HONORS:** Bd. & Officer-Community Housing for the Aged; **BUS ADD:** 19 W. Franklin St., Baltimore, MD 21201.

CHERIS, Samuel David——B: Nov. 14, 1945, Brooklyn, NY, *Part.*, Hall & Evans; **PRIM RE ACT:** Attorney; **SERVICES:** Tax aspects of RE transactions, indus. devel bonds; **REP CLIENTS:** Indiv., comml. & inst. investors in resid. rental & comml. props.; **PROFL AFFIL & HONORS:** ABA, on Real Prop., Probate & Trust, and Sect. on Taxation, Order of the Coif; Who's Who in Fin. & Ind.; **EDUC:** BS, 1967, Acctg. & Econ., Brooklyn Coll.; **GRAD EDUC:** JD, 1971, Stanford Univ. Sch. of Law; MBA, 1971, Fin., Stanford Univ. Grad. Sch. of Bus.; **EDUC HONORS:** Cum Laude, Hon. in Econ., Order of the Coif, Editor Stanford Law Review; **OTHER ACT & HONORS:** Member Dir's Comm. US Fencing Assn., 1980-; Bd. of Dir. Hearing Dog, Inc.; Jewish Community Ctr. of Denver; **HOME ADD:** 5730 Montview Blvd., Denver, CO 80207, (303)377-0504; **BUS ADD:** 2900 Energy Ctr., 717 17th St., Denver, CO 80202, (303)573-5022.

CHERNEY, Richard A.——B: June 25, 1912, Waterloo, IA, *Pres.*, Cherney and Associates, Inc.; **PRIM RE ACT:** Broker, Consultant, Appraiser, Developer, Syndicator; **REP CLIENTS:** Large indus., and large comml., primarily; **PROFL AFFIL & HONORS:** Battle Creek, and Kalamazoo Bd. of Realtors, Amer. Instit. of RE Appraisers, Soc. of RE Appraisers, MAI, SREA; **MIL SERV:** Med. Administrative, Capt.; **OTHER ACT & HONORS:** Calhoun Cty. Commnr. for 12 years; Elks; Masons; **HOME ADD:** 159 Stafford Ave., Battle Creek, MI 49015, (616)962-1047; **BUS ADD:** 159 Stafford Ave., Battle Creek, MI 48010, (616)962-1047.

CHEROS, John G.——B: Feb 10, 1939, Greenville, SC, *Atty.*, John G. Cheros, Atty.; **PRIM RE ACT:** Consultant, Attorney, Owner/Investor; **OTHER RE ACT:** Title insurance agent; **SERVICES:** Title examinations, closing all types of RE transactions, escrow services, issuing title insurance, investment counseling, devel. and synd., nat. and local levels, builders, realtors, and investors in comml. and resid. prop.; **PROFL AFFIL & HONORS:** Greenville Cty. Bar Assn.; SC Bar Assn.; Amer. Bar Assn.; Greenville Bd. of Realtors; Greenville & Nat. Homebuilders Assns.; Greenville C of C, Who's Who in American Law (Marquis Publ.); **EDUC:** BA, 1962, Pol. Sci. (major); English (minor), Furman Univ.; **GRAD EDUC:** MLL, 1964, Law, Univ. of SC; **EDUC HONORS:** Dean's List, Wig & Robe Honor Society; Claude Sapp Award; first in Grad. Class; Phi Beta Kappa; Recent Decisions Editor of S.C. Law Review; **MIL SERV:** US Army, Sp. 4; **OTHER ACT & HONORS:** Chmn. of SC Bar Assn. RE Sec. (1976); Overbrook So. Baptist Church; Bd. of Dir. of Mitchel Rd. Christian Ministries; **HOME ADD:** Route 2, Raven Rd., Greenville, SC 29607, (803)288-3916; **BUS ADD:** 1300 E. Washington St., Greenville, SC 29601, (803)233-7401.

CHERRY, James P.——B: Nov. 28, 1947, Detroit, MI, *VP*, Hall Real Estate, Inc., Acquisitions; **PRIM RE ACT:** Syndicator; **EDUC:** BSBA, 1969, Xavier Univ.; **GRAD EDUC:** MBA, 1971, Univ. of Detroit; **BUS ADD:** 18311 W. 10 Mile Rd., Southfield, MI 48075, (313)557-7700.

CHERTOK, Sumner J.——B: Feb. 17, 1927, Boston, MA, *Atty.*, Chertok & Chertok; **PRIM RE ACT:** Broker, Attorney, Syndicator, Consultant, Developer; **PREV EMPLOY:** Chertok & Chertok; Brookline Redev. Exec. Dir.; **PROFL AFFIL & HONORS:** NAHRO, MA Bay Fed. Bar; **EDUC:** AB, Gov., Harvard Coll.; **GRAD EDUC:** JD, Constitutional Litigation, Harvard Law School; **MIL SERV:** USN, 1C, South Pacific Theatre; **OTHER ACT & HONORS:** Chmn. Brookline Redev. Auth.; V Chmn. Brookline Housing Auth.; Exec. Dir. Brookline Redev. Auth.; **HOME ADD:** 142 Clinton Rd., Brookline, MA 02146, (617)277-1454; **BUS ADD:** 11 Beacon St., Boston, MA 02146, (617)523-0454.

CHESELDINE, Raymond M.——*Exec. VP*, Bank Marketing Assn.; **PRIM RE ACT:** Banker; **BUS ADD:** 309 W. Washington St., Chicago, IL 60606, (312)782-1442.*

CHESELDINE, Richard J., Jr.——B: Nov. 18, 1946, Montgomery, AL, *Pres.*, Rick's Lind-Davis RE Co., Inc.; **PRIM RE ACT:** Broker, Owner/Investor; **SERVICES:** Brokerage of resid. RE; brokerage of investment props.; **PROFL AFFIL & HONORS:** NAR, Realtors Natl. Mktg. Instit., Natl. Homebuilders Assn., CRS (Certi. Resid. Specialist) Realtor of the Yr. for the Montgomery Bd. of Realtors for 1981; Pres. of Montgomery Bd. of Realtors for 1981; **EDUC:** BA, 1960, Hist., Spring Hill Coll. Mobile, AL; **EDUC HONORS:** Summa Cum Laude, Class Valedictorian; **MIL SERV:** US Army; Capt.; **OTHER ACT & HONORS:** Commerce Exec. Soc., Univ. of AL; Rolling Hills Golf & Racquet Club; St. Bede's Catholic Church; **HOME ADD:** 3614 Lansdowne Dr., Montgomery, AL 36111; **BUS ADD:** 3666-C Debby Dr., P.O. Box 11265, Montgomery, AL 36111, (205)288-7665.

CHESLER, Earl R.——B: July 10, 1917, Elyria, OH, *Pres.*, Earl R. Chesler, Inc.; **PRIM RE ACT:** Consultant, Appraiser; **SERVICES:** RE consultant & appraiser; **REP CLIENTS:** Broward Cty. Downtown

Devel. Auth., Trust Dept Century Natl. Bank; **PROFL AFFIL & HONORS:** NAR, SREA, CRE (Gov.), SREA, Soc. of RE Appraisers; CRE, Amer. Soc. of RE Counselors; CRA, Nat. Assn. Review Appraisers; **EDUC:** BS, 1940, Bus. Admin., OH State Univ.; **MIL SERV:** USAF, Maj., 2 air medals; **HOME ADD:** 7401 SW 7th St., Plantation, FL 33317, (305)463-2415; **HOME TEL:** (305)791-5909; **BUS ADD:** 305 S Andrews, Las Olas Bldg., Suite 710, Ft. Lauderdale, FL 33301.

CHESNUT, Wayne D.——B: Oct. 18, 1937, Stuart, NE, *Broker - Owner*, Wagon Train Realty, Inc.; **PRIM RE ACT:** Broker, Property Manager, Syndicator; **OTHER RE ACT:** Exchangor; **SERVICES:** Represent builders and provide full-service prop. mgmt.; **PREV EMPLOY:** Producer of Commercials, documentary and educational films; **PROFL AFFIL & HONORS:** CA Assn. of Realtors, CA Apt. Assn., Building Industry Assn., Exchangors, State Dir. Investment Div. of C.A.R., Chmn. Dist. 12 Communications Comm., Educ. Comm., Investment Comm.; MLS Chairman, Dir. CA Apt. Assoc.; **EDUC:** BS, 1959, Radio/TV Broadcasting, Univ. of ID; **GRAD EDUC:** MBA, 1966, Communications, Columbia Coll.; **EDUC HONORS:** Dean's Honor Roll; **MIL SERV:** USMC, Sgt.; **OTHER ACT & HONORS:** AYSO, Rotary, Elks, JC's, C of C, Pres. of India Club, CB Radio Organization; **HOME ADD:** 6250 N. Fresno St., Fresno, CA 93726, (209)435-9277; **BUS ADD:** 610 Pico Suite B, Clovis, CA 93612, (209)292-3900.

CHEW, Richard J.——B: Jan. 3, 1934, Santa Maria, CA, *Pres.*, Richard Chew and Associates; **PRIM RE ACT:** Broker, Consultant, Appraiser, Banker, Owner/Investor; **SERVICES:** Consultation RE Fin. and Devel.; **REP CLIENTS:** Large RE Devels. and Investors; **PREV EMPLOY:** Coldwell Banker 1959-81; **PROFL AFFIL & HONORS:** Amer. Mort. Bankers; Intl. Council of Shopping Ctrs.; **EDUC:** BS, 1957, Bus., Mktg., Univ. of S. CA; **GRAD EDUC:** 1972, Mort. Fin., Stanford Univ., Northwestern Univ., MI State; **MIL SERV:** US Army, Signal Corps; **HOME ADD:** 8112 Zitola Terr., Playa del Rey, CA 90291, (213)823-4158; **BUS ADD:** 8112 Zitola Terr., Playa Del Rey, CA 90291, (213)823-4158.

CHICKEY, Joseph T.——B: May 9, 1946, Philadelphia, PA, *Mgr. Devel.*, Butler American Corp.; **PRIM RE ACT:** Developer; **SERVICES:** Design/const./devel.; **REP CLIENTS:** Carrier Corp., Proctor & Gamble, International Paper, US Steel; **PREV EMPLOY:** Carrier Corp. (RE Mgr.); Amer. Express Co., GTE; **PROFL AFFIL & HONORS:** NAIOP; **EDUC:** BA, 1968, Econ., Moravian Coll.; **GRAD EDUC:** Diploma in RE Analysis & Appraisal, 1977, New York Univ.; **MIL SERV:** USN, Lt.; **HOME ADD:** 2833 University Cir., Crestview Hills, KY 41017, (606)331-5000; **BUS ADD:** P.O. Box 282, Covington, KY 41017, (606)331-5000.

CHILCOTE, Lee A., Jr.——B: May 5, 1942, Cleveland, OH, *V.P., Sec. and Gen. Counsel*, First Union RE Investments; **PRIM RE ACT:** Attorney, Engineer; **SERVICES:** Corp. genl. counsel; **PREV EMPLOY:** Thompson, Hine and Flory, 1971-78; **PROFL AFFIL & HONORS:** ABA, OH Bar Assn.; **EDUC:** BA, 1964, Engrg.-mjr. and Eng.-mnr.; **GRAD EDUC:** BS,LLB, 1965, 1971, Engrg., Law, Thayer School of Engrg., Hastings Coll. of Law Univ. of CA.; **EDUC HONORS:** Order of Coif, Thurston Honor Soc., top 5 percent; **MIL SERV:** USMC, Capt., Bronze Star, Presidential Unit Citation, Vietnam Service Medal, Naval Unit Citation; **OTHER ACT & HONORS:** Councilman, V.Mayor, City of Cleveland Hgts., Trustee Fairmont Presbyterian Church; **HOME ADD:** 2322 Delamere Dr., Cleveland, OH 44106, (216)321-1747; **BUS ADD:** Suite 1900, 55 Public Sq., Cleveland, OH 44106, (216)781-4030.

CHILDRESS, Dennis E.——B: Feb. 21, 1936, Jefferson City, MO, *Pres.*, Realty World Grand Land; **PRIM RE ACT:** Broker, Architect, Builder; **PROFL AFFIL & HONORS:** Registered Architect, State of MI; **EDUC:** BArch, 1963, Arch, Auburn Univ., AL; **MIL SERV:** FL Nat. Guard, E7; **HOME ADD:** 1501 Union Ave. NE, Grand Rapids, MI 49508, (616)364-8335; **BUS ADD:** 3167 Kalamazoo Ave. SE, Grand Rapids, MI 49508, (616)243-7690.

CHILDS, Alvin, Jr.——B: Dec. 11, 1946, Jacksonville, TX, *Owner*, Childs Real Estate & DeveLopment; **PRIM RE ACT:** Developer, Owner/Investor, Property Manager; **SERVICES:** Feasibility analysis, devel. & mgmt. services; **REP CLIENTS:** Retail outlets & comml. users; **PROFL AFFIL & HONORS:** ICSC; BOMA; **EDUC:** BS, 1970, Commerce, Washington & Lee Univ.; **OTHER ACT & HONORS:** Former VP, Shreveport C of C; Chmn., Shreveport Housing Advisory Comm.; **HOME ADD:** 611 Southfield Rd., Shreveport, LA 71106, (318)865-0191; **BUS ADD:** 600 Hutchinson Bldg., Shreveport, LA 71101, (318)222-0847.

CHILES, Gene T.——B: Sept. 2, 1941, McCamey, TX, *Atty.*; **PRIM RE ACT:** Attorney, Owner/Investor; **SERVICES:** Legal; **REP CLIENTS:** Travis Bank and Trust; Travis Title Co.; Investors, Inc. (Mort. Co.); Numerous pvt. investors; **PREV EMPLOY:** 10 yrs. in comml. loans and income prop. financing with Ben G. McGuire & Co. (Houston), Lumberman's Investment Corp. (Austin), Investors, Inc. (Austin); **PROFL AFFIL & HONORS:** State Bar of TX; ABA; Travis Cty. Bar, Who's Who in TX, 1973-1974; Who's Who in So. & SW, 1978-1979; **EDUC:** BS, 1964, Bus./Econ., Austin Coll.; **GRAD EDUC:** JD, 1968, Law, Bates Coll. of Law, Univ. of Houston; **EDUC HONORS:** Dean's List; **HOME ADD:** 6207 Bend O'River, Austin, TX 78746, (512)327-6634; **BUS ADD:** 911 W. 38th St., Suite 400, Austin, TX 78705, (512)452-4424.

CHILTON, Gil——B: Mar. 15, 1944, *VP, Assets & Portfolio Mgr. Secondary Mktg.*, Guarantee S&L Assn.; **PRIM RE ACT:** Lender; **OTHER RE ACT:** Loan Purchaser; **SERVICES:** S&L Resid. and comml. lending and Purchasing, secondary loan mktg., and money mkt. analysis; **PREV EMPLOY:** Suburban Coastal Corp. (VP), PMI Mort. Ins. Co. (Mktg.), FHLMC (Sr. Underwriter & Account Rep.), State Mutual S&L Assn. (AVP); Far West Ins Agency (AVP & Mgr.); **PROFL AFFIL & HONORS:** CA S&L League, Secondary Mktg. Comm., GNMA Sub comm.; FNMA sub-comm.; FHLMC sub-comm.; CA Home Loan Mort. Assn., sub-comm.; Member, State Teacher's Retirement Board Member Gov. Public Investment Task Force and responsible investments sub-comm.; **GRAD EDUC:** BS, Bus. Admin., Fin., Univ. of San Francisco, CA; **OTHER ACT & HONORS:** Dir. Lakewood (CA) C of C, Dir. Lakewood Shopping Ctr. Merchants' Assn., Spec. Projects Member Long Bch. (CA) C of C, Jury Member Statewide Affordable Housing Competition (CA); **HOME ADD:** 3543 W Magill, Fresno, CA 93711, (209)432-0540; **BUS ADD:** Guarantee Fin. Ctr., W Tower, 1318 E Shaw Ave., Fresno, CA 93710, (209)226-9400.

CHIN, Roy——B: June 1950, NY, NY, *VP, Team Leader*, Chase Manhattan Bank, N.A., RE Fin., National West; **PRIM RE ACT:** Banker; **SERVICES:** Const. lending; **PREV EMPLOY:** Chase Bank 1973-; American Pioneer Corp. 1972; **PROFL AFFIL & HONORS:** Young Mort. Banker Assn., NAHB, ICSC; **EDUC:** BS, 1972, Engrg., Rensselaer Polytech. Inst.; **GRAD EDUC:** MBA, 1980, Fin., NY Univ.; **OTHER ACT & HONORS:** Who's Who in Fin. & Indus., 1981; **HOME ADD:** 80 Lafayette, Chatham, NJ 07928, (201)635-6724; **BUS ADD:** 1211 Ave. of Americas, New York, NY 10036, (212)730-3024.

CHING, Robert Soong——B: Aug. 25, 1936, Hollywood, CA, *Pres.*, Honolulu Mort. Co., Inc.; **PRIM RE ACT:** Attorney, Syndicator, Consultant, Lender; **SERVICES:** Comm'l. & resid. loan originations; loan admin. & servicing; **REP CLIENTS:** Aetna Life; NY Life; Metropolitan Life; Occidental Life; Trans Amer. Occidental Life; Crocker Nat. Bank; Citicorp, Inc.; Brooklyn Savings Bank; Lincoln Savings Bank; **EDUC:** BS, 1957, Univ. of MD/Univ. of HI; **GRAD EDUC:** JD, 1960, Harvard Law School; **EDUC HONORS:** Cum Laude; **MIL SERV:** US Army, Res; Cpl.; **OTHER ACT & HONORS:** Fin. Member, City of Seattle Landmarks Preservation, 1978 - 1979; Bd. of Dir., Honolulu Theater for Youth, 1980 - 1983; Tr., Historic HI Foundation, 1980 - 1983; **BUS ADD:** 820 Mililani St., POB 1464, Honolulu, HI 96806, (808)544-3400.

CHING, Wendell T.P.——B: Sept. 20, 1940, Wailuku, Maui, HI; **PRIM RE ACT:** Broker, Engineer, Builder, Owner/Investor; **PROFL AFFIL & HONORS:** CCIM; PE; **EDUC:** BS, 1963, Engrg., Univ. of HI; **MIL SERV:** US Army, Capt.; **HOME ADD:** 985 Ala Kapua St., Honolulu, HI 96818, (808)839-1813; **BUS ADD:** PO Box 19066, Honolulu, HI 96817, (808)524-5000.

CHINNOCK, Thomas G.——B: June 10, 1939, Evanston, IL, *VP Appraisal*, Strobeck, Reiss Co., Appraisal Div.; **PRIM RE ACT:** Broker, Consultant, Appraiser; **SERVICES:** Appraisals, Investment counseling; **REP CLIENTS:** Banks, major cos., indiv., attys.; **PROFL AFFIL & HONORS:** Member Amer. Inst. of RE Appraisers, Chicago and Nat. Assn. of Realtors, MAI designation, CRA designation; **EDUC:** BA, 1961, Fin., Econ., Univ. of IL; **MIL SERV:** US Army, SP-5; **OTHER ACT & HONORS:** Realtors 40 Club; Bd. of Gov., appraisal Div., of the Chicago RE Bd.; **HOME ADD:** 455 W. Oakwood Dr., Barrington, IL 60010, (312)526-2328; **BUS ADD:** 134 S. LaSalle St., Chicago, IL 60603, (312)644-4800.

CHIODO, Carol——*Mgr.*, Culbertson Co.; **PRIM RE ACT:** Property Manager, Developer; **OTHER RE ACT:** Investor's Rep.; **PREV EMPLOY:** Provident Nat. Bank, Philadelphia, PA; **EDUC:** BA, 1979, Intl. Bus., Lafayette Coll.; **EDUC HONORS:** Dean's List; **BUS ADD:** 12923 Ballsford Rd., Manassas, VA 22110, (703)631-0502.

CHIRURG, James Thomas——**B:** May 21, 1944, Wellesley, MA, *Lead Partner*, Catastasis Properties, Ltd. (1979-), Protasis Holdings (S.A.R.L.); **PRIM RE ACT:** Owner/Investor; **SERVICES:** Investment counseling, valuation, and mgmt.; **REP CLIENTS:** Instnl. and selected indiv. investors in comml. props.; **PREV EMPLOY:** First Boston Corp. (1969-70); Protasis Trust, Ltd. (1971-); **PROFL AFFIL & HONORS:** British Inst. of Mgmt.; Assn. for the Advancement of Appropriate Technol. for Developing Countries, Fellow, Inst. of Dirs. (UK); **EDUC:** AB, 1964, Asian Studies, Cornell Univ.; **GRAD EDUC:** MBA, 1969, Intl. Fin., Harvard Univ. Grad. School of Bus. Admin.; **EDUC HONORS:** Rotary Fellowship, Knox Fellowship; **MIL SERV:** USN; Lt. j.g.; Bronze Star w/combat "V"; **OTHER ACT & HONORS:** Royal Econ. Soc.; Amer. Econ. Assn.; Fellow, Salsburg Seminar (Austria); Fellow, Royal Asiatic Soc. (England), member, Inst. of Dir. European Assn. (IDEA); **HOME ADD:** 2115 Bush, San Francisco, CA 94115, (415)921-2382; **BUS ADD:** PO Box 4000, Berkeley, CA 94704, (415)346-2191.

CHISM, Earl——*Controller*, Washington Post Co.; **PRIM RE ACT:** Property Manager; **BUS ADD:** 15th St. NW, Washington, DC 20071, (202)334-6000.*

CHISWELL, S. James——**B:** Sept. 30, 1948, Buffalo, NY, *Staff VP*, National Association of Home Builders;, Association Mgmt. Servs.; **OTHER RE ACT:** Trade Assn. Exec.; **PREV EMPLOY:** Exec. VP, Niagara Frontier Builders Assn., Buffalo, NY; **PROFL AFFIL & HONORS:** Amer. Soc. of Assn. Execs.; Cleveland Soc. of Assn. Execs.; **EDUC:** BA, 1970, Pol. Sci., SUNY at Buffalo; **BUS ADD:** 15th St. NW, Wash., DC 20005, (202)822-0200.

CHITTAM, Dick——**B:** May 30, 1952, W. Palm Beach, FL, *Owner, Broker*, Dick Chittam Realty; **PRIM RE ACT:** Broker, Instructor, Property Manager, Banker, Appraiser, Builder; **OTHER RE ACT:** Auctioneer, Liquidator; **SERVICES:** Resid. brokerage & appraisal, rental mgmt.; **PROFL AFFIL & HONORS:** Athens Bd. of Realtors, AL Assn., NAR, Nat. Assn. of RE Appraisers, GRI, Realtor of Yr., 1981; **EDUC:** BS, 1973, Educ., Psych., Bus., Athens Coll.; **EDUC HONORS:** Magna Cum Laude; **OTHER ACT & HONORS:** Civitan, C of C, Indus. Devel. Comm.; **HOME ADD:** Rte. 4, Box 370-B, Athens, AL 35611, (205)232-0527; **BUS ADD:** 112 W. Wash., Athens, AL 35611, (205)232-6666.

CHODSKY, Val——*RE Rep. for Land*, Standard Oil of California; **PRIM RE ACT:** Property Manager; **BUS ADD:** 225 Bush St., San Francisco, CA 94104, (414)894-7700.*

CHODUR, Philip——**B:** May 22, 1947, Garner, IA, *Pres.*, Sunland Brokers; **PRIM RE ACT:** Broker, Consultant, Developer, Owner/Investor, Property Manager, Syndicator; **SERVICES:** Econ. analysis, synd., prop. mgmt., investment counseling; **PROFL AFFIL & HONORS:** Realtors Nat. Mktg. Inst.; BOMA; So. CA Chap.; CCIM, Broker, CA and TX; **EDUC:** 1974, Pol. Sci., Univ. of TX, Austin; **EDUC HONORS:** Grad. with Honors; **OTHER ACT & HONORS:** Toastmasters; **HOME ADD:** 4775 E. Mt. View, San Diego, CA 92116, (714)281-6259; **BUS ADD:** 3435 Camino del Rio, Suite 317, San Diego, CA 92108, (714)563-1823.

CHOMAS, J. Louis——**B:** Jan. 10, 1952, McKeesport, PA, *Atty.*; **PRIM RE ACT:** Attorney; **PROFL AFFIL & HONORS:** ABA; PA Bar Assn.; **EDUC:** BA, 1973, Pol. Sci., PA State Univ.; **GRAD EDUC:** JD, 1977, Univ. of Pittsburgh; **HOME ADD:** 207 Plum St., Elizabeth, PA 15037, (412)384-6181; **BUS ADD:** 103 Second St., Elizabeth, PA 15037, (412)261-3745.

CHOW, Steven Y.T.——**B:** Jan. 15, 1948, China, *Pres.*, American Investment Holding Co., Inc.; **PRIM RE ACT:** Broker, Developer, Syndicator; **SERVICES:** RE brokerage, comml., investment., devel.; **REP CLIENTS:** Far Eastern investors; **PREV EMPLOY:** Ritchie & Ritchie Corp.; Anderson, Chow & Assoc.; **PROFL AFFIL & HONORS:** Amer. Mktg. Assn.; Intl. Trade Council of San Francisco; San Francisco Bd. of Realtors; San Mateo Burlingam Bd. of Realtors; Amer. RE Exchange; **EDUC:** BA, 1974, Bus. Fin., San Francisco State Univ.; **GRAD EDUC:** MBA, 1976, Intl. Bus., Golden Gate Univ.; **HOME ADD:** 607 Bainbridge St., Foster City, CA 94404, (415)572-1765; **BUS ADD:** 153 Kearny St., Suite 409, San Francisco, CA 94108, (415)392-8700.

CHOWNING, John S.——**B:** Dec. 25, 1923, New Smyrna, FL, *Partner*, Shutts & Bowen, RE Div.; **PRIM RE ACT:** Attorney; **PROFL AFFIL & HONORS:** The FL Bar Assn.; Dade Cty. Bar Assn. and ABA; Amer. Soc. of Hospital Attys.; **EDUC:** BA, 1947, Univ. of FL; **GRAD EDUC:** LLB, 1950, Univ. of VA; **MIL SERV:** US Army; **OTHER ACT & HONORS:** Amer. Cancer Soc.; **HOME ADD:** 2603 Country Club Prado, Coral Gables, FL 33134, (305)665-6752; **BUS ADD:** 133 Sevilla Ave., Coral Gables, FL 33134, (305)444-3601.

CHRISTELLER, James R.——**B:** Apr. 13, 1924, Charleston, WV, *VP*, Joyner & Co. Realtors; **PRIM RE ACT:** Broker, Builder, Owner/Investor, Property Manager; **PREV EMPLOY:** Motel owner/operator '50-'74; **PROFL AFFIL & HONORS:** Inst. of RE Mgmt., CPM; **MIL SERV:** US Navy, PO 3/c; **HOME ADD:** 2616 Lafayette Ave., Richmond, VA 23228, (804)266-2228; **BUS ADD:** 2727 Enterprise Pkwy., Richmond, VA 23229, (804)270-9440.

CHRISTENSEN, Marvin——**B:** Sept. 15, 1939, Wheatland, WY, Realty World/Skyline Realty, Inc.; **PRIM RE ACT:** Consultant, Builder; **PREV EMPLOY:** Rancher/farmer; **PROFL AFFIL & HONORS:** NRA, FLI; **EDUC:** BS, 1961, Agriculture, Univ. of WY; **EDUC HONORS:** Alpha Zeta; **HOME ADD:** P.O. Box 798, Evansville, WY 82636, (307)265-5922; **BUS ADD:** 641 East 2nd, Casper, WY 82601, (307)265-5566.

CHRISTENSEN, William Lowell——**B:** Oct. 7, 1932, Salt Lake City, UT, *Appraiser & Counselor*, Christensen, Hewlett & Snell, Inc.; **PRIM RE ACT:** Consultant, Appraiser, Instructor; **REP CLIENTS:** Chevron, UT State Bldg. Bd., Citizens Bank, Mountain Fuel Supply Co., Bur. of Reclamation, Royal St. Corp.; **PREV EMPLOY:** VP of Zions Securities Corp. in charge of RE investments; **PROFL AFFIL & HONORS:** AIREA; MAI; CPM; SRPA; SR/WA; CRA; Sr. NARA; ASA; **EDUC:** BA, 1955, Econ., Westminster Coll., Fulton, MO; **MIL SERV:** US Army; Fin. Corp., Lt.; **OTHER ACT & HONORS:** Salt Lake Rotary Club; **HOME ADD:** 1407 Harvard Ave., Salt Lake City, UT 84105, (801)583-2408; **BUS ADD:** 455 E 400 S, Suite 308, Salt Lake City, UT 84111, (801)322-2436.

CHRISTENSON, Edward——**B:** Mar. 19, 1921, Menisino, MB, *Pres.*, Grand Forks Fed. S&L Assn.; **PRIM RE ACT:** Lender; **SERVICES:** Complete S&L plans; **PREV EMPLOY:** 10 yrs. - 1st Fed. S&L Assn., Grand Forks, ND; **PROFL AFFIL & HONORS:** US League of Savings Assns., Dir. - FHLB ND S&L League, Pres. - ND S&L League; **EDUC:** BS, 1943, Accounting & Bus., Univ. of ND; **GRAD EDUC:** Grad. School of S&L, IN; **EDUC HONORS:** Phi Eta Sigma - Hon. Freshman Frat., Beta Alpha Psi - Hon. Accounting Frat.; **MIL SERV:** USMC, Capt.; **OTHER ACT & HONORS:** Dir. C of C, United Fund, and Y Family Ctr.; **HOME ADD:** 2010 Oak St., Grand Forks, ND 58201, (701)772-0542; **BUS ADD:** 13 So. 4th St., Grand Forks, ND 58201, (701)775-5331.

CHRISTENSON, Robert E.——**B:** Sep. 29, 1936, Minneapolis, MN, The Towle R.E. Co.; **PRIM RE ACT:** Broker, Instructor, Consultant; **SERVICES:** Comml. Investment R.E. Sales, consulting, Comml. R.E. Inst.; **REP CLIENTS:** Corporate R.E. users, R.E. investors; **PROFL AFFIL & HONORS:** Upper Midwest CCIM Chapter, Past Pres., CIC, NAR, RNMI, OMEGA TAU RHO Service Medal, 1980, awarded by Natl. Assoc. of Realtors; **EDUC:** BS, 1958, Bus. Admin., Gustavus Adolphus Coll.,MN; **MIL SERV:** USNR, Lt. J.G., 1958-1961; **OTHER ACT & HONORS:** Past Chmn. BOD, The Health Central System, Bd. of Govs., Unity Medical Center, public speaker on hospital Trst. issues, Past Pres., West Metro Hospital Trustee Council, Bd. of Govs., Health Central Inst.; **HOME ADD:** 4920 Newton Ave,S., Minneapolis, MN 55409, (612)922-2324; **BUS ADD:** 600 Second Ave. S., Minneapolis, MN 55402, (612)341-4444.

CHRISTIAN, J.E.——**B:** May 20, 1954, San Francisco, CA, *Regional Land Mgr.*, Marathon Development California, Inc.; **PRIM RE ACT:** Developer, Builder, Owner/Investor, Property Manager; **SERVICES:** Hi-Rise office devel., land devel.; **PREV EMPLOY:** Bank America Appraisal, Grubb & Ellis Brokerage; **PROFL AFFIL & HONORS:** NAIOP, AIREA, ICSC, ULI; **EDUC:** BS, 1976, Mktg., Univ. CA at Berkeley; **GRAD EDUC:** MBA, 1979, Mktg., CA State Univ. at San Jose; **HOME ADD:** 42 Dorchester Dr., Daly City, CA 94015; **BUS ADD:** 595 Market St., Suite 1330, San Francisco, CA 94105, (415)495-8270.

CHRISTIAN, William R.——**B:** Mar. 18, 1950, Columbia, SC, *Partner*, Pepper, Hamilton and Sheetz, Los Angeles Office; **PRIM RE ACT:** Consultant, Attorney, Regulator, Owner/Investor, Syndicator; **OTHER RE ACT:** RE and corporate tax; **SERVICES:** Legal consultation; **REP CLIENTS:** RE Devel., RE Mgmt., groups and clients with income, estate or gift problems involving RE; full range of tax, securities, fin. and litigation services; **PREV EMPLOY:** Partner, Willis, Butler, Scheifly, Leydorf and Grant (Law Firm); **PROFL AFFIL & HONORS:** State Bar CA; Los Angeles Cty. Bar Assn. (Former Editor, Tax Sect. Newsletter, Tax Sect. Exec. Comm.), ABA, JD (1973) Coif; Law Review; **EDUC:** BA, 1969, Acctg., CA State Univ. at Fullerton; **GRAD EDUC:** JD, 1973, Tax Law, Hastings Coll. of the Law, Univ. of CA; **EDUC HONORS:** Coif; **OTHER ACT & HONORS:** Los Angeles Athletic Club; **HOME ADD:** 20855 Missionary Ridge St., Walnut, CA 91789; **BUS ADD:** 606 S. Olive St., Los Angeles, CA 90014, (213)617-8151.

CHRISTIANSEN, Paul A.——B: July 3, 1928, Detroit, MI, *Pres.*, Paul A. Christiansen and Company; **PRIM RE ACT:** Developer, Builder, Owner/Investor; **PREV EMPLOY:** Prof., Univ. of MO 1958-1980; **PROFL AFFIL & HONORS:** NAHB, HBA of Greater Kansas City, Eastern Jackson Cty. Bldrs. & Devels. Assn., CPA; **EDUC:** BS, 1948, Acctg., Wayne State Univ.; **GRAD EDUC:** MA, 1949, Econ., Wayne State Univ.; Grad. Studies, Harvard Univ.; **OTHER ACT & HONORS:** Jackson Cty. Bond Advisory Comm. 1969-1975; **HOME ADD:** 3333 Lake Shore Dr., Blue Springs, MO 64015, (816)229-7171; **BUS ADD:** 333 Lake Village Blvd., Blue Springs, MO 64015, (816)229-7171.

CHRISTIANSON, Bruce I.——B: Nov. 20, 1950, Minot, ND, *Prop. Mgr.*, Signal Realty; **PRIM RE ACT:** Broker, Consultant, Property Manager; **SERVICES:** Full service co.; **PROFL AFFIL & HONORS:** IREM, ND Bd. of Realtors, Minot Bd. of Realtors; **EDUC:** BA, 1973, Econ., Minot State Coll.; **OTHER ACT & HONORS:** City Alderman, elected 1980, Masonic Lodge, Shriner, Jaycees (Past Pres.), Rotary Club, Elks Club, C of C; **HOME ADD:** 1639 12th St. S.W., Minot, ND 58701, (701)839-3269; **BUS ADD:** 1541 S. Broadway PO Box 2189, Minot, ND 58701, (701)852-3505.

CHRISTIANSON, Michael J.——*Pres.*, Law Offices, Michael J. Christianson, Inc.; **PRIM RE ACT:** Attorney; **SERVICES:** Tax planning for US and for. RE investors; **REP CLIENTS:** US and foreign persons and corps.; **PREV EMPLOY:** Trial Atty., Internal Revenue Serv., US Dept. of Treas.; **PROFL AFFIL & HONORS:** Intl., ABA and CA Bar Assn.; **GRAD EDUC:** LLB, 1965, Law, State Univ. of IA; **EDUC HONORS:** Cum Laude; **BUS ADD:** 610 Newport Ctr. Dr., Ste. 550, Newport Beach, CA 92660, (714)644-9190.

CHRISTMAN, James R.——B: May 11, 1938, Dayton, OH, *Pres.*, Christman & Graddy Inc.; **PRIM RE ACT:** Consultant, Developer, Owner/Investor; **SERVICES:** Devel. of office and business parks in sunbelt; **REP CLIENTS:** First Equities Corp.; Peachtree Corners, Inc.; Southeastern Land Fund Inc.; **PREV EMPLOY:** Exec. VP, Wilwat Properties Inc., Atlanta, GA; **PROFL AFFIL & HONORS:** Bd. of Dirs., Gwinnett Cty. C of C; Nat. Assn. of Indus. & Office Parks; **EDUC:** BS, 1961, Bus. Admin./Econ., Wittenberg Univ.; **EDUC HONORS:** Grad. Cum Laude; **MIL SERV:** US Army Reserve, Lt., 1st Class; **HOME ADD:** 4678 S. Hope Springs Rd., Stone Mountain, GA, (404)294-6346; **BUS ADD:** POB 884, Norcross, GA 30091, (404)447-6734.

CHRISTOFF, Kenneth E.——B: Feb. 5, 1933, Pittsburgh, PA, *Pres.*, RE Appraisal Services, Inc.; **PRIM RE ACT:** Broker, Consultant, Appraiser, Owner/Investor; **OTHER RE ACT:** Expert witness in RE litigation; **SERVICES:** Appraisal of resid., comml. & indus. RE; **REP CLIENTS:** Fed., state and local govts., all major banks and other lending instns, and indiv. or inst. investors in appraisal of resid., comml. and indus. RE; **PREV EMPLOY:** RE broker since 1958, RE Appraisal Servs., Inc. since 1961; **PROFL AFFIL & HONORS:** NAR, PA Assn. of Realtors, Gr. Pittsburgh Bd. of Realtors, Nat. Inst. of RE Brokers, Amer. Right of Way Assn., NARA, CRA, Amer. Assn. of Cert. Appraisers, Cert. Appraiser, Sr., Intl. Org. of RE Appraisers (ICA), Intl. Cert. Appraiser, Sr. Member, Nat. Assn. of Cert. Real Prop. Appraisers (CPRA), Cert. Real Prop. Appraiser, Sr. Member, Who's Who in Amer., Who's Who in the East, Who's Who in RE, Notable Amers., Comm. Leaders and Noteworthy Amers., Book of Hon.; **EDUC:** RE & Ins., Univ. of Miami, Univ. of Pittsburgh; **OTHER ACT & HONORS:** Chmn. Scott Twp. Planning Comm., 1967-70; Chmn. Scott Twp. Zoning Hearing Bd., 1970-present; Pres. (1980-81) Amen Corner (Businessmen's club); Member The PA Soc. (NYC); **HOME ADD:** 2 Manorview Rd., Pittsburgh, PA 15220, (412)561-0994; **BUS ADD:** 1910 Lawyers Bldg., Pittsburgh, PA 15219, (412)261-2688.

CHRISTOFORO, John——B: Oct. 3, 1924, Revere, MA, *Sr. Partner*, Hale & Dorr; **PRIM RE ACT:** Attorney; **SERVICES:** Atty.; **GRAD EDUC:** LLB, 1949, Boston Univ. School of Law; **MIL SERV:** USN, Lt. Comdr.; **HOME ADD:** 30 Hillcrest Ave., Melrose, MA 02176, (617)665-5645; **BUS ADD:** 60 State St., Boston, MA 02109, (617)742-9100.

CHRISTOPH, Christine E.——B: July 18, 1951, Oak Park, IL, *Prop. Mgr.*, Barry Gillingwater Mgmt.; **PRIM RE ACT:** Property Manager, Broker; **PREV EMPLOY:** RE Broker, CPM, PCS Inc., Hinsdale, IL; Gillingwater Mgmt., Austin, TX; **PROFL AFFIL & HONORS:** IREM, RESSI, Chicago Bd. of Realtors, IL RE Broker, CPM; **EDUC:** BS, 1973, Interior Design, Purdue Univ.; **HOME ADD:** 1781 Spyglass #348, Austin, TX 78746, (512)327-6293; **BUS ADD:** 100 North International, Austin, TX 78746, (512)476-2633.

CHRISTOPHER, Michael C.——B: Oct. 15, 1947, San Diego, CA, *VP*, Trans-Continental Props. Inc.; **PRIM RE ACT:** Broker, Developer, Syndicator; **REP CLIENTS:** Investors in and devels. of comml. prop. and resid. housing projects; **EDUC:** BBA, 1972, RE & Urban Affairs, GA State Univ.; **HOME ADD:** 725 Cremona Ave., Coral Gables, FL 33146, (305)665-4798; **BUS ADD:** 255 Alhambra Cir., Suite 600, Coral Gables, FL 33134, (305)448-2766.

CHRISTOPOLIS, Nicholas V.——B: Sept. 21, 1949, Cleveland, OH, *VP*, Union Commerce Bank, RE Indus. Div.; **PRIM RE ACT:** Banker, Lender; **SERVICES:** Comml. RE Lender; **PROFL AFFIL & HONORS:** MBAA, Builders Exchange Inc., Builder Indus. Assn., Amer. Bankers Assn.; **EDUC:** BA, 1970, Bus., Baldwin/Wallace; **GRAD EDUC:** MBA, 1981, Bus., Baldwin, Wallace; **HOME ADD:** Berea, OH 44017, (216)234-8412; **BUS ADD:** 917 Euclid Ave. Ave., Cleveland, OH 44115, (216)344-6306.

CHRONLEY, James A.——B: July 31, 1930, Springfield, MA, *Exec. VP*, Burger Chef Systems, Inc., RE, Construction, Prop. Mgmt., Franchising; **OTHER RE ACT:** Corp. RE; **PREV EMPLOY:** Atlantic Richfield Co., National RE Dir. 1954-1974; Marriott Corp., VP RE Restaurant Operations; **PROFL AFFIL & HONORS:** Nat. Assn. of Corporate RE Execs., Intl. Council of Shopping Ctrs., Nat. Assn. of Review Appraisers; **EDUC:** AB, 1952, Econ., Brown Univ.; **MIL SERV:** US Army, Cpl., Amer. Spirit Honor Medal; **HOME ADD:** 745 Johnson Dr., Carmel, IN 46032, (317)846-1047; **BUS ADD:** College Park Pyramids, P O Box 927, Indianapolis, IN 46206, (317)875-8400.

CHU, Harold——B: Dec. 12, 1947, Pine Bluff, AR, *Pres.*, Harold Chu, Atty. at Law; **PRIM RE ACT:** Broker, Consultant, Attorney, Instructor; **SERVICES:** RE counseling & legal services related to RE;, Drafting of conveyancing documents; RE litigation; **PROFL AFFIL & HONORS:** Honolulu Bd. of Realtors, NAR, HI State Bar Assn., ABA; **EDUC:** BA, 1971, Psych., Stanford Univ.; **GRAD EDUC:** JD, 1974, NW Univ.; **EDUC HONORS:** Hons. in Psych.; **HOME ADD:** 900 Fort St. Mall, Suite 1260, Honolulu, HI 96813, (808)523-7544; **BUS ADD:** 900 Fort St. Mall, Suite 1260, Honolulu, HI 96813, (808)523-7544.

CHU, Hilbert——B: Oct. 17, 1950, Hong Kong, *Prin.*; **PRIM RE ACT:** Developer, Owner/Investor; **OTHER RE ACT:** CPA; **SERVICES:** Tax, audit, acctg., RE devel.; **REP CLIENTS:** KCOO Devel. Co., Inc.; Keng Fong For. Investment Co., Ltd.; Wolff Devel., Inc.; Kamp Devel., Inc.; Pac. Investment & Devel. Co., Inc.; **PREV EMPLOY:** Peat, Marwick, Mitchell & Co.; **PROFL AFFIL & HONORS:** AICPA; CA Soc. of CPA, CPA; **EDUC:** AB, 1972, Mathematics, Univ. of CA, Berkeley; **GRAD EDUC:** MBA, 1974, Acctg., Univ. of CA, Berkeley; Studying toward JD Degree at Univ. of San Diego - Expected to Graduate 1982; **EDUC HONORS:** Distinction in Gen. Scholarship, Phi Beta Kappa, Honors Program Completed with Distinction, Amer. Jurisprudence Award in Contracts; **OTHER ACT & HONORS:** Christian Businessmen Comm.; Kiwanis; Research Grant Award: Nat. Sci. Found. CA Heart Assn.; **BUS ADD:** 3434 Fourth Ave., Suite 120, San Diego, CA 92103, (714)297-6759.

CHUDNOW, I. Randall——*VP*, Lehigh Valley Industries, Inc.; **PRIM RE ACT:** Property Manager; **BUS ADD:** 200 East 42nd St., New York, NY 10017, (212)930-9600.*

CHULAK, Michael T.——B: Apr. 17, 1947, Los Angeles, CA; **PRIM RE ACT:** Syndicator, Consultant, Property Manager, Owner/Investor, Broker; **OTHER RE ACT:** Gen. Bldg. Contractor and Real Estate Instructor; **SERVICES:** Tax-sheltered RE investments and prop. mgmt.; **PROFL AFFIL & HONORS:** NAR; IREM; CPM; **EDUC:** BS, 1970, Bus. Admin., CA State Univ. at Los Angeles; **OTHER ACT & HONORS:** RE Inst. at Los Angeles Valley College and Moorpark College; **HOME ADD:** 272 Cedar Heights Dr., Thousand Oaks, CA 91360, (805)492-6386; **BUS ADD:** 9701 Wilshire Blvd. Seventh Floor, Beverly Hills, CA 90210, (805)492-6386.

CHUN, John Jason——B: Apr. 23, 1957, Honolulu, HI, *Realtor, Mortgage Broker, NASD-LRR*, John J. Chun, Inc.; **PRIM RE ACT:** Consultant, Owner/Investor; **OTHER RE ACT:** RE Paper Discounting, Mort. Banking & Serv.; **SERVICES:** Investment Consultation; **REP CLIENTS:** Drs., Dentist, Corp. Owners, ESQs, CPAs; **EDUC:** Fin. & RE, 1982, Non Taxable Transactions, Univ. of HI; **HOME ADD:** 3022 Hinano St., Honolulu, HI 96815, (808)734-2423; **BUS ADD:** Grosvenor Ctr., 733 Bishop St., Suite 1550, Honolulu, HI 96813, (808)523-7736.

CHUPP, O.L.——*VP Mfg.*, American Business Products, Inc.; **PRIM RE ACT:** Property Manager; **BUS ADD:** 2690 Lumberland Parkway, Ste. 500, Atlanta, GA 30339, (404)434-1000.*

CHURCH, Clayton——**B:** Mar. 3, 1930, Tacoma, WA, *Dir. of RE*, Grand Auto, Inc.; **PRIM RE ACT:** Broker, Developer, Owner/Investor, Property Manager; **SERVICES:** Site locations; **HOME ADD:** 24 Appian Ct., El Sobrante, CA 94803, (415)223-0570; **BUS ADD:** 7200 Edgewater Dr., Oakland, CA 94621, (415)568-6500.

CHURCHFIELD, P.M.——*Dir. Fac.*, Varian Assoc.; **PRIM RE ACT:** Property Manager; **BUS ADD:** 611 Hansen Way, Palo Alto, CA 94303, (415)493-4000.*

CHURCHILL, Robert W.——*Broker/Consultant*; **PRIM RE ACT:** Broker, Consultant, Owner/Investor, Property Manager; **SERVICES:** Investment counseling, prop. mgmt.; **REP CLIENTS:** Indiv. investors; **PROFL AFFIL & HONORS:** AICPA, CPA; **EDUC:** BS, 1974, Acctg.-Taxation, Metropolitan State Coll., Denver, CO; **BUS ADD:** 2342 Gillespie #3, Springfield, IL 62704, (217)787-7390.

CHUSED, Richard——**B:** Jan. 31, 1943, St. Louis, MO, *Assoc. Prof. of Law*, Georgetown Univ. Law Center; **OTHER RE ACT:** Teacher and writer; **PREV EMPLOY:** Rutgers Univ.; **PROFL AFFIL & HONORS:** Soc. of Amer. Law Teachers; **EDUC:** AB, 1965, Math, Brown Univ.; **GRAD EDUC:** JD, 1968, Univ. of Chicago Law School; **EDUC HONORS:** Deans List, Nat. Honor Scholar, Bowman C. Lingle Fellow in Urban Studies, Univ. Chicago Law Review; **HOME ADD:** 20 Ninth St. S.E., Washington, DC 20003, (202)544-6205; **BUS ADD:** 600 New Jersey Ave. NW, Washington, DC 20001, (202)624-8243.

CHYTROWSKI, Allan M.——**B:** June 4, 1931, Pszow, Poland, *Pres.*, Allan M. Chytrowski, Inc.; **PRIM RE ACT:** Owner/Investor, Syndicator; **SERVICES:** Investment & Venture banking; **PREV EMPLOY:** GS Grumman/Cowen, Paine Webber Jackson & Curtis; **PROFL AFFIL & HONORS:** Natl. Assn. of Securities Dealers; **EDUC:** BA, 1953, Econ., Univ. of Cracow; **GRAD EDUC:** MBA, 1955, Univ. of Vienna, Austria; PhD, 1965, Univ. of Vienna, Austria; **EDUC HONORS:** With great distinction; **OTHER ACT & HONORS:** Polish (1948-59) and Belgian (1959-65) rep. in bobsledding & luge, Olympic Games & World championships, Active in Luge; **HOME ADD:** 52 Surrey Dr., Belle Mead, NJ 08502, (201)874-5014; **BUS ADD:** 52 Surrey Dr., Belle Mead, NJ 08502, (201)874-5014.

CIANCIA, Jeremiah J.——**B:** Mar. 19, 1918, West Hoboken, NJ, *Pres. & Trustee*, Tamburelli Mgmt. Corp.; **PRIM RE ACT:** Broker, Owner/Investor, Property Manager, Insuror; **SERVICES:** Realtor of comml., recreation & apt. props.; **REP CLIENTS:** Investments & analysis for in house trusts, leasings, acquisitions of diverse real prop., owner & former operators of country clubs in Bergen Cty., NJ; **PREV EMPLOY:** 35 yrs. in present bus.; **PROFL AFFIL & HONORS:** NJ Homebuilders Assn., RE Broker State of NJ, Ins. Broker State of NJ, Reg. Pharmacist, State of NJ; **EDUC:** BS, 1939, Pharm., Chem., Columbia; **MIL SERV:** USN, Pharm. Mate, Petty Officer, 2nd. Cl., DD 474 Destroyer Despac 45, Amer. Theater, Asian Theater, 2 Bronze Stars, Japan Occupation; **OTHER ACT & HONORS:** Prime Ministers Club, Econ. Devel. of Israel, NY Medical Coll., Parents Council; **HOME ADD:** 10 Glenwood Ave., Leonia, NJ 07605; **BUS ADD:** 574 Grand Ave., Englewood, NJ 07631, (201)569-8255.

CIANI, Robert J.——**B:** Jan 31, 1936, Bronx, NY, *Pres.*, Feldman Lumber Co., Drywall Div.; **PRIM RE ACT:** Broker, Owner/Investor; **SERVICES:** RE for Bldg. Rennovations; **REP CLIENTS:** NY City Area Bldg. Material Supplier, Lumber & Drywall Partition Supplies; **EDUC:** BA, 1959, Queens Coll.; **OTHER ACT & HONORS:** Queens Cty. Const. & Builders Assn., Builders Inst. Westchester Cty.; **HOME ADD:** 33 Beechwood Dr., Glen Head, NY 11545, (516)671-1773; **BUS ADD:** 2 Woodward Ave., Ridgewood, NY 11385, (212)495-5000.

CIBULA, George——*VP*, Darwin Development Corp.; **PRIM RE ACT:** Developer; **BUS ADD:** 1800 N. 30th Ave., Melrose Park, IL 60160, (312)450-9100.*

CIK, Barry A.——**B:** Apr. 19, 1951, Cleveland, OH, *Pres.*, Bargina Assocs.; **PRIM RE ACT:** Consultant, Engineer, Developer; **SERVICES:** Engrg. & const. mgmt., self-sufficient communities; **REP CLIENTS:** Devels., lenders, forensic applications; **PREV EMPLOY:** Civil Engr. - Const., soils analysis, highways; **PROFL AFFIL & HONORS:** ASCE, NSPE, ASP, ULI NACORE; **EDUC:** BSCE, 1978, Land Devel., OH State Univ.; **GRAD EDUC:** Civil Engr. (MSCE), 1982, Land Devel. & Const., OH State Univ.; **EDUC HONORS:** Pres. ASP, Fellowship; 1981; **BUS ADD:** 3266 Desota Ave., Cleveland, OH 44118, (216)321-2733.

CILLUFFO, Vito——**B:** Jan. 31, 1935, Detroit, MI, *Fee Appraiser*; **PRIM RE ACT:** Appraiser; **SERVICES:** Resid. Appraisal; **REP CLIENTS:** H.U.D., Gen. Motors, Homequity; **PREV EMPLOY:** H.U.D., Amer. Fed. Savings Assn.; **PROFL AFFIL & HONORS:** SREA, SRA; **HOME ADD:** 25111 Normandy, Roseville, MI 48066, (313)772-4235; **BUS ADD:** 25111 Normandy, Roseville, MI 48066, (313)772-4235.

CITRANO, James P.——**B:** Jan. 2, 1942, Newark, NJ, *Pres.*, St. Johns Place, Joint Venture Fruehauf/Gulf United; **PRIM RE ACT:** Broker, Consultant, Developer, Owner/Investor, Property Manager; **PROFL AFFIL & HONORS:** North FL Chap. of IREM, Pres. 1981-82, CPM; **EDUC:** 1964, Eng., Colgate Univ.; **MIL SERV:** USMC, Capt.; **HOME ADD:** 3714 San Viscaya Dr., Jacksonville, FL 32217, (904)737-7728; **BUS ADD:** 1608 Gulf Life Tower, Jacksonville, FL 32207, (904)399-3625.

CIZEK, Jerome D.——**B:** July 29, 1947, Berwyn, IL, *VP/Treas.*, IMA Financial Corporation; **PRIM RE ACT:** Broker, Developer, Owner/Investor, Property Manager, Syndicator; **SERVICES:** Comml. RE acquisition, devel., & prop. mgmt.; **REP CLIENTS:** Substantial indiv. investors in CA; **PREV EMPLOY:** Peat, Marwick, Mitchell & Co., CPA's; **PROFL AFFIL & HONORS:** CA Soc. of CPA's, CPA & Betta Gamma Sigma; **EDUC:** BSBA, 1969, Acctg., Roosevelt Univ.; **GRAD EDUC:** MBA, 1970, Roosevelt Univ.; **MIL SERV:** USNR, Lt., Viet Nam Service; **HOME ADD:** 347 Semillon Cir., Clayton, CA 94517, (415)672-2010; **BUS ADD:** 381 Bush St., San Francisco, CA 94104, (415)398-3183.

CLABAUGH, Henry——**B:** Feb. 12, 1942, St. Louis, MO, *VP, Sr. Appraiser*, Affiliated Appraisers Co.; **PRIM RE ACT:** Consultant, Appraiser, Builder, Property Manager, Syndicator; **PROFL AFFIL & HONORS:** IFAS, CREA, CAS; **MIL SERV:** US Army, 1960-63; **OTHER ACT & HONORS:** Tr., Bel Ridge, 1964-65; Shriners; Masons; **HOME ADD:** 16065 Meadow Oak, Chesterfield, MO 63017, (314)532-7355; **BUS ADD:** 11552 St. Charles Rd., Bridgeton, MO 63404, (314)291-8454.

CLAFFEY, Joseph——*Corp. VP*, Peabody International Corp.; **PRIM RE ACT:** Property Manager; **BUS ADD:** 4 Landmark Sq., Stamford, CT 06901, (203)348-0000.*

CLAGGETT, Lewis E.——**B:** June 28, 1932, Newark, OH, *Realtor-Devel.*, The Land Office; **PRIM RE ACT:** Broker, Syndicator, Consultant, Appraiser, Developer, Owner/Investor, Insuror; **PROFL AFFIL & HONORS:** AACA, CA-S, RESSI, FLI, GRI, Realtor of the Yr. 1972; **MIL SERV:** USN, AT-3 (1952-1954); **HOME ADD:** 1142 Hilltop Drive, Newark, OH 43055, (614)366-1940; **BUS ADD:** 63 North 4th St., Newark, OH 43055, (614)345-1282.

CLAMAN, Jeffrey A.——**B:** Feb. 28, 1941, New York, NY, *Pres.*, JAC Enterprises Ltd.; **PRIM RE ACT:** Owner/Investor, Property Manager, Syndicator; **EDUC:** BS, 1964, Mgmt., NY Univ.; **GRAD EDUC:** MBA, 1968, Fin., NY Univ.; **EDUC HONORS:** Honor Scholarship, Dean's List; **BUS ADD:** 685 Broadway, Bayonne, NJ 07002, (201)858-2700.

CLANCY, Joseph P.——**B:** June 20, 1944, Seattle, WA, *Sr. VP*, Rauenhorst Corp., RE Div.; **PRIM RE ACT:** Developer; **SERVICES:** Development of comml. props.; **REP CLIENTS:** Olympus Camera; G.D. Searle; Bell & Howell; Mamiya Co.; Mitsubishi; Continental Can; **PREV EMPLOY:** VP and Mgr., Fund F., First Nat. Bank of Chicago, (RE service fund); **PROFL AFFIL & HONORS:** ABA, SIR, NACORE; **EDUC:** AB, 1966, Govt., Georgetown Univ.; **GRAD EDUC:** JD, 1969, Fordham Univ. Law School; MBA, 1971, Cornell Bus. School; **HOME ADD:** 2500 Simpson St., Evanston, IL 60201, (312)491-1197; **BUS ADD:** 411 Bus. Ctr. Dr., Mt. Prospect, IL 60056, (312)824-4444.

CLANCY, Peter J.——**B:** Jan. 12, 1940, Schenectady, NY, *Treas.*, SES Group Companies; **PRIM RE ACT:** Owner/Investor; **OTHER RE ACT:** Fin. Admin.; **SERVICES:** RE Acquisition and Fin. Mgmt.; **REP CLIENTS:** Attys., Physicians, Other Profl. and Corp. Pension Funds; **PREV EMPLOY:** Peat, Marwick, Mitchell & Co. (Miami); Spear, Sheldon, Safer & Co. (Miami); World Land & Investing Co., Ltd. (Nassau); **PROFL AFFIL & HONORS:** FL Instit. of CPA's, Assoc. Member; **EDUC:** BBA, 1962, Univ. of Miami; **EDUC HONORS:** Alpha Beta Psi, Order of Omega, Sigma Alpha Epsilon; **HOME ADD:** 13600 S.W. 79th Court, Miami, FL 33158, (305)235-4773; **BUS ADD:** 250 Catalonia Ave., Suite 404, Coral Gables, FL 33134, (305)448-5067.

CLAPP, John M.——**B:** Apr. 5, 1944, Washington, DC, *Assoc. Prof.*, Univ. of CT; **PRIM RE ACT:** Consultant, Instructor; **SERVICES:** Seaching/Research; **REP CLIENTS:** Dept. of S&L, CA; **PREV EMPLOY:** U.S. Gen. Acctg. Office, Univ. of CA, Citibank Econ. Dept.; **PROFL AFFIL & HONORS:** Rgnl. Sci. Assn.; Amer. RE and Urban Econ. Assn.; Amer. Econ. Assn., Brookings Econ. Policy Fellow, 1978 and 1979; Who's Who in CA RE; **EDUC:** BA, 1967, Econ., Harvard Coll.; **GRAD EDUC:** PhD, 1974, Bus. Econ., Columbia

Univ.; **EDUC HONORS:** Magna Cum Laude, Harvard Coll. Scholarship, Awarded NDEA IV Fellowship, Elected Beta Gamma Sigma; **OTHER ACT & HONORS:** 1979, Selected for Chancellor's Award, Univ. of CA; **HOME ADD:** 65 Auburn Rd., W. Hartford, CT 06119, (203)232-6524; **BUS ADD:** Dept. of Fin., U-4IRE, Univ. of CT, Storrs, CT 06268, (203)486-3228.

CLAREY, Frederick Joseph——B: Mar. 27, 1943, Youngstown, OH, *Exec. VP & CEO*, Murdock Realty Servs. Inc.; **PRIM RE ACT:** Broker, Property Manager; **SERVICES:** Comml. brokerage, prop. mgmt.; **PREV EMPLOY:** Cushman & Wakefield, Grubb & Ellis Co., IBM Corp.; **PROFL AFFIL & HONORS:** Los Angeles Bd. of Realtors, Rotary, Los Angeles C of C; **EDUC:** BSBA, 1966, Engrg., Mktg., Univ. of AZ, Tucson; **GRAD EDUC:** MBA, 1975, Bus. Admin., Pepperdine Univ.; **MIL SERV:** 3-A; **OTHER ACT & HONORS:** Amer. Youth Seminor Co. Chmn. CA Republican Party, co-chmn, Republican Assn. Tr.; Pepperdine Univeristy; **HOME ADD:** 400 S. Arden Blvd., Los Angeles, CA 90020, (213)936-0223; **BUS ADD:** 10900 Wilshire Blvd., Suite 1500, Los Angeles, CA 90024, (213)208-1661.

CLARK, Alfred L.——B: Aug. 4, 1945, Vicksburg, MS, *Appraiser (FEE)*, Alfred Clark RE, Inc.; **PRIM RE ACT:** Broker, Instructor, Consultant, Appraiser; **SERVICES:** Appraisals and Consultations relating to RE Prop. Housing and Urban Devel., City of Jackson-Legal Dept. and Indiv.; **PREV EMPLOY:** Staff Appraiser and Comm. Appraisal Super. City of Jackson Tax Assessors Office(1971-1974, 1975-1977); **PROFL AFFIL & HONORS:** Staff Appraiser, Local Saving and Loan (1974-1975) Member, Nat. Soc. of RE Appraiser, NAREB; **MIL SERV:** USAF, A1C(E-4); **OTHER ACT & HONORS:** Jackson Urban League, MS Ass. of Realists, Inc.(Jackson); **HOME ADD:** 1510 Schoolview Dr., Jackson State Univ.; **BUS ADD:** PO Box 2613, Jackson, MS 39207, (609)362-8769.

CLARK, Bonnie P.——B: May 23, 1924, Chicago, IL, *Owner*, Oakwood Realty; **PRIM RE ACT:** Broker, Consultant, Appraiser, Builder; **PROFL AFFIL & HONORS:** M.C. Board of R., IAR, NAR, RNMI, Realtor of Year 1977, Pres. of Local board 2 yrs.; State Dir. 5 yrs. GRI, CRS, CRB; **EDUC:** AA, 1944, Speech, Stephens Coll.; **GRAD EDUC:** Univ. of WI - 1 yr.; **EDUC HONORS:** Phi Theta Kappa Jr. year, student leg., treas. of Pan Hell; **OTHER ACT & HONORS:** Long Beach Ctry. Club, C of C, Mensa, Episcopal Church Vestry 3 years & Sr. Warden - 1 year; **HOME ADD:** 2201 Oakenwald Dr., Michigan City, IN 46360, (219)872-3779; **BUS ADD:** Tinkers Dam Arcade, N. Karwick Rd., Michigan City, IN 46360, (219)879-3328.

CLARK, Charles——*Commissioner*, Georgia Real Estate Commission; **PRIM RE ACT:** Property Manager; **BUS ADD:** 40 Pryor St., S.W., Atlanta, GA 30303, (404)656-3916.*

CLARK, Charles B.——B: Mar. 11, 1947, Anniston, AL, *Asst. VP*, Citicorp Real Estate, Inc. (CREI), Houston; **PRIM RE ACT:** Banker, Lender; **SERVICES:** Const., permanent and equity fin.; **REP CLIENTS:** Maj. RE devels. in southwest; **PREV EMPLOY:** Nat. Bank of FL 1978-80; First Nat. Bank of Commerce 1975-78; **PROFL AFFIL & HONORS:** AIREA, Econ. Soc. of FL; **EDUC:** BS, 1969, Math., Chem., Physics, Jacksonville State Univ.; **GRAD EDUC:** MBA, 1971, Fin., Operations Research, Tulane Univ.; **EDUC HONORS:** Deans List; **HOME ADD:** 11554 Riverview, Houston, TX 77077, (713)493-4233; **BUS ADD:** 1 Riverway, Suite 1800, Houston, TX 77056.

CLARK, Charles Edward——B: Sept. 10, 1949, Los Angeles, CA, *Atty. at Law*, Charles Edward Clark, Counsel to Gray, Whyte & Burkitt; **PRIM RE ACT:** Attorney; **SERVICES:** Legal serv. primarily in acquisition, synd. and, leasing of comml. and resid. real prop., RE fin., prop. mgmt.; **REP CLIENTS:** RE brokers, investors and private lenders; **PREV EMPLOY:** Tishman West Mgmt. Corp. Atty. (1979-80); **PROFL AFFIL & HONORS:** ABA, Los Angeles Cty. Bar Assn., Assn. of RE Attys., RESSI (Affiliate), Nat. Lawyers Club, Washington DC, CA State Bar, FL State Bar, US Sup. Ct., US Tax Ct., US Ct. of Claims, US Customs Ct., US Ct. of Mil. Appeals, US Dist. Ct., Central Dist., CA & So. Dist, FL; US Ct. of Appeals, 5th Cir. & 9th Cir., Pi Sigma Alpha, Nat. Hon Poli. Sci. Soc. through Univ. SC, Member of Steering Comm. of Gen. RE Practice Subsect. of Los Angeles Cty. Bar Assn., 1981 Member of Editorial Board of Securities Journal; **EDUC:** BA, 1971, Poli. Sci., Univ. SC; **GRAD EDUC:** JD, 1974, Law, Georgetown Univ. Law Ctr., Washington DC; **EDUC HONORS:** Pi Sigma Alpha; **OTHER ACT & HONORS:** Georgetown Alumni Admissions Program (Rngl. interviewer); Member of Bd. of Dir. Foothill Apt. Assn., Chmn. Pasadena Bar Assn., Annual Picnic 1981; **BUS ADD:** 301 E. Colorado Blvd., Ste. 600, Pasadena, CA 91101, (213)795-3640.

CLARK, Dennis B.——B: Mar. 20, 1934, Presque Isle, ME, *Dir. of Planning*, Gruen Assoc.; **PRIM RE ACT:** Consultant, Architect; **OTHER RE ACT:** Urban Planner; **SERVICES:** Site planning, pre-feasibility & feasibility studies; **REP CLIENTS:** Victor Palmieri & Co., Inc.; Winmar Co.; NY City Transit Authority; Urban Devel. Corp.; Campeau Corp.; **PROFL AFFIL & HONORS:** AIA; Amer. Inst. of Certified Planners; **EDUC:** AB, 1956, Columbia Coll.; **GRAD EDUC:** M.Arch., 1962, Arch., Columbia Univ.; MS, 1970, Urban & Rgnl. Planning, Pratt Inst.; **EDUC HONORS:** AIA Award; **MIL SERV:** U.S. Army, SP-4; **HOME ADD:** 27 Morningside Rd., Verona, NJ 07044, (201)239-1960; **BUS ADD:** 257 Park Ave. S., New York, NY 10010, (212)673-9200.

CLARK, Donald R.——B: May 1, 1935, Bangor, NY, *Exec. VP*, McCormick Properties, Inc., Mktg.; **PRIM RE ACT:** Consultant, Attorney, Developer, Owner/Investor, Property Manager; **SERVICES:** Site selection, bldg./rehab. analysis, land planning & devel., facility, design & constr., lease facilities; **PROFL AFFIL & HONORS:** NAIOP, N. Amer. Soc. for Corp. Planning, ABA, AIDC, MD Bar Assn.; **EDUC:** BEE, 1961, EE, MI State Univ.; **GRAD EDUC:** LLB/JD, 1968, Law, Univ. of MD; **MIL SERV:** USAF, SSgt.; **HOME ADD:** 11603 Mohr Rd., Kingsville, MD 21087, (301)592-2209; **BUS ADD:** 11011 McCormick Rd., Hunt Valley, MD 21031, (301)667-7708.

CLARK, E. M.——*SIR Mgr. Site Selection*, Campbell Soup Co.; **PRIM RE ACT:** Property Manager; **BUS ADD:** Campbell Place, Camden, NJ 08101, (609)964-4000.*

CLARK, Eddie——B: Mar. 26, 1942, Breckenridge, TX, *Partner*, Clark Brothers; **PRIM RE ACT:** Developer, Property Manager; **PROFL AFFIL & HONORS:** Dallas Bar Assn., Texas Bar Assn.; **EDUC:** BBA, 1964, Univ. of TX; **GRAD EDUC:** JD, 1967, Univ. of TX; **HOME ADD:** 4456 Belfort Pl., Dallas, TX 75205, (214)528-3963; **BUS ADD:** 8325 Walnut Hill Ln. #225, Dallas, TX 75231.

CLARK, Edward B.——B: Apr. 26, 1924, ID, *Pres.*, Sixth St. Prop.; **PRIM RE ACT:** Developer, Property Manager, Owner/Investor, Insuror; **SERVICES:** Comml. Bldgs./ Own & Lease; **PREV EMPLOY:** State Mgr. - Amer. Family Life Ins. Co., 1973 - 1976; **PROFL AFFIL & HONORS:** Pres. Club Award (2) Sales Mktg. Exec. Inst. Award; **EDUC:** BS, 1949, Econ., Univ. of Denver; **MIL SERV:** USAF; Cpl., 1942 - 1945; 2nd Lt., Reserves (1949); European Thratre; **OTHER ACT & HONORS:** Also affiliated with The Warehouse, Inc. (Pres.); **HOME ADD:** 2415 Mountain View Dr., Boise Id 83704, (208)377-0118; **BUS ADD:** 301 Idaho Bldg., Bose, ID 83701, (208)345-9805.

CLARK, E.H., Jr.——*President*, Baker International, Inc.; **PRIM RE ACT:** Property Manager; **BUS ADD:** PO Box 5500, Orange, CA 92667, (213)264-1221.*

CLARK, Foster L., III——B: Nov. 1, 1947, Birmingham, AL, *Chief Appraiser, S. Rgn.*, Eagle Appraisal Serv.; **PRIM RE ACT:** Appraiser; **SERVICES:** Appraisals for resid., comml., indus., land; **PREV EMPLOY:** 1973-81, Fee appraiser, Clark's RE and appraisals, Huntsville, AL; **PROFL AFFIL & HONORS:** AIREA, SREA, IRWA, MAI, SRPA, SRA; **EDUC:** BS Fin., 1972, RE and Ins., Univ. of AL; **EDUC HONORS:** Deans List; **MIL SERV:** USN, PO 2; **HOME ADD:** 5239 Palmyra, Las Vegas, NV 89102, (702)362-2159; **BUS ADD:** PO Box 5306, Las Vegas, NV 89102, (702)870-1434.

CLARK, Gavin C.——B: May 5, 1922, Toronto, Can., *Sr. V.P.*, H.N. Spenceley Assoc. Ltd.; **PRIM RE ACT:** Broker, Syndicator, Consultant, Appraiser, Developer, Property Manager, Owner/Investor; **PREV EMPLOY:** Former Dean of Bus. and Admin. Studies, Seneca Coll., Toronto. Formerly Managing Dir. the Ryerson Press (McGraw-Hill-Ryerson) Toronto, Formerly Exec. V.P. and Dir. Rolph Clark Stone Ltd. Toronto, Montreal, Halifax; **PROFL AFFIL & HONORS:** Cert. by the RE Inst. of Can. FRI Candidate; **EDUC:** BA, 1948, Law, Poli. Sci., Univ. of Toronto; **GRAD EDUC:** M. ED.(Toronto)M.M.P, M.D.P./I.E.M.(DIP.Harvard), Bus. Mgmt. and Educ. Admin., Harvard Bus. School and Harvard Grad. School of Educ.; **MIL SERV:** N, LCDR(g); **OTHER ACT & HONORS:** Bd. of Certification, Profit Planning and Mgmt. Inst. NY: Member Advisory Council, Can. School of Mgmt., Toronto; **HOME ADD:** 40 Kilbarry Rd., Toronto, M5G158, Ontario, (416)481-9463; **BUS ADD:** 439 Univ. Ave. Suite 1600, Toronto, MSG1Y8, Canada, (416)598-0375.

CLARK, George A.——B: Oct. 24, 1908, Jamaica, NY, *RE Broker (Owner)*, George A. Clark; **PRIM RE ACT:** Broker, Appraiser, Builder, Insuror; **SERVICES:** RE Brokerage; **PREV EMPLOY:** Rockefeller Ctr., Inc.; Bankers Trust Co.; **PROFL AFFIL & HONORS:** NAREB Long Island Bd. of Realtors, Distinguished Service Award by Long Island Bd. of Realtors, VP Libor Pres. Queens Div.

L.I.B.O.R.; **EDUC:** 1935, Trust Banking, Amer. Inst. of Banking; **GRAD EDUC:** Attended NY Univ. City Coll. Pace; **EDUC HONORS:** Cum Laude; **HOME ADD:** 55 Circle Rd., Muttontown, NY 11791, (516)364-9216; **BUS ADD:** 117-25 Jamaica Ave., Richmond Hill, NY 11418, (212)847-4224.

CLARK, Harper Scott——B: Mar. 7, 1945, Austin, TX, *Associate Broker*, Tyler-Roberts Realty Co., Inc.; **PRIM RE ACT:** Broker, Consultant, Appraiser, Owner/Investor; **SERVICES:** Investment counseling specialists for sales of older props. in hist. dist.; **REP CLIENTS:** Indiv. purch. of comml. and investment prop.; devels. and archs., hist. preservationists; **PROFL AFFIL & HONORS:** Greater Calcasieu Bd. of Realtors, GRI; **EDUC:** BS, 1971, Bus. Mgmt., GRI series, Investments analysis, resid. appraisal seminar, McNeese State Univ.; **MIL SERV:** USNR, Lt., 1965-81, Nat. Service Medal, Ten Yr. Naval Reserve Medal; **OTHER ACT & HONORS:** Pres., Calcasieu Historic Preservation Soc.; Pres. Lake Charles Little Theatre; Project Co-ordinator for Restoration of Arcade Opera House in Lake Charles, LA; **HOME ADD:** 1020 Pujo St., Lake Charles, LA, (318)439-4898; **BUS ADD:** 3510 Common St., Lake Charles, LA 70605, (318)477-5922.

CLARK, Howard S.——B: July 1, 1932, Salt Lake City, UT, *Gen. Partner (VP)*, Clark Leaming Props.; **PRIM RE ACT:** Banker, Developer, Owner/Investor, Property Manager; **SERVICES:** Develop turn key packages (land-building-furnishings-interiors); **EDUC:** 1953, Mktg., Univ. of UT; **GRAD EDUC:** 1955, Mktg., Univ. of UT; **MIL SERV:** USAF, Capt.; **OTHER ACT & HONORS:** Member, Salt Lake City C of C; Timpanogas Club, Salt Lake City, UT; Bd. of Dir., Davis Cty. Bank, Farmington, UT; **HOME ADD:** 3013 Sherwood Dr., Salt Lake City, UT 84108, (801)582-7665; **BUS ADD:** 375 W. 200 S., Salt Lake City, UT 84101, (801)532-1232.

CLARK, James K., Jr.——B: Nov. 17, 1942, Atlanta, GA, *Pres.*, Tri-City Commercial Sales, Inc.; **PRIM RE ACT:** Broker; **SERVICES:** Leasing & selling of comml., indus. and income props.; **PREV EMPLOY:** Comml. appraiser, Draper-Owens Co.; **PROFL AFFIL & HONORS:** Atlanta Bd. of Realtor, GA Assn. of Realtor, Inc., Assn. of GA RE Exchangors, NAR, Active Life Member of the Atlanta Bd. of Realtors Million Dollar Club; **EDUC:** BBA, 1965, RE, Univ. of GA; **HOME ADD:** 2335 Surrey Trail, College Park, GA 30349, (404)762-7825; **BUS ADD:** 5529 Old National Hwy., College Park, GA 30349, (404)768-8806.

CLARK, John B.——B: Aug. 2, 1936, Great Bend, KS, *Pres.*, Collins-Rancho Del Oro Co.; **PRIM RE ACT:** Developer; **SERVICES:** RE sales and land devel.; **PREV EMPLOY:** Law Partner, Pettit & Martin, San Francisco, CA; **PROFL AFFIL & HONORS:** San Diego & Oceanside Econ. Devel. Corp.; **EDUC:** BS, 1958, Engrg., Stanford Univ.; **GRAD EDUC:** LLB, 1961, Law, Stanford Law School; **EDUC HONORS:** Revising Editor, Stanford Law Review; **HOME ADD:** PO Box G, Rancho Santa Fe, CA 92067, (714)756-5620; **BUS ADD:** 11750 Sorrento Valley Rd., Suite 118, San Diego, CA 92121, (714)275-4621.

CLARK, John P.——B: July 17, 1927, Nyack, NY, *Atty. at law*, John P. Clark; **PRIM RE ACT:** Broker, Consultant, Attorney, Appraiser, Owner/Investor, Property Manager; **PROFL AFFIL & HONORS:** ABA, Nat. Realty Club, RE Bd. of City of NY; **EDUC:** BS, 1950, Acctg., Fordham Univ.; **GRAD EDUC:** JD, 1954, Fordham Univ.; **EDUC HONORS:** Deans List; **MIL SERV:** USN, SIC; **HOME ADD:** 20 Stuyvesant Oval, Box 10-H, New York, NY 1009, (212)260-2441; **BUS ADD:** 20 Stuyvesant Oval, Box 10-H, New York, NY 10009, (212)260-2441.

CLARK, Joyce W.——B: Aug. 6, 1938, Provo, UT, *Partner, Escrow Officer*, Valley Title Co.; **OTHER RE ACT:** Escrow Officer, Title Ins.; **SERVICES:** RE closing, exchanges, title ins.; Escrow Collections; **PREV EMPLOY:** 25 yrs., RE industry; **PROFL AFFIL & HONORS:** UT Cty. Bd. of Realtors; UT Valley Home Builders; WCR; Exec. Women Intl.; UT Cty. Mort. Bankers; UT Land Title Assn., Pres., Realtor's Credit Union; Bd. of Dir., Home Builders & EWI, Advisor Education Comm. UT Land Title; **HOME ADD:** 277 E. 340 S., Orem, UT, (801)224-3549; **BUS ADD:** 75 S. 200 E. St., Provo, UT 84601, (801)375-9900.

CLARK, Lawrence Sherman——B: Jan. 9, 1949, Freeport, IL, *Asst. Prof.*, Louisiana State Univ. Shreveport, Dept. of Bus. Admin.; **PRIM RE ACT:** Broker, Attorney, Instructor; **PREV EMPLOY:** N. IL Univ. DeKalb, J.A.G. Corps, US Army; **PROFL AFFIL & HONORS:** ABA, IL Bar Assn., Amer. Bus. Law Assn.; **EDUC:** BA, 1971, Acctg., Knox Coll.; **GRAD EDUC:** JD, 1974, Law, DePaul Univ., LLM in Taxation; **MIL SERV:** US Army, Capt., Army Commendation Award; **OTHER ACT & HONORS:** Commr. Geneva Park Dist. 2 years, 1979-81, Soc. of Automotive Historians; **HOME ADD:** 9238 Hillside Ave., Shreveport, LA 71118; **BUS ADD:** 8515 Youree Dr., Shreveport, LA 71115, (804)797-5017.

CLARK, Michael H.——B: Jan. 28, 1952, Nashville, TN, *Owner*, Mike Clark Realty Co., & Clark Devel.; **PRIM RE ACT:** Broker, Consultant, Appraiser, Developer, Owner/Investor, Property Manager; **REP CLIENTS:** Wash. Mfg. Co., Nashville, TN; Ely & Walker Corp., Memphis, TN; William R. Moore Corp., Memphis, TN; Numerous Nat. & Multi-Nat. Mfg., Retail & Devel. Concerns; **PREV EMPLOY:** 1972-73 Affiliate broker for Coleman, Boyd Realtors; **PROFL AFFIL & HONORS:** Nashville Bd. of Realtors, Legislative Comm., TN Assn. of Realtors, Gov. Affairs Comm., NAR, RNMI, Realtors FLI, Bd. Member & Dir. of Speakers Bur. for Nashville Area Chap. Amer. Red Cross, Consultant to Nature Conservancy; **EDUC:** 1970-73, Auburn Univ.; 1973-76, Attended Univ. of TN; **GRAD EDUC:** RE Cert, 1975; **MIL SERV:** Naval ROTC, Auburn Univ., Midshipman; **HOME ADD:** 3000 Hillsboro Rd., Nashville, TN 37215; **BUS ADD:** 2827 Columbine Pl., Nashville, TN 37204, (615)383-3420.

CLARK, Mitchell G.——B: Mar. 25, 1931, NC, *Pres.*, Vinson Realty Co. Inc.; **PRIM RE ACT:** Broker, Appraiser, Property Manager; **PROFL AFFIL & HONORS:** IREM, CPM; **EDUC:** BS, 1955, Soc. Studies & Physical Educ., Appalachian State Univ.; **MIL SERV:** USN, Sn.; **HOME ADD:** 6032 Rose Valley Dr., Charlotte, NC 28210, (704)553-1644; **BUS ADD:** 221 S. Church St., Charlotte, NC 28202, (704)375-7771.

CLARK, Peter L.——B: Aug. 30, 1945, Evanston, IL, *VP Commercial Development*, Campeau Corp. California; **PRIM RE ACT:** Developer, Owner/Investor; **PREV EMPLOY:** American Express Co. 1968-1982, Cummins Engine Co. 1969- 78, General Motors Corp. 1963-69; **PROFL AFFIL & HONORS:** ULI, Dir. Marin City Community Devel. Corp.; **EDUC:** BSME, 1968, General Motors Ins.; **GRAD EDUC:** MBA, 1971, Fin., Butler Univ.; **BUS ADD:** 681 Market St., Suite 401, San Francisco, CA 94105, (415)777-5151.

CLARK, Richard O.——B: Jan. 29, 1931, Kansas City, MO, *VP Regional Sales Mgr.*, Grubb and Ellis Comml. Brokerage Co., Oakland - Walnut Creek Region; **PRIM RE ACT:** Broker; **SERVICES:** Retail, office, and indus. leasing and investment counseling; **REP CLIENTS:** Major tenants, lenders, instnl. clients and investors; **PREV EMPLOY:** New York Life Ins. Co., Travelers Ins. Co., Farmers Ins. Group; **PROFL AFFIL & HONORS:** NAIOP; **EDUC:** BA, 1955, Eng., Hist., Econ., St. Mary's Coll., CA; **MIL SERV:** USMCR, Lt.C; **OTHER ACT & HONORS:** Mayor, City of Albany 1966-1971, S.F.B.A.R.T.D. Pres. '75; **HOME ADD:** 140 El Centro, PO Box 56, Diablo, CA 94528, (415)838-9448; **BUS ADD:** 1333 Broadway, Suite 700, Oakland, CA 94612, (415)444-7500.

CLARK, Robert J.——B: June 4, 1926, TX, *Pres.*, The Coronado Co., Inc.; **PRIM RE ACT:** Consultant, Developer, Builder, Owner/Investor, Property Manager; **SERVICES:** Fin., devel., brokerage; **REP CLIENTS:** Major retailers, corp. and indiv. investors; **PREV EMPLOY:** 12 yrs. of comml. banking; **PROFL AFFIL & HONORS:** BOMA, ICSC, Realtor; **EDUC:** BBA, 1949, Bus. & Fin., Univ. of TX; **GRAD EDUC:** All course work for MBA, 1949, RE and Banking, Univ. of TX; **EDUC HONORS:** T Assn. and member of Univ. Cowboy Assn.; **MIL SERV:** USN Air Corps.; **HOME ADD:** 2532 Cutler Ct. N.E., Albuquerque, NM 87106, (505)268-4678; **BUS ADD:** 4001 Indian School Rd. #310, Albuquerque, NM 87110, (505)262-2351.

CLARK, Robert T.——B: Nov. 8, 1942, St. Louis, MO, *VP of RE*, Fashion Bar, Inc.; **PRIM RE ACT:** Attorney; **OTHER RE ACT:** Mktg., site selection, lease negotiations; **SERVICES:** Acquisitions and consulting; **PREV EMPLOY:** VP, Worth's Stores, 1975-1977; **PROFL AFFIL & HONORS:** Intl. CSC DeveLopers; **EDUC:** BS, 1965, Math., St. Louis Univ.; **OTHER ACT & HONORS:** Bd. of Dir., YMCA; **HOME ADD:** 7505 S. Xanthia Pl., Denver, CO 80112, (402)463-6520; **BUS ADD:** 401 S. Buckley Rd., Aurora, CO 80017, (303)695-7979.

CLARK, Roger——B: Dec. 13, 1934, Madison, WI, *Owner*, Clarkson Co.; **PRIM RE ACT:** Syndicator, Developer, Owner/Investor; **SERVICES:** Rehab. of turn around multi-family and comml. prop.; **REP CLIENTS:** Indiv.; **PREV EMPLOY:** Johns - Manville Corp.; **PROFL AFFIL & HONORS:** Amer. Soc. of Mech. Engrs., Prof. Engineer, TX; **EDUC:** BME, 1956, TX A&M Univ.; **MIL SERV:** USA, 1st Lt.; **OTHER ACT & HONORS:** Boy Scouts of Amer.; **HOME ADD:** 3347 E. Geddes Dr., Littleton, CO 80122, (303)770-0965; **BUS ADD:** Box 2053, Littleton, CO 80122, (303)779-5647.

CLARK, Russell W.——B: May 6, 1942, Shelby, OH, *Treas.*, Wallick Construction Co.; **PRIM RE ACT:** Developer, Builder, Owner/Investor, Property Manager, Syndicator; **SERVICES:** Private placement of low income housing; **PROFL AFFIL & HONORS:** AICPA, OH

Soc. of CPA's, NAA, AMA, IMA, CPA; **EDUC:** BS, 1965, Acctg., Miami Univ., Oxford, OH; **GRAD EDUC:** MBA, 1977, Univ. of Dayton; **EDUC HONORS:** Dean's List; **MIL SERV:** USAF, Sgt.; **HOME ADD:** 2000 Riverhill Rd., Columbus, OH 43221, (614)457-2486; **BUS ADD:** 150 E. Mound St., Columbus, OH 43215, (614)464-4640.

CLARK, Stephen L.——B: Feb. 12, 1942, Wichita, KS, *Broker*, Clark Realtors; **PRIM RE ACT:** Broker, Property Manager, Developer; **OTHER RE ACT:** Lectures & Seminars on Investment Property; **PROFL AFFIL & HONORS:** NAR, RNMI, CCIM, past pres. of Wichita Metro. Area Bd. of Realtors, Recipient Wichita Realtor of Yr. Award (1976); **EDUC:** BA, 1965, Bus. Admin., Wichita State Univ.; **OTHER ACT & HONORS:** Bd. of Land User Econ., Adv. Bd. on RE matters to Wichita City Comm., Wichita, KS; **HOME ADD:** 7837 Pagent Ln., Wichita, KS 67206, (316)683-3568; **BUS ADD:** 201 S. Oliver, Wichita, KS 67218, (316)684-0533.

CLARK, William J.——B: Aug. 17, 1954, Elkton, MD, *Controller*, Capital Homes, Inc.; **PRIM RE ACT:** Developer, Builder; **SERVICES:** Retail home builder; **PREV EMPLOY:** Chesapeake Houses Inc.; Rouse Co.; **PROFL AFFIL & HONORS:** MD Assn. of CPA's, CPA; **EDUC:** BA, 1976, Acctg./Bus./Fin., Mt. St. Mary's Coll.; **EDUC HONORS:** Summa Cum Laude, Who's Who in Amer. Coll. & Univ.; **HOME ADD:** 1168 Long Valley Rd., Westminster, MD 21157, (301)848-8148; **BUS ADD:** 6500 Rock Spring Dr., Suite 200, Bethesda, MD 20034, (301)897-9200.

CLARKE, Charles F., Jr.——B: Mar. 3, 1929, Chicago, Il, *Exec. VP*, Sudler & Co.; **PRIM RE ACT:** Broker, Consultant, Property Manager, Owner/Investor; **PREV EMPLOY:** VP, Arthur Rubloff & Co., Chicago; **PROFL AFFIL & HONORS:** Chicago RE Bd.; BOMA, Pres. Greater N. MI Ave. Assn.; **EDUC:** BA, 1951, Classics, Brown Univ.; **MIL SERV:** US Army; Lt.; American Spirit of Honor Medal; **HOME ADD:** 234 W. Westminster, Lake Forest, IL 60045; **BUS ADD:** 875 N. Michigan Ave., Chicago, IL 60611.

CLARKE, Devane——B: Aug. 10, 1929, Ranger, TX, *Pres.*, Devane Clarke & Assoc. Inc.; **PRIM RE ACT:** Developer; **SERVICES:** Devel. for own account, devel. with investor partners, prop. mgmt., condo. conversion, brokerage; **PROFL AFFIL & HONORS:** Nat. Assn. of Builders, Nat. Apt. Assn., TX RE Broker, Pres. TX Apt. Assn., Pres. Dallas Apt. Assn., Appointed to State of TX Spec. Adv. Council on Housing; **EDUC:** BBA, 1951, Bus. & advertising, Univ. of TX; **OTHER ACT & HONORS:** Commadore of Chandlers Landing Yacht Club; **HOME ADD:** 4340 Alta Vista, Dallas, TX 75229, (214)352-5513; **BUS ADD:** Two Turtle Creek Village, Suite 606, Dallas, TX 75219, (214)559-0800.

CLARKE, Jack——B: June 26,1914, VA, Clarke Jack Wells; **PRIM RE ACT:** Broker, Developer, Owner/Investor; **PREV EMPLOY:** Freestate Indiv. Dev. Co., TX Eastern Transmision Co.; Lion Oil Co.; **PROFL AFFIL & HONORS:** Air Force Assn.; Amer. Indiv. Devel. Council; Amer. Ordinance Assn. ICSC; ULI; LA Realtor Assn.; NIREB, Who's Who in Amer., Fin. and Ind., S & SW; **EDUC:** AB, 1935, Williams Coll.; **GRAD EDUC:** 1937, NY Univ. Grad. School of Bus. Admin.; **MIL SERV:** US Naval Res., Lt., 5 stars; **BUS ADD:** Box 6, Shreveport, LA 71161, (318)221-5175.

CLARKE, James Brent, III——B: Jan. 2, 1950, Washington, DC, Weaver Bros., Inc., Comml. Sales and Leasing; **PRIM RE ACT:** Broker, Consultant, Appraiser; **SERVICES:** Consulting and brokerage of investment and comml. prop.; **REP CLIENTS:** Private and instnl. investors, local corp.; **PREV EMPLOY:** June 1974 to July 1978, H.L. Rust Co., Washington, DC, Prop. Mgr. and Salesman; **PROFL AFFIL & HONORS:** IREM, ICSC, Washington, DC Bd. of Realtors, CPM, Washington Bd. of Realtors 1978 Highest Volume for Indiv. in First Year as a Full Time Comml. Salesperson, Million Dollar Sales Club.; **EDUC:** BA, 1973, English, Ithaca Coll.; **HOME ADD:** 2212 Boxwood Dr., Falls Church, VA 22043, (703)241-8846; **BUS ADD:** 5530 Wisconsin Ave., Chevy Chase, MD 20815, (301)986-4384.

CLARKE, James J.——B: May 15, 1928, Ireland, *VP, Chief Appraiser*, Bankers Trust Co., RE; **PRIM RE ACT:** Consultant, Appraiser, Banker, Lender; **PROFL AFFIL & HONORS:** RE Bd. of NY; Peter Minuit Post 1247 Amer. Legion RE Post; AIREA; SREA (SRPA); NY State SREA; **EDUC:** AA, 1957, Bus., State Univ. of NY; **MIL SERV:** US Army; Sgt.; **HOME ADD:** 195 Woodsome Rd., Babylon, NY 11702, (516)587-7587; **BUS ADD:** 280 Park Ave., New York, NY 10017, (212)850-3040.

CLARKE, John Kirk——B: May 11, 1948, Maysville, KY, *Partner*, Clarke and Clarke, Attorneys; **PRIM RE ACT:** Attorney; **SERVICES:** Deed and mort. preparation, title examination, RE closings; **REP CLIENTS:** Lenders and indiv. or instnl. investors in resid. and comml. RE; **PROFL AFFIL & HONORS:** Mason Cty. Bar Assn., KY Bar Assn., and ABA (including real prop., probate, and trust div.); **EDUC:** AB, 1970, Poli. Sci., Hist., Centre Coll. of KY; **GRAD EDUC:** JD, 1973, Univ. of KY, Lexington; **EDUC HONORS:** Staff Member, KY Law Journal 1971-73; **OTHER ACT & HONORS:** Member, Maysville Independent Bd. of Educ. 1978-present, Chmn. 1981; **HOME ADD:** 510 E. 2nd St., Maysville, KY 41056, (606)564-3143; **BUS ADD:** PO Box 519, 119 Sutton St., Maysville, KY 41056, (606)564-5527.

CLARKE, Jon B.——B: May 5, 1943, Chicago, IL, *VP/Treas.*, Clarke & Waggener P.C.; **PRIM RE ACT:** Broker, Attorney, Syndicator, Owner/Investor; **SERVICES:** Legal; **REP CLIENTS:** Numerous land developers; **PROFL AFFIL & HONORS:** Denver, CO & ABA, Cont. Legal Educ. & Bar Assn.; Lecturer and Author on Business and RE Reorg. under Chapt. 11, 1976 to date; **EDUC:** BA, 1965, Hist., Duke Univ., Durham, NC; **GRAD EDUC:** JD, 1972, Bus. Law, Univ. of Denver, Coll. of Law; **EDUC HONORS:** Order of St. Ives (top 10% of class); **MIL SERV:** USNR, Comdr, 1965 to date; **HOME ADD:** 5908 E. Weaver Cir., Englewood, CO 80111, (303)770-6310; **BUS ADD:** 718 17th St., Suite 2400, Denver, CO 80202, (303)571-1600.

CLARKE, Phillips H., III——B: Sept. 24, 1945, Washington DC, *VP*, Donaldson, Lufkin & Jenrette, Inc., DLJ R.E., Inc.; **PRIM RE ACT:** Broker, Syndicator, Consultant, Owner/Investor; **PREV EMPLOY:** Chase Manhattan Bank; **EDUC:** BA, 1968, Williams Coll.; **GRAD EDUC:** MBA, 1974, RE.. Fin., Wharton; **MIL SERV:** USMC, 2nd Lt.; **HOME ADD:** 260 E. 78th St., New York, NY 10005; **BUS ADD:** 140 Broadway, New York, NY 10005, (212)747-9881.

CLARKE, Stephen F.——B: Oct. 12, 1946, Greenville, SC, *Pres.*, Lakeview Properties of Colorado, Inc.; **PRIM RE ACT:** Developer; **PREV EMPLOY:** Coldwell Banker Comml. RE Servs., Sr. Sales Consultant; **PROFL AFFIL & HONORS:** Nat. Assn. of Office and Indus. Parks, ICSC; **EDUC:** BS, 1968, Bus. Admin., The Citadel; **GRAD EDUC:** MBA, 1973, Mktg., Fin., Univ. of UT; **EDUC HONORS:** Distinguished Mil. Grad.; **MIL SERV:** USAF, Capt., 1968-72, Bronze Star, Vietnamese Cross of Gallantry with Silver Star; **OTHER ACT & HONORS:** Big Bros. of Amer.; **HOME ADD:** 382 Dexter St., Denver, CO 80220, (303)355-7596; **BUS ADD:** 1777 S. Harrison St., #509, Denver, CO 80210, (303)692-0790.

CLARSON, John J.——*VP RE*, Champion International Corp; **PRIM RE ACT:** Property Manager; **BUS ADD:** 16855 N. Chase Drive, Houston, TX 77060, (713)627-0360.*

CLASSEN, Don L.——B: Feb. 20, 1927, Newton, KS; **PRIM RE ACT:** Appraiser; **SERVICES:** 1 to 4 family resid. dwellings; **REP CLIENTS:** Lenders and relocating firms; **PROFL AFFIL & HONORS:** Designated SRA; **HOME ADD:** 1120 W. Broadway, Newton, KS 67114, (316)283-1821; **BUS ADD:** 1120 W. Broadway, Newton, KS 67114.

CLASSON, Stephen J.——B: Aug. 17, 1947, Ashland, WI, *Pres.*, BCR Capital Corporation; **PRIM RE ACT:** Broker, Property Manager; **SERVICES:** Large apt. project-acquisitions & mgmt. for investors (primarily synd.); **PREV EMPLOY:** Comml. RE Brokerage, Tax Consultation to RE Investors, spec. IRS Sec. 1031 Exchanging; **PROFL AFFIL & HONORS:** NARB, RESSI, Fox Valley Exchange Club; **EDUC:** BA Bus./Mktg., 1969, Econ., St. Norbert Coll.; **EDUC HONORS:** Dean's List; **HOME ADD:** 2381 Santa Barbara, Green Bay, WI 54304, (414)498-0689; **BUS ADD:** 424 S. Monroe Ave., Green Bay, WI 54301, (414)435-1245.

CLAUDE, Anthony B.——B: Feb. 18, 1936, Port-au-Prince, Haiti, *Supervisory Title Officer*, Title Guarantee Co.; **PRIM RE ACT:** Attorney, Owner/Investor, Insuror; **OTHER RE ACT:** Title Underwriter; **SERVICES:** Title Insurance; **EDUC:** 1959, French/Acctg., Hautes Etudes Commerciales Port-au-Prince, Haiti; **GRAD EDUC:** 1963, RE, Law School of Haiti Port-au-Prince; **OTHER ACT & HONORS:** International Entrepreneurs Assn.; Cert. in Title Examination and Reading, NY Univ., 1969-1970; Cert. in Mort. Banking, NY Univ., 1975-1978; **HOME ADD:** 223-24 113th Ave., Queens Village, NY 11429, (212)465-3742; **BUS ADD:** 120 Broadway, New York, NY 10271, (212)964-1000.

CLAUSEN, Rolland Budd——B: Oct. 6, 1930, Minneapolis, MN, *Sec./Treas.*, Red Carpet, Clausen & Assoc.; **PRIM RE ACT:** Broker, Instructor, Syndicator, Property Manager, Owner/Investor; **OTHER RE ACT:** AZ Accredited Instr. Brokers Lic.; **SERVICES:** Resid. Sales, Instr., Consulting, Prop. Investment & Managing; **PREV EMPLOY:** 12 years, Aerospace, Mgmt., Gen. Motors Corp, Hughes Aircraft; **PROFL AFFIL & HONORS:** NAR, RNMI, GRI, CRB, Chmn., Prof. Standards Comm., Tucson Bd. of Realtors, Past Chmn., Educ. Comm.; **EDUC:** BEE, 1958, Univ. of MN; **MIL SERV:** USA, PFC, Nat.

Defense; **HOME ADD:** 9261 E. Magoana, Tucson, AZ 85710, (602)198-4100; **BUS ADD:** 6475 E. 22nd St., Tucson, AZ 85710, (602)745-5252.

CLAUSSEN, Woodrow H.——B: Mar. 12, 1913, Chicago, IL, *Pres.*, Woodrow H. Claussen & Sons, Inc.; **PRIM RE ACT:** Consultant, Appraiser, Lender; **REP CLIENTS:** RE Loan Agents for Guarantee Savings & Loan Assn. since July 1959; **PREV EMPLOY:** Since April, 1947, in real estate lending with Buhler Mortgage Company, State Mortgage and Western Mortgage Company; **PROFL AFFIL & HONORS:** SREA, Chapter Pres. 1962, SRA; **OTHER ACT & HONORS:** Commr. Emeritus, Northern CA Federation Junior League Football; Recognized for outstanding service to Sacramento; Chap. SREA 1979-80; **HOME ADD:** 4891 Valletta Way, Sacramento, CA 95820, (916)455-4030; **BUS ADD:** 2701 Cottage Way, Suite 15, Sacramento, CA 95825, (916)485-5021.

CLAWSON, John W.——*Dir. of Area Devel.*, Rochester Gas & Electric Corp.; **PRIM RE ACT:** Developer; **BUS ADD:** 89 East Ave, Rochester, NY 14649, (716)546-2700.*

CLAY, Peter M.——B: Sept. 23, 1943, Englewood, NJ, *VP*, James W. Rouse & Co., Inc.; **OTHER RE ACT:** Mort. Banker; **SERVICES:** Debt & equity fin. for comml. RE; **REP CLIENTS:** Maj. Richmond area devels.; CT Gen.; State Farm; New England Mutual Life; John Hancock; Guardian Life; INA; TIAA; **PREV EMPLOY:** Howard Research & Devel., Columbia, MD; Equitable Trust Co., Baltimore, MD; **PROFL AFFIL & HONORS:** MBA, ICSC, NAIOP (Chapter Pres.), NAHB, Charter Registered Apt. Mgr.; **EDUC:** BA, 1965, Psych., Poli. Sci., C.W. Post Coll.; **MIL SERV:** USMC; Capt.; 1965-1968; **OTHER ACT & HONORS:** Founding Pres., Richmond RE Grp.; **HOME ADD:** 211 Riverwood Dr., Richmond, VA 23229, (804)740-8772; **BUS ADD:** 1108 E. Main St., Richmond, VA 23219, (804)780-1846.

CLAY, Robert J.——B: Aug. 28, 1927, Milwaukee, WI, *Pres.*, Clay Publicom, Inc.; **OTHER RE ACT:** Advertising/Public Relations Agency; **SERVICES:** Advertising, Public Relations, Marketing; **REP CLIENTS:** AFCOM, Butler Housing Corp., The Ramos/Jensen Co., Maurer Elliott Construction Co., Danielian Assoc., Socaland Devel., Zellner Communities; **PREV EMPLOY:** Similar Work; **PROFL AFFIL & HONORS:** NAHB, BIA, NAREE, Los Angeles and Orange Cty. Press Clubs, PRSA, Orange Cty. Advertising Fed., APR (Accredited in Public Relations); **EDUC:** BS, 1952, Journalism, Marquette Univ.; **MIL SERV:** US Army-AF, Pvt.; **OTHER ACT & HONORS:** Over two dozen, Press, Public Relations, and Advertising Awards; **HOME ADD:** 601 Calle Hidalgo, San Clemente, CA 92672, (714)498-7066; **BUS ADD:** 17801 Main St., Irvine, CA 92714, (714)557-5432.

CLAY, Willard H.——B: Feb. 3, 1936, Fort Smith, AR, *Pres./Broker*, Clay-Huss & Associates, Inc.; **PRIM RE ACT:** Broker, Consultant, Developer, Owner/Investor, Syndicator; **OTHER RE ACT:** Farm & land, land mgmt.; **SERVICES:** Investment RE brokerage and exchanging, plus full RE serv. and farm loan correspondent; **REP CLIENTS:** Indiv. investor, group investors, devels. and instnl. investors in high quality large projects, agric. props. and land projects; **PREV EMPLOY:** Pres. of medium size mfg. firm (founder); VP sales for major cosmetic firm; Staff Exec. for major mgmt. firm; **PROFL AFFIL & HONORS:** Multiple Listing Service, Intl. Inst. of Valuers, Grad. of RE Investment Brokerage and Tax Deferred Exchanges; **EDUC:** Acctg., Univ. of AR, School of Bus. Admin.; **MIL SERV:** US Army, Pvt.; **OTHER ACT & HONORS:** Numerous civic activities, trustee-United Methodist Church; **HOME ADD:** 4495 Sleeping Indian Rd., Fallbrook, CA 92028; **BUS ADD:** 2343 S. Mission Rd., Fallbrook, CA 92028, (714)728-8466.

CLAYPOOLE, J. Stanley——B: Aug. 12, 1947, Charleston, SC, *Attorney at Law*, Joye, Claypoole & Kefalos; **PRIM RE ACT:** Attorney; **SERVICES:** Title exams, of closing and Preparation of documents, conduct of closings and other legal services; **REP CLIENTS:** Lenders, devel., builders, and investors in Charleston, SC area; **PROFL AFFIL & HONORS:** ABA; **EDUC:** BA, 1969, Econ., Univ. of NC; **GRAD EDUC:** JD, 1975, Univ. of SC, **MIL SERV:** US Army, Cpt., Bronze Star, purple heart; **HOME ADD:** 88 Beaufain St., Charleston, SC 29401, (803)722-8726; **BUS ADD:** 5861 Rivers Ave., N. Charleston, SC 29405, (803)554-0351.

CLAYTON, Joe E.——B: June 27, 1981, Goshen, ID, *VP*, Wackerli Realty, Inc., Investments; **PRIM RE ACT:** Broker, Syndicator, Consultant; **SERVICES:** RE Investment Analysis; **REP CLIENTS:** Indiv. Corps., Synds., Banks, Attys., Drs.; **PREV EMPLOY:** Loan Officer, Amer. S&L, Sherman Oaks, CA; **PROFL AFFIL & HONORS:** NAR, Realtor of the Yr., 1975 & 1977; Dir. IAR, CCIM, GRI, Past Pres. I.F. Board of Realtors; **EDUC:** 1935, Pocatello, ID; **GRAD EDUC:** 1936, Bus., Univ. of ID; **MIL SERV:** USAF, Pvt.; **OTHER ACT & HONORS:** Lions, C of C, Dir. Exchange Counselors of Eastern ID; **HOME ADD:** 680 Gladstone, Idaho Falls, ID 83401, (208)529-2727; **BUS ADD:** 545 Shoup Ave., Idaho Falls, ID 83401, (208)522-7784.

CLAYTON, Kenneth M.——B: Sept. 28, 1948, Orlando, FL, *Atty. at Law*, Kenneth M. Clayton; **PRIM RE ACT:** Attorney, Owner/Investor; **SERVICES:** All aspects of RE law with emphasis on condo. law; **REP CLIENTS:** Devels., indiv. and instnl. investors, condo. and homeowner assns.; **PREV EMPLOY:** Law offices of Robert C. Matthias; **PROFL AFFIL & HONORS:** ABA; FL Bar Assn.; Orange Cty. Bar Assn.; Mid-FL Chap. of the Community Assn. Inst.; **EDUC:** BA, 1970, Liberal Arts, Washington & Lee Univ.; **GRAD EDUC:** JD, 1973, RE/Tax, Univ. of AL Law School; **EDUC HONORS:** John A. Campbell Moot Ct. Bd.; **MIL SERV:** US Army; Field Artillery, Capt.; **OTHER ACT & HONORS:** City of Orlando Bd. Reorg. Task Force; Local Govt. Comm., Orlando C of C; First Presbyterian Church; Infant Child Care Ctr., Bd. of Advisors; **HOME ADD:** 2410 Lake Shore Dr., Orlando, FL 32803, (305)894-7036; **BUS ADD:** Suite 600, Eola Office Ctr., 605 E. Robinson St., Orlando, FL 32801, (305)425-2125.

CLAYTON, Stuart D.——B: May 5, 1948, Berkeley, CA, *Mgr. of Office Leasing Div.*, Fuller and Co.; **PRIM RE ACT:** Broker; **OTHER RE ACT:** Office leasing; **SERVICES:** Office leasing, research of Denver mktg.; **REP CLIENTS:** Indivs. or instnl. investors in comml. prop., corps., and devel.; **PREV EMPLOY:** 1975-1980, Van Schaack and Co., Comml. Leasing Specialist; 1975, Highline Medical Bldg., Leasing Agent; 1974, John Madden Co., Leasing Agent for Greenwood Plaza; **PROFL AFFIL & HONORS:** CO Assn. of Realtors; NAR; Denver C of C; Profl. Bus. Women's Org., GRI; **EDUC:** BS, 1970, Univ. of SD; Chapman Coll. World Campus; GRI Univ. of CO; Xerox Profl. Selling Skills Course/Dale Carnegie Sales Course; **OTHER ACT & HONORS:** 1977, Named by CO/Bus. Magazine as one of CO's leading women in business in article entitled 'Women on Men's Turf'; 1979, Denver C of C Office Directory; 1981, Million dollar roundtable; one of CO's top producers in comml. RE; **HOME ADD:** 7250 Eastmoor Dr., 205, Denver, CO 80237, (303)759-1844; **BUS ADD:** 1515 Arapahoe, Suite 1600, Denver, CO 80202, (303)292-3700.

CLEARY, Martin——B: July 27, 1935, New York, NY, *Sr. V.P.*, Teachers Ins. & Annuity Assn.; **PRIM RE ACT:** Lender; **PROFL AFFIL & HONORS:** Member Mort. Advisory Comm. NYU, TR-ICSC, Member- Mort. Advisory Comm., NY State Teachers Retirement System; **EDUC:** BS, 1960, Acctg., Fordham Univ.; **GRAD EDUC:** MBA, 1963, Fin, NY Univ.; **BUS ADD:** 730 Third Ave., New York, NY 10271, (212)490-9000.

CLEARY, Terrence P.——B: Oct. 10, 1938, Milwaukee, WI, *Pres.*, Hopkins S&L Assn.; **PRIM RE ACT:** Banker, Lender, Insuror, Syndicator; **PREV EMPLOY:** With Hopkins S&L for the past 20 years; **PROFL AFFIL & HONORS:** Past Pres. of S&L League - Bd. Member Milwaukee S&L Council - Member of the Bd. of Dirs. of Hopkins S&L; **EDUC:** BA, 1960, Marquette Univ.; **OTHER ACT & HONORS:** United Fund, Red Cross, Easter Seal, St. Joseph's Hospital, Pres. of the Centurions of St. Joseph's Hospital 1978 and 1979; **HOME ADD:** 9207 Stickney Ave., Wauwatosa, WI 53226, (414)476-1275; **BUS ADD:** 2600 North Mayfair Rd., Wauwatosa, WI 53226, (414)475-5595.

CLEGG, Mark W.——B: Apr. 3, 1952, Boise, ID, *Owner/Broker*, Clegg Investments; **PRIM RE ACT:** Broker, Consultant, Owner/Investor, Syndicator; **SERVICES:** Investment prop. analysis, consultation, synd. & brokerage; **REP CLIENTS:** Indiv. and partnership grps. in analysis and acquistion of investment & devel. props.; **PREV EMPLOY:** States Investment Corp., 1975-1978, Acquisitions of investment props. and land devel.; **PROFL AFFIL & HONORS:** NAR (previously), Grad. Realtor Inst. (Previous); **EDUC:** BA, 1974, Econ., Boise State Univ.; **OTHER ACT & HONORS:** Nat. Rifle Assn.; Boise State Alumni Assn.; **HOME ADD:** 3371 Chickory Way, Boise, ID 83706, (208)342-6388; **BUS ADD:** 2402 W. Jefferson, Boise, ID 83702, (208)342-6633.

CLEMENT, Charles Frederic——B: Apr. 3, 1944, St. Louis, MO, *Pres.*, Clement Investment Associates, Inc.; **PRIM RE ACT:** Broker, Consultant, Appraiser, Banker, Developer, Owner/Investor, Property Manager; **SERVICES:** Diversified, full serv. RE corp.; **REP CLIENTS:** Indivs. as well as instns.; **PREV EMPLOY:** Northland Mort. Co., St. Louis 1972-1975; **PROFL AFFIL & HONORS:** MBAA; Home Bldrs. Assn.; **EDUC:** BA, 1966, Econ., Washington and Lee Univ., Lexington, VA; **EDUC HONORS:** Order of the Mongolian Minks; **OTHER ACT & HONORS:** Algonquin Golf Club; Member Bd. of Dirs.: Precious Metals, Inc.; C&B Investment Assocs., Inc.; Champion Springs Ranch Co., Inc.; **BUS ADD:** 111 W. Lockwood, Suite 209C, St. Louis, MO 63119, (314)962-1610.

CLEMENT, Clayton E.——**B:** Dec. 3, 1943, Oakland, CA, *Part.*, Clement, Fitzpatrick & Kenworthy; **PRIM RE ACT:** Attorney, Owner/Investor, Instructor; **SERVICES:** Legal; **REP CLIENTS:** Investors, synds., lenders, title insurers; **PROFL AFFIL & HONORS:** ABA (RE Problems Comm, Taxation Sect); Land Use Comm. (Litigation Sect.); State Bar of CA (RE Sect.); **EDUC:** BA, 1965, Hist., Univ. of the Pacific; **GRAD EDUC:** JD, 1968, Univ. of CA at Berkeley; **EDUC HONORS:** Cum Laude; **HOME ADD:** 1720 Proctor Dr., Santa Rosa, CA 95404, (707)528-2481; **BUS ADD:** 3333 Mendocino Ave., Suite 200, Santa Rosa, CA 95401, (707)523-1181.

CLEMENT, Daniel J.——**B:** Sept. 27, 1944, Bloomsburg, PA, *Part.*, Clement & Knight, Attys. at Law; **PRIM RE ACT:** Consultant, Attorney, Developer, Owner/Investor, Property Manager; **SERVICES:** Owner, devel. of resid. multi-family and comml. props.; **REP CLIENTS:** Consultant and legal advisor to various devel. and investor grps.; **PROFL AFFIL & HONORS:** PA Bar Assn.; Dist. of Columbia Bar Assn.; VA Bar Assn., Atty. at Law; approved atty. and policy writing agent for Berks Title Ins. Co.; **EDUC:** BS, 1966, Engrg. Mech., PA State Univ.; **GRAD EDUC:** JD, 1969, Law, George. Washington Univ., Nat. Law Ctr.; **EDUC HONORS:** Honors Grad.; **OTHER ACT & HONORS:** Lewisburg Kiwanis Club, Triangle Frat.; **HOME ADD:** Rt. 3, Box 251-B, Lewisburg, PA 17837, (717)524-7108; **BUS ADD:** 118 Market St., Lewisburg, PA 17837, (717)524-2277.

CLEMENT, Robert L., Jr.——**B:** Dec. 14, 1928, Charleston, SC, *Partner*, Young, Clement, Rivers & Tisdale; **PRIM RE ACT:** Broker, Attorney, Banker, Regulator, Owner/Investor, Instructor, Insuror, Syndicator; **REP CLIENTS:** Banking, mort. brokers, realtors; **PROFL AFFIL & HONORS:** Bar Assocs., Chmn. Corp., Banking and Tax. Sect., SC Bar, Asst. Corp. Counsel, City of Charleston, 1960; Judge, Municipal Court, City of Charleston, 1961-1963; **EDUC:** AB, 1948, Eng., The Citadel; **GRAD EDUC:** JD, 1951, Duke Univ. School of Law; **EDUC HONORS:** Distinguished Military Grad.; **MIL SERV:** USAF, Capt. (Res.); **OTHER ACT & HONORS:** Pres., Charleston Museum; numerous civic improvement organizations; **HOME ADD:** Townhouse 20, Dockside, 336 Concord St., Charleston, SC 29401, (803)723-4755; **BUS ADD:** 28 Broad St., POB 993, Charleston, SC 29402.

CLEMENTS, Teresa A.——**B:** Feb. 19, 1948, Richmond, IN, *2nd VP, Head of Prod.*, Phoenix Mutual Life Ins. Co., RE Investments; **PRIM RE ACT:** Lender, Property Manager, Syndicator; **OTHER RE ACT:** Purchaser; Joint Venture Partner; **SERVICES:** Purchase Joint Venture & Synd. of Comml. Prop. for Pension Funds, Indivs. and Gen. Acct.; **PREV EMPLOY:** CT Gen. Life Ins. Co.; **EDUC:** BA, 1970, Philosophy & Logic, Smith Coll.; **EDUC HONORS:** Phi Beta Kappa, High Distinction; **HOME TEL:** (203)521-7954; **BUS ADD:** One American Row, Hartford, CT 06115, (203)278-1212.

CLEMENTS, Thomas L.——**B:** Mar. 17, 1923, Detroit, MI, *Mgr., RE Servs.*, Shell Oil Co.; **OTHER RE ACT:** Oversee the buying, selling, leasing and mgmt. of all Real Assets for Shell Oil and Shell Chem. Cos.; **SERVICES:** Mktg., mfg., chemical research, distribution etc. (all in house); **PROFL AFFIL & HONORS:** Treas., Bd. of Dirs., Bd. of Trustees NACORE, Member of IDRC; **EDUC:** BA, 1947, Bus. Admin. and Econ., MI State Univ.; **MIL SERV:** USN, Lt.; **HOME ADD:** 12407 Old Oaks, Houston, TX 77024, (713)461-0879; **BUS ADD:** Two Shell Pl., PO Box 2099, Houston, TX 77001, (713)241-1394.

CLEMENTS, William D.——**B:** Dec. 30, 1939, Albany, NY, *VP*, Drexel Burnham Lambert Realty Inc.; **OTHER RE ACT:** Acquire RE projects for clients of firm; **SERVICES:** Investment & mgmt.; **REP CLIENTS:** Instns., pension funds, indivs.; **PREV EMPLOY:** VP - Transco Realty Trust (REIT) 1972-1978; **EDUC:** BA, 1961, Hist., Siena Coll.; **GRAD EDUC:** MBA, 1966, Fin., Wharton Grad.; **MIL SERV:** US Army, 1st Lt.; **HOME ADD:** 421 Wynnewood Rd., Pelham Manor, NY 10803, (914)738-2231; **BUS ADD:** 405 Lexington Ave., New York, NY 10017, (212)986-2800.

CLEMINSHAW, John G.——**B:** Aug. 16, 1937, Paterson, NJ, *Pres.*, John G. Cleminshaw, Inc.; **PRIM RE ACT:** Broker, Consultant, Appraiser, Property Manager, Owner/Investor; **SERVICES:** Appraisers for mkt. value and ad valorem purposes, feasibility studies; **REP CLIENTS:** Corps., instns, assessors; **PROFL AFFIL & HONORS:** AIREA, ASA, NARA, Pres. Natl. Assn. of Mass Appraisers, MAI, CRA; **EDUC:** AB, 1960, Eng. Lit., Arch., Univ. of PA; **GRAD EDUC:** 1981, Exec Educ., Smaller Co. Mgmt. Program; 1981, Harvard Univ. Grad. School of Bus. Admin; **MIL SERV:** USCG, Lt., USCG, Commendation Medal, 1960-64; **OTHER ACT & HONORS:** Publication: 'An Overview of Mass Appraisal', published by ASA; **HOME ADD:** 21 Cohasset Dr., Hudson, OH 44236, (216)650-0339; **BUS ADD:** 5 Atterbury Blvd., Hudson, OH 44236, (216)650-4300.

CLENNEY, Avery A.——**B:** June 10, 1946, Montgomery, AL, *Pres.*, Brentwood Properties; **PRIM RE ACT:** Broker, Developer, Owner/Investor, Property Manager; **SERVICES:** Prop. mgmt., investment counseling, devel. of comml. props.; **REP CLIENTS:** Instnl. and indiv. investors; **PREV EMPLOY:** Cobbs, Allen & Hall Mort. Co., Head of comml. loan dept.; **PROFL AFFIL & HONORS:** Bd. of Realtors, IREM C of C, CPM; **EDUC:** BS, 1968, Fin., Univ. of AL; **MIL SERV:** QMC, 2 Lt.; **OTHER ACT & HONORS:** Bd. of Dir. Colonial Trailways; **HOME ADD:** 203 Beech St., Birmingham, AL 35213, (205)870-4102; **BUS ADD:** 3940 Montclair Rd., Birmingham, AL 35213, (205)870-4157.

CLEVELAND, Newcomb——**B:** July 20, 1927, Bennington, VT, *Pres.*, Morland Devel. Co., Inc.; **PRIM RE ACT:** Broker, Developer; **PROFL AFFIL & HONORS:** Formerly NREB; **EDUC:** BA, 1950, Yale Univ.; **GRAD EDUC:** LLB, 1956, Univ. of CO, Law Sch.; **MIL SERV:** USN, 1945-46 (Eng.), USA, 1950-53, 1st Lt.; **OTHER ACT & HONORS:** Tr. Colby Sawyer Coll., New London, NH; **HOME ADD:** 2410 E. 34th St., Tulsa, OK 74105, (918)742-2354; **BUS ADD:** 1416-A E 38th St., Tulsa, OK 74105, (918)747-5964.

CLICK, David F.——**B:** Dec. 17, 1947, Miami Beach, FL, *Assoc. Prof.*, Univ. of MD School of Law; **PRIM RE ACT:** Instructor; **EDUC:** BA, 1969, Philosophy, Yale Univ.; **GRAD EDUC:** JD, MA, 1973, 1974, Law and Econ., Yale Univ.; **HOME ADD:** 1805 Thornton Ridge Rd., Towson, MD 21204, (301)321-1690; **BUS ADD:** 500 W. Baltimore St., Baltimore, MD 21201, (301)528-7194.

CLIFF, Patricia Warburg——**B:** Aug. 19, 1943, New York, NY, Patricia Warburg CLiff, P.C.; **PRIM RE ACT:** Broker, Attorney, Developer, Syndicator; **PROFL AFFIL & HONORS:** ABA, NYBA, Ct. of NY Bar Assn., Women's Bar Assn., NY RE Bd.; **EDUC:** AB, 1964, Mary Mount Coll., Tarrytown, NY; **GRAD EDUC:** MA, 1967, Ludwig Maximillian Univ., Munich, W. Germany; JD, 1980, Hofstra Law Sch.; **OTHER ACT & HONORS:** Founding Member of Lawyers Pro Choice; Assoc. with Douglas, Elliman, Gibbons & Ives; **HOME ADD:** Mt. Holly Rd., Katonah, NY 10536, (914)232-9413; **BUS ADD:** 575 Madison Ave., New York, NY 10022, (212)832-5899.

CLIFFORD, Jack M.——**B:** Mar. 28, 1914, Columbus, OH, *Pres.*, Jack M. Clifford & Co.; **PRIM RE ACT:** Developer, Owner/Investor; **SERVICES:** Raw land into totally improved indus. park and office park; **PREV EMPLOY:** Self-employed within own co.; **PROFL AFFIL & HONORS:** Realtor; **EDUC:** BBA, 1936, Fin., Ohio State Univ.; **MIL SERV:** US Army, Sgt.; **HOME ADD:** 910 Idlewilde Lane, SE, Albuquerque, NM 87108, (505)255-8918; **BUS ADD:** 2201 San Pedro Dr., NE, Building 2, Suite 201, Albuquerque, NM 87110.

CLIFTON, Russell B.——**B:** Jan 16, 1930, Maroa, IL, *VP for Mort. Programs*, FNMA; **OTHER RE ACT:** Secondary Mort. Mkt. Inv.; **PROFL AFFIL & HONORS:** NACMB; Natl. Academy of Conciliators; Bankers Former mem. of Adv. Comm.; Home Owners Warr. Corp.; voted 'Distinguished Fellow' of NACMB; **EDUC:** 1957, Acctg. & Fin., MI St. Univ.; **EDUC HONORS:** grad. Magna Cum Laude; **HOME ADD:** 15500 Straughn Dr., Laurel, MD 20810, (301)498-6537; **BUS ADD:** 3900 Wisconsin Ave., NW, Washington, DC 20014, (202)537-7404.

CLINE, James M.——**B:** Dec. 5, 1949, Bucyrus, OH, *Pres.*, J. Cline Realty, Inc.; **PRIM RE ACT:** Broker, Consultant, Owner/Investor, Instructor, Property Manager; **OTHER RE ACT:** Author; **SERVICES:** Investment counseling, devel. of comm. prop., nationally known lecturer on investing in RE & creative finance; **REP CLIENTS:** Have taught for CO Univ., Jones RE Colleges, and Lowry Seminars; and Robert Allen's Nothing Down Seminar; **PROFL AFFIL & HONORS:** RNMI; NAR; CO Springs Bd. of Realtors, CRB; CRS; GRI; RE Broker in States of CO and TX; **MIL SERV:** USAF, Sgt.; **HOME ADD:** 12325 Black Forest Rd., Colorado Springs, CO 80908, (303)495-4893; **BUS ADD:** 12325 Black Forest Rd., Colorado Springs, CO 80908, (303)495-4893.

CLINE, Leonard A.——**B:** Apr. 28, 1946, Brookline, MA, *Treasurer*, Eagle Management, Inc.; **PRIM RE ACT:** Broker, Property Manager, Owner/Investor, Syndicator; **PROFL AFFIL & HONORS:** IREM, Greater Boston RE Bd., ICSC, Realtor, CPM, Candidate; **EDUC:** BS, 1967, Mgmt. Sci., Case Inst. of Tech.; **GRAD EDUC:** MBA, 1969, RE Fin., Wharton Grad. Univ. of PA; **EDUC HONORS:** Deans List; **MIL SERV:** USAR, SP5; **HOME ADD:** 52 Temi Rd., Holliston, MA 01746, (617)429-1708; **BUS ADD:** 1576 A Washington St. Box 537, Holliston, MA 01746, (617)429-1708.

CLINE, Patricia A.——**B:** June 26, 1947, Louisville, KY, *Pres.*, Pace - Canfield Realtors; **PRIM RE ACT:** Broker; **SERVICES:** Resid. sales, investment counseling, exchange counsel; **REP CLIENTS:** Homeowners, investors seeking tax shelter, small bus. owners; **PROFL AFFIL**

& HONORS: KY RE Exchangors, Louisville Bd. of Realtors, C of C, Women's Council, GRI; **HOME ADD:** 7202 Boxwood Rd., Louisville, KY 40222, (502)425-1937; **BUS ADD:** 1156 Bardstown Rd., Louisville, KY 40204, (502)587-1121.

CLINE, Roger S.——B: May 4, 1946, London, England, *Sr. VP, Devel.*, Dunfey Hotels Corp.; **PRIM RE ACT:** Developer, Broker, Property Manager; **SERVICES:** Tech. Serv. for Hotel Devel.; Hotel Mgmt.; **PROFL AFFIL & HONORS:** AMA; Pacific Area Travel Assoc.; Amer. Assoc. Public Opinion Research; **EDUC:** MHCI, 1966, Hotel Admin., Westminster College, London, England; **GRAD EDUC:** MBA, 1970, Fin./Mktg., Columbia Business School; **HOME ADD:** 85 Roundhill Rd., Roslyn, NY 11577, (516)621-5394; **BUS ADD:** 515 Madison Ave., New York, NY 10022, (212)867-8000.

CLINKENBEARD, David E.——B: Apr. 9, 1927, Seattle, WA, *Pres. & CEO*, Peterborough Industrial Development Corp.; **PRIM RE ACT:** Attorney, Developer, Lender, Owner/Investor, Property Manager, Syndicator; **PREV EMPLOY:** VP - Amer. Express Co.; **PROFL AFFIL & HONORS:** Member of Bar - Washington; **EDUC:** AB, 1953, Bus. Admin., Univ. of WA; **GRAD EDUC:** JD, 1956, Law, Harvard Univ.; **MIL SERV:** USAR, Maj.; **OTHER ACT & HONORS:** Chmn. Bd. of Trustees; Intl. Action Learning Program; Bd. of Dir. - Athens Coll.; Dir. - Fishery Products Ltd.; Concepts, Inc.; Carlton Maintenance; **HOME ADD:** Temple, NH 0308, (603)878-2305; **BUS ADD:** 202 N. Bldg., Peterborough, NH 03458, (603)924-7121.

CLINTON, Curtis, Jr.——B: June 25, 1938, Muskagee, OK, *Pres.*, Devel. Mgmt. Assn. Ltd.; **PRIM RE ACT:** Syndicator, Consultant, Developer, Property Manager, Insuror; **OTHER RE ACT:** Investment banking & Ins. Broker props.; **SERVICES:** Devel. and Synd. of Comml. & Multi-family props.; **REP CLIENTS:** Broker Dealers, Lender Indivs., in comml. multi family and Indust. props.; **PREV EMPLOY:** Ex VP Swope Park BK. Dir. Special Projects, Dept. of Commerce EDA; **PROFL AFFIL & HONORS:** NASD, Young Man of Amer., Congressman Pampa Mitchell Capital Access Award, Leader of Month.; **EDUC:** BS, 1961, Bus. Educ., Univ of KS; **GRAD EDUC:** MBPA, 1975, Bus. & Mgmt., Central MI Univ.; **MIL SERV:** USA, Nov/Comm.; **OTHER ACT & HONORS:** Sr. Exec Service Dept. Commerce, Natl. Home Builders, Intl. Assn. Fin. Planners, C of C.; **HOME ADD:** 10224 Locust Rd., (202)484-3123; **BUS ADD:** 520 N. St. SW, Wash. DC 20024, (202)463-7383.

CLINTON, Richard P.——B: Aug. 24, 1934, Hartford, CT, *VP and Mgr.*, Hartford Nat. Bank, RE Div.; **PRIM RE ACT:** Banker; **SERVICES:** RE finance; **PREV EMPLOY:** FHA; **PROFL AFFIL & HONORS:** MAI, SRPA; **EDUC:** BS, 1960, Indus. Admin., Univ. of CT; **GRAD EDUC:** Grad. School of Banking, 1970, Banking, Rutgers Univ.; **MIL SERV:** US Army; **HOME ADD:** 1 Gold St., Hartford, CT 06103; **BUS ADD:** 777 Main St., Hartford, CT 06115, (203)728-2374.

CLONSER, Pierce——*Admin. Officer*, PA, Pennsylvania Real Estate Commission; **PRIM RE ACT:** Property Manager; **BUS ADD:** PO Box 2649, Harrisburg, PA 17105, (717)783-3658.*

CLONTZ, Eugene R.——B: Sept. 3, 1939, Marion, NC, *VP, Franchising and RE*, Volunteer Capital Corp., Corporate; **PRIM RE ACT:** Broker, Developer, Property Manager; **OTHER RE ACT:** In charge of devel. of fast food co. which now has 133 restaurants operating; **SERVICES:** Site Selection, construction, equipment and franchising; **PREV EMPLOY:** Self-employed restaurant owner and operator; **PROFL AFFIL & HONORS:** Nat. Assn. of RE Exec.; Intl. Franchise Assn.; **MIL SERV:** USAF, E4, Sgt.; **OTHER ACT & HONORS:** Who's Who in NC, 1973-74; **HOME ADD:** Route 2 Anderson Rd., Franklin, TN 37064, (615)794-1477; **BUS ADD:** Two Maryland Farms, Suite 100, PO Box 184, Brentwood, TN 37027, (615)373-5700.

CLOSSER, Bruce——B: Nov. 19, 1944, Marquette, MI, *Owner*, Closser Assoc.; **PRIM RE ACT:** Consultant, Appraiser; **SERVICES:** RE appraisals and counseling; **PROFL AFFIL & HONORS:** AIREA, Profl. Recognition Award, AIREA, 1980, Published Article, *Appraisal Journal, "Appraising the Ski Area"; MAI; SRPA*; **EDUC:** BA, 1967, Bus. Admin./Econ., Northern MI Univ., **EDUC HONORS:** Magna Cum Laude; **MIL SERV:** USA, 1967-1970, 1st Lt., Army Commendation Medal; **OTHER ACT & HONORS:** Bd. of Dir., Marquette Community Concert Assoc., Nat. Teaching Faculty, AIREA; **HOME ADD:** 1049 Allouez Rd., Marquette, MI 49855, (906)228-9629; **BUS ADD:** 224 Harlow Block, Marquette, MI 49855, (906)228-9133.

CLOUSER, John R.——B: Jan. 4, 1948, East Stroudsburg, PA, *Prop. Mgr.*, J. Milton & Associates, United Prop. Mgmt.; **PRIM RE ACT:** Consultant, Instructor, Property Manager; **SERVICES:** Taught courses in prop. mgmt., advised builder on his portfolio, specific recommendations on prop. disposition, implemented recommendations, wrote many reports & studies; **PREV EMPLOY:** Dir. of Prop. Mgmt., Midwest Mgmt. Co., Madison, WI, 1979-1980; **PROFL AFFIL & HONORS:** Instit. of RE Mgmt., Nat. Apt. Assn., Building Mgrs. & Owners Intl., Assn. of MBA's, Assn. of Profl. Prop. Mgrs., CPM, Real Prop. Admin., Cert. Apt. Mgr., IL RE Broker, FL RE Salesman; **EDUC:** BA, 1970, English, Hist., Philosophy, Millersville State; **GRAD EDUC:** MBA, 1981, RE, Nova Univ.; **EDUC HONORS:** Cum Laude, Class of 1895 Award, John K. Harley Award, A. G. Breidenstine Award, Class of 1910 Award, Wentzel-Wright Award, Dean's List - 5 times, Who's Who in American Colleges & Universities; **HOME ADD:** 6930 N.W. 186th St., Miami, FL 33015, (305)823-5476; **BUS ADD:** 18333 N.W. 68th Ave., Miami, FL 33015, (305)558-0060.

CLOYD, John A.——B: Nov. 25, 1937, Columbia, SC, *Assessor*, Richland Cty.; **PRIM RE ACT:** Appraiser, Assessor; **PREV EMPLOY:** Appraiser, SC Fed. S&L; **PROFL AFFIL & HONORS:** SREA, AIREA, IAAO, SRA, RM, RES; **EDUC:** BS, 1959, Mktg.; **MIL SERV:** USAF, Lt. Col., AF Outstanding Unit; **OTHER ACT & HONORS:** Bd. of Dir. Family Serv. Ctr., V Gov. 1978-1981 SREA; **HOME ADD:** 1415 Glenwood Rd., Columbia, SC 29204, (803)782-4274; **BUS ADD:** 2020 Hampton St., Columbia, SC 29204, (803)748-5013.

CLUBB, Michael W.——B: Oct. 11, 1951, Fairbanks, AK, *Pres.*, Michael Clubb & Co., Inc.; **PRIM RE ACT:** Broker, Consultant, Owner/Investor, Instructor, Real Estate Publisher; **OTHER RE ACT:** Specializing in small investment opportunities, non instnl. financing; **SERVICES:** Consultation, debt restructuring, acquisition and exchange, estate bldg.; **PROFL AFFIL & HONORS:** Bd. of Dirs., Puget Sound Exchangers; Member, Bd. of Realtors; **OTHER ACT & HONORS:** Advisor, econ. devel., real estate acquisition; Metropolitan Devel. Council, a federally funded non-profit corp.; **HOME ADD:** 2247 East Day Island Blvd. W., Tacoma, WA 98466, (206)565-0951; **BUS ADD:** 11208 44th Ave. E., Tacoma, WA 98446, (206)565-0951.

CLUM, Thomazine——B: Philadelphia, PA, *Pres.*, Stetson Management, Inc.; **PRIM RE ACT:** Broker, Consultant, Property Manager; **SERVICES:** Specializing in condo. & town house mgmt.; **REP CLIENTS:** Sheffield Manor; Brandenberry Park East; Westlake Ctry. Four; among many others; **PREV EMPLOY:** VP, Rowell, Inc. Roselle, IL, 1974-1977; Dir., Community Affairs, Larwin, IL, 1971-1974; **PROFL AFFIL & HONORS:** IREM; IL Chap., Elgin RE Bd.; Community Assn. Inst.; **EDUC:** BS, 1955, Goucher Coll., Baltimore; **HOME ADD:** 1730 Arlington Dr., Hanover Park, IL 60103, (312)289-2458; **BUS ADD:** 217 Main St., West Dundee, IL 60118, (312)428-5080.

CLUMPNER, Daniel C.——B: May 7, 1944, Chippewa Falls, WI, *Pres.*, Commonwealth Development Corp.; **PRIM RE ACT:** Engineer, Developer; **SERVICES:** Land & bldg. devel.; **PREV EMPLOY:** VP Owen Ayres & Assocs. (consulting engineers & architects); Pres., Keystone Corp (land developers); **PROFL AFFIL & HONORS:** NRA, WRA, ALDA, Profl. Engr., RE Broker; **EDUC:** BS, 1968, Civil Engrg., ND State Univ.; **MIL SERV:** USANG, Capt.; **OTHER ACT & HONORS:** Plan Commn., Tomah, WI, 1972-73, C of C, Luther Hosp. Devel. Council, small business council chmn.; **HOME ADD:** 2619 W. Princeton Ave., Eau Claire, WI 54701, (715)835-4831; **BUS ADD:** 3301 Golf Rd., Eau Claire, WI 54701, (715)832-8707.

CLURMAN, David——B: May 3, 1927, Jersey City, NJ, *Head of RE Dept.*, Phillips, Nizer, Benjamin, Krim & Ballon; **PRIM RE ACT:** Attorney; **PREV EMPLOY:** Asst. Atty. Gen., State of NY, in charge, Bureau of Securities & RE Fin., 1952-75; **PROFL AFFIL & HONORS:** Chmn., 1979-80, Real Prop. Sect. NY State Bar Assn.; Chmn. 1974-79, Condo. Comm., NY State Bar Assn.; **EDUC:** 1949, NYU; **GRAD EDUC:** JD, 1952, Law, Columbia Law School; **MIL SERV:** US Navy; **OTHER ACT & HONORS:** Author, *NY State RE Synd. Act, Coop. & Condo. Regulations*; *Bus. Condo.*; *Condo. & Cooperatives*; **BUS ADD:** 40 W. 57th St., New York, NY 10019, (212)977-9700.

CLUTSAM, Henry O., III——B: Jan. 6, 1947, New York, NY, *VP & Dir.*, Merrill Lynch Hubbard, Inc., MLMBS, Inc.; **PRIM RE ACT:** Banker, Lender; **SERVICES:** Master packager & servicer, Issuer of conventional mort. backed securities; **REP CLIENTS:** Thrift Instns., Mort. Bankers, other mort. originators; **PROFL AFFIL & HONORS:** Investment Assn. of NY; **EDUC:** BA, 1969, Bus., Hanover Coll., Madison, IN; **MIL SERV:** US Army Res.; Sgt.; 1st cl.; **OTHER ACT & HONORS:** Treas. of New Vernon Vol. Fire Dept.; **HOME ADD:** Village Rd., New Vernon, NJ 07976, (201)267-5761; **BUS ADD:** 2 Broadway, New York, NY 10004, (212)908-8464.

COAN, John A., Jr.——B: Aug. 2, 1948, South Amboy, NJ, *Appraiser-Consultant*, JC Associates; **PRIM RE ACT:** Consultant, Appraiser, Assessor; **OTHER RE ACT:** Manager; Assessor, township of Jackson; **SERVICES:** Appraisals and consultants in RE and prop.

tax matters; **REP CLIENTS:** Municipalities, orgs., and owners of all types of props. in both RE and prop. tax; **PREV EMPLOY:** Assessor, township of Lacey (1976-1981); NJ Div. of Taxation (1975-1976); **PROFL AFFIL & HONORS:** Member, Nat. Assn. of Indep. Fee Appraisers; Assoc. Member, Soc. of RE Appraisers; Assoc. of Mcpl. Assessors of NJ; Senior Member, NARA, IFA, CTA, CRA; **EDUC:** BA, 1970, Poli. Sci., LaSalle Coll.; **MIL SERV:** USANG, Capt., 1971-1981; **OTHER ACT & HONORS:** Lacey Township Jaycees (Pres. 1978-1979); **HOME ADD:** 483 Lake Barnegat Dr., Forked River, NJ 08731, (609)693-3722; **BUS ADD:** 483 Lake Barnegat Dr., Forked River, NJ 08731, (609)693-3722.

COATES, Jack P.——B: Apr. 1, 1928, Denver, CO, *VP, Resid. Mgr.*, Coldwell Banker Residential RE Services; **PRIM RE ACT:** Broker; **SERVICES:** Resid. RE brokerage; **REP CLIENTS:** Home sellers and purchasers, resid. land; corporate relocation of employees; **PREV EMPLOY:** Active in resid. RE since 1959; **PROFL AFFIL & HONORS:** Aurora Bd. of Realtors, CO Assn., Nat. Assn., RNMI, CRB; GRI; Pres., Aurora Bd. of Realtors 1982; **EDUC:** BS, 1947, Engrg., Univ. of CO; **OTHER ACT & HONORS:** Lt. Governor Optimist Intl. Assn. (CO-WY Dist.); **HOME ADD:** 5499 S. Waco, Aurora, CO 80015, (303)693-7373; **BUS ADD:** 1111 S. Abilene, Aurora, CO 80012, (303)696-0660.

COATES, Stephen J.——B: June 30, 1947, Berkeley, CA, *Pres.*, Coates & Sowards, Inc.; **PRIM RE ACT:** Broker, Instructor, Property Manager; **SERVICES:** Comml. Prop. Mgmt.; **REP CLIENTS:** Fin. Insts., corps., indivs., synds., foreign investors; **PREV EMPLOY:** Asst. VP & Reg. Prop. Mgr., Norris Begg & Simpson Ltd., Honolulu, HI, 1974-77; **PROFL AFFIL & HONORS:** Member Assoc. of S. Bay Brokers, IREM, CSM, ICSC, NAR, San Jose Bd. of Realtors, CPM, CSM; **EDUC:** BS, 1971, Bus. Indus. Mgmt., San Jose State Univ.; **GRAD EDUC:** MBA, 1972; **EDUC HONORS:** Dean's Scholar; **HOME ADD:** 15620 Palos Verdes Ave., Monte Setono, CA, (408)395-0646; **BUS ADD:** 1530 Meridian Ave., San Jose, CA 95125, (408)267-4600.

COATSWORTH, Betty C.——B: Apr. 6, 1923, Canada, *Mgr.*, Shepard & Morgan, Inc., Arcadia Office; **PRIM RE ACT:** Broker; **OTHER RE ACT:** Residential RE sales and mktg., mkt. analysis of single, family Residential prop.; sales training; **PREV EMPLOY:** Clara Clark RE, Sierra Madre, CA; **PROFL AFFIL & HONORS:** Arcadia Bd. of Realtors, RNMI; NAR; CA Assn. of Realtors, CRS, CRB, GRI; **EDUC:** Canadian Teachers Certificate, 1944, Elementary School Teacher, Moose Jaw Sask. Normal School and Univ. of Saskatoon, Sask., CAN.; **HOME ADD:** 1031 Monte Verde Dr., Arcadia, CA 91006, (213)446-5346; **BUS ADD:** 23 E. Huntington Dr., Arcadia, CA 91006, (213)145-1131.

COBB, Dana B.——B: July 22, 1948, Norwood, MA, *Sr. Atty. RE*, Volkswagen of Amer., Inc.; **PRIM RE ACT:** Attorney; **PREV EMPLOY:** Assoc. with Kelly Drye & Warren of NYC from 1973-79; **PROFL AFFIL & HONORS:** Member of Bar of States of NY & NJ; **EDUC:** BA, 1970, Econ., Yale Univ.; **GRAD EDUC:** JD, 1973, Law, Columbia Univ. Law Sch.; **HOME ADD:** 625 Albert Pl., Ridgewood, NJ 07450, (201)652-7911; **BUS ADD:** 818 Sylvan Ave., Englewood Cliffs, NJ 07632, (201)894-6635.

COBB, George W.——B: Mar. 17, 1928, Ft. Bend City, TX, *Pres.*, Heathergate Devel. Co.; **OTHER RE ACT:** Land Developer; **SERVICES:** Joint venture devel. of resid. & comml. land; **PREV EMPLOY:** Devel. Grande Oaks in Brazoria Cty., TX and Heathergate Estates in Harris Cty., TX; **EDUC:** BS, 1952, Bus. & Govt., Univ. of TX; **EDUC HONORS:** Athletic Scholarship; **MIL SERV:** USAF, Maj.; **HOME ADD:** 10225 Bissonnet #1297, Houston, TX 77036, (713)271-1212; **BUS ADD:** 10225 Bissonnet, #1297, Houston, TX 77036, (713)271-1212.

COBB, H. Hart, Jr.——*Mgr. RE Dept.*, West Point-Pepperell, Inc.; **PRIM RE ACT:** Property Manager; **BUS ADD:** PO Box 71, West Point, GA 31833, (205)756-7111.*

COBB, John B., Jr.——B: Aug. 8, 1915, Nashville, TN, *Atty.*; **PRIM RE ACT:** Attorney; **SERVICES:** Legal; **REP CLIENTS:** Title Ins. Co. of MN; Attys. Title Co.; **PREV EMPLOY:** Pres., Attys. Title Co.; Probate Club, Davidson Cty., TN; **PROFL AFFIL & HONORS:** ABA; TN & Nashville Bar Assns.; TN Trial Lawyers Assn., Citation in 1980 by Nashville Bar Assn.; **GRAD EDUC:** 1935, Law, Cumberland Law School; **MIL SERV:** Ordanance, Pvt.; **OTHER ACT & HONORS:** Probate Clerk, 14 yrs.; Dir., Mid-South Automobile Club; 26 yrs., Edler Gov. with Church of Christ (now resigned); Former Dir., Workman of the World Life Ins. Soc., NE; **HOME ADD:** Rte. 11, Moran Rd., Franklin, TN 37064, (615)373-8107; **BUS ADD:** 2200 Abbott Martin Rd., Nashville, TN 37215, (615)292-6585.

COBB, Ralph W., Jr.——B: May 26, 1922, Greenville, SC, *Sr. Partner*, Cobb-Lundquist, Realtors; **PRIM RE ACT:** Broker, Consultant, Appraiser, Developer, Owner/Investor; **SERVICES:** Realtor-Farm, Ranches, Comml. & Indus. Props.; **PREV EMPLOY:** Oil Co. VP; **PROFL AFFIL & HONORS:** Corpus Christi Bd. Realtors, TX Assn. Realtors NAR, FLI, TX Land MLS; **EDUC:** Bus. Admin., Univ. of TX, 1940-1942; **MIL SERV:** USN, (Pilot), Comdr., 12 yrs.; **OTHER ACT & HONORS:** Pres. - Bd. Realtors, State & Local Realtor Comm., Elder 1st Prebyterian Church, Dir. C of C; **HOME ADD:** 138 Lakeshore, Corpus Christi, TX 78413, (512)855-7450; **BUS ADD:** 5333 Everhart Ste 101, Corpus Christi, TX 78411, (512)854-4448.

COBB, Terrence L.——B: Dec. 2, 1949, Nashville, TN, *Pres.*, The Terrence Cobb Co.; **PRIM RE ACT:** Broker, Consultant, Property Manager, Syndicator; **SERVICES:** RE investments, consulting, fin., prop. mgmt.; **REP CLIENTS:** Indivs. and instl. investors; **PREV EMPLOY:** Equitable Mort. & Investment Corp., and Fidelity Capital Corp., Nashville, TN; **PROFL AFFIL & HONORS:** NARA, CRA; **EDUC:** BS, 1971, Bus. Mgmt., TN Tech. Univ.; **HOME ADD:** 2825 Glen Oaks Dr., Nashville, TN 37214, (615)889-0117; **BUS ADD:** 2 Music Cir. S, Nashville, TN 37203, (615)256-7778.

COBEAN, Robert H.——B: Feb. 23, 1911, Wellington, KS, *Partner*, Cobean, Weber & Renn; **PRIM RE ACT:** Attorney, Insuror; **OTHER RE ACT:** Title Insurance (Insured Titles); **SERVICES:** RE Contracts, Title Opinions, Title Insurance, Escrow; **PREV EMPLOY:** Self employed (1935-); **PROFL AFFIL & HONORS:** ABA, KS Bar Assn., Sumner Cty. Bar Assn.; **EDUC:** AB, 1935, Poli. Sci. & Hist., Washburn Univ.; **GRAD EDUC:** JD, 1935, Washburn Law School; **OTHER ACT & HONORS:** Prob. Judge (1939-1943) Cty. Atty. (1943-1949); KS Judicial Council (1947-); **HOME ADD:** 1018 West Harvey, Wellington, KS 67152, (316)326-2082; **BUS ADD:** 122 East Harvey, PO Box 188, Wellington, KS 67152, (316)326-7422.

COCHRAN, Douglas E.——*Pres.*, McDonough Co.; **PRIM RE ACT:** Property Manager; **BUS ADD:** PO Box 1744, Parkersburg, WV 26101, (304)422-8531.*

COCHRAN, Robert G.——B: Aug. 19, 1944, Daytona Beach, FL, *Atty.-at-Law*, MacFarlane, Ferguson, Allison & Kelly; **PRIM RE ACT:** Attorney; **SERVICES:** Legal; **REP CLIENTS:** Amer. Devel. Co., Doran Jason Co.; **PROFL AFFIL & HONORS:** Hillsborough Cty. Bar Assn., ABA, Editorial Bd. Member - FL Bar Journal/News; **EDUC:** BS, 1967, Biology, Univ. of FL; **GRAD EDUC:** JD, 1972, Law, Univ. of FL; **EDUC HONORS:** with Honors; Phi Kappa Phi; Order of the Coif Law Review; **MIL SERV:** US Navy, Lt., Vietnam Service Medal; **OTHER ACT & HONORS:** Legal author in FL Bar Journal and FL Real Prop. Practice (Chapter on Boundary Litigation); **HOME ADD:** 4110 Helene Pl., Valrico, FL 33594, (813)681-7125; **BUS ADD:** PO Box 1531, 512 N. Florida Ave., Tampa, FL 33601, (813)223-2411.

COCKE, James W.——*VP & Mgr. Economic Devel. Dept.*, Valley Nat. Bank of Arizona, So. Div.; **PRIM RE ACT:** Banker; **SERVICES:** Econ. information, housing, office, indus. and retail const. and growth trends, demographic Info.; **BUS ADD:** 2 E. Congress St., PO Box 311, Tucson, AZ 85702, (602)792-7388.

COCKERELL, C. Steven——B: Nov. 29, 1947, San Diego, CA, *Owner*, Sierra West Development Co./Far West Publications; **PRIM RE ACT:** Broker, Consultant, Developer, Builder, Owner/Investor, Instructor, Property Manager, Real Estate Publisher; **SERVICES:** Sales, Investment counseling, devel., publishing; **PREV EMPLOY:** Licensed RE Broker since 1970; **PROFL AFFIL & HONORS:** NAR, CAR, Life Credentials (2) CA Community Colls.; **GRAD EDUC:** BS-Fin., 1970, RE Fin. & Econ., San Diego State Univ.; **EDUC HONORS:** Dean's List; **OTHER ACT & HONORS:** CA Teacher's Assn.; **HOME TEL:** (916)626-4352; **BUS ADD:** PO Box 984, Placerville, CA 95667.

COCKRUM, William M., III——B: July 18, 1937, Indianapolis, IN, *VChmn.*, A.G. Becker-Warburg Paribas Becker; **PRIM RE ACT:** Consultant; **EDUC:** AB With Distinctions, 1959, Econ., DePauw Univ.; **GRAD EDUC:** MBA With Distinction, 1961, Harvard Univ.; **HOME ADD:** 666 Sarbonne Rd., Los Angeles, CA 90077, (213)472-8937; **BUS ADD:** One Century Plasa, Suite 3400, Los Angeles, CA 90067, (213)552-6115.

COCKS, Richard E.——B: Aug. 1, 1917, Coldwater, MI, *Corp. RE and Facil. Plan. Mgr.*, Miles Laboratories, Inc.; **PRIM RE ACT:** Property Manager, Engineer; **OTHER RE ACT:** Corp. RE; **REP CLIENTS:** All Co. Divs. and Depts.; **PREV EMPLOY:** Miles Laboratories, Inc. over 25 yrs.; **PROFL AFFIL & HONORS:** IN Devel. Res. Co.; NARA; **EDUC:** BA; Life Cert. Teaching, 1939, Chem., Math, Physics, W. MI Univ.; **GRAD EDUC:** BCE, 1942, Univ. of IL; **OTHER ACT & HONORS:** ACS, AIChE, etc.; **HOME ADD:** 1622 Victoria Dr.,

Elkhart, IN 46514, (219)264-3210; **BUS ADD:** PO Box 40, Elkhart, IN 46515, (219)264-8762.

COCO, Mark J.——B: May 27, 1951, Des Moines, IA, *Broker*, Quest Co.; **PRIM RE ACT:** Broker, Syndicator, Consultant, Property Manager, Owner/Investor; **OTHER RE ACT:** Mort. Brokering; **SERVICES:** RE Sales, investment, synd., prop. mgmt.; **REP CLIENTS:** Lenders and indiv. investors in Comml. Prop.; **EDUC:** BS in Bus. Admin., 1974, Mgmt., Kansas State Univ.; **HOME ADD:** 2410 Applewood Lane, Salina, KS 67401, (913)827-2558; **BUS ADD:** 1011 W. 103rd., Goeppert Bank Bldg., Kansas City, MO 64114, (816)941-9311.

COCOZIELLO, Peter J.——B: July 28, 1950, Uniontown, PA, *Pres.*, Advance Realty Advisors, Ltd.; **PRIM RE ACT:** Consultant, Developer, Owner/Investor, Property Manager, Syndicator; **REP CLIENTS:** Investors; **PREV EMPLOY:** J.I. Kislak Realty Corp., Midlantic Nat. Bank; **PROFL AFFIL & HONORS:** Nat. Builders Assn.; **EDUC:** BBA, 1973, Fin., PA State Univ.; **GRAD EDUC:** 1979, Mort. Fin. - Sr. Program, NY Univ. RE Instit.; **HOME ADD:** 9 Lenore Rd., Tewksbury, NJ, (201)832-5285; **BUS ADD:** 266 Main St., Gladstone, NJ 07934, (201)234-2950.

CODY, William J.——B: Jan. 30, 1952, Detroit, MI, *Prop. Mgr.*, Cushman & Wakefield of Michigan, Inc.; **PRIM RE ACT:** Property Manager; **PROFL AFFIL & HONORS:** RE Alumni of MI (Univ. of MI); Realtor-Assoc., S Oakland Cty. Bd. of Realtors, CPM, GRI; **EDUC:** BA, 1973, Econ., Wayne State Univ., Detroit, MI; **OTHER ACT & HONORS:** Sec., Rochester Jaycees; **HOME ADD:** 460 Evelyn Lane, Apt. 201, Rochester, MI 48063, (313)852-0045; **BUS ADD:** 27777 Franklin Rd., Suite 700, Southfield, MI 48034, (313)353-5880.

COE, James Thomas——B: Dec. 17, 1945, Royston, GA, *Mgr., RE Branch*, United States Postal Service, RE & Bldgs. Office; **PRIM RE ACT:** Consultant, Appraiser, Owner/Investor, Property Manager; **OTHER RE ACT:** Realty mgr. for approximately 2,000 facilities with 4.5 million sq. ft. of space; **SERVICES:** Real prop. acquisition, leasing, disposal and mgmt.; **REP CLIENTS:** US Postal Serv. (Fed. Govt.); **PREV EMPLOY:** US Army, Corps of Engrs., Supervisory Appraiser; **PROFL AFFIL & HONORS:** Nat. Assn. of Review Appraisers; Assn. of Govt. Appraisers, CRA; **EDUC:** BS, 1970, RE/Urban Devel., GA State Univ.; **OTHER ACT & HONORS:** Admin. Bd. & Fin. Chmn., United Methodist Church; BPOE Lodge 1602; Elks Nat. Found.; Published: chap. on Govt. Appraisal Review, Nat. Assn. of Review Appraisers Textbook; **HOME ADD:** 5336 O'Connel Ct., Stone Mountain, GA 30088, (404)469-3045; **BUS ADD:** 2245 Perimeter Park Dr., Suite 17, Atlanta, GA 30341, (404)221-5243.

COEN, George W.——B: Mar. 26, 1914, Lancaster, OH, *Atty at Law*, Coen and Wexler; **PRIM RE ACT:** Attorney; **PROFL AFFIL & HONORS:** OH Bar; US Supreme Ct. Bar; US Dist. Ct. Bar; US Circuit Ct. of Appeals Bar; US Military Ct. Bar; **GRAD EDUC:** JD, 1938, Univ. of VA; **OTHER ACT & HONORS:** Former Tr., Fairfield Cty. Chap. of the Amer. Red Cross; Former Appeal Agent, Selective Serv.; Former Chmn., Mental Health and Retardation Bd. 648; Former Law Dir., OH Commn. on Aging; Chmn., Bldg. Comm., Fairfield Cty. Handicapped Ctr.; Former Chmn., Lancaster Tax Review Bd.; Instr., Columbus Coll. of Art and Design, 1960-1979; Member of the OH State Library Bd., 1950-1972; Chmn., Amer. Library Tr. Assn. Endowment Comm., 1968; Past Pres., Amer. Library Tr. Assn.; Past Pres., OH State Library Bd. and the Fairfield Cty. Dist. Library Bd.; **HOME ADD:** 209 E. Mulberry St., Lancaster, OH 43130, (614)653-7961; **BUS ADD:** PO Box 1028, Lancaster, OH 43130, Suite 234 Equitable Federal Bldg., (614)653-7825.

COERPER, Milo G.——B: May 8, 1925, Milwaukee, WI, *Partner*, Coudert Bros. (Intl. Law Firm-Main Office-NY), Wash., D.C. Branch Office; **PRIM RE ACT:** Attorney; **SERVICES:** RE Law; **PROFL AFFIL & HONORS:** ABA: Section of Probate, Trust and RE Law; **EDUC:** BS, 1946, US. Naval Academy; **GRAD EDUC:** LLB, 1954, Univ. of MI Law School; MA, 1957, Georgetown Univ.; PHD, 1960, Georgetown Univ.; **MIL SERV:** USN, Lt.; **HOME ADD:** 7315 Brookville Rd., Chevy Chase, MD 20015, (301)652-8635; **BUS ADD:** One Farragut Sq. S., Washington, DC 20006, (202)703-3010.

COFFRIN, Peter Starbuck——B: Feb. 25, 1947, Ithaca, NY, *Devel. Co-ordinator and Prop. Mgr.*, So. Burlington Realty Corp.; **PRIM RE ACT:** Consultant, Developer, Property Manager, Syndicator; **EDUC:** BA, 1973, Hist., Univ. of VT; **GRAD EDUC:** AM, 1977, Hist., Japanese Econ., Univ. of Chicago; **EDUC HONORS:** All College Honors; **MIL SERV:** US Army, Communications; **OTHER ACT & HONORS:** Member, Winooski Zoning Bd. 1980-81; Vice-Chairperson Burlington Coll.; Treas. Spectrum Inc., Member, Community Council of Greater Burlington; **HOME ADD:** 434 S. Winooski Ave., Burlington, VT 05401, (802)863-3120; **BUS ADD:** 366 Dorset St., So. Burlington, VT 05401, (802)863-6391.

COGBURN, Martin A.——B: AR, *RE Broker, CCIM, CPA, Owner*, Cogburn Realty; **PRIM RE ACT:** Broker, Consultant, Appraiser, Developer, Owner/Investor, Property Manager, Syndicator; **OTHER RE ACT:** CPA, CCIM, Lecturer; **SERVICES:** Consulting, brokerage, synd., prop. mgmt., etc.; **REP CLIENTS:** Synd., indiv., banks, corps., partnerships; **PREV EMPLOY:** CPA, public practice, own office, 1945 to 1967; RE Broker, own office, 1967 to present; **PROFL AFFIL & HONORS:** CA Soc. of CPA's; NAR; RNMI; CA Assn. of Realtors; San Francisco Bd. of Realtors; Contra Costa Bd. of Realtors; Member, RE Synd. Div., CA Assn. of Realtors; N. CA Chap. No. 1 CCIM of RNMI, CPA; GRI; CCIM; Beta Alpha Psi; Tower and Flame, Univ. of CA Berkeley, CA; Chi Pi Alpha, Golden Gate Univ.; Teacher, G.G. Univ., 1945-1949; **EDUC:** 1936, Univ. of CA; 1940, Golden Gate Univ.; **EDUC HONORS:** Golden Gate Univ. Acctg. Honor Soc.; **OTHER ACT & HONORS:** Founding City Councilman, City of Lafayette, CA, 1968-1970; Aahmes Temple of Mystic Shrine; Lyons Club, San Francisco; Former Asst. Scout Master, Oakland, CA; Listed in Marquis Who's Who in the W. and Who's Who in Commerce and Indus.; **HOME ADD:** 3447 Black Hawk Rd., Lafayette, CA 94549, (415)283-6910; **BUS ADD:** 1901 Olympic Blvd., Suite 201, Walnut Creek, CA 94596, (415)945-6111.

COGGIN, Buena Vista, Mrs.——B: Jan. 8, 1928, Richmond County, NC, *Chief Exec. Officer, VP*, Richmond Fed. Savings & Loan Assn., Main Office - with two branch offices; **PRIM RE ACT:** Lender; **PREV EMPLOY:** Employed here for 35 years; **PROFL AFFIL & HONORS:** US League of Savings Assoc.; NC S&L League; S&L Found., Inc.; Fin. Mgrs. Soc. of Savings, Inst., NC Dir. for SE Conf. of US League; Dir. of NC S & L 1979-81; Chmn., NC S & L Scholarship Fund 1975-1982; Pres. of NC Group Fin. Mgrs. Soc.; Member of Nat. Nominating Comm. of Fin. Mgrs. 1980; **EDUC:** Grad. of Exec. Dev. Amer. S&L Inst., 1968/1969, Mgmt., Univ. of GA, Various Courses at Univ. of NC, Charlotte, NC through the Amer. S&L Inst. Chap; **OTHER ACT & HONORS:** Taught S&L courses at Applachain State Univ., Pres. of Rockingham C of C for 1981; Dir. for Rockingham C of C, 1977-1981; Pres. Richmond Cty. Heart Assn. 1969; Appointed to Vocational Educ. Advisory Council of the Richmond Cty. Schools, 3 yr. term 1979-1981; Appointed to Richmond Cty. Fair Housing Task Force 1979; Appointed a member of Applachain State Univ. Found. Bd. of Tr. 1978-1980; **HOME ADD:** 919 Roberdel Rd., Rockingham, NC 28379, (919)895-4489; **BUS ADD:** 115 S. Lawrence St., P.O. Box 1597, Rockingham, NC 28379, (919)895-6046.

COGIN, Walter——*Gen. Mgr.*, Port Authority of New York & New Jersey, Properties Division Port. Dept.; **PRIM RE ACT:** Developer; **BUS ADD:** One World Track Center, New York, NY 10048, (212)466-7978.*

COHAN, H.B.——B: Dec. 18, 1923, Seattle, WA, *Pres.*, A.H. Cohan Co.; **PRIM RE ACT:** Broker, Consultant, Owner/Investor; **SERVICES:** Comml. & indus. sales & leases; **PROFL AFFIL & HONORS:** NAR, GRI; **EDUC:** BA, 1946, Univ. of WA; **OTHER ACT & HONORS:** B'nai B'rith, Past Pres., Elks; **HOME ADD:** 2501 Canterbury Ln., Seattle, WA 98112, (206)322-5615; **BUS ADD:** 901 Vance Bldg., Seattle, WA 98101, (206)622-0193.

COHEN, Arthur C.——B: Jan. 26, 1940, New York, NY, *Prin. Agent*, Arthur Charles Cohen, Inc.; **PRIM RE ACT:** Consultant, Appraiser; **SERVICES:** Appraisals, consulting services, feasibility studies, market analyses and econ. studies; **REP CLIENTS:** Various inst., corp., accts., attys.; **PREV EMPLOY:** Dept. of HUD, 1965-1969; **PROFL AFFIL & HONORS:** Sr. Member, ASA; Member, AIREA; Member, NAIFA, MAI; IFAS; **EDUC:** BS, 1961, Hist., Univ. of WI; **GRAD EDUC:** MBA, 1971, Fin., Columbia Univ.; **EDUC HONORS:** Magna Cum Laude; **MIL SERV:** US Army Artillery, NCO; **OTHER ACT & HONORS:** Amer. Soc. of Appraisers, Co-Chmn. Bd. of Examiners - Real Prop.; **HOME ADD:** 110 Riverside Dr., New York, NY 10024, (212)873-8624; **BUS ADD:** 200 W. 57th St., New York, NY 10019, (212)757-7860.

COHEN, Earl H.——B: Mar. 24, 1948, St. Paul, MN, *Pres.*, Cohen & Bialick, P.A. Law Office; **PRIM RE ACT:** Attorney, Broker, Consultant, Owner/Investor, Property Manager, Syndicator; **SERVICES:** Synd., devel., consultation, brokerage & prop. mgmt.; **REP CLIENTS:** Kensington Props., Inc., Personal Props. Inc., Fingerman Ent., Moon Props., Noon Props.; **PREV EMPLOY:** 1973-76, NW Bank of MN Trust Dept.; **PROFL AFFIL & HONORS:** ABA, Real prop. and probate section, MN Bar Assn., DC Bar, Minneapolis Bd. of Realtors, Comml. Indus. MLS, Juris Doctor, RE Broker; **EDUC:** BS, 1970, Mgmt., Indus. relations, Univ. of MN, Coll. of Bus. Admin.; **GRAD EDUC:** JD, 1973, RE, Estate Planning, Bus. Planning, Univ. of MN; **EDUC HONORS:** Grad. With Distinction; **HOME ADD:** 3827 Zenith Ave. S., Minneapolis, MN 55410, (612)920-3906; **BUS ADD:**

200 Omni Bldg., 730 Hennepin, Minneapolis, MN 55403, (612)338-4850.

COHEN, Edward B.——**B:** Dec. 17, 1928, Chicago, IL, *VP*, The Northern Trust Co., Trust Dept. RE Services; **PRIM RE ACT:** Consultant, Property Manager, Banker, Owner/Investor, Insuror; **OTHER RE ACT:** Qualify RE Investments; **PROFL AFFIL & HONORS:** Realty Club of Chicago; Chicago RE Bd.; IREM, Ely Chap., Lambda Alpha Intl. Land Econ. Frat., Hon.; CPM; **EDUC:** BA, 1950, Poli.Sci., Law, Univ. of IL; **MIL SERV:** USA, Sgt., Korean Medal, UN Medal; **OTHER ACT & HONORS:** Life Member, Amer. Inst. of Banking; Tr., Lawrence Hall School For Boys; Bishop & Trustee, Episcopal Diocese of Chicago; **HOME ADD:** 5344 N. Lakewood Ave., Chicago, IL 60640, (312)334-8060; **BUS ADD:** 50 S. Lasalle St., Chicago, IL 60675, (312)444-3239.

COHEN, Gary J.——**B:** Apr. 20, 1946, New York, NY, *Partner*, Cohen & Ziskin; **PRIM RE ACT:** Attorney; **SERVICES:** RE Synd., securities and tax planning; **REP CLIENTS:** Natl. and Regl. synd., broker-dealers, indiv. investors; **PROFL AFFIL & HONORS:** CA Bar Assn., ABA Tax and Real Prop. Sections.; **EDUC:** BS, 1967,1969, Electical Engrg., Polytechnic Inst. of Brooklyn, Univ. of CA; **GRAD EDUC:** JD, BS, 1974, Univ. of CA, Berkeley; **EDUC HONORS:** Eta Kappa Nu, Order of the Coif, Law Review, Bartley Cavenaugh Crum Award (1st in Class of 1974); **BUS ADD:** 2029 Centry Park East 1700, Los Angeles, CA 90067, (213)552-2010.

COHEN, Herbert L.——**B:** Feb. 11, 1949, New York, NY, *Partner*, Liebowitz & Cohen; **PRIM RE ACT:** Attorney, Owner/Investor, Syndicator; **SERVICES:** All legal matters relating to acquisitions & fin.; **PREV EMPLOY:** Gen. Counsel/VP, XCOR Intl., Inc.; **PROFL AFFIL & HONORS:** ABA, Comm. on Real Prop.; Bar Assn. of the City of NY; **EDUC:** BA, 1970, Poli. Sci./Urban Planning, Brooklyn Coll., City Univ. of NY; **GRAD EDUC:** JD, 1973, Real Prop. Fin., Rutgers Univ.; **EDUC HONORS:** Cum Laude, Editor, Law Review; **BUS ADD:** 1290 Ave. of the Americas, Suite 4150, New York, NY 10104.

COHEN, Irving E.——**B:** Nov. 7, 1946, Brooklyn, NY, *Exec. VP*, Security Pacific Financial Services, Investment Real Estate Grp.; **PRIM RE ACT:** Consultant; **SERVICES:** RE asset mgmt., disposition of surplus land and buildings; **REP CLIENTS:** US corporations and fin. instit.; **PROFL AFFIL & HONORS:** Soc. for Indus. Archeology; RESSI; Nat. Assn. of Indus. and Office Parks; **EDUC:** BA, 1968, Econ., The City Coll. of NY; **GRAD EDUC:** MBA, 1973, Fin., NYU Grad. School of Bus. Admin.; **HOME ADD:** 9013 68th Ave., Forest Hills, NY 11375, (212)261-1609; **BUS ADD:** 100 Park Ave., New York, NY 10017, (212)883-0511.

COHEN, Jerome J.——**B:** July 25, 1918, New York, NY, Land Resources Corp.; **PRIM RE ACT:** Developer, Builder, Property Manager; **OTHER RE ACT:** Utility Operations; **PROFL AFFIL & HONORS:** Member of FL Bar; Member Amer. Land Devel. Assn.; Member ULI; **GRAD EDUC:** LLD, 1951, Univ. of Miami; **HOME ADD:** 11111 Biscayne Blvd., Miami, FL 33161; **BUS ADD:** 1125 NE 125th St., Miami, FL 33161, (305)895-6500.

COHEN, Jerome M.——*Pres. and CEO*, Williams RE Co., Inc.; **PRIM RE ACT:** Consultant, Appraiser, Property Manager, Developer; **OTHER RE ACT:** Sales, leasing, project coordination, fin.; **REP CLIENTS:** Prominent RE investors, major corporations; **PROFL AFFIL & HONORS:** Advisory Bd. of RE Inst. of NY Univ.; Comml. Panel of Amer. Arbitration Assn.; RE Bd. of NY; Bd of Dirs., Assn. for a Better NY; CRA of Nat. Assn. of Review Appraisers; VP of Exec. Comm. of Bd. of Dir. of Child Study Assn./Wel-Met Inc.; **OTHER ACT & HONORS:** Harmonie Club; Turnberry Yacht & Racquet Club; Jockey Club; Club of Clubs; **BUS ADD:** 1700 Broadway, New York, NY 10019, (212)582-8000.

COHEN, Jordan S.——**B:** Feb. 28, 1928, New York, NY, *Pres.*, J.S.C. Consulting Group, Pres. Intl. Equities, Inc., Investment; **PRIM RE ACT:** Consultant, Appraiser, Owner/Investor, Syndicator; **SERVICES:** Investment analyst RE, synd. evaluation; **REP CLIENTS:** Leonard L. Farber, Inc.; Shopping Center Associates, Ltd.; Gold Coast Capital Corp. SBIC; Walter P. Heller Intl.; Flushing National Bank; **PREV EMPLOY:** Sr. CRA; **PROFL AFFIL & HONORS:** ARA; **GRAD EDUC:** 1960, Civil Engrg., Univ. of VT, Rutgers Univ., School of Bus. 1964; **MIL SERV:** US Army, 1948-52, S/Sgt, Purple Heart, Bronze Star; **OTHER ACT & HONORS:** Boy Scouts of America; Boys Club; Advisory Board, Flushing National Bank; Advisory Board, FL Instit. of Tech.; **HOME ADD:** 2947 N.W. 68th St., Fort Lauderdale, FL 33309, (305)974-4649; **BUS ADD:** One Pompano Fashion Sq., Pompano Beach, FL 33062, (305)781-7100.

COHEN, Lawrence A.——**B:** Apr. 13, 1951, Chicago, IL, *VP*, Draper and Kramer, Inc.; **PRIM RE ACT:** Developer, Property Manager; **SERVICES:** Prop. mgmt., brokerage, dev., investment analysis; **REP CLIENTS:** State Farm Ins., NY Life, Prudential Ins.; **PROFL AFFIL & HONORS:** SORPA, BOMA, Natl. Realtors, CPM Candidate; **EDUC:** BA, 1973, Fin., Univ. of IL; **GRAD EDUC:** MBA, 1975, RE and Fin., Univ. of CA, Berkeley; **EDUC HONORS:** Cum Laude; **HOME ADD:** 331 S. Western, Park Ridge, IL 60068, (312)692-5713; **BUS ADD:** 33 W. Monroe, Chicago, IL 60603, (312)346-8600.

COHEN, Lee Allen——**B:** Sept. 13, 1926, Philadelphia, PA, *Chief Appraiser*, Philadelphia Savings Fund Sec., Appraisal; **PRIM RE ACT:** Appraiser, Banker, Lender; **PROFL AFFIL & HONORS:** AIREA, SREA, MAI, SRPA; **EDUC:** BS, 1949, Econ., Temple Univ.; **HOME ADD:** 138 W Walnut Park Dr., Philadelphia, PA 19120, (215)224-2540; **BUS ADD:** S. 12th St., Philadelphia, PA 19107, (215)629-2352.

COHEN, Leonard——**B:** Nov. 1, 1926, Hartford, CT, *VP*, Heyman Properties, Shopping Ctrs.; **PRIM RE ACT:** Developer; **OTHER RE ACT:** Development and Acquisition of Commercial Property; **SERVICES:** Devel. of shopping ctrs.; Purchase and Management; **REP CLIENTS:** K Mart, Grand Union, Path Mark, Woolco, Murphy's Mart, A&P, Rite Aid Drug, Shoe Town, Etc.; **PREV EMPLOY:** Self Employed - Leonard Cohen Assoc.; Pres. Sanndrel, Inc.,; VP RE Arlan's Dept. Stores; RE Broker, J.I. Kisak, Inc.; **PROFL AFFIL & HONORS:** Intl. Council of Shopping Ctrs., Cert. Shopping Ctr. Mgr. (CSM); **EDUC:** BS, 1948, RE & Fin., Wharton School of Fin. & Commerce, Univ. of PA; **GRAD EDUC:** Studies, 1948, Mktg., Univ. of CA at Los Angeles; **MIL SERV:** US Army, Pvt.; **OTHER ACT & HONORS:** Univ. of PA Secondary School Comm.; elected trustee, Tarrytown Bd. of Education, V. Chmn. Urban Renewal Admin., Tarrytown; **HOME ADD:** 10 River Terrace, Tarrytown, NY 10591, (914)631-6940; **BUS ADD:** 877 Post Rd. East, Box 7002, Westport, CT 06880, (203)226-1206.

COHEN, M. Richard——**B:** Oct. 16, 1938, Philadelphia, PA, *RE Appraiser/Valuation Engineer*, M. Richard Cohen Co.; **PRIM RE ACT:** Broker, Owner/Investor, Consultant, Engineer, Appraiser, Instructor; **SERVICES:** RE Appraisal and Consulting; **REP CLIENTS:** Prop. owners, lenders, all levels of govt. inst., etc.; **PROFL AFFIL & HONORS:** MAI, SRPA, ASA, R/W, PE; **EDUC:** BS, 1960, Civil Engrg., Univ. of PA; **GRAD EDUC:** MBA, 1962, RE & Fin., Univ. of PA, Wharton School; **OTHER ACT & HONORS:** Faculty - Wharton School, Univ. of PA; **BUS ADD:** 104 N. Camac St., Philadelphia, PA 19107, (215)564-0733.

COHEN, Marshall J.——**B:** Sept. 17, 1939, Newark, NJ, *Atty.*, Curtis, Mallet-Prevost, Colt & Mosle; **PRIM RE ACT:** Attorney; **SERVICES:** Legal; **PROFL AFFIL & HONORS:** The Assn. of the Bar of the City of NY, ABA, NY State Bar Assn.; **EDUC:** AB, 1961, Amer. Civ., Rutgers Univ.; **GRAD EDUC:** JD, 1976, Law, Columbia Law School; **EDUC HONORS:** Phi Beta Kappa, Summa Cum laude, Stone Scholar; **HOME ADD:** 531 Main St. 1420, Roosevelt Is., NY, (212)371-6286; **BUS ADD:** 100 Wall St., NY, NY 10005, (212)248-8111.

COHEN, Paul H.——**B:** July 23, 1948, Brooklyn, NY, *Managing Part.*, Cliff Realty Co., Cliff Data Systems, Inc.; **OTHER RE ACT:** RE Accounting & Mgmt., Comml. & indus. RE computer installations; **SERVICES:** Install computer base operating systems; **PREV EMPLOY:** Cushman & Wakefield Inc., The Mack Co., Owner Devels.; **PROFL AFFIL & HONORS:** AICPA, NY State Soc. of CPAs, CPA; **EDUC:** BS, 1970, Acctg., Fin. & Computers, Long Is. Univ.; **HOME ADD:** 340 E. 64th St., NY, NY 10021, (212)752-9653; **BUS ADD:** 200 E. 42nd St., New York, NY 10017, (212)867-0814.

COHEN, Paul J.——**B:** Aug. 6, 1953, Inyokern, CA, *VP, Synds.*, Adams Financial Corp.; **PRIM RE ACT:** Broker, Attorney, Syndicator; **OTHER RE ACT:** Fin. Planner; **PROFL AFFIL & HONORS:** ABA, CA Bar, Orange Cty. Bar, Intl. Fed. Fin. Planners, CA RE Broker; **EDUC:** BA, 1975, Univ. of CA, Irvine; **GRAD EDUC:** JD, 1979, Tax and Securities, Pepperdine Univ.; **EDUC HONORS:** with Honors; **HOME ADD:** 2288 Meyer Pl., Costa Mesa, CA 92627, (714)646-9929; **BUS ADD:** 3 Corporate Plaza, Newport Beach, CA 92660.

COHEN, Richard D.——**B:** Oct. 10, 1947, Boston, MA, *Pres.*, Cohen Props., Inc.; **PRIM RE ACT:** Syndicator, Developer, Property Manager, Owner/Investor; **PROFL AFFIL & HONORS:** IREM; Greater Boston RE Bd.; Rental Housing Assn., CPM; AMO; **EDUC:** BS, BA, 1969, Fin., Boston Univ.; **HOME ADD:** 40 Westerly Rd., Weston, MA 02193; **BUS ADD:** 1330 Beacon St., Brookline, MA 02146, (617)277-4202.

COHEN, Robert Jay——**B:** Aug. 27, 1952, Los Angeles, CA, *CPA*, Self-employed; **OTHER RE ACT:** CPA; **SERVICES:** Fin. statements, tax planning for devels., consulting services for condo. homeowners assns.; **PREV EMPLOY:** Kenneth Leventhal and Co.; **PROFL AFFIL & HONORS:** AICPA, CA Soc. of CPAs, Community Assns. Inst., CPA; **EDUC:** BA Econ., 1974, Econ., Acctg., UCLA; **HOME ADD:** 3350 Keystone Ave. #15, Los Angeles, CA 90034, (213)839-9697; **BUS ADD:** 2029 Century Park East, Suite 600, Los Angeles, CA 90067, (213)551-2896.

COHEN, Roger L.——**B:** Oct. 4, 1935, St. Joseph, MO, *Chmn. of the Bd.*, Roger L. Cohen & Co.; **PRIM RE ACT:** Broker, Syndicator, Consultant, Appraiser, Developer, Property Manager, Owner/Investor; **PROFL AFFIL & HONORS:** SIR; Omega Tau Rho; RESSI; ICSC; Urban Land Institute, Young Presidents Org.; Who's Who in the Midwest; **EDUC:** BS, 1957, Bus. Admin., Univ. of MO; **EDUC HONORS:** Sr. Men's Hon., Who's Who in Amer. Coll. & Univ.; **MIL SERV:** US Army; 1st Lt.; **HOME ADD:** 3700 W 64th, Mission Hills, KS 66109, (913)362-1774; **BUS ADD:** P.O. Box 26690, Kansas City, MO 64196, (816)471-0700.

COHEN, Ronald Marc——**B:** Feb. 7, 1951, Passaic, NJ, *Atty.*, Arthur and Speed, Ltd.; **PRIM RE ACT:** Attorney; **SERVICES:** RE settlements, contract negotiations and investment consultation; **PREV EMPLOY:** Donovan, Turnbull and Burns, 1976-1977; Donovan and Arthur, 1977-1979; **PROFL AFFIL & HONORS:** VA State Bar; Dist. of Columbia Bar; ABA; Arlington Bar Assn.; Fairfax Bar Assn., (RE Div.), Atty. at Law; **EDUC:** BA, 1973, Poli. Sci., Albright Coll.; **GRAD EDUC:** JD, 1976, The George Washington Univ. School of Law; **EDUC HONORS:** Cum Laude; **OTHER ACT & HONORS:** Arlington Jaycees, Outstanding Young Men of Amer., 1980; **BUS ADD:** 5549 Lee Hwy., Arlington, VA 22207, (703)241-7171.

COHEN, Sidney——**B:** Aug. 14, 1936, Boston, MA, *Pres.*, Suburban Trading Corp., New England Factory Outlet Ctrs., Inc.; **PRIM RE ACT:** Owner/Investor; **EDUC:** 1958, Acctg., Coll. of Bus. Admin., BU; **HOME ADD:** Framingham, MA 01701; **BUS ADD:** 12 Waverly St., PO Box 2130, Framingham, MA 01701, (617)872-0085.

COHEN, Stanley A.——**B:** Jan. 20, 1935, New York, NY, *Pres.*, Marco Management; **PRIM RE ACT:** Broker, Developer, Builder, Owner/Investor, Property Manager, Syndicator; **SERVICES:** Synd. of multi-family bldgs. Co-op conversions. New condo. const. co-op sales & mgmt.; **PROFL AFFIL & HONORS:** Builders Inst. of Westchester, Rockland Cty. Apt. Owners Assn., 3 Term VP of Apt. Owners Advisory Council; Legislative Chmn. Rockland Cty. AOA; **EDUC:** BA, 1956, Sociology, Univ. College, NY Univ; **HOME ADD:** 41 Clubway, Hartsdale, NY 10530; **BUS ADD:** 18 N. Central Ave., Hartsdale, NY 10530, (914)428-2360.

COHEN, Sylvan M.——**B:** July 28, 1914, Philadelphia, PA, *Pres.*, Pennsylvania Real Estate Investment Trust; **PRIM RE ACT:** Developer, Owner/Investor; **PREV EMPLOY:** Sr. Partner, Law firm of Cohen, Shapiro, Polisher, Shiekman & Cohen, Philadelphia, PA; Pres., Intl. Council Shopping Ctrs.; Pres., Nat. Assn. RE Investment Trusts; Chmn., Bd. of Govs., Philadelphia Bar Assn.; **EDUC:** BA, 1935, Univ. of PA; **GRAD EDUC:** JD, 1938, Law, Univ. of PA; **EDUC HONORS:** Cum Laude, Note & Legislation Editor of PA Law Review; **MIL SERV:** US Air Corps, 1st Lt., Combat Intelligence Officer; **OTHER ACT & HONORS:** Sr. Litigation Atty., Office Price Admin., 1941-1942; **HOME ADD:** 1820 Rittenhouse Sq., Philadelphia, PA 19103; **BUS ADD:** 12 S 12th St., Philadelphia, PA 19107.

COHN, Theodore R.——**B:** June 13, 1938, Newark, NJ, *Pres.*, T.R.C. Group; **PRIM RE ACT:** Developer, Owner/Investor, Property Manager, Syndicator; **SERVICES:** Rehab., prop. mgmt., private investments, equity participation; **PREV EMPLOY:** 10 yrs. as prin. of org., previously, RE atty.; **PROFL AFFIL & HONORS:** Member, Bd. of Dirs. NJ Apt. House Council; Member, NJ Prop. Owners Assn.; Member Nat. Apt. House Council; **EDUC:** BA, 1960, Univ. of MI; **GRAD EDUC:** JD, 1963, Univ. of MI Law School; **EDUC HONORS:** Jr. and Sr. Honor Socs.; **BUS ADD:** PO Box 196, Livingston, NJ 07039, (201)994-6606.

COHN, William A.——**B:** Oct. 10, 1950, Memphis, TN, *Atty.*, Irion, Cohn, and Kirsch; **PRIM RE ACT:** Attorney; **SERVICES:** Closing, litigation, title investigation; **PROFL AFFIL & HONORS:** ABA, TN Bar Assn., Comml. Law League of Amer., Memphis & Shelby Cty. Bar Assn., Memphis Trial Lawyers Assn.; **EDUC:** BS, 1972, Vertebrate Zoology, Univ. of TN 1968-70; Memphis State Univ. (1970-72, degree); **GRAD EDUC:** JD, 1977, Real Prop. & Estate Planning, Univ. of TN College of Law; Medical Microbiology, Univ. of TN Medical Units, 1972-1973; **EDUC HONORS:** Dean's List; **HOME ADD:** 410 Meadowcrest Cir., Memphis, TN 38117, (901)761-4594; **BUS ADD:** Suite 950, White Station Tower, 5050 Poplar Ave., Memphis, TN 38157, (901)682-5500.

COIN, Bruce J.——**B:** June 7, 1946, Philadelphia, PA, *Dir.*, Pro-Gressive Mortg. Corp.; **PRIM RE ACT:** Broker, Consultant, Appraiser; **OTHER RE ACT:** Fin., mort. banker; **SERVICES:** Tax free or conventional fin. for investment RE and/or counseling; **REP CLIENTS:** Devel., investors, instit.; **PREV EMPLOY:** Latimer & Buck Inc.; Advisor Fidelco Growth Investors; Kardon Investment/Peoples Bond & Mortgage; **PROFL AFFIL & HONORS:** Local Industrial Development Authorities; **EDUC:** Acctg., Temple Univ.; **MIL SERV:** US Army; 1966-68; **OTHER ACT & HONORS:** Write Column, 'The Financing Picture'; Published: RE Review, New York Times, Appraisal Journal; **HOME ADD:** 300 Seneca Dr., Wenonah, NJ 08090, (609)468-2514; **BUS ADD:** Western Savings Bank Bldg., Philadelphia, PA 19107, (215)735-4230.

COINER, Francis M.——**B:** Feb. 26, 1923, Newport News, VA, *Atty.*; **PRIM RE ACT:** Attorney, Instructor; **SERVICES:** Legal rep., buyer, seller, lender; **PROFL AFFIL & HONORS:** ABA; NC State Bar Assn.; Henderson Cty. Bar Assn.; Land of Sky Estate Planning Assn.; **EDUC:** BS, 1948, Eng., Hist., E Carolina Univ.; **GRAD EDUC:** LLB, 1951, Wake Forest Univ.; **MIL SERV:** USN; 1942-45, 1st Class PO; **HOME ADD:** 1616 Ridgewood Ave., Hendersonville, NC 28739, (704)693-9638; **BUS ADD:** 210 Third Ave. W, Hendersonville, NC 28739, (704)692-2507.

COLBERT, Charles R.——**B:** June 23, 1921, Dow, OK, *Owner*, Charles Colbert, Arch. Planner; **PRIM RE ACT:** Consultant; **OTHER RE ACT:** CBD Studies, City Planner; **SERVICES:** Site utilization studies, Central Bus. Dist. Studies; **REP CLIENTS:** Main Place, Dallas, TX; Worcester Cty. Natl. Bank; New Orleans School Bd., Webster Grove, MO Bd. of Educ.; LA Cities of Lafayette & Lake Charles, LA, etc.; **PREV EMPLOY:** Dean of Faculty of Arch., Columbia Univ., NY; TX A&M Univ., Coll. Sta., TX; Prof. LA State Univ. (Current); **PROFL AFFIL & HONORS:** AIA, LA Archs. Assoc. & Royal Society of Arts, Fellow AIA, Tau Beta Pi, AIA Nat. Design Hon. Award; **EDUC:** BArch., 1943, Arch., Univ. of TX; **GRAD EDUC:** 1946, Arch. & City Planning, Columbia Univ., Loyal Univ., Courses in School of Law; **MIL SERV:** USN, Lt., Atl. & Pac. Serv.; **OTHER ACT & HONORS:** Member LA State Bd. of Educ., 1972-78 (Elective), Presbyterian Church, Intl. House; **HOME ADD:** 510 Woodvine Ave., Metairie, LA 70005, (504)834-8151; **BUS ADD:** 4636 One Shell Sq., New Orleans, LA 70139, (504)522-6090.

COLBERT, Kenneth J.——**B:** June 29, 1945, Philadelphia, PA, *Pres.*, Colbert Engineering, Inc.; **PRIM RE ACT:** Engineer; **OTHER RE ACT:** Constr. Suprv. land devel. & mgmt.; **EDUC:** BCE, 1968, Univ. of MO, Rolla; **MIL SERV:** USAR, 1968-74, E-6, Sgt.; **HOME ADD:** 8603 Lucerne Rd., Randallstown, MD 21133, (301)655-5148; **BUS ADD:** P.O. Box 135, Millersville, MD 21108, (301)987-5294.

COLBERT, Robert Reed——**B:** Dec. 13, 1924, Wellsville, NY, *Chmn. and Pres.*, Institutional Equities Inc., Instnl. and Investors RE; **PRIM RE ACT:** Broker, Consultant, Engineer, Appraiser, Banker, Developer, Builder, Owner/Investor, Property Manager; **OTHER RE ACT:** Const. mgmt.; **SERVICES:** Devel., builder, mgr., consultant, mort. broker, const. mgmt., acquisitions, appraisals; **REP CLIENTS:** Lender and indiv. or instl. investors in comml. RE; **PREV EMPLOY:** Banking, Consultant and Mort. Officer, Comml. RE, 30 yrs.; **PROFL AFFIL & HONORS:** Lecturer, RE Investments, Cornell Univ., Who's Who in Fin. and Indus.; Who's Who in the East; **EDUC:** BS, 1948, Econ./Money and Banking/Civil Engrg./Labor Relations, Cornell Univ.; **OTHER ACT & HONORS:** Faculty Member, Advance Mort. School for Sr. Mort. Officers, Nat. Assn. of Mutual Savings Banks and Comm. on Mort. Investments; **HOME ADD:** 104 Homestead Rd., Ithaca, NY 14850, (607)277-4100; **BUS ADD:** PO Box 795, Ithaca, NY 14850, (607)277-4000.

COLBURN, Harry S., Jr.——**B:** Jan. 5, 1943, Buffalo, NY, *Partner; Tax Specialist*, Alley, Maass, Rogers, Lindsay & Chauncey, Taxation; RE; **PRIM RE ACT:** Broker, Consultant, Attorney; **SERVICES:** Legal, tax, advice and planning; RE selection and disposition; **PROFL AFFIL & HONORS:** ABA; The FL Bar; NY State Bar Assn.; Palm Beach Bd. of Realtors; **EDUC:** BA, 1965, Eng. Major; Math. & Philosophy Minors, Canjsius Coll.; **GRAD EDUC:** JD, 1968, Law, Harvard Law School; LLM(Taxation), 1975, Taxation, Univ. of FL., Law Sch.; **EDUC HONORS:** Summa Cum Laude; **OTHER ACT & HONORS:** Kiwanis Club of Palm Beach, FL, VP; Harvard Club of Beaches, VP; **HOME ADD:** 330 Franklin Rd., West Palm Beach, FL 33405, (305)588-6083; **BUS ADD:** 321 Royal Poinciana Plaza, Palm Beach, FL 33480, (305)659-1770.

COLBURN, Herbert William——**B:** Feb. 20, 1926, Huntington Park, CA, *Chartered Prop. Casualty Underwriter*, Colburn & Company; **PRIM RE ACT:** Insuror; **SERVICES:** Bus. & prop. ins.; **PROFL AFFIL &**

HONORS: Soc. of Chartered Prop. Casualty Underwriters; **EDUC:** BS, 1949, Econ., Univ. of CA, Berkeley; **MIL SERV:** US Army Air Force, Cadet; **HOME ADD:** 5100 via Dolce, #103, Marina del Rey, CA 90291, (213)823-3329; **BUS ADD:** 6320 Van Nuys Blvd., Ste 201, Van Nuys, CA 91401, (213)786-1342.

COLE, David L.——**B:** Apr. 26, 1939, Boston, MA, *Pres.*, Timberline Props.; **PRIM RE ACT:** Broker, Owner/Investor, Instructor; **OTHER RE ACT:** Resort Prop. Specialist; **SERVICES:** Mktg. of primary and resort props.; devel. opportunities; **PROFL AFFIL & HONORS:** Vail Bd. of Realtors; CO Assn. of Realtors; NAR, GRI; CRS; CRB; **EDUC:** BA, 1961, Econ., Bowdoin Coll.; **GRAD EDUC:** MBA, 1964, Mktg., Harvard Univ.; **MIL SERV:** US Army; 1st Lt.; **OTHER ACT & HONORS:** Bowdoin Coll. Alumni Council; **BUS ADD:** 286 Bridge St., Vail, CO 81657, (303)476-2113.

COLE, Frank M.——**B:** July 28, 1935, Cheyenne, WY, *Pres./Owner/Gen. Part.*, Cole Corp./Cole Dept. Store/The Bluffs Co.; **PRIM RE ACT:** Developer, Property Manager, Engineer, Owner/Investor; **PREV EMPLOY:** WY Hwy. Dept. (1958-1961); CA Hwy. Dept. (1957-1958); **PROFL AFFIL & HONORS:** ASCE; NSPE; ULI; ICSC; NRMA; NAHB, Reg. Prof. Engr., WY, CO; Land Surveyor, WY; CSM; **EDUC:** BS, 1957, Civ. Eng./Arch. Eng., Univ. of WY; **OTHER ACT & HONORS:** Cheyenne-Laramie Cty. Planning Commn. Member, 1981; Boy Scouts of Amer. Dist. Comm.; Cheyenne C of C; Transportation and Local Affairs Comm.; **HOME ADD:** 3400 Arrowhead Rd., Cheyenne, WY 82001; **BUS ADD:** 425 Cole Shopping Ctr., Cheyenne, WY 82001, (307)634-4577.

COLE, Gregory G.——**B:** Nov. 15, 1951, Childress, TX, *Assistant VP*, Coldwell-Banker, RE Fin. Services; **PRIM RE ACT:** Broker, Lender; **SERVICES:** Arrangement of equity & debt fin. structures; **REP CLIENTS:** Hancock, Aetna, Crocker Bank, T. Crow; **PREV EMPLOY:** United CA Mort. - San Francisco; **PROFL AFFIL & HONORS:** MBA, DYMBA, TMBA, DMBA, Pres. DYMBA; **EDUC:** Univ. of KS, 1975, Econ. Geog. & Bus., KU; **GRAD EDUC:** MBA, 1976, RE Fin., So. Methodist Univ.; **EDUC HONORS:** in Geog.; **MIL SERV:** USN, PO, Natl. Service Award; **HOME ADD:** 14760 Lochinvar, Dallas, TX 75240, (214)934-0821; **BUS ADD:** 5400 LBJ Freeway, Ste 1100, Dallas, TX 75240, (214)458-4852.

COLE, J. Ralph——**B:** Dec. 27, 1948, Owensboro, KY, *Consultant*; **PRIM RE ACT:** Consultant, Developer, Appraiser, Assessor; **SERVICES:** Consulting, devel. & valuation in multifamily RE; **REP CLIENTS:** Indiv. & corp. devel. cos., inst. (non-profit) entities interested in devel. of congregate housing & health care facilities; **PREV EMPLOY:** Consultant and prin. officer at Health Systems, Inc., of Boston, MA; VP of Devel. at Continental Wingate Co., Inc.; **PROFL AFFIL & HONORS:** Nat. Housing Rehab. Assn., Citizens Housing & Planning Assn., Nat. Leased Housing Assn.; **EDUC:** BS, 1970, Devel. & RE Fin., Urban Planning, Mgt., MIT; **MIL SERV:** USAF, S/Sgt.; **HOME ADD:** 167 Commonwealth Ave., Boston, MA 02116, (617)536-6538; **BUS ADD:** c/o Winn Devel. Co., Four Fanueil Hall Mktplace, Boston, MA 02109, (617)742-4500.

COLE, John N.——**B:** Apr. 15, 1951, New York, NY, *Ex Vice President*, Transcontinental Brokerage, Inc.; **PRIM RE ACT:** Broker, Insuror, Syndicator; **OTHER RE ACT:** National Brokerage; **SERVICES:** Commercial Insurance, RE Brokerage; **PREV EMPLOY:** Wm. A. White & Sons Comml. Leasing Long Island Division; **PROFL AFFIL & HONORS:** Westchester Bd. of Realtors; **EDUC:** BA, 1974, Pol. Sci., NY Univ.; **HOME ADD:** 2 Carlyle Place, Hartsdale, NY 10530, (914)428-0552; **BUS ADD:** 222 Mamaroneck Ave., White Plains, NY 10605, (814)948-7174.

COLE, Matthew B.——**B:** Aug. 5, 1928, New York, NY, *Dir. of Mktg.*, J.M. Jayson & Co. Inc., Mktg.; **PRIM RE ACT:** Syndicator; **SERVICES:** Private and public RE limited partnerships; **EDUC:** BA, 1954, Eng. & Mktg., Univ. of CT; **MIL SERV:** US Army, Signal Corp., 1951-53; **OTHER ACT & HONORS:** Pres. Buffalo Chapt. Amer. Mktg. Assn.; **HOME ADD:** 350 Frankhauser, Williamsville, NY 14221; **BUS ADD:** 680 Statler Bldg., Buffalo, NY 14202, (716)856-9777.

COLE, Patricia S.——*Ed.*, Real Estate News; **PRIM RE ACT:** Real Estate Publisher; **BUS ADD:** 720 S. Dearborn, Chicago, IL 60605, (312)922-7220.*

COLEMAN, B.——**B:** Dec. 7, 1946, Le Mars, IA, *Pres.*, Coleman Land Co.; **PRIM RE ACT:** Broker, Consultant, Developer, Syndicator, Real Estate Publisher; **REP CLIENTS:** UT State Wildlife Resources, Deer Valley Devel. Co., Huntsman Christensen Corp., City of Park City; **PREV EMPLOY:** Ski Area Devel. related employment and brokerage since 1971; **PROFL AFFIL & HONORS:** Broker-UT 1973; Broker-CO 1976, UT CCIM Chap.-Member; Member UT Indus. Devel. Exec. Assn.; **EDUC:** BS, 1969, Bus., Univ. of CO; **MIL SERV:** 4-F; **OTHER ACT & HONORS:** Park City Planning Commn. 1979-Present; Pres., Park City C of C 1980; Park City Visitors and Convention Bureau-Dir.; Park City C of C-Dir.; Rotary Club-Dir.; Chmn. of Sub Comm. for Agenda for the Eighties, Governors Special Task Force; **HOME ADD:** 1400 Lucky John, Park City, UT 84060, (801)649-9086; **BUS ADD:** PO Box 1800, Park City, UT 84060, (801)649-7171.

COLEMAN, Dennis J.——**B:** Dec. 6, 1939, Wichita, KS, *Owner*, Coleman & Assoc., Realtors; **PRIM RE ACT:** Broker, Appraiser, Property Manager, Owner/Investor; **SERVICES:** Residential Sale, Appraisals, and Prop. Mgmt.; **REP CLIENTS:** John Deere Co., Gen. Motors, Employee Transfer Corp.; **PREV EMPLOY:** Cert. Appraiser-Residential, AACA, RNMI; **PROFL AFFIL & HONORS:** RMNI, Johnson Cty. Bd. of Realtors, Pres. KS Assn. of Realtors, 1980; CRB; RNMI Realtor of the Yr., 1976; **EDUC:** BBA, 1963, Econ. & Mktg., Wichita State Univ.; **MIL SERV:** USAFR, E-5; **OTHER ACT & HONORS:** Bd. of Dir., Wichita State Univ. Alumni Assn.; **HOME ADD:** 14813 W 91st St., Lenexa, KS 66215, (913)888-8387; **BUS ADD:** 3500 W 75th St., Shawnee Mission, KS 66208, (913)384-1016.

COLEMAN, Ira J.——**B:** Aug. 2, 1903, San Francisco, CA, *Pres.*, Coleman Consulting Inc.; **PRIM RE ACT:** Consultant, Owner/Investor; **OTHER RE ACT:** On the Bd. of several resid. building corps.; **SERVICES:** Buy and sell RE for my own and client accts.; **PROFL AFFIL & HONORS:** Instit. of Mgmt. Consultants, Cert. Mgmt. Consultants; **EDUC:** BS, 1925, Econ., Univ. of CA; **GRAD EDUC:** MBA, 1927, Harvard Bus. School; **HOME ADD:** 6301 Castle Dr., Oakland, CA 94611, (415)531-8977; **BUS ADD:** 2401 Merced St., San Leandro, CA 94577, (415)482-4669.

COLEMAN, James H.——**B:** Mar. 15, 1944, San Antonio,TX, *Pres.*, Gaslight Sq. Devel. Corp.; **PRIM RE ACT:** Syndicator, Consultant, Appraiser, Developer; **OTHER RE ACT:** RE Research; **PREV EMPLOY:** VP Jagger Assoc. Austin, TX; Project Mgr. Devel. Research Assoc., L.A., CA; **EDUC:** BS, 1966, Bus. and RE, Trinity Univ. San Antonio, TX; **GRAD EDUC:** MS, Urban Land Econ., UCLA-School of Bus.; **EDUC HONORS:** Partial scholorship, Blue Key Nat. Honor Frat., Nat. Scholarship, Grad. studies in Fin. at Wharton School of Fin. and Commerce, Univ. of PA; **HOME ADD:** 300 S. Tumbleweed Trail, Austin, TX 78746, (512)263-2577; **BUS ADD:** 2724 E. Bee Caves Rd., Austin, TX 78746, (713)639-1515.

COLEMAN, Jennifer W.——**B:** Feb. 9, 1949, San Francisco, CA, *Devel. Accountant*, Dukes-Dukes & Assoc., Inc., RE; **OTHER RE ACT:** Accountant; **REP CLIENTS:** Dukes-Dukes & Assoc., Inc; San Francisco Housing Auth.; DD&A Consultants, Inc.; **PREV EMPLOY:** San Francisco Housing Auth., Sr. Rehabilitation Accountant; **PROFL AFFIL & HONORS:** Natl. Assn. of Black Accountants; **EDUC:** BA, 1973, Soc. Sci./Acctg., CA State Univ. at San Jose; **HOME ADD:** 4136 Carrington St., Oakland, CA 94601, (415)523-7922; **BUS ADD:** 1247 5th Ave., Oakland, CA 94606, (415)839-8633.

COLEMAN, Rod——**B:** June 3, 1957, Ft. Smith, AR, *Sr. VP*, ERC Peop. Inc.; **PRIM RE ACT:** Broker, Syndicator, Consultant, Developer, Builder, Property Manager, Owner/Investor; **PROFL AFFIL & HONORS:** NAHB, HBA, Acceptance for CPM; **OTHER ACT & HONORS:** Ft. Smith Planning Comm. 3 years; Ft. Smith Boys Shelter Dir.; **HOME ADD:** 10516 Riverview Dr, Ft. Smith, AR 72903, (501)542-6308; **BUS ADD:** 4720 Rogers Ave. Suite C, Ft. Smith, AR 72903, (301)452-9950.

COLEMAN, Ronald L.——**B:** Sept. 18, 1945, Wadena, MN, *Atty.*, Davies Pearson Anderson PS; **PRIM RE ACT:** Attorney; **SERVICES:** RE servs. and litigation, all areas; **REP CLIENTS:** Earl Mamlock Realty World; **PROFL AFFIL & HONORS:** ABA Real Prop. Sect.; WA State Bar Assn. Real Prop. Sect.; Pierce Cty. Bar Assn., City of Tacoma Planning Commn.; **EDUC:** BA, 1967, Philosophy, Sulpician Seminary of NW; **GRAD EDUC:** JD, 1972, Law, Willamette Univ. Coll. of Law; **EDUC HONORS:** Dean's List; Law Review Note Editor; **MIL SERV:** US Army; **BUS ADD:** PO Box 1657, 920 S Fawcett, Tacoma, WA 98401, (206)383-5461.

COLEMAN, U.L., III——**B:** Dec. 26, 1948, Marionville, MO, *Owner*, U.L. Coleman RE; **PRIM RE ACT:** Broker, Syndicator, Consultant, Developer, Builder, Property Manager, Owner/Investor; **SERVICES:** Prop. Mgmt., Gen. Contractor, Comml. RE; **PROFL AFFIL & HONORS:** IREM, Shreveport/Bossier Bd. of Realtors Boma ULI, CCIM, CPM; **EDUC:** Mathematics, Centenary Coll.; **HOME ADD:** 2409 Fairfield Ave., Shreveport, LA 71104, (318)424-7397; **BUS ADD:** 207 Milam St., Suite C, Shreveport, LA 71101, (318)221-0541.

COLEMAN, Walter L., III——**B:** Springfield, IL, *Chmn.*, Walco Realty Partners, Intl. Walco Consultants; **PRIM RE ACT:** Broker, Consultant, Developer, Owner/Investor, Syndicator; **SERVICES:**

Investment Counseling, RE workouts, Devel.; **REP CLIENTS:** Lenders & Investors; **PREV EMPLOY:** RE Devel./Consultant since 1964; Amer. Baptist Mgmt. Corp.; Non-profit Church Grps.; Harris Assocs. (Architects); Walco Realty Research Co. (Investor/Developer); **GRAD EDUC:** JD, Atlanta Law School; LLM, Prop., Woodrow Wilson Coll. of Law; **EDUC HONORS:** Delta Theta Phi Law Frat.; **OTHER ACT & HONORS:** Alumni Assn. Atlanta Law School & Woodrow Wilson Coll. of Law; A Founder: Christ the Mediator Lutheran Church, Chicago, IL; A Founder: Talent Assistance Program, Inc. (Chicago); A Founder: Chicago Community Ventures, Inc. (Venture Capital); Former Tres.: Home Investment Fund, Inc. Chicago IL (Second Mortgages); **HOME ADD:** PO Box 4330, Arlington, VA 22204; **BUS ADD:** 5550 Friendship Blvd. 250, Chevy Chase, MD 20815, (301)654-8977.

COLESSIDES, Nick J.——B: Jan. 14, 1938, Cavala, Greece, *Atty. at Law*; **PRIM RE ACT:** Consultant, Attorney, Syndicator; **SERVICES:** Legal servs. & consulting in connection with devel. const., leasing of comml. props., including all aspects thereof, and particularly in the area of planning zoning, and synd.; **REP CLIENTS:** FC Stangl Constr. & Devel., Hermes Assoc., Daines & Assoc., Mountain States Hospitality, Inc., Owners-Devels. of Comml. Props.; **PREV EMPLOY:** City Atty., City of W Jordan, UT, Asst. Cty. Atty., Salt Lake Cty., UT; **PROFL AFFIL & HONORS:** UT State Bar Assn.; **EDUC:** BS, 1963, Univ. of UT; **GRAD EDUC:** MS, 1967, Univ. of UT; JD, 1970, Univ. of UT; **OTHER ACT & HONORS:** UT Park City Atty., 1976-79; **HOME ADD:** 32 Haxton Pl., Salt Lake City, UT 84102, (801)364-2089; **BUS ADD:** 610 E South Temple, Salt Lake City, UT 84102, (801)521-4441.

COLIP, John R.——B: June 30, 1950, South Bend, IN, *Atty.*, Desenberg, Marrs, Colip & Carlin; **PRIM RE ACT:** Attorney; **SERVICES:** Review abstracts for title opinions, mort., foreclosures, condemnation representation; **REP CLIENTS:** State chartered bank, Fed. chartered S&L Assn., misc. land purchasers, misc. realtors; **PREV EMPLOY:** US Air Force, 1976-1980; **PROFL AFFIL & HONORS:** ABA; Berrien Cty. Bar Assn.; Admitted to Courts in State of MI, Western Fed. Dist. of MI, No. Fed. Dist. of IN, Ct. of Mil. Appeals; **EDUC:** Econ. - Liberal Arts, 1972, Econ., Univ. of Notre Dame; **GRAD EDUC:** JD, 1975, Law, Valparaiso Univ. School of Law; **MIL SERV:** USAF, Capt., 1976-1980, Commendation medal; **HOME ADD:** 510 W Fourth Street, Buchanan, MI 49107, (616)695-7497; **BUS ADD:** 223-225 E. Front St., PO Box 72, Buchanan, MI 49107, (616)695-1500.

COLLETTI, Paul J.——B: Oct. 28, 1939, New York, NY, *Principal & Counsel*, Preferred Land Services, Inc.; **PRIM RE ACT:** Consultant; **OTHER RE ACT:** Previous employment, sec. and counsel, First Hartford Corp. (RE Devel. & Textile Mfr.); Reg. Counsel, VP, Chicago Title Ins. Co., NY, NY; **PREV EMPLOY:** Chicago Title Ins. Co.; **PROFL AFFIL & HONORS:** NY State Bar Assn., NY City Lawyer's Assn., Assn. of the Bar of the City of NY, ABA, NY State Land Title Assn., Westchester-Fairfield Corp. Counsel Assn. (Chmn. RE Comm.), Member of NY, CT & Fed. Bars; **EDUC:** BA, 1962, Eng., Phil., St. John's Univ.; **GRAD EDUC:** JD, 1964, St. John's Univ., Sch. of Law; **EDUC HONORS:** Magna Cum Laude, Dean's List, Assoc. Ed. of Law Review, Recipient of Ins. and Practice Awards; **OTHER ACT & HONORS:** Author, Lecturer & Prof.; **HOME ADD:** RR 4, Kingswood Way, So. Salem, NY 10590, (914)533-2626; **BUS ADD:** 20 E 63rd St., New York, NY 10021, (212)308-1200.

COLLIE, H. Cris——*Exec. VP*, Employee Relocation; **OTHER RE ACT:** Profl. Assn. Admin.; **BUS ADD:** 1627 K St. NW, Washington, DC 20001, (202)857-0857.*

COLLIER, Russell——B: Apr. 10, 1923, St. Louis, MO, *Pres.*, Menlo Mgmt. Co.; **PRIM RE ACT:** Broker, Consultant, Developer, Owner/Investor, Property Manager; **OTHER RE ACT:** RE Mgmt.; **SERVICES:** RE investment & prop. mgmt.; **REP CLIENTS:** Pacific RE Investment Trust; **PREV EMPLOY:** Exec. VP - Pacific Plan, 1959-1970; **EDUC:** BA, 1946, Econ., Stanford Univ.; **GRAD EDUC:** MBA, 1948, Mktg., Stanford Univ.; **EDUC HONORS:** Cum Laude; **MIL SERV:** US Army, Lt., Bronze Star with Cluster, Purple Heart; **OTHER ACT & HONORS:** Treas., CA Rep. Party, 1972-1974; Bohemian Club; **HOME ADD:** 570 St. Francis, Menlo Park, CA 94025, (415)322-9723; **BUS ADD:** 770 Menlo Ave., Menlo Park, CA 94025, (415)327-7137.

COLLINS, Arthur F.——B: Nov. 11, 1943, Wellston, OH, *VP - Treas.*, United Realty Investors, Inc.; **PRIM RE ACT:** Broker; **OTHER RE ACT:** Chief Fin. Officer - RE Investment Co.; **PREV EMPLOY:** Treas. - Western Mort. Grp.; **PROFL AFFIL & HONORS:** AICPA, CA Soc. of CPA's, Cert. Pub. Acct.; **EDUC:** BS, 1966, Bus. Admin., CSU Nortridge; **HOME ADD:** 25620 Cielo Ct., Valencia, CA 91355, (805)255-0685; **BUS ADD:** 433 N. Camden Rd., Beverly Hills, CA 90210, (213)550-8791.

COLLINS, Bradfield J.——B: Jan. 30, 1924, Malden, MA, *RE Appraiser*, Brad Collins Agency; **PRIM RE ACT:** Appraiser; **SERVICES:** Appraisal of resid., comml. & indus. RE; **PREV EMPLOY:** Stone & Webster Engrg. Corp., New England Power Co., Gen. Electric Co.; **PROFL AFFIL & HONORS:** NAR, AIREA, MAI; **EDUC:** BS, 1950, EE, Univ. of MA; **MIL SERV:** US Army, Cpl.; **OTHER ACT & HONORS:** Chmn., Medford Housing Authority; Tr., Medford Savings Bank; **HOME ADD:** 58 Lincoln Rd., Medford, MA 02155, (617)396-5647; **BUS ADD:** 265 Salem St., Medford, MA 02155, (617)396-7590.

COLLINS, Charles L.——*VP*, Group One Development, Inc.; **PRIM RE ACT:** Broker, Developer; **SERVICES:** Site acquisition, devel. & leasing of comml. and indus. props.; **REP CLIENTS:** Lenders and indiv. or inst. investors in comml. & indus. props.; **PREV EMPLOY:** Coldwell, Banker & Co., Mission Viejo Co., CA; **PROFL AFFIL & HONORS:** NAIOP; **EDUC:** BS, 1957, Fin., Univ. of So. CAL; **MIL SERV:** USN, Lt. j.g.; **HOME ADD:** 30332 Benecia, Laguna Niguel, CA 92677, (714)831-0650; **BUS ADD:** 5160 Campus Dr., Newport Beach, CA 92660, (714)752-1005.

COLLINS, Frank——*Econ. Dev. Coord.*, Howard Cty. Econ. Development Office; **PRIM RE ACT:** Developer; **BUS ADD:** 3430 Cout House Dr., Ellicott City, MD 21043, (301)992-2345.*

COLLINS, John Gerald——B: Jan. 18, 1925, San Francisco, CA, *Sr. VP*, Ralph C. Sutro Co.; **PRIM RE ACT:** Broker, Consultant, Appraiser, Banker, Lender; **SERVICES:** Investment advisory, acquisition-sale major prop., fin.; **REP CLIENTS:** Pension funds, trusteed funds, instns.; **PREV EMPLOY:** Sr. VP, Emigrant Savings Bank, NY, NY; **PROFL AFFIL & HONORS:** AIREA; SREA; RE Bd. of NY, MAI; SRPA; **EDUC:** BS, 1947, Math., Stanford Univ.; **GRAD EDUC:** MBA, 1949, Bus., Stanford Univ.; **MIL SERV:** USN; Lt.; **HOME ADD:** 532 Adirondack Way, Walnut Creek, CA 94598, (415)932-5592; **BUS ADD:** 4900 Wilshire Blvd., Los Angeles, CA 90010, (213)932-1304.

COLLINS, John P.——B: Jan. 29, 1933, Seminole, OK, *Pres., CEO, Lexington Devel. Co.; Chmn. & CEO Transwestern Prop. Co.*, Lexington Development Co. and Transwestern Property Co.; **PRIM RE ACT:** Developer, Owner/Investor; **SERVICES:** Devel. office bldgs. & warehouses; land devel.; **PREV EMPLOY:** Sr. Partner, Trammell Crow Co., Dallas, TX; **PROFL AFFIL & HONORS:** Devels. Council GHHBA; **EDUC:** BBA, 1955, Mgmt., Univ. of Houston; **HOME ADD:** 5408 Westgrove Dr., Dallas, TX 75248, (214)931-6059; **BUS ADD:** 12201 Merit Dr., Ste. 170, Dallas, TX 75251, (214)233-1022.

COLLINS, LeRoy, Jr.——B: Sept. 3, 1934, Tallahassee, FL, *Broker/Pres.*, Dynamic Realty of Tampa, Inc.; **PRIM RE ACT:** Broker, Developer, Owner/Investor, Syndicator; **OTHER RE ACT:** Data Processor; **PREV EMPLOY:** Pres., Fin. Transaction Systems, Inc. since founding in 1969; **PROFL AFFIL & HONORS:** Tampa Bd. of Realtors, CCIM Candidate; SRS Candidate; **EDUC:** BS, 1956, US Naval Academy; **MIL SERV:** USN, Capt., US Naval Res.; **OTHER ACT & HONORS:** Who's Who in US; **HOME ADD:** 418 Blanca Ave., Tampa, FL 33606, (813)257-7762; **BUS ADD:** 15 Barbados Ave., Tampa, FL 33606, (813)251-5042.

COLLINS, Max——*VP Pers.*, Hon Industries, Inc.; **PRIM RE ACT:** Property Manager; **BUS ADD:** 414 E. Third St., Muscatine, IA 52761, (319)264-7100.*

COLLINS, Michael D.——B: July 4, 1943, Memphis, TN, *VP*, The Fairson Co., Inc.; **PRIM RE ACT:** Broker, Property Manager; **SERVICES:** Specialize in downtown leasing and prop. mgmt. plus gen. brokerage; **REP CLIENTS:** Owners of their own bus.; indiv. investors; corp. officers; **PREV EMPLOY:** Asst. Hosp. Administrator; Squadron Sec. Cmdr., USAF; **PROFL AFFIL & HONORS:** Bldg. Owners & Mgrs. Assn., Instit. of RE Mgmt.; Gr. Tulsa Bd. of Realtors; Air Force Assn.; Bd. of Dir. of Planned Parenthood of Northeastern OK, Inc., CPM; **EDUC:** BBA, 1965, Mktg./Bus. Mgmt., Univ. of OK; **GRAD EDUC:** Masters in Hosp. Admin., 1973, Mgmt. of Hospitals, Univ. of MN; **EDUC HONORS:** Outstanding Clerkship Paper; **MIL SERV:** USAF, Capt., Commendation Medal; **OTHER ACT & HONORS:** Pi Kappa Alpha Social Fraternity; Leadership Tulsa (Class VI); USAF - Admissions Liaison Officer; First Presbyterian Church Choir; Philcrest Tennis Club; **HOME ADD:** 1728 E 56th St., Tulsa, OK 74105, (918)743-5070; **BUS ADD:** 507 S. Main St., #401, Tulsa, OK 74103, (918)587-0303.

COLLINS, M.L.——*SIR Mgr. RE & Indus.*, Phillips Petroleum Company; **PRIM RE ACT:** Property Manager; **BUS ADD:** 546 Phillips Bldg. Annex, Bartlesville, OK 74004, (918)661-5185.*

COLLINS, Moseley——**B:** May 29, 1922, Tallahassee, FL, *Owner*, Collins & Co.; **PRIM RE ACT:** Engineer; **SERVICES:** Civil, Structural & Sanitary Engrg.; **PREV EMPLOY:** County Engr. Sarasota, Pinellas, Martin & Okeechobee; **PROFL AFFIL & HONORS:** FES, ASCE, NAPE; **EDUC:** BS, 1947, GA Tech.; **MIL SERV:** USAF, 1st Lt.; **HOME ADD:** 2684 Starwood Cir., Okeechobee, FL 33472, (305)964-7000; **BUS ADD:** 103 SW Third Ave., Okeechobee, FL 33472, (813)763-1600.

COLLINS, Ralph V.——**B:** Feb. 3, 1921, Herman, PA, *Pres.*, Ralph V. Collins Realty Inc.; **PRIM RE ACT:** Broker, Consultant, Appraiser, Property Manager, Owner/Investor; **OTHER RE ACT:** Past Pres. of Bd. of Realtors, now on Bd. of Dirs.; **SERVICES:** Counseling, qualifying, arranging financing, etc.; **PREV EMPLOY:** Salesman for McCalls RE prior to having my own office 10 yrs. ago; **PROFL AFFIL & HONORS:** Member of the local, state, & NAR, RE Broker, GRI, CRS & CRB; **EDUC:** RE, 1971, Penn. Grad. Realtors Inst.; **GRAD EDUC:** NAR CRB, 1980, Mgmt. of Brokerage Office, RNMI; **MIL SERV:** US Army Med., Sgt. 1942-45, Good Conduct Medal, African Mid-Eastern Campaign, Italian Campaign, France Campaign; **OTHER ACT & HONORS:** Butler Area School Bd. 1951 - 1962; Member Church Council, St. Andrews RC Church; Fourth Degree Knight, K of C; **HOME ADD:** 205 Cedar Rd., Butler, PA 16001, (412)287-7532; **BUS ADD:** 330 N. Main St., Butler, PA 16001, (412)287-0771.

COLLINS, Robert L.——**B:** Jan. 12, 1929, Bronx, NY, *Controller, Operating Servs.*, McGraw Hill, Inc., Corp.; **PRIM RE ACT:** Builder, Owner/Investor, Property Manager; **SERVICES:** Constr. lease admin., purchase, sales, relocation; **PROFL AFFIL & HONORS:** NACORE (Pres. NYC Chapt., 1979), Rho Epsilon; **EDUC:** BA, 1968, Hist., Rutgers Univ., Magna Cum Laude; **MIL SERV:** USMC, Cpl.; **OTHER ACT & HONORS:** Author book *Comml. Leasing, Atcom, Inc., NY 1977; Chapt. 36 'RE Planning & Control' in the Corporate Controller's Manual*, Warren Gorham & Lamont, Boston, 1981; Article 'Company Moving? How to Hold People', Administrative Mgmt., Nov. 1969; Article 'The Shrinking Square Foot', Admin. Mgmt., Oct, 1977; Article 'Rental Escalation, A New Threat to Office Costs', Admin. Mgmt., Dec. 1978; Article 'Energy Mgmt. & Post-Audits', The Journal of Prop. Mgmt., Sept., Oct. 1979; **HOME ADD:** 174 High St., Metuchen, NJ 08840; **BUS ADD:** 1221 Ave. of the Amers., New York, NY 10020, (212)997-6381.

COLLINS, Scott, Jr.——**B:** Sept. 2, 1931, Frankfort, KY, Scott Collins Co.; **PRIM RE ACT:** Consultant, Appraiser; **SERVICES:** RE Valuation & Consultation; **REP CLIENTS:** TVA, State of TN, various govt. agencies, banks, S&L's, major corps., oil cos., mort. brokers, etc.; **PROFL AFFIL & HONORS:** NAR; AIREA; Soc. of RE Appraisers; Amer. Soc. of Appraisers; Am. R.O.W. Assn., MAI, SRPA, Pres. local chaps. of these; Dist. Vice Gov., Soc. of RE Appraisers; **EDUC:** BS, 1958, Fin. & RE, Univ. of IN; **MIL SERV:** US Army, Lt. Col.; **OTHER ACT & HONORS:** Bd. Knoxville Symphony Soc.; **HOME ADD:** 5215 LaVesta Rd., Knoxville, TN 37918, (615)687-3024; **BUS ADD:** 2823 Essary Rd., PO Box 5444, Knoxville, TN 37918, (615)689-4334.

COLLINS, Susan Sonnek——**B:** Oct. 20, 1950, Mobridge, SD, *Atty.*, Finley, Kumble, Wagner, Heine, Underberg & Casey, Tax; **PRIM RE ACT:** Attorney; **SERVICES:** Tax atty.; **PREV EMPLOY:** Rainier Nat. Bank, Seattle, WA; **PROFL AFFIL & HONORS:** Delta Theta Phi, IA, WA & SD Bar Assns., ABA-Real Prop., Probate and Trust Sec., Outstanding Young Women of Amer.; **EDUC:** BA, 1973, Eng., Univ. of SD; **GRAD EDUC:** JD, 1976, Univ. of SD; **HOME ADD:** 6033 Liberty Bell Ct., Burke, VA 22015, (703)451-7278; **BUS ADD:** 1120 Connecticut Ave., NW, Suite 1010, Washington, DC 20036, (202)857-4470.

COLLINS, Terence P.——**B:** July 5, 1943, Philadelphia, PA, *Sr. VP*, Binswanger Co.; **PRIM RE ACT:** Broker, Consultant, Developer, Property Manager; **SERVICES:** Eval., devel., mktg., mgmt. of comml. & indus. bldgs.; **PREV EMPLOY:** IBM Corp., Sr. Mktg. Rep., Data Processing Div., 1968-1972; **PROFL AFFIL & HONORS:** Philadelphia BOMA; **EDUC:** BS, 1966, Mktg., LaSalle Coll.; **HOME ADD:** 13 Rotterdam E., Holland, PA 18966, (215)355-7987; **BUS ADD:** 1845 Walnut St., Philadephia, PA 19103, (215)448-6000.

COLLINS, Wm. Dennis——**B:** Oct. 17, 1942, *Sr. Facilities Planner*, Graco Inc., Corp. Facilities; **OTHER RE ACT:** Corp. RE Rep.; **SERVICES:** Full RE and facilities planning services; **PROFL AFFIL & HONORS:** MN Indus. Devel. Assoc.; **EDUC:** 1970, Ind. Psych./Bus. Admin., Univ. of MN; **HOME ADD:** 1508 143rd Ln. NE, Anoka, MN 55433, (612)755-3506; **BUS ADD:** 88 11th Ave. NE, Minneapolis, MN 55440, (612)623-6449.

COLLINS, William W.——**B:** Feb 20, 1931, Dallas, TX, *Senior VP*, Judson Realty, Inc.; **PRIM RE ACT:** Broker, Appraiser, Developer, Owner/Investor; **PREV EMPLOY:** William Pitt Real Estate, Stamford, CT; **PROFL AFFIL & HONORS:** RE Bd. of NY; **EDUC:** BA, 1953, Hist., Amherst Coll.; **MIL SERV:** USNR; **HOME ADD:** 47 Grace Church St., Rye, NY 10580, (914)967-5063; **BUS ADD:** 50 W 57th St., New York, NY 10019, (212)974-1900.

COLLIS, William A.——*Exec. VP*, RESSI; **OTHER RE ACT:** Profl. trade org. mgmt.; **BUS ADD:** 430 N. Michigan Ave., Chicago, IL 60611.

COLLISTER, Edward G., Jr.——**B:** Oct. 8, 1939, Bayshore, LI, NY, *Part.*, Collister & Kampschroeder; **PRIM RE ACT:** Attorney, Developer, Owner/Investor; **SERVICES:** Legal advice for clients, normal services for managing RE investment entities of which I am a part owner; **PROFL AFFIL & HONORS:** ABA, KS Bar Assn., Couglas Co. Bar Assn.; **EDUC:** BA, 1961, Poli Sci. & Hist., Univ. of KS; **GRAD EDUC:** LLB, 1964, Univ. of KS; **EDUC HONORS:** Summerfield Scholar, Honor Roll, Law Review including outstanding writing award; Nat. Moot Court Team; The class of 1937 scholarship; Rocky Mtn. Mineral Law found. scholarship; **OTHER ACT & HONORS:** Asst. Atty. Gen., State of KS 1969-1973; Chief Litigation Div. 1970-1973; Chief Criminal Div. 1972; Examiner, KS Commn. on Judicial Qualifications (1974-present); **HOME ADD:** 520 Millstone, Lawrence, KS 66044, (913)842-5918; **BUS ADD:** 2103 Orchard Lane, Lawrence, KS 66044, (913)842-3126.

COLLOPY, Eamonn E.——**B:** Dec. 4, 1944, New York, NY, *Sr. VP*, Draper and Kramer, Inc., Corp. Services Div.; **PRIM RE ACT:** Broker, Consultant, Developer, Property Manager; **SERVICES:** Corp. relocation, office bldg. devel., leasing and mgmt.; **REP CLIENTS:** Major insurance cos. and corporate clients; **PREV EMPLOY:** Intl. Bus. Machines and Control Data; **PROFL AFFIL & HONORS:** BOMA, IREM, NAIOP, RPA; **EDUC:** BS, 1978, Econ., Fordham; **GRAD EDUC:** MBA, 1976, Strategic Planning, Columbia Grad. School of Bus.; **EDUC HONORS:** Summa Cum Laude; **HOME ADD:** 2010 Glendale Ave., Northbrook, IL 60062, (312)272-3418; **BUS ADD:** 33 W. Monroe, Chicago, IL 60603, (312)346-8600.

COLLURA, Mario A.——**B:** May 5, 1940, Cleveland, OH, *Pres.*, MDR Development Company; **PRIM RE ACT:** Broker, Consultant, Engineer, Developer, Builder, Owner/Investor, Property Manager, Insuror, Syndicator; **OTHER RE ACT:** Timeshare devel., travel operation, media products, timeshare sales; **SERVICES:** Full Service in all above activities; **PREV EMPLOY:** Xerox Corp., Mgr. 1969-74; Hughes Aircraft Co., Mgr. 1962-69; **PROFL AFFIL & HONORS:** Venice Marina, Santa Monica and Culver City Bd. of Realtors, Venice, Marina and Culver C of C; **EDUC:** BSEE, 1962, Case Western Reserve Univ., Cleveland, OH; **GRAD EDUC:** Studies towards MBA, 1969-70, UCLA; **HOME ADD:** 4283 Moore St., Los Angeles, CA 90066, (213)397-8022; **BUS ADD:** 13470 Washington Blvd., Marina Del Rey, CA 90291, (213)823-1200.

COLMER, James H.——**B:** Oct. 28, 1923, Pascagoula, MS, *Atty.*, Sole Practitioner; **PRIM RE ACT:** Attorney; **SERVICES:** Loan closings, advising fed. RE regulations, invest. counseling; **REP CLIENTS:** Pascagoula S&L Assn.; Ingallas Employees Credit Union; Vickers Homes Inc.; **PROFL AFFIL & HONORS:** Amer. Judicature Soc.; ABA; MS State Bar; Jackson County Bar; Amer. Coll. of Mort. Attys.; MS Bar Found., Past Pres., Jackson Cty. Bar Assn.; Former City Atty. for Pascagoula & Moss Point, MS; **EDUC:** Univ. of MS, Columbia Univ., Univ. of MD, Millsaps Coll.; **GRAD EDUC:** JD, 1950, Law, Univ. of MS, George Washington Univ.; **MIL SERV:** USN, Lt.j.g.; **HOME ADD:** 2101 Beach Blvd., Pascagoula, MS 39567, (601)762-3321; **BUS ADD:** PO Box 1936, Pascagoula, MS 39567, (601)762-1414.

COLWELL, Peter F.——**B:** Oct. 21, 1943, Royal Oak, MI, *Assoc. Prof. of Fin.*, Univ. of IL at Champaign-Urbana; **OTHER RE ACT:** Consulting, Instruction, Research; **SERVICES:** Numerous journal articles, market studies; **PREV EMPLOY:** Univ. of GA, NBS, Howard Univ.; **PROFL AFFIL & HONORS:** AEA, Amer. RE & Urban Econ. Assn.; **EDUC:** BA, 1965, Econ. & Art, Albion Coll.; **GRAD EDUC:** MA, 1969, Urban Econ., Wayne State Univ.; Ph.D, 1973, Wayne State Univ.; **EDUC HONORS:** MI Scholars in Coll. Teaching, Omicron Delta Epsilon, NDEA Fellowship RFF-CUE Fellowship; **HOME ADD:** 2305 Barberry Dr., Champaign, IL 61820, (217)351-3007; **BUS ADD:** 1407 W. Gregory, Urbana, IL 61801, (217)333-2339.

COMBER, Frank J.——**B:** July 22, 1940, TN, *Dir. Design & Const.*, Homart Devel. Co.; **PRIM RE ACT:** Architect, Builder; **SERVICES:** Design & const. all projects; **PROFL AFFIL & HONORS:** Intl. Council of Shopping Centers, Regist. Architect; **EDUC:** BArch, 1963, Arch., Univ. of IL; **GRAD EDUC:** MBA, 1974, Fin., Loyca Univ.;

MIL SERV: US Air. Nat. Guard; **HOME ADD:** 42 Lea Rd., Barrington, IL 60010, (312)382-2519; **BUS ADD:** 55 West Monroe, Chicago, IL 60603, (312)875-9874.

COMBS, Ken——B: Nov. 30, 1950, Norfolk, VA, *Broker-Owner; Asst. Prof./Chmn.*, Dept. of RE, Del Mar Coll.; Ken Combs Realtors; **PRIM RE ACT:** Broker, Owner/Investor; **SERVICES:** Resid.-Comml.-RE Consultant; **PROFL AFFIL & HONORS:** Corpus Christi Bd. of Realtors; **EDUC:** BS, 1975, Psychology, TX A&I; **GRAD EDUC:** MBA, 1977, Mgmt. & Fin., Corpus Christi State Univ.; **OTHER ACT & HONORS:** Dir., Corpus Christi Teachers Credit Union Dir., RE Ed. Foundation; **HOME TEL:** (512)991-8991; **BUS ADD:** 4925 Everhart, Suite 120, Corpus Christi, TX 78411, (512)855-8483.

COMEY, J.B.——*Dir. RE*, Curtiss-Wright Corp.; **PRIM RE ACT:** Property Manager; **BUS ADD:** One Passaic St., Wood-Ridge, NJ 07075, (201)777-2900.*

COMFORT, Patrick C.——B: Sept. 21, 1930, Tacoma, WA, *Pres.*, Patrick C. Comfort, Inc., P.S.; **PRIM RE ACT:** Attorney, Developer, Syndicator; **REP CLIENTS:** Brownfield, Ltd.; Narrows Plaza; Regents Investment Co.; Meridian Devel. Group; **PREV EMPLOY:** Actively engaged in practice of the law for 25 yrs.; **PROFL AFFIL & HONORS:** ABA; WA State Bar Assn.; Tacoma Pierce Cty. Bar Assn., Member Bd. of Gov., WA State Bar Assn. (6th Dist.); Past Pres., Tacoma-Pierce Cty. Bar Assn.; **EDUC:** BA, 1952, Philosophy, Eng. Poli. Sci., Conzaga Univ.; **GRAD EDUC:** LLB, 1955, NY Univ. School of Law; **EDUC HONORS:** Cum Laude, Root-Tilden Fellow; **MIL SERV:** US Army, Sp/3; **OTHER ACT & HONORS:** Rep., State House of Reps., 1960-64; Bd. of Dir., Tumwater State Bank; W. WA State Univ. Bd. of Trustees 1970-77; **HOME ADD:** 1031 Crestwood Ln., Fircrest, WA 98466, (206)564-6046; **BUS ADD:** 1201 Regents Blvd., Fircrest, WA 98466, (206)564-8400.

COMMANDER, Charles E., III——B: Aug. 17, 1940, Jacksonville, FL, *Part.*, Commander, Legler, Werber & Dawes; **PRIM RE ACT:** Consultant, Attorney, Banker, Developer, Owner/Investor, Property Manager, Syndicator; **PREV EMPLOY:** Mahoney Hadlow Chambers & Adams, Barnett, Winston Co.; **PROFL AFFIL & HONORS:** FL Bar, ABA; **EDUC:** BS, 1962, Bus. & Econ., Commerce, Washington & Lee Univ.; **GRAD EDUC:** JD, 1965, Univ. of FL; **EDUC HONORS:** Law Review; **HOME ADD:** 3839 Ortega Blvd., Jacksonville, FL 32210, (904)388-1951; **BUS ADD:** 2000 Independent Sq., Jacksonville, FL 32202, (904)354-0424.

COMPOMIZZO, O. "Compy"——B: Sept. 19, 1928, Hartford, AK, *Deputy Dist. Dir.*, CA Dept. of Transportation; **PRIM RE ACT:** Broker, Appraiser; **OTHER RE ACT:** Mgr. Right of Way Dept.; **SERVICES:** Acquisition of R/W for state highways; **PREV EMPLOY:** 28 yrs. with Dept. of Trans.; **PROFL AFFIL & HONORS:** AIREA, MAI, Broker; **EDUC:** BA, 1953, Poli. Sci., CA State Univ. at Sacramento; **OTHER ACT & HONORS:** Member, Yuba City Planning Commn., 1960-1965; **HOME ADD:** 4025 Meander Dr., Redding, CA 96001, (916)246-0161; **BUS ADD:** 1657 Riverside Dr., Redding, CA 96001, (916)246-6267.

COMSTOCK, John B., II——B: June 20, 1924, Meriden, CT, *Owner/Broker*, Essex Real Estate Co.; **PRIM RE ACT:** Broker, Consultant, Appraiser, Developer, Builder, Owner/Investor, Instructor, Property Manager, Assessor; **PREV EMPLOY:** Have had own co. for 12 yrs.; previously was Comml. RE Broker for Allied Brokers of CT; **PROFL AFFIL & HONORS:** NAR; Lower CT River Bd. of Realtors; **EDUC:** BArch., 1944, Arch., Univ. of So. CA; **GRAD EDUC:** 1947, Metallurgy/Power Metal, Stevens Inst. of Tech.; **MIL SERV:** US ROTC; **HOME ADD:** 6 Cook Hill Woods Rd., Essex, CT 06426, (203)767-1718; **BUS ADD:** 63 N. Main St., Essex, CT 06426, (203)767-0979.

CON, Walter J.——B: Aug. 11, 1955, Chicago, IL, *Asst. VP/ Lending*, Bellflower S&L Assn., Lending; **PRIM RE ACT:** Owner/Investor; **SERVICES:** RE and Consumer Lending; **PREV EMPLOY:** 3 Yrs. Home Fed. S&L Assn.; **EDUC:** Bus. Admin., 1978, Fin., San Diego State Univ.; **GRAD EDUC:** 1981, Mgmt., Pepperdine Univ.; **HOME ADD:** 182 Tangelo, Irvine, CA 92714, (714)559-0683; **BUS ADD:** 16108 Bellflower Blvd., Bellflower, CA 90706, (213)867-7243.

CONDIOTTI, A.——B: Dec. 8, 1921, New York, NY, *Pres.*, Condiotti Enterprises, Inc., Debra Investment Corp.; **PRIM RE ACT:** Developer, Builder, Owner/Investor; **SERVICES:** Land devel., constr. of resid. and comml. props.; **PROFL AFFIL & HONORS:** Bldg. Indus. Assn., Nat. Assn. of Home Builders, Sonoma Cty. Alliance, Santa Rosa C of C; **EDUC:** BS, 1942, Econ., Brooklyn Coll.; **MIL SERV:** USN, Lt. Comdr.; **HOME ADD:** 1120 Wikiup Dr., Santa Rosa, CA 95401, (707)528-8214; **BUS ADD:** PO Box 6855, Santa Rosa, CA 95406, (707)544-7194.

CONDON, Donald S.——B: Dec. 26, 1930, Brooklyn, NY, *Chmn.*, The Condon Corp.; **PRIM RE ACT:** Broker, Consultant, Developer, Syndicator; **SERVICES:** Consulting, fin., org., feasibility studies, marketing serv. and devel.; **REP CLIENTS:** Chemical Bank, Morgan Guaranty Trust Co., Citicorp, Chase Manhattan Bank, Saloman Bros., Philadelphia Nat. Bank, Continental IL Bank; **PREV EMPLOY:** Chmn., Condyne Inc.; Bd. of Dir., Sterodyne Inc.; Chmn. of Parr, O'Mara, Condon Assoc. Inc.; Sales and Mktg., Owens-Coring Fiberglass Corp.; Condon Investment and Devel. Corp. (Howard & Kennith Co.); **PROFL AFFIL & HONORS:** Broward Cty. Planning Council; Who's Who Indus. & Fin.; Amer. Biographical Inst.; Intl. & Biographical Assn. - Men of Achievement; Intl. Platform Assn., Amer. Home Builders Award; Better Homes & Gardens Editors Award; Profl. Builders Top Merchandising Award; **EDUC:** BA, 1953, Hist./Educ., NW Univ.; **GRAD EDUC:** Grad. Work, Bus./Law, Univ. of Detroit/Oakland Univ./Univ. of Toledo; **EDUC HONORS:** Scholarship; **MIL SERV:** US Army, Cpl., 1953-1955; **OTHER ACT & HONORS:** Palm Beach Yacht Club; PGA Nat. Golf Club; The Beach Club; Birmingham AC; NY AC; Subject of Articles in House & Home, Profl. Builder, Business Week, Multi Housing News, Institl. Investor, RE Review; **HOME ADD:** 215 Jamaica Ln., Palm Beach, FL 33480, (305)848-9615; **BUS ADD:** PO Box 2007, Palm Beach, FL 33480, (305)659-3630.

CONDON, F. Milton——B: June 10, 1934, Brooklyn, NY, *Partner*, Condon and Condon; **PRIM RE ACT:** Attorney; **SERVICES:** Advice and counseling in connection with all types of RE matters and litigation.; **REP CLIENTS:** United Multiple Listing, local realty bds., pvt. devel. and RE brokers.; **PREV EMPLOY:** RE loan broker; **PROFL AFFIL & HONORS:** Instr. in RE Fin. at Santa Monica Coll.; local and CA state bar assn., lic. RE broker., JD; **EDUC:** 1956, Psych. and Bus., UCLA; **GRAD EDUC:** JD, 1959, School of Law, Univ. of Southern CA; **HOME ADD:** c/o 632 Arizona Avenue, Santa Monica, CA 90401, (213)393-0701; **BUS ADD:** 632 Arizona Avenue, Santa Monica, CA 90401, (213)393-0701.

CONDON, Gerald M.——B: Mar. 17, 1931, Minneapolis, MN, *Atty.*, Partner: Condon & Condon, Attys.; **PRIM RE ACT:** Attorney; **EDUC:** BA, 1954, UCLA; **GRAD EDUC:** LLB, 1957, Law, Loyola Law School; **MIL SERV:** USAF; **HOME ADD:** 1515 San Vicente Blvd., Santa Monica, CA 90402, (213)451-4130; **BUS ADD:** 632 Arizona Ave., Santa Monica, CA 90401, (213)393-0701.

CONDON, Warwick A.——B: May 14, 1937, Sydney, Australia, *Pres.*, Mgmt. Dusco Prop. Mgmt.; **PRIM RE ACT:** Developer, Property Manager; **REP CLIENTS:** Intl. income prop., US Lend Lease, F.G.I. Investors; **PREV EMPLOY:** Hooker-Barnes, Atlanta, GA; **PROFL AFFIL & HONORS:** Intl. Council of Shopping Ctrs., BSC; **EDUC:** BS; **GRAD EDUC:** B.Sc. (Tech), 1964, Civil. Engrg., Univ. of NSW; **HOME ADD:** 707 Berger Rd., Tampa, FL 33549, (813)963-2901; **BUS ADD:** Suite 73-730 5201 W. Kennedy Blvd., Tampa, FL 33609, (813)877-5588.

CONDORODIS, A. John——B: Apr. 13, 1933, Cincinnati OH, *VP*, Chelsea Moore Co., Comml. Indus. Div.; **PRIM RE ACT:** Broker, Consultant, Appraiser, Developer, Builder, Owner/Investor, Property Manager, Syndicator; **OTHER RE ACT:** Mergers and acquisitions; **SERVICES:** same as primary RE activities; **REP CLIENTS:** Gen. Electric, Kroger Co., Ford, Formica, Kenner Prods./Gen. Mills., Intl. Harvester, US Shoe, Firestone, Sperry & Hutchinson, DuBois Chem., Chemed Corp., Avon Products, Ralston Purina; **PREV EMPLOY:** Dietz Realty (1960-67), Theodore Mayer & Bro., Inc. (1967-73), Chelsea Moore Co. (1973 to present); **PROFL AFFIL & HONORS:** Cincinnati Bd. of Realtors, OH Assn. of Realtors, Nat. Assn. of Realtors, Alternate Tr. to OH Bd. of Realtors, SIR; **EDUC:** BBA, Acctg., Univ. of Cincinnati; **GRAD EDUC:** MBA, 1959, Mktg./Fin., Univ. of Cincinnati; **EDUC HONORS:** Dean's List, Dean's List & Beta Gamma Sigma; **MIL SERV:** ROTC, 2nd Lt.; **OTHER ACT & HONORS:** Retention/Expansion Comm., 1973-76, C of C, Indus. Revenue Bond Comm., 1978-present, local mktg. comm., Univ. of Cincinnati VP, Chmn Sesquiscentennial Fund, Team Capt. and Solicitor of Corp. Funds from 1961 to present, Past member UNOCIN, Present member UCATS; Church Bd. of Trs., VP, Sec. & Treas.; Order of AHEPA, Pres. & VP; also Bd. of Govs. on Dist. Lodge and Supreme Lodge levels. Sigma Chi Frat. and Sigma Sigma Frat., VP & Sec. OH Valley Ski Council, Past Pres. Cincinnati Ski Club, Member Cuvier Press Club, Kentucky Col., Assoc. of Yr. Finalist, Cincinnati Bd. of Realtors; **HOME ADD:** 831 Suire Ave., Cincinnati, OH 45205, (513)471-3618; **BUS ADD:** Suite 200, 105 W 4th St., Cincinnati, OH 45202, (513)621-1161.

CONE, Ray——*Corp RE Mgr.*, Textroix, Inc.; **PRIM RE ACT:** Property Manager; **BUS ADD:** PO Box 500, Beaverton, OR 97077, (503)644-0161.*

CONIGLIARO, Anthony S.——B: Apr. 25, 1950, New York, NY, *VP and COO*, Realty and Equipment Corp.; **PRIM RE ACT:** Owner/Investor; **PREV EMPLOY:** Coopers & Lybrand, 1974-1980; **PROFL AFFIL & HONORS:** AICPA; NY State Soc. of CPAs, CPA; **EDUC:** BSBA, 1972, Fin., Georgetown Univ.; **GRAD EDUC:** MBA, 1973, Acctg., Syracuse Univ.; **HOME ADD:** 70 Bayview Dr., Huntington, NY 11743, (516)549-8696; **BUS ADD:** 230 Park Ave., New York, NY 10169, (212)599-1925.

CONIGLIO, Vincent——*Pres.*, Champion Mortgage Company; **PRIM RE ACT:** Banker, Lender, Owner/Investor; **OTHER RE ACT:** Nat. Mortgage Banker/Debt Lender; **SERVICES:** Forward End-Loan Commitments on Residential (FHLMC); Forward Stand-By Commitments on Commercial Properties; **PREV EMPLOY:** First Financial mortgage serving Corp. & First New York Co.; **PROFL AFFIL & HONORS:** NY Credit Men's Assn., NAHB, SDBCA, Fin. Speaker at Various Nat. Fin. Shows, 16 times a year; **BUS ADD:** 3838 Camino Del Rio North, Suite 361, San Diego, CA 92108, (714)563-1650.

CONKLIN, Bruce Cox, Jr.——B: Feb. 11, 1947, Utica, NY, *Partner*, Greenwich Development Co.; **PRIM RE ACT:** Developer, Builder, Owner/Investor; **SERVICES:** Devel. of Comml., Indus. and Resid. Props.; **REP CLIENTS:** Lenders and indiv. and instnl. investors; **PREV EMPLOY:** Oxford Devel./Dunn Intl., 1977-1980, Peat, Marwick, Mitchell & Co., 1969-1976; **EDUC:** BS, 1969, Acctg., Lehigh Univ.; **HOME ADD:** 19432 Sierra Lago, Irvine, CA 92715, (714)955-3041; **BUS ADD:** 19762 MacArthur Blvd., Irvine, CA 92715, (714)851-8333.

CONKLIN, Robert B.——B: June 24, 1938, Shreveport, LA, *VP*, Smith-Ritchie/Landsing, Inc., Acquisitions; **PRIM RE ACT:** Broker, Consultant, Attorney, Owner/Investor, Syndicator; **PREV EMPLOY:** Partner: Lindsay, Hart, Neil & Weigler, Attys. At Law, Portland, OR; **PROFL AFFIL & HONORS:** OR State Bar, Amer. Bar Assn., Nat. Assn. of Realtors, Portland Bd. of Realtors, RNMI; **EDUC:** BA, 1962, Govt., Dartmouth Coll.; **GRAD EDUC:** JD, 1965, Law, Boalt Hall School of Law, Univ. of CA at Berkeley; **EDUC HONORS:** Cum Laude; **MIL SERV:** US Army, SP4; **HOME ADD:** 2744 S.W. Upper Dr., Portland, OR 97201, (503)222-4129; **BUS ADD:** 133 S.W. 2nd, Portland, OR 97204, (503)227-2654.

CONLEY, James C., Jr.——B: Apr. 11, 1947, Bethesda, MD, *VP Inv. Prop.*, The Carey Winston Co.; **PRIM RE ACT:** Broker; **SERVICES:** Sale of Inv. Prop.; **PROFL AFFIL & HONORS:** WA BR, Lifetime Member (WBR) Million Dollar Sales Club, Highest Gross Sales Vol. 1978 (WBR); **EDUC:** BSBA, Mgmt., Georgetown Univ., WA, DC; **EDUC HONORS:** Dean's List Jr. yr. (1968) & Sr. Yr. (1969); **MIL SERV:** Army Reserve, PFC; **OTHER ACT & HONORS:** Columbia Ctry. Club, Chevy Chase, MD; **HOME ADD:** 5318 Woodlawn Ave., Chevy Chase, MD 20015, (301)986-1329; **BUS ADD:** 4350 E-W Hwy., Ste. 200, Bethesda, MD 20014, (301)656-4212.

CONLEY, Kenneth S.——B: July 5, 1922, Holladay, TN, *Owner*, Conley and Company Architects; **PRIM RE ACT:** Architect, Owner/Investor; **OTHER RE ACT:** Landscape Architect; **SERVICES:** Planning, arch., landscape planning; **REP CLIENTS:** Medical facilities including hospitals, nursing homes, clinics, housing; **PROFL AFFIL & HONORS:** Arbitrator, Amer. Arbitration Assn.; Soc. Amer. Registered Architects, Licensed in TN, AR, LA, MS, AL, GA, SC, NC, KY and IN; **EDUC:** 1951, Arch., Tulane Univ.; **GRAD EDUC:** MArch., 1952, Arch., VA Polytechnic Inst. and State Univ.; **MIL SERV:** US Army, Tech. IV; WWII; Far East; **HOME ADD:** Rt. 5, Collins Rd., Nashville, TN 37221; **BUS ADD:** West 70 Bldg., 6922 Harding Rd., Nashville, TN 37221, (615)356-4799.

CONN, David——B: Jan. 21, 1946, Waynesburg, PA, *VP*, McFadden & Sprowis, Realtors; **PRIM RE ACT:** Broker, Instructor; **PREV EMPLOY:** Gen. Mgr. for two large RE Firms in Pittsburgh - Owner of RE Firm in Uniontown, PA; **PROFL AFFIL & HONORS:** NAR, CRB, CRS, GRI; **EDUC:** AB, 1967, Bus. Admin., Grove City Coll., Grove City, PA; **MIL SERV:** US Army, 1st Lt., Viet Nam Ribbons; **OTHER ACT & HONORS:** SAR - Pres. 1980 and 1981, Past Pres. Fayette Bd. of Realtors & Realtor of the Year 1974, Fayette Cty., PA; **HOME ADD:** 232 Baltusrol Dr., Naples, FL 33942, (813)774-0323; **BUS ADD:** 4700 Tamiami Tr. N, Naples, FL 33940, (813)261-1551.

CONNAUGHTON, William, Jr.——B: Boston, MA, *Pres.*, Algonquin Indus. Realty, Inc.; **PRIM RE ACT:** Broker, Consultant, Appraiser, Engineer, Syndicator; **SERVICES:** Specializing in Route 128 prop. for use or devel.; **REP CLIENTS:** A large firm servicing a broad spectrum of natl. and local clients; Also workout or surplus prop. specialists; **PROFL AFFIL & HONORS:** SIR, RESSI; **EDUC:** BS, 1958, Indus. Engrg., Northeastern Univ.; **GRAD EDUC:** MBA, 1970, Boston Coll.; **MIL SERV:** US Army, 1st Lt.; **OTHER ACT & HONORS:** Charitable Irish Soc. of Boston; **BUS ADD:** 19 Brook Rd., Needham Hts., MA 02194, (617)449-4949.

CONNELL, Robert——*VP Plng.*, Republic Corp.; **PRIM RE ACT:** Property Manager; **BUS ADD:** 1900 Avenue of the Stars, Ste. 2700, Century City, Los Angeles, CA 90067, (213)553-3900.*

CONNER, Leslie L., Jr.——B: July 15, 1939, Oklahoma City, OK, *Atty.*, Ungerman, Conner, & Little, OK City Office; **PRIM RE ACT:** Attorney, Owner/Investor; **PROFL AFFIL & HONORS:** OK City Title Attys., OK Cty. Bar, OK Bar Assn., Comml. Law League, ABA, Member Bd. of Gov. and Pres., Member House of Delegates; **EDUC:** BA, 1961, Govt. and Hist., OK Univ.; **GRAD EDUC:** LLB, 1963, OK Univ.; **EDUC HONORS:** Law Revue, Dean's Honor Roll; **MIL SERV:** USAF, Lt. Col.; **HOME ADD:** 19 Oakdale Farm Rd., Edmond, OK 73034, (405)478-4888; **BUS ADD:** 610 Colcord Dr., Oklahoma City, OK 73102, (405)235-1404.

CONNERS, John J., Jr.——B: July 6, 1934, Madison, WI, *Sr. VP, Mgr.*, Paine Webber RE Securities, Inc., Loan Brokerage Dept.; **OTHER RE ACT:** Secondary mkt. mort. loan brokerage; **SERVICES:** Secondary market mort. loan brokerage; **REP CLIENTS:** Mort. bankers, s&l's, mutual savings banks, comml. banks, life insurance co's., pension funds, state & local funds.; **PREV EMPLOY:** CMI Investment Corp.; Investors Mort. Insurance Co. (Founding officer); MGIC; FHA; **PROFL AFFIL & HONORS:** MBAA; SREA; USL; Nat. Legue, SRA; SREA; **EDUC:** BBA, 1957, Univ. of WI - Madison; **MIL SERV:** US Army; Capt.; **OTHER ACT & HONORS:** Bd. of Dirs., Lake Cty., Chaplainery Services, Inc.; **HOME ADD:** 100 Indian Rd., Lake Bluff, IL 60044, (312)234-0954; **BUS ADD:** 55 West Monroe St., Chicago, IL 60603, (312)580-8400.

CONNERY, Edmund M.——B: Nov. 2, 1918, Cohoes, NY, *Atty.*, Self; **PRIM RE ACT:** Attorney; **SERVICES:** Legal and Tax; **REP CLIENTS:** D.H. Overmyer Co., Inc.; Hadar Leasing Intl. Co., Inc.; **PREV EMPLOY:** VP, Sec. and General Counsel to D. H. Overmyer Co., Inc. 1964-1977.; **PROFL AFFIL & HONORS:** ABA - RE, Probate & Trust, Comm. and Corporate, Comml. & Banking Comm., JD, 1968; **EDUC:** BBA, 1941, Acctg., Siena Coll., Loudonville, NY; **GRAD EDUC:** LLB, 1948, Law, Albany Law School; **MIL SERV:** US Army, Sgt., 1942-46; **OTHER ACT & HONORS:** Admitted to Tax Ct. practice; **HOME ADD:** 6 Crossbar Rd., Hastings on Hudson, NY 10706, (914)478-1782; **BUS ADD:** 3 Park Ave; 29th Fl., New York, NY 10016, (212)889-5454.

CONNOLEY, William B.——B: Apr. 7, 1919, Wheeling, WV, *Exec. VP & Chief Operating Officer*, Shearson/American Express Mortgage Corp., Shearson/WesPac Realty & Devel.; **PRIM RE ACT:** Developer, Lender, Builder, Owner/Investor; **SERVICES:** Joint venture and constr. fin. capabilities for builders and devels. for resid., comml. and indus. projects.; **PREV EMPLOY:** Sr. VP & Chief Admin. RE Div. of USNB; **PROFL AFFIL & HONORS:** CMBA, MBA, Dir. Building Contr. Assn. & Assoc. Gen. Contr. Assn., Amer. Bankers Assn. Advisory Council on Housing & RE Fin., Past Pres. San Diego Mortgage Bankers Assn.; **EDUC:** BA, 1940, Bus. Admin., W. Liberty State Teachers Coll., WV; **GRAD EDUC:** Bus. Mgmt., Univ. of So. CA; Fin. of Comml. & Indus. Projects, Univ. of So. CA; **HOME ADD:** 1111 S. Coast Dr., Costa Mesa, CA 92626; **BUS ADD:** 1601 Dove St., Suite 275, Newport Bch., CA 92660, (714)752-7670.

CONNOLLY, George P.——B: Jan. 30, 1917, Chicago, IL, *Chmn. of Bd.*, Brown Nat. Bank; **PRIM RE ACT:** Broker, Banker; **PREV EMPLOY:** Banker; **HOME ADD:** 3016 85th St., Kenosha, WI 53142, (414)694-7157; **BUS ADD:** 3016 85th St., Kenosha, WI 53140, (414)658-1681.

CONNOLLY, Thomas K.——B: June 27, 1941, Winchester, MA, *VP*, First National Bank of Boston, RE; **PRIM RE ACT:** Owner/Investor; **SERVICES:** Acquisition, mgmt., valuation of prop.; **REP CLIENTS:** Major US pension accounts and indiv. investors; **PREV EMPLOY:** Arthur Andersen & Co.; **PROFL AFFIL & HONORS:** Member Urban Land, Shopping Ctr. Counsel, Mort. Bankers, CRA; **EDUC:** BS, 1963, Acctg. & Econ., Northeastern Univ.; **GRAD EDUC:** MBA, 1969, Fin. and Investment, Babson; **EDUC HONORS:** Cum Laude; **MIL SERV:** US Army; 1st Lt.; **HOME ADD:** 34 Coolidge Ave., Needham, MA 02192, (617)444-5811; **BUS ADD:** 100 Federal St., Boston, MA 02110, (617)434-4906.

CONNOR, H.C.——B: June 10, 1932, Hamilton, MO, *VP, Prop. Devel.*, The Prudential Insurance Co. of America, Western Div., RE Investment Dept.; **PRIM RE ACT:** Developer, Owner/Investor; **EDUC:** BA, 1958, Econ., Univ. of MO; **MIL SERV:** USN, Korean War; **HOME ADD:** 1600 Palisades Dr., Pacific Palisades, CA 90272, (203)459-2439; **BUS ADD:** Suite 2550, 2049 Century Park East, Los Angeles, CA 90067, (213)277-1400.

CONNOR, James J.——B: Mar. 18, 1944, Philadelphia, PA, *VP*, Beneficial Savings Bank; **PRIM RE ACT:** Banker, Lender; **PROFL AFFIL & HONORS:** Philadelphia Mort. Bankers Assn.; Amer. Assn. of Mort. Underwriters, Cert. Resid. Mort. Underwriter; **EDUC:** BS, 1973, Acctg. Bus. Admin., Villanova Univ.; **GRAD EDUC:** 1976, Grad. School of Mort. Banking, Northwestern Univ.; **BUS ADD:** 1200 Chestnut St., Philadelphia, PA 19107, (215)864-6126.

CONNOR, John B.——B: Jan. 2, 1946, New Bedford, MA, *Atty.*, Odin, Feldman & Pittleman, P.C.; **PRIM RE ACT:** Attorney; **EDUC:** BS, 1968, Bus. Mgmt./Econ., Georgetown Univ.; **GRAD EDUC:** JD, 1977, George Washington Univ.; **MIL SERV:** USN, LCDR; **HOME ADD:** 4209 Majestic Ln., Fairfax, VA 22030, (703)378-4616; **BUS ADD:** 10505 Jones St., Suite 300, P.O. Box 367, Fairfax, VA 22030, (703)385-7715.

CONNOR, Patrick T.——B: Sept. 5, 1946, Brooklyn, NY, *Sr. Sales Consultant, Assoc. Broker*, Coldwell Banker Comml. RE Services, Investments; **PRIM RE ACT:** Broker, Developer, Owner/Investor, Syndicator; **SERVICES:** Invest. planning, devel., leasing, sales & synd. of comml. prop.; **REP CLIENTS:** Private devel., instl. investors and found.; **PREV EMPLOY:** Pima Community Coll., Mktg. Dept., 1974-1976; **PROFL AFFIL & HONORS:** RESSI; Realtor, Recipient of the Bob Ellis Master of Investism Award, 1979; **EDUC:** BS, 1974, Mktg./Advtg., Univ. of AZ; **HOME ADD:** 8383 Tranque Verde, Tucson, AZ 85715, (602)749-1423; **BUS ADD:** 655 N. Alvernon Way 100, Tucson, AZ 85711, (602)881-6000.

CONNOR, William H.——B: May 20, 1929, Tichnor, AR, *Owner*, East Bay Co.; **PRIM RE ACT:** Broker, Consultant, Owner/Investor, Property Manager, Syndicator; **SERVICES:** RE packaging, exchanging; **REP CLIENTS:** Synd.; **PREV EMPLOY:** S&L Serv. Corp. VP; **PROFL AFFIL & HONORS:** Realtor - BOMA; **EDUC:** BA, 1968, Bus. Fin., Univ. of MD; **MIL SERV:** USAF, Maj., MSM; **OTHER ACT & HONORS:** Chmn. Cty. Bd. of Adjustment, Thurston, WA; Lions Intl.; **HOME ADD:** 6315 Gull Harbor Dr. NE, Olympia, WA 98506, (206)352-4941; **BUS ADD:** 6315 Gull Harbor Dr. NE, Olympia, WA 98506, (206)352-4941.

CONNORS, Francis A.——*Executive Director*, National Society of Professional Resident Managers; **OTHER RE ACT:** Profl. Assn. Admin.; **BUS ADD:** 1000 Vermont Ave. NW, Suite 1200, Washington, DC 20005, (202)628-4634.*

CONNORS, James——*Dir. RE*, Revlon, Inc.; **PRIM RE ACT:** Property Manager; **BUS ADD:** Rte. 27 & Talmade Rd., Edison, NJ 08817, (201)287-1400.*

CONNORS, Richard J.——B: Feb. 6, 1948, Philadelphia, PA, *Pres.*, Connors Investment Corp.; **PRIM RE ACT:** Broker, Consultant, Owner/Investor; **OTHER RE ACT:** Buyers broker, investment counselor, exchanger; **SERVICES:** Represent investors in acquisitions and dispositions; **PREV EMPLOY:** Tax accountant; **PROFL AFFIL & HONORS:** Tr., Puget Sound Exchangers; **EDUC:** BS, 1969, Acctg., Villanova Univ.; **MIL SERV:** USN; ENS.; **OTHER ACT & HONORS:** Kiwanis Intl., Chmn., Advisory Council, The Salvation Army of Pierce Cty.; **HOME ADD:** Rte. 1 Box 488, Vashon, WA 98070, (206)567-4204; **BUS ADD:** 404 W. Titus Bldg., Kent, WA 98031, (206)854-8640.

CONOLY, David Z.——B: July 19, 1953, Del Rio, TX, *Atty.*, Shaw, Thorpe & Conoly; **PRIM RE ACT:** Attorney; **REP CLIENTS:** San Jacinto Title Co., Pioneer Nat. Title Ins. Co., MN Title Co., Builders Assn. of Corpus Christi, Citicorp Homeowners, Inc., The Richard Gill Co.; **PROFL AFFIL & HONORS:** Nueces Cty. Bar Assn.; TX Bar Assn.; ABA, Comm. on New Devels. in RE Law; **EDUC:** 1975, Poli. Sci., S. Methodist Univ.; **GRAD EDUC:** JD, 1978, S. Methodist Univ.; **HOME ADD:** 438 Southern, Corpus Christi, TX 78404, (512)882-6316; **BUS ADD:** 5926 S. Staples, Suite D, Corpus Christi, TX 78413, (512)993-0201.

CONRAD, John F.——B: Feb. 5, 1933, Salisbury, MD, *Exec. VP*, Gabrielsen & Co.; **PRIM RE ACT:** Developer, Owner/Investor, Property Manager; **REP CLIENTS:** RE Trust of Amer.; Fifty Assoc.; Longs Drugs; Safeway; **PREV EMPLOY:** VP Operations, Wailea Land Corp., Devel. of 1500 Acre Resort; **PROFL AFFIL & HONORS:** ICSC, AIIE, Registered Professional Engineer - CA; **EDUC:** BS, 1955, Indus. Engrg., Purdue Univ.; **GRAD EDUC:** MBA, 1975, Fin., Univ. of HI; **EDUC HONORS:** Beta Sigma Phi; **MIL SERV:** US Army, 1st Lt.; **HOME ADD:** 677 Park Hill Rd., Danville, CA 94526, (415)820-8938; **BUS ADD:** Suite 910, Hearst Bldg., San Francisco, CA 94103, (415)495-3737.

CONRAD, Joseph, Jr.——B: Mar. 21, 1935, Rushville, IL, *VP*, Fred F. French of Maryland, Inc.; **PRIM RE ACT:** Broker, Instructor, Consultant, Property Manager; **OTHER RE ACT:** Leasing; **SERVICES:** Prop. Mgmt. & Leasing; **REP CLIENTS:** Builders, Office Space Users; **PREV EMPLOY:** Walker & Dunlop, Inc. 1975-1980; **PROFL AFFIL & HONORS:** IREM, BOMA, SORPA, Montgomery Cty. Bd. Realtors, CPM, RPA; **EDUC:** 1961- 1966, Amer. Univ., Wash., D.C.; **MIL SERV:** USMC, Sgt.,Korean PUC, United Nations Presidential Unit. Cit. Good Conduct American Defense; **HOME ADD:** 1300 E. Kennedy Rd., Sterling, VA 22170, (703)471-9044; **BUS ADD:** 11300 Rockville Pike, Rockville, MD 20852, (301)770-6960.

CONRAD, Kenneth——B: June 12, 1938, Dayton, IA, *VP*, Iowa Farms Associates, Inc.; **PRIM RE ACT:** Broker, Consultant, Appraiser, Property Manager; **SERVICES:** Specializing in farm mgmt. & land investment; **PREV EMPLOY:** Agriculture Econ., US Dept. of Agri. & US Tarriff Commn. 1962-69; **PROFL AFFIL & HONORS:** Amer. Soc. of Farm Mgrs. & Rural Appraisers; **EDUC:** BS, 1960, Agri. Educ., Agri. Econ., IA State Univ.; **HOME ADD:** 1023 25th Ave. N., Ft. Dodge, IA 50501, (515)576-4250; **BUS ADD:** M-15 Warden Plaza, Ft. Dodge, IA 50501, (515)576-1011.

CONROY, J. Michael, Jr.——B: Dec. 15, 1945, Wash. DC, *Princ. Atty.*, Conroy, Fitzgerald, Ballman & Ridgway; **PRIM RE ACT:** Attorney; **SERVICES:** Litigation, consultation, drafting; **REP CLIENTS:** Merrill Lynch Relocation Mgmt., Inc. US Home, Riggs Nat. Bank, Builders, brokers, banks; **PREV EMPLOY:** Public Defender's Office for MD, Staff Atty., 1976-79; **PROFL AFFIL & HONORS:** ABA, Amer. Trial Lawyers Assn., Admitted to US Supreme Court, JD; **EDUC:** 1967, Arts & Letters, Univ. of Notre Dame; **GRAD EDUC:** JD, 1971, Georgetown Univ. Law Ctr.; **MIL SERV:** US Army; **OTHER ACT & HONORS:** Chmn. Montgomery Cty. Bar, RE Sect.; Tr. Catholic Youth Org.; Member of Exec. Comm., Montgomery Cty. Bar Assn.; **HOME ADD:** 4806 Chevy Chase Blvd., Chevy Chase, MD, (301)656-7339; **BUS ADD:** Suite 202, 702 Russell Ave., Gaithersburg, MD 20877, (301)869-4300.

CONROY, John T., Jr.——B: June 23, 1937, Chicago, IL, *Pres.*, Investment Properties Corp.; **PRIM RE ACT:** Broker, Developer, Owner/Investor, Instructor, Property Manager, Syndicator; **SERVICES:** Specializing in comml. investment, RE devel. and synd. of comml. props.; **PROFL AFFIL & HONORS:** Pres., Naples Area Bd. of Realtors; Immediate past-pres., Naples Area C of C; Instructor, RNMI, CCIM; **EDUC:** BBA, 1959, Philosophy, Univ. of Notre Dame; **GRAD EDUC:** MA, 1961, Math, Fordham Univ.; **OTHER ACT & HONORS:** Member, Collier Cty. Housing & Fin. Authority; **HOME ADD:** 636 15th Ave. S., Naples, FL 33940, (813)261-7405; **BUS ADD:** 1391 Third St., S., Naples, FL 33940, (813)261-3400.

CONROY, Terence W.——B: Apr. 21, 1941, Boston, MA, *Pres.*, Carlson Development Corp.; **PRIM RE ACT:** Developer; **OTHER RE ACT:** RE Devel. & Const.; **PROFL AFFIL & HONORS:** Profl. Reg. Engr., RE Broker.; **EDUC:** BSCE, 1963, Princeton Univ.; **HOME ADD:** 21 Arnold Rd., Wellesley, MA 02181, (617)237-2258; **BUS ADD:** 321 Comm. Rd., Cochituate, MA 02121, (617)919-1200.

CONRY, Edward J.——B: Nov. 20, 1942, Toledo, OH, *Assoc. Professor of Law & Business*, State University, School of Bus.; **PRIM RE ACT:** Consultant, Attorney, Developer, Builder, Owner/Investor, Instructor, Real Estate Publisher; **PREV EMPLOY:** Asst. to the Sr. VP, Wells Fargo & Co.; **EDUC:** BA, 1969, Bus. Admin., CA State Univ., Fullerton; **GRAD EDUC:** MBA, 1972, RE, Univ. of CA - Berkeley; JD (RE), Univ. of CA - Davis; **EDUC HONORS:** Beta Gamma Sigma, Berkeley Honors Soc., Editor-in-Chief *UCD Barrister*; **OTHER ACT & HONORS:** 1981-1982 Research Rellow - Yale Univ., Author or co-author of numerous articles and 7 books, including "Utah Real Estate Law" and "Business Law Text and Cases"; **HOME ADD:** 1520 Sumac Dr., Logan, UT 84321, (801)750-2376; **BUS ADD:** Utah State Univ.-UMC 35, Logan, UT 84322, (801)750-2376.

CONSIGLI, Joseph A.——B: Nov. 19, 1926, New York, NY, *VP - RE*, Manville Properties Corp., Corp. RE; **PRIM RE ACT:** Developer, Owner/Investor, Property Manager; **PROFL AFFIL & HONORS:** Nat. Assn. of Corp. RE Execs.; Natl. Assn. Review Appraisers; Inst. of Bus. Appraisers; Coll. of RE Consultants, Dir. NACORE, AIA Awards 2 projects; **EDUC:** BS, 1951, Acctg., Bus. Law, Long Isl. Univ.; **MIL SERV:** USMC, Pvt.; **OTHER ACT & HONORS:** Dir., Youth League; Dir. Lakewood C of C; **HOME ADD:** 1364 E. Easter Circ., Littleton, CO 80122, (303)795-9175; **BUS ADD:** Ken Caryl Ranch, Denver, CO 80217, (303)978-2035.

CONSTABLE, William E.——B: Oct. 15, 1930, Bloomington, IN, *Partner*, Clark & Constable; **PRIM RE ACT:** Attorney; **SERVICES:** Representation of lenders and other parties in comml. RE transactions; **REP CLIENTS:** Aetna Life Ins. Co.; The Aetna Casualty and Surety

Co.; The Nat. Bank of Washington; **PREV EMPLOY:** Wilkes & Artis (Law Firm), Wash., DC 1971-1979; **PROFL AFFIL & HONORS:** ABA; IN State Bar Assn.; The Bar Assn. of the DC; the DC Bar; **EDUC:** AB, 1966, Govt., IN Univ.; **GRAD EDUC:** JD, 1969, Law, IN Univ School of Law; **EDUC HONORS:** Cum Laude, Phi Beta Kappa, Ford P. Hall Scholar in Govt., Order of the Coif; Weymouth Kirkland Scholar; **OTHER ACT & HONORS:** The MBA of Metropolitan Wash., Inc.; Apt. and Office Bldg. Assn.; The Gr. Wash. Bd. of Trade; **HOME ADD:** 3516 Pence Court, Annandale, VA 22003, (703)573-9677; **BUS ADD:** 1300 19th St.NW, Suite 250, Wash., DC 20036, (202)466-7171.

CONTI, Lou——B: Oct. 22, 1935, NY, *Pres.*, Combined Operators Corp.; **PRIM RE ACT:** Broker, Consultant, Engineer, Appraiser, Architect, Developer, Builder, Owner/Investor, Property Manager; **EDUC:** 1955, Engrg., NYS; **OTHER ACT & HONORS:** Investment Devel.; **HOME ADD:** 15 Weeks Rd., N Babylon, NY 11730, (516)586-7726; **BUS ADD:** 15 Weeks Rd., N Babylon, NY 11703, (516)586-7726.

CONTI, Richard C.——B: Mar. 25, 1950, Jamestown, NY, *Mgr.*, Laventhol & Horwath, Mgmt. Advisory Servs.; **PRIM RE ACT:** Consultant; **SERVICES:** Mkt. studies, fin. analyses; **REP CLIENTS:** Devels., lenders; **PROFL AFFIL & HONORS:** IL Mort. Bankers Assn.; **EDUC:** BA, 1973, Bus. Admin., State Univ. of NY at Brockport; **GRAD EDUC:** MBA, 1976, Bus. Admin., MI State Univ.; **EDUC HONORS:** Magna Cum Laude, Klare Fellowship; **HOME ADD:** 1819 N. McVicker, Chicago, IL 60639, (312)745-1023; **BUS ADD:** 111 E. Wacker, Chicago, IL 60601, (312)644-4570.

CONWAY, Daniel M.——B: Dec. 12, 1945, Janesville, WI, *Dir. of Mktg. & Econ. Research*, THK Assn. Inc.; **PRIM RE ACT:** Consultant; **SERVICES:** Planning & market research; **REP CLIENTS:** Mobil Land; City of Denver; Victorio Devel.; Chism Homes; **PREV EMPLOY:** H.O.H. Planning, Denver, CO; **PROFL AFFIL & HONORS:** ULI; Assn. of Land Econ.; Instr. at Denver Univ. & Univ. of CO; **EDUC:** BBA, 1968, Urban Land Econ., Univ. of WI; **HOME ADD:** 12550 E Bates, Denver, CO 80210, (303)755-7612; **BUS ADD:** 40 Inverness Dr. E, Denver, CO 80218, (303)932-5417.

CONWAY, E. Virgil——B: Aug. 2, 1929, Southampton, NY, *Chmn./Pres.*, The Seamen's Bank for Savings; **PRIM RE ACT:** Banker, Lender; **PROFL AFFIL & HONORS:** ABA; Assn. of the Bar of the City of NY; NY State Bar Assn.; **EDUC:** BA, 1951, Phil./Religion, Columbia Univ.; **GRAD EDUC:** LLB, 1956, Yale Univ., Law School; **EDUC HONORS:** Magna cum laude, Phi Beta Kappa, Cum Laude, Order of the Coif; **MIL SERV:** USAFR, Capt.; **OTHER ACT & HONORS:** Tr., Colgate Univ., 1970 - 1976; Pace Univ., Bd. of Tr.; NYC Police Foundation, Inc., Bd. of Tr.; **HOME ADD:** 345 Pondfield Rd., Bronxville, NY 10708, (914)779-3021; **BUS ADD:** 30 Wall St., NY, NY 10005, (212)797-5074.

CONWAY, E.R. (Bud)——B: Aug. 27, 1925, Concord, NH, *RE Investments Broker*, E.R. Conway, Realtor; **PRIM RE ACT:** Broker, Consultant, Instructor, Owner/Investor; **OTHER RE ACT:** Exchangor; **SERVICES:** Brokerage, fee counseling & consulting; **PREV EMPLOY:** Retired, US Army 22 yrs.; **PROFL AFFIL & HONORS:** CAR: NAR; Charter Member & Former 1st VP S. CA CCIM Chap.; Founder/Chmn. RE Forum, RECI, GRI; **EDUC:** BS, 1950, Bus. Admin., Univ. of NH; **MIL SERV:** US Army; Lt. Col., Legion of Merit and 4 Army Commendation Medals; **OTHER ACT & HONORS:** CA State Military Res.; **HOME ADD:** PO Box 1777, Rancho Santa Fe, CA 92067, (714)756-3422; **BUS ADD:** PO Box 1777, Rancho Santa Fe, CA 92067, (714)756-3422.

CONWAY, Patrick J.——B: Apr. 14, 1935, Janesville, WI, *VP*, Control Data Corp., R.E. & Facilities Admin.; **OTHER RE ACT:** Corp. Exec. R.E.; **EDUC:** BA, 1957, Fin., Univ. Of Notre Dame School of Commerce; **GRAD EDUC:** 1959, Marketing, Univ. of Stanford Grad. School of Bus.; **EDUC HONORS:** Cum Laude; **HOME ADD:** 8820 Crestwood Rd., Bloomington, MN 55437, (612)835-4663; **BUS ADD:** 8100 34th Ave. S., Minneapolis, MN 55440, (612)853-4950.

CONWAY, Robert M.——B: July 9, 1933, *Pres.*, Robert M. Conway and Associates, Inc.; **PRIM RE ACT:** Broker, Developer, Property Manager; **SERVICES:** RE Devel., Prop. Mgmt., Fin. Consulting, Sales; **PREV EMPLOY:** Pres. and Chmn. of the Bd. of Tower Grove Bank in St. Louis, Preceded by Sr. Lending Officer and Exec. VP of the Bank. The Prudential Ins. Co. of America-Sr. Investment Analyst; **PROFL AFFIL & HONORS:** Bd. of Dir.-United Student Aid Fund; Bd. of Trustees-Incarnate Word Hosp.; Former Bd. of Dir.-Landmarks Assn. of St. Louis; The Police Retirement Bd. of St. Louis; Former Bd. of Dir.-Midtown Medical Ctr. Redevel. Corp.; **EDUC:** BBA, 1955, Acctg. and Fin., St. Marys Univ., San Antonio TX; **GRAD EDUC:** MS in Commerce, 1968, St. Louis Univ. MO; **HOME ADD:** 2019 S. Grand, Unit 103, St. Louis, MO 63104, (314)771-2534; **BUS ADD:** 2019 S Grand Blvd., St. Louis, MO 63105, (314)771-8300.

CONWAY, William——*RE Mgr.*, California Portland Cement Co.; **PRIM RE ACT:** Property Manager; **BUS ADD:** 800 Wilshire Blvd., Los Angeles, CA 90017, (213)680-2316.*

CONWAY, William A., III——B: May 13, 1938, Jersey City, NJ, *VP*, Cushman & Wakefield; **PRIM RE ACT:** Broker, Consultant, Appraiser; **SERVICES:** Consultation on prop. values; sale & acquisition of income props. & devel. sites; **REP CLIENTS:** Lenders, pension fund & ins. co. owners & purchasers of income props., primarily office bldgs. Major devel. of office bldg. projects; **PREV EMPLOY:** Storage Tech. 73-75, Dir. of Fin., John Nuveen & Co., 1968-73, VP Corp. & Munic. Fin. Dept.; **PROFL AFFIL & HONORS:** NY Soc. of Security Analysts, Fin. Analysts Fed., Denver & CO Bd. of Realtors; **EDUC:** BA, 1960, Phil., Hist., Eng., Univ. of Notre Dame; **GRAD EDUC:** MBA, 1965, Econ., Mktg., NY Univ.; LLB/JD, 1965, Fordham Univ. Sch. of Law; **EDUC HONORS:** Great Books Honors Program, Scholarship, Munic. Bond Club of NY, Var. high grade awards; **MIL SERV:** USN, Ens.; **OTHER ACT & HONORS:** Denver Athletic Club, Downtown Denver Inc., Denver C of C; **HOME ADD:** 200 S Forest St., Denver, CO 80222, (303)320-6903; **BUS ADD:** 1125 17th St., Suite 1960, Denver, CO 80202, (303)573-5590.

COOCH, Robert A.——B: May 22, 1928, Ann Arbor, MI, *Pres.*, RA Cooch Co.; **PRIM RE ACT:** Appraiser; **SERVICES:** Appraisals; **REP CLIENTS:** Fed. govt., MI state govt., utility cos., oil cos., mort. cos., insurance & banking firms & indivs.; **PREV EMPLOY:** Ford Motor Co., Gen. Motors; **PROFL AFFIL & HONORS:** AIREA, ASA, NAREB, ULI, ARWA, SREA, MIRE Bd., IREF, ASA, MAI, SRPA; **EDUC:** BS, 1950, Sci. and Bus., Eastern MI Univ.; **GRAD EDUC:** MBA, 1951, Bus., Univ. of MI; **MIL SERV:** USN; **HOME ADD:** 2701 Dale View Dr., Ann Arbor, MI 48103; **BUS ADD:** 320 South Main St., Ann Arbor, MI 48104, (313)662-6577.

COOK, David H.——B: Dec. 25, 1948, Portland, OR, *Pres.*, L.B. Nelson Corp. of Oregon, OR Div.; **PRIM RE ACT:** Developer, Builder; **PREV EMPLOY:** VP Gen. Mgr., Columbia Custom Homes, BVTN, OR VP Amer. Bldg. ARB, San Diego, CA, Project Mgr.; **PROFL AFFIL & HONORS:** Centex Homes, Chicago, IL; **EDUC:** BS, 1971, Bus. Admin., MI State Univ.; **GRAD EDUC:** MS Resource Econ., 1973, Resource Econ. & Devel., Urban Planning, MI State Univ.; **HOME ADD:** 16470 S Glenwood Ct., Lake Oswego, OR 97034, (503)636-1380; **BUS ADD:** 11830 SW Kerr Parkway, Suite 302, Lake Oswego, OR 97034, (503)245-0701.

COOK, Donald A.——B: Aug. 19, 1930, OH, *Owner*, ERA D & J Cook Co.; **PRIM RE ACT:** Broker, Consultant, Appraiser; **OTHER RE ACT:** Resid. & comml. brokerage, appraisals & counseling; **SERVICES:** Indiv. & corp. investors; **PROFL AFFIL & HONORS:** NAR; NW Bergen Bd. of Realtors; Passaic County Bd. of Realtors; Nat. Assn of RE Appraisers & RE; Nat. Mktg. Inst., Grad. Realtor Inst., Cert. Resid. spec. & cert. RE appraiser; **MIL SERV:** US Army, Sig., 1949-69, Maj., BSM, ACM, GCM, ADM, NDSM, KSM, VSM, AFRM, UNSM, ROK PUC, PUCA, ROVCR, MUC, PUCN, CIB; **OTHER ACT & HONORS:** Dir. Ringwood C of C; Pres Ringwood Plaza Merchants Assn.; Tr. Kensington Wood Home Owners Assn.; **HOME ADD:** 36 Cheshire Ln., Ringwood, NJ 07456, (201)962-7761; **BUS ADD:** Ringwood Plaza, Ringwood, NJ 07456.

COOK, Donald L.——B: May 14, 1940, Wooster, OH, *Atty.*, Wood, Ris & Hames, P.C.; **PRIM RE ACT:** Attorney; **SERVICES:** Legal rep. and counseling; **REP CLIENTS:** The Equitable Life Assurance Soc., Mellon Bank, Geomex Enterprises, Roulier Enterprises, Gooch & Wagstaff Realtors; **PROFL AFFIL & HONORS:** ABA, Prop. & Probate Sect., CBA Real Prop. Sect., DBA; **EDUC:** BA, 1962, Pol. Sci., Wittenberg Univ.; **GRAD EDUC:** JD, 1971, Univ. of Denver; LLM, 1978, Law & Taxation, Univ. of Denver; **EDUC HONORS:** Law Journal; **MIL SERV:** USAF, Major, Bronze Star; **HOME ADD:** 3001 S. Gilpin St., Denver, CO 80210, (303)756-2169; **BUS ADD:** 1100 Denver Club Bldg., 518 17th St., Denver, CO 80202, (303)292-4060.

COOK, George W.——B: Aug. 31, 1922, Orlando, FL, *Pres.*, C.W.W. Construction Co.; **PRIM RE ACT:** Broker, Developer, Builder; **PROFL AFFIL & HONORS:** NE FL Builders Assn., Natl. Assn. of Home Builders; **EDUC:** BA, Univ. of Miami; **OTHER ACT & HONORS:** USMC, 1941-1945, 1st Lt.; **HOME ADD:** 1301 South 1st St. #901, Jacksonville Beach, FL 32250, (904)241-5759; **BUS ADD:** 3034 Pearl St., Jacksonville, FL 32206, (904)358-3816.

COOK, Glenn——B: Jan. 7, 1949, Los Angeles, CA, *Pres.*, Invest. Conversions, Inc.; **PRIM RE ACT:** Broker, Developer, Syndicator; **SERVICES:** Land Planning, devel., and brokerage of resid. subdiv. and hotels; **REP CLIENTS:** Major hotel mgmt. cos., hotel investors, and resid. builders; **EDUC:** BS Landscape Arch., 1974, Land Planning, CA Polytechnic State Univ.; **GRAD EDUC:** MBA, 1976, CA Polytechnic State Univ.; **HOME ADD:** 31501 Lindero Cyn. Rd. 4, Westlake Village, CA 91361; **BUS ADD:** 4764 Park Granada, Suite 212, Calabasas, CA 91302, (213)704-4200.

COOK, Jeffry J.——B: Nov. 25, 1943, Fairbanks, AK, *Pres. and Broker*, The Cook Co., Inc./Earl Cook, Realtors; **PRIM RE ACT:** Broker; **SERVICES:** RE brokerage and counseling; some devel.; **REP CLIENTS:** Safeway Stores, Inc.; LDS Church (Mormon); Laborers Local 492; State of AK; Fairbanks North Star Borough; NC Machiner (Skinner Industries); Doyon, Ltd.; **PREV EMPLOY:** Mgmt. Trainee with Seattle First Nat. Bank and Teaching Assist. while Grad. Student at Univ. of OR; **PROFL AFFIL & HONORS:** NAR, Fairbanks Bd. of Realtors, and AK Assn. Realtor. Fairbanks Rotary Club, GRI, designate from AK; CRS with Realtors Nat. Mktg. Inst.; **EDUC:** BBA from the Univ. of OR, 1966, RE and Banking. Non. Acad. CI 101, 102, 103 with Realtors Nat. Mktg. Inst.; Courses I, II, IV and VIII with AIREA.; **GRAD EDUC:** MBA, 1968, Urban Land Mgmt., Univ. of OR; **EDUC HONORS:** Beta Gamma Sigma, Univ. of OR; **OTHER ACT & HONORS:** Planning Commn. Chmn. Fairbanks 1972; VP Univ. of AK Bd. of Regents; Fairbanks Rotary Club; Salvation Army Advisory Bd. Member of Bd. of Dirs.; Exec. Comm. of the NAR; **HOME ADD:** SR 50079, Fairbanks, AK 99701, (907)456-6066; **BUS ADD:** P O Box 2134, Fairbanks, AK 99707, (907)456-5070.

COOK, John M.——B: Apr. 22, 1937, Detroit, MI, *Corp. Dir., RE & Facilities Mgmt.*, Burroughs Corp., RE & Facilities Mgmt.; **PRIM RE ACT:** Broker, Consultant, Engineer, Attorney, Appraiser, Architect, Builder, Owner/Investor, Property Manager; **PROFL AFFIL & HONORS:** NACORE (National Assn. of Corporate RE Execs.); **EDUC:** BS, 1959, Acctg. & Econ., E. MI Univ.; **OTHER ACT & HONORS:** Engrg. Soc. of Detroit; **HOME ADD:** 25333 Wykeshire Rd., Farmington Hills, MI 48018, (313)474-6238; **BUS ADD:** Burroughs Place, Detroit, MI 48232, (313)972-9682.

COOK, Kenneth J.——B: Sept. 17, 1936, Biloxi, MS, *RE Dir.*, K&B Inc.; **OTHER RE ACT:** Retail Super Drug Store (Rgn. Chain); **PROFL AFFIL & HONORS:** ICSC; NACORE; **EDUC:** BSC, 1958, Indus. Mgmt., Springhill Coll., Mobile, AL; **MIL SERV:** US Army; Maj., Joint Service Commendation, Bronze Star for Valor, Army Commendation for Valor, Bronze Star, Army Commendation; **OTHER ACT & HONORS:** Past Nat. VP for NACORE's Retail Grp.; **HOME ADD:** 5539 Hurst St., New Orleans, LA 70115, (504)895-3096; **BUS ADD:** K&B Plaza, Lee Circle, New Orleans, LA 70130, (504)586-1234.

COOK, Reuben Wright——B: Feb. 26, 1952, Auburn, AL, *Atty.*, Albrittons & Givhan; **PRIM RE ACT:** Attorney; **OTHER RE ACT:** Estate planning, tax area; **PROFL AFFIL & HONORS:** AL State Bar; GA State Bar; **EDUC:** BS, 1975, Acctg., Univ. of AL; **GRAD EDUC:** JD, 1978, Univ. of AL; LLM, 1980, Taxation, Emory Univ.; **MIL SERV:** US Army, Capt.; **HOME ADD:** PO Drawer 880, Andalusia, AL 36420, (205)222-8095; **BUS ADD:** PO Box 2191, Andalusia, AL 36420, (205)222-3177.

COOK, Robert——*Pres. Property Eastern Div.*, Roper Corp.; **PRIM RE ACT:** Property Manager; **BUS ADD:** 1905 W. Court St., Kankakee, IL 60901, (815)937-6000.*

COOK, Robert John——B: Mar. 23, 1951, Pittsburgh, PA, *Project Mgr. (Devel.) and Consultant*, Arthur Rubloff & Co., RE Devel.; **PRIM RE ACT:** Consultant, Developer; **SERVICES:** Devel. of comml. and resid. props., consulting to org. with RE needs or opportunities; **REP CLIENTS:** Amer. Med. Assn., Nat. Assn. of Realtors, Bell Fed. S&L, Hart Schaffner Marx, Beatrice Foods; **PREV EMPLOY:** City of Chicago, Dept. of Planning, 1978-1980; **EDUC:** BA, 1973, Arch./ Urban Design, Rice Univ.; **GRAD EDUC:** MArch., 1976, Arch./ Urban Design, Rice Univ.; MBA, 1981, Fin., Northwestern Univ.; **EDUC HONORS:** Pres. Honor Roll, Grad. Fellow, Dean's List; **HOME ADD:** 1360 N Lake Shore Dr. #203, Chicago, IL 60610, (312)642-0720; **BUS ADD:** 69 W Washington, Chicago, IL 60602, (312)368-5434.

COOK, Robert N.——B: Dec. 11, 1912, Vicksburg, PA, *Prof of Law*, Coll. of Law, Univ. of Cincinnati; **OTHER RE ACT:** Enviromnemtal and Land Data Systems; **PREV EMPLOY:** Sch. of Law, Western Reserve Univ. 1946-63, Prof. of Law; **PROFL AFFIL & HONORS:** ABA, PA Bar Assn., OH State Bar Assn., Cincinnati Bar Assn, Member Amer. Coll. of RE Lawyers; **EDUC:** AB, 1933, Pol. Sci., Bucknell Univ.; **GRAD EDUC:** JD, 1936, Law, Duke Law Sch.; **EDUC HONORS:** Cum Laude, (pres.) Pi Sigma Alpha, Tau Kappa Alpha, Law Review; **OTHER ACT & HONORS:** Originator and Prime Devel. of Comprehensive Unified Land Data System also known as Multi-purpose Land Data System or Multi-Purpose Cadastre; **HOME ADD:** 62 Rawson Woods Cir., Cincinnati, OH 45220, (513)961-9169; **BUS ADD:** Coll. of Law, Univ. of Cincinnati, Cincinnati, OH 45221, (513)475-2631.

COOK, Ted P.——B: Mar. 9, 1951, Louisville, KY, *VP/RE Dept. Head*, Temple National Bank, RE/Mort. Loan Dept.; **PRIM RE ACT:** Consultant, Appraiser, Banker, Property Manager; **SERVICES:** Servicing for investors, loan origination, investment counciling in RE; **REP CLIENTS:** Ins. Cos., REIT, S&L, Banks; **PROFL AFFIL & HONORS:** TX Bankers Assn.; TX Mort. Bankers Assn.; Temple Homebuilders Assn.; Amer. Bankers Assn., 1978 Assoc. Member of Year - Temple Homebuilders; **EDUC:** BS in Educ., 1974, Admin. of Educ./Pol. Sci., Baylor Univ.; **GRAD EDUC:** Nat. School of RE Fin., OH St. Univ.; **EDUC HONORS:** Dean's Distinguished List; **OTHER ACT & HONORS:** Bd. of Realtors, Member - TX Bankers Assn.; Mort. Fin. Comm.; Dir., Temple Jaycees; Campaign Mgr., Amer. Heart Assn.; Member, Mental Health & Mental Retardation Citizen Advisory Comm.; **HOME ADD:** 106 Ruggles Loop, Temple, TX 76501, (817)773-1028; **BUS ADD:** 100 W. Adams, P.O. Box 809, Temple, TX 76501, (817)778-8946.

COOKE, Jeffrey R.——*VP & General Counsel*, Sta-Rite Industries, Inc.; **PRIM RE ACT:** Property Manager; **BUS ADD:** 777 East Wisconsin Ave., Ste. 3300, Milwaukee, WI 53202, (414)276-6888.*

COOL, Stephen N.——B: June 9, 1940, Los Angeles, CA, *Pres.*, Stephen N. Cool, A Law Corp.; **PRIM RE ACT:** Attorney, Lender, Instructor; **SERVICES:** Law; **REP CLIENTS:** Mid-State Bank; Williams Bros. Mkts.; Pacific Improvements, Inc.; VIP Future Corp.; Vick Pace Const. Inc. Foremaster Const., Inc.; **PREV EMPLOY:** Interstate Commerce Commn. 1965-67. San Luis Obispo Cty. Dist. Atty.; **PROFL AFFIL & HONORS:** San Luis Obispo Cty. Bar Assn.; **EDUC:** Occidental Coll., 1962, Pol. Sci., UCLA Law Sch.; **GRAD EDUC:** LLB, 1965; **OTHER ACT & HONORS:** City Atty., Grover City, CA 1971-81; San Luis Obispo Cty. Republican Comm.; Pres., San Luis Obispo Cty. Bar Assn. 1980; **HOME ADD:** 254 Tolbert Pl., Arroyo Grande, CA 93420; **BUS ADD:** 1577 El Camino Real, Arroyo Grande, CA 93420, (805)489-8433.

COOLEY, Dorothy N.——B: Mar 4, 1929, Madison, WI, *Broker - Owner*, Cardinal Realty; **PRIM RE ACT:** Broker, Consultant, Appraiser, Owner/Investor; **SERVICES:** Homefinders and Investments too.- RE; **PROFL AFFIL & HONORS:** Southeastern Assn. of Realtors (IN); **EDUC:** Teaching, Income tax prep., Univ. of WI & IN Univ.; **HOME ADD:** 133 Woodlawn Dr., Batesville, IN 47006, (812)934-4809; **BUS ADD:** 3 Huntersville Rd., Batesville, IN 47006, (812)934-5544.

COOLICK, Wilma I.——B: June 3, 1917, Salisbury, MO, *Realtor Broker*, The Stanton Co. Inc.; **PRIM RE ACT:** Broker, Appraiser; **OTHER RE ACT:** Resid., Farms, Comml., Lake Homes; **SERVICES:** Inter-city relocation; **PREV EMPLOY:** Owner, Resort Hotel; **PROFL AFFIL & HONORS:** GRI; CRS; CRB, CRS Realtor of the Year 80 & 81; **EDUC:** 2 yr., Kirksville State Teachers Coll.; **OTHER ACT & HONORS:** Past Matron, Order of the Eastern Star; State President, Women's Council Realtors at 1980 State Gov. WCR 1981; CRS Pres., State AR 1981; Pres., Elect Fay B. of Realtors; **HOME ADD:** 2503 Elizabeth Ave., Fayetteville, AR 72702, (501)521-7087; **BUS ADD:** 1985 N. College Ave., Fayetteville, AR 72701, (501)521-7653.

COOLIDGE, Thomas E.T.——*Real Estate Financier*, Chase Eaton & Co.; **PRIM RE ACT:** Consultant, Developer, Owner/Investor, Syndicator; **PREV EMPLOY:** 1976-1977, Blyth, Eastman, Dillon & Co., Inc., Analyst in Corp. Fin. Dept.; 1973-1975, Native American, Inc., Supt. and Dir.; 1972-1973, Lagarita Land & Cattle Co., Co-Mgr.; **PROFL AFFIL & HONORS:** FL & OH RE Lic.; **EDUC:** AB, 1972, Hist., Univ. of PA; **GRAD EDUC:** MBA, 1980, Columbia Univ., School of Business; **OTHER ACT & HONORS:** Other Bus. Address: 28829 Chagrin Blvd., Cleveland, OH, 44122, (216)464-4300; **BUS ADD:** 242 Ocean Dr., Jupiter, FL 33458, (305)741-0720.

COOMBS, Edward H.——B: Aug. 20, 1943, Jamestown, NY, *Mgr.*, The Galvin Co. Realtors; **PRIM RE ACT:** Broker, Consultant, Appraiser; **OTHER RE ACT:** Office mgmt. training; **SERVICES:** Sales consulting, investment counseling, appraisals; **REP CLIENTS:** Lenders, attys., indivs., investors; **PROFL AFFIL & HONORS:** NAREA, Greater Boston RE Bd., and Affiliates, MLS Million Dollar Club, Phi Kappa Phi; **EDUC:** BA, 1965, Lib. Arts, Soc., Univ. of RI; **GRAD EDUC:** MA, 1969, Human Services, Andover Newton; **EDUC HONORS:** High Hon.; **OTHER ACT & HONORS:** Mass. Audubon Soc., Massapoag Yacht Club, Open Door Soc.; **BUS ADD:** 14 Common St., Wrentham, MA 02093, (617)384-3887.

COOMBS, James E.——B: Dec. 10, 1921, Morgantown, WV, *Pres.*, Baker & Coombs, Inc.; **PRIM RE ACT:** Developer, Builder, Owner/Investor, Property Manager; **PREV EMPLOY:** Pres. Wesco Equip. Inc., Pres. Morgantown Glass & Mirror, Pres. Coombs Enterprises Inc.; **PROFL AFFIL & HONORS:** Past Pres. A6C of WV, Past Pres. Morgantown C of C; **MIL SERV:** USAAF, Air Force, Capt.; **OTHER ACT & HONORS:** Beta Theta Pi; CIMS; Dir. - Farmers and Merchants Bank, Morgantown, WV; Westover Bank, Westover, Morgantown, WV; **HOME ADD:** 841 Sheldon Ave., Morgantown, WV 26505; **BUS ADD:** 601 E Brockway Ave., Morgantown, WV 26505, (304)296-4483.

COONEY, Kevin J.——B: Sept. 18, 1951, Chicago, IL, *Staff Atty.*, Title Guaranty Fund, Inc.; **PRIM RE ACT:** Attorney, Owner/Investor, Syndicator; **PROFL AFFIL & HONORS:** ABA, IL State Bar Assn., Chicago Bar Assn.; **EDUC:** BA, 1974, Bus.; Communications; Poli. Sci., Western IL; **GRAD EDUC:** JD, 1977, John Marshall Law School; **EDUC HONORS:** Dean's List; **OTHER ACT & HONORS:** Various community groups; **BUS ADD:** 29 S. LaSalle, Ste 540, Chicago, IL 60603, (312)372-8361.

COONS, C. Duane——B: Mar. 8, 1938, Greeley, CO, *Owner-Broker*, The Realty Exchange; **PRIM RE ACT:** Broker, Consultant, Lender, Owner/Investor; **OTHER RE ACT:** Exchanges; **EDUC:** BSBA, 1959, RE, Fin., Mgmt., Univ. of CO; **HOME ADD:** 430 Monroe St., Denver, CO 80206, (303)355-7109; **BUS ADD:** 430 Monroe St., Denver, CO 80206, (303)355-7109.

COONS, Richard A.——B: Dec. 11, 1938, Cherokee, OK, *Partner in Charge*, Touche Ross & Co., Honolulu, HI; **OTHER RE ACT:** CPA; **SERVICES:** Tax and Audit; **REP CLIENTS:** RE Devel., synd. and operators; **PROFL AFFIL & HONORS:** AICPA, HI Soc. of CPA's, RESSI, CPA; **EDUC:** 1960, Bus. Admin., Univ. of CA at Long Beach; **OTHER ACT & HONORS:** Planning Commn., Santa Rosa, CA 1962-1963, Hist. HI Found; **HOME ADD:** 881 Hahaione St., Honolulu, HI 96825; **BUS ADD:** 733 Bishop St. Suite 2000, Honolulu, HI 96813, (808)521-9591.

COOPER, Darrell M.——B: Apr. 18, 1939, Bangor, ME, *Pres.*, Property Investments, Inc., P.I. Realty Mgmt., Inc.; **PRIM RE ACT:** Broker, Consultant, Developer, Owner/Investor, Property Manager; **SERVICES:** Comml., Indus. Brokerage; RE Asset Mgmt. and consulting; **PROFL AFFIL & HONORS:** Realtors, Instit. of RE Mgmt., CPM; **EDUC:** BS, 1961, Corp. Fin., Wharton School of Fin. & Commerce, Univ. of PA; **HOME ADD:** 62 Meadowbrook Rd., Bangor, ME 04401, (207)942-6409; **BUS ADD:** 20 State St., PO Box 673, Bangor, ME 04401, (207)942-4815.

COOPER, Erwin E.——B: Oct. 7, 1918, Boston, MA, *Partner*, Kabatznick, Stern & Cooper; **PRIM RE ACT:** Attorney, Instructor; **OTHER RE ACT:** Pres. Overlook Condo. Assn.; **SERVICES:** Advice & representation of persons with RE problems in planning, implementation, and litigation and leasing, conveyances, title opinions, landlord and tenant problems; **REP CLIENTS:** Lenders, title cos., investors in comml. props., devels. and bldrs.; **PREV EMPLOY:** US Army, Legal Advisor to RE Contracting Officer, US Armed Forces in Middle East; **EDUC:** AB, 1939, Hist. & Govt., Univ. of NE at Orono; **GRAD EDUC:** JD, 1942, Harvard Law Sch.; **EDUC HONORS:** Dept. Hon.; **MIL SERV:** US Army, Col., USAR (Ret.), Meritorious Serv. Medal, Amer Theater Ribbons, ETO Ribbon with 5 Battle Stars; **OTHER ACT & HONORS:** Tau Epsilon Phi Frat., Past Intl. Pres., Adjunct Prof. New England Sch. of Law, 1953 to present (present subject), Modern RE Trans. Award, Distinguished Prof. Award by NESL Alumni; **HOME ADD:** Campton, NH 03223; **BUS ADD:** 212 Statler Office Bldg., Park Plaza, Boston, MA 02116, (617)542-3322.

COOPER, Fowler——B: Nov. 2, 1940, Jackson, MS, *Pres.*, The Fowler Cooper Co.; **PRIM RE ACT:** Broker, Consultant, Owner/Investor, Property Manager, Syndicator; **SERVICES:** Brokerage, consulting, prop. mgmt., synd.; **REP CLIENTS:** Cos., including lenders and indiv. owners and investors in comml. and investment props.; **PREV EMPLOY:** Federal Compress and Warehouse Co. (VP) and its affiliate Southwide Devel. Co. 1969-1975.; **PROFL AFFIL & HONORS:** IREM, Intl. Council of Shopping Centers, NAR; MS ORg. for Realty Exchange, Jackson Comml. RE Exchangers, FLI, Agricultural Comml. and Indus. Group., CPM; Chmn, Profl. Standards Comm. (past) Bd. of Dir. Jackson Bd. of Realtors Ad Hoc Comm. - Tennant/Landlord Act - MS Assn. of Realtors; Bd. of Dir. (past), Vice President M Chap. 80 - IREM; **EDUC:** BA, 1963, Hist., Univ. of the South (Sewanee); **GRAD EDUC:** MBA, 1967, Mktg., Wharton Grad. School of Fin. and Commerce (Univ. of PA); **EDUC HONORS:** Grad. with Honors in Hist., Dean's List, Grad. in top 10% of class, Sec. of Student Body, VP Assn. for Intl. Exchange of Students in Econ. and Commerce, Member Stearing Committee, MBA Club; **MIL SERV:** USAF, A2c; **OTHER ACT & HONORS:** Jackson C of C; Pascagoula Moss Point C of C; Past Pres., Big Bros./ Big Sisters of Memphis, Vestay (past) St. John's Episcopal Church, Memphis; **HOME ADD:** 1317 St. Ann, Jackson, MS 39202; **BUS ADD:** 2600 Lakeland Terr., Jackson, MS 39216, (601)362-3974.

COOPER, Glen J.——B: Dec. 13, 1947, Brush, CO, *Pres. & Assoc. Broker*, Maine Business Brokers, Inc.; **PRIM RE ACT:** Broker, Appraiser, Owner/Investor; **SERVICES:** Bus. opportunity brokerage; comml. appraisal; **REP CLIENTS:** Small bus. buyers & sellers; appraisal work for attys., accountants & lenders; **PREV EMPLOY:** Comml. Div., ERA; Floyd Ray Realty of Auburn, ME; **PROFL AFFIL & HONORS:** 1st VP, ME Assn. of Realtors; Local Bd. Pres. (1981); Member, Realtors Nat. Mktg. Inst., RESSI, 1981 Realtor of the Year, Local Bd.; **EDUC:** 1965, Econ., Hist., Univ. of CO; **GRAD EDUC:** 1973, Grad. School of Bank Mktg., Univ. of CO; **EDUC HONORS:** Student Senate; **OTHER ACT & HONORS:** Bd. of Dirs., Lewiston Tomorrow, Inc. and Lewiston-Auburn C of C; Auburn Bus. Devel. Corp.; Chmn. of Mayor's Mktg. Comm., Lewiston, ME 1981; Active Fundraiser for Muscular Dystrophy Assn.; **HOME ADD:** 393 Turner St., Auburn, ME 04210, (207)784-4822; **BUS ADD:** 393 Turner St., Auburn, ME 04210, (207)786-3636.

COOPER, Joel H.——B: Mar. 28, 1924, Brooklyn, NY, *Arch./Operations Officer*, National Bank of North America, Prop. Mgmt.; **PRIM RE ACT:** Architect; **SERVICES:** Design of bank branches, bank departmental offices; **PREV EMPLOY:** Private practice - Joel H. Cooper, AIA; **PROFL AFFIL & HONORS:** Past Pres. of Long Is. Chap. of the AIA; Member - NY Soc. of Archs., Registered Architect in NY, NJ, CT; NCARB; **EDUC:** BArch, 1948, Arch., Pratt Inst. School of Arch.; **EDUC HONORS:** Grad. with Honors; **MIL SERV:** Army Corps of Engrs., Active Service - 5/43 to 3/46, Tech. 4th Grade, European Theater of Operations - 5/44 to 2/46; **OTHER ACT & HONORS:** Member Ad. Comm.-Nassau Cty. Office for Aging; Adjunct Assoc. Prof. of Arch., NY Inst. of Tech., Old Westbury, NY; **HOME ADD:** 16 Ann Dr., Syosset, NY 11791, (516)921-2475; **BUS ADD:** 3161 Hempstead Turnpike, Levittown, NY 11756, (516)752-2439.

COOPER, John C.——*Coun*, Holly Sugar Corp.; **PRIM RE ACT:** Attorney, Property Manager; **BUS ADD:** PO Box 1052, Colorado Springs, CO 80901, (303)471-0123.*

COOPER, Kenneth V.——B: May 9, 1944, Winnipeg, Manitoba, *VP*, Campeau Corporation Texas, Campeau Corp., Ottawa, Ontario; **PRIM RE ACT:** Developer, Property Manager; **SERVICES:** Devel. and prop. mgmt. of multi-use comml. RE; **REP CLIENTS:** Comml./hotel/retail tenants; **PREV EMPLOY:** Great-West Life Assurance Co.; Equity and Joint Venture RE 1976-1980; Citibank NY Interim Fin. 1974-1976; Citadel Life Assurance Co.; Mort. Fin. 1971-1974; **PROFL AFFIL & HONORS:** The ULI; NAIOP; P. Eng. (Ontario); **EDUC:** BS, 1967, Civl Engrg., The Univ. of Manitoba; **GRAD EDUC:** MBA, 1971, Fin., RE, The Univ. of Western Ontario; **HOME ADD:** 4230 Beechwood Ln., Dallas, TX 75220, (214)357-9840; **BUS ADD:** Plaza of the Americas, LB342, 700 N. Pearl, Dallas, TX 75201, (214)745-1729.

COOPER, R. Jack——B: Aug. 1, 1933, Leatha, KY, *Investment Officer*, School Employees Retirement System of OH, Investment Div. Retirement Fund; **PRIM RE ACT:** Lender, Owner/Investor; **PROFL AFFIL & HONORS:** Fin. Analysts Federation, Partners, OH State Univ., State Investment Officers Assn.; **EDUC:** BS Bus Admin., 1960, Fin. & Credit, OH State Univ.; **GRAD EDUC:** MBA, 1967, Fin. & Investment, OH State Univ.; **EDUC HONORS:** Beta Gamma Sigma, Cum Laude; **MIL SERV:** USAF, 1st Lt.; **HOME ADD:** 1910 Langham Rd., Columbus, OH 43221, (614)457-0692; **BUS TEL:** (614)221-7012.

COOPER, R. Maurice——B: Sept. 27, 1915, Spokane, WA, *Atty. at Law, CPA*, Cooper Law Offices; **PRIM RE ACT:** Attorney, Instructor; **REP CLIENTS:** Spokane Cty. Bd. of Realtors, WA RE Educ. Found., Pacific Realty Co., Vic Lewis Realty, Tri State Realty, James S. Black & Co., Tomlinson Agency, F.S. Barrett Co., House & Home, Inc., Homes & Income, Inc., Century 21, A-Aladin Realty, Farihurst & Associates; **PROFL AFFIL & HONORS:** ABA, WA State Bar Assn., Spokane Cty. Bar; Amer. Inst. of Accountants, Doctor of Laws and CPA; **EDUC:** Gonzaga Univ., 1940, Pre-law & acctg.; **GRAD EDUC:** Gonzaga Univ., 1941, Law; **OTHER ACT & HONORS:** Past Pres. of Spokane Inter-State Fair, Past Intl. Pres. - Intl. Order of Moose, Past Dist. Gov. of Lions Intl., Past Pres. Spokane Jr. Chamber, Past VP & Dir. Spokane C of C; **HOME ADD:** S. 1519 Helena, Spokane, WA 99203, (509)435-7029; **BUS ADD:** N. 1522 Washington, Spokane, WA 99205, (509)326-3600.

COOPER, Robert B.——**B:** May 26, 1943, Somerville, NJ, *Exec. VP*, Molton/Cooper Mort. Investors, Inc.; **OTHER RE ACT:** Mort. banker; **SERVICES:** Fin. for large scale RE projects; **REP CLIENTS:** Various ins. cos., savings assns., pension funds & pvt. investors; **PREV EMPLOY:** Formerly loan officer with Nat. Life Ins. Co. of VT, Montpelier, VT, 1971-73; **PROFL AFFIL & HONORS:** Phi Delta Phi Intl. Legal Frat., Alpha Kappa Psi Profl. Bus. Frat., Exchoquev Phi Delta Phi; **EDUC:** BS, 1966, Fin. & RE, Bus. Admin., USC; **GRAD EDUC:** MBA, 1971, USC; JD, 1976, Loyola Univ. School of Law; **MIL SERV:** US Army; E-6, S/Sgt., 1967-69; **OTHER ACT & HONORS:** Jonathan Club, Los Angeles, since 1975; Published several articles, one involving usury law & wraparound morts., 1976; **BUS ADD:** 9800 S. Sepulveda Blvd., Suite 520, Los Angeles, CA 90045, (213)822-3011.

COOPER, Robert E.——**B:** Jan. 15, 1931, Portland, OR, *VP*, Blackfield Hawaii Corp., Devel.; **PRIM RE ACT:** Developer, Owner/Investor; **SERVICES:** Devel. of resid. and comml. props.; **PREV EMPLOY:** HI Housing Auth.; **EDUC:** 1958, Bus. Admin., San Jose State Univ.; **MIL SERV:** USAF; **HOME ADD:** 1035 Kainui Dr., Kailua, HI 96734; **BUS ADD:** 1221 Kapiolani Blvd., Suite 700, Honolulu, HI 96814, (808)538-3841.

COOPER, William H.——**B:** Feb. 23, 1951, St. Louis, MO, *Pres.*, William H. Cooper, Ltd.; **PRIM RE ACT:** Consultant, Owner/Investor; **OTHER RE ACT:** CPA; **SERVICES:** Income tax planning & consulting; **PROFL AFFIL & HONORS:** AICPA, ASCPA, Phoenix Tax Workshop, Estate Plannier Grp. of Phoenix, Delta Sigma Pi, Valley of the Sun RE Exchangors; **EDUC:** BS in BA, 1973, Acctg., Univ. of MO; **HOME ADD:** 5426 E. Roanoke, Phoenix, AZ 85008, (602)952-9494; **BUS ADD:** 3300 N. Central Ave., Suite 1300, Phoenix, AZ 85012, (602)241-1500.

COOPERSMITH, Henry J.——**B:** Mar. 17, 1943, Oakland, CA, *Shareholder*, Henry J. Coopersmith, Inc.; **PRIM RE ACT:** Attorney; **REP CLIENTS:** Investors, builders & devels.; **PROFL AFFIL & HONORS:** Member of the RE Sect. of the ABA; Member of the Tax Sect. of the Amer. Bar Assn.: Member of the Tax Sect. and RE Sect. of the Orange Cty. Bar Assn.; **EDUC:** BS, 1965, 1968, Acctg., CA State Coll. at Hayward JD, Univ. of CA at Berkeley; **GRAD EDUC:** LLM in Taxation, 1969, NY Univ.; **OTHER ACT & HONORS:** Previous Chmn. of Tax Sect., Orange Cty. Bar Assn.; Cert. Tax Law Specialist by Bd. of Legal Specialization of the CA State Bar; **BUS ADD:** 1200 N. Main St., Suite 800, Santa Ana, CA 92701, (714)834-1171.

COPE, Leland H.——**B:** June 18, 1929, Canton, OH, *Owner*, Leland H. Cope; **PRIM RE ACT:** Attorney, Developer, Owner/Investor, Property Manager; **SERVICES:** Legal services re: RE transactions; C.E.O. excavating co.; own and manage comml. RE; **REP CLIENTS:** Indiv. and corps. investing in RE; **PROFL AFFIL & HONORS:** ABA, OH State Bar Assn., Stark Cty. Bar Assn.; **EDUC:** BA, 1950, Bus. Admin. and Hist., Mount Union Coll.; **GRAD EDUC:** JD, 1953, Harvard Law School; **EDUC HONORS:** Cum Laude; **HOME ADD:** 130 44th St., NW, Canton, OH 44709, (216)492-3812; **BUS ADD:** 2800 Market Ave., North, Canton, OH 44709, (216)454-6183.

COPE, Robert Lloyd——**B:** Jan. 19, 1918, Richfield, UT, *Chief Appraiser*, Housing & Urban Devel., Fed. Housing Admin., Salt Lake City Insuring Office; **PRIM RE ACT:** Appraiser, Instructor; **PREV EMPLOY:** RE salesman; **PROFL AFFIL & HONORS:** Soc. of RE Appraisers; Pres., Soc. Salt Lake Chapter 41, 1976-1977, SRA; **EDUC:** Normal Degree, 1941, Educ./Eng., Brigham Young Univ.; BS, 1942, Educ./Eng., Brigham Young Univ.; **MIL SERV:** USAF; Capt.; Marksmanship; **OTHER ACT & HONORS:** High Priest in LDS Church; Bishop's Counselor, 1957-1962; Ward CLerk; Sunday School Supt.; Mission for the Church of Jesus Christ of Latter-day Saints, 1938-1940; **HOME ADD:** 1028 Mansfield Ave., Salt Lake City, UT, (801)467-3231; **BUS ADD:** 125 S. State St., Salt Lake City, UT 84111, (801)524-5225.

COPLAN, Ralph——*VP*, Robertshaw Controls Co.; **PRIM RE ACT:** Property Manager; **BUS ADD:** 1701 Byrd Ave., PO Box 26544, Richmond, VA 23261, (804)281-0700.*

COPLAND, Milton——**B:** Feb. 26, 1909, New York, NY, *VP*, Milton Copland, Uris 380 Madison Corporation; **PRIM RE ACT:** Attorney, Owner/Investor, Property Manager; **EDUC:** BS, 1929, Harvard Univ.; **GRAD EDUC:** LLB, 1932, Harvard Univ. Law School; **EDUC HONORS:** Cum Laude; **MIL SERV:** Transportation, 1st Lt.; **OTHER ACT & HONORS:** Harvard Club, NYC; **HOME ADD:** 190 E. 72 St., New York, NY 10021; **BUS ADD:** 300 Park Ave., New York, NY 10022, (212)407-9503.

COPPACK, Kenneth N.——**B:** June 1, 1927, England, *Asst. to the VP*, Montreal Engrg. Co., Ltd., Comml. Div.; **OTHER RE ACT:** RE Corporate Mgmt.: RE & Premises; **SERVICES:** Services to MONENCo. Grp.; **PROFL AFFIL & HONORS:** Can: MEIC, MCSEE, MCIM, MBOMA; MREBM; US: MNSPE; UK: MIERE; **EDUC:** BSc, 1967, Commerce, Sir George Williams Univ.; **MIL SERV:** Royal Air Force, Radar Engr., Berlin Airlift; Long Serv.; **OTHER ACT & HONORS:** Sec., Instn. of Electronic and Radio Engrs., MEI.; **BUS ADD:** PO Box 6088, Station "A", Montreal, H3C3Z8, Que., Canada, (514)286-3018.

COPPIN, Al——**B:** Sept. 10, 1943, Haywood, CA, *Pres.*, Keegan & Coppin Co., Inc.; **PRIM RE ACT:** Broker, Developer, Builder; **SERVICES:** RE brokerage, devel. of indus. and resid. projects, bldr. of resid. projects; **PREV EMPLOY:** Grubb and Ellis, Oakland and San Francisco; **PROFL AFFIL & HONORS:** Nat. Assn. of Realtors; BT Gen. Contractor; Constr. RE Broker; **EDUC:** BS, 1969, Engrg., Operations Mgmt., Univ. of CA - Berkeley; **GRAD EDUC:** MBA, 1970, Applied Econ., Univ. of CA - Berkeley; **EDUC HONORS:** Cum Laude, with honors; **MIL SERV:** US Army, Sgt.; **OTHER ACT & HONORS:** Phi Beta Kappa, CA Award; **HOME ADD:** 2754 Canterbury Dr., Santa Rosa, CA 95405, (707)544-3722; **BUS ADD:** 1335 N Dutton, Santa Rosa, CA 95405, (707)528-1400.

COPPOCK, Jerry K.——**B:** Jan. 9, 1932, Le Mars, IA, *Owner*, Crest Realty Service; **PRIM RE ACT:** Broker, Consultant, Appraiser, Property Manager, Insuror; **SERVICES:** Sales; **REP CLIENTS:** IBP; GM; Sioux Tools, NBT; **PROFL AFFIL & HONORS:** REMI; IAR; NAR, GRI; CRS; CRB; Past Pres., S.C. Bd.; VP, IA Assn. of Realtors, 1975-76; **MIL SERV:** USN, Den. Tech. 3rd Class, Korean, 1951-1955; **OTHER ACT & HONORS:** Lic. Lay reader, Episcopal Diocese of IA; **HOME ADD:** 610 14th St., Sioux City, IA 51105, (605)232-4397; **BUS ADD:** PO Box 1375, Sioux City, IA 51102, (712)252-3198.

COPPOLA, A. Gerard——**B:** Dec. 27, 1934, Mineola, LI, NY, *Pres.*, The Evan Group, Ltd.; **PRIM RE ACT:** Broker, Consultant, Developer, Builder, Property Manager; **OTHER RE ACT:** Mort. Broker; **SERVICES:** Packaging of Mort. Proposals for Presentation to Lending Instns.; Mgmt. of Condominium and Apt. Projects; Dev. Large Tracts of Land; **REP CLIENTS:** Developers, lenders and indiv. in Comml. Prop.; **PREV EMPLOY:** Axminster RE Corp., 602 42nd St., NY, NY; **PROFL AFFIL & HONORS:** NAHB, NAR, Bd. Dirs. Home Builders Assn. of Greater Springfield; Educ. Comm., Greater Springfield Bd. of Realtors; **EDUC:** Bergen Cty. Comm. Coll.; **MIL SERV:** USMC; Sgt., Good Conduct; European Occupation; **OTHER ACT & HONORS:** Guest Lecturer, Fairleigh Dickinson Univ., Fin. of Real Property, 1976; **HOME ADD:** 17 Brookside Cir., Wilbraham, MA 01095, (413)596-2234; **BUS ADD:** 17 Brookside Circle, Wilbraham, MA 01095, (413)596-9606.

COPSETTA, Norman G.——**B:** Mar. 11, 1932, Pennsauken, NJ, *Exec VP*, Cooper Abstract Co.; **OTHER RE ACT:** Title ins. agent; **SERVICES:** Full title ins. and settlement servs., spec. in researching, contested & ancient titles, also title work for easement acquisition; **REP CLIENTS:** Law firms, RE brokers, utility cos., maj. corps.; **PREV EMPLOY:** Mkt. St. Title & Abstract Co., 1949-53; Realty Abstract Co. 1953-64; Law firm of Davis & Reberkenny, 1964-present; Cooper Abstract Co., 1974-present; **PROFL AFFIL & HONORS:** NJ Land Title Assn.; Assn. of Legal Administrators; NJ Title Ins. Agents Assn.; Camden Cty. Bd. of Realtors; Charter Member Amer. Soc. of Notaries, S Jersey Exec. Assn., Pres. 1979 & 1980; **EDUC:** 1968, Intl. Accountants Soc. Sch. of Acctg.; **OTHER ACT & HONORS:** NJ For. Commnr. of Deeds for PA, 1961 to present; Mncpl. Treas. and Collector of Taxes for the Borough of Somerdale, 1961-64; United Fund Fair Share Chairperson Award, 1971 through 1981; **HOME ADD:** 212 S Browining Rd., Somerdale, NJ 08083, (609)783-0866; **BUS ADD:** 499 Cooper Landing Rd., Cherry Hill, NJ 08002, (609)667-6000.

CORALLINO, Robert L.——**B:** May 23, 1945, Fairmont, WV, *CPA*, Robert L. Corallino, CPA; **PRIM RE ACT:** Consultant; **OTHER RE ACT:** Accountant; **SERVICES:** Investment counseling, Synd. of comml. prop., ltd. partnershiPs, and Tax consultation; **PROFL AFFIL & HONORS:** AICPA; NH Soc. of CPA's; MD Soc. of CPA's; Exchange Club; Nat. Assn. of Accountants; Amer. Acctg. Assn., CPA; **EDUC:** BS, 1967, Acctg. and Taxes, WV Univ.; **GRAD EDUC:** MBA, 1969, WV Univ.; **HOME ADD:** 11 Matthew Patten Dr., Bedford, NH 03102, (603)668-4060; **BUS ADD:** 61 North St., Manchester, NH 03104, (603)623-5557.

CORBETT, Harry——*Dir. Space & Fac. Plng.*, The Gillette Co.; **PRIM RE ACT:** Property Manager; **BUS ADD:** Prudential Tower Bldg. 49th Floor, Boston, MA 02199, (617)421-7271.*

CORBIN, Lee D.——B: June 13, 1931, Phoenix, AZ, *Mg. Part.*, Property Management Assoc.; **PRIM RE ACT:** Property Manager, Owner/Investor; **OTHER RE ACT:** Owner, Pres., Space Mgmt. Corp.; **PREV EMPLOY:** Asst. Plant Maintenance AEROJET CORP., Sacramento, CA; **PROFL AFFIL & HONORS:** IREM, NAR, CA Assn. of Realtors, Sacramento Bd. of Realtors, Sacramento Co. Taxpayers League, Sacramento Apt. Assn., Most Outstanding Recreation Program in the USA awarded by the Natl. Indust. Rec. Assn.; **EDUC:** BS, 1953, Indus. Psych., Stanford Univ.; **MIL SERV:** US Army, Sp4; **HOME ADD:** 1448 Tradewinds Ave., Sacramento, CA 95822, (916)455-1192; **BUS ADD:** 601 University Ave., Ste. 100, Sacramento, CA 95825, (916)920-1021.

CORCORAN, Brian R.——B: May 20, 1948, Brooklyn, NY, *VP and Mgr., NY Region*, Cushman & Wakefield, Inc., Appraisal Div.; **PRIM RE ACT:** Appraiser, Instructor; **OTHER RE ACT:** Consultant; **SERVICES:** Valuation, Investment Counseling, Market Studies, Feasibility Studies; **REP CLIENTS:** Major Corps., Instit., Lenders and Law Firms; **PREV EMPLOY:** James H. Burns Co., Inc., Suburbia Fed. S&L Assn.; **PROFL AFFIL & HONORS:** Appraisal Instit., SREA, RE Bd. of NY, NY State Appraisal Soc., Indus. RE Brokers Assn., MAI, SRPA; **EDUC:** BA, 1970, Bus. Admin. & Econ., Marist Coll. Poughkeepsie, NY; **EDUC HONORS:** Outstanding student in Bus./Econ. Dept 1970; **HOME ADD:** 54 Westbury Rd., Garden City, New York, NY 11530, (516)746-0030; **BUS ADD:** 1166 Ave. of the Americas, New York, NY 10036, (212)841-7779.

CORCORAN, Christopher H.——B: Jan. 24, 1951, Rochester, NY, *Atty.*, Wiedman & Vazzana; **PRIM RE ACT:** Attorney; **PREV EMPLOY:** Harris, Beach, Wilcox, Rubin and Levey; **PROFL AFFIL & HONORS:** Monroe Cty. Bar Assoc., NY State Bar Assn., The Assn. of the Bar of the City of NY; **EDUC:** AB, 1973, Eng, Princeton Univ.; **GRAD EDUC:** JD, 1976, Albany Law School; **EDUC HONORS:** Bd. of Editors, Albany Law School; **HOME ADD:** 141 Brookside Dr., Rochester, NY 14614, (716)381-4534; **BUS ADD:** 5 S. Fitzhugh St., Rochester, NY 14614, (716)454-5850.

CORCORAN, Richard L.——B: June 18, 1941, Wheeling, WV, *Proprietor*, RLC & Co.; **PRIM RE ACT:** Consultant, Developer, Owner/Investor, Property Manager, Insuror; **OTHER RE ACT:** Fin. servs. consultant; **SERVICES:** Fin. Consultant; **REP CLIENTS:** Indiv.; Small Bus.; **PROFL AFFIL & HONORS:** Nat. Assn. Security Dealer, Million Dollar Round Table, NALU, NAHU, CLU, RHU, Reg. Representative; **EDUC:** Amer. Coll., Fin.; **MIL SERV:** USN, E-4, 1958-62; **OTHER ACT & HONORS:** Loyal Order of Moose, Knights of Columbus; **HOME ADD:** Midlothian, VA 23113, (804)794-8600; **BUS ADD:** 10400 Midlothian Tpk., Richmond, VA 23235, (804)794-8246.

CORDER, H. Robert——B: Mar. 13, 1920, Grand Junction, CO, *VP, Comml. Sales*, Latter & Blum, Inc., Comml. Sales; **PRIM RE ACT:** Broker, Consultant, Instructor, Syndicator; **SERVICES:** Investment counseling, indus. counseling, synd. of comml. prop.; **PROFL AFFIL & HONORS:** Soc. of Indus. Realtors (SIR); Intl. Inst. of Valuers, Sr. Member (SCV); **EDUC:** BA, 1941, Lib. Arts, Williams Coll.; **EDUC HONORS:** Cum Laude; **MIL SERV:** USN; Lt.; **OTHER ACT & HONORS:** Order of St. Lazarus; **HOME ADD:** 50 Orpheum Ave., Metairie, LA 70005, (504)835-4576; **BUS ADD:** 915 Common St., New Orleans, LA 70112, (504)525-1311.

CORDING, Robert——B: Apr. 17, 1925, Brooklyn, NY, *VP*, Long Island Trust Co., Mort. Dept.; **PRIM RE ACT:** Banker; **SERVICES:** Resid. & Comml. Mort. Loans in Long Island and Const. Loans & Mort. Warehouse Lines of Credit (Participations Natly. and Direct Locally); **PREV EMPLOY:** Marine Midland Bank - 23 yrs.; **PROFL AFFIL & HONORS:** ABA; Mort. Bankers of Amer.; Long Is. Bldg. Inst., Author - "Mort. Loan Warehousing in the NYC and Long Is. Area"; **GRAD EDUC:** Stonier Grad. School of Banking, 1967; **MIL SERV:** USAF, M/Sgt.; **HOME ADD:** 911 Old Britton Rd., North Bellmore, NY 11710, (516)221-4101; **BUS ADD:** 1401 Franklin Ave., Garden City, NY 11530, (516)294-2241.

CORDINGLEY, Bruce A.——B: Dec. 28, 1946, Chicago, IL, *Partner*, Ice Miller Donadio & Ryan; **PRIM RE ACT:** Attorney, Owner/Investor; **REP CLIENTS:** Local, regl. and nat. owners and dev. of RE; **PROFL AFFIL & HONORS:** Member of the Bar State of IN and Commonwealth of MA; **EDUC:** BS, 1968, Indus. Mgmt. and Econ., Purdue Univ.; **GRAD EDUC:** JD, 1971, Harvard Law School; **EDUC HONORS:** Distinction and Honors in Econ. Honors; **MIL SERV:** US Army, Capt.; **OTHER ACT & HONORS:** Pres., Indianapolis Fire Merit Bd.; **HOME ADD:** 332 N East St., Indianapolis, IN 46202, (317)635-3617; **BUS ADD:** 10th Floor, 111 Monument Circle, Indianapolis, IN 46202, (317)635-1213.

CORGEL, John B.——B: Mar. 16, 1948, Ithaca, NY, *Asst. Prof. of RE*, Univ. of FL, Dept. of Fin.; **OTHER RE ACT:** Academic Research; **SERVICES:** Teaching, research, serv.; **PROFL AFFIL & HONORS:** AREUEA; Amer. Econ. Assn.; **EDUC:** BBA, 1971, RE, Univ. of GA; **GRAD EDUC:** MS, 1976, Urban Geog., GA State Univ.; PhD, 1979, RE, Univ. of GA; **EDUC HONORS:** Beta Gamma Sigma; **HOME ADD:** 1852 N.W. 10th Ave., Gainesville, FL 32605, (904)374-8348; **BUS ADD:** 321 Bus., Univ. of FL, Gainesville, FL 32611, (904)392-1330.

CORLETT, G. Joseph——B: Mar. 11, 1951, Nampa, ID, *Owner/Partner*, Mountain States Appraisal & Consulting, Inc.; **PRIM RE ACT:** Consultant, Appraiser, Owner/Investor; **SERVICES:** Appraisal & consulting; **REP CLIENTS:** Comml. banks, s&l's, ins. co's., local & state Govts., Fed. govt., indivs.; **PREV EMPLOY:** Student, Univ. of ID; **PROFL AFFIL & HONORS:** MAI; SRPA; Intl. Right-of-Way Assn.; NAHB; Arbitrator (Amer. Arbitration Assn.), MAI; SRPA; SREA Natl. Young Adv. Council; Past Pres. Chapt. 157 Soc. of RE Appraisers; Past. Chmn. Assoc. Council of Home Builders Assn. of SW ID; **EDUC:** BS, 1973, Fin., Univ. of ID; **HOME ADD:** 11515 Wildrose Ct., Boise, ID 83704, (208)376-0916; **BUS ADD:** PO Box 1734, Boise, ID 83701, (208)336-1097.

CORLINS, Catherine——*Executive VP*, Women's Council of Realtors; **OTHER RE ACT:** Profl. Assn. Admin.; **BUS ADD:** 430 N. Michigan Ave., Chicago, IL 60611, (312)440-8083.*

CORMACK, George H.——*Dir. of Facilities and Real Prop.*, County of Orange, General Services Agency; **PRIM RE ACT:** Engineer, Appraiser, Architect, Builder, Property Manager; **OTHER RE ACT:** Facilities Planner; **SERVICES:** Engrg., design, const. mgmt., facilities planning, appraisal, prop. mgmt., acquisition, maint., alterations and leasing; **BUS ADD:** 628 N. Sycamore St., Santa Ana, CA 92701, (714)834-5739.

CORN, John H.——B: Mar. 7, 1941, New York, NY, *VP*, Tishman Midwest Mgmt. Corp.; **PRIM RE ACT:** Broker, Consultant, Developer; **OTHER RE ACT:** Comml. leasing, Midwest; **PROFL AFFIL & HONORS:** BOMA, Natl. Assn. of Indus. & Office Parks; **EDUC:** BA, 1963, Intl. Poli., Wesleyan Univ. Middletown, CT; **GRAD EDUC:** MBA, 1971, Fin./Urban Econs., Univ. of Chicago; **MIL SERV:** USAF, 1963-1969, Capt.; **OTHER ACT & HONORS:** Village Ctr. Study Grp., Chmn., Sr. Housing Site Selection Comm.; Pres. Deerfield Sr. Housing Corp. (nonprofit devel. corp.); **HOME ADD:** 339 Willow Ave., Deerfield, IL 60015, (312)945-7536; **BUS ADD:** 120 S. Riverside Plaza, Chicago, IL 60606, (312)641-7100.

CORNES, Phil M.——B: Feb. 20, 1924, Evanston, IL, *VP*, Cornes & Nielsen, Inc.; **PRIM RE ACT:** Broker, Developer, Owner/Investor, Property Manager; **OTHER RE ACT:** Devel. of Indus. Parks and Office Buildings; **REP CLIENTS:** Indiv. and inst. lenders and investors; **PROFL AFFIL & HONORS:** SIR, Chicago R.E Bd., NAR; **EDUC:** Commerce, NW Univ.; **OTHER ACT & HONORS:** Chicago Yacht Club, Bd. of Dir. Benefit Trust Life Ins. Co., Chicago, IL; **HOME ADD:** 1483 Shermer Rd., Northbrook, IL 60062, (312)564-4284; **BUS ADD:** 2020 Algonquin Rd., Schaumburg, IL 60195.

CORONA, Larry M.——B: Dec. 11, 1947, Birmingham, AL, *Owner*, L.M. Corona Inc.; **PRIM RE ACT:** Broker, Consultant, Builder, Owner/Investor, Property Manager, Syndicator; **PREV EMPLOY:** C-21 Jim Brister, Bris-Cor Homes, Inc.; **PROFL AFFIL & HONORS:** Houston Bd. of Realtors, Gulf Coast Bd. of Realtors, Gulf Coast Homes Bld. Assn., RESSI, ASPC, C-21 Investment Soc., Broker, Builder, Consultant; **MIL SERV:** US Army; **OTHER ACT & HONORS:** League City Planning Comm., Lions Club; **HOME ADD:** 410 Westminster, League City, TX 77573, (713)332-2277; **BUS ADD:** 410 Westminster, League City, TX 77573, (713)332-2277.

CORONTZOS, Robert——B: Oct. 27, 1937, Great Falls, MT, *Partner*, Jardine, Stephenson, Blewett & Weaver; **PRIM RE ACT:** Attorney; **PROFL AFFIL & HONORS:** ABA, State Bar of MT, Cascade Cty. Bar Assn., Fellow, Amer. Coll. of Probate Counsel; **EDUC:** BS, 1959, Bus. Admin., Coll. of Great Falls; **GRAD EDUC:** JD, 1962, Univ. of MT; **EDUC HONORS:** Magna Cum Laude, High Honors; **OTHER ACT & HONORS:** Rotary; **HOME ADD:** 9 Volk Terr., Great Falls, MT 59405, (406)453-7717; **BUS ADD:** PO Box 2269 7th fl. 1st Nat. Bank Bldg., Great Falls, MT 59403, (406)727-5000.

CORRADO, Nicholas A.——B: June 16, 1924, New York, NY, *Asst. Commnr.*, NYC Dept. of Gen. Services, Div. of Real Prop.; **PRIM RE ACT:** Consultant, Appraiser, Instructor; **OTHER RE ACT:** Specialist in municipal RE; **PREV EMPLOY:** Private gen. RE and insurance practice, Assessing experience; **PROFL AFFIL & HONORS:** SREA, Intl. Right of Way Assn., Columbia Soc. of Appraisers, AIREA, SRA, SRWA, CSA, Adjunct Lecturer in RE at Bernard M. Baruch Coll.;

EDUC: BA, 1949, Bus. and Liberal Arts, Columbia Coll. - NYC; **MIL SERV:** US Army, 1943-1946, Sgt., Good Conduct Medal - 2 Battle Stars; **HOME ADD:** 211 Allison Ave., Staten Island, NY 10306, (212)987-4267; **BUS ADD:** 2 Lafayette St., New York, NY 10007, (212)566-7565.

CORRIGAN, William G.——**B:** Oct. 2, 1933, St. Helena, CA, *Partner*, Bagshaw, Martinelli, Corrigan & Jordon; **PRIM RE ACT:** Attorney; **SERVICES:** Legal services; **REP CLIENTS:** First Amer. Title Insurance Co., St. Paul Title Insurance Co., First Amer. Title Co. of Marin, Marin Title Guaranty Co., Fox & Carskadon, Inc. Realtors, Frank Howard Allen & Co., Realtors, Amsco, Henry Hicks & Assocs.; **PROFL AFFIL & HONORS:** Marin Cty. Bar Assn., CA Bar Assn., ABA; **EDUC:** AB, 1955, Bus. Admin., Univ. of San Francisco; **GRAD EDUC:** JD, 1958, Univ. of San Francisco; **OTHER ACT & HONORS:** Bd. of Counselors, Univ. of San Francisco; **HOME ADD:** Kentfield, CA; **BUS ADD:** 950 Northgate Dr., San Rafael, CA 94903, (415)472-4500.

CORRODI, John T., Jr.——**B:** July 24, 1935, Columbus, OH, *Co-Owner*, Corrodi & Corrodi Realtors; **PRIM RE ACT:** Owner/Investor; **PREV EMPLOY:** General Telephone Co. of CA 1957-61; **PROFL AFFIL & HONORS:** Malibu Bd. of Realtors/Los Angeles Bd. of Realtors; **EDUC:** AB, 1957, Liberal Arts, Wesleyan Univ., Middletown, CT; **GRAD EDUC:** MBA, 1963, Mktg., Harvard Bus. School; **OTHER ACT & HONORS:** Cand./Malibu City Council, 1976; **HOME ADD:** Box 66, Malibu, CA 90265, (213)457-2584; **BUS ADD:** Box 66, Malibu, CA 90265, (213)456-6688.

CORROZI, John A.——**B:** Jan. 4, 1946, DE., *Pres.*, Corrozi Himes Inc.; **PRIM RE ACT:** Developer, Builder, Owner/Investor; **PREV EMPLOY:** Wilm. Housing Auth. - Comm. Housing Corp., Robino Ladd Corp.; **PROFL AFFIL & HONORS:** Home Builders, HOW; **MIL SERV:** USN, E-4; **HOME ADD:** 28 Welwyn Rd., Newark, DE; **BUS ADD:** 175 E. DE Ave., Newark, DE 19711, (302)737-8313.

CORSINI, Andrew C.——*Treas. & Secy.*, Swank, Inc.; **PRIM RE ACT:** Property Manager; **BUS ADD:** 6 Hazel St., Attleboro, MA 02703, (617)222-3400.*

CORSO, Anthony E.——**B:** Oct. 5, 1938, Chicago, *VP*, Site Location Specialists; **PRIM RE ACT:** Broker, Consultant, Developer, Property Manager; **SERVICES:** Marketing RE consulting, comm., brokerage, prop. mgmt.; **REP CLIENTS:** Retail Chains/comml. prop. devels. & investors/builders, architects, & attys. etc.; **PREV EMPLOY:** Nat. Tea Co. 1972-81, RE Research Corp. 1968-72; **PROFL AFFIL & HONORS:** Nat. Assn. Corp. RE Exec.; **EDUC:** BS, 1961, Marketing, DePaul Univ.; **GRAD EDUC:** MBA, DePaul Univ.; **EDUC HONORS:** Dean's List; **MIL SERV:** USAR, Sp4; **HOME ADD:** 5405 Groveside Ln., Rolling Meadows, IL 60008, (312)397-2323; **BUS ADD:** 1818 E Northwest Hwy., Arlington Hts., IL 60004, (312)394-0550.

COSE, Lexina——**B:** May 21, 1948, Hayden, CO, *Public Accountant/Realtor*, Lexina Cose, Public Accountant; **PRIM RE ACT:** Owner/Investor; **OTHER RE ACT:** Tax advisor & sales; **SERVICES:** Tax advice for RE investors & locating props.; **PROFL AFFIL & HONORS:** Upper CO Bd. of Realtors; **EDUC:** BA, 1974, Acctg., WI State Univ.; **HOME ADD:** 2202 Midland Ave., Glenwood Springs, CO 81601, (303)945-8305; **BUS ADD:** PO Box 1931, Glenwood Springs, CO 81602, (303)945-8305.

COSLICK, Merlin B.——**B:** Sept. 29, 1935, Asbury Pk., NJ, *V.P., Broker*, Terratec Corp.; **PRIM RE ACT:** Broker, Syndicator, Consultant, Appraiser, Developer, Owner/Investor; **OTHER RE ACT:** Demographer, site analyst; **SERVICES:** Miniwarehouse location studies; **PROFL AFFIL & HONORS:** NAR, NJAR, Somerset County Bd. of Realtors, Farm and Land Inst., NJ Comml. Investment Div. NARA, Sr. Member, GRI; **EDUC:** BS, 1958, Music, Trenton State Coll.; **GRAD EDUC:** MA, EDM, 1967,1971, Communication, Columbia Univ.; **EDUC HONORS:** Pres. Theta Nu Sigma Frat.; **OTHER ACT & HONORS:** Pres. Bd. of Trustees, Trinity United Church, Warren, NJ; Bd. Member, Watchung Arts Council (Founder); **HOME ADD:** 293 Mountain Blvd., Watchung, NJ 07060, (201)757-1211; **BUS ADD:** 67 Mountain Blvd., Warren, NJ 07060, (201)560-9713.

COSTA, David Francis, Jr.——**B:** July 27, 1929, Hayward, CA, *Arch./Planner*, David Francis Costa Jr. & Associates; **PRIM RE ACT:** Architect; **OTHER RE ACT:** Arbitrator, Amer. Arbitration Assn.; **SERVICES:** Architectural & planning services; structural, mechanical & electrical engrg.; master planning; econ. planning & research; **PREV EMPLOY:** Established architectural & planning offices in 1958, Oakland, CA; **PROFL AFFIL & HONORS:** Amer. Instit. of Arch., 1958; Salem Chap. of AIA (Past Pres. & Dir.); OR Council of Arch. (Delegate); Amer. Arbitration Assn., Licensed Arch.: CA (1958), OR (1968), WA (1970), and NCARB cert. (1972); **EDUC:** BA, 1955, Arch., Univ. of CA at Berkeley; **GRAD EDUC:** MA, 1956, Arch. & Planning, Univ. of CA at Berkeley; **EDUC HONORS:** Medal for Design, 1956; **MIL SERV:** U.S. Army, Sgt., Good Conduct; **OTHER ACT & HONORS:** Albany Rotary Club, Past Pres., 1978, Dir.; Rotary Intl., Paul Harris Fellow, 1980; Springhill Ctry. Club, 1968; **HOME ADD:** 3175 Independence Hwy., N.W., Albany, OR 97321, (503)928-8208; **BUS ADD:** 210 S. Ellsworth St., Albany, OR 97321, (503)926-2263.

COSTELLO, Daniel W.——**B:** June 17, 1930, Toledo, OH, *Sr. VP, Corp. RE & Gen. Services*, Amer. Express Co., Corp. RE & Gen. Services; **PRIM RE ACT:** Developer, Property Manager, Banker, Owner/Investor, Insuror; **SERVICES:** Travel & Fin. Services; **PREV EMPLOY:** Shell Oil Co., Sales & Mktg. and RE positions, 1955-63; Ford Motor Co., Dir.-RE & Const., 1963-70; Ford Motor Land Devel. Corp., Dir.-RE Devel. & Const 1970-74; **PROFL AFFIL & HONORS:** NARA, NAPA, NACORE, BOMA, Arch. & Design Awards for bldg. projects; **EDUC:** BS, 1952, Indus. Engrg./Mgmt., Purdue Univ.; **GRAD EDUC:** Extension courses, RE, Const, Fin., Univ. of MI; **MIL SERV:** US Army, 1st Lt., Korean Campaign Ribbon, U.N., Medal Distinguished Unit Citation, etc.; **HOME ADD:** 15 Princeton Rd., Allendale, NJ 07401, (201)825-1361; **BUS ADD:** American Express Plaza, NY, NY 10004, (212)323-2323.

COTNEY, John D.——**B:** June 26, 1926, Philadelphia, PA, *Pres.*, John D. Cotney; **PRIM RE ACT:** Appraiser, Lender, Owner/Investor; **SERVICES:** Appraisal, mort. fin., sales; **PROFL AFFIL & HONORS:** NAR (past Dir.); Past Pres. NJ Assn. of Realtors; **MIL SERV:** USN; **HOME ADD:** 7903 Lagoon Dr., Margate, NJ 08402, (608)823-6134; **BUS ADD:** 1 New York Ave., Atlantic City, NJ 08401, (609)344-7775.

COTSWORTH, C. Michael, CPM——**B:** Jan. 22, 1949, St. Louis, MO, *Pres.*, Capital Gain Investments; **PRIM RE ACT:** Consultant, Owner/Investor, Property Manager, Syndicator; **SERVICES:** Acquisition Analysis and Negotiation of Investement RE for Limited Partnership Interests, Prop. and/or Portfolio Mgmt.; **PREV EMPLOY:** Pres., Inter-Coast Mgmt. Corp.-Prop. Mgmt. firm, 1973-1979; VP, Essex Property Corp., Prop. Acquisitions and Syndication 1979-1981; **PROFL AFFIL & HONORS:** IREM; Apt. Owners & Mgrs. Assn.; NAR; BOMA, CPM; **EDUC:** BA, 1971, Psych.; Environmental Studies, Dartmouth Coll.; **GRAD EDUC:** Mgmt. and RE Grad. Courses, Univ. of CA at Berkeley; **EDUC HONORS:** Degree Cum Laude; Departmental Honors in Major; **HOME ADD:** 1436 Miramonte Ave., Los Altos, CA 94022, (415)961-1627; **BUS ADD:** 167 So. San Antonio Rd., Los Altos, CA 94022, (415)948-2857.

COTTINGHAM, Laurence M.——**B:** Oct. 17, 1932, Houston, TX, *Pres.*, Fincon Inc.; **PRIM RE ACT:** Consultant, Developer, Owner/Investor; **EDUC:** BA, 1955, Hist., So. Methodist Univ.; **GRAD EDUC:** JD, So. Methodist Univ.; MBA, Wharton Sch., Univ. of PA; **MIL SERV:** USAF, Lt.; **HOME ADD:** 6804 Northwood, Dallas, TX 75225, (214)369-4803; **BUS ADD:** 6510 Abrams Rd., Suite 240, Dallas, TX 75231, (214)341-0660.

COTTLE, J. Michael——**B:** June 13, 1937, Washington, DC, *Regl. Prop. Mgr.*, Equitable Life Assurance Soc.; **PRIM RE ACT:** Property Manager; **PROFL AFFIL & HONORS:** NACORE, IREM, Intl. Council of Shopping Ctrs., Wash. Bd. of Realtors; BOMA; **MIL SERV:** USNR; **BUS ADD:** 1875 Eye St. N.W., Suite 1140, Washington, DC 20006, (202)775-8340.

COTTON, John——**B:** Mar. 23, 1913, San Diego, CA, *Pres.*, Cotton-Ritchie Corp.; **PRIM RE ACT:** Broker, Appraiser, Property Manager; **OTHER RE ACT:** RE counselor, RE lecturer; **PROFL AFFIL & HONORS:** Mem. RE Adv. Comm., Univ. CA (1954-56, 1965-72); Awards Recipient Bronze Medal City of Paris (1975); Dist. Serv. Award Intl. RE Fed. (1968), Mem. NAR, Pres. (1969); San Diego Bd. Realtors, pres. (1951); CA Assn. Realtors, pres. (1956); IREF, pres. Amer. Chapt. (1973); Dep. world pres. (1977-79); IREM nat. VP. (1950); Pres. San Diego (1948); AIREA, nat. VP (1966), pres. San Diego (1962); Mem. ASREC, San Diego Apt. Owners Assn., Bd. Govs., 1978-80); Pres. (1944-46); CA Pres. (1948-49), Nat. Apt. Owners Assn. VP (1953), Amer. Arbitration Assn., Nat. Panel Arbitrators (1967-); **EDUC:** CA State Univ., Stanford Univ.; **OTHER ACT & HONORS:** San Diego Downtown Assn., pres. (1961); San Diego C of C, dir. (1970-74); VP Planning (1974); Amer. Right of Way Assn., Lions, Presbyterian; elder; **HOME ADD:** 2900 Nichols St., San Diego, CA 92106; **BUS ADD:** 233 A St., San Diego, CA 92101.

COTTONE, Daniel T.——**B:** Sept. 8, 1923, Union City, NJ, *Pres.*, D.C. Construction Co., Inc.; **PRIM RE ACT:** Developer, Builder; **SERVICES:** Resid., comml. & indus. bldg.; **PREV EMPLOY:** Const. engrg. consultant; **PROFL AFFIL & HONORS:** NAHB; **EDUC:** BS,

1949, Mech. Engrg., PA State; **GRAD EDUC:** MS, 1951, Mech. Engrg., PA State; **MIL SERV:** US Army, Sgt., ETO Victory Medal; **OTHER ACT & HONORS:** Union Cty. Planning Bd., 1970-76, Bd. of Dirs., Wychoff YMCA; **HOME ADD:** 76 Fardale Ave., Mahwah, NJ 07430, (201)327-9111; **BUS ADD:** 76 Fardale Ave., Mahwah, NJ 07430, (201)327-9111.

COTTONE, Philip S.——B: Nov. 19, 1939, New York, NY, *Pres. & Dir.*, IU Land Devel. Corp.; **PRIM RE ACT:** Consultant, Owner/Investor, Syndicator; **SERVICES:** Devel. & investment planning & implementation as principal and consultant; **REP CLIENTS:** Corps. and govt.; **PREV EMPLOY:** Mgr. RE Port of NY and NJ, 1966-72; **PROFL AFFIL & HONORS:** Gen. Counsel Intl Right of Way Assn. (past Pres of NY State Chapt. 1969), Member NACORE, Founder & Pres. Philadelphia Chapt., 1976-77, ULI, Philadelphia Bd. of Realtors, RESSI, SR/WA (1969), Right of Way Man of the Year (1976, PA Chapt.); **EDUC:** AB, 1961, Eng. Lit., Columbia Coll.; **GRAD EDUC:** LLB, 1966, NY Univ. Sch. of Law; **EDUC HONORS:** Kinne Memorial Prize for Humanities, Admin Law Prize; **OTHER ACT & HONORS:** Tr. Inc. Village of E Rockaway, NY (1970-72 Elective); Pres. Columbia Univ. Club of Philadelphia; Bd. Member Columbia Coll. Alumni Assn.; **HOME ADD:** 649 Clovelly Ln., Devon, PA 19333, (215)687-6147; **BUS ADD:** 1500 Walnut St., Philadelphia, PA 19102, (215)985-6538.

COTTRELL, Albert Peyton——B: Mar. 1, 1945, Pine Bluff, AR, *Owner/Partner*, Maxwell, Cottrell Development (owner of: Cottrell Development); **PRIM RE ACT:** Attorney, Developer, Owner/Investor; **SERVICES:** Office bldg. & shopping ctr. dev. investment quality; **PREV EMPLOY:** Coldwell, Banker Comm. Brokerage, Houston, TX for five years; **PROFL AFFIL & HONORS:** ICSC, ABA; **EDUC:** BS, BA, 1969, Fin., Eng., and Pol. Sci., Univ. of MS; **GRAD EDUC:** JD, 1972, Tax, RE Fin., Univ. of MS; **MIL SERV:** USANG; S/Sgt.; **OTHER ACT & HONORS:** Phi Delta Theta; Lamba Chi; **HOME ADD:** 221 Millbrook Ln., Houston, TX 77024, (713)974-4820; **BUS ADD:** 10,500 Richmond Ave., Houston, TX 77042, (713)977-9696.

COTTRELL, David, III——B: May 1, 1942, New Orleans, LA, *Pres.*, Cottrell Devel. Co.; **PRIM RE ACT:** Developer, Builder; **OTHER RE ACT:** Real Estate Investment Builders and Developers of Shopping Centers; **PROFL AFFIL & HONORS:** Houston Realty Breakfast Club, Intl. Council of Shopping Ctrs., ULI; **EDUC:** BS, 1965, Mktg. & Bus. Admin., Univ. S. MS; **EDUC HONORS:** Pres. Pi Sigma Epsilon Arkt. Frat.; V. Pres. Pan Amer. Student Assn.; **MIL SERV:** USN; CYN 3; **OTHER ACT & HONORS:** Boston Club, New Orleans Men's Club; **HOME ADD:** 222 Blalock, Houston, TX 77024, (713)974-7484; **BUS ADD:** 13711 W. Westheimer, Houston, TX 77077, (713)493-9700.

COTTRELL, Dudley P.——B: Jan. 16, 1922, Palos, AL, *Broker-Salesman*, Century 21, John W. Brooks Realty, Inc.; **PRIM RE ACT:** Consultant, Appraiser; **SERVICES:** Sales, Mgmt., Devel and Appraisals; **REP CLIENTS:** Mort. brokers, devels., banks, Merrill-Lynch, US Steel, Southern Co., S. Central Bell, Municipalities, attys.; **PREV EMPLOY:** Partner with Phillips, Rayfield & Cottrell Co., Appraisers & Consultants; **PROFL AFFIL & HONORS:** AIREA/MAI, SRPA, Realtor/Local and Nat., MAI and SRPA; **MIL SERV:** USAF, 1st. Lt.; **HOME ADD:** 909 Santa Rosa Blvd. 219, Ft. Walton Beach, FL 32548, (904)244-1563; **BUS ADD:** 106 Miracle Strip Pkwy., Ft. Walton Beach, FL 32548, (904)244-2121.

COUCH, Donald Paul——B: Jan. 9, 1930, Union, SC, *Owner & Broker in charge*, Don Couch Realtors & Don Couch Consultant; **PRIM RE ACT:** Broker, Consultant, Engineer, Developer, Builder, Owner/Investor, Instructor; **SERVICES:** Const. consultant & complete bldg. constr.; **REP CLIENTS:** Moderate size bldg. projects, office bldgs., warehousing & apts.; **PREV EMPLOY:** Field Engr. Heavy Airfield & Hwy Const. & Comml. Bldg. Contractor; **PROFL AFFIL & HONORS:** Realtor, Charleston Cty. Bd. of Charleston Civil Engrs. Club, SC Soc. of Engr., Nat. Speakers Assn., Licensed consultant, licensed realtor, DTM Speaking level, Toastmasters Hall of Fame, TM of yr. state of SC, 1975; **EDUC:** BS, 1952, Civil Engrg., The Citadel, Univ. SC, RE; **EDUC HONORS:** Who's Who in Coll. & Univs.; **MIL SERV:** US Army, Engrs., 1st lt., Korean Serv. Commendation Medals; **OTHER ACT & HONORS:** Baptist Deacon, Toastmasters Intl.; **HOME ADD:** 18 Norview Ct., Charleston, SC 29407, (803)556-3309; **BUS ADD:** Box 31192, Charleston, SC 29401, (803)556-3309.

COUCH, George J.——B: Aug. 5, 1932, San Francisco, CA, *Sec./Treas., Cal-Francisco Investment Corp.*, West Coast Properties; **PRIM RE ACT:** Broker, Developer, Owner/Investor, Property Manager, Syndicator; **SERVICES:** Devel., prop. mgmt., synd. of investment props., investor; **PROFL AFFIL & HONORS:** Nat. Assn. of RE Bds.; CAR, S.F. Bd. of Realtors, IREM, CPM; **EDUC:** BS, 1954, Bus. Admin. (Mktg.), Univ. of San Francisco; **MIL SERV:** US Army, 1st Lt.; **BUS ADD:** 1336 Polk St., San Francisco, CA 94109, (415)885-6970.

COUCH, Jay D.——B: Feb. 23, 1947, Norfolk, VA, *Pres.*, Couch & Associates, Inc.; **PRIM RE ACT:** Broker, Consultant, Appraiser, Developer, Property Manager, Owner/Investor; **SERVICES:** Full turn key project acquisition leasing; **REP CLIENTS:** Local investors and firms; **PROFL AFFIL & HONORS:** NAR, IREM, Nat. Home Builders, CPM, Pres. 2 yrs., Norfolk Chesapeake Bd. of Realtors; **EDUC:** Bus. Mgmt., Old Dominion Univ.; **MIL SERV:** USMC, E-5; **OTHER ACT & HONORS:** Comnr, Norfolk, Model Cities Commn., Kiwanis; **HOME ADD:** 1414 Trouville Ave., Norfolk, VA 23505, (804)423-4678; **BUS ADD:** 1300 First Virginia Bank Tower, Norfolk, VA 23510, (804)632-2323.

COUGHLIN, George Gordon, Jr.——B: Feb. 17, 1929, Binghamton, NY, *Partner*, Coughlin & Gerhart; **PRIM RE ACT:** Attorney; **SERVICES:** All legal services, RE, estate, corp., etc.; **PROFL AFFIL & HONORS:** NY Bar Assn., Broome Cty. Bar Assn., ABA, Fellow, Amer. Coll. of Probate Counsel; **EDUC:** BA, 1953, Colgate Univ.; **GRAD EDUC:** LLB, 1956, Univ. of VA; **OTHER ACT & HONORS:** Phi Alpha Delta; **BUS ADD:** One Marine Midland Plaza, PO Box 2039, Binghamton, NY 13902, (607)723-9511.

COUGHLIN, William G.——B: Boston, MA, *Pres.*, Ryan, Elliott & Coughlin; **PRIM RE ACT:** Broker, Property Manager; **PROFL AFFIL & HONORS:** CPM; **EDUC:** 1955, Harvard Coll.; **BUS ADD:** 24 Federal St., Boston, MA 02110, (617)357-8220.

COULTER, Larry E.——B: May 1, 1942, Marshalltown, IA, *Broker*, Tipton Corp.; **PRIM RE ACT:** Broker, Attorney, Consultant, Owner/Investor, Syndicator; **SERVICES:** Comml. & indus. broker, investment RE consultant; **PREV EMPLOY:** Practicing Atty.; **PROFL AFFIL & HONORS:** MN and Hennepin Cty. Bar Assns.; MN Prop. Exchangers, JD; **EDUC:** BSBA, 1964, Acctg., Drake Univ.; **GRAD EDUC:** JD, 1968, RE/Tax Law, Univ. of MN; **HOME ADD:** 6108 W. 99th St., Bloomington, MN 55438, (612)831-7810; **BUS ADD:** 1614 Harmon Pl., Minneapolis, MN 55403, (612)333-3455.

COURCHENE, Diane M.——B: Nov. 14, 1955, Detroit, MI, *Pres.*, Courchene Realty & Devel. Corp.; **PRIM RE ACT:** Broker, Builder, Owner/Investor; **OTHER RE ACT:** Gen. Contractor; **SERVICES:** Guidance to purchaser to particular site & home to their specific needs; Overall Supervision in Construction of Homes; **PREV EMPLOY:** General brokerage in Tallahassee, FL, devel. sales for large multi-family project in Pompano, FL; **PROFL AFFIL & HONORS:** Women's Council of Realtors; **EDUC:** BS, 1977, RE, FL State Univ.; **OTHER ACT & HONORS:** Charter Member of Advisory Bd. for Broward Cty Alumni & Foundation Office for FL State Univ., State Certified Gen. Contractor; **HOME ADD:** 4406 NW 20 St., Coconut Creek, FL 33066, (305)979-2734; **BUS ADD:** 2260 NE 1 Ave., Boca Ratan, FL 33431, (305)392-2285.

COURINGTON, Pat, Jr.——B: June 7, 1941, Birmingham, AL, *Pres.*, Courington, Inc., Realtors; **PRIM RE ACT:** Consultant, Property Manager, Appraiser; **SERVICES:** Investment counseling, valuation, prop. mgmt.; **REP CLIENTS:** Indivs. and corps.; **PROFL AFFIL & HONORS:** AL Assn. of Realtors, Inc.; NAR; AL Homebuilders Assn.; NAHB, CRB; CRS; CREA; **EDUC:** BA, 1963, Bus. Admin., Birmingham So. Coll.; **EDUC HONORS:** Wall Street Journal Econ. Award; **MIL SERV:** US Army, Pvt.; **OTHER ACT & HONORS:** Albertville Rotary Club; C of C; Rotary-Paul Harris Fellow; Community Resource Devel.; **HOME ADD:** 4 Sycamore Ln., Albertville, AL 35950, (205)878-1994; **BUS ADD:** PO Box 734, Downtown Mall, Albertville, AL 35950.

COURY, A. Sam——B: Aug. 8, 1936, Wichita, KS, *Pres.*, A. Sam Coury Enterprises; **PRIM RE ACT:** Consultant, Developer, Builder, Owner/Investor, Property Manager, Syndicator; **PROFL AFFIL & HONORS:** OK Homebuilders; OK City Chamber, U.S. Chamber/Com; **EDUC:** BS, 1961, OK Univ.; **GRAD EDUC:** DDS, 1961, Dentistry, Baylor Univ., Coll. of Dentistry; **HOME ADD:** Rte. 26, Edmond, OK 73112, (405)341-7416; **BUS ADD:** 2828 N.W. 57th, Oklahoma City, OK 73112, (405)842-6643.

COVERDALE, Glen E.——B: Jan. 9, 1930, Trafalgar, IN, *Sr. VP*, Metropolitan Life Ins. Co., RE Investments; **PRIM RE ACT:** Owner/Investor; **PROFL AFFIL & HONORS:** ULI; Tr., RE Inst. of NY Univ.; **EDUC:** AB, 1951, Econ., Franklin Coll.; **GRAD EDUC:** MBA, 1952, Mgmt., IN Univ.; **EDUC HONORS:** Cum Laude; **MIL SERV:** US Army, SFC, Commendation Ribbon; **HOME ADD:** 355 Heights Rd., Ridgewood, NJ 07450; **BUS ADD:** 1 Madison Ave., New York, NY 10010, (212)578-2051.

COVERT, Neil R.——**B:** Sept. 26, 1947, Chicago, IL, *Atty. at Law*, Gormin, Geoghegan, Covert & Green, P.A.; **PRIM RE ACT:** Attorney; **OTHER RE ACT:** Author; **SERVICES:** Legal rep.; **REP CLIENTS:** Gen. Electric Credit Corp., Knox Realty of FL, Inc., Rainbow Realty of Clearwater, Inc., Bank of Oldsmar, Merrill Lynch Realty, Pelican Point Realty; **PROFL AFFIL & HONORS:** Real Prop., Probate and Trust Law Section of the FL Bar Assn.; The Intl. Law Comms. of the FL Bar Assn.; ABA; Tampa Bay Intl. Trade Council; Pinellas Cty. RE Law Council, Member, Lawyers' Title Guaranty Fund; Who's Who of Amer. Univs. and Colls.; **EDUC:** BA, 1970, Bus. Admin., Simpson Coll.; **GRAD EDUC:** JD, 1976, Law, The John Marshall Law School; **EDUC HONORS:** Dean's List, Grad. with distinction; **HOME ADD:** 2977 Meadow Oak Dr. S., Clearwater, FL 33519, (813)796-5770; **BUS ADD:** 1212 S. Highland Ave., Clearwater, FL 33516, (813)441-3705.

COVEY, King L.——**B:** Sept. 20, 1943, Carthage, MO, *Partner*, Golden and Covey, Realtors/Hometrend; **PRIM RE ACT:** Broker, Consultant, Appraiser, Owner/Investor, Syndicator; **SERVICES:** Brokerage of investment and bus. props., consulting, mktg. of vacation condos. and resid. props.; **REP CLIENTS:** Investors, devels., retailers; **PROFL AFFIL & HONORS:** RNMI, FLI, Pres.-Littleton Indus. Devel. Corp., CRB; **EDUC:** BA, 1967, Econ., Harvard Coll.; **GRAD EDUC:** MBA, 1969, Fin., Harvard Bus. School; **EDUC HONORS:** Cum Laude; **MIL SERV:** USAF Res., S/Sgt.; **OTHER ACT & HONORS:** Gov's. Council on Growth (NH), Instr. - Univ. of NH School of Continuing Studies; **HOME ADD:** Summit Ave., Littleton, NH 03561, (603)444-7749; **BUS ADD:** 213 Main St., Littleton, NH 03561, (603)444-6737.

COVIELLO, Edmund T.——*Pres.*, DBG Management Corp., Div. of DBG Property Corp.; **PRIM RE ACT:** Developer, Property Manager, Syndicator; **BUS ADD:** 850 Third Ave., New York, NY 10022, (212)486-0077.

COVINGTIN, E.A., Jr.——**B:** Aug. 23, 1925, Springfield, TN, *Pres.*, Security Fed. S&L Assn.; **PRIM RE ACT:** Broker, Banker; **GRAD EDUC:** BS, Univ. of TN, Knoxville; **MIL SERV:** USAAF; **HOME ADD:** Rte. 11-Old Natchez Trace, Franklin, TN 37064, (615)646-0820; **BUS ADD:** 4235 Hillsboro Rd., Nashville, TN 37215, (615)383-6130.

COVINGTON, Dean——**B:** Mar. 14, 1916, Rome, GA, *Atty.*, Covington, Kilpatrick, Storey & Durham; **PRIM RE ACT:** Attorney, Owner/Investor; **SERVICES:** Atty. for buyers, lenders, sellers, title examinations, title opinions and insured title; **REP CLIENTS:** J. L. Todd Auction Co., Equitable Life Assurance Soc. of the U.S., Fed. Land Bank, Production Credit Assn., Natl. City Bank of Rome, Home Fed. S&L Assn., Rossville Fed. S&L Assn., Jefferson Standard Life Ins.; **PREV EMPLOY:** Engaged in same type bus. since 1939; **PROFL AFFIL & HONORS:** ABA, GA State Bar, Rome Bar Assn., Comml. Law League of Amer.; **EDUC:** AB, 1937, Econ. and Poli. Sci., Univ. of GA; **GRAD EDUC:** LLB and JD, 1939, Gen.; **EDUC HONORS:** Dean's List, Pres., Phi Delta Phi, Pres. SAE Frat., ODK Colonel, ROTC, Honor Grad.; **MIL SERV:** US Army, Lt. Col., Bronze Star, Action in Europe; **OTHER ACT & HONORS:** GA Ho. of Rep. 1947-52, Asst. Dist. Atty. (City Ct.) Cong. Dist. Comm. Member, Methodist Church, Defense Orientation Conference Assn. (Former VP), Law Coun., Univ. of GA Law School, VP, GA Alumni Soc., Charter Member of Rome Boys Club, Cty. Atty. 1970, Pres., Lt. Gov., state Sec., Kiwanis Club, Chosen Young Man of the Year of Rome, 1950; **HOME ADD:** 10 Forest Lane, Rome, GA 30161, (404)295-3002; **BUS ADD:** Suite 300, Citizens Federal Bldg., 701 Broad St., Rome, GA 30161, (404)291-8370.

COVINGTON, George M.——**B:** Oct. 4, 1942, Lake Forest, IL, *Partner*, Gardner, Carton & Douglas; **PRIM RE ACT:** Attorney; **REP CLIENTS:** Lenders and owners of comml., indus. and agric. prop.; **PROFL AFFIL & HONORS:** Chicago, IL and ABA; Member, RE Comm., Chicago Bar Assn.; **EDUC:** AB, 1964, Hist., Yale Univ.; **GRAD EDUC:** JD, 1967, Law, Univ. of Chicago; **MIL SERV:** US Army, SP-5; **BUS ADD:** One First Nat. Plaza, Chicago, IL 60603, (312)726-2452.

COVINGTON, J.E., Jr.——**B:** Feb. 23, 1935, Richmond, VA, *Pres.*, The Covington Co.; **PRIM RE ACT:** Attorney, Developer, Builder, Property Manager; **EDUC:** BA, 1956, Hist., Univ. of VA; **GRAD EDUC:** LLB, 1961, Univ. of VA; **MIL SERV:** US Army, Lt.; **BUS ADD:** Maple & York, Richmond, VA 23226, (804)288-8317.

COVINGTON, Virgil L.——**B:** Mar. 6, 1922, Chehalis, WA, *Gen. Mgr., Exec. VP*, Econ. Dev. Corp. of Shasta Cty., Superior CA Dev. Corp.; **PRIM RE ACT:** Developer, Lender, Property Manager; **SERVICES:** Devel. ind. land, 100% fin., land , bldg. & equip.; **REP CLIENTS:** Indus. & small bus. operate an SBA 502 & 503 devel. co.; **PREV EMPLOY:** 1945-65 Pres. & owner Covington LBR Co., & Covington Mfg. Co. (3) Lumber Mill Operations, Logging-Moulding Plant; **PROFL AFFIL & HONORS:** AIDC, AEDC member 16 yrs., Gen. Mgr., Econ. Dev. Corp. of Shasta Cty., Exec. VP, Superior CA Dev. Council, Cert. Indus. Devel. FM AIDC (CID Bd. Sec. 6 yrs.); **EDUC:** Bus., econ., Univ. of WA, Seattle, Whitman Coll, St. Marys, CA; **MIL SERV:** USN, Pilot, Cadet Training; **OTHER ACT & HONORS:** City Council, Mayor 6 yrs., Chmn. Bd. of Educ., Rotary (Past Pres.) , UMCA, Bd. Cty., Mercy Hospital VP Bd. 10 yrs.; **HOME ADD:** 3472 Thomas Ave., Anderson, CA 96007, (916)365-2333; **BUS ADD:** 1135 Pine St., Redding, CA 96001, (916)241-5361.

COWAN, Jim——*Exec. VP*, Vantage Cos.; **PRIM RE ACT:** Developer; **BUS ADD:** 2008 E. Randol Mill Rd., Arlington, TX 76011, (817)261-1031.*

COWAN, Wade——**B:** Dec. 21, 1936, El Dorado Springs, MO, *Supervisor, Special Projects Section, Land Branch*, TN Valley Auth., Prop. and Serv.; **OTHER RE ACT:** Land acquisition, TVA; **PROFL AFFIL & HONORS:** Nat. Mgmt. Assn.; **EDUC:** BA, 1963, Econs., Bus., Univ. of MO; **GRAD EDUC:** MBA, 1967, Econs., Univ. of MO; **MIL SERV:** US Army; Sp 5; **HOME ADD:** 212 Rolling Ridge Dr., Chattanooga, TN 37421, (615)894-1278; **BUS ADD:** 464 Lupton Bldg., Chattanooga, TN 37402, (615)751-2163.

COWELL, Richard W.——**B:** Aug. 12, 1943, Phillipsburg, NJ, *Pres.*, Cowell & Co. Inc.; **PRIM RE ACT:** Broker, Syndicator, Consultant, Appraiser, Developer, Property Manager; **SERVICES:** Investment Counseling, Devel., Valuation, Prop. Mgr. Synd. of Comml. Props., Appraising; **REP CLIENTS:** Banks, S&L, Homequity, Excutrans, Indivs. Investors RE; **PREV EMPLOY:** RE Devels. & Brokers; **PROFL AFFIL & HONORS:** E. Northampton Cty. Bd. of Realtors, NAR, CRB, CRS, GRI; **EDUC:** BA, 1970, Lib. Arts., Wm. & Mary Coll.; **MIL SERV:** USCG, E-4, Good Conduct Medal; **OTHER ACT & HONORS:** Bd. of Dir. C of C, Business, Indus./Profls.; **HOME ADD:** 3 York Place, Easton, PA 18042, (215)253-2684; **BUS ADD:** 3357 William Penn Hwy., Easton, PA 18042, (215)258-7234.

COWHEY, Robert E.——**B:** Aug. 19, 1937, Chicago, IL, *Pres.*, Cowhey Assoc., Ltd.; **PRIM RE ACT:** Engineer, Developer; **SERVICES:** Cowhey Assoc., Consulting Civil & Environ. Engr.; **REP CLIENTS:** RE devels., builders arch., land devel. cos., govt. agencies; **PREV EMPLOY:** Hartford Devel. Corp., 1966-75; Charles W. Greengard Assoc., Consultants, 1959-66; **PROFL AFFIL & HONORS:** ULI, NSPE, Nat. Tr. for Hist. Preservation, NAHB, Gold Key Award, Chicago Homebuilders, 1979; Outstanding Service Award, IL Soc. of Prof. Eng., 1965; **EDUC:** BSCE, 1959, Civil Engrg., Univ. of Notre Dame; **HOME ADD:** 6262 N Kirkwood Ave., Chicago, IL 60646, (312)545-6202; **BUS ADD:** 2200 E Devon Ave., Des Plaines, IL 60018, (312)635-7150.

COWLES, Ben W.——**B:** Feb. 20, 1928, Denver, CO, *Sr. Sales Consultant*, Coldwell Banker Commercial Real Estate Services; **PRIM RE ACT:** Broker, Consultant, Property Manager; **SERVICES:** Brokerage (sales and leasing) of devel. comml. and investment props., undevel. comml. and resid. land; **REP CLIENTS:** Corporate and indiv. investors and devels. in comml. props. and undevel. land; **PREV EMPLOY:** Employed by Coldwell Banker since 1949; **PROFL AFFIL & HONORS:** IREM, CPM, Recipient of William H. McCarthy Memorial Award (Coldwell Banker) 1980; **EDUC:** BA, 1949, Econ., Yale Univ.; **MIL SERV:** US Army, Cpl., 1950-1952; **OTHER ACT & HONORS:** Phoenix Kiwanis Club; Desert Forest Golf Club (Carefree, AZ); Los Angeles Ctry. Club; **HOME ADD:** 7654 E. Pasadena Ave., Scottsdale, AZ 85253, (602)945-5196; **BUS ADD:** 2346 No. Central Ave., Phoenix, AZ 85004, (602)262-5551.

COX, Charles Howard——**B:** Jan. 24, 1949, Ravenswood, WV, *Bldgs. Mgr.*, Charleston Area Med. Ctr. Inc., Memorial Div.; **PRIM RE ACT:** Consultant, Property Manager; **SERVICES:** Gen. Bldg. Mgmt for med. staff office bldg., Parking Garage, Office Design & relocation.; **REP CLIENTS:** Private Physicians, comml. retailers; **PREV EMPLOY:** Asst. Mgr, Edgewood Motel, Ravenswood, WV; **PROFL AFFIL & HONORS:** Carolinas-Virginias BOMA, W. VA Assoc. of Hospital Purchasing Agents & Materials Mgrs.; **EDUC:** BSBA, 1971, Indus. Mgmt, WV Univ.; **GRAD EDUC:** MBA, 1980, Mgmt., WV Coll. of Grad. Studies; **MIL SERV:** WV Natl. Guard, Capt., Pilot, 1971-present; **OTHER ACT & HONORS:** Optimist Club, Kanawha River Navy; **HOME ADD:** 1232 Paula Rd., Charleston, WV 25314, (304)342-4281; **BUS ADD:** 3000 MacCorkle Ave., SE, Charleston, WV 25304, (304)348-7991.

COX, Donald C.——**B:** Mar. 10, 1943, Cleburne, TX, *Pres.*, Cox, Imke & Proctor, Attys. at Law; **PRIM RE ACT:** Attorney; **SERVICES:** Legal servs. inc., subdiv. approvals; **REP CLIENTS:** Purchasers, sellers, land devels. & realtors resid & comml.; **PROFL AFFIL &**

HONORS: State Bar of NM; **EDUC:** BA, 1966, Fin., Bus. Admin., E TX State Univ.; **GRAD EDUC:** JD, 1969, Sch. of Law, Univ. of NM; **HOME ADD:** 525 Zia, Hobbs, NM 88240, (505)393-2311; **BUS ADD:** 1706 N Dal Paso, Hobbs, NM 88240, (505)393-1702.

COX, E. Harley, Jr.——B: Sept. 23, 1930, Fulton, AR, Coleman, Gantt, Ramsay & Cox; **PRIM RE ACT:** Attorney, Owner/Investor; **REP CLIENTS:** Simmons First Nat. Bank of Pine Bluff, First S. Fed. S & L Assn. of Pine Bluff, Theis-Smith Prop. Mgmt. Inc., The Midland Corp., Smithwick, Inc., Reliable Abstract & Title Co.; **PROFL AFFIL & HONORS:** Chmn. of Conveyancing Comm. of the Sect. on Real Prop., Probate and Trust Law of ABA - 1979 till present, Pres., AR Bar Assn., 1979-80; **EDUC:** JD, 1953, Law, Univ. of AR; **GRAD EDUC:** LLM, 1956, Law, Columbia Univ.; **MIL SERV:** USAF, 1953-1955, 1st Lt. (J. Adv. Sect.); **HOME ADD:** 10 Jefferson Pl., Pine Bluff, AR 71603, (501)535-0032; **BUS ADD:** PO Box 8509, Pine Bluff, AR 71611.

COX, F. Kim——B: Apr. 28, 1952, Vancouver, WA, *Atty.*, McClaskey, Horenstein & Wynne; **PRIM RE ACT:** Attorney; **SERVICES:** Legal services; **REP CLIENTS:** Thunderbird 1 Red Lion Motor Inns; **PREV EMPLOY:** Chief Counsel's Office of IRS, Arthur Anderson & Co., CPA's; **PROFL AFFIL & HONORS:** ABA (Real Prop. Sect.), WA & OR State Bars, AICPA's, CPA; **EDUC:** BS, 1974, Econ., Willamette Univ.; **GRAD EDUC:** JD, MBA, 1978, Law, Bus. Fin., Willamette Coll. of Law, Willamette School of Bus. Admin.; **HOME ADD:** 12116 SE 11th St., Vancouver, WA 98664, (206)254-8870; **BUS ADD:** 700 N. Hayden Island Dr., Portland, OR 97217, (503)283-5178.

COX, Frank D., II——B: Jan. 12, 1916, Philadelphia, PA, *Pres.*, Cox Realty Group Inc.; **PRIM RE ACT:** Broker, Appraiser; **SERVICES:** Brokerage, appraising, counseling, comml. props.; **REP CLIENTS:** Lenders, sellers & purchasers of indus. and comml. props.; **PROFL AFFIL & HONORS:** Natl. State & Philadelphia Bd. of Realtors; AIREA; Inst. Prop. Mgrs.; RNMI, MAI, CPM, CCIM; **EDUC:** BS, 1938, RE, Temple Univ.; **HOME ADD:** 1134 Hagues Mill Rd., Ambler, PA 19002, (215)643-5028; **BUS ADD:** 14 E German 19 Pike, Plymouth Meeting, PA 19462, (215)825-4222.

COX, Gilbert W., Jr.——B: Feb. 28, 1933, Stoneham, MA, *Atty.*, Cox & Horowitz; **PRIM RE ACT:** Attorney; **SERVICES:** Legal Services; **REP CLIENTS:** Several Banks in the Greater Boston Area; **PROFL AFFIL & HONORS:** ABA, MA Bar Assn. Norfolk Bar Assn.; **EDUC:** AB, 1955, Hist., Govt., Northeastern Univ.; **GRAD EDUC:** LLB, 1962, Law, Boston Univ.; **MIL SERV:** USN Reserve, Cdr.; **OTHER ACT & HONORS:** MA Legislator Needham-Wellesley 1968-1976; **HOME ADD:** 49 Colonial Rd., Needham, MA 02192, (617)444-5452; **BUS ADD:** 60 Dedham Ave., Needham, MA 02192, (617)444-2844.

COX, Hollis R.——B: Feb. 19, 1919, Holdenville, OK, *Broker-Appraiser*, Red Carpet Realtors; **PRIM RE ACT:** Broker, Appraiser, Owner/Investor, Instructor, Property Manager; **SERVICES:** All RE areas, plus resid. and comml. appraisals; **PREV EMPLOY:** House Realty, Williamson Realty; **PROFL AFFIL & HONORS:** NAR, RNMI, Nat. Assn. Independent Fee Appraisers, CRS; **EDUC:** BS, 1955, Social Sci., Sacramento State Coll., CA; **MIL SERV:** USAF Retired, 1939-1963, Maj., DFC, Air Medal; **HOME ADD:** 604 Helm, Midwest City, OK 73130, (405)769-3409; **BUS ADD:** 1819 S Air Depot, Midwest City, OK 73110, (405)737-7645.

COX, John M.——B: May 25, 1955, Owensboro, KY, *Assoc.*, Henry S. Miller Co., Commercial/Retail Division; **PRIM RE ACT:** Broker, Syndicator, Consultant, Owner/Investor; **SERVICES:** Retail Leasing, Site selection & eval., investment counseling, comml & retail prop. synd.; **PROFL AFFIL & HONORS:** NAR, TX Assoc. of Realtors, RESSI, San Antonio Bd. of Realtors; **EDUC:** BBA, 1973/77, Finance, So. Methodist Univ.; **GRAD EDUC:** MBA Program, 1977-79, Fin., RE, Univ. of TX at Austin; **OTHER ACT & HONORS:** Treas. & Bd. of Gov., Central TX Chap of RESSI 1981-82; **HOME ADD:** 2642 Lockhill-Selma Rd., San Antonio, TX 78230, (512)492-6687; **BUS ADD:** 8918 Tesoro Dr., Suite 118, San Antonio, TX 78217, (512)826-3251.

COX, Russell N.——B: Dec. 24, 1926, Boston, MA, *Pres.*, Resort Management, Inc.; **PRIM RE ACT:** Consultant, Developer, Owner/Investor, Property Manager; **REP CLIENTS:** First Nat. Bank of Boston, Bankers Trust Co., NY, Boston Univ., Cardinal Cushing Coll.; **PREV EMPLOY:** VP, Cabot, Cabot & Forbes Co. 1953-1963, Pres., Linnell & Cox, Inc. 1963-1971, Pres., Gen. Investment & Devel. Co. 1971-1977; **PROFL AFFIL & HONORS:** Realtor, Realtor; **EDUC:** BSEE, 1949, MIT; **GRAD EDUC:** MBA, 1951, Fin., Harvard Bus. School; **EDUC HONORS:** Tau Beta Pi, Sigma Xi, Baker Scholar; **MIL SERV:** US Army, T/5; **OTHER ACT & HONORS:** Chmn., Fin. Comm., Town of Weston, MA 1968-71; Chmn., Young Pres. Org., New England 1970-71; **HOME ADD:** Jennings Peak Rd., Waterville Valley, NH 03223; **BUS ADD:** Jennings Peak Rd., Waterville Valley, NH 03223, (603)236-8321.

COX, Warren C.——B: June 10, 1930, Hammond, IN, *Mgr., Dist. Facilities*, Motorola Inc., Communications; **OTHER RE ACT:** Negotiate leases, do logr., build to suit; **SERVICES:** Land searches & comml. site & land acquisition; **REP CLIENTS:** In house, 181 offices in US in all 50 states; **EDUC:** Tech. Degree, 1956, Radio Engrg., Valparsis Tech. Inst.; **MIL SERV:** USN, 3rd class aviation electrician (Korean War period); **OTHER ACT & HONORS:** Employed by Motorola Inc. 25 yrs. Worked from factory trainee through sales & serv. into RE & fin. Also analyzed 100 businesses & purchased 40 for Motorola; **HOME ADD:** 4205 Dixon Dr., Hoffman Estates, IL 60195, (312)359-5455; **BUS ADD:** 1303 E Algonquin Rd., Schaumburg, IL 60196, (312)576-6674.

COX, Willard J., Jr.——*Mgr. RE & Fac. Eng.*, Gould, Inc.; **PRIM RE ACT:** Property Manager; **BUS ADD:** 10 Gould Center, Rolling Meadows, IL 60008, (312)640-4000.*

COXWELL, Roy P.——B: Apr. 24, 1921, Phoenix, AZ, *Pres.*, Coxwell Building & Maintenance, Great Western Hosts, Rancho Grande Motel; Gold Nugget Restaurant; **PRIM RE ACT:** Developer, Builder, Owner/Investor, Property Manager; **SERVICES:** Hotel, restaurant, bars and apt. devels. and mgrs.; **PREV EMPLOY:** Have bought & sold hotels and motels for 40 yrs. in AZ, CA, CO & NM; **PROFL AFFIL & HONORS:** Amer. Hotel & Motel Assn.; Best Western & Quality Inns; Nat. Restaurant Assn., Past Pres., AZ Hotel & Motel Assn.; Gov., Best Western; **EDUC:** So. CA Military Academy; Long Beach Bus. Coll.; **MIL SERV:** USAF, M/Sgt., European Theater, Medal of Honor; **OTHER ACT & HONORS:** Wickenburg School Bd.; Wickenburg Town Council; Wickenburg Rotary Club, Past Pres.; El Zaribah Shrine; **HOME ADD:** 293 S. Jefferson, Wickenburg, AZ 85358, (602)684-2250; **BUS ADD:** PO Box 1328, 293 E. Center St., Wickenburg, AZ 85358, (602)684-2811.

COYLE, Timothy L.——B: Aug. 29, 1953, Los Angeles, CA, *Exec. Asst. to Assoc. Gen Dep. Assistant Security for Housing*, Dept. of HUD, Housing; **OTHER RE ACT:** Programs and operations mgr.; **SERVICES:** Policy formulation/dissemination/management; **REP CLIENTS:** All housing indus., state housing fin. agencies, 91 HUD field offices (housing staffs); **PREV EMPLOY:** Richert Steak Houses, Ins. 1973-1980; Reagan for President (Bush) Comm. 1979-1980; **PROFL AFFIL & HONORS:** Soc. of Profl. Journalists/Sigma Delta Chi; **EDUC:** BA, 1976, Journalism/Mktg., San Diego State Univ.; **HOME ADD:** 1302 Prince St., Alexandria, VA 22314, (703)836-4256; **BUS ADD:** 451 7th, SW, Washington, DC 20410, (202)755-7366.

COZZENS, Samuel——*Secy. & Asst. Treas.*, P.H. Glatfelter Co.; **PRIM RE ACT:** Property Manager; **BUS ADD:** 228 S. Main St., Spring Grove, PA 17362, (717)225-4711.*

CRABTREE, Gordon, W.——B: July 10, 1936, St. Vital, Manitoba, Canada, *Pres. and Chf. Exec. Officer*, Gordon Crabtree and Assoc., Inc.; **PRIM RE ACT:** Syndicator, Owner/Investor; **SERVICES:** synd., invest. analysis and counseling; **PROFL AFFIL & HONORS:** NAR, RNMI, RESSI, NASD, Omega Tau Rho-Realtors Frat. GRI Designation; **EDUC:** BSc.CE, 1961, Univ. of Manitoba, Canada; **OTHER ACT & HONORS:** Aloha Temple Shriner, Honolulu Elks Club, Pacific Club, Outrigger Canoe Club, Honolulu Club, Waialae Country Club; **HOME ADD:** 1829 Laukahi Pl., Honolulu, HI, (808)373-4542; **BUS ADD:** 932 Ward Ave., Ste. 480, Honolulu, HI 96814, (808)524-5822.

CRABTREE, Malcolm N.——B: Sept. 4, 1923, Hartford, CT, *Pres.*, The Southland Grp., Inc., Realtors; **PRIM RE ACT:** Broker, Architect, Owner/Investor; **OTHER RE ACT:** Cert. Gen. Contractor; Counselor; **SERVICES:** Comm'l. Investments; Counseling on RE; **REP CLIENTS:** Indiv. Investors & Fin. Instit.; **PROFL AFFIL & HONORS:** Realtor, Comm'l Investment Div. RNMI; RESSI; **EDUC:** B. Arch., 1949, Syracuse Univ.; **EDUC HONORS:** Sigma Epsilon Alpha; **MIL SERV:** US Army, 1st. Lt.; **OTHER ACT & HONORS:** Planning & Zoning Commn. (1954-1962), J.P. (1952-1973) Bloomfield CT, Nat. Const. Panel Amer. Arbitration Assn.; **HOME ADD:** 515 Siesta Way, P.O. Box 355, Stuart, FL 33495; **BUS ADD:** 614 SE Federal Hwy., FL 33457, (305)283-7900.

CRACCHIOLO, Peter——*Dir. of Corp. RE*, Masco Corp.; **PRIM RE ACT:** Property Manager; **BUS ADD:** 18450 Fifteen Mile Rd., Fraser, MI 48028, (313)293-9013.*

CRADDOCK, Thomas P.——B: Nov. 18, 1943, St. Louis Cty., MO, Thomas P. Craddock & Assocs.; **PRIM RE ACT:** Consultant, Appraiser; **SERVICES:** RE appraisals, investment analysis, market and feasibility studies and counseling; **PREV EMPLOY:** Mercantile Mort. Co. and St. Louis Cty. Assessor's Office; Valuation Counselors,

Inc.; **PROFL AFFIL & HONORS:** AIREA, Soc. of RE Appraisers, RE Bd. of St. Louis, MAI, SRPA; **EDUC:** BS, 1976, RE and Fin., Washington Univ.; **HOME ADD:** 7529 Lansdowne, St. Louis, MO 63119, (314)645-2406; **BUS ADD:** 2055 Craigshire Dr. Ste. 410, St. Louis, MO 63141, (314)576-3800.

CRAFT, Randal R.——B: July 13, 1918, Ellisville, MS, *Pres.*, Randal Craft Realty Co., Inc.; **PRIM RE ACT:** Broker, Consultant, Appraiser, Owner/Investor, Instructor, Property Manager; **SERVICES:** Acquisition and disposition, consulting, appraisals and prop. mgmt.; **REP CLIENTS:** Jackson Packing Co., American Public Life Ins. Co., Lamar Life Ins. , Deposit Guaranty Nat. Bank, First Nat. Bank, Jackson, Dyke Indus., Inc., George Bell Carpets, Inc., indiv. and corp. users/owners and investors in comml., indus. and multi-family resid. prop.; **PROFL AFFIL & HONORS:** Local, state & nat. Realtors; SIR; RNMI; NARA; FLI; MS CCIM Chap.; Jackson Comml. Exchange, Active Member, SIR; Cert. Comml. & Investment Member; RNMI; CRA; Exchange of the Yrs., 1968, RNMI; **MIL SERV:** USAF, Capt.; **OTHER ACT & HONORS:** V.Chmn., Hinds Cty. Zoning Commn., 1975-1982; Rotary; Knife & Fork; Heart Assn.; **HOME ADD:** 2310 Twin Lakes Cir., Jackson, MS 39211, (601)362-8911; **BUS ADD:** PO Box 4853, Jackson, MS 39211, (601)982-4101.

CRAIG, David W.——B: Oct. 11, 1937, Odessa, TX, *Owner*, David Craig & Co.; **PRIM RE ACT:** Consultant, Appraiser; **SERVICES:** RE Appraising and counseling, bus. valuation; **REP CLIENTS:** Lenders, comml. investors, state and fed. govt., indiv.; **PROFL AFFIL & HONORS:** AIREA, Soc. of RE Appraisers, Topeka Bd. of Realtors Bd. of Dir., NAR, MAI, SRPA, Nat. Education Chmn. for The AIREA; **EDUC:** BS, 1960, Civil Engrg., KS State Univ.; **GRAD EDUC:** JD, 1963, Washburn Univ.; **OTHER ACT & HONORS:** Bd. of Dir., Topeka C of C; **HOME ADD:** 1911 Westwood Dr., Topeka, KS 66604, (913)233-9807; **BUS ADD:** First Nat. Bank Tower #1420, Topeka, KS 66603, (913)233-2072.

CRAIG, R. Wayne——B: Mar. 1, 1947, Ft. Worth, TX, *Partner*, Moss & Craig Comml. RE; **PRIM RE ACT:** Broker, Consultant, Developer, Owner/Investor, Syndicator; **SERVICES:** Leasing, Sales & Investment, Shopping Ctr. Office & Indus. Projects; **PREV EMPLOY:** VP, Genie Devel. Corp., Univ. of the Pacific, Delta Coll., Lodi Unified School Dist.; **PROFL AFFIL & HONORS:** CA Assoc. of Realtors; Central Valley Mktg. Exchange; Member, ICSC; NAIOP; **EDUC:** BA, 1968, Comm. Arts, Westmont Coll.; **GRAD EDUC:** MA, 1973, Comm. Arts, Univ. of the Pacific, Stockton, CA; **MIL SERV:** US Army Natl. Guard, Sp. 5; **OTHER ACT & HONORS:** Lions Club Intl.; C of C; Teacher of the year 1975; Education of year 1976; **HOME ADD:** 703 W. Pine St., Lodi, CA 95240, (209)334-0550; **BUS ADD:** 222 W. Lockeford St., Suite 1, Lodi, CA 95240, (209)334-0550.

CRAIG, Robert A., III——B: Apr. 18, 1952, Portsmouth, VA, *Pres.*, Hallmark, Inc.; **PRIM RE ACT:** Broker, Appraiser, Owner/Investor, Property Manager; **SERVICES:** Appraisals, mgmt., sales; **PROFL AFFIL & HONORS:** AIREA, Soc. of RE Appraisers, RE Broker, Govt. Fee Appraiser; **EDUC:** Old Dominion Univ.; **OTHER ACT & HONORS:** Portsmouth Jaycees, Internal VP; **HOME TEL:** (804)484-1020; **BUS ADD:** 431 Cty. St., Portsmouth, VA 23704, (804)397-4661.

CRAIN, Charles Hugh——B: Mar. 31, 1949, Lafayette, LA, *Pres.*, Charles Hugh Crain Assoc., Archs.; **PRIM RE ACT:** Instructor, Developer, Builder, Owner/Investor, Architect; **PREV EMPLOY:** J. Giusti Assoc., Archs.-Planners, CO Springs, CO; M. Wayne Stoffle Archs., New Orleans, LA; **PROFL AFFIL & HONORS:** AIA, LAA, NCARB, LIBS; **EDUC:** BArch., 1972, Arch., Univ. of SW LA; **EDUC HONORS:** Dean's List; **OTHER ACT & HONORS:** Acadiana Arts Council, Fine Arts Foundation, Historic Landmarks Commn., Chmn. Laf. Bldg. Codes Comm., Member C of C; **HOME ADD:** 118 Island Pt., Lafayette, LA 70508, (318)981-9034; **BUS ADD:** PO Box 52148, Lafayette, LA 70503, (318)237-5918.

CRAIN, Thomas A.——B: July 18, 1947, Lexington, KY, *Pres.*, Crain Realty, Inc.; **PRIM RE ACT:** Broker, Instructor, Appraiser, Owner/Investor; **SERVICES:** Comml., resid., investment brokerage appraisals; **REP CLIENTS:** Merrill Lynch, Silver Dollar City, Taney Cty., City of Branson; **PREV EMPLOY:** Wade Bros. Realtors, Memphis, TN; **PROFL AFFIL & HONORS:** GRI, Candidate for CCIM, Tri Lakes Bd. Pres., 1977; MAR MLS Chmn. 1979; MAR Educ. Chmn. 1980-81; MAR instructor 1979; Pres. Instr. Rev. Comm. 1980-81; District VP, Homes for Living Regnl. VP; **EDUC:** BS, 1972, Mgmt., RE, Memphis State Univ.; **MIL SERV:** US Army, 1966-69, E-5; **OTHER ACT & HONORS:** Chmn. Taney Co. Rep. Party 1978 to present, Rotary, Church, Listed 1980 'Outstanding Young Men of Amer.'; **HOME TEL:** (417)334-1929; **BUS ADD:** 548 N. Hwy. 65, Branson, MO 65616, (917)334-6435.

CRAMER, Pat——B: Dec. 22, 1946, Los Angeles, CA, *Dir. of comml. prop.*, Ring Brothers Mgmt. Corp., Monogram Indus.; **PRIM RE ACT:** Property Manager; **OTHER RE ACT:** Leasing Agent; **SERVICES:** Leasing & mgmt. of comml. prop.; **REP CLIENTS:** Private indivs., ins. co., etc.; **PREV EMPLOY:** Over 10 yrs. previous experience handling comml. leasing; **PROFL AFFIL & HONORS:** BOMA, ICSC; **EDUC:** BA, 1968, Pol. Sci., Univ. of CA, Santa Barbara; **HOME ADD:** 2105 Hill Dr., Santa Monica, CA 90401; **BUS ADD:** 501 Santa Monica Blvd., Santa Monica, CA 90401.

CRAMER, Robert W.——*Corp. Dir. of Facilities*, Cubic Corp.; **PRIM RE ACT:** Property Manager; **BUS ADD:** 9233 Balboa Ave., San Diego, CA 92123, (714)277-6780.*

CRAMER, Steven E.——B: May 30, 1945, Denver, CO, *Pres.*, Ralmax Northwest Inc.; **PRIM RE ACT:** Broker, Syndicator; **SERVICES:** Resid. sales, synd., investment counseling; **REP CLIENTS:** Investors; **PROFL AFFIL & HONORS:** RNMI; RESSI, CRS, Past Pres.; N. Suburban Bd. of Realtors, ReaLtor of the Yr., 1979; **EDUC:** BBA, 1972, RE/Organ. Behavior, Univ. of CO; **MIL SERV:** USN, Petty Officer 2nd Class, Vietnam Campaign 3 Stars, Vietnam Serv. 3 Stars; **OTHER ACT & HONORS:** Adams Cty. Commnr., 1981-1985; Pres., Westminster C of C; Outstanding Young Coloradoan, 1979; **HOME ADD:** 11828 Vallejo St., Westminster, CO 80234, (303)466-7150; **BUS ADD:** 7255 Irving St., Suite 110, Westminster, CO 80030, (303)426-4200.

CRAMER, William D.——B: Sep. 9, 1924, Milton, OR, *Partner*, Cramer & Pinkerton; **PRIM RE ACT:** Attorney; **SERVICES:** Atty. services; **PROFL AFFIL & HONORS:** ABA, ATLA, OTLA; **EDUC:** BA, LLB, 1947-1949, Liberal Arts, OR Univ.; **GRAD EDUC:** JD, 1949, Law, Univ. of OR; **EDUC HONORS:** Phi Beta Kappa; **MIL SERV:** US Army, Sgt., Purple Heart; **OTHER ACT & HONORS:** City Atty. 25 yrs., ESD Bd. 7 yrs.; St. Water Policy Review Bd., School Bds. Assn., Bd. of Dir.; **HOME ADD:** 1598 Hillcrest Dr., Burns, OR 97720; **BUS ADD:** P.O. Box 646, Burns, OR 97720, (503)573-2066.

CRANDALL, F. Scott——B: Aug. 8, 1946, Columbus, OH, *VP*, Continental Nat. Bank, RE; **PRIM RE ACT:** Banker, Lender; **SERVICES:** Interim constr. loans, comml. resid.; **PREV EMPLOY:** Lomas & Nettleton, Pan Amer. Life Ins. (Permanent loans), First Commerce Corp.; **PROFL AFFIL & HONORS:** Mort. Bankers Assn.; Amer. Bankers Assn.; **EDUC:** BS/BA, 1969, Econ., Univ. of SW LA; **GRAD EDUC:** MBA, 1978, Econ., Fin., Univ. of New Orleans; **MIL SERV:** USN, E-5; **OTHER ACT & HONORS:** Rotary Club; **HOME TEL:** (817)265-2995; **BUS ADD:** PO Box 910, Ft.Worth, TX 76101, (817)334-9250.

CRANDALL, Gary J.——B: June 4, 1947, Pratt, KS, *Exec. VP*, Bruce J. Pierce & Assoc., Inc.; **PRIM RE ACT:** Developer, Owner/Investor, Syndicator; **OTHER RE ACT:** Proj. Mgr.; **SERVICES:** Venture Capital Activities; **PREV EMPLOY:** Oct. 71-Aug. 77, VP & Asst. Br. Mgr., Bank of NM (now First Interstate Bank of Albuquerque), 4th & Gold SW, Albuquerque, NM; **PROFL AFFIL & HONORS:** BOMA (Bldg. Owners & Mgrs. Assn. Intl.), Wash., DC; The Albuquerque Conservation Assn., Albuquerque; **EDUC:** BBA, 1969, Finance, Univ. of NM, Albuquerque, NM; **GRAD EDUC:** MBA, 1973, Acctg., Univ. of NM, Albuquerque, NM; **EDUC HONORS:** Wall Street Journal Achievement Award; Dean's List/Honor Roll, Sam Angel Memorial Scholarship; Dean's List/Honor Roll; **OTHER ACT & HONORS:** Petroleum Club; Pi Kappa Alpha Social Frat.; UNM Lobo Club, Past Dir. & Pres., Albuquerque Assn. of Credit Mgmt.; **HOME ADD:** 1701 Kit Carson SW, Albuquerque, NM 87104, (505)243-3405; **BUS ADD:** 320 Central SW, Suite 30, Albuquerque, NM 87102, (505)243-7723.

CRANE, Edward H.——B: Mar. 26, 1929, Brooklyn, NY, *VP and Gen. Counsel*, Jacobs, Visconsi & Jacobs Co.; **PRIM RE ACT:** Attorney, Owner/Investor; **SERVICES:** VP and Gen. Counsel; **PREV EMPLOY:** Partner, Thompson, Hine and Flory, Cleveland, OH (1956-73); **PROFL AFFIL & HONORS:** ABA; OH Bar Assn.; ICSC; **EDUC:** BS, 1951, Indus. Admin., Yale Univ.; **GRAD EDUC:** JD, 1956, Law, Yale Law School; **MIL SERV:** USAF, Lt.; **OTHER ACT & HONORS:** Cuyahoga Cty. Mental Health Bd. (1980-Present); Trustee, Joy Community Church; **HOME ADD:** 17408 Edgewater Dr., Lakewood, OH 44107, (216)521-2292; **BUS ADD:** 25425 Center Ridge Rd., Cleveland, OH 44145, (216)871-4800.

CRANE, Harold L.——B: Nov. 14, 1915, Flatbush, Brooklyn, NY, *Cert. Sr. Appraiser and Consultant*, The Crane Office; **PRIM RE ACT:** Broker, Consultant, Appraiser, Lender, Builder, Property Manager, Syndicator; **PROFL AFFIL & HONORS:** NAR; Long Island Assn. of Sr. Appraisers; New York State Realtors Assn., CRA; **EDUC:** 1940, NY Univ.; **GRAD EDUC:** 1939, Hofstra Coll., Hempstead, NY; **MIL SERV:** USAF; Capt.; **OTHER ACT & HONORS:** A.L. Lions; A OH RE Bd. P.I. NIREB; VP, Intl. Exchangers Assn.; Past VP of L.I.

Exchangers; Public Relation Chief of Nassau Cty. Ancient Order of Hibernias; Past Pres., South Shore Chap. of RE Bd. of Long Island, NY; **HOME ADD:** 2768 Beltagh Ave.,, Bellaire, NY, (516)785-8606; **BUS ADD:** 3285 Sunrise Hwy., Wantagh, NY 11793, (516)785-2525.

CRANE, Robert——**B:** Sept. 24, 1928, Lorain, OH, *Pres.*, Crane Realty & Management Co.; **PRIM RE ACT:** Broker, Consultant, Developer, Owner/Investor, Property Manager; **SERVICES:** Counseling, brokerage, mgmt., comml. leasing and joint ventures; **REP CLIENTS:** Indivs., synds., banks, REITS, partnerships and various other fin. instns.; **PROFL AFFIL & HONORS:** Amer Soc. of RE Counselors, IREM, Omega Tau Rho, CPM, CRE; **MIL SERV:** US Army, Cpl., 2 Battle Stars, Combat Infantrymans Badge, Korea Operations; **OTHER ACT & HONORS:** 1982 Sec-Treas., IREM; **HOME ADD:** 7006 W. Ocean Front, Newport Beach, CA 92663, (714)646-2903; **BUS ADD:** 500 643 S. Olive St., Los Angeles, CA 90014, (213)622-1856.

CRANHAM, William R.——**B:** Feb. 20, 1939, Los Angeles, CA, *Pres.*, LeRoy D. Owen Co.; **PRIM RE ACT:** Broker; **OTHER RE ACT:** RE Brokerage; **SERVICES:** Represents major mgrs. and comml. firms; **PREV EMPLOY:** LeRoy D. Owen Co.; **PROFL AFFIL & HONORS:** CA Assn. of Realtors, NAR, SIR, Los Angeles Bd. of Realtors, LA Cty. Bd. of RE, Coalition for Housing; **EDUC:** BS, Fin., Loyola Univ.; **OTHER ACT & HONORS:** Los Angeles Jr. C of C, Rotary Club of Los Angeles, Los Angeles Olympic Org. Comm., Los Angeles Cty. Rep. Comm., United Way, Nat. Safety Council, AAU; **BUS ADD:** 700 Wilshire Blvd., Los Angeles, CA 90017.

CRAVEDI, David L.——**B:** March 21, 1949, Worcester, MA, *Asst. VP*, Julien J. Studley, Inc., Washington Suburban; **PRIM RE ACT:** Broker, Consultant; **PROFL AFFIL & HONORS:** WA Bd. of Realtors; Rockville C of C; Million Dollar Leasing Club; **EDUC:** BA, 1971, Sociology, Univ. of MA; **GRAD EDUC:** MBA, 1975, Bus., Univ. of MA; **EDUC HONORS:** Phi Beta Kappa; **HOME ADD:** 3151 Tennyson St., Washington, DC 20015; **BUS ADD:** 4330 East-West Hwy. 909, Bethesda, MD 20814, (301)951-0014.

CRAVITZ, Alan R.——**B:** Jan. 14, 1947, NY, NY, *Pres.*, Developers Mortgage Corp.; **PRIM RE ACT:** Consultant, Developer, Lender; **SERVICES:** Specializing in FHA-insured and state housing authority multifamily loans; **REP CLIENTS:** Major apt. devels. in Chicago and IL; **PREV EMPLOY:** Mort. VP, Baird & Warner, Inc., Chicago; **PROFL AFFIL & HONORS:** IL Mort. Bankers Assn.; **EDUC:** BS, 1967, EE, Polytechnic Inst. of Brooklyn; **GRAD EDUC:** MBA, 1969, Fin., Univ. of Chicago; **EDUC HONORS:** Cum Laude; **OTHER ACT & HONORS:** Pres., Jr. Governing Bd., Chicago Symphony Orch.; Bd. Member, Chicago Opera Theater; **HOME ADD:** 2038 N. Orleans, Chicago, IL 60614, (312)248-1040; **BUS ADD:** 228 N. LaSalle St., Suite 2020, Chicago, IL 60601, (312)726-0083.

CRAWFORD, Clan., Jr.——**B:** Jan. 25, 1927, Cleveland, OH; **PRIM RE ACT:** Regulator; **SERVICES:** Zoning; **PROFL AFFIL & HONORS:** ABA, State Bar of MI; **EDUC:** BA, 1948, Econ, Bus. Admin., Oberlin Coll.; **GRAD EDUC:** JD, 1952, Univ. of MI; **OTHER ACT & HONORS:** City Councilman, 1957-8; Member Zoning Bd. of Appeals, 1973-6; Asst. Pros. Atty. 1955-7; **HOME ADD:** 2024 Geddes, Ann Arbor, MI 48104, (313)761-7180; **BUS ADD:** PO Box 7046, Ann Arbor, MI 48107, (313)761-7180.

CRAWFORD, Darroll F., Jr.——**B:** Jan. 31, 1943, Brenham, TX, *Pres.*, Guardian Builders, Inc.; **OTHER RE ACT:** Consultant, Builder, Comml. & Steel Bldgs.; **SERVICES:** Full Line of Const. related services from fin. consultation, arch., to const. & mgmt. consultation; **PREV EMPLOY:** US Home Corp., Div. Pres.; **PROFL AFFIL & HONORS:** Past member Greater Houston Builders Assn., VA/FHA Coordination Comm., Past member San Antonio Builders Assn., US Home Sales Consultant of the Year; **EDUC:** Bus. Admin., 1966, Indus. Mgmt., Univ. of TX, Austin, TX; **EDUC HONORS:** Teaching Assistant-mgmt. Area; Deans List Spring 1965; **OTHER ACT & HONORS:** Rotary Intl., Liberty C of C, Past Bd. member-Liberty Little League Baseball; **HOME ADD:** 1414 Bowie, Liberty, TX 77575, (713)336-9082; **BUS ADD:** PO Box 8008, Liberty, TX 77575, (713)336-9300.

CRAWFORD, David Creasor——**B:** June 25, 1933, Winnipeg, MB, *Chmn.*, A.E. LePage Capital Mgmt. Services, A Div of A.E.LePage Ltd.; **PRIM RE ACT:** Broker, Developer, Syndicator; **SERVICES:** RE pension fund investment, RE asset mgmt., devel. & synd. of comml. props.; **REP CLIENTS:** Indiv. and/or instnl. investors; **PREV EMPLOY:** Pres. of Guardian Mutual Investment Fund; Pres. Crawford Management Ltd.; Credit Officer, Industrial Development Bank; **PROFL AFFIL & HONORS:** Appraisal Inst. of Can.; Assn. of Ontario Land Econ.; Urban Devel. Inst.; Toronto RE Bd.; Assn. of Can. Pension Mgmt.; RE Inst. of Can., Fellow of RE Inst.; **EDUC:** Bachelor of Commerce, 1955, Fin., Univ. of MB; **MIL SERV:** Royal Can. Navy (Reserve); Lt.; **OTHER ACT & HONORS:** Naval Officers Assn.; Granite Club; Royal Can. Yacht Club; Vancouver Club; Alumni Member - Delta Kappa Epsilon; Bd. of Trade of Metropolitan Toronto; Alumni Assn. - Univ. of MB; Cambridge Club; Member - Wardroom Mess. HMCS York; ONT Underwater Council; **HOME ADD:** Apt. 3029, 33 Harbour Sq., Toronto, M5J 2G4, ON, (416)366-3921; **BUS ADD:** P.O. Box 100, Toronto Dominion Centre, Toronto, M5K 1G8, Can, (416)862-0611.

CRAWFORD, David L., Dr.——**B:** Mar. 2, 1931, PA, Real Property, Inc.; **PRIM RE ACT:** Consultant, Instructor; **OTHER RE ACT:** Software devel.; **SERVICES:** Investment counseling & consulting, instr. of RE schools & the public, buyer's broker, resid. income prop., project manager; **REP CLIENTS:** Indiv. investors, RE brokers & agents; **EDUC:** BS, Physics, Univ. of Pittsburgh; **GRAD EDUC:** PhD, 1958, Astronomy, Statistics, Univ. of Chicago; **EDUC HONORS:** Sigma Xi; **HOME ADD:** 3545 N Stewart, Tucson, AZ 85716, (602)327-9331; **BUS ADD:** 245 S Plummer, Tucson, AZ 85719, (602)792-3254.

CRAWFORD, Francine O.——**B:** Dec. 10, 1948, NJ, *Atty.*, Choate, Hall & Stewart; **PRIM RE ACT:** Attorney; **OTHER RE ACT:** Conveyancing; **SERVICES:** Representation of devel., buyers & banks, resid. market; **PREV EMPLOY:** Dellorfano, Greif & Feldman, P.C., 126 High St., Boston; **PROFL AFFIL & HONORS:** Boston Bar Assn.; **EDUC:** BA, 1970, Hist., Sarah Lawrence Coll., Bronxville, NY; **GRAD EDUC:** JD, 1976, NE School of Law; **EDUC HONORS:** Cum Laude, Grad. Tax Program, Boston Univ. Law School, L.L.M., 1981; **OTHER ACT & HONORS:** Bd. of Dir., Sarah Lawrence Alumn. Assn.; **HOME ADD:** 421 Beacon St., Boston, MA 02115, (617)267-8945; **BUS ADD:** 60 State St., Boston, MA 02109, (617)227-5020.

CRAWFORD, George——**B:** Oct. 30, 1943, Minneapolis, MN, *Partner*, Jones, Day, Reavis & Pogue; **PRIM RE ACT:** Attorney; **SERVICES:** All legal servs.; **REP CLIENTS:** Indiv. and instnl. investors, devels., lenders and synds. of comml. and resid. prop.; **PROFL AFFIL & HONORS:** ABA, RE Sect.; Los Angeles Cty. Bar, RE Sect.; **EDUC:** BA, 1965, Econ., Harvard Univ.; **GRAD EDUC:** JD, 1968, Harvard Law School; **EDUC HONORS:** Phi Beta Kappa, Magna Cum Laude, Magna Cum Laude; Pres., Harvard Law Review; **OTHER ACT & HONORS:** Law Clerk, Justice Byron R. White, US Supreme Ct., 1968; **HOME ADD:** 13417 Java Dr., Beverly Hills, CA 90210, (213)271-5514; **BUS ADD:** 2029 Century Park East, Suite 3600, Los Angeles, CA 90067, (213)553-3939.

CRAWFORD, H. R.——**B:** Jan. 18, 1939, Winston Salem, NC, *Pres.*, Crawford/Edgewood Managers; **PRIM RE ACT:** Consultant, Owner/Investor, Property Manager; **SERVICES:** Specializes in the turn around of problem projects; **PREV EMPLOY:** Former Asst. Secy. Dept. Hsg. Urban Level, 1973-1976 Hsg. Mgmt.; **PROFL AFFIL & HONORS:** IREM, WA Bd. of Realtors, Natl. Assn. RE Brokers (NAREB), NAR, CPM of Yr. 1973, J. Wallace Paletou 1974 (Highest Honor in Profession), Omega Tau Rho Award NAR 1979, numerous Natl. and Local Awards; **EDUC:** BA, 1975, Bus. Poli. Sci., Chicago State Univ.; **EDUC HONORS:** Registered Appointment Mngr., RAM NAH Mngr., RAM, NAHB; **MIL SERV:** USAF, Sgt.; **OTHER ACT & HONORS:** Chsg. Mgmt. Presently Serving DC City Councilmen elected 4 yr. term 1980; Asst. Sec., Dept. Hsg. Urban Dev. 73/76; Bed Dia Goodwill Indus., Jr. Citizens Corp., NAACP, Past Pres. Kiwanis - Eastern Branch; **HOME ADD:** 3195 Westover Dr., S.E., Wash., DC 20020, (202)583-7777; **BUS ADD:** 1443 PA Ave., SE, Wash., DC 20003, (202)547-4300.

CRAWFORD, Robert——*Mgr. RE*, International Minerals & Chemical Corp.; **PRIM RE ACT:** Property Manager; **BUS ADD:** 421 Hawley, Mundelein, IL 60060, (312)566-2600.*

CRAWFORD, Stephen L.——**B:** Oct. 2, 1954, Fort Worth, TX, *Pres.*, Cambridge Equities Corp.; **PRIM RE ACT:** Broker, Consultant, Developer, Owner/Investor, Instructor, Property Manager, Syndicator; **OTHER RE ACT:** Coll. Instr. at Northlake Coll.; **SERVICES:** Gen. Brokerage; Synd., Mgmt., Consulting; **PREV EMPLOY:** VP of Acquisitions for Brentwood Props., A Trammell Crow Affilliated Co.; **PROFL AFFIL & HONORS:** NAR; Dallas Bd. of Realtors, Realtors Natl. Mktg. Inst., Inst. of RE Mgmt., CPM, CCIM Candidate; **EDUC:** BBA, 1976, RE/Fin., TX Tech. Univ.; **OTHER ACT & HONORS:** Dallas Apt. Assn., Member of the RE Faculty at Northlake Coll. Coordination; **HOME ADD:** 6306 Galaxie Rd., Garland, TX 75042, (214)530-8829; **BUS ADD:** 4950 WestGrove Dr., Dallas, TX 75248, (214)931-1400.

CREANEY, C. Patrick——Howard Research & Devel. Corp.; **PRIM RE ACT:** Developer; **BUS ADD:** 10275 Little Patuxent Pkwy., Columbia, MD 21044, (301)992-6044.*

CREASEY, James S.——B: Nov. 16, 1951, Terre Haute, IN, *Atty.*, James S. Creasey, Attorney at Law; **PRIM RE ACT:** Consultant, Attorney, Builder, Owner/Investor, Property Manager; **SERVICES:** Legal; **PROFL AFFIL & HONORS:** Northwest CO Bar Assn, CO Bar Assn.; **EDUC:** Bus. Admin., 1973, IL State Univ.; **GRAD EDUC:** JD, 1976, Bus. RE, Univ. of CO - Boulder; **EDUC HONORS:** Grad. with Honors; **HOME ADD:** 748 Ashley Rd., Craig, CO 81625, (303)824-2859; **BUS ADD:** P O Box 1238, 580 Pershing, Craig, CO 81626.

CREGG, George W.——B: Oct. 22, 1916, Skaneateles, NY, *Pres.*, Cregg RE; **PRIM RE ACT:** Broker, Consultant, Attorney, Developer, Property Manager; **OTHER RE ACT:** Certified Indus. Devel.; **SERVICES:** Specialize in indus. & comml.; **REP CLIENTS:** Auburn I.D.A.; Genesee I.D.A.; Amsterdam I.D.A.; Cataragus I.D.A.; Cortland I.D.A.; Madis I.D.A.; Onondaga Cty. Water Authority; **PREV EMPLOY:** Pres., Upper NY Realty Corp.; **PROFL AFFIL & HONORS:** Dir. of Amer. Econ. Devel. Council; Counsel to NY Econ. Devel. Council, Past Chmn. Syracuse City Planning Commn.; **EDUC:** AB, 1938, Math. & Speech, Syracuse Univ.; **GRAD EDUC:** JD, 1941, Law, Harvard Law School; **EDUC HONORS:** Phi Beta Kappa, Phi Kappa Phi, Magna Cum Laude, Lincoln's Inn, Wilson Law Club; **MIL SERV:** USNR, Lt. Comdr.; Pacific Medal, European Medal, Amer. Medal; **OTHER ACT & HONORS:** 1969 to present, Administrative Dir. of Auburn Ind. Dev. Auth.; Village Atty. of N. Syracuse and Baldwinsville; 4th Degree Knights of Columbus; Past Pres. of NY State Assn. of Towns; Past Chmn. of March of Dimes; Past Comdr. of Post 41 of Amer. Legion; **HOME ADD:** 932 Onondaga Rd., Camillus, NY 13031, (315)468-1479; **BUS ADD:** 932 Onondaga Rd., Camillus, NY 13031, (315)468-1479.

CREMIEUX, Richard J.——B: Feb. 9, 1947, Chicago, IL, *Partner*, Joyce & Kubasiak, P.C.; **PRIM RE ACT:** Attorney; **SERVICES:** Legal rep. regarding sales, exchanges, acquisitions, devel., condo. conversions., fin., const., synd.; **REP CLIENTS:** Lenders, indiv. and inst. investors in comml. props.; **PROFL AFFIL & HONORS:** Chicago Bar Assn. (RE Law Comm., Condo. Law Subcomm.); IL State Bar Assn. (Real Prop. Law Comm.); ABA (Sect. on Real Prop., Probate and Trust Law, Condo Subcomm.); **EDUC:** BA, 1969, Pol. Sci., Loyola Univ.; **GRAD EDUC:** JD, 1976, Law, Loyola Univ. School of Law; **EDUC HONORS:** Law Review; **BUS ADD:** 3 First Nat. Plaza, Ste. 3900, Chicago, IL 60602, (312)641-2600.

CRESSY, David S.——B: July 6, 1937, New Orleans, LA, David S. Cressy & Assoc.; **PRIM RE ACT:** Attorney, Syndicator, Owner/Investor; **SERVICES:** Legal servs. in condo conversions & synds.; **PREV EMPLOY:** City Atty. for New Orleans, specializing in RE activities of city; **PROFL AFFIL & HONORS:** LA Bar Assn', La Trial Lawyers, Infernation House, RESSI, Active in several civil and Prof orgs.; **EDUC:** BS, 1963, Econ., Univ. of SW LA; **GRAD EDUC:** JD, 1967, Loyola Univ.; **EDUC HONORS:** Who's Who Amer. Coll. & Univ., Econ. Club; **MIL SERV:** USAF, E-5; **OTHER ACT & HONORS:** City Atty, New Orleans, Vista Shores Ctry Club, City Park Bd. of Dirs., New Orleans Museum of Art, Bd. of Dirs.; **HOME ADD:** 1734 Pressburg St., New Orleans, LA 70122, (504)283-9236; **BUS ADD:** 704 N Rampart St., New Orleans, LA 70116, (504)522-5239.

CREWS, Charles F.——B: June 27, 1932, Wichita, KS, *Partner*, Crews, Milliard & South; **PRIM RE ACT:** Attorney, Developer, Owner/Investor, Syndicator; **REP CLIENTS:** Provide legal services to builders, developers, architects & engrs., and mort. co.; **PROFL AFFIL & HONORS:** ABA, MO Bar Assn., Kansas City Bar Assn.; **EDUC:** BS, 1954, Bus. Admin. & Psychology, KS St. Univ.; **GRAD EDUC:** JD, 1959, Law, Harvard Univ.; **MIL SERV:** USAF, 1st Lt.; **OTHER ACT & HONORS:** Pres., Ctr. Bd. of Educ., 1969-71; Pres., Optimist Club; VP, So. K.C. C of C; **HOME ADD:** 711 W. Montcrew Dr., Kansas City, MO 64114, (816)942-0296; **BUS ADD:** 401 W. 89th St., Kansas City, MO 64114, (816)363-5466.

CREWS, William C.——B: Oct. 19, 1934, Manor, GA, *Asst. VP, Dir. of Sales*, Mondex Realty, Inc.; **PRIM RE ACT:** Broker, Builder, Instructor, Property Manager; **PREV EMPLOY:** Dir. of Sales, Northeast FL Mondex, Inc., 1981-present, Dir. of Mktg., Geo. W. Law Co., 1977-81; Sales Mgr. Harris Century 21, 1975-77; Pres. Chuck Crews & Assocs., 1971-75; Gen. Sales Mgr., WKTZ-FM Radio, 1968-71; Sales Mgr., WPDQ Radio, 1964-68; Sales Mgr., WIVY Radio, 1960-61; Sales Mgr., WMBR Radio, 1961-64; **PROFL AFFIL & HONORS:** FL Licensed RE Broker, Jacksonville Bd. of Realtors, NE FL Bldrs. Assn., Jacksonville C of C, Comm. of 100; Daytona Bch. C of C; Comm. of 100; **EDUC:** BA, 1957, Mktg./Bus., Univ. of FL; **HOME ADD:** 3030 Princeton Ave., Daytona Bch, FL 32018, (904)677-5056; **BUS ADD:** 595 N. Nova Rd., Ormond Beach, FL 32074, (904)672-9330.

CRISELL, Robert W.——B: Feb. 24, 1943, Los Angeles, CA, *Pres.*, Crisell Props. of CA, Inc., Crisell Bros. Devel., Inc.; **PRIM RE ACT:** Broker, Developer; **SERVICES:** Shop, ctr. dev., fin. consult., brokerage; **REP CLIENTS:** Dominicks; Jewel Food Stores; Walgreens; The Jolly Roger Rest.; **PREV EMPLOY:** Coldwell Banker, 1965-73; Howard S. Wright Dev. Co., 1973-76; **PROFL AFFIL & HONORS:** ICSC; **EDUC:** BS, 1965, RE, Univ. So. CA; **EDUC HONORS:** Coldwell Banker Top 10 Salesmen 1971; **OTHER ACT & HONORS:** Boy Scouts of Amer.; Athletic Club Operator; **HOME ADD:** 4938 San Jacinto Cir., Fallbrook, CA; **BUS ADD:** 4631 Teller Ave., Suite 130, Newport Bch., CA 92660, (714)752-1194.

CRISMAN, Bryan A.——B: Jan. 29, 1919, Chattanooga, TN, *Owner*, Bryan Crisman Co., Realtors; **PRIM RE ACT:** Broker, Appraiser, Owner/Investor, Syndicator; **SERVICES:** Investment analysis and consultations; **REP CLIENTS:** N. Amer. Rockwell, Sun Oil Co., Nat. Life Ins. Co., Holiday Inns of Amer., Amer. Elect. Power Co., Lennox Indus., K-Mart Stores, Amana Refrigeration Co., City of Memphis, shopping ctrs.; **PROFL AFFIL & HONORS:** AIREA, RESSI, RNMI, SIR., MAI, CCIM, GRI; **EDUC:** BS in Econ., 1940, Mktg.; **MIL SERV:** USN, Lt. Cmdr.; **OTHER ACT & HONORS:** Bd. of Dirs. of David Liscomb Coll., Nashville, TN; **HOME ADD:** 1025 Kings Park Dr., Memphis, TN 38117, (901)685-0811; **BUS ADD:** 4646 Poplar Ave., Memphis, TN 38117, (901)761-3327.

CRISWELL, Gary L.——B: May 27, 1938, York, PA; **OTHER RE ACT:** Acctg. in public practice, (self employed); **SERVICES:** Consultation, sales, exchanges, & tax advisory; **REP CLIENTS:** Varied: comml., agricultural, & non-comml.; **PREV EMPLOY:** Criswell & Assoc.; Commonwealth of KY, Kimberly Clark Corp.; **PROFL AFFIL & HONORS:** FLI; Nat. Soc. of Public Acctgs.; Nat. Assn. of Acctg.; KY Assn. of Acctgs., Enrolled to practice before the IRS; **EDUC:** BS, 1976, Acctg. & Taxation, Univ. of KY; **MIL SERV:** USAF; **HOME ADD:** 1628 Linstead Dr., Lexington, KY 40504, (606)277-8508; **BUS ADD:** 1628 Linstead Drive, Lexington, KY 40504, (606)278-7130.

CROCKER, William W.——B: Sept. 24, 1942, Troy, AL, *Pres.*, Philadelphia Investment, INA Corp.; **PRIM RE ACT:** Developer, Lender, Owner/Investor; **PREV EMPLOY:** Bankers Trust Co., NY; VP; Sea Pines Corp., Hilton Head Is., SC, Treas.; **PROFL AFFIL & HONORS:** ULI; **EDUC:** 1965, Math., Univ. of AL; **HOME ADD:** 621 S. 2nd St., Philadelphia, PA 19147, (215)627-7786; **BUS ADD:** 3 Parkway, Ste. 1220, Philadelphia, PA 19102, (215)241-3118.

CROFT, David James——*Dir.*, Department of Housing and Urban Development, Federal Home Loan Bank Board; **PRIM RE ACT:** Lender; **BUS ADD:** 451 Seventh St., S.W., Washington, DC 20410, (202)377-6505.*

CROKE, Jerome P.——B: June 15, 1933, Chicago, IL, *Sr. VP, Resid. Counsel & Corp. Sec.*, The Talman Home Federal Savings & Loan of IL; **PRIM RE ACT:** Attorney, Developer, Lender, Insuror; **OTHER RE ACT:** Counsel and sec. to subsidiary, Talman Home Investments Inc.; **SERVICES:** Engaged in RE devel. and ins.; **PREV EMPLOY:** Self-employed atty.; **PROFL AFFIL & HONORS:** ABA; IL Bar Assn.; Chicago Bar Assn.; **EDUC:** BS, 1956, Econ., Loyola Univ.; **GRAD EDUC:** JD, 1960, Law, DePaul Univ.; **MIL SERV:** US Army, Res.; Capt.; **OTHER ACT & HONORS:** Past Pres. Chicago Metro Area Comm. on S&L Assns. of Amer. Bar. Assoc. Corp. Banking & Bus. Law Sect. 1969-70; Dir. of Chicago Mort. Banks Assoc. 1974-; Vice Chmn., Attys. Comm. US League of Savings Assocs. 1981; Dir., St. George Hospital Corp. - currently; **HOME ADD:** 12850 Shoshone Rd., Palos Hts., IL 60463, (312)448-6221; **BUS ADD:** 31 W. Monroe, Chicago, IL 60603, (312)922-9775.

CROKE, Thomas F.——B: Aug. 12, 1927, Chicago, IL, *Pres.*, Centerpoint Corp.; **PRIM RE ACT:** Broker, Architect, Syndicator, Consultant, Developer, Property Manager; **REP CLIENTS:** Kidde, Inc., Nixdorf Computer, Talman Home Fed. S&L Assoc.; **PROFL AFFIL & HONORS:** NAR, NACORE, BOMA; **EDUC:** BS, 1950, Structural Design Civil Engineering, IL Inst. of Tech.; **HOME ADD:** 395 Berkeley Ave., Winnetka, IL 60093, (312)446-1694; **BUS ADD:** 500 N Michigan Ave., Chicago, IL 60611, (312)467-0333.

CROMMELIN, Jacques B.——B: Feb. 26, 1909, Spokane, WN, *Owner*, Jacques B. Crommelin & Assoc.; **PRIM RE ACT:** Broker, Consultant, Appraiser, Insuror; **SERVICES:** RE appraisal and counseling; limited brokerage & ins.; **REP CLIENTS:** USA National Park Service; Cty. of Riverside; City of Palm Springs; Morgan Guaranty Trust; 1st Wisconsin Bank; Standard Oil of CA; Columbia Univ.; Stanford Univ.; also indivs., corps. (local and nat.); **PREV EMPLOY:** Prudential Ins. Co. (1933-1943) (Mort. Loan Dept.); **PROFL AFFIL & HONORS:** AIREA; Amer. Soc. of RE Counselors; Soc. of RE Appraisers, MAI; CRE; SRPA; **EDUC:** BS-ME, 1932,

Engrg. (Indus.), Cornell Univ., Ithaca, NY; **OTHER ACT & HONORS:** Rotary Club of Palm Springs (1946-) (Pres. 1952-1953); Beta Theta Pi (Cornell Univ.); Boy Scouts of America, (1944 to present, Council Pres. 1969-1971); **HOME ADD:** Smoke Tree Ranch, Palm Springs, CA 92262, (714)327-2620; **BUS ADD:** 1800 S. Sunrise Way, Palm Springs, CA 92262, (714)327-2620.

CRONE, Jeffrey R.——B: Aug. 22, 1933, San Francisco, CA, *RE Appraiser and Consultant*, Independent - Self Employed; **PRIM RE ACT:** Broker, Consultant, Appraiser, Owner/Investor; **SERVICES:** Comml., indus., multi-resid. and rural appraisals and consultation; **REP CLIENTS:** Various banks, attornies, lenders, public agencies and numerous private clients; **PREV EMPLOY:** Supervising Appraiser, State of CA, Dept. of Gen. Services, RE Ser. Div.; **PROFL AFFIL & HONORS:** Member AIREA. Sr. Member, Intl. Right of Way Assn., MAI; **EDUC:** BS, 1961, Bus. and Indus. Mgmt., San Jose State Univ.; **MIL SERV:** US Army, E-5; **OTHER ACT & HONORS:** Boy Scouts of America; **HOME ADD:** 917 Sonoma Way, Sacramento, CA 95819, (916)451-5242; **BUS ADD:** 601 Univ. Ave., Suite 102, Sacramento, CA 95825, (916)920-5657.

CRONE, John T., III——B: Feb. 5, 1939, Cincinnati, OH, *VP*, Ray Ellison Devel., Inc., Comml. Prop.; **PRIM RE ACT:** Consultant, Developer, Owner/Investor, Property Manager; **SERVICES:** Devel. of comml. props., prop. mgmt. and consulting; **REP CLIENTS:** Office, warehouse, shopping ctr. and apt. tenants; indiv. as well as inst. lenders; **PREV EMPLOY:** Lomas & Nettleton Fin. Group (1971-81); Inter Capital Fin. Group (1968-71); **PROFL AFFIL & HONORS:** NAIOP; ICSC, Lic. RE Broker (TX); SREA 101 and 201 Exams; **EDUC:** BA, 1960, Physics, Engrg., Washington & Lee Univ., Lexington, VA; **GRAD EDUC:** Dipl. Engr., 1962, Mech. & Electrical Engrg., Edinburgh Univ., Edinburgh, UK; Cert. in RE, 1976, RE, So. Methodist Univ., Dallas, TX; **EDUC HONORS:** With Hons. (4.0 Average); **OTHER ACT & HONORS:** Guest Lecturer, So Methodist UNiv., N TX State Univ., and conferences sponsored by CERI & World Trade Inst.; **HOME ADD:** 3417 Stanford St., Dallas, TX 75225, (214)369-0805; **BUS ADD:** 4800 Fredericksburg at Loop 410, PO Box 5250, San Antonio, TX 78201, (512)349-1111.

CRONIN, Edmund B., Jr.——B: Apr. 11, 1937, Wheaton, MD, *Pres. and CEO*, H.G. Smithy Company; **OTHER RE ACT:** RE Servs. Co., fin., prop mgmt., leasing, consulting; **REP CLIENTS:** The Travelers Ins. Co., ManuLife (of Canada), IBM, Nat. Assn. of CTYS.; **PREV EMPLOY:** Sr. VP, B.F. Saul Co. 1960-76; **PROFL AFFIL & HONORS:** ULI, MBAA, Nat. Assn. of RE Bds.; **OTHER ACT & HONORS:** Member, Bd. of Dirs. First Amer. Bank, NA Wash. DC, Member, Bd. of Dirs., US Shelter Corp; Member, Bd. of Dir. Balt./Wash. Assn., Tr., Fed. City Council; **HOME ADD:** 16320 Batchellors Forest Rd., Olney, MD 20832; **BUS ADD:** 1110 Vermont Ave. NW, Washington, DC 20005, (202)775-9255.

CROOK, Richard, Jr.——*Secy.*, Champion Spark Plug; **PRIM RE ACT:** Property Manager; **BUS ADD:** PO Box 910, Toledo, OH 43661, (419)535-2567.*

CROOKALL, Charles E.——B: May 11, 1943, Brooklyn, NY, *VP*, Crookall, Shirley & Co.; **PRIM RE ACT:** Broker, Developer, Owner/Investor; **SERVICES:** Gen. brokerage of indus. and comml. office; **REP CLIENTS:** Instnl. real estate investors, devel. and corp. users of indus. and office prop.; **PREV EMPLOY:** Union Bank, 1973-1975; **PROFL AFFIL & HONORS:** Soc. of Indus. Realtors; Nat. Assn. of Realtors; CA Assn. of Realtors; **EDUC:** BA, 1965, Hist. and Govt., St. Lawrence Univ.; **MIL SERV:** USMC, Maj., 36 Air Medals, DFC, Pres. Unit Citation; **OTHER ACT & HONORS:** Rotary Intl.; **HOME ADD:** 419 Panorama Dr., Laguna Beach, CA 92651, (714)497-2914; **BUS ADD:** 12015 Slavson Ave., Suite D, Santa Fe Springs, CA 90670, (213)945-2921.

CROOKS, Patrick F.——*Gen. Mgr.*, Carma Developers (Wash.), Inc.; **PRIM RE ACT:** Developer, Lender, Builder, Owner/Investor, Insuror; **OTHER RE ACT:** Petro-Chemical, Restaurant, Hotel, Exec. Air Charter, Auto Dealership; **EDUC:** BA, 1969, Mktg. and R.E., Univ. of CA, Humboldt; **BUS ADD:** 910 Fifth Ave., Seattle, WA 98104, (206)623-1300.

CROSBY, R. Edward——B: Apr. 11, 1947, Baxley, GA, *Owner*, Crosby Financial; **PRIM RE ACT:** Consultant, Developer, Owner/Investor, Syndicator; **OTHER RE ACT:** Writer, RE related articles; **SERVICES:** Limited partnerships, general partnerships, joint ventures, consultation; **REP CLIENTS:** Instl., corp., pvt.; **PREV EMPLOY:** 10 yrs. of experience in RE devel., investment, consultation as principal; **EDUC:** BA, 1968, Bus. Admin., Univ. of So. FL; **MIL SERV:** US Army Nat. Guard, Sgt., 1965-1971; **OTHER ACT & HONORS:** US & Local Better Bus. Bureau; One of the founders of the Phoenix Camelback Kiwanis; Nat. Aircraft Owners Assn.; Private Pilot; Volunteer for M.D. Telethons; Easter Seal Fund Raiser; Advisory Bd. for Distributive Educ.; **HOME ADD:** PO Box 32981, Phoenix, AZ 85064, (602)954-5253; **BUS ADD:** PO Box 32981, Phoenix, AZ 85064, (602)954-5253.

CROSLAND, Lucien B.——B: June 15, 1946, Selma, AL, *Pres.*, The Crosland Co.; **PRIM RE ACT:** Developer, Owner/Investor; **SERVICES:** Retail; Ind. devel. expertise; Shopping centers and built-to-suit for natl. credit tenants throughout the SE & SW; **PROFL AFFIL & HONORS:** Bd. Member, Irving Flood Control Dist.; **EDUC:** BA, 1969, Econ.; Hist., Washington & Lee Univ.; **GRAD EDUC:** MBA, 1976, RE & Fin., So. Methodist Univ.; **EDUC HONORS:** Cum Laude, With Honors; **HOME ADD:** 3920 Gillon, Dallas, TX 75205; **BUS ADD:** 3131 Turtle Creek Blvd., Dallas, TX 75219, (214)522-0180.

CROSS, Carville Joseph——B: Sept. 7, 1926, Baltimore, MD, *Pres., C.J. Cross & Associates, Inc.*, C.J. Cross & Associates, Inc. Mortgage Bankers & Investment Real Estate Brokers Est. in 1969; **PRIM RE ACT:** Broker, Consultant, Appraiser, Banker; **SERVICES:** Seek and serv. funds from large instnl. investors, pension funds and life ins. cos. for large comml. devels. requesting equity and long term fin. and joint ventures; **REP CLIENTS:** Banks, ins. co., pension funds, builders and devels.; **PREV EMPLOY:** Mort. Banking since 1956; **PROFL AFFIL & HONORS:** Mort. Bankers Assn. of Amer. & Metropolitan Wash., DC Chap.; Nat. Assn. of Home Builders; N. VA Builders Assn.; NAR; Nat. Assn. of Indus. & Office Parks, NARA, Sr. Member CRA; **EDUC:** BA, 1946-49, Bus., Montgomery Cty. Jr. Coll.; George Wash. Univ.; Amer. Univ.; **GRAD EDUC:** LLD, 1953, Law, Univ. of Baltimore Law School; **MIL SERV:** USN; **OTHER ACT & HONORS:** Member Montgomery Cty. MD Devel. Advisory Bd. 3/71-12/71; Reciprocity Club of Bethesda, MD (Bus. Civic Club; twice Pres.); Guest Lecturer at Colls. and RE Bds.; **HOME ADD:** 4970 Sentinel Dr., Apt. 405, Bethesda, MD 20816, (301)229-9119; **BUS ADD:** 7657 Leesburg Pike, Falls Church, VA 22043, (703)893-9350.

CROSS, Easton, Jr.——B: Nov. 14, 1925, Bisbee, AZ, *Part.*, Cross & Adreon Architects; **PRIM RE ACT:** Architect; **SERVICES:** Planning; Arch. Design; Prod. Design; **REP CLIENTS:** Pvt. and Public for Comml. Instnl. and Resid. Projects Up to 10 Million; **PROFL AFFIL & HONORS:** Soc. Arch. Historians, AAA Arbitrator, N. VA Chap. AIA, Assoc. of Energy Engrs., Nat. Design Honor Awards, AIA, 1967, AISC 1955, AIA Mid Atlantic Resid. Design Awards, HUD., WA Center for Urban Studies Furn. Co., 4 Awards, 1971, VA Soc. of Energy Award, 1980; **EDUC:** BA, 1949, Arch. Sci., Harvard; **GRAD EDUC:** MArch., 1951, Harvard School of Design; **EDUC HONORS:** Ware Prize; **MIL SERV:** USNR, QM 3c 1943-1966; **OTHER ACT & HONORS:** Chmn. Advisory Comm. on Disposition of Surplus Schools, Fairfax, CA, 1981; Chmn. Fairfax Cty. Appeals Bd., 1969-1979; Chmn., Citizens Fairfax Cty. Crt; Arts Club of WA; Fairfax Cty. Comm. of 100; **HOME ADD:** 2309 Glassgow Rd., Alenandria, VA 22307, (703)765-8353; **BUS ADD:** 950 N. Glebe Rd., Arlington, VA 22203, (703)528-2311.

CROSS, Fenton E.——B: Aug. 18, 1944, Cleveland, OH, *Mgr., Western Rgnl. Appraisal Div.*, Cushman & Wakefield; **PRIM RE ACT:** Consultant, Appraiser; **SERVICES:** RE Appraisal & Consulting; **REP CLIENTS:** Corporate, Ins. Co., Pension Funds; **PROFL AFFIL & HONORS:** Member, AIREA, Amer. Arbitration Assn., Panel of Arbitrators, MAI; **EDUC:** BA, 1967, Urban Land Econ. & RE, OH State Univ.; **MIL SERV:** US Army, Capt.; **OTHER ACT & HONORS:** Jonathan Club, Lions Club; **BUS ADD:** 515 S. Flower St. 2200, Los Angeles, CA 90071, (213)485-1424.

CROSS, Richard A.——B: Mar. 25, 1951, Glendale, CA, *Assoc. Atty.*, Best, Best & Krieger; **PRIM RE ACT:** Attorney; **OTHER RE ACT:** Federal trial practice; Indian law; **REP CLIENTS:** Pvt. devels.; Naegele Outdoor Advertising Co.; De Anza Corp.; City of Corona; **PREV EMPLOY:** CA Ct. of Appeal, 4th District Div. 2, San Bernardino, CA; clerk to the Honorable Marcus Kaufman; **EDUC:** BA, 1973, Religious Studies, Pomona Coll.; **GRAD EDUC:** JD, 1979, Law, Univ. of S. CA, School of Law; **HOME ADD:** 1061 N. College Ave., Claremont, CA 91711; **BUS ADD:** Box 1028, 4200 Orange St., Riverside, CA 92502, (714)686-1450.

CROSS, Timothy D.——B: Feb. 11, 1947, Clarksburg, WV, *Pres.*, Syndicon Properties, Inc.; **PRIM RE ACT:** Broker, Consultant, Appraiser, Developer, Owner/Investor, Property Manager, Syndicator; **SERVICES:** Investment counseling, devel. feasibility and synd.; **REP CLIENTS:** Indiv., corporate, instnl. investors and users of comml. props.; **PREV EMPLOY:** Coral Ridge Properties, Inc. 1970-1973; **PROFL AFFIL & HONORS:** NAR; RNMI; RESSI; FL CCIM Chap.; NAREA, CCIM; CREA; **EDUC:** BS, 1969, WV Univ., Econ.; **GRAD EDUC:** MBA, 1977, Fin., Nova Univ.; **OTHER ACT & HONORS:** Coral Springs, Planning and Zoning Bd.; Bd. of Dirs., Bank of Coral Springs; Dir., FL Assn. of Realtors; Dir., Pompano

Beach-N. Broward Bd. of Realtors; **HOME ADD:** 9400 N.W. 40th St., Coral Springs, FL 33065, (305)752-2282; **BUS ADD:** 1881 University Dr., Suite 114, Coral Springs, FL 33065, (305)752-3940.

CROSSER, Daniel D.——B: Aug. 5, 1942, Kirkwood, MO, *Broker Assoc.*, Blakesley Comstock; **PRIM RE ACT:** Broker, Syndicator, Consultant, Owner/Investor, Developer; **SERVICES:** Investment Counseling, Synd. of Comml. & Resid. Prop., Exchanges; **REP CLIENTS:** Indiv. Investors; **PROFL AFFIL & HONORS:** NAR; **EDUC:** Aerospace Engrg., 1965, Structural Engrg., Texas A&M Univ.; **EDUC HONORS:** Grad. with Honors; **OTHER ACT & HONORS:** Tau Beta Pi; **HOME ADD:** 1014 The Strand, Manhattan Beach, CA 90266, (213)374-7590; **BUS ADD:** 321 12th St., Manhatten Beach, CA 90266, (213)546-3324.

CROTEAU, Gerald F.——B: Nov. 5, 1935, Somerville, MA, *Dir. of Marketing*, Armstrong Parsons; **PRIM RE ACT:** Broker, Consultant, Syndicator; **SERVICES:** Equity portfolio mgmt., investment counseling; **REP CLIENTS:** Insts., substantial indivs.; **EDUC:** BA, 1962, English, Univ. of CA, Santa Barbara; **MIL SERV:** US Army, Sgt., 1955-1958; **HOME ADD:** 1640 Grand Ave., Santa Barbara, CA 93103, (805)966-3241; **BUS ADD:** 1725 State St., Santa Barbara, CA 93101, (805)963-3325.

CROTTY, Jerome Francis——B: May 17, 1947, Chicago, IL, *Atty. at Law*, Rieck and Crotty, P.C.; **PRIM RE ACT:** Attorney; **REP CLIENTS:** Indiv. and Comml. RE Investors and Lending Instns.; **PREV EMPLOY:** Former Acting Advisor to State of IL Commnr. of Banks and Trust Co.; **PROFL AFFIL & HONORS:** ABA, IL State Bar Assn., Chicago Bar Assn., Chicago Assn. of Commerce & Indus.; **EDUC:** BS, 1970, Personnel Mgmt., So. IL Univ.; **GRAD EDUC:** JD, 1975, Law, John Marshall Law School; **EDUC HONORS:** Deans' List - School of Bus.; **HOME ADD:** 6505 N. Nashville Ave., Chicago, IL 60631, (312)763-8418; **BUS ADD:** 55 W. Monroe St., Suite 3660, Chicago, IL 60693, (312)726-4646.

CROUCH, C. David——B: May 15, 1951, Birmingham, AL, *Pres.*, The Dave Crouch Co., Inc.; **PRIM RE ACT:** Broker, Consultant, Appraiser, Property Manager, Insuror; **SERVICES:** Resid. brokerage, resid. investment counseling; prop. mgmt.; **REP CLIENTS:** Indiv. and investors; **PROFL AFFIL & HONORS:** Nashville Bd. of Realtors; NAR; **EDUC:** BA, 1975, Bus. Mgmt., David Lipscomb Coll.; **OTHER ACT & HONORS:** Pres., Exchange Club of Green Hills; **HOME ADD:** 5050 Hillsboro Rd., Nashville, TN 37215, (615)297-3847; **BUS ADD:** 2213 Bandywood Dr., Nashville, TN 37215, (615)383-4176.

CROUT, Robert L.——B: Dec. 24, 1949, Wichita Falls, TX, *Pres. - Chmn. of Bd. of Directors*, Crout Development Co.; **PRIM RE ACT:** Developer, Builder, Owner/Investor, Syndicator; **SERVICES:** Comml. & resid. bldr., devel., synd., investor; **PREV EMPLOY:** Acct. Exec., Merrill Lynch; **PROFL AFFIL & HONORS:** Mustang C of C; OKC Chamber, Nat. Homebuilders Assn., Central OK HBA, COHBA Developers Council; **EDUC:** BA, 1972, Fin. & Bus. Law, Univ. of OK; **OTHER ACT & HONORS:** Also affil. with: Nelms Crout Corp. and Plantation Devel. Corp.; **HOME ADD:** 708 Falcon Way, Mustang, OK 73064, (405)376-4437; **BUS ADD:** PO Box 250, Mustang, OK 73064, (405)376-3704.

CROW, Michael D.——B: June 1, 1946, Dallas, TX, *Pres.*, Crow Dev. Co.; **PRIM RE ACT:** Developer, Builder; **PROFL AFFIL & HONORS:** Home and Apt. Bldrs., Chmn. of Dev. Comm.; **EDUC:** BA, 1968, Econ., Univ. of PA; **GRAD EDUC:** MBA, 1970, Fin., Wharton School of Commerce, Univ. of PA; **MIL SERV:** US Army, Capt.; **OTHER ACT & HONORS:** New Arts Theatre Co., Chmn. of the Bd.; Historic Preservation League; **HOME ADD:** 3516 Harvard Ave., Dallas, TX 75205, (214)521-3258; **BUS ADD:** 2001 Bryan Tower, Suite 3150, Dallas, TX 75201, (214)742-1550.

CROW, Michael G.——B: Mar. 31, 1942, Los Angeles, CA, *Sales Assoc.*, R.C. Taylor Co., Investment & Comml.; **PRIM RE ACT:** Broker, Consultant; **OTHER RE ACT:** Indus. site location; **SERVICES:** RE investment counseling; indus. site location; **REP CLIENTS:** Indiv. investors, indus. users; **EDUC:** BA, 1964, Hist., Univ. of CA, Riverside; **GRAD EDUC:** MA, 1966, Hist., Univ. of CA, Riverside; PhD, pending, Econ. Hist., Univ. of CA; **OTHER ACT & HONORS:** Advisor, Newport Found. for Study of Econ. Issues; **HOME ADD:** 315 Signal Rd., Newport Beach, CA 92660, (714)645-3176; **BUS ADD:** 3 Corp. Plaza Dr., Newport Bch., CA 92660, (714)640-9900.

CROW, Steven T.——B: Apr. 10, 1949, St. Louis, MO, *Appraiser*; **PRIM RE ACT:** Appraiser; **REP CLIENTS:** Transamerica Relocation Sucs., Employee Transfer Corp., Kraft, Westinghouse; **PREV EMPLOY:** Porter Co., Ltd., Summit, NJ; Friday Agency, No. Brunswick, NJ; **PROFL AFFIL & HONORS:** Soc. of RE Appraisers; Nat. Assn. of Review Appraisers, SRA; CRA; CTA (Cert. Tax Assessor, NJ); **EDUC:** BA, 1971, Speech/Theatre/Educ., Marymount Coll., Salina, KS; **OTHER ACT & HONORS:** Adv. Bd. Member, Camp Merry Heart, (Easter Seals) Hackettstown, NJ; **HOME ADD:** Pennington Ave., Basking Ridge, NJ 07920, (201)766-4146; **BUS ADD:** PO Box 6, Basking Ridge, NJ 07920, (201)766-4146.

CROW, Ted F.——B: Mar. 3, 1947, Peoria, IL, *VP of Urban Devel.*, Southland Investment Properties, Inc., Prop. Devel./Comml.; **PRIM RE ACT:** Developer; **SERVICES:** In charge of $275 million of office devel. for Southland RE resources; **PREV EMPLOY:** Ted Crow Co. 9/76 to 6/79; Trammell Crow Co. 11/73-2/75; **PROFL AFFIL & HONORS:** Nat. Assn. of Indus. & Office Parks; **EDUC:** BBA, 1969, Fin., Univ. of TX at Austin; **GRAD EDUC:** MBA, 1973, Mktg. & Fin., Univ. of TX at Austin; **EDUC HONORS:** Dean's List, Nat. Honor Soc., Phi Kappa Phi, Beta Gamma Sigma, Dean's Award for Acad. Excellence; **HOME ADD:** 5540 Mercedes, Dallas, TX 75206, (214)821-9649; **BUS ADD:** 201 E. John W. Carpenter Fwy., Irving, TX 75062, (214)556-0244.

CROWELL, Ed.——*Special Project*, Galveston-Houston Co.; **PRIM RE ACT:** Property Manager; **BUS ADD:** 4900 Woodway, Houston, TX 77056, (713)966-2500.*

CROWELL, Robert M.——B: Feb. 24, 1932, Concord, MA, *Partner*, Town and Country Real Estate Associates; **PRIM RE ACT:** Broker, Consultant; **SERVICES:** Resid., comml., land, sales and listing; **PREV EMPLOY:** Merchandise Mgr., Spencer Gifts (Retail Div.); Pres., QCE of Pleasantville, Corp.; **PROFL AFFIL & HONORS:** Atlantic City., Cty. Bd. of Realtors, GRI; **EDUC:** BBA, 1953, Econ., Babson Coll.; **EDUC HONORS:** Dean's List; **MIL SERV:** US Army; Pfc.; **OTHER ACT & HONORS:** Rotary IntL., Treas.; Old Absecon Yacht Club, Treas.; **HOME ADD:** 707 New York Ave., Absecon, NJ 08201, (609)645-2159; **BUS ADD:** One Second Ave., Absecon, NJ 08201, (609)652-8800.

CROWLEY, John——*RE Asst. Secy. Legal & Senior Atty.*, Libbey-Owens-Ford Co.; **PRIM RE ACT:** Attorney, Property Manager; **BUS ADD:** 811 Madison Ave., Toledo, OH 43695, (419)247-3731.*

CROWLEY, Joseph——*Manager Prop. & RE*, Acton Corporation; **PRIM RE ACT:** Property Manager; **BUS ADD:** PO Box 407, Acton, MA 01720, (617)263-7711.*

CROWTHER, John H.——B: Mar. 21, 1932, Orange, NJ, *Arch.*, John H. Crowther; **PRIM RE ACT:** Architect, Developer, Owner/Investor; **PROFL AFFIL & HONORS:** AIA, NJ Soc. of Archs., Concrete Bldg. Award 1968, Masonry Bldg. of the Decade 1970; **EDUC:** BA, 1953, Humanities, St. Peters Coll.; **GRAD EDUC:** MArch, 1960, Arch, Columbia Univ.; **EDUC HONORS:** William Kinney Fellows Fellowship; **MIL SERV:** US Army, Cpl.; **OTHER ACT & HONORS:** Dir., Montclair Rehabilitation Org.; **HOME ADD:** 179 Midland Ave., Montclair, NJ 07042, (201)746-8492; **BUS ADD:** 10 S. Fullerton Ave., Montclair, NJ 07042, (201)744-8788.

CROXTON, Randolph R.——B: July 21, 1944, Danville, VA, *Dir.*, Croxton Collaborative, Architects; **PRIM RE ACT:** Architect; **SERVICES:** Planning, arch. & interior design; **REP CLIENTS:** Fifth Ave. Presbyterian Church, NYC; Amer. Stanhope Hotel, NYC; R.J. Reynolds Tobacco Co., Winston-Salem, NC; **PREV EMPLOY:** I.M. Pei and Part., Architects, 600 Madison Ave., NY, NY 10022; **PROFL AFFIL & HONORS:** AIA; NCARB; CSI, Arch. Record, Interiors Award, 1980; Residential Design Award, NY/AIA, 1981; **EDUC:** BArch, 1968, Arch./Bus., NC State Univ.; **GRAD EDUC:** Grad. Study, Bus./RE, NYU/RE Inst.; **EDUC HONORS:** Ed., 'Building Skeletons', SPSD, NCSU, 1968; **MIL SERV:** US Army, MI, Lt.; **OTHER ACT & HONORS:** Architectural League of NY; Municipal Art Soc.; **HOME ADD:** 16 E 84th St., NY, NY 10028, (212)794-1712; **BUS ADD:** 16 E 84th St., NY, NY 10028, (212)794-2285.

CROZIER, Robert W.——B: Sept. 7, 1921, NYC, *Architect*, Robert W. Crozier & Assoc.; **PRIM RE ACT:** Architect, Consultant, Owner/Investor; **SERVICES:** Architectural and Engineering; **PREV EMPLOY:** Self-employed since 1952; **PROFL AFFIL & HONORS:** Westchester Chap., AIA, NYSAA/AIA, CSI, Past Pres. Westchester Co., AIA, Past Pres., NYAA/AIA, Publications in several nat. Home Design magazines. Design Awards, 1957 Church Architectural Guild; 1958 and 1960, NYSAA; **GRAD EDUC:** BArch, 1948, Pratt Inst.; **OTHER ACT & HONORS:** Past Pres. Rye Lions, Lodge 1030 F&A Masons, Comdr. Rye Flotilla, USCGA, Vestryman Episcopal churches; **HOME ADD:** 21 Rocky Pt. Rd., Rowayton, CT 06853, (203)853-1766; **BUS ADD:** 41 Elm Pl., Rye, NY 10580, (914)967-6060.

CRUEA, Dudley——B: Sept. 6, 1956, Danville,IL, *Realtor*, Suiters RE; **PRIM RE ACT:** Broker, Appraiser; **SERVICES:** List, Appraise & Comml, Resid. & Farm Prop.; **PROFL AFFIL & HONORS:**

Fountain-Warren Bd. of Realtors; **GRAD EDUC:** BS, 1979, Mktg., IN State Univ.; **EDUC HONORS:** Rhod. Scholar - ISU, Deans List - Danville Jr. Coll.; **OTHER ACT & HONORS:** 7th District Chmn. Young Republicans, 1 Yr., Treas. - Fountain Cty. Republican Central Comm., Sec.-Treas. - Fountain - Warren Bd. of Realtors; **HOME ADD:** 707 10th St., Covington, IN 47932, (317)793-3200; **BUS ADD:** RR 2, Covington, IN 47932, (317)793-3754.

CRUME, Roy L.——B: Feb. 15, 1923, Howard, IN, *Owner*, Roy L. Crume, Auctioneer, Realtor & Appraiser; **PRIM RE ACT:** Broker, Appraiser; **OTHER RE ACT:** Auctioneer; **SERVICES:** Auctioneer and broker of RE & personal prop.; **REP CLIENTS:** Executors of estates, attys., banks, S&L Assns., corps. in transfer of employees; **PREV EMPLOY:** Auctioneer, Realtor and Appraiser for past 33 yrs.; **PROFL AFFIL & HONORS:** Nat. & State Auctioneers, RE Assn., NAR, FLI, RE Appraisers, Cert. Auctioneers Inst., Intl. Soc. of Appraisers, SRA, CAI, Auctioneer of year, State of IN, 1971. Past. Dir. Nat. Auctioneers Assn., Past Pres. of IN Auct. Assn., Past Pres. of Kokomo Bd. of Realtors and Metropolitan Kiwanis Club of Kokomo, IN, Pres. Kokomo Shrine Club (1982).; **EDUC:** Reppert Sch. of Auctioneering; **OTHER ACT & HONORS:** City of Kokomo C of C, Metro. Kiwanis Club of Kokomo Charter Member, Past Pres. & Dir.; Howard Lodge F&AM; Kokomo Eagles, POE, Loyal Order of Moose, Kokomo IN Lodge Life Member; Izaak Walton League of Amer.; Scottish Rite 32 deg. Mason, Valley of Indianapolis, Life Member; Scottish Rite Club of Howard Cty.; Murat Shrine, Indianapolis, IN; Kokomo Shrine Club, Past. Dir.; Kokomo Shrine Clowns; Howard Cty. Farm Bur. Co-op, Past. Pres. & Dir.; United Comml. Travelers of Amer.; Kokomo Elks Lodge BPOE, Life Member; Fraternal Order of Police, Kokomo, IN, Spec. Deputy Sheriff; **HOME ADD:** 2301 W Jefferson Rd., Kokomo, IN 46901, (317)452-6946; **BUS ADD:** 115 S. Dixon Rd., Kokomo, IN 46901, (317)457-8238.

CRUMP, G. Lindsay——B: Mar. 25, 1922, DeKalb, TX, *Exec. VP*, National Corp. for Housing Partnerships, Pres., NCHP Prop. Mgmt., Inc.; **PRIM RE ACT:** Developer, Builder, Property Manager, Syndicator; **SERVICES:** Build, Devel., Synd. & Mgr. Multi-Family Rental Housing; **PREV EMPLOY:** AMF Inc., 1956-1970, Div. VP, Asst. Grp. Exec., Chmn. of AMF Australia; **PROFL AFFIL & HONORS:** IREM, CPA; CPM; **EDUC:** BA, 1946, Public Acctg./Econ., Univ. of TX; **MIL SERV:** USAF, S/Sgt.; US Army, 1st Lt.; **OTHER ACT & HONORS:** Delta Sigma Pi; Beta ALpha Psi; New York Athletic Club; Nat. Housing Liaison Comm. of IREM; Nat. Advisory Council of Nat. Ctr. for Housing Mgmt.; Advisory Council of Nat. Multi-Housing Council; Multi-Family Housing Comm. of Nat. Assn. of Home Builders; Who's Who in Fin. and Indus., 1981-1982; **HOME ADD:** 1513 Snughill Ct., Vienna, VA 22180, (703)893-2187; **BUS ADD:** 1133 15th St., NW, Washington, DC 20005, (202)857-5737.

CRUMP, Thomas Richard——B: Oct. 24, 1945, Seguin, TX, *Pres.*, Crump & Knobles, Inc.; **PRIM RE ACT:** Attorney; **SERVICES:** Prof. legal services; **REP CLIENTS:** Countywide Title Co.; **PROFL AFFIL & HONORS:** Texas Trial Lawyers' Assn. Texas Assn. of Bank Counsel; Amer. Trial Lawyers' Assoc.; American, TX & San Antonio Bar Assns., Guadalupe Cty. Bar Assn.; South Central Bar Assn., ABA, Delta Theta Phi Law Frat.; **EDUC:** BS, 1969, Geology, St. Mary's Univ.; **GRAD EDUC:** J.D., 1971, St. Mary's Univ.; **EDUC HONORS:** Summa Cum Laude; **OTHER ACT & HONORS:** Delta Epsilom Sigma; New Braunfels C. of C.; TX Assn. of Realtors; **BUS ADD:** 109 W. Gonzales St., Seguin, TX 78155, (512)379-7610.

CRUTCHFIELD, Robert——*VP, Fin.*, Howell Corp.; **PRIM RE ACT:** Property Manager; **BUS ADD:** 800 Houston Natural Gas Bldg., Houston, TX 77002, (713)658-4000.*

CRUZ, Henry——B: Jan. 21, 1954, Manhattan, NY, *Project Director*, Urban League of Philadelphia, Homeowners/Homebuyers Counseling Program; **OTHER RE ACT:** Housing Consultant; **SERVICES:** Pre-Purchase Counseling, Default & Delinquency Mortgage Counseling, Credit/Finance and Money Management Counseling; **REP CLIENTS:** Currently low & moderate income housing consumers; **PREV EMPLOY:** June 1976 to March 1978 housing counselor, Urban League Housing Program; March 1978 to November 1979 Senior Counselor; **PROFL AFFIL & HONORS:** Nat. Fed. of Housing Counselors, US Dept. of Housing and Urban Devel., Certified Counselor; **EDUC:** Assoc. Degree, 1975, Bus. Admin., Temple Univ.; **GRAD EDUC:** Continue Studies on RE Educ., RE Education, Temple Univ. RE Inst.; **OTHER ACT & HONORS:** Counselor, Trainer, National Urban; National Paralegal Inst.; Board Member Housing Association of Delaware Valley; Mortgage Delinquency Committee Greater Philadelphia Partnership; Philadelphia Mortgage Plan; **HOME ADD:** 3651 Red Lion Rd., Apt. A-12, Philadelphia, PA 19114, (215)632-9741; **BUS ADD:** 5208 Chestnut Street, Philadelphia, PA 19139, (215)748-2020.

CRUZE, Harold——B: Sept. 21, 1931, New Orleans, LA, *Mgr., Prop. Mgmt. Dept.*, California State Automobile Assn.; **PRIM RE ACT:** Broker, Developer, Property Manager; **SERVICES:** All primary RE activities are accomplished for employer; **PREV EMPLOY:** RE Broker & Devel.; **PROFL AFFIL & HONORS:** San Francisco Bd. of Realtors & BOMA; **EDUC:** Attended Loyola Univ.; **MIL SERV:** US Army, S/Sgt., 1948-Apr. 1950; **OTHER ACT & HONORS:** Past Chmn. Hanford, CA Traffic Commn.; Past Member Planning Commn., Union City, CA; Director, Custom Chrome, Inc.; **HOME ADD:** 18724 Santon Ave., Castro Valley, CA 94546, (415)538-7206; **BUS ADD:** 150 Van Ness Ave., San Francisco, CA 94102, (415)565-2067.

CRYER, Clifford L.——B: July 27, 1948, Baltimore, MD, *Pres.*, Cryer & Co. Appraisers, Inc.; **PRIM RE ACT:** Consultant, Appraiser, Builder, Owner/Investor, Instructor, Property Manager; **SERVICES:** Valuation, feasibility studies, ltd. partnerships, investment counseling; **REP CLIENTS:** Nat. and local including lenders, new resid constr. investors and indivs.; **PREV EMPLOY:** The Arnold Co's., Appraiser & Resid. Devel., 1972-74; **PROFL AFFIL & HONORS:** Intl. Soc. of RE Appraisers; AIREA; Denver & CO Bds. of Realtors, SRPA; **EDUC:** BSBA, 1970, Bldg. Indus. & RE Fin., Univ. of Denver; **OTHER ACT & HONORS:** RE Appraisal Advisory Comm., Denver Public Schools, 1977-79; Instr. for GRI Realtor Course in cooperation with Univ. of CO; **HOME ADD:** 7110 S Cherry Dr., Littleton, CO 80122, (303)773-6308; **BUS ADD:** 1776 S Jackson, 406, Denver, CO 80210, (303)758-5774.

CRYER, Jeanne W.——B: May 20, 1925, Sharon, PA, *Investment RE Broker*, Jeanne Cryer Realty; **PRIM RE ACT:** Broker, Consultant, Owner/Investor; **PROFL AFFIL & HONORS:** NAR, Sierra Reno Exchangors, CCIM, NAR; **EDUC:** BA, 1945, Chem., Bus. Admin., Case Western Reserve Univ., Cleveland, OH; **EDUC HONORS:** Magna Cum Laude, Phi Beta Kappa; **HOME ADD:** 2580 Eastshore Pl., Reno, NV 89509; **BUS ADD:** 437 S. Sierra St., Reno, NV 89501, (702)322-7765.

CRYSTAL, Joel F.——B: Feb. 3, 1945, Brooklyn, NY, *Sr. Staff Atty.*, IPCO Corp.; **PRIM RE ACT:** Attorney; **SERVICES:** RE counsel for NYSE Corp. with 3 retail divs.; **PREV EMPLOY:** Pvt. legal practice, NYC 1968-76; **PROFL AFFIL & HONORS:** Assn. of Bar of City of NY, Westchester-Fairfield Cty. Corp. Counsel's Assn., NACORE; **EDUC:** BA, 1965, Hist., Brooklyn Coll.; **GRAD EDUC:** JD, 1968, Columbia Univ. Law School; **EDUC HONORS:** Cum Laude; **HOME ADD:** 19 Mt. Joy Ave., Scarsdale, NY 10583, (914)472-4731; **BUS ADD:** 1025 Westchester Ave., White Plains, NY 10604, (914)682-4532.

CRYSTAL, Richard——B: Oct. 29, 1940, New York, New York, *Partner*, Fenwick, Stone Davis & West; **PRIM RE ACT:** Attorney; **SERVICES:** Legal; **PREV EMPLOY:** Regan, Goldfarb, Heller, Wetzler & Quinn 1972-81; Wien Lane & Malkin Esq. 1966-1972; **PROFL AFFIL & HONORS:** ABA, City of New York Bar Assn.; **EDUC:** AB, 1962, Hist., Harvard Univ.; **GRAD EDUC:** LLB, 1966, Harvard Law School; **EDUC HONORS:** Cum Laude; **MIL SERV:** US Army, Pvt.; **OTHER ACT & HONORS:** 92nd St. YMYWHA, NYC., Dir.; **HOME ADD:** 41 Black Birch Ln., Scarsdale, NY 10583; **BUS ADD:** 488 Madison Ave., New York, NY 10022, (212)754-3000.

CUBBISON, Greg——B: Dec. 21, 1946, Pasadena, TX, *Leasing Agent*, The Horne Co., Prop. Mgmt.; **PRIM RE ACT:** Broker; **SERVICES:** Office space mktg.; **REP CLIENTS:** Corps. looking for office space; **PROFL AFFIL & HONORS:** Admin. Mgmt. Soc., Houston Bd. of Realtors, TX Assn. of Realtors, Nat. Assn. of Realtors, Cert. Admin. Mgr.; **EDUC:** BA, 1969, Hist., Univ. of TX at Austin; **MIL SERV:** US Air Force, Capt., Air Medals (3), Vietnamese Serv., Vietnamese Campaign; **OTHER ACT & HONORS:** Chapelwood United Methodist Church; **HOME ADD:** 853 Hickorywood Lane, Houston, TX 77024, (713)464-1604; **BUS ADD:** 1801 Main No. 600, Houston, TX 77002, (713)224-5595.

CUDA, Dan L.——B: April 7, 1945, Stromsburg, NE, *Pres.*, UMC Realty, Village Mano-Const. Inc.; **PRIM RE ACT:** Broker, Instructor, Syndicator, Consultant, Appraiser, Developer, Builder, Property Manager, Owner/Investor; **PROFL AFFIL & HONORS:** Bldr. Natl. Realtor, GRI, CRS, CAR, BAS; **EDUC:** BA, 1971, Bus. Admin & Educ., Univ. of NE; **MIL SERV:** US Army, E-5; **HOME ADD:** 2314 Sewell, Lincoln, NE 68522, (401)435-0818; **BUS ADD:** Suite 103, 501 West A, Lincoln, NE 68522, (402)475-4337.

CUDLIP, Peter M.——B: Feb. 2, 1954, Detroit, MI, *Project Mgr.*, Nu-West, Inc., CO Comml./Indus.; **PRIM RE ACT:** Developer; **PREV EMPLOY:** Devel., 5 yrs.; **PROFL AFFIL & HONORS:** Denver Bd. of Realtors, NMI, NAIOP; **EDUC:** BS, 1976, RE Investment and Devel., Univ. of UT; **HOME ADD:** 8101 E. Dartmouth, 73, Denver, CO, (303)755-1940; **BUS ADD:** 3035 S. Parker Rd., 509, Aurora, CO 80014, (303)696-1777.

CUIFFO, Frank W.——B: Oct. 13, 1943, Houston, TX, *Partner*, Carro, Spanbock, Londin, Fass & Geller; **PRIM RE ACT:** Attorney; **EDUC:** BS, 1964, Physics, Univ. of Notre Dame; **GRAD EDUC:** LLD, 1967, Fordham Univ. School of Law; **HOME ADD:** 14 Sturgis Rd., Bronxville, NY 10708, (914)337-8553; **BUS ADD:** 1345 Ave. of the Americas, NY, NY 10105, (212)757-2400.

CUKER, George——B: Feb. 24, 1934, Leningrad, Russia, *Pres.*, Kent Corp.; **PRIM RE ACT:** Consultant, Developer, Lender, Builder, Property Manager; **PROFL AFFIL & HONORS:** Soc. of Amer. Value Eng., Project Mgmt. Inst.; Amer. Mgmt. Assn.; Amer. Arbitration Assn.; Amer. Soc. Quality Control; **EDUC:** Franklin Inst., 1955, Engrg., Boston Univ.; **GRAD EDUC:** Harvard Bus. Sch., 1969, Bus.; **MIL SERV:** Avty., LTC; **OTHER ACT & HONORS:** Children's Museum Bd.; Children's Hospital Bd.; Hale House Bd.; HBSA Alumni; Handel & Mayor Bd., Provident Sav. Corp.; **HOME ADD:** 4 Newton St., Weston, MA 02139, (617)894-4003; **BUS ADD:** 45 Broad St., Boston, MA 02109, (617)482-0800.

CULBERTSON, Barry L.——B: June 2, 1938, Ft. Madison, IA, *VP, RE*, Atherton Indus., Inc., Pic-A-Dilly and It's-A-Dilly Stores; **OTHER RE ACT:** Retail Leasing; **PREV EMPLOY:** Circle K Corp 1965-68; Foodmaker, Inc. 1968-75; **PROFL AFFIL & HONORS:** Nat. Assn. of Corp. RE Execs., Intl. Council of Shopping Ctrs.; **EDUC:** BS, 1960, Fin., AZ State Univ.; **HOME ADD:** 614 Oregon Ave., San Mateo, CA 94402, (415)342-6392; **BUS ADD:** 260 Constitution Dr., Menlo Park, CA 94025, (415)328-5900.

CULP, Duane K.——B: Aug. 20, 1943, Rensselaer, IN, *Partner*, DCT Design Associates; **PRIM RE ACT:** Architect; **SERVICES:** Programming, land planning, arch. design, interior design; **REP CLIENTS:** Corps., pvt. devel., insts.; **PREV EMPLOY:** Planning & Design Firm; **PROFL AFFIL & HONORS:** AIA; KY Soc. of Arch.; E. KY Chap. AIA; Soc. for Mktg. Profl. Serv.; Lexington-Fayette Urban Cty. Landscape Review Comm.; **EDUC:** BS, 1967, Art/Arch., Ball State Univ.; BArch., 1970, Art/Arch., Univ. of KY; **OTHER ACT & HONORS:** Ashland Park Assn.; **HOME ADD:** 231 Catalpa Rd., Lexington, KY 40502, (606)266-8519; **BUS ADD:** 508 E. Main St., Lexington, KY 40508, (606)259-0303.

CULP, James F.——B: Feb. 14, 1918, Temple, TX, *Owner*, Culp RE; **PRIM RE ACT:** Broker, Consultant, Appraiser; **SERVICES:** RE counseling and appraising, brokerage, prop. mgmt., counseling and appraising services, TX and nearby states; **REP CLIENTS:** Lending and trust agents, estates, relocation cos., IRS, Dept. of Justice, Corps of Engineers, Intl. Boundary Commn., city and state agencies, corporate and pvt. clients; **PROFL AFFIL & HONORS:** AIREA; Temple - Belton Bd. of Realtors; TX and Nat. RE Assn.; Amer. Soc. of Farm Managers and Rural Appraisers; Amer. Soc. RE Counselors, MAI; CRE; Past VP and Governing Council AIREA; Past VP, TX Assn. of Realtors; Past Pres., Temple, TX, Bd. of Realtors; **EDUC:** BBA, 1939, Fin., Univ. of CO/Univ. of TX; **MIL SERV:** USN, Lt., Ret., 1940-1945; **HOME ADD:** 1408 N. 13th St., Temple, TX 76501, (817)773-5057; **BUS ADD:** 13 W. Central, Temple, TX 76501, (817)773-6833.

CUMBEST, Mark——B: Sept. 18, 1953, Pascagoula, MS, *Pres.*, Cumbest Realty, Inc.; **PRIM RE ACT:** Broker, Owner/Investor, Insuror; **SERVICES:** Resid. & land brokerage, exchanging, timberland and farms; **REP CLIENTS:** Investors in homes and land, exchangers; **PROFL AFFIL & HONORS:** FLI; Jackson Cty. Bd. of Realtors, Past Pres.; Rho Epsilon; Interex; MS Orgn. of Realty Exchangers, VP, Realtor of Yr. 1980, Jackson Cty. MS Bd. of Realtors, Candidate Accredited Farm & Land Member Designation; **EDUC:** BS, 1975, Bus. Admin., RE Ins., Univ. of S. MS; **OTHER ACT & HONORS:** Shriner, Rotary Intl., Dir. Jackson Cty. Econ. Devel. Found.; Outstanding Young Men of Amer., 1978; Charter Member, Pi Kappa Alpha Frat. Alumni Chap. at Univ. of S. MS; **HOME ADD:** Route 2, Box 150, Pasagoula, MS 39567, (601)588-6139; **BUS ADD:** Route 2, Box 150, Pascagoula, MS 39567, (601)588-6213.

CUMMINGS, Albert A.——B: June 21, 1927, Mesa, AZ, *Pres.*, Cummings Realty & Trust Co., Inc.; **PRIM RE ACT:** Broker, Consultant, Appraiser, Developer, Builder, Owner/Investor, Instructor, Property Manager, Syndicator; **SERVICES:** Investment counseling, valuation, devel. and synd. of comml. props., prop. mgmt.; **REP CLIENTS:** Indiv. or instnl. investors in comml. props., resid. sales and rentals; **PROFL AFFIL & HONORS:** RNMI, RESSI, FLI, CRB, CCIM, Accredited Farm & Land Member, GRI, Tucson Bd. of Realtors, Named Realtor of the year, 1973, Pres. 1972, VP 1971, Dir. 1969-74, Chmn. Membership Comm. 1970, Member Profl. Standards Comm., 1967 (Comm. of the Yr. Award), Pres. Tucson RE Exchange Club, 1967, Instr. Educ. Course Comm., 1969-73. MLS of Tucson, Inc. VP 1971, 1972, Treas. 1970, Sec. 1967, Dir. 1966-72. AZ Assn. of Realtors Dir. 1971, 1974, 1977, 1979, 1980, Chmn. Educ Comm., 1974 (Comm. of the Year Award), V. Chmn. 1973; Chmn. License Law Comm., 1971-72 (Comm. of Yr. Award); Chmn. Bd. of Govs. Realtors Inst., 1975, 1976, 1978, 1979; Member 1970-76, 1978, 1979, 1980, Inst. Realtors Inst. since 1970; Dir. AZ Assn. of RE Exchangors, 1966-67; Pres. Spec. Recognition Award, 1978, 1979; Member Editorial Review Bd., 1979, 1980; Second VP, 1981; **OTHER ACT & HONORS:** Distinguished Govs. Award, Sertoma Intl., Pres. John B. Wright PTA, 1969-70; Gov. AZ Dist. Sertoma Intl. 1968, 1969 (Distinguished Gov. Award); Chmn. of the Bd. Tucson Midtown Sertoma Club, 1969, 1970; Dir. Tucson Desert Sertoma Club, 1963, 1966; Chmn. of the Bd. Tucson Desert Sertoma Club, 1962, 1963; Pres. Tucson Desert Sertoma Club, 1961, 1962 (Superior Club Leadership Citation); Sec. Treas. Tucson Desert Sertoma Club, 1959-61 and part of 1963, Life Member Sertoma Intl., Served on Amer. Arbitration Assn. comml. panel since 1973; **HOME ADD:** 2324 N. Madelyn Cir., Tucson, AZ 85712, (602)326-4846; **BUS ADD:** 1725 N. Swan Rd., Tucson, AZ 85712, (602)881-3210.

CUMMINGS, Peter D.——B: Sept. 16, 1947, Montreal, Can., *Pres.*, First Southern Holdings, Inc.; **PRIM RE ACT:** Developer, Owner/Investor; **SERVICES:** RE Mgmt. and Dev.; **PROFL AFFIL & HONORS:** ULI; **EDUC:** BA, 1968, Eng. Lit., Yale Univ.; **GRAD EDUC:** MA, 1969, Eng. Lit., Univ. of Toronto; **OTHER ACT & HONORS:** Member, Bd. of Dir., Jewish Fed. of the Palm Beaches; **BUS ADD:** 501 S Flagler Dr., Suite 307, W Palm Beach, FL 33401, (305)659-2955.

CUMMINGS, Tom——B: Oct. 19, 1946, IA, *Pres.*, All State Management; **PRIM RE ACT:** Broker, Consultant, Owner/Investor, Property Manager; **SERVICES:** Apt. mgmt. services; **EDUC:** BBA - Mktg., 1969, Adver. Mktg., Univ. of IA, Iowa City, IA; **MIL SERV:** USMC, Cpl.; **HOME ADD:** 1415 Fairoaks Ct., East Lansing, MI 48823, (517)351-9370; **BUS ADD:** 241 East Saginaw, East Lansing, MI 48823, (517)351-1310.

CUMMINS, J.P.——*Mgr. Field RE*, Hoover Co.; **PRIM RE ACT:** Property Manager; **BUS ADD:** 101 E. Maple St., North Canton, OH 44720.*

CUMMINS, Neil J., Jr.——B: Sept. 14, 1945, CA, *Owner*, Self-employed consultant; **PRIM RE ACT:** Attorney, Engineer; **OTHER RE ACT:** Land Surveyor; **SERVICES:** Consultation regarding complex boundary and title problems; **PREV EMPLOY:** 10 yrs. land devel. engrg. and surveying with various So. CA Engrg. firms; **PROFL AFFIL & HONORS:** Registered Civil Engr.: AZ, CA, NV; Registered, Land Surveyor: CA, NV; Member, CA Bar; **EDUC:** Civil Engrg., Cal Poly Pomona; **GRAD EDUC:** JD, 1978, Mid-Valley Coll. of Law, Van Nuys, CA; **BUS ADD:** 18710 Serman Way, Suite 4, Reseda, CA 91335, (213)705-1255.

CUNNEEN, Charles T.——B: Jan. 13, 1928, Brooklyn NY, *VP*, Metropolitan Life Insurance Co., Co. Prop. and Services; **PRIM RE ACT:** Builder, Owner/Investor, Property Manager; **PROFL AFFIL & HONORS:** Amer. Arbitration Assn., Panel of Arbitrators; NY Building Congress, Dir., 23rd St. Assn., Inc., VP & Dir.; **EDUC:** BBA, 1955, Mgmt., St. John's Univ.; **GRAD EDUC:** MBA, 1960, Mgmt., New York Univ.; **MIL SERV:** US Army, Paratroopers, Technician Fifth Grade, Army of Occupation, Japan; **OTHER ACT & HONORS:** McBurney YMCA, Treas. & Dir.; **HOME ADD:** 200 Ocean Ave., Massapequa Park, NY 11762; **BUS ADD:** 1 Madison Ave., NYC, NY 10010, (212)578-2747.

CUNNINGHAM, G. Bruce——B: Jan. 26, 1947, Little Rock, AR, *Associate Counsel, VP*, Cousins Properties Inc.; **PRIM RE ACT:** Attorney; **PREV EMPLOY:** Lawyer with Alston, Miller & Gaines 1974-81; **PROFL AFFIL & HONORS:** ABA, State Bar of GA, Atlanta Bar Assn.; **EDUC:** BA, 1969, Govt., Columbia Coll., Columbia Univ.; **GRAD EDUC:** JD, 1974, Columbia Univ., NY; **EDUC HONORS:** Harlan Fiske Stone Scholar 1972- 73 and 1973-74; **MIL SERV:** US Army, SP-5, 1969-71; **OTHER ACT & HONORS:** Bd. of Dir., The Atlanta Virtuosi Found.; **HOME ADD:** 1259 Pasadena Ave. NE, Atlanta, GA 30306, (404)876-0982; **BUS ADD:** 300 Interstate N., Atlanta, GA 30339, (404)955-0000.

CUNNINGHAM, James F.——B: Apr. 2, 1943, Washington, DC, *Pres.*, Associated Housing Developers; Inc.; **OTHER RE ACT:** Real Est. Development; **PREV EMPLOY:** UMIC Props., Inc., 1978-1981; Nat. Housing Partnership, 1971-1978; **EDUC:** 1972, Acctg., Univ. of MD; **MIL SERV:** US Army, Sgt., 1966-1969; **HOME ADD:** 1503 Churu Rd., Southaven, MS 38671, (601)393-5026; **BUS ADD:** 2670 Union Ave. Ext., Memphis, TN 38112, (901)323-2450.

CUNNINGHAM, Michael J.——B: Mar. 7, 1945, Chicago, IL, *Sr. Sales Assoc. - Investments*, Coldwell Banker Co., Investment Dept.; **PRIM RE ACT:** Broker; **SERVICES:** Structuring of sales and joint ventures of comml. investment props, for devels., investors and synds.; **EDUC:** BS/BA, 1969, Mayor RE, Univ. of Denver; **MIL SERV:** USAR; **HOME ADD:** 29885 Monterey Lane, Evergreen, CO 80439, (303)674-3429; **BUS ADD:** Suite 200, 1050 17th St., Denver, CO 80439, (303)628-7400.

CUNNINGHAM, Richard G.——B: June 1, 1938, Rochester, NY, *Dir. of RE*, Wegmans Food Markets, Inc. & Wegmans Enterprises, Inc.; **PRIM RE ACT:** Broker, Consultant, Property Manager; **HOME ADD:** 586 Marsh Rd., Pittsford, NY 14534; **BUS ADD:** 1500 Brooks Ave., Rochester, NY 14603, (716)328-2550.

CURINI, Ronald A.——B: Oct. 12, 1935, Trenton, NJ, *Pres.*, Ronald A. Curini Appraisal Co., Inc.; **PRIM RE ACT:** Consultant, Appraiser; **SERVICES:** Resid, comml. & indus. appraising & consulting, all apsects of RE; **REP CLIENTS:** CITGO; Coca Cola; Exxon; Clorox Co.; 3M; Nabisco; IBM; Getty Oil; Shell Oil; **PROFL AFFIL & HONORS:** Member of SREA; Mercer Cty. Bd. of Realtors; Amer. Right of Way Assoc.; IFA; NARA, SRA, CRA, IFA, CTA & Int. V Gov. of SREA, District 16; **EDUC:** BA, 1958, Pol. Sci., Widener Coll., Chester, PA; **MIL SERV:** US Army, Capt.; **OTHER ACT & HONORS:** Chmn. Mercer Cty Overall Econ. Devel. Comm., Mercer Cty. C of C; **HOME ADD:** 725 Greenwood Ave., Trenton, NJ 08609; **BUS ADD:** 900 Kuser Road, Trenton, NJ 08619, (609)586-3500.

CURLEY, Andrew K.——B: Dec. 23, 1947, Cincinnati, OH, *Pres.*, Tower Commercial Corp., Synds. & investments; **PRIM RE ACT:** Broker, Syndicator, Consultant, Property Manager, Owner/Investor; **SERVICES:** Investment counseling, valuation, synd. of income prop., prop. mgmt.; **REP CLIENTS:** Indiv. or instnl. investors; **PREV EMPLOY:** NCPM, Inc. Cincinnati, OH, VP; Reinauer RE Corp., Lake Charles, LA, VP; **PROFL AFFIL & HONORS:** RESSI, RNMI, Greater Calcasieu Bd. of Realtors, Natl. Bd. of Realtors; **EDUC:** BBA, 1973, Mktg., Univ. of Cincinnati; **MIL SERV:** USMC, Cpl., Vietnam Service Medal, Vietnam Campaign Medal w/4 stars, Pres., Unit Citation, Natl. Defense Medal, Good Conduct Medal; **OTHER ACT & HONORS:** Young Men's Bus. Club; **HOME ADD:** 1804 Alvin St., Lake Charles, LA 70601, (318)439-6745; **BUS ADD:** 1011 Lakeshore Dr., Lake Charles, LA 70601, (318)436-9028.

CUROTTO, Ricky J.——B: Dec. 22, 1931, Lomita Park, CA, *Sr. Counsel*, Utah International Inc.; **PRIM RE ACT:** Consultant, Attorney; **SERVICES:** Devel., const., fin., leasing, sales and mgmt. counseling and consulting; **PREV EMPLOY:** Assoc., Peart, Baraty & Hassard, Attys. at Law, San Francisco, CA; **PROFL AFFIL & HONORS:** State Bar of CA; San Francisco Bar Assn.; ABA; Nat. Panel of Arbitrators of Amer. Arbitration Assn., Published "Conflict of Laws and Usury In CA: The Impact on Flow of Mort. Funds", Univ. of San Francisco Law Review, Vol. IX, No. 3, Winter 1975; **EDUC:** BS Cum Laude, 1953, Poli. Sci., Philosophy, Univ. of San Francisco; **GRAD EDUC:** JD, 1958, Law, Univ. of San Francisco Sch. of Law; **EDUC HONORS:** Pi Sigma Alpha, Poli. Sci. Frat.; Distinguished Mil. Student (R.O.T.C.), Bureau of Nat. Affairs Award; **MIL SERV:** US Army; 1st Lt.; 1954-1956; **OTHER ACT & HONORS:** Commonwealth Club of CA; Dir., Securities, Intermountain, Inc.; Dominican Homes, Inc.; Garden Hotels, Inc.; Simco Ind. Mort. Co.; also member of Bd. of Tr., Univ. of San Francisco; Capstone Capital Corp.; **HOME ADD:** 399 Sail Fish Isle, Foster City, CA 94404, (415)574-8087; **BUS ADD:** Room 800, 550 California St., San Francisco, CA 94104.

CURRIE, Edward A.——*SIR Dir. Corp. RE*, Uniroyal, Inc.; **PRIM RE ACT:** Property Manager; **BUS ADD:** World Headquarters, Benson Rd., Middlebury, CT 06749, (203)264-6516.*

CURRIE, William I.——B: Mar. 9, 1928, Staunton, VA, *Owner*, William I. Currie & Assoc.; **PRIM RE ACT:** Consultant, Appraiser, Property Manager; **SERVICES:** Comml. Indus., Resid. RE appraisals and consultation; **REP CLIENTS:** MD Food Market Authority; Gen. Services Admin.; MD Nat. Bank; David W. Kornblatt, Inc.; Baltimore Fed. S&L Assn.; **PREV EMPLOY:** Part. Wilson & Currie RE Appraisers & Consultants; VP, W,. Burton Guy & Co., Inc.; **PROFL AFFIL & HONORS:** Member AIREA, Member SREA, Past Pres. of MD Chap. No. 26, AIREA; Past Pres. of Balt. Chap. No. 24, SREA; Past Pres. of MD Chap. No. 16, IREM; **EDUC:** BS, 1949, Econ., Roanoke Coll.; **MIL SERV:** USN, Midshipman; **OTHER ACT & HONORS:** Past Pres. of Baltimore Jaycees; Past Pres. of United Nations Assn. of MD; Past Pres. Virginians of MD; Member of Soc. of Colonial Wars; **HOME ADD:** 1003 Woodson Rd., Baltimore, MD 21212, (301)435-6177; **BUS ADD:** 1101 N. Calvert St., Rm. 1806, Baltimore, MD 21202, (301)837-5121.

CURRIER, Barry Arthur——B: Apr. 16, 1946, Columbus, OH, *Prof. of Law*, Univ. of FL Coll. of Law; **PRIM RE ACT:** Attorney, Instructor; **PREV EMPLOY:** Latham & Watkins, Attys., Los Angeles, CA (1972-1973), Univ. of KY (1974-1976), Duke Univ. (1976-1977); **PROFL AFFIL & HONORS:** CA State Bar Assn., ABA (Sect. on Urban, State & Local Govt.); ULI; Planning and Law Div., Amer. Planning Assn., Order of the Coif, Pi Sigma Alpha; **EDUC:** BA, 1968, Pol. Sci., UCLA; **GRAD EDUC:** JD, 1971, Law, Univ. of So. CA; **HOME ADD:** 1848 N.W. 32nd Terr., Gainesville, FL 32605, (904)373-9739; **BUS ADD:** Coll. of Law, Univ. of FL, Gainesville, FL 32611, (904)392-2211.

CURRIER, Timothy J.——B: Apr. 18, 1952, Detroit, MI, *Atty.*, Dell, Shantz, Booker and Currier; **PRIM RE ACT:** Attorney; **SERVICES:** Legal counsel in RE transactions; **REP CLIENTS:** Indiv., bus. and school dists. in resid. and comml. RE transactions; **PROFL AFFIL & HONORS:** State Bar of MI, ABA, Oakland Cty. Bar. Assn.; Nat. School Bd. Assn., Council of School Attorneys; **EDUC:** BA, 1975, Govt., Univ. of Notre Dame; **GRAD EDUC:** JD, 1978, Univ. of Detroit, Sch. of Law; **HOME ADD:** 4145 Butternut Hill, Troy, MI 48098, (313)642-1342; **BUS ADD:** 3101 N. Woodward Ave., Suite 400, Royal Oak, MI 48072, (313)288-5800.

CURRY, Bryce——*Pres.*, Federal Home Loan Bank of New York; **PRIM RE ACT:** Banker; **BUS ADD:** One World Trade Center, Floor 103, NY, NY 10048, (212)432-2000.*

CURRY, Derrell R.——B: Jan. 25, 1933, Tampa, FL, *VP, Gen. Mgr.*, Burnett Real Estate, Inc.; **PRIM RE ACT:** Broker, Consultant, Appraiser, Owner/Investor; **SERVICES:** Sales, mgmt., appraising, consulting & investing; **REP CLIENTS:** Brandon State Bank, Barnett Bank; **PREV EMPLOY:** Sales, Graybar Electric Co., Inc.; **PROFL AFFIL & HONORS:** NAR, Amer. Assn. of Cert. Appraisers, Intl. Inst. of Valuers, CAS & SCV, Cert. Appraiser, Sr. & Sr. Cert. Valuer; **EDUC:** BS, 1958, Bus. Admin., Univ. of Tampa; **MIL SERV:** US Army, 1953-55, Cpl.; **OTHER ACT & HONORS:** Rotary Club, F&AM, Shriner; **HOME ADD:** 310 Greenview Dr., Brandon, FL 33511, (873)685-5563; **BUS ADD:** 1747 W Brandon Blvd., Brandon, FL 33511, (613)681-4676.

CURRY, Edna Tenhaaf——B: Sept. 27, 1928, St. Francisville, MO, *Pres.*, Home Realty, Inc., Resid. & Comml. Prop. - Specialty Farms; **PRIM RE ACT:** Broker, Consultant, Appraiser, Developer, Builder, Owner/Investor, Instructor, Property Manager, Syndicator; **SERVICES:** Homes, new const., indus., comml., acreages, rentals, farms; **PREV EMPLOY:** Salesman Peck RE, Galesburg, IL 1966-1969; Deets Realty Corp. & Western Estates Corp. Galesburg, IL 1969-1970; **PROFL AFFIL & HONORS:** IL Assn. RE Bds. (legis. com. 1972-1973); Galesburg C of C, Teacher Sandburg Jr. Coll. 1974-1978, GRI; **OTHER ACT & HONORS:** Bd. of Dir., First United Methodist Church 1974; Member Community Chorus 1974; Member People to People, IL Agricultural Leaders del. vs Hong Kong, China, Phillipines; Leader Brownies 1954-1957; Girl Scouts 1957-1961; Den Mother Boy Scouts of Amer. 1958; Active Heart Fund, March of Dimes, Community Chest 1954-1957; Pres. of Mother Singers Galesburg High School 1964-1965; Election Judge 1969-1967; Bd. of Dir. Girl Scouts 1969-1961; Campaign Dir., John W. Curry for State Rep. 1980; **HOME ADD:** 3247 Morningside Dr., Galesburg, IL 61401, (309)344-2242; **BUS ADD:** 501 E Losey, Galesburg, IL 61401, (309)342-9111.

CURRY, Kathryn A.——B: Nov. 29, 1947, Beatrice, NE, *Broker and lic. appraiser*, Professional Real Estate Investments, Inc.; **PRIM RE ACT:** Broker, Consultant, Appraiser, Developer, Owner/Investor, Instructor, Property Manager, Real Estate Publisher; **SERVICES:** Investment counseling, appraisal, exchange listing & selling of comml. investment props., prop. mgmt., speaker, writer & instr. on RE topics; **REP CLIENTS:** Indivs., and instnl. investors in comml. props.; **PREV EMPLOY:** Comml. Nat. Bank & Trust. Co.; **PROFL AFFIL & HONORS:** Bus. & Profl. Women's Clubs, Inc., Grand Is. Area C of C; Nat. Assn. of Realtors; **EDUC:** BA, 1970, Bus. Admin. & Econ., Doane Coll., Crete, NE; **GRAD EDUC:** MBA, 1980, Human Relations & Econ., Kearney State Coll., Kearney, NE; **OTHER ACT & HONORS:** YWCA; NE Coalition of Women; United Methodist Church; Received Basic Cert. from Amer. Banking Inst.; and a Grad. of the Nat. Installment Credit Sch.; Received Course Cert. from the RNMI for Completion of 2 Comml. Investment Courses; Bd. of Dir., Grand Isle Heritage Zoo; **HOME ADD:** 820 D Ave., Central City, NE 68826, (308)946-3965; **BUS ADD:** 307 N. Broadwell, Grand Isle, NE 68801, (308)381-7904.

CURRY, Paul L.——B: Feb. 10, 1953, Orlando, FL, *Commercial Loan Representative*, Stockton, Whatley, Davin & Co.; **PRIM RE ACT:** Appraiser, Lender, Broker, Consultant; **SERVICES:** Acquisition, appraisal, mort. fin., and joint ventures of comml. RE for Institutional Investors; **PREV EMPLOY:** Sales & leasing with Coldwell Banker & Co. 1978-1979; CPA with Arthur Young & Co. 1975-1978; Acquisition, financing, and property mgmt. with Travelers Ins. Co. 1979-1981; **PROFL AFFIL & HONORS:** Assoc. member of Mort. Bankers Assn., CPA; **EDUC:** BSBA, 1975, Bus. and Acctg., Univ. of FL; **EDUC**

HONORS: Grad. with Honors; **OTHER ACT & HONORS:** City Councilman 1971; Member of various honor soc. and clubs; Publication of an article in Real Estate Review; Guest speaker at BOMA's April conference; **HOME ADD:** 214 Brennen Rd., Orlando, FL 32806, (305)857-3179; **BUS ADD:** 300 N. Mills Ave., Orlando, FL 32803, (305)237-2342.

CURRY, William B., Sr.——B: Jan. 15, 1898, Philadelphia, PA, *Sec.*, Minard Solassin; **PRIM RE ACT:** Appraiser, Banker; **EDUC:** BS, 1916, Wharton Evening School V of P - 1923; **HOME ADD:** 233 Chestnut St., Philadelphia, PA 19106, (215)627-0990; **BUS ADD:** 233 Chestnut St., Philadelphia, PA 19106, (215)627-0990.

CURTIN, Daniel F.——B: Jan. 13, 1942, Beacon, NY, *Atty.*, Corbally, Gartland & Rappleyea; **PRIM RE ACT:** Attorney; **PROFL AFFIL & HONORS:** NY State Bar Assn.; Amer. Bus. Law Assn.; FL Bar Assn.; **EDUC:** BS, 1963, Acctg., Univ. of FL; **GRAD EDUC:** JD, 1966, Univ. of FL; **HOME ADD:** 10 Old English Way, Wappingers Falls, NY 12590, (914)297-8032; **BUS ADD:** 35 Market St., Poughkeepsie, NY 12601, (914)454-1110.

CURTIS, Berkeley H.——B: June 15, 1939, Los Angeles, CA, *Owner*, Berkeley H. Curtis and Assoc.; **PRIM RE ACT:** Instructor, Consultant, Appraiser, Developer, Builder; **REP CLIENTS:** Banks, const. cos., attys., devels., private investors; **PREV EMPLOY:** First Natl. Bank NV, Sr. Appraiser; **PROFL AFFIL & HONORS:** SREA, AIREA, SRPA; **EDUC:** AA, 1960, C.C., Citrus Coll., Glendora, CA; **EDUC HONORS:** yes; **OTHER ACT & HONORS:** Member, Clark Cty. Bd. of Equalization, 1979 to present; **HOME ADD:** 7512 Pasotral Pl., Las Vegas, NV 89128, (702)878-5471; **BUS ADD:** 2915 W. Charleston Blvd., Suite 3A, Las Vegas, NV 89102, (702)878-6224.

CURTIS, Charles M.——B: Jan. 24, 1926, Weatherford, TX, *Pres.*, Curtis & Assocs.; **PRIM RE ACT:** Broker, Developer, Builder, Owner/Investor, Property Manager; **OTHER RE ACT:** own 28 million sq. ft. of comml. land; **SERVICES:** Appraisals, purchase & sale of comml. RE; **REP CLIENTS:** Family Tr., Mgr.; **PREV EMPLOY:** Bldg. Material Mfr., Wholesale, dists.; **EDUC:** BBA, 1948, Bldg., Mktg., SMU Univ. of TX at Arlington, St. Mary's Coll.; **EDUC HONORS:** Pres. DKE Frat, VP Interfrat. council; **MIL SERV:** USN, Air Corp., Aviation Cadet; **HOME ADD:** 800 NE Loop 323, Tyler, TX 75708, (214)592-8528; **BUS ADD:** Boone Loop 323, Tyler, TX 75708, 14)592-0338.

CURTIS, David M.——B: Aug. 26, 1947, Frederick, OK, *Atty.*, Evans & Curtis; **PRIM RE ACT:** Consultant, Attorney, Owner/Investor, Property Manager; **SERVICES:** complete title, consulting and managerial services; **REP CLIENTS:** furnished upon request; **PREV EMPLOY:** City Attys. Office, OK City, OK; **PROFL AFFIL & HONORS:** ABA, OBA; **EDUC:** BA, 1969, Psych./Pol. Sci; **GRAD EDUC:** JD, 1972, RE, Univ. of OK; **EDUC HONORS:** OK Law Review; **MIL SERV:** JA, CPT, ARCOM; **OTHER ACT & HONORS:** City Councilman, City of Frederick; **HOME ADD:** 715 N. 11th, Frederick, OK 73542, (405)335-2408; **BUS ADD:** 121 N. 9th, Frederick, OK 73542, (405)335-2655.

CURTIS, James J.——B: July 13, 1953, Chicago, IL, *Prin.*, Bristol Group; **PRIM RE ACT:** Owner/Investor; **SERVICES:** RE Investment Mgmt.; **REP CLIENTS:** Major pension funds and large net worth indiv.; **PREV EMPLOY:** VP Acquisitions, Bank of Amer., Investment RE, 1976-1981; **PROFL AFFIL & HONORS:** ULI; SRA; **EDUC:** BS, 1975, Fin./Econ., Marquette Univ.; **GRAD EDUC:** MS, 1976, RE/Urban Land Econ., Univ. of WI; **HOME ADD:** 1467 Francisco, San Francisco, CA 94123; **BUS ADD:** 155 Montgomery St., San Francisco, CA 94104, (415)398-1022.

CURTIS, James J., Jr.——B: July 13, 1927, Oak Park, *Pres.*, James J. Curtis & Associates, Inc.; **PRIM RE ACT:** Consultant, Appraiser; **SERVICES:** Feasibility reports, appraisals, expert testimony "Highest and Best Use" analysis; **REP CLIENTS:** Intl. Harvester; Ford Motor Co.; Govt. Agencies; Continental Bank; Indiv. Law Firms; **PROFL AFFIL & HONORS:** AIREA; Soc. of RE Appraisers; Amer. Soc. of RE Counselors; Lambda Alpha; Chicago RE Bd., MAI; SRA; CRE; **EDUC:** BS Civil Engrg., 1950, Structural, Univ. of IL; **MIL SERV:** Navy, MM3/C; **HOME ADD:** 6170 Knoll Lane Ct., Willowbrook, IL 60514, (312)655-4357; **BUS ADD:** 223 W Jackson Blvd., Chicago, IL 60606, (312)922-5007.

CURTIS, Robert J.——B: Aug. 30, 1945, Trenton, NJ, *Dir. of Rgnl. Operations*, Arthur D. Little Inc.; **PRIM RE ACT:** Consultant, Appraiser; **PROFL AFFIL & HONORS:** AICPA, NJ Soc. of CPA's, Amer. Acctg. Assn., Nat. Assn. of Accountants, IMA, CPA, Cert. Mgmt. Accountant; **EDUC:** 1976, Bus. Admin., Acctg., Fin., Econ., Univ. of Miami; **GRAD EDUC:** 1971, Fin., Acctg., Mgmt., Wharton Grad. School of Fin., Univ. of PA; **EDUC HONORS:** Bache & Co. Scholar; **HOME ADD:** 21 Ivanhoe Dr., Robbinsville, NJ 08691, (609)259-3671; **BUS ADD:** 900 Rte. 9, Ste. 210, Woodbridge, NJ 07095, (201)750-2920.

CURTIS, William Henry——B: Aug. 6, 1936, Kansas City, MO, *Pres.*, CRI Properties; **PRIM RE ACT:** Broker, Developer, Owner/Investor, Property Manager, Syndicator; **SERVICES:** Devel., synd., leasing & prop. mgmt. of indus. bldgs.; **REP CLIENTS:** LSI Logic, Data Systems Design, Inc., Racal Vadic, Nicolet, Deckatrend Corp., Kamon Bearing; **PREV EMPLOY:** Grubb & Ellis Co.; **PROFL AFFIL & HONORS:** Assn. of S. Bay Brokers, San Jose C of C, Univ. Club, San Jose Athletic Club, Naval Reserve Assn., Rotary Club; **EDUC:** BA, 1958, Bus., Univ. of MO; **GRAD EDUC:** MBA, 1964, Indus. Mgmt., Wharton Grad. Sch.; **EDUC HONORS:** Dean's List; **MIL SERV:** USN, Cmdr.; **OTHER ACT & HONORS:** Bd. of Dir. O'Connors Hospital; **HOME ADD:** 15981 Grandview, Monte Sereno, CA 95030, (408)354-5695; **BUS ADD:** 2075A Bering Dr., San Jose, CA 95131, (408)998-8400.

CURTISS, Bruce D.——B: June 14, 1952, Curtiss & Baird; **PRIM RE ACT:** Broker, Attorney, Consultant, Owner/Investor; **OTHER RE ACT:** Abstractor; **SERVICES:** as licensed; **REP CLIENTS:** On request; **PROFL AFFIL & HONORS:** ABA, NBA, NE Land Title Assn., JD; BS with High Distinction, Univ. of NE; **EDUC:** UNL (above), 1973, Mgmt./RE, UNL Lincoln; **GRAD EDUC:** JD, UNL; **EDUC HONORS:** High Distinction; **OTHER ACT & HONORS:** Pres., Plainview C of C; **HOME TEL:** (402)582-3854; **BUS ADD:** Box 306, Plainview, NE 68769, (402)582-3838.

CURTISS, Joseph——*Secy.*, Susquehanna Corp.; **PRIM RE ACT:** Property Manager; **BUS ADD:** PO Box 5170, Denver, CO 80217, (303)779-0777.*

CURVEY, Bernard A.——B: June 21, 1933, Morrisonville, IL, *VP*, Craggs & Curvey Inc.; **PRIM RE ACT:** Broker, Consultant, Appraiser; **OTHER RE ACT:** Auctioneer; **SERVICES:** Investment counseling, 1031 tax free exchanges, farm sales; **PREV EMPLOY:** VP & Comml. Loan Officer 1965-1972, First Trust and Savings Bank, Taylorville; previously FDIC Bank Examiner; Admissions counselor for Coll. of Agriculture, Cornell Univ., NY; **PROFL AFFIL & HONORS:** RNMI; NAR; Farm & Land Inst.; currently serving as State Pres. IL Chap. 11 of the FLI, CRS; GRI; AFLM; Local Bd., Realtor of the Yr. Award 1980-1981; **EDUC:** BS, 1958, Agric. Indus., So. IL Univ., Carbondale IL; **GRAD EDUC:** MS, 1960, Agric. Econ., Cornell Univ., Ithaca, NY; **MIL SERV:** USAF; A2C, FEAF, Korean War, Ribbons & Misc.; **OTHER ACT & HONORS:** Kiwanis, Grad. School of Banking Madison WI; School of Banking Carbondale, IL; **HOME ADD:** 727 W. Vine St., Taylorville, IL 62568; **BUS ADD:** 907 Springfield Rd., Taylorville, IL 62568, (217)824-8131.

CUSHMAN, Robert Charles——B: Aug. 20, 1934, N.L., CT, *Pres.*, Cushman Realty; **PRIM RE ACT:** Broker, Appraiser; **SERVICES:** appraisal and brokerage of r.e.; **REP CLIENTS:** Groton Savings Bank, Hartford National Bank; **PROFL AFFIL & HONORS:** NAR, CAR, CID, NMI, Pres. N.L. Bd. of Realtors; **MIL SERV:** USN, 1CPO, National Defense, Good Conduct; **OTHER ACT & HONORS:** P. Pres. Mystic Community Ctr., P. Pres. Mystic Lions, Dir. of CID, Elks, Lions, St. Marks Church Vestry; **HOME ADD:** 2 Walter Fish Ave., Mystic, CT, (203)536-9591; **BUS ADD:** 20 Holmes St., Mystic, CT 06355, (203)536-3678.

CUSHWA, William——*Asst. Treas.*, Commercial Shearing & Stamping Col; **PRIM RE ACT:** Property Manager; **BUS ADD:** PO Box 239 1775 Logan Ave., Youngstown, OH 44501, (216)746-8011.*

CUSKER, Thomas J.——B: Mar. 24, 1940, Rochester, NY, *Part.*, Cusker & Cusker; **PRIM RE ACT:** Attorney; **PROFL AFFIL & HONORS:** ABA; Monroe City and NY State Bar Assn.; **EDUC:** BA, 1962, Pol. Sci., Univ. of Notre Dame; **GRAD EDUC:** JD, 1965, Albany Law Sch. of Union Univ.; **HOME ADD:** 396 Arnett Blvd., Rochester, NY 14619; **BUS ADD:** 605 Reynolds Arcade Bldg., Rochester, NY 14614, (716)546-5410.

CUTLER, Noah D.——*Atty.*, Noah D. Cutler P.C.; **PRIM RE ACT:** Attorney; **SERVICES:** Comprehensive rep. with regard to RE matters; **REP CLIENTS:** Pioneer Nat. Title Ins. Co., First Amer. Title Ins. Co., Bankers Trust Co., US Savings Bank of Newark, NJ; Rouse & Assocs.; **PREV EMPLOY:** Former VP and Assoc. Counsel of Commonwealth Land Title Ins. Co.; **PROFL AFFIL & HONORS:** Member, Amer., PA, Montgomery Cty. Bar Assns.; PA Bar Assn.: Land Transfers Comm., V. Chmn.; Vendors and Purchasers Comm., V. Chmn.; Condo. Law Comm., Member; Comm. to Improve Conveyancing

Practices, Member; Member of Montgomery Bar Assn. RE Land Use Planning Comm.; Founding Member and Dir., Main Line Lawyers' Forum, Principal Speaker for the PA Bar Assn. Real Prop. Sect. at the 1980 Mid-Yr. Meeting; **BUS ADD:** 2000 Valley Forge Cir. 118W, King of Prussia, PA 19406, (215)783-7150.

CUTLIP, Jack P.——**B:** May 3, 1951, Providence, RI, *Asst. V.P.*, RI Hospital Trust Natl. Bank, Corp. R.E.; **PRIM RE ACT:** Lender; **SERVICES:** Constr. Fin.; **EDUC:** BSBA, 1974, Acctg., Bryant Coll.; **GRAD EDUC:** MBA, 1979, Bus Admin., Providence Coll.; **HOME ADD:** 2 Burlingame Rd., Smithfield, RI 02901, (401)232-1694; **BUS ADD:** 1 Hospital Trust Plaza, Providence, RI 02903, (401)278-8621.

CYMROT, Allen——**B:** Nov. 9, 1936, Brooklyn, NY, *Pres., Member Bd. of Dir. 1977-Present*, The Robert A. McNeil Corp.; **PRIM RE ACT:** Syndicator, Property Manager; **SERVICES:** RE Investment and Mgmt.; **PREV EMPLOY:** Pres., Pacific Investments (now known as McNeil Securities); Div. VP, DuPont Walston, NYC; Dir.-Retail Sales;Cowen & Co., NYC; Branch Mgr., Bache & Co., NYC; **PROFL AFFIL & HONORS:** 1979 Pres. CA Synd. Forum, also served on Bd. of Gov., V. Chmn. CA; Vice Chairman and a member of the Board of Directors of the National Multi Housing Council; Director of the California Housing Council; Trustee for the National Apartment Association, Housing Council. Testified before Congress in Mar. 1980; again before House Ways and Means Comm., Mar. 1981.; **MIL SERV:** US Army; **BUS ADD:** 2855 Campus Dr., San Mateo, CA 94403, (415)572-0660.

CYR, John E.——**B:** Oct. 6, 1915, Missoula, MT, *Pres.*, John Cyr, Realtors, Inc.; **PRIM RE ACT:** Broker, Consultant, Appraiser, Instructor; **OTHER RE ACT:** RE book author; **SERVICES:** Gen. brokerage, appraising, consulting, articles; **REP CLIENTS:** Gen. public; **PREV EMPLOY:** Sims & Grupe, Realtors - Stockton; City of Stockton; Bank of Stockton; **PROFL AFFIL & HONORS:** Stockton Bd. of Realtors, CA Assn. Realtors, NAR, Farm & Land Institute, RNMI, RE Educators Assn., CA State C of C, GRI, CRS, AFLM - Honorary Director-For-Life of CA Assn. Realtors; **EDUC:** Univ. of CA Berkeley Extension; **EDUC HONORS:** Certificate in RE; **MIL SERV:** US Navy, Storekeeper 3/C; **OTHER ACT & HONORS:** Author: Book - "Training and Supervising RE Salesmen", P.H.T. no. 1973, Book - "Psychology of Motivation & Persuasion in RE Selling" - P.-H. 1975, Book, "RE Brokerage: A Success Guide" - R.E. Education Co. Chicago 1981; Member of Univ. of CA President's RE Advisory Comm.; **HOME ADD:** 4466 Denby Ln., Stockton, CA 95207, (209)477-0467; **BUS ADD:** 840 N. El Dorado St., Stockton, CA 95201PO Box 1567, (209)466-5311.

CYTRYNBAUM, Michael——**B:** Jan. 3, 1941, Montreal, Que., *Pres.*, First City Financial Corp. Ltd., First City Investments; **PRIM RE ACT:** Lender; **OTHER RE ACT:** Fin. servs., RE; **SERVICES:** Equity lender, in that our division lends into the equity portion of projects; **EDUC:** BA, 1962, McGill Univ.; **GRAD EDUC:** BCL, 1965, Civil Law, McGill Univ.; **HOME ADD:** 4036 Marine Dr., West Vancouver, V7V 1N6, BC, (604)926-9593; **BUS ADD:** 11th Floor, 777 Hornby St., Vancouver, V6Z 1S4, BC.

CZARNECKI, Walter, III——**B:** Sept. 15, 1945, Philadelphia, PA, *VP*, Franklin Realty Group of Pennsylvania, Inc., Comml. & Indus. Div.; **PRIM RE ACT:** Broker; **OTHER RE ACT:** VP in charge of Comml./Indus. Div.; **SERVICES:** Franklin Realty Grp. provides leasing, mgmt., sales, synd. and devel. servs.; **REP CLIENTS:** Prudential Ins. Co., Sun Life of CAN, Asplundh Enterprises, IBM; represent owners and devels.; **PREV EMPLOY:** Cushman & Wakefield, Reed & Stambaugh; **PROFL AFFIL & HONORS:** Bldg. Owners & Mgrs. Assn.; NAP; PA Assn. of Realtors; E. Montgomery Co. Bd. of Realtors; Rotary Club of Jenkintown, Dir.; Bd. member of Abington Township Indus. & Comml. Devel. Authority; union League of Philadelphia; **MIL SERV:** US Naval Air, Air Traffic Controller, PO2; **HOME ADD:** 638 Abington Ave., Glenside, PA 19038, (215)887-0685; **BUS ADD:** Rydal Executive Plaza, Rydal, PA 19046, (215)885-7440.

CZERWINSKI, Frank——**B:** Apr. 20, 1945, Elizabeth, NJ, *Consultant*, Frank Czerwinski Inc.; **PRIM RE ACT:** Consultant, Developer, Owner/Investor; **SERVICES:** Site selection, lease negotiation, fin. and project mgmt.; **REP CLIENTS:** Devels., private investor/owner and corps.; **PROFL AFFIL & HONORS:** MBAA, ICSG and NACORE; **EDUC:** BS, 1968, Bus., NYU - RE Inst., MI State - Mort. Banking; **MIL SERV:** US Army, Capt., Pilot; **HOME ADD:** One Knox Terr., Totowa, NJ 07512, (201)942-0967; **BUS ADD:** One Knox Terr., Totowa, NJ 07512, (201)942-0967.

DABNEY, John C.——**B:** Nov. 2, 1918, Atlanta, GA, *Owner*, Dabney & Assoc.; **PRIM RE ACT:** Consultant, Appraiser; **SERVICES:** Appraisals of all types of real props. and consultations regarding prop.; **REP CLIENTS:** Govt. agencies, indivs., corps., and trust depts. of banks, ins. cos., mort. lenders; **PROFL AFFIL & HONORS:** AIREA, Amer. Soc. of RE Counselors, Soc. of RE appraisers, MAI; CRE, SREA, John S. Schneider Award for contributions to appraisal education, AIREA; **EDUC:** BA, 1940, Pre-med. Sci., Emory Univ.; **GRAD EDUC:** MS, 1943, Physical Edu., Univ. of TN; **EDUC HONORS:** Phi Delta Kappa, Education-Honorary; **OTHER ACT & HONORS:** Rotary Club of Atlanta, First Presbyterian Church of Atlanta; **HOME ADD:** 3927 Parian Ridge Rd., NW, Atlanta, GA 30327, (404)233-8467; **BUS ADD:** 3525 Piedmont Rd., NE, 7 Piedmont Ctr., Ste. 210, Atlanta, GA 30305, (404)261-8284.

DADAKIS, G. Thomas——**B:** Nov. 4, 1949, NY, NY, *Pres.*, Dadakis & Co. Inc.; **PRIM RE ACT:** Broker, Consultant, Owner/Investor, Property Manager, Real Estate Publisher; **SERVICES:** Selling, leasing and managing corp. RE; **REP CLIENTS:** Corps. & instns. with office bldgs. for sale, lease or mgmt.; **EDUC:** BA, 1972, Communication, Fordham Univ.; **GRAD EDUC:** MA, 1977, Communication, Fairfield Univ.; **BUS ADD:** 255 Glenville Rd., Greenwich, CT 06830, (203)531-6821.

DAEM, Jean-Pierre——**B:** Jan. 11, 1945, Brussels, Belgium, *Pres.*, Bradson Management Services, Inc.; **PRIM RE ACT:** Consultant, Instructor, Property Manager; **OTHER RE ACT:** Background research for attys.; **SERVICES:** Prop. mgmt., arbitration services, transition services, condo. consultants; **REP CLIENTS:** Condo. assns.; developers; legal firms; Pres. CEO; Sudden Valley Props., Inc. ; land assembly, golf course mgmt., restaurant & country club mgr.; **PROFL AFFIL & HONORS:** NRPA; ULI; IREM; CAI; CPRA; C of C; Dean of Mgmt. Practices, PMOP Program; CAI, PCAM (Community Assns. Inst.); **EDUC:** BS, 1968, Zoology, Univ. of BC; **GRAD EDUC:** MSc, 1970, Simon Fraser Univ.; PhD, 1974, Simon Fraser Univ.; AA, 1976, Douglas Coll.; **EDUC HONORS:** Recipient of the C.D. Nelson Award for Outstanding Achievement, S.F.U.; **OTHER ACT & HONORS:** Chmn. GURD Liveable Region Policy Comm. (1973); Chmn., Burnaby Parks & Recreation Commn. (1973-80); S.F.U. Senate 1973; Chmn., Douglas Coll. Council (1973-74); Bd. of Govs., Western Can. Coll.; Bd. of Dirs., AUCC; Chmn., Housing; Parks & Land Comm., BC.COFC; **HOME ADD:** 7540 Carnleigh Pl., Burnaby, BC, (604)521-8596; **BUS ADD:** 7409 Conway Ave., Burnaby, BC, Can., (604)437-3336.

DAENZER, Peter B.——**B:** July 29, 1942, Mt. Vernon, NY, *Pres.*, Diversified Holdings Corp.; **PRIM RE ACT:** Syndicator; **PREV EMPLOY:** Intercapital Planning Corp., 1969-72; **PROFL AFFIL & HONORS:** RESSI, Charter Prop. Casualty Underwriter, CLU, Beta Gamma Sigma Hon. Soc.; **EDUC:** BS, 1964, Econ., Wharton Sch., Univ. of PA; **GRAD EDUC:** 1967 to 1968, Babson MBA Program; **MIL SERV:** US Army, Nat. Guard; **OTHER ACT & HONORS:** Union League Club, Silver Mine Golf Club, ATO Frat.; Harvard Bus. School - Exec. Educ. Program; Lloyds of London Underwriting Member; **HOME ADD:** Wilton, CT 06897New Canaan Rd.; **BUS ADD:** 475 Park Ave. S, NY, NY 10016, (212)684-7979.

DAGLE, C. Paul——**B:** Sept. 7, 1944, Hawarden, IA, *Lawyer*, Grebe, Gross, Jensen & Peek, PC; **PRIM RE ACT:** Attorney; **PROFL AFFIL & HONORS:** ABA, OR State Bar Assn.; **EDUC:** BA, 1966, Poli. Sci., Univ. of IA; **GRAD EDUC:** JD, 1969, Univ. of IA; **EDUC HONORS:** With Honors; **MIL SERV:** USAF, 1969-1972, Capt.; **HOME ADD:** 1927 NE Thompson St., Portland, OR 97212, (503)287-6782; **BUS ADD:** 1530 SW Taylor St., Portland, OR 97205.

D'AGOSTINO, A.R.——**B:** Dec. 5, 1916, Utica, NY, *Owner, Pres.*, A.R. D'Agostino Construction Co., Inc.; **PRIM RE ACT:** Developer, Builder, Owner/Investor; **OTHER RE ACT:** Golf course constr.; **SERVICES:** Complete constr. of championship golf courses; **REP CLIENTS:** Wollaston Golf Club, Milton, MA; Heritage Devel. of Westchester, NY; Dlryridge Golf Club, Ridgefield, CT; Smith-Richardson Golf Club, Fairfield, CT; and extensive re-modeling of EnJoie Golf Club for PGA Tour event, the BC Open; **PREV EMPLOY:** Resid. & comml. land devel. in Utica, NY area; **EDUC:** BS, 1939, Sci. & lang., Hamilton Coll.; **MIL SERV:** USAF, Lt., Air Medal, Purple Heart, 5 battles; **HOME ADD:** Weathervane Farm, Clinton, NY 13323, (315)853-2613; **BUS ADD:** D'Agostino Bldg., Deansboro, NY 13328, (315)841-4567.

DAHLBERG, Burton F.——**B:** Dec. 14, 1932, Ashland, WI, *Exec. VP*, Kraus Anderson, Inc.; **PRIM RE ACT:** Broker, Consultant, Developer, Builder, Property Manager, Owner/Investor, Insuror; **PREV EMPLOY:** Corporate RE Representative; **PROFL AFFIL & HONORS:** IREM, BOMA, Bd. of Realtors, CPM; **EDUC:** BA, 1960, Bus., Econ., Univ. of MN; **MIL SERV:** USAF, Sgt.; **OTHER ACT &**

HONORS: Past Pres. of Mpls. BOMA; **HOME ADD:** 8841 Southwood Dr., Bloomington, MN 55437, (612)831-8841; **BUS ADD:** 523 S. 8th St., Mpls., MN 55404, (612)332-1241.

DAHLEM, Bernard A.——B: July 21, 1929, Louisville, KY, *Chmn. of the Bd. & CEO*, The Dahlem Co.; **PRIM RE ACT:** Broker, Engineer, Developer, Builder, Owner/Investor, Property Manager; **SERVICES:** Realtor, design, const., prop. mgmt.; **PROFL AFFIL & HONORS:** Amer. Soc. Civ. Engr.; Nat., KY & Louisville Bd. of Realtors; Licensed Engineer KY, IN & TN, Cert. Shopping Ctr. Mgr.; Member of Initial Group Designated by InterCouncil of Shop. Ctrs. in 1964; **EDUC:** BCE, 1951, CE, Speed Scientific School of the Univ. of Louisville; **GRAD EDUC:** Master of Engrg., 1972, CE, Speed Scientific School of the Univ. of Louisville; **EDUC HONORS:** Tau Beta Pi; **MIL SERV:** USN, Civil Engr. Corps. Lt. jg; **OTHER ACT & HONORS:** Actors Theatre of Louisville Bd. Mbr. & Past Pres.; Overseer Univ. of Louisville; Bd. Mbr. Louisville Indus. Found. Intl. Council of Shopping Ctrs. Since 1958; **HOME ADD:** 604 Briar Hill Rd., Louisville, KY 40204, (502)895-2111; **BUS ADD:** 2330 S. Preston St., Box 17285, Louisville, KY 40217, (502)636-3344.

DAHLIN, Douglas A.——B: July 6, 1935, Max, ND, *Owner*, Gold Seal Mgmt. Co.; **PRIM RE ACT:** Broker, Instructor, Syndicator, Owner/Investor; **SERVICES:** RE Limited Partnerships; **PREV EMPLOY:** 16 yrs. in Casualty Ins.; **PROFL AFFIL & HONORS:** NAR, RESSI; **EDUC:** BBA, 1959, ND State Coll.; **HOME ADD:** 2806 S. 28th St., La Crosse, WI 54601, (608)788-0913; **BUS ADD:** 2806 S. 28th St., LaCrosse, WI 54601, (608)788-0913.

DAILEY, John H.——B: Oct. 26, 1945, Albany, NY, *VP*, Harold Hewitt Associates, Inc.; **PRIM RE ACT:** Broker, Developer, Owner/Investor, Instructor; **SERVICES:** Investment counseling, brokerage services including leasing, devel. and synd. of investment props.; **REP CLIENTS:** Indiv. investors, institl. investors and users of comml. props.; **PROFL AFFIL & HONORS:** ASSN, RICSC, Cert. Comml. Investment Member of the NAR #1156. Lifetime member of Sacramento Bd's. Master's Club; **EDUC:** BS, 1967, Bus. Admin., VA Polytechnic Inst., Blacksburg, VA; **GRAD EDUC:** MBA, 1973, Mgmt., Golden Gate Univ., San Francisco, CA; **MIL SERV:** USAF, Capt., Distinguished Flying Cross, Bronze Star, Air Medal - 7 clusters, Air Force Commendation Medal; **OTHER ACT & HONORS:** Sutter Club, Sacramento, CA; **HOME ADD:** 825 Treehouse Ln., Sacramento, CA 95825, (916)971-0902; **BUS ADD:** 601 University Ave., Suite 130, Sacramento, CA 95825, (916)929-9625.

DAILEY, John L.——B: Apr. 21, 1937, Casper, WY, *Atty. at Law (Pres.)*, Dailey, Goodwin & O'Leary, P.C.; **PRIM RE ACT:** Attorney, Owner/Investor; **SERVICES:** RE, legal and tax counsel servs., including tax deferred exchanges; **REP CLIENTS:** RE brokers and investors (including foreclosure); **PROFL AFFIL & HONORS:** ABA, CO and Denver Bar Assns.; **EDUC:** BS, 1959, Chem. Engrg., Univ. of CO; **GRAD EDUC:** JD, 1972, Univ. of Denver; **EDUC HONORS:** Order of St. Ives (Top 10% scholastically); **MIL SERV:** USN, Lt.; **OTHER ACT & HONORS:** Sigma Alpha Epsilon; **HOME ADD:** 9023 E. Eastman Pl., Denver, CO 80231, (303)755-0668; **BUS ADD:** 10957 E. Bethany Dr., Suite H., Aurora, CO 80014.

DAILEY, Kent——B: Feb. 14, 1954, Covington, KY, *Realtor*, Don Laake RE, Comml.-Investment; **PRIM RE ACT:** Broker, Instructor, Appraiser, Owner/Investor; **OTHER RE ACT:** Bus. Opportunities Broker; **SERVICES:** Investment analysis, gen. brokerage; **REP CLIENTS:** Indiv. investors, Atty's Clients, CPS's Clients; **PREV EMPLOY:** Mgr. of another R.E. Co. from 1976-1980, lic. full time agent since 1974; **PROFL AFFIL & HONORS:** Kenton Boone, KY & NAR; **EDUC:** BS, 1975, Educ. & R.E., N. KY Univ.; **OTHER ACT & HONORS:** N. KY C. of C., Covington-Kenton Cty. Jaycees, R.E. Instr. at N. KY Vocational School; **HOME ADD:** 3167 Royal Windsor, Edgewood, KY 41017, (606)727-1798; **BUS ADD:** 4209 Richardson Rd. Rd., Independence, KY 41051, (606)525-1157.

DAILEY, R. Marvin——B: Oct. 3, 1943, Rochester, NY, *Pres.*, Eastern Appraisal Associates; **PRIM RE ACT:** Consultant, Appraiser, Instructor, Property Manager; **SERVICES:** Gen. Appraisal & consulting practice; **REP CLIENTS:** Relocation firms, municipalities, US Govt.; **PREV EMPLOY:** 4 Yrs. as Law Clerk; **PROFL AFFIL & HONORS:** SREA; Genessee Valley RE Bd.; NAR; NY Assn. of Realtors; RE Bd. of Rochester NY; AIREA, SRA; MAI Candidate; **EDUC:** BS, 1966, Bus. Admin., Rochester Inst. of Tech.; **EDUC HONORS:** Dean's List; **OTHER ACT & HONORS:** Chmn. Bd. of Assessment Review; Victor 1975-1980; Victor C of C; Comml. pilot & flight instr.; **HOME ADD:** 6525 Boughton Hill Rd., Victor, NY 14564, (716)924-2737; **BUS ADD:** 251 West Main St., Victor, NY 14564, (716)924-7137.

DAILY, J. Allen——B: Feb. 3, 1941, Emporia, KS, *Pres.; Broker*, Look Realty of CO, Inc.; **PRIM RE ACT:** Broker, Lender, Owner/Investor; **SERVICES:** RE sales, prop. mgmt.; **PROFL AFFIL & HONORS:** GRI; **EDUC:** BA, 1968, Bus. & Econ., Emporia State Univ.; **MIL SERV:** USN, E-5; **HOME ADD:** 1230 Branding Iron Dr., Colorado Springs, CO 80915, (303)597-9086; **BUS ADD:** 2027 E Bijou St., Colorado Springs, CO 80909, (303)635-2537.

DAISLEY, E.T., Jr.——B: Aug. 11, 1928, Indianapolis, IN, *VP*, Don J. McMurray Co.; **PRIM RE ACT:** Broker, Appraiser; **OTHER RE ACT:** Mort. Banker (Primary); **SERVICES:** Originate Permanent Fin. on Comml. Loans; **PROFL AFFIL & HONORS:** Homebuilders; SREA; MBA; RE Bd., SRA; **EDUC:** BS, 1950, Zool., Chem., Math, Lang., Univ. of Iowa; **GRAD EDUC:** Certificate in RE, 1964, RE, Univ. of Neb. at Omaha; **MIL SERV:** US Army, Cpl. 1950-1952, Korean Medal and UN Medal; **OTHER ACT & HONORS:** Happy Hollow Club, Bd. of Dir. 1979 - 1981; Life Dir. Metropolitan Omaha Builders Assn.; Pres. Eastern Neb. Chap. III SREA 1962-1963; **HOME ADD:** 1121 So. 79th St., Omaha, NE 68124, (402)391-1446; **BUS ADD:** 10407 Devonshire Cir., Omaha, NE 68114, (402)391-2110.

DAITCH, Marvin C.——B: Nov. 22, 1940, Detroit, MI, *Pres.*, Daitch Mort. & Realty Co.; **PRIM RE ACT:** Broker, Developer, Lender, Builder; **SERVICES:** Fin. Acquisitions, Devel. of Comml. Proportions; **REP CLIENTS:** Life Ins. Cos. (Correspondent); **PREV EMPLOY:** Atty.; **PROFL AFFIL & HONORS:** MBAA-MI Mort. Bankers Assn.; State Bar of MI; ABA; Oakland Bar Assn.; **EDUC:** BS, 1962, Pharmacy, Wayne State Univ.; **GRAD EDUC:** JD, 1966, Univ. of Detroit Coll. of Law; **OTHER ACT & HONORS:** Member, White House Comm. on Ageing (ADHOC); Bd. Member, Founders Jr. Council, Detroit Inst. of Art; Member, Legislative Comm., MBAA, Lecturer, State Bar of MI, RSAC Property Seminar; **HOME ADD:** 7844 Huntington Rd., Huntington Woods, MI 48070, (313)353-6655; **BUS ADD:** 27777 Franklin Rd., 400 Amer. Ctr. Bldg., Southfield, MI 48034, (313)353-6655.

DALBY, Maxwell T.——B: Feb. 3, 1912, VA, *Broker-Owner*, Century 21 Dalby Realty & Investments Co.; **PRIM RE ACT:** Broker, Appraiser; **SERVICES:** Full serv. RE brokerage and appraisals; **REP CLIENTS:** Merrill Lynch, Home Equity, Goppert Bank, Laurel Bank; **PREV EMPLOY:** Builder & developer; **PROFL AFFIL & HONORS:** Kansas City Bd. of Realtors; MO Assn. of Realtors; NAR; Nat. Assn. of RE Appraisers; Amer. Coll. of RE Consultants, GRI, CREA, CREC; **EDUC:** BA, 1932, Law & Bus., Univ. of VA; **GRAD EDUC:** MBA, 1957, Univ. of TX; MPHA, 1963, Univ. of OK; **MIL SERV:** USN 1941-1946, Comdr.; **OTHER ACT & HONORS:** Bd. of Dir. Kansas City Crimes Prevention 1980-1981; C of C; Bd. of Dir. Mental Health Assn.; Bd. of Dir. Brokers Council; **HOME ADD:** 3700 Birchwood Dr., Kansas City, MO 64137, (816)966-9484; **BUS ADD:** 10518 Grandview Rd., Kansas City, MO 64137, (816)966-0123.

DALCOLMA, Thomas William——B: Apr. 18, 1944, Walnut Ridge, AR, *Pres.*, Dalcolma & Co., Inc.; **PRIM RE ACT:** Consultant, Developer; **SERVICES:** Mktg. and devel. counseling, devel.; **REP CLIENTS:** The Amer. City Corp., a div. of The Rouse Co., Columbia MD; **PREV EMPLOY:** Turner Constr. Co.; **EDUC:** BS, 1973, RE, Devel., Mgmt., Arch., Kent State Univ.; **EDUC HONORS:** Omicron Delta Kappa (Nat. Leadership Hon. Soc.); **MIL SERV:** US Army, SP-4; **HOME ADD:** 3601 Lytle Rd., Shaker Heights, OH 44122, (216)283-2243; **BUS ADD:** 3601 Lytle Rd,, Shaker Heights, OH 44122, (216)283-2243.

DALEY, Don J.——B: Oct. 3, 1920, Youngstown, OH, *Sr. VP*, First Hawaiian Bank, RE Div. Chmn.; **PRIM RE ACT:** Appraiser, Banker, Architect, Lender, Syndicator, Assessor; **SERVICES:** All phases of RE devel.; **REP CLIENTS:** Indivs. and/or cos., corps.; **PROFL AFFIL & HONORS:** IREM, Nat. Amer. Inst. of Landscape Arch., Legislative & Const. Income Comm., MBA, CPM; **MIL SERV:** USAF, Lt.; **OTHER ACT & HONORS:** AF Assn., HI Chapt.; HI Comm. Devel. Auth, Member, Bd. of Dir., Pearlridge Hosp., Downtown Imp. Assn., Oahu Devel. Conf., Air Force Assn., MBA Assn., HI Chapt; Co-Chmn Landscape Comm., Waialae Ctry. Club; Member Legislative Comm, C of C; Tennis Comm., Rotary Club, Facilities Comm., Bldg. Indus. Assn., Transp. Comm., C of C, Legislative Comm. HI Bd. of Realtors, Amer. Right of Way Assn.; **HOME ADD:** 367 Kawaihae St., Honolulu, HI 96825, (808)396-9310; **BUS ADD:** PO Box 3200, Honolulu, HI 96847, (808)525-6296.

DALEY, Vincent R., Jr.——B: June 21, 1940, Evanston, IL, *Pres.*, Daley & Associates; **PRIM RE ACT:** Broker, Consultant, Owner/Investor, Instructor, Property Manager, Syndicator; **OTHER RE ACT:** Condo. converter; **REP CLIENTS:** Private investors; **PREV EMPLOY:** Sears Roebuck Co., sales to store mgrs. 1961-1973; VP Retail Kenco Corp. (consultants) 1972-1973; **PROFL AFFIL & HONORS:** Intl. RE Fed.; NAR; IL Assn. of Realtors; RNMI; Chicago RE Bd.;

FL.; RESSI; Certified Comml. Investment member; **EDUC:** AA, 1961, Personnel, Lincoln Univ. & Loyola Univ.; **GRAD EDUC:** Law, Loyola Univ.; **MIL SERV:** US Army, Plt. Sgt.; **OTHER ACT & HONORS:** V. Chmn. Lincoln Education Council 1979-1980; Cent; Nat. Assn. Comm. on Public Relations Computer Marketing, Chicago Board Finance Committee, Board of Directors Commercial Investment MLS, Sales Council-Illinois Association of Realtors-Condominum Legislative Political Investment & RPAC (Realtors Political Involement Action Committee); **HOME ADD:** 2130 Lincoln Park W, Chicago, IL 60614, (312)327-3955; **BUS ADD:** 77 W. Washington Suite 1018, Chicago, IL 60602, (312)726-7387.

DALLAS, Carl E.——B: May 4, 1924, Carterville, IL, *Supr. of Assessments*, Randolph County; **PRIM RE ACT:** Broker, Appraiser, Instructor, Assessor; **SERVICES:** Valuation of all real prop. on a cty. wide basis for ad valorem tax purposes; **PREV EMPLOY:** Dep. Sup. of Assessments, Union Cty., IL; **PROFL AFFIL & HONORS:** Sr. Member Intl. Organ. of RE App., NARA, Intl. Assn., IL Assn. RE Educ., CIAO, ICA, CHHA, CRA, SCV, RE Broker; **EDUC:** Bus. Mgmt.; **MIL SERV:** USAF CMSgt. Ret.; **HOME ADD:** 101 Plum St., Box 73, Anna, IL 62906, (618)833-5975; **BUS ADD:** Courthouse, Chester, IL 62233, (618)826-3363.

DALLIANIS, Harry T.——B: Dec. 13, 1934, Tripolis, Greece, *Pres.-Gen. Mgr. Comml. Investment Div.*, Ideal Realty Co."'Your RE Ctr.", Comml. Investment Div.; **PRIM RE ACT:** Broker, Instructor, Syndicator, Consultant, Appraiser, Property Manager, Owner/Investor; **OTHER RE ACT:** Specialize in Larger Investments and Exchanges in Midwest and Coast-to-Coast; **REP CLIENTS:** Hotel, Motel Brokerage Investment and Mgmt.; **PREV EMPLOY:** Cert. teacher State of IL 20 yrs. (Pres.) of own Co. - Chicago Leand Area. (CRB) (CRS) (SRS) (GRI); **PROFL AFFIL & HONORS:** IFA, CRA, GRI; **EDUC:** BS, 1958, Commerce and Bus. Mktg. Mgmt., Comml. Investment Prop. and Synd. and Hotel/Motel Brokerage and Investment Synd. and Mgmt., Loyola Univ.; **EDUC HONORS:** Received many Professional Designations from Realtors Nat. Assns. over many yrs.; **MIL SERV:** US Army, All Weapons Concentrations; **OTHER ACT & HONORS:** Greek Orthodox Church; **HOME ADD:** 6831 N Tripp, Lincolnwood, IL 60646, (312)989-7766; **BUS ADD:** 3459 W Foster Ave., Chicago, IL 60625, (312)583-0100.

DALOISIO, James J., Esq.——B: May 20, 1947, Paterson, NJ, *Sec./Treas.*, Railroad Construction Co.; **PRIM RE ACT:** Attorney, Owner/Investor; **PROFL AFFIL & HONORS:** ASCE, NJSCE, ABA, NJBA, Camden Cty. Bar Assn., BCE, JD; **EDUC:** BCE, 1970, Civil Engrg., Vilanova Univ.; **GRAD EDUC:** JD, 1973, Law, Rutgers Law School; **EDUC HONORS:** Honor Roll, Am. Jur. Award Recipiant, Honor Roll; **HOME ADD:** 100 Avon Terrace, Moorestown, NJ 08057; **BUS ADD:** 700 Beideman Ave., Camden, NJ 08105, (609)964-1520.

DALTON, David W.——B: Aug. 12, 1947, Memphis, TN, *Pres.*, Bert Rodgers Schools of Real Estate; **PRIM RE ACT:** Instructor, Syndicator; **SERVICES:** Synd., license instr.; **PROFL AFFIL & HONORS:** RESSI, ABA, FL Bar, Certified RE Securities Sponsor, Sr. Instr., RESSI; **EDUC:** BA, 1970, Poli. Sci., Univ. of FL; **GRAD EDUC:** JD, 1972, Univ. of FL; **MIL SERV:** US Army, 1st Lt., Combat Infantryman's Badge, Bronze Star; **HOME ADD:** 5802 Shelburn Ct., Orlando, FL 32809, (305)859-5866; **BUS ADD:** 7201 Lake Ellenor Dr., Ste. 100, Orlando, FL 32809, (305)855-5441.

DALTON, James V.——B: June 3, 1944, Houston, TX, *Partner*, Cohen Brame & Smith, Professional Corp.; **PRIM RE ACT:** Attorney; **SERVICES:** Legal services to devels. and mort. lenders; **REP CLIENTS:** Aberdeen Land Co., Walter E. Heller & Co., Tabor Devel. Co.; **PROFL AFFIL & HONORS:** ABA, CO Bar Assn., Denver Bar Assn., State Bar of TX; **EDUC:** BSAE; BSEE, 1966; 1966, TX A&M Univ.; **GRAD EDUC:** MS, PhD, JD, 1968, 1971, 1976, Mechanical Engrg.; Law, TX A&M Univ., Rice Univ., Univ. of Houston; **EDUC HONORS:** Tau Beta Pi, Sigma Gamma Tau, Eta Kappa Nu, Dean's List, Member, Houston Law Review; Order of the Barons; **HOME ADD:** 1600 Grape St., Denver, CO 80220, (303)377-4839; **BUS ADD:** 1660 Lincoln St., Suite 1518, Denver, CO 80264, (303)837-8800.

DALY, Eugene F.——B: Apr. 4, 1940, Boston, MA, *Partner*, Realco Holdings (US), Ltd.; **PRIM RE ACT:** Developer, Owner/Investor; **SERVICES:** Devel. of comml. and resid. props.; **EDUC:** BA, 1962, Intl. Govt., Harvard Univ.; **GRAD EDUC:** MA, 1971, Urban Planning, Univ. of MD; **MIL SERV:** USN, Lt. JG, 1962- 1965; **HOME ADD:** 2950 Valera Ct., Vienna, VA 22180, (703)938-4821; **BUS ADD:** 210 N. Lee St., Alexandria, VA 22314, (703)684-0222.

DALY, Gerald W.——B: Aug. 26, 1935, Chicago, IL, *VP/Mgr. RE Fin. Div.*, Bank of Newport, RE; **PRIM RE ACT:** Banker; **OTHER RE ACT:** Const. Loans; **PROFL AFFIL & HONORS:** IL Mort. Bankers Assn., Mort. Bankers Assn., Chicago RE Bd.; **EDUC:** BBA, 1960, Acctg., Roosevelt Univ.; **BUS ADD:** 2101 E. Coast Hwy. at Avocado, PO Box 7890, Newport Beach, CA 92660, (714)760-6000.

DALY, Michael F.——B: Jan. 2, 1947, Afton, NY, *Partner*, DeGraff, Foy, Conway, Holt-Harris and Mealey, Taxation; **PRIM RE ACT:** Consultant, Attorney; **OTHER RE ACT:** Tax planning and counsel; **SERVICES:** Legal servs. incident to RE activity; **REP CLIENTS:** Mechanics Exchange Div. of the Dime Savings Bank of NY; Lenders and investors in RE projects; NY State Bd. of Realtors; **PREV EMPLOY:** NY State Senate; **PROFL AFFIL & HONORS:** ABA, NY State Bar Assn., Albany Cty. Bar Assn.; **EDUC:** BS, 1968, Indus. Engrg. and Admin. Sci., Yale Univ.; **GRAD EDUC:** JD, 1972, Albany Law School of Union Univ.; LLM(taxation), 1972, NY Univ. School of Law; **OTHER ACT & HONORS:** Frequent public speaker on tax topics; **HOME ADD:** 18 Chestnut Hill Rd. South, Loudonville, NY 12211, (518)436-1230; **BUS ADD:** 90 State St. 11th Fl., Albany, NY 12207, (518)462-5301.

D'AMANTE, Raymond P.——B: Mar. 16, 1943, Concord, NH, Law Offices of Raymond P. D'Amante; **PRIM RE ACT:** Attorney, Consultant, Developer, Owner/Investor; **SERVICES:** Legal advice related to all types of RE dev.; **REP CLIENTS:** Devel., brokers, consultants, engrs., owners, arch., investors in resid., comml. and indus. props.; **PROFL AFFIL & HONORS:** NH Bar Assn.,CA Bar Assn., NY Bar Assn., ABA; **EDUC:** B. Mgmt. Engr., 1966, Eng., RPI, Troy, NY; **GRAD EDUC:** JD, 1969, Law, Union Univ. Albany Law School; **EDUC HONORS:** Comments Editor - Law Review; **MIL SERV:** USAF, Capt. 1970-74; **OTHER ACT & HONORS:** Central NH Rgnl. Planning Commn.; Heights Bus. Alliance, Greater Concord C of C; **HOME ADD:** 41 Palm St., Concord, NH 03301, (603)228-1672; **BUS ADD:** 246 Loudon Rd., PO Box 494, Concord, NH 03301, (603)224-6777.

DAMANTI, Patrick J.——B: Apr. 6, 1947, Brooklyn, NY, *Partner / Officer Assoc. Counsel & Asst. Sec.*, Ahearn & Damanti / Greater NY Savings Bank; **PRIM RE ACT:** Attorney, Banker; **SERVICES:** Counsel to bank, drafting of legal documents, litigation; **REP CLIENTS:** The Greater NY Savings Bank; **PROFL AFFIL & HONORS:** ABA (RE Sect.), NY State Bar Assn. (RE Sect.), Brooklyn Bar Assn.; **EDUC:** AB, 1968, Hist./Poli. Sci., Holy Cross Coll.; **GRAD EDUC:** JD, 1972, Law, St. John's Univ. School of Law; **MIL SERV:** US Army, Spec. 4th; **HOME ADD:** 17 LaForge Rd., Darien, CT 06820, (203)655-1657; **BUS ADD:** 410 Madison Ave., New York, NY 10017, (212)752-7225.

DAMERON, Ben B., Jr.——B: June 7, 1949, Kodiak, AK, *Chmn. of Bd.*, Sunbelt Fin. Corp.; **PRIM RE ACT:** Broker, Syndicator, Property Manager; **OTHER RE ACT:** Apt. and office renovation, incl. fire restoration; **SERVICES:** Investment Brokerage, Renovation management and consulting; **REP CLIENTS:** W Coast Synd. and Underwriters; **PROFL AFFIL & HONORS:** RESSI, IREM, FIABCI, CPM candidate, CFP candidate; **EDUC:** Econ. Geog., 1973, Land Use and Trans., San Diego St. Univ.; **HOME ADD:** 8907 N 30th Way, Scottsdale, AZ 85258, (602)991-7759; **BUS ADD:** 301 E VA, Suite 1000, Phoenix, AZ 85004, (602)254-5400.

DAMIANI, Bruno——B: Feb. 1, 1915, Providence, RI, *Owner-Pres.*, J. Damiani & Son; **PRIM RE ACT:** Developer, Builder, Owner/Investor; **HOME ADD:** 31 Prentice Ave., Pawtucket, RI 02860, (401)723-4362; **BUS ADD:** 31 Prentice Ave., Pawtucket, RI 02860, (401)723-4362.

DAMMICCI, Anthony E.——B: Mar. 20, 1932, Raritan, NJ, *VP*, Kraus Anderson Realty Company; **PRIM RE ACT:** Broker, Developer, Builder, Owner/Investor, Property Manager; **SERVICES:** Devel., leasing, prop. mgmt., advertising; **REP CLIENTS:** Prudential Life Insurance Co., North Central Investment Co. & etc.; **PREV EMPLOY:** VP Leasing - Titus Inc.; **PROFL AFFIL & HONORS:** BOMA; ISSC; NAIOP, Amer. Mgmt. Assn.; **EDUC:** BA, 1953, Pre-Law and Bus., PA Military Coll.; **EDUC HONORS:** Distinguished Mil. Student - Head of Corps of Cadets; **MIL SERV:** US Army, Lt.; **HOME ADD:** 5812 Amy Dr., Edina, MN 55436, (612)926-6744; **BUS ADD:** 523 South Eighth St., Minneapolis, MN 55404, (612)332-1241.

DAMON, James R.——B: Sept. 24, 1945, Madison, WI, *Dir., Information Systems*, R.J. Frank & Associates, Info. Servs.; **OTHER RE ACT:** RE Office Mgmt. & Office Automation Consultant; **SERVICES:** Micro Computer Programming, Operational Plans Counseling, Computer Analysis for RE and Bus. Valuation; **REP CLIENTS:** Devels., Planners and Appraisers; **PREV EMPLOY:** First Nat. Bank of OR, 1972-1978; **EDUC:** BA, 1968, Speech-Bus., Eastern WA Univ.; **GRAD EDUC:** Applied Sci., 1981, Computer Programming/Computer Operations, Portland Community Coll.; **MIL SERV:** US Army, Capt., Air Medal, Bronze Star; **OTHER ACT & HONORS:** Bd. of

Dirs. Morrison Ctr. for Youth and Family Servs., Portland, OR; **HOME ADD:** 2344 SE 53rd, Portland, OR 97215, (503)238-3928; **BUS ADD:** Suite 150, 700 N Hayden Island Dr., Portland, OR 97217, (503)286-8989.

DANA, Donald E.——B: Nov. 20, 1948, San Francisco, CA, *Assoc. Counsel*, Wells Fargo Bank, Legal Dept.; **PRIM RE ACT:** Attorney; **SERVICES:** Legal counsel; **REP CLIENTS:** Wells Fargo Bank, Wells Fargo Mort. Co., Wells Fargo Realty Fin. Corp.; **PREV EMPLOY:** Chickering & Gregory; **EDUC:** MS, 1971, Psych., Univ. of San Francisco; **GRAD EDUC:** JD, 1978, Hastings Coll. of Law; **MIL SERV:** US Army, 1st Lt.; **HOME ADD:** 34 Paseo Mirasol, Tiburon, CA 94920, (415)435-4577; **BUS ADD:** 475 Sansome St., 8th Floor (AU 702), San Francisco, CA 94111, (415)396-7822.

DANCYGIER, Joseph——B: Feb. 19, 1949, Malimö, Sweden, *Sales/Operations, VP*, Help-U-Buy, Inc.; **PRIM RE ACT:** Broker, Consultant, Banker, Architect, Developer, Lender, Builder, Owner/Investor, Instructor, Property Manager, Syndicator, Real Estate Publisher; **OTHER RE ACT:** Seminars and training in "equity participation" through computer matching; **SERVICES:** Matching buyers with investors and with sellers of props.; **REP CLIENTS:** C-21, Red Carpets, Realty World, The Great 5% RE Cos., Title Ins. & Trust, Ticor Mort. Ins., Sunwest Devel. & Golden Rule Realty and many large independent RE firms; **PREV EMPLOY:** Dir. of Prop. Mgmt. and Pres. of D & K Devel.; **PROFL AFFIL & HONORS:** San Fernando Bd. of Realtors, IREM, Amer. Film Inst., AA - RE 1971, UCLA - RE, 1976, Cert. Program; **EDUC:** AA, 1971/1976, RE, Valley Coll. - UCLA; **OTHER ACT & HONORS:** Also assoc. with The Great 5% Real Estate Cos., Inc. - VP; **HOME ADD:** 16215 Dickens St., Encino, CA 91436, (213)784-3792; **BUS ADD:** 2802 Pacific Coast Hwy., Torrance, CA 90505, (213)326-4707.

DANEMAN, Steven Bradley——B: July 10, 1957, Chicago, IL, *Admn. Asst.; Prop. Devel. and Rehabilitation*, Sequoia Assoc., 7926 W. 3rd St.; L.A., CA; **PRIM RE ACT:** Syndicator, Developer, Property Manager, Owner/Investor; **OTHER RE ACT:** Rehabilitation; **SERVICES:** Devel., Synd., Rehab. Comml. and Res. Prop. and Prop. Mgmt.; **REP CLIENTS:** Amer. Income Prop., L.A., CA; **PROFL AFFIL & HONORS:** AELU, CED; **EDUC:** BS, 1979, Bus. Admon. and Poli. Sci., Lewis and Clark Coll., Portland, OK; **GRAD EDUC:** MBA, 1983, Mgmt., Fin., and Gov. Policy, UC Berkeley GSB; **HOME ADD:** 602 N. Bedford Dr., Beverly Hills, CA; **BUS ADD:** 102 Karry Ln., Pleasant Hill, CA 94523, (415)671-0947.

DANG, Theodore W.——B: Oct. 3, 1951, Oakland, CA, *Pres.*, Commonwealth; **PRIM RE ACT:** Broker, Consultant, Developer, Owner/Investor, Property Manager, Syndicator; **PROFL AFFIL & HONORS:** Local, state, and nat. Bd. of Realtors, CPM; RE Certificate Inst.; **EDUC:** BS, 1973, Bus. Admin., Univ. of CA, Berkeley; **OTHER ACT & HONORS:** Pres., East Bay Asian Local Devel. Corp.; Pres., Tomorrow Devel. Co., Inc.; **BUS ADD:** 164 11th St., Oakland, CA 94607, (415)832-5195.

D'ANGELO, Anthony J.——B: June 11, 1932, NY, *VP*, The Hammerson Prop. Corp.; **PRIM RE ACT:** Developer; **REP CLIENTS:** Var. leading nat. retail chains and maj. corps.; **PREV EMPLOY:** RE Manager, Xerox Corp., 1969-80; Dir. of Corp. RE, Standard Brands, 1965-69; **PROFL AFFIL & HONORS:** NACORE; **EDUC:** BA, 1953, Lib. Arts., Columbia; **GRAD EDUC:** Civil Engrg., Columbia; **HOME ADD:** 50 Quails Trail, Stamford, CT 06903, (203)322-1277; **BUS ADD:** 100 Park Ave., NY, NY 10017, (212)679-0275.

DANGLER, Martin S.——B: Sept. 27, 1926, L.I. City, NY, *Owner*, Martin S. Dangler; **PRIM RE ACT:** Broker, Consultant; **REP CLIENTS:** Consultant to attys. representing estates in disposition of holdings, leasing consultant to owners of shopping centers; **PROFL AFFIL & HONORS:** ICSC-NY R.E. Bd., Chmn. R.E. Practitioners Inst. at C.W. Post Centre, CSM With ICSC, "Man of the Year" in R.E. 1974-C.W. Post Centre; **MIL SERV:** USMC, Sgt., 1943-46; **BUS ADD:** 3510 Center View Ave., Wantagh, NY 11793, (516)785-4848.

DANIEL, Charles E.——B: Mar. 10, 1920, Texarkana, AR, *Pres.*, Salado Mountain Devel. Corp.; **PRIM RE ACT:** Consultant, Developer, Owner/Investor; **OTHER RE ACT:** Fin. packaging and start-up financing; **SERVICES:** Project investment & fin., interim consumer fin.; **REP CLIENTS:** Delta Devel. Grp., Suntree Design Grp., Ltd., Paugus Bay Condo Devel., all of NH; **PREV EMPLOY:** Investment Banking Underwriter, Bldg. & Devel. (Resid.) Advertising & Mktg., Financial Trust Transactions, all current and through ownership and/or contract; **EDUC:** Providence Academy; **MIL SERV:** US Army, Field Artillery, WW II; **HOME ADD:** 12410 Pleasant Forest Dr., Little Rock, AR 72212, (501)225-9186; **BUS ADD:** 500 Hall Bldg., Little Rock, AR 72201, (501)376-0491.

DANIEL, E. Ross——B: June 6, 1946, Americus, GA, *Pres.*, Sunbelt Investment Properties, Inc.; **PRIM RE ACT:** Broker, Syndicator, Consultant, Owner/Investor; **SERVICES:** RE brokerage & counselling regarding investment props.; **PROFL AFFIL & HONORS:** Atlanta Bd. of Realtors; **EDUC:** BS, 1968, Textiles, GA Inst. of Tech.; **GRAD EDUC:** MBA, 1971, Fin., GA State Univ.; **HOME ADD:** 5315 Mt. Vernon Pkwy., Atlanta, GA 30327, (404)257-0923; **BUS ADD:** 6201 Powers Ferry Rd., Suite 595, Atlanta, GA 30339, (404)955-4565.

DANIEL, William B.——B: Aug. 27, 1949, Charleston, SC, *Pres.*, Tidelands Realty, InC.; **PRIM RE ACT:** Broker, Property Manager, Owner/Investor; **SERVICES:** Mgmt. and sales of resort props. at Kiawah & Seabrook Is.; **REP CLIENTS:** Investors of resort props.; **PREV EMPLOY:** Medical Univ. of SC, 1972-1977, Human Resources Dir.; **PROFL AFFIL & HONORS:** Greater Charleston Bd. of Realtors; NAR; **EDUC:** BS, 1971, Mktg., Baptist Coll. at Charleston; **GRAD EDUC:** MBA, 1972, Mgmt., GA Southern; **EDUC HONORS:** Pres. of Student Body, Who's Who Among Students, Grad. with Distinction; **OTHER ACT & HONORS:** Chmn., Bd. of Tr. Opti-Isle, Optimist Club of Charleston, Optimist of the Year; Outstanding Young Men of Amer.; **HOME ADD:** 873 Stiles Dr., Charleston, SC 29412, (803)795-9138; **BUS ADD:** 143 St. Andrews Blvd., POB 30067, Charleston, SC 29407, (803)571-0214.

DANIELS, Derick——*President*, Playboy Enterprises; **PRIM RE ACT:** Property Manager; **BUS ADD:** 919 No. Michigan Ave., Chicago, IL 60611, (312)751-8000.*

DANIELS, Donald B.——B: June 11, 1938, Mt. Vernon, WA, *Chmn. of Bd. & CEO*, Shurgard Inc./Capital Northwest Management Corp.; **PRIM RE ACT:** Developer, Owner/Investor, Property Manager, Syndicator; **SERVICES:** Devel. & synd. of comml. props. (primarily Shurgard Mini-Storage); prop. mgmt.; **REP CLIENTS:** Indiv. investors in comml. props., and gen. partner and prop. mgr. for continuing –10M plus public offerings by rgnl. brokerage firms of Foster and Marshall (West Coast), Dain-Bosworth (Midwest); **PROFL AFFIL & HONORS:** Past Pres. & Dir. of Self Serv. Storage Assn.; The Nat. Assn. of Mini-Storage Owners and Devels.; **EDUC:** BA, 1961, Math., Univ. of WA; **GRAD EDUC:** MBA, 1963, Fin./Acctg./Statistics, Univ. of WA; **EDUC HONORS:** Math. Honorary, 2 yrs., Nat. Defense Educ. Act - Title IV Fellowship Award, 3 yrs.; **MIL SERV:** USAF, Capt., AF Commendation Medals for Merit. Serv.; **OTHER ACT & HONORS:** Bd. of Dirs., Olympia YMCA; **HOME ADD:** 114 W. 23rd, Olympia, WA 98501, (206)754-8485; **BUS ADD:** 2920 W. Harrison, Olympia, WA 98502, (206)943-7238.

DANIELS, Fred Peter——B: Nov. 12, 1908, NY, NY, *Pres. Chmn.*, Ace Realty Co.; **PRIM RE ACT:** Broker, Consultant, Appraiser; **SERVICES:** Investment counseling, comml. & indus. brokerage & appraising since 1951; **PROFL AFFIL & HONORS:** Sr. Cert. Valuer, Intl. Inst. Of Valuers, NAREA; **EDUC:** Univ. of AL; **MIL SERV:** US Army Engrs., Pvt.; **BUS ADD:** 1780 Sans Souci Blvd., N. Miami, FL 33181, (305)893-9595.

DANIELS, Robert H.——B: Aug. 24, 1947, Boston, MA, *Atty.*; **PRIM RE ACT:** Attorney; **SERVICES:** Litigation and Tax Consultation; **PREV EMPLOY:** Atty., McCutchen, Doyle, Brown & Enersen; **EDUC:** HB, 1969, Hist., Harvard; **GRAD EDUC:** JD, 1972, Harvard, Cum Laude; **EDUC HONORS:** Magna Cum Laude; **BUS ADD:** 555 California St. Suite 3180, San Francisco, CA 94104, (415)956-5400.

DANIELS, Robert S.——B: June 21, 1940, Brooklyn, NY, *Atty.*, Daniels & Daniels; **PRIM RE ACT:** Broker, Consultant, Attorney, Builder, Owner/Investor; **SERVICES:** Legal, Brokerage, Contracting; **REP CLIENTS:** By request; **PROFL AFFIL & HONORS:** Allegheny Cty. Bar Assn.; **EDUC:** BBA, 1962, Acctg., Univ. of Pittsburgh; **GRAD EDUC:** LLB, 1965, Law, Univ. of Pittsburgh; **HOME ADD:** 1200 Denniston Ave., Pittsburgh, PA 15213, (412)383-2606; **BUS ADD:** 2128 E. Carson St., Pittsburgh, PA 15203, (412)381-8809.

DANIELS, Walter C.——B: Nov. 6, 1940, New York, NY, *VP of Mktg. & New Project Devel.*, Hunt Development Corp.; **PRIM RE ACT:** Broker, Consultant, Developer, Owner/Investor, Property Manager; **SERVICES:** Joint Venture & Project Devel.; **PREV EMPLOY:** John W. Galbreath & Co.-RE Devel., Leasing, Mgmt. & Consultant; **PROFL AFFIL & HONORS:** BOMA Intl.; Realtor; **EDUC:** NA, 1963, Philosophy, Cathedral Coll.; **BUS ADD:** 1700 Atrium One, 201 E Fourth St., Cincinnati, OH 45202, (513)579-9700.

DANILUK, Daniel——B: Feb. 16, 1952, Warren, OH, *Asst. Legal Counsel*, The Cafaro Co.; **PRIM RE ACT:** Attorney; **SERVICES:** Legal counseling on acquiring, devel., managing, and disposing of comml. RE; **PROFL AFFIL & HONORS:** ABA; OH Bar Assn.; **EDUC:** BS, 1976, Geology, Youngstown State Univ.; **GRAD EDUC:** JD, 1979, Comml. and Prop. Law, Case Western Reserve Univ. School of Law; **EDUC HONORS:** Summa Cum Laude, Order of the Coif; **HOME ADD:** 2915 Warren Ave., McDonald, OH 44437; **BUS ADD:** 2445 Belmont Ave., Youngstown, OH 44504, (216)747-2661.

DANISH, John C.——B: Oct. 19, 1950, Dallas, TX, *Atty.*, Carlton and Danish; **PRIM RE ACT:** Attorney; **EDUC:** BA, 1972, Hist./Poli. Sci., Wheaton Coll.; **GRAD EDUC:** JD, 1975, S Methodist Univ., School of Law; **MIL SERV:** USMC, Pvt. (E-1); **HOME ADD:** 1801 Rusdell Dr., Irving, TX 75060, (214)253-6272; **BUS ADD:** 4640 Harry Hines Blvd., Dallas, TX 75235, (214)638-8044.

DANNER, John C.——B: May 27, 1950, Miami Beach, FL, *Comml RE Appraiser*, Marvin E. Meacham & Assoc., Inc.; **PRIM RE ACT:** Broker, Appraiser, Owner/Investor, Instructor, Property Manager; **SERVICES:** Primarily RE appraisals and consultants; **REP CLIENTS:** Numerous local municipalities, fin. instns., attys., private investors; **PREV EMPLOY:** Comml. RE Appraiser, Home Fed. S&L Assn., 1720 Harrison St., Hollywood, FL; **PROFL AFFIL & HONORS:** Member SREA, Previously SRA Member, SRPA, SRA; **EDUC:** BSBA, 1974, RE & Urban Land Studies, Univ. of FL; **HOME ADD:** 2426 SE 17th St., Ft. Lauderdale, FL 33316, (205)462-0659; **BUS ADD:** 1308 E Broward Blvd., Ft. Lauderdale, FL 33301, (305)463-3090.

DANT, Robert M.——B: Oct. 3, 1948, Portland, OR, *Pres.*, Dant Devel. Corp.; **PRIM RE ACT:** Consultant, Developer; **OTHER RE ACT:** Investor; **SERVICES:** Devel. & mgmt. of comml. prop. devel., consulting; **REP CLIENTS:** Indiv. investors; **PREV EMPLOY:** RE Mort. loan analyst, Standard Ins. Co.; **PROFL AFFIL & HONORS:** Portland Hist. Landmarks Comm., Wilsonville Planning Comm., Wilsonville Design Review Bd., Assoc. Soc. of RE Appraisers; **EDUC:** BBA, 1970, Fin. Mgmt., OR State Univ.; **MIL SERV:** OR Nat. Guard, S Sgt.; **OTHER ACT & HONORS:** Found. Bd. of Tr. Meridian Park Hospital; **HOME ADD:** PO Box 557, Wilsonville, OR 97070, (503)682-0905; **BUS ADD:** 1220 SW Morrison, Suite 1305, Portland, OR 97205, (503)227-4994.

DANZIG, Jeanette——B: Oct. 3, 1924, NYC, *Pres.*, Danzig Const. Co., Inc.; **PRIM RE ACT:** Builder; **OTHER RE ACT:** Sales of resid. housing; **PREV EMPLOY:** 20 yrs. RE sales; **PROFL AFFIL & HONORS:** St. Louis Home Builders Assn., Homer Award 1978 Best Home -200,000 to -225,000 Category; **BUS ADD:** 11601 Lakeshore Dr., Creve Coeur, MO 63141, (314)432-4434.

DANZIGER, Robert A.——B: Mar. 18, 1934, Springfield, MA, *Pres.*, Northland Investment Corp.; **PRIM RE ACT:** Consultant, Developer, Owner/Investor, Property Manager, Syndicator; **SERVICES:** Evaluating, synd., acquiring and man. income producing comml. RE; **PROFL AFFIL & HONORS:** Gr. Boston Bd. of Realtors, NAR; **EDUC:** AB, 1956, English Lit., Dartmouth Coll.; **GRAD EDUC:** MBA, 1957, Fin., Amos Tuck School of Bus. Admin.; **OTHER ACT & HONORS:** Dartmouth Coll. Alumni, Tuck School Alumni of Gr. Boston, Trustee - Beth Israel Hosp.; **HOME ADD:** 96 Temple St., W. Newton, MA 02165, (617)527-6203; **BUS ADD:** 20 Walnut St., Wellesley Hills, MA 02181, (617)235-2900.

DAOUD, George J.——B: Oct. 20, 1944, Beirut, *Pres.*, Motor Inn Management, Inc.; **PRIM RE ACT:** Consultant, Developer, Builder, Owner/Investor, Property Manager, Syndicator; **PREV EMPLOY:** Gen. Chmn. Holiday Inn, New London & Groton, CT 1974-75; Gentle Winds Beach Resort, St. Croix, VI, 1975-78; VP, VI Hotel & Motel Assn. 1976; **PROFL AFFIL & HONORS:** Member Amer. Hotel & Motel Assn.; Member, Educational Inst., cert. hotel admin.; **EDUC:** BS, 1967, NY Univ.; **GRAD EDUC:** MPS, 1969, Cornell Univ.; **HOME ADD:** 2960 Greencrest Dr., Kettering, OH 45432, (513)254-5446; **BUS ADD:** PO Box 1417, Dayton, OH 45401, (513)228-6656.

D'AOUST, Andre J.——B: Aug. 4, 1926, Alfred, Ontario, Can, *Exec. VP*, Quebec RE Assn.; **OTHER RE ACT:** Profl. Assn.; **SERVICES:** RE educ. program, forms, liaison with provincial govt.; **PREV EMPLOY:** Brinco, Ltd. Asst. Dir., Public Relations; Maclean-Hunter, Ltd., Editor in Chief, Revue-Moteur; **PROFL AFFIL & HONORS:** La Chambre de Commerce du Dist. de Montreal; La Chambre de Commerce de la Province de Quebec; The Montreal Bd. of Trade; FIABCI; CAN RE Assn.; **EDUC:** BA, 1949, Univ. of Ottawa; **MIL SERV:** Navy; seaman; **OTHER ACT & HONORS:** Pres., Duvernay School Bd. 1968-69; Member, Mirabel Racquet Club; Pres., Automotive Booster Club 1965; Pres., Bus. Paper Editors Assn. 1962; Pres., Cercle de la presse d'affaires 1966; **HOME ADD:** 2289 Coulonges, Duvernay, Quebec, CAN, (514)269-2093; **BUS ADD:** 1080 Beaver Hall Hill, Ste. 1100, Montreal, Que., CAN, (514)866-7641.

DARDEN, James W.——B: Jan. 19, 1944, Memphis, TN, *Mgr.-Land Dept.*, AL ByProducts Corp.; **PRIM RE ACT:** Property Manager; **PREV EMPLOY:** Darden & Asscs., Jefferson Co., Phg., Moore-Hardley; **EDUC:** BA, 1962-1966, Poli. Sci.; **GRAD EDUC:** MUP, 1968-1970, Land use Plrg.; **MIL SERV:** US Army, Ltc.; **HOME ADD:** 1 Ransom Rd., Birmingham, AL 35210, (205)838-1848; **BUS ADD:** P.O. Box 10246, Birmingham, AL 35202.

D'ARGENTO, Frank——*Dir. Corp. Fac.*, Tyco Laboratories, Inc.; **PRIM RE ACT:** Property Manager; **BUS ADD:** Tyco Park, Exeter, NH 03833, (603)778-7331.*

DARLING, Richard S.——B: Sept. 14, 1939, Bangor, ME, *Pres.*, Richard S. Sarling Co., Inc; **PRIM RE ACT:** Broker, Syndicator, Consultant, Appraiser, Developer, Builder, Property Manager, Assessor; **SERVICES:** Consultating for RE ad valorem prop. taxes and investments.; **PROFL AFFIL & HONORS:** Nat. Assn. Of Review Appraisers, BOMA, Nat. Assn. of Prop Tax Rep., Inst. of Taxation, So. AZ HBA; **EDUC:** Mktg. & Acctg., Univ. of Az; **GRAD EDUC:** BS, 1961; **MIL SERV:** USAFNG; **OTHER ACT & HONORS:** Mt. Oyster Club; Centurions; Old Pueblo Athletic Club River Racquet Club; **HOME ADD:** 5625 E. 8th., Tucson, AZ 85711, (602)745-6753; **BUS ADD:** 7000 E. Tanque Verde Rd., Suite 14, Tucson, AZ 85715, (602)296-6271.

DARNELL, Roger D.——B: July 19, 1943, Terrell, TX, *VP*, The Robert P. Warmington Co., RE; **PRIM RE ACT:** Attorney, Developer, Owner/Investor; **PREV EMPLOY:** Meserve, Mumper and Hughes, Los Angeles (Partner); **PROFL AFFIL & HONORS:** ABA, CA State Bar Assn. Bldg. Indus. Assn., Speaker: BIA, PCBC, ALI; **EDUC:** BS, 1965, Fin., Univ. of S. CA; **GRAD EDUC:** JD, 1968, Law, Univ. of S. CA; **EDUC HONORS:** Beta Gamma Sigma, Cum Laude; **OTHER ACT & HONORS:** City of Hope, Tuna Club, Newport Harbor Yacht Club; **HOME ADD:** 1300 E. Balboa Bldv., Balboa, CA 92661, (714)673-1300; **BUS ADD:** 3090 Pullman St., Costa Mesa, CA 92626, (714)966-1333.

DARR, Audrey E.——B: Oct. 2, 1921, Ross Cty., OH, *Pres.*, Darr Realty, Inc.; **PRIM RE ACT:** Broker, Owner/Investor, Syndicator, Property Manager; **SERVICES:** Synd., Prop. Mgmt., Resid. Brokerage; **PREV EMPLOY:** Arkay RE (Office Mgr.) 6 years; **PROFL AFFIL & HONORS:** Natl. Assn. Realtors, RESSI, OH Assn. Realtors, GRI; **EDUC:** BS, 1940, Journalism, Kent State Univ.; **GRAD EDUC:** 1975, RE, OH State Univ.; **OTHER ACT & HONORS:** Pres. Coshocton Cty. Bd. of Realtors, 1980, Bus. & Professional Women's Club, Trustee, Y.W.C.A., C of C, Coshocton; **HOME ADD:** 6321/2 Main St., Coshocton, OH 43812, (614)622-1389; **BUS ADD:** 632 Main St., Coshocton, OH 43812, (614)622-7537.

DARROW, Kenneth F.——B: June 24, 1945, Brooklyn, NY, Kenneth F. Darrow, P.A.; **PRIM RE ACT:** Attorney; **SERVICES:** Counseling, tax advice, negotiating, closing as to real prop. matters; **REP CLIENTS:** Buyers, sellers, synds., and brokers of comml. and resid. RE; **PREV EMPLOY:** Staff Atty., Chief Counsel, IRS, 1971-73, Atty.-Advisor US Tax Court, 1969-71; Associate, Pope, Ballard, Shepard & Fowle, Chicago, IL, 1973-73; Partner, Garlick, Cohn, Darrow & Hollander, N. Miami Beach, FL, 1976-80; **PROFL AFFIL & HONORS:** ABA, Real Prop. & Probate Sect., Tax Sect., Forum Comm. on Franchisting, FL Bar; **EDUC:** BS, 1966, Acctg., Lehigh Univ., Bethlehem, PA; **GRAD EDUC:** JD, 1969, Law, Fed. Income Tax., Georgetown Univ. Law Ctr., Washington, DC; **EDUC HONORS:** Cum Laude, Beta Alpha Psi, Law Review; **OTHER ACT & HONORS:** Outstanding Young Men of Amer., 1979; **HOME ADD:** 7850 SW 169th St., Miami, FL 33157, (305)233-4214; **BUS ADD:** 2600 Douglas Rd., Suite 1112, Coral Gables, FL 33134, (305)446-5000.

DARROW, Lawrence P.——*Pres.*, L.P. Darrow Realty Consultants, Inc.; **PRIM RE ACT:** Appraiser; **OTHER RE ACT:** Counselor; **SERVICES:** RE Appraising, Consulting, and Investment Analysis for All Types of Investment Props.; **REP CLIENTS:** First Nat. Bank of Chicago; Prudential Ins. Co.; Merrill Lynch Relocation; Marriott Corp.; Ford Motor Co.; Mobil Oil; TX Instruments; Intl. Harvester; Coca Cola Co.; Penn Central; McDonalds Corp.; **PREV EMPLOY:** First Chicago Realty Services, Inc.; Mort. Banking Subsidiary of First Natl. Bank; **PROFL AFFIL & HONORS:** AIREA; ASREC; SREA, MAI; CRE; **BUS ADD:** 414 Plaza Dr., Westmont, IL 60559, (312)986-9600.

DART, Henry Tutt——B: Oct. 8, 1948, New Orleans, LA, *Atty. at Law*; **PRIM RE ACT:** Broker, Attorney; **SERVICES:** For. RE investment counseling; **PROFL AFFIL & HONORS:** LA State Bar Assn., ABA, Real Prop. & Probate Sect. ABA, Comm. on For. Investment in US RE; **EDUC:** 1974, Poli. Sci., Univ. of New Orleans; **GRAD EDUC:** 1977, Civil Law, LA State Univ.; **MIL SERV:** USN, E5, Meritorious Unit Citation; **HOME ADD:** 3636 Jena St., New Orleans, LA 70125, (504)821-3074; **BUS ADD:** 317 Magazine St., New Orleans, LA 70130, (504)523-1001.

DASCENZI, Hazel Marie——**B:** Sept. 6, 1920, Palestine, TX, *RE Broker/Gen. Partner*, Hazel's Realty and Unity Devel. Co.; **PRIM RE ACT:** Broker, Developer, Builder, Owner/Investor, Property Manager, Syndicator; **SERVICES:** Presently the Gen. Partner in twenty synd.; **PROFL AFFIL & HONORS:** Nat. Assn. of Realtors; CAR; Soroptimist Club; Buena Park Bd. of Realtors, Pres., Buena Park, Cypress & La Palma Bd. of Realtors, 1963; Chmn., Credentials Comm. for CAR; Pres., two consecutive yrs., Soroptimist Intl. of Buena Park; Bus. Woman of the Yr.; Personalities of the West & Mid West; Intl. Biography; Women of the World; Several Cert. of Appreciation from CAR; Realtor of the Yr.; **OTHER ACT & HONORS:** Pres., Women's Div. C of C; **HOME ADD:** 14827 Brentstone Ave., Sunnymead, CA 92388, (714)653-2928; **BUS ADD:** 14827 Brentstone Ave., Sunnymead, CA 92388, (714)656-4884.

DATOR, William F.——**B:** Mar. 5, 1943, India, *Pres.*, The Dator Agency, Inc.; **PRIM RE ACT:** Broker, Appraiser, Developer, Owner/Investor, Property Manager, Syndicator; **REP CLIENTS:** TRW, IBM, Otis, Norelco, Lederle, Minolta, Faberge; **PROFL AFFIL & HONORS:** NAR, RESSI, Pres. NJ Chap. RESSI 1980-81; Realtor of the Year 1975; **EDUC:** 1964, Pol. Sci. & Bus., Monmouth Coll.; **OTHER ACT & HONORS:** Elected Charter Study Commr. 1978; Rotary; **HOME ADD:** 33 Olney Rd., Mahwah, NJ 07430, (201)529-4030; **BUS ADD:** 6E Ramado Ave., Mahwah, NJ 07430, (201)529-3000.

DAUGHERTY, William F.——**B:** June 12, 1939, Lexington, NC, *VP*, Wachovia Mortgage Co., Resid.; **PRIM RE ACT:** Lender; **SERVICES:** Originate FHA, VA, conventional and const. loans; **REP CLIENTS:** Gen. Public, Realtors and Builders; **PROFL AFFIL & HONORS:** MBAA; Wake Cty. Home Builders Assn.; Raleigh Bd. of Realtors, Wake Co. Lenders Assn.; **EDUC:** BS, 1961, Recreational Parks Admin., NC State Univ.; **MIL SERV:** US Army, Cpl.; **HOME ADD:** 5013 Tremont Dr., Raleigh, NC 27611, (919)876-7375; **BUS ADD:** PO Box 27886, Raleigh, NC 27611, (919)755-7737.

DAUM, Donald R.——**PRIM RE ACT:** Attorney; **SERVICES:** Legal and acctg. for RE devel.; **PREV EMPLOY:** Ernst & Whinney; **PROFL AFFIL & HONORS:** AAA/CPA, Treasurer, Houston Bar TX, AICPA, ABA, TX Soc. of CPA's; **BUS ADD:** 8300 Bissonnet Suite 600, Houston, TX 77074, (713)771-7000.

DAUSCH, William——*VP, Gen. Couns. & Secy.*, Eastmet Corp.; **PRIM RE ACT:** Attorney, Property Manager; **BUS ADD:** PO Box 507, Cockeysville, MD 21030, (301)666-1500.*

DAUTEL, Charles S.——*Secy.*, Eagle-Pichers Industries, Inc.; **PRIM RE ACT:** Property Manager; **BUS ADD:** PO Box 779-580 Walnut St., Cincinnati, OH 45202, (513)721-7010.*

DAVALLE, Al——*Corp. RE Mgr.*, DeSoto, Inc.; **PRIM RE ACT:** Property Manager; **BUS ADD:** 1700 South Mt. Prospect Rd., Des Plaines, IL 60018, (312)391-9000.*

DAVENPORT, Peter M.——**B:** Nov. 26, 1943, Joliet, IL, *Atty. at Law*; **PRIM RE ACT:** Attorney; **SERVICES:** Legal servs.; **PROFL AFFIL & HONORS:** Fayette Cty. Bar Assn.; KY Bar Assn.; ABA; **EDUC:** BA, 1965, Econ., Univ. of KY; **GRAD EDUC:** JD, 1966, Univ. of KY; LLM, 1973, Taxation, George Washington Univ.; **MIL SERV:** USAR JAGC, Maj; **BUS ADD:** 177 N. Limestone St., Lexington, KY 40507, (606)254-5531.

DAVENPORT, Stephen H., Jr.——**B:** Sept. 30, 1949, Norfolk, VA, *VP*, McGuire Properties, Inc., Devel.; **PRIM RE ACT:** Developer, Owner/Investor, Syndicator; **SERVICES:** Acquisition, constr., synd. of income props.; **REP CLIENTS:** Indiv. Investors as Ltd. Partners, Instnl. Investors; **PROFL AFFIL & HONORS:** RESSI; Charlotte Apt. Assn.; **EDUC:** BA, 1975, Eng., Univ. of NC at Chapel Hill; **MIL SERV:** USMC, Sgt. 1967-71; **OTHER ACT & HONORS:** Charlotte Athletic Club, Uptown YMCA, Mecklenburg Wildlife Club; **HOME ADD:** 1931 Ferncliff Rd., Charlotte, NC 28211, (704)366-1308; **BUS ADD:** 139 S. Tryon St., Charlotte, NC 28202, (704)334-7383.

DAVERMAN, James E.——**B:** Aug. 29, 1949, E. Grand Rapids, MI, *VP*, First Chicago Investment Corp.; **PRIM RE ACT:** Owner/Investor; **SERVICES:** RE Venture Capital Investment; **REP CLIENTS:** Devels. of and Investors in RE projects and RE cos.; **PREV EMPLOY:** Pres., W-G Devel. Corp.; Pres., Montwood, Inc.; VP, First Chicago Realty Serv., Inc. (all subsidiaries and affiliates of First Nat. Bank of Chicago), 1976-80; Advance Mort. Corp., 1973-76; **EDUC:** BBA, 1971, Econ. & Mktg., Univ. of MI; **GRAD EDUC:** MBA, 1973, Fin. & Acctg., The Wharton School, Univ. of PA; **HOME ADD:** 888 Valley Rd., Glencoe, IL 60022, (312)835-2093; **BUS ADD:** Ste. 2628, One First National Pl., Chicago, IL 60603, (312)732-8063.

DAVERSA, Frank——The FIP Corp.; **PRIM RE ACT:** Developer; **BUS ADD:** PO Box 354, Farmington, CT 06032, (203)677-1361.*

DAVES, Gerald D.——**B:** Mar. 15, 1946, NC, *Sr. VP*, Wood Properties, Inc.; **PRIM RE ACT:** Broker, Developer, Property Manager; **SERVICES:** Prop. mgmt., appraisal, devel., investment; **REP CLIENTS:** Owners of comml. & resid. props.; **PROFL AFFIL & HONORS:** Soc. of RE Appraisers; TN Assn. of Realtors; Nat. Assn. of Home Builders - Registered Apt. Mgr.; IREM; NAR, Pres., Knoxville Apt. Council, 1977; CPM - IREM; Bd. of Dir., Apt. Council of TN, 1981; Pres. E. TN Chapter IREM, 1981; Bd. of Dir. Knoxville Home Builders; **EDUC:** BS, 1968, Bus. Mgmt., E. TN State Univ.; **GRAD EDUC:** MBA, 1970, Mgmt., E. TN State Univ.; **MIL SERV:** U.S. Army, 1st Lt.; **HOME ADD:** 6908 Riverwood Dr., Knoxville, TN 37920, (615)579-0888; **BUS ADD:** 1300 United American Plaza, Knoxville, TN 37929, (615)637-7777.

DAVES, Mae E.——**B:** June 21, 1932, Reno, NV, *Pres.*, Capitol Area Marketing, Inc.; **PRIM RE ACT:** Broker, Consultant, Architect, Developer, Builder, Owner/Investor, Property Manager, Syndicator; **SERVICES:** Investment counseling, valuation, devel. and synd. of comml. props., prop. mgmt.; **REP CLIENTS:** Lenders and indiv. investors in comml. props.; **PROFL AFFIL & HONORS:** Bd. of Realtors; AIA; C of C, GRI; BA Bus.; **EDUC:** BA, 1968, Sacramento State Univ.; **OTHER ACT & HONORS:** Recipient of Distinguished Salesman Award from Sacramento Sales & Marketing Execs.; WCR; plus many other awards since 1970; Easter Seal Soc.; **HOME ADD:** 4216 Pocono Ct., Fair Oaks, CA 95628, (916)966-8109; **BUS ADD:** 2550 Fair Oaks Blvd. 123, Sacramento, CA 95825, (916)481-0916.

DAVEY, Richard W.——**B:** June 18, 1948, Pittsburgh, PA, *Dir. of RE*, Stop-N-Go Food Stores of Pittsburgh; **PRIM RE ACT:** Broker, Consultant, Appraiser, Owner/Investor, Property Manager; **SERVICES:** Valuation, devel., land use studies, prop. mgmt.; **REP CLIENTS:** Investors in comml. prop.; **PROFL AFFIL & HONORS:** Amer. Assn. of RE Appraisers, Nat. Assn. of Review Appraisers, Nat. Assn. of Corporate RE Execs., NAR, CRA, ICA; **EDUC:** BA, 1966, Bus. Admin, Monmouth Coll, Monmouth, IL; **GRAD EDUC:** 1974, RE, Duquesne Univ. School of RE; **OTHER ACT & HONORS:** Bd. of Dirs., St. Andrews - High Rise for the Elderly; Charter Member: Republican Presidential Task Force; **HOME ADD:** 7200 Baptist Rd., Apt. 105, Pittsburgh, PA 15102, (412)831-2919; **BUS ADD:** 2589 Boyce Plaza Rd., Pittsburgh, PA 15241, (412)257-1550.

DAVID, Leo——**B:** Feb. 24, 1912, Wash. DC, *VP - Prop. Mgmt.*, The Carey Winston Co.; **PRIM RE ACT:** Broker, Property Manager; **REP CLIENTS:** Indivs. and instnl. investors in comml. props.; **PROFL AFFIL & HONORS:** NAR; IREM; BOMA, CPM; RPA; Omega Tau Rho; DC Area Prop. Mgr. of the Yr. 1972; **EDUC:** BA, 1932, Fin., G. Wash. Univ.; **GRAD EDUC:** MBA, 1934, Retail Mgmt., Harvard Univ.; **MIL SERV:** USAF, T/Sgt. 1942-1946; **OTHER ACT & HONORS:** Lecturer and Profl. Lecturer in RE at The Amer. Univ., Wash., DC, 1950-1977; **HOME ADD:** 8506 Bradmoor Dr., Bethesda, MD 20034, (301)530-4017; **BUS ADD:** 4350 E. W. Hwy., Bethesda, MD 20014, (301)656-4212.

DAVID, Leonard J., CPM——Price Associates Inc.; **PRIM RE ACT:** Property Manager; **BUS ADD:** One North LaSalle St., Chicago, IL 60602, (312)641-1800.

DAVID, Dr. Mahlon R.——**B:** Feb. 24, 1945, Kewanee, IL, *Pres.*, David Enterprises, Inc.; **PRIM RE ACT:** Broker, Consultant, Appraiser, Developer, Owner/Investor, Builder, Instructor; **OTHER RE ACT:** Mort. Broker; Auctioneer; **SERVICES:** Indus. devel. & fin., bus. liquidations, farm liquidation; **REP CLIENTS:** Light indus. mfrs., comml. lenders, banks, indivs., municipalities, govt. agencies; **PREV EMPLOY:** Shamrock Land Co. 1971-73; **PROFL AFFIL & HONORS:** RNMI; IL FLI; IL Assn. of RE Educators; Federation of Indep. Bus.; IAA; NAA, Million Dollar Sales Club, IAR, Member ICA; **EDUC:** BME, 1968, Educ., Bus. Admin., IL Wesleyan Univ.; **GRAD EDUC:** MBA-DBA, 1981, Bus. Admin., Mktg. Maj., Pacific Western Univ.; **OTHER ACT & HONORS:** City Councilman/Oneida/3; District Dir./Boy Scouts/2; Phi Mu Alpha, Life Member, Experimental Aircraft Assn.; Nat. Rifle Assn.; Authored "Technical Assistance in R.E Mktg. - A Study Guide for the Perplexed" 2 Volumes; Assoc. Prof. of RE, Blackhawk Coll.; Jaycees - Outstanding Young Man of the Year; **HOME ADD:** 456 Circle Dr., Kewanee, IL 61443, (309)853-8744; **BUS ADD:** 320 Tenney St., Kewanee, IL 61443, (309)853-3070.

DAVIDS, Timothy J.——**B:** Oct. 24, 1945, MI, *Pres.*, Fogg Realty Co. Inc.; **PRIM RE ACT:** Broker, Consultant, Engineer, Developer, Owner/Investor, Property Manager, Syndicator; **OTHER RE ACT:** Condo. conversions; **SERVICES:** Prop. acquisition and devel., consulting, mgmt.; **REP CLIENTS:** Limited to several no. interests and a small number of CA profl. persons; **PREV EMPLOY:** Harris Corp., Engr.; **PROFL AFFIL & HONORS:** Melbourne Area Bd. of Realtors; State and Nat. Assn. of Realtors, Broker; **EDUC:** BS, 1969, Mech./Indus. Engrg., Univ. of So. FL; **OTHER ACT & HONORS:** St. Marks United Methodist Church; **HOME ADD:** 2711 S. Hwy. A1A, Melbourne Beach, FL 32937, (305)727-7935; **BUS ADD:** 404 N. Miramar, Indialantic, FL 32903, (305)723-5611.

DAVIDSMEYER, Gene——*VP, Treas. & Secy.*, Kroehler Mfg. Co.; **PRIM RE ACT:** Property Manager; **BUS ADD:** 747 Pratt Bldg., Elk Grove Village, IL 60007, (312)437-0710.*

DAVIDSON, Charles W.——**B:** Nov. 23, 1930, Bache, OK, *Pres.*, Charles W. Davidson Co.; **PRIM RE ACT:** Consultant, Engineer, Developer, Builder, Owner/Investor, Property Manager; **SERVICES:** Consulting Civil Engrs.; **REP CLIENTS:** Davidson & Kavanagh, Siffermann-Davidson, Standard Pacific, Kaufman & Broad, Ponderosa Homes, Broadmoor Homes, etc.; **PREV EMPLOY:** Civil Engr., City of San Jose; **PROFL AFFIL & HONORS:** CA Council Civil Engrs. & Land Surveyors; Assn. of Civil Engrs. & Land Surveyors, Santa Clara Valley; **EDUC:** Civil Engr., 1957, Engrg., San Jose State Univ.; **MIL SERV:** USAF, Cpl.; **OTHER ACT & HONORS:** San Jose Housing Authority, 1966-1969; Scottish Rite, San Jose, CA; **HOME ADD:** 1543 Peregrino Way, San Jose, CA 95125, (408)266-7520; **BUS ADD:** 90 E Gish Rd., San Jose, CA 95112, (408)295-9162.

DAVIDSON, Diane M.——**B:** Oct. 24, 1955, Des Moines, IA, *Atty.*, Central Life Assurance Co.; **PRIM RE ACT:** Attorney; **SERVICES:** Legal Inv. counsel to Central Life Assu. Co. and its subdivisions; **PROFL AFFIL & HONORS:** ABA; IA State Bar Assn., Young Lawyer Sec. RE Manuel Comm.; ABA Sect. of RP and Trust Probate Law; **EDUC:** BA, 1976, Hist./Pol. Sci., Morningside Coll., Sioux City, IA; **GRAD EDUC:** JD, 1979, Univ. of IA; **EDUC HONORS:** Summa Cum Laude, Grad. with honors; **HOME ADD:** 4815 Waterbury Rd., Des Moines, IA 50312, (515)277-9450; **BUS ADD:** 611 Fifth Ave., Des Moines, IA 50306, (515)283-2371.

DAVIDSON, Edward J.——**B:** Mar. 6, 1950, Cleveland, OH, *Mgr. of RE*, Diamond Shamrock Corp.; **PRIM RE ACT:** Attorney; **OTHER RE ACT:** Manages corp. RE; **PREV EMPLOY:** Gottlied & Schwartz (law firm); **PROFL AFFIL & HONORS:** ABA, IL Bar Assn., IDRC, Employee relocation council, JD; **EDUC:** BA, 1972, Hist., OH Univ.; **GRAD EDUC:** JD, 1975, Northwestern; **EDUC HONORS:** Summa Cum Laude, Grad. with Honors; **OTHER ACT & HONORS:** Published IDRC Project on sales-option contracts; **HOME ADD:** 7633 Fairmont Rd., Novelty, OH 44072, (216)338-6511; **BUS ADD:** 1100 Superior Ave., Cleveland, OH 44114, (216)694-4588.

DAVIDSON, Harold A.——**B:** Mar. 14, 1943, Los Angeles, CA, *Pres.*, Harold Davidson & Assoc., Inc., RE Research; **PRIM RE ACT:** Consultant, Instructor; **SERVICES:** RE research services emphasizing econ. & market feasibility studies and appraisal reports; **EDUC:** BS, 1965, Gen. Mgmt., Univ. of S CA; **GRAD EDUC:** MBA, 1968, Fin., Univ. of S CA; DBA, 1972, Fin./Urban Land Econ., Univ. of S CA; **EDUC HONORS:** Beta Gamma Sigma; **OTHER ACT & HONORS:** Member, Los Angeles Cty. Arch. Evaluation Bd.; Lambda Alpha (Honorary Land Econ. Frat.); **BUS ADD:** 1900 Ave. of the Stars, 2610, Los Angeles, CA 90067, (213)553-5551.

DAVIDSON, Marvin B.——**B:** Feb. 17, 1926, Plainfield, NJ, *Part.*, Halpern & Davidson Appraisal Co. Inc.; **PRIM RE ACT:** Broker, Syndicator, Appraiser, Property Manager, Owner/Investor; **SERVICES:** Appraisals; **REP CLIENTS:** J&J, IBM, RCA, Etc.; **PREV EMPLOY:** 12 yrs. Dist., Eng. NJ Highway Dept., 4 yrs, Appraiser, NY-NJ Port Authority, NYC; **PROFL AFFIL & HONORS:** SREA, Intnl. Right of Way Assoc. Senior Designations, SREA, AR/WA; **EDUC:** BS, Bus. Mgmt., Seton Hall Univ., Orange, NJ; **MIL SERV:** USAF, Air Cadet; **HOME ADD:** 17 Claire Dr., Bridgewater, NJ 08807, (201)722-4499; **BUS ADD:** 55 N. Gaston Ave., P.O. Box 932, Somerville, NJ 08876, (201)722-8199.

DAVIDSON, Phillip T.——**B:** Aug. 12, 1925, New Britain, CT., *Co-Chmn.*, D&L Venture Corp.; **OTHER RE ACT:** Retail bldg. & leasing; **PROFL AFFIL & HONORS:** VP & Dir. CT Bank Fed.; Natl. Retail Merchants Assn.; Dir. New Britain B&T Co.; First Bank, Comm. Expenditure Council; Greater Hartford Better Bus. Bur.; Gr. Hartford C of C Frederick Atkins, Inc. (Member of Exec. Comm.), Recipient of 'Indep. Retailer of Yr.' Award (NRMA, 1979); **EDUC:** BS, 1948, Trinity Coll.; **MIL SERV:** USN, Ensign, Gunnery Officer, 1942-45; **OTHER ACT & HONORS:** Dir. Control CT Rgnl. Heart Assn.; Family Counseling & Children's Servs. of Central CT; Corp. Wheeler Mental Health Clinic; New Britain Gen. Hospital; Inst. of Living; **HOME ADD:** 4 Eastview Dr., Simsbury, CT 06070; **BUS ADD:** 227 Main St., New Britain, CT 06051, (203)223-3655.

DAVIDSON, William G., III——**B:** Oct. 28, 1938, Fort Benning, GA, *Atty. at Law*; **PRIM RE ACT:** Consultant, Attorney; **SERVICES:** Settlement atty., fin., synd.; **REP CLIENTS:** corp. and indiv.; **PREV EMPLOY:** Premix Inc., Ashtabula, OH 1975-1978; Position Corp. Controller, Dennison Mfg. Co., Framingham, MA 1970-1975 Fin. Analyst.; **PROFL AFFIL & HONORS:** Fin. Exec. Inst., ABA, OH State Bar Assn., MD State Bar Assn., DC Bar, Atty. (Admitted in OH, MD and DC); **EDUC:** BS - US Naval Acad., 1960, Marine/Electrical Engrg.; **GRAD EDUC:** MBA, 1970, Corp. Fin. & Acctg., Wharton Univ. of PA; JD, 1974, Taxation, Suffolk Univ. Law Sch.; **EDUC HONORS:** Thesis: Econ. Benefits Attributable to Cooperative Housing - on file at US Dept. of HUD, Univ. of Toronto Library, Univ. of Montreal Library; **MIL SERV:** USN, 1960-1966, LCDR; **OTHER ACT & HONORS:** Kiwanis Club, Bd. of Dir., Ashtabula, OH; Volunteer in Technical Assistance ITA; Nat. Assn. of Accountants; **HOME ADD:** 4 Monroe St., Rockville, MD 20850, (301)340-7247; **BUS ADD:** 50 W. Montgomery Ave., Suite 340, Rockville, MD 20850, (301)340-7550.

DAVIES, Alan V.——**B:** Oct. 25, 1942, *Pres.*, J. Clarence Davies Realty Co., Inc.; **PRIM RE ACT:** Broker, Consultant, Appraiser, Instructor, Property Manager; **PROFL AFFIL & HONORS:** ASREC, ASA, NAR, IREM, NY Bd. of Realtors; **EDUC:** Dartmouth Coll., 1963; **OTHER ACT & HONORS:** Amer. Nat. Red Cross Disaster Services, Dir. Altro-Health & Rehab. Services; **HOME ADD:** 185 E 85 St., Apt. 27-K, New York, NY 10028, (212)369-8849; **BUS ADD:** 200 Madison Ave., New York, NY 10016, (212)661-2244.

DAVIES, Dean M.——**B:** Sept. 5, 1951, Salt Lake City, UT, *Pres.*, Equitec Properties Co.; **PRIM RE ACT:** Developer, Lender, Property Manager; **PREV EMPLOY:** Bus. Mgr. J.I. Case Co.; **PROFL AFFIL & HONORS:** Nat. Assn. of Corp. RE Execs., BOMA, Intl. Council of Shopping Centers, L.A. C of C, Oakland C of C, OACI; **EDUC:** BS, 1976, Econ., fin., Brigham Young Univ.; **HOME ADD:** 12976 Hawkins Dr., San Ramon, CA 94583, (415)829-8862; **BUS ADD:** 3732 Mt. Diablo Blvd., #360, Lafayette, CA 94549, (415)283-8900.

DAVIES, George——**B:** Oct. 17, 1944, Bloomington, IL, *Pres.*, George Davies Professsional Corp.; **PRIM RE ACT:** Attorney; **SERVICES:** Legal; **PROFL AFFIL & HONORS:** ABA (Sect. of Real Prop., Probate & Trust Law; Sect. of Taxation; Sect. of Corp., Banking, and Bus. Law), CO Bar Assn., Denver Bar Assn.; **EDUC:** BA, 1966, Poli. Sci., Parsons Coll.; **GRAD EDUC:** JD, 1969, Law, Univ. of Denver; **HOME ADD:** 1511 S. Genesee Ridge Rd., Golden, CO, (303)526-1105; **BUS ADD:** Ste. 1515, One Park Central, Denver, CO 80202, (303)571-1154.

DAVIES, John M., III——**B:** Jan. 14, 1941, Oak Park, IL, Davies Realty Shop; **PRIM RE ACT:** Broker, Attorney, Appraiser, Property Manager; **SERVICES:** Legal, investment counseling, appraising; **PROFL AFFIL & HONORS:** IL State Bar Assn., ABA, NAR, IL Assn. of Realtors; **EDUC:** BS, 1963, Bus., North Central Coll.; **GRAD EDUC:** JD, 1970, Law, John Marshall Law School; **HOME ADD:** 5637 Murray Dr., Berkeley, IL 60163, (312)547-5586; **BUS ADD:** 1812 Roosevelt Rd., Broadview, IL 60153, (312)343-4230.

DAVIES, Leslie E.——**B:** Nov. 3, 1928, Cleveland, OH, *Pres.*, Country Servs., Inc. Realtors; **PRIM RE ACT:** Broker, Appraiser, Insuror; **REP CLIENTS:** Investors, users; **EDUC:** BA, Econ., Univ. of MD; **HOME ADD:** Box 248 Rt 301, La Plata, MD 20646.

DAVIS, Alan J.——**B:** June 30, 1930, Butler, PA, Royal Palm Properties Corp., Investment and Comml.; **PRIM RE ACT:** Broker, Consultant, Owner/Investor, Syndicator; **SERVICES:** Investment counseling, investment analysis-valuation, preparation of pro-forms, synd. of comml. prop.; **REP CLIENTS:** Lenders-indivs.-instns. investing in comml. props.; **EDUC:** 1952, Bus., Dickinson Coll., Carlisle, PA; **MIL SERV:** US Army, 1952-1955, Cpl.; **HOME ADD:** 1036 Russell Dr., Highland Beach, FL 33134, (305)278-2717; **BUS ADD:** PO Box 548, Pompano Beach, FL 33061, (305)278-2717.

DAVIS, Barry M.——**B:** May 22, 1946, NY, NY, Barry M. Davis Realty Corp.; **PRIM RE ACT:** Broker, Consultant, Owner/Investor, Property Manager, Syndicator; **SERVICES:** Counseling, investment prop., acquisitions, mgmt.; **REP CLIENTS:** Instnl. & Indiv. clients; **PREV EMPLOY:** Arlen Realty & Devel. Corp. (1974-78), Smith Barney RE Corp. (1978-80); **EDUC:** BS, 1968, Fin., Univ. of Bridgeport; **GRAD EDUC:** MBA, 1974, Fin., Bernard Baruch Grad. Sch. of Bus. Admin.; **HOME ADD:** 215 E. 68th St., NY, NY 10021, (212)794-0319; **BUS ADD:** 215 E. 68th St., NY, NY 10021, (212)794-0319.

DAVIS, Billy H., Jr.——**B:** Nov. 2, 1951, Waco, TX, *Atty.*, Pakis, Cherry, Beard & Giotes, Inc.; **PRIM RE ACT:** Attorney; **SERVICES:** Complete - Negotiation, contract documentation, financing, closing;

REP CLIENTS: Jim Stewart Realtors, Inc.; **PROFL AFFIL & HONORS:** TX Young Lawyers Ass.; ABA RE Sect.; TX Bar Assn. RE Sect.; **EDUC:** BBA, 1974, Acctg., Baylor Univ.; **GRAD EDUC:** JD, 1976, Baylor Univ.; **EDUC HONORS:** Cum Laude; **MIL SERV:** USAR, E-5; **HOME ADD:** 8305 Woodcreek, Waco, TX 76710; **BUS ADD:** 800 First National Bldg., Waco, TX 76701, (817)753-4511.

DAVIS, B.J.——B: Sept. 21, 1940, Eufaula, OK, *Pres.*, Sebring Props., Inc.; **PRIM RE ACT:** Developer, Builder; **PROFL AFFIL & HONORS:** ULI, Nat. Assn. of Homebuilders, CO Assn of Homebuilders, Resid. Council, ULI; **EDUC:** BA, 1966, Far Eastern Studies, Univ. of OK; **MIL SERV:** USAF, Capt., Joint Services Commend. Medal; Air Force Commend. Medal; **HOME ADD:** 8232 E. Jamison Pl., Englewood, CO 80112, (303)770-6967.

DAVIS, Cantey P.——B: June 4, 1943, Albany, GA, *Exec. VP*, Spratlin, Realtors; **PRIM RE ACT:** Broker; **SERVICES:** Resid. RE brokerage; **PREV EMPLOY:** The Baier Corp.; **PROFL AFFIL & HONORS:** Atlanta Bd. of Realtors; GA Assn.; Nat. Assn.; RNMI, CRB; **EDUC:** BBA, 1966, Acctg., Univ. of GA; **EDUC HONORS:** Phi Kappa Phi; **OTHER ACT & HONORS:** CPA; **HOME ADD:** 2 Queen Anne Pl., Atlanta, GA 30318, (404)355-3496; **BUS ADD:** 96 E. Andrews Dr., N.W., Atlanta, GA 30305, (404)261-0216.

DAVIS, Charles H.——B: May 19, 1944, Melrose, MA, *Gen. Partner*, Davis Properties and Investments; **PRIM RE ACT:** Developer, Owner/Investor, Property Manager, Syndicator; **OTHER RE ACT:** Condo. conversion, manufacturing interests; **SERVICES:** Mgmt., brokerage, RE consulting; **REP CLIENTS:** private parties, private groups; **PREV EMPLOY:** Since age of 21, RE has been my only occupation and will remain such; **EDUC:** BA, 1972, Bus., Univ. of AZ; **GRAD EDUC:** various professional seminars and workshops, 2 years, Univ. of AZ; Coursework, Univ. of Chicago; **MIL SERV:** US Army, 1st Lt., Purple Heart, Bronze Star (2), Combat Infantryman's Badge, Ranger, Airborne; **OTHER ACT & HONORS:** Los Angeles Athletic Club, Olympic Club; **HOME ADD:** 355 Beacon St., Boston, MA 02116; **BUS ADD:** 435 S. LaCienega Blvd. 116, Los Angeles, CA 90048, (213)274-5192.

DAVIS, Clifford L.——B: Jan. 4, 1923, Mt. Erie, IL, *Asst. Sec. - VP*, Firestone RE Tire, RE Sakes/Mktg. Grp.; **PRIM RE ACT:** Property Manager; **SERVICES:** Primary Select sites Firestone Stores; **REP CLIENTS:** Manage props. leased or subleased; Work away surplus prop.; **PROFL AFFIL & HONORS:** NACORE-FL & OH Bar; **EDUC:** BSBA, 1948, Mktg. Fin., Univ. of Akron, OH; **GRAD EDUC:** JD, 1960, Univ. of Akron; **MIL SERV:** USN, Radio 2/C, 1942-45; **HOME ADD:** 255 Swartz Rd., Akron, OH 44319, (216)724-8172; **BUS ADD:** 1200 Firestone Pkwy., Akron, OH 44319, (216)379-4421.

DAVIS, Dennis D.——B: June 15, 1946, Riverside, CA, *Sr. VP*, Valley of California, Inc., Santa Clara County Operations; **PRIM RE ACT:** Broker; **SERVICES:** single family resales; **PROFL AFFIL & HONORS:** Realtor, Member of Los Altos Bd. of Realtors, San Jose RE Bd., CA Assn. of Realtors, NAR; **EDUC:** BS, 1971, Fin. & Prop. Mgmt., CA State Polytechnic Coll., San Luis Obispo; **EDUC HONORS:** Grad. with honors; **MIL SERV:** US Army 1965-68, E-5; **OTHER ACT & HONORS:** Advisory Bd., CA Land Title Co.; **HOME ADD:** 7555 Tierra Sombra Ct., San Jose, CA 95120, (408)268-3180; **BUS ADD:** 1374 E. Hamilton Ave., Campbell, CA 95008, (408)371-2100.

DAVIS, Don T., Sr.——B: July 20, 1935, Charlotte, NC, *Pres., CEO*, Davis and Davis RE Investments, Inc.; **PRIM RE ACT:** Broker, Property Manager, Syndicator; **OTHER RE ACT:** NASD broker/dealer (fin. princ.); **PROFL AFFIL & HONORS:** NAR; RNMI; RESSI; NASD, Awarded CCIM, and SRS; **EDUC:** BBA, 1972, RE, Fort Lauderdale Univ.; **MIL SERV:** USAF; Sgt.; Good Conduct/Purple Heart; **OTHER ACT & HONORS:** Also associated with Palm Beach Securities, Inc.; **HOME ADD:** 2300 Palm Beach Lakes Blvd., W Palm Beach, FL 33409, (305)689-8600; **BUS ADD:** 2300 Palm Beach Lakes Blvd., Suite #303, West Palm Beach, FL 33409, (305)689-8600.

DAVIS, Dwight W.——B: July 20, 1943, San Francisco, CA, *Pres.*, Leisure Lifestyle Corp.; **PRIM RE ACT:** Broker, Consultant, Builder, Owner/Investor, Property Manager; **SERVICES:** Mobile Home Park Mgmt., Planning, devel. & synd.; **REP CLIENTS:** IDS Mort. Trust; Boise Cascade Land Corp.; United CA Bank; United Bank of Denver; Del Webb Corp.; 1st Memphis Realty Trust; **PROFL AFFIL & HONORS:** Land Devel. Comm, Western Manufactured Housing Inst.; Western Mobile Home Assn.; IN Manufactured Housing Inst.; AZ Manufactured Housing Inst., Licensed CA RE Broker, Lic. CA Gen. Contractor, Lic. CA Ins. Agent and Lic. CA Manufactured Housing Dealer; **EDUC:** BS, 1966, Lib. Arts. & Econ., Univ. of OR; **OTHER ACT & HONORS:** Dir., San Diego Cty. Floot Control Commn. 1975-76; Dir. & VP Borrego Springs Water Dist. 1974-present; **BUS ADD:** 47 Quail Ct., Walnut Creek, CA 94596, (415)930-0810.

DAVIS, Frederick W.——B: June 16, 1944, *Pres.*, Weller-Davis, Inc.; **PRIM RE ACT:** Broker, Consultant, Developer, Builder, Owner/Investor, Property Manager, Syndicator; **SERVICES:** Brokerage services including mktg., promotion, sales and mgmt.; **REP CLIENTS:** VA in Washington, DC & Baltimore, MD; RE, mktg. consultants and sales brokers for US Steel Corp's Swan Point project in Charles Cty., MD Shannon & Luchs Realtors, 1972-74 marketing dir. of Swan Point; Davis & Assoc. 1969-72 pres. RE consulting; Korzendorfer Realty, Inc. 1969-69 asst. VP and associate broker-brokerage serv.; The Amer. RE Appraisal Corp. 1967-68 research analyst; **PROFL AFFIL & HONORS:** RE Brokerage for MD, DC and N. VA; Member of N. VA Bd. of Realtors, Licensed resid. gen. contractors for MD, DC & VA, Past VP of Rho Epsilon (Prof. RE Fraternity), Article published Oct. 1970 edition of The Appraisal Journal titled *Proximity to a Rapid Transit Station as a Factor in Residential Property Values*; **EDUC:** BS, 1967, Bus. Admin. - major RE, American Univ.; Certificate in RE - SBA, 1968; **GRAD EDUC:** MBA, 1968, RE, School of Bus. Admin.; **MIL SERV:** Army National Guard, honorable medical discharge; **OTHER ACT & HONORS:** MD Jr. C of C; **HOME ADD:** 225 11th St. SE, Washington, DC 20003, (202)543-0067; **BUS ADD:** PO Box 8895, Washington, DC 20003, (202)543-0067.

DAVIS, Gary E.——B: Nov. 11, 1947, Dayton, OH, *Atty.*, Vorys, Sater, Seymour & Pease; **PRIM RE ACT:** Attorney; **SERVICES:** Legal; **PROFL AFFIL & HONORS:** ABA, OH & Columbus Bar Assns.; **EDUC:** AB, 1970, Econs., Dartmouth Coll.; **GRAD EDUC:** JD, 1976, Univ. of MI; **EDUC HONORS:** Magna Cum Laude, Honors in Econs., Phi Beta Kappa, Cum Laude; **MIL SERV:** US Army Reserve, E-5; **HOME ADD:** 5310 Linworth Rd., Worthington, OH 43085, (614)457-8675; **BUS ADD:** 52 E Gay St., Columbus, OH 43215, (614)464-6386.

DAVIS, George W.——B: June 1, 1938, Blackwell, OK, *VP*, Raldon Homes; **PRIM RE ACT:** Broker, Developer, Builder; **SERVICES:** single family and attached for sale housing; **PREV EMPLOY:** Rossmoor Corp., E. Coast Mktg. Dir. 1970-72; Clarke-Frates Corp., Exec. VP in Mktg. 1973-75; **PROFL AFFIL & HONORS:** Member Inst. of Residential Mktg.; Member, Sales & Mktg. Execs. of Dallas; **EDUC:** BS, 1961, Mktg., Univ. of CA at Long Beach; **MIL SERV:** US Army, Sgt.; **OTHER ACT & HONORS:** Historic Preservation League, Museum of Fine Arts, Chmn. Trans. Advertising, United Way; **HOME ADD:** 713 Towne House Ln., Richardson, TX 75081, (214)783-9260; **BUS ADD:** 16901 Dallas Pkwy, Suite 110, Dallas, TX 75248, (214)931-1223.

DAVIS, Gregory L.——B: May 22, 1951, Buffalo, NY, *Gen. Counsel/Corp. Sec.*, Peter J. Schmitt Co., Inc.; **PRIM RE ACT:** Attorney, Property Manager; **PROFL AFFIL & HONORS:** ABA; NYSBA; Erie Cty. Bar Assn.; PA Bar Assn.; **EDUC:** BA, 1973, Poli. Sci., Ithaca Coll.; **GRAD EDUC:** JD, 1976, Corp. & RE, N.E. School of Law; **EDUC HONORS:** Student Body Pres., etc.; **HOME ADD:** 6846 Breen Rd., Amherst, NY 14226, (716)833-3321; **BUS ADD:** 678 Bailey Ave., Buffalo, NY 14206, (716)821-1430.

DAVIS, Helen——B: Sept. 6, 1931, Kershaw, SC, *Owner*, Helen Davis Realty & Insurance; **PRIM RE ACT:** Broker, Insuror; **SERVICES:** Brokerage, sales, etc.; **PREV EMPLOY:** Brackette Realty for 9 yrs., Started my bus. in April 1971; **PROFL AFFIL & HONORS:** Member-Lancaster Bd. of Realtors, Past Sec. & Treas. Lancaster Bd. of Realtors, Past member of Profl. Bus. Womens Club, Was first woman with RE Bus. in Lancaster, SC; **EDUC:** RE, Univ. of SC; **HOME ADD:** Rt. 8 Downing St., Lancaster, SC 29720, (803)285-9248; **BUS ADD:** 609 Great Falls Rd., Lancaster, SC 29720, (803)285-6996.

DAVIS, James——*Pres.*, Lone Star Industries, Inc.; **PRIM RE ACT:** Property Manager; **BUS ADD:** One Greenwich Plaza, Greenwich, CT 06830, (203)661-3100.*

DAVIS, James M.——B: Oct. 19, 1914, Columbus, OH, *Pres.*, James M. Davis, Inc. & Associates, Realtors; **PRIM RE ACT:** Broker, Consultant, Owner/Investor, Syndicator; **SERVICES:** Purchase, sale, asset mgmt., Gen. Partner; **PREV EMPLOY:** Coll. Pres.; **PROFL AFFIL & HONORS:** San Diego Bd. of Realtors; CA Assn. of Realtors; NAR; RNMI; San Diego Exchangors; **EDUC:** BSBA, 1937, Mktg., OH State Univ.; **GRAD EDUC:** MA, 1948, Educ., Columbia Univ.; EdD, 1953, Educ., Columbia Univ.; BDiv., 1942, Religion, Oberlin Grad. School of Theology; MDiv., 1974, Religion, Vanderbilt Univ.; **MIL SERV:** U.S. Army, Maj., Bronze Star w/OLC, 6 Campaign Medals; **OTHER ACT & HONORS:** Currently Pres., World Affairs Council of San Diego and Treas., Point Loma (San Diego) Rotary Club; Nat. Assn. for For. Student Affairs, Past Pres. & Life Member; **HOME ADD:** 4906 Pacifica Dr., San Diego, CA 92109, (714)272-6237;

BUS ADD: 4365 Mission Bay Dr., Suite 6, San Diego, CA 92109, (714)483-1100.

DAVIS, James V., Jr.——**B:** July 26, 1935, Booneville, MS, *Pres.*, Assoc. Appraisers, Inc.; **PRIM RE ACT:** Consultant, Appraiser, Owner/Investor; **SERVICES:** Appraisals, Feasibility Analysis and Counseling; **REP CLIENTS:** Lenders, Condemning Agencies and Investors; **PROFL AFFIL & HONORS:** SREA, Past Pres., Jackson Chap.; **EDUC:** BS, 1956, Agriculture and Econ., MS State Univ.; **HOME ADD:** P.O. Box 365, Madison, MS 39110, (601)856-8034; **BUS ADD:** Suite 106B, 5166 Keele St., Jackson, MS 39206, (601)982-5141.

DAVIS, Jeffrey A.——**B:** Mar. 9, 1953, Chicago, IL, *Sr. Mort. VP*, Baird & Warner, Inc.; **OTHER RE ACT:** Mort. Banker & Equity Sales; **REP CLIENTS:** Major Ins. Cos., Banks, Devels., Pension Funds; **PROFL AFFIL & HONORS:** IL Mort. Bankers Assn.; Nat. Assn. of Indus. & Office Parks; Jr. RE Bd.; **EDUC:** BS, 1975, Fin. & RE, Univ. of IL; **GRAD EDUC:** MS, 1976, Fin. & RE, Univ. of WI; **EDUC HONORS:** Dean's List; **HOME TEL:** (312)951-0622; **BUS ADD:** 115 S. LaSalle St., Chicago, IL 60603, (312)368-5802.

DAVIS, Jeffrey S.——**B:** July 20, 1949, Cleveland, OH, *VP/Partner*, Larry Davis Construction Co., Developer; **PRIM RE ACT:** Developer, Builder, Owner/Investor, Property Manager; **SERVICES:** General Contractor; **EDUC:** Bus. Mgmt., 1971, Gen. Bus., Northwood Inst., Midland, MI; **HOME ADD:** 2606 S. Green Rd., University Hts., OH 44122, (216)321-0007; **BUS ADD:** 32000 Solon Rd., Solon, OH 44139, (216)248-7770.

DAVIS, Jerry——**B:** June 2, 1944, Salt Lake City, UT, *Prin. Broker*, Jerry Davis, Realtor; **PRIM RE ACT:** Broker, Developer, Property Manager, Syndicator; **PROFL AFFIL & HONORS:** RNMI, GRI; CCIM, candidate; **EDUC:** BS Acctg., 1968, Computer Sci., Brigham Young Univ.; **GRAD EDUC:** MBA, 1969, Univ. of UT; **HOME ADD:** 47-595 Puapoo Pl., Kaneohe, HI 96744, (808)239-6368; **BUS ADD:** 1946 Young St. #200, Honolulu, HI 96826, (808)946-9037.

DAVIS, John H.——*Exec. Dir.*, Natl. Recreation and Park Assn.; **PRIM RE ACT:** Regulator; **BUS ADD:** 1601 N. Kent St., Arlington, VA 22209, (703)525-0606.*

DAVIS, John W.——**B:** Sept. 19, 1947, Houston, TX, Robinson & Davis; **PRIM RE ACT:** Broker, Consultant, Attorney, Developer; **REP CLIENTS:** Reliable Life Ins. Co., J.W. Robinson & Sons Mort., Metropolitan Life Ins. Co., US Life Title Co., Buffalo Title Co., Golden State Mutual Life Ins. Co.; **PROFL AFFIL & HONORS:** Houston RE Assn., Houston Mort. Bankers Assn., RE Law Comm.; **EDUC:** BS, 1971, Math, Univ. of Houston; **GRAD EDUC:** JD, 1975, Law, S. TX Coll. of Law; **EDUC HONORS:** Deans List 1970-1971; **OTHER ACT & HONORS:** ABA, State Bar of TX; US Supreme Ct. Bar; **HOME ADD:** 3340 So. MacGregor, Houston, TX 77021, (713)795-0462; **BUS ADD:** 2905 Elgin, Houston, TX 77004, (713)528-0581.

DAVIS, Joseph M.——**B:** Sept. 11, 1943, Columbia, SC, *Assoc. Prof of RE*, AZ State Univ., Fin. Dept.; **PRIM RE ACT:** Consultant; **OTHER RE ACT:** Re Prof., Seminar Leader; **SERVICES:** Investment Tax Credit Studies, RE Software; **REP CLIENTS:** Prudential Ins. Co.; Del Webb Devel.; Acctg. Firms; **PROFL AFFIL & HONORS:** Soc. of RE Appraisers Amer. Soc. of Appraisers Nat. Soc. of Review Appraisers Nat. Assoc. of Corp. RE Execs., SRPA, Amer. Soc. of Appraisers, CRA; **EDUC:** BS, 1965, Bus., Univ. of SC; **GRAD EDUC:** MBA, 1968, Bus., RE, TX A&I Univ.; PhD, 1975, Bus., RE, Univ. of GA; **EDUC HONORS:** Omicron Delta Kappa, Beta Gamma Sigma; **MIL SERV:** USN; LCDR, SC; **HOME ADD:** 1054 E. Buena Vista Dr., Tempe, AZ 85284, (602)839-2064; **BUS ADD:** Tempe, AZ 85251, (602)839-2064.

DAVIS, Judson R.——**B:** July 16, 1915, NJ, *Controller*, 800 East; **PRIM RE ACT:** Developer; **OTHER RE ACT:** Controller; **PREV EMPLOY:** CO Mort. Co., Boulder, CO; **EDUC:** BA, Acctg., Rider Coll.; **GRAD EDUC:** 1934, Rider Coll.; **HOME ADD:** 1410 Miracerros Lane N, Santa Fe, NM 87501, (505)983-6840; **BUS ADD:** PO Box 2046, Santa Fe, NM 87501, (505)983-2521.

DAVIS, Karl L., Jr.——**B:** July 30, 1930, Los Angeles, CA, *Partner*, Barger & Wolen; **PRIM RE ACT:** Attorney; **SERVICES:** Legal servs. in field of RE fin.; **REP CLIENTS:** Various instnl. lenders, including life ins. cos., banks, s & l assns., and trusts.; **PREV EMPLOY:** Former partner in Los Angeles law firm of Meserve, Mumper & Hughes; **PROFL AFFIL & HONORS:** Los Angeles Bar Assn. and ABA, The State Bar of CA and their sects. on Real Prop. and RE Fin., Assn. of RE Attys.; **EDUC:** BA, 1952, Econ., Stanford Univ.; **GRAD EDUC:** LLB, 1955, Law, UCLA-Law School; **OTHER ACT & HONORS:** Mort. Bankers Assn. of Amer., Amer. Land Title Assn.; **BUS ADD:** 530 W. Sixth St./Ninth Floor, Los Angeles, CA 90014, (213)680-2800.

DAVIS, Mark S., Esq.——**B:** Sept. 2, 1953, Kansas City, MO, *Special Asst. to the Mayor for Econ. Devel.*, Mayors Office; **PRIM RE ACT:** Attorney, Regulator, Syndicator, Consultant, Developer, Property Manager, Lender, Owner/Investor; **SERVICES:** Full range of govt. Services incl. tax abatement; **REP CLIENTS:** Gen. Motors, Intl. Harvestor, small bus.; **PREV EMPLOY:** City of S. Bend & Indianapolis C. of C.; **PROFL AFFIL & HONORS:** BA, Indiana State Bar Assoc., CUED; **EDUC:** BS, 1975, Criminal Justice, Indiana Univ.; **GRAD EDUC:** JD, 1979, Law School, IN Univ.; **EDUC HONORS:** Stu Bd. Member, Deans List, 2 semesters of Internship; **OTHER ACT & HONORS:** Chmn., Indpls. Overall Econ. Devel. Comm., Outstanding Young Men 1979; **HOME ADD:** 5833 N. Illinois St., Indianapolis, IN 46208, (317)255-0351; **BUS ADD:** 2521 City Cty. Bldg., Indianapolis, IN 46204, (317)236-3630.

DAVIS, M.G.——**B:** Nov. 11, 1930, Concho Cty, TX, *Atty. at Law*, Collin County Title Co.; **PRIM RE ACT:** Attorney; **OTHER RE ACT:** Pres., Title Ins. Agent; **SERVICES:** Legal service and title ins.; **REP CLIENTS:** Homeowners, builders, suppliers, lenders, realtors, investors; **PREV EMPLOY:** Pres. Dallas Title Co. of Houston; Pres. Guardian Title Co. of Houston; Owner of Security Land Title Co.; V.P. American Title Co. of Dallas; **PROFL AFFIL & HONORS:** Dallas Homebuilders, Dallas Bd. of Realtors, Collin Cty. Bd. of Realtors, State Bar of TX, Dallas News Involved Citizen Award, June 1980; **EDUC:** BBA, 1952, Fin., TX Tech. Univ.; **GRAD EDUC:** JD, 1958, Univ. of TX, School of Law at Austin; **MIL SERV:** USAFR; Retd., Maj.; **OTHER ACT & HONORS:** Sons of the Republic; Pres. Collin Cty. TX Ex. Assn.; State Dir. TX Tech Ex. Students; V.P. TX LTA; **HOME ADD:** 3708 Canoncita Lane, Plano, TX 75023, (214)596-3278; **BUS ADD:** Ste. B, 2129 West Parker Rd., Plano, TX 75074, (214)867-2000.

DAVIS, Monty——**B:** Jan. 4, 1941, NYC, NY, *Co. Bd. of Dir., Pres.*, Envicon Development Corp., Davis Realty Equities, Inc.; **OTHER RE ACT:** Real estate consulting, development and real estate law; **SERVICES:** RE Mgmt. & devel. consulting, and RE law; **REP CLIENTS:** Prin. consultant to the Envicon Grp. of Cos., RE Deve., Mgrs. & synds; **PREV EMPLOY:** VP & Counsel, Chief RE attorney; Bankers Trust Co.; **PROFL AFFIL & HONORS:** ABA, NY State Bar, Assn. of the Bar City of NY; **EDUC:** BA, 1963, Poli. Sci., CCNY; **GRAD EDUC:** JD, 1967, NYU Sch. of Law; **EDUC HONORS:** Phi Beta Kappa Cum Laude, Order of the Coif, Cum Laude, Editor *Law Review*, NYU Sch. of Law; **HOME ADD:** 60 Whippoorwill Lake Rd., Chappaqua, NY 10514, (914)238-5478; **BUS ADD:** Envicon-630 Fifth Ave., Suite 570, NY, NY 10111, (212)581-8818.

DAVIS, Richard H.——*Exec. Dir.*, San Diego Economic Development Corp.; **PRIM RE ACT:** Property Manager; **BUS ADD:** 1200 Third Ave., Ste. 600, San Diego, CA 92101.*

DAVIS, Richard S., Jr.——**B:** June 12, 1946, Nashville, TN, *Partner*, Richard S. Davis Assoc./Berger Realty, Inc.; **PRIM RE ACT:** Broker, Consultant, Developer, Owner/Investor; **SERVICES:** Shopping ctr. devel. & consulting, comml. brokerage; **PROFL AFFIL & HONORS:** ICSC; **EDUC:** BA, 1968, Hist., Middle TN State Univ.; **GRAD EDUC:** MBA, 1972, RE & Fin., GA State Univ.; **EDUC HONORS:** Pi Gamma Mu Honorary; **HOME ADD:** 2822 Lower Roswell Rd., Marietta, GA 30339, (404)971-1894; **BUS ADD:** 1785 The Exchange #150, Atlanta, GA 30339, (404)953-0940.

DAVIS, Richard Watkins——**B:** June 9, 1931, Lebanon, PA, *Partner*, Davis, Katz, Buzgon, Davis & Reed, Ltd.; **PRIM RE ACT:** Attorney, Engineer, Insuror; **OTHER RE ACT:** Agent for Title Insurance Corp. of PA; **SERVICES:** Legal - all phases including litigation; **REP CLIENTS:** Approved atty. for Berks Title Insurance Corp., Conestoga Title Insurance Co., Commonwealth Land Title Insurance Co., Chicago Title Insurance Co., etc.; **PREV EMPLOY:** Westinghouse Electric Corp. 1956-1959, Fourth United States Court of Appeals as law clerk to Judge Boreman 1962-1963; **PROFL AFFIL & HONORS:** Lebanon Cty, PA and ABA, VA State Bar, Lebanon Cty., PA and Nat. Societies of Profl. Engrs., Registered Profl. Engineer in PA, 1962-1963 Law Clerk to Hon. Herbert S. Boreman (4th U.S. Court of Appeals); **EDUC:** BA, BS, 1954, Ind. Engrg., Lehigh Univ., Bethlehem, PA; **GRAD EDUC:** LLB (JD), 1962, Univ. of VA School of Law; **EDUC HONORS:** Cum Laude, Tau Beta Pi, Cum Laude; **MIL SERV:** US Army, 1954-1956, Capt.; **OTHER ACT & HONORS:** VP Lebanon Cty. Bar Assn. 1980-, Bd. of Dirs., Abstracting Co. of Lebanon Cty. and Historic Preservation Trust of Lebanon Cty.; **HOME ADD:** 21 Walden Rd., Lebanon, PA 17042, (717)273-7219; **BUS ADD:** 525 S. Eighth St., PO Box 49, Lebanon, PA 17042, (717)274-1421.

DAVIS, Robert C.——B: Sept. 4, 1944, Rocky Mount, NC, *Partner*, Peat, Marwick, Mitchell & Co.; **OTHER RE ACT:** CPA; **SERVICES:** Tax and acctg.; **PROFL AFFIL & HONORS:** MBAA; **EDUC:** BS, 1966, Bus. Admin./Acctg., Univ. of NC, Chapel Hill; **EDUC HONORS:** Phi Beta Kappa; Beta Gamma Sigma; **HOME ADD:** 8616 Carlynn Dr., Bethesda, MD 20817, (301)229-8826; **BUS ADD:** 1990 K St. N.W., Wash., DC 20006, (202)223-9525.

DAVIS, Robert Lee, Jr.——*Pres.*, Lee Davis & Assoc., Inc.; **PRIM RE ACT:** Broker, Consultant, Developer, Property Manager, Syndicator; **OTHER RE ACT:** Fin. counseling & planning, and placement of term loans for bus.; **PROFL AFFIL & HONORS:** ICSC; **EDUC:** AB, Econ. & Bus., Duke; **GRAD EDUC:** AM, 1925, Vanderbilt; **OTHER ACT & HONORS:** 21 yrs. term officer Reconstruction Fin. Corp., V Chmn. Fin. Bldg. Fin. Comm. of TN Ind. Devel. Comm.; **HOME ADD:** 208 Imperial House Apts., Nashville, TN 37205, (615)383-3804; **BUS ADD:** 20th Fl., L&C Tower, Nashville, TN 37219, (615)244-5224.

DAVIS, Robert T.——B: May 1, 1936, Glen Cove, NY, *Exec. VP*, Eastdil Realty, Inc., Fin. Advisory; **PRIM RE ACT:** Broker, Consultant; **SERVICES:** RE counseling & brokerage; **REP CLIENTS:** Corp., fin. instns., devels., govt., found., indivs.; **PROFL AFFIL & HONORS:** ULI; **EDUC:** BS, 1958, Econ., Univ. of Miami; **MIL SERV:** US Navy, 1958-62, Lt.; **HOME ADD:** 107 Salisbury Ave., Garden City, NY 11530, (516)747-3076; **BUS ADD:** 40 W. 57th St., New York, NY 10019, (212)397-2735.

DAVIS, Roger B., Jr.——B: Feb. 16, 1943, Dayton, OH, *Pres.*, Hasbrouck & Graham, Inc. Realtors; **PRIM RE ACT:** Broker, Syndicator, Consultant, Appraiser, Developer, Property Manager, Owner/Investor; **OTHER RE ACT:** Investment Counseling, Land Dev., Prop. Mgmt., Land & Income Prop. Brokerage; **PROFL AFFIL & HONORS:** CPM, RESSI, RNMI, Realtor of the Year, Realtor best exemplifying Case of Exams, Outstanding Bd. Pres.; **EDUC:** BA, 1966, Eng., Pre-Med, Univ. of VA; **GRAD EDUC:** MBA, 1970, Mktg. and Fin., Daraen School of Bus. Admin., Univ. VA; **EDUC HONORS:** Pres. of Grad. Class, Raven Soc., Student Council, Tilka Hon. Soc.; **OTHER ACT & HONORS:** Pres., Dir. United Way, Dir. VA Student Aide Foundation; **HOME ADD:** 1010 Blue Redoe Rd., Charlottesville, VA 22905; **BUS ADD:** P.O. Box 5384, Charlottesville, VA 22901, (804)293-5102.

DAVIS, Ron——B: June 27, 1945, Dallas, TX, *VP Mktg.*, Gordon D. Browning Inc; **PRIM RE ACT:** Developer, Builder; **SERVICES:** Plan, mkt., & sell homes subdiv. in the –50 to –100,000 w/an annual volume of –48 million; **PROFL AFFIL & HONORS:** Sales & Mktg. Council; SMC Million Dollar Club, Nominated Sales Mgr. of the Yr.; **EDUC:** BBA, 1967, Mktg./Fin., E. TX State Univ.; **GRAD EDUC:** Advance Mgt. Studies, 1979, Mgt., Assertive Training for Mgrs., SMU, Cox School of Bus.; **OTHER ACT & HONORS:** Toast Masters, Charter Member; **HOME ADD:** 2715 N. Spring, Richardson, TX 75081, (214)690-8944; **BUS ADD:** 8515 Greenville Ave, Dallas, TX 75243, (214)341-8091.

DAVIS, Ronald A.——B: July 10, 1949, Rumford, ME, *Second VP, Mort. & Investment RE*, Union Mutual Life Ins. Co.; **PRIM RE ACT:** Lender, Owner/Investor; **SERVICES:** Fin., purch. & joint ventures; **PROFL AFFIL & HONORS:** CPA; **EDUC:** BS, 1971, Acctg., Univ. of ME; **GRAD EDUC:** MBA, 1977, Fin., Harvard Bus. Sch.; **HOME ADD:** 12 Woodland Rd., Gorham, ME 04038; **BUS ADD:** 2211 Congress St., Portland, ME 04122, (207)780-2270.

DAVIS, Russell Lewis——B: Mar. 8, 1903, Rocky Mt., VA, *Atty.-at-Law*, Davis, Davis, Davis & Welch; **PRIM RE ACT:** Attorney; **SERVICES:** RE practice; **REP CLIENTS:** First National Bank of Rocky Mount.; **PREV EMPLOY:** Have been practicing law for 54 years; **PROFL AFFIL & HONORS:** Davis, Davis, Davis & Welch - Atty.-at-Law, Rocky Mt., VA; **EDUC:** Three years at Roanoke Coll., 1920-1923; **GRAD EDUC:** Two years law at Univ. of VA; **OTHER ACT & HONORS:** Member of VA State Legislature for six years; **HOME ADD:** 116 Taliaferro, Rocky Mt., VA 24151, (703)483-5221; **BUS ADD:** 113 E. Court St., Rocky Mt., VA 24151, (703)483-5221.

DAVIS, Stuart——*Exec. Asst.*, Department of Housing and Urban Development, Multifamily Housing Programs; **PRIM RE ACT:** Lender; **BUS ADD:** 451 Seventh St., S.W., Washington, DC 20410, (202)755-6495.*

DAVIS, Thomas S.——B: Apr. 2, 1942, Lamesa, TX, *RE Repres.*, The Northwestern Mutual Life Insurance Co.; **PRIM RE ACT:** Developer, Owner/Investor, Property Manager; **SERVICES:** Prop. mgmt., devel. office indus. and resid.; **PREV EMPLOY:** Touche Ross & Co.; **PROFL AFFIL & HONORS:** AI CPA's, MN Soc. of CPA's, BOMA, NAIOP; **EDUC:** BA, 1968, Acctg. and Bus. Admin., Mankato State Coll.; **MIL SERV:** USMC, Corp.; **HOME ADD:** 15440 Edgewood Ct., Eden Prairie, MN 55344, (612)937-9246; **BUS ADD:** 4940 Viking Dr., Minneapolis, MN 55435, (612)835-4484.

DAVIS, Wallace R.——B: Mar. 21, 1935, Orange, CA, *Atty.*, Cohen Stokke & Davis, Head of Litigation Dept.; **PRIM RE ACT:** Consultant, Attorney, Owner/Investor, Property Manager, Syndicator; **OTHER RE ACT:** Spec. in RE litiation; **SERVICES:** Consultations, litigation, investment counseling; **REP CLIENTS:** Atlantic Richfield, Jess Ranch Corp., Oakridge Ranch & Cattle, U.S. Land & Cattle Corp., G. Wagner (land sales), H. Bruce Hanes (commn. collections); **PROFL AFFIL & HONORS:** CA Bar Assn., Orange Cty. Bar Assn., JD; **EDUC:** BA (Public Admin.), 1960, LBSC; **GRAD EDUC:** JD, 1963, Law, UCLA; **EDUC HONORS:** (upper 1/4); **MIL SERV:** US Army, Pfc. Special Serv.; **OTHER ACT & HONORS:** Candidate - CA Transportation Commn.; Friday Friars; Past Pres. Mexican Amer. Bar Assn. - Listed in *Who's Who in SW Poli.*; **HOME ADD:** 18502 Lincoln Cir., Villa Park, CA 92667; **BUS ADD:** 540 N. Golden Cir. Dr., Santa Ana, CA 92705, (714)835-1205.

DAVIS, W.R.——*Prop. Mgr.*, Florida Rock Industries, Inc.; **PRIM RE ACT:** Property Manager; **BUS ADD:** 155 E. 21st St., Jacksonville, FL 32201, (904)355-1781.*

DAVISON, David J.——B: Oct. 13, 1934, New York, NY, *Partner*, Davison & Company, CPA's; **PRIM RE ACT:** Consultant, Engineer, Owner/Investor; **OTHER RE ACT:** CPA; **SERVICES:** Evaluations, feasibility, fin. and tax planning; **REP CLIENTS:** Synds., lenders, investors, builders, and brokers; **PROFL AFFIL & HONORS:** AICPA, MO Soc. of CPA's, HBA, Cert. of Merit, Indus. Mgmt. Soc., CPA, Registered Profl. Engrg.; **EDUC:** BS, 1956, Indus. Engrg., Wash. Univ. (St. Louis); **GRAD EDUC:** MS/MBA, 1960, Indus. Engrg./Fin., Wash. Univ. (St. Louis); **EDUC HONORS:** Society of the Sigma Xi, Beta Gamma Sigma; **MIL SERV:** US Army (Ordnance Corps), Lt. (1959-60; **OTHER ACT & HONORS:** Officer, C of C; **HOME ADD:** 1703 Cordell Ct., Godfrey, IL 62035, (618)466-8074; **BUS ADD:** 120 Mill St., Bethalto, IL 62010, (618)377-2171.

DAWDA, Edward C.——B: June 7, 1952, Detroit, MI, *Atty.*, Clark, Klein & Beaumont; **PRIM RE ACT:** Attorney; **SERVICES:** Advice, RE sale and purchase of RE including fin. and tax aspects and attendance thereto; **REP CLIENTS:** First Fed. S&L Assn. of Detroit; Ford Motor Credit Co.; Massey-Ferguson, Inc.; J. I. Case Co., McBraw-Edison Co.; **PROFL AFFIL & HONORS:** Profl. affiliations member, Real Prop. Probate and Trust Sect., ABA; Member, Real Prop. Law Sect., State Bar of MI, Tax Aspects of RE Fin., *Who's Who in American Law*; **EDUC:** BA, 1974, Poli. Sci., MI State Univ.; **GRAD EDUC:** JD 1977, Law, Detroit Coll. of Law; **EDUC HONORS:** High Honors, Cum Laude; **BUS ADD:** 1600 First Fed. Bldg., 1001 Woodward Ave., Detroit, MI 48226, (313)962-6492.

DAWKINS, William J.——B: July 25, 1948, Gulfport, MS, *VP, Sec. and Gen. Counsel*, Selig Enterprises, Inc.; **PRIM RE ACT:** Broker, Attorney, Owner/Investor; **OTHER RE ACT:** Author; **PROFL AFFIL & HONORS:** RE Sect. of the Atlanta Bar Assn.; State Bar of GA; Amer. Bar Assn., Designated RE Law Specialist, State Bar of GA; **EDUC:** BA, 1970, FL State Univ.; **GRAD EDUC:** JD, 1974, The Emory Univ. School of Law; **OTHER ACT & HONORS:** Advisor, GA Gen. Assembly regarding Landlord/Tenant Law; Lecturer, Real Prop. Law Sect. of the State Bar of GA and Apt. Owners and Mgrs. Assn.; Television panelist, RE topics, Atlanta Bar Assn.; Author, Landlord and Tenant Series volumes *Breach and Remedies and Lease Forms and Clauses, The Law in GA*, published by The Harrison Co., 1979, and *Lease-Related Forms, The Law in GA*, published by The Harrison Co., 1980; **HOME ADD:** 2912 Blackwood Rd., Decatur, GA 30033, (404)633-6918; **BUS ADD:** Suite 550, 1100 Spring St., N.W., Atlanta, GA 30367, (404)876-5511.

DAWSON, G. C.——B: Dec. 3, 1922, Nokomis, VA, *Owner*, G.C. Dawson Real Estate; **PRIM RE ACT:** Broker, Appraiser, Developer; **MIL SERV:** USN, 2nd Class Gunners Mate; **OTHER ACT & HONORS:** Pres. of N. Neck Bd. of Realtors (2 yrs.); **HOME ADD:** White Stone, VA 22578, (804)435-1267; **BUS ADD:** PO Box 339, Kilmarnock, VA 22482, (804)435-3166.

DAWSON, John H., Jr.——B: Jan. 31, 1934, Rockville, MD, *Atty.*, Private Practice; **PRIM RE ACT:** Attorney; **SERVICES:** RE Conveyancing; **PREV EMPLOY:** Suburban Title & Investment Corp., (Successor to Chelsea Title & Guaranty Co.); Dist.-Realty Title Ins. Corp.; **PROFL AFFIL & HONORS:** ABA, MD State Bar Assn.; **EDUC:** BA, 1957, Govt. & Hist., CAS Amer. Univ.; **GRAD EDUC:** LLB, 1958, Law, Washington Coll. of Law of Amer. Univ.; **EDUC HONORS:** *Who's Who in Amer. Coll. & Univ.*, Editor of the Law Review; **MIL SERV:** US Army; Sp4; **HOME ADD:** 19111 Canadian Court, Gaithersburg, MD 20879, (301)869-2446.

DAY, Bennie R.——**B:** Nov. 11, 1939, Lynch, KY, *Exec. Dir.*, Foley Housing Authority; **PRIM RE ACT:** Broker, Regulator, Owner/Investor, Property Manager; **SERVICES:** Public Housing; **PREV EMPLOY:** RE Broker; Sun Ctry. Realty 1978-1980; Pres., Day Enterprises, Inc. 1969-1978; **PROFL AFFIL & HONORS:** IREM; ARM; APHADA; Nat. Assn. of Housing and Redevel. Officials; VP of Foley Local Devel. Cos.; Member of Community Housing Resource Bd., PHM; IREM ARM; RE Broker; **EDUC:** BS, 1976, Bus. Mgmt. and Admin., IN Univ.; **HOME ADD:** 205 W Pedigo Ave., Foley, AL 36535, (205)943-5981; **BUS ADD:** 302 Fourth Ave., Foley, AL 36535, (205)943-3901.

DAY, Christian C.——**B:** Jan. 22, 1946, Rochester, NY, *Asst. Prof. Legal Studies*, The Wharton Sch., Univ. of PA; **PRIM RE ACT:** Consultant, Attorney, Instructor; **SERVICES:** Ltd. consulting; **PREV EMPLOY:** Morgan, Lewis & Bockius, Philadelphia, PA, 1970-74; **PROFL AFFIL & HONORS:** ABA, Philadelphia Bar Assn.; Am. Bus. Law Assn.; **EDUC:** BA, 1967, Govt., Eng., Cornell Univ.; **GRAD EDUC:** JD, 1970, NY Univ. Sch. of Law; **EDUC HONORS:** Law Review, Dean's List; **MIL SERV:** USAR (MI), Capt., 1967-75; **OTHER ACT & HONORS:** Cornell Club of Philadelphia, Dir. 1972 to present; **HOME ADD:** 216 N Aberdeen Ave., Wayne, PA 19087, (215)658-5970; **BUS ADD:** 816 Centenary Hall, The Wharton Sch., Univ. of PA, Philadelphia, PA 19104, (215)243-5401.

DAY, Fairfield P., Jr.——**B:** Mar. 18, 1939, Short Hills, NJ, *Pres.*, Mobil Land Devel. (Texas) Corp.; **PRIM RE ACT:** Developer, Owner/Investor; **PREV EMPLOY:** VP, Joseph P. Day Realty, Inc.; **PROFL AFFIL & HONORS:** ULI, Home & Apt. Builders Assn., Nat. Assn. of Home Builders, TX Indus. Devel. Commn., Dallas Area Indus. Devel. Assn.; **EDUC:** BS, 1969, Bus. Mgmt., Fairleigh Dickinson Univ.; **EDUC HONORS:** Phi Omega Epsilon, Wall Street Journal Award; **MIL SERV:** US Army, Lt.; **OTHER ACT & HONORS:** Leadership Dallas Advisory Bd.; Dir., Dallas Cty. Community Coll. Dist. Foundn., Inc.,; Dir. Dallas Grand Opera Assn.; Dir. and VP, Dallas SPCA; Pres., TX Amateur Hockey Assn.; Dir. and Pres., Dallas Jr. Hockey Assn.; Dir., Dallas Theatre Center; Corp. Comm., Dallas Museum of Fine Arts; **HOME ADD:** 7325 Baxtershire Dr., Dallas, TX 75230, (214)368-4138; **BUS ADD:** PO Box 900, Dallas, TX 75221, (214)658-3262.

DAY, Robert M.——**B:** Feb. 8, 1952, Chicago, IL, *Mgr. Appraisal/Consulting Div.*, Merrill Lynch Realty, Appraiser/Consultant; **PRIM RE ACT:** Consultant, Appraiser; **SERVICES:** Valuation/consultation on all types of prop.; **REP CLIENTS:** Banks, Developers, Attys., etc.; **PROFL AFFIL & HONORS:** Nat. Assn. of Realtors; GA Assn. of Realtors, Atlanta Bd. of Realtors, Mtg. Bankers of GA; Soc. of RE Appraisers; AIREA, MAI, SRA; **EDUC:** 1974, RE, GA State Univ.; **HOME ADD:** 806 Wellesley Dr., Atlanta, GA 30305, (404)351-3954; **BUS ADD:** 233 Peachtree St., Suite 300, Atlanta, GA 30303, (404)658-5252.

DAZE, Douglas Edward——**B:** June 27, 1954, Jacksonville, FL, *Atty.*; **PRIM RE ACT:** Consultant, Attorney; **SERVICES:** Legal representation in all phases of real prop. devel., investment analysis and counseling; **PREV EMPLOY:** Staff Atty., FL Indus. Relations Commn.; **PROFL AFFIL & HONORS:** The FL Bar, ABA (Real Prop., Probate and Trust Sect.), Assn. of Trial Lawyers of Amer., Academy of FL Trial Lawyers; **EDUC:** AB, 1976, English, Univ. of GA; **GRAD EDUC:** JD, 1979, Law, FL State Univ., Coll. of Law; **EDUC HONORS:** Delta Omicron Tau Honor Soc., Cum Laude, Defender/Advocate Soc., with Honors; **BUS ADD:** 909 Garden Plaza, Orlando, FL 32803, (305)894-7114.

DEAL, Frank——*Fac. Serv. Mgr.*, National Semiconductor Corp.; **PRIM RE ACT:** Property Manager; **BUS ADD:** 2900 Semiconductor Dr., Santa Clara, CA 95051, (408)737-5000.*

DEAL, Robert J.——**B:** Dec. 7, 1941, Niagara Falls, NY, *Broker, Co-owner*, Brookside Realty, Inc.; **PRIM RE ACT:** Broker, Owner/Investor; **SERVICES:** RE Brokerage, investment, reloc. services; **REP CLIENTS:** Frito-Lay; Hewlett Packard; Burlington No.; VanRelco; Transamer.; etc.; **PROFL AFFIL & HONORS:** GRI, CRS, CRB, 1981 VP, WA CRS Chap.; 1982 President, Wa CRS Chap.; **EDUC:** RE, Clark Coll.; **EDUC HONORS:** Certificate in R.E., state of WA VIA Clark Coll.; **MIL SERV:** USN, E-5.; **OTHER ACT & HONORS:** Comml. pilot w/flight instr. & instrument ratings.; **HOME ADD:** 8511 N. E. 71st St., Vancouver, WA 98662, (206)892-8727; **BUS ADD:** 7301 N.E. Hwy 99, Vancouver, WA 98665, (206)699-4835.

DEAN, Howard M., Jr.——*Pres.*, Dean Foods; **PRIM RE ACT:** Property Manager; **BUS ADD:** 3600 North River Rd., Franklin Park, IL 60131, (312)625-6200.*

DEAN, Lawrence W.——**B:** Dec. 3, 1943, Wichita, KS, *Dev. Mgr.*, Great Plains Ventures, Inc., Great Plains Bus. Park; **PRIM RE ACT:** Broker, Syndicator, Consultant, Developer, Property Manager, Owner/Investor; **SERVICES:** Turnkey Build-To-Suit Lease or Purchase Indus., Also, Consultation on Indus. Revenue Bonds; **REP CLIENTS:** Manufacturers and Warehousers Needing Rail Siding; **PREV EMPLOY:** Owner of Apt. Finders Intl., Inc.; Part. in Prop. Mgmt. Firm; Const. Mgr. For Indus. Bldg.; **PROFL AFFIL & HONORS:** GRI; **EDUC:** BBA, 1966, Mgmt., Mktg., Engineering, Wichita State Univ.; **GRAD EDUC:** MBA, 1967, Mgmt., Mktg., Univ. of AZ; **EDUC HONORS:** Walter H. Beech Scholarship in Aeronautical Engineering; Dean's Hon. List, Grad. Scholarship; **OTHER ACT & HONORS:** Pres. Wichita Jaycees; Pres. - Wichita Assn. for Mgmt. Dev.; Bd. - Camp Fire Girls; Dist. Chief- Beta Theta Pi; **HOME ADD:** 9312 Briarwood Ct., Wichita, KS 67212, (316)722-2787; **BUS ADD:** 1711 Longfellow Ln., Wichita, KS 67207, (316)686-7361.

DEAN, Melvin——**B:** Feb. 20, 1952, CA, *Owner*, Dean Investment; **PRIM RE ACT:** Developer, Builder, Owner/Investor; **HOME ADD:** 607 E 4th St., Bakersfield, CA 93307, (805)324-2480; **BUS ADD:** 607 E 4th St., Bakersfield, CA 93307, (805)335-9020.

DEAN, Michael A.——**B:** Jan. 16, 1942, San Diego, CA, *Atty. At Law*, Wendel, Lawlor, Rosen & Black; **PRIM RE ACT:** Attorney; **REP CLIENTS:** Davidson & Licht Jewelry Co.; Quik Stop Mkts.; BankAmerica Realty Investors; Eastmont Mall Shopping Ctr.; Transpacific Devel. Co.; Lutheran Brotherhood; **PROFL AFFIL & HONORS:** Member: Intl. Council of Shopping Ctrs.; Nat. Assn. of Office And Indus. Parks; State Bar of CA (member Exec. Bd., Real Prop. Section); **EDUC:** BA, 1964, Social Sci., San Jose State Coll.; **GRAD EDUC:** JD, 1967, Law, Boalt Hall School of Law, Univ. CA; **OTHER ACT & HONORS:** Commnr., Community Devel. Advisory Commn., City of Oakland; Co-author, Comml. Real Prop. Lease Practice; CA Continuing Edu. of the Bar 1974; 1981 Supplement; **HOME ADD:** 5440 Fernhoff Rd., Oakland, CA 94619, (415)530-8377; **BUS ADD:** 20th Fl., Clorox Bldg., Oakland City Ctr., PO Box 2047, Oakland, CA 94604, (415)834-6600.

DEAN, Tod——**B:** Feb. 26, 1939, Chicago, IL, *Sales Agent*, Great City Realtors; **PRIM RE ACT:** Syndicator, Property Manager; **OTHER RE ACT:** Sales; **PROFL AFFIL & HONORS:** S.F. Bd. of Realtors, CA Assn. of Rates, NAR; **EDUC:** BA, 1961, Intl. Econ., Univ. of WI; **GRAD EDUC:** MA, 1971, Soc. Psych., Boston Univ.; **EDUC HONORS:** Dean's List, Teaching Fellowship 1969-71; **MIL SERV:** USN, Lt.; **HOME ADD:** 224a Noe St., San Francisco, CA 94114; **BUS ADD:** 1764 Haight St., San Francisco, CA 94117, (415)751-0737.

DEANER, Charles W.——**B:** Nov. 16, 1922, Erie, PA, *Sr. Partner*, Deaner & Deaner; **PRIM RE ACT:** Attorney; **REP CLIENTS:** Title Insurance and Trust Co.; MN Title; Safeco Title; Margaretten Mort. Co.; Sherwood & Roberts; Security Pacific Mort. Co.; Lomas & Nettleton; **PROFL AFFIL & HONORS:** State Bar of NV, ABA, Amer. Coll. of RE Lawyers, Pres. of NV State Bar 1980-81; **EDUC:** BA, 1948, Amer. Hist., Gannon Univ.; **GRAD EDUC:** JD, 1951, Syracuse Coll. of Law; **MIL SERV:** USAF; Sgt.; **HOME ADD:** 1208 Westlund, Las Vegas, NV 89102, (702)878-8700; **BUS ADD:** 300 S. Fourth St. 600, Las Vegas, NV 89101, (702)382-6911.

DE ARIAS, Louis C.——**B:** Jan. 9, 1954, Cuba, *VP Fin.*, CHG International Inc.; **PRIM RE ACT:** Developer, Builder, Property Manager, Syndicator; **SERVICES:** Joint venture negotiations, devel. of comml. and resid. props.; **REP CLIENTS:** Cadillac Fairview, Carma Developers, Marathon Realties; **PREV EMPLOY:** Price Waterhouse & Co., 1973-1977; **PROFL AFFIL & HONORS:** Seattle Master Builders Assn., Amer. Inst. of Spanish Speaking CPA's, AICPA; **EDUC:** BA, 1975, Acctg., Univ. of WA; **EDUC HONORS:** Magna Cum Laude; **HOME ADD:** 30717 5th Pl. S., Federal Way, WA 98003, (206)941-7377; **BUS ADD:** 200 S. 333rd, Federal Way, WA 98003, (206)838-1200.

DEARING, G.C.——**B:** May 29, 1920, Wynne, AR, *Independent Fee, Appraiser*, G.C. Dearing Appraisal Services; **PRIM RE ACT:** Appraiser; **SERVICES:** RE Appraisals all types; **REP CLIENTS:** Banks, law firms, corps., s&l's private indivs.; **PREV EMPLOY:** I have been an Appraiser for the past 16 yrs. Prior to this I was involved in const. heavy, ind. comm. & lt. res.; **PROFL AFFIL & HONORS:** N.A.I.F.A.; Assoc. of Cert. Appraisers Intl.; Inst. of Valuers, Member of Governmental Appraisers Assn., IFA; C.A.S.; S.C.V.; **GRAD EDUC:** Have completed many courses, Sponsored by AIREA, SREA, NAIFA and others; **HOME ADD:** 10 Shannon Dr., Wynne, AR; **BUS ADD:** 10 Shannon Dr., 363 E. Union Ave., Wynne, AR 72396, (501)238-2427.

DEARMORE, Roy F.——**B:** Nov. 9, 1934, TX; **PRIM RE ACT:** Owner/Investor; **EDUC:** BS, 1958, TX Wesleyan, Fort Worth, TX; **GRAD EDUC:** MD, 1958, Univ. of TX; MPH, 1960, Tulane Univ.;

MIL SERV: USPHS, Asst. Surg.; **HOME ADD:** PO Box 40639, Garland, TX 75040; **BUS ADD:** PO Box 40639, Garland, TX 75040.

DEARNER, R. Milton——*VP Engr.*, National Steel Corp.; **PRIM RE ACT:** Property Manager; **BUS ADD:** 2800 Grant Bldg., Pittsburgh, PA 15219, (412)263-4100.*

DEASON, Marshall C., Jr.——**B:** Jan. 19, 1947, Takoma Park, MD, *Of Counsel*, Diecidue, Ferlita, Prieto and Nutter, P.A.; **PRIM RE ACT:** Attorney; **PREV EMPLOY:** VP/Gen. Coun., Cheezem Devel. Corp., 1979-81; Pres., Coastal Title Co., 1979-81; US Dept. HUD, 1972-1974; **PROFL AFFIL & HONORS:** ABA; FL Bar; Md Bar; MD Bar; Am. Soc. of Intl. Law; **EDUC:** BA, 1968, Hist., Denison Univ.; **GRAD EDUC:** JD, 1972, Law, Cumberland School of Law, Samford Univ.; **EDUC HONORS:** Cum Laude, Exec. Editor, Law Review; **OTHER ACT & HONORS:** Bd. of Dir., FL Lung Assn.; **HOME ADD:** 13859 Feather Sound Drive, Clearwater, FL 33520, (813)576-3782; **BUS ADD:** 612 Horatio St., Tampa, FL 33606, (813)251-0124.

DEATHERAGE, Gerald H.——**B:** June 26, 1935, Sanders, KY, *Developer*; **PRIM RE ACT:** Developer, Owner/Investor; **OTHER RE ACT:** Rental Housing; **SERVICES:** Devel. of Resid. Lots, Leasor of Office Space; **REP CLIENTS:** Indiv., Comml., Bus., Profls.; **PREV EMPLOY:** Dir. of Food Distr., KY Dept. of Agriculture; **EDUC:** BS, 1957, Agri., Univ. of KY; **MIL SERV:** US Army, Pvt.; **HOME ADD:** 1015 Highland Ave, Carrollton, KY 41008, (502)732-5122; **BUS ADD:** 601 Sycamore St., Box 364, Carrollton, KY 41008, (502)732-5750.

DEBENEDETTO, Anthony J.——**B:** Nov. 14, 1936, San Jose, CA, *Branch Mgr.*, Lomas and Nettleton Co.; **PRIM RE ACT:** Broker, Lender; **SERVICES:** RE Loans of all types; **PROFL AFFIL & HONORS:** CMBA; MBA; Fresno Bd. of Realtors; **EDUC:** RE, CA State Univ. of Fresno; **EDUC HONORS:** Award; **MIL SERV:** CA Air NG/T/Sgt.; **HOME ADD:** 1502 E Calimyrna, Fresno, CA 93710, (209)439-0412; **BUS ADD:** 135 W Shaw, Suite 106, Fresno, CA 93704, (209)226-2881.

DEBUSK, Edith——**B:** Apr. 12, 1912, Waco, TX, *Owner*, Edith DeBusk, Atty. at Law; **PRIM RE ACT:** Attorney, Owner/Investor; **PROFL AFFIL & HONORS:** TX Bar Assn., ABA Sects. on Real Prop., Amer. Judicature Soc., Intl Legal Soc., Past Gov. of Dist. 9, Past Pres. Altrusa Intl Inc.; **GRAD EDUC:** Cert. in Law, So. Methodist Univ.; **EDUC HONORS:** Magna Cum Laude; **OTHER ACT & HONORS:** Comm. Council of Dallas, TX Soc on Aging, United Cerebal Palsy Assn., Citizens Traffic Comm. of Dallas, Women's Council of Dallas Cty.; **HOME ADD:** 7365 Elmridge Dr., Dallas, TX; **BUS ADD:** 777 S Central Expwy, Ste. 7-P, Richardson, TX 75080.

DECESARIS, Domenic F.——**B:** Mar. 7, 1940, Philadelhpia, PA, *Sr. VP*, Central Mortgage Co.; **PRIM RE ACT:** Broker, Banker, Lender; **SERVICES:** Interim and long-term mort. fin.; **PREV EMPLOY:** Fidelity Bond & Mort. Co. 1958-1970; **PROFL AFFIL & HONORS:** Delaware Cty. Bd. of Realtors; Mort. Bankers Assn.; Home Bldrs. Assn. of SE PA; Past Chmn. Exec. Assoc. Council HBA of Philadelphia; Lic. PA RE Broker; Lic. PA Fire Ins. Agent; **EDUC:** BA, 1971, Econ., LaSalle Coll.; **EDUC HONORS:** Cum Laude; **OTHER ACT & HONORS:** Member: Unico Nat.; Hold Cert. of Registered Apt. Mgr. sponsored by the Nat. Assn. of Home Bldrs; Hold designation as Cert. Mort. Banker sponsored by the MBA of Amer; approved as Level 1 Underwriter by Fed. Nat. Mort. Assn.; received designation as Fee Inspector by US Dept. of Housing and Urban Devel.; **HOME ADD:** 246 Gibbons Rd., Springfield, PA 19064, (215)328-6450; **BUS ADD:** 1700 Market St., Philadelphia, PA 19103, (215)496-4441.

DE CHADENEDES, Guy B.——**B:** Sept. 2, 1929, Flushing, NY, *Owner*, The de Chadenedes Co.; **PRIM RE ACT:** Broker, Developer, Builder, Owner/Investor; **SERVICES:** Listing, selling and managing prop. for local & overseas clients; **PREV EMPLOY:** Surveying, insp., consultation, advising on rehab. of war-ravaged areas with Dept. of Def.; **PROFL AFFIL & HONORS:** Bd. of Realtors, NAR, Assn. of Realtors, CRS; **EDUC:** BS-Agr., 1951, Eng., Cornell Univ.; **MIL SERV:** US Army 1951-1971, Lt. Col., Meritorious Achievement Med., Bronze Star Med., Army Commendation Med..; **OTHER ACT & HONORS:** Optimist Intl. - Past Lt. Gov., Pres. Elect of Local Club; **HOME ADD:** 948 Allegheny Drive, Colorado Springs, CO 80919, (303)598-7183; **BUS ADD:** 5520 N. Union Blvd, Colorado Springs, CO 80918, (303)593-8888.

DECIMA, Jay P.——**B:** May 17, 1934, Cheyenne, WY, *Gen. Mgr.*, JMK Traders; **PRIM RE ACT:** Consultant, Developer, Owner/Investor, Real Estate Publisher; **OTHER RE ACT:** Owner, Landlord Consultant, Advisor, Tax Specialist; **SERVICES:** Landlord Property Managment, Owner, Tax Shelter; **REP CLIENTS:** Developer Rehab Specialist, Private Indivs. high income who require shelter plus management; **EDUC:** Trade, 2 yrs. Jr. Coll.; **MIL SERV:** US Army, Sgt.; **OTHER ACT & HONORS:** Own and Operate 120 Homes and Residential Rentals; **HOME ADD:** PO Box 3051, Redding, CA 96099; **BUS ADD:** PO Box 3039, Redding, CA 96049.

DECKER, Quentin M.——**B:** Sept. 11, 1936, Huron, SD, *Exec. Inv. Mgr.*, Monetary Investment Co.; **PRIM RE ACT:** Broker, Owner/Investor; **SERVICES:** Services to Banks and Savings Institutions (Courtesy Deposits); **REP CLIENTS:** Banks and Savings Instns.; **PROFL AFFIL & HONORS:** NAFCO, ISF, CRA, FMS, AFA, AAii, AEA, CRA (Sr. Member); **EDUC:** 3 yrs. coll.; **MIL SERV:** Army, 2 yrs., Spl. 4; **HOME ADD:** 1959 West 33rd St., Sioux Falls, SD 57105, (605)334-6462; **BUS ADD:** P.O. Box 1273, Sioux Falls, SD 57101, (605)334-3417.

DECKER, Roland A.——*Air Products & Chemicals, Inc.*; **PRIM RE ACT:** Property Manager; **BUS ADD:** PO Box 538, Allentown, PA 18105, (215)481-4511.*

DECKER, Ronald O.——**B:** Oct. 21, 1932, Weston, WV, *Dir., Corp. RE*, Air Products and Chemicals, Inc.; **OTHER RE ACT:** Corp. RE Dept.; **PREV EMPLOY:** Mgr., RE, Stewart-Warner Corp., 1972-1974, Atty., NY Central RR, 1959-1965, Consultant, The Fantus Co. - 1965-1971, Counsel, Inst. of Gas Technology, 1974-77; Gen. Counsel, Gas Research Inst., 1977-1980; **PROFL AFFIL & HONORS:** Indus. Devel. Research Council, ABA, IL State Bar Assn., Fed. Energy Bar Assn., Amer. Gas. Assn., Admitted to IL bar, 1959; **EDUC:** BA, 1955, Swarthmore Coll.; **GRAD EDUC:** JD, 1959, Univ. of Chicago Law School; **OTHER ACT & HONORS:** Dir., Chicago Council on Foreign Relations, 1965-71; Dir., Chicago Map Soc., 1978-80; Dir., Lehigh Cty. Hist. Soc.; **HOME ADD:** 2031 Greenwood Rd., Allentown, PA 18103; **BUS ADD:** P O Box 538, Allentown, PA 18105, (215)481-8977.

DECKER, Victor A., III——**B:** Sept. 1, 1935, Hawley, PA, *Atty.*; **PRIM RE ACT:** Attorney; **SERVICES:** Title work, closings; **REP CLIENTS:** First State Bank, Citizens Savings Assn.; **EDUC:** AB, 1957, Psych., Princeton Univ.; **GRAD EDUC:** JD, 1960, Yale Univ.; **HOME ADD:** 1719 Main St., Honesdale, PA 18431, (717)253-3913; **BUS ADD:** 300 Keystone St., Hawley, PA 18428, (717)226-4581.

DEEB, Edward——**B:** May 28, 1927, Lebanon, *Pres.*, Deeb Investments Inc.; **PRIM RE ACT:** Broker, Developer, Builder, Owner/Investor, Property Manager; **SERVICES:** Devel. mgmt. and develop.; **REP CLIENTS:** Profls. & businessmen in comml. and condos.; **PROFL AFFIL & HONORS:** SFV Bd. of Realtors, Realtor; **EDUC:** BA, 1950, Psych., UCLA; **GRAD EDUC:** MA, 1951, Psych., Univ. of OR; **MIL SERV:** Army, Sgt.; **OTHER ACT & HONORS:** Past Lt. Gov. Kiwanis, Bd. of Govs., YMCA; **BUS ADD:** 10700 Burbank Blvd., N. Hollywood, CA 91601, (213)984-2484.

DEEN, Bill W.——**B:** Oct. 26, 1952, Shreveport, LA, *Appraiser*, Deen RE Appraising & Consultants; **PRIM RE ACT:** Appraiser; **SERVICES:** Single family RE appraising; **REP CLIENTS:** Equitable Relocation Service; Home Equity; Merrill Lynch; Numerous Mort. Cos.; S&Ls; **PROFL AFFIL & HONORS:** Sr. Member of SREA, Pres., Shreveport Chap. of SREA; **EDUC:** BS, 1975, Bldg. Const., NE LA Univ.; **OTHER ACT & HONORS:** Benevolent and Protective Order of Elks; **HOME ADD:** 4822 Longstreet Pl., Bossier City, LA 7112, (318)742-0619; **BUS ADD:** POB 5627, Shreveport, LA 71105, (318)868-5968.

DEEN, Curtis M.——**B:** Oct. 24, 1946, Memphis, TN, *Asst. VP of Prop. Mgmt.*, Elkington & Keltner Mgmt., Inc., Prop. Mgmt.; **PRIM RE ACT:** Property Manager; **PROFL AFFIL & HONORS:** Exec. Comm. Memphis Chap. of IREM, CPM; **EDUC:** BS, 1969, Tech., Memphis State Univ.; **GRAD EDUC:** MS, Tech. engrg., Memphis State Univ.; **HOME ADD:** 1050 Kernstown Cir., Collierville, TN 38017, (901)853-4527; **BUS ADD:** 564 Colonial, Memphis, TN 38117, (901)767-4290.

DEEN, James——**B:** June 10, 1947, Miami, FL, *Pres.*, James Deen AIA Arch., Planner & Assocs. Inc.; **PRIM RE ACT:** Consultant, Architect, Developer, Owner/Investor; **OTHER RE ACT:** Planner; **SERVICES:** Design & devel. high density resid. communities; **REP CLIENTS:** Investors and devels. of comml. & resid. props; **PROFL AFFIL & HONORS:** ULI, AIA, Amer. Planning Assn.; **EDUC:** BArch, 1950, Arch., Univ. of FL; **EDUC HONORS:** Highest Honors, **HOME ADD:** 3 Grove Isle, Miami, FL 33143, (305)856-6996; **BUS ADD:** 7500 Red Rd., S Miami, FL 33143, (305)661-5121.

DEESE, Larry Keith——**B:** Dec. 29, 1946, Charlotte, NC, *Rgnl. Planning Dir.*, Post, Buckley, Schuh & Jernigan, Inc.; **PRIM RE ACT:** Consultant; **OTHER RE ACT:** Landscape Arch.; **SERVICES:** Planning, engrg., construction mgmt.; **REP CLIENTS:** US Home Corp., The Calibre Cos., Bessemer Props.; **PROFL AFFIL & HONORS:** Amer. Soc. of Landscape Arch., ULI, Amer. Planning Assn., ASLA; **EDUC:** Bach. Landscape Arch., 1971, NC State Univ.;

HOME ADD: 1186 Lake Colony Dr., Marietta, GA 30067, (404)992-6635; **BUS ADD:** 3715 Northside Pkwy., Suite 606-100 Northcreek, Atlanta, GA 30327, (404)261-2360.

DEESE, Robert E.——**B:** May 3, 1934, Chicago Heights, IL, *VP*, Metro Prop. Mgmt. Co.; **PRIM RE ACT:** Broker, Developer, Builder, Property Manager; **SERVICES:** All leasing for project, coordinate remodeling, design, new const.; **REP CLIENTS:** One-half of 190 tenants listed in Fortune 1000; **PREV EMPLOY:** Pemtom-Home Builder 1969-1972; **PROFL AFFIL & HONORS:** IREM, CPM; **EDUC:** BA, 1961, Econ., Univ. of WA; **MIL SERV:** US Army, Cpl.; **OTHER ACT & HONORS:** C of C; **HOME ADD:** 1865 Meadowview Rd., Bloomington, MN 55420, (612)854-1978; **BUS ADD:** 7850 Metro Pkwy. Suite #211, Minneapolis, MN 55420, (612)854-8500.

DEFANO, Bernard M.——**B:** Dec. 1, 1927, Chicago, IL, *RE Mgr., MW Terr.*, Sears Roebuck & Co., Handle 13, MW States; **PRIM RE ACT:** Consultant, Appraiser, Builder, Property Manager, Engineer; **PREV EMPLOY:** 37 yrs with Sears, 1955 to 1967 Elect Eng., 1968 to 1977 Const. Mgr. MW Terr., 1977 to 1980 Facilities Planning Mgr., 1980 to New RE Mgrs.; **GRAD EDUC:** BA/EE, 1955, Chicago Tech.; **MIL SERV:** USAF, Sgt., 1945-46; **OTHER ACT & HONORS:** ICSC; **HOME ADD:** 1602 Cedar Ln, Mt. Prospect, IL 60056; **BUS ADD:** 7447 Skokie Blvd., Skokie, IL 60077, (312)967-3232.

DEFAZIO, Dominic——**B:** July 10, 1938, New Britain, CT, *Exec. VP*, The Sierra Grizzly Corporation; **PRIM RE ACT:** Broker, Developer, Owner/Investor, Syndicator; **SERVICES:** Locate, devel., buy sell or synd. investment props.; **REP CLIENTS:** Own company and selected clients; **EDUC:** BS, 1963, Mktg. & Merchandising, Univ. of Hartford; **MIL SERV:** USMC.; **HOME ADD:** 714 Cross Ave., Los Angeles, CA 90065; **BUS ADD:** 294 St. Albans Ave., South Pasadena, CA 91030, (213)792-3551.

DEFINE, William T.——**B:** July 23, 1941, Baltimore, MD, *Partner*, Miles & Stockbridge; **PRIM RE ACT:** Attorney; **SERVICES:** Lender & borrower representation, comml. RE transactions; **REP CLIENTS:** MD Nat. Bank, Union Trust Co. of MD, Citicorp RE, Inc.; **PROFL AFFIL & HONORS:** ABA - Real Prop. & Bus. Assn. Sections; State & Local Bar Assn.; Corp., Banking & Bus. Sect., Council of MD State Bar Assn.; **EDUC:** BA, 1963, Pol. Sci., Loyola Coll.; **GRAD EDUC:** JD, 1966, Villanova Univ. School of Law; **EDUC HONORS:** Magna Cum Laude, Order of Coif, Law Review; **MIL SERV:** Army Artillery, Capt.; **HOME ADD:** 4300 Conifer Court, Glen Arm, MD 21057, (301)668-6787; **BUS ADD:** 10 Light St., Baltimore, MD 21202, (301)727-6464.

DEFOYD, W.L. (Bob)——**B:** Feb. 20, 1936, Frederick, OK, *Pres.-Owner*, East Texas Development, Indian Creek Lodge, Pawnee's Wind Point Park, Defoyd Investments, W.L.Defoyd Insurance Agency, Inc.; **PRIM RE ACT:** Broker, Consultant, Developer, Builder, Owner/Investor, Property Manager, Insuror, Syndicator; **PROFL AFFIL & HONORS:** Amer. Land Devel. Assn.; TX RE Assn.; TX Apt. Assn.; Piney Woods Apt. Assn.; Nat. Federation of Independent Bus.; Amer. Water Works Assn.; Nat. Apt. Assn.; TX Independent Agent's Assn.; **EDUC:** Univ. of Houston: G.B.A.; **MIL SERV:** USN; F 1st; **HOME ADD:** 1516 Copeland Dr., Lufkin, TX 75901, (713)632-5238; **BUS ADD:** 3110 S. 1st., P O Box 1298, Lufkin, TX 75901, (713)639-4451.

DEFRANCE, William P.——**B:** Jan. 24, 1926, Elizabeth, NJ, *Owner*, Accent Realty Co.; **PRIM RE ACT:** Broker, Consultant; **OTHER RE ACT:** Money Broker; **SERVICES:** Complete design of sales environment for new communities; **REP CLIENTS:** U.S. Home; Levitt Homes Florida; Sanzari Ent.; Muss Developers; Pizzo & Pizzo; Builders of new communities, lenders, investors; **PROFL AFFIL & HONORS:** NJ Comm. Inv. Div., GRI; **MIL SERV:** Navy Air Corps, ARM 3/C, 1944-1946; **OTHER ACT & HONORS:** Optimist Club of S PLfd., Charter Member, Past Pres.; Amer. Academy of Aerospace Educ., Founding Father, Charter Member, Present VP; **HOME ADD:** 137 Kenwood Ave., S Plainfield, NJ 07080, (201)755-5597; **BUS ADD:** 1305 Roller Rd., Ocean, NJ 07712, (201)493-3777.

DEFRANCEAUX, George W.——**B:** Mar. 12, 1913, Wash., DC, *Chmn.*, National Corp. for Housing Partnerships; **PRIM RE ACT:** Developer, Lender, Builder, Property Manager; **OTHER RE ACT:** We purchase equities & joint venture with builders and/or devels.; **PROFL AFFIL & HONORS:** Home Builders Assn.; Mortg. Bankers Assn.; NAR; **OTHER ACT & HONORS:** Chmn. of DRG Fin. Corp. & DeFranceaux Realty Grp.; **HOME ADD:** 4343 Westover Pl., NW, Washington, DC 20016, (202)244-4901; **BUS ADD:** 1133 15th St., NW, Washington, DC 20005, (202)857-5710.

DEFREN, Burton——*Ed.*, Inst. for Business Planning, Inc., Real Estate Investment Planning; **PRIM RE ACT:** Real Estate Publisher; **BUS ADD:** U.S. Hgway 9, Englewood Cliffs, NJ 07632, (201)592-2040.*

DEGEORGE, James B.——**B:** Jan. 21, 1932, Houston, TX, *Owner*, J.B. DeGeorge Interests; **PRIM RE ACT:** Developer, Owner/Investor, Property Manager; **EDUC:** RE & Gen. Bus., Univ. of TX, Univ. of Houston; **MIL SERV:** Marine Corps., Cpl. 1950-51; **OTHER ACT & HONORS:** Intl. Wine & Food Soc. (Past Pres.); Knights of the Vine (Treas.); Les Amis De Escoffier (Bd. of Dir.); **HOME ADD:** 6023 Crab Orchard St., Houston, TX 77057, (713)780-9765; **BUS ADD:** 3520 Montrose Blvd., Houston, TX 77006, (713)526-3036.

DEGOFF, Robert——*Dir. Fac. Plng.*, Levi Strauss & Co.; **PRIM RE ACT:** Property Manager; **BUS ADD:** 1155 Battery St., San Francisco, CA 94106, (415)544-6000.*

DE GRAAUW, Frank R.——**B:** Jan. 14, 1950, Abbeville, LA, *Broker/Pres.*, Southwestern Realty Services; **PRIM RE ACT:** Broker, Consultant, Developer, Syndicator; **SERVICES:** Income prop. devel., investment consultation, comml. brokerage; **REP CLIENTS:** Partnership and instl. investors; **PROFL AFFIL & HONORS:** RNMI, RESSI, NAR; **EDUC:** BS, 1974, Biology & Chemistry, LA State Univ., Baton Rouge, LA; **GRAD EDUC:** MS, 1976, Counseling Psych., Univ. of Southwestern LA, Lafayette, LA; **OTHER ACT & HONORS:** Rotary Intl.; LSU Varsity Club,; Delta Tau Delta Alumni Assn.; Greater Lafayette C of C; LSU Alumni Assn.; **HOME ADD:** 215 Third St., Abbeville, LA 70510, (318)898-2072; **BUS ADD:** PO Box 4-3949, Lafayette, LA 70504, (318)264-9200.

DEGRILLA, Robert J.——**B:** July 29, 1942, San Francisco, CA, *Pres.*, Wells Fargo Asset Mgmt. Co.; **OTHER RE ACT:** Asset Mgt.-"Owner", Prop. Mgr. and Leasing Agent; **SERVICES:** Insurance, Leasing, Strategy & Acquisitions; **REP CLIENTS:** Wells Fargo REIT; Wells Fargo Bank Pension Fund; Off Shore Funds; **PREV EMPLOY:** Coldwell, Banker & Co.; **PROFL AFFIL & HONORS:** NACORE; **EDUC:** BA, Bus., RE, CA State Univ. at San Francisco; **MIL SERV:** US Army, 1965-1967, Sgt., ARCOM; **HOME ADD:** 10065 Sunn Circle, Fountain Valley, CA 92708; **BUS ADD:** 330 Washington St., Marina del Rey, CA 90291, (213)822-2032.

DE HAAN, Neil——**B:** June 4, 1948, Amsterdam, Netherlands, *Dir.*, City of Elizabeth, NJ, Dept. of Community Development; **OTHER RE ACT:** Local Govt.; **SERVICES:** Asst. in site location; processing for local approvals; fin. packaging; **EDUC:** BA, 1970, Hist., George Washington Univ.; **GRAD EDUC:** Masters of Social Work, 1973, Social Policy and Planning, Rutgers Univ.; **EDUC HONORS:** Phi Beta Kappa; **HOME ADD:** 243 Browning Ave., Elizabeth, NJ 07208, (201)353-1473; **BUS ADD:** 50 Winfield Scott Plaza, Elizabeth, NJ 07201, (201)353-5992.

DEHAAN, Ronald M.——**B:** Apr. 29, 1942, Evergreen Park, IL, *Pres.*, DeHaan & Richter, P.C.; **PRIM RE ACT:** Attorney; **SERVICES:** negotiation, documentation, arbitration and litigation in connection with purchase, sale, construction, fin. or conversion of real prop.; **REP CLIENTS:** Central Nat. Bank in Chicago; MI Ave. Nat. Bank of Chicago; First Nat. Bank of Des Plaines; Capitol Cos., Inc.; Service Electric Co.; McLennan Co.; Klefstad Co., Inc.; **PROFL AFFIL & HONORS:** Amer. Bar Assn., IL State Bar Assn., Chicago Bar Assn., Amer. Arbitration Assn.; **EDUC:** Liberal Arts, 1964, Poli. Sci., Northwestern Univ.; **GRAD EDUC:** Juris Doctorate, 1967, Univ. of IL Law Sch.; **EDUC HONORS:** Jr. and Sr. Men's Honorary; **HOME ADD:** 1801 A. W. Estes Ave., Chicago, IL 60626, (312)262-1029; **BUS ADD:** 55 W. Monroe St., Suite 1000, Chicago, IL 60603, (312)726-2660.

DEHN, John J.——**B:** Oct. 31, 1920, Canton, OH, *Proprietor*, John J. Dehn; **PRIM RE ACT:** Broker, Appraiser, Property Manager; **OTHER RE ACT:** Mort. Broker; **SERVICES:** Condo. devel. & mgmt.; **PREV EMPLOY:** Gen. Atty., Amer. States Ins. Co.; **EDUC:** AB, 1943, Poli. Sci., Univ. of AL; **GRAD EDUC:** LLB, 1948, Univ. of AL Law School; **MIL SERV:** US Army Air Force, Cpl., 1943-1946; **HOME ADD:** 4274 South Landar Dr., Lake Worth, FL 33463, (305)439-1986; **BUS ADD:** 350 S. County Rd., Suite 10, Palm Beach, FL 33480, (305)659-3642.

DEININGER, Colleen——*Owner/Broker*, Century 21, Colleen Realty Corp.; **PRIM RE ACT:** Broker, Consultant, Appraiser, Developer, Builder, Owner/Investor, Instructor, Property Manager, Syndicator; **PROFL AFFIL & HONORS:** Pres., Women's Network; Dir. of Kenosha Bd. of Realtors; NAR, WRA, Cent. 21-Invest. Soc., CRS; CCIM; **EDUC:** BA, 1966, Elem. Educ./Physiology/Acctg. & Fin., Carthage Coll.; **OTHER ACT & HONORS:** AAUW; **HOME ADD:** 4905 70th St., Kenosha, WI 53142, (414)694-9550; **BUS ADD:** 4721 70th St., PO Box 744, Kenosha, WI 53142, (414)694-9550.

DEIS, George——*VP & Gen. Coun.*, Collns & Aikman Corp.; **PRIM RE ACT:** Attorney, Property Manager; **BUS ADD:** 210 Madison Ave., New York, NY 10016, (212)578-1200.*

DEISENROTH, Craig——*Corp. Secy.*, Campbell Taggart, Inc.; **PRIM RE ACT:** Property Manager; **BUS ADD:** 6211 Lemmon Ave., PO Box 222640, Dallas, TX 75221, (214)358-9375.*

DEJEAN, Milton——*Dir. Capital Plng. Fac.*, Ingersoll-Rand Co.; **PRIM RE ACT:** Property Manager; **BUS ADD:** 200 Chestnut Ridge Rd., Woodcliff Lake, NJ 07675, (201)573-0123.*

DE LA GARZA, Connie——**B:** Feb. 22, 1942, Raymondville, TX, *Pres.*, Bahnman Realty, Inc.; **PRIM RE ACT:** Broker, Appraiser, Property Manager; **SERVICES:** Appraisals, sales, prop. mgmt.; **REP CLIENTS:** Lenders, indivs., corps.; **PREV EMPLOY:** Only job since being tax assessor (1963-71); **PROFL AFFIL & HONORS:** Nat. State & local Bd. of Realtors, Member SREA, TX Assn. of Assessing Officers, GRI, 1968 Outstanding Assessor of TX, Cert. TX Assessor (CTA), Reg. Profl. Assessor (RPA); **EDUC:** 2yrs., Bus. & Gov., TX A&M Univ.; **OTHER ACT & HONORS:** Tax Assessor City of Harlingen, 1967-71; Mayor Protem 1976; Member Lions Club, C of C, Boy's Club, etc.; **HOME ADD:** 2814 Lotus, Harlingen, TX 78550, (512)423-8063; **BUS ADD:** 503 E Harrison, PO Box 1749, Harlingen, TX 78550, (512)423-3488.

DELANEY, Charles——*Treas.*, Ocean Spray Cranberries, Inc.; **PRIM RE ACT:** Property Manager; **BUS ADD:** Water St., Plymouth, MA 02360, (617)747-1000.*

DELANEY, Dexter——*Chrmn of Brd.*, Montana Real Estate Commission; **PRIM RE ACT:** Property Manager; **BUS ADD:** 1424 9th Ave., Helena, MT 59620, (406)449-2961.*

DELANEY, James J.——**B:** May 7, 1944, NYC, NY, *Pres.*, James J. Delaney & Associates, Inc.; **PRIM RE ACT:** Consultant; **SERVICES:** RE, facilities, office systems; **REP CLIENTS:** Profl. firms seeking to expand or relocate; **PREV EMPLOY:** Paine Webber Jackson & Curtis Inc.; **PROFL AFFIL & HONORS:** NACORE; **EDUC:** AB, 1964, Hist., Fordham; **GRAD EDUC:** JD, 1967, Fordham Univ. School of Law; **HOME ADD:** 1036 Lakeside Pl., Baldwin, NY 11510, (516)223-6556; **BUS ADD:** 114 Liberty St., NY, NY 10006, (212)267-8032.

DELANEY, John A.——**B:** June 13, 1936, Mt. Vernon, NY, *VP and Mgr., Corporate RE*, Foremost-McKesson, Inc.; **OTHER RE ACT:** Corp. RE Mgr.; **SERVICES:** Purchase, sale, leasing, const. indus. prop.; **PREV EMPLOY:** Xerox Corp., Otis Elevator, Allstate Ins. Co.; **PROFL AFFIL & HONORS:** Ind. Devel. Research Council, NACORE, SIR; **EDUC:** BA, 1958, Hist./Pol. Sci., Iona Coll.; **GRAD EDUC:** MBA, Exec. Devel., Fin., Grad. School Bus., Univ. of MI; **HOME ADD:** 83 Santa Maria Dr., Novato, CA 94947, (415)892-1295; **BUS ADD:** 1 Post St., San Francisco, CA 94104, (415)983-8646.

DELANEY, John W.——**B:** May 9, 1948, WA, *Pres.*, City Mortgage Services, Inc., W Div.; **OTHER RE ACT:** Mort. banking; **SERVICES:** Home mort.; **REP CLIENTS:** Lenders & inst. investors on the secondary mkt.; **PREV EMPLOY:** Seafirst Mort. Corp/. vp, 1976-78; **PROFL AFFIL & HONORS:** MBA, Seattle Masterbuilders, US League of S&L, Nat. Assn. of RE Appraisers; **EDUC:** BA, 1970, Bus. Admin., Central WA St. Coll.; **GRAD EDUC:** 1974, Mort. Banking, NW Univ.; **HOME ADD:** 9605 SE 72nd, Mercer Is, WA 98040, (206)232-8592; **BUS ADD:** 11110 NE 8, Bellevue, WA 98004, (206)453-2288.

DELANEY, Michael F.——**B:** May 21, 1942, Philadelphia, PA, *Pres.*, The Delaney Co. & First National Realty Corp.; **PRIM RE ACT:** Broker, Appraiser, Builder, Owner/Investor, Instructor, Property Manager, Insuror; **SERVICES:** Realtor, brokerage, mgmt., ins., appraisals; **REP CLIENTS:** Banks, S & L Assns., attys., govt. agencies and investors for comml. resid. and indus. RE; **PREV EMPLOY:** RE instr., LaSalle Coll.; PA State Univ.; **PROFL AFFIL & HONORS:** Soc. RE Appraisers; Amer. Soc. Appraisers; Nat. Assn. RE Bds.; Right of Way Assn., SRPA; **EDUC:** BA, 1963, Pre-Law, Liberal Arts, Villanova Law School, LaSalle Coll.; **HOME ADD:** 87 Briarwood Rd., Holland, PA 18966, (215)968-5491; **BUS ADD:** 7269 Rising Sun Ave., Philadelphia, PA 19111, (215)728-1776.

DELANEY, Thomas——*RE Manager*, American Petrofina Co. of Texas; **PRIM RE ACT:** Property Manager; **BUS ADD:** PO Box 2159, Dallas, TX 75221, (214)750-2400.*

DELANY, Robert——**B:** May 16, 1926, Platte, SD, *Owner*, Gold Cup Agency; **PRIM RE ACT:** Broker, Appraiser, Developer, Builder, Owner/Investor; **PREV EMPLOY:** Self-employed 30 yrs.; **HOME ADD:** 111 E. New York Ave., Gunnison, NY 81230, (303)641-3399; **BUS ADD:** 111 E. New York Ave., Gannison, CO 81230, (303)641-3800.

DEL CAMPO, Martin——**B:** Nov. 27, 1922, Guadalajara, Mex., *Arch./Partner*, Del Campo Associates, Architects/Planners; **PRIM RE ACT:** Banker, Architect; **SERVICES:** Design, admin. of constr.; **REP CLIENTS:** State of CA; City of San Francisco; City of San Jose; East Bay Mcpl. Utility Dist. US Postal Service; USN; **PREV EMPLOY:** Lecturer in Design, UC, Coll. of Environmental Design; Mgr., Hotel Victoria S.A., Mex.; Pres., City Federal S&L, Oakland/Berkeley; **PROFL AFFIL & HONORS:** AIA; **EDUC:** BS, 1940, Colegio Frances de Mexico; **GRAD EDUC:** BArch, 1948, Arch., Univ. of Mexico; **OTHER ACT & HONORS:** Listed in *Marquis' Who's Who in Bus. & Fin.*; US-Mex. C of C; Assn. of Latin Amer. Businessmen; Pres., City Fed. S&L, Oakland; Exec. Chmn. of the Bd., City Fed. S&L, Oakland; **HOME ADD:** 1601 Shrader St., San Francisco, CA 94117, (415)664-4379; **BUS ADD:** 507 Howard St., San Francisco, CA 94105, (415)777-4025.

DEL CASINO, Anthony A.——**B:** Oct. 24, 1919, NYC, NY, *Asst. VP*, Citibank, N.A.; **PRIM RE ACT:** Broker, Consultant, Appraiser, Property Manager; **OTHER RE ACT:** Site/lease, locator/negotiator; **SERVICES:** Site locations, lease negotiator, leasing/lease admin., valuation, prop. mgmt.; **REP CLIENTS:** Citicorp, Citibank and its clients, customers, investors in comml. and resid. prop.; **PREV EMPLOY:** United Cigar-Whelan Stores Corp., 1950-1958; Century Theatres, Inc., 1959; **PROFL AFFIL & HONORS:** Grand Central Rental Conditions Comm.; RE Bd. of NY; CPM; IREM; FIABCI (Intl. RE Fed.); NACOR: NAR; CSA; Lic. RE Broker, NY State; Peter Minuit RE Chapt. #1247; Amer. Legion, CPM; CSA; NRA; FIABCI; **EDUC:** 1948/49, RE, Columbia Univ.; 1957, RE, Pace ColL.; **MIL SERV:** US Army; 7th Armored Div., Sgt.; 1942-1946, Bronze Star, European Theatre Ribbon (4); **HOME ADD:** 801 W. 181st St., NY, NY 10033, (212)927-7557; **BUS ADD:** 153 E. 53rd St., NY, NY 10043, (212)559-1896.

DELHAISE, Jean-Claude——**B:** Apr. 23, 1942, Chatelet, Belgium, *Pres.*, Monde Investments & Trading Corp.; **PRIM RE ACT:** Builder, Owner/Investor, Syndicator; **GRAD EDUC:** MBA, 1977, Law & Adm., Inst. d'Enseignement Superieur Lucien Cooremans, Brussels, Belgium; **EDUC HONORS:** Cum laude; **BUS ADD:** 639 E. Ocean Ave., Boynton Bch., FL 33435, (305)428-7211.

D'ELIA, Vincent——**B:** Nov. 19, 1949, NY, *Atty.*, Beck & D'Elia; **PRIM RE ACT:** Attorney; **REP CLIENTS:** Orleans Builders & Developers, Canetic Corp., Commerce Bank of NJ, Community Title Abstract Co.; **PROFL AFFIL & HONORS:** Camden Cty. Bar Assn., NJ State Bar Assn., Burlington Cty. Bar Assn.; **EDUC:** BA, 1971, Econ., Harper Coll., State Univ. of NY at Binghamton; **GRAD EDUC:** JD, 1974, Law, Rutgers School of Law; **EDUC HONORS:** with honors; **HOME ADD:** 2036 Tuckerton Rd., Medford, NJ 08055, (609)654-6623; **BUS ADD:** 10 Grove St., Cherry Hill, NJ 08034, (609)663-0051.

DELISA, John——**B:** Dec. 28, 1939, Queens, NY, *VP*, Bache & Co.; **PRIM RE ACT:** Consultant, Syndicator; **SERVICES:** Equity Fin., Joint Ventures; **PREV EMPLOY:** Partner in Shopping Center Devel. Co.; **PROFL AFFIL & HONORS:** Soc. RE Appraisers; RE Securities & Synd. Inst., Lic. RE Broker, NY; **EDUC:** BS, 1961, Engrg., Bucknell Univ.; **GRAD EDUC:** MS, 1968, Engrg., Yale Univ. & Polytechnic Inst. of Brooklyn; **HOME ADD:** Box 46, Stony Brook, NY 11790, (516)751-6464; **BUS ADD:** 222 Middle Country Rd., Smithton, NY 11787.

DELISLE, Richard A.——**B:** Apr. 13, 1949, Holyoke, MA, *Chmn. of the Bd.*, D & D Developments, Inc.; **PRIM RE ACT:** Consultant, Developer, Owner/Investor, Property Manager, Syndicator; **PROFL AFFIL & HONORS:** BOMA; **EDUC:** 3 years, Mgmt., GA State Univ.; **OTHER ACT & HONORS:** Kiwanis Club, Bank Advisory Bd.; **HOME ADD:** 521 Sleepy Hollow Rd., Shreveport, LA 71115; **BUS ADD:** 3010 Knight St., Suite 230, Shreveport, LA 71105, (318)869-3117.

DELL, Marilyn——**B:** Apr. 18, 1943, CA, *Pres./Owner*, McMinnville Realty, Inc.; **PRIM RE ACT:** Broker, Instructor; **SERVICES:** RE investment, my firm handles resid. and comml. props., my personal spec. is aviation related RE; **REP CLIENTS:** Evergreen Aviation, Inc.; **PROFL AFFIL & HONORS:** Yamhill Cty. Bd. of Realtors, OR Assn. of Realtors, NAR, Yamhill Cty. Comml. Investment Div., Yamhill Cty. Planning Comm., Yamhill Cty. Realtor of the Year, 1979, Chmn. for Comm. for redevel., McMinnville, OR; **EDUC:** BS, 1969, Eng., UCLA; **EDUC HONORS:** Cum Laude; **OTHER ACT & HONORS:** Member Yamhill Cty. Task Force on Land Use Planning, Member Bd. of Dirs. Valley Comm. Bank in Org., Member Adv. Comm. Gallery Players, McMinnville, OR; **HOME ADD:** 707 Alder, McMinnville,

OR 97128, (503)472-4565; **BUS ADD:** 419 E 6th, McMinnville, OR 97128, (503)470-0581.

DELLA VALLE, Petra C.——B: June 29, 1954, West Berlin, Germany, *Appraiser*, RSI Appraisal Grp.; **PRIM RE ACT:** Appraiser; **SERVICES:** Appraisals of Indus. & Co-ml. RE; **REP CLIENTS:** Chem. Bank, Assoc. Barclays, Bancorp of Amer.; **PREV EMPLOY:** Campus Realty, Philadephia, PA, Income Producing Prop. Mgmt.; **PROFL AFFIL & HONORS:** Amer. Soc. for Info. Sci.; **EDUC:** BA, 1976-77, German, KS State Univ.; **GRAD EDUC:** MLS, 1979, Inf. Sci.; **EDUC HONORS:** Phi Betta Kappa, Magna Cum Laude; **HOME ADD:** 2727 Hudnull St., #117, Dallas, TX 75235; **BUS ADD:** 2520 W. Mockingbird Ln., Dallas, TX 75235, (214)350-2381.

DELMAN, James B.——B: Apr. 6, 1947, San Francisco, CA, *Pres.*, Delman Co.; **PRIM RE ACT:** Broker, Consultant, Appraiser, Owner/Investor, Property Manager; **REP CLIENTS:** S&L and Comml. Banks, Pvt. and Synd. Investors in Comml. Props., Comml. Leasing; **PREV EMPLOY:** Chief Appraiser for S&L Assn., Prop. Mgmt. and Comml. Leasing for S&L Assn.; **PROFL AFFIL & HONORS:** Sr. Member of the Natl. Assn. of Review Appraisers; Affiliate San Francisco Bd. of Realtors, CRA; **EDUC:** BA, 1970, Poli. Sci. and Hist., Univ. of San Francisco; **GRAD EDUC:** MBA, RE, Golden Gate Univ.; **OTHER ACT & HONORS:** San Francisco Planning and Urban Research (SPUR); Appraiser approved by state of CA to work for state chartered S&L's. Approved by FNMA and FHMC; **BUS ADD:** 342-Fifth Ave., San Francisco, CA 94118, (415)668-6363.

DELORENZO, Ken——B: Aug. 2, 1944, NY, *VP - Operations*, Century Devel. Corp., Operations; **PRIM RE ACT:** Developer, Builder, Property Manager; **SERVICES:** Prop. Mgmt.; **PREV EMPLOY:** Prop. Mgmt. System; **PROFL AFFIL & HONORS:** Cert. Prop. Mgr.; **EDUC:** BS, 1968, Arch., Math., The Univ. of Tx at Austin; **HOME ADD:** 10103 Cedar Creek, Houston, TX 77042, (713)782-2111; **BUS ADD:** Suite 1700, Five Greenway Plaza, Houston, TX 77046, (713)621-9500.

DELTZ, Jack C.——B: Apr. 22, 1950, Ronceverte, WV, *RE Officer*, Maryland Nat. Bank., Props. Mgmt.; **PRIM RE ACT:** Banker, Property Manager; **OTHER RE ACT:** Site location, lease negotiation; **PROFL AFFIL & HONORS:** Nat. Assn. of Corp. RE Execs; **EDUC:** BS, 1972, Mktg., WV Univ.; **OTHER ACT & HONORS:** Dir. of Youth Activities, Prince Georges Assn. of the Baptist Convention; **HOME ADD:** 9248 Greenwood Ln., Lanham, MD 20706, (301)459-4754; **BUS ADD:** PO Box 987, Baltimore, MD 21202, (301)244-5782.

DE LUCA, Joseph P.——B: Jan. 24, 1931, Messina, Italy, *Pres*, Aculed Financial Services, Inc.; **PRIM RE ACT:** Broker, Consultant, Owner/Investor; **SERVICES:** Mort. fin., counseling, devel. & brokerage comml. prop.; **REP CLIENTS:** Pension funds, instnl. lenders, devel. & investors of comml. props.; **PREV EMPLOY:** Comml. Bank 1961-68, Union Pension Funds Admin, 1968-77; **PROFL AFFIL & HONORS:** W Pension Conf., Bay Area Mort Assoc., Bankers Assn., Phi Alpha Delta (Law), Golden Gate Univ., State Bar of CA, Estate Planning, Tr. & Probate Sect., Member CA Dept. of RE, Broker; **EDUC:** BA, 1961, Pol. Sci., Econ., Univ. of CA at LA (UCLA); **GRAD EDUC:** LLB, 1963, Law, Van Norman Coll. of Law; MBA, current, RE, Golden Gate Univ.; **EDUC HONORS:** Student of Yr.; **MIL SERV:** USN, CPO, Pres. Citation (Unit); **OTHER ACT & HONORS:** Il Cenacola, Sons of Italy in Amer., Serra Intl.; **HOME ADD:** 5372 Hilltop Cres, Oakland, CA 94618, (415)547-0281; **BUS ADD:** Rincon Annex, Box 3571, San Francisco, CA 94119, (415)653-8474.

DELUCA, Mark P.——B: Jan. 25, 1944, Olean, NY, *Broker*, Fourman Organization; **PRIM RE ACT:** Consultant, Owner/Investor, Property Manager, Syndicator; **SERVICES:** Investor, synd., mgmt. of prop.; **PROFL AFFIL & HONORS:** Bd. of Dirs., Bd. of Realtors; MLS, IFA; Nat. Assn. Indep. Fee Appraisers; **EDUC:** 1967, Engrg., Manhattan Coll.; **GRAD EDUC:** 1973, Law, Seton Hall Univ., School of Law; **HOME ADD:** 204 Wayfair Ln., Wyckoff, NJ 07481; **BUS ADD:** 241 Cedar Ln., Teaneck, NJ 07666, (201)836-2400.

DEMMITT, Richard Joseph——B: July 4, 1952, Baltimore, MD, *Investment Specialist*, The Caton Realty Co.; **PRIM RE ACT:** Consultant, Owner/Investor, Property Manager, Syndicator; **OTHER RE ACT:** Analyst, tax planning; **SERVICES:** Selling investment prop., consulting buyers & sellers, synd. of comml. props.; **PREV EMPLOY:** H&R Block, Tax Consultant; **PROFL AFFIL & HONORS:** CCIM; **EDUC:** BS, Comml., Indus., Investment Prop., Howard Community Coll.; **EDUC HONORS:** Phi Dheta Kappa; **OTHER ACT & HONORS:** Member of RESSI; Howard Cty. Bd.; **HOME ADD:** 9966 Route 99, Ellicott City, MD 21043, (301)465-4544; **BUS ADD:** 9339 Balto. Nat. Pike, Ellicott City, MD 21043, (301)465-0842.

DEMOUTH, R.M.——*Secy. & Counsel*, Stewart-Warner; **PRIM RE ACT:** Property Manager; **BUS ADD:** 1826 Diversey Parkway, Chicago, IL 60614, (312)883-6000.*

DEMPSEY, Charles L.——*Inspector Gen.*, Department of Housing and Urban Development, Ofc. of Inspector General; **PRIM RE ACT:** Lender; **BUS ADD:** 451 Seventh St., S.W., Washington, DC 20410, (202)755-6430.*

DEMPSEY, D. Kevin——B: Jan. 18, 1946, NYC, NY, *Pres.*, Dempsey & Co.; **PRIM RE ACT:** Consultant, Appraiser; **SERVICES:** RE Appraisals and Consulting Servs.; **REP CLIENTS:** Var. comml. banks and thrift instns., indiv. investors, ins. co's., municipalities, reloc. co's.; **PREV EMPLOY:** Citicorp Realty Comm. (1974-75), Manhattan Savings Bank (1971-74); **PROFL AFFIL & HONORS:** Member RE Bd. NY, MAI Designation from AIREA, SRPA and SRA designation from SREA; **EDUC:** BA, 1969, Gen. Soc. Sci., Villanova Univ., Villanova, PA; **MIL SERV:** US Army, Nat. Guard, US Air Nat. Guard, Sgt.; **OTHER ACT & HONORS:** Active Member Amer. Yacht Club, Rye, NY; **HOME ADD:** 3 Pol Rd., Rye, NY 10580, (914)967-4989; **BUS ADD:** 184 Purchase St., Rye, NY 10550, (914)967-0236.

DEMPSEY, Jack——B: June 4, 1935, Providence, RI, *Pres.*, Jack Dempsey's RE Assoc., Inc.; **PRIM RE ACT:** Broker, Consultant, Appraiser; **PROFL AFFIL & HONORS:** RI Realtors Assoc; Nat. Assoc. Realtors, CRB; **EDUC:** BA, 1957, Pol. Sci./Pre Law, Providence Coll.; **HOME TEL:** (401)934-1400; **BUS ADD:** 89 1/2 Rocky Hill Rd., N. Scituate, RI 02857, (401)934-1400.

DEMSON, Robert D., CPM——B: July 21, 1931, Cleveland, OH, *Pres.*, Demson & Assoc. Inc.; **PRIM RE ACT:** Broker, Instructor, Syndicator, Consultant, Developer, Property Manager, Owner/Investor; **SERVICES:** Prop. Mgmt, Consulting, Sales, Leasing; **PROFL AFFIL & HONORS:** Natl. Apt. Assn., Natl. Apt. Council, NAREB, IREM, Pres. Chap 47 IREM, CPM of Yr.; **EDUC:** BA, 1960, Pol. Sci., Hist., AZ State Univ.; **MIL SERV:** USAF, S/Sgt.; **OTHER ACT & HONORS:** American Arbitration Assn., Phoenix Housing Comm., Phoenix Bd. Realtors Court of Ethics; **HOME ADD:** 1225 E. Encantada Pl., Phoenix, AZ 85014; **BUS ADD:** 5201 N. 19th Ave., 124, Phoenix, AZ 85015, (602)246-8586.

DENICOLA, L. Lawrence——B: Nov. 10, 1924, Brooklyn, NY, *Owner*, L. Lawrence de Nicola; **PRIM RE ACT:** Attorney, Owner/Investor; **SERVICES:** Title settlements, counseling devels. and investors, forming various entities as vehicles for devel. or ownership; **PROFL AFFIL & HONORS:** VA Bar Assn.; Alexandria Bar Assn.; **EDUC:** AB, 1950, Eng., Georgetown Univ., Coll. of Arts & Sciences; **GRAD EDUC:** JD, 1953, Georgetown Univ., Law School; LLM, 1956, Govt. Contracts/Anti Trust, Georgetown Univ., Law School; **OTHER ACT & HONORS:** USN, PO 3rd Class, 1943-1946, Submarine Service; **HOME ADD:** 8114 Bainbridge Rd., Alexandria, VA 22308; **BUS ADD:** Suite 235, 6911 Richmond Hwy., Alexandria, VA 22306, (703)660-6642.

DENMEAD, Robert G.——B: Apr. 27, 1908, W Liberty, OH, *Treas.*, The Denmead Co., Realtors; **PRIM RE ACT:** Broker, Consultant, Owner/Investor; **SERVICES:** Counseling & brokerage, indus. & investment props.; **REP CLIENTS:** Indiv. & corp. owners or users of comml., indus., investment RE; **PREV EMPLOY:** First Lic. as RE salesman, 1933, with Wm. P. Zinn & Co., est. own brokerage 1945; **PROFL AFFIL & HONORS:** SIR, ASREC, CRE, Columbus Realtor of Yr., 1968; **EDUC:** BS, 1930, Engrg., Arch., Antioch Coll.; **OTHER ACT & HONORS:** Chmn. Franklin Cty. Reg. Planning Comm., 62-67; Univ. Club, Faculty Club, Upper Arlington Art League; **HOME ADD:** 3880 Surrey Hill Pl., Columbus, OH 43220, (614)451-4024; **BUS ADD:** 22 E Gay St., Columbus, OH 43215, (614)224-1492.

DENNEE, Glen——B: Apr. 9, 1936, CA, *Pres.*, Red Carpet Realtors of San Jose; **PRIM RE ACT:** Broker, Developer, Owner/Investor; **SERVICES:** New & resales; **PROFL AFFIL & HONORS:** San Jose RE Bd., Los Gatos Saratoga Bd., CA Assn. of Realtors, NAR; **MIL SERV:** US Air Nat. Guard, 1st class; **HOME ADD:** PO Box 408, Saratoga, CA 95071, (408)867-2699; **BUS ADD:** 369 Winchester Blvd., San Jose, CA 95128, (408)248-2440.

DENNERY, Moise W.——B: New Orleans, LA, *Senior Partner*, McCloskey, Dennery, Page & Hennesy; **PRIM RE ACT:** Attorney; **SERVICES:** Gen. legal advice and rep., corp. sec.; **REP CLIENTS:** Latter & Blum, Inc., New Orleans, LA; **PROFL AFFIL & HONORS:** New Orleans, LA, Amer. Bar Assns.; **EDUC:** BA, 1935, Arts & Sci., Tulane Univ.; **GRAD EDUC:** LLB (JSD), 1937, Law, Tulane Univ.; **EDUC HONORS:** Order of the Coif; Bd. of Editors, Tulane Law Review; **OTHER ACT & HONORS:** Delegate & Sec'y., LA Const. Conv. - 1973; **BUS ADD:** 505 Hibernia Bldg., New Orleans, LA 70112,

(504)586-1323.

DENNEY, K. Duane——**B:** May 27, 1923, Plattsburg, OH, *Sr. VP*, Automation Indus., Inc., Corp. Office; **OTHER RE ACT:** In charge of Real Prop. purchases & leases for all of our co. RE requirements; **PREV EMPLOY:** With this co. 1949 to present; **PROFL AFFIL & HONORS:** Los Angeles Treas. Club & Fin. Ex. Inst., Outstanding Alumnus Award 'Franklin Univ.' Franklin Alumnus Assn. Hon. 1980 Award; **EDUC:** BS, 1948, Acctg. & Taxes, Franklin Univ., OH; **MIL SERV:** USN, PFC, Bronze Star medal with 4 oak leaf clusters; **OTHER ACT & HONORS:** Bd. of Gov. Hosp. for Crippled Children, Life Member Pepperdine Univ. Assoc., Life Member of Univ. of So. CA Assoc., Member of LA Ctry. Club, Shrine Temple (LA); **HOME ADD:** 146 Via Monte Doro, Redondo Beach, CA 90277, (213)375-6372; **BUS ADD:** 1901 Ave. of the Stars, Los Angeles, CA 90067, (213)879-2222.

DENNIS, C.W.L. (Dub)——**B:** May 23, 1922, Duster, Comanche Co, TX, *Owner*, The Dennis Co.; **PRIM RE ACT:** Broker, Consultant, Developer, Builder, Property Manager, Lender, Owner/Investor; **PROFL AFFIL & HONORS:** Wichita Falls Realtors, TX Realtors, NAR, NT Homebuilders, TX Builders, NAHB, Past Pres. NTHBA, TAB, Past VP NAHB, Life Dir. NAHB, 1980 Builder of the Yr. NTHBA; **EDUC:** 1939, Bus., Abilene Christian Coll., Abilene, TX; **GRAD EDUC:** 1940, Bus., Hardin Coll., Wichita FaLls, TX; **MIL SERV:** USAF, Capt.; **OTHER ACT & HONORS:** SW Rotary, Wichita Falls (Past. Pres.), Wichita Falls Bd. of Commerce & Indus.; **HOME ADD:** 2020 Hiawatha, Wichita Falls, TX 76309, (817)692-5563; **BUS ADD:** Old Town Ctr., Wichita Falls, TX 76308, (817)692-0410.

DENNIS, Jack V., Jr.——**B:** July 3, 1951, Little Rock, AR, *VP & Mgr.*, Lincoln First Mortgage Inc., an affiliate of Lincoln First Banks NA, Houston Office; **PRIM RE ACT:** Lender; **SERVICES:** Const. lender income 1-20 millions; **PREV EMPLOY:** River Oaks Bank & Trust, Houston, TX; Union Planters Nat. Bank, Memphis, TN; **EDUC:** BS/BA, 1973, Fin. & Banking, Univ. of AR; **GRAD EDUC:** MBA, 1977, RE, Fin., Memphis State Univ.; **HOME ADD:** 2321 Steel St., Houston, TX 77098, (713)523-7831; **BUS ADD:** 11 Greenway Plaza, Suite 2806, Houston, TX 77046, (713)877-1728.

DENNIS, William H.——**B:** Sept. 6, 1920, Marion, MD, *Gen. Mgr.*, South Town Plaza Assoc., RE Mgmt.; **PRIM RE ACT:** Consultant, Banker, Owner/Investor, Property Manager; **SERVICES:** All forms of prop. mgmt., consultation, fin. consultation & const. consultation; **REP CLIENTS:** Culver Ridge Shopping Ctr., Inc., CFLV Assoc., S. Town Plaza, CV Assn., Merchants Main Shopping Ctr. All Rochester NY Firms; **PREV EMPLOY:** VP Lincoln First Bank; RE Mgr., Rochester, NY; **EDUC:** BA, 1941, Econ. & Bus. Admin., W. MD Coll.; **MIL SERV:** USAF, Maj., Combat Stars, Pacific Theatre WW II; **HOME ADD:** 47 W. Church St., Fairport, NY 14450, (716)723-0381; **BUS ADD:** 3385 Brighton-Henrietta Town Line Rd., Rochester, NY 14623, (716)442-9872.

DENNISON, Dan——**B:** Sept. 19, 1945, Minn, MN, *VP, Mgr. of Operations*, Trafalgar Developers of FL, Isla Del Sol (St. Pete) Plantation (Tampa) Ventura (Orlando); **PRIM RE ACT:** Broker, Developer, Builder, Property Manager; **OTHER RE ACT:** Marketing; **PREV EMPLOY:** AVP, General Devel. Corp. (1974-79); General Manager, Port Charlotte; **PROFL AFFIL & HONORS:** FL RE Broker, FL Class C Contractor; **EDUC:** BA, 1968; **GRAD EDUC:** MBA, 1974, Vanderbilt Univ.; **MIL SERV:** USN, Lt., 1968-72; **HOME ADD:** 1029 43rd Ave. No., St. Petersburg, FL 33703, (813)525-4974; **BUS ADD:** 6025 Sun Blvd., St. Petersburg, FL 33715, (813)867-1191.

DENNY, Richard A., Jr.——**B:** Oct. 13, 1931, Atlanta, GA, *Partner*, King & Spalding; **PRIM RE ACT:** Attorney, Owner/Investor; **SERVICES:** Legal servs.; **REP CLIENTS:** Devel. and investors, including post props., inc. (apt. devel.), Carter & Assoc. (office and shopping ctr. devels.), Fed. Dept. Stores; **PROFL AFFIL & HONORS:** Amer., GA, Atlanta Bar Assns., Lawyers Club of Atlanta, Past Pres., Lawyers Club of Atlanta; **EDUC:** BA, 1952, Econ., Washington & Lee Univ.; **GRAD EDUC:** LLB, 1954, Emory Univ.; **EDUC HONORS:** Law Review, Honor Grad.; **OTHER ACT & HONORS:** COB, The Lovett Sch., Past Pres., Washington & Lee Alumni; **HOME ADD:** 650 W. Paces Ferry Rd., NW, Atlanta, GA 30327, (404)237-0060, **BUS ADD:** 2500 Trust Co. Tower, Atlanta, GA 30327, (404)572-4600.

DENSBORN, Donald K.——**B:** July 25, 1951, Logansport, IN, *Atty.-at-Law*, Henderson, Daily, Withrow, Johnson & Gross; **PRIM RE ACT:** Attorney; **SERVICES:** Legal; **REP CLIENTS:** Counsel to const. and permanent lenders, devel., brokers and synd. (comml., indus., multi-family, single family); **PROFL AFFIL & HONORS:** ABA; IN State Bar Assn.; Indianapolis Bar Assn.; RESSI; Bd. of Editors of RE Securities & Syndication Journal; **EDUC:** BS, 1973, Bus./Fin., IN Univ.; **GRAD EDUC:** JD, 1976, Law, IN Univ.; **EDUC HONORS:** Magna Cum Laude, Beta Gamma Sigma, Phi Eta Sigma Hon. Frat., Magna Cum Laude; **HOME ADD:** 5168 N. IL St., Indianapolis, IN 46208, (317)257-2352; **BUS ADD:** One Indiana Sq., Suite 2450, Indianapolis, IN 46204, (317)639-4121.

DENSMORE, Larry A.——**B:** Feb. 25, 1949, Cumberland, MD, *Mgr.-RE*, So. Bell Tel. & Tel. Co.; **OTHER RE ACT:** Acquisition, disposition, leasing for corp. RE dept.; **EDUC:** BA, 1971, Econ., Stetson Univ.; **GRAD EDUC:** MA, 1972, Econ., Univ. of MI; **EDUC HONORS:** Magna Cum Laude; **BUS ADD:** PO Box 390, Jacksonville, FL 32201, (904)350-3583.

DENSMORE, Robert R.——**B:** Apr. 13, 1948, Detroit, MI, *Chief Fin. Officer, Controller*, Manufacturers Hanover Mortgage Corp., Fin. Operations; **PRIM RE ACT:** Banker; **PREV EMPLOY:** 4 yrs. Touche Ross & Co.; **PROFL AFFIL & HONORS:** AICPA, MACPA, NAA, AMBA, MBA, CPA; **EDUC:** BA, 1970, Acctg., Univ. of Detroit; **GRAD EDUC:** MBA, 1972, Acctg., Univ. of Detroit; **EDUC HONORS:** Key Club Member (outstanding Sr.), Cum Laude; **OTHER ACT & HONORS:** Alpha Kappa Psi, Manuscript Award; **HOME ADD:** 6282 Quaker Hill Dr., W. Bloomfield, MI 48033, (313)661-9093; **BUS ADD:** 27555 Farmington St., Farmington Hills, MI 48018, (313)661-7522.

DENSMORE, Thomas H.——**B:** Dec. 27, 1934, *Realtor*, Densmore Realty; **PRIM RE ACT:** Broker, Owner/Investor; **PROFL AFFIL & HONORS:** Local, State & Nat. RE Board, GRI, CRB; **EDUC:** BS, 1960, Bus., FL State Univ.; **MIL SERV:** USAF; **HOME ADD:** PO Box 338, Inverness, FL 32650, (904)726-3442; **BUS ADD:** PO Box 338, Inverness, FL 32650, (904)726-3442.

DENSON, Theodore D.——**B:** Feb. 12, 1932, Detroit, MI, *Pres.*, State 12 Plaza, Inc.; **PRIM RE ACT:** Developer; **SERVICES:** Devel./owner - comml. light indust. devel.; **PREV EMPLOY:** (1970-1978) Owner, T & M Chevrolet, Inc.; **PROFL AFFIL & HONORS:** Pi Tau Sigma (Hon. Mech. Eng. Frat.); **EDUC:** BS, 1958, Mech. Engrg., MI State Univ.; **MIL SERV:** USN; Aviation Machinist Mate 3rd Class; **OTHER ACT & HONORS:** Rotary; **HOME ADD:** 5644 Blue Grass Ln., Saline, MI 48176, (313)429-5006; **BUS ADD:** 5644 Blue Grass Ln., Saline, MI 48176, (313)429-5006.

DENZEL, Ken J.——**B:** Jan. 21, 1940, Chicago, IL, *Pres./Atty.*, S.A. International; **PRIM RE ACT:** Attorney, Owner/Investor, Syndicator; **SERVICES:** Synd., mgmt., investment, consultant; **REP CLIENTS:** Profl. and athletes; **PROFL AFFIL & HONORS:** ABA; IL Bar Assn.; Chicago Bar Assn.; Chairman, Sports Law Committee; **EDUC:** BA, 1962, Econ/Bus. Admin., St. Ambrose Coll.; **GRAD EDUC:** LLD, 1967, Law, Loyola Univ.; **EDUC HONORS:** Outstanding Leadership & Scholastic Achievement; **BUS ADD:** POB 141, Park Ridge, IL 60068.

DEPASCALE, Fred A.——**B:** Mar 5, 1928, NY, *Sr. Real Prop. Appraiser*, Emigrant Savings, RE; **PRIM RE ACT:** Instructor, Appraiser, Assessor; **PREV EMPLOY:** NYC Real Prop. Assessment Bureau; **PROFL AFFIL & HONORS:** SREA, SRPA; **MIL SERV:** USA, PFC; **HOME ADD:** 2469 Fortesque Ave., Oceanside, NY 11572, (516)536-3279; **BUS ADD:** 5 E. 42nd St., NYC, NY 10017, (212)883-7814.

DEPEW, Robert G.——Robert G. Depew & Assoc.; **PRIM RE ACT:** Developer; **BUS ADD:** 9711 F. George Plamer Hwy., Lanham, MD 20706, (301)459-1255.*

DEPIETRI, Robert J., Jr.——**B:** July 22, 1957, Framingham, MA, *VP/Controller*, Casper Corporation, RE Devel.; **PRIM RE ACT:** Developer, Owner/Investor, Property Manager; **OTHER RE ACT:** Planners; **SERVICES:** Devel., Mgmt., Planner, Investors, Comml./Props.; **REP CLIENTS:** Devels., Investors, Maj. Corps., Lenders Dealing with Respect to Comml. Props.; **PROFL AFFIL & HONORS:** BOMA, Amer. Mgmt. Assn., Inst. of Mgmt. Acctg.; **EDUC:** BS, 1979, Acctg., Univ. of Lowell; **HOME ADD:** 10 Wyndemere Dr.,, Southboro, MA 01772, (617)881-4951; **BUS ADD:** 254 Cochituate Rd., Framingham, MA 01701, (617)872-8838.

DERBES, David S.——**B:** Sept. 4, 1951, New Orleans, LA, *Pres.*, David S. Derbes, Inc.; **PRIM RE ACT:** Broker; **OTHER RE ACT:** Comml. Feasibility Analysis; **SERVICES:** Prop. mgmt.; **PROFL AFFIL & HONORS:** NAR, St. Tammany Bd. of Realtors, G.R.I., Pres. St. Tammany Bd. of Realtors; **EDUC:** BS Forestry & Wildlife Mgmt., 1974, LA State Univ., Baton Rouge; **OTHER ACT & HONORS:** Chmn. St. Tammany Parish Zoning Commn., Pres. St. Tammany Parish Planning Advisory Bd.; **HOME ADD:** Rte 5, Box 88, Covington, LA 70433; **BUS ADD:** Rte 3, Box 603, Covington, LA 70433, (504)892-8980.

DEREGT, John S.——B: San Fran., CA, *Pres.*, Holvick deRegt Koering, 1960 to Pres.; **PRIM RE ACT:** Developer, Builder; **OTHER RE ACT:** Commercial, indus. & mixed-use; **PROFL AFFIL & HONORS:** Indus. & Office Park Council of ULI; NAIP;ICSC; **EDUC:** BCE, 1950, Univ. of Santa Clara; **MIL SERV:** US Army, Sgt., 1951-1953; **HOME ADD:** 97 Elena, Atherton, CA 94025, (415)326-1887; **BUS ADD:** 1230 Oakmead Pkwy., Suite 210, Sunnyvale, CA 94086, (415)493-0111.

DERNAGO, Theodore P., Jr.——B: July 17, 1942, Springfield, MA, *Leasing Agt.*, The Pyramid Cos.; **PRIM RE ACT:** Broker, Attorney, Regulator, Instructor, Syndicator, Developer, Builder, Property Manager, Owner/Investor, Insuror; **SERVICES:** Legal, leasing, and prop. mgmt. of comml. prop.; **REP CLIENTS:** The Pyramic Cos.; **PREV EMPLOY:** Counsel. Aetna Life & Casualty, Hartford, CT (1970-79), RE Broker, Dernago RE, MA & CT; **PROFL AFFIL & HONORS:** ABA, NC Bar Assn., Wash. IREM, Wash. Bar Assn., Various State & local RE, E Bds. Greater Springfield (MA), Homebuilders Assn CPM, Fellowship from Admin Mgmt. Assn.; **EDUC:** BBA, 1966, Mgmt, Fin. Econ., W. NE Coll., Springfield, MA.; **GRAD EDUC:** MA, Econ. Fin., Univ. of NE, Lincoln, NE; JD, 1970, Econ. Fin., Univ. of Nebraska Law Sch.; **EDUC HONORS:** Class Pres., Frat. Pres., Student Govt. Pres., Grad. Cum Laude, Moot Court Winner/Part.; **OTHER ACT & HONORS:** Bd. of Health Elected Member Town of Southwick (1977-79), Greater Springfield (MA) Homebuilders, CO Chapt. No. 51, CPM's, Gvt. Relations Liaison for City of Northampton C of C, and the Pyramid Cos.; **HOME ADD:** 697 College Hwy, Southwick, MA 01077, (413)569-6863; **BUS ADD:** 5795 Widewaters Pkwy, P.O. Box 98, Dewitt, NY 13214, (413)586-5700.

DERRICK, Bill D.——B: Jan. 18, 1949, Dallas, TX, *Sr. VP & Partner, Mktg./Leasing Nat.*, Treptow Murphree & Co., Nat. Headquarters; **PRIM RE ACT:** Developer; **SERVICES:** Complete devel. services: design, fin., construction, mktg.; **PREV EMPLOY:** Coldwell Banker, Salesman of the Yr., High Rise Office Bldg. Spec., 1978-1980; Nat. Salestrainer & Regnl. Dir. of The Gillette Co., Boston, MA, 1971-1978; **PROFL AFFIL & HONORS:** Houston Developers Assn.; TX RE Broker; Deacon, Bethany Christian Church; **EDUC:** BBA, 1970, Mgt./Fin., Univ. at TX, Arlington; **EDUC HONORS:** Dean's List; **HOME TEL:** (713)784-8500; **BUS ADD:** 5858 Westheimer, Suite 800, Houston, TX 77057, (713)784-8500.

DERRICK, William J.——B: Mar. 24, 1934, El Paso, TX, *Pres.*, Derrick & Schaefer Inc.; **PRIM RE ACT:** Broker, Attorney, Developer, Owner/Investor, Syndicator; **SERVICES:** Devel. & synd. comml., apt., resid., buy & sell props. for investory; **PREV EMPLOY:** Partner, Kemp, Smith, Duncan & Hammond, 1961-1978; **PROFL AFFIL & HONORS:** ABA; TX Bar Assn., Fellow, TX Bar Assn.; Chmn., TX Bd. of Legal Specialization, 1972-1976; **EDUC:** BA, 1956, Univ. of TX at Austin; **GRAD EDUC:** LLB, 1958, Univ. of TX School of Law; **EDUC HONORS:** Phi Delta Phi; **MIL SERV:** USAF, Capt., 1958-1961; **HOME ADD:** 858 River Oaks, El Paso, TX 79912, (915)584-0083; **BUS ADD:** 6006 N. Mesa, Suite 600, El Paso, TX 79912, (915)581-8161.

D'ERRICO, John A.——B: Sept. 3, 1954, NY, *RE Admin.*, The Bank of New York, Trust RE; **PRIM RE ACT:** Banker; **OTHER RE ACT:** Trust RE; **SERVICES:** Holding, managing, and distributing a portfolio of accounts containing RE of varying complexities and types. Full control over these props. for acquisition, mgmt., leasing and ultimate disposal, review appraiser; **PREV EMPLOY:** Dime Savings Bank of NY RE Dept., Prop. Mgr./Appraiser; **PROFL AFFIL & HONORS:** Soc. of RE Appraisers, Assn. of MBA Execs.; **EDUC:** BS, 1976, Bus. Mgmt./Fin./Mktg., St. Francis Coll.; **GRAD EDUC:** NYU School of Continuing Education, Mortgage Institute, RE Finance New School for Social Research: Real Estate Finance; **HOME ADD:** 530 4th St., Brooklyn, NY 11215; **BUS ADD:** 90 Washington St., New York, NY 10015, (212)530-8525.

DESANCTIS, Leo J.——B: Apr. 19, 1924, Boston, MA, DeSanctis Realty; **PRIM RE ACT:** Broker; **SERVICES:** Comml./Indus. Sales and Leasing; **EDUC:** BA, 1946, Psych./Soc., Harvard Univ.; **GRAD EDUC:** Babson Institute—'49 & '50; **HOME ADD:** 230 E. Eagle St., E. Boston, MA 02128, (617)567-6176; **BUS ADD:** 230 E. Eagle St., E. Boston, MA 02128, (617)567-7568.

DESANTIS, James L.——B: Aug. 9, 1927, Trenton, NJ, *Real Estate Appraiser - Consultant*, Tri-Val Appraisals; **PRIM RE ACT:** Consultant, Appraiser; **PREV EMPLOY:** NJ Trans. Dept.; **PROFL AFFIL & HONORS:** SREA; NARA; ARWA, SRA; CRA; SR/WA; **HOME ADD:** 212 Mott St., Trenton, NJ 08611, (609)393-2773; **BUS ADD:** 212 Mott St., Trenton, NJ 08611, (609)394-5766.

DESANTIS, Joseph John——B: June 19, 1916, Brooklyn, NY, *Owner*, DeSantis Bros.; **PRIM RE ACT:** Property Manager, Owner/Investor; **SERVICES:** Investment & devel. of comml. & resid. props.; **PREV EMPLOY:** DeSantis Despatch, Local trucking and warehousing; **OTHER ACT & HONORS:** Community Bd. for Ambulatory Ser. of Maimondes Medical Ctr.; Parish Council St. Catharine of Alexandria; **HOME ADD:** 941 46th St., Brooklyn, NY 11219; **BUS ADD:** 23 W. 31st St., NY, NY 10001, (212)279-3669.

DESAUTELS, David A.——B: June 26, 1947, Burlington, VT, *Pres.*, Desautels Real Estate, Inc.; **PRIM RE ACT:** Broker, Owner/Investor, Instructor; **SERVICES:** Relocation service; **PROFL AFFIL & HONORS:** NAR, CCIM, CRB, CRS, GRI; **EDUC:** BS, 1969, Bus., Univ. of VT; **HOME ADD:** E. Rd., Colchester, VT 05446, (802)879-6175; **BUS ADD:** 85 Main St., Colchester, VT 05446, (802)878-5371.

DESIDERIO, Fred L.——B: July 26, 1924, Reno, NV, *Owner*, Desiderio Prop. & Sierra Nevada Ins., Inc.; **PRIM RE ACT:** Broker, Consultant, Developer, Property Manager, Owner/Investor, Insuror; **SERVICES:** Devel. of Income & Comml. Prop, Prop. Mgmt.; **PREV EMPLOY:** Sierra Realty, Inc., & Sierra Prop. Mgmt. Co. Note, sold above firms 1979 & 1980, Title Pres. & Owner.; **PROFL AFFIL & HONORS:** Reno Bd. of Realtors, NAR, IREM, CPM, GRI, Pres. Reno Bd. of Realtors 1966, Pres. Nevada Assn. Of Realtors 1971, Pres. N. Nevada/Tahoe Chap. of IREM, 1981; **EDUC:** 1945-1948, Bus. Admin., Univ. of NV, Reno; **OTHER ACT & HONORS:** Commnr, Reno Housing Authority, 1974-78, Druids, Elks; **HOME ADD:** 2170 Skyline Blvd., Reno, NV 89509, (702)826-1410; **BUS ADD:** 1750 Locust St., Suite D, Reno, NV 89502, (702)329-8330.

DESLAURIERS, Charles——B: Dec. 3, 1952, Burlington, VT, *Mgr. Devel. and Analysis*, The Sheraton Corp., North Amer.; **OTHER RE ACT:** Hotel Devel.; **SERVICES:** Hotel mgmt., acquisition, devel. and joint venture of hotel props.; **REP CLIENTS:** Lenders and major indivs. or instit. investors in hotel props.; **PREV EMPLOY:** Cornell Univ. School of Hotel Admin., Bolton Valley Corp., Bolton VT; **PROFL AFFIL & HONORS:** The Cornell Soc. of Hotelmen; Triad Comm., Cornell School of Hotel Admin., Bd. of Dirs., Bolton Valley Corp.; **EDUC:** BA, 1974, Econ. and Bus. Admin., Univ. of VT, Coll. of Arts and Sci.; **GRAD EDUC:** Master of Profl. Studies, 1978, Hotel Admin., Cornell Univ., School of Hotel Admin.; **EDUC HONORS:** Dean's List, Dean's List, Phi Kappa, Phi, Ye Hosts; **OTHER ACT & HONORS:** Amer. Yacht Club; **HOME ADD:** 9A Mechanic St., Marblehead, MA 01945, (617)631-8123; **BUS ADD:** 60 State St., Boston, MA 02109, (617)367-3600.

DESMOND, Michael J.——B: Sept. 12, 1949, Washington, DC, *Sales Mgr., Nat. Title Service*, Commonwealth Land Title Ins. Co.; **PRIM RE ACT:** Insuror; **SERVICES:** Title Ins. and Consulting in MA, NH & ME; **REP CLIENTS:** Mort. Lenders, Conveyancing Law Firms, Devels., Investors, and Major Corps.; **PREV EMPLOY:** Title Abstracter; Construction; **PROFL AFFIL & HONORS:** New England Land Title Assn., ALTA; NACORE; **EDUC:** AB; AB, 1971, Georgetown Univ.; **HOME ADD:** 4 Bristol Dr., Duxbury, MA 02332, (617)585-6166; **BUS ADD:** 50 Federal St., Boston, MA 02110, (617)542-0800.

DESPAIN, J.C.——*Dir. Real Prop. Mgmt. & Fac.*, Northrop Corp.; **PRIM RE ACT:** Property Manager; **BUS ADD:** Century Park East, Century City, Los Angeles, CA 90067, (213)553-6262.*

DESPAIN, Larry C.——B: Nov. 29, 1939, Los Angeles, CA, *RE Rep.*, Atherton Indus., Inc.,, dba Pic-A-Dilly and It's-A-Dilly Stores; **OTHER RE ACT:** Site selection and lease negotiation; **PREV EMPLOY:** Fotomat Corp. 1968-1977 - Rgnl. RE Mgr.; **PROFL AFFIL & HONORS:** Intl. Council of Shopping Centers; **EDUC:** BA - Hist., 1963, Univ. of CA, Santa Barbara; **OTHER ACT & HONORS:** Victorian Alliance (S.F.), Secretary - Bd. of Dirs. - Martin Luther Tower - San Francisco (Non-profit Apartment Project for Srs.); **HOME ADD:** 911 Central Ave., San Francisco, CA 94115, (415)563-7278; **BUS ADD:** 260 Constitution Dr., Menlo Park, CA 94025, (415)328-5900.

DESPAIN, Willis N.——B: Dec. 19, 1915, New London, IA, *Owner*, Despain Investment Co.; **PRIM RE ACT:** Broker, Consultant, Appraiser, Lender, Owner/Investor, Property Manager; **PREV EMPLOY:** Self-employed Ins. Agent; **PROFL AFFIL & HONORS:** Burlington RE Bd.; FLI; Nat. Assn. of RE Appraisers; **MIL SERV:** US Army, Tech. Sgt., Bronze Star; **OTHER ACT & HONORS:** Lions Club; Amer. Legion; Indian Hills Country Club; United Methodist Church; Elks; **HOME ADD:** 219 S. Northfield, Mediapolis, IA 52637, (319)394-3453; **BUS ADD:** 627 Main St., Mediapolis, IA 52637, (319)394-3969.

DETHLEFSEN, R.M.——B: Aug. 18, 1926, Watsonville, CA, *Owner*, Dick's Equipment Appraisal Service; **OTHER RE ACT:** Appraiser of Machinery and Equipment; **SERVICES:** Consultations, useful lives, residuals, equip. appraisals; **PREV EMPLOY:** Bank of Amer. 31 yrs., Equip. Guide Book Co. & F.S Equip. Mgmt. Corp.; **PROFL AFFIL & HONORS:** ASA, Review Appraisers, On Bd. of Examiners ASA, State Dir. for Region 13; Amer. Arbitration Assn., Annual Pres. Trophy 1977; **OTHER ACT & HONORS:** Masons, Scottish Rite; **HOME ADD:** 1131 Monica Ln., San Jose, CA 95148, (408)246-5378; **BUS ADD:** 1131 Monica Ln., San Jose, CA 95128, (408)246-5378.

DEUTSCH, Edward R.——B: Aug. 31, 1937, NY, NY, *Sr. VP*, National Bank of N. America, General Services; **PRIM RE ACT:** Banker, Builder, Property Manager; **SERVICES:** Facilities planning, acquisition and mgmt.; **PROFL AFFIL & HONORS:** RE Bd. of NY; Building Owners and Mgrs. Assn.; **EDUC:** BA, 1960, Econ., Queens Coll.; **GRAD EDUC:** MBA, 1965, Indus. Mgmt., City Coll., Baruch School; **MIL SERV:** Air Nat. Guard, A1C; **HOME ADD:** 87 Bellows Ln., Manhasset, NY 11030, (516)365-8909; **BUS ADD:** 3161 Hempstead Tpk., Levittown, NY 11756, (516)752-2428.

DEUTSCH, Isaac——B: July 5, 1950, NY, *CPA, Tax Mgr.*, Jaffe, Haft & Spring, CPA's; **OTHER RE ACT:** CPA, Tax Mgr.; **SERVICES:** Tax planning, tax return preparation, tax advice, conversion of prop. to cooperative and/or condo. operations; **REP CLIENTS:** RE Ltd. Partnerships, Cont. Contractors, Cooperative Corps.; **PROFL AFFIL & HONORS:** AICPA; NYSSCPA; NYSSCPA Tax Comm. on Profl. Serv. Corps., Lecturing at 1981 Acctg. Symposium, NY; **EDUC:** BA, 1972, Acctg., Brooklyn Coll.; **GRAD EDUC:** MBA, 1974, Taxation, Bernard M. Garuch; **EDUC HONORS:** Dean's List; **OTHER ACT & HONORS:** Instruction in Acctg., Touro Coll., 1979; **HOME ADD:** 453 FDR Dr., NY, NY 10002, (212)260-3771; **BUS ADD:** The Towers, 111 Great Neck Rd., Great Neck, NY 11021, (516)466-4233.

DEUTSCH, Jerome——B: Feb. 8, 1929, New York City, NY, *President*, Consultants for Property & Resources, Inc.; **PRIM RE ACT:** Consultant, Developer, Owner/Investor, Syndicator; **PREV EMPLOY:** Exec. VP, Realty Equities Corp. 1958-1970; **EDUC:** BA, 1951, Econ., CCNY; **MIL SERV:** US Army, Sgt.; **HOME ADD:** 177 Hillair Cir., White Plains, NY 10605, (914)949-4419; **BUS ADD:** 311 E. 50th St., New York, NY 10022, (212)758-0842.

DEVANEY, Thomas R.——B: Sept. 11, 1948, Bayonne, NJ, *Assistant General Counsel*, Pembrook Management, Inc.; **PRIM RE ACT:** Attorney; **SERVICES:** Legal & Fin. Counseling, Devel. & Synd. of Comml. Props. (including hotels, apts., indus. bldgs.) Devel. of resid. props. (including major resid. subdivs., & condos.); **REP CLIENTS:** Lenders and indiv. partnership clients for devel., sale and lease, synd. of comml. props.; **PREV EMPLOY:** Prime Motor Inns, Inc. Clifton, NJ; United Jersy Mort. Co., Hackensack, NJ; **PROFL AFFIL & HONORS:** ABA, NJ & NY Bar Assns., Admitted to practice NJ, NY and Fed. Bars; **EDUC:** BA, 1971, Amer. Hist., Univ. of Detroit, Detroit, MI 48221; **GRAD EDUC:** JD, 1974, Law, St. John's Univ. School of Law, Jamaica NY; **EDUC HONORS:** St. Thomas More Scholarship, Sr. Activities Award; **MIL SERV:** USA Reserve, Capt.; **OTHER ACT & HONORS:** Morris Cty. Republican Cty. Committeeman 1978 to Date; VChmn., Pequamock Twp. Envionmental Commn.; **HOME ADD:** 11 Park Ave., Pompton Plains, NJ 07444, (201)839-9698; **BUS ADD:** 355 Lexington Ave., New York, NY 10017, (212)557-8495.

DEVINE, Charles V., Jr.——B: Feb. 1, 1948, Pittsburgh, PA, *Dir. of New Stores, Central Rgn.*, F.W. Woolworth Co.; **OTHER RE ACT:** Corp. RE devel. (mgmt.); **PREV EMPLOY:** Tenneco, 1979-1980; Dunkin Donuts, 1974-1979; Grand Union, 1971-1974; **PROFL AFFIL & HONORS:** Intl. Council of Shopping Ctrs.; Nat. Assn. of Corp. RE Execs.; **EDUC:** BA, 1970, Math., Duquesne Univ.; **EDUC HONORS:** Dean's List; **MIL SERV:** US Army, Green Berets, Capt., NDCC Medal Heroism; **OTHER ACT & HONORS:** Parsippany Twp., NJ, Bd. of Educ. Task Force, 1977; Washington Twp., NJ, Zoning Bd. of Adjustment, 1982; **HOME ADD:** 478 Monroe Ave., Washington Twp., NJ 07675, (201)664-7020; **BUS ADD:** 233 Broadway, New York, NY 10279, (212)553-2043

DEVINE, James D.——B: June 8, 1944, Chicago, IL, *Pres.*, Superior Investment & Dev. Corp. (SIDCOR); **PRIM RE ACT:** Attorney, Syndicator, Consultant, Developer, Builder, Owner/Investor; **PREV EMPLOY:** VP, Arthur Rubloff & Co. 1973-1980; **PROFL AFFIL & HONORS:** IL, Chicago Bar Assns.; ICSC; Natl., IL Assns. of Realtors, RE Bd., RESSI; **EDUC:** BS, 1962, Bus. Admin., Marquette Univ.; **GRAD EDUC:** JD, 1973, Law, Loyola Univ.; **MIL SERV:** USN, Lt., Naval Commendation; **HOME ADD:** 820 Arthur Ave., Libertyville, IL 60048, (312)362-0551; **BUS ADD:** 4930 W. Oakton, Skokie, IL 60077, (312)982-9600.

DE VINNIERE, Dominique Rocoffort——B: Aug. 5, 1946, France, *Owner*, ROC Consulting Co.; **PRIM RE ACT:** Builder; **OTHER RE ACT:** Designer, gen. contractor; **REP CLIENTS:** IF Devel. Inc., Maisons Francaises; **GRAD EDUC:** Arch. Sch. (France); **HOME ADD:** 1527 10th St. #21, Santa Monica, CA 90401, (213)393-8392; **BUS ADD:** 1527 10th St. #21, Santa Monica, CA 90401, (213)393-8392.

DEVITO, Joseph John——B: Feb. 19, 1934, NY, NY, *Pres.*, Innovax Construction Corp.; **PRIM RE ACT:** Consultant, Developer, Builder; **OTHER RE ACT:** Const. Mgrs.; **SERVICES:** Construction; **PREV EMPLOY:** Architect; **PROFL AFFIL & HONORS:** Astronomical Soc.; **GRAD EDUC:** Arch., 1960, Pratt Univ.; **MIL SERV:** US Army, Electorincs, SP-4; **OTHER ACT & HONORS:** Opened INNOVAX - East Construction Corp. new office in NY; 146 Broadway, Suite 1404, NY, NY 10036; **HOME ADD:** 274 Buttery Rd., New Canaan, CT 06840, (203)972-1332; **BUS ADD:** 10835 Santa Monica Blvd., Los Angeles, CA 90025, (213)475-9565.

DEVITO, Richard A.——B: Nov. 30, 1940, Boston, MA, E.F. DeVito Realty Trust, Const. Div.; **PRIM RE ACT:** Broker, Developer, Builder, Owner/Investor, Real Estate Publisher; **EDUC:** BS, 1961, Public Comm./Econ., Boston Univ.; **HOME ADD:** 706 Boston Post Rd., Weston, MA 02193, (617)899-2702; **BUS ADD:** 470 Boston Post Rd., Weston, MA 02193, (617)899-2702.

DEVLIN, George A.——B: June 23, 1913, Detroit, MI, *Consultant*, National Planning, Inc., Allright Auto Parks, Inc.; **PRIM RE ACT:** Consultant; **SERVICES:** Parking feasibility, functional design, project coordination & operation; **REP CLIENTS:** Owners and devels. of office bldgs., retail store, large shopping ctr., multi-use complexes, hospitals in USA, Can. W. Europe; **PREV EMPLOY:** Nat. Garages, Inc., 1935-75; **PROFL AFFIL & HONORS:** ULI, Nat. Parking Assn., US C of C; **GRAD EDUC:** ME, 1935, Mech. Engrg., Cornell Univ.; **HOME ADD:** 19495 Lighthouse Pointe, Grosse Ile, MI 48138, (313)676-3864; **BUS ADD:** 35950 Industrial Rd., Livonia, MI 48150, (313)591-0665.

DEWAR, Donald J., III——B: Sept. 19, 1948, Baltimore, MD, *VP*, Merrill Lynch Realty/Chris Coile Inc.; **PRIM RE ACT:** Broker, Owner/Investor, Instructor, Property Manager; **PREV EMPLOY:** RE resid. & comml. sales; **PROFL AFFIL & HONORS:** NAR; Greater Baltimore Bd. of Realtors, Cert. Resid. Broker Mgr.; **EDUC:** BA, 1973, Law/Soc., Essex Community Coll., Univ. of Baltimore; **MIL SERV:** USN, PO 3, Nat. Service Award, 1965-1969; **HOME ADD:** 8816 Goldentree Ln., Baltimore, MD 21221, (301)686-3331; **BUS ADD:** 7846 Eastern Blvd., Baltimore, MD 21224, (301)288-4300.

DEWAR, William D.——B: May 6, 1944, Baltimore City, MD, *Broker*, CARE Realty, Inc.; **PRIM RE ACT:** Broker, Consultant, Engineer, Attorney, Appraiser, Developer, Lender, Builder, Owner/Investor, Property Manager, Syndicator, Assessor; **SERVICES:** Investment Consulting & Dev.; Prop. Mgmt.; **REP CLIENTS:** Investors and indiv. primarily in area of distress props.; **PREV EMPLOY:** Admitted to the practice of Law in MD, PA, and FL, RE Broker in MD; **EDUC:** BS, 1970, Physics, Math, Liberal Arts Arts, Loyola Coll. of Baltimore, Baltimore, MD; **GRAD EDUC:** JD, 1975, Prop. and Bus. Law and Taxation, Univ. of Baltimore, Baltimore, MD; **MIL SERV:** US Nat. Guard, Sp5; **OTHER ACT & HONORS:** Church and Alumni Grps.; **HOME ADD:** 1684 Grandview Rd., Pasadena, MD 21122, (301)437-1978; **BUS ADD:** PO Box 275, Severn, MD 21144, (301)437-1889.

DEWEEVER, Petrus Leroy——B: April 1, 1954, St. Maarten, *Managing Dir., VP*, Temdal Holdings N.V.; **PRIM RE ACT:** Broker, Consultant, Syndicator; **SERVICES:** Investment consultants, devel. and synd. of resort prop.; **PROFL AFFIL & HONORS:** Kiwanis Internatinal; **EDUC:** BBA, 1978, Econ., George Washington Univ.; **OTHER ACT & HONORS:** Member of Democratic Party (Present Govt. of St. Maarten); **HOME ADD:** Saunders 2, Philipsburg, St. Maarten; **BUS ADD:** Frontstreet 11, Philipsburg, St. Maarten, Bahamas, (305)854-2415.

DEWEY, Robert——B: Nov. 22, 1922, Chicago, IL, *COB & Broker*, The Devonshire Co.; **PRIM RE ACT:** Broker, Appraiser, Developer, Builder, Owner/Investor, Instructor, Syndicator; **EDUC:** 1941-43, Arch., Cornell Univ.; **MIL SERV:** USAF, Capt., Air medal w/4 clusters; **OTHER ACT & HONORS:** Dir., IL Dept. of Aeronautics 1945-49; **HOME ADD:** 131 S. Clermont St., Denver, CO 80222, (303)758-7611; **BUS ADD:** 2833 S. CO Blvd., Denver, CO 80222, (303)758-7611.

DEWOLFE, Richard B.——B: Mar. 15, 1944, NY, NY, *Pres.*, The Dewolfe Companies; **PRIM RE ACT:** Broker, Consultant, Appraiser, Property Manager, Syndicator; **SERVICES:** RE brokerage, appraisal, mgmt. relocation services and investment synd.; **REP CLIENTS:**

Indiv. clients, banks, lawyers, corps.; **PREV EMPLOY:** First Nat. Bank of Boston; **PROFL AFFIL & HONORS:** NAR; MA Assn. of Realtors; Boston RE Bd; RESSI; RNMI; ERC, GRI; CRS; Greater Boston Realtor of Yr., 1978; MA Realtor of Yr., 1978; GRI Bd. of Govs.; Dir., Pres., Greater Boston RE BD.; Dir., MA Assn. of Realtors; **EDUC:** BA, 1971, Bus. Admin., Boston Univ.; **GRAD EDUC:** Metropolitan Coll., Boston Univ.; **MIL SERV:** USAF, E6; **OTHER ACT & HONORS:** Treas., Public Library Milton; Town Meeting Member; Dir., Milton Hospital; Corporator, Milton Savings Bank; Past Pres., Milton Rotary; Milton Yacht Club; **HOME ADD:** 33 Russell St., Milton, MA 02187; **BUS ADD:** 17 Canton Ave., Milton, MA 02186, (617)698-0075.

DEWOSKIN, William——B: Dec. 22, 1941, Chicago, IL, *Pres.*, William DeWoskin & Associates; **PRIM RE ACT:** Broker, Developer, Owner/Investor, Property Manager, Syndicator; **PROFL AFFIL & HONORS:** NAR, CREB, IAREB, IREM, CPM; **EDUC:** BS, 1963, Univ. of PA-Wharton School; **MIL SERV:** US Army N.G., Sgt.; **HOME ADD:** 246 Melba Lane, Highland Park, IL 60035, (312)432-4229; **BUS ADD:** 408 S Oak Park Ave., Suite 222, Oak Park, IL 60302, (312)782-9890.

DEXTER, Donald P.——B: Aug. 12, 1932, Detroit, MI, *Owner*, Dexter Associated Enterprise; **PRIM RE ACT:** Appraiser, Builder, Owner/Investor, Property Manager; **SERVICES:** Restoration of old homes; **EDUC:** Bus. & Indus. Arts, Western MI Univ.; **EDUC HONORS:** VP Indus. Arts Assn.; **MIL SERV:** USA 1952-1954, Cpl.; **OTHER ACT & HONORS:** Pres., Kalamazoo Landlords Assn. 1975-1976; **HOME ADD:** 408 Main St., Battle Creek, MI 49017, (616)965-2584; **BUS ADD:** 408 Main St., Battle Creek, MI 49017, (616)965-2584.

DE YAMPERT, Thomas K.——B: Nov. 21, 1948, Albuquerque, NM, *Rgnl. Mgr.*, R&B Commercial Mgmt., R&B Enterprises; **PRIM RE ACT:** Consultant, Developer, Owner/Investor, Property Manager; **SERVICES:** High rise project mgmt., devel. & acquisition; **REP CLIENTS:** Mt. Bell Telephone, Gulf Oil, Teneco, and Major Ins. Cos.; **PREV EMPLOY:** Mgr. Comml. Devel., ITT; **PROFL AFFIL & HONORS:** Nat. Assn. of Office & Indus. Parks, Intl. Council of Shopping Ctrs., Urban & Other Rgnl. and Local RE Orgs.; **EDUC:** 1973, Bus. Admin. Min., Fin., Acctg. & Mktg., CA Poly Tech Univ. at Pomona, CA; **GRAD EDUC:** MBA, 1980, Fin., Univ. of N FL; **MIL SERV:** USN Res., Lt., Nat. Defense Ribbon, Forces Res. Medal, Naval Res. Ribbon, Meritorious Unit Commendation, ARM; **HOME ADD:** 6495 Happy Canyon Rd., #68, Denver, CO 80237, (303)757-1490; **BUS ADD:** 1355 S Colorado Blvd., Suite 111, Denver, CO 80222, (303)759-9579.

DIAMOND, R. Patrick——B: Aug. 25, 1947, Dumas, AR, *Pres.*, R. Patrick Diamond, Inc.; **PRIM RE ACT:** Broker, Appraiser; **SERVICES:** Valuation of resid. & comml. propls., comml. brokerage; **REP CLIENTS:** Mort. lenders, home-buying cos., indivs.; **PROFL AFFIL & HONORS:** AIREA, RNMI, NAR, GRI, CRS; **EDUC:** Vanderbilt Univ., 1966; McNeese State Univ., 1967-70; **EDUC HONORS:** Student Union Bd. Pres., 1970; **OTHER ACT & HONORS:** Pres. Grt. Calcasieu Bd. of Realtors, 1977; **HOME ADD:** 2435 20th St., Lake Charles, LA 70601, (318)478-2668; **BUS ADD:** 1835 Oak Park Blvd., Suite 4, Lake Charles, LA 70601, (318)478-5716.

DIAMOND, Robert M.——B: Dec. 23, 1948, NY, NY, Thomas & Fiske, P.C.; **PRIM RE ACT:** Attorney; **SERVICES:** Condo. and community assn. law & devel.; **REP CLIENTS:** Devels., lenders, condo. converters, mgmt. cos., apt. owners, homeowner's assns., tenants' assn., indiv. unit owners; **PREV EMPLOY:** Fried, Frank, Harris, Shriver & Kampelman 1974-76; **PROFL AFFIL & HONORS:** ABA; VA State Bar; DC Bar; VP, Metropolitan Washington Chap., Community Assns. Inst., Reporter, Uniform Condo. Act, Nat. Conference on Uniform State Laws; **EDUC:** BA, 1970, Pol. Sci. & Eng., Colgate Univ.; Vassar Coll.; **GRAD EDUC:** JD, 1974, Law, Columbia Univ. School of Law; **MIL SERV:** U. S. Army, Sp/5; **OTHER ACT & HONORS:** Consultant and draftsman: WV, PA, LA, VA, DC Condo. Acts; Author and lecturer regarding condo. conversion and devel.; Articles re the development process - *The Ideal Development Team*; Articles re condominium warranties - *Developer Warranties in the Sale of Residential Condominiums*; *The Magnuson-Mass Act and the Virginia and District of Columbia Condominium Act Warranties*; **HOME ADD:** 3117 Ravensworth Pl., Alexandria, VA 22302, (703)379-1222; **BUS ADD:** 510 King Street, Suite 200, Alexandria, VA 22314, (703)836-8400.

DIAZ, Eddie C.——B: Dec. 5, 1926, Chile, So. Amer., *Pres.*, Land/Tech Corp.; **PRIM RE ACT:** Broker, Consultant, Developer, Owner/Investor, Property Manager; **PREV EMPLOY:** Diaz, Seckinger & Assocs., VP; **PROFL AFFIL & HONORS:** Comm. of 100; Amer. Planning Commn.; Tampa C of C; Tampa Bd. of Realtors; Lic. Mort. Broker; **EDUC:** Bus. Admin., Univ. of Tampa; **MIL SERV:** US Army, T/5; **OTHER ACT & HONORS:** Chmn., Hillsborough Cty. Aviation Authority Member, 2 yrs.; **HOME ADD:** 3818 Ridge Ave., Tampa, FL 33603, (813)223-1645; **BUS ADD:** 2001 Pan Am Cir., Tampa, FL 33607, (813)879-4478.

DIAZ, Jean Michael, (Mr.)——B: Oct. 26, 1949, Oxnard, CA, *Real Prop. Admin.*, City of Palo Alto, RE Div.; **PRIM RE ACT:** Consultant, Appraiser, Instructor, Property Manager; **SERVICES:** All RE serv. including acquisition, mgmt. & disposition of RE assets - counseling & instruction; **REP CLIENTS:** Public agencies; **PREV EMPLOY:** Cty. of Orange, CA/RE Div, Bd. of Supervisors, (asst. to board member); **PROFL AFFIL & HONORS:** Assoc. member, ULI; IR/WA, Intl. Instit. of Valuers (IIV); Assoc. member, NARA; ASPA; WGRA; Designated Sr. Member IR/WA; Designated Sr. member IIV; Cert. instr. IR/WA; Chmn. Intl. Prop. Mgmt. Comm. IR/WA 1981-1982; various offices IR/WA & ASPA; **EDUC:** BA, 1972, CA State Univ., Fullerton, CA; **GRAD EDUC:** MPA, 1981, Public Admin., CA State Univ., Fullerton, CA; **EDUC HONORS:** Dean's List; **HOME ADD:** 1166 Sunnyvale-Saratoga, 34, Sunnyvale, CA 94087, (408)739-4181; **BUS ADD:** 250 Hamilton Ave., P.O. Box 10250, Palo Alto, CA 94303, (415)329-2472.

DICK, Donald F.——B: Mar. 13, 1929, Toledo, OH, *Dir. Area Devel. Div.*, Toledo Edison Co., Area Devel. Div.; **OTHER RE ACT:** Econ. Devel.; **SERVICES:** Econ. Information - Sites, Cldgs., Labor, Taxes, Amenities-all information and contacts needed to decide to expand or locate new facility; **PREV EMPLOY:** Nopper Homes (Builders), Reynold Constr., RE Lic. State of OH, Assoc. SIR; **PROFL AFFIL & HONORS:** Amer. Indus. Devel. Council, Past Pres. Great Lakes Area Devel. Research Council, Indust. Devel. Research Council, Past Chmn. OH Econ. Devel. Council, Instr. RE, Toledo Univ.; **EDUC:** 1963, Bus. Admin. - RE, Univ. of Toledo; **GRAD EDUC:** Univ. of OK, Indus. Devel. Inst.; **MIL SERV:** USN, 2nd Class; **OTHER ACT & HONORS:** Past Pres. Anthony Wayne Bd. of Educ.; **HOME ADD:** 9900 Dutch Rd., Whitehouse, OH 43571, (419)877-5430; **BUS ADD:** 300 Madison Ave., Toledo, OH 43652, (419)259-4045.

DICK, Michael L.——B: Jan. 22, 1942, Bremerton, WA, *Chmn. of Bd.*, Spot Realty, Inc. and Inter Development Corp.; **PRIM RE ACT:** Broker, Consultant, Banker, Developer, Builder, Owner/Investor, Property Manager, Insuror; **SERVICES:** Full serv. RE; **REP CLIENTS:** Nat. and intl. investors; **PREV EMPLOY:** Smith Corona Marchant 1965-1967; Teledyne 1967-1969; **PROFL AFFIL & HONORS:** NAR, CRB; **EDUC:** BA, 1965, Econ., Western WA Univ.; **MIL SERV:** USNG; E-5; **OTHER ACT & HONORS:** Navy League; Army Assn.; **HOME ADD:** 10810 Gravelley Lake Dr., Tacoma, WA 98499, (206)582-0945; **BUS ADD:** 1020 Sea/Tac, 17930 Pacific Hwy S., Seattle, WA 98188, (206)246-9761.

DICK, Neil A.——B: June 15, 1942, Cleveland, OH, *VP/ Dir. of Mktg.*, Cannon Design Inc.; **PRIM RE ACT:** Consultant, Engineer, Architect, Developer, Property Manager; **OTHER RE ACT:** Devel. consulting, planning; **SERVICES:** Arch., engrg., planning const. mgmt.; **REP CLIENTS:** Hooker Chem., Moore Bus. Consulting Forms, Buffalo Savings Bank, St. Mary's Hosp., Evansville, IN; Atlantic City Med. Ctr., Atlantic City, NJ; **PREV EMPLOY:** Nat. Housing Consultants, Cleveland, OH; CT Gen. Ins. Co.; Stirling Homex Corp., Avon, NY; Inland Steel Co.; **PROFL AFFIL & HONORS:** SMPS, Prof. Serv. Mgmt. Assn., AMA, BOMA, Amer. Hosp. Assn., AHCA, C of C, Who's Who in Fin. & Indus., Dir. of SMPS, Currently elected official Cty. Dem. Comm. & Exec. Comm.; **EDUC:** BArch, 1965, Arch., OH State Univ.; **GRAD EDUC:** MBA, 1967, Mktg., Cleveland State Univ.; **EDUC HONORS:** APX Merit of Hon., Class VP; **MIL SERV:** USAR, 1965-70, Sgt. E-7; **OTHER ACT & HONORS:** Town Comm., Zone Leader, Treas. & Member of Exec. Comm., many religious & civil orgs.; **HOME ADD:** 97 Koster Row, Amherst, NY 14226, (716)835-4211; **BUS ADD:** 2170 Whitehaven Rd., Grand Island, NY 14072, (716)773-6800.

DICK, William M.——B: Aug. 29, 1946, Quantico, VA, *VP*, First Interstate Mortgate Co., Resid. Loans; **PRIM RE ACT:** Lender; **PROFL AFFIL & HONORS:** Bay Area Mort. Assn., MBAA, Past Sec. of Bay Area Mort. Assn., Co-chairperson of the Young Mort. Bankers of Amer.; **EDUC:** BA, 1969, Eng., Univ. of Southern CA, Los Angeles; **GRAD EDUC:** MBA, 1971, San Diego State Univ.; **HOME ADD:** 1450 Reibli Rd., Santa Rosa, CA 95404, (707)545-8158; **BUS ADD:** 1 Embarcadero Center, Suite 2401, San Francisco, CA 94111, (415)544-5933.

DICKENSON, David B.——B: July 25, 1942, Ashland, KY, *RE Atty.*, Scott, Dickenson and Linus, Chartered Attorneys; **PRIM RE ACT:** Attorney; **SERVICES:** Atty, Boca Raton Bd. of Realtors, Inc.; **PROFL AFFIL & HONORS:** So. Palm Beach Cty., Palm Beach Cty., and ABA's; The FL Bar; **EDUC:** BBA, 1965, Univ. of Cincinnati; **GRAD EDUC:** JD, 1968, Univ. of Miami Law School; **EDUC HONORS:** Pres., Student Bar Assn.; Bar & Gavel Legal Soc.; **OTHER**

ACT & HONORS: Trustee, Gulfstream School; Pres., Exchange Club of Boca Raton; FL Atlantic Univ. Found.; Boca Raton Hist. Soc.; Bankers' Club, John's Island Club; Boca Raton Hotel & Club; FL League of Anglers; **HOME ADD:** 1240 Coconut Rd., Boca Raton, FL 33432, (305)391-4372; **BUS ADD:** Suite 600, 150 E. Palmetto Park Rd., Boca Raton, FL 33432, (305)391-1900.

DICKERMAN, Allen F.——**B:** Jan. 19, 1934, Somerville, MA, *Owner Mgr.*, Belmont Props.; **PRIM RE ACT:** Owner/Investor, Property Manager; **PREV EMPLOY:** Engr. Polaroid Corp., 1962-69; Quality Control Mgr., Compugraphic Corp., 1970-73; **EDUC:** BS, 1957, Mech. Engrg., Tufts Univ.; **GRAD EDUC:** MBA, 1959, Indus. Mgmt., Boston Univ.; **MIL SERV:** USAF, Capt., 1959-62; **HOME ADD:** 23 Heritage Dr., Lexington, MA 02173, 17)862-8813; **BUS ADD:** PO Box 354, Lexington, MA 02173, (617)862-2862.

DICKERSON, Richard F.——**B:** Feb. 20, 1945, Temple, TX, *VP & Mgr.*, SW Bank, RE Div.; **PRIM RE ACT:** Banker; **PREV EMPLOY:** San Diego Fed., 1972-77, Bank of Amer., 1970-72; **PROFL AFFIL & HONORS:** Member of the Bd. (Liaison Comm.) for local RE lenders & realtors, 4 yrs., FNMA Level II underwriter; **EDUC:** BS, 1970, Bus. Admin. & Fin., Brigham Young Univ.; **OTHER ACT & HONORS:** Member Sch. Bd. Health & Safety Comm., 1 yr., Leader in local church group representing Spanish speaking membership (5 yrs.); **HOME ADD:** 4600 Park Dr., Carlsbad, CA 92008, (714)729-4733; **BUS ADD:** 1737 W. Vista Way, Vista, CA 92083, (704)726-5870.

DICKINSON, Mark C.——**B:** April 24, 1947, Brookline, MA, *Pres.*, Dickinson Devel. Corp.; **PRIM RE ACT:** Broker, Developer, Owner/Investor; **SERVICES:** Full Service Devel./Mktg. Co. involved in Commercial RE.; **REP CLIENTS:** Hospital Mort. Group, Inc.; Transco Realty Trust, Grossman Ind. Prop., Inc. Burlington Northern Air Freight, Shaws Supermarkets, OSCO Drug, T.J. Max etc.; **PREV EMPLOY:** Grossman Indus. Prop., Inc. (6yrs.) Director of Devel. MacBro Const. (2 1/2) yrs. Land Aquisition & Project Devel.; **PROFL AFFIL & HONORS:** ICSC; South Shore C of C; Progress Downtown Quincy; MA RE Broker; **EDUC:** BA, 1969, Amer. Studies, Amherst Coll.; **GRAD EDUC:** Attended Boston Coll. Grad. School of Mgmt., Fin.; **EDUC HONORS:** Pres.-Rugby Club/ Lord Jeff Soc./ Football; **OTHER ACT & HONORS:** Assoc. Class Agent & Reunion Chmn. at Amherst Coll.; **HOME ADD:** 30 Travis Dr., Chestnut Hill, MA 02167, (617)964-5943; **BUS ADD:** 142 Union St., Braintree, MA 02167, (617)848-1955.

DICKINSON, William——**B:** Oct. 9, 1933, S Gate, CA, *Regional Mgr.*, Kilroy Ind.; **PRIM RE ACT:** Developer, Property Manager; **PREV EMPLOY:** VP and Mgr., RE Admin. Dept. Seattle First Nat. Bank; **PROFL AFFIL & HONORS:** Pres., NW Chap. of NACORE; Member Seattle Chap. BOMA, and Former Tr. thereof; **EDUC:** Poli. Sci., 1955, Russian and Portuguese, Univ. of WA; **MIL SERV:** USAF, Capt.; **OTHER ACT & HONORS:** Seattle Tennis Club; **HOME ADD:** 4939-NE 86th, Seattle, WA 98115, (206)525-6524; **BUS ADD:** 17930 Pacific Highway So., Seattle, WA 98188, (206)242-8970.

DICKMAN, Samuel D.——**B:** Mar. 23, 1941, Chicago, IL, *VP*, Robert A Polacheck Co., Inc.; **PRIM RE ACT:** Broker, Consultant; **SERVICES:** Brokerage, counseling, assemblage; **REP CLIENTS:** Leading local & nat. fin. instns.; Fortune 500; Mgrs., private investors; **PROFL AFFIL & HONORS:** Soc. of Indus. Realtors, WI & Milwaukee Bd. of Realtors, Urban Land Inst., SIR; **EDUC:** 1962, Northwestern Univ.; **OTHER ACT & HONORS:** Treas. Village of Smorewood, 1981; **HOME ADD:** 4326 N. Wildwood Ave., Smorewood, WI 53211, (414)964-3862; **BUS ADD:** 777 E. Wisconsin Ave., Milwaukee, WI 53202, (414)273-0880.

DIEHL, Richard A.——**B:** Feb. 24, 1941, New York, NY, *Facilities Coordinator*, Guardian Life; **PRIM RE ACT:** Property Manager; **PROFL AFFIL & HONORS:** CPM NY RB, Rheo Epi So; **EDUC:** bus., CUNY; **MIL SERV:** USN, Seamen, 2 yrs. reservist; **HOME ADD:** 173 Fifty Acre Rd. S., Southtown, NY 11787, (516)724-8696; **BUS ADD:** 201 Park Ave. S., New York, NY 10003, (212)598-1984.

DIERDORFF, Jack L.——**B:** Aug. 24, 1918, Wolf Point, MT, *Exec. VP*, UNICO Prop., Inc.; **PRIM RE ACT:** Developer, Property Manager; **SERVICES:** Full managerial services, **REP CLIENTS.** Only operate our own prop.; **PREV EMPLOY:** Metropolitan Bldg. Corp. - Seattle, WA; **PROFL AFFIL & HONORS:** BOMA, Past Pres. BOMA, RPA, WSBCAC; **EDUC:** BA, 1940, Poli. Sci. and Bus., Univ. of WA, Seattle, WA; **MIL SERV:** US Army, 1941-1945, 1st Lt.; **OTHER ACT & HONORS:** Washington Athletic Club, Rainier Club, 101 Club, Univ. of WA Alumni Assn., Better Business Bureau, Jerry Lorentzon Foundation, C of C, Downtown Seattle Development Assn., Ducks Unlimited, King County Humane Society, Big Brothers of Seattle, Seattle Rotary Club, WA State Forest Practices Advisory Comm.; **HOME ADD:** 18241 14th N.W., Seattle, WA 98177, (206)542-2971; **BUS ADD:** 3300 Rainier Bank Tower, Seattle, WA 98101, (206)628-5093.

DIESSNER, Michael F.——**B:** Jan. 30, 1952, *Atty.*, Storey & Ross; **PRIM RE ACT:** Attorney; **EDUC:** AB, 1974, Hist., Creighton Univ.; **GRAD EDUC:** JD, 1977, Creighton Univ.; LLM, 1978, NY Univ.; **EDUC HONORS:** Cum Laude; **HOME ADD:** 2302 East Cortez, Phoenix, AZ 85028, (602)992-6595; **BUS ADD:** 2100 North Central Ave., Phoenix, AZ 85004, (602)252-7500.

DIETRICH, Robert E.——**B:** July 15, 1947, Salinas, CA, *RE Appraiser*, Burke, Hansen, Homan & Klafter; **PRIM RE ACT:** Consultant, Appraiser; **SERVICES:** Appraisal of farms and ranches, comml., subdivs., indus., multi-family resid.; **PROFL AFFIL & HONORS:** AIREA; Amer. Soc. of Farm Mgrs. and Rural Appraisers; SREA; Assoc. Member, So. AZ Home Builders Assn.; **EDUC:** BS, 1969, Bus. Admin., Univ. of AZ; **MIL SERV:** US Army, 1st Lt., 1970-1973; **OTHER ACT & HONORS:** Tucson C of C; Treas. and Exec. VP of Burke, Hansen & Moman; **BUS ADD:** 6245 E. Broadway, Ste. 690, Tucson, AZ 85711, (602)790-8555.

DIETZ, Rowland——**B:** Oct. 26, 1920, Cincinnati, OH, *Pres.*, R.E. Dietz and Co., Inc.; **PRIM RE ACT:** Broker, Syndicator, Consultant, Property Manager; **REP CLIENTS:** Fort Washington Trust; **PREV EMPLOY:** Asst. Prof., Western Coll. for Women, Oxford, OH; Visiting lecturer, 1962-1967, Northern KY Univ. 1975; **PROFL AFFIL & HONORS:** Inst. of RE Mgmt., CPM; **EDUC:** BA, 1942, Poli. Sci., Swarthmore Coll.; **GRAD EDUC:** MA, PhD, 1962, Public Law, Columbia Univ.; **MIL SERV:** USNR, Ens.; **OTHER ACT & HONORS:** Dir. Charter Comm., Cincinnati, 1953-1978; VP Council on World Affairs, 1955-56; Consultant, Brookings Inst., 1964; Pres., Cincinnati Inst. of RE Mgmt., 1972; Cincinnati Assn. 1972 to present; **HOME ADD:** 544 Milton St., Cincinnati, OH 45202, (513)241-4434; **BUS ADD:** 225 E. 6 St, Cincinnati, OH 45202, (513)241-3375.

DIEZ, Jim, Jr.——**B:** Jan. 26, 1943, San Francisco, CA, *Chmn. of the Bd.*, Diez Associates; **PRIM RE ACT:** Lender, Owner/Investor, Property Manager; **EDUC:** BS, 1966, Fin., Univ. of CO; **BUS ADD:** PO Box 32590, Phoenix, AZ 85064.

DIFIORE, Richard James——**B:** July 16, 1950, Chicago, IL, *Devel. Dir.*, Cousins Properties Inc.; **PRIM RE ACT:** Developer, Owner/Investor, Property Manager; **OTHER RE ACT:** Leasing Dir., Prop. Mgr.; **PREV EMPLOY:** Kern & Padgett Co., Portman Props.; **PROFL AFFIL & HONORS:** IREM, ICSC, CPM; **EDUC:** BS, 1972, Mktg., Univ. of VA; **HOME ADD:** 687 Willow Mill Ct., Marietta, GA 30067, (404)971-4047; **BUS ADD:** 300 Interstate N., Atlanta, GA 30339, (404)955-0000.

DIGENNARO, Frank——**B:** Aug. 8, 1919, New York, NY, *Dir. of RE*, United Artist Theatre Corp.; **PRIM RE ACT:** Broker, Appraiser; **OTHER RE ACT:** Site expert; **PROFL AFFIL & HONORS:** Long Island Bd. of Realtors; **GRAD EDUC:** Long Island Univ., 1940; **OTHER ACT & HONORS:** Pres. Kiwanis Club, Member Pioneer's Club, Motion Picture Industry; **HOME ADD:** 94-07 156th Ave., Howard Beach, NY 11414, (212)641-5113; **BUS ADD:** 2545 Hempstead Tpk., East Meadow, NY 11554, (516)579-8400.

DIGERONIMO, Richard J.——**B:** July 3, 1950, Brooklyn, NY, *VP*, Howard Jackson Assoc., Inc.; **PRIM RE ACT:** Consultant, Appraiser; **SERVICES:** RE appraising & consulting, nationwide basis; **REP CLIENTS:** JMB; McNeil; Integrated Resources; R.A. Meneil Corp.; Stonehenge; Commonwealth Pacific; Citicorp; URNS Realty Inc.; **PROFL AFFIL & HONORS:** MAI; SRPA; IFAS; CRA; **EDUC:** BS, 1973, Psychology, RE Valuation & Fin., SUNY, Stonybrook; **OTHER ACT & HONORS:** Stonybrook Alumni Assn.; **HOME ADD:** 32 Roxbury Rd., Garden City, NY, (516)741-2987; **BUS ADD:** 129 Front St., Mineola, NY 11501, (516)248-2844.

DIGIORNO, John B.——**B:** Dec. 18, 1927, Pittsburgh, PA, *Pres.*, Century 21, DiGiorno Realty, Inc.; **PRIM RE ACT:** Broker, Consultant, Appraiser, Owner/Investor, Property Manager, Insuror, Syndicator; **SERVICES:** Investment counseling, prop. mgmt., prop. evaluation, comml. packaging, insurance, appraisal service; **REP CLIENTS:** Attys., banking instns., housing opportunities, org., investors in comml. projects; **PREV EMPLOY:** Designer & Mech. Engr. in pvt. indus. 1949-1969; **PROFL AFFIL & HONORS:** NAR; PAR; Greater Pittsburgh Bd. of Realtors; McKeesport Bd. of Realtors; Century 21 Comml./Investment Bd.; **MIL SERV:** USN; Fireman 1/c; South Pacific Duty, Marksmans; **OTHER ACT & HONORS:** Clairton Rifle Club; W. Mifflin Vol. Fireman; Elks; Thompson Run Athletic Assn.; **HOME ADD:** 1061 Huston Dr., West Mifflin, PA 15122, (412)466-6510; **BUS ADD:** 4401 Kennywood Blvd., West Mifflin, PA 15122, (412)462-7300.

DIJULIUS, Dr. Leonard G.——**B:** Oct. 30, 1923, Lowellville, OH, *Pres.*, Tudor Enterprises; **PRIM RE ACT:** Broker, Syndicator, Consultant, Developer; **SERVICES:** Investment Counseling & Analysis, Dev. Synd.; **PROFL AFFIL & HONORS:** Comml. & Investment Div. of CAR; RESSI; **EDUC:** 1946-1947, Pre-Med., Univ. of Akron, OH; **GRAD EDUC:** DDS, 1951, Pediatric Dentistry, Northwestern Univ.; **EDUC HONORS:** Dean's Hon. List; **MIL SERV:** US Army, WW II, Sgt; Korean War, Capt.; **HOME ADD:** PO Box 2441, Rancho Santa Fe., CA 92067, (714)481-3221; **BUS ADD:** 15930 Via de las Palmas, PO Box 2441, Rancho Santa Fe, CA 92067, (714)481-3221.

DILBECK, Harold Roy——**B:** May 28, 1932, Taft, CA, *Prof.*, CA State Univ. at Long Beach; **PRIM RE ACT:** Broker, Instructor; **OTHER RE ACT:** CPA; **PREV EMPLOY:** Visiting Assoc. Prof., Escula de Administration de Negocios Para Granuados (Stanford) USAID Project, Lime Peru; Asst. & Assoc. Prof. in Fin., USC, 1961-1966; Grad. Research Economist, UCLA, 1960-1961; **PROFL AFFIL & HONORS:** AICPA; CA State Soc. of CPA's; Amer. Fin. Assn.; Fin. Mgmt. Assn., Amer. Men & Women of Science (12th Edition); Who's Who in the W., 1980-1981; Who's Who in CA Bus. & Fin., 1980-1981; Who's Who in CA, 1981-1982; **EDUC:** BS, 1956, Fresno State Coll.; **GRAD EDUC:** MBA, 1958, Univ. of CA at Los Angeles; PhD, 1961, Univ. of CA at Los Angeles; **MIL SERV:** USMC; **OTHER ACT & HONORS:** Published in: Journal of Fin., March, 1962; Public Utilities Fort-Nightly, March 26, 1964; The Journal of Business of the Univ. of Chicago, July, 1964; The Journal of Accountancy, October, 1967 with Robert Seiler; **HOME ADD:** 18722 Vanderlip, Santa Ana, CA 92705, (714)731-7370; **BUS ADD:** Harold Dilbeck Accountants, Inc., 1442 Irvine Blvd., Suite 219, Tustin, CA 92680, (714)730-1661.

DILL, B. John——**B:** Dec. 3, 1951, Milton, MA, *Pres.*, Center Square Inc., Springfield Inst. for Savings; **PRIM RE ACT:** Broker, Developer, Lender, Owner/Investor, Property Manager; **SERVICES:** Devel., leasing & mgmt. of comml.; **REP CLIENTS:** Resid. RE for the account of Springfield Instn. for Savings & others; **PREV EMPLOY:** Asst. VP Springfield Instn. for Savings; **PROFL AFFIL & HONORS:** ULI, SREA, Mort. Bankers Assn., ICSC, BOMA; **EDUC:** BA, 1974, Williams Coll.; **HOME ADD:** 132 Overlook Dr., Springfield, MA 01118; **BUS ADD:** Suite 2406, 1500 Main St., Springfield, MA 01103, (413)781-0065.

DILL, Leonard C.——**B:** May 10, 1931, Philadelphia, PA, *Sr. VP & Treas.*, Hotel Investors Corp.; **PRIM RE ACT:** Developer, Owner/Investor, Property Manager; **SERVICES:** Devel. or acquisition of mgmt. of hotels; **PREV EMPLOY:** Hotel Investors Trust, 1971-1980; **EDUC:** BA, 1956, Eng., Univ. of PA; **MIL SERV:** US Army 1951-1954; **HOME ADD:** 18125 Cattail Rd., Poolesville, MD 20837, (301)972-8446; **BUS ADD:** 5530 Wisconsin Ave., Chevy Chase, MD 20815, (301)654-9200.

DILLENBECK, Steven R.——**B:** Aug. 8, 1940, Los Angeles, CA, *Prop. Mgr.*, Port of Los Angeles; **PRIM RE ACT:** Appraiser, Developer, Property Manager; **OTHER RE ACT:** Leasing of comml. port facilities; **SERVICES:** All port facilities and land and water; **REP CLIENTS:** All port users - 550 leases; **PROFL AFFIL & HONORS:** Propeller Club, Intl. Right of Way Assn., CPM - IREM; **EDUC:** BS, 1964, Public Admin., Univ. of S. CA; **OTHER ACT & HONORS:** Wilmington C of C, Harbor Assn. of Indus. & Commerce; **BUS ADD:** 425 Palos Verdes Ave., San Pedro, CA 90731, (213)519-3860.

DILLINGHAM, William W.——**B:** Feb. 26, 1941, Ogdensburg, NY, *Pres.*, Centry 21 Dillingham; **PRIM RE ACT:** Broker, Consultant, Appraiser; **SERVICES:** Relocation counseling, Valuation and gen. RE brokerage including all types of props.; **PROFL AFFIL & HONORS:** VP, SW MI Bd. of Realtors; VP Bd. of Dirs., Twin Cities area C of C, GRI, RAM, CRS; **EDUC:** 1963, Econ. and Psych., DePauw Univ. - Greencastle, IN; **GRAD EDUC:** 1968, Aeronautical Scis., USNR; **MIL SERV:** USNR, Lt. Comdr., 1966-1974; **OTHER ACT & HONORS:** St. Joseph - Benton Harbor, Rotary Club; **HOME ADD:** 303 S. Veronica Ct., St. Joseph, MI 49085, (616)983-3003; **BUS ADD:** 2024 Washington Ave., St. Joseph, MI 49085, (616)983-6371.

DILLMAN, Rodney J.——**B:** July 3, 1952, Lima, OH, *Assoc. Counsel*, Massachusetts Mutual Life Insurance Co., Law; **PRIM RE ACT:** Attorney; **PROFL AFFIL & HONORS:** MA Bar Assn., ABA (Real Pro. Sect.); **EDUC:** BS Educ., 1974, Mathematics and Social Studies, Kent State Univ.; **GRAD EDUC:** MA Econ., 1975, Kent State Univ.; JD, 1978, Duke Univ.; **HOME ADD:** 77 Peekskill Ave., Springfield, MA 01129, (413)783-6289; **BUS ADD:** 1295 State St., Springfield, MA 01111, (413)788-8411.

DILLON, Joseph G.——**B:** Sept. 1, 1934, Chicago, IL, *Pres.*, Joseph Dillon & Company; **PRIM RE ACT:** Broker, Consultant, Appraiser, Developer, Owner/Investor, Property Manager, Syndicator; **SERVICES:** Full service RE specializing in indus. and comml. props.; **PREV EMPLOY:** Gen. Dynamics Corp., Henry Crown & Co., Harrington, Tideman, & O'Leary, Arthur Rubloff & Co., Joseph Dillon & Co.; **PROFL AFFIL & HONORS:** Society of Industrial Realtors (Past National Director) Assn. of Industrial RE Brokers (Past President) NAIOP (Past Chapter President) Industrial Development and Research Counsel, Urban Land Institute, Realty Club of Chicago, Realtors' Forty Club; **EDUC:** BA, 1956, Loyola Univ.; **MIL SERV:** US Army, Capt.; **HOME ADD:** 551 Monroe St., Glencoe, IL 60022; **BUS ADD:** 631 Busse Rd., Bensenville, IL 60106, (312)860-5300.

DILLON, Peter——*Pres.*, Northwestern Steel & Wire Co.; **PRIM RE ACT:** Property Manager; **BUS ADD:** 121 Wallace St., Sterling, IL 61081, (815)625-2500.*

DI MARIA, Philip A.——**B:** May 19, 1914, Chicago, IL, *Partner*, Di Maria & Ferguson; **OTHER RE ACT:** Law Practice; **SERVICES:** Counsel and litigation in RE matters; **REP CLIENTS:** RE Brokers, RE sales and RE devel.; **PREV EMPLOY:** Self employed in law firm; **PROFL AFFIL & HONORS:** CA Trial Lawyers Assn., Order of the Coif at Stanford Law School; **EDUC:** BA, 1935, Econ., Stanford; **GRAD EDUC:** JD, 1938, Law, Stanford Law School; **EDUC HONORS:** Phi Beta Kappa, Order of the Coif; **MIL SERV:** USAF, Capt.; **OTHER ACT & HONORS:** Bd. of Dir. - Peninsula Mfr. Assn.; Bd. of Dir. Palo Alto C of C; **HOME ADD:** 330 Sunkist Lane, Los Altos, CA 94022, (415)948-6357; **BUS ADD:** 425 Sherman Ave., Palo Alto, CA 94306, (415)321-4460.

DIMARTINO, Arthur——**B:** Mar. 15, 1946, New York, NY, *Partner*, Trammell Crow Co., OH Valley; **PRIM RE ACT:** Developer, Owner/Investor; **SERVICES:** Devel.,leasing and mgmt. of indus. and comml. props.; **PREV EMPLOY:** Bankers Trust Co., NYC; **PROFL AFFIL & HONORS:** Industrial Devel. Council; **EDUC:** BA, 1968, Poli. Sci., Brown Univ.; **GRAD EDUC:** MBA, 1973, Fin., Wharton Grad. Div.; **MIL SERV:** USAR; **OTHER ACT & HONORS:** Commnr., Brown Club of KY; Louisville Energy Commn., Advisory Bd., Christ Church United Methodist; **BUS ADD:** 7601 National Tpk., Louisville, KY 40214, (502)361-0101.

DIMICELLI, Vincent——**B:** Apr. 26, 1952, New York, NY, *Consultant*, Woodway Realty Corp.; **PRIM RE ACT:** Consultant, Developer, Owner/Investor, Syndicator; **OTHER RE ACT:** Computer analyses, joint ventures; **SERVICES:** Serving foreign clients investing in, buying or selling US RE; **REP CLIENTS:** MM. Worms & Cie (Paris), foreign banks, RE devels., and private investors; **EDUC:** BA, 1976, Hist., Rutgers Univ.; **GRAD EDUC:** MBA, 1978, RE, Fin., Rutgers Grad. School of Bus. Admin.; **HOME ADD:** 20 Winding Way, Little Silver, NJ 07739, (201)530-4004; **BUS ADD:** 450 Park Ave., New York, NY 10022, (212)355-5050.

DIMOND, Jack——**B:** Jan. 26, 1942, Asheville, NC, *Pres.*, Timbercreek Development Corp.; **PRIM RE ACT:** Consultant, Engineer, Developer, Builder, Owner/Investor, Property Manager, Syndicator; **SERVICES:** Complete planning & devel. capabilities; **PREV EMPLOY:** Bruce Williams Consulting Engrs.; Black & Ueatch Consulting Engrs.; Gillenwaters Devel.; Engrg. Design; **PROFL AFFIL & HONORS:** MSPE, NSPE, ASME, Registered; **EDUC:** BSME, 1969, Energy, Univ. MO Rolla; **GRAD EDUC:** MS Engrg. Administration, 1970, Fin., Univ. MO Rolla; **HOME ADD:** 4650 S. Kelley, Springfield, MO 65807, (417)883-4502; **BUS ADD:** 982 S. Timbercreek Ave., Springfield, MO 65807, (417)864-7557.

DINA, Nizar——**B:** Jan. 23, 1938, Tanzania, *Pres.*, Eurocommerce Realty Ltd.; **PRIM RE ACT:** Broker, Consultant, Owner/Investor; **PROFL AFFIL & HONORS:** RE Bd. of Gr. Vancouver, ICI Div.; Intl. Inst. of Valuers; **EDUC:** 1952, Language, Cambridge; **HOME ADD:** 1211-2016 Fullerton Ave., N. Vancouver, B.C., Can., (604)926-3008; **BUS ADD:** Suite 411-717 W. Pender St., Vancouver, B.C., Can., (604)685-7246.

DINKELMAN, Jerard H.——**B:** July 14, 1954, Salt Lake City, UT, *Broker*, Trade- West Devel. Corp., RE; **PRIM RE ACT:** Broker, Developer, Builder, Owner/Investor; **SERVICES:** New home builder; **REP CLIENTS:** First time home buyers & retirerees; **PREV EMPLOY:** Realtor Assoc. 1977-80; **PROFL AFFIL & HONORS:** NHBA, Salt Lake Bd. of Realtors, HOW Builder, Member of the Million Dollar Club; **EDUC:** BA, 1972, Trade Tech. of UT; **HOME ADD:** 6370 Higate Ave., Salt Lake City, UT 84107, (801)968-5388; **BUS ADD:** 6526 S. State St., Salt Lake City, UT 84107, (801)268-3200.

DINOTE, Daniel A., Jr.——**B:** Oct. 2, 1927, Philadelphia, PA, *Principal*, Dinote & Associates; **PRIM RE ACT:** Broker, Consultant, Attorney, Appraiser; **SERVICES:** Comml. and indus. prop. valuation and investment counsel; **REP CLIENTS:** Institl. and corp. lenders and investors; **PREV EMPLOY:** Income, mort., loan depts. of First Pennsylvania Bank, 1963-1966; Equitable Life Assurance Soc., 1956-1963; **PROFL AFFIL & HONORS:** AIREA; SREA; ABA; ULI, MAI; **EDUC:** AB, 1950, Psych./Poli. Sci., Coll. of Liberal Arts, Temple Univ.; **GRAD EDUC:** JD, 1961, Law, Univ. of Baltimore Law School; **EDUC HONORS:** Magna Cum Laude; **MIL SERV:** USNR; HA1/c, WWII; **HOME ADD:** 2813 Marshall Rd., Drexel Hill, PA 19026, (215)259-9082; **BUS ADD:** 2813 Marshall Rd., Drexel Hill, PA 19026, (215)259-9082.

DINSMORE, John A.——B: June 27, 1933, Wauwatosa, WI, *Mgr. of RE & Risk Mgmt.*, Jos. Schlitz Brewing Co.; **PRIM RE ACT:** Broker, Consultant, Appraiser, Builder, Property Manager, Insuror; **OTHER RE ACT:** Ad valorem tax rep.; **SERVICES:** Investment counseling, valuation, tax rep., prop. mgmt., bldg. admin. and risk mgmt.; **REP CLIENTS:** Mgmt. of Indus. Corps.; **PREV EMPLOY:** Right-of-way acquisitions of electric utility; **PROFL AFFIL & HONORS:** NACORE; Nat. Assn. of Prop. Tax Reps.; AR/WA; Intl. Assn. of Assessing Officers, Cert. Prop. Tax Rep.; **EDUC:** BS, 1959, Econ., Univ. of WI; **MIL SERV:** USAF, Sgt., 1951-1955; **OTHER ACT & HONORS:** Alderman, City of Cedarburg, 1974-1979; AOPA; **HOME ADD:** N78 W. 7064 Oak St., Cedarburg, WI 53212, (414)377-3202; **BUS ADD:** PO Box 614, Milwaukee, WI 53201, (414)224-5626.

DINSMORE, Richard H.——B: June 12, 1943, Indianapolis, IN, *Broker, Mgng. Partner*, Cushman, Wakefield of Kentucky, Ramco Props., Part.; **PRIM RE ACT:** Broker, Consultant, Developer, Owner/Investor, Property Manager; **SERVICES:** RE brokerage, investor devel.; **REP CLIENTS:** Prudential Ins. Co. of Amer.; Ramco Props.; **PREV EMPLOY:** Dist. Mgr., Amer. Telephone & Telegraph; 8 yrs.; **PROFL AFFIL & HONORS:** Louisville Bd. of Realtors; NAIOP, MBA; BEE; MBEE; Broker; **EDUC:** BEE, 1966, EE, Univ. of Louisville, Louisville, KY; **GRAD EDUC:** MBA, 1968, Univ. of KY; MBEE, 1975, Univ. of Louisville; **EDUC HONORS:** Omicron Delta Kappa, Dean's List; **MIL SERV:** US Army; SP-5; **OTHER ACT & HONORS:** Pres. Countryside Homeowners Assn., 155 homes; **HOME ADD:** 13105 Blossom Way, Prospect, KY 40059, (502)228-8856; **BUS ADD:** PO Box 35576, Louisvil, KY 40232, (502)897-2571.

DINSMORE, Robert——*Manager Office Administration*, Amstar Corporation; **PRIM RE ACT:** Property Manager; **BUS ADD:** 1251 Avenue of the Americas, New York, NY 10020, (415)367-2011.*

DIPRETE, Andrew A.——*Member*, Department of Housing and Urban Development, Federal Home Loan Bank Baord; **PRIM RE ACT:** Lender; **BUS ADD:** 451 Seventh St., S.W., Washington, DC 20410, (202)377-6270.*

DIRIENZO, Gregory C.——B: Feb. 4, 1947, Burlington, NJ, *Partner*, Greenwich Development Co.; **PRIM RE ACT:** Developer, Builder, Syndicator; **SERVICES:** Investment counseling, valuation, devel. and synd. of comml. props., prop. mgmt.; **PREV EMPLOY:** VP Development, Oxford Props. Inc., Newport Beach, CA; **EDUC:** BS, 1972, Fin. & RE, San Diego State Univ.; **HOME ADD:** 23 Pinehurst, Newport Beach, CA 92660; **BUS ADD:** 19762 MacArthur Blvd., Irvine, CA 92715, (714)851-8333.

DISABATO, Ray R.——B: Aug. 12, 1948, Evergreen Park, IL, *Asst. VP*, Western Amer. Mort., Comml. Loans; **PRIM RE ACT:** Lender; **SERVICES:** Comml. R.E. lending & devel.; **REP CLIENTS:** Devels. & instnl. investors in comml. props.; **PREV EMPLOY:** Supervisor, Appraisal Dept., Western S & L; **PROFL AFFIL & HONORS:** SRA-SREA, MBA, Candidate for MAI, AIREA; **EDUC:** BS, 1972, Fin., Univ. of AZ; **MIL SERV:** AZ AirNG, S/Sgt.; **HOME ADD:** 4602 E., 9th, Tucson, AZ, (602)326-1548; **BUS ADD:** P.O. Box 12547, Tucson, AZ, (602)886-1258.

DISCALA, Joseph V.——B: Jan. 21, 1950, Norwalk, CT, *CEO*, DiScala Fairfield Co.; **PRIM RE ACT:** Consultant, Owner/Investor, Property Manager; **PROFL AFFIL & HONORS:** SIR; NACORE, CRE FIABCI Board of Realtors; RE Brokers Assn.; **EDUC:** Principals & Practices in RE (Certificate), 1970, Office Leasing, Univ. of CT; **HOME ADD:** 14 Norport Dr., E. Norwalk, CT 06855, (203)866-7218; **BUS ADD:** 101 Merritt 7 Corporate Park, Norwalk, CT 06855, (203)853-0200.

DISERA, Bonnie——B: Mar. 29, 1934, Joliet, IL, *Realtor Assoc.-Broker*, Bell Realty; **PRIM RE ACT:** Broker, Appraiser, Owner/Investor, Property Manager, Real Estate Publisher; **SERVICES:** RE saleswoman; **HOME ADD:** 555 Westminster, Joliet, IL 60435, (815)725-8584; **BUS ADD:** 2122 W. Jefferson, Joliet, IL 60435, (815)725-1251.

DISNEY, Fred——B: Mar. 11, 1946, Tuscaloosa, AL, *Exec. VP*, James A. Sammons Co.; **PRIM RE ACT:** Developer; **PROFL AFFIL & HONORS:** ULI; **MIL SERV:** USMCR, Sgt.; **HOME ADD:** 2454 Lofton Terr., Fort Worth, TX 76109, (817)927-8203; **BUS ADD:** 2630 W. Freeway 218, Fort Worth, TX 76102, (817)335-3216.

DISTELL, Stephen A.——B: Mar. 12, 1935, Philadelphia, PA, *Owner*, S.A. Distell Realtors; **PRIM RE ACT:** Broker, Consultant, Appraiser, Developer, Builder, Owner/Investor, Property Manager, Insuror; **SERVICES:** Relocation brokerage, Brokerage Div., Custom Home Building; **REP CLIENTS:** Bell S&L Assoc.; Jos. Beller Esq., Donald Artzt Esq.; FHA Fee Appraiser; **PREV EMPLOY:** Fox Builders; Colonial Mrtg. Service Co.; **PROFL AFFIL & HONORS:** NAR; PA Assn. of Realtors; ERC - Employee Relocation Council; Mainline Bd. of Realtors; Delaware Cty. Bd. of Realtors; **EDUC:** BS, 1959, Temple Univ.; **OTHER ACT & HONORS:** Mason; **HOME ADD:** 307 Barwynne Ln., Wynnewood, PA 19151, (215)642-0741; **BUS ADD:** 337 Montgomery Ave., Bala Cynwyd, PA 19004, (215)667-7400.

DITMANS, Frederick S.——B: Apr. 20, 1951, Aberdeen, MD, *Controller*, Bradley Industrial Park; **PRIM RE ACT:** Developer, Builder, Property Manager; **OTHER RE ACT:** Lic. RE Salesperson; **EDUC:** BS, 1978, Fin., Lehigh Univ.; **GRAD EDUC:** MBA, 1980, Fin. and Mgmt. of Org., Columbia School of Bus.; **EDUC HONORS:** High Honors; **OTHER ACT & HONORS:** Rotary of Blauvelt; **HOME ADD:** 626 So. Pascack Rd., Spring Valley, NY 10913, (914)735-3268; **BUS ADD:** 500 Bradley Hill Rd., Blauvelt, NY 10913, (914)358-7300.

DITZ, William W.——*Northern CA Proj. Mgr.*, Cabot, Cabot & Forbes; **PRIM RE ACT:** Developer; **BUS ADD:** 1 Maritime Plaza, Ste 1300, San Francisco, CA 94111, (415)981-5180.*

DIXON, Carl F.——B: Jan. 21, 1934, Trenton, NJ, *Broker*, Dixon Realty, Inc.; **PRIM RE ACT:** Broker, Consultant, Appraiser, Owner/Investor, Property Manager, Insuror; **SERVICES:** Sales, consultation; **PREV EMPLOY:** Mktg.; **PROFL AFFIL & HONORS:** NAR, CO Assn. of Realtors, RE Exchangors, GRI Designation; **EDUC:** BS, 1956, Pre-Dental, Wilberforce Univ.; **GRAD EDUC:** Grad. School of Bus., 19 hrs., Bus. Mgmt., Univ. of CO; **MIL SERV:** US Army, E-5; **OTHER ACT & HONORS:** Commnr. - Aurora Housing Authority, United Way Mile-Hi Board; **HOME ADD:** 11551 E. Cedar Ave., Aurora, CO 80012, (303)341-2324; **BUS ADD:** 1532 Galena Ste #301, Aurora, CO 80010, (303)343-6660.

DIXON, Don R.——B: Nov. 20, 1938, Vernon, TX, *Chief Exec. Officer*, Dondi Group, Inc.; **PRIM RE ACT:** Developer, Builder; **SERVICES:** Resid. merchant bldg. & investment propl. devel.; **PREV EMPLOY:** Raldon Corp., Dallas, TX; **PROFL AFFIL & HONORS:** Nat. Assn. of Homebuilders; **EDUC:** BS, 1960, Mktg., Univ. of CA at Los Angeles, Highest Hon.; **HOME ADD:** 6515 Clubhouse Cir., Dallas, TX 75251, (214)387-8941; **BUS ADD:** 7995 LBJ Frwy. 118, Dallas, TX 75251, (214)385-7300.

DIXON, John E.——B: Apr. 3, 1955, Sandusky, OH, *Mgr.*, Landlord Credit, Inc.; **PRIM RE ACT:** Appraiser, Property Manager, Owner/Investor; **PROFL AFFIL & HONORS:** Member of OH Realtors, Erie Cty. Bd. of Realtors, MLS, Candidate for CPM, NAR, Notary of Public, Cleveland Branch of IREM; **EDUC:** Toledo Univ., Lorain Community Coll., Firelands Coll.; **HOME ADD:** 928 Hayes Ave., Sandusky, OH 44870, (419)626-0751; **BUS ADD:** 1002 Tiffin Ave. Box 2059, Sandusky, OH 44870, (419)625-2713.

DIXON, Paul H., Jr.——B: Feb. 21, 1935, Little Rock, AR, *VP*, The Danny Thomas Co.; **PRIM RE ACT:** Broker, Syndicator; **SERVICES:** Comml. Brokerage, Sund. of Comml. Props. and raw land; **REP CLIENTS:** Indiv. investors in comml. props.; **PREV EMPLOY:** 7 yrs. in Securities/Tax shelter sales; **PROFL AFFIL & HONORS:** NAR; RESSI; Little Rock/N. Little Rock Bd. of Realtors, 1980 Million Dollar Sales Club of Little Rock/N Little Rock Bd. of Realtors; **EDUC:** BA, 1956, Econ., Henderson State Univ.; **GRAD EDUC:** Acctg., Univ. of AR at Little Rock; **MIL SERV:** US Army, Capt., Active Duty 56/57, 61/62; **HOME ADD:** 3200 Montrose Dr., Little Rock, AR 72212, (501)225-7943; **BUS ADD:** Suite 400, 212 Ctr., Little Rock, AR 72201, (501)374-2231.

DIXON, Stephen J.——B: Aug. 12, 1942, Atlanta, GA, *Pres.*, Clover, Realtors; **PRIM RE ACT:** Broker; **SERVICES:** Full serv. resid. & comml. RE; **PROFL AFFIL & HONORS:** NAR, GA Assn. of Realtors, RNMI, CRB, GRI; **EDUC:** BBA, 1964, RE, Univ. of GA; **OTHER ACT & HONORS:** Tr., Joseph T. Walker School; **HOME ADD:** 1011 Clubland Ct., Marietta, GA 30067, (404)971-7076; **BUS ADD:** 257 Mt. Vernon Hwy. NE, Atlanta, GA 30363, (404)255-6122.

DOAN, Gregory K.——B: July 26, 1947, Auburn, NY; **PRIM RE ACT:** Broker, Consultant, Appraiser; **SERVICES:** Sales, appraisal, and consulting; **PREV EMPLOY:** VP in charge of Corp. RE Dept. of RI Hospital Trust, Nat. Bank, Providence; **PROFL AFFIL & HONORS:** Member of NY State Soc. of RE Appraisers; Member,

Cayuga Cty. Bd. of Realtors; **EDUC:** BS, 1969, RE/Urban Devel., Syracuse Univ.; **GRAD EDUC:** MBA, 1973, Fin., Univ. of RI; **HOME ADD:** 5892 E. Lake Rd., Auburn, NY 13021, (315)255-1882; **BUS ADD:** 25 E. Genesee St., Auburn, NY 13021, (315)253-7371.

DOBB, Herbert——*Sr. VP Adm.*, Western Gear Corp.; **PRIM RE ACT:** Property Manager; **BUS ADD:** PO Box 182, Lynwood, CA 90262, (213)638-7821.*

DOBRIN, Stanley R.——**B:** Oct. 14, 1942, MN, *Pres.*, The Highland Fin. Group, Inc.; **PRIM RE ACT:** Broker, Consultant, Syndicator; **OTHER RE ACT:** Mort. Broker; **SERVICES:** RE consulting & mort. placement; **REP CLIENTS:** RE owners & investors; **PREV EMPLOY:** Mort. Assocs., Inc. 1969-74; **PROFL AFFIL & HONORS:** Mort. Bankers Assn./Apt. Assn. MN, Licensed MN RE Broker; **EDUC:** BA, 1964, Econ., Oberlin Coll.; **GRAD EDUC:** MBA, 1969, Fin. & RE, Harvard Bus. School; **OTHER ACT & HONORS:** Olympic Hills C of C; Past Dir. Mpls. Fed. for Jewish Serv.; Dir., Talmud Torah School; Past Pres. Indian Foothills Assn., Pres., BDH-Ohio Inc.; Pres., Tsl Inc. (oil co's.); Dir., Tabor Mining & Metals Corp.; Dir., Wheel & Axle Serv. Corp.; **HOME ADD:** 7001 Sally Ln., Edina, MN 55435, (612)941-7787; **BUS ADD:** 6100 Green Valley Dr., Bloomington, MN 55438, (612)831-2275.

DOBRIS, Joel C.——**B:** Jan. 19, 1940, Albany, NY, *Prof. of Law*, Univ. of CA at Davis; **PRIM RE ACT:** Attorney, Instructor; **SERVICES:** Law teacher; **PREV EMPLOY:** Lawyer, Milbank, Tweek, Hadley & McCloy, NY, 1966-76; **PROFL AFFIL & HONORS:** ABA, NY State Bar Assn., Assn. of the Bar of the City of NY; **EDUC:** BA, 1963, Eng., Yale; **GRAD EDUC:** LLB, 1966, Univ. of MN; **EDUC HONORS:** Law Review; **HOME ADD:** 1508 Lemon Ln., Davis, CA 95616, (916)756-6359; **BUS ADD:** Sch. of Law Univ. of CA, Davis, CA 95616, (916)752-1600.

DOBROTH, Dale——**B:** July 9, 1949, Chicago, IL, *Vice President*, Balcor Mortgage Advisors; **PRIM RE ACT:** Broker, Lender, Property Manager, Syndicator; **SERVICES:** Wrap around mort. loand; 1st mort. loans; **REP CLIENTS:** Comml. prop. owners valued in excess of $2,000,000; **PREV EMPLOY:** C.N.A. Ins.-Mort. Loan and RE; **PROFL AFFIL & HONORS:** Chicago Jr. RE Bd.; Chicago N. Shore RE Bd.; Accredited Mgmt. Org.-Institute of RE Mgmt., CPM; CSM; RPA; **EDUC:** Bus., 1976, Fin., Northwestern Univ.; **HOME ADD:** 552 Greystone, Wheeling, IL 60090, (312)454-1954; **BUS ADD:** 10024 Skokie Blvd., Skokie, IL 60077, (312)677-2900.

DOBSON, Tom W.——**B:** Jan. 25, 1914, Lewiston, ME, *Self-employed - owner*, Tom Dobson Realty - Realtor; **PRIM RE ACT:** Broker, Appraiser, Banker, Insuror; **SERVICES:** U.S.D. Dir. 1942-1944; **PREV EMPLOY:** Travelers Ins. Co., Wash, DC, Self-employed - Tom Dobson Realty & Ins. since 1944; **PROFL AFFIL & HONORS:** Gainesville Bd. Realtor of the Year Award 1974; **EDUC:** 1940, George Washington & Southeastern Univ. DC; **GRAD EDUC:** AA, 1940, Poli. Sci., Southeastern Univ., Washington, DC; **MIL SERV:** Dir. U.S.O. Tallahassee FL (1942-1943) & Avon Park FL (1943-1944); **OTHER ACT & HONORS:** ASA, Intl. RE Fed. Amer. Chap.; **HOME ADD:** 1049 SW 11th Terrace, Gainesville, FL 32601, (904)372-8296; **BUS ADD:** 1219 W. University Ave., PO Box 1066, Gainesville, FL 32602, (904)372-1473.

DODD, James H.——**B:** Mar. 8, 1931, Belmont, NC, *Realtor*, Lord Real Estate; **PRIM RE ACT:** Broker, Owner/Investor; **REP CLIENTS:** Investors (for synds.) and apt. exchangors; **PREV EMPLOY:** Coll. instr.; **PROFL AFFIL & HONORS:** NAR, ME Assn. of Realtors; **EDUC:** BS Education, 1956, Eng.; **GRAD EDUC:** MA, 1967, Eng.; **EDUC HONORS:** Phi Delta Kappa; **MIL SERV:** US Army, Pfc, Four Bronze Stars with Arrow Head; **OTHER ACT & HONORS:** Pres. of two investment clubs, Pres. Bath Brunswick Rental Assn., Bd. of Dirs., YMCA; **HOME ADD:** Mere Point Road, RFD 3, Box 3095, Brunswick, ME 04011, (207)725-5001; **BUS ADD:** 159 Pleasant St., Brunswick, ME 04011, (207)729-9912.

DODDS, Dorothy Gillespie——**B:** Nov. 21, 1921, Wichita, KS, *Broker, Owner*, Dorothy Dodds Realtors; **PRIM RE ACT:** Broker, Owner/Investor, Property Manager; **SERVICES:** Resid. sales and prop. mgmt.; **PREV EMPLOY:** RE saleslady from Jan. 1964 to 1969; RE Sales Mgr., 1969 - 1978; **PROFL AFFIL & HONORS:** CRB; CRS; Women's Council of Realtors; NAR; RNMI, Salesman of the Yr., 1967; KS WCR Woman of the Yr., 1970; Omega Tau Rho Award, 1975; MLS Broker of the Yr., 1979; **EDUC:** 1941, Elem. Educ., Friends Univ.; **OTHER ACT & HONORS:** Life Membership, Harry St. PTA; Past Pres., Wichita and KS Chap. of Women's Council of Realtors; Gov. of KS WCR, 1977 & 1978; Pres., KS CRS Chap., 1981; Dir. of Wichita Bd. of Realtors, 1971-1973; Who's Who of Amer. Women, 1977-1978 edition; Reorganized Church of Jesus Christ of Latter Day Saints; Dir. of Wichita Metro. Area Bd. of Realtors, 1980-82; Dir. of KS Assn. of Realtors, 1981; **HOME ADD:** 1724 S. Waco Ave., Wichita, KS 67213, (316)263-7138; **BUS ADD:** 714 N. West St., Wichita, KS 67203, (316)943-9339.

DODEK, Aaron Willard——**B:** Sept. 6, 1935, Washington, DC, *VP*, Hugh T. Peck, Inc., Prop. Mgmt.; **PRIM RE ACT:** Consultant, Owner/Investor, Property Manager; **SERVICES:** Profl. prop. mgmt. and leasing; **REP CLIENTS:** Univ. of MD, various embassies; **PREV EMPLOY:** Beers Bros., Inc. - Realtors; **PROFL AFFIL & HONORS:** IREM, W. Central Chap. #92; Montgomery Cty. Bd. of Realtors, CPM; **EDUC:** Richmond Profl. Inst. & Amer. Univ.; **GRAD EDUC:** Southeastern Univ.; **MIL SERV:** USCG, Seaman 3rd; **OTHER ACT & HONORS:** Pres. W. Central MD Chap. of IREM, Shillelagh Air Travel Club, Inc.; **HOME ADD:** 19512 Desmet Pl., Gaithersburg, MD, (301)948-6444; **BUS ADD:** 10808 Connecticut Ave., Kensington, MD 20795, (301)933-0081.

DODGE, Donald G.——*Dpty. Asst. Secy.*, Department of Housing and Urban Development, Program Mgmt.; **PRIM RE ACT:** Lender; **BUS ADD:** 451 Seventh St., S.W., Washington, DC 20410, (202)755-6267.*

DODGE, Nathen P.——**B:** Oct. 5, 1910, Boston, MA, *CEO*, N.P. Dodge Co.; **PRIM RE ACT:** Broker, Consultant, Developer, Builder, Owner/Investor, Property Manager, Insuror, Syndicator; **PROFL AFFIL & HONORS:** Omaha RE Bd., Past. Pres.; NE RE Assn., Past Pres.; Nat. Assn. RE Bds., Past VP; **EDUC:** A, 1933, Harvard Coll.; **MIL SERV:** USAF, Lt.; **OTHER ACT & HONORS:** Omaha City Council 1956-62; Metropolitan Utlities Dist. Chmn. 19; Past Pres. Omaha Urban League; Bd. of Govs.; Boys Clubs of Omaha; Past Pres. NE Harvard Clubs; Assoc. Harvard Clubs (US); **HOME ADD:** 10250 Fieldcrest Dr., Omaha, NE 68114; **BUS ADD:** 8701 W. Dodge Rd., Omaha, NE 68114, (402)397-4900.

DODGE, Robert I.——*Dir.*, Department of Housing and Urban Development, Urban Rehab.; **PRIM RE ACT:** Lender; **BUS ADD:** 451 Seventh St., S.W., Washington, DC 20410, (202)755-5685.*

DODSON, Valerie E.——**B:** May 18, 1939, Winston-Salem, NC, *Broker/Owner*, Blue Ridge Properties/Better Homes and Gardens; **PRIM RE ACT:** Broker, Appraiser, Owner/Investor; **SERVICES:** Primarily Resid. RE Sales; **REP CLIENTS:** All price ranges; **PROFL AFFIL & HONORS:** RNMI; Kingsport Bd. of Realtors; TN Assn. of Realtors, GRI, CRS, CRB Mgr.; **EDUC:** Katherine Gibbs School, Boston, MA; Agnes Scott Coll.; **HOME ADD:** 2064 Canterbury Rd., Kingsport, TN 37660, (615)247-2747; **BUS ADD:** 444 E. Center St., Kingsport, TN 37660, (615)247-4181.

DOERFLIER, Ronald J.——*Chief Fin. Officer*, Capital Cities Communications, Inc.; **PRIM RE ACT:** Property Manager; **BUS ADD:** 485 Madison Ave., New York, NY 10022, (212)421-9595.*

DOERGER, Gerald L.——*Mgr. Corp. Commun. & Dev.*, Carlisle Corp.; **PRIM RE ACT:** Property Manager; **BUS ADD:** 1700 DuBois Tower, Cincinnati, OH 45202, (513)241-2500.*

DOERN, David A.——**B:** July 17, 1940, *Exec. VP*, Rostenberg-Doern Company, Inc.; **PRIM RE ACT:** Broker, Consultant; **SERVICES:** Corp. & Inst. RE; **REP CLIENTS:** Represent Fortune 1,000 cos.: corp. RE requirement, and major devels. as exclusive agents; **PROFL AFFIL & HONORS:** RE Bd. of NY, Indus. RE Brokers Assn., ULI, Southwestern Area Commerce & Indus. Assn. of CT, Inc.; **EDUC:** BS, 1962, Econ., Holy Cross Coll.; **OTHER ACT & HONORS:** Kiwanis; **HOME ADD:** 8 Burling Ave., White Plains, NY 10601, (914)428-4364; **BUS ADD:** 1 North Broadway, White Plains, NY 10601, (914)761-4000.

DOERR, Marga E.——**B:** Nov. 14, 1935, Germany, *VP*, Flagship Natl. Bank of Miami, Mort. and RE; **PRIM RE ACT:** Banker, Lender; **SERVICES:** Const. lending, permanent fin., standing loans, asset-based fin.; **REP CLIENTS:** Devel., mfrs., wholesalers; **PROFL AFFIL & HONORS:** N.A.B.W., Econ. Soc. of S. FL, MBAA, Mort. Bankers Assn. of Greater Miami; **EDUC:** BA, 1980, Mgmt.; **EDUC HONORS:** Departmental Honors; **OTHER ACT & HONORS:** League of Women Voters; **HOME ADD:** 7804 S.W. 103 Pl, Miami, FL 33173, (305)279-0410; **BUS ADD:** 777 Brickell Ave., Miami, FL 33131, (305)579-7328.

DOERSCH, Richard C.——*Corp. Atty.*, Interlake Inc.; **PRIM RE ACT:** Attorney, Property Manager; **BUS ADD:** 2015 Spring Rd., Oak Brook, IL 60521, (312)986-6600.*

DOHERTY, D.A.——*Gen. Mgr.*, Texaco, Inc.; **PRIM RE ACT:** Property Manager; **BUS ADD:** 2000 Westchester Ave., White Plains, NY 10650, (914)253-4000.*

DOHERTY, Edward W.——**B:** Dec. 16, 1946, NYC, NY, *Sr. Regional Dir., MRO RE*, Marriott Corp., Marriott Restaurant Operations; **OTHER RE ACT:** RE Dev. of Corp. Restaurants; **PREV EMPLOY:** Pillsbury Corp., 1973-75; **PROFL AFFIL & HONORS:** NACORE; ICSC (Assoc. Member); Nat. Assn. of Review Appraisers (CRA); **EDUC:** BS, 1968, Mktg., St. John's Univ., Jamaica, NY; **GRAD EDUC:** MBA, 1972, Mktg., Mt. John's Univ., Jamaica, NY; **HOME ADD:** 866 Roslyn Rd., Ridgewood, NJ 07450, (201)447-2133; **BUS ADD:** 625 From Rd., Paramus, NJ 07652, (201)262-1000.

DOHERTY, James L.——**B:** Dec. 29, 1932, Springfield, MA, *Pres.*, Elam & Funsten; **PRIM RE ACT:** Broker, Consultant, Appraiser, Property Manager; **SERVICES:** Brokerage, prop. mgmt., ins., appraisals; **PROFL AFFIL & HONORS:** AIREA, NAR, VA Assn. Realtors, Richmond Bd. of Realtors, MAI; **EDUC:** BA, 1955, Econ., Bowdoin; **GRAD EDUC:** MBA, 1959, Mktg., Columbia; **MIL SERV:** US Army, 1st. Lt.; **OTHER ACT & HONORS:** Bds. - Central Richmond Assn., United Negro Colleges, First VA Bank Colonial, Nat. Conference of Christians & Jews; **HOME ADD:** 43 Willway Ave., Richmond, VA 23226, (804)358-0905; **BUS ADD:** 619 E. Main St., Richmond, VA 23219, (804)644-9451.

DOHRMAN, Fred——*Mgr. Realty Div.*, Winnebago Industries, Inc.; **PRIM RE ACT:** Property Manager; **BUS ADD:** PO Box 152, Forest City, IA 50436, (515)582-3535.*

DOHT, John A.——**B:** Feb. 10, 1925, Hempstead, NY, *Dir., of RE & Servs, Div. VP*, Doubleday & Co., Inc.; **OTHER RE ACT:** Mgmt. of corporate RE; **PROFL AFFIL & HONORS:** Nat. Assn. of Corporate RE Execs.; **MIL SERV:** USAF, 1st Sgt.; **OTHER ACT & HONORS:** VP & Tr., NY Chap. Leukemia Soc. of Amer., Inc.; **HOME ADD:** 67 Pickwick Lane, North Babylon, NY 11703, (516)669-7315; **BUS ADD:** 245 Park Ave., New York, NY 10167, (212)953-4405.

DOIRON, J. Russell——**B:** Apr. 17, 1908, Baton Rouge, LA, *VP*, J.T. Doiron, Inc., Realtor; **PRIM RE ACT:** Broker, Consultant, Appraiser, Developer, Owner/Investor, Property Manager; **SERVICES:** All services required in the above categories; **REP CLIENTS:** Indivs., corps., partnerships, attys., lending instns., etc.; **PREV EMPLOY:** Continuous employment in RE bus. since 1916; **PROFL AFFIL & HONORS:** AIREA; IREM; Soc. of RE Appraisers; NAR, MAI; CPM; SRPA; Recipient, 1980 J. Wallace Paletou Award from IREM; **EDUC:** BBA, 1930, Comml./Gen. Bus., LA State Univ.; **EDUC HONORS:** Delta Sigma Pi, Beta Gamma Sigma; **OTHER ACT & HONORS:** Chmn., Exec. Parish Democratic Exec. Comm., 1936-1975; Kiwanis Club; C of C; Knight Comdr., Order of the Holy Sepulchre of Jerusalem; **HOME ADD:** 1001 Drehr Ave., Baton Rouge, LA 70806, (504)383-2285; **BUS ADD:** 620 Florida St., PO Box 3213, Baton Rouge, LA 70821, (504)343-5721.

DOLAN, Earl T., Jr.——**B:** Sept. 9, 1947, Baltimore, MD, *Pres.*, E.T. Dolan & Associates, Inc.; **PRIM RE ACT:** Broker, Consultant, Appraiser; **OTHER RE ACT:** Right-of-way Negotiator; **SERVICES:** RE sales & appraisals of resid. & comml. prop.; **REP CLIENTS:** Lenders, Indivs., investors and public agencies in resid. and comml. props.; **PROFL AFFIL & HONORS:** SREA, NARA, ARWY, RE Bd. of Gr. Baltimore, SRA, CRA, Realtor; **EDUC:** BS, 1971, Bus. Mgmt., Univ. of Baltimore; **OTHER ACT & HONORS:** Member of Bd. of Dirs. for Soc. of RE Appraiser Local Chap. 24, Pres. of Manor Glen Improvement Assn. Inc.; **HOME ADD:** 4 Edgarwood Court, Phoenix, MD 21131, (301)667-1564; **BUS ADD:** 305 E. Joppa Rd., Towson, MD 21204, (301)296-9313.

DOLAN, Harry L., Jr.——**B:** Jan. 18, 1942, Chicago, IL, *Pres.*, Dolan Associates; **PRIM RE ACT:** Broker, Developer, Owner/Investor, Syndicator; **PROFL AFFIL & HONORS:** IREM, ICSC, Chicago RE Bd., CPM, CSM; **EDUC:** BS, 1963, Soc. Studies, Loyola Univ.; **EDUC HONORS:** Who's Who Blue Key Hon. Soc.; **MIL SERV:** USMC, Sgt.; **OTHER ACT & HONORS:** Pres., Cambridge Forest Assn. 1979; **HOME ADD:** 36 Cumberland Dr., Lincolnshire, IL 60015, (312)945-3264; **BUS ADD:** 2275 Half Day Rd., Bannockburn, IL 60018, (312)945-6600

DOLAN, Paul R.——**B:** Feb. 25, 1931, Hollywood, CA, *Pres.*, Inter-Investments; **PRIM RE ACT:** Broker, Consultant, Developer, Owner/Investor; **PREV EMPLOY:** Pres. (sub.) of Xerox; Consultant - McKinsey & Co.; **PROFL AFFIL & HONORS:** FIABCI; **EDUC:** BS, 1953, Bus. Admin., Univ. of CA (Berkeley); **GRAD EDUC:** MBA, 1955, Bus. Admin., Univ. of CA (Berkeley); **MIL SERV:** US Army; Sgt., Commendation medals; **OTHER ACT & HONORS:** Pres. - Executive seminars; **BUS ADD:** 34 Malaga Cove Plaza, Palos Verdes Estates, CA 90274, (213)373-0692.

DOLBEARE, Cushing N., Ms.——*Dir.*, Natl. Low Income Housing Coalition; **PRIM RE ACT:** Regulator; **BUS ADD:** 1346 Connecticut Ave., NW, Washington, DC 20036, (202)296-4944.*

DOLBY, Cornelius A.——**B:** Jan. 9, 1943, Columbus, OH, *VP*, Long & Foster RE, Inc., Comml.; **PRIM RE ACT:** Broker, Consultant, Instructor, Syndicator; **SERVICES:** Sell & lease comml. prop., builder land sales; **PROFL AFFIL & HONORS:** RMNI, RESSI, NVBR, DC Bd. of Realtors, WA Bd. of Trade, RMNI Faculty, CCIM; **EDUC:** 1965, Govt., IA State Univ.; **MIL SERV:** USN, Lt.; **OTHER ACT & HONORS:** RNMI Snyder Trophy, 1978, No. VA Bd. of Realtors Top Producer Award, RNMI Sr. Instructor; **HOME ADD:** 8911 Lynnhurst Dr., Fairfax, VA 22031, (703)280-4024; **BUS ADD:** 3918 Propserity Ave., Fairfax, VA 22031, (703)849-1007.

DOLIN, Richard A.——**B:** Dec. 10, 1944, Greensboro, NC, *Asst. Prof.*; **PRIM RE ACT:** Consultant; **SERVICES:** Capital budgeting, project analysis & evaluation; **REP CLIENTS:** Lenders & investors in projects; **PREV EMPLOY:** Atty. in private practice with extensive work for banks and constr. cos.; **PROFL AFFIL & HONORS:** KY Bar Assn., IN Bar Assn., ABA, Midwest Fin. Assn., Fin. Mgmt. Assn.; **EDUC:** BS, 1970, Microbiology, OH State Univ.; **GRAD EDUC:** MBA, 1979, Bus., Bellarmine Coll.; JD, 1973, Law, Univ. of Louisville; **OTHER ACT & HONORS:** Exec. Council, Presbytery of Louisville, Exec. Council Synod of Mid-South, Dir. Westminster Terr.; **HOME ADD:** 1306 Old Taylor Tr., Goshen, KY 40026, (502)228-4048; **BUS ADD:** Bus. Admin., Bellarmine Coll., Louisville, KY, (502)452-8245.

DOLL, Denis E.——**B:** Apr. 19, 1935, Saskatchewan, *Mgr., Prop. Mgmt. Div.*, Block Bros. Industries, Ltd., Pres. Napier Services Ltd. (a subsidiary); **PRIM RE ACT:** Property Manager; **SERVICES:** Prop. Mgmt. office, shopping centers, Indus., Condo, Apts.; **REP CLIENTS:** Co. owned projects & client (investor) owned; **PREV EMPLOY:** Great West Life Assurance Co. 1963-1969, The Baxter Group 1969-74; **PROFL AFFIL & HONORS:** VP BOMA BC; VP Pama. (Pacific Apt. Mgrs. Assn.), Member ICSC, RPA through BOMI Wash., DC; **EDUC:** BA, 1963, Engrg., Econ., Fin., Univ. of Saskatchewan, Saskatoon; **HOME ADD:** 1586 McNair Dr., North Vancouver, (604)980-3376; **BUS ADD:** 208-1030 West GA St., Vancouver, V6E-2Z8, BC, Canada, (604)685-8511.

DOLLENBERG, P. Douglas——**B:** Dec. 12, 1939, Baltimore MD, *Pres. and CEO*, Nottingham Properties, Inc.; **PRIM RE ACT:** Developer; **SERVICES:** Devel. of land and buildings for resid., comml., indus. use; **REP CLIENTS:** The Rouse Co., The Ryland Grp., Inc., Weyerhaeuser RE Co., Centex Corp., Mercantile Bank & Trust Co.; **PREV EMPLOY:** Whiting-Turner Contracting Co.; **PROFL AFFIL & HONORS:** Registered Profl Engr. - MD, Nat./Profl. Engrs., MD Soc. of Profl. Engrs., ASCE - Dir., Engrg. Soc. of Baltimore, Cert. Fallout Shelter Analysist, Tau Beta Pi Soc. (Nat. Engrg. Honorary), Chi Epsilon (Civil Engrg. Honorary); NAIOP; ULI; **EDUC:** BS, 1961, Civil Engrg., Univ. of MD - Coll. Park; **GRAD EDUC:** MS, 1962, Civil Engrg., Purdue Univ.; **OTHER ACT & HONORS:** Greater Baltimore Medical Ctr. - Tr.; Dir. of Towson Devel. Corp., Baltimore Cty. C of C; Past Dir. and VP of Baltimore Cty: Planning & Advisory Comms.; **HOME ADD:** 1010 Fallscroft Way, Lutherville, MD 21093; **BUS ADD:** 100 W. Pennsylvania Ave., Towson, MD 21204, (301)825-0545.

DOLLNIG, Richard D., IFA——**B:** Apr. 3, 1928, Chicago, IL, *RE Appraiser*, Richard D. Dollnig, IFA; **PRIM RE ACT:** Appraiser; **SERVICES:** RE appraisal reports on resid., comml. & vacant land; **REP CLIENTS:** Lending Inst., Veterans Admin., Attys., Private clients; **PROFL AFFIL & HONORS:** Nat. Assn. of Indep. Fee Appraisers, IFA; **MIL SERV:** USNR, Yeoman; **HOME ADD:** 2160 Kalanianaole St., Hilo, HI 96720, (808)935-1464; **BUS ADD:** 2160 Kalanianaole St., Hilo, HI 96720, (808)935-1464.

DOLMAN, Jack A., Jr.——**B:** Jan. 7, 1944, OK City, OK, *Pres.*, Dolman & Company, Inc.; **PRIM RE ACT:** Broker, Syndicator, Consultant, Developer, Property Manager, Owner/Investor; **SERVICES:** Comml. investment brokerage, consulting, prop. mgmt.; **REP CLIENTS:** Pvt. investors, ltd. partners; **PREV EMPLOY:** ERC Props. Inc., Asst. VP Operations; Fiann Hills Devel. Corp., Broker & Contoller; Fairfield Communities, Inc., Sales Mgr.; **PROFL AFFIL & HONORS:** NAHB, Pres. local assn. 1979-81; NAR; **EDUC:** BS, 1967, Mktg., Radio & TV, Adv. & Pub. Rel., OK State Univ.; **MIL SERV:** USMC; **HOME ADD:** 2500 So. 56th, Fort Smith, AR 72903, (501)452-4094; **BUS ADD:** 2120 Weldron Rd., Suite 112-A, PO Box 3892, Fort Smith, AR 72913, (501)452-8193.

DOLMAN, John P.——**B:** June 15, 1915, Swarthmore, PA, *Chmn.*, Jackson-Cross Co.; **PRIM RE ACT:** Broker, Consultant, Appraiser; **OTHER RE ACT:** Appraisal & counseling, broker; **SERVICES:** Provides services in Appraisal & counseling, Brokerage, Prop. Mgmts.

Prop. Maintenance.; **REP CLIENTS:** Phila. Nat. Bank, Provident Nat. Bank, Continental B&T. Co.; **PREV EMPLOY:** Began career with Jackson-Cross in 1937; **PROFL AFFIL & HONORS:** ASREC, AIREA, ULI, Intl. Right of Way Assn., Amer. Inst., of RE, Amer. Chap. (FIABCI), Fed. Intl. Des Geometres (FIG); **EDUC:** AB, 1937, Econ., Univ. of PA; **MIL SERV:** USN, LCDR, Letter of Commendation; **OTHER ACT & HONORS:** Bd. Member YMCA of Phila. & Vicinity, Member Bds. of Univ. City Assoc., Franklin Maintenance Co., Payroll Services, Inc., Jackson Cross 121, Inc.; Member Union League of Phila.; Natl. College Frat. Pi Kappa Alpha.; **HOME ADD:** 212 Dogwood Ln, Wallingford, PA 19086, (215)566-3236; **BUS ADD:** 2000 Market St., Philadelphia, PA 19103, (215)561-8900.

DOMBROSKI, William E.——B: Aug. 10, 1942, Wilkes-Barre, PA, *Broker, Pres.*, America Realty Co.; **PRIM RE ACT:** Broker, Consultant, Appraiser, Owner/Investor, Instructor, Property Manager; **SERVICES:** Investment analysist, consultant, appraiser, educator, synd. of comml. props., prop. mgmt.; **PREV EMPLOY:** General Electric Corp.; Burroughs Corp.; **PROFL AFFIL & HONORS:** Asst. Prof. (Current), Luzerne Cty. Community Coll., Devel. Full RE Program, NAR; PA Realtors Assn.; Wilkes-Barre Bd. of Realtors; **EDUC:** BS, 1964, Bus. Admin. & Acctg., King's Coll.; **GRAD EDUC:** MBA, 1965, Mgmt. & Fin., The Univ. of Scranton; **MIL SERV:** US Army; Sgt.; **OTHER ACT & HONORS:** 32nd degree Mason & Shriner; **HOME ADD:** 1110 Wyoming Ave., Forty Fort, PA 18704; **BUS ADD:** 1110 Wyoming Ave., Forty Fort, Wilkes-Barre, PA 18704, (717)288-1422.

DOMBROWSKI, Garrett James——B: Aug. 19, 1949, Jersey City, NJ, *Atty. at Law*, Garrett J. Dombrowski; **PRIM RE ACT:** Attorney; **SERVICES:** Examination and closing of title in resid. transactions; **PROFL AFFIL & HONORS:** ABA; NJ State Bar Assn.; Essex Cty. Bar Assn.; NY State Bar Assn.; NY Co. Bar, Approved Atty; Chi. Title Ins., Title Guar. Co.; **EDUC:** BA, 1971, Poli. Sci., Rutgers Univ.; **GRAD EDUC:** 1976, Brooklyn Law Sch.; 1981, Taxation Law, Temple Univ., School of Law, Grad. Studies Div.; **EDUC HONORS:** Dean's List; Who's Who in Amer. Coll.; Leadership Recognition Soc., RE Practice Course - Top 10% of class; **OTHER ACT & HONORS:** Committeeman, Hudson Co. Democratic Comm., 1972-1976; Rutgers Univ. Alumni Assn.; **HOME ADD:** 68 Eighth Ave., Passaic, NJ 07055, (201)472-1295; **BUS ADD:** One Liberty Plaza, 31st Floor, New York, NY 10080.

DOMNICK, Terrence M.——B: Nov. 19, 1948, Peoria, IL, *Pres.*, United States Development Corp.; **PRIM RE ACT:** Consultant, Developer, Owner/Investor; **OTHER RE ACT:** Marina devel., golf course & mktg. RE; **SERVICES:** Mktg., devel. and consulting; **PREV EMPLOY:** Merifield Acres, Inc.; **PROFL AFFIL & HONORS:** Amer. Land Devels. Assn.; **EDUC:** So. IL Univ.; **HOME ADD:** 32 Palmetto Dr., Wrightsville Beach, NC, (919)256-3958; **BUS ADD:** Belvedere Plantation, PO Box 4055, Hampstead, NC 28443, (919)270-2761.

DONAHUE, Charles B, III——B: Apr. 17, 1937, Hampton, IA, *Partner*, Donahue & Scanlon; **PRIM RE ACT:** Attorney; **SERVICES:** Full legal servs.; **REP CLIENTS:** Ostendorf - Morris Co.; King James Group Condo Devel.; Pacer Construction Corp.; Prescott, Ball & Turben RE Div.; Walter E. Heller Mort. Fin.; **PREV EMPLOY:** Calfee, Halter & Griswold, 1967-79; TRW Inc., 63-67; Westinghouse, 1962-63; **PROFL AFFIL & HONORS:** ABA, OH State Bar Assn., FL Bar Assn., Gr. Cleveland Bar Assn., Harvard Club of Cleveland; **EDUC:** AB, 1959, Econ., Harvard Coll.; **GRAD EDUC:** JD, 1967, Cleveland Marshall Law Coll. of Cleveland State Univ.; **EDUC HONORS:** Cum Laude; **MIL SERV:** USAF, Capt.; **OTHER ACT & HONORS:** Cleveland Athletic Club, Who's Who in Amer. Law; **HOME ADD:** 800 Brick Mill Run, Westlake, OH 44145, (216)331-3232; **BUS ADD:** One Erieview Plaza, Cleveland, OH 44114, (216)696-0022.

DONAHUE, Daniel W.——B: Feb. 4, 1942, Los Angeles, CA, *Pres.*, John S. Griffith & Co.; **PRIM RE ACT:** Developer; **SERVICES:** Const., brokerage and Prop. mgmt.; **PREV EMPLOY:** 1966-1968, Coldwell Banker & Co. Comml. Brokerage Co., Newport Beach, CA; **PROFL AFFIL & HONORS:** Intl. Council of Shopping Ctrs.; Bank of Amer. RE Investment Trust, Pres., Intl. Council of Shopping Ctrs., 1981-1982; Tr., Bank of Amer. RE Investment Trust, 1980 to Present; **EDUC:** BS, 1963, Bus. and Indus. Mgmt., San Jose State Univ.; **MIL SERV:** USAR, PFC, 1963-1964; **OTHER ACT & HONORS:** Honors UCLA Sch. of Arch. & Urban Planning/Dean's Council; Newport Harbor Yacht Club, 552 Club/Hoag Memorial Hospital, Hon. Editorial Bd. of Nat. Mall Monitor; **HOME ADD:** 1903 Yacht Colinia, Newport Beach, CA 92660, (714)644-1017; **BUS ADD:** 3200 Bristol St., Suite 660, Costa Mesa, CA 92626, (714)979-2230.

DONALDSON, Francis——B: July 12, 1921, Westkilbride, Scotland, *Sr. VP*, Mobil Land Development Corp., Design and Engrg.; **PRIM RE ACT:** Developer; **OTHER RE ACT:** Architect, Land Planner; **PREV EMPLOY:** Grosvender Intl. Member Royal Arch. Institute of Can., Registered Architect, HI; **PROFL AFFIL & HONORS:** Recipient of Massey Medal; **EDUC:** Aradossan Academy; **GRAD EDUC:** Glasgow Sch. of Arch. Royal Engrs., Sgt.; **OTHER ACT & HONORS:** Amer. Planning Assn., ULI; **HOME ADD:** 500 Almer Rd. #301, Burlingame, CA 94010, (415)343-9889; **BUS ADD:** 1515 Spear St. Tower, One Market Plaza, San Francisco, CA 94105, (415)764-1503.

DONDORFER, C. H.——B: Sept. 24, 1939, Graz, Austria, *Associate Broker*, Century 21 Launders, Investment Properties; **PRIM RE ACT:** Broker, Consultant, Appraiser, Developer, Builder, Owner/Investor, Property Manager, Syndicator; **SERVICES:** Land purchase, approve for devel. including zoning changes; **PREV EMPLOY:** Gen. pvt. contractor; **PROFL AFFIL & HONORS:** Lake Cty. Bd. of Realtors; **EDUC:** High School, 2 years of Coll. (Bus. Admin.); **MIL SERV:** Army N.G., Pvt.; **HOME ADD:** 7756 King Memorial, Mentor, OH 44060, (216)255-7450; **BUS ADD:** 7295 Center St., Mentor, OH 44060, (216)255-1111.

DONEGAN, James C.——B: May 21, 1939, New Orleans, LA, *Pres.*, Donegan Realty Co., Inc.; **PRIM RE ACT:** Broker, Consultant, Owner/Investor, Property Manager, Syndicator; **SERVICES:** Brokerage, investment & mgmt.; **REP CLIENTS:** Lenders and indiv. or instnl. investors in comml. props.; **PREV EMPLOY:** Reg. Rep., NYSE Firm 1968-74; Associated with largest RE firm (commercial) in S.E. 74-77; Broker & consultant & mgmt. 77-present; **PROFL AFFIL & HONORS:** RNMI, IREM, NAR; **EDUC:** BA, 1963, Sociology, LA State Univ.; **MIL SERV:** USAF, 1st Lt.; **HOME ADD:** 2715 E. Sudbury Ct., Atlanta, GA 30360, (404)455-6793; **BUS ADD:** PO Box 723776, Atlanta, GA 30339, (404)435-6165.

DONEIT, Peter——B: June 23, 1948, Marktredwitz, Germany, *Mgr. Props.*, RWI Properties Ltd.; **PRIM RE ACT:** Consultant, Owner/Investor, Property Manager, Syndicator; **SERVICES:** Acquisition, synd. of income props., property mgmt.; **PREV EMPLOY:** Chief Prop. Mgr. CMHC; **PROFL AFFIL & HONORS:** Can. RE Assn.; Inst. of RE Mgmt.; Appraisal Inst. of Can., CPM, FRI; **OTHER ACT & HONORS:** Member of Municipal Planing Bd. and Council; Soc. of Mgmt. Accts.; Member of Educ. Advisory Bd., Algonquin Coll.; Dir. RE Inst. of Can.; **HOME ADD:** 1285 Cahill Dr., 702, Ottawa, KiV-9A7, Ontario, Canada, (613)523-8951; **BUS ADD:** 3460 Drumond St., Montreal, H3G-1Y1, Quebec, Canada, (514)287-9734.

DONELSON, F.M.——B: May 2, 1927, Chicago, IL, *Pres./COB*, Don Donelson & Assoc. Inc.; **PRIM RE ACT:** Broker, Syndicator, Consultant, Developer, Builder; **OTHER RE ACT:** Joint venture specialist dealing with European and US investors; **PROFL AFFIL & HONORS:** NAHB; FIABCI; NAR ALDA, Life Dir., NAHB; Pres., OH HBA; Pres., C of C; **MIL SERV:** Air Force, Sgt.; **OTHER ACT & HONORS:** Rotary, C of C of US, FL, Holland, Germany; **HOME ADD:** 9 Emerald Pointe Blvd., Punta Gorda, FL 33950, (813)639-0927; **BUS ADD:** 1200 W. Relta Esplanade, Punta Gorda, FL 33950, (813)639-8721.

DONG, Donald D.——B: Apr 25, 1939, Hong Kong, *Senior Partner*, Investment Associates; **PRIM RE ACT:** Broker; **OTHER RE ACT:** Instructor; **SERVICES:** Real Estate Brokerage, Instructor City Coll. of S.F.; **REP CLIENTS:** Other real estate firms; **PREV EMPLOY:** Lecturer, San Francisco State Univ., S.F., CA, 94132, 1971-77; **PROFL AFFIL & HONORS:** San Francisco Bd. of Realtors, Member Grievance Comm., Bd. Member, Continental Savings and Loan Assn.; **EDUC:** BA, 1961, English Literature, Havard Univ.; **GRAD EDUC:** MA, 1967, Theatre Art, San Francisco State; PhD Candidate, 1970, Comparative Literature, Univ. of WA; MBA, Real Estate, Golden Gate Univ.; **MIL SERV:** US Army, E-5; **HOME ADD:** 164 Seacliff Ave., San Francisco, CA 94121, (415)386-2788; **BUS ADD:** N. One Haight St., San Francisco, CA 94102, (415)431-3394.

DONLEY, Roger T.——B: May 25, 1937, Superior, WI, *VP & Div. Mgr.*, Northwestern National Bank of St. Paul, RE Div.; **PRIM RE ACT:** Banker, Lender; **SERVICES:** Origination, underwriting, loan admin., secondary market act.; **REP CLIENTS:** Consumers, builder/devel., investors; **PROFL AFFIL & HONORS:** Mort. Bankers Assn. of Amer./MN; Amer. Inst. of Banking; St. Paul Area Builders Assn.; **EDUC:** BS, 1960, Geology/Geography, Univ. of WI, Superior; **GRAD EDUC:** 1974, Grad. School of Banking, Univ. of WI, Madison; 1979, School of Mort. Banking, Univ. of Northwestern; **MIL SERV:** US Air Force Reserve; **BUS ADD:** Northwestern National Bank, 55 E. 5th St., St. Paul, MN 55101, (612)291-2144.

DONNELL, Jack——*Pres.*, Charter Co.; **PRIM RE ACT:** Property Manager; **BUS ADD:** 21 W. Church St., Charter Security Life Building, Jacksonville, FL 32202, (904)358-4111.*

DONNELLY, Allan P.——**B:** Feb. 26, 1944, CA, *Atty. at Law*, Allan P. Donnelly, A Professional Law Corp.; **PRIM RE ACT:** Attorney, Developer, Builder, Syndicator; **SERVICES:** Legal counseling and representation, devel. and synd. of comml. props.; **REP CLIENTS:** Indiv. investors and devels. in comml. props.; **PROFL AFFIL & HONORS:** ABA, CA State Bar, Los Angeles Cty. Bar Assn., San Gabriel Valley Bar Assn., Listed, Marquis, Who's Who In American Law; CA Hist. Soc., Who's Who in CA; **EDUC:** Bus. Admin., 1968, Mgmt., CA State Univ., Los Angeles; **GRAD EDUC:** JD, 1974, Univ. of W. Los Angeles; **EDUC HONORS:** Managing Editor, Law Review, 1974; Staff, Law Review, 1973; **OTHER ACT & HONORS:** Member, Bd. of Educ., San Gabriel School District, 1977-present; San Gabriel Rotary Club; sponsor of bill in CA State Legislature regarding comml. condo. taxation; testimony before CA State Legis.; **HOME ADD:** 115 W. Lime Ave., San Gabriel, CA 91776, (213)573-3671; **BUS ADD:** 1381 E. Las Tunas Dr., Suite 8, San Gabriel, CA 91776, (213)283-2886.

DONNENBERG, Milton——**B:** Feb. 20, 1923, *Pres.*, Milton Donnenberg Assoc.; **PRIM RE ACT:** Broker, Consultant, Appraiser, Property Manager; **SERVICES:** Prop. Mgmt., Consulting, Appraising, Sales; **REP CLIENTS:** Lenders, Individual & Corporate Clients; **PROFL AFFIL & HONORS:** IREM, Atlantic City, Cty. Bd. of Realtors, Past Pres. Atlantic City Cty. Bd. of Realtors; **EDUC:** Certificate Bus. Admin., 1948, RE, Rutgers Univ.; **MIL SERV:** USAF, S/Sgt.; **OTHER ACT & HONORS:** BNAI, Brith, Temple Beth El Dir.; **HOME ADD:** 225 N. Swarthmore Ave., Ventnor City, NJ 08406, (609)823-3186; **BUS ADD:** 1421 Atlantic Ave., Atlantic City, NJ 08401, (609)348-2280.

DONOVAN, Michael——**B:** Oct. 4, 1935, Chicago, IL, *Dist. Sales Mgr.*, United Farm Agency; **PRIM RE ACT:** Broker, Consultant; **OTHER RE ACT:** Trainer; **SERVICES:** Set up offices for United, train reps., run sales training programs, some consultant work and appraising; **PROFL AFFIL & HONORS:** Nat. and Local Bd. of Realtors; **EDUC:** AB, 1959, Sci. Educ., San Jose Univ.; **OTHER ACT & HONORS:** School Bd. Chmn.; **HOME ADD:** 886N 2E, American Fork, UT 84003, (801)756-8331; **BUS ADD:** 612 W. 47th St., Herber City, UT 84032, (801)756-8331.

DOODY, James P.——**B:** June 10, 1946, Ireland, *RE Counsel*, American Standard Inc.; **PRIM RE ACT:** Attorney; **PREV EMPLOY:** RE Atty., Mudge Rose Guthrie & Alexander, NY City; **PROFL AFFIL & HONORS:** NY and NJ State Bar Assns., Assn. of the Bar of the City of NY; **EDUC:** BA, 1968, History, Fordham Coll.; **GRAD EDUC:** JD, 1972, Columbia Law School; **OTHER ACT & HONORS:** President, Tuckahoe Union Free School District Board of Ed., Westchester Cty., NY; **HOME ADD:** 65 Stebbins Ave., Eastchester, NY 10707, (914)337-9419; **BUS ADD:** 40 West 40th St., New York, NY 10018, (212)840-5123.

DOOLAN, Devin John——**B:** Aug. 28, 1940, Port Chester, NY, *Partner*, Furey, Doolan, Abell & Hogan; **PRIM RE ACT:** Attorney; **SERVICES:** Gen. legal counsel to lenders, devel., homeowners assns. including condo. and cooperatives; **REP CLIENTS:** Comml. banks, S&L Assns., Mort. banking indus., condo. assns. and resid. coop. corps.; **PROFL AFFIL & HONORS:** ABA, MD State Bar Assn., Bar Assn. of DC, Montgomery Cty. Bar Assn.; **EDUC:** Liberal arts, Eng., Fairfield Univ., CT; **GRAD EDUC:** JD, 1965, Catholic Univ. Law Sch.; **OTHER ACT & HONORS:** MD States Legislature 1970, 1974; **HOME ADD:** 3509 Windsor Pl., Chevy Chase, MD 20815, (301)652-1051; **BUS ADD:** 8401 Connecticut Ave., 1, Chevy Chase, MD 20815, (301)652-6880.

DORAN, Camille V.——**B:** Dec. 28. 1953, Wichita, KS, *Attorney at Law*; **PRIM RE ACT:** Attorney; **SERVICES:** Legal services, including counseling; **REP CLIENTS:** Private investors, sellers in commercial, residential, undeveloped props., Developers; **PROFL AFFIL & HONORS:** ABA, MN State Bar; **EDUC:** BA, 1976, Hist., Relig., Bus. & Econ., College of St. Scholastica, Duluth, MN; **GRAD EDUC:** JD, 1980, Wm. Mitchell College of Law, St. Paul, MN; **OTHER ACT & HONORS:** Audubon Soc., Natl. Wildlife Assn.; **HOME ADD:** 5236 London Rd., Duluth, MN 55804, (218)525-5394; **BUS ADD:** 608 Board of Trade Bldg., Duluth, MN 55802, (218)727-5591.

DORCHESTER, John D., Jr.——**B:** July 12, 1935, OK City, OK, *Pres.*, The Dorchester Cos.; **PRIM RE ACT:** Consultant, Appraiser, Owner/Investor, Instructor; **SERVICES:** RE appraisal, mkt. analysis; **REP CLIENTS:** Banks, S&L and other thrift instns; corps., govt. agencies, pvt. indivs.; **PREV EMPLOY:** Asst. Dir. Tulsa Urban Renewal Auth., 1962-64; Chief, Comml. Loans (Eastern OK) for OK Mort. Co., 1964-68; Formed Dorchester Cos. (partnership with John D. Dorchester, Sr.), in 1968; **PROFL AFFIL & HONORS:** AIREA, Amer. Soc. of RE Counselors, NAR, OK Assn. of Realtors, Metro. Tulsa Bd. of Realtors, Realtor Member VP Tulsa Bd., 1968; ULI, Amer. Right of Way Assn., Intl. Assn. of Assessing Officers, RESSI, MAI, CRE; **EDUC:** BBA, 1957, Fin. (RE), Acctg., Univ. of OK; **GRAD EDUC:** MA, 1963, Land Econ., with spec. study in appraising & urban devel., Univ. of OK; **EDUC HONORS:** Grad. with Honors, Outstanding Male Grad.; **MIL SERV:** US Army, Capt., Ranger, Expert Infantryman's Badge; **OTHER ACT & HONORS:** SPOKE Award, Top 5 First Yr. Jaycees in US, 1965; Numerous civic awards for participation in comm. affairs; **HOME ADD:** 8455 South Coll., Tulsa, OK 74136, (918)481-1708; **BUS ADD:** 1722 S. Carson, Suite 3005, Tulsa, OK 74119, (918)583-0102.

DORDICK, Beverly——*Ed.*, Gale Research Co., Real Estate Information Sources; **PRIM RE ACT:** Real Estate Publisher; **BUS ADD:** 1400 Book Tower, Detroit, MI 48226, (313)961-2242.*

DORFMAN, Joel——*Exec. VP*, Frederick & Herrud, Inc.; **PRIM RE ACT:** Property Manager; **BUS ADD:** 18700 W. Ten Mile Rd., Southfield, MI 48075, (313)552-0700.*

DORFMAN, Michael——*Dir. Fac. Engr.*, Compo Industries; **PRIM RE ACT:** Property Manager; **BUS ADD:** 125 Roberts Rd., Waltham, MA 02254, (617)899-3000.*

DORGAN, Kathleen A.——**B:** Sept. 1, 1956, Mankato, MN, *Exec. Dir.*, Capitol Hill Improvement Corp., N.A.; **OTHER RE ACT:** Non-Profit Housing Planning & Design; **SERVICES:** Homeownership, design, RE list & Sec. 8 Dev.; **REP CLIENTS:** City of Albany, Historic Albany Found., Inc., Urban League of the Albany Area, Inc., neighborhood assns. and indivs.; **PREV EMPLOY:** 312 Consultant, Arch. Designer; **PROFL AFFIL & HONORS:** Nat. Trust for Historic Pres. member, RE Salesperson NYS; **EDUC:** BS, 1981, Building Sci., Rensselaer Polytechnic Inst.; **GRAD EDUC:** BArch., 1981, Rensselaer Polytechnic Inst.; **EDUC HONORS:** Who's Who in Amer. Colls. & Univs. 1976, Dean's Award in Arch. Theory 1976; **OTHER ACT & HONORS:** Steering Comm. - Lark St. Area Merchants Grp.; **HOME ADD:** 206 Jay St., Albany, NY 12210, (518)436-1129; **BUS ADD:** 260 Lark St., Albany, NY 12210, (518)462-9696.

DOROUGH, James Steven——**B:** Mar. 22, 1948, Birmingham, AL, *Dir. of Synds.*, Metropolitan Properties, Inc., Synds.; **PRIM RE ACT:** Broker, Consultant, Syndicator; **SERVICES:** Primarily synd. and brokerage; **PREV EMPLOY:** Birmingham Area C of C; **PROFL AFFIL & HONORS:** RNMI; RESSI, CCIM; **EDUC:** BA, 1970, Drama and Speech, Birmingham-Southern Coll.; **EDUC HONORS:** Omicron Delta Kappa; **MIL SERV:** US Army Res., S/Sgt.; **OTHER ACT & HONORS:** Pres., Nat. Alumni Assn., Birmingham-Southern Coll.; 1981 Outstanding Young Men of Amer.; Rotary; Birmingham Bd. of Realtors; **HOME ADD:** 1745 Wellington Rd., Birmingham, AL 35209, (205)871-7698; **BUS ADD:** Suite 500, 2 Metroplex Dr., Birmingham, AL 35209, (205)870-9960.

DORSET, Richard T.——**B:** March 17, 1935, York, PA, *Pres.*, West York Realty; **PRIM RE ACT:** Broker, Appraiser, Builder, Property Manager, Owner/Investor; **SERVICES:** All RE Related Services to above Activities; **PROFL AFFIL & HONORS:** Nat., PA, York Realtors Assn., GRI, CRS, CRB, MILLION DOLLAR CLUB, Special Recognition from York Bd. of Realtors for Pres. of Salesman's Assn.; **MIL SERV:** USN; **OTHER ACT & HONORS:** School Bd. Dir., 4 Yrs. Lions Intl.; **HOME ADD:** 1761 W. Market St., York, PA 17404, (717)848-1831; **BUS ADD:** 1761 W. Market St., York, PA 17404, (717)848-1831.

DORSEY, Leighton C.——**B:** Oct. 3, 1930, Wilmington, DE, *Partner*, Bader, Dorsey - Kreshtool; **PRIM RE ACT:** Attorney; **PROFL AFFIL & HONORS:** Delaware, ABA, Nat. Assn. of Housing & Rehab. Officials, NAHB; **EDUC:** BA, 1952, Poli. Sci., Dartmouth Coll.; **GRAD EDUC:** LLB, 1955, Harvard Law School; **HOME ADD:** 1224 Tatnall St., Wilmington, DE 19801, (302)652-8850; **BUS ADD:** 1102 West St., PO Box 2202, Wilmington, DE 19899, (302)656-9850.

DORSEY, Robert K.——**B:** Jan. 20, 1931, NYC, *Atty. at Law*, Robert K. Dorsey; **PRIM RE ACT:** Attorney; **SERVICES:** All legal services; **REP CLIENTS:** Stocks Mill and Supply, Vegas Paint Co.; **PREV EMPLOY:** Own firm for 18 yrs.; **PROFL AFFIL & HONORS:** NV Bar Assn., CA Bar Assn., NY Bar Assn., US Supreme Ct., ABA, Court of Claims, US Tax Court; **EDUC:** AB, 1953, Hist., Princeton; **GRAD EDUC:** LLB, 1958, Law, Univ. of VA; **MIL SERV:** US Army, Intelligence; **OTHER ACT & HONORS:** Elks; **HOME ADD:** 2204 Plaza del Puerto, Las Vegas, NV 89102, (702)871-2799; **BUS ADD:** 300 E. Fremont, #105, Las Vegas, NV 89101, (702)384-2763.

DOSTART, Paul J.——**B:** Nov. 12, 1951, Riceville, IA, *RE Tax Atty.*, Gray, Cary, Ames & Frye; **PRIM RE ACT:** Broker, Attorney, Owner/Investor; **OTHER RE ACT:** RE Tax Counsel; **REP CLIENTS:** Domestic & for. investors, devel., instnl. lenders, agribus.;

PROFL AFFIL & HONORS: CA & TX Bars, AICPA, CA Soc. of CPA (San Diego Chapt. RE Sect.), ABA Tax Sect., CPA (IL, 1974); **EDUC:** BS, 1973, Acctg., IA State Univ.; **GRAD EDUC:** JD, 1977, Univ. of Houston; LLM, 1978, NY Univ.; **OTHER ACT & HONORS:** Cuyamaca Club of San Diego, Editor, 'Tax and Bus. Tips', Monthly Column in *Avocado Grower Magazine*, several other pubs. in profl. journals; **HOME ADD:** 4382 Pavlov Ave., San Diego, CA 92122; **BUS ADD:** 525 'B' St., Suite 2100, San Deigo, CA 92101, (714)236-1661.

DOSWELL, Menard——Rouse & Assoc.; **PRIM RE ACT:** Developer; **BUS ADD:** Ste 100 Potomac Bldg., 8600 LaSalle Rd., Baltimore, MD 21204, (301)828-6655.*

DOTY, Sharon N.——**B:** May 6, 1938, Monterey Park, CA, *VP*, Wells Fargo Bank, N.A., RE Indus. Grp.; **PRIM RE ACT:** Lender; **SERVICES:** Our Group provides interim const. financing; **EDUC:** BA, 1960, Poli. Sci., Scripps Coll., Claremont, CA; **BUS ADD:** 770 Wilshire Blvd., Los Angeles, CA 90017, (213)683-7531.

DOTZOUR, G. Gordon——**B:** Jan. 28, 1924, Wichita, KS, *Chmn. of Bd.*, Dotzour, Inc., Realtors; **PRIM RE ACT:** Broker, Appraiser, Developer, Owner/Investor; **SERVICES:** Relocation specialist with 3rd party transfer corps.; **REP CLIENTS:** Executrans; Equitable Relocation Service; Homequity; Relocation Realty Service Corp.; Employee Transfer Corp.; Bank of St. Louis; **PROFL AFFIL & HONORS:** NAR; KS Assn. of Realtors; Wichita Metropolitan Bd. of Realtors; RNMI; FLI, CRB; CRS; GRI; **EDUC:** BA, 1946, Econ., Stanford Univ.; **MIL SERV:** USAAF; 1943-1945; **OTHER ACT & HONORS:** Wichita Bd. of Park Commnrs., Pres., 1964-1972; Dir., Wichita Crime Commn.; Dir., Better Business Bureau; Dir., Nat. Bank of Wichita, 1964-1981; Dir., Wichita Metro Bd. of Realtors; **HOME ADD:** 110 N. Maize Rd., Wichita, KS 67212, (316)722-1272; **BUS ADD:** 9100 W. Central Ave., Wichita, KS 67212, (316)722-2345.

DOUB, James C.——**B:** Aug. 20, 1947, Baltimore, MD, *Partner*, Miles & Stockbridge; **PRIM RE ACT:** Attorney; **SERVICES:** Legal rep. of foreign investors in US RE, banks in RE Fin. and other clients in indus. devel. revenue bonds; **PROFL AFFIL & HONORS:** ABA, Banking Law Comm., Energy Law Comm.; **EDUC:** AB, 1969, Econ., Cornell Univ.; **GRAD EDUC:** JD, 1972, Univ. of VA; **MIL SERV:** US Army, Cpt.; **HOME ADD:** 322 Broxton Rd., Baltimore, MD 21212; **BUS ADD:** 10 Light St., Baltimore, MD 21202, (301)727-6464.

DOUGHERTY, James W.——**B:** Mar. 5, 1946, Jersey City, NJ, Sole Practitioner; **PRIM RE ACT:** Attorney; **SERVICES:** Contract negotiations & formation - thru closing; **REP CLIENTS:** Most clients are resid. buyers - sellers; **PREV EMPLOY:** US Dept. of Justice, 1972-1975, US Ct. Appeals - 3d Cir.- Law Secy. (1971-1972); County Asst. D.A. (1975-1978); **PROFL AFFIL & HONORS:** ABA, NJ SBA, Hudson & Passaic Cty. Bar Assns.; **EDUC:** BA, 1967, Liberal Arts, Fordham Univ.; **GRAD EDUC:** JD, 1971, Law, Seton Hall Univ.; **OTHER ACT & HONORS:** United States Dept. of Justice/Organized Crime Strike Force, employed as a United States Attorney from 1972 to 1975; Attorney General's Office, Trenton, NJ from July 1975 to Sept. 1975; Passaic Cty. Prosecutor's Office, 77 Hamilton St., Passaic, NJ from Oct. 1975 to May 1977 employed as Assistant Prosecutor in charge of the Gambling and narcotics Unit; Union Cty. Prosecutor's Office employed as Assistant Prosecutor from July 1977 to April 1978; Private Practice: since April 24, 1978, sole practitioner; **HOME ADD:** 114 Oakwood Dr., Wayne, NJ 07470, (201)628-9778; **BUS ADD:** 921 Bergen Ave., Jersey City, NJ 07306, (201)656-4357.

DOUGHERTY, John——*Mgr. RE*, Teledyne, Inc., Real Estate Dept.; **PRIM RE ACT:** Property Manager; **BUS ADD:** Avenue of the Stars, Los Angeles, CA 90067, (213)277-3311.*

DOUGLAS, Charles——**B:** Oct. 27, 1944, Kiowa, CO, The First Nat. Bank of Strasburg, RE Loan; **PRIM RE ACT:** Consultant, Banker, Lender, Owner/Investor, Syndicator; **SERVICES:** Const. & mort. lending; **REP CLIENTS:** Indiv. borrowers, builders & contrs. and indus. & instnl. investors in ltd. partnership synds.; **PREV EMPLOY:** Examiner FDIC 1972-77; **PROFL AFFIL & HONORS:** ABA, CO Bankers Assn., Advisory Member Eastern CO Realtors Assn.; **EDUC:** 1971, Acctg., Econ., ABA Nat. Sch. for RE Fin. at OH State Univ.; **EDUC HONORS:** Superior acad. achievement at school for RE fin.; **MIL SERV:** USN, E-5, Vietnam Serv.; **HOME ADD:** PO Box 382, Strasburg, CO 80136, (303)622-4280; **BUS ADD:** PO Box 536, Strasburg, CO 80136, (303)622-4201.

DOUGLAS, Howard J.——**B:** May 8, 1946, NYC, NY, *Pres.*, Hobar Group, Inc.; **OTHER RE ACT:** RE Synd.; Prop. Mgmt.; Lecturing; **SERVICES:** Tax and fin. consulting; RE consultation; **PROFL AFFIL & HONORS:** IAFP; NAA, Who's Who in Fin.; **EDUC:** BS, 1968, Indus. Engrg., Syracuse Univ.; **GRAD EDUC:** MBA, 1970, Fin., NYU, Dean's List; APC, 1976, Taxation, NYU; **EDUC HONORS:** Dean's List, Dean's List; **HOME ADD:** 55 Buttonwood Dr., Dix Hills, NY 11756, (516)499-3460; **BUS ADD:** 1800 Northern Blvd., Roslyn, NY 11576, (516)484-3460.

DOUGLAS, Paul W.——*Pres.*, Freeport Mineral Co.; **PRIM RE ACT:** Property Manager; **BUS ADD:** Zoo Park Ave., New York, NY 10166, (212)578-9200.*

DOUGLASS, Allan M.——**B:** Apr. 7, 1912, Dallas, TX, *VP*, Exec. RE Serv. Inc., Comml.; **PRIM RE ACT:** Broker, Developer, Syndicator; **OTHER RE ACT:** Mort. Broker; **SERVICES:** Brokerage, synd. devel., mort. brkge.; **PREV EMPLOY:** Officer of Exec. Material Serv. Div., Gen. Dynamics Corp., Chicago, Borg-Warner, Chicago, Nat. Gypsum Buffalo; **PROFL AFFIL & HONORS:** NAR, FAR, Sarasota Bd. of Realtors, RESSI, FL Assn. Morg. Brokers, CCIM, SRS, SMC; **GRAD EDUC:** MBA, 1955, Bus. Admin., Univ. of Chicago; **OTHER ACT & HONORS:** Bird Key Yacht Club, Dir. Snelling & Snelling Intl., Sarosota, FL; **HOME ADD:** 5790 Midnight Pass Rd., Apt. 402-A, Sarasota, FL 33581, (813)349-5953; **BUS ADD:** 1770 Wood St., Sarasota, FL 33577, (813)365-0900.

DOUGLASS, Jean H.——**B:** Oct. 23, 1946, St. Louis, MO, *Dir. of Tax Sheltered Investments*, Stifl, Nicolaus and Company, Incorporated, Tax Shelter Div.; **PRIM RE ACT:** Broker, Consultant, Owner/Investor, Instructor, Syndicator; **OTHER RE ACT:** Marketer of RE securities; **SERVICES:** Structuring and mktg. investment prop. offerings; **REP CLIENTS:** Numerous clients in 13 state region serviced by 30 branch offices of NYSE member firm; **PREV EMPLOY:** Parnter in Wolk/Douglass RE Preparation Courses, an accredited pre-license school; Office in Wolk/Douglass, Inc. a RE brokerage firm; Owner of J.H. Douglass, Realtor; **PROFL AFFIL & HONORS:** MO Chap. Pres., RESSI; Past Dir., MO Assn. of Realtors and RE Bd. of Metro. St. Louis, GRI; AFLM; NAR; **EDUC:** AB, 1968, Poli. Sci., St. Louis Univ.; **HOME ADD:** 730 Crab Thicket Lane, St. Louis (Des Peres), MO 63131, (314)821-7286; **BUS ADD:** 500 N. Broadway, St. Louis, MO 63102.

DOUGLASS, Mark——**B:** Feb. 9, 1951, Minneapolis, MN, *Atty. at Law*; **PRIM RE ACT:** Attorney, Owner/Investor, Syndicator; **PROFL AFFIL & HONORS:** ABA, MN State Bar Assn.; **EDUC:** AB, 1976, Hist., Harvard Univ.; **GRAD EDUC:** JD, 1979, Law, Hamline Univ. Sch. of Law; **EDUC HONORS:** Departmental Honors in Hist.; **HOME ADD:** 1400 Spruce Pl., Minneapolis, MN 55403, (612)870-4948; **BUS ADD:** 3109 Hennepin Ave. S., Minneapolis, MN 55408, (612)827-3563.

DOUTHIT, David V.——**B:** Dec. 27, 1938, NY, NY, *Partner*, Lincoln Property Co.; **PRIM RE ACT:** Broker, Developer, Owner/Investor; **SERVICES:** Devel. of indus. & comml. props.; **REP CLIENTS:** Maj. nat., rgnl. & local users of indus. and comml. facilities.; **PREV EMPLOY:** D.H. Overmyer Co., Bell & Norfleet, Coldwell Banker; **PROFL AFFIL & HONORS:** Portland C of C, N. Clackamas C of C, Nat. Assoc. of Office & Indus. Parks, Speaker at SIR Conference; **EDUC:** Econ., CCNY; **MIL SERV:** US Army, 1957-59, Pfc.; **HOME ADD:** 15990 SW Colony Ct., Tigard, OR 97223, (503)620-2666; **BUS ADD:** 2660 SE Mailwell Dr., PO Box 22166, Milwaukie, OR 97222, (503)652-1661.

DOVE, Aytan Alexander——**B:** Dec. 20 1943, Philadelphia, PA, *Broker Associate*, Century 21 Great American Reality, Investment Services Div.; **PRIM RE ACT:** Broker, Instructor, Syndicator; **OTHER RE ACT:** Mort. Broker; **SERVICES:** Investment Counseling, Loan Placement, Leasing, Comml. Sales & Devel.; **REP CLIENTS:** Investors, developers, mostly in Comml. RE and rehabilitaion programs; **PROFL AFFIL & HONORS:** NAR; RNMI; AZ Assoc. Realtors; Dir., 3 yr. term, Bd. of Dirs., Cochise Bd. of Realtors, CCIM; **EDUC:** BA Recreation Admin., 1971, CA State at Long Beach CA; **GRAD EDUC:** MA: Psych., Counseling & Guidance, 1973, Counseling and Guidance for youth-oriented programs, and Leisure Time Counseling. Retirement Counseling, and Family Counseling, Univ. of N. CO, CSAP at Fort Huachuca, AZ; **EDUC HONORS:** Dean's Honor Roll; **MIL SERV:** USAF; E-3 (Airman) Standard In-Service, 1961-1965; **OTHER ACT & HONORS:** Commnr. on the Sierra Vista Parks and Recreation Commn.; VP, Kiwanis, Past Dir. of Cochise Bd. of Realtors Multiple Listing Service; Instr. for Western Coll. School of RE, Instructor for GRI program; AZ Assn. of Realtors Instr., Speakers Caravan, RE Dept., AZ Assn.; **HOME ADD:** 340 Duchess Dr., Sierra Vista, AZ 85635, (602)485-4618; **BUS ADD:** 741 E. Blvd., Sierra Vista, AZ 85635.

DOVE, Bruce Lee——**B:** Dec. 21, 1946, Wash. DC, *Corp. Counsel, Atty.*, East Bay Devel. Corp.; **OTHER RE ACT:** Leasing and acquisitions; **EDUC:** BA, 1968, Mktg., MI State Univ.; **GRAD EDUC:** MBA, 1972, Mktg., MI State Univ.; JD, 1972, Georgetown Law Sch.; **MIL SERV:**

USA; **HOME ADD:** 3 Overlook Way, Winchester, MA 01890, (617)729-3627; **BUS ADD:** 5 Middlesex Ave., Somerville, MA 02145, (617)628-8600.

DOW, Victor W.D.——**B:** Jan. 5, 1957, Taipei, Taiwan, *Partner*, Dow & Co.; **PRIM RE ACT:** Developer, Builder, Owner/Investor; **SERVICES:** Devel. of condo. & tract housing; **PROFL AFFIL & HONORS:** ASCE; **EDUC:** BS, 1979, Construction, Univ. of Southern CA; **HOME TEL:** (213)288-1398; **BUS ADD:** 901 Berkebile Ct., Monterey Park, CA 91754, (213)571-8707.

DOWD, John E.——**B:** May 30, 1946, Vermillion Co., IN, *Atty.*, Ringer and Dowd; **PRIM RE ACT:** Attorney; **SERVICES:** All types of RE transactions, closings, document preparations; **REP CLIENTS:** VA, FHA, John Hancock Mutual Life Ins. Co., Prudential Life Ins. Co., Warren Cty. Fed. S&L Assn.; **PROFL AFFIL & HONORS:** ABA, IN State Bar Assn., Warren Cty. Bar Assn.; **EDUC:** BA, 1969, Poli. Sci., IN Univ.; **GRAD EDUC:** JD, 1972, Law, IN School of Law at Indianapolis; **OTHER ACT & HONORS:** Prosecuting Atty., Warren Cty. 1978- ; Bd. Child Adult Resource Serv. Center; **HOME ADD:** 302 Falls St., Williamsport, IN 47993, (317)762-6593; **BUS ADD:** 110 N. Monroe St., PO Box 194, Williamsport, IN 47993, (317)762-2625.

DOWD, Michael J.——**B:** July 30, 1941, Boston, MA, *Pres.*, Investment Services Inc.; **PRIM RE ACT:** Broker, Consultant, Developer, Owner/Investor, Syndicator; **SERVICES:** Synd. of Comml. and Subsidized Resid. prop., arrange debt for credit tenants and govt. assisted housing, particular interest in Hist. Props.; **PREV EMPLOY:** VP RE, Nomburger Loeb and Co.; (Member NY Stock Exchange)-VP Corp. Analysis, Amer. Express Co.; Pres. Amer. Realty Team; **EDUC:** BA, 1963, Eng. Lit., Columbia Coll.; **GRAD EDUC:** MBA, 1967, Harvard Bus. School; **HOME ADD:** 192 Meadowbrook Rd., Weston, MA, (617)899-1978; **BUS ADD:** 11 Beacon St., Boston, MA 02108, (617)742-2022.

DOWLING, Donald R.——**B:** Aug. 23, 1945, Jacksonville, FL, *Pres.*, Don Dowling Realty - Gallery of Homes; **PRIM RE ACT:** Broker, Appraiser, Builder, Property Manager; **SERVICES:** Counseling, relocation, property mgmt.; **REP CLIENTS:** Third party relocation cos., indus. (corporate) clients; **PREV EMPLOY:** Former Motel Owner; **PROFL AFFIL & HONORS:** SC Assn. of Realtors; NAR; **EDUC:** BA, 1967, Bus. Admin./Econ., Newberry Coll.; **EDUC HONORS:** Outstanding Young Alumnus Award 1978; **MIL SERV:** US Army, S/Sgt.; **OTHER ACT & HONORS:** City Councilman - current Deacon of First Baptist Church; A Member of the Newberry City Council; Past Pres. of the Newberry Rotary Club; Past Pres. of the Newberry Cty. Devel. Bd. C of C; Bd. of Dirs. of SC State C of C; Bd. of Tr. of Newberry Coll.; Former Member of the City of Newberry Planning Commn.; Former campaign Chmn. for the Easter Seal Soc.; Founder of the Recent "Shop Newberry Cty. First" Promotion; Member of the Advisory Bd. of Citizens and So. Nat. Bank in Newberry; Former Member of the Newberry Parks and Recreation Dept. Advisory Council; Coordinator of the "Great" town program; **HOME ADD:** Pondwood, Newberry, SC 29108, (803)276-0992; **BUS ADD:** 384 Wilson Rd., PO Box 553, Newberry, SC 29108, (803)276-9700.

DOWLING, Geoffrey W.——**B:** July 3, 1952, Evanston, IL, *Mrg., Indus. RE*, Kraft, Inc.; **PRIM RE ACT:** Broker, Consultant, Appraiser, Developer, Owner/Investor, Property Manager, Syndicator; **SERVICES:** Acquisition & disposition of corp. RE, counseling, synd.; **REP CLIENTS:** Kraft, indiv. investors, small bus.; **PROFL AFFIL & HONORS:** NACORE, AIDC, NARA, CRA; **EDUC:** BS, 1974, Mktg., RE, AZ State Univ.; **OTHER ACT & HONORS:** Sigma Nu Frat., H.O. Club; **HOME ADD:** 129 S. Glendale Ave., Barrington, IL 60010, (312)381-4679; **BUS ADD:** Kraft Court, Glenview, IL 60025, (312)998-2466.

DOWLING, Owen Q.——**B:** Apr. 21, 1950, Chicago, *Prop. Mgr.*, Dowling and Company Realtors; **PRIM RE ACT:** Broker, Property Manager; **SERVICES:** Income prop. mgmt., condo. mgmt.; **REP CLIENTS:** profls.; investors; **PREV EMPLOY:** Sales, National Safety Council, US C of C, Dun & Bradstreet; **PROFL AFFIL & HONORS:** Realtor; **EDUC:** BA, 1972, Liberal Arts, Univ. of Denver; **GRAD EDUC:** MBA, 1979, Fin., Keller Grad. School of Mgmt.; **MIL SERV:** USMC, 1st Lt.; **HOME ADD:** 437 Home Ave., Oak Park, IL 60302, (312)383-9202; **BUS ADD:** 1101 Lake St., Oak Park, IL 60302, (312)383-6600.

DOWLING, Terence D.——**B:** Aug. 13, 1946, Chicago, IL, *Pres.*, Dowling & Co.; **PRIM RE ACT:** Broker, Developer, Property Manager, Syndicator, Owner/Investor; **SERVICES:** Brokerage, mgmt., condo. conversion; **PREV EMPLOY:** Farnsworth Palmer & Co., Office leasing specialist, comml. brokerage; **PROFL AFFIL & HONORS:** RE, RESSI, Pres. IL Chapt. of RESSI, Sec. of Oak Park Bd. of Realtors, Past Officer Jr. RE Bd. of Chicago; SRS Candidate; **EDUC:** BA, 1969, Hist. & Eng., Univ. of Denver; **GRAD EDUC:** 1969-71, Law, John Marshall Law School; **HOME ADD:** 1025 N. East, Oak Park, IL 60302, (312)848-7456; **BUS ADD:** 101 Lake St., Atrium on the Mall, Oak Park, IL 60301, (312)383-6600.

DOWLING, Thomas W.——*VP Mktg.*, British American Development Corp.; **PRIM RE ACT:** Developer; **BUS ADD:** 423 Loodonville Rd., NY, NY 12211, (518)462-5331.*

DOWNING, Robert S.——**B:** Dec. 28, 1953, Phoenix, AZ, *VP-Controller*, Marquis Development Co., Inc.; **OTHER RE ACT:** Controller; **SERVICES:** Accounting, tax and fin. planning; **PREV EMPLOY:** Main Lafrentz and Co., CPA; **PROFL AFFIL & HONORS:** AICPA, CPA, AZ; **EDUC:** BS, 1975, Acctg., AZ State Univ.; **EDUC HONORS:** Cum Laude; **HOME ADD:** 12625 N. 34th St., Phoenix, AZ 85032, (602)992-3775; **BUS ADD:** 1250 E. Missouri Ave., Phoenix, AZ 85014, (602)248-8842.

DOWNS, James——*Ed.-Publ.*, Real Estate Research Corp., The National Letter; **PRIM RE ACT:** Real Estate Publisher; **BUS ADD:** 72 W. Adams Street, Chicago, IL 60603, (312)346-5885.*

DOWNS, Joseph M.——**B:** May 17, 1921, Chicago, IL, *Pres.*, Joseph M. Downs Investments; **PRIM RE ACT:** Broker, Syndicator, Consultant, Developer, Property Manager, Owner/Investor; **SERVICES:** Investment counseling, sales, synd., Mgmt.; Coast to Coast comml. props., office bldgs., shopping ctrs., apt. complexes, hotels/motels; **REP CLIENTS:** Lenders Pension Funds, Devel., Investors, European/Far East Investors; **PREV EMPLOY:** Major Ins. Co.; **PROFL AFFIL & HONORS:** IREM, Intl. Fed. of RE; **EDUC:** DePaul Univ., 1951, Bus. Admin./RE; **MIL SERV:** USN, CPO; **OTHER ACT & HONORS:** Admin. Asst. to Commn. of City Planning, City of Chicago; **BUS ADD:** 18538 Cowing Ct., Homewood, IL 60430, (312)798-5366.

DOWTY, Navi J.——**B:** Apr. 4, 1945, MI, *Pres.*, Capital Security Investments, Inc.; **PRIM RE ACT:** Broker, Syndicator, Developer, Property Manager; **OTHER RE ACT:** Mkt. Analysis; **SERVICES:** Creation of RE Investments; **REP CLIENTS:** Investors; **PROFL AFFIL & HONORS:** Intl. Assn. of Exchangors, CCIM, RESSI; **EDUC:** BS, 1968, Chem./Paper Engr., W. MI Univ.; **OTHER ACT & HONORS:** Pres. of Wausau Toastmasters, Pres. Wausau Apt. Assn.; **HOME ADD:** 2410 Jeffrey Ln., Schofield, WI 54476, (715)359-4941; **BUS ADD:** 700 Grand Ave., Wausau, WI 54401, (715)845-4367.

DOYLE, Allan M., Jr.——*Treas.*, Koll Morgen Corp.; **PRIM RE ACT:** Property Manager; **BUS ADD:** 60 Washington St., Hartford, CT 06106, (203)547-0600.*

DOYLE, C. Richard——**B:** Mar. 26, 1930, MI, *Atty.*, Gess Mattingly Saunier & Atchison; **PRIM RE ACT:** Attorney; **SERVICES:** General; **PROFL AFFIL & HONORS:** ABA; KY State Bar Assn.; Fayette Cty. Bar Assn.; **EDUC:** AB, 1952, Journalism, Univ. of MI; **GRAD EDUC:** LLB, 1955, Univ. of KY; **EDUC HONORS:** Order of Coif, Law Journal Editor in Chief; **MIL SERV:** US Army, E-5; **HOME ADD:** Rte. One, 4907 Tates Creek Pike, Lexington, KY 40515, (606)272-5464; **BUS ADD:** 201 W. Short St., Lexington, KY 40507, (606)255-2344.

DOYLE, John T.——*Fin. VP & Dir.*, Daniel O'Connell Sons Inc.; **OTHER RE ACT:** Prop. Mgmt., Const., Devel.; **PREV EMPLOY:** Main Hurdman, Springfield, MA - CPA; Treas., Nonotuck Mfr. Co., S. Hadley, MA; **PROFL AFFIL & HONORS:** MA Soc. of CPA's; Amer. Instit. of CPA's; Fin. Exec. Instit., CPA - MA; **EDUC:** BBA, 1953, Fin./Acctg., School of Mgmt., Boston Univ.; **MIL SERV:** US Army; **OTHER ACT & HONORS:** VP & Trustee, Holyoke Hospital; Advisory Bd., Holyoke Office Third Nat. Bank & Trust Co.; Dir., Mt. Tom Ski Area Inc., Holyoke, MA; Dir., Sales Tech. Corp., Holyoke, MA; **BUS ADD:** 480 Hampden St., Holyoke, MA 01041, (413)534-5667.

DOYLE, Marc H.——**B:** July 11, 1951, Rochester, NY, *Indus. Specialist*, Grubb & Ellis Commercial Brokerage Co., Indus. Div.; **PRIM RE ACT:** Broker; **SERVICES:** Indus. brokerage; **REP CLIENTS:** Avco Community Devel., Inc.; **PREV EMPLOY:** City of San Diego, Assistant Devel. Admin.; **PROFL AFFIL & HONORS:** San Diego Bd. of Realtors; **EDUC:** BS, 1974, Mktg., San Diego State Univ.; **EDUC HONORS:** Dean's List; **HOME ADD:** 2004 Countrywood Court, Encinitas, CA 92024, (714)942-2984; **BUS ADD:** 2121 Palomar Airport Rd., Carlsbad, CA 92008, (714)438-1333.

DOYLE, Robert A.——**B:** Nov. 19, 1926, Chicago, IL, *Pres.*, Doyle and Assoc.; **PRIM RE ACT:** Broker, Consultant, Developer, Banker, Owner/Investor; **SERVICES:** devel. and mgmt. of comml. RE; **REP CLIENTS:** Indus. and Indiv. Investors in Indust. and Comml. Props.; **PREV EMPLOY:** Nat. Sales Mgr., Nelson Co., Rockford, IL; **PROFL AFFIL & HONORS:** IREM, CCIM; **EDUC:** PhD, Phil, Bus., Marquette Univ.; **MIL SERV:** USNAC; **OTHER ACT & HONORS:** Public Bldg. Comm., Winnebago Cty., 1966-1975; Pres., Rockford Comm. Trst., 1972-1981; President, Rockford Board of Realtors, 1966; **HOME ADD:** 1724 Old Wood Rd., Rockford, IL 61107, (815)399-6446; **BUS ADD:** 205 7th St.,PO Box 4477, Rockford, IL 61110, (815)968-5826.

DRAGOO, Douglas——**B:** Aug. 13, 1957, Colorado Springs, CO, *Pres.*, Paragon Properties, Ltd.; **PRIM RE ACT:** Broker, Consultant, Developer, Builder; **SERVICES:** Comml. and resid. devel. consulting and brokerage; **REP CLIENTS:** Consulting for United Bank of Denver Boychuk Devel., Paragon Props.; **PREV EMPLOY:** Selection Research, Dragoo Const., Passive Heat Products; **EDUC:** Bus. Admin., 1976, 1980, RE, Const. Mgmt., Univ. of UT, Univ. of NE; **HOME ADD:** 155 Glencrest Ct., Colorado Springs, CO 80907, (303)526-6641; **BUS ADD:** 3512 N. Tejon, Colorado Springs, CO 80907, (303)634-5564.

DRAGOS, Stephen F.——**B:** Aug. 30, 1936, Chicago, IL, *Exec. VP*, Milwaukee Redevel. Corp.; **PRIM RE ACT:** Developer; **PREV EMPLOY:** Gen. Mgr. of Planning & Design for Mondev, Ltd. of Montreal, Exec. Dir. of the non-profit Valley Devel. Foundation in upstate NY (1965-1973); **PROFL AFFIL & HONORS:** AIA, Urban Devel./Mixed Use Council, ULI, Washington, D.C.; **EDUC:** BA Architecture (5 year program), 1961, Univ. of Notre Dame; **MIL SERV:** USNG; **OTHER ACT & HONORS:** Immediate Past Pres., Friends of Art of the Milwaukee Art Ctr.; BOD, Milwaukee Forum; Member of the Board, The Park People of Milwaukee Cty., Inc.; Member, Goals for Milwaukee 2000, Steering Comm.; **HOME ADD:** 2810 N. Hackett Ave., Milwaukee, WI 53211, (414)352-8183; **BUS ADD:** 161 W. Wisconsin Ave., Milwaukee, WI 53203, (414)276-5995.

DRAKE, James D.——**B:** Mar. 9, 1943, Raymondville, TX, *VP & Gen. Mgr.*, Schulgen Props., Inc.; **PRIM RE ACT:** Broker, Developer, Property Manager, Owner/Investor; **PREV EMPLOY:** S-D Mgmt Corp., 1979-81, Westvaco Corp., 1974-79, H.J. Heinz Co., 1973-74, US. Dept. of Agric., 1970-72; **PROFL AFFIL & HONORS:** BOMA, Dev. of Houston; **EDUC:** BS, 1972, Urban Dev., The Amer. Univ.; **GRAD EDUC:** MBA, 1973, Fin., Univ. of Chicago, Grad. School of Bus.; **MIL SERV:** USN, 1966-70, 2nd class PLO; **OTHER ACT & HONORS:** The Windsor Club; **HOME ADD:** 12131 Gladewick Dr., Houston, TX 77077, (713)496-0945; **BUS ADD:** 9055 Katy Fwy., Suite 302, Houston, TX 77024, (713)465-5802.

DRAKE, Reynolds——**B:** Oct. 11, 1924, New York, NY, *Pres./Owner*, Drake Associates; **PRIM RE ACT:** Broker, Consultant, Appraiser, Developer, Builder, Owner/Investor, Instructor, Syndicator; **PROFL AFFIL & HONORS:** NAR; NH Assn. of Realtors; S. Bd. of Realtors; SC Bd. of Realtors, GRI; VP of NH Assoc. of Realtors; **EDUC:** BS, 1949, Math., Dartmouth Coll.; **MIL SERV:** USAF; Capt.; Air Medal; **OTHER ACT & HONORS:** Sec. NH Assn. of Realtors 1980; Treas. NH Assn. of Realtors 1981; **HOME ADD:** Ocean Rd., Portsmouth, NH 03801, (603)436-7050; **BUS ADD:** Route 101, Greenland, NH 03840, (603)436-7050.

DRAKE, Richard W.——**B:** Aug. 30, 1932, Omaha, NE, *Sr. VP*, Union Commerce Bank, RE Indus. Div.; **PRIM RE ACT:** Banker; **SERVICES:** Construction/Homebuilder Credits/Mort. Bankers Warehousing Credits, Residential Lending/Long-term Comml. Lending. Also Condo-conversion Lending; **REP CLIENTS:** Homebuilders, Mort. Bankers, Condominium Converters; **PREV EMPLOY:** VP Continental IL Nat. Bank & Trust Co., Chicago; **PROFL AFFIL & HONORS:** ABA, MBAA Mort. Bankers Assn. of Greater Cleveland, Intl. Frat. of Lambda Alpha. Builders Exchange, I Robert Morris Assoc.; **EDUC:** BS, 1954, Indus. Econ., IA State Univ.; **GRAD EDUC:** Mort. Banking Certificate, 1960-62, N. Western Univ.; **OTHER ACT & HONORS:** Golden Age Ctrs. of Greater Cleveland, Inc. Member Bd. of Tr. and Past Pres.; Neighborhood Housing Services of Cleveland, Member Bd. of Tr. and Treas., Member: Mayfield Ctry. Club; **HOME ADD:** 2675 Wrenford Rd., Shaker, OH 44122, (216)464-5087; **BUS ADD:** 917 Euclid Ave., Cleveland, OH 44101, (216)344-6300.

DRANE, Phillip D.——**B:** Oct. 24, 1941, Mobile, AL, *Exec. VP*, White-Spunner & Associates, Inc.; **PRIM RE ACT:** Broker, Consultant, Developer, Owner/Investor, Property Manager, Syndicator; **SERVICES:** Comml. brokerage; comml., resid., indust. devel.; **REP CLIENTS:** Indiv., pension funds, trusts, investors; **PROFL AFFIL & HONORS:** Mobile RE Exchange Club; South Al Regional Planning Comm. Transp. Advisory Council; Damphin Island Park & Beach Bd.; **EDUC:** BS, 1965, Bus. Admin., Auburn Univ.; **HOME ADD:** 304 Dogwood Ln., Mobile, AL 36616, (205)343-3596; **BUS ADD:** PO Box 16227, Mobile, AL 36616, (205)476-6000.

DRAPER, Daniel Clay——**B:** Jun 7, 1920, Boston, MA, *Partner, Atty.*, Cadwalader, Wickersham & Taft, RE; **PRIM RE ACT:** Attorney; **OTHER RE ACT:** Banking and RE; **PREV EMPLOY:** Assoc. Firm, Kelley, Drye & Warren, NYC 1947-1955; **EDUC:** BA, 1940, W. VA Univ.; **GRAD EDUC:** MA, 1941, W. VA Univ.; LLB, 1947, Harvard Univ.; **MIL SERV:** USN, LtC., Bronze Star, European Service Ribbon Three Star; **OTHER ACT & HONORS:** Pilgrims, St. George Soc., Harvard, Downtown Assn.; **HOME ADD:** 124 Lloyd Rd., Montclair, NJ 07042, (201)744-7804; **BUS ADD:** One Wall St., New York, NY 10005, (212)785-1000.

DRAPER, Malcolm, Jr.——*Chmn.*, Department of Housing and Urban Development, Federal Home Loan Bank Board; **PRIM RE ACT:** Lender; **BUS ADD:** 451 Seventh St., SW, Washington, DC 20410, (202)377-6273.*

DRATH, Richard——**B:** Sept. 7, 1942, Brooklyn, NY, *Partner*, Rachlin & Cohen, Ft. Lauderdale Office; **PRIM RE ACT:** Owner/Investor; **OTHER RE ACT:** CPA; **SERVICES:** Bus. and tax consultation; **PREV EMPLOY:** Drath & Sheinfeld, CPA's 1973-1974; **PROFL AFFIL & HONORS:** AICPA; FL Inst. of CPA's; NY State Soc. of CPA's; **EDUC:** BS, 1965, Fin., Miami Univ., OH; **HOME ADD:** 560 S. Lake Dasha Dr., Plantation, FL 33324, (305)473-1915; **BUS ADD:** 3101 N. Federal Highway, Ft. Lauderdale, FL 33306, (305)565-1065.

DREHER, Ralph M.——**B:** Aug. 26, 1930, Tubingen, CO, *Pres.*, The Dreher Corp., CO; **PRIM RE ACT:** Developer, Owner/Investor, Insuror, Syndicator; **SERVICES:** Devel. & ins. multi-family resid.; **EDUC:** 1960, Engr. & Public Relations, Omaha Univ.; **GRAD EDUC:** 1965, Technology, N.W. M State Univ.; **MIL SERV:** US Army, Sgt., various decorations; **OTHER ACT & HONORS:** Fire Marshall I.C. Fire Dept.; **HOME ADD:** 19378 Hill Dr., Morrison, CO 80465, (303)697-4765; **BUS ADD:** 5748 S. Gallup St., Littleton, CO 80120, (303)795-5200.

DRESNICK, David W.——**B:** Feb. 16, 1941, NY, NY, *Pres.*, Glendale Grp. Inc.; **PRIM RE ACT:** Consultant, Developer, Lender, Syndicator; **SERVICES:** RE consultant servs. & devel.; **PREV EMPLOY:** Exec. VP and COO US Life S&L, Exec VP Grosvenor Props., Pres. Sequoia Mort. Co., Pres. Pan Pacific Devel. Co.; **PROFL AFFIL & HONORS:** Former Dir. Home Loan Counseling Ctr., Sr. ABA, Who's Who in CA; **EDUC:** 1962, Bus. Admin., Univ. of CA, Berkeley; **HOME ADD:** 2112 Lenore Dr., Glendale, CA 91206, (212)790-2951; **BUS ADD:** 2112 Lenore Dr., Glendale, CA 91206, (213)790-1851.

DRESSER, Winifred H.——**B:** Nov. 8, 1932, Clay Cty., IN, *Pres.*, Toni's Enterprises of Pasco, Inc.; **PRIM RE ACT:** Builder; **SERVICES:** New Home Custom Constr.; **PROFL AFFIL & HONORS:** Hernando Builders Assn., FHBA, NAHB, Pres. Hernando Builder's Assn., (Current), 1978 Pasco Cty. Builder of Yr.; **MIL SERV:** USWMC, Sgt.; **OTHER ACT & HONORS:** W. Hernando C. of C., Amer. Legion Comm. of 100; **HOME ADD:** 19 Dan River Dr., Spring Hill, FL 33526, (904)683-3895; **BUS ADD:** 301 Landmark Dr., Hudson, FL 33568, (813)868-1422.

DRESSLER, David C., Jr.——**B:** Oct. 2, 1953, *Project Mgr. - Resid. Devel.*, Arvida Corp., Weston Communities; **PRIM RE ACT:** Developer; **EDUC:** BA, 1975, Yale Univ.; **GRAD EDUC:** MBA, 1979, Harvard Univ.; **BUS ADD:** 901 E. Las Olas Blvd., Fort Lauderdale, FL 33301, (305)761-1808.

DREW, Michael B.——**B:** Apr. 25, 1950, Sedalia, MO, *Pres.*, M.B. Drew Co.; **PRIM RE ACT:** Broker, Consultant, Developer, Property Manager; **SERVICES:** Investment counseling, site selection & analysis, prop. mgmt.; **REP CLIENTS:** Indiv., corporate, and instnl. investors and users of comml. and investment RE; **PROFL AFFIL & HONORS:** NAR, IN Assn. of Realtors, Metro. Indpls. Bd. of Realtors, Nat. Assn. of Corporate RE Execs., RNMI; **EDUC:** BS, 1972, Mgmt. and RE, IN Univ.; **BUS ADD:** 1111 East 54th St., Indianapolis, IN 46220, (317)255-3900.

DREW, Robert (Trader)——**B:** Feb. 1, 1924, Creston, IA, *Broker*, Drew and Drew Real Estate Exchangors; **PRIM RE ACT:** Broker, Consultant, Developer, Builder, Owner/Investor, Instructor, Syndicator; **SERVICES:** Investment counseling for nationwide exchanging; synd., investor, devel.; **REP CLIENTS:** Lenders and indiv. or instnl. investors in FL props., as buyer agent or joint venture; **PROFL AFFIL & HONORS:** Nat. VP of INTEREX, FL RE Exchangors Editor in Chief; **EDUC:** Drake Univ., 1947; **MIL SERV:** US Army, 1942-1945; **HOME ADD:** 8120-Diagonal Rd., St. Petersburg, FL 33702, (813)577-6762; **BUS ADD:** 8120-Diagonal Rd. N., St. Petersburg, FL

33702, (813)577-6762.

DREWS, Donald Frederick——**B:** Dec. 3, 1928, Minneapolis, MN, *Asst. VP - Props. & Facilities*, Western Airlines, Legal Div.; **PRIM RE ACT:** Architect, Property Manager; **SERVICES:** Corporate Mgr. - RE and const. devel.; **PREV EMPLOY:** The Cerny Assoc., Architects/Engineers, VP, Minneapolis, MN, 1953-1968; **PROFL AFFIL & HONORS:** AIA, Amer. Transport Assn., Past Chmn. Airport Affairs, Registered Architect/CA & MN; **EDUC:** BA & BArch, 1951 & 1953, Arch., Univ. of MN; **EDUC HONORS:** Alpha Roe Chi Honor Medal, Ellerbe Prize in Arch.; **MIL SERV:** USAF, 1st Lt.; **OTHER ACT & HONORS:** Rotary Intl., Past Pres.; LA Airport Club; **HOME ADD:** 5826 Flambeau Rd., Rancho Palos Verdes, CA 90274; **BUS ADD:** 6060 Avion Dr., Los Angeles, CA 90045, (213)646-2330.

DREWS, John R.——**B:** Aug. 4, 1942, Okla City, OK, *Pres.*, John Drews Co.; **PRIM RE ACT:** Broker, Developer, Property Manager, Syndicator; **SERVICES:** RE Brokerage, Devel., Synd., & Mgmt. - All Comml.; **REP CLIENTS:** Investors and uses of comml. RE; **PREV EMPLOY:** Henry S. Miller Co. 1972-73; **PROFL AFFIL & HONORS:** NAR, RNMI, IREM, ULI, CCIM, CPM; **EDUC:** BBA, 1964, Mktg. & Acctg., Southern Methodist Univ.; **GRAD EDUC:** MBA, 1972, Mktg., TX Christian Univ.; **MIL SERV:** USAF, S/Sgt.; **OTHER ACT & HONORS:** Bd. of Dir., Family Services Agency of Tarr Cty.; **BUS ADD:** 2204 Forest Park Blvd., Ft. Worth, TX 76110, (817)926-2600.

DREZNER, David——**B:** July 4, 1938, Brooklyn, David Drezner Real Estate; **PRIM RE ACT:** Broker; **SERVICES:** Sale, leasing, fin. & devel. of Hotels, motels, and multi-use projects; **PROFL AFFIL & HONORS:** Rho Epsilon, Urban Land Inst.; **EDUC:** 1961, Const., State Univ., Farmingdale; **HOME TEL:** (212)832-3495; **BUS ADD:** 122 East 42th St., New York, NY 10168, (212)687-8660.

DRILLER, Jay——*Mgr. Surplus Fac.*, International Paper Co.; **PRIM RE ACT:** Property Manager; **BUS ADD:** 77 W. 45th St., New York, NY 10036, (212)536-6000.*

DRIMER, Walter——**B:** Mar. 16, 1941, Montreal, Can., *VP Devel.*, Sage Devel. Corp.; **PRIM RE ACT:** Broker, Consultant, Developer, Syndicator; **SERVICES:** Consult with health care and investment community; **REP CLIENTS:** Indivs., synds., and non-profit organizations in health care field; **PREV EMPLOY:** Pres., First Continental Realty Investment Corp., 1972-1976; **PROFL AFFIL & HONORS:** Consultant to chapter for Co-operative Global Devel.; Member, Amer. Assn. Health for the Aged; **HOME ADD:** 28 Levering Cir., Bala Cynwyd, PA, (215)667-6594; **BUS ADD:** 2 Bala Cynwyd Plaza, Bala Cynwyd, PA 19004.

DRISCOLL, Arthur E.——**B:** Sept. 17, 1932, Brooklyn, NY, *VP*, Citibank NY, Corp. RE; **PRIM RE ACT:** Banker; **SERVICES:** VP in charge of corp. RE; **REP CLIENTS:** Citibank, NA; **PREV EMPLOY:** US Trust Co., RE Investments; **PROFL AFFIL & HONORS:** NY RE. Bd., NACORE, BOMA, NARA, Intl. RE Fed., Intl. Council Shopping Ctrs.; **MIL SERV:** US Army, Sgt., Korean Svc. Med., Good Conduct; **HOME ADD:** 15 Palmer Dr., Sayville, NY 11782, (516)567-0331; **BUS ADD:** 153 E. 53 St., New York, NY 10043, (212)559-1890.

DROBISCH, Edward C.——**B:** Nov. 13, 1914, Decatur, IL, *Chmn. of Bd.*, Realty World, Ed Drobisch & Co.; **PRIM RE ACT:** Broker, Consultant, Appraiser, Instructor, Property Manager; **SERVICES:** RE consulting and appraisal, brokerage, prop. mgmt.; **REP CLIENTS:** Merrill Lynch; Employee Transfer Corp.; Firestone; **PROFL AFFIL & HONORS:** Realtors, GRI; CRB; CRPA; **EDUC:** BS, 1938, Math. and Econs., Adm. Engrg., Millikin Univ., Decatur, IL; **MIL SERV:** USN; LCDR.; Amer. European WWII Naval Reserve; **OTHER ACT & HONORS:** Past Pres. Lions Club; Masonic; Shrine; Silver Beaver-Boy Scouts; **HOME ADD:** 3360 Dell Oak Dr., Decatur, IL 62526, (217)877-6645; **BUS ADD:** 363 S. Main St., Decatur, IL 62523, (217)428-0943.

DROEGE, J. Robert——**B:** Nov. 3, 1925, KY, *VP RE*, Marriott Corp.; **PRIM RE ACT:** Attorney, Developer, Builder, Owner/Investor; **SERVICES:** Hotel, restaurant, in-flight feeding; **PREV EMPLOY:** Kroger Co.; **PROFL AFFIL & HONORS:** Phi Delta Phi (Legal); **EDUC:** BS, 1947, Pre-Legal, Miami Univ.; **GRAD EDUC:** LLB - JD, 1949, Law, Univ. of Cincinnati; **MIL SERV:** US Army Air Corp, 1944-1945; **HOME ADD:** 10901 Burbank Dr., Potomac, MD 20854; **BUS ADD:** Marriott Dr., Bethesda, MD 20058, (301)897-7496.

DROESCH, David W.——**B:** Dec. 2, 1942, Cincinnati, OH, *VP*, Chelsea Moore Co.; **PRIM RE ACT:** Broker, Consultant, Property Manager; **PROFL AFFIL & HONORS:** CPM - IREM, Nat. Gov. Counsellor - IREM; RPA-BOMA; **EDUC:** BS, 1965, Indus. Mgmt., Univ. of Dayton; **GRAD EDUC:** MBA, 1967, Econ., Fin., Univ. of Dayton; **HOME ADD:** 5300 Hamilton Ave., 1610, Cincinnati, OH 45224, (513)541-4422; **BUS TEL:** (513)671-1600.

DROPKIN, Allen H.——**B:** Oct. 26, 1930, Chicago, IL, *Partner*, Arvey, Hodes, Costello & Burman; **PRIM RE ACT:** Attorney; **SERVICES:** All Servs. of a Legal Nature; **PROFL AFFIL & HONORS:** Chicago, IL State Bar Assns., Member, Real Prop. Comm.; **EDUC:** AB, 1948, Liberal Arts, Univ. of Chicago; **GRAD EDUC:** JD, 1951, Law, Univ. of Chicago; **OTHER ACT & HONORS:** Spec. Counsel, Sub Comm. on Housing Comm. on Banking, Currency; US House of Rep. 1956; **HOME ADD:** 990 N. Lake Shore Dr., Chicago, IL 60611, (312)440-1523; **BUS ADD:** 180 N. LaSalle St., Chicago, IL 60601, (312)855-5008.

DROSSLER, Richard A.——**B:** Dec. 1, 1937, Baltimore, MD, *VP, Acquisitions*, Drever, McIntosh & Co., Inc.; **PRIM RE ACT:** Owner/Investor, Syndicator; **SERVICES:** Purchase and manage props. (own account); **PREV EMPLOY:** Pres., Drossler Investment Co., 1964-1981; Pres., Drossler Research Corp., 1969-1981; **PROFL AFFIL & HONORS:** CA Apt. Assn.; Amer. Mktg. Assn.; **EDUC:** BS, 1959, Indus. Mgmt./Math., MIT; **OTHER ACT & HONORS:** Bd. of Trs., Lamplighters; **HOME ADD:** 3140 Jackson St., San Francisco, CA 94115, (415)563-0783; **BUS ADD:** 110 Sutter St., Suite 905, San Francisco, CA 94104, (415)433-1773.

DROSTE, Edward C.——**B:** Apr. 22, 1951, New Hampton, IA, *Pres.*, Bieder Management Services, Inc.; **PRIM RE ACT:** Broker, Consultant, Instructor, Property Manager; **SERVICES:** RE asset mgmt. condo. conversion, devel. & mgmt., resort mktg.; **REP CLIENTS:** Continental Bank of IL, Housing Investment Corp. of Chase Manhattan; **PREV EMPLOY:** VP, Mgmt., Subsidiary of US Home Corp.; **PROFL AFFIL & HONORS:** CPM; Past Pres., Suncoast Chap. of Community Assns. Inst., CPM; **EDUC:** BS, 1973, Indus. Admin./Mktg./Poli. Sci., IA State Univ.; **EDUC HONORS:** Grad. Class Pres.; **OTHER ACT & HONORS:** Chmn., Indian Shores Code Enforcement Bd.; **HOME ADD:** 19450 Gulf Blvd., Indian Shores, FL 33535, (813)595-0533; **BUS ADD:** 1452 U.S. 19 S., Suite 500, Clearwater, FL 33516, (813)535-9681.

DRUCKER, A. Norman——**B:** Aug. 23, 1930, Brooklyn, NY, *Broker*, Norman A. Drucker; **PRIM RE ACT:** Attorney; **SERVICES:** Legal rep.; **PROFL AFFIL & HONORS:** ABA; FL Bar Assn.; Amer. Academy of Matrimonial Lawyers; **EDUC:** BS, 1953, Univ. of WI; **GRAD EDUC:** JD, 1958, Univ. of Miami Law School; **MIL SERV:** US Army-Judge Advocate General's Corps 1953-1980, Lt.Col., Army Commendation Medal; **HOME ADD:** 7940 West Dr., N. Bay Village, FL 33139, (305)756-7535; **BUS ADD:** 420 Lincoln Rd., Suite 601, Miami Beach, FL 33139, (305)538-1401.

DRUCKER, Cecily A.——**B:** Aug. 31, 1944, VT, *Part.*, Skjerven, Morrill, MacPherson & Drucker; **PRIM RE ACT:** Consultant, Attorney, Owner/Investor, Syndicator; **REP CLIENTS:** Becker & Yaconelli, Winchester Investments; **PROFL AFFIL & HONORS:** ABA, State Bar of CA; **EDUC:** 1966, Poli. Sci., Univ. of Rochester; **GRAD EDUC:** 1974, Hastings Coll. of the Law, Univ. of CA; **BUS ADD:** 601 Montgomery St., Suite 1900, San Francisco, CA 94111, (415)986-8383.

DRUCKER, Erwin B.——*Partner*, Drucker & Falk; **PRIM RE ACT:** Broker, Consultant, Owner/Investor, Instructor, Property Manager, Insuror, Syndicator; **REP CLIENTS:** Mellon Nat. Mort. Corp.; Monumental LIfe Ins. Co.; maj. resid. apt. complexes, Bel Meade Shopping Ctr.; Glenwood Ctr.; Recoughton Shopping Ctr.; Langley Cir. Shopping Ctr.; Parkview Ctr.; **PROFL AFFIL & HONORS:** IREM, NAR; Nat. Pres., IREM, 1978, Realtor of the year, 1968, 1981; Newport News Chap., Bd. of Realtors; **EDUC:** AB, 1950, Univ. of VA; **GRAD EDUC:** JD, Harvard Univ. Law Sch.; **MIL SERV:** USAR, Capt.; **OTHER ACT & HONORS:** Peninsula C of C, Newport News Rotary Club, Bd. of Dirs., United VA Citizens & Marine Bank; **HOME ADD:** 23 Garland Dr., Newport News, VA 23606; **BUS ADD:** 9286 Warwick Blvd., PO Box 96, Newport News, VA 23607, (804)245-1541.

DRUEHL, Josephine Torres——**B:** May 14, 1948, Manila, Philippines, *Atty.*, Law Offices of Josephine Torres Druehl; **PRIM RE ACT:** Attorney; **PREV EMPLOY:** Santa Clara Cty. Counsel, Land Use Sect.; **PROFL AFFIL & HONORS:** ABA, CA State Bar, Land Use Sect.; **EDUC:** BS, 1972, Biological Sci., San Jose State Univ.; **GRAD EDUC:** JD, 1975, Univ. of CA, Hastings; **OTHER ACT & HONORS:** Legal Advisor, Philippine Professional & Bus. Soc. of Santa Clara Valley, Inc.; **BUS ADD:** Suite 480, 95 S. Market, San Jose, CA 95113, (408)298-1505.

DRURY, Charles E.——*Pres.*, Hayes-Albien Corp.; **PRIM RE ACT:** Property Manager; **BUS ADD:** 1999 Wildwood Ave., Jackson, MI 49202, (517)782-9421.*

DRUSKIN, Victor——**B:** Nov. 10, 1944, San Diego, CA, *Gen. Counsel & VP/RE*, Consolidated Capital; **PRIM RE ACT:** Attorney, Instructor; **SERVICES:** overseeing acquisitions, sales, mort. loans, condo. conversions, leasing and other gen. RE matters; **PREV EMPLOY:** Gen. Counsel, Johnstown Properties 1976-78; Cook Investment Props. 1974-75, VP; Jenkins & Perry 1969-73, Assoc. & Part.; **PROFL AFFIL & HONORS:** Member of the State Bar of CA, ABA, Alameda Cty. Bar Assn. and the San Diego Cty. Bar Assn.; **EDUC:** BA, 1966, Poli. Sci., Hist. & Econ., San Diego State Univ.; **GRAD EDUC:** JD, 1969, Univ. of CA, Berkeley; **HOME ADD:** 105 Golden Hills Ct., Danville, CA 94526; **BUS ADD:** 1900 Powell St., Suite 1000, Emeryville, CA 94608, (415)652-7171.

DRYDEN, Willia——*Dir. Fac. & Mgmt. Plng.*, Heublein Inc.; **PRIM RE ACT:** Property Manager; **BUS ADD:** Munson Rd., Farmington, CT 06032, (203)677-4061.*

DUBERSTEIN, James S.——**B:** Jun. 3, 1934, Dayton, OH, *VP*, Duberstein Investment, Inc.; **PRIM RE ACT:** Broker, Consultant, Syndicator; **SERVICES:** Acquisitions for pvt. and public buyers (Shopping Ctr./Offices/Apts.); **REP CLIENTS:** Pension funds/synd./public & pvt. offerings; **EDUC:** BA, 1958, Bus., Univ. of PA (Wharton) OH State Univ.; **GRAD EDUC:** OH State/Harvard (MBA-Audit); **HOME ADD:** 3112 Hilliard Ave., Dayton, OH 45415, (513)278-2361; **BUS ADD:** 111 West 1st St. #810, Dayton, OH 45415, (513)223-7337.

DUBIN, Arthur N.——**B:** Sept. 9, 1952, Wash., DC, *Pres.*, Dubin & Associates, Prop. Mgmt.; **PRIM RE ACT:** Consultant, Property Manager; **SERVICES:** Full Serv. and Limited Serv. for Condo., Co-Ops, HOA; **REP CLIENTS:** Condo. in MD, Wash, DC & VA; **PREV EMPLOY:** 1977-81 Brenneman Assoc., Inc.; **PROFL AFFIL & HONORS:** CPM, IREM; Lic. Salesman in MD; Member of Montgomery Cty. MD Bd. of Realtors; Member of CAI; **EDUC:** BS, 1974, Bus. Mgmt., Univ. of MD; **EDUC HONORS:** Grad. with Honors; **HOME ADD:** 5308 Yorktown RD., Bethesda, MD 20816, (301)654-5308; **BUS ADD:** 5272 River Road; Suite 490, Bethesda, MD 20014, (301)656-5808.

DU BOIS, Reyn——**B:** Apr. 16, 1940, Troy, NY, *VP*, Vanguard Props. of AZ, Inc. & VPA Realty, Inc.-Broker; **PRIM RE ACT:** Broker, Consultant, Owner/Investor; **SERVICES:** Brokerage, RE research and analysis; **REP CLIENTS:** Land investors and devels., office and indus. investors; **PREV EMPLOY:** Mountain West Research 1973-1974; **PROFL AFFIL & HONORS:** AZ Assn. of Indus. Devels.; Amer. Assn. of Applied Geographers; ULI; Underground Space Assn.; **EDUC:** BA, 1974, Computer Applications, Resource Analysis, AZ State Univ.; **GRAD EDUC:** MS, Georaphy, 1975, Computer Graphics and Land Use Analysis, AZ State Univ.; **EDUC HONORS:** AZ Academy of Sci., Outstanding Service Award; **MIL SERV:** USN, E-5; **OTHER ACT & HONORS:** Amer. Futurist Soc.; Citizens for Space; Phoenix Ski Club; **HOME ADD:** 8016 E. Earll Dr., Scottsdale, AZ 85251, (602)941-5015; **BUS ADD:** 3014 N. Hayden Rd., Suite 109, Scottsdale, AZ 85251, (602)994-1920.

DUBS, Kenneth P., Sr.——**B:** Oct. 29, 1948, Chicago, IL, *Pres.*, Countrywood Realty Inc.; **PRIM RE ACT:** Broker, Consultant, Appraiser, Developer, Builder, Property Manager; **OTHER RE ACT:** Interior and exterior design and land planning; **SERVICES:** Sales, Investment, Appraisals, Bldg.; **REP CLIENTS:** Lenders, Devels., Attys., Misc. Corps.; **PROFL AFFIL & HONORS:** Barrington Bd. of Realtors (State and Nat.), AACA, CRPAA, GRI, CRS, CRB Cand., Misc. Multi Million Dollar Sales Awards; **EDUC:** Pre-Med. and Bus., Northern IL Univ.; **MIL SERV:** USN, Hosp. Corps, VietNam Camp Good Conduct; **OTHER ACT & HONORS:** Dir. Barrington Bd. of Realtors; Officer, Barrington Board of Realtors; **HOME ADD:** 45 Witt Rd., S. Barrington, IL 60010; **BUS ADD:** 65 S. Barrington Rd., S. Barrington, IL 60010, (312)381-8070; **BUS TEL:** (312)382-1815.

DUCA, Sam——**B:** Dec. 9, 1920, Ossining, NY, *Assessor*, City & Cty of San Francisco; **PRIM RE ACT:** Assessor; **SERVICES:** Prop. tax admin.; **PROFL AFFIL & HONORS:** AIREA; Intl. Assn. of Assessing Officers; CA Assessors Assn.; San Francisco RE Bd., MAI; **EDUC:** AA, BS, 1949, RE Appraisal, Land Econ., Bus. Admin., Univ. of CA-Berkeley, Stanford Univ.; **GRAD EDUC:** MBA, 1952, Land Econ., Univ. of CA-Stanford; **MIL SERV:** USMC; S Major; various; **OTHER ACT & HONORS:** Elected Assessor 1978; Bd. of Dir., St. Mary's Hosp. Comm. Bd.; Bd. of Dir., USO; Bd. of Dir., UNICO; Olympic Club; **HOME ADD:** 16 Wawona St., San Francisco, CA 94127, (415)558-4351; **BUS ADD:** 101 City Mall, San Francisco, CA 94102, (415)558-4351.

DUCHARME, Jacque——**B:** May 7, 1949, Pasadena, CA, *Corp. VP*, Julien J. Studley, Inc., Chicago; **PRIM RE ACT:** Broker, Consultant; **SERVICES:** Office space - office bldgs.; **PROFL AFFIL & HONORS:** Assoc. of Commerce and Indus.; **EDUC:** BS, 1971, Econ./Eng., Univ. of NE; **GRAD EDUC:** MBA, 1980, Univ. of Chicago; **EDUC HONORS:** With Honors; **HOME ADD:** 1132 W. Drummond Pl., Chicago, IL 60614, (312)525-8233; **BUS ADD:** 35 E. Wacker, Chicago, IL 60601, (312)641-0055.

DUCKER, Stuart R., III——**B:** July 1, 1945, Pensacola, FL, *Corp. Sec.*, Zachariae Realty; **PRIM RE ACT:** Broker; **SERVICES:** Brokerage Serv. for Resid. & Comml. Prop.; **PROFL AFFIL & HONORS:** NAR, RNMI, NJ Assn. of Realtors, GRI, CRB; **EDUC:** BA, 1967, Poli. Sci., Duke Univ.; **OTHER ACT & HONORS:** Stafford Township Bd. of Educ. 1976-1977, Deer Lake Park Lake Assn., Tr.; **HOME ADD:** 104 Temple Ave., Manahawkin, NJ 08050, (609)597-8737; **BUS ADD:** 595 E. Bay Ave., Manahankin, NJ 08050, (609)597-1172.

DUCKWORTH, W. Joseph——**B:** Nov. 14, 1948, Philadelphia, PA, *Exec. VP*, Toll Bros. Inc.; **PRIM RE ACT:** Developer, Builder; **PREV EMPLOY:** Sr. Consultant, Day & Zimmerman RE Services; **PROFL AFFIL & HONORS:** ULI, NAHB; **EDUC:** BS, 1970, Mech. Engrg. - Econs., Carnegie - Mellon Univ.; **GRAD EDUC:** MBA, 1972, Fin., Univ. of PA, Wharton School; **EDUC HONORS:** Scimithrs, Pi Tau Sigma, Omicron Delta Kappa, Student Body Pres.; **HOME ADD:** 1500 Laurie Ln., Yardley, PA 19067, (215)493-0395; **BUS ADD:** 101 Witmer Rd., Horsham, PA 19044, (215)441-4400.

DUDENEY, Peter N.——**B:** Jan. 25, 1926, London England, *Pres.*, Centry 21 Homes, Inc.; **PRIM RE ACT:** Broker, Engineer, Appraiser, Owner/Investor, Instructor; **SERVICES:** Resid. & Comml. RE Brokerage Full Service, Relocation, Appraising & Investment Counseling; **PROFL AFFIL & HONORS:** RNMI, NAR, WCR, SREA, Assoc. Prof. Engrs., CRB, CRS, GRI; **EDUC:** BSEE, 1955, Gen. Electronics, Univ. of London; **GRAD EDUC:** MSC, 1956, Physics, Univ. of London; **HOME ADD:** 38 Dorethy Rd., W. Redding, CT 06896, (203)938-3053; **BUS ADD:** 642 Danbury Rd., Ridgefield, CT 06877, (203)438-9649.

DUDLEY, George E.——**B:** July 14, 1922, Earlington, KY, *Partner*, Brown, Todd & Heyburn; **PRIM RE ACT:** Attorney; **SERVICES:** All types of legal serv. relating to devel. and fin. RE; **PROFL AFFIL & HONORS:** Amer., KY and Louisville Bar Assns.; Sixth Circuit Judicial Conf.; **EDUC:** BS, 1947, Commerce, Univ. of KY; **GRAD EDUC:** LLB, 1950, Law, Univ. of MI; **EDUC HONORS:** ODK, Barristers Soc.; **MIL SERV:** US Army; 1943-46, 1951-52, Capt.; **OTHER ACT & HONORS:** 1st VP, Nat. Easter Seal Soc.; Dir., Norton-Children's Hospitals; Advisory Bd., Jefferson Community Coll.; **HOME ADD:** 1905 Crossgate Ln., Louisville, KY 40222, (502)425-2135; **BUS ADD:** 1600 Citizens Plaza, Louisville, KY 40202, (502)589-5400.

DUDLEY, Mark M.——**B:** Apr. 6, 1947, Shelbyville, IN, *Broker/Owner*, Johnson, Dudley & Dishman, Better Homes & Gardens Real Estate; **PRIM RE ACT:** Broker, Appraiser; **SERVICES:** Resid., farm, comml. sales & evaluation; **PROFL AFFIL & HONORS:** NAR, Hancock Cty. Bd. of Realtors (Pres. 1980); Indianapolis Metropolitan Bd. of Realtors; **EDUC:** AB, 1971, Poli. Sci., IN Univ., I.V. Found.; **GRAD EDUC:** Grad. Work, 1972-73, Poli. Sci., IN Univ.; **MIL SERV:** USAF Res. 1970-71; **OTHER ACT & HONORS:** Greenfield Park Bd., 1975 - present (Pres., 1981), Hancock Cty. Unit Amer. Cancer Soc. (Pres. 1979); Greenfield C of C (Bd. Member 1978-79); Greenfield Jaycees (Bd. member 1981); Elks Club; Acadia Alumni Assn.; In Univ., Alumni Assn.; **HOME ADD:** 115 McClellan Rd., Greenfield, IN 46140, (317)462-6415; **BUS ADD:** 1215 N. State St., Greenfield, IN 46140, (317)462-5533.

DUDLEY, Seth——**B:** Mar. 29, 1956, Los Angeles, CA, *Asst. VP*, Julien J. Studley, Inc.; **PRIM RE ACT:** Broker, Consultant; **SERVICES:** Consulting & brokerage servs. for users and devels. of office space & office bldgs.; **REP CLIENTS:** Ins., Data Processing, Law & Acctg. Firms; **PREV EMPLOY:** Regents of the Univ. of CA; **EDUC:** BA, 1976, Eng., Univ. of CA, Berkley; **EDUC HONORS:** Phi Beta Kappa; **HOME ADD:** 11027 Blix St., N. Hollywood, CA 91602, (213)760-7517; **BUS ADD:** 10850 Wilshire Blvd., Los Angeles, CA 90024, (213)475-5761.

DUERKOP, Stephen P., CPM——**B:** Jan. 21, 1943, Chicago, IL, *Grp. VP*, JMB Prop. Mgmt. Corp.; **PRIM RE ACT:** Property Manager; **PROFL AFFIL & HONORS:** IL Broker, CPM; **EDUC:** BBA, 1965, Mktg., Univ. of IA; **BUS ADD:** 875 MI Ave. Suite 1350, Chicago, IL 60611, (312)440-5050.

DUES, John J.——*Dir.*, The Mead Corp.; **OTHER RE ACT:** Site selection, leasing, acquisitions, disposals, asset mgmt.; **SERVICES:** Forest products, pulp, paper, packing; **HOME ADD:** 1222 Hathaway Rd., Dayton, OH 45419; **BUS ADD:** Courthouse Plaza NE, Dayton, OH 45463, (513)222-6323.

DUETSCH, John E.——**B:** Sept. 25, 1915, Newark, NJ, *Partner*, Morris & McVeigh; **PRIM RE ACT:** Attorney; **SERVICES:** Legal; **REP CLIENTS:** Klockner Companies; **PROFL AFFIL & HONORS:** NY State Bar; ABA; **EDUC:** Fordham Univ.; **GRAD EDUC:** 1941, RE, Fordham Law School; **MIL SERV:** U.S. Army, Pvt.; **OTHER ACT & HONORS:** Mayor and Councilman, Livingston, NJ; **HOME ADD:** 11 Pond Hill Rd., Convent Station, NJ 07961, (201)267-1231; **BUS ADD:** 767 Third Ave., New York, NY 10017, (212)593-6200.

DUFAULT, Peter D.——**B:** Oct. 21, 1936, Trenton, NJ, *VP*, McBride Enterprises, Inc.; **PRIM RE ACT:** Developer; **OTHER RE ACT:** Project Mgr., Condo. Devel., turnkey devel. of office, indus. & comml. bldgs. for sale or lease, planning & devel. of office/research parks, devel. & sales of condo.; **PREV EMPLOY:** Trammell Crow Co. 1974-1976 - Prop. Mgr.; **EDUC:** BS, 1959, Bus. Admin., Rider Coll.; **MIL SERV:** US Army, 1960-1961, Pfc.; **OTHER ACT & HONORS:** Mahwah Planning Bd. 1972-1976, Mahwah Zoning Bd. 1971-1977, C of C, Pres. & Dir., Bd. of Governors, Ramapo Coll. of NJ, Bd. of Dirs., Friends of Ramapo Coll.; Dir., Ramapo Ridge Condo. Assn.; **HOME ADD:** 72 Oweno Rd., Mahwah, NJ 07430, (201)529-4271; **BUS ADD:** 808 High Mountain Rd., Franklin Lakes, NJ 07417, (201)891-3900.

DUFF, Robert W.——*VP, Nat. Subdiv. Devel.*, First Amer. Title Ins. Co., Nat. Staff; **OTHER RE ACT:** Title Ins. (Tech. Coordinator); **SERVICES:** Nat. title ins.; **REP CLIENTS:** Builders, devels., attys., engrs., brokers; **PROFL AFFIL & HONORS:** Dir., CA Bldg. Indus. Assn.; Dir., Orange Cty. Bldg. Indus. Assn.; **EDUC:** AA, RE/Fin., Santa Ana Coll.; **MIL SERV:** US Army, Sgt. First Class, Combat Inf. Badge; **OTHER ACT & HONORS:** Intl. Footprint Assn.; Moose Lodge; **HOME ADD:** PO Box 1242, Santa Ana, CA 92702; **BUS ADD:** PO Box 267, Santa Ana, CA 92702.

DUFFIELD, Lee——*Mgr. RE*, Fairchild Industries, Inc.; **PRIM RE ACT:** Property Manager; **BUS ADD:** 2301 Century Blvd., Germantown, MD 20767, (301)428-6000.*

DUFFNER, C. E.——**B:** Mar. 13, 1927, Oklahoma City, OK, *Partner*, Duffner-Schafer; **PRIM RE ACT:** Broker, Developer, Owner/Investor, Property Manager; **SERVICES:** Comml. brokering, prop. mgmt., land devel. mgmt. with joint venture partners; **PREV EMPLOY:** Pres., C. E. Duffner Co.; **PROFL AFFIL & HONORS:** Central OK Homebuilders Assn., Inc., Nat. Assn. of Homebuilders, BOMA, Intl. Council of Shopping Centers, ULI, Past Pres., OKC Homebuilder's Assn. (1967), Nat. Dir., Nat. Assn. of Homebuilders (10 years); **EDUC:** BS, 1951, Structural Engrg., Univ. of TX and Univ. of OK; **EDUC HONORS:** ASIE Hist. Award, Dean's Honor Roll; **OTHER ACT & HONORS:** V Chmn., Public Housing Auth. (2 years); Phi Gamma Delta; Univ. of OK Alumni Assn.; Past Bd. of Trs. - Phi Gamma Delta; Jr. League of Oklahoma City; Cir. Club; Founding Dir. - The Greens Ctry. Club; Optimist Club; Oklahoma Mental Health Assn., and C of C; **HOME ADD:** 1110 Sherwood Ln. #202, Oklahoma City, OK 73116, (405)840-4174; **BUS ADD:** 1140 NW 63, Suite 300, Oklahoma City, OK 73116, (405)848-5617.

DUFFY, Frederick J.——**B:** Sept. 6, 1934, Hoboken, NJ, *Pres.*, Duffy Realty Inc.; **PRIM RE ACT:** Broker, Appraiser, Property Manager; **OTHER RE ACT:** Summer vacation rentals; **SERVICES:** Sales, rentals of resid. & comml. RE; **PREV EMPLOY:** CT Gen. Life Ins.; Sunset Harbor Realty, Sales Mgr.; **PROFL AFFIL & HONORS:** NAR; Ocean Cty. Bd. of Realtors (CRS & CRB - NJ Chapts.), CRI; CRS; CRB; **EDUC:** BA, 1957, Communication Arts, Seton Hall Univ.; **EDUC HONORS:** Who's Who in Amer. Colls., Pres. of Class, 1956 & 1957; **MIL SERV:** US Army-Res., Capt.; **HOME ADD:** 295 12th St., Surf City, NJ 08008, (609)494-3032; **BUS ADD:** 5112 Long Beach Blvd., Brant Beach, NJ 08008, (609)494-5353.

DUFFY, James O., Jr.——**B:** Aug. 29, 1949, Long Branch, NJ, *VP*, Laidlaw Realty, Inc.; **OTHER RE ACT:** Investment consultation and mgmt. comml. prop. acquisition and synd.; **REP CLIENTS:** Indiv. and instnl. investors; **PREV EMPLOY:** Chemical Bank (RE Div.); **PROFL AFFIL & HONORS:** ICSC; NAIOP; **EDUC:** BA, 1971, Econ., Georgetown Univ.; **GRAD EDUC:** MBA, 1974, Fin., Univ. of PA, Wharton School; **EDUC HONORS:** Dean's List, 1971; **HOME ADD:** 45 Ridge Rd., Rumson, NJ 07760; **BUS ADD:** 20 Broad St., New York, NY 10005, (212)363-3267.

DUFFY, Mark Alan——**B:** Aug. 5, 1952, Kirstishov, OK, *In-House Counsel, Asst. Sec.*, Continental Federal Savings and Loan Assn.; **PRIM RE ACT:** Attorney; **SERVICES:** Federal compliance, litigation, comml., consumer lending and title; **PROFL AFFIL & HONORS:** OK Bar Assn.; Federal Bar for Eastern and Western Districts, OK; ABA; OK Cty. Bar Assn.; OK Cty. Title Lawyers Assn.; **EDUC:** BA, 1974, E. Asian Studies, OK State Univ.; **GRAD EDUC:** JD, 1977, Law, OK City Univ.; **EDUC HONORS:** Dean's Roll; **HOME ADD:** 1513 Pine Oak Dr., Edmond, OK 73034, (403)348-5543; **BUS ADD:** 101 Park Ave., Oklahoma City, OK 73102, (405)236-3641.

DUFFY, Richard B.——**B:** Oct. 26, 1932, Chicago, IL, *Asst. VP*, Equitable Life Assurance Soc., Realty Operations; **PRIM RE ACT:** Owner/Investor, Property Manager; **SERVICES:** Supervise investment portfolio of real prop.; **REP CLIENTS:** Employer only; **PREV EMPLOY:** First National Bank of Denver 1957-74; **PROFL AFFIL & HONORS:** San Francisco Chap. IREM; San Francisco BOMA, CPM, Pres. Denver Chap. BOMA 1974; Pres. Denver Chap. IREM 1971; **EDUC:** BA, 1954, Poli. Sci., Univ. of IL; **MIL SERV:** US Army, Cpl.; **HOME ADD:** 6 Descanso Dr., Orinda, CA 94563, (415)376-5650; **BUS ADD:** One Market Pl., San Francisco, CA 94563, (415)541-5140.

DUFFY, Stephen L.——**B:** May 29, 1940, NY, NY, *VP*, Mgmt. Assoc. Inc.; **PRIM RE ACT:** Consultant, Appraiser, Owner/Investor; **SERVICES:** Prop. tax admin. & consulting, RE feasibility studies, mkt. analyses appraisals; **REP CLIENTS:** The Hertz Corp; Lifetime Communities; US Life Realty Co.; Kaufman & Broad Inc.; N. Amer. Mort. Investors; United Jersey Mort. Co.; US Home Corp.; Bellemeade Dev. Co.; Cushman & Wakefield, Inc.; **PREV EMPLOY:** 5 years, Indep. RE consultant, 8 years, Corp. VP Indus. RE; **PROFL AFFIL & HONORS:** Lic. RE Broker, Member, Indus. Dev. Research Council; **EDUC:** BS, 1962, Sci., Fordham Coll.; **GRAD EDUC:** 1964, Fin., NY Inst. of Fin.; **HOME ADD:** Route 22, Bedford, NY 10506, (914)234-5726; **BUS ADD:** 149 Route 46, Clifton, NJ 07012, (201)546-2912.

DUGAN, James W.——**B:** July 31, 1948, Pittsburgh, PA, *Exec. VP*, Gregory-Grace and Associates, Inc.; **PRIM RE ACT:** Consultant, Engineer, Architect; **OTHER RE ACT:** Land Planner; **SERVICES:** Land Planning, Site Engrg., Arch. Design; **REP CLIENTS:** Indiv., lenders and instnl. investors in planned residential communities, comml. and office ctrs. and indus. parks; **PROFL AFFIL & HONORS:** Amer. Soc. of Landscape Archs; Amer. Consulting Engrs. Council; Urban Land Inst.; **EDUC:** BA, 1970, Environmental Design, Point Park Coll.; **GRAD EDUC:** MLA, 1972, Landscape Arch./Land Planning, LA State Univ.; **EDUC HONORS:** Cum Laude; **HOME ADD:** 9539 Autumn Trail Cove, Memphis, TN 38134, (901)388-5253; **BUS ADD:** 2969 Elmore Park Road, Memphis, TN 38134.

DUGGAN, Arthur L.——**B:** Dec. 1, 1931, Everett, MA, *Pres.*, Inn America Corporation; **OTHER RE ACT:** Devel. own and operate Sheraton and Hilton hotels; **SERVICES:** Full range of services normally found in first-class hotels; **REP CLIENTS:** Franchise with Sheraton and Hilton; **PREV EMPLOY:** Exec. VP, Archris Hotel Corp., Boston, MA; Sr. VP, Fed. Home & Mort. Co., State College, PA; **PROFL AFFIL & HONORS:** Amer. Hotel & Motel Assn., NY Hotel Assn., PA Hotel Assn., MA Hotel Assn., DE Hotel Assn., MA C of C, PA C of C, NY C of C, DE C of C; **EDUC:** BBA, 1960, Bus., Bryant Coll., Providence, RI; **GRAD EDUC:** MBA, 1964, Bus., Northeastern Univ., Boston, MA; **MIL SERV:** USAF, Capt.; **OTHER ACT & HONORS:** Plymouth Yacht Club, Plymouth, MA, Eel River Swim & Tennis Club, Plymouth, MA, Ocean Reef Club, Key Largo, FL, The Bay Club (House Comm.), Boston, MA, Past Jr. C of C (1960 listed in Outstanding Young Men of the Year), Cat Cay Club, Cat Cay, Bahamas; **HOME ADD:** 216 Warren Ave., Plymouth, MA 02360; **BUS ADD:** 140 Wood Rd., Braintree, MA 02184, (617)848-9266.

DUGGAN, James——*Secy. & Gen. Counsel*, Fansteel, Inc.; **PRIM RE ACT:** Property Manager, Attorney; **BUS ADD:** Tantalum Place, North Chicago, IL 60064, (312)689-4900.*

DUGGAN, Randolph F., IV——**B:** Jan. 29, 1954, Dallas, TX, *Sec. - Dir.*, Far W. Equities Inc.; **PRIM RE ACT:** Broker, Syndicator, Developer, Owner/Investor; **SERVICES:** Acquisition of speculative and income prop.; **PROFL AFFIL & HONORS:** RESSI; **HOME ADD:** 20241 20th Pl. NE, Seattle, WA 98155, (206)363-2713; **BUS ADD:** PO Box 719, Lynnwood, WA 98036, (206)771-5160.

DUGGAR, Rolfe D.——**B:** May 18, 1931, Chicago, IL, Rolfe D. Duggar, P.A.; **PRIM RE ACT:** Attorney, Consultant, Developer, Owner/Investor; **SERVICES:** Consultation on dev., managing and owning apts., as well as providing legal services in RE areas; **REP CLIENTS:** Indiv. and instns. involved in RE; **PROFL AFFIL & HONORS:** Nat. Apt. Assn. (formerly Consul, Officer, Exec. Bd. 5 yrs.); Two term Pres., FL Apt. Assn.; Three terms, Pres., Pinellas Apt. Assn.; Amer., FL & St. Petersburg Bar Assn's.; NAHB; **GRAD EDUC:** LLB, 1957, Stetson Coll. of Law; **OTHER ACT & HONORS:** Rotary (Past Pres., W. St. Petersburg - Dist. Gov. Nominee '82-'83 Dist. 695); Bd. of Dir., Goodwill Indus.; Pres., GIS Housing (sub. of Goodwill Indus.);

Dir. & former Crusade Chmn., Amer. Cancer Soc. of Pinellas Cty; Former Officer, Comm. of 100 Pinellas Cty; Served 5 yrs, Pinellas Indus. Council; **HOME ADD:** 1324 Park St. N., St. Petersburg, FL 33710; **BUS ADD:** 4699 Central Ave., St. Petersburg, FL 33713, (813)321-4700.

DUGICK, Angela E.——**B:** Aug. 9, 1949, Lueneburg, W. Germany, *Devel. Mgr.*, Quadrant Devel.; **PRIM RE ACT:** Developer; **SERVICES:** Acquire, analyze, devel. real prop. for resid., comml. and indus. uses; mkt. research; fin. analysis; **PREV EMPLOY:** Cook Inlet Rgn., Inc., Special Projects Coordinator, 1976-1981; **PROFL AFFIL & HONORS:** Nat. Assn. of Bus. Econ.; NAR; Anchorage NAR, Planning & Zoning Comm., Editor, 'Anchorage RE Research Report'; **EDUC:** BA, 1977, Econ., Univ. of AK; **OTHER ACT & HONORS:** Who's Who in Amer. Women, since 1979; **HOME ADD:** 3331 Evergreen St., Anchorage, AK 99504, (907)337-1400; **BUS ADD:** 6000 C St., Suite D, Anchorage, AK 99503, (907)274-8509.

DUKELLIS, E. Nicholas——**B:** Aug. 11, 1938, King City, CA, *Broker-Owner*, Dukellis Realty; **PRIM RE ACT:** Broker, Owner/Investor, Property Manager; **PROFL AFFIL & HONORS:** RESSI, CAR Investment Div., RE Nat. Mktg. Assn., GRI Cert., and several Million Dollar Club Awards; **EDUC:** 2 yr. Chabot Co.., 1969, RE - 2 yr. San Jose State Univ.; **MIL SERV:** USN, 3rd class petty officer; **OTHER ACT & HONORS:** Pleasanton Rotary Club, C of C, Pleasanton Downtown Merchants Assn., Homeowner's Assn. Pres.; **HOME ADD:** 3407 Brandy Ct., Pleasanton, CA 94566, (415)846-6083; **BUS ADD:** 401 Main St., Pleasanton, CA 94566.

DUKELOW, William H.——**B:** Jan. 30, 1943, Hot Springs, SD, *Exec. VP*, Charter Mort. Co., Comml. Div.; **PRIM RE ACT:** Broker; **SERVICES:** Mort. Banking and RE Sales; **PREV EMPLOY:** 11 yrs. with Charter Mort. Co.; **PROFL AFFIL & HONORS:** Member Mort. Bankers Assn. ICSC, NAIOP, Registered RE Broker, Registered Mort. Broker; **EDUC:** BS, 1965, Chem. Engrg., SD Sch. of Mines & Technology; **GRAD EDUC:** MBA, 1970, Mktg., Univ. of FL; **EDUC HONORS:** Cum Laude; **MIL SERV:** US Army Engrg., 1 Lt., Bronze Star-Vietnam; **OTHER ACT & HONORS:** YMCA Bd. of Dir., Bd. of Dir. March of Dimes; **HOME ADD:** 7678 Hollyndge Cir., Jacksonville, FL 32216, (904)641-1556; **BUS ADD:** 25 W. Forsyth St., Jacksonville, FL 32202, (904)359-2053.

DUKES, John E.——**B:** Dec. 29, 1935, GA, *Pres.*, Dukes-Dukes and Assoc., Inc.; **PRIM RE ACT:** Consultant, Developer, Property Manager; **SERVICES:** Resid. and Comml. structures; **PREV EMPLOY:** Dir. of San Francisco Poverty Program, Econ. and Community Devel.; **EDUC:** BA, 1964, Econ., Golden Gate Univ.; **MIL SERV:** USAF, 2nd Cl. Airman; **HOME ADD:** 762 E. Marshall Blvd., San Bernardino, CA, (714)882-2483; **BUS ADD:** 1875 W. Highland Ave., San Bernardino, CA 92405, (714)887-6491.

DULUDE, D.O.——*Pres.*, Kuhlman Corp.; **PRIM RE ACT:** Property Manager; **BUS ADD:** 2565 W. Maple Rd., Troy, MI 48084, (313)649-9300.*

DUMONT, C. Donald——**B:** Sept. 22, 1914, Ridgefield Park, NJ, *Sec.*, Dow & Condon, Inc.; **PRIM RE ACT:** Broker, Appraiser, Property Manager; **SERVICES:** Sale and lease of land and improved props., appraisals; **PROFL AFFIL & HONORS:** SIR, MAI; **EDUC:** BA, 1937, Econ., Dartmouth Coll.; **MIL SERV:** Signal Corps., Capt.; **HOME ADD:** 79 Mountain Terr. Rd., W. Hartford, CT 06107, (203)521-5333; **BUS ADD:** 111 Pearl St., Hartford, CT 06103, (203)249-6521.

DUMONT, James W.——**B:** Feb. 2, 1952, Avon Park, FL, *Marketing/Leasing Mgr.*, Oxford Properties, Inc., Western Rgn.; **OTHER RE ACT:** Leasing of office and retail space, Comml. Devel.; **SERVICES:** Complete in-house devel. & mgmt. of large, downtown integrated projects; **PREV EMPLOY:** 2 yrs. as resid. RE sales in FL, 5 yrs. Prop. Mgr. in CO; **PROFL AFFIL & HONORS:** Dewer Bd. of Realtors, Downtown Denver, Inc., Inst. of RE mgmt. and Urban Land Inst., CPM; **EDUC:** BS, 1974, RE and Urban Devel., Univ. of FL; **OTHER ACT & HONORS:** Smithsonian Inst., Cousteau Soc., Phi Delta Theta Frat.; **HOME ADD:** 1245 Grape St., Denver, CO 80220, (303)355-0740; **BUS ADD:** 1675 Broadway, Suite 1600, Denver, CO 80202, (303)623-0433.

DUMPER, Robert S.——**B:** Sept. 22, 1940, Chicago, IL, *VP and Div. Mgr.*, Kacor Development Co.; **PRIM RE ACT:** Developer; **PREV EMPLOY:** Kaiser - Aetna VP 1964-76; **PROFL AFFIL & HONORS:** Member of Intl. Council of Shopping Centers; HI RE Broker; **EDUC:** BA, 1962, Econ., Princeton Univ.; **GRAD EDUC:** MBA, 1964, Acctg., Stanford Univ.; **EDUC HONORS:** Cum Laude; **OTHER ACT & HONORS:** Dir., Greater Oakland YMCA; N. CA Regional Dir. Princeton Annual Giving; **HOME ADD:** 51 Stark Knoll Pl., Oakland, CA 94618, (415)653-0178; **BUS ADD:** 300 Lakeside Dr., Oakland, CA 94643, (415)271-3010.

DUNCAN, Freeman B.——**B:** Dec. 27, 1946, Los Angeles, CA, *Atty.*, Freeman B. Duncan, Atty. at Law; **PRIM RE ACT:** Attorney, Instructor; **SERVICES:** Legal rep. and instr. on law subjects; **REP CLIENTS:** Coeur d'Alene Bd. of Realtors, First Amer. Title Co., Coeur d'Alene, ID; **PREV EMPLOY:** USAF as Judge Advocate; **PROFL AFFIL & HONORS:** ABA, ID Trial Lawyers Assn., Cert. instr. for the ID RE Comm; **EDUC:** 1970, Bus. Admin., Univ. of WY; **GRAD EDUC:** JD, 1973, Univ. of WY; **MIL SERV:** USAF, Capt.; **OTHER ACT & HONORS:** Rotary, Past Pres.; **HOME ADD:** 388 Ponderosa Dr., Post Falls, ID 83854, (208)773-7279; **BUS ADD:** 388 Ponderosa Dr., Post Falls, ID 83854, (208)773-7279.

DUNCAN, James W., Jr.——**B:** May 1, 1952, Newton, MA, *Pres.*, Duncan - Byrnes, Inc.; **PRIM RE ACT:** Broker, Attorney, Developer, Owner/Investor; **SERVICES:** Site location; investment analysis & valuation; dev. and acquisition of comml. prop.; **REP CLIENTS:** Instnl. investors and indiv.; **PROFL AFFIL & HONORS:** CCIM; NAR; RESSI; **EDUC:** BA, 1974, Econ., Wheaton Coll., IL; **GRAD EDUC:** JD, 1978, RE/Tax., Univ. of MD; **EDUC HONORS:** Magna Cum Laude; Omicron Delta Epsilon- Econ. Hon. Soc, Magna Cum Laude; AMJUR Book Award; **MIL SERV:** USMC; OCS; Commandant's Honor Roll; **OTHER ACT & HONORS:** Nat. Bd. of Dir., Search Ministries; **HOME ADD:** 5 Forest Ridge Ct., Timonium, MD 21093, (301)252-1873; **BUS ADD:** 6071 Falls Rd., Baltimore, MD 21209, (301)377-4284.

DUNCAN, Roderick——**B:** June 11, 1944, Toronto, Can., *Chartered Accountant*; **PRIM RE ACT:** Syndicator; **OTHER RE ACT:** Intl. tax problem-solving & planning; **SERVICES:** Fin. and tax structuring; **REP CLIENTS:** Profund Fin. Corp; Equity Trust Co. Ltd; Tridel Corp.; **PROFL AFFIL & HONORS:** Can. Tax Found.; Fiscal Logic Group; Intl. Fiscal Assn.; Intl. Tax Planning Assn.; Ontario Inst. of Chartered Accts.; Tax Executives Inst.; **EDUC:** BA, 1967, Poli. Econ., Univ. of Toronto; **GRAD EDUC:** MA, 1968, Univ. of Guelph; **HOME ADD:** 60 Apricot St., Ontario, Can. L3T1C8, Thornhill; **BUS ADD:** Suite 1904, One Yonge St., Toronto, M5E1E5, Can., (416)362-4696.

DUNCAN, Thomas A.——**B:** May 23, 1944, Lansing, MI, *Broker/Salesman*, Merrill Lynch Realty, Rodgers & Cummings, Comml.-Investment; **PRIM RE ACT:** Broker; **OTHER RE ACT:** Conversion of motel-apt. properties to condo. and co-op., Broker of Beach Area Income Prop.; **SERVICES:** Coordination of entire conversion activities; **REP CLIENTS:** Property owners, investment groups, limited partnerships; **PROFL AFFIL & HONORS:** NAR; FL Assn. of Realtors; **EDUC:** BS, 1967, Mktg., FL State Univ.; **MIL SERV:** USN, E-5, Vietnam Medal, Vietnam Campaign; **HOME ADD:** 756 Eldorado Ave., Clearwater Beach, FL 33515, (813)446-0116; **BUS ADD:** 1988 Gulf to Bay Blvd., PO Box 6600, Clearwater, FL 33518, (813)442-4111.

DUNCAN, W.M.C.——**B:** Feb. 11, 1929, Toronto, Ontario, Can., *VP and Gen. Mgr.*, Genstar Devel. Co., Land Devel. Toronto Rgn.; **PRIM RE ACT:** Developer; **PREV EMPLOY:** Dir., Town Planning Consultants Ltd.; Mgr., Project Planning Assn., Mgr., W.L. Wardrop & Assoc.; **PROFL AFFIL & HONORS:** Assn. Prof. Engr. of Ont., Can. Inst. of Planners, Urban Devel. Inst., BASC, PE, MCIP, Bd. of Dir., Urban Devel. Inst. 1981-82; **EDUC:** BASC, 1952, Civil., Univ. of Toronto; **EDUC HONORS:** 2nd Class; **MIL SERV:** Can. Army, Reserve, Lt.; **HOME ADD:** 39 Montressor Dr., Willowdale, M2P 1Y9, Ontario, Canada, (416)222-2191; **BUS ADD:** 502 302 The East Mall, Islington, M9B 6C7, Ont., Canada, (416)232-2280.

DUNHAM, Howard W.——**B:** July 15, 1927, Dallas, TX, *Pres.*, H.W. Dunham & Assoc., Inc.; **PRIM RE ACT:** Broker, Consultant, Appraiser; **SERVICES:** Comml. RE; **REP CLIENTS:** Corp. clients - more than 100 listed on NYSE or otherwise well known public cos.; large banks; attys; CPAs; realtors; **PROFL AFFIL & HONORS:** Amer. Soc. of RE Counselors; AIREA; Soc. of RE Appraisers; NAR; Amer. Right of Way Assn., CRE; MAI; **EDUC:** BBA, 1951, So. Methodist Univ./UCLA; **MIL SERV:** US Navy Reserves; **HOME ADD:** 6738 Briar Cove, Dallas, TX 75240, (214)239-5270; **BUS ADD:** 8350 Meadow Rd., Suite 268, Dallas, TX 75231, (214)987-4433.

DUNHAM, James K.——**B:** Mar. 20, 1938, *Asst. VP, Corporate RE Officer*, Rainier National Bank; **PRIM RE ACT:** Consultant, Banker, Property Manager; **PROFL AFFIL & HONORS:** IREM, NACORE; BOMI; **EDUC:** BS, Econ., Univ. of ID; **GRAD EDUC:** Cert. of Grad., Pacific Coast Banking School, Univ. of WA, Amer. Inst. Banking; **MIL SERV:** US Air Force, Lt. Col., Retired; **OTHER ACT & HONORS:** Boy Scout Chmn., Seattle C of C; **BUS ADD:** PO Box 3966, NO6-2, Seattle, WA 98124, (206)621-5551.

DUNHAM, Robert W.——**B:** Aug 24, 1943, New Castle, PA, *Owner, Part.*, Realty Appraisal & Consulting Serv.; **PRIM RE ACT:** Consultant, Appraiser; **SERVICES:** Appraisal, consulting activities & feasibility studies; **REP CLIENTS:** Comml. Banks, S&L Insts., Devels., Synds., etc.; **PROFL AFFIL & HONORS:** AIREA, MAI; **EDUC:** BSBA, 1973, Fin., Econ., FL Tech. Univ.; **MIL SERV:** US Army, E-5, Army Commendation Medal; **HOME ADD:** 1919 Boyce St., Sarasota, FL 33579, (813)366-5662; **BUS ADD:** 635 S. Orange Ave., Suite 10, Sarasota, FL 33579, (813)366-5854.

DUNLEVIE, Ernie——**B:** Aug. 3, 1923, NY, NY, *Pres.*, Dunray Land Co., Inc.; **PRIM RE ACT:** Broker, Developer; **PROFL AFFIL & HONORS:** Palm Springs Bd. of Realtors (Past Pres.); CA RE Assn.; Nat. Assn. of RE Bds., Past VP CREA; **MIL SERV:** USAF, WWII; **OTHER ACT & HONORS:** Past Bd. Member Riverside Cty. Dept. of Devel.; Bermuda Dunes Cty. Club (founder); Ber. Dunes Racquet Club; Balboa Bay Club; Catalina Is. Yacht Club; **HOME ADD:** 42555 Stardust Pl., Bermuda Dunes, CA 92201; **BUS ADD:** 79050 Ave. 42, Bermuda Dunes, CA 92201, (714)345-2694.

DUNN, Larry B.——**B:** Aug. 9, 1938, Minneapolis, MN, *Pres.*, Marketing Network, Inc.; **PRIM RE ACT:** Broker, Consultant, Developer, Builder, Owner/Investor, Syndicator; **SERVICES:** Bldg. & devel. joint ventures/gen. brokerage; **REP CLIENTS:** Investors/bldg. & devel. firms; **PREV EMPLOY:** US Home Corp. Regional Pres.; Pres., Coachman Realty & Investments; IBM Corp.; State of FL Dept. of Admin.; **PROFL AFFIL & HONORS:** FL Econ. Club; FL Assn. Realtors; NAR; FL Homebuilders Assn.; Nat. Assn. Homebuilders; **EDUC:** BBA, 1968, Indus. Mgmt., FL State Univ.; **MIL SERV:** USN, Lt.; **OTHER ACT & HONORS:** founding Dir., FL Econ. Club; Listed in Who's Who in the South and Southeast; **HOME ADD:** 914 S. Town and River Dr., Fort Meyers, FL 33907, (813)481-6655; **BUS ADD:** 3949 Evans Ave., Fort Meyers, FL 33901, (813)481-6655.

DUNN, Leo——**B:** Nov. 28, 1930, *Sr. Planner*, IBM, GPD; **PRIM RE ACT:** Owner/Investor; **PREV EMPLOY:** USAF; **EDUC:** BS, 1959, Gen. Sci., Univ. of WA; **GRAD EDUC:** MBA, 1975, Mgmt., Golden Gate Univ.; **EDUC HONORS:** Cum Laude; **MIL SERV:** USAF, 1/Lt.; **HOME ADD:** 6743 Crystal Springs Dr., San Jose, CA 95120.

DUNN, Philip C.——**B:** Oct. 4, 1948, Middletown, CT, *Pres.*, Philip C. Dunn & Assoc., Inc.; **PRIM RE ACT:** Broker, Consultant, Developer, Owner/Investor, Property Manager, Syndicator; **OTHER RE ACT:** Pension fund RE advisor; **SERVICES:** Investment counseling synd., asset mgmt., consultant, devel.; **REP CLIENTS:** Private investors, fin. insts., and pension funds; **PREV EMPLOY:** Bank OH Advisory, 1973-76; Fox & Carskdin Fin. Corp., VP, 1976-78; Univ. Grp. Inc., 1978-79; Landsing Props., 1979-80; **PROFL AFFIL & HONORS:** IREM; RESSI; NASD; Rgn. Investment Advisor; **EDUC:** AB, 1970, Soc. Sci., Arts & Sci., Villanova Univ.; **GRAD EDUC:** MBA, 1976, Intl. Fin., Golden Gate Univ., San Francisco, CA; **MIL SERV:** US Army, SP-4; **HOME ADD:** 703 Cabin Dr., Mill Valley, CA, (415)383-0765; **BUS ADD:** 700 Larkspur Landing Cir., Suite 199, Larkspur, CA 94939, (415)461-2170.

DUNN, Rodney P.——**B:** Sept. 27, 1949, Dallas, TX, *VP - Prop. Mgr.*, Elbert Aldrich Realtor, Inc.; **PRIM RE ACT:** Appraiser, Property Manager, Owner/Investor; **OTHER RE ACT:** Sale of comml., industrial, farm & ranch props.; **SERVICES:** Prop. mgmt., appraisal, sale of comml., farm & ranch indus. props.; **PREV EMPLOY:** Senter Realtors, Abilene, TX 1972-74; **PROFL AFFIL & HONORS:** NAR, TX Assn. of Realtors, IREM, Pres., Temple-Belton Bd. of Realtors, 1978; Realtor of the Yr.; Realtor Assoc. of the Year, 1976; **EDUC:** BS, 1972, Mktg.-Advertising, Abilene Christian Univ.; **EDUC HONORS:** Mr. ACU; V.W. Kelly Award; Pres. of Student Assn.; **OTHER ACT & HONORS:** Served two years as Pres. of Abilene Christian Univ. Natl. Alumni Assn., 1976-78; **HOME ADD:** 3406 Cottonwood Ln., Temple, TX 76501, (817)773-0335; **BUS ADD:** 18 N. Third St., Temple, TX 76501, (817)773-4901.

DUNN, Wallace E.——**B:** Mar. 3, 1920, Chicago, IL, *COB*, DMC, Inc., RE Devel.; **PRIM RE ACT:** Consultant, Developer, Builder, Owner/Investor, Property Manager, Syndicator; **SERVICES:** Project devel.; **PREV EMPLOY:** Tishman Realty, E.F. Hutton Realty, Dillingham Realty; **PROFL AFFIL & HONORS:** CPM, CSM, IREM, BOMA; **EDUC:** BS, Bus., NYU; **MIL SERV:** US Army Capt., Bronze Star; **OTHER ACT & HONORS:** Bd. Educ. Pres., 5 yrs.; SAE Chamber Wilshire Blvd., Westwood Bel Air Bay Club, Jonathan Club; **HOME ADD:** 1731 San Fernando Rd., Atascadero, CA 93422, (805)466-5010; **BUS ADD:** 1731 San Fernando Rd., Atascadero, CA 93422, (805)466-5040.

DUNN, Wesley Brankley——**B:** Oct. 9, 1951, Baskerville, VA, *Atty.*, Levine, D'Alessio, Mullins & Stone; **PRIM RE ACT:** Consultant, Attorney, Owner/Investor, Instructor; **SERVICES:** Comml. and resid. loan closings, document review and devel., truth in lending, condo. documentation and gen. corp. representation; **REP CLIENTS:** Indiv., inst. and pvt. lenders, builders, devel., brokers, realtor bds. and pvt. and inst. investors; **PREV EMPLOY:** Assoc. Atty. with Atlanta Law Firm of Hansell, Post, Brandon & Dorsey, Specializing in Gen. RE; **PROFL AFFIL & HONORS:** Atlanta Bar Assn., real prop. sect., NAR, GA Bar Assn., real prop. sect., ABA, GA Assn. Realtors, Fayette & Clayton Cty. Bd. of Realtors, GRI, Current faculty member; **EDUC:** BA, 1974, Hist. and Psych., GA State Univ.; **GRAD EDUC:** Doctor of Law, 1978, Emory Univ. Law Sch.; **EDUC HONORS:** Omicron Delta Kappa, Who's Who, Most Outstanding Student, Pres. Student Bar Assn. 1977-78; **OTHER ACT & HONORS:** Henry Cty. C of C, Fayette Cty. C of C, Henry Cty. Landmarks, McDonough Kiwanis Club, McDonough Youth Association; **HOME ADD:** 125 Wellington Dr., McDonough, GA 30253, (404)957-4735; **BUS ADD:** 1597 Phoenix Blvd., 8, College Park, GA 30349, (404)521-1624.

DUNN, William B.——**B:** Dec. 2, 1939, Newark, NJ, Clark, Klein & Beaumont; **PRIM RE ACT:** Attorney; **SERVICES:** Acquisition, financing, leasing, devel. of RE, secured transactions; **REP CLIENTS:** Lenders, instnl. and indiv. investors and users; **PROFL AFFIL & HONORS:** ABA Real Prop., Probate & Trust Section (Member of Council); State Bar of MI Real Prop. Law Section (Chmn. Elect); Amer. Coll. of RE Lawyers (Member, Bd. of Govs.); Anglo-Amer. Real Prop. Inst.; **EDUC:** AB, 1961, Eng./Pol. Sci., Muskingum Coll.; **GRAD EDUC:** JD, 1964, Law, Univ. of MI Law School; **HOME ADD:** 611 University Pl., Grosse Pointe, MI 48230, (313)886-8510; **BUS ADD:** 1600 First Fed. Bldg., Detroit, MI 48226, (313)962-6492.

DUNNE, James C.——**B:** Nov. 23, 1923, New York, NY, *Managing Atty.*, J. C. Penney Co., Inc., RE; **PRIM RE ACT:** Attorney; **PREV EMPLOY:** RE VP, Sec. and genl counsel W.T. Grant Co.; **PROFL AFFIL & HONORS:** RE Comm. Westchester-Fairfield Cty. Corp. Counsel Assn., JD; **EDUC:** BA, 1949, Phil./Econ., Fordham Univ.; **GRAD EDUC:** JD, 1952, Harvard Law School; **MIL SERV:** US Army, S/Sgt., 1942-46; **HOME ADD:** Talmadge Hill, Darien, CT 06820; **BUS ADD:** 1301 Ave. of the Americas, New York, NY 10019, (212)957-7760.

DUNSTON, Ronald G.——**B:** June 8, 1941, Laurel, MS, *Pres. (Owner)*, RE Investments; **PRIM RE ACT:** Broker, Developer, Builder, Owner/Investor, Syndicator; **SERVICES:** Investment analysis, investment mgmt., brokerage; **REP CLIENTS:** Profls. who wish to invest, instnl. investors, lending instns. wishing joint venture project mgrs.; **PROFL AFFIL & HONORS:** NAR, GRI; **OTHER ACT & HONORS:** Elks, Singing River Yacht Club; **HOME ADD:** 3310 Washington Ave., Pascagoula, MS 39567, (601)762-8275; **BUS ADD:** PO Box 28, Pascagoula, MS 39567, (601)474-2769.

DUPREE, Thomas B., Jr.——**B:** Nov. 30, 1925, Baton Rouge, LA, *Pres.*, Waguespack, Dupree and Felts, Inc., Shreveport, New Orleans and Baton Rouge Offices; **PRIM RE ACT:** Consultant, Appraiser, Owner/Investor, Syndicator; **OTHER RE ACT:** RE Econ.; **SERVICES:** RE appraisals, market studies, expert witness testimony. counseling for site acquisition, prop.; **REP CLIENTS:** Attys., banks and other lenders, fed., state and local agencies, corp. RE owners, private investors, sales, leasing and financing; **PREV EMPLOY:** Engrg., construction and RE brokerage; **PROFL AFFIL & HONORS:** ASREC, AIREA, LA Realtors Assn. RE Bd. of New Orleans, MAI, CRE, Realtors; **EDUC:** BS, 1948, Engrg., LA State Univ.; **GRAD EDUC:** MBA, 1951, Bus. and Fin., Wharton School of Bus., Univ. of PA; **OTHER ACT & HONORS:** Past Pres., LA/MS Chapter, AIREA; **HOME ADD:** 5599 Mirador Circle, Shreveport, LA 71119, (318)631-5388; **BUS ADD:** 1301 Petroleum Tower, Shreveport, LA 71101, (318)221-2588.

DUPUIS, Richard P.——**B:** July 24, 1952, Lafayette, LA, *Sales Mgr.*, John Knight Real Estate; **PRIM RE ACT:** Broker, Developer, Property Manager; **SERVICES:** Comml. - investments brokerage; **PROFL AFFIL & HONORS:** Mid-South Chap. of CCIM; RNMI; NAR, CCIM; **EDUC:** BA, 1977, Mgmt., Univ. of SW LA; **HOME ADD:** 51 Audubon Oaks, 100 Edmonia St., Lafayette, LA 70506, (318)233-7784; **BUS ADD:** 221 Rue De Jean, Suite 102, Lafayette, LA 70508, (318)233-8713.

DURAN, Timothy C.——**B:** June 23, 1943, Los Angeles, CA, *Pres.*, Arlington Land & Investment Co., Inc.; **PRIM RE ACT:** Broker, Consultant, Developer, Owner/Investor, Property Manager, Syndicator; **SERVICES:** Assistance in maximizing income with minimum risk for selected clients; **REP CLIENTS:** (Previous) - Burger King; Motel 6; National Can; numerous devel. & local firms; **PREV EMPLOY:** Coldwell Banker & Co.; Grubb & Ellis; **PROFL AFFIL & HONORS:** Assn. of South Bay Brokers; Various RE Bds.; **EDUC:** BS, 1966, Bus., Fin., Univ. of S. CA; **OTHER ACT & HONORS:** Bd. of Dir. Clark Found.; Amer. Auto Leasing; Georight Industries; Member several pvt. organizations; **HOME ADD:** 25 Zapata Way, Portola Valley, CA, (415)851-3377; **BUS ADD:** 330 Commercial St., PO Box 1237, San Jose, CA 95108, (408)275-1555.

DURBIN, Joseph W.——B: May 15, 1925, Sunfish, KY, *CRB*, Century 21 Grammer & Moore Realtors; **PRIM RE ACT:** Broker; **PROFL AFFIL & HONORS:** Louisville Bd. of Realtors; KY Assn. of Realtors; NAR, CRB; **EDUC:** BS, 1951, Agriculture, Western KY Univ.; **GRAD EDUC:** MPH, 1959, Public Health, Tulane Univ., New Orleans, LA; **MIL SERV:** US Army, Sgt., Purple Heart; **HOME ADD:** 6701 Concord Hill Rd., Louisville, KY 40228, (502)239-8421; **BUS ADD:** 5908 Bardstown Rd., Louisville, KY 40228, (502)239-2100.

DURDEL, Sonna M.——B: Apr. 12, 1949, Portland, OR, *VP and Gen. Mgr. Oregon*, The Koll Co., NW; **PRIM RE ACT:** Developer, Property Manager; **OTHER RE ACT:** Marketing, leasing; **SERVICES:** Construction, prop. mgmt., and devel., leasing; **PROFL AFFIL & HONORS:** NAIOP, ULI; **EDUC:** BS, 1971, Humanities & Social Sci., Home Econ.; **EDUC HONORS:** OR State Univ. Woman of Achiev., Omicron Nu (Honorary), Mortar Board, Dean's List & Honor Roll; **HOME ADD:** 5175 SW Elm Ave., Beaverton, OR 97005, (503)644-4844; **BUS ADD:** 10110 SW Nimbus Ave. B-11, Portland, OR 97223, (503)684-0510.

DURFEE, David Allen——B: Nov. 8, 1949, Holbrook, AZ, *Assoc. Atty.*, Wentworth & Lundin; **PRIM RE ACT:** Attorney; **SERVICES:** Aquisition, Fin., Devel., Disposition; **REP CLIENTS:** Resid., Comml. and Indus. Prop. Devels.; **PREV EMPLOY:** RE Broker; **PROFL AFFIL & HONORS:** ABA, Real Prop., Probate and Trust Sect.; **EDUC:** BS, 1971, Physics, Brigham Young Univ.; **GRAD EDUC:** MBA, 1973, Brigham Young Univ.; JD, 1978, AZ State Univ.; **EDUC HONORS:** Cum Laude, Law Journal, Editorial Bd.; **MIL SERV:** USAF, Capt.; **HOME ADD:** 2457 W. Portobello, Mesa, AZ 85202; **BUS ADD:** 3500 Valley Bank Center, Phoenix, AZ 85073, (602)257-7622.

DURFEE, Waite D., Jr.——B: May 12, 1920, Council Bluffs, IA, *VP*, Jensen Durfee & Assoc. Inc.; **PRIM RE ACT:** Property Manager; **SERVICES:** Office bldg. mgmt.; **PROFL AFFIL & HONORS:** BOMA, RPA Soc. of Real Prop. Admin.; **EDUC:** BA, 1942, Econ., Coe Coll. Cedar Rapids, IA; **GRAD EDUC:** MA, 1948, Econ., Univ. of MN; **EDUC HONORS:** Magna Cum Laude; **MIL SERV:** US Army, Capt., Bronze Star, Purple Heart with Cluster, 3 theatre ribbons; **OTHER ACT & HONORS:** City Council Appointee Nicollet Mall Advisory Comm., 1969-date Kiwanis, Downtown Council of Minneapolis, Minneapolis City Assessors Land Value Advisory Comm., 1968-date; **HOME ADD:** 2423 Sheridan Ave. N., Minneapolis, MN 55411, (612)588-9073; **BUS ADD:** Suite 802, Midwest Plaza Bldg., 801 Nicollet Mall, Minneapolis, MN 55402, (612)372-6014.

DURHAM, Clyde O.——B: Oct. 14, 1931, Omaha, NE, *Dir. RE*, Union Pacific Railroad Co., RE Dept.; **PRIM RE ACT:** Broker, Appraiser, Developer, Builder, Property Manager; **OTHER RE ACT:** NE RE Broker & Appraiser licenses; **PROFL AFFIL & HONORS:** Amer. Econ. Dev. Council, Amer. Railway Dev. Assn., Employee Relocation Council, Soc. of Ind. Realtors; **MIL SERV:** US Army, SFC 11-17-52/9-28-54; **HOME ADD:** 5305 Raven Oaks Dr., Omaha, NE 68152, (402)571-2240; **BUS ADD:** 1416 Dodge St., Room 306, Omaha, NE 68179, (402)271-3960.

DURHAM, James F., II——B: June 14, 1931, Madisonville, KY, *Partner*, Shutts & Bowen, Real Estate; **PRIM RE ACT:** Attorney; **REP CLIENTS:** New England Mutual Life Ins. Co.; New England Gen. Life Ins. Co.; Victoria Station; **PROFL AFFIL & HONORS:** KY Bar; FL Bar; Dade Cty. Bar; Inter- Amer. Bar; Intl. Bar Assn.; Amer. Soc. of Intl. Law; **EDUC:** BA, 1952, Vanderbilt Univ.; **GRAD EDUC:** LLB, 1954, Vanderbilt Univ.; **MIL SERV:** US Army, Lt. Legal Officer; **HOME ADD:** 3508 Segovia Ave., Coral Gables, FL 33134, (304)448-7055; **BUS ADD:** 133 Sevilla Ave., Coral Gables, FL 33134, (304)444-3601.

DURKEE, Bert R.——B: Mar. 11, 1912, Chatham, Ont., Can., *Atty. at Law*, Katz, McAndrews, Durkee, Balch & Lefstein; **PRIM RE ACT:** Attorney; **SERVICES:** Gen. RE practice; **PROFL AFFIL & HONORS:** ABA, IL Bar Assn. and Rock Is. Cty. Bar Assn.; **GRAD EDUC:** LLB, 1938, Univ. of NE; **EDUC HONORS:** Cum laude, Order of the Coif; **MIL SERV:** USN, Lt.; **HOME ADD:** 1336 21st Ave., Rock Island, IL 61201, (309)788-1424; **BUS ADD:** 2OO Plaza Office Bldg., Rock Island, IL 61201, (309)788-5661.

DURKIN, Phyllis E.——B: Nov. 22, 1947, New York, *Pres.*, Durkin Co.; **PRIM RE ACT:** Consultant; **SERVICES:** Investment Counseling, feasibility analysis, valuation, land planning resid. and non-resid. props.; **REP CLIENTS:** Devels., lenders, instnl. and indiv. investors in comml., indus. and resid. props.; **PREV EMPLOY:** Asst. VP Dir. of Mkt. Research, R&B Enterprises, (a Los Angeles-based RE Devel.) and prop. mgr., VP, The Russell Co.; **PROFL AFFIL & HONORS:** CDMC, Soc. of RE Appraisers; **EDUC:** BA, 1968, Eng., Mkt. Econ., Rutgers Univ.; **BUS ADD:** 2810 2nd St., Santa Monica, CA 90405, (213)399-8463.

DURRETT, John Richard, Jr.——B: Feb. 22, 1929, Springfield, OH, *Owner*, John R. Durrett, Jr. & Assoc.; **PRIM RE ACT:** Broker, Appraiser, Developer, Regulator; **OTHER RE ACT:** Residential Builder; **PROFL AFFIL & HONORS:** Kenneth Keyes Award 1968-1977-1979; CCIM; CRB; CRS; GRI; **EDUC:** BS, Bus., Jacksonville Univ.; **MIL SERV:** USAF, A/1/C, Various ribbons pertaining to Japan occupation, Korean campaign & Good Conduct; **OTHER ACT & HONORS:** Membership in Private Club - Ponte Vedra Club, Ponte Vedra, Fl.; **HOME ADD:** 2871 Forest Mill Ln., Jacksonville, FL 32217, (904)737-1921; **BUS ADD:** 6215 St. Augustine Rd., Jacksonville, FL 32217, (904)737-6722.

DURST, Stephen——*VP Operations*, Cooper Laboratories, Inc.; **PRIM RE ACT:** Property Manager; **BUS ADD:** 3145 Porter Dr., Palo Alto, CA 94304, (415)856-5000.*

DURTSCHI, Walter L.——B: Sept. 30, 1919, Barneveld, WI, *VP*, Century 21 Pfister Farm Agency Inc.; **PRIM RE ACT:** Broker, Appraiser, Developer, Builder, Owner/Investor, Property Manager; **SERVICES:** Investment Counseling, Valuation, Prop. Mgmt.; **REP CLIENTS:** Lenders and indiv. investors in Farm & Comml. Props.; **PROFL AFFIL & HONORS:** NAR; Century 21 Investment Soc., WI Realtors Assn. Honor Soc.; GRI; CRS; CRB; **MIL SERV:** US Army, S/Sgt., 1942-1946; **HOME ADD:** PO Box 104, Mt. Horeb, WI 53572, (608)437-8795; **BUS ADD:** 106 E. Main St., Mt. Horeb, WI 53572, (608)437-3044.

DUSCHATKO, William L.——B: Mar. 26, 1944, NY, NY, *Managing Partner*, Thoreau's Landing Assoc.; Mill River Assocaites; **PRIM RE ACT:** Developer, Owner/Investor, Syndicator; **SERVICES:** Full scale comml. and resid. devel.; **PREV EMPLOY:** Pres. First NH Mort. Corp.; **PROFL AFFIL & HONORS:** Soc. of Review Appraisers, CRA; **EDUC:** AB, 1965, Gvt., Dartmouth Coll.; **GRAD EDUC:** MBA, 1967, Fin., Amos Tuck Sch. of Bus. Admin.; **OTHER ACT & HONORS:** Tr., Spaulding Youth Ctr., Manchester Girls Club; **HOME ADD:** 5 Olde English Rd., Bedford, NH 03102, (603)472-5393; **BUS ADD:** 5 Olde English Rd., Bedford, NH 03102, (603)472-5393.

DUSEK, Jaroslav——B: Apr. 8, 1922, Pecky, Czechoslovakia, *Owner*, Dusek Investment Realty; **PRIM RE ACT:** Broker, Syndicator, Consultant, Owner/Investor; **OTHER RE ACT:** Econ.; **SERVICES:** RE consulting, brokerage & investing; **PREV EMPLOY:** Research Econ. Columbia Univ., NY, Dep. Nat. Dev.; **PROFL AFFIL & HONORS:** NAR RNMI, CCIM; **GRAD EDUC:** 1962, Econ, Univ. of Melbourne, Australia; MA, 1969, Econ, CCNY; **HOME ADD:** FDD 1, New Milford, CT; **BUS ADD:** Meeting House Terr, New Milford, CT 06776, (203)355-2406.

DUSENBURY, C.F.——B: Jan. 5, 1950, Conway, SC, *Pres.*, Associated Appraisers; **PRIM RE ACT:** Consultant, Appraiser; **REP CLIENTS:** HUD, Lenders, Relocation Servs., Attys., Accountants and Ins. Cos.; **PREV EMPLOY:** Dusenbury RE Appraisal Co.; **PROFL AFFIL & HONORS:** Amer. Assn. of Cert. Appraisers, Nat. Assn. of Review Appraisers, Nat. Assn. of Indep. Fee Appraisers, NAR, CA-S, CRA, IFA; **EDUC:** AA, 1970, Univ. of SC; BA, 1972, Francis Marion Coll.; **EDUC HONORS:** Dean's List Student; **OTHER ACT & HONORS:** Grand Strand Sertoma Club; **HOME ADD:** 74th Ave. N., Myrtle Beach, SC 29577, (804)449-9340; **BUS ADD:** 401 79th Ave. N., Myrtle Beach, SC 29577, (803)449-9340.

DUTEL, William J.——B: Nov. 11, 1947, New Orleans, LA, *Partner*, Dutel & Dutel, Attys. at Law; **PRIM RE ACT:** Attorney; **REP CLIENTS:** Central States SE & SW Areas Health & Welfare Fund; Central States SE and SW Areas Pension Fund; Colonial Savings Assn. of Wrightsville, PA; Dixie Fed. S&L Assn.; DHSA, Inc.; Dutel Title Agency; Inc.; First City Mort. Co.; First Homestead Fed. Savings Assn.; FHSA; Inc.; First Natl. Mort. Corp.; Harris Mort. Corp.; Hertz Realty Corp.; Intl. Fidelity Insurance Co.; Rockwood Insurance Co.; Tonti Devel. Corp., Inc.; United Fidelity Life Insurance Co.; Western Southern Life Insurance Co.; **PROFL AFFIL & HONORS:** New Orleans, LA, Fed. and Amer. Bar Assns.; ABA Comm., Nominations, Legal Needs of the Public, Real Prop. & Probate Sect.; Discovery (Sect. on Litigation); LA Trial Lawyers Assn., The Assn. of Trial Lawyers of Amer., Natl. Assn. of Accts., Amer. Land Title Assn., Mort. Bankers Assn. of Amer.; **EDUC:** BS, 1974, Acctg., Univ. of New Orleans; **GRAD EDUC:** JD, 1976, Law, Tulane Univ. School of Law; **EDUC HONORS:** Member, Beta Alpha Psi; **OTHER ACT & HONORS:** Pres., Alumni Assn., Univ. of New Orleans; 1980-1981; **HOME ADD:** 1216 Broadway, New Orleans, LA 70118, (504)866-7571; **BUS ADD:**

309 Baronne St., New Orleans, LA 70112, (504)581-7115.

DUTKOWSKY, Andrew D.——B: Jan. 30, 1945, Pittsburgh, PA, *Pres.*, Island Resort Prop. Mgmt., Inc. 1979 - Present; **PRIM RE ACT:** Broker, Property Manager; **OTHER RE ACT:** Condo. Mgr.; **SERVICES:** Manage Resort Condo., Long Term Rental Village; **REP CLIENTS:** Resort Condos. controlled by owner elected Bd. of Dirs., indiv. owned rental units; **PREV EMPLOY:** Condo. Mgr., Oliver Realty Inc. Pittsburgh, PA; **PROFL AFFIL & HONORS:** IREM, CAI, CPM; **EDUC:** 1966, Math, Gannon Coll. Erie, PA; **MIL SERV:** US Army, 1st Lt., Army Commendation Medal; **HOME ADD:** 3 Camellia St., Hilton Head Island, SC 29928, (803)785-3459; **BUS ADD:** Sea Cabin Ocean Club, PO Box 4868, Hilton Head Island, SC 29938, (803)785-8702.

DUVAL, David B.——B: Aug. 30, 1939, Bronxville, NY, *Partner*, The Linpro Co.; **PRIM RE ACT:** Developer, Builder, Owner/Investor, Property Manager; **PREV EMPLOY:** Grubb and Ellis Comml. Brokerage Co.; **EDUC:** BA, 1961, Pol., Princeton Univ.; **BUS ADD:** 5353 W. Dartmouth Ave., Suite 312, Denver, CO 80227, (303)985-8701.

DVES, John J.——B: Jan. 22, 1948, Greenville, OH, *Dir., Corporate RE/Pres.*, The Mead Corp., Mead Land Services Inc.; **OTHER RE ACT:** User of Real Prop.; **SERVICES:** Negotiation, Valuation, Site Selection, Asset Mgmt.; **REP CLIENTS:** Mead Corp. Operating Unit; **PREV EMPLOY:** Dues Development Co.; **PROFL AFFIL & HONORS:** IDRC, SIR, ULI, NACORE, AICAM.; **EDUC:** BBA, 1970, Fin., Univ. of Note Dame; **GRAD EDUC:** MBA, 1976, Fin. Mktg., Univ. of Dayton; **OTHER ACT & HONORS:** Exec. Comm.-Dayton Devel. Council; Facilities Comm.-Datyon Bd. of Educ.; **HOME ADD:** 1222 Hathaway Rd., Dayton, OH 45419, (513)299-0716; **BUS ADD:** Courthouse Plaza N.E., Dayton, OH 45463, (513)222-6323.

DWYER, Gerald E.——B: June 14, 1949, Kekst and Co., Inc.; **OTHER RE ACT:** Fin. Relations Consultant; **SERVICES:** Investor and fin. relations and corp. communications; **REP CLIENTS:** United Realty Investors, CT Gen. Mort. & Realty Investors, Marsh & MacLennan RE Advisors, Inc., Paine Webber Properties, Inc.; **EDUC:** BA, 1971, Eng. and Philosophy, Univ. of CT; **OTHER ACT & HONORS:** Advisor to Nat. Assn. for the Endowment of Humanities; **HOME ADD:** Rocky Dell Farm, Brewster, NY 10509; **BUS ADD:** 430 Park Ave., New York, NY 10022, (212)593-2655.

DWYER, Jeffry R.——B: May 14, 1946, Union City, NJ, *Partner, Comml. RE Fin.*, Lane and Edson P.C.; **PRIM RE ACT:** Attorney; **PROFL AFFIL & HONORS:** Member of the Dist. of Columbia and NY Bar; Member of the ABA; **EDUC:** BSFS, 1967, Intl. Affairs, Edmund A. Walsh School of Foreign Serv., Georgetown Univ.; **GRAD EDUC:** 1970, Law, Georgetown Univ.; **OTHER ACT & HONORS:** Co-Author, The Law of RE Fin., 1981; Adjunct Prof., RE Planning, Georgetown Univ. Law School; **BUS ADD:** 1800 M St., Washington, DC 20036, (202)457-6800.

DWYER, Michael——*VP Market Res. & Prod. Devel.*, Peavey Co.; **PRIM RE ACT:** Property Manager; **BUS ADD:** Peavey Bldg., 730 Second Ave. South, Minneapolis, MN 55402, (612)370-7500.*

DWYER, Stephen I.——B: Jan. 15, 1949, New Orleans, LA, *Atty. (Partner)*, Gordon, Arata, McCollan & Stuart; **PRIM RE ACT:** Attorney; **SERVICES:** Negotiation, documentation, title, fin.; **REP CLIENTS:** First Nat. Bank of Jefferson Parish; Allied Bancshares, Diversified Mort. Investors; Coldwell Mort. Trust; etc.; **PROFL AFFIL & HONORS:** ABA (Real Prop., Probate & Trust Div.), Pres. - Loyola Law Alumni; Dean's Advisory Council - Loyola Univ. School of Law (New Orleans); LA Law Inst.; **EDUC:** AB, 1970, Eng. & Pre-Med., Holy Cross, Worcester, MA; **GRAD EDUC:** JD, 1976, Loyola Univ. School of Law; MA, 1972, Eng., Univ. of New Orleans; **EDUC HONORS:** Dean's List, Magna Cum Laude, Summa Cum Laude (with Distinction); **OTHER ACT & HONORS:** Bd. of Dirs., Alumni, Loyola Univ.; **HOME ADD:** 1185 Robert E. Lee Blvd., New Orleans, LA 70124; **BUS ADD:** 24th Floor, Pan American Life Center, New Orleans, LA 70130, (504)581-1636

DYER, John J., Jr.——B: June 27, 1929, Flint, MI, *Pres.*, Dyer Financial Co.; **OTHER RE ACT:** Mort. Banker; **PROFL AFFIL & HONORS:** MBAA; **EDUC:** BA, 1951, Econ., Poli. Sci., Univ. of MI; **MIL SERV:** USMC, Sgt.; **HOME ADD:** 2644 West Park Blvd., Shaker Hts., OH 44122, (216)932-0654; **BUS ADD:** 23200 Three Commerce Park Sq., Suite 850, CLeveland, OH 44122, (216)464-7172.

DYER, T. Stephen——B: June 25, 1952, Richmond, VA, *Atty. at Law*, Bryan, Cave, McPheeters & McRoberts; **PRIM RE ACT:** Attorney; **SERVICES:** Legal representation, counsel and advice; **REP CLIENTS:** Firm represents lenders, indivs. and instnl. investors and devels. in all aspects of comml. RE; **PREV EMPLOY:** Schiff Hardin & Waite, Chicago IL law firm, 1979-1981; **PROFL AFFIL & HONORS:** ABA; MO Bar Assn.; Metro. St. Louis Bar Assn.; **EDUC:** BA, 1974, Anthropology, Northwestern Univ.; **GRAD EDUC:** JD, 1979, Law, Univ. of Chicago; **EDUC HONORS:** Phi Beta Kappa; Grad. With Highest Distinction; **OTHER ACT & HONORS:** Member, Real Property, Probate and Trustee Law Section of ABA; Member, Corporation, Banking and Business Law Section of ABA; Member, Real Estate Committee of Business Law Section of Bar Assn. of Metropolitan St. Louis; Member, Nat. Health Lawyers Assn.; **HOME ADD:** 6803 Waterman, St. Louis, MO 63130, (314)721-7752; **BUS ADD:** 500 N. Broadway, St. Louis, MO 63102, (314)231-8600.

DYER, W. Dale——B: Nov. 1, 1933, Elwood, NE, *Pres.*, Double D Contractors, Inc.; **PRIM RE ACT:** Broker, Developer, Builder, Property Manager; **PREV EMPLOY:** 12 yrs. electronic engr.; **PROFL AFFIL & HONORS:** NAHB, OR State Homebuilders, NAR, Corvallis C of C; **EDUC:** BEE, 1957, Elect. Engrg., Univ. of NE; **GRAD EDUC:** MBA, 1963, Mgmt., Fin., Univ. of Santa Clara; **EDUC HONORS:** Eta Kappa Nu, Sigma Tau; **HOME ADD:** Rt. 2, Box 146, Corvallis, OR 77330, (503)753-3059; **BUS ADD:** 999 N.W. Circle Blvd., Corvallis, OR 97330, (503)757-1654.

DYESS, William G.——B: Dec. 31, 1925, Akron, OH, *Appraiser*, W.G. Dyess Appraisals; **PRIM RE ACT:** Appraiser, Banker; **SERVICES:** Appraisals/consultant; **REP CLIENTS:** Security Pacific Bank, Crocker Bank, Merrill Lynch Relocation; **PREV EMPLOY:** 27 yrs. with S&L; **PROFL AFFIL & HONORS:** Sr. Member IFAS, Sr. Member NARA Member AAA, CRA; **EDUC:** Univ. of Akron; **MIL SERV:** US Army, Sgt., Pacific Theater, Good Conduct; **OTHER ACT & HONORS:** Public Works Comm., City of La Canada; **HOME ADD:** PO Box 201, La Canada, CA 91011, (213)290-4460; **BUS ADD:** PO Box 201, La Canada, CA 91011, (213)790-6553.

DYKSTRA, Daniel D.——B: Oct. 29, 1955, Paterson, NJ, *Atty.*, Gleysteen, Harper, Eidsmoe, Heidman & Redmond; **PRIM RE ACT:** Attorney; **SERVICES:** Title opinions, contracts, deeds, probate sales, estate planning; **PROFL AFFIL & HONORS:** ABA; Real Prop. and Probate Div.; IA St. Bar Assn.; Amer. Judicuture Soc.; Greater Siouxland Estate Planning Council; **EDUC:** AB, 1977, Soc. Sci., Dordt Coll.; **GRAD EDUC:** JD, 1980, Univ. of IA Coll. of Law; **EDUC HONORS:** Dordt Coll. Alumni Award, Amer. Jurisprudence Award; Managing Editor, Journal of Corp. Law; **OTHER ACT & HONORS:** Reformed Church of Amer.; **HOME ADD:** 3372 Stone Park Blvd., Sioux City, IA 51104, (712)255-2418; **BUS ADD:** Suite 200, Home Federal Bldg., Sioux City, IA 51102, (712)255-8838.

DYSON, Robert——*Pres.*, Red Carpet Realtors Corp.; **PRIM RE ACT:** Syndicator; **BUS ADD:** 1111 Civic Dr., Suite 300, Walnut Creek, CA 94596.*

DZIADUL, W. John——B: Nov. 14, 1947, Ipswich, MA, *Mort. Officer*, Boston Mutual Life Ins. Co., RE Div.; **PRIM RE ACT:** Lender; **SERVICES:** Comml. prop. construction and permanent mort. loans; **PREV EMPLOY:** Citizens Savings Bank, Providence RI 1978-1980; Erie Savings Bank, Buffalo, NY 1971-1978; **PROFL AFFIL & HONORS:** MBA; **EDUC:** BS, 1970, Fin.; **GRAD EDUC:** 1978, Brown Univ., Grad. School of Savings Banking; **MIL SERV:** US Army; 2nd Lt.; **OTHER ACT & HONORS:** RI Red Cross; Looking Glass Theatre; **HOME ADD:** 6 Briarwood Dr., Barrington, RI 02806, (401)245-2898; **BUS ADD:** 120 Royall St., Canton, MA 02021, (617)828-7000.

DZIAMBA, Nancy C.——B: Jan. 30, 1952, Hudson, NY, *Managing Agent*, Walter Uccellini Enterprises, Inc.; **PRIM RE ACT:** Property Manager; **PROFL AFFIL & HONORS:** NYS RE Lic., Notary Public; **HOME ADD:** 2103 Sausse Ave. #1D, Troy, NY 12180, (518)274-0991; **BUS ADD:** 5 Broadway, Box 305, Troy, NY 12181, (518)271-7564.

EACRET, Dr. David T.——B: Feb. 10, 1941, Bozeman, MT, *Pres.*, Research Economics; **PRIM RE ACT:** Consultant, Syndicator; **SERVICES:** RE feasibility studies, RE synd.; **REP CLIENTS:** Newman Bretton Props. (Long Beach), State of WA; **PREV EMPLOY:** Economist, First Nat. Bank of Chicago, Sr. Economist, RE Research Corp. (LA); **PROFL AFFIL & HONORS:** RESSI; **EDUC:** BS, 1963, Bus., Fin., Univ. of MT; **GRAD EDUC:** MBA, 1966, Bus.,

Econ., Univ. of Denver; PhD, 1972, Econ., CO State Univ.; **MIL SERV:** US Army, 1st Lt.; **OTHER ACT & HONORS:** Rotary Club of Spokane, C of C; **HOME ADD:** 2109 Southeast Blvd., Spokane, WA 99203, (509)534-0745; **BUS ADD:** 245 Spokane Falls Blvd., Spokane, WA 99201.

EADS, Lorenzo Dow——B: Mar. 1, 1932, Georgetown, KY, *Owner-Broker*, Eads Realty; **PRIM RE ACT:** Broker; **SERVICES:** RE Brokerage; **PROFL AFFIL & HONORS:** NAR; KY and Frankfort, Franklin Cty. Bd. of Realtors; **EDUC:** BS, 1978, Police Admin., E. KY Univ.; **GRAD EDUC:** MPA, 1981, Mgmt., KY State Univ.; **MIL SERV:** USAF; 1951-1971, M.Sgt.; AF Commendation Medal w/Oak Leaf Cluster; **OTHER ACT & HONORS:** Kiwanis Club, Bd. of Dir., Past Chmn. of Bd.; First United Methodist Church; Past Pres. of Men's Club; Shriner; Mason; **HOME ADD:** 1037 Sioux Trail, Frankfort, KY 40601, (502)695-3176; **BUS ADD:** 200 McClure Bldg., Frankfort, KY 40601, (502)875-3845.

EAKIN, Robert D.——B: Sept. 22, 1938, Floydada, TX, *Shareholder*, Robert D. Eakin, P.C.; **OTHER RE ACT:** CPA; **SERVICES:** Fin and Tax Advisory Servs.; **REP CLIENTS:** Brokers, Devels., Indiv. and Grp. Investors; **PROFL AFFIL & HONORS:** AICPA, TX Soc. of CPA, Central Chap. of CPAs, CPA; **EDUC:** BBA, 1961, Acctg., Univ. of TX; **OTHER ACT & HONORS:** Rotary Club of Temple Texas; Water Quality Advisory Council of CT COG; Temple C of C; TX Assn. of Bus.; Temple Ctry. Club; Longhorn Club; Univ. of TX Ex-Students Assn.; **HOME ADD:** 2809 Pecan Valley Dr., Temple, TX 76502, (817)778-5628; **BUS ADD:** 2005 Bird Creek Dr., Suite 113, Temple, TX 76501, (817)774-8868.

EAMES, Gary A.——B: Feb. 11, 1948, Detroit, MI, *VP*, FCH Services Inc.; **PRIM RE ACT:** Appraiser, Developer, Property Manager, Syndicator; **SERVICES:** Devel. of multi-family props.; **PROFL AFFIL & HONORS:** IREM, Washington Bd. of Realtors, CPM; **EDUC:** BS Econ., 1970, Acctg., Wharton School Univ. of PA; **GRAD EDUC:** MBA, 1974, Acctg., Case Western Reserve Univ.; **MIL SERV:** US Army, 1st Lt.; **HOME ADD:** 6808 Haycock Rd., Falls Church, VA 22043, (703)536-5263; **BUS ADD:** 2101 L St. N.W., Suite 409, Washington, DC 20037, (202)857-4123.

EARNEST, G. Lane——B: May 12, 1938, Pueblo, CO, *Partner*, Caplan and Earnest; **PRIM RE ACT:** Attorney; **REP CLIENTS:** Banks, S&L, Bds. of Realtors, Realtor Firms; **PROFL AFFIL & HONORS:** ABA, RE Law Section; Boulder Cty. Bar RE Section; **EDUC:** A&S, 1960, Econ./Hist., Univ. of CO; **GRAD EDUC:** LLB, 1963, Univ. of CO Sch. of Law; **EDUC HONORS:** Blue Key; **MIL SERV:** US Army, Cpt., Army Commendation Medal; **OTHER ACT & HONORS:** Municipal Judge (City of Boulder) 1972-76; Bd. of Dirs., Arapahoe Nat. Bank; **HOME ADD:** 2255 Bluebell Ave., Boulder, CO 80302, (303)447-1291; **BUS ADD:** Suite 300, 1301 Spruce St., Boulder, CO 80302, (303)443-8010.

EARP, Gary D.——B: Dec. 23, 1946, Richland, WA, *VP*, AARO Real Estate Center, Inc., Better Homes & Gardens, Corp. Headquarters, Columbia Plaza; **PRIM RE ACT:** Broker, Developer, Owner/Investor, Syndicator; **PROFL AFFIL & HONORS:** NAR, WA Assn. of Realtors, Tri-City Bd. of Realtors, State Dir. and Tri-City Bd. of Realtors, 1982 VP; **EDUC:** 1970, Bus. Mgmt. & Admin.; **HOME ADD:** 3326 W. 24th St., Kennewick, WA 99336, (509)586-6503; **BUS ADD:** 6855 Clearwater, Kennewick, WA 99336, (509)735-2535.

EARP, Orson K., Jr.——B: Oct. 21, 1934, Memphis, TN, *COB*, Marx & Bensdorf RE & Investment Co.; **PRIM RE ACT:** Broker, Syndicator, Consultant, Property Manager, Owner/Investor; **SERVICES:** Comml. and resid. RE Sales, leasing, synd. of income props., investment counseling, prop. mgmt.; **REP CLIENTS:** Indiv. investors in income props., trust depts. of local fin. insts. & estates; **PREV EMPLOY:** The Galbreath Co., Memphis, TN, 1959-77, Pres. CEO, 1973-77; **PROFL AFFIL & HONORS:** CPM, RAM NAREB, Pres., Memphis IREM, Exec. Comm, IREM (Regional VP, Sr. VP & Treas), Omega Tau Rho, Million Dollar Sales Club; **EDUC:** BA, 1956, Econ. Hist., Wash. & Lee, Lexington, VA; **OTHER ACT & HONORS:** Pres. Phoenix Club, Pres. TN Club, Memphis C of C, Memphis Rotary Club Officer, Bd. of Dir. Exec. Comm., Memphis Reg. Cancer Ctr., Deacon Idlewild Presbyterian Church; **HOME ADD:** 2938 Garden Ln., TN 38111, (901)324-1688; **BUS ADD:** 1407 Union Ave., Memphis, TN 38104, (901)725-1121.

EARP, Susan L.——B: Aug. 17, 1942, Wash., DC, *Assoc. Broker*, Lewis & Silverman, Realtors; **PRIM RE ACT:** Broker, Consultant; **PREV EMPLOY:** Shannon & Luchs RE Sales Assoc.; **PROFL AFFIL & HONORS:** NAR; MCBR; Gaithersburg C of C, CRB; **HOME ADD:** 21501 Davis Mill Rd., Germantown, MD 20874, (301)365-7425; **BUS ADD:** 8401 Connecticut Ave., Chevy Chase, MD 20015, (301)656-1323.

EASLEY, George W., Jr.——B: Apr. 5, 1949, Prescott, AR, *Owner*, Easley RE; **PRIM RE ACT:** Broker, Insuror; **PROFL AFFIL & HONORS:** GRI, CRS, CRB; **EDUC:** BS, RE, Univ. of AR; **GRAD EDUC:** BS, 1971; **OTHER ACT & HONORS:** Broken Arrow Planning Commn., Apr. 1980 to pres.; **HOME ADD:** PO Box C, Broken Arrow, OK 74012, (918)455-3225; **BUS ADD:** PO Box C, Broken Arrow, OK 74012, (918)258-7666.

EAST, James D.——*RE Adm.*, Federal-Mogul Corp.; **PRIM RE ACT:** Property Manager; **BUS ADD:** PO Box 1966, Detroit, MI 48235, (313)354-7700.*

EAST, William J.——B: Dec. 6, 1937, Rochester, NY, *Pres. & Chmn.*, Reed & Stambaugh Co. and Affiliates; **PRIM RE ACT:** Broker, Consultant, Property Manager; **SERVICES:** RE, sales, leasing, prop. mgmt.; **PREV EMPLOY:** Controller, Hoeganaes Corp., 1963-68; Dir. of Fin. & Acctg., The West Co., 1968-69; Asst. Corp. Controller, Leasco Data Processing Equipment Corp., 1969-70; **PROFL AFFIL & HONORS:** Pres., BOMA & Philadelphia; VP Building Operators' Labor Relations, Inc.; **EDUC:** BA, 1959, Econ., Princeton Univ.; **GRAD EDUC:** MBA, 1961, Fin., Harvard Bus. School; **EDUC HONORS:** Cum Laude; **MIL SERV:** US Army; **OTHER ACT & HONORS:** Treas. & Member of Bd., Easter Seal Soc.; **HOME ADD:** 528 W. Moreland Ave., Philadelphia, PA 19118, (215)247-7716; **BUS ADD:** 4 Penn Ctr. Plaza, Philadelphia, PA 19103, (215)568-2727.

EASTLUND, Gary——B: Jan. 8, 1944, Alexandria, MN, *Exec. VP*, Scottland, Inc.; **PRIM RE ACT:** Broker, Developer, Builder, Property Manager; **SERVICES:** Construction, prop. mgmt., site selection, fin. and land devel.; **REP CLIENTS:** Indiv. and instnl. investors, and owners of various types of comml. and indus. businesses; **PROFL AFFIL & HONORS:** Nat. Assn. of Indus. and Office Parks; MN Indus. Devel. Assn.; **EDUC:** Bus. Admin., St. Cloud State Coll./MN School of Bus.; **OTHER ACT & HONORS:** Shakopee Indus. Comml. Commn.; Officer and Dir., Shakopee C of C; Shakopee Subdiv. Ad Hoc Comm.; **HOME ADD:** PO Box 222, Shakopee, MN 55379, (612)445-8724; **BUS ADD:** 5244 VaLLey Industrial Blvd., Shakopee, MN 55379, (612)445-3242.

EASTMAN, Thomas G.——B: July 28, 1946, Los Angeles, CA, *Principal-Owner*, Aldrich, Eastman & Waltch, Inc.; **PRIM RE ACT:** Owner/Investor; **SERVICES:** Investment mgmt., primarily for tax exempt insts.; **REP CLIENTS:** Corp. pension plans and endowments; **PREV EMPLOY:** The Boston Co. (1979-1981); Coldwell Banker Mgmt. Corp. (1972-1979); **EDUC:** BA, 1968, Hist., Stanford Univ.; **GRAD EDUC:** MBA, 1970, Harvard Bus. School; **BUS ADD:** 234 Congress St., Boston, MA 02110, (617)542-9300.

EASTMENT, George T, III——B: May 1, 1945, Brooklyn, NY, *Financial VP*, Long & Foster RE, Inc.; **PRIM RE ACT:** Broker, Owner/Investor, Property Manager; **SERVICES:** Resid. resale and new home brokerage; **PROFL AFFIL & HONORS:** AICPA's, VA Soc. of CPA's; **EDUC:** BBA, 1967, Acctg., Manhattan Coll.; **GRAD EDUC:** MBA, 1972, Fin., Colgate, Darden Grad. Sch. of Bus. Admin, Univ. of VA; **EDUC HONORS:** Epsilon Sigma Phi Hon. Frat.; Grad., Cum Laude; **MIL SERV:** USMC; Capt.; **HOME ADD:** 5195 Dungannon Rd., Fairfax, VA 22030, (703)278-8230; **BUS ADD:** 3918 Prosperity Ave., Fairfax, VA 22031, (703)849-1003.

EASTON, John J.——B: Aug. 26, 1918, Mt. Vernon, NY, *Principal*, J. J. Enterprises; **PRIM RE ACT:** Broker, Consultant, Instructor; **OTHER RE ACT:** Exchangor; **REP CLIENTS:** Buyer broker; **PREV EMPLOY:** Continental Realtors, Associate; Bristol Myers Co., Dir. Staff Admin.; ITT Intelcom, Dir. Admin.; Col, USAF; Ret'd.; **PROFL AFFIL & HONORS:** Academy of RE; INTEREX; CT RE Exchangors, GRI; **EDUC:** BS, 1941, US Military Academy; **MIL SERV:** USAF; Col.; **BUS ADD:** 520 West Ave., Suite 201, Norwalk, CT 06850, (203)838-3121.

EASTON, Steven K.——B: May 28, 1946, NY, *Pres., Owner*, Easton Realty, Inc. Realtors; **PRIM RE ACT:** Broker, Consultant, Developer, Owner/Investor, Instructor, Property Manager; **SERVICES:** Consultant to profls., Jr. Coll. instructor, devel. of office condos.; **REP CLIENTS:** Medical Profl. People, Investors; **PROFL AFFIL & HONORS:** IREM, FL Assn. of Realtors, St. Petersburg Bd. of Realtors, NAR, CPM, GRI; **EDUC:** BA, 1968, Foreign Languages, Univ., of Tampa, Univ. of S. FL; **OTHER ACT & HONORS:** St. Petersburg Yacht Club, St. Petersburg Power Squadron; **HOME ADD:** PO Box 11077, Saint Petersburg, FL 33733, (813)822-2824; **BUS ADD:** 25 56th St. S., Saint Petersburg, FL 33707, (813)347-2148.

EATON, K.J.——*Pres.*, Small Business Management Investors; **PRIM RE ACT:** Consultant, Owner/Investor, Syndicator; **PROFL AFFIL & HONORS:** Profl. Engr., Cert. Mgmt. Consultant; **EDUC:** BS, 1947, Indus. Engrg.; BS, 1944, Mech. Engrg.; **GRAD EDUC:** M.Bus. Econ.,

1950; **MIL SERV:** US Army, G-2; **BUS ADD:** 17 E. Chestnut, Chicago, IL 60611, (312)943-1355.

EATON, Wm. Lee——**B:** May 14, 1947, Effingham, IL, *Partner*, Boyle, Eaton & Pecharich; **PRIM RE ACT:** Attorney; **SERVICES:** Gen. and comprehensive legal advice in connection with RE investment and development, including condo. and townhouse devel. projects; **REP CLIENTS:** Indiv. and corps. involved in comml. props. Corp. devel. in condo. and townhouse devel.; **PREV EMPLOY:** Yavapai Community Coll., Instr. in Real Prop. and Bus. Law; **PROFL AFFIL & HONORS:** AS Assn.; Bd. of Legal Specialization; Comm. on Continuing Legal Educ.; Comm. on Unauthorized Practice of Law, Univ. of AZ, JD with distinction; **EDUC:** BA, 1969, Hist. and Russian Language and Area Studies, Univ. of IL; **OTHER ACT & HONORS:** Chmn., Mayor's Ad Hoc Tax Review Comm., City of Prescott Past Rgnl. Commr.; AYSO, Region 172; **HOME ADD:** 1975 Shadow Valley Dr., Prescott, AZ, (602)778-0363; **BUS ADD:** 100 E. Union St., PO Box 1549, Prescott, AZ 86302, (602)445-0122.

EAVES, Cary L.——**B:** July 6, 1950, Lubbock, TX, *Realtor*, Morgan Eaves Agency; **PRIM RE ACT:** Broker, Insuror; **SERVICES:** Independent Ins. Agent; **PROFL AFFIL & HONORS:** Outstanding Young Man of America, 1978; Candidate CCIM; **EDUC:** BBA, Resid. RE, Bus. Admin., Gen. Ins., West TX State Univ.; **OTHER ACT & HONORS:** Plainview TX C of C, Bd. of Dir. United Way, Past Pres. Toastmasters Intnl.; **HOME ADD:** 2408 W. 14th, Plainview, TX 79072, (806)293-8904; **BUS ADD:** 109 W. 7th, PO Drawer K, Plainview, TX 79072, (806)296-5514.

EBELING, Leslie G.——**B:** July 31, 1936, Spokane, WA, *Pres.*, Legg Fin. Services, Inc.; **PRIM RE ACT:** Consultant, Developer, Owner/Investor, Syndicator; **OTHER RE ACT:** Mort. broker; **SERVICES:** Re investment counseling, devel., joint venturs, mort. brokering, RE brokerage, synd.; **REP CLIENTS:** Devels., investors, instnl. lenders, bldrs.; **PREV EMPLOY:** Investment Services, Inc.; **EDUC:** BS, 1958, Engrg., Univ. of PortLand; **MIL SERV:** USAF, Capt., 1959-1964; **BUS ADD:** 3550 N Central Ave., Suite 1506, Phoenix, AZ 85012, (602)265-0291.

EBERHARD, Gary L.——**B:** Dec. 29, 1935, Los Angeles, CA, *Pres. & CEO*, Fuller Commercial Brokerage Co.; **PRIM RE ACT:** Broker, Consultant, Developer; **PREV EMPLOY:** VP, Regional Dir. of Mktg., Coldwell Banker; **PROFL AFFIL & HONORS:** ULI, NAIOP, Nat. Bd. of Realtors, Top sales honors, Coldwell Banker; **EDUC:** BS, 1960, Fin., Univ. of So. CA; **EDUC HONORS:** Scroll of Honor; **HOME ADD:** 772 Lincoln Ave., Winnetka, IL 60093, (312)446-3479; **BUS ADD:** 122 South LaSalle St., Chicago, IL 60605, (312)726-1500.

EBERHARDT, James——*Acquisitions Officer*, J.M. Jayson & Co., Inc.; **PRIM RE ACT:** Owner/Investor, Property Manager, Syndicator; **OTHER RE ACT:** Investment counseling; **SERVICES:** Private and public underwriting of RE equities; **REP CLIENTS:** REIT's, instns., public mkt.; **EDUC:** 1966, Bus. Admin., Univ. of Buffalo; **OTHER ACT & HONORS:** Councilman, Town of Pembroke, NY; **HOME ADD:** 1242 Meiser Rd., Corfu, NY 14036, (716)762-8720; **BUS ADD:** 680 Statler Bldg., Buffalo, NY 14202, (716)856-9562.

EBERHART, Laurence L.——**B:** Mar. 26, 1924, Chicora, PA, *Sec.*, Forell Consolidated Corp.; **PRIM RE ACT:** Syndicator, Consultant, Developer, Builder, Property Manager, Engineer, Lender, Owner/Investor; **SERVICES:** Comml., indus., resid.; **PREV EMPLOY:** COB, Peabody Noise Control, Inc.; **PROFL AFFIL & HONORS:** ASHRAE, INCE, NCPMA, ASA, OH Small Businessman of Year Award, Who's Who in Fin. and Ind.; **EDUC:** BS, 1948, Engrg.-Indus., PA State Univ.; **EDUC HONORS:** Tau Beta Pi, Sigma Tau; **MIL SERV:** USAC, Capt., South Pacific Theater WWII; **OTHER ACT & HONORS:** Tr. - Wash. Township, Franklin County, OH - 12 years; Shriner, Masons, Tr. - Dublin Community Church; Nimrods, Dublin Historical Soc.; C of C; **HOME ADD:** 7078 Dublin Rd., Dublin, OH 43017, (614)889-8963; **BUS ADD:** 4770 Sawmill Rd., Columbus, OH 43220, (614)764-9986.

EBERT, Larry P.——**B:** Apr. 10, 1952, Sandusky, OH, *Mgr., Corporate RE*, The Mead Corp.; **PRIM RE ACT:** Consultant, Attorney, Developer, Owner/Investor; **OTHER RE ACT:** Corp. RE Exec./Facility Planner; **SERVICES:** Acquisitions, Disposals, Leases, Fin. Analysis, RE Devel., etc.; **REP CLIENTS:** Divs. and subs. of The Mead Corp.; **PREV EMPLOY:** Dargusch & Hutchins Law Offices; **PROFL AFFIL & HONORS:** Industrial Devel. Research Council; Nat. Assn. of Corp. RE Execs.; ABA; OH Bar Assn.; **EDUC:** BA, 1974, Hist., Case Western Reserve Univ.; **GRAD EDUC:** JJD, 1977, Corporate/Tax, OH State Univ. School of Law; **EDUC HONORS:** Magna Cum Laude, Honors in History, Deans List 1970-1974, etc., Cum Laude, Chief Justice-OH State Univ., CT; **OTHER ACT & HONORS:** Paper Published: "The Role of In-house Legal Consulting Servs." Indus. Devel. January/February, 1981; **HOME ADD:** 9128 Normandy Ln., Centerville, OH 45459, (513)885-3198; **BUS ADD:** Courthouse Plaza, N.E., Dayton, OH 45463, (513)222-6323.

EBERWEIN, A.M.——**B:** Mar. 6, 1932, Montreal, Can., *Building Services Manager*, ESSO Resources Canada Ltd.; **PRIM RE ACT:** Owner/Investor, Property Manager; **SERVICES:** In-house Serv. only; **REP CLIENTS:** Parent Co. and Affiliates; **PROFL AFFIL & HONORS:** UDI, Calgary; BOMI; NACORE; **EDUC:** B. Commerce, 1955, Fin., Univ. of MB; **MIL SERV:** Navy, S. Lt.; **HOME ADD:** 1416 Joliet Ave. SW, Calgary, Alberta, Canada; **BUS ADD:** 237 4th Ave., SW, Calgary, Alberta, Canada, (403)237-4024.

EBLEN, James H.——**B:** Oct. 2, 1929, KY, *Pres.*, Eblen Industries Inc.; **PRIM RE ACT:** Broker, Developer, Builder, Owner/Investor, Syndicator; **SERVICES:** Devel. and synd. of resid. props.; **REP CLIENTS:** Lenders and indiv. investors in resid. props.; **PROFL AFFIL & HONORS:** CA Assn. of Realtors; NAR; Who's Who in the W.; Fin. & Indus. Intl. Register of Profiles, GRI; **EDUC:** AA, 1972, RE, Orange Coast Coll.; **MIL SERV:** USAF, M/Sgt., 1948-1968, AF-Commendation w/OLC; **OTHER ACT & HONORS:** Realtor of the Yr., 1975; **BUS ADD:** 1825 De La Cruz Blvd., Suite 12, Santa Clara, CA 95050, (408)727-7166.

EBY, Christopher S.——**B:** Apr. 9, 1948, Pittsburgh, PA, *VP, Broker, Mgr.*, Copper Mountain Real Estate, Inc.; **PRIM RE ACT:** Broker; **SERVICES:** Specialize in new & resale resort condo.; **REP CLIENTS:** Copper Mt. Corp.; **PROFL AFFIL & HONORS:** NAR, CO Assn. of Realtors, Summit Co. Bd. of Realtors, GRI; **EDUC:** BS, 1973, Communications, S. IL Univ.; **OTHER ACT & HONORS:** Member, Town of Frisco Planning & Zoning, Past Instructor, RE CO Mt. Coll., Past Dir., Secretary, Summit Cty. Bd. of Realtors; **HOME ADD:** Box 1, Frisco, CO 80443, (303)668-5444; **BUS ADD:** Box 3001, Copper Mt., CO 80443, (303)668-2320.

ECCLES, Noëlla L.——**B:** Dec. 24, 1929, Pawtucket, RI, *Mgr.*, Gallery of Homes; **PRIM RE ACT:** Broker; **SERVICES:** Resid. Sales & Rentals; **PROFL AFFIL & HONORS:** NAR, RIAR, NCBR, GFRBR, WCR, RNMI, 1976 Realtor of Yr., GRI, CRS, CRB, RIAR State Pres. 1981-82; **EDUC:** Univ. of RI; **OTHER ACT & HONORS:** C of C; **HOME ADD:** 317 Highland Rd., Tiverton, RI, (401)625-5685; **BUS ADD:** 1048 Stafford Rd., Tiverton, RI 02878, (401)624-6631.

ECHELBARGER, Lindsey L.R.——**B:** June 15, 1952, Everett, WA, *Partner*, Echelbarger Land Co.; **PRIM RE ACT:** Developer, Builder, Owner/Investor, Property Manager; **SERVICES:** Devel., bldg. and ownership of comml. props.; **REP CLIENTS:** Indiv. investors in comml. props.; **PROFL AFFIL & HONORS:** Puget Sound Council of Govts. Task Force on Housing, BOMA, Nat. Assn. of Indus. & Office Parks; **EDUC:** BA, 1975, Hist., Amherst Coll.; **OTHER ACT & HONORS:** Coll. Club, Seattle; Exec. Bd., Snohomish Cty. Republican Party; **HOME ADD:** 23614 107th Pl. W., Edmonds, WA 98020, (206)542-1067; **BUS ADD:** PO Box 30, Lynnwood, WA 98036, (206)774-0205.

ECK, George N., Jr.——**B:** May 17, 1924, S. Weymouth, MA, *Assessor*, Town of Framingham; **PRIM RE ACT:** Assessor; **REP CLIENTS:** 17,000 Parcels; **PREV EMPLOY:** 30 yrs. Fuel Bus. & Heating & Air Cond. Equip.; **PROFL AFFIL & HONORS:** Past Pres. Framingham Kiwanis Club, IAAO, MAA, Legion of Honor; **MIL SERV:** US Army, Cpl., E.T.O. - 4 Battle Stars; **OTHER ACT & HONORS:** Assessor - 18 Yrs., Amer. Legion, D.A.V., Founder of Henderson Trauma Fund, Framingham Union Hosp. Corporator; **HOME ADD:** 34 Salem End Rd. 19B, Framingham, MA 01701, (617)875-5678; **BUS ADD:** Memorial Bldg., Framingham, MA 01701, (617)875-7417.

ECKEL, John——**B:** July 27, 1936, Houston, TX, *Atty.*, Mills, Shirley, McMicken & Eckel; **PRIM RE ACT:** Attorney; **REP CLIENTS:** First Hutchings-Sealy Nat. Bank of Galveston; **PROFL AFFIL & HONORS:** State Bar of TX, Member Sect. RE, Probate and Trusts; **EDUC:** BA, 1958, Eng., Princeton Univ.; **GRAD EDUC:** LLB, 1961, Law, Univ. of TX School of Law; **OTHER ACT & HONORS:** Bd. of Trs., Galveston Wharves 1978 to present; **HOME ADD:** 6500 Bayou Front Drive, Galveston, TX 77551, (713)744-6807; **BUS ADD:** 700 First Hutchings-Sealy National Bank Bldg., Galveston, TX 77550, (713)763-2341.

ECKELS, William P.——**B:** Jan. 29, 1946, Atchison, KS, *Atty.*, Shughart, Thomson & Kilroy, PC; **PRIM RE ACT:** Attorney; **PROFL AFFIL & HONORS:** ABA, Kansas City Bar Assn., Lawyers Assn. of Kansas City; **EDUC:** BA, 1969, Hist., Franklin & Marshall Coll.; **GRAD EDUC:** JD, 1973, Univ. of MO; **EDUC HONORS:** Law Review, Bus. Editor; **MIL SERV:** US Army Res., S/Sgt.; **HOME ADD:** 1217 W. 59th St., Kansas City, MO 64113, (816)444-1144; **BUS ADD:** 900 Commerce Bank Bldg. 922 Walnut, Kansas City, MO

64106, (816)421-3355.

ECKHARDT, John H.——**B:** Mar. 18, 1943, Madison, WI, *Pres.*, First National Bank & Trust Co.; **PRIM RE ACT:** Banker; **SERVICES:** Banking; **PROFL AFFIL & HONORS:** ABA, IBAA, WBA, Sank Co., Bankers; **EDUC:** 1967, Educ., Southern IL Univ.; **MIL SERV:** US Army, Cpt.; **HOME ADD:** 540 Pine Acres, Baraboo, WI 53913, (608)356-5915; **BUS ADD:** PO Box 129, Baraboo, WI 53913, (608)356-3901.

ECKHART, Walter E.——**B:** May 10, 1925, Hackensack, NJ, *Pres.*, Eckhart Associates Inc. Realtors; **PRIM RE ACT:** Broker, Appraiser, Property Manager, Insuror; **SERVICES:** RE brokerage - sales - leases - prop. mgmt. appraisals - resid. & comml. RE; **REP CLIENTS:** Serving major corps., banks, S&L; **PROFL AFFIL & HONORS:** Westfield Bd. of Realtors, NJ Assn. of Realtors, Nat. Assn. of Realtors, Amer. Assn. of Cert. Appraisers, Licensed RE Broker state of NJ, Cert. Appraiser-Sr.-Amer. Assn. of Cert. Appraisers; **EDUC:** BS, 1949, Commerce & Fin., Bucknell Univ.; **MIL SERV:** USMC, 1943-46, Cpl.; **OTHER ACT & HONORS:** Past Pres. Rotary Club of Union, NJ; **HOME ADD:** 20 Burrington Gorge, Westfield, NJ 07090, (201)232-7954; **BUS ADD:** 223 Lenox Ave., Westfield, NJ 07091, (201)233-2222.

ECKMAN, J.W., II——**B:** Mar. 25, 1950, Fountain Hill, PA, *Pres./VP*, Mahoning Manor Estates, Inc./Eckman Lumber Co., Inc.; **PRIM RE ACT:** Engineer, Developer, Builder, Owner/Investor; **SERVICES:** Devel. & bldg. on own prop., bldg. materials dist., mfg. of bldg. components; **PROFL AFFIL & HONORS:** Amer. Chem. Soc.; AIChE, Mid Atlantic Lumbermen's Assn.; Truss Plate Inst.; PA Bldrs. Assn.; Amer. For. Assn.; **EDUC:** BS, 1972, Lehigh Univ.; **GRAD EDUC:** MBA, 1973, Econ. & Fin., Lehigh Univ.; **EDUC HONORS:** Cum Laude; **OTHER ACT & HONORS:** Pres. Lehigh Area School Bd. 1976-1978; NFIB Action Council; US Sen. Bus. Adv. Bd.; **HOME ADD:** R1, Box 393, Lehighton, PA 18235, (717)386-4427; **BUS ADD:** R3, Box 117, Lehighton, PA 18235, (325)377-2460.

ECONOMOPOULOS, James——**B:** Jan. 18, 1925, Brooklyn, NY, *Owner*, James Econ Realty; **PRIM RE ACT:** Broker, Consultant, Appraiser, Builder, Owner/Investor, Property Manager; **MIL SERV:** USMC, 1943-46, S/Sgt., O/Seas Asia Theater; **HOME ADD:** 44 Murray Dr., Westbury, NY 11590, (516)334-8505; **BUS ADD:** 343 Maple Ave., Westbury, Long Is., NY 11590, (516)334-9030.

EDELMAN, Gilbert, Esquire——**B:** Oct. 7, 1932, Philadelphia, PA, *Atty.*, Stuzin and Camner, P.A.; **PRIM RE ACT:** Attorney; **SERVICES:** Legal; **REP CLIENTS:** Fed. Savings and Loan; Comml. Banks; Gen. Contractors; **PROFL AFFIL & HONORS:** FL Bar Assn. and ABA; **EDUC:** BBA, 1954, Univ. of Miami; **GRAD EDUC:** JD, 1967, Temple Univ.; **MIL SERV:** US Army; **HOME ADD:** 11740 SW 113th Place, Miami, FL 33176; **BUS ADD:** 999 Brickell Ave., Suite 400, Miami, FL 33131, (305)577-0600.

EDEN, Ernie——*Ed.*, Nat'l. Assn of Housing Cooperatives, Cooperative Housing Bulletin; **PRIM RE ACT:** Real Estate Publisher; **BUS ADD:** 1828 L St., NW, Washington, DC 20036.*

EDFORS, Hugh T.——**B:** Nov. 7, 1946, Saginaw, MI, *Atty.*, Roan & Grossman, also self-employed; **PRIM RE ACT:** Broker, Consultant, Attorney, Appraiser, Owner/Investor; **SERVICES:** Investment Counseling, Valuation, Legal, Brokerage; **REP CLIENTS:** Natl. Inst. Investors, Indivs., Devels., Consulting Firms; **PREV EMPLOY:** Prin. Counselor, RE Research Corp., 1975-1980; **PROFL AFFIL & HONORS:** Chicago Bar Assn., Real Prop. Law Comm., and RE Synd. Sub-Comm., IL State Bar Assn., Member of Sect. on Federal Taxation; ABA, Sect. of Real Prop., Probate & Trust Law, MAI Candidate, Amer. Inst. of RE Appraisers, Candidate, Soc. of RE Appraisers; **EDUC:** BA, 1969, Geology, Northwestern Univ.; **GRAD EDUC:** MS, 1974, RE Investment Analysis and Appraisal, Univ. of WI, Madison; MBA, 1975, Fin., Univ. of Chicago; JD, 1979, Law, DePaul Univ.; **EDUC HONORS:** Academic Scholarships, Awarded Full Year's Stipend for Graduate Work in Geology, Dean's List; **HOME ADD:** 1150 N. Lake Shore Dr., 18K, Chicago, IL 60611, (312)266-6338; **BUS ADD:** 55 W. Monroe St., Chicago, IL 60603, (312)263-3600.

EDGE, J. Dexter, Jr.——**B:** June 7, 1942, Newport News, VA, *Atty.*, Henkel, Hackett, Edge & Fleming, P.C.; **PRIM RE ACT:** Attorney; **SERVICES:** Legal; **PROFL AFFIL & HONORS:** GA Bar; ABA; DC Bar; Lawyers Club; Atlanta Bar Assn.; **EDUC:** BSIM, 1964, Indus. Mgmt., GA Tech.; **GRAD EDUC:** JD, 1973, Emory Law School; MBA, 1977, GA State Univ.; **MIL SERV:** USN, Lt.; **HOME ADD:** 1973 Castleway Ln., Atlanta, GA 30345, (404)321-3331; **BUS ADD:** 1900 Peachtree Ctr. Tower, 230 Peachtree St., Atlanta, GA 30303, (404)577-2900.

EDGE, Lawrence L.——**B:** Aug. 11, 1945, Atlanta, GA, *Pres.*, Consolidated Equities Corp.; **PRIM RE ACT:** Broker, Consultant, Developer, Owner/Investor, Property Manager; **SERVICES:** RE investment, devel. and mgmt.; **REP CLIENTS:** Lenders and indivs. or instnl. investors in comml. props.; **PROFL AFFIL & HONORS:** Dir. Consolidated Equities Corp., Chmn. Bd. Amer. Reservation Systems, Inc., VP Gran Crique Investment Corp., Treas. & Dir. Northwest Atlanta Motor Inn, Inc.; **EDUC:** BS, 1967, Indus. Admin., Yale Univ.; **GRAD EDUC:** MBA, 1969, Fin., Harvard Univ.; **OTHER ACT & HONORS:** Campus Crusade for Christ, Assoc. Staff, Listed in 'Outstanding Young Men of Amer., 1978', Elder, First Presbyterian Church of Atlanta; **HOME ADD:** 3219 Rockingham Dr., NW, Atlanta, GA 30327, (404)355-0863; **BUS ADD:** 1280 W. Peachtree St., NW, Ste. 300, Atlanta, GA 30367, (404)873-1941.

EDINGER, Sid——*VP Admin. Services*, Kimberly-Clark Corp.; **PRIM RE ACT:** Property Manager; **BUS ADD:** Neenah, WI 54956, (414)721-2000.*

EDINGTON, Jack L.——**B:** Feb. 4, 1945, Detroit, MI, *Pres.*, Jack L. Edington, Inc.; **PRIM RE ACT:** Consultant; **PREV EMPLOY:** Dir. of RE, Sports Illustrated Court Clubs; VP RE One of Washtenaw; **PROFL AFFIL & HONORS:** RNMI; NAR; MI Assn. of Realtors; RESSI; **EDUC:** BS, 1972, Poli. Sci., Eastern MI Univ.; **HOME ADD:** 8225 W. Huron River Dr., Dexter, MI 48130, (313)426-2592; **BUS ADD:** 103 E. Liberty, PO Box 7301, Ann Arbor, MI 48104, (313)665-0616.

EDLER, Robert W.——**B:** June 25, 1936, Davenport, IA, *Partner*, Rudnick & Wolfe; **PRIM RE ACT:** Attorney, Owner/Investor; **PROFL AFFIL & HONORS:** RESSI; ABA; Chicago and IL Bar Assns.; **EDUC:** 1958, DePauw Univ.; **GRAD EDUC:** MA, 1959, Hist., Univ. of Chicago; LLB, 1962, Law, Stanford Univ.; **EDUC HONORS:** Phi Beta Kappa; **HOME TEL:** (312)835-1374; **BUS ADD:** 30 N. LaSalle St., Chicago, IL 60602, (312)368-4051.

EDMISTON, Helen——**B:** Feb. 4, 1922, Fort Smith, AR, *Pres.*, Edmiston-Prewitt Development Co., Inc.; **PRIM RE ACT:** Broker, Developer, Owner/Investor, Builder, Property Manager; **PROFL AFFIL & HONORS:** NARAB, Fayetteville Bd. of Realtors; **EDUC:** BA, 1943, Journalism, Univ. of AR; **EDUC HONORS:** Phi Beta Kappa, Pi Kappa, Mortar Board; **OTHER ACT & HONORS:** Who's Who in Amer. Univ., Member of Planning Commn., 1972-1979; **HOME ADD:** #3 Greenbriar, Fayetteville, AR 72701, (501)521-4532; **BUS ADD:** #9 Township, Fayetteville, AR 72701, (501)521-3933.

EDMONDSON, James T.——**B:** Oct. 30, 1925, NY, *Pres.*, Albion Corp.; **PRIM RE ACT:** Broker, Owner/Investor, Instructor, Syndicator, Real Estate Publisher; **SERVICES:** Investment counseling; **REP CLIENTS:** Instns., indivs.; **PREV EMPLOY:** Pres., Albion Publishing Co., San Francisco, CA; **PROFL AFFIL & HONORS:** NAR; CA Assn. of Realtors, Marin Cty. Bd. of Realtors; RESSI; REMNI, CBC; (CCIM Candidate; SRS Candidate); **EDUC:** AB, 1949, Psych., Cornell Univ.; **GRAD EDUC:** MA, 1950, Psych., Counseling, Cornell Univ.; **MIL SERV:** USNR, Cmdr.; **HOME ADD:** 4174 Redwood Hwy., San Raphael, CA 94903, (415)479-1000; **BUS ADD:** 4174 Redwood Hwy., San Raphael, CA 94903, (415)479-1000.

EDMUNDS, David E.——**B:** Apr. 8, 1922, Ann Arbor, MI, *Pres.*, Edmunds And Assoc. Inc. Realtors; **PRIM RE ACT:** Broker, Syndicator, Consultant, Owner/Investor; **SERVICES:** Sales, Exchanging a little mgmt.; **PROFL AFFIL & HONORS:** Clearwater Largo Dunedin Bd. of Realtors, St. Petersburg BOR, Gulf Beach BOR, Pasco BOR, FL RE Exchangors, GA RE Exchangors, INTEREX, The Academy of RE; **EDUC:** BS, ME, 1948, Univ. of MI; **MIL SERV:** US Army Air Corp, Pilot/1st Lt., 7 Air Medals, 2 DFC's; **OTHER ACT & HONORS:** Past Pres., founding Dir. and current Dir. of our local YMCA; **HOME ADD:** 709 Harbor Is., Clearwater, FL 33515, (813)442-1491; **BUS ADD:** 1878 Drew St., Clearwater, FL 33515, (813)446-8504.

EDMUNDS, Kenneth E.——**B:** Jan. 16, 1927, Salt Lake City, UT, *Owner*, Kenneth E. Edmunds, Realtor; **PRIM RE ACT:** Broker, Consultant, Developer, Owner/Investor, Instructor, Property Manager, Syndicator; **SERVICES:** Investment Counseling; Synd. of Comml. & Indus. Props.; Props. Mgmt. and Tax Deferred Real Prop. Exchanges; **REP CLIENTS:** Devel., RE Brokers; **PROFL AFFIL & HONORS:** Realtors Assns., Contra Costa Bd.; CA Assn. of Realtors; Nat. Assn. of Realtors, CCIM, RNMI, NAR Member of the Nat. Soc. of Exchange Counselors (SEC); **EDUC:** BS, 1974, Mgmt., RE, Golden Gate Univ. (BS); Univ. of UT; **EDUC HONORS:** Skull & Bones, Jr. Soc., Univ. of UT; **MIL SERV:** Army 1946-48; 50-52; 65-67, Col., Air Medal w/3 Oak Leaf Clusters; **OTHER ACT & HONORS:** Rotary Club of Alamo, CA, Past Pres., 1978-79; **HOME ADD:** 54 Winding Glen, Danville, CA 94526, (415)837-2026; **BUS ADD:** 1910 Olympic Blvd.,

Suite 205, Walnut Creek, CA 94596, (415)930-9111.

EDWARDS, Barry A.——B: Oct. 24, 1945, San Mateo, CA, *RE Mgr.*, McCall Properties Inc. (A wholly owned sub. of McCall Oil & Chemical Corp); **PRIM RE ACT:** Developer, Property Manager, Owner/Investor; **PREV EMPLOY:** Prudential Ins. Co. of Amer. 1976-80; **EDUC:** BA, 1968, Wesleyan Univ.; **GRAD EDUC:** MBA, 1976, RE, Fin., Stanford Grad. School of Bus.; **BUS ADD:** 808 SW 15th Ave., Portland, OR 97205, (503)228-2600.

EDWARDS, Daniel P.——B: Apr. 15, 1940, Enid, OK, *VP*, Cole, Helox, Tolley, Edwards & Keene, P.C.; **PRIM RE ACT:** Attorney, Owner/Investor, Instructor, Syndicator; **SERVICES:** Legal counseling in RE and synd. MA; **PROFL AFFIL & HONORS:** CO Bar Assn.; ABA; RESSI; **EDUC:** BA, 1962, Univ. of OK; **GRAD EDUC:** JD, 1965, Harvard Law School; **EDUC HONORS:** Phi Beta Kappa, Magna Cum Laude; **OTHER ACT & HONORS:** Lecturer in Law, Colorado Coll., Who's Who in the West, Who's Who in Amer. Law; **HOME ADD:** 5 Cheyenne Mountain Blvd., CO Springs, CO 80903, (303)635-0244; **BUS ADD:** 3 South Tejon, Colo Springs, CO 80903, (303)473-4444.

EDWARDS, David A.——B: May 26, 1937, Canton, OH, *Exec. Dir.*, Fairfax Cty. Econ. Devel. Auth.; **OTHER RE ACT:** Econ. devel., bus. promotion (local govt.); **SERVICES:** One stop source of detailed market RE and devel. data; **REP CLIENTS:** Bus. considering the possibility of locating or expanding their operations in Fairfax Cty., VA, Realtors, builders, and devels. of comml. and indus. RE; **PREV EMPLOY:** Dir. of Long Range Plans, Fairfax Co., VA; **PROFL AFFIL & HONORS:** NAIOP, IDRC, NCUED, ULI, ABDC, SIDC, APA; **EDUC:** B Chem., 1959, Chem. Engrg., Purdue Univ.; **GRAD EDUC:** MP, 1966, City & Reg. Planning, Univ. of NC; **MIL SERV:** USN, Lt.; **HOME ADD:** 2000 Lakewinds Dr., Reston, VA 22091, (703)860-1169; **BUS ADD:** 8330 Old Courthouse Rd., Suite 800, Vienna, VA 22180, (703)790-0600.

EDWARDS, David R.——*Secy.*, Cessna Aircraft; **PRIM RE ACT:** Property Manager; **BUS ADD:** PO Box 1521, Wichita, KS 67201, (316)685-9111.*

EDWARDS, Donald L.——B: Aug. 19, 1947, Lexington, KY, *VP*, The Kissel Co., Lexington; **PRIM RE ACT:** Lender; **SERVICES:** FHA, VA, Conv. mort.; **PREV EMPLOY:** Citizens Fidelity Mortg. Co.; **PROFL AFFIL & HONORS:** Lexington MBA, NY State MBA, Past Pres. Lex. MBA, 1976; **EDUC:** BBA, 1971, Fin., Eastern KY Univ.; **BUS ADD:** 373 Waller Ave., Lexington, KY 40504, (606)254-8051.

EDWARDS, George D.——B: July 11, 1934, Providence, RI, *RE Broker, Comml.*, Hurwit and Simons, Realtors, Comml.; **PRIM RE ACT:** Broker, Consultant; **SERVICES:** Office leasing, local banks, urban instns.; **REP CLIENTS:** Maj. ins. & other nat. corps., as well as indiv. investors; **PREV EMPLOY:** City mgr. HUD., back-to-city promotion, counseling & mortgaging; **PROFL AFFIL & HONORS:** Intl. City Mgmt. Assoc., Realtor; **EDUC:** BA, 1955, Govt., Psych, French, Wesleyan Univ., CT; **GRAD EDUC:** MBA, 1959, Local State Govt. Admin., Univ. of PA; **EDUC HONORS:** Fels Inst. of Local and State Govt.; **MIL SERV:** USN Res., Lt., 1955-57; **HOME ADD:** 142 Whiting Ln., W. Hartford, CT 06119, (203)236-5128; **BUS ADD:** 125 LaSalle Rd., W Hartford, CT 06107, (203)561-2340.

EDWARDS, H. William——B: Aug. 22, 1937, Newark, NJ, *Dir., Corp. RE*, Amer. Aggregates Corp.; **PRIM RE ACT:** Broker, Consultant, Engineer, Developer, Builder, Owner/Investor, Instructor, Real Estate Publisher; **SERVICES:** RE & human behavior seminars, RE consulting, resid. & comml. devel.; **PROFL AFFIL & HONORS:** NJ Soc. of Profl. Planners; NJ Soc. of Profl. Engrs.; Nat. Assn. of Realtors, Lic. Profl. Planner; Lic. Profl. Land Survey; RE Broker; **EDUC:** 1962, Engrg., Newark Coll.; **GRAD EDUC:** 1979, OH State Univ.; **MIL SERV:** US Army; Sgt.; **HOME ADD:** 7418 Rt. 49 N., Greenville, OH 45331; **BUS ADD:** Garst Ave., Greenville, OH 45331, (513)548-2111.

EDWARDS, Harry L.——B: Apr. 30, 1948, Kansas City, KS, *Pres.*, H.L. Edwards Realty Co.; **PRIM RE ACT:** Broker, Consultant, Syndicator; **SERVICES:** Brokerage of multi-family and comml. prop.; **REP CLIENTS:** Indiv. investors in multi-family and comml. prop.; **PROFL AFFIL & HONORS:** RESSI; IREM, CPM; **EDUC:** BA, 1971, Bus. Admin., Ottawa Univ.; **BUS ADD:** 7225 Prospect, Kansas City, MO 64132, (816)363-1700.

EDWARDS, James A.——B: Nov. 11, 1947, Gallipolis, OH, *Atty.*, Edwards & Edwards; **PRIM RE ACT:** Attorney; **SERVICES:** Deed, title insurance, litigation; **REP CLIENTS:** Fairfield Fed. S&L Assn. of Lancaster, OH; BankOhio Nat. Bank; **PROFL AFFIL & HONORS:** OH State Bar Assn.; ABA; AZ Bar Assn.; Fairfield Cty. Bar Assn.; **EDUC:** BA, 1970, Econ., OH Wesleyan; **GRAD EDUC:** JD, 1974, Univ. of MI; **EDUC HONORS:** Phi Beta Kappa, Cum Laude; **MIL SERV:** USAR; **OTHER ACT & HONORS:** Asst. Prosecuting Atty., Fairfield Cty., OH, 1979 to present; **HOME ADD:** 360 Kemper Ave., Lancaster, OH 43130, (614)687-0440; **BUS ADD:** 136 E. Main St., Lancaster, OH 43130, (614)687-5803.

EDWARDS, Kenneth G.——B: Nov. 6, 1943, Alhambra, CA, *Sr. VP & Sr. Credit Officer*, Wells Fargo Bank, RE Ind. Grp.; **PRIM RE ACT:** Banker; **SERVICES:** Construction loans and mortgage warehousing; **PROFL AFFIL & HONORS:** Urban Land Inst.; **EDUC:** BS, 1967, Bus. Admin., CA State Univ. at Los Angeles; **GRAD EDUC:** MBA, 1969, Bus. Admin. - Fin., Univ. of S. CA; **BUS ADD:** 770 Wilshire Blvd., Los Angeles, CA 90017, (213)683-7365.

EDWARDS, Mark B.——B: Nov. 14, 1939, Asheville, NC, *Atty.*, Berry, Hogewood, Edwards & Freeman, P.A.; **PRIM RE ACT:** Attorney; **SERVICES:** All legal services, tax analysis; **REP CLIENTS:** Inst. lenders, devel., owners; **PROFL AFFIL & HONORS:** Amer. Coll. of Probate Counsel; **EDUC:** AB, 1961, Math., Duke Univ.; **GRAD EDUC:** JD, 1963, Law, Duke Univ., Sch. of Law; **EDUC HONORS:** Phi Beta Kappa, Order of the Coif; **MIL SERV:** US Army, Sgt.; **OTHER ACT & HONORS:** Bd. of Mgrs., The Methodist Home for the Aged., Inc.; **HOME ADD:** 2326 Whilden Ct., Charlotte, NC 28211, (704)366-4873; **BUS ADD:** Suite 3601, One NCNB Plaza, Charlotte, NC 28280, (704)374-1566.

EDWARDS, Norma——B: Apr. 14, 1930, Bartlett, IA, *Dir. of Key RE School; Broker-Assoc. (salesperson)*, Key Real Estate Co., Council Bluffs Branch Office; **PRIM RE ACT:** Broker, Instructor; **SERVICES:** Brokerage and schooling; **REP CLIENTS:** Resid. and comml. clients all price ranges - represent corporate relocation clients; instr. for pre-license training and sales-training classes; **PREV EMPLOY:** Public school teacher for 15 years; **PROFL AFFIL & HONORS:** WCR; **EDUC:** BS, 1970, Educ., Univ. of NE at Omaha; **EDUC HONORS:** Cum Laude; **HOME ADD:** 330 Spencer Ave., Council Bluffs, IA 51501, (712)323-9728; **BUS ADD:** 229 S. Main St., Council Bluffs, IA 51501, (712)328-3133.

EDWARDS, Richard——B: Oct. 29, 1947, MD, *Gen. Partner*, Amsted Associates; **PRIM RE ACT:** Syndicator; **SERVICES:** Prop. mgmt., investment counseling, devel.; **REP CLIENTS:** Indivs.; **PROFL AFFIL & HONORS:** AICPA, CPA; **EDUC:** BA, 1968, Econ., Univ. of CA, Santa Barbara; **GRAD EDUC:** MBA, 1970, Fin., Univ. of OR; **HOME ADD:** 1628 Durango Ave., Los Angeles, CA 90035, (213)552-4900; **BUS ADD:** 1801 Century Park East, Suite 730, Los Angeles, CA 90067, (213)552-4900.

EDWARDS, Roger A.——B: Aug. 11, 1944, Decatur, IL, *VP*, West Shell, Inc. Realtors, Comml./Indus. Div.; **PRIM RE ACT:** Consultant; **OTHER RE ACT:** Acquisitions; **SERVICES:** Brokerage, leasing, consulting, feasibility & asset mgmt. analysis; **REP CLIENTS:** Indiv. & instnl. investors and users; **PROFL AFFIL & HONORS:** RNMI; Nat. Assn. of Review Appraisers; Amer. RE & Urban Econ. Assn., CCIM; CRA; Omega Tau Rho; **EDUC:** BA, 1966, Humanities, Wheaton Coll.; **GRAD EDUC:** MA, 1970, Emory Univ.; **HOME ADD:** 6714 Miami Bluff, Cincinnati, OH 45227, (513)271-5184; **BUS ADD:** Three E. Fourth St., Cincinnati, OH 45202, (513)721-4200.

EDWARDS, Stephen Allen——B: July 12, 1953, Battle Creek, MI, *Assoc.*, Pepper, Hamilton & Scheetz; **PRIM RE ACT:** Attorney; **PROFL AFFIL & HONORS:** Amer., PA, WI, & MI Bar Assns.; **EDUC:** BA, 1975, Philosophy, Univ. of MI; **GRAD EDUC:** JD, 1978, Univ. of MI; **EDUC HONORS:** High Honors, Grad. with High Distinction, James B. Angell Scholar, Max H. Cutcheon Award, Grad. Cum Laude; **HOME ADD:** 517 S. 6th St., Philadelphia, PA 19147, (215)627-0958; **BUS ADD:** 123 S. Broad St., Philadelphia, PA 19109, (215)893-4553.

EDWARDS, Weston E.——B: May 13, 1934, Flushing, NY, *COB*, Merrill Lynch Realty Assoc. and Merrill Lynch Relocation Mgmt.; **OTHER RE ACT.** Parent Co. for a nationwide network of full-service RE firms; **PREV EMPLOY:** Pres. and Founder, TICOR Relocation Mgmt. Co.; **PROFL AFFIL & HONORS:** Chmn. Nat. Advisory Council, Grad. School of Mgmt., Brigham Young Univ.; **EDUC:** BS, 1954, Bus. Admin., Brigham Young Univ.; **GRAD EDUC:** MBA & DBA, 1958, 1961, Harvard Univ. Grad. School of Bus. Admin.; **EDUC HONORS:** Baker Scholar; received MBA with High Distinction; **MIL SERV:** USAF,1st Lt.; **OTHER ACT & HONORS:** former member of Econ. Advisory Bd. of Dept. of Commerce, Served on research faculty of Harvard Bus. School (1958-61); **HOME ADD:** 95 Ferris Hill Rd., New Canaan, CT 06840, (203)966-0651; **BUS ADD:** Four Landmark Sq., Stamford, CT 06901, (203)356-1400.

EFFINGER, Charles H.W., Jr.——**B:** Dec. 28, 1935, Baltimore, MD, *VP*, The Equitable Trust Co., Comml. Banking; **PRIM RE ACT:** Banker, Lender, Instructor; **SERVICES:** RE fin.; **PREV EMPLOY:** The Rouse Co. (James W. Rouse & Co., Inc.); **PROFL AFFIL & HONORS:** MBA (Wash., DC & MD); Baltimore Bd. of Realtors; Nat. Assn. of Indus. & Office Parks; **EDUC:** BS, 1961, Econ., Loyola Coll.; **GRAD EDUC:** 1964, Law, Univ. of Baltimore; **MIL SERV:** USMC; Cpl.; Good Conduct; **HOME ADD:** 7301 Yorktowne Dr., Towson, MD 21204, (301)286-6809; **BUS ADD:** PO Box 1556, Baltimore, MD 21203, (301)547-4513.

EGAN, John——**B:** May 15, 1910, Chicago, IL, *RE Consultant*, Macy's CA; **PRIM RE ACT:** Broker, Attorney, Consultant; **PROFL AFFIL & HONORS:** Dir. CA Bus. Props. Assn., Tr., Golden Gate Univ., SF, Former Trustee ICSC; **EDUC:** BS, 1932, Teaching, De Paul Univ.; **GRAD EDUC:** JD, 1936, John Marshall Law School; MA, 1940, NW Univ.; **MIL SERV:** USN, Lt. Comdr., Pres. Unit Citation; **HOME ADD:** 35 Locksly Ln., San Rafael, CA 94901, (415)454-0699; **BUS ADD:** PO Box 7888, San Francisco, CA 94120, (415)393-3360.

EGAN, Joseph V., III——**B:** Sept. 28, 1941, Staten Island, NY, *Managing Partner*, Wright Egan Assoc.; **PRIM RE ACT:** Broker, Developer, Builder, Owner/Investor, Property Manager, Syndicator; **EDUC:** Bucknell, 1963; **MIL SERV:** USAR, Sgt.; **HOME ADD:** 5 Martins Cir., Newtown Sq., PA 19073, (215)353-5943; **BUS ADD:** 500 E. Lancaster Ave., Saint Davids, PA 19087, (215)964-9282.

EGAN, Michael M., III——**B:** Jan. 9, 1943, Jacksonville, FL, *Pres.*, RF & D Corp.; **PRIM RE ACT:** Developer, Owner/Investor, Syndicator; **PREV EMPLOY:** Mort. Banker, McElvain-Reynolds Mort. Bankers, Chicago, IL; **EDUC:** AB, 1965, English Lit., Georgetown Univ., Washington DC; **OTHER ACT & HONORS:** Pres., Goodman Theatre Bd. of Dirs., Chicago; **HOME ADD:** 1450 N. Astor St., Chicago, IL 60610; **BUS ADD:** RE Development, PO Box N-438, Northfield, IL 60093.

EGBERT, Clark R.——**B:** Jan. 1, 1942, Salt Lake City, UT, *Realtor*, John Hall & Associates, Comml. & Resid.; **PRIM RE ACT:** Broker, Owner/Investor, Property Manager; **SERVICES:** Resid. & comml. sales, prop. mgmt.; **REP CLIENTS:** Indiv. investors and raw land speculators; **PREV EMPLOY:** US Govt. - IRS; **PROFL AFFIL & HONORS:** Phoenix Bd. of Realtors, AZ Assn. of Realtors; **MIL SERV:** USMC, Cpl.; **HOME ADD:** 6501 N. Black Canyon, Phoenix, AZ 85015, (602)992-4485; **BUS ADD:** 6501 N. Black Canyon, Suite 03, Phoenix, AZ 85015, (602)242-6377.

EGELHOFF, David C.——**B:** Dec. 15, 1948, Milwaukee, WI, *Pres.*, Macadam Forbes, Inc., Comml. Brokerage Co.; **PRIM RE ACT:** Broker; **SERVICES:** Comml. RE Brokerage; **PREV EMPLOY:** Coldwell Banker Comml. Brokerage Co.; **EDUC:** BA, 1971, Bus., Mktg. & Fin., Univ. of WI; **MIL SERV:** USAF; **OTHER ACT & HONORS:** Multnomah Athletic Club, Univ. Club, Portland Golf Club; **HOME ADD:** 8025 SW Maple, Portland, OR 97225; **BUS ADD:** 5441 SW Macadam Ave., Portland, OR 97201.

EGGERS, Richard L.——**B:** June 15, 1942, Princeton, IL, *Area Devel. Supervisor*, IL Power Co.; **PRIM RE ACT:** Consultant, Developer, Instructor; **SERVICES:** Assist clients in their expansion efforts; **REP CLIENTS:** Anchor Hocking, Owens IL, Ralston Purina, Chromolloy Amer. Corp., Coca-Cola; **PREV EMPLOY:** Corp. Research Analyst, Montgomery Ward & Co.; **PROFL AFFIL & HONORS:** IL Devel. Council, Gr. Lakes Area Devel. Council, Amer. Econ. Devel. Council, CID; **EDUC:** BS, 1965, Econ., N. IL Univ.; **OTHER ACT & HONORS:** Decatur C of C, Decatur Youth Hockey Assn.; **HOME ADD:** 485 Robinson Ave., Decatur, IL 62521, (217)428-9630; **BUS ADD:** 500 S. 27th St., Decatur, IL 62525, (217)424-6801.

EGGLESTON, James Duane, Jr.——**B:** Nov. 22, 1955, Alva, OK, *Gen. Counsel*, Preferred Properties Corp.; **PRIM RE ACT:** Attorney; **PREV EMPLOY:** Seay, Gwinn, Crawford, Mebus & Blakeney, 1980-1982; **PROFL AFFIL & HONORS:** ABA; State Bar of TX; Dallas Bar Assn.; ABA Sections of: Taxation, Real Property, Probate and Trust, Corporate, Banking and Bus.; **EDUC:** BS, 1977, Bus., OK Christian Coll.; **GRAD EDUC:** JD, 1980, RE/Securities, Univ. of KS; **EDUC HONORS:** Magna Cum Laude; Who's Who in Amer. Universities; Student Senate Treas., Order of the Coif; KS Law Review; **OTHER ACT & HONORS:** Turnpike Church of Christ, Deacon; US Tax Court - Admitted to Practice; Legal Counsel to Turnpike Christian School; **HOME ADD:** 1505 Canterbury Ct., Grand Prairie, TX 75050, (214)641-6932; **BUS ADD:** 4230 L.B.J. Freeway, Ste. 207, Dallas, TX 75234, (214)387-4460.

EGUINA, Steven G.——*Exec. VP*, Diversified Prop., Inc.; **PRIM RE ACT:** Syndicator, Property Manager, Owner/Investor; **SERVICES:** Gen. Part. for Investment Clients, Provides Mgmt. to Investment Grps. & Third Parties; **PREV EMPLOY:** VP, Fox & Carsicadon Financial Corp.; Tax Staff, Arthur Anderson & Co.; **EDUC:** BS, 1970, Bus. Admin./Acctg., CA State Univ. of Hayward, CA; **GRAD EDUC:** MBA, Bus. Admin./Fin., CA State Univ. at Hayward; **MIL SERV:** US Army, Military Police, Cpl.; **BUS ADD:** 18952 MacArthur Blvd., Suite 400, Irvine, CA 92715, (714)833-7767.

EHMER, Robert G.——**B:** Jan. 10, 1921, Dubuque, IA, *Sr. VP*, College Park Corp., RE; **PRIM RE ACT:** Broker, Developer, Owner/Investor, Property Manager, Insuror; **PROFL AFFIL & HONORS:** State of IN RE Broker; Marion Cty. State of IN Gen. Contractor; **EDUC:** BS, 1942, Econ./Mech. Engr., Purdue Univ.; **MIL SERV:** USN; Lt.s.g., Pacific Theater, 7 Battle Stars, Philippine Theater, 3 Battle Stars; **HOME ADD:** 201 Bluffs Cir., Noblesville, IN 46060, (317)877-3941; **BUS ADD:** 3500 DePauw Blvd., Indianapolis, IN 46268, (317)871-4394.

EHN, C. Lennart——**B:** Feb. 2, 1941, Hartford, CT, *Mgr., Headquarters Project*, International Telecommunications Satellite Org.; **PRIM RE ACT:** Engineer, Architect, Developer, Builder, Property Manager; **PREV EMPLOY:** VP, Oxford Devel. 1977-1980; Proj. Mgr. Aberthaw Const. 1975-1976; Kay-Locke, Inc. 1973-1975; Morse/Diesel 1969-1973; **PROFL AFFIL & HONORS:** Chi Epsilon, Hon. Civil Engrg. Frat.; **EDUC:** BSCE, 1963, Structures/Const., MIT; **GRAD EDUC:** MS, 1964, Const. Mgmt., Stanford Univ.; **EDUC HONORS:** Chi Epsilon, Hon CE Frat; **HOME ADD:** 9245 Three Oaks Dr., Silver Spring, MD 20901, (301)587-1035; **BUS ADD:** 490 L'Enfant Plaza SW, Washington, DC 20024, (301)488-0184.

EICHHORN, Richard E.——**B:** Aug. 16, 1946, Sioux City, IA, *Prop. Mgt. and Devel.*, Oxford Props., Inc.; **PRIM RE ACT:** Developer, Property Manager; **PREV EMPLOY:** Asst. VP - IDS Mort. Devel. Co.; **PROFL AFFIL & HONORS:** BOMA; IREM; ICSC, Cert. Prop. Mgr.; **EDUC:** BA, 1969, Mktg., St. Cloud State Univ.; **GRAD EDUC:** Mgmt. Internship Program, 1969-1970, Mgmt., Amer. Mgmt. Assn.; **OTHER ACT & HONORS:** Pres. Milwaukee Ave. Home Owners Assn.; **HOME ADD:** 2115 22nd Ave. S., Minneapolis, MN 55404, (612)375-9106; **BUS ADD:** 400 Baker Bldg., Minneapolis, MN 55402, (612)372-1574.

EICHLER, Eric Y.——**B:** Aug. 4, 1935, Newark, NJ, *Pres., Chmn. of the Bd.*, The Linpro Co.; **PRIM RE ACT:** Developer, Builder, Owner/Investor, Property Manager; **SERVICES:** Consulting, mgmt., const., land devel.; **PREV EMPLOY:** Lincoln Prop. Co.; The Austin Co.; **PROFL AFFIL & HONORS:** Nat. Realty Comm.; Nat. Multi Housing Council; ULI; **EDUC:** Philosophy-Religion, Dartmouth Coll.; **HOME ADD:** 1061 Waterloo Rd., Berwyn, PA 19312, (215)647-1749; **BUS ADD:** Irwin Bldg. Gulph Rd., King of Prussia, PA 19406, (215)265-5700.

EICHLER, Sol Alexander, Esq.——**B:** Mar. 25, 1915, NJ, *Counsellor at Law of NJ*, Sol Alexander Eichler; **PRIM RE ACT:** Attorney, Owner/Investor, Syndicator; **PROFL AFFIL & HONORS:** Comm. on Intl. RE Law of the World Assn. of Law; **EDUC:** 1935, Univ. of NC; **GRAD EDUC:** LLB, 1938, Rutgers Univ.; NY Univ. School of Grad. Law, School of Intl. Law - Peace Palace, The Hague, Holland; **HOME ADD:** Claridge House One, Claridge Dr., Verona, NJ 07462, (201)239-5605; **BUS ADD:** 744 Broad St., Newark, NJ 07102, (201)622-5678.

EIDELMAN, Gene——**B:** June 20, 1956, Russia, *Partner*, First Pacific Group; **PRIM RE ACT:** Consultant, Developer, Owner/Investor, Property Manager, Syndicator; **SERVICES:** Synd. of resid. investment prop., investment counseling, prop. mgmt.; **REP CLIENTS:** Indiv. investors in comml. props.; **PROFL AFFIL & HONORS:** Atlanta Owners & Mgrs. Assn.; Beverly Hills Bd. of Realtors; **BUS ADD:** 5775 Peachtree-Dunwoody Rd. Ste. 200E, Atlanta, GA 30342, (404)255-6954.

EIGEL, Christopher J.——**B:** May 22, 1945, Evanston, IL, *Sr. VP & Gen. Mgr.*, Koenig & Strey, Inc.; **PRIM RE ACT:** Broker, Owner/Investor, Instructor; **OTHER RE ACT:** Relocation Assistance; **SERVICES:** Full resid. RE serv.; **REP CLIENTS:** Merrill Lynch Relocation Mgmt.; Abbott Laboratories; Allstate Insurance Co.; **PREV EMPLOY:** The Northern Trust Co., 1969-1974; **PROFL AFFIL & HONORS:** NAR; RNMI; Member of RE Advisory Comm., Oakton Community Coll., GRI; **EDUC:** 1967, Liberal Arts, Econ., Univ. of IL; **GRAD EDUC:** MBA, 1969, Mktg., Univ.of Chicago; **EDUC HONORS:** James Scholar; Grad. with Honors, Pillsbury Fellow; **MIL SERV:** US Army National Guard, Sgt.; **HOME ADD:** 630 Windsor Road, Glenview, IL 60025, (312)729-1262; **BUS ADD:** 999 Waukegan Rd., Glenview, IL 60025, (312)729-5050.

EINHORN, Stephen E.——B: June 25, 1943, NY, *Partner*, Mertz, Einhorn & Associates; **PRIM RE ACT:** Broker, Consultant; **SERVICES:** Specialists in Mergers and Acquisitions and Appraisals of mfg., retail and distrib. activities; concentrating in the Midwest; **PREV EMPLOY:** 1964-1975 VP of Adelphi Indus., a manufacturer of paints, adhesives and coatings; **PROFL AFFIL & HONORS:** Nat. Assn. of Merger and Acquisition Consultants; **EDUC:** BA, 1964, Chem., Cornell Univ.; **GRAD EDUC:** Masters, 1966, Chem. Engrg., Brooklyn Polytech; 1965, Wharton Grad. School; **HOME ADD:** 8049 North Links Way, Milwaukee, WI 53217, (414)351-3169; **BUS ADD:** 2401 N. Mayfair Rd., Suite 104, Milwaukee, WI 53226, (414)258-2288.

EINIG, Richard J.——B: Jan. 6, 1951, St. Louis, *Pres.*, Einig & McGuire, Inc.; **PRIM RE ACT:** Broker, Appraiser, Property Manager, Owner/Investor; **REP CLIENTS:** Bank of St. Louis-Various investors, Dealing in Comml. & investment prop.; **PREV EMPLOY:** Ira E. Berry, Inc., Realtors Sr. VP; **PROFL AFFIL & HONORS:** IREM (CPM) NAIFA, Mgr. of the Yr. IREM, Million Dollar Round Table-NAHB; **MIL SERV:** US Army, Sgt.; **OTHER ACT & HONORS:** 2nd VP Tr. Normandy Osteopatic Hospitals, St. Louis; Dir. RE Bd. of Metropolitan St. Louis; Dir. & Member Exec. Comm. MO Assn. Realtors; **HOME ADD:** 84 Forest Crest, Chesterfield, MO 63017, (314)469-1419; **BUS ADD:** 11820 Tesson Ferry Rd., St. Louis, MO 63128, (314)849-3900.

EISEN, Dr. Dennis——B: Nov. 18, 1935, Brooklyn, NY, *Pres.*, Dennis Eisen & Assoc.; **PRIM RE ACT:** Consultant, Owner/Investor; **OTHER RE ACT:** Computer software devel.; **SERVICES:** Customized RE & mort. computer software packages; **REP CLIENTS:** Major realtors, govt. agencies, mort. lenders, synds., housing devel. corps.; **PROFL AFFIL & HONORS:** Amer. RE & Urban Econ. Assn., The Inst. of Mgmt Scis.; **EDUC:** BS, 1956, Engrg., NYU; **GRAD EDUC:** PhD, 1965, Applied Math., Adelphi Univ.; **HOME ADD:** 1612 Auburn Ave., Rockville, MD 20850, (301)762-1474; **BUS ADD:** 1612 Auburn Ave., Rockville, MD 20850, (301)762-1441.

EISENBERG, Harry——B: Apr. 10, 1941, NYC, *VP*, O'Keefe & Eisenberg of Westchester Inc.; **PRIM RE ACT:** Broker; **SERVICES:** RE investments sales & consultant broker; **REP CLIENTS:** Specializing in the sale of props. leased to the US Post Office; **PROFL AFFIL & HONORS:** Pres.-'CID' Dir. of Realty Bd.; **EDUC:** Bus. Admin., Baruch School of Bus. Admin., CCNY; **GRAD EDUC:** BBA, Bus.; **MIL SERV:** USMC, 1963-1970, Sgt.; **HOME ADD:** Guinea Rd., North Salem, NY 10509, (914)961-6262; **BUS ADD:** 646 Tuckahoe Rd., Yonkers, NY 10710.

EISENBERG, Lawrence D.——B: July 3, 1943, NY, NY, *Partner*, Hess Segall Guterman Pelz & Steiner; **PRIM RE ACT:** Attorney; **SERVICES:** Counseling and representation of clients; **REP CLIENTS:** Owners, investors & lenders, both indiv. & inst.; **PREV EMPLOY:** Gen. council, Feist & Feist, NJ; Marshall, Bratter, Greene, Allison & Tucker, NYC; **PROFL AFFIL & HONORS:** NYS Bar Assn.; Panel of Arbitrators, Amer. Arbitration Assn.; **EDUC:** BA, 1965, Poli. Sci., Syracuse Univ.; **GRAD EDUC:** JD, 1968, Cornell Law Sch.; **EDUC HONORS:** Deans List, Editor- Cornell Law Review, Phi Kappa Phi; **HOME ADD:** Vetere Pl., Mt. Kisco, NY 10549, (914)241-0270; **BUS ADD:** 230 Park Ave., New York, NY 10169, (212)689-2400.

EISENBERG, Leo——B: July 24, 1921, Kansas City, MO, *Chmn. of the Bd.*, Leo Eisenberg & Co. Realtors; **PRIM RE ACT:** Broker, Owner/Investor, Insuror, Property Manager, Syndicator; **SERVICES:** Sales, leases and devel. of comml. & indus. RE props.; joint ventures, investments, prop. mgmt., ins.; **PROFL AFFIL & HONORS:** Intl. Council of Shopping Ctrs., State Dir., MO & KS, 1969-1973; RNMI; BOMA, Dir., 1959-1960; Apt. Owner's & Mgr's. Assn.; IREM; FIABCI; Intl. Trader's Club; NAR; Nat. Assn. of RE Investment Funds; MO Assn. of Realtors; RE Bd. of KS City, MO, Dir., 1967-1969, Only person in the hist. of RNMI to receive both top annual awards; Snyder Trophy (1974) for Exchange-of-the-yr. and Campbell Trophy (1972) RE transaction of the yr.; **MIL SERV:** US Marine Corps, Staff Sgt.; **OTHER ACT & HONORS:** Member and Former Chmn. of Bd., Zoning Adjustment of Kansas City, 1965-1975; Greater Kansas City Sports Commn., 1970 1973; Kansas City C of C; Honorary Col. of Gov. Hearnes (SO) staff, 1965-1972; Mayor's Corps of Progress, 1971-1973; Bd. of Dir., Heart of Amer. Eye Ctr., Kansas City, 1954-1973; Honorary Bd. Dir., Rockhurst Coll., Kansas City, 1967-1973; Red Coaters of Kansas City Chiefs, Dir., 1970-1973; **HOME ADD:** 1226 W. 64th Terr., Kansas City, MO 64113, (816)523-5899; **BUS ADD:** 1101 Walnut, Suite 800, Kansas City, MO 64106, (816)221-8000.

EISINGER, Errol——B: June 18, 1945, NY, NY, *VP*, Pyms-Suchman RE Co., Investment Div.; **PRIM RE ACT:** Broker, Syndicator, Developer, Property Manager, Owner/Investor; **SERVICES:** Devel. and synd. of comml. props.; prop. mgmt.; **PREV EMPLOY:** Cost Accountant, Bahama Cement Co. (Subs. of US Steel); Banking, Atl. Nat. Bank; **PROFL AFFIL & HONORS:** IREM, RE Assn. of Profls., CPM; **EDUC:** BSBA, 1967, Acctg. and Fin., Univ. of FL; **OTHER ACT & HONORS:** Civitan; **HOME ADD:** 14565 SW 75th St., Miami, FL 33183, (305)382-2320; **BUS ADD:** 9205 So. Dixie Hwy., Miami, FL 33156, (305)667-6461.

EISNER, Ralph H.——B: Aug. 11, 1930, Milwaukee, WI, *Deputy Cost Chief*, US Dept. of HUD, Cost Branch; **PRIM RE ACT:** Consultant, Engineer, Appraiser, Lender; **PREV EMPLOY:** First WI Mort. Co. 1971-1978; Amer. Appraisal Co. (Boeckh Div.) 1967-1971; **PROFL AFFIL & HONORS:** Amer. Soc. of Appraisers; Amer. Assn. of Cost Engrs., ASA (Sr. member); Cert. Cost Engr.; **EDUC:** 1954, Constr. Technol., Milwaukee Tech. Inst./Chicago Tech.; **MIL SERV:** US Army, Cpl 1951-1953; **HOME ADD:** 4979 N. 107th St., Milwaukee, WI 53225, (414)464-1698; **BUS ADD:** 744 N. 4th St., Milwaukee, WI 53203, (414)291-1057.

EKER, Andrew H.——B: May 7, 1940, Seattle, WA, *Partner*, EG Enterprises/Gamel Homes, Inc.; **PRIM RE ACT:** Developer, Builder, Owner/Investor; **PREV EMPLOY:** M-B Contracting Co., Inc. - VP Gen. Mgr. 1963-1981; **EDUC:** BA, 1963, Const. Mgmt., Univ. of WA; **HOME ADD:** 1901 Parkview Circle, Anchorage, AK 99504, (907)276-0632; **BUS ADD:** 2702 Gambell St., Suite 202, Anchorage, AK 99503, (907)279-0574.

EKHOLM, Vicki F.——B: June 16, 1938, Houston, TX, *VP - Southwest*, Omnia Properties, Inc.; **PRIM RE ACT:** Property Manager; **OTHER RE ACT:** RE salesperson; **SERVICES:** Supervision of income producing props.; search for acquisitions; buying and selling of income producing props.; **REP CLIENTS:** Investors (indiv. and inst.) in comml. props.; **PREV EMPLOY:** Asst. Mgr. 248 Unit Apt. prop. for 1 1/2 yrs. - Mgr. of same 1 yr.; Prop. supervisor for 2000 apt. units and 56,000 sq. ft. of comml. space for 5 years; **PROFL AFFIL & HONORS:** Houston Apt. Assn. - National Apt. Assn., Candidate for CPM; **EDUC:** BA, 1960, Foreign Language, Rice Univ.; **EDUC HONORS:** Best Pledge-Owen Wister Literary Soc.; **OTHER ACT & HONORS:** Houston Livestock Show and Rodeo Comm. person - 15 years; **HOME ADD:** 5030 Autumn Forest Dr., Houston, TX 77091, (713)688-0357; **BUS ADD:** 8989 Westheimer, Suite 306, Houston, TX 77063, (713)780-9849.

EKLOF, Phil——B: Sept. 14, 1928, Los Angeles, CA, *Pres.*, Southwest Property Research; **PRIM RE ACT:** Consultant, Appraiser; **SERVICES:** RE consultation and valuation; **REP CLIENTS:** Nat. Corps., City, Cty., State and Fed. Govts., Local Devel.; **PREV EMPLOY:** VP, RE Research Corp. 1969-1979; Dir. of Appraisals, Econ. Research Assocs. 1979-1981; **PROFL AFFIL & HONORS:** Member of the AIREA; MAI; **EDUC:** BA, 1953, Econ. and Bus. Admin., Univ. of CA at Los Angeles; **GRAD EDUC:** MBA, 1959, RE and Fin., Univ. of Southern CA; **MIL SERV:** US Army; Sgt.; Good Conduct; **OTHER ACT & HONORS:** Past Pres., Lone Star High School Rodeo Assn.; Member, Dallas Hist. Landmark Preservation Comm.; **HOME ADD:** 6131 Royal Crest Dr., Dallas, TX 75230, (214)692-1658; **BUS ADD:** 7616 LBJ Frwy., Dallas, TX 75240, (214)960-0888.

EKLUND, Douglas N.——B: May 17, 1930, Cumberland, WI, *Rgnl. Exec. VP*, Crocker Port. Co., Crocker Nat. Corp.; **PRIM RE ACT:** Banker, Lender; **OTHER RE ACT:** Mort. Banker, RE Finance; **SERVICES:** Placement of permanent & const. fin.; **PREV EMPLOY:** Amer. Fletcher Mort. Co., MA Mutual Life Ins. Co., Metropolitan Life Ins. Co.; **PROFL AFFIL & HONORS:** Mort. Bankers of Amer., Intl. Council of Shopping Ctrs., Nat. Assn. of Indus. and Office Parks; **EDUC:** BS, 1952, Econ., Univ. of WI, Hamline Univ.; **GRAD EDUC:** Masters, 1955, Hist., Univ. of Frankfurt (Germany), Univ. of MD; **MIL SERV:** US Army, Staff Sgt.; **HOME ADD:** 1008 Tuckahoe, Indianapolis, IN 46260, (317)255-0506; **BUS ADD:** 9100 Meridian Pl., 20 E. 91st St., Indianapolis, IN 46240, (317)844-4944.

ELAFROS, Bernard——*Treas.*, Commerce Clearing House, Inc.; **PRIM RE ACT:** Property Manager; **BUS ADD:** 4025 W. Peterson Ave., Chicago, IL 60646, (312)583-8500.*

ELAM, Gene——*Pres.*, Pacific Lumber Co.; **PRIM RE ACT:** Property Manager; **BUS ADD:** 1111 Columbus Ave., San Francisco, CA 94133, (415)771-4700.*

ELANDER, William August——B: July 31, 1934, Worcester, MA, *Lawyer, Conveyancer*, Self-employed; **PRIM RE ACT:** Attorney; **OTHER RE ACT:** Conveyancer; **SERVICES:** RE title research leading up to & including transfer & mort. of RE; **REP CLIENTS:** All lawyers and banks in Worcester Cty., title cos. in Worcester Cty. not exclusively for one bank; **PROFL AFFIL & HONORS:** MA Conveyancers Assn.; New England Land Title Assn.; ABA; **EDUC:**

AB, 1956, Amer. Hist., Harvard Univ.; **GRAD EDUC:** JD, 1961, Law, Boston Univ., School of Law; **MIL SERV:** US Army; Spec. 2, 1956-1958; **OTHER ACT & HONORS:** Central Electric Railfans Assn.; Soc. of American Baseball Research; Intl. Naval Research Org.; US Naval Inst.; CO Reailroad Hist. Found., Inc.; Thursday Night League (basketball); **HOME ADD:** 3 Roseland Rd., Worcester, MA 01609, (617)752-3515; **BUS ADD:** 2 Court House, Worcester, MA 01608, (617)754-4078.

ELCOCK, Ronald M.——B: May 21, 1943, Trinidad, WI, *Econ. Devel. Spec.*, NAACP, Economic Development; **PRIM RE ACT:** Broker, Assessor; **SERVICES:** Tech. Asst. RE: planning and implementation of econ. devel. projects. Prop. Mgr. RE: my own investments in housing. RE sales which include both resid. and comml. as well as FL communities; **PREV EMPLOY:** Bushwick Stuyvesant Heights Rehab Ctr: planning as well as securing fin. RE: the rehab. of resid. buildings.; AWI Consultants, Inc: economic Devel. project.; **PROFL AFFIL & HONORS:** Nat. Assn. of Redevel. Officals (NAHRO) Ctr. for Community Econ. Devel.; **EDUC:** BA, 1967, Poli. Sci., Econ., Central State Univ.; **GRAD EDUC:** MA, 1969, Poli. Sci., Secondary Educ., Atlanta Univ.; **OTHER ACT & HONORS:** Trustee, Townhouse Intl. School; Bd. Member, Fulton Commons Revitalization Corp.; **HOME ADD:** 515 Macon St., Brooklyn, NY 12233, (212)574-6916; **BUS ADD:** 1790 Broadway, New York, NY 10019, (212)245-2100.

ELFSTROM, Scott——B: Dec. 25, 1948, St. Paul, MN, *Pres.*, Key Prop. Mgmt. Co.; **PRIM RE ACT:** Broker, Owner/Investor, Property Manager; **PROFL AFFIL & HONORS:** IREM, CPM; **EDUC:** AA, AS, BA, BS, 1972, Engrg. Mgmt., Univ. of WI; **OTHER ACT & HONORS:** CPM; **HOME ADD:** 728 W. Cty. Rd. C, Roseville, MN 55113; **BUS ADD:** 728 W. Cty. Rd. C., Roseville, MN 55113, (612)483-8381.

ELKINS, George W.——B: Nov. 30, 1899, Sante Fe, NM, *COB*, George Elkins Co.; **PRIM RE ACT:** Broker, Syndicator, Developer, Property Manager, Lender, Owner/Investor, Insuror; **SERVICES:** Comml. Sales & Leasing, Resid., Escrow, Mort. Loan Prop. Mgmt., Mort. Banking, Devel. Synd.; **REP CLIENTS:** Various Ins. Cos.; Private Indivs.; **PROFL AFFIL & HONORS:** L.A. Realty Bd.; Beverly Hills Realty Bd.; CA RE Assn.; Nat. Assn. of RE Bds., Realtor of the Yr. - 1974; Man of the Yr. - 1978; **EDUC HONORS:** Awarded Hon. Doctorate of Laws by Pepperdine Univ. in 1971; **MIL SERV:** US Army '18; **OTHER ACT & HONORS:** Bel-Air Bay Club; Men's Garden Club; Balboa Club; Econ. Round Table; Amer. Educ. League; Newcomen Soc.; Bd. of Regents, Pepperdine Univ., Tr. CA State Parks Found.; Americanism Educ. League - Tr.; **HOME ADD:** 632 N. Alta Dr., Beverly Hills, CA 90210, (213)276-3062; **BUS ADD:** 499 N. Canon Dr., Beverly Hills, CA 90210, (213)272-3456.

ELLBERGER, Stan——B: Feb. 9, 1943, Bronx, NY, *Pres. & Chmn. of the Bd.*, Sterling National Realty Group, Inc. & Equity Sharing Plan Corp.; National School of RE, RE Sales Profile Div.; **PRIM RE ACT:** Consultant; **OTHER RE ACT:** Franchisor, Licensor, Trainer & Author; **SERVICES:** Mktg. Training, advertising, creative fin. & recruiting; **REP CLIENTS:** programs to RE Brokers; **PREV EMPLOY:** Exec. VP, The Sterling Thompson Group 1972-80; **PROFL AFFIL & HONORS:** NAR; RE Leaders of Amer., Bd. of Advisors, Author of 'Proven Success Methods for Listing & Selling RE'; **EDUC:** BS, 1965, Chem. Engrg., Drexel Univ., Phila, PA; **EDUC HONORS:** Blue Key Scholarship; **HOME ADD:** 18 Framingham Rd., Ocean, NJ 07712, (201)493-8519; **BUS ADD:** Ocean Park Profl. Bldg., 1602 Lawrence Ave., Ocean, NJ 07712, (201)493-2110.

ELLEDGE, Harold W.——B: Apr. 7, 1937, Como, TX, *VP*, Synergism, Inc., Senter, Realtors Comml.; **PRIM RE ACT:** Broker, Instructor, Syndicator, Consultant, Developer, Property Manager, Owner/Investor; **SERVICES:** Investment Counseling, Synd., Prop. Mgmt.; **PROFL AFFIL & HONORS:** RNMI, IREM, CCIM, CPM; **EDUC:** BS, 1958, Mathematics, E. TX State Univ.; **GRAD EDUC:** MS, 1966, Mathematics, E. TX State Univ.; **HOME ADD:** 3486 Santa Monica, Abilene, TX 79605, (215)698-2116; **BUS ADD:** One Energy Sq., Suite 20 C, Abilene, TX 70604, (915)676-5725.

ELLENBERGER, Robert——B: Oct. 23, 1929, Wells Cty., IN, *Pres.*, Ellenberger Bros, Inc.; **PRIM RE ACT:** Broker, Consultant, Appraiser, Developer, Property Manager; **OTHER RE ACT:** Auctioneer; **SERVICES:** All under above classifications; **PROFL AFFIL & HONORS:** IN & Nat. Auctioneers-Realtors Assns.; FLI; Adams, Jay, Wells Co. Bd. of Realtors; Ft. Wayne Bd. of Realtors; Fort Wayne MLA; Adams, Jay, Wells Country MLS., Cert. Auctioneers Inst.; (CAI) Designation; **MIL SERV:** IN Natl. Guard, SFC; **OTHER ACT & HONORS:** Bluffton C of C, Fort Wayne BBB; **HOME ADD:** R.R. No. 3, Bluffton, IN 46714, (219)824-0148; **BUS ADD:** 130 1/2 West Market St., Bluffton, IN 46714, (219)824-2426.

ELLENBOGEN, Bernard——B: Feb. 15, 1929, Brooklyn, NY, *Partner*, Ellenbogen, Freeman & Co., P.C.; **OTHER RE ACT:** CPA; **SERVICES:** Acctg., analysis and tax services; **REP CLIENTS:** RE brokerage and mgmt. and RE owners; **PROFL AFFIL & HONORS:** AICPA, NY State Soc. of CPA's, NY Bar Assn., CPA; **EDUC:** BBA, 1951, Acctg., City Coll. of NY; **GRAD EDUC:** LLB, 1957, Law, Brooklyn Law School; **MIL SERV:** US Army, Cpl.; **HOME ADD:** 425 E. 79th St., New York, NY 10021, (212)737-2106; **BUS ADD:** 225 W. 34th St., New York, NY 10022, (212)564-7500.

ELLENBOGEN, Steven W.——B: June 5, 1943, Baltimore, MD, *Regional Devel. Mgr.*, CMD (Central Manufacturing District); **PRIM RE ACT:** Developer, Owner/Investor; **SERVICES:** Indus. and office land devel., speculative and build-to-suit bldgs.; **REP CLIENTS:** Nat., regional and local indus. and light mfg. users; **PREV EMPLOY:** Del E. Webb Corp., Phoenix, AZ, 1973-1974; Charter Properties, Inc., Chicago, IL, 1975-1981; **PROFL AFFIL & HONORS:** NAR; Assn. of Indus. RE Brokers; Nat. Assn. of Indus. & Office Parks; **EDUC:** BS, 1965, Gen. Engrg., US Mil. Acad., West Point; **GRAD EDUC:** MBA, 1972, Harvard Bus. School; **MIL SERV:** US Army, Capt.; **HOME ADD:** 456 Belmont Ave., Chicago, IL 60657, (312)281-7168; **BUS ADD:** One First National Plaza, Suite 4950, Chicago, IL 60603, (312)726-2232.

ELLER, James J.——*Atty.*, Pitto & Ubhaus, P.C.; **PRIM RE ACT:** Attorney; **SERVICES:** Purchase & sale of real property, leases, fin., partnerships bus. counseling, contracts, devel.; **REP CLIENTS:** Devel., investors, hotel owners and operators; **EDUC:** BA, 1974, Biology, Univ. of CA at San Diego; **GRAD EDUC:** JD, 1977, Law, Univ. of Santa Clara; **EDUC HONORS:** Cum Laude; **BUS ADD:** 2 N. 2d St., San Jose, CA 95113, (408)287-9001.

ELLIAS, Myra——*VP Gen. Couns. & Secy.*, Monfort of Colorado, Inc.; **PRIM RE ACT:** Attorney, Property Manager; **BUS ADD:** Box G, Greeley, CO 80632, (303)353-2311.*

ELLIOT, Joseph K.——B: Oct. 19, 1925, Boston, MA, *Sr. VP*, Galbreath-Ruffin Corp., Construction and Devel. Grp.; **OTHER RE ACT:** Contracting and leasing consultation; Project Devel., Civil Engr.; **SERVICES:** Project devel., project mgr., construction consultant for office buildings and hotels; **REP CLIENTS:** Banks, insurance cos., mfr. firms, natural resource firms, transp. cos., fin. firms and investors in major office bldgs. and hotels; **PREV EMPLOY:** Walter Kidde Constructors Inc., 1950-1952; The Thompson Construction Corp., 1946-1950; **PROFL AFFIL & HONORS:** Sustaining Member, ULI, Profl. Engr., NY State; **EDUC:** BCE, 1947, Civil Engrg., Rensselaer Polytech. Inst., Troy, NY; **EDUC HONORS:** Phalanx; **MIL SERV:** USN, CEC, Const. Btln., Lt.; **OTHER ACT & HONORS:** Trustee, Sunnyside S&L Assn., Irvington, NY; Pres./Bd. of Trustees, Irvington Presbyterian Church, Irvington, NY; Comm. Chmn., Westchester-Putnam Council, Boy Scouts of Amer.; **HOME ADD:** 45 Circle Dr., Irvington-on-Hudson, NY 10533, (914)591-7952; **BUS ADD:** 633 Third Ave., New York, NY 10017, (212)986-4888.

ELLIOT, Raymond H.——*Pres.*, Federal Home Loan Bank of Boston; **PRIM RE ACT:** Banker; **BUS ADD:** PO Box 2196, Boston, MA 02106, (617)223-3206.*

ELLIOTT, David L.——B: Oct. 14, 1943, Orange, NJ, *Owner*, Elliott Investments; **PRIM RE ACT:** Consultant, Developer, Owner/Investor, Syndicator; **EDUC:** BS, 1967, Math., Univ. of AZ; **OTHER ACT & HONORS:** Treas., The Wayflete School, Portland, ME; **BUS ADD:** 22 Ash St., Hollis, NH 03049, (603)465-7333.

ELLIOTT, Jon A.——B: July 23, 1948, Lincoln, NE, *Atty. at Law*, Nelson & Harding, Corporate Comml. Section Head, Omaha Office; **PRIM RE ACT:** Attorney; **SERVICES:** Acquisition, lease, subdiv., fin., comml. & indus. RE; **REP CLIENTS:** Lending instns., investors, devels., mfrs., contractors and suppliers; **PREV EMPLOY:** Lic. RE salesman 1969-1970; **PROFL AFFIL & HONORS:** ABA (Member, Sects. on RE, Corps., Banking & Bus. Law); NE State Bar Assn., Exec. Comm., Young Lawyers Sec., NSBA (1974-1978); **EDUC:** BA, 1970, His., Eng., Poli. Sci., Univ. of NE; **GRAD EDUC:** JD, 1972, Prop. and Bus. Law, Univ. of NE; **EDUC HONORS:** JD with Distinction; **MIL SERV:** USAR 1972-1980, Capt.; **OTHER ACT & HONORS:** Tr./Clerk, Sanitary & Improvement Dist. No. 155 Douglas Cty., NE 1973-present; SW Sertoma Club of Omaha, NE - President; **HOME ADD:** 3717 N. 114 Circle, Omaha, NE 68164, (402)493-1415; **BUS ADD:** 800 Nebraska Savings Bldg., 1623 Farnam St., Omaha, NE 68102, (402)348-0832.

ELLIOTT, Ward——B: June 9, 1932, Nicholasville, KY, *Broker/Part.*, Western Realty Co.; **PRIM RE ACT:** Broker, Instructor, Consultant, Owner/Investor; **SERVICES:** Co. offers RE specialists in resid., comml., & agri.-auction props.; **PREV EMPLOY:** HEW, 1956-1968;

HUD, 1968-1972; **PROFL AFFIL & HONORS:** MBR, NAR, KAR, 1980 KY Realtor of Yr.; Past Pres. of Local Bd.; Dir. KY Assn. of Realtors; CRB; **EDUC:** BS, 1956, Geog. & Biol., W. KY Univ.; **GRAD EDUC:** Fellowship N.I.P.A., 1965-66, Woodrow Wilson School of Public & Intl. Affairs, Princeton Univ.; **OTHER ACT & HONORS:** Dir., KY C of C, KY Coll.; **HOME ADD:** R.D. #3, Box 164, Bowling Green, KY 42101, (502)782-3189; **BUS ADD:** 1411 Scottsville Rd., Bowling Green, KY 42101, (502)781-1234.

ELLIOTT-GRUEN, Kate——B: Jan. 28, 1954, *Associate*, Laventhol & Horwath; **PRIM RE ACT:** Consultant; **SERVICES:** RE Advisory Serv.; **EDUC:** 1976, Purdue Univ.; **GRAD EDUC:** MD, 1979, RE Appraisal/Investment Analysis, Univ. of WI; **HOME ADD:** 6810 Broadway Terr., Oakland, CA 94611, (415)654-7156; **BUS ADD:** 50 California St., Ste. 2450, San Francisco, CA 94111, (415)989-0110.

ELLIS, Arlen O.——*Prin.*, Ellis & Co.; **PRIM RE ACT:** Broker, Consultant, Owner/Investor; **SERVICES:** Indus. Comml. brokerage (emphasis on office leasing); **REP CLIENTS:** Instnl. and Pvt. investors & users; **PREV EMPLOY:** CA Licensed RE Broker since 1955; **PROFL AFFIL & HONORS:** BOMA, Past Sec./Treas. BOMA Intl.; Past Pres. BOMA San Francisco; Past Pres. San Francisco/ Chap. of IREM; **OTHER ACT & HONORS:** Advisory Bd. San Francisco Salvation Army; **BUS ADD:** PO Box 516, Sausalito, CA 94965, (415)332-7924.

ELLIS, Delbert R.——B: June 11, 1932, Newberg, OR, *Pres.*, AMFAC Mort. Corp.; **PRIM RE ACT:** Developer, Lender; **SERVICES:** Residential Land Dev., Seller/Servicer Residential & Comml. Mort.; **REP CLIENTS:** Life Ins. Co., Ins. Cos. S&L; **PREV EMPLOY:** Ernst & Ernst (Ernst & Whinney) Staff Acct. to Mgr.; **PROFL AFFIL & HONORS:** MBAA, OR MBA, AICPA, OSCPA; **GRAD EDUC:** BS, 1955, Bus. Admin., OR State Univ.; **MIL SERV:** USAF 1955-57, Capt.; **OTHER ACT & HONORS:** Bd. of Gov., MBA 1980-1981, Pres., OMBA 1977-1979; **HOME ADD:** Rte. 2, Box 40A, Newberg, OR 97132, (503)538-6081; **BUS ADD:** 2525 SW Third Ave., Portland, OR 97201, (503)243-1705.

ELLIS, Dorothy J.——B: Aug. 20, 1938, Philadelphia, PA, *VP*, Rich Port, Realtor; **PRIM RE ACT:** Broker; **SERVICES:** Full service, resid. spec.; **PREV EMPLOY:** Baird & Warner, Realtor, Assoc., 1968-70; **PROFL AFFIL & HONORS:** NW Sub. Bd. of Realtors, Chicago Bd. of Realtors, IL Assn. Realtors, NAR, RNMI, IREF, Women's Council, CRB, CRS, GRI; **EDUC:** 1956, ME Twp. HS, Park Ridge, IL; 1957, NW Univ., Chicago; 1963, Univ. of Miami, FL; 1978, Harper Jr. Coll., Palatine; 1981, DePaul Univ., Chicago; **OTHER ACT & HONORS:** Elk Grove Twp. Reg. Republican Org., Dep. Comml. & Precinct Capt., 1979-; Bd. Dir. YMCA (Park Ridge), 1978-81; Daughters of Amer. Revolution; Adv. Counsel & Guest lecturer for Oakton Comm. Coll., Biography in Marquis Who's Who in the World, Who's Who of Amer. Women, Who's Who in Fin. & Indus., Bd. of Dirs. REEF of IAR (RE Educ. Found. of IL Assn. Realtors) 1981-83, Chmn. Political Involvement Comm. of IAR (IL Assn. Realtors) 1980-82, Articles published: 1978 "Illinois Realtors Headlines", 1979 *Real Estate Today*, 1981 *Real Estate Advertiser*; **HOME ADD:** 461 W. Kathleen Dr., Des Plaines, IL 60016, (312)439-6353; **BUS ADD:** 210 W. Northwest Hwy., Arlinton Hts., IL 60004, (312)253-3800.

ELLIS, F. Ross——B: Dec. 18, 1907, Cleveland, OH, *Owner*, Ross Ellis Appraisal Serv.; **PRIM RE ACT:** Appraiser; **SERVICES:** Appraisal of all types of RE; **REP CLIENTS:** Major Corps., Attys., Govt. Bodies & Pvt. Indivs.; **PREV EMPLOY:** Nat. City Bank of CLeveland, OH 14 yrs.; **PROFL AFFIL & HONORS:** Cleveland Area Bd. of Realtors, OH Assn., Nat. Assn. IFA, CRB, CRS, GRI, IFAS; **MIL SERV:** USMC, Good Conduct Medal, Expert Rifleman; **OTHER ACT & HONORS:** Masonic Lodge, Gaston G. Allen #629, Lake Erie Consistory, Al Koran Shrine; **HOME ADD:** 2021 King James Pkwy. #217, Westlake, OH 44145, (216)871-1867; **BUS ADD:** 17825 Detroit Ave., Lakewood, OH 44107, (216)228-7402.

ELLIS, Kenneth A.——B: Jan. 29, 1935, US, *Dep. for Operations*, Parish of Trinity Church, Operations Div; **PRIM RE ACT:** Broker, Property Manager, Owner/Investor; **PREV EMPLOY:** Kenneth D. Laub Co., Inc., VP; **PROFL AFFIL & HONORS:** RE Bd. of NY, Downtown Lower Manhattan Assn.; **EDUC:** BA, Math/Physics, Wagner Coll., Staten Is.; **MIL SERV:** USN; **HOME ADD:** 56 Copperleaf Terr, Staten Is., NY 10304, (212)351-5545; **BUS ADD:** 74 Trinity Place, New York, NY 10006, (212)285-0814.

ELLIS, Richard C.——B: June 7, 1947, Waterbury, CT, *VP*, Main Street South Corp., The Hydraulic Co.; **PRIM RE ACT:** Consultant, Lender, Developer, Builder, Property Manager; **PREV EMPLOY:** Dir. 4 yrs., Middlesex Cty. Devel. Council; Pres., Bridgeport Econ. Devel. Corp.; **EDUC:** BA, 1969, Econ., Hist., Univ. of CT; **OTHER ACT & HONORS:** Fin. Advisory Bd., City of Bridgeport; **HOME ADD:** 26 Overland Ave., Bridgeport, CT 06606; **BUS ADD:** 835 Main St., Bridgeport, CT 06601, (203)367-6421.

ELLIS, Robert B.——B: Mar. 19, 1954, De Witt, AR, *Loan Officer*, First Nat. Bank in Stuttgart; **PRIM RE ACT:** Consultant, Appraiser, Banker, Owner/Investor; **SERVICES:** Home and home improvement loans, const. loans; **PREV EMPLOY:** Examiner with Fed. Home Loan Bank Bd. (1976-77), First Fed. S&L Stuttgart (1977-79); **PROFL AFFIL & HONORS:** Mort. Bankers Assn. of AR; **EDUC:** BSBA, 1976, Fin. & Banking, Investments, Acctg., Univ. of AR at Fayetteville; **OTHER ACT & HONORS:** Lions Club, Baptist Men's Club; **HOME ADD:** 1901 Cherry St., Stuttgart, AR 72160, (501)673-6497; **BUS ADD:** PO Box 908, Stuttgart, AR 72160, (501)673-3545.

ELLIS, Terrance C.——B: Nov. 1, 1927, Buffalo, NY, *Branch Mgr.*, Great Western Industrial Realty, Los Angeles Office; **PRIM RE ACT:** Consultant, Builder, Owner/Investor; **PROFL AFFIL & HONORS:** AIREA; CA Assn. of Realtors; NAR; **EDUC:** Fin., RE, Const., Loyola Univ., LA; UCLA; **MIL SERV:** USN; **HOME ADD:** 402 El Centro #9, South Pasadena, CA 91030, (213)682-3276; **BUS ADD:** 926 Stanford Ave., Los Angeles, CA 90021, (213)627-2711.

ELLIS, William C.——B: Nov. 3, 1944, LeRoy, KS, William C. Ellis, CPA; **OTHER RE ACT:** CPA; **SERVICES:** Income tax planning & services, fin. planning, acctg. systems and serv.; **REP CLIENTS:** Devel., bldrs., prop. mgrs. & brokers, owners & investors; **PROFL AFFIL & HONORS:** AICPA, CPA Soc., KS Soc. of CPA's; **EDUC:** BBA, 1965, Acctg., Emporia State Univ., Emporia, KS; **OTHER ACT & HONORS:** Rotary Intl.; **HOME ADD:** 1129 Michigan Blvd., Zion, IL 60099, (312)662-8272; **BUS ADD:** 1129 Michigan Blvd., Zion, IL 60099, (312)662-8272.

ELLISON, Kenneth C.——B: Aug. 2, 1933, Wyandotte, OK, *Partner*, Ellison, Gresham & Nelson; **PRIM RE ACT:** Attorney; **SERVICES:** Legal servs. in RE; **PREV EMPLOY:** Self Employed since 1962; **PROFL AFFIL & HONORS:** Tulsa Cty. & OK Bar Assn.; Tulsa Cty. & OK Soc. of CPA's, CPA; **EDUC:** Bus. Admin., 1962, Acctg., Tulsa Univ.; **GRAD EDUC:** LLB, 1965, Law, Tulsa Univ., Coll. of Law; **EDUC HONORS:** Dean's Honor Roll; **MIL SERV:** US Army; Cpl.; 1953-1955; **HOME ADD:** 5016 E. 39th Pl., Tulsa, OK 74135; **BUS ADD:** 4815 S. Harvard, Suite 534, Tulsa, OK 74135, (918)749-1673.

ELLMAN, Martin——B: Feb. 19, 1942, Bronx, NY, *Pres.*, Ellman Enterprises; **PRIM RE ACT:** Consultant, Owner/Investor, Property Manager, Syndicator; **SERVICES:** Investment Counseling, Devel. and Synd. of Resid. Props., Prop. Mgmt.; **REP CLIENTS:** Indiv. investors; **PREV EMPLOY:** IBM Corp.; **PROFL AFFIL & HONORS:** Lowry-Nickerson Assn.; **EDUC:** BS, 1963, Mktg., NY Univ.; **GRAD EDUC:** MBA, 1968, Mgmt. Information Systems, Amer. Univ.; **BUS ADD:** PO Box 5814, Bethesda, MD 20814, (202)363-5397.

ELLSWORTH, David G.——B: Jan. 20, 1941, Los Angeles, CA, *Sr. Partner, RE Dept.*, Memel, Jacobs, Pierno & Gersh, RE; **PRIM RE ACT:** Attorney; **OTHER RE ACT:** Complete legal services pertaining to all types of RE matters, including local, state, nat. and intl. real prop. transactions; fin., acquisition, devel., disposition and major landlord-tenant representation; **REP CLIENTS:** Real Estate Developers and Investors both domestic & foreign, Banks, mort. bankers, RE investment trusts and other instnl. investors; McDonnell Douglas Corp., MDC Realty Co.; Welton Becket Assoc. (arch. & engrs.); Lloyd's Bank; Wells Faro & Co.; Wells Fargo Realty Services, Inc.; Grupo Industrial ALFA, S.A. and CASOLAR; Fondo Nacional de Fomento al Turismo (FONATUR); Societe Tahitienne d'Amenagement de Condominiums; **PREV EMPLOY:** Law firm of Meserve, Mumper & Hughes; **PROFL AFFIL & HONORS:** ABA; State Bar of CA; Los Angeles Cty. Bar Assn.; Amer. Land Devel. Assn. (Dir.); ULI (Member, Exec. Grp. of Recreational Devel. Council); Nat. Timeshare Council; Devel. Council of Pacific Area Travel Assn.; and International Council of American Land Devel., LLB/JD; **EDUC:** BS, 1962, Bus. Admin., Univ. of So. CA; **GRAD EDUC:** LLB/JD, 1965, Law, Univ. of So. CA; **OTHER ACT & HONORS:** Chmn., Bd. of Commnrs., Los Angeles Cty. Housing Authority; Los Angeles Cty. Beach Advisory Commn.; Commn. of the CA's; Los Angeles County Community Development Commission; US/Mexico Quadriparte Commission; Wilshire Ctry. Club; The Vintage Club; San Carlos Ctry. Club; Malibu Riding and Tennis Club; **HOME ADD:** 31974 Pacific Coast Hwy., Malibu, CA 90265, (213)457-2365; **BUS ADD:** 1801 Century Park E., 25th Floor, Los Angeles, CA 90067, (213)556-2000.

ELLSWORTH, John D.——B: Nov. 13, 1944, Clarion, IA, *Part.*, Kutak, Rock & Huie; **PRIM RE ACT:** Attorney; **SERVICES:** Firm provides full range of legal serv., specialize in RE tax and securities; **REP CLIENTS:** Underwriters, devel. and synd. of RE and oil and gas programs; **PREV EMPLOY:** SEC 1972-1974; **PROFL AFFIL &**

HONORS: DC and BE Bar Assns., RESSI, ABA; **EDUC:** BA, 1966, Gov. Econ., Carleton Coll., Northfield, MN; **GRAD EDUC:** JD, 1969, Harvard Law School; LLM (Tax), 1974, Georgetown Univ. Law School; **EDUC HONORS:** Phi Beta Kappa, Magna Cum Laude; **MIL SERV:** USAR, Capt., Army Commendation Medal; **OTHER ACT & HONORS:** Member, Advisory Comm. to N. Amer. Securities Administrators Assn.; **HOME ADD:** 9749 Fieldcrest Dr., Omaha, NE 68114, (402)391-0104; **BUS ADD:** 1650 Farnam St., Omaha, NE 68102, (402)346-6000.

ELLSWORTH, Thomas A.——B: Nov. 19, 1938, Boston, MA, *VP, RE Operations*, The Sheraton Corp.; **OTHER RE ACT:** Adm. of Corp. Real Estate Brokerage Hotel & Motor Inns; **SERVICES:** Responsible for acquisition, disposal and financing of all Sheraton RE plus negotiation of shop leases and prop. taxes in Sheraton operated hotels; additionally through Sheraton Realty, a subsidiary of Sheraton Corp. we operate a full line brokerage service for hotels and motor inns; **PROFL AFFIL & HONORS:** Nat. Assn. of Corporate RE Executives; **EDUC:** 1961, Hotel Admin., Cornell Univ., School of Hotel Admin.; **MIL SERV:** USN, Lt.j.g.; **HOME ADD:** 9 Western Ave., Essex, MA 01929, (617)768-7513; **BUS ADD:** 60 State St., Boston, MA 02109, (617)367-3600.

ELMAN, Harvey——B: Nov. 27, 1946, Montreal, *Pres.*, Luarca Corp.; **PRIM RE ACT:** Owner/Investor; **SERVICES:** Represent substantial private clients; **REP CLIENTS:** Interested in providing equity for devel. situations; **PREV EMPLOY:** 10 Years in RE banking; Partner has const. and banking background; **EDUC:** BS, 1968, Psych., McGill Univ.; **GRAD EDUC:** MBA, 1970, Fin., Columbia Univ.; **HOME ADD:** 21 Aldred Ct., Hampstead, Que, Canada, (514)487-0323; **BUS ADD:** 1000 Sherbrooke St. W., Montreal, H3A 2R6, Que, Canada, (514)844-1061.

ELMENDORF, C. Lindsay——*Ed.*, Foundation for Cooperative Housing, FCH News Briefs; **PRIM RE ACT:** Real Estate Publisher; **BUS ADD:** 2101 L St., NW, Washington, DC 20037, (202)857-4100.*

ELMORE, Kit——B: July 12, 1947, Wheeler, IL, *Owner*, Elmore Housing Co.; **PRIM RE ACT:** Appraiser, Owner/Investor, Syndicator; **OTHER RE ACT:** Rental housing since 1969, mobile home parks, houses, apts.; **SERVICES:** Fee appraisers, synd., rentals; **EDUC:** BS, BA, 1972-1974, Soc. Sci., Univ. of NC; **MIL SERV:** USAF, A1C Sgt., Nat. Defense Serv. Medal Vietnam 1966; **HOME ADD:** Rt. 1, Box 318, Camden, NC 27921, (919)335-1078; **BUS ADD:** Rt.1, Box 318, Camden, NC 27921, (919)335-1078.

ELMORE, S. Churchill——B: Sept. 6, 1921, Wash. DC, *Part.*, Williams, Myers & Quiggle; **PRIM RE ACT:** Attorney; **SERVICES:** Legal advice to clients in respect to real prop.; representation of clients before RE comms. & before trial and appellate courts; **REP CLIENTS:** RE brokers, RE investors, builders, renovators & owners; **PREV EMPLOY:** Counsel, US House of Reps. Appropriations Comm.; Practice of Law for 31 yrs.; spec. in real prop. matters; **PROFL AFFIL & HONORS:** Amer. Law Inst., DC Judicial Conference, ABA, DC Bar; **EDUC:** BA, 1943, Liberal arts, pre-law, Wash. & Lee Univ.; **GRAD EDUC:** LLB, 1950, GNU; **MIL SERV:** US Army, Capt., Presidential Unit Citation, European Theater Ribbons; **OTHER ACT & HONORS:** DC RE Comm., 1960-71; Chevy Chase Club; **HOME ADD:** 5142 Tilden St. NW, Washington DC 20016, (202)244-8994; **BUS ADD:** 888 17th St. NW, Suite 900, Washington DC 20006, (202)333-5900.

ELROD, Paul F., Jr.——B: Nov. 18, 1944, Cleveland, TN, *Senior Appraiser*, Chattanooga Federal Service Co., Inc.; **PRIM RE ACT:** Appraiser; **SERVICES:** Resid., small comml. & indus. appraising; **PREV EMPLOY:** Mass Appraisal Firms; Appraiser Co. Assessors Office; 4 yrs.; **PROFL AFFIL & HONORS:** Soc. of RE Appraisers, SRA; **EDUC:** AS, Gen. Bus., Cleveland State Comm. Coll.; **MIL SERV:** US Navy, PO2; **HOME ADD:** Rt. 9, Box 534A, Cleveland, TN 37311, (615)472-7660; **BUS ADD:** Broad & 9th St., Chatly, TN 37402, (615)756-6161.

ELROD, W. Kenneth——*Pres.*, J. C. Bradford Properties, Inc., Affiliate of J. C. Bradford & Co.; **PRIM RE ACT:** Consultant, Developer, Syndicator; **PREV EMPLOY:** Elrod, Beal & Co., Pine St. Equity Corp.; **GRAD EDUC:** MBA, Univ. of TN; **BUS ADD:** 170 4th Ave., N., Nashville, TN 37219, (615)748-9490.

ELSEA, Richard——*Pres.*, Real Estate One Licensing Co.; **PRIM RE ACT:** Syndicator; **BUS ADD:** 29630 Orchard Lake Rd., Farmington Hills, MI 48018, (313)851-2600.*

ELTINGE, Kennard M.——B: Aug. 27, 1944, San Francisco, CA, *Pres.*, Tower RE; **PRIM RE ACT:** Broker, Syndicator, Developer, Owner/Investor; **SERVICES:** Devel. of Comml. Prop., Synd.; **REP CLIENTS:** Major devel., tenants; **PREV EMPLOY:** John Price and Assoc.; **PROFL AFFIL & HONORS:** Salt Lake Bd. of Realtors; **EDUC:** BA Poli. Sci., 1976, Intl. Relations - Econ., Univ. of UT; **MIL SERV:** USMC; **HOME ADD:** 32446 S. 1700 E, Salt Lake City, UT 84106, (801)486-2530; **BUS ADD:** 180 E. 2100 S, #101, Salt Lake City, UT 84115, (801)486-5057.

ELWOOD, George H.——B: May 19, 1927, Hancock, NY, *Atty. at Law*; **PRIM RE ACT:** Attorney; **SERVICES:** Legal; **REP CLIENTS:** The First National Bank of Hancock, Hancock, NY; Blueberry Lake, Inc.; **PROFL AFFIL & HONORS:** DE Cty. and NY Bar Assns.; ABA, Past Chmn. of Real Prop. Law Section of NY State Bar Assn.; **EDUC:** AB, 1949, Hist., Rutgers Univ., New Brunswick, NJ; **GRAD EDUC:** LLB, 2952, Fordham Univ. - School of Law, New York, NY; **MIL SERV:** USN, Seaman 1st Class (SKD); **HOME ADD:** 49 E. Main St., Hancock, NY 13783, (607)637-2645; **BUS ADD:** 10 W. Main St., Hancock, NY 13783, (607)637-4791.

ELWOOD, James C.——B: Feb. 22, 1951, Key West, FL, *Gen. Mgr.*, Arvida Corp., Arvida So.; **PRIM RE ACT:** Developer, Builder; **OTHER RE ACT:** Prop. acquisition, joint ventures; **SERVICES:** Acquisition, land improvement, const.; **PREV EMPLOY:** Dir. of Acquisitions, Arvida Corp.; Sr. Auditor, Peat, Marwick, Mitchell & Co., CPA's; **PROFL AFFIL & HONORS:** Gen. Contractor, State of FL; CPA, State of FL; **EDUC:** BS, 1972, EE, Univ. of PA; **GRAD EDUC:** MBA, 1974, Fin./Acctg., Univ. of Chicago; **EDUC HONORS:** Cum Laude; **HOME ADD:** 77 Crandon Blvd. #2-E, Key Biscayne, FL 33149, (305)361-3502; **BUS ADD:** 9400 S. Dadeland Blvd., Penthouse Suite, Miami, FL 33156, (305)667-1124.

ELY, Edward A.——B: July 22, 1947, Baltimore, MD, *Manager, Devel. & Operations*, McCormick Prop., Inc.; **PRIM RE ACT:** Developer, Builder, Owner/Investor; **SERVICES:** Office & indus. park devel. & design/build gen. contractor; **REP CLIENTS:** Gen. Instrument, Exxon, PHH, Westinghouse, Western Electric, McCormick & Co.; **PREV EMPLOY:** Exxon Co. USA 6 yrs. 1971-1976; **PROFL AFFIL & HONORS:** NAIOP, NACORE, Amer. Mktg. Assn., NAR; **EDUC:** BS, 1975, Mktg.; **GRAD EDUC:** MBA, 1980, Johns Hopkins Univ.; **EDUC HONORS:** Cum Laude, SS; **MIL SERV:** US Army, SP-5; **HOME ADD:** 1911 Clifden Rd., Catonsville, MD 21228, (301)744-4145; **BUS ADD:** 1616 McCormick Dr., Landover, MD 20785, (301)386-2500.

EMBREE, H. Gene——B: Nov. 27, 1932, Chicago, IL, *Pres.*, Teninga-Bergstrom Realty; **PRIM RE ACT:** Broker, Property Manager, Owner/Investor; **SERVICES:** RE Sales & Prop. mgmt.; **PREV EMPLOY:** Mort. banking, Heitman Mort. Co.; **PROFL AFFIL & HONORS:** NAR, IAR, IREM, RNMI, CPM, Realtor of Yr. 1979; **EDUC:** BA, 1968, RE Bus. Admin., Northwestern Univ.; **HOME ADD:** 3446 W. 218th St., Matteson, IL 60443, (312)748-1137; **BUS ADD:** 8544 S. Ashland Ave., Chicago, IL 60620, (312)779-8100.

EMERSON, Gordon E., Jr.——B: Nov. 2, 1916, Medford, MA, *Chmn.*, Bay Finance Corp. (NYSE); **PRIM RE ACT:** Developer, Property Manager, Lender, Owner/Investor; **PREV EMPLOY:** Sr. VP, John Hancock Mutual Life Ins. Co.; Exec. VP, Cabot, Cabot & Forbes Co.; **EDUC:** AB, 1940, Econ., Middlebury Coll.; **GRAD EDUC:** Adv. Mgmt. Cert., 1963, Gen. Mgmt, Harvard Bus. School; **MIL SERV:** USCG (res.); **OTHER ACT & HONORS:** Chmn., MA Housing Finance Ag., 1968-1977; Chmn., MA Home Mort. Finance Ag., 1974-1977; Chmn., Rockport Sch. Comm., Rockport, MA; Chmn., Boston Municipal Research Bur., 3 yrs; **HOME ADD:** Highland Rd. RFD 2, Box 395, S. Hampton, NH 03827, (603)394-7412; **BUS ADD:** 2 Faneuil Hall Mktpl., Boston, MA 02109, (617)742-7550.

EMERSON, Peter S.——B: Dec. 7, 1952, Annapolis, MD, *Asst. Assessor*, Assessors Dept.; **PRIM RE ACT:** Consultant, Appraiser, Instructor, Assessor; **PROFL AFFIL & HONORS:** Assn. of MA Assessors; Intl. Assoc. Assessing Officers; Assoc. Soc. of RE Appraisers; Nat. Assn. Review Appraisers, MAA; CRA; **EDUC:** BSBA, Bus. Admin., Northeastern Univ. School of Bus. Admin.; **EDUC HONORS:** Grad. with Honors; **OTHER ACT & HONORS:** Notary Public since 1978; **HOME ADD:** 32 Tremont St., Stoneham, MA 02180, (617)438-2859; **BUS ADD:** Town Hall, 1 Lafayette St., Wakefield, MA 01880, (617)245-0310.

EMERTON, Lawrence A., Sr.——B: Oct. 1, 1928, Concord, NH, *Owner*, Larry Emerton, Appraisers; **PRIM RE ACT:** Appraiser; **SERVICES:** Resid. & comml. appraisals throughout So. NH; **REP CLIENTS:** Most major banks in So. NH and many other large and medium sized clients in the area, comml., indus. & resid.; **PREV EMPLOY:** Present full time office for 10 yrs.; **PROFL AFFIL & HONORS:** Assoc. SREA, Member Manchester C of C; **EDUC:** BA, 1952, Bus. & Eng., New England Coll., Henniker, NH; **MIL SERV:** USMC; **OTHER ACT & HONORS:** Sch. Dist. Moderator/Planning

Bd., Member Indus. Council, Past Dist. Gov. of Lions Clubs of New Hampshire, Active Member Lions, Pres. of Lions Twin-State Soccer Game (NH & VT); **HOME ADD:** 5 Wallace Rd., Goffstown, NH 03045, (603)497-2158; **BUS ADD:** 69 Bay St., Manchester, NH 03104, (603)622-6020.

EMERY, James H.——**B:** Mar. 10, 1942, Whittier, CA, *Pres.*, Century 21 Emery RE Inc., Southland Fin. Corp., Coastal Counties Escrow, Orange Cty. Escrow Corp.; **PRIM RE ACT:** Broker, Lender, Owner/Investor, Insuror; **SERVICES:** Multi office resale RE Brokerage, Escrow Service, Loan Brokerage (1st & 2nd Trust Deed), Ins. Agency; **PROFL AFFIL & HONORS:** Member CAR & NAR, Member Nat. Brokers Comm. Congress of Century 21, GRI; **EDUC:** BA, 1964, Bus. Admin., Whittier Coll.; **HOME ADD:** 1307 Denise Ct., Brea, CA 92621, (714)529-4762; **BUS ADD:** Corp. Headquarters, 2545 E. Chapman Ave, Suite 200, Fullerton, CA 92631, (714)879-1101.

EMERY, Patrick G.——**B:** Apr. 3, 1950, Seoul, Korea, *VP, Leasing*, Willaims Realty Corp., Willco Props. Inc.; **PRIM RE ACT:** Broker, Developer; **SERVICES:** Office and retail leasing; **REP CLIENTS:** Cos. requiring office or retail space in Tulsa, Denver, Charlotte, Houston or Overland Park; **PREV EMPLOY:** Cushman & Wakefield; **PROFL AFFIL & HONORS:** NACORE; NAIOP; Metro. Tulsa Bd. of Realtors; **EDUC:** BA, Fin., Univ. of OK; **MIL SERV:** US Army, Sgt.; **HOME ADD:** 1527 E. 36th Pl., Tulsa, OK 74105, (918)749-6490; **BUS ADD:** PO Box 2400, Suite 3800, Tulsa, OK 74101, (918)588-2850.

EMIG, John W.——**B:** Nov. 28, 1954, Denison, OH, *VP*, Ohio Real Estate Appraisers Inc.; **PRIM RE ACT:** Appraiser; **SERVICES:** Resid. & income prop. appraising; **REP CLIENTS:** Local lenders, relocation firms; **PROFL AFFIL & HONORS:** Soc. of RE Appraisers, SRPA; **EDUC:** BBA, 1977, Fin. & RE, Kent State Univ.; **GRAD EDUC:** MBA, 1981, Kent State Univ.; **EDUC HONORS:** Summa Cum Laude; **HOME ADD:** 1183 Garth Dr., Kent, OH 44240, (216)673-4354; **BUS ADD:** 326 S. Main St., Suite 307, Akron, OH 443083, (216)253-8023.

EMMI, Joseph, Jr.——**B:** Mar. 6, 1923, Rochester, NY, *VP & Chief Appraiser*, First Nationwide Savings & Loan Assoc., Loan Div.; **PRIM RE ACT:** Broker, Consultant, Appraiser, Developer, Lender, Owner/Investor, Property Manager; **SERVICES:** Review Appraiser, RE Investment Consultant; **PROFL AFFIL & HONORS:** SREA, NARA, RE Broker; SRA; CRA; **EDUC:** AA, 1949, Bus., Econ. & Arch., E.L.A. Community Coll.; **MIL SERV:** USN, P.O., 7 Battle Stars, So. Pacific Theatre; **HOME ADD:** 12342 Brock Ave., Downey, CA 90242, (213)923-3152; **BUS ADD:** 9800 Sepulveda Blvd., Los Angeles, CA 90045, (213)642-0309.

EMPEY, Gene F.——**B:** July 13, 1923, Hood River, OR, *Owner/Mgr.*, Empey & Co., Inc.; **PRIM RE ACT:** Broker, Appraiser, Instructor, Property Manager; **SERVICES:** RE investment counselling, devel. and sales, appraising; **PROFL AFFIL & HONORS:** NAR, State Pres. CCIM, NV Chap.(3 times), CRS, GRI; **EDUC:** BS, 1949, Animal Husbandry, OR State Univ.; **GRAD EDUC:** MS, 1950, Tech. Journalism, IA State Univ.; **MIL SERV:** US Army, Capt., Inf. PTO; **OTHER ACT & HONORS:** Member, NV State Planning Bd.; Chmn., (6 yrs.) NV State Higher Education Advisory Comm., Chmn. 4-yrs.; Tahoe-Douglas C of C Pres.; Heavenly Valley Ski Club, Pres.; **HOME ADD:** 1258 Tamarack Dr., Zephyr Cove, NV 89448, (702)588-2823; **BUS ADD:** 512 S. Curry St., Carson City, NV 89701, (702)882-6000.

END, David B.——**B:** Jan. 25, 1949, Milwaukee, WI, *Relocation Coordinator*, Bruce, Barry & Gleysteen, Inc.; **PRIM RE ACT:** Broker; **SERVICES:** Residential specializing in relocation; **PROFL AFFIL & HONORS:** RNMI, WI Realtors Assn., Milwaukee Bd. of Realtors; Designations: GRI, CRB, CRS, WRA Hon. Soc. 1980, 1981; **EDUC:** BA, 1971, Poli. Sci., Marquette Univ.; **HOME ADD:** 2212 N. Lake Dr., Milwaukee, WI 53202, (414)277-0738; **BUS ADD:** 4491 N. Oakland Ave., Shorewood, WI 53211, (414)962-4413.

ENDERLE, Alan G.——**B:** Aug. 22, 1942, San Antonio, TX, *Atty.*, Kreis, Enderle, Halpert & Etter, P.C.; **PRIM RE ACT:** Attorney; **SERVICES:** Legal Counsel; **REP CLIENTS:** Jacobs, Visconsi and Jacobs; MI Natl. Bank; Homebuilders Assn. of Kalamazoo; Ltd. partnerships in the multi-family housing field; realtors, builders and devels.; **PREV EMPLOY:** Deming, Hughey, Keiser, & Allen Kalamazoo, MI (1972-1978); **PROFL AFFIL & HONORS:** State Bar of MI (RE Sect.); ABA (RE Sect.); Home Builders Assn. of Kalamazoo; Kalamazoo Cty. Bar Assn.; **EDUC:** BS, 1964, Journalism, Rutgers Univ.; **GRAD EDUC:** JD, 1972, Coll. of William and Mary; **MIL SERV:** US Army, Capt., Bronze Star, ACM, MSM; **HOME ADD:** 2513 Law Ave., Kalamazoo, MI 49008, (616)343-2831; **BUS ADD:** 800 Industrial State Bank Bldg., Kalamazoo, MI 49007, (616)383-3784.

ENDERS, W. Dean——**B:** Mar. 23, 1948, Milwaukee, WI, *Pres.*, Remanco, Inc., Subsidiary of Inland Steel; **PRIM RE ACT:** Property Manager; **SERVICES:** Mgmt. of Invest. RE; **PREV EMPLOY:** Grootemaat Co., Milwaukee,WI, VP Prop. Mgmt.; **PROFL AFFIL & HONORS:** IREM, Realtors; BOMA; NAA, CPM; Broker in WI, WV, IN; Realtor; **EDUC:** AA, 1968, Bus., Univ. W. MI, Univ. of WI; **HOME ADD:** 1636 Ferndale, Northbrook, IL 60062, (312)564-4636; **BUS ADD:** 6160 N. Cicero Ave., Chicago, IL 60646, (312)736-3136.

ENEN, David A.——**B:** Sept. 27, 1950, Lakewood, OH, *RE Analyst*, Moore Handley, Inc.; **OTHER RE ACT:** Site Selection; **SERVICES:** Site selection; sales forecasting for retail facilities; **PREV EMPLOY:** Montgomery Ward; Facilities Analyst; **EDUC:** BA, 1972, Poli. Sci./Soc., Univ. of KY; **GRAD EDUC:** M. Urban Planning & Policy, 1975, Univ. of IL - Chicago; **EDUC HONORS:** Research Assistantship; Activities: Hon. Soc. Serv. Award; **HOME ADD:** 1302 15th Ave. S., Birmingham, AL, (205)252-6013; **BUS ADD:** PO Box 2607, Birmingham, AL 35202, (205)663-8233.

ENEVER, C. Robert——**B:** Jan. 22, 1928, UK, *Exec. Officer*, Mountain Resorts, Inc.; **PRIM RE ACT:** Developer, Property Manager; **OTHER RE ACT:** Hotel Owner; **PROFL AFFIL & HONORS:** CPA; **EDUC:** BS, 1952, Econ., Univ. of London, England; **GRAD EDUC:** MBA, 1959, Fin., Northwestern Univ., Chicago; **EDUC HONORS:** With Distinction; **MIL SERV:** Brit. Army; **OTHER ACT & HONORS:** Planning Comm. Member, 2 yrs.; **HOME ADD:** Box 239, Steamboat Springs, CO 80477, (303)879-2017; **BUS ADD:** Box 6350, Steamboat Village, CO 80499, (303)879-3700.

ENGEL, Cal——**B:** Oct. 11, 1912, SD, *Exec. VP*, Aberdeen Development Corp.; **PRIM RE ACT:** Developer, Builder, Property Manager; **SERVICES:** Site selection & devel.; **PREV EMPLOY:** Public School Admin.; **PROFL AFFIL & HONORS:** AEDC; NASSP; **EDUC:** BS, 1937, Hist., Dakota Wesleyan; **GRAD EDUC:** MS, 1957, Admin., Northern State Coll.; **MIL SERV:** US Army, TSgt.; **OTHER ACT & HONORS:** Kiwanis, Lt. Gov.; Fourth Planning Bd.; **HOME ADD:** 1621 S. Lincoln, Aberdeen, SD 57401, (605)225-3023; **BUS ADD:** PO Box 1179, Aberdeen, SD 57401, (605)229-5335.

ENGEL, Donald——*Secy.*, Clow Corp.; **PRIM RE ACT:** Property Manager; **BUS ADD:** 1211 West 22nd St., Oak Brook, IL 60521, (312)325-6000.*

ENGEL, Mark F.——**B:** Apr. 11, 1947, Philadelphia, PA, *Controller*, Ralph Langsam Associates, Inc.; **PRIM RE ACT:** Broker, Developer, Owner/Investor, Property Manager, Insuror; **OTHER RE ACT:** Gen. Contractor; **SERVICES:** Prop. mgmt., rehabs.; **PROFL AFFIL & HONORS:** Bronx Bd. of Realtors, VP, Member, Tr., BP, CPM, CPA, Ins. Broker, Who's Who in Amer. Colls., Serv. Medal, Senate Key; **EDUC:** BA, 1967, Acctg., Queens Coll.; **MIL SERV:** US Army Res., S/Sgt., 1968-73; **HOME ADD:** 25 Schooner Ln., Port Washington, NY 11050, (516)883-5807; **BUS ADD:** 3550 Jerome Ave., Bronx, NY 10467, (212)881-7770.

ENGELBERG, Burt W.——**B:** Oct. 9, 1954, Harvey, IL, *Atty.*, Kamensky & Landan; **PRIM RE ACT:** Attorney; **SERVICES:** Investment advice, RE closings, tax consulting; **PROFL AFFIL & HONORS:** ABA (Section on RE, Probate and Trust Law), IL Bar Assn., and Chicago Bar Assn., CPA; **EDUC:** BS, 1976, Acctg., Univ. of IL; **GRAD EDUC:** JD, 1979, Univ. of IL; **EDUC HONORS:** Grad. with High Honors; **OTHER ACT & HONORS:** Author: "The Amer. Phoenix - New Incentives for Old Bldgs.", The Journal of RE Taxation, Spring 1980; **HOME ADD:** 2454 N. Geneva Terr., Chicago, Il 60614; **BUS ADD:** 120 S. LaSalle St., Chicago, IL 60603, (312)368-1776.

ENGELSTAD, Wendell E.——**B:** July 24, 1945, Kasson, MN, *Broker - Owner*, Westate Services; **PRIM RE ACT:** Broker, Appraiser; **SERVICES:** Farm, comml. & res. sales, farm & comml. appraising, prop. mgmt., tax consulting, acctg.; **REP CLIENTS:** Indiv., attys., lending inst., estate planners, municipalities; **PREV EMPLOY:** Research Farm Mgr., Land O'Lakes, Inc., 1969-1974; **PROFL AFFIL & HONORS:** NAR; FLI; MN Farm & Comml. Multiple, Comml. Listing Serv.; Amer. Soc. of Farm Mgrs. & Rural Appraisers; Nat. Assn. of Tax Practioners; **EDUC:** BS, 1969, Animal Sci./Agric. Econ., Univ. of MN; **OTHER ACT & HONORS:** Nat. Exchange Club, US Jaycees; **HOME ADD:** 655 20th St. N.E., Owatonna, MN 55060, (507)451-7759; **BUS ADD:** 285 SE 18th St., Owatonna, MN 55060, (507)451-4989.

ENGLANDER, Morris K.——*VP RE*, General Cinema Corp.; **PRIM RE ACT:** Property Manager; **BUS ADD:** PO Box 1000-27 Boylston St., Chestnut Hill, MA 02167, (617)232-8200.*

ENGLERT, John A.——**B:** Sept. 1, 1929, Syracuse, NY, *Broker*, Carolantic Realty, Inc.; **PRIM RE ACT:** Broker; **SERVICES:** Sales, leasing, synd., valuation of comml. & indus. props.; **REP CLIENTS:** Indivs., corps. & instnl. owners, purchasers, lessees and lessors of indus. and comml. props.; **PROFL AFFIL & HONORS:** SIR, Raleigh Bd. of Realtors, NC Indus. Devel. Assn., VP, Syracuse Bd. of Realtors (1978), VP, NY Chap. of Soc. of Indus. Realtors (1978); **EDUC:** BS, 1956, Bus. Admin. - Sales Mgmt./Advertising, Syracuse Univ.; **MIL SERV:** USN, 1948-52, PO 2nd Class, Four decorations; **OTHER ACT & HONORS:** Capital City Club of Raleigh, Chapel Hill Ctry. Club; **HOME ADD:** 4104 Glen Laurel Dr., Raleigh, NC 27612, (919)782-6068; **BUS ADD:** PO Drawer 1550, Raleigh, NC 27602, (919)832-0594.

ENGLERT, Richard G.——**B:** Jan. 19, 1932, Pittsburgh, PA, *RE Mgr.*, Englert Properties Ltd.; **PRIM RE ACT:** Appraiser, Property Manager, Insuror; **OTHER RE ACT:** Leasing mgr., devel.; **PREV EMPLOY:** Friendly Ice Cream Corp., RE Site Developer, Graham Realty Co.; **PROFL AFFIL & HONORS:** NACORE, 1981 Pres. of Pittsburgh Chap., 1979-1980 Sec./Treas.; **EDUC:** BBA, 1954, Banking/Econ., Univ. of Pittsburgh; **MIL SERV:** US Army; Military Police, 1st Lt.; **OTHER ACT & HONORS:** State of PA, Govt. Advisory Bd. for Health Care; Pittsburgh Athletic Assn.; Allegheny Club; **HOME ADD:** 235 Outlook Dr., Mt. Lebanon, PA 15228, (412)563-6016; **BUS ADD:** 235 Outlook Dr., Pittsburgh, PA 15228, (412)563-6016.

ENGLER-WIGBELS, Dixie Lee——**B:** May 15, 1939, Wadsworth, OH, *Assoc. VP*, AFCO Realty Assoc. Inc., Prop. Mgmt.; **PRIM RE ACT:** Property Manager; **OTHER RE ACT:** Leasing; **SERVICES:** Prop. mgmt., leasing, consulting lenders; **REP CLIENTS:** Instnl. and indiv. investors; **PREV EMPLOY:** Prop. Mgr., Northside Air terminal, Chamblee, GA, 1975-1979; **PROFL AFFIL & HONORS:** NAR, IREM, BOMA, Atl. Bd. of Realtors, CPM, 1980 Geo. F. Richardson Award from BOMA Atl. for outstanding contributions to Assoc., Secy. Treas. BOMA Atl., Bd. of Dir. Atl. Chap. of IREM; Officer Atl. chap. of IREM; guest lecturer GA State Univ. dept. of RE; **EDUC:** 1957; **HOME ADD:** 425 Wavetree Dr., Roswell, GA 30075, (404)993-8112; **BUS ADD:** 148 International Blvd., Suite 660, Atlanta, GA 30303, (404)659-4811.

ENGLISH, Allan J.——**B:** Nov. 3, 1925, New Britain, CT, *Partner*, Riva Ridge Assoc. & Bay Assoc.; **PRIM RE ACT:** Property Manager, Owner/Investor; **PREV EMPLOY:** US Army 1944-79; **EDUC:** BS, 1949, Military Engrg., USMA, West Point, NY; **GRAD EDUC:** MS, 1970, Intl. Affairs, GW Univ., Wash., DC; **MIL SERV:** US Army, Col.; DSSM, LM, MSM(3), ARCOM (3), PH(2); **HOME ADD:** 2916 Southwater Point Dr., Annapolis, MD 21401, (301)224-3059; **BUS ADD:** 2916 Southwater Point Dr., Annapolis, MD 21401, (301)266-5317.

ENGLISH, Jim, Jr.——**B:** Apr. 4, 1919, Vineland, NJ, *VP*, English Realty, Inc.; **PRIM RE ACT:** Broker, Consultant, Developer, Builder, Property Manager, Insuror; **OTHER RE ACT:** Mort. Broker; Title Insurance; **PREV EMPLOY:** Pres. Eng. Co., Dir. of Fairlanes, Inc.; Pres., Pocomoke Realty, HC; VP, Pioneer Title of MD; **HOME ADD:** Route 1, Box 24, Salisbury, MD 21801, (301)749-6836; **BUS ADD:** 3800 Ocean Hwy., Ocean City, MD 21842, (301)289-5366.

ENGLISH, Leonard M.——**B:** Jan. 1, 1943, Cleveland, OH, *Admin. Officer, Mgr. RE & Const.*, Central National Bank of Cleveland, RE & Const.; **PRIM RE ACT:** Broker, Consultant, Builder, Instructor, Property Manager; **OTHER RE ACT:** Chippewa Valley Realty (Lic. Broker); **SERVICES:** Negotiate all Bank RE/Coordinate Const.; **PREV EMPLOY:** 1968-1977 Manage over 2 million sq. ft. of income prop. - Mall, Shop. Ctr., Apts., Office Bldgs. & Condos.; **PROFL AFFIL & HONORS:** IREM, Nat. Assn. of Corporate RE Execs., Cleveland Area Bd. of Realtors, CPM, Designated Prop. Mgmt. Instr. for OH Assoc. of Realtors; Vice Chmn. Assoc. Bd. of Dir. Cleveland Bd. of Realtors; **EDUC:** BS, 1966, Labor Econ., OH State Univ.; **OTHER ACT & HONORS:** Mayor, Briarwood Beach, OH; VP Amer. Cancer Soc. of Medina Cty.; VP Medina Cty. Rgnl. Planning Commn.; Mentioned in Congressional Record for Making St. Patrick's Day A Legal Holiday (in Briarwood Beach, OH); **HOME ADD:** 485 Shorefield Dr., Chippwea Lake, OH 44215, (216)769-3041; **BUS ADD:** 800 Superior Ave., Cleveland, OH 44114, (216)344-5233.

ENNIS, B.M.——*VP Adm.*, United Foods, Inc.; **PRIM RE ACT:** Property Manager; **BUS ADD:** 106 Dawson Ave., Bells, TN 38006, (901)663-2341.*

ENNIS, Bruce C.——**B:** Mar. 22, 1941, Dover, DE, *Atty. at law*, Schmittinger & Rodriguez, PA; **PRIM RE ACT:** Attorney; **PROFL AFFIL & HONORS:** Kent Cty. Bar Assn., DE State Bar Assn.; **EDUC:** BA, 1963, Poli. Sci., WV Wesleyan Coll., Buckhannon, WV; **GRAD EDUC:** JD, 1966, Dickinson Sch. of Law, Carlisle, PA; **MIL SERV:** US Army, Spec. 5 (E5); **OTHER ACT & HONORS:** Wesley United Methodist Church, Dover, DE; Lecturer Wesley Coll., Dover, DE; Lecturer DE Tech. & Comm. Coll., Dover, DE; **HOME ADD:** 444 Troon Rd., Dover, DE 19901, (302)653-6773; **BUS ADD:** 414 S. State St., PO Box 497, Dover, DE 19901, (302)674-0140.

ENNIS, William M.——**B:** June 4, 1949, Philadelphia, PA, *VP*, Indus. Valley Bank & Trust Co., Const. Lending; **PRIM RE ACT:** Banker, Lender; **SERVICES:** Const. loans for indus., comml. & resid. projects; **REP CLIENTS:** RE devels.; **PREV EMPLOY:** Continental Bank, Philadelphia, PA, Const. Loan Dept., 1972-80; **PROFL AFFIL & HONORS:** Philadelphia Mort. Bankers Assn.; **EDUC:** BS, 1971, Acctg., Bus. Admin., PA State Univ.; **MIL SERV:** Army Res., SSgt.; **OTHER ACT & HONORS:** Lawncrest Comm. Assn., Penn State Alumni Assn.; **BUS ADD:** 1700 Market St., Philadelphia, PA 19103, (215)496-4496.

ENOCH, Ann——*Dir.*, TN Real Estate Commission; **PRIM RE ACT:** Property Manager; **BUS ADD:** The Doctor's Bldg., Rm 428, Church St., Nashville, TN 37219, (615)741-2273.*

ENSZ, Paul——**B:** Apr. 3, 1950, Reedley, CA, *Owner/Part.*, ERA Kings River Realtors; **PRIM RE ACT:** Syndicator, Developer, Builder, Property Manager, Owner/Investor; **SERVICES:** RE sales plus const., devel. and prop. mgmt.; **PROFL AFFIL & HONORS:** Bd. of Realtors, Multiple Listing Service, Top listing agent, 1st quarter 1981 E.R.A. RE; **EDUC:** BA, 1972, Soc. Sci., CA State Univ., Fresno; **GRAD EDUC:** Life Teaching Credential, 1973, Soc. Sci., CA State Univ.; **OTHER ACT & HONORS:** VP, Reedley C of C; Dir. Reedley Jaycees; Dir. Sunrise Kiwanis; **BUS ADD:** 1540 'G' St., Reedley, CA 93654, (209)638-9220.

EPHGRAVE, Bert., III——**B:** Aug. 19, 1948, Birmingham, AL, *VP*, First AL RE Fin., Income Prop.; **PRIM RE ACT:** Broker; **SERVICES:** Mort. banking, debt and equity placements, sales; **REP CLIENTS:** Lenders and inst. investors in comml. props., devels. and synd. of comml. props.; **PREV EMPLOY:** Prudential Ins. Co., RE Investment Dept., 1971-76; Ackerman & Co., 1976-77; **PROFL AFFIL & HONORS:** MBA; **EDUC:** BBA, 1971, RE, Fin., S. Methodist Univ.; **EDUC HONORS:** Dean's List; **HOME ADD:** 428 Paddock Ct., Mobile, AL 36608, (205)343-6665; **BUS ADD:** PO Box 9880, Mobile, AL 36609, (205)342-7562.

EPLEY, Donald R.——**B:** Jan. 30, 1942, Kingman, KS, *Prof. of Fin.*, Univ. of AR, Fin. Dept.; **PRIM RE ACT:** Consultant, Appraiser, Instructor, Real Estate Publisher; **PREV EMPLOY:** Univ. of AL, Univ. of MO, Wichita State Univ., Westminster Coll.; **PROFL AFFIL & HONORS:** AREUEA, SREA, SW Fin. Assn.; **EDUC:** BA, 1964, Econ., Math., Soc., Wichita State Univ.; **GRAD EDUC:** PhD, 1972, Urban & Reg. Econ., Univ. of MO; **OTHER ACT & HONORS:** Beta Gamma Sigma; Omicron Delta Epsilon; 1977-79 AR Realtors Assn.; Pres. Award, 1980-81 Coll. of Bus.; Distinguished Faculty Award for Research, 1975 Soc. of RE Appraisers Acad. Intern; **HOME ADD:** 2232 Sheridan, Fayetteville, AR 72701; **BUS ADD:** BA 302 Coll. of Bus., Univ. of AR, Fayetteville, AR 72701, (501)575-4505.

EPPERSON, E. Russell, III——**B:** May 3, 1947, Atlanta, GA, *VP*, Arthur Rubloff & Co., Indus. Prop. Group; **PRIM RE ACT:** Broker; **SERVICES:** Indus. RE Servs.; **REP CLIENTS:** Brinks Warehousing; Bellwether Automatic, Inc.; Atlantic Canadian Corp.; **PREV EMPLOY:** Adams-Cates Co.; **PROFL AFFIL & HONORS:** SIR; **EDUC:** BBA, 1969, Bus., Univ. of GA; **EDUC HONORS:** Varsity Football 1966-68; **HOME ADD:** 2815 Mornington Dr., Atlanta, GA 30327, (404)351-8620; **BUS ADD:** 134 Peachtree St. NW, Ste. 1500, Atlanta, GA 30043, (404)577-5300.

EPPERSON, Kraettli Q.——**B:** May 2, 1949, Ft. Eustis, VA, *Gen. Counsel, VP and Sec.*, American First Land Title Insurance Co.; **PRIM RE ACT:** Attorney; **OTHER RE ACT:** Title Ins.; **SERVICES:** Real prop. title ins.; **PREV EMPLOY:** Lawyers Title of OK City, Inc., VP and Atty.; **PROFL AFFIL & HONORS:** ABA; OK Bar Assn; OK Bar Assn. Real Prop. Section (Title Examination Standards Comm.-Vice Chairman), OK City Soc. of Title Attys.; **EDUC:** BA, 1971, Poli. Sci., Univ. of OK; **GRAD EDUC:** JD, 1978, Law, OK City Univ.; **EDUC HONORS:** Merit Scholarship, Dean's Honor Roll, Phi Delta Phi (Pres.), Nat. Order of Barristers; **MIL SERV:** US Army, Capt. (1971) (Reserves 1975-81); **HOME ADD:** 5724 NW 83rd St., OK City, OK 73132, (405)722-8910; **BUS ADD:** 133 W. Main, PO Box 25225, Oklahoma City, OK 73102, (405)270-5421.

EPSTEIN, Alvin J.——*Pres.*, Epstein Funding, Inc.; **OTHER RE ACT:** Investment and Mort. Banking and Brokerage and Corp. Prop.; **SERVICES:** Arranges equity & dept. fin. of prime income-producing; **REP CLIENTS:** Corp. prop. users, private devel. and instnl.

investor/lenders; **PROFL AFFIL & HONORS:** ICSC, MBA of NY, NYU Bus. Forum; **EDUC:** BS, 1966, Sci., Penn State; **GRAD EDUC:** MBA, 1972, Fin., NY Univ.; **EDUC HONORS:** NYU Club Award, Beta Gamma Sigma; **MIL SERV:** US Navy, Lt.; **BUS ADD:** PO Box 5003 (33 Riverside Ave.), Westport, CT 06881, (203)226-8171.

EPSTEIN, David L.——**B:** Mar. 30, 1933, Indianapolis, IN, *Pres.*, David Epstein Co., Inc. Realtors & Devels., Comml.; **PRIM RE ACT:** Broker, Consultant, Developer, Owner/Investor, Syndicator; **REP CLIENTS:** Pop Shoppes of Can., Payless, Cashways, Wendy's & Jo Jo's, Taco Bell, Steak n Shake, Burger Chef Systems, Inc., C. A. Muer Corp., Melvin Simon & Assoc., Inc., Godfather's Pizza, Inc., Indiana National Bank; **PROFL AFFIL & HONORS:** Indianapolis Bd. of Realtors, Comml. Indus. Multiple Listings; **HOME ADD:** 8921 Sourwood Ct., Indianapolis, IN 46260; **BUS ADD:** 8925 N. Meridian St., Suite 111, Indianapolis, IN 46260.

EPSTEIN, Gilbert——**B:** Oct. 13, 1929, Brooklyn, NY, *Pres.*, The Epstein Co.; **PRIM RE ACT:** Consultant, Appraiser, Developer, Owner/Investor, Syndicator; **SERVICES:** Appraisal, Const., Mgmt.; **REP CLIENTS:** Banks, Ins. Cos., Various Lenders; **PROFL AFFIL & HONORS:** AIREA; Soc. of RE appraisers, MAI, SREA; **EDUC:** BS, BPA, 1957, Univ. of AZ; **GRAD EDUC:** MBA, 1962, RE, Fin., Univ. of S. CA; **MIL SERV:** US Army, Cpl.; **HOME ADD:** 6027 Lindley Ave., #21, Tarzana, CA 91356; **BUS ADD:** 5430 Van Nuys Blvd., 303, Van Nuys, CA 91401, (213)872-1905.

EPSTEIN, Harry——*Beneficial Standard Properties, Inc.*; **PRIM RE ACT:** Developer; **BUS ADD:** 3700 Wilshire Blvd. Ste. 220, Los Angeles, CA 90010, (213)381-8766.*

EPSTEIN, Joel E.——*Sr. VP*, Apt. Mgrs. Inc.; **PRIM RE ACT:** Broker, Consultant, Developer, Owner/Investor, Instructor, Property Manager; **SERVICES:** Brokerage, Prop. Mgmt., Investment Counseling; **REP CLIENTS:** Pvt. Investors, Prop. Owners and Management Cos.; **PROFL AFFIL & HONORS:** Natl. and IN Apt. Assns., 1982 Nat. Chmn., Natl. Apartment Mgmt. Accreditation Bd.; Natl. Cert. Inst. and Speaker, Natl. Apt. Assn. Certified Apartment Mgmt. and Certified Apartment Maintainance technician; **EDUC:** BA, 1971, Pol. Sci., Crim. Justice, Psych. & Soc., IN Univ.; **GRAD EDUC:** MA & MBA in progress 1972, Clinical Psych., Butler Univ.; **MIL SERV:** USAF; **HOME ADD:** 2112 Burningtree Ln., Carmel, IN 46032, (317)846-3885; **BUS ADD:** 5480 N. Michigan Rd., Indianapolis, IN 46208, (317)255-0300.

EPSTEIN, Joseph S.——**B:** Oct. 28, 1943, Freeport, NY, *Pres. & Dir.*, First Amer. Realty Assn. Inc.; **PRIM RE ACT:** Broker; **SERVICES:** RE Fin. Sales & Consulting; **REP CLIENTS:** Lenders and indiv. or inst. investors in comml. props.; **PREV EMPLOY:** VP Prime Mort. Co. 1970-76; **PROFL AFFIL & HONORS:** Dir. Prime Motor Inns, Inc.; Dir. Cindy's Inc.; **EDUC:** BA, 1965, English and Hist., Lafayette Coll.; **GRAD EDUC:** JD, 1968, Tax and Constitutional Law, Univ. of Cincinnati; **EDUC HONORS:** Nat. Moot Court Team; **HOME ADD:** 120 N. Mountain Ave., Montclair, NJ 07042, (201)783-3791; **BUS ADD:** 1030 Clifton Ave., Clifton, NJ 07013, (201)778-7767.

EPSTEIN, Michael David——**B:** Jan. 15, 1945, Washington, DC, *Part.*, Epstein Assoc. and US Service Industries; **PRIM RE ACT:** Owner/Investor; **SERVICES:** Fin. analysis & Eval. of office bldgs. & apt. houses; **REP CLIENTS:** Various Indiv. Investors & Self.; **PROFL AFFIL & HONORS:** AOBA, PMA, Bldg. Ser. Contr. Assn., Dir. Capital Assn. of Bldg. Serv. Cntr., Cert. Bldg. Serv. Exec.; **EDUC:** BS, 1967, Bus. Admin., Univ. of MD, Coll. Pk.; **OTHER ACT & HONORS:** Nat. Advisory Council, Weizman Inst. of Sci., Outstanding Young Men of Amer., 1970; **BUS ADD:** 4th Fl., 1424 K St. NW, Wash. DC 20005, (202)283-2030.

EPSTEIN, Robert——*VP & Corp. Secy.*, W.F. Hall Printing Co.; **PRIM RE ACT:** Property Manager; **BUS ADD:** 4600 Diversey Ave., Chicago, IL 60639, (312)794-4600.*

EPTER, Bernard A.——**B:** Mar. 20, 1924, New York, NY, *VP*, First National Savings and Loan Assn., Mort. Banking; **PRIM RE ACT:** Banker; **SERVICES:** Resid. RE fin.; **REP CLIENTS:** Mort. Cos. and Fin. Instit.; **PREV EMPLOY:** Lawrence A. Epter & Assocs., Inc. 1945-1974, So. Mort. Assocs., Inc. 1974-78; **PROFL AFFIL & HONORS:** MBAA; Mort. Bankers Assn. of FL; Mort. Bankers Assn. of Miami; FL Assn. of Mort. Bankers, SMC (Nat. Assn. of Mort. Bankers); "Broker of the Year", 1973 (FL Assn. of Mort. Bankers); **EDUC:** 1949, New York Univ.; **MIL SERV:** USAF, Cpl.; **OTHER ACT & HONORS:** Pres., Mort. Bankers Assn. of Greater Miami, 1976/77; Pres., FL Assn. of Mort. Bankers, 1979; **HOME ADD:** 20020 N. E. 21st Ave., N. Miami Beach, FL 33179; **BUS ADD:** 633 N.E. 167th St., N. Miami Beach, FL 33162, (305)651-2841.

ERBESFIELD, Carl S.——**B:** Sept. 24, 1948, Atlanta, GA, *VP/Managing Broker*, Crest Realtors/Better Homes & Gardens; **PRIM RE ACT:** Broker, Appraiser, Instructor; **SERVICES:** Resid. RE brokerage; **PROFL AFFIL & HONORS:** Atlanta Bd. of Realtors; GA Assn. of Realtors; NAR; RNMI, GRI; CRS; CRB; **EDUC:** AB, 1971, Mktg./Bus. Educ./Public Relations, Univ. of GA; **EDUC HONORS:** Student Liaision; **HOME ADD:** 6451 N. Hampton Dr. N.E., Atlanta, GA 30328, (404)252-4334; **BUS ADD:** 865 Holcombe Bridge Dr., Roswell, GA 30076.

ERENBERG, Douglas D.——**B:** Apr. 5, 1951, Los Angeles, CA, *Corp. Sec., Chief Fin. Officer, Legal Counsel, Managing Officer*, Erenberg Enterprises, Erenberg Brothers Partnership; **PRIM RE ACT:** Broker, Attorney, Developer, Owner/Investor, Property Manager, Syndicator; **SERVICES:** Devel. Wholly-Owed Props. in CA, AZ & HI; **PROFL AFFIL & HONORS:** State Bar of CA, Atty. (Master of Estate Planning); **EDUC:** BA, 1973, Psych./Econ., Stanford Univ.; **GRAD EDUC:** JD; LLM, 1976; 1978, Family Estate Planning, Pepperdine Univ. School of Law; Univ. of Miami, FL; **BUS ADD:** 2525 Medford St., Los Angeles, CA 90033, (213)225-5651.

ERGANIAN, Richard——**B:** May 18, 1941, Fresno, CA, *VP*, The Vineyard; **PRIM RE ACT:** Developer, Property Manager; **SERVICES:** Comml. RE devel.; **REP CLIENTS:** Valley Fed. Savings, San Diego Fed. Savings, Peppermill Restaurants, Bank of Amer., & other retail & office space users; **PREV EMPLOY:** Pepsi Co. Inc., Wells Fargo Leasing, Intercoast Devel.; **PROFL AFFIL & HONORS:** Intl. Council of Shopping Centers; **EDUC:** BS, 1968, Fin. & RE, CA State Univ., Fresno; **GRAD EDUC:** MBA, 1969, RE, CA State Univ., Fresno; **HOME ADD:** 660 "O" St., Fresno, CA 93721, (209)222-0182; **BUS ADD:** 660 "O" St., Fresno, CA 93721, (209)222-0182.

ERICH, John A.——**B:** Apr. 4, 1947, Milwaukee, WI, Reinhart, Boerner, Van Deuren, Norris & Rieselbach, SC; **PRIM RE ACT:** Syndicator; **PROFL AFFIL & HONORS:** ABA; WI State Bar Assn.; Milwaukee Bar Assn.; **EDUC:** AB, 1969, Philosophy, Ripon Coll.; **GRAD EDUC:** JD, 1972, Law, Univ. of Chicago; **EDUC HONORS:** Phi Beta Kappa, Magna Cum Laude; **HOME ADD:** 1229 N. Jackson St., Unit 306, Milwaukee, WI 53202, (414)272-3644; **BUS ADD:** 1800 Marine Plaza, Milwaukee, WI 53202, (414)271-1190.

ERICKSEN, Grover G.——**B:** Feb. 20, 1936, Moultrie, GA, *Pres.*, Caldwell Equity FL, Inc., Condo. Apt. Devel.; **PRIM RE ACT:** Broker, Developer; **PREV EMPLOY:** VP/ Gen. Mgr., Pelican Bay, Naples, FL; Coral Ridge Props., Westinghouse; **PROFL AFFIL & HONORS:** ULI, Bd. of Realtors, Realtor; **EDUC:** BA, 1959, Naval Sci., US Naval Acad.; **GRAD EDUC:** MBA, 1968, Gen. Bus., Colgate-Darden, Univ. of VA; **MIL SERV:** USN, Cmdr., DFC, 7 Air medals, Purple Heart; **HOME ADD:** 160 Carica Rd., Naples, FL 33940, (813)597-4724; **BUS ADD:** 9600 S. Tamiami Trail, Suite 217, Ft. Myers, FL 33907, (813)936-3696.

ERICKSON, Charles A.——**B:** Jan. 8, 1939, Maryville, MO, *Corp. Atty.*, Interstate Brands Cor.; **PRIM RE ACT:** Attorney, Property Manager; **SERVICES:** Corp. atty. in charge of RE; **PREV EMPLOY:** Previously engaged in private practice of law and RE devel. and construction; **PROFL AFFIL & HONORS:** ABA; Kansas City Bar Assn.; MO Bar Assn.; Lawyer's Assn.; Clay County Bar Assn.; **EDUC:** AB, 1961, Poli. Sci., Bus. Admin., Psych., Sociology, Drury Coll., Springfield, MO; **GRAD EDUC:** JD, 1964, Law, Wash. Univ., St. Louis, MO; **EDUC HONORS:** Fr., Soph. Jr. Class Presidents, Student Body President, Student Bar Assn. Pres.; **HOME ADD:** 4118 NE Davidson Rd., Kansas City, MO 64116, (816)454-0680; **BUS ADD:** 12 E Armour Blvd., PO Box 1627, Kansas City, MO 64141, (816)561-6600.

ERICKSON, Franklin E.——**B:** Jan. 22, 1911, Minneapolis, MN, *Pres./Owner*, Erickson Construction Co.; **PRIM RE ACT:** Developer, Builder, Owner/Investor; **SERVICES:** Bldg. and devel. for large comml. projects; **REP CLIENTS:** Bank of Amer., Sheraton Hotel, Lucky Super Markets, John Ascuaga's Nugget, Sparks NV, Sears Roebuck, Granny Goose; **PROFL AFFIL & HONORS:** Assoc. Gen. Contractors Assn.; **EDUC:** N. Sacramento; **OTHER ACT & HONORS:** 1957 Pres. of Assoc. Gen. Contractors Assn.; Comodore of Port of Sacramento; Sutter Club; Grandfathers; Del Paso Ctry. Club; Rotary Club; Duck Club; **HOME ADD:** POB 15167, Sacramento, CA 95851, (916)925-6588; **BUS ADD:** POB 15167, Sacramento, CA 95851, (916)448-5316.

ERIKSSON, John V.——**B:** Jan. 6, 1940, Galveston, TX, *VP*, Gulf Coast Investment Corp.; **PRIM RE ACT:** Broker, Banker, Lender, Owner/Investor, Insuror; **SERVICES:** Gen. mort. lending-joint ventures; **PREV EMPLOY:** Amer. Nat. Ins. Co./Mort. Div., Peat, Marwick, Mitchell & Co.; **PROFL AFFIL & HONORS:** Nat. Assn. of Review Appraisers; Dir. Houston Mort. Bankers Assn., CRA; **EDUC:**

BBA, 1963, Acctg., Sam Houston State univ.; **GRAD EDUC:** MBA, 1966, Marketing/Fin., Sam Houston State Univ.; **HOME ADD:** 1203 El Dorado, Houston, TX 77062, (713)488-6021; **BUS ADD:** 1903 Hermann Dr., Houston, TX 77004, (713)525-6103.

ERKSON, Ronald L.——B: Jan. 17, 1946, San Francisco, CA, *Pres.*, Capital Shelter Fund, Inc.; **PRIM RE ACT:** Broker, Consultant, Developer, Owner/Investor, Property Manager; **SERVICES:** RE Synd. of Income Prop. in the Western US; **PREV EMPLOY:** Design and Devel. for Pac. Telephone Co. (67-70); **PROFL AFFIL & HONORS:** NAR, CA Assoc. of Realtors, WA Assoc. of Realtors, RESSI Member, Dir. of Dartnell Corp., GRI, CA; GRI, WA; CCIM Candidate; Cert. of RE WA State; RE Broker CA and WA; **EDUC:** 1972, Bus./Mktg./Govt., Univ. of CA, San Francisco; **GRAD EDUC:** MBA, 1974, Bus., Univ. of CA, Berkeley; **MIL SERV:** USMC, Capt., Navy Commendation Navy/Marine Corp. Medal Vietnam Flying Cross; **OTHER ACT & HONORS:** Delta Sigma Pi, Lyons Club, Young Realtors; **HOME ADD:** 14602 NE 174th, Woodinville, WA 98072, (206)483-8237; **BUS ADD:** 10001 NE 4th, Bellevue, WA 98009, (206)454-1446.

ERMLER, Richard——B: July 3, 1946, New York, NY, *Partner*, Tree Group; **PRIM RE ACT:** Broker, Developer, Builder, Owner/Investor, Property Manager, Syndicator; **OTHER RE ACT:** CPA; **SERVICES:** Own, Build, Manage, synd. market rate multi-family housing; **REP CLIENTS:** Self & investor grps.; **PROFL AFFIL & HONORS:** AICPA; NYSSCPA; CSCPA; RESSI; NAR; **EDUC:** BS, 1969, Acctg., C.W. Post Coll.; **HOME ADD:** 11 Wood Pond, Old Saybrook, CT 06475, (203)388-3713; **BUS ADD:** 48 Main St., Old Saybrook, CT 06475, (203)388-1241.

ERNEST, Michael J.——B: Nov. 14, 1954, Los Angeles, CA, *Appraiser/Inspector*, Ernest & Assoc. Ltd., Fred L. Blair & Assoc.; **PRIM RE ACT:** Consultant, Appraiser; **OTHER RE ACT:** Bldg. inspector and prop. tax; **REP CLIENTS:** Texaco, Inc.; Amer. Petro.; Executrans; Eastman Kodak Co.; Reliance Ins. Co.; Bank of OK; Republic Nat. Bank, etc.; **PREV EMPLOY:** Field Appraiser, Dallas Cty. Tax Office; Market Research & Analysis-Dresco, Inc., Dallas; Field Appraiser, City of Dallas, Dept. of Taxation; Fee Appraiser & Home Inspector-Clyde Crum Appraisal Consultants, Dallas; Fee Appraiser & Home Inspector, Fred L. Blair & Assoc., Dallas; Bldg. Inspector-Ernest & Assoc. Ltd., Dallas; **PROFL AFFIL & HONORS:** Intl. Org. of RE Appraisers, Sr. Member (ICA); Cert. Manufactured Housing Appraiser (CMHA); TX RE Commn., Reg. RE Inspector (RREI); Amer. Soc. of Profl. Consultants; Intl. Assn. of Electrical Inspectors; Nat. Notary Assn.; The Dallas Black C of C; TX Manufactured Housing Assn.; Dallas C of C; The Greater Dallas Bd. of Realtors Affiliate; International Inst. of Values, Sr. Member (SCV), GRI, SCV, ICA, CMHA, RREI; **EDUC:** BFA, LA Tech. Univ., Ruston, LA; **OTHER ACT & HONORS:** USPA, SCR-8614, Listed in *Who's Who in RE: The Directory of the RE Professions* - RE Review; **HOME ADD:** PO Box 57, Grambling, LA 71245, (318)247-6117; **BUS ADD:** 5844 Prospect, Dallas, TX 75206, (214)826-4816.

ERNST, Henry J.——*Treas.*, Moog; **PRIM RE ACT:** Property Manager; **BUS ADD:** Seneca St. at Jamison Rd., E. Aurora, NY 14052, (716)652-2000.*

ERNST, Jerome W.——B: Mar 10, 1933, Chicago, IL, *Sr. VP*, Charterhouse Investment Co.; **PRIM RE ACT:** Consultant, Appraiser, Owner/Investor; **SERVICES:** RE investments, mortgage loans; **REP CLIENTS:** Major eastern insurance cos.; **PREV EMPLOY:** Crocker Natl. Bank, Los Angeles & Newport Beach, CA Asst. VP; **PROFL AFFIL & HONORS:** AIREA; Natl. Assn. of Review Appraisers; Intl. Instit. of Valuers; Assn. of Military Appraisers; Natl. Assn. of RE Bds., MAI; **EDUC:** BS, 1957, RE, Univ. of AZ; **GRAD EDUC:** Graduate work toward MBA, 1957, RE, Econs., Univ. of AZ; **MIL SERV:** US Army, Res., Col. 1979-present; **OTHER ACT & HONORS:** K of C; Alpha Kappa Psi; Phi Kappa Theta; Alpha Delta Sigma; **HOME ADD:** 8191 Burnham Circle, Huntington Beach, CA 92646; **BUS ADD:** 1801 Ave. of the Stars, Suite 525, Los Angeles, CA 90067, (213)277-2100.

ERNST, John W., Jr.——B: Sept. 18, 1934, Indianapolis, IN, *Pres.*, Ernst/Eaton & Associates, Inc.; **PRIM RE ACT:** Broker, Developer, Owner/Investor, Property Manager; **SERVICES:** Bldg., devel. and mgmt. of comml. props; **REP CLIENTS:** Prudential Ins. Co., AmNedVast, Inc. (Atlanta), J.T. Holding Co. (Atlanta), local banks and privates.; **PREV EMPLOY:** Comml. Props. Assn.; Div. od Keiser-Aetna; **PROFL AFFIL & HONORS:** Intl. Council of Shopping Ctrs., Indianapolis C of C, Chmn. Design Review Comm. of Dept. of Metropolitan Devel. of Indianapolis; **OTHER ACT & HONORS:** Ernst/Eaton was awarded Excellence in Devel. by Design Review Comm. for their Lakewood 6801 Office Park and the Architectural Award by the Noblesville C of C for the Klubhaus of Amer.; **HOME ADD:** 4626 Somerset Way S., Carmel, IN; **BUS ADD:** 6801 Lake Plaza Dr., Suite A-103, Indianapolis, IN, (317)842-0020.

ERVANIAN, Armen——*VP RE*, Greyhound Corp.; **PRIM RE ACT:** Property Manager; **BUS ADD:** Greyhound Tower, Phoenix, AZ 85077, (602)248-4000.*

ERWIN, Mark Wylea——B: Mar. 30, 1944, Coral Gables, FL, *Pres.*, First Prop. Grp.; **PRIM RE ACT:** Broker, Syndicator, Consultant, Developer, Builder, Property Manager, Owner/Investor; **SERVICES:** Dev. & Synd. of Comml. & Residential Projects; **PREV EMPLOY:** 1969-1978 - RE Admin., UPS; **PROFL AFFIL & HONORS:** Cert. Review Appraisers, Adjunct Prof. Winthrop Coll.; **EDUC:** 1969, Bus., Univ. of TN; **MIL SERV:** USAF, A1c, Unit citation, good conduct, marksman; **OTHER ACT & HONORS:** Past JP 1976-78 Ridgeford, CN, Planning Commn. 1977-1978; Dir. Bank of Fort Mill; Past Pres. 1980, C of C; Dir. York County Econ. Dev. Bd.; Pres. Local Dev. Bd.; Lions, Chamber, River Hills Country Club, Spring Lake Country Club; **HOME ADD:** 10 Wood Hollow Road, River Hills Plantation, Clover, SC 29710, (803)831-2031; **BUS ADD:** The Marino River Hills Plantation, Clover, SC 29710, (803)831-2001.

ESACOVE, Donald——B: Mar. 31, 1932, Los Angeles, CA, *Pres.*, Investment Training Inst.; **PRIM RE ACT:** Consultant; **SERVICES:** Office Support, Training, Follow-Up; **REP CLIENTS:** Physicians; **PREV EMPLOY:** 10 yrs.-Property Mgt.; **EDUC:** BS, 1954, Chemistry, UCLA; **GRAD EDUC:** MS, 1963, Journalism, UCLA; **EDUC HONORS:** Sigma Delta Chi Honorary; **MIL SERV:** USAF, 1/Lt.; **HOME ADD:** PO Box 25399, Houston, TX 77005, (713)526-3429; **BUS ADD:** PO Box 25399, Houston, TX 77005, (713)782-9974.

ESHELMAN, Darwin K.——B: Feb. 13, 1928, Ft. Wayne, IN, *Pres.*, Eshelman Appraisal & Consulting; **PRIM RE ACT:** Appraiser; **SERVICES:** Resid. Appraisals; **REP CLIENTS:** Relocation Cos., i.e. Merrill Lynch Relocation Mgmt., Inc.; Homequity; Equitable Relocation Mgmt.; Banks; S & L; **PROFL AFFIL & HONORS:** Soc. of RE Appraisers, SREA; **GRAD EDUC:** BS, 1954, IN Univ.; **MIL SERV:** USN, Underwater Demolition Team 3; **OTHER ACT & HONORS:** Masonic Lodge; **HOME ADD:** 2213 La Amatista Rd., Del Mar, CA 92014, (714)755-3440; **BUS ADD:** 3071 El Cajon Blvd. Suite 201, San Diego, CA 92104, (714)283-0227.

ESHLEMAN, James A.——B: Aug. 25, 1932, Champaign, IL, *Regional Dir. of RE*, The Kroger Co., Gen. Office; **OTHER RE ACT:** Corp. RE; **SERVICES:** Site selection, lease neg., land acquisition & prop. mgmt.; **PREV EMPLOY:** USAF; **PROFL AFFIL & HONORS:** RE Broker; **EDUC:** BS, 1954, Acctg., IN Univ.; **MIL SERV:** USAF, Capt.; **HOME ADD:** 1132 N. Irving Hghts. Dr., Irving, TX 75061, (214)579-1022; **BUS ADD:** P O Box 226388, Dallas, TX 75266, (214)438-5161.

ESKENAZI, Jack J.——B: June 9, 1941, NY, *Broker*, Investment Equities Co.; **PRIM RE ACT:** Broker; **SERVICES:** Investment broker; **REP CLIENTS:** Westwood Fin.; County 6, Los Angeles; Beneficial Life Ins.; Pvt. parties; **PREV EMPLOY:** RSVP Realtors; **PROFL AFFIL & HONORS:** Var. local bds.; **EDUC:** BA, 1963, Econ., OH State Univ.; **GRAD EDUC:** 1963-79, Taxation, UCLA, USC; **OTHER ACT & HONORS:** Acct., Never out of Escrow; **HOME ADD:** 4109 Alemman Dr., Tarzana, CA 91356, (213)996-0756; **BUS ADD:** 10960 Wilshire Blvd., Suite 1426, Los Angeles, CA 90067, (213)473-1558.

ESKIE, Dennis J.——B: Mar. 17, 1944, Ft. Dix, NJ, *Owner*, Dennis J. Eskie & Associates; **PRIM RE ACT:** Consultant, Developer; **OTHER RE ACT:** Land planning & feasibility studies; **SERVICES:** Devel. consultant with emphasis on comml.; **REP CLIENTS:** Dept. stores, food stores, land owners; **PREV EMPLOY:** Maisel and Associates; **PROFL AFFIL & HONORS:** CCIM; Bd. of Realtors; ICSC; **EDUC:** BA, 1970, Poli. Sci., Psych., Washburn Univ.; **MIL SERV:** USMC; Sgt.; 62-66; **OTHER ACT & HONORS:** Bd. of Dirs., Downtown Topeka, Inc.; **HOME ADD:** 1213 Western, Topeka, KS, (913)232-0209; **BUS ADD:** 525 Topeka Blvd., Topeka, KS 66603, (913)232-2473.

ESPELAND, Terrance I.——B: Apr. 9, 1944, Duluth, MN, *Pres.*, Tieco Insurance Agency, Inc.; **PRIM RE ACT:** Builder, Owner/Investor, Insuror; **SERVICES:** Lic. gen. contractor; **PROFL AFFIL & HONORS:** Profl. Ins. Agents Assn., Indep. Ins. Agents. Assn., Soc. of CLU, Soc. of Chartered Prop. & Casualty Underwriters, CLU, Chartered Prop. & Casualty Underwriters; **EDUC:** BA, 1966, Mathematics, San Jose State Univ.; **GRAD EDUC:** MBA, 1970, Fin., Univ. of Santa Clara; **OTHER ACT & HONORS:** Pres. of the Univ. of Santa Clara Grad. School of Bus. Alumni Assn.; **HOME ADD:** 1766 Patio Dr., San Jose, CA 95125, (408)266-3724; **BUS ADD:** P O Box 5789, San Jose, CA 95150, (408)241-6683.

ESSIG, William J.——**B:** July 13, 1938, S. Bend, IN, *Asst. Gen. Counsel*, Benefit Trust Life Ins. Co.; **PRIM RE ACT:** Attorney; **PREV EMPLOY:** Pioneer Nat. Title Ins., Lawyers Title Ins Corp.; **PROFL AFFIL & HONORS:** ABA IL State Bar Assn., Chicago Bar Assn.; **EDUC:** BA, 1959, Hist., Yale Univ.; **GRAD EDUC:** JD, 1965, The Law School, Univ. of Chicago; **MIL SERV:** US Army, SP 4, 1961 - 1962; **OTHER ACT & HONORS:** Fellow, Life Mgmt. Inst., CLU; **HOME ADD:** 2942 Greenleaf Ave., Wilmette, IL 60091, (312)251-8763; **BUS ADD:** 1771 Howard St., Chicago, IL 60626, (312)274-8100.

ESSNER, David——*VP Fin. & Treas.*, Universal Foods Corp.; **PRIM RE ACT:** Property Manager; **BUS ADD:** 433 E. Michigan St., Milwaukee, WI 53202, (414)271-6755.*

ESSNER, Gene——**B:** Sept. 2, 1928, McKeeport, PA, *Atty. at Law*, Fine Jacobson Block Klein Colan & Simon, P.A., RE; **PRIM RE ACT:** Attorney; **PROFL AFFIL & HONORS:** ABA; FL Bar; Dade Cty. Bar Assn.; **EDUC:** BBA, 1948, Univ. of Miami; **GRAD EDUC:** JD, 1951, Univ. of Miami; LLM, 1971, Univ. of Miami; **OTHER ACT & HONORS:** Author; **HOME ADD:** 6240 S.W. 86th St., Miami, FL 33143, (305)666-9865; **BUS ADD:** 2401 Douglas Rd., Miami, FL 33145, (305)446-2200.

ESTERLINE, Jerrold——*Acquisition Dept.*, Sheller-Globe; **PRIM RE ACT:** Property Manager; **BUS ADD:** 1505 Jefferson, PO Box 962, Toledo, OH 43697, (419)255-8840.*

ESTERN, Jay S.——**B:** May 29, 1915, Omaha, NE, *Pres.*, Century 21 Estern, Inc.; **PRIM RE ACT:** Broker, Owner/Investor, Instructor, Property Manager; **OTHER RE ACT:** Dir. Boca Raton, Bd. of Realtors; **PREV EMPLOY:** Pres. Estro Inc., A CA Corp.; **PROFL AFFIL & HONORS:** Realtor, GRI; **GRAD EDUC:** 1943, Radio Engrg., Radio Electronic Inst., Wash. DC; **MIL SERV:** USMS, Lt. JG; **OTHER ACT & HONORS:** 32 deg. Mason, Sr. Member US Power Squadron; **HOME ADD:** 500 S. Ocean Blvd., 601, Boca Raton, FL 33432, (305)392-8155; **BUS ADD:** 140 N Federal Hwy., PO Box 188, Boca Raton, FL 33432, (305)395-8155.

ESTES, Doyle D.——**B:** June 11, 1949, Wall, SD, *Partner*, Gunderson, Farrar, Aldrich, Warder & De Merssemen; **PRIM RE ACT:** Attorney, Developer, Owner/Investor; **EDUC:** BS, Poli. Sci., 1971, Govt., Bus. Admin., Univ. of SD; **GRAD EDUC:** JD, LLM, 1975, 1978, Univ. of SD, NY Univ.; **HOME ADD:** 2724 W. St. Anne, Rapid City, SD 57701, (605)341-2952; **BUS ADD:** P O Box 1820, Rapid City, SD 57709, (605)342-2814.

ESTES, George E., Jr.——**B:** June 4, 1928, Gulfport, MS, *Atty.*, Estes, Estes & Alexander, P.A.; **PRIM RE ACT:** Attorney, Banker, Owner/Investor; **SERVICES:** Sale and Loan Closings, Title Examinations, Synd.; **REP CLIENTS:** Merchants Bank and Trust Co., lenders and indiv. investors; **PREV EMPLOY:** City Atty., Gulfport, MS; **PROFL AFFIL & HONORS:** Harrison Cty. & MS State Bar Assns.; MS Trial Lawyers Assn.; Amer. Land Title Assn.; **EDUC:** 1948, MS Coll.; **GRAD EDUC:** 1950, Univ. of MS; **OTHER ACT & HONORS:** First Baptist Church; Gulfport Yacht Club; **HOME ADD:** 20 Bayou View Dr., Gulfport, MS 39501, (601)896-5654; **BUS ADD:** 1611 23rd Ave., Gulfport, MS 39501, (601)863-5582.

ESTES, John P.——**B:** March 8, 1945, Greenville,MS, *Pres.*, John P. Estes, Inc.; **PRIM RE ACT:** Broker, Consultant, Property Manager; **SERVICES:** Prop. mgmt., Envestment Analysis, Consulting, Rehabilitation; **PREV EMPLOY:** Founded and operated Cactus Mgmt., Inc. from 1977 to 1980; **PROFL AFFIL & HONORS:** IREM, Advisory Bd. Western Intnl., Univ. of Phoenix; **EDUC:** BBA, 1967, Banking and Fin., Univ. of MS; **MIL SERV:** US Army, E-5; **OTHER ACT & HONORS:** Sigma Alpha Epsilon Alumni; **HOME ADD:** 1097 E. Carter, Tempe, AZ 85282; **BUS ADD:** 1097 E. Carter, Tempe, AZ 85282, (602)831-1718.

ESTIS, Dennis A.——**B:** May 4, 1947, Newark, NJ, *Partner*, Greenbaum, Greenbaum, Rowe & Smith, Litigation; **PRIM RE ACT:** Attorney; **REP CLIENTS:** Parker Imperial Condo., Island House Condo. Assn., Kaufman & Broad Devel. Co.; **PROFL AFFIL & HONORS:** ABA, NJ Bar Assn.; **EDUC:** BA, 1969, Poli. Sci., Johns Hopkins Univ.; **GRAD EDUC:** JD, 1972, Law, NY Univ. School of Law; **EDUC HONORS:** Omicron Delta Kappa, Pi Sigma Alpha, Root-Tilden Scholar; **OTHER ACT & HONORS:** Councilman - Bor. of Roselle Park, NJ 1976-1981; Chmn., Union Cty. Democratic Party, 1980-1981.; **HOME ADD:** 300 E Westfield Ave., Roselle Park, NJ 07204; **BUS ADD:** Gateway I, Newark, NJ 07102, (201)623-5600.

ESTOPINAL, Stewart Joseph——**B:** Dec. 10, 1957, New Orleans, LA, *Dir. of Leasing*, Coldwell Banker/Michael J. Lipsey; **PRIM RE ACT:** Broker, Consultant, Property Manager; **SERVICES:** Brokerage, leasing, prop. mgmt., consulting; **EDUC:** BBA, 1979, Mktg., Loyola Univ. of the South; **GRAD EDUC:** Pres. enr. in MBA Program, Loyola Univ. of the South; **HOME ADD:** 400 Metairie Rd., Metairie, LA 70005, (504)835-5554; **BUS ADD:** 4405 N I-10 Service Rd., Suite 100, Metairie, LA 70002, (504)455-1900.

ESTRIN, Dianne G.——**B:** July 11, 1944, San Francisco, CA, *Atty.*, The Gap Stores, Inc.; **PRIM RE ACT:** Attorney, Owner/Investor; **SERVICES:** Advice, Re-structuring of var. RE transactions, Negotiation & Documentation; **PREV EMPLOY:** RE Atty. Heller, Ehrman, White & McAuliffe, San Francisco, CA; **PROFL AFFIL & HONORS:** CA Bar, ABA, San Francisco Bar Assn., Member RE Sect. ABA; **EDUC:** BA, 1968, Psych., Univ. of CA, Berkeley; **GRAD EDUC:** JD, 1977, RE, Golden Gate Univ. Law Sch.; **EDUC HONORS:** Summa cum Laude; **BUS ADD:** 900 Cherry Ave., San Bruno, CA 94066, (415)952-4400.

ETIENNE, Cynthia——**B:** May 17, 1950, TX, *Assoc. Counsel*, Southwestern Life Insurance Co., Legal Dept.; **PRIM RE ACT:** Attorney, Lender; **SERVICES:** Investment counsel to ins. co.; **PREV EMPLOY:** Private practice, Houston, Waco, TX; **PROFL AFFIL & HONORS:** Amer. Land Title Assn., TX Land Title Assn., ABA, TX Bar Assn., Dallas Bar Assn.; **EDUC:** BS, 1972, Psych./Physics, Univ. of Houston; **GRAD EDUC:** JD, 1977, Legal, Baylor Univ. School of Law; **EDUC HONORS:** Dean's List, Magna Cum Laude, Delta Theta Phi Law Fraternity, Dean, Vice-Dean; **HOME ADD:** 5636 Spring Valley, Dallas, TX 75240, (214)644-1203; **BUS ADD:** P O Box 2699, Dallas, TX 75221, (214)655-5181.

ETKIN, Alex J.——**B:** Sept. 25, 1918, Detroit, MI, *Chmn. of the Bd.*, A.J. Etkin Construction Co.; **PRIM RE ACT:** Engineer, Developer, Builder, Owner/Investor; **SERVICES:** Gen. Contracting; Owner-Devel. Office Bldgs, Apts., Indus. Bldgs.; **PROFL AFFIL & HONORS:** Past Pres. Associated Gen. Contractors, Detroit Chapter; Assoc. Gen. Contractors (Wash, DC) - Nat. Dir. Engrg. Soc. of Detroit; **EDUC:** Detroit Inst. of Technol.; **MIL SERV:** US Army, Non-Com; **OTHER ACT & HONORS:** Dir, Amer. Technion Soc.; Amer. Arbitration Assn.; **HOME ADD:** 25040 Roycourt, Huntington Woods, MI 48070; **BUS ADD:** 10111 Capital Ave., Oak Park, MI 48237, (313)548-8500.

ETKIN, Douglas M.——**B:** Dec. 26, 1952, Detroit, MI, *VP*, Schostak Brothers & Co., Inc.; **PRIM RE ACT:** Attorney, Developer, Owner/Investor, Property Manager; **SERVICES:** Devel. and Mgmt. of comml. props.; **REP CLIENTS:** Corp. and Indiv. Investors, TIAA, Schroder RE Corp., Dayton Hudson Corp.; **PROFL AFFIL & HONORS:** ABA, State Bar of MI, Intl. Council of Shopping Centers, MI Assn. of Realtors, Pres., Univ. of MI RE Club (1974); **EDUC:** BBA, 1974, RE, Univ. of MI; **GRAD EDUC:** JD, 1977, Wayne State Univ. Law School; **BUS ADD:** 17515 W. Nine Mile Rd., Southfield, MI 48075, (313)559-2000.

ETTNER, Larry W.——**B:** Feb. 16, 1951, Salem, OR, *Pres.*, Costain Seattle Inc., Costain Ltd.; **PRIM RE ACT:** Developer, Builder; **SERVICES:** Resid. & Comml. Devel.; **PREV EMPLOY:** Pres. of Landura Corp. of the NW; **PROFL AFFIL & HONORS:** Nat. Homebuilders; **EDUC:** BS, 1973, Pol. Sci. & Govt., Willamette Univ.; **GRAD EDUC:** Masters, 1975, Urban Planning, Univ. of OR, School of Arch.; **OTHER ACT & HONORS:** City Councilman, Woodburn, OR 1972-1974; Bd. of Dir., Amer. Inst. of Planners, OR Chapter; **HOME ADD:** 4002 W. Lake Sammamish Pkwy, Redmond, WA 98052, (206)881-5743; **BUS ADD:** 12301 NE 10th Pl., Bellevue, WA 98005, (206)455-1969.

EUDALY, Dick——**B:** July 7, 1943, Gulfport, MS, *Pres.*, Camelot Properties Corp.; **PRIM RE ACT:** Consultant, Developer, Owner/Investor; **SERVICES:** Income prop. devel. & consultant servs.; **REP CLIENTS:** Local and natl. investors and personal account; **PREV EMPLOY:** Instr., TX A & M Univ. 1966-69; **PROFL AFFIL & HONORS:** Ft. Worth Bd. of Realtors; Dir., TX Prop. Exchangors 1974; Pres., N. TX Exchangors; Chmn. of Civic Affairs Commn.; Ft. Worth Bd. of Realtors; Charter Member, N. TX Chap. of CCIM, GRI; **EDUC:** BS, 1964, TX Tech. Univ.; **GRAD EDUC:** MS, 1966, OK State Univ.; **OTHER ACT & HONORS:** Shady Oaks Ctry. Club; Petroleum Club; Dir. Southwest YMCA; CEF of Tarrant Cty.; Pres. Downtown Republican of Tarrant Cty.; Metropolitan Diners Club, *Who's Who in Fin. & Indus.*; *Who's Who in TX*; *Outstanding Young Men of Amer.*; *Who's Who in the S & SW*; **BUS ADD:** 915 Oil & Gas Bldg., Ft. Worth, TX 76102, (817)335-1998.

EURING, George A., Jr.——**B:** Mar. 20, 1941, Floral Park, NY, *Chief of Planning*, Ralph Burke Associates; **PRIM RE ACT:** Consultant; **SERVICES:** Planning, Design, Feasibility Studies; **PROFL AFFIL & HONORS:** Amer. Econ. Assn.; **EDUC:** AB, 1963, Econ., Math., English, Blackburn Coll.; **GRAD EDUC:** AM, 1965, Econ., Univ. of MD (Columbia); **EDUC HONORS:** Wallstreet Journal Student

Achievement Award in Econ., NSF Summer Fellowship; **MIL SERV:** USMC Res., Pvt.; **HOME ADD:** 423 Carter St., Libertyville, FL 60048, (312)362-1767; **BUS ADD:** 1550 Northwest Highway, Suite 400, Park Ridge, IL 60068, (312)297-1172.

EVANS, Allan V.——B: Apr. 24, 1916, Great Britain, *Realtor & Land Planner*, Allan Evans Assoc.; **PRIM RE ACT:** Broker, Consultant, Appraiser, Developer, Property Manager; **OTHER RE ACT:** Specialize in Land; **PREV EMPLOY:** Dir. NH Div. of Econ. Devel. 1959-65; **PROFL AFFIL & HONORS:** Bd. Realtors, Home Builders Assn.; **EDUC:** BArch., 1939, State and Local land planning, UNH; **MIL SERV:** Corps of Engineers, Capt.; **OTHER ACT & HONORS:** Member Zoning Bd. of Adjustment - Concord, NH, 8 yrs.; **HOME ADD:** Box 40, Main St., New London, NH 03257, (603)526-4066; **BUS ADD:** PO Box 40, Main St., New London, NH 03257, (603)526-4066.

EVANS, Charles C.G., Jr.——B: Jan. 31, 1940, Baltimore, MD, *Pres.*, Evans Development Co.; **PRIM RE ACT:** Consultant, Developer, Owner/Investor, Property Manager; **SERVICES:** RE devel. and consultant and mgmt.; **PREV EMPLOY:** The Rouse Co.; **PROFL AFFIL & HONORS:** Intl. Council of Shopping Ctrs.; **HOME ADD:** 6422 Pratt Ave., Baltimore, MD 21212, (301)377-4079; **BUS ADD:** Suite 253, World Trade Ctr., Baltimore, MD 21202, (301)727-7270.

EVANS, Clifford S., Jr.——*Dir. RE & Const.*, Litton Industries; **PRIM RE ACT:** Property Manager; **BUS ADD:** 360 North Crescent Dr., Beverly Hills, CA 90210, (213)273-7860.*

EVANS, Donald L.——B: Apr. 22, 1933, Madison, WI, *Pres.*, D. L. Evans Co. Inc.; **PRIM RE ACT:** Consultant; **SERVICES:** Investment RE - consultant & brokerage; **REP CLIENTS:** First WI Nat. Bank; Xerox; Univ. of WI; St. Mary's Medical Center; **PREV EMPLOY:** Formerly associated with The Amer. Appraisal Co. - Milwaukee; **PROFL AFFIL & HONORS:** Amer. Soc. of RE Counselors; AIREA; Amer. Soc. of Appraisers; NAR; **EDUC:** BS, 1959, Const. Admin., Univ. of WI; **GRAD EDUC:** MS, 1964, Appraisal & Investment Analysis, Univ. of WI; **MIL SERV:** US Army, 1953-1954, Sgt., Korean Serv.; **HOME ADD:** 105 Ozark Tr., Madison, WI 53705, (608)233-2658; **BUS ADD:** 6409 Odana Rd., Madison, WI 53719, (608)274-4141.

EVANS, James——*Pres.*, Media General, Inc.; **PRIM RE ACT:** Property Manager; **BUS ADD:** 333 E. Grace St., Richmond, VA 23219, (804)649-6000.*

EVANS, John——*Dir. Fac. Plng. & Engr.*, Marion Laboratories, Inc.; **PRIM RE ACT:** Property Manager; **BUS ADD:** 10236 Bunker Ridge Rd., Kansas City, MO 64137, (816)761-2500.*

EVANS, M. D.——B: Feb. 27, 1930, NY, NY, *Owner*, M.D. Evans Real Estate; **PRIM RE ACT:** Broker, Consultant, Developer, Owner/Investor; **SERVICES:** Comml. props. only; **PROFL AFFIL & HONORS:** Various Realtor Bds.; **EDUC:** BS, 1951, Aero. Engrg., St. Louis Univ.; **GRAD EDUC:** 2 yrs., Fin. & Econ., FL Univ. (Jacksonville); **MIL SERV:** USAF, 1st Lt.; **HOME ADD:** 116 Live Oak, Metairie, LA 70005, (504)834-1708; **BUS ADD:** 3221 Behrman Pl., New Orleans, LA 70114, (504)368-7039.

EVANS, Roger W.——B: Jan. 8, 1944, CA, *VP - Regional Dir. of Mktg., Indust. Props.*, Coldwell Banker, Comml. RE Services; **PRIM RE ACT:** Broker, Consultant; **SERVICES:** Provide prof. brokerage servs. in the acquisition, dev. and disposal of indust. props.; **REP CLIENTS:** The Fortune 1000 Cos. & others; Maj. Natl. & For. Dev. firms; Major Natl. & For. Investors; **PROFL AFFIL & HONORS:** Soc. of Indus. Realtors; ULI; NAIOP, 1976 Coldwell Banker Distinguished Sales Achievement Award; 1977 Indus. Broker of the Year, Adams Cty. CO; **EDUC:** BS, 1966, Soc., AZ State Univ.; **GRAD EDUC:** MA, 1968, Psych., AZ State Univ.; **EDUC HONORS:** Grad with Distinction; **MIL SERV:** USAR; **OTHER ACT & HONORS:** Boston Racquet Club, Museum of FA; **HOME ADD:** 40 Mt. Vernon St., Boston, MA 02108, (617)367-9092; **BUS ADD:** 50 Staniford St., Boston, MA 02114.

EVANS, Shirley A.——*Dir.*, Department of Housing and Urban Development, Finance and Accounting; **PRIM RE ACT:** Lender; **BUS ADD:** 451 Seventh St., S.W., Washington, DC 20410, (202)755-6310.*

EVATT, Thomas M.——B: Jan. 13, 1948, San Jose, CA, *Sr. Sales Consultant*, Western Props. Brokerage Inc.; **PRIM RE ACT:** Broker; **SERVICES:** Indus. sales & leasing greater bay area; **EDUC:** BS, 1974, San Jose State Univ.; **MIL SERV:** USN, E-5; **HOME ADD:** 1302 Gros Ventures Ct., Fremont, CA 94538; **BUS ADD:** 3393 Arden Rd., Hayward, CA 94545.

EVENSON, Gregory Dean——B: Mar. 29, 1950, St. Paul, MN, *Atty. at Law*; **PRIM RE ACT:** Attorney; **SERVICES:** Closing servs., title work; **REP CLIENTS:** Gen public, lending instns., devels.; **PROFL AFFIL & HONORS:** ABA, MN Bar Assn., Carlton Cty. and Pine Cty. Bar Assns.; **EDUC:** BA, 1972, Econ. & Hist., Univ. of MN; **GRAD EDUC:** JD, 1975, Univ. of MN; **OTHER ACT & HONORS:** Sturgeon Lake Area Lion's Club; **HOME ADD:** Moose Lake, MN 55767; **BUS ADD:** PO Box 492, 309 Arrowhead Ln., Moose Lake, MN 55767, (218)485-8167.

EVERAGE, Gordon L.——B: July 27, 1930, Sapulpa, OK, *Pres.*, Grimmer-Erker Better Homes and Gardens Realtors; **PRIM RE ACT:** Broker, Builder, Instructor; **SERVICES:** Resid., Comml., Synd., RE Mgmt.; **REP CLIENTS:** Indivs. in resid. props. & investors in comml. props.; **PROFL AFFIL & HONORS:** Metro. Tulsa RE Bd., NAR, RNMI, RE Sales Assn. of Tulsa, GRI, CRS, CRB; **EDUC:** BS, 1956, Mktg. & Mgmt., Univ. of Tulsa; **OTHER ACT & HONORS:** Pres. of Oil Capitol C of C; Bd. of Dir. of Metro. Tulsa C of C; **HOME ADD:** 7402 E. 70th, Tulsa, OK 74133, (918)252-4419; **BUS ADD:** 3601 East 51st St., Tulsa, OK 74135, (918)745-0123.

EVERETT, James——*Asst. VP*, Murray Ohio Manufacturing; **PRIM RE ACT:** Property Manager; **BUS ADD:** PO Box 268, Franklin St., Brentwood, TN 37027, (615)373-6500.*

EVERETT, N.L.——B: June 17, 1911, Palmer, TX, *Owner*, N.L. Everett Appraiser/Broker; **PRIM RE ACT:** Broker, Consultant, Appraiser, Property Manager, Owner/Investor; **OTHER RE ACT:** Income projections on prop.; **SERVICES:** Appraise, Project, Sell, Manage; **REP CLIENTS:** Attys., Banks, Ellis Cty., Indiv's., Investor Groups; **PREV EMPLOY:** Operated 3000+ acre farm & cattle operation, plus feed lot & order buying since about 1931 until retirement, & going into RE & appraising in 1972; **PROFL AFFIL & HONORS:** Amer. Soc. Rural App. & Farm Mgrs.; TX Soc.; **EDUC:** 1929-1931, Pre-med., Trinity Univ.; **GRAD EDUC:** 1972-1973, RE, Fin., Law, Appraisal; **OTHER ACT & HONORS:** Served as VP of Corsicana Pro. Credit Assn., 9 yrs.; Exec. Loan Comm., NRA (life); Ellis Co. Farm Bureau; S.W. Cattle Raisers Assn.; Amer. Security Council; Sheriffs' Assn. of TX; TX State Rifle Assn. (life); Masonic Lodge 459; OES 508; **HOME ADD:** Rt. 1, Box 63, Palmer, TX 75152, (214)449-3101; **BUS ADD:** Rt. 1 Box 63, Palmer, TX 75152, (214)449-3101.

EVERETT, Wilson Earl, Jr.——B: Dec. 28, 1952, Weldon, NC, *Indus. Ins. Appraiser (resident)*, Factory Mutual; **PRIM RE ACT:** Consultant, Appraiser, Insuror; **SERVICES:** Boiler & machinery inspection, fire & safety investigations; **PROFL AFFIL & HONORS:** AASA; **EDUC:** BS, 1976, Drafting, VA State Univ., Petersburg, VA; **OTHER ACT & HONORS:** Kappa Alpha Psi; **HOME ADD:** 3022 Boring Ct., Decatur, GA 30034, (404)288-2436; **BUS ADD:** 1151 Rt. 1, Norwood, MA 02062, (617)762-4300.

EVERHAM, George R.——B: Jan. 15, 1945, Detroit, MI, *Mort. Loan Officer*, MI Nat. Bank of Detroit, RE; **PRIM RE ACT:** Banker, Lender, Builder, Property Manager; **OTHER RE ACT:** Mort. loan warehousing; **SERVICES:** RE workouts; **PREV EMPLOY:** VP JT. Barnes & Co., 1973-81; **PROFL AFFIL & HONORS:** Mort. Bankers Assn.; **EDUC:** BBA, 1974, Fin., RE, Eastern MI Univ.; **GRAD EDUC:** 1981, RE Ext., Univ. of MI; **MIL SERV:** US Army, 1967-69, SP/5, Good Conduct; **HOME ADD:** 1383 Whittier, Grosse Pointe Park, MI 48230, (313)881-8529; **BUS ADD:** 22595 W. 8 Mile Rd., Detroit, MI 48219, (313)255-6400.

EVERSOLE, Otis H.——B: July 30, 1917, Yonkers, OK, Appraisal Associates; **PRIM RE ACT:** Appraiser; **OTHER RE ACT:** RE Condemnation and Damage Specialist; **SERVICES:** Appraisal of resid., multi-family, apts. and condo. resid. props., and indus., comml., and farm and ranch prop.; **REP CLIENTS:** Southwestern Bell Tele. Co., OK Gas & Electric Co., OK Natural Gas Co., Grand River Dam Auth., State of OK, and various municipalities; various and many law firms; **PREV EMPLOY:** 30 continuous years offering complete RE appraisal; **PROFL AFFIL & HONORS:** Nat. Assn. of Indep. Fee Appraisers, Nat. Assn. of Cert. Review Appraisers, Amer. Right-of-Way Assn., ASRA, IFAC, CRA; **EDUC:** Anoka-Ramsey Coll., 1971, Instr. Cert., Nat. Assn. of Indep. Fee Appraisers; **HOME ADD:** 116 South 4th Street, Muskogee, OK 74401, (918)682-5656; **BUS ADD:** 116 S. Fourth St., Muskogee, OK 74401, (918)682-6640.

EVERSOLE, Otis H., Jr.——B: July 20, 1939, Muskogee, OK, *VP, Real Estate Services*, Williams Realty Corp., Willco Properties, Inc.; **PRIM RE ACT:** Broker, Consultant, Attorney, Appraiser; **PREV EMPLOY:** Atty. in pvt. practice; **PROFL AFFIL & HONORS:** ABA; OK Bar Assn.; Tulsa Bar Assn.; Nat. Assn. of Review Appraisers; Intl. Council of Shopping Ctrs.; Nat. Council for Urban Econ. Devel.; Intnl. Inst. of Valuers, Serves on the bd. of dir. for neighborhood housing serv.

in Tulsa; **EDUC:** BA, 1962, Educ., Hist., Eng., Northeastern OK State Univ.; **GRAD EDUC:** JD, 1966, Univ. of Tulsa; **EDUC HONORS:** Deans Honor Roll; **OTHER ACT & HONORS:** Dist. Atty. of Muskogee Cty. 1974-75; OK Chap. of the Nat. Multiple Sclerosis Soc.; Muskogee Cty. Council of Youth Servs.; Muskogee C of C; **HOME ADD:** 5213 E 99th St., Tulsa, OK 74136, (918)299-6753; **BUS ADD:** PO Box 2400 1 Williams Ctr., Tulsa, OK 74101, (918)588-2893.

EVERSON, Gordon A.——B: Oct. 27, 1941, Grand Forks, ND, *Chief Appraiser & VP*, Metropolitan Federal S&L; **PRIM RE ACT:** Appraiser; **SERVICES:** RE appraisals for mort. purpose and investment counseling; **PROFL AFFIL & HONORS:** Soc. of RE Appraisers, SRA; **EDUC:** 1962, Arch. Drafting & Estimating, Univ. of ND & State School of Sci.; **MIL SERV:** US Army Nat. Guard; **OTHER ACT & HONORS:** First Lutheran Church; BPOE 260; **HOME ADD:** 3507 Evergreen Rd., Fargo, ND 58102, (701)293-0602; **BUS ADD:** Box 2687, Third and Fifth St., Fargo, ND 58108, (701)293-2600.

EVERY, Russell B.——*Pres.*, Lamson & Sessions Co.; **PRIM RE ACT:** Property Manager; **BUS ADD:** 2000 Bond Court, Cleveland, OH 44114, (216)781-5000.*

EVILSIZER, Norman E.——B: June 19, 1941, Pilots Knob, IL, *Midwest Region Agency Dir., A.V.P.*, Title Ins. Co. of Minnesota Region; **OTHER RE ACT:** Title ins., Abstracting servs. in Minn., WI, IL, ND, SD, NB, WY, & MT; **SERVICES:** Title ins., escrow & abstract services; **REP CLIENTS:** Lenders, devels., investors, attys., realtors and all related RE fields; **PREV EMPLOY:** St. Paul Title Ins.; Title Ins. Co. of St. Louis; Title Ins. Co. of Los Angeles; Great Western Escrow Co's.; **PROFL AFFIL & HONORS:** Various state land title assns.; **EDUC:** E. IL Univ.; **HOME ADD:** 6733 1st Ave. So., Richfield,, MN, (612)861-1004; **BUS ADD:** 400 2nd Ave. So., Minneapolis, MN 55401, (612)371-1199.

EVKENAZI, S.——*Ed.*, Standard Abstract Corp., Manhattan Apt. House Directory; **PRIM RE ACT:** Real Estate Publisher; **BUS ADD:** 132 Nassua St., New York, NY 10038, (212)732-0225.*

EWERS, Ormond C.——*Sr. Appraiser, Instructor in RE & RE Appraisal*, Ormond C. Ewers Assoc., Suffolk Community Coll.; **PRIM RE ACT:** Consultant, Appraiser, Instructor; **SERVICES:** Appraisals, Educ.; **PREV EMPLOY:** Ins. Co. Appraiser, RE Broker; **PROFL AFFIL & HONORS:** Nat. Trust for Historic Preservation, Nature Conservancy; Past Pres., Wading River Civic Assn.; New Pres., Wading River Historical Soc.; Past Pres., Suffolk Com. Coll. Faculty Sen.; **EDUC:** BS, 1940, Educ., Rutgers Univ.; **GRAD EDUC:** Courses, Univ. of CT, C.W. Post Coll., Adelphi Univ., Southhampton Coll.; **EDUC HONORS:** Public Speaking Medal; **MIL SERV:** USN, Chief; **OTHER ACT & HONORS:** Member Planning Bd. & Zoning Bd. of Appeals; Cont. Ed. Advisory Bd.; Member Republican Nat. Comm.; Former Scoutmaster & Comm. Chmn.; Charter Member Clinton, NY Kiwanis; Rgn. 1, SUNY, Regionalization Comm. (elected); RE Life Experience Evaluator, SUNY (Empire State College), Old Westbury, NY; RE Course Evaluator, Amer. Council on Educ., Wash. DC; **HOME ADD:** Oliver St., Wading River, NY 11792, (516)929-4080; **BUS ADD:** Box 584, Wading River, NY 11792, (516)929-4080.

EWING, P. Van, III——B: May 31, 1946, Columbia, MO, *Owner/Broker*, Century 21 Ewing-Bachman, Inc.; **PRIM RE ACT:** Broker, Developer; **OTHER RE ACT:** Exchangor; **SERVICES:** Exchange counseling, devel. consulting; **PROFL AFFIL & HONORS:** RESSI, Inst. of Creative Mktg.; **EDUC:** BS, 1968, Bus. Admin. & Econ., Drury Coll.; **MIL SERV:** US Army, Lt.; **HOME ADD:** 1115 Eagle Dr., Whiskey Hill, Vail, CO; **BUS ADD:** 2271 N Frontage Rd. W., Vail, CO 81657, (303)476-4721.

EWING, Thomas G.——B: Aug. 21, 1951, Avon, IL, *Managing Agent*, United Realty Corp.; **PRIM RE ACT:** Broker, Property Manager, Insuror; **SERVICES:** Manage office bldgs., indus. bldg., & shopping malls; **PREV EMPLOY:** Comml. banker 1975-1979; **PROFL AFFIL & HONORS:** IREM currently working towards CPM (2/2 complete); **EDUC:** BS Bus Admin., 1974, Bus. Fin., Math and Law, IL State Univ.; **OTHER ACT & HONORS:** Member of the Bd. of Realtors; **HOME ADD:** 104 Oak Knolls Ave. So., Rockford, IL 61100, **BUS ADD:** 120 W. State, Rockford, IL 61101, (815)987-2177.

EXAMITAS, Ronald——*Gen. Coun. & Secy.*, Tasty Baking Co.; **PRIM RE ACT:** Property Manager; **BUS ADD:** 2801 Hunting Park Ave., Philadelphia, PA 19129, (215)221-8500.*

EYRING, Phillip Max——B: Aug. 9, 1934, Berkeley, CA, *Pres.*, Eyring Realty Inc.; **PRIM RE ACT:** Broker, Instructor, Syndicator, Consultant, Appraiser, Developer, Owner/Investor; **SERVICES:** Exchange Realtor; Invest. Counselor; **PREV EMPLOY:** USAF, Chaplain (Capt.); **PROFL AFFIL & HONORS:** Rotary, CCIM, RECI, CRS, GRI; **EDUC:** BS, 1958, Fin. & Banking, Brigham Young Univ.; **GRAD EDUC:** MBA, 1963, RE & Urban Land Econ., UC Berkeley; **EDUC HONORS:** Glenn Willaman Scholarship; **MIL SERV:** USAF, Capt., Chaplain; **OTHER ACT & HONORS:** Pres. El Sobrante C of C; LDS Church; **HOME ADD:** 342 Constance Pl., Moraga, CA 94556, (415)376-6980; **BUS ADD:** 1657 No. California Blvd., "E", Walnut Creek, CA 94596.

FABER, Edward——*Dir.*, Wisconsin Bureau of Real Estate; **PRIM RE ACT:** Property Manager; **BUS ADD:** Box 7921, Madison, WI 53707, (608)266-2135.*

FABIAN, JoAnne——B: Apr. 14, 1934, NJ, *Atty.*, Vailarino McNeil & Fabian; **PRIM RE ACT:** Broker, Attorney, Banker, Owner/Investor, Instructor; **SERVICES:** Exchanges, bus. condo., devel. packages; **PROFL AFFIL & HONORS:** ABA, CA Bar Assn.; **EDUC:** BS, 1955, Biology & Chemistry, Ursinus Coll.; **GRAD EDUC:** MA, 1962, Eng. Lit., Seton Hall Univ.; JD, 1974, Law, Hasting Coll. of Law; **EDUC HONORS:** Law Journal; **OTHER ACT & HONORS:** Dir. & Sec., New Horizons Savings & Loan Assn.; **HOME ADD:** 226 Magnolia Ave., San Rafael, CA 94901, (415)454-6837; **BUS ADD:** 55 Professional Ctr. Pkwy, San Rafael, CA 94903, (415)472-3434.

FABIAN, Samuel T.——B: Feb. 6, 1908, Meriden, CT, *Consultant to Fabian Assoc.*, Fabian Assoc., Const. RE App.; **PRIM RE ACT:** Broker, Consultant, Appraiser; **REP CLIENTS:** Wesleyan Univ., Middletown, Ct., Town of Portland, Portland, CT, Lending Inst., Lawyers; **PREV EMPLOY:** Self & Middletown Housing Auth.; **PROFL AFFIL & HONORS:** Am. Arbitration Assn. Ct. Assn. of Housing & Redevel. Auth., Am. Soc. of Appraisers, Life Member of Salvation Army, awards for outstanding services; **EDUC:** Grinnell Coll., Class of 1933; **OTHER ACT & HONORS:** Exec. Dir. of Middletown, CT. Housing Auth., 1953-68 Exchange Club Past Pres., Past Pres. CT ASA, CT Assoc. of Housing Redev., Middletown RE Bds., Comdr. of Putnam Phalenx, Many Community Service Awards; **HOME ADD:** 162 Old Mill Rd., Middletown, CT 06457, (203)346-8945; **BUS ADD:** 698 Wash St., Middletown, CT 06457, (203)347-3329.

FACEY, John A., III——B: June 14, 1950, Springfield, MA, *Partner*, Keyser, Crowley, Banse, Abell & Facey; **PRIM RE ACT:** Attorney; **SERVICES:** Legal serv. in RE devel. and fin.; **PROFL AFFIL & HONORS:** ABA; VT Bar Assn.; VT & MA Bar; New England Land Title Assn.; **EDUC:** BA, 1972, Hist., Coll. of the Holy Cross; **GRAD EDUC:** JD, 1975, Suffolk Univ. School of Law; **OTHER ACT & HONORS:** Chmn., Subcomm. on Title Ins., VT Bar Assn.; **HOME ADD:** 199 Clematis Ave., Rutland, VT 05701, (802)775-1895; **BUS ADD:** 29 S. Main St., Box 975, Rutland, VT 05701, (802)775-2100.

FADEM, Jerrold A.——B: Jan. 19. 1926, St. Louis, MO, *Partner*, Fadem, Berger & Norton; **PRIM RE ACT:** Attorney; **SERVICES:** Real prop. litigation, eminent domain, construction, environmental, urban affairs, and zoning; trial and appellate practice; **REP CLIENTS:** Western Fed. Savings & Loan, Texaco, Inc., Intl. Telephone & Telegraph Co., Southern Pacific Railroad Co., Title Insurance and Trust Co., Monogram Indus., Inc., Carlsberg Fin. Corp.; **PREV EMPLOY:** Corps. of Engrs., RE Div. 1951-1953; **PROFL AFFIL & HONORS:** Consultant on Eminent Domain for CA Law Revision Comm., Chmn. State Bar Assn. Comm. on Condemnation (Law & Procedure) 1977-1978, Los Angeles Cty. Bar Assn. Comm. on Condemnation Law; **EDUC:** BS, 1947, Indus. Mgmt. and Econ., Univ. of CA at Los Angeles, Wash. Univ., St. Louis; **GRAD EDUC:** JD, 1953, Law, Loyola Univ., Los Angeles; **MIL SERV:** Adjutant Gen. Corp., S. Sgt., 2nd Lt. Reserve; **HOME ADD:** 33 Sea Colony Dr., Santa Monica, CA 90405, (213)396-9292; **BUS ADD:** 501 Santa Monica Blvd., Suite 600, Santa Monica Blvd., Santa Monica, CA 90406, (213)451-9951.

FADIMAN, James——B: May 27, 1939, NY, *Pres.*, Fadiman Corp.; **PRIM RE ACT:** Consultant, Owner/Investor; **SERVICES:** Consulting; **REP CLIENTS:** Crosby Trusts, Indivs.; **PROFL AFFIL & HONORS:** Amer. Psych. Assn.; **EDUC:** BA, 1960, Soc. Relations, Harvard Univ.; **GRAD EDUC:** MA, 1963, Psych., Stanford Univ.; PhD, 1965, Psych., Stanford Univ.; **OTHER ACT & HONORS:** Edited 5 books, co-authored one text book; **HOME ADD:** 1070 Colby Ave., Menlo Park, CA 94025; **BUS ADD:** 1070 Colby Ave., Menlo Park, CA 94025, (415)329-0862.

FAFARD, Madlyn A.——**B:** Nov. 11, 1934, Framingham, MA, *VP*, Fafard Co.; **PRIM RE ACT:** Property Manager; **OTHER RE ACT:** Sales, Mktg., Interior Decorating; **PROFL AFFIL & HONORS:** Nat. Assn. of Home Builders, MA Assn. of Home Builders, MA Assn. Realtors, NAR, Woman of the Year Award 1980; **EDUC:** BS, 1964, Educ., Framingham State Coll.; **GRAD EDUC:** MS, 1970, Reading & Language Arts, Framingham State Coll.; **HOME ADD:** 1060 Grove St., Framingham, MA 01701, (617)877-9350; **BUS ADD:** 290 Eliot, Ashland, MA 01721, (617)881-1600.

FAGAN, Barbara——**B:** Apr. 13, 1938, NY, *Bldg. Mgr.*, Mendix Realty; **PRIM RE ACT:** Property Manager; **PROFL AFFIL & HONORS:** BOMA, 34 Midtown Assn.; **EDUC:** BS, 1959, Hist., NY Univ.; **OTHER ACT & HONORS:** Bd. Member, 9 yrs., Friends Seminary Sch. Comm., Bd. Member 5 yrs., Assn. for Help of Retarded Children; **HOME ADD:** 200 E 78th St., NY, NY, (212)628-5258; **BUS ADD:** 20 Broad St., NY, NY 10005, (212)269-8171.

FAGIN, Robert F.——*Dir. (Actg.)*, Department of Housing and Urban Development, Personnel; **PRIM RE ACT:** Lender; **BUS ADD:** 451 Seventh St., S.W., Washington, DC 20410, (202)755-5500.*

FAIA, Kenneth W.——**B:** Oct. 20, 1927, Houston, TX, *VP*, Security Homestead Assn., Comml. Loan Coordinator; **PRIM RE ACT:** Lender; **SERVICES:** Lender, income producing prop.; **PREV EMPLOY:** First National Bank of Commerce 4 yrs., Delta Mortgage Corp. 20 yrs.; **PROFL AFFIL & HONORS:** Past Pres., Mort. Bankers Assn. of Greater New Orleans; **EDUC:** PhB, 1950, Phil., Loyola Univ. of the South; **MIL SERV:** USMC; Capt.; Korea, 5 Battle stars; **OTHER ACT & HONORS:** Lakeside Ctry. Club; **HOME ADD:** 3904 Ferran Dr., Metairie, LA 70002, (504)455-7766; **BUS ADD:** 221 Carondelet St., New Orleans, LA 70130, (504)587-1311.

FAIGIN, Larry B.——**B:** Nov. 10, 1942, Cleveland, OH, *Gen. Counsel & Sr. VP*, Shapell Industries, Inc.; **PRIM RE ACT:** Attorney, Developer; **SERVICES:** Shapell Indus. is a major devel. of single family dwellings, condos. and comml. sites in the state of CA; **PREV EMPLOY:** Alston, Gaines & Miller, Atlanta, GA and Willkie, Farr and Gallagher, NYC, specializing in RE Law; **PROFL AFFIL & HONORS:** Member, Visiting Comm., Case Western Reserve Univ.; Friends of Beta Falasha Community in Ethiopia; Alpha Epsilon Pi; Phi Alpha Delta; ABA; CA Bar Assn.; Beverly Hills Bar Assn.; NY Bar Assn., Dir., Shapell Indus., Inc.; Dir., First Nat. Bank of Beverly Hills; Citizens Advisory Council, 1984 Olympic Games; **EDUC:** AB, 1965, Law, Case Western Reserve Univ.; **GRAD EDUC:** JD, 1968, Law, Case Western Reserve Univ.; **EDUC HONORS:** Dewit Scholar, 1966, Alumni Scholar, 1967; **BUS ADD:** 8383 Wilshire Blvd., Suite 700, Beverly Hills, CA 90211, (213)655-7330.

FAILLA, Charles Vincent——**B:** Nov. 26, 1939, NY, *Pres.*, Charles V. Failla & Associates, Inc., RE Appraiser; **PRIM RE ACT:** Appraiser; **SERVICES:** RE appraisal, marketability & feasibility studies; **REP CLIENTS:** Lenders, devels., entrepreneurs, investors - nationally; **PREV EMPLOY:** VP & Rgnl. Mgr., So. US for large nat. appraisal co.; **PROFL AFFIL & HONORS:** Member, Appraisal Inst.; Sr. Member, Columbia Soc. of Appraisers, MAI, CSA, GRI, REI; **EDUC:** BA, 1962, Hist., Univ. of Notre Dame; **GRAD EDUC:** MSM, 1977, RE, FL Intl. Univ.; **MIL SERV:** USMC, Capt.; **HOME ADD:** 6580 Santona St., Coral Gables, FL 33134, (305)666-1914; **BUS ADD:** 2911 Bridgeport Ave., Miami, FL 33133, (305)445-5155.

FAIR, J. Henry, Jr.——*Partner*, Holcombe & Fair Realtors; **PRIM RE ACT:** Broker, Consultant, Appraiser, Developer, Syndicator; **SERVICES:** Comml. indus. props., appraisal of RE; **REP CLIENTS:** Gulf Oil, First Nat. Bank, Uniroyal, Eastman Kodak, IBM, Esso, Nestle Co., etc. service stations, shipyard props., office bldgs., condos., apts., motels, etc.; **PROFL AFFIL & HONORS:** AIREA, Soc. of RE Appraisers, Nat. Assn. of RE Bds., SC Assn. of Realtors, Greater Charleston Bd. of Realtors, Pres., Charleston Chap. Soc. of RE Appraisers 1972-3 and 1976-7; **EDUC:** BIE, 1952, GA Tech.; **MIL SERV:** USN, 1952-1954; **BUS ADD:** 205 King St., PO Box 668, Charleston, SC 29402, (803)772-2642.

FAIRCHILD, Kenneth (Ken) H., Jr.——**B:** Apr. 9, 1924, Brooklyn, NY, *Comml. Sales Assn. (Comml. Coordinator)*, Red Carpet, Michael Shinn & Assoc., Inc. (Formerly Century-21), Comml. Div.; **PRIM RE ACT:** Consultant, Owner/Investor, Instructor; **OTHER RE ACT:** Comml. Investment & Indus. Props.; **SERVICES:** Full resid. & comml. & referral through 10 metro offices; **PREV EMPLOY:** Commodities both Grains & Lumber; **PROFL AFFIL & HONORS:** GRI & Candidate for CCIM, Local Bd. of Realtor of the Year Comml. Sales 1974, Pres. Club past 4 years, Top Comml. producer for firm 1980; **EDUC:** BBA, 1950, Law & Econs., Univ. of Denver; **GRAD EDUC:** Statistics, Commodity Trading, RE, Various; **MIL SERV:** USN, 1943-1946, P/O 3/c, Theaters all; **HOME ADD:** 3300 So. Tamarac Dr. #C-206, Denver, CO 80231, (303)752-2698; **BUS ADD:** 6850 East Evans Ave., Denver, CO 80224, (303)758-2880.

FAIRCLOTH, Bradley——*Mktg. Mgr.*, Bessemer Improvement Co.; **PRIM RE ACT:** Developer; **BUS ADD:** 822 N. Elm St., PO Box 6367, Greensboro, NC 27405, (919)272-8179.*

FAIRFIELD, Al——**B:** Aug. 26, 1934, Blytheville, AR, *Pres.*, Fairfield Co.; **PRIM RE ACT:** Developer, Builder, Owner/Investor; **SERVICES:** Devel. office bldgs., subdivs., build various housing; **PROFL AFFIL & HONORS:** ULI, Natl. Assn. of Homebuilders, Houston C of C; **EDUC:** BBA, 1958, Mgmt., So. Methodist Univ.; **MIL SERV:** US Army, Sgt., Various Decorations; **OTHER ACT & HONORS:** Houston Racquet Club, Houston Ski Club; **HOME ADD:** 5001 Woodway, Suite 1802, Houston, TX 77056, (713)623-8248; **BUS ADD:** 9575 Katy Freeway, Suite 300, Houston, TX 77024, (713)461-6142.

FAITH, Peter J.——**B:** Aug. 3, 1912, Austria, *Owner*, Faith Realty Co.; **PRIM RE ACT:** Broker, Appraiser; **OTHER RE ACT:** Farm Specialist, Auctioneer, Tax Practitioner, RE Auctioneer; **PREV EMPLOY:** In RE and farm operation for 25 yrs.; **EDUC:** RE-Tax, Bookkeeping, Acctg., Tax Acctg., 6 years up-dating tax work H & R Block, Univ. of WI; **OTHER ACT & HONORS:** Former member of Realtors Assn. Auctioneers Assn., Member of the State and National Auctioneers Assn. for the past twenty years; **HOME ADD:** Route 2, Whitewater, WI 53190, (414)473-2779; **BUS ADD:** Rte 2 Hwy 12, Parker Rd., Whitewater, WI 53190, (414)473-2779.

FALCK, Randall F.——**B:** June 26, 1947, Los Angeles, CA, *Sr. VP*, Kilroy Industries; **PRIM RE ACT:** Appraiser, Developer, Builder; **OTHER RE ACT:** Project fin.; **SERVICES:** Full range office & indust. devel; **REP CLIENTS:** Tenants include Hughes Aircraft, Rockwell, Northrop, NCR, Honeywell, Security Pacific Bank, Pacific Mutual Life; **PREV EMPLOY:** Security Pacific Bank Corp., Banking Dept., RE Ind. Div and Investment Dept.; **PROFL AFFIL & HONORS:** NARA, CRA; **EDUC:** BS, 1970, Fin., USC; **GRAD EDUC:** MBA, 1971, Fin., USC; **EDUC HONORS:** Cum Laude; **OTHER ACT & HONORS:** L.A. Philharmonic Men's Committee; **BUS ADD:** 2230 E. Imperial Hwy., El Segundo, CA 90245, (213)772-1193.

FALIK, Thomas A.——**B:** June 10, 1951, Houston, TX, *Partner*, Hiller, Kornfeld & Falik; **OTHER RE ACT:** Gen. Bus. and RE; **SERVICES:** Representation in all areas of RE including devel. and for. investors; **PROFL AFFIL & HONORS:** Member, ABA Comm. on RE Tax Problems, and Comm. on For. Investment in US RE, CPA, TX, 1976; **EDUC:** BS, 1973, Econ./Acctg., Univ. of PA, Wharton School; **GRAD EDUC:** JD, 1976, Univ. of TX; **EDUC HONORS:** Beta Alpha Psi, Phi Delta Phi; **OTHER ACT & HONORS:** UJA Nat. Young Leadership Cabinet; **HOME ADD:** 8015 Duffield Ln., Houston, TX 77071, (713)777-8999; **BUS ADD:** 1908 Summit Tower, Eleven Greenway Plaza, Houston, TX 77046, (713)621-6310.

FALK, Emanuel E.——**B:** July 23, 1904, Newport News, VA, *Sr. Partner*, Drucker & Falk; **PRIM RE ACT:** Broker, Consultant, Appraiser, Property Manager, Insuror, Syndicator; **REP CLIENTS:** City Corp. RE, Inc. - John Hancock Ins. Co., Arlen Realty; **PROFL AFFIL & HONORS:** MAI, CRE, CPM, 1960 Natl. Pres. IREM, Past Pres. Newport News Bd. of Realtors, 1962 Realtor of Year - State of VA; **EDUC:** 2 years Univ. of VA, 1921-23; **OTHER ACT & HONORS:** Past Commnr. Peninsula Port Authority of VA, Past Pres. United Way; **HOME ADD:** 27 Garland Dr., Newport News, VA 23606, (804)595-5397; **BUS ADD:** 9286 Warwick Blvd., Newport News, VA 23607, (804)245-1541.

FALKENBERG, Mary Ann——**B:** Dec. 8, 1931, Chicago, IL, *Broker, Mgr. & Co-Owner*, Associates Realty Corporation; **PRIM RE ACT:** Broker, Consultant, Instructor, Owner/Investor, Property Manager; **SERVICES:** Relocation consultant, mgr.; **REP CLIENTS:** Union Oil, Motorola, Gould, Victor Comptometer, Chrysler Corp.; **PREV EMPLOY:** Top producer with Quinlan & Tyson, Inc.; **PROFL AFFIL & HONORS:** NAR, Cert. Home Protection Consultant, IL Assn. of RE Bds., Exec. Female, Life member in both One & Two Million Dollar Clubs, The 10th Member of the MAP MLS to attain a life membership in the two Mill. Dollar Club in the History of the MAP serv. (25 yrs.); **EDUC:** 1953, Music, Barat Coll. and Northwestern Univ.; **EDUC HONORS:** Always grad. with highest honors, attained scholarship; **OTHER ACT & HONORS:** Served in capacities of leadership in politics, local profl. groups, membership in Women's Clubs, etc.; Actively serves as organist and adult choir dir. for 25 yrs. at local church; **HOME ADD:** 517 Warwick Dr., Palatine, IL 60067, (312)358-2273; **BUS ADD:** 630 N. Court, Palatine, IL 60067, (312)991-6500.

FALKER, Michael J.——B: June 21, 1946, NY, NY, *Gen. Part.*, Cambridge Assoc.; **PRIM RE ACT:** Developer; **PREV EMPLOY:** Gen. Counsel to F.I.P. Corp., CT's largest indus. dev.; **PROFL AFFIL & HONORS:** Member of the CT Bar Assn.; **EDUC:** BA, 1968, Eng., Rutgers Coll.; **GRAD EDUC:** JD, 1971, Univ. of CT School of Law; **EDUC HONORS:** Law Review; **BUS ADD:** 750 Main St., Hartford, CT 06103, (203)727-1854.

FALLENBAUM, Sam——B: Mar. 28, 1941, Montreal, Can., *VP of Fin.*, Peel Properties International, Inc.; **PRIM RE ACT:** Developer, Builder; **OTHER RE ACT:** CPA; **SERVICES:** Builder/devel.; **PREV EMPLOY:** Private practice; **PROFL AFFIL & HONORS:** Inst. of Chartered Accountants, FL Atlantic Bldrs. Assn.; **EDUC:** BA, 1963, Acctg. & Fin., McGill Univ.; **HOME ADD:** 1361 NW 94th Terr., Plantation, FL 33322, (305)475-9894; **BUS ADD:** 5820 N Federal Hwy, Suite A, Boca Raton, FL 33431, (305)997-7022.

FALLIS, Barry E.——B: Mar. 9, 1935, NYC, NY, *Pres.*, Britton Devel. Ltd.; **PRIM RE ACT:** Developer; **SERVICES:** Site selection, investment, arch., fin., constr. and mktg.; **REP CLIENTS:** For. & Domestic investors; **PROFL AFFIL & HONORS:** NYS Soc. CPA, AICPA, CPA; **EDUC:** BS, 1956, Acctg., NY Univ.; **MIL SERV:** US Army, Cpl.; **HOME ADD:** 305 E. 70th St., NY, NY 10021, (212)288-4157; **BUS ADD:** 501 E. 75th St., NY, NY 10021, (212)734-5600.

FALLON, Michael P.——B: Aug. 19, 1940, Baltimore, MD, *Pres.*, Northwest Realty; **PRIM RE ACT:** Broker, Consultant, Engineer, Attorney, Appraiser, Developer, Builder, Syndicator; **SERVICES:** Consulting and devel.; **REP CLIENTS:** Mfrs., comml. bldgs., const. firms; **PREV EMPLOY:** Ford Motor Co.; MCC Powers; Square D Co.; **PROFL AFFIL & HONORS:** NAR; Nat. Assn. of Business Economists; Nat. Assn. of Profl. Engrs., Who's Who in Fin.; Chmn., Mayors Youth Council; **EDUC:** BS, 1968, Eng./Econ., Univ. of MD; **GRAD EDUC:** MBA, 1978, Univ. of Chicago; **EDUC HONORS:** Delta Mu Delta; **OTHER ACT & HONORS:** Pres., Park Ridge Park Dist.; Kahkawa Ctry. Club; Plaza Club; **HOME ADD:** 300 Talcott Pl., Park Ridge, IL 60068, (312)825-0087; **BUS ADD:** 361 W. 11th St., Erie, PA 16512, (814)454-8101.

FALLS, Edward Joseph——B: Feb. 24, 1920, NYC, NY; **PRIM RE ACT:** Attorney; **PROFL AFFIL & HONORS:** NY State Bar; IL State Bar; CA State Bar Assn.; ABA, RE section; **EDUC:** BS, 1940, St. Johns Univ.; **GRAD EDUC:** JD, 1946, St. Johns; **BUS ADD:** 695 Town Ctr. Drive, #640, Costa Mesa, CA 92626.

FALTZ, Richard A.——B: Sept. 12, 1946, Sandwich, IL, *VP*, Don L. Dise, Inc.; **PRIM RE ACT:** Developer, Builder, Property Manager, Syndicator; **OTHER RE ACT:** Land planning & devel., const.; **SERVICES:** Land planning, const. mgmt.; **PROFL AFFIL & HONORS:** Nat. Assn. Home Bldrs., Urban Land Inst.; **EDUC:** BS, 1968, Mktg., Bus., Northern IL Univ., Dekalb, IL; **OTHER ACT & HONORS:** 5 Yrs., City Govt., City Council Member; **HOME ADD:** 405 E. Dekalb St., Somonauk, IL 60552, (815)498-2663; **BUS ADD:** PO Box 1107, Aurora, IL 60552, (312)897-6900.

FAN, Albert C.——B: May 26, 1945, An-Whei, China, *Bus. Mgr.*, Houston International Success Realty; **PRIM RE ACT:** Broker, Consultant, Appraiser, Architect, Developer, Builder, Owner/Investor, Property Manager, Syndicator; **REP CLIENTS:** T.D. Enterprises, ACF Interest, Houston Intl. RE Research & Investment; **EDUC:** BArch, 1968, Arch. & City Planning, Coll. of Chinese Culture; **GRAD EDUC:** MArch, 1972, Arch. & Urban Devel., Univ. of NE, Lincoln NE; **EDUC HONORS:** Teaching Scholarship; Regency Fellowship; Honorable Citizen of the State of NE 1973; **OTHER ACT & HONORS:** Supervision of Construction, NJDOD; NCARB; **HOME ADD:** 8811 Wind Side Dr., Houston, TX 77040; **BUS ADD:** Box 40622, Houston, TX 77040, (713)466-4750.

FANCERA, Anthony J.——B: Mar. 2, 1956, Elizabeth, NJ, *VP*, Robeng, Inc.; **PRIM RE ACT:** Consultant, Builder, Owner/Investor, Syndicator; **OTHER RE ACT:** Investment counseling; **SERVICES:** Conversion and mgmt. of resid. prop.; **REP CLIENTS:** Indivs. & profls. in resid. props.; **PROFL AFFIL & HONORS:** Amer. Mgmt. Assn., Amer. Entrepreneur Assn.; **HOME ADD:** 243 Scotland St., Scotch Plains, NJ 07076, (201)322-1736; **BUS ADD:** 243 Scotland St., Scotch Plains, NJ 07076, (201)322-1736.

FANCY, Sidney E.C.——B: July 3, 1937, England, *Mgr. Econ. Devel.*, City of Vancouver, Econ. Devel.; **PRIM RE ACT:** Consultant; **OTHER RE ACT:** Member, Indus. Park Mktg. Comm.; **SERVICES:** Brief industrialists on available indus. land in Vancouver, and on the local economy in general; **PREV EMPLOY:** Manitoba Dept. of Indus. & Commerce, Consultant; Publisher, Dauphin Herald, Dauphin, Manitoba; City of Saskatoon, SK - Indus. Parks; City of Brandon, MB - Indus. Parks; **PROFL AFFIL & HONORS:** Member & Dir. - Indus. Devels. Assn. of CAN., Member, Amer. Econ. Devel. Council, Member, Pacific NW Indus. Devel. Council, Member, Econ, Develop. Assn. of BC; **EDUC:** BA, 1960, Geography and English, Univ. of BC; **MIL SERV:** Can. Army (Regular), Lt. 1956-1963; Can. Army (Militia), Capt., 1967-1969; **HOME ADD:** Delta, BC, (604)943-8093; **BUS ADD:** Ste721-601 W. Broadway Ave., Vancouver, V5Z4C2, BC, (604)873-7212.

FANNING, Ronald H., AIA,PE——B: Oct. 5, 1935, Evanston, IL, *Pres.*, Fanning/Howey Associates, Inc.; **PRIM RE ACT:** Engineer, Architect, Developer, Owner/Investor, Property Manager, Syndicator; **SERVICES:** Complete devel. serv. from concept to completion of project with prop. mgmt.; **PROFL AFFIL & HONORS:** AIA; Nat. Soc. of Profl. Engrs.; **EDUC:** BArch., 1959, Arch., Miami Univ.; **MIL SERV:** USMC 1960-1968, Pvt.; **OTHER ACT & HONORS:** Elks; **HOME ADD:** 422 Magnolia St., Celina, OH 45822, (419)586-3879; **BUS ADD:** 540 E Market St., Celina, OH 45822, (419)586-7771.

FANT, Francis R., Jr.——B: Oct. 28, 1940, Anderson, SC, *Atty.*; **PRIM RE ACT:** Attorney, Developer, Owner/Investor; **SERVICES:** Legal Ser; **PROFL AFFIL & HONORS:** ABA, SC State Bar; Anderson Cty. Bar Assn. (Pres. 1980); **EDUC:** BA, 1962, Erskine Coll.; **GRAD EDUC:** JD, 1962, Univ. of SC Law School; **EDUC HONORS:** Order of Wig and Robe; **OTHER ACT & HONORS:** Dir., Montessori School of Anderson; **HOME ADD:** Anderson, SC; **BUS ADD:** P.O. Box 498, Anderson, SC 29622, (803)226-3444.

FANTLE, Charles——B: Sept. 4, 1942, Ft. Dodge, IA, *Pres.*, Unicorn Properties, Inc.; **PRIM RE ACT:** Broker, Consultant, Owner/Investor, Property Manager; **OTHER RE ACT:** Condo converter; **SERVICES:** RE brokerage, condo conversion and prop. mgmt.; **PREV EMPLOY:** Builder/devel.; **PROFL AFFIL & HONORS:** IREM, Bd. of Realtors; **EDUC:** BS, 1968, Mktg., Univ. of S. FL; **OTHER ACT & HONORS:** CPM Designation; **HOME ADD:** 4334 Outrigger Ln., Tampa, FL 33615, (813)885-3653; **BUS ADD:** 2117 S. Dale Mabry, Tampa, FL 33609, (813)253-0212.

FARARD, Howard——B: Nov. 25, 1939, Milford, MA, *Pres.*, Farard Cos.; **PRIM RE ACT:** Consultant, Developer, Builder, Owner/Investor, Property Manager, Broker; **OTHER RE ACT:** Contracting; **SERVICES:** All above plus engr.; **PROFL AFFIL & HONORS:** Nat. Assn. of Home Builders, MA Assn. of Home Builders, Chmn, of the Bd. of Investment, Milford Savings Bank, Milford, MA; **HOME ADD:** Onset Avenue, Buzzards Bay, MA 02532, (617)881-1600; **BUS ADD:** 290 Eliot St., Ashland, MA 01721, (617)881-1600.

FARHA, George S.——B: Feb. 2, 1918, Lebanon, *Owner/Mgr.*, George Farha & Co.; **PRIM RE ACT:** Broker, Attorney, Developer, Owner/Investor, Property Manager; **PROFL AFFIL & HONORS:** OK City Metro. Bd. of Realtors, Urban Redev. Comm., CCIM Candidate; **EDUC:** LLB, 1955, Law, OK Univ., W VA Tech, Univ. of Grenoble, OK City Univ.; **GRAD EDUC:** JD, 1973, OK City Univ. Sch. of Law; **EDUC HONORS:** 3rd in grad. class; **MIL SERV:** USAF, Capt., 1941-45, 1950-52, Air Medal with 5 clusters & sev. lesser medals; **OTHER ACT & HONORS:** OK City Rotary Club, C of C, Sr. Warden St. John's Episcopal Church (highest layman office); **HOME ADD:** 5513 N Billen, OK City, OK 73112, (405)842-5706; **BUS ADD:** 4101 N Classen, Suite F, Oklahoma Cty, OK 73118, (405)525-5072.

FARKAS, Robin L.——B: Oct. 13, 1933, NY, NY, *Chmn. of the Board*, Alexander's Inc.; **OTHER RE ACT:** Administration; **SERVICES:** Site selection, market analysis, negotiation, mgmt.; **PREV EMPLOY:** Staff consultant-Arthur D. Little; **PROFL AFFIL & HONORS:** ICSC, NY RE bd.; **EDUC:** BA, 1954, Social Relations, Harvard Univ.; **GRAD EDUC:** MBA, 1961, Harvard Grad. School of Bus.; **MIL SERV:** US Army, SP3; **OTHER ACT & HONORS:** 1972 Cert. of Appreciation, City of NY; **HOME ADD:** 730 Park Ave., NY, NY 10021, (212)249-0815; **BUS ADD:** 500 7th Ave., NY, NY 10018, (212)560-2137.

FARLEY, Jack L.——B: Apr. 23, 1937, Henderson, KY, *Pres.*, Village Green Subdivision, Inc.; **PRIM RE ACT:** Broker, Developer, Builder, Property Manager; **PROFL AFFIL & HONORS:** Home Builders Assn. of Louisville (Past Pres., VP, Treas., Sec and Dir.); Nat. Home Builder's Assn., Life Dir.; Home Builder's Assn. of KY, Past Dir. and Past Chmn. of the VA-FHA Commn., KIPDA, Housing Commn. member; Mayor's Task Force on Housing, 1977 Home Builder of the Year Award, HBAL; **EDUC:** Civil Engr. (3 yrs.) RE (2 yrs.), Univ. of Louisville, Speed Scientific Sch.; **MIL SERV:** US Army, Pvt. SP-4, Distinguished Pistol Badge; **OTHER ACT & HONORS:** Kosair Shrine; **HOME ADD:** 7540 Riva Ridge Rd., Louisville, KY 40214, (502)361-1541; **BUS ADD:** 7540 Riva Ridge Rd., Louisville, KY 40214, (502)361-1541.

FARLEY, William H.——**B:** Dec. 17, 1936, Brockton, MA, *Pres.*, The Farley Co.; **PRIM RE ACT:** Broker, Consultant, Developer, Property Manager; **PREV EMPLOY:** Meredith & Grew, Inc.; **PROFL AFFIL & HONORS:** Pres. CT Valley BOMA, VP & Bd. of Dir., Office Network, Inc.; **EDUC:** BS, 1958, Econ., Holy Cross Coll.; **GRAD EDUC:** MBA, 1963, Fin., Univ. of CT; **OTHER ACT & HONORS:** Town of Simsbury Library Bd., Chmn. 1972-81, Chmn. of Bd. Hartt Coll. of Music, Bd. of Regents, Univ. of Hartford, Bd. of Trustees, State Bank for Savings; **HOME ADD:** 16 Saw Mill Rd., W. Simsbury, CT 06092, (203)658-5948; **BUS ADD:** 100 Pearl St., Hartford, CT 06103, (203)525-9171.

FARMER, Fred——**B:** May 25, 1946, Mayfield, KY, *Asst. VP*, DeRand Investment Corporation, Tax Shelters; **PRIM RE ACT:** Broker, Lender, Instructor, Syndicator; **OTHER RE ACT:** Financial Planner; **SERVICES:** Synd. RE on a nat. basis; sale of securities to investors; financial planning; **REP CLIENTS:** Private and instnl. investors, builders; **PREV EMPLOY:** Unity Mort. Corp., Asst. VP, 1978-1981; **PROFL AFFIL & HONORS:** MBAA; MD Bd. of Realtors; Nat. Assn. of RE Educators; International Association of Financial Planners; **EDUC:** BS, 1972, Bus. Mgmt., Univ. of MD; **MIL SERV:** USAF; 1966-1968; **OTHER ACT & HONORS:** Gaithersburg Jaycees; **HOME ADD:** 11 Bouldercrest Ct., Rockville, MD 20850, (301)279-2265; **BUS ADD:** 2201 Wilson Boulevard, Arlington, VA 22201, (703)527-3827.

FARNEY, Duncan R.——**B:** Oct. 30, 1941, Carthage, NY, *Principal*, Johnson, Mullan, Brundage & Keigher, P.C.; **PRIM RE ACT:** Attorney, Instructor; **SERVICES:** All gen. RE legal serv., including preparation of offering plans for condo. and townhouse assns.; **REP CLIENTS:** The Cabot Grp., Inc.; Mendon Valley, Inc.; Bristol Mountain Village; **PREV EMPLOY:** Harter Secrest & Emery, Rochester N.Y. 1966-1973; **PROFL AFFIL & HONORS:** Monroe Cty. Bar Assn.; NY State Bar Assn.; Community Assns. Inst., Justinian Soc.; **EDUC:** BA, 1963, Hist., Hamilton Coll.; **GRAD EDUC:** LLB, 1966, Prop. & Estates, Syracuse Univ. Coll. of Law; **EDUC HONORS:** Justinian Soc., Comments Editor-Syr Law Review; **OTHER ACT & HONORS:** Trustee - Fairport Public Library 1971-75; Trustee-Chi Psi Assn. of Hamilton Coll.; Asbury First United Methodist Church, Rochester, NY; 1982 Chairman - Real Estate Section, Monroe County Bar Assn.; **HOME ADD:** 319 San Gabriel Dr., Rochester, NY 14610; **BUS ADD:** 47 S. Fitzhugh St., Rochester, NY 14614, (716)262-5700.

FARNSWORTH, Larry A.——**B:** Jan. 27, 1935, Bunkerville, NV, *Owner*, Farnsworth Co.; **PRIM RE ACT:** Consultant; **OTHER RE ACT:** Resid., Designer, Artist, 200 Newspaper Synd. Column, Publisher: Southwest Home Review; **SERVICES:** House Plans; **REP CLIENTS:** 6000 Small contractors and realtors; **EDUC:** Arch, Engrg., Univ. of OR, Univ. of UT; **MIL SERV:** US Army, Cpl.; **OTHER ACT & HONORS:** LVWD 5 yrs. Rgnl. Planning; **BUS ADD:** PO Box 1841, Las Vegas, NV 89125, (702)384-4202.

FARR, Dennis P.——**B:** Sept. 12, 1947, Kansas City, MO, *Mgr., Appraisal Servs.*, Coldwell Banker, Appraisal Servs.; **PRIM RE ACT:** Consultant, Appraiser; **SERVICES:** RE Appraisals, consultation; **REP CLIENTS:** Prop. owners, devels., investors; **PREV EMPLOY:** Winius-Montandon, Inc.; **PROFL AFFIL & HONORS:** AIREA; SREA; **EDUC:** BS, 1978, RE, AZ State Univ.; **MIL SERV:** US Army, SP-5, 1966-69; **HOME ADD:** 3001 N 47th St., Phoenix, AZ 85018, (602)959-2984; **BUS ADD:** 2346 N Central Ave., Phoenix, AZ 85004, (602)262-5588.

FARR, Gary L.——**B:** Apr. 26, 1942, Seattle, WA, *Prop. Mgr.*, Seattle City Light, Prop. Mgmt.; **PRIM RE ACT:** Regulator, Owner/Investor, Property Manager; **OTHER RE ACT:** Governmental (Utility) Acquisition, Mgmt. & Sales; **SERVICES:** Purchase Rights of Way for Electrical Transmission, manage R's/W & other props., sale of surplus props.; **PREV EMPLOY:** Right of Way, Sr. Real Prop. Agent (City of Seattle); Asst. Engr., City of Seattle, Engrg. Dept (1961-1975); **PROFL AFFIL & HONORS:** Senior Member, Intl. Right of Way Assn.; Seattle Mgmt. Assn.; **EDUC:** Assoc. RE Degree, 1977, RE, Shoreline Community Coll., Seattle; **HOME ADD:** 1912 NE 127th, Seattle, WA 98125, (206)364-8392; **BUS ADD:** 1015 3rd Ave., Seattle, WA 98125, (206)625-3394.

FARRAR, David W.——**B:** Aug. 25, 1942, Clifton Forge, VA, *Partner*, Sheppard, Mullin, Richter & Hampton; **PRIM RE ACT:** Attorney; **SERVICES:** Sale and loan documentation and negotiation; **REP CLIENTS:** Fin. instns., devels., for. investors; **PROFL AFFIL & HONORS:** CA and Amer. Bar Assns.; Real Prop. and Taxation Sects., Lecturer, CA Continuing Educ. of the Bar; **EDUC:** BA, 1964, Eng./Physchology, Univ. of VA; **GRAD EDUC:** JD, 1973, Univ. of VA; **MIL SERV:** USN, Lt. Comdr., Distinguished Flying Cross; **HOME ADD:** 214 N. Gower St., Los Angeles, CA 90004, (213)467-5317; **BUS ADD:** 333 South Hope St., 48th Floor, Los Angeles, CA 90071, (213)620-1780.

FARRELL, Reid D.——**B:** Sept. 26, 1927, Gastonia, NC, *Pres.*, Farrell Realty, Inc.; **PRIM RE ACT:** Broker; **SERVICES:** Marketing resid. & vacant land, fin.; **REP CLIENTS:** Indiv. sellers primarily; Also General Motors, General Telephone, IBM, 3M, Employee Transfer Corp.; **PREV EMPLOY:** Volume builder and devel.; **PROFL AFFIL & HONORS:** Nat. Assn. of Realtors; Realtors Nat. Marketing Instit.; FL Assn. of Realtors; Sarasota Bd. of Realtors; All Points Relocation Service, Inc., CRB & CRS ; GRI ; Treas., FAR; Dir., NAR; Realtor of the Yr.; Pres., Sarasota Bd. of Realtors; **EDUC:** BS, 1949, Yarn Mgmt./Textile Engrg., NC State Univ.; **EDUC HONORS:** Cum Laude; **MIL SERV:** USN, PO 3rd Class; **OTHER ACT & HONORS:** RE Consultant to Sarasota Hospital Bd.; Dir., C of C & Kiwanis; **HOME ADD:** 1703 Bay View Dr., Sarasota, FL 33579, (813)955-5331; **BUS ADD:** 2065 Constitution Blvd., Sarasota, FL 33581, (813)924-1293.

FARRELL, Robert J., Jr.——**B:** Buffalo, NY, *Mgr.*, R.J. Farrell & Co., Inc., RE Investment; **PRIM RE ACT:** Syndicator; **REP CLIENTS:** Pension Funds; **EDUC:** AB, 1981, Fin., St. Michael's Coll., Winooski, VT; **BUS ADD:** Suite 616, Lewis Wharf, Boston, MA 02110, (617)523-0828.

FARREN, John B., Jr.——**B:** Oct. 18, 1942, Boston, MA, *Sr. VP and Chief of Operations*, Cadillac Fairview Urban Development, Inc., S. Rgn.; **PRIM RE ACT:** Developer, Owner/Investor, Property Manager; **SERVICES:** Devel. for own account and in joint ventures; **REP CLIENTS:** Joint ventures with TX E. Corp. and Frost Natl. Bank; **PREV EMPLOY:** Paramount Equities Ltd., Pres Trizee S. Ltd., VP Crow Carter Assoc. Devel. Officer; **PROFL AFFIL & HONORS:** ULI, NACORE, AM Fin. Assn., Forum Club of Houston; **EDUC:** BS, 1965, Acctg., Boston Coll., Sch. of Mgmt.; **GRAD EDUC:** MBA, 1971, Fin. and RE, Univ. of CA at Berkeley; **EDUC HONORS:** Magna cum laude, with distinction; **MIL SERV:** USN, Sub. Serv., Lt. 0-3, Presidential Unit Citation; **OTHER ACT & HONORS:** Bd. Member, Houston Ctr. Club; **HOME ADD:** The Warrington, 3831 Turtle Creek Blvd., Suite 4G, Dallas, TX 75219, (214)528-0136; **BUS ADD:** 5252 First International Bldg., 1201 Elm St., Dallas, TX 75270, (214)748-0441.

FARRIS, David——*Mgr. Branch Plants*, Trane Co.; **PRIM RE ACT:** Property Manager; **BUS ADD:** 3600 Pammel Creek Rd., LaCrosse, WI 54601, (608)787-2000.*

FASANO, Michael V.——**B:** Oct. 30, 1948, Teaneck, NJ, *VP*, General Investment Funds (unit of the General Tire & Rubber Co.); **PRIM RE ACT:** Consultant, Owner/Investor, Property Manager; **OTHER RE ACT:** Articles published include (1) "Why Public Buildings Cost So Much", *RE Review*, Spring 1981 and (2) "Commingled RE Funds Capture Investor's Interest", *Pension & Investments*, March 26, 1979; **PREV EMPLOY:** 1972-1976; Exec. Office of the Pres., Office of Mgmt. & Budget, Sr. Budget Examiner responsible for the Gen. Serv. Admin.; **PROFL AFFIL & HONORS:** Instit. of RE Mgmt.; Wash. Bd. of Realtors; CPM; **EDUC:** BA, 1970, Econ., NW Univ.; **GRAD EDUC:** MA, 1970, Public Admin., Univ. of WI, Madison; **HOME ADD:** 1536 17th St., NW, Wash., DC 20036, (202)232-1756; **BUS ADD:** 5454 Wisconsin Ave., Suite 710, Washington, DC 20015, (301)657-2880.

FATE, Gary A.——**B:** Jan. 9, 1943, Columbus, OH, *Asst. VP*, Citicorp RE, Inc.; **PRIM RE ACT:** Broker, Banker; **SERVICES:** Const. and Interim loans, placement of long term debt; **REP CLIENTS:** RE Devels. and Instnl. Lenders; **PREV EMPLOY:** Advance Mort. Corp., Manufacturers Hanover Mort. Corp., Citizens Mort. Investment Trust, Buckeye Federal S&L Cols. OH; **PROFL AFFIL & HONORS:** MBAA; **EDUC:** BS, Bus. Admin., 1965, RE, OH State Univ.; **GRAD EDUC:** MBA, 1971, RE & Fin., OH State Univ.; **MIL SERV:** US Army, 1st Lt.; **HOME ADD:** 1030 W. Chicago Ave. Apt. 104, Oak Park, IL 60302, (312)383-7819; **BUS ADD:** 200 S. Wacker Dr., Chicago, IL 60606, (312)993-3213.

FAUBUS, Donald E.——**B:** Jan. 20, 1944, Santa Barbara, CA, *Atty.*, Law Office of Donald E. Faubus; **PRIM RE ACT:** Attorney; **SERVICES:** RE contracts/negotiation; Litigation; **PROFL AFFIL & HONORS:** ABA, Los Angeles Bar Assn., Whittier Bar Assn.; **EDUC:** BS, 1966, Bus. Admin, UCLA; **GRAD EDUC:** JD, 1974, Law, McGeorge School of Law, Univ. of the Pacific; **EDUC HONORS:** CA Scholarship Fed. and UCLA Alumni Scholarships, Traynor Soc. (Life Member), Amer. Jurisprudence Award (Civil Procedure); **MIL SERV:** USAF, Capt., Bronze Star; **HOME ADD:** 2149 Las Lomitas, Hacienda Hgts., CA; **BUS ADD:** 16131 E. Whittier Blvd., Suite 100, Whittier, CA 90603, (213)947-4628.

FAULCONER, Michael N.——B: Dec. 21, 1941, Norfolk, VA, *VP*, Yeargin Properties, Inc.; **PRIM RE ACT:** Broker, Consultant, Appraiser, Developer, Owner/Investor; **SERVICES:** Devel. of prop., prop. evaluation, mktg., leasing & mgmt., referrals for other servs., site selection & analysis; **PREV EMPLOY:** Liberty Life Ins. Co., 1968-1972; Gulfco Capital Mgmt., 1972-1980; **PROFL AFFIL & HONORS:** Intl. Assn. of Fin. Planners; Inst. of Cert. Fin. Planners (provisional member); Nat. Assn. of Real Prop. Appraisers; Nat. Assn. of Review Appraisers; **EDUC:** BA, 1964, Bus./Hist., Davidson Coll.; **MIL SERV:** US Army Intelligence, 1st Lt., Special Forces; **HOME ADD:** 208 Dove Tree Rd., Greenville, SC 29607, (803)288-4673; **BUS ADD:** POB 6508, Greenville, SC 29606, (803)242-6960.

FAUST, Robert L.——B: Feb. 28, 1938, Dallas, TX, *Pres.*, Robert Faust Mort. Co.; **PRIM RE ACT:** Broker, Lender; **PREV EMPLOY:** Glenn Justice Mort. Co.; **PROFL AFFIL & HONORS:** SRA Affiliate Member, Dallas Bd. of Realtors; Dallas Home & Apt. Builders, OK RE License; **EDUC:** BBA, 1960, Econ. & Fin., Southern Methodist Univ.; **MIL SERV:** US Army; PFC, 1960-1962; **OTHER ACT & HONORS:** Bent Tree Ctry. Club, Dallas Gun Club; **HOME ADD:** 7607 Rambler Rd., Dallas, TX 75231, (214)363-9200; **BUS ADD:** 6060 N. Central Expwy, Suite 734, Dallas, TX 75206, (214)691-1545.

FAVERO, Paul J.——B: May 18, 1948, Los Angeles, CA, *VP*, First Los Angeles Bank, RE; **PRIM RE ACT:** Banker, Lender; **SERVICES:** RE loans, interim fin., AITD loans, second TD loans; **PREV EMPLOY:** Bank of Amer., NT & SA, 1971-78; **PROFL AFFIL & HONORS:** So. CA Mort. Bankers Assn.; **EDUC:** BA, 1973, Psych., CA State Univ., Los Angeles; **HOME ADD:** 961 Brightwood St., Monterey Park, CA 91754, (213)268-9686; **BUS ADD:** 1950 Ave. of the Stars, Los Angeles, CA 90067, (213)557-1211.

FAWCETT, J. Scott——B: Nov. 5, 1937, Pittsburgh, PA, *Exec. VP*, Marinita Dev. Co.; **PRIM RE ACT:** Broker, Appraiser, Developer, Builder, Owner/Investor; **PREV EMPLOY:** Shell Oil Co., Land Investment Mgr. (1970-1976); **PROFL AFFIL & HONORS:** Bldg. Indus. Assoc.; Intl. Right of Way Assoc.; NARA; Intl. Inst. of Valuers; **EDUC:** BS, 1959, Mktg., Ohio State Univ.; **MIL SERV:** US Army; 1960-62; **OTHER ACT & HONORS:** Univ. Athletic Club; **HOME ADD:** 8739 Hudson River Cir., Fountain Valley, CA 92708, (714)968-5000; **BUS ADD:** 3835 Birch St., Newport Beach, CA 92660, (714)549-5111.

FAWLSTICH, James R.——*Pres.*, Federal Home Loan Bank of Seattle; **PRIM RE ACT:** Banker; **BUS ADD:** Seattle, WA 98101, (206)624-3980.*

FEATHERSTON, Charles V.——B: Nov. 24, 1919, Richmond, VA, *Pres.*, Commercial Financing Corp.; **PRIM RE ACT:** Broker, Appraiser, Developer, Lender, Insuror; **PROFL AFFIL & HONORS:** Gen. Agents and Mgrs. Conference of NALU; Nat. Assn. of Review Appraisers; Intl. Inst. of Valuers; Intl. Assn. Fin. Planners, CRA; Scv; **EDUC:** BA, 1945, Univ. of MD/Air Univ. (USAF); **GRAD EDUC:** 1981, Successful Investing and Money Mgmt. (RE, Life Ins., Mort., Fed. Taxes, Stocks, Bonds), Fin. Educ. Services; **EDUC HONORS:** Officer's courses; **MIL SERV:** US Army/USAF, Capt., Purple Heart, ETO w/Arrowhead, Five Stars and Many other decorations; **OTHER ACT & HONORS:** Masonic Orders; The Amer. Defense Preparedness Assn.; Amer. Security Council; **HOME ADD:** 2942 Rosalind Ave. S.W., Roanoke, VA 24014, (703)342-8026; **BUS ADD:** 502 30th St. N.W., Roanoke, VA 24017, (703)982-0323.

FEATHERSTON, Harley G.——B: Dec. 21, 1926, Shawnee, OK, *Owner-Broker*, Harley G. Featherston RE; **PRIM RE ACT:** Broker, Appraiser, Builder, Owner/Investor; **OTHER RE ACT:** Notary Public, JP, Auctioneer; **SERVICES:** Buy & Sell RE; **PREV EMPLOY:** Mitchell's RE, Salem, NH; **PROFL AFFIL & HONORS:** Salem Contractors Assn.; **EDUC:** BA, 1951, Liberal Arts, Univ. of OK; **MIL SERV:** US Army, Sgt.; **OTHER ACT & HONORS:** Trustee Derry-Salem Elks for past 8 years; **HOME ADD:** 16 Pleasant St., Salem, NH 03079, (603)898-2826; **BUS ADD:** 16 Pleasant St., Salem, NH 03079, (603)898-7501.

FEATHERSTON, Larry G.——B: Aug. 19, 1912, Mt. Ida, AR, *Co-Owner (Co)*, Fran Shelton and Assoc. Inc.; **PRIM RE ACT:** Broker, Consultant, Syndicator, Owner/Investor; **OTHER RE ACT:** Farm & ranches, securities; **SERVICES:** Full serv.; **REP CLIENTS:** Investors, farmers, ranchers, businessmen, natl. cos.; **PROFL AFFIL & HONORS:** Chico Bd. of Realtors; CA Assn. of Realtors; NAR; Notary Public, Treas., VP, Chico Bd. Realtors 1982; **EDUC:** AA, 1962, Soc., Ysba Jr. Coll.; **GRAD EDUC:** CA State Univ. at Chico; **MIL SERV:** US Army; E-5, Good Conduct; **OTHER ACT & HONORS:** Dist. Chmn., Fin. Chmn., Ranchero Bidwell Boy Scouts of Amer, Mt. Lasser Area Council; **HOME ADD:** 167 Terr. Dr., Chico, CA 95926, (916)345-2980; **BUS ADD:** 180 Cohasset Rd., Chico, CA 95926, (916)891-6786.

FECHTMAN, George——*Director Office Services*, Amax, Inc.; **PRIM RE ACT:** Property Manager; **BUS ADD:** AMAX Center, Greenwich, CT 06830, (203)622-3000.*

FEDER, Gerald——B: Aug. 2, 1941, Belleville, *Owner*, Gerald Feder Builder & Rental; **PRIM RE ACT:** Builder; **SERVICES:** Rentals, builder; **EDUC:** Grad. High Sch.; **HOME ADD:** 123 Sundew, Belleville, IL, (618)235-1809; **BUS ADD:** 123 Sundew, Belleville, IL 62221, (618)235-1809.

FEDER, Leonard H.——*VP and NY State Counsel*, Commonwealth Land Title Insurance Co.; **PRIM RE ACT:** Attorney; **PROFL AFFIL & HONORS:** NY State Bar; NY State Land Title Assn.; **BUS ADD:** 1290 Ave. of Americas, New York, NY 10104, (212)246-7900.

FEDER, Steven B.——B: Feb. 25, 1949, Cedar Rapids, IA, *Sec. of Corp., Legal Counsel*, Fed. Devel., Inc.; **OTHER RE ACT:** Legal, Devel. and Mgmt.; **SERVICES:** RE devel. and prop. mgmt.; **PREV EMPLOY:** General Growth Properties, Des Moines, IA; **PROFL AFFIL & HONORS:** ABA, IA Bar Assn., Cty. Condemnation Bd., Chmn. of Cedar Rapids C of C; Apt. Owners Comm.; **EDUC:** AB, 1971, Intl. Politics and Latin American Studies, Tulane Univ. and Victoria Univ. of Manchester (England); **GRAD EDUC:** JD, 1974, Univ. of IA Coll. of Law; **EDUC HONORS:** Phi Beta Kappa, Pi Sigma Alpha, Cum Laude with honors in Pol. Sci., V Chmn. of Moot Court Bd.; **OTHER ACT & HONORS:** Tulane Univ. Alumni Admissions Comm.; **HOME ADD:** 7014 Surrey Dr. NE, Cedar Rapids, IA 52402, (319)377-5258; **BUS ADD:** PO Box 2846, 2200 Buckingham Dr. NW, Cedar Rapids, IA 52406, (319)396-8300.

FEDEWA, Bernard E.——B: Oct. 3, 1944, St. Johns, MI, *Housing Supervisor*, Michigan Housing Devel. Authority, Fin.; **PRIM RE ACT:** Broker, Developer, Lender; **SERVICES:** Housing fin., multi & single family, condos., housing rehab.; **PROFL AFFIL & HONORS:** MBA of MI; Nat. Assn. of Housing & Redevel. Officials; Rotary Intl.; Urban Affairs Assn., Co-Author *Housing for the Elderly* Van Nostrand Reinhold, 1975; **EDUC:** 1968, Packaging Engrg./Building Constr., MI State Univ.; **GRAD EDUC:** 1970, Mktg. Research, MI State Univ.; **OTHER ACT & HONORS:** E. Lansing Econ. Devel. Corp.; **HOME ADD:** 324 Chesterfield, E. Lansing, MI 48823, (517)351-1762; **BUS ADD:** 401 S. Washington Sq., POB 30044, Lansing, MI 48909, (517)373-8016.

FEEHAN, John J., Jr.——B: Aug. 2, 1945, Jersey City, NJ, *Devel. Officer*, Medical Building Corp.; **PRIM RE ACT:** Developer; **SERVICES:** Complete synd., fin. devel., design & const. medical office bldgs and clinics; **REP CLIENTS:** Hospitals, medical grp. practices, investors; **PREV EMPLOY:** Devel., dir. Amer. Medical Bldgs.; **PROFL AFFIL & HONORS:** US Naval Academy Alumni Assn.; Harvard Bus. School Alumni Assn.; **EDUC:** BS, 1967, For. Affairs, US Naval Academy; **GRAD EDUC:** MBA, 1974, Intl. Bus. RE, Harvard Bus. School; **EDUC HONORS:** Superintendent's List, Second Yr. Academic Honors; **MIL SERV:** USN; Lt.; Viet Nam Service Medal, Air Medal, Korean Medal Active Duty, 1967-72; **OTHER ACT & HONORS:** San Diego Track Club, Comdr., USN, Res.; 1972-present; **HOME ADD:** 326 E St., Olivenhain, CA 92024, (714)436-7264; **BUS ADD:** 7777 Girard Ave., La Jolla, CA 92037, (714)454-3196.

FEENEY, John——*Dir. RE*, United Technologies Co.; **PRIM RE ACT:** Property Manager; **BUS ADD:** One Financial Plaza, Hartford, CT 06101, (203)728-7000.*

FEENEY, M. James——B: Aug. 5, 1946, Fort Wayne, IN, *Mgr., Domestic Fin. Analysis/RE*, Monsanto Co.; **PRIM RE ACT:** Consultant; **PREV EMPLOY:** Monsanto, 11 yrs.; **PROFL AFFIL & HONORS:** NACORE; **EDUC:** BS, 1969, Acctg., IN Univ.; **GRAD EDUC:** MBA, 1970, Fin., MI State Univ.; **HOME ADD:** 1229 DuMotier Dr., Manchester, MO 63011, (314)527-8274; **BUS ADD:** 800 N. Lindbergh Blvd., St. Louis, MO 63167, (314)694-7581.

FEENEY, Paul R.——B: Oct. 6, 1944, NJ, *VP*, Alexander Summer Inc.; **PRIM RE ACT:** Property Manager; **SERVICES:** Asset mgmt.; **REP CLIENTS:** Ins. & banking Instns. and indiv. owners; **PROFL AFFIL & HONORS:** NAR; RNMI; IREM; **EDUC:** BSBA, Edison State Coll.; **MIL SERV:** USN; **BUS ADD:** 222 Cedar Ln., Teaneck, NJ 07666, (201)836-4500.

FEENEY, Thomas J.——B: Feb. 28, 1915, Yonkers, NY, *Sr. VP*, Tombrock Corp.; **PRIM RE ACT:** Owner/Investor, Property Manager; **OTHER RE ACT:** RE matters for nat. restaurant chain; **PROFL AFFIL & HONORS:** Founding Member, Nat. Assn. of Corp. RE Execs.; **EDUC:** AB, 1935, Philosophy, St. Joseph's Seminary & Coll.; **GRAD EDUC:** MA, 1938, Soc. Studies, Columbia Univ.; **EDUC**

HONORS: Phi Delta Kappa; **OTHER ACT & HONORS:** Citizen of the Yr., Stamford, CT; Pres. of Stamford Rotary Club; Pres. of Stamford Chap. of Amer. Cancer Soc.; 1st VP of Soc. of Former Special Agents of the FBI; Chmn. of Bd. of Educ. of Diocese of Bridgeport; Keynote Speaker for United Way; **HOME ADD:** 82 E Cross Rd., Stamford, CT 06907, (203)322-5835; **BUS ADD:** 580 Main St., Stamford, CT 06904, (203)324-5707.

FEENSTRA, Derek P.——**B:** March 29, 1935, Netherlands, *VP, Proj. Dev. & Mgmt.*, Stewart Construction/Consultants, Inc.; **PRIM RE ACT:** Consultant, Engineer; **OTHER RE ACT:** Corp. RE, Specifically new construction; **SERVICES:** Leasing facilities, designing & constructing new facilities for corp clients; **PREV EMPLOY:** Combustion Engrg., Inc., Mgr. of Dev. of Comml. & Industrial RE, Design and Building of Industrial and Corp. RE; **PROFL AFFIL & HONORS:** PE; CT, ONT (Canada); **EDUC:** CE, 1959, Structural design & engineering, MIT; **GRAD EDUC:** MSCE, 1964, Construction Mgmt., Harvard Bus. School; **MIL SERV:** Royal Dutch Air Force; **HOME ADD:** 2418 S. Voss Rd., Houston, TX 77057, (713)974-6581; **BUS ADD:** PO Box 94138, Houston, TX 77018, (713)688-8665.

FEIGENBERG, Louis A.——**B:** Mar. 18, 1943, Chicago, IL, *Atty.*; **PRIM RE ACT:** Consultant, Attorney; **SERVICES:** RE prop. tax reductions and consultation; **REP CLIENTS:** Owners and mgrs. of various comml., indus. and multi-unit resid. props.; **PREV EMPLOY:** Asst. State's Atty. of Cook Cty., IL - RE Tax Div. (1972-1978); **PROFL AFFIL & HONORS:** ABA, IL Bar Assn., Chicago Bar Assn., IL CPA Soc., CPA; **EDUC:** BBA, 1964, Acctg., Univ. of WI; **GRAD EDUC:** JD, 1972, DePaul Univ.; **MIL SERV:** US Army, Lt., Bronze Star; **HOME ADD:** 1310 N. Ritchie Ct., Chicago, IL 60610, (312)944-5552; **BUS ADD:** 11 S. LaSalle St., Suite 1315, Chicago, IL 60603, (312)346-7518.

FEIN, Bernard——*Pres.*, United Industrial Corp.; **PRIM RE ACT:** Property Manager; **BUS ADD:** 660 Madison Ave., NY, NY 10021, (212)752-8787.*

FEINBERG, Allen H.——**B:** May 6, 1932, NY, *Pres.*, Allen H. Feinberg Architects & Allen H. Feinberg Associates; **PRIM RE ACT:** Architect, Developer, Builder, Syndicator; **SERVICES:** Arch., const. mgmr., devel.; **PROFL AFFIL & HONORS:** AIA; **EDUC:** BArch., 1954, MIT; **MIL SERV:** USAF, Capt., Retired; **BUS ADD:** 116-55 Queens Blvd., Forest Hills, NY 11375, (212)261-8333.

FEINBERG, Jeffrey——**B:** Dec. 13, 1947, Philadelphia, PA, *Atty. at Law*, Law Offices of Jeffrey Feinberg, P.A.; **PRIM RE ACT:** Attorney; **SERVICES:** Documentation, litigation, closings, title ins.; **REP CLIENTS:** Devels., gen. contractors, subcontractors, owners; **EDUC:** BA, 1970, Eng., Temple Univ.; **GRAD EDUC:** JD, 1978, RE Law, Temple Univ.; **EDUC HONORS:** Law Review; **OTHER ACT & HONORS:** MENSA; **HOME ADD:** 71 N.W. 170th St., N. Miami Beach, FL 33169, (305)651-4567; **BUS ADD:** 2500 E. Hallandale Beach Blvd., Suite 707, Hallandale, FL 33009, (305)457-7744.

FEINBERG, Norman M.——**B:** Nov. 18, 1934, New York City, NY, *Pres.*, Gateside Corp.; **PRIM RE ACT:** Consultant, Developer, Owner/Investor, Builder, Property Manager; **SERVICES:** Devel. of Apt. Houses, Office Bldgs., Indus. Parks, Shopping Ctrs., Marinas; **PROFL AFFIL & HONORS:** Nat. Apt. Council; Delaware Valley Apt. Owners Assn.-Member Bd. of Dir. and VP, Recipient Mayor's Award Outstanding Bldg. Renovation City of White Plains, NY; **EDUC:** BS, 1956, Econ., New York Univ.; **EDUC HONORS:** Deans List 4 Times; Student Hall of Fame; **OTHER ACT & HONORS:** Arbitrator: Amer. Arbitration Assn.; Young Presidents Organization; Bd. of Dir. and VP-Assn. of Mentally Ill Children; **HOME ADD:** 748 Long Hill Rd., W Blaircliff Manor, NY 10510, (914)762-1322; **BUS ADD:** 150 White Plains Rd., Tarrytown, NY 10591, (914)631-7575.

FEINERMAN, Milton——*Pres.*, Federal Home Loan Bank of San Francisco; **PRIM RE ACT:** Banker; **BUS ADD:** PO Box 7948, San Francisco, CA 94120, (415)393-1000.*

FEINSTEIN, Edward——**B:** June 21, 1923, NY, NY, *Pres.*, Heritage Corp. of S. FL; **PRIM RE ACT:** Consultant, Appraiser, Banker, Developer, Lender, Owner/Investor, Instructor, Property Manager, Syndicator; **SERVICES:** Mort. banking, title ins., life & A&H ins.; **REP CLIENTS:** 40 inst. investors, var. devel. builders and brokers; **PROFL AFFIL & HONORS:** MBAA; Mort. Bankers Sustaining Realtor, Mort. Banker of Yr., 1966; Cert. Mort. Banker; Cert. Mort. Underwriter; Cert. Review Appraiser; Intl. Coll. of RE Consulting Profls.; Intl. Inst. of Valuers; Sr. Cert. Valuer; Past Pres. MBA of Gr. Miami 1971-72; **EDUC:** BBA, 1947, Fin. & Econ., Acctg., Univ. of Miami; **EDUC HONORS:** Iron Arrow Hon. Soc., Soc. Univ. Founders; **MIL SERV:** USN, Res.; Lt. j.g.; European Theatre; **OTHER ACT & HONORS:** NCCU; Dir. Multiple Schlerosis Soc.; **HOME ADD:** 120 S Prospect Dr., Coral Gables, FL 33133, (305)661-4575; **BUS ADD:** 1318 NW 7th St., Miami, FL 33135, (305)324-4000.

FEIRMAN, Jerome B.——**B:** Aug. 6, 1944, NY, NY, *Pres.*, Feirman Bros., J-M-H Realty, Papillon Realty; **PRIM RE ACT:** Consultant, Owner/Investor, Property Manager, Syndicator; **SERVICES:** Prop. Mgmt. & Consultation serv., synd. of comml. props.; **REP CLIENTS:** The Rosebud Farms; **EDUC:** BS, 1965, Social Studies, Educ., NY Univ., School of Educ.; **OTHER ACT & HONORS:** Beta Sigma Rho Frat.; VP 9th Precinct Council; **HOME ADD:** 64 East 7th St., NY, NY 10003, (212)260-2839; **BUS ADD:** 36 East 7th St., NY, NY 10003, (212)228-3370.

FEIRMAN, Robert I.——**B:** Nov. 22, 1942, Bronx, NY, *Owner*, The Feirman Co.; **PRIM RE ACT:** Owner/Investor, Property Manager, Syndicator; **PREV EMPLOY:** The Robert A. McNeil Corp., Sr. VP & Dir. Legal Counsel; **PROFL AFFIL & HONORS:** Member NY and CA Bar; CA RE Broker; Member ABA; US C of C, Who's Who in CA Hist. Soc.; **EDUC:** BBA, 1964, Acctg., Bernard Baruch Sch. of Bus.; **GRAD EDUC:** LLB, LLM, 1967, 1969, Law & Corp. Law, Brooklyn Law Sch., NYU Sch. of Law; **EDUC HONORS:** Tuition Scholarship to Brooklyn Law; **OTHER ACT & HONORS:** Thoroughbred Horse Owner, Member CA Horsemen's Protective Benevolent Assn.; **HOME TEL:** (415)851-7741; **BUS ADD:** 750 Welch Rd., Suite 325, Palo Alto, CA 94304, (415)326-8220.

FELDER, Bruce B.——**B:** Sept. 27, 1937, Cleveland, OH, *Pres./CEO*, Record Data Inc.; **PRIM RE ACT:** Appraiser; **OTHER RE ACT:** Title reporting & title ins.; **SERVICES:** Ltd. title reports, title ins. policies & appraisals; **REP CLIENTS:** Second mort. lenders, banks, S&L, credit unions; **PREV EMPLOY:** Deputy Clerk, Ct. of Common Pleas, Cuyahoga Cty., Cleveland, OH; **PROFL AFFIL & HONORS:** Nat. Second Mort. Assn.; Nat. Cons. Fin. Assn.; Amer. Land Title Assn.; OH Land Title Assn.; **EDUC:** 1958, Pre-Law, John Carroll Univ.; **GRAD EDUC:** 1961, Cleve Marshall Law School; **OTHER ACT & HONORS:** Who's Who in the Midwest, 1978; TR., Cleveland Mt. Sinai Medical; Chmn. of Communication of Jewish Community Fed. Ctr. of Cleveland; 1977 - Most Interesting Cleveland Resident; 1981 - Leadership - Cleveland Comm.; 1982 - Elected Cleveland Hts. High School Hall of Fame; **HOME ADD:** Winding Creek Estate, Pepper Pike, OH 44124, (216)464-1880; **BUS ADD:** 725 St. Clair Ave., N.W., Cleveland, OH 44113, (216)696-2100.

FELDMAN, Earl N.——**B:** June 22, 1943, Cleveland, OH, *Pres.*, Feldman & Steres, PC; **PRIM RE ACT:** Attorney; **SERVICES:** Legal Counsel; **PROFL AFFIL & HONORS:** CA Bar Assn., CA CPA Soc., Cert. Taxation Specialist; **EDUC:** BS, 1965, Acctg., UCLA; **GRAD EDUC:** MBA, 1966, UCLA; JD, 1969, Harvard Law School; **EDUC HONORS:** Cum Laude, Beta Gamma Sigma, Ernst & Whinney Acctg. Award 1966; **BUS ADD:** 1200 Third Ave. 1324, San Diego, CA 92101, (714)239-1151.

FELDMAN, Leslie——**B:** Apr. 9, 1942, NY, NY; **PRIM RE ACT:** Attorney, Syndicator; **PROFL AFFIL & HONORS:** ABA, NY City Lawyers; **EDUC:** BA, 1964, Hist., Colgate Univ.; **GRAD EDUC:** LLB, 1967, Brooklyn Law School; **BUS ADD:** 325 Broadway, New York, NY 10017.

FELDMAN, Marc H.——**B:** Oct. 17, 1953, NY, *Atty.*; **PRIM RE ACT:** Attorney, Owner/Investor; **SERVICES:** All closing servs. including title examination and title ins., document prep., escrow serv., ltd. partnerships and corps., mort. foreclosures & counseling; **REP CLIENTS:** RE Devel., Condo. Assns., RE brokers, pvt. mort. lenders, indiv. owners and purchasers; **PROFL AFFIL & HONORS:** FL Bar, ABA, Lawyers Title Guaranty Fund, Sarasota Cty. Bd. of Realtors, Manatee Cty. Bar Assn.; **EDUC:** BA, 1975, Philosophy, Tulane Univ.; **GRAD EDUC:** JD, 1978, Univ. of FL; **HOME ADD:** 1524 84 St. NW, Bradenton, FL 33529, (813)792-5306; **BUS ADD:** 6221 14 St. W, Bradenton, FL 33507, (813)755-3731.

FELDMAN, Michael J.——**B:** Dec. 22, 1946, Holyoke, MA, *Sr. VP, Lending Services*, NYS Mort. Loan Enforcement and Admin. Corp.; **OTHER RE ACT:** Loan Workouts; Tax Shelter; Synds.; **SERVICES:** Mort. loan portfolio workouts using tax shelters as a principal workout tool; **PREV EMPLOY:** Princeton Univ., Asst. Treas.; Chase Manhattan Bank, N.A., VP; **EDUC:** AB, 1969, Econ., Clark Univ., Worcester; **GRAD EDUC:** MBA, 1971, NY Univ.; **HOME ADD:** 56 E. 87th, #3D, New York, NY 10028, (212)289-7284; **BUS ADD:** 11 W. 42nd St., 21st Floor, New York, NY 10036, (212)790-2487.

FELDMAN, Saul J.——**B:** May 31, 1939, Boston, MA, *RE and Condo. Atty.*, Law Office of Saul J. Feldman; **PRIM RE ACT:** Attorney; **SERVICES:** RE and Condo. Atty.; **PROFL AFFIL & HONORS:**

Boston Bar Assn.; MA Bar Assn.; ABA; MA Conveyances Assn.; NEw England Land Title Assn.; **EDUC:** BA, 1962, Govt., Harvard Coll.; **GRAD EDUC:** 1966, Harvard Law School; **EDUC HONORS:** Cum Laude; **OTHER ACT & HONORS:** Pres., New England Realty Lodge; Legal Editor, *New England RE Journal*; **HOME ADD:** 18 Shepard Ave., Swampscott, MA 01907, (617)599-1463; **BUS ADD:** 50 Congress St., Boston, MA 02109, (617)523-1825.

FELDSHUE, Alan M.——B: Apr. 24, 1953, Pittsburgh, PA, *Sales Rep., Prop. Mgr.*, The Denmead Co.; **PRIM RE ACT:** Property Manager; **OTHER RE ACT:** Sales & leasing rep.; **SERVICES:** Sales, leasing, prop. mgmt. of comml. & indus. RE; **EDUC:** BS, 1976, Bus. Educ., OH State Univ.; **HOME ADD:** 6356 Chippenhook Ct., Dublin, OH 43017, (614)764-2757; **BUS ADD:** 22 E Gay St., Columbus, OH 43215, (614)224-1492.

FELIX, Steven——B: July 13, 1948, NYC, *Sr. VP*, Harold Siegelaub Co., Inc.; **PRIM RE ACT:** Banker, Broker, Consultant, Developer, Property Manager, Owner/Investor; **SERVICES:** Value Enhancement of RE through analysis and Mktg. of Surplus, Distressed, Problem Props.; **REP CLIENTS:** Financial Instns., Public Corps. and Govt. Agencies in Shopping Ctrs, Indust. Complexes, Land; **PREV EMPLOY:** Grand Union Supermarkets (RE Mgr.), A&P (disposal of closed stores, site loc. negot. & research new stores); VW of Amer. (disposal of surplus prop.); **PROFL AFFIL & HONORS:** RE Bd. of NY, Research Comm.; Young Mens RE Assn., International Council of Shopping Centers; **EDUC:** BS, 1971, Bus. Journ., Fairleigh Dickinson Univ.; **HOME ADD:** 123 Cypress St., Millburn, NJ 07041, (201)761-5522; **BUS ADD:** 100 E 42 St., Suite 2501, NY, NY 10017, (212)867-6545.

FELL, Leo B.——B: Dec. 12, 1938, Council Bluffs, IA, *Mgr., Corp. Facilities*, Memorex Corp.; **OTHER RE ACT:** Corp. RE Mgr.; **SERVICES:** Lease nego., site location studies, RE asset mgmt; **REP CLIENTS:** Internal corp. div.; **PROFL AFFIL & HONORS:** Member of IDRC; AIIE; **EDUC:** BS, 1961, Indus. Engrg.; **MIL SERV:** US Army; SP-4, 1961-1963; **HOME ADD:** 10166 English Oak Way, Cupertino, CA 95014, (408)257-2674; **BUS ADD:** M/S 06-01, San Tomas at Central Expressway, Santa Clara, CA 95052, (408)987-2668.

FELL, Martin——*VP Fin.*, Scholastic Magazines, Inc.; **PRIM RE ACT:** Property Manager; **BUS ADD:** 50 W. 44th St., New York, NY 10036, (212)944-7700.*

FELLMAN, Lesli Denyse——B: Feb. 22, 1957, Miami, FL, *Tax Consultant*, Touche Ross & Co.; **PRIM RE ACT:** Consultant; **OTHER RE ACT:** Accountant; **PROFL AFFIL & HONORS:** CA CPA Soc., Los Angeles Chapter RE Comm., Touche Ross & Co.-RE Comm.; **EDUC:** BGS, 1978, Acctg., Univ. of MI; **GRAD EDUC:** Master in Bus. Taxation, to be completed in 1982, Taxation, Univ. of Southern CA; **HOME ADD:** 11645 Montana Ave. #235, Los Angeles, CA 90049, (213)476-8071; **BUS ADD:** 3700 Wilshire Blvd., Los Angeles, CA 90010, (213)381-3251.

FELTOVIC, John A.——B: Sept. 11, 1934, Perth Amboy, NJ, *Mgr., RE & Gen. Services*, Research-Cottrell, Inc., Corporate Staff; **PRIM RE ACT:** Consultant, Engineer, Appraiser, Builder, Property Manager; **OTHER RE ACT:** Space planning, facility planning; **SERVICES:** Gen. services, dept. structured to provide Research-Cottrell with complete task from determining need to completely operational facility; **PREV EMPLOY:** Pan American World Airways, Alcoa; **PROFL AFFIL & HONORS:** NACORE; IDRC; AIIE; **EDUC:** BSME, 1957, ME, NJ Inst. of Tech.; **GRAD EDUC:** MS, 1965, Mgmt., NJ Inst. of Tech.; **EDUC HONORS:** 3.45/4.00; **MIL SERV:** USAF, Capt.; **OTHER ACT & HONORS:** Dir., Metuchen Rec. Comm.; NJIT Alumni Advisory Bd.; St. Joseph's High School Fathers Club Advisory Bd.; **HOME ADD:** 67 Salem Court, Metuchen, NJ 08840, (201)494-0392; **BUS ADD:** POB 1500, Somerville, NJ 08876, (201)685-4751.

FELTS, Ernest T., Jr.——B: Aug. 3, 1946, Tupelo, MS, *Pres.*, Banyan Realty Corp.; **PRIM RE ACT:** Developer, Owner/Investor, Property Manager, Syndicator; **SERVICES:** Acquisition & Devel. of Hotels and Comml. Props. Investment Advisor, Prop. Mgmt.; **REP CLIENTS:** Indiv. and Corp. Investors in Hotels and Comml. Props.; **PREV EMPLOY:** NW Mutual Life Ins. Co., RE Investment Dept. 1973-1979; **PROFL AFFIL & HONORS:** Bldg. owners and mgrs. Assn., Amer. Hotel and Motel Assn.; **EDUC:** BS, 1969, Mktg., RE, Univ. of TN; **HOME ADD:** 9334 Clearhurst Dr., Dallas, TX 75238, (214)349-2921; **BUS ADD:** 7515 Greenville Ave., Suite 1000, Dallas, TX 75231, (214)691-3800.

FELTS, Jean C.——B: Feb. 16, 1933, Sanilac Cty., MI, *VP*, Waguespack, Dupree & Felts, Inc.; **PRIM RE ACT:** Consultant, Appraiser; **SERVICES:** RE counseling and appraisal; **REP CLIENTS:** Prudential Ins. Co., Monsanto Chemical, Getty Oil, Hibernia Nat. Bank, Corps of Engrs., Home Loan Bank Bd.; **PROFL AFFIL & HONORS:** Amer. Soc. of RE Counselors; AIREA; RE Bd. of New Orleans; **EDUC:** BS, 1953, Bus. Admin./Acctg., Univ. of Detroit; **OTHER ACT & HONORS:** Intl. House; The Chamber - New Orleans and the River Rgn.; The Legal Center; Historic Faubourg St. Mary; **HOME ADD:** 1468 Calhoun St., New Orleans, LA 70118, (504)895-0573; **BUS ADD:** 822 Perdido St., New Orleans, LA 70112, (504)581-6947.

FENDLER, Ryan D.——B: Aug. 29, 1926, NY, NY, *Partner*, D.R.T. Co.; **PRIM RE ACT:** Developer, Builder, Owner/Investor, Syndicator; **EDUC:** BA, 1951, Econ., Hobart Coll.; **MIL SERV:** USN; ROM 3/C; **HOME ADD:** RFD 1, Newport, ME 04953, (207)938-4958; **BUS ADD:** Box 148, Pittsfield, ME 04967, (207)487-3232.

FENICHEL, Saul M.——B: Nov. 10, 1952, Lakewood, NJ, *Tax Supervisor*, Coopers & Lybrand, Nat. Tax Serv.; **OTHER RE ACT:** Accountant; **PREV EMPLOY:** NJ Div. of Taxation, 1974, Coopers & Lybrand, 1976, 9/77 to present; **PROFL AFFIL & HONORS:** Member NJ Bar, NJ Soc. of CPA, JD, CPA; **EDUC:** BS, 1974, Acctg., Wharton Sch. of Univ. of PA; **GRAD EDUC:** JD, 1977, Rutgers Sch. of Law, Newark, NJ; **EDUC HONORS:** Cum Laude, Beta Alpha Psi; **BUS ADD:** 1800 M St., NW, Suite 400 N, Wash. DC 20036, (202)822-4253.

FENMORE, Donald M.——B: Apr. 9, 1939, Los Angeles, CA, *Partner*, Loeb & Loeb, RE Dept.; **PRIM RE ACT:** Attorney; **SERVICES:** RE atty.; **REP CLIENTS:** Devel., lenders, brokers, synd.; **PREV EMPLOY:** Asst. US Atty., US Dept. of Justice - Tax Div.; **PROFL AFFIL & HONORS:** LA Cty. Bar Assn., CA Soc. of CPA's, Amer. Assoc. of Atty. - CPA's, Atty., CPA, RE Broker; **EDUC:** BS in Econ., 1961, RE and Fin., Wharton School of Fin. & Commerce, Univ. of PA; **GRAD EDUC:** JD, 1965, Law, Univ. of So. CA Sch. of Law; **EDUC HONORS:** Award in Acctg. (UCLA); Beta Gamma Sigma; Wm. Mirkel Award for Top Sr. Thesis in RE; **MIL SERV:** US Army Res., Sp-4; **OTHER ACT & HONORS:** Author of book *Condensed CPA Tax Review, 4th ed.*; **BUS ADD:** 10100 Santa Monica Blvd., 22nd Floor, Los Angeles, CA 90067, (213)552-7700.

FENNELL, Ruth——*RE Specialist*, California Dept. of RE, Publications Sect.; **PRIM RE ACT:** Regulator; **BUS ADD:** 1719 24th St., Sacramento, CA 95816, (916)322-9740.

FENNIMORE, C. Thomas——B: Mar. 6, 1947, Indianapolis, IN, *VP and Div. Counsel*, NC Nat. Bank, RE Lending Div./Law Sect.; **PRIM RE ACT:** Attorney, Banker, Lender; **SERVICES:** Comml. RE lending; **PREV EMPLOY:** Chicago Title Insurance Co.; **PROFL AFFIL & HONORS:** ABA, NC Bar and Bar Assn.; **EDUC:** BS, 1969, Industrial Engrg., Purdue Univ. (West Lafayette, IN); **GRAD EDUC:** JD, 1972, Law, IN Univ. (Bloomington, IN); **OTHER ACT & HONORS:** Pres., St. Mark's Ctr. Inc.; Charlotte Historic Dist. Commn.; **HOME ADD:** 323 West Ninth St., Charlotte, NC 28202, (704)372-1091; **BUS ADD:** One NCNB Plaza, Charlotte, NC 28255, (704)374-5258.

FENTON, Edgar——B: Oct. 29, 1921, Detroit, MI, *Pres.*, Cadroy Management; **PRIM RE ACT:** Broker, Developer, Builder, Owner/Investor, Property Manager, Syndicator; **PROFL AFFIL & HONORS:** Dir. of Builder's Assn. of So. MI, VP of Apt. Assn. of MI; **EDUC:** BA, 1943, Univ. of MI; **GRAD EDUC:** Attended Wayne State Univ. Law School; **MIL SERV:** USAF, enlisted man, 1942-1945; **OTHER ACT & HONORS:** Bd. of Jewish Family Servs., Franklin Hills Ctry. Club, Standard Club; **HOME ADD:** 27545 Gateway Dr. S., Farmington Hills, MI 48010, (313)477-5566; **BUS ADD:** 26555 Evergreen #618, Southfield, MI 48076, (313)353-1420.

FERACO, Ray, Jr.——B: July 10, 1950, Bartow, FL, *Asst. VP*, SE Mort. Co., Comml. Div.; **PRIM RE ACT:** Consultant, Appraiser; **PREV EMPLOY:** Chief Appraiser, Coral Gables Fed. S&L 1972-1981; **PROFL AFFIL & HONORS:** SRPA Designation SREA, AIREA, Candidate FL RE Broker, SRPA Designation - Soc. of RE Appraisers; **EDUC:** BA, Bus. Admin., 1972, Parsons Coll., IA; **HOME ADD:** 7910 SW 19th St., Miami, FL 33155, (305)264-2749; **BUS ADD:** 1390 Brickell Ave., Miami, FL 33131, (305)350-9120.

FERBER, Roman——*Exec. Dir.*, Indus. & Comml. Incentive Bd., Office of Econ. Devel.; **OTHER RE ACT:** Govt. Admin.; **SERVICES:** Tax Exemption Granting Agency; **BUS ADD:** 17 John St., 15th Fl., NY, NY 10038, (212)566-0207.

FERGUSON, Debra——B: July 5, 1952, Castroville, TX, *Realtor-Pres.*; **PRIM RE ACT:** Broker; **EDUC:** AA, 1973, Univ. of AK; **HOME ADD:** 410 E. 46th, Anchorage, AK 99503, (907)276-4764; **BUS ADD:** 4325 Laurel, Anchorage, AK 99503.

FERGUSON, Harry Don——B: Mar. 12, 1940, Poplar Bluff, MO, *Owner/Broker*, Ferguson RE; **PRIM RE ACT:** Broker, Consultant, Appraiser, Owner/Investor, Property Manager; **SERVICES:** RE Sales, Appraisals, & Mgmt.; **REP CLIENTS:** Livingston Const. Co.; **PREV EMPLOY:** Homequity, Livingston Const. Co., First Presbyterian Church; **PROFL AFFIL & HONORS:** Three Rivers Bd. of Realtors, MO Assn. of Realtors, NAR, GRI, Pres., Three Rivers Bd. Realtors 1977 & 1978; Chmn., State Affairs Comm. Mar 1978; NAR Nominating Comm. 1980; NAR Profl. Standards Comm. 1982; **EDUC:** 1963, Bus. Admin. and Math, Univ. of TX; **MIL SERV:** US Army; Pvt. E-3, Sharp Shooter; **OTHER ACT & HONORS:** Sec. Planning & Zoning Comm. City of Poplar Bluff 1967-1979, First V. Comdr., Amvets Post 29,1982; **HOME ADD:** Lake Lock Loma, PO Box 4115, Poplar Bluff, MO 63901, (314)785-3980; **BUS ADD:** 2895 Hwy. 67 N., PO Box 4115, Poplar Bluff, MO 63901, (314)785-0156.

FERGUSON, Jane——*Adm. Off. Services & RE*, Westvaco; **PRIM RE ACT:** Property Manager; **BUS ADD:** 299 Park Ave., New York, New York2s10171, (212)688-5000.*

FERGUSON, Lewis H., III——B: Oct. 22, 1944, Abilene, TX, *Part.*, Williams & Connolly; **PRIM RE ACT:** Attorney, Syndicator, Owner/Investor; **PROFL AFFIL & HONORS:** ABA, Sect. of Taxation, Adjunct Prof., Georgetown Univ. Law Ctr.; **EDUC:** BA, 1966, Econ., Yale Coll.; **GRAD EDUC:** MA, 1973, Econ., Kings Coll., Cambridge Univ., U.K.; JD, 1971, Harvard Law School; **EDUC HONORS:** Cum Laude, High Honors in Pol. & Econ., Member, Bd. of Editors, *Harvard Law Review*; **HOME ADD:** 5309 Burling Terr., Bethesda, MD 20018, (301)986-1008; **BUS ADD:** 839 17th St., NW, Wash., DC 20006, (202)331-5540.

FERGUSON, Robert William——B: Dec. 3, 1935, Portland, ME, *Atty.*; **PRIM RE ACT:** Attorney, Banker, Owner/Investor, Insuror; **OTHER RE ACT:** Dir.; **SERVICES:** Titles, closing serv., devel. and taxation of RE; **REP CLIENTS:** Depositors Trust Co. of So. Maine, Jagger Bros., Inc., Maineland, Inc., Central Maine Power Co.; **PROFL AFFIL & HONORS:** ABA, member Bus. Law and RE Sections; ME Bar Assn.; Member, RE Section; Member, Title Standards Comm.; **EDUC:** BS, 1960, Math/Physics, Northeastern Univ/Gordon Coll.; **GRAD EDUC:** JD, 1963, Law, Univ. of ME School of Law; **EDUC HONORS:** Law Review; **OTHER ACT & HONORS:** Chmn., Shapleigh Planning Bd.; Civic; Masonic; **HOME ADD:** Shapleigh, ME, (207)324-2615; **BUS ADD:** 180 Main St., Depositors Bank Bldg., POB 97, Springvale, ME 04083, (207)324-5357.

FERGUSON, Ronald C.——B: Aug. 20, 1946, W. Palm Beach, FL, *Pres.*, Ferguson Realty, Ltd.; **PRIM RE ACT:** Broker, Consultant, Owner/Investor, Syndicator; **REP CLIENTS:** Indiv. and partnerships; **PROFL AFFIL & HONORS:** CCIM; FL Assn. of Realtors; RESSI; RNMI; MI Assn. of Realtors; Exchange Div.; Pensacola C of C; **EDUC:** BA, 1969, Econ., Univ. of OK; **EDUC HONORS:** Omicron Delta Kappa, BMOC; **MIL SERV:** US Army; 1st Lt., 69-71; **BUS ADD:** 9030 Woodrun Rd., Pensacola, FL 32504, (904)477-2123.

FERGUSON, William P.——B: Nov. 20, 1923, El Segundo, CA, *Dir. of Bus. Devel.*, Brown Realtors, Bus. Devel.; **PRIM RE ACT:** Broker, Instructor; **SERVICES:** Valuation, Prop. Mgmt., Servicing Third Party Cos., Corporate moves; **PREV EMPLOY:** Indus. Engrg., 1960-71; **PROFL AFFIL & HONORS:** CAR, NAR, RNMI, CRB, CRS, GRI; **MIL SERV:** USN, SK2C; **OTHER ACT & HONORS:** Pres. Conejo Valley Bd. of Realtors, Coll. Instr. of RE Broker Courses, 5 yrs; **HOME ADD:** Thousand Oaks, CA 91361, (805)495-1276; **BUS ADD:** 110 E. Thousand Oaks Blvd., Thousand Oaks, CA 91360, (805)495-2175.

FERNALD, Parker——*Mgr. Corp. RE*, Hercules Inc.; **PRIM RE ACT:** Property Manager; **BUS ADD:** 910 Market St., Wilmington, DE 19899, (302)575-5000.*

FERNELIUS, Earl W.——B: Dec. 22, 1927, Detroit, MI, *Pres.*, Earl Fernelius RE Appraisal Service & Consultant; **PRIM RE ACT:** Broker, Instructor, Consultant, Appraiser; **OTHER RE ACT:** Analyst; **SERVICES:** Appraisal, consultant, analyst, instr., broker; **REP CLIENTS:** Attys, state of MI, Dept. Nat. Resources, Chrysler Corp., GM Corp., GE Co.; **PREV EMPLOY:** Bloomfield Hills School Dist.; **PROFL AFFIL & HONORS:** ASA, SRA, SRPA, Realtor of Yr., Pres. Birmingham-Bloomfield Bd. of Realtors, VP MI Assn. of Realtors, V. Gov. SREA; **EDUC:** BS, 1952, Hist., Speech & Teaching, E. MI Univ.; **MIL SERV:** US Army, Pfc.; **HOME ADD:** 520 Wellesley, Birmingham, MI 48009, (313)644-8456; **BUS ADD:** 520 Wellesley, Birmingham, MI 48009, (313)642-4100.

FERNWOOD, Grail O.——B: May 31, 1915, Bluffton, AL, *Appraiser - Farm Mgmt. Consultant*, Self-employed; **PRIM RE ACT:** Broker, Consultant, Appraiser, Property Manager; **OTHER RE ACT:** Farm Mgr.; **SERVICES:** Valuation & mgmt.; **PROFL AFFIL & HONORS:** AIREA, MAI; **EDUC:** BS Agriculture, 1940, Natural Resources - Econ., Univ. of CA & Columbia Univ., NY; **MIL SERV:** US Air Corp, Sgt., Weather Serv. - WWII; **OTHER ACT & HONORS:** Elks - Marin; Listed Who's Who in the West - 1966-1968; **HOME ADD:** 131 Legend Rd., San Anselmo, CA 94960, (415)457-9208; **BUS ADD:** 131 Legend Rd., San Anselmo, CA 94960, (415)457-9208.

FERON, Richard L.——B: Jan. 25, 1943, Philadelphia, PA, Strouse Greenberg & Co., Indus.; **PRIM RE ACT:** Broker, Consultant, Developer, Owner/Investor; **SERVICES:** RE Brokerage, Shopping Ctr.; Indus. Comml. Investment; Indus., Devel. Appraisals; Fin. Prop. Mgmt.; **REP CLIENTS:** Sears; Prudential; Metro. Life; Amer. Steel; Abbott Labs; Tyco Labs.; Merrill Lynch; Travelers; Penn Mutual Life Ins. Co.; R.H. Meyer Inc.; Wanamakers; Hoeckingers; **PROFL AFFIL & HONORS:** NAR, SIR; **EDUC:** 1965, Acctg., Commerce & Fin., Villanova Univ.; **OTHER ACT & HONORS:** Germantown Cricket Club, Big Bros. of Amer., V Chmn. - Phila. Board of Realtors; **HOME ADD:** 844 Ivy Rd., Ambler, PA 19002, (215)643-4878; **BUS ADD:** 1626 Locust St., Philadelphia, PA 19103, (215)985-1100.

FERRAGAMO, Anthony E.——B: June 10, 1948, Boston, MA, *Reg. Arch.*, A.E. Ferragamo, Reg. Arch.; **PRIM RE ACT:** Architect; **SERVICES:** Arch. Land Use & Environmental Planning, Alternative Energy Consultants; **PROFL AFFIL & HONORS:** AIA, Boston Soc. Archs., NCARB, MA HBA, Amer. Arbit. Assn.; **EDUC:** BS, 1970, MIT; **GRAD EDUC:** MArch, 1972, MIT; **OTHER ACT & HONORS:** Assoc. Prof., Cape Cod Community Coll.; **BUS ADD:** 478 Rte. 6A, P.O. Box 332, E. Sandwich, MA 02537, (617)888-0869.

FERRARA, Alfred J.——B: Mar. 29, 1939, New York City, NY, *Gen. Mgr.*, Alaska Valuation Serv., Inc.; **PRIM RE ACT:** Consultant, Appraiser, Instructor; **SERVICES:** Consultation and valuation of Bus. and RE; **REP CLIENTS:** Corp. and fin. instns., fed. and state govt. agencies; **PREV EMPLOY:** Alaska Dept. of Natural Resources, Bureau of Land Mgmt. (US Dept. of the Interior); **PROFL AFFIL & HONORS:** Bldg. Indus. Assn. (Dir.); SREA (Pres. 1973, 1981); Amer. Inst. of RE Appraisers (Pres. 1980) Alaska Chap., MAI, SRPA, CRA, Profl. Recognition Award 1980 AIREA; **EDUC:** BA, 1966, Mgmt. & Fin., Univ. of AK; **OTHER ACT & HONORS:** Rotary; **HOME TEL:** (907)344-3617; **BUS ADD:** 550 W. 54th Ave., Anchorage, AK 99502, (907)278-3537.

FERRARA, Anthony J.——B: Sept. 29, 1919, Jeffrey City, NJ, *Owner, Pres.*, Ferrara Marchese & Co.; **OTHER RE ACT:** RE Tax Consultant; **SERVICES:** Tax advisor for owners & investors of RE; **PREV EMPLOY:** Self employed for past 35 years; **PROFL AFFIL & HONORS:** Licensed Public Acct.; **EDUC:** BS Acctg., 1949, Law School; **GRAD EDUC:** LLB, John Marshall Law Sch.; **MIL SERV:** US Army; Sgt.; 1941-1945; **OTHER ACT & HONORS:** Dir. of Pensions & Dir. of Fin. - 4 years, Jersey City, NJ; **HOME ADD:** 20 Stegman, Jersey City, NJ 07305, (201)659-6668; **BUS ADD:** 574 Newark Ave., Jersey City, NJ 07305, (201)798-6666.

FERRARA, Donald F.——B: Jan. 2, 1938, NY, *Vice President, Group Executive, Real Estate Investment*, Chase Investors Management Corporation, Real Estate Investment Group; **PRIM RE ACT:** Owner/Investor; **SERVICES:** Commercial Real Estate, Investment Advisory, Investment Acquisition, Investment Management; **REP CLIENTS:** Institutional/Governmental; Domestic/Foreign; Minimum Account size $100 Million; **PREV EMPLOY:** Directed RE operations of General Foods Corp., 1970-74; Equitable Life Assurance Society, RE investments, 1960-70; **PROFL AFFIL & HONORS:** Urban Land Inst.; Int'l. Council of Shopping Ctrs., Licensed RE Broker; **EDUC:** BS, 1959, Fin., Bucknell Univ.; **GRAD EDUC:** Various RE courses; **EDUC HONORS:** Distinguished Military Grad; Amer. Legion Award; **MIL SERV:** US Army, Lt.; **OTHER ACT & HONORS:** Int'l. Oceanographic Found.; Int'l. Game Fish Assn.; **HOME ADD:** 36 Berkshire Rd., Rockville Centre, NY 11570, (516)678-1446; **BUS ADD:** 1211 Avenue of the Americas, New York, NY 10036, (212)730-3714.

FERRER, Gonzalo——B: Aug. 2, 1936, Hato Rey, PR, *Partner*, R. F. McCloskey Assocs., RE Appraisers & Consultants; **PRIM RE ACT:** Consultant, Engineer, Appraiser; **REP CLIENTS:** Most fin. inst. in PR and many lge. state side cos.; **PREV EMPLOY:** Rominez de Arellano & Co. Inc., Box 485, San Juan, PR 00902, Bldrs. & Devels.; **PROFL AFFIL & HONORS:** MAI; AIREA, SREA, Soc. of RE Appraisers; **EDUC:** BCE, 1956, Cornell Univ.; **EDUC HONORS:** Member Chi Epsilon, Honorary Frat. in Civil Engrg.; **MIL SERV:** USANG, AMN; **HOME ADD:** 4 Meadow Ln., Georgetown, Guaynabo, PR 00657, (809)783-2459; **BUS ADD:** Box 10537 Caparra Hts. Sta., San Juan, PR 00922, (809)754-6520.

FERRIER, Dennis C.——B: Oct. 4, 1948, Manhattan, NY, *Sr. Appraiser*, Lane Appraisals Inc.; **PRIM RE ACT:** Appraiser; **OTHER RE ACT:** Consultant; **SERVICES:** Complete Appraisal Services; **REP CLIENTS:** Investors, Instns., Mcpl. & Govt. Agencies, Attys., Corps. and Individuals; **PREV EMPLOY:** Sr. Appraiser, Doern Appraiser - 1978-1980; Chief Appraiser - Westchester Fed. Savings, 1976-1978; Sr. Appraiser - Peoples Savings Bank, 1973-1976; Staff Appraiser - NY Savings Bank, 1971-1973; **PROFL AFFIL & HONORS:** AIREA, SREA, MAI, SRPA; **EDUC:** BS, Bus. Admin., Pacific Western Univ.; **MIL SERV:** US Army, 1968-1971, Spec. 5th Class, Good Conduct Medal, Army Commendation Medal; **HOME ADD:** 3407 Lorelei Dr., Yorktown Hgts., NY 10598, (914)962-3185; **BUS ADD:** 2180 Boston Post Rd., Larchmont, NY 10538, (914)834-1400.

FERRIS, Don——B: Apr. 23, 1943, Baltimore, MD, *Indep. Contractor*, Grubb & Ellis Commercial Brokerage Co., Investment/Office Buildings; **PRIM RE ACT:** Broker, Consultant, Owner/Investor, Instructor, Syndicator; **SERVICES:** Sales and leasing of office bldgs; investments; **REP CLIENTS:** Domestic and for. investors, syndicators, owners/users; **PREV EMPLOY:** Exec., Xerox Corp., 1967-1977; **PROFL AFFIL & HONORS:** Beverly Hills Bd. of Realtors; **EDUC:** BBA, 1972, Intl. Bus., George Washington Univ.; **GRAD EDUC:** MBA, 1974, Intl. Bus., George Washington Univ.; **MIL SERV:** USASA, Capt., 1962-1967; **OTHER ACT & HONORS:** Bd. Member, Kidney Found. of So. CA; **HOME ADD:** 19 Ketch, Marena Delrey, CA 90291, (213)396-4985; **BUS ADD:** 9606 Santa Monica Blvd., Beverly Hills, CA 90210, (213)278-2190.

FERRIS, Louise——*Mgr. RE*, CPC International, Inc.; **PRIM RE ACT:** Property Manager; **BUS ADD:** International Plaza, Englewood Cliffs, NJ 07632, (201)894-4000.*

FERRIS, Robert J.——B: June 1, 1941, Cortland, NY, *Prin. Broker & Owner*, Ferris RE; **PRIM RE ACT:** Broker, Consultant, Appraiser, Owner/Investor; **PROFL AFFIL & HONORS:** NAR, NY State Assn. of Realtors, Nat. Assn. Comml. Investment Div. Member, NY Society of RE Appraisers; **HOME ADD:** 16 Bellevue Ave., Cortland, NY 13045; **BUS ADD:** 99 Groton Ave., Cortland, NY 13045, (607)753-6723.

FERRO, Jeffrey, E.——B: May 25, 1946, Evanston, IL, *Pres.*, Heart of the Ozarks Builders, Inc.; **PRIM RE ACT:** Builder; **SERVICES:** Gen. Contractor for Custom Residential Homes; **PREV EMPLOY:** (Broker), First Real Estates, 1972-74 Amer. Nat. Bank, 1970-72; **PROFL AFFIL & HONORS:** NAHB, AHBA, Twin Lakes Bldrs. Assn., VP of Builders Assn., (1980); Director of Builders Assoc. (1982); **EDUC:** BS, 1968, Gen. Bus. Admin. Specializing in Mgmt., No. IL Univ.; **GRAD EDUC:** 27 hrs. Grad. work, 1970, Bus. Admin., No. IL Univ.; **EDUC HONORS:** Faculty Asst., Honor Roll, Pres. of Society for the Advancement of Mgmt. (1 ChapUSA,1969); **OTHER ACT & HONORS:** Officer in Knights of Columbus, (1980); **HOME ADD:** P.O. Box 89, Mountain Home, AR 72653, (501)425-4538; **BUS ADD:** P.O. Box 89, Mountain Home, AR 72653, (501)425-4538.

FERRON, David V.——B: Dec. 16, 1944, Westbrook, ME, *VP Properties.*, Consumer Value Stores (CVS), Melville Corp.; **OTHER RE ACT:** Store expansion and asset mgt. programs; **SERVICES:** RE, const., prop. mgmt., fixture manufacturing, warehousing, capital expenditure planning, long term growth planning, energy, store planning and design; **PROFL AFFIL & HONORS:** NACORE (Current Bd. Dir.), Int. Council of Shopping Ctrs., Spec's Advisory Bd. Member (Store Planning, Equipment, Const. Serv.), Chain Store RE Exec. Assn.; Lic. RE Broker (MA), The Marquis Who's Who in the E - 18th Ed. 1981-82, Who's Who in New England by N.E. RE Journal - 1978, Personalities of Amer. 1982 Ed.; **EDUC:** 1968, Mktg. & Bus. Admin., Northeastern Univ.; **EDUC HONORS:** Marketing Major; **OTHER ACT & HONORS:** Notary Public (MA), Holliston Newcomers Club, Holliston Fathers Club; **HOME ADD:** 340 Winter St., Holliston, MA 01746, (617)429-1184; **BUS ADD:** 400 Founders Dr., Woonsocket, RI 02895, (401)765-1500.

FERSTL, Tom M.——B: Apr. 19, 1939, Fort Smith, AR, *Owner*, Ferstl Enterprises; **PRIM RE ACT:** Broker, Attorney, Appraiser, Instructor, Property Manager; **SERVICES:** Prop. Mgmt., RE Appraisal, RE Law; **REP CLIENTS:** Consultation work and appraisals for all local lenders and life ins. cos.; **PREV EMPLOY:** Asst. Regional Dir. & Regional Appraiser of the Fed. Home Loan Mort. Corp.; **PROFL AFFIL & HONORS:** IREM, SREA, AIREA, ABA, MAI, CPM, SREA, Atty. at Law; **EDUC:** BBA, 1966, Gen. Bus., Univ. of AR at Little Rock; **GRAD EDUC:** JD, 1972, RE Law, Univ. of AR School of Law; **EDUC HONORS:** Sword and Shield Honor Soc., Phi Alpha Delta Law Frat.; **OTHER ACT & HONORS:** Justice of the Peace, Pulaski Cty. 1965-1970; **HOME ADD:** 7 Lou Ellen Dr., Little Rock, AR 72202, (501)666-1439; **BUS ADD:** 7 Lou Ellen Dr., Little Rock, AR 72202, (501)666-1439.

FESS, Michael D.——B: Sept. 25, 1935, Haynesville, LA, *Pres.*, Fess Assn.; **PRIM RE ACT:** Broker, Consultant, Developer, Builder, Owner/Investor, Property Manager, Syndicator; **PROFL AFFIL & HONORS:** Realtor, CCIM; **EDUC:** BS, 1958, Centenary Coll.; **HOME ADD:** 31 Springlake Way, Shreveport, LA 71106, (318)868-9422; **BUS ADD:** 2620 Centenary Blvd., Shreveport, LA 71104, (318)221-7827.

FESSEL, Norbert——B: June 22, 1929, Berlin, Germany, *Part.*, Fessel and Goldman; **PRIM RE ACT:** Attorney; **OTHER RE ACT:** Title ins.; **SERVICES:** Gen. legal service, title exam, title ins. and rpts.; **PROFL AFFIL & HONORS:** ABA, RI Bar Assn., CT Bar Assn.; **EDUC:** BA, 1951, Poli. Sci., Brown Univ., Providence, RI; **GRAD EDUC:** LLB, 1954, Harvard Law School; **MIL SERV:** US Army; **OTHER ACT & HONORS:** Sec. Jewish Home for the Aged; VP Bridge Club of RI; **HOME ADD:** 26 Meadowbrook Dr., Barrington, RI 02806, (401)245-6289; **BUS ADD:** 11 Park Row, Providence, RI 02903, (401)331-2300.

FETSCH, William B.——B: Feb. 5, 1948, East Chicago, IN, *Dir. Comml. Devel.*, Edw. R. Carr & Assoc., Inc.; **PRIM RE ACT:** Developer, Lender, Builder, Owner/Investor, Property Manager, Syndicator; **SERVICES:** Build/own/manage comml. props.; **PROFL AFFIL & HONORS:** BOMA, Nat. Assn. of Home Builders, ULI, NAIOP; **EDUC:** BS, 1970, Econometrics/Statistics, IN Univ.; **GRAD EDUC:** MS, 1973, Micro-Econ. Theory, IN Univ.; **EDUC HONORS:** Dean's List; **HOME ADD:** 6535 Copact, Falls Church, VA 22044; **BUS ADD:** 7535 Little River Tpk., Annandale, VA 22003, (703)941-7710.

FEUER, Bruce R.——B: June 2, 1948, Miami, FL, *Sr. VP - Prop. Devel.*, Butler Shoe Corp.; **PRIM RE ACT:** Attorney, Property Manager; **OTHER RE ACT:** Comml. leasing, mgmt.; **PREV EMPLOY:** Feuer and Feuer, Attys., 1972-74, Maimi, FL; **PROFL AFFIL & HONORS:** State Bar of GA, FL Bar, ABA, ICSC, NACORE; **EDUC:** BA, 1970, Bus., Law, Oglethorpe Univ.; **GRAD EDUC:** JD, 1972, Emory Univ. Law School; **HOME ADD:** 3720 Mayfair Rd., Atlanta, GA 30342, (404)262-1951; **BUS ADD:** 1600 Terrell Mill Rd., P.O. Box 105535, Atlanta, GA 30348, (404)955-6400.

FEUERSTEIN, Howard Michael——B: Sept. 16, 1939, Memphis, TN, *Atty.*, Stoel, Rives, Boley, Fraser & Wyse; **PRIM RE ACT:** Attorney; **SERVICES:** Legal Services in RE transactions and matters; **PROFL AFFIL & HONORS:** OR State Bar, Multnomah Cty. Bar Assn., ABA, Listed in Marquis, Who's Who in American Law; FNMA approved atty. for condos. and planned unit devel.; **EDUC:** BA, 1961, Vanderbilt Univ.; **GRAD EDUC:** JD, 1963, Law, Vanderbilt Univ.; **EDUC HONORS:** Founder's Medal for first honors; Editor-in-Chief, Law Review; Order of the Coif; **OTHER ACT & HONORS:** Amer. Land Devel. Assn.; Community Assn. Instit.; OR Bd. of Realtors Condo Study Comm.; **HOME ADD:** 4815 SW Stonebrook Ct., Portland, OR 97201, (503)246-4702; **BUS ADD:** 23rd Floor, 900 SW 5th Ave., Portland, OR 97204, (503)224-3380.

FICK, Edmund J.——*VP Fin. & Treas.*, Easco Corp.; **PRIM RE ACT:** Property Manager; **BUS ADD:** 201 North Charles St., Baltimore, MD 21201, (301)837-9550.*

FICK, Wayne E.——B: Oct. 20, 1930, St. Louis, MO, *Leasing Rep./Bldg. Mgr.*, Trammell Crow Co., St. Louis; **PRIM RE ACT:** Property Manager; **OTHER RE ACT:** Leasing Rep.; **PREV EMPLOY:** RE Depts. - 2 Nat. Cos. Site Location & Mgmt.; **PROFL AFFIL & HONORS:** BOMA-St. Louis, BOMA Chap. Pres. 1980-81; **EDUC:** Po.S., 1953, Geography, history, philosphy, St. Louis Univ., St. Louis, MO; **MIL SERV:** USAF, Capt., Korean Service; **OTHER ACT & HONORS:** SME - St. Louis; **HOME ADD:** 12183 Hibler Dr., Creve Coeur, MO 63141, (314)878-5817; **BUS ADD:** 4203 Earth City Expressway, Earth City, MO 63045, (314)291-3373.

FIEBICK, Gary A.——B: Dec. 30, 1942, Richmond, CA, *Broker, Sales Mgr., Pres.*, Sunriver Realty; **PRIM RE ACT:** Broker, Consultant, Developer, Instructor; **OTHER RE ACT:** Recreation land devel.; **SERVICES:** Sales, sales org., valuation, project consultant; **REP CLIENTS:** Mid-high income investors, recreation land devel. comm., devels.; **PROFL AFFIL & HONORS:** OAR; NAR; RNMI; ULI; Amer. Land Devel. Assn., GRI; CRB; **EDUC:** BS, 1968, Bus. Educ., Univ. of ID; **GRAD EDUC:** MBA, Acctg., RE, Portland State Univ.; **EDUC HONORS:** Phi Beta Lambda, Sr., 68; **MIL SERV:** USN; CT3; **OTHER ACT & HONORS:** Church Council Member, 1981; Member Sch. Dist. Facilities Planning Comm., 1980-81; Chmn. Bldg. Comm. Sunriver Comm. Church, 1981-82; **HOME ADD:** PO Box 3324, Sunriver, OR 97702, (503)593-1111; **BUS ADD:** Great Hall, Ctr. Dr., Sunriver, OR 97702, (503)593-1626.

FIEHLER, Thomas L.——**B:** Aug. 19, 1951, Perryville, MO, *Reg. Supervisor*, Realty Appraisal & Mgmt. Corp., Appr. Div.; **PRIM RE ACT:** Appraiser, Lender; **SERVICES:** Appraisals of resid. & comml. RE; **REP CLIENTS:** Lenders, indivs. & privt. cos.; **PROFL AFFIL & HONORS:** SRA, SREA, Review appraiser for Nat. Assn. of Review Appraisers; **EDUC:** BS, 1974, Mktg. Mgmt, Psych., S. MO State Univ.; **MIL SERV:** USANG, SP4; **HOME ADD:** 6224 Clematis Dr., Dayton, OH 45449, (513)433-3647; **BUS ADD:** 915 Elliott Dr., Middletown, OH 45042, (513)424-7022.

FIELD, Dr. Irving M.——**B:** Jan. 21, 1934, Green Bay, WI, *Prof. of Bus. Admin.*, WA State Univ., RE & Insurance; **PRIM RE ACT:** Broker, Consultant, Appraiser, Instructor, Insuror; **SERVICES:** Univ. teaching research, publication and extension activities. Pvt. appraising & consulting; **REP CLIENTS:** Port of Whitman Cty., Pullman School Dist., City of Palouse, & Area Fin. Instit.; **PREV EMPLOY:** The Equitable Life Assurance Soc. of the US, The Univ. of OR; **PROFL AFFIL & HONORS:** Amer. Soc. of Appraisers; Whitman Cty., State of WA and NAR; The Amer. RE and Urban Econ. Assn., ASA designation & Past Pres. Spikane Chap., Past Pres. Whitman Cty. Bd. of Realtors; **EDUC:** BS, 1956, RE, Univ. of MO; **GRAD EDUC:** MBA, 1960, Mktg., WA State Univ.; Dr. of Business Admin., 1966, Insurance & Urban Geography, Univ. of OR; **EDUC HONORS:** Beta Gamma Sigma, Bus. Academic Honorary, Teaching Asst.; **OTHER ACT & HONORS:** Acocia Fraternity; Past Nat. Pres. United Church of Christ; Past Chmn. Bd. of Tr.; **HOME ADD:** Box 595, Pullman, WA 99163, (509)334-3921; **BUS ADD:** Todd Hall 123, Pullman, WA 99164, (509)335-2322.

FIELD, Maxwell John——**B:** June 1, 1934, London, Eng., *Chmn., Pres. & CEO*, Marathon US Realties, Inc.; **PRIM RE ACT:** Developer, Owner/Investor; **OTHER RE ACT:** Executive; **PREV EMPLOY:** Can. Marathon Realty Co. Ltd, Monarch Investments Ltd., MEPC Can. Props., Ltd., WH Bosley & Co., Ltd., UK Gerald Eve & Co., Howell & Brooks; **PROFL AFFIL & HONORS:** Royal Inst. of Chartered Surveyors, (Fellow); Ass. of Ont. Land Econ., FRICS, OLE; **EDUC:** ARICS, 1957, Valuations, Coll. of Estate Mgmt., London Univ.; **BUS ADD:** One First Natl. Plaza, Suite 2550, Chicago, IL 60603, (312)782-5114.

FIELDS, Charles L.——**B:** Aug. 19, 1936, Gloucester, MA, *Pres.*, New England Lobster Co., Inc.; **PRIM RE ACT:** Broker, Owner/Investor; **EDUC:** BS, 1958, Marine Engrs., Duke Univ., MA Maritime Academy; **MIL SERV:** USN, Lt.(j.g.); **OTHER ACT & HONORS:** Marine Fisheries Advisory Comm. 1968-1981, New England Sculptor's Assn., Rockport Art Assn., Cambridge Art Assn.; **HOME ADD:** 43 Pigeon Hill St., Rockport, MA 01966, (617)546-6059; **BUS ADD:** Break Water Ave., Rockport, MA 01966, (617)546-9488.

FIELDS, David E., Jr.——**B:** Dec. 5, 1929, Tulsa, OK, *Pres.*, Fields RE Securities Co.; **PRIM RE ACT:** Broker, Consultant, Developer, Lender, Owner/Investor, Syndicator; **SERVICES:** Consulting, devel. & mort. brokerage; **REP CLIENTS:** Profls. & physicians; **PREV EMPLOY:** All in investment RE; **PROFL AFFIL & HONORS:** Rotary, Local Devel. Comm., Reg. RE Broker - SC & NC, Reg. Principal; **EDUC:** BA, 1953, OK Univ.; **EDUC HONORS:** BS in Chem.; **MIL SERV:** Exempt for Atomic Energy Work - SRP Project; **OTHER ACT & HONORS:** SBA Regional Council; Ctry. Club of Charleston, Southern Hills C. of C., Tulsa, OK; Former Dir. of Occoneeche Council of Boy Scouts of Amer.; Eagle Scout; Past Dir., Bd. of Bethel Methodist Church; Who's Who in SE; **HOME ADD:** One King St., Charleston, SC 29401, (803)722-3305; **BUS ADD:** 18 Broad St., Charleston, SC 29401, (803)723-8249.

FIELDS, Gerald S.——**B:** Oct. 14, 1947, Montreal, Que., *Gen. Counsel*, Fidinam (Can.)Ltd.; Fidinam USA Inc.; **PRIM RE ACT:** Consultant, Attorney, Owner/Investor, Instructor, Real Estate Publisher; **SERVICES:** Legal; **PREV EMPLOY:** Practices in the areas of RE and taxation. Author of numerous works relating to RE and mort. fin.; **PROFL AFFIL & HONORS:** Law Soc. of Upper Can.; Can. Tax Found.; Can. Bar Assn.; ABA; Intl. Council of Shopping Ctrs.; **EDUC:** BA with distinction, 1969, Concordia Univ., Montreal; **GRAD EDUC:** LLB, 1972, Osgoode Hall Law Sch.; **EDUC HONORS:** Prizewinner while as Osgoode Hall; **OTHER ACT & HONORS:** Editor-in-Chief of Can. Mort. Practice Reporter series; Lectures for Law Soc. of Upper Canada, Ontario RE Assn.; Ontario Mort. Brokers Assn.; **HOME ADD:** 61 Loganberry Crescent, Willowdale, ON, Canada, (416)498-1210; **BUS ADD:** Ste. 2703, 2 Bloor St. E., Toronto, ON, Canada, (416)962-5600.

FIELDS, Mary Bryan——**B:** Nov. 15, 1949, Macon, Bibb Cty., GA, *Broker/Partner*, Commercial Investment Management Corp./Atlantic Land & Development Corp.; **PRIM RE ACT:** Broker, Developer, Owner/Investor, Instructor; **OTHER RE ACT:** Devel. of timeshare resorts; **SERVICES:** Devel., sales & leasing of comml./investment props., devel. & sales of timeshare resorts; **REP CLIENTS:** Indiv. & instnl. investors; **PROFL AFFIL & HONORS:** Pres. - Brunswick Glynncounn Bd. of Realtors; Exec. Bd. of Dirs. - GA Assn. of Realtors; Member - Realtors Nat. Mktg. Inst., Faculty Member - Brunswick Junior Coll. (RE); Post-Licensing Inst. - GA RE Commn., CCIM Candidate; Realtor of the Year 1980; **EDUC:** BBA, 1971, Fin., Univ. of GA; **GRAD EDUC:** MA, 1973, RE, Univ. of GA; **EDUC HONORS:** Phi Kappa Phi, Cum Laude Grad.; **OTHER ACT & HONORS:** Pres. - Brunswick Jr. Woman's Club; Charter Bd. Member - GA Coalition to Prevent Shoplifting; Brunswick Devel. Task Force; Charter Member - Leadership Brunswick; GA Clubwoman of the Year 1979; Advisory Council - Volunteer Serv., Inc.; **HOME ADD:** 203 Military Rd., St. Simons Island, GA 31522, (912)638-4429; **BUS ADD:** 100 Redfern Village, St. Simons Island, GA 31522, (915)638-9941.

FIELDS, William A.——**B:** Mar. 30, 1939, Parkersburg, WV, *Partner*, Fields & Hollister; **PRIM RE ACT:** Attorney; **OTHER RE ACT:** Title Ins. Agent; **SERVICES:** for Lawyers Title Ins. Corp.; **REP CLIENTS:** Central Trust Co., Marietta, Dime Bank of Marietta; Homequity (numerous other banks); **PROFL AFFIL & HONORS:** OH Bar Assn., Mid-Ohio Valley Estate Planning Council; **EDUC:** BS, 1961, Fin., OH State Univ.; **GRAD EDUC:** JD, 1964, Law, Harvard Univ. Law School; **EDUC HONORS:** Magna Cum Laude, Beta Gamma Sigma,Outstanding Senior Man at OSU; **OTHER ACT & HONORS:** Acting Judge, Marietta Municipal Court; MENSA, Marquis' Who's Who in America; **HOME ADD:** 129 Hillcrest Dr., Marietta, OH 45750, (614)373-1240; **BUS ADD:** 217 2nd St., Marietta, OH 45750, (614)374-5346.

FIETZ, Charles H.——**B:** Dec. 10, 1933, Milwaukee, WI, *Pres.*, State-line Appraisals, Ltd.; **PRIM RE ACT:** Consultant, Appraiser, Assessor; **SERVICES:** Appraisal of resid. & small comml. props., consultant for ad valorum tax matters, city assessor for three communities; **REP CLIENTS:** Mutual S&L, Beloit Savings Bank, Merrill Lynch Relo., Executrans Relo.,Transamerica Relo., First Savings of WI, First Savings of So. Beloit, etc.; **PREV EMPLOY:** Have been in appraisal and assessment field since 1957; **PROFL AFFIL & HONORS:** SREA; WI Assn. of Assessing Officers; Beloit Bd. of Realtors, Sr. Resid. Appraiser; Cert. WI Assessor 2 & 3; **OTHER ACT & HONORS:** City Assessor, W. Bend, WI, 1957-1960; Deputy Village Assessor, Edina, MN, 1960-1964; Deputy Assessor, Janesville, WI, 1970-1974; City Assessor, Beloit, WI, 1974-1978; **HOME ADD:** POB 983, Beloit, WI 53511, (608)364-0096; **BUS ADD:** POB 693, Beloit, WI 53511, (608)364-0096.

FIFIELD, Charles H.——**B:** July 13, 1946, St. Louis, MO, *Pres./CEO*, Southwest Financial Group, Inc.; **PRIM RE ACT:** Broker, Owner/Investor, Syndicator; **SERVICES:** Investment counseling and synd. of comml. properties; **REP CLIENTS:** Individuals and instit. investors in comml. properties; **PREV EMPLOY:** Bank of Amer., 1969-1970; CapitaL Analysts, Inc., 1970-1973; **EDUC:** BBA, 1968, Econ., S Methodist Univ.; **GRAD EDUC:** MBA, 1969, Fin./Intl. Bus., NW Univ.; **EDUC HONORS:** Dean's List; **HOME ADD:** 1702 North Blvd., Houston, TX 77098; **BUS ADD:** 3336 Richmond Ave. #200, Houston, TX 77098, (713)526-3051.

FIFIELD, Otto R.——**B:** Oct. 31, 1922, Crown Point, IN, *Pres.*, First Assoc. Inc.; **PRIM RE ACT:** Broker, Developer, Owner/Investor; **OTHER RE ACT:** Lake Cty, IN; **SERVICES:** Listing, selling, devel. - resid.; **PROFL AFFIL & HONORS:** Pres. of S. Lake Bd. of Realtors, CRS & CRB; **EDUC:** Purdue Univ.; **GRAD EDUC:** GRI, 1975, IN Univ.; **MIL SERV:** US Army, Sgt.; **OTHER ACT & HONORS:** Pres., Gary Rotary Club - 1980; **HOME ADD:** 8228 W. 82nd Ct., Crown Point, IN 46307, (219)365-8541; **BUS ADD:** 182 W. North St., Crown Point, IN 46307, (219)769-3439.

FIFIELD, Steven D.——**B:** Jan. 29, 1948, Gary, IN, *Exec. VP*, Fifield Palmer & Co.; **PRIM RE ACT:** Broker, Developer, Owner/Investor; **SERVICES:** Manage, lease & devel. office bldgs. in IL; **REP CLIENTS:** Lenders & indiv. or instnl. clients in office devels.; **PREV EMPLOY:** Urban Investment & Devel.; **PROFL AFFIL & HONORS:** ULI, BOMA, Nat. Assn. of Indus. and Office Parks; **EDUC:** AB, 1970, Math. & Econ., IN Univ.; **GRAD EDUC:** MBA, 1972, Fin., Mktg., Univ. of Chicago; **EDUC HONORS:** Cum Laude, High Honors; **OTHER ACT & HONORS:** Member Schaumburg Devel. Comm.; Trustee, Lake Forest Academy; co-chmn., memberships Econ. Club of Chicago; **HOME ADD:** 35 Indian Hill Rd., Winnetka, IL 60093; **BUS ADD:** 101 N. Wacker Dr., Chicago, IL 60606, (312)853-3700.

FIGG, Dorothy R.——**B:** Oct. 11, 1935, Lynchburg, VA, *Dir., Mktg. & Relocation*, Savage & Company, Realtors, Better Homes and Gardens; **PRIM RE ACT:** Broker, Instructor; **OTHER RE ACT:** Corporate relocation; **SERVICES:** Resid. RE including "Settling-In" services; **PREV EMPLOY:** VP, Robert L. Figg & Sons Insurance Agency;

PROFL AFFIL & HONORS: Richmond Bd. of Realtors, Old Dominion Chap.; Rho Epsilon RE Fraternity, CRB, RE Broker; **OTHER ACT & HONORS:** Outstanding Young Women in America, 1968; Bd. Tr., Trinity Episcopal School; Past Dir. of Lee District JWC, VFWC; Past Dir., Richmond YWCA; **HOME ADD:** 4444 Hickory Rd., Richmond, VA 23235, (804)272-0307; **BUS ADD:** 9400 Midlothian Tpke, P.O. Box 3055, Richmond, VA 23235, (804)320-7191.

FIGUEREDO, Antonio B.——B: Aug. 20, 1934, Havana, Cuba, *Sec./Treas.*, Lomas Santa Fe Inc.; **PRIM RE ACT:** Developer, Builder Owner/Investor, Property Manager; **SERVICES:** Prop. mgmt., devel. of comml. properties; **REP CLIENTS:** Indiv. investors; **PREV EMPLOY:** Amer. Housing Guild, 1971-1975; **PROFL AFFIL & HONORS:** AICPA; CA Soc. of CPA's; **EDUC:** BA, 1967, Acctg., Havana Univ.; **GRAD EDUC:** Masters, 1969, Fin., Havana Univ.; **HOME ADD:** 14365 Janal Way, San Diego, CA 92129, (714)485-6791; **BUS ADD:** 265 Santa Helena, Solana Beach, CA 92075, (714)755-1552.

FILLINGIM, Larry K.——B: Apr. 6, 1947, Pensacola, FL, *Partner*, Fillingim & Assoc., P.A.; **PRIM RE ACT:** Consultant, Attorney, Property Manager; **OTHER RE ACT:** CPA; **SERVICES:** Counselor to Builders, Devel., as to tax questions; **REP CLIENTS:** CKM Builders, Ridgeway Enterprises; **PREV EMPLOY:** Various CPA Firms - Partner for seven yrs.; **PROFL AFFIL & HONORS:** Bd. of Dir. member of eleven investment & RE Devel. corps., Devel.-Nat. Hist. & Bus. Review; **EDUC:** BA, 1973, Econ., Fin., FL Intl.; BA, 1976, Univ. of Miami (FL).-Finance; **GRAD EDUC:** MBA, 1975, FL Intl. Univ.; JD-Woodrow Wilson Coll. of Law, 1979, Taxation, RE; **EDUC HONORS:** Received 'Ruddy Investment Counseling Award'-1974; **MIL SERV:** USMC, Cpl., Ordinary decorations; **OTHER ACT & HONORS:** AOPA; **HOME ADD:** 416 Riverlake Ct., Woodstock, GA 301881; **BUS ADD:** PO Box 263, Roswell, GA 30077, (404)475-1544.

FILLIP, G. Stephen——B: Sept. 15, 1951, Falls County, TX, *V.P.*, First National Bank of Lubbock, R.E. Div., Mgr.; **PRIM RE ACT:** Banker, Lender; **SERVICES:** Permanent residential, placement of permanent comml., interim coust. loans, dev. loans; **REP CLIENTS:** contractors, devlprs.; **PROFL AFFIL & HONORS:** Assoc. mgr. West TX HBA, SREA, ABA, TX Bankers Assn., MBA, Lubbock Assn. of Credit Mgmt., Grad. Natl. School of R.E. Fin., OH State Univ.; **EDUC:** BBA, 1974, RE, TX Tech Univ.; **EDUC HONORS:** Deans List, Mbr. Alpha Kappa Psi, Honorary Fin. Frat.; **OTHER ACT & HONORS:** Rotary; **HOME ADD:** 4422 88th St., Lubbock, TX 79424, (806)794-5521; **BUS ADD:** P.O. Box 1241, Lubbock, TX 79408, (806)765-8861.

FILLMORE, Tom D.——B: Oct. 17, 1942, Cedar Rapids, IA, *RE & Ins. Mgr.*, Wilson Foods Corp.; **PRIM RE ACT:** Property Manager, Insuror; **SERVICES:** Buy-sell-lease prop. & buy & admin. total ins. program; **EDUC:** BBA RE, 1979, Bus. & Acctg., Central State Univ. - Edmond, OK; **MIL SERV:** USNR, E4; **HOME ADD:** 10713 Condor Terr., Oklahoma City, OK 73132, (405)722-7205; **BUS ADD:** 4545 Lincoln, Oklahoma City, OK 73105, (405)525-4641.

FILOON, John W., Jr.——B: Oct. 7, 1936, Boston, MA, *VP*, Integrated Resources Equity Corp.; **PRIM RE ACT:** Broker, Syndicator; **PROFL AFFIL & HONORS:** RESSI; **EDUC:** BA, 1959, Eng., Harvard Coll.; **GRAD EDUC:** MBA, 1966, Bus., Northeastern Univ.; **MIL SERV:** USMC, Lt.; **HOME TEL:** (212)799-0229; **BUS ADD:** 666 Third Ave., NY, NY 10017, (212)878-9415.

FINCH, Brian A.——B: Sept. 28, 1951, Chicago, IL, *Owner*, Finch RE Appraisal; **PRIM RE ACT:** Appraiser; **SERVICES:** Appraisal of comml., indus., resid. & farm prop., expert witness; **REP CLIENTS:** Fortune 500 Cos., S&L, banks, relocation cos., municipal redevel. agencies; **PREV EMPLOY:** 5 yrs. (1976-1981) with MCSC, an indep. fee appraisal co.; 2 yrs. (1974-1976) with Peoria Savings & Loan Assn.; **PROFL AFFIL & HONORS:** Member, SREA; Affiliate Member, Peoria Bd. of Realtors, SRPA by the SREA; **EDUC:** BBA, 1973, Gen. Bus. Admin., Western IL Univ.; **GRAD EDUC:** MBA, 1974, Fin., Grad. School of Bus., Western IL Univ.; **OTHER ACT & HONORS:** Current Member, Bd. of Dir., Peoria Chap. 28, Soc. of RE Appraisers; Past Pres., Peoria Chap. 28, Soc. of RE Appraisers (1978-1979); **HOME ADD:** 336 E. Edgewood, Morton, IL 61550, (309)266-9692; **BUS ADD:** 336 E. Edgewood, Morton, IL 61550, (309)266-9692.

FINCH, Robert M.——B: Nov. 30, 1919, Lebanon, KS, *Chmn. of the Bd.*, Bob Finch & Associates, Inc.; **PRIM RE ACT:** Broker, Appraiser, Builder; **SERVICES:** Gen. brokerage; **PROFL AFFIL & HONORS:** NAR, Local, State Assns. of Realtors, Home Builders Assn., CRS, MIRM (Homebuilders), Former State Pres.; Former Nat. Dir. of NAR; R. O. T. Y. for KS 1974; **EDUC:** BS, 1947, Bus. Admin. and Econ., Ft. Hays State Univ.; **MIL SERV:** Sig Corps, 1st Sgt.; **HOME ADD:** 3601 C Fairway Dr., Hays, KS 67601, (913)625-2744; **BUS ADD:** 13th & Pine, P O Box 935, Hays, KS 67601, (913)625-7313.

FINCH, Ruth W.——B: Jan. 28, 1914, Arkansas City, KS, *Mgr./Broker*, R.W. Finch RE; **PRIM RE ACT:** Broker, Consultant, Property Manager; **SERVICES:** Rental Mgr., Resid.-Acreages; **OTHER ACT & HONORS:** 20 yrs. in the field of Optometry; Life Membership in Optometric Assoc. for Assistance for the 8 last years of outstanding services in the field of Optometry.; **HOME ADD:** 1703 Brenthereen St., Idaho Falls, ID 83401, (208)522-2970; **BUS ADD:** 1703 Brenthaven - PO Box 641, Idaho Falls, ID 83401, (208)524-0900.

FINDLAY, John G.——B: June 11, 1944, Montclair, NJ, *Pres.*, Re/Max of Albuquerque; **PRIM RE ACT:** Broker, Developer, Owner/Investor; **SERVICES:** Investment counseling, devel., land brokerage; **REP CLIENTS:** Indiv. and instns. interested in investment RE; **PREV EMPLOY:** Broadcasting 1968-1976; **PROFL AFFIL & HONORS:** NAR; Albuquerque Bd. of Realtors; RNMI; **EDUC:** BA, 1966, Soc., Princeton Univ.; **GRAD EDUC:** Course work completed (no thesis), 1968, Mass Communications, Univ. of Denver; **OTHER ACT & HONORS:** Charlie Pride Golf Fiesta Comm.; Princeton Alumni Schools Comm.; **HOME ADD:** 8925 7th St. NW, ALbuquerque, NM 87114, (505)897-2324; **BUS ADD:** 4175 Montgomery NE, Albuquerque, NM 87109, (505)881-9700.

FINE, Alvin M.——B: Dec. 30, 1926, Boston, MA, *Assoc.*, Allen Assoc.; **PRIM RE ACT:** Developer, Property Manager, Engineer; **SERVICES:** Prop. Mgmt.; **REP CLIENTS:** Comml.-Shopping Ctrs.; **PROFL AFFIL & HONORS:** Boston Soc. of Civil Engineers; **EDUC:** BS in Civil Engrg., 1950, Const., Northeastern Univ.; **MIL SERV:** USN, S/1/C 1943-1944; **HOME ADD:** 12 Sylvan Rd., Sharon, MA 02067, (617)784-2524; **BUS ADD:** 131 State St., Boston, MA 02109, (617)742-2250.

FINE, Mark L.——B: Feb. 10, 1946, Cleveland, OH, *Pres.*, American Nevada Corp., Inc.; **PRIM RE ACT:** Broker, Developer, Owner/Investor; **PREV EMPLOY:** Loeb, Rhoades & Co., 42 Wall St., NY, NY; **PROFL AFFIL & HONORS:** NV Devel. Authority-Tr.; Las Vegas Bd. of Realtors-Member; S. MV Home Builders-Dir.; ULI; **EDUC:** BS, Bus. Admin., 1968, R.E., Univ. AZ, Tucson; **OTHER ACT & HONORS:** Jewish Family Servs., Big Brothers, Boy Scouts of Amer.; **HOME ADD:** 2241 Geronimo, Las Vegas, NV 89109, (702)733-3909; **BUS ADD:** 2501 N. Green Valley Pkwy., Suite 101, Henderson, NV 89015, (702)458-8855.

FINE, Milton——B: May 18, 1926, Pittsburgh, PA, *President*, Interstate Hotels Corporation; **PRIM RE ACT:** Property Manager; **OTHER RE ACT:** Develops and manages hotel properties; **EDUC:** AB, 1949, Econ., Univ. of Pittsburgh; **GRAD EDUC:** LLB, 1950, Law School, Univ. of Pittsburgh; **EDUC HONORS:** Magna Cum Laude; **MIL SERV:** United States Army, Sgt.; **HOME ADD:** 5365 Darlington Rd., Pittsburgh, PA 15217, (412)521-3054; **BUS ADD:** 218 Frick Building, Pittsburgh, PA 15217, (412)227-6700.

FINE, William I.——B: May 26, 1928, St. Paul, MN, *Pres.*, Fine Associates Inc.; **PRIM RE ACT:** Developer; **PREV EMPLOY:** Asst. District Atty., Dallas, TX, 1950-1951; USAF, 1952-1953; Sr. Partner, Fine, Simon & Schneider, 1953-1968; Chmn. of the Bd., Fine Properties Corp., 1969-1970; Chmn. of the Exec. Comm. of the Bd. of Trustees, Meitman Mortgage Investors, 1970-1971; **EDUC:** BSL, 1948, Univ. of MN; **GRAD EDUC:** LLB, 1950, Univ. of MN Law School; **MIL SERV:** USAF; Capt.; 1952-1953; **OTHER ACT & HONORS:** AAAS; **HOME ADD:** 21 Greenway Gables, Minneapolis, MN 55403, (612)338-2444; **BUS ADD:** 1916 IDS Tower, Minneapolis, MN 55402, (612)332-2561.

FINEHIRSH, Richard——B: Mar. 5, 1933, NY, *Pres.*; **PRIM RE ACT:** Broker, Consultant, Appraiser, Developer, Builder, Owner/Investor, Property Manager, Syndicator; **OTHER RE ACT:** Creative mort. fin.; **SERVICES:** Consulting, creating joint venture partnerships; **REP CLIENTS:** All phases of RE from land selection to finished project; Consultant to RE investors, lenders, joint ventures; **PREV EMPLOY:** RE & Mort. Consulting to Lehman Bros. Loeb Rhoades & other Wall St. Houses and Leading Banks; **PROFL AFFIL & HONORS:** AABB, AAT, **GRAD EDUC:** LLG, NYU; **MIL SERV:** US Army; **OTHER ACT & HONORS:** Adv. to Israel/Indus. Devel.; **HOME ADD:** POB 315, Roslyn, NY 11576, (516)484-2381; **BUS ADD:** POB 315, Roslyn, NY 11576, (516)484-2381.

FINERTY, Patrick J.——B: Aug. 27, 1944, Napoleon, OH, *VP, Fin.*, Robert B. Aikens & Assoc., Inc.; **PRIM RE ACT:** Developer, Owner/Investor, Property Manager; **OTHER RE ACT:** Acctg. and Fin.; **SERVICES:** Acctg. and Fin., Prop. Mgmt.; **PREV EMPLOY:** Arthur Andersen & Co.; **PROFL AFFIL & HONORS:** AICPA; MACPA; ICSC; **EDUC:** BA, 1966, Bus., Acctg., Fin. & Econ., MI State Univ.; **MIL SERV:** U.S. Army, Sgt.; **HOME ADD:** 10420 Cedar

Point Dr., Union Lake, MI 48085, (313)698-4485; **BUS ADD:** 911 W Big Beaver Rd., Suite 201, Troy, MI 48084, (313)362-1360.

FINGERHUT, Paul M.——**B:** June 10, 1929, Brooklyn, NY, *VP Mgmt.*, Kraz Mgmt. Inc.; **PRIM RE ACT:** Attorney; **PROFL AFFIL & HONORS:** Brooklyn Bar Assn.; **EDUC:** BBA, 1951, Acctg., CCNY; **GRAD EDUC:** LLB(JD), 1959, Brooklyn Law Sch.; **MIL SERV:** US Army, DFC; **HOME ADD:** 2411 Mill Ave., Brooklyn, NY 11234, (212)968-1477; **BUS ADD:** 445 Park Ave., NY, NY 10022, (212)753-8000.

FINK, Alan——**B:** Nov. 19, 1946, Baltimore, MD, *Atty.*; **PRIM RE ACT:** Attorney; **SERVICES:** Legal; **REP CLIENTS:** Fairfax S&L; **PROFL AFFIL & HONORS:** ABA; Sect. of RE & Trust Law; MD State Bar Assn.; Baltimore City Bar Assn.; **EDUC:** BA, 1968, Govt./Politics, Univ. of MD; **GRAD EDUC:** JD, 1972, Law, Univ. of MD; **MIL SERV:** US Army Reserve, Honorary Discharge; **HOME ADD:** 8220 Streamwood Dr., Pikesville, MD 21208, (301)484-0024; **BUS ADD:** 22 West Road, Suite 200, Towson, MD 21204, (301)321-8500.

FINK, Henry A.——**B:** Feb. 19, 1941, Springfield, IL, *Pres.*, Henry Fink & Assoc., Inc.; **PRIM RE ACT:** Broker, Consultant, Developer, Owner/Investor; **SERVICES:** Hotel devel. servs.; **REP CLIENTS:** The Trammell Crow Co., Lincoln Prop. Co., Banco Mexicano Somex S.A.; **PREV EMPLOY:** Inns. of the Amer., Inc., VP; Wynncor Ltd., Gen. Mgr.; Club Corp. of Amer., VP; **PROFL AFFIL & HONORS:** Amer. Hotel & Motel Assn., Lecturer on Hotel planning at Intl. Seminars; **EDUC:** BA, 1963, Intl. Econ., Univ. of TX; **HOME ADD:** 3820 Miramar Ave., Dallas, TX 75205, (214)528-1816; **BUS ADD:** 5115 McKinney Ave., Dallas, TX 75205, (214)528-0846.

FINKE, Robert Lawrence——**B:** Chicago, IL, *VP*, Hawthorn Realty Group, Devel.; **PRIM RE ACT:** Developer, Property Manager; **SERVICES:** Devel. and synd. of comml. props., prop. mgmt.; **REP CLIENTS:** Indiv. and instnl. investors in resid. and comml. props.; **PREV EMPLOY:** First Nat. Bank of Chicago 1974-1977; **EDUC:** BS Engrg., 1971, Civil Engrg. and ME, Univ. of IL; **GRAD EDUC:** MBA, 1974, Fin., Univ. of IL; **HOME ADD:** 1718 E. Illinois, Wheaton, IL 60187, (312)665-3931; **BUS ADD:** 8 E. Huron, Chicago, IL 60611, (312)266-8100.

FINKELSTEIN, Don——**B:** Sept. 25, 1954, Montreal, Que., *VP*, Concordia City Properties Ltd., Resid.; **PRIM RE ACT:** Property Manager; **SERVICES:** Prop. mgmt.; **EDUC:** BA, 1977, Indus. Relations/Org. Deve., McGill Univ.; **HOME ADD:** 350 Prince Arthur St., West Apt. 2902, Montreal, H2X3R4, Que., Canada, (514)849-8456; **BUS ADD:** 300 Leo Pariseau-Suite 2500, Montreal, H2W2P4, Que., Can., (514)845-6231.

FINNEY, Parker W.——*Mgr. RE Services*, Koppers Co., Real Estate Section; **PRIM RE ACT:** Property Manager; **BUS ADD:** Koppers Bldg., Pittsburgh, PA 15219, (412)227-2621.*

FINNEY, Stuart L.——**B:** Aug. 28, 1940, Detroit, MI, *Partner*, Fuller & Finney; **PRIM RE ACT:** Attorney, Owner/Investor, Syndicator; **PROFL AFFIL & HONORS:** MN Bar Assn., Hennepin Cty. Bar Assn.; **EDUC:** BA, 1962, hist., Univ. of MI, Ann Arbor; **GRAD EDUC:** JD, 1965, Wayne State Univ., Detroit; **EDUC HONORS:** Law Review; **HOME ADD:** 4410 W 98th St. Cir., Bloomington, MN 55437, (612)831-2427; **BUS ADD:** 1910 Northwestern Fin. Ctr., Bloomington, MN 55437, (612)835-9980.

FIORENTINO, Michael E.——**B:** Dec. 18, 1947, Boston, MA, *VP*, First Mall Management; **PRIM RE ACT:** Consultant, Owner/Investor, Property Manager; **SERVICES:** Shopping centers consulting, mgmt., leasing and rehab.; **REP CLIENTS:** Individual and instnl. investors, owners of shopping centers; **PREV EMPLOY:** Dir. of Property Management Consultant Realty, 1977-79 Clearwater, FL; VP Loeb Rhoades and Co., 1974-77, South Daytona Beach, FL; MA & FL Broker; **PROFL AFFIL & HONORS:** CSM from ICSC; **EDUC:** BS, 1971, Bus. Admin., Univ. of CT; **HOME ADD:** 19 West 070 Avenue La Tours, Oakbrook, IL 60521, (312)964-3900; **BUS ADD:** 10 South LaSalle St., Suite 1338, Chicago, IL 60603, (312)630-1075.

FIRCHER, Leo J.——**B:** Jan. 4, 1933, Berkeley, CA, *Sr. Partner*, Lawler, Felix & Hall; **PRIM RE ACT:** Attorney; **REP CLIENTS:** JMB Realty Corp.; Carlyle RE Ltd. Partnerships; JMB Income Props., Ltd.; JMB Realty Trust; Cabot, Cabot & Forbes; Winthrop Securities Co., Inc.; Standard Oil Co. of CA; Huntington Bch. Co., Varco Intl. Inc.; The Bank of CA; Brunswick Corp.; **PROFL AFFIL & HONORS:** State Bar of CA; Los Angeles; Cty. Bar Assn. (Member 1970 Sec. 1971, Exec. Comm, Sect. of Comml. Law & Bankruptcy); ABA (Sub-comm. on Gen. Provisions, Sales, Bulk Transfers and Documents of Title; Comm. on Partnership; Sects. of Taxation, Corps. Banking and Bus. Law; Real Prop. Probate & Trust Law); Nat. Assn. of RE Investment Trusts, Inc., Cert. Spec. Taxation Law; CA Bd. of Legal Spec.; **EDUC:** BS, 1954, Acctg., Bus. Admin., Univ. of CA, Berkeley; **GRAD EDUC:** JD, 1957, Univ. of CA, Berkeley (Boalt Hall); **EDUC HONORS:** Phi Beta Kappa; **OTHER ACT & HONORS:** Town Hall of CA (Chmn. 1970-71, Public Fin. & Taxation Sect.); CA Club.; Author 'Tax Sheltered Investments: What, Who, When and Which', The Bus. Lawyer, Vol. 28, No. 3, Apr., 1973; 'The Enforcement of Environmental Standards-Problems of Compliance and Defense,' Syllabus, 10th Annual Corp. Council Inst. of Northwestern Univ. Law Sch., 1971; 'Definition and Utility of Leases,' CA Continuing Educ. of the Bar Project on Real Prop. Leases, 1968.; Instr. 1959, 1961, Loyola Univ. Sch. of Law, Los Angeles, CA; **BUS ADD:** 700 S Flower St., 30th Fl., Los Angeles, CA 90017, (213)629-9330.

FIRESTONE, J.——*VP Fin. & Treas.*, Elixir Industries; **PRIM RE ACT:** Property Manager; **BUS ADD:** 17925 S. Broadway, Gardena, CA 90248, (213)321-1191.*

FIRSEL, Michael D.——**B:** Apr. 16, 1949, Chicago, IL, *Partner*, Kamensky & Landan; **PRIM RE ACT:** Attorney; **SERVICES:** Conversions, Land Devel., Synds., Troubled Prop.; **REP CLIENTS:** Devel., Condo. Assns., Banks and Synds.; **PROFL AFFIL & HONORS:** ABA, Chicago Bar Assn., IL State Bar Assn., Community Assn. Inst., Chicago RE Bd., Licensed RE Broker; **EDUC:** Univ. of WI, 1970, History & Pol. Sci., Liberal Arts; **GRAD EDUC:** DePaul Univ. Coll. of Law, 1973; **EDUC HONORS:** Cum Laude Grad.; **OTHER ACT & HONORS:** President, Beth Tikvah Congregation, Hoffman Estates, IL; **HOME ADD:** 1611 E Burr Oak, Arlington Hts., IL 60004, (312)398-0355; **BUS ADD:** 120 S LaSalle, Chicago, IL 60603, (312)368-1776.

FIRTEL, Irving——**B:** July 30, 1912, NYC, NY; **PRIM RE ACT:** Broker, Consultant, Attorney; **PROFL AFFIL & HONORS:** ABA, The FL Bar, Miami Bch. Bar Assn.; **EDUC:** BS, 1932, NY Univ.; **GRAD EDUC:** JD, 1934, NY Univ. Law Sch.; **OTHER ACT & HONORS:** Pres. Miami Bch. Jr. C of C, 2 X Pres. MB Optimists, Exalted Ruler MB Elks, 1601; Pres. Gr. Miami Hebrew Acad. 4 yrs.; **HOME ADD:** 820 Arthur Godfrey Rd., Miami Bch., FL 33140, (305)866-6391; **BUS ADD:** 820 Arthur Godfrey Rd., Miami Bch., FL 33140, (305)673-3000.

FIRTH, Malcolm——**B:** May 20, 1915, S. Orange, NJ, *Owner*; **PRIM RE ACT:** Broker, Developer, Owner/Investor, Property Manager; **OTHER RE ACT:** Comml. & Indus. RE Spec.; **PROFL AFFIL & HONORS:** MAI, SIR, (Retired); **EDUC:** BS, 1937, Econs., Univ. of VA; **MIL SERV:** Ordnance, Capt.; **OTHER ACT & HONORS:** City Commnr., Sea Ranch Lakes, FL, Past Pres. Charleston, UM Bd. of Realtors, & Pompano Beach Bd. of Realtors, Past Pres. WV, Realtors, Past VP, NAR, Dir. NAR; **HOME ADD:** 16 Gate House Rd., Ft. Lauderdale, FL 33308, (305)942-2442; **BUS ADD:** 1305 NE. 23rd Ave., Pompano Beach, FL 33062.

FISCHBACH, Peter C.——**B:** Dec. 10, 1941, NY, NY, *Pres.*, Office Enterprises, Inc.; **PRIM RE ACT:** Broker; **SERVICES:** Office leasing (spec.); **PROFL AFFIL & HONORS:** CCIM Candidate; **EDUC:** Civil Engr., Univ. of Denver; **MIL SERV:** USAFR; **HOME ADD:** 203 Doby Dr., Mandeville, LA 70448, (904)626-5002; **BUS ADD:** Latter & Blum, Inc., 916 Gravier St., New Orleans, LA 70112, (504)529-4779.

FISCHBACH, Robert A.——**B:** June 29, 1943, NYC, NY, *Pres.*, Metro Atlanta Prop.; **PRIM RE ACT:** Syndicator, Property Manager; **SERVICES:** Acquisitions, synd., mktg., prop. mgmt., leasing; **REP CLIENTS:** Lenders and indiv. or instl. investors; **PREV EMPLOY:** Robert A. McNeil Corp., Regional VP; Great Amer. Mgmt. & Investment, Asst. VP; **PROFL AFFIL & HONORS:** CPM; Bd. of Dir., Apt. Owners and Mgrs. Assn.; IREM; IAFP; **EDUC:** BS, 1966, Comm. Planning, Univ. of Cincinnati; **OTHER ACT & HONORS:** Big Brother Assn; **HOME ADD:** 380 Earlston Dr., Atlanta, GA 30328, (404)393-4274; **BUS ADD:** 6075 Barfield Rd., Suite 108, Atlanta, GA 30328, (404)252-6116.

FISCHBEIN, Carl——**B:** Aug. 26, 1921, New York City, *CPA*, Sartain Fischbein & Co. (Partner); **PRIM RE ACT:** Consultant, Attorney, Owner/Investor; **OTHER RE ACT:** CPA; **SERVICES:** Tax Consultant; **REP CLIENTS:** Contractors,Developers, and RE Owners; **PREV EMPLOY:** IRS; **PROFL AFFIL & HONORS:** OK Bar Assn., Amer. Soc. CPA's, OK Soc. CPA, AR Soc. CPA, CPA Assoc., Amer. Assn. Attys., CPA, Tulsa Estate Planning Forum; **EDUC:** BS Bus., 1943, Acctg., Univ. of OK; **GRAD EDUC:** JD, 1948, Tax Law, Univ. of OK; **MIL SERV:** US Army Field Artillery, Capt., Bronze Star; **BUS ADD:** 3010 S. Harvard Suite 400, Tulsa, OK 74114, (918)749-6601.

FISCHER, John W.——**B:** Aug. 1, 1943, Cincinnati, OH, Peck Shaffer & Williams; **PRIM RE ACT:** Attorney; **SERVICES:** Bond Counsel, Hospital Revenue Bond Fin., FHA Counsel, Indus. Devel Bond Fin.; **PROFL AFFIL & HONORS:** Amer. Soc. of Hospital Attys.; Amer. Arbitration Assn.; Cincinnati OH State Bar Assns.; ABA; **EDUC:** AB, 1965, Univ. of MI; **GRAD EDUC:** JD, 1968, Univ. of MI; **EDUC HONORS:** Phi Delta Phi Frat.; **BUS ADD:** 2200 First National Bank Center, 425 Walnut St., Cincinnati, OH 45202, (513)621-3394.

FISCHER, Thomas B.——**B:** Feb. 22, 1947, Omaha, NE, *VP & Gen. Counsel*, First Nat. Bank & Trust Co. of Lincoln, Legal; **PRIM RE ACT:** Attorney, Banker, Lender; **PROFL AFFIL & HONORS:** ABA, NE State Bar Assn., Amer. Inst. of Banking; **EDUC:** BA, 1970, Univ. of NE at Omaha; **GRAD EDUC:** JD, 1973, Univ. of NE Coll. of Law; **EDUC HONORS:** ODK; **HOME ADD:** 3421 S 76th St., Lincoln, NE 68506, (402)483-2419; **BUS ADD:** 13th & "M" St., Lincolm, NE 68506, (402)471-1241.

FISH, John E., Jr.——**B:** Jan. 21, 1949, Baltimore, MD, *Pres.*, J.E. Fish & Assoc., Inc.; **PRIM RE ACT:** Broker, Consultant, Appraiser, Owner/Investor, Property Manager, Insuror, Syndicator; **SERVICES:** Any R.E. or Bus. opportunities; **REP CLIENTS:** Several area banks, nat. corps., numerous indiv.; **PREV EMPLOY:** Dist. Appraiser for E. Div. 4 for The Fed. Home Loan Bank Bd.; **PROFL AFFIL & HONORS:** Sr. member Soc. of R.E. Appraisers; Res. member of AREA & Cert. Bus. Consultant, SRA, RM, CBC; **EDUC:** BS, 1971, Bus. and mktg., Loyola Coll., Baltimore, MD; **GRAD EDUC:** MS, Taxation, Univ. of Baltimore; **HOME ADD:** 12286 Carroll Mill Rd., Ellicott City, MD 21043, (301)988-9338; **BUS ADD:** 5200 Ritchie Hwy., Baltimore, MD 21225, (301)789-2112.

FISHER, B.H.——*Dir. Mktg. Services*, Century Development Corp.; **PRIM RE ACT:** Developer; **BUS ADD:** 5 Greenway Plaza, Ste 1700, Houston, TX 77046, (713)621-9500.*

FISHER, Bob——**B:** Mar. 21, 1945, Vallejo, CA, *VP*, RE/Max of America; **PRIM RE ACT:** Broker, Consultant, Owner/Investor, Instructor, Syndicator; **OTHER RE ACT:** Franchisor; **PROFL AFFIL & HONORS:** NAR, CO Assn. of Realtors, S Suburban Bd. RNMI, RESSI, CRB; **EDUC:** BA, 1968, Mktg., Bus., Adams State Univ.; **GRAD EDUC:** MA, 1969, Mktg., Econ., Adams State Univ.; **HOME ADD:** 1601 W 116th Ct., Denver, CO 80234; **BUS ADD:** 5251 S Quebec St., Englewood, CO 80111, (303)770-5531.

FISHER, Carl D.——*Mgr. Lease Operations*, International Paper Co.; **PRIM RE ACT:** Property Manager; **BUS ADD:** 77 W. 45th St., New York, NY 10036, (212)536-6000.*

FISHER, David A.——**B:** June 25, 1951, Pasadena, CA, *Partner*, Long, Fisher and Miller; **PRIM RE ACT:** Broker, Consultant, Attorney, Regulator, Owner/Investor, Instructor, Syndicator; **SERVICES:** Lawyer/broker/investment counselor/educator; **REP CLIENTS:** Privileged; **PROFL AFFIL & HONORS:** IAFP - Tax - RE - Bus. Sects. ABA, CA and San Diego Bar Assns. - NASD - RESSI; **EDUC:** BA, 1973, Legal Systems and Language, Univ. of CA, San Diego; **GRAD EDUC:** JD, 1976, Law, Western State Univ.; **EDUC HONORS:** Provosts Honor List, Exec. Editor Law Review/Dean's Honor List; **BUS ADD:** 2515 Camino Del Rio S., Suite 238, San Diego, CA 92108, (714)297-0932.

FISHER, George——**B:** Feb. 3, 1925, NY, NY, *Exec. VP*, Jerome Belson Assoc.; **PRIM RE ACT:** Broker, Appraiser, Instructor, Property Manager; **PROFL AFFIL & HONORS:** Pres. NY Chap. Registered Apt. Mgrs., Member, RAM Bd. of Govs., Washington, DC; **EDUC:** 1947, Soc. Sci., Brooklyn Coll.; **GRAD EDUC:** 1967, RE Valuations, Adelphi Univ., Hofstra Univ.; **EDUC HONORS:** Principles of RE; **OTHER ACT & HONORS:** Member Advisory Comm. Apt. House Inst., CPM Desig., Dir., NYSAHRO, Bd. of Governors, NAHRO; **BUS ADD:** 39 Broadway, NY, NY 10006, (212)269-5958.

FISHER, Herbert H.——**B:** Mar. 24, 1927, Rome, NY, *Atty. at Law*, Herbert H. Fisher; **PRIM RE ACT:** Consultant, Attorney; **SERVICES:** Legal representation and housing cooperative consulting services; **REP CLIENTS:** Housing cooperatives, owners of HUD insured mort. and HUD held multi-family props., owners of conventionally mort. multi-family props.; **PROFL AFFIL & HONORS:** Chicago Bar Assn.; VP, Nat. Assn. of Housing Coops.; Midwest Assn. of Housing Coops.; IL Housing Coops. and Assoc., Lifetime membership award issued by Midwest Assn. of Housing Cooperatives; Certificate of Merit issued by Federation of Section 213 Cooperatives, NY, NY; **EDUC:** BS, 1949, Econ., Univ. of WI; LLB, 1953, Univ. of WI; **EDUC HONORS:** Grad. Senior Honors; **MIL SERV:** US Army, Sgt.; **HOME ADD:** 2130 Lincoln Park W., Chicago, IL 60614; **BUS ADD:** One N. LaSalle St., Suite 1111, Chicago, IL 60602, (312)346-9690.

FISHER, Jeffrey D.——**B:** Nov. 10, 1947, Lancaster, PA, *Asst. Prof.*, IN Univ., Dept. of RE; **PRIM RE ACT:** Consultant, Instructor; **OTHER RE ACT:** Computer Software; **REP CLIENTS:** Ins. Cos.; Appraisers; Brokers; **PROFL AFFIL & HONORS:** Amer. RE and Urban Econ. Assn.; American Finance Assn.; Financial Management Assn.; **EDUC:** BS, 1970, Bus., Purdue Univ.; **GRAD EDUC:** PhD, 1980, RE, OH State Univ.; **EDUC HONORS:** Phi Kappa Phi; Beta Gamma Sigma; **HOME ADD:** 2526 Spicewood Lane, Bloomington, IN 47401, (812)336-9029; **BUS ADD:** Indiana Univ. School of Business, Bloomington, IN 47401, (812)335-3297.

FISHER, Patricia A.——**B:** July 29, 1946, Sioux City, IA, *Atty.*, Sears, Roebuck and Co., Western Territory; **PRIM RE ACT:** Attorney; **SERVICES:** Negotiate & document acquisition, devel. & constr. transactions, legal advice; **PROFL AFFIL & HONORS:** CA State Bar (RE Sect.), Los Angeles Bar (RE & Corp. Counsel Sects.), Intl. Council of Shopping Ctrs, ABA (Trust, Prop. & Probate Sect & forum comm. on constr), Assn. of RE Attys.; **GRAD EDUC:** JD, 1977, Whittier Coll. Sch. of Law; **EDUC HONORS:** Dean's List, Honor Roll, Valedictorian; **HOME ADD:** 690 E. California Blvd., Pasadena, CA 91106, (213)449-5807; **BUS ADD:** 900 S. Fremont Ave., Alhambra, CA 91802, (213)576-4454.

FISHER, Peter——*Pres.*, Medalist Industries, Inc.; **PRIM RE ACT:** Property Manager; **BUS ADD:** 10218 N. Port Washington Rd., Meguan, WI 53092, (414)241-8500.*

FISHER, Phillip T.——**B:** Feb. 25, 1948, Concord, NC, *Sec.-Treas.*, North Carolina RE Licensing Bd.; **PRIM RE ACT:** Regulator; **PREV EMPLOY:** VP, Fisher RE; **EDUC:** AB, 1970, Pol. Sci., Univ. of NC, Chapel Hill; **MIL SERV:** US Army Res., Sgt.; **HOME ADD:** 1608 Sherburg Ct., Raleigh, NC 27606, (919)851-6410; **BUS ADD:** PO Box 17100, 1200 Navaho Dr., Raleigh, NC 27619, (914)872-3450.

FISHER, Robert B.——**B:** Mar. 21, 1945, Vallejo, CA, *VP*, RE/MAX of Amer., Inc.; **PRIM RE ACT:** Broker, Instructor, Syndicator, Consultant, Owner/Investor; **OTHER RE ACT:** Franchisor; **PROFL AFFIL & HONORS:** NAR, CAR, RESSI, RNMI, Local chapters of CRB, CCIM, RESSI, CRB; **EDUC:** 1968, Mktg, Adams State Coll.; **GRAD EDUC:** 1969, Econ, Adams State Coll.; **HOME ADD:** 1601 W 116th Ct., Denver, CO 80234; **BUS ADD:** 5251 S Quebec St, Englewood, CO 80111.

FISHER, Roy R., Jr.——**B:** Mar. 25, 1923, Davenport, IA, *Pres.*, Appraisal Services International, Ltd.; **PRIM RE ACT:** Consultant, Appraiser; **SERVICES:** Consultant servs. & appraisal servs. US, Can.; **REP CLIENTS:** Runzheimer and Co.; **PREV EMPLOY:** Runzheimer & Co., Dir. of Housing; **PROFL AFFIL & HONORS:** Soc. of RE Appraisers 160; AACI 1032, MAI 1927; CRE 490; **EDUC:** BS, 1947, Forestry, IA State Univ.; **EDUC HONORS:** Cardinal Key, Alpha Zeta; **MIL SERV:** USAF, 1st Lt., Air Medal w/5 OLC; **HOME ADD:** 8585 N. Manor Ln., Fox Point, WI 53217, (414)351-2490; **BUS ADD:** 2050 W. Good Hope Rd., Milwaukee, WI 53209, (414)352-5660.

FISHER, Walter——*VP Corp. Dev.*, Ex-Cell-O Corp.; **PRIM RE ACT:** Property Manager; **BUS ADD:** 2855 Coolidge St., Troy, MI 48084, (313)649-1000.*

FISHER, William——*Architect, Solar Design Spec.*, William Fisher Arch.; **PRIM RE ACT:** Architect, Developer, Builder; **OTHER RE ACT:** Energy efficient arch. spec.; **PROFL AFFIL & HONORS:** AIA; CSI; APA; **HOME ADD:** CA; **BUS ADD:** 607 Riverview Dr., Capitola, CA 95010.

FISK, Jack G.——**B:** Feb. 22, 1925, McDade, TX, *Pres.*, Southwestern Gen. Land Co.; **PRIM RE ACT:** Broker, Appraiser, Developer, Builder, Owner/Investor, Property Manager, Syndicator; **SERVICES:** Investment & fin. counseling, devel. & synd. of comml. props. & raw land, appraisal of comml. props. & ranch lands, prop. mgmt.; **REP CLIENTS:** Lenders & indiv. or inst. investors in comml. props. and raw land; **MIL SERV:** US Army, Purple Heart & cluster, Bronze Star, European Theatre of ops., 5 stars etc., Commanding Gen., TX State Guard; **OTHER ACT & HONORS:** State Legislature, House of Reps., 4 yrs., Campaign staff of Hubert H. Humphrey for Pres., Nat. Rifle Assn., Heart Assn., Cancer Assn., Hon. Dr. of Laws, Univ. of TX at San Antonio, TX; **HOME ADD:** PO Box 1368, El Campo, TX 77437, (713)648-2905; **BUS ADD:** 1926 Tracy Lynn Ln., Alvin, TX 77511, (713)585-4527.

FITCH, Donald G.——**B:** June 14, 1935, *Sr. VP, RE. and Prop. Devel.*, Zale Corp.; **OTHER RE ACT:** RE Officer-Retail Co.; **SERVICES:** RE & prop. devel. activities for Zale Corp.; **PROFL AFFIL & HONORS:** Intl. Council of Shopping Ctrs. State Dir.; **EDUC:** Attended TX Tech. and Arlington St.; **HOME ADD:** 4012 Amherst, Dallas, TX 75225, (214)691-0950; **BUS ADD:** 3000 Diamond Pk.,

Dallas, TX 75247, (214)634-4157.

FITE, Judge B.——**B:** Mar. 7, 1917, Dallas, *Judge Fite Land Assoc. (Prop.) Judge Fite Co., Inc. (Chmn. Bd.)*, Judge Fite Land Associates & Judge Fite Co., Inc.; **PRIM RE ACT:** Broker, Consultant, Appraiser, Developer, Lender, Builder, Owner/Investor, Instructor, Property Manager, Insuror, Syndicator; **OTHER RE ACT:** Departmentalized servs. gen. RE brokerage; **PREV EMPLOY:** RE Ins. since 1937; **PROFL AFFIL & HONORS:** FLI; NAR, Acc. Farm & Land Member; Greater Dallas Bd. of Realtors - Dir., 1956-1970, Chmn. - MLS Comm. 1957-1958, Pres. - Dallas Realtors Educ. Found 1967, Exec. Comm. of Bd. 1965-1970, Pres. - 1968-1969, Realtor of the Year 1970, Prof. Standards 1976-1977, Goals and Planning 1972-1979; TX Assn. of Realtors - Tr. - TX Realtors Found. 1971-1979, Pres. - Tr. - TX Realtors Found. 1975-1976, Dir. - TAR (2 terms) and as NAR Dir. (2 terms), Legislative Comm. 1967-1979, Educ. comm. 1967-1980, Faculty - TX Realtors Inst.; NAR - Dir. - NAR 1976-1981, Lic. Law Comm. 1967-1981, Realtors Comm. 1971-1974, Omega Tau Rho - Nat. RE Frat., Fed., Dir. - The Realtors Found. of NAR; FLI of NAR - Bd. of Govs. 1971-1981, Rgnl. VP - TX/LA - 1972, Pres. - TX Chap. - FLI - 1973, Legislative Comm., Educ. Comm., Convention Comm. 1976-1977, Chmn. - Long Range & Fin. Comm. 1978-1979, Faculty - FLI of NAR, Pres - FLI of NAR 1981, TX Farm & Land Broker of the Year 1979; **MIL SERV:** US Army, WW II, 1st Lt., Bronze Star, Purple Heart; **OTHER ACT & HONORS:** Mensa Interel; Oak Cliff - Dallas & US C of C-Legislative Comm.; Dallas Sales & Mktg. Execs. (Past Chmn. - Jr. Achievement Sales Training); TX & Southwestern Cattle Raisers Assn.; Christ Episcopal Church; Diocese of Dallas; Who's Who in the Southwest and Who's Who in TX; **HOME ADD:** 2920 Woodmere, Dallas, TX 75233, (214)339-8343; **BUS ADD:** 2754 W. Davis St., Dallas, TX 75211, (214)339-6537.

FITTIPALDI, Frank N.——*VP Corp. Counsel & Secy.*, Midland-Ross Corp.; **PRIM RE ACT:** Property Manager; **BUS ADD:** 20600 Chagrin Blvd., Cleveland, OH 44122, (216)491-8400.*

FITTS, Jay T.——**B:** Jan. 11, 1936, Chicago, IL, *Pres.*, Jay T. Fitts & Assocs., Inc.; **PRIM RE ACT:** Consultant, Appraiser, Developer; **SERVICES:** Prop. selection, fin. feasibility & mktg. studies; **REP CLIENTS:** Fin. instit.; **PROFL AFFIL & HONORS:** SREA Designation Soc. of RE Appraisers, MAI Designation Amer. Inst. of RE Appraisers; **EDUC:** BS, 1957, Agric./Econ., Univ. of IL; **EDUC HONORS:** Alpha Zeta; **HOME ADD:** 920 Eddy Ct., Wheaton, IL 60187, (312)668-3252; **BUS ADD:** 1419 N. State Parkway, Chicago, IL 60610, (312)649-5700.

FITZGERALD, John W.——**B:** July 19, 1948, Minneapolis, MN., *Pres.*, Realty Designs Inc.; **PRIM RE ACT:** Broker, Consultant, Developer, Owner/Investor; **SERVICES:** Comprehensive Comml. Investment RE serv.; **REP CLIENTS:** Misc. law firms, RE Co's., indiv.; **PROFL AFFIL & HONORS:** RNMI; MN Prop. Exchangors, Soc. of Exchange Counselors, CCIM; **OTHER ACT & HONORS:** Past Pres. (1980), MN Prop. Exchangors, Chmn.; Prior Lake Planning Commn.; **HOME ADD:** 14120 Orchard Cr., Prior Lake, MN 55372, (612)445-4466; **BUS ADD:** 12940 Harriet Ave. S, Burnsville, MN 55337, (612)894-1140.

FITZGERALD, J.P.——*Mgr. RE*, Merck & Co., Inc.; **PRIM RE ACT:** Property Manager; **BUS ADD:** PO Box 2000, Rahway, NJ 07065, (201)574-4000.*

FITZGERALD, Michael F.——**B:** Apr. 24, 1945, Rockville Ctr., NY, *VP*, William J. Gill & Co. Inc.; **PRIM RE ACT:** Consultant, Appraiser; **SERVICES:** appraisals, feasibility studies; **REP CLIENTS:** Banks, S & L Assns.; **PROFL AFFIL & HONORS:** AIREA; Soc. of RE Appraisers, MAI, SRPA; **EDUC:** Bus., 1967, Fin., Univ. of Notre Dame; **OTHER ACT & HONORS:** Knights of Columbus, Boy Scouts; **HOME ADD:** 22 Magnolia St., Westbury, NY 11590, (516)333-1606; **BUS ADD:** 600 Old Country Rd., Garden City, NY 11530, (516)746-4590.

FITZGERALD, Mike——**B:** Sept. 4, 1918, London, Eng., Mike Fitzgerald RE; **PRIM RE ACT:** Broker; **PROFL AFFIL & HONORS:** Realtor-Assoc.; **EDUC:** Sr. Mgmt. Prop. Devel., 1972, Capetown Univ., S. Africa; **MIL SERV:** Brit. Army, Maj., Military Cross, Mention in Dispatches; **OTHER ACT & HONORS:** Rotarian; **HOME ADD:** 7412 High Ave., La Jolla, CA 92037, (714)459-8797; **BUS ADD:** 7412 High Ave., La Jolla, CA 92037, (714)459-0793.

FITZPATRICK, Daniel W.——**B:** Nov. 11, 1946, St. Albans, NY, *CPM*, Robert Goldberg RE Mgmt. Co.; **PRIM RE ACT:** Syndicator, Property Manager; **SERVICES:** Long Range Mgmt. Plans; **PROFL AFFIL & HONORS:** IREM, POA, Apt. House Council, CPM; **EDUC:** BS, 1969, Bus., RE, Commerce, Rider Coll.; **OTHER ACT & HONORS:** Long Valley Environmental Commn. (1980); **HOME ADD:** 5 Appletree Way, Long Valley, NJ 07853, (201)852-3634; **BUS ADD:** 12 S. Orange Ave., S. Orange, NJ 07079, (201)763-4566.

FITZSIMMONS, James R.B.——**B:** Sept. 27, 1939, Wilmington, DE, *VP, Prop. & Facilities*, Avis, Inc.; **PRIM RE ACT:** Consultant, Attorney, Property Manager; **OTHER RE ACT:** Negotiator; **PROFL AFFIL & HONORS:** New York State Bar Assn.; **EDUC:** BA, 1961, Columbia Coll; **GRAD EDUC:** LLB, 1964, Fordham Univ. School of Law; **HOME ADD:** 315 East 72nd St., New York, NY 10021, (212)535-6358; **BUS ADD:** 900 Old Country Rd., Garden City, NY 11530, (516)222-3491.

FITZWILLIAM, Michael F.——**B:** Aug. 30, 1945, Memphis, TN, *VP & Comptroller*, The Equitable Life Mort. & Realty Investors; **PRIM RE ACT:** Lender, Owner/Investor; **OTHER RE ACT:** CPA; **PROFL AFFIL & HONORS:** AICPA, MA Soc. of CPA's, Fin. Execs. Inst.; **EDUC:** BS, BA, 1967, Acctg., Stonehill Coll.; **EDUC HONORS:** Dean's List; **HOME ADD:** 5 Hemlock Dr., Canton, MA 02021; **BUS ADD:** 1 Federal St., Boston, MA 02110, (617)542-0592.

FIUMARA, John——**B:** May 22, 1952, Boston, MA, *Deputy Dir.*, City of Boston, Office of Prop. Equalization, Educ.; **PRIM RE ACT:** Broker, Consultant, Assessor; **OTHER RE ACT:** On leave from RE bus. to participate in court mandated revaluation project in Boston; **SERVICES:** Investment counseling and valuation; **PROFL AFFIL & HONORS:** Licensed MA RE Broker; **EDUC:** BS, 1974, Bio., Boston Coll.; **GRAD EDUC:** MBA, 1978, Acctg., taxation, Suffolk Univ.; **EDUC HONORS:** Cum Laude; **OTHER ACT & HONORS:** Bd. of Dir. of North End Comm. Health Ctr., K of C; **HOME ADD:** 165 Endicott St., Boston, MA 02113, (617)742-3569; **BUS ADD:** 147 Milk St., Boston, MA 02109, (617)725-4887.

FIX, Wayne——**B:** Feb. 7, 1927, Lafayette, IN, *Pres.*, Wayne Fix Agricultural Consulting Firm; **PRIM RE ACT:** Broker, Consultant, Attorney, Appraiser, Owner/Investor, Instructor; **OTHER RE ACT:** Agricultural Land Supr., IN Univ.; **SERVICES:** Appraisal, brokerage, land use analysis, estate planning, investment planning, agriculture taxation; **REP CLIENTS:** Owners, lenders, investors, mgrs. of agriculture property; **PREV EMPLOY:** US Dept. Agric., 1951-1971, Soil Conservation Service; **PROFL AFFIL & HONORS:** ABA; IN State Bar Assn.; IN RE Educators Assn.; Soil Conservation Soc. of Amer., Cert. RE Instr., Inst. for RE Instruction; **EDUC:** BS, 1951, School of Agric., Purdue Univ.; **GRAD EDUC:** MS, 1965, Outdoor Recreation, IN Univ.; JD, 1972, Law, IN Univ.; **OTHER ACT & HONORS:** City Council, 1972-1976, BLoomington, IN; **HOME ADD:** 3611 Parkview Dr., Bloomington, IN 47401, (812)332-5228; **BUS ADD:** 409 S. Walnut St., POB 1194, Bloomington, IN 47402, (812)336-1311.

FLAD, J. Michael——**B:** Aug. 26, 1946, Norristown, PA, *Sr. VP Columbia Residential Mgmt., Inc.*; **PRIM RE ACT:** Broker, Developer, Owner/Investor, Property Manager, Syndicator; **SERVICES:** Resid. mgmt. (rental & condo.), interior const.; **REP CLIENTS:** Shelter Corp. of Can., The Rouse Co.; **PREV EMPLOY:** Draper & Kramer, Chicago; **PROFL AFFIL & HONORS:** BOMA; CAI; IREM; **EDUC:** BS, 1974, Fin., LaSalle CoLl., Philadelphia, PA; **MIL SERV:** USN, E-5; **HOME ADD:** 9511 Gray Mouse Way, Columbia, MD 21046, (301)596-4688; **BUS ADD:** 9050-KY Red Branch Rd., Columbia, MD 21045, (301)995-0999.

FLAKE, John J.——**B:** Jan. 31, 1948, Little Rock, AR, *Pres.*, Flake & Co.; **PRIM RE ACT:** Broker, Consultant, Developer, Property Manager, Owner/Investor; **PROFL AFFIL & HONORS:** CCIM, Nat. Assoc. of Realtors; **EDUC:** AB, 1970, Poli. Sci., Univ. of IL; **GRAD EDUC:** MBA, 1971, Fin., Babson Coll.; **OTHER ACT & HONORS:** Bd. of Dir. AR Orchestra Soc., United Way, Boy Scouts; **HOME ADD:** 4917 E. Crestwood, Little Rock, AR 72207, (501)663-9546; **BUS ADD:** 200 Comml. Nat. Bank Bldg., Little Rock, AR 72201, (501)376-8005.

FLAMME, John Eric——**B:** Feb. 15, 1942, MI, *Owner*, Investor's Mort. Co.; **PRIM RE ACT:** Consultant, Broker; **OTHER RE ACT:** RE Lecturer; **SERVICES:** RE Investment Analysis and Brokerage, Mortgage Brokerage, and Consulting; **REP CLIENTS:** Investors in small to medium residential & commerical properties; **PREV EMPLOY:** Fin. Analysis; Engineering; **PROFL AFFIL & HONORS:** CAR; NAR; RNMI, CCIM; **EDUC:** BS, 1967, Indus. Engrg., San Jose State Univ.; **GRAD EDUC:** MBA, 1975, Fin., San Francisco State Univ.; **OTHER ACT & HONORS:** RE Investment Lecturer, Univ. of CA, Berkeley, and other colleges; **HOME ADD:** 6680 Pineneedle Dr., Oakland, CA 94611, (415)668-7550; **BUS ADD:** 22693 Hesperian Blvd. Suite 240, Hayward, CA 94541, (415)887-4343.

FLANAGAN, John W.——**B:** May 8, 1948, Boston, MA, *VP Operations*, US Home Corp., Sarasota/Manatee; **PRIM RE ACT:** Syndicator, Consultant, Developer, Builder, Owner/Investor; **PREV EMPLOY:** Pres., Greenmoss Builders, Inc.; **EDUC:** BA, 1971, Fin., Econ., Acctg., Rutgers Univ.; **HOME ADD:** 99 Sunset Dr., Sarasota, FL 33577, (813)792-6866; **BUS ADD:** 6715 16th Ave. Dr. W, Bradenton, FL 33505, (813)366-4569.

FLANDERS, Donald——*Corp. Mgr. Pers.*, Pantesote Co.; **PRIM RE ACT:** Property Manager; **BUS ADD:** Greenwich Office Park, Box 1800, Greenwich, CT 06830, (203)661-0400.*

FLATO, Clark Courtney——**B:** May 12, 1946, Corpus Christi, TX, *Owner*, Clark C. Flato Co.; **PRIM RE ACT:** Broker, Consultant, Developer, Builder, Owner/Investor, Property Manager; **SERVICES:** Brokerage, investment consultant., prop. mgmt., devel. and redevel.; **REP CLIENTS:** Indivs. and corp. clients; **PREV EMPLOY:** Flato Realty Investment Trust (1972-81); **PROFL AFFIL & HONORS:** NAREIT, Int. Council of Shopping Ctrs.; **EDUC:** BBA, GBA, Univ. of Houston; **MIL SERV:** US Army, Sgt., 1968-70; **OTHER ACT & HONORS:** MENSA; **HOME ADD:** 3321 San Antonio St., Corpus Christi, TX 78411, (512)852-6660; **BUS ADD:** PO Box 1999, Corpus Christi, TX 78403, (512)881-8625.

FLATT, Nachman——**B:** July 7, 1953, Amsterdam, Holland; **PRIM RE ACT:** Consultant; **SERVICES:** Tax consultation, investment analysis; **PREV EMPLOY:** Sr. Tax consultant, Touche Ross & Co.; **PROFL AFFIL & HONORS:** AICPA, CA Soc. CPA's; **EDUC:** BA, 1975, Poli. Sci., Econ.; **GRAD EDUC:** MBT, 1977, Taxation, Univ. of S. CA; **EDUC HONORS:** Beta Gamma Sigma; **BUS ADD:** 15207 Magnolia Blvd. #207, Sherman Oaks, CA 91403, (213)981-0986.

FLEER, Arnold J.——**B:** Dec. 20, 1926, St. Louis Cty., MO, *Sr. VP*, KMS Mortgage and Investment Co., Mort. and Banking and RE Brokerage; **PRIM RE ACT:** Broker, Consultant, Appraiser, Banker; **OTHER RE ACT:** Mort. banking; **REP CLIENTS:** CT Mutual Life Ins. Co., Equitable Life Ins. Co. of IA, John Hancock Mutual Life Ins. Co., Sam S. Schahet Co., Cardinal Indus., The Travelers Ins., Capitol Holding Corp.; **PREV EMPLOY:** VP - National City Bank of Cleveland, OH, Asst. VP - Amer. Fletcher Nat. Bank; **PROFL AFFIL & HONORS:** Nat. Assn. of RE Bds., IN RE Assn., Metropolitan Indianapolis RE Bd., MBAA, MAI; **EDUC:** BSBA, 1949, Bus. Admin./Fin., WA Univ., St. Louis, MO; **MIL SERV:** USN, S 1/C; **OTHER ACT & HONORS:** Ctry. Club of Indianapolis, Carmel Racquet Club; **HOME ADD:** 10303 Lakeshore Dr. E., Carmel, IN 46032, (317)844-1596; **BUS ADD:** Indianapolis, IN 46204620 Guaranty Building, (317)875-7900.

FLEISCHMAN, William O.——**B:** Sept. 21, 1945, Alhambra, CA, *Partner*, Fleischman, Enriquez & Magloff; **PRIM RE ACT:** Attorney, Owner/Investor; **SERVICES:** RE and corporate law; **REP CLIENTS:** Nakam Corp.; Const. Consultants Co., an affiliate of Continental IL Bank; Pioneer Theatres, Inc.; Beverly Wilshire Hotel; **PREV EMPLOY:** Manatt, Phelps, Rothenberg & Tunney; Loeb and Loeb; Beverly Hills Nat. Bank; **PROFL AFFIL & HONORS:** Los Angeles Cty. Bar Assn.; ABA; **EDUC:** BA, 1967, Speech, Univ. of CA, Berkeley; **GRAD EDUC:** LLB, 1970, UCLA; **MIL SERV:** US Army; Pfc.; **OTHER ACT & HONORS:** Arbitrator - Amer. Arbitration Assn.; United Jewish Welfare Fund; **HOME ADD:** 1553 Tower Grove Dr., Beverly Hills, CA 90210, (213)550-1751; **BUS ADD:** 1900 Ave. of the Stars, Suite 2450, Los Angeles, CA 90067, (213)553-7176.

FLEISCHMANN, Barry——**B:** Feb. 11, 1940, Reading, PA, *Pres.*, V.I.P. Inns of America, Inc.; **PRIM RE ACT:** Consultant, Developer, Owner/Investor, Property Manager; **SERVICES:** Hotel & Motor Inn devel. and operations; **REP CLIENTS:** Goodman Co., Cambria Savings & Loan Assn., Innovative Hospitality, Ltd.; **PROFL AFFIL & HONORS:** Amer. Hotel & Motel Assn.; PA Hotel & Motor Inn Assn.; PA Travel Council; Nat. Restaurant Assn.; **EDUC:** BS, 1962, Math./Fin., E. Stroudsburg State; **OTHER ACT & HONORS:** Bd. Member, PA Hotel-Motor Inn Assn.; PA Travel Council; **HOME ADD:** Rose Hill, Wernersville, PA 19565, (215)678 6661; **BUS ADD:** POB 4008, 3100 Oregon Pike, Lancaster, PA 17604, (717)656-2727.

FLEISHER, Robert H.——**B:** Dec. 6, 1912, Phila., PA, *Pres.*, National Mobile Industries, Inc.; **PRIM RE ACT:** Developer, Owner/Investor; **EDUC:** Attended, Univ. of VA & Johns Hopkins Univ.; **OTHER ACT & HONORS:** Hon. Dir. and former pres. Jewish Family Serv. of Phila., Hon. Dir. and former Pres. Locust Club of Phila, Exec. comm. member and former chmn. of bldgs. & grounds comm. of Childrens Hospital of Phila.; **HOME ADD:** 8363 Fisher Rd., Elkins Pk., PA 19117, (215)884-7579; **BUS ADD:** 101 Mill Creek Rd., Ardmore, PA 19003.

FLEISHMAN, Harvey R.——**B:** June 2, 1934, Boston, MA, *Partner in charge of RE Taxation*, Tofias, Fleishman, Shapiro & Co.; **OTHER RE ACT:** Tax Accountant; **SERVICES:** Tax Acctg.; **REP CLIENTS:** RE devels., owners, mgrs., condo. conversion, synds.; **PROFL AFFIL & HONORS:** MA Soc. CPA, AICPA, MBA, Natl. CPA Grp.; **EDUC:** BS, 1956, Acctg., Univ. of PA; **GRAD EDUC:** JD, 1963, Law, Suffolk Univ. Law School; LLM, 1979, Taxation, Boston Univ. Law School; **HOME ADD:** 97 Arlington Rd., Brookline, MA, (617)277-7736; **BUS ADD:** 1320 Soldiers Field Rd., Boston, MA 02135, (617)254-1700.

FLEISHMAN, Irving——**B:** Jan. 12, 1926, Wash. DC, *Pres.*, Manchester Builders, Ltd.; **PRIM RE ACT:** Broker, Consultant, Developer; **SERVICES:** Also mort. packaging & providing equity funds; **PREV EMPLOY:** Const. of comml. & apts., mort. broker; **EDUC:** AABA, 1950, Gvt. & Law, George Wash. Univ.; **GRAD EDUC:** 1951, George Wash. Law Sch.; **MIL SERV:** USN, Radioman 2/C; **OTHER ACT & HONORS:** Elks, Masons, Chevy Chase Athletic Club; **BUS ADD:** 4450 S. Park Ave., 1008, Chevy Chase, MD 20815, (301)986-8555.

FLEMING, Arthur N.——**B:** May 15, 1924, Princeton, IL, *Pres.*, The Fleming Co.; **PRIM RE ACT:** Broker, Engineer, Appraiser, Architect, Developer, Builder, Owner/Investor, Instructor, Property Manager, Syndicator; **SERVICES:** Devel. & Synd. of comml. props., valuation, investment counseling, prop. mgmt.; **PROFL AFFIL & HONORS:** Life Dir. Natl. Assn. of Home Builders, Natl. Assn. of Realtors, Community & Cty. Area Plan Commns., Realtor of yr.; **EDUC:** BS, 1947, ME, Univ. of IL; **GRAD EDUC:** MS, 1948, ME, Univ. of IL; **EDUC HONORS:** Grad. with high hons., Tau Beta Pi Scholastic Hon.; **MIL SERV:** USAF, Cpl. Nominal; **OTHER ACT & HONORS:** Cty. Bd. Member, 1970's School Bd. Member, 1960's, Named Damville First Citizen, 1977; **HOME ADD:** 1 Logan Terr., Danveille, IL 61832, (217)446-4553; **BUS ADD:** PO Box 596, 3100 N Vermillion St., Danville, IL 61832, (217)443-2500.

FLEMING, John C.——**B:** Mar. 10, 1949, Wichita Falls, TX, *Atty.*, Zeleskey, Cornelius, Rogers, Hallmark & Hicks; **PRIM RE ACT:** Attorney; **SERVICES:** Legal services, including acquisition, fin., leasing; **REP CLIENTS:** Lenders, shopping ctr. devel.; apt. devel.; retail tenants; instnl. investors; other comml. and indus. devel. or owners; **PROFL AFFIL & HONORS:** State Bar TX (Real Estate Probate & Trust Law Sect.); ABA; TX Assn. of Bank Counsel; **EDUC:** BA, 1971, Liberal Arts, Cleveland, Lee Coll.; **GRAD EDUC:** JD, 1975, Law, Univ. of Houston; **EDUC HONORS:** Summa Cum Laude; Alpha Chi; Who's Who in Amer. Coll. & Univ., Order of Barons; **OTHER ACT & HONORS:** Pres., Angelina Cty. Child Welfare Bd.; **HOME ADD:** 806 Markus, Lufkin, TX 75901, (713)632-3381; **BUS ADD:** 1616 S. Chestnut, P.O. Drawer 1728, Lufkin, TX 75901, (713)632-3381.

FLEMING, Reginald——*RE Dept.*, Stauffer Chemical Co.; **PRIM RE ACT:** Property Manager; **BUS ADD:** Westport, CT 06880, (203)222-3000.*

FLEMING, Robert H.——**B:** July 22, 1929, Brooklyn, NY, *Dist. Mgr., RE & Ins.*, 195 Broadway Corp.; **PRIM RE ACT:** Engineer, Builder, Property Manager, Insuror; **OTHER RE ACT:** Corp. RE; **SERVICES:** RE subs. of AT&T; **REP CLIENTS:** AT&T; **PROFL AFFIL & HONORS:** NACORE; ASME, VP, NACORE (NY) 1982; **EDUC:** BSME, 1957, Polytech. Inst. of NY; **GRAD EDUC:** NY Univ./Pace Univ.; **HOME ADD:** 1405 Harmon Cove Towers, Secaucus, NJ 07094, (201)864-3111; **BUS ADD:** 195 Broadway - 30-C1810, NY, NY 10007, (212)393-3952.

FLETCHER, James C., III——**B:** Sept. 21, 1938, Brooklyn, NY, *Sr. VP*, Mortgage Guaranty Ins. Corp.; **PRIM RE ACT:** Insuror; **SERVICES:** Pool and primary mort. ins.; **REP CLIENTS:** Investment bankers, housing fin. agencies, savings and loans, comml. banks, pension funds; **PREV EMPLOY:** Metro. Life Ins. Co., Mort. Dept., 1960-68; Comml. Loan Ins. Corp., 1968-78; **PROFL AFFIL & HONORS:** NAHB, MBA; **EDUC:** BA, 1966, RE & Fin., City Coll. of NY, Baruch Sch. of Bus.; **MIL SERV:** US Army, Sgt., Good Conduct Medal; **OTHER ACT & HONORS:** Bd. of Dir. VP of Easter Seal Soc. of Milwaukee Cty., Bd. of Dir. Waukesha Cty. Council on Alcoholism and other drug abuse; **HOME ADD:** 18495 Gate Post Rd., Brookfield, WI 53005, (414)782-3618; **BUS ADD:** MCIC Plaza, PO Box 488, Milwaukee, WI 53201, (414)347-6815.

FLETTRICH, Edward Frederick——**B:** July 19, 1915, New Orleans, LA, *Chmn. & CEO Natl. Fence Corp.*, Owner E.F. Flettrich Co.; **PRIM RE ACT:** Owner/Investor; **PREV EMPLOY:** Pres. R.D. Pitard Hardware Co., Inc.; **PROFL AFFIL & HONORS:** Const. Indus. Assn.-New Orleans C of C - Young Men's Bus. Club of New Orleans; **OTHER ACT & HONORS:** Exec. Club - Co-operative Club as Past Sec.; Treas. Chain Link Fence Assn. of New Orleans; Bd. of Greater New Orleans, Inc.; **HOME ADD:** 1231 Sixth St., New Orleans, LA

70115, (504)895-9837; **BUS ADD:** P.O. Box 15347-3449 Tchoupitoulas St., New Orleans, LA 70175, (504)899-8255.

FLEURY, Frederick M.——*VP Fin.*, Giddings & Lewis, Inc.; **PRIM RE ACT:** Property Manager; **BUS ADD:** Doty St., Fond du Lac, WI 54935, (414)921-9400.*

FLEXNER, Richard D.——**B:** May 18, 1940, New York, NY, *Prin.*, Bird, Scherffius, Flexner & Cronkright, P.C.; **PRIM RE ACT:** Attorney; **SERVICES:** All legal services associated with the acquisition, devel., fin. and conveyancing of RE, including securities and tax matters; **PROFL AFFIL & HONORS:** State Bar of GA, RE Law Sect., Atlanta Bar Assn., Atlanta Lawyers Club, Intl. Shopping Ctr. Council; **EDUC:** BA, 1962, Poli. Sci., Emory Univ.; **GRAD EDUC:** JD, 1967, Emory Univ., School of Law; **EDUC HONORS:** Bryan Soc., (pred. to Order of the Coif); member, Journal of Public Law, recipient, Appellate Advocacy Award; **HOME ADD:** 4685 Northside Dr., NW, Atlanta, GA 30327, (404)252-8479; **BUS ADD:** 701 Harris Tower, 233 Peachtree St., NE, Atlanta, GA 30303, (404)577-2400.

FLEXNER, Thomas M.——**B:** Aug. 15, 1954, Bronxville, NY, *Associate*, Corporate Property Investors; **PRIM RE ACT:** Owner/Investor; **SERVICES:** Acquisition, devel. and mgmt. of income-producing RE; **REP CLIENTS:** Pension funds, comml. banks, private found.; **PREV EMPLOY:** AT&T - Supervisor of Pension Planning, RE; **EDUC:** BA, 1976, Econ., Southwestern at Memphis; **GRAD EDUC:** MBA, 1978, Fin., Amos Tuck School, Dartmouth Coll.; **EDUC HONORS:** Honors and Dist., Phi Beta Kappa, Amos Tuck Scholar, Grad. with High Distinction; **HOME ADD:** 300 East 40th St., New York, NY 10016, (212)599-0317; **BUS ADD:** 230 Park Ave., New York, NY 10169, (212)725-2150.

FLINT, James W.——**B:** June 10, 1941, Oakland, CA, *VP and Assoc. Dir.*, L. F. Rothschild, Unterberg, Towbin Prop.; **PRIM RE ACT:** Broker, Syndicator, Consultant, Owner/Investor; **OTHER RE ACT:** R.E. investment banking; **SERVICES:** Investments in R.E. and R.E. Securities; **REP CLIENTS:** Indiv. and inst. investors; **PREV EMPLOY:** Sr. VP, Dain Corp, 1975-1976; VP B.F. Saul R.E.I.T 1972-1975; **EDUC:** BBS, 1963, Bus. Admin., Univ. of CA; **GRAD EDUC:** MBA, 1979, Finance, Fairleigh Dickenson Univ.; **HOME ADD:** 35 Brookfield Way,, Morristown, NJ 07960, (201)538-4143; **BUS ADD:** 55 Water St., N Y, NY 10041, (212)425-3300.

FLIPPIN, G. Franklin——**B:** July 15, 1947, Mt. Airy, NC, *Mgng. Part.*, Wetherington, Flippin, Melchionna & Burton; **PRIM RE ACT:** Attorney; **REP CLIENTS:** United VA Bank, NCR Corp., Executrans, Inc., Investors Relocation Grp.; **PROFL AFFIL & HONORS:** Bd. of Govs., Bus. Law Sect., VA State Bar, ABA, VA & Roanoke Bar Assn.; **EDUC:** BS, 1969, Econ., Hampden-Sydney Coll.; **GRAD EDUC:** JD, 1973, Univ. of VA; **EDUC HONORS:** Epsilon Sigma Phi; **HOME ADD:** 401 Clydesdale St., Roanoke, VA 24014, (703)343-6847; **BUS ADD:** 1100 United VA Bank Bldg., Roanoke, VA 24011, (703)982-3800.

FLODIN, Mark W.——**B:** Apr. 6, 1951, Chicago, IL, *Gen. Mgr.*, Century 21, Cahill Bros. Realtors, Comml.-Investment; **PRIM RE ACT:** Broker, Property Manager; **SERVICES:** Sales, mgmt., analysis; **PREV EMPLOY:** The Littlestone Co., Mgmt., 1974-1975; **PROFL AFFIL & HONORS:** CREB; RNMI; CCIM Candidate; RESSI; IREM, ARM; **EDUC:** BS, 1973, Pol. Sci./Econ., Miami Univ., Oxford, OH; **HOME ADD:** 6327 S. Knox, Chicago, IL 60636, (312)581-6670; **BUS ADD:** 5501 So. Ashland Ave., Chicago, IL 60636, (312)776-0580.

FLOOD, T. Patrick——**B:** July 14, 1935, San Francisco, CA, *Partner*, Jennings, Strouss & Salmon; **PRIM RE ACT:** Attorney; **SERVICES:** Legal RE real prop. transactions & litigation; **REP CLIENTS:** Sellers & buyers of real prop., RE devels., archs. and engrs.; **PROFL AFFIL & HONORS:** State Bar of AZ; Maricopa Cty. Bar Assn. (Bd. of Dirs. 1978-80); Forum Comm. of the Const. Indus. - ABA; Fidelity & Surety Comm. - ABA; Defense Research Inst.; **EDUC:** BS, 1958, Engrg., US Naval Acad. Also attended Univ. of Notre Dame (1953-54); **GRAD EDUC:** JD, 1965, Law, Univ. of AZ; **EDUC HONORS:** Grad. with Distinction, Battalion Commdr., Pres. of N-Club, Lettered in Football & Swimming, Ralph E. Love Memorial Award, Martin Gentry Scholarship, Phi Delta Phi, Phi Delta Theta; **MIL SERV:** USN (1958-1962), Lt.; **OTHER ACT & HONORS:** Western Athletic Conference Football Official, Phoenix Thunderbirds (Outstanding Thunderbird 1979-80), Chmn. HI-Y Model Legis. Comm.; **HOME ADD:** 7220 N. 12th Ave., Phoenix, AZ 85021, (602)943-7591; **BUS ADD:** 111 W. Monroe, Suite 1600, Phoenix, AZ 85003, (602)262-5817.

FLOOR, Emanuel A.——**B:** Dec. 3, 1935, Salt Lake City, UT, *Pres.*, Triad Utah; **PRIM RE ACT:** Consultant, Developer, Owner/Investor, Property Manager; **OTHER RE ACT:** Executive; **SERVICES:** Project mgmt., maintenance, marketing, planning; **EDUC:** BS, 1957, Econ./Statistics, Univ. of UT; **EDUC HONORS:** Cum Laude, Wall St. Journal Award; **OTHER ACT & HONORS:** Member, Bd. of Govs., S.L. Area C of C; Member, Public Utilities Advisory Bd.; **HOME ADD:** 2205 Country Club Dr., Salt Lake City, UT 84109, (801)484-1429; **BUS ADD:** 221 Charles Lindbergh Dr., Salt Lake City, UT 84116, (801)532-3668.

FLORA, William D.——**B:** Nov. 6, 1939, Chicago, IL, *Part.*, Coopers & Lybrand, Tax; **PRIM RE ACT:** Consultant, Instructor; **OTHER RE ACT:** Atty., Taxation, CPA; **SERVICES:** Tax consultation; **REP CLIENTS:** Investors, devels. prop. mgmt., firms, bldrs, engrg. firms, bankers; **PROFL AFFIL & HONORS:** CA Soc. of CPA's, CA Bar Assn.; **EDUC:** BBA, 1961, Acctg., Univ. of Notre Dame; **GRAD EDUC:** JD, 1964, Taxation, Univ. of MI Sch. of Law; **EDUC HONORS:** Cum Laude; **HOME ADD:** Mill Valley, CA 94941; **BUS ADD:** 333 Market St., San Francisco, CA 94105, (415)957-3204.

FLORENCE, James E.——**B:** Sept. 22, 1946, Atlanta, GA, *Pres.*, Century 21 East Metro Realty; **PRIM RE ACT:** Broker, Consultant, Appraiser, Developer, Owner/Investor, Property Manager, Insuror, Syndicator; **SERVICES:** Resid./comml. brokerage, investment counseling synd.; **PROFL AFFIL & HONORS:** NAR, GA Assn. of Realtors, Rockdale Co. Bd. of Realtors, Dekalb Co. Bd. of Realtors, RNMI, NAIFA, CCIM, IFA; **EDUC:** BBA, 1968, RE/Bus. Admin., Univ. of GA; **MIL SERV:** US Army Reserves, Sp. 4/C; **OTHER ACT & HONORS:** Appointee: Rockdale Cty. Planning Comm. 1977/1978; Dir., Rockdale Cty. C of C 1979; State Dir., GA Assn. of Realtors 1974, 1979; Local Bd. Pres. 1974, 1978 - Local Bd. of Dir. 1971 thru 1979; Outstanding Realtor Award 1979; **HOME ADD:** 2242 Cedar Mill Ct., Conyers, GA 30207, (404)483-1589; **BUS ADD:** 2948 Woodrow Dr., Lithonia, GA 30058, (404)482-2121.

FLOURNOY, John F.——**B:** Sept. 10, 1940, Columbus, GA, *Pres*, Flournoy Construction co.; **PRIM RE ACT:** Developer, Builder, Owner/Investor, Property Manager, Syndicator; **SERVICES:** Construction, devel. and synd. of multifamily housing projects, prop. mgmt.; **PROFL AFFIL & HONORS:** Nat. Bd. of Realtors; **EDUC:** Univ. of NC Bus. School; **MIL SERV:** USMC, Capt.; **OTHER ACT & HONORS:** GA Area council pres. for Boys Clubs of Amer, Past Pres. & Bd. of Dir. Metropolitan Boys Club of Columbus, GA; **HOME ADD:** Rte. 1 Box 139 Fulton Rd., Upatoi, GA 31829; **BUS ADD:** 3810 Buena Vista Rd., Columbus, GA 31995, (404)687-4301.

FLOWER, Paul——*Dir.*, Kansas, KS Real Estate Commission; **PRIM RE ACT:** Property Manager; **BUS ADD:** 535 Kansas, Rm. 1212, Topeka, KS 66603, (413)296-3411.*

FLOWER, Robert J.——**B:** Nov. 9, 1939, Yonkers, NY, *Pres.*, Robert J. Flower, Ltd., Main Office; **PRIM RE ACT:** Consultant, Appraiser, Owner/Investor; **OTHER RE ACT:** RE analyst; **SERVICES:** Full range of servs. for all RE endeavors; **REP CLIENTS:** Ford Motor Co., Chrysler Realty, Bank of NY, ABKO Prop., HELM Resources; **PREV EMPLOY:** salesman, Dunwoodie Agency, 1962-4; **PROFL AFFIL & HONORS:** NAR, Profl. Org. of RE Appraisers, NY Assn. Realtors Westchester Cty. Bd. Realtors (dir 1971-), Nat. Assn. RE Counselors, AFA, CAS, IVR; **EDUC:** BS, 1967, Fordham Univ.; **OTHER ACT & HONORS:** Chmn. Yonkers Assessment Rev. Bd., 1970-4, Co-founder Neighborhood Improvement Program, Yonkers Urban Renewal Agency, Created forerunner to the Shared Appreciation Mort.; Registered in Who's Who in the East (1977-82); Designed Inner City Mortgage Guarantee Program; Adjunct Prof., RE Econ. at West Point, 1979 (by Appt.); **HOME ADD:** 136 Bobolink Rd., Yonkers, NY 10701; **BUS ADD:** Biltmore Ave., Ste. 217, Rye, NY 10580, (914)423-2122.

FLOWERS, Hal C.——**B:** June 15, 1947, Oak Ridge, TN, *VP*, Paragon Group, Inc.; **OTHER RE ACT:** Comml. Devel. and Mktg.; **SERVICES:** Full Serv. Devel. and Prop. Mgmt.; **PREV EMPLOY:** Adams-Cates Co., Atlanta, GA; **PROFL AFFIL & HONORS:** BOMA, Inst. of RE Mgmt., Natl. Assn. of Corp. RE Exec., Comm. of 100 (C of C); **EDUC:** BBA, 1969, RE, GA State Univ.; **MIL SERV:** US Army, 2nd Lt.; **HOME ADD:** 4405 Beach Park Dr., Tampa, FL -3609, (813)877-1236; **BUS ADD:** 201 E. Kennedy Blvd., Suite 1800, Tampa, FL 33602, (813)229-6200.

FLOWERS, Raymond P.——**B:** Sept. 26, 1920, Philadelphia, PA, Cy Jordan Realty, Inc.; **PRIM RE ACT:** Broker, Consultant, Appraiser; **SERVICES:** Appraisal of all forms of RE, brokerage and counseling; **REP CLIENTS:** Bankers Trust Co., NY; Union Dime Savings; Wachovia Mort. Co.; Nat. Bank N. Amer.; Jamaica Savings Bank; Continental Bank, Chicago; Detroit Bank & Trust Co.; Union Mutual Ins., Portland, ME; **PREV EMPLOY:** Pres., Raymond P. Flowers & Assoc., Ft. Lauderdale, FL; **PROFL AFFIL & HONORS:** AIREA-Pres., 1973; NAR; NC Assn. of Realtors; Yancey-Mitchell Bd. of Realtors-Pres. Elect, MAI, formerly held SRPA and Amer. Soc. of

Appraisers but resigned; **OTHER ACT & HONORS:** Active in Rotary Club and Lions Intl.; **HOME ADD:** Rte. 5 Box 958, Burnsville, NC 28714, (704)675-4884; **BUS ADD:** 51 West Blvd., Burnsville, NC 28714, (704)682-6166.

FLOYD, Wendell C.——B: Jan. 6, 1945, Houston, TX, *Pres.*, Hawaiiana Mgmt. Co., Ltd.; **PRIM RE ACT:** Consultant, Developer, Owner/Investor, Property Manager; **SERVICES:** Principally mgmt. of condos.; **PREV EMPLOY:** Comml. Mgmt. with Payless Drugs and Service Merchandise; **PROFL AFFIL & HONORS:** IREM, BOMA, Realtor; **EDUC:** BA, 1968, Eng., Math., Baylor Univ.; **MIL SERV:** US Army; E-5, Vietnam, Korea; **OTHER ACT & HONORS:** Jaycees, USCPFA; **HOME ADD:** PO Box 27541, Honolulu, HI 96827, (808)955-0744; **BUS ADD:** PO Box 88025, Honolulu, HI 96815, (808)955-0744.

FLYNN, Edmund W.——B: Oct. 12, 1933, Hartford, CT, *VP, Operations and Fin.*, Crown Ctr. Redev. Corp., Subs. of Hallmark Cards, Inc.; **PRIM RE ACT:** Developer, Property Manager, Owner/Investor; **PREV EMPLOY:** VP Chrylser Realty Corp.; **PROFL AFFIL & HONORS:** ULI; NACORE, Reg. Broker (MO); **EDUC:** 1955, Yale Univ.; **GRAD EDUC:** 1961, Harvard Bus. School; **MIL SERV:** US Navy; Lt.; **HOME ADD:** 3410 W 89th St., Leawood, KY 66206, (913)341-1782; **BUS ADD:** 2440 Pershing Rd., Kansas City, MO 64105, (816)274-5930.

FLYNN, J. Michael——B: July 19, 1946, Pittsfield, MA, *VP*, Meredith & Grew Inc., Comml. Brokerage; **PRIM RE ACT:** Broker; **PREV EMPLOY:** M & G, Inc., 8 yrs.; William H. Dolben & Sons, 2 yrs.; **PROFL AFFIL & HONORS:** Greater Boston RE Bd.; Dir., Comml. Investment Council; **EDUC:** BA, 1969, Mktg., Boston Coll.; **OTHER ACT & HONORS:** Longwood Cricket Club; Blue Chips; **HOME ADD:** 45 Old England Rd., Chestnut Hill, MA 02167, (617)734-3250; **BUS ADD:** 125 High St., Boston, MA 02110, (617)482-5330.

FLYNN, Jack C.——*Pres.*, Anchor Pacific Co.; **PRIM RE ACT:** Broker, Appraiser, Developer, Instructor, Syndicator; **SERVICES:** Acquisition and devel.; **PROFL AFFIL & HONORS:** CAR, NAR, ASA, SREA, IFAS, CRA; **EDUC:** BS, 1951, Bus. & Fin., Univ. of So. CA; **BUS ADD:** 2047 Huntington Dr., S. Pasadena, CA 91030, (213)441-1171.

FLYNN, James J.——B: May 22, 1931, Jersey City, NJ, *Part.*, The Flynn-Ramage Co.; **PRIM RE ACT:** Appraiser; **SERVICES:** Appraisals of real prop.; **REP CLIENTS:** Chase Manhattan, Merrill Lynch, Summit and Elizabeth Trust Co.; **PREV EMPLOY:** Self employed for 13 yrs.; **PROFL AFFIL & HONORS:** SREA, SRA Designation; **MIL SERV:** US Army, Cpl.; **OTHER ACT & HONORS:** V. Chmn. Verona Bd. of Adjustment, 1978; Mbr. Verona Planning Bd., 1976-77 Past Pres. N. NJ Chap.No. 37 SREA; **HOME ADD:** 74 Harrison St., Verona, NJ 07044, (201)239-7593; **BUS ADD:** PO Box AA, Summit, NJ 07901, (201)273-0750.

FLYNN, Ramsey W.J.——B: Mar. 8, 1927, *Pres.*, O'Conor & Flynn, Inc.; **PRIM RE ACT:** Broker, Consultant, Appraiser, Instructor, Property Manager, Insuror; **SERVICES:** Relocation Dept., New Homes and Land Sales Div., Ins. Co., Comml. and Indus. Div.; **PROFL AFFIL & HONORS:** NAHB; MD Assn. Homebuilders; MD Assn. of Realtors; NAR; **EDUC:** BS, Arch. Engrg., Catholic Univ.; **MIL SERV:** USNAF; **BUS ADD:** 22 W. Padonia Rd., Timonium, MD 21093, (301)252-2111.

FLYNN, Robert J.——B: Aug. 11, 1927, NY, NY, *Sr. VP-Shopping Ctrs.*, R. H. Macy & Co., Inc., R. H. Macy Prop.; **PRIM RE ACT:** 11 for Corp. owned shopping ctrs.; **PROFL AFFIL & HONORS:** ICSC, CSM, Chmn. of CSM Admissions and Governing Committee; **EDUC:** BS, 1949, Civil Engineering, Bucknell Univ.; **MIL SERV:** USN, Lt. J.G.; **OTHER ACT & HONORS:** Councilman, Town of N. Castle 1975-79, Nyack Boat Club; **HOME ADD:** 51 Whipporwill Rd. E, Box 68, Armonk, NY 10504, (914)273-9329; **BUS ADD:** Garden State Plaza, Paramus, NJ 07652, (201)843-3690.

FLYNN, Stephen A., Jr.——B: Jan. 3, 1951, Norwalk, CT, *Pres.*, S.A. Flynn Associates Inc.; **PRIM RE ACT:** Consultant, Developer, Builder, Owner/Investor; **SERVICES:** Gen. contractor, resid. and comml.; **PREV EMPLOY:** Loan Mktg. Rep., Empire Savings and Loan Assn.; **EDUC:** BSBA, 1974, RE/Const. Mgmt., Univ. of Denver; **OTHER ACT & HONORS:** Denver Athletic Club; **HOME ADD:** 12689 E Bates Cir., Aurora, CO, (303)751-7422; **BUS ADD:** 3531 S. Pennsylvania St., Englewood, CO 80110, (303)761-6440.

FLYNN, Ted——B: Oct. 12, 1933, Hartford, CT, *VP Operations and Fin.*, Crown Center Redevelopment Corp.; **PRIM RE ACT:** Developer; **PREV EMPLOY:** VP Chrysler Realty Corp., Troy, MI 1970-77; **PROFL AFFIL & HONORS:** ULI, Nat. Assn. of Corp. RE Execs.; Intl. Council of Shopping Ctrs.; **EDUC:** BA, 1955, Yale Univ.; **GRAD EDUC:** MBA, 1961, Harvard Bus. School; **MIL SERV:** USN, Lt., Aviation; **HOME ADD:** 3410 W. 89th St., Leawood, KS 66206, (913)341-1782; **BUS ADD:** 2440 Pershing Rd., Suite 500, Kansas City, MO 64608, (816)274-5930.

FOCHT, John C.——B: Oct. 13, 1945, Lebanon, PA, *Pres.*, Land Title Agency of Florida, Inc.; **PRIM RE ACT:** Broker, Consultant, Developer, Owner/Investor; **OTHER RE ACT:** RE Land Title; **SERVICES:** Consultant, devel. comml. RE, and condos. and issue title ins.; **PROFL AFFIL & HONORS:** FL Land Title Assn.; Assoc. Builders & Contractors, Gold Coast Chap.; Mort. Bankers Assn.; Forum Club of Palm Beach, Who's Who in the S & SW & Who's Who in Fin.; **EDUC:** BS, Bus. Admin., Columbia Union Coll.; Law, Stetson Univ. Coll. of Law; **MIL SERV:** USN; **OTHER ACT & HONORS:** Zoning Commn. Town of Golfview; Past Pres. Kiwanis Club of WPB - Sunrise; BBA; **HOME ADD:** 20 Country Club Rd., W. Palm Beach, FL 33406; **BUS ADD:** 471 Spencer Dr., W. Palm Beach, FL 33409, (305)686-1499.

FOGEL, Danny L.——B: Mar. 16, 1933, Omaha, NE, *Pres.*, Danny L. Fogel CCIM, Inc.; **PRIM RE ACT:** Broker, Consultant, Developer, Owner/Investor, Instructor, Syndicator, Real Estate Publisher; **OTHER RE ACT:** Author of two RE Books, lectures nationally; **PROFL AFFIL & HONORS:** NAR; CA Assn. Realtors, CCIM; Sr. Instr., NAR; Master Instr., CA Assn. Realtors; **EDUC:** BS, 1955, Univ. of NE; **HOME ADD:** 17243 Cloudcroft Dr., Poway, CA 92064, (714)485-6238; **BUS ADD:** 16766 Bernardo Ctr. Dr. Suite 103, San Diego, CA 92128, (714)566-6220.

FOGEL, Harold——B: March 19, 1919, NY, NY, *V.P. Leasing - Sales*, First Hartford Realty Corp.; **OTHER RE ACT:** Commercial Leasing; **EDUC:** 1950, R.E., Pace Inst.; **MIL SERV:** US Army; Pvt.; **HOME ADD:** 49B Cliffside Dr., Manchester, CT 06040, (203)643-6857; **BUS ADD:** 49B Cliffside Dr., Manchester, CT 06040, (203)646-6555.

FOGG, Kathy——B: July 19, 1957, Allentown, PA, *Asst. to the Pres., RE*, Ray Fogg Building Methods, Inc.; **PRIM RE ACT:** Developer, Property Manager; **OTHER RE ACT:** Realtor, General Contractor; **PROFL AFFIL & HONORS:** Sales License; **EDUC:** BBA, 1979, RE/Bus. Admin., Kent State Univ.; **HOME ADD:** 651 Vineyard Dr., Broadview Hts., OH 44147, (216)237-1655; **BUS ADD:** 4913 Van Epps Rd., Cleveland, OH 44131, (216)351-7976.

FOGG, Raymon B.——B: Jan. 6, 1930, Cleveland, OH, *Pres.*, Ray Fogg Building Methods Inc.; **PRIM RE ACT:** Engineer, Developer, Builder; **PROFL AFFIL & HONORS:** Natl. Assn. of Indus. & Office Parks, Natl. Soc. of PE, PE; **EDUC:** BSCE, 1953, Civil Engrg., OH Univ.; **MIL SERV:** USAF; 1st Lt.; **HOME ADD:** 8023 Skyline Dr., CLeveland, OH 44141, (216)526-1663; **BUS ADD:** 4913 Van Epps Rd., Cleveland, OH 44131, (216)351-7976.

FOLDES, Paul G.——B: Apr. 10, 1947; **PRIM RE ACT:** Broker, Attorney, Owner/Investor; **SERVICES:** Consultant; **PROFL AFFIL & HONORS:** JD; CCIM, Candidate; **EDUC:** BE, 1969, EE, NY Univ.; **GRAD EDUC:** JD, 1973, Law, Georgetown Univ. Law Ctr.; **HOME ADD:** PO Box 2963, Arlington, VA 22202; **BUS ADD:** PO Box 2963, Arlington, VA 22202, (703)684-9249.

FOLEY, Daniel J.——B: Aug. 3, 1918, NYC, *Pres.*, 1st Federal Savings & Loan; **PRIM RE ACT:** Lender; **SERVICES:** RE Loans; **PREV EMPLOY:** VP, Gen. Counsel; **EDUC:** BS, 1943, Law, Pol. Sci., Fordham Univ.; **GRAD EDUC:** LLB, JD, 1951, St. John's Univ. Law School; **MIL SERV:** USMC, Navigator; **HOME ADD:** 1430 Martin Rd., Albert Lea, MN 16007; **BUS ADD:** 143 W. Clark St., Albert Lea, MN 16007, (507)377-4400.

FOLEY, Robert J.——B: Dec. 3, 1917, St. Helena, CA, *RE Appraiser*; **PRIM RE ACT:** Appraiser; **SERVICES:** Gen. appraisal services including condemnation; **REP CLIENTS:** US Govt., State of CA, Cty. of Contra Costa, all city govts. in cty., most school districts, and most all other public or quasi-public agencies in cty.; **PREV EMPLOY:** RE brokerage, construction and subdiv. devel., securities analysis; **PROFL AFFIL & HONORS:** Sr. Member, ASA; **EDUC:** Appraisal Courses, Univ. of CA Ext.; **MIL SERV:** USAAF, Contract Flight Instr.; **OTHER ACT & HONORS:** Pres., W.C. C of C, 1953; Pres., Diablo Ctry. Club, 1963; **HOME ADD:** 42 Sharmar Court, Walnut Creek, CA 94595, (415)934-9352; **BUS ADD:** 42 Sharmar Court, Walnut Creek, CA 94595, (415)934-9352.

FOLLENSBEE, James——B: June 3, 1935, Waukegan, IL, *Pres.*, James Follensbee & Assoc. Ltd.; **PRIM RE ACT:** Consultant, Engineer, Architect, Owner/Investor; **SERVICES:** Arch. Planning & engrg. and econ. feasibility analysis; **REP CLIENTS:** Private, public & instnl. clients; **PROFL AFFIL & HONORS:** Corp. Member AIA,

NCARB Cert.; **EDUC:** BS, 1959, Univ. of IL; **MIL SERV:** US Naval Res., Lt.; **HOME ADD:** 916 N Fuller Rd., Gurnee, IL 60031, (312)336-2763; **BUS ADD:** 311 W Hubbard St., Chicago, IL 60610, (312)467-4767.

FOLSE, William Lee——**B:** Feb. 21, 1931, Beaumont, TX, *Chmn. of the Bd. 1976*, First Metroplex Corporation; **PRIM RE ACT:** Consultant, Banker, Developer, Builder, Owner/Investor, Property Manager, Syndicator; **SERVICES:** RE investment and devel., prop. mgmt.; **REP CLIENTS:** Lenders and investors in resid. and comml. props.; **PREV EMPLOY:** Exec. VP, Rockwall Estates, Inc. 1968-1974; **PROFL AFFIL & HONORS:** Nat. Home & Apt. Bldrs. Assn.; Dallas Historic Preservation League, Amer. Mgmt. Assn.; Historic Preservation League Vinyard-Fairmount Project Tour Award; **EDUC:** BS, 1952, Mathematics-Bus., Southwestern Univ.; **EDUC HONORS:** Blue Key, Nat. Honor Frat., Who's Who in American Univ. and Coll., Pres. Pan-Hellenic Council; **MIL SERV:** USMC 1952-1955, Capt.; **OTHER ACT & HONORS:** Chmn. Rockwall Estates Planning Comm. 1970-1974; Dallas Ctry. Club; Dallas Council on World Affairs; Dallas Hist. Soc.; Amer. Bus. Club; **HOME ADD:** 3905 Miramar, Dallas, TX 75205, (214)521-9213; **BUS ADD:** 2717 McKinney Ave., Dallas, TX 75204, (214)698-9800.

FOLSOM, John R.——**B:** Dec. 30, 1918, Hartsville, SC, *Pres.*, SC Fed. S&L Assn.; **PRIM RE ACT:** Broker, Lender; **SERVICES:** S&L Customer Serv.; **PREV EMPLOY:** Aiken Loan & Security Co. 1940-1941; Liberty Life Ins. Co., 1941-1960; **PROFL AFFIL & HONORS:** Dir. & Exec. Comm., SC S&L League; Dir. SC Heart Assn.; Amer. Heart Assn., One of 10 most influential men in Columbia, SC - 1979; Special Citation of Merit from Columbia Bd. of Realtors, 1970; Award for chairing Study Comm. on Taxation by Richland County Council; **EDUC:** BA, 1940, Furman Univ., Greenville, SC; **MIL SERV:** USN, Lt. j.g.; **OTHER ACT & HONORS:** Chmn., Richland-Lexington Airport Commn., 1980--, The Summit Club, Forest Lake Club, Poinsett Club; Bd. of Trs. - Columbia Coll.; **HOME ADD:** 1515 Adger Rd., Columbia, SC 29205, (803)256-0612; **BUS ADD:** 1500 Hampton St., Columbia, SC 29201, (813)254-1500.

FONSHILL, Ira William, III——**B:** May 16, 1930, Baltimore, MD, *Owner/Broker*, Fonshill & Company; **PRIM RE ACT:** Broker, Developer, Owner/Investor, Syndicator; **OTHER RE ACT:** Sec. broker/dealer (NASD); Gen. Partner Boisl Geothermal, Ltd.; **SERVICES:** Direct participation programs (RE & Drilling); **REP CLIENTS:** High cash flow private investors; **PREV EMPLOY:** Acquisitions - Boise Cascade Corp., Boise, ID Long-Range Fin. Planning - Monsanto (Chemstrand Div.); **PROFL AFFIL & HONORS:** Nat., State, Boise Bds. of Realtors; Nat. Assn. of Securities Dealers; Intl. RE Fed., CCIM, SRS, CRS, GRI, MBA; **EDUC:** BS Indust. Mgmt., Methods, Motion & time study, minor in mktg., NYU; **GRAD EDUC:** MBA, Policy and Admin.; Long-range Planning, Univ. of WA, Seattle, WA; **MIL SERV:** USAF, S/Sgt.; **HOME ADD:** 200 Coston St., Boise, ID 83702, (208)344-4552; **BUS ADD:** 331 W. Idaho St., P O Box 1228, Boise, ID 83701, (208)336-8700.

FOOTE, Gene——**B:** Sept. 16, 1927, Brainerd, MN, *Owner*, Gene Foote - RE Appraiser; **PRIM RE ACT:** Broker, Appraiser, Instructor; **OTHER RE ACT:** Instructor of several RE related courses; **SERVICES:** Profl. RE appraisals; **PROFL AFFIL & HONORS:** SRA - IFAS - GRI; **EDUC:** RE, IN Univ., Univ. of GA, Univ. of NE, Univ. of IN; **MIL SERV:** US Navy, Rdm. 2, 6 decorations; **OTHER ACT & HONORS:** Municipal Judge - 1958-1970, Pres. Brainard Bd. of Realtors, Pres. Crosby C of C, Pres. Crosby PTA, Pres. Lions Club, Pres. Firemans Relief Club; **HOME ADD:** Lakeshore Dr., Crosby, MN 56441, (218)546-5352; **BUS ADD:** Box 217, 132 W. Main St., Crosby, MN 56441, (218)546-5353.

FOOTE, William D.——**B:** July 23, 1934, Oakland, CA, *Partner*, Cadillac Fairview Homes West; **PRIM RE ACT:** Developer; **PREV EMPLOY:** Kaiser Aetna/Asset Mgmt. Div., VP and Gen. Mgr. 1973-76; **EDUC:** Econ. & Pol. Sci., Univ. of So. CA; **GRAD EDUC:** Bus., Univ. of CA in Los Angeles; **MIL SERV:** USCG; **BUS ADD:** 500 Newport Center Dr., Suite 815, Newport Beach, CA 92660, (714)640-5771.

FORCUCCI, Dino Dean, Jr.——**B:** Mar. 12, 1954, Chicago, IL, *Pres.*, Dean Realty & Investment Co.; **PRIM RE ACT:** Broker, Developer, Syndicator; **SERVICES:** RE investment synd., mgmt. and brokerage; **REP CLIENTS:** Indiv. and inst. investors; **PREV EMPLOY:** Department of Revenue; **PROFL AFFIL & HONORS:** NAR; RESSI; **EDUC:** BS, 1977, Fin./RE, Univ. of IL; **GRAD EDUC:** JD, 1981, Law, John Marshall Law School; **HOME ADD:** 1616 N. Sayre, Chicago, IL 60635; **BUS ADD:** 6120 W. North Ave., Chicago, IL 60639, (312)637-3182.

FORD, Donald D.——*VP, Lending*, Seaway National Bank of Chicago, Loan Dept.; **PRIM RE ACT:** Lender; **BUS ADD:** 645 E 87th St., Chicago, IL 60619, (312)487-4800.

FORD, Frank B.——**B:** Dec. 20, 1948, Springfield, MO, *Atty. at Law*, Rock and Borgelt, P.C.; **PRIM RE ACT:** Attorney; **SERVICES:** Closings, litigation, counsel concerning zoning and planning, probate transfers; **REP CLIENTS:** City of Dearborn Heights MI Planning Commn., Pvt. indivs.; **PROFL AFFIL & HONORS:** ABA including Sect. of Real Prop., Probate and Trust Law; State Bar of MI including Real Property Law Section and Probate and Trust Law Sect.; **EDUC:** AB, 1970, Drama, Washington Univ. in St. Louis; **GRAD EDUC:** MFA, 1972, Playwrighting, Univ. of CT; JD, 1977, Law, Wayne State Univ.; **EDUC HONORS:** Omicron Delta Kappa; Cum Laude, Sam S. Shubert Playwrighting Fellowship; **OTHER ACT & HONORS:** Asst. Corp. Counsel, City of Dearborn Heights, MI; Fairlane Club (Social and Athletic Club; **HOME TEL:** (313)565-9289; **BUS ADD:** 24500 Ford Rd., Dearborn Heights, MI 48127, (313)274-4064.

FORD, Gabriel——**B:** Oct. 15, 1945, Ravenna, OH, *RE Broker-Owner*, Brownstone Properties; **PRIM RE ACT:** Broker, Appraiser, Property Manager; **PROFL AFFIL & HONORS:** RE Bd. of Brooklyn; **EDUC:** BA, Phil., Maryknoll Coll.; **GRAD EDUC:** Diploma, 1976, RE Inst. of NYU; **HOME ADD:** 112 Prospect Park W, Brooklyn, NY 11215, (212)768-2554; **BUS ADD:** 106 Montague St., Brooklyn, NY 11201, (212)875-1289.

FORD, Herbert S.——**B:** May 24, 1946, *Law Firm Partner*, Fink, Lynette & Ford; **PRIM RE ACT:** Attorney; **SERVICES:** RE Synd., devel. Brokers-dealers; Legal representation in acquisition and fin. of all types of comml. indus. and multi-family resid. prop., including all phases of RE synd. including securities law regulation, broker-dealer regulation and mort. financing; **PROFL AFFIL & HONORS:** ABA, Essex Cty. Bar Assn.; **EDUC:** BA, 1968, Amer. Studies, Lehigh Univ.; **GRAD EDUC:** JD, 1972, NYU Law School; **EDUC HONORS:** Cum Laude; **BUS ADD:** Gateway 1, Newark, NJ 07102, (201)624-3000.

FORD, James A.——**B:** Jan. 4, 1940, USA, *VP*, Continental Wingate Co., Inc., Rush Management Co., Inc.; **PRIM RE ACT:** Consultant, Property Manager; **OTHER RE ACT:** Prop. Mgmt.; Mgmt. Consultant; **PREV EMPLOY:** Housing Consultant Suffolk Community Devel. Corp. Coram, NY; **PROFL AFFIL & HONORS:** Soc. of Architects & Planners; **EDUC:** Pol. Sci., 1970, Pre Law, City Coll. NY; **GRAD EDUC:** Urban Planning, 1973, Housing, NY Univ.; **MIL SERV:** US ARmy, Pfc; **HOME ADD:** 741 Colonial St., Uniondale, NY 11553, (516)538-5121; **BUS ADD:** 747 Riverside Dr., New York, NY 10031, (212)368-8104.

FORD, Michele——**B:** Nov. 26, 1950, Ardmore, OK, *Pres.*, Sunbelt Equities, Inc.; **PRIM RE ACT:** Broker, Syndicator, Property Manager; **SERVICES:** Comml. RE Tax Shelters, Mktg. Research; **REP CLIENTS:** Indiv. clients interested in income-producing prop. located in Sunbelt area; **PROFL AFFIL & HONORS:** RESSI; **EDUC:** BS, 1972, Intl. Mktg. & French, LSU, Baton Rouge, LA, Universite de l'Ouest, Angers, Fr.; **GRAD EDUC:** MBA, 1981, Mktg. & Fin., Univ. of S. Western LA; **OTHER ACT & HONORS:** FORUM Women's Network, 100 Club of Lafayette, Inc. (Charter Member & Dir.); **HOME ADD:** 303 Feu Follet Rd., Lafayette, LA, (318)237-7572; **BUS ADD:** 222 Rue DeJean, P.O. Box 53934, Layfayette, LA 70505, (318)269-7000.

FORD, Paul M.——**B:** July 17, 1928, Easton, PA, *Pres.*, Paul Ford Agency, Inc.; **PRIM RE ACT:** Broker; **SERVICES:** RE brokerage - insurance brokerage; **REP CLIENTS:** Local indivs. and bus.; **PROFL AFFIL & HONORS:** Past Pres. Easton RE Bd. Past VP - PA Assn. of Realtors, Past President - Lehigh Valley Soc. of Appraisers, GRI, CRS, SRA; **EDUC:** BA, 1950, English, Colgate Univ. Hamilton, NY; **MIL SERV:** USAF, Col., Meritorious Service Medal, Air Medal - Combat Theatre Awards; **OTHER ACT & HONORS:** Northampton Cty. Bd. of View - 12 years, Local Charities, Past Dir. C of C, Past Pres. - Easton Rotary Club, Trustee - PA Assn. of Realtors Educ. Found.; **HOME ADD:** 509 Acorn Dr., Easton, PA 18042, (215)252-1341; **BUS ADD:** 126 Bushkill St. PO Box 309, Easton, PA 18042, (215)253-6123.

FORD, Robert S.——**B:** Aug. 19, 1936, Indianapolis, IN, *Partner*, Main Hurdman, CPA's, Indianapolis Office; **PRIM RE ACT:** Consultant; **OTHER RE ACT:** CPA; **SERVICES:** Fed. tax consult., econ. feasibility studies, fin. and tax reporting; **PROFL AFFIL & HONORS:** AOCPA, IN Soc. of CPA's, CPA; **EDUC:** BS, Mgmt. and Acctg., IN Univ.; **OTHER ACT & HONORS:** Columbia Club, Indianapolis, IN, Visiting Lecturer, IN Univ.; **HOME ADD:** 112 C. Shoreline Ct., Noblesville, IN 46060, (317)377-2993; **BUS ADD:** 11 S. Meridian St., Suite 815, Indianapolis, IN 46204, (317)635-2228.

FORD, Stanley——*Exec VP*, Gabriel Realty; **PRIM RE ACT:** Developer; **BUS ADD:** PO Box 547, Paramus, NJ 07652, (201)262-5300.*

FORD, Thomas S.——**B:** Jan. 22, 1944, Vicksburg, MS, *Pres.*, Madison Investment Co.; **PRIM RE ACT:** Broker, Lender, Insuror, Syndicator; **SERVICES:** Complete fin. including construction, permanent & equity; **REP CLIENTS:** So. Housing Partners, Inc.; Kirkland Homes; CN Co.; Constructors, Inc.; **PREV EMPLOY:** Peat, Maick, Mitchell & Co.; **PROFL AFFIL & HONORS:** Bd. of Realtors; RESSI, CPA, Silver Medal May '67 exam; **EDUC:** BBA, 1966, Acctg., Univ. of MS; **GRAD EDUC:** MA, 1967, Acctg., Univ. of MS; **OTHER ACT & HONORS:** Valley Hill Ctry. Club; Vestry Church of the Nativity - Episcopal; **HOME ADD:** 7808 Shadowbend, Huntsville, AL 35802, (205)881-8596; **BUS ADD:** 2315 Bob Wallace Ave. 2, Huntsville, AL 35805, (205)533-0200.

FORD, Wesley C.——**B:** Apr. 22, 1933, NY, *Pres.*, W.C. Ford Real Estate Corp.; **PRIM RE ACT:** Broker, Appraiser, Instructor, Property Manager; **OTHER RE ACT:** Conversions to co-op; **SERVICES:** Comml. and indus. RE; **PROFL AFFIL & HONORS:** Amer. Assn. Cert. Appraisers; RNMI; LIBOR; NY State Assn. of Realtors; NAR, GRI; CRS; **MIL SERV:** USAF, A1-C, 1952-1956; **OTHER ACT & HONORS:** Past Pres., Floral Park Lions Club; VP, Floral Park C of C; **HOME ADD:** 120 Kildare Rd., Garden City, NY 11530; **BUS ADD:** 206 Jericho Tpk., Floral Park, NY 11001, (516)354-1833.

FORDE, George S., Jr.——**B:** Jan. 17, 1934, Plainfield, NJ, *Atty.*, Stradley, Ronon, Stevens & Young; **PRIM RE ACT:** Attorney; **SERVICES:** Legal; **REP CLIENTS:** Instit. and Pvt. owners, investors, devels.; **PROFL AFFIL & HONORS:** ABA, PA Bar Assn., Philadelphia Bar Assn., Amer. Arbitration Assn.; **EDUC:** BS, 1955, St. Joseph's Univ.; **GRAD EDUC:** JD, 1958, Villanova Univ., School of Law; **EDUC HONORS:** Dougherty Fellowship, Law Review; **MIL SERV:** USAF Res., S.Sgt.; **OTHER ACT & HONORS:** Serra Club of Philadelphia; St. Thomas More Soc.; Catholic Philopatrian Literary Inst.; Amer. Civil Liberties Union; Friendly Sons of St. Patrick; Cardinal's Comm. on Human Relations (1970-78); Conference on the Holocaust; **HOME ADD:** 8401 Seminole Ave., Philadelphia, PA 19118, (215)242-8332; **BUS ADD:** 1100 One Franklin Pl., Philadelphia, PA 19102, (215)564-8019.

FORE, Richard——**B:** April 9, 1945, Lynchburg, VA, *Partner*, Lincoln Prop. Co. 1976-; **PRIM RE ACT:** Developer, Builder, Property Manager, Syndicator; **SERVICES:** Apt. devel.; **PREV EMPLOY:** Admin. Asst. to the Sec. of H.U.D., Dep. Admin. New Comm. Admin. HUD; **PROFL AFFIL & HONORS:** Immediate Past Pres. Nat. Multi Housing Council - Nat. Assn. of Home Builders Member; **EDUC:** BS, 1968, Criminology & Corrections, FL State Univ.; **GRAD EDUC:** MPA, 1970, Public Admin., AZ State Univ.; **OTHER ACT & HONORS:** Pres. Housing Commn. 1981, Vice Chmn. Govt. Regulations Comm., NV Republican Party Fin. Chmn., Reagan Housing Task Force - Reagan Transition Team; **HOME ADD:** 3155 Loma Vista Ave., Las Vegas, NV 89120, (702)798-2911; **BUS ADD:** Suite 216 1500 E. Tropicana, Las Vegas, NV 89109, (702)798-2911.

FOREMAN, Robert Lee——**B:** Dec. 3, 1934, Los Angeles, CA, *Pres.*, RE Analysts of Newport, Inc.; **PRIM RE ACT:** Consultant, Appraiser, Instructor; **OTHER RE ACT:** Author; **SERVICES:** RE appraisal, feasibility analysis, consultation; **REP CLIENTS:** S&L Assns. and banks, govt. agencies, devels.; **PROFL AFFIL & HONORS:** MAI; Amer. Inst. of RE Appraisers; 1981-1982, Member of Nat. Exec. Comm. and (ex officio) Governing Council, SREA; **EDUC:** BA, 1956, Philosophy, Occidental Coll.; **OTHER ACT & HONORS:** Member of Govs. Task Force on Solid Waste Mgmt., 1969-1970; **HOME ADD:** 1507 Kathleen Ln., Newport Beach, CA 92660, (714)646-4958; **BUS ADD:** 3700 Campus Dr., Suite 209, Newport Beach, CA 92660, (714)540-2062.

FORESTER, David E.——**B:** Sept. 17, 1936, Dekalb, IL, *Sr. Devel. Dir.*, The Rouse Co., Comm. Devel.; **PRIM RE ACT:** Developer; **PREV EMPLOY:** Simon Enterprises, Inc., Scott Forester; **PROFL AFFIL & HONORS:** ULI, Nat. Assn. of Home Builders; **EDUC:** BA, 1958, Econ. & City Planning, Rutger's Univ.; **GRAD EDUC:** MRP, 1961, City & Reg. Planning, Cornell Univ.; **EDUC HONORS:** Phi Beta Kappa, Welhofer Scholarship, Univ. Fellowship; **HOME ADD:** 10233 Thistle Brook Ct., Columbia, MD 21044, (301)730-7074; **BUS ADD:** 10275 Little Patuxent Pkwy, Columbia, MD 21044, (301)992-6033.

FORESTER, Kenneth P., Jr.——**B:** Jan. 20, 1936, Sumter, SC, *Exec. VP*, SYNCO, Inc.; **PRIM RE ACT:** Broker, Developer, Builder, Owner/Investor, Property Manager, Syndicator; **SERVICES:** Devel. and synd. of comml. & resid. prop., prop. mgmt.; **REP CLIENTS:** Lenders and indiv. or institutional investors in comml. prop.; **PROFL AFFIL & HONORS:** Bd. of Realtors, IREM, Found. Dir. of Charlotte Apt. Assn. CPM; **EDUC:** BA, 1958, Bus. & Econ., Davidson Coll.; **EDUC HONORS:** O.D.K.; **MIL SERV:** US Army, Capt., D.M.S.; **HOME ADD:** 2611 Lemon Tree Ln., Charlotte, NC 28211, (704)366-8592; **BUS ADD:** Po Box 34487, Charlotte, NC 28234, (704)376-9500.

FORHAN, John F.——**B:** Sep. 15, 1948, Dayton, OH, *Assoc.*, Holland & Hart; **PRIM RE ACT:** Attorney; **SERVICES:** Legal rep.; **REP CLIENTS:** Major land devel./sellers and lenders; **PROFL AFFIL & HONORS:** ABA, CO Bar Assn., Denver Bar Assn.; **EDUC:** BA, 1970, Econ., MI St. Univ.; **GRAD EDUC:** JD, 1978, Law, Univ. of IL, Coll. of Law; **EDUC HONORS:** Grad. with honor, Summa Cum Laude; Order of the Coif; Law Forum; **MIL SERV:** USAF, Capt., Commendation Medal; **HOME ADD:** 2264 Glencoe St., Denver, CO 80207, (303)322-0980; **BUS ADD:** Denver, CO 80201PO Box 8749, (303)575-8169.

FORMAN, R. Edward——**B:** Mar. 27, 1948, Savannah, GA, *Resid. RE Sales Mgr.*, Nyman Gallery of Homes; **PRIM RE ACT:** Broker; **OTHER RE ACT:** Resid. RE Sales Mgr.; **SERVICES:** RE sales, RE training; **PREV EMPLOY:** Sen. Herman E. Talmadge; US Senate 1969-1977; **PROFL AFFIL & HONORS:** CRB, NAR, PC Cty. Bd. of Realtors; **HOME ADD:** 13717 Piscataway Dr., Ft. Washington, MD 20022, (301)292-4559; **BUS ADD:** 10905 Ft. Washington Rd., Suite 100, Ft. Washington, MD 20744, (301)292-9500.

FORNES, Mark S.——**B:** Feb. 21, 1956, Dayton, OH, *Gen'l. Mgr.*, Danis Industries Corp., RE; **PRIM RE ACT:** Broker, Developer; **SERVICES:** Devel. of comml. & indus. props., prop. mgmt., brokerage & leasing; **PROFL AFFIL & HONORS:** Nat. Assn. of Indus. & Office Parks (Legislative Chmn.), BOMA; **EDUC:** BS, 1977, Fin., Univ. of Dayton; **GRAD EDUC:** MBA, 1981, Univ. of Dayton; **EDUC HONORS:** Omicron Delta Epsilon (Nat. Hon. Soc., Fin. & Econ.); **OTHER ACT & HONORS:** Dayton Area C of C (Legislative comm.), Wash. Township, Centerville C of C (fin. comm. chmn.); **HOME ADD:** 1602 Pinetree Ln., Dayton, OH 45449, (513)866-2212; **BUS ADD:** 1801 E First St., Dayton, OH 45403, (513)228-1225.

FORRESTER, Mark A.——**B:** Dec. 1, 1947, Watertown, NY, *VP RE*, Ramada Inns, Inc.; **PRIM RE ACT:** Developer, Owner/Investor; **PROFL AFFIL & HONORS:** NACORE, Broker; **EDUC:** BA, 1969, Gov't, Notre Dame Univ.; **GRAD EDUC:** MBA, 1972, AZ State; **EDUC HONORS:** Cum Laude, Beta Gamma Sigma; **HOME ADD:** 6833 N. 3rd Pl., Phoenix, AZ 85012, (602)248-0568; **BUS ADD:** PO Box 590, Phoenix, AZ 85001, (602)273-4590.

FORRESTER, Robert M.——*Secy. & Treas.*, Farmer Bros. Co.; **PRIM RE ACT:** Property Manager; **BUS ADD:** 20333 S. Normandie Ave., Torrance, CA 90509, (213)775-2451.*

FORSHEÉ, Eugene "Beau"——**B:** July 9, 1946, Kingstree, SC, *Pres.-Broker in Charge*, Garden City Realty, Inc.; **PRIM RE ACT:** Broker, Owner/Investor; **OTHER RE ACT:** Sales Mgr.; **SERVICES:** Vacation Rentals-Resort Sales-Comml. Sales; **PREV EMPLOY:** 1970-Banking; **PROFL AFFIL & HONORS:** SC Chap. of CCIM, SC Chapter of IREM, SC Assn. of Realtors, GRI, Realtor of Year, S. Grand Strand Bd. of Realtors 1978 & 1980; **EDUC:** BS, 1969, Indus. Mgmt., GA Tech.; **MIL SERV:** 1-y; **HOME ADD:** US Bus. 17, Murrells Inlet, SC 29576, (803)651-7290; **BUS ADD:** Atlantic Ave., Garden City, SC 29576, (803)651-2121.

FORSYTHE, Lynn M.——**B:** Oct. 2, 1949, Chicago, IL, *Assoc. Prof.*, CA State Univ., Fresno, Dept. of Fin. and Indus.; **PRIM RE ACT:** Attorney, Owner/Investor; **SERVICES:** Legal servs. including contract negotiation and drafting, tax counseling, and estate planning; **REP CLIENTS:** Prop. Mgrs.; indiv. investors; **PREV EMPLOY:** Faculty member at NM State Univ., CA State Univ. Long Beach, CA; **PROFL AFFIL & HONORS:** ABA Sect. of Tax.; ABA Sect. of Real Prop., Probate and Trust Law, Admitted to the CA and PA State Bars; **EDUC:** BA, 1970, Sociology, PA State Univ.; **GRAD EDUC:** JD, 1973, Law, Univ. of Pittsburgh School of Law; **EDUC HONORS:** Alpha Kappa Delta, Pi Gamma Mu, John H. Sorg Scholarship; **OTHER ACT & HONORS:** Estate and Gift Tax Atty. at IRS, 1973-1975; Amer. Assn. of Univ. Women; Intl. Fed. of Women Lawyers; **HOME ADD:** 712 W. Indianapolis Ave., Clovis, CA 93612, (209)291-3315; **BUS ADD:** School of Bus., Dept. of Fin. and Indus., Fresno, CA 93740, (209)294-2151.

FORTE, Joseph Philip——**B:** Dec. 19, 1947, NY, NY, *Atty.*, Trubin Sillcocks Edelman & Knapp; **PRIM RE ACT:** Attorney; **REP CLIENTS:** Lenders and mort. bankers; **PREV EMPLOY:** Cadwalader, Wickersham & Taft 1973-75; **PROFL AFFIL & HONORS:** NY State Bar Assn., Comm. RE Fin. & liens, NY Cty. Lawyers Assn. Comm. on Banking, Assn. Bar of City of NY, ABA; **EDUC:** BA, 1969, Pol. Sci., St. Francis Coll.; **GRAD EDUC:** JD, 1973, St. John's Univ.;

EDUC HONORS: Franciscan Scholar, magna cum laude, Managing Editor, Law Review, Cum Laude, Thomas More Scholar; **MIL SERV:** Natl. Guard; **OTHER ACT & HONORS:** Dir., Light Opera of Manhattan; **HOME ADD:** 4117 Westmoreland St., Little Neck, NY 11363, (212)423-6179; **BUS ADD:** 375 Park Ave., NY, NY 10152, (212)759-5400.

FORTNER, Seymour S.——B: Feb. 23, 1917, Denver, CO, *Pres.*, S.S. Fortner & Co. Inc.; **PRIM RE ACT:** Broker, Attorney, Developer, Owner/Investor, Property Manager; **SERVICES:** Comml. prop. mgr., sales, leasing; **REP CLIENTS:** Insurance Exch. Bldg., Denver; World Savings Bldg., Denver; United Bank of Lakewood, Denver; **PREV EMPLOY:** S.S. Fortner Inc., 1958 to present; **PROFL AFFIL & HONORS:** IREM; CPM, CPM, Arbitrator, Amer. Arbitration Assn.; **EDUC:** BA, 1938, Pol. Sci., Denver Univ.; **GRAD EDUC:** LLD, 1941, Law, Denver Univ.; **MIL SERV:** Intelligence, 1st Lt.; **OTHER ACT & HONORS:** Sr. Corps. of Retired Execs., US Govt. SBA; **HOME ADD:** 3991 S. Magnolia Way, Denver, CO 80237, (893)758-0795; **BUS ADD:** 466 Ins. Exch. Bldg., Denver, CO 80202, (303)893-1505.

FORTUNATO, Donald L.——B: Oct. 30, 1927, Chicago, IL, *VChmn*, The Balcor Co.; **PRIM RE ACT:** Broker, Lender, Owner/Investor, Property Manager, Syndicator; **SERVICES:** RE investment mgmt., evaluation and acquisition; prop. mgmt., and mort. fin.; **REP CLIENTS:** RE mgmt. investments for instit1. investors, indivs., and corps.; **PREV EMPLOY:** 20 years with Fidelity Mutual Life Insurance Co., Philadelphia; **PROFL AFFIL & HONORS:** NAR; RESSI; Nat. Assn. of Securities Dealers; **EDUC:** BS, 1949, N. IL Univ.; **OTHER ACT & HONORS:** Italian/Amer. Sports Hall of Fame; **HOME ADD:** 715 Glen Court, Glenview, IL 60025, (312)724-8512; **BUS ADD:** 10024 Skokie Blvd., Skokie, IL 60077, (312)677-2900.

FORTUNE, Kenneth S.——B: Oc.t 8, 1918, Montreal Can., *Owner*, K.S. Fortune Assoc.; **PRIM RE ACT:** Broker, Consultant, Appraiser; **OTHER RE ACT:** Land-use planning-subdividing; **REP CLIENTS:** Nat. Capital Commn., Ottawa, Can., IBM, NE Tele.; **PREV EMPLOY:** NCC Ottawa, public works Can., IBM & NE Tele.; **PROFL AFFIL & HONORS:** Soc. of RE Appraisers, NAREA, Int. R. of W. Assn., SRA, RRA, IR/WA; **EDUC:** BS, 1942, Chem. Engrg., McGill Univ. Montreal; **GRAD EDUC:** Diploma, 1976, American Law & Procedure, Lasalle Extension Univ.; **OTHER ACT & HONORS:** Jaguar North America Assn.; **HOME TEL:** (802)933-2373; **BUS ADD:** Enosburg, VT 05450, (802)933-2373.

FORWARD, Robert H., Jr.——B: Feb. 3, 1945, Orange, CA, *Ofcl. Counsel (also, partner, Forward, Smith & Assoc., RE investment counselors)*, Parker, Milliken, Clark & O'Hara; **PRIM RE ACT:** Consultant, Attorney; **SERVICES:** Legal services and real estate investment counseling; **PROFL AFFIL & HONORS:** Real Property Sects., Los Angeles Cty. and CA State Bar Assns.; **EDUC:** BA, 1966, Eng., Stanford Univ.; **GRAD EDUC:** JD, 1969, Harvard Law School; **EDUC HONORS:** Honors in English; **OTHER ACT & HONORS:** Trustee, Raymond M. Alf Museum, Claremont, CA; Dir., Theatre Exchange Soc., Inc., N. Hollywood, CA; **BUS ADD:** 2049 Century Park E, Suite 3490, Los Angeles, CA 90067, (213)203-0080.

FOSKIE, Bryan F.——B: Oct. 31, 1944, *Pres.*, Bryan Foskie RE Inc.; **PRIM RE ACT:** Broker, Instructor, Appraiser; **PROFL AFFIL & HONORS:** RNM, CRB, CRS, GRI, Realtor of the year 1978; **EDUC:** BS, 1969, Mgmt. Econ., Youngstown State Univ.; **EDUC HONORS:** Yes; **OTHER ACT & HONORS:** C of C, YMCA, Red Cross; **HOME ADD:** 1963 Henn Hyde Rd., Warren, OH 44484, (216)372-3333; **BUS ADD:** 1O78 Elm Rd., Warren, OH 44483, (216)372-3333.

FOSTER, Daniel G.——B: Sept. 3, 1943, New York, NY, *Pres.*, Foster & Foster Enterprises (F&FE); **PRIM RE ACT:** Broker, Consultant, Developer, Owner/Investor, Property Manager, Syndicator; **OTHER RE ACT:** Mort. Broker, CPA, MBA; **SERVICES:** F&FE has brokered more than $6,000,000 of RE since May 1980 inception; **PREV EMPLOY:** Alexander & Alexander, Inc. 1975-79 - Managing VP - Western US; Price Waterhouse, 1967-75, Mgr., Mgmt. Advisory Services; **PROFL AFFIL & HONORS:** Tucson Bd. of Realtors, AICPA, ASCPA, CSCPA, CPA; **EDUC:** BA, 1965, Econ. and Poli. Sci., Stanford Univ.; **GRAD EDUC:** MBA, Acctg., Columbia Univ. Grad. School of Bus.; **EDUC HONORS:** Econ.; **OTHER ACT & HONORS:** Skyline Ctry. Club, Tucson Tomorrow, Tucson C of C; **HOME ADD:** 4840 E. Placita Tres Vidas, Tucson, AZ 85718; **BUS ADD:** 4840 E. Placita Tres Vidas, Tucson, AZ 85718, (602)299-5040.

FOSTER, D.D.——B: Nov. 17, 1942, Kinston, NC, *Pres.*, Foster Realty Co., Inc.; **PRIM RE ACT:** Broker; **SERVICES:** Brokerage, Prop. Mgmt. & Appraisals; **PROFL AFFIL & HONORS:** Realtor Assoc., RNMI, CRS, GRI; **EDUC:** AB, 1965, Social Studies, Univ. E Carolina; **GRAD EDUC:** MAI Courses: Univ. of MD, Univ. of GA, Univ. San Francisco, Appraisal; **MIL SERV:** US Guard, E-5; **OTHER ACT & HONORS:** Mayor City of Kinston; **HOME ADD:** 2204 Sparre Dr., Kinston, NC 28501, (919)522-1036; **BUS ADD:** 802 Nelson St., PO 888, Kinston, NC 28501, (919)523-2132.

FOSTER, John D.——B: Sept. 30, 1942, NY, NY, *Sr. VP, AZ Branch Mgr.*, Cushman & Wakefield of AXM Ubc.; **PRIM RE ACT:** Broker, Consultant, Property Manager; **OTHER RE ACT:** AZ Branch mgr. (responsible for C&W activities); **PROFL AFFIL & HONORS:** NAR, Phoenix Bd. of Realtors; **EDUC:** BS, 1965, Govt. Pol. Sci., AZ State Univ.; **EDUC HONORS:** Departmental Hons.; **OTHER ACT & HONORS:** Member Exec. Bd. Boy Scouts of Amer., Theodore Roosevelt Council; **HOME ADD:** 3022 E Columbus, Phoenix, AZ 85016, (602)957-3540; **BUS ADD:** Suite 400, 4747 N 22nd St., Phoenix, AZ 85016, 02)957-0111.

FOSTER, John M.——B: Jan. 21, 1941, Vance Co., *Pres.*, Davis-Foster Realty; **PRIM RE ACT:** Broker, Developer, Builder; **SERVICES:** RE devel.; **PREV EMPLOY:** Banking, mort. fin.; **PROFL AFFIL & HONORS:** Kerr Lake Bd. of Realtors; **OTHER ACT & HONORS:** Past Pres. Henderson Jaycees; Past Chmn. Vance Co. Heart Fund; Past Dir. of Vance-Henderson C of C; Red Cross; **HOME ADD:** P O Box 594, Henderson, NC 27536, (919)438-6057; **BUS ADD:** P O Box 1738, Henderson, NC 27536, (919)492-4066.

FOSTER, Ronald S.——B: June 27, 1945, Spartanburg, SC, *RE Appraiser and Consultant*, Ronald S. Foster, RE Appraisals; **PRIM RE ACT:** Consultant, Appraiser; **SERVICES:** RE appraisals, feasibility study, investment counseling; **REP CLIENTS:** Lending inst., corps., employee relocation cos., mort. cos.; **PREV EMPLOY:** James Robinson & Assoc., RE Appraisals; **PROFL AFFIL & HONORS:** AIREA; GA Bd. of Realtors; Gwinnett Co. Bd. of Realtors, MAI; **EDUC:** Bus. Admin./Econ., Furman Univ.; **MIL SERV:** SC Nat. Guard, 1966-1972; **OTHER ACT & HONORS:** Toastmasters Intl.; **HOME ADD:** 4703 Marc Ct., Lilburn, GA 30247, (404)923-5539; **BUS ADD:** 4703 Marc Court, Lilburn, GA 30247, (404)923-6411.

FOSTER, Ruth E.——B: Aug. 27, 1950, Raleigh, NC, *Prop. Mgr.*, Braedon Prop. Mgmt., Inc., Prop. Mgmt.; **PRIM RE ACT:** Property Manager; **PREV EMPLOY:** Encyclopedia Sales, Global Indus.; **PROFL AFFIL & HONORS:** #1 Rep. E Coast Fall '75; **EDUC:** BA, 1972, Hist. - Elem. Educ., Mary Washington Coll.; **GRAD EDUC:** Real Prop. Admin. Candidate; **EDUC HONORS:** Pi Gamma Mu; **HOME ADD:** 4256 Buckman Rd., Alexandria, VA 22309; **BUS ADD:** 1150 17th St., NW, Wash., DC 20036, (202)466-2130.

FOTI, Jack R.——B: Mar. 7, 1946, NY, NY, *Mgr. Corp. Dev.*, The Bekins Co.; **OTHER RE ACT:** Manage Co's. 4,000,000 Sq. Ft. of Warehouse, Handle disposition of $30,000,000 RE, All Leasing, Merger, & Acquisition of Cos. for Diversifications; **PREV EMPLOY:** Asst. to Sr. VP, Corp. Dev., Whittaker Corp. 1969-1977; **PROFL AFFIL & HONORS:** Assn. Corp. Growth (Member), Indus. Dev. Research Council (Member); **EDUC:** BS, 1967, Econ. & Hist., Univ. of CA, Riverside; **GRAD EDUC:** MBA, 1968, Bus., UCLA; **EDUC HONORS:** High Honor at Grad.; **MIL SERV:** US Army, M/Sgt.; **HOME ADD:** 3342 Troy Dr., LA, CA 90068, (213)874-0866; **BUS ADD:** 777 Flower St., Glendale, CA 91201, (213)507-1200.

FOUNTAIN, Edmund M., Jr.——B: Aug. 14, 1948, Montreal, Can., *Pres.*, Fountain Appraisal Co., Inc.; **PRIM RE ACT:** Consultant, Appraiser; **SERVICES:** Valuation, investment consulting; **REP CLIENTS:** Major lenders, accountants and instit. investors interested in comml. props.; **PREV EMPLOY:** RE Research Corp; **PROFL AFFIL & HONORS:** AIREA; SREA; Houston Bd. of Realtors, MAI; SRPA; GRI; **EDUC:** BBA, 1971, Mgmt and Arch., Texas Tech. Univ.; **EDUC HONORS:** Dean's List; **HOME ADD:** Box 112, Cypress, TX 77429, (713)890-0102; **BUS ADD:** 12337 Jones Rd., Suite 200, Houston, TX 77070, (713)890-0102.

FOUNTAIN, Michael——*Treasurer*, Armstrong Rubber Company; **PRIM RE ACT:** Property Manager; **BUS ADD:** 500 Sargent Dr., New Haven, CT 06707, (203)562-1161.*

FOUNTAIN, Milton O.——B: Dec. 18, 1909, Warren, MA, *Appraiser, Realtor*; **PRIM RE ACT:** Broker, Consultant, Appraiser, Developer, Builder, Owner/Investor; **OTHER RE ACT:** Inspector; **SERVICES:** Resid., Indus., Comml. appraisals of farm prop., shopping ctrs., land takings, resids.; **REP CLIENTS:** US Govt., banks, corps., indivs.; **PROFL AFFIL & HONORS:** MA Assn. of Ins. Agents, SREA, Past. Pres & Member of Bd.of Dir. NAREB, Wash. Realtor Comm., MA Assn. of RE Bds., Past State Dir. Hampshire Cty. Bd. of Realtors, Northampton, MA; Past Pres. & Past Member of Bd. of Dirs., Pres. 1973-4, Propf. Realty Lodge, SRA, AFA, NARA, ACA Sr. Realtor of the Yr., 1963, 1969; **EDUC:** Appraisal & RE courses, Univ. of MA; **OTHER ACT & HONORS:** Over 25 yrs. on Warren Bd. of Health & Warren Sch. Comm., Warren Planning Bd., Chmn. Advisory Bd.

Upper Quaboag River Watershed, Quaboag Reg. High Sch. Comm. Member, Commn. on Central Reg. Planning Bds., Sewer Comm. Chmn., Bd. of Selectmen 1975/1976/1977/Chmn.; **HOME ADD:** Boston Post Rd., Warren, MA 01083, (413)436-5608; **BUS ADD:** One Winthrop Terr., Warren, MA 01083, (413)436-5530.

FOURNIER, Walter F.——B: Feb. 26, 1912, Northampton, MA, *Broker*, Walter F. Fournier Assoc.; **PRIM RE ACT:** Broker, Consultant, Appraiser; **SERVICES:** Counselor, exchanger; **PREV EMPLOY:** Sales Prefabs Sears, 1948-49, Western MA; **PROFL AFFIL & HONORS:** Past Pres. AK Creative RE, Past Pres AK Assoc. Mort. Consultants, Soc. of Exchange Counselors, Cert. Bus. Counselors, Nat. Assn. of Review Appraisers (Sr.); **MIL SERV:** USN, 1944-45, 1st class Elect. 5 engagement star, both theatres; **OTHER ACT & HONORS:** Pres. Fairview Comm. Counsel, Dir. Sea Scouts, Spec. Police Flood, 1938 Northampton, Elks 45 yrs., K of C 4th Degree, Pres. IBEW 1937, Commdr. VFW Post 3836, 1956-57; Sr. Listing Who's Who in Creative RE, 1975-81; **HOME ADD:** 603 E 22nd Ave., Anchorage, AK 99503, (907)272-8960; **BUS ADD:** 613 E 22nd Ave., Anchorage, AK 99503, (907)277-7474.

FOUTCH, James R.——B: July 18, 1936, Omaha, NE, *Partner*, Dibrell, Dibrell, Greer and Brown; **PRIM RE ACT:** Attorney; **REP CLIENTS:** Amer. Nat. Ins. Co.; Moody Nat. Bank; US Nat. Bank; Galveston Hist. Found.; **PROFL AFFIL & HONORS:** ABA, TX & Galveston Cty. Bar Assns.; **EDUC:** BBA, 1958, Mgmt., Creighton Univ., Omaha, NE; **GRAD EDUC:** LLB, 1962, Law, Univ. of TX School of Law, Austin, TX; **MIL SERV:** US Army, Capt.; **OTHER ACT & HONORS:** Galveston Hist. Found.; Pres. (1980); **HOME ADD:** 47 Colony Park Cir., Galveston, TX 77551, (713)744-6945; **BUS ADD:** One Moody Plaza, Galveston, TX 77550, (713)765-5525.

FOWLER, Christy Seip——B: Apr. 17, 1953, Erie, PA, *Associate, Management Advisory Services*, Laventhol & Horwath; **PRIM RE ACT:** Consultant; **SERVICES:** Market expansion strategy and site selection; **REP CLIENTS:** Fin. insts., shopping ctrs., retailers, restaurants; **PREV EMPLOY:** George R. Frerichs & Assoc., Inc., 1976-1981; **PROFL AFFIL & HONORS:** Amer. Mktg. Assn.; RE Broker - IL; Intrl. Council of Shopping Ctrs.; **EDUC:** BA, 1975, Econ., Dension Univ.; **OTHER ACT & HONORS:** Junior League of Chicago, Inc.; **BUS ADD:** 111 E. Wacker Dr., Chicago, IL 60601, (312)644-4570.

FOWLER, Edward H., Jr.——B: June 28, 1932, Santa Monica, CA, *Mgr., Prop., Sales & Excise Taxes*, Aluminum Co. of America; **OTHER RE ACT:** Responsible for advalorem taxes and directly involved in valuations of all facilities and operations in US and Can.; **PROFL AFFIL & HONORS:** Inst. of Prop. Taxation, 2nd VP and Chmn. of Educ. Comm.; Amer. Soc. of Appraisers; Intl. Assn. of Assessing Officers, Member; Nat. Assn. of Review Appraisers; Nat. Assn. of Corp. RE Execs.; Intl. Inst. of Valuers, CRA; SCV; CMI; **EDUC:** Cert. of Completion, 1953, Acct., Bus. and Tax Law, Robert Morris Bus. School; **MIL SERV:** USN, SKSN; **HOME ADD:** 317 First Ave., Belle Vernon, PA 15012, (412)929-6271; **BUS ADD:** 1501 Alcoa Bldg., Pittsburgh, PA 15219, (412)553-2874.

FOWLER, Jack W.——B: Mar. 24, 1932, Vinton, IA, *Pres.*, Fowler Real Estate & Ins., Inc.; **PRIM RE ACT:** Broker, Developer, Builder, Property Manager, Insuror; **SERVICES:** Ex. Comm. Amer. Baptist Homes; **PREV EMPLOY:** Const. Co., Pres. to 1954 then RE & Const.; **PROFL AFFIL & HONORS:** NAR; CAR, CPM; CRB; GRI; **EDUC:** BA, 1954, Chemistry, Park Coll.; **OTHER ACT & HONORS:** Pres., Boulder Bd. of Realtors; Realtor of the Yr., Boulder; **HOME ADD:** 5501 Jay Rd., Boulder, CO 80302, (303)530-3165; **BUS ADD:** 2400 28th St., Boulder, CO 80301.

FOWLER, James T.——B: Oct. 24, 1944, Hagerstown, MD, *Pres.*, Fowler & Fowler, Inc.; **PRIM RE ACT:** Broker, Consultant, Owner/Investor, Property Manager; **OTHER RE ACT:** Specializing in Mktg. and Sales in Business and RE Props.; **SERVICES:** Mktg., Adv., synd., purchasing, selling, development; **REP CLIENTS:** Maj. condo. devels., time share condo. land devels., single family housing, nat. and intl. marketing of land sales, shelter sales and time sharing; **PREV EMPLOY:** 18 yrs. broadcast communications, 6 yrs. mktg. land and shelter, advertising agency ownership - 3 yrs., RE specialist for over 5 yrs.; **PROFL AFFIL & HONORS:** Amer. Soc. of Profl. Consultants, Lic. RE Broker; **EDUC:** BA, 1974, Mktg./Communications, Univ. of S. FL; **MIL SERV:** USMC; **OTHER ACT & HONORS:** Rotarian, BSA, Poli. grps., etc.; **HOME ADD:** 12405 River Rd. S.E., Ft. Myers, Lee Cty., FL 33905; **BUS ADD:** PO Box 05759, Ft. Myers, Lee Cty., FL 33905, (813)694-8211.

FOWLKES, W.C.——B: Nov. 1, 1948, Madison, NC, *Mort. L.O.*, Piedmont Trust Bank; **PRIM RE ACT:** Appraiser, Banker; **OTHER RE ACT:** Mktg. - Secondary Mort.; **REP CLIENTS:** E.I. DuPont, Inc.; **PREV EMPLOY:** VP - Loans w/Lincoln S&L Assoc., Richmond, VA; **PROFL AFFIL & HONORS:** VA MBA, MBAA, Exec. VP Martinsville - Henry Cty. HBA, SREA, M-HC Bd. of Realtors, Who's Who in Fin. & Ind. (1981), Who's Who S & SW (1978-80); **EDUC:** AS, 1972, RE, Middle GA Coll.; BS, 1974, RE, VA Commonwealth Univ.; **GRAD EDUC:** School of Mort. Banking, 1978, RE Fin., Northwestern Univ. - Grad. Sch. of Business; **MIL SERV:** USAF 1968-72, USAR 1979-pres., Sp/5, Outstanding unit award, Good Conduct, Expert Marksman; **OTHER ACT & HONORS:** Pres. - Martinsville Jaycees 1980-81, Kappa Sigma (VCU) Alumni of the yr. 1977, Rho Epsilson - RE Frat.; **HOME ADD:** 1404 Spruce St., Martinsville, VA 24112, (703)632-3251; **BUS ADD:** PO Box 4751, Martinsville, VA 24112, (703)632-2971.

FOWLKES, W.W.——B: Apr. 30, 1913, Danville, VA, *Atty.*, W.W. Fowlkes, Atty.; **PRIM RE ACT:** Attorney; **SERVICES:** Legal servs. and estate planning; admin. of estates; **PROFL AFFIL & HONORS:** Member, San Antonio Bar Assn.; State Bar of TX; VA Bar; ABA, Pres., San Antonio Bar Assn.; Dir., State Bar of TX; **EDUC:** Washington and Lee Univ.; **GRAD EDUC:** LLB, 1935, Real Prop., Washington and Lee Univ.; **EDUC HONORS:** Pres., Frat. House Corp.; **OTHER ACT & HONORS:** Rotary Intl.; Amer. Arbitration Assn.; TX State Wide Credit Assn.; Order of the Alamo; Chmn., TX Legal Forms Comm. published two RE legals forms, conveyancing manuals; **HOME ADD:** 412 Canterbury Hill, San Antonio, TX 78209, (512)826-4142; **BUS ADD:** 1824 Frost Bank Tower, San Antonio, TX 78205, (512)224-5234.

FOWLKS, Robert C.——B: Feb. 9, 1936, Los Angeles, CA, *Dist. Mgr.*, Grubb & Ellis Property Service Co.; **PRIM RE ACT:** Broker, Consultant, Property Manager; **OTHER RE ACT:** Const. mgr.; **SERVICES:** Prop. mgr., const. mgmt., consulting; **REP CLIENTS:** Agent for public and pvt. owners of office bldgs., shopping ctrs., and indus. parks; **PROFL AFFIL & HONORS:** BOMA; IREM; Los Angeles C of C; Los Angeles Realty Bd., CPM; **EDUC:** BS, 1958, Econ/Sci., Univ. of CA at Davis; **GRAD EDUC:** MBA, 1960, RE, UCLA; **MIL SERV:** USAF; **HOME ADD:** 809 El Medio Ave., Pacific Palisades, CA 90272, (213)459-1536; **BUS ADD:** 1126 Wilshire Blvd., Los Angeles, CA 90017, (213)481-2350.

FOX, Arthur E.——B: Sept. 3, 1920, New York, NY, *Atty.*, Arthur E. Fox, Tax Atty.; **PRIM RE ACT:** Attorney; **OTHER RE ACT:** CPA; **SERVICES:** Tax law, tax planning; **REP CLIENTS:** Investors, devels., synds., builders, mort. bankers, lenders, estates, heirs, trusts; **PROFL AFFIL & HONORS:** ABA, FL Bar Assn., Dade Cty. Bar Assn., Amer. Inst. CPAs, FL Inst. of CPAs, NY State Soc. of CPAs; **EDUC:** BBA, 1940, Acctg., City Coll. - NY; **GRAD EDUC:** JD, 1954, Law, Univ. of Miami; **EDUC HONORS:** Insignium Award, Cum Laude; **MIL SERV:** US Army; **HOME ADD:** Key Biscayne, FL; **BUS ADD:** 240 Crandon Blvd., Miami, FL 33149, (305)361-7719.

FOX, Claire R.——B: Dec. 15, 1937, Albany, CA, *Broker-Owner*, Fox Realtors; **PRIM RE ACT:** Broker, Instructor, Syndicator, Property Manager, Owner/Investor, Real Estate Publisher; **PROFL AFFIL & HONORS:** NAR, CA Assn. Realtors, RNMC, GRI; **EDUC:** BS, 1966, Bus. Educ., CA State Univ.; **OTHER ACT & HONORS:** Published, *Introduction to Syndication: Syndicating Single Family Homes*; **HOME ADD:** 103 Mt. Trinity Ct., Clayton, CA 94517, (415)672-0351; **BUS ADD:** 103 Mt. Trinity Ct., Clayton, CA 94517, (415)672-2020.

FOX, David——*Commissioner*, California, CA Real Estate Dept.; **PRIM RE ACT:** Property Manager; **BUS ADD:** 1719 24th St., Sacramento, CA 95816, (916)445-3996.*

FOX, Frederick W.——B: Oct. 17, 1928, Milwaukee, WI, *VP*, Stone & Webster Appraisal Corp.; **PRIM RE ACT:** Appraiser; **SERVICES:** Valuation and tax services relating to RE; **REP CLIENTS:** Many fortune 500 Cos.; **PREV EMPLOY:** The American Appraisal Co., 1960-74; **PROFL AFFIL & HONORS:** Amer. Soc. of Appraisers, Amer. Assn. of Cost Engineers, Columbia Soc. of RE Appraisers, NY State Soc. of RE Appraisers, Broker, States of CT & NY; RE Bd. of NY, Inc.; **EDUC:** BS, 1952, Fin., Statistics, Univ. of WI, Madison; **MIL SERV:** USMC; **HOME ADD:** 14 Twin Brooks Ln., Fairfield, CT 06430, (203)259-0257; **BUS ADD:** 90 Broad St., NY, NY 10004, (212)269-4224.

FOX, George G.——B: Sept. 25, 1938, Detroit, MI, *Mgr. of RE*, General Motors Corp.; **OTHER RE ACT:** Mgr. of RE providing all of the services provided herein; **SERVICES:** Intl. Indus., Comml., and Residential; **PROFL AFFIL & HONORS:** SIR, IDRC; **EDUC:** BA, 1962, Bus. Admin., Eastern Univ.; **MIL SERV:** US Army, SP4; **HOME ADD:** 18818 Lincoln Re., Lathrup Village, MI 48076, (313)559-0683; **BUS ADD:** 485 W Milwaukee, Detroit, MI 48202, (313)556-2712.

FOX, Howard L.——*Pres.*, Howard L. Fox, Inc.; **PRIM RE ACT:** Broker; **PROFL AFFIL & HONORS:** NAR; Two Profl. Designations: Accredited Farm and Land Member; CCIM; **EDUC:** BS, Wharton School, Univ. of PA; **MIL SERV:** USAF; 1st Lt.; **BUS ADD:** 196 Clinton Ave., Kingston, NY 12401, (914)338-3444.

FOX, James E.——**B:** New Brunswick, NJ, *Mgr. RE*, Allied Corp.; **OTHER RE ACT:** Mgr. RE; **SERVICES:** Leasing, subleasing, acquisitions, sales, consulting, corp. prop.; **PREV EMPLOY:** RE Agent, PA Railroad; Mgr., Prop., Lehigh Valley Railroad; Mgr., Field Offices, Amer. Express Co.; **PROFL AFFIL & HONORS:** Pres. and Dir., The Indus. Devel. Research Council; **EDUC:** BS, 1952, Commerce, Rider Coll.; **MIL SERV:** USN, R.Adm. 2nd/C, USN Unit Citation; **HOME ADD:** 2307 Weinmann Way, Yardley, PA 19067, (215)493-2823; **BUS ADD:** POB 2251 R, Morristown, NJ 07960, (201)455-4451.

FOX, Matthew C.——**B:** Apr. 18, 1943, *CEO*, Burnham Dev. Co.; **PRIM RE ACT:** Syndicator, Developer, Property Manager; **PREV EMPLOY:** Exec. V. P./Brucarla Corp. (Subs. of Amer. Home Products Corp. NY), Part./Coopers & Lybrand, NY; **PROFL AFFIL & HONORS:** Lic. RE Broker, IL Lic. Engineer, CA, CPM; **EDUC:** BS, 1955 & 1958, Mgmt. Engineering/Civil Engineering, Rensellaer Polytech. Inst.; **GRAD EDUC:** MBA, 1961, Fin., NY U.; **MIL SERV:** USN, Lt. J.G.; **OTHER ACT & HONORS:** Elected to 9 Nat. Soc. for Engineering & Fin. Winner of 2 Nat. Design Awards - 20 yr. exp. with HUD Programs and Systems; **HOME ADD:** 1210 N. Astor St., Chicago, IL 60610, (312)787-8246; **BUS ADD:** 111 East Wacker Dr., Suite 2930, Chicago, IL 60601, (312)938-2281.

FOX, Michael E.——**B:** Apr. 14, 1938, Chicago, IL, *Partner*, Adams, Fox, Marcus, Adelstein & Gerding; **PRIM RE ACT:** Attorney; **SERVICES:** All aspects of legal rep.; **REP CLIENTS:** BSF Devel. Inc. (condo converters), Downs, Mohl & Co. (mgmt.); **PREV EMPLOY:** Atty., staff, joint comm. on Internal Revenue Taxation 1965-68; **PROFL AFFIL & HONORS:** Amer., fed., IL and Chicago Bar Assns., CPA; **EDUC:** BS, 1959, Acctg., Univ. of IL; **GRAD EDUC:** JD, 1962, Harvard Law School; **EDUC HONORS:** high honors; **MIL SERV:** US Army, SP 4th Class; **HOME ADD:** 315 Auburn, Winnetka, IL 60093, (312)446-8756; **BUS ADD:** 208 S. La Salle St., 1278, Chicago, IL 60604, (312)368-1900.

FOX, Wayne Noland——**B:** June 20, 1952, Brooklyn, NY, *VP*, National Corp. for Housing Partnershps, Prop. Mgmt.; **PRIM RE ACT:** Broker, Consultant, Developer, Owner/Investor, Instructor, Property Manager; **SERVICES:** Investment counseling, devel., packaging and synd. of resid. props., prop. mgmt.; **PREV EMPLOY:** Grenadier Realty Corp., (Starrett Housing Corp.), 1230 Pennsylvania Ave., Brooklyn, New York 11239; **PROFL AFFIL & HONORS:** Assn. of Black Psychologists (Bd. of Dir.); NY RE Bd. member; Apt. Owners Advisory Council of Westchester, Outstanding Young Men of America (1981); IREM; **EDUC:** BA, 1973, Psychology, City Coll. of NY, New York, NY; **GRAD EDUC:** MBA, 1977, Bus. Mgmt., New School for Social Research, New York, NY; **OTHER ACT & HONORS:** Kings Cty.; Cty. Comm. Member 1979-1980; Lions Club (Bd. of Dirs.); Bd. Member of New York City Planning Board; Tri-State Rgnl. Planning Commn., Bd. Member; **HOME ADD:** 393 Parkside Ave., Brooklyn, NY 11226, (212)941-5297; **BUS ADD:** 156 William St., New York, NY 10038, (212)227-6112.

FOXMAN, Stephen Mark——**B:** Aug. 10, 1946, Youngstown, OH, *Member (Shareholder)*, Goodman & Ewing; **PRIM RE ACT:** Attorney, Owner/Investor; **SERVICES:** RE Atty.; **REP CLIENTS:** Lenders, indiv. investors, lessors and lessees, RE brokerage firms, mort. brokers and mort. bankers; **PROFL AFFIL & HONORS:** ABA, Philadelphia Bar Assn., DC Bar Assn.; **EDUC:** BS, 1968, Fin./econ., Wharton School of Fin. and Commerce, London School of Econ.; **GRAD EDUC:** JD, 1971, Harvard Law School; **EDUC HONORS:** Beta Gamma Sigma, cum laude; **OTHER ACT & HONORS:** Faculty Member, Inst. for Paralegal Training; **HOME ADD:** 828 Lombard St., Philadelphia, PA 19147; **BUS ADD:** 1429 Walnut St. 14th Fl., Philadelphia, PA 19102, (215)864-7722.

FOY, John N.——**B:** Oct. 1, 1943, Monroe, MI, *Sr. VP & Assoc.*, CBL & Associates, Inc.; **PRIM RE ACT:** Developer, Builder; **SERVICES:** Devel. & mgmt. of shopping ctrs.; **PREV EMPLOY:** Sr. VP, Fin. Serv. Div., Arlen Shopping Ctrs. Co. 1972-77; **PROFL AFFIL & HONORS:** Intl. Council of Shopping ctrs., TN and Amer. Bar Assns.; **EDUC:** BS, 1965, Hist., Austin Peay State Univ.; **GRAD EDUC:** JD, 1967, Univ. of TN; **MIL SERV:** US Army, 1968-77, Capt.; **OTHER ACT & HONORS:** Member of Pres. Scholar Comm. 1978-80 as appointed by Pres. Jimmy Carter; **HOME ADD:** 1025 Hibbler Cir., Chattanooge, TN 37412, (615)624-9547; **BUS ADD:** One Northgate Park, Chattanooga, TN 37415.

FOYTEK, Dan——*Site Location Cons.*, Detroit Edison, Area Development; **PRIM RE ACT:** Developer; **BUS ADD:** 2000 Second Ave., Rm. 308 WCB, Detroit, MI 48226, (313)237-7795.*

FRAIOLI, Lawrence A.——*Partner*, The Appraisal Services Group; **PRIM RE ACT:** Consultant, Appraiser, Owner/Investor, Property Manager; **SERVICES:** RE Appraisal & consulting, prop. mgmt.; **REP CLIENTS:** Major banks, ins. cos., corps., attys., devels.; **PREV EMPLOY:** RE Consultant in the RE Investment Dept. Morgan Guaranty Trust Co. of NY; **PROFL AFFIL & HONORS:** NY RE Bd., Amer. Soc. of Appraisers; NY State Soc. of RE Appraisers; Sr. Member of Nat. Assn. of Review Appraisers, CRA; **OTHER ACT & HONORS:** Member of Local Planning Bd.; Was instructor of appraisal for RE Course at Mercy Coll.; **BUS ADD:** 400 Bedford Rd., Armonk, NY 10504, (914)273-9754.

FRALIN, David——*Mgr. RE & Ins.*, Dan River, Inc.; **PRIM RE ACT:** Property Manager; **BUS ADD:** Box 261, Danville, VA 24541, (804)799-7000.*

FRANCE, Ralph H., II——**B:** July 9, 1941, Baltimore, MD, France & Metzner, P.A.; **PRIM RE ACT:** Attorney, Developer, Owner/Investor; **SERVICES:** Legal, devel. and synd. of multi-family and comml. props.; **REP CLIENTS:** Indiv. investors in real prop.; **PROFL AFFIL & HONORS:** ABA; State Bar Assn.; Washington Cty. Bar Assn.; PA State Landlords Assn.; **EDUC:** AB, 1962, Govt., Franklin and Marshall Coll.; **GRAD EDUC:** LLB, 1965, Real Prop./Zoning, Univ. of MD Law Sch.; **EDUC HONORS:** Henning Webb Prentis Memorial Prize; **MIL SERV:** US Navy Res., Cmdr., 1966 - present; **HOME TEL:** (301)797-7992; **BUS ADD:** 81 W. Washington St., Hagerstown, MD 21740, (301)797-0100.

FRANCE, William——*Chmn. & CEO*, Tower Marc; **PRIM RE ACT:** Broker, Consultant, Developer, Owner/Investor, Property Manager; **SERVICES:** Devel. & ownership, suburban office bldgs. & distribution centers, Brokerage & Prop. Mgmt.; **PREV EMPLOY:** First TN Banks, 1963-1980; **PROFL AFFIL & HONORS:** MBA; Nat. Assn. of RE Investment Trusts; Nat. Assn. of Indus. and Office Parks; SREA, CRA; **EDUC:** 1959, Bus., MS State Univ.; **MIL SERV:** US Naval Res., Lt. Comdr.; **OTHER ACT & HONORS:** Tr., Tower Marc; Editorial Advisory Bd., S.E. RE News; **BUS ADD:** Suite 1000, 6263 Poplar Ave., Memphis, TN 38119, (901)683-2444.

FRANCIS, Charles T.——**B:** Oct. 9, 1942, Boston, MA, *Pres.*, Ryan, Elliott & Co. of RI, Inc.; **PRIM RE ACT:** Broker; **PROFL AFFIL & HONORS:** Soc. of Indus. Realtors, DIR; **EDUC:** BA, 1964, Music, Trinity Coll.; **MIL SERV:** USN, Lt.; **HOME ADD:** 182 Everett Ave., Providence, RI 02906, (401)331-2325; **BUS ADD:** 111 Westminster St., Providence, RI 02903, (401)331-0350.

FRANCIS, Gene W.——**B:** Nov. 13, 1941, Kansas City, MO, *Part.*, Durant, Mankoff, Davis, Wolens & Francis; **PRIM RE ACT:** Attorney; **PROFL AFFIL & HONORS:** Dallas Bar, Texas Bar, ABA, Chmn, Real Prop. Sec. Dallas Bar Assn., 1978; Chmn, Texas Bar Assn. Condo. Subcomm. Faculty Member, ALI-ABA Condo. & Planned Devel. Inst.; **EDUC:** BSIE, 1963, KS State Univ.; **GRAD EDUC:** LLB, 1966, So. Methodist Univ.; **EDUC HONORS:** Phi Alpha Delta Frat., SMU Endowment Scholar 1963-65; **OTHER ACT & HONORS:** Pres. SMU Law Alumni Assn. - 1980; **HOME ADD:** 5548 Wateka, Dallas, TX 75209, (214)350-8164; **BUS ADD:** Dallas, TX 752023900 First Nat. Bank Bldg., (214)748-0074.

FRANCIS, John Patrick, Jr.——**B:** Dec. 20, 1947, Boston, MA, *Leasing Dir.*, Gigliotti Corp., Comml. Div.; **PRIM RE ACT:** Broker, Consultant, Developer, Builder, Owner/Investor, Property Manager, Syndicator; **OTHER RE ACT:** Lease negotiator, work-out specialist; **SERVICES:** Devel. of comml. props., site acquisition, rehab.; **REP CLIENTS:** Retail chain stores, comml. (investors)/landowners, devel. of shopping ctrs.; **PREV EMPLOY:** J.I. Kislak Realty Corp., S/C Div., Newark, NJ; Korman Corp., Philadelphia, PA; Quaker State Realty, Newtown, PA; **PROFL AFFIL & HONORS:** Bucks Cty. Bd. of Realtors (PA); PA Assn. of Realtors; Intl. Council of Shopping Ctrs.; **EDUC:** BA, 1970, Soc. Sci., Villanova Univ., Villanova, PA; **HOME ADD:** RD#2 Box 284-D Thompson Mill Rd., Newtown, PA 18940, (215)598-3800; **BUS ADD:** Suite #500 One Oxford Valley, 2300 E Lincoln Hwy., Langhorne, PA 19047, (215)752-7600.

FRANCIS, Leroy A.——**B:** June 14, 1910, Terre Haute, Vigo Cty., IN, *Atty. at Law*, Francis, Cook & Rider; **PRIM RE ACT:** Attorney, Developer, Builder, Owner/Investor; **OTHER RE ACT:** Examining titles and handling negotiations and closings of RE matters; **SERVICES:** Develop land through corp. known as Sunset Harbor, Inc., of which the above named person is Pres.; **REP CLIENTS:** Sunset Harbor, Inc.; agent for Chicago Title Insurance Company; U. S. Life; and Amer. Title Ins. Co.; **PROFL AFFIL & HONORS:** Terre Haute

Bar Assn.; IN Bar Assn.; ABA; **EDUC:** BS in Bus., 1948, IN Univ.; **GRAD EDUC:** JD, 1949, IN Univ.; **MIL SERV:** US Army, 1940-45, Col. Retd., Bronze Star; **OTHER ACT & HONORS:** Judge of Vigo Superior Ct. - 1958, Delta Tau Delta; Sigma Delta Kappa; **HOME ADD:** 2220 N. 10th St., Terre Haute, IN 47804, (812)234-0845; **BUS ADD:** 19 South Sixth St., Terre Haute, IN 47807, (812)232-9501.

FRANCIS, Merrill R.——B: Jan. 28, 1932, Iowa City, IA, *Part.*, Sheppard, Mullin, Richter & Hampton; **PRIM RE ACT:** Attorney; **SERVICES:** Negotiation & documentation of RE sales & loans, representation of lenders in foreclosing upon RE loans, rep. of lenders & borrowers; **REP CLIENTS:** Lenders and inst. investors, lessors; **PROFL AFFIL & HONORS:** State Bar of CA; ABA; LA County Bar; Chm. subcomm. on secured creditors, Business Bankruptcy, ABA; Mem. Exec. Comm. Comml. Law & Bank Sect. LA County Bar, Fellow ABA; **EDUC:** BA, 1954, Econ., Phi Beta Kappa, Magna Cum Laude, Pom Coll.; **GRAD EDUC:** JD, 1959, Stanford Law Sch.; **EDUC HONORS:** Order of the Coif; **MIL SERV:** US Naval Res., Lt.; **OTHER ACT & HONORS:** Member Jonathin Club; **HOME ADD:** 4812 Gould Ave., La Canada, CA 91011, (213)790-2400; **BUS ADD:** 333 S. Hope St., 48th Fl., Los Angeles, CA 90071, (213)620-1780.

FRANCIS, Richard N.——*Executive V. President*, National Multi Housing Council; **OTHER RE ACT:** Profl. Assn. Admin.; **BUS ADD:** 1800 M St. NW Suite 285-5, Washington, DC 20036, (202)659-3381.*

FRANCIS, Stephen J.——B: Sept. 13, 1944, San Mateo, CA, *Dir. RE Div.*, Dept. of Bus. Regulation, RE Div.; **OTHER RE ACT:** Administrator; **SERVICES:** Licensing, testing, regulation of RE; **PREV EMPLOY:** Deputy dir. of RE div. (2 yrs.), Appraiser State Tax Comm.; **PROFL AFFIL & HONORS:** Pres., Nat. Assn. of RE, Lic. Law Officials, 1981, current member; **EDUC:** BS, 1969, 1968, Weber BS, Weber State Coll., Ogden, UT; **MIL SERV:** USMC, Cpl.; **OTHER ACT & HONORS:** Dir. of RE Div, 8 yrs.; **HOME ADD:** 776 10th Ave, Salt Lake City, UT 84103, (801)531-6680; **BUS ADD:** 500 State Cap. Blvd., Salt Lake City, UT 84114, (801)533-5661.

FRANCISCO, M. Robi——B: Apr. 1907, Iowa, *Owner/Broker*, R & R RE; **PRIM RE ACT:** Broker, Developer, Appraiser, Owner/Investor; **PREV EMPLOY:** 25 years in RE; RE & prop. mgmt. 10 yrs.; **PROFL AFFIL & HONORS:** Accredited Farm & Land Broker Emeritus; Intl. Instit. of Valuers; Sr. Cert. Review Appraiser, Amer. Council Econ. Devel., Amer. Soc. of Profl. Consultants; **OTHER ACT & HONORS:** Econ. Devel. Council; Riverside Co.; Inland Manpower Comm.; Flood Commissioner, Riverside Co. (4 yrs.); Housing Auth. Adv. Commissioner; Soreptomists; Nat. League Amer. Women; Pres. Lake Elsnore Branch; Overall Econ. Devel. Projects; **BUS ADD:** 28235 E. Worcester, Sun City, CA 92380, (714)679-3129.

FRANCK, Donald G.——B: June 26, 1935, Detroit, MI, *VP*, First Federal Savings & Loan Assn. of Detroit, Mgr., Comml. Loan Div.; **PRIM RE ACT:** Appraiser, Lender; **SERVICES:** Mort. lending on multi-family, comml. & indus. props.; **REP CLIENTS:** Indivs., partnerships, & corps.; **PREV EMPLOY:** VP - Detroit Mort. & Realty Co.; **PROFL AFFIL & HONORS:** Soc. of RE Appraisers, Amer. Soc. of Appraisers, SRA, ASA; **EDUC:** BBA, 1957, RE, Univ. of MI; **MIL SERV:** USAF, 1st Lt.; **OTHER ACT & HONORS:** Moslem Temple Shrine; Acacia Lodge F&AM 477; **HOME ADD:** 1115 Balfour, Grosse Pointe Park, MI 48230, (313)822-6372; **BUS ADD:** 1001 Woodward Ave., Detroit, MI 48226, (313)965-1400.

FRANCY, Robert E.——B: July 27, 1930, Flagstaff, AZ, *Appraiser*, Appraisal Sciences, Ltd.; **PRIM RE ACT:** Consultant, Appraiser, Owner/Investor; **OTHER RE ACT:** Machinery & equipment valuation; **SERVICES:** RE appraisals, consultation; **REP CLIENTS:** US Govt., State of AZ, Cities, Utility Co., Law Firms, Banks & Indivs.; **PREV EMPLOY:** 16 years indep. appraiser; **PROFL AFFIL & HONORS:** Sr. member, Amer. Soc. of Appraisers; Sr. Member, Intl. Right of Way Assn., Coll. of Fellows, ASA, SR/WA, CRA, IRUA; **EDUC:** BS, 1952, Agriculture, Univ. of AZ; **OTHER ACT & HONORS:** Past Intl. Pres. Amer. Soc. of Appraisers 1979-1980; **HOME ADD:** 20644 N 39th Ave., Glendale, AZ 85308, (602)843-5036; **BUS ADD:** 4414 N 19th Ave., Suite C, Phoenix, AZ 85015, (602)248-0005.

FRANDSEN, Jerald L.——B: Feb. 29, 1932, Sioux City, IA, *Pres.*, Frandsen & Frandsen Ltd., Realtors; **PRIM RE ACT:** Broker, Appraiser, Instructor, Property Manager; **SERVICES:** Gen. Brokerage, Appraisal, Mgmt., Instruction; **REP CLIENTS:** Buyers, sellers, investors, owners, students; **PREV EMPLOY:** Pre. Reno Bd. of Realtors 1978; Dir. (NV) FLI; NV Assn. of Realtors; **PROFL AFFIL & HONORS:** Nat., State, and Local Bd. of Realtors; Nat. Soc. of Profs.; Nat. Educ. Assn.; FIABCI; FLI; Bus. Law Assn., Dept. Chmn. (RE, ins., hotel, motel casino at Truckee Meadows Comm. Coll.); GRI; **EDUC:** BS, 1955, Hist./Eng., Univ. of NE; **MIL SERV:** USMC, Capt.; **OTHER ACT & HONORS:** Dir. Stewart Title Co.; Dir. Navy League of US, NV; **HOME ADD:** 2922 Randolph Dr., Reno, NV 89502, (702)825-3015; **BUS ADD:** 1135 Terminal Way, Suite 207, Reno, NV 89502, (702)786-0500.

FRANK, Stephen——B: Dec. 10, 1934, Brooklyn, NY, *Pres.*, Stephen Frank Assoc., Inc.; **PRIM RE ACT:** Broker, Consultant, Owner/Investor; **PREV EMPLOY:** Frank Wittman, Inc. 1958-1968; **PROFL AFFIL & HONORS:** RE Bd.; **EDUC:** 1956, RE Major, Baruch Coll., CCNY; **EDUC HONORS:** RE Award; **MIL SERV:** US Army, sp3, 1956-1958; **HOME ADD:** 1125 San Pedro Ave., Coral Gables, FL 33156, (305)665-7565; **BUS ADD:** 2000 S. Dixie Hwy., Suite 214, Miami, FL 33133, (305)854-5500.

FRANK, William S.——B: Sept. 18, 1939, Mineola, NY, *Sr. RE Analyst*, ITT; **PRIM RE ACT:** Consultant; **SERVICES:** Legal and Bus. for Acquisitions and dispositions; **EDUC:** BA, 1963, Econ., C.W. Post Coll.; **GRAD EDUC:** JD, 1967, Brooklyn Law School; **EDUC HONORS:** Pi Gamma Mu, Soc. Sci. Honor Soc.; Dean's List; **HOME ADD:** 36 W. 84th St., NY, NY 10024, (212)799-4335; **BUS ADD:** 320 Park Ave., NY, NY 10022, (212)940-2834.

FRANKEL, James B.——B: Feb. 25, 1924, IL, *Counsel*, Cooper White & Cooper; **PRIM RE ACT:** Attorney; **PREV EMPLOY:** Lecturer in law, Yale Law Sch., RE Fin.; **EDUC:** US Naval Acad., 1945; **GRAD EDUC:** LLB, 1952, Yale Law Sch.; **EDUC HONORS:** with distinction, Law Journal/Asst. in instr.; **MIL SERV:** USN; **BUS ADD:** 44 Montgomery St., San Francisco, CA 94123, (415)433-1900.

FRANKEL, Jay L.——B: Aug. 7, 1930, New York, NY, *Pres.*, Solar Realty Group, Ltd. & Solar Management Co.; **PRIM RE ACT:** Broker, Consultant, Developer, Owner/Investor, Property Manager, Syndicator; **SERVICES:** Synd., brokerage, prop. mgmt.; **REP CLIENTS:** Indiv. investors in comml. props. and condo. assns.; **PREV EMPLOY:** Milton M. Schwartz & Assoc., Inc. 1953-1977; **PROFL AFFIL & HONORS:** Chicago RE Bd., Community Assns. Inst., Licensed RE Broker; **EDUC:** BA, 1951, Mktg., Commerce, Univ. of IL; **GRAD EDUC:** MA, 1956, Poli. Sci., Northwestern Univ.; **EDUC HONORS:** High Honors, Beta Gamma Sigma; **MIL SERV:** US Army, 1st Lt., 1951-1953; **OTHER ACT & HONORS:** Exec. Club of Chicago; Chi. Assn. of Comm. & Ind.; **HOME ADD:** 95 Lakeside Pl., Highland Park, IL 60035, (312)433-2258; **BUS ADD:** 2 N. Riverside Plaza, Chicago, IL 60606, (312)559-0225.

FRANKHAUSER, Wayne——*RE Mgr.*, Alberto-Culver Co.; **PRIM RE ACT:** P.operty Manager; **BUS ADD:** 2525 Armitage Ave., Melrose Park, IL 60160, (312)681-5200.*

FRANKLIN, Edward O.——B: Nov. 10, 1937, Memphis, TN, Franklin Development & Investment Co.; **PRIM RE ACT:** Syndicator; **EDUC:** 1961, Auburn Univ.; **GRAD EDUC:** Bachelor of Law VM MD, 1964, LaSalle Univ.; **MIL SERV:** Army, Capt. 1964; **OTHER ACT & HONORS:** Port & Harbor Comn. Memphis & Shelf Cty.; Amer. Vet. Medical Assn.; Cook Convention Ctr.-Comnr.; Chmn. Bd.-Lifeline Intl. Inc. (Medical Equip. Mfr.); Bd. of Dir.-Nat. Anesthesia & Respiratory Dealers Assn.; **BUS ADD:** 3126 Sandbrook, Memphis, TN 38116, (901)396-2980.

FRANKLIN, George——*Secretary*, Automatic Switch Co.; **PRIM RE ACT:** Property Manager; **BUS ADD:** Hanover Rd., Florham, NJ 07932, (201)466-2000.*

FRANKLIN, Gerry M.——B: May 6, 1943, Wilson, NC, *VP*, Frank S. Phillips, Inc., Pro. Mgmt. Dept.; **PRIM RE ACT:** Property Manager; **SERVICES:** Condo. apt. bldgs., office bldgs. shopping ctrs.; **REP CLIENTS:** New England Mutual Life Inc. Co., Midland Mutual Life Ins. Co.; **PROFL AFFIL & HONORS:** CPM, IREM, RPA Candidate with Apt. & Office Bldg. Assn., Member Wash. Bd. Realtors; **HOME ADD:** 2800 Duvall Rd., Burtonsville, MD 20730, (301)384-5510; **BUS ADD:** 6106 MacArthur Blvd., Wash. DC 20016, (301)229-9000.

FRANKOVIC, R.L.——B: June 21, 1920, Red Lodge, MT, *Owner, Broker*, Frankovic Realty; **PRIM RE ACT:** Broker, Appraiser, Owner/Investor, Property Manager; **SERVICES:** Selling, managing, appraising, owner of props.; **REP CLIENTS:** First Nat. Bank, Homequity, Merrill/Lynch Relocation; **PREV EMPLOY:** 21 yrs. RE Bus. in Buffalo, WY; **PROFL AFFIL & HONORS:** Buffalo Bd. of Realtors, WY Assn. Realtors, NAR; **EDUC:** 1947-48, Bus. Admin., Billings Bus. Coll., Billings, MT; **MIL SERV:** USAF, S/Sgt., Air Medal, Asiatic Pac. Campaigns; **OTHER ACT & HONORS:** Kiwanis, Vet. of For. Wars, Knights of Columbus, Amer. Legion; **HOME ADD:** West of Buffalo, Buffalo, WY 82834, (307)684-5579; **BUS ADD:** 407 N Main, Buffalo, WY 82834, (307)684-5579.

FRANSEN, Kenneth J.——**B:** Nov. 3, 1952, Toronto, Can., *Atty.*, Baker, Manock & Jensen; **PRIM RE ACT:** Attorney; **SERVICES:** Legal services regarding most phases of RE and water law; **PROFL AFFIL & HONORS:** ABA, Sect. of Real Prop., Probate and Trust Law; State Bar of CA, Real Prop. Sect., Order of the Coif; **EDUC:** BA, 1974, Hist., CA State Univ. at Fresno; **GRAD EDUC:** JD, 1977, UCLA Law School; **EDUC HONORS:** President's List, Summa Cum Laude, Order of the Coif; **BUS ADD:** Sixth Floor, Security Bank Bldg., Fresno, CA 93721, (209)442-0550.

FRANZ, Lydia T.——**B:** Jan. 11, 1924, Chicago, IL, *Pres.*, Century 21 - Country Squire; **PRIM RE ACT:** Broker; **SERVICES:** Brokerage (primarily resid.); **REP CLIENTS:** Kraftco, Dupont, Executrans, Merrill Lynch, ERS, etc; **PREV EMPLOY:** 21 yrs. in RE; **PROFL AFFIL & HONORS:** NAR, Dir.; IL Assn. of Realtors, Treas., 1982; RNMI, Bd. of Gov.; Barrington Bd. of Realtors, Pres., GRI; CRS; CRB; Omega Tau Rho; **EDUC:** BMusic, 1944, Piano/Theory, IL Wesleyan Univ.; **GRAD EDUC:** MMusic, 1948, Piano, Northwestern Univ.; **EDUC HONORS:** 3.76 average out of possible 4.0; **MIL SERV:** WAC; Sgt.; Pres. Citation; **OTHER ACT & HONORS:** Barrington Area C of C, Pres.; MENSA; **HOME ADD:** 76 Lakeview Pkwy., Timberlake, Barrington, IL 60010, (312)526-7540; **BUS ADD:** 209 Park Ave., Barrington, IL 60010, (312)381-6464.

FRANZ, Roger C.——**B:** Oct. 31, 1949, Portland, OR, *Asst. VP*, BA Mortgage of Denver, BA Mort. and International Realty Corp., A BankAmerica Corp.; **PRIM RE ACT:** Broker, Consultant; **OTHER RE ACT:** Mort. banker; **SERVICES:** Income prop. mort. banking serv.; **REP CLIENTS:** Maj. Denver devel. of income prop. , represent inst. investors for mort., joint ventures, purchases; **PREV EMPLOY:** Comml. loan officer, Bank of America, San Francisco, CA; **PROFL AFFIL & HONORS:** MBA; **EDUC:** BBA, 1971, Fin. and Mktg., Univ. of OR, Eugene; **GRAD EDUC:** M Mgmt., 1975, Fin., Northwestern Univ., Evanston, IL; **HOME ADD:** 7188 S Magnolia Cir., Englewood, CO 80112, (303)771-2159; **BUS ADD:** 4700 S Syracuse Pkwy., Denver, CO 80237, (303)770-3883.

FRASCO, James A.——**B:** Aug. 13, 1945, Peoria, IL, *VP*, Beaumont Co.; **PRIM RE ACT:** Broker, Syndicator, Appraiser, Property Manager; **OTHER RE ACT:** Lic. Salesman CA; **PREV EMPLOY:** VP of Major Bank RE Operation located in Chicago, IL; **PROFL AFFIL & HONORS:** Inst. of RE mgmt.; Nat. Assoc. of Review Appraisers, CPM; CRA; **MIL SERV:** Army, E-6; **HOME ADD:** 18948 Harwett, Northridge, CA 91376; **BUS ADD:** 541 N Larchmont Blvd., Los Angeles, CA 90004, (213)466-9761.

FRAUSTRO, Jerry——**B:** Sept. 28, 1952, McAllen, TX., *Pres.*, Las Mitras Devel. Corp.; **PRIM RE ACT:** Broker, Consultant, Developer, Owner/Investor, Syndicator; **SERVICES:** Leasing, site acquisitions, joint ventures; **PROFL AFFIL & HONORS:** NAR, RNMI, CCIM; **EDUC:** Bus., 1977, Pan Amer. Univ., Edinburg, TX 78539; **HOME ADD:** 2101 Kerria #4, McAllen, TX 78501, (512)687-7384; **BUS ADD:** 600 S. 27th, McAllen, TX 78501, (512)687-8427.

FRAZIER, John E.——**B:** Apr. 29, 1941, Birmingham, AL, *Assistant VP and Regional RE Mgr.*, Philadelphia Investment Corp., INA Corp.; **PRIM RE ACT:** Consultant, Developer, Lender, Owner/Investor, Property Manager; **SERVICES:** Purchase and/or joint venture devel. of comml. props.; **REP CLIENTS:** Owners, devels.; **PREV EMPLOY:** The Philadelphia Nat. Bank, 1977-1981; **PROFL AFFIL & HONORS:** ULI; **EDUC:** BA, 1964, Eng. & Econ., Univ. of AL; **GRAD EDUC:** MA, 1974, Intl. Relations, Univ. of AR; PhD (ABO), 1977, Poli. Sci., PA State Univ.; **MIL SERV:** USAF; Capt., DFC, AM; **BUS ADD:** 3 Parkway, Ste. 1220, Philadelphia, PA 19102, (215)241-2134.

FRAZIER, Larry David——**B:** Dec. 26, 1931, Muskegon, MI, *Pres.*, The Frazier Company; **PRIM RE ACT:** Broker, Instructor, Syndicator, Consultant, Appraiser, Developer, Builder; **SERVICES:** General RE brokerage serv., appraisals; **PROFL AFFIL & HONORS:** NAR, MI Assn. of Realtors, GRI, RAM, CRB Multi Million Award; Million Award; Sr. Award; **EDUC:** BA, 1953, Acct. and Mktg., Davenport Coll.; **GRAD EDUC:** MA, 1967, RE, Univ. of MI; **EDUC HONORS:** Cum Laude; **MIL SERV:** US Army, M/Sgt., Bronze Star, Purple Heart; **HOME ADD:** 9800 Whitneyville, Caledonia, MI 49316, (616)891-8121; **BUS ADD:** 3226 28th SE, Grand Rapids, MI 49508, (616)942-8630.

FRAZIER, Thomas B., II——**B:** June 15, 1947, Minden, LA, *Project Coord.*, JCP Realty, Inc. (JC Penney Co., Inc., Devel. Div.); **PRIM RE ACT:** Developer, Owner/Investor, Property Manager; **SERVICES:** Devel. and ownership of major rgnl. shopping ctrs.; **PREV EMPLOY:** In-House Counsel for Michael Baker, Jr., Inc.; **PROFL AFFIL & HONORS:** ABA; MS State Bar Assn.; LA State Bar Assn.; **EDUC:** BSME, 1970, LA Tech. Univ.; **GRAD EDUC:** JD, 1974, Law, LA State Univ.; **EDUC HONORS:** Jr. and Sr. Class Pres.; **HOME ADD:** 103 Columbus Dr., Tenafly, NJ 07670, (201)568-1842; **BUS ADD:** 1301 Ave. of the Americas, NY, NY 10019, (212)957-5055.

FREDA, Edward M.——*Exec. VP*, People's Savings Bank - Bridgeport, Lending; **PRIM RE ACT:** Banker; **PROFL AFFIL & HONORS:** MAI; SRPA; Mort. Bankers Assn; **EDUC:** BS, Econ., Wharton School - Univ. of PA; **MIL SERV:** USAF, Capt.; **BUS ADD:** 899 Main St. PO Box 1580, Bridgeport, CT 06602, (203)579-7282.

FREDERICK, Paul S.——**B:** Oct. 2, 1945, Nashville, TN, *Sr. Sales Consultant*, Coldwell Banker Comml. RE Servs.; **PRIM RE ACT:** Broker; **PREV EMPLOY:** US Naval Intelligence Officer; **EDUC:** BS, 1967, Syracuse Univ.; **MIL SERV:** USN; Lt. Comdr.; **HOME ADD:** 1053 W. Sierra, Fresno, CA 93711, (209)439-5970; **BUS ADD:** 1510 E. Shaw 103, Fresno, CA 93710, (209)226-4321.

FREDERICKS, T. Douglas——**B:** Mar. 31, 1949, Detroit, MI, *VP*, Warmington Development, Inc., Investment Prop. Div.; **PRIM RE ACT:** Developer, Owner/Investor, Property Manager; **SERVICES:** Develop & purchase comml. prop.; **PROFL AFFIL & HONORS:** Intl. Council of Shopping Centers; BOMA; **EDUC:** BA, 1971, Communications, MI State Univ.; **OTHER ACT & HONORS:** Newport Harbor Yacht Club; Royal Ocean Racing Club; **HOME ADD:** 72 Sandpiper, Irvine, CA 92714; **BUS ADD:** 17100 Gillette Ave., Irvine, CA 92714, (714)557-5511.

FREDERKING, George H.——**B:** Apr. 26, 1929, Gibson City, IL, *Pres.*, Frederking & Associates; **PRIM RE ACT:** Consultant; **SERVICES:** Investment RE, mgr. housing, (all phases), nat. mktg. for bldg. products; **PREV EMPLOY:** VP and Gen. Mgr. W. G. Best Homes Co., Exec. VP - Sales Housing, The Klingbeil Co., Nat. Sales Mgr. Woodcarv Div. of Nutone Inc.; **PROFL AFFIL & HONORS:** NAHB, HMA, NKCA, Was selected to write the chap. on "prefabricated housing" in the "RE Encyclopedia" published by Prentice-Hall; **EDUC:** Attended Bradley Univ. for 2 years, also attended several service schools, personal library & have taken many RE & Business courses - I have also attended many seminars; **MIL SERV:** USAF, SSgt., Letter of Commendation for Leadership & hgh. grades; **HOME ADD:** 3417 Summer Set Way, Oceanside, CA 92054, (714)439-6903; **BUS ADD:** 3417 Summer Set Way, Oceanside, CA 92054, (714)439-6903.

FREDRICK, Arnold A.——**B:** Oct. 31, 1927, Strawberry Point, IA, *Sr. VP, Investments*, Lutheran Mutual Life; **PRIM RE ACT:** Appraiser, Lender, Owner/Investor; **SERVICES:** Mort. Loans & RE for Investment; **REP CLIENTS:** Various correspondents around the ctry.; **PROFL AFFIL & HONORS:** Iowa Chap. 34 Amer. Instit. of RE appraisers (Pres. 1976), MAI, CMB; **EDUC:** BS, 1953, Labor & Ind. Mgmt., Univ. of IA; **MIL SERV:** US Army, Sgt.; **HOME ADD:** 221 2nd St. SE, Waverly, IA 50677, (319)352-4070; **BUS ADD:** Heritage Way, Waverly, IA 50677, (319)352-4090.

FREE, Liston, Jr.——**B:** Apr. 30, 1941, Tuscaloose, AL, *VP*, Jackson, Co., Mort. Banker; **PRIM RE ACT:** Broker, Consultant, Appraiser, Lender; **SERVICES:** Mort. loans, equity, appraisal, consultation; **REP CLIENTS:** Inst. investors, indiv. synds.; **PROFL AFFIL & HONORS:** MBAA, Nat. & Local Bd. of Realtors; **EDUC:** BS, 1964, Banking, Univ. of AL; **MIL SERV:** US Army, Pvt.; **HOME ADD:** 6451 Old Shell Rd., Mobile, AL 36608, (205)344-5937; **BUS ADD:** 2970 Cottage Hill Rd., Suite 147, PO Box 16875, Mobile, AL 36616, (205)476-5516.

FREED, Donald E.——**B:** May 18, 1931, NYC, NY, *Architect*, Donald E. Freed - Architect; **PRIM RE ACT:** Architect; **SERVICES:** Complete arch. serv. including planning, supervision, interiors and design functions; **PREV EMPLOY:** Former partner Harry M. Prince & Assoc.; Private practice since 1957; **PROFL AFFIL & HONORS:** Pres., NY Soc. of Architects; Past Pres., Amer. Registered Architects; Amer. Arbitration Assn.; Fine Arts Fed.; NY Council of Architects, Serv. Award from Amer. Registered Architects; **EDUC:** B Arch., 1953, Arch., Syracuse Univ.; **MIL SERV:** US Army, Sgt.; **OTHER ACT & HONORS:** Former Commnr., Boy Scouts of Amer.; Past Pres., Edgemont E Club; Past Pres., Hartsdale Lawns Civic Assn.; **HOME TEL:** (914)723-7844; **BUS ADD:** 10 Fort Hill Ln., Scarsdale, NY 10583, (914)725-4063.

FREED, Eric R.——**B:** July 8, 1980, *Pres.*, Dera Corporation; **PRIM RE ACT:** Syndicator; **OTHER RE ACT:** Intl. Fin.; **PREV EMPLOY:** Grubbs & Ellis Comml. Investment Broker; **EDUC:** Williams Coll.; **GRAD EDUC:** Western State Univ., College of Law; **BUS ADD:** 4578 Vista De La Patria, Del Mar, CA 92014, (714)481-5213.

FREED, Kenneth L.——**B:** Apr. 26, 1942, Cambridge, MA, *Partner*, PF Devel. Co.; **PRIM RE ACT:** Consultant, Developer, Owner/Investor, Property Manager; **SERVICES:** RE investment analysis, devel.

planning; **REP CLIENTS:** Investors in comml. & resid. props.; **PREV EMPLOY:** Boston Redev. Auth., 1967-70; Housing Innovations, Inc., 1970-77; Beal Co., 1977-78; **EDUC:** AB, 1963, Phil., Harvard Coll.; **EDUC HONORS:** Cum Laude; **MIL SERV:** US Army Res., 1964-70; **HOME ADD:** 103 Beacon St., Boston, MA 02116, (617)267-2469; **BUS ADD:** 280 Summer St., Boston, MA 02210, (617)426-1879.

FREEDENBERG, Charles——**B:** Sept. 20, 1943, Chicago, IL, *Pres.*, Charles Freedenberg & Assoc., Inc.; **PRIM RE ACT:** Broker, Consultant, Instructor, Syndicator; **OTHER RE ACT:** RE Software Devel.; **SERVICES:** Comml. investment brokerage, appraisal, consulting, synd.; **REP CLIENTS:** Pension funds, pvt. clients; **PREV EMPLOY:** Former IRS Atty.; **PROFL AFFIL & HONORS:** Nat. Instructor CID Courses of Realtors Nat. Mktg. Inst., CCIM; **EDUC:** BS, 1967, Bus. Mktg., Univ. of IL, Urbana, IL; **GRAD EDUC:** JD, 1970, Law, The John Marshall Law Sch., Chicago, IL; **HOME ADD:** 4501 NE 55th St., Seattle, WA 98105, (206)525-9896; **BUS ADD:** 216 First Ave. S., Suite 320, Seattle, WA 98104, (206)587-0688.

FREEDMAN, Robert W.——**B:** Mar. 5, 1950, Philadelphia, PA, *Gen. Counsel*, Construction Consultants Company; **PRIM RE ACT:** Developer, Builder, Owner/Investor, Property Manager; **SERVICES:** Devel., construction and investment in RE; **PREV EMPLOY:** Cohen, Shapiro, Polisher, Shiekman & Cohen Attys. at Law, 1976-1978; **EDUC:** BS, 1972, Econ., Univ. of PA; **GRAD EDUC:** JD, 1975, Univ. of PA School of Law; **EDUC HONORS:** Grad. Cum Laude; **BUS ADD:** 1000 Maplewood Dr., Maple Shade, NJ 08052, (609)667-6810.

FREELAND, Barry——**B:** June 23, 1948, Sebastopol, CA, *Pres.*, Freeland/Fowles Assoc., Inc.; **PRIM RE ACT:** Broker, Consultant, Appraiser, Developer, Builder, Owner/Investor, Instructor, Property Manager, Syndicator; **PROFL AFFIL & HONORS:** Somona Cty. Bd. of Realtors/RE Mktg. Inst., CRS, Lifetime member Million Dollar Club; **EDUC:** BA/AA, 1970, Hist., Sonoma State, CA; **MIL SERV:** USMC, Cprl.; **OTHER ACT & HONORS:** Santa Rosa Lions Club; Dir. Sonoma Cty. Bd. of Realtors; **HOME ADD:** 325 Candlelight Dr., Santa Rosa, CA 95404, (707)542-7197; **BUS ADD:** 1418 4th St., Santa Rosa, CA 95404, (707)544-4343.

FREEMAN, Claire——*Dpty. Asst. Secy.*, Department of Housing and Urban Development, Program Policy Dev. & Evaluation; **PRIM RE ACT:** Lender; **BUS ADD:** 451 Seventh St., S.W., Washington, DC 20410, (202)755-6082.*

FREEMAN, Herbert L.——**B:** Dec. 12, 1946, Omaha, NE, *VP*, CBS Real Estate Co.; **PRIM RE ACT:** Broker, Broker in NE and IA; NAR; Realtor memb; **SERVICES:** Research & Devel. of new programs; controlling & forecasting, admin., implemented 100% commn. concept; **PREV EMPLOY:** Broker in NE and IA; **PROFL AFFIL & HONORS:** Served on the Citizens Adv. Bd. to the Central Bus. Dist. Task Forof the Omaha River Front Devel. Comm. Taught RE Principles and Practices for the Univ. of NE at O; **EDUC:** BS, 1965, Secondary Educ., Eng. and Hist., Univ. of NE at Omaha; **GRAD EDUC:** MBA, 1981, Univ. of NE; **EDUC HONORS:** Summa Cum Laude; **HOME ADD:** 15310 Jones Circle, Omaha, NE 68154, (402)333-4950; **BUS ADD:** 9202 West Dodge Rd., Suite 302, Omaha, NE 68114, (402)397-6222.

FREEMAN, James E.——*Owner*, Freeman & Associates, Realtors; **PRIM RE ACT:** Broker, Developer, Syndicator; **PROFL AFFIL & HONORS:** Nashville Assn. of Realtors; RNMI; TN Assn. of Realtors, CCIM; GRI; **EDUC:** Emory Univ.; **GRAD EDUC:** 1946, GA Tech.; **HOME ADD:** 5912 Sedberry Rd., Nashville, TN 37205, (615)352-5720; **BUS ADD:** 109 Fairfax Ave., Nashville, TN 37203, (615)383-3111.

FREEMAN, James P.——**B:** Apr. 1, 1952, Seattle, WA, *Pres.*, Associated Design-Construct, Inc.; **PRIM RE ACT:** Developer, Builder, Owner/Investor, Property Manager, Syndicator; **SERVICES:** Synd. services for pvt. indivs. into comml. RE projects that we devel./build/manage; **REP CLIENTS:** Pvt. indivs.; **PROFL AFFIL & HONORS:** Seattle C of C; **EDUC:** (Degree not received), 1975, Math, Univ. of CA, Berkeley; Univ. of WA; **EDUC HONORS:** U.C. Regents Scholar, 1971, U.W. Scholar 1973; Dean's List various quarters; **OTHER ACT & HONORS:** Adv. Bd. Seattle Housing Resources Group; Housing Issues Comm., Seattle C of C, Fremont Community Council; **HOME ADD:** 949 N. 35th St., #301, Seattle, WA 98103, (206)632-5895; **BUS ADD:** 449 N. 34th St., Seattle, WA 98103, (206)632-5662.

FREEMAN, Jeffrey Bruce——**B:** May 7, 1948, Newark, NJ, *Pres.*, Brian Scott Realty, Inc., Farm & Acreage Brokerage Firm; **PRIM RE ACT:** Broker; **SERVICES:** Broker, Large RE Trans. - Farms & Acreage; **REP CLIENTS:** Redi Plants, Inc.; Sir L's Packing Co.; Johnny Johnson Farms; Chappclaine Inv. N/V; United Telephone Serv.; United Parcel Serv.; So. Diesel Co.; William K. Carpenter; David Lee; **PREV EMPLOY:** Farm Acreage; **PROFL AFFIL & HONORS:** RE Broker; **HOME ADD:** 9220 SW 142nd St., Miami, FL 33176, (305)251-0900; **BUS ADD:** 9000 SW 87th Ct., Suite 215, Miami, FL 33176, (305)270-0200.

FREEMAN, Kemper——**B:** Apr. 10, 1910, Seattle, WA, *Gen. Partner*, Bellevue Properties, a limited partnership; **PRIM RE ACT:** Developer, Banker, Owner/Investor, Property Manager; **OTHER RE ACT:** Chmn. of Bd. and CEO, First Mutual Savings Bank; Partner, Auburn Props.; **PREV EMPLOY:** Mgr., Miller Freeman Publications; Pres., Olympic Shipbuilders; Pres., Seattle Helicopters; V.P., Concrete Conduit Co.; **EDUC:** Stanford Univ.; **OTHER ACT & HONORS:** Member WA State Planning Council 1940-46; Pres., Stanford Univ. Alumni Assn., 1959-60; **HOME ADD:** Bellevue, WA 98009PO Box 908; **BUS ADD:** PO Box 908, Bellevue, WA 98009, (206)454-2431.

FREEMAN, Leon L.——**B:** May 10, 1902, St. Louis, MO, *Chmn. of the Bd., CEO*, L.L. Freeman, Inc.; **PRIM RE ACT:** Broker, Consultant, Appraiser, Developer, Lender, Owner/Investor, Property Manager, Insuror, Syndicator; **PREV EMPLOY:** Founder of Org. in 1935; **PROFL AFFIL & HONORS:** NAR; Nat. Mort. Bankers Assn.; WI Mort. Bankers Assn.; Natl. Assn. of Ins. Agents; **EDUC:** BS, 1923, Econ., For. Affairs, Dartmouth Coll.; **GRAD EDUC:** 1933, Intl. Relations, Marquette Univ.; **MIL SERV:** USN, Lt. Cmdr., Pres. Citations; **OTHER ACT & HONORS:** Chmn. Racine Community Chest, 1948; Past Pres. Racine Art Assn.; Racine Royal Federalists; Past Member Build Amer. Better Comm.; Past Chmn. Urban Affairs Comm.; MBA; Milwaukee Univ. Club; **HOME ADD:** 1115 W. Green Tree Rd., Milwaukee, WI 53217, (414)351-4153; **BUS ADD:** 2829 Durand Ave., Racine, WI 53403, (414)554-6100.

FREEMAN, R. Carter, Jr.——**B:** Mar. 6, 1937, LaGrange, GA, *Pres.*, Freeman, Penrose & Associates, Inc.; **PRIM RE ACT:** Consultant, Syndicator; **SERVICES:** Mgmt. Consulting and Econ. Feasibility, Synd. Structuring and Funding; **PREV EMPLOY:** Touche Ross & Co., Pannell, Kerr, Fortser & Co.; **PROFL AFFIL & HONORS:** AICPA; HI, GA MT Soc. of CPA's; Nat. Assn. of Securities Dealers; Inst. of Mgmt. Cons., Intl. Assn of Fin. Planners, CPA, Cert. Mgmt. Consultant; **EDUC:** BBA, 1959, Bus. Admin., Emory Univ., Atlanta; **HOME ADD:** 235 Kulamanu Pl, Honolulu, HI 96816, (808)737-4320; **BUS ADD:** 745 Ft. St. Suite 1414, Honolulu, HI 96813, (808)524-5490.

FREEMAN, Roland D.——**B:** Oct. 12, 1941, Lynchburg, VA, *Sr. VP*, Amer. Republic Realty Corp.; **PRIM RE ACT:** Syndicator, Developer, Property Manager, Owner/Investor; **SERVICES:** Devel., Acquisition & Synd. of Investment RE; **REP CLIENTS:** Individuals; **PROFL AFFIL & HONORS:** IREM, RE Fin. Exec. Assn., Several Apt. Assn., CPM; RAM; CAM; Multihousing Leadership Award - 1978; **EDUC:** BS, 1964, Bus. Admin. - Econ., Carroll Coll., Waukesha, WI; **GRAD EDUC:** 1968, Bus., Marquette Univ.; **EDUC HONORS:** Top Teke Scholar, AKY Scholarship Award, Dean's List, Who's Who in Amer. Coll. and Univ.; **OTHER ACT & HONORS:** Officer of numerous local and nat. industry groups; Author of *Encyclopedia of Apt. Manager* and numerous articles; Frequent Speaker to Assns. and Conventions; Who's Who in Amer. Fin. and Industry; **HOME ADD:** 6508 Briarmeade Dr., Dallas, TX 75240, (214)233-2582; **BUS ADD:** 14841 Coit Rd., Suite 315, Dallas, TX 75248, (214)233-9064.

FREEMANN, John W.——**B:** Mar. 30, 1948, Bryn Mawr, PA, *VP, Fin.*, Pulte Home Corp., GA Div.; **PRIM RE ACT:** Developer, Builder; **SERVICES:** Single & MuLti Family Housing; **PREV EMPLOY:** Mfg.; **EDUC:** BBA, 1973, Business Admin., Roanoke Coll, Salem, VA; **GRAD EDUC:** MBA, 1974, Fin., Lehigh Univ., Bethlehem, PA; **EDUC HONORS:** Dean's List; **MIL SERV:** USN, PO3; **HOME ADD:** 11905 Fox Rd., Alpharetta, GA 30201; **BUS ADD:** 6675 Peachtree Industria Blvd., Atlanta, GA 30360.

FREER, L. Raymond, III——**B:** June 15, 1941, Pasadena, CA, *VP*, First Interstate Mortgage Co.; **PRIM RE ACT:** Appraiser; **SERVICES:** Appraisal serv. for comml./indus. prop. in conjunction with obtaining fin.; **PREV EMPLOY:** Coldwell, Banker and Co.; **PROFL AFFIL & HONORS:** AIREA, MAI; **EDUC:** BA, 1964, Econ., Univ. of So. CA; **MIL SERV:** U.S. Army, Non-comm. officer; **OTHER ACT & HONORS:** Bd. of Dir. of Pasadena Foothill Tennis Patrons Assn.; Bd. of Dir., Sierra Madres Girl Scout Council; Member, Econ. Devel. Council; Member, Pasadena C of C; **HOME ADD:** 4150 Cambridge Rd., Flintridge, CA 91011, (213)790-4720; **BUS ADD:** 245 S. Los Robles Ave., Pasadena, CA 91109, (213)356-7612.

FREI, Michael C.——**B:** Apr. 4, 1946, Salt Lake City, UT, *Partner*, Snow, Christensen & Martineau; **PRIM RE ACT:** Attorney; **SERVICES:** Complex RE Devel., Shopping Ctrs., Rgnl. Malls, Office and Condo. mixed use Devel., fin. of RE; **REP CLIENTS:** Price Devel. Co.,

Busch Devel. Inc., Cottonwood Mall Co., Christiansen Brothers Construction; **PREV EMPLOY:** Asst. General Counsel, Arbertsons Inc. Boise, ID (Maj. Grocery Chain-NYSE); Gen. Counsel, Price Devel. Co. Salt Lake City, UT (Maj. RE Devel.-Intermountain West); **PROFL AFFIL & HONORS:** ABA, CA Bar Assn., UT Bar Assn., Order of the Coif; **EDUC:** 1965,1968,, Math, Humanities, Univ. of UT; **GRAD EDUC:** 1971, Law, Univ. of UT, Coll. of Law; **EDUC HONORS:** Honors Program, Asst. Editor, UT Law Review; **MIL SERV:** US Army Res.; **HOME ADD:** 4962 Stanford Ln., Salt Lake City, UT 84117, (801)278-8787; **BUS ADD:** 10 Exchange Place, Eleventh Floor, PO Box 3000, Salt Lake City, UT 84110, (801)521-9000.

FREILICH, Samuel C.——B: Jan. 2, 1934, Cleveland, OH, *VP*, Ring Brothers Corp.; **PRIM RE ACT:** Developer; **SERVICES:** Devel. of comml. & resid. RE; **PREV EMPLOY:** Del E. Webb Corp. - Mgr. Comml. RE Div.; **EDUC:** BS, 1956, Mktg., Miami Univ.; **HOME ADD:** 3715 Dixie Lyn Ave., Sherman Oaks, CA 91423, (213)783-7166; **BUS ADD:** 501 Santa Monica Blvd., 7th Floor, Santa Monica, CA 90401, (213)393-7276.

FREIMOR, Jack——B: Dec. 4, 1931, New York, New York, *Asst. VP*, Citicorp Real Estate, Inc.; **PRIM RE ACT:** Architect, Lender; **SERVICES:** Mgr. technical services for construction lending; **PREV EMPLOY:** Hy Blueweiss Consultants, Inc., 1966-1974; **PROFL AFFIL & HONORS:** The Construction Specifications Inst.; **EDUC:** BArch., 1960, Design and Urban Planning, Pratt Inst., Brooklyn, NY; **MIL SERV:** US Army, Cpl., Good conduct; **HOME ADD:** 13740 S.W. 82 Court, Miami, FL 33158, (305)235-0753; **BUS ADD:** Miami, FL 33131One Southeast Third Ave., (305)377-4384.

FREMGEN, William H.——B: Mar. 17, 1932, Chicago, IL, *VP*, Talman Home Federal Savings & Loans Assn. of IL, Special Lending; **PRIM RE ACT:** Attorney, Developer, Lender; **SERVICES:** Mort. & consumer lending; **PREV EMPLOY:** Chicago Title & Trust Co.; **PROFL AFFIL & HONORS:** Home Builders Assn. of Greater Chicagoland (Dir.), IL Mort. Bankers Assn.; **EDUC:** BA, 1954, Econ., St. Josephs Coll. of IN; **GRAD EDUC:** JD, 1960, Loyola Univ. of Chicago; **MIL SERV:** US Army, PFC; **HOME ADD:** 240 Hampton Ct., Palatine, IL 60067, (312)991-0631; **BUS ADD:** 201 S. State St., Chicago, IL 60604, (312)922-9600.

FRENCH, Alfred G., II——B: April 21, 1951, Belton, TX, *Architect*, McCarthy Mgmt. & Devel. Co.; **PRIM RE ACT:** Architect, Developer; **SERVICES:** Design and devel. of comml. props.; **PREV EMPLOY:** Construction Management West, Inc., 1978-1980; Sherwood & Roberts Real Estate 1977-1978; **PROFL AFFIL & HONORS:** Amer. Instit. of Arch., Spokane Bd. of Realtors; **EDUC:** B Arch., 1977, Architecture-Business, Univ. of ID; **EDUC HONORS:** Alpha Rho Chi, Phi Kappa Phi, Outstanding Student, 1975, 1976, 1977; **MIL SERV:** US Marines, Sgt. E-5; **HOME ADD:** East 124 Walton, Spokane, WA 99207, (509)487-7137; **BUS ADD:** 217 Northtown Office Bldg., N. 4407 Div., Spokane, WA 99207.

FRENCH, Hans T.——B: Nov. 18, 1932, Chicago, IL, *Pres.*, P.R. Duke Realty Corp.; **PRIM RE ACT:** Broker, Developer; **SERVICES:** Devel. & leasing of shopping centers; **PREV EMPLOY:** F.C. Tucker, Co., Inc. 1973-1979; L.S. Ayres & Co. 1963-1973; **PROFL AFFIL & HONORS:** Intl. Council of Shopping Centers; Nat. Assn. of Corporate RE Execs. (founding member); **EDUC:** BA, 1961, Social Studies, OH State Univ.; **EDUC HONORS:** Cum Laude; **MIL SERV:** USAF; **HOME ADD:** PO Box 291, Zionsville, IN 46077, (317)873-5336; **BUS ADD:** 8900 Keystone Crossing, Suite 1122, Indianapolis, IN 46240, (317)846-4700.

FRENCH, Taylor N.——B: Apr. 26, 1939, Brownsville, TN, *Realtor*, French & Co.; **PRIM RE ACT:** Broker; **SERVICES:** Brokerage; **PREV EMPLOY:** VP, First TN Bank; **PROFL AFFIL & HONORS:** Memphis Bd. of Realtors, TN. Assn. of Realtors, NAR, GRI, CRS, CRB; **EDUC:** BA, 1962, Eng., Univ. of OK; **GRAD EDUC:** JD, 1965, Law, Memphis State Univ.; **OTHER ACT & HONORS:** Kiwanis Intl., Univ. Club of Memphis, Memphis City Beautiful Comm.; **HOME ADD:** 424 Goodland Circle, Memphis, TN 38111, (901)458-9622; **BUS ADD:** 5159 Wheelis, Suite 108, Memphis, TN 38117, (901)767-0020.

FRENKIL, Leonard I.——B: Feb. 2, 1938, Baltimore, MD, *Pres.*, Development & Construction Co., Inc.; **PRIM RE ACT:** Broker, Owner/Investor, Developer, Builder, Syndicator; **PREV EMPLOY:** Chief Exec. Officer - Kone Lotus Corp., devel. of resort props.; **PROFL AFFIL & HONORS:** Greater Baltimore Bd. of Realtors, The Engineering Soc. of Baltimore, Soc. of Mil Engrs., Johns Hopkins Ctr. for Metropolitan Planning and Research, Broker, Certificate of Recognition, Baltimore Afro American; **EDUC:** Pre-Law, Johns Hopkins Univ.; **GRAD EDUC:** LLB, 1968, Law, Mount Vernon Law School; JD, 1970, Law, Univ. of Baltimore; **OTHER ACT & HONORS:** Commnr. MD Health & Higher Educ. Facilities Auth.; Chmn., Baltimore County State Central Comm., Second District; Boy Scouts of Amer.; The Hopkins Club; Merchants Club; Advertising Club; Bd. of Dir., Linwood Children's Ctr.; Selected by State Dept. as Part of a Team to Inspect Progress Being Made Under Marshall Plan; former Justice of Peace; Bd. of Dirs., North Charles General Hosp.; Also affiliated w/Kone Lotus Corp., Victor Devel. Co.; **HOME ADD:** Fleetwood Farms, 9245 Dolfield Rd., Owings Mills, MD 21117, (301)363-0995; **BUS ADD:** 1 E. Chase Street, Baltimore, MD 21202, (301)539-0320.

FRESHMAN, Samuel K.——B: Sept. 8, 1932, Pottstown, PA, *Sr. Part.*, Freshman, Mulvaney, Marantz, Comsky, Forst, Kahan & Deutsch; **PRIM RE ACT:** Broker, Attorney, Syndicator, Developer, Property Manager, Owner/Investor, Real Estate Publisher; **PREV EMPLOY:** Adjunct prof. of RE at USC Grad School of Fin. (1977-79), Chmn. Bd. of Trans-State Title Co., & Bank of LA Advisory Dir. of Banco Popular de Peurto Rico & Amer. City Bank; **PROFL AFFIL & HONORS:** Beverly Hills Bar Assn., ABA, LABA, RESSI, Amer. Right of Way, LA Realty Bd.; **EDUC:** BA, 1954, Pre Law, Stanford Univ.; **GRAD EDUC:** JD, 1956, RE, Stanford Law School; **EDUC HONORS:** Phi Sigma Alpha, Alpha Delta Sigma, Phi Alpha Delta; **HOME ADD:** 29119 Cliffside Dr., Malibu, CA 90265, (213)457-9703; **BUS ADD:** 9100 Wilshire Blvd., 8th fl., E Tower, Beverly Hills, CA 90212, (213)273-1870.

FREUND, Fredric S.——*Pres.*, Hanford-Freund & Co.; **PRIM RE ACT:** Broker, Consultant, Property Manager; **SERVICES:** Spec. in comml. and retail investment props. and coops and condos. and rental apts.; **PROFL AFFIL & HONORS:** Pres. Hanford Freund & Co., San Francisco RE Brokers & Mgrs; San Francisco Bd. of Realtors, Pres, 1974 & 1975; Dir. CA Assn. of Realtors 1967 through 1977; NAR, Lambda Alpha, Hon. Land Econ. Frat.; BOMA of San Francisco, San Francisco C of C; Better Bus. Bur. of San Francisco; RNMI; IREM; Amer. Soc. of RE Counselors, 1975 Realtor of the Year as awarded by the San Francisco Bd. of Realtors; Inst. in RE Mgmt. Univ. of CA Ext.; Guest Lecturer on RE Investments, Stanford Univ. Sch. of Bus. Admin.; **EDUC:** Brown Univ., Providence, RI; **OTHER ACT & HONORS:** Dir. of United Fed. S&L Assn., San Francisco, CA; **BUS ADD:** 47 Kearny St., San Francisco, CA 94108, (415)981-5780.

FREW, William J., Jr.——B: Aug. 10, 1945, NYC; **PRIM RE ACT:** Attorney; **PROFL AFFIL & HONORS:** NYS, Richmond Cty. Bar Assns., ABA, SI Trial Lawyers Assn.; **EDUC:** Grad. Degree, 1967, Bio-Chem., Univ. of Dayton; **GRAD EDUC:** MBA,, Investments & Fin., Brooklyn Law School; **OTHER ACT & HONORS:** SI Rotary Club, Legal Council & Bd. Member of SI Amer. Red Cross & Meals on Wheels of SI, Inc.; Tr. & Treas. of SI Zoological Soc., Dir SI Chap. Amer. Cancer Soc.; **HOME ADD:** 34B Seth Ct., SI, NY 10301, (212)273-6354; **BUS ADD:** P.O. Box 179, Staten Island, NY 10314, (212)447-8300.

FREY, Bruce J.——B: Apr. 11, 1941, Chicago, IL, *Chmn. of the Bd., CEO*, Downs, Mohl & Co.; **PRIM RE ACT:** Broker, Syndicator, Consultant, Developer, Property Manager, Owner/Investor, Insuror; **OTHER RE ACT:** Condominium conversion; **SERVICES:** r.e. prop. mgmt., condominium conversion, synd.; **PREV EMPLOY:** V.P. McKey and Poague; **PROFL AFFIL & HONORS:** IREM; Chicago RE Board, Accredited mgmt., IREM, CPM; **EDUC:** BA, 1962, Bus., Guilford Coll., Greensboro, NC; **MIL SERV:** USMC, Lt.; **OTHER ACT & HONORS:** Board of Directors, Mt. Sinai Hospital; **BUS ADD:** One N. LaSalle St., Ste. 2900, Chicago, IL 60602, (312)236-3806.

FREY, Robert E., Jr.——B: Mar. 26, 1944, Evanston, IL, *Cert. Fin. Planner*, KMS Fin. Services, Inc.; **PRIM RE ACT:** Broker, Instructor, Syndicator, Consultant, Owner/Investor, Real Estate Publisher; **SERVICES:** Complete Fin. Planning, Instr. of Securities & Synd. Courses; Mktg. of RE and other direct participation program securities; **PREV EMPLOY:** Realty Specialist, Corps. of Engineers, owner-broker of RE firm; **PROFL AFFIL & HONORS:** RESSI, Life Member Intl. Assn. of Fin. Planners, Past Pres. Wash. Assn. of Fin. Planners, Inc., Seattle C of C; President's Club; GRI; **EDUC:** BS, 1965, Chem., IL Inst. of Tech.; **GRAD EDUC:** MS, 1967, Chem., Univ. of WA; **EDUC HONORS:** Phi Eta Sigma Natl. Hon. Frat.; **OTHER ACT & HONORS:** Bd. of Dir. Washington Feminist Fed. Credit Union; **HOME ADD:** 7331 Dibble Ave. NW, Seattle, WA 98117, (206)783-7105; **BUS ADD:** 1125 Denny Bldg., Seattle, WA 98121, (206)623-2885.

FRIBERG, Emil E.——B: Apr. 11, 1935, Wichita Falls, TX, *Pres.*, Friberg, Alexander, Maloney, Gipson, Weir Inc.; **PRIM RE ACT:** Engineer, Owner/Investor; **SERVICES:** Engr. design for new and existing bldg., energy conservation; **REP CLIENTS:** Esco Elevators,

Inc. Ft. Worth; C.W. Rogers Co., Ft. Worth; The Univ. of TX System, Austin, TX; **PROFL AFFIL & HONORS:** Amer. Soc. Heating, Refrigerating & Air Conditioning Engr., Amer. Soc. Mechanical Engrs., TX & Nat. Soc. of Profl. Engrs., Amer. Consulting Engrs. Council, Profl. Engr.; **EDUC:** BS, 1958, Mechanical Engr., Univ. of TX; **MIL SERV:** US Army Corps of Engineers, 1st Lt.; **OTHER ACT & HONORS:** Rotary Club of Fort Worth, Fort Worth Club, Who's Who in S. & S.W., Engr.; **HOME ADD:** 3406 Woodford Dr., Arlington, TX 76013, (817)265-4497; **BUS ADD:** 206 E. 8th St., Fort Worth, TX 76102, (817)336-0543.

FRIDAY, Victor——B: Feb. 20, 1918, MI, *Owner*, Horizon Hills; **PRIM RE ACT:** Developer; **SERVICES:** Devel. resid. lots; **PREV EMPLOY:** Self employed; **EDUC:** BS, 1946, MI State Univ.; **EDUC HONORS:** Alpha Zeta; **OTHER ACT & HONORS:** Past Dist. Gov. Lions Intl.; **HOME ADD:** PO Box 157-6500 Carmody Rd., Coloma, MI 49038, (616)468-6360; **BUS ADD:** PO Box 157, Coloma, MI 49038, (616)946-9008.

FRIED, Martin L.——B: Feb. 11, 1934, Brooklyn, NY, *Assoc. Dean & Prof. of Law*, Syracuse Univ. Coll. of Law; **PRIM RE ACT:** Instructor; **SERVICES:** Classroom instr.; **PROFL AFFIL & HONORS:** ABA, NY State Bar Assoc., Onondago Cty. Bar Assoc.; **EDUC:** BA, 1955, Econ., Antioch Coll.; **GRAD EDUC:** LLB, 1958, Columbia Law School; LLM, 1968, NY Univ. School of Law; **EDUC HONORS:** Harlan Fiske Stone Scholar; **MIL SERV:** USAFR, Sgt.; **HOME ADD:** 102 Woodside Dr., Syracuse, NY 13224, (315)446-0130; **BUS ADD:** Ernest I. White Hall, Syracuse, NY 13210, (315)423-2392.

FRIEDLAN, Larry D.——B: May 24, 1947, Furth, Germany, *Pres.*, The Merriam Co., Inc.; **PRIM RE ACT:** Broker, Consultant, Developer, Owner/Investor, Property Manager; **SERVICES:** Selling improved lots, maintaining rds. for 425 residences and 3,000 prop. owners. Also do condo, devel. of comml. & resid. props.; **REP CLIENTS:** Indiv. lenders & instnl. investors in comml. props., and published book; **PREV EMPLOY:** Self employed as RE broker in MO & OK, with ownership in sev. comml. resort, and resid. condo projects. Also do consulting for feasibility of converting existing units into condos; **PROFL AFFIL & HONORS:** Nat. Apt. Assn., (Founder of Springfield Apt. Assn.); Inst. of Bus. Appraisers of Amer.; **EDUC:** BS, 1971, Econ., Cbem., Phys. Sci., Kearney State Coll., Kearney, NE; **OTHER ACT & HONORS:** C of C; **HOME ADD:** Skyline Hills, Forsyth, MO 65653, (417)546-6214; **BUS ADD:** Rockaway Beach, MO 65740, (417)561-4142.

FRIEDLAND, Richard, CPM——B: Nov. 26, 1924, Indianapolis, IN, *Pres.*, The Heritage Grp; **PRIM RE ACT:** Broker, Syndicator, Property Manager, Owner/Investor; **SERVICES:** Specializing in the acquiring, synd., and mgmt. of turnaround apts., comml. and off. prop.; **REP CLIENTS:** fin. planners; **PREV EMPLOY:** Mgr. acquiring dept., Property Research Corp., Exec. V.P. Wilson Const. and Dev. Corp., Gen. Part., Burton Smith, Friedland and Assoc.; **PROFL AFFIL & HONORS:** RESSI, IREM, State Chmn. Synd. Div. of CA Assoc. of Realtors; **EDUC:** BA, 1948, Gen. Bus., IN Univ.; **MIL SERV:** US Army Med. Dept., Sgt., Pacific Theatre; **HOME ADD:** 3301 Club Dr., Los Angeles, CA 90064, (213)836-2800; **BUS ADD:** 8701 Wilshire Blvd., Beverly Hills, CA 90211, (213)659-1620.

FRIEDMAN, Abraham P.——B: July 24, 1930, New Orleans, LA, *Atty.*, Dow Cogburn & Friedman; **PRIM RE ACT:** Attorney; **REP CLIENTS:** Continental IL Nat. Bank, Treptow Murphree Co., Republicbank- Spring Branch, MacGregor Park Nat. Bank, Brookhollow Nat. Bank, Systech Props., USA Props. Fund, Ltd.; **PROFL AFFIL & HONORS:** Amer, TX, LA & Houston Bar Assns., Lecturer TX State Bar Seminars, RE; **EDUC:** BBA, 1951, Acctg., Tulane Univ.; **GRAD EDUC:** JD, 1956, Tulane Coll. of Law; **MIL SERV:** US Army, Maj., 1952-54, Bronze Star; **HOME ADD:** 5118 Braesheather, Houston, TX 77096, (713)723-9720; **BUS ADD:** 9 Greenway Plaza, Suite 2300, Houston, TX 77046, (713)626-5870.

FRIEDMAN, B.——*Ed.*, Western Real Estate News & Investor; **PRIM RE ACT:** Real Estate Publisher; **BUS ADD:** 1335 S. Flower, Los Angeles, CA 90015, (213)749-0151.*

FRIEDMAN, Brian K.——B: Dec. 3, 1953, Richland, WA, *Pres.*, Assoc. Prop.; **PRIM RE ACT:** Broker, Consultant, Owner/Investor, Property Manager, Syndicator; **OTHER RE ACT:** Comml. Invest.; **SERVICES:** Investment counseling, devel. of limited partnerships, profl. asset mgmt., leasing, condo. convers.; **REP CLIENTS:** Indiv., partnership & inst. investors in income producing prop.; **PROFL AFFIL & HONORS:** IREM of Nat. Bd. of Realtors; Camden Cty. Bd. of Realtors; IREM, DE Valley Chap., CPM, Realtor; **EDUC:** BS, 1975, Bus. & RE, Monmouth Coll.; **OTHER ACT & HONORS:** C of C; Apt. Owners Assn.; **HOME ADD:** 707 Kings Croft, Cherry Hill, NJ 08034, (609)667-6698; **BUS ADD:** Suite 514, One Cherry Hill, Cherry Hill, NJ 08002, (609)667-4116.

FRIEDMAN, Burt——*Director, Real Estate*, AM International; **PRIM RE ACT:** Property Manager; **BUS ADD:** 130 E. Randolph St., Chicago, IL 60602, (312)565-2800.*

FRIEDMAN, David A.——B: June 26, 1937, NJ, *Pres.*, Interstate Realty, Inc.; **PRIM RE ACT:** Broker, Developer, Owner/Investor; **SERVICES:** Income producing RE investments nationwide; **REP CLIENTS:** Pension funds, overseas investors, indiv., inst., synd.; **PREV EMPLOY:** General Electric Co., RE Dept.; Xerox Corp.; Mgr. of RE; **PROFL AFFIL & HONORS:** Soc. of RE Mgrs.; IREM; NY RE Bd.; **EDUC:** 1959, Geology; **MIL SERV:** US Army; **HOME ADD:** 165 E. 72nd St., New York, NY 10021; **BUS ADD:** Suite 1006, 50 Rockefeller Plaza, New York, NY 10020, (212)752-6020.

FRIEDMAN, Edward A.——B: Mar. 24, 1948, Bellefonte, PA, *Owner*, Appraisal Assoc.; **PRIM RE ACT:** Broker, Attorney, Syndicator, Appraiser, Developer; **SERVICES:** Legal, re consulting, appraising, brokerage; **REP CLIENTS:** Corp., lenders, attys.; **PROFL AFFIL & HONORS:** Centre Co. Bd. of Realtors, PA Assn. of Realtors, Realtors Natl. Mktg. Inst., IREM, SREA, AIREA; County Bar Assn., PA Bar Assn., ABA, CPM, CCIM, SRPA, MAI, MBA, JD; **EDUC:** BS, 1970, Bus. RE, OH State; **GRAD EDUC:** MBA, 1975, R.E., SFO State Univ.; **EDUC HONORS:** Deans List, Phi Eta Sigma; **OTHER ACT & HONORS:** RE Instr., PA State Univ.; **HOME ADD:** 743 W. Hamilton Ave., State College, PA 16801, (814)234-2225; **BUS ADD:** P.O. Box 798, 248 Calder, State College, PA 16801, (814)234-6004.

FRIEDMAN, Jack P.——B: Mar. 13, 1945, Chester, PA, *Head of Research Div.*, TX RE Research Ctr.; **PRIM RE ACT:** Consultant, Instructor; **SERVICES:** Teaching, income prop. analysis; **REP CLIENTS:** US Justice Dept.; LA Bd/ of Regents; TX Assn. of Realtors; **PREV EMPLOY:** CPA, 1967-71; **PROFL AFFIL & HONORS:** AICPA's; AREVEA; SRPA, CPA, Broker; **EDUC:** BBA, 1966, Fin., Wake Forest Univ.; **GRAD EDUC:** PhD, 1975, RE, GA State Univ.; MBA, Acctg., Pace; **OTHER ACT & HONORS:** Author of sev. RE texts and journal articles; **HOME ADD:** 1709 Todd Trail, College Station, TX 77840, (713)696-0737; **BUS ADD:** TX A&M Univ., College Sta, TX 77843, (713)845-2078.

FRIEDMAN, Joseph N.——B: Sept. 5, 1931, New York, NY, *VP and Chief Underwriting Counsel - Natl. Accts.*, First Amer. Title Ins. Co.; **PRIM RE ACT:** Attorney, Insuror; **SERVICES:** Title commitments and title ins.; **REP CLIENTS:** Lenders, devel., purchasers of real prop.; **PREV EMPLOY:** Attys. Abstract Inc., 1966-1973; Schwartz, Friedman, Schwartz & Friedman, 1966-1973; law firm representing L.I. City S&L Assn., 1959-1966; **PROFL AFFIL & HONORS:** Amer., NY, and Queens Bar Assns.; Amer., NY, PA & New England Land Title Assns.; **EDUC:** 1949, NYU; 1952, Wesleyan Univ.; **GRAD EDUC:** LLB, 1958, NY Law School; **EDUC HONORS:** Cum Laude; **MIL SERV:** US Army, Cpl., European Theatre, Marksmanship, Good Conduct; **OTHER ACT & HONORS:** Tr., Richmond Hill Savings Bank; Neponsit Prop. Owners Assn.; Temple Bethel of Rockaway Park; Formerly Chmn., Local Draft Bd. 67; Tr., Peninsula Hospital Ctr.; **HOME ADD:** 139 Beach 147 St., Neponsit, NY 11694, (212)634-8970; **BUS ADD:** 170 Broadway, New York, NY 10038, (800)221-7965.

FRIEDMAN, Milton R.——B: Jan. 16, 1940, Hartford, CT, *Owner*; **PRIM RE ACT:** Attorney; **PREV EMPLOY:** Taylor, Blanc, Capron & Marsh, Amer. Law Inst. Lecturer; **PROFL AFFIL & HONORS:** ABA, Assn. of the Bar of City of NY; Amer. Coll. of RE Lawyers; **EDUC:** BA, Yale; **GRAD EDUC:** LLB, Law, Yale; **OTHER ACT & HONORS:** Various books and publications dealing with RE law, organized Practicing Law Inst. Panel on Commer. RE Leases; **HOME TEL:** (212)787-0028; **BUS ADD:** 115 W. 73rd St., NY, NY 10023, (212)787-0028.

FRIEDMAN, Penny——*Dir. Prop. Dev.*, Taft Broadcasting Co.; **PRIM RE ACT:** Property Manager; **BUS ADD:** 1718 Young st., Cincinnati, OH 45210, (513)721-1414.*

FRIEDMAN, Richard L.——B: Dec. 6, 1940, Cambridge, MA, *Pres.*, Carpenter & Co. Inc.; **PRIM RE ACT:** Broker, Developer, Consultant, **PROFL AFFIL & HONORS:** IREM, RE Bd., C of C, ICSC, CPM; **EDUC:** BA, 1963, Philosophy, Dartmouth Coll.; **MIL SERV:** US Army; Lt.; **OTHER ACT & HONORS:** Numerous Bd. of Dirs. and Trusteeships; **HOME ADD:** 22 Wellesley St., Weston, MA 02193, (617)899-8822; **BUS ADD:** 175 Federal St., Boston, MA 02110, (617)542-7506.

FRIEDMAN, Richard S.——B: Apr. 19, 1944, Milwaukee, WI, *Atty.*, Rifkind & Sterling Inc., RE; **PRIM RE ACT:** Attorney; **SERVICES:** Legal services in acquisition, devel., fin., synd. of comml. props.; **REP CLIENTS:** Devel., underwriters/investment bankers, lenders, retail chains; **PREV EMPLOY:** Sr. VP & Gen. Counsel, Shopping Ctr. Devel. Co. 1972-74; Assoc. at Loeb & Loeb 1970-72; **PROFL AFFIL & HONORS:** CA, Los Angeles, Beverly Hills & IL Bar Assns.; Intl. Council of Shopping Ctrs.; **EDUC:** BA, 1965, Pol. Sci. & Econ., Univ. of IL; **GRAD EDUC:** JD, 1968, Univ. of IL, Coll. of Law; **MIL SERV:** US Army 1968-69, 1st. Lt., Army Commendation Medal; **BUS ADD:** 9454 Wilshire Blvd., 6th Fl., Beverly Hills, CA 90212, (213)278-0970.

FRIEDMAN, Robert B.——B: July 29, 1935, Trenton, NJ, *Exec. VP*, First City Properties; **PRIM RE ACT:** Developer, Property Manager; **OTHER RE ACT:** Condo. convertor; **SERVICES:** Devel., prop. mgr., work out specialist; **REP CLIENTS:** Land owners, lenders, inst. investors; **PREV EMPLOY:** Pres., Carl M. Freeman Assoc., Silver Spring, MD; **PROFL AFFIL & HONORS:** Nat. Assn. of Home Builders; **EDUC:** 1957, Civil Engrg., Princeton Univ.; **GRAD EDUC:** MBA, 1965, RE/Fin., Amer. Univ.; **MIL SERV:** USN, Lt., Civil Eng. Corps; **HOME ADD:** 16401 Tudor Dr., Encino, CA 91316, (213)906-2066; **BUS ADD:** 9171 Wilshire Blvd., Beverly Hills, CA 90211, (213)274-5553.

FRIEDMAN, Robert N.——Friedman-Fogel Inc.; **PRIM RE ACT:** Developer; **BUS ADD:** 1515 Winters Bank Tower, Dayton, OH 45402, (513)228-1101.*

FRIEDMAN, Robert P.——B: Sept. 21, 1952, Los Angeles, CA, *Assoc.*, Dreisen, Kassay & Freiberg; **PRIM RE ACT:** Attorney; **PROFL AFFIL & HONORS:** State Bar of CA; **EDUC:** AB, 1975, History, Univ. of CA,Berkeley; **GRAD EDUC:** JD, 1978, Law, Georgetown Univ. Law Ctr.; **EDUC HONORS:** Cum Laude; **HOME ADD:** 1914 Corinth Ave. #111, Los Angeles, CA 90025, (213)478-7432; **BUS ADD:** 1801 Century Park East, Suite 740,, Los Angeles, CA 90067, (213)277-2171.

FRIEDMAN, Stanford J.——B: June 27, 1927, Cleveland, OH, *Pres.*, The Solar Group Inc.; **PRIM RE ACT:** Developer; **SERVICES:** Devel. of comml. prop.; **EDUC:** BS, 1949, Mech. Engrg. & Indus. Engrg., Univ. of MI; **OTHER ACT & HONORS:** City of Cleveland Advisory Comm., Port Auth.; **HOME ADD:** 5200 Three Village Dr., Lyndhurst, OH 44124, (216)449-0668; **BUS ADD:** 1210 E. 55t St., Cleveland, OH 44103, (216)431-9000.

FRIEDMAN, Stephen B.——B: Dec. 17, 1945, Philadelphia, PA, *Deputy Dir., RE Consulting Grp.*, Laventhol & Horwath; **PRIM RE ACT:** Consultant; **SERVICES:** Mkt. & fin. analysis; devel. programs; urban revitalization programs; **REP CLIENTS:** devels., local govt.; **PREV EMPLOY:** RE Research Corp.; APA; WI State Planning Office; **PROFL AFFIL & HONORS:** APA; Metropolitan Housing and Planning Council (Chicago), AICP; **EDUC:** BA, 1968, Urban & Comm. Studies, Goddard Coll.; **GRAD EDUC:** MS, 1971, Urban & Regional Planning, Univ. of WI; **HOME ADD:** 2014 N. Clifton Ave., Chicago, IL 60614, (312)871-7697; **BUS ADD:** 111 E. Wacker Dr., Chicago, IL 60601, (312)644-4570.

FRIGON, William——*Fac. Manager*, Avgat, Inc.; **PRIM RE ACT:** Property Manager; **BUS ADD:** 33 Perry Avenue, PO 799, Attleboro, MA 02703, (617)222-2202.*

FRILLMAN, Louis W.——B: Oct. 30, 1952, Chicago, IL, *VP*, Robert Boblett Assoc., Inc., RE Appraisal Servs.; **PRIM RE ACT:** Broker, Consultant, Appraiser, Property Manager; **OTHER RE ACT:** RE devel., counseling & mgmt. servs.; **SERVICES:** RE counseling and appraisals for lenders, investors, devels., govt. agencies, and others; **REP CLIENTS:** Union Oil Co. of CA, Honeywell, Inc., 3M, First Nat. Bank of St. Paul, Northwestern Nat. Bank of Minneapolis; **PROFL AFFIL & HONORS:** AIREA, Nat. Assn. of Indus. & Office Parks, ULI, Nat. Assn. of Corp. RE Execs., MAI; **EDUC:** BBA, 1973, Fin., Coll. of St. Thomas; **HOME ADD:** 18632 Taconite Tr., Eagan, MN 55122, (612)452-2843; **BUS ADD:** 1007 First Bank Place, W., Minneapolis, MN 55402, (612)333-6515.

FRISSELL, Robert N.——B: Feb. 2, 1918, Thief River Falls, MN, *Pres.*, The Frissell Co., Inc.; **PRIM RE ACT:** Broker, Consultant, Appraiser, Developer, Owner/Investor; **SERVICES:** Brokerage, consulting, appraisals; **PROFL AFFIL & HONORS:** AIREA; MAI; Soc. of RE Appraisers; CRA; Nat. Assn. of RE Bds.; **EDUC:** BS, 1947, Econ./Pol. Sci., Univ. of ND; **MIL SERV:** USAF, Lt. Col. Retd., several medals; **OTHER ACT & HONORS:** Elks; Amer. Legion; Shrine.; Retired Officers Assn.; **HOME ADD:** 1433 S. 19th St., Fargo, ND 58103, (701)237-5160; **BUS ADD:** 1330 Gateway Dr., Box 1821, Fargo, ND 58107, (701)235-1189.

FRITSCHE, Ernest G.——B: Westerville, OH, *Pres.*, The Fritsche Corp.; **PRIM RE ACT:** Broker, Developer, Builder, Owner/Investor, Property Manager; **REP CLIENTS:** J.C. Penney Co.; Federated Dept. Stores Inc.; York Steak Systems Inc.; Banc Ohio Corp.; Huntington Nat. Bank; Flickinger Corp.; Exxon Corp.; SOHIO; Marathon Oil Co.; **PROFL AFFIL & HONORS:** Pres., Columbus Home Builders Assn.; Pres., Assoc. Builders of Columbus; Trustee, Columbus RE Bd.; Pres., OH Home Builders Assn.; NAHB; **EDUC:** Otterbein Coll., Franklin Univ.; **MIL SERV:** US Army; Lt. Col.; **BUS ADD:** 6245 Sunderland Dr., Columbus, OH 43229, (614)436-5995.

FROELICH, Cezar M.——B: Jan. 1, 1946, Deutschkrone, Germany, *VP*, Shefsky, Saitlin & Froelich, Ltd.; **PRIM RE ACT:** Attorney; **EDUC:** 1964-1967, Loyola of Chicago; **HOME ADD:** 19 Meadowood Ln., Northfield, IL 60093, (312)729-0091; **BUS ADD:** 444 N. Michigan Ave., Suite 2300, Chicago, IL 60611, (312)527-4000.

FROHM, James M.——*Assoc. Broker (Partner)*, Belcher Realty & Auction Co.; **PRIM RE ACT:** Broker, Appraiser, Developer, Builder, Owner/Investor, Insuror; **BUS ADD:** 303 W. Columbia Ave., Battlecreek, MI 49015, (616)963-0084.

FROST, Fredric W.——B: Mar. 26, 1934, Chappaqua, NY, *Dir. Corp. Facilities Mgt.*, Pitney Bowes, Inc.; **PRIM RE ACT:** Developer; **OTHER RE ACT:** Corp. RE & prop. mgmt.; **SERVICES:** All corp. props. acquisition & mgmt.; **REP CLIENTS:** Company employees & mgmt.; **PROFL AFFIL & HONORS:** NACORE, SIR, IDRC, BOMA; **EDUC:** BA, 1956, Govt., Wesleyan Univ.; **MIL SERV:** USMC, Lt. Col., 1956-61; **OTHER ACT & HONORS:** Marine Corps. Res. Officers Assn., Marine Corps. League; **HOME ADD:** 46 Minute Man Rd., Ridgefield, CT 06877, (203)438-4265; **BUS ADD:** 69 Walter Wheeler Dr., Stamford, CT 06926, (203)356-5315.

FROST, Richard Nelson——B: Jan. 14, 1947, Los Angeles, CA, *Partner*, Frost Spence Trinen; **PRIM RE ACT:** Broker, Consultant; **OTHER RE ACT:** Specializing in major comml./retail projects; **SERVICES:** Leasing, sales and consulting; **REP CLIENTS:** The Prudential Insurance Co., C.J. Segerstrom & Sons, Daon Corp., IBM, Exxon, and other major corp. and serv. firms; **PREV EMPLOY:** 1973-80, Rgnl. Mgr./Partner, Charles Dunn Co., Newport Beach; 1970-1973, Broker, Asst. of Sr. VP; Cushman & Wakefield, Los Angeles; **PROFL AFFIL & HONORS:** Home Builders Counsel, Past Member Bd. of Dir.; Los Angeles Bd. of Realtors; **EDUC:** BS, 1968, Bus. Admin. & Fin., CA State Coll, San Luis Obispo; **GRAD EDUC:** MBA, 1971, Fin./RE, Univ. S. CA; JD, 1978, Western States Univ.; **EDUC HONORS:** Pres., Blue Key Nat. Honor Frat., Amer. Juris Prudence Award, Bancroft Whitney Publishing 1978; **OTHER ACT & HONORS:** Phi Kappa Psi, Frat. member; S. Coast Repertory Theater, Benefactors Comm.; **BUS ADD:** Ground Floor, 695 Town Ctr. Dr., Costa Mesa, CA 92626, (714)641-1111.

FRUECHTENICHT, A.W.——B: Feb. 2, 1947, Fort Wayne, IN, *Part.*, Fruechtenicht Law Office; **PRIM RE ACT:** Broker, Attorney, Instructor; **SERVICES:** Legal advice, title exams., document prep.; **REP CLIENTS:** S&L, bldrs., devels.; **PROFL AFFIL & HONORS:** ABA, IN State Bar Assn., Allen Cty. IN Bar Assn., JD; **EDUC:** BS, 1968, Acctg., IN Univ.; **GRAD EDUC:** JD, 1971, Law, IN Univ. Sch. of Law; **MIL SERV:** USAR, First Lt.; **HOME ADD:** 13916 Spring Hollow Rd., Fort Wayne, IN 46804, (219)672-2326; **BUS ADD:** 421 Standard Bldg., Fort Wayne, IN 46802, (219)422-8414.

FRUTKIN, William J.——B: Jan. 31, 1946, New York, NY, *Atty.*, Spector Cohen Gadon & Rosen, P.C.; **OTHER RE ACT:** Representation of developers and lenders; **SERVICES:** Full range of comml. RE legaL services; **PROFL AFFIL & HONORS:** Philadelphia, Pennsylvania & ABA.; **EDUC:** BA, 1967, Univ. of Rochester; **GRAD EDUC:** JD cum laude, 1971, Univ. of PA School of Law; **BUS ADD:** 29th Floor, 1700 Market St., Philadelphia, PA 19103, (215)241-8888.

FRY, Harry——*Sr. VP Adm.*, Snap-On Tools Corp.; **PRIM RE ACT:** Property Manager; **BUS ADD:** 80th St., Kenosha, WI 53140, (414)656-5200.*

FRY, John U.——B: June 19, 1941, San Francisco, CA, *Pres.*, J. Ulick Associates; **PRIM RE ACT:** Developer, Owner/Investor, Instructor, Property Manager; **SERVICES:** RE proj. mgmt.; **REP CLIENTS:** RE brokerages and lending inst.; **PREV EMPLOY:** Saga Corporation, Operations Mgr., 1970-1974; RLS Associates, VP, 1974-1978; **PROFL AFFIL & HONORS:** IREM, CPM; **EDUC:** BA, 1963, Hist., Arts & Sci., Univ. of San Francisco; **GRAD EDUC:** MBA, 1967, Fin., Santa

Clara Univ.; **MIL SERV:** US Army, E-7, Sgt.; **BUS ADD:** 387 Belle Monti Ave., Aptos, CA 95003, (408)688-9234.

FRYDMAN, Ronald——Frydman & Assoc., Realtors; **PRIM RE ACT:** Developer; **BUS ADD:** 2349 Stanley Ave., Dayton, OH 45404, (513)223-4261.*

FRYE, David A.——*VP and Sr. Mort. Off.*, Orange Savings Bank; **PRIM RE ACT:** Banker, Lender; **PREV EMPLOY:** Asst. City Mort. Super., The Mutual Benefit Life Ins. Co.; **EDUC:** BS, U.S. Merchant Marine Acad.; **GRAD EDUC:** MBA, Rutgers, State Univ.; **BUS ADD:** 340 Main St., Madison, NJ 07940, (201)822-2770.

FRYER, Malcolm F., Jr.——**B:** Apr. 3, 1934, Melrose, MA, *Owner*, The Fryer Co., Inc.; **PRIM RE ACT:** Broker, Consultant, Property Manager; **OTHER RE ACT:** All activity related specifically to comml. & indus. props. and clients; **SERVICES:** Dev./const. consulting, site searches; **PREV EMPLOY:** Dir., Admin. & Mktg., Leggat McCall & Werner, Boston (1973-1974); VP, Spaulding & Slye Corp. (1974-1976); **PROFL AFFIL & HONORS:** Greater Lowell, MA & Nat. Bds. of Realtors; No. Middlesex C of C & Indus.; Assn. Bldrs. & Contractors, Yankee Chap.; **EDUC:** BLA, 1959, Eng., Univ. of NH; **MIL SERV:** US Army, Sgt. (1955-1957); **HOME ADD:** 200 Proctor Rd., Chelmsford, MA 01824, (617)256-5839; **BUS ADD:** 134 Middle St., Lowell, MA 01852, (617)453-3352.

FRYKLUND, Richard K.——**B:** Dec. 31, 1945, Revere, MA, *Pres.*, Dick Ellen Props., Inc.; **PRIM RE ACT:** Broker, Syndicator, Consultant, Property Manager, Owner/Investor; **SERVICES:** Prop. Mgmt., Investment Counseling; **REP CLIENTS:** Home Buyers, Investors, Devels.; **PREV EMPLOY:** Gen. RE 1974-1979; **PROFL AFFIL & HONORS:** GRI, 1978; CRS, 1979; CRB, 1980; **EDUC:** BA, 1971, Geog., Lit., Univ. of CA, Berkeley; **MIL SERV:** USMC, Cpl. 1964-68; **OTHER ACT & HONORS:** 1st VP CA Bike Club 1971; **HOME ADD:** 24737 Aden Ave., Newhall, CA 91321, (805)259-0579; **BUS ADD:** 24006 Lyons Ave., Newhall, CA 91321, (805)254-0303.

FRYMARK, Herbert F.——**B:** Aug. 30, 1932, Oak Park, IL; **PRIM RE ACT:** Syndicator, Owner/Investor; **OTHER RE ACT:** Agent, J.D. Williams Century 21; **SERVICES:** Authorship of Synd. Offerings; Investment Adviser; **PREV EMPLOY:** S.E.C.; Eximbank; FAA Securities Analysis; **PROFL AFFIL & HONORS:** RESSI, CCIM (Designate), P. G. Bd. Realtors; **EDUC:** BS, 1960, RE, Corp. Finance, Marquette Univ.; **MIL SERV:** USN; MM2, Korean War 1952-1956; **OTHER ACT & HONORS:** Toastmasters, Amer. Legion; **HOME ADD:** 3515 Susquehanna Dr., Beltsville, MD 20705; **BUS ADD:** P.O.Box 44, Beltsville,, MD 20705, (301)572-5077.

FUCHS, David——**B:** Feb. 26, 1935, Flushing, NY, *Owner/Broker*, Help-U-Sell of Mission Viejo; **PRIM RE ACT:** Broker; **SERVICES:** All resid. sales serv. except escrow; **EDUC:** BS, 1955, Engr., MA Inst. Technol.; **BUS ADD:** 23881 Via Fabricante, Ste. #507, Mission Viejo, CA 92691, (714)951-3855.

FUCHS, Steven L.——**B:** Feb. 18, 1954, NYC, *Pres.*, Hartman Investment Grp., Inc.; **PRIM RE ACT:** Broker, Banker; **SERVICES:** Financing Consultant; **PREV EMPLOY:** Atty.; **PROFL AFFIL & HONORS:** ABA, MA Bar Assoc.; **EDUC:** BA, 1977, Poli., NY Univ.; **GRAD EDUC:** JD, 1980, Law, Boston Univ., School of Law; **EDUC HONORS:** Founders Day Award; **HOME ADD:** 151 Tremont St. #16E, Boston, MA 02111; **BUS ADD:** 151 Tremont, PO Box 108, Boston, MA 02112, (617)542-2727.

FUELBERTH, John H.——**B:** Dec. 1, 1941, Pekin, IL, *VP*, The Herget National Bank of Pekin, RE Loan Dept.; **PRIM RE ACT:** Banker, Lender; **EDUC:** BS, 1963, Agricultural Bus., CO State Univ.; **GRAD EDUC:** MS, 1964, Agricultural Bus., CO State Univ.; **MIL SERV:** US Army, Capt.; **HOME ADD:** 2125 Highwood, Pekin, IL 61554, (309)346-8418; **BUS ADD:** 33 S Fourth St., Pekin, IL 61554, (309)347-1131.

FUHRER, Larry——**B:** Sept. 23, 1939, Ft. Wayne, IN, *Private Investment Banker*, The Cent RE Capital Group; **PRIM RE ACT:** Broker, Consultant, Owner/Investor, Instructor, Syndicator; **OTHER RE ACT:** Investment Banker; **SERVICES:** Strategic and corp. planning, financing, capital formation, org., mgmt. counsel, short term exec. roles, mktg., communications, acquisitions, sale and corp. control; **REP CLIENTS:** Investors, divisional execs., attys., accountants, bankers, private bus. owners, KFC Corp., MTI Teleprograms Inc., The QMedia Group Inc., Evans Indus. and numerous other indus. and corps.; **PREV EMPLOY:** Pres., 1975-1980, Equibanque Ltd.; Pres., 1971-1975, Killian Associates Inc.; Sec., 1972-1973, Forward Planning Commn., Taylor Univ.; Pres., 1971-1972, Council Member, 1969-1979, Taylor Univ. Alumni Council; Assocs., 1968-1972, Chmn. of Assocs., 1969-1970, Taylor Univ.; Exec. Asst. to the Pres., 1966-1970 , Ihe Robert Johnston Corp., Los Angeles, Chicago and NY, 1968-1969; Publications Manager, 1961-1965, "Youth for Christ" Magazine, 1962-1965; **PROFL AFFIL & HONORS:** RE Broker, IL; NAR; DuPage Bd. of Realtors, Outstanding Young Man in Amer., 1971; Who's Who in the Midwest, 1977 and later; Who's Who in Fin. and Indus., 1981; Men of Achievment, 980, Cambridge, England; **EDUC:** AB, 1961, Psych./Religion, Taylor Univ., Upland, IN; **GRAD EDUC:** MBA, No. IL Univ.; **OTHER ACT & HONORS:** Managing Dir., Presidential Services Inc., 1966 to present; Dir., The Equity Realty Group Ltd., 1971 to present; Chmn., The Financial Services Group Ltd., 1973 to present; Managing Dir., The Craftsmen's Clearing House, 1979 to present; First Presbyterian Church of Glen Ellyn; Civil Air Patrol Certificate of Proficiency (Former Cadet Major); AAU Class IV swimming official; Chmn., West Suburban swim conference; **BUS ADD:** 226 E. Roosevelt Rd., Wheaton, IL 60187, (312)668-6501.

FUHRMAN, Howard D.——**B:** Sept. 4, 1944, NY, *VP & Controller*, Lesny Development Co.; **PRIM RE ACT:** Developer, Builder, Owner/Investor; **OTHER RE ACT:** Financial Officer; **PREV EMPLOY:** Kenneth Lesenthal & Co.; CPA's; **PROFL AFFIL & HONORS:** AICDA, CA Soc. of CPAs; **EDUC:** BS, 1966, Acctg., UCLA; **GRAD EDUC:** MS, 1972, Fin., CA State Univ. Long Beach; **HOME ADD:** 6251 Halm Ave., Los Angeles, CA 90051, (213)641-6737; **BUS ADD:** PO Box 5526, Beverly Hills, CA 90210, (213)653-7117.

FUJISHIMA, Burt S.——**B:** Sept. 11, 1953, Chicago, IL, *Pres.*, Condo. Resources Group, Inc.; **PRIM RE ACT:** Broker, Developer, Owner/Investor; **PREV EMPLOY:** Sales mgr. for condo. conversions for Stein & Co.; **EDUC:** BS, 1977, Psych. & Biology; **HOME ADD:** 635 W Armitage, Chicago, IL 60614, (312)642-0795; **BUS ADD:** 635 W Armitage Ave., Chicago, IL 60614, (312)951-8567.

FULCHER, Wanda Jo——**B:** Sept. 10, 1947, Wash., NC, *Branch Mgr.*, Mort. Corp. of the South, Residential; **PRIM RE ACT:** Banker, Lender; **SERVICES:** Mort. banking, full service; **PREV EMPLOY:** Ray McCotter Realty, New Bern, NC, First Citizens Bank, Commercial Credit Corp.; **PROFL AFFIL & HONORS:** Jacksonville Bd. of Realtors, Morehead Bd. of Realtors, New Bern Bd. of Realtors, Havelock Bd. of Realtors, Jacksonville Home Builders Assoc., MBA, 1979 Outstanding Service Award from Home Builders, 1980 Assoc. Builder of the Year Award from Home Builders; **EDUC:** 1966, Exec. Sec. training, Carteret Tech. Inst., Morehead City, NC; **OTHER ACT & HONORS:** 1st Pres. of Ladies Auxilliary of Home Builders, Exec. Officer of Jacksonville Home Builders, Organizer of the Ladies Aux.; **HOME ADD:** 110 Princess Pl., Jacksonville, NC 28540, (919)353-7391; **BUS ADD:** P.O. Box 658, Jacksonville, NC 28540, (919)455-8222.

FULLER, Charles R.——**B:** Sept. 29, 1924, Grand Rapids, MI, *Owner*, Fuller Appraisals; **PRIM RE ACT:** Developer; **SERVICES:** R.E. Appraisals; **PREV EMPLOY:** 32 yrs. in RE appraising, Instr., Univ. of MI, ext. courses in appraisals, 1955-70; **PROFL AFFIL & HONORS:** SREA, MAI; Bd. of Governors 1967-69; Pres., Grand Rapids Chptr. SREA; Pres., Univ. of MI Alumni Assoc.; **EDUC:** BS, 1950, Indust. Engrg., Univ. of MI; **MIL SERV:** US Army, 1943-46; **OTHER ACT & HONORS:** Grand Rapids University Club, Grand Rapids Rotary Club; **HOME ADD:** 1125 Santa Cruz S.E., Grand Rapids, MI 49506, (616)452-8228; **BUS ADD:** 501 Waters Bldg., Grand Rapids, MI 49503, (616)451-0761.

FULLER, Donn M.——**B:** Sept. 7, 1946, Minneapolis, MN, *VP*, MEPC American Properties Inc.; **PRIM RE ACT:** Developer, Owner/Investor, Property Manager; **REP CLIENTS:** Comml. office & retail centers; **PREV EMPLOY:** Touche Ross & Co. - Public Acctnt.; **PROFL AFFIL & HONORS:** AICPA, Soc. for Fin. Officers; **EDUC:** BS, 1976, Acctg./Fin., Mankato State Univ.; **MIL SERV:** US Navy, E-5, 1970-1974; **HOME ADD:** 3631 Diamond Head Dr., Plano, TX 75075, (214)867-0631; **BUS ADD:** 700 N. Pearl LB 400, Dallas, TX 75201, (214)749-0000.

FULLER, Michael——**B:** Apr. 7, 1946, Evanston, IL, *Pres.*, The Real Estate Shoppe, Ltd.; **PRIM RE ACT:** Broker, Owner/Investor, Syndicator; **SERVICES:** Resid. & comml. sales, investments; **PREV EMPLOY:** North Shore Partnership; Fuller-Krassner; Plum Creek Partners; Sales Mgr., Hogan, Farwell/Marken Realty Grp.; Northbrook Estates; Fuller-Rogatz; Koenig & Strey Realtors; Hyacinth Pl. Assn.; RecreAcres Ltd.; Woodall's Park Devel. Serv.; Woodall Publishing Co.; Michael Fuller Realty; **PROFL AFFIL & HONORS:** Life Member, Million Dollar Club and IL Assn. of Realtors; NAR; Northshore Bd. of Realtors; **EDUC:** BBA, 1970, Bus. Mgmt./Econ., Univ. of WI, Whitewater; **OTHER ACT & HONORS:** Bd. of Dirs., Woodall Publishing Co.; **HOME ADD:** 3022 Cherry Ln., Northbrook, IL 60062, (312)564-4457; **BUS ADD:** 3022 Cherry Ln., Northbrook, IL 60062, (312)272-7070.

FULLER, Walter Erwin, Jr.——B: July 23, 1938, Guilford Cty., NC, *Partner*, Brooks, Pierce, McLendon, Humphrey & Leonard; **PRIM RE ACT:** Attorney; **SERVICES:** Legal; **PROFL AFFIL & HONORS:** Greensboro, NC and ABA; Real Prop. Sec. of NC and ABA; NC Land Title Assn.; **EDUC:** BS, 1960, Bus. Econ., Univ. of NC; **GRAD EDUC:** LLB, 1964, Duke Univ. School of Law; **EDUC HONORS:** Phi Beta Kappa, Beta Gamma Sigma, Student Govt. officer, Grad. with Honors, Order of the Coif, Duke Law Journal - Articles Editor; **HOME ADD:** 2105 Medford Ln., Greensboro, NC 27408, (919)275-2111; **BUS ADD:** 1400 Wachovia Bldg., 201 N. Elm St., PO Drawer U, Greensboro, NC 27402, (919)373-8850.

FULLER, William Norman——B: Feb. 17, 1948, Savannah, GA, *Arch. and Princ./Reg. Arch. State of GA*, The Fuller Group and Brockway & Co.; **PRIM RE ACT:** Consultant, Architect, Developer, Builder, Owner/Investor; **OTHER RE ACT:** Agent, Design Network, Inc.; **SERVICES:** Arch., planning, bldg. consultant, devel. and engrg.; **REP CLIENTS:** Amoco Oil Co., Gen. Motors, The McCarthy Co. of GA; **PREV EMPLOY:** Jova Daniels Busby, Arch., Atlanta, GA, Tenneco Oil Co., Atlanta, GA; The Austin Co., Atlanta, GA; **PROFL AFFIL & HONORS:** Soc. of Amer. Reg. Arch., AIA, Who's Who in the South and SE; Cert. Nat. Council of Arch. Rge. Bds.; **EDUC:** BArch, 1973, GA Inst. of Tech.; **OTHER ACT & HONORS:** Member city of Atlanta Zoning Review Bd. 1976-1979, Friends of the Library Bd., Atlanta, GA, Member City of Atlanta Legislative Study Commn. 1980-present; Member Fulton Council, GA; Private Industry Council Bd., 1981-present; **HOME ADD:** 2444 Poole Rd. SW, Atlanta, GA 30311, (404)758-4852; **BUS ADD:** 1626 E Virginai Ave., College Park, GA 30337, (404)761-6686.

FULOP, Irwin M.——B: 1904, Salt Lake City, UT, *Of Counsel*, Fulop and Hardee; **PRIM RE ACT:** Attorney; **OTHER RE ACT:** Arbitrator at American Arbitration.; **SERVICES:** In const. indust. cases; **PROFL AFFIL & HONORS:** ABA, State Bar of CA, Los Angeles Bar Assn., Beverly Hills Bar Assn.; **EDUC:** AB, 1925, Univ. of CA; **GRAD EDUC:** JD, 1928, Harvard Law School; **OTHER ACT & HONORS:** Lecturer - RE - Continuing Educ. of Bar - CA; **HOME ADD:** 518 N. Crescent Dr., Beverly Hills, CA 90210, (213)274-3926; **BUS ADD:** 9665 Wilshire Blvd., Beverly Hills, CA 90212, (213)278-6500.

FULTON, Charles L.——B: Dec. 11, 1927, Highlands, NC, *Sr. RE Partner*, Manning, Fulton & Skinner; **PRIM RE ACT:** Attorney; **SERVICES:** Gen. legal servs. to devels., builders, brokers and lenders; **REP CLIENTS:** IBM; R.J. Reynolds Indus.; Amoco Oil Co.; Rheem Mfg. Co.; Siemens-Allis, Inc.; Carolantic Realty, Inc.; **PROFL AFFIL & HONORS:** ABA; NC and Wake Cty. Bar Assns.; Amer. Coll. of Mort. Attys.; NC Land Title Assn.; **EDUC:** AB, 1947, Pol. Sci./Math., Univ. of NC; **GRAD EDUC:** JD, 1950, Univ. of NC; **EDUC HONORS:** Order of the Golden Fleece, Order of the Holy Grail, Order of the Coif, Assoc. Editor Law Review, With Honors; **MIL SERV:** USN, Lt.; **OTHER ACT & HONORS:** Visiting Lecturer in Law, UNC Law School; Guest Lecturer, Georgetown Univ.; Instr., NC RE Found. (10 yrs.); **HOME ADD:** 3624 Williamsborough Ct., Raleigh, NC 27609, (919)781-2379; **BUS ADD:** 800 Wachovia Bank Bldg., POB 1150, Raleigh, NC 27602, (919)828-8295.

FULTON, George A.——B: Mar. 18, 1933, Reading, PA, *Sr. VP, Corp. Mktg.*, Walker Lee Inc., Mktg.; **PRIM RE ACT:** Consultant; **OTHER RE ACT:** Research-staff of 30; **SERVICES:** Feasibility studies for devel. nat. residential consumer preference surveys; **REP CLIENTS:** Housing Magazine(McGraw-Hill), Centex, Presley Corp., McKeon Housing Corp.; **PREV EMPLOY:** Adv. Mgr.-Del E. Webb Corp.; **PROFL AFFIL & HONORS:** Bd. of Dir., Orange Cty. Devel. Corp. NAHB member; **EDUC:** BA, 1955, Mktg., Univ. of AZ; **MIL SERV:** US Army, 1st Lt.; **HOME ADD:** 5071 Stone Canyon, Yorba Linda, CA 92656, (714)970-7417; **BUS ADD:** 1901 E. 4th St., Santa Ana, CA 92705, (714)835-4242.

FUNK, Daniel M.——B: Oct. 21, 1948, New Brunswick, NJ, *Cty. Solicitor*, Cty. of Newton, Law Dept.; **PRIM RE ACT:** Attorney; **SERVICES:** Legal Advice, Research, Drafting, Title Work, Litigation; **REP CLIENTS:** Mayor, Bd. Of Alderman, School Comm., All Comms., Bds., Commns. and Dept.; **PREV EMPLOY:** Maher McCann & Talcott, Worcester, MA; **PROFL AFFIL & HONORS:** NIMLO; **EDUC:** BA, 1970, Hist., Rutgers Univ., NJ; **GRAD EDUC:** JD, 1973, Law, Northeastern School of Law; **EDUC HONORS:** Phi Beta Kappa, Cum Laude; **OTHER ACT & HONORS:** Cty. Solicitor, 1977 to present; **HOME ADD:** 36 Hamlin Rd., Newton Centre, MA 02159, (617)527-0617; **BUS ADD:** Newton Centre, MA 02159City Hall, (617)552-7050.

FUNT, Harold——B: Oct. 9, 1917, NYC, NY, *VP, Dir. RE Div.*, Wometco Enterprises, Inc.; **PRIM RE ACT:** Appraiser, Developer, Builder, Property Manager; **SERVICES:** Site selections, leasing, sales & purchasing; **PROFL AFFIL & HONORS:** VP NACORE, ULI, Sr. Member NARA, CRA; **EDUC:** OH Univ., NY Univ.; **HOME ADD:** 1880 NE 208th Terr., N Miami Bch., FL 33179, (305)932-4683; **BUS ADD:** 306 N Miami Ave., Miami, FL 33128.

FURBUSH, David M.——*Atty. at Law*, Brobeck, Phleger & Harrison; **PRIM RE ACT:** Broker, Attorney; **SERVICES:** Concentrating in litigation, including RE-related litigation; **BUS ADD:** One Market Plaza, Spear St. Tower, San Francisco, CA 94105, (415)442-0900.

FURBUSH, Donald M.——B: Apr. 13, 1935, Oakland, CA, *Sr. VP*, BankAmerica Realty Services, Inc.; **PRIM RE ACT:** Property Manager, Lender, Owner/Investor; **OTHER RE ACT:** RE asset mgr.; **PREV EMPLOY:** Arthur Rubloff & Co. 1974-78; Grubb & Ellis Co. 1964-74; **PROFL AFFIL & HONORS:** IREM; ICSC; BOMA, CPM, RPA; **EDUC:** BS, 1957, General Curriculum, Univ. of CA, Berkeley; **GRAD EDUC:** MBA, 1960, Hosp. Admin., Univ. of Chicago, IL; **MIL SERV:** US Army, 2nd Lt.; **OTHER ACT & HONORS:** Pres. Amer. Lung Assn. of CA, 1981; **HOME ADD:** 2951 Gibbons Dr., Alameda, CA 94501, (415)523-4033; **BUS ADD:** 555 California St., Suite 4275, San Francisco, CA 94104, (415)622-8094.

FURMAN, Robert R.——B: Aug. 21, 1915, Trenton, NJ, *Pres.*, Furman Builders, Inc.; **PRIM RE ACT:** Developer, Builder; **SERVICES:** Site acquisition & devel, const. fin., leasing, mgmt. of completed bldgs.; **PROFL AFFIL & HONORS:** Bethesda/Chevy Chase C of C; Assn. Bldrs & Contrs.; United Way; Montgomery Cty. C of C; Rotary Club of Bethesda/Chevy Chase, Reg. Civil Engr. & Surveyor in the Dist of Columbia & the State of OH; **EDUC:** BSCE, 1937, Civil Engrg., Princeton Univ.; **MIL SERV:** US Army, Lt. Col.; **OTHER ACT & HONORS:** Member & Past Pres. of the Bethesda-Chevy Chase C of C; Member and Past Pres. of Rotary Club of Bethesda-Chevy Chase; Member of Assoc. Bldrs. & Contrs.; Active Member and Past Chmn. for United Way for Montgomery Cty.; Member of the Montgomery Cty. C of C; Member of St. John's Church, Bethesda; Member and Past Pres. of Edgemoor Club, Bethesda; **HOME ADD:** 6745 Greentree Rd., Bethesda, MD 20817; **BUS ADD:** 1151 Seven Locks Rd., Rockville, MD 20854, (301)424-1800.

FURTICK, Michael H.——B: Dec. 24, 1949, Humbolot, TN, *VP, Broker*, Century 21, First Realty of Sarasota, Inc., Comml. Investment Div.; **PRIM RE ACT:** Broker, Consultant, Developer, Owner/Investor, Property Manager, Syndicator; **SERVICES:** Comml. & investment brokerage, consulting; **REP CLIENTS:** Devels., investors, domestic and off-shore; **PREV EMPLOY:** Palmer 1st Natl. Bank (Comml. Banking); Green Tree Communities, Inc. (Land Devel.); **PROFL AFFIL & HONORS:** NAR, FL Assn. of Realtors, RESSI, RE License in TX and FL; **EDUC:** BBA, 1972, RE & Fin., Univ. of MS; **OTHER ACT & HONORS:** Member Million Dollar Sales Club of Century 21 RE Network; **HOME ADD:** 1555 Tarpon Center Dr., Apt. 134-E, Venice, FL 33595, (813)484-8679; **BUS ADD:** 2999 South Tamiami Trail, Sarasota, FL 33579, (813)953-2121.

FUSSELL, Patrick H.——B: Mar. 19, 1928, San Augustine, TX, *Pres.*, Pat Fussell & Associates, Inc. (Branch offices in Dallas, TX & Shreveport, LA); **PRIM RE ACT:** Broker, Developer, Builder, Owner/Investor, Property Manager, Syndicator; **OTHER RE ACT:** Specializing in motel/hotel props.; **SERVICES:** Brokerage, site selection, new prop. devel., synds., joint ventures; **REP CLIENTS:** Indivs., corps., investor grps., lenders and other synds.; **PREV EMPLOY:** RE and devel. since 1954; **PROFL AFFIL & HONORS:** NAR, TX Assn. of Realtors, RESSI, GRI; **EDUC:** Bus. Admin., Stephen F. Austin Univ. and Univ. of VA; **MIL SERV:** US Army, Infantry, Capt., Combat Infantry Badge, Korean Conflict Medal, Unit Citation; **OTHER ACT & HONORS:** Rotary Intl.; **HOME ADD:** 201 Baxter Lane, San Augustine, TX 75972, (713)275-3491; **BUS ADD:** 119 E. Columbia St. (Mail: P O Drawer P), San Augustine, TX 75972, (713)275-3491.

FUTTERMAN, Philip G.——B: July 28, 1933, Yonkers, NY, *Pres.*, Futterman Organization Inc.; **PRIM RE ACT:** Broker, Consultant, Owner/Investor; **SERVICES:** Retail & office leasing/consulting, shopping ctr. planning & devel.; **REP CLIENTS:** Maj. high-end intl. retailers and corporate space users; shopping ctr. devels.; investment bldrs. & owners; **PREV EMPLOY:** Julien J. Studley Inc.; **PROFL AFFIL & HONORS:** RE Bd. of NY; Stores & Leasing Comm.; Intl. Council of Shopping Ctrs.; **EDUC:** BA, 1955, Intl. Studies/French, OH State Univ.; Diplome d'Etudes, Univ. of Paris (La Sorbonne); **GRAD EDUC:** 1957, Johns Hopkins School of Advanced Intl. Studies, (Wash. DC & Bologna, Italy); **OTHER ACT & HONORS:** Who's Who in the East; **HOME ADD:** 7 W 81st St., NY, NY 10024, (212)362-5677; **BUS ADD:** 565 Fifth Ave., NY, NY 10024, (212)661-6200.

GABALAC, Frank——*Prop. Mgr.*, Van Dorn Co.; **PRIM RE ACT:** Property Manager; **BUS ADD:** 2700 East 79th St., Cleveland, OH 44104, (216)361-5234.*

GABBARD, Thomas L.——**B:** Apr. 10, 1946, Lexington, KY, *Pres.*, Medico Realty Corp.; **PRIM RE ACT:** Broker, Consultant; **SERVICES:** Portfolio investment planning for clients; **PROFL AFFIL & HONORS:** GRI; **EDUC:** BSBA, 1968, RE/Urban Planning, Univ. of FL; **MIL SERV:** US Army, 1st Lt., 1969-1971, (2) Bronze Stars in Vietnam; **OTHER ACT & HONORS:** Member, Gainesville Exchange Club; **HOME ADD:** G & G Farm, County Line Rd., McIntosch, FL 32664, (904)591-2860; **BUS ADD:** 2300 SW 34th St., Gainesville, FL 32608, (904)373-3166.

GABEL, Kenneth G.——**B:** Apr. 3, 1942, E. St. Louis, IL, *Pres.*, Greyhound Leasing & Financial Corp.; **PRIM RE ACT:** Broker, Developer, Lender, Owner/Investor, Property Manager; **SERVICES:** RE Fin. and Equity Servs.; **REP CLIENTS:** Corp., partnerships, and props.; **PREV EMPLOY:** Pres., CCDC 1980-Present Sr. VP, CCDC, 1979-1980; VP Underwriting CCDC, 1975-1979; VP Admin., CCDC, 1972-1975; Mgr. Corp. Facilities Admin. Control Data Corp. 1971-1972; Supervisor Corp. Fac. Adm., Con. Data Corp. 1969-1971; Sr. Adm. Specialist Corp. Fac. Adm. Con/ Data Corp. 1968-1969; USAF, Capt. 1963-1969; **PROFL AFFIL & HONORS:** Amer. Mgmt. Assn., Homebuilders Assn. of MD, MBA, Baltimore Edon. Soc., Natl. Assn. of Bus. Econ.; **EDUC:** BS, 1963, Aeronautical Admin., Parks Coll. of Aeronautical Technol. of St. Louis Univ.; **GRAD EDUC:** MBA, 1968, Mgmt., Grad. School of Bus. Admin., Univ. of Miami; **MIL SERV:** USAF, Capt.; **HOME ADD:** 6 Skipjack Ct., Baltimore, MD 21221; **BUS ADD:** Phoenix, AZ 85013.

GABRIEL, David H.——**B:** Feb. 22, 1948, San Francisco, CA, *Asst. VP*, Lloyds Bank CA, RE Indus. Div.; **PRIM RE ACT:** Broker, Banker, Lender; **SERVICES:** Indus./comml. RE const., fin., private RE acquisition TX and CA; **REP CLIENTS:** Major rgnl. devels., high income personal assocs.; **PREV EMPLOY:** Sr. Mort. Loan Analyst, Farmers Ins. Grp., Los Angeles; Assoc., Marcus & Millichap Investment RE Brokers; **PROFL AFFIL & HONORS:** Bay Area Mort. Assn.; NCA Mort. Bankers Assn.; MBA; Member, San Francisco Planning & Urban Renewal, JCC Outstanding Young Man of the Year, 1980; **EDUC:** Communication Theory, 1970, Bus. Communication and Org., San Francisco State Univ.; **GRAD EDUC:** Credential, Business/Education, 1972, Bus., Univ. of CA, Berkeley; **OTHER ACT & HONORS:** Admin. Asst., Mayor of S.F. 1968-1970; Intern, CA Assembly, 1970-71; Lic. RE Broker State of CA and State of TX; **HOME ADD:** 7 Sheldon Terr., San Francisco, CA 94122, (415)564-1886; **BUS ADD:** 444 Market St., 22nd Floor, San Francisco, CA 94111, (415)765-9519.

GABRIEL, Eberhard J.——**B:** Mar. 22, 1942, Rumania, *Sr. VP & Gen. Counsel*, Govt. Employees Fin. Corp. & Subs.; **PRIM RE ACT:** Attorney, Lender, Regulator; **REP CLIENTS:** In-House Counsel for Consumer Fin. and Banking Firm; **PREV EMPLOY:** Atty. with Govt. Employees Ins. Co. (GEICO) 1968-1970; **PROFL AFFIL & HONORS:** ABA, Sect. on Bus. Law and Real Prop. Law, MD Bar Assn.; PHI ALPHA DELTA, JD; **EDUC:** BA, 1963, Eng., Hist., St. Joseph's Coll., IN; **GRAD EDUC:** JD, 1966, Law, Georgetown Univ. Law Ctr.; **OTHER ACT & HONORS:** Secr.-Treas. & Dir., Indus. Bank Savings Guaranty Corp. of ; NCFA Law Forum & Law Comm.; Lecturer - Current Legal Problems at Univ. of CO - NCFA Installment Banking School 1974-1981; **BUS ADD:** 7551 W. Alameda Ave., PO Box 5555, Denver, CO 80217, (303)234-8380.

GADD, John L.——**B:** Oct. 21, 1933, Chicago, IL, *VP*, Lloyd Thomas/Coats & Burchard Co.; **PRIM RE ACT:** Appraiser, Consultant; **SERVICES:** Appraisals for sale, fin., mergers, condemnation, etc.; **REP CLIENTS:** Fortune 500 Co's., plus leading corps. in Can. and Mexico; **PREV EMPLOY:** Two yrs. experience as mort. negotiator, Equitable Life Assurance Soc. of US, 1960-1961; **PROFL AFFIL & HONORS:** Sr. Member, MAI; AIREA; Amer. Soc. of Appraisers; Soc. of RE Appraisers; Appraisal Inst. of Can.; Fellow. Inc. Soc. of Valuers & Auctioneers of England; Realtor Member, Nat. Assn. of RE Brokers; **EDUC:** 1956, Mktg., Loyola Univ.; **MIL SERV:** U.S. Army, Cpl., 1956-1958; **OTHER ACT & HONORS:** Member, Indus./Comml. Devel. Comm. of The Village of Arlington Hts., IL; Intl. Sr. VP, Amer. Soc. of Appraisers; Intl. Relations Comm. AIREA; **HOME ADD:** 843 S Burton Pl., Arlington Hts., IL 60005, (312)392-1148; **BUS ADD:** 6676 Howard St., Niles, IL 60648, (312)470-1800.

GADD, Richard V., Jr.——**B:** Jan 4, 1946, Atlanta, GA, *Pres., Western Div.*, Homecraft Land Dev. Inc., SW Div.; **PRIM RE ACT:** Developer; **SERVICES:** Land Dev. Mgmt.; **REP CLIENTS:** Affiliated with US Home Corp.; **PREV EMPLOY:** Cousins Props., Atlanta, GA.; **EDUC:** BS, 1969, Industrial Mgmt., GA Tech; **MIL SERV:** US Army, 1st Lt.; **HOME ADD:** 12805 Arroyo De Vista, Albuquerque, NM 87107, (505)296-1094; **BUS ADD:** 4001 Carlisle NE, Albuquerque, NM 87107, (505)883-6228.

GAERTNER, Robert——*Corp. Adm. Dir.*, Medtronic, Inc.; **PRIM RE ACT:** Property Manager; **BUS ADD:** 3055 Old Highway Eight, PO Box 1453, Minneapolis, MN 55440, (612)574-4000.*

GAGE, John——*SIR Dir. Corp. RE*, Perkin-Elmer Corp.; **PRIM RE ACT:** Property Manager; **BUS ADD:** 761 Main Ave., Norwalk, CT 06856, (203)762-1000.*

GAGE, Peter, Jr.——**B:** Mar. 11, 1941, Minden, IA, *VP*, The Omaha National Bank, Comml. RE Dept.; **PRIM RE ACT:** Banker, Lender; **SERVICES:** Const., land devel., and term comml. RE loans; **PREV EMPLOY:** Prudential Ins. Co., RE Investment; **PROFL AFFIL & HONORS:** Member, AIREA, MAI; **EDUC:** BS, 1964, RE, Univ. of Omaha; **MIL SERV:** US Army, Spec. 4; **OTHER ACT & HONORS:** Optimist; **HOME ADD:** 201 Bowman Ave., Glenwood, IA, (712)527-4137; **BUS ADD:** 1700 Farnam St., Omaha, NE 68102, (402)348-6310.

GAICH, Michael G.——**B:** Feb. 23, 1944, Greensburg, PA, *Pres. and Chmn. of the Bd.*, Brevard Realty, Inc./Better Homes and Gardens; **PRIM RE ACT:** Broker, Consultant, Developer, Owner/Investor, Property Manager, Syndicator; **SERVICES:** Investment counseling, Devel. and Synd. of Comml. prop., Prop. Mgmt., Gen. Brokerage plus Project Sales; **REP CLIENTS:** Indiv. clients; **PROFL AFFIL & HONORS:** Realtors Natl. Mktg. Inst., Nat. Assoc. of Realtors, Nat. RE Exchange Inc., Intern. Immobilia, Inc., CCIM; **EDUC:** BS, 1966, Flight Text Eng, WA Univ., Morgantown, WV; **GRAD EDUC:** MS, 1970, Bus. Mgmt., FL Inst. of Technology, Melbourne, FL; **HOME ADD:** 1700 S Atlantic Ave., Apt.#306, Cocoa Beach, FL 32931, (305)783-4198; **BUS ADD:** 1811 E Merritt Island Cswy., Merritt Island, FL 32952, (305)453-4200.

GAINER, Stephen R.——*Atty.*; **PRIM RE ACT:** Broker, Attorney, Instructor; **SERVICES:** RE purchases; comm'l. leasing; invmt. (legal aspects; **PROFL AFFIL & HONORS:** ABA, St. Bar CA; **EDUC:** BA, 1964, Econ., Univ. of MI; **GRAD EDUC:** J.D., 1968, Law, Univ. of Chicago; **EDUC HONORS:** Grad. Honors., Ed., Univ. of Chicago Law Review; **OTHER ACT & HONORS:** Counsel of Marvin County Inc. Prop. Assoc.; **BUS ADD:** 172 Golden Gate, San Francisco, CA 94102, (415)928-3213.

GAINES, Irving D.——**B:** Oct. 14, 1923, Milwaukee, WI, *Atty.*, Irving D. Gaines, S.C.; **PRIM RE ACT:** Attorney; **SERVICES:** Legal; **REP CLIENTS:** First Bank-Milwaukee; Family S&L Assn.; Title Ins. Co. of MN, Inc.; Chicago Title Ins. Co.; **PROFL AFFIL & HONORS:** Amer. Judicature Soc.; ABA; WI State Bar; FL State Bar; Milwaukee Bar Assn.; WI Academy of Trial Lawyers; **EDUC:** BA, 1943, Univ. of WI; **GRAD EDUC:** JD, 1947, Univ. of WI Law School; **MIL SERV:** US Army, Cpl., Intelligence Interpreter, 1943-1946; **HOME ADD:** 7821 N. Mohawk Rd., Milwaukee, WI 53217, (414)352-5575; **BUS ADD:** Suite 726, 735 N. Water St., Milwaukee, WI 53202, (414)271-1938.

GAINES, Jack W.——**B:** Aug. 7, 1921, Greensboro, NC, *Pres.*, Gaines-Curland Corp. & Hamlet Devel. Corp.; **PRIM RE ACT:** Developer, Builder, Syndicator; **SERVICES:** Land Dev., home builder, apt. builder; **PREV EMPLOY:** Pres. of Haft-Gaines Co.; **PROFL AFFIL & HONORS:** NAHB; **EDUC:** BS, 1943, Univ. of NC; **MIL SERV:** USN; Lt.; **HOME ADD:** 4800 Wildewood Dr., Delray Beach, FL 33445, (305)498-7831; **BUS ADD:** 4701 Cocoplum Way, Delray Beach, FL 33445, (305)498-0900.

GAISER, J. Raymond——*Atty. at Law*; **PRIM RE ACT:** Attorney; **SERVICES:** RE sales and purchases, title searches, RE closings; **REP CLIENTS:** Local banks and credit union; **PREV EMPLOY:** IRS (US); **PROFL AFFIL & HONORS:** ABA, MI Bar, Local Bar Assns.; **EDUC:** BA, 1949, Law, Univ. of MI; **MIL SERV:** US Army, 1st Lt.; **OTHER ACT & HONORS:** Acting and Asst. Prosecuting Atty., Friend of the Ct. 18 years; **BUS ADD:** 426 Cayuga St., PO Box 31, Iron River, MI 49935, (906)265-2619.

GAJADHAR——**B:** May 10, 1935, Guyana - S Amer.; **PRIM RE ACT:** Owner/Investor; **PREV EMPLOY:** Self; **EDUC:** BA, 1960, Bio. & Chem., Univ. of Evansville, IN; **GRAD EDUC:** MD, 1971, Univ. of SK, Can.; **HOME ADD:** 9909 Hurstwood Ct., Louisville, KY 40222; **BUS ADD:** 722 Medical Towers, N Louisville, KY 40202, (502)589-5846.

GAJDEK, Matthew——**B:** Oct. 20, 1924, Brooklyn, NY, *Acting Regional Real Estate Officer*, NY State Dept. of Transportation, RE Div.; **PRIM RE ACT:** Regulator; **OTHER RE ACT:** Office Mgr.; **PREV EMPLOY:** Engrg.; **PROFL AFFIL & HONORS:** SRA; CSA; CRA; **HOME ADD:** POB 1058, Stony Brook, NY 11790; **BUS ADD:** NY

State Office Bldg., Veterans Memorial Hwy., Hauppauge LI, NY 11788, (516)979-5095.

GAJJAR, Navin J.——**B:** June 7, 1927, India, *VP*, Nilima Properties; **PRIM RE ACT:** Owner/Investor, Property Manager, Syndicator; **OTHER RE ACT:** Mfr.; **PREV EMPLOY:** DuPont Co. of Wilmington, DE - 25 yrs.; **EDUC:** BS, Chem./Tex. Engrg., Phila. Coll. of Textile & Science; **GRAD EDUC:** MS, Mech. Engrg., MIT; **OTHER ACT & HONORS:** VP, Thunderbird Indus., Inc.; Also affiliated with Jayson's Construction; **HOME ADD:** 2827 Walnut Rd., Norman, OH 73069, (405)364-7020; **BUS ADD:** POB 1390, Norman, OK 73070, (405)364-8854.

GALBREATH, W. Percy——**B:** Dec. 26, 1946, Memphis, TN, *Pres.*, The Galbreath Company, Inc.; **PRIM RE ACT:** Broker, Appraiser, Developer, Builder, Property Manager, Lender, Owner/Investor; **SERVICES:** Sales, leasing, mgmt., devel. of comml., indus., investment, and multi-family prop., mortgage banking; **PROFL AFFIL & HONORS:** NAR, IREM, Memphis Bd. of Realtors, Million Dollar Sales Club - 1975, 1976, 1978, 1979, 1980; Pres. of Memphis Chap. IREM; Lamda Alpha; **EDUC:** BBA, 1973, RE, Fin., Memphis State Univ.; **MIL SERV:** USNR, Lt. j.g.; **OTHER ACT & HONORS:** Bd. of Dir. - Stratton YMCA; Bd. of Dir. - The TN Club; Member - The Memphis Country Club; **HOME ADD:** 2133 Rolling Valley Dr., Germantown, TN 38138, (901)754-3216; **BUS ADD:** 100 N. Main, #2200, Memphis, TN 38103, (901)525-3681.

GALE, Jack L.——**B:** Jan. 13, 1927, Toledo, OH, *VP*, Real Estate One, Inc.; **PRIM RE ACT:** Broker, Consultant, Owner/Investor, Real Estate Publisher, Instructor; **SERVICES:** Gen. brokerage, author, lecturer; **PREV EMPLOY:** Builder-Retailer; **PROFL AFFIL & HONORS:** Orlando, Winter Park Bd. of Realtors; Realtors Nat. Mktg. Inst.; FL Assn. of Realtors, NAR, Paul Harris Rotary Fellow; Grad. Realtors Inst.; CRS; CRB; AFLM; **EDUC:** BS, 1949, Journalism, Ohio Wesleyan; **MIL SERV:** US Navy; **OTHER ACT & HONORS:** Maitland Rotary - Past Pres.; **HOME ADD:** 1517 Westchester Ave., Winter Park, FL 32789, (305)628-8234; **BUS ADD:** 340 N. Maitland Ave., POB 156, Maitland, FL 32751, (305)644-6244.

GALE, Robert J.——**B:** July 23, 1926, Green Bay, WI, *Pres.*,, Robert Gale Enterprises, Inc.; **PRIM RE ACT:** Developer, Builder; **OTHER RE ACT:** Land Devel., Office Bldgs., Small Shopping Ctrs.; **SERVICES:** Devel. of resid. housing, condominiums, single family townhouses, etc., joint-ventures and sole ownership; **PREV EMPLOY:** Gale Org. - Joint venture with Allstate Ins. Co., ITT Levitt & Sons, Pres. of Levitt Multihousing Corp.; **PROFL AFFIL & HONORS:** Builders Assn. of S. FL; **EDUC:** 1949, Education, Northwestern Univ.; **OTHER ACT & HONORS:** Dade Cty., FL Indus. Advisory Bd., Dade Cty., FL Urban Renewal Comm.; **HOME ADD:** 1000 Quayside Terr., Miami, FL 33138, (305)893-1634; **BUS ADD:** 501 Bonaventure Blvd., Ft. Lauderdale, FL 33326, (305)472-2800.

GALEY, Michael H.——**B:** June 19, 1947, Ottumwa, IA, *VP and Gen. Mgr.*, Kennedy Devel. Group, Inc.; **PRIM RE ACT:** Developer, Builder, Owner/Investor; **SERVICES:** Devel. of Comml. Prop.; **REP CLIENTS:** Investors in Comml. Prop.; **PROFL AFFIL & HONORS:** Natl. Assn. of Home Builders, Intnl. Council of Shopping Ctrs.; **EDUC:** BS, 1970, Civil Engrg., IA State Univ.; **HOME ADD:** 4160 N. Terramere Ave., Arlington Heights, IL 60004, (312)870-9585; **BUS ADD:** 10 E. Coll. Dr., Arlington Heights, IL 60004, (312)394-4800.

GALINDO, Ramiro A.——**B:** Oct. 5, 1938, Bolivia, *Pres. and CEO*, Galindo Group of Companies; **PRIM RE ACT:** Engineer, Developer, Builder, Owner/Investor, Banker; **SERVICES:** Land devel.; res. const.; **PREV EMPLOY:** 10 yrs. as Consulting Engr.; 8 yrs. as Developer; **PROFL AFFIL & HONORS:** Fellow, ASCE; TX Soc. of Profl. Engrs., PE; Reg. Public Surveyor; **EDUC:** BSCE, 1960, TX A&M; **GRAD EDUC:** MSCE, 1962, TX A&M; **EDUC HONORS:** Nat. & Civil Engrg. Honor Soc., Chi Epsilon; **OTHER ACT & HONORS:** Sch. Bd. Pres., Cochabamba Bolivia, 1970-1973; Dir., Girls Club of Bryan; Danish Consul to Bolivia; Knight of the Royal Order of the Danebrog (Denmark), C of C Bryan TX; **HOME ADD:** 3015 Hummingbird Cir., Bryan, TX 77801, (713)779-4714; **BUS ADD:** 4103 S TX Ave., Bryan, TX 77801, (713)846-8759.

GALIP, Ronald——**B:** Feb. 28, 1934, Youngstown, OH, *Partner*, Galip & Manos; **PRIM RE ACT:** Attorney; **SERVICES:** Legal servs. for comml. RE devels. & retailers; **REP CLIENTS:** Edward J. DeBartolo Corp., Oxford Devel. Co.; LeRoy Jewelers; Arby's; **PREV EMPLOY:** Gen. Counsel for the Cafaro Co. 1957-1978; **PROFL AFFIL & HONORS:** ABA, OH State Bar Assn., Intl. Council of Shopping Centers, Landlord, Tenant Comm. ABA; Law Conference Comm.; ICSC; **EDUC:** BA, 1957, Liberal Arts, Youngstown State Univ.; **GRAD EDUC:** JD, 1957, Law, OH State Univ.; **OTHER ACT & HONORS:** Chmn., ICSC Law Conferences; Author, ICSC Shopping Center Report & "The Shopping Center as a Public Forum-Revisited" (1981); **HOME ADD:** 3445 Logan Way, Youngstown, OH 44505, (216)759-1508; **BUS ADD:** 422 City Centre One, PO Box 28, Youngstown, OH 44501, (216)743-6600.

GALLAGHER, James J.——*Pres.*, Eastdil Advisers, Inc.; **OTHER RE ACT:** Investment Adviser to Corp. Pension Funds; **SERVICES:** R.E. Investment and Asset Mgmt.; **REP CLIENTS:** Maj. Domestic Corp. Pension Funds; **BUS ADD:** 40 W. 57 St., NY, NY 10019, (212)977-4505.

GALLAGHER, James V.——**B:** July 12, 1933, Peekskill, NY, *Pres.*, Gallagher Associates, Inc.; **PRIM RE ACT:** Broker, Consultant, Appraiser, Lender, Builder, Property Manager; **SERVICES:** Data processing consulting service; **REP CLIENTS:** Basser & Kaufman, Hartford Provisions Co.; **PROFL AFFIL & HONORS:** Bd. of Realtors - CT; Nat. & Norwalk CT Bds. of Realtors, RE Broker - CT & NY; **EDUC:** BA, 1955, Econ., Villanova - Iona; **GRAD EDUC:** MA, 1965, Bus., NYU Grad. Sch. of Bus.; **MIL SERV:** US Army, SP3; **OTHER ACT & HONORS:** Bd. of Election, School Bd.; **HOME ADD:** 2605 N.W. 114th Ave., Coral Springs, FL 33065, (305)753-8568; **BUS ADD:** 399 Ringgold St., Peekskill, NY 10566, (203)866-1679.

GALLAGHER, Margaret Parr——**B:** Apr. 5, 1939, Baltimore, MD, *VP*, Melbourne Feagin J. Hammersmith, Inc., Residential Resales; **PRIM RE ACT:** Broker, Instructor; **OTHER RE ACT:** Manager of Sales Assoc.; **SERVICES:** Advertising; **PREV EMPLOY:** Tchr., Sales Assoc., Asst. Mgr., Trainer, Taught RE Courses for Howard Comm. Coll.; **PROFL AFFIL & HONORS:** GRI, RESSI, Realtor Howard Cty. MD, Million Dollar Club Howard Cty. Greater Baltimore, MD; **EDUC:** BS, 1961, Educ., Geography, Towson Univ.; **EDUC HONORS:** Geography-LED Class; **OTHER ACT & HONORS:** Chief Judge Elections Howard Cty., League of Women Voters; **HOME ADD:** 9226 Mellenbrook Rd., Columbia, MD, (301)730-5114; **BUS ADD:** 306 Second St., Laurel, MD 20810, (301)725-5278.

GALLAGHER, Ralph——**B:** April 30, 1939, NY, Atty. at Law; **PRIM RE ACT:** Attorney; **SERVICES:** Title Ins. & Escrow Claims Litagation; **REP CLIENTS:** Title Ins. Cos.; **PREV EMPLOY:** Asst. VP & Rgnl. Counsel, Safeco Tile Ins. Co., Firemans Fund Amer. Ins. Co., CA Casualty Mgmt. Co., US Dept. of State; **PROFL AFFIL & HONORS:** State Bar of CA; **EDUC:** BA, 1961, Area Studies & Physics, Harvard; **GRAD EDUC:** JD, 1976, Law, Hastings Coll. of Law, Univ. of CA; **BUS ADD:** 2408 California St., San Francisco, CA 94115, (415)929-0252.

GALLAGHER, Terence J.——**B:** Sept. 5, 1938, Philadelphia, PA, *Gen. Part.*, Gallagher Maher Assoc.; **PRIM RE ACT:** Attorney, Regulator, Owner/Investor, Syndicator; **SERVICES:** RE investment, consulting, & synd.; **REP CLIENTS:** Indivs. & instnl. investors, broker/dealer security firms; **PREV EMPLOY:** Asst. VP Citibank, NYC, VP Bessener Trust Co., Newark, NJ; **PROFL AFFIL & HONORS:** Bar NJ & VA, Intl. Assn. of Fin. Planners; **EDUC:** 1960, Georgetown Univ.; **GRAD EDUC:** LLB, 1963, Univ. of VA; **HOME ADD:** Long Hill Rd., Green Village, NJ, (201)539-7679; **BUS ADD:** 310 S. St., Morristown, NJ 07960, (201)455-1118.

GALLAGHER, William C.——**B:** July 29, 1929, Philadelphia, PA, *Sales Assoc.*, Roadrunner Agency; **PRIM RE ACT:** Broker, Consultant, Owner/Investor, Property Manager; **OTHER RE ACT:** Indus. Devel.; **SERVICES:** Market Analysis; **PREV EMPLOY:** Gallery of Homes 3 1/2 yrs.; NM Dept. of Devel. (Indus. & Resort Devel. Mgr.), Mgr. Intl. Bus.; **PROFL AFFIL & HONORS:** CID; GRI; **EDUC:** BA, 1951, Econ., Psych., Ursinus Coll., Collegville, PA; **GRAD EDUC:** MBA, 1975, Mktg., Intl. Trade, Univ. of NM, Albuquerque; **EDUC HONORS:** Grad., Exec. Prog.; **MIL SERV:** USN; AG3; **HOME ADD:** 212 Corona St., Santa Fe, NM 87501, (505)982-0444; **BUS ADD:** P.O. Box 1208, Santa Fe, NM 87504, (505)982-4251.

GALLANTER, Sanford——**B:** May 4, 1928, Newark, NJ, *Pres.*, The Aspen Grp., Inc.; **PRIM RE ACT:** Developer, Owner/Investor; **PROFL AFFIL & HONORS:** Pres. & Dir. - Nat. Housing Rehab. Assn.; **EDUC:** BS with honors, 1951, Bus. Admin., Rutgers Univ.; **GRAD EDUC:** JD, 1955, Law, Rutgers Univ. School of Law; **EDUC HONORS:** Elected to Nat. Bus. School Honor Soc.; **BUS ADD:** 56 Park Pl., Newark, NJ 07102, (201)623-0300.

GALLEGOS, Richard L.——**B:** Oct. 21, 1940, Albuquerque, NM, Richard L. Gallegos, Atty. at Law; **PRIM RE ACT:** Attorney; **EDUC:** BA, 1966, Chemistry, Univ. of NM; **GRAD EDUC:** JD, Law, Western State; **EDUC HONORS:** Emmanual Kent Scholarship Award, Jurisprudence Award Real Prop.; **HOME ADD:** 10905 Riesling Dr., San Diego, CA 92131, (714)271-7837; **BUS ADD:** 9225 Mira Mesa Blvd., Stet. 204, P O Box 26577, San Diego, CA 92126, (714)578-2850.

GALLEHER, E. Grice——**B:** June 16, 1935, Richmond, VA, *Sr. RE Officer*, First & Merchants National Bank, Trust RE Div.; **PRIM RE ACT:** Consultant, Banker, Property Manager; **SERVICES:** Acquisition, mgmt. & disposition of prop. for trust & estates; **PROFL AFFIL & HONORS:** IREM, VA Assn. of Realtors, CPM, GRI; **EDUC:** BA, 1956, Sociology, Univ. of VA; **MIL SERV:** USMC, Capt.; **HOME ADD:** 307 Roslyn Rd., Richmond, VA 23226, (804)285-1843; **BUS ADD:** PO Box 26903, Richmond, VA 23261, (804)788-2697.

GALLET, Jeffry H.——**B:** Nov. 18, 1942, New York City, NY, *Atty.*, Yavner Gallet & Dreyer; **PRIM RE ACT:** Attorney; **OTHER RE ACT:** Litigation; **PROFL AFFIL & HONORS:** Amer. Bar. Assn., NY State Bar Assn. (Chairperson, committee on the warranty of habitability), Assn. of the Bar of the City of NY, Award for Outstanding Service to Cooperative Housing Movement from Federation of Sect. 213s, Inc.; **EDUC:** BA, 1964, Pol. Sci., Wilkes Coll.; **GRAD EDUC:** JD, 1967, Brooklyn Law School; **OTHER ACT & HONORS:** Judge, Civil Court of the City of NY (1980); Commissioner New York State Temporary Commission on Rental Housing (1977-1980), President, New York Metropolitan Council of the American Jewish Congress (1981-); Adjunct Assistant Professor of Law, Brooklyn Coll. (1978-79); Co-Author of two books and author or co-author of 18 articles on RE subjects; **HOME ADD:** 222 West 83rd St., New York, NY, (212)724-5811; **BUS ADD:** 42 Broadway, Rm. 1701, New York, NY 10004, (212)269-5566.

GALLETTI, Michael Lawrence——**B:** Apr. 25, 1952, Montreal, CAN., *VP - Triangle Realties, Inc.*, Triangle Realties, Inc., Triangle Properties Ltd. Etc.; **PRIM RE ACT:** Broker, Consultant, Developer, Builder, Owner/Investor, Syndicator; **PREV EMPLOY:** Marathon Realties, Ltd., Marcil Mort. Corp., R.W.I. Properties, Ltd.; **PROFL AFFIL & HONORS:** Montreal Bd. of Trade, Montreal RE Bd., Can. RE Assn., Bachelor of Commerce, F.R.I. Retail Merchandising Diploma; **EDUC:** BS, 1976, Admin. and Fin., Concordia Univ.; **HOME ADD:** 4041 Grey Ave., Montreal, H4A3N9, Quebec, (514)487-3051; **BUS ADD:** 1509 Sherbrooke St. W, Suite 4B, Montreal, H3GIMI, Quebec, Canada, (514)932-1166.

GALLIER, Theo A.——**B:** Oct. 29, 1947, Liberty, TX, *Sr. VP*, Henry S. Miller Management Corp.; **PRIM RE ACT:** Property Manager; **SERVICES:** Complete Mgmt. of all types of comml. props.; **REP CLIENTS:** Major fin. instns., for. investors, devels., synds.; **PROFL AFFIL & HONORS:** Candidate for CPM & MAI Designations; **EDUC:** BA, 1969, Econ., TX Tech. Univ. - Lubbock, TX; **GRAD EDUC:** MBA, 1973, Fin., Univ. of TX at Austin; **EDUC HONORS:** Grad. with Honors; **HOME ADD:** 9816 Amberton Pkwy, Dallas, TX 75243, (214)690-5274; **BUS ADD:** 2001 Bryan Tower, 30th Fl., Dallas, TX 75201, (214)748-9171.

GALST, Lester R.——**B:** Sept. 9, 1918, Milwaukee, WI, *Owner, Broker*, Ticket of Arizona; **PRIM RE ACT:** Broker, Consultant, Instructor; **OTHER RE ACT:** Equity-Share Program; **PREV EMPLOY:** Owner, Expectation Shops, retail chain, Phoenix, 1947-1965; Buyer, Bon Marche group Allied Stores Corp., Seattle, 1966-1968; Owner, Broker, Londonderry Realty, Gallery of Homes, Lake Havasu City, AZ, 1968-1980; Les Galst & Assocs., Realtors, Lake Havasu City, 1980-1981; **PROFL AFFIL & HONORS:** NAR; RNMI; FLI; AZ Assn. pg Realtors; Scottsdale Bd. of Realtors Honorary Life Member Lake Havasu Bd. of Realtors, CRB; CRS; GRI; **MIL SERV:** US Army, First Lt.; **OTHER ACT & HONORS:** Bd. of Dir., Lake Havasu Assn. for Retarded and Handicapped, VP, 1976, Pres., 1977-1978; Bd. of Dir., Lake Havasu Community Devel. Corp., 1979-1981 Bd. of Directors Lake Havasu City Chamber of Commerce 1970-1972 and president 1972; Bd. of Directors Arzona Assn Realtors 1974 to present 2nd V. Pres. Arizona Assn Realtors 1978 1st V. Pres. Arizona Assn Realtors 1979 President Ariz. Assn Realtors 1980 Treasurer Ariz. Assn Realtors 1982 Bd. of Directors Nat'l Assn of Realtors 1980 to present Realtor of year 1975 Lake Havasu Bd. of Realtors; **HOME ADD:** 5566 N. 76th Pl., Scottsdale, AZ 85253; **BUS ADD:** 7323 E. Shoeman Ln., Scottsdale, AZ 85251, (602)941-0641.

GALSTON, John Wood——**B:** Nov. 5, 1940, New York, NY, *Pres.*, Envicon Development Corp.; **PRIM RE ACT:** Architect, Developer, Owner/Investor, Syndicator; **SERVICES:** Devel. and Investment in RE Props.; **REP CLIENTS:** Indiv. and Corporate Investors; **PREV EMPLOY:** 1966-1967; Dir., Pres.'s Commn. on PA Ave., Washington, DC; '67-'73: Assoc. Partner & Dir. of Washington Office - Skidmore, Owings & Merrill (Arch. & Urban Planning); **PROFL AFFIL & HONORS:** AIA, Amer. Inst. of Certified Planners, Psi Chi (Nat. Hon. Psych. Soc.), AIA, Amer. Inst. of Certified Planners - Recipient of AIA Student Medal, 1966; Fulbright Scholar, 1966-67; Winchester Traveling Fellow, Recipient HUD Design Award for Operation Breakthrough 1968; **EDUC:** BS, 1962, Psych., Tufts Univ.; **GRAD EDUC:** BArch; MArch, 1966, Arch. and Planning, Yale Univ.; **EDUC HONORS:** Cum Laude, Winchester Traveling Fellowship; AIA Student Medal, Alpha Rho Chi Medal; **OTHER ACT & HONORS:** Dir., Pres. Commn. on Pennsylvania Ave., Washington, DC-1966-67; Young Pres. Org.; Racquet & Tennis Club (NY); Yale Club; Metropolitan Club (DC); Sec. Cold Spring Harbor Beach Club (NY); Phillips Exeter Acaedmy, Rgnl. Alumni Council; Nat. Trust for Hist. Preservation; **HOME ADD:** 101 Woodchuck Hollow Rd., Huntington, NY 11743, (516)423-7251; **BUS ADD:** 630 Fifth Ave.; Suite 570, New York, NY 10111, (212)581-8818.

GALUSH, Robert J.——**B:** Jan. 18, 1930, Minneapolis, MN, *Asst. Sec.*, Twin City Federal Savings & Loan, Prop. Mgmt.; **PRIM RE ACT:** Appraiser, Instructor, Property Manager; **PROFL AFFIL & HONORS:** Soc. of RE Appraisers, SRA; **HOME ADD:** 1115 Raleigh St., St. Paul, MN 55108, (612)645-9741; **BUS ADD:** 1300 Twin City Federal Tower, 801 Marquette Ave., Minneapolis, MN 55402, (612)370-7085.

GALVIN, John Patrick——**B:** July 5, 1933, Detroit, MI, *Atty.*, (Owner) Law Offices of John Patrick Galvin Esq; **PRIM RE ACT:** Attorney; **SERVICES:** RE & construction law (all phases); **REP CLIENTS:** Dresser Indus. (Dallas), Crecent Corp. (Chicago); **PREV EMPLOY:** VP & Counsel, Title Ins. & Trust Co., L.A., CA; **PROFL AFFIL & HONORS:** CA State Bar, Los Angeles Cty. Bar, Orange Cty. Bar, ABA, Assn. Trial Lawyers of Amer.; **EDUC:** BS Cum Laude, 1956, Univ. of Detroit; **GRAD EDUC:** JD, 1967, Law, Univ. of Detroit Law School; **EDUC HONORS:** Cum Laude; **MIL SERV:** USN, Lt., Aviator; **OTHER ACT & HONORS:** Big Canyon CC, Irvine Coast CC, John Wayne Tennis Club; **HOME ADD:** 10941 Lake Court Rd., (Lemon Heights), Santa Ana, CA 92705; **BUS ADD:** 4299 MacArthur Blvd, Suite 200, Newport Beach, CA 92660, (714)752-0456.

GAMBLE, Gerald L.——**B:** Feb. 22, 1941, Jefferson, TX, *Pres. and Owner*, Gerald L. Gamble Co., Inc.; **PRIM RE ACT:** Broker, Consultant; **SERVICES:** Brokerage of comml. and indus. RE and counseling; **REP CLIENTS:** Nat. and local indus. clients; fin. inst.; investors; fast food and retail chains; **PROFL AFFIL & HONORS:** SIR; Amer. Soc. of RE Counselors; RNMI; ABA; OK Bar Assn., SIR; CRE; CCIM; JD; **EDUC:** BA, 1963, Univ. of OK; **GRAD EDUC:** MA, 1964, Econ. History, Stanford Univ.; JD, 1968, Law, OK City Univ.; **EDUC HONORS:** Phi Beta Kappa; Pres., Student Body; Outstanding Sr. Man, Woodrow Wilson Fellow; **MIL SERV:** USAF, Capt.; **OTHER ACT & HONORS:** Rotary Club; C of C; Econ. Club; OK City Golf and Ctry. Club; Petroleum Club; **HOME ADD:** 8514 Waverly, Oklahoma City, OK 73120, (405)842-2519; **BUS ADD:** 1102 Midland Ct.,, Oklahoma City, OK 73102, (405)232-1138.

GAMBLE, William Ellis——**B:** Apr. 10, 1945, Memphis, TN, *Asst. VP*, Depositors Savings Association, Mort. Loan Div.; **PRIM RE ACT:** Appraiser, Lender; **SERVICES:** Income prop. valuation and fin.; **REP CLIENTS:** Indiv. and/or inst. investors in income producing RE; **PREV EMPLOY:** UniFirst Fed. S&L Assn., Income Prop. Loan Officer; **PROFL AFFIL & HONORS:** Bd. of Dir., Greater Jackson Apt. Assn.; **EDUC:** BA, 1968, Pol. Sci., Millsaps Coll., Jackson, MS; **MIL SERV:** US Army, SP/5, Vietnam Service Medal; **OTHER ACT & HONORS:** Bd. of Dir., Sertoma Club; Pres., River Place I Homeowners Assn.; **HOME ADD:** 118 River PL., Jackson, MS 39211, (601)956-6655; **BUS ADD:** POB 918, Jackson, MS 39205, (601)354-0521.

GAMBRILL, J. Matthew——**B:** July 18, 1947, MN, *Pres. & Counsel*, Natl. Capital Realty Corp.; **PRIM RE ACT:** Consultant, Attorney, Owner/Investor; **SERVICES:** Office bldg., apt. & marine investments; **PROFL AFFIL & HONORS:** ABA, DC Bar Assn., Congressional Ctry. Club, City Tavern Club; **EDUC:** BA, 1969, Hist., Hobart Coll.; **GRAD EDUC:** JD, 1972, Law, Catholic Univ. Law Sch.; **HOME ADD:** 6716 Fairfax Rd., Chevy Chase, MD 20015, (301)656-3863; **BUS ADD:** 1511 K St. NW Suite 1100, Washington, DC 20005, (202)783-4113.

GAMEZ, Barbara M.——*Dir. Book Publishing*, Realtors Nat. Mktg. Inst.; **PRIM RE ACT:** Real Estate Publisher; **SERVICES:** Educ. reading mat. for RE profls.; **PROFL AFFIL & HONORS:** Assoc. of Amer. Publishers, Chicago Book Clinic; **BUS ADD:** 430 N Michigan Ave., Chicago, IL 60611, (312)670-3520.

GAMMON, Terrance——*Dir. RE*, Stride Rite Corp.; **PRIM RE ACT:** Property Manager; **BUS ADD:** 5 Cambridge Center, Cambridge, MA 02142, (617)491-8800.*

GANGE, Jack——*Chmn*, South Dakota, SD Real Estate Bd.; **PRIM RE ACT:** Property Manager; **BUS ADD:** PO Box 490, Pierre, SD 57501, (605)773-3600.*

GANGLOFF, Gerard P.——B: Jan. 9, 1948, Chicago, IL, *Auditor and Bus. Consultant*, Partner; Chulock, Sherwani & Gangloff, CPA's; **OTHER RE ACT:** Auditor and consultant; **SERVICES:** Examination of financial statements, bus. & tax consulting; **REP CLIENTS:** Various RE partnerhips, RE brokers, investors; **PREV EMPLOY:** 8 yrs. with large local (Chicago) CPA firm; 3 yrs. indus. acctg.; **PROFL AFFIL & HONORS:** French-Amer. C of C; Amer. Inst. of CPA's; IL Soc. of CPA's, Member of Fin. Mgmt. Assn.; Nat. Honor Soc.; **EDUC:** BBA, 1970, Public Acctg., Loyola Univ.; **GRAD EDUC:** MBA, 1981, RE Fin., DePaul Univ.; **OTHER ACT & HONORS:** Officer positions in charitable organizations and clubs; **HOME ADD:** 3826 W. Jarvis, Skokie, IL 60076, (312)677-3254; **BUS ADD:** 221 N. La Salle, Chicago, IL 60601, (312)372-4141.

GANGLOFF, Peter A.——B: Nov. 1, 1942, Albany, NY, *Dir., VP and Treas.*, Midtown Holdings Corp.; **PRIM RE ACT:** Developer, Property Manager; **SERVICES:** Devel., leasing and mgmt. of downtown shopping ctr./office complex; **PROFL AFFIL & HONORS:** AICPA; NYS Soc. of CPA's; Intl. Council of Shopping Ctrs.; Building Owners and Mgrs. Assn., CPA; **EDUC:** BS, 1964, Acctg., Univ. of Rochester; **OTHER ACT & HONORS:** Rochester C of C; Univ. Club of Rochester; **HOME ADD:** 17 Lookout View Rd., Fairport, NY 14450, (716)223-1970; **BUS ADD:** 300 Midtown Tower, Rochester, NY 14604, (716)454-2070.

GANLY, David M.——B: Nov. 15, 1937, Ridgewood, NJ, *Atty.*, Gudger, Reynolds & Patton; **PRIM RE ACT:** Attorney; **PREV EMPLOY:** Pres. & Chief Op. Officer, Comp-U-Card of Amer., Inc.; **PROFL AFFIL & HONORS:** ABA, NC Bar Assn.; **EDUC:** BA, 1959, Arch., Yale Univ.; **GRAD EDUC:** JD, 1980, NCCU; **MIL SERV:** US Army, Capt., Purple Heart, Armed Forces Expeditionary Medal (Vietnam); **OTHER ACT & HONORS:** Member of Advisory Comm. to Orange Cty., NC, on Land Title Records Mgmt., 1979-81; Dir. & Treas. Land Conservancy of Ridgefield, CT.; **HOME ADD:** 22 Forest Ridge Dr., Arden, NC 28704, (704)684-5224; **BUS ADD:** One Oak Plaza, Suite 203, Asheville, NC 28801, (704)253-5671.

GANN, Gregg——B: July 6, 1948, Los Angeles, CA, *VP/Dist. Mgr.*, Grubb & Ellis Comml. Brokerage Co.; **PRIM RE ACT:** Broker, Attorney; **PREV EMPLOY:** Atty.; **PROFL AFFIL & HONORS:** CA Bar, Amer. Bar Assn.; **EDUC:** BA, 1976, Amer. Studies, CA State Univ. at LA; **GRAD EDUC:** JD, 1979, Law, Loyola Law School; **EDUC HONORS:** Dean's List, All semesters, Hon. Scholarship; **MIL SERV:** USAF; **HOME ADD:** 2837 Glendon Ave., Los Angeles, CA 90064, (213)475-6846; **BUS ADD:** 9606 Santa Monica Blvd., Suite 200, Beverly Hills, CA 90210, (213)278-2190.

GANS, Daniel J.——B: June 8, 1954, NYC, *Gen. Part.*, Hoboken Restorations, 210 Project; **PRIM RE ACT:** Developer; **SERVICES:** Condo conversions; **PREV EMPLOY:** Asst. Foreman for Arch. Builder, Project Coord. NYC Subcontractor; **PROFL AFFIL & HONORS:** Hoboken Condo. Devels. Assn., spokesman; **EDUC:** 1977, Eng., Gettysburg Coll.; **GRAD EDUC:** 1981, Int. Env. Design, Pratt Univ.; **OTHER ACT & HONORS:** Top freestyle skier; **HOME ADD:** Leonia, NJ 07605348 Highwood Ave, (201)944-7476; **BUS ADD:** 210 3rd St., Hoboken, NJ 07030, (201)792-1739.

GANS, Peter M.——B: Aug. 22, 1943, NY, *Pres.*, Gans Realty and Investment Co.; **PRIM RE ACT:** Broker, Syndicator, Property Manager, Owner/Investor; **SERVICES:** Full service prop. mgmt. and leasing, investment analysis and counseling; **REP CLIENTS:** Indiv., devel., instl. investors, and investment grps.; **PROFL AFFIL & HONORS:** NAR, IREM, ICSC, BOMA, RESSI, CPM; **EDUC:** BA, 1965, Econ., Stanford Univ.; **GRAD EDUC:** MBA, 1973, Fin., Univ. of S. CA; **MIL SERV:** USMC, Capt.; **BUS ADD:** 600 Imogen Ave., Suite 108, Los Angeles, CA 90026, (213)662-3101.

GANS, Ray J.——*Pres.*, The Commodore Corp.; **PRIM RE ACT:** Property Manager; **BUS ADD:** PO Box 295-400W. Brooklyn St., Syracuse, IN 46567, (219)457-4431.*

GANS, Robert——B: Aug. 28, 1916, Dunkard, PA, *Prop. Mgr.*, Robert Gans, Realtor; **PRIM RE ACT:** Broker, Developer, Owner/Investor, Property Manager; **SERVICES:** Devel., mgmt. and sale of income producing props.; **PROFL AFFIL & HONORS:** NAR, IREM, Intl. Council of Shopping Ctrs., Olympic Peninsula Rental Assn., CPM, CSM, CCIM; **EDUC:** 1937, PA State Univ.; **EDUC HONORS:** Nat. Pres. of IREM, 1966; Pres. of Seattle King Cty. Bd. of Realtors, 1974; **HOME ADD:** 275 Dungeness Meadows, Sequim, WA 98382, (206)683-7036; **BUS ADD:** 209 Sunnyside Sq. Bldg., PO Box 850, Sequim, WA 98382, (206)683-7094.

GANTZ, John G., Jr.——*Dir. Adm.*, Wheelabrator-Frye, Inc.; **PRIM RE ACT:** Property Manager; **BUS ADD:** Liberty Lane, Hampton, NY 03842, (603)926-5911.*

GANZ, Erwin——*Exec. VP Ind. Opers.*, Ronson Corp.; **PRIM RE ACT:** Property Manager; **BUS ADD:** One Ronson Rd., Bridgewater, NJ 08807, (201)526-5900.*

GARAFALO, Joseph——B: Aug. 31, 1940, New York, NY, *Asst. VP*, Baird & Warner, Inc., Comml./Investment Div.; **PRIM RE ACT:** Broker, Consultant; **SERVICES:** Mktg. & sales of investment prop.; investment advisory serv.; consulting serv.; **REP CLIENTS:** Comml. & resid. prop. owners; instns.; pension funds; synd.; indiv. investors; **PREV EMPLOY:** RE Research Corp., VP; Citicorp Realty Consultants, Exec. Dir.; **PROFL AFFIL & HONORS:** Chicago RE Bd.; Nat. Assn. of Corporate RE Execs.; NAR; International Council of Shopping Centers; **EDUC:** BS, 1961, EE, Manhattan Coll., NY; **GRAD EDUC:** MBA, 1967, Mgmt. & Mktg., NY Univ.; **EDUC HONORS:** Eta Kappa Nu Honor Frat.; **HOME ADD:** 7330-11 Winthrop Way, Downers Grove, IL 60515, (312)754-2433; **BUS ADD:** 115 S LaSalle St., Chicago, IL 60603, (312)368-5769.

GARBISCH, Harold P.——B: Sept. 13, 1922, Jackson, WI, *Owner*, Jackson Realty; **PRIM RE ACT:** Broker, Appraiser, Property Manager; **OTHER RE ACT:** RE Security Sales; **SERVICES:** Investment counseling, comml., investment, farm sales; **PREV EMPLOY:** RE devel., restaurant owner, farm operator and owner; **PROFL AFFIL & HONORS:** RMNI, NAR, WRA, FLI, WI Exchange Club, Milwaukee Traders, GRI;CCIM Candidate; **EDUC:** 1954, Agric.; **MIL SERV:** Mil. Govt. 1943-45, T/5, ETO; **HOME ADD:** 1845 Sherman Rd., Jackson, WI 53037, (414)677-3139; **BUS ADD:** 1845 Sherman Rd., Jackson, WI 53037, (414)677-3139.

GARCIA, Bernie I.——B: June 8, 1939, Taos, NM, *Owner*, Bernie I. Garcia & Assoc.; **PRIM RE ACT:** Consultant, Appraiser, Instructor; **SERVICES:** Consultant, appraiser; **REP CLIENTS:** 3M Co., Merrill Lynch, Homequity Inc., FHA VA Dept. Affairs, Firestone, Imperial Bank, Coca Cola, Paramount Pictures, City of Los Angeles, TRW; **PREV EMPLOY:** Valuation Engr. for LA Cty. Flood Control, Civil Engr.; **PROFL AFFIL & HONORS:** Sr. Member of both ASA, NAIFA; **EDUC:** BS, Civil Engrg., Loyola Univ., Los Angeles; **EDUC HONORS:** Academic Scholarship; **HOME ADD:** 3748 Woodhurst Dr., Covina, CA 91724, (213)332-3129; **BUS ADD:** 266 S. Glendora Ave., Ste 5, W. Covina, CA 91790, (213)919-3307.

GARCIA, Dr. Gaspar V.——B: Jan. 7, 1946, Carolina, PR, *Exec. VP*, LRF Developers, Inc.; **PRIM RE ACT:** Consultant, Developer, Owner/Investor, Syndicator; **SERVICES:** Prop. Devel.; **REP CLIENTS:** Battery Park City; **PREV EMPLOY:** Consultant, fin.; **PROFL AFFIL & HONORS:** AMA, IAUP, Nat. Hispanic Housing Coalition, DCS Honoris Causa, Amer. Univ.; **EDUC:** BA, 1971, Econ., Queens Coll.; **GRAD EDUC:** MBA, 1977, Fairleigh Dickinson Univ.; **OTHER ACT & HONORS:** Counsel, Chmn. Ways & Means, NYS Assembly, 1977; Chmn. RE Comm. NHHC-NYC; Biographed: Who's Who Indus. and Fin.; Bronx C of C; Bd of Dirs. Hostos Community Coll.; **HOME ADD:** 2138 Haviland Ave., Bronx, NY 10472, (212)829-4941; **BUS ADD:** 384 E. 149th St., Bronx, NY 10455, (212)993-1000.

GARD, Scott——B: Dec. 25, 1942, Kansas City, MO, *Program Mgr., Econ.*, Midwest Research Inst.; **PRIM RE ACT:** Consultant; **SERVICES:** Location and market studies; **REP CLIENTS:** Banks, RE devels.; **EDUC:** BA, 1965, Econ., Univ. of MO, Kansas City; **GRAD EDUC:** 1971, Econ.; **MIL SERV:** US Army; E-4; **HOME ADD:** 2919 W. 51st, Westwood, KS 66205, (913)432-6940; **BUS ADD:** 425 Volker Blvd., Kansas City, MO 64110, (816)597-3357.

GARDEMEYER, Dennis Alan——B: Feb. 19, 1949, San Francisco, CA, *VP*, Cemo Development, Inc.; **PRIM RE ACT:** Developer, Builder, Owner/Investor; **PREV EMPLOY:** Partner, Fulcrum Assocs.; VP-Fulcrum Const.; Pres., Capitol Pacific Construction, Inc.; **PROFL AFFIL & HONORS:** Bldg. Indus. Assn. of Superior CA; **EDUC:** BS, 1971, Fin., CA State Univ. Sacramento; **GRAD EDUC:** MBA, 1975, Fin., CA State Univ., Sacramento; **EDUC HONORS:** Outstanding Male Grad., Wall Street Journal Award, Outstanding Bus. Student; **MIL SERV:** US Army Res., E-5; **OTHER ACT & HONORS:** Tr., Delta Farms Reclamation Dist. 2030, San Joaquin Cty. 5 yrs.; Ducks Unlimited and Big Bros.; **HOME ADD:** 3215 Stanford Lane, El Dorado Hills, CA 95630, (916)933-1229; **BUS ADD:** 2893 Sunrise Blvd., Suite 201, Rancho Cordova, CA 95670, (916)635-1300.

GARDNER, Mark S——B: June 28, 1953, Fredsbg., VA, *Atty.*, Gardner & Maupin; **PRIM RE ACT:** Attorney; **SERVICES:** Title exam. & settlement servs.; **PROFL AFFIL & HONORS:** ABA, Real Prop. Sect.; **EDUC:** AB, 1975, Hist., Davidson Coll.; **GRAD EDUC:** JD, 1978, TC Williams Sch. of Law, Univ. of Richmond; **EDUC HONORS:** Ed. in Chief of Law Review, Outstanding Grad in 1971; **OTHER ACT & HONORS:** Spotsylvania Cty. Comm. Atty., 1980; **HOME ADD:** PO Box 486, Spotsylvania, VA 22553, (703)582-5192;

BUS ADD: PO Box 129, Spotsylvania, VA 22553, (703)582-6333.

GARFIELD, Joseph A.——B: Aug. 19, 1906, NY, *Part.*, Garfield-Triester Props.; **PRIM RE ACT:** Developer; **PREV EMPLOY:** Utilities & R.E. Devel.; **EDUC:** BS, 1925, N.Y.U.; **GRAD EDUC:** LLB, 1927, St. Lawrence Univ.; **EDUC HONORS:** Summa Cum Laude; **OTHER ACT & HONORS:** Also associated with Mayfair in the Grove; **HOME ADD:** 2901 S. Bayshore Dr., Coconut Grove, FL 33133, (305)443-0495; **BUS ADD:** 2699 Bayshore Dr., Coconut Grove, FL 33133, (305)858-2414.

GARFIELD, Louis N.——B: May 7, 1939, Orange, NJ, *Partner*, Barkan Properties; **PRIM RE ACT:** Developer; **SERVICES:** Comml., indus., resid. RE devel.; **PROFL AFFIL & HONORS:** Natl. Leased Housing Assoc.; **EDUC:** BSME, 1960, Lehigh Univ.; **GRAD EDUC:** MBA, 1963, Mktg., U. of MI; **EDUC HONORS:** Grad. w/Distinction; **HOME ADD:** 72 Highland St., W. Newton, MA 02165, (617)244-3528; **BUS ADD:** 1330 Boylston St., Chestnut Hill, MA 02167, (617)734-9600.

GARFIELD, M. Robert——B: Feb. 5, 1922, Cincinnati, OH, *Exec. VP*, West Shell, Inc., Comml./Indus. & Prop. Mgmt. Divs.; **PRIM RE ACT:** Broker, Consultant, Appraiser, Instructor, Property Manager; **SERVICES:** Full service in all phases of Comml./Indus. RE; **PREV EMPLOY:** The Carew Tower; **PROFL AFFIL & HONORS:** Cincinnati Bd. of Realtors, OH Assn. of Realtors, NAR, IFAS, Senior, Amer. Assn. Cert. Appraiser, Sr., GRI, Amer. Arbitration Assn., Honors: OH Assn. of RE Bds. "Associate of the Year, State of OH 1962"; **EDUC:** BS, 1946, Bus. Admin., OH State Univ.; **MIL SERV:** US Army, Lt., 1942-46; **HOME TEL:** (513)631-0865; **BUS ADD:** 3 E. Fourth St., Cincinnati, OH 45202, (513)721-4200.

GARFINKEL, Arnold——B: Sept. 19, 1937, KS City, MO, *Pres.*, Quality Hill New Town Redevelopment Corp.; **PRIM RE ACT:** Developer, Owner/Investor, Property Manager; **PROFL AFFIL & HONORS:** RESSI; Nat. Trust for Hist. Preservation; Victorian Soc. of Amer.; Hist. House Assn. of Amer.; Hist. KS City Foundation, Realtor; **EDUC:** BA, 1959, Colonial Amer. Hist. & Arch., Univ. of PA; **GRAD EDUC:** MA, 1962, Foreign Area Studies/Japan, Yale Univ.; **EDUC HONORS:** Cum Laude, Yale Univ. Fellowship, Ford Found. Grant, NDEA Scholarship; **OTHER ACT & HONORS:** Landmarks Commn., KS City, MO, 1978-1980; Univ. of PA Alumni Club of KS City; Yale Club of KS City; Japan America Soc.; **HOME ADD:** 4629 Mercier, KS City, MO 64112, (816)931-7372; **BUS ADD:** 1030 Washington, KS City, MO 64105, (816)842-5682.

GARFINKEL, Marvin——B: Mar. 23, 1929, Philadelphia, PA, Garfinkel & Volpicelli; **PRIM RE ACT:** Consultant, Attorney, Developer, Owner/Investor, Instructor; **PROFL AFFIL & HONORS:** ABA Fed. Bar; PA Bar; Philadelphia Bar; Intl. Bar; Intl. Law Assns.; Am. Coll. RE Lawyers; **EDUC:** BA, 1951, Pomona Coll.; **GRAD EDUC:** LLB, 1954, Law, Univ. of PA; LLM, 1962, Law, NY Univ.; **EDUC HONORS:** Magna Cum Laude; **OTHER ACT & HONORS:** Order of the Coif; **HOME ADD:** Cobble Court, Haverford, PA 19041; **BUS ADD:** 308 Walnut St., Philadelphia, PA 19106, (215)923-5678.

GARIBALDI, Joseph J., Jr.——B: Dec. 8, 1914, NJ, *Chmn. of the Bd.*, Garibaldi Realty Corp.; **PRIM RE ACT:** Broker, Consultant, Appraiser, Owner/Investor, Insuror; **PROFL AFFIL & HONORS:** Soc. of Indus. Realtors (Charter Member); Amer. Soc. of RE Counselors; NAR; NJ Assn. of Realtors; Indus. RE Broker Assn., Past Pres., NJ Chapt., SIR; Past Pres., IREBA; Treas., Bd. of Realtors; **EDUC:** BA, 1937, Fordham Univ.; **MIL SERV:** U.S. Army, Capt.; **OTHER ACT & HONORS:** Member of Exec. Comm. & Bd. of Dir. of Fidelity Union Ban Corp.; **HOME ADD:** 60 Hilltop Rd., Short Hills, NJ 07078, (201)379-2728; **BUS ADD:** 2 Edison Pl., POB 517, Springfield, NJ 07081, (201)467-3000.

GARLAND, Rebecca T.——B: Mar. 17, 1947, Erwin, TN, *Gen. Counsel*, Tennessee Housing Devel. Agency, Legal; **PRIM RE ACT:** Attorney; **SERVICES:** The agency is a leader for single-family,multi-famiLy rental apts.; **REP CLIENTS:** The agency raises funds thru tax-exempt bonds for these purposes; **PREV EMPLOY:** Asst. Gen. Counsel, TN Housing Devel. Agency; Garland Law Firm, Erwin, TN; Title & closing work for FHA, S&L, Banks; **EDUC:** BA, 1968, Chem., Vanderbilt Univ.; **GRAD EDUC:** JD, 1975, Law, Univ. of TN Law School; **HOME ADD:** 818 Todd, Nashville, TN 37221, (615)646-9207; **BUS ADD:** 706 Church St., Suite 226, Nashville, TN 37203, (615)741-2936.

GARLAND, William E.——B: Sept. 18, 1944, Summit, NJ, *Prof., Seton Hall Law School*, Seton Hall Univ., School of Law; **PRIM RE ACT:** Consultant, Attorney, Owner/Investor, Instructor; **SERVICES:** Representation, consultation, drafting; **PREV EMPLOY:** Partner, Stanziale & Garland, Newark, NJ 07102; **EDUC:** AB, 1966, Econ., Fairfield Univ.; **GRAD EDUC:** JD, 1969, Law, Seton Hall Univ., School of Law; **OTHER ACT & HONORS:** Author, *NJ Legal Bus. Forms*, Third Edition in progress; "Purchaser's Increased Interest Rates: Caveat Venditor"; **HOME ADD:** 251 Washington St., Jersey City, NJ 07302, (201)432-8549; **BUS ADD:** 1111 Raymond Blvd., Newark, NJ 07102, (201)642-8825.

GARNER, Douglas——B: Apr. 1, 1941, San Francisco, CA, *Pres.*, Douglas Devel. Co.; **PRIM RE ACT:** Consultant, Developer, Syndicator; **SERVICES:** Devel. and synd. of RE, comml. & indus. props.; **REP CLIENTS:** Investors & instns.; **PREV EMPLOY:** M.H. Golden Co., 12 yrs., 1967-79; **EDUC:** BS, 1964, Civil Engrg., Stanford Univ.; **GRAD EDUC:** MS, 1967, Civil Engrg., Const., Stanford Univ.; **MIL SERV:** USN, 1964-66, Lt.; **HOME ADD:** 3584 Moultrie Ave., San Diego, CA 92117, (714)274-4056; **BUS ADD:** PO Box 80068, San Diego, CA 92138, (714)293-7556.

GARNER, J. Randall——B: Dec. 9, 1948, Atlanta, GA, *Pres.*, Peachtree Crossing Realty and J. R. Garner Homes, Inc.; **PRIM RE ACT:** Developer, Builder, Broker, Property Manager; **SERVICES:** Brokerage & mgmt. in Comml. and Resid. RE Development & Consulting; **PREV EMPLOY:** Atlanta Merchandise Mart (owned by John Portman, Willowick Mgmt. Co., Div. of Amer. Invsco); **PROFL AFFIL & HONORS:** Gwinnett Bd. of Realtors, GA Assn. Realtors, NAR, Metro Atl. Homebuilders Assn., Named to Outstanding Young Men of Amer. in 1980; **EDUC:** Acctg. & RE, GA State Univ.; **MIL SERV:** GA Nat. Guard E-5; **OTHER ACT & HONORS:** Gwinnett C of C, Atlanta C of C, Member Atlanta Athletic Club; **HOME ADD:** 5224 Amhurst Dr., Norcross, GA 30092, (404)449-8868; **BUS ADD:** 3459 Holcomb ., Norcross, GA 30092, (404)448-0437.

GARNER, Michael R.——B: Oct. 22, 1950, Montebello, CA, *Atty.*, Sax & MacIver; **PRIM RE ACT:** Attorney; **PROFL AFFIL & HONORS:** ABA, WA State Bar Assn.; **EDUC:** AB, 1971, Poli. Sci., Stanford Univ.; **GRAD EDUC:** JD, 1976, Law, Boalt Hall, Univ. of CA, at Berkeley; **EDUC HONORS:** Grad. w/Distinction; **BUS ADD:** 1415 Fifth Ave., Seattle, WA 98171, (206)624-1940.

GAROFALO, Albert A.——B: Aug. 24, 1911, Southport, CT, *Owner*, Pequot Realty Company; **PRIM RE ACT:** Developer, Owner/Investor; **PROFL AFFIL & HONORS:** Ct. Bar Assn.; Bridgeport Bar Assn.; **EDUC:** AB, 1933, Fordham Univ.; **GRAD EDUC:** JD, 1937, Harvard Law School; **MIL SERV:** US Army, Inf., 1st Lt.; **OTHER ACT & HONORS:** Judge, Fairfield Town Ct. 1949-1951; **HOME ADD:** 291 Mill Hill Rd., Southport, CT 06490, (203)255-2926; **BUS ADD:** 53 Unquowa Place, Fairfield, CT 06430, (203)259-5202.

GAROFALO, Ronald J.——B: Nov. 24, 1934, Chicago, IL, *VP*, The Siteman Org., Inc.; **PRIM RE ACT:** Broker, Developer, Property Manager; **OTHER RE ACT:** Dir. of Leasing - Denver Region; **SERVICES:** Comml. RE Devel., Leasing & Prop. Mgmt.; **REP CLIENTS:** For own account; **PREV EMPLOY:** VP and Dir. of Comml. Leasing for Van Schaack & Co. - Denver, VP and Dir. Leasing & Prop. Mgmt. for Seay & Thomas, Inc. - Chicago; **PROFL AFFIL & HONORS:** IREM (CPM), BOMA (RPA), Aurora Bd. of Realtors; **EDUC:** BS, 1957, Bus. Admin., Loyola Univ. - Chicago; **MIL SERV:** US Army, Sgt.; **HOME ADD:** 6940 S. Steele St., Littleton, CO 80122, (303)770-2158; **BUS ADD:** 1330 S. Potomac St., Suite 100, Aurora, CO 80012, (303)752-1775.

GARRETSON, Ronald B——B: Sep. 18, 1920, Salem, IA, *Pres.*, Garretson Mort. Co.; **PRIM RE ACT:** Broker, Lender, Insuror; **SERVICES:** Mort. banking; **REP CLIENTS:** Life ins. lenders; **PROFL AFFIL & HONORS:** MBAA; **EDUC:** BA, 1943, Hist. & Pol. Sci., Univ. of WA, Seattle; **MIL SERV:** US Army, USAR, Retired 1977, Col., Legion of Merit; **OTHER ACT & HONORS:** Past Pres. Univ. of WA, Club of So. Cal. IA, Assn. of So. CA; **HOME ADD:** 176 Glen Summer Rd., Pasadena, CA 91105, (213)793-4227; **BUS ADD:** 61 S. Lake Ave., Pasadena, CA 91109, (213)681-8741.

GARRETT, Devry Walker——B: June 14, 1949, Houston, TX, *Partner*, Childs, Fortenbach, Beck & Guyton; **PRIM RE ACT:** Attorney; **OTHER RE ACT:** Practice includes RE devel. and fin.; **REP CLIENTS:** First International Bank in Houston, N.A.; So. Nat. Bank of Houston; Greenway Bank and Trust of Houston; Turboff Interests; Barry Lotz Investments, Inc.; **PROFL AFFIL & HONORS:** State Bar of TX, Section on RE Law; ABA; Sections on RE and Corporate & Banking; TX Bank Lawyers Assn.; Houston Bar Assn.; **EDUC:** BA, 1971, Eng., Univ. of Houston, Magna Cum Laude; **GRAD EDUC:** JD, 1975, Law, Univ. of Houston; **EDUC HONORS:** Summa Cum Laude; Article Editor, *Houston Law Review*, 1974-5; **BUS ADD:** 402 Pierce, Houston, TX 77002, (713)659-6681.

GARRETT, Edwin B.——B: Dec. 19, 1938, Winston-Salem, NC, *Rgnl. VP*, Fairfield Communities, Inc., Eastern Div.; **PRIM RE ACT:** Broker, Developer, Builder; **PROFL AFFIL & HONORS:** NC Realtors; ALDA; **EDUC:** BA, 1964, Sales Mgmt., E. TN State Univ.; **MIL SERV:** USAF; **HOME ADD:** Fairfield Mountains, Lake Lure, NC 28746, (704)625-9111; **BUS ADD:** 408 Cedar Bluff, Knoxville, TN 37923, (615)691-9090.

GARRETT, Jack P.B., Jr.——B: Aug. 22, 1920, Waco, TX, *Owner*, Garrett Realty Co. & Jack Garrett & Co.; **PRIM RE ACT:** Broker, Consultant, Appraiser, Developer, Owner/Investor, Property Manager, Insuror, Syndicator; **OTHER RE ACT:** NASD Lic.; Ins. Lic.; **SERVICES:** RE Broker; **REP CLIENTS:** Fin. Planner, Waddell & Reed Co., Kansas City; **PREV EMPLOY:** 23 yrs., in RE Comml.; **PROFL AFFIL & HONORS:** Nat. RE Bd.; TX Bd.; Dallas Bd. of Realtors; Intl. Assn. of Fin. Planners, NASD Ins. Broker; **EDUC:** 1941, RE, So. Methodist Univ.; **MIL SERV:** US Naval Res., Lt.j.g., 1942-1945; **HOME ADD:** 4312 Belclaire, Dallas, TX 75205, (214)528-7729; **BUS ADD:** 604 Oakwood Tower, 3626 N. Hall, Dallas, TX 75219, (214)528-8290.

GARRETT, John C.——B: Dec. 17, 1939, Los Angeles, CA, *Atty.*, Drummy Garrett King & Harrison; **PRIM RE ACT:** Attorney; **REP CLIENTS:** Confidential; **PROFL AFFIL & HONORS:** ABA; Orange Cty. Bar Assn., Current Pres., Orange Cty. Bar Assn.; **EDUC:** AB, 1961, Stanford Univ.; **GRAD EDUC:** 1966, Univ. of CA, Hastings Coll. of Law; **MIL SERV:** USMC, Capt.; **HOME ADD:** Newport Beach, CA 92660; **BUS ADD:** 4041 MacArthur Blvd., Newport Beach, CA 92660, (714)833-8151.

GARRETT, Joseph——B: May 24, 1948, Berkeley, CA, *VP - Project & Subdiv. Fin.*, First California Mortgage Co.; **OTHER RE ACT:** Mortgage banker; **SERVICES:** Takeout fin. on condo. projects, PUDs & single-family subdivs.; **REP CLIENTS:** Citation Homes, Centex Homes; **PREV EMPLOY:** Baldwin & Howell Mort. Banking Co.; **PROFL AFFIL & HONORS:** No. CA Mort. Bankers Assn., FNMA level 2; **EDUC:** AB, 1970, Poli. Sci., Univ. of CA; **GRAD EDUC:** MA, 1972, Poli. Sci., Univ. of WA; MBA, 1975, Univ. of CA; **OTHER ACT & HONORS:** Chmn., Berkeley Housing Authority 1973-77, Commnr., Berkeley Redevel. Agency 1973-77, Commnr., Berkeley Planning Commn. 1977-78; **HOME ADD:** 1429 Spruce St., Berkeley, CA 94709, (415)540-8848; **BUS ADD:** 1100 Larkspur Landing Cir., Larkspur, CA 94939, (415)461-7090.

GARRETT, Larry Eugene——B: June 16, 1943, Memphis, TN, *Chmn. of Bd.*, Regal Realty of Memphis, Inc.; **PRIM RE ACT:** Broker, Instructor, Syndicator, Consultant, Appraiser, Property Manager, Owner/Investor; **REP CLIENTS:** HUD; 1st TN Bank, N.A., Memphis; Union Planters Natl. Bk., Memphis; **PROFL AFFIL & HONORS:** NAR; RESSI; NAIFA; **EDUC:** BBA, 1975, RE, Memphis State Univ.; **MIL SERV:** US Army; 1965-1969, Capt.; Bronze Star, Army Commendation; **HOME ADD:** 3966 Weaver Rd., Memphis, TN 38109, (901)789-0753; **BUS ADD:** 1188 Minna Pl., Memphis, TN 38104, (901)725-5400.

GARRETT, Richard——*Treas*, H.P. Hood, Inc.; **PRIM RE ACT:** Property Manager; **BUS ADD:** 500 Rutherford Ave., Boston, MA 02129, (617)242-0600.*

GARRETT, Van Holt, Jr.——B: Mar. 2, 1922, Augusta, GA, *Pres.*, Garrett Realty Investments Co.; **PRIM RE ACT:** Broker, Consultant, Developer, Property Manager, Owner/Investor; **SERVICES:** Prop. Mgmt., Assigned Brokerage, Counselling; **PREV EMPLOY:** Pres., Garrett-Bromfield & Co., RE Ins.; **PROFL AFFIL & HONORS:** IREM; ASREC; RNMI-CRB, CCIM; **EDUC:** BBA, 1948, RE, Univ. of Denver; **MIL SERV:** USAF, 1st Lt.; **OTHER ACT & HONORS:** Dir. United Bank of Denver N.A.; **HOME ADD:** 3220 E Kentucky Ave., Denver, CO 80209, (303)777-4646; **BUS ADD:** 1385 S. CO Blvd., Denver, CO 80209, (303)758-8088.

GARRIGAN, Richard Thomas——B: Mar. 4, 1938, Cleveland, OH, *Assoc. Prof.*, DePaul Univ., Dept. of Fin.; **PRIM RE ACT:** Consultant, Owner/Investor, Instructor, Real Estate Publisher; **SERVICES:** RE consulting; bus. school-level RE instr.; RE pub.-author and ed.; **REP CLIENTS:** RE invest. adviser, private mort. ins., mort. banker; **PREV EMPLOY:** Presidential Exchange Exec., Fed. Home Loan Bank Bd., 1977-1978; **PROFL AFFIL & HONORS:** Amer. Fin. Assn., Amer. RE and Urban Econ. Assn., Intl. Frat. of Lambda Alpha, Pres. of the U.S. Award for Achievement, 1978; **EDUC:** BS, summa cum laude, 1961, Acctg., The OH State Univ.; **GRAD EDUC:** MS, PhD, 1966, 1973, RE, Univ. of WI - Madison; **EDUC HONORS:** Beta Gamma Sigma, Haskins and Sells Award for Excellence in Acctg., Ford Found. Fellow, Phi Kappa Phi; **HOME ADD:** 51 Crescent Place, Wilmette, IL 60091, (312)251-8076; **BUS ADD:** 25 East Jackson Blvd., Chicago, IL 60604, (312)321-7834.

GARRISON, Burl L.——B: Feb. 28, 1924, St. Louis, MO, *Pres.*, General Mortgage Co.; **PRIM RE ACT:** Broker, Consultant, Appraiser, Banker, Lender, Instructor, Syndicator; **SERVICES:** Mort. lending, appraising, consulting; **REP CLIENTS:** John Hancock Life Insurance, Provi. Mutual Life Insurance, Coll. Life Ins.; **PREV EMPLOY:** RE Mortgage, Comml. Banking, Appraisal Indus. since 1945; **PROFL AFFIL & HONORS:** NAREB, AIREA, SREA, Mort. Bankers Assn., HBA, Cert. Mort. Underwriters Assn., RESSI, MAI, SRPA, CMB; **EDUC:** Various, Econ., Washington Univ., So. Methodist Univ.; **MIL SERV:** USAF, S/Sgt., North Africa, Italy, India, Burma, China; Battle area ribbons; **OTHER ACT & HONORS:** Mason, Dir. "Woods Mill 40 Bank", has authored many articles in trade journals or newspapers on RE subjects; **HOME ADD:** 419 Tamarack, Ballwin, MO 63011, (314)391-9711; **BUS ADD:** 14323 S. Outer Rd., Chesterfield, MO 63017, (314)878-6600.

GARRISON, Junius H., Jr.——B: Nov. 27, 1924, Greenville, SC, *Pres.*, The Furman Co.; **PRIM RE ACT:** Broker, Syndicator, Consultant, Appraiser, Developer, Builder, Property Manager, Owner/Investor; **PROFL AFFIL & HONORS:** IREM; CPM; ASREC; SIR; URI, Past Regnl. VP, IREM; Omego Tau Rh.; **EDUC:** BA, 1942-1943, Econ., Clemson Univ.; BA, 1946-1949, Econ., Furman Univ.; **EDUC HONORS:** Magna Cum Laude; **MIL SERV:** USAF; **OTHER ACT & HONORS:** Past Pres., Greenville Symphony; United Way; **BUS ADD:** Daniel Bldg., Greenvile, SC 29602, (803)242-5151.

GARRISON, R. Leonard, Jr.——B: Sept. 7, 1937, Ontario, OR, *Pres.*, Garrison Pacific Properties; **PRIM RE ACT:** Consultant, Developer, Builder, Owner/Investor, Property Manager; **SERVICES:** Devel., own & manage shopping ctrs.; **PROFL AFFIL & HONORS:** ICSC, CA Bus. Props., ICSC State Dir.; Bd. CA Bus. Props.; **EDUC:** BS, 1959, Agricultural Econ., OR State Univ.; **GRAD EDUC:** MBA, 1963, RE, Univ. of CA at Berkeley; **EDUC HONORS:** Alpha Zeta Honorary Soc., Willamen Fellowship; **MIL SERV:** USN, Lt.; **OTHER ACT & HONORS:** Univ. Club, Commonwealth Club; **HOME ADD:** 300 Summit Ave., San Rafael, CA 94901; **BUS ADD:** 1050 Northgate Dr., San Rafael, CA 94903, (415)479-7300.

GARROTE, Angel J.——B: Jan. 20, 1936, Cuba, *Partner*, Gama Investing Co.; **PRIM RE ACT:** Owner/Investor, Property Manager, Syndicator; **SERVICES:** RE investment analysis; **PREV EMPLOY:** General Electric Credit Corp. of PR, VP - Operations; **EDUC:** 1955, Acctg., Professional Bus. School, Cardenas, Cuba; **GRAD EDUC:** MBA, 1959, Acctg., Univ. of Havana, Cuba; **HOME ADD:** Sirena Q-3, Dorado Del Mar, Dorado, PR 00646; **BUS ADD:** POB 208, Sabana Seca, PR 00749, (809)795-0520.

GARSON, Kent H.——B: Mar 3, 1936, Phila., PA, *Mgr., Corp. RE*, Curtiss Wright Corp.; **PRIM RE ACT:** Property Manager, Owner/Investor; **PREV EMPLOY:** Mobil Oil Corp., 1967-1972; **PROFL AFFIL & HONORS:** Nacore (founding member), Bergen Cty., NJ Dev. Council, So. NJ Dev. Council, NJ Farm Bureau; **EDUC:** BS, 1960, Bus. Admin., Univ. of Delaware; **MIL SERV:** USA, Sgt.; **HOME ADD:** RD 1, Box 327B, Blairstown, NJ 07825; **BUS ADD:** 1 Passaic St., Wood Ridge, NJ 07095, (201)777-2900.

GARTHOEFFNER, George——B: Oct. 18, 1938, St. Louis, MO, *Pres.*, George Garthoeffner Assoc.; **PRIM RE ACT:** Consultant, Appraiser; **SERVICES:** Comml., Indus., Resid. Appraising and Consulting; **REP CLIENTS:** Lenders and Devels., Fed. Agencies; **PREV EMPLOY:** Appraiser, Metro RE Serv.; VP, Appraiser, Paul U. Holzen & Assoc.; **PROFL AFFIL & HONORS:** NAR; AIREA; SREA, RM - Amer. Inst.; SRA; **EDUC:** BA, 1960, Philosophy, Physics; Educ., Math., Cardinal Glennon Coll., St. Louis Univ.; **OTHER ACT & HONORS:** Eagle Scout Assn.; **HOME ADD:** 1530 Froesel, Ellisville, MO 63011, (314)227-7937; **BUS ADD:** 1353 Manchester, Ellisville, MO 63011, (314)227-9555.

GARTLEY, Jayne D.——B: Aug. 11, 1946, *Mgr. RE Admin.*, Rockwell Intl. Corp.; **OTHER RE ACT:** Corp/RE; **SERVICES:** Total Site Selection Appraisal Lease Negotiations, acquisitions, Dispositions; **PROFL AFFIL & HONORS:** NACORE; VP-Pittsburgh Chap., Amer. Soc. of Profl. & Exec. Women; Nat. Assn. of Review Appraisers, Sr. Member, SRA; **EDUC:** BS, 1969, Econ., Robt. Morris Coll., Duquesne Univ.; **BUS ADD:** 600 Grant St., Pittsburgh, PA 15219, (412)565-7435.

GARUFI, Anthony T.——B: Apr. 9, 1953, Albany, NY, *Lic. RE Broker*, The Howard Companies, Investment; **PRIM RE ACT:** Broker, Consultant; **SERVICES:** Investment counseling & brokerage; **REP CLIENTS:** Indiv. and instnl. prop. owners and investors; **PREV EMPLOY:** Price Waterhouse & Co. 1975-1977; **PROFL AFFIL & HONORS:** NAR; RNMI; NY State Assn. of Realtors; **EDUC:** BA, 1975, Econ./Urban Studies, Dartmouth Coll.; **HOME ADD:** 14 Bethwood Dr., Londonville, NY 12211, (518)783-1854; **BUS ADD:** 50

State St., Albany, NY 12207, (518)434-8181.

GARVIN, John R.——**B:** May 9, 1935, Bellefontaine, OH, *Pres.*, Continental Appraisal Co.; **PRIM RE ACT:** Broker, Consultant, Appraiser; **SERVICES:** Investment analysis & consultation; comml., indus. and investment prop.; **REP CLIENTS:** Pension funds, trusts, major corps., attys., pvt. investors; **PROFL AFFIL & HONORS:** MAI; **EDUC:** BBA, 1959, RE, OH State Univ.; **HOME ADD:** 775 Loch Lomond Ln., Worthington, OH 43085; **BUS ADD:** 50 W. Broad St., Columbus, OH 43215, (614)221-5173.

GARZA, Paul, Jr.——**B:** June 11, 1935, Laredo, TX, *Pres.*, Rio Vista, Inc.; **PRIM RE ACT:** Consultant, Engineer, Developer, Owner/Investor; **SERVICES:** Land devel., housing projects, comml. props.; **REP CLIENTS:** Tesoro Devel. Corp., Laredo; Lasby Park Terrace, Ltd.; City of Laredo; US Postal Service; **PREV EMPLOY:** City of Laredo, Dir. of Planning; Paul Garza & Assocs., Principal Consultant; City of Waco, TX, Traffic & Planning Engr.; **PROFL AFFIL & HONORS:** TX Soc. of PE; Nat. Soc. of PE; Amer. Inst. of Cert. Planners; Inst. of Traffic Engrs., White House Fellows Program 1963; Engr. of the Year, Gateray Chapter, 1966; **EDUC:** BSCE, 1955, Civil Engrg. & Urban Planning, TX A & M Univ.; **OTHER ACT & HONORS:** Bd. of Dirs., Tesoro S & L Assn., Laredo; Nat. Pres., League of United Latin Amer. Citizens, 1970-71; **HOME ADD:** 1402 Market St., Laredo, TX 78040, (512)724-6214; **BUS ADD:** P.O. Box 902, 1601 Matamoros St., Laredo, TX 78040, (512)722-7731.

GASK, Michael——**B:** Nov. 6, 1934, Brooklyn, NY, *Claims Atty.*, The Title Guarantee Co., Claim Dept.; **PRIM RE ACT:** Attorney; **SERVICES:** Legal consultant; **REP CLIENTS:** Staff Atty., The Title Guarantee Co.; **PREV EMPLOY:** Chicago Title Ins. Co., legal research, title clearance, reading, examining; **EDUC:** BA, 1967, Eng. Lit./Philosophy, CCNY; **GRAD EDUC:** JD, 1971, Law, School of Law, Fordham Univ., Amer. Jurisprudence Prize; **OTHER ACT & HONORS:** Chmn., Liturgy Comm., St. Margaret Mary's Parish, Bronx, NY; Member, Catholic Alumni Club, NYC; **HOME ADD:** 255 E. 176 St., Bronx, NY 10457, (212)299-7108; **BUS ADD:** 120 Broadway, NY, NY 10271, (212)964-1000.

GASKILL, John B., Jr.——**B:** Jan. 23, 1950, Glendale, CA, *Owner*, Monarch Realty Services; **PRIM RE ACT:** Broker, Consultant, Developer, Property Manager; **SERVICES:** Comml. and indus. brokerage, mgmt. and consulting; **PREV EMPLOY:** Dir. of Operations, Multi-Family Div.; Rgnl. Prop. Mgr., Asset Mgmt. Div.; Kaufman & Broad, Inc., 1973-1975; **EDUC:** BBA, 1973, Fin./Acctg., CA State Univ.; **EDUC HONORS:** Cum Laude; **OTHER ACT & HONORS:** Supervisor of Volunteers, Community TV of So. CA (KCET); **HOME ADD:** Burbank, CA 91505; **BUS ADD:** 4421 Riverside Dr., Suite 200, Burbank, CA 91505, (213)841-6298.

GASKINS, Steve P., III——**B:** Feb. 21, 1947, New York, NY, *Principal Broker*, Holley, Hargett & Spain, Better Homes & Gardens, Pres., G&L Mgmt. Corp., Pres., Fin. Investors Group, Inc., Pres.; **PRIM RE ACT:** Broker, Owner/Investor, Property Manager, Syndicator; **SERVICES:** Resid. RE Brokerage, Prop. Mgmt., Synd. of resid. props.; **PROFL AFFIL & HONORS:** N. VA Bd. of Realtors; RESSI; **EDUC:** BS, 1969, Biology, Coll. of William & Mary; **GRAD EDUC:** JD, 1980, Law, Geo. Mason Univ. School of Law; **MIL SERV:** US Army, Capt. 1970-1974; **HOME ADD:** 5721 Heming Ave., Springfield, VA 22151, (703)451-5718; **BUS ADD:** 803 W. Broad St., Suite 245, Falls Church, VA 22046, (703)532-7505.

GASPARINI, Frederick Vincent Marratto——**B:** Nov. 28, 1948, Los Angeles, CA, *Pres.*, Exclusive Realtors; **PRIM RE ACT:** Broker, Consultant, Instructor; **OTHER RE ACT:** RE sales trainer/writer; **PREV EMPLOY:** Head Sales Trainer for Day Realty, 1977; Training Manuals, Seminars; **PROFL AFFIL & HONORS:** San Fernando Valley, Burbank, E. Orange, Los Angeles, Santa Clarita Valley United Multiple Listing Service, Top Selling Agent - Top Listing Agent; **OTHER ACT & HONORS:** VChprsn./Chmn., Educ. Comm. SFVBR; **BUS ADD:** 4922 Vineland Ave., N. Hollywood, CA 91601, (213)760-0897.

GASPARRO, Peter William——**B:** Mar. 27, 1938, New York, NY, *RE/Facilities Mgr.*, Xerox Corp., N.E. Operations - BSG; **PRIM RE ACT:** Property Manager; **OTHER RE ACT:** Site selection, lease negotiating, const.; **PREV EMPLOY:** Equitable Life Assurance Society; **PROFL AFFIL & HONORS:** NACORE; **EDUC:** BS, 1968, Arch./Const., Pratt Inst., Brooklyn, NY; **MIL SERV:** US Army, Sgt., 1962-64; **HOME ADD:** 214-15 33 Ave., Bayside, NY 11361, (212)428-1171; **BUS ADD:** Two Pickwick Plaza, Greenwich, CT 06830, (203)622-5382.

GASPERONI, Emil, Sr.——**B:** Nov. 13, 1926, Hillsville, PA, *Owner*, Gasperoni Real Estate; **PRIM RE ACT:** Appraiser, Developer, Owner/Investor, Property Manager, Syndicator; **OTHER RE ACT:** Realtor; **PROFL AFFIL & HONORS:** Nat. Soc. of Fee Appraisers; RE Securities and Synd. Inst.; Nat. Assn. of RE Brokers; **EDUC:** 1956, RE, Univ. of Pittsburgh; **MIL SERV:** US Army; 1945-1946, Europe; **OTHER ACT & HONORS:** Coral Ridge Golf & Ctry. Club, Ft. Lauderdale, FL; Lake Toxaway Ctry. Club, Lake Toxaway, NC; **HOME ADD:** 4201 N.E. 25 Ave., Ft. Lauderdale, FL 33308, (305)566-2613; **BUS ADD:** 2501 E. Commerical Blvd., Ft. Lauderdale, FL 33308, (305)776-7100.

GATES, Allen F.——**B:** July 17, 1928, New York, NY, *Pres.*, Gates Real Estate, Inc.; **PRIM RE ACT:** Broker, Consultant, Appraiser, Developer, Owner/Investor, Instructor; **SERVICES:** Indus. park & single family devel., indus. brokerage; **REP CLIENTS:** Leeds & Northrup, GTE, Bendix, Walter Kidde, Hooker Barnes Homes; other indus. users and resid. builders; **PREV EMPLOY:** 20 yrs. in elec. engrg., sales, and mktg.; **PROFL AFFIL & HONORS:** FL Indus. Devel. Council; Pinellas Indus. Assn., Past Pres., GRI; Candidate, CCIM; **EDUC:** BSEE, 1950, Electronic Engrg., Johns Hopkins Univ.; **GRAD EDUC:** MSEE, 1955, Aeronautics/Math., Johns Hopkins Univ.; **EDUC HONORS:** Tau Beta Pi in Jr. yr.; **MIL SERV:** USAF, Maj.; **OTHER ACT & HONORS:** Chmn., Indus. Advisory Comm. to City of Pinellas Park; Chmn., Water Quality Mgmt.; Tampa Bay Rgnl. Pl. Council; Comm. of 100 of Pinellas Cty.; St. Petersburg Yacht Club; Contractors & Builders Assn.; St. Petersburg Bd. of Realtors; **HOME ADD:** 4143 51st Ave. S, St. Petersburg, FL 33711, (813)867-4010; **BUS ADD:** 3500 Bldg., 3530 First Ave., N, St. Petersburg, FL 33713, (813)822-5444.

GATES, Robert Pfarr——**B:** May 16, 1942, Cedar Rapids, IA, *Atty.*, Erskine & Tulley; **PRIM RE ACT:** Developer, Regulator; **SERVICES:** Purchases, exchanges, limited partnerships, devel., leasing; **REP CLIENTS:** Boston Fin. Tech. Grp. Inc.; Business Men's Assurance Co. of Amer.; Wong Props.; Indiv. & synd. investors & devel. of comml. props.; **PREV EMPLOY:** Hancock, Rothert & Bunshoft, 1972-80, part.; **PROFL AFFIL & HONORS:** SF Bar, State Bar of CA, ABA; **EDUC:** AB, 1964, Econ, Math., Occidental Coll.; **GRAD EDUC:** JD, 1969, Law, Univ. of MI; **OTHER ACT & HONORS:** Peace Corps. Volunteer, Philippines, 1965-67; **HOME ADD:** 8 Palm Ct., Menlo Park, CA 94025, (415)326-7914; **BUS ADD:** 625 Market St., Suite 719, San Francisco, CA 94105, (415)392-5431.

GATHERS, Charles E.——**B:** Sept. 1, 1931, Mahattan, KS, *Pres.*, Charles Gathers & Assoc. Inc., Western Summit Development Corp.; **PRIM RE ACT:** Architect, Developer, Owner/Investor, Property Manager; **SERVICES:** Architect/Planning and Devel.; **GRAD EDUC:** BArch, 1955, Univ. of IL; **EDUC HONORS:** Bronze Tablet Scholar; **MIL SERV:** USA, Engr., 1st Lt.; **HOME ADD:** 8729 E. Kettle Pl., Englewood, CO 80112; **BUS ADD:** 1825 Lawrence St., Denver, CO 80112, (303)892-1324.

GATHMAN, J. Denis——**B:** Dec. 23, 1941, Chicago, IL, *VP and Dir. of Appraisal, Chicago*, Real Estate Research Corp., RE Appraisal; **PRIM RE ACT:** Consultant, Appraiser; **SERVICES:** Investment counseling and valuation; **REP CLIENTS:** Lenders and indiv. or instnl. investors in comml. props.; **PREV EMPLOY:** Talman Home Fed. S&L Assn. 1963-1974; **PROFL AFFIL & HONORS:** AIREA, Soc. of RE Appraisers; Intl. Fraternity of Lambda Alpha; Intl. Inst. of Valuers, SCV; MAI; **EDUC:** BBA, 1963, Fin., Loyola Univ., Chic.; **OTHER ACT & HONORS:** Member of the Comml. and Indus. Devel. Comm. of the Chicago Assn. of Commerce and Indus.; **HOME ADD:** 614 S. Roosevelt, Arlington Heights, IL 60005, (312)870-1548; **BUS ADD:** 72 W. Adams, Chicago, IL 60603, (312)346-5885.

GATLEY, R.H.——*Pres.*, Commerce Communities Corp.; **PRIM RE ACT:** Broker, Consultant, Developer, Owner/Investor, Property Manager, Syndicator; **SERVICES:** Prop. mgmt. & fee devel; **PREV EMPLOY:** Norris, Beggs & Simpson 1957-1964; Bothin RE Co. 1964-1970; **PROFL AFFIL & HONORS:** NAIOP; **EDUC:** BS, 1954, Indus. Mgmt. & RE Bus., Univ. So. CA; **BUS ADD:** 3000 Sandhill Rd. #-210, Menlo Park, CA 94025.

GAUDETTE, Arthur T.——**B:** Jan 26, 1939, St. Paul, MN, *RE Appraiser*, Appraisal Assoc.; **PRIM RE ACT:** Appraiser; **REP CLIENTS:** Relocation Firms MGIC, AVCO, U.S. Bankruptcy Court Trustee's Assoc. Finance, Ford Motor Credit; **PREV EMPLOY:** Elections Mktg. Engineer, FHA Staff appraiser, AR Hwy Riteway Dept.; **PROFL AFFIL & HONORS:** Associate Member SRA; **EDUC:** BS, 1966, Electronics Engrg., AR State Univ.; **GRAD EDUC:** 1967-69, Bus. Admin., AR State Univ.; **MIL SERV:** USAF, Sgt; **OTHER ACT & HONORS:** SWAP; **HOME ADD:** 7914 E. Palm Ln, Scottsdale, AZ 85257; **BUS ADD:** Residential Relocation, 7914 E. Palm Ln., Scottsdale, AZ 85257, (602)990-0291.

GAUEN, Charles F.——**B:** Sept. 21, 1947, Dallas, TX, *Pres.*, Charles Gauen & Company, Land/Comml.-Acquisition; **PRIM RE ACT:** Broker, Consultant, Appraiser, Developer, Builder, Owner/Investor, Instructor, Property Manager, Syndicator; **OTHER RE ACT:** Specializing in comml. downtown props. for lease or investment, oil & gas leasing and comml. land acquisition; **SERVICES:** Utilizing advanced RE techn. for proper transaction support for the client; **REP CLIENTS:** Centex Const. Co., Homart Dev. Corp., Raldon Corp.; **PREV EMPLOY:** Hoffman Realtors, Head Comml. Div., 1978-81; **PROFL AFFIL & HONORS:** Amer. Inst. of Bldg. Design and TX Inst. of Bldg. Design, Top producer, Hoffman Realtors; **EDUC:** AA & BA, 1969, Bus. Mgmt., personnel admin., Southern Methodist Univ.; **HOME ADD:** 1189 Tranquilla Dr., Dallas, TX 75218, (214)327-1394; **BUS ADD:** 10010 Miller Rd., L.B.J. Freeway, Dallas, TX 75238, (214)341-5900.

GAUGHEN, Thomas W.——**B:** June 17, 1946, Harrisburg, PA, *Dir. of Prop. Devel.*, Gaughen Latham Prop. Devel.; **PRIM RE ACT:** Developer; **SERVICES:** Prop. Mgmt., appraiser, broker; **PROFL AFFIL & HONORS:** ASHRAE; CCIM; RENMI; GRI, CCIM: GRI; **EDUC:** BS Mech. Engrg., 1972, Villanova Univ.; **GRAD EDUC:** MS Econometrics, 1973, Math, UCLA; **EDUC HONORS:** Engrg. Honor Soc., Pi Tau Sigma; **MIL SERV:** USMC, Cpl., Purple Heart; **OTHER ACT & HONORS:** Chmn. Hampden Township Bi-Centennial Comm.; Toastmasters, Optimist Intl.; Advisory Bd. Keystone Council of Boy Scouts of Amer.; **HOME ADD:** 140 Bryce Rd., Camp Hill, PA 17011, (717)737-3030; **BUS ADD:** 3800 Market St., P.O. Box 686, Camp Hill, PA 17011, (717)763-1800.

GAULDING, Jon C.——**B:** Jan. 15, 1953, Dallas, TX, *VP*, Vantage Cos., Corp.; **PRIM RE ACT:** Consultant, Appraiser, Developer, Owner/Investor, Instructor, Property Manager, Syndicator; **OTHER RE ACT:** on copr. staff of vertical integrated development co.; **PROFL AFFIL & HONORS:** Nat. Assoc. of Indus. & Office Parks, BOMA Nat. Advisory Council, MBA; **EDUC:** BA, 1975, Bus., Austin Coll.; **GRAD EDUC:** MBA, 1976, RE & Fin., So. Methodist Univ.; **HOME ADD:** 7047 Brookshire Dr., Dallas, TX 75230, (214)368-3713; **BUS ADD:** 2525 Stemmons Frwy, Dallas, TX 75230, (214)631-0600.

GAUNAURD, Henry——**B:** Sept. 9, 1946, *VP*, Draper and Kramer, Inc.; **PRIM RE ACT:** Broker, Consultant, Appraiser, Developer, Owner/Investor, Property Manager; **REP CLIENTS:** Major Ins. Cos., Corps., Investors; **PROFL AFFIL & HONORS:** Chicago RE Bd.; NAR; Soc. of RE Appraisers, IREM; IL Mort. Bankers Assn., CPM, SRPA; **EDUC:** BS, Loyola Univ.; **HOME ADD:** 1143 S. Plymouth Ct. #506, Chicago, IL 60605, (312)939-4914; **BUS ADD:** 33 West Monroe St., Suite 1900, Chicago, IL 60603, (312)346-8600.

GAUTHIER, Joseph H.——**B:** Dec. 6, 1935, Los Angeles, CA, *Pres.*, Diversified Realty, Inc.; **PRIM RE ACT:** Broker; **SERVICES:** Comml. investment brokerage; **REP CLIENTS:** Indiv. clients in comml. investment props.; **PREV EMPLOY:** Sole prop. in comml. investment RE, 1977-79; gen. brokerage, prop. mgmt., loan brokerage, 1972-77; **PROFL AFFIL & HONORS:** RNMI, NAR, NV Assn. of Realtors, Reno Bd. of Realtors, CCIM; **EDUC:** BS, 1964, Bus. Admin., UCLA; **MIL SERV:** US Army Res., SP-4, 1958-64; **OTHER ACT & HONORS:** Served as Worshipful Master, 1973, Larchmont Lodge, 614, F&AM, Los Angeles, CA; Los Angeles Scottish Rite Bodies, Al Malaikah Shrine Temple, Los Angeles, CA; **HOME ADD:** 3165 Reanon Ct., Reno, NV 89509, (702)826-6021; **BUS ADD:** 232 Court St., Reno, NV 89501, (702)322-5088.

GAUTSCH, Donald H.——**B:** Jan. 30, 1923, LaCrosse, WI, *Assoc. Broker*, Century 21, Jim Vaughn Associates, Inc.; **PRIM RE ACT:** Broker, Consultant, Engineer, Instructor; **OTHER RE ACT:** Comml. investments and exchanging; **PREV EMPLOY:** Bus. counseling, GBS Area Dir.; Cert. Mfg. Engr.; **PROFL AFFIL & HONORS:** Amer. Mgmt. Assn.; Soc. of Mfg. Engrs.; Intl. Exchangors Assn.; NAR; RNMI; SCREMEC, AAAS; Listed in Who's Who in Creative RE, a Profl. Director; **EDUC:** 1943, Chem., Univ. of WI; BSME, 1956, Sci./Math., Tri State Univ.; **EDUC HONORS:** Member, Skull & Bones; Pres., ME Soc.; Pres., SAE; **MIL SERV:** US Army Res.; Ret., Capt. AG, GCM, AR, ATS, w/Bronze Star, WW II Victory, Korean Victory; **OTHER ACT & HONORS:** AOPA; ROA; Soc. of Commn. Officers; Nat. Assn. of Small Businesses; **HOME ADD:** 317 Richbourg Rd., Greenville, SC 29615, (803)244-3741; **BUS ADD:** 3110 Wade Hampton Blvd., 14 Gallery Ctr., Taylors, SC 29687, (803)292-1946.

GAVEY, James E.——**B:** June 6, 1942, Buffalo, NY, *Founder and Pres.*, Gavey & Co., Inc.; **PRIM RE ACT:** Syndicator, Appraiser, Developer, Builder, Property Manager, Owner/Investor; **SERVICES:** Investment counseling, valuation, devel. and synd of apt. props. nationwide; investment portfolio prop. mgmt.; **REP CLIENTS:** Indiv. and instnl. investors; **PREV EMPLOY:** Arthur Andersen & Co. (1965-1973), Firmwide part., investment and tax shelter consulting; **PROFL AFFIL & HONORS:** AICPA; NY Soc. CPA; Nat. Apt. Assn.; NAHB; NARA; Intl. Inst. Valuers, Who's Who in Indus. and Fin.; **EDUC:** BA, 1964, Liberal Arts, Le Moyne Coll.; **GRAD EDUC:** MBA, 1965, Fin. and Acctg., Columbia Bus. School; **EDUC HONORS:** Dean's list; **OTHER ACT & HONORS:** Chmn. United Fund, NY; Chmn/Commne. Housing Authority, NY; Cooperstown Ctry. Club; Union League Club; Siwanoy Ctry. Club; **HOME ADD:** 98 Park Ave., Bronxville, NY 10708, (914)337-5032; **BUS ADD:** 80 Park Ave., N.Y., NY 10016, (212)867-0130.

GAY, Donald——**B:** Feb. 14, 1941, Abington, PA, *Pres.*, Donald Gay & Assoc., Inc.; **PRIM RE ACT:** Broker, Instructor, Consultant, Developer, Property Manager; **PREV EMPLOY:** Richard B. Herman & Co. - Binswamger/Herman Co. 1961-1977; **PROFL AFFIL & HONORS:** NAREB, BOMA; **EDUC:** BS, 1962, Econ., Albright Coll. - Reading, PA; **HOME ADD:** 3260 Masons Mill Rd., Huntington Valley, PA 19006, (215)657-0887; **BUS ADD:** 1601 Church Rd., Glenside, PA 19038, (215)885-3805.

GEAHLEN, Donald——**B:** July 13, 1945, Perrysburg, OH, *Broker/Mgr.*, AZ West Realty & Investment Co.; **PRIM RE ACT:** Broker, Consultant, Developer, Builder, Owner/Investor, Property Manager; **SERVICES:** Sales and Mgmt. of mostly resid. props. & land; **REP CLIENTS:** Thomas Devel. and investors of income props.; **PREV EMPLOY:** Past VP Mesa Sertona Club, Million Dollar Club Realty Execs.; **PROFL AFFIL & HONORS:** Mesa Chandler Tempe Multiple listing service, AZ Assn. of Realtors, NAR, Mesa C of C, Realtor; **MIL SERV:** USAR, E-4; **HOME ADD:** 1559 G. Hampton Circ., Mesa, AZ 85204, (602)892-9001; **BUS ADD:** 309 E. 10th Dr., Mesa, AZ 85202, (602)833-8444.

GEBERT, Jerry R.——**B:** Mar 7, 1947, Wisconsin Rapids, WI, *Asst. VP*, Security First National Bank; **PRIM RE ACT:** Banker, Instructor; **PREV EMPLOY:** Branch mgr. S & L Assn. for 10 years; **PROFL AFFIL & HONORS:** WBA; ABA; Realtor Assn.; **EDUC:** BAA, 1969, Acctg., Spencarian Coll., Milwaukee, WI; **OTHER ACT & HONORS:** Sheboygan Parking and Transit Utility; Sheboygan Retirement Home, Inc. Bd. of Dir.; **HOME ADD:** 130 Long Ct., Sheboygan, WI 53081, (414)452-9384; **BUS ADD:** 605 Plaza 8, Sheboygan, WI 53081, (414)459-6051.

GECHTER, Lawrence R.——**B:** Oct. 3, 1940, Detroit, MI, *Part., Tax Dept.*, Touche Russ and Co.; **PRIM RE ACT:** Consultant; **OTHER RE ACT:** CPA; **SERVICES:** Tax consult.; **REP CLIENTS:** Unable to disclose info.; **PROFL AFFIL & HONORS:** Det. R.E. Bd., AGC Homebuilders Assn.; **EDUC:** BBA, 1968, Acctg. and Fin., Univ. of MI; **EDUC HONORS:** Dean's List; **BUS ADD:** 200 Renaissance Ctr., Detroit, MI 48243, (313)446-1500.

GEEBEL, Paul R.——**B:** Jan. 21, 1951, Ba Axe, MI, *Asst. Prof. of Fin.*, TX Tech Univ.; **PRIM RE ACT:** Consultant, Instructor, Real Estate Publisher; **SERVICES:** Teach, research, and publish in RE fin., investments, and appraisal; **REP CLIENTS:** Consulting for indiv. investors in RE, Conduct seminars in RE investment analysis; **PROFL AFFIL & HONORS:** Amer. RE and Urban Econ. Assn.; Southwest Fin. Assn.; Fin. Mgmt. Assn.; TX RE Teachers, Outstanding Young Men of Amer., 1981; Sigma Iota Epsilon, Rho Epsilon; **EDUC:** 1975, Mgmt., MI State Univ.; Augusta Coll. GA; **GRAD EDUC:** MBA, 1975, Univ. of GA, Athens, GA; 1980, RE & Urban Devel./Fin. minor, Univ. of GA; **EDUC HONORS:** Mary Bates Chatham, William Shenkel, Atlanta Bd. of Realtors Scholarships; **MIL SERV:** US Army; Spec. 4, Recreation Servs.; **HOME ADD:** 5210 27th St., Lubbock, TX 79407, (806)793-6966; **BUS ADD:** Box 4320, Area of Fin., TX Tech Univ., Lubbock, TX 79407, (806)742-3340.

GEER, Lewis F.——**B:** June 18, 1946, New York, NY, *Owner-Broker*, First Realty Assn.; **PRIM RE ACT:** Broker, Consultant, Developer, Owner/Investor, Instructor; **PROFL AFFIL & HONORS:** RNMI, NAR, FLI, RESSI, RANM, GRI; **EDUC:** BA, 1970, Hist., Yale Univ.; **HOME ADD:** 1041 Governor Dempsey Dr., Santa Fe, NM 87501, (505)988-3704; **BUS ADD:** 524 Don Gaspar, Santa Fe, NM 87501, (505)988-9683.

GEER, Thomas L.——**B:** Sept. 26, 1951, Johnstown, PA, *Partner*, Carson, Vieweg & Gerr; **PRIM RE ACT:** Attorney, Owner/Investor; **SERVICES:** Tax planning and counseling; **PROFL AFFIL & HONORS:** State Bar of MI; ABA; PA Bar Assn., Real Property Law Sects.; **EDUC:** BA, 1973, Psych., Boston Univ.; **GRAD EDUC:** JD, 1976, Univ. of Pittsburgh School of Law; LLM, 1978, Taxation, Georgetown Univ. Law Center; **EDUC HONORS:** Cum Laude; **HOME ADD:** 1891 Kirts, N. 216, Troy, MI 48084, (313)649-2972; **BUS ADD:** 860 W. Long Lake Rd., Ste. 333, Bloomfield Hills, MI 48013, (313)644-2000.

GEERING, Christina Z.——**B:** Apr. 11, 1946, New York, NY, *Dir.*, Varney Street Publishing; **PRIM RE ACT:** Regulator, Real Estate Publisher; **SERVICES:** Multiple listing newsletter for New England area RE, also private publishing service to professionals; **REP CLIENTS:** In all phases of RE; **PROFL AFFIL & HONORS:** Nat. Bd. of RE Publishers; **EDUC:** BA, 1968, Journalism/Communications, Boston Univ.; **GRAD EDUC:** MA, 1970, Business, Harvard Business School; **EDUC HONORS:** Summa Cum Laude, Magna Cum Laude; **OTHER ACT & HONORS:** League of Women Voters; US Ski Assn.; **HOME ADD:** 102 Rockview St., Jamaica Plain, MA 02130; **BUS ADD:** 10 Varney St., Jamaica Plain, MA 02130, (617)522-8478.

GEHLBACH, Gary R.——**B:** Mar. 8, 1949, Lincoln, IL, *Atty.*, Dixon, Morin, Ehrmann & Gehlbach; **PRIM RE ACT:** Attorney; **SERVICES:** As atty. with respect to RE synds., condo. devels. and most other aspects of RE practice; **REP CLIENTS:** Various instnl. lenders (e.g. Dixon Nat. Bank, First Nat. Bank in Amboy, Dixon Home S&L Assn.), private devels., contractors, various RE brokers and firms; **PREV EMPLOY:** Atty. for Law Offices of Pesmen & Weil, P.C., Chicago, IL, specializing in RE synds., acquisitions and sales of comml. prop.; **PROFL AFFIL & HONORS:** Amer. Judicature Soc.; ABA; IL State Bar Assn.; Lee Cty. Bar Assn.; **EDUC:** BA, 1971, Math./Econ., Knox Coll.; **GRAD EDUC:** JD, 1978, Law, IIT/Chicago-Kent College of Law; **EDUC HONORS:** Alfred P. Sloan Found. Scholar, Grad. with High Honors, Bar and Gavel Award, Amer. Jurisprudence Award, Corpus Juris Secondum Award; **OTHER ACT & HONORS:** Bd. of Trs. of Dixon Public Library; Bd. of Dirs. of Bradford Mutual Fire Ins. Co.; **HOME ADD:** 222 S. Ottawa Ave., Dixon, IL 61021, (815)288-4957; **BUS ADD:** 121 E. First St., Dixon, IL 61021, (815)284-2288.

GEIGER, Paul Joseph——**B:** Oct. 1, 1949, Glendale, CA, *RE Counsel*, Denny's Inc., All Div.; **PRIM RE ACT:** Consultant, Attorney, Property Manager; **SERVICES:** Review and prepare all RE contracts, inst. and arrange litigation, const. disputes, escrows and prop. mgmt. for corporate office bldgs. and Denny's restaurants; **PREV EMPLOY:** Coldwell Banker & Co. (Assoc. Gen. Counsel), 1975-1978; **PROFL AFFIL & HONORS:** ABA, LA Cty. Bar Assn., Phi Alpha Delta Law Fraternity; **EDUC:** BBA, 1972, Bus. Admin., Loyola Univ. of Los Angeles; **GRAD EDUC:** JD, 1975, Law, Loyola Univ. of Los Angeles; **EDUC HONORS:** Dean's List; **HOME ADD:** 2220 E. Chapman #41, Fullerton, CA 92631; **BUS ADD:** 14256 E. Firestone Blvd., La Mirada, CA 90637, (716)739-8100.

GEIGER, Robert J.——*Chmn. of the Bd.*, Jefferson Nat. Mort.; **PRIM RE ACT:** Broker, Consultant, Appraiser, Banker, Developer, Instructor, Syndicator; **OTHER RE ACT:** Mort. banker primarily & is active in the RE and devel. field serv. as a consultant to European grps. regarding land purchase and income props. and is starting RE synd. on income props.; **BUS ADD:** 6000 W. Greentree Exec. Campus, Ste. 200, Marlton, NJ 08053, (609)596-0300.

GEIS, Joseph R.——**B:** Aug. 21, 1947, Minneapolis, MN, *Owner*, Joe Geis Inc.; **PRIM RE ACT:** Broker, Instructor, Developer, Builder, Property Manager, Owner/Investor; **SERVICES:** Residential/Comml. Bldg.-sales, leasing, mgmt.; **PROFL AFFIL & HONORS:** NAHB, NAR, Certified Comml. Investment Mem.; **EDUC:** BA, 1969, Mktg., OK St. Univ.; **GRAD EDUC:** MBA, 1971, Bus., OK State Univ.; **EDUC HONORS:** Blue Key; **MIL SERV:** USAR, S/Sgt.; **HOME ADD:** 3514 Wynn Cir., Edmond, OK 73034, (405)341-1728; **BUS ADD:** 3431 S Wynn Dr., Edmond, OK 73034, (405)348-7900.

GEIS, Norman——**B:** July 13, 1925, St. Paul, MN, *Atty.*, Greenberger, Krauss & Jacobs, Chartered; **PRIM RE ACT:** Attorney; **SERVICES:** Rep. of RE devels. and instl. lenders; **REP CLIENTS:** Talman Home Fed. S&L Assn. of IL; First Nat. Bank of Chicago; Romanek-Golub & Co.; Comml. Credit Devel. Corp.; McHugh Levin Assocs.; **PROFL AFFIL & HONORS:** ABA; IL State Bar Assn.; Chicago Bar Assn.; Amer. Coll. of RE Lawyers, Bd. of Gov's.; Amer. Coll. of RE Lawyers; Past Chmn., Chicago Bar Assn. Condominium Comm.; Past Chmn., ABA Comm. on Condominiums, Cooperatives and Homeowner Assns.; Asst Secretary, ABA Section of Real Property, Probate & Trust Law; **EDUC:** AB, 1947, Univ. of Chicago; **GRAD EDUC:** JD, 1951, Univ. of Chicago Law School; **EDUC HONORS:** With Honors, Ed., Law Review; **MIL SERV:** Infantry, 1943-1945, PFC, Bronze Star; **OTHER ACT & HONORS:** Acting Chmn., Bd. of Zoning Appeals, Highland Park, IL, Who's Who in America; **HOME ADD:** 1530 Green Bay Rd., Highland Park, IL 60035, (312)432-0684; **BUS ADD:** 180 N. LaSalle St., Suite 2700, Chicago, IL 60601, (312)346-1300.

GEISINGER, Edward I.——**B:** Dec. 19, 1946, New York, NY, *Corp. VP*, Julien J. Studley, Inc.; **PRIM RE ACT:** Broker, Consultant; **SERVICES:** Comml. lease analysis & negotiation, feasibility studies; **REP CLIENTS:** Assns. (non-profit), law firms and major cos. in the acquisition of comml. props. or space; **PREV EMPLOY:** Ely-Crinkshank Co., Inc. NYC (1971-1972); **PROFL AFFIL & HONORS:** WA Bd. of Realtors; WBR Mortgage & Finance Comm.; RE Bd. of NY, WA Bd. of Realtors Million Dollar Sales and Leasing Clubs; **EDUC:** BS, 1969, Econ., NY Univ.; **OTHER ACT & HONORS:** NYU Alumni; Smithsonian Inst.; **HOME ADD:** 12033 Trailridge Dr., Potomac, MD 20854, (301)279-7141; **BUS ADD:** 1333 New Hampshire Ave., NW, Washington, DC 20036, (202)296-6360.

GEIST, Donald D.——**B:** Jan. 31, 1948, Chicago, IL, *Leasing and Building Mgr.*, L.J. Sheridan & Co.; **PRIM RE ACT:** Broker, Consultant, Appraiser, Developer, Property Manager; **SERVICES:** Investment and leasing advice, devel. and prop. mgmt.; **REP CLIENTS:** Comml. and indus. clients, pension and ins. co.; **PROFL AFFIL & HONORS:** Chicago RE Bd.; BOMA; **EDUC:** BA, 1970, Business Management, Lewis Univ.; **GRAD EDUC:** RPA Program/Bldg. Mgmt., BOMA; **MIL SERV:** US Army Reserve; **HOME ADD:** 2815 W. Estes Ave., Chicago, IL 60645, (312)761-6477; **BUS ADD:** 111 W. Washington St., Chicago, IL 60602, (312)726-7743.

GELARDIN, Robert——*Treas.*, Gelardin, Bruner, Cott, Inc., G/B/C Devel. Corp.; **PRIM RE ACT:** Consultant, Developer, Property Manager, Syndicator; **SERVICES:** Devel., synd. of comml. & residential.; **EDUC:** BA, Swarthmore Coll.; **GRAD EDUC:** MA, Urban Planning, MIT; **HOME ADD:** 15 Maple Ave., Cambridge, MA 02139; **BUS ADD:** 75 Cambridge Pkwy., Cambridge, MA 02142, (617)492-8400.

GELFOND, Lawrence P.——**B:** May 21, 1942, Brooklyn, NY, *Partner-in-Charge*, Laventhol & Horwath; **PRIM RE ACT:** Consultant, Owner/Investor; **OTHER RE ACT:** CPA; **SERVICES:** Court Appointed Receiver; **EDUC:** BSBA, 1964, Acctg., Univ. of Denver; **EDUC HONORS:** Beta Alpha Psi; **HOME ADD:** 13 Cherrymoor Dr., Englewood, CO 80110, (303)781-2700; **BUS ADD:** 1800 Emerson St., Denver, CO 80218, (303)861-2500.

GELHAUS, Melvin F.——**B:** Sept. 10, 1920, Oakland, CA, *Sr. Appraiser*, Bank of Amer., Sacramento Appraisal Dist.; **PRIM RE ACT:** Appraiser; **SERVICES:** Valuation of agri-bus., farm, ranch & other rural props.; **REP CLIENTS:** Staff appraiser for Bank of Amer.; **PREV EMPLOY:** Self-emp. dairyman & cattleman; **PROFL AFFIL & HONORS:** Amer. Soc. of Appraisers, Sr. Member Amer. Soc. of Appraisers; **EDUC:** AA, 1940, Pre-Legal, Univ. of CA, Berkeley; **MIL SERV:** USN Air Corp., Lt. JG, 1943-45; **HOME ADD:** 2172 Montecito Way, Sacramento, CA 95822, (916)421-5786; **BUS ADD:** 1541 Merkley Blvd., W Sacramento, CA 95691, (916)449-4362.

GELINA, Maurice R.——**B:** May 27, 1947, New York, *Office Mgr.*, Julien J. Studley, Inc.; **PRIM RE ACT:** Broker, Consultant, Owner/Investor; **SERVICES:** Office Bldg. Leasing, consulting and devel.; **PREV EMPLOY:** Clark-Biondi Co.; **PROFL AFFIL & HONORS:** NAR; FL Assn. of Realtors; **EDUC:** BA, 1971, Bus. Admin./Math/Educ., Univ. of NY; **EDUC HONORS:** Cum Laude; **OTHER ACT & HONORS:** Various Civic Orgs.; **HOME ADD:** 701 Swan, Miami Springs, FL 33166, (305)883-8227; **BUS ADD:** One Biscayne Tower, Suite 3640, Miami, FL 33131, (305)374-2200.

GELLER, David J.——**B:** Oct. 9, 1949, New York, NY, *In-house Counsel*, Wilder-Manley Associates, Inc.; **PRIM RE ACT:** Broker, Consultant, Attorney, Developer, Owner/Investor, Property Manager; **PROFL AFFIL & HONORS:** ABA, Sect. on Corporate Banking and Bus. Law; **EDUC:** AB, 1970, Amer. Studies, Wesleyan Univ.; **GRAD EDUC:** JD, 1975, Law, Northeastern Univ. Law School; **EDUC HONORS:** Dept. Honors; **HOME ADD:** 119 Freeman St., Brookline, MA 02146, (617)232-0331; **BUS ADD:** 66 Long Wharf, Boston, MA 02110, (617)726-1524.

GELLER, Guy G.——**B:** Sept. 15, 1907, Lebanon, PA, *Partner*, Geller Real Estate Co.; **PRIM RE ACT:** Broker, Appraiser, Banker, Property Manager; **MIL SERV:** USAF, 1941-53, Maj.; **HOME ADD:** Lebanon Ct. Apts., C-208, Jackson Blvd., Lebanon, PA 17042, (717)272-7963; **BUS ADD:** 773 Cumberland St., Lebanon, PA 17042, (717)272-5637.

GELLER, Leonard——**B:** Apr. 11, 1933, Newark, NJ, *Owner*, Leonard Geller; **PRIM RE ACT:** Broker; **SERVICES:** Sales; **PREV EMPLOY:** Salesman-A. Schwarz Co., E. Orange, NJ (2 yrs.); Geller-Marks Co., E. Orange, NJ (10 yrs.); **EDUC:** BS, 1955, Bus. Mgmt., Seton Hall Univ.; **EDUC HONORS:** Dean's List; **MIL SERV:** USA, Sgt.; **HOME ADD:** 17 Rippling Brook Dr., Short Hills, NJ 07078, (201)376-6970; **BUS ADD:** 24-26 Park Ave., W. Orange, NJ 07078.

GELLERT, Donald N.——**B:** Oct. 21, 1938, London, England, *Member of Firm*, Otterbourg, Steindler, Houston & Rosen, P.C.; **PRIM RE ACT:** Attorney; **PROFL AFFIL & HONORS:** ABA; NY State Bar Assn. (Landlord/Tenant Comm.); Bar Assn. of the City of NY; **EDUC:** 1960, History, Harvard Coll.; **GRAD EDUC:** 1963, Harvard Law School; **EDUC HONORS:** Magna Cum Laude; **HOME ADD:** Lewis

Rd., Irvington, NY 10533, (914)591-6565; **BUS ADD:** 230 Park Ave., NY, NY 10169, (212)661-9100.

GELLING, Louis——**B:** May 6, 1921, Springdale, AR, *Pres.*, St. Petersburg Realty Corp.; **PRIM RE ACT:** Broker, Consultant, Appraiser, Owner/Investor, Property Manager; **OTHER RE ACT:** Specializing in comml. invest. prop.; **SERVICES:** Full serv. RE; **PREV EMPLOY:** Reg. Army Officer 31 years; **PROFL AFFIL & HONORS:** Realtors Nat. Mktg. Inst.; NAR; FL Assn. of Mort. Brokers, Candidate, CCIM; **EDUC:** BS Mil. Sci. & Physical Ed., 1949, Govt. & Pol., Univ. of MD, College Park, MD; **GRAD EDUC:** MA, 1963, Public Admin., Univ. of MD, College Park, MD; **EDUC HONORS:** Phi Kappa Phi, Pi Sigma Alpha; **MIL SERV:** US Army, Col., Silver Star (2), Bronze Star (2), Legion of Merit (2), Distinguished Flying Cross; **OTHER ACT & HONORS:** 32 Mason & Shriner; Past Pres. of Sunshine City Kiwanis Club; Member Coast Guard Auxiliary; Member Assn. of the US Army; Member Dioscean Comm. Episcopal Diocese of SW FL. Chmn. Comml./Investment Comm., St. Petersburg Bd. of Realtors; **HOME ADD:** 1313 80th St. So., St. Petersburg, FL 33707, (813)347-3923; **BUS ADD:** 4554 Central Ave., St. Petersburg, FL 33711, (813)321-7575.

GELLMAN, Yale H.——**B:** Sept. 16, 1934, Yonkers, NY, *Partner-Atty.*, Proskauer Rose Goetz & Mendelsohn, RE Dept.; **OTHER RE ACT:** RE Law; **PROFL AFFIL & HONORS:** NY State Bar Assn.; Assn. of the Bar of the City of NY; NY County Lawyer's Assn.; **EDUC:** BA, 1954, New York Univ.; **GRAD EDUC:** JD, 1957, Harvard Law School; **HOME ADD:** 131 Schenck Ave., Great Neck, NY 11021; **BUS ADD:** 300 Park Ave., NY, NY 10022, (212)909-7172.

GENDLER, H. Lee——**B:** Oct. 20, 1930, Omaha, NE, *Pres.*, Marathon Realty Corp.; **PRIM RE ACT:** Broker, Developer, Owner/Investor, Syndicator; **OTHER RE ACT:** Condo. conversion; **SERVICES:** Mktg. indus. prop. and bus., devel. and synd. comml., indus. prop.; **REP CLIENTS:** Indiv. and institl. investors; **PREV EMPLOY:** Pres., Great Day Devel. Corp.; **PROFL AFFIL & HONORS:** NAIOP; ICSC; **EDUC:** 1952, Econ./Psych., Yale Univ.; **MIL SERV:** USCG-R, Lt.j.g.; **HOME ADD:** 9820 Spring St., Omaha, NE 68124, (402)391-1919; **BUS ADD:** 11128 John Galt Blvd., Suite 575, Omaha, NE 68137, (402)592-1940.

GENDREAU, Richard——**B:** Sept. 7, 1946, Minneapolis, MN, *Pres.*, R&C Realty; **PRIM RE ACT:** Broker, Consultant, Instructor; **SERVICES:** Feasibility studies; **PROFL AFFIL & HONORS:** RNMI, Bus. Admin. Assn.; **EDUC:** BS, 1968, Gen. Bus., St. Cloud St. Univ.; Course work for a Doctorate Degree, completed Spring 1977, Bus. Admin., Univ. of KY, Lexington, KY,; **GRAD EDUC:** MBA, 1969, Fin. & Mgmt., St. Cloud State Univ.; **HOME ADD:** 1421 Birchmont Dr., Bemidji, MN 56601, (218)751-8595; **BUS ADD:** 1421 Birchmont Dr., Bemidji, MN 56601, (218)751-8595.

GENT, Philip D.——**B:** May 17, 1943, IA, *VP/Appraisals*, Bohemian S&L Assoc.; **PRIM RE ACT:** Appraiser; **SERVICES:** Gen. appraisals and counseling services.; **REP CLIENTS:** Reloc., lenders, owners and investors; **PREV EMPLOY:** 15; **PROFL AFFIL & HONORS:** SREA, SRPA, ARA; **EDUC:** BS, 1965, Econ., IA State Univ.; **OTHER ACT & HONORS:** Cedar Rapids Rotary Club; **HOME ADD:** 2160 Coldstream Ave., NE, Cedar Rapids, IA 52402, (319)362-9650; **BUS ADD:** 3910 Ctr. Pt. Rd., NE, Cedar Rapids, IA 52402, (319)364-0153.

GENT, Raymond D.——**B:** Mar. 7, 1940, Long Beach, CA, *Regional VP for RE Investments*, Mutual Life Ins. Co. of NY (MONY), Dallas RE Investment Office; **PRIM RE ACT:** Lender, Owner/Investor; **OTHER RE ACT:** Refinance; **PREV EMPLOY:** MONY - Atlanta RE Invest. Office, 10 yrs.; **EDUC:** BS, 1962, Indus. Mgmt., GA Tech., Atlanta, GA; **GRAD EDUC:** MBA, 1974, RE, GA State Univ., Atlanta, GA; **MIL SERV:** USN, Lt., Joint Serv. Commendation Medal; **HOME ADD:** 2101 Stardust Court, Euless, TX 76039, (817)571-9199; **BUS ADD:** 1230 Riverbend Dr., Suite 220, Dallas, TX 75247, (214)630-5972.

GENTILE, Anthony R.——**B:** July 1, 1942, Philadelphia, PA, *Mgr. Building Services*, Beverage Mgmt. Inc., Corp.; **PRIM RE ACT:** Consultant, Engineer, Developer, Builder, Owner/Investor, Property Manager; **REP CLIENTS:** Work for employer only; **PREV EMPLOY:** IU Intl. Scott Paper Co.; **PROFL AFFIL & HONORS:** Amer. Inst. of Plant Engrs.; **EDUC:** BSME, 1964, Machinery design, Machi-BSME, PA Military Coll.; **GRAD EDUC:** MBA, 1968-72, Bus. Admin., Glassboro State Coll.; **MIL SERV:** PA Air Nat. Guard, 1964-70, S/Sgt., Honor Grad.; **OTHER ACT & HONORS:** US Patent granted; **HOME ADD:** 7250 Cubbage Rd., Westerville, OH 43081, (614)882-0458; **BUS ADD:** 1001 Kingsmill Pkwy., Columbus, OH 43229, (614)846-9800.

GENTILOZZI, Albert E.——**B:** June 11, 1927, Clarksburg, VA, *Co-Owner*, Gentilozzi Real Estate & Mgt. Co.; **PRIM RE ACT:** Broker, Consultant, Developer, Owner/Investor, Property Manager, Syndicator; **OTHER RE ACT:** CPM; **SERVICES:** Leasing, mgmt. - mkt. analysis, feasibility studies, income-expen. analysis gnt. proj.; **PREV EMPLOY:** Walter-Neller Co. - Lansing, MI; **PROFL AFFIL & HONORS:** Lan. Bd. of Realtors, IREM, Constr. Specifications Inst., CPM; **EDUC:** Henry Ford C/C, 1950, Indus. Tr. Inst.; **MIL SERV:** A.A.F., Sgt., A.M.; **HOME ADD:** 5517 River Ridge, Lansing, MI 48917, (517)323-4155; **BUS ADD:** Suite 300, 501 South Capital Ave., Lansing, MI 48933, (517)371-3230.

GENTRY, Allan S.——**B:** Feb. 14, 1941, Fresno, CA, *RE Analyst*, Real Estate Services Ctr., Phoenix; **PRIM RE ACT:** Consultant, Appraiser, Owner/Investor; **OTHER RE ACT:** RE Analyst; **SERVICES:** Studies of RE; **REP CLIENTS:** Devel., lenders, owner/investors, synds., prop. mgrs., archs., brokers; **PREV EMPLOY:** Local, Nat. & Intl. firms; **PROFL AFFIL & HONORS:** Assoc. Member of Soc. of RE Appraisers; Candidate for membership to AIREA, RE Analyst; **EDUC:** Stockton Coll., Phoenix Coll., IN Univ., Purdue Univ.; **MIL SERV:** USAF, Maj.; **BUS ADD:** 3900 E. Camelback Rd., #108, Phoenix, AZ 85018, (602)957-8116.

GENTRY, Richard N., Jr.——**B:** Sept 27, 1944, Wichita, KS, *Atty.*, Clem, Triggs & Gentry; **PRIM RE ACT:** Attorney; **SERVICES:** Legal representation and counseling; **PROFL AFFIL & HONORS:** ABA, IL State Bar Assn., Peoria Cty. Bar Assn., Member Attys. Title Guaranty Fund, Inc., Chmn., Prepared Legal Serv. Standing Comm., IL State Bar Assn.; **EDUC:** BA, 1966, Econ., Univ. of MI; **GRAD EDUC:** JD, 1969, Univ. of IL; **OTHER ACT & HONORS:** Heart of Il United Way-Planning Panel; **HOME ADD:** 332 Wood Ridge Dr., Dunlap, IL 61525, (309)243-9249; **BUS ADD:** 300 NE Perry Ave., Peoria, IL 61603, (309)673-2600.

GEORGE, Charles D.——**B:** Aug. 4, 1936, Hamilton, OH, *Atty.*, MacFarlane, Ferguson, Allison & Kelly; **PRIM RE ACT:** Attorney; **SERVICES:** Closings, title ins., condos.; **REP CLIENTS:** Bank of Clearwater; NE Bank of Clearwater; **PROFL AFFIL & HONORS:** FL Bar (Real Prop., Probate & Trust Law Section); ABA (Real Prop., Probate & Trust Law Section), FL Bar Designation Plan - Real Prop.; **EDUC:** BS, 1958, Bus. Admin., OH State Univ.; **GRAD EDUC:** JD, 1960, OH State Univ.; **MIL SERV:** U.S. Air Force Res., Col., AFCM; **HOME ADD:** 2346 Haddon Hall Pl., Clearwater, FL 33516, (813)531-7232; **BUS ADD:** 900 Bank of Clearwater Bldg., PO Drawer 2197, Clearwater, FL 33517, (813)441-1763.

GEORGE, Gerald——*Treas.*, Houston Oil & Minerals Corp.; **PRIM RE ACT:** Property Manager; **BUS ADD:** 1100 Louisiana St., Houston, TX 77002, (713)658-3000.*

GEORGE, James Wesley——**B:** Feb. 5, 1917, Minneapolis, MN, *Broker*, Century 21 Real Estate; **PRIM RE ACT:** Broker, Consultant, Property Manager; **SERVICES:** RE urban sales, consultants, prop. mgmt. relocation; **REP CLIENTS:** Absentee owners, transferred execs.; **PREV EMPLOY:** VP Marketing, Ideal Mfg. Co., Marketing Consultants Services, Ltd.; **PROFL AFFIL & HONORS:** IA Assn. of Realtors, NAR Political Action Comm., GRI Broker; **EDUC:** BA, 1938, Econ.-Soc., Wm. Penn Coll., Oskallosa, IA; **GRAD EDUC:** MA, 1942, Bus. Admin., State Univ. of IA; **EDUC HONORS:** Pi Kappa Delta; **OTHER ACT & HONORS:** Rotary Club, C of C, Automotive Boosters Club, City Devel. Comm.; **HOME ADD:** 812 Penn Blvd., Oskallosa, IA 52577, (515)673-7449; **BUS ADD:** 812 Penn Blvd., Oskallosa, IA 52577, (515)673-7449.

GEORGE, Paula R.——**B:** June 29, 1947, DuQuoin, IL, *Pres.*, Stewart Title of LA, Inc.; **PRIM RE ACT:** Consultant, Attorney, Insuror, Syndicator; **SERVICES:** Abstract & title examination of RE; **REP CLIENTS:** Investors, realtors, sellers & homebuyers, builders, lenders, comml. investors; **PREV EMPLOY:** Profl. Oil and Gas Landman, 1977-1978; **PROFL AFFIL & HONORS:** LA Bar Assn.; Jefferson Bar Assn.; ABA; RESSI; Jefferson Bd. of Realtors; Women's Council; C of C, JD; GRI; **EDUC:** BA, 1969, Speech, LA State Univ.; **GRAD EDUC:** JD, 1978, Law, Loyola Law School; **OTHER ACT & HONORS:** Who's Who in Women; Who's Who in Law; **HOME ADD:** 7500 Stoneleigh Dr., New Orleans, LA 70123, (504)737-7177; **BUS ADD:** 3131 Harvard Ave., Suite 101, Metairie, LA 70002, (504)887-6911.

GEORGE, Robert——**B:** Dec. 9, 1921, RI, *VP*, Sherwood & Roberts, Inc., Portland Comml. Office; **PRIM RE ACT:** Banker, Lender; **SERVICES:** Const. loans, permanent loans, joint ventures, participations; **REP CLIENTS:** builders, devel., contractors, RE investors; **PREV EMPLOY:** Other Mort. Cos.; **PROFL AFFIL & HONORS:** Mort. Bankers Assn.; **EDUC:** Math, Univ. of FL; **EDUC HONORS:** Phi Eta Sigma, Dean's List; **MIL SERV:** US Army & AF, Maj., Dist.

Flying Cross, 6 Air Medals; **BUS ADD:** 1335 SW Fifth, Portland, OR 97232, (503)243-1835.

GEORGE, Robert J.——B: Aug. 11, 1944, Paterson, NJ, *Pres.*, Boston Publishing Co.; **PRIM RE ACT:** Real Estate Publisher; **SERVICES:** Founded and published "Investing in Real Estate" and "The Real Estate Investing Letter"; **EDUC:** BA, 1967, Eng./Sociology, MO Univ.; **OTHER ACT & HONORS:** Somerset Club; Knickerbocker; Tennis & Racquet Club; **HOME ADD:** 60 Washington St., Sherborn, MA 01770, (617)653-8868; **BUS ADD:** 306 Dartmouth St., Boston, MA 02116, (617)267-7100.

GEORGE, Sid——B: July 17, 1943, Houston, TX, *Pres.*, Sid George, CPA, PC & Sheltered Investments, Inc.; **PRIM RE ACT:** Broker, Consultant, Owner/Investor, Instructor, Property Manager, Syndicator; **SERVICES:** Tax planning, investment counseling & synd. of tax advantaged RE; **PROFL AFFIL & HONORS:** Houston Bd. of Realtors, Greater Houston Bldrs. Assn., Nat. Assn. of Home Bldrs.; **EDUC:** BS, 1961, Physics, Univ. of Houston; **GRAD EDUC:** MBA, 1971, Bus., Sam Houston State Univ.; **MIL SERV:** USA, 1st Lt., Purple Heart; **BUS ADD:** One Allen Ctr., Suite 3010, Houston, TX 77002, (713)759-9920.

GEORGI, John M.——B: Oct. 2, 1942, Milan, TN, *Pres.*, Ski & Shore Properites, Inc.; **PRIM RE ACT:** Broker, Owner/Investor, Syndicator; **OTHER RE ACT:** Franchisor; **SERVICES:** Counseling on a referral basis; Synd. of comml. investment props., franchisor of resort RE franchises; **REP CLIENTS:** Indiv. and instnl. investors; **PROFL AFFIL & HONORS:** MI Assn. of Realtors; NAR; MI Assn. RE Exchange Div.; FL RE Exchange, CCIM; **EDUC:** BS, 1964, Acctg., Econ., Univ. of MD; **MIL SERV:** USMC, Capt.; **HOME ADD:** Tannery Creek, Petoskey, MI 49770, (616)347-1984; **BUS ADD:** 1231 U.S. 31 N., Petoskey, MI 49770, (616)347-7600.

GEORGIANA, Joseph S., Esq.——B: Oct. 18, 1933, Woodbury, NJ, Capehart & Scatchard, P.A.; **PRIM RE ACT:** Attorney; **SERVICES:** Legal services; **REP CLIENTS:** Continental Title Insurance Co., Brokers Mort. Service, Tri-County Savings and Loan Assn., Unity Savings Assn., Chigago, IL; **PREV EMPLOY:** Ware & Georgiana, Esqs., Pitman, NJ (1960-1963); **PROFL AFFIL & HONORS:** US, NJ, Camden Cty. Bar Assns., Phi Beta Kappa, Gettysburg, 1955; **EDUC:** BA, 1955, Gettysburg Coll., PA; **GRAD EDUC:** LLB, 1958, Univ. of MI; **EDUC HONORS:** Magna Cum Laude; **MIL SERV:** US Army, S-5; **OTHER ACT & HONORS:** Atty., Cherry Hill Zoning Bd. - 1971-75; Pres., Cherry Hill Democrat Club, 1970-71; **HOME ADD:** 1109 Winding Dr., Cherry Hill, NJ 08003, (609)428-4715; **BUS ADD:** 304 Harper Dr., Moorestown, NJ 08057, (609)234-6800.

GERAGHTY, Martin P.——B: Mar. 4, 1945, Chicago, IL, *VP*, Collins Tuttle & Co., Inc.; **PRIM RE ACT:** Broker, Consultant, Developer, Owner/Investor; **OTHER RE ACT:** Leasing Dir., Comml. Props.; **SERVICES:** Office relocation counseling & brokerage, sale and leasing of office props., devel. of major comml. props.; **REP CLIENTS:** Major users of office space, owners of substantial office props., investors in major comml. props.; **PREV EMPLOY:** Arthur Rubloff & Co. 1973-1976, Draper & Kramer & Co. 1976-1980; **EDUC:** BA, 1967, Poli. Sci., Loyola Univ. (Chicago); **GRAD EDUC:** MA, 1969, Latin Amer. Studies, Univ. of MO (Columbia); **EDUC HONORS:** Numerous Honorary Soc., NDEA Title IV, Fellowship; **MIL SERV:** ILARNG, Sgt.; **OTHER ACT & HONORS:** Alderman, 4th Ward City of Evanston, IL 1973-1975; Pres., Consumers' Health Grp., Evanston, IL; Various Political, Govt. and Religious Comms.; **HOME ADD:** 1527 Washington, Evanston, IL 60202, (312)328-6425; **BUS ADD:** 20 N. Clark St., Chicago, IL 60602, (312)427-6400.

GERECHOFF, Russell L.——B: July 5, 1956, Neptune, NJ, *Broker Salesman*, G&G Realtors; **PRIM RE ACT:** Broker, Property Manager; **PROFL AFFIL & HONORS:** CRS, CRB; **EDUC:** BS, 1978, Bus., Monmouth Coll.; **OTHER ACT & HONORS:** VP of Jr. C of C of Ocean Township; **HOME ADD:** 414 Parker Ave., Deal Park, NJ 07723; **BUS ADD:** Box I, Norwood & Roosevelt Ave., Deal, NJ 07723, (201)531-2000; **BUS TEL:** (201)531-0044.

GERECHT, Ach——*Publ.*, Community Development Services, Inc., Washington Report on Real Estate; **PRIM RE ACT:** Real Estate Publisher; **BUS ADD:** 399 Natl. Press Bldg., Washington, DC 20045, (202)638-6113.*

GEREND, Robert P.——B: Feb. 7, 1938, Memphis, TN, *Chmn.*, The Pace Corp.; **PRIM RE ACT:** Broker, Consultant, Developer, Builder, Owner/Investor, Instructor, Property Manager, Real Estate Publisher, Syndicator; **SERVICES:** Synd., comml. brokerage, devel.; **PREV EMPLOY:** Mgr., The Boeing Co.; **PROFL AFFIL & HONORS:** WA Assn. of Realtors; Nat. Assn. of Fin. Consultants; NAR; Pres. Assn.; Intl. Platform Assn., The Nat. Speakers' Assn.; Toastmasters Intl., Best Section Award, AIAA, 1974, Chmn.; Who's Who in Fin. and Indus.; Who's Who in the World, and Men of Achievement; Pres., WA Sect. of RESSI; Author, various RE articles and newsletters; nat. lecturer on RE investment strategy and RE Commentator for KIRO radio in Seattle, WA; **EDUC:** BS, 1961, Engrg., Univ. of WI; **GRAD EDUC:** MS, 1968, Engrg., Seattle Univ.; **EDUC HONORS:** With Honors; **HOME ADD:** 14877 SE 50th St., Bellevue, WA 98008, (206)746-1415; **BUS ADD:** 16301 NE 8th St., Suite 251, Bellevue, WA 98008, (206)746-4743.

GERENT, Harry R.——B: Feb. 3, 1933, Germany, *Owner*, Gerent RE Investments; **PRIM RE ACT:** Broker, Instructor, Syndicator, Developer, Builder, Owner/Investor; **OTHER RE ACT:** RE Partnerships; **SERVICES:** Assemble Land Parcels - Dev. - Build-Synd.; **REP CLIENTS:** Prof. People; **PREV EMPLOY:** RE Salesman & Broker Athletic Dir. - Mgr.; **PROFL AFFIL & HONORS:** RNMI, RESSI, GRI, CRS, CCIM, Exchangor of the Yr. - Cleveland Area Realty Exchangors; **EDUC:** BA, 1961, W Reserve Univ.; **MIL SERV:** USA, Pfc.; **OTHER ACT & HONORS:** Pres. Nat. Assn. of Athletic Dir., Tr. Westlake Sportsman's Chb., Tr. Bidele Fellowship; **HOME ADD:** 31403 Avon Rd., Westlake, OH 44145, (216)835-1745; **BUS ADD:** 31403 Avon Rd., Westlake, OH 44145, (216)835-3350.

GERFIN, Thomas Joseph——B: July 27, 1949, Milwaukee, WI, *Asst. VP*, Metro Financial Group, Ltd.; **PRIM RE ACT:** Consultant, Developer, Lender; **SERVICES:** Mort. fin., equity, prop. devel.; **PREV EMPLOY:** Project Mgr., Carsam Group, Inc., Housing Devel. Officer, IL Housing Devel. Auth.; **PROFL AFFIL & HONORS:** IL Mort. Bankers Assn., Oak Park Plan. Commn.; **EDUC:** BCE, 1971, Purdue Univ.; **GRAD EDUC:** MS, 1973, RE Investment analysis and appr., Univ. of WI, Madison; **HOME ADD:** 616 Gunderson Ave., Oak Park, IL 60304, (312)848-4603; **BUS ADD:** 55 W. Monroe St. #3550, Chicago, IL 60603, (312)346-9235.

GERHARD, Ronald H.——B: July 24, 1942, New York, NY, *Pres.*, Arenberg Sage, Inc.; **PRIM RE ACT:** Architect, Developer, Builder, Engineer, Owner/Investor; **PROFL AFFIL & HONORS:** AIIE; **EDUC:** Indus. Engr., 1964, Penn. State; **BUS ADD:** PO Box 250, 57 Cornwall St., Jamaica Plain, MA 02130, (617)522-2800.

GERHARDT, Sidney J.——B: Feb. 22, 1925, Mobile, AL, *Pres.*, Gerhardt Investment Group, Inc. & Marketing America, Inc.; **PRIM RE ACT:** Consultant, Appraiser, Owner/Investor, Property Manager; **OTHER RE ACT:** Comml. Mort. Broker; Comml. fin.; **SERVICES:** Pvt. Mort. Placements; Feasibility Studies, Appraising; **REP CLIENTS:** Mort. & Money Brokers, RE devels., Nationwide; **PROFL AFFIL & HONORS:** Nat. Assn. of Review Appraisers, CRA; **EDUC:** BE, 1945, Mech. Engrg., Yale Univ., Carnegie Inst. of Tech.; **GRAD EDUC:** Commissioned Officer, 1945, USNR Midshipmens School, Columbia Univ.; **MIL SERV:** USNR, Ensign, Amer. Defense ribbon, Phil. Sea Frontier ribbon; **HOME ADD:** 3814 Claridge Rd., Mobile, AL 36608, (205)342-1955; **BUS ADD:** 917 Western Amer. Circ., Mobile, AL 36609, (205)343-5410.

GERHART, Bruce P.——B: Dec. 14, 1949, Chicago, IL, Burnham Realty; **PRIM RE ACT:** Broker, Syndicator; **SERVICES:** Investment Counseling, Comml. Realty Synd.; **REP CLIENTS:** Indiv. & Instnl. Investors; **PREV EMPLOY:** Mgr. - Neighborhood Serv. (Public Agency Specialized in Residential & Comml. Realty Rehabilitation); **PROFL AFFIL & HONORS:** CCIM & SRS Candidacies, RNMI, RESSI; **EDUC:** BA, 1972, Pol. Sci., Wittenberg Univ.; **GRAD EDUC:** MPA, 1975, Kent State Univ.; **HOME ADD:** 812 Manor Ct., Joliet, IL 60436; **BUS ADD:** 111 E. Wacker, Chicago, IL 60601, (312)938-2250.

GERICKE, John J., Jr.——*Grp. VP*, Reed & Stambaugh Co., Prop. Mgmt. Div.; **PRIM RE ACT:** Property Manager; **SERVICES:** Complete Prop. Mgmt. for Comml. Prop.; **REP CLIENTS:** Indiv. or Instnl. Prop. Owners; **BUS ADD:** 4 Penn Ctr. Plaza, Philadelphia, PA 19103, (215)568-2727.

GERINGER, A.C.——*Dir. Admin. & Human Services*, PVO International; **PRIM RE ACT:** Property Manager; **BUS ADD:** World Trade Center, San Francisco, CA 94111, (415)362-0990.*

GERITY, Mark B.——B: Oct. 16, 1945, Charleston, SC, *VP/Treas.*, Intown Development Corp.; **PRIM RE ACT:** Broker, Consultant, Developer, Builder, Owner/Investor, Property Manager, Syndicator; **PREV EMPLOY:** Northeast Utilities 1975-77; **EDUC:** BA, 1967, Latin Amer. Studies, Yale Univ.; **GRAD EDUC:** MBA, 1974, Fin., Babson Coll.; **MIL SERV:** USMC, 1968-71, Capt.; **HOME ADD:** 18 Cone St., Hartford, CT 06105, (203)233-0309; **BUS ADD:** 1 Frederick St., Hartford, CT 06105, (203)247-3009.

GERMAIN, Craig D.——*Pres.*, Craig Germain Company; **PRIM RE ACT:** Broker, Developer, Builder; **BUS ADD:** 433 Las Colinas Blvd., Irving, TX 75062, (214)659-1525.

GERMAK, Ralph A.——**B:** Apr. 3, 1949, Wilkes-Barre, PA, *Pres.*, Century 21 Roush-Germak Real Estate, Inc.; **PRIM RE ACT:** Broker, Attorney, Appraiser; **SERVICES:** RE sales, appraisals, and legal servs.; **PREV EMPLOY:** Commonwealth of PA, Dept. of Revenue; **PROFL AFFIL & HONORS:** ABA; PA Bar Assn.; Juniata Cty. Bar Assn.; Century 21 RE Investment Club; **EDUC:** BA, 1971, Econ./Bus., Kings Coll.; **GRAD EDUC:** JD, 1974, Law, Dickinson School of Law; **EDUC HONORS:** Cum Laude; **OTHER ACT & HONORS:** Knights of Columbus, Fayette Area Lions Club; **HOME ADD:** Box 249, S. Main St., McAlisterville, PA 17049, (717)463-3686; **BUS ADD:** Box 167, Suite 2, Washington Ave., Mifflintown, PA 17059.

GERMONY, Geoffrey G.——*Pres.*, Marc Equity Corp., New Resid. Div. of W. NY; **PRIM RE ACT:** Engineer, Developer, Builder, Owner/Investor, Property Manager; **SERVICES:** Devel. and const. of resid. and comml. prop.; active in condo conversion projects; **PREV EMPLOY:** Roblin Indus., Indus. Housing Div., Devel. & Mgmt. Consultant to Investors; **PROFL AFFIL & HONORS:** NAHB, Niagara Frontier Builders Assn., NHBA; **EDUC:** Engrg., Syracuse Univ.; **HOME ADD:** 9550 Sisson Hwy., Eden, NY 14057, (716)992-3925; **BUS ADD:** 2730 Transit Rd., Buffalo, NY 14224, (716)675-1200.

GEROULD, Ann K.——**B:** Mar. 20, 1938, Kalamazoo, MI, *Pres. and Managing Broker*, Prop. Resource Center; **PRIM RE ACT:** Broker, Developer, Owner/Investor; **OTHER RE ACT:** Rehab. & Adaptive Reuse; **SERVICES:** Sales, Investment Counseling; **PROFL AFFIL & HONORS:** RESSI; RMNI; NHIC; Kalamazoo City Planning Commiss.; Downtown Kalamazoo Assn.; Stuart Area Rehab. Assn., Private Prop. Rehabilitation Award, 1980; **HOME ADD:** 308 Stuart, Kalamazoo, MI, (616)381-1439; **BUS ADD:** 628 South Park, Kalamazoo, MI 49007, (616)385-4444.

GERSCHEFSKE, Charles——**B:** Mar. 14, 1951, Waukegan, IL, *Pres.*, Charles Gerschefske RE Research and Appraisal Co.; **PRIM RE ACT:** Consultant, Appraiser, Assessor; **OTHER RE ACT:** Appraisal Review, Assessment Admin.; **SERVICES:** RE Research and Appraisals; **REP CLIENTS:** Lenders, Brokers, Builders, Indiv. of all Professions; **PREV EMPLOY:** 15 yrs. Deputy Assessor, Town of Vernon Lake Cty., IL; **PROFL AFFIL & HONORS:** Intl. Assn. of Assessing Officers, IL Prop. Assessment Inst. Assn. of Governmental Appraisers, Cert. IL Assessing Officer, CRA, ICA; **EDUC:** BS, 1974, Indus. Education, Univ. of WI; **OTHER ACT & HONORS:** Village Trustee, Buffalo Grove, Vernon Township Assessor; **HOME ADD:** 111 Circle Dr., Buffalo Grove, IL 60090, (312)459-1565; **BUS ADD:** 111 Circle Dr., Buffalo Grove, IL 60090, (312)634-4600.

GERSHENSON, Harry——**B:** July 8, 1910, St. Louis, MO, *Lawyer*, Gershenson & Gershenson; **PRIM RE ACT:** Attorney; **SERVICES:** Legal; **PROFL AFFIL & HONORS:** Past Pres., Amer. Coll. of Probate Lawyers; Past Pres., MO Bar; Past Pres., St. Louis Bar, Past Pres., Scribes Law Writers Soc.; **GRAD EDUC:** LLB, 1924, Benton Coll. of Law; **HOME ADD:** 542 Warder, University City, MO 63130, (314)727-2973; **BUS ADD:** 7733 Forsyth Blvd., St. Louis, MO 63105, (314)725-2545.

GERSON, Donald A.——**B:** Apr. 24, 1927, NY, *Pres.*, Sun Land Industries, Inc.; **PRIM RE ACT:** Attorney, Developer, Builder; **SERVICES:** RE devel. & builder; **PROFL AFFIL & HONORS:** Nat. Assn. Home Builders, Nat. Assn. RE Appraisers; **EDUC:** BS, Pre-Law, NY Univ.; **GRAD EDUC:** LLB (JD), Law, NY Univ.; **EDUC HONORS:** Honor Roll, Moot Court; **MIL SERV:** USAF, Capt.; **HOME ADD:** Rte 940 HCRB113, Pocono Summit, PA 18346, (717)839-7910; **BUS ADD:** Rte 940 HCRB113, Pocono Summit, PA 18346, (717)839-7910.

GERSTEN, Harry R.——**B:** Apr. 10, 1946, Reno, NV, *Prop. Mgr.*, CA First Bank, Trust RE; **PRIM RE ACT:** Broker, Property Manager; **SERVICES:** Prop. Mgmt., Investment Counseling, Valuation, Sales; **PREV EMPLOY:** The Gersten Cos., 1971 to 1980; **PROFL AFFIL & HONORS:** Amer. Mgmt. Assn, CA RE Broker; **EDUC:** BS, 1973, RE, San Diego State Univ.; **EDUC HONORS:** Dean's List, Rio Hondo Coll. Whittier; **MIL SERV:** USA, SP 4; **OTHER ACT & HONORS:** Chula Vista Assn. for Gifted Children, Natl. Wildlife Fed., CA RE Broker; **HOME ADD:** 230 Camino Entrada, Chula Vista, CA 92010, (714)425-7688; **BUS ADD:** 530 B St., Suite 700, San Diego, CA 92101, (714)294-4650.

GESSLING, Donald C.——**B:** Dec. 11, 1921, Bronx, NY, *VP, Broker/Mgr.*, RE/MAX of Fort Myers, Inc.; **PRIM RE ACT:** Broker; **SERVICES:** Gen. RE brokerage; **REP CLIENTS:** Third Party Buying Co's. and indiv.; **PREV EMPLOY:** Self employed prof. photographer 1948-1969; **PROFL AFFIL & HONORS:** RNMI, GRI, CRS, CRB; **MIL SERV:** USAF, Lt. Col., Air Medal, DUC (1942-1945); **OTHER ACT & HONORS:** Past Pres. Ft. Myers Bd. of Realtors; **HOME ADD:** Rt. 13, Box 718-A, Ft. Myers, FL 33908, (813)481-7395; **BUS ADD:** 5448 S US 41, Fort Myers, FL 33907, (813)936-4494.

GETTEL, Ronald——*RE Appraiser*; **PRIM RE ACT:** Consultant, Appraiser; **OTHER RE ACT:** Author; Instructor; **SERVICES:** Counsel to minimize RE Taxes, Appraisal of major income properties throughout US; **PROFL AFFIL & HONORS:** AIREA; Sr. RE Analyst Member (SREA), Soc. of RE Appraisers; CRE, Amer. Soc. of RE Counselors; Member ASA, Amer. Soc. of Appraisers (Past Pres. of AIREA and SREA Chapters), MAI; **EDUC:** IN Univ.; **EDUC HONORS:** Devised method of selecting capitalization rates used by some appraisers (The Gettel Method); **OTHER ACT & HONORS:** Have written books on RE Subjects (Example: *RE Guidelines and Rules of Thumb*, McGraw-Hill, 1976) and shorter pieces (Example: Chapter in *The RE Handbook*, Dow Jones-Irwin, 1980); Widely interviewed and quoted on methods to reduce prop. taxes; **BUS ADD:** 6715 Quail Ridge, Ft. Wayne, IN 46804, (219)432-2482.

GETZ, Bert A.——**B:** May 7, 1937, Chicago, IL, *Pres.*, Globe Corp.; **PRIM RE ACT:** Owner/Investor; **EDUC:** BBA, 1959, Univ. of MI; **OTHER ACT & HONORS:** Dir. Fed. Nat. Mort. Assn., Dir. AZ Bank, Pres & Dir. AZ Comm. Found., Tr. Lawrenceville Sch., NJ; **HOME ADD:** 7223 Black Rock Tr., Scottsdale, AZ 85253, (602)948-1117; **BUS ADD:** 3634 Civic Ctr. Plaza, Scottsdale, AZ 85253, (602)947-7888.

GETZEN, William E.——**B:** May 9, 1932, Elkhorn, WI, *Partner*, Williams, Parker, Harrison, Dietz & Getzen, RE; **PRIM RE ACT:** Consultant, Attorney, Owner/Investor; **SERVICES:** Counselor to RE devel., RE mort. lenders and investors; **REP CLIENTS:** Ramar Group Companies, Inc.; Taylor Woodrow Homes, Ltd.; Arvida Corp.; United First Federal S & L Assn.; Ellis B & T Co.; **PREV EMPLOY:** RE Atty.; **PROFL AFFIL & HONORS:** ABA; The FL Bar; Sarasota Cty. Bar Assn., Past Pres., Sarasota Cty. Bar Assn.; **EDUC:** BS, 1954, Gen. Engrg., Univ. of IL; **GRAD EDUC:** JD, 1959, Univ. of IL; **EDUC HONORS:** Pres. of Gen. Engrg. Soc., Pres., Phi Delta Phi - Outstanding Grad. Award; **MIL SERV:** USAF; Capt.; **OTHER ACT & HONORS:** Rotary Club of Sarasota (Past Pres.); The Field Club (Past Commodore); **HOME ADD:** 1421 Westbrook Dr., Sarasota, FL 33581, (813)922-8581; **BUS ADD:** 1550 Ringling Blvd., Sarasota, FL 33578, (813)366-4800.

GETZOV, Joel Merril——**B:** Nov. 1, 1943, Chicago, IL, *Partner*, Wolin & Getzov; **PRIM RE ACT:** Attorney; **SERVICES:** Legal rep. & consultation; **REP CLIENTS:** Curto Reynolds Oelerich, Inc., Corm Associates, McElvain Reynolds Co., Mid Continental Realty Corp, Wolin-Levin, Inc., Marian Realty, Inc.; **PROFL AFFIL & HONORS:** ABA, IL State Bar Assn.; **EDUC:** BS, 1966, Acctg., Univ. of IL; **GRAD EDUC:** JD, 1970, DePaul Univ. Law Sch.; **HOME ADD:** 2904 W. Lunt Ave., Chicago, IL 60645, (312)274-8777; **BUS ADD:** 111 W. Washington St. #1527, Chicago, IL 60602, (312)372-9832.

GEWERTER, Harold Phillip——**B:** Oct. 1, 1953, Los Angeles, CA, *Atty.*, Gewerter & Breedlove, Chartered; **PRIM RE ACT:** Attorney, Instructor; **SERVICES:** RE & Tax Atty., Faculty Univ. of NV, Las Vegas; **REP CLIENTS:** RE Synd., devel. & brokers; **PREV EMPLOY:** Faculty, Univ. of NV, Las Vegas, Lecturer in areas of RE & Taxation; Lecturer for NV State Bd. of Realtors; **PROFL AFFIL & HONORS:** ABA, Sect. of Taxation and Real Prop., Probate & Trust, Award for Profls. in Taxation, Univ. of CA, Los Angeles, 1979; **EDUC:** BA, 1975, Psych., Univ. of S CA; **GRAD EDUC:** MS, 1977, Educ. Psych., Univ. of S CA; JD, 1979, Southwestern Univ. Sch. of Law; **EDUC HONORS:** CA State Scholar, Grad. with Honors; **HOME ADD:** 6221 Shadywood Las Vegas, NV 89102; **BUS ADD:** 333 N. Rancho Dr., Ste. 570, Las Vegas, NV 89106, (792)647-6023.

GEYSER, Lynne, M.——**B:** Mar. 28, 1938, NY, *Atty. at Law, Pres.*, Lynne M. Geyser, A Profl. Corp.; **PRIM RE ACT:** Broker, Attorney, Instructor, Syndicator, Owner/Investor; **SERVICES:** Legal Services, Specializing in Synd., Partnerships, all R.E. & Gen. Bus. & Contract Matters; **REP CLIENTS:** The Biddle Grp., Sauers Bros. Constr. Co.; The Irvine Co.; **PROFL AFFIL & HONORS:** AIREA; **EDUC:** BA, 1960, Econ, Queens Coll., NY; **GRAD EDUC:** JD, 1968, UCLA; **EDUC HONORS:** Order of the Coif; **OTHER ACT & HONORS:** Westwood Art Assn., Contmp. Art Council, Law Prof., Malibu CA, IA City.; **BUS ADD:** 647 Camino De Los Mares, Suite 206, San Clemente, CA 92672, (714)493-1555.

GHERARDI, James C.——**B:** Oct. 19, 1933, New York, NY, *Pres.*, Point Management Co., Inc.; **PRIM RE ACT:** Broker, Developer, Builder, Owner/Investor, Property Manager, Syndicator; **PREV**

EMPLOY: S. Charles Gherardi, Inc., Pres.; **PROFL AFFIL & HONORS:** Queens Cty. Builders.; L.I. Home Builders; L.I. Bd. of Realtors, Queens Cty. Builders, 1980 Best Bldg. award; Queens Cty. C of C, 1972 award for Outstanding Church Bldg.; **EDUC:** BA, 1955, Chem., Columbia Coll.; **MIL SERV:** USN; Lt.j.g.; **OTHER ACT & HONORS:** NY State RE Advisory Bd., 1965-1973; Bd. of Dir., Holy Cross High School; Man of the Yr., Flushing Boys Club; Queens C of C; **HOME ADD:** Shore Dr. E., Amagansett, NY 11930, (212)463-4589; **BUS ADD:** 188-12 Northern Blvd., Flushing, NY 11358, (212)353-3224.

GHIM, Youngje Paul——B: May 15, 1932, Seoul, Korea, *Mgmt. Analyst*, Real Property Div., Dept. of General Services, State of OR; **OTHER RE ACT:** Prop. Administration; **SERVICES:** Mgmt. of Real Prop. for State Agencies, planning and analysis; **PROFL AFFIL & HONORS:** Amer. Soc. for Public Admin.; **EDUC:** BA, 1957, Public Admin., Poli. Sci., Seoul; **GRAD EDUC:** MA, 1964, Public Admin., Univ. of WA, Seattle; PhC, 1966, Public Admin., Univ. of WA; **HOME ADD:** 1025 Fernwood Ct NW, Salem, OR 97304, (503)364-3554; **BUS ADD:** 1225 Ferry St., Salem, OR 97310, (503)378-4080.

GIACINTI, Ralph A.——B: Sept. 19, 1933, Racine, WI, *Franchise Salesman*, Electronic Realtor, Assoc., Franchise Div.; **PRIM RE ACT:** Consultant, Developer, Builder, Instructor, Syndicator; **OTHER RE ACT:** Franchise Salesman; **SERVICES:** Training in fin. R.E. & R.E. Brokers Mgmt. Training; **REP CLIENTS:** 50 ERA Brokers in Central IL; **PREV EMPLOY:** Owner, Builder, Douglopor-Subdivision & Apts.; **EDUC:** 1956, Eng./Salesmanship, Univ. WI; Electronics, Devry Sch. of Electronics; **HOME ADD:** 216 Stanley Ave., Morton, IL 61550, (309)266-5065; **BUS ADD:** 216 Stanley Ave., Morton, IL 61550, (309)266-5065.

GIAGNOCAVO, J. Gregory——B: Feb. 8, 1953, Quakertown, PA, *Pres.*, Coquina Shores Developments Inc.; **PRIM RE ACT:** Broker, Developer, Owner/Investor, Syndicator; **SERVICES:** Synd. of investment props., devel. of oceanfront condo projects from assembling land to build-out; **REP CLIENTS:** Indiv. investors in comml. or build to suit projects; **PROFL AFFIL & HONORS:** ULI; NAFP; **EDUC:** Univ. of W. ON, Can., 1974, Bus. Admin.; **OTHER ACT & HONORS:** 1981 Outstanding Young Men of Amer. Recipient by Jaycees; **HOME ADD:** 3640 N. 34th Ave., Emerald Hills Ctry. Club, Hollywood, FL 33021, (305)864-2999; **BUS ADD:** 210 S. Atlantic Ave., Box 1767, Ormond Beach, FL 32074, (904)673-0181.

GIALAMAS, George——B: Oct. 20, 1938, Chicago, IL, *Pres.*, The Gialamas Co.; **PRIM RE ACT:** Broker, Consultant, Appraiser, Developer, Owner/Investor, Property Manager, Syndicator; **PROFL AFFIL & HONORS:** WI Bd. of Realtors; Madison Bd. of Realtors, GRI; **EDUC:** 1960, Liberal Arts, Marquette Univ.; **GRAD EDUC:** 1962, Marquette; **HOME ADD:** 1830 Thurstrand Rd., Madison, WI 53705, (608)238-8817; **BUS ADD:** 427 Grand Canyon Dr., Madison, WI 53719, (608)833-8100.

GIAMPAOLI, Peter G.——B: June 30, 1947, Chico, CA, *Pres.*, Ingram Realtors, Inc.; **PRIM RE ACT:** Broker, Consultant, Developer, Builder, Property Manager, Owner/Investor; **OTHER RE ACT:** Investment Broker; **SERVICES:** Investment analysis, site analysis, devl. and counseling; **REP CLIENTS:** Indiv. corps., Pension plans, and partnerships; **PREV EMPLOY:** 11 years as licensed CA R.E. Broker; **PROFL AFFIL & HONORS:** NAR, CA Assn. of Realtors, CCIM; **EDUC:** BS, 1969, Bus. Admin., CA State Univ., Chico; **OTHER ACT & HONORS:** CA Trout, Trout Unltd., Ducks Unltd.; **HOME ADD:** 20 Covell Park, Chico, CA 95926, (916)891-1531; **BUS ADD:** 352 Vallombrosa Ave., Chico, CA 95926, (916)891-1531.

GIAMPAOLO, Joseph A.——B: Mar. 20, 1946, Brooklyn, NY, *Pres.*, JB Properties, Giampaolo & Assoc. Inc.; **PRIM RE ACT:** Developer, Owner/Investor, Property Manager, Syndicator; **SERVICES:** Devel. for both turnkey projects for owner & owner/investor, synd. packages, prop. mgmt.; **REP CLIENTS:** Indus. owner, instnl. investments grp. in comml. & indus. props.; **EDUC:** BS, 1964, Const. Engrg., Gonzaga Univ.; **GRAD EDUC:** MBA, 1971, Fin., Claremont Univ.; **HOME ADD:** 1250 Kenilworth Ave., San Marino, CA 91108, (213)572-7575, **BUS ADD:** 3907 N. Rosemead Blvd., Suite 100, Rosemead, CA 91770, (213)572-7575.

GIANCOLA, Richard D.——B: Oct. 5, 1952, Brooklyn, NY, *RE Broker*, Arthur Realty Co.; **PRIM RE ACT:** Broker, Consultant, Owner/Investor; **SERVICES:** Investment counseling, prop. mgmt.; **REP CLIENTS:** Indiv., prof.; **EDUC:** BS, 1974, Acctg., Fordham Univ.; **EDUC HONORS:** Beta Alpha Psi, GM Business Scholarship; **HOME ADD:** 90 79th St., Brooklyn, NY 11209, (212)833-4197; **BUS ADD:** 7419 13th Ave., Brooklyn, NY 11228, (212)259-5400.

GIANNONE, Edward J.——B: Aug. 27, 1942, Norristown, PA, *Gen. Partner*, Ispec Assoc.; **PRIM RE ACT:** Developer, Owner/Investor, Property Manager, Syndicator; **SERVICES:** Advertising, rentals, acctg., investment counseling; **REP CLIENTS:** De Kalb Ct. Assoc.; Campus Hill Assoc.; **PREV EMPLOY:** Hayes Assoc. (R.E. Sales); **PROFL AFFIL & HONORS:** Montgomery Cty. Estate Planners Assn.; **EDUC:** BA, 1970, Fin., Ursinus Coll.; **OTHER ACT & HONORS:** Committeeman Plymouth 2-1, 3 yrs. 1975-78; Bd. of Dir. Smith Kline Fed. Credit Union; **HOME ADD:** 7385 Ridge Ave., Philadelphia, PA 19128, (215)483-8735; **BUS ADD:** 1705 Sandy Hill Rd., Norristown, PA 19401, (215)272-8858.

GIBBON, John Thomas——B: Aug. 10, 1953, Astoria, OR, *Staff Counsel; Secretary*, The Robert Randall Co., NLT, Investment Inc.; **PRIM RE ACT:** Attorney, Developer; **OTHER RE ACT:** Planner; **SERVICES:** Legal and plan processing; **REP CLIENTS:** Corp. atty. and some pvt. practice; **PREV EMPLOY:** Pvt. Law Practice; **PROFL AFFIL & HONORS:** ABA, Sect. of Real Prop. Probate & Trust; OR State Bar, RE & Land Use Section, Editor, Chapter of OR CLE Land Use Manual; **EDUC:** BA, 1975, Legal and Govt. Serv., Pacific Univ.; **GRAD EDUC:** JD, 1978, Nat. Resources Law, Lewis & Clark - Northwestern Coll. of Law; **OTHER ACT & HONORS:** Sec., Northwest Environmental Defense Ctr.; **HOME ADD:** 15280 S.W. 100th, Tigard, OR 97223, (503)620-9622; **BUS ADD:** 9500 S.W. Barbur Blvd., Portland, OR 97219, (503)245-4336.

GIBBONS, Earle J.——B: Oct. 28, 1929, Coalinga, CA, *Pres.*, Elmer F. Karpe, Inc.; **PRIM RE ACT:** Broker, Consultant; **PREV EMPLOY:** Judge, West Kern Municipal Ct.; **PROFL AFFIL & HONORS:** Bakersfield Bd. of Realtors, CA Bar Assn.; **EDUC:** AB, 1951, Poli. Sci., Univ. of CA, Berkeley; **GRAD EDUC:** JD, 1961, Univ. of CA, Los Angeles; **MIL SERV:** USA, Lt.; **HOME ADD:** Star Rte Box 39A, Granite Sta., Bakersfield, CA 93301, (805)399-6081; **BUS ADD:** 4000 Ming Ave., Bakersfield, CA 93309, (805)832-1806.

GIBBONS, Meigs Christian——B: Nov. 15, 1947, Anthony, KS, *Pres.*, Towne Research; **PRIM RE ACT:** Consultant, Developer, Owner/Investor, Syndicator; **SERVICES:** Market research, public agency coordination, devel. mgmt., downtown redevel.; **REP CLIENTS:** Anderson RE Co., City of Brighton, CO, City of Golden, CO; **PREV EMPLOY:** Partner, Environmental Resources Grp.; Urban Planner, San Bernardino Cty. Planning Dept. (CA); **EDUC:** BS, 1970, Social Studies, Univ. of OK; **GRAD EDUC:** Masters, 1972, Urban Planning, Univ. of OK; **EDUC HONORS:** Grad. with Honors, 4.0/4.0 GPA; **HOME ADD:** Clear Creek Cty., CO, (303)764-3680; **BUS ADD:** 87 Sawmill Rd., POB 2583, Evergreen, CO 80439, (303)674-3680.

GIBSON, Ben T., Jr.——B: July 26, 1929, Union, SC, *Pres.*, AIMCO, Inc.; **PRIM RE ACT:** Broker, Consultant, Owner/Investor, Instructor, Insuror; **SERVICES:** Consulting and brokerage; **PROFL AFFIL & HONORS:** Amer. Soc. of RE Consultants; Farm and Land Inst., CRE; AFLM; **EDUC:** BS, 1951, Bus. Admin., Davidson; **MIL SERV:** USN; **OTHER ACT & HONORS:** Paul Harris Fellow; Rotary Intl.; **HOME ADD:** Rt. 1, Box 67, Union, SC 29379, (803)427-8145; **BUS ADD:** POB 130, Union, SC 29379, (803)427-9061.

GIBSON, G. Darcy——B: May 1, 1928, New York, *Architect-Owner*, Architects Planners Associates; **PRIM RE ACT:** Engineer, Architect; **SERVICES:** Planning, site engrg., arch.; **REP CLIENTS:** Indus. devel., housing devel.; **PREV EMPLOY:** NYS Facilities Devel. Corp. 65-72; **PROFL AFFIL & HONORS:** AIA, Nat. Council of Arch. Reg. Bds., Member Zoning Appeals Bd., Amer Arbitration Assn., Columbia Univ., RA, AIA, 1980 Concrete Indus. Award for a Cultural Facility; **EDUC:** BA, Pre Arch., Columbia Coll.; **GRAD EDUC:** MArch, 1957, Columbia School of Planning & Arch.; **EDUC HONORS:** W.K. Fellows Fellowship; **MIL SERV:** USMC, Sgt., Sharpshooter, Victory Medal; **HOME ADD:** Kirby Land North, Rye, NY 10580, (914)967-4770; **BUS ADD:** 129 Broadway, Amityville, NY 11701, (516)598-0330.

GIBSON, Herbert C.——B: Jan. 13, 1945, W Palm Beach, FL, *Lawyer*, Gibson and Gibson; **PRIM RE ACT:** Attorney; **SERVICES:** RE Legal Services; **REP CLIENTS:** FL Nat. Bank of Palm Beach Cty.; **PROFL AFFIL & HONORS:** Amer., FL, Palm Beach Cty. Bar Assns., Who's Who in Amer. Law; **EDUC:** BA Cum Laude, 1967, Pol. Sci., Econ., Univ. of the South, Sewanee, TN; **GRAD EDUC:** JD, 1970, Law, Univ. of FL; **EDUC HONORS:** Cum Laude grad., Phi Delta Phi; **MIL SERV:** USAR, Judge Advocate, Capt. 1970-1978 Active; Ready Reserve Service; **OTHER ACT & HONORS:** Member, V Chmn., Chmn. City of W Palm Beach Planning Bd.; Bd. of Dir., Palm Beach Blood Bank; **HOME ADD:** 6309 Washington Rd., W Palm Beach, FL 33405, (305)588-1118; **BUS ADD:** PO Box 1629, West Palm Beach, FL 33402, (305)655-8686.

GIBSON, Marjory F.——B: Brooklyn, NY, *Atty.*, law Offices of Joel Zebrack; **PRIM RE ACT:** Attorney; **SERVICES:** Legal servs.;

PROFL AFFIL & HONORS: Alameda Cty. Bar Assn., CA State Bar Assn.; **EDUC:** Poli. Sci., Brooklyn Coll.; **GRAD EDUC:** LLB, 1964, Harvard Law Sch.; **EDUC HONORS:** Magna Cum Laude, Phi Beta Kappa, Honors in Poli. Sci.; **OTHER ACT & HONORS:** Oakland City Council Member, former member, Oakland Planning Commn.; **BUS ADD:** Suite 1615 405-14th St., Oakland, CA 94612, (415)763-1615.

GIBSON, Maury E., Jr.——B: Oct. 28, 1924, Oakland, CA, *Owner/Broker/Realtor*, Gibson investment Props.; **PRIM RE ACT:** Broker, Consultant, Property Manager, Syndicator; **SERVICES:** Comml. investment brokerage and synd.; **REP CLIENTS:** Pvt. investors in RE income producing props.; **PREV EMPLOY:** Corp. RE Mgr., 12 yrs; Part. RE Projects Consulting firm, 2 yrs.; **PROFL AFFIL & HONORS:** NAR, CA Assn. of Realtors, RNMI, CCIM, CPM, GRI, RECI; **EDUC:** BS, 1950, Indus. Engrg. and Bus. Mgmt., Univ. of CA at Berkeley, CA; **GRAD EDUC:** Adv. RE Cert., 1964, RE Econ., Law, Practice, Univ. of CA At Berkeley; **MIL SERV:** USAF, Cpl., WWII; **HOME ADD:** 2425 Wilbur St., Pacific Bch., CA 92109, (714)270-9966; **BUS ADD:** PO Box 2148, La Jolla, CA 92038, (714)270-0400.

GIBSON, Thomas C.——B: Jan. 23, 1950, Plymouth, IN, *VP, Commercial Division*, Cressy and Everett Relators, Inc., Prop. Mgmt. Leasing; **PRIM RE ACT:** Consultant, Property Manager; **OTHER RE ACT:** Leasing agent (office building); **SERVICES:** Leasing, brokerage, property mgmt., consulting; **REP CLIENTS:** Amer. States Insurance, Gen. Accident Group, Holliday Corp., FBT Bancorp; **PREV EMPLOY:** St. Joseph Bank & Trust Co. RE Development Officer; **PROFL AFFIL & HONORS:** IREM, South Bend-Mishawaka Bd. of Realtors, CPM; **EDUC:** BS, 1973, RE, IN Univ., Bloomington; **GRAD EDUC:** 12 hrs. of grad. work in Bus., IN Univ., South Bend, IN; **EDUC HONORS:** Made the Deans List on two occasions; **OTHER ACT & HONORS:** Marshall County Horse Assn., Thi Delta Theta Frat; **HOME ADD:** 9696 Sycamore Rd., Plymouth, IN 46563, (219)936-2095; **BUS ADD:** 332 N Ironwood Dr., South Bend, IN 46615, (219)233-6141.

GIBSON, Thomas H., Jr.——B: Mar. 22, 1930, Cleveland, OH, *Pres.*, Gibson Development Co., Inc.; **PRIM RE ACT:** Consultant, Developer, Owner/Investor; **SERVICES:** Full scale devel. consultation; **REP CLIENTS:** Gentry Co., San Diego, CA; **PREV EMPLOY:** VP of Mktg., Fox & Carskadon Fin. Corp., Menlo Park, CA; **EDUC:** BS, 1953, Bus. Admin., Stetson Univ.; **MIL SERV:** US Army, 1st Lt.; **HOME ADD:** 7765 Via Capri, La Jolla, CA 92037, (714)459-8640; **BUS ADD:** 8535 Commerce Ave., San Diego, CA 92121, (714)578-7676.

GIBSON, Wayne R.——B: July 4, 1941, IL, *VP, RE*, White Hen Pantry, Jewel Cos., Inc.; **OTHER RE ACT:** Retail chain store RE; **PROFL AFFIL & HONORS:** IREM; Chicago RE Bd.; Nat. Assn. of Corporate RE Execs.; Nat. Assn. of Review Appraisers, CPM; CRA; Lic. RE Broker; **EDUC:** BBA, 1965, Mgmt., Roosevelt Univ.; **EDUC HONORS:** Dean's List; **MIL SERV:** US Army, E-5; **HOME ADD:** 717 Shoreline Cir., Schaumburg, IL 60194, (312)882-4131; **BUS ADD:** 666 Industrial Dr., Elmhurst, IL 60126, (312)833-3100.

GIBSON, William S., II——B: June 1, 1934, Seco, KY, *Pres.*, Action Prop. Corp.; **PRIM RE ACT:** Broker, Appraiser, Developer, Builder, Property Manager; **SERVICES:** Res. and Comml. sales, appraisal and mgmt.; **PREV EMPLOY:** S. Cent. Bell Telephone Co., 1954-68; **PROFL AFFIL & HONORS:** V.P. Big Sandy Bd. of Realtors, Dir. KY Assoc. of Realtors; **MIL SERV:** USN, Seaman; **OTHER ACT & HONORS:** Mbr. Pike Cty. C of C and Pikeville Rotary Club; Past local and state offices in Jaycees; Past Pres. Paintsville, KY Rotary Club and C of C; **HOME ADD:** Box 477, Harold, KY 41635, (606)478-9987; **BUS ADD:** Rte. 3, Box 673, Pikeville, KY 41501, (606)432-8181.

GIDDENS, Earle A.——B: May 24, 1926, Tampa, FL, *Owner-Pres.*, Earle A. Giddens and Assoc., Inc.; **PRIM RE ACT:** Consultant, Appraiser; **SERVICES:** RE Appraiser, consultant, analyst; **REP CLIENTS:** Local, State & Fed. Govts., HUD, Attys., Devels., Indivs.; **PROFL AFFIL & HONORS:** SREA-MAI, Past Intl. VP SREA; **EDUC:** BS, 1951, RE, Univ. of FL, Gainsville; **MIL SERV:** USAF, Sgt.; **HOME ADD:** 14100 SW 92 Ave., Miami, FL 33138, (305)251-1935; **BUS ADD:** 8045 NW 36 St. Suite 517, Miami, FL 33166, (305)591-9328.

GIDWITZ, Peter E.——B: Jan. 13, 1950, Chicago, IL, Burnham Companies; **PRIM RE ACT:** Broker, Developer, Owner/Investor, Property Manager; **SERVICES:** Multi-Family Indus. & Commercial Devel., Indus. & Comml. Brokerage Management; **REP CLIENTS:** Brokerage for Helene Curtis Indus., Inc., Continental Materials Corp., Consolidated Packaging Corp.; **PROFL AFFIL & HONORS:** Chicago RE Bd., IREM, NAR, Life Member - RPAC, CPM; **EDUC:** AB, 1973, Pol. Sci., Brown Univ.; **MIL SERV:** USAF Res., Sgt. 1969-1974; **OTHER ACT & HONORS:** Vice Chairman, IL Indus. Devel. Authority 1976-Present, Dir./VP GNPDC; **HOME ADD:** 70 E Cedar St., Chicago, IL 60611; **BUS ADD:** 111 E. Wacker Dr., Suite 2930, Chicago, IL 60601, (312)938-2250.

GIFFORD, Joan D.——B: Mar. 4, 1923, Devonshire, England, *Pres.*, Gifford Realty, Inc.; **PRIM RE ACT:** Broker, Consultant, Owner/Investor, Instructor, Property Manager, Insuror; **PROFL AFFIL & HONORS:** WCR; Million Dollar Sales Club; Realtor Promotion Comm.; Build. Norfolk Better Comm., Publicity Comm., Realtor of the Yr. 1981; first woman to receive this award in 61 yr. history; **HOME ADD:** 1923 Bayview Blvd., Norfolk, VA 23503, (804)587-7070; **BUS ADD:** 1547 E. Little Creek Rd., Norfolk, VA 23518, (804)583-5976.

GILBANE, Robert V.——B: June 4, 1948, Providence, RI, *Exec. VP*, Gilbane Prop. Inc.; **OTHER RE ACT:** Investment Builder; **SERVICES:** RE Dev. Serv. - Comml, Indus., & Retail, Multi family Dev.; **REP CLIENTS:** Aetna, Equitable, CT; **PREV EMPLOY:** Gilbane Bldg. Co.; **PROFL AFFIL & HONORS:** NACORE; NAIOP, NAHB; BOMA; **EDUC:** BA, 1971, Brown Univ.; **HOME ADD:** Rumford, RI; **BUS ADD:** 7 Jackson Walkway, Providence, RI 02940, (401)438-5650.

GILBER, C. Gordon, Sr.——B: July 31, 1918, Baltimore, MD, *Owner*, C. Gordon Gilbert Assocs.; **PRIM RE ACT:** Consultant, Appraiser; **REP CLIENTS:** Govt. agencies (fed., state and local), lending instns., lawyers, corps. and indivs.; **PROFL AFFIL & HONORS:** AIREA, SREA, The Bar Assn. of Baltimore City, MAI, SREA; **EDUC:** BA, 1940, Educ. and Math., Western MD Coll; **GRAD EDUC:** JD, 1969, Law, Univ. of MD; **MIL SERV:** Engrs., 1st Lt., Overseas Serv. & Battle Stars; **OTHER ACT & HONORS:** Gr. Baltimore Bd. of Realtors, MD Assn. of Realtors, Nat. Assn. of Realtors; **HOME ADD:** 1 Roundridge Rd., Timonium, MD 21093, (301)252-1771; **BUS ADD:** 204 N Liberty St., Rm 511, Baltimore, MD 21201, (301)685-5717.

GILBERG, Kenneth R.——B: Feb. 2, 1951, Philadelphia, PA, Pechner, Dorfman, Wolffe, Rounick & Cabot; **PRIM RE ACT:** Consultant, Owner/Investor, Syndicator; **PROFL AFFIL & HONORS:** ABA, PA Bar Assn., Philadelphia Bar Assn., Member RE Div.; **EDUC:** BS, 1973, Poli. Sci., Lebanon Valley Coll.; **GRAD EDUC:** JD, 1976, Law, DE Law School; **BUS ADD:** Suite 1300, 1845 Walnut St., Philadelphia, PA 19103, (215)561-7100.

GILCHRIST, Fred C., Jr.——B: Aug. 17, 1898, Laurens, IA, *Atty.*, Gilchrist & Gilchrist; **PRIM RE ACT:** Attorney; **SERVICES:** Examination of abstracts, preparing RE contracts and probate of estates; **PROFL AFFIL & HONORS:** IA State Bar Assn.; Amer. Coll. of Probate Counsel; **EDUC:** BA, 1920, Univ. of IA; **GRAD EDUC:** LLB, 1922, Univ. of IA; **MIL SERV:** US Army, 2nd Lt.; **OTHER ACT & HONORS:** City Atty., City of Laurens, IA; Masonic Lodge; Lions Club; **HOME ADD:** 340 S. 1st St., Laurens, IA 50554, (712)845-4531; **BUS ADD:** 147 North 3rd St., Laurens, IA 50554, (712)845-4518.

GILE, Albert, Jr.——B: July 1, 1939, Rochester, NH, *Pres.*, Towne & Country Realty; **PRIM RE ACT:** Broker, Consultant, Appraiser, Developer, Owner/Investor; **SERVICES:** Gen. agency with emphasis on investment & development; **REP CLIENTS:** Investors; **PREV EMPLOY:** Asst. Prof. - Univ. of NH; **PROFL AFFIL & HONORS:** Member Local, MT State Assn. of Realtors, NAR, Amer. Soc. Agri. Engrs., Past Pres. Bittenroot Valley Bd. of Realtors, 1st Chmn. Bittenroot Valley Multiple Listing Serv.; **EDUC:** BS, 1964, Agri. Engrg. - Structures, Univ. of NH; **GRAD EDUC:** MS, 1971, Soil & Water Sci., Univ. of NH; **OTHER ACT & HONORS:** Vice Chmn. - Ravalli Cty. GOP, Member Grange, Elks, Kiwanis; **HOME ADD:** 15 Skyline Dr., Hamilton, MT 59840, (406)363-3874; **BUS ADD:** 716 S. 1st, Hamilton, MT 59840, (406)363-4630.

GILES, Ron——B: Nov. 26, 1939, Shelby, NC, *Partner*, Giles Agency, Ins. & RE; **PRIM RE ACT:** Broker, Appraiser, Owner/Investor, Property Manager, Insuror; **PROFL AFFIL & HONORS:** NAR, Ind. Ins. Agents, GRI; **EDUC:** AB, 1962, Univ. of NC, Chapel Hill; **HOME ADD:** 610 Brookwood Dr., Spindale, NC 28160, (704)286-3625; **BUS ADD:** 611E Main St., Spindale, NC 28160, (704)286-4181.

GILINSKY, Stanley E.——B: July 7, 1918, Trenton, NJ, *Sr. VP Corporate RE*, Batus - Retail Division, Saks Fifth Avenue; Gimbels, Kohl's, Thimbles; **OTHER RE ACT:** Corporate RE Dept.; **SERVICES:** Handle RE affairs of 2,000,000,000 retail groups; **PROFL AFFIL & HONORS:** RE Bd. of NY, AMA; **EDUC:** BBA, 1940, Fin. and Acctg., Lehigh Univ.; **GRAD EDUC:** JD, 1944, Law, Univ. of PA; **EDUC HONORS:** Phi Beta Kappa - Graduated with Honors; **OTHER ACT & HONORS:** Teaneck Redevelopment Bd. 1970-74; **HOME ADD:** 32 Grayson Place, Teaneck, NJ 07666, (201)833-1704; **BUS ADD:** 1270 Ave. of Americas, Rockefeller Center, New York, NY

10020, (212)399-4283.

GILL, Ellen F.——**B:** Dec. 2, 1950, Long Branch, NJ, *Partner*, K.S. Sweet Assoc.; **PRIM RE ACT:** Consultant, Developer, Owner/Investor; **OTHER RE ACT:** Devel., fin.; **SERVICES:** Asst. Gen. Mgr., Princeton Forrestal Ctr. (land devel.); **REP CLIENTS:** Both instit. and indiv. investors (e.g., Princeton Univ., Fidelity Mutual Life); **PREV EMPLOY:** Citibank, Marine Midland Bank, Corp. Lending; **PROFL AFFIL & HONORS:** Indus. RE Brokers Assn.; **EDUC:** BA, 1973, Econ., Wellesley Coll.; **GRAD EDUC:** MBA, 1977, Fin., Stanford Univ.; **HOME ADD:** 74 Parker Rd. S., Plainsboro, NJ 08536, (609)799-4640; **BUS ADD:** Princeton Forrestal Ctr., 105 College Rd. E., 3rd Fl., Princeton, NJ 08540, (609)452-7720.

GILL, George——*Treas.*, General Host. Corp.; **PRIM RE ACT:** Property Manager; **BUS ADD:** 22 Gate House Rd., Stanford, CT 06902, (203)357-9900.*

GILL, Harpal S.——**B:** May 7, 1937, Rampur Punjab, India, *Owner-Mgr.*, Tahlequah RE; **PRIM RE ACT:** Broker, Appraiser, Owner/Investor, Property Manager; **PREV EMPLOY:** Prof., Northeastern State Univ., Tahlequah, OK; **PROFL AFFIL & HONORS:** Nat. Assn. of Realtors, OK Assn. of Realtors; **EDUC:** BA, 1956, Econ., Pol. Sci., Punjab Univ., India; **GRAD EDUC:** MA, Pol. Sci., Econ., Adams State Coll.; MS, Pol. Sci., Econ., KS State Univ.; PhD, Pol. Sci., Univ. of ID; **HOME ADD:** Rt. 2, Box 33, Tahlequah, OK 74464, (918)456-5044; **BUS ADD:** Rt. 2, Box 33, Tahlequah, OK 74464, (918)456-6609.

GILL, Kevin——*Mgr. Adm. & RE*, Spring Mills, Inc.; **PRIM RE ACT:** Property Manager; **BUS ADD:** Executive Office Bldg., Fort Mill, SC 29715, (803)547-2901.*

GILL, Steve T.——**B:** Mar, 11, 1946, Spokane, WA, *Comml./ Investment Dept. Mgr.*, Tomlinson Agency, Inc., Comml./ Investments Div.-Spokane Area; **PRIM RE ACT:** Broker, Owner/Investor, Instructor, Syndicator; **SERVICES:** Brokerage and synd. of comml./invenstment props., instruction, supervision & training of comml. salespeople; **REP CLIENTS:** Indiv. and instnl. investors in comml. RE; **PROFL AFFIL & HONORS:** Bd. of Realtors, Member Realtors Nat. mktg. inst., CCIM Candidate; **EDUC:** BA, 1972, Mktg., Bus., Econ., Eastern Wash. State Univ.; **MIL SERV:** US Army 1967-69, S/Sgt., E-6, Purple Heart, Good Conduct; **HOME ADD:** W. 714-20th Ave., Spokane, WA 99203, (509)838-6900; **BUS ADD:** W 606 3rd Ave., Spokane, WA 99204, (509)624-9131.

GILLE, Thomas William——**B:** Aug. 2, 1948, San Francisco, CA, *Dir. of Prop.*, Hogland, Bogart & Bertero; **PRIM RE ACT:** Consultant, Property Manager; **SERVICES:** Prop. mgmt. for comml. bldgs.; **REP CLIENTS:** Pvt. and instit. investors in comml. props.; **PREV EMPLOY:** Norris, Beggs & Simpson, 1975-1980, City Coll. of San Francisco, 1971-1980; **PROFL AFFIL & HONORS:** San Francisco Bd. of Realtors, The Instit. of RE Mgmt., Intl. Council of Shopping Ctrs., Bldg. Owners and Mgrs. Intl., CPM; **EDUC:** BS, 1969, Amer. Govt. and Hist., San Francisco State Univ.; **GRAD EDUC:** MA, 1971, Constitut. Law, San Francisco State Univ.; **EDUC HONORS:** Deans List, Grad. with distinction; **HOME ADD:** 650 CA St., San Francisco, CA 94708; **BUS ADD:** 650 CA St., San Francisco, CA 94108, (415)398-1010.

GILLEN, Robert D.——**B:** Nov. 28, 1954, Hinsdale, IL, *Partner*, Collander & Gillen; **PRIM RE ACT:** Attorney, Consultant; **SERVICES:** Consulting & prep. in all aspects of RE; **REP CLIENTS:** Resid. & comml. investors, purchasers, and sellers; **PROFL AFFIL & HONORS:** American Bar Assn.-Real Prop., Probate & Trust Division, IL State Bar Assn., Dupage Cty. Bar Assn., Assn. of Trial Lawyers, Attorney at Law Licensed by State of IL, and US Federal Court; **EDUC:** BS Bus. Admin., 1976, Bus. w/Topical Minor Pre-Law, Univ. of IL; **GRAD EDUC:** JD, 1979, Law, IIT/Chicago-Kent Coll. of Law; **EDUC HONORS:** Grad. with Honors; **OTHER ACT & HONORS:** Naperville Rotary Club, Bd. of Dir., Businessmans Flying Club, Delta Sigma Pi Profl. Bus. Frat.; **BUS ADD:** 111 E Jefferson Ave., Suite Two N, Napierville, IL 60546, (312)420-8025.

GILLER, Ben——**B:** Aug. 15, 1897, Grand Forks, ND, *Pres.*, Beach Builders Serv., Inc.; **PRIM RE ACT:** Broker, Appraiser, Banker, Owner/Investor; **SERVICES:** RE Appraisal; **REP CLIENTS:** Jefferson Nat. Bank of Miami Bch., FL; **PREV EMPLOY:** Head of Appraisal Dept., WA Fed. S&L Assn.; **PROFL AFFIL & HONORS:** SREA, NARA, Miami Bch. Bd. of Realtors, Nat. Assn. of RE Bds., FL Chapt. 71, SREA, Nat. Assn. of Review Appraisers, Reg. RE Broker, State of FL; Lic. Bldg. Contr., City of Miami Bch., since 1934; SRPA, CRA; **EDUC:** Courses 101 and 201 SREA; **OTHER ACT & HONORS:** Chief Appraiser of WA Fed. S&L Assn. of Miami Bch. since 1952; **HOME ADD:** 5151 Collins Ave., Apt. 533, Miami Bch., FL 33140, (305)866-6443; **BUS ADD:** 523 Michigan Ave., Miami Bch., FL 33139, (305)673-2948.

GILLESPIE, James H.——**B:** Mar. 26, 1937, St. Paul, MN, *Chmn.*, Cosmopolitan State Bank; **PRIM RE ACT:** Broker, Attorney, Banker, Owner/Investor; **SERVICES:** Synd. of comml. prop., financing; **PREV EMPLOY:** Pres., Rio Verde Devel., Inc., Rio Verde, AZ (1975-80); VP & Counsel, Eden Land Corp., Eden Prairie, MN (1973-75); **PROFL AFFIL & HONORS:** Past Pres., MN Housing Inst., 1975; ABA; MN Bar Assn.; **EDUC:** BBA, 1959, Econ., Univ. of MN; **GRAD EDUC:** LLB, 1963, RE, Yale Law School; **EDUC HONORS:** High Distinction, Order of Coif; **HOME ADD:** 2635 Interlachen Dr., Stillwater, MN 55082, (612)439-7338; **BUS ADD:** 101 S. Main St., Stillwater, MN 55082, (612)439-3050.

GILLESPIE, K.H.——**B:** May 19, 1942, Melfort, SK, Can., *Pres.*, Gillespie Investments Ltd.; **PRIM RE ACT:** Consultant, Developer, Owner/Investor, Property Manager, Syndicator; **SERVICES:** Investment consulting prop. mgmt.; **REP CLIENTS:** Pvt. and inst. investors; **PROFL AFFIL & HONORS:** Fellow RE Inst. of Can.; Profl. div., RE Inst. of BC, RE Bd. Greater Vancouver, FRI, RI (BC); **EDUC:** B. Commerce, 1968, Urban land econ. and fin., Univ. of BC; **EDUC HONORS:** Urban Land & Fin.; **HOME TEL:** (604)263-1392; **BUS ADD:** 626 W. Pender St., Vancouver, V6B1V9, BC, Canada, (604)685-0361.

GILLETT, Victor——**B:** Feb. 4, 1932, El Paso, TX, *Sr. VP & Natl. Mktg. Dir.*, Stewart Title Guaranty Co.; **OTHER RE ACT:** Title Ins. Underwriter; **SERVICES:** Title Ins.; **PREV EMPLOY:** Pres. & CEO, Stewart Title & Trust of Phoenix, 1961-1977; Stewart Title Guaranty Co.-Corpus Christi, TX 1955-1961; **PROFL AFFIL & HONORS:** Amer. Land Title Assn.; Natl. Assn. of Corp. RE Exec.; Natl. Assn. of Indus. & Office Parks; Intl. Council of Shopping Ctrs.; **EDUC:** BBA, 1953, TX A&M Univ.; **EDUC HONORS:** Student Senate; Commander "B" Armor; Ross Volunteers; **MIL SERV:** US Army, Lt.; **OTHER ACT & HONORS:** Assn. of US Army; Navy League; Sugar Creek Ctry. Club; Houstonian Club; Aggie Club; Bd. of Dirs. of Stewart Title Guaranty Co.; **HOME ADD:** 2803 Fairway Dr., Sugar Land, TX 77478, (713)494-1427; **BUS ADD:** 2200 W Loop S, Suite 840, Houston, TX 77027, (713)871-1100.

GILLIAM, Larry L.——**B:** Aug. 13, 1947, OK, The Homesteaders, Inc.; **PRIM RE ACT:** Broker; **PROFL AFFIL & HONORS:** CPA, CCIM; **EDUC:** BS, 1969, Accounting, OK City Univ.; **HOME ADD:** 2113 Bois de Arc, Normal, OK 73069; **BUS ADD:** 102 E Eufula, Norman, OK 73069, (425)329-6976.

GILLIES, Roderick M.——**B:** Feb. 1, 1943, Washington, DC, *Dir. of Comml. Mgmt.*, JBG Properties, Inc.; **PRIM RE ACT:** Developer, Builder, Property Manager, Owner/Investor; **SERVICES:** Devel., leasing and mgmt.; **PREV EMPLOY:** Gulf Reston, Inc., The Braedon Co., Pomponio Brothers RE & Construction Co., Inc.; **PROFL AFFIL & HONORS:** Washington Bd. of Realtors; Inst. of RE Mgmt.; Apt. & Office Bldg. Assn.; Bldg. Owners & Mgrs. Inst.; Soc. of Real Prop. Adm., CPM; Real Prop. Admin. (Candidate); **EDUC:** BBA, 1964, Pers. Mgt. & Indus. Relations, TX Christian Univ.; **MIL SERV:** USAF, 1/Lt.; **HOME ADD:** 4220 Holborn Ave., Annandale, VA 22003; **BUS ADD:** 1220 19th St., NW, Washington, DC 20036, (202)659-0730.

GILLIGAN, Robert G.——**B:** July 8, 1942, Hartford, CT, *Partner*, Clark, Mayo & Gilligan; **PRIM RE ACT:** Attorney; **SERVICES:** Comml. RE law & fin.; **PROFL AFFIL & HONORS:** ABA; CT Bar Assn. (Real Prop. Sect.); Hartford Cty. Bar Assn., Omicron Delta Epsilon; **EDUC:** BA, 1969, Econ., Univ. of Hartford; **GRAD EDUC:** JD, 1972, Univ. of CT School of Law; **EDUC HONORS:** George Affleck Scholarship, Cum Laude, Amer. Jurisprudence Award, Honors; **OTHER ACT & HONORS:** Asst. Majority Leader, CT State House of Rep. 1975-Present; House Chmn. Banks Comm.; **HOME ADD:** 60 Washington St., Hartford, CT 06106; **BUS TEL:** (203)247-3297.

GILLILAN, William J., III——**B:** June 20, 1946, Pittsburgh, PA, *Pres.*, Center Homes Inc.; **PRIM RE ACT:** Developer, Builder; **PREV EMPLOY:** Center Homes Inc., 1974 to present; **PROFL AFFIL & HONORS:** Who's Who in Fin. and Indus., **EDUC:** BS, 1968, Indus. Engrg., Purdue Univ.; **GRAD EDUC:** MBA, 1970, Bus., Harvard Univ.; **EDUC HONORS:** High Honors, Tau Beta Pi, Omicron Delta Kappa; **MIL SERV:** USN, Lt.; **OTHER ACT & HONORS:** Westmorland Ctry. Club; **HOME ADD:** 6115 Shadycliff Dr., Dallas, TX 75240, (214)980-6788; **BUS ADD:** 4600 Republic Nat. Bank Tower, Dallas, TX 75208, (214)748-7901.

GILLINOV, Lynda J.——**B:** Nov. 17, 1941, Cleveland, OH, *RE Appraiser*, Samuel H. Weiser & Associates, Realtors, Appraisal Dept.; **PRIM RE ACT:** Appraiser, Instructor; **SERVICES:** Valuation and evaluation of RE; **REP CLIENTS:** Various agencies for the US Govt., maj. indus. corps., insurance cos., and mort. instits.; **PREV EMPLOY:** Assignments for Cuyahoga Metropolitan Housing Authority, City of Cleveland Buckeye Block Grant Acquisition, Hopkins Intl. Airport Expansion; **PROFL AFFIL & HONORS:** AIREA, SREA, ASA, NAR, NAIFA, RNMI, CABOR; International Board of Examiners, ASA; Division of Course Administration: RM Required Exam Subcomm., AIREA; Editorial Advisory Comm., SREA; Comms. of the OH Chap., AIREA, MAI, SRPA, ASA, IFAS, GRI, CRS, RE Brokers Lic.; **EDUC:** Four years of coll. at OH State Univ., Cleveland State Univ. & Cuyahoga Community Coll., RE; **EDUC HONORS:** GRI (Grad. Realtors Inst.), Cert. in RE; **OTHER ACT & HONORS:** Bd. of Dirs., Cleveland Academy of Medicine (Women's Comm.), Cleveland Inst. of Music and various religious organizations; **HOME ADD:** 4346 Univ. Pkwy., Cleveland, OH 44118, (216)291-0414; **BUS ADD:** 14429 Cedar Rd., Cleveland, OH 44121, (216)291-0415.

GILLIS, John Winfred——B: July 13, 1947, Chicago, IL, *Prin.*, Anthem Props.; John Gillis, Architects; **PRIM RE ACT:** Architect, Developer, Builder, Owner/Investor; **SERVICES:** Arch.; constrc. mgmt.; **PROFL AFFIL & HONORS:** Soc. of Amer. Reg. Archs.; **EDUC:** Univ. of IL, IL Inst. of Tech., F.L. Wright Sch. of Arch.; **OTHER ACT & HONORS:** Metropolitan Museum, PA Acad. of Arts; **HOME ADD:** 25 Joraleman St., Brooklyn Hts., NY 11201, (212)237-1261; **BUS ADD:** 25 Joralemon St., Brooklyn Hts., NY 11201, (212)246-5040.

GILMAN, Marvin S.——B: Jan. 15, 1922, New York, NY, *Exec. VP*, Leon N. Weiner & Associates, Inc.; **PRIM RE ACT:** Attorney, Developer, Builder, Owner/Investor, Syndicator; **PREV EMPLOY:** Lecturer, US Dept. of State; **PROFL AFFIL & HONORS:** FNMA, NAHB, Homebldrs. of DE, Who's Who in the East; **EDUC:** AB, 1942, Econ., Brooklyn Coll.; **GRAD EDUC:** JD, 1951, Brooklyn Law School; **EDUC HONORS:** Fellowship in Econ.; **MIL SERV:** US Army, S/Sgt.; **OTHER ACT & HONORS:** DE Trust for Historic Preservation; **HOME ADD:** 17 Woodbrook Circ., Wilmington, DE 19810, (302)475-6398; **BUS ADD:** Edgemart Bldg., Four Deney Rd., Wilmington, DE 19809, (302)764-9430.

GILMARTIN, Wayne S.——B: May 28, 1948, New York, NY, *Principal*, Goldberg, Kohn, P.C.; **PRIM RE ACT:** Attorney, Owner/Investor; **SERVICES:** Legal services (synd., fin., acquisition); **PROFL AFFIL & HONORS:** ABA - Real Prop. Comm.; Chicago Bar Assn. - Real Prop. Comm., JD; **EDUC:** BA, 1970, Hist., Notre Dame; **GRAD EDUC:** JD, 1975, Univ. of Chicago; **EDUC HONORS:** Magna Cum Laude; **OTHER ACT & HONORS:** Union League Club of Chicago; **HOME ADD:** 9225 S. Hoyne, Chicago, IL 60620, (312)239-6836; **BUS ADD:** 55 E. Monroe, Suite 3950, Chicago, IL 60603, (312)332-2177.

GILMORE, Carl P.——B: Apr. 21, 1943, Tulsa, OK, *Dir.*, Weinrich, Gilmore & Adolph, PS; **PRIM RE ACT:** Attorney; **SERVICES:** Legal counsel to lenders, contractors, devels.; **REP CLIENTS:** Wells Fargo Mort. Co., John Graham Devel. Servcs., Pac. Component Homes, Inc., Norco Const. Co., Pac. West Realty Trust; **PREV EMPLOY:** Law specialist U.S. Coast Guard, 1968-1972; **PROFL AFFIL & HONORS:** ABA; Amer. Trial Lawyers Assn.; WA Bar Assn.; Seattle King Cty. Bar Assn., Chairperson and speaker at various CLE seminars; **EDUC:** Math/Econ., MO Southern Coll.; **GRAD EDUC:** JD, Univ. of MO; **EDUC HONORS:** Pres., Student Body, Finalist Moot Ct. Competition; **MIL SERV:** US Coast Guard, Lt.; **OTHER ACT & HONORS:** Rainier Club; WA Athletic Club; **HOME ADD:** 3118 Lakewood Ave. S., Seattle, WA 98144, (206)722-2685; **BUS ADD:** Suite 4000, SeaFirst Fifth Ave. Plaza, 800 Fifth Ave., Seattle, WA 98104, (206)623-9100.

GILMORE, G. Calvin——B: May 8, 1948, Lebanon, MO, *Owner*, Calvin Gilmore Investments; **PRIM RE ACT:** Broker, Consultant, Developer, Builder, Owner/Investor; **OTHER RE ACT:** Investor (income props.); **PROFL AFFIL & HONORS:** Local, State and Nat. Assn. of Realtors; Nat. Mktg. Instit., CCIM Candidate; **HOME ADD:** 392 Panoramic Dr., Camdenton, MO 65020, (314)346-2046; **BUS ADD:** POB 745, Camdenton, MO 65020, (314)346-2234.

GILMORE, John F.——B: May 9, 1929, Compton, IL, *Pres.*, Investors Incentives, Inc.; **PRIM RE ACT:** Consultant, Developer, Owner/Investor, Syndicator; **EDUC:** BA, 1952, Bus., Speech, MI State Univ.; **BUS ADD:** Fed. Sq. Bldg. Suite #1, Grand Rapids, MI 49503, (616)774-7071.

GILMORE, Michael D.——B: Oct. 12, 1950, Philadelphia, PA, *Sr. Atty.*, INA Service Co.; **PRIM RE ACT:** Attorney; **SERVICES:** Legal Counseling; **PREV EMPLOY:** Alco Standard Corp.; 1976-1979; **PROFL AFFIL & HONORS:** ABA, PA & Philadelphia Bar Assns.; **EDUC:** BS, 1971, Secondary Educ., W Chester State Coll., W Chester, PA; **GRAD EDUC:** JD, 1974, Law, Univ. of PA; **EDUC HONORS:** Cum Laude; **MIL SERV:** US Army Res., Capt.; **HOME ADD:** 718 Vernon Rd., Philadelphia, PA 19119, (215)848-1360; **BUS ADD:** 1600 Arch St., Philadelphia, PA 19101, (215)241-5018.

GILPIN, Thomas T.——B: Jan. 5, 1953, Winchester, VA, *Treasurer*, Lenoir City Co.; **PRIM RE ACT:** Developer, Property Manager; **SERVICES:** Investments, devel., prop. mgmt.; **PROFL AFFIL & HONORS:** S. Indus. Devel. Council; **EDUC:** BA, 1975, Amer. Hist., Princeton Univ.; **EDUC HONORS:** Cum Laude; **OTHER ACT & HONORS:** Bd. of Dir., Local United Way; **HOME ADD:** 126 S. Church St., Berryville, VA 22611, (703)955-4216; **BUS ADD:** Box 117, Boyce, VA 22620, (703)955-4217.

GILSTER, A.H., Jr.——B: Dec. 22, 1945, Chicago, IL, *Owner*, The Gilster Co.; **PRIM RE ACT:** Broker, Consultant, Appraiser; **SERVICES:** Full serv. brokerage, valuation, recreation prop.; **PROFL AFFIL & HONORS:** Door Cty. Bd. of Realtors; WI Realtors Assn.; NAR; RNMI, GRI; CRB; Door Cty. Realtor of the Yr., 1981; Pres., Door Cty. Bd. of Realtors, 1979; **EDUC:** BA, 1967, Eng. Lit., Knox Coll.; **OTHER ACT & HONORS:** Door Cty. C of C.; **HOME ADD:** Fish Creek, WI 54212, (414)868-3704; **BUS ADD:** POB 303, Fish Creek, WI 54212, (414)868-3245.

GILVESENKAMP, Lester O.——*Asst. Treas.*, Malinckrodt, Inc.; **PRIM RE ACT:** Property Manager; **BUS ADD:** PO Box 5840, St. Louis, MO 63134, (314)895-2000.*

GIMBERT, Clement H.——B: Feb. 7, 1930, Huntington, WV, *Pres.*, H.L. Rust Co., Wash. D.C.; **PRIM RE ACT:** Broker, Appraiser, Developer, Property Manager, Lender, Owner/Investor, Insuror; **PREV EMPLOY:** Peoples Life Ins. Co. 1965-81, Jefferson Life Ins. Co. 1963-65, Prudential Ins. Co. 1954-63; **PROFL AFFIL & HONORS:** Met. Wash. Bd. of Trade and Mort. Bankers Assoc. of Wash. D.C.; **EDUC:** BS, 1952, Bus. Admin., VA Poly. Inst.; **MIL SERV:** USA, 1st Lt.; **OTHER ACT & HONORS:** Member, BOD, First Fed. S&L Assn. of Arlington, VA; Member Advisory Board of Tr., Columbia Title Ins. Co., Wash., D.C.; Member BOD, Jackson Cross Co., Philadelphia PA; **HOME ADD:** 2026 Forest Hill Drive, Silver Spring, MD 20903, (301)434-6277; **BUS ADD:** 1800 K St. N.W., Wash., DC 20006, (202)862-3000.

GINGELL, Robert A.——B: July 23, 1923, Alexandria, VA, *Lawyer*, Law Offices of Robert A. Gingell; **PRIM RE ACT:** Attorney, Owner/Investor; **SERVICES:** Legal advice; **REP CLIENTS:** Bethesda Realty Co., Photo Science, Inc., Union Trust Co. of MD, Airflow Co., H&R Enterprises, Inc., DRG Assocs.; **PROFL AFFIL & HONORS:** ABA, MD State Bar Assn, Montg. Co. Bar Assn., Fellow, Amer. Coll. of RE Attys.; **EDUC:** AB, 1947, Lib. Arts, G. Wash. Univ.; **GRAD EDUC:** JD, 1949, G. Wash. Univ.; **MIL SERV:** USMC, Capt., USMCR, retd.; **OTHER ACT & HONORS:** Rotary club(Kensington Wheaton Dist. #762); **HOME ADD:** 5220 Parkway Dr., Chevy Chase, MD 20815, (301)652-1918; **BUS ADD:** Suite 214, 11151 Viers Mill Rd., Silver Spring, MD 20902, (301)949-0100.

GINGREY, James F., Jr.——B: Feb. 28, 1941, Augusta, GA, *Partner*, Johnston & Gingrey Law Firm; **PRIM RE ACT:** Attorney; **PROFL AFFIL & HONORS:** ABA, GA Bar Assn., Atlanta Bar Assn.; **EDUC:** Univ. of GA, 1964, Bus. Admin.; **GRAD EDUC:** Emory Univ. Law Sch., 1971, RE; **HOME ADD:** 4 Bohler Ln., Atlanta, GA 30327, (404)351-3054; **BUS ADD:** P O Box 20781, Atlanta, GA 30320, (404)997-1880.

GINGRICH, Henry F.——B: Sept. 12, 1923, Elizabethtown, PA, *Partner*, Gingrich & Smith; **PRIM RE ACT:** Attorney; **SERVICES:** RE Settlements & RE legal advice; **REP CLIENTS:** Banks & Municipal corps. & Pvt. indiv.; **PROFL AFFIL & HONORS:** PA & Amer. Bar Assns. RE Sections, 3 related sections, PA Bar Assn. Lancaster Cty. Bar Assn. RE Comm.; **EDUC:** 1946, Psych. & Eng., Elizabethtown Coll.; **GRAD EDUC:** JD, 1952, Temple Univ. Sch. of Law; **EDUC HONORS:** Law Review, 2nd yr.; **MIL SERV:** US Air Force, infantry, Cpl.; **OTHER ACT & HONORS:** Inspector of Elections 1954-60; **HOME ADD:** 151 E. High St., Elizabethtown, PA 17022, (717)367-3068; **BUS ADD:** 133 E. High St., Elizabethtown, PA 17022, (717)291-1118.

GINLEY, William A.——B: Jul. 6, 1930, Kittanning, PA, *Pres.*, McGinley Real Estate, Inc.; **PRIM RE ACT:** Broker, Appraiser, Developer, Owner/Investor, Instructor, Insuror; **SERVICES:** Prop. mgmt.; appraisals; sales; **REP CLIENTS:** S & L; fin. instns.; providing mgmt. of investment portfolios of comml. props.; **PROFL AFFIL & HONORS:** IREM; Amer. Assn. Cert. Appraisers; NAR, CPM; Sr.

Appraiser; **OTHER ACT & HONORS:** Kiski Area School Authority Vice Chmn. 1961-63; Allegheny Twp. Munic. Sewerage Auth. Vice Pres., 1968-70; Dir. Moraine Trails Boy Scouts of America; Instr. of RE for PA State Univ. (1963-Present); Indiana Univ. of PA (1977-Present); Pres., Greater Alle-Kiski Area Bd. Realtors 1979; **HOME ADD:** Moreland Manor RD3, Leechburg, PA 15656, (412)842-7831; **BUS ADD:** Corner 56 at 356, Box 257-A, Vandergrift, PA 15690, (412)568-3677.

GINSBURG, Sheldon H.——B: Mar. 22, 1938, Chicago, IL, *Pres.*, Shell Devel. Corp.; **PRIM RE ACT:** Consultant, Developer, Builder, Owner/Investor, Syndicator; **EDUC:** BS, 1959, Acctg., DePaul; **EDUC HONORS:** Beta Gamma Sigma, Pi Gamma Mu, Beta Alpha Psi; **BUS ADD:** 4849 W Golf Rd., Skokie, IL 60077, (312)679-2000.

GINTHER, Noble C., III——*Pres.*, Big Three Realty; **PRIM RE ACT:** Broker, Appraiser, Property Manager; **SERVICES:** Mgmt., Resid. & Comml. Sales; **PREV EMPLOY:** Mgmt. of several office bldgs. including leasing and const.; **EDUC:** RE Bus. Admin., 1980, Real Estate, Univ. of Tx at Austin; **HOME ADD:** 211 Castillo, San Antonio, TX 78210, (512)533-0077; **BUS ADD:** 705 E. Houston # 900, San Antonio, TX 78205, (512)222-0984.

GIOFFRE, Bruno J.——B: June 27, 1934, Port Chester, NY, *Sr. Partner*, Gioffre & Gioffre, P.C.; **PRIM RE ACT:** Consultant, Attorney, Developer, Owner/Investor, Property Manager, Syndicator; **OTHER RE ACT:** Closing Atty. and Member of Bd. of Dir. to Lending Inst.; Member, Advisory Bd. to Title Co.; **SERVICES:** Legal representation and counseling, prop. mgmt., devel. and synd. of comml. and resid. props., representation of clients in rezoning of props.; **REP CLIENTS:** Sound Fed. S&L Assn.; Lyon Farm Village; Longview Terr. Cooperative Owners Assn.; Rye Town Hilton Inn; Waters Edge Homeowners Assn.; Luxo Lamp Corp.; Shalom Nursing Home; Port Chester Nursing Home; **PROFL AFFIL & HONORS:** US, NY, Westchester Cty. and Port Chester-Rye Bar Assns.; NY and Westchester Cty. Magistrates Assns.; Member, Bd. of Dir., Westchester Cty. Magistrates Assn.; **EDUC:** BA, 1956, Govt./Philosophy, Cornell Univ.; **GRAD EDUC:** JD, 1958, Cornell Law School; **OTHER ACT & HONORS:** Justice, Town of Rye, 1965 to present; Member, Bd. of Dir., United Hospital, Port Chester Public Library; Sound Fed. S&L Assn.; Shalom Nursing Home; Port Chester Nursing Home; **HOME ADD:** 18 Beechwood Blvd., Port Chester, NY 10573, (914)939-5134; **BUS ADD:** 220 Westchester Ave., Port Chester, NY 10573, (914)939-1860.

GIORDANO, Robert A.——B: Nov. 10, 1948, Newark, NJ, *Asst. VP*, Howco Investment Corp., Sub. of Howard Savings Bank; **PRIM RE ACT:** Appraiser, Lender, Owner/Investor; **OTHER RE ACT:** Investment analyst; **SERVICES:** RE Devel., investor, joint ventures, direct devel., acquisitions, sales, leasing of resid., comml. & indus. props.; **PREV EMPLOY:** 1970-72 J.I Kislek Mort. Corp., Newark, NJ, 1973-77 Veterans Admin. Loan Guaranty Div., Newark, 1977-80 Broadway Bank, Patersway Mort. Lending; **EDUC:** BS, 1977, Bus. Admin. & Fin., Upsals Coll., E Orange, NJ; **HOME ADD:** 22 West View Rd., W Orange, NJ 07052, (201)731-8464; **BUS ADD:** 768 Broad St., Newark, NJ 07101, (201)624-9111.

GIRARD, Gene F.——B: Oct. 26, 1923, Bayonne, NJ, *Pres.*, Girard Realty, Inc.; **PRIM RE ACT:** Broker, Appraiser, Developer, Property Manager, Insuror; **OTHER RE ACT:** RE sales. Wrote book on Policy Manual & Training for Salesmen - 1966.; **PROFL AFFIL & HONORS:** Nat. & NY State Assn. of Realtors; RNMI; Albany, Saratoga & Schenectady RE Bds. of Realtors, Cert. Resid. Mgmt. Broker; CRS; GRI; **EDUC:** BA, 1949, RE Civil Engrg., Union Coll.; **MIL SERV:** US Army, Cpl., Purple Heart with Oak Leaf Cluster, Combat Badge, Conspicuous Service Cross, Victory Medal; 3 yrs. WWII; **OTHER ACT & HONORS:** 1948 Lacrosse goalie of the year for NY State; Chmn. Schenectady Off-Track Betting Commn.; Schenectady Curling Club; Taught Lapidary Classes; Eagle Scout & Former Scoutmaster & Post Advisor; Pres. of Albany Cty. Bd. of Realtors, Inc. 1980; Pres. of Schenectady Bd. of Realtors, Inc. 1963-64; Rgnl. VP, NY State Assn. Realtors, Inc. 1973; Pres., The Vikings Restaurant & Lounge, since 1966; **HOME ADD:** 120 Shirley Dr., Schenectady, NY 12304, (518)370-5556; **BUS ADD:** 1001 State St., Schenectady, NY 12307, (518)374-7711.

GITELSON, Stanley H.——B: Dec. 13, 1942, Wash., DC, *VP*, Charles E. Smith Mgmt. Inc., Comml. Mgmt. Dept.; **PRIM RE ACT:** Property Manager; **SERVICES:** Mgmt. of Comml. & Retail space; **PROFL AFFIL & HONORS:** Wash., DC Bd. of Realtors; Inst. of RE Mgmt., 1980 Prop. Mgr. of Yr., Wash., DC; **EDUC:** Attended Amer. Univ., Univ of MD, & Montgomery Coll.; **MIL SERV:** USN; **HOME ADD:** 11425 Beechgrove Lane, Potomac, MD 20854, (301)340-2244; **BUS ADD:** 1735 Jefferson Davis Hwy., Arlington, VA 22202, (703)920-8500.

GITLEN, Gordon P.——B: Feb. 12, 1953, Hartford, CT, *Atty. at Law*, Law Office of Gordon P. Gitlen; **PRIM RE ACT:** Attorney; **PREV EMPLOY:** In-house counsel, Fred Sands Realtors, Legal staff of Coldwell Banker & Co; Partner, Michaels, Getz & Gitlen; **PROFL AFFIL & HONORS:** Assn. of RE Attys.; Santa Monica Bay Dist. Bar Assn.; ABA; Beverly Hills Bar Assn.; **EDUC:** BS, 1975, Philisophy & Bus., Claremont Men's Coll.; **GRAD EDUC:** JD, 1978, Law, Southwestern Univ.; **EDUC HONORS:** Dean's List 1975; **BUS ADD:** 1299 Ocean Ave., Ste. 300, Los Angeles, CA 90401, (213)277-3456.

GJOVIG, Bruce——B: Mar. 24, 1951, Crosby, ND, *Exec. Off.*, Grand Forks Bd. of Realtors, Inc., NAR; **OTHER RE ACT:** Trade assn. mgmt.; **SERVICES:** MLS, Lobbying, Edu., Para-legal Advice, Infor.; **EDUC:** BS, BA, 1974-1975, Zoology, Math, Chem., Univ. of ND, Coll. of Arts & Sciences; **EDUC HONORS:** Blue Key, Dean's List; **OTHER ACT & HONORS:** Chmn. Grand Forks Rep.; Urb. Dev. Comm. Grand Forks Dev. Found.; Delta Tau Delta; Rotary; Elks; **HOME ADD:** 2215 Univ. Ave., Grand Forks, ND 58201, (701)775-3484; **BUS ADD:** Box 1371, 600 DeMers Ave., Ste. 201, Grand Forks, ND 58201, (701)775-4231.

GLACKIN, Dorothy M.——B: Feb. 12, 1926, Bloomingdale, NJ, *Pres.*, Paul L. Glackin, Inc.; **PRIM RE ACT:** Broker, Owner/Investor; **PREV EMPLOY:** Admin., Harford Co. Library, 1948-1958; **PROFL AFFIL & HONORS:** NAR/MD Assn. of Realtors, Dir., Harford Co. Bd. of Realtors; **EDUC:** BA, 1947, Library Sci., Rutgers Univ. (Douglass Coll.); **OTHER ACT & HONORS:** Dir., Citizens Nursing Home Bd., Member, Adv. Bd., Harford Community Coll.; **HOME ADD:** 1613 Chestnut St., Cardiff, MD 21024, (301)452-5400; **BUS ADD:** 332 S. Main St., Bel Air, MD 21014, (301)838-3500.

GLAD, Charles R.——B: Aug. 8, 1948, Sterling, CO, *Sec./Tres.*, West Chase Development; **PRIM RE ACT:** Consultant, Developer, Owner/Investor, Builder, Property Manager, Syndicator; **OTHER RE ACT:** Arrange fin., anchor tenants; **SERVICES:** Acquisition, synd. and related comml. props.; **PREV EMPLOY:** Owner public acctg. firm, Office bldg. owner & prop. mgmt.; **PROFL AFFIL & HONORS:** Nat. Assn. of Account., RE Agents Lic.; **EDUC:** BS, 1970, Acctg., Mktg., Univ.; **HOME ADD:** 9277 W. Wesley Dr., Lakewood, CO 80227, (303)986-6161; **BUS ADD:** 1300 Glenarm Pi, The Penthouse, Denver, CO 80204, (303)623-1560.

GLASER, Barry——*Asst. Treas.*, McQuay-Perfex, Inc.; **PRIM RE ACT:** Property Manager; **BUS ADD:** 5401 Gamble Dr., PO Box 9316, Minneapolis, MN 55440, (612)553-5000.*

GLASER, Dennis C.——B: Nov. 26, 1944, Caldwell, KS, *VP*, Banner Development Co., Inc.; **PRIM RE ACT:** Broker, Developer, Owner/Investor, Property Manager; **PREV EMPLOY:** Controller, Large Natl. Apt. Devel.; **PROFL AFFIL & HONORS:** NAA, AICPA, KS CPA; **EDUC:** BS-Acctg., 1967, Bus., KS State Univ.; **MIL SERV:** Army Reserve, E-6; **OTHER ACT & HONORS:** Woodlawn United Methodist Church; **HOME ADD:** 1022 Bodine, Derby, KS 67037, (316)788-0603; **BUS ADD:** 707 N. Waco, Suite 106, Wichita, KS 67203, (316)265-6616.

GLASER, Herbert——B: Aug. 1, 1927, NJ, *Owner*, Glaser Development Co.; **PRIM RE ACT:** Developer, Attorney, Owner/Investor; **PROFL AFFIL & HONORS:** ABA; Beverly Hills, LA Cty. Bar Assn.; RE Sects. for various Bar Assns.; **EDUC:** BA, 1947, Pol. Sci., UCLA; **GRAD EDUC:** LLB, 1951, Harvard Law School; **EDUC HONORS:** Pi Kappa Sigma, Pi Kappa Delta; **OTHER ACT & HONORS:** Pres., City of Los Angeles Bd. of Fire Commnrs. (1962-1970); Real Estate Advisory Comm.; CA Commr. of Corp.; **HOME ADD:** 719 N. Linden Dr., Beverly Hills, CA, (213)550-0125; **BUS ADD:** 924 Westwood Blvd., Los Angeles, CA 90024, (213)824-1444.

GLASGALL, Franklin——B: Nov. 23, 1932, Newark, NJ, *VP RE*, Restaurant Assoc. Ind., Inc.; **PRIM RE ACT:** Broker, Developer, Property Manager; **OTHER RE ACT:** Admin.; **SERVICES:** Site sel., acquist., divest., dev., admin.; **PREV EMPLOY:** VP Sanndrel Inc., Shopping Center Devel.; **PROFL AFFIL & HONORS:** RE Bd. of NY, NACORE, ICSC; **EDUC:** BS, 1954, Acctg., Econ., OH State Univ.; **MIL SERV:** USAF, Capt., 1954-56; **HOME ADD:** 165 W. 66th St., NY, NY 10023, (212)874-2397; **BUS ADD:** 1540 Broadway, NY, NY 10036, (212)997-1350.

GLASS, Marc Jerome——B: Dec. 9, 1945, CA, *Partner*, Glass & Lebovitz; **PRIM RE ACT:** Attorney, Owner/Investor, Instructor; **OTHER RE ACT:** Title Ins. Agent; **SERVICES:** Complete Legal Servs., including Title, Regulatory, Zoning, Fin. & Closing Documents; **PROFL AFFIL & HONORS:** Various Bar Assns., Tax Instr., Univ. of Hartford Bus. School; **EDUC:** BA, 1967, Econ., Harvard Coll.; **GRAD EDUC:** JD, 1970, Tax, Harvard Law School; **EDUC HONORS:** Honors; **OTHER ACT & HONORS:** Instr. in Tax Law, Austin Barney School of Bus., Univ. of Hartford, 1976-present; **HOME ADD:**

54 Buckingham St., Hartford, CT 06106, (203)728-0053; **BUS ADD:** 101 Pearl St., Hartford, CT 06103, (203)728-5858.

GLASS, Naomi G.——**B:** Apr. 16, 1949, New York, NY, *Partner*, Guggenhime & Glass; **PRIM RE ACT:** Syndicator; **SERVICES:** Form partnerships for small investors; **PREV EMPLOY:** Comml. brokerage - sales & leasing between 1977-1980; **EDUC:** BA, 1970, Univ. of Pittsburgh; **GRAD EDUC:** Master in Bus. Admin., 1976, Harvard Bus. School; **EDUC HONORS:** Magna Cum Laude; **HOME ADD:** 1725 Taylor St., San Francisco, CA 94133, (415)885-6802; **BUS ADD:** 26 Presidio Terrace, San Francisco, CA 94118, (415)928-3412.

GLASSMAN, Donald L.——**B:** Apr. 24, 1932, Philadelphia, PA, *Pres.*, Style Craft Builders Inc.; **PRIM RE ACT:** Developer, Builder, Owner/Investor, Syndicator; **SERVICES:** Devel. and Synd. of Commerce Props., Prop. Mgmt.; **REP CLIENTS:** Land Acquisition; **PROFL AFFIL & HONORS:** Amer. Arbitration Assn.; **EDUC:** BS, Bus., Univ. of PA; **OTHER ACT & HONORS:** Chmn. of Bd., Devel. Ctr. for Autistic Children, Lu Lu Temple Shrine; **HOME ADD:** Melrose Park, PA; **BUS ADD:** Gwynedd Plaza, Springhouse, PA 19477, (215)643-3280.

GLATSTIAN, Charles——**B:** Sept. 28, 1927, New York, NY, *Pres.*, Glatstian R.E. Agency, Inc.; **PRIM RE ACT:** Broker, Consultant, Owner/Investor; **PREV EMPLOY:** Self employed; **HOME ADD:** 45 Trommel Dr., Mahwah, NJ 07430, (201)529-2822; **BUS ADD:** 417 Main St., Hackensack, NJ 07601, (201)489-7050.

GLATZER, Sanford B.——**B:** Apr. 1, 1936, New York, NY, *Atty.*, Glatzer & Belovin; **PRIM RE ACT:** Attorney, Owner/Investor; **REP CLIENTS:** Indiv. investors, FHA lenders, builders and 'rehab' specs.; **PROFL AFFIL & HONORS:** Var. bar assns.; **EDUC:** BS, 1957, Acctg., NYU Sch. of Commerce; **GRAD EDUC:** LLB, 1960, Brooklyn Law Sch.; LLM, 1965, Tax, NYU Law Sch.; **MIL SERV:** US Army; Cpl.; **HOME ADD:** 24 Gillies Ln., Norwalk, CT 06854, (203)838-3563; **BUS ADD:** 2311 White Plains Rd., Bronx, NY 10467, (212)655-2000.

GLAWE, Rick S.——**B:** May 21, 1949, Green Bay, WI, *Dir.*, Glawe Inc.; **PRIM RE ACT:** Broker, Consultant, Appraiser, Developer, Builder, Instructor, Property Manager, Syndicator; **SERVICES:** Investment counseling, synd., feasibility studies, prop. mgmt., devel. and builder; **REP CLIENTS:** Indivs., partnerships, corps. and lenders; **PROFL AFFIL & HONORS:** Registered Rep., Nat. Assn. of Securities Dealers, WI Realtors Honor Soc., CCIM, CRS, GRI; **EDUC:** AA, 1971, Mgmt., Cornell Univ.; **HOME ADD:** 135 W. Mission Rd., Green Bay, WI 54301, (414)437-3092; **BUS ADD:** 2020 Riverside Dr., Green Bay, WI 54301, (414)435-4266.

GLAZE, Phyllis Laser——**B:** Nov. 26, 1947, Little Rock, AR, *Prop. Mgr. & Assoc. Part.*, Barnes, Quinn, Flake & Anderson, Inc., Prop. Mgmt.; **PRIM RE ACT:** Broker, Syndicator, Consultant, Appraiser, Developer, Property Manager, Owner/Investor; **PROFL AFFIL & HONORS:** Little Rock Bd. of Realtors, IREM, BOMA, Bd. of Dir. Little Rock Bd. of Realtors, CPM; **OTHER ACT & HONORS:** Treas., Amer. Cancer Soc., No. Little Rock; Treas., IREM - AR Chapter-1982; **HOME ADD:** 901 Regal, North Little Rock, AR 72118, (501)758-4220; **BUS ADD:** 2100 First Natl. Bldg., Little Rock, AR 72201, (501)372-6161.

GLAZER, Larry——**B:** Oct. 12, 1945, Mt. Vernon, NY, *Partner*, Buckingham Properties; **PRIM RE ACT:** Developer, Builder, Owner/Investor, Property Manager, Syndicator; **EDUC:** 1966, Accountant, Univ. of Buffalo; **GRAD EDUC:** MBA, 1968, Fin., Columbia Univ.; **EDUC HONORS:** Phi Beta Kappa, Bisonhead Soc.; **HOME ADD:** 89 Stuyvesant Rd., Pittsford, NY 14534, (716)385-3166; **BUS ADD:** 687 Monroe Ave., Rochester, NY 14607.

GLAZER, Ronald B.——**B:** Jan. 13, 1943, Philadelphia, PA, *Atty.*, Cohen, Shapiro, Polisher, Shiekman and Cohen; **PRIM RE ACT:** Attorney, Instructor; **SERVICES:** Client rep. in all aspects of RE transactions; **REP CLIENTS:** FPA Corp., PA RE Investment Trust; **PROFL AFFIL & HONORS:** ICSC, ABA, PA Bar Assn., Philadelphia Bar Assn.; **EDUC:** AB, 1964, Poli. Sci., Dickenson Coll.; **GRAD EDUC:** JD, 1967, Univ. of PA; **EDUC HONORS:** Cum Laude; **OTHER ACT & HONORS:** Author of *PA Condo. Law and Practice*, Bisel, Phila., 1981, 2nd edition; **HOME ADD:** 304 Hedgerow Ln., Wyncote, PA 19095, (215)576-5506; **BUS ADD:** 2700, 12 S. 12th St., Philadelphia, PA 19107, (215)922-1300.

GLAZIER, Margaret F.——**B:** Apr. 19, 1939, Osage Cty., MO, *Gen. Mgr., Co owner*, Consolidated Realty Inc.; **PRIM RE ACT:** Broker, Appraiser, Developer, Owner/Investor; **PROFL AFFIL & HONORS:** Rho Epsilon RE Frat., WCR, Assn. of Realtors, RNMI, Past. Pres. WCR, 1977, Dir. Wichita Bd. of Realtors, Vlntr. of the Yr., KS Chap. Arthritis Found., 1969; **EDUC:** Wichita State Univ. Continuing ed. community and RE; **HOME ADD:** 6116 Legion, Wichita, KS 67204, (316)838-6242; **BUS ADD:** 1107 N. Broadway, Wichita, KS 67214, (316)264-0653.

GLEASON, Gary M.——**B:** Feb. 22, 1940, Elmira, NY, *Partner*, Spencer, Gleason & Hebe; **PRIM RE ACT:** Attorney; **REP CLIENTS:** Lenders and investors in RE; **PROFL AFFIL & HONORS:** ABA, PA Bar Assn., Tioga Cty. Bar Assn.; **EDUC:** Colgate Univ., 1962, Econ.; **GRAD EDUC:** JD, 1966, Law, Marshall-Wythe Sch. of Law, Coll. of William & Mary; **HOME ADD:** R.D. 12+5, Box 236, Wellsboro, PA 16901, (717)724-4001; **BUS ADD:** 17 Central Ave., Wellsboro, PA 16901, (717)724-1832.

GLENN, Patrick O.——**B:** Aug. 24, 1947, Wichita, KS, Appraisal, feasibility, investment analysis; **PRIM RE ACT:** Broker, Consultant, Appraiser, Developer; **SERVICES:** Appraisal, feasibility, investment analysis; **PREV EMPLOY:** First Nat. Bank of OKC, Liberty Nat. Bank of OK, RE Lending, mort. underwiting, appraising; **PROFL AFFIL & HONORS:** Candidate AIREA, Assoc. SREA, NAR; **EDUC:** BS, 1969, Econ., Univ. of Denver; **MIL SERV:** USA, E-3; **HOME ADD:** 1120 Huntington Ave., Oklahoma City, OK 73116, (405)848-6366; **BUS ADD:** 511 Couch D., Suite 200, Olkahoma City, OK 73102, (405)239-6000.

GLENN, Robert T.——**B:** Sept. 17, 1945, NJ, *Pres.*, Robert Glenn Assocs., Inc.; **PRIM RE ACT:** Broker, Appraiser, Developer; **SERVICES:** appraisal, brokerage, devel.; **REP CLIENTS:** Banks, devel., pension funds, instnl. investors; **PROFL AFFIL & HONORS:** AIREA; Soc. of RE Appraisers; Realtor, MAI; SRPA; **EDUC:** BA, 1971, Econ., NC State Univ.; **GRAD EDUC:** MA, current, Econ., NC State Univ.; **MIL SERV:** US Army; E-5, PH, GCM, USM, UDM; **OTHER ACT & HONORS:** Hist. Preservation; **HOME ADD:** 339 Awake Field Dr., Charlotte, NC 28209, (704)527-5559; **BUS ADD:** 118 Latta Arcade, Charlotte, NC 28202, (704)375-5549.

GLESNER, Richard C.——**B:** Aug. 23, 1941, Sturgeon Bay, WI, *Shareholder*, Ross & Stevens, S.C.; **PRIM RE ACT:** Consultant, Attorney, Owner/Investor; **SERVICES:** Legal serv. in the acquisition, sale and exchange of prop. interests; **REP CLIENTS:** PDQ Corp. Tuscarora Plastics; Rocky Rococo Corp.; Kinsman Devel. Co.; Randall Bank; First Wisconsin Nat. Bank of Madison; **PROFL AFFIL & HONORS:** ISCS, ABA, Real Pro. Sect.; **EDUC:** Bus. Adm., Hist., 1963, St. Norbert Coll.; **GRAD EDUC:** JD, 1966, Univ. of WI; **EDUC HONORS:** Delta Epsilon Sigma Honor Soc.; Who's Who in American Univ. & Coll.; Honors Grad., Order of Coif; **MIL SERV:** USA, 1st. Lt.; **HOME ADD:** 3322 Leyton Ln., Madison, WI 53703, (608)274-6800; **BUS ADD:** 801 First Wisconsin Plaza, 1 S. Pinckney, Madison, WI 53703, (608)257-5353.

GLICK, Eugene B.——**B:** Aug. 29, 1921, Indianapolis, IN, *Pres.*, Gene B. Glick Co., Inc.; **PRIM RE ACT:** Developer, Builder, Owner/Investor, Property Manager; **SERVICES:** Exec. Dir. of the Co.; **PREV EMPLOY:** Mort. Loan Officer, Peoples State Bank, Indianapolis, IN; **EDUC:** BS, 1942, Bus. Admin./Psych., IN Univ.; **MIL SERV:** US Army, 45th Infantry 7th Div.; **HOME ADD:** 215 Williams Ct., Indianapolis, IN 46260, (317)255-2184; **BUS ADD:** 9102 N. Meridian St., Indianapolis, IN 46240, (317)844-7741.

GLICK, Kenneth J.——**B:** Feb. 14, 1933, Chicago, IL, *Atty.*, Ray & Glick, Ltd.; **PRIM RE ACT:** Attorney; **REP CLIENTS:** Lenders, synd., builders and devel. on an indiv. basis; **EDUC:** BS, 1954, Econ., Univ. of IL; **GRAD EDUC:** LLB, 1956, Univ. of IL; **HOME ADD:** 1110 Sandstone, Libertyville, IL 60048, (312)680-7131; **BUS ADD:** 611 S. Milwaukee Ave., P.O. Box 400, Libertyville, IL 60048, (312)680-9600.

GLICK, Marvin M.——**B:** Nov. 25, 1943, Brookline, MA, *Prin.*, Marvin M. Glick CPA, Jamar Prop., Chateau Estates, Back Bay Condo. Corp.; **PRIM RE ACT:** Developer, Property Manager, Lender, Owner/Investor; **PREV EMPLOY:** IRS, Dept. of Treas.; **PROFL AFFIL & HONORS:** Amer. Inst. CPA's & Soc. of CPA's; **EDUC:** BBA, 1966, Acctg., Univ. of MA; **EDUC HONORS:** Dean's List; **MIL SERV:** USA Nat. Guard; **BUS ADD:** 233 Needham St., Newton, MA 02164, (617)965-6050.

GLICK, Michael I.——**B:** Oct. 22, 1935, NY, *Pres.*, Michael I. Glick Co., Inc.; **PRIM RE ACT:** Consultant, Owner/Investor, Syndicator; **SERVICES:** Acquisitions, synd. and mgmt. of investment props.; **REP CLIENTS:** Consultant: Citicorp, Chase Manhattan Bank, Gerald D. Hines Interests, CPAs, Attys.; **PREV EMPLOY:** Helmsley-Spear Inc., 1959; Swig, Weiller-Arnow, 1959-1967; **PROFL AFFIL & HONORS:** RE Bd. of NY, Former Chmn., Bd. of Govs., Young Men's RE Assn. of NY; **EDUC:** AB, 1957, Eng. Lit., Williams Coll.; **GRAD EDUC:** MBA, 1959, RE/Fin., Columbia Univ. Grad. Sch. of Bus.; **EDUC**

HONORS: 1975-80 Assoc. Class Agent, VP, Grad. Bus. Assn.; **OTHER ACT & HONORS:** Harmonie; Birchwood Ctry. Club; Beachpoint Club; Williams Coll. Club; Columbia Univ. Club; **HOME ADD:** 1111 Park Ave., NY, NY, (212)369-1898; **BUS ADD:** 60 E 42nd St., Suite 2825, NY, NY 10165, (212)661-7660.

GLICK, Paul M.——B: Dec. 7, 1948, New York, NY, *Part.*, Friedman & Koven; **PRIM RE ACT:** Attorney; **SERVICES:** Legal counseling-all phases of R.E.; **PROFL AFFIL & HONORS:** US Supreme Ct., US Court of Claims, US Tax Ct., Amer., IL, Chicago Bar Assns., Professor, DePaul Univ. Grad. School of Law; **EDUC:** 1970, Pol. Sci.; **GRAD EDUC:** 1973, De Paul Univ. Coll. of Law; **EDUC HONORS:** Grad. with Honors, Cum Laude; **BUS ADD:** 208 S. La Salle St., Chicago, IL 60604, (312)346-8500.

GLICKFELD, Bruce——B: Mar. 9, 1948, NY, *Atty.*, De Castro, West & Chodorow, Inc.; **PRIM RE ACT:** Attorney; **REP CLIENTS:** US and for. RE investors and devels.; **PROFL AFFIL & HONORS:** ABA; CA, Beverly Hills and Los Angeles Cty. Bar Assns.; **EDUC:** BA, 1969, Poli. Sci., UCLA; **GRAD EDUC:** JD, 1972, UCLA; **EDUC HONORS:** Dean's List, Order of Coif; Law Review; **HOME ADD:** 21132 Las Flores Mesa Dr., Mailbu, CA 90265, (213)456-2217; **BUS ADD:** 10960 Wilshire Blvd. Suite 1800, Los Angeles, CA 90024, (213)478-2541.

GLICKMAN, Edwin J.——B: Apr. 1, 1932, NY, *Exec. VP*, Sybedon Corp.; **PRIM RE ACT:** Broker, Consultant, Developer, Syndicator; **SERVICES:** Arrange joint ventures, synd. props., act as developer; **REP CLIENTS:** Indivs., instit.; **PREV EMPLOY:** Madison Equities, Partner - Major RE Devel. in NY; **PROFL AFFIL & HONORS:** Dir.; Resources Pension Shares, Inc. - 5th Avenue Assn.; **EDUC:** Dartmouth Coll., 1953, Liberal Arts; **MIL SERV:** US Army, First Lt.; **HOME ADD:** 45 East 89th St., New York, NY 10028, (212)289-6660; **BUS ADD:** 1211 Ave. of Americas, New York, NY 10036, (212)354-5756.

GLICKMAN, Robert——*VP*, Norton Simon, Inc.; **PRIM RE ACT:** Property Manager; **BUS ADD:** 277 Park Ave., New York, NY 10017, (212)832-1000.*

GLICKSON, Scott L.——B: Mar. 28, 1950, Chicago, IL, *Atty.*, Gordon, Schlack, Glickson, Gordon & Davidson, PC; **PRIM RE ACT:** Broker, Attorney, Owner/Investor, Instructor; **SERVICES:** Legal, tax and investment planning; **PROFL AFFIL & HONORS:** Amer., IL and Chicago Bar Assns., Chicago RE Bd.; **EDUC:** BA, 1972, Fin., Univ. of IL; **GRAD EDUC:** JD, 1975, Northwestern Univ. Law Sch.; **EDUC HONORS:** High Honors; **BUS ADD:** 444 N Michigan Ave. 36th fl., Chicago, IL 60611, (312)321-1700.

GLIDDEN, Allan H.——B: April 19, 1920, Waltham, MA, *V.P.*, Mutual of NY, RE; **PRIM RE ACT:** Developer, Lender, Owner/Investor; **SERVICES:** Investment area of ins. Co.; **PREV EMPLOY:** Prudential Life Ins. Co.; **PROFL AFFIL & HONORS:** SIR, NY RE Bd., ULI, ICSC; **MIL SERV:** USA, M/Sgt.; **OTHER ACT & HONORS:** Pres. Tr., Mony Mort. Investors; Tr., Dry Dock Savings Bank; Dir., A&A Investment Corp.; Dir., Greerco Corp.; Advisory Bd., Citibank; Advisory Bd., Lincoln First Credit Corp.; Advisory Bd., NY State Employees Retirement System; **HOME ADD:** 50 Aiken St. Apt. 293, Norwalk, CT 06851, (203)846-0364; **BUS ADD:** 1740 Broadway, NY, NY 10019, (212)708-2035.

GLOSS, Paul H.——*Mgr., RE*, Timken Co.; **PRIM RE ACT:** Property Manager; **BUS ADD:** 1835 Duebar Ave. SW, Canton, OH 44706, (216)453-4511.*

GLOVER, J. Littleton, Jr.——B: Dec. 14, 1942, Newnan, GA, *Atty.*, Glover & Davis, P.A.; **PRIM RE ACT:** Attorney; **SERVICES:** Legal; **REP CLIENTS:** Atl.-Can. Corp.; Batson-Cook Devel. Co.; Bailey & Assoc.; Powers Ferry-Nautilus; **PROFL AFFIL & HONORS:** ABA; **EDUC:** BA, 1964, Econ., Vanderbilt Univ.; **GRAD EDUC:** LLB/JD, 1967, Law, Univ. of VA; **EDUC HONORS:** Magna Cum Laude, Phi Beta Kappa, Order of the Coif; **MIL SERV:** U.S. Army, Capt., Bronze Star, 1969-1971; **HOME ADD:** 18 Woodlane, Newnan, GA 30263, (404)253-1951; **BUS ADD:** 10 Brown St., POB 1038, Newnan, GA 30264, (404)253-4330.

GLUCK, Michael——B: Dec. 4, 1928, New York, NY, *COB*, Agora Industries, Inc.; **PRIM RE ACT:** Developer, Builder, Owner/Investor, Property Manager; **EDUC:** BBA, 1950, Mgmt., CCNY; **EDUC HONORS:** Cum Laude; **MIL SERV:** USN; **OTHER ACT & HONORS:** Young Pres. Org.; World Business Council, NY C of C & Indus., World Trade Club; **HOME ADD:** 531 Main St., New York, NY 10044, (212)838-2642; **BUS ADD:** 45-50 Court Sq., Long Island City, NY 11101, (212)361-2121.

GLUPKER, Warren D.——B: Jan. 3, 1935, Chicago, IL, *V.P., Chief Appraiser*, Allstate Savings and Loan; **PRIM RE ACT:** Appraiser; **PREV EMPLOY:** Gibraltar S and L, 20 yrs.; **PROFL AFFIL & HONORS:** SREA, NARA, SRA, CRA; **EDUC:** 1955-57, Pre-Med, Thornton Coll., Harvey, IL; **GRAD EDUC:** Bus. and R.E., UCLA Ext., Pierce Coll.; **MIL SERV:** USA, SPC-3; **OTHER ACT & HONORS:** Treas. CA Mkt. Data Co-op Bd. of Dir.-C.M.D.C.; **HOME ADD:** 2443 Loma Vista, Pasadena, CA 91104, (213)797-2821; **BUS ADD:** 701 North Brand Blvd., Glendale, CA 91201, (213)956-1800.

GLUSAK, John Bruce——B: Oct. 14, 1949, Chicago, IL, The Equitable Life Assurance Society of the United States, RE; **PRIM RE ACT:** Property Manager; **SERVICES:** Prop. mgmt.; **PREV EMPLOY:** L. J. Sheridan & Co., Prop. Mgmt. 1971-77; **PROFL AFFIL & HONORS:** Bldg. Owners and Mgrs. Assn. of Chicago, Chicago RE Bd., RPA; RE Broker; CPM; **EDUC:** BS, 1970, Mgmt., DePaul Univ.; **EDUC HONORS:** Cum Laude; **HOME ADD:** 8820 W. 100 St., Palos Hills, IL 60465; **BUS ADD:** 401 N. Michigan Ave., Chicago, IL 60611, (312)321-4850.

GLYNN, John P., Jr.——B: Apr. 13, 1937, Lincoln, NE, *Atty.*, John P. Glynn, Jr. Atty.; **PRIM RE ACT:** Attorney; **SERVICES:** Subdiv. resid. comml. indus. zoning; **REP CLIENTS:** Cherry Hill RE Inc., Cherry Hill Const. Co., Cherry Hill Devel. Co., Cherry Hill Mgmt. Co.; **PROFL AFFIL & HONORS:** Lincoln and NE Bar Assn., ABA; **EDUC:** BS, 1959, Hist., Eng., Univ. of NE; **GRAD EDUC:** LLB, 1962, Univ. of NE; **HOME ADD:** 2943 Sheridan Blvd., Lincoln, NE 68502, (402)435-5707; **BUS ADD:** 245 S 84th, Lincoln, NE 68510, (402)483-2897.

GLYNN, Neil H.——*VP*, The Green Co., Inc.; **PRIM RE ACT:** Broker, Developer, Builder, Owner/Investor, Instructor; **SERVICES:** Builder, devel. of resid. housing, condo projects; **PROFL AFFIL & HONORS:** Dir. of Nat. Assn. of Home Builders, RNMI, Bd. of Trs. of Nat. Council of Housing Indus., Dir. Cape Cod Contractors & Builders Assn., NAHB Sales Mgr. of the Yr, Bill Molster Award, Best Idea of the Year Award, Life time member of Million Dollar Cir. since 1971, Hon. Member of Indus. Adv. Bd. for 1982 Multi-Housing World, Member of Nat. Assn. of RE Eds., Who's Who in the East, The Dictionary of Intl. Biography, Comm. Leaders and Noteworthy Amers. & Men of Achievement; **EDUC:** Univ. of NH; **GRAD EDUC:** Grad., Gen. Motors Inst.; **OTHER ACT & HONORS:** Former Dir. Cape Cod C of C & Home Owners Warranty Council; Charter Member and Past Pres. of the Inst. of Resid. Mktg.; Bd. of Trs. of the Nat. Sales and Mktg. Council; **BUS ADD:** 1 Belmont Rd., W Harwich, MA 02671, (617)432-1500.

GLYNN, Paul C.——B: Apr. 26, 1952, Boston, MA, *Atty.*, Paul C. Glynn, Attorney at Law; **PRIM RE ACT:** Attorney; **SERVICES:** Legal Servs.; **REP CLIENTS:** Falmouth Nat. Bank; Old Colony Bank; Plymouth Savings Bank; Title Ins. Co.; **PREV EMPLOY:** Title Examiner - Holland, Delaney & Perpall, 141 Main St., Falmouth, MA 02540; **PROFL AFFIL & HONORS:** MA Continuing Legal Educ. - Sponsor; ABA; MA Bar Assn.; Plymouth Cty. Bar Advocates; Barnstable Cty. Bar Advocates; Rotary Intl., Falmouth C of C; Falmouth Youth Hockey; **EDUC:** BA, 1977, Econ., Boston Coll.; **GRAD EDUC:** JD, 1978, Suffolk Univ. Law School; **OTHER ACT & HONORS:** Chmn., Falmouth Retirement Bd.; Falmouth Town Meeting Member; **HOME ADD:** 131 Siders Pond Rd., Falmouth, MA 02540, (617)548-8232; **BUS ADD:** 465 Main St., E. Falmouth, MA 02536, (617)548-8232.

GOCHMAN, John J.——B: Mar. 16, 1933, New York, NY, *Atty. at Law*; **PRIM RE ACT:** Attorney; **REP CLIENTS:** Conte Elec. Inc., Sleepy Hollow Medical Grp. P.C.; **PROFL AFFIL & HONORS:** ABA; NY State Bar Assn.; Westchester Cty. Bar Assn.; Peekskill Bar Assn., Acting Village Justice, Village of Croton; **EDUC:** 1954, Pol. Sci., Brooklyn Coll.; NYU; **GRAD EDUC:** JD; MA; LLB, NY Law School; New School for Social Research; **MIL SERV:** US Army, SP4; **OTHER ACT & HONORS:** Croton C of C, Pres. 1976-77; Croton Rotary Club, Pres. 1978; F & A Masons; **HOME ADD:** 19 Piney Pt. Ave., Croton on Hudson, NY 10520, (914)271-5606; **BUS ADD:** PO Box 7, 36 Oneida Ave., Croton on Hudson, NY 10520, (914)271-6236

GOCKERMAN, Bruce C.——B: July 1, 1947, Detroit, MI, *Atty.*, Gockerman & Swain; **PRIM RE ACT:** Attorney, Owner/Investor, Syndicator; **PROFL AFFIL & HONORS:** ABA, MI Bar Assn.; **EDUC:** BS, 1969, Econ., Acctg.; **GRAD EDUC:** JD, 1972, Wayne State Univ.; **EDUC HONORS:** Honors; **MIL SERV:** USA, Capt.; **HOME ADD:** 819 Locust St., Ministee, MI 49660, (616)723-3258; **BUS ADD:** 414 Water St., Manistee, MI 49660, (616)723-8333.

GODBOUT, Arthur R., Jr.——B: Oct. 7, 1957, Hartford, CT, *VP, Devel.*, Universal Structures, Inc.; **PRIM RE ACT:** Developer, Builder, Owner/Investor, Property Manager; **SERVICES:** Comml. & resid.

devel., prop. mgmt.; **PROFL AFFIL & HONORS:** Assoc. member, Hartford Cty. Home Builders Assn.; Nat. Assn. of Home Builders, Manufactured Housing Subcomm. of the Single Family Housing Comm., Nat. Assn. of Home Builders (Elected March 1981); **EDUC:** BSBA, 1979, Fin., Georgetown Univ., Washington, DC; **HOME ADD:** 98 Mountain Terr. Rd., West Hartford, CT 06107, (203)521-5757; **BUS ADD:** 550 Wilbur Cross Hwy., Berlin, CT 06037, (203)828-6513.

GODDARD, Geoff——B: Mar. 26, 1938, Surrey, England, *VP*, Grosvenor International CA, Inc.; **OTHER RE ACT:** Valuation, Negotiation; **SERVICES:** Acquisition of income producing investment RE; **REP CLIENTS:** For Grosvenor Intl. and its partners (maj. U.K. Pension Funds); **PREV EMPLOY:** Sr. VP, Mobil Land Devel. Corp. (Subsidiary of Mobil Oil); **HOME ADD:** 145 Bayview Ave., Belvedere, CA 94920, (415)435-0572; **BUS ADD:** 44 Montgomery St., San Francisco, CA 94104, (415)434-0175.

GODIN, R. J., Jr.——B: Mar. 5, 1943, Montgomery, AL, *Partner*, Southern Development Co.; **PRIM RE ACT:** Consultant, Developer, Property Manager; **SERVICES:** Apt. devel. and mgmt., consultant; **REP CLIENTS:** Consultant for various housing auth. in AL; **PROFL AFFIL & HONORS:** Nat. Leased Housing Assn.; Council for Rural Housing and Devel.; **EDUC:** BA, 1965, Pre-Law, Univ. of AL; **OTHER ACT & HONORS:** VP & Bd. of Dir. of Nat. Leased Housing Assn.; Sec. & Bd. of Dir. of Council for Rural Housing & Devel.; **HOME ADD:** 3142 Highfield Dr., Montgomery, AL 36111, (205)265-0921; **BUS ADD:** 2 Dexter Ave., (P O Box 407), Montgomery, AL 36104, (205)834-1283.

GODINHO, Joseph J.——B: Feb. 4, 1953, Ferndale, CA, *Broker/Buyer*, Cal-Real Realty; **PRIM RE ACT:** Broker, Consultant, Owner/Investor, Instructor, Syndicator; **OTHER RE ACT:** Equity sharing investor; **SERVICES:** Opinions in regard to tax implications; tax/acctg. instr.; **PREV EMPLOY:** IRS Field Agent; Coll. of Notre Dame; Modesto Jr. Coll.; W. Profl. Seminars; **PROFL AFFIL & HONORS:** Inland Soc. of Tax Consultants, Teaching Creditals in Acctg./Tax; **EDUC:** BA, AS, 1976, Acct./Econ., Stanislaus State Coll.; **HOME ADD:** 10101 Del Almendra Dr., Oakdale, CA 95361, (209)847-6362; **BUS ADD:** PO Box 711, Modesto, CA 95353, (209)847-6362.

GOEHRING, Robert W.——B: June 24, 1945, Pittsburgh, PA, *Atty.*, Craig, Goehring & Harrison; **PRIM RE ACT:** Attorney; **REP CLIENTS:** Lenders and Multi-Family Devels.; **PROFL AFFIL & HONORS:** ABA - Condo. Comm.; **EDUC:** AB, 1967, Econ., Bucknell Univ.; **GRAD EDUC:** JD, 1970, Duguesne Univ. Law School; **HOME ADD:** 1703 Georgetown Pl., Pittsburgh, PA 15235, (412)243-5479; **BUS ADD:** 1508 Law & Fin. Bldg., Pittsburgh, PA 15219, (412)281-6501.

GOETSCHEL, Arthur——*Assistant Treasurer*, Amsted Industries, Inc.; **PRIM RE ACT:** Property Manager; **BUS ADD:** 3700 Prudential Plaza, Chicago, IL 60601, (312)645-1670.*

GOETSCHIUS, James R.——B: June 1, 1931, Ramsey, NJ, *VP*, Merrill Lynch Realty, Comml. Servs.; **PRIM RE ACT:** Broker, Property Manager, Syndicator; **SERVICES:** Sale of Investment RE; leasing, sales, mgmt. of comml. RE; **PREV EMPLOY:** TIAA; Prudential; Morgan Stanley & Co. (RE Depts.); **PROFL AFFIL & HONORS:** REBNY, IREM, CPM; Pres. NJ Chap. 1 of IREM; **EDUC:** BA, 1953, Econ., Princeton Univ.; **MIL SERV:** US Army CIC, Special Agent, Korean Unit Citation; **HOME ADD:** 931 Hillcrest Rd., Ridgewood, NJ, 07450, (201)445-1070; **BUS ADD:** 919 3rd Ave., New York, NY 10022, (212)421-7000.

GOETTLICH, Faith Katcher——B: Dec. 7, 1956, Newark, NJ, *VP*, Custodial Bldg. Serv., Inc.; **OTHER RE ACT:** Bldg. cleaning contr.; **SERVICES:** Janitorial serv., window cleaning, floor serv. and new const. clean-up; **REP CLIENTS:** Anheuser Busch, Chevron USA, DuPont, First Jersey Nat. Bank Ctr.; **PREV EMPLOY:** Levinson-Zaprauskis Assoc., Philadelphia, PA, summer employment, 1979 (Arch.); **PROFL AFFIL & HONORS:** Bldg. Serv. Contrs. of Amer., ULI, Amer. Planning Assn.; **EDUC:** AB, 1978, Urban Studies, Washington Univ., St. Louis, MO; **GRAD EDUC:** Master of City Planning, 1980, Housing, RE Law & Fin., Univ. of PA, Philadelphia, PA; **EDUC HONORS:** Dean's List Distinctions; **OTHER ACT & HONORS:** Washington Univ. Alumni Assn.; **HOME ADD:** 187 Crestwood Dr., S. Orange, NJ 07079, (201)763-7939; **BUS ADD:** PO Box 97, Maplewood, NJ 07040, (201)763-3320.

GOETZ, Donald H.——B: Aug. 25, 1932, IN, *Dir. of RE*, Whirlpool Corp.; **PRIM RE ACT:** Engineer, Property Manager; **PROFL AFFIL & HONORS:** Construction Research Council, Registered Prof. Engr., Registered Pat. Agent; **EDUC:** BS, 1959, Structural Engrg., Purdue Univ.; **MIL SERV:** USA, Cpl.; **OTHER ACT & HONORS:** Pres. of School Bd. 1962-1964; V.P Construction Research Council 1982; **HOME ADD:** 5773 Ponderosa Dr., Stevensville, MI 49127, (616)429-9863; **BUS ADD:** 2000 US 33N, Benton Harbor, MI 49022.

GOETZ, Donald L.——B: Aug. 11, 1936, Phila., PA, *Pres.*, Fidelity Enterprises, Inc.; **PRIM RE ACT:** Developer, Lender, Owner/Investor; **PROFL AFFIL & HONORS:** Fin. analysts of Phila; Mort. Bankers Assn.; ULI; Life Office Mgmt. Assn.; **EDUC:** AB, 1958, Princeton Univ.; **GRAD EDUC:** LLB, 1963, Temple Univ. Law Sch.; **MIL SERV:** USAR, Capt.; **OTHER ACT & HONORS:** Dir., Arena Operating Co., Atlanta Coliseum, Inc., CAPCO, Exchange Nat. Bank, Southeastern Land Fund, Inc., White Cap, Inc.; Also affiliated with Fidelity Mutual Life Subs., Fidelity Standard Life Ins. Co., Dir., Capital Enterprises Corp., VP & Dir., FML Financial Corp., Dir. & Pres., Fidelity Enterprises, Inc., Dir. & Pres.; Dir. of various other RE wholly-owned subsidiaries of Fidelity Enterprises, Inc.; **HOME ADD:** 1232 Valley Rd., Rydal, PA 19046, (215)572-0792; **BUS ADD:** Fidelity Mutual Life Bldg., PA, S. Penn Sq., Philadelphia 19101, (215)977-8250.

GOETZ, Lewis J.——B: Nov. 27, 1945, Passaic, NJ, *Dir.*, Greenwell Goetz Architects, PC; **PRIM RE ACT:** Architect; **SERVICES:** Architecture, space planning, cost; analyses, interior design, arch. graphics, furniture design; **REP CLIENTS:** Boston Properties, Inc., Toyota, TX Eastern, Dun & Bradstreet, John Akridge Co., Leggat, McCall & Werner, Nat. Council on the Aging, Inc., Morrison & Foerster, Nat. Fire Protection Assn., Planning Research Corp.; **PREV EMPLOY:** Leo A. Daly Co. 1975&1979, In charge of design & planning, Washington, DC office; **PROFL AFFIL & HONORS:** AIA, NCARB, Nat. Trust for Historic Preservation; **EDUC:** BArch, 1970, OH State Univ., Columbus OH; **EDUC HONORS:** Recipient of Reynolds Metals Award 1970; **HOME ADD:** 3318 20th St, NE, Washington, DC 20018, (202)526-2244; **BUS ADD:** 1606 20th St., NW, Washington, DC 20009, (202)466-4610.

GOFF, Lyman——B: June 30, 1943, Providence, RI, Lyman Goff Crch.; **PRIM RE ACT:** Architect, Developer, Builder, Owner/Investor; **PREV EMPLOY:** Carlin/Pozzi Archs. 1968-1971, New Haven, CT; **PROFL AFFIL & HONORS:** AIA; CT Soc. of Archs. NCARB; Registered MA, CT, RI; **EDUC:** BA, 1965, Arch., Princeton Univ.; **GRAD EDUC:** MFA, 1968, Arch., Princeton Univ.; **EDUC HONORS:** Cum Laude; **HOME ADD:** Sequan Rd., Watch Hill, RI 02891, (401)596-5139; **BUS ADD:** 10 Water St., Mystic, CT 06355, (203)572-0514.

GOGGANS, Travis P.——B: Nov.11, 1929, Littlefield, TX, *Prof. of Acctg.*, University of Oklahoma; **PRIM RE ACT:** Consultant, Owner/Investor, Property Manager, Real Estate Publisher; **PROFL AFFIL & HONORS:** OK Soc. of CPA's, Amer. Acctg. Assn., CPA, PhD, Author of over 50 articles dealing with taxation and author of textbook to be published by Prentice Hall in 1982 titled *Estate Planning and Practice Handbook*; **EDUC:** BBA, 1957, Acctg., Econ, RE, Fin., OK Univ.; **GRAD EDUC:** MBA, 1958, Acctg., fin., OK Univ.; PhD, 1963, Econ., OK Univ.; **EDUC HONORS:** Grad. with Distinction, Beta Gamma Sigma, Omicron Chi Epsilon; **MIL SERV:** USAF, SGT.; **OTHER ACT & HONORS:** Past Grand Patron OK Order of E. Star, All Masonic Orders; **HOME ADD:** 742 Terrace Pl., Norman, OK 73069, (405)329-6409; **BUS ADD:** 200 W. Brooks, Norman, OK 73069, (405)325-4221.

GOHL, Eugene G.——B: Nov. 15, 1931, Cumberland, WI, *Owner and Pres.*, G-G Appraisals, Ltd.; **PRIM RE ACT:** Consultant, Appraiser, Instructor, Assessor; **REP CLIENTS:** Numerous municipalities, lending instns., banks, corps., and indivs.; **PREV EMPLOY:** WI Dept. of Revenue (Appraiser) 16 yrs.; **PROFL AFFIL & HONORS:** Soc. of RE Appraisers; Intl. Assn. of Assessing Officers; Indianhead Assn. of Assessing Officers, SRPA and CAE; **EDUC:** BS, 1950, Agriculture, Univ. of WI; **HOME ADD:** 1203 Lee St., Rice Lake, WI 54868, (715)234-4079; **BUS ADD:** 321 N. Main St., Rice Lake, WI 54868, (715)234-4093.

GOIHMAN, David——B: July 27, 1939, Caracas, Venezuela, *Partner Mgr.*, G&D Enterprises Ltd.; **PRIM RE ACT:** Consultant, Developer, Builder, Owner/Investor, Property Manager, Syndicator; **SERVICES:** Provide consultation for foreign investors; **PREV EMPLOY:** Head of Public Relations Dept., First Nat. City Bank, Miranda Branch, Caracas-Venezuela (1970-1971); **PROFL AFFIL & HONORS:** Union Federal S & L Assn. of Miami, Dir. Advisory Bd.; **EDUC:** Lee Inst., Boston MA; AA, 1961, Univ. of Hartford; **OTHER ACT & HONORS:** Young Pres. Club; Mt. Sinai Hospital; **HOME ADD:** 6370 Allison Rd., Miami Beach, FL 33141, (305)868-1556; **BUS ADD:** 2125 Biscayne Blvd., Miami, FL 33137, (305)573-6514.

GOING, James M.——**B:** Mar. 14, 1940, Portland, OR, *VP/Sec.*, Alhadeff/Going & Associates, Inc.; **OTHER RE ACT:** Real Estate Developement, Consulting, Investment; **SERVICES:** Prop. devel. & mgmt., consultation; **REP CLIENTS:** Seattle First Nat. Bank, RE Trust Dept; Piers Assocs.; Town Center Assoc.; Winmar; Red Robin Enterprises; Lasher & Johnson; Everett Marina Village Assoc.; Pacific West Realty Trust; Pentagram, Inc.; Bellevue Downtown Assn.; King Cty. East Tourist & Convention Bureau; Bell, Isaki & Assocs.; Tulalip Tribes; **PREV EMPLOY:** Town Center Assocs.; Piers Assocs.; Pentagram Props., Inc.; Olympia Highlands; Mill Park Assocs.; Valley River Devel., Inc.; Inlet Devel. Assoc.; Consultant - LCF Assoc.; Intl. Council of Shopping Centers; State Dir., WA, AK & ID; **PROFL AFFIL & HONORS:** Tr., Pacific West Realty Trust, Elected member of Lambda Alpha hon. frat.; **EDUC:** AB, 1963, Econ., Whitman Coll.; **GRAD EDUC:** MBA, 1965, Gen. Program, Univ. of Chicago; **EDUC HONORS:** Who's Who in Amer. Univs. and Colls.; **HOME ADD:** 4726 91st S.E., Mercer Island, WA 98040, (206)232-2302; **BUS ADD:** 100 S King St., Suite 350, Seattle, WA 98104.

GOLANTY, George C.——**B:** Nov. 5, 1913, Pittsburgh, PA, *Broker*; **PRIM RE ACT:** Broker, Consultant, Owner/Investor, Syndicator; **SERVICES:** Counseling & devel. synd. for comml. props. & land deals; **EDUC:** BS, 1935, Bus. Admin., Univ. of Pittsburgh; **HOME ADD:** 16500 N Park Dr., Suite 1514, Southfield, MI 48075, (313)559-5059; **BUS ADD:** 16500 N. Park Dr., Suite 1514, Southfield, MI 48075, (313)559-5059.

GOLANTY, James S.——**B:** May 31, 1940, Detroit, MI, *VP, Gen. Counsel*, Lambrecht Realty Co., Lambrecht Mort. Co.; **PRIM RE ACT:** Broker, Consultant, Attorney, Lender, Owner/Investor; **SERVICES:** FHA Multifamily Packaging & Lending; **PROFL AFFIL & HONORS:** MI & CO Bar, Mort. Bankers of Amer.; **EDUC:** BA, 1962, Univ. of MI; **GRAD EDUC:** JD, 1965, Wayne State Univ.; **HOME ADD:** 756 Race, Denver, CO; **BUS ADD:** 770 Grant, Suite 218, Denver, CO 80203, (303)832-4000.

GOLD, Annette M.——**B:** Feb. 18, 1939, Albion, NE, *Assoc. Broker*, Woods Bros. Realty, Lincolnshire Office; **PRIM RE ACT:** Broker; **SERVICES:** Selling & listing; **PREV EMPLOY:** Banking-First Mid Amer.; **PROFL AFFIL & HONORS:** Lincoln Bd. of Realtors-NAR, Woods Bros. Realtor of the Yr. (1979), GRI; **OTHER ACT & HONORS:** Charter Women's Pool League; Sunrise Toastmasters; **HOME ADD:** 4035 Teri Lane, Lincoln, NE 68502, (402)489-3580; **BUS ADD:** 1630 S. 170th, Suite 100, Lincoln, NE 68506, (402)483-4741.

GOLD, Herbert Z.——**B:** Feb. 16, 1915, New York, NY, *Partner*, Stackler, Frank & Gold; **PRIM RE ACT:** Developer, Builder, Owner/Investor, Property Manager; **OTHER RE ACT:** Self-employed as Builder and Urban Renewal, Developer & Sponsor; **PROFL AFFIL & HONORS:** Life Dir., LI Builders Inst.; Life Dir., NAHB, Organizer & Chmn. Apt. House Council LIBI; **EDUC:** BS in Econ., 1936, Wharton School, Univ. of PA; **GRAD EDUC:** JD, 1940, NY Univ. Law School; **OTHER ACT & HONORS:** Woodmere Bay Y.C. Commodore; Dir., Nassau Cty. Day Care Council and Rockville Ctr. Headstart Programs; **HOME ADD:** 1332 Boxwood Dr., Hewlett Harbor, NY 11557, (516)374-3606; **BUS ADD:** PO Box 319, 77 No. Centre Ave., Rockville Ctr., NY 11571, (516)678-3888.

GOLD, Jeffrey M.——**B:** Dec. 30, 1954, Brooklyn, NY, *RE Exec.*, Tenzer Greenblatt Fallon & Kaplan; **PRIM RE ACT:** Broker, Consultant, Attorney, Developer, Property Manager; **PREV EMPLOY:** Tax Spec., Deloitte Haskins & Sells; **PROFL AFFIL & HONORS:** Assn. of The Bar of the City of NY; **EDUC:** BS, 1976, Acctg., Brooklyn Coll.; **GRAD EDUC:** JD, 1979, Law, Boston Univ. Sch. of Law; **EDUC HONORS:** Cum Laude, Moot Court, Best Brief, Best Overall; **HOME ADD:** 69-40 108th St., Forest Hills, NY 11375, (212)268-1596; **BUS ADD:** 405 Lexington Ave., NY, NY 10174, (212)573-4362.

GOLD, Seymour B.——**B:** Sept. 3, 1922, New York, NY, *Pres.*, Gold Mort. Co.; **PRIM RE ACT:** Broker, Consultant, Appraiser, Lender, Instructor; **OTHER RE ACT:** Mort. consultant Mortage Broker; **SERVICES:** Mort. portfolio mgmt., evaluation & consultation in regards to real prop. and existing mort.; **REP CLIENTS:** Prop. owners seeking fin. investors and lenders offering fin. and holders of existing morts.; **PROFL AFFIL & HONORS:** Past Pres. Nat. Assn. of Mort. Brokers; Past. Pres. FL Assn. of Mort. Brokers; Past. Chmn., Bd. of Govs., Soc. of Mort. Consultants; Nat. Assn. of Indep. Fee Appraisers, Nat. Assn of Review Appraisers, IFAS, CRA, SMC, GRI; **MIL SERV:** USAF, S/Sgt., 1943-45, Air Medal with 5 clusters; **OTHER ACT & HONORS:** Adjunct Prof. for RE Univ. of FL & Broward Comm. Coll.; RE Brown Comm. Coll; **BUS ADD:** 2610 W Oakland Park Blvd., Ft. Lauderdale, FL 33311.

GOLD, Steven H.——**B:** Apr. 30, 1940, Los Angeles, CA, *Chmn.*, Center Financial Group; **PRIM RE ACT:** Lender, Owner/Investor, Syndicator; **OTHER RE ACT:** Mort. banking; Mort. broker; **SERVICES:** joint venture fin.; **PROFL AFFIL & HONORS:** UCLA RE Advisory Comm.; UCSD Advisory; UCLA Sch. of Arch. & Urban Planning; ICSC; RE Cabinet USF; **EDUC:** BS, 1961, Bus., CSULA; **GRAD EDUC:** MBA, 1963, Fin., UCLA; **EDUC HONORS:** Dean's List; **MIL SERV:** US Army, Sp.4; **HOME ADD:** 3336 Dona Rosa, Studio City, CA 91607; **BUS ADD:** 1888 Century Park E., Los Angeles, CA 90067, (213)553-2353.

GOLDBERG, Arnold——**B:** Dec. 22, 1944, Norwich, CT, *Pres., Broker*, CA Lake Lands, Inc., RE, Prefabricated Homes, Recreation Props.; **PRIM RE ACT:** Broker, Consultant, Appraiser, Owner/Investor; **OTHER RE ACT:** Bldg. coordinator, notary public; **SERVICES:** Spec. in recreation lake props.; **PROFL AFFIL & HONORS:** Nevada Cty. Bd. of Realtors, CA Assoc. of Realtors & NAR; **EDUC:** AA, 1964, Bus., Sacramento City Coll.; **OTHER ACT & HONORS:** Loyal Order of Moose; Secretary, R.G. Cooley, Construction, Inc.; **HOME ADD:** 14907 Lake Ln., Cascade Shores, CA 95959, (916)265-5775; **BUS ADD:** PO Box 1272, Nevada City, CA 95959, (916)265-4488.

GOLDBERG, Arthur M.——*President*, Triangle Industries, Inc.; **PRIM RE ACT:** Property Manager; **BUS ADD:** PO Box 850, Holmdel, NJ 07733, (201)946-8500.*

GOLDBERG, George——**B:** May 25, 1921, Brooklyn, NY, *Dir. of Housing*, The DeMatteis Organizations; **PRIM RE ACT:** Broker, Consultant, Insuror, Syndicator; **OTHER RE ACT:** CPA (NY); **SERVICES:** Tax, Ins., Synds., Banking, Consulting; **PREV EMPLOY:** Partner in Kandel Schaeffer Co. CPAs; **PROFL AFFIL & HONORS:** Member of AICPA, NY State Soc. of CPAs; **EDUC:** BBA, 1943, Acctg., City Coll. of NY; **GRAD EDUC:** 1950, Taxes, NY Univ.; **HOME ADD:** 1590 W 8th St., Brooklyn, NY 11204, (212)232-4835; **BUS ADD:** 820 Elmont Rd., Elmont, NY 11003, (516)285-5500.

GOLDBERG, Jack——*Ed.*, Apt. Owners & Mgrs. Assn of America, Apartment Management Report, Apt. Owners & Mgrs of Amer. Newsletter; **PRIM RE ACT:** Real Estate Publisher; **BUS ADD:** 65 Cherry Ave., Watertown, CT 06795, (203)274-2589.*

GOLDBERG, James Stone——**B:** Feb. 4, 1950, Louisville, KY, Goldberg & Simpson, PSC; **PRIM RE ACT:** Attorney; **SERVICES:** Gen. legal serv. concerning comml. & resid. RE transactions and RE foreclosure litigation on behalf of various fin. instns.; **REP CLIENTS:** Portland Fed. S&L, Louisville, KY; Cowger & Miller Mort. Co., Inc., Louisville, KY; Lomas & Nettleton Co., Philadelphia, PA; Realty Mort. Inc., Atlanta, GA; **PREV EMPLOY:** 1976-1977 Asst. Atty. Gen. Commonwealth of KY; **PROFL AFFIL & HONORS:** ABA, KY Bar Assn., Louisville Bar Assn.; **EDUC:** BS, 1972, Bus. & Econ., School of Bus., IN Univ.; **GRAD EDUC:** JD, 1976, Law, Univ. of Louisville, School of Law; **EDUC HONORS:** Dean's List; **HOME ADD:** 11021 Bretchin Rd., Louisville, KY 40243, (502)245-4852; **BUS ADD:** 2800 First National Tower, Louisville, KY 40202, (502)589-4440.

GOLDBERG, Michael A.——**B:** Aug. 30, 1941, Brooklyn, NY, *Herbert R. Fullerton Prof. of Urban Land Policy and Assoc. Dean*, Faculty of Commerce and Bus. Admin., Univ. of BC; **OTHER RE ACT:** Academic; **SERVICES:** Teaching and research in a broad range of fields related to RE and urban devel.; **PREV EMPLOY:** Research Assoc., Center for RE and Urban Econ., Univ. of CA at Berkeley from 1965-68. At UBC since 1968; **PROFL AFFIL & HONORS:** Amer. RE and Urban Econ. Assn., Rgnl. Sci. Assn., Amer. Planning Assn., Amer. Econ. Assn., Can. Econ. Assn., Can. Rgnl. Sci. Assn., ULI; **EDUC:** BA, 1962, Econ., Brooklyn Coll.; **GRAD EDUC:** MA, 1965, Econ., Univ. of CA at Berkeley; PhD, 1968, Econ., Univ. of CA at Berkeley; **EDUC HONORS:** Cum Laude; **OTHER ACT & HONORS:** Chmn., Transportation Research Bd. Comm. on Urban Acitivity Systems; Vancouver Econ. Advisory Commn.; various editorial bds. of journals; Dir., Amer. RE and Urban Econ. Assn.; **HOME ADD:** 5587 Olympic St., Vancouver, V6N 1Z4, BC, Can., (604)263-4764; **BUS ADD:** 2053 Main Mall, Vancouver, V6T 1Y8, BC, Can, (604)228-2749.

GOLDBERG, Nathan M.——**B:** June 16, 1924, Albany, NY, *Atty./CPA*, Goldberg & Gottheim; **PRIM RE ACT:** Attorney; **SERVICES:** Legal; **PROFL AFFIL & HONORS:** ABA; Amer. Assn. of Atty.-CPA's; AICPA; all state and Local chap.; NYS Soc. of CPA's, Albany Cty. Bar Assn., NYS Bar Assn., JD, LLB, CPA; **EDUC:** BBA, 1946, Acctg., Siena Coll.; **GRAD EDUC:** JD, 1949, Law, Albany Law Sch. of Union Univ.; **EDUC HONORS:** Magna Cum Laude; **MIL SERV:** USN, Ens.; **OTHER ACT & HONORS:** Past Nat. Cmdr., Jewish War Veterans of USA; Member of Nat. Exec. Comm. of a number of orgs. and Past Pres. of local comm. agencies; **HOME ADD:** 175 Tampa Ave., Albany, NY; **BUS ADD:** 75 State St., Albany, NY 12207.

GOLDBERGER, Melvin T.——B: June 6, 1919, Knoxville, TN, *Pres.*, GIC Corp.; **PRIM RE ACT:** Consultant, Developer, Owner/Investor; **EDUC:** BS in Bus. Admin., 1940, OH State Univ.; **MIL SERV:** Med. Adm. Corps., 1st Lt.; **HOME ADD:** 901 E. Camino Real, Boca Raton, FL 33432, (305)426-1250; **BUS ADD:** 1700 S. Dixie Hwy., Royal Palm Tower I, Boca Raton, FL 33432, (305)392-9777.

GOLDEN, D. Daniel——B: Oct. 9, 1921, Milwaukee, WI, *Sr. Partner*, Laventhol & Horwath; **PRIM RE ACT:** Consultant; **OTHER RE ACT:** CPA; **REP CLIENTS:** Consolidated Capital RREEF; **EDUC:** BS, 1942, Commerce, Acctg., Northwestern Univ.; **EDUC HONORS:** BAY; **MIL SERV:** USN, Res.; Lt. SC; **BUS ADD:** 50 California St., 2450, San Francisco, CA 94111, (415)989-0110.

GOLDEN, E. Ted——B: Sept. 9, 1920, Wheeling, WV, *Owner*, E. Ted Golden, MAI; **PRIM RE ACT:** Consultant, Appraiser; **SERVICES:** Valuation reports, ct. testimony, consultations, mkt. research; **REP CLIENTS:** Resid., comml., office, shopping ctr., indus., instnl., recreational, rural props. in WV, OH, Western PA, Western MD; **PREV EMPLOY:** Musician (trumpet) with NBC Wheeling Steel Musical Steelmakers, 1937-1942; **PROFL AFFIL & HONORS:** Member, Nat. Appraisal Review Comm.; Dir. and past Chmn. of OH Chap. AIREA; Morgantown Bd. of Realtors; Wheeling Bd. of Realtors; Belmont Cty. Bd. of Realtors, MAI, RE Broker, States of OH & WV; **EDUC:** BS, 1942, Biology/Chemistry, Bethany Coll., Bethany, WV; **GRAD EDUC:** MS, 1947, Biology/Hist., Case Western Reserve Univ., Cleveland, OH; **EDUC HONORS:** Honors in Hist.; **MIL SERV:** USN Res.; 1943-1946, Lt.; **OTHER ACT & HONORS:** AF&FM; Scottish Rite; and AAONMS (Osiris Temple); Kappa Alpha Order; **HOME ADD:** Harewood, Box 3, Morgantown, WV 26505, (304)594-1700; **BUS ADD:** Harewood, Box 3, Morgantown, WV 26505, (304)594-1700.

GOLDENBERG, Mark C.——B: June 12, 1949, St. Louis, MO, *Atty.*, Ross Constr. Co.; **PRIM RE ACT:** Attorney, Developer, Builder, Syndicator; **OTHER RE ACT:** Tax planning & fin. acctg.; **SERVICES:** Acquisition, devel., legal & tax planning; **REP CLIENTS:** Land owners, investors in comml. & devel. resid. projects; **PREV EMPLOY:** Peat, Marwick, Mitchell & Co., CPA's; **PROFL AFFIL & HONORS:** ABA, IL State Bar Assn., Madison Cty. Bar Assn., CPA, Atty. at Law; **EDUC:** BS, 1970, Acctg., Univ. of IL; **GRAD EDUC:** JD, 1973, Univ. of IL; **EDUC HONORS:** Dean's List; **HOME ADD:** 2637 Westmoreland St., Granite City, IL 62040, (618)931-6450; **BUS ADD:** 3701 Nameoki Rd., Granite City, IL 62040, (618)452-0600.

GOLDENHERSH, Robert S.——B: July 23, 1922, St. Louis, MO, *Partner*, Rosenblum, Goldenhersh, Silverstein & Zafft; **PRIM RE ACT:** Attorney; **SERVICES:** Gen. RE, constr. co., fin. commitments, synd.; **REP CLIENTS:** The Michelson Org.; Paragon Group (formerly Lincoln Prop.); Pioneer Nat. Title Ins. Co.; **PROFL AFFIL & HONORS:** ABA; MO Bar Assn.; St. Louis Bar Assn.; St. Louis County Bar Assn.; Prop. Comm., MO & St. Louis Bar Assns.; **GRAD EDUC:** LLM, 1948, Taxation, NYU; JD, Washington Univ.; **MIL SERV:** USAC, 1943-1946; **HOME ADD:** 211 Rondelay Ct., St. Louis, MO 63141, (314)432-2222; **BUS ADD:** 777 Bonhomme, Suite 1414, St. Louis, MO 63105, (314)726-6868.

GOLDFIELD, Alfred S.——B: July 5, 1939, Hartford, CT, *Part.*, Herzfeld & Rubin, P. C.; **PRIM RE ACT:** Attorney; **REP CLIENTS:** Large number of domestic and intl. clients dealing in RE; **PROFL AFFIL & HONORS:** NY State Bar Assn; Assn. of the bar of the Cty of NY; Member of Manhattan Community Bd. 8; **EDUC:** BA, 1961, Psych./Bio., Yale Univ.; **GRAD EDUC:** JD, 1964, Columbia Law School; **EDUC HONORS:** Elizabethan Soc., Scroll & Key Soc., Dean's List; **OTHER ACT & HONORS:** Bd. of Dirs., Manhattan Theatre Club, Yale Alumni Fund; **HOME ADD:** 155 E. 76th St., NY, NY 10021; **BUS ADD:** 40 Wall St., NY, NY 10005, (212)344-0680.

GOLDFINE, Jerald L.——B: Oct. 8, 1954, Philadelphia, PA, *Controller*, Cynwyd Investments; **PRIM RE ACT:** Owner/Investor; **PREV EMPLOY:** Arthur Andersen &. Co. 1978-1980; **PROFL AFFIL & HONORS:** AICPA, PICPA; **EDUC:** BA, 1976, Econs., Dickinson Coll.; **GRAD EDUC:** MBA, 1978, Acctg., NY Univ.; **HOME ADD:** 48 Llanfair Rd. #11, Ardmore, PA 19003; **BUS ADD:** 725 Conshohocken State Rd., Bala Cynwyd, PA 19003, (215)839-4100.

GOLDIN, Edward S.——B: Apr. 13, 1930, Providence, RI, *VP*, Pucci & Goldin, Inc., Attys. at Law; **PRIM RE ACT:** Attorney, Developer, Owner/Investor; **SERVICES:** Sect. of Ltd. Partnerships, title, leasing; **REP CLIENTS:** Hillcrest Village Associates, BGS Realty Co., The One Fifty-Eight Partnership, BO Realty Associates, P&G Realty Associates, Fin. Investors, Inc., Local Banks, Local Counsel for Arco Loan and Investment Co.; **PROFL AFFIL & HONORS:** ABA; RI Bar Assn.; RI Realtors Assn.; Comml. Law League of Amer.; ATLA, BS, JD; **EDUC:** BS, 1952, URI; **GRAD EDUC:** JD, 1955, BU Law School; **OTHER ACT & HONORS:** City Councilman, Providence, 1962-1974; Pres., Temple Beth El; Providence, RI United Way; Jewish Fed. of RI; **HOME ADD:** 51 Harwich Rd., Providence, RI 02906, (401)272-9757; **BUS ADD:** 123 Dyer St., Providence, RI 02903, (401)861-7400.

GOLDING, Jerome——B: Dec. 24, 1913, New York, NY, *Owner*, Jerome and Rachel Golding; **PRIM RE ACT:** Broker, Property Manager, Owner/Investor; **EDUC:** 1935, PreMed.; **GRAD EDUC:** BA, 1935, NYC; **HOME ADD:** 46 E. 65th St., New York, NY, (212)988-9128; **BUS ADD:** 46 E. 65th St., NY, NY 10021, (212)988-9128.

GOLDMAN, Aaron——B: Jan. 13, 1919, Brooklyn, NY, *Partner*, Goldman & Goldman; **PRIM RE ACT:** Broker, Consultant, Engineer, Appraiser, Developer, Lender, Builder, Owner/Investor, Syndicator; **OTHER RE ACT:** RE & Morts., Mort. Bankers, Consulting Engrs., Construction Mgrs., Gen. Contractors, Electrical Contractors; **SERVICES:** Const., RE, fin., planning, construction, consulting; **REP CLIENTS:** Consulting Engrs.; Attys.; Devels.; Investors; Condo. Assns.; **EDUC:** BCHE, 1940, Sch. of Tech., Coll. of NYC; **GRAD EDUC:** MBA, 1971, Gen. Bus., FL Atlantic Univ.; DBA, 1982, Nova Univ.; **MIL SERV:** USAF, Signal Corps., Capt.; **HOME ADD:** 1101-88th St., Surfside, FL 33154, (305)866-7334; **BUS ADD:** 1123-71st St., Miami Beach, FL 33141, (305)866-7334.

GOLDMAN, Elwin J.——B: June 5, 1922, Chicago, IL, *CPA*, Mittenthal Goldman & Co.; **PRIM RE ACT:** Consultant; **OTHER RE ACT:** CPA; **SERVICES:** Consultation, Tax Advice, Synd.; **EDUC:** Commerce, 1948, Northwestern Univ.; **MIL SERV:** Signal Corps, Sgt. Mjr., Purple Heart; **HOME ADD:** 9520 Tripp, Skokie, IL 60076, (312)674-5652; **BUS ADD:** 5214 W. Main St., Skokie, IL 60077, (312)673-0930.

GOLDMAN, Gary——B: July 13, 1953, Toronto, *VP*, Goldfan Holdings Ltd.; **PRIM RE ACT:** Broker, Appraiser, Builder, Owner/Investor, Property Manager; **OTHER RE ACT:** Development Expeditor, Acquisitions, Marketing; **SERVICES:** Develop, build & market; **PREV EMPLOY:** The Cadillac Fairview Corp., A.E. LePage (Ont) Ltd.; **PROFL AFFIL & HONORS:** Can. Inst. of Planners, Toronto RE Assn.; **EDUC:** BA, 1975, Soc., Acadia Univ.; **GRAD EDUC:** MES, 1978, Urban Planning, Environ. Studies, York Univ.; **MIL SERV:** Cadet Corp., Kings Coll. Sch., Windsor, NS; **HOME ADD:** 33 Stillwater Cres., Willowdale, Ont., Can, (416)665-5787; **BUS ADD:** 250 Madison Ave., Toronto, M4T 1X3, Ont., Can., (416)962-9080.

GOLDMAN, Jay——B: July 3, 1943, Charleston, WV, *Owner*, Goldman Associates; **PRIM RE ACT:** Broker, Consultant, Attorney, Appraiser; **SERVICES:** RE comml./indus. brokerage, appraising; **REP CLIENTS:** Union Carbide, Carbon Indus., McJunkin Corp., Bethlehem Steel; **PROFL AFFIL & HONORS:** NAR, RNMI, SIR, CCIM; **EDUC:** BS, 1966, Bus. Admin. RE, Morris Harvey Coll./Univ. of Charleston; **GRAD EDUC:** JD, 1970, WV Univ. Coll. of Law; **EDUC HONORS:** Wall Street Journal Award; **MIL SERV:** US Army, Officer; **OTHER ACT & HONORS:** Judge, City of Charleston, 1975-1981; **HOME ADD:** P.O. Box 3184, Charleston, WV 25332, (304)343-5695; **BUS ADD:** P.O. Box 3184, Charleston, WV 25332, (304)343-5695.

GOLDMAN, Merton B.——B: June 16, 1948, El Paso, TX, *Atty.*, Sole Practitioner; **PRIM RE ACT:** Attorney; **SERVICES:** Legal Services Re: Acquisition, Devel., Fin., Sydication, Sale of Comml. and Resid. Prop.; **REP CLIENTS:** Lenders, Devels., Synd.; **PREV EMPLOY:** US Securities & Exchange Comm., Wash., D.C. - Enforcement Div.) Lackshin & Nathan, Esqs., Houston, Tx (1977-1980); **PROFL AFFIL & HONORS:** State Bar of TX (Real Prop. Sect.); ABA (Real Prop. Sect.); **EDUC:** BA, 1970, Econ.-Acctg., Claremont Men's Coll., Claremont, CA; **GRAD EDUC:** JD, 1973, Law, Univ. of Houston - Bates Coll. of Law; **EDUC HONORS:** Stag (Honor-Service Grp.), Baron's (Scholastic Honor Grp.); Honor Court Judge; **HOME ADD:** 7133 Gran Vida, El Paso, TX 79912, (915)581-1571; **BUS ADD:** 4849 North Mesa, Ste. 220, El Paso, TX 79912, (915)532-1222.

GOLDMAN, Nathan——B: May 2, 1909, USA, *VP of the Bd.*, Sonnenblick-Goldman Corp.; **PRIM RE ACT:** Broker; **HOME ADD:** 778 Park Ave., New York, NY 10021, (212)879-5971; **BUS ADD:** 1251 Avenue of the Americas, New York, NY 10020, (212)541-4321.

GOLDMAN, S. Howard——B: Jan.2, 1930, Brooklyn, NY, *Part.*; **PRIM RE ACT:** Developer, Builder, Owner/Investor; **PREV EMPLOY:** M. Robert Goldman & Sons, Mort. Bankers (owner/partner); **PROFL AFFIL & HONORS:** RE Bd. of NY; **EDUC:** BS, 1951, RE, Syracuse Univ.; **GRAD EDUC:** MBA, 1953, Indus. Mgmt., Wharton School of the Univ. of PA; **EDUC HONORS:** Dean's List; **OTHER**

ACT & HONORS: Member, Bd. of Dirs., Diagnostic Data, Inc.; **HOME ADD:** 214 Good Hill Rd., Weston, CT 06883, (203)226-7771; **BUS ADD:** 1860 Broadway, New York, NY 10023, (212)307-0404.

GOLDNER, Arthur——**B:** Aug. 5, 1950, Haifa, Israel, *Pres.*, Arthur Goldner & Associates, Inc.; **PRIM RE ACT:** Broker, Developer, Owner/Investor, Property Manager, Syndicator; **PREV EMPLOY:** RE Salesman; **PROFL AFFIL & HONORS:** No. Side RE Bd., Evanston N. Shore Bd. of Realtors, Chicago RE Bd., RESSI, NAR; **EDUC:** 3 yrs. Univ. of IL, 1969-72, Arch.; **HOME ADD:** 40 Maple Hill Rd., Glencoe, IL 60022, (312)835-1782; **BUS ADD:** 914 Chicago Ave., Evanston, IL 60202, (312)475-5100.

GOLDSTEIN, Barry J.——*VP*, Property Services, Inc.; **PRIM RE ACT:** Developer; **BUS ADD:** 815 South Main St., Ste. 333, Jacksonville, FL 32207, (904)396-1782.*

GOLDSTEIN, Gilbert——**B:** Jan. 21, 1931, Philadelphia, PA, *Pres.*, Raymond Goldstein & Co.; **PRIM RE ACT:** Broker, Developer, Owner/Investor, Property Manager; **OTHER RE ACT:** Condo. Conversion; **SERVICES:** Investment prop. devel., brokerage, purchasing and mgmt.; **PREV EMPLOY:** Self employed; **PROFL AFFIL & HONORS:** NARB; PA Assoc. RE Bds.; Philadelphia Bd. of Realtors; ICSC; **EDUC:** BA, 1951, Bus., PA State Univ.; **MIL SERV:** USAF, 1st. Lt., 1951-53; **OTHER ACT & HONORS:** Green Valley Country Club, Philadelphia; Hunters Run Country Club, Del Rey Beach, FL; Chmn. Jewish Sr. Adult Activities & Research, Greater Philadelphia area; **HOME ADD:** 1830 Rittenhouse Sq., Philadelphia, PA 19103, (215)732-1212; **BUS ADD:** 1808 Rittenhouse Sq., Philadelphia, PA 19103, (215)735-0770.

GOLDSTEIN, Howard——**B:** Jan. 16, 1942, Wilkes-Barre, PA, *Pres.*, GFI Development Co.; **PRIM RE ACT:** Developer; **SERVICES:** Devel. of comml. and indusl. props.; **PREV EMPLOY:** VP and Gen. Counsel, Watt Indusl., Inc.; **PROFL AFFIL & HONORS:** Members of VA, Dist. of Columbia and CA Bars; **EDUC:** BS, 1963, Econ., PA State Unv.,; **GRAD EDUC:** JD, 1966, Georgetown Univ. Law Ctr.; **EDUC HONORS:** Omicron Delta Kappa, Beta Gamma Sigma; **MIL SERV:** US Army; Capt.; 1966-1968; **HOME ADD:** P.O. Box 2652, Rancho Santa Fe, CA 92067, (714)756-5521; **BUS ADD:** P.O. Box 1624, Rancho Santa Fe, CA 92067, (714)756-3707.

GOLDSTEIN, James F.——**B:** Jan. 1, 1940, Milwaukee, WI, *VP*, Carlsberg Fin. Corp., Acquisitions-investments; **PRIM RE ACT:** Consultant, Owner/Investor; **OTHER RE ACT:** Income prop. acquisition specialist; **SERVICES:** Negotiation and acquisition of large income props. for profl. buyers, particularly mobile home parks; **REP CLIENTS:** Profl. income prop. investors, synd. and devels.; **PREV EMPLOY:** VP of Carlsberg Fin. for 15 years; **EDUC:** BA, 1962, Econ., Stanford Univ.; **GRAD EDUC:** MBA, 1964, UCLA Bus. School; **HOME ADD:** 10104 Angelo View, Beverly Hills, CA 90210; **BUS ADD:** 2800 28th St., 2nd Floor, Santa Monica, CA 90405, (213)450-6800.

GOLDSTEIN, Joel——*Dir. RE & Contract Mgr.*, Mohawk Data Sciences Corp.; **PRIM RE ACT:** Property Manager; **BUS ADD:** 7 Century Dr., Parsippany, NJ 07054, (201)540-9080.*

GOLDSTEIN, Larry A.——**B:** June 9, 1947, Wilkes Barre, PA, *VP*, Berger/Berman Group, Berger/Berman Builders, Inc.; **PRIM RE ACT:** Developer, Builder, Owner/Investor; **SERVICES:** Comml. & resid. const. & devel. mgmt.; **REP CLIENTS:** Lending Instns.; **PREV EMPLOY:** Planner, Anne Arundel Cty. (1971-73); Dir. of Land Planning, Dewberry, Nealon & Davis, Annapolis, MD (1973-76); Berger/Berman (1976-81); **EDUC:** BA, 1969, Poli. Sci., PA State Univ.; **GRAD EDUC:** MUP, 1971, Land Planning, Univ. of Pittsburgh; **EDUC HONORS:** Parmi Nous & Blue Key Hon. Socs.; **HOME ADD:** 2605 Oakenshield Dr., Potomac, MD 20854; **BUS ADD:** 6101 Montrose Rd., Rockville, MD 20852, (301)770-2280.

GOLDSTEIN, Laurence S.——**B:** Nov. 4, 1946, Los Angeles, CA, *Pres.*, Laurence S. Goldstein and Co., Inc.; **PRIM RE ACT:** Developer; **OTHER RE ACT:** Broker; **PREV EMPLOY:** 1974-1977 Self-employed investment consultant; 1971-1974 Acct. Exec. Merrill Lynch; **PROFL AFFIL & HONORS:** Bldg. Industry Assn./So. CA; **EDUC:** BA, 1968, Hist., CA State Univ. - Northridge; **BUS ADD:** 8601 Wilshire Blvd., Suite 601, Beverly Hills, CA 90211, (213)659-1556.

GOLDSTEIN, Leonard R.——**B:** Apr. 15, 1943, Washington, DC, Goldstein & Ahalt, Chartered; **PRIM RE ACT:** Attorney; **EDUC:** BA, 1964, Govt. & Politics, Univ. of MD; **GRAD EDUC:** JD, 1967, Law, Georgetown Univ. Law Ctr.; **HOME ADD:** 6900 Wells Pkwy., Univ. Pk., MD 20742, (301)699-5283; **BUS ADD:** 4321 Hartwick Rd., College Pk., MD 20740.

GOLDSTEIN, Martin——*Pres.*, DPF, Inc.; **PRIM RE ACT:** Property Manager; **BUS ADD:** 141 Central Park Ave. S., New York, NY 10530, (212)428-5000.*

GOLDSTEIN, Michael S.——**B:** Dec. 29, 1949, Los Angeles, CA, *Asst. VP*, Countrywide Funding Corp.; **PRIM RE ACT:** Lender; **SERVICES:** FHA, VA, Conv. loans; **REP CLIENTS:** FHA VA, FNMA, FHLMC; **PREV EMPLOY:** S-G Mortgage Corp. 1978-80; **PROFL AFFIL & HONORS:** SCMBA, CMBA, MBA; **HOME ADD:** 10531 Garden Grove Ave., Northridge, CA 91326, (213)368-7142; **BUS ADD:** 3440 Wilshire Blvd., Los Angeles, CA 90010, (714)835-5752.

GOLEC, Janice——*Staff Asst.*, Department of Housing and Urban Development, Ofc. of Secy./Undersecy.; **PRIM RE ACT:** Lender; **BUS ADD:** 451 Seventh St., S.W., Washington, DC 20410, (202)755-8063.*

GOLICZ, Lawrence J.——**B:** Feb. 21, 1944, Detroit, MI, *Pres.*, American Appraisal & Feasibility Corp.; **PRIM RE ACT:** Consultant, Appraiser, Owner/Investor, Assessor; **SERVICES:** Appraisal, feasibility studies; **REP CLIENTS:** Fed., State, Municipal, Indus., Comml.; **PROFL AFFIL & HONORS:** AIREA, SREA, MAI, SRPA; **EDUC:** BA, 1966, Hist., Univ. of MI; **GRAD EDUC:** MA, 1968, Hist., Washington State Univ.; PhD, 1973, Urban/Bus./Demographic Hist., Univ. of ME/Univ. of WI; **EDUC HONORS:** Regents Scholarship, Teaching Assistantships, Grad. School Scholarship, Grant by Social Science Research Council; **OTHER ACT & HONORS:** Who's Who Fin. and Indus.; **HOME ADD:** 1619 Elderwood Cir., Middleton, WI 53562, (608)836-9277; **BUS ADD:** 6510 Schroeder Rd., Madison, WI 53711, (608)274-3744.

GOLLAHER, Raymond Clifford——**B:** Mar. 29, 1949, Kennett, MO, *VP*, Barter Systems, Inc.; **PRIM RE ACT:** Broker, Instructor, Syndicator, Consultant, Appraiser, Developer, Builder, Property Manager, Lender, Owner/Investor, Real Estate Publisher; **PREV EMPLOY:** Asst. Mgr., Abide Realtors 1975-76, Gen. Mgr. Harold Jones Co., 1976-79, Gen. Mgr. Harris Realty, 1979-81; **PROFL AFFIL & HONORS:** CRS, NAR, Assn. of Realtors, OK Assn., OK City Metropolitan Bd. of Realtors, Central OK Homebuilders Merit Award, 1980; **EDUC:** 1968, Mgmt., Central State Univ.; **MIL SERV:** USAFR, T. Sgt., Unit Pres., Citation, Meritorious Award; **OTHER ACT & HONORS:** Boy Scouts of Amer., OK City C of C, Central Homebuilders Assn.; **HOME ADD:** 1919 NW 33 Rd., OK City, OK 73118, (405)528-5996; **BUS ADD:** 4848 N. MacArthur, OK City, OK 73122, (405)495-4600.

GOLLEHON, Ellene M.——**B:** Nov. 21, 1928, Omaha, NE, *Pres. - Owner*, Genelco, Inc.; **PRIM RE ACT:** Broker, Owner/Investor; **SERVICES:** RE brokerage resid. - comml.; **PREV EMPLOY:** 2 1/2 yrs. RE previous to starting Genelco, Inc.; **PROFL AFFIL & HONORS:** NAR, NE Realtors, Omaha Bd. of Realtors, Womens Council of Realtors (1981 Pres. Omaha Chap.); **EDUC:** Med. Tech. RE, Univ. of Omaha; **OTHER ACT & HONORS:** Profl. Engrs. of NE Auxiliary, Metro. Omaha Builders Assn., Metro. Omaha Builders Assn. Women's Auxiliary, Zonta Intl. (Sec. Omaha Chap.); **HOME ADD:** 2416 South 97th Ave., Omaha, NE 68124, (402)397-5443; **BUS ADD:** 2603 S 160 St., Omaha, NE 68130, (402)330-2000.

GOLUB, Kenneth, L.——**B:** May, 31, 1945, Ft. Knox, KY, *Pres.*, K.L. Golub Co.; **PRIM RE ACT:** Appraiser; **SERVICES:** RE Valuation, analysis & consulting; **PROFL AFFIL & HONORS:** Published various RE articles in 'The Appraisal Journal' and 'The Real Estate Appraiser & Analyst', MAI, SRPA, ASA, CRA; **EDUC:** BA, 1966, Eng., SUNY (Harpur Coll.); **OTHER ACT & HONORS:** Amer. Mensa; **HOME ADD:** Hickory Ln., Mt. Kisco, NY 10549; **BUS ADD:** PO Box 523, 444 Main St., Mt. Kisco, NY 10549, (914)666-0033.

GOMBERG, Mandel——**B:** July 9, 1924, Chicago, IL, *Partner*, Angell, Kaplan, Zaidman & Gomberg; **PRIM RE ACT:** Consultant, Owner/Investor; **PROFL AFFIL & HONORS:** AICPA, IL CPA Soc., ULI, NAREC, NAREIT, NRC, NAR; **EDUC:** BS, 1947, Acctg., Univ. of IL; **GRAD EDUC:** MS, 1948, Econ., Univ. of IL; **MIL SERV:** US Army, S/Sgt., 1943-45; **OTHER ACT & HONORS:** Mensa, Giraffe Soc.; **HOME ADD:** 3325 Wilder, Skokie, IL 60076, (312)674-9545; **BUS ADD:** 105 W. Madison, Chicago, IL 60602, (312)641-2555.

GOMEZ, Frank P.——**B:** Sept. 16, 1902, Rio Florido Sinaloa, Mexico, *Realtor*; **PRIM RE ACT:** Consultant, Appraiser, Instructor; **PREV EMPLOY:** Self employed since 1952; **PROFL AFFIL & HONORS:** SIR since 1951, Hon. Member San Francisco RE Bd.; **HOME ADD:** 61 Lane Pl., Atherton, CA 94025, (415)325-6507; **BUS ADD:** 351 CA St., San Francisco, CA 94104, (415)788-0454.

GOMINGER, George W.——*Mgr. Ins. & RE*, Owens-Corning Fiberglas; **PRIM RE ACT:** Property Manager; **BUS ADD:** Fiberglas Tower, 15th Fl., Toledo, OH 43659, (419)248-8468.*

GONCZY, Stephen I.——**B:** Mar. 17, 1913, Hungary, *Prop. Mgr.*, Wirtz Realty Corporation; **PRIM RE ACT:** Property Manager; **SERVICES:** Mgmt. of 35 story comml. bldg.; **PROFL AFFIL & HONORS:** Inst. of RE Mgmt.; Dir., Chicago RE Bd., CPM, Mgr. of the Yr., 1980; **EDUC:** 1933, Royal Military Academy of Hungary; **GRAD EDUC:** LLD, 1937, Elizabeth Univ., Hungary; **MIL SERV:** US Army, Mil. Int., Lt. Col.; **OTHER ACT & HONORS:** Amer. Legion, Vice Comdr., Post 38; **HOME ADD:** 5227 N. Magnolia, Chicago, IL 60640, (312)271-9675; **BUS ADD:** 333 N. Michigan Ave. Bldg., Chicago, IL 60601, (312)726-8333.

GONSALVES, Jose Antero——*VP*, Trafalgar Developers of Florida, Inc.; **PRIM RE ACT:** Developer; **BUS ADD:** 275 Fountainbleau Blvd., Miami, FL 33172, (305)223-7110.*

GONZALES, Richard——*Pres.*, Realty Co. of America; **PRIM RE ACT:** Syndicator; **BUS ADD:** 550 West Colfax Ave., Denver, CO 80204, (303)623-1218.*

GONZALEZ, Rafael——**B:** Oct. 25, 1937, Mayaguez, PR, *VP & Gen. Mgr.*, Compania Puerto Kai, Inc.; **PRIM RE ACT:** Developer; **PREV EMPLOY:** Santa Juanita Devel., Bayamon PR (4,000 units); EBEC Housing Corp., San Juan, PR; **PROFL AFFIL & HONORS:** Home Builders Assn., PR Inst. of Civil Engrgs.; **EDUC:** BCE, Civil Engrg.; **MIL SERV:** USA, Capt.; **OTHER ACT & HONORS:** PR Nat. Guard; **HOME ADD:** D-43 B St., Colinas de Monte Carlo, Rio Piedras, PR 00924, (809)768-5290; **BUS ADD:** PO Box 898 Canovanas, PR 00629, (809)724-2900.

GONZALEZ, Richard J.——**B:** Mar. 8, 1928, Grosse Pointe, MI, *Partner*, Fiddler, Gonzalez & Rodriguez; **PRIM RE ACT:** Attorney; **REP CLIENTS:** The Chase Manhattan Bank, N.A.; Housing Investment Corp.; The Equitable Life Assurance Soc. of the US; **EDUC:** BSS, 1949, Hist., Georgetown Univ. Coll. of Arts and Sci.; **GRAD EDUC:** JD, 1951, Georgetown Law School; **MIL SERV:** US Army, Lt.; **HOME ADD:** 10 Candina St., Victoria Plaza Condo., Apt. 3A, Condado, Santurce, PR 00907, (809)724-8568; **BUS ADD:** GPO Box 3507, San Juan, PR 00936, (809)753-3150.

GOOD, Sheldon F.——**B:** June 4, 1933, Chicago, IL, *Pres.*, Sheldon F. Good & Co., Inc. Real Estate Auctions, Inc.; **PRIM RE ACT:** Broker, Consultant, Instructor; **OTHER RE ACT:** RE auction; **SERVICES:** Comml. & indus. RE; **PREV EMPLOY:** Sales mgr. Baird & Warner, Inc.; **PROFL AFFIL & HONORS:** Chicago RE Bd., IL Assn. of Realtors, NAR, Lambda Alpha, Nat. Assn. of Auctioneers; Past Pres. Comml. Invest. Div., NAR, CCIM; **EDUC:** BS, 1955, Urban land Econ., Univ. of IL; **MIL SERV:** USA, E-5; Hon. Discharge; **OTHER ACT & HONORS:** Winner of Synder Trophy; Selected One of Chicago's 10 Outstanding Young Men 1968; Pres. Gastro-Intestinal Found. at Univ. of Chicago; Recipient of the 'Crown of a Good Name'; awarded by Jewish Nat. Fund RE 'Man of the Year'; State of Israel Bonds; 1981 Univ. of IL, Outstanding Grad. Alumni Award; **BUS ADD:** 11 N Wacker Dr., Chicago, IL 60606, (312)346-1500.

GOODACRE, Kenneth Robert, CPM——**B:** Jan. 21, 1943, San Antonio, TX, *Pres. & CEO*, Camelback Management Company; **PRIM RE ACT:** Broker, Consultant, Property Manager, Syndicator; **PREV EMPLOY:** Del E. Webb Realty & Mgmt. Co. 1970-1976; Mgr. Resid. Props. Div.; **PROFL AFFIL & HONORS:** Cert. Prop. Mgr. 1975; **EDUC:** BS, 1970, Fin. specialization in RE, AZ State Univ.; **MIL SERV:** USA, Sp-5; **HOME ADD:** 5124 E Desert Park Lane, Paradise Valley AZ 85253, (602)991-8746; **BUS ADD:** 2515 N Third St., Phoenix, AZ 85004, (602)255-7441.

GOODE, Howard C.——**B:** Mar. 28, 1940, Chicago, IL; **PRIM RE ACT:** Attorney; **SERVICES:** Legal servs. related to devel., zoning, fin., const., sales & acquisition, condos., synd. of RE and local tax matters; **REP CLIENTS:** Devels. of comml., indus. and resid. props. and synds.; **PROFL AFFIL & HONORS:** Chicago Bar Assn.; IL Bar Assn.; **EDUC:** BS, 1961, Acctg., Northwestern Univ.; **GRAD EDUC:** JD, 1964, Northwestern Univ.; **HOME ADD:** 2100 Valencia Dr., Northbrook, IL 60062, (312)564-5825; **BUS ADD:** 108 Wilmot Rd., Suite 207, Deerfield, IL 60015, (312)948-7980.

GOODE, Ronald A.——**B:** Sept. 20, 1940, Wash., DC, *Vice President*, The Oliver T. Carr Co.; **OTHER RE ACT:** Comm. Leasing; Prop. Mgmt; Devel.; Const.; **SERVICES:** Devel., Leasing, Prop. Mgmt.; **REP CLIENTS:** Indiv. or Instit. Investors in Comml. Dev. Projects; **PREV EMPLOY:** Gen. Engrg. Assoc., Washington, DC (1967-70) York Div., Borg Warner Corp., York PA (1965-67); **PROFL AFFIL & HONORS:** Wash. Bd. of Realtors, American Society of Heating, Refrigerating and Air Conditioning Engineers, Registered Profl. Engr. (DC, VA, MD), Licensed RE Broker (DC); **EDUC:** BS Mechanical Engrg., 1963, Univ. of VA; **MIL SERV:** USN, Comdr.; **HOME ADD:** 6048 Edgewood Terrace, Alexandria, VA 22307, (703)765-7971; **BUS ADD:** 1700 Pennsylvania Ave., NW, Washington, DC 20006, (202)624-1750.

GOODER, Donald M.——**B:** June 30, 1925, Chicago, IL, *Pres.*, Donald M. Gooder & Assoc., Inc.; **PRIM RE ACT:** Consultant, Appraiser; **SERVICES:** Resid., Comml., and Indus. Appraisals; **REP CLIENTS:** Lending instns., devels., Chemical Bank Exec. Relocation Service, Transamerica Relocation, I.B.M., Digital, Arco, Equitable Life Assurance, and others; **PREV EMPLOY:** Swango Appraisal & Research Consultants, head of RE Trust Dept. of Lawyers Title of AZ (17 yrs.); **PROFL AFFIL & HONORS:** Soc. of RE Appraisers, (Member of Bd), Southern AZ Home Builders Assn., SRPA; MAI Candidate; **EDUC:** BSBA, 1952, Bus. Econ., Univ. of AZ; **EDUC HONORS:** Blue Key - Natl. Sr. Men's Honorary; **MIL SERV:** USAAF; **OTHER ACT & HONORS:** AZ Acad. - AZ Town Halls; Exec. Bd. - Catalina Council Boy Scouts of Amer. (20Yrs.); United Way Bd. (past); St. Josephs Hospital Advisors Council (past); **HOME ADD:** 6901 E. Edgemont, Tucson, AZ 85710, (602)298-0833; **BUS ADD:** 4901 E. 5th St., Suite 204, Tucson, AZ 85711, (602)325-3304.

GOODFRIEND, Herbert J.——**B:** Sept. 9, 1926, New York, NY, *Pres.*, Otterbourg, Steindler, Houston & Rosen PC; **PRIM RE ACT:** Attorney; **SERVICES:** Legal servs. in all RE matters; **REP CLIENTS:** Chem. Bank, Farm Credit Assn., Manufacturers Trust Co.; **PROFL AFFIL & HONORS:** ABA, NY State Bar Assn., NYC Lawyers Assn., Counsel NY Bd. of Trade, Fellow of ABA, Rep. NYC Lawyers Joint Conference with RE Bd. of NY; **EDUC:** AB, 1947, Econ., NY Univ.; **GRAD EDUC:** LLB, 1950, NY Univ., Law Review; LLM, 1953, Taxation, NY Univ.; **MIL SERV:** USA, 1945-46; **OTHER ACT & HONORS:** Fin. Mgmt. Comm. Amer. Apparel Assn.; Tr., Temple Beth El of Great Neck; **HOME ADD:** 122 Pine Hill Rd., Great Neck, NY 10020, (516)466-4523; **BUS ADD:** 230 Park Ave., NY, NY 10169, (212)661-9100.

GOODING, Walter L.——**B:** Oct. 31, 1939, Grant, OK, *Broker Assoc.*, Hallmark Realty, Inc.; **PRIM RE ACT:** Broker, Syndicator; **SERVICES:** Brokerage for raw land and synd.; **REP CLIENTS:** Devels., indiv. investors and grps. of investors when synd.; **PREV EMPLOY:** Dist. Mgr. for an oil co.; **PROFL AFFIL & HONORS:** San Antonio Bd. of Realtors, Greater San Antonio Builders Assn., their State and Nat. Affiliates; **EDUC:** 1961-1963, Geology, Univ. of OK; **MIL SERV:** US Marine Corps, 1958-1961, Corporal E-4, Letter of Commendation from Commanding Gen., 1959; **OTHER ACT & HONORS:** Member, Castle Hills First Baptist Church; **HOME ADD:** 2607 Whisper Hill, San Antonio, TX 78230, (512)492-9278; **BUS ADD:** 1635 NE Loop Suite 910, San Antonio, TX 78209, (512)828-9261.

GOODJOIN, Albert Thomas——**B:** March 19, 1952, New York, NY, *R.E. Ins. Broker, Tax Consultant*, Carter Realty; **OTHER RE ACT:** Tax Advisor; **SERVICES:** R.E., Tax, Ins., Legal; **REP CLIENTS:** Indiv., small bus., profls.; **PREV EMPLOY:** 5 yrs. with present firm; **PROFL AFFIL & HONORS:** Nat. Realtors, Member; Amer. Appraisers, Member, Summa Cum Laude, John Jay College of Criminal Justice; **EDUC:** BS, 1973, Urban Planning; **GRAD EDUC:** MBA, 1982, Mgmt., Columbia Business School, Grad. School of Business; **MIL SERV:** USMC; Sgt.; **OTHER ACT & HONORS:** Bronx Burrough Pres. Advisory Bd.; **HOME ADD:** 45 E. 233rd St., Bronx, NY 10470, (212)991-1156; **BUS ADD:** 1101 Mt. Vernon Ave., Yonkers, NY 10504, (914)289-5900.

GOODLOE, John D., Jr.——**B:** Jan. 1, 1935, Washington, DC, *President*, Adams/Cates Co.; **PRIM RE ACT:** Broker, Developer, Property Manager; **SERVICES:** Sales, leasing, mgmt., consulting, devel.; **REP CLIENTS:** Indiv., corp., fin. instns., owners, tenants; **PROFL AFFIL & HONORS:** ULI, SIR, Intl. Council of Shopping Centers, FIABCI, SIR Nat. Intercity Transaction Award 1971; **EDUC:** AB, 1957, Pre-Law; **MIL SERV:** US Navy, Lt.JG; **OTHER ACT & HONORS:** Rotary; Dir. & Past Pres. of Atlanta Bd. of Realtors; Past Pres. of GA Chap. of SIR; Current Chmn. of Bd. of Amer. Realty Services Group; **HOME ADD:** 210 Townsend Pl. NW, Atlanta, GA 30327, (404)261-2044; **BUS ADD:** 225 Peachtree St. NE, Atlanta, GA 30303, (404)522-5477.

GOODMACHER, Maxine——*Atty. at Law*; **PRIM RE ACT:** Attorney; **SERVICES:** Legal; **PREV EMPLOY:** RE Law & Fin., Safeway Stores, Inc., Oakland, CA; RE Atty.; Legal Dept., Montgomery Ward & Co., Oakland, CA, Sr. Atty.; **PROFL AFFIL & HONORS:** ABA, Real Prop. & Probate Sec.; CA State Bar, RE Sect.; Contra Costa Bar Assn.; **EDUC:** AB, 1972, Pol. Sci., Bus. Admin., Univ. of CA, Berkeley; **GRAD EDUC:** JD, 1975, Univ. of San Francisco Sch. of Law; **EDUC**

HONORS: Phi Beta Kappa; **HOME ADD:** Orinda, CA; **BUS ADD:** 706 Main St., Ste. B, PO Box 867, Martinez, CA 94553, (415)229-4320.

GOODMAN, I. Michael——B: Feb. 10, 1937, New York, NY, *Pres.*, Samada RE Co. Inc.; **PRIM RE ACT:** Instructor, Consultant, Developer, Property Manager, Owner/Investor; **OTHER RE ACT:** Owner-Mgr.; **PROFL AFFIL & HONORS:** IREM, Member Legislative Comm.; VP NY Chap. of IREM; RE Bd., Member Legislative Comm. of RE Bd. of NY, CPM; **EDUC:** 1959, Hist./Bus. Adm., Colby Coll.; **MIL SERV:** USA Res.; **OTHER ACT & HONORS:** Lecturer, NY Univ., Hunter Coll., New School; Member Natl. Trust for Hist. Preservation, Preservation League of NY; Former Past Chmn. Jewish Big Brothers of NY; **BUS ADD:** 400 Madison Ave., NY, NY 10017, (212)873-1100.

GOODMAN, Larry L.——B: Aug. 8, 1944, Cincinnati, OH, *Partner*, Walton, Matlock & Goodman; **PRIM RE ACT:** Attorney; **REP CLIENTS:** Synds., Devels., Architects, Contractors; **PROFL AFFIL & HONORS:** ABA, Cincinnati Bar Assn.; **EDUC:** BA, 1968, Hist., Univ. of Cincinnati; **GRAD EDUC:** JD, 1973, Law, Univ. of Toledo; LLM, 1974, Law, NY Univ.; **MIL SERV:** US Army, SP4, Army Commendation; **HOME ADD:** 834 Clifton Hills Terrace, Cincinnati, OH 45220, (513)961-3495; **BUS ADD:** 414 Walnut St., Suite 910, Cincinnati, OH 45202, (513)241-1430.

GOODMAN, Richard A.——B: June 17, 1949, Oakland, CA, *Sole Proprietor*, Law Offices of Richard A. Goodman; **PRIM RE ACT:** Attorney; **OTHER RE ACT:** Practice of RE Law; **REP CLIENTS:** St. Mary's Hosp., So. Alameda Cty. Bd. of Realtors, RE devels., synds., investors; **PREV EMPLOY:** Loube & Lewis, Attys. at Law; **PROFL AFFIL & HONORS:** CA State Bar Assn., RESSI; **EDUC:** BA, 1970, Lit., UC San Diego; **GRAD EDUC:** JD, 1974, UCLA Sch. of Law; **EDUC HONORS:** Editor, UCLA, Alaska Law Review; **HOME ADD:** 2090 Manzanita Dr., Oakland, CA 94611, (415)339-0895; **BUS ADD:** One Kaiser Plaza, Suite 701, Oakland, CA 94612, (415)763-2300.

GOODMAN, Robert L.——B: Apr.9, 1948, Knoxville, TN, *Pres.*, The Goodman Group, Inc.; **PRIM RE ACT:** Syndicator, Consultant, Property Manager, Owner/Investor; **SERVICES:** RE Computing; **REP CLIENTS:** Synd. & Mgmt. of Income Prop.; **PROFL AFFIL & HONORS:** TX Apt. Assoc., Intl. Assoc. of Fin. Planners; RESSI; **EDUC:** BS, 1971, Engineering Physics, Univ. of TN; **GRAD EDUC:** MBA, 1977, RE, Pepperdine Univ.; **EDUC HONORS:** with Honors, Pres./Key Exec. Program; **BUS ADD:** 12900 Preston Rd., Dallas, TX 75230, (214)387-2327.

GOODMAN, Ronald David——B: Mar. 25, 1953, Portland, OR, *Pres.*, Ron Goodman RE Seminars; **PRIM RE ACT:** Broker, Instructor, Real Estate Publisher; **SERVICES:** Courses and seminars in all areas of real estate, publish nat. recognized real estate texts; **REP CLIENTS:** Current and prospective licensees; investors; trade and coll. bookstores; and prop. schools; **PROFL AFFIL & HONORS:** RE Educ. Assn.; RE Securities and Synd. Instit.; Farm and Land Instit.; NAR, Grad., Realtors Instit.; **HOME ADD:** 3536 N.E. Holman, Portland, OR 97217, (503)288-1408; **BUS ADD:** Weston Plaza, Suite 110, 2154 N.E. Broadway, Portland, OR 97232, (503)284-6675.

GOODMAN, Walt——B: July 2, 1937, San Francisco, CA, *Sales Mgr.*, Bryski Realty; **OTHER RE ACT:** Exchangor; **SERVICES:** Knowledge of exchanging; **HOME ADD:** 641 Fenley Ave., San Jose, CA 95117, (408)248-1144; **BUS ADD:** 215 Echo Dr., Campbell, CA 95008, (408)248-1144.

GOODMAN, William G.——B: Sept. 30, 1931, Enterprise, AL, *Owner*, Registered RE Broker; **PRIM RE ACT:** Broker, Owner/Investor, Property Manager; **SERVICES:** Condo. & resid. sales, rentals; **REP CLIENTS:** Primary & secondary home buyers, renters; **PREV EMPLOY:** VP, Pinnacle Port Devels., Panama City Beach, FL, 1976-1978; **EDUC:** BS, 1959, Chem., Univ. of AL; **GRAD EDUC:** MBA, 1966, Mgmt., Syracuse Univ.; **MIL SERV:** US Army, Col., LOM w/OLC, BS, MSM w/OLC, JSCM, ACM, 1953-1974; **OTHER ACT & HONORS:** Pi Kappa Phi Frat.; **HOME ADD:** 23223 W. Hwy. 98, Panama City Beach, FL 32407, (904)234-8211; **BUS ADD:** 23223 W. Hwy. 98, Panama City Beach, FL 32407, (904)234-8211.

GOODRICH, Charles——*Corp. Mgr. Fac. Plng.*, Geosource, Inc.; **PRIM RE ACT:** Property Manager; **BUS ADD:** 2700 S. Post Oak Rd., Ste. 2000, Houston, TX 77056, (713)961-1111.*

GOODRICH, Chris M.——B: June 16, 1955, Omaha, NE, *Atty.*, Kennedy, Holland, DeLacy & Svoboda; **PRIM RE ACT:** Attorney; **SERVICES:** RE synd. and partnerships; conveyances; **EDUC:** BA, 1976, Econ., Univ. of NE; **GRAD EDUC:** LLM-JD, 1978-1979, Law and Taxation, Univ. of NE-Wash. Univ.; **OTHER ACT & HONORS:** Contributing author of book soon to be published entitled *Legal Compliance Annual for Business*; **HOME ADD:** 9412 Laurel St., Omaha, NE 68134, (402)571-8455; **BUS ADD:** 1900 One First Nat. Ctr., Omaha, NE 68102, (402)342-8200.

GOODRIDGE, Edwin N.——B: Mar. 5, 1945, Princeton, NJ, *Sr. Appraiser & Corp. Banking Officer, RE*, First of Denver, RE Constr.; **PRIM RE ACT:** Appraiser, Lender; **SERVICES:** Comml. Constr. Loan underwriting & Mkt. Analysis; **REP CLIENTS:** Major owner-devels. of Comml. projects in Metro. Denver & other growth areas along both slopes of the Rocky Mtns.; **PREV EMPLOY:** H.G. Bowes & Son, Denver, CO 1971-1975; Aspen RE & Investment Co.; Pres. & Fee Appraiser, Jackson, WY, 1977-79; **PROFL AFFIL & HONORS:** CO RE Broker since 1970, Candidate AIREA; **GRAD EDUC:** BA, 1968, RE Fin. & Valuation, Univ. of AZ, Tucson, AZ; **HOME ADD:** 422 Dexter St., Denver, CO 80220, (303)355-8011.

GOODSITT, Robert D.——B: Feb. 18, 1933, Milwaukee, WI, *VP*, Arthur Rubloff, Co.; **PRIM RE ACT:** Property Manager; **PROFL AFFIL & HONORS:** Bd. of Dir. Greater N. Michigan Ave. Assoc., IREM, Chicago RE Bd., NAR; **EDUC:** BS, 1954, Econ., Univ. of WI; **MIL SERV:** USA, 1st Lt.; **HOME ADD:** 1460 Sandburg Tr., Chicago, IL 60610; **BUS ADD:** 69 W. Washington, Chicago, IL 60610, (312)787-5700.

GOODSTEIN, Barnett M.——B: Oct. 1, 1921, Dallas, TX, *Pres.*, Goodstein & Starr, P.C.; **PRIM RE ACT:** Attorney, Owner/Investor, Instructor; **OTHER RE ACT:** Title Co. Fee Office Mgr.; **SERVICES:** Counseling and litigation in real prop. matters; closings for Title Co.; **PREV EMPLOY:** Self-employed since 1957 in law; **PROFL AFFIL & HONORS:** Dallas, TX and American Bar Assns.; American Arbitration Assn.; Nat. Acad. of Arbitrators; Indus. Relations Research Assn.; **EDUC:** BA, 1942, Econ., Univ. of TX at Austin; **GRAD EDUC:** MA, 1942, Econ., Univ. of TX at Austin; JD, 1957, Law, So. Methodist Univ.; **EDUC HONORS:** Cum Laude; **MIL SERV:** AACS, T/Sgt.; **OTHER ACT & HONORS:** Dallas Cty. School Bd., 1980 to present (term to 1985); Hearing Officer for City of Dallas; Panel Member for Amer. Arbitration Assn. and for Fed. Mediation and Conciliation Serv.; **HOME ADD:** 5002 De Loache Ave., Dallas, TX 75220, (214)369-7286; **BUS ADD:** 5925 Forest Ln., Ste. 200, Dallas, TX 75230, (214)387-4303.

GOODWIN, Harold D.——B: Jan. 30, 1920, Waterloo, IA, *Pres.*, Goodwin Consulting Service; **PRIM RE ACT:** Consultant; **SERVICES:** Comml. RE investment prop.; **PROFL AFFIL & HONORS:** Cert. Indus. Devel.; **MIL SERV:** USAF; Capt.; Several; **HOME ADD:** 8350 Roe Ave., Prairie Village, KS 66207, (913)649-1503; **BUS ADD:** 8350 Roe Ave., Prairie Village, KS 66207, (913)341-4200.

GOODWIN, J.B.——B: Dec. 15, 1949, San Antonio, TX, *Pres.*, J.B. Goodwin Co.; **PRIM RE ACT:** Broker, Instructor, Property Manager, Owner/Investor, Insuror; **PROFL AFFIL & HONORS:** TX Assn. of Realtors; RNMI, Tr., Tax Realtors Foundation; CRB; Outstanding Young Men in America, 1978; **OTHER ACT & HONORS:** Austin C of C; Faculty Advisory Bd., Austin Community Coll.; **HOME ADD:** 2607 B River Hills Rd., Austin, TX 78746, (512)263-1764; **BUS ADD:** 124 W Anderson, Austin, TX 78752, (512)837-7880.

GOODWIN, Ronald——B: Dec. 18, 1943, Birmingham, AL, *Cert. Prop. Mgr.*, Polinger Co.; **PRIM RE ACT:** Consultant, Instructor, Property Manager, Syndicator; **PROFL AFFIL & HONORS:** WA Bd. of Realtors; IREM; Prop. Mgmt. Assn.; **MIL SERV:** USAF, E-5; **OTHER ACT & HONORS:** Rental Accomodations Commn., Landlord Rep.; Kiwanis Club; YMCA; Amer. Cancer Soc.; **HOME ADD:** 3746 Southern Ave. S.E., Washington, DC 20020, (202)584-0427; **BUS ADD:** 5530 Wisconsin Ave., Suite 1000, Chevy Chase, MD 20015, (202)561-5702.

GOODWIN, Ronald R.——B: Jan. 9, 1941, Phillips, TX, *Partner*, Goodwin & Stewart; **PRIM RE ACT:** Attorney; **SERVICES:** RE legal work and litigation; **REP CLIENTS:** San Angelo Bd. of Realtors; First City Nat. Bank; local realtors; **PREV EMPLOY:** Philadelphia Eagles Football Club (6 yrs.), First Nat. Bank of Odessa; **PROFL AFFIL & HONORS:** ABA; TX Bar Assn., Chmn of Agric. Tax Sect., member of Agric. Tax Law Comm., Member of RE Probate Sect.; Tom Green Cty. Bar Assn., former dir.; **EDUC:** BBA, 1964, Fin., gen. bus., Baylor Univ.; **GRAD EDUC:** JD, 1969, Baylor Univ. Law Sch.; **EDUC HONORS:** All SWC & All Amer. football and baseball; Omicron Delta Kappa, Men's Leadership Frat.; Who's Who in Amer. Colls. & Univs., Phi Delta Phi Frat; **OTHER ACT & HONORS:** Chmn. Civil Service Comm. and Treas. San Angelo Bd. of Educ.; Elder & Chmn. of Bd. of First Christian Church; Former Dir. of YMCA Bd. & March of Dimes Bd.; **HOME ADD:** 3702 Sul Ross, San Angelo, TX 76901, (915)949-5221; **BUS ADD:** PO Drawer 31, San Angelo, TX 76902, (915)655-7331.

GOPMAN, Howard Z.——**B:** Oct. 29, 1940, Kansas City, MO, *Atty.*, Reif and Gopman; **PRIM RE ACT:** Attorney, Syndicator; **SERVICES:** Securities law and RE law servs.; **REP CLIENTS:** Synd., RE cos., securities broker/dealers, investors; **PROFL AFFIL & HONORS:** ABA; IL Bar Assn.; WI Bar Assn.; Chicago Bar Assn.; NAR; IL Assn. of Realtors; Chicago RE Bd., Arbitrator-Amer. Arbitration Assn.; Hearing Officer, IL Pollution Control Bd.; Hearing Officer, IL Office of Educ.; **EDUC:** BS, 1962, Econ., Univ. of WI; **GRAD EDUC:** JD, 1965, Law, Univ. of WI; MBA, 1967, Fin. Banking & Invest., Univ. of WI; **EDUC HONORS:** Non-res Scholar; **HOME ADD:** 226 Millbrook Ln., Wilmette, IL 60091, (312)251-5031; **BUS ADD:** 205 W Randolph St., Suite 1340, Chicago, IL 60606, (312)263-0270.

GORDEN, Thomas——*Dir. RE Mgmt.*, Consolidated Foods Corp.; **PRIM RE ACT:** Property Manager; **BUS ADD:** 135 So. LaSalle St., Chicago, IL 60603, (312)726-6414.*

GORDEN, William——**B:** Aug. 1, 1923, Espever, Norway, *Dir. of RE*, Sun Company Inc.; **OTHER RE ACT:** RE Management; **SERVICES:** Corporate admin.; **REP CLIENTS:** Corporate; **PREV EMPLOY:** RE - engrg., Facilities Mgr.; **PROFL AFFIL & HONORS:** Nat. Assn. of Corporate RE, SAE, Nat. Assn. of Review Appraisers; Nat. Assn. of Prop. Tax Rev., CRA, CPTR; **EDUC:** BS, 1949, ME, Wayne State Univ.; **MIL SERV:** USN Aviator, 1942-1945, Lt., Naval Av.; **OTHER ACT & HONORS:** Waynesborough CC. - Edgmont CC - Franklin Inst.; **HOME ADD:** 22 Andrews Rd., Malvern, PA 19355, (215)644-4476; **BUS ADD:** 100 Matsonford Rd., Radnor, PA 19087, (215)293-6160.

GORDON, Benny W., Jr.——*Pres.*, Benny Gordon Realty Co.; **PRIM RE ACT:** Broker, Consultant, Appraiser, Developer, Property Manager, Insuror; **PROFL AFFIL & HONORS:** NAIFA, NAACP, IFAS, CRA, CREM NARER - Nat. Realtors; **BUS ADD:** 4144 Lindell, Suite 220, St. Louis, MO 63108, (314)531-8020.

GORDON, Bernard——**B:** June 13, 1916, Albany, NY, *Pres.*, Arrowhead Assoc. Inc.; **PRIM RE ACT:** Consultant, Developer, Builder, Owner/Investor, Property Manager; **SERVICES:** RE, Bus. problems counseling; **PREV EMPLOY:** Owner, Pres. Super Mkt. Chain, Saveway Super Mkt. Inc., Sold. 1971; **PROFL AFFIL & HONORS:** Albany Bldrs., NAHB, Nat. Assn. of Fin. Consultants; **OTHER ACT & HONORS:** SCORE, Serv. of Ret. Execs., Spons. by US Bus. Admin., Masons; **HOME ADD:** 44 Milner Ave., Albany, NY 12203, (518)482-8190; **BUS ADD:** Twin Towers, 99 Washington Ave., Suite 1102, Albany, NY 12210, (518)462-7411.

GORDON, Charles L.——**B:** Mar. 27, 1938, Indianapolis, IN, *Chmn.*, Monetary Investment Group; **PRIM RE ACT:** Broker, Appraiser, Developer, Owner/Investor, Property Manager, Syndicator; **OTHER RE ACT:** CEO RE investment trust; **PREV EMPLOY:** 1971-1974, Multivest, Inc., VP, RE Investments; 1969-1971, Bank of the Commonwealth, Asst. VP, Comml. Mort.; 1962-1969, Equitable Life Assurance Soc. of the US; **PROFL AFFIL & HONORS:** RESSI; Amer. Inst. of RE Appraisers; Soc. of RE Appraisers; Nat. Assn. of RE Brokers; S. Oakland Cty. Bd. of Realtors, Assoc. Member; Nat. Assn. of RE Investment Trusts; ULI; **EDUC:** BS, Bus./RE, IN Univ.; **MIL SERV:** US Army; **OTHER ACT & HONORS:** Grosse Pointe Yacht Club; **BUS ADD:** 23777 Southfield Rd., Suite 224, Southfield, MI 48075, (313)569-4545.

GORDON, Donald J.——**B:** Aug. 20, 1928, New York, NY, *Partner*, Digby Management Co.; **PRIM RE ACT:** Instructor, Property Manager, Owner/Investor; **SERVICES:** Owner mgmt.; **PROFL AFFIL & HONORS:** RE Bd. of NY, Rent Stabilization Bd. (Dir.); Dir., Realty Advisory Bd. on Labor Relations, CHIP, CPM; CPM of the Year 1978; Greater NY Chap. Award for Outstanding serv. from NY Univ.; RE Inst. 1980; **EDUC:** 1949, Poli. Sci., Econ., Swarthmore Coll.; **OTHER ACT & HONORS:** Westchester Cty. Rent Guidelines Bd., 1977-80, Owner Member; Adjunct Assoc. Prof. of RE at NY Univ., The RE Inst.; **HOME ADD:** 142 Tewkesbury Rd., Scarsdale, NY 10583, (914)472-1814; **BUS ADD:** 59 E 54th St., NY, NY 10022, (212)755-3063.

GORDON, Hank——**B:** Sept. 9, 1934, San Antonio, TX, *Chmn. of the Bd.*, The Rainier Fund, Inc.; **PRIM RE ACT:** Developer; **OTHER RE ACT:** Shopping Center Devel.; **PREV EMPLOY:** Partner ITT Levitt & Sons (Levitt Investment Props.); **PROFL AFFIL & HONORS:** ICSC; **EDUC:** BA, 1956, Psych., Univ. of S. CA; **MIL SERV:** USNR, HM 2 no. class; **OTHER ACT & HONORS:** 7 yrs. L.A. County Narcotics and Dangerous Drugs Commn., Chmn. 3 yrs.; **HOME ADD:** 101 101st St. SE B104, Bellevue, WA 98004, (206)455-4440; **BUS ADD:** 12400 S.E. 38th St., Bellevue, WA 98006, (206)643-1010.

GORDON, John R.——**B:** Apr. 20, 1948, Lansing, MI, *Pres.*, Gordon & Associates, Inc.; **PRIM RE ACT:** Engineer; **OTHER RE ACT:** Surveyor; **SERVICES:** Surveying, land devel. design; **REP CLIENTS:** Resid. & indus. devel.; **PREV EMPLOY:** Becker & Assoc., St. Louis, MO 1969-74; **PROFL AFFIL & HONORS:** Amer. Planning Assn., Amer. Congress Surveying & mapping; **HOME ADD:** 1306 E. Compton Blvd., Springfield, MO 65807; **BUS ADD:** 2244 S. Campbell, Springfield, MO 65807, (417)883-4736.

GORDON, Michael——**B:** Mar. 28, 1942, New York, NY, *Chmn.*, GLM Corp.; **PRIM RE ACT:** Developer, Builder, Owner/Investor; **SERVICES:** Builder/dev. of comml. props., condo. conversion; **EDUC:** BA, 1962, Univ. of MN; **GRAD EDUC:** JD, 1965, Univ. of Chicago Law Sch.; **EDUC HONORS:** Summa Cum Laude, Phi Beta Kappa, Law Review Editor; **HOME ADD:** 2242 Cathedral Ave. NW, Washington DC 20008, (202)667-6003; **BUS ADD:** 2531 P St., NW, Washington DC 20007, (202)337-7800.

GORDON, Nicholas N.——*RE Manager*, Anderson, Clayton & Co.; **PRIM RE ACT:** Property Manager; **BUS ADD:** 1100 Louisiana, Houston, TX 77002, (504)733-7550.*

GORDON, Victor M.——**B:** Sept. 15, 1911, New Haven, CT, *Sr. & Managing Partner*, Gordon & Hosen, Attys.; **PRIM RE ACT:** Consultant, Attorney, Lender, Owner/Investor, Real Estate Publisher; **SERVICES:** Legal Services, Loans; **PROFL AFFIL & HONORS:** various Bar Assns., Chief Sr. Editor, CT Bar Journal; **EDUC:** BA, 1935, John Hopkins Univ.; **GRAD EDUC:** JD, 1938, Boston Univ., Sch. of Law; **MIL SERV:** Counterintelligence Corps., Spec. Agent, ETO Bronze Star; Combat Infantry Badge; **OTHER ACT & HONORS:** Editorial Bd. 1946-81, CT Bar Journal - Editor in Chief 1960-70; **HOME ADD:** 190 McKinley Ave., New Haven, CT 06515, (203)387-3617; **BUS ADD:** 1570 Chapel St., New Haven, CT 06511, (203)777-3408.

GORDON, Wallace E.——**B:** Oct. 24, 1929, Scranton, PA, *Partner*, G & G Realty Co., Realtors; **PRIM RE ACT:** Broker, Appraiser, Property Manager, Insuror; **SERVICES:** Gen. Brokerage, RE Appraising, Gen. Ins.; **REP CLIENTS:** Local & Out of Area Banks, Attys., Corps., Indivs.; **PROFL AFFIL & HONORS:** Realtors Assns.; Profl. RE Brokers Assn.; Natl. Assn. of Independent Fee Appraisers; Amer. Assn. of Cert. Appraisers; Intl. Inst. of Valuers, IFA, CAS, SCV; **EDUC:** BS, 1954, Bus. Admin., Keystone Jr. Coll., Susquehanna Univ.; **EDUC HONORS:** Phi Theta Kappa, Frat. Pres.; Who's Who in Amer. Coll. & Univ.; **MIL SERV:** US Army, 1st. Sgt., Good Conduct Medal; Amer. Defence; German Occupation; **OTHER ACT & HONORS:** Rotary; VFW; Amer. Legion; F & AM; Elks; Amer. Choral Dirs. Assn.; Bd. Dir. & Past Pres. Scranton Community Concert Assn.; Listed Who's Who in the E.; Listed Intl. Dictionary Biography; Wm. Connell Award for 'Significant Contribution to Area Culture' 1977; **HOME ADD:** 317 Crest Dr., Clarks Green, PA 18411, (717)586-4126; **BUS ADD:** 206 Miller Bldg., 422 Spruce St., Scranton, PA 18530, (717)344-6148.

GOREE, Janace H.——**B:** Jan. 6, 1950, Pelahatchie, MS, *Asst. Prof. of Fin. & Gen. Bus.*, Jackson State Univ., Fin. & Gen. Bus.; **PRIM RE ACT:** Broker, Attorney, Appraiser; **OTHER RE ACT:** Teaching RE & RE Appraising; Lawyer; **PREV EMPLOY:** Golden Deed Realty; **PROFL AFFIL & HONORS:** ABA, TX Bar Assn., MS Bar Assn.; **EDUC:** BA, 1971, Acctg., Jackson State Univ.; **GRAD EDUC:** JD/MBA, 1971, Law, Thurgood Marshall School of Law/MS Coll.; **EDUC HONORS:** Jurisprudence Awards, Nominated Outstanding Young Woman of the Year, 1979, 1980, & 1981; **OTHER ACT & HONORS:** VP PTA; **HOME ADD:** 945 Metarie Rd., Jackson, MS 39209, (601)948-2499; **BUS ADD:** Jackson State Univ., Dept. of Fin. & Gen. Bus., Jackson, MS 39209, (601)968-2531.

GORHAM, Howard N.——**B:** June 12, 1927, Brooklyn, NY, *VP & Sr. Assoc. Counsel*, The Chase Manhattan Bank, Legal and RE Fin.; **PRIM RE ACT:** Attorney, Banker, Lender, Owner/Investor; **PREV EMPLOY:** Dreyer & Traub - Partner; **EDUC:** BS, 1949, Acctg., NY Univ.; **GRAD EDUC:** LLB & LLM, 1953 & 1958, Legal, NY Univ.; **EDUC HONORS:** Beta Gamma Sigma; **MIL SERV:** US Army, T-5; **HOME ADD:** 8 Sylvan Ln., Scarsdale, NY 10583, (914)472-1621; **BUS ADD:** 1 Chase Manhattan Pl., 22nd Fl., NY, NY 10081, (212)552-3581.

GORKA, Francis L.——**B:** Feb. 24, 1921, Springfield, MA, *Chief Valuation Engr.*, Indus. Risk Insurers; **PRIM RE ACT:** Appraiser, Insuror; **OTHER RE ACT:** Machinery & equipment; **SERVICES:** Insurance (fire ins.); **PROFL AFFIL & HONORS:** ASA, Fellow ASA; **EDUC:** BME, 1955, W. New England Coll.; **MIL SERV:** US Army; Corp. of Engrs., Sgt.; 1946-48; **HOME ADD:** 16 Seymour Rd., Windsor Locks, CT 06096, (203)623-1288; **BUS ADD:** 85 Woodland St., Hartford, CT 06096, (203)525-2601.

GORMAN, Daniel F.——B: Apr. 23, 1942, Boston, MA, *Dir. of RE Dev.*, Franklin Realty Group, Inc., RE Dev.; **PRIM RE ACT:** Broker, Instructor, Syndicator, Consultant, Developer, Property Manager, Owner/Investor; **OTHER RE ACT:** Mort., banking; **SERVICES:** Brokerage, constr., consulting, devel. leasing, mort. banking, prop. mgmt., and synd. of comml. and multifamily rental props.; **REP CLIENTS:** Instnl., and indiv. investors and owners, developers of comml. and multifamily props.; **PREV EMPLOY:** The Fox Co., Office Bldg., Devel. and prop. mgmt., 1977-1980; **PROFL AFFIL & HONORS:** CPM, Instr. at RE Inst., Temple Univ.; **EDUC:** BS, 1964, Civil Engr., Worcester Poly. Inst.; **GRAD EDUC:** MBA, 1970, Intl. Bus, Wharton Grad. Div., Univ. of PA; **EDUC HONORS:** Dean's List; **MIL SERV:** CEC-USNR, Lt., Navy Achievement Medal; **OTHER ACT & HONORS:** Rep. committeeman, Cheltenham Twp. 1980 to present; **HOME ADD:** 328 Gribbel Rd., Wyncote, PA 19095, (215)576-1055; **BUS ADD:** Rydal Exec. Plza., Rydal, PA 19046, (215)885-7440.

GORMAN, John D.——B: Apr. 17, 1933, Daisytown, PA, *Exec. VP*, Broadscope, Inc.; **PRIM RE ACT:** Developer, Builder; **SERVICES:** Founder, Officer and Dir., Chief Fin. Officer of Broadscope, Inc., Dir. of PA Vacation Land Devel. Assn.; **PROFL AFFIL & HONORS:** Amer. Land Devel. Assn., RESSI; **EDUC:** 1954, Mathematics, CA State Coll.; **GRAD EDUC:** 1958, Mathematics, Univ. of Pittsburgh; **HOME ADD:** 808 Pine St., Philadelphia, PA 19107, (215)928-1519; **BUS ADD:** Towamensing Trails, Albrightsville, PA 18210, (717)722-0192.

GORMAN, William R.——B: July 29, 1935, Chicago, IL, *Pres.*, W.R. Gorman & Associates, Investment Realtors, Inc.; **PRIM RE ACT:** Broker, Consultant, Owner/Investor, Instructor, Property Manager, Syndicator; **SERVICES:** Real prop. sales, counseling, estate planning, synd., tax deferment, exchanging, prop. mgmt.; **REP CLIENTS:** Indiv. investors; **PREV EMPLOY:** Beckman Instrument; Armour Brach Found.; **PROFL AFFIL & HONORS:** Apt. Assn. of Orange Cty., City Assn. Realtors, Fullerton Rotary Club, Fullerton C of C, Cert. Comml. investment member, CCIM, MBA, BSME; **EDUC:** BSME, 1957, Purdue Univ.; **GRAD EDUC:** MBA, 1964, Northwestern Univ.; **HOME ADD:** 300 E Las Palmas Dr., Fullerton, CA 92635, (714)870-0689; **BUS ADD:** 1335 W. Valencia Dr., Suite A, Fullerton, CA 92633, (714)992-0111.

GORRA, John J.——B: Apr. 20, 1947, Minneapolis, MN, *Princ.*, R.S.M. Co.; **PRIM RE ACT:** Broker, Consultant, Instructor, Owner/Investor, Property Manager, Syndicator; **SERVICES:** Owner occupied Multi-family devel.; Consulting, initiation, orientation and implementation of Home Owner Assns.; Mktg. & sales consultant, prop. mgmt. devel. Converters, Investors, Lenders, Homeowners Assns.; **PREV EMPLOY:** Recreational Investors, Inc., Ski Area Condo. Devel.; **PROFL AFFIL & HONORS:** IREM, NAR, Natl. Apt. Assn., MN Multi-Housing Assn., Community Assns. Inst., ULI, Community Assns. Inst., MN chap. Minneapolis Bd. of Realtors, BOMA, Outstanding Bd. Member, MN Multi- Housing Assn., Distinguished Serv., Community Assns. Inst.; **EDUC:** BA, 1970, Bus. Psych., Univ. of MN; **OTHER ACT & HONORS:** Planning Comm., Luther Church; Smithsonian Inst.; Dir. on numerous Non-Profit & Bus. Corp.; **HOME ADD:** 5144 Valley View, Edina, MN 55436, (612)920-4690; **BUS ADD:** 6400 Flying Cloud Dr., Eden Prairie, MN 55344, (612)941-9050.

GORROW, Charles R.——B: Sept. 11, 1933, Ogdensburg, NY, *Pres.*, Continental Realty Co., Div. of C.I.R. Investors, Inc.; **PRIM RE ACT:** Broker, Consultant, Developer, Owner/Investor, Instructor, Property Manager; **SERVICES:** Investment counseling, prop. analysis, devel., prop. mgmt.; **PROFL AFFIL & HONORS:** Greater Buffalo Bd. of Realtors, NY State Assn. of Realtors, NAR, RNMI, RESSI, Intl. RE Exchange, CCIM; **MIL SERV:** USA, Cpl., Purple Heart; **HOME ADD:** 5795 S. Abbott Rd., Hamburg, NY 14075, (716)648-0468; **BUS ADD:** 2959 Genesee St., Buffalo, NY 14225, (716)891-9111.

GOSLINE, Norman A.——B: Nov. 6, 1935, Gardiner, ME, *Owner*, Norman A. Gosline, Realtor; **PRIM RE ACT:** Consultant, Appraiser; **SERVICES:** RE appraiser and consultant to various private, corporate and govt. entities; **REP CLIENTS:** Digital, U.S. Postal Serv., ME Dept. of Transportation; Nature Conservancy; Bowdin Coll.; Merrill Lynch Relocation; Exxon Corp.; Canal Bank; M.G.I.C.; Casco Bank; Webber Petroleum; **PROFL AFFIL & HONORS:** Past Pres., ME Assn. and Kennebec Valley Realtors; Pres., State of ME Chap. SREA; Secretary, New England Chap. AIREA, MAI, SRPA, GRI; **EDUC:** BA, 1957, Bus. and Econ., Univ. of ME (Orono); **OTHER ACT & HONORS:** Rotarian, Mason; **HOME ADD:** 87 West Hill Rd., Gardiner, ME 04345, (207)582-1100; **BUS ADD:** PO Box 290, Gardiner, ME 04345, (207)582-1100.

GOSS, Darr L.——B: Nov. 7, 1932, Salem, OR, *Sr. Consultant*, Grabenhorst Bros. Realtors, Comml./Indus. Div.; **PRIM RE ACT:** Consultant, Appraiser; **OTHER RE ACT:** Farm & timber land tract spec.; **SERVICES:** Site acquisition, agricultural & airfield land planning; **REP CLIENTS:** Indiv. and inst. investors in comml., indus., agricultural and timberland props.; **PREV EMPLOY:** RE Mgr., Beri, Inc.; **PROFL AFFIL & HONORS:** FLI, Oregon Soc. of Farm Mgrs. and Rural Appraisers; **EDUC:** BS, 1956, Philosophy, Univ. of OR; **GRAD EDUC:** MPA, 1964, Land Use Planning, George Washington Univ.; **MIL SERV:** USAF; Col., Legion of Merit Air Medal; **OTHER ACT & HONORS:** Member, Linn Cty. Planning Advisory Comm.; FAA Licensed Airline Transport Pilot; Director, Santiam Valley Bank; **HOME ADD:** P.O. Box 376, Aumsville, OR 97325, (503)749-1252; **BUS ADD:** 198 Liberty St., SE, Salem, OR 97301, (503)362-2471.

GOSS, James W.——*Dir. Corp RE*, Pennzoil Co.; **PRIM RE ACT:** Property Manager; **BUS ADD:** PO Box 2967, Houston, TX 77001, (713)236-7878.*

GOSSETT, Donald Ira——B: Apr. 11, 1941, *Owner*, Gossett & Assocs., Realtors; **PRIM RE ACT:** Broker, Owner/Investor; **PREV EMPLOY:** Fishman & Co.; Oppenheimer Indus.; Charles F. Curry RE Co.; **PROFL AFFIL & HONORS:** RE Bd. of Kansas City, MO; Kansas RE Assn.; NAR; Nat. Inst. of RE Mgmt.; KS, MO, NE, WY RE Brokers Lic.; **OTHER ACT & HONORS:** Lenexa C of C; Mission C of C; Masonic Lodge #325; AF & AM; **BUS ADD:** 11308 W. 71 St., Shawnee, KS 66202, (913)362-0556.

GOSSETT, James F.——B: Sept. 11, 1951, Iowa City, IA, *Research and Assessing Counsel and Acting Dir. of Publications*, International Association of Assessing Officers; **PRIM RE ACT:** Attorney; **OTHER RE ACT:** Real Estate Publications; **PREV EMPLOY:** Assn. Exec., NAR; **PROFL AFFIL & HONORS:** ABA, Comms. relating to taxation and exempt orgs.; **EDUC:** BSJ, 1973, Journalism, Northwestern Univ.; **GRAD EDUC:** JD, 1976, Northwestern Law School; **EDUC HONORS:** With Honors, Editorial Bd., Journal of Criminal Law and Criminology; **HOME ADD:** 600 N. McClurg Ct. #3605 A, Chicago, IL 60611, (312)337-7522; **BUS ADD:** 1313 E. 60th St., Chicago, IL 60637, (312)947-2053.

GOTSHALL-MAXON, Lee F., Esq.——B: Dec. 20, 1953, Elgin, IL, *Atty. at Law*, Lillick McHose & Charles, RE Grp.; **PRIM RE ACT:** Attorney; **SERVICES:** Advice regarding all RE matters with emphasis on lge. RE devels./acquisitions and for. investors; **PREV EMPLOY:** Environmental Protection Agency, 1973; **PROFL AFFIL & HONORS:** ABA, State Bar of CA; **EDUC:** BA, 1975, Govt. & Urban Regional Studies, Dartmouth Coll.; **GRAD EDUC:** JD, 1980, Real Prop., Hastings Coll. of Law; **EDUC HONORS:** Cum Laude, Order of the Coif; **HOME ADD:** 1201 Vallejo St., San Francisco, CA 94109, (415)474-3731; **BUS ADD:** 2 Embarcadero Ctr., Suite 2600, San Francisco, CA 94111, (415)421-4600.

GOTTHELF, Beatrice F.——B: May 4, 1951, New York, NY, *Dir., Investments & Sales*, Julien J. Studley, Inc.; **PRIM RE ACT:** Broker, Consultant, Owner/Investor; **PREV EMPLOY:** Chase Manhattan Bank, NA; Urban Devel. Corp.; **PROFL AFFIL & HONORS:** ULI, Municipal Art Soc.; MBAA; RE Bd., Tr. RE Instl of NY; **EDUC:** BA, 1973, Amer. Studies/Music, Williams Coll.; **HOME ADD:** 415 E 85 St., New York, NY 10028, (212)472-0086; **BUS ADD:** 342 Madison Ave., New York, NY 10173, (212)949-1982.

GOTTHELP, Don——*Mgr. RE Div.*, Xerox Corp.; **PRIM RE ACT:** Property Manager; **BUS ADD:** Long Bridge Rd., Stamford, CT 06904, (203)329-8711.*

GOTTLIEB, Albert J.——B: Nov. 15, 1931, Chicago, IL, *VP*, Hemsley-Spear, Inc., Comml. Sales, leasing, & mgmt.; **PRIM RE ACT:** Broker, Property Manager; **PROFL AFFIL & HONORS:** Lecturer RE Inst. NYU, RE Bd. of NY; **EDUC:** BA, 1952, Yale Univ.; **GRAD EDUC:** MBA, 1954, Harvard Bus. Sch.; **HOME ADD:** 6 Roger Pl., White Plains, NY 10605, (914)949-9558; **BUS ADD:** 60 E. 42nd St., NY, NY 10165, (212)880-0408.

GOTTLIEB, Jerome Robert——B: Dec. 8, 1923, Minneapolis, MN, *Pres.*, Gottlieb Properties; **PRIM RE ACT:** Broker, Consultant, Attorney, Developer, Owner/Investor, Syndicator; **PROFL AFFIL & HONORS:** SIR, Amer. Soc. of RE Counselors, Inst. of RE Mgmt., RE Security & Synd. Inst., IL State Bar Assn., Chgo. Bar Assn., SIR, CRE, CPM; **EDUC:** BS, 1947, Bus., Northwestern Univ.; **GRAD EDUC:** MBA, JD, 1951, 1978, Fin. and Law, Northwestern Univ.; **MIL SERV:** US Army, 2nd Lt., 1943-1946; **HOME ADD:** 180 E. Pearson St., Apt. 6507, Chicago, IL 60611, (312)337-7714; **BUS ADD:** One E. Superior St., Rm. 304, Chicago, IL 60611, (312)782-6735.

GOTTLIEB, Sam B.——**B:** July 15, 1937, Dallas, TX, *Pres.*, Hilltop Real Estate Investment & Sales Corp.; **PRIM RE ACT:** Broker, Developer, Builder, Owner/Investor, Property Manager, Syndicator; **PREV EMPLOY:** Sam B. Gottlieb Devel. Corp., Pres., 1969-1978; J.R. Gottlieb & Co. RE Devels., VP, 1960-1969; **PROFL AFFIL & HONORS:** Houston Bd. of Realtors; Comml. MLS; IL and TX RE Broker; ULI; RESSI; **EDUC:** BS, 1958, Geology/Chem., OK Univ.; BBA, 1960, RE/Acctg. and Fin., So. Methodist Univ.; **MIL SERV:** USMC Res., Honorable Discharge; **OTHER ACT & HONORS:** Bd. of Dir., Westwood Ctry. Club, Houston; **HOME ADD:** 12334 Kitty Brook Dr., Houston, TX 77071, (713)729-5585; **BUS ADD:** 10101 Fondren, Suite 226, Houston, TX 77096, (713)270-7600.

GOTTSCHALK, Robert O.——**B:** Nov. 4, 1927, Rochester, IN, *VP*, Gottschalk Realty, Inc.; **PRIM RE ACT:** Broker, Consultant, Appraiser, Developer, Owner/Investor, Property Manager; **PREV EMPLOY:** Casualty Ins., Life Ins. Sales and Mgmt., Farmer, Mutual Fund Sales; **PROFL AFFIL & HONORS:** Fulton Cty. Bd. of Realtors, IN Assn. of Realtors, NAR, FLI, GRI, CRS, CRB, Accredited Farm & land Member; **OTHER ACT & HONORS:** Rochester Township Tr., 1970-74; Rochester School Bd. 1970-1974; First Christian Church, Masonic Lodge, Shrine, Rotary Club, Dir. First Nat. Bank, Dir. Fulton Cty. Family YMCA, Dir. Rochester Vocation Trades, Inc.; **HOME ADD:** PO Box 544, Rochester, IN 46975, (219)223-3587; **BUS ADD:** 122 E. 8th St., Rochester, IN 46975, (219)223-3179.

GOTTUSO, Josephine M.——**B:** Sept. 10, 1927, Scranton, PA, *Atty. at Law; Designated Broker*, Ex VP, Gene Hart Realty, Inc.; **PRIM RE ACT:** Broker, Consultant, Attorney, Owner/Investor, Instructor; **OTHER RE ACT:** Public Speaker; **SERVICES:** RE Legal Servs., RE Consultant, RE Broker; **REP CLIENTS:** RE Brokers and Salespersons, Investors, Attys., Indiv., RE Devel., Escrow Cos.; **PROFL AFFIL & HONORS:** NAR, CA State Bar Assn., Eastern Bar Assn., Christian Legal Soc., Bd. of Realtors Pomona Valley; State CA Bd. of Registered Nurses, Nat. Council of Exchangers, CA Assn. Realtors, WCR; **EDUC:** BA, 1968, Amer. Studies, CA State Univ., Los Angeles; **GRAD EDUC:** JD, 1973, Univ. of LaVerne Sch. of Law; **OTHER ACT & HONORS:** Order Eastern Star, Star of the West Chap. 468; Amer. Red Cross Volunteer Reg. Nurse; **HOME ADD:** 737 W. Tenth St., Claremont, CA 91711; **BUS ADD:** 145 N. Indian Hill Blvd., Claremont, CA 91711, (714)624-3521.

GOULD, Arthur——**B:** Apr. 12, 1917, Natl. City, CA, *Pres.*, The Argo Co.; **OTHER RE ACT:** Devels. primarily and brokers for specific things and/or people/entities/investors/corps., 35 yrs., all phases; **EDUC:** AB, 1940, Bus. Admin. & Foreign Languages, Dominantly Latin and Spanish, BYU, Provo, UT; **MIL SERV:** US Army, Sgt., Hon. Dischg.; **BUS ADD:** 2382 Camino Vida Roble, Suite C, Carlsbad, CA 92008, (714)438-4046.

GOULD, Glenn——*RE Dept.*, Hillenbrand Industries, Inc.; **PRIM RE ACT:** Property Manager; **BUS ADD:** Hwy. 46, Batesville, IN 47006, (812)934-7000.*

GOULD, Jay——**B:** June 4, 1940, Brooklyn, NY, *Pres.*, Majestic Prop. Mgmt. Corp.; **PRIM RE ACT:** Broker, Consultant, Attorney, Owner/Investor, Property Manager; **SERVICES:** Prim. mgmt. and leasing of shopping ctrs., apt. complexes, office bldgs. & indus. prop.; **REP CLIENTS:** Gould Investors Trust, NY Life & few indiv. investors; **PREV EMPLOY:** VP, Gould Investors Trust; Assoc., Tom H. Matthew, Esq.; Elmer Fox Westheimer, CPA's; **PROFL AFFIL & HONORS:** Assoc. Member, Soc. of RE Appraisers, Member, NY & NC State Bars; Admitted to practice law before several fed. courts including the US Supreme Ct.; Certificate in Real Prop. Law from RE Inst. of NY Univ.; **EDUC:** BA, 1962, Acctg., Univ. of NC; **GRAD EDUC:** JD, 1964, Comml. Law, Univ. of NC, Law School; **MIL SERV:** US Army Reserve, Pfc.; **HOME ADD:** 363 E. 76th St., NY, NY 10021; **BUS ADD:** 60 Cutter Mill Rd., Great Neck, NY 10021, (516)466-3100.

GOULD, Thomas L.——**B:** Dec. 26, 1930, St. Louis, MO, *Dir. of RE*, Commonwealth Edison Co.; **PRIM RE ACT:** Attorney; **OTHER RE ACT:** Acquisition, sale and mgmt. of RE; **PROFL AFFIL & HONORS:** Chicago RE Bd., Chicago Bar Assn., IL State Bar Assn., Amer. Right of Way Assn.; **EDUC:** BS, 1953, Forestry, Univ. of MO; **GRAD EDUC:** JD, 1962; **MIL SERV:** USAF, 1954-56, 1st Lt.; **HOME ADD:** 6200 N. Mandell, Chicago, IL 60646, (312)631-1943; **BUS ADD:** PO Box 767, Chicago, IL 60690, (312)294-3233.

GOULDING, Gerald L.——**B:** May 12, 1949, Provo, UT, *Lawyer*, Frome & Goulding; **PRIM RE ACT:** Attorney, Owner/Investor; **OTHER RE ACT:** Accountant; **SERVICES:** Legal, taxation, acctg.; **REP CLIENTS:** Star Valley Realty, Ellis Big Game Realty, Hoffman & Assoc., Realtors & Appraisers, Star Valley State Bank; **PREV EMPLOY:** Public Acctg. Firm of Coopers & Lybrand, Law firm of Moyle & Draper; **PROFL AFFIL & HONORS:** WY, UT, Amer. Bar Assns., AICPA; **EDUC:** BS, 1972, Acctg., Brigham Young Univ.; **GRAD EDUC:** JD, 1975, Univ. of UT Coll. of Law; **EDUC HONORS:** Cum Laude, Honors Program; **OTHER ACT & HONORS:** Delegate State Pol. Conventions, Cty. hospital Bd., Elder in LDS Church, Missionary in Germany for LDS Church, 68-70; **HOME ADD:** 680 Jackson, Afton, WY 83110, (307)886-3904; **BUS ADD:** PO Box 968, Afton, WY 83110, (307)886-5430.

GOULDSBURY, William C.——*VP & Secy.*, Coca-Cola Bottling of NY, Inc.; **PRIM RE ACT:** Property Manager; **BUS ADD:** 425 E. 34th St., NY, NY 10016, (201)487-8650.*

GOULET, Richard C——**B:** Oct. 24, 1946, Berlin, NH, *Mgr. Fin & Admin., Corp. RE*, Computervision Corp.; **PRIM RE ACT:** Owner/Investor; **SERVICES:** Fin. & Admin. of Corp. RE activities; **PREV EMPLOY:** Sanders Assn. 1967-1980; **EDUC:** BSBA, 1976, Gen. Mgmt., Univ. of Lowell; **GRAD EDUC:** MBA, 1977, Fin., Babson Coll.; **EDUC HONORS:** Summa Cum Laude; **MIL SERV:** USN, E-4; **OTHER ACT & HONORS:** Lecturer, Rivier Coll.; **HOME ADD:** 58 King St., Nashua, NH 03060, (603)889-7695; **BUS ADD:** 6 Crosby Dr., Bedford, MA 01730, (617)275-1800.

GOURLEY, John D.——**B:** Oct. 19, 1938, Ellsbury, MO, *Exec. VP and Gen. Counsel*, Lehndorff Group of Companies; **PRIM RE ACT:** Attorney, Owner/Investor, Instructor; **PROFL AFFIL & HONORS:** ABA; Member of the Bar in MO, MN, IL, TX; **EDUC:** BS, Econ., Drake Univ.; **GRAD EDUC:** JD, St. Louis Univ.; **EDUC HONORS:** Cum Laude; **HOME ADD:** 5335 Waneta, DaLlas, TX 75209, (214)352-3235; **BUS ADD:** 3737 Noble Ave., Suite 200, Dallas, TX 75204, (214)670-0422.

GOUTAS, Edward M.——**B:** Sept. 12, 1942, Bellows Falls, VT, *Owner*, Edward M Goutas Law Office; **PRIM RE ACT:** Attorney; **SERVICES:** Rep. of Buyers and Sellers of all types of RE; **REP CLIENTS:** Cersosimo Lumber Co., Inc., Burlington Savings Bank; **PROFL AFFIL & HONORS:** ABA, VT Bar Assn. and Windham County Bar Assn.; **EDUC:** BA, 1964, Pol. Sci., St. Michael's Coll.; **GRAD EDUC:** JD, 1968, John's Univ. of Law; **EDUC HONORS:** St. Thomas More Scholar; **OTHER ACT & HONORS:** Member of Bellows Falls Village Trustees 1974-1976, BPOE 1619, Bellows Falls, VT, Bellows Falls Country Club, Bellows Falls, VT, Windham Dist. Probate Ct. Judge 1979 to present; **HOME ADD:** A Atkinson St., Bellows Falls, VT 05101, (802)463-3618; **BUS ADD:** 18 Sq., Bellows Falls, VT 05101, (802)463-4522.

GOVE, Robert C.——**B:** June 13, 1921, St.Paul, MN; **PRIM RE ACT:** Broker, Attorney, Owner/Investor, Property Manager; **EDUC:** BS, 1947, Law, Univ. of MN; **GRAD EDUC:** JD, 1949, Law, Univ. of MN; **MIL SERV:** USAF, Sgt.; **HOME ADD:** 5505 Westbrook Rd., Golden Valley, MN 55422, (612)546-7524; **BUS ADD:** 2155 N. Lilac Dr., Golden Valley, MN 55422, (612)546-7524.

GOW, James E.——**B:** Sept. 29, 1923, Endicott, NY, *Atty. and VP of Profl. Corp.*, Leasure, Gow & Rizzuto, P.C.; **PRIM RE ACT:** Attorney; **SERVICES:** Represent lenders, buyers, sellers and contractors on resid. and comml. transactions; **REP CLIENTS:** Citizens Savings Bank, F.S.A., Endicott Trust Co., Marine Midland Bank, NA, Howard & Teeter Home Builders, Inc.; **EDUC:** BA, 1949, Pol. Sci., Econ., Hamilton Coll.; **GRAD EDUC:** LLB, 1952, Cornell Law School; **MIL SERV:** US Army, T5; **OTHER ACT & HONORS:** United Way of Broome Cty., Inc.; **HOME ADD:** 3724 Wildwood Dr., Endwell, NY 13760, (607)785-5917; **BUS TEL:** (607)748-7351.

GOW, Robert H.——*VP Corp. Dev.*, Gulf Resources & Chemical Corp.; **PRIM RE ACT:** Property Manager; **BUS ADD:** 1100 Milam, 47th Floor, Houston, TX 77002, (713)658-0471.*

GRACE, W.M.——**B:** Sept. 10, 1934, Burlington Jct., MO, *Pres.*, W.M. Grace Development Co.; **PRIM RE ACT:** Developer, Builder; **PROFL AFFIL & HONORS:** ICSC; **EDUC:** BA, 1957, Indus. Econ., Univ. of AZ; **GRAD EDUC:** MBA, Econ., Univ. of AZ; **MIL SERV:** USA; **OTHER ACT & HONORS:** Other Bus. Address, 7575 N. 16th St. Ste. 1, Phoenix, AZ 85020; (602)956-8254; **HOME ADD:** 2400 Lucille Ave., St. Joseph, MO, (816)233-8218; **BUS ADD:** 1900 N Belt., St. Joseph, MO 64502, (816)233-8218.

GRAEPER, Michael R.——**B:** May 6, 1940, Portland, OR, *Pres.*, Shelter Prop. Corp., Realtors; **PRIM RE ACT:** Broker, Architect, Instructor, Syndicator, Consultant, Appraiser, Developer, Builder, Property Manager, Owner/Investor; **SERVICES:** Full brokerage service; **PROFL AFFIL & HONORS:** Portland Bd. of Realtors, Clackamas Cty. Bd. of Realtors, GRI; **EDUC:** BS, 1962, Hist., Bus., Sci, Univ. of OR; **OTHER ACT & HONORS:** Trustee, Epsilon Omicrom Assn. of Phi Gamma Delta; **HOME ADD:** 2 Britten Ct, Lake

Oswego, OR 97034, (503)636-6724; **BUS ADD:** 16063 S.W. Boones Ferry Rd., Oswego, OR 97034, (503)635-9295.

GRAF, Jenny H.——B: July 7, 1933, Somerset, KY, *VP*, Palm Beach Assocs., Inc., Gould Florida Inc. (Parent-Gould, Rolling Meadows, Inc.); **PRIM RE ACT:** Broker, Developer, Builder, Owner/Investor, Property Manager; **OTHER RE ACT:** Devel. of 10,300 acre "New Town"; **SERVICES:** Market Research and Product Planning; **REP CLIENTS:** Home of Palm Beach Polo & Ctry. Club (Whitman Cup, Men's 35+ Tennis, Girl's 12-under Tennis), Soc. Register Top Corp. Office & (CEO, Ch. Bd. purchasers); **PREV EMPLOY:** Investment Corp. of FL & subsidiaries i.e., joint venture w/ALCOA, Breakwater Housing Corp., West Plantation Devel. Corp.; **PROFL AFFIL & HONORS:** Amer. Marketing Assn., National Assn. of Home Builders, Zonta, MIRM-Member Institute of Residential Marketing (Honorarily 1st Women in US to be designated); Reg. R.E. Broker, former Reg. Mort. Broker; **EDUC:** Attended Univ. of MI and NY Univ., Self-educated, extensive personal and professional library, 100's of hours of undergraduate and graduate level audited, plus professional seminars; **OTHER ACT & HONORS:** Mgmt. Bd. - 1st American Bank of Palm Beach Cty.; Bd. of Dirs. - Assn. of Special Dists.; Member, Citizens Advisory Bd. to Palm Beach Legislative Delegation; State Comm. Person of Libertarian Party of FL and Previously in NY; **HOME ADD:** 12326 Westhampton Cir. Wellington, W. Palm Beach, FL 33411, (305)793-5816; **BUS ADD:** 12230 Forest Hill Blvd., W. Palm Beach, FL 33411, (305)793-5100.

GRAHAM, James B.——B: Aug. 28, 1942, Vulcan, AB, *Pres.*, J.B. Graham & Assoc., Ltd.; **PRIM RE ACT:** Consultant, Instructor; **SERVICES:** Mktg. consulting & mktg. research; **REP CLIENTS:** NuWest Devel. Ltd., Carma Devel., Allarco Devel., New Home Cert. Program of AB; **PREV EMPLOY:** Assoc. Prof. Faculty of Mgmt., Univ. of Calgary; **PROFL AFFIL & HONORS:** Amer. Mktg. Assn.; **EDUC:** BS, 1965, Gen. Sci., Univ. of AB; **GRAD EDUC:** MBA, 1970, Mktg., Univ. of W. ON; PhD, 1978, Univ. of W. ON; **HOME ADD:** 98 Chinook Dr., Cochrane, AB, Canada, (403)932-2366; **BUS ADD:** Box 276, Cochrane, AB, Canada, (403)932-2366.

GRAHAM, Joe M.——B: Apr. 4, 1940, Midland, TX, *Pres.*, Graham Investments, Inc.; **PRIM RE ACT:** Consultant, Owner/Investor; **REP CLIENTS:** Boothe Fin. Rep.; Fikes Found., RE Advisor; **PREV EMPLOY:** VP, IDS Mort.; **PROFL AFFIL & HONORS:** Past Pres., No. TX Chap. NACORE; **EDUC:** BBA, 1963, Univ. of TX; **GRAD EDUC:** MBA, 1964, Univ. of SC; **BUS ADD:** Suite 504, Two Turtle Creek Village, Dallas, TX 75219, (214)522-6400.

GRAHAM, Ralph V.——B: Mar. 6, 1914, Tuscoha, TX, *Owner*, Ralph V. Graham, Realtors; **PRIM RE ACT:** Broker, Consultant, Appraiser, Instructor, Property Manager, Insuror; **REP CLIENTS:** Homequity, CT, City of Plainview, Salvation Army, RE Clients (Listors) for Some Appraising; **PROFL AFFIL & HONORS:** Plainview Bd. of Realtors, TX Assn. of Realtors, NAR, RNMI, FLI, TX RE Teachers Assn., GRI, CRS, Pres., Plainview Bd. of Realtors (1976); **EDUC:** BA, 1944, Psych., Education, Theology, Abilene Christian Univ.; **GRAD EDUC:** STM, DM, 1949,1952, Counseling, Theology, Education, Princeton Theological Seminary, Temple Sch. of Theology (Philadelphia); **EDUC HONORS:** Magna Cum Laude, Who's Who in Amer. Coll. and Univ.; **OTHER ACT & HONORS:** Lions Club, Rotary Club, One Time Pres., Plainview Ministeriah Assn.; **HOME ADD:** 1607 Travis, Plainview, TX 79072, (806)296-9734; **BUS ADD:** 504 Joliet, Plainview, TX 79072, (806)293-4246.

GRAHAM, Thomas M., Jr.——B: May 2, 1941, Rockville Centre, NY, *Pres.*, Thomas M. Graham & Co., Inc.; **PRIM RE ACT:** Broker, Owner/Investor; **SERVICES:** Appraisal, Consulting, Synd., Investment Counseling; **REP CLIENTS:** Indiv. or instln. investors in real prop.; **PREV EMPLOY:** Pres. and V Chmn. Realty Growth Investors RE Investment Trust, Towson, MD 1979-1981; **PROFL AFFIL & HONORS:** YMREA; RE Bd. of NY; Natl. Realty Club, REI; GRI; **EDUC:** AB, 1963, Hist., Georgetown Univ.; **MIL SERV:** USA, 1st Lt., 1963-1965; **OTHER ACT & HONORS:** Univ. Club of NYC; Natl. Golf Links of Amer.; Tr., St. David's School, 12 E. 89th St.; Catholic Big Brothers; **HOME ADD:** 1155 Park Ave., New York, NY 10028, (212)289-4041; **BUS ADD:** 509 Madison Ave., New York, NY 10022.

GRAHAM, William J.——B: Nov. 8, 1935, Brainerd, MN, *Pres.*, Vector, Ltd.; **PRIM RE ACT:** Broker, Consultant, Developer, Owner/Investor, Property Manager, Syndicator; **SERVICES:** Consultant service & primarily leasing indus. space; **REP CLIENTS:** RREEF Corp., The Boston Co.; **PREV EMPLOY:** Broker for Coldwell Banker; **PROFL AFFIL & HONORS:** Phoenix Ctry. Club; AZ Assn. of Indus. Devel.; **EDUC:** BS, Econ.; **BUS ADD:** 2920 N. 7th St., #10, Phoenix, AZ 85014, (602)263-5585.

GRAHN, Melvin——Bellemead Devel. Corp.; **PRIM RE ACT:** Developer; **BUS ADD:** 1717 No. Naper Blvd., Naperville, IL 60540, (305)369-1800.*

GRAINGER, LeRoy "Cecil"——B: Jan. 23, 1932, Conway, SC, *Pres.*, G-H Devel. & Realty, Inc.; **PRIM RE ACT:** Broker, Appraiser, Developer, Builder, Owner/Investor, Instructor, Property Manager, Insuror; **PROFL AFFIL & HONORS:** CRB; **EDUC:** 1958, Agricultural Econ., Clemson Univ.; **MIL SERV:** US Army, Cpl.; **OTHER ACT & HONORS:** Jaycees, VP, Pres., State VP, Natl. Dir.; Kiwanis; **HOME ADD:** 488 Hwy. 905, Conway, SC 29526, (803)248-4888; **BUS ADD:** 1400 Church St., (Hwy. 501), P O Box 710, Conway, SC 29526, (803)248-2204.

GRAMER, Clifford C., Jr.——B: Dec. 24, 1942, Chicago, IL, *Atty.*, Gerber, Ives & Gramer; **PRIM RE ACT:** Attorney; **PROFL AFFIL & HONORS:** ABA, NM State Bar Assn.; **EDUC:** BA, 1965, Eng., Yale Univ.; **GRAD EDUC:** JD, 1968, Northwestern Univ. School of Law; **HOME ADD:** 335 E. Buena Vista, Santa Fe, NM 87501, (505)982-0843; **BUS ADD:** Suite I, 320 Paseo de Peralta, P.O. Box 2325, Santa Fe, NM 87501, (505)988-9646.

GRANAHAN, Joseph A., Jr.——B: July 1, 1929, Phila., PA, *Part.*, Granahan, Martin E. Campbell Realtors; **PRIM RE ACT:** Broker, Consultant, Appraiser, Property Manager; **SERVICES:** Residential Sales, Appraising, Mgmt.; **PROFL AFFIL & HONORS:** GRI, CRB; **EDUC:** BA, 1951, Econ., La Salle Coll.; **MIL SERV:** USA; **HOME ADD:** 624 Lindley Rd., Glenside, PA 19038, (215)887-8531; **BUS ADD:** 7706 Ogontz Ave., Phila., PA 19150, (215)927-7700.

GRANDCOLAS, Wayne E.——B: Dec. 10, 1931, Belleville, IL, *Pres.*, Construction Escrow Serv., Inc.; **OTHER RE ACT:** Disbursing and Escrow; **SERVICES:** Disbursing & Escrowing of Construction Funds; **PROFL AFFIL & HONORS:** MBAA, Homebuilders Assn., Construction Indus. Credit Bureau, RE League of Greater St. Louis; **EDUC:** BS, 1954, Industrial Arts Design, S IL Univ.; **MIL SERV:** USA, Sgt.; **OTHER ACT & HONORS:** Greenbriar Hills Ctry. Club; **HOME ADD:** #9 Cedarbrook Ln., Kirkwood, MO 63122, (314)822-1962; **BUS ADD:** 215 N Meramec, St. Louis, MO 63105, (314)725-4810.

GRANT, Anne R.——*Exec. Editor*, Realtors National Marketing Institute, Publishing Div.; **PRIM RE ACT:** Real Estate Publisher; **BUS ADD:** 430 N. Michigan, Chicago, IL 60611, (800)621-9522.

GRANT, Eugene M.——B: July 17, 1918, New York, NY, *Pres.*, Eugene M. Grant & Co.; **PRIM RE ACT:** Owner/Investor; **PROFL AFFIL & HONORS:** Gov. NY RE Bd., VP Nat. Realty Club, Treas. & Tr. NY Realty Found.; **EDUC:** BA, 1938, Univ. of MI; **GRAD EDUC:** LLB, 1941, Law, Columbia Law Sch.; **MIL SERV:** USAF, Maj., Air Medal, Croix de Guerre, Pres. Unit Citation; **OTHER ACT & HONORS:** 1981-82 Campaign Chmn. NY UJA/Fed.; **HOME ADD:** 839 Orienta Ave., Mamaroneck, NY 10543, (914)698-7052; **BUS ADD:** 200 Park Ave., NY, NY 10166, (212)682-0480.

GRANT, Gerald P.——B: Apr. 11, 1925, Milwaukee, WI, *Mgr., Warehousing & Marketing Services*, Great Northern Nekoosa Corp., Butler Paper Co. & Nekoosa Envelopes, Inc.; **PRIM RE ACT:** Consultant, Engineer, Architect, Property Manager; **SERVICES:** Site selection, design, contract negotiation, construction; **REP CLIENTS:** Mgmt. of owned and/or leased multi-div. plant, warehouse & office facilities; **PROFL AFFIL & HONORS:** Chmn., Warehouse Operations Comm., Nat. Paper Trade Assn.; **EDUC:** BS, 1950, Naval Arch., Engrg., US Merchant Marine Acad.; **MIL SERV:** USN, 1942-46, QM; **HOME ADD:** 7933 S. Pennsylvania Dr., Littleton, CO 80122, (303)797-0118; **BUS ADD:** 23 Inverness Way E. Box 3359, Englewood, CO 80155, (303)773-8343.

GRANT, J. Kirkland——B: Feb. 14, 1943, Monroe, MI, *Dean & Prof. of Law*, Delaware Law School of Widener University; **PRIM RE ACT:** Attorney, Owner/Investor, Instructor; **SERVICES:** Consultant; **REP CLIENTS:** Hotel and private investors; **PROFL AFFIL & HONORS:** ABA; Bar in MI, NY, SC, Scribes; **EDUC:** BBA, 1965, Acctg. & Fin., Univ. of MI, **GRAD EDUC:** JD, 1967, Univ. of MI Law School; **EDUC HONORS:** Cum Laude; **OTHER ACT & HONORS:** Bd. of Dir. Wilmington Opera Society; **HOME ADD:** 5 Quail Crossing, Centreville, DE 19807, (302)655-5600; **BUS ADD:** Box 7474 Concord Pike, Wilmington, DE 19803, (302)478-3000.

GRANT, Michael A.——B: Mar. 25, 1947, Montreal, CAN, *VP*, Republic Realty Mortgage Corp.; **OTHER RE ACT:** Mort. Banker; **SERVICES:** RE Fin. & RE Portfolio Investment Advisory Servs.; **REP CLIENTS:** Ins. Cos., Pension Funds & Depository Instns.; **PREV EMPLOY:** 10 yrs RE Fin. exper. with same firm; **PROFL AFFIL & HONORS:** Chicago Mort. Bankers Assn., Chicago RE Bd.; **EDUC:**

BS, 1970, Mktg. & Adv., Univ. of IL; **OTHER ACT & HONORS:** Published Author; **HOME ADD:** 839 N. Brainard, Naperville, IL 60540, (312)355-1969; **BUS ADD:** 111 W. Washington, Suite 1737, Chicago, IL 60602, (312)558-8248.

GRANT, Miles R.——B: Feb. 14, 1952, Denver, CO, *Construction Mgr./Broker*, Wood Bros. Homes/Miles R. Grant Realty, N Denver; **PRIM RE ACT:** Broker, Consultant, Builder, Property Manager, Engineer, Owner/Investor; **PREV EMPLOY:** Prop. Mgmt. (Faith Realty), Ft. Collins, CO; **PROFL AFFIL & HONORS:** HBA Energy Comm. - Thornton, Westminister & Denver Coordinating Comm.; **EDUC:** Construction Mgmt. & Engr., 1974, Mgmt. & Engineering, CO State Univ.; **OTHER ACT & HONORS:** YMCA - Sporting house, NRA, Big Brothers; **HOME ADD:** 9854 W Polk Pl, Littleton, CO 30123, (303)973-0874; **BUS ADD:** 9854 W Polk Pl., Littleton, CO 80123, (303)455-9392.

GRANT, Richard C.——B: Sept. 6, 1943, Philadelphia, PA, *Partner*, Mershon Sawyer Johnston Dunwody & Cole; **PRIM RE ACT:** Attorney; **REP CLIENTS:** Devels., investors, brokers, lenders; **PROFL AFFIL & HONORS:** ABA, FL Bar, VP Collier Cty. RE Attys., Inc.; **EDUC:** BA, 1965, Lib. Arts, Univ. of FL; **GRAD EDUC:** JD, 1972, Law, Univ. of FL; **EDUC HONORS:** Order of the Coif; **MIL SERV:** USA, Capt., Bronze Star; **HOME ADD:** 158 Caribbean Rd., Naples, FL 33940, (813)597-7759; **BUS ADD:** Ste. 201, 600 5th Ave. S, Naples, FL 33940, (813)262-7302.

GRANT, Robert B.——B: Oct. 24, 1929, Springfield, MA, *Pres. (Prin. Broker)*, Syndex Financial Corp.; **PRIM RE ACT:** Broker, Consultant, Syndicator; **OTHER RE ACT:** Exchanger; **SERVICES:** Synd. and brokerage to accomplish coordinated tax-deferred exchanges; investment counseling; **REP CLIENTS:** Indiv. investors in comml. props.; **PREV EMPLOY:** USCG, Fin. Mgmr., 1951-1971; **PROFL AFFIL & HONORS:** Local, State and Nat. Assn. of Realtors; RNMI, CCIM; GRI; **EDUC:** BS, 1951, Gen. Engrg., USCG Academy; **GRAD EDUC:** MBA, 1961, Fin. Mgmt. (Comptrollership), George Washington Univ.; **MIL SERV:** USCG, Comdr, 1947-1971; **HOME ADD:** 60 Aalapapa Pl., Kailua, HI 96734, (808)261-2653; **BUS ADD:** 1750 Kalakaua Ave., Suite 3701, Honolulu, HI 96826, (808)944-5530.

GRANT, Stanley Charles——B: Dec. 2, 1928, Brooklyn, NY, *Prin.*, Stanley Charles Grant A.I.A., Architect; **PRIM RE ACT:** Architect; **SERVICES:** Planning, Architectural, Interior Design; **REP CLIENTS:** Corp. and Private; **PROFL AFFIL & HONORS:** AIA, Inst. Store Planners, NCARB Certified, Amer. Arbitration Assn.; **EDUC:** BBA, RE, CCNY; **MIL SERV:** USANG; Cpl., 42nd Infantry Div.; **OTHER ACT & HONORS:** Soc. of Amer. Military Engineers, Instr. in Architecture - Inst. of Design and Construction; **HOME ADD:** NY, NY; **BUS ADD:** 41 Union Sq., NY, NY 10003, (212)929-0944.

GRANTHAM, Russell A.——B: Oct. 25, 1920, Tamms, IL, *Pres.*, Greenway, Inc.; **PRIM RE ACT:** Broker, Attorney, Developer, Owner/Investor; **PREV EMPLOY:** VP, Gen. Counsel Fee Trunk Sewer, Inc.; **PROFL AFFIL & HONORS:** MO Bar Assn.; **EDUC:** BS, 1947, Bus. Admin, So. IL Univ.; **GRAD EDUC:** JD, 1950, St. Louis Univ.; **MIL SERV:** USAF; Capt., Distinguished Flying Cross, 5 air medals; **OTHER ACT & HONORS:** Chmn., St. Louis Cty Council, 1958-62; **HOME ADD:** 14269 Trailtop Dr., Chesterfield, MO 63017; **BUS ADD:** 6577 Cortena Dr., St. Louis, MO 63042, (614)731-5323.

GRANTON, Samuel Richard——B: Sept. 3, 1922, Buffalo, NY, *RE Counselor, Mort. Broker, Owner, Exec. VP*, Gran Terra Realty Inc.; **PRIM RE ACT:** Broker, Consultant, Instructor, Real Estate Publisher; **OTHER RE ACT:** Seminar spec. (RE & Profl. Fields) and RE Exchanger; **SERVICES:** Consulting, Seminar Work Shops, Mort. Brokerage, Paralegal Consulting; **REP CLIENTS:** Title ins. cos., escrow cos., attys.; **PREV EMPLOY:** Sr. Escrow Office & Title Officer Safeco Title Ins. Co., 1952-68; Nat. Escrow Officer, Title Group with US Fin., 1971-75; Mort. Broker & NASD Rep., 1968-71; **PROFL AFFIL & HONORS:** Sr. Cert. Escrow Officer designated by CA Escrow Assn., Intl. Exchangers Assn., Intnl. Bus. & Exchange Assn., London, England, Member Amer. Escrow, Achievement Inst., Member of Synd. Research Assn. (5 states), CA Escrow Assn., CSEO, Cert. Sr. Escrow Officer, CA Assn. of RE Teachers; **EDUC:** BS, 1950, Soc. Sci., CCNY; US Armed Forces Inst.; Graduate, Weaver School of RE (MO); **GRAD EDUC:** Candidate for MA, 1955-56, Hist. & Educ., Claremont Grad. Sch.; **MIL SERV:** USA, Tech. Sgt., USAF 2nd Lt., Direct comm. from Pres. Truman; **OTHER ACT & HONORS:** Co-author in nationwide RE Magazine "First Tuesday" August 1981 issue Nominee, 'A Name Only'; **HOME ADD:** 1652 Traveld Way, Encinitas, CA 92024, (714)436-0728; **BUS ADD:** 2157 Newcastle Ave., Suite A, Cardiff by the Sea, CA 92007, (714)436-5177.

GRANVILLE, Irwin E.——B: Oct. 24, 1934, New York, NY, *VP*, Lefrak Organization, Inc.; **PRIM RE ACT:** Developer, Builder, Owner/Investor, Property Manager; **SERVICES:** Prop. devel., const., prop. mgmt.; **PREV EMPLOY:** R&H Mgmt. Co., IBM, ITT; **PROFL AFFIL & HONORS:** RE Bd. of NY; **EDUC:** BSCE, 1957, CUNY; **GRAD EDUC:** MBA, 1969, Fin. and Investments, CUNY; **HOME ADD:** 320 West 76 St., New York, NY 10023, (212)724-8947; **BUS ADD:** 97-77 Queens Blvd., Rego Park, NY 11374, (212)459-9021.

GRASSER, George R.——B: Oct. 21, 1939, Staten Island, NY, Albrecht, Maguire, Heffern & Gregg, P.C.; **PRIM RE ACT:** Attorney, Instructor; **PROFL AFFIL & HONORS:** Erie Cty. Bar Assn., Chmn RE Comm., 1978-; NY State Bar Assn., RE Sect. Comm. on Condos and Coops., Subcomm. on Revision to Condo Act; Comm. Assn. Inst. VP Western NY Chapt.; Acad. of Authors Comm. Assn. Inst., Outstanding Achievement Award, Niagara Frontier Builders Assn., 1978; **EDUC:** BBA, 1960, Acctg., Iona Coll.; **GRAD EDUC:** JD, 1964, Fordham Univ. Sch. of Law; **MIL SERV:** USA, E-6; **OTHER ACT & HONORS:** Instr. broker's course and cont. educ. course of Buffalo Bd. of Realtors; Author *Prop. Taxes and HOAs* published Apr. 1980 by Comm. Assn. Inst.; **HOME ADD:** 40 Garden Ct., Amherst, NY 14226, (716)837-7755; **BUS ADD:** 2100 Main Place Tower, Buffalo, NY 14202, (716)853-1521.

GRASSI, Sebastian V., Jr.——B: July 8, 1954, Portsmouth, NH, *Atty.*, Law Offices of William M. Wright; **PRIM RE ACT:** Attorney; **SERVICES:** RE sales and purchase of legal counseling; RE devel. (legal counseling), business & tax planning, estate admin.; **REP CLIENTS:** indiv. sellers and purchasers, home building construction and RE devels., numerous religious organizations; **PREV EMPLOY:** IRS, Appellate Div.; **PROFL AFFIL & HONORS:** MI Bar Assn., Amer. Bar Assn., Christian Legal Soc.; **EDUC:** BS, 1976, Mgmt. and Labor Econ., Lehigh Univ., Bethlehem, PA; **GRAD EDUC:** JD, 1979, Tax Planning, Corp. and Bus. Planning, Univ. of Detroit Law Sch.; **EDUC HONORS:** Deans List, Beta Gamma Sigma, Law Review (member 'Journal of Urban Law'); **MIL SERV:** USMCR, Pvt. 1974-75; **HOME ADD:** 23890 Middlebelt, Apt. 2208, Farmington Hills, MI 48024, (313)474-2515; **BUS ADD:** 19500 Middlebelt, Suite 106W, Livonia, MI 48152, (313)478-5882.

GRASSO, James V.——B: Sept. 29, 1919, Newton, MA, *Dir., RE Devel.*, The Continental Corp., Corp. RE; **OTHER RE ACT:** Corp. RE Mgr., devel.; **SERVICES:** Plan, develop, lease, equip corp. premises; **PREV EMPLOY:** Building Constr. Consultant, 1967-80; Mgr./Sup. Bldgs. & Grounds, Harvard Univ., 1960-65; Geo. A. Fuller & Co., 1950-60; **PROFL AFFIL & HONORS:** ULI, Amer. Mgmt. Assn.; **EDUC:** AB, 1950, Govt., Harvard Coll.; **EDUC HONORS:** Cum Laude; **MIL SERV:** US Army, 1st Lt.; **OTHER ACT & HONORS:** Write, Lecture on Building, Real Estate, and Conservation; **HOME ADD:** 234 Rockland Ave., River Vale, NJ 07675, (201)666-1818; **BUS ADD:** 80 Malden Ln., NY, NY 10038, (212)440-3507.

GRAU, Franklin E.——B: Dec. 15, 1942, Havana, Cuba, *Pres.*, Grau Construction Co., Inc., Franklin E. Grau & Associates; **PRIM RE ACT:** Architect, Consultant; **OTHER RE ACT:** Planning. gen'l. contracting; **SERVICES:** Arch., Engrg. & Construction Services, Feasibility Studies; **REP CLIENTS:** Private and Instit. Investors; **PREV EMPLOY:** Planning Dir. for large RE development Corp.; **PROFL AFFIL & HONORS:** APA, NCARB Certified; **EDUC:** BArch., Design, Pratt Institute; **GRAD EDUC:** MArch./MS, Design/RE Devel., Pratt Instit./NYU/Univ. of Manchester, England; **MIL SERV:** US Army, Capt., Bronze Star; **OTHER ACT & HONORS:** Chmn., Miami Shores Code Enforcement Bd.; Member, N. Miami Arch. Review Bd.; Member, N.M. Mayor's task force; Board of Dir. L.R. Chamber of Commerce; **HOME ADD:** 857 N.E. 98th St., Miami, FL 33138, (305)754-6065; **BUS ADD:** 857 N.E. 98th St., Miami Shores, FL 33138, (305)751-8796.

GRAVATT, Larry G.——*Pres.*, Master Craft, Inc., Realtors; **PRIM RE ACT:** Broker, Developer, Builder, Owner/Investor; **PROFL AFFIL & HONORS:** FLI, NAR.; **EDUC:** Agric. Educ./Indus. Arts, SD State Univ.; **GRAD EDUC:** Bus. Admin., Black Hills State Coll, SD; **OTHER ACT & HONORS:** Chmn, Rapid City Planning Comm; Pres., Home Builders Assn.; Pres., Black Hills Board of Realtors; Pres., Rapid City Multiple Listing Service; **BUS ADD:** P.O. Box 2083, 36 E. Chicago, Rapid City, SD 57701, (605)343-6666.

GRAVERS, Renate——B: Sept. 4, 1944, Riga, Latvia, *Sr. VP*, UNI Realty Corp.; **PRIM RE ACT:** Broker, Property Manager; **SERVICES:** Sales, joint venture structuring, prop. mgmt., investment counseling; **REP CLIENTS:** European Investors; **EDUC:** BA, 1966, Poli. Sci. and Intl. Relations, NY Univ.; **EDUC HONORS:** Grad. with Honors; **HOME ADD:** 1561 Cooper Rd., Scotch Plains, NJ 07076, (201)889-1799; **BUS ADD:** 300 Lanidex Pl., PO Box 179, Parsippany, NJ 07054, (201)884-1166.

GRAVES, Darryl——B: Feb 13, 1947, Neodesha, KS, *Sec.-Treas.*, Graves & McGill, P.C.; **PRIM RE ACT:** Attorney, Owner/Investor; **SERVICES:** Counsel to builders, devels., lenders, brokers, realtors, bankers, arch. surveyers & engrs.; **PREV EMPLOY:** Ind. ins. adjuster; **PROFL AFFIL & HONORS:** CO & KS Bar; **EDUC:** BS, 1971, Business Administration, Kansas State Univ.; Garden City Jr. Coll.; **GRAD EDUC:** JD, 1975, Washburn Law Sch.; **OTHER ACT & HONORS:** Eagle Scout; Tr. Euzoa Bible Church; Sigma Alpha Epsilon Scholarship Award; **BUS ADD:** Box 772810, Steamboat Springs, CO 80477, (303)879-6200.

GRAVES, Ed——B: Feb. 6, 1944, Vancouver, WA, *Asst. Prof.*, American Coll.; **PRIM RE ACT:** Instructor, Insuror; **SERVICES:** Teach fin., law, ins. of RE; **PREV EMPLOY:** Prop. Mgr. 1965-1968; **PROFL AFFIL & HONORS:** Amer. Risk and Ins. Assn.; CLU Soc.; **EDUC:** BBA, 1971, Mktg., CA State Univ. at Los Angeles; **GRAD EDUC:** MA, 1975, Ins. and RE, Wharton School of Univ. of PA; **EDUC HONORS:** S.S. Huebner Fellowship 1972-1975; **MIL SERV:** US Army, 1968-1970, Sgt.; **HOME ADD:** 3787 Woodland Ave., Drexel Hill, PA 19026, (215)623-7355; **BUS ADD:** 270 Bryn Mawr Ave., Bryn Mawr, PA 19010, (215)896-4514.

GRAVES, James M.——B: July 31, 1935, Newark, NJ, *VP*, Loeb Partners Realty, Synd.; **PRIM RE ACT:** Broker, Syndicator; **OTHER RE ACT:** Handle apts., office bldgs., shopping ctrs.; **SERVICES:** Acquire props. as principal for investment or syndication; **REP CLIENTS:** Indivs., inst.; **PREV EMPLOY:** VP RE Loeb Rhoades Hornblower & Co. 1978-79, VP RE Shearson Hayden Stone 1966-78; **EDUC:** BA, 1957, History, Harvard; **GRAD EDUC:** JD, 1960, Law, Columbia; **EDUC HONORS:** Cum Laude; **HOME ADD:** 49 E. 96th St., New York, NY 10028, (212)883-0375; **BUS ADD:** 521 5th Ave., New York, NY 10175.

GRAVES, Philip F——*Dir. RE*, GAF Corp.; **PRIM RE ACT:** Property Manager; **BUS ADD:** 140 W. 51st St., New York, NY 10020, (212)621-5000.*

GRAVES, Richard W.——B: Feb. 27, 1936, Texarkana, TX, *Mgr.-Dallas RE Investment Office*, Northwestern Mutual Life Insurance Co., RE investments; **OTHER RE ACT:** RE Portfolio mgr.; **SERVICES:** Fin., devel., prop. mgmt., RE investments; **PROFL AFFIL & HONORS:** T. Mort. Bankers Assn.; Dallas Mort. Bankers Assn.; Dallas C of C; **EDUC:** BBA, 1958, Acctg., fin., econ., Baylor Univ.; **MIL SERV:** US Army, 1st Sgt.; **OTHER ACT & HONORS:** Metro Businessmen's Assn., Baylor Alumni Council, Who's Who in Fin. & indus. 1978-80, Personalities in the South 1978, MT Club; Boy Scouts Committee; Baptist Deacon - VChmn. of Deacons, 1st Baptist Plano, Past Bd. Member, FL Baptist Children's Home; Cty. Task Force; Amer. Securities Council; **HOME ADD:** 3615 N. Echo Trail, Plano, TX 75023, (214)596-7069; **BUS ADD:** 7616 LBJ Frwy., Suite 727, Dallas, TX 75251, (214)387-9014.

GRAVES, Thomas W., Jr.——*Secy.*, Fieldcrest Mills; **PRIM RE ACT:** Property Manager; **BUS ADD:** 326 E. Stadium Dr., Eden, NC 27288, (919)623-2123.*

GRAVES, William G., III——B: Apr. 8, 1942, Miami Beach, FL, *Pres.*, William Graves & Assoc. Ltd.; **PRIM RE ACT:** Broker, Owner/Investor, Property Manager, Syndicator; **SERVICES:** Investment counseling, brokerage & synd. of investment prop., prop. mgmt.; **PROFL AFFIL & HONORS:** Member Instit. of RE Mgmt., Community Assns. Instit., NAR, AZ Assn. of Realtors, Cert. Prop. Mgr., Accredited Mgmt. Org.; **EDUC:** Poli. Sci., 1967, Intl. Bus., Sophia Univ., Tokyo; **EDUC HONORS:** Cum Laude; **OTHER ACT & HONORS:** Lions Club, YMCA Comm., JCC Comm.; **BUS ADD:** 5119 N. 19th Ave. W, Phoenix, AZ 85015, (602)242-6644.

GRAY, Edward W., Jr.——B: Mar. 15, 1946, Gary, IN, *Sr. Atty.*, R.R. Donnelley & Sons Co., Corp. Headquarters; **PRIM RE ACT:** Attorney, Instructor; **SERVICES:** Full range of RE counseling; drafting; **REP CLIENTS:** R.R. Donnelley & Sons Co.; NAR; **PREV EMPLOY:** Kirkland & Ellis Assoc. 1970-73, specialized in RE litigation; **PROFL AFFIL & HONORS:** ABA; Chicago Bar Assn.; Chicago Council of Lawyers, Chmn., Hearing Bd., IL; Atty., Registration and Disciplinary System of Supreme Ct. of IL; **EDUC:** BA, 1970, Sociology, Univ. of Chicago; **GRAD EDUC:** JD, 1970, Columbia Univ.; **OTHER ACT & HONORS:** Bd. of Chicago Child Care Soc.; **HOME ADD:** 5400 S. Hyde Park Blvd., 13, Chicago, IL 60615, (312)955-8916; **BUS ADD:** 2223 S. Martin L. King Dr., Chicago, IL 60616, (312)326-8012.

GRAY, Jan Charles——B: June 15, 1947, Des Moines, IA, *VP & Gen. Counsel, Public Affairs*, Ralphs Grocery Co., Legal Dept.; **PRIM RE ACT:** Broker, Attorney, Owner/Investor, Instructor; **OTHER RE ACT:** Author; **PREV EMPLOY:** Assoc. Kindel & Anderson, LA; Assoc. Halstead, Baker & Sterling (now HaLstead & Baker), LA; **PROFL AFFIL & HONORS:** ABA, State Bar of CA, Los Angeles Cty Bar Assn., San Fernando Valley Bar Assn., CA RE Broker, Arbitrator, Amer. Arbitration Assn., Judge Pro Tem, Los Angeles Municipal Court; **EDUC:** AB, 1969, Econ., emphasis Indus. Organ., Univ. of CA (Berkeley); **GRAD EDUC:** JD, 1972, Harvard Law Sch.; **EDUC HONORS:** Summa cum laude; **MIL SERV:** USA, Hon. discharge; **OTHER ACT & HONORS:** Member Democratic Central Comm., LA Cty. 1980-82; Amer. Econ. Assn., Phi Beta Kappa of S CA, Harvard Club of S. CA, Univ. of CA (Berkeley) Alumni Assn., Town Hall of Los Angeles, Los Angeles World Affairs Council, Publications: "Tax Aspects of Real Estate Developments & Reacquisitions", American Bar Association, Section of Real Property, Probate and Trust Law Publications, "Real Estate in Mid-Century: Transition, Taxation and Trends" (1974); "Issues in Rent Control: Or, Law Isn't Everything", Public Law Section of the State Bar of California Fourth Annual Program Syllabus, Vol. 4, No. 1 (1979); "Rent Control: An Analysis for the 80's Part I: An Historical Perspective", Apartment Business Outlook, Vol. 2, No. 5 (1980); "Part II: Implications for the Future", Apartment Business Outlook, Vol. 2, No. 7 (1981); **HOME ADD:** PO Box 470, Beverly Hills, CA 90213; **BUS ADD:** PO Box 54143, Los Angeles, CA 90054, (213)637-1101.

GRAY, Leslie B.——B: Apr. 8, 1924, E. Springfield, NY, *Pres.*, Pomeroy Appraisal Assoc., Inc.; **PRIM RE ACT:** Consultant, Appraiser; **SERVICES:** RE appraising and counseling; **REP CLIENTS:** Lenders, attys., govt. agencies; **PREV EMPLOY:** NY State Bd. of Equalization & Assessment, 1960-1964; **PROFL AFFIL & HONORS:** AIREA; ASREC; ULI, MAI; CRE; **EDUC:** AS, 1943, Agric. Engrg., Cornell Univ.; **OTHER ACT & HONORS:** Bd. of Educ., 1950-1956; Kiwanis; Metropolitan Devel. Assn.; Meals on Wheels Bd. Member; **HOME ADD:** 4458 Sunset Dr., Syracuse, NY 13215, (315)469-0978; **BUS ADD:** One Lincoln Ctr., Syracuse, NY 13202, (315)422-7106.

GRAY, Loren Gene——B: Dec. 28, 1931, Moundsville, WV, *Owner Broker*, Sun Valley Realty; **PRIM RE ACT:** Broker, Appraiser; **SERVICES:** Offering complete RE serv.; **PROFL AFFIL & HONORS:** NAR, AACA, GRI, CRS, CAR; **MIL SERV:** USA, Cpl.; **OTHER ACT & HONORS:** Bd. of Dir. Mercantile Bank; **HOME ADD:** 1027 Grandview Rd., Glen Dale, WV 26038, (304)845-6987; **BUS ADD:** 703 5th St., Moundsville, WV 26041, (304)845-8500.

GRAY, Michael R.——B: Mar. 7, 1943, Stamford, CT, *Pres.*, Pyramid Real Estate & Mgmt. Co.; **PRIM RE ACT:** Broker, Owner/Investor, Property Manager, Syndicator; **SERVICES:** Brokerage, Mgmt., Repair and Maint. Mgmt., Synd.; **PREV EMPLOY:** VP, Lomas & Nettleton Co.; **EDUC:** BBA, 1966, Mktg./Fin., Univ. of Cincinnati; **OTHER ACT & HONORS:** Bd. of Taxation, City of Stamford, CT; Dir. Cosmepak Corp.; **HOME ADD:** 65 Flint Rock Rd., Stamford, CT 06903, (203)329-0884; **BUS ADD:** 20 Summer St., Stamford, CT 06901, (203)348-8566.

GRAY, V. Allen——B: Feb. 25, 1943, Denver, CO, *Gen. Mgr.*, The Harvey Canal, Land and Improvement Co.; **PRIM RE ACT:** Developer, Owner/Investor, Property Manager; **REP CLIENTS:** McDermott, Inc.; Combustion Engrg., Inc.; Halliburton, Inc.; Winn-Dixie; TG & Y; Volume Shoe; K & B Drugs; Revco; **PREV EMPLOY:** Point Clear Co., Mobile, AL 1977-1980; Univ. of WA, Seattle, WA 1975-1977; Dept. of Defense, 1965-1975; **EDUC:** BA, 1965, Hist./Pol. Sci., Univ. of CO, Boulder, CO; **GRAD EDUC:** M.Lib., 1977, Information Sci., Univ. of WA, Seattle, WA; **OTHER ACT & HONORS:** Harvey Canal Indus. Assn.; **HOME ADD:** 3908 Perrier St., New Orleans, LA 70115, (504)891-8701; **BUS ADD:** 1016 First Nat. Bank of Commerce Bldg., New Orleans, LA 70112, (504)529-2989.

GRAYBIEL, Allan C.——*Chmn. of the Bd.*, First Fed. S&L of Lenawee Cty.; **PRIM RE ACT:** Appraiser, Developer, Syndicator, Instructor; **PROFL AFFIL & HONORS:** SRA; **BUS ADD:** 202 N Main St., Adrian, MI 49221, (517)265-6126.

GRAYBILL, Michael A.——B: June 9, 1947, Augusta, GA, *Pres.*, Trotter Realty Comml. & Investment Div.; **PRIM RE ACT:** Broker, Syndicator, Developer, Builder, Property Manager; **SERVICES:** Div. and synd. of commercial prop., exchanges, valuation, prop. mgmt.; **PREV EMPLOY:** Exec. VP, CSRA Capital Corp.; **PROFL AFFIL & HONORS:** CCIM Candidate; **EDUC:** BBA, 1970, Finance, George Washington Univ., Wash., DC; **GRAD EDUC:** MBA, Finance and Investments, George Washington Univ., Wash. DC; **EDUC HONORS:** Claude F. Stokes Memorial Scholarship; **OTHER ACT & HONORS:** Past Pres., W. Augusta Rotary; Chrmn. Boy Interact Club; **HOME ADD:** 354 Habersham Rd., Augusta, GA 30907, (404)860-5755; **BUS ADD:** 3512 Wheeler Rd., Augusta, GA 30909, (404)736-4211.

GRAYSON, James Y.——**B:** Mar. 21, 1943, Paterson, NJ, *Atty. at Law*; **PRIM RE ACT:** Broker, Attorney; **SERVICES:** Counsel, investments, fin. & retirement planning; **PROFL AFFIL & HONORS:** CA Bar Assn., ABA, Section on Real Prop, probate & trust law; **EDUC:** 1965, Econ., Educ., Calvin Coll.; **GRAD EDUC:** MA, 1968, Education, MI State Univ.; JD, 1977, W. State Univ. Coll. of Law-San Diego; **HOME ADD:** 703 Bonita Dr., Folsom, CA 95630, (916)933-2953; **BUS ADD:** 5200 Sunrise Blvd. #3, Fair Oaks, CA 95630, (916)961-2227.

GRAYSON, John A.——**B:** Oct. 14, 1930, Lowell, IN, *Part.*, Ice Miller Donadio & Ryan; **PRIM RE ACT:** Attorney, Consultant; **SERVICES:** Gen. legal services to all facets of RE indus.; **REP CLIENTS:** Lenders, devels., retail store tenants & gen. indus. & comml. users of RE; **PREV EMPLOY:** Visiting Asst. Prof of Law, IN Univ. School of Law 1957-58; **PROFL AFFIL & HONORS:** Amer. IN State & Indianapolis Bar Assns., Charter Fellow of the Indiana Bar Foundation; **EDUC:** BS, 1952, Public Speaking & Comm., Northwestern Univ.; **GRAD EDUC:** JD, 1955, Univ. of MI School of Law; **EDUC HONORS:** Hardy Scholar 1948-52; **OTHER ACT & HONORS:** Bds. of Dirs., Greater Indianapolis Progress Comm, Crossroads Rehab. Ctr. Inc., Indiana Repertory Theatre, Inc.; **HOME ADD:** 6836 Cricklewood Rd., Indianapolis, IN 46220, (317)849-1509; **BUS ADD:** 111 Monument Cir., Indianopolis, IN 46204, (317)635-1213.

GRAYSON, Michael A.——**B:** Mar. 18, 1943, Detoit, MI, *Partner*, Flame, Sanger, Grayson & Ginsburg, A Profl. Corp.; **PRIM RE ACT:** Attorney; **SERVICES:** Full legal serv. in connection with real prop.; **REP CLIENTS:** Indiv. investors, devels. and brokers; **PROFL AFFIL & HONORS:** Los Angeles Cty. Bar Assn. (Member Real Prop. Law Sect.), ABA, State Bar of CA; **EDUC:** BS, 1964, Bus. Admin., Univ. of CA Los Angeles; **GRAD EDUC:** JD, 1967, Univ. of CA Los Angeles; **BUS ADD:** 16633 Ventura Blvd., Ste. 600, Encino, CA 91436, (213)788-3720.

GRAYSON, Stephen R.——**B:** May 21, 1938, New York, NY, *Pres.*, Stephen R. Grayson Realty, Inc.; **PRIM RE ACT:** Broker, Attorney, Developer, Builder, Property Manager, Owner/Investor, Syndicator, Engineer; **SERVICES:** Devel. and Synd. of Office and Indus. Bldgs.; Prop. Mgmt. of Owned RE Investments; Residential Construction; **PREV EMPLOY:** IBM, Penril Data Communications, Inc., Honeywell Grp., Sanders Associates, Inc.; **PROFL AFFIL & HONORS:** ABA, NAHB, SMHBA, DC Bar Assoc., ABA-Real Prop. Div., US Court of Claims, US Court of Customs and Patent Appeals, US Supreme Court, US Court of Appeals, B.I.E., L.L.B.; **EDUC:** BS, 1959, Indus. Engrg.-Constr., GA Inst. of Technol.; **GRAD EDUC:** LLB, 1963, Patent and Trademark Law, George Washington Univ. Natl. Law Ctr.; **EDUC HONORS:** VP-Student Bar Assn.; **OTHER ACT & HONORS:** Montgomery Cty., MD; WSSC Task Force and Housing Policy Comm.; Bd. of Dirs., Jewish Community Ctr. of Greater Washington; Bd. of Dirs., Woodmont Country Club; Luxmanor Citizens Assn. Bd. of Dirs.; Builders Design & Leasing, Inc. Bd. of Dirs.; **BUS ADD:** 6276 Montrose Rd., Rockville, MD 20852, (301)770-7566.

GRAYSON, W. Cabell, Jr.——**B:** Nov. 4, 1953, Wash., DC, *Apt. Spec.*, Coldwell Banker Comml. Brokerage Servs., Apt. and Investments; **PRIM RE ACT:** Broker; **SERVICES:** Sales and brokerage of apt. and investment prop.; **REP CLIENTS:** Indiv. and instnl. investors in apt. and investment prop., condo. converters; **PREV EMPLOY:** Spec. Asst., Conservation Foundation, Wash. DC; **PROFL AFFIL & HONORS:** Nat. Multi Housing Council; N. VA Apt. Assn.; Apt. and Office Bldg. Assn.; NAA; **EDUC:** BA, 1977, Hist. and Environmental Science, Yale Univ.; **GRAD EDUC:** 1975-1976, Danish, Krabbesholm Hojskole, Skive, Denmark; **HOME ADD:** 1222 N. Meade St., Arlington, VA 22209, (703)276-9660; **BUS ADD:** 2020 K Street N.W., Ste. 340, Washington, DC 20006, (202)457-5700.

GRAZIANO, Anthony——**B:** Dec. 7, 1943, Newark, NJ, *Pres.*, Atlantic Coast Realty APpraisal Group; **PRIM RE ACT:** Consultant, Appraiser; **SERVICES:** Consultation, valuation; **REP CLIENTS:** Public agencies and private investors; **PROFL AFFIL & HONORS:** AIREA; NAR, MAI; IFAS; CTA; **OTHER ACT & HONORS:** Bd. of Dir., NJ Chap. AIREA; Bd. of Dir., Toms River Area YMCA; **HOME ADD:** 1365 Silverton Rd., Toms River, NJ 08753, (201)341-4496; **BUS ADD:** 201 Hooper Ave., Toms River, NJ 08753, (201)244-7000.

GREBLER, Arthur R.——**B:** May 21, 1918, Brooklyn, NY, *COB each co.*, Universal Cities Real Estate Co., Inc. - Wram Development Co., Inc.- Grebler & Sons, Inc.; **PRIM RE ACT:** Broker, Consultant, Appraiser, Developer, Builder, Owner/Investor, Syndicator; **OTHER RE ACT:** Professor, Lecturer, Writer; **PROFL AFFIL & HONORS:** NARA, Sr. Member San Fernando Valley Bd. of Realtors; Urban Land institute, Staff - CA State Univ.; Lifetime Community College Credential; **EDUC:** PhB, 1940, Urban Land Econ. & Labor Econ., Univ. of WI; **GRAD EDUC:** PhM, 1941, City Mgmt., Univ. of WI; **MIL SERV:** US Army, T. Sgt.; **OTHER ACT & HONORS:** Amer. Film Instit.; **HOME ADD:** 5831 Wish Ave., Encino, CA 91316, (213)881-5382; **BUS ADD:** 4386 Lankershim Blvd., Toluca Lake, CA 91602, (213)763-8481.

GREEK, Frank, Jr.——**B:** Mar. 1941, NJ, *Pres.*, Frank A. Greek & Son, Inc.; **PRIM RE ACT:** Developer, Builder, Owner/Investor, Property Manager; **SERVICES:** Design/build, lease/sell in indus. field; **PROFL AFFIL & HONORS:** NAIOP, C of C, PE; **EDUC:** BSCE, 1963, GA Tech.; **MIL SERV:** US Army, Lt.; **BUS ADD:** 158 Tices Ln., East Brunswick, NJ 08816.

GREELEY, Larry——**B:** Sept. 1, 1933, Toledo, OH, *Salesman*, NEAL Realty; **PRIM RE ACT:** Owner/Investor; **OTHER RE ACT:** RE Salesman-investor; **PREV EMPLOY:** Educ.-School Band Dir. 22 yrs. 1956-78; **PROFL AFFIL & HONORS:** Member MEich Ed. Assn.-Nat., MI School Band & Orchestra Assn.; **EDUC:** Univ. of Toledo, 1956, Music Ed., Ed.; **GRAD EDUC:** 1966, Music Ed., Wayne State Univ.; **MIL SERV:** USA, Signal Corp., 1st Lt.; **OTHER ACT & HONORS:** Toledo Federation of Musicians; **HOME ADD:** 1966 W. Temperance Rd., Temperance, MI 48182, (313)847-8264; **BUS ADD:** 3102 Sylvania Ave., Toledo, OH 43613, (419)473-2433.

GREEMANN, Harvey W.——**B:** Nov. 9, 1946, IN, *VP*, Waterfield Mort. Co., Inc., Comml. loans; **PRIM RE ACT:** Broker, Banker, Lender; **PROFL AFFIL & HONORS:** W. MI Mort. Lenders Assn.; **EDUC:** BS, 1969, Fin., IN Univ.; **HOME ADD:** 6050 Adaway Ct. S.E., Grand Rapids, MI 49506, (616)676-0280; **BUS ADD:** 3445 Lake Eastbrook Blvd., S.E., Grand Rapids, MI 49506.

GREEN, Grant D.——**B:** Dec. 31, 1927, Syracuse, NY, *Sr. VP*, Landauer Assocs., Inc., Mktg. & Fin. Servs.; **PRIM RE ACT:** Consultant; **PREV EMPLOY:** Princeton Univ.; Huberth & Huberth, Inc.; Albert B. Ashforth Inc.; Brown, Harris & Stevens Inc.; **PROFL AFFIL & HONORS:** Amer. Land Devel. Assn.; **MIL SERV:** USN, R.T. 1 Cl.; **OTHER ACT & HONORS:** Chmn., Princeton Township Zoning Bd. of Adjustment; **HOME ADD:** 44 Rollingmead, Princeton, NJ 08540, (609)921-8155; **BUS ADD:** 200 Park Ave., NY, NY 10166, (212)687-2323.

GREEN, Harvey E.——**B:** Aug. 21, 1947, Los Angeles, CA, *Rgnl. Mgr.*, Marcus & Millichop Inc., Investment Brokers; **PRIM RE ACT:** Broker, Developer; **SERVICES:** Investment broker; **REP CLIENTS:** Don Koll, Grubbard Ellis Realty, Ford Mfrs. Life Ins. Co., Empire S&L, Equitec Fin. Corp., US Nat. Bank of OR, So. Pacific RR; **PREV EMPLOY:** Coldwell Broker Investment Props., First VP Investment props.; **EDUC:** 1968, Bus. Admin., Univ. of CA; **MIL SERV:** USA, Sgt., Army Commendation Medal, 1968-70; **HOME ADD:** 12243 Huston St., Studio City, CA 91604, (213)506-4080; **BUS ADD:** 16530 Ventura Blvd., Encino, CA 91436, (213)907-0600.

GREEN, Herbert J.——**B:** June 10, 1927, NY, *Chief Expeditor*, Lone Star Ind. Inc.; **PRIM RE ACT:** Broker; **OTHER RE ACT:** Advisor - Counseling; **SERVICES:** Planning; **REP CLIENTS:** Internal; **EDUC:** BS, 1948, NYU; **EDUC HONORS:** Mgmt., Psych. Fin. Awards; **MIL SERV:** USN, WWII; **OTHER ACT & HONORS:** Rep. Town Mgr., Greenwich, CT - 12 yrs, Pres. Exped. Mgr. Assn. 1979-1981, Faculty: NYU, Faculty: Hunter Coll. (CUNY); **HOME ADD:** 66 Halsey Dr., Old Greenwich, CT 06870, (203)637-9958; **BUS ADD:** PO Box 2880, Greenwich, CT 06830, (203)661-3100.

GREEN, Jeffrey S.——**B:** Feb. 8, 1948, Chicago, *Sr. VP*, First Nat. Realty-Devco, First Nat. Realty & Devel.; **PRIM RE ACT:** Broker, Syndicator, Consultant, Developer; **SERVICES:** Comml. RE Investment Devel., Brokerage and Synd.; **REP CLIENTS:** Instl. Lenders, User and Indiv. Investors in Comml. RE; **PREV EMPLOY:** Coldwell, Banker Fin. & Devel. Serv. 1978-1980; Strouse-Greenberg Chicago, Dir. of Leasing 1975-2978; Jack Jacobs & Co., VP Comml. Prop. Acquisitions; **PROFL AFFIL & HONORS:** ICSC; Nat. Conf. of Off Price Malls; NAR; **EDUC:** BS, 1971, Econ., Mkt. Research, N. IL Univ.; **GRAD EDUC:** MBA, 1973, Econ., N. IL Univ.; **OTHER ACT & HONORS:** Open Lands Project, Friends Chicago River Devel.; **HOME ADD:** 3959 W. Glenlake Ave., Chicago, IL 60659, (312)478-8583; **BUS ADD:** 5230 W. 159th, Oak Forest, IL 60452, (312)687-7600.

GREEN, Jerome——**B:** May 15, 1922, Morgan, MN, *Pres.*, Apt. Consulting, Inc.; **PRIM RE ACT:** Consultant, Appraiser, Developer, Owner/Investor, Property Manager, Syndicator; **PREV EMPLOY:** Self, RE, farming; **PROFL AFFIL & HONORS:** MN Farm Mgrs. & Appraisers; **EDUC:** Cont. educ., Bus. & Fin.; **EDUC HONORS:** Valedictorian; **OTHER ACT & HONORS:** Sch. Bd. Member, 5 yrs., V Chmn.; **HOME ADD:** Morgan, MN 56266, (507)249-3315; **BUS ADD:** Morgan, MN 56266, (507)249-3315.

GREEN, John——B: June 14, 1945, Evanston, IL, *Owner*, Century 21 Bill Green Realtors; **PRIM RE ACT:** Broker, Property Manager; **SERVICES:** Resid. sales; **PROFL AFFIL & HONORS:** Century 21; **EDUC:** BS, Bus. Admin., Univ. of KS, Sch. of Bus.; **MIL SERV:** USA, 2nd Lt.; **HOME ADD:** 3708 SW 33rd, Topeka, KS 66614, (913)273-6295; **BUS ADD:** 3100 W 10th, Topeka, KS 66604, (913)233-2020.

GREEN, Marvin——B: Jan. 1, 1921, Louisville, KY, *VP*, Bass & Weisberg Realtors, Prop. Mgmt.; **PRIM RE ACT:** Consultant, Property Manager; **SERVICES:** Prop. Mgmt. & Counseling; **REP CLIENTS:** Investor in resid. & comml. props.; **PROFL AFFIL & HONORS:** IREM, Louisville Bd. Realtors, BOMA, CPM; **HOME ADD:** 3307 Cawein Way, Louisville, KY 40218, (502)458-4686; **BUS ADD:** 3411 Bardstown Rd., Louisville, KY 40218, (502)459-1928.

GREEN, Robert W.——B: Nov. 10, 1934, Lynn, MA, *Eastern Regional Sales Mgr.*, Western Digital Corp.; **PRIM RE ACT:** Owner/Investor; **EDUC:** BS, 1956, Marine & Electrical Engineering, MA Maritime; **MIL SERV:** USN, Lt. JG; **OTHER ACT & HONORS:** Elks, Boston Yacht Club; **HOME ADD:** 7 Calumet Ln., Marblehead, MA 01945, (617)631-0962; **BUS ADD:** 70 Atlantic Ave., Marblehead, MA 01945, (617)631-6466.

GREEN, Walter P.——B: June 25, 1921, New York, NY, *Sr. VP*, EI Realty, Inc.; **PRIM RE ACT:** Broker, Engineer, Developer, Builder, Owner/Investor, Property Manager; **SERVICES:** Promotion, devel., const. mgmt.; **REP CLIENTS:** A props. developer per our own grp.; **PREV EMPLOY:** Sr. VP Engr. Inc., Turnkey Contractors; **PROFL AFFIL & HONORS:** Licensed Profl. Engr.; Lic. RE Broker, Nat. Soc. of Profl. Engrs., Rensselaer Alumni Assn.; **EDUC:** BS, 1942, Civil Engrg., RPI; **GRAD EDUC:** MBA, 1955, Bus. Admin., Rutgers Univ.; **EDUC HONORS:** Tau Beta Pi, Chi Epsilon, Honorary Engrg. Socs.; **OTHER ACT & HONORS:** Chmn., Millburn Short Hills Democratic Party; Advisory Bd. Essex Cty. Vocational Schools; **HOME ADD:** 39 Merrywood Ln., Short Hills, NJ 07078, (201)379-6360; **BUS ADD:** 50 Park Pl., Newark, NJ 07101.

GREEN, William Trimble——B: Feb. 6, 1947, Laurel, MS, *Pres.*, The Green Lumber Co.; **PRIM RE ACT:** Broker, Developer; **PROFL AFFIL & HONORS:** Amer. Forestry Assn., Nat. Consumer Fin. Assn., Real Estate Broker #6997, Registered Forester #356; **EDUC:** BS, 1971, Bus. Admin., Centenary Coll. of LA; **HOME ADD:** 750 N 6th Ave., Laurel, MS 39440, (601)649-4285; **BUS ADD:** PO Box 2097, Laurel, MS 39440, (601)649-9023.

GREENBAUM, David Roy——B: Dec. 7, 1951, Rockville Ctr., NY, *Atty.*, Weil, Gotshal & Manges, Tax, RE Depts.; **PRIM RE ACT:** Attorney, Instructor; **PROFL AFFIL & HONORS:** Instr. NY Univ. RE Inst., School of Continuing Educ.; **EDUC:** BA, 1973, Soc. Scis, Univ. of Rochester; **GRAD EDUC:** JD, 1976, Law, Taxation & RE, Univ. of Chicago; **EDUC HONORS:** Summa Cum Laude, Phi Beta Kappa; **HOME ADD:** 233 E 70th St., NY, NY 10021, (212)628-5527; **BUS ADD:** 767 Fifth Ave., NY, NY 10153, (212)310-8436.

GREENBERG, Emerson P.——B: May 6, 1922, Litchfield, MN, *VP of RE & Facilities*, Gelco Corp.; **PRIM RE ACT:** Builder, Property Manager; **OTHER RE ACT:** Owner; **EDUC:** BBA, 1947, Univ. of MN, School of Bus. Admin.; **HOME ADD:** 5248 Know Ave., South, Minneapolis, MN 55419, (612)926-1978; **BUS ADD:** 1 Gelco Dr., Eden Prairie, MN 55344, (612)828-2666.

GREENBERG, Gerald Morton——B: April 7, 1930, Denver, CO, *Pres.*, Environmental Community Development Co.; **PRIM RE ACT:** Developer, Builder, Owner/Investor, Property Manager; **PREV EMPLOY:** During late 60s and early 70s, Mr. Greenberg founded Environmental Community Devel. Co., which emphasized the devel. of resid. facilities; **PROFL AFFIL & HONORS:** W. Regnl. Pres. of Self Storage Assn., In early 1974, Mr. Greenberg carried a successful proxy fight for Denver's largest REIT (Denver RE Investment Assn.); Supervised RE prop. worth over $130 million; **EDUC:** Exec. Program, 1979, Advanced Study of Bus., Amos Tuck Sch. & Univ. of CO (1948); **OTHER ACT & HONORS:** Member of C of C in 6 cities in CO; W. Rgnl. Pres. of Self Serv. Storage Assn.; Served 7 yrs. as a Bd. of Tr. with REIT (Denver RE Investment Assn.) & supervised RE prop. worth over $130 million; has Gen. Electric Award of Recognition for Leadership in Resid. Constr.; **HOME ADD:** 8101 E. Dartmouth #39, Denver, CO 80231, (303)340-2430; **BUS ADD:** 50 South Havana, Denver, CO 80012.

GREENBERG, Harvey——B: Oct. 22, 1945, Portland, OR, *Pres.*, Harvey Greenberg Financial Corp.; **PRIM RE ACT:** Broker, Developer, Syndicator; **OTHER RE ACT:** Mort. Broker and Consultant; **SERVICES:** Mort. brokering and consulting for maj. RE projects; **PREV EMPLOY:** Bache & Co, Stockbroker, 1969-1974; State of WA - Securities Fraud Investigator, 1974-1976; Sonnenblick-Goldman Corp., 1977-1980, Rgn. VP; **PROFL AFFIL & HONORS:** Mort. Bankers Assn.; NAIOP; **EDUC:** 1968, Bus. Admin./Fin., Univ. of WA; **HOME ADD:** 4126 50th Ave. S., Seattle, WA 98118, (206)725-6514; **BUS ADD:** 130 Lakeside Ave., Seattle, WA 98122, (206)325-8940.

GREENBERG, Howard, Esq.——B: Feb. 22, 1946, New Rochelle, NY, *Atty. (partner)*, Kleinbard, Bell & Porecker, Esqs.; **PRIM RE ACT:** Attorney; **SERVICES:** legal; **PREV EMPLOY:** Contracting Officer, USNR 1969-72; **PROFL AFFIL & HONORS:** Philadelphia Bar Assn., ABA, Probate and RE Div.; **EDUC:** BS, 1967, M.E., Towne School, Univ. of PA; **GRAD EDUC:** JD, 1973, Law, Univ. of PA; **EDUC HONORS:** Sigma Tau; **MIL SERV:** US Navy, Lt; **HOME ADD:** 7610 Mountain Ave., Elkins Park, PA 19117, (215)635-3599; **BUS ADD:** Suite 1550, United Engrs. Bldg., 30 S. 17th St., Philadelphia, PA 19103, (215)568-2000.

GREENBERG, Martin J.——B: Aug. 5, 1945, Milwaukee, WI, *Atty.; Adjunct Prof. of Law*, Strauss & Greenberg; **PRIM RE ACT:** Broker, Owner/Investor, Instructor, Syndicator, Real Estate Publisher; **OTHER RE ACT:** Author; **SERVICES:** Legal, investment consulting, synd., publishing, teaching; **PREV EMPLOY:** Hoyt, Green & Meissner, 1971-74; Weiss, Steuer, Berzowski & Kriger, 1974-76; Greenberg & Boxer, 1976-78; Private Practice, 1978; Asst. Prof. of Law, Marquette Univ. Law School, 1976 - ; RE Investments Consultant, Inter/Design Investments, Inc., 1976 -; **PROFL AFFIL & HONORS:** WI and Milwaukee Bar Assns.; ABA; Milwaukee Bd. of Realtors, WI Chap.; Shorewood Bd. of Review, 1977 - ; Woolsack Soc., 1978 - ; WI RE Examining Bd., Book Revisions Comm., 1978 -, Lawyers Pro Bono Publico Award 1978; WI Bar Found., "Project Inquiry" Lecturer; Dir. and Pres., Law Projects, Inc.; Who's Who in Amer. Law; **EDUC:** BS, 1967, Pol. Sci. and Hist., Univ. of WI; **GRAD EDUC:** JD, 1971, Marquette Univ. Law School; **EDUC HONORS:** With Honors, Pi Sigma Alpha; Pi Gamma Mu; Alpha Sigma Nu, honorary frats.; **OTHER ACT & HONORS:** Campaign Cabinet, United Fund Drive 1972-73; Tr., Marquette Univ. Law Alumni Assn.; Milwaukee Masonic Lodge No. 261; Chancellor, Tau Epsilon Rho Graduate Chap., 1972-3; Brotherhood Board, Congregation Emanu-El B'ne Jeshurun, 1976-78, 1979-present; Corporate Member, Jewish Vocational Service; Bd. of Dirs., Community Coordinated Child Care, 1976-77; **HOME ADD:** 9429 North Broadmoor St., Bayside, WI, (414)352-8918; **BUS ADD:** 1139 East Knapp St., Milwaukee, WI 53202, (414)271-4849.

GREENBERG, Stuart L.——B: Aug. 22, 1941, Chicago, IL, *Exec. VP*, The Abacus Group; **PRIM RE ACT:** Lender; **OTHER RE ACT:** Full service mort. banker; **SERVICES:** All forms of income prop. fin. services; **REP CLIENTS:** Devels., archs., lawyers, corps.; **PREV EMPLOY:** In mort. banking for 12 yrs.; Previously a teacher; **PROFL AFFIL & HONORS:** MBA, IMBA, CREB, AIREB, CMB, CRA; **EDUC:** BA, 1965, Educ., Fin., Roosevelt Univ.; **GRAD EDUC:** Sch. of Mort. Banking, Northwestern Univ., Post grad. work; **OTHER ACT & HONORS:** Past Pres., Jr. RE Bd. of Chicago; Past Director, IL Mort. Bankers Assn.; Lecturer, Mort. Bankers Assn. of America; Chmn., Planning Comm., IL Mort. Bankers Assn.; **HOME ADD:** Long Grove, IL 60047; **BUS ADD:** 10 S. Lasalle St., Chicago, IL 60603, (312)346-9172.

GREENBERT, Arnold C.——*Pres.*, Coleco Industries, Inc.; **PRIM RE ACT:** Property Manager; **BUS ADD:** 945 Asylum Ave, Hartford, CT 06105, (203)278-0280.*

GREENBURGER, Francis——B: Feb. 13, 1949, New York, NY, *Pres.*, Time Equities, Inc.; **PRIM RE ACT:** Developer, Owner/Investor, Property Manager, Syndicator; **SERVICES:** Resid. and comml., owner-mgr.; cooperative conversions; synds.; **EDUC:** BS, 1973, Pol. Sci., Baruch Coll.; **BUS ADD:** 825 Third Ave., New York, NY 10022, (212)371-6512.

GREENE, Earle W.——B: May 10, 1925, Salem, VA, *Managing Broker*, Earle Greene, Realtor; **PRIM RE ACT:** Broker, Consultant, Developer, Builder, Property Manager, Owner/Investor; **SERVICES:** Locate Sites For Users, Consulting; **REP CLIENTS:** Convenience Stores, Dev., Food Franchisors; **PROFL AFFIL & HONORS:** RNMI Comml./Investment Div., CCIM Designation; **EDUC:** BCS, 1948, Acctg., Nat. Bus. Coll.; **MIL SERV:** USAF, 1943-1945, S/Sgt., 5 Air Medals; **OTHER ACT & HONORS:** City Planning Commn.; **HOME ADD:** 1503 White Oak Ct., Martinsville, VA 24112, (703)638-8056; **BUS ADD:** 234 E Church St. (Box 3746), Martinsville, VA 24112, (703)632-6461.

GREENE, Gordon J.——B: Aug. 18, 1945, Chicago, IL, *VP*, Sheldon F. Good & Co.; **PRIM RE ACT:** Broker; **OTHER RE ACT:** RE Auctions; **SERVICES:** Comml. RE Brokerage & RE Auctions; **PREV EMPLOY:** Continental IL Nat. Bank; **PROFL AFFIL & HONORS:** Chicago RE Bd.; RESSI; Assn. of Indus. RE Brokers, Two time recipient of Campbell Trophy from NAR - outstanding comml. RE transaction in U.S., 1974 & 1975; **EDUC:** BS, 1968, Fin., Univ. of IL - Champaign; **MIL SERV:** USA, SP5-E5, 1968 - 1970; **OTHER ACT & HONORS:** Dir., Alpha Beta Chapt., Theta Xi Frat.; **HOME ADD:** 292 Shenstone, Riverside, IL 60546, (312)447-2781; **BUS ADD:** 11 N. Wacker Dr., Chicago, IL 60546, (312)346-1500.

GREENE, H. Theodore——B: Mar. 19, 1926, Boston, MA, *Pres.*, Glenrock Devel. Corp.; **PRIM RE ACT:** Developer, Builder, Property Manager, Engineer, Owner/Investor; **SERVICES:** Devel. of Residential Indus. & Comml. Prop., Prop. Mgmt., Consultation; **REP CLIENTS:** Individual & Instnl. Investors; **PREV EMPLOY:** Xerox Corp., 1965-1976, Corp. Dir.; **PROFL AFFIL & HONORS:** Bldg. Indus. Assn.; **EDUC:** BS Indus. Engineering, 1948, Production Mgmt., Econ., Univ. of CA, Berkeley, CA; **GRAD EDUC:** MBA, 1950, Marketing, Advertising, Stanford Univ.; **MIL SERV:** USN; 1st Class PO; **HOME ADD:** 710 N. Maple Dr., Beverly Hills, CA 90210, (213)274-5878; **BUS ADD:** 10000 Santa Monica Blvd., Los Angeles, CA 90067, (213)556-1833.

GREENE, Hiram J., III——B: Dec. 31, 1939, Wash., DC, *VP*, Edgewood Mgmt. Corp.; **OTHER RE ACT:** Prop. Mgmt.; **SERVICES:** Mgmt. resid. & multi family housing; **REP CLIENTS:** Lenders and investors of resid. props.; **PREV EMPLOY:** Pres., Union States Mgmt. Co.; Exec. VP H.S.I. Mgmt. Inc.; **PROFL AFFIL & HONORS:** Inst. of RE Mgmt., Chpt. 8, Wash, DC; Prop. Mgmt. Assn. of Metropolitan Wash., DC; Wash. Bd. of Realtors, CPM; **EDUC:** BS, Econ., Law, Prop. Mgmt., Engrg., Auburn Univ.; Amer. Univ., Wash., DC Univ. of MD, Coll. Pk., MD; **OTHER ACT & HONORS:** Prop. Mgr. of the Year 1974, Inst. of RE Mgmt.; Past Pres., N. GA Chpt. Inst. of RE Mgmt., Atlanta, GA 1974; **HOME ADD:** 13811 Castle Blvd. 22, Silver Spring, MD 20904; **BUS ADD:** 5454 Wisconsin Ave., Suite 1450, Chevy Chase, MD 20815, (301)654-9110.

GREENE, Randall Frederick——B: Apr. 17, 1949, Florida, *Pres.*, Greene Realty, Inc.; **PRIM RE ACT:** Broker, Syndicator, Developer, Builder; **SERVICES:** Condominium and suburban office bldg. dev.; **REP CLIENTS:** Instl. and Pvt. Investors; **PREV EMPLOY:** Pres., Coastland Corp. of FL (Over-the-Counter) 1977-80, Public RE builder and dev.; **PROFL AFFIL & HONORS:** IREM, Nat./State/Local Bds. of Realtors, Young Pres. Org.; Who's Who in the South; Who's Who in Finance; **EDUC:** AA, 1971, Eng., Univ. of FL; **EDUC HONORS:** FL Blue Key; Omicron Delta Kappa; Savant; Pres. Phi Kappa Tau Frat.; **OTHER ACT & HONORS:** Dir., Lee Co.; YMCA; Dir., Big Brothers of Lee Co. (FL); Aircraft Owners and Pilots Assn.; MENSA; **HOME ADD:** 344 Blanca Ave., Tampa, FL 33606; **BUS ADD:** 344 Blanca Ave., Tampa, FL 33606, (813)254-1031.

GREENE, Sheldon——B: June 25, 1933, Brooklyn, NY, *Pres.*, Sheldon Greene & Assoc., Inc.; **PRIM RE ACT:** Broker; **SERVICES:** Hotel-Motel Spec.; **PREV EMPLOY:** 1956-66, The Futterman Corp., NY, VP; 1966-68, Elk Realty, NY, VP; 1968-70, Keyes Nat. Investors, Miami, VP; **PROFL AFFIL & HONORS:** Miami Beach Bd. Realtors, Dir. (5 yrs.); Motel Brokers Assn. of Amer., Officer & Dir.; FL Motel Brokers, Inc., Pres., Hon. Community Prof. at FL Intl. Univ.; **EDUC:** BBA, 1954, Acctg./RE, CCNY; **MIL SERV:** USA, PFC; **OTHER ACT & HONORS:** Elks Club; Author, articles "A Modern Approach to Hotel Divesting in Hotel & Motel Mgmt." (1976); "What is Your Prop. Worth," in Can. Resort & Motel; **HOME ADD:** 7441 Wayne Ave., Miami Beach, FL 33141, (305)865-6701; **BUS ADD:** 1720 79 St. Causeway, Miami, FL 33141, (305)865-6932.

GREENE, Stanley H.——B: Aug. 13, 1934, New York, NY, *Architect*, Progressive Design Inc.; **PRIM RE ACT:** Architect, Developer, Builder; **SERVICES:** Complete arch. serv., planning and devel.; **REP CLIENTS:** Participation with land owners or investors in multiple housing or comml. projects; **EDUC:** BArch., 1957, Univ. of FL; **EDUC HONORS:** Gargoyle (Arch. Hon. Soc.), Phi Kapp Phi (Eng. Hon. Soc.); **OTHER ACT & HONORS:** Nat. Council of Arch. Registration Bds. Certificate holder; **HOME ADD:** 6855 E. Edgewater Dr., Coral Gables, FL 33133; **BUS ADD:** 1451 Brickell Ave. #303, Miami, FL 33131, (305)371-0272.

GREENE, Thomas——*Adm. VP*, Soundesign Corp.; **PRIM RE ACT:** Property Manager; **BUS ADD:** 34 Exchange Place, Jersey City, NJ 07302, (201)434-1050.*

GREENFIELD, Gerald——B: Sept. 9, 1939, Cohoes, NY, *Part.*, Jenner & Block; **PRIM RE ACT:** Attorney; **SERVICES:** All legal phases of comml. RE; **REP CLIENTS:** Lenders, devels., brokers, inst., investors, foreign invest., prop. mgrs., maj. corps.; **PROFL AFFIL & HONORS:** ABA; IL State Bar Assn.; NY State Bar Assn.; Chicago Bar Assn.; Chicago Mort. Attys. Assn.; **EDUC:** BA, 1961, Union Coll.; **GRAD EDUC:** JD, 1964, Albany Law Sch. of Union Univ.; **EDUC HONORS:** Law Review; **HOME ADD:** 1318 Edgewood Ln., Northbrook, IL 60062; **BUS ADD:** One IBM Plaza, Chicago, IL 60611, (312)222-9350.

GREENMAN, Andrew B.——B: Aug. 5, 1934, New Yok, NY, *Pres.*, Greenman Corporate Consultants, Inc.; **PRIM RE ACT:** Consultant; **EDUC:** BA, 1956, Journalism, Washington & Lee Univ.; **MIL SERV:** US Army, 1st Lt.; **HOME ADD:** 910 Jefferson St., Hollywood, FL 33019, (305)921-8017; **BUS ADD:** 307 S. 21st Ave., Hollywood, FL 33020, (305)929-2213.

GREENMAN, Karl——B: Jan. 9, 1933, Boston, MA, *Part.*, Greenman, Grossman and Duffy; **PRIM RE ACT:** Attorney, Syndicator; **REP CLIENTS:** Ryan, Elliott and Co., Spaulding and Co., Inc., Stride Rite; **PROFL AFFIL & HONORS:** Boston Bar Assn.; **EDUC:** BA, 1954, Poli. Sci., Univ. of VT; **GRAD EDUC:** LLB, 1957, Law, Harvard Law School; **MIL SERV:** USNR, Lt. Comm.; **OTHER ACT & HONORS:** Harvard Club of Boston; **HOME ADD:** 595 Clapboardtree St., Westwood, MA 02090, (617)326-3874; **BUS ADD:** 185 Devonshire St., Boston, MA 02110, (617)542-0297.

GREENSPAN, Arnold S.——B: Apr. 3, 1921, New York, NY, *Partner*, Greenspan Bros.; **PRIM RE ACT:** Developer, Builder, Owner/Investor; **SERVICES:** Build to suit, build for own acct., condo. & coop conversion; **PREV EMPLOY:** Const. laborer; **PROFL AFFIL & HONORS:** Pres. Westchester-Putnam Home Builders Assn.; **EDUC:** BA, 1941, Journalism, NY Univ.; **MIL SERV:** US Army Air Force, NCO, Bronze Star; **HOME ADD:** 75 Long Hill Rd., Briarcliff Manor, NY 10510, (914)941-6063; **BUS ADD:** 10 Franklin Ave., White Plains, NY 10601, (914)761-0820.

GREENSTEIN, Abraham J.——B: Sept. 23, 1945, New York, NY, *Partner*, Pohoryles Goldberg Forester Staton & Harris, P.C.; **PRIM RE ACT:** Attorney; **SERVICES:** Legal services (counseling & representation); **REP CLIENTS:** Devels., builders, permanent and construction lenders, condo. & cooperative converters; **PREV EMPLOY:** Acting Admin., DC Dept. of Housing & Community Dev's. Neighborhood Improvement Admin. (Housing Rehab., Code enf., condo. and co-op regulation), Chmn., Bd. of Condemnation; **PROFL AFFIL & HONORS:** ABA Sect. on Real Property, Probate & Trust Law; Wash. Bd. of Realtors Condo-Coop Comm.; DC Builders Assn. Legislation Comm., DC Builders Assn. Special Achievement Award; **EDUC:** BA, 1965, Spanish (Major), History (Minor), NY Univ.; **GRAD EDUC:** JD, 1968, The Geo. Washington Univ. Law Ctr.; **HOME ADD:** 7530 13th St., N.W., Wash., DC 10012, (202)726-2386; **BUS ADD:** 1801 K St., N.W. - Suite 1105 L, Wash., DC 20006, (202)785-2940.

GREENSTEIN, Gary G.——B: July 5, 1949, NY, *VP*, Quadrelle Realty Services, Inc.; **PRIM RE ACT:** Broker, Consultant, Appraiser, Property Manager; **OTHER RE ACT:** Rehab. of comml. prop.; **REP CLIENTS:** Weight Watchers Intl., Inc.; **PREV EMPLOY:** Wm. A. White & Sons, Inc.; **EDUC:** AAS, 1971, Communications, NY Inst. of Technology; **HOME ADD:** RD2 Box 69, Moseman Ave., Katonah, NY 10536, (914)245-6566; **BUS ADD:** 2 East Ave., Larchmont, NY 10538, (914)834-2600.

GREENSTEIN, Mitchell M.——B: June 4, 1952, Bronx, NY, *VP-Gen. Counsel Atty.*, Quadel Group, Inc.; **PRIM RE ACT:** Attorney, Syndicator; **SERVICES:** Synd., ownership & mgmt. of multi-family and hotels; **REP CLIENTS:** Indiv. and pension plans; **PROFL AFFIL & HONORS:** Member-PA Bar; **EDUC:** BBA, 1974, Acctg., Baruch Coll.-City Univ. of NY; **GRAD EDUC:** JD, 1977, Duquesne Univ. School of Law; **EDUC HONORS:** Cum Laude, Salutatorian; **HOME ADD:** 907 Sixth St., SW, Washington, DC 20024, (202)484-3318; **BUS ADD:** 11300 Rockville Pike, Eleventh Floor, Rockville, MD 20852, (301)468-9400.

GREENWALD, Charles K.——B: Jan. 21, 1929, Chicago, IL, *Dir. of Corp. RE*, Dart & Kraft, Inc.; **OTHER RE ACT:** Corp.; **SERVICES:** Gen.; **PREV EMPLOY:** IBM, Tishman Realty & Const., Kraft, Inc.; **PROFL AFFIL & HONORS:** NACORE, IDRC, Indust. RE Mgrs. Council; **EDUC:** BA, 1952, Pol. Theory, IN Univ.; **MIL SERV:** USA; **OTHER ACT & HONORS:** Dir. Corlands Corp. For Open Lands, Chicago, IL; **HOME ADD:** 702 Waukegan Rd., Glenview, IL 60025, (312)724-3659; **BUS ADD:** 2211 Sanders Rd., Northbrook, IL 60062, (312)498-8000.

GREENWOOD, Carl J.——B: Jan. 15, 1943, Orange, CA, *Pres./Owner*, Greenwood & Son, Real Estate Investments; **PRIM RE ACT:** Broker, Developer, Owner/Investor, Property Manager, Syndicator; **SERVICES:** Synd. of Income Producing RE props.; **REP CLIENTS:** Indiv. investors; **PROFL AFFIL & HONORS:** RESSI, CA Assn. of Realtors, NAR; **EDUC:** BA, 1964, Econ., Stanford Univ.; **MIL SERV:** USN, Lt.-j.g.; **OTHER ACT & HONORS:** Tustin Rotary Club; **HOME ADD:** 12575 Redhill Ave., Tustin, CA 92680, (714)838-4578; **BUS ADD:** 17452 Irvine Blvd. #A, Tustin, CA 92680, (714)544-4000.

GREER, Dennis F.——*Dir.*, Department of Housing and Urban Development, Administrative Services; **PRIM RE ACT:** Lender; **BUS ADD:** 451 Seventh St., S.W., Washington, DC 20410, (202)755-5123.*

GREER, Gaylon E.——**B:** Oct. 21, 1936, AR, *Prof.*, DePaul Univ., Grad. School of Bus.; **PRIM RE ACT:** Broker, Consultant, Instructor; **OTHER RE ACT:** Author; **SERVICES:** Investment counseling, tax planning, training; **REP CLIENTS:** Indiv. investors, profl. assns.; **PROFL AFFIL & HONORS:** Amer. RE and Urban Econ. Assn.; Fin. Mgrs. Assn.; RE Educators Assn.; Nat. Assn. of Corporate RE Execs.; **EDUC:** BS, 1963, Acctg., AZ State Univ.; **GRAD EDUC:** PhD, 1971, Econ., Univ. of CO; **MIL SERV:** USAF, Capt.; **HOME ADD:** Nine Stonehearth Square, Indian Head Park, IL 60525, (312)238-2542; **BUS ADD:** 25 East Jackson Blvd., Chicago, IL 60604, (312)321-8351.

GREER, Glenn E.——**B:** Oct. 20, 1926, Wilber, NE, *Branch Mgr.*, Benton McCarthy Realty, Bellevue E. Office; **PRIM RE ACT:** Broker; **SERVICES:** Full service resid. office; **PROFL AFFIL & HONORS:** RNMI, CRS, CRB; **MIL SERV:** USA (21 yrs.), Lt. Col., Bronze Star; **HOME ADD:** 16426 SE 21st Place, Bellevue, WA 98008, (206)747-6586; **BUS ADD:** 10 148th Ave. NE, Bellevue, WA 98007, (206)643-7333.

GREER, John L.——**B:** Aug. 24, 1934, St. Paul, MN, *Sec./Treas.*, Southwind Investments; **PRIM RE ACT:** Owner/Investor, Property Manager, Syndicator; **SERVICES:** RE Counseling; **REP CLIENTS:** Local Investors; **PREV EMPLOY:** Stockbroker, Ins. Sales, Rgnl. Sales Mgr. Nat. Co., Marriage, Family, Child Counselor (Licensed); **PROFL AFFIL & HONORS:** NAR, CA Assn. of Realtors, Investment Div.; **EDUC:** BA, 1957, Phil., Don Bosco Coll., Newton, NJ; **GRAD EDUC:** MA, 1977, Psych., Univ. of Santa Clara, Santa Clara, CA; **EDUC HONORS:** Magna Cum Laude; **MIL SERV:** USA, E-5, Good Conduct, CIC; **HOME ADD:** 848 Upton Way, San Jose, CA 95136, (408)265-4640; **BUS ADD:** 6472 Camden Ave. #203, San Jose, CA 95210, (408)268-3611.

GREER, Miles——Savannah Port Authority; **PRIM RE ACT:** Developer; **BUS ADD:** PO Box 128, Savannah, GA 31402, (912)233-9604.*

GREER, Richard B.——**B:** Apr. 3, 1931, Asheville, NC, *Realtor Assoc.*, Heritage Real Estate and Development Co., Cocoa Beach Office; **OTHER RE ACT:** Sales; **PREV EMPLOY:** US Army, Lt. Col. Retd.; **PROFL AFFIL & HONORS:** Cape Kennedy Bd. of Realtors, NAR; **EDUC:** BS, 1953, Hist., Eng., Jacksonville State Univ.; **MIL SERV:** US Army, Lt. Col., Legion of Merit W/OLC, Bronze Star, Joint Serv. Comm. W/OLC, Comm. Medal W/30LC; **HOME ADD:** 650 N. Atl. Ave., Cocoa Beach, FL 32931, (305)783-8157; **BUS ADD:** 130 Canaveral Pl., Cocoa Beach, FL 32931, (305)783-8157.

GREER, Sally W.——**B:** June 13, 1947, Charleston, SC, *Pres.*, Century 21 Port Realty, Inc.; **PRIM RE ACT:** Broker; **SERVICES:** Primarily resid. brokerage, some comml. devels.; **REP CLIENTS:** Kraft Inc., Litton Bionetics, Amer. Mutual Life Ins.; **PROFL AFFIL & HONORS:** Greater Charleston Bd. of Realtors, GRI, Dir. Charleston Bd. of Realtors, Dir. State Bd. of Realtors; **EDUC:** BA, 1970, Hist., Poli. Sci., Jacksonville Univ., Jacksonville, FL; **OTHER ACT & HONORS:** Charleston C of C; **HOME ADD:** 660 Sloan Dr., Charleston, SC 29412, (803)795-4709; **BUS ADD:** 628 St. Andrews Blvd., Charleston, SC 29407, (803)556-3810.

GREFE, Richard H.——**B:** July 15, 1935, Des Moines, IA, *Sec. & Gen. Mgr.*, Grefe Contractors, Inc.; **PRIM RE ACT:** Builder; **SERVICES:** Gen. Contractor, Single Family Custom Homes; **PREV EMPLOY:** Columbia Fed. S&L Assn. RE Appraiser, DC, RE Div.; **EDUC:** BS, 1958, Bus. Admin., VA Poly. Inst., Blacksburg, VA; **MIL SERV:** USA, SP-4, Good Conduct Award Commendation Award; **OTHER ACT & HONORS:** Nat. Rifle Assn.; Alaskan Malamute Club of Amer., BOD; **HOME ADD:** 4138 Virginia St., Fairfax, VA 22032, (703)273-1931; **BUS ADD:** 10010 Main St., Fairfax, VA 22031, (703)273-5616.

GREFFET, Charles V.——**B:** Oct. 16, 1920, Charleston, SC, *Pres.*, Greffet Realty; **PRIM RE ACT:** Broker; **SERVICES:** Specialize in unimproved land and comml. prop.; **PREV EMPLOY:** Retired from USAF; **PROFL AFFIL & HONORS:** NAR; RNMI; FLI; Tucson Bd. of Realtors; Tucson C of C, CCIM; AFLM; **EDUC:** BA, 1960, Pol. Sci., Univ. of MD; **GRAD EDUC:** MA, 1967, Latin Amer. Studies, Georgetown Univ.; **EDUC HONORS:** Distinction; **MIL SERV:** USAF; Col.; DFC, Legion of Merit, Air Medal; **OTHER ACT & HONORS:** Military decorations from the Governments of Argentina, Peru, and Venezuela; **HOME ADD:** 4630 Hacienda del Sol, Tucson, AZ 85718, (602)299-1337; **BUS ADD:** 5151 No. Oracle Rd., Tucson, AZ 85704, (602)887-2036.

GREGORY, Carl C., III——**B:** Aug. 20, 1944, Los Angeles, CA, *Pres.*, Amer. Western Realty Co.; **PRIM RE ACT:** Broker; **REP CLIENTS:** Major instns.; **PROFL AFFIL & HONORS:** ICSC; **EDUC:** BBA, 1967, Acctg., So. Methodist Univ.; **GRAD EDUC:** MBA, 1968, Fin., Univ. of So. CA; **OTHER ACT & HONORS:** Bd. of Trustees, The UMET Trust; **HOME TEL:** (213)454-0050; **BUS ADD:** 523 W 6th St., Los Angeles, CA 90014, (213)680-0880.

GREIF, J. H.——**B:** May 1, 1934, Leipzig, Germany, *Chmn.*, The Griffin Group of Co's.; **PRIM RE ACT:** Consultant, Developer, Owner/Investor, Property Manager, Syndicator; **SERVICES:** Investment, mgmt., fin., synds.; **REP CLIENTS:** Indivs., pension funds; **PREV EMPLOY:** Standard Oil Co., Exxon Nuclear Co.; **PROFL AFFIL & HONORS:** Fin. Execs. Inst.; Amer. Econ. Assn.; Amer. Fin. Assn., Who's Who in Fin. and Indus.; **EDUC:** 1954, Northwestern Univ.; **GRAD EDUC:** MBA, 1956, Fin., Univ. of Chicago; **HOME ADD:** 4714 E. Mercer Way, Mercer, WA 98040; **BUS ADD:** Professional Ctr. Bldg., Mercer Island, WA 98040, (206)232-4685.

GREIG, D. Wylie——**B:** Aug. 21, 1944, Washington, DC, *Dir., RE Industries Prog.*, SRI Intl. (formerly Stanford Research Institute); **PRIM RE ACT:** Consultant; **OTHER RE ACT:** mgmt; **SERVICES:** Market and fin. analysis, strategic planning and mgmt., consulting; **REP CLIENTS:** Devel., Major Corps., Fin. Instit., Inst. Investors; **EDUC:** BA, 1966, Eng., Juniata Coll., Huntingdon, PA; **GRAD EDUC:** MBA, 1972, Land Devel. & RE Fin., Wharton School, Univ. of PA; MCP, 1972, Grad. School of Fine Arts, Univ. of PA; **HOME ADD:** 2040 Edgewood Dr., Palo Alto, CA 94303, (415)858-2552; **BUS ADD:** 333 Ravenswood Ave., Menlo Park, CA 94025, (415)859-5276.

GREISINGER, Richard——*Admin. Sec. to Brd. of RE*, Michigan, Michigan Real Estate Div.; **PRIM RE ACT:** Property Manager; **BUS ADD:** PO Box 30018, Lansing, MI 48909, (517)373-0490.*

GRENDE, Michael R.——**B:** May 11, 1944, Missoula, MT, *Mgr. of Lands & Leases*, Western Energy Co.; **PRIM RE ACT:** Property Manager; **OTHER RE ACT:** Mineral and surface lease acquisition, land, purchase; **PREV EMPLOY:** MT Dept. of State Lands 1971-74; **PROFL AFFIL & HONORS:** Intl. Right of Way Assn.; **EDUC:** Agriculture Production, 1971, Range Mgmt., MT State Univ.; **MIL SERV:** USN, E-5, Antartic Serv. Award, Hon. Discharge; **OTHER ACT & HONORS:** City Council, Chmn., 1976-1980, MT Mining Assn.; **HOME ADD:** 1809 Bannack Dr., Billings, MT 59101, (406)259-5079; **BUS ADD:** 113 N. Broadway, Billings, MT 59101, (406)252-2277.

GRENIER, Michel——**B:** Apr. 28, 1943, Province of Que., *VP*, Larry Smith & Assoc. Ltd., Part of Coopers & Lybrand, Chartered Accts.; **PRIM RE ACT:** Consultant; **SERVICES:** Market analysis, feasibility studies, site selection; **REP CLIENTS:** Major devel., retailers, fin. insts., govts. archs. engrgs.; **PREV EMPLOY:** 1968-73 Larry Smith & Assoc., 1973-76 Mondev Intnl., 1976- Larry Smith & Assoc., Ltd.; **PROFL AFFIL & HONORS:** ICSC, Retail Council of Canada, Assoc. Quebec D'urbanisme; **EDUC:** BA, 1965, Coll. Ste.-Marie; **GRAD EDUC:** MA, 1968, Geog., Univ. de Montreal; **HOME ADD:** 869 Hardy St., Ste Therese, J7E 3Y8, Que, Can, (514)430-5293; **BUS ADD:** 630 Dorchester Blvd. W., Suite 2600, Montreal, H3B 1W5, Que, Canada, (514)866-0594.

GRENNAN, Thomas A.——**B:** Oct. 12, 1953, Grand Island, NE, *Atty.*, Gross, Welch, Vinardi, Kauffman & Day, P.C.; **OTHER RE ACT:** Litigation and Corporate; **REP CLIENTS:** East Const., Inc., Corkol Const., Inc.; **PREV EMPLOY:** Asst. to the Mayor, Papillion, NE; **PROFL AFFIL & HONORS:** ABA, NE Bar Assn., Omaha Bar Assn. (editor, Omaha Bar Newsletter 1979-present), Alpha Sigma Nu; **EDUC:** 1975, Creighton Univ.; **GRAD EDUC:** 1978, Law, Creighton Univ.; **EDUC HONORS:** Cum Laude, Alpha Sigma Nu; **HOME ADD:** 12327 Cuming St., Omaha, NE 68154, (402)493-2765; **BUS ADD:** 800 Commercial Federal Tower, 2120 S. 72nd St., Omaha, NE 68124.

GREW, Robert R.——**B:** Mar. 25, 1931, Metamora, OH, *Part.*, Carter, Ledyard & Milburn; **PRIM RE ACT:** Attorney; **REP CLIENTS:** Instnl. lenders, instnl. and individual investors; **PROFL AFFIL & HONORS:** ABA; Fed. Bar Assn., Lecturer, Practicing Law Inst.; **EDUC:** AB, Letters and Law, 1953, Univ. of MI; **GRAD EDUC:** JD, 1955, Univ. of MI; **MIL SERV:** USAF; 1st Lt.; **HOME ADD:** 8 E. 96th St., NY, NY 10028, (212)427-2617; **BUS ADD:** 2 Wall St., NY, NY 10005, (212)732-3200.

GREY, Francis J.——**B:** Nov. 30, 1931, Yeadon, PA, *Managing Part. Tax Serv.*, Coopers & Lybrand; **OTHER RE ACT:** CPA; **SERVICES:** Tax Serv.; **PREV EMPLOY:** 22 yrs. with C & L; **PROFL AFFIL & HONORS:** AICPA, PICPA, NAHB & PHBA, Dir. - Phila. C of C; Chmn. - U. of PA Tax Conf.; **EDUC:** BS, 1958, Accounting, Econ.,

Villanova Univ.; **EDUC HONORS:** Distinguished & PICPA Leadership Award; **MIL SERV:** USA, Sgt., 3 Battle Stars Korean War; **OTHER ACT & HONORS:** Bd. of Gov., Phila. Country Club & Union League; Lecturer in Law - Villanova Univ., Grad. Tax Program; **HOME ADD:** 2021 Waynesborough Rd., Paoli, PA 19301, (215)647-4625; **BUS ADD:** 2100 Three Girard Plaza, Philadelphia, PA 19102, (215)582-5186.

GREYTAK, Lee J.——**B:** Sept. 14, 1949, CT, *Controller*, Trammell Crow Co.; **PRIM RE ACT:** Consultant, Developer, Builder, Owner/Investor, Property Manager; **SERVICES:** Devel. of indus. & comml. parks, prop. managed.; **REP CLIENTS:** Indiv., instnl., pension investors in comml. & indus. props.; **PROFL AFFIL & HONORS:** Nat. Assn. of Accountants, Bd. of Dir. Nat. Assn. of Accountants, 1978-79; **EDUC:** BA, 1973, Acctg., Fin., RE, CA State Univ. of Fullerton; **EDUC HONORS:** Co-chmn. of the Acctg. Soc.; **OTHER ACT & HONORS:** Eagle Scout, Boy Scout Merit Badge Counselor, Jr. Achievement; **HOME ADD:** 1106 Angelcrest Dr., Hacienda Heights, CA 91745, (213)330-6534; **BUS ADD:** 6200 Peachtree St., Los Angeles, CA 90040, (213)724-2246.

GRIEME, Ralph B., Jr.——**B:** Jan. 16, 1943, Covington, KY, *Broker, Comml. & Industrial, RE, Pres.*, Grieme Devel. Corp.; **PRIM RE ACT:** Broker, Consultant, Developer, Owner/Investor; **OTHER RE ACT:** Gen. econ. devel. programs for local govts., broker, acquisitions, sales, leasing of comml. indus. & investment prop., devel. resid. and office projects; **REP CLIENTS:** IDC, City of Cincinnati, OH; **PREV EMPLOY:** VP RE Devel., VP Butler Co., Crescent Springs, KY; **EDUC:** AB, 1965, Bus. Admin., Thomas More Coll., Covington, KY; **GRAD EDUC:** MBA, 1969, Bus. Admin., Xavier Univ., Cincinnati, OH; **MIL SERV:** USA, Lt.; **OTHER ACT & HONORS:** Vice Mayor City of Covington, KY; Chmn. Northern KY area Planning Comm; Former Pres. and current member of Exec Comm. of the OH, KY, IN Rgnl. Council of Govts.; **HOME ADD:** 1012 Hillcrest Ln., Park Hills, KY 41011, (606)297-7565; **BUS ADD:** 1012 Hillcrest Ln., Park Hills, KY 41011, (606)291-7565.

GRIER, David C.——**B:** Jan. 27, 1928, Albion, MI, Neal, Grier, Hanson & Hanson; **PRIM RE ACT:** Attorney; **SERVICES:** All conventional atty. servs.; **REP CLIENTS:** Citizens Trust & Savings Bank of South Haven; **PROFL AFFIL & HONORS:** State Bar of MI; ABA; **EDUC:** AB, 1954, Hist. & Econ., Albion Coll., Albion, MI; **GRAD EDUC:** JD, 1957, Univ. of MI Law School; **EDUC HONORS:** With High Honors; Phi Beta Kappa; **MIL SERV:** US Army, S/Sgt., 1946-1952, Army Security Agency; **OTHER ACT & HONORS:** Van Buren Cty. Public Admin., 1967 to date; South Haven City Council 1964-1965; **HOME ADD:** 316 Clinton St., South Haven, MI 49090, (616)637-1096; **BUS ADD:** 401 Center St., South Haven, MI 49090, (616)637-1191.

GRIFFIN, Charles R.——**B:** March 5, 1943, Anchorage, AK, *Certified Public Accountant*, Charles R. Griffin, CPA; **PRIM RE ACT:** Consultant, Owner/Investor, Property Manager; **SERVICES:** Income tax analysis, property management; **REP CLIENTS:** Individual investors; **PREV EMPLOY:** Arthur Young & Co. (CPA's), San Jose, CA; **PROFL AFFIL & HONORS:** Army Inst. of CPA's; AK Society of CPA's; Amer. Acctg. Assn., CPA in AK & CA; **EDUC:** BS, 1970, Bus. Admin., San Jose State Coll., San Jose, CA; **EDUC HONORS:** BS with Distinction; Dean's List; Beta Alpha Psi; Beta Gamma Sigma; **MIL SERV:** US Army Reserves, Pvt., 1962; **OTHER ACT & HONORS:** Moose; Elks; AK State Fair, Director & Secretary; Palmer C of C, Dir. Treasurer; Mat-Su Baseball, Dir. & Treasurer; AK Independent Baseball League, Treasurer; **HOME ADD:** Star Route B, Box 7486, Palmer, AK 99645, (907)745-4421; **BUS ADD:** PO Box 670, Palmer, AK 99645, (907)745-3239.

GRIFFIN, Fred B.——**B:** Sept. 12, 1938, Houston, TX, *Pres.*, Griffin/Juban Interests Inc.; **PRIM RE ACT:** Developer, Owner/Investor, Property Manager; **EDUC:** 1960, Physics/Engrg., Washington & Lee; **GRAD EDUC:** 1962, Fin./Acctg., Univ. of TX; **BUS ADD:** 1502 Augusta #240, Houston, TX 77057, (713)975-1756.

GRIFFIN, George——*Pres.*, Michigan General Corp.; **PRIM RE ACT:** Property Manager; **BUS ADD:** Dallas Federal Savings Tower, 8333 Douglas, Dallas, TX 75225, (214)369-1500.*

GRIFFIN, James K., Jr.——**B:** Mar. 14, 1950, Holyoke, MA, *VP*, La Bonte Diversified Devel., Ind., New England; **PRIM RE ACT:** Broker, Developer, Builder, Owner/Investor, Property Manager; **EDUC:** BS, 1973, Bus. Admin., Georgetown Univ.; **GRAD EDUC:** MBA, Mktg. Mgmt., Suffold Univ.; **HOME ADD:** 3 Bacon Pl., Newton, MA 02164; **BUS ADD:** PO Box 1098, Plymouth, MA 02360, (617)888-7800.

GRIFFIN, John F.——**B:** Oct. 13, 1940, Washington, DC, *Pres. and Partner*, Mulligan/Griffin Associates, Inc.; **PRIM RE ACT:** Broker, Developer, Owner/Investor, Property Manager; **SERVICES:** Develop office & HiTech R&D Facilities; **REP CLIENTS:** Wholly owned or controlled RE Props.; **PREV EMPLOY:** Pres., DANAC Assoc. Inc.-Comml and RE Brokerage Firm; VP, DANAC RE Investment Corp., (comml. & indus. RE devel. firm); **EDUC:** BSBA, 1962, Gen. Bus.; **MIL SERV:** US Army, 1st Lt.; **BUS ADD:** 1700 Research Blvd., Rockville, MD 20850, (301)762-7070.

GRIFFIN, Ken——**B:** Feb. 3, 1931, Dallas, TX, *Atty.*, Ken Griffin, Atty.; **PRIM RE ACT:** Attorney, Owner/Investor; **SERVICES:** Legal; **REP CLIENTS:** Odessa Savings Assn.; Permian Bank & Trust; Murphy & Rochester, Inc.; **PROFL AFFIL & HONORS:** State Bar of TX; ABA; Ector Cty. Bar Assn.; **EDUC:** BBA, 1956, Univ. of TX at Austin, TX; **GRAD EDUC:** LLB, 1957, Univ. of TX at Austin, TX; **MIL SERV:** USMC, S/Sgt.; **OTHER ACT & HONORS:** Rotary Club; Church of Christ, Odessa, TX; **HOME ADD:** 116 Conet, Odessa, TX 79763, (915)337-8076; **BUS ADD:** Suite A, Odessa Savings Bldg., PO Drawer 4109, Odessa, TX 79760, (915)337-3535.

GRIFFIN, Mark Gerard——**B:** Mar. 30, 1947, Port Chester, NY, *Part.*, Lambert, Griffin and McGovern; **PRIM RE ACT:** Attorney, Instructor, Syndicator, Owner/Investor; **OTHER RE ACT:** Author; **SERVICES:** Legal Rep., Synd. of Comml. and residential prop.; **REP CLIENTS:** RE Dev., Lenders and Investors; **PREV EMPLOY:** RE Instr., Howard Univ and Strayer Coll.; **PROFL AFFIL & HONORS:** DC and MD Bar Assns.; Wash. Bd. of Realtors; **EDUC:** BA, 1969, Gov., Georgetown Univ.; **GRAD EDUC:** JD, 1973, Georgetown Univ.; **OTHER ACT & HONORS:** Member, DC RE Commn. 1977-1980; Member Advisory Bd. of Dirs., Madison Nat. Bank; Member Bd. of Dirs. of Columbia Hist. Soc., The Edes Home and the Bureau of Rehab. of the Nat. Capitol Area; **HOME ADD:** 3108 33rd Place, Wash., DC 20008, (202)244-5647; **BUS ADD:** 1629 K St. NW, Suite 200, Wash., DC 20006, (202)296-9000.

GRIFFIN, Mike G.——**B:** Aug. 2, 1948, TX, *Pres.*, Griffin Mortgage Co., Greener & Sumner Devel. Co.; **PRIM RE ACT:** Broker, Consultant, Developer; **SERVICES:** Comml. mort. banker; equity broker; packages to be built devel.; **PREV EMPLOY:** Murray Realty; First City Mort. Co.; **PROFL AFFIL & HONORS:** TX RE Broker; **EDUC:** BA, 1970, Econ. and Bus. Admin., TX C. Univ.; **BUS ADD:** 9500 Forest Lane, Suite 531, Dallas, TX 75243, (214)348-9631.

GRIFFIN, Paul E., Jr.——**B:** June 7, 1930, Los Angeles, CA, *Pres.*, Griffin Devel. Co.; **PRIM RE ACT:** Developer, Builder, Owner/Investor; **SERVICES:** Devel. of a variety of resid. projects, as well as comml. and indus. projects; **PREV EMPLOY:** Fourth generation homebuilder in S CA; **PROFL AFFIL & HONORS:** Bd. of Dir. of Building Indus. Assn.; V Chmn., Exec. Comm., BIA-Political Action Comm. (1981); Bd. of Dir. of Natl. Assn. of Home Builders; **EDUC:** BCE, 1953, Civil Engrg., UCLA; **MIL SERV:** USAF, Lt. Korean; **OTHER ACT & HONORS:** Bd. of Dir. of Moorpark Coll. Found.; Bd. of Trustees of UCLA Found.; Member of UCLA Chancellor's Assoc. State of CA Commission of the CA; **HOME ADD:** 19436 Kinzie St., Northridge, CA 91324, (213)349-1108; **BUS ADD:** 19436 Ventura Blvd., Tarzana, CA 91356, (213)881-5200.

GRIFFIN, Richard P.——**B:** July 12, 1938, St. Louis, MO, *Pres.*, Grifton, Inc.; **PRIM RE ACT:** Syndicator, Property Manager, Owner/Investor; **PROFL AFFIL & HONORS:** Apt. Assn. of MI; **EDUC:** BS, 1960, Chem. Engrg., Univ. of Notre Dame; **GRAD EDUC:** MBA, 1965, Fin., NY Univ.; **HOME ADD:** 1353 Shevchenko Dr., Ann Arbor, MI 48103, (313)994-6314; **BUS ADD:** 320 S. Main St., Ann Arbor, MI 48108, (313)995-2343.

GRIFFIN, Stephen L.——**B:** May 4, 1949, Atlanta, GA, *Branch Mgr.*, Mfr. Life Ins. Co., Dallas RE Off.; **PRIM RE ACT:** Property Manager; **OTHER RE ACT:** Inv. analysis; **SERVICES:** Prop. mgmt., acquisitions, dev. site loc.; **REP CLIENTS:** Co. portfolio; **PROFL AFFIL & HONORS:** IREM, Bd. of Realtors, CPM, BOMA; **EDUC:** BA, 1971, Econ, Bus. Admin., Vanderbilt Univ.; **GRAD EDUC:** MBA, 1975, RE, GA St. Univ.; **MIL SERV:** USA, E-4; **OTHER ACT & HONORS:** Neighborhood Planning Commn., Vanderbilt Club; **HOME ADD:** 5827 Waggoner, Dallas, TX 75230, (214)691-8437; **BUS ADD:** 2730 Stemmons Frwy., Dallas, TX 75207, (214)631-1970.

GRIFFIN, W.A.——*Pres.*, Daniel Industries, Inc.; **PRIM RE ACT:** Property Manager; **BUS ADD:** One River Way, Ste. 2200, Houston, TX 77056, (713)960-1300.*

GRIFFIN, William L.——**B:** Mar. 25, 1924, Kansas City, MO, *VP & Regional Operations Mgr.*, CIT Corp.; **PRIM RE ACT:** Lender; **SERVICES:** Intermediate fin.; **EDUC:** BS, 1948, Bus. Admin., Univ. of MO, Columbia, MO; **MIL SERV:** USNR; **HOME ADD:** 19

Cornwall Rd., Freehold, NJ 07728; **BUS ADD:** 1481 Oak Tree Rd., Iselin, NJ 08830, (201)283-3210.

GRIFFIS, Jack L.——**B:** July 1, 1932, Rossville, IN, *RE Broker*, Griffis Realty Investments; **PRIM RE ACT:** Broker, Owner/Investor; **OTHER RE ACT:** Exchangor, counselor; **EDUC:** BS, 1960, Bus. Admin., St. Joseph's Coll., Rensselaer, IN; **MIL SERV:** USAF, A/3c; **HOME ADD:** 2481 Ridge Park Lane, Orange, CA 92667, (714)637-6266; **BUS ADD:** 726 East Katella Ave., Orange, CA 92667, (714)633-6633.

GRIFFITH, Charles Richard, Jr.——**B:** Mar. 19, 1934, Altoona, PA, *VP, RE Devel. Co.*, Rosso & Mastracco Inc.; **PRIM RE ACT:** Broker, Developer, Builder, Property Manager, Instructor; **PREV EMPLOY:** Goodman, Segar, Hogan, Inc. 1100 VA Nat. Bank Bldg., Norfolk, VA 23510; VP-Leasing and Mgmt.; **PROFL AFFIL & HONORS:** Nat. Assoc. Realtors, Tidewater Assoc. Realtors, Instit. of Real Mgmt., CPM; Past VP Tidewater of Realtors; Past Pres. Chap. 39 (IREM); Past Pres. Mid-City Merchants Assoc.; Pres., Rosso & Mastracco Employee Credit Union; **EDUC:** BS, 1957, Acctg., Univ. of MD; **MIL SERV:** US Army, Sgt., Asst. Chief of Staff, Intelligence, Pentagon, Wash., DC; **OTHER ACT & HONORS:** "Office Building Feasibility Study for Medium-size Metropolitan Area", *Journal of Property Management*, Nov.-Dec., 1969; Contributing Editor, 12th Ed. *Principles of Prop. Mgmt.*, Inst. of RE Mgt. 1980; Lic. Resid. Ins. Agent, VA; Adjunct Faculty, Tidewater Community College, Faculty, Insti. of RE Mgmt., Chicago, IL; **HOME ADD:** 4640 Helensburgh Dr., Chesapeake, VA 23321; **BUS ADD:** 1187 Azalea Garden Rd., Norfolk, VA 23502, (804)855-6011.

GRIFFITH, Christopher G.——**B:** Dec. 24, 1946, Orlando, FL, *VP*, Pan American Mort. Corp., Div. Head, Income Prop. Div.; **PRIM RE ACT:** Broker, Consultant, Appraiser, Banker, Lender; **SERVICES:** Investment counseling; mort. financing; joint venture and construction financing; equity, valuation analysis; **REP CLIENTS:** Individuals, lenders, inst. investors, pension funds investing in comml. RE; **PREV EMPLOY:** Dir., Income Prop. Dept., Mort. Bankers Assn. of Amer., 1977-1980; The Northwestern Bank, 1975-1977; Cameron Brown Co., 1972-1975; **PROFL AFFIL & HONORS:** NARA; Income Prop. Comm., Mort. Bankers Assn. of Amer.; NAREA; Delta Sigma Pi Profl. Bus. Frat., CRA; Sr. Member, Charles P. Landt Award, 1973; **EDUC:** BS, 1972, Mgmt./Mktg., Univ. of SC; **MIL SERV:** US Army, 1st Lt., 1965-1969; **HOME ADD:** 9129 SW 72nd Ave., Miami, FL 33156, (305)661-0309; **BUS ADD:** 150 SE Third Ave., Miami, FL 33131, (305)577-5800.

GRIFFITH, Darlene Inez——**B:** June 14, 1938, South Gate, CA, *Owner*, Griffith Investment Consultant; **PRIM RE ACT:** Broker, Consultant, Owner/Investor, Property Manager, Syndicator; **OTHER RE ACT:** Consular for bus., Investment Consultant; **SERVICES:** Fin. planning; **REP CLIENTS:** Investors, Bus. owners; **PREV EMPLOY:** Bus. owner; **PROFL AFFIL & HONORS:** Whittier Dist. Bd. of Realtors, NAR, CA Assn. of Realtors, RESSI, LA Bus. Marketers grp., CA Synd., GRI, CBC; **EDUC:** Teaching credential, 1974, Bus. & PE, Compton Jr. Coll., Cerritas Jr. Coll., N Hondo Jr. Coll., Univ. of CA, Berkeley; **OTHER ACT & HONORS:** 1981-82 Who's Who in Fin. & Indus.; Pres. and Past Sec. of Los Angeles Bus. Assn.; **HOME ADD:** 14130 Caswood St., Whittier, CA 90602, (213)693-1431; **BUS ADD:** 13400 E. Whittier Blvd., Suite E, Whittier, CA 90605, (213)693-4384.

GRIFFITH, H. William——**B:** Oct. 28, 1929, Utica, NY, *RE Broker*, H. William Griffith; **PRIM RE ACT:** Broker, Consultant, Appraiser, Developer; **SERVICES:** Appraisals, Marketing, Investment Analysis; **PREV EMPLOY:** RE Salesman; **PROFL AFFIL & HONORS:** NATFA, NARA, NAR; **EDUC:** Univ. of Syracuse (Utica Coll.); **GRAD EDUC:** 3 yrs., Public Rel. & Bus., Univ. of Syracuse; **MIL SERV:** USAF, A/1C; **OTHER ACT & HONORS:** PGA - Former; **HOME ADD:** 926-A Blvd., New Milford, NJ 07646, (201)967-9171; **BUS ADD:** 10 McKinley St., Dumont, NJ 07628, (201)664-2400.

GRIFFITH, Harry F.——**B:** Aug. 11, 1930, Chicago, IL, *Pres.*, Crandall Realty, Inc.; **PRIM RE ACT:** Broker, Appraiser; **SERVICES:** Sales, appraisals, acquisitions; **REP CLIENTS:** Banks, local municipalities, relocation cos., attys, cts. and indiv.; **PROFL AFFIL & HONORS:** Assoc. Member SREA, Livingston Cty. Bd. of Realtors, MI Assn. of Realtors, NAR, Realtor of the Year 1963 & 1976, Past Pres. Livingston Cty. Bd. of Realtors, Dir. MI Assn. Realtors; **EDUC:** BS, 1952, Math., MI State Univ.; **GRAD EDUC:** MA, 1956, Bus., RE, MI State Univ.; **EDUC HONORS:** Dist. Mil. Student; **MIL SERV:** USAF Res. Ret., Capt.; **OTHER ACT & HONORS:** VChmn. of Bd. of Dir., 1st Nat. Bank in Howell; **HOME ADD:** 5950 Challis Rd., Brighton, MI 48116, (313)229-9467; **BUS ADD:** 322 E. Grand River Ave., Howell, MI 48843, (517)546-0906.

GRIFFITH, James B., Jr.——**B:** May 9, 1954, Mansfield, LA, *Asst. VP*, Pioneer Mortgage Corp., Loan Production; **PRIM RE ACT:** Lender; **SERVICES:** Mort. banking, specializing in FHA/VA loans; **REP CLIENTS:** FNMA, GNMA and other instl. investors; **PREV EMPLOY:** Field Rep., Fed. Land Bank of Baton Rouge; **PROFL AFFIL & HONORS:** Affiliate Member, Shreveport & Bossier Bd. of Realtors, Assoc. Member, Shreveport Bossier Homebuilders Assn., 1981 Grad. School of Mort. Banking; **EDUC:** BS, 1976, RE & Fin., Bus. Admin., LA Tech Univ., Ruston, LA; **HOME ADD:** 256 Hanging Moss Tr., Shreveport, LA 71106, (318)797-2932; **BUS ADD:** 1400 Line Ave., Shreveport, LA 71104, (318)221-1547.

GRIFFITH, Jimmy C.——**B:** Feb. 14, 1941, Timpson, TX, *Pres.*, Greenway Enterprises, Inc., Greenway Enterprises Construction, Inc., Greenway Associates; **PRIM RE ACT:** Developer, Builder, Owner/Investor; **SERVICES:** Turn-key comml./indus. devel. of bldgs. for lease or sale; **REP CLIENTS:** Hertz, Fuqua Indus. (TSC), Federal Express, Rollins, Diamond Mfg.; **PREV EMPLOY:** Mutual of NY, loan dept.; CT Mutual, loan dept.; **PROFL AFFIL & HONORS:** TX Indus. Devel. Council, Ft. Worth Bd. of Realtors, GRI; **EDUC:** BS, 1963, Animal Sci., TX A&M; **GRAD EDUC:** MS, 1971, Econ., LA State Univ.; **EDUC HONORS:** Distinguished Student; Phi Kappa Phi, Gamma Sigma Delta; **HOME ADD:** 4201 Marys Creek, Ft. Worth, TX 76116, (817)244-8084; **BUS ADD:** 4201 Marys Creek, Ft. Worth, TX 76116, (817)244-8084.

GRIFFITHS, George——*Treas.*, Consolidated Aluminum Corp.; **PRIM RE ACT:** Property Manager; **BUS ADD:** PO Box 14448, St. Louis, MO 63178, (314)878-6950.*

GRIFFITHS, O. Wayne——**B:** Sept. 8, 1938, Oklahoma City, OK, *Pres.*, Griff Homes & Griff Construction Corp.; **PRIM RE ACT:** Developer, Builder; **SERVICES:** Custom & spec. homes, comml. & devel.; **PREV EMPLOY:** City of Oklahoma City; **PROFL AFFIL & HONORS:** Sr. Planner Community Devel. 17 yrs.; **OTHER ACT & HONORS:** Newcastle Planning Commn.; **HOME ADD:** Rte 1 Box 379A, Newcastle, OK 73065, (405)387-4999; **BUS ADD:** 4229 Royal Ave. #100, Oklahoma City, OK 73108, (405)943-9310.

GRIMBALL, William H., Jr.——**B:** Sept. 3, 1946, Charleston, SC, *Partner*, Grimball, Cabaniss, Vaughan & Robinson, Attys.; **PRIM RE ACT:** Attorney; **SERVICES:** Legal counseling, title research, title insurance, closing serv.; **REP CLIENTS:** SC St. Ports Authority, Charleston Cty. Park, Recreation and Tourist Comm., Southern Railway System; **PROFL AFFIL & HONORS:** ABA; Real Prop. Probate and Trust Law Sect.; **EDUC:** BA, 1968, Eng., Univ. of the South; **GRAD EDUC:** JD, 1975, Univ. of SC; **MIL SERV:** US Naval Reserve, Lt. Cmdr.; **OTHER ACT & HONORS:** VP Membership, Charleston Council, US Navy League; Mbr. Rotary Group Study Team to India, 1980; Mbr. Sea Power Speaker's Team since 1972 (Two Awards); **HOME ADD:** 5 Colonial St., Charleston, SC 29401, (803)722-1407; **BUS ADD:** Box 816, 39 Broad St., Charleston, SC 29402, (803)577-9440.

GRIMES, Robert S.——**B:** Dec. 9, 1943, New York, NY, *Gen. Part.*, Cowen & Co., RE Services; **PRIM RE ACT:** Broker, Attorney, Consultant, Owner/Investor; **SERVICES:** Selection & structuring of RE investments for indivs., instl. clients & pension funds; **REP CLIENTS:** Indiv. and/or instl. clients, parts. and/or personal clients of firm; **PREV EMPLOY:** Loeb Rhoades & Co., RE, 1973-76; Marshall, Bratter, Greene, Allison & Tucker, Atty., 1968-73; **PROFL AFFIL & HONORS:** Assoc. of Bar of City of NY, RESSI; **EDUC:** BS, 1965, Econ. & Fin., The Wharton School of Econ. & Fin. of Univ. of PA; **GRAD EDUC:** JD, 1968, Law School of Univ. of PA; **EDUC HONORS:** Magna cum Laude, Beta Gamma Sigma; **HOME ADD:** 415 E 52nd St., NYC, NY 10022; **BUS ADD:** 545 Madison Ave., NYC, NY 10022, (212)688-7400.

GRIMM, James——*Sr. VP Fin. & Admin.*, MAPCO, Inc.; **PRIM RE ACT:** Property Manager; **BUS ADD:** 1800 S. Baltimore Ave., Tulsa, OK 74119, (918)584-4471.*

GRIMM, Norman E.——**B:** June 20, 1915, Crescent City, FL, *Realtor*, Grimm & Assoc. Realty; **PRIM RE ACT:** Broker, Syndicator, Developer, Property Manager, Owner/Investor; **PREV EMPLOY:** US Govt. Serv., Prop. Mgmt., Utilization, and Disposal; **PROFL AFFIL & HONORS:** TAR, NAR, RESSI; **EDUC:** Math, Hendrix Coll., Conway, AR; **MIL SERV:** USAF, Lt. Col., Air Medal (Two Clusters), Various Theater Ribbons; **HOME ADD:** 5111 Donna Dr., San Antonio, TX 78228, (512)732-8076; **BUS ADD:** 2415 Castroville Rd., San Antonio, TX 78228, (512)433-2064.

GRIMM, W. Thomas——**B:** Feb. 23, 1940, PA, *Sr. Counsel*, Westinghouse Electric Corp., Community Devel. Grp; **PRIM RE ACT:** Attorney; **SERVICES:** Land Devel.; **REP CLIENTS:** Coral Ridge

Props., Half Moon Bay Props., Coral Ridge-Collier Props., Inc., Treasure Lake Coy. and subs. cos. which together constitute Westinghouse's Community Devel. Grp.; **PREV EMPLOY:** Investment Corp. of FL; **PROFL AFFIL & HONORS:** ABA, Assn. of the Bar of the City of NY, NJ Bar, FL Bar, CA Bar, Amer. Land Devel. Assn.; **EDUC:** BA, 1961, Pol. Sci., Lafayette Coll.; **GRAD EDUC:** LLB, Law, Univ. of VA; **EDUC HONORS:** Honors in Govt.; **MIL SERV:** NJ ANG, S/Sgt.; **HOME ADD:** 1530 N.E. 63rd Ct., Ft. Lauderdale, FL 33308; **BUS ADD:** 3300 University Dr., Coral Springs, FL 33065, (305)752-1100.

GRING, Clayton G.——B: Sept. 1, 1932, Reading, PA, *Pres.*, Fairfield, Inc., Comml. Div.; **PRIM RE ACT:** Broker, Builder, Property Manager, Syndicator; **SERVICES:** Synd. realtor, devel., prop. mgr.; **REP CLIENTS:** Indiv. or inst. investors in comml. RE; **PREV EMPLOY:** Computer Prop. Corp.; **PROFL AFFIL & HONORS:** NAR, Inst. of RE Mgmt., Who's Who in Data Processing; **EDUC:** BS, 1960, Acctg., Fin., Fairleigh Dickenson Univ., Rutherford, NJ; **GRAD EDUC:** MS, 1965, Fin., Acctg., Fairleigh Dickenson Univ.; **EDUC HONORS:** Cum Laude; **MIL SERV:** Army, SFC; **OTHER ACT & HONORS:** Lions Club, VFW; **HOME ADD:** 33 River Ridge Cir., Little Rock, AR 72207, (501)227-6494; **BUS ADD:** 1207 Robsomen Park Rd., Little Rock, AR 72207, (501)664-6000.

GRISHAM, Bob——B: June 1, 1926, Bonne Terre, MO, *Pres.*, Grisham, Inc.; **PRIM RE ACT:** Broker, Consultant, Developer, Owner/Investor; **SERVICES:** Comm. & Investment brokerage, Farm and Ranch, Indus.; **REP CLIENTS:** Hanna Mining Co., Martin Marietta, small manufactures, fast food RE Reps., Investors; **PREV EMPLOY:** Lumber yard operation, builder; **PROFL AFFIL & HONORS:** NAR, RMNI, St. Louis RE Exchange, MO Pres. of Farm and Land Inst., Pres. of Mineral Area Board of Realtors, CCIM of Nat. Assoc., Realtors; **EDUC:** Attended Univ. of MO and Flat River Jr. Coll.; No Degrees; **MIL SERV:** USN, Radioman; **HOME ADD:** 709 Mulberry, Bismarck, MO 63624, (314)734-2562; **BUS ADD:** 907 Cedar St., Bismarck, MO 63624.

GRISHMAN, Milton——B: Dec. 4, 1949, Gulfport, MS, *Pres.*, Moody Grishman Agency, Inc.; **PRIM RE ACT:** Broker, Consultant, Appraiser; **SERVICES:** Resid. and comml. brokerage, relocation specialist, appraisal, consultant; **REP CLIENTS:** Dupont, Equitable Relocation Serv., Merrill-Lynch Relocation, Homequity; **PROFL AFFIL & HONORS:** Assoc. Member, Soc. of RE Appraisers; Candidate, Amer. Inst. of RE Appraisers; Realtors Nat. Marketing Inst.; Nat. Assn. of Realtors, GRI; 1980 recipient of Martha Helm Memorial Award for serv. to Realtor Bd., Biloxi-Ocean Springs Bd. of Realtors; **EDUC:** BA, 1973, Eng., Univ. of AL; **EDUC HONORS:** Grad. Asst., Eng. Dept., 1974-1975; **HOME ADD:** 303 St. Charles Ave., Biloxi, MS 39530, (601)436-6988; **BUS ADD:** 1312 W. Howard Ave., Biloxi, MS 39530, (601)432-2671.

GRISNIK, Francis J., III——B: Feb. 6, 1944, *Pres.*, F.J. Grisnik, Inc.; **PRIM RE ACT:** Consultant, Developer, Property Manager; **SERVICES:** Devel., synd. & mgmt. of multi-family res. props.; **REP CLIENTS:** Indiv. investors in multi-family res. props.; **PROFL AFFIL & HONORS:** Nat. Assn. of Home Builders, Apt. Assn. of Metropolitan Pittsburgh, Registered Apt. Mgr.; **EDUC:** BArch, 1967, Carnegie Inst. of Tech.; **MIL SERV:** USN, Lt.; **OTHER ACT & HONORS:** Boy Scouts of America; **HOME ADD:** 410 Robinhood Ln., McMurray, PA 15317, (412)941-5091; **BUS ADD:** PO Box 10807, Pittsburgh, PA 15236, (412)384-4744.

GRODETSKY, Murray H.——B: Feb. 6, 1934, Jamaica, NY, *Gen. Counsel*, Fisher Brothers; **PRIM RE ACT:** Consultant, Attorney, Developer, Builder, Owner/Investor, Property Manager; **EDUC:** BS, 1955, Acctg., Wharton School, Univ. of PA; **GRAD EDUC:** LLD, 1958, Columbia Law School; **MIL SERV:** USA, Pvt.; **HOME ADD:** 360 E 72nd St., New York, NY 10021, (212)734-3958; **BUS ADD:** 299 Park Ave., New York, NY 10017, (212)752-5000.

GRODT, Paul O.——B: June 15, 1926, IA, *Pres.*, Grodt & McKay, Realtors; **PRIM RE ACT:** Broker, Attorney, Instructor, Consultant, Appraiser, Owner/Investor, Insuror; **SERVICES:** RE Brokerage 2 offices - 50 salespersons; **PREV EMPLOY:** RE 25 yrs.; **PROFL AFFIL & HONORS:** IA State Bar Assn., Des Moines, IA; NAR, Realtor of the Yr. 1970 Des Moines Assn. Realtors; Distinguished Serv. Award, Jaycees; GRI; CRS; CRB; **EDUC:** B Comml. Sci., 1947, Bus. Adm. & Acctg., Drake Univ., Des Moines, IA; **GRAD EDUC:** JD, 1950, Drake Univ.; **MIL SERV:** USN, Lt. (jg); **OTHER ACT & HONORS:** Alpha Tau Omega, Social Frat. & Phi Alpha Delta, Law frat.; Embassy Club, Des Moines; Rotary Club, W Des Moines; **HOME ADD:** 4000 Grand, W Des Moines, IA 50265; **BUS ADD:** 1100 Grand, W Des Moines, IA 50265, (515)223-5050.

GROENE, Carl——*Ed.*, Security Title Ins. Co., Security News; **PRIM RE ACT:** Real Estate Publisher; **BUS ADD:** 3700 Wilshire Blvd., Los Angeles, CA 90010, (213)873-7788.*

GROFF, Anna——B: Apr. 4, 1929, Canon City, CO, *Pres.*, B&A Inc., Realtors; **PRIM RE ACT:** Broker, Developer, Builder, Owner/Investor; **SERVICES:** RE sales, resid., comml & investment collection dept.; **PREV EMPLOY:** First Nat. Bank of Fairbanks, AK; Nat. Bank, City Finance, Fairbanks, AK; **PROFL AFFIL & HONORS:** NAR; RMMI; C of C (Gtr. Fbks. and Nat.), Realtor of Year, NAR; RNMI; **HOME ADD:** Anderson Rd., Fairbanks, AK 99707; **BUS ADD:** 544 9th Lower Level, PO Box 927, Fairbanks, AK 99707, (907)452-1811.

GROFF, Milton——*VP Control & Adm.*, Chelsea Industries, Inc.; **PRIM RE ACT:** Property Manager; **BUS ADD:** 1360 Soldiers Field Rd., Boston, MA 02135, (617)878-9010.*

GROLEAU, Carol A.——B: July 24, 1940, Mobile, AL, *Pres.*, Roscoe Inc. Realtors; **PRIM RE ACT:** Broker, Developer, Builder, Owner/Investor; **SERVICES:** Brokerage, developing, bldg.; **PROFL AFFIL & HONORS:** Bd of Dir, Rockford Bd. Realtors; State & Nat'l. Mktg. Inst.; Rockford Homebuilders, GRI; CRS; 5 yr Member Arbitration Comm.; **HOME ADD:** 6511 Elevator Rd, Roscoe, IL 61073, (815)623-2449; **BUS ADD:** 11405 Main St, Roscoe, IL 61073, (815)623-2182.

GRONVALL, John——B: June 29, 1957, Cincinnati, OH, *Pres.*, Renaissance Developers, Inc.; **PRIM RE ACT:** Builder, Owner/Investor, Property Manager, Syndicator; **OTHER RE ACT:** Mortgage and Finance Programs; Venture Capital; **SERVICES:** Sale of Programs; **PROFL AFFIL & HONORS:** Nat. Home Builders Assn.; Mahoning Cty. Home Builders Assn., Speaker at 1981 Nat. Home Builders Convention; **EDUC:** BS Bus. Admin., 1979, Mgmt. & Fin., Youngstown State Univ.; **EDUC HONORS:** Dean's List, Honors Composition; **OTHER ACT & HONORS:** Kentucky Colonel; **HOME ADD:** 4484 Devonshire Dr., Boardman, OH 44512, (216)788-5810; **BUS ADD:** 3736 Boardman-Canfield Road, Canfield, OH 44406, (216)533-2283.

GROSBY, Robert N.——B: Jan. 13, 1927, New York, NY, *Partner*, Grosby & Grosby; **PRIM RE ACT:** Consultant, Attorney, Owner/Investor; **SERVICES:** Tax Shelter Consultant (CT, NY and FL); **PROFL AFFIL & HONORS:** CT & NV Bar Assns.; **EDUC:** AB, 1947, Harvard Univ.; **GRAD EDUC:** LLD, 1950, Cornell Univ.; **MIL SERV:** US Navy, Lcdr.; **OTHER ACT & HONORS:** counsel to CT House of Representatives, 1964-66; **HOME ADD:** 154 East Rocks Rd., Norwalk, CT 06850, (203)847-9735; **BUS ADD:** 11 Isaac St., Norwalk, CT 06852, (203)853-3300.

GROSS, Earl L. (Mick)——B: May 2, 1938, Pasadena, CA, *Chmn.*, U S Mortgage; **PRIM RE ACT:** Broker, Banker, Developer, Lender, Owner/Investor, Property Manager, Syndicator; **SERVICES:** Mort. banking; comml. & single family; **REP CLIENTS:** Trusts - S&L - Banks - Ins. Cos.; **PREV EMPLOY:** Integrity Fin. Corp. - Current Pres., Associated Co. 1975-present; **MIL SERV:** USMC; **HOME ADD:** 1524 Antigua, Newport Beach, CA 92661; **BUS ADD:** 1913 E. Seventeenth St., Santa Ana, CA 92701, (714)547-8845.

GROSS, Gordon R.——B: Apr. 14, 1931, Buffalo, NY, *Sr. Part.*, Gross, Shuman, Brizdle, Laub & Gilfillan, P.C.; **PRIM RE ACT:** Attorney, Developer, Owner/Investor, Syndicator; **SERVICES:** Legal; **REP CLIENTS:** Numerous devels., synds. & lending inst.; **PREV EMPLOY:** Past Pres. & Chmn. of Dominion Mort. & Realty Tr.; **PROFL AFFIL & HONORS:** Amer. & NY State Bar Assns.; **EDUC:** Poli. Sci., Hist., Oberlin Coll., State Univ. of NY at Buffalo; **GRAD EDUC:** LLB, 1955, Law; **HOME ADD:** 585 Lebrun Rd., Amherst, NY 14226, (716)835-4567; **BUS ADD:** 2600 Main Pl. Tower, Buffalo, NY 14202, (716)854-4300.

GROSS, Irwin A.——B: Mar. 17, 1938, Oak Park, IL, *RE Counsel*, Combined Ins. Co. of Amer.; **PRIM RE ACT:** Attorney, Lender; **SERVICES:** Investment Analysis - Atty. Role and Underwriting; **REP CLIENTS:** RE Loan/Equity positions; **PREV EMPLOY:** Practicing RE Atty., Mort. Banking Background, Pension Fund, Asset Admin.; **PROFL AFFIL & HONORS:** Chicago Mort. Attys. Assn., Contributor - Contin. Legal Educ.; **EDUC:** BS in B.A., 1960, Fin., Univ. of AZ; **GRAD EDUC:** LLB, 1964, Univ. of De Paul, Coll. of Law; **HOME ADD:** 1636 Birch Rd., Northbrook, IL 60062, (312)564-1636; **BUS ADD:** 707 Stokie Blvd., Northbrook, IL 60062, (312)564-8000.

GROSS, James E.——B: Apr. 29, 1950, Duluth, MN, *Mgr. Trust RE, Pres.*, United Bank of Az, Trust Div.; Gross & Williams, Inc.; **PRIM RE ACT:** Broker, Consultant, Appraiser, Property Manager, Banker; **SERVICES:** As Pres. of Gross & Williams, Inc. - Prop. Mgmt. Feasibility Studies; As Trust Officer United Bank - Prop. Mgmt. &

Lending; **PREV EMPLOY:** Trust RE Admin. - First Nat. Bank of AZ; **PROFL AFFIL & HONORS:** NAR/IREM, CPM; **EDUC:** BS, 1973, Fin. & RE, AZ State Univ., Tempe; **MIL SERV:** US Army 1968-1970, Spec. 4; **HOME ADD:** 1347 W. Pecos, Mesa, AZ 85202, (602)838-6742; **BUS ADD:** 1347 W. Pecos, Mesa, AZ 85202, (602)248-2159.

GROSS, Jerry A.——B: Mar. 25, 1941, Hartford, CT, *Pres.*, Ambassador Square, Inc.; **PRIM RE ACT:** Attorney, Developer, Owner/Investor; **SERVICES:** Condo. devel., condo. conversion; **PREV EMPLOY:** Atty. at Law; **PROFL AFFIL & HONORS:** FL Condo. Commn.; ABA; FL Bar Assn., Cert. of Appreciation Real Prop., Probate & Trust Law Section of FL Bar; Recognition as Outstanding Member, FL Condo. Commn.; **EDUC:** BA, 1963, Bus., Univ. of Miami; **GRAD EDUC:** LLB/JD, 1966, Univ. of Miami Sch. of Law; **EDUC HONORS:** Cert. of Meritorious Serv., Student Govt., Pi Lambda Phi, Order of Omega; **OTHER ACT & HONORS:** Greater Miami Jewish Federation; Lecturer, NY Law Journal; Lecturer, FL Bar Assn.; **HOME ADD:** 2901 Bayshore Dr., Miami, FL, (305)448-4266; **BUS ADD:** 825 S. Bayshore Dr., Suite 1643, Miami, FL 33131, (305)374-1744.

GROSS, Norman S.——B: Dec. 14, 1941, Orlando, FL, *Realtor Associate*, Portner & Portner, Inc.; **PRIM RE ACT:** Broker, Syndicator, Consultant, Developer, Property Manager, Owner/Investor; **SERVICES:** Ev. & Synd., Consulting, Prop. Mgmt., Comml. & Resid. Brokerage; **PREV EMPLOY:** VP, Loeb Rhoades, Hornblower & Co., 1974-79; **PROFL AFFIL & HONORS:** RESSI, Investment Div. FL Assoc. of Realtors; **GRAD EDUC:** 1968, Investments, Amer. Inst. of Banking; **OTHER ACT & HONORS:** V Chmn. City of Hollywood Civil Service Bd., Broward Forum, Chmn. Elect, Greater Hollywood C of C PAC, Chmn. 1980, V Chmn., Gold Coast Free Enterprise Coalition, 1981-82; **HOME ADD:** 2925 Pierce St., Apt. 3, Hollywood, FL 33020, (305)920-1736; **BUS ADD:** 4302 Hollywood Blvd., Hollywood, FL 33021, (305)922-4488.

GROSS, Ronald J.——B: Oct. 11, 1937, Yakima, WA, *Prop.*, CA Indus.; **PRIM RE ACT:** Broker, Engineer; **SERVICES:** Site location, indus. facilities, advanced fac. planning, sales & leasing of indus.; **REP CLIENTS:** Elect./mfr. bus.; **PREV EMPLOY:** Hewlett Packard Co., Amer. Thermoform Corp., Xerox Data Systems, Indus. Engrg. Supervisor for Memorex Corp., Memorex, Indus. Prop. Co.; **PROFL AFFIL & HONORS:** Soc. of Indus. Engrg., Amer. Inst. of Indus. Engrg., Assn. of South Bay Brokers; **EDUC:** BS, 1960, Indus. Engrg., San Jose State Univ.; Advanced studies at UCLA, 1962-64 in Computer Sci.; **HOME ADD:** 351 Neal St., Pleasanton, CA 94566, (415)846-1093; **BUS ADD:** 3375 Scott Blvd., Suite 200, Santa Clara, CA 95051, (408)496-6633.

GROSS, Sheldon A.——*Pres.*, Sheldon Gross Realty, Inc.; **PRIM RE ACT:** Broker, Consultant, Appraiser, Developer, Owner/Investor, Instructor, Property Manager; **PREV EMPLOY:** Seton Hall Univ.; Mallor-McCabe Gross & Co.; Gross Devel. Co.; Berkley Fed. S&L Assn.; Berkeley Fin. Corp.; **PROFL AFFIL & HONORS:** AAA; AMA; ASA; FLI; IREA; NAREA; NAR; RNMI; SIR, Pres. Annual Award; **EDUC:** BS, Econ., Univ. of IL; **GRAD EDUC:** MBA, Mktg., Seton Hall Univ.; **OTHER ACT & HONORS:** Past Pres., NJ Chap. Society of Indus. Leasing; Past Pres., NJ Chap. Amer. Society of Appraisers; **BUS ADD:** 80 Main St., W. Orange, NJ 07052, (201)672-3900.

GROSSE, Ernest J.——B: May 5, 1925, NY, *Second VP*, The Chase Manhattan Bank, NA, Legal; **PRIM RE ACT:** Attorney, Banker, Lender; **PROFL AFFIL & HONORS:** ABA; NY Cty. Lawyers Assn.; NY State Bankers Assn.; **GRAD EDUC:** LLB, 1955, St. John's Univ.; **MIL SERV:** USN, MM/2C; **HOME ADD:** 606 Knollwood Ct., Valley Cottage, NY 10989, (914)268-3452; **BUS ADD:** 1 Chase Manhattan Plaza, New York, NY 10081, (212)552-3583.

GROSSEIBL, Eric H.——B: Jan. 5, 1945, NJ, *VP & Treas.*, Bellemead Development Corp., Wholly Owned Sub. of The Chubb Corp.; **PRIM RE ACT:** Developer, Builder, Owner/Investor; **PREV EMPLOY:** Arthur Young & Co., CPAs; **PROFL AFFIL & HONORS:** AICPA; **EDUC:** BS, 1967, Acctg., Fairleigh Dickinson Univ., **MIL SERV:** US Army, Sgt., 1967-1969, Air Medal; **BUS ADD:** 210 Clay Ave., Lyndhurst, NJ 07071, (201)438-6880.

GROSSGOLD, Richard——B: Dec. 5, 1933, Bronx, NY, *Pres.*, Grossgold Associates Inc.; **PRIM RE ACT:** Broker, Architect; **PROFL AFFIL & HONORS:** Santa Barbara RE Exchangors; **EDUC:** BArch., 1958, Arch., Cornell Univ.; **EDUC HONORS:** Received Henry Adams Award for excellence in the study of arch.; **MIL SERV:** USNR, Lcdr.; **HOME ADD:** 1429 Shoreline Dr., Santa Barbara, CA 93109, (805)966-9394; **BUS ADD:** 1429 Shoreline Dr., Santa Barbara, CA 93109, (805)966-9394.

GROSSMAN, Allan H.——B: Nov. 21, 1927, New Jersey, NJ, *Pres.*, Cadillac Fairview Building Development, Inc.; **PRIM RE ACT:** Developer, Builder; **SERVICES:** Builders, devel. & mktg. of condos.; **PREV EMPLOY:** Pres., Centex Homes of NJ; Pres., Centex Homes of FL; **PROFL AFFIL & HONORS:** AIA; **EDUC:** BS, 1949, Arch., PA State Univ.; **HOME ADD:** Apt. 3109, 300 Winston Dr., Cliffside Park, NJ 07010, (201)224-9751; **BUS ADD:** 2050 Center Ave., Fort Lee, NJ 07010, (201)947-9200.

GROSSMAN, Charles——B: Sept. 13, 1943, Houston, TX, *Pres.*, Schroder Real Estate Corp.; **PRIM RE ACT:** Owner/Investor; **SERVICES:** Prop. investment and mgmt.; **REP CLIENTS:** North Amer. Prop. Unit Trust, Sarakreek Holding N.V., British Post Office Staff, Superann. Fund; **PROFL AFFIL & HONORS:** ABA; RE Bd. of NY; **EDUC:** BA, 1965, Govt./Econ., Harvard Coll.; **GRAD EDUC:** MBA/JD, 1969, Bus./Law, Columbia Univ. School of Bus., School of Law; **EDUC HONORS:** Magna Cum Laude, Dean's List; **HOME ADD:** 115 Central Park W., NYC, NY 10023, (212)595-5794; **BUS ADD:** One State St., NYC, NY 10004, (212)269-6500.

GROSSMAN, Everett P.——B: June 10. 1924, Boston, MA, *Exec. VP*, Evans Products Co. - Retail Grp., Grossman's; **OTHER RE ACT:** Bldg. Material Chain; **SERVICES:** Corp. RE Exec. 350 stores; **PROFL AFFIL & HONORS:** NACORE, Realty Lodge Binai Brith, ARCA Engrs. & INAI Brith; **EDUC:** AB, 1946, Arch., Harvard; **MIL SERV:** USA, Sgt. 1943-1946; **OTHER ACT & HONORS:** Dir. - Quincy Coop. Bank, Past Pres. MA Retail Lumber Dealers Assoc.; **HOME ADD:** 141 Montvale Rd., Weston, MA 02193, (617)894-8387; **BUS ADD:** 200 Union St., Braintree, MA 02184, (617)848-0100.

GROSSMAN, Ezra——*VP*, Goldman Sachs Realty Corp., Asset Redeployment; **PRIM RE ACT:** Broker, Consultant; **SERVICES:** Assist corporations and owners in prop. dispositions and raising capital; **REP CLIENTS:** Dayton Hudson, The Carlson Companies, Urban Investment and Devel. Co., Oxford Devel. Co., Copaken White & Blitt; **BUS ADD:** 60 Broad St., NY, NY 10004, (212)794-8847.

GROSSMAN, Jay M.——B: Mar. 2, 1946, NJ, *Sr. VP*, The Codman Co. Inc., Resid.; **PRIM RE ACT:** Broker, Consultant, Developer, Builder, Owner/Investor; **PROFL AFFIL & HONORS:** Greater Boston RE Bd., Nashua Re Bd., Natl. Assn. of Home Builders; **EDUC:** BA, 1968, Econ., Dickinson Coll.; **GRAD EDUC:** MBA, 1972, Boston Univ.; **EDUC HONORS:** Cum Laude; **HOME ADD:** Boston, MA; **BUS ADD:** 211 Congress St., Boston, MA 02110, (617)423-6500.

GROSSMAN, Robert M.——B: Jan. 19, 1944, Chester, PA, *Pres.*, Case Capital Corp.; **PRIM RE ACT:** Broker, Consultant, Lender, Owner/Investor, Instructor, Property Manager, Syndicator; **OTHER RE ACT:** Arrange Mort. Fin.; **SERVICES:** Consulting, broker comml. fin., morts.; **REP CLIENTS:** Private and instnl. lenders and investors; **PROFL AFFIL & HONORS:** NY Univ. - Joint Ventures/RE Div. of Career Devel., Lic. RE Broker; Who's Who Long Island RE; Amer. Arbitration Assn.; **EDUC:** BA, 1965, Econ. and Fin., Queens Coll.; **GRAD EDUC:** MS, 1971, Psych., C.W. Post Coll., Long Island Univ.; **EDUC HONORS:** Cum Laude, Pres. Econ. Award 1964, Dean's List, Cum Laude; **OTHER ACT & HONORS:** Instr./Lecturer - RE/Fin. - CUNY; **BUS ADD:** One Old Country Rd., Carle Place, NY 11514, (516)747-4242.

GROSSMANN, George A.——B: Feb. 10, 1936, Waverly, IA, *Broker*, Fausett & Co., Inc.; **PRIM RE ACT:** Broker, Appraiser, Instructor; **SERVICES:** RE brokerage and appraisals; **REP CLIENTS:** Merrill Lynch Relocation Mgmt., Inc.; Homequity; Mountain Home School Bd.; Local attys.; **PREV EMPLOY:** Owner/Mgr., Fox Realtors (seven offices in the western suburbs of Chicago); ERA Highlander Realty Inc.; **PROFL AFFIL & HONORS:** RNMI; FLI; Nat. Assn. of RE Appraisers; Nat. Assn. of Review Appraisers; NAR; TX Assn. of Realtors; Greater Dallas Bd. of Realtors, CRB; CRS; Accredited Farm & Land Member; CRA; Cert. RE Appraiser; GRI; **EDUC:** BS, 1956, Bio-Chem., Wartburg Coll.; **MIL SERV:** US Army; E-5; **OTHER ACT & HONORS:** Elks; Moose; Fianna Hills Ctry. Club; USPS; AR Realtors Assn., President's Awards in 1978, 1979 and 1980; Outstanding Serv. Award from N. Central Bd. of Realtors; NCBOR, Past Pres., 1977 & 1978; AR FLI, Past Pres., 1978; Chmn., AR Assn. Forms Comm.; **HOME ADD:** 17601 Preston Rd. #148, Dallas, TX 75252, (214)248-6888; **BUS ADD:** 4050 Westgrove-St. 100, Dallas, TX 75248, (214)931-9911.

GROSZEK, Marlene——B: Apr. 20, 1942, Chicago, IL, *Pres. Chmn. of the Bd.*, Groszek Realty, Inc.; **PRIM RE ACT:** Broker, Builder, Owner/Investor; **SERVICES:** Investment counseling; **REP CLIENTS:** Indivs. & lenders; **PREV EMPLOY:** Landview Construction Co., Groszek Construction Co.; **PROFL AFFIL & HONORS:** GRI, CRB, NAR, IL Assn. of Realtors, Life Member RPAC; **EDUC:** Gen. Educ.; **OTHER ACT & HONORS:** Commnr. Will Cty. Reg.

Planning Comm., Pres. Will Cty. Bd. of Realtors, Stockholder & Dir. of Groszek Constr. Co., Inc., Chmn. IL Assn. of Realtors, Public Information Coucil, Dir. at Large, IL Assn. of Realtors, Will Cty. Zoning Bd. of Appeals Member; **HOME ADD:** 976 Shetland Dr., Frankfort, IL 60423, (815)469-3595; **BUS ADD:** 340 W. Lincoln Hwy., Frankfort, IL 60423, (815)469-4700.

GROTH, Duane A.——B: June 2, 1940, W. St. Paul, MN, *Part Owner - Mgr.*, F's GMA.O Investments; **PRIM RE ACT:** Consultant, Appraiser, Developer, Builder, Owner/Investor, Property Manager, Insuror; **OTHER RE ACT:** Farming, RE & Ins. sales; **REP CLIENTS:** Estates, farmers, lenders; **PREV EMPLOY:** RE sales - ins. underwriter; **PROFL AFFIL & HONORS:** Realtor Bds. & Farm Orgs., Indep. Ins. Agent Assn.; **EDUC:** Bus. & Liberal Arts, Univ. of MN; **MIL SERV:** US Army; Cpl., Disabled Amer. Veteran; **HOME ADD:** 6850 170th St., E, Hastings, MN 55033, (612)437-5382; **BUS ADD:** 308 Vermillion St., Hastings, MN 55033, (612)435-5000.

GROTRIAN, Dennis J.——B: Jan. 26, 1944, Ft. Wayne, IN, *Sr. Partner*, Grotrian & Boxberger; **PRIM RE ACT:** Attorney, Owner/Investor; **SERVICES:** Legal counsel; **REP CLIENTS:** Peoples Trust Bank, Anthony Wayne Bank, Farmers Home Admin. - USDA; **PREV EMPLOY:** Lawyers Title Ins. Co.; **PROFL AFFIL & HONORS:** City of Ft. Wayne Planning Commn.; Ft. Wayne C of C - Indus. Comm., Fellow, IN Bar Found.; Who's Who in Amer. Law, 1979; **EDUC:** BA, 1967, Pre-Law, IN Univ.; **GRAD EDUC:** JD, 1970, RE, IN Univ.; **EDUC HONORS:** Dean's List, The Order of Barristers; **OTHER ACT & HONORS:** City of Ft. Wayne - Park Comm.; Allen Cty., IN State, Amer. and Intl. Bar Assn. Member; Outstanding Young Men of Amer., 1974; **HOME ADD:** 1310 W. Sherwood Terr., Ft. Wayne, IN 46807, (219)456-4208; **BUS ADD:** Suite 200, Metro Building, Fort Wayne, IN 46802, (219)423-3595.

GROVER, Courtney P., III——B: July 15, 1947, Bay City, TX, *Atty.*, Crain, Caton, James & Womble; **PRIM RE ACT:** Attorney; **SERVICES:** All legal servs. for RE devel., investment and tax problems; **REP CLIENTS:** Indiv. and corp. investors in RE; **PROFL AFFIL & HONORS:** Member State Bar of TX, ABA, Houston Bar Assn.; **EDUC:** BS, 1977, Bus. & Fin., Univ. of TX & Univ. of Houston; **GRAD EDUC:** JD, 1981, RE & Oil & Gas, Whittier Coll. Sch. of Law; **EDUC HONORS:** Cum Laude , Law Review; **OTHER ACT & HONORS:** Bd. of Dirs. Grover & Assoc. Inc.; **HOME ADD:** 8048 Oakwood Forest Dr., Houston, TX 77040, (713)937-4609; **BUS ADD:** 3300 Two Houston Ctr., Houston, TX 77010, (713)658-2323.

GROVES, Paul A.——B: Aug. 15, 1947, Ft. Wayne, IN, *Pres.*, Allen P Assoc.; **PRIM RE ACT:** Broker, Syndicator; **OTHER RE ACT:** Reg. Gen. Securities Principal; **SERVICES:** RE synd., limited partnership formation; **REP CLIENTS:** Pvt. investors, inst. investors; **PROFL AFFIL & HONORS:** Member, RESSI; Member Nat. Assn. of Securities Dealers, Inc. Wash., DC, Registered Gen. Securities Principal; **EDUC:** BS, 1972, Bio., Psys. Chem., Purdue Univ., W. Lafayette, IN; **EDUC HONORS:** Recipient, Nat. Sci. Found. Grant in Bio. 1971; **MIL SERV:** USAF, Capt., Meritorious Service Award; **OTHER ACT & HONORS:** Ft. Wayne Futures, Transp. Task Force; Member, Nat. Guard Assn. of the US/IN; Also affiliated with Goldleaf Investments, Inc.; **HOME ADD:** 2416 Preston Dr., Ft. Wayne, IN 46815, (219)484-3421; **BUS ADD:** 6012 Stellhorn Rd., Ft. Wayne, IN 46815, (219)484-6981.

GROWNEY, Louis P.——B: Dec. 25, 1919, Conception Jct., MO, *Indus. Devel. Dir.*, Pacific Power & Light Co.; **OTHER RE ACT:** Econ. Devel.; **SERVICES:** Site location assistance; **PROFL AFFIL & HONORS:** AEDC; AIR; **EDUC:** BS, 1943, Indus. Engrg., Univ. of AL; **MIL SERV:** USN, Lt.; **HOME ADD:** 11815 S.W. Terra Linda St., Beaverton, OR 97005, (503)644-3440; **BUS ADD:** Public Serv. Bldg., Portland, OR 97204, (503)243-4698.

GRUBB, Donald J.——B: Aug. 15, 1924, Berkeley, CA, *Pres.*, The Grubb Co., Inc.; **PRIM RE ACT:** Broker, Consultant, Developer, Property Manager; **PREV EMPLOY:** Grubb and Ellis Co., VP 1955-1967; **PROFL AFFIL & HONORS:** Oakland Bd. of Realtors, CA Assn. of Realtors, NAR; **EDUC:** BS, 1949, Bus. Admin., Univ. of CA at Berkeley; **MIL SERV:** USAAF, 1943-1946; **HOME ADD:** 5834 McAndrew Dr., Oakland, CA 94611; **BUS ADD:** 1960 Mountain Blvd., Oakland, CA 94611, (415)339-0400.

GRUBE, Charles H.——B: Oct. 12, 1937, Bellville, TX, *Pres.*, Charles Grube Properties, Inc.; **PRIM RE ACT:** Owner/Investor, Syndicator; **PROFL AFFIL & HONORS:** TX RE Commn., Broker, Salesman; States of TX and LA, Reg. Profl. Engr.; **EDUC:** BS, 1960, Petroleum Engrg., TX A&M Univ.; **OTHER ACT & HONORS:** Houston C of C, Downtown Comm.; Past Dir., Post Oak YMCA Bd.; Assn. of Former Students, TX A&M Univ.; First United Methodist Church, Downtown Houston; Amer. Heart Assn. Fund Raising; **HOME ADD:** 11617 Blalock Forest, Houston, TX 77024, (713)783-9940; **BUS ADD:** 2027 Bank of the Southwest Bldg., Houston, TX 77002, (713)652-5932.

GRUBER, Arnold A.——B: Jan. 14, 1942, NY, *Partner*, Marks Shron & Co., CPA's; **OTHER RE ACT:** CPA; **SERVICES:** Acctg.; **REP CLIENTS:** Indivs. and cos. primarily in the RE indus.; **PROFL AFFIL & HONORS:** AICPA, NY State Soc. of CPA; **EDUC:** BBA, 1963, Acctg., CCNY; **HOME ADD:** 35 Cow Ln., Great Neck, NY 11024, (516)829-5757; **BUS ADD:** 111 Great Neck Rd., Great Neck, NY 11021, (516)466-6550.

GRUCHOT, Thaddeus J.——B: July 23, 1930, Chicago, IL, *VP*, Household Merchandising, Inc., Ben Franklin; **OTHER RE ACT:** Retail Store Devel.; Franchising-Merchandising; **PROFL AFFIL & HONORS:** Intl. Council of Shopping Centers; AMA; IL State Bar Assn.-Chicago Bar Assn.; **EDUC:** BS, 1956, Mgmt., DePaul Univ.; **GRAD EDUC:** JD, 1959, Law, DePaul Univ.; **EDUC HONORS:** Pres., Student Council and Blue Key Nat. Honor Frat., Pres. Phi Kappa Alpha Frat., Editor, Law Review; **MIL SERV:** USAF, S/Sgt.; **HOME ADD:** 680 35 Revere Ct., Deerfield, IL 60015, (312)945-8069; **BUS ADD:** 1700 S Wolf Rd., Des Plaines, IL 60018, (312)298-8800.

GRUENHAGEN, Melvin P.——B: May 13, 1923, Napa, CA, *Assoc. Appraiser*, CA State Bd. of Equalization, Assessment Standards; **PRIM RE ACT:** Appraiser; **SERVICES:** Prop. Tax Admn.; **PREV EMPLOY:** Placer Cty. Assessor's Office; **PROFL AFFIL & HONORS:** Nat. Assn. of Review Appraisers, Soc. of R.E. Appraisers, SRA; CRA; **EDUC:** BS, 1963, Bus. Admin., CA State Univ., Sacramento; **GRAD EDUC:** MS, 1969, RE Appraisal & Investment Analysis, Univ. of WI, Madison; **EDUC HONORS:** Grad. With Honors; **HOME ADD:** P.O. Box 2568, El Macero, CA 95618, (916)753-7172; **BUS ADD:** 1020 N. St., Sacramento, CA 95814, (916)445-4982.

GRUNWALD, Jack——*VP Fin. Treas. & Secy.*, Pentair Industries, Inc.; **PRIM RE ACT:** Property Manager; **BUS ADD:** 1700 W. Highway 36, St. Paul, MN 55113, (612)636-7920.*

GRUSKIN, Arthur——B: Feb. 17, 1932, New York, NY, *Mort. Broker, Placer*, Sonnenbuck-Goldman Corp.; **PRIM RE ACT:** Broker, Consultant; **OTHER RE ACT:** RE Sales, RE Fin.; **SERVICES:** Sales, fin.; **PREV EMPLOY:** Friedman Drew Corp., NYC (1970-74); Art Gruskin Assoc., NYC (1974-77); **PROFL AFFIL & HONORS:** Mort. Bankers Assn., NY, YMBA, NY; **EDUC:** 1954, Bus., Advertising, CCNY; **GRAD EDUC:** Art, Whitman Sch. Design; **OTHER ACT & HONORS:** Bd. of Dir. Free Synagogue of West, Pres. Men's Club; **HOME ADD:** 61 Carwall Ave., Mt. Vernon, NY 10552, (914)667-0555; **BUS ADD:** 1251 Ave. of Amer., NY, NY 10020, (212)541-4321.

GSOTTSCHNEIDER, Richard——B: June 4, 1944, New York, NY, *Pres.*, RKG Associates, Inc.; **PRIM RE ACT:** Consultant, Developer, Property Manager; **SERVICES:** Primarily consulting; **PREV EMPLOY:** Econ. Research Assoc. in Boston and Touche Ross & Co. in Washington, DC; **PROFL AFFIL & HONORS:** Amer. Planning Assn.; **EDUC:** BS, 1967, Resource Econ., Univ. of NH; **GRAD EDUC:** MS, 1969, Resource Econ. and Bus., Univ. of NH; **MIL SERV:** US Army, Capt.; **HOME ADD:** Ambler's Acres, Durham, NH 03824, (603)868-2376; **BUS ADD:** Durham Point Rd., Durham, NH 03824, (603)868-5513.

GUARD, Alan H.——*Chief, Bureau of Leases*, NY State Office of General Services; **OTHER RE ACT:** State Govt.; **SERVICES:** Leasing Real Prop. for St. Agencies; **PREV EMPLOY:** Field Supr. (Appraising) NY State Bd. of Equalization and Assessment 1958-1961; **PROFL AFFIL & HONORS:** Licensed RE Broker, NY State; **EDUC:** BS in Commerce, 1947, Bus. Admin., Univ. of Notre Dame, S. Bend, IN; **MIL SERV:** USN, Lt.; **OTHER ACT & HONORS:** Univ. Club, Albany NY Bethlehem Sportsmens Club; **HOME ADD:** 66 St. Clair Dr., Delmar, NY 12054, (518)439-4223; **BUS ADD:** Empire State Plaza Tower Bldg., (26th Floor), Albany, NY 12242, (518)474-4720.

GUARINO, Alfred A., Jr.——B: Mar. 16, 1952, Hanover, NH, *Partner*, Guarino & Bean; **PRIM RE ACT:** Attorney; **SERVICES:** Title search and opinion, prep. of documents, closing trans.; **REP CLIENTS:** Marble Savings Bank, Rt. 4, Woodstock, VT, First Interstate Bank, 10 Gates St., White River Jct., VT; **PREV EMPLOY:** Clerk Assoc. & Part., Guarino & Bean; **PROFL AFFIL & HONORS:** ABA, VT Bar Assn., FL Bar Assn.; **EDUC:** BA, 1974, Pol. Sci. & Hist., Univ. of VT; **GRAD EDUC:** JD, 1977, Stetson Univ. Coll. of Law; **HOME ADD:** White River Jct., VT, (802)295-6510; **BUS ADD:** Box 367, White River Jct., VT 05001, (802)295-2575.

GUARINO, Salvatore F.——B: March 13, 1937, Philadelphia, PA, *V.P.*, Hilton Hotels Corp., Corp. Prop.; **PRIM RE ACT:** Developer; **SERVICES:** Hotel dev. or indiv. in hotel dev.; **PROFL AFFIL &**

HONORS: Amer. Hotel and Motel Assn., Intl. Assn. of Hotel Acctg.; **EDUC:** BA, 1960, Acctg, Bus. Adm., Drexel Univ. and Pierce Coll.; **MIL SERV:** USANG, S/Sgt.; **OTHER ACT & HONORS:** Knights of Columbus, Sr. VP Hilton Inns Inc.; **HOME ADD:** 444 Philadelphia Ave., Westmont, IL 60559, (312)323-5529; **BUS ADD:** 27 E. Monroe St., Chicago, IL 60603, (312)443-1500.

GUARTON, Gonzalo A.——**B:** Mar. 26, 1940, Havana, Cuba, *Pres.*, Gentry Realty Inc.; **PRIM RE ACT:** Broker, Consultant, Developer, Builder, Property Manager, Owner/Investor, Insuror; **EDUC:** BS, 1957, Bio., Coll. De Belon; **GRAD EDUC:** Engrg., 1960, Electrical, Havana Univ.; **BUS ADD:** 37-56 76th St., Jackson Heights, NY 11373, (212)476-2318.

GUCCI, Dominick E.——*VP Fac. Plng. & Costr.*, Johnson & Johnson; **PRIM RE ACT:** Property Manager; **BUS ADD:** 501 George St., New Brunswick, NJ 08903, (201)524-0400.*

GUERRA, Albert P.——**B:** July 23, 1923, Puerto Rico, *Pres.*, Century 21 Camelot Realty, Inc.; **PRIM RE ACT:** Broker, Consultant, Engineer, Developer, Builder, Owner/Investor, Instructor, Property Manager; **SERVICES:** List, sell, mgmt., build, investments(personal); **PREV EMPLOY:** Sr. Tool design engr. for The Boeing Co. 20 yrs.; **PROFL AFFIL & HONORS:** Grad. RE Inst., CRB, Past Realtors Bd., MLS Pres., Bd. Pres.; **EDUC:** 1951, Engrg., Math, Wichita State Univ.; **MIL SERV:** USN, 1943-45, 2CPO, Radioman, gunner, Air Medal; **OTHER ACT & HONORS:** Moose Lodge, Amer. Legion; **HOME ADD:** 2616 Bob White, Wichita, KS 67204, (316)838-1283; **BUS ADD:** 706 N. Main, Wichita, KS 67203, (316)264-7341.

GUERRA, George L.——**B:** June 22, 1937, Philadelphia, PA, *Pres.*, Integrated Industries, Inc.; **PRIM RE ACT:** Engineer, Developer, Builder, Owner/Investor, Property Manager, Syndicator; **SERVICES:** Full serv. RE Co.; **REP CLIENTS:** Atlantic City Trans. Authority, State of PA Dept. of Health, Erwin Indus.; **EDUC:** BSME, 1966, Mech. Engrg., Drexel Univ.; **GRAD EDUC:** MSME, 1969, Mech. Engrg., Renesselaer Polytechnic Inst.; **EDUC HONORS:** Tau Beta Phi; **MIL SERV:** USN, Lt. j.g., Navy Pilot; **OTHER ACT & HONORS:** Township Auditor, 2 yrs.; **HOME ADD:** Rd. 1, Glenmoore, PA 19343, (215)942-2701; **BUS ADD:** 110 Pickering Way, Exton, PA 19341, (215)363-6100.

GUERRERA, Sam——*Dir. Fin.*, Valspar Corp.; **PRIM RE ACT:** Property Manager; **BUS ADD:** 1101 South Third St., Minneapolis, MN 55415, (612)332-7371.*

GUESS, Robert E.——**B:** June 19, 1948, Union, SC, *Atty. at Law*; **PRIM RE ACT:** Attorney; **SERVICES:** Legal, Title Examinations, Drafting & Prep. of sales and debt instruments, exchange agreements, joint ventures & partnership agreements; **PREV EMPLOY:** Previous Pvt. Law Practice, Greenville, SC and Charleston, SC; **PROFL AFFIL & HONORS:** ABA, SC Union Cty. Bar Assns., Member Real Prop. Section ABA & SCBA; **EDUC:** AB, 1970, Eng., Presbyterian Coll., Clinton, SC; **GRAD EDUC:** JD, 1974, Univ. of SC, School of Law; **EDUC HONORS:** Blue Key Honor Frat; **OTHER ACT & HONORS:** Bd. of Dirs., Piedmont Chap., Amer. Red Cross; **HOME ADD:** 114 Park Dr., Union, SC 29379, (807)427-9352; **BUS ADD:** 201 E. Main St., PO Box 278, Union, SC 29379, (803)427-9352.

GUGLE, George L., III——**B:** May 24, 1928, Columbus, OH, *Sr. VP*, Chemical Mortgage Co., Insured Project Dept.; **PRIM RE ACT:** Lender; **SERVICES:** Process HUD Projects for devel., deliver insured loans to investors; represent investors in auctions; **REP CLIENTS:** Devels., ins. cos. & pension funds; **PREV EMPLOY:** Citizens Financial Corporation; **PROFL AFFIL & HONORS:** Mortgage Bankers Assn. of America, Soc. of RE Appraisals, NHRA, Dir. NAHB, SRA; **EDUC:** BA, 1950, Pre Law, Miami Univ.; **HOME ADD:** 45 S. Stanwood Rd., Columbus, OH 43209, (614)231-6158; **BUS ADD:** 101 East Town St., Columbus, OH 43215, (614)460-3058.

GUIDERA, Richard T.——**B:** Nov. 14, 1928, *Sr. VP, Operations & Leasing*, The Center Companies; **PRIM RE ACT:** Broker, Developer, Property Manager; **OTHER RE ACT:** Shopping center leasing man and broker; **REP CLIENTS:** The Equitable, Shell Pension Funds, CT Gen. Telmari, Ford Motor Land & Devel. Co., Prudential, J.C. Realty, Dayton Hudson; **PROFL AFFIL & HONORS:** Intl. Council of Shopping Centers; **EDUC:** BA, 1950, Physical Sci., Harvard Coll.; **MIL SERV:** USMC, Capt.; **HOME ADD:** 173 Ridgeview Dr., Wayzata, MN 55391, (612)473-6071; **BUS ADD:** 330 Second Ave., S., Minneapolis, MN 55401, (612)343-2606.

GUILBEAU, Harry——**B:** Nov. 1, 1943, LA, *Pres.*, Oakleaf Fin. Inc.; **PRIM RE ACT:** Broker, Consultant, Owner/Investor, Instructor, Syndicator; **SERVICES:** Investment counseling, investment synd.; **REP CLIENTS:** Indiv. & instnl. investors in investment props.; **PREV EMPLOY:** IBM 10 yrs.; **PROFL AFFIL & HONORS:** CA Assn. RE Teachers, CCIM; **EDUC:** BS, 1969, Mktg., Econ., LA State Univ.; **OTHER ACT & HONORS:** Toastmasters, Orange Cty. Sheriff Deputy, Reserve Pilot; **BUS ADD:** 180 Newport Ctr. Dr., Suite 180, Newport Bch., CA 92660, (714)752-7828.

GUILD, Jeffrey W.——**B:** Dec. 14, 1951, Baltimore, MD, *VP & Council*, Fletcher Bright Co.; **PRIM RE ACT:** Attorney; **SERVICES:** Counsel to Fletcher Bright Co. A RE Dev. and Syn. Co.; **PREV EMPLOY:** Counsel, Gulfco Capital Mgmt., Inc., A Subsidiary of Gulf United Corp.; **PROFL AFFIL & HONORS:** ABA, TN Bar Assn.; **EDUC:** BS, 1973, Poli. Sci., Univ. of TN; **GRAD EDUC:** JD, 1976, Law, Univ. of TN Coll. of Law; **EDUC HONORS:** Grad. with Hon., Deans List; **OTHER ACT & HONORS:** Phi Delta Phi Legal Frat.; **HOME ADD:** 403 Ashwood Ter., Chattanooga, TN 37415; **BUS ADD:** 1520 First TN Bldg., Chattanooga, TN 37402, (615)765-4042.

GUILDERSON, Paul H.——**B:** Mar. 28, 1925, Boston, MA, *Dir. NH Office of Industrial Devel.*, Department of Resources and Econ. Devel., Div. of Econ. Devel.; **OTHER RE ACT:** State devel. agency; **SERVICES:** Plant location services; **REP CLIENTS:** Digital Equip. Corp., ECA; **PREV EMPLOY:** Jos. T. Ryerson & Son Inc. (Steel and Aluminum distr.); **PROFL AFFIL & HONORS:** Northeastern Indus. Devels. Assn. (Past Pres.); **EDUC:** BA, 1947, Econ., Dartmouth Coll.; **MIL SERV:** USMC Res., Capt.; **HOME ADD:** 16 Blueberry Ln., Bow, NH 03301, (603)244-5162; **BUS ADD:** P O Box 856, Concord, NH 03301, (603)271-2591.

GUILLORY, John Lee——**B:** July 28, 1945, Oakland, CA, *VP Dist. Mgr.*, Grubb & Ellis Co.; **PREV EMPLOY:** 1977-79 VP & Sales Mgr. for Grubb & Ellis, 0akland CA; 1975-76, Sales Mgr. & Asst. Dist. Mgr. for Grubb & Ellis Co., San Jose, CA; 1970-75 Gubb & Ellis Co. RE Comml. Leasing Spec.; 1969-70, Played profl. football with Cincinnati Bengals; 1968 worked during off season with CT Gen. Life Ins. Co. in the estate, business and pension planning dept. in conjunction with this, has life ins. and mutual fund lic.; 1967-68 Lockheed Electronics Downey, CA as Prod. Control Coordinator; 1967-68 played profl. football with Oakland Raiders; **EDUC:** BA, 1967, Pol. Sci., Stanford Univ.; **GRAD EDUC:** MBA, 1977, Pepperdine Univ.; **EDUC HONORS:** Affiliated with Phi Kappa Sigma Frat., while at Stanford won All-Coast hons. for 3 yrs. in football, Member of Block 'S' Letter Soc.; **OTHER ACT & HONORS:** Sec. to Bd. of Dirs. Charilla Found.; **HOME ADD:** 5 Sereno Cir., Oakland, CA; **BUS ADD:** 1333 Broadway, Oakland, CA 94619.

GULBIN, Robert B.——**B:** Mar. 4, 1927, Brooklyn, NY, *Asst. VP, Leasing Mgr.*, Irving Trust Co., RE Servs. Div.; **OTHER RE ACT:** Landlord & tenant leasing; **SERVICES:** lease negotiations and admin., landlord representation; **REP CLIENTS:** Primarily 'Irving Trust', numerous tenants of 'Irving Trust'; **PREV EMPLOY:** Leasing mgr. for Merrill Lynch, Pierce, Fenner & Smith, Inc.; **PROFL AFFIL & HONORS:** RE Bd. of NY; BOMA of Gr. NY, Inc.; **EDUC:** BBA, 1955, Mgmt. & Econ., Bus. Admin, St. John's Univ.; **GRAD EDUC:** MBA, 1961, Indus. Relations & Econ., NYU Grad Sch. of Bus.; **EDUC HONORS:** Magna Cum Laude; **HOME ADD:** 6810 6th Ave., Brooklyn, NY 11220, (212)745-3247; **BUS ADD:** One Wall St., NY, NY 10015, (212)487-6657.

GULLEDGE, Keith A.——**B:** June 11, 1946, Greensboro, NC, *Pres.*, The Gulledge Corporation; **PRIM RE ACT:** Syndicator; **SERVICES:** Acquisition of multi-family housing, existing, new const., conventional & govt. assisted nationwide; Public and private offerings; **PREV EMPLOY:** Dir. of conventional acquisitions for Kaufman & Broad Asset Mgmt., Inc., Wash., DC; **EDUC:** BA, 1970, Poli. Sci., Brigham Young Univ.; **GRAD EDUC:** Masters Degree, 1972, Bus. Admin., Brigham Young Univ.; **OTHER ACT & HONORS:** Was named Youth of the Yr. in the City of Greensboro by the Mayor's Office; Graduated from BYU High Honors with Distinction; Bishop, Alexandria Ward, The Church of Jesus Christ of Latter-day Saints; **HOME ADD:** 4528 Peacock Ave., Alexandria, VA 22304, (703)370-2717; **BUS ADD:** 5203 Leesburg Pike, Ste. 701, Falls Church, VA 22041, (703)931-6000.

GULLEY, Wilbur P., Jr.——**B:** Aug. 8, 1923, Little Rock, AR, *Pres.*, Savers Federal Savings and Loan Assoc.; **PRIM RE ACT:** Banker, Lender, Owner/Investor, Insuror; **SERVICES:** Mort. Lending & Hazard Ins.; **PROFL AFFIL & HONORS:** Bd. of Dir., C of C; Bd. of Trs. Hendrix Coll., Lantie R. Martin Award, Arkansas S & L League, 1974; **EDUC:** AB, 1947, Bus., Duke Univ.; **EDUC HONORS:** Phi Beta Kappa; **MIL SERV:** USN, 1943-46, Line Officer; **HOME ADD:** 2 Sunset Dr., Little Rock, AR 72207, (501)663-3306; **BUS ADD:** Capitol at Spring St., Little Rock, AR 72201, (501)372-3311.

GULLO, Russell J.——B: June 12, 1956, Buffalo, NY, *Pres.*, Gullo Enterprises, Inc. Investment Real Estate Brokerage; **PRIM RE ACT:** Broker, Consultant, Developer, Owner/Investor, Property Manager, Syndicator; **OTHER RE ACT:** Investment Counselor, handing the acquisition and disposition of income; **SERVICES:** Producing props. nationwide for instnl. and private clients; **PREV EMPLOY:** VP, Computerized Apt. Rentals Inc.; **PROFL AFFIL & HONORS:** RNMI, Candidate for C.C.I.M.; **EDUC:** BS, 1978, Fin., Canisius Coll.; **BUS ADD:** 35 Standish Rd., Buffalo, NY 14216, (716)834-6742.

GUNDY, Thames——B: Oct. 19, 1949, Prairie City, OR, *Pres.*, Thames Gundy corp. (formerly Design-Research Inc.); **PRIM RE ACT:** Broker, Developer, Builder, Owner/Investor, Property Manager, Syndicator; **SERVICES:** Devel. and synd. of resid. investment props.; **REP CLIENTS:** Indiv. investors; **PROFL AFFIL & HONORS:** NAR, Home Builders Assn. of SW ID; **EDUC:** AS, 1974, RE, Santa Barbara City Coll.; AA, 1975, Econ., Santa Barbara City Coll.; **MIL SERV:** USAFA, C4; **HOME ADD:** 4901 Bitterbrush, Boise, ID 83703, (208)342-5802; **BUS ADD:** One Capital Center, 999 Main St. Suite 801, Boise, ID 83702, (208)336-4466.

GUNNS, Stephen Richard——B: Oct. 20, 1950, Dallas, TX, *Pres.*, Union Nat. Investment Grp.; **PRIM RE ACT:** Syndicator, Consultant, Developer, Property Manager, Owner/Investor; **SERVICES:** Investment Counseling, Investments RE; **REP CLIENTS:** Instl., Foreign Investors; **PREV EMPLOY:** Portfolio Mgmt., Union Nat. Life Ins. Co.; **EDUC:** 1972, Ins., Bus., Univ. of TX; **OTHER ACT & HONORS:** Dir., Union Nat. Life Ins. Co.; **BUS ADD:** 9100 Wilshire Blvd. Wilshire-Doheny Plaza, Beverly Hills, CA 90212, (213)276-3482.

GUNSTEENS, Kenneth M.——B: June 19, 1921, Chicago, IL, *Owner, Mgr.*, Bice Realtors; **PRIM RE ACT:** Broker, Appraiser; **SERVICES:** RE Brokerage; **PROFL AFFIL & HONORS:** NW Suburb. IAR and NAR, RNMI, GRI, CRB, CRS; **EDUC:** BS, 1950, Mktg., Univ. of IL; **EDUC HONORS:** Chi Gamma Iota Honorary Frat., Univ. Honors, 1948; **MIL SERV:** USN, Y1c, Overseas; **OTHER ACT & HONORS:** Author of "RE Today" pub. Articles, Computer Acctg. for RE Ofc., Feature Cover Story, Back to Basics, Authored Weighted Av. Money Mort. 1.3p art. in the "IL Realtor", 1981 IL CRB Chapter Pres., 1971 NW Suburban Bd. of Realtors Pres.; **HOME ADD:** 209 N. Aldine, Park Ridge, IL 60068; **BUS ADD:** 17 N. N.W. Hwy., Park Ridge, IL 60068, (312)823-5139.

GUNTER, Howard M., Jr.——B: Sept. 24, 1935, Columbia, SC, *Pres.*, Gunter Realty, Inc.; **PRIM RE ACT:** Broker, Instructor; **PROFL AFFIL & HONORS:** Rotary, CCIM, CRB, AFLM, GRI; **EDUC:** BS, 1957, Mgmt., Univ. of SC; **MIL SERV:** USAF, 1st Lt., Commendation Medal; **HOME ADD:** 4661 Parker Ct., Maitland, FL 32751, (305)628-2228; **BUS ADD:** 807 W. Morse Blvd., Winter Park, FL 32789.

GUNTER, Hubert F.——B: Oct. 20, 1925, Aiken Cty., SC, *Retd. Regl. Mgr. VP*, Cameron-Brown Co., Resid.; **PRIM RE ACT:** Owner/Investor; **PREV EMPLOY:** Mort. Banking 30 yrs.; **PROFL AFFIL & HONORS:** MBA; **EDUC:** AB, 1950, Poli. Sci.-Acctg., Wofford Coll. Spartanburg, SC; **MIL SERV:** USNR, AFC3C; **HOME ADD:** Carriage Hill Condos., Apt. 131, 5225 Clemson Ave., Columbia, SC 29206, (803)782-5195; **BUS TEL:** (803)782-5195.

GUNTHER, Stephen C.——*Mgr., Pasadena Office*, Barry S. Slatt Mortgage Co., Pasadena; **PRIM RE ACT:** Lender; **OTHER RE ACT:** Mort. banker, investment banker; **SERVICES:** Comml. and indus. RE mort. loans & equities; **PROFL AFFIL & HONORS:** Barry S. Slatt Mort. Co. is a member of the Mort. Banker's Assn. of Amer. & the CA Mort. Bankers Assn.; **BUS ADD:** 251 S. Lake Ave., Suite 107, Pasadena, CA 91101, (213)449-3507.

GUPTON, Joe W.——B: Jan. 28, 1943, Paducah, KY, *Mgr., RE Serv. Dept.*, Citizens B&T Co.; **PRIM RE ACT:** Regulator, Banker, Lender; **EDUC:** BS, 1966, Bus., W. KY Univ.; **OTHER ACT & HONORS:** Pi Kappa Alpha; Dir., Reidland Optimist Club 80-81; Pres. Elect, Reidland Optimist Club 81-82; **HOME ADD:** 121 Nickell Hts., Puducah, KY 42001, (502)898-7448; **BUS ADD:** PO Box 2400, Paducah, KY 42001, (502)444-6321.

GURIN, Dr. H. Gerry——B: Apr. 6, 1917, Atlanta, GA, *VP, Jett Forest Estates, Inc.*, Jett Forest Estates Inc./Besser Construction Co. Partner; **PRIM RE ACT:** Developer, Builder, Owner/Investor, Property Manager; **SERVICES:** Devel., builder, mgmt., consultation; **REP CLIENTS:** Banks, lenders, investors; **PROFL AFFIL & HONORS:** Amer. Optometric Assn., GA Optometric Assn., Fifth Dist. Optometric Assn.; **EDUC:** PhG, Mercer School Pharmacy, 1937, IL Coll. Optometry 1939; **MIL SERV:** US Trans. Corps, 1st Lt., Pacific Theater, 4th Inf. Reg. Ribbon; **HOME ADD:** 5140 Jett Forest Trail NW, Atlanta, GA 30327, (404)252-4060; **BUS ADD:** 100 Peachtree, Atlanta, GA 30303, (404)688-7398.

GURMAN, Marvin T.——B: Mar. 13, 1928, New York, NY, *Pres.*, Woodstock Heritage Ltd. and Norwich Realty Co., Inc.; **PRIM RE ACT:** Broker, Consultant, Appraiser, Developer, Builder, Owner/Investor, Property Manager, Syndicator; **OTHER RE ACT:** Arch. designer; **SERVICES:** Creation and devel. of RE Projects (purchase, design, approvals, fin., const.); **PROFL AFFIL & HONORS:** NAR, Pres.-Hanover Lebanon Bd. of Realtors; **EDUC:** 1948, SUNY, Inst. of applied Arts and Sci.; **EDUC HONORS:** Tau Phi Sigma; **MIL SERV:** USA, Tech. 4; **OTHER ACT & HONORS:** Scoutmaster-BSA; **HOME ADD:** Woods End, Etna, NH 03750, (603)643-2442; **BUS ADD:** Box 541 - 1820 House, Main St., Norwich, VT 05055, (802)649-1786.

GURWITCH, Harry——B: Oct. 2, 1934, Mobile, AL, *Assoc.*, Brian Scott Realty, Inc.; **PRIM RE ACT:** Consultant, Assessor, Instructor, Appraiser, Owner/Investor; **OTHER RE ACT:** Sales Assoc.; **SERVICES:** RE brokerage, valuation & synd.; **REP CLIENTS:** US & for. investors in comml. prop.; **PREV EMPLOY:** Over 20 yrs. experience in all phases of RE; **PROFL AFFIL & HONORS:** Nat. Assn. of Review Appraisers; Sr. Member, NARB, CRA; **EDUC:** BA, 1955, Vanderbilt Univ.; **OTHER ACT & HONORS:** Founding Partner, Union Ctr. Venture, a partnership formed for the redevel. of Union Station, St. Louis, MO; **HOME ADD:** 2525 Sunset Dr., Miami Beach, FL 33140, (305)532-2876; **BUS ADD:** 9000 S.W. 87th Court, Suite 215, Miami, FL 33176, (305)270-0200.

GUSHUE, Patrick F.——B: July 6, 1943, Quincy, MA, *Prin./Owner*, Patrick F. Gushue Assoc.; **PRIM RE ACT:** Architect, Consultant, Property Manager, Engineer; **OTHER RE ACT:** Landscape arch.; **SERVICES:** Design Service for interior/exterior landscape & site engrg.; **REP CLIENTS:** Beck Stoffer & Assoc., Spectra Systems, Barry A. Rose, W.R. Grace & Co., Allendale Mutual Ins. Co., Dimeo Const. Co., Leinthal Eisenberg Anderson, Various Town Govt. in Newfoundland; **PREV EMPLOY:** C.E. Maguire, Landscape Architect, 1968-72; **PROFL AFFIL & HONORS:** AILA, CSLA, 3 design awards, 1973-74 for Allendale Mutual Ins. Co., RI, Pres. AILA, 1978-79, VP AILA 1976-77; **EDUC:** AA, 1969, Agric., Agric. Coll.; **GRAD EDUC:** AA, 1970, Bus., Morrow Bus. Prog., Alexander Hamilton Inst., NY, NY; **MIL SERV:** USN, EAD-3, 1960-64; **OTHER ACT & HONORS:** Notary Public, 1974-88, K of C Council 180; **HOME ADD:** 33 Ashmont St., Boston, MA, (617)288-5183; **BUS ADD:** 33 Ashmont St., Boston, MA 02124, (617)282-4022.

GUSTAFSON, Craig——B: Feb. 4, 1953, Lynwood, CA, *Pres.*, Pacific Investment Brokers; **PRIM RE ACT:** Broker, Developer, Owner/Investor, Property Manager; **SERVICES:** Investment counseling, development and syndication of comml. properties; **REP CLIENTS:** Individual and instnl. investors; **PROFL AFFIL & HONORS:** San Diego Bd. of Realtors; State of CA Dept. of Real Estate, Realtor; **EDUC:** RE Law and Fin., San Diego State Univ.; **OTHER ACT & HONORS:** VP, Del Cerro Community Assn., 1 yr.; Del Cerro Community Assn.; **HOME ADD:** 6419 Pasa Tiempo Ave., San Diego, CA 92120, (714)286-2498; **BUS ADD:** 7860 Mission Center Ct., Ste. 107, San Diego, CA 92108, (714)294-9040.

GUSTAFSON, Don A.——B: Oct. 23, 1945, Bellingham, WA, *RE Appraiser and Consultant*, Edward H. Miller Co.; **PRIM RE ACT:** Consultant, Appraiser; **SERVICES:** Appraising and consulting; **PROFL AFFIL & HONORS:** MAI and SRPA Designations; **EDUC:** BA, 1968, Hist./Pol. Sci., Univ. of Puget Sound; **HOME ADD:** 628 Fieldston, Bellingham, WA 98225, (206)734-7124; **BUS ADD:** 1400 Broadway St., Bellingham, WA 98225, (206)734-3420.

GUSTAFSON, Russell——B: July 26, 1925, Northfield, MN, *Mgr. of Valuation Sect.*, MN Dept. of Transportation, Tech. Services; **PRIM RE ACT:** Consultant, Appraiser; **OTHER RE ACT:** Mgr. of appraisal activities for govt. agency; **SERVICES:** Valuation of prop. to be acquired or sold , consultation in any RE decision; **REP CLIENTS:** Other agencies served: State Planning Agency, Metropolitan Airport, Dept. of Natural Resources; **PREV EMPLOY:** Farm Mgr. and Rural Appraiser from 1953-59 with Doane Agricultural Services, Inc., St. Louis, MO; **PROFL AFFIL & HONORS:** AIREA, AFM, ARA, Amer. Soc. of Farm Mgrs. & Rural Appraisers, Past Pres. Award, SREA of St. Paul, Minn Farm Mgrs. & Rural Appraisers Inc., MAI; **EDUC:** BS, 1953, Agric. Econ., Coll. of Agric., Univ of MN; **MIL SERV:** USA, SFC, 1951-52; **HOME ADD:** 353 Christine Ln., West St. Paul, MN 55118, (612)457-1747; **BUS ADD:** 511 Transportation Bldg., MN Dept. of Transportation, St. Paul, MN 55155, (612)296-1135.

GUSTINE, Frank W., Jr.——*VP*, Oliver Realty Inc.; **PRIM RE ACT:** Developer; **BUS ADD:** 2800 - Two Oliver Place, Pittsburgh, PA 15222, (412)281-0100.*

GUTERL, Joseph N.——B: May 7, 1947, Jersey City, NJ, *Managing Editor, Current Legal Forms with Tax Analysis*, Matthew Bender & Co., Inc., Law and Tax Publishers; **OTHER RE ACT:** Law and Tax Publishing (Current Legal Forms with Tax Analysis contains six (6) RE volumes dealing with Entities, Sales, Const., Partnerships, Condos., and Coops., and Leases; **PREV EMPLOY:** Carb, Luria, Glassner, Cook & Kufeld, NY, NY '74 - 76, Wharton, Stewart & Davis, Somerville, NJ '76 - '79; **PROFL AFFIL & HONORS:** ABA; **EDUC:** BA, 1969, Hist., The Catholic Univ. of Amer., Wash., DC; **GRAD EDUC:** JD, 1974, Law, Rutgers Law School; **EDUC HONORS:** Humanities Hon. Program (Seton Hall Univ., S Orange, NJ), degree awarded cum laude; **HOME ADD:** 551 Winsor St., Bound Brook, NJ 08805, (201)356-0887; **BUS ADD:** 235 E 45th St., NY, NY 10017, (212)661-5050.

GUTHEIL, John——B: Sept. 10, 1944, New York, NY, *Partner*, Trubin Sillcocks Edelman & Knapp; **PRIM RE ACT:** Attorney; **REP CLIENTS:** Citibank, N.A., Kings Plaza Shopping Ctr.; **PROFL AFFIL & HONORS:** NY State Bar Assn.; Assn. of the Bar of the City of NY; **EDUC:** BA, 1965, Eng., Columbia Univ.; **GRAD EDUC:** JD, 1968, Harvard Law School; **EDUC HONORS:** Phi Beta Kappa; Magna Cum Laude; **HOME ADD:** 10 Derby Ln., Ossining, NY 10562, (914)762-4253; **BUS ADD:** 375 Park Ave., NY, NY 10152, (212)759-5400.

GUTHRIE, Mark G.——B: Sept. 28, 1943, Lawton, OK, *Consulting Forester*, Self Employed; **PRIM RE ACT:** Consultant, Appraiser, Owner/Investor; **OTHER RE ACT:** Acquisition; **SERVICES:** Timberland Serv.; **REP CLIENTS:** Principals; **PREV EMPLOY:** Forest Industry, Univ., Govt.; **PROFL AFFIL & HONORS:** ACF, SAF, AAII, TFA, OFA, NFIB, XI Sigma Pi, Registered Forester; **EDUC:** BS, 1972, Forest Mgmt.-Gen., Stephen F. Austin St. Univ. Nacogdoches, TX; **GRAD EDUC:** MSF, Pending, Forest Econ., SFASU; **EDUC HONORS:** Magna Cum Laude (pending); **MIL SERV:** USAF, Sgt.; **OTHER ACT & HONORS:** Planning com./zoning Broken Bow, OK 3 yrs., State V-Chmn. Amer. Tree Farm System, OK; **HOME ADD:** PO Box 872, Broken Bow, OK 74728, (405)584-6233; **BUS ADD:** 22½ N. Main, Broken Bow, OK 74728, (405)584-6233.

GUTHRIE, Paul R.——B: Sept. 21, 1948, Yonkers, NY, *Exec. VP*, Amer. Continental Property, Inc.; **PRIM RE ACT:** Consultant, Developer, Owner/Investor, Property Manager; **SERVICES:** Investment analysis, devel. and prop. mgmt.; **PREV EMPLOY:** Second VP, Chase Manhattan Bank, NA, Responsible for mgmt. and sale of all owned RE in Chase Manhattan's Mort. and Realty Trust portfolio, 1977-1980; RE rep. for A&P Co.; Vornado, Inc. and Grand Union Co., 1972-1977; **PROFL AFFIL & HONORS:** Lic. RE Broker, NY State; Intl. Council of Shopping Ctrs.; IREM; **EDUC:** BBA, 1971, Econ., Pace Univ., NY; **GRAD EDUC:** MBA, 1979, Mgmt., Pace Univ. Grad. School; **EDUC HONORS:** Grad. with Distinction, Published Honors Thesis; **HOME ADD:** 95 Plymouth Ave., Yonkers, NY 10708, (914)779-9518; **BUS ADD:** 620 Fifth Ave., NY, NY 10020, (212)245-5770.

GUTLEBER, John J.——B: Sept. 16, 1946, NY, *Asst. VP*, Marine Midland Bank, Constr. Loan Dept.; **PRIM RE ACT:** Banker, Lender; **SERVICES:** Constr. loan financing; **PREV EMPLOY:** Corwin Gutleber Agency, Inc.; **PROFL AFFIL & HONORS:** L.I. Bd. of Realtors, Suffolk Cty. RE Bd. of Dirs., MAI Candidate; **EDUC:** BBA, 1968, Law and Fin., Adelphi Univ.; **GRAD EDUC:** MBA, 1970, Fin., Adelphi Univ.; **HOME ADD:** Box 643 Old Field Rd., Setauket, NY 11733, (516)751-2782; **BUS ADD:** 534 Broad Hollow Rd., Melville, NY 11747, (516)752-4391.

GUTMACHER, Norman William——B: Dec. 21, 1946, Cleveland, OH, *Partner*, Benesch, Friedlander, Coplan & Aronoff; **PRIM RE ACT:** Attorney; **REP CLIENTS:** Devel., synd., comml. RE brokers and sponsors of FHA proj.; **PROFL AFFIL & HONORS:** Appointed member of the RE Synd. Comm. of the OH Div. of Securities; former appointed member of the Legislation, Policy and Rules Comm. of the OH Div. of Securities; elected member of the Governing Bd. of the RE Section of the Cleveland Bar Assn.; elected member of the Governing Bd. of the Securities Law Sec. of the Cleveland Bar Assn. and Chmn of the Blue Sky Subcomm. thereof; member of the Apt. and Home Owners Assn. of Greater Cleveland; **EDUC:** BS, 1968, Chemistry, OH State Univ.; **GRAD EDUC:** JD, 1971, Univ. of Cincinnati Coll. of Law; **EDUC HONORS:** Order of Coif; Editor of the Univ. of Cincinnati Law Review; **HOME ADD:** 23203 Beachwood Blvd., Beachwood, OH 44122, (216)381-8227; **BUS ADD:** 1100 Citizens Bldg., Cleveland, OH 44114, (216)696-1600.

GUTMAN, Ralph J.——B: Aug. 18, 1907, NY, *Part.*, Steckler, Frank & Gutman; **PRIM RE ACT:** Attorney; **PROFL AFFIL & HONORS:** Assn. of the Bar of the City of NY, ABA; **EDUC:** BS, 1927, Wash. Sq. Coll., NYU; **GRAD EDUC:** LLB, 1928, NYU Law School; **HOME ADD:** 441 W. End Ave., NY, NY 11235, (212)787-5756; **BUS ADD:** 60 E. 42nd St., NY, NY 10165, (212)682-7744.

GUTSTEIN, Solomon——B: June 18, 1934, Newport, RI, *Member*, Gutstein & Schwartz, Ltd.; **PRIM RE ACT:** Attorney; **SERVICES:** Law; **PREV EMPLOY:** Sr. Member, Gutstein & Schwartz; **PROFL AFFIL & HONORS:** ABA; IL State Bar Assn.; Chicago Bar Assn., Lectured in RE programs since 1963 for IL State Bar Assn & Chicago Bar Assns. & planned seminar & educational programs; Editorial Advisor for Bar Assn. RE Handbooks, 1967-1971; Author articles on Title, Homestead Rights (1972), RE Tax Problems (1974); Co-Author *Construction Law in IL*, 1980 and 1981 (2nd edition); **EDUC:** AB, 1953, Liberal Arts, Univ. of Chicago; **GRAD EDUC:** JD, 1956, Law, Univ. of Chicago; **EDUC HONORS:** Grad. with Honors, Fuerstenberg Scholar, Assoc. Editor, The Law Review; Kosmerl Fellow; Fuerstenberg Scholar; **OTHER ACT & HONORS:** Alderman, 40th Ward, Chicago, 1975-1979; Many civic & community groups; Many community awards & citations; **BUS ADD:** 180 N. LaSalle St., Suite 3018, Chicago, IL 60601, (312)368-4343.

GUTTENBERG, Larry L.——B: Aug. 23, 1919, Rumania, *Pres.*, Republic Mort. Corp.; **PRIM RE ACT:** Lender; **SERVICES:** Produce FHA, VA & Conv. Morts.; **PROFL AFFIL & HONORS:** MI MBA; MBAA, Cert. Mort. Banker; VP of MBA of MI; **EDUC:** BS, 1940, Acctg., Detroit Inst. of Tech.; **MIL SERV:** USA, S/Sgt., Battle Stars - 1942-1946; **OTHER ACT & HONORS:** Treas. of Jewish Nat. Fund of Detroit; Sustaining Member of the Boy Scouts of Amer.; **HOME ADD:** 18617 Walmer Ln., Birmingham, MI 48009, (313)540-2278; **BUS ADD:** 18800 Wio Mile Rd., Box 2110, Southfield, MI 48037, (313)559-1010.

GUTTMAN, Barney C.——B: June 7, 1939, Pittsburgh, PA, *Pres.*, Barney C. Guttman and Assoc., Inc.; **PRIM RE ACT:** Broker, Consultant, Owner/Investor, Property Manager, Syndicator; **SERVICES:** Synd. of comml. prop., investment and financial consulting; **PREV EMPLOY:** Natl. Steel Corp.; Merrill Lynch, Pierce, Fenner & Smith; **PROFL AFFIL & HONORS:** Greater Pittsburgh Bd. of Revisions; Natl. Assn. of Realtors; Intl. Assn. of Financial Planners, Realtor; **EDUC:** BS, 1961, RE/Econ., Wharton School of Fin. and Comm.; **MIL SERV:** US Air Natl. Guard, 1961-1967; **OTHER ACT & HONORS:** Concordia Club; Westmoreland C of C; Press Club; Bd., Squirrel Hill Urban Coalition/Housing Task Force; Bd., Pittsburgh Center for the Arts; **HOME ADD:** 11 Darlington Cr., Pittsburgh, PA 15217, (412)521-1112; **BUS ADD:** 13th Floor, Investment Bldg., 239 Fourth Ave., Pittsburgh, PA 15222, (412)281-1666.

GUY, William L., III——*Partner*, Gunhus, Grinnell, Jeffries, Klinger, Vinje & Swenson; **PRIM RE ACT:** Attorney; **SERVICES:** Legal Services-Estate Planning, Corps.; **REP CLIENTS:** Anderson-Jordahl Devel. Co., Dynamic Indus. Inc., Pierce Mobile Homes Sales Inc.; **PROFL AFFIL & HONORS:** MN, ND State Bar Assns., Amer. Instit. of CPAs; Admitted to US Tax Court Apr. 27, 1946, Minneapolis, MN; **EDUC:** BS Bus. Admin., 1968, Acctg., Univ. of ND; **GRAD EDUC:** JD, 1976, Law-Tax, Univ. of ND Law School; **MIL SERV:** USNR, Lt.; **OTHER ACT & HONORS:** CPA (1973); **HOME ADD:** RR3, Freedom Way, Moorhead, MN 56560, (218)233-5187; **BUS ADD:** 512 Center Ave., Moorhead, MN 56560, (218)236-6462.

GWINN, William——*Commissioner*, Oregon, Oregon Real Estate Div.; **PRIM RE ACT:** Property Manager; **BUS ADD:** 158 12th St., N.E., Salem, OR 97310, (503)378-4170.*

GYPTON, James C.——B: Nov. 3, 1935, Newark, NJ, *Exec. VP, RE*, Victor Palmieri & Co. Inc., Penn Central Props. Div.; **PRIM RE ACT:** Consultant, Property Manager; **REP CLIENTS:** The Penn Central Corp.; **PREV EMPLOY:** Mgr. Corp. RE Amerada Hess Corp.; **EDUC:** BBA, 1961, Econ., Upsala; **HOME ADD:** 13 E Ridge Rd., Pennington, NJ 08531, (609)737-0164; **BUS ADD:** 1700 Market St., Philadelphia, PA 19103, 15)561-1650.

HAAG, George Alva——B: Aug. 18, 1939, San Antonio, TX, *Pres.*, Haag Development Corp.; **PRIM RE ACT:** Developer, Builder; **PREV EMPLOY:** VP, First Souther, Inc.; Profl. Campaign Mgr., US Rep. James M. Collins, Gov. William Cahill, US Rep. William Windall; **PROFL AFFIL & HONORS:** Who's Who in Amer. Politics, 1970-1976; Who's Who in Amer. Govt., 1971-1976; Personalities of the S., 1971-1980; Outstanding Jaycee (TX), 1971; Notable Amer. of the Bicentennial Era, 1976-1980; US Community Leaders, 1976-1980;

Dictionary of Intl. Biography, Volume XIV, 1977-1980; **EDUC:** BS, Pol. Sci., TX A&I Univ.; **GRAD EDUC:** MA, Pol. Sci., Univ. of MO; **EDUC HONORS:** Magna Cum Laude, Summa Cum Laude; **MIL SERV:** USAF, Capt.; **HOME ADD:** 5 Arrowood Terr., Bethesda, MD 2O034, (301)469-6063; **BUS ADD:** 2506 Iverson St., Hillcrest Heights, MD 20031, (301)423-7411.

HAAS, Donald E.——**B:** Oct. 5, 1933, Pittsburgh, PA, *Owner*, D.E. Haas Associates; **PRIM RE ACT:** Consultant, Owner/Investor; **SERVICES:** Planning, Community Devel., Housing; **REP CLIENTS:** Local Units of Govt.; Other Consultants; **PREV EMPLOY:** Redevel. Dir., City of Mount Clemens, MI; VP, Multiple Servs., Inc. (Muskegon, MI); **PROFL AFFIL & HONORS:** Nat. Assn. of Housing and Redevel. Officials; Metropolitan Assn. of Urban Designers and Environmental Planners; **EDUC:** BS, 1956, Agricultural Econ. and Rural Sociology, PA State Univ.; **GRAD EDUC:** MS, 1958, Rural Sociology, PA State Univ.; **MIL SERV:** USAF Res., Maj. (Active Duty 1959-61); **OTHER ACT & HONORS:** Res. Officers Assn. of the US (Life Member); **HOME ADD:** 3087 Knollwood Ct., Muskegon, MI 49441, (616)755-6629; **BUS ADD:** PO Box 733, Muskegon, MI 49443, (616)726-3111.

HAAS, John E.——**B:** Jan. 6, 1945, Greenville, SC, *Dir., Exec. VP*, First Citizens Mort. Corp., First Citizens Bank; **PRIM RE ACT:** Lender; **SERVICES:** Mort. banking; **PROFL AFFIL & HONORS:** MBAA, MBA of the Carolinas, HBA, Columbia Urban Lending Project; **EDUC:** AB, 1967, Bus. Admin. & Econ., Wofford Coll.; **GRAD EDUC:** MBA, 1970, Acctg., Univ. of SC; **EDUC HONORS:** Dean's List; **MIL SERV:** US Army; Lt.; **HOME ADD:** PO Box 11703, Columbia, SC 29211, (803)736-0280; **BUS ADD:** 1015 Lady St., PO Box 11257, Columbia, SC 29211, (803)799-9465.

HAASE, Dennis J.——**B:** July 15, 1951, Eugene, OR, *Pres.*, Bankers Land Co.; **PRIM RE ACT:** Broker, Syndicator, Developer, Builder, Owner/Investor; **PROFL AFFIL & HONORS:** NAR; **EDUC:** Bus., Law & R.E., R.E., Investments; **BUS ADD:** 354 W. 6th., Eugene, OR 97401, (503)686-1921.

HABACK, Peter L.——**B:** July 25, 1951, New York, NY, *VP*, Helmsley-Spear of IL, Inc.; **PRIM RE ACT:** Broker; **SERVICES:** Mgmt. and leasing of six office bldgs. in downtown Chicago, gen. brokerage; **PREV EMPLOY:** with Helmsley-Spear since 1976; **PROFL AFFIL & HONORS:** BOMA-CREB, Who's Who in Fin. and Indus. 1981 Edition; **EDUC:** BA, 1973, Poli. Sci., Public Admin., Amer. Univ.; **GRAD EDUC:** 1974-1976, Law, John Marshall Law School; **EDUC HONORS:** Member Faculty Council-School of Govt.; **HOME ADD:** 1852 N. Hudson, Chicago, IL 60614; **BUS ADD:** Suite 210, One N. Dearborn St., Chicago, IL 60602, (312)781-2400.

HABEGGER, Edward P.——**B:** May 12, 1925, Monroe, IN, *RE Consultant*, Gray Drug Stores, Inc.; **OTHER RE ACT:** RE Consulting Services; **PREV EMPLOY:** Gray Drug Stores Inc. (RE VP, 17 Years), Kroger (RE, 13 yrs), Colonial Stores (RE 4 yrs.); **PROFL AFFIL & HONORS:** ICSC; **EDUC:** 1947, Acctg. & Bus. Law, Intl. Bus. Coll.; **EDUC HONORS:** Honor Grad.; **MIL SERV:** USA; **OTHER ACT & HONORS:** Bd. B.L.I. & WCRF Radio; **HOME ADD:** 9173 Dogwood Rd., Brecksville, OH 44141, (216)526-3806; **BUS ADD:** 9173 Dogwood Rd., Brecksville, OH 44141, (216)526-3806.

HABER, Miles J.——**B:** June 19, 1942, New York, NY, *Sr. VP, Dir. of Const., Eastern Div.*; **PRIM RE ACT:** Developer, Builder; **SERVICES:** Devel., Bldg., Prop. Mgmt.; **PREV EMPLOY:** HRH Const. Corp., New York, NY, 1968-1977; **PROFL AFFIL & HONORS:** Amer. Soc. of Civil Engrs., N VA Home Builders, Surburban MD Home Builders; **EDUC:** BCE, 1965, Const. Mgmt., Civil Engrg., Cornell Univ.; **GRAD EDUC:** M Engr., 1966, Const. Mgmt., Civil Engr., Cornell Univ.; **MIL SERV:** US Army, 1st Lt.; **HOME ADD:** 3507 Bradley Ln., Chevy Chase, MD 20815, (301)656-8787; **BUS ADD:** 4351 Garden City Dr., Suite 300, Landover, MD 20785, (301)459-8700.

HABER, Murray——*Pres.*, Maxwell Management Corp.; **PRIM RE ACT:** Owner/Investor, Property Manager, Syndicator; **OTHER RE ACT:** Syndication Mgmt.; **EDUC:** 1949, Bus., Miami Univ.; **BUS ADD:** 101 West 55th St., New York, NY 10019, (212)757-5632.

HABERMAN, Howard M.——**B:** Sept. 17, 1943, Newark, NJ, *VP*, Haberman Bldg. Corp.; **PRIM RE ACT:** Developer, Builder, Property Manager, Owner/Investor; **SERVICES:** Prop. Mgmt.; **PROFL AFFIL & HONORS:** Amer. Inst. of CPA's; CPA: NY, NJ, IL, SRPA; **EDUC:** BBA, 1965, Acctg., Univ. of Pittsburgh, Pittsburgh, PA; **GRAD EDUC:** MBA, 1967, Acctg., Univ. of Chicago; **MIL SERV:** USAFR, Sgt.; **OTHER ACT & HONORS:** NJ Zoological Socl, Dir. 1981; **BUS ADD:** 59 Main St., W. Orange, NJ 07052, (201)736-0330.

HABIF, Moreno——**B:** Oct. 11, 1937, Havana, Cuba; **PRIM RE ACT:** Syndicator; **PREV EMPLOY:** Founder and VP Sales, Oriental Trading Div. of Suave Shoe (NY Stock Exchange); **PROFL AFFIL & HONORS:** VP Temple Menorah Miami Beach; **EDUC:** BBA, 1963, Acctg., Miami Univ.; **HOME ADD:** 1440 S. Biscayne Pt. Rd., Miami Beach, FL 33141, (305)866-9793; **BUS ADD:** 4593 E. 10th Ave., Hialeah, FL 33102, (305)687-1660.

HABIG, Douglas A.——*Pres.*, Kimball International, Inc.; **PRIM RE ACT:** Property Manager; **BUS ADD:** 1549 Royal, Jasper, IN 47546, (812)482-1600.*

HACHENBURG, Robert——**B:** May 7, 1918, Philadelphia, PA, *Prof. of Law*, Temple Univ. School of Law, Specializing in Comml. & RE Law; **PRIM RE ACT:** Consultant, Attorney, Instructor; **REP CLIENTS:** Shopping center owners & devels.; **PREV EMPLOY:** Sr. VP, Counsel, Secretary & Dir. of Albert M. Greenfield & Co. Inc. 1949-1969; **PROFL AFFIL & HONORS:** Brokers Lic. in PA, NJ and NY until 1969, Att. at Law; **EDUC:** AB, 1939, Eng., Univ. of PA; **GRAD EDUC:** JD, 1943, Law, Univ. of PA Law School; **EDUC HONORS:** Grad. w/Hon., Phi Beta Kappa, Book Awards, Editor of Law Review; **MIL SERV:** Navy Intelligence: Jap. Language Spec., Lt.; **HOME ADD:** 138 Royal Ave., Wyncote, PA 19095, (215)887-1414; **BUS ADD:** Broad and Montgomery Sts., Philadelphia, PA 19122, (215)787-7422.

HACKBARTH, Raymond William, Jr.——**B:** Sept. 24, 1947, Syracuse, NY, *Pres.*, RHA Props.; **PRIM RE ACT:** Broker; **SERVICES:** Prop. mgmt, real estate invest. & consultant; **REP CLIENTS:** Various RE investors; **PREV EMPLOY:** Pres. Monarch Securities; Dir. of Ins. Services Ticor Mort. Ins.; Assoc. VP Umet Trust; Asst. Atty. MacKenzie, Smith, Lewis, Michelle & Hughes; **PROFL AFFIL & HONORS:** ABA, NY State Bar Assn., Who's Who in CA, Who's Who in Bus. & Fin.; **EDUC:** BA, 1969, Lib. Arts, Allegheny Univ.; **GRAD EDUC:** JD, 1974, RE & Bus. Law; **MIL SERV:** USA, Sgt.; **OTHER ACT & HONORS:** VP Syracuse Univ. Alumni Grp. of S. CA; Roosters of Chanteclair; Phi Gamma Delta; **HOME ADD:** Capistrano Beach, CA; **BUS ADD:** PO Box 4466, San Clemente, CA 92672, (714)661-7113.

HACKETT, Gerard L.J.——**B:** Nov. 27, 1921, Quebec City, Can., *Engr.*, Consultant; **PRIM RE ACT:** Consultant, Engineer, Regulator; **SERVICES:** Engrg. bids, contracts & specifications, project mgmt.; expertise in code standards and standardization.; **PREV EMPLOY:** James Bay Energy Corp., Montreal; **PROFL AFFIL & HONORS:** Standards Engrg. Soc., Const. Specifications Can., Engr., Master of Engrg.; **EDUC:** BS, 1951, Mech. Engrg., McGill Univ.; **GRAD EDUC:** MS, 1977, Civil/Mech., Concordia Univ.; **MIL SERV:** RCAF, Sgt., CVSM; **OTHER ACT & HONORS:** Cert. in Standards Engrg. by SES; **HOME ADD:** 1740 Edgewood, St. Bruno, J3V4N9, Que., Can., (514)653-9337; **BUS ADD:** 1740 Edgewood, St. Bruno, J3V4N9, Que., Can, (514)653-9337.

HACKETT, Paul——*Dir. Corp. Services*, Harper & Row Publishers, Inc.; **PRIM RE ACT:** Property Manager; **BUS ADD:** 10 E. 53rd St., New York, NY 10022, (212)593-7000.*

HACKMANN, John S.——**B:** Mar. 31, 1927, East St. Louis, IL, *Pres.*, Illinois Federal Savings and Loan Assn.; **PRIM RE ACT:** Attorney, Appraiser, Lender; **SERVICES:** Lending; **REP CLIENTS:** S&L Assn.; **PROFL AFFIL & HONORS:** Soc. of RE Appraisers, Nat. Assn. of Review Appraisers, CRA, SRA; **EDUC:** BA, 1949, Poli. Sci. & Econ., Wash. Univ., St. Louis, MO; **GRAD EDUC:** JD, 1955, Law, St. Louis Univ., St. Louis, MO; **MIL SERV:** USN, Seaman; **HOME ADD:** 38 Signal Hill Blvd., Belleville, IL 62223, (618)397-0741; **BUS ADD:** 6550 N Illinois St., Fairview Heights, IL 62208, (618)397-5300.

HACKNEY, Thomas A.——**B:** May 30, 1953, Lincoln, AL, *Owner*, Remo Bros.; **PRIM RE ACT:** Developer, Owner/Investor, Property Manager; **PROFL AFFIL & HONORS:** ACHA, FAH; **EDUC:** Biology/Chemistry, 1975, Auburn Univ.; **GRAD EDUC:** MHA, 1978, Hospitals - Health Admin., Univ. of AL in Birmingham; **OTHER ACT & HONORS:** Treas. of the Bd. - Amer. Rural Health Assn.; **HOME ADD:** P O Box 221, Lincoln, AL 35096, (205)323-8494; **BUS ADD:** 1109 Cullom St., Birmingham, AL 35205, (205)250-7103.

HADDAD, Lawrence——**B:** July 12, 1931, Clinton, IA, *Pres./CEO*, New Frontier Developments Co./New Frontier Mgmt. Corp.; **PRIM RE ACT:** Developer, Owner/Investor, Property Manager; **PREV EMPLOY:** U.S. Dept. of HUD; U.S. Office of the Sec. of Defense; VP, Shelter Devel. Corp.; **PROFL AFFIL & HONORS:** Nicholas Award, Dak Park, IL for multi-family devel.; **EDUC:** BA, 1958, Journalism/Pol. Sci., Univ. of MN; **GRAD EDUC:** MA, 1961, Middle E. Studies, Amer. Univ. of Beirut; **MIL SERV:** USN; PO 3rd Class, 1951-1955; **OTHER ACT & HONORS:** Dir. of Production Low

Income Housing, Region 5, US Dept. HUD; Area Dir., Indianapolis, IN, 1971-1972; **HOME ADD:** River Forest, IL 60305; **BUS ADD:** 307 N. Michigan, Chicago, IL 60601, (312)236-0189.

HADDAD, Leo Gus——B: June 10, 1951, El Paso, TX, *Pres.*, Haddad Properties, Inc.; **PRIM RE ACT:** Broker, Developer, Owner/Investor, Syndicator; **SERVICES:** Income prop. devel., investment, brokerage; **REP CLIENTS:** El Paso Electric Co., Franklin Land and Resources, Lanchart Industries, LGH Investment Corp., Haddad Trust Investors, Synd., and Devel. of Income producing prop.; **PREV EMPLOY:** E.F. Hutton & Co.; **PROFL AFFIL & HONORS:** El Paso Housing Rehab Bd.; RNMI; **EDUC:** BSA, 1974, Fin./Econ., Univ. of TX, El Paso; **OTHER ACT & HONORS:** Bd. of Dirs., Kiwanis Club of El Paso; Chmn., Bd. of Dirs., El Paso State Ctr. of Human Devel.; **HOME ADD:** 935 Rim Rd., El Paso, TX 79902; **BUS ADD:** 101 Arizona Ave., El Paso, TX 79902, (915)533-8400.

HADDOCK, Douglas R.——B: Apr. 7, 1942, Idaho Falls, ID, *Assoc. Prof.*, St. Mary's Univ., School of Law; **PRIM RE ACT:** Consultant, Attorney, Instructor; **PREV EMPLOY:** Pvt. Law Practice; **PROFL AFFIL & HONORS:** ABA; **EDUC:** BA, 1967, Pol. Sci., Univ. of UT; **GRAD EDUC:** JD, 1970, Univ. of UT, Coll. of Law; **EDUC HONORS:** Honors Prog.; Phi Beta Kappa, Schiller Scholarship; Managing Editor, UT Law Review; Coif; **HOME ADD:** 8418 Timber Mill, San Antonio, TX 78250, (512)684-4237; **BUS ADD:** One Camiro Santa Maria, San Antonio, TX 78284.

HADDOW, David Forbes——B: Nov. 28, 1953, New York, NY, *Mort. Loan Officer*, Banco Mortgage Co., Income Loan Div.; **OTHER RE ACT:** Mort. banker; **SERVICES:** Permanent and interim fin. for comml. RE projects; **REP CLIENTS:** Lenders and devels. investing in comml. RE; **PREV EMPLOY:** Atlanta Dept. of Budget and Planning; **PROFL AFFIL & HONORS:** Mort. Bankers Assn. of GA; **EDUC:** BA, 1979, Hist., Emory Univ.; **GRAD EDUC:** Master of City Planning, 1979, City Planning, GA Inst. of Tech.; MBA, 1982, GA State Univ.; **OTHER ACT & HONORS:** Nat. Trust for Hist. Preservation; George E. Manners Award for Grad. Study in Bus. for 1981 (GA State Univ.); **HOME ADD:** 4755 Millbrook Dr., NW, Atlanta, GA 30327, (404)252-3452; **BUS ADD:** 2100 Powers Ferry Rd., Suite 460, Atlanta, GA 30339, (404)955-2921.

HADFIELD, Michael James——B: Jan. 25, 1934, Waukesha, WI, *Pres. & Bd. Chmn.; RE Broker*, Oconee Devel. Corp.; Luten Properties, Inc.; **PRIM RE ACT:** Broker, Developer, Owner/Investor; **SERVICES:** Recreational & resid. devel., comml. investment, RE sales (primary); **REP CLIENTS:** Private investors, indus. firms, wholesalers & retailers, chain stores, restaurants; **PREV EMPLOY:** Salesman, then VP, Real Prop. Center, Inc., Largo, FL, 1974-79; Bd. Chmn. & Pres. FM Enterprises, Inc. (WQXM Radio Sta.), Clearwater, FL, 1968-69; **PROFL AFFIL & HONORS:** Fl Assn. Realtors, Clearwater-Largo-Dunedin Bd. of Realtors, NAR, Nat. Marktg. Inst. (CCIM Candidate), Who's Who in Aviation (1981), Who's Who in RE in Amer. (1981), Who's Who in Amer. Colls. & Univs. (1954-55); **EDUC:** BEE, 1955, Comm. Electronics, Marquette Univ.; **GRAD EDUC:** MEE, incompl., Electronics, Univ. of WI, Milwaukee; MBA, incompl., Mgmt., Univ. of So. FL; **EDUC HONORS:** Tau Beta Pi, Alpha Sigma Nu, Pi Mu Epsilon, Eta Kappa Nu, Scabbard & Blade, SAME & AFCEA Gold Medals; **MIL SERV:** USMC; Capt.; **OTHER ACT & HONORS:** Republican Party, Pres. of Parish Council St. Cecelia's Church (1973-75), Author of nine tech. papers in engrg. field; **HOME ADD:** 12449 84th Way N., Largo, FL 33543, (813)531-5715; **BUS ADD:** 615 S Missouri Ave., Clearwater, FL 33516, (813)446-4280.

HADLEY, Joann Jody——B: Nov. 2, 1934, IL, *Pres., Consultant, Prop. Mgmt., Ins., Fin.*, J.J. Enterprises; **PRIM RE ACT:** Consultant, Property Manager, Insuror; **PROFL AFFIL & HONORS:** Triple C. Bus. Club., Amer. Legion, C of C, Biniki City Radio, IL Law Envo Enforcement; **EDUC:** AA/AS, Long Beach City College, BCC Community College; **HOME TEL:** (305)631-5324; **BUS ADD:** P.O. Box 958, Cocoa, FL 32922, (305)631-5324.

HAEGER, Warren J.——*Secretary Treasurer*, Real Estate Aviation Chapter; **OTHER RE ACT:** Profl. Assn. Admin.; **BUS ADD:** 5440 St. Charles Rd., Berkeley, IL 60163, (312)547-7100.*

HAERING, Joseph——*Dir. of Fac. & RE*, Harris Corp.; **PRIM RE ACT:** Property Manager; **BUS ADD:** Melbourne, FL 32919, (305)727-9100.*

HAESSLER, George W.——B: Jan. 2, 1922, Leshara, NE, *Partner*, Haessler Sullivan & Inbody; **PRIM RE ACT:** Attorney; **SERVICES:** Legal; **REP CLIENTS:** Comml. state Bank, Cedar Bluffs, NE, State Bank of Colon; **EDUC:** 1946, Midland Coll., ME; **GRAD EDUC:** LLB, 1949; JD, 1968; **MIL SERV:** US Army, Cpl., 3 campaigns; **OTHER ACT & HONORS:** Cty. Atty. Saunders Co. 1951-62; Member Coll. of Probate Counsel; **HOME ADD:** 444 E 16th, Wahoo, NE 68066, (402)443-3220; **BUS ADD:** 666 N Broadway, Wahoo, NE 68066, (402)443-4181.

HAFF, Dr. Courtney A.——B: June 24, 1946, Portland, OR, *RE Advisor*, The Equitable Life Assurance Society of the US, Investment Evaluation Dept.; **PRIM RE ACT:** Consultant, Appraiser; **OTHER RE ACT:** Mkt./Investment Analyst, Asst. Prof.; **SERVICES:** Correspondent, Eton Journal of RE Investment; **REP CLIENTS:** City of NY, Lincoln Inst. of Land Policy, Center for Local Tax Research, State of HI, MA Environmental Design; **PREV EMPLOY:** Sr. Analyst, ABT Assocs.; Pres., Public Policy Research; Dir. of Research, Fin., Office of Appraisal Research, City of NY; **PROFL AFFIL & HONORS:** ULI; Amer. Inst. of Cert. Planners; AREUEA; Nat. Assn. of Review Appraisers, AICP; CRA; **EDUC:** BS, 1968, Urban and Rgnl. Econ., Univ. of OR; **GRAD EDUC:** MPA, 1972, RE/Urban Land Econ., NY Univ.; PhD, 1976, RE/Urban Land Econ., NY Univ.; **EDUC HONORS:** Grad. Fellowship; **MIL SERV:** Armor, 1st Lt.; **OTHER ACT & HONORS:** Intl. Ctr. for Land Policy Studies; Lincoln Inst. Fellowship; Consultant to the City of NY, Fovt. of the Dominican Republic, State of HI & Ctr. for Local Tax Research; **HOME ADD:** 16 Hudson St., NY, NY 10013, (212)227-3255; **BUS ADD:** 1285 Ave. of the Americas, NY, NY 10020, (212)554-3908.

HAFFNER, Robert——*Tax Mgr.*, Vernitron; **PRIM RE ACT:** Property Manager; **BUS ADD:** 2001 Marcus Ave., Lake Success, NY 11042, (516)775-8200.*

HAFNER, William Lincoln——B: Apr. 15, 1939, Cleveland, OH, *Exec. VP*, Heitman Advisory Corp.; **PRIM RE ACT:** Consultant, Appraiser; **SERVICES:** Analysis and appraisal of props. for pension fund acquisition; **REP CLIENTS:** Amer. Tel. & Tel. Pension Fund, Brit. Postal Workers Retirement Fund; **PREV EMPLOY:** R.A. Cooch Co.; Grad. School of Bus. Admin., The Univ. of MI; **PROFL AFFIL & HONORS:** AIREA; Soc. of RE Appraisers; Amer. Inst. of Planners; Nat. Assn. Corp. RE Execs., MAI; SRPA; AICP; **EDUC:** BA, 1961, Econ., OH Univ.; **GRAD EDUC:** MS, 1978, RE/Fin. Analysis, Grad. School of Bus., Univ. of WI; MA, 1965, Bus. Econ., Vanderbilt Univ.; **HOME ADD:** 1100 N. Dearborn #1212, Chicago, IL 60610; **BUS ADD:** 180 N. LaSalle St., Chicago, IL 60601.

HAGAMAN, John F.——B: May 1, 1939, New Orleans, LA, *VP and Gen. Mgr.*, Marco Developers, Inc.; **PRIM RE ACT:** Broker, Consultant, Developer, Owner/Investor, Property Manager, Syndicator; **SERVICES:** Prop. evaluation, cash flow analysis, land planning, devel. planning; **REP CLIENTS:** Various corps., resid. devels., estates, pension trusts, comml. devels.; **PREV EMPLOY:** Humble Oil & Ref. (now Exxon); RE Mgr., R.T. Marshall Co., Inc.; RE Brokerage; **PROFL AFFIL & HONORS:** Houston Bd. of Realtors; TX Assn. of Realtors, Various local Houston honors; **EDUC:** 1961, Eng./Econ., Dartmouth Coll.; **MIL SERV:** US Army Nat. Guard, E-5; **OTHER ACT & HONORS:** Champions Golf Club; Metropolitan Racquet Club; Warwick Club; **HOME ADD:** 3614 Montrose Blvd., Apt. 507, Houston, TX 77006, (713)520-9971; **BUS ADD:** 601 Jefferson, Suite 3505, Houston, TX 77002, (713)759-1258.

HAGEE, Joseph G.——B: Aug. 3, 1936, Indianapolis, IN, *Pres.*, Century 21 Mitchell Bros.; **PRIM RE ACT:** Broker, Consultant, Appraiser, Developer, Property Manager, Owner/Investor; **OTHER RE ACT:** Specialty & Condo. Conversions, IL, MO, CO, AZ; **REP CLIENTS:** First Nat. Bank of Evanston & Others; **PROFL AFFIL & HONORS:** Leading IL Century 21 Office (5 yrs.); **EDUC:** BS, 1959, Mgmt., IN Univ., Bloomington; **GRAD EDUC:** MBA, 1960, Mgmt. & Fin., IN Univ., Bloomington, IN; **EDUC HONORS:** SEC of the S.I.E. Mgmt. hon. soc., Mgmt. Assistantship; **MIL SERV:** USA, 1st Lt.; **OTHER ACT & HONORS:** Pres. United Fund, Past Plan Commnr. City of Evanston, Phi Delta Theta, N Lite Bd.; **HOME ADD:** 2623 Lincoln St., Evanston, IL 60201, (312)864-7478; **BUS ADD:** 2528 Greenbay Rd., Evanston, IL 60201, (312)492-9660.

HAGEN, David B.——B: Mar. 12, 1953, Sacramento, CA, *Pres.*, TYT Corp.; **PRIM RE ACT:** Consultant, Owner/Investor, Instructor, Property Manager; **SERVICES:** Investment consulting, prop. mgmt., educ. services; **EDUC:** Bus. Mgmt., 1979, Fin. Acctg., Univ. of MD, Coll. Park; **HOME ADD:** 13213 Superior St., Rockville, MO 20853, (301)942-8458; **BUS ADD:** PO Box 6486, Silver Spring, MD 20906, (301)933-3978.

HAGEN, Kenneth E.——B: 1929, Berkeley, CA, *Atty.*, Law Offices of Kenneth E. Hagen; **PRIM RE ACT:** Consultant, Attorney, Owner/Investor, Syndicator; **OTHER RE ACT:** Attorney; Owner/Investor; Community Associations including CC&Rs to collections; Litigation on all matters pertaining to RE; Governmental clearances including departments of RE and corp.; SEC exemptions and limited offerings; related business matters such as limited partnerships and corporations;

EDUC: BA, 1952, Speech, Univ. of CA, Berkeley; **GRAD EDUC:** JD, 1955, Boalt Hall, Univ. of CA, Berkeley; **HOME ADD:** 3270 Santa Marie, Fullerton, CA 92635; **BUS ADD:** 100 West Valencia Mesa Dr. #210, Fullerton, CA 92635, (714)879-7070.

HAGEN, Stephen C.——B: Feb. 21, 1942, Great Bend, KS, *VP*, Merrill, Lynch Hubbard, Inc., Hubbard Adv. Grp.; **PRIM RE ACT:** Consultant, Owner/Investor; **OTHER RE ACT:** New Investments; **REP CLIENTS:** Hubbard RE Investments; **EDUC:** BA, 1964, Journalism, Univ. of KS; **GRAD EDUC:** MBA, 1968, Bus. Mgmt., Wharton Sch. of Fin.; **BUS ADD:** 2 Broadway, NY, NY 10004, (212)908-8483.

HAGENAH, W.——*Sr. VP & Treas.*, Wrigley, Wm. Jr. Co.; **PRIM RE ACT:** Property Manager; **BUS ADD:** 410 N. Michigan Ave, Chicago, IL 60611, (312)644-2121.*

HAGERICH, Robert, Jr.——B: Jan. 23, 1952, Johnstown, PA, *Partner*, Hagerich and Son Real Estate; **PRIM RE ACT:** Broker, Appraiser; **REP CLIENTS:** Bethlehem Steel, Merrill-Lynch, Texaco, Sun Oil Co., Westinghouse, Johnstown Bank and Trust Co., US National Bank; **PROFL AFFIL & HONORS:** Soc. of RE Appraisers; Bd. of Realtors, SRPA; **EDUC:** Bus. Admin., 1973, RE, PA State Univ.; **OTHER ACT & HONORS:** Bd. of Dirs. C of C; **HOME ADD:** RD 3, Box 159, Johnstown, PA 15904, (814)266-9406; **BUS ADD:** 337 Stonycreek St., Johnstown, PA 15901, (814)536-3569.

HAGESTAD, Grant K.——B: July 20, 1937, San Mateo, CA, *Pres.*, Estate Homes of Northern CA, Inc.; **PRIM RE ACT:** Engineer, Developer, Builder; **SERVICES:** Land Devel. and Construction serv.; **PREV EMPLOY:** Oceanic Prop., Bldrs. Resources Corp., Private Consultant; **PROFL AFFIL & HONORS:** Bd. of Dir., BIA of Northern CA; ASCE, Lic. Civil Eng., State of CA; **EDUC:** BS, Master of Science, 1960, Civil Engrg./Engrg. Econ., Stanford Univ.; **GRAD EDUC:** MBA, 1964, Econ. & Fin., Stanford Univ.; **EDUC HONORS:** Tau Beta Pi, Dean's List; **OTHER ACT & HONORS:** Bd. of Dir., YMCA; **HOME ADD:** 31 Coquito Ct., Portola Valley, CA 94025; **BUS ADD:** 3001 So. Winchester Blvd., Campbell, CA 95008, (408)374-7910.

HAGGARTY, Kevin F.——B: Dec. 10, 1942, New York, NY, *VP*, Salomon Brothers, RE Group; **PRIM RE ACT:** Broker, Consultant, Developer, Owner/Investor; **SERVICES:** Consulting, advising, financing; **REP CLIENTS:** Corp., fin. instit., foreign investors, pension funds and major devel.; **PREV EMPLOY:** Equitable Life Assurance Soc.; **PROFL AFFIL & HONORS:** ICSC; NACORE; ULI; Young Mort. Bankers; RE Bd. of NY; **EDUC:** BBA, 1968, Fin./Econ., St. Francis Coll.; **BUS ADD:** 1 NY Plaza, NY, NY 10004, (212)747-7373.

HAGOOD, Wayne D.——B: Dec. 3, 1924, Fort Worth, TX, *Pres.*, Hagood & Associatees, Inc.; **PRIM RE ACT:** Consultant, Appraiser, Owner/Investor; **SERVICES:** Appraisals, feasibility, investment - market; **REP CLIENTS:** Fin., Govtl., Bus., Indus., Attys., Accts., Indiv.; **PREV EMPLOY:** Same since 1953, appraiser for Mortgage Co. 1950-1953; **PROFL AFFIL & HONORS:** AIREA; ASREC, MAI, CRE; **EDUC:** TCU; **MIL SERV:** USN; 1942-1946; Adm(g)2C, Air Medal; **HOME ADD:** 4308 Balboa, Fort Worth, TX 76133, (817)292-6991; **BUS ADD:** 800 No. Freeway, Fort Worth, TX 76102, (817)335-8686.

HAGOPIAN, John——*Dir. RE*, Fruehauf Corp.; **PRIM RE ACT:** Property Manager; **BUS ADD:** 10900 Harper, PO Box 238, Detroit, MI 48232, (313)267-1000.*

HAHN, Richard F.——B: May 20, 1909, Chicago, IL, *Partner*, Halfpenny, Hahn & Roche; **PRIM RE ACT:** Attorney; **SERVICES:** Legal serv.; **REP CLIENTS:** Purchasers and sellers of RE; **PROFL AFFIL & HONORS:** Chicago Bar Assn.; IL Bar Assn.; ABA, Who's Who in World; **EDUC:** BS, 1930, Bus. Admin., Univ. of IL, Coll. of Commerce; **GRAD EDUC:** JD, 1933, Univ. of IL, Coll. of Law; **OTHER ACT & HONORS:** Member Woodstock City Council; Woodstock Indsl. Devel. Commn.; Woodstock City Planning Commn.; **HOME ADD:** 415 Laurel Ave., Woodstock, IL 60098, (815)338-1485; **BUS ADD:** 111 W. Washington St., Chicago, IL 60602, (312)782-1829.

HAID, Linda L.——B: May 23, 1952, Rochester, NY, *Pres.*, Branford Realty Corp.; **PRIM RE ACT:** Broker, Property Manager; **SERVICES:** Primarily prop. mgmt.; **PROFL AFFIL & HONORS:** Inst. of RE Mgmt.; Nat. Assn. of Home Builders; Nat. Assn. of Realtors, CPM; **EDUC:** 1975, Merchandising, Univ. of AZ; **HOME ADD:** 76 Clintwood Ct., Rochester, NY 14620, (716)442-4300; **BUS ADD:** 56 Clintwood Ct., Rochester, NY 14620, (716)442-4300.

HAIK, Mac——B: Jan. 19, 1946, Meridian, MS, *Owner*, Mac Haik Enterprises; **PRIM RE ACT:** Developer, Broker, Consultant, Owner/Investor, Property Manager; **OTHER RE ACT:** Leasing; **SERVICES:** Consulting, Comm. RE brokerage, investments, mgmt., leasing, space planning, arch., janitorial construction; **PREV EMPLOY:** 1968-1972, Houston Oilers Professional Football; 1973-1976, Co-owner and Managing Partner of Mafridge/Haik Investments Realty Co.; **PROFL AFFIL & HONORS:** Delta Sigma Pi, Pi Sigma Epsilon, Houston C of C; Spring Branch C of C; Broker, TX RE Commission; Omicron Delta Kappa; **EDUC:** BBA, 1967, Mktg./Sales Mgmt., Univ. of MS; **EDUC HONORS:** Univ. Leadership Award, Pres. Lettermen's Club, Pres. Fellowship of Christian Athletes, Mr. Ole Miss, Dean's List, Academic All S.E. Conference (Twice), Academic All-American (Twice); **OTHER ACT & HONORS:** Member, NFL Alumni Assn.; Dir., Univ. of MS Alumni Assn. (Houston Chapter); Football (College--All Southeastern Conference, All American); **BUS ADD:** 11777 Katy Freeway, Suite 495 North Bldg., Houston, TX 77079, (713)496-7788.

HAINES, John P.——B: Jan. 13, 1930, Sacramento, CA, *Asst. VP, Mgr., Profl. Servs.*, American Appraisal Associates, Inc., No. CA; **PRIM RE ACT:** Broker, Engineer, Appraiser, Builder; **SERVICES:** Indus. and comml. prop. valuation; **PREV EMPLOY:** Marshall and Stevens, Inc., 1961-1965; Real Estate Research Corp., 1968-1971; **PROFL AFFIL & HONORS:** Soc. of RE Appraisers; Amer. Assn. of Cost Engrs.; NARA, SRA; CRA; AACE; **EDUC:** BS, 1953, Marine Engrg., CA Maritime Acad.; **EDUC HONORS:** Pi Sigma Phi; **MIL SERV:** USN, Res.; Comd.; **OTHER ACT & HONORS:** Naval Order of the US Assn. of Naval Aviation; Naval Res. Assn.; **HOME ADD:** 576 Moraga Way, Orinda, CA 94563, (415)376-1099; **BUS ADD:** 1221 Broadway, Ste. 800, Oakland, CA 94612, (415)832-3650.

HAISLIP, Diane——B: Nov. 9, 1951, Kansas City, KS, *Asst. VP, Internal Audit Mgr.*, Charles F. Curry Co.; **PRIM RE ACT:** Banker, Lender; **OTHER RE ACT:** Mort. Banker; **SERVICES:** Fin. homes & HUD Servicing; **PREV EMPLOY:** Internal Auditor - Anchor Savings Assn.; **HOME ADD:** 13445 W. 51st St., Shawnee, KS 66216, (913)631-2738; **BUS ADD:** 20 W. Ninth St., Kansas City, MO 64152, (816)471-8300.

HAITBRINK, Richard F.——B: Sept. 7, 1941, Salina, KS, *Counselor at Law*, Richard F. Haitbrink, Esq.; **PRIM RE ACT:** Attorney, Owner/Investor, Syndicator; **SERVICES:** Legal serv.; **REP CLIENTS:** Investors, builders and devel. in comml. prop.; **PREV EMPLOY:** Legislative Asst., U.S. Senator James B. Pearson (R-KS), 1966-1968; **PROFL AFFIL & HONORS:** ABA; ABA RE Sect.; KS and MO Bar Assns.; **EDUC:** BA, 1963, Econ./Eng., Univ. of KS; **GRAD EDUC:** JD, 1966, Law, Univ of KS; **EDUC HONORS:** Owl Soc. (Jr. Men's Honorary); Sachem (Sr. Men's Honorary); Honor Roll, Grad. with Distinction; Order of the Coif; **OTHER ACT & HONORS:** U.S. Tennis Assn., Chmn. - Credentials Comm.; Member, Constitution and By-Laws Comm.; **HOME ADD:** 8226 Monrovia, Lenexa, KS 66215, (913)888-8762; **BUS ADD:** 2000 Johnson Dr., Suite 100, Mission Woods, KS 66205, (913)384-6767.

HAITH, Lawrence L.——B: Oct. 11, 1948, Kansas City, MO, *Pres.*, Haith & Co., Inc.; **PRIM RE ACT:** Broker, Syndicator, Consultant, Developer, Property Manager, Owner/Investor; **SERVICES:** Full Serv. RE Co.; **PROFL AFFIL & HONORS:** Kansas Cfty, MO.; MO & Nat. Realtors, CPM; **EDUC:** BA, Econ., Univ. of MO-Kansas City; **OTHER ACT & HONORS:** Jewish Nat. Fund-Pres.; **HOME TEL:** (816)931-4818; **BUS ADD:** 4635 Wyandotte, Suite 203, Kansas City, MO 64112.

HALE, William W.——B: Oct. 4, 1938, Portland, OR, *Pres.*, Hale Associates Realty, Ltd.; **PRIM RE ACT:** Broker, Consultant, Developer, Owner/Investor, Property Manager, Syndicator; **SERVICES:** Synd. of apt. prop., rehab. hist. structures, forming joint ventures; **REP CLIENTS:** Wealthy indiv. seeking tax shelter and capital gain opportunities; **PROFL AFFIL & HONORS:** Nat. Assn. of RE Brokers; OR Assn. of Realtors; Portland Bd. of Realtors; RE Securities & Synd. Inst.; OR Apt. Owners Assn.; OR State Homebuilders Assn.; Portland C of C; **EDUC:** BS, 1964, Bus./Psych., Portland State Univ./OR State Univ.; **OTHER ACT & HONORS:** Dir., Mult. Cty. Republican Central Comm.; Bd. Member, Catlin Gabel School & Newtown Coast Found., Nature Conservancy; **HOME ADD:** 255 S.W. Harrison, Portland, OR 97201, (503)226-6505; **BUS ADD:** 320 SW Oak St., Portland, OR 97204, (503)222-7000.

HALES, Karen A.——B: Dec. 4, 1939, Saginaw, MI, *Pres.*, Ski & Shore Robert R. Hale, Inc.; **PRIM RE ACT:** Broker; **REP CLIENTS:** Devel. with following clients: Holbrook & Bicknell, Clare, MI, J. Gower Chapman, Lansing, MI, T. Beatrice Buchner, Harrison, MI; **PREV EMPLOY:** In real estate since 1968, salespersons lic. 1969, Broker's License w/Harper & Young, Inc. 1970 or 71, bought Harper

& Young out in 1973; **PROFL AFFIL & HONORS:** Clare-Cladwin Bd. of Realtors, Harrison Area C of C, Harrison Ladies Auxiliary, 1974 Realtor of the Yr., 1980 Woman of the Year (Harrison); **EDUC:** RE I, II, III, GRI of MI on Dec. 4, 1975; **HOME ADD:** 3139 Bischoff, Harrison, MI 48625, (517)539-7988; **BUS ADD:** 492 N. Clare Ave., Harrison, MI 48625, (517)539-6461.

HALEY, James L.——B: Dec. 11, 1933, Rochester, NY, *Sales VP*, West Shell, Inc.; **PRIM RE ACT:** Broker, Consultant, Appraiser; **SERVICES:** Sale and leasing of comml. and indus. props., investment sales, property devel. counseling; **REP CLIENTS:** Comml. and indus. prop. owners, users and investors; **PREV EMPLOY:** Federated Dept. Stores; J.C. Penney Co., Property Devel.; **PROFL AFFIL & HONORS:** NAR, GRI; **EDUC:** BA, 1956, Liberal Arts, Univ. of TX; **GRAD EDUC:** 1958, Urban Planning, Univ. of BC; **HOME ADD:** 8365 Indian Hill Rd., Cincinnati, OH 45243, (513)561-5889; **BUS ADD:** 3 E. Fourth St., Cincinnati, OH 45202, (513)721-4200.

HALEY, John——*Dir. Corp. Dev.*, Dayco Corp.; **PRIM RE ACT:** Property Manager; **BUS ADD:** PO Box 10043, Dayton, OH 45401, (513)226-7000.*

HALL, A. Stanley——B: Jan. 29, 1932, Kendallville, IN, *VP*, Bear Realty, Inc.; **PRIM RE ACT:** Broker, Consultant, Appraiser, Instructor; **PROFL AFFIL & HONORS:** GRI, CRS, CRB; **EDUC:** BA, 1958, Police Admin., IN Univ.; **MIL SERV:** USN, YN2; **OTHER ACT & HONORS:** Exec Bd. BSA, Rotary, Past Pres. Mason; Also affiliated w/Gallery of Homes; **HOME ADD:** 1318 9th Ave., Kenosha, WI 53142, (414)859-3000; **BUS ADD:** 715 56th St., PO Box 338, Kenosha, WI 53141, (414)657-7194.

HALL, Adolphus, Jr.——B: Feb. 15, 1947, Chicago, IL, *Pres.*, Urban Vistas Realty & Mgmt., Inc.; **PRIM RE ACT:** Broker, Attorney, Property Manager, Syndicator; **SERVICES:** Synd. of multi-family/comml. props., prop. mgmt.; **PREV EMPLOY:** US Securities & Exchange Commn. 1975-77; **PROFL AFFIL & HONORS:** NAR, RE Securities & Synd. Inst.; **EDUC:** BS ED., 1968, Chicago State Univ.; **GRAD EDUC:** JD, 1975, Law, DePaul Univ.; MPA, 1972, Public Admin., Roosevelt Univ.; LLM, 1982, Taxation, John Marshall Law School; **BUS ADD:** 1 N. LaSalle St., Chicago, IL 60602, (312)263-2079.

HALL, Allan J.——B: Apr. 12, 1936, Krakow, Poland, *Pres.*, Moon, Hall & Associates, Inc.; **PRIM RE ACT:** Attorney, Developer, Builder, Owner/Investor; **REP CLIENTS:** Pizza Hut, Intl. Paper, Wendys, Consultant Prop. Mgmt., Inc., Bally, Inc.; **PREV EMPLOY:** Allan J. Hall Const. Corp.; **PROFL AFFIL & HONORS:** GA Bar Assn., FL Bar Assn., FL Broker, GA RE Broker; **EDUC:** Bachelor of Bldg. Const., 1958, Const., Univ. of FL; **GRAD EDUC:** JD, 1968, Law, Univ. of FL; **EDUC HONORS:** Gargoyle Soc., Dean's List; **OTHER ACT & HONORS:** Chattahoochee Fliers; **HOME TEL:** (404)256-0987; **BUS ADD:** Ste. 905 Northside Tower, Atlanta, GA 30326, (404)255-5900.

HALL, Betsy——B: July 19, 1943, Hartford, CT, *Prop. Mgr.*, Fox & Carskadon Mgmt. Corp.; **PRIM RE ACT:** Property Manager; **PROFL AFFIL & HONORS:** Inst. of RE Mgmt., Intl. Council of Shopping Centers, Certified Prop. Mgr. (CPM); **EDUC:** AA, 1965, Bus., Advert., Pasadena City Coll.; **HOME TEL:** (714)641-5990; **BUS ADD:** 5140 Campus Dr., Newport Beach, CA 92660, (714)752-8326.

HALL, Charles E.——B: Aug. 17, 1915, Peoria, IL, *Owner*, Charles E. Hall, Realtor; **PRIM RE ACT:** Owner/Investor; **SERVICES:** Investment & resid. counseling; **PROFL AFFIL & HONORS:** Intl. Exchangors Assn., Cape Coral Bd. of Realtors; **EDUC:** Bus., Bradley Univ.; **GRAD EDUC:** Sales & Mktg., Syracuse Univ.; **OTHER ACT & HONORS:** Cape Coral Rotary Club, VP; Cape Coral Power Squadron, Commdr.; Intl. Yachting Fellowship of Rotarians, Commodore; FL West Offshore Power Boat Racing Assn., Commodore; **HOME ADD:** 4945 Triton Court W., Cape Coral, FL 33905, (813)542-5032; **BUS ADD:** 4020 Del Prado Blvd., Cape Coral, FL 33904, (813)542-5032.

HALL, Charles T.——B: Oct. 23, 1920, Campti, LA, *Pres.*, Charles T. Hall & Sons; **PRIM RE ACT:** Broker, Consultant, Appraiser, Developer, Builder, Owner/Investor, Property Manager; **SERVICES:** Complete RE Serv.; **REP CLIENTS:** Home Federal Savings & Loan Assn. of Shreveport, Contract Negotiator for City of Shreveport, LA; many attys. & investors, maj. reloc. cos.; **PREV EMPLOY:** Mgr., Shelby Investment Corp.; Mgr. Sklar Bldg.; Mgr. Petroleum Towers; Commnr. Shreveport Housing Authority; **PROFL AFFIL & HONORS:** CPM from IREM; SRA; CRA, CPM; SRA; Realtor of Year of Local Assn. of Realtors; Nat. Speakers Bureau; **EDUC:** BS, 1943, Chemistry-Physics, Northwestern St. Univ.; **MIL SERV:** US Army, 1st Lt.; 1942-1946; **OTHER ACT & HONORS:** Past Pres., Alumni Assn. of Northwestern St. Univ.; Past Pres., Broadmoor Kiwanis Club; Past Pres., Community Council of Social Agencies of Shreveport, LA; Norwela Council, Boy Scouts of Amer.; Metropolitan YMCA; Broadmoor YMCA; Active Deacon, Broadmoor Baptist Church; **HOME ADD:** 8312 Suffolk Dr., Shreveport, LA 71106, (318)868-8364; **BUS ADD:** P.O. Box 5577, Shreveport, LA 71105, (318)869-2592.

HALL, Cline S.——B: Jan. 2, 1945, Christiansburg, VA, *Sr. RE Appraiser*, Fairfax Cty. of Assessments; **PRIM RE ACT:** Appraiser, Owner/Investor, Instructor, Assessor; **PREV EMPLOY:** McNeil RE, Christiansburg, VA; **PROFL AFFIL & HONORS:** IAAO, VAAO, SREA, SRA, RES; **EDUC:** BS, 1971, Bus. Admin., VA Polytechnic Inst. & State Univ.; **HOME ADD:** 2707 Clarkes Landing Dr., Oakton, VA 22124, (703)620-4085; **BUS ADD:** 4100 Chain Bridge Rd., 4th Fl., Fairfax, VA 22030, (703)691-2371.

HALL, Craig——B: Apr. 10, 1950, Ann Arbor, MI, *Chmn. of the Bd.*, The Hall RE Group; **PRIM RE ACT:** Broker, Developer, Owner/Investor, Property Manager, Syndicator; **PROFL AFFIL & HONORS:** NAR; RESSI (Founder of the MI Chap. and Pres., in 1977); S. Oakland Cty. Bd. of Realtors; Nat. Realty Comm.; Nat. Apt. Assn.; VChmn., MI State C of C; Past Member, Taxation Legislation Subcomm.; Member of the Bd. of Consultants, Career Horizons at E. MI Univ., One of America's Ten Outstanding Young Men in 1979 by the US Jaycees; **OTHER ACT & HONORS:** Member and VChmn., State Bldg. Authority (Appointed by the Gov. of MI); Member of the State of MI Securities Law Advisory Comm. to the MI Corp. and Securities Bureau; Author of books entitled *The RE Turnaround*, 1979, Prentice Hall, Inc. and *Craig Hall's Book of RE Investing*, Holt-Rinehart & Winston, Feb. 1982; Tr. of the MI Opera Theater; Tr. of the Detroit Chap. of the March of Dimes. Other Bus. Address: 8340 Meadow Rd. Ste. 134, Dallas, TX, 75231; **HOME ADD:** Bloomfield Hills, MI; **BUS ADD:** 18311 W. Ten Mile Rd., Southfield, MI 48075, (313)557-7700.

HALL, David M.——B: 1952, Racine, WI, Wilson Hall, P.C., Attorneys and Counselors at Law; **PRIM RE ACT:** Attorney; **SERVICES:** Condo. org.; gen. RE practice; **PROFL AFFIL & HONORS:** Lake Cty. Bar Assn., IL Bar Assn., ABA; **EDUC:** BA, 1973, Hist. and Eng., Carthage Coll.; **GRAD EDUC:** JD, 1976, Loyola Univ. of New Orleans; **EDUC HONORS:** Editor of Law Review; **OTHER ACT & HONORS:** Treas. of Lake Cty. Bar Assn., Pres. of Waukegan YMCA; **HOME ADD:** 1906 N. Sheridan Rd., Waukegan, IL 60087; **BUS ADD:** 4 S. Genesee St., Waukegan, IL 60085.

HALL, Denison M.——B: Aug. 12, 1945, Boston, MA, *Exec. VP*, Greater Boston Development, Inc.; **PRIM RE ACT:** Syndicator; **OTHER RE ACT:** RE Investment Mgr.; **SERVICES:** Equity Synd. of low income housing, comml. props. & investment counseling; **REP CLIENTS:** Indiv. investors and pension funds; **PREV EMPLOY:** The Rouse Co., Columbia, MD 1971-73; Mitchell Energy Div. Corp., The Woodlands, TX 1973-75; **PROFL AFFIL & HONORS:** ULI; Comm. for Rural Housing & Devel.; **EDUC:** BA, 1971, Amer. Soc. Hist., Yale Univ.; **EDUC HONORS:** Honors in maj.; **MIL SERV:** USA, E-5; **BUS ADD:** Old City Hall - 45 School St., Boston, MA 02108, (617)227-7915.

HALL, Duncan Wayne——B: Nov. 19, 1952, Corpus Christi, TX, *Atty.*, Simmang & Hall; **PRIM RE ACT:** Attorney; **SERVICES:** Legal representation during all phases of various RE transactions; **PROFL AFFIL & HONORS:** State Bar of TX; Amer. Bar Assn. (Sect. of Real Prop., Probate and Trust Law); Lee Cty. Bar Assn.; **EDUC:** BBA, 1975, Gen. Bus., Univ. of TX at Austin; **GRAD EDUC:** JD, 1978, Law, St. Mary's Univ. School of Law, San Antonio, TX; **OTHER ACT & HONORS:** Giddings Volunteer Fire Dept. (Secretary 1980 - pres.); **HOME ADD:** P.O. Box 441, Giddings, TX 78942, (713)542-3496; **BUS ADD:** 127 E. Austin, PO Box 480, Giddings, TX 78942, (713)542-3123.

HALL, Edwin C.——B: Nov. 3, 1943, Greensboro, NC, *Pres.*, Edwin C. Hall Associates Inc.; **PRIM RE ACT:** Broker, Consultant, Property Manager; **PREV EMPLOY:** Mgmt. Div., Mgr. C.W. Francis & Son, Realtors, Roanoke, VA, Managing and leasing comml. & resid. prop. Jan. 1967-June 1975; **PROFL AFFIL & HONORS:** SIR, First annual 'Realtor of the Yr.' 1978 - Roanoke Valley Bd. of Realtors; CPM; CCIM; GRI; **MIL SERV:** USMC; **OTHER ACT & HONORS:** Pres., Downtown Roanoke, Inc., 1979, 1980; Dir., C of C, 1976-1977, 1980-1981; VA RE Commnr., 1978-1986; **HOME ADD:** 2810 Avenham Ave. SW, Roanoke, VA 24014, (703)344-3103; **BUS ADD:** 1007 FNEB Bldg., Roanoke, VA 24011, (703)982-0011.

HALL, George E., Jr.——B: Nov. 20, 1946, Sterling, IL, *Gen. Part.*, Security Fin Services; **PRIM RE ACT:** Syndicator, Owner/Investor; **SERVICES:** R.E. synd.; **EDUC:** Pol. Sci., 1972, Brigham Young Univ.; **OTHER ACT & HONORS:** Pres., Republican Men's Club, 2 yrs.; **HOME ADD:** 203 B. 600 N., Alpine, UT 84003, (801)756-3131; **BUS ADD:** 57 W. 200 S., Salt Lake City, UT 84101, (801)359-7601.

HALL, H. Glen——**B:** Apr. 28, 1933, Ossining, NY, *Atty.*, Brown & Hall; **PRIM RE ACT:** Consultant, Attorney; **SERVICES:** Rep. of sellers/purchasers of resid. and comml. RE; **PREV EMPLOY:** Closing Atty., Intercounty Title Co., 1966-1969; Town of Greenburgh as Dep. Town Atty., 1969-1973; Atty., Greenburgh Planning Bd., 1969-1973; Lic. RE Broker, 1969; **PROFL AFFIL & HONORS:** Member, Bd. of Dir., Briarcliff Woods Condo., 1981-date; Pres.-Elect., Westchester Cty. Bar Assn., 1981-date; Member, Advisory Council, Pace Univ., School of Law 1975-date; Pres., Tarrytown Hist. Soc., 1973-1975; Member, House of Delegates, NY State Bar Assn., 1978-date; Editor, WCBA official magazine, Westchester Bar Topics, 1976-1979; **EDUC:** BA, 1955, Govt., Principia Coll.; **GRAD EDUC:** LLB/JD, 1958, NY law, Albany Law School, Union Univ.; **MIL SERV:** US Army; (NYNG) Signal Corp; **OTHER ACT & HONORS:** Dep. Town Clerk, Town of Greenburgh, 1972; Special Investigator, Election Frauds Bureau, Dept. of Law, NY State Atty. Gen., 1956; Salvation Army, Advisory Bd., Westchester Cty., 1972 to date; **HOME ADD:** 81 Briarcliff Dr. S., Ossining, NY 10562, (914)762-1790; **BUS ADD:** 351 Manville Rd., Box 243, Pleasantville, NY 10570, (914)769-4635.

HALL, Jay A.——**B:** Feb. 16, 1951, Little Rock, AR, *VP*, Savers Federal Savings & Loan Assn.; **PRIM RE ACT:** Appraiser, Lender; **REP CLIENTS:** S&L, lenders, indiv.; **PROFL AFFIL & HONORS:** Soc. of RE Appraisers, AIREA, Bd. of Realtors, RM-AIREA; SRA; **EDUC:** BBA, 1973, Fin., Univ. of AR; **MIL SERV:** US Air NG, Sgt.; **HOME ADD:** 430 Ivory Dr., Little Rock, AR, (501)663-2616; **BUS ADD:** 5th & Spring Sts., Little Rock, AR 72201, (501)372-3311.

HALL, Katherine Post——**B:** Nov. 2, 1945, Los Angeles, CA, *VP*, BranWest Corp.; **PRIM RE ACT:** Developer, Builder; **SERVICES:** Development of major comml. RE as owner builder; **PREV EMPLOY:** Architect, structural engr., Builder; **PROFL AFFIL & HONORS:** AIA, Certified Condo. Expert, Nat. Assn. of Homebuilders; **EDUC:** BA, 1965, Arch. and Engrg., Univ. of CA at Los Angeles; **GRAD EDUC:** MEE, 1969, Arch. and Engrg., Univ. of S. CA; **BUS ADD:** 201 Ocean Ave. #1101B, Santa Monica, CA 90402, (213)451-8181.

HALL, Lawrence E.——**B:** April 13, 1925, San Diego, CA, *VP, Pres.*, VP - Corp. Facilities, Puget Sound Power & Light Co., Pres. - Puget Western, Inc.; **PRIM RE ACT:** Engineer, Developer, Owner/Investor, Property Manager; **SERVICES:** Responsible for all RE matters for Puget Sound Power & Light Co., Pres. & Chief Exec. Officer of Puget Western, Inc., land devel. co. (wholly owned subs. of Puget Sound Power & Light Co.); **PREV EMPLOY:** Corps of Engrs. 1946-1954, WA State Power Commn. 1954-1957; **PROFL AFFIL & HONORS:** Member, Amer. Soc. of Mech. Engrs., Member, Amer. Soc. of Civil Engrs., VP and Dir., Bellevue Downtown Devel. Assn., Bd. Member of WA State Research Council, King Cty. Policy Devel. Commn., Steering Comm., Licensed Profl. Engr. - WA & OR; **EDUC:** BSME, 1946, Mech. Engrg., Univ. of WA; **MIL SERV:** USN, Lt. (j.g.); **OTHER ACT & HONORS:** WA Athletic Club, Seattle, WA Rainier Club, Seattle, WA, Bellevue Athletic Club, Bellevue, WA; **HOME ADD:** 428 - 168th Ave. S.E., Bellevue, WA 98008, (206)746-3257; **BUS ADD:** Puget Power Bldg., Bellevue, WA 98009, (206)453-6883.

HALL, Lea R.——**B:** Oct. 28, 1937, Shreveport, LA, *Devel.*, Pierremont Office Park; **PRIM RE ACT:** Developer, Owner/Investor, Property Manager; **SERVICES:** RE Devel., Mgmt. (C.P.M.), Investor; **PREV EMPLOY:** Comml. Loan Officer with mort. banker; **PROFL AFFIL & HONORS:** Shreveport Bd. of Realtors, Bd. of Appeals, NAREM; **EDUC:** BS, 1959, Bus.-Fin.; **MIL SERV:** US Army, Maj.; **OTHER ACT & HONORS:** Shreveport Club, City Club of Baton Rouge, Univ. Club and Petroleum Club; **HOME ADD:** 1040 Erie, Shreveport, LA 71106, (318)865-8836; **BUS ADD:** 910 Pierremont, Suite 117, Shreveport, LA 71106, (318)865-3552.

HALL, Lyle W., Jr.——**B:** Aug. 12, 1944, Schnectady, NY, *Sr. VP*, Butcher & Singer, Soverign Realty; **PRIM RE ACT:** Consultant, Developer, Owner/Investor, Property Manager, Syndicator; **SERVICES:** RE equity synd.; **REP CLIENTS:** Various NY stock exchange member firms, investment advisors; **PROFL AFFIL & HONORS:** CPA; **EDUC:** BBA, 1970, Acctg., Temple; **MIL SERV:** US Army; **HOME ADD:** 1056 King of Prussia Rd., Radnor, PA 19102, (215)688-7140; **BUS ADD:** 211 S. Broad St., Philadelphia, PA 19107, (215)985-5120.

HALL, Michael B.——**B:** Aug. 12, 1949, Langdale, AL, *Comml. Broker*, Caine Co., Comml./Investment Prop.; **PRIM RE ACT:** Broker, Consultant, Developer, Owner/Investor; **SERVICES:** Devel., sale & leasing of comml./investment prop.; **REP CLIENTS:** Investors, banks, corp. owners of comml., office & indus. prop.; **PREV EMPLOY:** Greenville Cty. Planning Commn., 1972-1974; Caine Co., 1974-1976; Michael Hall & Assoc., Inc., 1976-1981; **PROFL AFFIL & HONORS:** Amer. Planning Assn.; Nat. Assn. of Home Builders; NAR; **EDUC:** BA, 1971, Public Admin./Econ., Univ. of KS; **HOME ADD:** 11 Rock Creek Dr., Greenville, SC 29605, (803)242-1045; **BUS ADD:** POB 2287, Greenville, SC 29602, (803)242-6840.

HALL, Orvin J.——**B:** Jan. 31, 1927, Virginia, MN, *Sales Assoc.*, Towle Real Estate Co.; **PRIM RE ACT:** Broker; **PREV EMPLOY:** IDS Mort., 1966-1980; **PROFL AFFIL & HONORS:** AIREA; Gov. Councilor, 1981-1983, MAI; **EDUC:** BBA, 1950, Bus./Indus. Admin., Univ. of MN; **MIL SERV:** US Navy; Petty Officer 2nd Class; **HOME ADD:** 5929 Wooddale Ave., Edina, MN 55424, (612)922-5632; **BUS ADD:** 600 2nd Ave. S., Minneapolis, MN 55402, (612)341-4444.

HALL, Peter V.——**B:** Apr. 14, 1934, Ft. Wayne, IN, *Chmn.*, Argus Financial Corp.; **PRIM RE ACT:** Owner/Investor; **SERVICES:** Venture capital money for builders & devels.; **PREV EMPLOY:** Chmn., Colonial Mort. Co. 1968-73; Sr. VP, PMI Mort. Ins. Co. 1973-78; Pres., PMI Mort. Corp. 1979-80; **PROFL AFFIL & HONORS:** Nat. Assn. of RE Brokers; **EDUC:** BA, 1957, Econ., Georgetown Univ., Washington, DC; **GRAD EDUC:** MBA, 1962, Fin., Stanford Univ.; **MIL SERV:** USN, Ens.; **HOME ADD:** 600 Eucalyptus, Hillsborough, CA 94010, (415)342-0479; **BUS ADD:** 3190 Clearview Way, San Mateo, CA 94402.

HALL, Peter William——**B:** Aug. 14, 1941, Rahway, NJ, *Pres.*, Point Wylie Prop., Inc.; **PRIM RE ACT:** Broker, Developer; **PREV EMPLOY:** Regional Mgr. with Carolina Caribbean Corp.; **PROFL AFFIL & HONORS:** NAR, Most productive Realty World office in NC & SC; **EDUC:** Psych./Soc., 1964, Human Dev., Rutgers Univ.; **GRAD EDUC:** Econ., 1973, NC State Univ.; **EDUC HONORS:** Deans List; **MIL SERV:** USA, Capt., 3 Bronze Stars; **HOME ADD:** 7018 Chelsea Day Lane, Tega Cay, Ft. Mill, SC 29715, (803)548-4476; **BUS ADD:** One Tega Cay Dr., Fort Mill, SC 29715, (803)548-3551.

HALL, R. Douglas, III——**B:** Mar. 29, 1941, Glen Ridge, NJ, *Pres., CEO*, Bay Colony Prop. Co. Inc.; **PRIM RE ACT:** Developer, Property Manager, Owner/Investor; **PREV EMPLOY:** Mgr. RE Fin., Ford Motor Credit Co. 1970-74; Mort. LO, John Hancock; **EDUC:** Yale Univ., 1963, Econ.; **OTHER ACT & HONORS:** Chmn. Fin. Comm., Manchester, MA; **HOME ADD:** 5 Running Ridge Rd., Manchester, MA 01944, (617)526-7433; **BUS ADD:** 2 Faneuil Hall Market, Boston, MA 02109, (617)742-7550.

HALL, Ralph C.——**B:** Mar. 28, 1928, Chicago, IL, *VP and RE Counsel*, H.E. Butt Store Prop. Co's - 1966 to present; **PRIM RE ACT:** Attorney, Developer, Property Manager; **PREV EMPLOY:** Hall Investment Co.; Amer. Oil Co.; The Kroger Co.; scope of work included RE mort. banking, appraising, prop. mgmt., RE investment devel., consultant, and legal work related thereto, during period 1948-1966; **PROFL AFFIL & HONORS:** Amer., TX, OK, and Nueces Cty. Bar Assns.; ICSC; **EDUC:** Pre-Law, Univ. of OK, Univ. of Tulsa; **GRAD EDUC:** LLB, 1952, Law, Univ. of OK, Univ. of Tulsa; **MIL SERV:** USCG; Seaman 1st Class; **OTHER ACT & HONORS:** Goodwill Industries of Corpus Christi; Pharaohs Ctry. Club; **HOME ADD:** 6826 Aswan Dr., Corpus Christi, TX 78412, (512)991-4726; **BUS ADD:** PO Box 9216, Corpus Christi, TX 78408, (512)881-1218.

HALL, Robert W.——**B:** June 22, 1924, Philadelphia, PA, *VP*, Andrews, Dickinson, & Pinkstone, Inc., Appraisal & Counseling; **PRIM RE ACT:** Consultant, Appraiser; **SERVICES:** Appraisal & Counseling; **REP CLIENTS:** Indus., Banks, Ins. Co's.; **PROFL AFFIL & HONORS:** AIREA; SREA; SRWA, Prof. Recognition Award - Hirea SREA; Lambda Alpha; MAI; CCIM; **EDUC:** BS Temple Univ., 1949, RE, Bus. Admin.; **HOME ADD:** 527 Featherbed Lane, Glen Mills, PA 19342, (215)459-3961; **BUS ADD:** PO Box 175, Chadds Ford, PA 19317, (215)459-5651.

HALL, Susan M.——**B:** Sept. 29, 1947, Stamford, CT, *Atty.*, Goodwin, Procter & Hoar; **PRIM RE ACT:** Attorney; **REP CLIENTS:** Lending inst. & pvt. devel.; **PREV EMPLOY:** NY State Urban Devel. Corp. 1973-74; Dept. of HUD, 1969-1973; **PROFL AFFIL & HONORS:** ABA, MA Bar Assn.; **EDUC:** BA, 1969, Govt., Smith Coll.; **GRAD EDUC:** JD, 1977, Law, Boston Univ. School of Law; **HOME ADD:** Old Concord Rd., Lincoln, MA 01773; **BUS ADD:** 28 State St., Boston, MA 02109, (617)523-5700.

HALL, William——*Dir. Corp RE*, PPG Industries, Inc.; **PRIM RE ACT:** Property Manager; **BUS ADD:** Gateway Ctr., Pittsburgh, PA 15222, (412)434-3131.*

HALL, William O.——**B:** July 31, 1944, New Bedford, MA, *Asst. Dir.*, New Bedford Industrial Development Commission; **PRIM RE ACT:** Consultant; **OTHER RE ACT:** Govt. - Econ. Devel.; **SERVICES:** Provide assistance in plant relocation or expansion; **PROFL AFFIL &**

HONORS: New Bedford C of C; **EDUC:** BS, 1967, Mktg. - Mgmt., Bryant Coll.; **OTHER ACT & HONORS:** Bristol Cty. Devel. Council Bd. of Dirs., Waterfront Area Hist. League (WHALE); **HOME ADD:** 101 Armour St., New Bedford, MA 02740, (617)994-7440; **BUS ADD:** 1213 Purchase St., New Bedford, MA 02740, (617)997-6501.

HALLBERG, Frank D., Jr.——B: Sept. 9, 1931, Boston, MA, *RE Mgr.*, American Mutual Liability Insurance Co., Home Office; **PRIM RE ACT:** Broker, Property Manager; **SERVICES:** Monitor and provide staff assistance in RE negotiation for all co. office leasing. Manage in-house office space planning and design activity for co. offices; **PROFL AFFIL & HONORS:** Greater Boston RE Bd., former Exec. Comm. mbr. of Inst. of Bus. Designers; **EDUC:** BFA, 1956, Interior Design, Arch., Boston Univ., SFAA; **MIL SERV:** USAF, A1C; **OTHER ACT & HONORS:** Burlington Land Use Committee, 1979 to date; Burlington Bd. of Registrars, 1980 to date; Burlington Republican Town Committee; Exec. Comm. Burlington 4th of July parade committee; Past. chmn. Standing School Bldg. Committee; Capital Budget Comm.; coach; scout leader; fund raiser; church school teacher; **HOME ADD:** 56 Macon Rd., Burlington, MA 01803, (617)272-2920; **BUS ADD:** Quannapowitt Pkwy., Wakefield, MA 01880, (617)245-6000.

HALLENBORG, Harris——*Exec. Dir.*, NH, New Hampshire Real Estate Commission; **PRIM RE ACT:** Property Manager; **BUS ADD:** 3 Capital St., Concord, NH 03301, (603)271-2701.*

HALLORAN, Leo B.——*VP*, Spaulding & Slye; **PRIM RE ACT:** Developer; **BUS ADD:** Two Broadway Executive Park, 205 NW 63rd, Oklahoma City, OK 73116, (405)848-1000.*

HALLORAN, Thomas C.——B: May 19, 1941, Hartford, CT, *RE Mgr.*, Combined Ins. Co. of Amer., Hearthstone Div.; **PRIM RE ACT:** Broker, Consultant, Property Manager, Insuror; **SERVICES:** Prop. Mgmt. & leasing, in house consulting, ins., mgmt. facilities; **PREV EMPLOY:** C.W. Whittier & Bro., Children's Hospital Med. Ctr.; **PROFL AFFIL & HONORS:** IREM, Greater Boston RE Bd., CPM; **EDUC:** Trinity Coll., 1963, Hist. & Psych.; **GRAD EDUC:** MBA, 1965-68, Univ. of Hartford; **MIL SERV:** USANG, E-4; **OTHER ACT & HONORS:** Union Hosp. Bd. of Corps.; **HOME ADD:** 9 Phillips Cir., Swampscott, MA 01907, (617)592-0048; **BUS ADD:** 111 WA St., Brookline, MA 02146, (617)731-9000.

HALPER, Emanuel B.——B: June 24, 1933, New York, NY, *Partner*, Zissu Berman Halper Barron & Gumbinger; **PRIM RE ACT:** Attorney, Developer; **OTHER RE ACT:** Writer, Lecturer; **PROFL AFFIL & HONORS:** Chmn. of the Bd. Intl. Inst. for RE Studies; Chmn. Intl. RE Comm. World Assn. of Lawyers; Member, panel of Arbitrators, Amer. Arbitration Assn.; Chmn. of the Editorial Policy Comm.; Intl. Prop. Investment Journal, Contributing Editor, RE Review; Adjunct Prof. of RE NY Univ.; Gavel Award for Contribution to understanding of law and justice, ABA; Award for Teaching Excellence, NYU; **EDUC:** BA, 1954, Eng., Phil., Hist., The City Coll.; **GRAD EDUC:** JD, 1957, Columbia Law School; **EDUC HONORS:** Grad. with special honors; **MIL SERV:** US Army, Spec. 5; **OTHER ACT & HONORS:** Amer. Acad. of Political Science, Metropolitan Opera Guild; **HOME ADD:** 770 Bryant Ave., Roslyn Harbor, NY 11576, (516)621-1062; **BUS ADD:** 450 Park Ave., NY, NY 10022, (212)371-3900.

HALTOM, Robert Ballard——B: May 2, 1925, Batesville, MS, *Pres.*, Bob Haltom & Co.; **PRIM RE ACT:** Broker, Instructor, Consultant, Appraiser, Owner/Investor; **OTHER RE ACT:** Mkt. Maker in Historic Prop.; **SERVICES:** Appraisals - Consultant - Marketer; **REP CLIENTS:** Owners & Their Agents, Buyers of Pre-Civil War Bldgs.; **PREV EMPLOY:** Owner & Mgr. of Pine Lumber Mfg. Operation for 17 yrs.; **PROFL AFFIL & HONORS:** FLI, RNMI, FIABCI, AIREA, GRI, CRS, CRB; **EDUC:** BA History & BS Pharmacy, Univ. of MS; **MIL SERV:** USN, Ens.; **HOME ADD:** 108 Dana Rd., Natchez, MS 39120; **BUS ADD:** 113 Jefferson Davis Blvd., Natchez, MS 39120, (601)442-3718.

HAMES, Bernard A.——B: Aug. 20, 1939, Fort Dodge, IA, *VP*, First Nat. Bank of MN, Prop. Mgmt. Dept.; **PRIM RE ACT:** Builder, Property Manager, Engineer; **PREV EMPLOY:** The Crosby Co. 1967-72; **PROFL AFFIL & HONORS:** IREM, BOMA, CPM, RPA; **EDUC:** BS Mech. Engin., 1963, Indus. Eng., State Univ. of IA; **OTHER ACT & HONORS:** Bd. of Educ. District 277 - 1968-72; **HOME ADD:** 4455 Bayside Rd., Maple Plain, MN 55359, (612)472-4615; **BUS ADD:** 120 S. 6th St., Minneapolis, MN 55480, (612)472-4615.

HAMILTON, Bill F.——B: June 3, 1946, Ft. Worth, TX, *Dir. of Acquisitions*, Income Properties NW Corp.; **OTHER RE ACT:** Prop. Mgmt.; Income Prop. Synd.; **SERVICES:** Syndication; **PREV EMPLOY:** Amfac Mort. Corp., Asst. VP, 1976-80; Office & Warehouse Propertier, Inc. 1980-1981; **PROFL AFFIL & HONORS:** Soc of RE Appraisers; **EDUC:** BA, 1968, Public Admin, CA State Univ., Sacramento; **MIL SERV:** USA, 1968-71, Sgt.; **HOME ADD:** 12933 SE 69th Pl., Bellevue, WA 98006, (206)641-4199; **BUS ADD:** Plaza 600, Seattle, WA 98232, (206)623-9538.

HAMILTON, David Lawrence——B: Oct. 19, 1944, San Francisco, *Mgr., Collateral Securities Operation, General Electric Credit Corp. VP & Dir., Trafalgar Credit Corp.*; **PRIM RE ACT:** Developer, Lender, Builder, Owner/Investor, Insuror; **OTHER RE ACT:** Mort. Banker; Mort.-Backed Securities Program, Comml. & Single-Family Lender, Equity Investor, devel./bldg., of single-family prop., private mort. ins.; **PREV EMPLOY:** VP, Blyth Eastman Paine Webber; Economist/Senior Financial Analyst, Federal Reserve Board; **PROFL AFFIL & HONORS:** National Association of Home Builders; Mortgage Bankers Assn. (member Business Development Committee); Urban Land Instit., Novick's Who's Who of Mortgage-Backed Securities; **EDUC:** BA, 1971, Econ., Stanford Univ.; **GRAD EDUC:** MBA, 1973, Fin./Mktg., Harvard Grad. School of Bus.; **HOME ADD:** 1425 Bradford St. #3A, Stamford, CT 06905, (203)348-4874; **BUS ADD:** 260 Long Ridge Rd., Stamford, CT 06902, (203)357-4414.

HAMILTON, Irvin L.——B: July 24, 1949, Abilene, TX, *Owner*, Hamilton Props.; **PRIM RE ACT:** Broker, Consultant; **SERVICES:** Comml. Investment Prop. Sales, Investment Counseling & Institutional; **REP CLIENTS:** Indiv. & Investors in Comml. Investment RE; **PROFL AFFIL & HONORS:** Natl. RE Exchange, TX Prop. Exchangers, Comml.-Investment Div.-Austin Bd. of Realtors (Pres.), Austin Comml. RE Soc., C.C.I.M. (Cert. Comml. Investment Member-RNMI; **EDUC:** BS, 1971, Chemistry, McMurry Coll., Abilene, TX; **EDUC HONORS:** Who's Who in American Colls. and Univ., Gamma Sigma Epsilon; **OTHER ACT & HONORS:** Austin Aqua Festival; **HOME ADD:** 8619 Honeysuckle, Austin, TX 78759, (512)345-5312; **BUS ADD:** 1008 Mopac Circle, Suite 202, Austin, TX 78746, (512)327-8540.

HAMILTON, Joe F.——B: Jan. 20, 1938, Russellville, Franklin, AL, *Pres.*, Russellville Realty & Insurance Co., Inc.; **PRIM RE ACT:** Broker, Consultant, Appraiser, Developer, Lender, Owner/Investor, Instructor, Property Manager, Insuror; **SERVICES:** Sales (RE & Ins.), mgmt., appraisals, mort. loans; **REP CLIENTS:** Lenders, indivs., estates; **PREV EMPLOY:** Sales - H&A Ins. Co.; Salaried supervision with mfg. plant; instruction of RE in coll. curriculum; chemist; **PROFL AFFIL & HONORS:** Rotary Intl.; Assoc. Member SRA; PIA of AL & USA, Kemper Ins. Co. Agent of Month; Kemper Ins. Co. Scholarships 1978; Kemper Ins. Co. Top H&A Agent 1979; Pres. Club Kemper Ins. Co. 1979; Rotarian of the Year 1980-1981; **EDUC:** BS, 1960, Math. & Chemistry (double major), Florence State Coll., now Univ. of N. AL, Florence, AL; **OTHER ACT & HONORS:** Juvenile Court Advisory Comm.; Pres., Baptist Church Deacon; Teacher of Youths, Trustee; **HOME ADD:** Rt. #3, Box 209, Russellville, Franklin, AL, (205)332-1540; **BUS ADD:** 616 "B" US Highway 43, B Pass S, Russellville, AL 35653, (205)332-0624.

HAMILTON, Lea——*Dir.*, Department of Housing and Urban Development, Info. Policies & Systems; **PRIM RE ACT:** Lender; **BUS ADD:** 451 Seventh St., S.W., Washington, DC 20410, (202)755-5306.*

HAMILTON, Thomas J.——B: Oct. 5, 1931, Springfield, IL, *Part.*, Tom Hamilton RE; **PRIM RE ACT:** Broker; **SERVICES:** RE sales - primarily residential - appraisals consulting; **PREV EMPLOY:** 25 hrs. full time RE bus.; **PROFL AFFIL & HONORS:** Past Pres. Spfld. Bd. of Realtors; Past Chmn. MLS; GRI, CRB; **EDUC:** BS, 1953, Bus. Admin., Notre Dame Univ.; **MIL SERV:** USA, Sgt., Overseas medal (1953-1955); **OTHER ACT & HONORS:** Elks, K.C., Sertoma, Island Bay Yacht Club, State, Nat. Bd. of Realtors - Notre Dame Alumni Club of Cent. IL; **HOME TEL:** (217)546-6789; **BUS ADD:** 111 Chatham Rd., Springfield, IL 62704, (217)787-1551.

HAMILTON, William C.——*VP Mfg.*, Mine Safety Appliances Co.; **PRIM RE ACT:** Property Manager; **BUS ADD:** 600 Penn Center Blvd., Pittsburgh, PA 15235, (412)325-1313.*

HAMISTER, Mark E.——B: Oct. 18, 1949, Buffalo, NY, *Pres.*, Hamister & Associates, Inc.; **PRIM RE ACT:** Consultant, Engineer, Developer, Owner/Investor, Property Manager; **SERVICES:** Complete serv. firm to devel. health care facilities, housing, hotels/motels, etc. (including fin.); **REP CLIENTS:** Large and small investor grps. & non-profit grps. throughout the US; **PREV EMPLOY:** COO of NY Upstate largest chain of health care and housing facilities; **PROFL AFFIL & HONORS:** NCOA, NISH, AHA, AAHA, NYAHA, Appointed to 1981 White House Conference on Aging, and numerous fed. and state advisory posts; **EDUC:** Bus./Fin. Admin., 1972, Bus. Mgmt., Fin. Mgmt., Bus. Law, Rochester Inst. of Technol.; **OTHER**

ACT & HONORS: Mem. Advent Episcopal Church; Found. of Amherst Elderly Transp. Corp.; **BUS ADD:** 651 Delaware Ave., Buffalo, NY 14202, (716)882-2852.

HAMLIN, Clay W., III——B: Mar. 6, 1945, Buffalo, NY, *Atty.*, Hunt Kerr, Bloom & Hitchner PC; **PRIM RE ACT:** Attorney, Syndicator; **SERVICES:** Tax Planning, structuring limited part. synds., tax opinions, due diligence; **PREV EMPLOY:** Pepper, Hamilton & Scheetz, Attys., Arthur Anderson & Co., CPA's; **PROFL AFFIL & HONORS:** Amer. & PA Bar Assn.; Amer. & PA Inst. of CPA's, Author of var. tax articles, books & tax mgmt. portfolios; **EDUC:** BS, 1967, Econ., Univ. of PA; **GRAD EDUC:** MBA, 1972, Wharton; JD, 1979, Temple Univ.; **EDUC HONORS:** Outstanding scholar athlete in class of 1967, Class of 1975 award, distinction, Law Review, Cum Laude; **MIL SERV:** USN, LTJG; **OTHER ACT & HONORS:** Lecturer in law, Temple Univ., Masters in Law in Taxation Program; **HOME ADD:** 2036 Delancey St., Philadelphia, PA 19103, (215)735-5703; **BUS ADD:** Drexel Bldg., 15th & Walnut St., Philadelphia, PA 19102, (215)864-0800.

HAMLIN, Dale A.——B: May 30, 1942, Yuba City, CA, *Dir. RE Operations*, Pinehurst, Inc.; **PRIM RE ACT:** Developer, Builder; **PREV EMPLOY:** Boise Cascade (Land Dev.); Dir. various Divs. 68-75 Diamondhead Corp.; **PROFL AFFIL & HONORS:** ULI, Broker NC; **EDUC:** AB, 1965, Pol. Sci., Bethel Coll., St. Paul, MN; **MIL SERV:** USANG, Sgt.; **OTHER ACT & HONORS:** Bd. Member Ctry. Day School; **HOME ADD:** 190 Briarwood Circle, Pinehurst, NC 28374, (919)295-6147; **BUS ADD:** PO Box 938, Pinehurst, NC 28374, (919)692-6100.

HAMLIN, F. Gordon, Jr.——B: Apr. 21, 1943, Orange, NJ, *Pres.*, Northeast Capital Corp.; **PRIM RE ACT:** Consultant, Owner/Investor, Syndicator; **OTHER RE ACT:** Mort. broker; **SERVICES:** Structure and market real estate synd.; **REP CLIENTS:** Devel.; **PREV EMPLOY:** VP, Shelter Group, Inc., RE Devel.; VP, Canal Nat. Bank, Portland, ME; **PROFL AFFIL & HONORS:** MBA; **EDUC:** BA, 1968, Govt., Dartmouth Coll.; **GRAD EDUC:** MBA, 1971, Fin., NYU Grad. School of Bus. Admin.; **EDUC HONORS:** Full Scholarship; **MIL SERV:** U.S. Army, E-5; **OTHER ACT & HONORS:** Trustee, Gr. Portland Landmarks; Trustee, Osteopathic Hosp. of ME; **HOME ADD:** 14 Chapel St., Freeport, ME 04032, (207)865-4618; **BUS ADD:** 97-A Exchange St., POB 189 DTS, Portland, ME 04112, (207)774-6754.

HAMM, D. Michael——B: Oct. 30, 1938, *Atty.*; **PRIM RE ACT:** Attorney, Owner/Investor; **OTHER RE ACT:** CPA; **EDUC:** BA, 1961, Baylor Univ.; **GRAD EDUC:** MBA, Acctg., SMU; JD, Texas; **BUS ADD:** 3000 South Post Oak Blvd., Suite 1500, Houston, TX 77056, (713)965-9091.

HAMM, Thomas M.——B: 1944, NY, Wilder Resnick, Inc.; Thomas M. Hamm & Company, Inc.; **PRIM RE ACT:** Broker, Consultant; **PREV EMPLOY:** Managing Dir. EIC Devel. Corp., VP The Chase Manhattan Bank; **PROFL AFFIL & HONORS:** Motel Brokers Assn. of Amer.; **EDUC:** BS, 1967, Bus. Admin., Boston Univ.; **GRAD EDUC:** MBA, 1970, Fin., Intl. Bus., Columbia Univ.; **MIL SERV:** Army ROTC; **HOME ADD:** PO Box 4013, Springdale, CT 06907; **BUS ADD:** Suite 3105, 1270 Ave. of the Americas, New York, NY 10020, (212)247-5321.

HAMMANN, Arthur H.——B: Apr. 27, 1914, Chicago, IL, *Realtor*, Hammann Realty Assoc.; **PRIM RE ACT:** Broker, Consultant, Attorney, Appraiser, Banker, Lender, Owner/Investor, Instructor, Property Manager, Syndicator; **SERVICES:** Lender rep.; **PREV EMPLOY:** Mort. Loan Officer, Mgr.-Mort. Dept., Sherwood & Roberts, Inc.; VP, 1963; Sherwood & Roberts, Inc.; **EDUC:** BS, 1935, Econ./Bus., NW Univ.; **GRAD EDUC:** JD, 1938, NW Univ.; **MIL SERV:** USN, Lcdr.; **OTHER ACT & HONORS:** Lt. Gov. of Hawaii; Kiwanis Intl., VP, HI Chapter The Retired Officers Assn.; **HOME ADD:** 427 Opihikao Pl., Honolulu, HI 96825, (808)396-9432; **BUS ADD:** 427 Opihikao Pl., Honolulu, HI 96825, (808)396-9432.

HAMME, D. Eugene——B: Nov. 8, 1939, York, PA, *Exec. VP*, Walker & Dunlop; **PRIM RE ACT:** Property Manager; **PREV EMPLOY:** The Fidelity Mutual Life Ins. Co., 1967 Asst. Controller, 1969 Investment Controller, 1970 Asst. VP, 1971 2nd VP; **PROFL AFFIL & HONORS:** Greater Wash. Bd. of Trade: Comm. Devel. Bur. Steering Comm., Chmn. 1981 Task Force on Metro related RE Devel., AICPA, PA Inst. of CPA's, MBA of Amer., 1980-81 Personnel Subcomm. Chmn., Wash. Bd. of Realtors; **EDUC:** BS, 1962, Bus. Admin., Drexel Univ.; **GRAD EDUC:** MBA, 1970, Drexel Univ.; **OTHER ACT & HONORS:** Combined Health Appeal, Nat. Capital Area, 1981, V Chmn. Cultural Alliance of Gr. Wash.; **BUS ADD:** 1156 15th St., NW, Washington DC 20005, (202)872-5511.

HAMMEL, Richard F.——B: May 30, 1923, Owatonna, MN, *Chmn*, Greenspan, Inc.; **PRIM RE ACT:** Architect, Developer; **SERVICES:** Planning design; **REP CLIENTS:** AIA; MN Soc. of Archs.; Soc. of Coll. & Univ. Planners; **PROFL AFFIL & HONORS:** Fellow AIA; **EDUC:** Univ. of MN, 1944, Arch., Univ. of MN; **GRAD EDUC:** MArch, 1947, Arch., Harvard; **EDUC HONORS:** Dist. Achievement Award; **MIL SERV:** USN Res., Ens.; **HOME ADD:** 13709 Wood Ln., Minnetonka, MN 55343, (612)544-4500; **BUS ADD:** 1201 Harmon Pl., Minneapolis, MN 55403, (612)332-3944.

HAMMEL, Robbie J.——B: Feb. 12, 1942, Atlanta, GA, *CPA*, Robbie J. Hammel, CPA; **PRIM RE ACT:** Consultant; **OTHER RE ACT:** Acctg.; **SERVICES:** Tenant sales examinations, project of feasibility studies, special accounting reports, admin. & org. consulting; **REP CLIENTS:** Office bldgs., shopping ctrs., devel. & prop. mgrs.; **PREV EMPLOY:** Weingarten Realty, Inc.; **PROFL AFFIL & HONORS:** Amer. Soc. of Women Accountants; TX Soc. of CPA's; Intl. Council of Shopping Ctrs., Recipient of Citizens Appreciation Award from USAF, 1967 and from USN; **EDUC:** Acctg., Univ. of Houston; Miami Dade Univ.; GA State Coll.; **OTHER ACT & HONORS:** First Baptist Church N.W.; **HOME ADD:** 5902 Caruso Forest Dr., (713)445-4409; **BUS ADD:** 5415 Antoine, Houston, TX 77092, (713)957-3800.

HAMMER, Alan R.——B: Sept. 3, 1946, Brooklyn, NY, *Partner*, Brach, Eichler, Rosenberg, Silver, Bernstein & Hammer, P.A.; **PRIM RE ACT:** Attorney, Owner/Investor, Property Manager, Syndicator; **REP CLIENTS:** Gebroe-Hammer Assoc.; Muroff Assoc.; NJ Realty Co.; **PROFL AFFIL & HONORS:** NJ Prop. Owners Assn.; ABA; NJ Bar Assn.; Essex Cty. Bar Assn.; **EDUC:** BS, 1968, RE, Rider Coll.; **GRAD EDUC:** JD, 1971, RE, Rutgers Law School, Newark; **HOME ADD:** Three Fawn Dr., Livingston, NJ 07039, (201)994-3320; **BUS ADD:** 101 Eisenhower Pkwy., Roseland, NJ 07068, (201)228-5700.

HAMMER, Charles——*Dir. Mfg. Serv.*, Standard-Coosa-Thatcher Co.; **PRIM RE ACT:** Property Manager; **BUS ADD:** 18th & Watkins St., PO Box 791, Chattanooga, TN 37401, (615)622-3131.*

HAMMER, Jack T.——B: Aug. 20, 1941, New York, NY, *Chmn. of the Bd.*, Housing Systems, Inc.; **PRIM RE ACT:** Broker, Consultant, Developer, Owner/Investor, Property Manager, Syndicator; **OTHER RE ACT:** Profl. devel., ownership and mgmt. of RE for others; **SERVICES:** Housing Systems manages over 200 million dollars of RE in 8 SE states and is a public co. traded; **REP CLIENTS:** OTC; Maj. corporate execs. and other profls. in the high income tax bracket; **PREV EMPLOY:** Founder, Major stock holder since 1969; **PROFL AFFIL & HONORS:** IREM; NAR, CPM; Who's Who in RE; **EDUC:** BS, 1962, Bus. Admin., Amer. Univ.; **GRAD EDUC:** BS, 1964, RE/Fin., Amer. Univ.; **EDUC HONORS:** RE Frat., Grad. of NY Inst. of Fin.; **OTHER ACT & HONORS:** US Senatorial Advisory Bd.; **HOME ADD:** 440 Pine Valley Dr., Marietta, GA 30067, (404)953-3135; **BUS ADD:** 1000 Cir. 75 Parkway, Suite 701, Atlanta, GA 30339, (404)952-2233.

HAMMERBACK, William J., Jr.——B: July 20, 1920, San Francisco, CA, *Appraiser*, Hammerback Appraisal Co.; **PRIM RE ACT:** Consultant, Appraiser, Owner/Investor; **SERVICES:** Appraisal & consulting; **REP CLIENTS:** Crocker Bank, Barclays Bank, VA, CPA firms; **PREV EMPLOY:** FHA, 1955-59, Amer. S & L 1960-71; **PROFL AFFIL & HONORS:** SREA, Nat. Assn. of Review Appraisers, SRA, CRA; **EDUC:** Univ. of CA. Ext.; **EDUC HONORS:** Cert. in R.E., MAI courses 1,2,4, and 6. Numerous R.E. courses; **MIL SERV:** USA, CPL. 1952-53, CIB; **OTHER ACT & HONORS:** San Mateo Golf Club; **HOME ADD:** 32 Eddystone Ct., Redwood City, CA 94065, (415)592-3251; **BUS ADD:** 32 Eddystone Ct., Redwood City, CA 94065, (415)592-3251.

HAMMES, David C.——Rouse & Assoc.; **PRIM RE ACT:** Developer; **BUS ADD:** 5955 Richard St., Jacksonville, FL 32216, (904)731-7277.*

HAMMES, Jerry——B: Dec. 13, 1931, Kankakee, IL, *Pres./Dir.*, Romy Hammes, Inc., Peoples Bank Marycrest, Marycrest S&L Assn.; **PRIM RE ACT:** Developer, Banker, Owner/Investor; **EDUC:** 1949 - 1952, Bus. Admin., Univ. of Notre Dame; **MIL SERV:** USA, S/Sgt. 53-55, G.B.; **OTHER ACT & HONORS:** Pres., S Bend Econ. Devel. Comm.; Dir., C of C; Treas., Better Bus. Bureau; Dir., Michiana Pub. Broadcasting Corp.; **HOME ADD:** 2330 Topsfield Rd., S. Bend, IN 46614, (219)291-0361; **BUS ADD:** 2015 Western Ave., S. Bend, IN 46629, (219)288-0621.

HAMMITT, J. Neil——B: Aug. 17, 1933, Woodbine, IA, *Sr. VP*, Banco Mortgage Co., Income Loan Div.; **OTHER RE ACT:** Mort. Banker; **SERVICES:** Consultant, morts., JV's, wraps, standbys; **PROFL AFFIL & HONORS:** MA; Nat. Assn. of Indus. and Office Parks; Intl. Council of Shopping Centers; **HOME ADD:** 5200

Glengarry Parkway, Edina, MN 55436, (612)926-4234; **BUS ADD:** 7901 Xerxes Ave., So., Bloomington, MN 55431, (612)881-4200.

HAMMON, Coral L.——B: May 31, 1921, Garner, IA, *Mgr. Appraisal Dept.*, Harold A. Allen Co.; **PRIM RE ACT:** Appraiser, Developer; **SERVICES:** Investment, purchasing & selling counseling, feasibility studies valuation; **REP CLIENTS:** Govt., corps. and indivs. for comml. indus. devel. and undevel. props.; **PROFL AFFIL & HONORS:** AIREA, Soc. of RE Appraisers, MAI, SRPA; **EDUC:** BSC, 1942, Univ. of IA; **MIL SERV:** USMC, 1st Lt.; **OTHER ACT & HONORS:** Past Pres. Tacoma Chapter No. 61 Soc. of RE Appraisers; **HOME ADD:** 202 Ramsdell, Fircrest, WA 98466, (206)564-7230; **BUS ADD:** 9805 Gravelly Lake Dr. SW, Tacoma, WA 98499, (206)582-6111.

HAMMOND, Charles A.——B: Dec. 15, 1947, Ogden, UT, *Pres.*, Ogden Title Co., Bonneville Title Co., Inc.; **OTHER RE ACT:** Title ins.; **SERVICES:** Title ins., escrow closings, oil and mineral leases; **REP CLIENTS:** Mort. lenders, comml. lenders, realtors, devels., pvt. investors, oil firms; **PROFL AFFIL & HONORS:** Member Amer. Land Title Assn., UT Land Title Assn., Ogden Bd. of Realtors, Weber Basin Home Builders Assn., 1st VP UT Land Title Assn.; **EDUC:** 1972, Bus. Admin., Mktg. Acctg., Brigham Young Univ.; **MIL SERV:** USAF, 1st Lt.; **HOME ADD:** 665 N Foxtail Ln., Kaysville, UT 84037, (801)766-1495; **BUS ADD:** 2520 Jefferson Ave., Ogden, UT 84401, (801)627-2770.

HAMON, Richard G.——B: Dec. 30, 1937, Corpus Christi, TX, *VP & Dir.*, Winstead, McGuire, Sechrest & Minick, A Profl. Corp.; **PRIM RE ACT:** Attorney; **SERVICES:** Legal Serv.; **PROFL AFFIL & HONORS:** ABA, TX Bar Assn., Dallas Bar Assn.; **EDUC:** BBA, 1959, Acctg. and Econ., Baylor Univ.; **GRAD EDUC:** JD, 1962, Law, Baylor Univ.; **OTHER ACT & HONORS:** Rotary Club of Dallas; **HOME ADD:** 9619 Brentgate, Dallas, TX 75238; **BUS ADD:** 1700 Mercantile Dallas Bldg., Dallas, TX 75201, (214)742-1700.

HAMPION, Kent F.——B: Sept. 24, 1947, Ypsilanti, MI, *Admin. Mgr.*, The Hilton Head Co., Inc.; **PRIM RE ACT:** Developer; **SERVICES:** Land devel. & related amenities, inc. golf, tennis, restaurants & hospitality; **PREV EMPLOY:** Div. Controller Marathon Pipeline Co., Martinsville, IL; **EDUC:** BA, 1969, Econ., OH N. Univ.; **GRAD EDUC:** MBA, 1975, Fin., Bowling Green Univ.; **EDUC HONORS:** Cum Laude; **MIL SERV:** USA, Signal Corps., SP4; **HOME ADD:** 74 Barony Ln., Port Royal Plantation, Hilton Head Is., SC 29928, (803)842-3075; **BUS ADD:** PO Drawer 1304, Hilton Head Is., SC 29928, (803)785-4211.

HAMPSON, Richard P.——B: Apr. 3, 1938, Waltham, MA, *Consultant*, Sole Practitioner, Mgmt. Consulting Servs.; **PRIM RE ACT:** Consultant; **SERVICES:** Computerized and manual bus. systems devel.; **REP CLIENTS:** Resid. and comml. prop. devels. and mgrs.; **PROFL AFFIL & HONORS:** Cert. Data Processer, Cert. Information Systems Auditor; **EDUC:** BA, 1959, Econ., Univ. of NH; **GRAD EDUC:** MBA, 1975, Mgmt. Sci., Pace Univ.; **EDUC HONORS:** Alumni Assn. Bd.; **OTHER ACT & HONORS:** Dist. and local scouting; **HOME ADD:** 6 Meadow Rd., Montrose, NY 10548, (914)737-8669; **BUS ADD:** 6 Meadow Rd., Montrose, NY 10548, (914)737-8669.

HAMPTON, Barbara E.——B: May 3, 1951, Chestertown, MD, *Staff Spec., Training*, S Central Bell Telephone Co., Corporate Learning Ctr.; **PRIM RE ACT:** Instructor; **SERVICES:** RE instr. for Bell System Ctr. for Tech. Educ.; **PREV EMPLOY:** S Central Bell, Nashville, TN, RE Leasing Negotiator; **PROFL AFFIL & HONORS:** BOMA; **EDUC:** BA, 1973, Math., Econ., Vanderbilt Univ., Nashville, TN; **EDUC HONORS:** Magna Cum Laude, Phi Beta Kappa; **HOME ADD:** 3620 Hunters Hill Dr., Birmingham, AL 35210, (205)956-7032; **BUS ADD:** Rm. 303, 200 Beacon Pkwy W, Birmingham, AL 35209, (205)942-0156.

HAMPTON, Carl L.——B: Mar. 31, 1937, Lexington, OH, *VP, Mgr. Mort. Lending*, Ohio Citizens Bank; **PRIM RE ACT:** Banker, Lender; **SERVICES:** Const. lending, mort. banking; **PREV EMPLOY:** Reviewing appraiser; Prudential Ins. Co. of Amer. 7 yrs.; **PROFL AFFIL & HONORS:** Sr. Member, Nat. Assn. of Review Appraisers; **EDUC:** BS, 1960, Agricultural Econ. & Fin., OH State Univ.; **GRAD EDUC:** MS, 1962, Agriculture, Econ. and Fin., OH State Univ.; **MIL SERV:** USAF, Capt.; **OTHER ACT & HONORS:** Member, Bd. of Educ., Genoa Local Schools 1976-78; **HOME ADD:** 22323 W. Elmwood Pkwy., Genoa, OH 43430, (419)855-4446; **BUS ADD:** 1 Levis Sq., Toledo, OH 43603, (419)259-7723.

HAMPTON, Marguerite M.——B: June 3, 1942, Marysville, OH, *Pres.*, Marguerite & Associates; **PRIM RE ACT:** Broker, Consultant, Insuror; **OTHER RE ACT:** Mort. Broker; **SERVICES:** Consultation on Packaging, Devel.; **REP CLIENTS:** Specializing in comml., indus./hotel-motel and large resid. tracts, land devel.; **PREV EMPLOY:** RE Broker, Owner of Marguerite & Assoc. for 3 yrs.; **PROFL AFFIL & HONORS:** Toastmaster's International; NAR; CAR & SD Bd. of Realtors; **HOME ADD:** 9714 Cam. Del. Marfil, San Diego, CA 92124, (714)565-4783; **BUS ADD:** 920 Kline St. Suite 100, La Jolla, CA 92037, (714)459-0534.

HAMRE, Hadley A.——B: Sept. 11, 1930, Granite Falls, MN, *Asst. Sec.*, Twin City Fed. Serv. Corp.; **PRIM RE ACT:** Appraiser; **SERVICES:** RE appraisals, feasibility reports (for Twin City Fed. only); **PREV EMPLOY:** Newcombe & Lawrence Appraisals, Inc., 1960-65; **PROFL AFFIL & HONORS:** SREA, SRPA & SRA; **EDUC:** BA, 1955, Geog., Univ. of MN; **MIL SERV:** USA, Cpl., 1952-54; **HOME ADD:** 8201 Harrison Cir., Minneapolis, MN 55437, (612)831-7816; **BUS ADD:** 801 Marquette Ave., Minneapolis, MN 55437, (612)370-7470.

HAMREN, Arnold M.——B: Aug. 13, 1923, Thompson, IA, *Dir., Prop. Mgmt.*, Kentucky Fried Chicken; **PRIM RE ACT:** Property Manager; **PREV EMPLOY:** 15 yrs Shell Oil Co., RE Rep.; 5 yrs. Mgr. RE Northwestern Refining Co.; 2 yrs own RE Bus.; 6 yrs. Dir. of RE RFC Corp.; **PROFL AFFIL & HONORS:** NACORE; **EDUC:** BA, Accounting Econ., ST. Olaf Coll., Northfield, MN; **MIL SERV:** USA Inf., (Platoon) Sgt., 1943-1946; **HOME ADD:** 8810 Nottingham Pkwy, Louisville, KY 40232, (502)426-3985; **BUS ADD:** PO Box 32070, Louisville, KY 40232, (502)456-8476.

HAMRICK, Larry Dean——B: May 30, 1931, Cleveland Cty., Shelby, NC, *Sec. & Treas.*, Warlick & Hamrick Assoc., Ins. & RE, Corp.; **PRIM RE ACT:** Broker, Consultant, Appraiser, Owner/Investor, Insuror; **OTHER RE ACT:** Hospitality Bus., Motel Owner; **PREV EMPLOY:** Self employed as indicated since 1966; **PROFL AFFIL & HONORS:** NAR, Profl. Ins. Agents, Nat. Assn. Ind. Ins. Agents., NC Realtors Assn., Ind. Ins. Agents of NC, Carolina Assn. of Profl. Ins. Agents; **EDUC:** BS, 1953, Bus. Admin., Mktg. and Advertising, Univ. of NC at Chapel Hill; **MIL SERV:** USMC, Capt.; **OTHER ACT & HONORS:** Past member Planning & Zoning Bd., City of Kings Mountain; Kings Mountain Rotary Club, Kings Mountain Ctry. Club, Past Pres. Kings Mountain Rotary Club, Past Pres. Cleveland Cty. Bd. of Realtors, Past. Sec. Kings Mountain Ctry. Club, Past. Chmn. Admin. Bd. of Central United Methodist Church of Kings Mountain; **HOME ADD:** 1202 Townsend, Kings Mountain, NC 28086, (704)739-6613; **BUS ADD:** PO Box 552, 106 E Mountain St., Kings Mt., NC 28086, (704)739-3611.

HAMS, Robert C.——*VP*, Liberty Life Insurance Co., Liberties Property Group; **PRIM RE ACT:** Developer; **BUS ADD:** PO Box 789, Greenville, SC 29602, (803)268-8333.*

HAMWEY, Charles H.——B: Jan. 17, 1941, Oneonta, NY, *Pres.*, RE By Hamwey, Inc.; **PRIM RE ACT:** Broker, Consultant, Appraiser, Owner/Investor, Instructor; **OTHER RE ACT:** RE Auction Div.; **SERVICES:** ICR - Relocation, resid., comml. appraisal, RE Auction Div.; **REP CLIENTS:** Relocation Realty, Executrans., Employee Transfer, US Steel; **PROFL AFFIL & HONORS:** RNMI, NAR, MT Assn. of Realtors, Billings Bd. of Realtors, Big Sky Marketers, Condemnation Comm. for State of MT, Qualified in Dist. Ct. as expert on RE value, Salesman of Yr., Billings Bd. of Realtors, 1975; Member of Million Dollar Club since 1975; Dir. Billings Bd. of Realtors; Member of Advisory Comm., Billings MLS; Chmn. Grievance Comm., Billings Bd. of Realtors; RE Broker; Pres. Billings Bd. of Realtors; State Dir. for Billings Bd. of Realtors CRB, CRS, GRI; **EDUC:** BA, 1964, Bus., Hist. & Physical Educ., Rocky Mountain Coll., Billings, MT; **OTHER ACT & HONORS:** Little League Chief Umpire, City of Billings, 1975-81; Member of the Little League Program, City of Billings, 1975-81; Member of Advisory Bd. of Billings Childrens Receiving Home Found.; Member of St. Patricks Church; Volunteer help for school projects at the Fratt Sch.; Member of Hiland Golf Club; Member of Nat. Republican Party; Fund Raiser and Campaign Comm.; Assistance District Administrator of Little League in Montana; Director on the Billings Chamber Commerce; **HOME ADD:** 3025 Beech Ave., Billings, MT 59102, (406)656-5684; **BUS ADD:** 1010 Grand Ave., Billings, MT 59102, (406)248-2020.

HAN, John D.——B: May 2, 1940, Seoul, Korea, *Pres.*, H-D Development Co., Inc.; **PRIM RE ACT:** Architect, Developer, Builder, Owner/Investor; **PREV EMPLOY:** Los Angeles Cty. Engrs., Facilities Dept.; **EDUC:** BArch Engr, 1962, Arch, Seoul Natl. Univ.; **GRAD EDUC:** MArch, Urban Design, UCLA; **OTHER ACT & HONORS:** Cty. of Los Angeles, Cty. Engr., 7 yrs.; **HOME ADD:** 1852 Silverwood Ter., Los Angeles, CA 90026, (213)663-4214; **BUS ADD:** 1654 Wilshire Blvd., Los Angeles, CA 90017, (213)483-7760.

HANAHAN, Ingraham H.——**B:** Nov. 4, 1937, Dothan, AL, *Owner*, Century 21; **PRIM RE ACT:** Broker; **PROFL AFFIL & HONORS:** Dothan Bd. of Realtors, AL and Nat., Pres. Dothan Bd. of Realtors; **EDUC:** BS, 1960, Profl. Selling, Univ. of AL; **MIL SERV:** USAF, A1C; **OTHER ACT & HONORS:** Bd. of Dirs. Boys Club of Dothan, AL; **HOME ADD:** 106 Camelia Dr., Dothan, AL 36303, (205)794-5115; **BUS ADD:** 2967 Ross Clark Cir. SW, Dothan, AL 36301, (205)793-4000.

HANAUER, Peter H.——**B:** Mar. 7, 1939, New York, NY, *Treas., Chief Fin. Officer*, Crestwood Village, Inc.; **PRIM RE ACT:** Builder, Owner/Investor; **SERVICES:** Devel. of adult communities; **PREV EMPLOY:** Corporate Prop. Investors, S.D. Leidesdorf & Co.; **PROFL AFFIL & HONORS:** AICPA; NJ Soc. of CPAs; **EDUC:** BS, 1960, Acctg., NYU; **MIL SERV:** US Army, Pfc., Army Reserve; **OTHER ACT & HONORS:** Member, Planning Bd., Howell, NJ, 1979-1980; **HOME ADD:** 45 Newbury Rd., Howell, NJ 07731, (201)367-6422; **BUS ADD:** POB 166, Whiting, NJ 08759, (201)350-1500.

HANAWAY, Richard J.——**B:** Oct. 15, 1934, Providence, RI, *Pres.*, Hanaway Management Co., Inc. and Hanaway Investment Co.; **PRIM RE ACT:** Broker, Consultant, Owner/Investor, Property Manager; **OTHER RE ACT:** RE Exchangor; **PROFL AFFIL & HONORS:** Intl. Exchangors Assn.; FL RE Exchangors; NE RE Exchangors, Cert. Exchangor; Listed: Who's Who in Creative RE; **EDUC:** AB, 1956, Colgate Univ.; **GRAD EDUC:** MAT, 1963, RI Coll.; **MIL SERV:** USAF Res., Lt. Col.; **HOME ADD:** Williamsburg Sq., Plymouth, NH 03264, (603)536-3176; **BUS ADD:** Williamsburg Sq., Plymouth, NH 03264, (603)536-1218.

HANCOCK, George W.——**B:** Jan. 9, 1931, Randolph, NE, *Co-owner*, Hancock, King, Robinson & Co.; **PRIM RE ACT:** Broker, Appraiser; **SERVICES:** Sales and appraisals of comm'l./investment prop.; **PROFL AFFIL & HONORS:** Soc. RE Appraisers, Pres., Lincoln Bd. of Realtors, 1974; Pres., NE Chap. SREA, 1981-1982; SRA; **EDUC:** BS, 1953, Bus. & Speech, Univ. of NE; **MIL SERV:** USA, Infantry, Capt.; **OTHER ACT & HONORS:** Bds. of Dir.: USO; Campfire Girls; Reserve Officers Assn.; YMCA; Better Lincoln Comm.; Lions Club; Phi Gamma Delta; **HOME ADD:** 2340 Woodsdale, Lincoln, NE 68502, (402)435-0969; **BUS ADD:** 1120 K St., Lincoln, NE 68508, (402)474-3130.

HANCOCK, James B.——**B:** Apr. 18, 1952, New Albany, IN, *Part.*, Hancock and Hancock Attys. at Law; **PRIM RE ACT:** Attorney, Instructor, Builder, Owner/Investor; **SERVICES:** Deeds, Abstracts, Real Contracts, Purchase and Sale of RE; **REP CLIENTS:** Realtors, Corp. and Indiv. Investors; **EDUC:** BA, 1973, Poli. Sci., Purdue Univ.; **GRAD EDUC:** JD, 1979, John Marshall Law School (Chicago); **EDUC HONORS:** AVA Estate, Assn. of Trail Lawyers; **OTHER ACT & HONORS:** Public Defender - 1 Yr.; **HOME ADD:** R 2 Box 152F, Floyd Knobs, IN 47119, (812)923-3395; **BUS ADD:** 413 W. First St., New Albany, IN 47150, (812)923-7032.

HANCOCK, William G.——**B:** June 3, 1950, Richmond, VA, *Partner*, Mays, Valentine, Davenport & Moore, Bus. Sect.; **PRIM RE ACT:** Attorney; **SERVICES:** Legal rep. of comml. and resid. RE investors, brokers, lenders and devels.; **REP CLIENTS:** Nat. bank, fed. S&L assn., life ins. co., realtors trade assn. and indiv. investors and devel., condo homeowner's assns.; **PROFL AFFIL & HONORS:** ABA; VA State Bar; City of Richmond Bar Assn.; Real Prop. Sects., VA Continuing Legal Educ.; Author and speaker, GRI, Inst. Lecturer; Who's Who in South and Southwest; Exec. Committee of Young Lawyers Sect. of VA Bar Assn.; **EDUC:** BA, 1972, Econ., Univ. of VA; **GRAD EDUC:** JD, 1975, Comml. Law, Real Prop., Tax, TC Williams School of Law, Univ. of Richmond; **EDUC HONORS:** Deans List, Editorial Bd. of Law Review, Moot Court Judge; **OTHER ACT & HONORS:** Articles published in Univ. of Richmond Law Review, Richmond Ronald McDonald House, Counsel, VA State Bar News, VA CLE RE Handbook; Who's Who in the South & Southwest; **HOME ADD:** 111 Tempsford Ln., Richmond, VA 23226, (804)285-3578; **BUS ADD:** 23rd fl. F&M Ctr., Richmond, VA 23219, (804)644-6011.

HANDLER, Steven D.——**B:** Dec. 9, 1947, New London, CT, *VP, Planning and Control*, Amer. Invsco Corp.; **OTHER RE ACT:** Specialist in RE, Acctg., Analysis and Systems, Accountant, Fin. Analyst; **SERVICES:** Consulting on financially related matters to condo. assns.; **PREV EMPLOY:** S.D. Leidesdorf & Co. CPA's (Subsequently merged with Ernst & Whinney); **PROFL AFFIL & HONORS:** Amer. Inst. of CPA's; IL CPA Soc.; Amer. Mgmt. Assn.; Exec. Club of Chicago, CPA; MBA; **EDUC:** BBA, 1971, Acctg., Univ. of IA; **GRAD EDUC:** MBA, 1981, Information Systems, DePaul Univ.; **EDUC HONORS:** Grad. with honors, 4.0 GPA on a scale of 4.0; Delta Mu Delta, Nat. Honor Soc. of Bus. Admin.; **HOME ADD:** 980 Summit Dr., Deerfield, IL 60015, (312)948-0485; **BUS ADD:** 120 S LaSalle, 23rd Flr., Chicago, IL 60603, (312)621-4132.

HANDLER, Stuart——**B:** Jan. 13, 1939, Detroit, MI, *Pres.*, Stuart Handler R.E. Co.; **PRIM RE ACT:** Broker, Syndicator; **OTHER RE ACT:** Investor; **SERVICES:** Specialize in the sale of comml., investment and indus. R.E.; **PROFL AFFIL & HONORS:** Member NAR, RESSI, RNMI, CCIM; Past Pres. 1980 IL Chap. of CCIM; **EDUC:** BA, 1960, Univ. of MI; **GRAD EDUC:** MBA, 1962, Mktg., N.W. Univ.; **HOME ADD:** 9410 N. Central Park Ave., Evanston, IL; **BUS ADD:** 205 W. Randolph St., Suite 1350, Chicago, IL 60603, (312)236-6538.

HANDY, Michael R.——**B:** Sept. 25, 1946, Flint, MI, *Sr. VP*, Nygaard, Mims & Hoffman, P.C., Taxes; **PRIM RE ACT:** Consultant, Owner/Investor, Instructor; **SERVICES:** Tax, Fin. and Acctg. Consultation, Review and Audit of Fin. Statements; **REP CLIENTS:** Bldg. Cont., RE Devel., Investors, RE Brokerage; **PREV EMPLOY:** Tax Mgr., Main Hurdman, 1974-1979; **PROFL AFFIL & HONORS:** AICPA, OSCPA, NW Tax Inst. Comm., CPA, OR and CA; **EDUC:** BS, Bus. Admin., 1969, Acctg., Univ. of NV, Reno; **GRAD EDUC:** M of Bus. Taxation, 1976, Univ. of S. CA; **MIL SERV:** USA, Capt.; **BUS ADD:** 700 NE Multnomah St. Suite 1200, Portland, OR 97232, (503)239-8000.

HANES, Mildred——*Mgr.*, Community Development Services, Inc., Housing Affairs Letter; **PRIM RE ACT:** Real Estate Publisher; **BUS ADD:** 399 Nat'l. Press Bldg., Washington, DC 20045, (202)638-6113.*

HANFORD, Lloyd Dr., Jr.——**B:** Apr. 14, 1928, San Francisco, CA, *Pres.*, Lloyd Hanford Jr. & Co.; **PRIM RE ACT:** Consultant, Appraiser; **SERVICES:** RE Consultation and Appraisal; **REP CLIENTS:** Banks, S & L's, Pension Funds, Natl. Retailers, Attys., Accts., REIT's., maj. investors & nat. corps.; **PROFL AFFIL & HONORS:** AIREA, SREA, Amer. Soc. of RE Counselor, IREM, BOMA, MAI, CRE, CPM; **EDUC:** BA, 1950, Econ.-Poli. Sci., Univ. Ca at Berkeley; **MIL SERV:** USA, Cpl.; **OTHER ACT & HONORS:** 1969 Natl. Pres., Inst. of RE Mgmt., Dir. - Growth Realty Cos. (YSE - SYM GRW); **BUS ADD:** 369 Pine St. Suite 416, San Francisco, CA 94104, (415)391-6155.

HANFORD, Timothy Lloyd——**B:** Oct. 24, 1955, San Francisco, CA, Cooley, Godward, Castro, Huddleson & Tatum; **PRIM RE ACT:** Attorney; **PROFL AFFIL & HONORS:** ABA, Sect. of Taxation; Sect. of Real Prop., Probate & Trust Law; CA State Bar; **EDUC:** BS, 1977, Math., Stanford Univ.; **GRAD EDUC:** JD, 1980, Law, Harvard Law Sch.; **EDUC HONORS:** Cum Laude; **HOME ADD:** 282 18th Ave., 6, San Francisco, CA 94121, (415)221-3811; **BUS ADD:** One Maritime Plaza, 20th Fl., San Francisco, CA 94111, (415)981-5252.

HANKIN, Lowen K.——**B:** Philadelphia, PA, *Partner*, Hankin, Hankin & Hankin; **PRIM RE ACT:** Attorney, Developer, Lender, Owner/Investor, Regulator; **SERVICES:** Attys. Specializing in RE and Litigation Matters; Devel., Investor of Real Prop.; **PROFL AFFIL & HONORS:** PA Bar Assns., Phila. and Montgomery Cty. Bar Assns., JD; **EDUC:** BA, 1971, Econ., Trinity Coll. (CT); **GRAD EDUC:** JD, 1974, Law, Yale Law School; **EDUC HONORS:** Valedictorian of Class, Phi Beta Kappa; **BUS ADD:** Profl. Ctr. Bldg., Willow Grove, PA 19090, (215)659-3500.

HANKIN, Mark——**B:** Feb. 20, 1949, Philadelphia, PA, *Pres.*, Hankin Organ.; **PRIM RE ACT:** Syndicator, Consultant, Developer, Builder, Property Manager, Owner/Investor; **SERVICES:** Builder-Devel., Mgr. Indus., & Comml. Prop.; **EDUC:** Pol Sci - Intl. Relations and Econ., 1971, Swarthmore Coll.; **EDUC HONORS:** Fellowship, Univ. of Pittsburgh, School of Public Affairs, Grad.; **BUS ADD:** P. O. Box 26767, Elkins Park, PA 19117, (215)674-9660.

HANKIN, Stephen, Esq——**B:** June 15, 1944, Philadelphia, PA, Hankin, D'Amato & Sandson; **PRIM RE ACT:** Attorney; **SERVICES:** Legal; **REP CLIENTS:** Atlantic County Improvement Authority; Ramada Inns, Inc.; Tropicana Hotel/Casino; **PROFL AFFIL & HONORS:** ABA, NJ Bar Assn.; **EDUC:** BA, 1966, Dickinson Coll., Carlisle, PA; **GRAD EDUC:** JD, 1969, Washington Coll. of Law, Amer. Univ., Wash., DC; **EDUC HONORS:** Salutatorian; Amer. Jurisprudence Award for Constitutional Law; **HOME ADD:** 8 Point Dr., Longport, NJ 08403, (609)823-4653; **BUS ADD:** 30 South NY Ave., Atlantic City, NJ 08401, (609)344-5161.

HANKINS, Russell——*Mgr. Human Res.*, Camco; **PRIM RE ACT:** Property Manager; **BUS ADD:** 7010 Ardmore St., Houston, TX 77024, (713)747-4000.*

HANKS, E. Ralph——**B:** Dec. 11, 1918, Corning, CA, *Owner/Investor*; **PRIM RE ACT:** Developer, Owner/Investor; **SERVICES:** Sales of mountain land lots to tracts; **REP CLIENTS:** Recreation lot buyers, small investors; **PREV EMPLOY:** Income prop. owner; **PROFL AFFIL & HONORS:** RE Investors; RE Intelligence Amer Forestry Assn.; Nat. Rifle Assn.; Amer. Fighter Aces Assn.; Assn of Naval Aviation, Ex Blue Angel; **EDUC:** CA Poly, Univ of S. CA, UCLA (RE Courses); **MIL SERV:** USN, Capt., Navy Cross Legion of Merit, DFC, AM, PUC; **OTHER ACT & HONORS:** Who's Who in the West; **HOME ADD:** Christmas Tree Canyon Box 239, Mora, NM 87732, (505)387-5126; **BUS ADD:** Christmas Tree Canyon Box 239, Mora, NM 87732, (505)387-5126.

HANLEY, Michael J.——B: May 30, 1950, Providence, RI, *Atty.*, Gould, Cooksey, Fennell & Appleby; **PRIM RE ACT:** Attorney; **PROFL AFFIL & HONORS:** ABA; The Assn. of Trial Lawyers of Amer.; FL Bar Assn.; FL Trial Lawyers; **EDUC:** BA, 1972, Sociology, Coll. of the Holy Cross; **GRAD EDUC:** JD, 1976, Suffolk Univ. Law Sch.; **EDUC HONORS:** Dean's List; **HOME ADD:** 2105 Buena Vista Blvd., Vero Beach, FL 32960, (305)569-5844; **BUS ADD:** 979 Beachland Blvd., Vero Beach, FL 32960, (305)231-1100.

HANLON, Kathleen Marie——B: Mar. 22, 1956, Clevland, OH, *Project Planner*, Walt Disney Productions, Wed Ent./Land Use Planning Dept.; **OTHER RE ACT:** Urban Designer; Landscape Architect; **SERVICES:** Land Use planning: physical, financial, computer-aided; **REP CLIENTS:** Walt Disney World, Walt Disney Land; **PROFL AFFIL & HONORS:** Member-Amer. Soc. of Landscape Arch.; Amer. Planning Assn.; Amer. Photogrametry Soc.; **EDUC:** BArch, 1979, OH State Univ.; **GRAD EDUC:** Masters, Urban Design, Harvard Graduate School of Design, Harvard University; **HOME ADD:** 710 Copeland Ct., Santa Monica, CA 90405, (213)396-3736; **BUS ADD:** 1401 Flower St., Burbank, CA 91201, (213)956-4244.

HANNA, Harry M.——B: Jan. 13, 1936, Portland, OR, *Partner*, Wheelock, Niehaus, Hanna, Murphy, Green & Osaka; **PRIM RE ACT:** Attorney; **SERVICES:** RE, Tax, Corp., & Banking Law; **REP CLIENTS:** Instnl. Lenders, Indiv. and Corp. Bus.; **PROFL AFFIL & HONORS:** OR, Multnomah Cty., Amer. and Fed. Bar Assns., OR Licensed RE Broker; **EDUC:** BS, 1958, Univ. of OR; **GRAD EDUC:** JD, 1966, Northwestern School of Law of Lewis and Clark Coll.; **OTHER ACT & HONORS:** Dist. CT. Judge Pro Tempore, Multnomah Cty., OR 1973-1980; **BUS ADD:** One SW Columbia, Portland, OR 97258, (503)224-5930.

HANNA, John Paul——B: July 12, 1932, New York, NY, *Pres.*, John Paul Hanna, A Prof. Corp.; **PRIM RE ACT:** Attorney; **PROFL AFFIL & HONORS:** Real Prop. Sect., ABA; Comm. on Condos. & Planned Unit Devel. Housing, CA State Bar Assn.; **EDUC:** BA, 1954, Stanford Univ.; **GRAD EDUC:** JD, 1959, Stanford Law School; **MIL SERV:** USA, Reserve, Capt.; **OTHER ACT & HONORS:** Author of *CA Condo. Handbook*, Bancroft-Whitney; **HOME ADD:** 137 Atherton Ave., Atherton, CA 94025, (415)328-7280; **BUS ADD:** 525 Univ. Ave., Suite 1400, Palo Alto, CA 94301, (415)321-5700.

HANNAFIN, Lawrence——*Dir.*, , Connecticut Real Estate Commission; **PRIM RE ACT:** Property Manager; **BUS ADD:** State Capital, 210 Capital Ave., Hartford, CT 06115, (203)566-5197.*

HANNAY, Robert E.——B: Jan. 19, 1926, Seattle, WA, *Pres.*, Wildwood Realty & Investments; **PRIM RE ACT:** Broker, Consultant, Developer, Owner/Investor; **PROFL AFFIL & HONORS:** Realtors; Amer. Real Estate Exchange; **EDUC:** BA, 1947, Econ., Univ. of WA; **GRAD EDUC:** MS, 1963, Mgmt., AZ State Univ.; **OTHER ACT & HONORS:** Dir. AZ Econ. & Dev. Bd.; Pres. Rotary Club of Prescott; Dir. Yavasai Cty./Indus. Devel. Auth.; **HOME ADD:** 15 Highland Terr., Prescott, AZ 86301; **BUS ADD:** 1 Wildwood Dr., Prescott, AZ 86301, (602)445-1119.

HANNER, Erik R.——B: May 4, 1938, Holyoke, MA, *Broker - Sr. Consultant*, Erik Hanner & Associates; **PRIM RE ACT:** Broker, Consultant, Developer, Owner/Investor, Property Manager, Syndicator; **SERVICES:** Specializing in representing purchaser (lessee) in real prop. acquisition; design/build project manager; **REP CLIENTS:** Zayre Dept. Stores, Pizza Inn, Inc.; Volume Shoe Corp.; Striderite Corp.; Hamill-McKinney Architects; Store-Tek Inc.; Commonwealth Investment Corp.; **PREV EMPLOY:** Pizza Inn, (Corp), Sr. RE Consultant 1978-1982; General Growth Properties, Proj. Dir. 1974-1978; Zayre Corp., Mgr. RE Construction Div. 1970-1974; ITT - Sheraton Corp., A/Mgr. New Construction 1967-1970; **PROFL AFFIL & HONORS:** Nat. Assn. of Corporate RE Execs.; Intl. Council of Shopping Centers, Broker in MA, IA, MO & TX; **EDUC:** BS, 1961, ME, Northeastern Univ.; **EDUC HONORS:** DMG; **MIL SERV:** US Army, 1st Lt., Corps of Engrs.; **HOME ADD:** 3561 Green Acres Terr., Dallas, TX 75234, (214)247-4711; **BUS ADD:** 3561 Green Acres Terrace, Dallas, TX 75234, (214)620-1600.

HANNESSON, Paul——*Sr. VP Fin.*, Overhead Door Corp.; **PRIM RE ACT:** Property Manager; **BUS ADD:** 6250 LBJ Freeway, PO Box 22285, Dallas, TX 75240, (214)233-6611.*

HANNI, Walter S.——*Pres.*, Nat. Assn. of Review Appraisers; **PRIM RE ACT:** Appraiser; **SERVICES:** Valuation consultant, reviewing appraisals; **HOME ADD:** 1374 40th Ave., San Francisco, CA 94122; **BUS ADD:** Suite 410 Midwest Fed. Bldg., St. Paul, MN 55101, (415)564-4955.

HANS, David Michael——B: Dec. 8, 1937, Lewisburg, PA, *VP*, NDC Mgmt. Corp., Mgmt. and Leasing; **PRIM RE ACT:** Property Manager; **OTHER RE ACT:** Retail & Comml. Leasing; **SERVICES:** Full Serv. RE Activities; **REP CLIENTS:** Parent Co. Owed Prop.; **PREV EMPLOY:** Gen. Electric Co., Food Fair Stores, Inc.; **PROFL AFFIL & HONORS:** APT Assoc. of Pittsburgh; IREM; NAR DGH - Bd. of Realtors, CPM; **MIL SERV:** USARNG, ES-Sgt.; **OTHER ACT & HONORS:** Boy Scouts of Amer., Trinity United Methodist Church; **HOME ADD:** 323 Squire Lane, McMurray, PA 15213, (412)941-9674; **BUS ADD:** Webster Hall, 4415 Fifth Ave., Pittsburgh, PA 15213, (412)578-7733.

HANSEN, Brian N.——B: Jan. 11, 1950, Waukegan, IL, *Executive VP*, Attorneys' Title Guaranty Fund, Inc.; **OTHER RE ACT:** Title Insurance; **PREV EMPLOY:** Sole practitioner; **PROFL AFFIL & HONORS:** ABA, CBA, DBA; **EDUC:** AB, 1972, Biology, Drake Univ.; **GRAD EDUC:** JD, 1979, John Marshall Law Sch.; **EDUC HONORS:** Dean's List; **HOME ADD:** 4135 A Monroe Dr., Boulder, CO 80303, (303)440-0086; **BUS ADD:** 1726 Champa, Suite 520, PO Box 869, Denver, CO 80201, (303)893-3055.

HANSEN, Cletus J.——B: May 6, 1938, Dubuque, IA, *Dir.*, Wisconsin Dept. of Regulation and Licensing, RE Bureau; **PRIM RE ACT:** Regulator; **SERVICES:** Lic. & consumer protection; **REP CLIENTS:** Lic. and consumers; **PREV EMPLOY:** WI Dept. of Justice, 1973-1978; **PROFL AFFIL & HONORS:** Amer. Soc. of Training and Devel.; **EDUC:** BA, 1956, Educ., Loras Coll.; **GRAD EDUC:** MS, 1972, Adult Educ., Univ. of WI; **EDUC HONORS:** Magna Cum Laude; **HOME ADD:** 1106 Ellen Ave., Madison, WI 53716, (608)222-5146; **BUS ADD:** P O Box 8936, Madison, WI 53708, (608)266-5514.

HANSEN, Erik Lars——B: Mar. 29, 1949, Lakewood, OH, *Partner*, Peat, Marwick, Mitchell & Co., Mgmt. Consulting; **PRIM RE ACT:** Consultant; **SERVICES:** Market, econ. and fin. planning services; **REP CLIENTS:** Devel., arch. & engrs., land planners, fin. instit., govt. agencies; **PROFL AFFIL & HONORS:** Exec. Group Member of ULI Recreational Devel. Council; Amer. Hotel & Motel Assn.; Amer. Inst. of CPAs, CPA; **EDUC:** BS, 1971, Hotel Admin., Cornell Univ.; **HOME ADD:** 7727 Woodrow Wilson Dr., Los Angeles, CA 90046, (213)874-2642; **BUS ADD:** 555 S. Flower St., Los Angeles, CA 90071, (213)972-4000.

HANSEN, George I.——B: Mar. 17, 1930, Seattle, WA, *Pres.*, George I. Hansen, PC; **PRIM RE ACT:** Attorney, Regulator, Appraiser, Property Manager, Banker; **OTHER RE ACT:** Developer of Condos.; **SERVICES:** Agent, undisclosed prin., legal, consultant & devel.; **PREV EMPLOY:** Mort. co's house counsel; **PROFL AFFIL & HONORS:** JD, LLB; **EDUC:** BA, 1951, Bus., Univ. of WA; **GRAD EDUC:** LLB, 1959, Law, Northwestern Sch. of Law; JD, 1970, Law, Northwestern Sch. of Law; **MIL SERV:** Army, Lt. Col.; **OTHER ACT & HONORS:** Planning Commn.; **HOME ADD:** 17107 S Cliffview Rd., Oregon City, OR 97045; **BUS ADD:** 1000 SW Third Ave., Portland, OR 97204, (503)224-5445.

HANSEN, Kent——*Staff Attorney*, Interpace Corp.; **PRIM RE ACT:** Attorney, Property Manager; **BUS ADD:** 260 Cherry Hill Rd., Parsippany, NJ 07054, (201)335-1111.*

HANSEN, Mike——*Fac. Mgr.*, Measures Corp.; **PRIM RE ACT:** Property Manager; **BUS ADD:** One Results Way, Cupertino, CA 95014, (408)255-1500.*

HANSEN, R. Edwin——B: Jan. 1, 1947, Davenport, IA, *VP*, Security Pacific Bank, RE Fin. - Const. Loans; **PRIM RE ACT:** Banker, Lender; **SERVICES:** Const. fin. - major comml. and resid. projects; **PROFL AFFIL & HONORS:** Building Indus. Assn. of So. CA, Licensed RE Broker; **EDUC:** BS, 1971, Bus. Admin., AZ State Univ.; **MIL SERV:** USMC, Cpl., 1965-1967; **HOME ADD:** 1421 Superior Ave., Newport Beach, CA 92663, (714)646-2142; **BUS ADD:** 4000 MacArthur Blvd., Suite 660, Newport Beach, CA 92660, (714)759-4216.

HANSEN, Richard——B: Dec. 5, 1924, Marshfield, OR, *Owner*, Richard Hansen & Assoc.; **PRIM RE ACT:** Broker, Developer, Builder, Owner/Investor; **PROFL AFFIL & HONORS:** Placer Cty.

Bd. of Realtors, CAR; RNMI; Soc. RE Exchange Gr.; ICSC; **MIL SERV:** USN; S1/c 1941-1945; **HOME TEL:** (916)885-4878; **BUS ADD:** 11245 Dry Creek Rd., Auburn, CA 95603, (916)885-4878.

HANSEN, Royal I.——**B:** Aug. 26, 1948, Salt Lake City, UT, *Atty. at Law*, Moyle & Draper; **PRIM RE ACT:** Attorney; **SERVICES:** Legal services relating to RE practice; **PREV EMPLOY:** DC Court of Appeals 1975-76; US House of Reps. 1971-72; **PROFL AFFIL & HONORS:** ABA, Section: Real Prop; Fed. Bar Assn. Sections: Natural Resources & Public Lands; UT State Bar Assn., Sections: Energy & Natural Resources and Real Prop., Admission to practice: UT, DC and US Supreme Ct.; **EDUC:** BS, 1972, Pol. Sci. and Eng., Univ. of UT; **GRAD EDUC:** JD, 1975, Law, Univ. of UT; **EDUC HONORS:** Dean's List; Pacesetter Award; Skull & Bones Honorary; ASUU Student Senate, Asst. Ed., UT Bar Journal; Norton Scholarship for Law; Presidential Merit Scholarship; Chief Justice Moot Court Honors Bd.; **HOME ADD:** 2026 Herbert Ave., Salt Lake City, UT 84108, (801)582-1342; **BUS ADD:** 600 Deseret Pl., Salt Lake City, UT 84111, (801)521-0250.

HANSON, Alden M.——*VP & Treas.*, Munsingwear, Inc.; **PRIM RE ACT:** Property Manager; **BUS ADD:** 718 Glenwood Ave., Minneapolis, MN 55405, (612)340-4700.*

HANSON, Bruce H.——**B:** Nov. 11, 1945, Milwaukee, WI, *President*, RLC Investments,Inc.; **PRIM RE ACT:** Consultant, Developer, Lender, Property Manager, Owner/Investor; **PREV EMPLOY:** Division Manager, United Farm Agency, Inc.; **PROFL AFFIL & HONORS:** WI and MO Bar Assns. (Member Real Prop. Committee MO Bar); **EDUC:** BS, 1967, International Relations, Univ. of WI; **GRAD EDUC:** JD, 1970, Law, George Washington Univ. Law School; **EDUC HONORS:** Trustee Scholarships All 3 years; **OTHER ACT & HONORS:** Amer. Angus Assn.; Former Chmn. Richland Cty. (WI) Democratic Party; Past Pres. Richland Cty. (WI) Bar Assn.; **HOME ADD:** Red Rock Ranch, Rt. 1 Box 57, Oskaloosa, KS 66066, (913)863-2719; **BUS ADD:** 612 W. 47th St., Kansas City, MO 64112, (816)753-6260.

HANSON, JoAnn——**B:** June 7, 1952, Toledo, OH, *Asst. VP*, Morgan Guaranty Trust Co., RE Investment Dept.; **PRIM RE ACT:** Owner/Investor; **OTHER RE ACT:** Purchase RE for bank clients; **SERVICES:** Acquisition and mgmt. of client's RE assets, indiv. and pension funds; **PROFL AFFIL & HONORS:** ICSC, Assn. of RE Women (NYC); **EDUC:** BA, 1974, Urban Planning, Yale Univ.; **GRAD EDUC:** MBA, 1978, Fin./RE, Wharton, Univ. of PA; **EDUC HONORS:** Summa Cum Laude, Phi Beta Kappa; **BUS ADD:** 9 W 57 St. 11th Fl., New York, NY 10019, (212)826-7115.

HANSON, Mark J.——**B:** Aug. 2, 1953, Philadelphia, PA, *Sr. Invest. Analyst*, Penn Mutual Life Ins. Co., Mort. & Joint Vent. Div.; **OTHER RE ACT:** Inst. invest. counselling; **SERVICES:** Mort./Joint venture; **REP CLIENTS:** Penn Mutual Life Ins. Co.; **PREV EMPLOY:** NY Life Ins. Co., 1978-81; **PROFL AFFIL & HONORS:** Associate Member, Soc. of RE Appraisers Candidate; AIREA; Amer. RE and Urban Econ. Assn.; **EDUC:** BA, 1975, Poli. Sci./Econ., Rutgers Univ.; **HOME ADD:** PO Box 3732, Cherry Hill, NJ 08034, (609)547-8399; **BUS ADD:** Independence Sq., Philadelphia, PA 19172, (215)629-0600.

HANSON, Peter O.——*Pres.*, James E. Hanson Inc.; **PRIM RE ACT:** Developer; **BUS ADD:** 235 Moore St., Hackensack, NJ 07601, (201)488-5800.*

HANSON, Richard A.——**B:** Oct. 14, 1941, Chicago, IL, *Nat. Dir. of RE*, Coopers & Lybrand; **OTHER RE ACT:** Accountants; **SERVICES:** Auditing, Taxation & RE Consulting; **REP CLIENTS:** RE Partnerships, syndications, developers; **PROFL AFFIL & HONORS:** Chicago RE Bd.; AICPA, IL CPA Soc.; Chicago Mort. Bankers Assn.; RESSI, NAR, CPA; **EDUC:** BS, 1963, Acctg., St. Joseph's Coll.; **GRAD EDUC:** MS, 1976, DePaul Univ.; **HOME ADD:** 14729 S. Menard, Oak Forest, IL 60452, (312)687-2257; **BUS ADD:** 222 S. Riverside Pl., Chicago, IL 60606, (312)559-5559.

HANTGAN, Richard S.——**B:** Mar. 6, 1956, New York, NY, *Assoc.*, Hammer, Siler, George Assoc.; **PRIM RE ACT:** Consultant; **OTHER RE ACT:** Planner; **SERVICES:** Mkt. feasibility & fin. analysis for comml., retail, resid. and indus. devel.; project evaluation & disposition strategies; **REP CLIENTS:** Devels., lenders, investors and public agencies; **PREV EMPLOY:** Internships with NYC Dept. of City Planning; Univ. of PA RE Dev. Office, NJ Dept. of Community Affairs; **PROFL AFFIL & HONORS:** Amer. Planning Assn.; **EDUC:** AB, 1978, Urban Studies, Univ. of PA; **GRAD EDUC:** MCP, 1979, Land-use, Real Estate and Urban Devel., Univ. of PA; **EDUC HONORS:** Chosen as Teaching Asst. under grant from NEH, Selected by faculty of City Planning Dept. for accelerated studies; course work at the Wharton School; **HOME ADD:** 2800 Quebec St. NW, Washington, DC 20008, (202)244-0014; **BUS ADD:** 1140 Connecticut Ave., NW, Washington, DC 20036, (202)223-1100.

HAPPEL, H. William——**B:** Feb. 19, 1943, New York, NY, *Asst. VP*, Irving Bus. Ctr., Inc., Affiliate of Irving Trust Co.; **PRIM RE ACT:** Banker; **SERVICES:** Provide const. and interim fin. with well defined sources of repayment; **PREV EMPLOY:** Wells Fargo Bank, Chemical Bank; **EDUC:** BA, 1965, Hist., Univ. of NC; **GRAD EDUC:** MBA, 1970, Fin., Cornell Univ.; **MIL SERV:** USA, E-4, Bronze Star; **HOME ADD:** 31 Sunflower, Irvine, CA 92714; **BUS ADD:** 800 W 6th St., Los Angeles, CA 90017, (213)628-2511.

HARA, Sol J.——**B:** Aug. 12, 1936, Chicago, IL, *VP*, Cantor Fitzgerald Realty Corp.; **PRIM RE ACT:** Broker, Owner/Investor, Syndicator; **SERVICES:** Synd. of comml. propl., prop. mgmt., brokerage of comml. props. not for company use; **REP CLIENTS:** Individuals and companies in tax oriented synd. of comml. prop.; **PREV EMPLOY:** Instnl. Investors Trust (1977-1979), Investors Funding Corp. of NY (1968-1977); **PROFL AFFIL & HONORS:** Licensed Broker - NY; **EDUC:** BS, 1958, Mktg., Mgmt., NY Univ.; **GRAD EDUC:** MBA, 1960, Mgmt., Fin., Columbia Univ.; **EDUC HONORS:** Honors Day Award; **HOME ADD:** 331 E. 71st St., NY, NY 10021, (212)737-9604; **BUS ADD:** 1 World Trade Ctr., New York, NY 10048, (212)938-5131.

HARBIN, Jim——**B:** Aug. 13, 1932, Knox Cty., TN, *Pres.*, Jim Harbin & Co., Inc.; **PRIM RE ACT:** Broker, Appraiser, Developer, Builder, Property Manager, Owner/Investor, Insuror; **SERVICES:** Comml. & Indus. Constr., Mktg. and Dev.; **PREV EMPLOY:** Self-Employed Since 1955; **PROFL AFFIL & HONORS:** Assn. Builders & Contractors - Realtors Bd., CCIM CRB, CRS, GRI; **MIL SERV:** USN; 2nd Cl., Capt. Citation; Korean War; **OTHER ACT & HONORS:** Knox Cty. Commissioner - 1980 to Present; Panel of Arbitrations of Amer.; Designated TN Col. by the Gov. of TN; **HOME ADD:** W. Emory Rd., Powell, TN 37849, (615)947-6988; **BUS ADD:** 6408 Clinton Hwy., Knoxville, TN 37912, (615)938-2961.

HARDEMAN, James C., Sr.——**B:** Mar. 24, 1924, Alpharetta, GA, *RE Dir.*, Gulf Oil Co. - U.S., Div. of Gulf Oil Corp.; **PRIM RE ACT:** Developer, Property Manager, Owner/Investor; **OTHER RE ACT:** Support and Admin., Consultants for Dist. RE Personnel; **PREV EMPLOY:** Pres., Old Salem, Inc., and Salem S, Inc., RE Dev. and Investment Co's., Atlanta, GA; **PROFL AFFIL & HONORS:** State of GA RE Lic; Member of NACORE; **HOME ADD:** 9231 Westheimer Rd., #115, Houston, TX 77001, (713)977-4397; **BUS ADD:** 2240 Two Houston Ctr., Houston, TX 77001, (713)754-4162.

HARDIN, Charles R., Jr.——**B:** June 18, 1921, Newark, NJ, *Partner*, Pitney, Hardin, Kipp & Szuch; **PRIM RE ACT:** Attorney; **PROFL AFFIL & HONORS:** Amer., NJ, Morris Cty. (NJ) and Essex Cty. (NJ) Bar Assns.; **EDUC:** BA, 1942, Econ., Princeton Univ.; **GRAD EDUC:** 1948, Columbia Univ. Law School; **MIL SERV:** USN; Lt.; **OTHER ACT & HONORS:** Chester Twp Planning Bd., 1969-1981, Chmn. 1970-1981; **HOME ADD:** RFD 2, Box 1184, Chester, NJ 07930; **BUS ADD:** 163 Madison Ave., P.O. Box 2008, Morristown, NJ 07960, (201)267-3333.

HARDIN, David R.——**B:** Dec. 14, 1944, Louisville, KY, *Pres.*, Luxor Realty; **PRIM RE ACT:** Broker, Owner/Investor, Property Manager, Syndicator; **PROFL AFFIL & HONORS:** PhD; **EDUC:** BA, 1965, Pol. Sci., Univ. of PA; **GRAD EDUC:** PhD, 1972, Mgmt., Northwestern Univ.; **MIL SERV:** USAF Res., 1st Lt.; **BUS ADD:** 2675 Cumberland Pkwy, Suite 225, Atlanta, GA 30339, (404)433-8389.

HARDIN, Richard D.——**B:** May 19, 1924, Stephenville, TX, *Pres.*, Hardin Corp.; **PRIM RE ACT:** Developer, Owner/Investor, Property Manager; **SERVICES:** Comm. real estate, prop. devel., leasing and management; **REP CLIENTS:** Primarily joint venture projects, total of 100 million in 10 yrs. and current projects totaling 50 million, Major lenders and corp. investors in comml. projects; **PROFL AFFIL & HONORS:** BOMA; Assoc. General Contractors Assn.; Urban Land Institute; Austin C of C; **EDUC:** BFA, 1951, Art & Archeology, Univ. of TX/Austin TX/Princeton Univ.; **GRAD EDUC:** Victoria College, New Zealand; **EDUC HONORS:** Fulbright Scholarship; **MIL SERV:** USMC; Sgt.; So. Pacific, 1942-1945; **OTHER ACT & HONORS:** Board Member TX Institute for Rehabilitation & Research; TX Medical Ctr., Houston; Headliners Club, Austin; **HOME ADD:** 2300 Pease Rd., Austin, TX 78703, (512)476-8748; **BUS ADD:** 315 Nueces, Austin, TX 78701, (512)472-3333.

HARDING, Chester R., Jr.——**B:** Feb. 26, 1931, Washington, DC, *Exec. VP*, North American Doctors Investment Fund, Inc., Exec. Offices; **OTHER RE ACT:** RE Investment and Pension Trust; **SERVICES:** Investment counseling, valuation, devel. & synd. comml. props., tax shelters; **REP CLIENTS:** Participating Physicians and

Investors throughout the U.S., Can. and Overseas; **PREV EMPLOY:** Amer. Realty Trust (REIT), 1970-1976; **EDUC:** BBA, 1957, Fin. Mgmt./Acctg., SE Univ.; **MIL SERV:** USN, SN (1st), 1952-1953; **OTHER ACT & HONORS:** Key Man Award, Jaycees; **HOME ADD:** 6034 North 22nd St., Arlington, VA 22205, (703)536-7872; **BUS ADD:** 1750 K St. N.W. Suite M100, Washington, DC 20006, (202)466-7760.

HARDMAN, Walt——B: Mar. 4, 1928, Seattle, WA, *Pres.*, The Hardman Co.; **PRIM RE ACT:** Broker, Consultant, Appraiser, Developer, Property Manager; **SERVICES:** Devel., mgmt., appraisals; **REP CLIENTS:** Indiv. and instit.; **PREV EMPLOY:** W. T. Grant Co., RE Dept.; **PROFL AFFIL & HONORS:** IREM, SREA (Assoc.), Seattle-King Cty. Bd. of Realtors, CPM; **EDUC:** BA, 1950, RE & Bus. Admin., Univ. of WA, Seattle, WA; **EDUC HONORS:** Oval Club; **MIL SERV:** US Army; **HOME ADD:** 1812 14th St., Bremerton, WA 98310, (206)377-7055; **BUS ADD:** 415 Bell St., Seattle, WA 98121, (206)624-2724.

HARDWICK, Charles V., Jr.——B: May 28, 1941, Richmond, VA, *VP*, National Lending Group, Inc.; **PRIM RE ACT:** Lender, Builder; **SERVICES:** Acquisition, const., devel., permanent loans & joint ventures; **REP CLIENTS:** Ryan, Capital Homes; builders & condo. converters, comml. devels.; **PREV EMPLOY:** James T. Barnes, Washington, DC, 1977-1981; **PROFL AFFIL & HONORS:** Nat. Assn. of Home Builders, Washington, DC; Suburban MD Home Builders; No. VA Home Builders, CRA; **EDUC:** BA, 1962, Bus./Public Admin., VA Polytech. Inst.; **GRAD EDUC:** 1966, T.C. Williams School of Law; **EDUC HONORS:** Corps of Cadets, Arnold Air. Soc.; **MIL SERV:** USAF; 1st; **OTHER ACT & HONORS:** Masons; Scottish Rites; Shriner; Multifamily Fin. Comm.; **HOME ADD:** 2031 Royal Fern Ct. 11C, Reston, VA 22091, (703)860-8297; **BUS ADD:** 11300 Rockville Pike, Rockville, MD 20852, (301)468-9300.

HARDWICK, James O.——B: Mar. 7, 1940, SC, *Pres.*, Hardwick & Co.; **PRIM RE ACT:** Consultant, Architect, Developer, Owner/Investor; **SERVICES:** Design & planning feasibility analysis, const. mgmt. & devel. of resid. projects; **REP CLIENTS:** Sea Pines Co.; **PROFL AFFIL & HONORS:** Registered Architect in GA; **EDUC:** BArch, 1963, Arch., Clemson; **GRAD EDUC:** MBA, RE, GA State Univ.; **EDUC HONORS:** Alpha Rho Chi Arch. Award; **MIL SERV:** Corps of Engr., Capt., Army Accomodation Award; **HOME ADD:** 13 Lands End Way, Hilton Head, SC 29928, (803)671-5955; **BUS ADD:** PO Drawer 11, Hilton Head, SC 29938, (803)842-3955.

HARDY, John——*Dir. Econ. Dev. Dept.*, Indianapolis Power & Light Co.; **PRIM RE ACT:** Developer; **BUS ADD:** 25 Monument Circle, PO Box 1595B, Indianapolis, IN 46206, (317)261-8395.*

HARDY, Walter B.——B: July 25, 1933, Indianapolis, IN, *Owner*, Walter B. Hardy RE Investments; **PRIM RE ACT:** Broker, Owner/Investor; **SERVICES:** RE Investing - Income Prop., Apts., Comm.; **EDUC:** BA, 1973, Soc., CA State Univ., L.A.; **GRAD EDUC:** RE Fin. and Mktg., UCLA; **HOME ADD:** 1810 E. Linda Vista St., W. Covina, CA 91791, (213)919-2504; **BUS ADD:** 5525 E. St., Long Beach, CA 90804, (213)498-1377.

HARKEY, Willard W.——B: Mar. 24, 1925, Phoenix, AZ, *Owner*, Willard W. Harkey Realty; **PRIM RE ACT:** Broker; **OTHER RE ACT:** Realtor; **PROFL AFFIL & HONORS:** No. AZ Bd. Realtors Pres.; Pres. Flagstaff MLS Bd. Dirs. of AAR; Bd. Govs. of Realtor Inst. of AZ, CRB; CRS; AZ RE Broker; Realtor of Year 1971 - No. AZ Bd.; 1st Pres. Grand Canyon Council - AZ Certified Residential Brokers; **EDUC:** BS, 1950, Bus. Admin., AZ State Coll., Flagstaff; **MIL SERV:** US Army; **OTHER ACT & HONORS:** Flagstaff Rotary Club; Flagstaff C of C; City of Flagstaff Firemen's and Policemen's Retirement Bd.; Bishop, Church of Jesus Christ of Latter Day Saints, Flagstaff, AZ; **BUS ADD:** 219 N. Humphreys, Flagstaff, AZ 86001, (602)774-1412.

HARKINS, Harry H. Jr.——B: May 29, 1951, Buckhannon, WV, *Asst. Atty. Gen.*, NC Dept. of Justice, RE; **PRIM RE ACT:** Attorney, Regulator; **SERVICES:** legal advice & broker lic. revocation proceedings; **REP CLIENTS:** NC RE Commn.; **PREV EMPLOY:** pvt. legal practice; **PROFL AFFIL & HONORS:** ABA, NC Bar Assoc., FL Bar, NARELLO (member legal comm.); **EDUC:** AB, 1973, Hist., Duke Univ.; **GRAD EDUC:** JD, 1976, Vanderbilt Univ. Law School; **EDUC HONORS:** Magna cum laude; **OTHER ACT & HONORS:** Exec. Comm. Duke Univ. Annual Fund, Comm. Advisory Bd., WCPE-FM, Raleigh, NC; **HOME ADD:** Rt. 7, Box 223-E, Durham, NC 27707, (919)493-2320; **BUS ADD:** PO Box 17100, Raleigh, NC 27619, (919)872-3450.

HARKINS, Richard C.——B: Apr. 21, 1941, Montgomery, AL, *Dir., Investment Sales, FL Div.*, Cardinal Industries, Inc.; **PRIM RE ACT:** Developer, Owner/Investor, Property Manager, Syndicator; **SERVICES:** Turn-Key Devel. of Apts. & Mgmt. Co.; **REP CLIENTS:** Buyer Grps. & Equity Investor Indivs. & Grps.; Broker/Dealers; Pension Funds for Purchase of Second Morts. and Land Sale/Lease-backs; **PREV EMPLOY:** Econ. Analyst, Gulf Oil RE Devel. Corp, Orlando, FL; VP, Environmental Design Grp., Constructors, Winter Park, FL; **PROFL AFFIL & HONORS:** CPA; **EDUC:** EE (Electrical Engrg.), 1965, Antenna & Waveguide Systems, San Diego State; BS, Acctg., 1971, Univ. of AL; **GRAD EDUC:** MA, Masters Acctg., 1973, Univ. of AL; **MIL SERV:** USN, Lt. (R); **HOME ADD:** 351 Isabella Dr., Longwood, FL 32750, (305)831-4652; **BUS ADD:** 3701 S. Sanford Ave., PO Box U, Sanford, FL 32771, (305)321-0220.

HARLAN, Donald L.——B: July 25, 1933, Chicago, IL, *Partner*, Harlan and Myles Company; **PRIM RE ACT:** Broker, Consultant, Developer, Owner/Investor, Instructor, Syndicator; **SERVICES:** Devel. and synd. of comml. props., RE consulting, investment counseling, valuation & mktg. advisors; **REP CLIENTS:** Denver Union Terminal Railway Co., Silverado S&L, Univ. Natl. Bank of Denver, indiv. and instnl. investors in comml. props.; **PREV EMPLOY:** Sr. VP/Sales Mgr. for Frederick Ross Co., 6/75 to 12/80; **PROFL AFFIL & HONORS:** Denver Bd. of Realtors - Pres. 1980, CO and NAR, RESSI, RNMI Advisory Bd., Chicago Title Co., CCIM Chapter #6, Comml. Listing Service of Denver, CCIM, RNMI; **EDUC:** BS, 1956, Mktg. Mgmt., Univ. of CO; **GRAD EDUC:** MBA, 1970, Univ. of Denver; **MIL SERV:** USAF, Capt. 57-63, Outstanding Unit Award; **OTHER ACT & HONORS:** Univ. of CO Bus. Alumni Advisory Council; Bd. of Dirs. - Spalding Rehab. Hospital; Alumni Recognition Award - Univ. of CO, 1978; **HOME ADD:** 5757 South Ivanhoe St., Englewood, CO 80111, (303)771-6808; **BUS ADD:** 1777 South Harrison St., Suite P-305, Denver, CO 80210, (303)753-9988.

HARLAN, Leonard Morton——B: June 1, 1936, Newark, NJ, *Chmn.*, The Harlan Co., Inc.; **PRIM RE ACT:** Consultant, Developer, Owner/Investor, Instructor; **PREV EMPLOY:** RE partnerships; Donaldson, Lufkin & Jenrette, Inc., VP; **PROFL AFFIL & HONORS:** Columbia Bus. School, Adjunct Prof.; NY Univ. RE Inst., Adj. Assoc. Prof.; 1979-80 Pres. Advisory Comm. Indus. Innovation; Lic. RE Broker NY, NJ, Shattuck Memorial Award; Amer. Inst. RE Appraisers; RE Inst. NYU; Disting. Teacher Award; Who's Who in Fin. and Indus.; **EDUC:** BME, 1959, Indus. and Engrg. Admin., Cornell Univ.; **GRAD EDUC:** MBA, 1961, Harvard Grad. School of Bus. Admin.; Doctor of Bus. Admin., 1965, Harvard Grad. School of Bus. Admin.; **EDUC HONORS:** with Distinction; **OTHER ACT & HONORS:** Past VP Harvard Bus. School Club, NY; Harvard Club, NY; Member Executive Board, Amer. Jewish Comm.; Zeta Beta Tau Frat.; **HOME ADD:** Windmill Farm, Cranbury, NJ 08512; **BUS ADD:** 150 E. 58th St., New York, NY 10055, (212)980-9400.

HARLAN, Thomas P.——B: Oct. 31, 1944, Lebanon, PA, *Partner*, Henry, Beaver Wolf & Mesics; **PRIM RE ACT:** Attorney; **SERVICES:** Full legal services re sales purchase, financing; **REP CLIENTS:** Lebanon Valley National Bank, Farmers Trust Co., Commonwealth National Bank, U.S. Life Title Ins. Co., Commonwealth Land Title, Palmyra Zoning Hearing Bd.; **PROFL AFFIL & HONORS:** PA Bar Assn., Lebanon Cty. Bar Assn.; **EDUC:** BA, 1966, Gen. Arts & Sciences, PA State Univ.; **GRAD EDUC:** JD, 1970, General Law, Villanova Law School; **MIL SERV:** USMC, L/Cpl.; **OTHER ACT & HONORS:** Lions Club, General Counsel, PA Sports Hall of Fame; **HOME ADD:** 1st & Maple Sts., Mt. Gretna, PA 17064, (717)964-3141; **BUS ADD:** 937 Willow St., Lebanon, PA 17042, (717)274-3644.

HARLE, Larry J.——B: May 6, 1947, Wenatchee, WA, *Pres.*, L.J. Harle Properties, Inc.; **PRIM RE ACT:** Consultant, Developer, Owner/Investor, Property Manager, Syndicator; **SERVICES:** Synd. & Devel. of Residential & Comml. Props., investment counseling & Prop. Mgmt.; **REP CLIENTS:** Indiv. investors in resid. & comml. props.; **PREV EMPLOY:** Safeco Ins. Co. 1970-79; **PROFL AFFIL & HONORS:** Seattle Apt. Operators Assn.; Rental Housing Owners of Seattle; Alpha Kappa Psi; **EDUC:** BA, 1970, Bus. & Fin., Eastern WA State Univ.; **OTHER ACT & HONORS:** BPOE; NW Div. Paul Bunyan Club; **BUS ADD:** 17204 Brook Blvd., Bothell, WA 98011, (206)481-8535.

HARLOWE, William I.——B: Jan. 2, 1934, Alexandria, VA, *Pres.*, Potomac Land Co.; **PRIM RE ACT:** Broker, Developer, Syndicator; **SERVICES:** Gen. brokerage, land brokerage, devel.; **PROFL AFFIL & HONORS:** NAR, Dir. VA Assn., Realtor Land and Farm Inst., ULI, Comm. Chmn. Northern VA Bd. of Realtors; **EDUC:** BS, 1970, Law Enforcement, Amer. Univ.; **GRAD EDUC:** Tech. of Mgmt., Data Processing, Amer. Univ.; **MIL SERV:** USA, Sgt. 1st Class, Korea; **OTHER ACT & HONORS:** Intl. Assn. Chief's of Police; **HOME ADD:** 822 Walker Rd., Great Falls, VA 22066, (703)759-3237; **BUS**

ADD: 1447 Dolley Madison Blvd., McLean, VA 22101, (703)821-1745.

HARMAN, Joseph H.——B: Jan. 22, 1934, High Point, NC, *Pres.*, Commonwealth Investment Mortgage Corp.; **PRIM RE ACT:** Banker, Developer, Lender, Builder, Owner/Investor, Insuror; **SERVICES:** Bldg. devel. ins. RE loans; **PREV EMPLOY:** First Mort. Corp.; **PROFL AFFIL & HONORS:** MBAA, NAHB, Community Assns. Inst., ULI; **EDUC:** BS, 1957, Mktg., Univ. of Richmond; **GRAD EDUC:** MA, 1961, Eng. Lit., Univ. of MI; **HOME ADD:** P.O. Box 560, Fairfax, VA 220300, (703)691-8520; **BUS ADD:** PO Box 368, Falls Church, VA 22046, (703)536-3600.

HARMON, Albert C.——B: Sept. 23, 1925, New York, NY, *Dir. of Mgmt.-Waterside Plaza*, Dwelling Managers, Inc.; **PRIM RE ACT:** Property Manager; **SERVICES:** Resid. complex, garage, stores, comml. space; **PROFL AFFIL & HONORS:** IREM; CPM, V Chmn. Educ. Div.; **EDUC:** BBA, 1949, Acctg., mgmt., Duquesne Univ.; **EDUC HONORS:** Cum Laude; **MIL SERV:** USN, ETM 2/c; **OTHER ACT & HONORS:** Bd. of Dirs. Snug Harbor Cultural Ctr., Staten Is.; **HOME ADD:** 231 Sprain Brook Rd., Woodbury, CT 06798, (212)689-1577; **BUS ADD:** 30 Waterside Plaza, NY, NY 10010.

HARMON, Gilbert M.——B: Mar. 20, 1928, Gt. Barrington, MA, *VP, Branch Mgr. CT*, Cross & Brown Co.; **PRIM RE ACT:** Broker; **SERVICES:** All phases of Comml. RE; **HOME ADD:** 241-23 Hamilton Ave., Stamford, CT 06902, (203)327-6239; **BUS ADD:** 253 Riverside Ave., Westport, CT 06880, (203)226-8989.

HARMON, Robert T.——B: Dec. 11, 1946, Bayonne, NJ, *Managing Gen. Part.*, Berg. Harquel Assoc.; **PRIM RE ACT:** Consultant, Owner/Investor, Syndicator; **SERVICES:** Tax planning; **REP CLIENTS:** Execs., principles of closely-held corps., other profls.; **PREV EMPLOY:** 1975-80 Part. of Finkle and Co., CPA; **PROFL AFFIL & HONORS:** NJ Soc. of CPA, AICPA; **EDUC:** BA, 1971, Acctg. & Bus. Admin., Univ. of Tampa, FL; **GRAD EDUC:** MBA, 1974, Acctg. & Taxation, St. John's Univ., NYC; **HOME ADD:** 11 Shawnee Trail, Montville, NJ 07045, (201)263-0185; **BUS ADD:** One Exec. Dr., Fort Lee, NJ 07024, (201)592-6700.

HARMS, Barbara——*Ed.*, Chicago Title & Trust Co., Guarantor; **PRIM RE ACT:** Real Estate Publisher; **BUS ADD:** 111 W. Washington St, Chicago, IL 60602, (312)630-2461.*

HARMSEN, Mark D.——B: Apr. 4, 1955, Grand Rapids, MI, *Pres.*, Westmark Properties; **PRIM RE ACT:** Consultant, Developer, Property Manager, Owner/Investor; **SERVICES:** Investment counseling, grp. investment formation, prop. mgmt.; **REP CLIENTS:** Indiv. investors in comml. props.; **EDUC:** BBA, 1978, Mkth. & RE, Univ. of MI; **HOME ADD:** 1736 Lotus SE, Grand Rapids, MI 49506, (616)245-8463; **BUS ADD:** 500 Peoples Bldg., Grand Rapids, MI 49503, (616)454-9529.

HARP, William C.——B: Mar. 25, 1943, San Diego, CA, *VP, Acquisitions Mgr.*, Coldwell Banker, Capital Mgmt. Servs.; **PRIM RE ACT:** Appraiser, Developer, Banker; **OTHER RE ACT:** Investment Acquisition Mgr.; Fin. Investment Review; **SERVICES:** Pension Fund Investment Mgmt.; **REP CLIENTS:** Corporate, Municipal and Union Pension Funds; **PREV EMPLOY:** Nat. Accounts Comml. Loan Officer with First Interstate Bank, RE Investment Brokerage; **EDUC:** BS, 1966, Bus. Admin., San Diego State Univ.; **GRAD EDUC:** MBA, 1974, RE & Fin., Univ. Southern CA; **HOME ADD:** 1316 Crest Rd., Del Mar, CA 92014; **BUS ADD:** 1365 Fourth Ave., San Diego, CA 92101, (714)721-1570.

HARPER, Allen C.——B: Apr. 10, 1945, St. Louis, MO, *Pres.*, Amer. Community RE, Inc.; **PRIM RE ACT:** Broker, Consultant, Developer, Builder, Property Manager; **PROFL AFFIL & HONORS:** Natl. Assn. of Home Builders, Miami Bd. of Realtors, Coral Gables Bd. of Realtors; **EDUC:** Principia Coll.; **MIL SERV:** Air Force, Capt.; **OTHER ACT & HONORS:** Greater Miami C of C.; Leadership Chmn., Transportation Action Comm.; New World Center Action Comm.; Citizens Transportation Comm., Dade County; Bd. of Trs., Adventure/Unlimited; **HOME ADD:** 7875 S.W. 141 Terr., Miami, FL 33158, (305)253-0803; **BUS ADD:** 999 Brickell Ave., Suite 620, Miami, FL 33131, (305)377-0666.

HARPER, C.R.——B: Apr. 14, 1934, Wash., DC, *Pres.*, Accredited RE Appraisal Service, Inc.; **PRIM RE ACT:** Appraiser; **REP CLIENTS:** Attys.; fin. instns.; govt. agencies; non-profit org.;indivs.; **PROFL AFFIL & HONORS:** NARA; NAIFA, IFAS, CRA; **EDUC:** AB, 1955, Lib. Arts, Princeton Univ.; **MIL SERV:** USNR, Lt. j.g.; **HOME ADD:** 5907 Frazier Lane, McLean, VA 22101; **BUS ADD:** 6869 Elm Street, McLean, VA 22101, (703)790-5522.

HARPER, James L.——B: Mar. 26, 1925, Nashville, TN, *Owner*, James L. Harper & Associates; **PRIM RE ACT:** Broker, Consultant, Appraiser, Developer, Owner/Investor, Property Manager; **PROFL AFFIL & HONORS:** AIREA; SREA; NAR; ASREC, MAI; SREA; CRE; **EDUC:** BA, 1949, Physics/Math., Vanderbilt Univ.; **GRAD EDUC:** LLB, 1955, Nashville YMCA Night Law Sch.; **MIL SERV:** USN; **HOME ADD:** 688 Timber Ln., Nashville, TN 37215, (615)383-7347; **BUS ADD:** 15th Floor, Third Nat. Bank Bldg., Nashville, TN 37219, (615)244-4300.

HARPER, James M.——B: Dec. 18, 1936, Moultrie, GA, *Pres.*, J. M. Harper & Assoc., Inc.; **PRIM RE ACT:** Broker, Consultant, Appraiser; **SERVICES:** R.E. Consulting and Appraising; **PROFL AFFIL & HONORS:** MAI, SRPA, Intl. Right of Way Assoc., Member Jacksonville and Natl. Assoc., of Realtors, Past Pres. Jacksonville Chap. of SREA; **EDUC:** GA So. Coll. - Statesburo, Ga and Jacksonville Univ., Jacksonville, Fl; **HOME ADD:** 12354 Ft. Caroline Rd., Jacksonville, FL 32225, (904)641-7438; **BUS ADD:** 2503 Rogero Rd., Jacksonville, FL 32211, (904)743-5300.

HARPER, Nolan Sidney——B: June 22, 1940, Jackson, MS, *Pres.*, Mississippi Valley Leasing Corp.; **PRIM RE ACT:** Owner/Investor; **SERVICES:** Comml. props. - owner/manager; **PROFL AFFIL & HONORS:** MS Bar Assn., ABA; **EDUC:** BA, 1962, Pre-Law/Poli. Sci., MS State Univ.; **GRAD EDUC:** JD, 1965, Law, Univ. of MS; **EDUC HONORS:** Pres. Sigma Phi Epsilon, Vice Justice Phi Alpha Delta; **OTHER ACT & HONORS:** Lions Club; **HOME ADD:** 5445 Brianfield Road, Jackson, MS 39205, (601)956-1342; **BUS ADD:** PO Box 1791, Jackson, MS 39205, (601)948-2812.

HARPS, Richard R.——B: June 27, 1949, Washington, DC, *VP Appraisals*, John R. Pinkett, Inc.; **PRIM RE ACT:** Appraiser; **SERVICES:** Investment counseling and valuations; **REP CLIENTS:** Lenders, instnl. & indiv. investors, govt. agencies; **PROFL AFFIL & HONORS:** AIREA, Wash. Bd. of Realtors, MAI; **EDUC:** BA, 1972, Econ. & Math., The Amer. Univ.; **BUS ADD:** 1507 Ninth St., NW, Washington DC 20001, (202)797-4740.

HARPS, William S.——B: July 3, 1916, Philadelphia, PA, *1st VP*, John R. Pinkett, Inc.; **PRIM RE ACT:** Consultant, Appraiser, Instructor; **SERVICES:** RE Appraisals and Counseling; **REP CLIENTS:** All branches of Fed. Govt. and DC Govt., Major Banks, Major Corps., Attys. and Investors; **PROFL AFFIL & HONORS:** MAI, 1981 Nat. Pres. AIREA Lambda Alpha, Joseph Allard Award 1974, Howard Univ. Alumni Award; **EDUC:** BS, 1943, Chem.-Math, Howard Univ.; **OTHER ACT & HONORS:** DC Bd. of Zoning Adjustment 1963-1977; Dir., WA Bd. of Trade; Fed. City Council; Nat. BK of WA, Perpetual Amer. Fed. S&L; **HOME ADD:** 1736 Shepherd St. NW, Washington, DC 20011, (202)882-5841; **BUS ADD:** 1507 9th St. NW, Wash., DC 20001, (202)797-4742.

HARRAH, Margaret 'Peg'——B: May 19, 1928, Elkhart, IN, *Partner*, Dunn Gallery of Homes; **PRIM RE ACT:** Broker, Appraiser, Property Manager; **PROFL AFFIL & HONORS:** Nat., State & Local Bds. of Realtors; FLI; RNMI, CRB; **EDUC:** 1950, RE, IN Univ. Bus. School; **HOME ADD:** RR 5, Box 40B, Bloomfield, IN 47424, (812)384-8505; **BUS ADD:** 23 S. Washington, Bloomfield, IN 47424, (812)384-3551.

HARRELSON, Robert——*Exec. Secy.*, New Mexico, New Mexico Real Estate Commission; **PRIM RE ACT:** Property Manager; **BUS ADD:** 4000 San Pedro, N.E., Suite A, Albuquerque, NM 87110, (505)842-3226.*

HARRICK, Joseph W.——B: Apr. 4, 1930, Johnstown, PA, *Pres.*, Harrick Realty Co.; **PRIM RE ACT:** Broker, Consultant, Owner/Investor, Property Manager; **SERVICES:** Consulting & brokerage, site finding; **REP CLIENTS:** Westinghouse Electric (New Community Devel. Grp. & Coral Ridge Properties); Citizens Gas & Coke Utility; Norris Foods (Burger Chef Franchisee); Eagle Highlands Joint Venture (W. German Investor); **PREV EMPLOY:** Self-employed realtor since Feb. 1962; Prior to 1962, Indus. Dist. Sales Mgr., IN, Scott Paper Co.; **PROFL AFFIL & HONORS:** Metro. Indpls. Bd. of Realtors; State & Nat. Bds., Past Chmn., Comml.-Indus. Div., Metro. Indpls. Bd. of Realtors; **EDUC:** BS, 1952, Gen. Bus., WV Univ.; **EDUC HONORS:** Mountain-Ranking Men's Hon., Sphinx, Scabbard & Blade, Distinguished Military Student, 4 Yr. Letter Winner - Varsity Football; **MIL SERV:** US Army Inf., Korea, 1953-1954, 1st Lt., Bronze Star; **OTHER ACT & HONORS:** Past Chmn., Design Review Comm., Metro. Planning Commn.; Tabernacle Pres. Church; Indianapolis Men's Teaching Leader - Bible Study Fellowship; **HOME ADD:** 321 W. Kessler Blvd., Indianapolis, IN 46208, (317)253-9094; **BUS ADD:** 321 W. Kessler Blvd., Indianapolis, IN 46208, (317)257-0506.

HARRIGAN, Jon P.——**B:** Jan. 12, 1948, Pittsburgh, PA, *Acct. Exec.*, Cushman & Wakefield of PA, Inc.; **PRIM RE ACT:** Broker, Consultant; **SERVICES:** Corp. housing studies, comml. & indus. brokerage; **REP CLIENTS:** IBM, Mellon Bank, Westinghouse Electric, TWA, Quadrex, Allegheny International, comml. & instnl. owners; **PREV EMPLOY:** Rockwell Intl. Corp., Mgr. RE, 1974-81; **PROFL AFFIL & HONORS:** NACORE; **EDUC:** BS, 1969, Bus. Admin., WV Wesleyan; **MIL SERV:** Nat. Guard, S/Sgt., 1969-75; **HOME ADD:** 2243 Gray Ridge Rd., Allison Pk., PA 15101, (412)487-4089; **BUS ADD:** Pittsburgh Nat. Bldg., Fifth & Wood Sts., 24th Fl., Pittsburgh, PA 15222, (412)261-9050.

HARRINGTON, Carroll S.——**B:** Apr. 11, 1932, Providence, RI, *Exec. VP*, Howard Realty Co.; **PRIM RE ACT:** Owner/Investor; **OTHER RE ACT:** Lease negotiator and prop. mgr.; **SERVICES:** Major office building owner; **REP CLIENTS:** Tennants: Grinnell Fire Protection; **PROFL AFFIL & HONORS:** BOMA, NFPA Life Safety Code for office occupancies; **EDUC:** BA, 1953, Econ., Harvard Univ.; **GRAD EDUC:** MBA, 1958, Finance, Wharton; Extension schools: Harvard School of Architecture, RI School of Design for Space Planning; **MIL SERV:** USN, Lt., Airborne Combat Information Officer; **OTHER ACT & HONORS:** Chmn. Glocester School Comm., Past Chmn. Glocester Budget Comm., RI Brokers License; **HOME ADD:** Long Entry Rd., Glocester, RI 02814; **BUS ADD:** 10 Durrance St., Providence, RI 02903, (401)421-5337.

HARRINGTON, Curtis G.——**B:** Dec. 23, 1932, Grayson Cty., *Pres.*, Tri-County R.E.; **PRIM RE ACT:** Broker, Instructor, Consultant, Appraiser, Insuror; **OTHER RE ACT:** Part time instr.-Wytheville Community Coll.; **PROFL AFFIL & HONORS:** Bd. of Dir.-Mountain Security S & L; Bd. of Dirs.-C OF C, CRS; CRA; CRB; **EDUC:** R.E., Wytheville Community Coll.; **HOME ADD:** Rt.1, Independence, VA 24348, (703)773-3925; **BUS ADD:** P.O. Box 398, Independence, VA 24348, (703)773-3632.

HARRIS, D. Michael——**B:** Aug. 14, 1950, Atlanta, GA, *Pres.*, D. Michael Harris, M.A.I.; **PRIM RE ACT:** Consultant, Appraiser; **SERVICES:** RE appraising and consulting; **REP CLIENTS:** Lend Lease, Inc.; Scott Hudgens Co.; Bank of Amer.; Realty Services, Inc.; Bankers Life Ins. Co.; Citizens & So. Nat. Bank; First Nat. Bank of Chicago; McDonald's; Ford Leasing Devel. Co.; Nat. Park Serv.; **PREV EMPLOY:** Breedlove & Harris, Inc.; **PROFL AFFIL & HONORS:** AIREA; Soc. of RE Appraisers; NAR, MAI; SRPA; GRI; 1977 & 1981 Young Advisory Council; Soc. of RE Appraisers; **EDUC:** BS, 1972, Bus. Admin., W. GA Coll.; **HOME ADD:** 1678 Terrell Ridge Dr., Marietta, GA 30067, (404)952-8725; **BUS ADD:** 1945 The Exchange, Suite 120, Atlanta, GA 30339, (404)952-4008.

HARRIS, David P.——**B:** June 23, 1937, Boston, MA, *Pres.*, Harris Development Corp.; **PRIM RE ACT:** Developer; **SERVICES:** Land devel.; **REP CLIENTS:** Various; **EDUC:** BS, 1959, Chemistry (math minor), Univ. of Rochester; **GRAD EDUC:** MBA, 1963, Fin., Wharton School of Univ. of PA; **MIL SERV:** US Army, 1st Lt.; **HOME ADD:** 548 Douglas Dr., Lake Forest, IL 60045, (312)295-2397; **BUS ADD:** 548 Douglas Dr., Lake Forest, IL 60045, (312)831-9410.

HARRIS, Earl L.——**B:** Aug. 20, 1942, NY, *Pres.*, Martins Development Company, Inc.; **PRIM RE ACT:** Developer, Attorney; **PREV EMPLOY:** PA Housing Fin. Agency, 1975-78; Federal Nat. Mort. Assn., 1973-75; Dept. of Housing and Urban Devel., 1972-73; **EDUC:** BS, 1963, Psych., Howard Univ.; **GRAD EDUC:** JD, 1968, Univ. of Pittsburgh School of Law; **BUS ADD:** 603 Payne Shoemaker Building, 240 North Third St, Harrisburg, PA 17101, (717)233-3394.

HARRIS, Ernest A.——**B:** July 29, 1939, AR, *VP & Div. Mgr.*, John D. Lusk & Son, Lusk Hawaii; **PRIM RE ACT:** Broker, Developer, Builder, Engineer, Lender; **OTHER RE ACT:** Gen. Contractor; **SERVICES:** RE Devel.; **PREV EMPLOY:** VP Pacific Const. Co.; **PROFL AFFIL & HONORS:** NSPE, ASCE, AGC, CILO, VFW; **EDUC:** BCE, 1961, OR State Univ.; **EDUC HONORS:** Full Tuition, Room & Board Scholarship; **MIL SERV:** USMC; Capt., Bronze Star, Purple Heart; **OTHER ACT & HONORS:** Member Oahu Ctry. Club, Quartermaster Vietnam Post of VFW, Structures Chm. Oahu Ctry.. Club; **HOME ADD:** 2937 Kalakaua Ave. #28, Honolulu, HI 96815, (808)922-1113; **BUS ADD:** 841 Bishop St., Ste. 1618, Honolulu, HI 96813, (808)537-4972.

HARRIS, Harvey A.——**B:** Nov. 5, 1936, St. Louis, MO, *Partner*, Stolar, Heitzmann, Eder, Seigel & Harris; **PRIM RE ACT:** Attorney; **SERVICES:** Legal consultation and counseling; **REP CLIENTS:** Devels., synds., builders, lenders and investors; **PROFL AFFIL & HONORS:** ABA, MO Bar Assn., St. Louis Bar Assn., Admitted before US Supreme Ct.; **EDUC:** AB, 1958, Econ., Harvard; **GRAD EDUC:** JD, 1961, Law, Harvard; **EDUC HONORS:** Magna Cum Laude; **OTHER ACT & HONORS:** Treas. Harvard Club of St. Louis; VP & Dir. Jewish Fed. of St. Louis; **HOME ADD:** 31 Westmoreland Pl., St. Louis, MO 63108, (314)361-0676; **BUS ADD:** 515 Olive, 17th Fl., St. Louis, MO 63101, (314)231-2800.

HARRIS, Howard——**B:** Apr. 9, 1933, Chicago, IL, *Sr. VP*, Unity Savings Assn.; **PRIM RE ACT:** Attorney, Developer, Lender; **SERVICES:** Devel. Loans; **REP CLIENTS:** Unity Savings Assn.; Bank of Commerce & Industry; **PROFL AFFIL & HONORS:** Chicago Bar Assn., IL Bar Assn., ABA, Juris Doctorate DePaul Univ.; **EDUC:** BA, 1955, Pol. Sci., Drake Univ.; **GRAD EDUC:** LLB & JD, 1957, Law, DePaul Univ.; **HOME ADD:** 6137 N. Lauderdale, Chicago, IL 60634, (312)463-1517; **BUS ADD:** 4242 N. Harlem, Chicago, IL 60634, (312)456-0400.

HARRIS, Hugh D.——*Pres.*, State Wide Real Estate; **PRIM RE ACT:** Syndicator; **BUS ADD:** 2209 Ludington St., Escanaba, MI 49829, (906)786-1308.*

HARRIS, Jack J.——**B:** Jan. 3, 1924, Detroit, MI, *Realtor*, E.F. Thompson; **PRIM RE ACT:** Consultant, Developer, Owner/Investor, Syndicator; **OTHER RE ACT:** Investment counselor, valuation, land specialist; **SERVICES:** Land acquisition, devel. of resid. res.; **REP CLIENTS:** Income, comml. and indus. prop.; **PREV EMPLOY:** Sales Mgr., Dist. Nat. concern insulation, builder and devel. in So. CA, Licensed Realtor for 23 Yrs.; **PROFL AFFIL & HONORS:** Realty Inv. Assn. Or. Cty.; Or. Cty. A. RE Brokers Nat. Coun. of Exchangors; Or. Coast Exchangors; E.O.C. Bd. of Realtors; CA Assn. of Realtors; NAR, GRI; **EDUC:** 2 yrs. U. of MI interrupted by Army Service, Bus. Admin.; **MIL SERV:** US Army; 1943-46, Master Sgt.; EAME Theater Medal, Good Conduct Medal, Amer. Theater Med., WWII Victory Medal; **OTHER ACT & HONORS:** Jr. C of C; **HOME ADD:** 2202 N. Baker St., Santa Ana, CA 92706, (714)543-7134; **BUS ADD:** 2202 N. Baker St., Santa Ana, CA 92706, (714)731-3826.

HARRIS, James W.——**B:** Sept. 29, 1949, Atlanta, GA, *Part.*, Smith, Cohen, Ringel, Kohler & Martin; **PRIM RE ACT:** Attorney; **SERVICES:** Lenders to inst. & indiv. investors in RE; also spec. in RE sales & marketing; **PROFL AFFIL & HONORS:** Atlanta Bar Assn., GA Bar Assn. & ABA; **EDUC:** AB, 1971, Pol, Princeton Univ.; **GRAD EDUC:** JD, 1974, Duke Univ. Sch. of Law; **EDUC HONORS:** Magna cum Laude; **BUS ADD:** 2400 First Atlanta Tower, Atlanta, GA 30383, (404)656-1800.

HARRIS, Jeff D.——**B:** Dec. 8, 1947, Albuquerque, NM, *VP/Controller*, Mitchell Devel. Corp. of the SW, a wholly owned sub. of Mitchell Energy & Devel. Corp.; **PRIM RE ACT:** Developer, Builder, Owner/Investor, Property Manager; **SERVICES:** Devel. of The Woodlands, a 23,000 acre new town near Houston; **PREV EMPLOY:** Fin. VP, Superior Homes, Inc., (1977-79); Audit Mgr., Arthur Andersen & Co. (1969-77); **PROFL AFFIL & HONORS:** AICPA, TX Soc. of CPA's, NAREC, Amer. Acctg. Assn., Bd. of Dir. Houston Chap. of CPA's, Bd. of Dir. Texas CPA's; **EDUC:** 1969, Acctg., Bus. Admin., Univ. of NM; **EDUC HONORS:** Dean's List, 1965-69; Three Men's Hon. Socs., including Blue Key; **MIL SERV:** USA, SG/E6; **OTHER ACT & HONORS:** Bd. of Dir. The Woodlands Comm. Assn.; Univ. of NM Alumni Assn., Bd. of Dir.; **HOME ADD:** 3858 Villa Ridge, Houston, TX 77068, (713)440-1760; **BUS ADD:** PO Box 4000, 2201 Timberloch Pl., The Woodlands, TX 77380, (713)363-6123.

HARRIS, John A.——**B:** Mar. 28, 1936, Washington, DC, *Pres.*, Potomac Ventures, Inc.; **PRIM RE ACT:** Broker, Consultant, Owner/Investor, Property Manager; **OTHER RE ACT:** Consultant on recreation facilities; **PROFL AFFIL & HONORS:** Washington Bd. of Trade; Nat. Indoor Tennis Assn.; **EDUC:** BA, 1958, Hist., Univ. of MI; **GRAD EDUC:** MBA, 1960, Mktg., Univ. of MI; **EDUC HONORS:** Fielding Yost Scholar; **MIL SERV:** US Army; Pvt.; Soldier of Day, Ft. Knox, KY; **OTHER ACT & HONORS:** Bd. of Dir., Washington Area Tennis Patrons Found., Inc.; Elected to Nat. Capital Area Tennis Hall of Fame; Co-Chmn., Washington Star Intl. Tennis Championships, 13 yrs.; **HOME ADD:** 10401 Buckboard Pl., Potomac, MD 20854, (301)299-7022; **BUS ADD:** 3300 Whitehaven St., N.W., Suite 501, Washington, DC 20007, (202)338-7712.

HARRIS, John C., Jr.——**B:** Mar. 13, 1946, Scottsboro, AL, *Part.*, Harris & Hasseltine; **PRIM RE ACT:** Attorney, Owner/Investor; **SERVICES:** Atty.; **PROFL AFFIL & HONORS:** ABA; Homebuilders Assn. of the Muscle Shoals Area; Lauderdale Cty. Bar Assn.; **EDUC:** BA, 1969, Pol. Sci., Wash. & Lee Univ.; **GRAD EDUC:** JD, 1972, Univ. of AL; **OTHER ACT & HONORS:** Member Lauderdale Cty. Dem. Exec. Comm.; Kiwanis Club; Civil Serv. Bd. for the City of Florence, AL; **HOME ADD:** 217 Forest Hills Dr., Florence, AL 35630, (205)764-1358; **BUS ADD:** 407 S. Court St., Florence, AL 35630, (205)764-1358.

HARRIS, Nelson——*President*, Pittway Corp.; **PRIM RE ACT:** Property Manager; **BUS ADD:** 333 Skokie Blvd., Northbrook, IL 60062, (312)498-1260.*

HARRIS, R. Lee——**B:** Mar. 18, 1954, Kansas City, MO, *Rgnl. Prop. Mgr.*, Robert E. Esrey and Co.; **PRIM RE ACT:** Broker, Consultant, Property Manager; **SERVICES:** Prop. mgmt., leasing, brokerage, consulting; **REP CLIENTS:** Prudential Ins. Co. of Amer., Jefferson S&L, Urban Equities; **PROFL AFFIL & HONORS:** Nat. Apt. Assn.; IREM; NAR, CPM; Member, IREM - Acad. of Authors; Past VP of Kansas City Multi-Family Housing Assn.; **EDUC:** BS, 1975, Econ./ Bus., KS State Univ.; **EDUC HONORS:** Dean's List; **OTHER ACT & HONORS:** Boy Scouts of Amer.; **HOME ADD:** 3815 W. 84th Terr., Leawood, KS 66206, (913)642-3996; **BUS ADD:** 3100 Broadway, Penntower, Kansas City, MO 64111, (816)531-8100.

HARRIS, Richard——*Treas.*, Nortek, Inc.; **PRIM RE ACT:** Property Manager; **BUS ADD:** 815 Reservoir Ave., Cranston, RI 02910, (401)943-1500.*

HARRIS, Robert S.——**B:** June 22, 1938, Miami, FL, *Rgnl. Mgr.*, Post, Buckley, Schuh & Jernigan, Inc.; **PRIM RE ACT:** Consultant, Engineer, Regulator; **OTHER RE ACT:** Real Estate Analyst, Engineering, Planning, Surverying; **SERVICES:** Profl. engrg., planning, surveying, environmental analysis; RE feasibility analysis, mgmt. consulting; **REP CLIENTS:** Major land devels., Cty., City & State Gvts.; **PREV EMPLOY:** Harry C. Schwebke & Assoc. (1957-62), Consult. Engrgs. & Surveyors; **PROFL AFFIL & HONORS:** Soc. of Amer. Mil. Engrgs., Amer. Congress on Surveying & Mapping; Nat. Hist. Soc.; FL Soc. of Profl. Land Surveyors; FL Planning & Zoning Assn.; Amer. Soc. of Photogrammetry, FL Reg. Profl. Land Surveyor 1869, Elected State Pres. of FL Soc. of Profl. Land Surveyors (1976-77); Received FL Land Surveyor of Yr. Award (1976); **EDUC:** Civil. Engrg., Land Surveying, land planning, Intl. Correspondence Sch., Dade Cty. Adult Educ.; **GRAD EDUC:** Bus. Admin., Univ. of Miami (1956-58), Alexander Hamilton Inst. (1963-65); **MIL SERV:** USA, Corps. of Engrs., S/Sgt., E-6, (1958-66), Active Res.; **OTHER ACT & HONORS:** Serve as consulting engr. to Montoe Cty. FL Govt. (1974-78 & 1981-present); appointed by former Gov. Askew & FL Cabinet as first Chmn. FL Public Land Survey Adv. Bd. (1976-78), Rotary Club of Homestead, Homestead, FL City C of C; Nat. Rifle Assn.; **HOME ADD:** 16095 SW 84th Ave., Miami, FL 33157, (305)233-1351; **BUS ADD:** 10 Palms Plaza, Homestead, FL 33030, (305)248-4750.

HARRIS, Russell A., Jr.——**B:** Nov. 6, 1934, Albany, NY, *Regional Dir., Local Assessment Serv.*, NY State Div. of Equalization and Assesment; **PRIM RE ACT:** Consultant, Assessor; **SERVICES:** Mass. Appraisal advice and serv. to local assessment officials; **PROFL AFFIL & HONORS:** SREA; IAAO, SRA, designation; **EDUC:** BPS, 1975, Econ. majoring in RE, SUNY; **MIL SERV:** USN, PNA2; **HOME ADD:** 45 8rescia Blvd., Highland, NY 12528, (914)691-7967; **BUS ADD:** 2180 North Plank Rd., Newburgh, NY 12550, (914)561-2068.

HARRIS, Sam O., Jr.——**B:** Dec. 20, 1935, Dallas, TX, *Broker Consultant*, Preston RE Services, Owner; **PRIM RE ACT:** Broker, Instructor, Consultant, Property Manager, Owner/Investor, Insuror, Real Estate Publisher; **OTHER RE ACT:** Bus. consultant to RE Brokers; **SERVICES:** Brokerage of residential and investment props. in the N. TX area; **REP CLIENTS:** Hoyt R. Matise Co., Guio Gregg Realtors, Inc., Martha Gideon Realtors, Inc.; **PREV EMPLOY:** V.P. & Resident Mgr. Coldwell Banker Residential Brokerage Co.; **PROFL AFFIL & HONORS:** Greater Dallas Bd. of Realtors-TAR-NAR, Past TAR Dir., Past Education Chmn. GDBR; **EDUC:** BBA, 1958, RE and Bus. Law, So. Methodist Univ.; **MIL SERV:** USMC, E-4,Honors; **OTHER ACT & HONORS:** 12 yrs. and elected Cty. of Dallas Exec. Comm., Tech. Club of Dallas Past Pres., Producers' Council, Past Pres.; Const. spec. Inst., Mcgraw Hill F.W. Dodge Adv. Comm.(Royal Oaks C.C.-Rock Creek Life Mem.); **HOME ADD:** 3242 Bryn Mawr, Dallas, TX 75225, (214)368-0935; **BUS ADD:** 8235 Douglas #1000, Dallas, TX 75225, (214)750-0000.

HARRIS, William Steven——**B:** Feb. 23, 1934, St. Louis, MO, *Exec. VP*, Westmoreland Capital Corp.; **PRIM RE ACT:** Consultant, Property Manager, Syndicator; **SERVICES:** Formation and underwriting of Ltd. partnerships; **REP CLIENTS:** Investing in comml. props., including acquisition and mgmt. of props.; **PREV EMPLOY:** Former officer of NY Stock Exchange member firm, VP of investment advisory subs. (1959-74); **EDUC:** BS, 1956, Bus. Admin., Commerce, St. Louis Univ.; **EDUC HONORS:** Who's Who Among Students; **MIL SERV:** USA, 1957-59, Admin. Spec., Commend. Ribbon; **HOME ADD:** 12438 Huntingwick, Houston, TX 77024, (713)465-1341; **BUS ADD:** 680 Statler Bldg., Buffalo, NY 14202, (716)856-9777.

HARRIS, William W.——**B:** May 3, 1918, Houston County, TX, *RE Appraiser & Counsellor*, William W. Harris, MAI, CRE; **PRIM RE ACT:** Consultant, Appraiser; **SERVICES:** Appraisals, Consultation, Income Prop.; **REP CLIENTS:** Instns., Attys., Trusts; **PREV EMPLOY:** Chmn., Harris & Gates Mort. Bankers; **PROFL AFFIL & HONORS:** MAI, CRE, Realtor, Past Pres., TN Chap. AIREA, Past Int. VP, SREA; **EDUC:** AB, 1938, Hist., Univ. of AK; **GRAD EDUC:** JD, 1940, Univ. of AK; **MIL SERV:** USN; WWII, LCDR.; **OTHER ACT & HONORS:** Elder Presbyterian Church; **HOME ADD:** 1108 Kings Park Dr., Memphis, TN 38117, (901)685-6582; **BUS ADD:** 6263 Poplar Suite 928, Memphis, TN 38119, (901)761-3940.

HARRISON, David T.——**B:** 1942, Detroit, MI, *Sr. VP*, First Nat. Bank & Trust Co.; **PRIM RE ACT:** Banker; **PROFL AFFIL & HONORS:** RMA; MBA; Chmn. Kalamazoo Small Bus. Devel. Corp.; Treas., Kalamazoo Neighborhood Housing Corp.; **EDUC:** BA, W. MI Univ.; **MIL SERV:** USN; **HOME ADD:** 3110 Polaris, Kalamazoo, MI 49006, (616)349-7313; **BUS ADD:** 108 E Michigan Ave., Kalamazoo, MI 49006, (616)383-9074.

HARRISON, Henry S.——**B:** June 19, 1930, New Haven, CT, *Pres.*, Real Property Analysts, Inc.; **PRIM RE ACT:** Consultant, Appraiser, Owner/Investor, Instructor, Insuror, Real Estate Publisher; **OTHER RE ACT:** Author; **PROFL AFFIL & HONORS:** AIREA; Soc. of RE Appraisers; RE Educ. Assn.; Greater New Haven Bd. of Realtors; Literary Guild, Realtor of the Yr., Greater New Haven Bd. of Realtors, 1979; Profl. Recognition, AIREA; **EDUC:** US, Econ., Univ. of PA - Wharton School; **GRAD EDUC:** MA, RE & Appraising, Goddard Coll.; **BUS ADD:** 315 Whitney Ave., New Haven, CT 06511, (203)562-3159.

HARRISON, James——*Asst. to Pres.*, Standex International; **PRIM RE ACT:** Property Manager; **BUS ADD:** Manor Parkway, Salem, NH 03079, (603)893-9701.*

HARRISON, Joseph H.——**B:** July 16, 1947, Fairbury, IL, *Salesman, Broker*, Heart of America Better Homes & Gardens, Resid.; **PRIM RE ACT:** Broker, Consultant, Appraiser, Syndicator; **OTHER RE ACT:** Sales; **PREV EMPLOY:** Investigator State of IL; **PROFL AFFIL & HONORS:** GRI, CRS, CRB, Lifetime Member 2 Million Dollar Club; **EDUC:** BA, 1971, Soc., Southern IL Univ. Carbondale; **OTHER ACT & HONORS:** Shriners (Bloomington); **HOME ADD:** 5 Pembroke Cr., Bloomington, IL 61701, (309)662-1675; **BUS ADD:** 2301 E Washington, Bloomington, IL 61701, (309)662-8464.

HARRISON, Milton——**B:** Sept. 11, 1942, Greenville, SC, *Pres.*, Milton Harrison & Associates; **PRIM RE ACT:** Broker, Developer, Instructor, Owner/Investor, Property Manager; **SERVICES:** Investment counseling, comml. sales; **PROFL AFFIL & HONORS:** Greater Minneapolis Bd. of Realtors, multi housing assn.; **EDUC:** BA, 1965, Wayne State Univ.; **GRAD EDUC:** MA, 1966, Univ. of MN; **OTHER ACT & HONORS:** Columbia Univ. School of Bus. Exec. Program, Stanford Univ. Exec. Program; **HOME ADD:** 1640 Spring Valley Rd., Golden Valley, MN 55422, (612)588-5417; **BUS ADD:** 4335 Excelsior Blvd., Minneapolis, MN 55416, (612)920-5755.

HARRISON, Peter R.——**B:** Feb. 23, 1947, Miami, FL, *VP & Branch Mgr.*, Cushman & Wakefield; **PRIM RE ACT:** Broker, Syndicator; **REP CLIENTS:** Numerous; **PREV EMPLOY:** Mtg. Banking; **PROFL AFFIL & HONORS:** Amer Soc. of Appraisers; **EDUC:** BA, 1969, Econ., Denison Univ., OH; **GRAD EDUC:** MBA, 1971, Gen. Bus., Univ. of Miami; **HOME ADD:** 7810 SW 51 Ave., Miami, FL 33143, (305)371-4411; **BUS ADD:** 800 Brickell Ave., Miami, FL 33131, (305)371-4411.

HARRISON, Stanley L.——*Sr. VP*, S.L. Nusbaum & Co., Inc., Apt. Div.; **PRIM RE ACT:** Broker, Developer, Owner/Investor, Property Manager; **SERVICES:** RE Co. - Leasing, mgmt., devel.; **PROFL AFFIL & HONORS:** Tidewater Apt. Council, Tidewater Builders, IREM, VP Norfolk RE Bd., Past Pres. MAI; **EDUC:** BS, 1949, Univ. of VA; **MIL SERV:** USAF, Lt.; **OTHER ACT & HONORS:** Bd. of Dir. of Medical Ctr. Hospitals, Ohef Sholom Temple; **HOME ADD:** 7305 Barberry Ln., Norfolk, VA 23505, (804)423-0928; **BUS ADD:** P.O. Drawer 2491, Norfolk, VA 23501, (804)627-8611.

HARRISON, William H.——**B:** Aug. 1, 1910, Cape Girardeau, MO, *Owner*, William H. Harrison, Realtor; **PRIM RE ACT:** Broker, Consultant, Appraiser, Developer, Property Manager; **SERVICES:** Broker, Prop. Mgr., Appraiser, Indus. and Comml. prop., Devel. (land only); **REP CLIENTS:** G.T.E., Amer. Foods, McQuay-Norris, Midwest Rubber Reclaiming Co., Atlas Mfg. Co.; **PREV EMPLOY:** VP, Sr. VP (RE Fin.) and Exec. VP of First Nat. Bank in St. Louis; **PROFL AFFIL & HONORS:** RE Bd. of Metropolitan St. Louis; SIR, AIREA; **EDUC:** AB, 1932, Econ., Univ. of MO; **GRAD EDUC:** MA, 1933, Pol. Sci., Univ. of MO; **MIL SERV:** US Army, Maj. Gen.,

Legion of Merit with Oak Leaf Cluster; **OTHER ACT & HONORS:** See *Who's Who in America* (since 1968); **HOME ADD:** 8101 Edinburgh Dr., Clayton, MO 63105, (314)721-2206; **BUS ADD:** 11 S Meramec, Suite 700, Clayton, MO 63105, (314)727-3300.

HARROWER, Robert M.——B: Oct. 9, 1933, Batavia, NY, *Pres.*, Batavia Homes & Development Corp.; **PRIM RE ACT:** Developer, Builder; **SERVICES:** Lot costs & sales, new home estimates; **PREV EMPLOY:** Genesee Lumber Co., Inc.; **EDUC:** Hobart Coll. - 2 years; Bryant & Stratton Bus. Inst. 2 years; **MIL SERV:** USA, Sgt.; **OTHER ACT & HONORS:** Rotary Club, Batavia Club, Stafford Ctry. Club; **HOME ADD:** 115 Naramore Dr., Batavia, NY 14020, (716)343-4091; **BUS ADD:** 76 Franklin St., Batavia, NY 14020, (716)343-0777.

HARRS, Leland Allen——B: Oct. 6, 1936, Chicago, IL, *AVP*, The Union Labor Life Ins. Co.; **PRIM RE ACT:** Lender; **PREV EMPLOY:** MONY 1965-1975; **PROFL AFFIL & HONORS:** NYC Mort. Bankers Assn., L.I. R.E.A.; **EDUC:** BA, 1958, Econ., Northwestern Univ.; **GRAD EDUC:** MBA, 1974, Investments, New York Univ.; **MIL SERV:** US Navy, Lt.; **HOME ADD:** 209-06 39th Ave., Bayside, NY 11361, (212)224-2325; **BUS ADD:** 850 Third Ave., New York, NY 10022, (212)752-5200.

HARSHEY, William R.——B: Sep. 27, 1921, Kokomo, IN, *VP*, Floyd Cty. Bank; **PRIM RE ACT:** Appraiser, Banker; **OTHER RE ACT:** Mgr. Mort. Dept.; **PROFL AFFIL & HONORS:** IN MBA; Assoc. Member S. IN Bd. of Realtors; Assoc. Member S. IN Home Builders Assoc.; Assoc. Member SRA; **EDUC:** BS, 1948, Bus. Admin., Butler Univ. IN; **HOME ADD:** 1005 Harbrook Dr., New Albany, IN 47150, (812)944-3858; **BUS ADD:** 1702 E. Spring St., PO Box 1148, New Albany, IN 47150, (812)944-8421.

HARSSON, Kenn——B: Feb. 13, 1949, Knoxville, TN, *Pres.*, West Wind Realty, Inc.; **PRIM RE ACT:** Broker; **SERVICES:** RE Sales; **PROFL AFFIL & HONORS:** Sales and Mktg. Execs. of Knoxville; Dir., Home Builders Assn. of Greater Knoxville; KBR; TAR; NAR; RNMI, GRI; CRS; Candidate for CRB; 1980 Assoc. of the Year - Home Builders Assn. of Knoxville; Pres. 1981-1982 of Sales and Mktg. and Exec. of Knoxville; **EDUC:** Liberal Arts, 1971, Latin, Sweet Briar Coll.; **HOME ADD:** 1727 Blackwood Dr., Knoxville, TN 37923, (615)693-1849; **BUS ADD:** 10826 Kingston Pike, P.O. Box 22711, Knoxville, TN 37922, (615)966-3000.

HART, Dennis M.——B: Sept. 3, 1944, Three Rivers, MI, *Pres.*, First California Mortgage Co.; **PRIM RE ACT:** Developer, Lender, Insuror; **EDUC:** BS, Econ., Math, Golden Gate Univ.; **GRAD EDUC:** MBA, 1970, Fin., U.C. Berkeley; **MIL SERV:** USA, Capt., Bronze Star; **HOME ADD:** 95 Peacock Dr., San Rafael, CA 94901; **BUS ADD:** P.O. Box 9149, San Rafael, CA 94912, (415)461-7090.

HART, Frank——*Office Manager*, Revere Copper & Brass; **PRIM RE ACT:** Attorney, Property Manager; **BUS ADD:** 605 Third Ave., New York, NY 10016, (212)578-1500.*

HART, George M.D., Jr.——B: Aug. 25, 1948, Pensacola, FL, *VP*, First National Bank of Florida, First FL Banks; **PRIM RE ACT:** Consultant, Developer, Property Manager; **SERVICES:** Planning, devel., prop. mgmt.; **PROFL AFFIL & HONORS:** IREM, BOMA; **EDUC:** BA, 1970, Econ., Univ. of the South; **GRAD EDUC:** MBA, 1972, Acctg., Fin., Emory Univ.; **HOME ADD:** 923 Terra Mar Dr., Tampa, FL 33612, (813)961-3582; **BUS ADD:** PO Box 1810, Tampa, FL 33601, (813)224-1339.

HART, Jay A.——B: Apr. 16, 1923, Rockford, IL, *Owner*, Jay Hart Realtors; **PRIM RE ACT:** Broker, Consultant, Appraiser, Banker, Developer, Lender, Builder, Owner/Investor, Instructor, Property Manager, Insuror, Syndicator; **OTHER RE ACT:** Computer systems analyst; **SERVICES:** Counseling, valuation, brokerage, consulting, devel., fin., synd., mgmt., & computer systems; **PREV EMPLOY:** Pres., Intl. Serv. Co., 1952-1960; VP Hart Oil Co., 1947-present; **PROFL AFFIL & HONORS:** SIR; NAR; Nat. Assn. of Review Appraisers, SIR; CRA; **EDUC:** 1943, Math/Bus., Univ. of IL/Univ. of MO/Univ. of Miami; **EDUC HONORS:** Phi Eta Sigma; **MIL SERV:** US Army, Cavalry, US Air Force, Civil Employee War Dept.; **OTHER ACT & HONORS:** Author, Real Estate Buyers & Sellers Guide; **HOME ADD:** 2406 E. Lane, Rockford, IL 61107, (815)877-1533; **BUS ADD:** 3701 E. State St., Rockford, IL 61108, (815)398-6550.

HART, Loren F.——B: May 27, 1981, Mitchell, SD, *VP*, Dougherty, Dawkins, Strand & Yost; **PRIM RE ACT:** Syndicator; **OTHER RE ACT:** Investment Banking; **PREV EMPLOY:** Atty. - Faegre & Benson, Minneapolis, MN, Shearman & Sterling, New York, NU; **EDUC:** BA, 1972, Poli. Sci., Grinnell Coll.; **GRAD EDUC:** JD, 1975, Law, Columbia Univ. School of Law; MBA, 1981, Bus., Harbard Bus. School; **EDUC HONORS:** Phi Beta Kappa, Harlan Fiske Scholar, Grad. with distinction; **HOME ADD:** 7350 York Ave. South, Edina, MN 55435, (612)835-5232; **BUS ADD:** 700 Lumber Exchange Bldg., Minneapolis, MN 55401, (612)341-6020.

HART, R. Morey——B: Feb. 25, 1908, Uniontown, AL, *Pres.*, Hart Realty Co., Inc.; **PRIM RE ACT:** Broker, Consultant, Appraiser; **PROFL AFFIL & HONORS:** Local, state & nat. RE Bds., Pres. of Pensacola Bd. of Realtors, 1957; Pres. of Appraisal Inst. Chapt., 1968; **EDUC:** BA, Eng., Hist., Math., Lang., Univ. of the South, Sewanee, TN; **EDUC HONORS:** Member Bd. of Tr., 15 yrs., and Bd. of Regents for 6 yrs., Nat. Alumni Pres. 2 yrs (1966-67); **MIL SERV:** USN, Lt. Cmdr.; **OTHER ACT & HONORS:** Rotary Club (Paul Harris Fellow), Pensacola Country Club, Member Bd. of Dir. local savings assoc.; **HOME ADD:** 1428 Lemhurst Dr., Pensacola, FL 32507, (904)453-5262; **BUS ADD:** Suite 334, Brent Bldg., PO Box 12711, Pensacola, FL 32575, (904)433-3156.

HART, Ross C.——B: Dec. 18, 1950, Roanoke, VA, Hart and Hart, Attys., Ltd.; **PRIM RE ACT:** Attorney; **SERVICES:** Full legal and title services in RE purchase and devel.; **REP CLIENTS:** Lenders, purchasers and investors in resid. and comml. props.; **PROFL AFFIL & HONORS:** ABA, VA State Bar, Roanoke Bar Assn.; **EDUC:** BA, 1973, Bus. Admin., Monmouth Coll., IL; **GRAD EDUC:** JD, 1976, Univ. of VA School of Law; **OTHER ACT & HONORS:** Member, VA Fifth Dist. Planning Commn. (1981-pres.), VP, Rke. Valley SPCA (1977-1979), Member, Bd. of Dirs., Consumer Credit Counseling Service of Roanoke Valley, Inc (1979 - pres.), VP, Consumers Credit Counseling Service of Roanoke Valley, Inc. (1980 - pres.), Pres., Medmont Lake Homeowners Assn. (1980 - present); **HOME ADD:** 5110 Medmont Circle, SW, Roanoke, VA 24018, (703)774-3022; **BUS ADD:** 308 Second St., SW, Roanoke, VA 24011, (703)344-3278.

HART, Tom W.——B: May 15, 1942, Boise, ID, *Airport Mgr. and Dir. of Indus. Devel.*, Cty. of Yuba Airport; **PRIM RE ACT:** Property Manager; **OTHER RE ACT:** Dir. of Indus. Devel. and Airport Mgmt.; **SERVICES:** Site location serv. for ind.; **REP CLIENTS:** Major indust., aviation bus.; **PREV EMPLOY:** Dir. of Indus. Dev., City of Baltimore, MD; Ex. Dir., Santa Maria Valley Devel., Inc.; Ex. Dir. of Indus. Devel., Superior-Douglas Cty., WI; **PROFL AFFIL & HONORS:** Amer. Assn. of Airport Exec.; CA Assn. of Airport Exec.; Amer. Indus. Devel. Council; Sigma Alpha Epsilon, Fellow Member, Amer. Indus. Devel. Council; **EDUC:** BA, 1965, Soc., Univ. of NV; **GRAD EDUC:** AIDC, 1971, Econ. Devel., Univ. of OK; **OTHER ACT & HONORS:** CA State Gas Commnr., 1971-1973; Dir. of Kiwanis, 1981; Santa Maria Rotary; Boys Club; Taxpayers Assn.; Ctry. Club; **HOME ADD:** 102 E. 18 St., Marysville, CA 95901, (916)742-0493; **BUS ADD:** 1364 Sky Harbor Dr., Yuba Cty. Airport, Marysville, CA 95901, (916)674-6463.

HART, William A.——B: Dec. 9, 1940, Baton Rouge, LA, *Owner*, C-21 Wm. Hart & Assoc.; **PRIM RE ACT:** Broker, Developer, Builder; **PROFL AFFIL & HONORS:** Baton Rouge Bd. Realtors, LRA, NAR, GRI, CRS, CRB; **EDUC:** Attended L.W.U., 1958-1962, RE & Ins.; **MIL SERV:** USA, Sgt.; **OTHER ACT & HONORS:** S.M.E., NAHB; **HOME ADD:** 1747 Applewood Rd., Baton Rouge, LA, (504)766-1967; **BUS ADD:** 13906 Perkins Rd., Baton Rouge, LA 70810, (504)293-7171.

HARTE, Stanley J.——B: July 7, 1910, New York, NY, *Owner*, Stanley J. Harte RE; **PRIM RE ACT:** Developer, Owner/Investor, Property Manager; **PREV EMPLOY:** At all times self-employed; **PROFL AFFIL & HONORS:** NY Univ. Alumni, Columbia Univ. Law School Alumni; **EDUC:** BS, 1930, NY Univ.; **GRAD EDUC:** BBL, 1933, Columbia Univ. Law School; **OTHER ACT & HONORS:** Palm Beach Club, Westchester Ctry. Club, ' Man of the Year" Award, Palm Beach FL, 1981; **HOME ADD:** 1072 N. Lake Way, Palm Beach, FL 33480, (305)848-3653; **BUS ADD:** 255 Sunrise Ave., Palm Beach, FL 33480, (305)833-1611.

HARTEL, Paul J.——B: Apr. 23, 1950, Boston, MA, *Real Estate Officer*, Plymouth Savings Bank, Mort. Loan Dept.; **OTHER RE ACT:** Mortgage Banker; **PREV EMPLOY:** Indep. RE Appraiser and Consultant, **PROFL AFFIL & HONORS:** R.M. Amer. Inst. of RE Appraisers; **EDUC:** BBA Bus. and Fin., 1971, RE and Urban and Reg. Studies, Univ. of MA; **GRAD EDUC:** MBA, 1974, RE Fin., Univ. of MA; **OTHER ACT & HONORS:** Faculty of School of Savings Banking; Savings Bank Assn. of MA; Member Falmouth Indus. Dev. Commn.; Pres. of Real Property Services, Inc., a subs. of Plymouth Savings Bank; **HOME ADD:** 11 Creighton Pk., Falmouth, MA 92540; **BUS ADD:** 226 Main St., Wareham, MA 02571, (617)295-3800.

HARTELIUS, Channing J.——B: Oct. 2, 1946, Great Falls, MT, *Pres.*, Hartelius and Associates, P.C.; **PRIM RE ACT:** Consultant, Attorney, Owner/Investor; **OTHER RE ACT:** Aside from emphasis on RE in law practice, I am involved in a motel, oil and gas investments, farming, apts. and other misc. RE investments; **REP CLIENTS:** RE brokers, indiv. investors, farm and ranch; **PREV EMPLOY:** Asst. Atty. Gen., MT 1971, Asst. City Atty., Great Falls, MT 1972-76; **PROFL AFFIL & HONORS:** ABA, Amer. Trial Lawyers Assn., MT Bar Assn., ABA Sec. on Real Prop., Assn. of Trial Lawyers, Asst. City Atty. 1972-76; **EDUC:** BA, 1968, Econs., Hist., Poli. Sci., Univ. of MT; **GRAD EDUC:** JD, 1971, George Washington Univ.; **EDUC HONORS:** Honors; **MIL SERV:** USMC, Capt.; **OTHER ACT & HONORS:** Bd. of Dirs. Consumer Credit Counsellors, Great Falls C of C, Montana Hist. Soc., Smithsonian Inst., U.S. Jaycees Pres. Award of Distinction; **HOME ADD:** 315 4th Ave. N., Great Falls, MT 59401, (406)452-9260; **BUS ADD:** 600 Central Plaza, Suite 408, Great Falls, MT 59401, (406)727-4020.

HARTFORD, Ed——*Director Facility*, Amdahl Corp.; **PRIM RE ACT:** Property Manager; **BUS ADD:** 1250 E. Arques Ave., Sunnyville, CA 94086, (408)746-6000.*

HARTIGAN, John T.——**B:** Mar. 3, 1933, Chicago, IL, *VP*, Acme Markets, Inc.; **PRIM RE ACT:** Attorney, Owner/Investor; **PROFL AFFIL & HONORS:** NACORE; ICSC; **EDUC:** BA, 1958, Hist., Loyola Univ.; **GRAD EDUC:** JD, 1962, Loyola Univ.; **EDUC HONORS:** Cum Laude; **MIL SERV:** USA, Sp4; **HOME ADD:** 425 Woodcrest Rd., Wayne, PA 19087, (215)687-1007; **BUS ADD:** 124 N 15th St., Philadelphia, PA 19101, (215)568-3000.

HARTIGAN, Thomas J.——**B:** Sept. 23, 1921, Lowell, MA, *Trustee*, The Twenty Seven Trust; **PRIM RE ACT:** Consultant, Appraiser, Property Manager; **OTHER RE ACT:** RE Liquidations; **SERVICES:** Gen. RE consultant servs.; **REP CLIENTS:** Current assignment includes liquidation of 150 million dollars of RE assets of the former Chase Manhattan Mort. and Realty Tr. The beneficiaries are 26 maj. US banks and the FDIC; **PREV EMPLOY:** Officer of the NY Life Ins. Co., RE and Mort. Loan Dept. from 1956-68; Pres. of First Union REIT, Cleveland, OH 1968-78; **PROFL AFFIL & HONORS:** AIREA, MAI; **EDUC:** 1948, RE, Northwestern Univ., Mort. Banking; **MIL SERV:** US Army, Ninth Air Force, S/Sgt.; **OTHER ACT & HONORS:** Union Club of Cleveland; Canterbury Golf Club; **HOME ADD:** 31749 S. Woodland, Pepper Pike, OH 44124, (216)831-8464; **BUS ADD:** Nat. City Ctr., 1900 E. 9th St., Ste. 1520, Cleveland, OH 44114, (216)696-1111.

HARTLAUB, R. Jeffrey——**B:** Sept. 27, 1947, Trenton, NJ, *Atty.*, Hartlaub and Dotten; **PRIM RE ACT:** Attorney; **SERVICES:** Legal and investment counseling; **REP CLIENTS:** Summit, New Providence, Berkeley Heights, Bd. of Realtors, Num. corps. and indivs. maintaining extensive RE investment portfolios; **PROFL AFFIL & HONORS:** NJ State Bar Assn., Tr. Summit Home for Children, Cheseborough Found., Tr. William & Sadie R. Cutter Trust Fund., Inc., Biographical Ref., Who's Who in the East, 1981; **EDUC:** BS, 1969, Econ., Franklin & Marshall, Lancaster, PA; **GRAD EDUC:** JD, 1972, Temple Univ.; **EDUC HONORS:** Dean's List, Law Review; **HOME ADD:** 22 Plymouth Rd., Summit, NJ 07901; **BUS ADD:** 573 Springfield Ave., Summit, NJ 07901, (201)273-5730.

HARTLEY, Donald L., Sr.——**B:** Mar. 21, 1941, Savannah, GA, *Pres.*, D. L. Hartley & Associates, Inc.; **PRIM RE ACT:** Broker, Consultant, Owner/Investor, Property Manager; **REP CLIENTS:** Nat./intl. investors, lenders, indivs., est. on comml. props.; **PREV EMPLOY:** Lockheed-Georgia Co. (Legal Dept.); GA Dept. of Industry & Trade; Coldwell-Banker Co.; **PROFL AFFIL & HONORS:** Nat. Assn. of Indus. and Office Parks; Amer. Indus. Devel. Council; GA Indus. Devel. Assn.; GA RE Commn., Cert. Indus. Devel. (AIDC); Exodus Finis Award 1974 & 1975; Outstanding Serv. Award 1974; **EDUC:** BBA; AA, 1965, Econ., Physics, Univ. of GA & Armstrong State Coll.; **GRAD EDUC:** LLB, 1968, Contracts & RE, Atlanta Law School; **MIL SERV:** USN; **OTHER ACT & HONORS:** Elder - Presbyterian Church; **HOME TEL:** (404)461-2574; **BUS ADD:** PO Box 490096, Atlanta, GA 30349.

HARTMAN, Ardin G.——**B:** Feb. 22, 1927, Madison, WI, *Owner - Broker*, Hartman Assoc.; **PRIM RE ACT:** Broker, Consultant, Developer, Owner/Investor; **SERVICES:** Full serv. to prop. owners, buyers and developers; **PREV EMPLOY:** Principal - owner of Hartman Assoc. a management consulting firm; **PROFL AFFIL & HONORS:** Amer. Mgmt. Assn.; Soc. for Advancement of Mgmt.; **EDUC:** BBA, 1951, Indus. Mgmt., Univ. of WI - Madison; **EDUC HONORS:** Phi Beta Kappa; Beta Gamma Sigma; Phi Kappa Phi; **MIL SERV:** USA, T-5; **OTHER ACT & HONORS:** Rotary Intl., Club Pres.; Elder in Presbyterian Church, US; **HOME ADD:** 3483 Vista Trail, Lilburn, GA 30247, (404)972-9529; **BUS ADD:** 494 Blvd. SE, Atlanta, GA 30312, (404)622-1064.

HARTMAN, Burton A.——**B:** Oct. 11, 1924, Brooklyn, NY, *Part.*, Morgan, Lewis & Bockius; **OTHER RE ACT:** Real Prop. Law; **REP CLIENTS:** NY Life Ins. Co., Teachers Ins. & Annuity Assn., NW Mutual Life Ins. Co., Can. Imperial Bank of Commerce; **PREV EMPLOY:** Asst. Gen Counsel, NY Life Ins. Co., 1963-77; **PROFL AFFIL & HONORS:** RE Fin. Comm., Sect. of Real Prop, Probate & Trust Law, ABA, Amer. Coll. of RE Lawyers, Amer. Coll. of Mort. Attys., Amer. Land Title Assn.; **EDUC:** AB, 1947, Eng., Allegheny Coll., Wash. Sq. Coll., NY Univ.; **GRAD EDUC:** LLB, 1950, Law, NY Univ. Sch. of Law; **MIL SERV:** USMC, 1st Lt., Pres. Unit Citation, Navy Unit Commendation; **HOME ADD:** 8231 SW 82 Pl., Miami, FL 33143, (305)271-4744; **BUS ADD:** One Biscayne Tower, Miami, FL 33131, (305)579-0340.

HARTMAN, Donald J.——**B:** Mar. 15, 1926, Detroit, MI, *Exec. VP*, Carl Rosman & Co.; **PRIM RE ACT:** Broker, Consultant, Appraiser; **SERVICES:** consultation, investment analysis, prop. analysis, appraisal brokerage, site selection; **REP CLIENTS:** specializing in industrial, comml. and investment RE and tax matters; **PROFL AFFIL & HONORS:** NAR, SIR, AIREA, RNMI, Amer. Soc. Appraisers, SIR, MAI, CRE, ASA; **EDUC:** BS, 1949, EE, Univ. of MI; **MIL SERV:** US Army Air Force, Aviation Cadet; **OTHER ACT & HONORS:** Adjunct lecturer, Univ. of MI RE Program; **HOME ADD:** 5128 Whispering Oak, West Bloomfield, MI 48O33, (313)626-6698; **BUS ADD:** Ste. 717, 26555 Evergreen Rd., Southfield, MI 48076, (313)353-2100.

HARTMAN, Gary L.——**B:** Nov. 17, 1943, Wadsworth, OH, *Exec. Dir.*, Akron Area Bd. of Realtors; **OTHER RE ACT:** Exec. Dir. of trade assn.; **SERVICES:** Trade assn. for membership of approximately 3,000; **PREV EMPLOY:** Dir. of Public Relations, Akron Rgnl. Devel. Bd.; **PROFL AFFIL & HONORS:** NAR; OH Assn. of Realtors; Amer. Soc. of Assc. Execs.; **EDUC:** BA, 1966, Journalism, Kent State Univ.; **OTHER ACT & HONORS:** Akron Rgnl. Devel. Bd., Cascade Club; **HOME ADD:** 1539 Belle Meade Rd., Copley, OH 44321, (216)666-8278; **BUS ADD:** 405 S High St., PO Box 1663, Akron, OH 44308, (216)434-6677.

HARTMAN, Richard R.——**B:** Mar. 19, 1926, Schuylkill Haven, PA, *VP*, Mass Mutual Life Insurance Co., Major Props.; **PRIM RE ACT:** Owner/Investor; **EDUC:** BA, 1946, Bus. Admin., Dartmouth Coll.; **GRAD EDUC:** MSC, 1948, Fin., Dartmouth; **MIL SERV:** US Navy, Officer Candidate; **OTHER ACT & HONORS:** Elected Member of Wilbraham School Comm., Bd. of Governors, NAREIT; Also affil. with Mass Mutual Mort. and Realty Investors (VP and Treas.); **HOME ADD:** 18 Ruth Dr., Wilbraham, MA 01095, (413)596-6484; **BUS ADD:** 1295 State St., Springfield, MA 01111, (413)788-8411.

HARTMAN, Stephen J.——**B:** June 10, 1946, St. Paul, MN, *Partner*, Maryland Industrial Enterprises; **PRIM RE ACT:** Broker, Developer, Owner/Investor; **SERVICES:** Site selection, design, build, lease, sell; **REP CLIENTS:** Frank Parsons Paper Co., White-Rose Paper Co., Lee Electric Co. of Baltimore, Becton-Dickenson, General Motors, Gross Mechanical Laboratories, John-Jeffrey Corp.; **PREV EMPLOY:** Control Data Corp., Sr RE Analyst 5 years; Comml. Credit Devel. Corp., VP-RE Equities 3-1/2 years; Industrial Realty Co., Inc. VP Assoc. Broker 4 years; **PROFL AFFIL & HONORS:** Soc. of Indus. Realtors; Greater Baltimore Bd. of Realtors; Nat. Assn. of Indus. and Office Parks, SIR; **EDUC:** BA, 1968, Econ., St. John's Univ. of Collegeville, MN; **OTHER ACT & HONORS:** Rotary Club of Baltimore; **HOME ADD:** 2202 Rockwell Ave., Catonsville, MD 21228, (301)788-3679; **BUS ADD:** PO Box 11845, 6665 Security Blvd., Baltimore, MD 21207, (301)265-5500.

HARTMAN, William J.——**B:** May 21, 1927, Three Rivers, MI, *Mgr., RE*, Chrysler Corp.; **PRIM RE ACT:** Attorney, Property Manager; **PROFL AFFIL & HONORS:** MI State Bar, Assoc., SIR; **EDUC:** AB, 1951, Eng. and Hist., Univ. of MI; **GRAD EDUC:** JD, 1955, Univ. of MI; **MIL SERV:** US Army, 1945-1947, T/5; **HOME ADD:** 633 Madison, Birmingham, MI 48008, (313)646-7637; **BUS ADD:** P O Box 1919, Detroit, MI 48288, (313)956-2556.

HARTNETT, Michael James——**B:** Mar. 21, 1940, Ireland, *Pres. and CEO*, Tillyard & Partners, Inc.; **PRIM RE ACT:** Consultant; **SERVICES:** Intl. prop. consultatnts to fin. instns.; **REP CLIENTS:** Pension funds (RE investment advice), banks and mort. lenders (RE loan inspector); **PROFL AFFIL & HONORS:** Inst. of Quantity Surveyors, Amer. Inst. of Arbitrators, FIQS, ACI Arb.; **EDUC:** BA, 1961, Bldg. Econ., Oxford School of Bldg., Oxford, England; **GRAD EDUC:** MS, 1972, Econ., Aston Univ., Birmingham, England; **HOME ADD:** R.R. #1, Alton, LONIAO, Ont., Canada, (519)941-9214; **BUS ADD:** 5 Hanover Plaza, Suite 1001, NY, NY 10004, (212)363-7333.

HARTSTEIN, Elliott D.——**B:** Aug. 18, 1948, Indianapolis, IN, *Partner*, Cohon Raizes & Regal; **PRIM RE ACT:** Attorney; **SERVICES:** Condo. law, mechanics liens, const. disputes & litigation, tax protests of comml. and resid. props.; **REP CLIENTS:** Condo. assns., gen. and subcontractors, suppliers, devel.; **PROFL AFFIL & HONORS:** Chicago Bar Assn., Condo. Mechanic liens commn., IL State Bar, Sec. on Real Prop., Amer. Assn. of Trial Lawyers; **EDUC:** BA, 1970, Poli. Sci., Univ. of IL; **GRAD EDUC:** JD, 1974, DePaul Univ. Coll. of Law; **EDUC HONORS:** Law Review, Bd. of Editors; **OTHER ACT & HONORS:** Buffalo Grove Zoning Bd. 1977-79, Buffalo Grove Village Bd. 1979-date; **HOME ADD:** 908 Providence, Buffalo Grove, IL 60090, (312)634-0665; **BUS ADD:** 208 S LaSalle #1860, Chicago, IL 60604, (312)726-2252.

HARTUNG, Charles Anthony——**B:** May 26, 1955, Durand, WI, *Mgr.*, Chippewa Valley Appraisal Service, Inc.; **PRIM RE ACT:** Consultant, Appraiser; **SERVICES:** Appraisal of RE and consultation; **PREV EMPLOY:** Worked as an appraiser for Robert Anderson and Associates, Inc. in Eau Clair, WI; **PROFL AFFIL & HONORS:** Candidate for the RM designation offered by the AIREA. I also hold a WI RE Broker's License Certified on the Assessor I level; **EDUC:** BBA, 1977, RE and Urban Land Econ., Univ. of WI; **EDUC HONORS:** Gradepoint average was approximately 3.3; **OTHER ACT & HONORS:** Member of Durand-Arkansaw Jaycees; **HOME ADD:** 645 Main St., Arkansaw, WI 54721, (715)285-5158; **BUS ADD:** 308 3rd Ave. West, Durand, WI 54736, (715)672-5269.

HARTVET, R.A.——*SIR Corp. Dir. RE*, Smith, A.O. Corp.; **PRIM RE ACT:** Property Manager; **BUS ADD:** 3533 No. 27th St., PO Box 584, Milwaukee, WI 53201, (414)447-4435.*

HARTY, John T.——**B:** Apr. 12, 1942, Chicago, IL, *Partner/President*, Harty & Harty/Shamrock Ventures, Inc.; **PRIM RE ACT:** Consultant, Attorney, Developer, Property Manager, Syndicator; **OTHER RE ACT:** Investment Brokerage and RE Devel.; **SERVICES:** Legal, Real Estate Consulting & Development; Investment Brokerage; **PREV EMPLOY:** Pres., Acacia Equities, Inc.; Pres. & Counsel, Lincoln Mortgage Investors; VP & Sec., Dunn Properties Corp.; **PROFL AFFIL & HONORS:** CA State Bar; IL State Bar; **EDUC:** BA, 1964, Liberal Arts, Univ. of Notre Dame; **GRAD EDUC:** JD, 1967, Law, Univ. of Notre Dame; **EDUC HONORS:** Law Review; **OTHER ACT & HONORS:** ACLU; **HOME ADD:** 14 Mountain View, Irvine, CA, (714)833-0315; **BUS ADD:** 14 Mountain View, Irvine, CA 92715, (714)851-0352.

HARTY, Maureen A.——**B:** Mar. 4, 1944, Salt Lake City, UT, *VP and Gen. Counsel*, Shamrock Ventures Inc.; Partner - Harty & Harty, Attys. at Law; **PRIM RE ACT:** Consultant, Attorney, Developer, Property Manager, Syndicator; **PREV EMPLOY:** Partner - Marlin & Harty, Attys. at Law; **PROFL AFFIL & HONORS:** ABA, CA State Bar Assn., CA Bar Sections-RE & Bus.; Orange Cty. Bar Assn., Orange Cty. Bar Sections-RE & Bus.; **EDUC:** BA, 1966, Mathematics, St. Mary's Coll., Notre Dame, IN; **GRAD EDUC:** JD, 1979, Western State Univ., Coll. of Law; **EDUC HONORS:** with Scholastic Merit; **OTHER ACT & HONORS:** Charter 100, Citizens Task Force for O.C.T.C., Santa Ana Trans. Corridor; **HOME ADD:** 14 Mountain View, Irvine, CA 92715, (714)833-0315; **BUS ADD:** 14 Mountain View, Irvine, CA 92715, (714)851-0352.

HARTZ, J. Ernest, Jr.——**B:** Apr. 8, 1935, Berkeley, CA, *VP and Gen. Counsel*, Genstar Corp.; **PRIM RE ACT:** Attorney; **SERVICES:** Legal; **PREV EMPLOY:** Sr. VP, Southeast Banking Corp., Miami, FL; **PROFL AFFIL & HONORS:** Member of the CA, FL and DC Bar Assns.; **EDUC:** BA, 1957, Hist., Stanford Univ.; **GRAD EDUC:** LLB, 1961, Law, Univ. of CA at Berkeley; **EDUC HONORS:** Law Rev. & Order of Coif; **MIL SERV:** US Army, Capt.; **HOME ADD:** 48 Sunnyside Lane, Orinda, CA 94563, (415)254-4038; **BUS ADD:** Suite 3900, Four Embarcadero Ctr., San Francisco, CA 94111, (415)986-7200.

HARVEY, Frank M.——**B:** Nov. 28, 1939, Boston, MA, *RE Mgr.*, The Stanley Works; **PRIM RE ACT:** Property Manager; **OTHER RE ACT:** Corp. RE; **SERVICES:** Acquisition, financing, disposition and mgmt. of corp. RE; **PREV EMPLOY:** Sr. RE Administrator; GTE; **PROFL AFFIL & HONORS:** Active Member, Indus. Devel. Research Council; **EDUC:** AB, 1963, Govt./Econ., Boston Coll.; **GRAD EDUC:** LLB, 1967, Law, Boston Univ.; **HOME ADD:** 76 Dover Rd., New Britain, CT 06050, (203)225-1972; **BUS ADD:** 195 Lake St., New Britain, CT 06050, (203)225-5111.

HARVEY, Perry A.——**B:** July 13, 1944, Cleveland, OH, *VP Mktg., Office Broker*, Interwest, Inc.; **PRIM RE ACT:** Broker, Consultant, Developer, Builder, Owner/Investor, Syndicator; **SERVICES:** Sales, Devel. Origination, Funding, & Mgmt.; **EDUC:** BA, 1967, Eng., Yale Univ.; **OTHER ACT & HONORS:** Aspen Planning & Zoning Commn. 1978-Present; **HOME ADD:** 990 E. Hyman Ave., Aspen, CO 81611, (303)925-2182; **BUS ADD:** 710 E. Durant St., Aspen, CO 81611, (303)925-2772.

HARVEY, Phillip Anthony——**B:** Nov. 1, 1945, Houston, TX, *Owner*, Houston Investment; **PRIM RE ACT:** Broker, Consultant, Owner/Investor, Property Manager, Syndicator; **SERVICES:** Brokerage, investment consulting, synd.; **REP CLIENTS:** Indiv. investors and groups; **PREV EMPLOY:** Xerox Corp., Grubb and Ellis Corp., Coldwell Banker Corp.; **PROFL AFFIL & HONORS:** Sales and Mktg. Council of Bldg. Indus. Assn.; Los Angeles Bd. of Realtors; NAR; CA Assn. of Realtors; San Fernando Valley Bd. of Realtors; **EDUC:** BS, 1969, Mktg., Woodbury Univ.; **OTHER ACT & HONORS:** Los Angeles World Affairs Council; **HOME ADD:** 8787 Shoreham Dr., Los Angeles, CA 90069, (213)854-6612; **BUS ADD:** 1100 Glendon Ave., Suite 1250, Los Angeles, CA 90024, (213)208-2623.

HARWARD, Coralynn Y.——**B:** May 7, 1925, Raleigh, NC, *Atty. at Law*, Individual Practitioner; **PRIM RE ACT:** Attorney; **PROFL AFFIL & HONORS:** ABA, NC Bar Assn., NC Assn. CPA's, CPA; **EDUC:** AB, 1946, Econ., Duke Univ.; **GRAD EDUC:** JD, 1978, Duke Univ. Law Sch.; **HOME ADD:** 2502 Sevier St., Durham, NC 27705, (919)489-9877; **BUS ADD:** 2502 Sevier St., Durham, NC 27705, (919)489-9877.

HARWOOD, David J.——**B:** Mar. 5, 1946, Worcester, MA, *Partner*, Paxton & Seasongood; **PRIM RE ACT:** Attorney; **REP CLIENTS:** Constr. & long term mort. lenders, devels. & indiv. and instnl. investors in comml. and resid. RE; **PROFL AFFIL & HONORS:** ABA, OH State Bar Assn., Cincinnati Bar Assn., Real Prop. Trust & Probate Law Sect. of the ABA (Comm. on Creditors' Rights); **EDUC:** BS, 1968, Econ. & Hist., Miami Univ., Oxford, OH; **GRAD EDUC:** JD, 1971, Univ. of MI; **EDUC HONORS:** Dean's List., High Honors, With Honors; **MIL SERV:** USN, Lt.; **HOME ADD:** 722 Yorkhaven, Cincinnati, OH 45246, (513)851-4954; **BUS ADD:** 1700 Central Trust Tower, Cincinnati, OH 45202, (513)352-6746.

HARWOOD, William James——**B:** Mar. 27, 1941, Harbor Beach, MI, *Owner*, Diversified Services; **PRIM RE ACT:** Assessor; **OTHER RE ACT:** Real prop. tax consultant/representative; **SERVICES:** Prop. tax consultant/assessors to corp./govt.; **REP CLIENTS:** Fast food chains; devels.; shopping ctr. owners; office owners; super market chains; mfg. co.; **PREV EMPLOY:** Equalization Dir., Tax Assessor for Cities, Charter Townships, and General Law Townships; **PROFL AFFIL & HONORS:** Society of RE Appraisers; Intl. Assn. of Assessing Officers; MI Assessors Assn., MI Cert. Level III Assessor; MI RE Broker; **EDUC:** BA, 1963, Hist. and Pol. Sci., Parsons Coll.; **GRAD EDUC:** 3 yrs, 1965, Law, Detroit Coll. of Law; 1979-80, AIREA; 1981, SREA; 1981, IAAO; **OTHER ACT & HONORS:** Jaycees; Lions; Saginaw Soap Box Derby Comm.; Delta College's Property Tax Advisory Bd.; **HOME ADD:** 3251 Columbine, Saginaw, MI 48603, (517)790-0591; **BUS ADD:** 3251 Columbine, Saginaw, MI 48603, (517)790-0135.

HASENSTAB, J. Michael——**B:** Jan. 20, 1949, Beaver Dam, WI, *Mktg. Dir.*, American Medical Buildings; **PRIM RE ACT:** Consultant, Architect, Developer, Builder; **SERVICES:** AMB devel., design, fin., build, and lease medical office bldgs. for hospitals nationwide; **REP CLIENTS:** Hospitals, clinics, physicians; **PREV EMPLOY:** Uni Shelter, Inc., 1975-1981, Resid. Devel., Dir. of Devel. and Mktg.; **PROFL AFFIL & HONORS:** Nat. Assn. of Home Builders; Univ. of WI RE Alumni Assn.; **EDUC:** BA, 1973, Urban Land Econ./Pol. Sci., Univ. of WI; **OTHER ACT & HONORS:** Past Dir., Community Assns., Inst. of WI; **HOME ADD:** 4121 N. Newhall, Shorewood, WI 53211, (414)961-8784; **BUS ADD:** 735 N. Water St., Milwaukee, WI 53202, (414)276-2277.

HASHIOKA, Christopher E.——**B:** Jan. 19, 1948, Chicago, IL, *Sr. VP*, The Balcor Co., Acquisition; **PRIM RE ACT:** Broker, Lender, Owner/Investor, Property Manager, Syndicator; **PROFL AFFIL & HONORS:** Chicago RE Bd., AICPA, IL CPA Soc., IREM; **EDUC:** BA, 1970, Gen. Studies, Harvard Univ.; **GRAD EDUC:** MBA, 1972, Bus., Univ. of Chicago; **EDUC HONORS:** Cum Laude; **OTHER ACT & HONORS:** Univ. Club of Chicago, Harvard Club; **HOME ADD:** 3240 N. Lake Shore Dr., Chicago, IL 60657, (312)935-4662; **BUS ADD:** 10024 Skokie Blvd., Skokie, IL 60077, (312)677-2900.

HASKINS, C.O.——**B:** Jan. 9, 1929, Humphrey Cty., MS, *Pres.*, Comml. Developers, Inc.; **PRIM RE ACT:** Consultant, Developer, Builder, Owner/Investor; **OTHER RE ACT:** Shopping Ctr. Devel./ Owner; **SERVICES:** Devel., ownership & mgmt. of shopping ctrs. and comml. props.; **PREV EMPLOY:** Shell Oil Co., 1954-63; **PROFL AFFIL & HONORS:** Intl. Council of Shopping Ctrs., NY, NY; Intl. House, New Orleans, LA; MS Econ. Council; **EDUC:** BBA, 1953, Tulane Univ.; **MIL SERV:** USMC, Cpl.; **HOME ADD:** 1610 Ellen

Dr., McComb, MS 39648, (601)684-8226; **BUS ADD:** PO Box 681, McComb, MS 36648, (601)684-4809.

HASLACH, Frank——*Dir. Assets*, Evans Products; **PRIM RE ACT:** Property Manager; **BUS ADD:** PO Box 3295, Portland, OR 97208, (503)222-5502.*

HASSAN, Yahya M.A.——**B:** Sept. 14, 1947, Washington, DC, *Arch./Pres.*, Hassan Associates, Architecture; **PRIM RE ACT:** Architect; **OTHER RE ACT:** Prop. Devel. consultant; Interior Arch.; **PREV EMPLOY:** MAAP Arch. & Planners. 1977-80; **PROFL AFFIL & HONORS:** Const. Spec. Inst.; **EDUC:** BArch., 1971, Arch., Howard Univ.; **GRAD EDUC:** MArch, 1976, Arch., GA Inst. of Tech.; **OTHER ACT & HONORS:** Bd. of Trustees Neighborhood Arts Ctr.; Tech. Advisor Steering Comm. Member Toney Valley Neighborhood Org.; Outstanding Young Men of Amer., 1980; Bd. of Dir. CPM Intnl.; **HOME ADD:** 3356 Casa Linda Dr., Decatur, GA 30032, (404)284-4429; **BUS ADD:** PO Box 32519, Decatur, GA 30032, (404)284-4429.

HASTIE, J. Drayton, Jr.——**B:** July 21, 1942, Savannah, GA, *Atty. at Law*, J. Drayton Hastie, Jr., Attorney at Law; **PRIM RE ACT:** Attorney; **SERVICES:** RE taxation, including exchanges, partnership and corporate taxation related to RE; title work; RE synd.; **PREV EMPLOY:** Davis, Polk & Wardwell, New York City, NY; **PROFL AFFIL & HONORS:** ABA, SC Bar Assn. and Charleston Cty. Bar Assn.; **EDUC:** 1964, Hist., Princeton Univ.; **GRAD EDUC:** 1967, Harvard Law School; **EDUC HONORS:** Summa Cum Laude, Cum Laude; **MIL SERV:** US Army, Capt.; **HOME ADD:** 40 Legare St., Charleston, SC 29401, (803)577-2113.

HASTINGS, James A.——**B:** Dec. 30, 1936, Minneapolis, MN, *Chief Appraiser, WY, KS, NE*, Bureau of Land Mgmt., Tech. Servs.; **PRIM RE ACT:** Appraiser; **OTHER RE ACT:** Negotiator; **SERVICES:** Appraisals and appraisal review; **REP CLIENTS:** Govt. and pvt.; **PREV EMPLOY:** US Fish and Wildlife; **PROFL AFFIL & HONORS:** Amer. Soc. of Farm Mgrs. and Rural Appraisers; Nat. Assn. of Review Appraisers; Intl. Right-of-Way Assn.; Soc. of RE Appraisers, Accredited Rural Appraiser 555; Cert. Review Appraiser; Sr. Right-of-Way Agent 2929; **EDUC:** BS, 1962, Economics and Forestry, Univ. of MN; **MIL SERV:** US Army; M/Sgt.; **OTHER ACT & HONORS:** Elks, Amer. Legion; **HOME ADD:** 6602 Willshire Blvd., Cheyenne, WY 82001, (307)632-4274; **BUS ADD:** 2515 Warren Ave., PO Box 1828, Cheyenne, WY 82009, (307)778-2220.

HASTINGS, Robert C.——**B:** Aug. 4, 1938, Omaha, NE, *Gen. Part. Graham Wong Hastings and President*, Hastings Martin Chew and Assoc., Ltd.; **PRIM RE ACT:** Broker, Appraiser, Developer; **SERVICES:** Valuation, mktg. analysis, fin. analysis of resort hotel, comml. projects and condo. projects; **REP CLIENTS:** Lenders, investment bankers; **PREV EMPLOY:** RE Research Corp., 1965-69; **PROFL AFFIL & HONORS:** AIREA, SREA, ULI, MAI, SRPA, AIREA Profl. Recognition Award; **EDUC:** BS, 1960, Acctg., Univ. of AZ; **GRAD EDUC:** MBA, 1965, Fin., Univ. of AZ; **HOME ADD:** 425 Portlock Rd., Honolulu, HI 96825, (808)395-2704; **BUS ADD:** Suite 1800, 841 Bishop St., Honolulu, HI 96813, (803)524-1700.

HASTINGS, Robert L.——**B:** May 18, 1925, Kenosha, WI, *Pres.*, Foremost Guaranty Corp.; **OTHER RE ACT:** Mort. guaranty ins., RE; **SERVICES:** Consultant; **PREV EMPLOY:** Exec. VP Continental Mort. Ins.; **PROFL AFFIL & HONORS:** AIREA, SREA, Mort. Ins. Cos. of Amer., MAI, SREA, 1978 Intl. Pres. of SREA; **EDUC:** BS, 1949, Econ., Univ. of WI; **GRAD EDUC:** 1964, Univ. of WI, Grad. Sch. of Banking; **MIL SERV:** Army Air Force, S/Sgt., Air Medal with 2 clusters, European Theatre, 7 Battle Stars; **OTHER ACT & HONORS:** Kenosha, WI Bd. of Educ., 1956-62; Tr. Village of Shorewood Hills, WI, 1981; Rotary Club of Downtown Madison; **HOME ADD:** 3549 Lake Mendota Dr., Madison, WI 53705, (608)238-0468; **BUS ADD:** 131 W Wilson St., Madison, WY 53703, (608)251-2200.

HATCH, Henry R.——*Secy.*, Acme Cleveland Corp.; **PRIM RE ACT:** Property Manager; **BUS ADD:** 1242 East 49th St., PO Box 5617, Cleveland, OH 44101, (216)431-3120.*

HATCH, Michael W.——**B:** Nov. 19, 1949, Pittsfield, MA, *Partner*, Foley & Lardner; **PRIM RE ACT:** Attorney; **SERVICES:** Atty. and counselor to RE lenders, investors, developers; **REP CLIENTS:** Instnl. lenders, instnl. and indiv. investors in comml. and multi-family resid. props.; **PROFL AFFIL & HONORS:** WI Mort. Bankers Assn.; ABA; WI and NY State Bar Assns.; **EDUC:** BS, 1971, Econs., St. Lawrence Univ., Canton, NY 13617; **GRAD EDUC:** JD, 1974, Bus., Tax, RE, Yale Law School, New Haven, CT; **EDUC HONORS:** Magna Cum Laude, Phi Beta Kappa, Omicron Delta Kappa; **OTHER ACT & HONORS:** Dir. of Milwaukee Mgmt. Servs. Org.; Sigma Chi Frat; **HOME ADD:** 324 E. Lexington Blvd., Milwaukee, WI 53217, (414)962-8608; **BUS ADD:** 777 E. Wisconsin Ave., Milwaukee, WI 53202, (414)271-2400.

HATCH, Philip E.——**B:** Mar. 30, 1945, Neptune, NJ, *RE Mgr.*, McDonald's Corp.; **PRIM RE ACT:** Developer; **OTHER RE ACT:** Retail site devel.; **SERVICES:** Site & market analysis, prop. analysis, negotiations, zoning & planning reviews; **REP CLIENTS:** McDonald's Corp.; **PREV EMPLOY:** Hanson Devel. Co. 1973-1974; Chase Manhattan Bank 1971-1973; **PROFL AFFIL & HONORS:** RE Bd. of NY, Mu Gamma Tau (Mgmt. - honors) NY Univ.; **EDUC:** BS, 1971, Mgmt., NY Univ.; **GRAD EDUC:** MBA, 1978, Fin., Fairleigh Dickinson Univ.; **EDUC HONORS:** Dean's List; **MIL SERV:** USAF, Sgt.; **HOME ADD:** 137 Montclair Ave., Montclair, NJ 07042, (201)746-3673; **BUS ADD:** 1455 Broad St., Bloomfield, NJ 07003, (201)338-5300.

HATCH, William M.——**B:** Apr. 3, 1937, Spokane, WA, *Dir., RE Sch. of WA*, Audio Educational Systems, Inc.; **PRIM RE ACT:** Consultant, Owner/Investor, Instructor, Insuror, Syndicator; **OTHER RE ACT:** Educ. mgr. & counselor; **SERVICES:** RE & ins. license prep., continuing educ., counseling & spec. seminars; **PREV EMPLOY:** Lecturer, Univ. of MD, Germany; Instr. Univ. of OR; Asst. Prof. Allegheny Coll., Meadville, PA; **PROFL AFFIL & HONORS:** Affiliate Member Spokane Bd. of Realtors & member of RE Educators Assn., Hold licenses in life/health ins., prop., & casualty ins., securities & RE; **EDUC:** BA, 1963, Hist & Languages, Gonzaga Univ. & Whitworth Coll., Spokane, WA; **GRAD EDUC:** MA, 1966, Central European, Soviet & Near Eastern Hist., Univ. of WA & Stanford Univ.; PhD, 1973, Stanford Univ.; **EDUC HONORS:** Cum Laude, Stanford Grad. Scholarship & Ford Foundation Study Grant; **MIL SERV:** US Army, Parachutist; **OTHER ACT & HONORS:** Spokane C of C; **HOME ADD:** W. 414 Euclid, Spokane, WA 99205; **BUS ADD:** N. 4601 Monroe, Suite 306, Spokane, WA 99205, (509)325-2587.

HATHAWAY, Daniel A.——**B:** Sept. 25, 1952, Detroit, MI, *Gen. Counsel*, Boileau & Johnson, RE Investment Co.; **PRIM RE ACT:** Consultant, Attorney, Instructor, Syndicator; **SERVICES:** Counsel to the firm in RE, synd., taxation; **PREV EMPLOY:** Law firm - Jennings & Campbell, La Jolla, CA; **PROFL AFFIL & HONORS:** CA State Bar Assn., San Diego Cty. Bar Assn.; **EDUC:** BA, 1976, Poli. Sci., San Francisco State Univ.; **GRAD EDUC:** JD, 1979, RE, Taxation, Univ. of San Diego; **EDUC HONORS:** Member Pi Sigma Alpha Nat. Poli. Sci. Honors Soc., Magna Cum Laude, Member San Diego Law Review 1978-79; **HOME ADD:** 4885 Lorraine Dr, San Diego, CA 92115, (714)287-6240; **BUS ADD:** 1347 Broadway, El Cajon, CA 92101, (714)579-8401.

HATHAWAY, James E., Jr——**B:** Aug. 18, 1935, Kansas City, MO, *Pres.*, Hathaway, Moore & Assoc.; **PRIM RE ACT:** Broker, Instructor, Syndicator, Consultant, Developer, Property Manager; **PREV EMPLOY:** IBM, VP Pathfinder Ins. Co., Exec. VP Rector, Phillips Morse, Inc.; **PROFL AFFIL & HONORS:** NAR, RNMI, AR Realtors Assoc.; **EDUC:** BA, 1956, Univ. of KS; **OTHER ACT & HONORS:** Little Rock C of C, Past VP, United Way, YMCA (Past Dir.), Past VP Little Rock Jaycees; **HOME ADD:** 3901 Cedar Hill Rd., Little Rock, AR 72202; **BUS ADD:** 1210 Worthen Bank Bldg., Little Rock, AR 72201, (501)372-1700.

HATHAWAY, Louis E., III——**B:** Sept. 16, 1936, Springfield, MA, *VP, RE and Morts.*, The Manhattan Life Insurance Co.; **PRIM RE ACT:** Consultant, Appraiser, Lender, Property Manager; **OTHER RE ACT:** Leasing; **PREV EMPLOY:** VP, RE and Mort. at The Union Dime Savings Bank, 1960-1977; **PROFL AFFIL & HONORS:** Amer. Arbitra. Assn.; Bd. of Dir., Nat. Assn. of Cert. Mort. Bankers; Treas., MBA of NY; RE Bd. of NY (Past Chmn., Mort. Comm.); MBAA, Distinguished Fellow, Nat. Assn. of Cert. Mort. Bankers; **EDUC:** BA, 1960, Intl. Relations, Brown Univ.; **MIL SERV:** U.S. Army, SP-4, 1958-1964; **OTHER ACT & HONORS:** Union League Club; Wee Burn Ctry. Club; Advisory Bd., NY Univ. Mort. Inst.; **HOME ADD:** 39 Leeuwarden Rd., Darien, CT 06820, (203)327-3890; **BUS ADD:** 111 W. 57th St., NY, NY 10019, (212)484-9525.

HATHORNE, Gerald——*Mgr. RE Dept.*, Polaroid Corp.; **PRIM RE ACT:** Property Manager; **BUS ADD:** 575 Technology Square, Cambridge, MA 02139, (617)577-2000.*

HATTER, Larry L.——**B:** May 1, 1948, Gratz, PA, *Secretary Treasurer*, Stor-Mor Warehousing; **PRIM RE ACT:** Broker, Developer, Builder, Owner/Investor, Property Manager; **SERVICES:** Develop & gen. contract ind. & comml. warehousing, prop. mgmt.; **PREV EMPLOY:** Self employed in own RE devel. or brokerage firm since grad. from coll.; **PROFL AFFIL & HONORS:** RESSI; Self Service Storage Assn.; NAR; **EDUC:** BS in Bus. Admin., 1970, Acctg. & Econ., PA State Univ.; **HOME ADD:** 833 Meadow Ln., Camp Hill, PA 17011; **BUS ADD:** 191 Salem Church Road, Mechanicsburg, PA 17055, (717)697-

4476.

HATTIS, Bernard S.——B: Dec. 8, 1920, Chicago, IL, *Pres.*, The Hattis Associates, Inc.; **PRIM RE ACT:** Engineer, Developer; **OTHER RE ACT:** Planner; **SERVICES:** Studies, design, devel., mgmt. and operation; **PREV EMPLOY:** C of E, USA; **PROFL AFFIL & HONORS:** ASME; ASHRAE; **EDUC:** BS, 1939, Mech. Engrg., Univ. of IL; BS, 1941, Mil. Sci. and Tactics, Northwestern Univ.; **GRAD EDUC:** MCE, 1941, Heat/Power Engr., Northwestern Univ., CO School of Mines; ED, 1943, Mil. Engr., Northwestern Univ., CO School of Mines; **EDUC HONORS:** Eshbach Award, Chas. T. Main Award; **MIL SERV:** USA & USN, Brig. Gen., 27 decorations and awards; **OTHER ACT & HONORS:** Bds. & Comms. of 7 Nat. and Intl. Orgs.; **HOME ADD:** 100 Wilmot Rd., Deerfield, IL 60015, (312)945-8104; **BUS ADD:** POB 44, 100 Wilmot Rd., Deerfield, IL 60015, (312)945-8100.

HAUCH, Larry——*Mgr. RE*, Whirlpool Corp.; **PRIM RE ACT:** Property Manager; **BUS ADD:** Administrative Center, 2000 U.S. 33 N., Benton Harbor, MI 49022, (616)926-3354.*

HAUCK, Adam L.——B: Sept. 6, 1931, W. Germany, *Realtor*, Adam L. Hauck, Realtor, Investment; **PRIM RE ACT:** Broker, Consultant, Syndicator; **SERVICES:** Buyer's broker; motels, shopping centers, office bldgs.; **PROFL AFFIL & HONORS:** NAR, FL Assn. of Realtors, RNMI, RESSI, FL RE Exchangors, VP Brevard RE Exchange; **EDUC:** AAS, 1978, Sci., Rollins Coll., Air Univ.; **MIL SERV:** USAF, Numerous Decorations; **OTHER ACT & HONORS:** Amer. Meteorological Soc.; **HOME ADD:** 445 Island Dr., Merritt Island, FL 32952, (305)453-0582; **BUS ADD:** 445 Island Dr., Merritt Island, FL 32952, (305)453-0582.

HAUER, James A.——B: Apr. 3, 1924, Fond du Lac, WI, *Atty.*, James A. Hauer, P.C.; **PRIM RE ACT:** Broker, Consultant, Attorney, Developer, Syndicator; **SERVICES:** Legal & fin. consulting; **PREV EMPLOY:** Self employed atty., Patent engr., consultant; **PROFL AFFIL & HONORS:** ABA, WI Bar Assn., Waukesha Cty. Bar Assn., Doctor of Laws, Bachelor of Civil Engrg.; **EDUC:** BCE, 1947, Marquette Coll. of Engrg.; **GRAD EDUC:** JD, Marquette Univ. Law Sch.; **EDUC HONORS:** Licensed US Patent Atty.; **HOME ADD:** 1090 Red Barn Ln., Elm Grove, WI 53122; **BUS ADD:** 1090 Red Barn Ln., Elm Grove, WI 53122, (414)786-6747.

HAUETER, Jack——B: Nov. 30, 1924, Milwaukee, WI, *Chmn. of Bd.*, Semco Corp., Forest Hill Assoc.; **PRIM RE ACT:** Broker, Consultant, Developer, Instructor, Syndicator; **REP CLIENTS:** Corps. and ind. investors; **EDUC:** BS, 1950, Civil and Soils Engrg., Agr., Univ. of WI, Madison; **MIL SERV:** USN, OM2/c, Afr-Eur, Aisa Pac- Phil. GCM, PH, LSM; **BUS ADD:** 2800 S Chicago Ave., S Milwaukee, WI 53152, (414)762-0212.

HAUGEN, Odd E.——B: Jan. 16, 1950, Norway, *Pres.*, Albany Hill Fin. Corp., ERA Albany Hill Realty; **PRIM RE ACT:** Broker, Syndicator; **OTHER RE ACT:** Comml. investment; **SERVICES:** Brokerage & Consulting; **REP CLIENTS:** Indivs.; **PROFL AFFIL & HONORS:** NAR, CAR, RESSI, CAI, FIABCI, CCIM of RNMI; **EDUC:** BS, 1973, Physiology of Exercise, W. MD Coll.; **GRAD EDUC:** MBA, 1977, Fin. & RE, Univ. of CA, Berkeley; **EDUC HONORS:** Dept. Hon., Cum Laude; **HOME ADD:** 513 Melinda Ct., El Sobrante, CA 94803, (415)222-4894; **BUS ADD:** 555 Pierce St., CML 4, Albany, CA 94706, (415)525-7640.

HAUGHEY, Philip C.——B: Mar. 25, 1935, Waltham, MA, *Pres.*, The Haughey Company; **PRIM RE ACT:** Syndicator, Developer, Property Manager, Owner/Investor; **PREV EMPLOY:** Jewel Cos.(Star Market Div., Boston MA); **PROFL AFFIL & HONORS:** ICSC; **EDUC:** AB, 1957, Hist.-Govt., Harvard Coll.; **HOME ADD:** 201 Kent Rd., Waban, MA 02168, (617)527-2883; **BUS ADD:** 2464 Mass. Ave., Cambridge, MA 02168, (617)491-8500.

HAUS, J. Gilbert, Jr.——B: May 31, 1937, Baltimore, MD, *Dir. of Sales*, Dickinson-Heffner, Inc.; **PRIM RE ACT:** Consultant, Engineer, Architect, Developer, Builder, Owner/Investor, Property Manager; **SERVICES:** Builder, devel., investor, prop. mgmt.; **PREV EMPLOY:** VP Sales & Mktg., Howard Research & Devel. Co.; **PROFL AFFIL & HONORS:** Nat. Assn. of Indus. and Office Parks; SIR; **EDUC:** BA, 1959, Econ., Univ. of VA; **EDUC HONORS:** Imp Society, TILKA; **MIL SERV:** US Army, Infantry, 1st Lt.; **HOME ADD:** 1818 Ruxton Rd., Ruxton, MD 21204, (301)828-8522; **BUS ADD:** POB 8691, B.W.I. Airport, Baltimore, MD 21240, (301)796-2550.

HAUSMAN, Bruce——B: Mar. 4, 1930, New York, NY, *Sr. VChmn., Chmn. of the Exec. Comm.*, Belding Heminway Co., Inc.; **PRIM RE ACT:** Attorney, Owner/Investor; **PROFL AFFIL & HONORS:** Counsel to Herschcopf & Stevenson, 230 Park Ave., NYC, NY 10169; **EDUC:** BA, 1951, Econ., Brown Univ.; **GRAD EDUC:** MS, 1952, Mgmt. & Mktg., Columbia Univ. - Grad. School of Bus.; JD, 1979, NY Law School; **HOME ADD:** 860 United Nations Plaza, New York, NY 10017; **BUS ADD:** 1430 Broadway, New York, NY 10018, (212)944-6040.

HAUSMAN, Nancy Harrelson——B: Nov. 30, 1954, Paris, TN, *Atty. at Law*, Nancy Harrelson Hausman; **PRIM RE ACT:** Attorney; **PROFL AFFIL & HONORS:** ABA, Div. of RE, Probate and Trust, Banking Div.; TX Bar Assn., Div. of RE, Probate and Trust; **EDUC:** BA, 1975, Pol. Sci. and French, Univ. of MS; **GRAD EDUC:** JD, 1977, Univ. of MS; LLM, 1979, Yale Univ.; **EDUC HONORS:** Who's Who in Amer. Colls.; Hall of Fame; Phi Kappa Phi; Mortar Bd.; Magna Cum Laude, Valedictorian; Honor Council; 9 Amer. Jurisprudence Awards; Dean Farley Award; West Publishing Co. Award for hightest 2nd and third year average; **OTHER ACT & HONORS:** Bd. of Dirs., Frontier State Bank, Eagle Pass, TX; **HOME ADD:** 675 Main, Eagle Pass, TX 78852, (512)773-8873; **BUS ADD:** 675 Main St., Eagle Pass, TX 78852, (512)773-6700.

HAUSMAN, Sidney——B: Dec. 11, 1919, Bethlehem, PA, *Pres.*, Property Equities Corp.; **PRIM RE ACT:** Broker, Consultant, Owner/Investor, Syndicator; **SERVICES:** Investment Counseling, Synd. of Comml. Prop.; **EDUC:** BS, 1941, Bus. and Journalism, PA State Univ.; **EDUC HONORS:** Alpha Delta Sigma; **MIL SERV:** USAF, Lt.; **HOME ADD:** 6831 SW 147th Ave., Miami, FL 33193, (305)382-2020; **BUS ADD:** Sunset Center, 10300 S.W. 72nd St., Suite 165, Miami, FL 33173, (305)598-1333.

HAUSMANN, John E.——*VP*, Continental Bank, RE - Comml. Division; **PRIM RE ACT:** Banker, Lender; **EDUC:** BA, 1966, Econ., Union Coll.; **GRAD EDUC:** MBA, 1970, Univ. of VA; **OTHER ACT & HONORS:** Village Pres., LaGrange; **BUS ADD:** 231 S. LaSalle St., Chicago, IL 60693, (312)828-6270.

HAVEL, William A.——B: July 25, 1941, Detroit, MI, *Dir.*, Oakland Property Managers; **PRIM RE ACT:** Consultant, Owner/Investor, Instructor, Property Manager, Syndicator; **OTHER RE ACT:** Tax Consultant, Fin. Planner, RE Sales; **SERVICES:** RE synd., exchanges, tax planning; **REP CLIENTS:** High tax bracket investors; **PREV EMPLOY:** Tax consultant, fin. planner, RE sales; **PROFL AFFIL & HONORS:** CDP; **EDUC:** BS, 1964, Purchasing & Material Control, Gen. Motors Instit., Flint, MI; **GRAD EDUC:** MBA, Bus. Admin., 1970, Operations Research, Wayne State Univ., Detroit, MI; **OTHER ACT & HONORS:** Jaycees, VP of Oakland Landlords Assn., Legislative Rep. to MLA (MI Landlords Assn.), Jr. Achievement Advisor; **HOME ADD:** 4610 Fiddle Lake Rd., Pontiac, MI 48054, (313)682-8844; **BUS ADD:** 611 N. Lapeer Rd. P O Box 555, Lake Orion, MI 48035, (313)682-8844.

HAVEMEYER, John F., III——B: May 26, 1939, Syracuse, NY, *Pres.*, Appraisal Research, Inc./Upstate Home Inspection; **PRIM RE ACT:** Appraiser; **OTHER RE ACT:** Building inspections; **SERVICES:** Appraisals and inspections; **REP CLIENTS:** Homequity, Bank of NY, Binghamton Savings, Key Bank, Equitable Life, NYS Teachers Retirement Executrans; **PREV EMPLOY:** Pomeroy Appraisal Associates; **PROFL AFFIL & HONORS:** AIREA; Soc. of RE Appraisers, MAI; SRPA; **EDUC:** BS, 1963, Psych./Econ., Allegheny Coll.; **GRAD EDUC:** MAI, 1977, Appraisal, Univ. of GA; SRPA, 1978, Appraisal, Univ. of DE, Univ. of CT; **OTHER ACT & HONORS:** Pres., Chap. 148, Soc. RE Appraisers, 1979-1980; **HOME ADD:** Eibert Rd., Skaneafeles, NY 13152, (315)685-7573; **BUS ADD:** Loew Bldg., Suite 405, Syracuse, NY 13202, (315)471-3840.

HAVERTY, Harold——*Exec. VP & Chief Oper. Officer*, Deluxe Check Printers, Inc.; **PRIM RE ACT:** Property Manager; **BUS ADD:** PO Box 43399, St. Paul, MN 55164, (612)483-7111.*

HAWEKOTTE, John William, Jr.——B: Feb. 26, 1948, Chicago, IL; **PRIM RE ACT:** Broker, Consultant, Attorney, Syndicator; **OTHER RE ACT:** CPA; **SERVICES:** Tax & investment counseling, synd.; **PREV EMPLOY:** Arthur Andersen & Co., PMA Props. & Investments; **PROFL AFFIL & HONORS:** ABA, CA State Bar Assn., AICPA, Atty., CPA, RE Broker; **EDUC:** BS, 1970, Acctg., Univ. of Santa Clara; **GRAD EDUC:** JD, 1978, UCLA Sch. of Law; **EDUC HONORS:** Beta Gamma Sigma, Managing Ed., UCLA Law Review 1977-78; **MIL SERV:** USA, 1st Lt., 1971-73; **HOME TEL:** (714)773-4339; **BUS ADD:** 230 Kensington Ln., La Habra, CA 90631, (714)870-1155.

HAWES, George D.——B: July 17, 1944, Neptune, NJ, *VP*, Citibank, NA, Govt. Securities Dealer Div.; **OTHER RE ACT:** RE Fin.; **SERVICES:** Dealer in Govt. Guaranteed Mort. Backed Securities; **REP CLIENTS:** Lomas and Nettleton, Mort. Assocs., Colonial Mort. Serv. Co., Cameron Brown Co., Bankers Mort.; **PREV EMPLOY:** Lending Officer, Citibank Portfolio Mgr., Citibank; **EDUC:** BS, 1966,

Fin., Lehigh Univ., Bethlehem, PA; **MIL SERV:** USMC, Maj., DFC, Navy Commendation; **OTHER ACT & HONORS:** USMC Public Affairs Unit, NYC, NY; Phi Gamma Delta Alumni Assn.; **HOME ADD:** 29 Hemlock Dr., N. Tarrytown, NY 10591, (914)631-2606; **BUS ADD:** 55 Water St., NYC, NY 10043, (212)668-3917.

HAWK, James J.——B: Apr. 4, 1942, Long Beach, CA, *VP*, Hoffman Assocs., Incorporated; **PRIM RE ACT:** Consultant, Property Manager; **OTHER RE ACT:** Bus. Mgmt. RE, Investment Mgmt., RE Counseling; **SERVICES:** Acquisition & private placement, RE asset mgmt. and investment counseling for pension funds; **REP CLIENTS:** Family Trusts & Found., Pension Funds, Corp. & other bus mgrs.; **PREV EMPLOY:** Prop. Research Fin. Corp.; **PROFL AFFIL & HONORS:** ASREC, LA Bd. of Realtors, CA Assn. of Realtors, NAR, Counselor of RE (CRE); **EDUC:** BA, 1966, Poli. Sci. Bus., Univ. of S. CA; **GRAD EDUC:** MBA, 1971, Fin. & Acctg., Univ. of S. CA; **OTHER ACT & HONORS:** Chmn. & Past Pres. of Commerce Assn., Support group for the Univ. of S. CA School of Bus. Admin.; **HOME ADD:** 2126 Courtland Ave., San Marino, CA 91108, (213)799-4444; **BUS ADD:** 626 Wilshire Blvd., Suite 1024, Los Angeles, CA 90017, (213)620-0621.

HAWKE, Richard D.——B: Apr. 10, 1951, St. Paul, MN, *Atty.*, Roedler, Bellows & Hughes; **PRIM RE ACT:** Attorney, Syndicator; **SERVICES:** Legal Services, Title Opinions, Investment Counseling, and Synd.; **REP CLIENTS:** Lenders and Indiv. Investors; **PREV EMPLOY:** Prop. Mgmt. and Acctg. Work; **PROFL AFFIL & HONORS:** ABA, RE and Trust Sect. and Tax Sect., MN State Bar Assn., MA Bar Assn., the Assn. of Trial Lawyers of Amer.; **EDUC:** BA, 1973, Poli. Sci., St. Olaf Coll.; **GRAD EDUC:** JD, 1976, Boston Univ.; **EDUC HONORS:** Blue Key Honor Soc.; **OTHER ACT & HONORS:** Admitted to practice before the MN Supreme Ct., MA Supreme Judicial Ct., US Dist. Ct., US Tax Ct., Citizens League; **HOME ADD:** 293 Ryan Ave., St. Paul, MN 55102, (612)225-0084; **BUS ADD:** 435 Hamm Bldg., St. Paul, MN 55102, (612)291-8015.

HAWKEY, G. Michael——B: Apr. 17, 1941, Montclair, NJ, *Atty. (Partner)*, Sullivan & Worcester; **PRIM RE ACT:** Broker, Attorney, Owner/Investor; **REP CLIENTS:** Fidelity Mgmt. & Research Co. (FMR Props., Inc.); Prospect Hill Exec. Office Park; Newton-Wellesley Exec. Office Park; Victor Realty Devel. Co.; Raymond Cattle Co.; Bay Bank Harvard Trust Co.; Bay Bank Boston; Boston Water & Sewer Commission; Boscom; **PROFL AFFIL & HONORS:** Greater Boston RE Bd. (firm membership); MA Convegancers Assn.; **EDUC:** BA, 1963, Econ., Princeton Univ.; **GRAD EDUC:** LLB, 1967, Law, Cornell Univ.; **EDUC HONORS:** Cum Laude; **OTHER ACT & HONORS:** Various directorships & local Mcpl. Bds.; **HOME ADD:** 26 Arlington Rd., Wellesley, MA, (617)235-7074; **BUS ADD:** Post Office Square, Boston, MA 02109, (617)338-2800.

HAWKINS, Adolphus W., Jr.——B: Mar. 4, 1922, Culpeper, VA, *VP*, Scott & Strinefellow Inc., RE/Corp. Fin.; **PRIM RE ACT:** Broker; **OTHER RE ACT:** Merger/acquisition specialist of co. selling/buying; **SERVICES:** Brokerage; **EDUC:** BA, 1948, Econ., The Univ. of VA; **GRAD EDUC:** Poli. Sci., Balliol Coll., Oxford Univ., England; **MIL SERV:** USN, Pac. in WWII; **HOME ADD:** 3808 Dover Rd., Windsor Farms, Richmond, VA 23221, (804)353-6485; **BUS ADD:** 909 E. Main St., Mutual Bldg., PO Box 1575, Richmond, VA 23213, (804)643-1811.

HAWKINS, Barry C.——B: Oct. 7, 1943, Portland, ME, *Partner*, Tyler Cooper Grant Bowerman & Keefe, Managing Partner of Stanford Office; **PRIM RE ACT:** Attorney; **SERVICES:** Represent assns., devels. and lenders; **REP CLIENTS:** Fountainwood Condominium; Ocean View Condominium; Rivers Edge Development Company; CT Savings Bank; The Ledges (Planned Unit Development) Assn.; **PROFL AFFIL & HONORS:** Bd. of Dir., CT Chap. Community Assn., Inst., Inc.; ABA and CT Bar Assn.; **EDUC:** BA, 1965, Hist., Bowdoin Coll.; **GRAD EDUC:** JD, 1968, edg JD, Univ. of VA Law School; **EDUC HONORS:** Honors in Hist.; **MIL SERV:** US Army, Capt., Bronze Star; **OTHER ACT & HONORS:** Chmn., United Way Allocations Comm.; Quinnipiack Club; Landmark Club; **HOME ADD:** 4 Rainey Lane, Westport, CT 06880, (203)222-0120; **BUS ADD:** 3 Landmark Sq., Stamford, CT 06901, (203)348-5555.

HAWKINS, Barry Michael——B: Nov. 20, 1945, Charlottesville, VA, *VP, Mortg. Loan Dept.*, Liberty Life Insurance Co., Investment Div.; **PRIM RE ACT:** Appraiser, Lender; **SERVICES:** First mort. loans; comml. income props., SE USA and on a limited basis income prop. joint venture fin.; **REP CLIENTS:** Indiv. and/or instit. investors in comml. income props.; **PROFL AFFIL & HONORS:** Member of the MBA of America and the MBA of the Carolinas, A Lic. RE Broker (South Carolina), Sr. Member (CRA) of the NARA; **EDUC:** BA, 1968, Econ., Univ. of VA; **GRAD EDUC:** MBA, 1972, Mktg., Univ. of VA - Colgate Darden Grad. School of Bus. Admin.; **MIL SERV:** US Army, E-5 Sgt., 1968-1970; **HOME ADD:** 198 Hudson Rd., Greenville, SC 29615, (803)288-7686; **BUS ADD:** P O Box 789, Greenville, SC 29602, (803)268-8230.

HAWKINS, Paul Minor, Jr.——B: July 22, 1923, Snow Hill, MD, *Gen. Mgr.*, Grossklag/Better Homes and Gardens, Resid.; **PRIM RE ACT:** Broker, Appraiser, Instructor; **OTHER RE ACT:** Relocation Dir.; faculty member, RE Educ. Co.; **PREV EMPLOY:** Priest of the Episcopal Church (active 24 years); **PROFL AFFIL & HONORS:** Pres., Fox Valley Bd. of Realtors, GRI, CRB; **EDUC:** BA, 1947, Eng. Lit., Univ. of the South, Sewanee, TN; **GRAD EDUC:** M.Div., 1950, Theology, Seabury-Western Theological Seminary, Evanston, IL; **EDUC HONORS:** Optime Merins; **MIL SERV:** US Army, Cpl., E.T.O. & G.C.; **OTHER ACT & HONORS:** Hinds Cty. Bd. of Mental Health (MS) 1970-72, Sons of the Amer. Revolution, Lions Club, V.F.W.; **HOME ADD:** 1596 Kirkwood Dr., Geneva, IL 60134, (312)232-4432; **BUS ADD:** 401 W. State St., Geneva, IL 60134, (312)232-6100.

HAWKINS, Preston——B: Apr. 2, 1951, Pasadena, CA, *Pres.*, Herbert Hawkins Co., Inc.; **PRIM RE ACT:** Broker, Consultant, Attorney; **PREV EMPLOY:** CA Land Title Co., Trinity Mort. Co.; **PROFL AFFIL & HONORS:** NAR, CA Assn. Realtors, ABA, CA State Bar Assn., Fed. Bar, JD; **EDUC:** BSBA, 1973, Fin./RE, Univ. S CA; **GRAD EDUC:** JD, 1978, Pepperdine Univ. School of Law; **EDUC HONORS:** Dean's List; **BUS ADD:** 5770 N Rosemead Blvd., Temple City, CA 91780, (213)285-9811.

HAWKINS, Richard M.——B: July 23, 1949, Nevada City, CA, Richard M. Hawkins; **PRIM RE ACT:** Attorney; **SERVICES:** RE law, probate, estate planning; **PROFL AFFIL & HONORS:** CA State Bar Assn., ABA, NV Cty. Bar Assn.; **EDUC:** BS, 1971, Math., Univ. of CA at Davis; **GRAD EDUC:** JD, 1974, Univ. of CA, Hastings Coll. of the Law; **EDUC HONORS:** Phi Kappa Phi, Top 10% of grad. class, Order of the Coif, Thurston Hon. Soc. of Hastings Coll. of the Law, Top 10% of grad. class; **HOME ADD:** 13343 Red Dog Rd., NV City, CA 95959, (916)265-5667; **BUS ADD:** 305 Railroad Ave., Suite 10, NV City, CA 95959, (916)265-6908.

HAWLEY, Clifton H., III——B: Apr. 8, 1947, Savannah, GA, *VP-RE*, Watkins Associated Industries, Pres.-First South Realty, Inc., VP-Wilwat Properties; **PRIM RE ACT:** Broker, Developer; **SERVICES:** Devel., Mgmt., Fin. & Brokerage; **REP CLIENTS:** Primarily for various subsidiaries of Watkins Assn. Inc.; **PREV EMPLOY:** 1973-1978, VP-Cousins Prop., Inc.; **PROFL AFFIL & HONORS:** NAOIP; **EDUC:** 1965-1968, Poli. Sci., Princeton; BA, 1968-1970, Econ., Univ. of GA; **GRAD EDUC:** MBA, 1974, Bus.-Fin., GA State; **HOME ADD:** 156 Lake Forrest Ln. NE, Atlanta, GA 30342, (404)255-7364; **BUS ADD:** PO Box 1738, Atlanta, GA 30371, (404)448-1033.

HAWTHORNE, R. Bradley——B: Sept. 12, 1948, Detroit, MI, *VP, Mgr.*, Cushman & Wakefield of MI, Inc.; **PRIM RE ACT:** Broker; **SERVICES:** Comml., office, indus., retail sales & leasing and investment sales; **PROFL AFFIL & HONORS:** Detroit Athletic Club, Econ. Club of Detroit, NACORE, S Oakland Cty. Bd. of Realtors; **EDUC:** BS, 1970, E MI Univ.; **GRAD EDUC:** MS, 1972, E MI Univ.; **OTHER ACT & HONORS:** Renaissance Club; Founders Soc. of Detroit Inst. of Arts; **HOME ADD:** 3861 Mystic Valley Dr., Bloomfield Hills, MI 48013, (313)642-1174; **BUS ADD:** American Ctr., 27777 Franklin Rd., Suite 700, Southfield, MI 48034, (313)353-5880.

HAWTHORNE, Randolph G.——B: Dec. 9, 1949, Ft. Lee, VA, *VP*, Boston Financial Technology Group, Inc.; **PRIM RE ACT:** Consultant, Owner/Investor, Property Manager, Syndicator; **REP CLIENTS:** Devels. and Investors of Multi-family Props.; **PREV EMPLOY:** With BFTG Since 1973; **EDUC:** SB, 1971, Mgmt., MIT; **GRAD EDUC:** MBA, 1973, Fin., Harvard Bus. School; **EDUC HONORS:** w/distinction; **MIL SERV:** US Army Res., Capt.; **OTHER ACT & HONORS:** Alumni Officer, MIT; **HOME ADD:** 99 Mason Terr., Brookline, MA 02146, (617)738-7618; **BUS ADD:** One Post Office Sq., Boston, MA 02109, (617)482-9790.

HAY, Jerry——B: Dec. 14, 1935, San Diego, CA, *Pres.*, Hawkins Devel. Co.; **PRIM RE ACT:** Syndicator; **OTHER RE ACT:** Devel., Prop. Mgmt.; **SERVICES:** Comml., indus. & resid. devel., synd. and prop. mgmt.; **PREV EMPLOY:** Pres. Dillingham Devel. Co.; **PROFL AFFIL & HONORS:** ULI, ICSC, Stanford Grad. Sch. of Bus. Alumni Assn.; **EDUC:** BA, 1957, Pol. Sci. & Econ., San Diego Univ.; **GRAD EDUC:** For. Serv., French Lang., European Pol. Sci., Univ. of Paris (Sorbonne); Adv. Mgmt., Stanford Grad. Sch. of Bus.; **MIL SERV:** USA, Lt.; **HOME ADD:** 7331 Stone Creek Ln., Anaheim, CA 92807, (714)998-3645; **BUS ADD:** 2001 E 1st St., Santa Ana, CA 92705, (714)953-0310.

HAY, Jess Thomas——**B:** Jan. 22, 1931, Forney, TX, *Chmn. and CEO*, Lomas & Nettleton Financial Corp.; **PRIM RE ACT:** Lender; **SERVICES:** Lomas & Nettleton Fin. Corp. provides comprehensive fin. serv. to the RE indus.; **PREV EMPLOY:** Law firm of Locke, Purnell, Boren, Laney & Neely, Dallas, TX - Assoc. from 1955 to 1961 and Partner from 1961 to 1965; **PROFL AFFIL & HONORS:** Amer., TX and Dallas Bar Assns.; Amer. Judicature Soc.; (Newcomer) Soc. of N. Amer.; **EDUC:** BBA, 1953, So. Methodist Univ., Dallas, TX; **GRAD EDUC:** JD, 1955, So. Methodist Univ. School of Law; **EDUC HONORS:** Magna Cum Laude; **OTHER ACT & HONORS:** Bd. of Tr. and Bd. of Govs., So. Methodist Univ.; Bd. of Regents, The Univ. of TX System; Member, Dallas Citizens Council, Dallas Council on World Affairs; Bd. of Dir., TX Research League; Treas., Greater Dallas Planning Council; **HOME ADD:** 7236 Lupton Cir., Dallas, TX 75225, (214)368-4059; **BUS ADD:** 2001 Bryan Tower, Suite 3600, Dallas, TX 75201, (214)746-7100.

HAYAKAWA, T. George——**B:** July 4, 1924, Los Angeles, CA, *Pres.*, Hayakawa Associates; **PRIM RE ACT:** Consultant, Engineer; **SERVICES:** Consulting mechanical and electrical engrg.; **REP CLIENTS:** CA State Univ. and Colls.; Jet Propulsion Lab.; **PROFL AFFIL & HONORS:** Amer. Soc. of Heating, Refrigerating & Air Conditioning Engrs.; CA Engrs. Assn. of CA; Mech. Engrs. Assn.; Amer. Consulting Engrs. Council; Nat. Soc. of Profl. Engrs.; CA Soc. of Profl. Engrs.; Inst. for Advancement of Engrg.; So. CA Solar Energy Assn., Fellow, Amer. Soc. of Heating, Refrigerating, and Air Conditioning Engrs., Inc.; Fellow, Inst. for the Advancement of Engrg.; **EDUC:** Bach. of Engrg., 1949, ME, Univ. of So. CA; **MIL SERV:** US Army, Sgt., 1944-1946; **OTHER ACT & HONORS:** Optimist Club; **HOME ADD:** 140O Via Del Rey, Pasadena, CA 91030, (213)258-1892; **BUS ADD:** 1180 S. Beverly Dr., Los Angeles, CA 90035, (213)879-4477.

HAYAUD DIN, M.A.——**B:** Feb. 6, 1947, Peshawer, Pakistan, *Project Mgr.*, Gerald D. Hines Interests, Devel.; **PRIM RE ACT:** Broker, Developer, Owner/Investor; **REP CLIENTS:** Shell Oil, TWA, Pillsbury, SE First Nat. Bank, First Nat. Bank of Chicago, Huntington Bank, United Bank of Denver, Texas Commerce Bank; **PREV EMPLOY:** McKinsey and Co., Inc., LaSalle Partners Inc., Citicorp; **PROFL AFFIL & HONORS:** AMASCE, AMICE, IL RE Broker; **EDUC:** B. Eng., 1968, Civil Engrg., Univ. of Peshawer; **GRAD EDUC:** 1970, Concrete Structures, City & Guilds Inst., Imperial Coll., London; 1975, Bus. Admin., Harvard Univ. Bus. Sch.; **EDUC HONORS:** 1st class hons., Aga Khan Fellow; **OTHER ACT & HONORS:** Univ. Club of Chicago, Harvard Club of NYC; **HOME ADD:** 3700 Alhambra Ct., Coral Gables, FL 33134; **BUS ADD:** Suite 3270, One Biscayne Tower, Miami, FL 33131, (305)371-6458.

HAYDEN, Bruce P.——**B:** Sept. 9, 1915, Saginaw, MI, *Pres.*, Hayden Associates, Inc.; **OTHER RE ACT:** RE Counselor; **SERVICES:** Place fin. for major projects; acquire income prop. for investors, including devel. strategies and programs, finding suitable prop., evaluating props. potentials, and in negotiations; evaluate RE problems and opportunities, the pros & cons of possible actions, recommend action to be taken; **REP CLIENTS:** corps., fin. inst., public agencies, investors, foreign and domestic, and devel.; **PREV EMPLOY:** CT Gen. Life Ins. Co., Mort. & RE Dept. 1938-72, Elected VP in 1965; **PROFL AFFIL & HONORS:** Amer. Soc. of RE Counselors; Tr. ULI; Corp. Prop. Investors; Dir. Schroder RE Corp. in NY and CBT Realty Co. in Hartford; RE Bd. of NY, Resid. appointment to Nat. Rent. Control Bd. 1972-73; **EDUC:** BS, 1938, US Naval Acad.; **MIL SERV:** USNR, Lt. C.; **HOME ADD:** 48 Mountain Terrace Rd., W Hartford, CT 06107, (203)521-6526; **BUS ADD:** 1 Regency Dr., PO Drawer 708, Bloomfield, CT 06002, (203)243-1481.

HAYDEN, J. Anthony, Jr.——**B:** Apr. 8, 1944, Philadelphia, PA, *Sr. VP, Branch Mgr. NE Rgnl. Dir.*, Cushman & Wakefield, Inc., Cushman & Wakefield of PA, Inc.; **PRIM RE ACT:** Broker, Consultant, Appraiser, Developer, Property Manager; **SERVICES:** Mgr. of full serv. nat. RE firm; **REP CLIENTS:** Buyers, sellers, tenants and landlords, all phases of RE; **PREV EMPLOY:** Partner in Indus. & Comml. RE Devel. firm; **PROFL AFFIL & HONORS:** SIR, Philadelphia Bd. of Realtors, Nat. Assn. of RE Brokers, PA Bd. of Realtors; **EDUC:** BS, 1967, Acctg., LaSalle Coll.; **MIL SERV:** USN, 3 yrs., Lt., Navy Commendation Medal, Vietnam; **OTHER ACT & HONORS:** Dir. St. Edmonds Home for Crippled Children, Dir. of Amer. Diabetes Assn.; **HOME ADD:** 1435 Monk Rd., Gladwyne, PA 19035, (215)649-3989; **BUS ADD:** 2000 Market St., 18th Fl., Philadelphia, PA 19103, (215)564-2400.

HAYDEN, J. David——**B:** Jan. 8, 1947, St. Louis, MO, Fox & Co., Taxation; **PRIM RE ACT:** Consultant, Regulator, Syndicator; **OTHER RE ACT:** CPA - Acct., Counselor, Securities & taxation; **SERVICES:** Investment counseling, structuring of RE synd.; **REP CLIENTS:** RE Dev. & promoters, owners/investors, builders of multi family & comml. props. (private placements); **PROFL AFFIL & HONORS:** RESSI; **EDUC:** BS, 1975, Bus. (Acctg.), So. IL Univ.; **MIL SERV:** USN, PO1, 1968-72; **OTHER ACT & HONORS:** Delta Sigma Pi; **HOME ADD:** 9038 Harvest Ln., Wichita, KS 67212, (316)722-2978; **BUS ADD:** 800 Fourth Fin. Ctr., Wichita, KS 67202, (316)265-3231.

HAYDEN, Mrs. Lee——**B:** Jan. 9, 1923, Norwood, CO, *Pres./Broker*, Hayden Realty, Inc.; **PRIM RE ACT:** Broker; **SERVICES:** Residential RE; **PREV EMPLOY:** Banking, Secretarial, RE Sales; **PROFL AFFIL & HONORS:** Dir. Boise Bd. of Realtors, Member of State and Nat. Bds., Member Million Dollar Club, CRS, CRB, GRI; **EDUC:** AS, 1942, Secretarial Sci., CO Women's Coll., Denver, CO; **GRAD EDUC:** Currently, Sr. Status, part-time, Bus. Admin., Boise State Univ., Boise, ID; **EDUC HONORS:** Dean's Honor Roll, 1941 & 1942, Delta Tau Kappa (Hon.); **HOME ADD:** 3116 Woodbrook Pl., Boise, ID 83706, (208)345-8189; **BUS ADD:** 1789 Broadway Ave., Boise, ID 83706, (208)344-7885.

HAYDEN, Ralph F.——**B:** Jan. 15, 1922, New York, NY, *Sr. VP*, King Kullen Grocery Co. Inc.; **PRIM RE ACT:** Consultant, Owner/Investor, Property Manager; **EDUC:** BBA, 1951, Acctg., Pace Univ.; **MIL SERV:** US Coast Guard, 1940-1944; **OTHER ACT & HONORS:** Sr. Partner, Hayden & Hayden, Public Acctg.; **BUS ADD:** 1194 Prospect Ave., Westbury, NY 11743, (516)333-7100.

HAYES, Byron, Jr.——**B:** July 9, 1934, Los Angeles, CA, *Part.*, McCutchen, Black, Verleger & Shea; **PRIM RE ACT:** Attorney; **SERVICES:** Represent mort. lenders and end users of RE; **PROFL AFFIL & HONORS:** ABA; CA Bar; Los Angeles Cty. Bar Assn. (VP of RE Sect.); Fin. Lawyers Conf., Assn. of RE Attys.; **EDUC:** BA, 1956, Econ., Pomona Coll.; **GRAD EDUC:** LLB, 1959, Law, Harvard Law School; **EDUC HONORS:** Magna Cum Laude, Phi Beta Kappa, Cum Laude; **MIL SERV:** US Army Res. Nat. Guard, Capt.; **HOME ADD:** 4256 Navajo St., Toluca Lake, CA 91602; **BUS ADD:** 600 Wilshire Blvd., Los Angeles, CA 90017, (213)624-2400.

HAYES, Daniel P.——**B:** Sept. 19, 1946, Flint, MI, *Pres.*, Ramsey-Shilling Comml. Brokerage Co.; **PRIM RE ACT:** Broker, Developer, Owner/Investor; **REP CLIENTS:** Union Fed. S&L Assn., Operating Engrs. Tr. Funds, Jacobs Engrg. Grp., Wolff-Sensen-Buttery, Classic Projects Corp.; **PROFL AFFIL & HONORS:** Los Angeles Realty Bd., NAR; **EDUC:** BS, 1970, Mktg., San Diego State Univ.; **HOME ADD:** 675 Magnolia Ave., Pasadena, CA 91106, (213)449-1819; **BUS ADD:** 3360 Barham Blvd., Los Angeles, CA 90068, (213)851-6666.

HAYES, Jed——**B:** May 18, 1955, Hartford, CT, *Pres.*, Sullivan, Hayes, & Company; **PRIM RE ACT:** Broker, Developer; **SERVICES:** Retail brokerage and devel., indus. brokerage and office bldg. devel.; **EDUC:** BA, 1978, RE and Const. Mgmt., Univ. of Denver; **HOME ADD:** 6483 B South Havana St., Englewood, CO 80111, (303)741-4180; **BUS ADD:** 1624 Market St., Suite 202, Denver, CO 80202, (303)534-5429.

HAYES, John P.——*Pres.*, National Gypsum Co.; **PRIM RE ACT:** Property Manager; **BUS ADD:** 4100 First International Bldg., Dallas, TX 75270, (214)653-8511.*

HAYES, Kerry——**B:** Nov. 17, 1947, Ashtabula, OH, *Mgr.*, Peat, Marwick, Mitchell & Co., RE and Recreation Practice; **PRIM RE ACT:** Consultant; **SERVICES:** Feasibility Market, Valuation, Fin. Studies; **REP CLIENTS:** Public and Pvt. Sector; **PROFL AFFIL & HONORS:** Inst. of Mgmt. Consultants, Cert. Mgmt. Consultant; **EDUC:** BIE, 1970, GA Inst. of Tech.; **GRAD EDUC:** MS Ind. Mgmt., 1973, GA Inst. of Technology; **EDUC HONORS:** AIIE, Alpha Pi Mu; **HOME ADD:** 300 Greenwood Dr., Key Biscayne, FL 33149, (305)361-1571; **BUS ADD:** 800 Brickell Ave., Miami, FL 33131, (305)358-2300.

HAYES, Larry G.——**B:** Nov. 16, 1941, Batesville, IN, *Exec. VP*, Amer. Institute of RE Appraisers; **OTHER RE ACT:** CEO-Assn.; **PREV EMPLOY:** Dir., Moser Bus. School, 1969-1974; **PROFL AFFIL & HONORS:** Member, Amer. Soc. of Assn. Execs.; Chicago Soc. of Assn. Execs.; Execs. Club of Chicago; **EDUC:** BA, 1965, Asbury Coll.; **HOME ADD:** 425 W. Wellington, Chicago, IL 60657, (312)327-3212; **BUS ADD:** 430 N. Michigan Ave., Chicago, IL 60611, (312)440-8161.

HAYES, William F.——**B:** Sept. 1, 1921, New Richmond, WI, *Pres.*, Hayes & Ferg, SC; **PRIM RE ACT:** Broker, Consultant, Developer, Builder, Owner/Investor, Property Manager, Insuror; **SERVICES:** Legal; **REP CLIENTS:** Modern Pole Bldrs., Inc., Ripon, WI; Zimmerman Bros., Inc., Marshfield, WI; Amer. Family Ins., Madison, WI; Ripon Devel. Co., Inc., Ripon; M&I Bank, Ripon, WI; First Nat. Bank of Ripon, WI; **PROFL AFFIL & HONORS:** Amer., WI, Fonddular Cty. Bar Assns.; WI Academy of Trial Lawyers; Amer. Trial

Lawyers; Defense Research Inst.; Member, Panel of Arbitrators, Amer. Arbitration Assn.; **EDUC:** BS, 1949, Sci., German & Econ., Univ. of WI, River Falls, WI; **GRAD EDUC:** LLD, 1954, Law, Marquette Univ.; **EDUC HONORS:** Silver R, Scholastic Achievement; **MIL SERV:** USMC; S/Sgt; 1942-1945 Pacific Theater; **HOME ADD:** Skyline Cir., Ripon, WI 54971, (414)748-3312; **BUS ADD:** 104 W. Jackson, Ripon, WI 54971, (414)748-5187.

HAYMAKER, Timothy L.——B: Aug. 30, 1947, Parkersburg, WV, *Mgr./RE Operations*, Ashland Oil, Inc.; **PRIM RE ACT:** Regulator, Consultant, Developer, Owner/Investor; **OTHER RE ACT:** Lease, sale & purchase of co. assets, tax deferred prop. exch.; **SERVICES:** Site eval., valuations, inv. analysis, dev., permits, involuntary condemnation proceedings; **REP CLIENTS:** Ind. & Mfg. Co.; Dev. & Inv. Co.; **PREV EMPLOY:** Broker & Part., Gainer, Kirtley, Haymaker & Co., Huntington, WV; **PROFL AFFIL & HONORS:** Ind. Dev. Research Council; Central OH Valley Ind. Council; ULI; **EDUC:** AB, 1969, Ed. Admin., Marshall Univ.; **EDUC HONORS:** Pres., Sigma Phi Epsilon; Omega Greek Honorary; U. Grant Dubach Award; **OTHER ACT & HONORS:** Bd. of Dir., Blue Grass Cerebral Palsy Ctr.; Marshall Univ. Alumni Assn.; Sigma Phi Epsilon Alumni Assn.; **HOME ADD:** 2016 Des Cognets Ln., Lexington, KY 40502, (606)266-0006; **BUS ADD:** POB 14000, Lexington, KY 40512, (606)268-7348.

HAYMAN, Alan J.——B: Aug. 19, 1942, Detroit, MI, *Sec./Treas.*, The Hayman Co.; **PRIM RE ACT:** Broker, Consultant, Attorney, Owner/Investor, Property Manager, Syndicator; **SERVICES:** Real prop. mgmt., brokerage, leasing; **REP CLIENTS:** Instnl. i.e., Equitable Life Assur.; Soc. of the US Mutual of NY; Great West Life; NY State Employees Retirement System; Grand Trunk R.R.; also, indivs. and investment grps. and investment ltd. partnerships; **PROFL AFFIL & HONORS:** MI State Bar; **EDUC:** BS, 1964, Hist., Wayne State Univ.; **GRAD EDUC:** JD, 1967, Law, Univ. of Detroit; **HOME ADD:** W. Bloomfield, MI 48033; **BUS ADD:** 22255 Greenfield, Southfield, MI 48075, (313)569-5555.

HAYMAN, Stephen P.——B: Aprl. 27, 1940, *Pres.*, The Hayman Co.; **PRIM RE ACT:** Broker, Consultant, Attorney, Owner/Investor, Property Manager, Syndicator; **REP CLIENTS:** Gr. W Life Assurance, NY State Employees Retirement System, Bank of Amer., Equitable Life Assurance Soc. of US; **GRAD EDUC:** JD, 1964, Univ. of Detroit; **BUS ADD:** 22255 Greenfield, Southfield, MI 48075, (312)569-5565.

HAYMES, Allan——B: Mar. 16, 1927, New York, NY, *Pres.*, Allan Haymes Assoc.; **PRIM RE ACT:** Broker, Consultant, Appraiser, Developer, Owner/Investor, Instructor, Syndicator; **OTHER RE ACT:** Author-*Homeowners Digest of RE Secrets* and writer of RE articles (gen.), "Wheeling & Dealing in Real Estate"; **PREV EMPLOY:** Consultant to the NY State Urban Devel. Corp. 1977-1978 for their indus., condo. in NYC; **PROFL AFFIL & HONORS:** NYS Soc. of RE Appraisers since 1958, Assoc. ass't prof. of RE, NYU; Contributing editor to the RER; **GRAD EDUC:** Defacto PHD; **MIL SERV:** USN; 1943-1945, Med. Corps. 1st Class, Europe/D Day Ribbon; **HOME ADD:** 210 Central Park S., NY, NY 10019, (212)586-8404; **BUS ADD:** 1776 Broadway, NY, NY 10019, (212)586-8404.

HAYNES, Richard R.——B: Jan. 19, 1932, Washington, IN, *Sr. VP & Chief Appraiser*, Workingmens Federal Savings & Loan Assn.; **PRIM RE ACT:** Lender; **PREV EMPLOY:** Equitable Life Assurance Soc. of the US; **PROFL AFFIL & HONORS:** MAI; Soc. of RE Appraisers; **EDUC:** BS, 1959, RE, IN Univ.; **GRAD EDUC:** 1971, S&L, IN Univ.; **MIL SERV:** US Air Force; S/Sgt.; **HOME ADD:** 1112 Nota Dr., Bloomington, IN 47401, (812)332-9915; **BUS ADD:** P O Box #906, Bloomington, IN 47401, (812)332-9465.

HAYS, William E.——B: July 6, 1926, Fairview, KS, *Pres.*, Northwest Christian Coll.; **PRIM RE ACT:** Broker, Developer, Owner/Investor, Instructor, Property Manager, Syndicator; **PREV EMPLOY:** Owner - Oakbrook Props.; **EDUC:** BA, 1957, Northwest Christian Coll.; **GRAD EDUC:** BD, 1966, LLD, 1978, Theology, Bus., Texas Christian Univ.; **HOME ADD:** 2896 Lydick Way, Eugene, OR 97401, (503)484-6157.

HAYWARD, Frank E.——B: Sept. 4, 1908, Sayville, NY, Coldwell Banker & Co.; **PRIM RE ACT:** Broker, Consultant, Banker; **PREV EMPLOY:** 30 yrs. with Coldwell Banker & Co.; **EDUC:** 1932, Petroleum Prod./Engrg., CO School of Mines; **GRAD EDUC:** MBA, 1934, Fin./Prod., Stanford Grad. School of Bus.; **MIL SERV:** USN; Cmdr., Unit Citation, Letter of Commendation, Service and Battle Decorations; **OTHER ACT & HONORS:** Tr., MA Mutual Mortgage & Realty Investors; Tr., CA Acad. of Sci.; Dir., Bowest Corp. (Subsd. Bowery Savings Bank); Dir., Dodge & Cox Stock Fund; Tr., Dodge & Cox Balanced Fund; **HOME ADD:** 5 W. Shore Rd., Benedere, CA 94920, (415)435-9950; **BUS ADD:** 351 California St., San Francisco, CA 94104, (415)397-7798.

HAYWARD, Sailing K.——B: Nov. 23, 1934, New York, NY, *VP - RE*, Crum & Forster Insurance Companies; **PRIM RE ACT:** Owner/Investor, Property Manager; **OTHER RE ACT:** Manage corp. const. projects, lease mgmt.; **PROFL AFFIL & HONORS:** RE Bd. of NY; NACORE; NY C of C; **EDUC:** BA, 1960, Indus. Psych., Lehigh Univ.; **MIL SERV:** USMC, Cpl.; **HOME ADD:** 236 Lurline Dr., W. Millington, NJ 07946, (201)647-5666; **BUS ADD:** 305 Madison Ave., Morristown, NJ 07960, (201)285-7451.

HAYWOOD, Robert A.——B: July 20, 1944, Durham, NC, *VP*, Wilma Realty Services, Inc., Asset Mgmt.; **PRIM RE ACT:** Broker, Consultant, Appraiser, Owner/Investor, Instructor, Property Manager; **SERVICES:** RE Mgmt., Leasing, Consulting; **PREV EMPLOY:** 10 yrs. The RE Bus., B.F. Saul R.E.I.T., First Union R.E.I.T., Coldwell Banker; **PROFL AFFIL & HONORS:** IREM, BOMA, Atlanta Bd. of Realtors, Soc. of Review Appraisers, SORPA, RPA, CRA; **EDUC:** BA, 1967, Geog. & Pol. Sci., Univ. of NC, Chapel Hill; **GRAD EDUC:** MBA, 1973, RE & Fin., GA State Univ.; **HOME ADD:** 1633 Eagles Mr., Marietta, GA 30067, (404)992-1179; **BUS ADD:** Suite 500, 233 Peachtree St., Atlanta, GA 30043, (404)953-4600.

HAZEN, Kenneth K.——B: Mar. 23, 1941, Newark, NJ, *Mgr. RE Devel.*, Aetna Life & Casualty, RE Investment Dept.; **PRIM RE ACT:** Developer, Owner/Investor, Property Manager; **SERVICES:** Selection of prop. for RE purchase and/or devel.; **REP CLIENTS:** Devel. & owners of investment grade RE; **EDUC:** BA, 1963, Lib. Arts., Econ. & Govt., Hamilton Coll.; **HOME ADD:** Mountain Ln., Farmington, CT 06032, (203)677-8143; **BUS ADD:** One Civic Ctr. Plaza, PO Box 1414, Hartford, CT 06143, (203)273-2373.

HAZEN, Russell J.——B: May 26, 1955, Brooklyn, NY, *Mort. Acctg.*, Troy Savings Bank, Mort.; **PRIM RE ACT:** Consultant, Appraiser, Banker, Lender, Owner/Investor, Property Manager; **OTHER RE ACT:** Salesman; **SERVICES:** Consulting, investment, mort. serv.; **REP CLIENTS:** Investors, gen. public; **PREV EMPLOY:** Del Palmer Appraisal Corp., Albany, NY; Moffit Hollis Realtors, Latham, NY; **EDUC:** AA, 1976, Acctg., Albany Bus. Coll.; **OTHER ACT & HONORS:** Cert. of Mort. Law I & II sponsored by MBA; **HOME ADD:** 4 Grotto Ct., Waterliet, NY 12189, (518)271-1131; **BUS ADD:** State & 2nd St., Troy, NY 12180, (518)272-3800.

HAZEWINKEL, William Charles——B: June 5, 1940, Los Angeles, CA, *Pres.*, Wm. Hazewinkel & Co.; **PRIM RE ACT:** Broker, Consultant, Appraiser, Property Manager; **REP CLIENTS:** Coast Community Coll. Dist.; 1st Interstate Mort. Co.; CA 1st Bank; **PREV EMPLOY:** Prop. Directions; Lincoln S&L; Santa Barbara S&L; **PROFL AFFIL & HONORS:** SREA, IREM, SCV, Realtor, Newport Harbor Bd. of Realtors, CPM, SRPA; **EDUC:** BS, 1962, Bus. Admin., RE Major, USC; Certificates, 1966, RE, Univ. of CA; Certificates, 1969, RE, Orange Coast Coll.; **OTHER ACT & HONORS:** Chmn., Newport Beach Planning Commn., 4 yrs.; **BUS ADD:** 2700 W. Coast Hwy., Suite 280, Newport Beach, CA 92663, (714)645-5555.

HAZZARD, Roger Philip——B: Dec. 12, 1949, Seattle, WA, *Pres.*, Western Commercial Real Estate; **PRIM RE ACT:** Broker; **SERVICES:** Comml. RE brokerage in office buildings, apts., marketing services and development of multi-unit complexes; **REP CLIENTS:** Synds., devels. and indiv. clients in comml. investments; **PREV EMPLOY:** Sales Mgr. 1975-1980, Spartus Comml. Corp., Sales Mgr. for the Comml. RE Div. of the Quadrant Corp. A Weyer Timber Comp.; **PROFL AFFIL & HONORS:** Bd. of Realtors, King Cty.; **EDUC:** BS; **GRAD EDUC:** In Bus. Admin., 1972, Bus. Mgmt. & Mktg., Univ. of WA; **HOME ADD:** 36503 32nd Ave. So., Auburn, WA 98002, (206)952-2731; **BUS ADD:** 33719 9th Ave. S., Suite 1, Federal, WA 98003, (206)838-6000.

HEAD, J. Reginald——B: Feb. 12, 1930, Chambers Cty., AL, *Pres.*, ERA Head Realty Co.; **PRIM RE ACT:** Broker, Appraiser, Developer, Owner/Investor, Syndicator; **PROFL AFFIL & HONORS:** Rockdale Bd. of Realtors, past pres.; GA Assn. of Realtors; NAR, GRI, 1979 Realtor of the Year; **EDUC:** LaGrange Coll., So. Tech. Inst., GA State Univ.; **MIL SERV:** USN, Electrician Mate; **OTHER ACT & HONORS:** Outstanding Young Man of the Year 1966; City Council Member 1962-1964; Rotary Club; Bd. of Trustees Salem Campground, Inc.; **HOME ADD:** 1277 Shadowlawn Dr., Conyers, GA 30207, (404)483-7407; **BUS ADD:** 1070 Iris Dr., Conyers, GA 30207, (404)483-3939.

HEAD, Nelson H.——B: July 13, 1946, Birmingham, AL, *Pres.*, Hill Realty Co.; **PRIM RE ACT:** Developer, Owner/Investor; **OTHER RE ACT:** RE Devel.; **SERVICES:** Leasing comml. RE, devel. comml. RE; **EDUC:** BS, 1968, Commerce, Washington & Lee Univ.; **MIL SERV:** USN, Lt.; **OTHER ACT & HONORS:** Foreign Relations Comm.; Redstone Club; Chmn., Big Brother, Big Sisters of Birmingham; Chmn. AL School of Fine Arts Found.; **HOME ADD:** 2411

Henrietta Rd., Birmingham, AL, (205)933-9588; **BUS ADD:** POB 2323, Birmingham, AL 35201, (205)251-1206.

HEADLEE, William A.——**B:** May 28, 1928, Fort Dodge, IA, *Pres.*, OR Mgmt. Grp.; **PRIM RE ACT:** Broker, Consultant, Developer, Owner/Investor; **OTHER RE ACT:** Counselor-Problem RE; **SERVICES:** Full RE counselor, work out, and equity recovery services; **REP CLIENTS:** All major lending instit. in Northwest, lawyers, and courts; **PROFL AFFIL & HONORS:** NAR, OAR, Clackamas Cty. Bd. of Realtors, Lake Oswego Redevelopment Policy Bd., Land Use Comm. C of C., Chairman; **EDUC:** BS, 1951, Bus. Admin. and Mktg., UT State Univ.; **GRAD EDUC:** MBA, 1955, Mktg., Havard Grad. Sch. of Bus. Admin.; **MIL SERV:** USAF, Lt.; **OTHER ACT & HONORS:** Rotary Intl.; Pres. Lakewood Ctr. Lake Oswego Community Theatre; **HOME ADD:** 1874 Glenmorrie Terrace, Lake Oswego, OR 97034, (503)636-6721; **BUS ADD:** 47 N. State St., Lake Oswego, OR 97034, (503)636-8433.

HEADLUND, Donald C.——**B:** July 26, 1933, Salt Lake City, UT, *Exec. VP*, Valley Federal Savings; **PRIM RE ACT:** Lender; **SERVICES:** RE Loans; **EDUC:** BA, 1955, Econ., Occidental Coll.; **GRAD EDUC:** S & L Grad. School, 1980, IN Univ.; **MIL SERV:** USAF, Capt.; **HOME ADD:** 5800-72 Owensmouth, Woodland Hills, CA 91367, (213)704-5455; **BUS ADD:** 6842 Van Nuys Blvd., Van Nuys, CA 91405, (213)786-7220.

HEAGERTY, Chris——**B:** July 25, 1948, Jersey City, NJ, *Exec. VP and Dir. of Sales and Mktg.*, The Heagerty Co., Realtors; **PRIM RE ACT:** Broker, Consultant, Property Manager; **OTHER RE ACT:** Relocation Specialist; **SERVICES:** Sales, Mktg., Resid. and Comml. Leasing, Prop. Mgmt., Relocation Counseling; **REP CLIENTS:** Indiv. and Corp. Relocation in area; owners of Comml., investment, and resid. props.; **PREV EMPLOY:** Univ. of TX; **PROFL AFFIL & HONORS:** TX Assn. of Realtors, NAR, WCR, GRI, CRB; **EDUC:** BA, 1970, Biology, Notre Dame; **GRAD EDUC:** MA, 1973, Microbiology, Univ. of TX; **OTHER ACT & HONORS:** Chmn., Education Comm., Austin Bd. of Realtors; **HOME ADD:** 8711 Crest Ridge Cir., Austin, TX 78750, (512)258-4037; **BUS ADD:** 8705 Shoal Creek Suite 100, Austin, TX 78758, (512)458-3531.

HEAGERTY, James J.——**B:** Dec. 18, 1929, St. Petersburg, FL, *Pres.*, First City Federal Savings and Loan Assn.; **PRIM RE ACT:** Lender; **OTHER RE ACT:** Investor, Synd.; **PROFL AFFIL & HONORS:** Manatee Cty. Bd. of Realtors; CRA; Nat. S & L League; US League Savings Assn.; **EDUC:** BS, 1957, Mktg., FL State Univ.; **OTHER ACT & HONORS:** Pres., Nat. S & L League; Bd. of Tr. New Coll. and St. Leo; Past Pres. C of C and United Fund; **HOME ADD:** 4919 Riverview Blvd., W, Bradenton, FL 33529, (813)748-1099; **BUS ADD:** PO Box 1969, Bradenton, FL 33506, (813)748-0811.

HEAGERTY, Stephen P.——**B:** Feb. 18, 1948, Baltimore, MD, *Pres.*, Heagerty Co., Realtors; **PRIM RE ACT:** Broker, Instructor; **OTHER RE ACT:** Relocation Consultant; **SERVICES:** Residential comml. sales and mktg.; prop. mgmt; leasing, relocation consulting; **PROFL AFFIL & HONORS:** Austin Bd. of Realtors, TAR, NAR, TRANSLO Dir., Realtors Mktg. Inst. CRB; TRANSLO 1981 Realtor of the Year; **EDUC:** BA, 1970, Poli Sci., John Hopkins; **GRAD EDUC:** 1970-75, Mgmt.-Psych, Univ. of TX; **HOME ADD:** 8711 Crest Ridge Dr., Austin, TX 78750, (512)258-4037; **BUS ADD:** 8705 Shoal Creek Blvd., Suite 100, Austin, TX 78758, (512)458-3531.

HEAGY, John A., III——**B:** Sep. 12, 1952, Alburquerque, NM, *Project Dir.*, Interstate North Assoc. (W.B. Johnson Prop.); **PRIM RE ACT:** Attorney, Consultant, Developer, Builder, Property Manager, Real Estate Publisher; **PREV EMPLOY:** Kager Prop. Inc.; **PROFL AFFIL & HONORS:** BOMA, NAIOP, C of C., Editorial Adv. Bd. Atlanta Office Guide; **EDUC:** BS, 1974, RE, Pol. Sci., Univ of GA; **HOME ADD:** 4900 Hampton Farms Dr., Matta, GA 30067, (404)971-8853; **BUS ADD:** 300 Interstate N., Suite 285, Atlanta, GA 30339, (404)955-0842.

HEALY, Gerald F.——**B:** Oct. 14, 1893, Watertown, NY, *Owner*, Healy Realty Co.; **PRIM RE ACT:** Broker, Consultant, Engineer, Appraiser, Developer, Owner/Investor, Property Manager; **SERVICES:** Counseling on comml. and indus. RE; **PROFL AFFIL & HONORS:** Amer. Soc. of RE Counselors, SIR, AIREA; (Ret'd), Past Pres., MI Assn. of Realtors; **EDUC:** 1915, Civil Engrg., Cornell Univ.; **MIL SERV:** 303rd Engr., Capt.; **OTHER ACT & HONORS:** Rotary Club, Flint City Club, Univ. Club, Flint Golf Club; **HOME ADD:** 3806 Wroxton Road, Flint, MI 48504, (313)732-7576; **BUS ADD:** Suite 102, Northbank Center, 400 N. Saginaw St., Flint, MI 48502, (313)239-5824.

HEALY, John J., Jr.——**B:** Aug. 1, 1946, New York, NY, *VP*, Manufacturers Hanover Trust Co.; **PRIM RE ACT:** Consultant, Appraiser; **PROFL AFFIL & HONORS:** AIREA, Soc. of RE Appraisers, Young Men's RE Assn., Rho Epsilon RE Frat., MAI, SRPA; **EDUC:** BBA, 1969, Fin. and Investments, Hofstra Univ.; **GRAD EDUC:** MBA, 1977, Fin., Hofstra Univ.; **HOME ADD:** 84 Downing St., East Williston, NY 11596, (516)742-0339; **BUS ADD:** 270 Park Ave., New York, NY 10017, (212)286-6491.

HEALY, Thomas R.——**B:** May 23, 1930, Boston, MA, *Pres.*, Healy Co., Inc., Realtors & Counselors; **PRIM RE ACT:** Broker, Consultant, Appraiser, Lender, Owner/Investor; **OTHER RE ACT:** Arbitrator; **SERVICES:** Leasing, selling, exchanging comml. and indus. prop., site/space selection, buyers/lessee broker, arbitrator, fee consulting, investment counseling; **REP CLIENTS:** Bus., inst. and indiv. investors; **PROFL AFFIL & HONORS:** San Francisco RE BD, VP 1981, Dir.; CCIM Chapter One; RNMI; CA Assn. of Realtors; Nat. Assn. of Realtors; **EDUC:** BA, 1952, Econ., Brown Univ.; **GRAD EDUC:** MBA, 1959, Mktg./Fin., Northwestern Univ.; **MIL SERV:** USN, Lt.; **OTHER ACT & HONORS:** St. Francis Yacht Club; Marin Yacht Club; Marin Tennis Club; **HOME ADD:** 195 Stanford Ave., Mill Valley, CA 94941, (415)332-9355; **BUS ADD:** 351 CA St., San Francisco, CA 94104, (415)421-9355.

HEARD, Drayton——**B:** Jan. 9, 1941, New Haven, CT, *Pres.*, CNB Equity Corp.; **PRIM RE ACT:** Lender; **SERVICES:** Construction and intermediate term loans; **REP CLIENTS:** Devels. and owner/investors; **PREV EMPLOY:** Barclay Amer. Bus. Credit 1973-1980; MA Mutual Life Ins. Co. 1968-1973; **EDUC:** BA, 1963, Hist., Univ. of NC (Chapel Hill); **MIL SERV:** USMC, Sgt.; **HOME ADD:** 25 Westborough Dr, W. Hartford, CT 06107; **BUS ADD:** 33 Church St., PO Box 1946, Waterbury, CT 06720, (203)756-7218.

HEARD, Joe——**B:** Oct. 3, 1913, Itta Bena, MS, *Owner*, Joe Heard, Realtor; **PRIM RE ACT:** Broker; **SERVICES:** Resid. Sales; **PROFL AFFIL & HONORS:** CRB; **EDUC:** 1938, LA State Univ.; **MIL SERV:** US Army Artillery Infantry; Lt. Col., 5 Battle Stars, European Theater, Bronze Star; **OTHER ACT & HONORS:** Lions Club; Bass Club; TRCA; SPEB; SQSA; **HOME ADD:** 203 Broadmoor, Jackson, MS 39206, (601)362-2900; **BUS ADD:** 203 Broadmoor, Jackson, MS 39206, (601)362-2900.

HEARN, Arlene——**B:** Dec. 6, 1925, Shawano, WI, *VP, Gen. Mgr.*, O'Malley Realty Associates; **PRIM RE ACT:** Broker; **OTHER RE ACT:** Lic. Mort. Broker; **SERVICES:** Selling, leasing & exchanging comml. & indus. props., raw land, and bus. opportunities; **REP CLIENTS:** Devels., investors & users; **PREV EMPLOY:** 15 years in RE profession; **PROFL AFFIL & HONORS:** Phoenix Bd. of Realtors, ICSC, RE Broker, Mort. Broker; **OTHER ACT & HONORS:** Phoenix C of C; Phoenix Ctry. Club; Soroptimist Intl. of Phoenix; **HOME ADD:** 8445 E. San Marino Dr., Scottsdale, AZ 85258, (602)998-4236; **BUS ADD:** 1800 N. Central Ave., Phoenix, AZ 85004, (602)258-8411.

HEARN, Robert E.——**B:** July 5, 1930, Jackson, TN, *Owner*, Hearn Cons. Co.; **PRIM RE ACT:** Broker, Banker, Owner/Investor, Property Manager, Syndicator; **OTHER RE ACT:** Gen. Const. Design & Build., 2nd Generation in Bus. in Jackson Since 1920; **PROFL AFFIL & HONORS:** Jackson Bd. of Realtors; **EDUC:** Special Student, Engrg., Univ. of TN; **MIL SERV:** USN, Petty Officer; **OTHER ACT & HONORS:** also affiliated with Hearn-Haynes developments, Hearn Realty Co. & Hearn Properties; **HOME ADD:** 701 N Parkway, Jackson, TN 38301, (901)668-5421; **BUS ADD:** 1903 N Highland, Jackson, TN 38301, (901)423-9204.

HEARN, Robert L., III——**B:** Nov. 25, 1927, Birmingham, AL, *Pres.*, Hearn Co.; **PRIM RE ACT:** Consultant, Appraiser; **REP CLIENTS:** Attys., Corps., State of AL, Banks, US Govt.; **PREV EMPLOY:** Cobbs, Allen, Hall Mort. Co., Now Mort. Corp. of South, 1960 - 1964, Staff Appraiser; **PROFL AFFIL & HONORS:** AIREA; SREA; Intl. Right of Way, NAR; MAI; **EDUC:** 1946 - 1949, Univ. of AL; **MIL SERV:** USA, Cpl.; **OTHER ACT & HONORS:** Vestavia Country Club; The Club; Downtown Club; **HOME ADD:** 10 Ridge Dr., Birmingham, AL 35213, (205)271-8937; **BUS ADD:** 2101 Magnolia Ave. S. Suite 509, Birmingham, AL 35205, (205)251-7304.

HEARN, Thomas N.——**B:** Apr. 21, 1937, Amherst, OH, *VP*, Knutson Mort. & Fin. Corp., Comml. Div.; **PRIM RE ACT:** Lender; **SERVICES:** Const. loans, equity sales, long term loans; **REP CLIENTS:** Life Ins. cos., banks, pension funds and other investors; **PREV EMPLOY:** First WI Nat. Bank (Milwaukee), Women's Fed. S&L (CLeveland); **PROFL AFFIL & HONORS:** NAIOP, MBA; **EDUC:** BA, 1959, Hist. & Bus. Admin., OH Wesleyan Univ., Delaware, OH; **GRAD EDUC:** 1965, Mgmt. Acctg., Whittenberg Univ., Springfield, OH; **MIL SERV:** USAF, 1st Lt.; **OTHER ACT &**

HONORS: Troop Chmn. Boy Scouts, various church activities, Nat. Office Comm. on Bldg. & Loan for Assn. of Congregational Churches; **HOME ADD:** 17210 6th Ave., N., Plymouth, MN 55447, (612)476-0890; **BUS ADD:** 17 Wash. Ave., N., Minneapolis, MN 55401, (612)371-3635.

HEATH, George Delton——B: May 11, 1932, Houston, *Broker-Owner*, Heath RE; **PRIM RE ACT:** Broker, Instructor, Developer, Owner/Investor; **PROFL AFFIL & HONORS:** NAR, RNMI, FLI, TX Indus. Council, Wood Cty. Bd., Kaufman-Vanzandt Bd., GRI, CRB, CRS; **EDUC:** BA RE, 1954, RE, Ins., Univ. of TX; **MIL SERV:** US Army, Paratrooper, PFC; **HOME ADD:** Rte. 2, Box 212, Grand Saline, TX 75140, (214)962-4377; **BUS ADD:** 509 W. Garland, Grand Saline, TX 75140, (214)962-3080.

HEATH, Jesse B., Jr.——B: May 25, 1940, Madisonville, TX, *Partner*, Heath & Knippa; **PRIM RE ACT:** Attorney; **REP CLIENTS:** Crocker Nat. Bank, Growth Realty Cos., Weyerhauser Co., Hilton Intl., Realfin Co., First City Devels. Corp., First TX Savings Assn., West Houston Props. Inc.; **PREV EMPLOY:** Carrington, Coleman, Sloman, & Blumenthal, Dallas, TX (1968-70); **PROFL AFFIL & HONORS:** ABA, Sect. of Real Prop., Probate & Trust Law; Council Member of Sect. on Real Prop. Probate & Trust Law (1981-); Chmn. Comm. on New Devels. in RE law and Practice (1979-81); V. Chmn. Comm. on Creation and Evaluation of Div. Projects (1978-79); V. Chmn. of Special Comm. on Uniform Land Trans. Act (1976-78); Member Nominating Comm. (1979-80), State Bar of TX, Council Member, RE Probate & Trust Law Sect., (1978-); Houston Bar Assn., Chmn. of RE Law Sect. (1980-81), Co-author "Real Prop. Annual Survey of TX Law", 31 SW Law Journal 27 (1977), 32 SW Law Journal 27 (1978), and 33 SW Law Journal 48 (1979); Co-author "Summary of the Uniform Land Transactions Act", 13 Real Prop., Probate & Trust Journal 672 (1978); Author "1977 Legal Devels. in Real Prop. Law", *The Houston Lawyer 1978*; Author "Land Acquisition for an Income Project", State Bar of TX, First Advanced RE Law Course (1979); Author "Recent Devels. in TX RE Law", State Bar of TX, Second Advanced RE Law Journal 815 (1981); Author "Sale-Leasebacks and Leasehold Mortgages, Fin. RE during the Inflationary 80's" (ABA Nat. Inst. 1981), Author, "New Developments in Real Estate Financing", 12 St. Mary's Law J. 811 (1981); Bd. of Govs. and Member of Exec. Comm. of Amer. Coll. of RE Lawyers (1980-), Member, Anglo-Amer. Real Prop. Ins. (1981-), Founder and Member of Houston RE Lawyers Council (1979-); **EDUC:** BBA, 1963, RE, So. Methodist Univ.; **GRAD EDUC:** LLB, 1966, So. Methodist Univ. Sch. of Law; **EDUC HONORS:** Barristers Phi Delta Phi, Managing Editor of SW Law Journal; **OTHER ACT & HONORS:** Bd. of Visitors So Methodist Univ. Sch. of Law (1976-80); **HOME ADD:** 3434 Del Monte, Houston, TX 77019, (713)523-8850; **BUS ADD:** 2800 Texas Commerce Tower, Houston, TX 77002, (713)224-3330.

HEATH, R. Terry——B: June 22, 1953, Muncie, IN, *Atty.*, Heath, Bell & Lyman, Prof. Corp.; **PRIM RE ACT:** Attorney; **SERVICES:** Legal services; **PROFL AFFIL & HONORS:** ABA, Real Prop. Probate & Tr. Law Sect.; **EDUC:** BS, 1975, Bus., Purdue Univ.; **GRAD EDUC:** JD, 1978, Indiana Univ. Law Sch.; LLM, Georgetown Univ. Law Ctr.; **EDUC HONORS:** Dist. student, Cum Laude; **HOME ADD:** 6315 N. Evanston Ave., Indianapolis, IN 46220, (317)842-7272; **BUS ADD:** 7007 N Graham Rd., PO Box 55267, Indianapolis, IN 46205, (317)842-7272.

HEATH, Robert H.——*Partner*, Alabama Realty; **PRIM RE ACT:** Developer, Owner/Investor, Property Manager; **BUS ADD:** 3322 South Memorial Pkwy., Huntsville, AL 35805, (205)883-2800.

HEBERS, Frank J.——B: Jan. 30, 1921, St. Louis, MO, *Pres.*, Kemmons Wilson Realty, Co.; **PRIM RE ACT:** Broker, Owner/Investor, Property Manager; **SERVICES:** Selling, Leasing, Devel.; **PREV EMPLOY:** Memphis REB Pres., 1975; TN Assn. of Realtors, Pres., 1981; **PROFL AFFIL & HONORS:** Memphis Realtor of Yr., 1976, TN Realtor of Yr., 1976; **MIL SERV:** USN, 1st Cl., PO; **HOME ADD:** 2501 Windy Oaks, Germantown, TN 38138, (901)754-9444; **BUS ADD:** 1629 Winchester, Memphis, TN 38130, (901)346-8800.

HECHT, Emil——B: July 6, 1924, Svalva, Czechoslovakia, *Pres.*, MDC Corp.; **PRIM RE ACT:** Broker, Developer, Builder, Property Manager; **PREV EMPLOY:** Sr. Accountant - J.K. Lasser & Co. CPAs and Its Predecessor - Denver, CO 1952-1971; **EDUC:** 2 semesters Med. School - Charles Univ., Prague, Czechoslovakia, 1945-1946; **GRAD EDUC:** Int. Acctg. Soc., Chicago, IL, Correspondent School in Acctg., 1952-1954; **OTHER ACT & HONORS:** V. Chmn. - Mountain Fin. Serv. Inc., Denver, CO - Holding Co. for 4 banks & Dir. of Holding Co. and Banks; **HOME ADD:** 3695 S. Poplar, Denver, CO 80237; **BUS ADD:** 3600 S. Yosemite, Suite 900, Denver, CO 80237, (303)773-1100.

HECK, Richard A.——B: June 27, 1938, NJ, *Pres.*, J. Arthur Neck & Son; **PRIM RE ACT:** Broker, Consultant, Appraiser, Property Manager; **SERVICES:** Sales, Rentals, Appraisals, Fin. and Mgmt. for Comml. and Resid. Prop.; **REP CLIENTS:** Honequity, Merrill Lynch, Transamerica, Equitable, Gen. Motors, Executrans, Corporate Relocation Agency; **PROFL AFFIL & HONORS:** Soc. of RE Appraisers, NAR, NJ Assn. of Realtors, Pascack Valley Bd. of Realtors; **EDUC:** BA Bus. Admin., 1960, Fin. and Econ., Rutgers Univ.; **EDUC HONORS:** Wall St. Journal Fin. Award, 1960; **OTHER ACT & HONORS:** Dir. of a number of institutions and corporations.; **BUS ADD:** 206 Center Ave., Westwood, NJ 07675, (201)664-4505.

HECKENDORN, John G.——B: Nov. 6, 1947, Bryn Maur, PA, *Assoc. Broker*, Seattle Pacific Realty, Inc.; **PRIM RE ACT:** Broker, Consultant, Owner/Investor; **SERVICES:** Complete servs. for Retail Users & Syndicators; **REP CLIENTS:** Maj. retail & restaurant chains Syndicators; **PREV EMPLOY:** Broker-co-owner, Heim, Heckendorn, & Bauce, Realtors, State Coll., PA; **PROFL AFFIL & HONORS:** Seattle, King Cty., WA, Assn. of Realtors, NAR, RNMI, CCIM; **EDUC:** XS, 1969, Food Serv. & Hotel Admin., PA State Univ.; **OTHER ACT & HONORS:** Alpha Sigma Phi Frat., Delta Beta XI Award; **HOME ADD:** 414 Lakeside So., Seattle, WA 98144, (206)325-4043; **BUS ADD:** 400 Securities Bldg., Seattle, WA 98101, (206)682-3100.

HEDBERG, Jon B.——B: Nov. 26, 1935, Sioux City, IA, *Exec. VP & Managing Officer*, The Pacifica Corp.; **PRIM RE ACT:** Developer, Builder; **OTHER RE ACT:** Supervision of all building activities; **SERVICES:** Res. Homebuilder & Land Devel. for Sale to Other Builders; **REP CLIENTS:** Weyerhauser-Pardee, Ring Bros., 1st Fed. of Santa Monica; McKeon Const. Co., Inc.; **PREV EMPLOY:** Boise Cascade Corp., 1968-1973; **PROFL AFFIL & HONORS:** Dir., Bldg. Indus. Assn., Gov. Affairs Council; **EDUC:** Geology, IA State Univ. & Valley Coll.; **HOME ADD:** 32054 Canterhill Pl., Westlake Village, CA 94015, (213)889-8905; **BUS ADD:** 33100 Via Colinas 104, Westlake Village, CA 94015, (213)991-9150.

HEDEN, Thomas F.——B: Oct. 29, 1933, Minneapolis, MN, *Dir. Assets Mgmt.*, Otis Elevator Co.; **PRIM RE ACT:** Attorney, Owner/Investor, Property Manager; **OTHER RE ACT:** Corporate RE and Mgr., Manage RE portfolio and Capital Plan; **SERVICES:** Buying, Selling, Leasing, Constr. of existing and new facilities; **PREV EMPLOY:** Ogden Corp., Litton Indus., Penn Central Transportation Co.; **PROFL AFFIL & HONORS:** CA Bar; Nat. Assn. of Corporate RE Execs.; **EDUC:** BS, 1956, Educ., Univ. of MN; **GRAD EDUC:** JD, 1961, Law, UCLA; **EDUC HONORS:** Grad. with Distinction, Moot Court Honors Program; **MIL SERV:** US Army, 1956-1958; **HOME ADD:** 144 E. Brittany Farms Rd., New Britain, CT 06053, (203)225-1669; **BUS ADD:** 1 Farm Springs, Farmington, CT 06032, (203)677-6000.

HEDLUND, C.J.——B: Dec. 24, 1937, Clear Lake, WI, *Pres.*, Colorado Bighorn Corp.; **PRIM RE ACT:** Broker, Syndicator, Developer, Builder, Property Manager, Owner/Investor; **SERVICES:** Spec. in Selfstorage & Office Bldgs. including Renovations; **PROFL AFFIL & HONORS:** SSSA; **HOME ADD:** 7225 W. Box Canyon Rd., Sedalia, CO 80135; **BUS ADD:** 7790 E. Arapahoe Rd. #210, Englewood, CO 80112, (303)773-0315.

HEDRICK, Janet L.——B: July 9, 1948, LA, CA, *VP*, J.H. Hedrick & Co.; **PRIM RE ACT:** Developer, Builder, Syndicator; **SERVICES:** Land devel.; **PREV EMPLOY:** City of El Cajon; **PROFL AFFIL & HONORS:** Bldg. Contractors Assn.; **EDUC:** BA, 1970, Soc., UCLA; **GRAD EDUC:** MBA, 1975, Public Admin., San Diego St.; **OTHER ACT & HONORS:** Charter 100; **HOME ADD:** 5580 Lake Parkway, 13, La Mesa, CA 92041, (714)469-8317; **BUS ADD:** 1516 W. Redwood St., San Diego, CA 92101, (714)298-9960.

HEFFERAN, T. William——B: Aug. 9, 1949, Wash. DC, *VP*, Investors' Incentives, Inc.; **PRIM RE ACT:** Consultant, Developer, Property Manager; **SERVICES:** Prop. Mgmt.; RE investment counseling; **PROFL AFFIL & HONORS:** Inst. of RE Mgmt., Candidate for Cert. as a Prop. Mgr.; Member RE Bd; Pres. BOMA 81-82; Bd. of Dir. Downtown, Inc., CPM Candidate; **EDUC:** BS, 1977, Grand Valley State Coll.; **MIL SERV:** US Army, Sgt.; **HOME ADD:** 7014 Leonard Rd., Eastmanville, MI 40503, (616)837-6439; **BUS ADD:** Suite 1 Fed. Sq. Bldg., Grand Rapids, MI 49503, (606)774-9595.

HEFFERNAN, E. Michael——B: June 25, 1942, Ann Arbor, MI, *Gen. Part*, Heffernan, Freiberg & Assoc.; **PRIM RE ACT:** Consultant, Developer, Owner/Investor; **SERVICES:** Consult on problem props., work out/dispose of same; **REP CLIENTS:** Instns. & indivs.; **PREV EMPLOY:** VP BankAmerica Capital Corp., (venture capital fund), 555 California St., San Francisco, CA; **PROFL AFFIL & HONORS:** Fin. Exec. Inst. (Bd. of Dir), CPA (CA); **EDUC:** BA, 1964, Lib. Arts,

Stanford Univ.; **GRAD EDUC:** MBA, 1966, Fin., Univ. of MI; **MIL SERV:** USN, Lt., Navy Achievement Award; **OTHER ACT & HONORS:** BSA, San Mateo Cty. Council (Bd. of Dir.); **BUS ADD:** 151 Upper Terr., San Francisco, CA 94117, (415)861-5305.

HEGER, Mr. Jan M.——**B:** Nov. 25, 1942, Lincoln, NE, *Atty. at Law - Partner*, Heger & Heger; **PRIM RE ACT:** Attorney; **OTHER RE ACT:** Real Estate Investment and Sales; **SERVICES:** RE litigation & negotiations; **REP CLIENTS:** Stockly & Popou, Structural & Design Engrs., Newport Beach, CA; **PREV EMPLOY:** Counsel - Chicago Title Ins. Co., Pacific Mutual Life Ins. Co. (Real Estate Acquisitions and Sales); **PROFL AFFIL & HONORS:** Southeast Bar Assn.; ABA; Los Angeles Cty. Bar Assn.; Delta Theta Phi Law Frat.; Long Beach Bar Assn.; **EDUC:** BA, 1961, Bus. & Engr., CA State Polytechnic; Univ. of Uppsala; Intl. Law, Sweden; **GRAD EDUC:** JD, 1977, RE, Southwestern Univ. School of Law; **MIL SERV:** US Army, 1966-1969, 1st Lt.; **BUS ADD:** 9418 Alondra, Bellflower, CA 90706, (213)867-7247.

HEIBERG, Robert Alan——**B:** June 29, 1943, St. Cloud, MN, *Atty. (Part.)*, Dorsey, Windhorst, Hannaford, Whitney & Holladay; **PRIM RE ACT:** Attorney, Instructor; **SERVICES:** Legal Rep.; **REP CLIENTS:** RE Sunds., Constr. and Permanent Lenders; **PREV EMPLOY:** Law Clerk to Mr. Justice Walter E. Roqosheske, MN Supreme Court, 1968-69; **PROFL AFFIL & HONORS:** Hennepin Cty., MN Bar Assn. & ABA; **EDUC:** BA, 1965, Pol. Sci., Univ. of MN; **GRAD EDUC:** JD, 1968, Univ. of MN Law School; **EDUC HONORS:** Phi Beta Kappa, Summa Cum Laude, Order of the Coif, Articles Editor, MN Law Review; Summa Cum Laude; **HOME ADD:** 4510 Wooddale Ave., Edina, MN 55424, (612)926-4762; **BUS ADD:** 2200 First Bank Pl. E, Minn., MN 55402, (612)340-2751.

HEIDORN, Donald G.——**B:** May 6, 1928, Evanston, IL, *Pres.*, CENTURY 21 Ctry. Squire IL, Inc.; **PRIM RE ACT:** Broker, Instructor, Consultant, Appraiser, Owner/Investor; **OTHER RE ACT:** Relocation of transferring corp. personnel, Prop. Mgmt.; **SERVICES:** RE Mktg., Appraising, & Investment Counseling; **REP CLIENTS:** Continental Bank-Equitable Relocation Serv., Executrans, Law firms engaged in RE; **PROFL AFFIL & HONORS:** NAR, NW Suburban Bd. of Realtors (Dir.); RNMI, SREA, Nat. Relocation Consultants, Inc. (Dir.) 1981; Chicago Relocation Connection, Inc. Pres. 1981, RE Advisory Bd. Harper Coll. 1972 to present, CRB, CRS, GRI, SRA; **EDUC:** BA, 1950, Bus. Admin., Knox Coll. Galesburg, IL; **MIL SERV:** USA, 1st Lt., 1951-1953; **OTHER ACT & HONORS:** NW Suburban Council Boy Scouts of Amer. Exec. Bd.: 1965 to pres., Bd. of Dir., Mt. Prospect Crusade of Mercy 1974-1975; **HOME ADD:** 517 S. Main St., Mt. Prospect, IL 60056, (312)255-6465; **BUS ADD:** 906 S. Roselle Rd., Schaumburg, IL 60172, (312)894-4000.

HEIDRICK, G. A., Jr.——**B:** Apr. 4, 1940, Baltimore, MD, *Pres.*, Fidelity Federal Savings & Loan Assn.; **PRIM RE ACT:** Consultant, Appraiser, Banker, Developer, Lender, Owner/Investor, Syndicator; **SERVICES:** Devel. Consulting, Debt and Equity Synd.; **REP CLIENTS:** Lenders, Investors and Devel. of Comml. and Resid. RE; **PREV EMPLOY:** Peat, Marwick, Mitchell & Co.; **PROFL AFFIL & HONORS:** ABA, AICPA, Amer. Assn. of Mort. Underwriters; **EDUC:** BA, 1962, Univ. of VA; **GRAD EDUC:** JD, MBA, 1969, 1972, Taxation, Finance, Univ. of MD, Loyola Coll.; **BUS ADD:** 16 E. Lombard St., Baltimore, MD 21202, (301)244-8241.

HEIFETZ, Alan W.——*Chf. Admin. Law Judge*, Department of Housing and Urban Development, Ofc. of Administrative Law Judge; **PRIM RE ACT:** Lender; **BUS ADD:** 451 Seventh St., S.W., Washington, DC 20410, (202)673-6128.*

HEILBRUNN, Jerome——**B:** May 22, 1949, Chicago, IL, *Asst. VP; Condo. Div.*, Amer. Invsco. Mgmt. Inc.; **PRIM RE ACT:** Property Manager; **REP CLIENTS:** Condo. Prop. Mgmt.; **PROFL AFFIL & HONORS:** IREM; NAR; Chicago RE Bd., CPM, RE Broker; **EDUC:** Engr.-Acctg., Univ. of IL, Chicago Circle Campus; **HOME ADD:** 1306 W. Cornelia Ave., Chicago, IL 60657, (312)929-5186; **BUS ADD:** 120 S. LaSalle St., Rm 507, Chicago, IL 60603, (312)621-2176.

HEILMANN, Frank M.——*VP*, McBridge Enterprises; **PRIM RE ACT:** Developer; **BUS ADD:** 808 High Mountain Rd., Franklin Lakes, NJ 07417, (201)891-3900.*

HEIM, Bruce K.——**B:** Nov. 7, 1941, Glen Cove, NY, *Pres.*, H H & B Realtors; **PRIM RE ACT:** Broker, Instructor, Property Manager, Owner/Investor; **SERVICES:** Comml. Brokerage, Consulting, Prop. Mgmt. Lenders, Indiv. Inv. Corp.; **PROFL AFFIL & HONORS:** CPM, CCIM; **EDUC:** BS US Mil. Acad., 1963, West Point; **GRAD EDUC:** MBA, 1970, RE & Fin., Penn. St.; **MIL SERV:** Infantry, Capt., Bronze Star, Air Medal, Army Commendation Medal, Combat Infantryman Badge; **HOME ADD:** 1600 Fox Hollow Rd., St. College, PA 16901, (814)238-6660; **BUS ADD:** 1840 N. Atherton St., State College, VA 16801, (814)237-0311.

HEIMAN, Fred——*VP Administrator*, Allen Group, Inc.; **PRIM RE ACT:** Property Manager; **BUS ADD:** 534 Broadhollow Rd., Melville, NY 11746, (513)293-5500.*

HEIMAN, Kenneth——**B:** Nov. 4, 1920, Seattle, WA, *RE Officer*, City of Tacoma, Comm. Devel. Dept.; **PRIM RE ACT:** Broker, Appraiser; **SERVICES:** Acquisition & Disposition of Prop. Appraisals, Consulting; **PREV EMPLOY:** Broker, Ken Heiman Realty, 1972-78, VP Tacoma Realty, 1962-72; **PROFL AFFIL & HONORS:** CCIM; **EDUC:** BA, 1943, Econ., Univ. of Wash.; **MIL SERV:** US Army, Lt., Purple Heart, Eto Medal; **OTHER ACT & HONORS:** Pres. Kiwanis, Pres. Municipal League, Pres. Chmn. Nat. Conf. of Christians & Jews, Awarded Distinguished Citizen Tacoma Pierce Cty. Municipal League, 1972, Citizen of Yr., Nat. Conf. of Christians & Jews, 1979; **HOME ADD:** 1901 N. Cedar, Tacoma, WA 98406, (206)759-5881; **BUS ADD:** 740 St. Helens, 10th Fl., Tacoma, WA 98406, (206)593-4960.

HEIMSATH, Charles H.——**B:** July 23, 1950, New Haven, CT, *Sr. Econ.*, Rice Ctr.; **PRIM RE ACT:** Consultant, Property Manager, Owner/Investor; **SERVICES:** RE Research, Mkt. Analysis, Urban Demography & Contract Research in Urban Econ. problems; **REP CLIENTS:** Exxon, Getty Oil Co., Cameron Iron Works, Houston C of C; **PREV EMPLOY:** Office of Mayor, City of Houston, Econ. Dev. Div.; **PROFL AFFIL & HONORS:** Houston Bd of Realtors, APA, Houston Old Town Dev., Corp VP, 1980, 1981; **EDUC:** BA, 1972, Econ., Univ. of VT; **GRAD EDUC:** MS, 1976, Urban Planning RE Investment, Univ. of TX; **EDUC HONORS:** Grad. with hon.; **HOME ADD:** 2103 Bartlett, Houston, TX 77098, (713)521-1478; **BUS ADD:** 9 Greenway Plaza, Suite 1900, Houston, TX 77046, (713)965-0100.

HEINDRICHS, Robert W.——**B:** July 12, 1942, E. Grand Rapids, MI, *VP*, Westdale's Better Homes & Gardens; **PRIM RE ACT:** Broker, Instructor, Consultant; **SERVICES:** RE Broker & Mgr.; **PROFL AFFIL & HONORS:** Pres. Sales Mktg., Exec., 15 million dollar Sales Award (1980), VP & Bd. of Dir. Grand Rapids Bd. of Realtors (1979-82), CCIM, CRB, GRI, RAM; **EDUC:** 1970, RE, Univ. of MI; **MIL SERV:** USMC, E-5, 1960-63; **OTHER ACT & HONORS:** Pres. Dean Lake Assoc., 1980, Member, Advisory Bd. Grand Valley State Coll.; **HOME ADD:** 2555 Audubon Ct. NE, Grand Rapids, MI 49506, (616)364-9415; **BUS ADD:** 4350 Plainfield Ave., NE, Grand Rapids, MI 49505, (616)363-3853.

HEINEMAN, G. Wendell——**B:** Feb. 24, 1931, VA, *Pres.*, Heineman Co. Ltd.; **PRIM RE ACT:** Broker, Instructor, Syndicator, Consultant, Developer, Builder, Property Manager, Real Estate Publisher; **OTHER RE ACT:** Real Prop. Asset Mgmt., Fortune 1,000 Public Corp.; **REP CLIENTS:** Gen. Accidental Corp., Grand Union Stores, Baltimore Gas & Electric Co., Intl. Paper Co., McCormick Prop., Inc.; **PREV EMPLOY:** Pres. Intl. Paper Realty Corp., VP McCormick Prop. Inc.; **PROFL AFFIL & HONORS:** Dir. NACORE, Pres. Baltimore Cty. C of C; **EDUC:** BS, 1957, Indus. Mgmt., Certificate-Labor Relations, Univ. of Baltimore; **GRAD EDUC:** MBA, 1964, Fin., Mktg., Human Relations, Amer. Univ. - Wash., DC; **EDUC HONORS:** Cum Laude; **OTHER ACT & HONORS:** Dir. Baltimore Area Boy Scouts, Mil. Order of Foreign Wars, Intl. Wine and Food Soc.; **BUS ADD:** 500 Wyneate Rd., Timonium, MD 21093, (301)252-5670.

HEINER, Hal——*Mgr. Corp. Fac.*, Copeland Corp.; **PRIM RE ACT:** Property Manager; **BUS ADD:** Campbell Rd., Sidney, OH 45365, (513)498-3392.*

HEINRICHS, Jerry——**B:** May 8, 1939, Halbur, IA, *Pres.*, Investors Realty, Inc.; **PRIM RE ACT:** Broker; **SERVICES:** Sales, Leasing, Mgt., Counseling, Portfolio Mgt.; **PROFL AFFIL & HONORS:** CCIM; **EDUC:** BS,BA, 1961, Creighton Univ.; **HOME ADD:** 11730 Howard Rd., Omaha, NE 68154, (402)333-1035; **BUS ADD:** 10855 W. Dodge Rd., Omaha, NE 68154, (402)334-7560.

HEINS, Robert August William——**B:** July 30, 1945, Long Island, NY, *Pres.*, Robert Heins AIA, Architect; **PRIM RE ACT:** Architect, Builder; **SERVICES:** Arch., Interior Design, Constr., Constr. Mgmt., Export Consultation; **PROFL AFFIL & HONORS:** AIA; NYS AIA; **EDUC:** BA Arch., 1968, Arch., Syracuse Univ.; **OTHER ACT & HONORS:** 1976, 1978 MIA Arch. Awards Assns.; Village of Bellport Arch. Review Bd.; Bd. of Dir., Brookhaven Memorial Med. Ctr.; **BUS ADD:** 43 Main St., Westhampton Beach, NY 11978, (516)288-5556.

HEIPLE, Don W.——**B:** Oct. 25, 1917, St. Louis, MO, *Pres.*, Red Carpet-Don Heiple & Associates; **PRIM RE ACT:** Broker, Consultant, Instructor, Property Manager; **SERVICES:** Gen. Brokerage - Resid. Comml. Investment; **PROFL AFFIL & HONORS:** Pres., AZ Chap.

CRB's; Past Pres., Phoenix Bd. of Realtors; Past Pres. Nat. Council of Red Carpet Realtors; **EDUC:** AB, 1939, St. Louis Univ.; **GRAD EDUC:** GRI, 1974, Graduate Realtors Inst., AZ State Univ.; **MIL SERV:** US Army, Capt., 1941-1946; **OTHER ACT & HONORS:** American Red Cross, Chap. Pres.; **HOME ADD:** 5530 N. 2nd St., Phoenix, AZ 85012, (602)277-2756; **BUS ADD:** 2601 W. Dunlap, Phoenix, AZ 85021, (602)242-5551.

HEISE, G. Fred——B: July 19, 1931, El Paso, TX, *Pres.*, LR Property Management Inc.; **PRIM RE ACT:** Broker, Consultant, Developer, Owner/Investor, Property Manager; **SERVICES:** All phases consultation for all types shopping ctrs.; **PROFL AFFIL & HONORS:** Pres. FL Council of Shopping Ctrs., Intl. Council of Shopping Ctrs.; **EDUC:** BS, 1953, Bus., CO State Univ.; **GRAD EDUC:** 1965, RE Devel., Mgmt., Shopping Ctr. Mgmt., MI State Univ.; **MIL SERV:** US Army, 1st Lt.; **OTHER ACT & HONORS:** Awarded Lifetime Membership Jaycees 1966; **HOME ADD:** 6 Iroquois Tr., Ormond Beach, FL 32074, (904)673-0999; **BUS ADD:** PO Box 4417, South Dayton, FL 32021, (904)767-7433.

HEISLER, M.G.——B: Dec. 21, 1932, Cleveland, OH, *Pres.*, M.G. Heisler & Co.; **PRIM RE ACT:** Broker, Consultant, Builder, Owner/Investor, Instructor, Property Manager; **PREV EMPLOY:** Same co. 25 yrs.; **PROFL AFFIL & HONORS:** Realtor, IREM, SIR; **EDUC:** 1956, Bys., OH State Univ.; **HOME ADD:** 3916 Ashford Dunwoody Rd., Atlanta, GA 30319, (404)457-3030; **BUS ADD:** Suite One, 2964 Peachtree Rd., NW, Atlanta, GA 30305, (404)237-1537.

HEISTER, J.W.——B: Oct. 23, 1929, Brady, TX, *Pres.*, SHWC, Inc.; **PRIM RE ACT:** Architect, Developer; **SERVICES:** Arch./Engr./Planning; **PROFL AFFIL & HONORS:** AIA, Texas Soc. of Archs., Dallas Chapter AIA, Dallas RE Ex. Assoc. Profl. Serv., Mgmt. Assoc.; **GRAD EDUC:** BA Arch., TX A&M, 1953; **HOME ADD:** 9543 Spring Branch Dr., Dallas, TX 75238, (214)341-0124; **BUS ADD:** 10300 N. Central Expressway, Bldg. 4, Suite 100, Dallas, TX 75231, (214)691-6299.

HEIT, William S.——B: Oct. 9, 1917, Lyons, NY, *CEO*, Foremost Group - Lolita Enterprises; **PRIM RE ACT:** Broker, Consultant; **OTHER RE ACT:** Hunting & Wildlife Resource; **SERVICES:** Ecological Surveys; **REP CLIENTS:** Hunting Clubs; client who desires wildlife resource prop.; **PREV EMPLOY:** Wildlife & Waterfowl Biologist, U.S. Fish & Wildlife Serv.; Asst. Prof., TX A & M; **PROFL AFFIL & HONORS:** Wildlife Soc.; Ducks Unltd.; Pheasants Unltd.; Houston Conservation Grp.; **EDUC:** BS, 1939, Wildlife Mgmt/Conserva., Cornell Univ.; **GRAD EDUC:** 1949, Law, KS Univ.; **EDUC HONORS:** Dir. of Intramural Athletics, Letter - Lacrosse; **MIL SERV:** Army Inst. of Pathology, Coll.; **OTHER ACT & HONORS:** Houston Livestock & Rodeo; Greater Houston Rod & Gun Club; **HOME ADD:** 9227 Vickijohn, Houston, TX 77031, (713)774-5370; **BUS ADD:** 9227 Vickijohn, Houston, TX 77071.

HEJL, David A.——B: Nov. 3, 1948, Midland, TX, *VP Prop. Mgr.*, All-Rich Inc., Mgmt. Div.; **PRIM RE ACT:** Property Manager; **SERVICES:** Prop. Mgmt., Devel., Bldg., & Synd.; **PROFL AFFIL & HONORS:** NAR, TX RE Assn., Midland Home Builders Assn.; **EDUC:** BA, 1971, Religion & Secondary Educ., Abilene Christian Coll.; **GRAD EDUC:** BS ED, 1972, Religion & Secondary Educ., Abilene Christian Coll.; **HOME ADD:** 3624 W. Shandon, Midland, TX 79702, (915)697-5282; **BUS ADD:** 205 E. Michigan, P.O. Box 1721, Midland, TX 79701, (915)683-4864.

HEKTNER, George W.——B: Apr. 26, 1923, Fargo, ND, *VP*, Carr Smith & Associates Inc.; **PRIM RE ACT:** Broker, Consultant, Engineer, Appraiser; **SERVICES:** Bldg. Design & Const. Mgmt., Land Planning; **PROFL AFFIL & HONORS:** NAIOP; NACORE; ASA; CRA; IAREC; **EDUC:** BS, 1950, Engr./Econ./Acctg., Univ. of ND/Univ. of WI; **GRAD EDUC:** Exec. Academy, Univ. of MI; Grad. School - Const. Mgmt., GA State Univ.; **MIL SERV:** U.S. Army, Sgt.; **OTHER ACT & HONORS:** Kiwanis; Task Force Master Plan, Dade Co., FL; **HOME ADD:** 3600 Alhambra Ct., Coral Gables, FL 33134, (305)665-9593; **BUS ADD:** 123 Almeria Ave., Coral Gables, FL 33134, (305)442-0035.

HELBERT, Michael C.——B: Dec. 30, 1950, Wichita, KS, *Treas.*, Guy, Helbert, Bell & Smith, Chartered; **PRIM RE ACT:** Attorney, Owner/Investor; **SERVICES:** Counseling; Title Examinations; **REP CLIENTS:** McCracken RE, Emporia, KS; Farm & Home RE, Citizens Nat. Bank of Emporia, KS; Rural Housing Developers, Ltd.; **PROFL AFFIL & HONORS:** ABA, Sect. Real Prop., Probate & Trust Law; **EDUC:** AB, 1972, Pol. Sci., Univ. of KS; **GRAD EDUC:** JD, 1975, Univ. of KS; **HOME ADD:** 1721 Hammond Dr., Emporia, KS 66801, (316)343-2688; **BUS ADD:** 519 Comml. St., Emporia, KS 66801, (316)343-6500.

HELD, Edward H.——*Pres.*, Land Mart of America; **PRIM RE ACT:** Syndicator; **BUS ADD:** 1400 W. 3rd St., North Little Rock, AR 72114, (501)376-0303.*

HELD, Gilbert——B: July 19, 1943, NY, NY, *Dir.*, 4-Degree Consulting; **PRIM RE ACT:** Consultant; **SERVICES:** Operations Research Analysis, Fin. Analysis, Survey/Questionaires, Gen. Consulting; **REP CLIENTS:** Tymnet, Citicorp, Exxon Instnl.; **PREV EMPLOY:** Honeywell Information Systems, Shell Oil, IBM, US Govt.; **PROFL AFFIL & HONORS:** Inst.of Electrical & Electronic Engrs.; **EDUC:** BSEE, 1965, Math, Operations Research, Electrical Engr., PA Military Coll. Chester,PA; **GRAD EDUC:** MSEE,MSTM MBA, 1966, 1973,1977, Operations Research, Fin., NY Univ., American Univ.; **EDUC HONORS:** Dome Prize, Distinguished Military Student, Phi Kappa Phi; **MIL SERV:** US Army, USAR,Maj.; **OTHER ACT & HONORS:** Author of 3 books, 40 articles, Market Research Advisor to Nat. Publication, Contributing Editor; **HOME ADD:** 4736 Oxford Rd., Macon, GA 31210, (912)477-0293; **BUS ADD:** 4736 Oxford Rd., Macon, GA 31210, (912)477-0293.

HELDERRAD, James E.——*Mgr. Ind. Dev.*, Illinois Metro East; **PRIM RE ACT:** Developer; **BUS ADD:** P. O. Box 596, Edwardsville, IL 62025, (314)231-5555.*

HELGESEN, Andrew——B: Feb. 17, 1952, Ft. Lauderdale, FL, *Atty.*, Bratten and Harris, P.A.; **PRIM RE ACT:** Attorney; **SERVICES:** Legal Counsel, Contract Preparation and Closing; **REP CLIENTS:** Bay Harbor RE, Inc.; Hatton Prop.; **PROFL AFFIL & HONORS:** FL Bar; Palm Beach Cty. Bar Assn.; Palm Beach Cty. Realtors-Atty. Comm. Designated Specialty in Area of Real Prop. Law Under FL Bar Plan; **EDUC:** BA-Pol. Sci., 1973, Pol. Sci., Univ. of S. FL; **GRAD EDUC:** JD, 1977, Law, Univ. of FL; **EDUC HONORS:** Grad. with Highest Honors, Grad. with Honors; **HOME ADD:** 4128 Catalpha Ave., Palm Beach Gardens, FL 33410, (305)622-2538; **BUS ADD:** 707 Comeau Bldg., W. Palm Beach, FL 33401, (305)659-2400.

HELGESEN, Jack C.——B: Aug. 2, 1949, Ogden, UT, *Assoc.*, Bethancourt & Fuller, P.C.; **PRIM RE ACT:** Attorney, Owner/Investor; **REP CLIENTS:** Various RE Devel. Synds., Brokers and Agents; **PREV EMPLOY:** Lic. RE Agent, State of UT 1977-79; **PROFL AFFIL & HONORS:** ABA, Sect. on Taxation and Real Prop., Probate & Trust Law; **EDUC:** BA, 1977, Fin., Bus. Admin., Weber State Coll., Ogden, UT; **GRAD EDUC:** JD, 1980, Brigham Young Univ., J.R.C. School of Law; **EDUC HONORS:** Cum Laude, Author, Editor of "BYU Journal of Legal Studies"; Co-author of "Treatise on Land use and zoning"; **HOME ADD:** 437 E. 10th Ave., Mesa, AZ 85204, (602)833-4649; **BUS ADD:** 20 E. Main, Ste. 600, Mesa, AZ 85201, (802)833-0709.

HELLER, Howard E.——B: June 29, 1950, Brooklyn, NY, *Pres.*, Heller & Heller, P.C.; **PRIM RE ACT:** Broker, Attorney; **REP CLIENTS:** Kinney Shoe Corp.; Am-Cal Const. Corp.; **PROFL AFFIL & HONORS:** ABA, NY State Bar Assn.; **EDUC:** BA Summa Cum Laude, 1971, Hist., Politics, NY Univ.; **GRAD EDUC:** 1974, NY Univ. School of Law; **EDUC HONORS:** Phi Beta Kappa, Founders Day Award, Order of the Coif, Goodman Scholarship Award, Founders Day Award, Pomeroy Prize, JD Cum Laude; **HOME ADD:** 320 East 23rd St., New York, NY 10010; **BUS ADD:** 233 Broadway, New York, NY 10279, (212)233-3466.

HELLER, Roger——B: Aug. 3, 1931, SC, *VP*, Realty Market, Inc.; **PRIM RE ACT:** Broker; **SERVICES:** Private Treaty & Auction Sales, Exchanges, Buyer Brokerage, Mgmt.; **PROFL AFFIL & HONORS:** Farm & Land Inst. of NAR, NAR; Amer. Soc. of Farm Mgrs., Rural Appraisers, Accredited Farm Manager; Accredited Farm & Land Broker; **EDUC:** BS Agriculture, 1953, Educ. & Farm Mgmt., SD State Univ.; **GRAD EDUC:** MS Agriculture, 1957, Educ. & Farm Mgmt., SD State Univ.; **BUS ADD:** 822 E. Lincoln, Box 26, Olivia, MN 56277, (612)523-1951.

HELLGETH, Thomas G.——B: Nov. 13, 1943, Chicago, IL, *Mgr., Comml. Investment Dept.*, Haderlein & Co., Realtors; **PRIM RE ACT:** Broker, Consultant, Owner/Investor; **SERVICES:** Investment Counseling, Site Acquisitions, Exchanges; **REP CLIENTS:** Indiv. or inst. investors for comml. investment prop.; **PROFL AFFIL & HONORS:** Realtors Nat. Mktg. Inst.; Dir. of the IL Chap. 14 CCIM, CCIM; **EDUC:** BBA, 1966, Mktg., Loyola Univ.; **HOME ADD:** 5445 N. Oketo Ave., Chicago, IL 60656, (312)763-7801; **BUS ADD:** 3413 N. Paulina St., Chicago, IL 60657, (312)525-9121.

HELLMAN, Dennis I.——B: July 7, 1946, NY, NY, Baer, Marks & Upham; **PRIM RE ACT:** Attorney; **PROFL AFFIL & HONORS:** ABA, Real Prop. Sect.; NY State Bar Assn., Real Prop. Comm.; **EDUC:** BA, 1967, Pol. Sci., City Coll. of NY; **GRAD EDUC:** JD, 1974, NYU Law Sch.; **EDUC HONORS:** Cum Laude, Spec. Hons. in

Pol. Sci., Articles Editor of Law Review; **HOME ADD:** 23 Old Colony Dr., Larchmont, NY 10538, (914)834-1735; **BUS ADD:** 299 Park Ave., NY, NY 10171, (212)832-1700.

HELLMUTH, Andrew P.——B: Jan. 12, 1946, Springfield, OH, *Broker*, Link-Hellmuth, Inc.; **PRIM RE ACT:** Broker, Consultant, Appraiser, Developer, Owner/Investor, Property Manager, Insuror; **SERVICES:** Resid. and Comml. Brokerage, Devel. and Mgmt.; **PROFL AFFIL & HONORS:** GRI; CRS; **EDUC:** BBA, 1968, Fin., Notre Dame Univ.; **GRAD EDUC:** MBA, 1971, RE/Intl. Fin., Columbia Univ.; **EDUC HONORS:** Beta Gamma Sigma; **MIL SERV:** US Army; 1st Lt.; **HOME ADD:** 202 Hawthorne, Springfield, OH 45504, (513)390-0410; **BUS ADD:** The Riverbend Bldg., 333 N. Limestone St., Springfield, OH 45503, (513)323-6426.

HELM, F. Del——B: Mar. 15, 1930, Montrose, CO, *VP, RE Mgr.*, Lucky Stores, Inc., Midwest Food Div.; **OTHER RE ACT:** Devel. new supermarkets; **PREV EMPLOY:** Chief Branch locations analyst, Bank of Amer.; **PROFL AFFIL & HONORS:** Food Mktg. Inst., ICSC; **EDUC:** BA, 1951, Econ., Univ. of Pacific, Stockton, CA; **MIL SERV:** USA, Sgt.; **HOME ADD:** 3410 49th St., Moline, IL 61265, (309)797-1230; **BUS ADD:** PO Box 67, Rock Island, IL 61201, (309)787-7650.

HELM, Nelson,, Jr.——B: Feb. 16, 1940, Louisville, KY, *Lawyer*, McCoy Gathright & McCoy; **PRIM RE ACT:** Attorney, Syndicator; **SERVICES:** Closings, Title Searches, Document Prep.; **PROFL AFFIL & HONORS:** KY Bar Assn.; **EDUC:** AB, 1962, Econ., Princeton Univ.; **GRAD EDUC:** JD, 1969, Law, Univ. of Louisville; **HOME ADD:** 555 Sunnyside Dr., Louisville, KY 40206; **BUS ADD:** 3626 First Nat. Tower, Louisville, KY 40202, (502)584-4191.

HELM, P. Ralph——*Pres.*, Manitowac Co.; **PRIM RE ACT:** Property Manager; **BUS ADD:** PO Box 66, Manitowac, WI 54220, (414)684-6621.*

HELMKE, Edward——*Dir. RE*, RCA Corp.; **PRIM RE ACT:** Property Manager; **BUS ADD:** 30 Rockefeller Plaza, New York, NY 10020, (212)621-6000.*

HELMS, Charles B.——*VP Fin.*, Crompton & Knowles Corp.; **PRIM RE ACT:** Property Manager; **BUS ADD:** 345 Park Ave., New York, NY 10154, (212)754-1660.*

HELMS, Donald W.——B: Jan 30, 1931, Cleveland, OH, *Pres.*, Helms Realty, Inc.; **PRIM RE ACT:** Broker, Consultant, Developer, Owner/Investor, Instructor, Property Manager; **OTHER RE ACT:** Exchanger, Buyers Broker, Chief Moderator; **SERVICES:** Exchanging, Mgmt. Buyers Broker, Counseling; **PREV EMPLOY:** Comml/Indus. Mgr.; **PROFL AFFIL & HONORS:** Pres. and Chief Moderator of Amer. Property Exchange (APX); Pres. and Chief Moderator of OH Comml. Residential Exchange Assn.; Past Pres. and Chief Moderator of Cleveland Area Realty Exchangers, Exchanger of the Year; **MIL SERV:** US Airborne (Paratroopers), Sgt.; **OTHER ACT & HONORS:** Past Pres. of Medina Rotary; Pres. Gloria Glens Assoc.; Oktoberfest Comm. 4 yrs., Church Council Chmn.; **HOME ADD:** 1 Beachside Blvd., Chippewa Lake, OH 44215, (216)769-3100; **BUS ADD:** 72 Public Square, Medina, OH 44256, (216)725-1800.

HELMS, J.C.——B: May 24, 1941, Bryn Mawr, PA, *Owner, J.C. Helms Interests; Gen. Partner, HN Props. & HN Mgmt.*, J.C. Helms Interests, HN Props., HN Mgmt.; **PRIM RE ACT:** Developer, Owner/Investor, Property Manager; **SERVICES:** Devel., Mgmt.; **PREV EMPLOY:** 1971-1974: Gerald D. Hines Interests; **EDUC:** BA, 1963, Classics & Allied Fields, Harvard Coll.; **GRAD EDUC:** MA, 1966, Classical Philosophy, Harvard Univ.; PhD, 1970, Harvard Univ.; **EDUC HONORS:** Phi Beta Kappa; Detur Prize (3 times); **HOME ADD:** 4530 Briar Hollow Place, Apt. 313, Houston, TX 77027, (713)621-8537; **BUS ADD:** 2425 W. Loop S., Suite 480, Houston, TX 77027, (713)961-9999.

HELMS, Marc Douglas——*Pres.*, The Marc of Excellence Investments, Inc.; **PRIM RE ACT:** Broker, Property Manager, Syndicator; **OTHER RE ACT:** 1031 Tax Deferred Exchanger 3 nat. organizations; **SERVICES:** Buyers, Broker, Mort. Broker, Investor, Cert. Bus. Counselor; **PROFL AFFIL & HONORS:** FL Real Estate Exchangers, RESSI, CBC, AMREX, Academy of RE; **BUS ADD:** Box 4243, Pensacola, FL 32507, (904)434-7460.

HELPERN, Martin W.——B: May 28, 1928, NYC, NY, *Partner*, Laventhol & Horwath, Tax; **OTHER RE ACT:** Accountant CPA; **SERVICES:** Tax and Cash Flow Projections, Tax Analysis, etc.; **REP CLIENTS:** Minskoff, Founders Properties, S & S Development, Pan Am Building, etc.; **PROFL AFFIL & HONORS:** AICPA, NY Society of CPA's, RESSI; **EDUC:** 1951, Acctg., Pace Univ.; **GRAD EDUC:** LLM, 1961, Taxation, School of Law, NY Univ.; JD, 1957, School of Law, NY Univ.; **EDUC HONORS:** Dean's List; **HOME ADD:** 11 Fifth Ave., New York, NY, (212)228-2781; **BUS ADD:** 919 Third Ave., New York, NY 10022, (212)980-3100.

HELPERN, Robert E.——B: Feb. 13, 1946, NYC, *Partner*, Newman Tannenbaum Helpern & Hirschtritt; **PRIM RE ACT:** Attorney; **SERVICES:** Legal Services; **PROFL AFFIL & HONORS:** NY State Bar Assn. (Comm. on RE Fin. and Liens); **EDUC:** BA, 1967, Poli. Sci., Brown Univ.; **GRAD EDUC:** JD, 1971, NYU School of Law; **EDUC HONORS:** Dean's List, Editor, Law Review; **MIL SERV:** US Army Res., E-4; **HOME ADD:** 71 Raymond Pl., Hewlett, NY 11557, (516)569-2125; **BUS ADD:** 310 Madison Ave., New York, NY 10017, (212)986-9700.

HELSTEN, Charles T.——B: Apr. 30, 1933, Duluth, MN, Fortune Real Estate, Inc.; **PRIM RE ACT:** Broker, Owner/Investor; **SERVICES:** Investment and Comml. Prop. Brokerage and Counseling; **REP CLIENTS:** Investors and users - comml. prop.; **PREV EMPLOY:** USAF, 1952-1976; **PROFL AFFIL & HONORS:** Comml. Investment Div. El Paso Bd. of Realtors, CCIM W. TX Chap.; **EDUC:** Bus. Admin., 1975, Louisiana Tech; **MIL SERV:** USAF, Colonel, Distinguished Flying Cross (2), Air Medal (11), Distinguished Service Medal; **HOME ADD:** 5469 La Estancia, El Paso, TX 79932, (915)581-4871; **BUS ADD:** 4849 N. Mesa, Ste. 206, El Paso, TX 79912, (915)544-6208.

HELWIG, Charles E.——B: Jan. 23, 1946, Allentown, PA, *Sr. Dev. Dir.*, The American City Corp.; **PRIM RE ACT:** Consultant; **SERVICES:** Tech. Asst. to Public Sector on Downtown Devel.; **REP CLIENTS:** Secondary market cities, Dir. of Comm. Devel.; **PREV EMPLOY:** Devel. Sales & Mktg.; **PROFL AFFIL & HONORS:** ULI; Lic. MD State RE Broker; **EDUC:** BS, 1968, Econ. & Corp. Fin., Babson Coll., Wellesley Hills, MA; **HOME ADD:** 5325 Night Roost Ct., Columbia, MD 21045, (301)730-1336; **BUS ADD:** The Amer. City Bldg., Suite 701, Columbia, MD 21044, (301)992-6077.

HELYFIELD, R.L.——*Exec. Dir.*, Southeast Mississippi Industrial Council; **PRIM RE ACT:** Developer; **BUS ADD:** P. O. Box 280 County Courthouse, Ellisville, MS 39440, (601)477-8617.*

HEMMER, Edgar H.——B: Sept. 8, 1923, Seymour, IN, *Pres., Prof. of RE*, Hemmer Enterprises, IN Univ.; **PRIM RE ACT:** Consultant, Developer, Owner/Investor, Instructor; **SERVICES:** Consulting, Feasibiltiy & Leasing; **REP CLIENTS:** Small fin. inst. and devel. cos.; **PREV EMPLOY:** US Naval Aviator; **PROFL AFFIL & HONORS:** Amer. RE & Urban Econ. Assn., Fin. Mgmt. Assn., PhD.; **EDUC:** BS, BSAE, 1946, 1954, Engr., US Naval Academy, US Naval Postgrad. Sch.; **GRAD EDUC:** MS, MSIE, PhD., 1955,1969, 1971, Indus. Engr., Fin. & RE, Purdue Univ.; **MIL SERV:** USN, Cmdr.; **HOME ADD:** 16ll Sheridan Rd., W. Lafayette, IN 47906, (317)463-4809; **BUS ADD:** 801 W. MI St., IndianapoLis, IN 46223, (317)264-4121.

HEMRY, Richard M.——B: Feb. 6, 1931, Springfield, OH, *Owner*, Hemry Realty Co.; **PRIM RE ACT:** Broker, Consultant, Appraiser, Instructor; **SERVICES:** Valuation Resid., Comml. & Indus., Mktg. of same; **REP CLIENTS:** Lenders, employee transfer co's. & indiv. corporate clients as well as indivs. in both valuation & mktg.; **PREV EMPLOY:** Self employed since Feb., 1959; **PROFL AFFIL & HONORS:** Soc. of RE Appraisers; AIREA; NAR; Amer. Soc. of Appraisers; Amer. RE and Urban Econ. Assn.; RNMI, SRA; RM #401 Sr. Member, Urban Prop.; GRI; CRS; **EDUC:** BS, 1953, Mktg./Merchandising, Miami Univ., Oxford, OH; **OTHER ACT & HONORS:** Various Masonic Orders & Nobles of the Mystic Shrine; Troop Comm. member, BSA; COB, of Zoning Appeals, Springfield Township; **HOME ADD:** 401 Capri Cir., Springfield, OH 45505, (513)325-9101; **BUS ADD:** 401 Capri Cir., Springfield, OH 45505, (513)325-6959.

HENDERSON, Dean R.——B: Oct. 17, 1948, Sparta, IL, *Partner*, Peat, Marwick, Mitchell & Co.; **OTHER RE ACT:** CPA; **SERVICES:** Tax Consulting; review of proposed transactions; **REP CLIENTS:** Partnerships; indiv.; corp.; S & L assns. participating in joint ventures and gen. partners synd. RE tax shelters; projects include housing, office buildings, apts., industrial parks & restoration of hist. structures; **PROFL AFFIL & HONORS:** AICPA; FL Inst. of CPAs; **EDUC:** BBA, 1970, Acctg., Univ. of MO, Columbia; **HOME ADD:** 11006 Ridgedale Rd., Tampa, FL 33617; **BUS ADD:** P.O. Box 1439, Tampa, FL 33601, (813)223-1466.

HENDERSON, J. Harrison, III——B: Aug. 13, 1946, Alexandria, LA, *Atty.*, Guste, Barnett & Shushan; **PRIM RE ACT:** Consultant, Attorney, Developer, Builder, Owner/Investor, Property Manager; **EDUC:** BA, 1968, Bus. Admin., The Citadel; **GRAD EDUC:** JD, 1971, Civil Law, Tulane Law School; **MIL SERV:** US Army Res., Capt.; **HOME ADD:** 820 Third St., New Orleans, LA 70130,

(504)899-7838; **BUS ADD:** 1624 1st Nat. Bank of Comm. Bldg., New Orleans, LA 70112, (504)529-4141.

HENDERSON, R. Stephen——**B:** Sept. 19, 1942, OH, *Owner/Mgr.*, Henderson Land Investment Co.; **PRIM RE ACT:** Broker, Appraiser, Property Manager, Owner/Investor; **PROFL AFFIL & HONORS:** FLI; OH Chap. Amer. Soc. Farm Mgrs. & Rural Appraisers; RESSI; Ohio Assn. of Realtors; Champaign Cty. Bd. of Realtors; **EDUC:** BS, 1970, CA State Poly. Univ.; **MIL SERV:** US Army, Spec. 4, Purple Heart, Air Medal; **OTHER ACT & HONORS:** Champaign Co. Repub. Exec. Comm.; **BUS ADD:** 6911 W. Rte. 36, St. Paris, OH 43072, (513)652-1974.

HENDERSON, Ray——*VP, Treas. & Secy.*, Imperial Sugar; **PRIM RE ACT:** Property Manager; **BUS ADD:** P. O. Box 9, Sugar Land, TX 77478, (713)491-9181.*

HENDERSON, Tom——**B:** Oct. 15, 1942, Mackinaw, IL, *Owner*, Henderson Real Estate; **PRIM RE ACT:** Broker, Consultant, Appraiser, Instructor, Real Estate Publisher; **PREV EMPLOY:** RE Instructor, IL State Univ.; **PROFL AFFIL & HONORS:** Bloomington-Normal Bd. of Realtors; IL Assn. of Realtors; NAR; IREA; Natl. RE Educ. Assn.; Assn. of IL RE Educ., Pres., ICA Intl. Org. of RE Appraisers; **EDUC:** BS, 1964, Univ. of IL.; **GRAD EDUC:** MS, 1971, Fin. & Mktg., IL St Univ.; **MIL SERV:** USMC, Capt.; **OTHER ACT & HONORS:** Co-author of "RE Principles and Practices" by Ficek, Henderson & Johnson; "IL Supplement for RE Priniciples and Practices" by Carlon, Henderson & Johnson; "RE License Examination Guide" by Henderson Ficek, Johnson & Kruse; all pub. by Merrill Publishing Co.; **HOME ADD:** 29 Univ. Ct., Normal, IL 61761, (309)452-8763; **BUS ADD:** 309 W. Beaufort, Normal, IL 61761, (309)454-1241.

HENDRIAN, Tom——**B:** July 27, 1953, Detroit, MI, *Devel. Assoc.*; **OTHER RE ACT:** RE Devel.; **REP CLIENTS:** Hotel corps., mgmt. cos., clubs, devels.; **PREV EMPLOY:** 10 yrs. Holiday Inns., Inc., Mgmt.; 3 yrs Pannell Kerr Forster, Consultant; **PROFL AFFIL & HONORS:** CPA, GA; **EDUC:** BA, 1975, Hotel, Rest. & Instl. Mgmt., MI State Univ.; **GRAD EDUC:** MBA, 1979, Acctg., Wayne State Univ.; **EDUC HONORS:** Beta Gamma Sigma; **HOME ADD:** 2479 St. Augustine Tr., Marietta, GA 30067, (404)853-0479; **BUS ADD:** 225 Peachtree St., Atlanta, GA 30303, (404)688-7541.

HENDRY, John L., III——**B:** Dec. 3, 1930, China, *Owner*, Hendry Investments; **PRIM RE ACT:** Developer, Owner/Investor, Property Manager; **SERVICES:** Devel. and const. of comml. props., apts., and the mgmt. thereof; **PREV EMPLOY:** 1954-1962, Asst. Mgr., Mtg. Loan Dept., Maxson, Mahoney, Turner; 1962-1965, Mgr., Ptr., Trinity Investments (RE); 1965-1967, Ptr., Hendry & Merritt (RE); 1967 to present, Hendry Investments (RE Devel.); **PROFL AFFIL & HONORS:** AIREA; Econ. Devel. Found.; IREM; Soc. of Resid. Appraisers; NAR; Local Assn. of RE Bds.; San Antonio Apt. Assn.; NAHB; C of C (San Antonio & N. San Antonio), MAI; CPM; **EDUC:** BBA, 1963, Bus. Admin./Banking/RE, So. Methodist Univ.; **GRAD EDUC:** MBA, 1963, Bus. Admin., So. Methodist Univ.; **EDUC HONORS:** Cert. of Achievement in RE, 1959; **HOME ADD:** 401 Terrell Rd., San Antonio, TX 78209, (512)826-6105; **BUS ADD:** 8700 Crownhill Blvd., 500 Crown Tower, San Antonio, TX 78209, (512)824-2322.

HENER, Karla——*Ed.*, American Inst. of Real Estate Appraisers, Appraiser; **PRIM RE ACT:** Real Estate Publisher; **BUS ADD:** 430 N. Michigan Ave., Chicago, IL 60611, (312)440-8141.*

HENKEL, Edward, Jr.——**B:** Jan. 18, 1924, Detroit, MI, *Pres.*, Edward Henkel Realty Co.; **PRIM RE ACT:** Broker; **OTHER RE ACT:** Land Contract Investments; **SERVICES:** servicing mort. correspondent for 4 life ins. cos.; **PROFL AFFIL & HONORS:** MBA of MI, NAR, MI Assn. of Realtors, RNMI, Past Pres. Detroit Bd. of Realtors, Detroit Realtor of the Year; **EDUC:** BA, 1949, Econ., Forensics, Kenyon Coll, Gambier, OH; **EDUC HONORS:** Tau Kappa Alpha, Forensic honor soc.; **MIL SERV:** USCG, Seaman; **OTHER ACT & HONORS:** Former mbr., Grosse Pointe Park Bd. of Review, Ctry Club of Detroit, Grosse Point Hunt Club; **HOME ADD:** 27 Preston Pl., Grosse Pointe Farms, MI 48236, (313)886-6167; **BUS ADD:** 500 Executive Pk Bldg., 500 Stephenson Hwy., Troy, MI 48236, (313)583-9700.

HENLEY, J. Rudy——**B:** Aug. 28, 1949, S. Charleston, WV, *Broker, VP*, McCabe-Henley Properties Inc., Comml. Investment; **PRIM RE ACT:** Broker, Developer, Syndicator; **SERVICES:** Investment Counseling, Brokerage, Devel. and Synd. of Comml. Investment Prop.; **REP CLIENTS:** Bank trust depts. and indiv. investors; **PROFL AFFIL & HONORS:** Charleston Municipal Planning Commn.; RESSI; RNMI, CCIM; CRS; **EDUC:** BBA, 1971, Mktg., WV Univ.; **HOME ADD:** 807 Oakwood Rd., Charleston, WV 25314, (304)343-9676; **BUS ADD:** POB 3708, Charleston, WV 25335, (304)342-4415.

HENRY, J. Donald——*Pres.*, PGO Realty; **PRIM RE ACT:** Broker, Owner/Investor; **SERVICES:** Complete Resid. Sales, Appraisals, Devel, ME MLS, York Cty. MLS, Homefinders, Inc. and Nat. Home Relocation; **PROFL AFFIL & HONORS:** NAR, Cert. Resid. Mgmt. and SREA, Portland Bd. of Realtors, Realtor of the Year 76 & 78, ME Assn. Realtor of the Year 1978, NAR Omeaga Tau Rho, 2 term NAR Dir. from ME, 10 yr. Legislative NAR, Presid. & Charter Member Gorham C of C, Chmn. ME RE Commn. Continuing Educ. Comm. 1979-1980; **EDUC:** Univ. of NH and Boston Univ.; **MIL SERV:** USAF, Sgt.; **OTHER ACT & HONORS:** Chmn. of Bd. member Gorham Planning Bd., Founder & Pres. Gorham C of C, Pres. 78-80 Gorham Hist. Soc., Past Pres. Gorham Lions Intl.; **HOME ADD:** 21 Alden Ln., Gorham, ME 04038, (207)839-2701; **BUS ADD:** 39 Main St., Gorham, ME 04038, (207)839-3309.

HENRY, John J.——**B:** Apr. 11, 1944, Wilmington, DE, *VP/Gen. Mgr.*, Century 21, Hubbell RE Co.; **PRIM RE ACT:** Broker, Instructor, Consultant, Appraiser, Property Manager; **OTHER RE ACT:** Gen. Mgmt.; **SERVICES:** Consulting, Appraising, Investment Analysis, Prop. Mgmt.; **REP CLIENTS:** Private & instnl. investors, lenders; **PREV EMPLOY:** 10 yrs. RE exp.; **PROFL AFFIL & HONORS:** SREA, RESSI, RNMI, Top Century 21 co. for entire state of MI in 1979 and 1980; **EDUC:** BA, 1972, Mgmt., MI State Univ.; **GRAD EDUC:** MBA, 1972, Fin. (26 hrs. toward degree), MI State Univ.; **EDUC HONORS:** Grad. with hon.; **MIL SERV:** US Army, SP/5, Vietnam Service Medal, Vietnam Campaign Medal; **OTHER ACT & HONORS:** MI State Univ. Alumni Assn., Past member of Lions Club, Rotary Club, and Jaycees, Outstanding Young Man of Amer. (1979); **HOME ADD:** 5619 Bearcreek Dr., Lansing, MI 48917, (517)323-4800; **BUS ADD:** 4515 W. Saginaw Hwy, Lansing, MI 48917, (517)321-1000.

HENRY, Richard Lee——**B:** Mt. Vernon, IL, *Atty. at Law*, Richard Lee Henry; **PRIM RE ACT:** Attorney; **SERVICES:** Title Work Purchase/Sale of Comml. and Resid. Props., Comml. Prop. Devel.; **REP CLIENTS:** Mort. loan div. of fin. inst., indiv. purchasers/sellers of comml. & resid. props., indiv. investors in comml. props., comml. material suppliers, title co.; **PROFL AFFIL & HONORS:** Garland Cty. Bar Assn., Phi Alpha Delta, AR Bar Assn., ABA (RE section); **EDUC:** BA, 1971, Psych. and Drama, Henderson State Coll.; **GRAD EDUC:** JD, 1974, Banking and Comml. Law, Univ. of AR.; **EDUC HONORS:** Honor Student, Honor Role; **MIL SERV:** U.S. Army, Sgt.; **OTHER ACT & HONORS:** Hot Springs Downtown Lions Club, St. Lukes Episcopal Church; **HOME ADD:** 206 Shawnee, Hot Springs, AR 71901, (501)623-8843; **BUS ADD:** 405 ABT Towers Bldg., Hot Springs, AR 71901, (501)624-1401.

HENSELER, Gerry——*Treasurer*, Banta, George, Company; **PRIM RE ACT:** Property Manager; **BUS ADD:** Curtis Reed Plaza, Merasha, WI 54952.*

HENSHAW, N.D.——**B:** June 20, 1922, Madill, OK, *Owner*, N.D. Henshaw, Investments; **PRIM RE ACT:** Developer, Builder, Owner/Investor; **SERVICES:** Land Devel., Prop. Rental, Resid., Comml., Indus.; **PROFL AFFIL & HONORS:** Urban Land Inst.; NAIOP; NAHB; Tulsa C of C; Broken Arrow C of C; **EDUC:** BS, 1948, Bus. Mgmt., Univ. of Tulsa; **MIL SERV:** USAAC, Cadet; **OTHER ACT & HONORS:** Tulsa Symphony; Opera; Center for Physically Limited; **HOME ADD:** 3132 Columbia Cir., Tulsa, OK 74105, (918)742-8894; **BUS ADD:** 9511 E. 46th, Tulsa, OK 74145, (918)622-2313.

HENSLEE, S. Elmo——**B:** Oct. 22, 1924, Birmingham, AL, *Pres.*, Pecos Development Corp.; **PRIM RE ACT:** Broker, Engineer, Architect, Developer, Owner/Investor, Syndicator; **PREV EMPLOY:** Pecos Devel. Corp. - 33 years; **PROFL AFFIL & HONORS:** NAHB, NAR, Soc. of Profl. Engrs.; **EDUC:** BA, 1948, Arch., TX Tech Univ.; BS, 1948, Civil Engr., TX Tech. Univ.; **HOME ADD:** 150 W. Editis, Los Altos, CA 94022, (425)941-5409; **BUS ADD:** 349 First St., Los Altos, CA 94022, (415)948-0407.

HENSON, E. Eddie——**B:** June 7, 1936, Elk City, OK, *Pres.*, Williams Realty Corp.; **PRIM RE ACT:** Developer, Property Manager; **SERVICES:** Dev. of mixed use projects and Mgmt. of same and Restoration of hist. structures; **PREV EMPLOY:** Prop. Dev. Exec. for Helmerich & Payne; **PROFL AFFIL & HONORS:** ULI, Cert. Shopping Ctr. Mgr. Org., IREM, Young Presidents Org., ICSC, NAR; **EDUC:** BME, 1959, Texas Tech.; **GRAD EDUC:** MBA, 1963, Harvard Bus. School; **OTHER ACT & HONORS:** Dir. Tulsa C of C, Dir. Indian Nat. Council of Boy Scouts of Amer., Pres., Downtown Tulsa Unltd.; **HOME ADD:** 1520 E. 26 Place, Tulsa, OK 74114, (918)747-7895; **BUS ADD:** P.O. Box 2400, Tulsa, OK 74101, (918)588-2840.

HENSON, William R.——B: Sept. 30, 1924, AR, *Pres.*, Bill Henson Co., Inc., dba Superior Home Loans; **PRIM RE ACT:** Broker; **SERVICES:** Home Loan Brokerage Firm; **REP CLIENTS:** Borrowers and Investors; **PROFL AFFIL & HONORS:** NAR, CA Assn. of Realtors, CA Indep. Mort. Brokers Assn., So. Alameda Cty. Bd. of Realtors, Realtor of the Year 1980-SACBOR; **MIL SERV:** US Army, Maj., Bronze Star w/ Oak Leaf Cluster and Combat Inf. Badge; **OTHER ACT & HONORS:** Rotary Club. BBB & Hayward C of C; **HOME ADD:** 18650 Brickell Way, Castro Valley, CA 94546, (415)886-0127; **BUS ADD:** 21344 Mission Blvd., Hayward, CA 94541, (415)889-1900.

HENTSCHEL, John Joseph——B: Apr. 30, 1950, Baltimore, MD, *Pres.*, The Hentschel Org.; **PRIM RE ACT:** Broker, Consultant, Appraiser, Instructor, Syndicator; **OTHER RE ACT:** Assoc. Prof. of RE, Univ. of Baltimore; **SERVICES:** RE Appraisal & Counseling; Investment Prop. Brokerage; Synd. of Income Producing Prop.; **REP CLIENTS:** Mort. lenders & indiv. & instit. investors in RE; govt. agencies; **PROFL AFFIL & HONORS:** Soc. of RE Appraisers (Assoc.); Nat. Assn. of Realtors; RE Securities & Synd. Instit.; **EDUC:** BSBA, 1973, Fin., Towson State Univ.; **MIL SERV:** MD Air Nat. Gd., Sgt., Nat. Defense Ribbon, Meritorious Unit Citation, Good Conduct Ribbon; **HOME ADD:** 3110 Lawnview Ave., Baltimore, MD 21213, (301)276-4439; **BUS ADD:** 2838 Kentucky Ave., Baltimore, MD 21213, (301)483-5522.

HENWARD, DeBanks M., III——B: June 26, 1931, Syracuse, NY, *Pres.*, The Franchise Group, Inc., Hometels of America Franchising, Inc.; **PRIM RE ACT:** Attorney, Developer, Owner/Investor; **OTHER RE ACT:** Franchising; **SERVICES:** Franchise, RE, Arch. Training; **REP CLIENTS:** Hometels of America Franchising, Inc,; Granada Royale Hometels (hotel chain); **PREV EMPLOY:** Ramada Inns, Inc.; **PROFL AFFIL & HONORS:** NACORE (past); **EDUC:** BA, 1953, Eng. & Poli. Sci., Syracuse Univ.; **GRAD EDUC:** JD, 1958, Syracuse Univ.; **MIL SERV:** USMC, 1st Lt.; **OTHER ACT & HONORS:** Asst. Counsel, Corp. Comm. City of Syracuse; Comm. Counsel, NY State Senate; NY State and AZ Bar; **BUS ADD:** 3644 E. McDowell, Suite 214, Phoenix, AZ 85008, (602)267-9409.

HENZE, Mark E.——B: Sept. 22, 1956, Wilmington, DE, *Atty. at Law*, Sole Practitioner; **PRIM RE ACT:** Attorney; **SERVICES:** Legal Serv. for Devels. & Bldrs.; **PROFL AFFIL & HONORS:** Amer. Bar Assn., CO Bar Assn., Licensed to practice in CO, Var. scholastic awards; **EDUC:** BA, 1978, Sci. & Pol. Sci., No. Central Coll., Naperville, IL; **GRAD EDUC:** JD, 1981, Legal (Real Prop. conc.), Univ. of Denver, Coll. of Law; **EDUC HONORS:** Cum Laude, Ed. of yr. Award (Newspaper), Distinguished Student Service Award, Cum Laude, Independent Research on Time-Sharing Accepted for Publication; **OTHER ACT & HONORS:** Published article on Alcohol Fuels in 1977, used by US Senate; Published book entitled "The Law of Time-Shared Property", Clark Boardman & Co., Ltd., (1982); **HOME ADD:** 1810 S. Williams Ave., Denver, CO 80210, (303)722-3419; **BUS ADD:** 1810 S. Williams Ave., Denver, CO 80210.

HEPBURN, Brian——*Vice President Fac. Planning*, Bard, C.R., Inc.; **PRIM RE ACT:** Property Manager; **BUS ADD:** 731 Central Ave., Murray Hill, NJ 07974, (201)277-8000.*

HEPNER, Patricia R.——B: July 4, 1938, Ellsworth, KS, *Sec./Treas.*, Hepner Realty, Inc.; **PRIM RE ACT:** Broker, Consultant, Appraiser, Developer, Builder, Property Manager, Owner/Investor, Insuror; **PROFL AFFIL & HONORS:** Natl., State, Local Bd. of Realtors, GRI, CRS; **OTHER ACT & HONORS:** Outstanding Young Woman of Amer., Life Membership Org. Jr. Auxil. Volunteer Council VP; **HOME ADD:** Hwy 60 W, Conway, AR 72032, (501)329-6393; **BUS ADD:** Hwy 64 E, Conway, AR 72032, (501)329-6856.

HERAMB, Brent R.——B: May 24, 1947, San Diego, CA, *Owner*, Brent R. Heramb, Attorney at Law; **PRIM RE ACT:** Broker, Consultant, Attorney, Owner/Investor, Property Manager; **OTHER RE ACT:** CPA; **SERVICES:** Prop. Mgmt., Consulting, Legal; **REP CLIENTS:** Homeowner Assns. & RE Devels.; **PREV EMPLOY:** Deloitte Haskins & Sells, CPA's, 1968-1973; **PROFL AFFIL & HONORS:** AICPA; CA Soc. of CPA's; ABA; CA State Bar Assn.; San Diego Cty. Bar Assn.; Community Assn. Inst., CPA, Atty., RE Broker; **EDUC:** BS, 1968, Acctg., San Diego State Univ.; **GRAD EDUC:** JD, 1977, Law, CA Western School of Law; **EDUC HONORS:** Cum Laude; **MIL SERV:** USN Res.; PO2; **BUS ADD:** 5551 Toyon Rd., San Diego, CA 92115, (714)566-3340.

HERBERG, Roland L.——B: July 29, 1927, ND, *Pres.*, Hawaiiana Investment Co., Inc., Sub. of C. Brewer & Co. Ltd.; **OTHER RE ACT:** Corp. Asset Mgr.; Gen. Mgr.; Policy Devel.; Broler; Strategist; Appraiser; Negotiator; **SERVICES:** Strategy, Planning, Devel., Operations, Mktg.; **REP CLIENTS:** Lge. corps. & indiv. investors; **PREV EMPLOY:** Pres. Snowmass Amer. Corp., devels. of snowmass Resort Comm., Aspen, CO; VP James Corp., S. CA Comm.; **PROFL AFFIL & HONORS:** ULI, Recreational Devel. Council, Honolulu Bd. of Realtors; **EDUC:** BS, 1950, Acctg., San Diego State Univ.; **GRAD EDUC:** MBA, 1952, Indus. & Const. Mgmt., Stanford Grad. Sch. of Bus.; **MIL SERV:** USNR, AEM 3/c; **OTHER ACT & HONORS:** HI Resort Devel. conference, State Citizen's Advisory Comm. on Coastal Zone Mgmt., Tr. Pacific & Asian Affairs Council; **HOME ADD:** 1627 Kamole St., Honolulu, HI 96821, (808)373-2979; **BUS ADD:** P. O. Box 1826, Honolulu, HI 96805, (808)544-6165.

HERBST, Dr. Lawrence——B: Aug. 8, 1946, Haverhill, MA, *Pres. and Adm.*, L. Herbst Farms/Larry's Western Supply, Lawrence Herbst; **PRIM RE ACT:** Consultant, Developer, Lender, Owner/Investor; **PREV EMPLOY:** Dr. Lawrence Herbst: rancher, trucker, vet, businessman; **PROFL AFFIL & HONORS:** US Sports Clubs; SCM; Who's Who in Amer.; Who's Who in the West; **EDUC:** UCLA/Cornell/Fairfax; **BUS ADD:** P. O. B. 1659, Beverly Hills, CA 90213.

HERD, Alan A. (Scotty)——B: May 11, 1938, Los Angeles, CA, *Prin.*, A. Scott Herd Associates; **PRIM RE ACT:** Broker, Consultant, Developer, Owner/Investor, Instructor, Syndicator; **SERVICES:** RE Investment Counseling, Investment and Brokerage; **REP CLIENTS:** Corps. and private investors; **PROFL AFFIL & HONORS:** Los Angeles and Beverly Hills Bd. of Realtors; Amer. Soc. of RE Counselors; RE Cert. Inst., GRI, CRE, RECI; **EDUC:** BS, 1960, Urban Land Econ., Univ. of CA at Berkeley; **MIL SERV:** USMCR, Cpl. (E-4); **BUS ADD:** 144 S. Beverly Dr., #403, Beverly Hills, CA 90212, (213)273-8168.

HERD, Jon T.——B: June 2, 1936, Chicago, IL, *Pres.*, Prop Mgmt. of Amer., Inc., Herd Mgmt. Co.; **PRIM RE ACT:** Property Manager; **OTHER RE ACT:** all related to mgmt, acquisition, sales, rentals; **SERVICES:** All including market surveys & ins. & tax rendering; **REP CLIENTS:** Drs., lawyers, realtors; **PREV EMPLOY:** 26 yrs. prop. mgmt.; **PROFL AFFIL & HONORS:** IREM, NAHB, NAR, CPM, RAM; **EDUC:** 1956, Acctg., Wright Coll., Chicago & La Salle Ext. Univ., Chicago; **OTHER ACT & HONORS:** City Chrm., Political 8 yrs. Gov. Housing Commn. Sheriff's Assn., Shriner, Girl Scout, C of C, Instr. El Paso Apt. Assn., Intl. Bus. Coll. and Univ. of TX at El Paso, TX Apt. Assn., El Paso Apt. Assn., Natl. Apt. Assn.; **HOME ADD:** 8408 Whitus Dr., El Paso, TX 79925, (915)779-1469; **BUS ADD:** 8408 Whitus Dr., El Paso, TX 79925, (915)779-1460.

HERING, J. Clayton——B: Mar. 5, 1941, Portland, OR, *VP*, Norris, Beggs & Simpson, Portland & Tacoma Rgnl. Offices; **PRIM RE ACT:** Broker; **SERVICES:** Comml./Indus. Sales & Leasing, Prop. Mgmt., Real Estate Finin.; **REP CLIENTS:** New England Mutual Life, John Hancock Mutual Life, Farmers New World Life, Manufacturers Life, Quadrant Corp., A Weyerhauser Subs., Equitable Life Ins., Olympia & York, Lincoln Props., Orbanco Fin. Servs., Tacoma S&L, First Interstate Bank of WA; **PREV EMPLOY:** Zellerbach Paper Co., 1967-1972; **PROFL AFFIL & HONORS:** NAR; Portland Bd. of Realtors; Portland BOMA; ICSC; **EDUC:** BA, 1963, Econ., Dartmouth Coll.; **EDUC HONORS:** Grad. with Distinction in Econ.; **MIL SERV:** USMC, Capt., Navy Commendation with Combat V; **OTHER ACT & HONORS:** Multnomah Athletic Club; Racquet Club; Univ. Club; Good Samaritan Bd. of Tr.; OR Symphony, Bd. Member; Pres., Artquake Festival Bd.; Portland Better Business Bd. Member; Assoc. for Portland Progress Bd.; **HOME ADD:** 1708 S.W. Highland Rd., Portland, OR 97221, (503)223-5201; **BUS ADD:** 720 S.W. Washington, Portland, OR 97205, (503)223-7181.

HERINK, Robert V.——B: Feb. 28, 1927, Leigh, *Indep. Fee Appraiser & Broker*; **PRIM RE ACT:** Broker, Syndicator, Consultant, Appraiser, Builder, Property Manager, Lender, Owner/Investor, Insuror; **SERVICES:** Prim. Resid. Brokerage & Appraisals; **PROFL AFFIL & HONORS:** SREA, Bd. of Dir., SREA Chapt., CRS, GRI; **EDUC:** BS, 1950, Commerce, Creighton Univ.; **GRAD EDUC:** MBA, 1965, Gen. Bus. Major, Acctg. & Mktg. Minors, Creighton Univ.; **MIL SERV:** US Army, Pvt.; **OTHER ACT & HONORS:** Former Parish council member, St. Robert's Parish, Omaha, NE; Past Omaha MLS Chmn.; **HOME TEL:** (402)571-2500; **BUS ADD.** 9521 Spencer St., Omaha, NE 68134, (402)571-2500.

HERITAGE, Jack W.——B: Nov. 5, 1919, Perry, OH, *Chmn. of Bd.*, Heritage Co. of FL; **PRIM RE ACT:** Broker, Consultant, Insuror; **SERVICES:** Gen. RE and Ins.; **REP CLIENTS:** Home buyers, investors; **PREV EMPLOY:** Coach and teacher (1951-56), RE Ins. (1956 to present); **PROFL AFFIL & HONORS:** CRB Mgr. (CRB), CRS, GRI, Past Pres. Sarasota Bd. of Realtors; 1970 Realtor of the Year (Sarasota Bd.); Past Pres. CRB, State Chapt.; **EDUC:** BS, 1949, Educ. PE, Bowling Green State Univ.; **GRAD EDUC:** MS, 1951, Educ. PE, George Willaims Coll.; **MIL SERV:** US Army, 3 and half yrs., pvt.; **OTHER ACT & HONORS:** City Comm. (1971-74); Dir.

Southeast First. Nat. Bank of Sarasota (1972 to present); Past Pres. Sarasota Cty. C of C (1980); Past Pres. Sarasota YMCA (1966-67); Past Pres. Civitan (1968-69); Chmn. Van Wezel Performing Arts Bd. of Dir.; Past Chmn. Sarasota Cty. Better Bus. Council; **HOME ADD:** 2152 Wood St., Sarasota, FL 33577, (813)955-8517; **BUS ADD:** 1859 Main St., Sarasota, FL 33577, (813)366-5190.

HERMAN, A.——*Dir. Store Dev.*, Ethan Allen, Inc.; **PRIM RE ACT:** Property Manager; **BUS ADD:** Ethan Allen Dr., Danbury, CT 06810, (203)743-8000.*

HERMANN, Richard C.——B: Sept. 26, 1947, Chicago, IL, *Pres.*, Traverse Realty & Devel.; **PRIM RE ACT:** Syndicator, Developer, Property Manager; **SERVICES:** Devel. & Synd. of Comml. Props.; **REP CLIENTS:** Pvt. Investment Grps.; **PREV EMPLOY:** Coopers & Lybrand 1969-1975; **PROFL AFFIL & HONORS:** AICPA, RESSI, Chicago RE Bd., NASD; **EDUC:** BS, BA, 1969, Acctg., MI Tech. Univ.; **GRAD EDUC:** MST, 1975, Taxation, DePaul Univ., Chicago; **EDUC HONORS:** Magna Cum Laude; **MIL SERV:** US Army, Spec. 4; **OTHER ACT & HONORS:** Univ. Club of Chicago; **HOME ADD:** 1109 W. Webster, Chicago, IL 60614, (312)477-8729; **BUS ADD:** 850 N. DeWitt 4E, Chicago, IL 60611, (312)951-8440.

HERMELINK, Herman M.——B: May 26, 1917, Kansas City, KS, *Pres. (Retd.)*, Crescent Land & Timber Corp.; **PRIM RE ACT:** Developer, Property Manager; **OTHER RE ACT:** Timber Mgmt.; **PROFL AFFIL & HONORS:** Soc. of Amer. Foresters, Forest Farmers Assn., NC Forestry Assn., Forest Conservationist of the yr.: 1972-NC, 1980-SC; **EDUC:** BS, 1939, Forest Mgmt., Univ. of MI; **GRAD EDUC:** M of Forestry, 1940, Forest Mgmt.; Minor in Bus., Duke Univ.; **EDUC HONORS:** Attended on Fellowship; **MIL SERV:** US Army Corps Engineers, Maj.; **OTHER ACT & HONORS:** Present Member Charlotte Tree Commn., State of NC Forest Council - 2 yrs. in the '70s, Advisory Bd., Medklenburg Council of Boy Scouts, Member Bd. of Directors, Mecklenburg 4-H Foundation; **HOME ADD:** 5701 Lansing Dr., Charlotte, NC 28211, (704)366-8583; **BUS ADD:** Box 30817, Charlotte, NC 28230, (704)372-9640.

HERNANDEZ, Franklyn C.——B: Mar. 3, 1947, Trinidad, *Asst. VP*, Freedom Nat. Bank of NY; **PRIM RE ACT:** Banker, Lender; **PROFL AFFIL & HONORS:** Young Mort. Bankers Assn., Amer. Mgmt. Assn.; **EDUC:** 1975, Soc. Sci. and Econ., Fordham Univ.; **GRAD EDUC:** RE Fin., 1977, NY Univ.; **OTHER ACT & HONORS:** Tr., Malcolm-King Coll.; **HOME ADD:** 345 W. 145th St., NYC, NY 10027; **BUS ADD:** 275 W. 125th St., NYC, NY 10027.

HERRIMAN, Charles E.——B: Sept. 15, 1941, Gary, IN, *Pres.-Mohican Properties, Inc.; Practicing Atty.*, Mohican Properties, Inc.; **PRIM RE ACT:** Attorney, Developer, Syndicator; **SERVICES:** Legal and Profl. advice; **REP CLIENTS:** Multiple; **PREV EMPLOY:** Practicing Atty.; **PROFL AFFIL & HONORS:** ABA; IN State Bar Assn.; Grant Cty. Bar Assn., LLB; **EDUC:** AB, 1963, Pre-Law, Franklin Coll., Franklin, IN; **GRAD EDUC:** LLB, 1966, Law, IN Univ. School of Law; **EDUC HONORS:** Blue Key; Class Officer; **HOME ADD:** 709 West Fourth St., Marion, IN 46952, (317)664-3649; **BUS ADD:** P. O. Box 927, 122 E. Fourth St., Marion, IN 46952, (317)664-7307.

HERRING, Coy K.——B: July 11, 1935, Limestone Co., TX, *Pres.*, West Prop. Serv.; **PRIM RE ACT:** Broker, Consultant, Instructor, Property Manager; **SERVICES:** Property Mgmt., Sales, Leasing, Consulting; **REP CLIENTS:** Indiv.-Partnerships-Corp.; **PREV EMPLOY:** Bixby Ranch C., RE Operations Mgr.; **PROFL AFFIL & HONORS:** IREM; Apt. Assn. CA So. Cities-Long Beach Dist. Bd. of Realtors, C.P.M.; **EDUC:** AA, 1969, RE, Pierce Coll.; **OTHER ACT & HONORS:** Pres.-Apt. Assn. CA S Cities-1982; Pres.-L.A. Chapter IREM-1978; Downtown Long Beach Assoc.; Downtown Long Beach Lions; **HOME ADD:** 14269 Baker St., Westminster, CA 92683, (714)897-3247; **BUS ADD:** 3722 Atlantic Ave., Long Beach, CA 90807, (213)595-7471.

HERRMANN, J. Robert——B: Feb. 19, 1930, Syracuse, NY, *VP*, The Hayner Hoyt Corp., Devel.; **PRIM RE ACT:** Broker, Syndicator, Consultant, Developer, Builder, Property Manager, Engineer, Owner/Investor, Insuror; **SERVICES:** Devel., Const., Mgmt. and Synd.; **REP CLIENTS:** Indiv. Investors and/or Owners of Comml. and Multi-family Props.; **PREV EMPLOY:** Production Mgr., Community Tech., Inc.; Pres., Herrmann Bros., Inc.; **PROFL AFFIL & HONORS:** NAHB; NYS Bldrs. Assn.; Tech. Club of Syracuse; Nat. Soc. Prof. Engrs.; Assoc. Bldrs. & Constr. Inc.; Onon Co. Planning Fed., Lic. Prof. Eng. (PE); Lic. RE Broker; Lic. Ins. Broker; Lic. Gen. Contr. in NC; Reg. Apt. Mgr. (RAM), (HUD); **EDUC:** BCE, 1951, Syracuse Univ.; **GRAD EDUC:** Grad. Work, RE, Syracuse Univ/Univ. Coll.; **EDUC HONORS:** Magna Cum Laude, Tau Beta Pi; Sigma Tau Sigma Award, physics; **MIL SERV:** USN, Seabees, BUL 3; **OTHER ACT & HONORS:** Valley Men's Club; Onondaga C of C; Boy Scouts; **HOME ADD:** 4980 Tenterden Dr., Syracuse, NY 13215, (315)469-4918; **BUS ADD:** 1820 LeMoyne Ave., Syracuse, NY 13208, (315)455-5941.

HERRON, Steven Freddy——B: May 23, 1952, Houston, TX, *Assoc.*, M. Donald Forman; **PRIM RE ACT:** Attorney; **SERVICES:** Negotiations, Agreements of Sale, Prep. of Documents, Attendance at Closing; **REP CLIENTS:** Indiv. and corp., clients in both resid. and comml. prop.; **PROFL AFFIL & HONORS:** Member, Camden County Bar; Dist Court Comm.; ABA; NJ Bar Assn.; Camden Cty. Bar Assn., Approved Atty., Chicago Title Ins. Co., ABA Real Prop. Probate Trust Sect.; **EDUC:** BA, 1974, Poli. Sci., Hist., Tulane Univ.; **GRAD EDUC:** JD, 1977, Tulane Univ.; **OTHER ACT & HONORS:** B'Nai B'rith, AZA Chap. Advisor; **HOME ADD:** 1608 Cedar Dr., Medford, NJ 08055, (609)953-1433; **BUS ADD:** Ste 3, Barclay House Apt., 1200 E. Marlton Pike, Cherry Hill, NJ 08034.

HERSCHENFELD, Richard S.——B: Mar. 15, 1948, NYC, NY, *House Counsel*, Americana Properties; Richard S. Herschenfeld, Inc.; **PRIM RE ACT:** Broker, Consultant, Attorney, Developer, Lender, Builder, Property Manager, Syndicator; **PROFL AFFIL & HONORS:** NY State Bar; Beverly Hills Bar; L.A. Cty. Bar; State Bar of CA; Beverly Hills Bd. of Realtors; ABA; CA Assn. of Realtors; Nat. Assn. of Realtors; L.A. Cty. Bd. of Realtors; L.A. Cty. Bar; Malibu Bd. of Realtors; **EDUC:** BS, 1970, Econ./Indus. Relations, Univ. of Bridgeport, CT; **GRAD EDUC:** JD, 1973, NY Law School; **HOME ADD:** 2015 Castle Heights Ave., Los Angeles, CA 90034, (213)202-1363; **BUS ADD:** 2001 S. Barrington Ave., Suite 300, Los Angeles, CA 90025, (213)476-2244.

HERSKOWITZ, Robert S.——B: Oct. 21, 1931, Phila., PA, *Pres.*, Jay Martin Const. Co. & Robert S. Herskowitz RE Broker; **PRIM RE ACT:** Broker, Developer, Builder, Owner/Investor, Insuror; **REP CLIENTS:** Fast Food Cos.; **PROFL AFFIL & HONORS:** Homebuilders League of S. Jersey RE; **EDUC:** BS, 1953, Liberal Arts, Univ. of PA; **EDUC HONORS:** With Honors; **MIL SERV:** US Army, SP-2, Good Conduct 8th Army; **HOME ADD:** 515 Fireside Ln., Cherry Hill, NJ 08003, (609)428-2569; **BUS ADD:** 108 Parkville Rd., Woodbury, NJ 08096, (609)468-0900.

HERTEL, Theodore B., Jr.——B: Jan. 23, 1947, Milwaukee, WI, Saichek & Hertel, S.C.; **PRIM RE ACT:** Attorney, Instructor; **SERVICES:** Legal Serv. pertaining to RE transactions; **REP CLIENTS:** Adam Mayer RE Co., Inc.; Family S&L Assn.; **PROFL AFFIL & HONORS:** WI Bar Assn., ABA, Assn. of Trial Lawyers of Amer., WI Academy of Trial Lawyers; **EDUC:** BA, 1969, Poli. Sci., Carroll Coll.; Freie Univ., Berlin, Germany; **GRAD EDUC:** 1972, Law, Univ. of WI; **HOME ADD:** 4754 N. Hollywood Ave., Whitefish Bay, WI 53211, (414)332-1779; **BUS ADD:** Ste. 6032, 161 W. Wisconsin Ave., Milwaukee, WI 53203, (414)271-8875.

HERTZ, Mel R.——B: Feb. 26, 1945, Toronto, Canada, Leonardo/Luria, Inc.; **PRIM RE ACT:** Broker, Syndicator, Owner/Investor; **SERVICES:** Invest. Counciling, Syndi., for small investors; **PROFL AFFIL & HONORS:** Honolulu Bd. of Realtors, RESSI, TIGR; **EDUC:** BS, 1966, Mktg. & Advertising, Wayne State Univ., Detroit, MI; **GRAD EDUC:** MBA, 1968, Fin., Wayne State Univ.; **HOME ADD:** 237 Kuumele Pl, Kailua, HI 96734, (808)262-4610; **BUS ADD:** 190 S. King St. Suite 1730, Honolulu, HI 96813, (808)523-7751.

HERTZ, Thomas W.——B: Mar. 7, 1946, Viborg, SD, *Atty. at Law*, Thomas W. Hertz, P.C., a Corp. Part. in the Partnership of Ulmer & Hertz; **PRIM RE ACT:** Attorney; **PROFL AFFIL & HONORS:** ABA; SD Bar Assn., Who's Who in Amer. Law; Martindale-Hubbell; **EDUC:** BS, 1968, Metalurgical Engr., SD School of Mines and Tech.; **GRAD EDUC:** JD, 1977, Univ. of SD; **EDUC HONORS:** Various scholarships; **HOME ADD:** 201 N. 5th St., Menno, SD 57045, (605)387-5696; **BUS ADD:** Menno State Bank Bldg., Menno, SD 57045, (605)387-5658.

HERTZMARK, Sidney S.——B: Dec. 21, 1915, Denver, CO, *Chmn., Bd. of Dir.*, Hertzmark-Parnegg Realty, Inc.; **PRIM RE ACT:** Broker, Consultant, Owner/Investor, Property Manager; **PROFL AFFIL & HONORS:** ASREC, ICSC, ASA, CRE, CSM; **EDUC:** BA, 1939, Bus. Admin. & Econ., Univ. of NM; **GRAD EDUC:** Post Grad. work, 1939-40, George. Wash. Law Sch.; 1943-44, Univ. of VA & Stanford; **EDUC HONORS:** Sr. Honors. Program; **MIL SERV:** UVS, Capt.; **OTHER ACT & HONORS:** Albuquerque Planning Comm., 1968-73; Albuquerque Petroleum Club, Albuquerque Ctry. Club; **HOME ADD:** 1612 Cardenas NE, Albuquerque, NM 87110, (505)883-6161; **BUS ADD:** 7301 Indian Sch. Rd., NE, Albuquerque, NM 87110, (505)883-6161.

HERZ, Andrew L.——B: Nov. 12, 1946, NY, NY, *Partner*, Richards, O'Neil & Alleqaert; **PRIM RE ACT:** Attorney; **SERVICES:** Legal services; **PREV EMPLOY:** Gen. Counsel, NY State Mort. Loan

Enforcement & Admin. Corp.; **PROFL AFFIL & HONORS:** NY State Bar Assn. (Real Prop. Sect.); Assn. of the Bar of the City of NY (Real Prop. Comm.) 1977-80; Housing & Urban Devel. Comm. 1980-81; ABA, Cert. of Merit, NY State Mort. Loan Enforcement & Admin. Corp. 1981; **EDUC:** AB, 1968, Govt., Columbia Coll.; **GRAD EDUC:** JD, 1971, Columbia Law School; **EDUC HONORS:** Harlan Fiske Stone Scholar; articles editor, Columbia Journal of Law and Social Problems; **OTHER ACT & HONORS:** Chmn., Village of Ossining Zoning Bd. of Appeals 1980-now; Alumni Class Pres., Columbia Law School Class of 1971; Dir., Interfaith Council for Action, Inc.; Dean's Advisory Comm., Univ. of WVA Law School; **HOME ADD:** 46 Justamere Dr., Ossining, NY 10562, (914)941-6780; **BUS ADD:** 660 Madison Ave., NY, NY 10021.

HERZBERGER, Robert Charles——B: Apr. 4, 1954, Baltimore, MD, *Mort. Officer*, The Savings Bank of Baltimore, Secondary Mort. Mkt.; **PRIM RE ACT:** Banker, Lender, Regulator; **PROFL AFFIL & HONORS:** Young Mort. Bankers Assn. of MD, Treas.; Econ. Advisory Comm., Univ. of Baltimore; Baltimore Econ. Soc.; **EDUC:** BS, 1976, Mktg./Econ., Univ. of MD; **GRAD EDUC:** MS, In Progress, Econ., Univ. of Baltimore; **BUS ADD:** Baltimore and Charles Sts., Baltimore, MD 21201, (301)244-3349.

HERZOG, Sam——B: July 9, 1929, Brooklyn, NY, *Part.*, Deb Assoc.; **PRIM RE ACT:** Developer, Builder; **OTHER RE ACT:** Apt. owner and Mgmt.; **PROFL AFFIL & HONORS:** RAM, CPM Candidate NAHB Life Dir. (past V.P. for NY & NJ); Past Pres. of Bldrs. Assoc. of Mer. NJ, Past pres. NJ Bldrs. Assoc., Founding Pres. of NJ Apt. House Council; **GRAD EDUC:** 1951, Geology, CCNY; **OTHER ACT & HONORS:** E. Brunswick Rent Control Bd., Chmn. NJ State Hotel and Multiple Family Comm. (Natl. V. Chmn.), Member, Comm. On Civil Rights, State of NJ 1969-72; **HOME ADD:** 6 Lohman Rd., Convent Station, NJ 07961, (201)538-1699; **BUS ADD:** 15 Civic Ctr., E. Brunswick, NJ 08816, (201)257-7504.

HESS, Peter A.——B: Nov. 5, 1938, Chicago, IL, *Atty.*, Hess & Karlan, Ltd.; **PRIM RE ACT:** Attorney; **SERVICES:** Legal Spec. in RE, Mort. & Const. Lending; **REP CLIENTS:** Mort. bankers, banks, S & L Assn., Ins. cos., & devels.; **PROFL AFFIL & HONORS:** ABA, IL, FL, Chicago Bar Assns., Chicago MAA, MAAA, MBA of Chicago; **EDUC:** BS, Econ & Fin., Univ of IL; **GRAD EDUC:** JD, IL Inst. of Tech., Chicago, Kent Coll. of Law; **MIL SERV:** US Army, 1st Lt.; **OTHER ACT & HONORS:** IL Inst. for cont legal ed, Publs & Lecturer, Lecturer for MBAA, Dir. McCormick Boy's Club, Dir. IL Mortgage Bankers Assn., Exec. VP, Chicago Mortgage Attorney's Assn.; **HOME ADD:** 568 Hill Terr., Winnetka, IL 60093, (312)446-2228; **BUS ADD:** 180 N. LaSalle St., Ste 2525, Chicago, IL 60601, (312)332-1100.

HESS, Robert L.——B: Jan. 11, 1930, Tacoma, WA, *Owner*, Robert L. Hess Realty; **PRIM RE ACT:** Broker, Appraiser, Developer, Builder, Owner/Investor, Instructor; **OTHER RE ACT:** Counselling; **SERVICES:** Counselling, Estate Planning; **PREV EMPLOY:** Licensed RE Broker; **PROFL AFFIL & HONORS:** NAR, WA Assn. of Realtors, Tacoma-Pierce Co. Bd. of Realtors, Chapter II Cert. Comml. Invstmt. Member, Amer. Chapter Intl. RE Fed., CCIM, SEC (Councilor Member of Nat. Soc. of Exchange Counselors); **EDUC:** 1981, Real Estate School, Fort Steilacoom Community Coll.; **EDUC HONORS:** 3.5 grade average GA; **MIL SERV:** US Army, Cop., GCM; **OTHER ACT & HONORS:** Tacoma Yacht Club, Tacoma Club, Tacoma Lawn Tennis Club, Elks, Apt. Assn. of Pierce Cty, WA Apt. Assn.; **HOME ADD:** 525 Broadway #205, Tacoma, WA 98402; **BUS ADD:** 730 Fawcett Ave. Ste. 1A, Tacoma, WA 98402, (206)383-1507.

HESSE, Michael——B: Aug. 21, 1939, Buffalo, NY, *VP*, Sec Pac Inc., Security Pacific RE; **PRIM RE ACT:** Broker, Developer, Owner/Investor, Syndicator; **OTHER RE ACT:** Full Serv. Resid./Investment Brokerage; **PREV EMPLOY:** Investor's Property Acquisition, Inc., Pres.; Barristers Investment Servs., Inc., Pres.; **PROFL AFFIL & HONORS:** Intl. RE Fed.; RESSI; RNMI, Realtor; **EDUC:** BA, 1962, Hist./Eng., Univ. of AZ; **OTHER ACT & HONORS:** Who's Who in CA 1981-82; **HOME ADD:** 3336 Hillside Terr., Lafayette, CA 94549, (415)935-1245; **BUS ADD:** 587 Ygnacio Valley Rd., Walnut Creek, CA 94596, (415)933-7900.

HESSEN, Neal J.——B: July 19, 1952, Duluth, MN, *Atty.*, Fryberger, Buchanan, Smith and Frederick, P.A.; **PRIM RE ACT:** Attorney; **SERVICES:** All areas of RE Law; **REP CLIENTS:** Instnl. and Pvt. Lenders, Realtors, Devels., Investors; **PROFL AFFIL & HONORS:** ABA, MN Bar Assn.; **EDUC:** BA, 1974, Speech Communication, Univ. of MN; **GRAD EDUC:** JD, 1977, Drake Univ. School of Law; **EDUC HONORS:** Cum Laude; **OTHER ACT & HONORS:** Bd. of Dirs.-Downtown Bus. and Profl. Assn.; Bd. of Dirs.-Duluth Art Int.; Bd. of Dirs.-Jr. Archievement of Duluth; Duluth Area C of C; Skyline Rotary Club of Duluth; **HOME ADD:** 5227 Tioga St., Duluth, MN 55804, (218)525-3965; **BUS ADD:** 700 Lonsdale Bldg., Duluth, MN 55802, (218)722-0861.

HESTER, Robert W.——B: Nov. 11, 1918, Toledo, OH, *Owner, Broker*, Gaslight Comml. R.E.; **PRIM RE ACT:** Broker, Syndicator, Consultant, Owner/Investor; **OTHER RE ACT:** Bus. mergers, Acquist.; **SERVICES:** Brokerage; **PREV EMPLOY:** Sales dir., same firm; **PROFL AFFIL & HONORS:** CCIM; **MIL SERV:** US Army Corps, Tech/Sgt.; **OTHER ACT & HONORS:** Rotary Intl.; **HOME ADD:** 5934 Stearns, Shawnee Mission, KS 66203, (913)631-8505; **BUS ADD:** 3170 Mercier, Kansas City, MO 64111, (816)931-0742.

HETLAND, John R.——B: Mar. 12, 1930, Minneapolis, MN, *Pres.*, John R. Hetland, PC; **PRIM RE ACT:** Attorney, Instructor, Real Estate Publisher; **OTHER RE ACT:** Prof. of Law, Univ. of CA, Berkeley, Author of the following books: Hetland, "CA Real Prop. Secured Transactions", 1970; Hetland, "Secured RE Transactions", 1974; "CA Cases on Secured Transactions in land", 1975; Hetland, "Secured RE Transactions", 1977; **PROFL AFFIL & HONORS:** CA and MN State Bars; ABA; **EDUC:** BSL, 1952, Univ. of MN; **GRAD EDUC:** JD, 1956, Univ. of MN; **EDUC HONORS:** Summa Cum Laude, Order of Coif; **MIL SERV:** USN, Lt. Cmdr. (Active Duty 1953-55); **HOME ADD:** 20 Redcoach Lane, Orinda, CA 94563, (415)254-5130; **BUS ADD:** 2600 Warring St., Berkeley, CA 94704, (415)548-5900.

HETRICK, Patrick K.——B: Mar. 11, 1945, Milwaukee, WI, *Prof. of Law*, Campbell University School of Law; **PRIM RE ACT:** Consultant, Attorney, Instructor; **OTHER RE ACT:** Author of NC RE Law Textbooks; **PREV EMPLOY:** Marquette Univ. Sch. of Law 1972-78; **EDUC:** 1967, Univ. of WI, Milwaukee; **GRAD EDUC:** JD, 1971, Marquette Univ.; **EDUC HONORS:** Magna Cum Laude; **HOME ADD:** P. O. Box 584, Buies Creek, NC 27506, (919)893-3856; **BUS ADD:** P. O. Box 158, Buies Creek, NC 27506, (919)893-4111.

HEUER, Charles R., AIA, Esq.——B: Jan. 15, 1949, Youngstown, OH, *Staff Architect Attorney.*, The Architects Callabrative, Inc., Cambridge, MA; **PRIM RE ACT:** Attorney, Architect; **SERVICES:** Architectural; **REP CLIENTS:** Bldg. owners, developers; **PREV EMPLOY:** Hill International, Inc. 1980-1982; AIA 1978-1980; Dor., Documents/Graphic; Charles R. Heuer Arch. 1977-1979; Dalton - Dalton - Newport, Inc. 1974-1977; Schwab & Twitty Arch. 1972-1974; **PROFL AFFIL & HONORS:** AIA; Wash. Metro Chap., AIA; ABA; VA State Bar; **EDUC:** BArch., 1971, Arch., Carnegie-Mellon Univ., Pittsburgh, PA; **GRAD EDUC:** MArch., 1972, Arch. Structures, OH State Univ.; JD, 1979, Law, Amer. Univ. (Also studied at Cleveland State Univ.); **EDUC HONORS:** Law Review at Cleveland State; **BUS ADD:** 46 Brattle St., Cambridge, MA 02138, (617)868-4200.

HEUER, Robert Emerson——B: June 16, 1932, NYC, *Pres.*, Aegean Devel. Corp.; **PRIM RE ACT:** Architect, Developer, Builder, Owner/Investor, Property Manager; **SERVICES:** Archit., Design, Constr., Devel.; **PROFL AFFIL & HONORS:** Amer. Instit. of Arch.; Nat. Council of Arch. Registrations Bds.; CA Licensed Contractors Assn.; CSI; NCARB, AIA; **EDUC:** BA, 1959, Arch., Fairleigh Dickinson Univ.; **MIL SERV:** USN; **OTHER ACT & HONORS:** NAHB Grand Award for Design 1978, Recipient of Gold Nugget Award for Design 1979; **BUS ADD:** 5525 Oakdale Ave., Suite 225, Woodland Hills, CA 91364, (213)703-7580.

HEUGEL, Kenneth E.——B: Jan. 2, 1933, Evansville, IN, *Pres.*, Heugel Realty, Inc.; Heugel & Assoc., Inc.; Tri-State Securities, Inc.; **PRIM RE ACT:** Broker, Syndicator, Consultant, Developer, Property Manager; **OTHER RE ACT:** Securities (RE); **SERVICES:** RE Org. & Tax Consulting; **PROFL AFFIL & HONORS:** CCIM; **EDUC:** BS, 1954, RE, Indiana Univ.; **MIL SERV:** USAF, Capt.; **OTHER ACT & HONORS:** Rotary; Ctry. Club; **HOME ADD:** 420 S. Hebron Ave., Evansville, IN 47715; **BUS ADD:** Suite 302, 101 Plaza E. Blvd., Box 5476, Evansville, IN 47715, (812)479-8966.

HEVERT, Doris——*Mgr. Office Adm.*, International Flavors & Fragrances, Inc.; **PRIM RE ACT:** Property Manager; **BUS ADD:** 521 W. 57th St., New York, NY 10019, (212)765-5500.*

HEYDORN, Munn W.——B: Mar. 8, 1938, Chicago, IL, *Sr. VP*, Lake MI Financial Group; **PRIM RE ACT:** Broker, Lender, Insuror; **SERVICES:** Mtge. Banking, Sales, Const. Lending; **PREV EMPLOY:** 1969-1970 Pioneer Tr. & Svgs. Bk., Chicago RE Dept.; 1964-1969 Pacific Mut'l. Life Ins. RE Dept.; **PROFL AFFIL & HONORS:** IL Mtge. Bankers, Mtge. Bankers of Amer.; **EDUC:** BS, Fin.; **HOME ADD:** P. O. Box 456, Winfield, IL 60190, (312)690-8587; **BUS ADD:** 69 W. Washington St., Chicago, IL 60602, (312)236-2545.

HEYLAND, E. Bruce——**B:** Dec. 7, 1936, Toronto, CAN., *Pres.*, Hammerson Canada Inc.; **PRIM RE ACT:** Developer; **PREV EMPLOY:** Bramalea Ltd. 1976-1978; **PROFL AFFIL & HONORS:** CIPREC, BOMA; **EDUC:** BA, 1959, Econ. and Pol. Sci., Univ. of Toronto; **GRAD EDUC:** MSA, 1962, Admin. & Mktg., Univ. of Toronto; **EDUC HONORS:** Alumni Award, 1962; **OTHER ACT & HONORS:** Pres., The Adult Cerebral Palsy Inst. of Metropolitan Toronto; **HOME ADD:** 104 Esgore Dr., Toronto, Can. M5M 3S2, (416)483-1474; **BUS ADD:** P. O. Box 252, Toronto-Dominion Centre, Toronto, Canada M5K 1J5, (416)364-6902.

HIBAN, Arthur W.——**B:** Aug. 25, 1935, NY, *Pres.*, Hiban, Graffius & McKee Ltd.; **PRIM RE ACT:** Property Manager; **SERVICES:** Mgmt. of Community Assns. & Consulting Services; **PREV EMPLOY:** Dir. of Community Mgmt., Shannon & Luchs Co., Wash., DC; **PROFL AFFIL & HONORS:** IRM, CAI, Academy of Authors, CPM, IREM; **EDUC:** BS, 1957, Econ., Univ. of MD; **MIL SERV:** USN, Cmdr., Supply Cords; **HOME ADD:** 5725 Harpers Farm Rd., Columbia, MD 21044, (301)596-4012; **BUS ADD:** 5272 River Rd., Wash., DC 20016, (201)656-1938.

HIBBERD, Donald H.——**B:** Mar. 4, 1954, Philadelphia, PA, *Pres./Broker/Owner*, C21 Donald H. Hibberd - Realtors; **PRIM RE ACT:** Broker, Instructor, Consultant, Appraiser, Property Manager, Owner/Investor, Insuror; **SERVICES:** Prop. Mgmt., Investment Counseling; **REP CLIENTS:** Indiv., Lenders, Appraisers, Investment Grps., Attys.; **PROFL AFFIL & HONORS:** NAR PA Assn. of Realtors, Delaware Cty. Bd. of Realtors, CRB, GRI, AIM Awards; **EDUC:** Univ. of PA, 1975, Econ., Bus., R.E., Wharton; **OTHER ACT & HONORS:** Rotary; **HOME ADD:** 360 Kirk La., Media, PA 19063; **BUS ADD:** 1167 A W. Baltimore Pike, Media, PA 19063, (215)565-7770.

HIBST, Dale V.——*Asst. to VP Fin.*, Newell Companies, Inc.; **BUS ADD:** 29 E. Stephenson St., Freeport, IL 61032, (815)235-4171.*

HICKERSON, Philip H.——**B:** July 2, 1938, Richmond, VA, *Pres.*, Philip H. Hickerson, Inc.; **PRIM RE ACT:** Broker; **SERVICES:** Resid. Resale, New Home Sales, Land and Subdiv. devel.; **REP CLIENTS:** Reynolds Metals, Philip Morris, USA, Chesapeake & Potomic Telephone Co., VA Electric and Power Co., American Tobacco Co., ATO, Medical Coll. of VA; **PREV EMPLOY:** Partner & Secretary for Bowers, Nelms & Fonville, Inc.; **PROFL AFFIL & HONORS:** Dir. Richmond Bd. of Realtors, GRI, CRB, CRS; **EDUC:** BS Bus. Admin., 1960, Construction, Engr., VA Polytechnic Inst.; **OTHER ACT & HONORS:** Chmn. and Number of the Diaconite - St. Giles Church; **HOME ADD:** 11 Dahlgren Rd., Richmond, VA 23233, (804)784-3511; **BUS ADD:** 1403 Pemberton Rd., Suite C-304, Richmond, VA 23229, (804)740-7522.

HICKEY, Cornelius (Neil) A.——**B:** July 22, 1934, San Francisco, CA, *Pres.*, Plan-A-Visions, Inc.; **PRIM RE ACT:** Instructor, Consultant, Builder; **OTHER RE ACT:** Plan-A-Visions, Inc. main activity is Const. Fin. Planning and Bldg. Consultant for the "Do it yourself" Builder; **REP CLIENTS:** People who want to do some of the work in order to get affordable housing; **PREV EMPLOY:** VP of a small const. co.; Regional Mgr. of a large RE land co.; **PROFL AFFIL & HONORS:** Better Bus. Bureau, Certificate of Achievement from Chabot Coll. in Housing Inspection and Bldg. Inspection; **EDUC:** BA, 1964, Bus. and Econ., San Francisco State Univ.; **MIL SERV:** US Army, PFC; **OTHER ACT & HONORS:** Valley Spokesmen's Touring Club, Lecturer for the Owner/Builder Ctr. in Berkeley, CA on Const. Fin.; **HOME ADD:** 4414 Bacon St., Pleasanton, CA 94566, (415)846-7798; **BUS ADD:** P. O. Box 1973, Pleasanton, CA 94566, (415)462-1153.

HICKMAN, James R. (Bob)——**B:** Dec. 31, 1931, Centerview, MO, *Gen. Mgr.*, Santee-Cooper Resort, Inc.; **PRIM RE ACT:** Broker, Consultant, Property Manager; **SERVICES:** RE Brokerage, Prop. Mgmt., Appraisals; **REP CLIENTS:** Santee-Cooper Resort, Inc.; **PREV EMPLOY:** Gen. Mgr., Santee Shores, Inc., Former Exec. Dir., SC Dept. of Parks Recreation and Tourism; **PROFL AFFIL & HONORS:** Orangeburg (S.C.) Bd. of Realtors, Nat. Assn. of Realtors; **EDUC:** BA, 1957, Broadcast Journalism, Univ. of MO; **EDUC HONORS:** Sigma Delta Chi Award, Outstanding Male Grad. in Journalism; **MIL SERV:** USAF, S/Sgt.; **OTHER ACT & HONORS:** News Sec. to SC Gov. Robert E. McNair 1965-1967; Santee Lions Club; Charity Lodge No. 62; A.F.M. Lay Leader; Elloree United Methodist Church, Elloree, SC; Former Member: SC Pollution Control Authority; Gov's. Beautification and Community Improvement Bd.; **HOME ADD:** Saluda Dr., Santee-Cooper Resort, Santee, SC 29142, (803)854-2508; **BUS ADD:** S.C. Highway 6, Santee, SC 29142, (803)854-2111.

HICKMAN, Dr. J.W.——**B:** Dec. 11, 1917, Lousiville, KY, *Pres.*, Spaceport USA, Inc.; **PRIM RE ACT:** Broker, Developer, Builder, Owner/Investor, Property Manager; **SERVICES:** Lease, Construct, Devel.; **REP CLIENTS:** NCR, Stromberg Carlson, Gould, Inc., Emerson Radio, Nat. Chem.; **PREV EMPLOY:** Devel.-Seminole Indus. Park; Devel. W. Orange Indus. Park; **PROFL AFFIL & HONORS:** DDS; Lic. Realtor; **GRAD EDUC:** DDS, 1947, Emory Univ.; **MIL SERV:** USAF, Capt., 1950-52; **OTHER ACT & HONORS:** Bd. of Adjustment-Cty.; **HOME ADD:** 203 Riverbend Rd., Longwood, FL 32750; **BUS ADD:** I-4 & ST Rd. 46, Sanford, FL 32771, (305)323-0061.

HICKMAN, Robert Emmett——**B:** Oct. 21, 1922, Wilmington, DE, *Pres.*, Jackson Cross Appraisal Co., Jackson Cross Co.; **PRIM RE ACT:** Consultant, Appraiser; **PREV EMPLOY:** Farmers Bank, State of DE; Robert E. Hickman RE Co.; Jackson Cross of Delaware; **PROFL AFFIL & HONORS:** AIREA; ASREC; SIR; IREM; RNMI, Realtor of the Yr., DE, 1969; Lambda Alpha, 1981; **EDUC:** BS, 1943, Civil Engr., Cornell Univ.; **MIL SERV:** USN, Res.; Lt.j.g.; **OTHER ACT & HONORS:** Listed in Who's Who in Amer.; **HOME ADD:** 1001 Kensington Ln., Wilmington, DE 19807, (302)655-7494; **BUS ADD:** 2000 Market St., Philadelphia, PA 19103, (215)561-8787.

HICKOX, Charles——*Mgr. Mfg. Engr.*, Tappon Co.; **PRIM RE ACT:** Property Manager; **BUS ADD:** Tappon Park, P. O. Box 606, Mansfield, OH 44901, (419)755-2011.*

HICKS, Alec, Jr.——**B:** July 27, 1941, Philadelphia, PA, *Sr. VP*, Jackson Cross Co., Prop. Mgmt.; **PRIM RE ACT:** Consultant, Property Manager, Engineer; **SERVICES:** Planning, Budgeting, Energy Mgmt., Mgmt. Surveys; **REP CLIENTS:** Prudential, UIDC, Scagate Investments, Mutual Life Ins. Co., Thos. Jefferson Univ., Mellon Bank; **PREV EMPLOY:** Reed & Strombaugh Co., 1974-80, Intl. Capital Corp., 1974, Granton's Realtors 1970-74; **PROFL AFFIL & HONORS:** IREM, BOMA, Pres. Delaware Valley Chap. IREM, 1979 & 1980; **EDUC:** BME, 1963, Villanova Univ.; **GRAD EDUC:** MBA, 1969, Mktg., MI State Univ.; **OTHER ACT & HONORS:** Scoutmaster, Boy Scouts of Amer.; **HOME ADD:** 60 Lodges Ln., Bala Cynwyd, PA 19004, (215)667-4741; **BUS ADD:** 2000 Market St., Philadelphia, PA 19103, (215)561-8991.

HICKS, C. Flippo——**B:** Feb. 24, 1929, Fredericksburg, VA, *Pres.*, Martin, Hicks & Ingles, Ltd.; **PRIM RE ACT:** Attorney; **SERVICES:** Title examination, closing, escrow for both purchasers and sellers of RE and fin. instns.; **REP CLIENTS:** Middle Peninsula, Northern Neck S & L Assn., United VA Bank of Gloucester, Fed. Land Bank of Baltimore; **PREV EMPLOY:** Asst. Atty. Gen. of VA 1953-59; **PROFL AFFIL & HONORS:** ABA, VA Bar Assn.; **EDUC:** BS, 1950, Commerce, Univ. of VA; **GRAD EDUC:** LLB, 1952, Univ. of VA; **EDUC HONORS:** Beta Gamma Sigma, The Raven Soc., Member of Law Review, Omicron Delta Kappa; **MIL SERV:** USN, Lt.; **HOME ADD:** 'Pinewold', Gloucester, VA 23061, (804)693-2782; **BUS ADD:** Court Cir., P. O. Box 708, Gloucester, VA 23061, (804)693-2500.

HICKS, Floyd J.——**B:** June 18, 1908, Torrington, CT, *Self-employed Fee Appraisal*; **PRIM RE ACT:** Broker, Syndicator, Consultant, Appraiser; **SERVICES:** Appraisals, Residential Foreclosures, Commercial & Industrial; **PREV EMPLOY:** US Civil Service FHA appraiser (Deputy Chief), Deputy Dir.; Deputy Asst. Agcy. Mgr. F.N.M.A.; **PROFL AFFIL & HONORS:** ASA; **EDUC:** Univ. of IN; **MIL SERV:** US Army, S/Sgt., ETO; **OTHER ACT & HONORS:** W. Hartford Town Council, 1948-51, Amer. Legion; V.F.W., Masonic Order; Shriners, Sphinx Temple; St. John's Episcopal Church, W. Hartford; **HOME ADD:** 97 Little City Rd., Killingworth, CT 06417, (203)345-2514; **BUS ADD:** P.O. Box 65, Madison, CT 06443, (202)345-2514.

HICKS, Marion Lawrence (Larry), Jr.——**B:** Sept. 5, 1945, Bethlehem, PA, *Partner*, Thompson & Knight; **PRIM RE ACT:** Attorney; **REP CLIENTS:** Lenders and other RE clients, Buying, Selling, Bldg. and Financing Comml. RE; **PREV EMPLOY:** 1970-1971, Employment with US Courts; **PROFL AFFIL & HONORS:** State of TX Bar; ABA Real Prop. Sect.; Local Bar; **EDUC:** BA, 1967, Hist., Duke Univ.; **GRAD EDUC:** JD, 1970, Law, Univ. of TX, Austin; **EDUC HONORS:** Sigma Delta Pi, JD with Honors; Order of the Coif; Article Editor, TX Law Review; **OTHER ACT & HONORS:** Law Clerk, US Court of Appeals for Ninth Circuit; Member of Amer. Arbitration Assn., Panel of Arbitrators; **HOME ADD:** 9946 Rockbrook, Dallas, TX 75220, (214)352-2386; **BUS ADD:** 2300 Republic National Bank Bldg., Dallas, TX 75201, (214)655-7606.

HICKS, Tyler G.——**B:** June 21, 1921, New York, NY, *Pres.*, IWS, Inc.; **PRIM RE ACT:** Consultant, Engineer, Real Estate Publisher; **PROFL AFFIL & HONORS:** ASME;IEEE; Intl. Oceanographic Found.; **EDUC:** 1948, Mech. Engr.; **OTHER ACT & HONORS:** Also associated with McGraw-Hill Book Co., as Publisher, Profl. & Reference Book Div.; **HOME ADD:** 24 Canterbury Rd., Rockville Centre, NY 11570, (516)766-1070; **BUS ADD:** 24 Canterbury Rd., Rockville Centre, NY 11570, (516)766-5850.

HIEFIELD, Betty Lyn——B: Aug. 14, 1928, Indianapolis, IN, *Realtor*, Realty World, Southwest Props.; **PRIM RE ACT:** Broker; **SERVICES:** Resid. Specialist; **REP CLIENTS:** Specializing in Transferees and First Time Buyers; **PREV EMPLOY:** H.W. Kothe & Assoc.; Realtors; **PROFL AFFIL & HONORS:** NAR; RNMI; WCR; CA Assn. of Realtors; Long Beach Dist. Bd. of Realtors; Metro-Indianapolis Bd. of Realtors; Rolling Hills Bd. of Realtors, (MLS only), CRB, CRS, GRI, 1978 Indianapolis Disting. Woman Realtor of the Year; **EDUC:** BA, 1953, Eng., Butler Univ.; **EDUC HONORS:** Cum Laude; **OTHER ACT & HONORS:** Women's Council of the Long Beach Area C of C; Nat. Soc. of Colonial Dames in the State of IN; Jr. League of Indianapolis; The Dramatic Club; Woodstock Club; Officers Wives Club of the Long Beach Naval Station; The Madhatters; **HOME ADD:** 207 Termino Ave., Long Beach, CA 90803, (213)438-2942; **BUS ADD:** 4115 E. Broadway Suite B, Long Beach, CA 90803, (213)439-0271.

HIERONYMUS, Edward W.——B: June 13, 1943, Davenport, IA, *Partner*, O'Melveny & Myers; **PRIM RE ACT:** Attorney; **SERVICES:** Legal Servs. with respect to Comml. RE and Natural Resources Transactions; **REP CLIENTS:** Devels. of major comml. projects and instnl. lenders; **PROFL AFFIL & HONORS:** ABA, CA and Los Angeles Bar Assns.; **EDUC:** AB, 1965, Econ., Knox Coll., Galesburg, IL; **GRAD EDUC:** JD, 1968, Duke Univ. School of Law; **EDUC HONORS:** Cum Laude, With distinction; **MIL SERV:** US Army, Capt., Army Commendation Medal, Meritorious Service Medal; **BUS ADD:** 611 W Sixth St., Los Angeles, CA 90017, (213)620-1120.

HIGBE, Clifton M.H.——B: Sept. 13, 1932, Columbia, SC, *Atty.*, Law Office of Clifton M.H. Higbe/Clifton M.H. Higbe RE; **PRIM RE ACT:** Broker, Attorney; **SERVICES:** Legal Services; Sales and Purchase Counseling; Synd. of Comml. Props.; **PROFL AFFIL & HONORS:** ABA; CA Bar Assn.; Sacramento Co. Bar Assn.; Nat. Assn. of Home Builders; Building Industry Assn.; **EDUC:** AA, 1962, Soc. Sci./Bus. Admin., Amer. River Coll., FL State Univ.; **GRAD EDUC:** JD, 1970, Law, Univ. of the Pacific, McGeorge School of Law; **EDUC HONORS:** Amer. Jurisprudence Certificate of Award; **MIL SERV:** USAF, Lt., 1950-1958; **HOME ADD:** 836 Commons Dr., Sacramento, CA 95825, (916)929-9586; **BUS ADD:** Woodside Office Park, 800 Howe Ave., Suite 270, Sacramento, CA 95825, (916)920-2022.

HIGDON, Dallis——B: Nov. 30, 1945, Bakersfield, CA, *RE Appraiser & Consultant*, Dallis Higdon & Assoc.; **PRIM RE ACT:** Broker, Consultant, Appraiser, Developer; **SERVICES:** RE Appraisals & Synds. Investment Analysis; **REP CLIENTS:** Banks, investors; **PREV EMPLOY:** Karpe Fisher Appraisal Co.; **PROFL AFFIL & HONORS:** Soc. of RE Appraisers, MGA Assn. of Gov. Appraisers; **EDUC:** BS, 1970, Bus. Mktg., Fresno State Univ.; **MIL SERV:** US Marine Corps., Res., Corp.; **HOME ADD:** 3918 Garnsey Ln., Bakersfield, CA, (805)325-5300; **BUS ADD:** 819 H St., Bakersfield, CA 93304, (805)323-2760.

HIGGINBOTHAM, Fred C., Jr.——*Sr. VP & Treas.*, General American Oil Co. of Texas; **PRIM RE ACT:** Property Manager; **BUS ADD:** Meadows Bldg., Dallas, TX 75206, (214)368-5811.*

HIGGINS, Alan M.——B: Jan. 10, 1945, Cincinnati, OH, *Mgr., Corp. RE; Pres., The General Tire Realty Co.*, The General Tire & Rubber Company, Corp.; **PRIM RE ACT:** Consultant, Appraiser, Developer, Owner/Investor, Instructor, Property Manager; **PREV EMPLOY:** 5 years with Standard Oil Co., oil industry RE experience; **PROFL AFFIL & HONORS:** NACORE Indus. Devel. Research Council; SREA; Soc. of Indus. Realtors; Bus. Devel. Council for First Union Natl. Bank NC; Member of the Editorial Review Bd. of "Corp. Design" Magazine; Member of Indus. RE Mgrs. Council; Founder - Amer. Inst. of Corporate Assett Mgrs.; Chmn. and Founder of "Amer. Indus. Acquisition Consultants"; Member Nat. Bd. of Realtors; Member Akron Area Bd. of Realtors; Member of Faculty Schools of Continuing Education Univ. of OK, 1977-1980, Univ. of WI, 1978, Univ. of NC, 1980-; Who's Who-Fin. & Indus. '79-'80; Who's Who-Midwest '80-'81; Who's Who-World '80-'81, Chmn. of the Bd. of NACORE; **EDUC:** BS, 1967, Bus. Admin., Miami Univ. - Oxford, OH; **OTHER ACT & HONORS:** Akron Regional Dev. Bd. and Akron Prop. Corp. Task Force; **HOME ADD:** 495 Bath Hills Blvd., Akron, OH 44313, (216)864-4704; **BUS ADD:** One General St., Akron, OH 44329, (216)798-3142.

HIGGINS, James G.——B: Oct. 11, 1930, San Mateo, CA, *VP*, Embarcadero Center, Inc.; **PRIM RE ACT:** Broker, Consultant, Property Manager; **SERVICES:** Leasing & Mgmt. Supervision; **PREV EMPLOY:** VP in charge of RE Negotiations, Wells Fargo Bank, San Francisco; **PROFL AFFIL & HONORS:** IREM, San Francisco RE Bd.; **EDUC:** BS Commerce, 1952, Acctg., Fin., Univ. Santa Clara, Santa Clara, CA; **MIL SERV:** USMC, 1st Lt.; **OTHER ACT & HONORS:** Pres. Bay Area USA; **HOME ADD:** 15 Oak Ave., Kentfield, CA 94904, (415)453-8581; **BUS ADD:** Suite 2360, Three Embarcadero Center, San Francisco, CA 94111, (415)772-0555.

HIGH, Barbara Anne——B: Oct. 9, 1941, Palm Beach, FL, *Supervising Editor*, American Institute of Real Estate Appraisers, The Appraisal Journal; **PRIM RE ACT:** Real Estate Publisher; **SERVICES:** Manuscript Solicitation, Author Liaisons Writing, Editing, Scheduling Production; **PREV EMPLOY:** Dartnell Corp.-Bus. publishers; **EDUC:** BA, 1976, Eng. Lit. & Lang., Loyola Univ., Chicago, IL; **GRAD EDUC:** MA, 1978, Eng. Lit. & Lang., Univ. of Chicago; **EDUC HONORS:** Summa Cum Laude, Edward L. Surtz Award for Literary Excellence; **HOME ADD:** 606 W. Aldine, Chicago, IL 60657, (312)327-7532; **BUS ADD:** 430 N. Michigan, Chicago, IL 60611, (312)440-8174.

HIGNELL, Fred W.——B: Mar. 3, 1943, Oakland, CA, *Prin.*, Hignell & Hignell, Inc.; **PRIM RE ACT:** Broker, Syndicator, Developer, Property Manager, Owner/Investor; **SERVICES:** Group Investments, Prop. Mgmt, Devel.; **PROFL AFFIL & HONORS:** CPM, IREN, GCIM, NAREB; **EDUC:** BS, 1966, Civil Engr., Cal. State Univ., Chico; **GRAD EDUC:** MS, 1967, Civil Engr., Stanford; MBA, Ph.D., 1969,1971, Long Range Planning, Stanford Grad. School of Bus; **HOME ADD:** Rt. 5, Box 79I, Chico, CA 95926; **BUS ADD:** 1382 Longfellow Ave., Chico, CA 95926, (916)342-0182.

HILDEBRAN, Robert C.——B: Dec. 28, 1939, Baltimore, MD, *V.P.*, Grubb & Ellis Co., Comm. Brokerage Co.; **PRIM RE ACT:** Broker; **SERVICES:** Comml. R.E. Brokerage; **PREV EMPLOY:** Solar Div. of Intl. Harvester; **EDUC:** BS, 1961, Mechanical Engr., Lehigh Unlv.; **HOME ADD:** 140 Albion St., Denver, CO 80220, (303)320-0520; **BUS ADD:** 1512 Larimer St., Denver, CO 80202, (303)572-7700.

HILDEN, Rod——B: Mar. 31, 1949, Vancouver, WA, *Rgnl. Mgr. - Asset Mgmt. Div.*, The Koll Co., Northwest Div.; **PRIM RE ACT:** Broker, Developer, Owner/Investor, Property Manager; **SERVICES:** Const., Devel., Mgmt.; **PREV EMPLOY:** Coldwell Banker, Prop. Mgmt. Systems, Joseph Lynch & Co.; **PROFL AFFIL & HONORS:** IREM, BOMA, Nat. Assn. of Indus. Park Operators, Intl. Council of Shopping Centers; **EDUC:** Bus., 1973, Fin., Univ. of WA; **MIL SERV:** US Army, S/Sgt.; **BUS ADD:** 2021 152nd Ave. NE, Redmond, WA 98052, (206)643-1776.

HILEMAN, R.D.——*Corp. RE Dir.*, Lockheed Corp.; **PRIM RE ACT:** Property Manager; **BUS ADD:** P. O. Box 551-2555 N. Hollywood Way, Burbank, CA 91520, (213)847-6607.*

HILER, Ken, Jr.——B: Jan. 17, 1946, Lexington, KY, *Pres.*, Ken Hiler Builder Inc.; **PRIM RE ACT:** Developer, Builder, Owner/Investor; **SERVICES:** Custom Homes; **PROFL AFFIL & HONORS:** Lexington Home Builders Assn., Pres. 1977; **EDUC:** Maj. Bus. Mgmt., 1969, Bus., W. KY Univ.; **MIL SERV:** USN, Lt.; **HOME ADD:** 1404 Meganwood Ct., Lexington, KY 40502, (606)266-6371; **BUS ADD:** 183 Moore Dr., Lexington, KY 40503, (606)276-1424.

HILL, Charles——B: July 8, 1949, CO, *Pres.*, Hill Equities, Inc.; **PRIM RE ACT:** Consultant, Developer, Lender, Owner/Investor, Syndicator; **SERVICES:** Consultation, Valuation, Devel. & Synd. of Comml. Prop., Project Financing for Comml. Projects; **REP CLIENTS:** Pension funds, indiv. and instl. investors; **EDUC:** BA, 1972, UCLA; **GRAD EDUC:** JD, 1976, Southwestern Univ. School of Law; **EDUC HONORS:** Hornbook Award in Prop. Law; **OTHER ACT & HONORS:** Also affiliated with the Hill Stewart Co. (Pres.); **HOME ADD:** 15314 DePauw St., Pacific Palisades, CA 90272, (213)454-3188; **BUS ADD:** 2001 Wilshire Blvd, Suite 501, Santa Monica, CA 90403, (213)453-1961.

HILL, Dale——*RE Consultant*, E-Systems, Inc.; **PRIM RE ACT:** Consultant, Property Manager; **BUS ADD:** PO Box 226030, Dallas, TX 75226, (214)661-1000.*

HILL, Dez R.——B: Sept. 24, 1947, Shreveport, LA, *Part., Bronner-Hill Construction; VP, Bronner-Hill, Ltd.*, Bronner-Hill; **PRIM RE ACT:** Broker, Developer, Builder, Property Manager, Owner/Investor; **SERVICES:** RE Sales, Home and Comml. Construction, Prop. Mgmt.; **PROFL AFFIL & HONORS:** Shreveport Bossier Bd. of Realtors, Bd. Member, LA Realtors Assn. Exec. Comm.; SIR; CRB, GRI; **GRAD EDUC:** BS, 1970, Mktg., LA State Univ.; **MIL SERV:** USN; **OTHER ACT & HONORS:** Bd. of Dir. - YMCA, Young People's Advisory Bd. - Bank of Commerce, Greater Shreveport Econ. Devel. Foundation; **HOME ADD:** 601 Oneonta, Shreveport, LA 71105, (318)865-0881;

BUS ADD: 3958 Youree Dr., PO Box 5357, Shreveport, LA 71105, (318)865-0291.

HILL, Frank D.——B: Dec. 30, 1940, Ardmore, OK, *Partner*, McAfee & Taft; **PRIM RE ACT:** Attorney; **PROFL AFFIL & HONORS:** ABA; OK Bar Assn.; State Bar of TX; **EDUC:** BBA, 1963, Acctg. and Fin., Univ. of OK; **GRAD EDUC:** LLB, 1966, Law, Univ. of TX at Austin; LLM, 1969, Taxation, The George Washington Univ.; **MIL SERV:** US Army; Cpt., 1967-70; **HOME ADD:** 1841 NW 56, Oklahoma City, OK 73118, (405)842-0835; **BUS ADD:** 100 Park Ave., Oklahoma City, OK 73102, (405)235-9621.

HILL, Jerel J.——B: July 28, 1952, Sherman, TX, *SW Regnl. Counsel*, Title Insurance Co. of MN; **PRIM RE ACT:** Attorney, Insuror; **SERVICES:** Handle Underwriting Decisions and Policy Claims; **PREV EMPLOY:** Staff Counsel, Gulf Interstate Engr. Co., Houston, TX; **PROFL AFFIL & HONORS:** State Bar RE, Probate & Trust Sect., NM Title Ins. Rating Bureau; **EDUC:** BA, 1974, Poli. Sci., N. TX State Univ.; **GRAD EDUC:** JD, 1977, Law, Univ. of TX; **EDUC HONORS:** Magna Cum Laude, top 10% of class; **HOME ADD:** 3226 Brookgreen, Kingwood, TX 77339, (713)358-9296; **BUS ADD:** 652 East North Belt, Suite 126, Houston, TX 77060, (713)447-1780.

HILL, Jerry E.——B: Mar. 2, 1938, Memphis, TX, *Partner*, Woodland Development; **PRIM RE ACT:** Architect, Developer, Owner/Investor; **OTHER RE ACT:** Planner; **PROFL AFFIL & HONORS:** AIA; NE TX AIA, Past Pres., of NE TX AIA; **EDUC:** BArch, 1961, Design, TX Tech. Univ.; **OTHER ACT & HONORS:** Past Pres. Lufkin Noon Lions Club; Crown Colony Ctry. Club; **HOME ADD:** 1208 Lotus Lane, Lufkin, TX 75901, (713)634-6851; **BUS ADD:** 1208 Lotus Lane, Lufkin, TX 75901, (713)632-3353.

HILL, Lloyd H.——B: Dec. 22, 1934, Brookfield, MO, *Pres.*, Lloyd H. Hill Realtors; **PRIM RE ACT:** Broker, Syndicator, Appraiser, Developer; **OTHER RE ACT:** RE Auctioneer; **SERVICES:** RE Sales, Appraisals of Land, and Land Devel.; **PROFL AFFIL & HONORS:** Kansas City, MO Bd. of Realtors, NAR, FLI, Realtor of the Yr., Kansas City, MO 1970, Farm & Land Realtor of the Yr. 1977; **EDUC:** Univ. of Kansas City; **MIL SERV:** US Army, 1954-1957, Sgt.; **OTHER ACT & HONORS:** Pres., Kansas City C of C - 1972, Bd. of Zoning Adjustment; Lee's Summit Bd. of Dirs.; Lee's Summit C of C; **HOME ADD:** 715 Montgomery, Lee's Summit, MO 64063, (816)524-6611; **BUS ADD:** 18 E. 3rd St., Lee's Summit, MO 64063, (816)524-9000.

HILL, Max L., Jr.——B: Aug. 15, 1927, Belleville, IL, *Pres.*, Max L. Hill Co., Inc.; **PRIM RE ACT:** Broker; **SERVICES:** Resid. & Comml. Brokerage, Devel., Prop. Mgmt., Insurance, Consulting; **PROFL AFFIL & HONORS:** Nat. Assn. of Realtors, Regnl. VP; C & S Nat. Bank Advisory Bd.; Univ. of SC Center for RE and Urban Econ. Studies, Ex. Comm., CRB; Charleston Realtor of the Yr., 1971; SC Realtor of the Yr., 1978; **EDUC:** BS, 1951, Engrg., U.S. Naval Academy; **EDUC HONORS:** Who's Who Among Students in Amer. Univs. and Colls.; **MIL SERV:** U.S. Army/U.S. Navy/U.S. Air Force, Private/Appren. Seaman & Midshipman/1st Lt. Pilot, SAC, Select Crew; **HOME ADD:** 109 Tradd St., Charleston, SC 29401, (803)577-6010; **BUS ADD:** 33 Broad St., Charleston, SC 29401, (803)577-3830.

HILL, Neil——Duncan Properties, Ltd.; **PRIM RE ACT:** Developer; **BUS ADD:** 100 Park Ave. Bldg., Suite 1200, Oklahoma City, OK 73102, (405)239-6727.

HILL, Richard G.——B: Apr. 17, 1924, IA, *Mgr.*, R.B. Purdum RE; **PRIM RE ACT:** Broker, Consultant, Engineer, Appraiser, Owner/Investor; **PROFL AFFIL & HONORS:** Lamoine Valley Bd. of Realtors, Charter Pres., 1968, GRI; Lifetime Member-Million Dollar Circle.; **EDUC:** BA, 1949, Mech. Engrg., Univ. of Cincinnati; **EDUC HONORS:** Pres. of Amer. Soc. of Mech. Engrg., 1948-49, undergrad. div.; **MIL SERV:** US Army, Air Force, Lt., DFC, WWII; **OTHER ACT & HONORS:** Charter Pres. Lamoine Valley Bd. of Realtors, 1968; **HOME ADD:** 703 Auburn Dr., Macomb, IL 61455, (309)833-2869; **BUS ADD:** 211 E. Jackson St., Macomb, IL 61455, (309)833-4577.

HILL, Robert E.——B: May 10, 1946, Elgin, IL, *Pres.*, Bob Hill RE, Inc.; **PRIM RE ACT:** Broker; **SERVICES:** Resid. (Rental & Serv.); **PROFL AFFIL & HONORS:** NAR, RNMI, GRI, Realtors Inst. of IL, CRS, CRB; **MIL SERV:** USAF, E-4, Serv. Medal; **OTHER ACT & HONORS:** Sec., The Elgin Bd. of Realtors, Fox Valley Kiwanis Club Elgin, N. Eng. Bus. Assn., The Elgin Area C of C; **HOME ADD:** 850 Douglas Ave., Elgin, IL 60120, (312)965-4709; **BUS ADD:** 606 Dundee Ave., Elgin, IL 60120, (312)742-5566.

HILL, Roderick——B: June 6, 1943, Detroit, MI, *Loan Spec.*, Housing & Urban Devel., Housing Mgmt. Multi Family; **PRIM RE ACT:** Regulator, Property Manager; **SERVICES:** Housing Consultant, Devel. & Prop. Mgmt.; **PREV EMPLOY:** FCH Services, Inc., 1968-72; **PROFL AFFIL & HONORS:** IREM, Detroit RE Bd., Optimist Club; Amer. Entrepreneurs Assn., CPM; **EDUC:** BA, 1969, Soc., Acctg., & Urban Planning, Wayne State Univ.; **MIL SERV:** US Army, SP-5, 2 overseas medals (Vietnam); **OTHER ACT & HONORS:** VP Jim Pandy Ski Club; **HOME ADD:** 19165 Freeland, Detroit, MI 48235, (313)342-5087; **BUS ADD:** 477 Michigan Ave., Detroit, MI 48226, (313)226-7534.

HILL, Sherman E.——B: Sept. 26, 1926, West Branch, IA, *Owner/Appraiser*, Profl. Appraisers; **PRIM RE ACT:** Appraiser; **OTHER RE ACT:** Sec. Charlev Co. Inc., FL; **SERVICES:** IFA of Resid., Income Prop., Comml.; **REP CLIENTS:** Barks Corp., Cape Girardeau, MO; **PREV EMPLOY:** Fed. Civil Service, USDA, Army Corps of Engr. (1968 - 1976); also Bldg. Contractor and retail bus. owner; **PROFL AFFIL & HONORS:** Nat. Assn. of Ind. Fee Appraisers, IFA; **EDUC:** Appraisal & Construction Inspection Training from US Govt. Arch. & Engrs. and Profl. Appraisers, also NAIFA training; RE course S.E. MO Univ.; **EDUC HONORS:** Outstanding Achievement Award (USDA); **MIL SERV:** USMC, Cpl., WWII, Purple Heart, Bronze Star, Presidential Citation.; **OTHER ACT & HONORS:** Shrine, East St. Louise, IL, VFW, DAV, BMPIW; **HOME ADD:** East Cape Park, McClure, IL 62957, (618)661-1647; **BUS ADD:** East Cape Park, McClure, IL 62957, (618)661-1647.

HILL, T. Bowen, III——B: Oct. 21, 1929, Montgomery, AL, Hill, Hill, Carter, Franco, Cole & Black; **PRIM RE ACT:** Attorney; **EDUC:** BS, 1951, Univ. of AL; **GRAD EDUC:** LLB, 1953, Univ. of AL; **HOME ADD:** 3721 Vaughn Rd., Montgomery, AL 36106, (205)272-7881; **BUS ADD:** PO Box 116, Montgomery, AL 36195, (205)834-7600.

HILL, Victor J., CPM——B: July 26, 1922, Sayre, OK, *Pres.*, Condominium Properties, Inc.; **PRIM RE ACT:** Broker, Consultant, Developer, Property Manager; **PREV EMPLOY:** Annuitant, Exxon Co., USA, VP, Whiteside & Grant, Realtors - Tulsa, OK; **PROFL AFFIL & HONORS:** Loca, State Bd. of Realtors, NAR, IREM, CPM; **EDUC:** BS, 1949, Bus., OK Baptist Univ.; **EDUC HONORS:** Pres., Baptist Student Union; **MIL SERV:** US Army Air Force, S/Sgt.; **OTHER ACT & HONORS:** Mason, Knights Templar; **HOME ADD:** 8215 E. 58th St., Tulsa, OK 74145, (918)252-4086; **BUS ADD:** 3105 E. Skelly Dr., Suite 515, Tulsa, OK 74105, (918)749-9743.

HILLBROOK, Roger William, Jr.——B: Dec. 15, 1943, Enid, OK, Hillbrook Props.; **PRIM RE ACT:** Consultant, Developer, Owner/Investor, Syndicator; **SERVICES:** Develop Prop. Comml. & Indus. as Gen. Part.; **PREV EMPLOY:** VP The Naiman Co. (Devel. of US & Can. RE), 1971-77; **EDUC:** BS, 1965, Acctg., Econ., Univ. of WY; **GRAD EDUC:** RE, Univ. of CA, Extension, La Jolla, CA; **MIL SERV:** USAF, Capt., Vietnam Serv. Medal & similar; **HOME ADD:** PO Box 1994, Rancho Santa Fe, CA 92067; **BUS ADD:** 777 S. Pacific Coast Hwy, Suite 208 E, Solana Beach, CA 92075, (714)481-5535.

HILLDRUP, James W.——B: Aug. 7, 1955, Fredericksburg, VA, *Atty.*; **PRIM RE ACT:** Attorney; **SERVICES:** RE Closings, Deeds, Deed Correction Suits; **REP CLIENTS:** Buyers of homes; **PROFL AFFIL & HONORS:** VA State Bar; VA Bar Assn., ABA; **EDUC:** BA, 1977, Pol. Sci., Univ. of Richmond; **GRAD EDUC:** JD, 1980, T.C. Williams School of Law of the Univ. of Richmond; **EDUC HONORS:** Phi Beta Kappa, Honor Grad., Pol. Sci. Honorary Frat., Am. Jur. Book Award; **OTHER ACT & HONORS:** Dir. Chancellor Ruritan Club; Deacon of Fredericksburg Baptist Church; **HOME ADD:** 312 Clay St., Fredericksburg, VA 22401, (703)898-2023; **BUS ADD:** 5314 Plank Rd., Fredericksburg, VA 22401, (703)786-6670.

HILLE, Richard——B: Jan 12, 1945, Sacto, CA, *Mgr. Devel. & Fin.*, E.F. Hutton & Co., Inc., RE Investment Dept.; **PRIM RE ACT:** Broker, Attorney, Lender, Syndicator; **PREV EMPLOY:** Teachers Ins. & Annuity Assn. of Amer.; **PROFL AFFIL & HONORS:** ABA; **EDUC:** BA, 1966, Soc. Sci., San Jose State; **GRAD EDUC:** MUP/JD, 1970/1976, Urban Planning, NYU & St. John's Univ.; **HOME ADD:** 25 Tudor City Pl., NY, NY 10017; **BUS ADD:** 1 Battery Park Plaza, NY, NY 10004, (212)742-3203.

HILLEMEYER, William C.——B: Aug. 11, 1934, Chicago, IL, *Sr. VP*, Daseke & Co.; **OTHER RE ACT:** RE Equity Investment Banker; **PREV EMPLOY:** IBM Corp., Armonk, NY; **PROFL AFFIL & HONORS:** Nat. Assn. of Profl. Engineers; CT Soc. of Profl. Engrs.; **EDUC:** BS, 1957, Chem. Engrg., MI State Univ.; **GRAD EDUC:** Statistics, Purdue Univ.; **EDUC HONORS:** Phi Eta Sigma, Scholastic Honorary Soc.; **MIL SERV:** US Army; 1st Lt.; **HOME ADD:** 209 Brushy Ridge Rd., New Cannan, CT 06840 06840, (203)972-1070;

BUS ADD: 3003 Summer St., Stamford, CT 06905, (203)324-9500.

HILLESTAD, Charles A.——B: Aug. 30, 1945, McCurtain, OK, *Partner*, DeMuth, Kemp & Backus, Chmn. of RE Dept.; **PRIM RE ACT:** Attorney; **SERVICES:** RE Corp., Partnership and Gen. Bus. Legal Services, Comml. Leasing; **REP CLIENTS:** Brokers, arch., consultants, devel., builders, prop. mgrs., bankers, lenders, owners and investors in RE; **PREV EMPLOY:** CO Supreme Ct. Clerk; **PROFL AFFIL & HONORS:** Amer., CO and Denver Bar Assns., Amer Arbitration Assn., P.O.E.T.S. (an ad hoc grp. of RE Attys.); **EDUC:** BS, 1967, Pol. Sci. & Hist., Univ. of OR; **GRAD EDUC:** JD, 1972, Univ. of MI Law Sch.; **MIL SERV:** US Army, S/Sgt.; **OTHER ACT & HONORS:** Dir. Hist. Denver, Leadership Denver, Nat. Trust for Hist. Preservation, Downtown Denver, Inc., Housing Task Force, CO Assn. of Commerce and Indus., Nature Conservancy.; **HOME ADD:** 2151 Tremont Pl., Denver, CO 80205, (303)534-5454; **BUS ADD:** Denver, CO 80202718-17th St., Suite 1600, (303)629-1800.

HILLGER, Dave——B: June 28, 1933, NM, *Pres.*, Globe Property Exchange, Inc.; **PRIM RE ACT:** Broker; **SERVICES:** Problem Solving, Estate Bldg., Equity Exchanges; **PROFL AFFIL & HONORS:** Soc. of Exchange Counselors; AZ Assn. of RE Exchangors; Nat. Assn. of Realtors, Cert. AZ Exchangor; **EDUC:** BA, 1956, Chem. Engrg., NM State Univ.; **MIL SERV:** US Army, Pvt.; **HOME ADD:** 1545 E. Ivyglen, Mesa, AZ 85203, (602)833-3147; **BUS ADD:** 659 E. Main, Suite A, Mesa, AZ 85203, (602)962-0940.

HILLHOUSE, Richard A.——B: June 25, 1943, Denver, CO, *Atty./Partner*, Lewis and Roca; **PRIM RE ACT:** Attorney; **SERVICES:** Specialist - RE Law; **REP CLIENTS:** Inspiration Consolidated Copper Co., State Farm Ins. Co., Prudential, Union Bank, Saguaro S&L, Occidental Land, Inc.; **PROFL AFFIL & HONORS:** ABA, AZ Bar Assn., WY Bar Assn., Maricopa Cty. Bar Assn., Law Clerk, Tenth Circuit Court of Appeals 1968-1969; **EDUC:** BS, 1966, Bus. Admin., Univ. of WY, San Jose St. Univ.; **GRAD EDUC:** JD, 1968, Univ. of WY; **EDUC HONORS:** grad. w/hon.; Editor-in-Chief, Land & Water Law Review (1967-1968); **OTHER ACT & HONORS:** Bd. of Dir., AZ Lawyers Credit Union; Author, Arizona Real Estate Sales Act: A Developer's View, 1977 AZ Bar Journal 42; **HOME ADD:** 6720 N. 19th Pl., Phoenix, AZ 85016, (602)248-0159; **BUS ADD:** 100 W. Washington, Phoenix, AZ 85003, (602)262-5366.

HILLIKER, Richard——*Mgr. Land Res. Dev.*, Consolidated Papers, Inc.; **PRIM RE ACT:** Property Manager; **BUS ADD:** PO Box 50, Wisconsin Rapids, WI 54494, (715)422-3111.*

HILLYARD, Richard——B: July 15, 1945, Wash., DC, *Chief, Acquisition Branch*, General Services Administration, Space Mgmt. Div.; **OTHER RE ACT:** Managing 20 Leasing Specialists Activities; **SERVICES:** Leasing of Office, Storage, and Special Facilities; **REP CLIENTS:** All fed. agencies in IL, OH, MI, MN, WI, IN; **EDUC:** BA, 1967, Soc., Wheeling Coll., Wheeling, WV; **GRAD EDUC:** Courses in RE, Amer. Univ.; **MIL SERV:** USN, Lt.; **HOME ADD:** 2113 Hull Court, Naperville, IL 60565; **BUS ADD:** 230 South Dearborn St., Chicago, IL 60604, (312)353-5600.

HILYARD, David C.——B: Jan. 9, 1923, Circleville, OH, *Assoc.*, Hartigan Assoc., Inc.; **PRIM RE ACT:** Broker, Consultant, Appraiser, Property Manager; **SERVICES:** Large Comml. RE, over 50 yrs. experience; **PREV EMPLOY:** Sr. Officer, First Union RE Investment Trust; **PROFL AFFIL & HONORS:** BOMA; Shopping Ctr. Assn.; Cleveland Area Bd. of Realtors, RPA; RE Broker/Salesman; **EDUC:** 1948, Mktg./Acctg., OH State Univ.; **MIL SERV:** US Army, Medic, PFC, Unit & Merit Citation; **HOME ADD:** Aurora, OH 44202, (216)562-6640; **BUS ADD:** National City Ctr., Suite 1520, 1900 E. 9th St., Cleveland, OH 44114, (216)696-0777.

HIMELSTEIN, Mandel E.——B: Jan. 4, 1933, Ft. Wayne, IN, *Pres.*, Mandel E. Himelstein, P.C., Lawyers; **PRIM RE ACT:** Attorney; **SERVICES:** All Legal Servs. Concerning RE & Gen. Corp. & Bus.; **PREV EMPLOY:** RE & Gen. Bus. pvt. practice; **PROFL AFFIL & HONORS:** Amer., AZ, IL, Maricopa Cty., Chicago Bar Assns., Am. Judicature Soc., Intl. Assoc. Jewish Lawyers & Jurists, Phi Delta Phi Legal Frat., Lawyer-Pilot Bar Assn., Lawyer to Lawyer Consultation Panel, Northwestern Univ. Law Alumni Assn., AZ State & Univ. Law Alumni Assn., JD, Spec. Asst. Atty. Gen. State of IL; **EDUC:** BS, 1954, Lit., Hist., Language, Northwestern Univ.; **GRAD EDUC:** JD, 1959, Northwestern Univ. Law Sch.; **EDUC HONORS:** Dean's List, Oustanding Junior, 1953, Research Staff, 1958; Sec-Treas., Class of 1959; **MIL SERV:** US Army, Sgt., Korea; **OTHER ACT & HONORS:** Legal Columnist 10 yrs, Trade Magazine, lecturer panelist Real Prop. subjects, civic & legal corps., Mayor's Comm. on Cable TV, 1974, Nat. Council on Alcoholism, 1972; Many Bds. of Dir. Civil, legal & religious grps.; **HOME ADD:** 7211 N. 11th Pl., Phoenix AZ 85020, (602)944-3819; **BUS ADD:** 1110 E. Missouri, Phoenix, AZ 85014, (602)248-9192.

HINDERY, Leo J.——B: Oct. 31, 1947, Springfield, IL, *Treas.*, Natomas Company; **PRIM RE ACT:** Owner/Investor; **PREV EMPLOY:** UT Intl. Inc., SF, CA 1971-80; **EDUC:** BA, 1968, Econ., Pol. Sci., Seattle Univ.; **GRAD EDUC:** MBA, 1971, Fin, Systems, Stanford Univ.; **EDUC HONORS:** Alpha Sigma Nu, Beta Gamma Sigma; **MIL SERV:** USAR; **OTHER ACT & HONORS:** Univ. Club, Commonwealth Club; **BUS ADD:** 601 CA St., San Francisco, CA 94108, (415)981-5700.

HINDY, George V.——B: Aug. 17, 1941, Brooklyn, NY, *Part.*, Adler, Hindy, Turner & Glasser, P.C.; **PRIM RE ACT:** Attorney; **SERVICES:** Fin. & Tax Structuring; Drafting & Reviewing RE Legal Document & Synd. Memoranda; **REP CLIENTS:** Rep. several synd.; **PROFL AFFIL & HONORS:** Legislative & Regulation Comm. - RESSI of NAR; NY County Lawyers Assn.; Amer. Judges Assn.; Brooklyn Bar Assn., Member - Who's Who in Amer. Law; **EDUC:** BS, 1963, Pol. Sci., Econ., Fordham Univ.; **GRAD EDUC:** MBA, 1973, Fin., St. John's Univ. Grad. School of Bus.; JD, 1966, Fin., St. John's Univ. Law School; **EDUC HONORS:** Top 10%; **MIL SERV:** US Army; **OTHER ACT & HONORS:** Chmn. Traffic & Transportation Comm. & Member Exec. Bd. of NYC Community Board 10; Arbitrator for Small Claims Div. - NYC Civil Court.; **HOME ADD:** 467 - 82nd St., Brooklyn, NY 11209; **BUS ADD:** 150 East 58th St., NY, NY 10155, (212)752-6610.

HINERFELD, Sydney——B: Apr. 7, 1915, Scranton, PA, *Pres.*, Hinerfeld Realty Co.; **PRIM RE ACT:** Broker, Consultant, Appraiser, Banker, Property Manager; **SERVICES:** Comml. - Indus. - Resid. and Appraisals; **PREV EMPLOY:** Always self-employed realtor; **PROFL AFFIL & HONORS:** NAR; PA Assn. of Realtors; Intl. Council of Shopping Ctrs.; Soc. of Indus. Realtors; Scranton Bd. of Realtors; RENMI, SIR; **EDUC:** BA, 1937, Univ. of Scranton; **GRAD EDUC:** BA, 1937, Phil. in Soc. Sci., Univ. of Scranton; **OTHER ACT & HONORS:** Dir., Fidelity Deposit & Discount Bank, Dunmore, PA; **BUS ADD:** 224 Adams Ave., Scranton, PA 18503, (717)342-8312.

HINES, Bruce——*Treas.*, Duriron Co., Inc.; **PRIM RE ACT:** Property Manager; **BUS ADD:** 425 N. Findlay St., Dayton, OH 45401, (513)226-4000.*

HINES, Jack L.——B: June 10, 1947, Houston, TX, *Pres.*, Clarion Corp.; **PRIM RE ACT:** Consultant, Developer, Property Manager; **SERVICES:** Gen. Part.; RE Devel.; **PREV EMPLOY:** Exec. VP Cullen Ctr., Inc.; VP Deauville Props.; **PROFL AFFIL & HONORS:** ULI; IREM; ICSC; **EDUC:** BS, 1971, Bus. RE, Univ. of Houston; **BUS ADD:** 4233 W. Alabama, Houston, TX 77027, (303)878-7160.

HINES, Dr. Mary Alice——B: Feb. 19, 1936, Muncie, IN, *Prof. of RE and Fin.*, The Univ. of Alabama, Tuscaloosa, College of Commerce and Bus. Admin.; **OTHER RE ACT:** Prof. of RE and Fin./Author of many RE books; **SERVICES:** Feasibility Studies, Mkt. Studies, Author of Text and Trade Books; **REP CLIENTS:** RE devel., nationwide distributors and publishers of RE books; **PROFL AFFIL & HONORS:** Amer. RE and Urban Econ. Assn.; AIREA; Soc. of RE Appraisers; Fin. Mgmt. Assn.; Amer. Fin. Assn.; So. Fin. Assn.; Midwest Fin. Assn., Numerous research grants, faculty internships for the School of Mort. Banking, Stonier Grad. School of Banking, WI School of Banking; **EDUC:** BS, 1957, Bus. Ed. and Math., IN Univ.; **GRAD EDUC:** MS, 1960, Fin./Mktg./Econ., IN Univ.; PhD, 1967, Quantitative Methods, The OH State Univ.; **EDUC HONORS:** Alpha Lambda Delta Freshman Hon., Delta Pi Epsilon Grad. Hon., Published doctoral dissertation (Nat. Retail Merchants Assn. of NY); Grad. Assistantships through the Master's and PhD Degree work; **OTHER ACT & HONORS:** Indian Hills Country Club; Univ. Club; First Presbyterian Church; Pres., 2nd VP, 1st VP - Midwest Fin. Assn.; **HOME ADD:** 6 Academy Dr., Tuscaloosa, AL 35406, (205)758-4988; **BUS ADD:** Box J, University, AL 35486, (205)348-6094.

HINKEL, Richard——*VP Ind. Rels. & Personnel*, Homestake Mining Co.; **PRIM RE ACT:** Property Manager; **BUS ADD:** 650 California St. 9th Fl., San Francisco, CA 94108, (415)981-8150.*

HINSDALE, Wayne——B: Aug. 31, 1941, CA, *Atty.*, Taylor, Hinsdale & Williamson, Inc.; **PRIM RE ACT:** Attorney; **REP CLIENTS:** Sutter-Yuba Bd. of Realtors; **PROFL AFFIL & HONORS:** State Bar, Real Prop. Sect.; **EDUC:** BA, 1963, Poli. Sci., Univ. of CA at Davis; **GRAD EDUC:** JD, 1971, Univ. of Pacific, McGeorge School of Law; **OTHER ACT & HONORS:** Yuba City Unified School Dist., Bd. of Trustees, 1977 to present; **HOME ADD:** 1596 Upland Dr., Yuba City, CA 95991, (916)674-9139; **BUS ADD:** 520 Olive St., Suite C, PO Box 467, Marysville, CA 95901, (916)743-2026.

HINSHAW, Robert L.——**B:** Aug. 11, 1930, Sacramento, CA, *Broker*, same; **PRIM RE ACT:** Broker, Consultant, Lender, Instructor, Real Estate Publisher; **EDUC:** BS, 1953, Bus. Admin., Univ. of San Francisco; **MIL SERV:** US Army, Lt., Korea; **HOME ADD:** PO Box 834, Benicia, CA 94510, (707)745-9735; **BUS ADD:** PO Box 834, Benicia, CA 94510, (707)745-9735.

HINTON, M.C.——**B:** Nov. 1, 1928, Warren Cty., KY, *Pres.*, M.C. Hinton Home Builders, Inc.; **PRIM RE ACT:** Developer, Builder; **PROFL AFFIL & HONORS:** Home Bldrs. Assn., Past Pres. Local Home Bldrs. Assn.; **MIL SERV:** USN, F1; **OTHER ACT & HONORS:** 2 yrs. Planning and Zoning Comm.; **HOME ADD:** 1509 Highland Way, Bowling Green, KY 42101, (502)781-6538; **BUS ADD:** 512 E. 12th St., Bowling Green, KY 42101, (502)842-1625.

HIRD, Kenneth L.——**B:** Apr. 24, 1956, Wichita, KS, *Atty.*, Williams, Hird & White, Inc.; **PRIM RE ACT:** Attorney; **SERVICES:** Title Work, Preparation of RE Documents; **REP CLIENTS:** Numerous local RE firms, Exchange Bank of Skiatook, OK; **PROFL AFFIL & HONORS:** ABA; Real Prop., Probate and Trust Section of the ABA; OK Bar Assn.; **EDUC:** BS, 1977, Bus. Admin., OK Christian Coll.; **GRAD EDUC:** JD, 1980, Univ. of Tulsa; **EDUC HONORS:** Who's Who in Amer. Coll. and Univ.; **HOME ADD:** 2020 S. 120th E. Ave., Tulsa, OK 74128, (918)437-0756; **BUS ADD:** 1595 S. Utica, Tulsa, OK 74104, (918)744-0266.

HIRSCHBERG, Marvin L.——**B:** Dec. 8, 1939, New York City, *Pres.*, Country Brook, Inc.; **PRIM RE ACT:** Consultant, Engineer, Developer, Owner/Investor; **SERVICES:** Computerized Project Mgmt. Control Systems; **PREV EMPLOY:** Developer, Synd., RE Analyst; **PROFL AFFIL & HONORS:** MBAA, RE Advisors; **EDUC:** BSCE, 1962, Engrg./RE Law, New England Coll.; **GRAD EDUC:** MBA, 1964, Corporate Fin., Adelphi Univ.; **EDUC HONORS:** Sr. Class Pres., Honor Soc.; **OTHER ACT & HONORS:** Assn. of MBA; **HOME ADD:** 43 E. Cheryl Rd., Pine Brook, NJ 07058, (201)227-2906; **BUS ADD:** 43 E. Cheryl Rd., Pine Brook, NJ 07058, (212)697-3800.

HIRSCHTRITT, Joel S.——**B:** June 1, 1945, MD, *Partner*, Newman Tannenbaum Helpern & Hirschtritt; **PRIM RE ACT:** Attorney; **SERVICES:** Legal Services; **PROFL AFFIL & HONORS:** Assn. of the Bar, City of NY, NY State Bar Assn. (Comm. on RE Fin.); **EDUC:** BA, 1967, Econs., CCNY; **GRAD EDUC:** JD, 1971, NYU; **EDUC HONORS:** Who's Who in Amer. Coll. & Univ., Econ. Honor Soc., Dean's List, Moot Ct. Bd.; **MIL SERV:** US Army Res., E-4; **HOME ADD:** 1 Washington Square Village, New York, NY 10003, (212)533-9861; **BUS ADD:** 310 Madison Ave., New York, NY 10017, (212)986-9700.

HIRSH, Joan C.——**B:** July 30, 1929, Harrisburg, PA, *Pres.*, Morton Hirsh Inc.; **PRIM RE ACT:** Broker; **PROFL AFFIL & HONORS:** Realtor, Women's Council of Realtors; NAR; PAR; Greater Harrisburg AR, Pres., Local Council WCR, 1978; **EDUC:** Univ. of Miami; **OTHER ACT & HONORS:** Member-NCJW-JCC-Several time board member Hbg. Hadassah-(not currently) board member-Hemlock Coucil Girl Scouts; **HOME ADD:** 4027 N. 2nd St., Harrisburg, PA 17110, (717)232-2101; **BUS ADD:** 1998 W. Harrisburg Pike, Middletown, PA, P.O. Box 1623, Harrisbur, PA 17105, (717)232-1945.

HIRT, Helen L.——**B:** Apr. 11, 1909, Cedarville, OH, *VP*, A.H.M. Graves Co., Inc.; **PRIM RE ACT:** Broker; **SERVICES:** Mktg. Resid. RE; **PROFL AFFIL & HONORS:** Metropolitan-Indianapolis Bd. of Realtors; NAR; Assn. of Realtors, 1972 Realtor of Year - Indianapolis; 1975 Nat. Pres. Women's Council of Realtors; **EDUC:** RE; **HOME ADD:** 605 Sugarbush Dr., Zionsville, IN 46077, (317)873-4268; **BUS ADD:** 1119 Keystone Way, Carmel, IN 46032, (317)844-4545.

HISE, William P.——**B:** Aug. 6, 1936, Des Moines, IA, *Asst. Gen. Counsel*, Dayton-Hudson Corp.; **PRIM RE ACT:** Attorney; **REP CLIENTS:** Dept. Stores Dayton, Hudson, Browns Diamonds Specialty Stores Mervyns; B. Dalton Booksellers; Target Stores; All Dayton-Hudson Corp. Operating Cos.; **PREV EMPLOY:** The Rouse Co., Columbia, MD 21044; **PROFL AFFIL & HONORS:** MN, IA, MD, and ABA Assns.; **EDUC:** BA, 1958, Hist. - Poli. Sci., State Univ. of IA; **GRAD EDUC:** JD, 1966, Amer. Univ.; **MIL SERV:** US Army, Capt., 1958-60; **OTHER ACT & HONORS:** Member City Council - Minnetonka, MN 1977 to present; **HOME ADD:** 15834 Randall Ln., Minnetonka, MN 55343, (612)934-2619; **BUS ADD:** 777 Nicollet Mall, Minneapolis, MN 55402, (612)370-6884.

HISKEN, Steven G.——**B:** Nov. 17, 1952, Tacoma, WA, *Leasing Assoc.*, UNICO Properties, Inc.; **PRIM RE ACT:** Property Manager; **OTHER RE ACT:** Leasing Agent; **PREV EMPLOY:** Alaska Gen. Const. Co./managed office at Prudhoe Bay, AK and at Camp Lonely, AK; **PROFL AFFIL & HONORS:** BOMA, Seattle C of C; **EDUC:** BBA, 1976, Fin., Univ. of WA, Seattle; **GRAD EDUC:** MBA, 1979, Fin., Mgmt. Systems, Univ. of WA, Seattle; **EDUC HONORS:** Phi Beta Kappa (Cum laude), Phi Eta Sigma; **OTHER ACT & HONORS:** Beta Theta Pi Fraternity; WA State RE Lic.; **HOME ADD:** 2032 43rd E., Apt. 10, Seattle, WA 98112, (206)322-2119; **BUS ADD:** 3300 Rainier Bank Tower, Seattle, WA 98101, (206)628-5083.

HISLE, DeWitt T.——**B:** July 26, 1934, Lexington, KY, *Managing Partner*, Hisle & Co., CPA's; **OTHER RE ACT:** CPA; **PROFL AFFIL & HONORS:** KY Soc. of CPA's, AICPA; **EDUC:** BS, 1956, Acctg., Univ. of KY; **EDUC HONORS:** Beta Alpha Psi Acctg. Honorary; **MIL SERV:** US Army, 1st. Lt.; **OTHER ACT & HONORS:** Rotary Club, C of C, Comml. Prop. Assn. of Lexington; Bd. of Dirs., Jerrico, Living Arts & Sci. Center, Lexington Center Corp.; **HOME ADD:** 624 Lakeshore Dr., Lexington, KY 40502; **BUS ADD:** PO Box 927, 277 E. High St., Lexington, KY 40588, (606)259-3403; **BUS TEL:** (606)266-5094.

HISSAM, Dallas E.——**B:** Dec. 29, 1937, MN, *Broker*, United Farm Agency, Comml. & Investment; **PRIM RE ACT:** Broker, Consultant, Appraiser, Developer, Owner/Investor, Instructor, Syndicator; **PREV EMPLOY:** VP United Farm Agency, Inc.; **PROFL AFFIL & HONORS:** Cert. Bus. Counselor, CRA; **EDUC:** Bus. Admin., Psych., Univ. of CA, Univ. of MO; **GRAD EDUC:** Art of RE Neg., Profl. Counseling Technique, Counselor Selling, Amer. Acad. of RE Exchange, Wilson Learning Corp., Paul Mock & Assoc.; Bus. Fin. for the Non-Fin. Exec, RE Trusts, Corp. Use and Formations, Taxation, RE Appraisal, Bus. Brokerage, Acctg. Gen. Econ.; **OTHER ACT & HONORS:** Lic. as broker in GA & MO; **HOME ADD:** 5452 Chanel Ct., Dunwoody, GA 30338, (404)394-5718; **BUS ADD:** 1534 Dunwoody Village Parkway, Atlanta, GA 30338, (404)396-2122.

HITCH, Peter——**B:** May 6, 1947, Indianapolis, IN, *VP*, Wells Fargo Realty Advisors; **PRIM RE ACT:** Lender, Owner/Investor; **PREV EMPLOY:** First Bank System; N.W. Mutual Life; **PROFL AFFIL & HONORS:** Urban Land Inst.; Mort. Bankers; NAIOP; **EDUC:** BA, 1970, Econ., Univ. of WI; **GRAD EDUC:** MS, 1971, RE/Urban Land Econ., Univ. of WI; **HOME ADD:** 9400 Cedar Ave., Minneapolis, MN 55420; **BUS ADD:** 4604 IDS Ctr., Minneapolis, MN 55402, (612)339-2565.

HITCHCOCK, Douglas R.——**B:** July 3, 1945, Atlanta, GA, *RE Assoc.*, Sherwood & Roberts, Inc., RE; **PRIM RE ACT:** Consultant, Owner/Investor, Syndicator; **OTHER RE ACT:** Realtor; **SERVICES:** Investment Counseling; **PREV EMPLOY:** PNW Bell Tel. Co., 1963-81; **PROFL AFFIL & HONORS:** NAR, RESSI, Candidate CCIM, SRS; **EDUC:** BA, 1972, Bus., Univ. of WA; **MIL SERV:** US Army, SP4, 1965-67; **HOME ADD:** 15307 SE 43 Pl., Bellevue, WA 98006, (206)747-4888; **BUS ADD:** 17422 108th Ave. SE, Renton, WA 98006, (206)255-2511.

HITCHCOCK, Thomas K.——**B:** Oct. 4, 1945, Houston, TX, *Pres.*, Hitchcock Props. Inc.; **PRIM RE ACT:** Broker, Consultant; **SERVICES:** Sales & Acquisition of Investment Prop. and Devel. Sites; **REP CLIENTS:** Instnl. investors in comml. prop., office, and multi-family resid. devels.; **PREV EMPLOY:** 8 yrs., Brokerage, Laguarta, Gavrel & Kirk, Consistent Top Sales Awards; **PROFL AFFIL & HONORS:** Houston Bd. of Realtors, NAR, Nat. Inst. of RE Brokers, CCIM, Nat. Inst. of RE Brokers; **EDUC:** BBA, 1968, Fin., Law, TX Christian Univ., Ft. Worth, TX; **HOME ADD:** 3922 Oberlin, Houston, TX 77005, (713)668-4380; **BUS ADD:** 3100 Weslayan, Suite 250, Houston, TX 77027, (713)871-9141.

HITT, James L.——**B:** Feb. 12, 1944, Bartlesville, OK, *Trust Officer*, The First Nat. Bank of Chicago, Personal Banking and Trust Dept. RE Div.; **PRIM RE ACT:** Consultant, Property Manager, Banker, Owner/Investor; **SERVICES:** Acquisition Consulting to Investors; Equity Purchasing for RE Equity Fund, and Customer Accounts; Asset Mgmt. for Equity Fund Account and Customer Accounts; **PREV EMPLOY:** Nat. Asset Mgmt. of Comml. Prop. for Large Chicago Fin. Instn.; Prop. Mgmt. for Maj. Chicago RE Serv. Co.; Nat. Prop. Mgmt. of Resid. Props. for Devels.; **PROFL AFFIL & HONORS:** Chicago RE Bd., NAR, IL Assn. of Realtors, IREM, CPM; **EDUC:** BS, 1972, Bus. and Music, IN Univ.; **MIL SERV:** USN, E-5; **HOME ADD:** 29 W. 426 Tanglewood, Warrenville, IL 60555, (312)393-2960; **BUS ADD:** 1 First Nat. Plaza, Chicago, IL 60670, (312)732-2498.

HIVELY, James A.——**B:** Dec. 26, 1948, Canton, OH, *VP*, Morgan Guaranty Trust Co., RE Dept.; **PRIM RE ACT:** Banker; **OTHER RE ACT:** Fin. Advisory and Placement Serv.; **EDUC:** BS, 1970, Econ., Univ. of PA; **GRAD EDUC:** Master of City Planning, 1973, Univ. of PA; MBA, 1976, The Wharton School, Univ. of PA; **HOME ADD:** 40 E. 89th St., NY, NY 10028, (212)348-7827; **BUS ADD:** 23 Wall St., NY, NY 10015, (212)483-3930.

HIXSON, E.C., Jr.——*VP Land*, Superior Oil Co.; **PRIM RE ACT:** Property Manager; **BUS ADD:** City National Bank Building, PO Box 1521, Houton, TX 77001, (713)751-4111.*

HLAVACEK, Leopold——**B:** Oct. 4, 1933, Czechoslovakia - Kosice, *Pres.*, Velur Props. Inc.; **PRIM RE ACT:** Broker, Lender, Owner/Investor, Property Manager, Syndicator; **OTHER RE ACT:** Land investment co.; **SERVICES:** Sales, Loans, Synd., Mgmt., Coordination; **PREV EMPLOY:** Gen. Mgr. for Orbis Props., Materials Manager for Silmar Div. of Vistron Corp.; **PROFL AFFIL & HONORS:** San Fernando Valley Bd. of Realty, Antelope Valley Bd., San Francisco Bar, SFV & AV & SF & San Diego MLS, Master Degree, Marketing; PhD, Marketing; **GRAD EDUC:** MBA, 1957, Mktg. & Quality Control & Testing, Prague School Of Econ.; **MIL SERV:** In Czechoslovakia; **HOME ADD:** 17161 Autumn Cir., Huntington Beach, CA 92647, (714)842-9175; **BUS ADD:** 15335 Morrison St., Suite 145, Sherman Oaks, CA 91403.

HOAG, John Clark——**B:** May 2, 1944, Beverly Hills, CA, *Assoc. Title Counsel*, Title Insurance & Trust Co., Corporate Law; **PRIM RE ACT:** Attorney, Insuror; **SERVICES:** Local problems dealing with real prop.; **PREV EMPLOY:** Hoag, Overholt & Bonaparte 1975-77; **PROFL AFFIL & HONORS:** State Bar of CA; ABA; Los Angeles Cty. Bar Assn. (Vice-Chairperson, Land Use Comm.), Phi Delta Phi, Editor; Coastal Devel. Planning Techniques, Los Angeles Cty. Bar (1979); **EDUC:** AB, 1967, English, USC; **GRAD EDUC:** CA Western School of Law; **EDUC HONORS:** Labor Law award, tax law award; **HOME ADD:** Westwood, CA; **BUS ADD:** 6300 Wilshire Blvd., Suite 804, Los Angeles, CA 90048, (213)852-6157.

HOAG, Myron L.——**B:** May 12, 1909, Sioux City, IA, *Appraiser*, Self Employed; **PRIM RE ACT:** Consultant, Appraiser; **OTHER RE ACT:** Assessment Appeals Board Hearing Officer; **SERVICES:** Gen. Appraising, RE Loans and Consultant; **REP CLIENTS:** Resid. bus. hotel, apt., indus.,church, dairy, farm, and acreage prop.; attys., corps., fin. inst., indiv. and the Superior Court of L.A. Cty.; **PREV EMPLOY:** Citizens S&L Assn. of Santa Barbara, CA; CA Fed. Savings; **PROFL AFFIL & HONORS:** NARA; L.A. Realty Board; NAR; CAR; NAIFA; **MIL SERV:** USAF; Maj.; **HOME ADD:** 3750 Canfield Rd., Pasadena, CA 91107, (213)351-8022; **BUS ADD:** 14545 Victory Blvd., Van Nuys, CA 91411, (213)782-1494.

HOAG, Richard J.——**B:** Sept. 9, 1946, NY, *Pres.*, RSJ Devel. Inc.; **PRIM RE ACT:** Broker, Consultant, Attorney, Developer, Owner/Investor, Property Manager, Syndicator; **SERVICES:** Devel. of Master Planned Communities & Comml. RE; Prop. Mgmt.; Tax Planning; Comml. Site Selection, Constructions; **REP CLIENTS:** City Equities, Rigel Ltd., Edaw Inc.; **PREV EMPLOY:** 1974-77 Pres. Cal-American Inc.; 1972-74, ROSSCO Inc., Dir. of Acquisitions; 1972 Corp. Counsel, Fortune Fund., Inc., USF Partners, Inc., USF Securities, Inc., San Diego, CA; 1971-72 World Leisure Time Mgmt. Co.; 1969-71 Prop. Research Fin. Corp.; **PROFL AFFIL & HONORS:** CA Bar Assn., US Dist. Ct. Bar Assn., Intl. Council of Shopping Ctrs., Lectured at UC Irvine on RE Synd., Who's Who in CA; **EDUC:** BA, 1967, Pol. Sci., CA State Northridge, Loyola of Los Angeles; **GRAD EDUC:** JD, 1970, Univ. of So. CA; **EDUC HONORS:** Dean's List, Honors Program, Delta Sigma Phi Frat., Phi Delta Phi (Legal Frat); **OTHER ACT & HONORS:** Jonathan Club, Rancho Las Palmas Ctry. Club, Malibu Racquet Club, Delegate, Amer. Legion, IN (Hoosier Boys State 1963); **BUS ADD:** 2800 28th St., Ste. 325, Santa Monica, CA 90405, (213)450-7871.

HOALEY, Mary——*Atty.*, Insilco Corp.; **PRIM RE ACT:** Attorney, Property Manager; **BUS ADD:** 1000 Research Pkwy., Meriden, CT 06450, (203)634-2000.*

HOBART, K. Bruce——**B:** Apr. 8, 1949, Richwood, WV, *Pres.*, Urban Development & Investment, Ltd.; **PRIM RE ACT:** Broker, Consultant, Developer, Owner/Investor, Syndicator; **SERVICES:** Investment Counseling, Devel. & Synd. of Income Props., Leasing, Mort. Fin. & Sales Brokerage; **REP CLIENTS:** Inst. investors in debt & equity positions re: comml. props., offshore investment groups; **PREV EMPLOY:** H.G. Smithy Company, 1977-81; VNB Mortgage Corp., 1969-77; **PROFL AFFIL & HONORS:** Mort. Bankers Assn., Home Builders Assn., Richmond Apt. Council, Richmond RE Group; **EDUC:** BA, 1971, Econ. & Bus., King Coll., Bristol, TN; **HOME ADD:** 2119 Rocky Point Ct., Richmond, VA 23229, (804)740-4126; **BUS ADD:** Suite 203, 2727 Enterprise Pkwy., Richmond, VA 23229, (804)747-0690.

HOBBS, Edward P.——**B:** May 24, 1940, Norwalk, CT, *Exec. VP*, Albert B. Ashforth, Inc.; **OTHER RE ACT:** Commercial Broker; **PROFL AFFIL & HONORS:** NACORE; **EDUC:** BA, 1962, Languages, Washington & Lee Univ.; **GRAD EDUC:** MBA, 1965, Mktg., Columbia Univ.; **EDUC HONORS:** Dean's List; **MIL SERV:** US Army, Infantry, Capt.; **HOME ADD:** 10 Colonial Ct., New Canaan, CT 06840, (203)966-5208; **BUS ADD:** 3001 Summer St., Stamford, CT 06905, (203)324-4844.

HOBBS, Robert L.——**B:** Sept. 19, 1911, Velpen, IN, *Builder-Devel.*, Hobbs Realty Co.; **PRIM RE ACT:** Developer, Builder; **EDUC:** Univ. IL; **GRAD EDUC:** B of Bus. Educ., 1938; **MIL SERV:** USN, Lt., Leis; **OTHER ACT & HONORS:** Pres., Decatur area Bridge Assn.; **BUS ADD:** Rt. 1 535 Loma, Decatur, IL 62526, (217)877-6486.

HOBBS, Robert S.——**B:** Jan. 6, 1934, Newark, NJ, *Pres.*, The Hall RE Group, SW Operations; **PRIM RE ACT:** Broker, Property Manager, Owner/Investor, Syndicator; **PROFL AFFIL & HONORS:** Nat. Assn. of Realtors, RE Securities and Sund. Inst.; **EDUC:** BBA, 1958, Acctg., The Univ. of MI; **GRAD EDUC:** MBA, 1950, Fin., Univ. of MI; **HOME ADD:** 11259 Shelterwood, Dallas, TX 75229; **BUS ADD:** 8340 Meadow Rd., Suite 134, Dallas, TX 75231, (214)373-4822.

HOBBS, Roger C.——**B:** Mar. 9, 1950, Orange, CA, *Pres.*, Century Amer. Corp.; **PRIM RE ACT:** Broker, Consultant, Developer, Builder, Instructor, Syndicator; **REP CLIENTS:** Indiv. & inst. investors, fast food, major retailors; **PROFL AFFIL & HONORS:** Faculty, CA State Univ., Univ. of CA, CPM; MAI Teaching Credential; **EDUC:** BS, 1972, Fin., Univ. of S CA; **GRAD EDUC:** MBA, 1974, Univ. of S CA; **HOME ADD:** 6622 LaCumbre, Orange, CA 92666; **BUS ADD:** 1440 E. Chapman, Orange, CA 92666, (714)633-2780.

HOBBY, Eddie——**B:** Mar. 28, 1942, Atlanta, GA, *VP & SE Reg. Mgr.*, The Abacus Grp.; **PRIM RE ACT:** Broker, Lender; **SERVICES:** All areas of RE Fin.; **REP CLIENTS:** The Paragon Grp., Lincoln Prop. Co., Captran Devel. Corp., Ocean Props. Ltd.; **PREV EMPLOY:** VP Branch Mgr., BA Mort. Co.; **PROFL AFFIL & HONORS:** MBA, NAIOP; **EDUC:** BS, 1972, Fin., FL State Univ.; **HOME ADD:** 1979 Castille Dr., Palm Harbor, FL 35563; **BUS ADD:** 5401 W. Kennedy Blvd., Tampa, FL 33609, (813)879-4252.

HOCHMAN, James A.——**B:** July 8, 1949, New York, NY, *Atty.*, James A. Hochman, Attorney at Law; **PRIM RE ACT:** Attorney, Owner/Investor; **SERVICES:** Full legal representation in RE and other legal matters; **PREV EMPLOY:** Counsel to Lawyers Title Ins. Corp., and counsel to Downs, Mohl & Co., Counsel to 535 N Michigan Ave. Associates; **PROFL AFFIL & HONORS:** Chicago Bar Assn., ABA, and Real Prop. Law Comm.; **EDUC:** AB, 1971, Eng./Amer. Lit., Brown Univ.; **GRAD EDUC:** JD, 1977, RE Law, Boston Univ. School of Law; **EDUC HONORS:** Cum Laude, Dean's List, Amer. Jurisprudence Award for Excellence in Criminal Law; **MIL SERV:** USN, Lcdr., USNR; **OTHER ACT & HONORS:** Lecturer in Law, Chicago-Kent Coll. of Law, Chicago, IL; **HOME ADD:** 512 West Belden, Chicago, IL 60614, (312)248-5726; **BUS ADD:** One IBM Plaza, Suite 1414, Chicago, IL 60611, (312)527-1666.

HOCKENYOS, Mark G.——**B:** July 22, 1945, Springfield, IL, *Pres.*, Hockenyos Real Estate & Development Co.; **PRIM RE ACT:** Broker, Developer, Owner/Investor, Syndicator; **SERVICES:** Full Serv. Comml./Investment Brokerage; **REP CLIENTS:** Specializing in lodging props. site acquisitions, and sale leasebacks; **PROFL AFFIL & HONORS:** RESSI, RNMI, FLI, Interstate Motel Brokers USA, CCIM Candidate; **EDUC:** BA Communications, 1968, Speech, English, Mktg., So. IL Univ.; **GRAD EDUC:** MEd, 1973, Admin., Sangamon State Univ.; **HOME ADD:** 14 West Hazel Dell, Springfield, IL 62707, (217)529-7886; **BUS ADD:** 211 South Grand Ave., W., Springfield, IL 62704, (217)525-2687.

HOCKER, David E.——**B:** Jan. 1, 1938, Owensboro, KY, *Owner & Pres.*, David Hocker & Assocs.; **PRIM RE ACT:** Developer; **PREV EMPLOY:** Owner of Shopping Ctr.; **PROFL AFFIL & HONORS:** ICSC, State Dir., KY/WV; Cert. Shopping Ctr. Mgr., ICSC; **EDUC:** BA, 1959, KY Wesleyan Coll.; **OTHER ACT & HONORS:** Chmn., Bd. of Tr., KY Wesleyan Coll.; Member Council of Indep. KY Coll. & Univ., KY C of C, Bd. of Dir.; **HOME ADD:** 2057 Bittel Rd., Owensboro, KY 42301, (502)926-1275; **BUS ADD:** 500 Wesleyan Park Plaza, Owensboro, KY 42301, (502)926-2616.

HOCKERSMITH, Steven C.——**B:** June 19, 1950, Little Rock, AR, *Pres.*, Medifax Investments; **PRIM RE ACT:** Broker, Developer, Syndicator; **REP CLIENTS:** Indiv. Investors, Emphasing Medical Investors primarily; **PREV EMPLOY:** Fawcett & Co., 10 yrs., Devel. and Synd. of Comml. Prop.; **PROFL AFFIL & HONORS:** AR Bd. of Realtors; BOMA of AR, Grad. of RE Inst.; CCIM Candidate; **EDUC:** 1972, Bus. Law, Univ. of AR; **OTHER ACT & HONORS:** Charter Pres. of Optimist Club; Bd. of Dir. of BOMA; **HOME ADD:** 1824 N. Hughes, Little Rock, AR 72204, (501)664-1987; **BUS ADD:** Suite 1000, Medical Towers Bldg., Little Rock, AR 72207, (501)225-3216.

HODDER, Donald W.——**B:** Oct. 18, 1928, Lincoln, NE, *Owner*, Don Hodder, Realtor; **PRIM RE ACT:** Broker, Consultant, Owner/Investor, Property Manager; **SERVICES:** Investment Counseling, Buyer and Seller Brokerage; **REP CLIENTS:** Indiv. and group investors in comml. RE; **PREV EMPLOY:** Fin. and planning mgmt. of projects ranging from less than –100,000 to in excess of –1 Billion, 1957-1979; **PROFL AFFIL & HONORS:** RNMI; RESSI; CCIM Chap. 6; Metro-Denver Comml. Listing Serv. Comm. Member; FLI; Denver and Jefferson Cty. Exchangers Organizations; NAR; CAR; **EDUC:** BScME, 1951, Univ. of NE; **MIL SERV:** USAR, Capt.; **HOME TEL:** (303)278-2949; **BUS ADD:** 13915 W. 31st Ave., Golden, CO 80401, (303)279-8709.

HODGES, James W.——**B:** Apr. 16, 1940, Newark, NJ, *VP*, The Colwell Co., Comml. Loans; **PRIM RE ACT:** Broker, Consultant, Lender; **SERVICES:** Mort. Banking, Comml. RE, Fin.; **REP CLIENTS:** Life ins. cos., pension funds, S&L's, indiv. & instl. investors in comml. prop.; **PREV EMPLOY:** Citicorp RE Inc., 1976-1981; Advance Mort. Corp., 1973-1976; **PROFL AFFIL & HONORS:** MBA; CA MBA; **EDUC:** BA, 1962, Bus. Admin./Psych., Drury Coll.; **GRAD EDUC:** 1971, Mgmt. Systems, NYU Grad. School of Bus.; **EDUC HONORS:** Pi Gamma Mu; **MIL SERV:** USN, Lt. (SC), 1962-1966; **HOME ADD:** 20361 Tomlee Ave., Torrance, CA 90503, (213)316-3934; **BUS ADD:** 3223 W. 6th St., Los Angeles, CA 90020, (213)380-3170.

HODIES, Robert M.——**B:** May 7, 1938, Newark, NJ, *Part.*, Finkel/Hodies Assoc.; **PRIM RE ACT:** Broker, Instructor, Consultant, Appraiser, Lender; **SERVICES:** R.E. Fin., Consulting, Appraisal, Brokerage; **REP CLIENTS:** Devel., investors, synds., instns., S & L , banks, Ins. cos.; **PROFL AFFIL & HONORS:** MAI, AIREA, Lic., CA R.E. Broker; **EDUC:** BA, 1960, 1962, Philosophy, Univ. of CA Berkeley, R.E. Certificate, Univ. CA Berkeley; **GRAD EDUC:** MBA, 1978, Bus., CA State Univ. Dominguez Hills; **HOME ADD:** 10625 Youngworth Rd., Culver City, CA 90230, (213)559-3789; **BUS ADD:** 049 Century Pk. E.Suite 1200, L.A., CA 90067, (213)557-2000.

HODSDON, Stan——**B:** Oct. 18, 1924, Wales, ME, *Owner*, Hodsdon Realty; **PRIM RE ACT:** Broker, Consultant, Appraiser, Owner/Investor, Property Manager, Insuror, Syndicator; **PROFL AFFIL & HONORS:** Realtor, Athens, GA (Local Bd.); GA - Nat. Appl. (NIA); Sr. Member, AACA; NA of REA; CRA; **EDUC:** AB, 1949, Educ./Soc. Sci., Atl. Christian Coll.; **GRAD EDUC:** MEd, 1950, Ed./Phys. Ed./Soc. Sci., Univ. of FL; **MIL SERV:** US Army, WW II, Pvt., ETO, 6 Battle Stars; **OTHER ACT & HONORS:** Member, Local Planning Commn.; Past Chmn., State Advisory Comm. Arco Planning and Devel.; State Offices in VFW And Amer. Legion; Silver Beaver BSA; **HOME ADD:** 462 S. Elm St., Commerce, GA 30529; **BUS ADD:** 462 S. Elm St., PO Drawer 180, Commerce, GA 30529, (404)335-3194.

HOEHN, Elmer L.——**B:** Dec. 19, 1915, Memphis, IN, *Chmn.*, Spectrum Properties Inc. (and) Commercial Logistics Corp.; **PRIM RE ACT:** Broker, Attorney, Developer, Owner/Investor, Property Manager; **SERVICES:** Mgmt. of Comml. Props., Warehousing; **PROFL AFFIL & HONORS:** So. IN Bd. of Realtors, ABA; Indiana & D.C. Bar Assoc., Admitted to the US Supreme Ct.; IN RE Comm. Lic.; **EDUC:** BS, 1936, Bus., Canterbury Coll.; **GRAD EDUC:** JD, 1940, Law, Univ. of Louisville; **OTHER ACT & HONORS:** Administrator, US Oil Import Admin.; Dir. Oil and GAs; IN Dept. Natural Resources; State Rep. IN Gen. Assembly; Nat. Press Club, Washington, DC; Nat. Lawyers Club, Washington, DC; **HOME ADD:** 19 Blanchel Terr., Jeffersonville, IN 47130, (812)282-2055; **BUS ADD:** 1415 Clark Blvd., Jeffersonville, IN 47130, (812)288-9057.

HOERNIG, Glenn Alenn——**B:** Sept. 7, 1952, Chicago, IL, *Bd. Member*, Harvard Hall; **PRIM RE ACT:** Consultant, Regulator, Builder, Owner/Investor, Property Manager, Syndicator; **SERVICES:** Prop. Mgmt., Rehab. of Resid. Dwellings, Advice on Purchasing, Fin. and Struct. Lay-outs; **REP CLIENTS:** Tenant Assn., self; **PROFL AFFIL & HONORS:** Assn. Photography Intl., Nat. Speleological Soc.; **EDUC:** BS, 1980, Bus. Admin., Amer. Univ.; **OTHER ACT & HONORS:** MENSA, Intertel; **HOME ADD:** 1222 N. Meade St., 14, Arlington, VA 22209; **BUS ADD:** 1222 N. Meade St., 14, Arlington, VA 22209, (703)235-1630.

HOFERT, Alvin H.——**B:** Jan. 17, 1895, St. Paul, MN, *Pres.*, J. Hofert Co., Scot C. Scott, J. Hofert Co. PO Box 88 Olympia WA 98507; **PRIM RE ACT:** Owner/Investor; **OTHER RE ACT:** Land Purchasing for Tree Planting; **SERVICES:** Lee Shepard, J. Hofert Maritimes Ltd., PO Box 480, Bridewater, NS (902)54307189; J. Hofert Co., PO Box 228 Cadillac, MI 40601 (616)775-4871; J. Hofert Maritimes Ltd. PO Box 415 Midland, Ontario L4R 4L1; **REP CLIENTS:** Alan Little Forestry and Tree growing Acreage; **HOME ADD:** 313 S. McCadden P., Los Angeles, CA 90020, (213)934-0314; **BUS ADD:** 5955 S. Western Ave., PO Box 47719, Los Angeles, CA 90047, (213)740-6500.

HOFFMAN, Arnold L.——**B:** Dec. 21, 1945, NY, NY, *VP*, Drexel Burnham Lambert Realty; **PRIM RE ACT:** Syndicator, Consultant; **SERVICES:** Investment Counseling, Synd. of RE; **PREV EMPLOY:** Nat. Dir.; Tax Advantaged Investments, Dean Witter Reynolds; **PROFL AFFIL & HONORS:** Chmn., Dist. Comm., NASD; Member of RE Comm., NASD; **EDUC:** AB, 1967, Econ., Cornell Univ.; **GRAD EDUC:** MBA, 1969, Fin., Stanford Bus. School; **EDUC HONORS:** US Steel Fellowship; **MIL SERV:** USAR, Sgt.; **HOME ADD:** 306 Buckeye Ct., Lafayette, CA 94549, (415)938-9794; **BUS ADD:** 555 California St. #2540, San Francisco, CA 94104, (415)981-7030.

HOFFMAN, Clive——**B:** July 20, 1937, Capetown, South Africa, *Pres.*, Clive Hoffman Assoc., Inc.; **OTHER RE ACT:** Exec. Dir., CA mort. brokers inst., Public Relations Counsel; **SERVICES:** Public Relations Mktg., Advertising, Ltd. Partner; **REP CLIENTS:** MCA Devel. Co., Cushman Realty Corp., O'Donnell, Brigham & Partners, Central Pacific Corp.; **PROFL AFFIL & HONORS:** Nat. Investor Relations Inst., Nat. Assn. of RE Editors; **EDUC:** BA Telecommunications, 1959, UCLA; **EDUC HONORS:** Dean's List/Cum Laude; **OTHER ACT & HONORS:** Bd. Member/Temple Isaiah/Past Chmn.; Community affairs comm., Los Angeles Bd. of Educ., Founding Pres. Community School, Los Angeles; **HOME ADD:** 9149 Larke Ellen Cir., Los Angeles, CA 90035, (213)553-3790; **BUS ADD:** 3348 Overland Ave. 101, Los Angeles, CA 90034, (213)202-1133.

HOFFMAN, Lawrence L.——**B:** Oct. 21, 1938, Los Angeles, CA, *Atty. & Broker*, Hoffman & Linde, Attys. at Law; **PRIM RE ACT:** Broker, Consultant, Attorney, Syndicator; **SERVICES:** Atty. Spec. in RE and Public Agency Land Use Matters, Broker Spec. in Investment Props.; **REP CLIENTS:** The Tahoe-Sierra Preservation Council (Prop. Owners Assn.), The Modland Corp., Tahoe-Donner Prop. Owner Assn., etc.; **PREV EMPLOY:** Formerly Chief Asst. City Atty., City of Los Angeles; 15 yrs. exp. in RE matters and RE and public agency repres.; **PROFL AFFIL & HONORS:** Admitted US Supreme Court, CA Supreme Court, CA Assn. of Realtors, Tahoe Sierra Bd. of Realtors; **EDUC:** BA, 1960, Pol. Sci., Stanford Univ.; **GRAD EDUC:** JD, 1967, Univ. of So. CA Sch. of Law; **MIL SERV:** USNR, Lt., 1960-63; **OTHER ACT & HONORS:** Chief Asst. City Atty. Los Angeles, 1973-77; Deputy Cty. Counsel, Los Angeles, 1967-71; **HOME ADD:** Tahoe Vista, CA; **BUS ADD:** 3000 Northlake Blvd., Suite 8, PO Box 7740, Tahoe City, CA 95730, (916)583-8542.

HOFFMAN, Leigh David——**B:** Sept. 12, 1957, Bridgeport, CT, *Mgr., Admin. Services*, Bailey and Casey Management Co.; **OTHER RE ACT:** Lease Administration; **PREV EMPLOY:** Investors Mort. Co. Bridgeport, CT. Asst. Prop. Mgr.; Creative Mgmt. and Realty Co., Inc. Waterbury CT; **PROFL AFFIL & HONORS:** IREM; **EDUC:** BS, 1979, Fin. Mgmt. Computers, Univ.of CT; **EDUC HONORS:** Deans List; **HOME ADD:** 4102 Inverrary Blvd., Lauderhill, FL 33319, (305)739-0762; **BUS ADD:** 1220 Amerifirst Bldg. 1 SE 3rd Ave., Miami, FL 33131, (305)374-0600.

HOFFMAN, L.M.——*VP Materials*, National Can; **PRIM RE ACT:** Property Manager; **BUS ADD:** 8101 W. Higgins Rd., Chicago, IL 60631, (312)399-3000.*

HOFFMAN, Melvyn L.——*Atty. at Law*, McArdle, Hoffman & McArdle; **PRIM RE ACT:** Attorney; **SERVICES:** All Phases of RE Law, Devel., Synd., Consulting; **REP CLIENTS:** Indivs., partnerships, corps., trusts, estates; **PREV EMPLOY:** Tax Consultant, C.C.H. Computax, Inc.; **PROFL AFFIL & HONORS:** La Crosse Cty. Bar Assn.; WI State Bar Assn.; La Crosse Area C of C, JD; CFP; **BUS ADD:** 205 Fifth Ave. S., Suite 204, PO Box 1503, La Crosse, WI 54601, (608)782-8098.

HOFFMAN, Nathan Paul——**B:** Jan. 19, 1947, Beaver Dam, WI, *VP*, Woody, Gumm, Hoffman & Heintz, P.C.; **PRIM RE ACT:** Attorney, Developer, Owner/Investor; **OTHER RE ACT:** Own Interest in TX Titles, an Abstract & Title Co.; **SERVICES:** Legal, Title, Devel. & Prop. Mgmt.; **REP CLIENTS:** Numerous builders and RE Cos.; **PROFL AFFIL & HONORS:** Builders Assn. of Victoria; State Bar of TX Sales & Mktg. Council; **EDUC:** BA, TX, 1969, Eng., Univ. TX - Austin; **GRAD EDUC:** JD, 1973, TX Tech Univ., Lobbock; **EDUC HONORS:** Editor of "Dictum"; **HOME ADD:** 117 Chimney Rock, Victoria, TX 77901, (512)578-4342; **BUS ADD:** 1208 E. Mockingbird Ln., PO Box 4526, Victoria, TX 77901, (512)578-3579.

HOFFMAN, Stuart K.——**B:** Dec. 16, 1949, Philadelphia, PA, *Partner*, Schwartz and Nash, P.A.; **PRIM RE ACT:** Attorney; **SERVICES:** Legal Representation in all Phases in RE Investment and Devel.; **REP CLIENTS:** Indiv. and corporate investors in resid. and comml. prop.; **PROFL AFFIL & HONORS:** The FL Bar (Real Prop. Probate and Trust Sect.); A.B.A. (Real Prop., Robate and Trust Sect.), Real Prop.

Law Designation; **EDUC:** BS, 1971, Acctg., NY Univ. School of Commerce; **GRAD EDUC:** JD, 1974, Law, Amer. Univ. WA Coll. of Law; **EDUC HONORS:** Dean's Honor Key, Law Review; **HOME ADD:** 4115 Toledo St., Coral Gables, FL 33146; **BUS ADD:** 777 Brickell Ave., Suite 700, Miami, FL 33131, (305)374-1200.

HOFFMAN, Thomas Rick——B: June 26, 1947, Los Angeles, CA, *Pres.*, ERA-The Property Store; **PRIM RE ACT:** Broker, Consultant, Developer; **SERVICES:** Devel., Resid. Comml. & Investment; **EDUC:** BS, 1971, Consumer Mktg. & Product Strategy, San Diego State Univ.; **HOME ADD:** 11751 La Colina Rd., San Diego, CA 92131, (714)566-3542; **BUS ADD:** 7094 Miramar Rd., Suite 113, San Deigo, CA 92121, (714)578-5510.

HOFFMAN, William H.——B: Sept. 17, 1930, Phillipsburg, NJ, *Sr. VP, Construction*, National Corp. for Housing Partnerships; **PRIM RE ACT:** Engineer, Developer, Builder, Owner/Investor; **SERVICES:** RE Devel. & Const., Design Review, Purchasing; **PREV EMPLOY:** AMF, Inc.; **PROFL AFFIL & HONORS:** Nat. Inst. of Bldg. Sci.; Bldg. Research & Advisory Bd., Nat. Exec. Council, NIBS; **EDUC:** BSEE, 1952, Elec. Engrg., Lafayette Coll., Easton, PA; **HOME ADD:** 6113 Walhonding Rd., Bethesda, MD 20816, (301)229-6062; **BUS ADD:** 1133 15th St., NW, Washington, DC 20005, (202)857-5771.

HOFFORD, Ray——*Ed.*, Greater Boston Real Estate Bd., The Realtor Roster; **PRIM RE ACT:** Real Estate Publisher; **BUS ADD:** 24 School St., Boston, MA 02108, (617)523-2910.*

HOFKIN, Mark——B: Aug. 4, 1946, Poland, *Gen. Mgr.*, Air Line Corp.; **OTHER RE ACT:** Energy Conservation Consultant; **SERVICES:** Consultation and Implementation of Energy Conservation Products and Ideas; **REP CLIENTS:** Joseph Cutler & Sons; David Marshall & Co.; Basil Corp.; Franklin Chemical; Gerit J. Lewisch A.I.A.; **PREV EMPLOY:** Bordentown Mil. Inst., 1970-1972, Air Mart Corp. 1972-1975; **PROFL AFFIL & HONORS:** Home Builders Assn. Refrigeration Serv. Engrs. Soc.; **EDUC:** BA, 1970, Econometrix, Temple Univ.; **GRAD EDUC:** MBA, 1977, Taxation, Pace Univ.; **OTHER ACT & HONORS:** 1980 Who's Who in Bus.; 1980-81 Who's Who in the World; 1981-82 Who's Who in the East; **HOME ADD:** 1067 Hillview Turn, Huntingdon Valley, PA 19006, (215)947-1622; **BUS ADD:** 2187 E. Huntingdon St., Philadelphia, PA 19125, (215)634-6633.

HOFSLETTER, Lois——*Executive Vice President*, American Society of Real Estate Counselors; **OTHER RE ACT:** Profl. Assn. Admin.; **BUS ADD:** 430 N. Michigan Ave., Chicago, IL 60611, (312)440-8091.*

HOGAN, John J.——B: Jan 26, 1918, NY, NY, *RE Appraiser/Consultant*, John T. Hogan SREA; **PRIM RE ACT:** Broker, Consultant, Appraiser; **PREV EMPLOY:** Assoc. Regl. Appraiser for Genl. Serv. Admin. (US Govt.) NY, NJ, PA, DE, VA & PR; **PROFL AFFIL & HONORS:** SREA, Pres., Chmn. SREA NY Chap.; **MIL SERV:** US Army Engrg.; **OTHER ACT & HONORS:** Peter Minuet Post Amer. Legion; **HOME ADD:** 178 Strathmore Gate Dr., Stony Brook, NY 11790, (516)751-6373; **BUS ADD:** 23 Green St., Huntington, NY 11743, (516)427-1156.

HOGAN, John J.——B: Feb. 10, 1940, NY, NY, *VP*, William J. Gill & Co., Inc.; **PRIM RE ACT:** Consultant, Appraiser; **SERVICES:** Nationwide RE Appraisals & Consultations; **REP CLIENTS:** Maj. fin. instns., corporate clients and indiv. income producing props.; **PROFL AFFIL & HONORS:** AIREA; Soc. of RE Appraisers; Long Island Bd. of Realtors, MAI, SRPA; **EDUC:** BA, 1962, Philosophy, Cathedral Coll.; **OTHER ACT & HONORS:** School Bd. Tr., Carle Place Schools - 6 yrs.; Nassau-Suffolk School Bds. Assn.; NY State School Bds. Assn.; **HOME ADD:** 329 Rushmore Ave., Carle Place, NY 11514, (516)997-7277; **BUS ADD:** 600 Old Country Rd., Garden City, NY 11530, (516)746-4590.

HOGAN, Robert W.——B: Sept. 14, 1920, Newburgh, NY, *VP & Sec.*, D'Ambrosia, Hogan, Oppenheimer, Saperston & Voit Real Estate Associates, Inc.; **PRIM RE ACT:** Broker; **PREV EMPLOY:** 1950-1959 Sun Oil Co., Exec. Training Program; **PROFL AFFIL & HONORS:** SIR, Active Member; **EDUC:** BA, 1950, Econ. & Bus. Admin., Hope Coll., Holland, MI; **GRAD EDUC:** Some courses Syracuse Univ. toward Advanced Degree; **MIL SERV:** US Army, 1940-45, S/Sgt., Amer. Defense Service Medal; Asiatic Pac. Service Medal; World War II Victory Medal; **HOME ADD:** 13 Vernon Cr., Cheektowaga, NY 14225, (716)836-0339; **BUS ADD:** 560 Delaware Ave., Buffalo, NY 14202, (716)884-7000.

HOGARD, Earl——*Corp. Secy.*, Witco Chemical Co., Inc.; **PRIM RE ACT:** Property Manager; **BUS ADD:** 277 Park Ave., NY, NY 10017, (212)872-4200.*

HOGE, Andrew E.——B: Aug. 7, 1938, Willoughby, OH, *Atty.*, Hoge & Lekisch; **PRIM RE ACT:** Attorney; **REP CLIENTS:** Wash. Mort. Co., Inc.; Aetna Life Ins. Co.; John Hancock Ins. Co.; Nat. Bank of AK; **PROFL AFFIL & HONORS:** ABA, Sect. of Real Prop., Probate & Trust Law, Pres. Anchorage Estate Planning Council; Chmn. Admin. Law Sect. of the AK Bar Assn.; **EDUC:** BS, 1960, Acctg. & Fin., OH Univ.; **GRAD EDUC:** LLB, 1963, NYU; **EDUC HONORS:** Cum Laude, Beta Gamma Sigma, Beta Alpha Psi; **HOME ADD:** SRA Box 2138, Anchorage, AK 99507, (907)344-8248; **BUS ADD:** 437 'E' St., Suite 500, Anchorage, AK 99501, (907)276-1726.

HOHMAN, Charles——*Treas.*, Halstead Industries, Inc.; **PRIM RE ACT:** Property Manager; **BUS ADD:** W. New Castle St., Zelienople, PA 16063, (412)452-9400.*

HOKANSON, Stephen P.——B: Dec. 5, 1946, Indianapolis, IN, *VP*, Hokanson Co's., Inc.; **PRIM RE ACT:** Broker, Syndicator, Consultant, Developer, Property Manager; **OTHER RE ACT:** Leasing Agent; **SERVICES:** Full Service Comml. Investment RE; **REP CLIENTS:** Amer. Fletcher Nat. Bank, St. Vincent Hospital and HeaLth Care Ctr., Coll. Life Ins. Co. of Amer.; **PROFL AFFIL & HONORS:** BOMA, IREM, NAR, 1976, Pres. of Indpls. IREM, 1979, Pres. N Central Regional Conf. BOMA, 1981, Pres. Metropolitan Indpls. Bd. of Realtors; **EDUC:** BS, 1969, Admin. & Mgmt, IN Univ.; **OTHER ACT & HONORS:** 1977 Outstanding Young Man of Amer.; **HOME ADD:** 5616 Audubon Ridge, Indianapolis, IN 46250, (317)842-0857; **BUS ADD:** 45 N. Pennsylvannia St., #200, Indianapolis, IN 46204, (317)638-3576.

HOLBROOK, Joseph C.——B: Aug. 22, 1921, Royston, GA, *VP*, Mount Vernon Realty, Inc.; **PRIM RE ACT:** Broker, Instructor, Property Manager; **SERVICES:** Resid. Comml., Prop. Mgmt.; **PREV EMPLOY:** USAF - 30 years; **EDUC:** BS, 1962, Indus. Admin., N. GA Coll.; **GRAD EDUC:** LLB, 1963, LaSalle Univ.; **MIL SERV:** USAF, Col., Legion of Merit; **OTHER ACT & HONORS:** Daedalians; **HOME ADD:** 4112 Orleans Place, Alexandria, VA 22304; **BUS ADD:** 6000 Stevenson Ave., Alexandria, VA 22304, (703)370-4600.

HOLCER, Thomas E.——B: Nov. 27, 1949, Chicago, IL, *Sr. Consultant*, The Marling Group; **PRIM RE ACT:** Consultant, Appraiser; **SERVICES:** Valuation, Feasibility Studies, Mkt. Analysis, Condo. Conversion Studies; **REP CLIENTS:** Lenders, devels. of comml. props.; **PROFL AFFIL & HONORS:** AIREA, MAI; **EDUC:** BA, 1971, Poli. Sci., W. IL Univ.; **HOME ADD:** 3411 Venard, Downers Grove, IL 6O515, (312)852-5032; **BUS ADD:** One Northfield Pl., Northfield, IL 60093, (312)446-9380.

HOLCHER, Donald R.——B: Nov. 16, 1943, Berkeley, CA, *Prin. and Dir. of RE*, Rreef Corp.; **OTHER RE ACT:** Investment Advisor for Pension Funds; Mgr. of Portfolio; **PREV EMPLOY:** VP, Grubb and Ellis Co.; **PROFL AFFIL & HONORS:** IREM, ICSC and Bd. of Realtors; **EDUC:** BBA, 1966, Fin., Golden Gate Univ.; **GRAD EDUC:** MBA, 1969, Fin., Golden Gate Univ.; **EDUC HONORS:** Dean's list 3 semesters; **MIL SERV:** USAR, E-6; **OTHER ACT & HONORS:** Olympic Club-San Francisco; **HOME ADD:** 650 CA. St.,Suite 1800, San Francisco, CA 94108; **BUS ADD:** 650 CA St., Suite 1800, S.F., CA 94108, (415)781-3300.

HOLCOMB, Lyle Donald, Jr.——B: Feb.3, 1929, Miami, FL, *Partner*, Therrel, Baisden, Stanton, Wood & Setlin; **PRIM RE ACT:** Attorney; **SERVICES:** Rep. of Buyers and Sellers in Spot Sales, Rep. of Instnl. Lender; **REP CLIENTS:** Chase Fed. S & L Assn., Flaghsip Natl. Bank of Miami; **PREV EMPLOY:** Law firm of Holcomb & Holcomb, Miami, FL 1955-72, involved in real prop. work; **PROFL AFFIL & HONORS:** The FL Bar, Exec. Council of the Real Prop., Probate & Trust Law Sect. of The FL Bar, Real Prop. probate & trust law section of ABA; Fellow, American College of Probate Counsel; **EDUC:** BA, 1951, Pol. Sci., Univ. of MI; **GRAD EDUC:** JD, 1954, real prop., probate, Univ. of FL Coll. of Law; **EDUC HONORS:** Editor in Chief, Univ. of FL Law Review; **OTHER ACT & HONORS:** Silver Beaver Award from S. FL Council, Boy Scouts of Amer., Past pres., Miami Beach Bar Assn.; **HOME ADD.** 700 Malaga Ave., Coral Gables, FL 33134, (305)445-7584; **BUS ADD:** Suite 600, 111 Lincoln Rd., Miami Beach, FL 33139, (305)672-1921.

HOLDER, Carol L.——B: Jan. 6, 1956, Waco, TX, *VP Dir. of Leasing*, T-Shirts Plus; **OTHER RE ACT:** Secure retail space in enclosed malls & shopping ctrs.; **REP CLIENTS:** 100 franchise stores per yr.; **HOME ADD:** Rt. Box 1108, Waco, TX 76710, (817)848-4014; **BUS ADD:** P.O. Box 1049, Waco, TX 76703, (817)662-5050.

HOLDERITH, Emeric R.——B: June 29, 1941, Elizabeth, NJ, *Partner*, The Linpro Company; **PRIM RE ACT:** Developer, Builder, Owner/Investor, Property Manager; **PREV EMPLOY:** Grubb & Ellis Comml. Brokerage Co.; **EDUC:** BS, 1963, Mktg., Econ., Miami Univ., Oxford,

OH; **BUS ADD:** 5353 West Dartmouth Ave., Suite 312, Denver, CO 80227, (503)985-8701.

HOLEMAN, Jack R.——B: June 8, 1929, South Bend, IN, *Pres.*, Condomimium Consultants, Inc.; **PRIM RE ACT:** Consultant, Instructor, Property Manager, Syndicator; **OTHER RE ACT:** Author of "Condominium Mgmt." Published 1980 - Prentice-Hall (Hard cover text); **SERVICES:** Instr. - Univ. of Miami 1980-81 on Basic and Advanced Condominium Mgmt. Synd. Columinist for the Knight-Ridder Newspapers - "Condo-Line" - *Miami Herald*; **PREV EMPLOY:** Author of synd. column "Condo-Living" 1978-1981, Tampa Tribune, Palm Beach Post; **PROFL AFFIL & HONORS:** Community Assn. Inst., Bldg. Mgrs. Intl., FL Assn. Realtors, Cert. Bldg. Admin.; **EDUC:** BA, 1953, Western KY State Teachers Coll.; **MIL SERV:** USN, Mdshpmn.; **HOME ADD:** 201 Crandon Blvd., Key Biscayne, FL 33149, (305)433-0337; **BUS ADD:** 201 Crandon Blvd., Key Biscayne, FL 33149, (305)361-5725.

HOLGUIN, Henry A.——B: Sept. 10, 1951, Ft. Benning, GA, *Atty.*, Spierer and Woodward; **PRIM RE ACT:** Consultant, Attorney, Owner/Investor, Syndicator; **OTHER RE ACT:** Exchanges, Syndications; **SERVICES:** Fed. and State Securities and Sund. Consulting; Drafting of Synd. Offering Documents, Qualification and Registration with Fed. & State Regulatory Agencies; **REP CLIENTS:** Title Ins. and Trust, Transamer. Title Ins., Spring Realty, and other RE Agencies, Brokers, Synd. and indiv.; **PREV EMPLOY:** CA Dept. of Corps., Staff Counsel; **EDUC:** BS, 1973, Bus. Admin., Univ. of So. CA; 1971, Univ. of Cambridge, England; **GRAD EDUC:** JD, 1976, Corp./Bus., Univ. of CA at Davis; **HOME ADD:** 706 Vincent Park, No. 3, Redondo Beach, CA 90277, (213)374-1485; **BUS ADD:** 21535 Hawthorne Blvd. Ste 532, Torrance, CA 90503, (213)540-3199.

HOLLAND, James J.——B: Dec. 29, 1935, Chelsea, MA, *Pres.*, James Holland Realtor, Better Homes and Gardens; **PRIM RE ACT:** Broker, Appraiser; **SERVICES:** Resid. and Comml. Brokerage; **PREV EMPLOY:** Assoc. with Harrison Assoc. Realtors as a realtor from 6/73 to 3/76; Sales Mgr. of Cape Realty from 3/76 to 9/77; **PROFL AFFIL & HONORS:** NAR; MA Assn. of Realtors; Cape Cod Bd. of Realtors; Realtors Nat. Mktg. Inst.; AIREA, CRB; CRS; GRI; **OTHER ACT & HONORS:** Formerly on the Advisory Comm. of the Rgnl. Tech. High School, Harwich, MA; **HOME ADD:** 8 McNamara Ave., W. Yarmouth, MA 02673, (617)394-6749; **BUS ADD:** 550A Rt. 28, W. Yarmouth, MA 02673, (617)771-4202.

HOLLAND, Woodrow A.——B: Oct. 24, 1947, Houston, TX, *Sec. and Counsel*, Champion Realty Corp.; **PRIM RE ACT:** Attorney; **SERVICES:** Legal and Bus. Counseling; **REP CLIENTS:** Champion Realty Corp. and Champion Intl. Corp.; **PREV EMPLOY:** Dyche & Wright, 1600 Mellie Esperson Bldg., Houston, TX; **PROFL AFFIL & HONORS:** State Bar of TX, ABA, Houston Bar Assn., Houston Young Lawyers Assn.; **EDUC:** BSCE, 1970, S. Methodist Univ.; **GRAD EDUC:** Dr. of Jurisprudence, 1974, Univ. of TX School of Law; **EDUC HONORS:** Outstanding Civil Engr. Grad. 1970; **MIL SERV:** US Army Res., Sgt. 1970-76; **HOME ADD:** 11802 Fidelia Ct., Houston, TX 77024, (713)781-0528; **BUS ADD:** One Greenspoint Plaza, Suite 500, 16855 Northchase, Houston, TX 77060, (713)931-6161.

HOLLANDER, Sherman S.——B: Mar. 7, 1920, Cleveland, OH, *Atty.*, Terrell, Salim, Hollander & Esper; **PRIM RE ACT:** Attorney; **OTHER RE ACT:** Legal Rep. as to RE Title and other RE matters; **REP CLIENTS:** Safeco Title Ins. Co., Title Ins. Co. of MN, Schmidt Mort. Co.; **PREV EMPLOY:** Pres. and Chief Title Officer of Hollander Abstract Co., 1954-68; OH Title Corp., 1968-72; **PROFL AFFIL & HONORS:** Past Pres. & Life Member OH Land Title Assn.; Treas. Cuyahoga Cty. Bar Assn.; VP Real Prop. Sect. OH State Bar Assn.; Member Cleveland Bar Assn.; ABA; **EDUC:** AB, 1941, Case Western Res. Univ.; **GRAD EDUC:** LLB, 1946, Case Western Res. Univ. Sch. of Law; **EDUC HONORS:** Phi Beta Kappa; **MIL SERV:** USA Air Corps., First Lt. Navigator; **OTHER ACT & HONORS:** Beachwood Bd. of Educ., 1960-73, Pres. 1964, 1968, 1970; Heights Area C of C Citizen of Year, 1960; Beachwood Civic League Citizen of Yr., 1973; **HOME ADD:** 23902 Woodway Rd., Cleveland, OH 44122, (216)381-5685; **BUS ADD:** 1620 Standard Bldg., Cleveland, OH 44113, (216)621-6784.

HOLLEMAN, L. Worth, Jr.——B: Apr. 26, 1948, Raleigh, NC, *Attorney*, Tuggle Duggins Meschan Thornton & Elrod, P.A. (Dir.-Partner); **PRIM RE ACT:** Attorney; **SERVICES:** Gen. Real Prop. Practice: all Types of Resid. Comml. and Investment Prop.; **REP CLIENTS:** Lenders, title ins. cos., indiv., devels., investors, all types of comml. props.; **PROFL AFFIL & HONORS:** ABA; NC Bar Assn., Real Prop. Sect.; NC State Bar Assn.; Greensboro Bar Assn., past Pres., Young Lawyers Sect., Rating by Martindale-Hubbell Law Dir.; **EDUC:** 1970, Bus. Admin., Univ. of NC, Chapel Hill; **GRAD EDUC:** JD, 1974, School of Law, Univ. of NC, Chapel Hill; **EDUC HONORS:** Dean's List; Student Legislature; Counsel to Honor Ct., Dean's List; **HOME ADD:** 802 Dover Rd., Greensboro, NC 27408, (919)273-0941; **BUS ADD:** P.O. Drawer X, Greensboro, NC 27402, (919)378-1431.

HOLLENBECK, Don——B: Dec. 7, 1949, Albuquerque, NM, *Salesman*, NY Life; **PRIM RE ACT:** Consultant, Owner/Investor; **SERVICES:** Consulting; **PROFL AFFIL & HONORS:** Million Dollar Round Table, Nat. Assn. of Life Underwriters; **EDUC:** BS, 1973, Educ., Univ. of NM; **MIL SERV:** US Army, E-5; **OTHER ACT & HONORS:** Prof. Bowlers Assn.; **HOME ADD:** 13509 Witcher NE, Albuquerque, NM 87112, (505)293-5306; **BUS ADD:** 6400 Uptown Blvd. NE, Suite 600W, Albuquerque, NM 87112, (505)883-5757.

HOLLERAN, W.E.——B: Oct. 29, 1925, Fairmont, WV, *Mgr., RE Servs.*, Standard Oil Co. of IN; **PRIM RE ACT:** Attorney, Property Manager; **PROFL AFFIL & HONORS:** MI State Bar; VP Educ., Nat. Assn. of Corporate RE Execs.; Intl. Right of Way Assn.; **EDUC:** BSEd, 1948, Social Studies, OH State Univ.; **GRAD EDUC:** MA, 1949, Social Studies, OH State Univ.; JD, 1956, Law, Wayne State Univ.; **EDUC HONORS:** Prize Law School, Conflict of Laws; **MIL SERV:** US Army, 1st Lt.; **HOME ADD:** 1521 Swallow, Naperville, IL 60565, (312)357-3689; **BUS ADD:** 200 E. Randolph Dr., Chicago, IL 60601, (312)856-5603.

HOLLIDAY, Morton——B: Aug. 7, 1937, Ansonia, CT, *Sr. VP*, Sonnenblick-Goldman Corp., Affil. of Lehman Bros., Kuhn Loeb Inc.; **PRIM RE ACT:** Broker, Consultant; **SERVICES:** Fin. & Sale of Income Producing Prop.; **REP CLIENTS:** Instl. lenders & indiv. or instnl. investors in comml. props.; **PREV EMPLOY:** Counsel Teachers Ins. & Annuity Assn., 1965-67; **PROFL AFFIL & HONORS:** RE Bd. of NY; MBA; NY State Bar Assn.; **EDUC:** BA, 1958, Bus., UConn.; **GRAD EDUC:** JD, 1961, Boston Univ.; **OTHER ACT & HONORS:** Adv. Dir. & Shareholder of Lehman Bros.; **HOME ADD:** 150 E. 61st St., NY, NY 10021, (212)753-1476; **BUS ADD:** 1251 Ave. of the Americas, NY, NY 10020, (212)541-4321.

HOLLINS, Harry——*Exec. Dir.*, Lousiana, LA Real Estate Commission; **PRIM RE ACT:** Property Manager; **BUS ADD:** P.O. Box 14785, Baton Rouge, LA 70808, (504)925-4771.*

HOLLIS, Austin O., Jr.——B: Aug. 30, 1952, Jacksonville, FL, *VP*, Miller, Rogers, Hollis Inc.; **PRIM RE ACT:** Broker, Consultant, Appraiser, Developer, Builder; **SERVICES:** Primary, Appraiser/Consultant; Secondary, Devel./Bldr./Mktg. Brokerage; **REP CLIENTS:** Major oil co's. & banks; **PROFL AFFIL & HONORS:** Jacksonville Bd. of Realtors; AIREA; Soc. of RE Appraisers; NAR; FL Assn. of Realtors, MAI; SRPA; **EDUC:** AA, Bus., N. FL Jr. Coll.; BA, 1974, Land Econ., Univ. of N. FL; **EDUC HONORS:** Summa Cum Laude, Pres. - Phi Theta Kappa, Cum Laude; **OTHER ACT & HONORS:** Mort. Broker, Resid. Contractor; **HOME ADD:** 2131 Sweet Briar Ln., Jacksonville, FL 32217, (904)731-1294; **BUS ADD:** 1755 Univ. Blvd. W., Jacksonville, FL 32217, (904)737-3232.

HOLLOHAZY, Attila N.——B: May 26, 1943, Hungary, *Pres.*, Atlantic Mgmt. & Devel. Inc.; **PRIM RE ACT:** Engineer, Architect, Developer, Builder, Owner/Investor, Property Manager, Syndicator; **HOME ADD:** 716 The West Mall, Suite 1802, Etobicoke, Ont., Can., (416)621-1275; **BUS ADD:** 2901 S. Ocean Blvd., Highland Bch., FL 33431, (305)276-6700.

HOLLORAN, Joseph W.——B: Nov. 15, 1924, Pueblo, CO, *VP*, Holloran Realty & Investment Co., Resid. Brokerage; **PRIM RE ACT:** Broker, Consultant, Lender, Owner/Investor, Property Manager; **SERVICES:** RE Sales & Exchanges (Trades); **REP CLIENTS:** Employee Transfer Corp., Relo Realty, Transamerica, Van Relco; **PROFL AFFIL & HONORS:** Nat. & State Realtor Assns., Pueblo Bd. of Realtors, GRI, CO Realtor of the Yr., 1978; Many yrs. Dir., NAR; Served on Nat. Legislative Comm. of NAR; **EDUC:** BSBA, 1949, RE, Univ. of Denver; **OTHER ACT & HONORS:** Pres., CO Prop. Tax Limitation Comm.; **HOME ADD:** 2310 Coronado Rd., Pueblo, CO 81003, (303)544-5495; **BUS ADD:** 305 N. Santa Fe, Pueblo, CO 81003, (303)544-4562.

HOLLOWAY, William B.——B: Oct. 13, 1934, Tuscaloosa, AL, *VP*, McGraw Breckinridge Realtors, Comml./Investment; **PRIM RE ACT:** Broker, Consultant, Engineer, Appraiser, Owner/Investor, Property Manager, Syndicator; **SERVICES:** Brokerage, Synd., Investment Consulting; **PREV EMPLOY:** VP Mktg./Andro Corp. Tulsa OK 1970-1976; Pres., Holloway Nolte Inc. 1966-1969; **PROFL AFFIL & HONORS:** NAR; RNMI; RESSI, Reg. Profl. Engr.; **EDUC:** BS Mech. Engr., 1956, Air conditioning & Heating, Univ. of OK; **EDUC HONORS:** Hughes Tool Co. Scholarship; Tau Beta Pi membership; **MIL SERV:** USAF/SAC, Capt., 1956-1959; **OTHER ACT & HONORS:** CCIM Candidate; **HOME ADD:** 3847 S. Troost, Tulsa,

OK 74105, (918)749-1153; **BUS ADD:** 819 S. Denver Ave., Tulsa, OK 74119, (918)583-1000.

HOLLWAY, Paul J.——B: Nov. 29, 1926, Philadelphia, PA, *Pres.*, Hollway Associates; **PRIM RE ACT:** Developer, Owner/Investor, Property Manager, Syndicator; **SERVICES:** Synd. and Devel. of Indus. & Comml. RE; **REP CLIENTS:** Indiv. investors and synd. groups; **PREV EMPLOY:** Indus. & Comml. RE Sales, J. Russell Winder, Realtors, 1970-1978; **PROFL AFFIL & HONORS:** NABR, State and Local Bds., U of P RE Soc. (Life Member); **EDUC:** 1973, RE, Wharton School of Bus. & Fin.; **MIL SERV:** US Army, MSgt.; **OTHER ACT & HONORS:** Dir. Bus. Assn. of Germantown, P.E.C.O. Consumer Council, Dir. & Past Pres. Lions Club of Germantown, Exec. Comm. Gtn. Devel. Council, Greater Philadelphia C of C, Penjerdel Council, John T. Clary, Chairman, Energy Advisory Committee; **HOME ADD:** 3126 W. Penn St., Philadelphia, PA 19129, (215)848-8736; **BUS ADD:** P.O. Box 25603, Philadelphia, PA 19144, (215)849-6431.

HOLMAN, Kenneth——B: Aug. 7, 1949, Rexburg, ID, *CEO*, Kenman Corp.; **PRIM RE ACT:** Broker, Syndicator, Property Manager; **SERVICES:** RE Investments for indiv. corps. & pension grps., brokerage, prop. mgmt.; **REP CLIENTS:** Hughes Aircraft Co., Petrominerals, Inc., Mutual Benefit Life Ins., Nabisco; **PREV EMPLOY:** VP for Natl. RE Synd Co., Pres. of multi state prop mgmt. co.; **PROFL AFFIL & HONORS:** NAR, RESSI, IREM, NASD, NAA, Past Pres. UT Apt. Assn., RE Broker UT & CO, Securities Broker & Dealer, Certified Property Manager; **EDUC:** BS, 1973, Acctg., Brigham Young Univ.; **GRAD EDUC:** MBA, 1974, Bus., Univ. of UT; **EDUC HONORS:** Member Alpha Beta Psi, MBA Council; **OTHER ACT & HONORS:** Centerville City Council, 1980-83, Centerville Farmington Rotary Intl.; **HOME ADD:** 109 W. Ricks Creek Way, Centerville, UT 84014, (801)292-9330; **BUS ADD:** Beneficial Life Tower, Suite 850, 36 S. State St., Salt Lake City, UT 84111, (801)363-6170.

HOLMAN, R.W., Jr.——B: Oct. 7, 1943, Berkeley, CA, *Pres.*, Holman Grp. Ltd.; **PRIM RE ACT:** Consultant, Developer, Owner/Investor; **OTHER RE ACT:** Devel. mgmt.; **SERVICES:** Devel. feasibility analysis & project mgmt.; **REP CLIENTS:** Parts. Pacific Bank, Bank of Amer., Bank of Tokyo, Bank of New South Wales (Aust.), HI State Housing Auth., City & Cty of Honolulu; **PREV EMPLOY:** C. Brewer & Co./Adm. Honolulu, Oakland Redev. Agency, Asst. Prof. Univ. of HI School of Bus.; **PROFL AFFIL & HONORS:** Amer. Inst. of Planners; **EDUC:** BA, 1966, Econ., Univ. of CA, Berkeley; **GRAD EDUC:** MA, 1969, Econ., Planning, Univ. of Lancaster, England; **EDUC HONORS:** Cord Fellowship, Brit. Council Fellow; **HOME ADD:** 4116 Black Point Rd., Honolulu, HI 96816, (808)737-5366; **BUS ADD:** 570 Auahi St., Honolulu, HI 96813, (808)533-6041.

HOLMAN, Steven G.——B: July 3, 1951, Vancouver, WA, *Leased Prop. Mgr.*, The Boeing Co., Boeing Computer Services Co.; **OTHER RE ACT:** Leased prop. acquisition & Mgmt.; **PREV EMPLOY:** RE Broker & CPM (Certified Property M brokerage 1973-1980; **PROFL AFFIL & HONORS:** IREM, NAR, WA Assn. of Realtors, Seattle-King Co. Bd. of Realtors Legislative Chmn. (1978); BCS Facilities cost savings winner, 1980; **EDUC:** Comm., 1973, Mktg. & Adv. (minor in RE & Econ.), WA State Univ.; **EDUC HONORS:** Preisner Academic Scholarship; **OTHER ACT & HONORS:** Bellevue Kiwanis, Delta Sigma Phi Frat., Past RE Instr. at Edmonds & N. Seattle Comm. Colls.; **HOME ADD:** 10304 NE 186th St., Bothell, WA 98011, (206)486-4972; **BUS ADD:** P.O. Box 24346, Mailstop 7c-30, Seattle, WA 98124, (206)763-5365.

HOLMES, David F.——B: Oct. 30, 1952, Orlando, FL, *Atty.*, Braverman & Holmes, Attys. & Counselors at Law; **PRIM RE ACT:** Attorney; **SERVICES:** Authorized agent for Lawyers Title Guaranty Fund; all types of RE, collections, and litigation; **REP CLIENTS:** Perrone and Cramer Realty Corp., other private lenders and small instl. lenders; **PROFL AFFIL & HONORS:** Member, FL Bar, Real Prop. Sect.; Broward Bar Assn.; **EDUC:** BA, 1975, Econ., FL State Univ.; **GRAD EDUC:** JD, 1970, Law/Comml., Nova Law Ctr.; **EDUC HONORS:** Law Review Editor, 1976 to 1978; Author Comment Nova L.J. 101, 1977; Moot Court 1977; **MIL SERV:** US Army; SP 4, 1972-1974; **HOME ADD:** 920 S.W. 74th Ave., N. Lauderdale, FL 33068, (305)722-9557; **BUS ADD:** P.O. Box 14185, Ft. Lauderdale, FL 33302, (305)524-0505.

HOLMES, J. David——B: May 16, 1946, Palestine, TX, *Exec. VP*, Adams & Holmes Mort. Co., Inc.; **PRIM RE ACT:** Broker, Consultant, Appraiser, Developer, Builder; **OTHER RE ACT:** Mort. Banker; Title Ins. Exec.; **SERVICES:** Comml. Loan Brokerage and Serv.; Consulting to Both Devels., Builders and Lenders; Fee Appraisal Work; Comml. Sales; **REP CLIENTS:** Life Ins. Cos., Thrift Instns.; Pension Funds; Reit's Indiv. Investors; **PREV EMPLOY:** San Jacinto Savings Assn. (Houston, TX); Bank of the Southwest, N.A. (Houston, TX); First Continental Mort. Co. (Houston, TX); **PROFL AFFIL & HONORS:** Austin MBA; TX MBA; MBAA; TX Land Title Assn., CMB; SREA; AIREA; NARA (candidate); (CRA); **EDUC:** BBA, 1968, RE & Banking, N. Tx State Univ., Denton; **GRAD EDUC:** Certificate; MBA, 1975, Mort. Banking School of Mort. Banking, Northwestern Univ., Chicago, IL; **MIL SERV:** US Army; USAR Fin. Corps., Maj (Reserve) 1968-Pres., Service Award; Good Conduct Award; **OTHER ACT & HONORS:** Lions Club; Austin Ctry. Club; Austin Club; Headliners Club; Westwood Ctry. Club; St. David's Episcopal Church; **HOME ADD:** 2509 El Greco Cove, Austin, TX 78703, (512)479-8447; **BUS ADD:** 507 W. Ave., P.O. Box 1356, Austin, TX 78767, (512)476-6248.

HOLMES, John B.——*Mktg. Mgr.*, McCormick Properties, Inc.; **PRIM RE ACT:** Developer; **BUS ADD:** 11011 McCormick Rd., Hunt Valley, MD 21031, (301)667-7736.*

HOLMES, Peter C.——B: Aug. 19, 1949, Hartford, CT, *Exec. VP - Principal*, The Farley Co.; **PRIM RE ACT:** Broker, Consultant, Property Manager; **REP CLIENTS:** Aetna Life & Casualty; Travelers; Heublein; IBM; UTC; City of Hartford; Urban Inv. & Devel. Co.; **PROFL AFFIL & HONORS:** Nat. Assn. of Realtors; NACORE; **EDUC:** AB, 1971, Econ., Coll. of the Holy Cross; **GRAD EDUC:** MBA, 1976, Fin., Univ. of CT; **OTHER ACT & HONORS:** Univ. Club; Conn. Trust for Hist. Preservation, Trustee & Chmn. of RE Comm.; **HOME ADD:** 14 W. Hill Dr., W. Hartford, CT 06119, (203)236-3331; **BUS ADD:** 100 Pearl St., Hartford, CT 06103, (203)525-9171.

HOLMES, Phillip H.——B: July 20, 1933, Akron, OH, *Pres.*, Amer. Cities Corps.; **PRIM RE ACT:** Broker, Consultant, Developer, Builder, Owner/Investor, Property Manager, Syndicator; **EDUC:** BS, 1955, Indus. Mgmt., Univ. of Akron, Akron, OH; **GRAD EDUC:** MBA, 1963, Econ. & Fin., Univ. of Akron, Akron, OH; **MIL SERV:** US Army, Transportation, 1st Lt.; **HOME ADD:** 1512 Candlewood Dr., Worthington, OH 43085, (614)888-6229; **BUS ADD:** 1080 Kingsmill Parkway, Suite 120, Columbus, OH 43229, (614)885-7020.

HOLMES, Robert J.——B: May 18, 1935, Salt Lake City, UT, R.J. Holmes, MAI & Assoc.; **PRIM RE ACT:** Appraiser; **SERVICES:** RE appraisals & feasibility studies; **REP CLIENTS:** Instl. lenders, devel.; **PREV EMPLOY:** Sr. loan officer on west coast for large fin. instn.; **PROFL AFFIL & HONORS:** AIREA; Soc. of RE Appraisers, MAI; SRPA; **EDUC:** Bach., 1976, Gen. Studies, Brigham Young Univ.; **HOME ADD:** 1558 Devonshire Dr., Salt Lake City, UT 84108, (801)581-1245; **BUS ADD:** 41311 E. Florida Ave., Hemet, CA 92343, (213)384-0076.

HOLOD, Mark A.——B: Mar. 8, 1949, NY, NY, *Mgr., Corp. RE*, PepsiCo, Inc.; **PRIM RE ACT:** Consultant, Property Manager; **OTHER RE ACT:** Corp. RE Mgmt.; **PREV EMPLOY:** Penn Central Corp.; **PROFL AFFIL & HONORS:** Nat. Assn. of Corp. RE Execs, Indus. Devel. Research Council, Licensed RE Broker, NY State; **EDUC:** BA, 1970, Pol. Sci., City Coll. of NY; **GRAD EDUC:** MBA, 1982, Mktg., Baruch Coll.; **HOME ADD:** 401 E. 65th St., NY, NY 10021, (212)794-1415; **BUS ADD:** Anderson Hill Rd., Purchase, NY 10577, (914)253-1108.

HOLSCHER, Richard H.——B: Dec. 18, 1928, Columbus, OH, *First VP, Div. Head*, First WI Nat. Bank of Milwaukee, RE Fin. Div.; **PRIM RE ACT:** Banker, Lender; **REP CLIENTS:** Comml. & resid. RE loans and mort. banking; **PREV EMPLOY:** RE Mgr. Amer., Oil Co.; **PROFL AFFIL & HONORS:** Mortgage Bankers; BOMA; **EDUC:** BS, 1951, Commerce, Bus. Admin., Univ. of IL; **GRAD EDUC:** JD, 1955, Univ. of IL; **MIL SERV:** US Army, 1st Lt.; **OTHER ACT & HONORS:** Alderman, City of Sunset Hills, MO, 1960-64; Pres. WI Humane Soc.; Dir. Milwaukee Cty. Hist. Soc.; Ozawkee Ctry. Club; **HOME ADD:** 2220 W. Applewood Ln., Glendale, WI 53209, (414)352-5238; **BUS ADD:** 777 E. WI Ave., Milwaukee, WI 53202, (414)765-4809.

HOLSINGER, Donald G.——B: June. 21, 1940, Ellendale, ND, *Owner/Part.*, General Homes; **PRIM RE ACT:** Developer, Builder, Owner/Investor; **SERVICES:** Devel. land resid., indus.; **EDUC:** BSME, 1963, Bus. & Math., Univ. of WA; **HOME ADD:** 26101 NW 31st Ave., Ridgefield, WA 98642, (206)887-3012; **BUS ADD:** 406 NW 139th St., Vancouver, WA 98665, (206)574-4225.

HOLST, Norman D.——B: Jan. 26, 1943, St. Louis, MO, *VP Dir. of Corp. RE*, Commerce Banchares Inc.; **OTHER RE ACT:** Corp. RE Mgmt.; **SERVICES:** Facilities planning, design and constr., property mgmt.; **PREV EMPLOY:** Econ.-Planner, Mid-Amer. Reg. Council, Kanses City, MO 1967-1972; **PROFL AFFIL & HONORS:** NACORE, BOMA, AIB, Bd. of Dirs. of NACORE; **EDUC:** BS, 1966,

Bus. Admin. and Poli. Sci., Univ. of MO, Columbia; **OTHER ACT & HONORS:** Greater Kansas City C of C; **HOME ADD:** 211 E. 73rd Terr., Kansas City, MO 64114, (816)444-5123; **BUS ADD:** 720 Main St., Kansas City, MO 64105, (816)234-2384.

HOLSTEN, Theodore W.——B: Aug. 12, 1934, Minneapolis, MN, *Pres.*, Exemplar, Inc.; **PRIM RE ACT:** Broker, Developer; **SERVICES:** Res. lot devel. for bldrs.; **PREV EMPLOY:** Engr. w/ HoneyweLl, Inc.; **PROFL AFFIL & HONORS:** IEEE, NAHB; **EDUC:** BS, 1957, Mech. Engr., Univ. of MN; **MIL SERV:** US Army, Pvt.; **OTHER ACT & HONORS:** Kiwanis; **HOME ADD:** 3213 Townview Ave. NE, Minneapolis, MN 55418, (612)781-1429; **BUS ADD:** 3213 Townview Ave. NE, Minneapolis, MN 55418, (612)781-1429.

HOLT, Adrian J.——B: Sept. 1, 1936, Amsterdam, Holland, *Dir. of Prop. Mgmt.*, Wm. A. White & Sons; **PRIM RE ACT:** Consultant, Broker; **OTHER RE ACT:** Management; **SERVICES:** Full serv. RE Co.; **PREV EMPLOY:** 1968-74, Rgnl. Dir. of Prop. Mgmt., Tishman Realty & Const. Co., Inc.; **PROFL AFFIL & HONORS:** Dir., RE Bd. of NY; Dir., IREM; Dir., BOMA, CPM; **EDUC:** BS, 1959, Structural Engr., Gore Hill Coll., Sydney, Australia; **OTHER ACT & HONORS:** Pres., East Side Assn.; **HOME ADD:** 425 Davenport Ave., New Rochelle, NY 10805, (914)576-3959; **BUS ADD:** 51 E. 42nd St., NY, NY 10017, (212)682-2300.

HOLT, Darrel M.——B: Aug. 18, 1915, Saskatchewan, CAN, *COB*, The Towle Co.; **PRIM RE ACT:** Broker, Consultant, Appraiser, Owner/Investor; **REP CLIENTS:** Can. Life Assurance Co., CT Mutual Life Ins. Co., NY LIfe Ins. Co.; **PROFL AFFIL & HONORS:** AIREA, ULI, BU Gov's - NIREB, Regl. VP, MBA, MAI, CCIM, CPM; **EDUC:** BA, 1936, Hamline Univ.; **GRAD EDUC:** Hamline Univ., St. Paul MN, 1936; **OTHER ACT & HONORS:** Tr. Hamline Univ., Comm. chmn. commr.; **HOME ADD:** 5416 Stauder Cir., Edina, MN 55436, (612)935-7979; **BUS ADD:** 600 Second Ave. S., Minneapolis, MN 55402, (612)341-4444.

HOLT, Philetus Havens, III——B: Aug. 19, 1928, Summit, NJ, *Prin.*, Holt & Morgan Assoc., P.A.; **PRIM RE ACT:** Architect, Consultant, Developer, Owner/Investor; **OTHER RE ACT:** Hist. Preservation & Restoration; **SERVICES:** Planning, Arch., Devel. Consulting; **REP CLIENTS:** Indiv., Instns., State & Other Govt. Divs.; **PREV EMPLOY:** C.K. Agle AIA-AIP Arch. & Planner 1955-1965; **PROFL AFFIL & HONORS:** Member AIA, Soc. of Arch. Hist., Nat. Trust for Hist. Preserv., Recd. 5 Design Awards - NJSA-AIA; **EDUC:** BArch, 1950, Princeton Univ.; **GRAD EDUC:** MFA in Arch., 1952, Princeton Univ., School of Arch. & Urban Planning; **EDUC HONORS:** Honors, AIA Medal, Lloyd Warren Prize; **OTHER ACT & HONORS:** Pres., Hist. Soc. of Princeton, 1981- ; Advisory Council, Dept. of Arch., Mercer Co. Community Coll.; **BUS ADD:** 350 Alexander St., Princeton, NJ 08540, (609)924-1358.

HOLTZMAN, David——B: July 6, 1934, NY, NY, *Pres.*, Dabar Mgmt. Co., Inc.; **PRIM RE ACT:** Broker, Consultant, Lender, Owner/Investor, Instructor, Property Manager, Syndicator; **SERVICES:** Prop. mgmt., consulting, synd. of mort., comml. & resid. props.; **REP CLIENTS:** Pvt. investors; **PROFL AFFIL & HONORS:** IREM, Apt. Owners Advisory Council of Westchester Cty., Amer. Arbitration Assn., Advisor to Westchester Cty. Rent Guidelines Bd., CPM, Comml. arbitrator; Accredited Management Organization; **EDUC:** BA, 1956, Botany, Chem., Hunter Coll.; **OTHER ACT & HONORS:** Judicial Convention Delegate, Chmn. Endowment Fund of Riverdale Yonkers Soc. for Ethical Culture; **HOME ADD:** 4425 Manhattan Coll. Pkwy., Bronx, NY 10471, (212)549-1200; **BUS ADD:** 3865 Cannon Pl., Bronx, NY 10463, (212)796-3600.

HOLZEL, Stephen E.——B: Aug. 5, 1942, Berlin, Germany, *Pres.*, Strive, Inc.; **PRIM RE ACT:** Owner/Investor, Property Manager; **PREV EMPLOY:** Amax, Inc.; **EDUC:** BA, 1966, Econ., Upsala Coll.; **OTHER ACT & HONORS:** Explorers Club, Circumnavigators Club; **HOME ADD:** P.O. Box 871, Upper Montclair, NJ 07043, (201)429-0122; **BUS ADD:** 26 Park St., Montclair, NJ 07042, (201)744-4470.

HOLZER, Robert L.——B: Jan. 16, 1938, Chicago, IL, *Sr. VP*, North West Federal Savings & Loan of Chicago, Lending; **PRIM RE ACT:** Lender; **SERVICES:** Resid. lending; **PROFL AFFIL & HONORS:** US Savings & Loan League, National Savings & Loan League, Sr. Loan Underwriter, Soc. of Loan Underwriters; **EDUC:** BS, Mgmt. & Fin., Univ. of IL; **MIL SERV:** US Army, Lt.; **OTHER ACT & HONORS:** Pres. Park Ridge Kiwanis 1977; Dir. Park Ridge YMCA 1980; **HOME ADD:** 2109 Glenview Ave., Park Ridge, IL 60068; **BUS ADD:** 2454 Dempster, Des Plaines, IL 60016, (312)296-0900.

HOMER, Dean R.——B: Dec. 30, 1944, Joliet, IL, *Pres.*, Royal Harbour Mgt. Corp.; **PRIM RE ACT:** Broker, Consultant, Owner/Investor, Property Manager, Syndicator; **OTHER RE ACT:** CPA; **SERVICES:** Consulting for investment & tax aspects synd.; **REP CLIENTS:** Various indiv., parts., corps.; **PROFL AFFIL & HONORS:** AICPA, ISCPA, CPA; **EDUC:** BS, 1966, Acctg., Fin. Mgt., S. IL Univ.; **GRAD EDUC:** CPA, 1973, Univ. of IL; **MIL SERV:** US Army, Lt.; **HOME ADD:** 22400 Butterfield Rd., Richton Park, IL 60471, (312)747-3179; **BUS ADD:** 22400 Butterfield Rd., Richton Park, IL 60471, (312)747-3179.

HOMER, Irving E.——B: Jan. 10, 1915, Jeffersonville, NY, *Pres.*, Irving Homer Assoc., Inc.; **PRIM RE ACT:** Broker, Consultant, Appraiser, Banker, Owner/Investor; **PROFL AFFIL & HONORS:** IFA, Intl. Inst. of Valuers (SCV); **EDUC:** AA, RE Law, RE procedure, Orange Cty. Community Coll.; **MIL SERV:** USN, CCS; **OTHER ACT & HONORS:** Sr. VP, First Fed. S & L Assn., Dir., West Side Fed. S & L Assn., NY; Retired; **HOME ADD:** 9 W. Main St., Port Jervis, NY 12771, (914)856-7655; **BUS ADD:** 9 W. Main St., Port Jervis, NY 12771, (914)856-6310.

HON, Jack D.——B: Aug. 8, 1930, Bristow, OK, *Broker-Owner*, Hon & Assoc.; **PRIM RE ACT:** Broker, Instructor, Syndicator, Consultant, Developer, Property Manager, Owner/Investor; **SERVICES:** Co. provides all gen. brokerage serv.; I specialize in indus. siting and location; Co. has full Comml./Investment Dept. and full Resid. Dept.; **REP CLIENTS:** Nat. Cos., Devels. and Investors; **PROFL AFFIL & HONORS:** RNMI, GRI; NV Assn. of Realtors; CRB; **EDUC:** Business, Univ. MD - SMU; **MIL SERV:** USAF, M/Sgt., 11 Decorations & Awards; **OTHER ACT & HONORS:** Lions; B.S.A.; Elks Lodge Outstanding Citizen of the Yr., N. Las Vegas, NV 1977; Assoc. of the Yr., Las Vegas Bd. of Realtors, 1971; Shrine; C of C Past Pres.; **HOME ADD:** 1901 Oakleaf Ln., Las Vegas, NV 89102, (702)871-6690; **BUS ADD:** 5030 Paradise Rd., Suite C-112, Las Vegas, NV 89119, (702)736-6526.

HONEGGER, William——B: June 23, 1922, Portland, OR, *Mgr., RE*, Orange and Rockland Utilities, Inc.; **PRIM RE ACT:** Broker, Appraiser, Property Manager; **SERVICES:** Buy, manage and sell co. prop.; **PROFL AFFIL & HONORS:** Intl. Right of Way Assn., Sr. Member; **EDUC:** BS, 1949, Civil Engr., Columbia Univ.; **MIL SERV:** USN, Lt. JG, 1943-45; **HOME ADD:** 98 Westminster Dr., Pearl River, NY 10965, (914)735-2177; **BUS ADD:** One Blue Hill Plaza, Pearl River, NY 10965, (914)627-2584.

HONEYCUTT, Kent——B: Mar. 7, 1930, Oakboro, NC, *Owner-Mgr.*, ERA-Regency Realty; **PRIM RE ACT:** Broker, Appraiser, Builder, Instructor, Property Manager, Insuror; **PROFL AFFIL & HONORS:** RNMI, GRI, CRS, CRB; **EDUC:** BS, 1972, Bus. Studies, NAOAC Post Grad. School, Monterey, CA; **GRAD EDUC:** MBA, 1977, Mgmt., Middle TN State Univ.; **MIL SERV:** USN, CDR; **HOME ADD:** Rt. #1, Cumberland, Furnace, TN 37051, (615)387-3682; **BUS ADD:** 1715 Fort Campbell Blvd., Clarksville, TN 37040, (615)552-7070.

HONIG, Marvin I.——B: Mar. 12, 1938, Albany, NY, *Atty.*, Marvin I. Honig, Attorney at Law; **PRIM RE ACT:** Broker, Consultant, Attorney, Developer, Builder, Owner/Investor; **OTHER RE ACT:** Comml. real prop. tax reduction proceedings; **SERVICES:** Legal and advisory serv. to devel.; **REP CLIENTS:** Niagara Mohawk Power Corp.; **PROFL AFFIL & HONORS:** ABA; NYS Bar Assn.; Rensselaer Cty. Bar Assn.; Amer. Arbitration Assn.; **EDUC:** AB, 1959, Bus./Liberal Arts, Syracuse Univ.; **GRAD EDUC:** 1963, Gen. Law, Albany Law School; **MIL SERV:** Army, 1st Lt.; **OTHER ACT & HONORS:** Cty. Atty., 1972-date; **HOME ADD:** RD 3, Box 257-A, Troy, NY 12180; **BUS ADD:** 54 Second St., Troy, NY 12180.

HONIG, O. Charles——*President*, Alaska Interstate Co.; **PRIM RE ACT:** Property Manager; **BUS ADD:** 2200 Post Oak Tower, 5051 Westheimer Rd., Houston, TX 77056, (713)621-8710.*

HONIG, Robert M.——B: June 3, 1925, Flint, MI, *Sr. VP*, First National Bank of Evergreen Park; **PRIM RE ACT:** Consultant, Appraiser, Banker, Lender; **OTHER RE ACT:** Lic. RE Broker, Lic. Ins. Broker, inactive; **SERVICES:** Resid., comml. RE lending, consulting, appraisal review; **REP CLIENTS:** Self-employed RE and Ins. Broker, Land Title Ins. Co. (Los Angeles, CA, now SAFECO); **PROFL AFFIL & HONORS:** Chicago RE Bd., Southwest Suburban Bd. of Realtors, Soc. of Loan Underwriters, Sr. Loan Underwriter, Soc. of Loan Underwriters; **EDUC:** BA, 1978, BOG, Governors State Univ., Park Forest South, IL; **EDUC HONORS:** Lincoln Academy of IL Medal, Who's Who in Amer. Colleges and Univs.; **MIL SERV:** USN, HM2 (ORT), American Defense, Asiatic-Pacific Theatre of War, Phillipine Liberation, China Service, WW II Victory medals; Nat. Defense Service Medal; **OTHER ACT & HONORS:** Alderman, City of Palos Heights, IL 1966-1969, Amer. Mensa Ltd., Ordained Elder, Reformed Church in Amer.; **HOME ADD:** 12332 Richard Ave., Palos Heights, IL 60463, (312)448-7552; **BUS ADD:** 3101 West 95th St., Evergreen Park, IL 60642, (312)779-6700.

HONKE, Dennis O.——B: Sept. 23, 1948, Alton, IL, *Bldg. Mgr., Prop. Mgr.*, Dennis O. Honke; **PRIM RE ACT:** Broker, Owner/Investor, Property Manager; **SERVICES:** Prop. mgmt., comml. leasing, resid. mgmt.; **EDUC:** BS, 1973, Pharmacy, St. Louis Coll. of Pharmacy; **MIL SERV:** US Army Res., Sgt. First Class; **OTHER ACT & HONORS:** Alton-Godfrey Rotary Club; **HOME ADD:** Rte. 1, Box 294, Alton, IL 62002, (618)466-4588; **BUS ADD:** 307 Henry St., Alton, IL 62002, (618)462-3372.

HONNER, Robert A.——B: Dec. 28, 1896, Detroit, MI, *Owner*, Robert A. Honner Co.; **PRIM RE ACT:** Broker, Consultant, Appraiser, Owner/Investor, Property Manager; **OTHER RE ACT:** Tr. of Charles A. Widmann Trust; Hon. Life Member, Beverly Hills Bd. of Realtors; **SERVICES:** State of CA, RE Lic., 1920 to date; **REP CLIENTS:** City Nat'l. Bank; Buckeye Cos., Devels; **PREV EMPLOY:** Asst. Comptroller, Univ. of So. CA; **PROFL AFFIL & HONORS:** IREM, Hon. Life Member, Beverly Hills Bd. of Realtors; **OTHER ACT & HONORS:** Past Pres., Half Century Club, Univ. of So. CA; Beverly Hills Bd. of Realtors; Beverly Hills Men's Club; Kiwanis Club of Beverly Hills; **HOME ADD:** 655 Ocampo Dr., Pacific Palisades, CA 90272, (213)459-1122; **BUS ADD:** 655 Ocampo Dr., Pacific Palisades, CA 90272, (213)454-7219.

HOOD, James V.——B: Apr. 22, 1947, Covington, KY, *Pres.*, Hood & Assoc.; **PRIM RE ACT:** Consultant, Owner/Investor; **SERVICES:** Valuation analysis, fin. counseling; **EDUC:** BSBA, 1969, Mgmt., Xavier Univ., Cincinnati, OH; **GRAD EDUC:** MBA, 1973, Fin., Xavier Univ., Cincinnati, OH; **MIL SERV:** US Army, Capt.; **HOME ADD:** 1856 Summerland Ave., Winter Park, FL 32789, (305)629-1128; **BUS ADD:** 225 E. 6th St., Cincinnati, OH 45224, (513)421-5900.

HOOD, Lloyd——*Pres.*, Lloyd Hood, Inc.; **PRIM RE ACT:** Instructor, Owner/Investor, Syndicator; **SERVICES:** Consultant, appraiser, devel., builder & prop. mgr.; **PROFL AFFIL & HONORS:** IREM, Fellow of Realtors Inst., CPM; **HOME ADD:** P.O. Box 11987, Chicago, IL 60611, (312)878-0780; **BUS ADD:** P.O. Box 11987, Chicago, IL 60611, (312)878-0780.

HOOD, Theodore——*Corp. Risk Manager*, Applied Power, Inc.; **PRIM RE ACT:** Property Manager; **BUS ADD:** P.O. Box 325, Milwaukee, WI 53201, (414)784-7900.*

HOOKER, Harry——B: June 20, 1938, Rocky Mount, NC, *Pres.*, Harry Hooker Constr. Co. Inc.; **PRIM RE ACT:** Broker, Developer, Builder; **SERVICES:** Design/Build; **REP CLIENTS:** Butler Buildership; **PROFL AFFIL & HONORS:** M.B.D.A., A.B.C. San Antonio C of C, N. San Antonio C of C, Advisory Council Member, San Pedro Bank; Only RE Broker Member Only Design/Build Member; **EDUC:** BS, Constr., 1960, Bus., Trinity Univ., San Antonio, TX; **GRAD EDUC:** 1967, RE, Fin. & Constr., Dyer School of RE; **MIL SERV:** US Army Reserves, 1960-1962, Lt.; USAF, Capt., 1962-1968; **HOME ADD:** 14327 Turtle Rock, San Antonio, TX 78232, (512)494-3922; **BUS ADD:** 13620 NW Mil Hwy, San Antonio, TX 78231, (512)492-9411.

HOOPER, Stanton K.——*Pres.*, Carma Developers Inc.; **PRIM RE ACT:** Developer, Owner/Investor, Property Manager; **OTHER RE ACT:** Merchant bldr.; **SERVICES:** Devel. of office towers, bus. parks, condos., single family, land devel., medical clinics, shopping ctrs., joint venture or synd. of above; **BUS ADD:** 595 Market St., San Francisco, CA 94105, (415)495-7575.

HOOPER, William L.——B: Nov. 1, 1935, New Haven, CT, *Owner*, Hooper & Associates; **PRIM RE ACT:** Consultant, Developer, Property Manager, Owner/Investor; **SERVICES:** Comml. & resid. devel. & mgmt.; **EDUC:** BCE, 1957, structural design, MIT; **GRAD EDUC:** MS, 1960, Mgmy., Sloan School of Mgmt., MIT; **EDUC HONORS:** Tau Beta Pi, Chi Epsilon, Sigma XI; **BUS ADD:** Suite 200 5801 Peachtree, Dunwoody Rd., Atlanta, GA 30342, (404)256-0900.

HOOPES, Claude B.——B: Aug. 22, 1949, Columbus, GA, *VP, Devel. Dir.*, Spaulding & Slye Corp., NE Region; **PRIM RE ACT:** Broker, Consultant, Developer, Builder, Owner/Investor; **SERVICES:** Devel. of comml. props., investment counseling, construction of comml. props.; leasing; prop. mgmt.; **REP CLIENTS:** Fortune 500 cos., especially hi-tech indus.; **PREV EMPLOY:** Mktg. Dir., Sea Pines Co., Hilton Head, SC; **PROFL AFFIL & HONORS:** BOMA, CBREB; **EDUC:** BA, 1972, Poli. Sci./Socio., Princeton Univ.; **EDUC HONORS:** Magna Cum Laude; **HOME ADD:** 24 Pine St., Dover, MA 02030 02030; **BUS ADD:** 15 New England Executive Park, Burlington, MA 01803, (617)523-8000.

HOOPES, Harriet——B: Aug. 1, 1937, Natchex, MI, *Broker*, ERA-Vista, Realtors; **PRIM RE ACT:** Broker; **SERVICES:** Total RE Brokerage; **PROFL AFFIL & HONORS:** Charter mem. Million Dollar Club; Women of the Yr. 1980 UT St. Realtors; CRS; GRI; WCR; Omega Tau Rho; **EDUC:** BS, 1959, Sec. Ed., Math, Univ. of UT; **OTHER ACT & HONORS:** WJ C of C, Church Women United; **HOME ADD:** 3603 Macintosh La., Salt Lake City, UT 84121, (801)943-1043; **BUS ADD:** 9394 S. Redwood Rd., W. Jordan, UT 84084, (801)566-2493.

HOOPES, John N.——B: May 17, 1944, Newport, RI, *Mgr. - Asst. VP*, Wilshire Appraisal Services, S. Section; **PRIM RE ACT:** Consultant, Appraiser; **SERVICES:** Consultation and appraisal services; **REP CLIENTS:** Glendale Fed. Savings, Wilshire Mort. Corp., Wilshire Diversifed Inc., other investment lenders; **PROFL AFFIL & HONORS:** 9 yrs. member SREA, SRA; **EDUC:** BA, 1966, Hist., CA State Univ. at Long Beach; **MIL SERV:** US Air Force 1967-1971, S. Sgt.; **HOME ADD:** 2170 Gondar Ave., Long Beach, CA 90815, (213)596-9577; **BUS ADD:** 9030 Stonewood St., Downey, CA 90241, (213)861-9267.

HOOVER, Andrew S.——B: Mar. 21, 1955, Altoona, PA, *Assoc. Broker*, Hoover Realtors; **PRIM RE ACT:** Broker, Instructor, Appraiser, Assessor, Consultant; **SERVICES:** Course instructor, investment counseling, valuation, resid. devel., Hotel-Motel Sales; Commercial Sales; Residential Sales; **REP CLIENTS:** Lenders, indiv. investors; **PROFL AFFIL & HONORS:** NAR; RNMI; Independent Fee Appraisers, GRI; CRA; Intl. Cert. Appraiser; **OTHER ACT & HONORS:** Bd. of Dir., C of C; Navy League; Kiwanis; Jaycees; Board of March of Dimes; **HOME ADD:** 313 31st St., Altoona, PA 16602, (814)946-4312; **BUS ADD:** 1904 Union Ave., Altoona, PA 16601, (814)944-6169.

HOOVER, Rex Neal——B: Sept. 10, 1948, Perrytown, TX, *Owner-Broker*, Hoover & Hoover Realty; **PRIM RE ACT:** Broker, Consultant, Appraiser, Developer, Owner/Investor, Property Manager, Syndicator; **SERVICES:** Comml. & resid., sales, prop. mgmt., synd. of comml/prop.; **PREV EMPLOY:** Century 21, Golden Spread Realty - Salesman & Broker; **PROFL AFFIL & HONORS:** RESSI; **EDUC:** AA, Indus. Electronics & RE, Amarillo Coll.; **MIL SERV:** USN, ET2; **HOME ADD:** 52 Pioneer, Booker, TX 79005, (806)658-4883; **BUS ADD:** 601 S. Main, Perrytown, TX 79010, (806)435-6873.

HOOVER, Richard I.——B: Feb. 1, 1926, St. Paul, MN, *Owner*, Hoover & Associates; **PRIM RE ACT:** Consultant, Appraiser, Instructor, Property Manager; **SERVICES:** Investment counseling, valuation, prop. mgmt., instr. of valuation techniques; **REP CLIENTS:** Lenders and indiv. or instl. investors and govt. agencies; **PREV EMPLOY:** Dept. of Hwys., State of WA; US Dept. of Interior; **PROFL AFFIL & HONORS:** Member, Amer. Inst. of RE Appraisers; Soc. of RE Appraisers; **MIL SERV:** USN; 1st Class PO; **BUS ADD:** N. 1010 Woodward Rd., Spokane, WA 99206, (509)924-4771.

HOOVER, Steven G.——B: Oct. 11, 1942, Ottumwa, IA, *Counsel, Corporate Law Dept.*, Hughes Aircraft Co., Exec. Offices; **PRIM RE ACT:** Consultant, Attorney; **PROFL AFFIL & HONORS:** Nat. Assn. of Corporate RE Execs., ABA, Los Angeles Cty. Bar Assn., San Fernando Valley Bar Assn., Themis Soc. of Southwestern Univ.; **EDUC:** BA, 1966, Econ., Claremont Men's Coll.; **GRAD EDUC:** JD, 1972, Law, Southwestern Univ.; **OTHER ACT & HONORS:** Certificate in Govt. Contract Mgmt., UCLA; **HOME ADD:** 5546 Paradise Valley Rd., Hidden Hills, CA 91302, (213)348-0816; **BUS ADD:** Hughes Aircraft Co., Centinela & Teale Sts., 1/A190, Culver City, CA 90230, (213)391-0711.

HOPE, John T.——*Dir. of RE*, RCA Corp.; **OTHER RE ACT:** Leasing and purchasing, disposal of corp. assets; **PREV EMPLOY:** Appraiser and loan negotiator, Mony-Mutual Life Ins. Co. of NY; RE Broker, Cross & Brown Co., NYC; **EDUC:** BA, Rutgers Univ.; **BUS ADD:** 30 Rockefeller Ctr., NY, NY 10020, (212)621-6186.

HOPE, Kent S.——B: Oct. 2, 1955, Dallas, TX, *Investment/Prop. Mgr.*, HWC, Inc.; **PRIM RE ACT:** Broker, Developer, Property Manager; **SERVICES:** Lease or sale of comml. investment props., income props. mgmt., build to suit; **PREV EMPLOY:** Comml. investment RE broker, Hank Dickerson and Co.; **PROFL AFFIL & HONORS:** RNMI, Nat. Assn. of Indus. and Office Parks; Greater Dallas Bd. of Realtors, TAR, NAR; **EDUC:** BBA, 1979, Econ., Fin., RE, Baylor Univ.; **OTHER ACT & HONORS:** Dallas C of C, N. Dallas C of C, Young Life; **BUS ADD:** P.O. Box 427, Addison, TX 75001, (214)239-1324.

HOPKINS, Alyin C.——B: Sept. 14, 1918, Philadelphia, PA, *VP*, Jos. L. Muscarelle, Inc.; **PRIM RE ACT:** Consultant, Developer, Builder, Owner/Investor, Property Manager; **SERVICES:** Build-lease indus. comml. & office; **REP CLIENTS:** ATT; Aetna Ins.; Crum & Foster; Jones & Laughlin; US Steel; Tenneco Chemicals Pitney Bowes; Prudential Ins.; Xerox, AllTrans Intl., BASF, IBM, Etc.; **PREV EMPLOY:** Land & indus. devel., E.L. Rwy. 14 Years; **PROFL AFFIL & HONORS:** NJIDA, IREBA, NEIDA; **EDUC:** BS, 1940, Econ., Trinity Coll.; **MIL SERV:** USN, Lt.; **OTHER ACT & HONORS:** Mountain Lakes Bd. of Ed.; Planning Bd., 1960-65; Tr., Riverside Hospital (Past Pres.); Former Pres., NJIDA; **HOME ADD:** Scott Road, R.D.1, Boonton, NJ 07005, (201)334-7681; **BUS ADD:** Essex St.

at Route 17, Maywood, NJ 07607, (201)845-8100.

HOPKINS, Guy M.——**B:** Mar. 1, 1926, Janesville, WI, *Pres.*, Realty World - G.M. Hopkins, Inc.; **PRIM RE ACT:** Broker, Appraiser; **SERVICES:** Appraisal of Resid. Prop.; **PREV EMPLOY:** Self-employed; **PROFL AFFIL & HONORS:** Soc. of RE Appraisers, Sr. Resid. Appraiser; **EDUC:** BBA, 1949, RE, Univ. of WI, Madison, WI; **MIL SERV:** USAF, PFC; **OTHER ACT & HONORS:** Chmn. Rockton Planning Commn. - 12 yrs.; **HOME ADD:** 419 Bleecher St., Rockton, IL 61072, (815)624-6261; **BUS ADD:** 206 W. Main St., Rockton, IL 61072, (815)624-8151.

HOPKINS, J. William, Jr.——**B:** Dec. 31, 1938, Kansas City, MO, *Pres.*, Nutter & Associates; **PRIM RE ACT:** Broker, Consultant, Owner/Investor, Instructor, Property Manager, Syndicator; **REP CLIENTS:** Indiv. and Inst. Investors; **PROFL AFFIL & HONORS:** Natl. Assn. Realtors; Inst. of RE Mgt., Cert. Prop. Mgr.; Formerly Sr. VP IREM; **EDUC:** BS, 1960, Bus., Univ. of MO at Col.; **MIL SERV:** US Army, 1st Lt.; **OTHER ACT & HONORS:** Chmn., Jackson Cty. Sports Complex Authority, 1975-1979; **HOME ADD:** 211 W. 67th, Kansas City, MO 64113, (816)361-5199; **BUS ADD:** 4153 Broadway, KS City, MO 64111, (816)531-6811.

HOPKINS, Peter——*VP, RE*, Time, Inc.; **PRIM RE ACT:** Property Manager; **BUS ADD:** Time & Life Building, Rockefeller Center, New York, NY 10020, (212)586-1212.*

HOPKINS, Richard C.——**B:** May 28, 1926, Montevideo, Uruguay, *Owner/Mgr.*, United Farm RE; **PRIM RE ACT:** Broker, Attorney, Owner/Investor; **SERVICES:** Mktg. Real Prop. and bus. opportunities; **PREV EMPLOY:** Practicing atty.; **PROFL AFFIL & HONORS:** ABA, CO Bar Assn., Ft. Collins Bd. of Realtors; **EDUC:** AB, 1948, Econ., Coll. of William & Mary; **GRAD EDUC:** LLB, 1954, Harvard Law Sch.; JD, Harvard Law Sch.; **EDUC HONORS:** Phi Beta Kappa; **MIL SERV:** US Army, Maj.; **HOME ADD:** 3013 E Mulberry, Ft. Collins, CO 80524, (303)493-2498; **BUS ADD:** 3013 E Mulberry, Ft. Collins, CO 80524, (303)493-2493.

HOPKINS, Roland——*Ed. - Publ.*, New England Real Estate Journal; **PRIM RE ACT:** Real Estate Publisher; **BUS ADD:** 57 Washington St., Norwell, MA 02018, (617)749-6947.*

HOPKINS, Wesley L.——**B:** Sept. 9, 1937, Miami, FL, *Pres.*, Big Canoe Corp.; **PRIM RE ACT:** Developer; **OTHER RE ACT:** R.E. sales(land, timeshare, shelter(primary & secondary) & conference); **SERVICES:** Golf, tennis, boating, fishing etc.; **EDUC:** BS, 1964, Acctg. & Fin., L.A. State Univ.; **MIL SERV:** USN, E-5; **OTHER ACT & HONORS:** FL C of C; **HOME ADD:** Ridgeview Dr., Big Canoe, GA 30143, (404)579-3357; **BUS ADD:** Hwy 53, Big Canoe, GA 30143, (404)522-8437.

HOPPE, William E.——**B:** Feb. 18, 1921, Buffalo, NY, *VP*, Realty Growth Grp.; **PRIM RE ACT:** Developer, Owner/Investor, Property Manager, Syndicator; **PREV EMPLOY:** Trust RE Mgr. and AVP, San Diego Trust & Savings Bank; **PROFL AFFIL & HONORS:** IREM, CPM, CA RE Broker; **EDUC:** BS, 1961, Bus., USIU; **GRAD EDUC:** MS, 1966, Intl. Affairs, George Washington Univ.; **MIL SERV:** USN, Capt., Legion of Merit; **HOME ADD:** 6530 El Camino del Teatro, LaJolla, CA 92037; **BUS ADD:** 1263 Greenfield Dr., El Cajon, CA 92021, (714)579-3902.

HOPPER, Davis T.——*Manager Corp. Risk & Real Estate*, ACF Industries, Inc.; **PRIM RE ACT:** Property Manager; **BUS ADD:** 750 Third Ave., New York, NY 10017, (212)986-8600.*

HORINBEIN, Larry B.——**B:** Dec. 30, 1950, Marion, SC, *Sales Mgr.*, Horinbein Agency; **PRIM RE ACT:** Broker, Consultant, Appraiser, Property Manager, Insuror; **SERVICES:** Counseling, appraising, prop. mgmt.; **REP CLIENTS:** Lenders; **PROFL AFFIL & HONORS:** NAR, SCAR, NAHB, GRI; **EDUC:** BS, 1973, Bus. Admin., The Citadel; **EDUC HONORS:** Round Table, 1st Battalion Cmdr., Jr. Sword Drill; **MIL SERV:** US Army, 1st Lt.; **HOME ADD:** P.O. Box 990, Marion, SC 29571, (803)651-3505; **BUS ADD:** 221 N. Main St., Marion, SC 29571, (803)423-3955.

HORN, Dennis M.——**B:** Apr. 10, 1950, Elmira, NY, *Atty.*, Dunnells, Duvall, Bennett & Porter; **PRIM RE ACT:** Attorney, Owner/Investor; **SERVICES:** Legal counseling, devel. & synd. of comml. trans.; **REP CLIENTS:** Devels, synds., indiv. & instnl. investors in comml. props.; **PREV EMPLOY:** Fried, Frank, Harris, Shriver & Kampelman, Wash. DC, Levitt Homes, Inc., VP & Reg. Counsel; **PROFL AFFIL & HONORS:** ABA, FL Bar, DC Bar; **EDUC:** BA, 1972, Econ. Hist., Univ. of Rochester, Rochester, NY; **GRAD EDUC:** JD/MS, 1973, Econ., Urban Planning, Law, London School of Econ.; JD, 1976, Law, Univ. of PA Law Sch.; **EDUC HONORS:** Phi Beta Kappa, Magna Cum Laude; **HOME ADD:** 4300 Chesapeake St., NW, Wash. DC, 02)363-8920; **BUS ADD:** 1220 Nineteenth St., NW, Suite 400, Washington DC 20036, (202)861-1422.

HORN, Larry E.——**B:** Aug. 7, 1925, Doylestown, OH, *Owner*, Larry Horn & Co.; **PRIM RE ACT:** Broker, Appraiser, Instructor, Property Manager, Owner/Investor; **OTHER RE ACT:** Rehab. Prop. (40-60 bldgs. yearly); **REP CLIENTS:** Veterans admin.; **PREV EMPLOY:** Construction; **PROFL AFFIL & HONORS:** Bd. of Realtors: Columbus, OH Assn., NAR, GRI, CRS, CRB; **EDUC:** BA, 1952, RE/Mktg.; **EDUC HONORS:** two RE Scholarships; **MIL SERV:** USAF, S/Sgt., Air Medal w/1 Oak Leaf, Asiatic Pacific Tbeater Ribbon w/8 Bronze Stars, S. Phillipine Ribbon Liberation, Good Conduct Ribbon, Victory Medal; **OTHER ACT & HONORS:** Univ. Club of Columbus, Perry Cty. Historical Soc.; **HOME ADD:** 8285 Township Rd. 51NE RD 1, Somerset, OH 43783, (614)743-1590; **BUS ADD:** 863 S. High St., Columbus, OH 43206, (614)444-6843.

HORN, Ralph D.——**B:** Aug. 13, 1942, Dayton, OH, *Pres.*, Horn Enterprises, Inc.; **PRIM RE ACT:** Consultant, Attorney, Developer, Owner/Investor, Property Manager, Syndicator; **SERVICES:** Investment counseling, valuation, devel. and synd. of comml. prop.; prop. mgmt.; **PROFL AFFIL & HONORS:** ICSC; **EDUC:** BA, 1964, Eng. Literature, OH State Univ.; **GRAD EDUC:** JD, 1967, Law, OH State Univ. Coll. of Law; **OTHER ACT & HONORS:** Asst. Cty. Prosecutor 1967-1969; **HOME ADD:** 4140-G Idle Hour Cir., Dayton, OH 45415, (513)277-3064; **BUS ADD:** Suite 2360, Winters Bank Bldg., Dayton, OH 45423, (513)223-3168.

HORNE, Charles D.——*VP Realty*, United States Steel Corp.; **PRIM RE ACT:** Property Manager; **BUS ADD:** 600 Grant St., Rm. 2656, Pittsburgh, PA 15230, (412)433-1121.*

HORNE, Charles W.——**B:** Dec. 14, 1935, Fort Smith, AR, *Chmn. of Bd./CEO*, Angel Fire Corp. (Four Season Resort); **OTHER RE ACT:** Resort Operations, Real Estate Development and Sales, Timeshare; **PREV EMPLOY:** RE Consultant (Clients: Midland Natl. Bank, Ralston Purina's Keystone), Pres. Larwin Devel. Inc.; **PROFL AFFIL & HONORS:** Profl. Civil Engr.; **EDUC:** BS, 1960, Civil Engr, Fresno State Univ., CA; **GRAD EDUC:** MBA, 1968, Mktg, Univ. of Santa Clara, CA; **EDUC HONORS:** Dean's List; **HOME ADD:** Angel Fire, NM 87710, (505)377-6813; **BUS ADD:** Angel Fire, NM 87710, (505)377-2301.

HORNE, Frederick R., III——**B:** Feb. 4, 1951, Kansas City, MO, *Cashier*, Sloan State Bank; **PRIM RE ACT:** Banker; **SERVICES:** Loan Off.; **PROFL AFFIL & HONORS:** Sioux City Bd. of Realtors; **EDUC:** Bus. Admin. & Econ., 1973, Graceland Coll.; **HOME ADD:** Box 16, Sloan, IA 51055, (712)428-3931; **BUS ADD:** Box AC, Sloan, IA 51055, (712)428-3344.

HORNE, M.S.——**B:** Jan. 8, 1910, Richfield, UT, *Pres.*, James Stewart Co.; **PRIM RE ACT:** Developer, Builder, Owner/Investor; **EDUC:** BS, 1940, Econ. & Acctg., Geo. Wash. Univ., Wash. DC.; **HOME ADD:** 144 E. Country Club. Dr., Phoenix, AZ 85014, (602)274-6116; **BUS ADD:** 3033 N. Central Ave., Phoenix, AZ 85012, (602)264-2181.

HORRELL, Hugh H.——**B:** Aug. 1, 1934, Louisville, KY, *Pres.*, Leo Brokerage Corp., Horrell & Assoc.; **PRIM RE ACT:** Broker, Attorney, Owner/Investor; **REP CLIENTS:** Nu-West Grp., Amer. Home Mort., Cordary Investments; **PREV EMPLOY:** Turf Vac Corp., Pres.; **PROFL AFFIL & HONORS:** CA Assn. of Realtors, NAR, Nat. Inst. of Exchange Counselors; **EDUC:** BS, 1956, Bus. Mgmt., Univ. of Louisville; **EDUC HONORS:** NROTC Scholarship; **HOME ADD:** 44 Neapolitan Ln. E, Long Beach, CA 90803, (213)439-2429; **BUS ADD:** 911 Studebaker Rd., Ste 270, Long Beach, CA 90815, (213)493-1416.

HORTON, David T.——**B:** Aug. 21, 1946, Detroit, MI, *Pres.*, Anthony S. Brown/Eric Yale Lutz Management Group Inc., Prop. Mgmt.; **PRIM RE ACT:** Broker, Developer, Builder, Property Manager; **SERVICES:** Comml. devel., acquisition and prop. mgmt.; **REP CLIENTS:** Indiv. and instnl. investors in comml. and multi-family devel.; **PREV EMPLOY:** Sr. VP, Schostak Bros. & Co., Inc., 1971-1981; **PROFL AFFIL & HONORS:** IREM; ICSC, CPM; **EDUC:** BA, 1969, Econ., Wayne State Univ.; **HOME ADD:** 5646 Perrytown, W. Bloomfield, MI 48033, (313)661-1818; **BUS ADD:** 800 S. Worth St., Birmingham, MI 48011, (313)540-2900.

HORTON, Donald H.——**B:** June 7, 1950, New York, *VP, Acquisitions*, V.M.S. Realty, Inc.; **PRIM RE ACT:** Owner/Investor, Syndicator; **SERVICES:** Private placements, public limited partnerships, investing for inst. clients & pension fund consulting; **PREV EMPLOY:** Smith Barney RE Group, Chase Manhattan Bank; **PROFL AFFIL & HONORS:** Young Mtge. Bankers Assn., NY Broker, IREM; **EDUC:** AB, 1972, English - Bus., Villanova Univ.; **GRAD EDUC:** Cert. in RE

Studies, 1976, NY Univ.; **OTHER ACT & HONORS:** M.B.Y.C.; **BUS ADD:** 69 W. Washington St., Suite 1747, Chicago, IL 60602, (312)263-3636.

HORTON, Edward B., Jr.——B: Aug. 23, 1922, Denver, CO, *VP*, Bennett Horton Realtor, Inc.; **PRIM RE ACT:** Broker, Consultant, Appraiser, Lender, Property Manager; **OTHER RE ACT:** Dir., Midland Federal S&L Assn.; **SERVICES:** Valuation, investment counseling, sales, mgmt. & loans; **REP CLIENTS:** Lawyers, indiv. and investors in RE in metro. Denver; **PROFL AFFIL & HONORS:** Denver Bd. of Realtors; Amer. Inst. of RE Appraisers; Soc. of RE Appraisers, MAI; SREA; **MIL SERV:** USN; Lt.j.g.; 1942-1945; **OTHER ACT & HONORS:** Rotary; **HOME ADD:** 4995 Larkspur, Littleton, CO 80123, (303)794-4819; **BUS ADD:** 1761 Ogden St., P.O.B. 18307, Denver, CO 80218, (303)861-4122.

HORTON, G. Michael——B: May 31, 1944, Long Beach, CA, *Pres., Chief Exec. Officer*, The G.M. Horton Corp.; **PRIM RE ACT:** Developer, Builder, Owner/Investor, Property Manager; **PROFL AFFIL & HONORS:** AZ Assn. of Realtors; Dir. AZ Multi-Housing Assn.; Intl. Council of Shopping Ctrs., City Beautification Award, Tempe, AZ; **EDUC:** BA, Lit., Univ. of CA, Berkeley; **EDUC HONORS:** Phi Beta Kappa, Woodrow Wilson Fellowship Nominee Honors Prog., Maxima Cum Laude; **MIL SERV:** US Army, 1st Lt., Bronze Star, Army Commendation, Nat. Defense Medal & Vietnam Serv. Medal; **OTHER ACT & HONORS:** Dir., Boys Clubs of Phoenix; Carl Hayden Soc.; AZ State Univ.; **HOME ADD:** 615 W. Lawrence Rd., Phoenix, AZ 85013, (602)265-7000; **BUS ADD:** 2100 N. Central Ave., Suite 100, Phoenix, AZ 85004, (602)258-0700.

HORTON, George H.——B: Nov. 24, 1910, Oakland, CA, *Owner - Indiv.*, Self-employed; **PRIM RE ACT:** Broker, Consultant; **PROFL AFFIL & HONORS:** ASREC, RNMI, CCIM; **EDUC:** Bus. Admin., UC - Berkeley; **MIL SERV:** US Army, Lt. Col.; **OTHER ACT & HONORS:** Amer. Arbitration Assn. Panelist, Omega Tau Rho; **BUS ADD:** 42 Truitt Ln., Oakland, CA 94618, (415)444-2611.

HORTON, Hooker——*Sr. Corp. Buyer*, Corning Glass Works; **PRIM RE ACT:** Property Manager; **BUS ADD:** Corning, NY 14830, (607)974-9000.*

HORTON, James C.——*VP & Secy*, Portec Inc.; **PRIM RE ACT:** Property Manager; **BUS ADD:** 300 Windsor Drive, Oak Brook, IL 60521, (312)920-4600.*

HORTON, Larry A.——B: July 17, 1935, Mt. Vernon, IL, *Onwer*, Larry Horton Real Estate & Investment Co.; **PRIM RE ACT:** Appraiser, Builder, Owner/Investor, Property Manager; **SERVICES:** Investment counseling, prop. mgmt., devel. of comml. props., valuation; **REP CLIENTS:** Lenders - indivs., investors in comml. props.; **PREV EMPLOY:** Robinson's Ltd. RE; **EDUC:** BS, 1959, Univ. of Evansville - School of Bus.; **MIL SERV:** IN Nat. Guard, 2nd Lt.; **OTHER ACT & HONORS:** Pres. of Ridgecrest Conco. Resale Assn., Steamboat Springs, CO; **HOME ADD:** 628 Walnut St., Mt. Vernon, IN 47620, (812)838-3906; **BUS ADD:** P.O. Box 502, Mt. Vernon, IN 47620, (812)838-3906.

HORTON, William Pharis——B: June 15, 1934, Kansas City, MO, *Atty.*, Murphy, Stolper, Brewster & Desmond, S.C.; **PRIM RE ACT:** Attorney; **SERVICES:** Legal; **PREV EMPLOY:** Admin. Asst. to Hon. Thos. B. Curtis (R-Mo) (1959-1963); Instr. in Condo. Law - WI; IL Realtors Inst.; State Bar of WI; **PROFL AFFIL & HONORS:** State, local, ABA; State, local, NAR, Amer. Coll. of RE Counsel; **EDUC:** AB, 1956, Intl. Relations, Dartmouth Coll.; **GRAD EDUC:** LLB, 1963, Georgetown Univ. Law Ctr.; **EDUC HONORS:** Phi Beta Kappa, Magna Cum Laude, Staff, Georgetown Law Journal; **MIL SERV:** USN, LT(JG); **HOME ADD:** 6421 Antietam Ln., Madison, WI 53705, (608)233-5765; **BUS ADD:** Suite 2000, 150 E. Gilman St., Madison, WI 53703, (608)257-7181.

HORVITZ, Carl——B: Sept. 10, 1924, Boston, MA, *Pres.*, Horvitz Enterprises; **PRIM RE ACT:** Broker, Consultant, Developer, Owner/Investor, Syndicator; **SERVICES:** Counseling, joint venturing with clients, rehab.; **PROFL AFFIL & HONORS:** NAREB; **MIL SERV:** US Army, Sig. Corps., S/Sgt., Silver Star; **BUS ADD:** 4151 Middlefield Rd., Palo Alto, CA 94303, (415)493-5555.

HORWITZ, Louis A.——B: Apr. 29, 1899, Newark, NJ, *Chmn. of Bd.*, Mayflower S&L; **PRIM RE ACT:** Appraiser, Banker, Lender; **PREV EMPLOY:** Teacher, Secondary Schools Coaching Football Basketball & Track; **PROFL AFFIL & HONORS:** Rotary Club; C of C; Masonic Order; Tall Cedars ZOA; ELKS; **EDUC:** BS, 1939, Rutgers Univ., Bucknell, Tufts Coll.; **GRAD EDUC:** 1939, Rutgers Univ.; **EDUC HONORS:** Phi Beta Kappa; **MIL SERV:** USN; Seaman 1st Class; World War I 1918; **OTHER ACT & HONORS:** Pres. Rotary Club, Pres. ZOA, Pres. School Mens Masonic Club; **HOME ADD:** 320 So. Harrison St., E. Orange, NJ 07052, (201)678-3355; **BUS ADD:** 72 So. Livingston Ave., Livingston, NJ 07039, (201)992-6262.

HOSACK, John L.——B: Jan. 3, 1944, Tacoma, WA, *Partner*, Tobin & Tobin; **PRIM RE ACT:** Attorney; **REP CLIENTS:** Lenders, RE investors & title insurers; **PROFL AFFIL & HONORS:** ABA, CA St. Bar, The Bar Assn. of San Francisco, Chmn. Real Prop. Sect., The Bar Assn. of San Francisco (1978-80); **EDUC:** Poli. Sci., U. of WA; **GRAD EDUC:** JD, 1968, Univ. of San Francisco; **OTHER ACT & HONORS:** Dir. Palace of Fine Arts League, Author CA Title Ins. Practice (1980); Lecturer for Practicing Law Inst., NY Law Journal Seminars & CA Continuing Educ. of the Bar; **HOME ADD:** 625 Belvedere St., San Francisco, CA 94114, (415)661-1341; **BUS ADD:** One Post St., 2600 Crocker Plaza, San Francisco, CA 94104, (415)433-1400.

HOTCHKIN, Edgar E.——B: July 23, 1926, Jackson, MI, *Pres.*, Anchor West Fin.; **PRIM RE ACT:** Broker, Developer, Owner/Investor, Property Manager; **SERVICES:** Group Investments & Small Comml. Devel.; **PROFL AFFIL & HONORS:** NAR; Listed in: Who's Who in Creative RE, Who's Who in Comml.-Investment RE, RE Securities Members, CCIM; **EDUC:** BS, 1951, Electronics; **MIL SERV:** USN; **BUS ADD:** 1044 E. Green St., Pasadena, CA 91106, (213)795-7066.

HOUCK, H.F.——*Mgr. RE*, Emhart Corp.; **PRIM RE ACT:** Property Manager; **BUS ADD:** P.O. Box 2730, Hartford, CT 06101, (203)677-4631.*

HOUDE, Donald I.——*Under Secy.*, Department of Housing and Urban Development, Ofc. of Secy./Under S ecy.; **PRIM RE ACT:** Lender; **BUS ADD:** 451 Seventh St., S.W., Washington, DC 20410, (202)755-7123.*

HOUFEK, Dennis F.——B: Sept. 2, 1944, Omaha, NE, *Atty. and Counselor at Law*; **PRIM RE ACT:** Attorney; **SERVICES:** Legal; **REP CLIENTS:** WESCO Investments, Inc., GC Cole Corp., Tatco Investments, Inc., Teneris, Inc.; **PREV EMPLOY:** Life Investors, Inc. 1973-78, Lehndorff USA Grp., 1978-79; **PROFL AFFIL & HONORS:** State Bar of TX, RE., probate and trust sect., State Bar of NE, ABA real prop. probate and trust sect.; **EDUC:** BS, 1966, Bus. Admin., Univ. of NE; **GRAD EDUC:** JD, 1969, Univ.of NE; **OTHER ACT & HONORS:** Soc. of Former Special Agents of the Fed. Bureau of Investigation; **HOME ADD:** 10119 Betty wood Ln., Dallas, TX 75243, (214)231-7598; **BUS ADD:** 9400 N. Central Exp. 1210, Dallas, TX 75231, (214)368-6595.

HOUSE, Norman R.——B: Oct. 19, 1931, Louisville, KY, *Designated Broker*, Norm House Realty, Inc.; **PRIM RE ACT:** Broker, Consultant, Syndicator; **OTHER RE ACT:** Exchanger; **PREV EMPLOY:** USAF, US Army; **PROFL AFFIL & HONORS:** Cochies Bd. of Realtors, Pres. 1978 & 79; RESSI, Sierra Vista RE Exchangors, Pres. 1980; Inst. of Cert. Bus. Counselors, CBC, GRI, CRS; **EDUC:** AB, 1953, Soc. sci. & educ., Western KY Univ.; **GRAD EDUC:** MA, 1954, Educ., Western KY Univ.; EdS, 1967, Counseling, guidance, The George Washington Univ.; **MIL SERV:** US Army, Ltc. (R); **OTHER ACT & HONORS:** City of Sierra Vista City Council 1981 to present; Chmn. Grievance Comm., AZ Assn. of Realtors 1980; Realtor of the Year, Cochise Bd. of Realtors 1981; AZ Assn. of Realtors, Exec. Comm. 1982; **HOME ADD:** 113 Plaza Azul, Sierra Vista, AZ 85635, (602)459-1270; **BUS ADD:** 11 E. Wilcox Dr., Ste. B, Sierra Vista, AZ 85635, (602)459-0123.

HOUSE, Steve——B: July 23, 1953, Farmville, NC, *Asst. VP*, Cambron-Brown Co., Resid. Div.; **PRIM RE ACT:** Banker; **SERVICES:** Const. Loans, Permanent Loans; **REP CLIENTS:** Realtors, Builder, Indivs.; **PROFL AFFIL & HONORS:** MBA, Clayton & Fayette Cty Bd. of Realtors Tri-Cty Homebuilders; **EDUC:** BA, 1975, Econ., NC State Univ., Raleigh; **GRAD EDUC:** Working on MBA, Fin, Georgia State Univ., Atlanta, GA; **OTHER ACT & HONORS:** Bethany Presbyterian Church; **HOME ADD:** 115 Bradley Ct., Fayetteville, NC 28300, (404)461-4250; **BUS ADD:** 1587 Phoenix Blvd., Suite 1, Atlanta, GA 30349, (404)996-1364.

HOUSER, William J.——B: Mar. 18, 1946, Homestead, PA, *Dir. of Land Acquisition*, Cardinal Industries Inc., FL; **PRIM RE ACT:** Broker, Attorney, Developer, Builder, Property Manager, Syndicator; **SERVICES:** Shelter Indus.; **PREV EMPLOY:** Nat. Dir., RE, Ponderosa Steakhouses; **PROFL AFFIL & HONORS:** ABA; PA Bar Assn.; OH Bar Assn.; Nat. Assn. of Corporate RE Execs.; Intl. Council of Shopping Ctrs., RE Broker, OH, PA; Atty. at Law, OH, PA; **EDUC:** BS, 1968, Fin., Univ. of PA, Wharton School of Fin. & Commerce; **GRAD EDUC:** JD, 1975, Suffolk Univ. School of Law; **HOME ADD:** 3770 Sutter's Mill Cir., Casselberry, FL 32707, (305)331-6695; **BUS ADD:** 3701 S. Sanford Ave., P.O.B. U, Sanford, FL 32771, (305)321-

0220.

HOUSTON, David T., Jr.——*Prs.*, David T. Houston Co.; **PRIM RE ACT:** Developer; **BUS ADD:** 1025 Broad St., Bloomfield, NJ 07003, (201)429-8000.*

HOUSTON, James——**B:** March 13, 1945, Atlanta, GA, *Pres.*, Hardin, Inc.; **PRIM RE ACT:** Broker, Consultant, Property Manager; **SERVICES:** Comml. Brokerage & Full Ser. Prop. Mgmt., specializing in multi-family; **PREV EMPLOY:** Redman Ind. Inc., Arthur Anderson & Co.; **PROFL AFFIL & HONORS:** NAR (State Bd.) IREM, TX Apt. Assoc., CAI CPA, CPM Candidate; **EDUC:** BA/BA, 1972, Acctg. & Fin., Univ. of FL; **EDUC HONORS:** High Honors; **HOME ADD:** 20 Hickory Hills, Lake Dallas, TX 75065; **BUS ADD:** 420 S. Carroll, Denton, TX 76201, (817)383-2388.

HOUSTON, John C.——**B:** Aug. 10, 1937, Graceville, MN, *Pres.*, Houston Const. Inc.; **PRIM RE ACT:** Broker, Developer, Builder, Engineer, Owner/Investor; **REP CLIENTS:** Builders, Indivs.; **PREV EMPLOY:** Houston Eng., US Bureau of Public Roads; **PROFL AFFIL & HONORS:** ASCE, MN Prop. Exchangers, Tau Beta Pi Assoc.; **EDUC:** BSCE, 1960, Civil Engrg., ND Agricultural Coll; **GRAD EDUC:** MSCE, 1962, Civil Engr., ND State Univ.; **EDUC HONORS:** Tau Beta Pi; **HOME ADD:** 13009 Diamond Path W., Apple Valley, MN 53124, (612)423-2995; **BUS ADD:** 13009 Diamond Path W., Apple Valley, MN 55124, (612)423-2995.

HOUSTON, Lee——**B:** Nov. 25, 1938, Indisuola, IA, *Chmn.*, Lee Houston & Assoc., Ltd.; **PRIM RE ACT:** Broker, Consultant, Owner/Investor, Instructor, Insuror, Syndicator; **SERVICES:** RE Brokerage, investment prop. synd., RE education (The RE Sch.) Ins. (Clement-Houston Ins., Inc.); **PROFL AFFIL & HONORS:** Realtors/Ind. Agents/NALU, C.L.U., Amer. Coll. Bryn Mawr PD 1968; **EDUC:** BA, 1970, Poli. Sci., Drake Univ.; **GRAD EDUC:** J.D., 1972, Drake Univ. Law Sch.; **HOME ADD:** 2611 W. 100th, Anchorage, AK 99502, (907)344-6376; **BUS ADD:** 507 W. Northern Lights Blvd., Anchorage, AK 99503, (907)276-5909.

HOUSTON, Peter C.——**B:** Jan. 24, 1935, St. Marys, PA, *Dir. of Prop. Mgmt.*, ARA Services, Inc., Corp. Staff; **PRIM RE ACT:** Broker, Consultant, Attorney, Property Manager; **SERVICES:** Prop. mgmt., counseling, acquisition evaluation, dispositions, documentation, leasing; **PREV EMPLOY:** SL Triester Intl. Mgmt. Corp. 1969-72, Houston and Daghir Attys. at Law 1959-60; **PROFL AFFIL & HONORS:** LLB; **EDUC:** BA, 1956, Hist., Westminster Coll., PA; **GRAD EDUC:** LLB, 1959, Dickinson School of Law, PA; **EDUC HONORS:** Phi Alpha Theta; **OTHER ACT & HONORS:** Lic. RE Salesman (PA); **HOME ADD:** 14 Andrews Rd., Malver, PA 19355, (215)647-6279; **BUS ADD:** Independence Sq. W., 16th & Walnut Sts., Philadelphia, PA 19106, (215)574-5406.

HOVDE, Donald I.——*Under Sec. of HUD*, US Dept. of HUD; **OTHER RE ACT:** Oversee day to day operations of HUD; **PREV EMPLOY:** Owner & Pres. of Hovde Realty, Inc., Madison, WI; Partner RE Inc., Nat. Sr. VP; 122 Bldg. Corp.; **PROFL AFFIL & HONORS:** NAR; Local & State Assns. of Realtors, Realtor of Year, WI-1976; Pres. of NAR; **EDUC:** BBA, 1953, Fin., Univ. of WI; **MIL SERV:** US Army, US Army Res. 1953-1963, Pilot's Wings; **OTHER ACT & HONORS:** Past Pres. of Greater Madison C of C; Past Dir. of Methodist Hospital Found.; **BUS ADD:** HUD Bldg., 451 7th St., SW, Washington, DC 20410, (202)755-7123.

HOVEY, Winthrop T.——**B:** Mar. 26, 1919, Seattle, WA, *Pres.*, Carr-Gottstein Props., Inc.; **PRIM RE ACT:** Developer, Owner/Investor; **PREV EMPLOY:** Pres.-Beneficial Standard Props.; **PROFL AFFIL & HONORS:** I.C.S.C.-U.L.I.; **HOME ADD:** 665 Highlander Cir., Anchorage, AK 99502, (907)344-0396; **BUS ADD:** 1341 Fairbanks St., Anchorage, AK 99501, (907)276-4470.

HOVIK, Byron F.——*Pres.*, Menlo Mort. Investment Co.; **PRIM RE ACT:** Broker, Syndicator, Appraiser, Developer, Property Manager, Banker, Owner/Investor; **PREV EMPLOY:** Northwestern Mutual Life Ins. Co., Mort. Loan Supr.; VP Wilshire Mort. Co.; **PROFL AFFIL & HONORS:** MBAA, NCMBA, CMBA, NACMB, CMB, SCR; **EDUC:** BA, 1948, Stanford Univ.; **HOME ADD:** 385 Fletcher Dr., Atherton, CA 94025; **BUS ADD:** 430 Sherman Ave., Palo Alto, CA 94306, (415)326-4515.

HOWARD, Bradley Duke——**B:** Apr. 29, 1952, LA, CA, *Pres. owner of Classic Props.*, Classic Props. (Duke Enterprises Inc.); **PRIM RE ACT:** Broker, Consultant, Developer, Builder, Owner/Investor, Property Manager; **SERVICES:** RE Sales Comml. Indus. & Devel. Builder; **REP CLIENTS:** Heltzer Enterprises; Jackbilt Inc.; **PREV EMPLOY:** R.E. Mgmt. "Garden Apts"; **PROFL AFFIL & HONORS:** Lakeside Golf Club, San Fernando Bd. of Realtor; Burbank Bd. of Realtors, Toluca Lake C of C, Broker, B1 Contractor; **EDUC:** BA, 1974, RE & Acctg., UCLA, CSUN, UCSB; **BUS ADD:** 3300 W. Olive Ave., Burbank, CA 91505, (213)841-0881.

HOWARD, Daggett H.——**B:** Mar. 20, 1917, NYC, NY, *Sr. Partner*, Howard, Poe & Bastian (law firm), and Pres. Bristol Property Management and Sers., Inc.; **PRIM RE ACT:** Attorney, Owner/Investor, Property Manager, Syndicator; **SERVICES:** Legal services, synd., prop. mgmt.; **REP CLIENTS:** L'Enfant Plaza Props., Inc., Bristol Associates, Monroe Associates, Amtrak, Morgan Guaranty Trust Co. of NY; **PROFL AFFIL & HONORS:** ABA, Fed. Bar Assn., DC Bar, AOBA, Fed. Dist., Circuit and Supreme Court Bars, JD Degree; **EDUC:** BA, Yale Univ., 1938, Econs., Moses Brown School, Providence, RI, Cum Laude Soc.; **GRAD EDUC:** JD, 1941, Law, Yale Law School; **EDUC HONORS:** Magna Cum Laude, Phi Beta Kappa, High Distinction in Econs., Bd. of Editors of Yale Law Journal; **MIL SERV:** US Navy, Ensign, USNR; **OTHER ACT & HONORS:** Gen. Counsel, Fed. Aviation Agency (1958-62), Deputy Gen. Counsel, US Air Force (1953-58), Asst. to Spec. Counsel to the Pres., White House (1945), Metropolitan Club, Chevy Chase Club, Yale and Yale Law School Clubs, Wash., DC; **HOME ADD:** 4554 Klingle St., NW, Wash., DC 20016, (202)363-3854; **BUS ADD:** 1701 PA Ave., NW, Washington, DC 20006, (202)298-8333.

HOWARD, James W.——**B:** Sept. 17, 1925, IN, *Pres.*, The Home Mart; **PRIM RE ACT:** Broker, Consultant, Engineer, Attorney, Developer, Builder, Owner/Investor, Syndicator; **PROFL AFFIL & HONORS:** ABA; CA Bar Assn.; SD Bar Assn.; Cordonado & SD Bd. of Realtors; CA Assn. of Realtors; NAR, ASME; **EDUC:** BSME, 1949, Production Mgmt./Mech. Engr., Purdue Univ.; **GRAD EDUC:** MBA, 1962, Banking & Fin., Western Reserve Univ.; JD, 1976, Law, Western State Univ.; **EDUC HONORS:** Pi Tau Sigma, Beta Sigma Phi, Law Honorary; **MIL SERV:** US Army; Sgt.; Bronze Star, Com. Inf. Badge, Parachutist Badge, 1943-1946; **OTHER ACT & HONORS:** Co-Chmn., Chicago, IL Sesquicentennial Comm., 1968; Amer. Mgmt. Assn.; Tau Kappa Epsilon; Dir.; Boys Club, Boy Scouts, Rehabilitation Inst., Mercy Hospital, Chicago; **HOME ADD:** P.O.B. A-80427, San Diego, CA 92138; **BUS ADD:** 2605 Camino Del Rio S., Suite 300, San Diego, CA 92138, (714)291-9520.

HOWARD, Norman A.——**B:** June 29, 1915, NYC, NY, *Counsel*, Burns Jackson Summit Rovins & Spitzer; **PRIM RE ACT:** Attorney; **REP CLIENTS:** Builders, owners,/investors, lenders, synds.; **PREV EMPLOY:** Partner in Kahr & Spitzer & Howard Now merged into Burns, Jackson, Summit Rovins Spitzer & Feldesman; **PROFL AFFIL & HONORS:** New York Cty. Lawyers Assn., Member Comm. on Real Prop. Law 1967-1973, Former lecturer at Practicing Law Institute. Author "The Essential Elements of a Net Lease."; Co-author of following PLI publications: "Real Estate Financing" (1971), "Sale and Leaseback Financing" (1969), "Commercial Real Estate Leases" (1963); **EDUC:** Fordham Teachers Coll. & City Coll. of City of New York; **GRAD EDUC:** Fordham Law School, 1941; **MIL SERV:** US Army, MSgt.; **OTHER ACT & HONORS:** Member, Traffic & Parking Comm. Hempstead, NY 1952-54, Former Pres. of (1) Univ. Gardens Prop. Owners Assn. and (2) U.G. Pool and Tennis Club; **HOME ADD:** 56 Somerset Dr., Great Neck, NY 11280, (516)482-4895; **BUS ADD:** 445 Park Ave., New York, NY 10022, (212)980-3200.

HOWARD, Norris C.——**B:** Aug. 10, 1938, Crisfield, MO, *Broker/Owner*, Howard Real Estate; **PRIM RE ACT:** Broker, Consultant, Appraiser, Owner/Investor, Property Manager, Syndicator; **SERVICES:** Gen. Brokerage, prop. mgmt., investment advising; **REP CLIENTS:** Indiv. lenders & instl. accts. and special comml./investment projects; **PREV EMPLOY:** Bus. operator and Direct sales mgmt.; **PROFL AFFIL & HONORS:** NAR, RNMI, RESSI; **EDUC:** 1956, Crisfield High School; **OTHER ACT & HONORS:** Past Pres. of Allen Lions Club; **HOME ADD:** P.O. Box 56, Allen, MD 21810, (301)742-6795; **BUS ADD:** P.O. Box 386, Salisbury, MD 21801, (301)546-1977.

HOWARD, Peggy Ann——**B:** July 15, 1944, Shelley Cty., TX, *Asst. Rgnl. Counsel, RE Operations*, Prudential; **PRIM RE ACT:** Attorney; **SERVICES:** All phases of RE devel., leasing and mgmt. of comml. real prop.; **PREV EMPLOY:** Represented a S&L in lending, construction, devel.; **PROFL AFFIL & HONORS:** ABA; TX Bar Assn.; **EDUC:** 1969, Eng./Math., Baylor Univ.; **GRAD EDUC:** Masters, 1972, Univ. of Houston; 1978, S. TX Coll. of Law; **HOME ADD:** 1111 S. Post Oak Blvd. 729, Houston, TX 77056, (713)840-9806; **BUS ADD:** 1111 Post Oak Blvd. 729, Houston, TX 77056, (713)627-2100.

HOWARD, Robert B.——**B:** June 12, 1934, Saranac Lake, NY, *Partner*, The Howard Companies, Comml.-Investment Div.; **PRIM RE ACT:** Broker, Consultant, Appraiser, Developer, Builder, Owner/Investor, Syndicator; **SERVICES:** Complete appraisal, feasibility studies, purchase and synd.; **REP CLIENTS:** Chemical Bank, Bankers Trust,

Ely Lilly Drug Co., G.D. Searle & Co., Chrysler Credit Corp., Dime Savings Bank of NY, (Mechanics Exchange Bank, Albany, New York); **PROFL AFFIL & HONORS:** RESSI, NYSAR, NAR; **MIL SERV:** US Army, E-4; **HOME ADD:** 127 Chancellor Dr., Guilderland, NY 12084, (518)456-6852; **BUS ADD:** 50 State St., Albany, NY 12207, (518)434-8181.

HOWARD, Roger H., Esq.——B: Dec. 5, 1944, Los Angeles, *Atty.*, Law Offices of Boren, Elperin, Howard & Sloan; **PRIM RE ACT:** Attorney; **SERVICES:** Condo./stock cooperative and subdiv. law; **REP CLIENTS:** Major lenders and devel. in So. CA; **PROFL AFFIL & HONORS:** ABA; Los Angeles Bar Assn.; Beverly Hills Bar Assn.; Century City Bar; CA Bar, Member of State of CA Comm. on Stock Cooperatives, Condo. and Subdiv. Law Speaker at numerous seminars held by title companies, univ., and mort. brokerage co.; **EDUC:** BS, 1967, Poli. Sci., UCLA; **GRAD EDUC:** JD, 1971, Law, UCLA; **EDUC HONORS:** selected by UCLA Alumni Assn., as outstanding gradg. Sr.; **OTHER ACT & HONORS:** Benjamin Crocker Symposium (1981); selected as member of CA State Bar Comm. on Stock Cooperatives; Condo. & Subdiv. Law; **HOME ADD:** 320 Homewood Rd., Los Angeles, CA 90049, (213)476-3176; **BUS ADD:** Century Park Ctr., 9911 W. Pico Blvd., Suite 1150, Los Angeles, CA 90035, (213)556-1032.

HOWARD, Ronald M.——B: Feb. 24, 1940, Seattle, WA, *Comm'l. Sales Mgr.*, Cameo Prop., Inc., Comm'l. Investments; **PRIM RE ACT:** Syndicator, Consultant, Developer, Property Manager, Owner/Investor; **SERVICES:** Synd. of comm'l. investment prop., apt. & condo. dev., full service RE sales, leasing & exchanging; **PREV EMPLOY:** Owner First Hill Holding Co. - Synd. & Prop. Mgmt. - RE Investments.; **PROFL AFFIL & HONORS:** Realtor, RESSI; **MIL SERV:** USN, PO4; **OTHER ACT & HONORS:** Past Pres. Lake Ballinger Community Club; **HOME ADD:** 23823 74 Ave. W., Edmonds, WA, (206)778-1272; **BUS ADD:** 22019 HiWay 99, Edmonds, WA 9802O, (206)775-7591.

HOWARD, Roy M.——B: Feb. 17, 1921, Emmett, ID, *Owner*, RE Data Servs.; **PRIM RE ACT:** Consultant, Appraiser; **OTHER RE ACT:** RE Market analyst; **SERVICES:** Market feasibility, location, higher & best use studies, investment counseling; **REP CLIENTS:** Lenders, synds., devels., indiv. state & local govts.; **PREV EMPLOY:** Mort Invest. Dept., Prudential Ins., Co. 7 yrs.; Valuation Supervisor, Fed. Housing Admin, 4 yrs.; Sr. Loan officer, Maj. mort. banking firm, 5 yrs.; VP RE Appraisal firm, 5 yrs.; Ind. RE consultant 11 yrs.; **EDUC:** 1949, OR State Univ.; **MIL SERV:** US Army, Maj., 1940-46, 1951-53, Several decorations; **HOME ADD:** 3711 Wren, Lake Oswego, OR 97034, (503)636-1760; **BUS ADD:** Box 583, Lake Oswego, OR 97034, (503)636-8771.

HOWARD, Susanne C.——B: July 14, 1951, White Plains, NY, *Atty.*, Choate, Hall & Stewart; **PRIM RE ACT:** Attorney; **SERVICES:** Land use and Environmental law; **PREV EMPLOY:** Tyler & Reynolds 1980; Thomas & Howard 1978-80; Environmental Law Inst. 1976-77; **PROFL AFFIL & HONORS:** Environmental Law Comm. of the Boston Bar Assn.; Board Member, Women's Bar Assn.; Member, MA Bar Assn.; ABA Natural Resources Div.; **EDUC:** AB, 1973, Hist., Washington Univ.; **GRAD EDUC:** JD, 1977, Catholic Univ. of Amer.; **EDUC HONORS:** Author, Note, "Future Land & Water Recreation Resources and the Fund That Supports Them", Env.Law Reporter 50034, Apr. 1977; **HOME ADD:** 5 Craigie Circ., 56, Cambridge, MA 02138; **BUS ADD:** 60 State St., Boston, MA 02109, (617)227-5020.

HOWARTH, Robert R.——B: Apr. 15, 1921, Chatham, NY, *Pres.*, Howarth Realty, Inc.; **PRIM RE ACT:** Broker, Consultant, Appraiser, Property Manager; **OTHER RE ACT:** Bus. Broker; **SERVICES:** Investment counseling, bus. & prop. evaluation, mort. procurement & comml. prop. sales, appraisals & mgmt.; **REP CLIENTS:** Bus. exec., banks, accountants, and investors or buyers of comml. props.; **PREV EMPLOY:** Pres., Columbia Corp., Chatham, NY, 1945-1963; Pres., Howarth Board Sales, Inc., Utica, NY, 1963-1971; **PROFL AFFIL & HONORS:** NAR; NY St. Assn. of Realtors; Greater Utica Bd. of Realtors, NY St. Soc. RE Appraisers; Paper Indus. Mgmt. Assn., U.S. Exec. Res., U.S. Dept. of Commerce; **EDUC:** 1940, Bus., Albany Bus. Coll.; **MIL SERV:** U.S. Army Air Force, Maj., 1940-1946; **OTHER ACT & HONORS:** Past Chmn., Nat. Paperboard Assn. (E.); Past Treas., Univ. of ME, Pulp & Paper Found.; Past Pres. & Treas., Columbia Memorial Hospital, Hudson, NY; **HOME ADD:** RD 1, Higby Rd., New Hartford, NY 13413, (315)797-2387; **BUS ADD:** Security Bldg., 120-124 Bleecker St., Utica, NY 13501, (315)797-1438.

HOWARTH, Thomas G.——B: May 5, 1921, Fitchburg, MA, *Atty.*; **PRIM RE ACT:** Attorney; **PROFL AFFIL & HONORS:** ABA; MA Bar Assn.; ME Bar Assn.; Essex Cty. (MA) Bar Assn.; **EDUC:** AB, 1942, Pol. Sci., Bates Coll; **GRAD EDUC:** LLB, 1952, Northeastern Univ.; AM, 1961, Pol. Sci., Boston Univ.; **MIL SERV:** US Army; Capt.; **OTHER ACT & HONORS:** Town Counsel, Manchester, MA, 1965-70; Rotary Club, Beverly, MA; Var religious and frat. orgs.; **HOME ADD:** 51 Union St., Manchester, MA 01944, (617)526-7992; **BUS ADD:** 49 Union St., Manchester, MA 01944, (617)526-1578.

HOWDEN, John F.——B: Aug. 1, 1941, El Paso, TX, *Pres.*, Southwest Appraisal Co., Inc.; **PRIM RE ACT:** Appraiser; **SERVICES:** Appraisals, counseling, mkt. studies; **REP CLIENTS:** Albuquerque Fed. Savings; Security Fed. Savings; Amrep; First Nat. Bank; **PROFL AFFIL & HONORS:** Member, AIREA; Soc. of RE APpraisers; Realtors Assn., MAI; SRPA; **EDUC:** BA, 1964, Hist., Stanford Univ.; **MIL SERV:** US Army; Capt.; Bronze Star; **OTHER ACT & HONORS:** Sr. Warden, St. Michael's Episcopal Church; Past Pres., Chap. 114 Soc. of RE Appraisers; **HOME ADD:** 517 Roehl N.W., Albuquerque, NM 87107, (505)898-1263; **BUS ADD:** P.O.B. 25000, Albuquerque, NM 87125, (505)883-3420.

HOWE, Mitchell B., Jr.——B: Nov. 14, 1941, Chicago, IL, *Pres.*, Howe & Herrador Enterprises; **PRIM RE ACT:** Broker, Consultant, Engineer, Owner/Investor, Property Manager; **SERVICES:** Real Prop. consultation, prop. mgmt., building engr.; **PROFL AFFIL & HONORS:** Pasadena Bd. of Realtors; Amer. Soc. for Metals; **EDUC:** Bus. Mgmt.; **MIL SERV:** Army, SP-5; **OTHER ACT & HONORS:** Christian Bus. Men's Comm. USA (Pasadena Central); **HOME ADD:** 2670 Devonport Rd., San Marino, CA 91108, (213)796-8890; **BUS ADD:** 180 S. Lake Ave., Pasadena, CA 91101, (213)792-0514.

HOWE, Randolph R.——B: Dec. 25, 1935, Hollywood, CA, *Owner*, Randolph R. Howe Co.; **PRIM RE ACT:** Broker, Consultant, Owner/Investor, Instructor, Syndicator, Real Estate Publisher; **OTHER RE ACT:** Foreign and out of state serv.; **SERVICES:** Acquisition and marketing of investment prop. - one million dollars plus; **REP CLIENTS:** Confidential; **PROFL AFFIL & HONORS:** NAR, CA Assn. of Realtors, Realtors Nat. Mktg. Instit., E. San Diego Cty. Bd. of Realtors, CCIM and GRI; **EDUC:** RE, San Diego State Univ./Univ of CA at San Diego; **OTHER ACT & HONORS:** Two lifetime teaching credentials, Comm. Coll. and Adult Educ., author of RE investment analysis and exchange text, "Real estate is Now!" and audio cassette training program, "Experience-Now!" for the training of investment RE specialist; **BUS ADD:** 480 N. Magnolia Ave., El Cajon (San Diego), CA 92020, (714)442-2553.

HOWE, Richard P.——B: Oct. 19, 1944, Manchester, NH, *Pres.*, Richard P. Howe & Assoc., Inc.; **OTHER RE ACT:** RE Investment; **SERVICES:** Investments, mgmt., leasing; **REP CLIENTS:** Inst. investors and pvt. investors in comml. office bldgs.; **EDUC:** BA, 1967, Bowdoin Coll.; **HOME ADD:** 8910 Vista View, Dallas, TX 75243, (214)349-4925; **BUS ADD:** 18601 LBJ Frwy., Mesquite, TX 75150, (214)270-6561.

HOWELL, A. Harold——B: Apr. 30, 1941, Boston, MA, *Managing Dir.*, Boston Fin. Technology Group, Inc.; **PRIM RE ACT:** Owner/Investor, Property Manager, Syndicator; **PROFL AFFIL & HONORS:** CPM; IREM; Reg. Securities Principal; Reg. RE Broker; **EDUC:** AB, 1963, Phys. Sci., Harvard Coll.; **GRAD EDUC:** MBA, 1968, Bus., Amos Tuck School of Bus. Admin.; **EDUC HONORS:** Highest Distinction; **MIL SERV:** USN, Lt., 1964-1966; **HOME ADD:** 81 Walnut St., Winchester, MA 01890, (617)729-9486; **BUS ADD:** One Post Office Square, Boston, MA 02109, (617)482-9790.

HOWELL, Bill——B: June 15, 1942, Corpus Christi, TX, *Owner*, Bill Howell R.E.; **PRIM RE ACT:** Broker, Consultant, Developer, Owner/Investor; **SERVICES:** Investment counseling, devel. of comml. props., creative fin. consultation, brokerage; **EDUC:** BS, 1965, Phys. Sci., Univ. of TX-Austin; **HOME ADD:** 3519 E. Glen, El Paso, TX 79905, (915)592-0945; **BUS ADD:** 6028 Surety Dr., El Paso, TX 79905, (915)779-3725.

HOWELL, Floyd——B: Jan. 13, 1927, Clearfield, PA, *Broker*, Howell Associates, Inc., Century 21; **PRIM RE ACT:** Broker, Consultant, Lender, Owner/Investor; **OTHER RE ACT:** RE Exchanger; **SERVICES:** Counseling & RE tax free exchanges; **REP CLIENTS:** Investors; **PREV EMPLOY:** RE Investor and Tax Accountant (Public); **PROFL AFFIL & HONORS:** GRI, Enrolled Agent (to practice before IRS) Director NMCF, NAR, NSPA, RANM, NMCF, NCF; **EDUC:** Grad., Higher Acctg. & Bus. Admin., 1950, DuBois Business Coll.; **MIL SERV:** Army, Cpl., WW II, European Theatre Operations, Etc.; **OTHER ACT & HONORS:** President TM Inst.; **HOME ADD:** 906 Yocca, Truth or Consequences, NM 87901; **BUS ADD:** 110 Clancy, Truth or Consequences, NM 87901, (505)894-6611.

HOWELL, Jerry——*Mgr. RE Dept.*, Graniteville Co.; **PRIM RE ACT:** Property Manager; **BUS ADD:** PO Box 128, Graniteville, SC 29829, (803)663-7231.*

HOWELL, John Mackey——**B:** Mar. 27, 1946, Hannibal, MO, *Fin. VP & Gen. Counsel*, The Mason Cassilly Cos.; **PRIM RE ACT:** Attorney, Developer, Builder, Owner/Investor, Property Manager, Syndicator; **SERVICES:** Largest resid. devel. in MO, also active in comml. devel.; **PREV EMPLOY:** Price Waterhouse & Co., CPA's, 5 yrs., Pvt. law practice, 5 yrs.; **PROFL AFFIL & HONORS:** Var. RE Accts. and fed. and MO Bar; **EDUC:** BS, 1967, Acctg., Univ. of MO. Sch. of Bus. & Public Admin.; **GRAD EDUC:** JD, 1971, Law, St. Louis Univ. Sch. of Law; **MIL SERV:** USMC, Sgt.; **HOME ADD:** 14950 Greenleaf Valley Dr., Chesterfield, MO 63017; **BUS ADD:** 15510 Olive Blvd., Suite 200, Chesterfield, MO 63017, (314)532-1100.

HOWELL, Pamela Sue——**B:** June 11, 1952, Danville, IL, *Partner*, Doyle and Howell, Attys. at Law; **PRIM RE ACT:** Attorney; **SERVICES:** Represent buyers, sellers, lenders and landlord/tenants; **PROFL AFFIL & HONORS:** ABA, ISBA, VCBA; **EDUC:** BA, 1974, Mathematics, DePaul Univ., Greencastle, IN; **GRAD EDUC:** JD, 1977, Notre Dame Law School, Notre Dame, IN; **EDUC HONORS:** Phi Beta Kappa, Magna Cum Laude, Cum Laude; **OTHER ACT & HONORS:** Delta Delta Delta Sorority; **HOME ADD:** RD 3, Danville, IL 61832, (217)443-4360; **BUS ADD:** 4 N. Vermilion, Suite 805, Danville, IL 61832, (217)446-3844.

HOWELL, Ronald A.——*Partner*, George, Whitfield and Howell Realty Co.; **PRIM RE ACT:** Broker, Appraiser; **SERVICES:** Sales, appraising, consultation, feasibility studies; **PROFL AFFIL & HONORS:** RNMI; NAR; FLI, CRS; GRI; **EDUC:** AAS, 1976, RE, Tidewater Community Coll.; **EDUC HONORS:** Cum Laude; **OTHER ACT & HONORS:** Bd. of Dir., Central YMCA; Past Pres., Ports. Jaycees; **HOME ADD:** 4934 Briarwood Ln., Portsmouth, VA 23703, (804)484-0404; **BUS ADD:** 3219 Stamford Rd., Portsmouth, VA 23703, (804)483-4880.

HOWELL, Thomas G.——**B:** Mar. 1, 1951, Wash., DC, *Sr. Atty.*, Kellogg Company; **PRIM RE ACT:** Attorney; **SERVICES:** Consulting & Advising Corp., all local RE matters; **PREV EMPLOY:** US Patent & Trademark Office; **PROFL AFFIL & HONORS:** ABA; **EDUC:** BA, 1973, Econ. and Hist., NC Wesleyan Coll.; **GRAD EDUC:** JD, 1977, Law, George Mason Univ. School of Law; **EDUC HONORS:** Deans List 4 Semesters, Omicron Delta Kappa Honor Frat.; **OTHER ACT & HONORS:** Order of DeMolay - Chevalier, Past Mast Councilor, Representative Demolay Award, 1970 Intl. Oratorical Runnerup; 1969 VA state Oratorical Champion; 1970 VA State Flower Talk Champion; Outstanding Young Men of Amer. 1981; **HOME ADD:** 120 Greentree Ln. 37B, Battle Creek, MI 49015, (616)979-9813; **BUS ADD:** 235 Porter St., Battle Creek, MI 49016, (616)966-2170.

HOWELL, Wes——**B:** Sept. 25, 1923, San Francisco, *Broker*, Howell Lake Tahoe Realty; **PRIM RE ACT:** Broker, Owner/Investor, Assessor; **PROFL AFFIL & HONORS:** NAR, RNMI, NV Assn. Realtors, CA Assn. Realtors, GRI; **EDUC:** BA, 1944, Engr., Stanford Univ.; **MIL SERV:** US Army, 1st Lt.; **OTHER ACT & HONORS:** Pres. N. Tahoe C of C, 1974-75; **HOME ADD:** Box 3177, Incline, NV 89450; **BUS ADD:** Box 3177, Incline, NV 89450, (702)831-0334.

HOWES, Edward B.——**B:** Sept. 13, 1921, San Bernardino, CA, *VP, Corp. RE Mgr.*, Redlands Fed. S&L Assn., Admin.; **PRIM RE ACT:** Consultant, Appraiser, Property Manager; **PREV EMPLOY:** Deputy Assessor; **PROFL AFFIL & HONORS:** SREA, NARA, SRA, CRA; **MIL SERV:** USAF, Lt., Col., DFC, Air Medal; **OTHER ACT & HONORS:** Arrowhead Ctry. Club; **HOME ADD:** 3371 Broadmoor Blvd., San Bernardino, CA 92404, (714)886-4195; **BUS ADD:** 300 E. State St., Redlands, CA 92373, (714)793-2391.

HOWINGTON, Ezra Frank, Jr.——**B:** Dec. 12, 1924, Atlanta, GA, *Partner*, Massell and Howington; **PRIM RE ACT:** Broker, Consultant, Owner/Investor, Syndicator; **SERVICES:** Mktg. of RE, brokerage, mkt. feasibility, consulting; **EDUC:** BBA, 1949, Univ. of GA; **MIL SERV:** USAF, 1st Lt. Pilot; **HOME ADD:** 3469 Knollwood Dr., NW, Atlanta, GA 30305, (404)233-7349; **BUS ADD:** 3330 Peachtree Rd. 339, Atlanta, GA 30326, (404)237-5777.

HOY, David R.——**B:** Nov. 5, 1938, Ely, NV, *Pres. & Atty.*, Hoy & Miller, Chtd.; **PRIM RE ACT:** Attorney, Builder, Owner/Investor; **SERVICES:** Legal serv. to builders, devel. & title insurers; **REP CLIENTS:** Capriotti Const. Co.; Varibuild, Inc.; Stewart Title Co.; Transamerica Title Co.; **PROFL AFFIL & HONORS:** ABA - Comm. on RE; Probate & Trust Law, Subcomm. on Time Sharing; NV State Bar, CA State Bar; **EDUC:** BSBA, 1960, Acctg., Univ. of NV, Reno; **GRAD EDUC:** JD, 1963, Law, UCLA; **HOME ADD:** 1545 Meadowview Lane, Reno, NV 89501, (702)825-8619; **BUS ADD:** 350 S. Center St., Suite 550, Reno, NV 89501, (702)786-8000.

HOYES, Louis W.——**B:** Oct. 8, 1948, NYC, NY, *VP*, Citibank, N.A., RE Industries Div.; **PRIM RE ACT:** Banker; **OTHER RE ACT:** RE investment advisor; **SERVICES:** Comml. RE fin., acquisition and sale; **REP CLIENTS:** Instl. investors in comml. RE; **EDUC:** BS, 1970, Econ., The City Coll. of NY; **GRAD EDUC:** MBA, 1972, Fin., Harvard Bus. School; **OTHER ACT & HONORS:** Dir., Amer. Cancer Soc., L.I. Div.; **HOME ADD:** 2340 Hampton Court, Northbrook, IL 60062, (312)993-3000; **BUS ADD:** 200 South Wacker Dr., Chicago, IL 60606, (312)993-3201.

HOYT, Lawrence F.——**B:** Apr. 19, 1941, Perrsburg, OH, *Pres.*, L.F. Hoyt & Assoc.; **PRIM RE ACT:** Broker, Consultant, Instructor, Property Manager, Syndicator; **SERVICES:** Brokerage, consulting, prop. negotiation, indus. RE; **PREV EMPLOY:** Pres. Vantage Realty, Inc., Columbus Div. of Vantage Co., Dallas, TX; **PROFL AFFIL & HONORS:** NAR, OAR, Columbus Bd. of Realtors, Bldg. Owners & Mgrs. Assn., Soc. of Real Prop. Admin., Columbus Comml. Indus. Investment Realtors, Columbus RE Exchangers, GRI, RPA, Real Prop. Admin (BOMA), Columbus Bd. of Realtors, Million Dollar Club; **EDUC:** Bus. Admin., Toledo Univ.; **MIL SERV:** USMCR 1961-67, Sgt.; **OTHER ACT & HONORS:** Columbus Area C of C; **HOME ADD:** 1976 Andover Rd., Columbus, OH 43212, (614)488-0954; **BUS ADD:** 1631 Northwest Profl. Plaza, Columbus, OH 43220, (614)451-9204.

HOYT, Richard W.——**B:** Apr. 16, 1939, Winchester, MA, *Assoc. Prof. of RE, Chmn. Dept. of Fin.*, Coll. of Bus. & Econ., Dept. of Fin.; **PRIM RE ACT:** Broker, Consultant, Appraiser, Instructor; **SERVICES:** Investment counseling; **REP CLIENTS:** Indiv. investors; **PREV EMPLOY:** State of CA, Dept. of Trans. 1966-68; **PROFL AFFIL & HONORS:** Amer. RE & Urban Econ. Assn.; Alpha Kappa Psi; **EDUC:** BA, 1966, Bus. Adm., CA State Univ. at Long Beach; **GRAD EDUC:** MBA & PhD, 1970 & 1977, Bus. Adm., CA State Univ. & Univ. of AK; **MIL SERV:** US Army, SP4 1959-62; **HOME ADD:** 1920 Hallwood Dr, Las Vegas, NV 89120, (702)798-4612; **BUS ADD:** Univ. of NV, Las Vegas, NV 89154, (702)739-3493.

HRIN, Arthur J.——**B:** Mar. 8, 1943, Plainfield, NJ, *Assoc. Broker, Owner*, Block Bros. Industries; (USA) Inc., I C & I; **PRIM RE ACT:** Broker, Owner/Investor, Instructor; **SERVICES:** Agent for Downtown Prop. Acquisition; **REP CLIENTS:** Cabot, Cabot & Forbes; Diamond Parking; Metropolitan Fed. Savings; DAON; Lincoln Prop. Co.; **PREV EMPLOY:** Grubb & Ellis, Agent - 6 yrs.; **PROFL AFFIL & HONORS:** CCIM Cand.; FIABCI, Intl. Assn.; Nat. & State Assns. of Realtors; Seattle-King Ctry. Bd. of Realtors (Dir.); **EDUC:** Fin., RE, Acctg., Rider Coll., Trenton, NJ; **OTHER ACT & HONORS:** Bd. of Ed., Fieldsboro, NJ 1967-69; **HOME ADD:** 1531 Seattle W., Seattle, WA 98101, (206)285-5115; **BUS ADD:** 1918 Terry Ave., Seattle, WA 98116, (206)625-9500.

HRUSKA, Elias N.——**B:** July 7, 1943, San Francisco, CA, *Owner/Operator*, Investment Planning & Research, Financial Planner Resource Counseling Corp.; **PRIM RE ACT:** Consultant, Appraiser, Owner/Investor, Instructor, Insuror; **OTHER RE ACT:** Registered Princ., NASD; Life, Disability, Casualty Ins. Licensed; Variable annuities; Fin. planning; **SERVICES:** Comprehensive fin./investment planning; **PREV EMPLOY:** Pres., Apex Fin. Corp., a securities firm; **PROFL AFFIL & HONORS:** Intl. Assn. of Fin. Planners; **EDUC:** Italian/Spanish, 1966, Univ. of CA, Berkeley; **GRAD EDUC:** MA, 1968, Italian, Univ. of CA, Berkeley; **EDUC HONORS:** Grad. with Honors; Departmental Citation, Teaching Fellowship; **OTHER ACT & HONORS:** Toastmaster; **HOME ADD:** 139 Salice Way, Campbell, CA 95008, (408)866-8106; **BUS ADD:** 139 Salice Way, Campbell, CA 95008, (408)249-4462.

HU, Jackson K.——**B:** Dec. 3, 1913, Jackson Hu & Associates, Inc.; **PRIM RE ACT:** Broker, Consultant, Appraiser; **PREV EMPLOY:** Indep. RE Appraiser; Mort. Loan RE Appraiser, Bank of Canton, Hongkong Bank of CA, Bank of the Orient, Mitsubishi Bank of CA, Sanwa Bank of CA; Inheritance Tax Appraiser, State of CA; Member of Tax Appeal Bd., San Francisco; **PROFL AFFIL & HONORS:** Soc. of RE Appraisers; MAI; Nat. Assn. of Review Appraisers; Nat. Assn. of RE Bds.; CA RE Assn.; San Francisco Bd. of Realtors, 1980-1981, MAI, Minority Relation Comm., Chmn.; **EDUC:** AB, 1937, Econ./Bus. and Educ., San Francisco State Coll.; **GRAD EDUC:** 1940, Econ./Bus. Admin., NYU/Univ. of CA, Berkeley; **HOME ADD:** 5 17th Ave., San Francisco, CA 94121; **BUS ADD:** 619 Clay St., San Francisco, CA 94111, (415)986-1370.

HUBBARD, Evelyn S.——**B:** Mar. 30, 1953, Atlanta, GA, *Atty.*; **PRIM RE ACT:** Attorney; **SERVICES:** RE closings; **PROFL AFFIL & HONORS:** GA Bar Assn.; CORE Estate Planning Council; **EDUC:** BS, 1974, Psychology, Emory Univ.; **GRAD EDUC:** JD, 1977, Law, Univ. of GA; **EDUC HONORS:** Cum Laude; **HOME ADD:** 205 Camellia Dr., Sylvania, GA 30467, (912)564-9290; **BUS ADD:** 121 N.

Main St., PO Box 1704, Sylvania, GA 30467, (912)564-7421.

HUBER, George B.——**B:** Apr. 12, 1957, Ft. Wayne, IN, *Project Mgr.*, Southland RE Resources, Southland Investment Props.; **PRIM RE ACT:** Developer; **SERVICES:** Comml. Prop. Devel.; **PREV EMPLOY:** RE & Mtg. Investment Dept. of Mutual Life Ins. Co. at NY, 1980; **PROFL AFFIL & HONORS:** Fin. Mgmt. Assn.; **EDUC:** BA, 1979, Bus. Admin., Vanderbilt Univ.; **GRAD EDUC:** MBA, 1981, RE/Fin., Univ. of MI; **EDUC HONORS:** Awarded Grad. with Dist.; **OTHER ACT & HONORS:** Beta Gamma Sigma Nat. Bus. Hon.; Fin. Mgmt. Assn., Nat. Hon. Soc.; **HOME ADD:** 4351 Normandy, Dallas, TX 75205, (214)526-2615; **BUS ADD:** 201 E. John Carpenter Frwy., Suite 401, Irving, TX 75062.

HUBER, J. Neil, Jr.——**B:** Oct. 20, 1943, Albany, NY, *Partner*, Peper, Martin, Jensen, Maichel and Hetlage; **PRIM RE ACT:** Attorney; **PREV EMPLOY:** Partner, Gallop, Johnson, Crebs & Neuman, Clayton, MO 1979-81; Counsel, Temporary Study Comm. on the Future of the Adirondacks 1969-71; **PROFL AFFIL & HONORS:** MO Bar Assn., NY Bar Assn.; ABA; Metropolitan Bar Assn. of St. Louis; **EDUC:** AB, 1965, Govt., Hamilton Coll.; **GRAD EDUC:** JD, 1968, Law, Syracuse Univ. Coll. of Law; **EDUC HONORS:** Law Review, Justinian Honorary Soc.; **HOME ADD:** 2320 Camberwell, Des Peres, MO 63131, (314)966-5884; **BUS ADD:** 720 Olive, St. Louis, MO 63101, (314)421-3850.

HUBERT, Frank D.——**B:** Oct. 7, 1908, Yugoslavia, *Pres.*, Frank D. Hubert Real Estate - Investments; **PRIM RE ACT:** Broker, Consultant, Developer, Owner/Investor; **EDUC:** Bus. Adm. 2 years in Vienna, Austria; **HOME ADD:** 1312 N. Harper Ave., Los Angeles, CA 90046, (213)657-7797; **BUS ADD:** 1312 N. Harper Ave., Los Angeles, CA 90046, (213)657-7797.

HUBERT, James H.——**B:** Apr. 25, 1943, Lawton, OK, *VP Economist*, Federal Home Loan Bank of Seattle; **PRIM RE ACT:** Appraiser, Instructor; **OTHER RE ACT:** Economist; **SERVICES:** Economic analysis; **PREV EMPLOY:** Great NW Fed. S & L Assn. 1967-69; **PROFL AFFIL & HONORS:** Amer. Fin. Assn.; Amer. Econ. Assn.; Soc. of RE Appraisers; Lambda Alpha, SRA; **EDUC:** Bus. Admin., 1971, Urban Devel., Univ. of WA; **GRAD EDUC:** MA, 1973, Economics, Univ. of WA; **MIL SERV:** USMC, 1961-65; **OTHER ACT & HONORS:** Pres., NW Fed. Credit Union; Editor, Seattle-Everett RE Research Report; **HOME ADD:** 10660 Riviera Pl., NE, Seattle, WA 98125, (206)367-0133; **BUS ADD:** 600 Stewart St., Seattle, WA 98125, (206)624-3980.

HUBIN,, Dr. Vincent J.——**B:** July 26, 1918, NYC, *Pres.*, Hubin Assoc.; **PRIM RE ACT:** Instructor, Consultant, Appraiser, Assessor; **SERVICES:** Appraisals, Consulting, Expert Witness, etc.; **PREV EMPLOY:** NYU, NYC; **PROFL AFFIL & HONORS:** ASA, Corp.; **EDUC:** BS, 1947, Bus. Admin., NYU; **GRAD EDUC:** MBA, PhD, 1948, 1959, Land Econ., NYU; **OTHER ACT & HONORS:** Assessor, Saddle River Borough, NJ, 11 yrs.; **HOME ADD:** 211 W. Saddle River Rd., Saddle River, NH 07458; **BUS ADD:** 663 Fifth Ave., NYC, NY 10022, (201)327-2435.

HUBKA, Verne Robert——**B:** Oct. 15, 1925, Diller, NE, *Atty.*, Hubka & Hubka; **PRIM RE ACT:** Engineer, Attorney; **OTHER RE ACT:** Planner & land use; **SERVICES:** Real prop. law, land devel., leases and unlawful detainers; **REP CLIENTS:** Land owners, devels., special dists.; **PREV EMPLOY:** Civil Engr., San Diego Cty. Sanitation Dist.; Planning & Land Use Dept., San Diego Cty.; **EDUC:** BS, 1946, 1963, Naval Sci.; Civil Engr.; Aero Engr.; Metallurgy; Mathematics, Univ. of NE; IA State Univ.; Univ. of Notre Dame; Univ. of So. CA; San Diego State Univ.; **GRAD EDUC:** JD, 1978, Law, Western State Univ.; **MIL SERV:** USN, Cmdr., DFC; 8 Air Medals; US Naval Aviator; Jet Pilot 7000 Hours Flight Time; **OTHER ACT & HONORS:** Notre Dame Man of the Year; San Diego Trial Lawyers Assn.; NASA M.O.L. Project; **HOME ADD:** 4656 56th St., San Diego, CA 92115, (414)583-3328; **BUS ADD:** 5837 El Cajon Blvd., San Diego, CA 92115, (714)583-3366.

HUDDLESTON, Joseph R.——**B:** Feb. 5, 1937, Glasgow, KY, *Partner*, Huddleston Brothers & Duncan; **PRIM RE ACT:** Consultant; **SERVICES:** Conveyance and title opinions; title ins.; **PROFL AFFIL & HONORS:** ABA; KY Bar Assn.; Assn. of Trial Lawyers of Amer.; KY Acad. of Trial Attys.; Bowling Green Bar Assn.; **EDUC:** AB, 1959, Hist. and Amer. Civilization, Princeton Univ.; **GRAD EDUC:** JD, 1962, Law, Univ. of VA; **HOME ADD:** 2626 Smallhouse Road, Bowling Green, KY 42101, (502)842-9253; **BUS ADD:** 1032 College St., PO Box 2130, Bowling Green, KY 42101, (502)842-1659.

HUDGINS, C. Reid, III——**B:** Oct. 30, 1945, Summit, NJ, *Atty. Shareholder, Dir., VP*, Combs, Huff, Carey, Callander & Hudgins; **PRIM RE ACT:** Attorney; **SERVICES:** Legal servs.; **REP CLIENTS:** Devels., synds., indivs. & instn. investors, mgmt. cos.; **PROFL AFFIL & HONORS:** ABA, State Bar of MI, Kalamazoo Cty. Bar Assn.; **EDUC:** BA, 1967, Psych., Olivet Coll.; **GRAD EDUC:** JD, 1970, Law, Vanderbilt Univ. Sch. of Law; **HOME ADD:** 2348 Bronson Blvd., Kalamazoo, MI 49008, (616)382-3383; **BUS ADD:** 3503 Greenleaf Blvd., Kalamazoo, MI 49008, (616)375-2002.

HUDSON, James H.——*Trust Officer RE*, 1st Natl. Bank of Chicago, Trust RE Investments; **PRIM RE ACT:** Banker; **OTHER RE ACT:** RE Acquisitions for Institut. RE Fund F; **BUS ADD:** 900 Two Turtle Creek Village, Dallas, TX 75219, (214)559-2170.

HUDSON, L. Richard——**B:** June 11, 1923, Davenport, IA, *Exec. Dir.*, Community Interfaith Housing, Inc.; **PRIM RE ACT:** Broker, Consultant, Developer, Owner/Investor, Property Manager; **SERVICES:** Prop. mgmt., home repair, multi-family devel., consult.; **PROFL AFFIL & HONORS:** Apt. Assn.; **EDUC:** AB, 1945, Sociology, Drake Univ.; **GRAD EDUC:** MDiv., 1948, Homeletics, Union Theological Seminary; **HOME ADD:** 4579 N. Illinois, Indianapolis, IN 46208, (317)283-3689; **BUS ADD:** 2401 N. Central, Indianapolis, IN 46205, (317)923-1314.

HUDSON, William Campbell, III——**B:** May 7, 1951, NY, NY, *Atty.*, Tighe and Senning; **PRIM RE ACT:** Attorney; **SERVICES:** Legal counseling regarding RE matters; **PROFL AFFIL & HONORS:** ABA (member, Section of RE Prop., Probate); Trust Law; CT Bar Assn.; Middlesex Cty. Bar Assn.; **EDUC:** BA, 1973, Hist., Tulane Univ.; **GRAD EDUC:** JD, 1976, Tulane Univ. School of Law; **OTHER ACT & HONORS:** Rep., CT River Estuary Rgnl. Planning Agency; Pres., Essex Hist. Soc.; VP, Visiting Nurses of Lower Valley; VChmn., Essex Democratic Town Comm.; **HOME ADD:** Book Hill Rd., Essex, CT 06426, (203)767-0333; **BUS ADD:** 71 Main St., POB 757, Essex, CT 06426, (203)767-2195.

HUEY, Arthur T.——**B:** Feb. 15, 1941, Traverse City, MI, *VP*, Michael Latas & Asociates, Exec. Search Div.; **PRIM RE ACT:** Consultant; **SERVICES:** Exec. search servs. for RE indus.; **PREV EMPLOY:** Partner, Mason Woods Co., St. Louis (Carriage trade strip center devel.); Mall Mgr., Plaza Frontenac, Frontenac; Leasing Rep., Crow, Pope & Land, St. Louis; Comml RE Broker, Town & Ctry.; Controller, Leelanau Homestead/Leelanau Schools, Glen Arbor, MI; Auditor, Arthur Anderson & Co., Chicago; **PROFL AFFIL & HONORS:** MO RE Broker, Member Beta Alpha Psi; Member Beta Gamma Sigma; **EDUC:** BA, 1963, Liberal Arts, Middlebury Coll., Middlebury, VT; **GRAD EDUC:** MBA, 1966, Acctg., MI State Univ.; **HOME ADD:** 2501 Oak Springs Lane, St. Louis, MO 63131, (314)567-4725; **BUS ADD:** 2 Lindbergh Plaza Square, St. Louis, MO 63132, (314)993-6500.

HUFFMAN, R. Engene——**B:** Dec. 21, 1925, St. Paul, MN, *Pres.*, L. Bruce Stallard Co., Inc.; **PRIM RE ACT:** Broker, Consultant, Developer, Builder, Owner/Investor, Property Manager; **OTHER RE ACT:** Leasing specialist; **SERVICES:** Indus. & comml. leasing, valuation, mgmt.; **PREV EMPLOY:** Lease Dept. Mgr. for outdoor advertising Firm; **PROFL AFFIL & HONORS:** SIR; Active Member San Diego Bd. of Realtors; **GRAD EDUC:** BA, 1949, Intl. Fin., Univ. of MN; **MIL SERV:** USAF; 2nd Lt.; **HOME ADD:** 1907 W. California St., San Diego, CA 92110, (714)235-6171; **BUS ADD:** 1222 India St., San Diego, CA 92101, (714)235-6171.

HUFFMASTER, William M.——**B:** Sept. 3, 1932, Tebbetts, MO, *VP*, NY Life Ins. Co., RE; **PRIM RE ACT:** Appraiser, Developer, Property Manager, Lender, Owner/Investor; **EDUC:** BS, 1959, Univ. of MO, Columbia, MO; **MIL SERV:** US Army; 1953-1955, Sgt.; **HOME ADD:** 184 Mountain Rd., Wilton, CT 06897, (203)762-3944; **BUS ADD:** 51 Madison Ave., NY, NY 10010, (212)576-7223.

HUFFT, John——*VP Corp. Fac.*, Couchmen Industries, Inc.; **PRIM RE ACT:** Property Manager; **BUS ADD:** PO Box 30, Middlebury, IN 46540, (219)825-5821.*

HUGGARD, Victor A., Jr.——**B:** Sept. 24, 1936, Jamaica, NY, *Dir., Div. of Contract Admin.*, Office of Gen. Serv., State of NY, Design and Constr. Group; **PRIM RE ACT:** Engineer, Attorney, Architect, Builder, Owner/Investor; **SERVICES:** Complete devel., design, constr. & mgmt.; **REP CLIENTS:** All agencies of state, facilities devel. corp. & state univ. constr. fund.; **PREV EMPLOY:** Gen. Counsel, LeCraig Devel. Corp.; Commnr. Public Works, Schenectady Cty.; City Bldg. Inspector, City of Schenectady; **PROFL AFFIL & HONORS:** ABA, NY State Bar Assn., Schenedtady Cty. Bar Assn., Amer. Soc. of CE, Lic. Profl. Engr., Atty.; **EDUC:** BCE, 1962, CE, Valparaiso, Univ.; **GRAD EDUC:** JD, 1967, Law, Brooklyn Law School; **MIL SERV:** US Army, PFC; **OTHER ACT & HONORS:** Pres., Summit Avenue Lutheran Church; Bd. of Dir., Schenectady Community Action Program; **HOME ADD:** 1055 Morningside Ave., Schenectady, NY

12309, (518)346-7196; **BUS ADD:** Empire State Plaza, Tower Bldg., Albany, NY 12242, (518)474-0201.

HUGGINS, Harold H.——**B:** Oct. 17, 1944, Charleston, SC, *Realtor/Appraiser*, Huggins and Harrison, Inc.; **PRIM RE ACT:** Broker, Instructor, Consultant, Appraiser, Developer, Owner/Investor, Insuror; **PROFL AFFIL & HONORS:** NAR, MD. Assn. of Realtors, IREM, RNMI, CPM, CRB, CRS, GRI; **MIL SERV:** USNR, Aviation Cadet; **OTHER ACT & HONORS:** V.-Chmn. Montgomery Cty. Landlord Tenant Comm., Pres.-Lions Eye Bank, Kensington Lions Club, Kensington Baptist Church, Past. Pres. & Dir. - Lions Preschool Center for the Visually Handicapped; **HOME ADD:** 15112 Watergate Rd., Silver Spring, MD 20904, (301)384-0812; **BUS ADD:** 10615 Connecticut Ave., Kensington, MD 20795, (301)949-2800.

HUGHEN, Lowell H.——**B:** Aug. 11, 1937, Wetumpka, AL, *Atty.*, Hansell, Post, Brandon & Dorsey; **PRIM RE ACT:** Attorney; **PROFL AFFIL & HONORS:** ABA, State Bar of GA, GA Mort. Bankers Assn., Atlanta Lawyers Club, Exec. Comm. and Sec. of RE Section of State Bar of GA; **EDUC:** BA, 1959, Liberal Arts, Auburn Univ.; **GRAD EDUC:** LLD, 1968, Law, Emory Univ.; **EDUC HONORS:** Managing Editor, Law Review; **MIL SERV:** USMC, Capt.; **HOME ADD:** 166 W. Wesley Rd., NW, Atlanta, GA 30305, (404)351-6417; **BUS ADD:** 3300 First Natl. Bank Tower, Atlanta, GA 30303, (404)581-8087.

HUGHES, Carey J.——*Pres.*, Hughes Devel. Corp.; **PRIM RE ACT:** Broker, Consultant, Appraiser, Developer, Builder, Owner/Investor, Property Manager, Syndicator; **SERVICES:** Investment counseling, appraisals, valuation, devel., prop. mgmt.; **REP CLIENTS:** Lenders, attys., indiv. investors; **PROFL AFFIL & HONORS:** Burlington Cty. Realtors; SREA; NAREB; NJ Assn. of RE Bds., GRI; **MIL SERV:** US Army; **OTHER ACT & HONORS:** Broker/Pres. Carlyn Realtors, income & investment Real Estate; **HOME ADD:** 261 Sunny Jim Dr., Medford, NJ 08055, (609)654-6400; **BUS ADD:** Suite One, Heritage Lbdg., Rte. 541, Medford, NJ 08055, (609)983-4288.

HUGHES, Daniel M.——*Deputy Under Secy./Field Coordination*, Department of Housing and Urban Development, Office of The Secy/Under Secy.; **PRIM RE ACT:** Lender; **BUS ADD:** 451 Seventh St., S.W., 20410, Washington, DC, (202)755-7426.*

HUGHES, F. Patrick——**B:** Mar. 5, 1948, Baltimore, MD, *Controller, Project Devel.*, BTR Realty, Inc.; **PRIM RE ACT:** Developer, Regulator, Owner/Investor, Property Manager; **OTHER RE ACT:** Fin., promotion, controls; **SERVICES:** Controls, mgmt., prop. mgmt., indus. devel., mort. fin.; **PROFL AFFIL & HONORS:** Natl. Assn. of Indus. & Office Parks; Intl. Council of Shopping Ctrs., CPA; **EDUC:** BA, 1970, Acctg., Loyola Coll.; **GRAD EDUC:** MBA, 1982, Loyola Coll.; **OTHER ACT & HONORS:** Hibernian Soc. of Baltimore; Member of Bd., Light Street S&L; Alumni Bd., Loyola Coll.; **HOME ADD:** 134 Newburg Ave., Baltimore, MD 21228, (301)788-8344; **BUS ADD:** 4646 Wilkens Ave., Baltimore, MD 21229, (301)247-4991.

HUGHES, Fred——**B:** Aug. 4, 1930, Queens, NY, *CFP, Pres.*, Fred Hughes Co.; **PRIM RE ACT:** Broker, Consultant, Owner/Investor, Instructor, Insuror, Syndicator; **OTHER RE ACT:** Certified Fin. Planner; **SERVICES:** Tax Shelters, Overall Planning, Tax Free Exchanges; **PROFL AFFIL & HONORS:** VP & Dir. L.I. Chap., Int. Assn. of Fin. Planners, DDE, CFP, AE; **HOME ADD:** Box 95, Centerport, NY 11721; **BUS ADD:** 295 East Main St., Centerport, NY 11721, (516)673-0660.

HUGHES, George G.——**B:** Feb. 1, 1941, Columbus, OH, *Pres.*, Oakwood Corp.; **PRIM RE ACT:** Consultant, Developer, Owner/Investor, Property Manager, Syndicator, Real Estate Publisher; **SERVICES:** Investment counseling, devel. and synd. of comml. props., prop. mgmt.; Restoration; **REP CLIENTS:** Lenders and indiv. investors in comml. props.; **PROFL AFFIL & HONORS:** RESSAI, Columbus Bd. of Realtors, SRS - Specialist in RE Synd.; **EDUC:** BA, 1963, Hist. and Philosophy, St. Charles Coll.; **GRAD EDUC:** MA, 1967, Theology, Catholic Univ., Washington, DC; **OTHER ACT & HONORS:** Leathlerkips Yacht Club, Metropolitan Club of Columbus, Bd. Member - Northwest Mental Health Center; OH Div. of Securities' RE Syndication Comm.; **HOME ADD:** 1161 Lincoln Rd., Columbus, OH 43212, (614)486-5800; **BUS ADD:** 7792 Olentangy River Rd., Worthington, OH 43085, (614)846-7792.

HUGHES, J. Michael——**B:** May 1, 1944, Jacksonville FL, *Atty.*, Mahoney, Hadlow & Adams; **PRIM RE ACT:** Attorney; **REP CLIENTS:** Lenders, dev., indiv. investors in R.E.; **PROFL AFFIL & HONORS:** ABA, FL Bar Assn., Jacksonville Bar Assn.; **EDUC:** BA, 1967, Coll. of Arts & Sci., Univ. of VA; **GRAD EDUC:** JD, 1970, Coll. of Law, FL State Univ.; **OTHER ACT & HONORS:** Dir., Childrens Home Soc. of FL, Pres., Univ. of VA Alumni of Jacksonville; **BUS ADD:** 100 Laura St., PO Box 4099, Jacksonville, FL 32201, (904)354-1100.

HUGHES, James A.——**B:** Mar. 21, 1949, Pikeville, KY, *Pres.*, James A. Hughes & Associates; **PRIM RE ACT:** Developer, Owner/Investor, Property Manager; **SERVICES:** Shopping Ctr. Devel. and Leasing; **REP CLIENTS:** Equity Investors and Natl. Retail Chains; **PROFL AFFIL & HONORS:** Intl. Council of Shopping Ctrs.; C of C; **EDUC:** BBA, 1971, Mktg. & Acctg., Morchand State Univ.; **EDUC HONORS:** Deans List; **OTHER ACT & HONORS:** Member KY Colonels, Sigma Pi Frat., Lt. Gov. KY-TN Dist. Key Club Intl.; **HOME ADD:** 27 Greer St., Prestonsburg, KY 41653, (606)886-8141; **BUS ADD:** 1292 Riverview, Prestonsburg, KY 41653, (606)886-2403.

HUGHES, Ronald——**B:** Apr. 26, 1932, Bryn Mawr, PA, *Gen. Partner*, Hadly Hughdak Ventures; **PRIM RE ACT:** Developer, Owner/Investor, Property Manager; **SERVICES:** Devel., lease, manage office bldgs.; **EDUC:** BS, 1959, Bus. Admin., Univ. AZ, Tucson, AZ; **MIL SERV:** US Army; **HOME ADD:** 67 Prospect Ave., Montclair, NJ 07042; **BUS ADD:** 799 Bloomfield Ave., Verona, NJ 07044, (201)239-3777.

HUGHES, Ryland James——**B:** Dec. 23, 1929, Richmond, VA, *Pres.*, Ryland J. Hughes, Real Estate Appraiser/Consultant; **PRIM RE ACT:** Broker, Consultant, Appraiser; **SERVICES:** Indep. appraisals, ct. testimony, rights-of-ways; **REP CLIENTS:** Indiv. and Comml. Landowners; **PREV EMPLOY:** VA Dept. of Highways; **PROFL AFFIL & HONORS:** Nat. Assn. of RE Appraisers; Nat. Assn. of Review Appraisers; Assoc. Member, VA Assoc. of Assessing Officers, CRA, CREA; **EDUC:** Urban Studies, 1981, Urban planning, VA Commonwealth Univ.; **MIL SERV:** USMC, Sgt., Good Conduct; **HOME ADD:** 15200 Midlothian Turnpike, Midlothian, VA 23113, (804)794-8130; **BUS ADD:** 15200 Midlothian Turnpike, Midlothian, VA 23113, (804)794-8130.

HUGHES, Stephen M.——**B:** July 29, 1945, San Francisco, CA, *V.P. Resid. Mgr.*, Coldwell Banker Comml. RE Services; **PRIM RE ACT:** Broker; **SERVICES:** Comml., Indust., Investments; **PROFL AFFIL & HONORS:** NAIOP, Dir. Phila. Chap.; Phila. Bd. of Realtors, C&I Div., Dir; ICSC; **EDUC:** BA, 1967, Bus. Admin., Univ. of the Pacific; **GRAD EDUC:** MBA, 1968, Univ. of S. CA; **MIL SERV:** USMC, Sgt.; **HOME ADD:** 1330 Partridge Lane, Villanova, PA 19085, (215)527-3856; **BUS ADD:** 2000 Market St. 1415, Philadelphia, PA 19103, (215)299-3210.

HUGHES, Stephen V., Jr.——**B:** Sept. 27, 1924, Lawrence, MA, *Mgr. of RE*, New England Electric System, New England Power Serv. Co.; **PRIM RE ACT:** Broker, Appraiser, Property Manager, Engineer; **SERVICES:** RE & Land planning, site investigation & review, acquisition & project mgmt.; **PROFL AFFIL & HONORS:** Reg. Prof. Engr., Reg. Land Surveyor, Sr. Member IR/WA, Past Pres. & Nat. Dir., New England Chapter IR/WA; **EDUC:** BS in Civil Engr., 1950, Civil & Sanitary (Environmental), MI State Univ.; **MIL SERV:** US Army, Capt. Bronze Star & Misc.; **OTHER ACT & HONORS:** Bd. of Dir. - Amer. Red Cross; **HOME ADD:** 15 Wachusett Ave., Lawrence, MA 01841, (617)686-0950; **BUS ADD:** 25 Research Dr., Westboro, MA 01581, (617)366-9011.

HUGHES, Vester Thomas, Jr.——**B:** May 24, 1928, San Angelo, TX, *Partner*, Hughes & Hill; **PRIM RE ACT:** Attorney, Owner/Investor; **SERVICES:** Legal advice on RE taxation; **REP CLIENTS:** Trammell Crow Co., W.W. Caruth, Jr.; **PREV EMPLOY:** Jackson, Wlaker, Winstead, Cantwell & Miller, 1955-58; Partner 1958-76; **PROFL AFFIL & HONORS:** Amer. Law Inst., Exec. Council; ABA; **EDUC:** BA, 1949, Pre-law, Rice Univ.; **GRAD EDUC:** LLB, 1952, Tax law, Harvard Law School; **EDUC HONORS:** With distinction, Harvard Law Review, Cum Laude; **MIL SERV:** US Army, 1st Lt.; **OTHER ACT & HONORS:** Various Speeches and articles on RE taxation; **HOME ADD:** 1222 Commerce St. #2215, Dallas, TX 75202, (214)748-1969; **BUS ADD:** 1000 Mercantile Dallas Bldg., Dallas, TX 75202, (214)651-0477.

HUGO, Martin A., Jr.——**B:** Apr. 5, 1948, Oconto, WI, *RE Dir.*, Safeway Stores, Inc., Kansas City; **OTHER RE ACT:** Retail RE, new store devel. & surplus prop. mktg.; **SERVICES:** Retail site selection, lease negotiation, site acquisition, etc.; **REP CLIENTS:** I work exclusively for Safeway, where I manage their Kansas City Div., RE Dept.; **PREV EMPLOY:** US Postal Serv, RE Dept., 1975; Continental Mort. Ins., 1974-75; WI Dept. of Transportation Appraiser, 1973-74; **PROFL AFFIL & HONORS:** Intl. Counsel of Shopping Centers, MO RE Broker & KS RE Broker; **EDUC:** BBA, 1973, RE & Urban Land Econ., Univ. of WI, Madison & Green Bay Campuses; **MIL SERV:** US Army, E-5, Air Medal with 'V' Service; **HOME ADD:** 131 W. 61st Terr., Kansas City, MO 64113, (816)361-8968; **BUS ADD:** PO Box 461, Kansas City, MO 64141, (816)932-8222.

HUGUET, Terry N.——B: July 19, 1939, Alhambra, CA, *Chief Appraiser*, Huguet & Associates; **PRIM RE ACT:** Broker, Consultant, Appraiser, Instructor; **SERVICES:** Urban Land Econ. and Valuation Servs.; **REP CLIENTS:** Firestone Co., Bethlehem Steel Corp., Exxon Oil Corp., Investors Mort. Ins. Corp., Merrill-Lynch Co., Executrans, Inc., Transamerica Relocation Corp.; **PREV EMPLOY:** Locke Land Servs., Long Beach, CA; Appraisal Assocs., Long Beach, CA; **PROFL AFFIL & HONORS:** Sr. Member, Amer. Assn. of Cert. Appraisers; Sr. Member, NARA, Cert. Appraiser, Sr.; CRA; **EDUC:** AA, 1974, Physical Sci., CA State Univ. at Long Beach/Long Beach City Coll.; BS, 1977, Physical Sci., CA State Univ. at Long Beach; **MIL SERV:** USN, E-2; **OTHER ACT & HONORS:** Rotary Club of Amer.; Elks Club of Amer.; CA RE Teachers Assn.; CA Appraisal Council; **HOME ADD:** 4318 Deeboyar Ave., Lakewood, CA 90712; **BUS ADD:** 6754 Paramount Blvd., Long Beach, CA 90805, (213)633-7299.

HUI, Kane K.——B: Feb. 17, 1949, China, *Pres.*, Amcor Devel. Inc.; **PRIM RE ACT:** Owner/Investor; **SERVICES:** Devel. prop. mgmt., synd., investment counseling; **REP CLIENTS:** Intl. Investors & insts.; **PROFL AFFIL & HONORS:** Honolulu Bd. of Realtors; **EDUC:** BBA, 1973, Acctg., Travel Indus. Mgmt., Univ. of HI; **OTHER ACT & HONORS:** Rotary Club of Honolulu; **HOME ADD:** 1197 Lunalilo Home Rd., Honolulu, HI 96825, (808)395-7882; **BUS ADD:** 1164 Bishop St., Suite 1512, Honolulu, HI 96813, (808)536-7061.

HULL, Lewis A.——B: July 7, 1916, Clinton, IL, *Sr. Partner*, Hull, Campbell, Robinson & Gibson; **PRIM RE ACT:** Broker, Attorney; **GRAD EDUC:** JD, 1939, Univ. of MO; **MIL SERV:** US Air Corp., Capt.; **HOME ADD:** R.R. #11, Hammond, IL 61929, (217)677-2353; **BUS ADD:** PO Box 1765, 500 Millikin Ct., Decatur, IL 62525, (217)429-4296.

HULSEBERG, Edmund W.——B: Aug. 3, 1932, Cook Cty., IL, *Land Devel. Consultant*; **PRIM RE ACT:** Broker, Consultant, Owner/Investor; **OTHER RE ACT:** Land surveyor & planner, constr. mgmt.; **SERVICES:** Prop. mgmt. & consultant; **PREV EMPLOY:** 20 yrs. of exp. of surveying, RE constr. and facilities engr.; **PROFL AFFIL & HONORS:** NSPE; AIPE; SORPA; RE broker; RLS; CPE; RPA Candidate; **MIL SERV:** USN, TM-3 (SS), Submarine Servs.; **OTHER ACT & HONORS:** W. Springfield Planning Bd., since 1978; **HOME ADD:** 60 Tatham Hill Rd., W. Springfield, MA 01089, (413)734-0817; **BUS ADD:** 60 Tatham Hill Rd., West Springfield, MA 01089.

HULT, James M.——B: July 15, 1951, Denver, CO, *Pres.*, Venture Grp, Ltd.; **PRIM RE ACT:** Broker, Consultant, Attorney, Owner/Investor; **SERVICES:** RE legal serv., and fin. analysis & feasibility; **PROFL AFFIL & HONORS:** CO Bar Assn., CO Broker; **EDUC:** BS, 1973, Bus. & Fin., Univ. of CO, Boulder; **GRAD EDUC:** JD, 1978, Bus./Law, Univ. of CO, Boulder; **OTHER ACT & HONORS:** Other bus. tel. (303)443-7447 (Real Estate); **HOME ADD:** 4000 Carlock, Boulder, CO 80303, (303)494-5269; **BUS ADD:** 2040 Broadway, Ste 200, Boulder, CO 80302, (303)447-1632.

HULTING, Frederick B., Jr.——B: Jan. 25, 1933, Oakland, CA, *Atty. at Law*; **PRIM RE ACT:** Broker, Attorney, Syndicator; **SERVICES:** Legal, all phases of RE; **REP CLIENTS:** RE devel., owners & investors; **PREV EMPLOY:** Atty., RE Div., Safeway Stores; Counsel, Kaiser Aetna; **PROFL AFFIL & HONORS:** CA State Bar, ABA, Fallbrook Bd. of Realtors; **EDUC:** AB, 1956, Stanford Univ.; **GRAD EDUC:** LLB, 1960, Hastings Coll. of the Law; **HOME ADD:** 27759 Tierra Vista, Rancho California, CA 92390, (714)676-4776; **BUS ADD:** 27403 Ynez Rd., Suite 207, Rancho California, CA 92390, (714)676-6196.

HUME, Gregory R.——B: Nov. 28, 1946, *VP, Marketing*, The Koll Co.; **PRIM RE ACT:** Developer, Builder, Property Manager; **OTHER RE ACT:** Contractor; **PREV EMPLOY:** Coldwell Banker - Broker; **PROFL AFFIL & HONORS:** NAIOP, Reg. VP; **EDUC:** BA, 1971, Bus. Admin., Univ. of WA, Seattle, WA; **HOME ADD:** 5811 111th Ave., SE, Bellevue, WA 98006, (206)746-6359; **BUS ADD:** 2021 152nd Ave., NE, Redmond, WA 98052, (206)643-1776.

HUMFELD, Patricia A.——B: Dec. 1, 1934, St. Louis, MO, *RE Analyst*, Monsanto Co., Treasury; **OTHER RE ACT:** Acquisition, Disposition & Analysis; **PREV EMPLOY:** Pioneer Nat. Title Ins. Escrow and Title Officer; Ridgewood Const. Co., VP; Associate Broker; **PROFL AFFIL & HONORS:** NACORE; St. Louis Women's Commerce Assn., VP, Indus. Council, NACORE; Pres., St. Louis Chap., NACORE; Broker, State of MO; **EDUC:** BA, 1963, Fine Arts/RE, Washington Univ.; **OTHER ACT & HONORS:** St. Louis Art Museum; Valley Sailing Assn.; Monsanto Corporate Pac, member of contributions comm.; **HOME ADD:** 71 Greendale Dr., St. Louis, MO 63121, (314)851-1898; **BUS ADD:** 800 N. Lindbergh, St. Louis, MO 63166, (314)694-7582.

HUMPHREY, Robert F.——B: May 25, 1947, Batavia, NY, *J.D.*, Cooney, Fussell and Humphrey; **PRIM RE ACT:** Attorney; **SERVICES:** Gen. RE and banking; **REP CLIENTS:** Comml. and savings banks, limited partnerships, indivs.; **PREV EMPLOY:** Instr., Genessee Community Coll., "RE Salesperson" and "RE Broker"; **PROFL AFFIL & HONORS:** ABA, NY State Bar Assn.; **EDUC:** BA, 1968, Eng., Canisius Coll.; **GRAD EDUC:** JD, 1971, Univ. of VA, School of Law; **EDUC HONORS:** Editor, VA Legal Research Grp.; **OTHER ACT & HONORS:** Pres., Genessee Cty. C of C 1981; Dir., Community Chest, Junior Achievement, etc.; **HOME ADD:** 6543 Prentice Rd., Stafford, NY 14143, (716)768-6259; **BUS ADD:** 3 Main St., LeRoy, NY 14482, (716)768-6259.

HUMPHREYS, Richard L.——B: Oct. 6, 1943, Sacramento, CA, *Exec. VP, Loan Admin.*, First Fed. S&L Assn. of HI, Loan Admin.; **PRIM RE ACT:** Lender; **SERVICES:** Resid. loans, comml. const. interim & takeout loans; **REP CLIENTS:** Devel. indiv.; **PREV EMPLOY:** Amfac Fin. Corp., 1973-79, Sr. VP Mgr. Interim Lending/Mort. Banking Div.; **PROFL AFFIL & HONORS:** Mort. Bankers Assn., Nat. S&L League, US League of Savings Assns., C of C; **EDUC:** BS, 1967, Bus. Admin., Menlo Coll., Menlo Park, CA; **HOME ADD:** 55 Nawiliwill St., Honolulu, HI 96825; **BUS ADD:** 851 Fort St., Honolulu, HI 96813, (808)531-9404.

HUNKER, George H., Jr.——B: Sept. 1, 1914, Las Vegas, NM, *Pres. (Sr. Partner)*, Hunker - Fedric, P.A., Law Offices; **PRIM RE ACT:** Attorney; **OTHER RE ACT:** Counselor; **SERVICES:** Specializing in problems relating to US oil and gas leases; **REP CLIENTS:** FL Exploration Co., Cotton Petroleum Corp., J.C. Williamson (Ind. Oil Operator); **BUS ADD:** 210 Hinkle Bldg., Roswell, NM 88202, (505)622-2700.

HUNN, Erich A. L.——B: April 26, 1929, Heidelberg, Germany, *Pres.*, Hunn Enterprises, Inc.; Calabash Realty Co.; **PRIM RE ACT:** Broker, Consultant, Appraiser, Developer, Builder, Owner/Investor, Property Manager; **PREV EMPLOY:** Hunn Enterprises, Inc., Pres. Hunn Enterprises, Intl., Pres.; **PROFL AFFIL & HONORS:** Bd. of Realtors, C of C, Licensed RE Broker in NC & SC, Gen. Cont. - Devel.; **EDUC:** BS, 1962, Econ., Europe; **HOME ADD:** 5724 Springs Ave., Myrtle Beach, SC 29577, (803)449-5590; **BUS ADD:** Rt. 1-Box 148, Shallotte, NC 28459, (919)579-6590.

HUNNICUTT, Richard D.——B: Jan. 2, 1947, Macon, Bibb Co., GA, *VP*, Sun Bank, N.A., RE Loan Dept. - Resid. Loans; **PRIM RE ACT:** Banker; **SERVICES:** Resid. counseling, acq. & dev. loans, valuation, const. loans, permanent loans; **REP CLIENTS:** Inst. investors, FNMA, GNMA; **PREV EMPLOY:** James T. Barnes Mort. Co., Fickling & Walker Mort. Inc., SunBank Mort. Co.; **PROFL AFFIL & HONORS:** Instr. - Amer. Institute of Banking (AIB), Past Pres. - MBA of Cent. FL, Member Bd. of Gov's. MBA of FL, Past Dir. - Home Bldr. Assn. of Mid FL, Member Bd. of Realtors, FL & Orlando - Winter Park, Various Awards as Comm. Chmn.; **MIL SERV:** USN, Radarman 2, Various Decorations - Vietnam; **OTHER ACT & HONORS:** 32 Degree Mason; W. Master of Masonic Lodge; **HOME ADD:** 1212 Sunshine Tree Blvd., Longwood, FL 32750, (305)862-5951; **BUS ADD:** PO Box 3467, 200 South Orange Ave., Orlando, FL 32802, (305)237-5010.

HUNNICUTT, Warren, Jr.——B: May 15, 1924, Columbus, GA, *Pres. & Chmn.*, Warren Hunnicutt, Jr., Inc.; **PRIM RE ACT:** Broker, Consultant, Appraiser, Developer, Instructor, Syndicator, Assessor; **SERVICES:** RE Appraiser/Consultant; **REP CLIENTS:** Banks, ins. cos., S & L indivs., corps.; **PREV EMPLOY:** Pres., Hunnicutt & Assoc., Inc. (sold co.); **PROFL AFFIL & HONORS:** AIREA (Past Chap. Pres.); Amer. Soc. of RE Counselors; St. Petersburg Bd. of Realtors (Past Pres.); Former Chap. Pres.) Soc. of RE Appraisers, MAI, CRE; **HOME ADD:** 7946 Ninth Ave. So., St. Petersburg, FL 33707, (813)347-6683; **BUS ADD:** 5511 Central Ave., St. Petersburg, FL 33710, (813)381-9222.

HUNT, Harry H., III——B: Oct. 5, 1933, *Pres.*, Snyder-Hunt Corp., Exec. Offices; **PRIM RE ACT:** Developer, Builder, Owner/Investor, Property Manager; **PROFL AFFIL & HONORS:** AIREA: Member, Alumni Assn., Univ. of VA; Student Aid Found., Member, Univ. of VA; Member, Hokie Club, VA Polytechnic Inst. and State Univ.; Member, Ctry. Club of VA; Member, Sons of Amer. Revolution;

Member, Blacksburg C of C; Member, Apt. Owners and Mgrs. Assn. of Amer.; Member, Mgmt. Exchange Grp., Nat. Profl. Apt. Devel. Grp.; Dir., Blacksburg Apt. House Council; Member, Roanoke Valley Chapt., Nat. Assn. of Home Builders; Member, Roanoke Valley Apt. House Council; Past Pres., Profl. Govt. League, Local Civic Org.; Member, Bd. of Adjustment and Appeals, Montgomery Cty., VA; Speaker, Apt. Builder-Devel. Nat. Conference and Exposition, Miami, FL, sponsored by Multi-Family Housing News; Dir., First Nat. Exchange Bank of Montgomery Cty.; Chmn., Bd. of Trustees, Montgomery Cty. Hospital; MAI; Grad., Mort. Banking School of Amer., Mort. Bankers Assn. of Amer.; **EDUC:** BA, 1958, Commerce/Bus., Univ. of VA; **GRAD EDUC:** Northwestern Univ.; **MIL SERV:** US Army; **HOME ADD:** Rte. 1, Box 427-A, Blacksburg, VA 24060, (703)552-8887; **BUS ADD:** 800 Hethwood Blvd., Blacksburg, VA 24060, (703)552-3515.

HUNT, Philip——**B:** Dec. 29, 1935, Mobile, AL, *VP, General Counsel & Asst. Secy.*, Morrison Inc., Legal; **PRIM RE ACT:** Appraiser; **PROFL AFFIL & HONORS:** FL Bar; ABA; Natl. Rest. Assn.; Natl. Assn. of Mfgrs; Assoc. Ind. of AL; Food Serv. & Lodging Inst.; US Chamber of Comm.; Natl. Right to Work Comm. of 1000; NACORE; Amer. Mgmt. Assn.; **EDUC:** BS, 1960, Geology, FL State Univ.; MS, 1961, Bus. Admin., FL State Univ.; **GRAD EDUC:** JD, 1966, Law, Stetson Univ.; **MIL SERV:** USAF; **OTHER ACT & HONORS:** Bd. of Mgmt., YMCA; Rotary Club; **HOME ADD:** 203 Tuthill Ln., Mobile, AL, (205)342-6356; **BUS ADD:** 4721 Morrison Dr., POB 160266, Mobile, AL 36625, (205)344-3000.

HUNT, R.A.——*Realty Mgr.*, Western Electric Co., Inc.; **PRIM RE ACT:** Property Manager; **BUS ADD:** 222 Broadway, NY 10038, (212)571-3605.*

HUNT, Thomas B.——**B:** July 4, 1934, Columbia, MO, *Pres.*, T.B. Hunt & Associates; **PRIM RE ACT:** Broker, Developer, Owner/Investor; **PREV EMPLOY:** Trust banking; **EDUC:** AB, 1956, Econ., Univ. of MO, Columbia; **GRAD EDUC:** JD, 1959, Univ. of MO, Columbia; **MIL SERV:** US Army, JAGC, Capt.; **HOME ADD:** Rt. 3 Box 73A, Santa Fe, NM 87501, (505)988-1094; **BUS ADD:** Rt. 3 73A, PO Box 4963, Santa Fe, NM 87502, (505)988-1094.

HUNT, Vard Stephen——**B:** Mar. 15, 1948, Los Angeles, CA, *Principal/Gen. Partner*, V. Stephen Hunt & Assoc. & Separate Ltd. Partnerships for each Devel.; **PRIM RE ACT:** Broker, Consultant, Developer, Appraiser; **OTHER RE ACT:** Investor; **SERVICES:** Acquisition, devel., land planning, devel. & feasibility consulting; **REP CLIENTS:** CA, HI & Intl.: Banks, S&L's, Devels. & Investors; **PREV EMPLOY:** VP, Dir. of RE & Research, Gibraltar S&L, Beverly Hills; UCLA, RE Instr.; **PROFL AFFIL & HONORS:** Nat. Assn. of Bus. Econs.; CA RE Assn., Recipient of So. CA MAI Award; **EDUC:** BS, 1970, Econ./Fin., Univ. of So. CA; **GRAD EDUC:** MBA, 1971, RE, Univ. of So. CA; **EDUC HONORS:** Magna Cum Laude, Beta Gamma Sigma Hon. Soc.; **OTHER ACT & HONORS:** Bd. of Dirs., United Realty Investors (Amer. Stock Exchange); **HOME ADD:** 910 Strand, Hermosa Beach, CA 90254, (213)379-6832; **BUS ADD:** 9595 Wilshire Blvd., Beverly Hills, CA 90212, (213)379-7842.

HUNTER, Charles H.——*Exec VP*, Kissinger/Hunter Co.; **PRIM RE ACT:** Developer; **BUS ADD:** 300 Bryant Bldg., 1102 Grand Ave., Kansas City, MO 64106, (816)842-2690.*

HUNTER, Donald E.——**B:** Jan. 13, 1941, Chicago, IL, *Exec. VP*, Zuchelli, Hunter & Associates, Inc., Co-owner, Amer. RE Investments, Inc.; Toombs Devel. Co.; **PRIM RE ACT:** Consultant, Developer, Owner/Investor; **OTHER RE ACT:** RE Economist; **SERVICES:** Negotiating/packaging large-scale comml. mixed-use projects (–50 million–-250 million range); **REP CLIENTS:** Rockefeller Center Devel. Corp., Gerald D. Hines Interests, Daniel Intl., Cities of Jacksonville, Fort Worth, Cleveland, New Haven; **PREV EMPLOY:** Devel. Project Mgr., Westinghouse Electric Corp. 1969-1973; Developed Jakarta Indus. Estate in Indonesia; **PROFL AFFIL & HONORS:** Bd. of Dir. Nat. Council for Urban Econ. Devel., Several projects described in Urban Land Institute's Downtown Development Handbook as innovative public/private Partnerships; **EDUC:** BArch., 1963, Arch./RE Econ., Univ. of KS; **GRAD EDUC:** MCP, 1967, RE Econ., Housing, Univ. of CA - Berkeley; **EDUC HONORS:** Honor Roll, AIA Scholarship, Laverne Noyes Scholarship; **MIL SERV:** USN, Lt., Vietnam Service Medal Unit Commendation; **HOME ADD:** 104 Fogle Dr., Annapolis, MD 21403, (301)268-3551; **BUS ADD:** MD Nat. Bank Bldg., 160 South St., Annapolis, MD 21401, (301)269-6565.

HUNTER, Ernest H.——**B:** Oct. 20, 1944, Baraboo, WI, *Pres.*, Hunter Realty Inc.; **PRIM RE ACT:** Broker, Developer, Builder, Owner/Investor; **PROFL AFFIL & HONORS:** NAR, RNMI, GRI, CRS; **HOME ADD:** 3906 Eaton Dr., Rockford, IL 61111, (815)877-1611; **BUS ADD:** 4616 E. State St, Rockford, IL 61108, (815)397-6146.

HUNTER, J. Edwin——**B:** Jan. 12, 1935, Statesville, NC, *Pres.*, Hunter Realty & Construction; **PRIM RE ACT:** Broker, Appraiser, Builder, Property Manager; **SERVICES:** RE counseling and third party corporate relocations, land devel.; **REP CLIENTS:** Equitable Relocation, Merril Lynch, Homequity, Exec. Relocation, 3M, FMC, So. Bell, Exectrans; **PREV EMPLOY:** So. Bell, 1957-1962; Shelburne Mfg. Co., Gen. Mgr., 1962-1973; **PROFL AFFIL & HONORS:** Member, Past Pres., State Dir., Iredell Cty. Bd. of Realtors; NC Assn. of Realtors; NAR; NC & Nat. Homebuilders; Candidate, Amer. Inst. of RE Appraisers, GRI; **EDUC:** BS, 4yrs., Bus., The Citadel; **MIL SERV:** US Army, 1st Lt.; **OTHER ACT & HONORS:** Elected Member, Statesville School Bd., Current (12 yrs.); Tr., So. Baptist Annuity Bd., Dallas, TX; Rotary Club, Past Treas. & Dir.; **HOME ADD:** 1100 Lake Side Dr., Statesville, NC 28677, (704)872-6748; **BUS ADD:** 956 Davie Ave., Statesville, NC 28677, (704)872-0923.

HUNTER, Joseph R.——**B:** Feb. 26, 1946, *Owner*, Joe R. Hunter RE; **PRIM RE ACT:** Broker, Consultant, Developer, Property Manager; **SERVICES:** Leasing, mgmt., tenant improvements, sales, devel.; **PREV EMPLOY:** LA Oil & Marine Ctr.; RE Mgmt. Corp.; **PROFL AFFIL & HONORS:** BOMA; **EDUC:** BS, 1968, Commerce, Ferris State Coll.; **OTHER ACT & HONORS:** United Way Div. Chmn.; Real Prop. Administrator by BOMA Intl.; Founder Office Bldg. Assn. in Metairie, LA; **HOME ADD:** 1209 High Ave., Metairie, LA 70001, (504)455-6166; **BUS ADD:** 1209 High Ave., Metairie, LA 70001, (504)455-6166.

HUNTER, Robert N.——**B:** June 5, 1930, Palmer, MA, *VP*, CM Mutual Life Ins. Co., Urban Investments; **PRIM RE ACT:** Lender, Owner/Investor; **PROFL AFFIL & HONORS:** AIREA, MAI; **EDUC:** BA, 1952, Econ., Trinity Coll., Hartford, CT; **GRAD EDUC:** MBA, 1956, Fin., Univ. of MI; **MIL SERV:** USAF; 1st Lt.; **BUS ADD:** 140 Garden St., Hartford, CT 06115, (203)727-6537.

HUNTER, Still, Jr.——**B:** Apr. 26, 1939, Jasper, AL, *Pres.*, Still Hunter & Associates, Inc.; **PRIM RE ACT:** Consultant, Developer, Owner/Investor; **SERVICES:** RE Devel.; **PREV EMPLOY:** Mgr. RE, Harbert Corp. 1968-80; Project Mgr., Riverchase, The Harbert-Equitable Joint Venture 1974-76; **PROFL AFFIL & HONORS:** Birmingham C of C; **EDUC:** BSME, 1961, Mech. Engr., Univ. of AL; **GRAD EDUC:** MBA, 1968, Mgmt., Harvard Grad. Sch. of Bus. Admin.; **EDUC HONORS:** Grad. 1st in Engr. Class (Tau Beta Pi Soph. & Sr. Award); **MIL SERV:** US Army, 1st. Lt.; **HOME ADD:** 3112 Sharpsburg Circ., Birmingham, AL 35210, (205)951-2519; **BUS ADD:** PO Box 76079, Birmingham, AL 35253, (205)870-3700.

HUNTER, William——*Executive Director*, National Realty Club; **OTHER RE ACT:** Profl. Assn. Admin.; **BUS ADD:** 12E 41st St., New York, NY 10017, (212)532-3100.*

HUNTER, William A.——**B:** June 23, 1927, Pittsburgh, PA, *VP*, Major Realty Corp.; **PRIM RE ACT:** Broker, Consultant, Developer, Property Manager; **SERVICES:** Devel. of comml., resid. and indus. prop., consultant; **REP CLIENTS:** Nat. investors and devel. (hotels, restaurants, etc.); office bldgs. devel. and indus. devel. as well as devel. for our own account; **PREV EMPLOY:** Gulf Oil RE Devel. Co.; **PROFL AFFIL & HONORS:** NACORE; IREM; Advisory Bd. Member City of Orlando; FL Planning & Zoning Assn.; Nat., State and City Bd. of RE; AOPA, Cert. Prop. Mgr.; Man of the Yr., Gulf Oil RE Devel. Corp.; **EDUC:** BS, 1950, Fin./Econ., Univ. of Pittsburgh; **GRAD EDUC:** MBA, 1954, RE/Fin., Univ. of Pittsburgh; **EDUC HONORS:** Sigma Cum Laude, Phi Beta Kappa, Phi Beta Sigma, Order of Artus (Econ.); **HOME ADD:** 6158 Yarrow Ct., Orlando, FL 32811, (305)351-9400; **BUS ADD:** 5750 Major Blvd., Suite 500, Orlando, FL 32805, (305)351-1111.

HUNTER, William E., Jr.——**B:** Sept. 24, 1943, Detroit, MI, *Broker*, Barnes Realtors; **PRIM RE ACT:** Broker, Appraiser; **SERVICES:** Residential Sales, Residential Appraiser; **PREV EMPLOY:** Church of Christ Minister; **PROFL AFFIL & HONORS:** TN Assn. of Realtors, State Energy Chmn. (1981), CRB, CRS, & CREA Designations; **EDUC:** Falls Bus. Coll.; **GRAD EDUC:** Bus., 1963; **EDUC HONORS:** Pres. Student Body; **HOME ADD:** 173 Delvin Dr., Antioch, TN 37013, (615)833-0507; **BUS ADD:** 417 Welshwood Dr., Nashville, TN 37211.

HUNTLEY, Steven T.——**B:** Apr. 12, 1952, Los Angeles, CA, *VP - Acquisitions*, Triton Fin. Corp., Triton Prop. Div.; **PRIM RE ACT:** Developer, Owner/Investor, Property Manager, Syndicator; **SERVICES:** Investment counseling, devel. and synd. of comml. props., prop. mgmt.; **REP CLIENTS:** Indiv. and instl. investors in comml. props.; **PREV EMPLOY:** Corp. lending officer - Wells Fargo Bank, San Francisco, CA; **PROFL AFFIL & HONORS:** CA RE Broker, Phi Kappa Phi - National Honor Soc., Omicron Delta Epsilon - National Soc. of Economics; **EDUC:** BA, 1974, Econs./Mathematics, CA State

Univ., Long Beach; **GRAD EDUC:** MBA, 1978, Fin./Intl. Mgmt., UCLA; **EDUC HONORS:** Magna Cum Laude, Recipient of GSM Investment Club Award 1977; **OTHER ACT & HONORS:** Member, Alumni Comm. - UCLA Grad. School of Mgmt., San Francisco Chapter; **HOME ADD:** 2032 Monroe Ave., Belmont, CA 94002, (415)591-3416; **BUS ADD:** 375 Diablo Rd., Suite 200, Danville, CA 94526, (415)838-8484.

HUNTSMAN, Frank C.——*Pres., Escrow Officer*, Escrow Consultants, Inc.; **PRIM RE ACT:** Consultant; **OTHER RE ACT:** Escrow lic., State of CA; **SERVICES:** Escrow agent in the non-residential RE transaction, consultant in structure of major RE props. for synd./sale/trusteeship; **BUS ADD:** 4041 MacArthur Blvd., 170, Newport Beach, CA 92660, (714)833-7642.

HUNZIKER, Dean E.——**B:** Sept. 2, 1942, Ames, IA, *Real Estate Broker*, Hunziker & Furman Inc., Realtors; **PRIM RE ACT:** Broker, Developer, Owner/Investor; **SERVICES:** Brokerage, land devel., const.; **PROFL AFFIL & HONORS:** NAR, Iowa AR, Ames Bd. of Realtors, RNMI, GRI, CRS; **OTHER ACT & HONORS:** Dir.- C of C, Dir. Econ. devel.; Commn., Pres.-Multiple Sclerosis; **HOME ADD:** 2624 Cleveland, Ames, IA 50010, (515)232-7848; **BUS ADD:** 803 24th St., Ames, IA, (515)232-4214.

HURLBURT, Thomas H.——**B:** Mar. 82, 1946, San Diego, CA, *Pres.*, The Hurlburt Co., Inc.; **PRIM RE ACT:** Broker, Consultant, Developer, Property Manager, Syndicator; **SERVICES:** Investment Consulting, Synd. and Devel. of Investment Props., Prop. Mgmt.; **REP CLIENTS:** Indiv. Investors in Comml. & Resid. Props.; **EDUC:** BS, 1968, Bus., Univ. of CO; **GRAD EDUC:** MBA, 1969, Fin., Univ. of SO. CA; **EDUC HONORS:** Deans List; **HOME ADD:** 3090 Franklin Canyon Dr., Beverly Hills, CA 90210, (213)858-7681; **BUS ADD:** 10653 Riverside Dr., NO. Hollywood, CA 91602, (213)761-6109.

HURLEY, John M., Jr.——**B:** May 26, 1944, Brooklyn, NY, *Dir. of Dev.*, Westport Restaurants, Inc.; **OTHER RE ACT:** Corporate RE and Construction; **PREV EMPLOY:** McDonald's Corp. 1973-1978, RE Rep., RE Analyst, RE Mktg. Analyst, Magic Pan, Inc., 1978-1981, Mgr. of RE; **PROFL AFFIL & HONORS:** Intl. Council of Shopping Centers; **EDUC:** BBA, 1965, Bus., St. Francis Coll., B'klyn, NY; **MIL SERV:** US Army, E-5; **HOME ADD:** 26 Cedar Lake East, Denville, NJ 07834, (201)627-2087; **BUS ADD:** 285 Riverside Ave., Westport, CT 06880, (201)625-5123.

HURLEY, John P.——**B:** Jan. 26, 1921, Morris Town, NJ, *Realtor-Owner*, Realty World, John P. Hurley; **PRIM RE ACT:** Broker, Appraiser; **PROFL AFFIL & HONORS:** GRI, CREA, SCV, Realtor; **EDUC:** BE, 1950, Univ. of VT; **GRAD EDUC:** MEd, 1951, Springfield Coll., Springfield, MA; **MIL SERV:** USMC, Sgt.; **OTHER ACT & HONORS:** Past Pres. of Morris Plains Kiwanis; Chrmn. Lafayette Club, Univ. of VT Alumni Fund; Elected to the University of Vermont Athletic Hall of Fame, 1981; **HOME ADD:** 55 Old Farmhouse Rd., Millington, NJ 07946, (201)647-0884; **BUS ADD:** 381 Speedwell Ave., Morris Plains, NJ 07950, (201)539-6407.

HURLEY, Patrick W.——**B:** July 6, 1942, St. Cloud, MN, *Sr. Fin. Analyst*, American Appraisal Co., Southern Region; **PRIM RE ACT:** Consultant, Appraiser; **SERVICES:** RE equities and business appraisals; **REP CLIENTS:** Synds., major corps., private companies, attys.; **PREV EMPLOY:** Pres., Northwest Securities Corp.; **PROFL AFFIL & HONORS:** RESSI; ASA, SRS; **EDUC:** BS Fin. Mgmt., 1966, Fin., Acctg., and Econ., So. IL Univ.; **GRAD EDUC:** 1969 and 1970, Post Grad. Study in Econ. and Acctg., So. IL Univ. and Lyola Univ.; **MIL SERV:** US Army, Sp 4; **OTHER ACT & HONORS:** 1975 - Fin. Prin. Broker/Dealer NASD; **HOME ADD:** 4770 Cambridge Dr., Dunwoody, GA 30338, (404)396-6247; **BUS ADD:** 1819 Peachtree Rd., NE, Atlanta, GA 30309, (404)352-2167.

HURR, Myron——*Manager, RE*, Amerace Corp.; **PRIM RE ACT:** Property Manager; **BUS ADD:** 555 Fifth Avenue, New York, NY 10017, (212)986-8282.*

HURST, Hollis C.——**B:** July 26, 1924, Ochlochnee, GA, *Pres.*, H. Square Corp., Inc.; **PRIM RE ACT:** Engineer, Builder, Owner/Investor, Property Manager; **SERVICES:** Pres. & Chmn. of Bd., 21 yrs.; **PREV EMPLOY:** Lockheed GA Co., 28 yrs., Engr.; **PROFL AFFIL & HONORS:** Sr. Member IEEE, PE 6555, GA, Electrical Engr.; **EDUC:** BEE, 1950, EE, GA Inst. of Tech.; **GRAD EDUC:** MS, 1957, Mgmt., GA Inst. of Tech.; **MIL SERV:** USAF, Lt. Col., Distinguished Unit Citation, With Pacific Theater and 2 battlebattle stars; **OTHER ACT & HONORS:** Dist. Gov. GA Toastmasters, Pres. Lockheed GA Co., NMA Chapter; **HOME ADD:** 2130 Roswell Rd., Smyrna, GA 30080, (404)435-7211; **BUS ADD:** 2130 Roswell Rd., Smyrna, GA 30080, (404)435-7211.

HURST, O. Byron, Sr.——**B:** Sept. 21, 1918, Hot Springs, AR, *RE Broker & RE Appraiser, Cert.*, Hurst Realty, Inc. & HP Mass Appraisal, Inc.; **PRIM RE ACT:** Broker, Consultant, Appraiser, Assessor; **SERVICES:** Mass Appraisals for Pol. Subdiv.; **REP CLIENTS:** HP Mass Appraisal Co., Inc.; **PREV EMPLOY:** Licensed Ins. Agent for Amer. Foundation Life Ins. Co., Okla. City, OK; NFC Mktg., E. Little Rock, AR; **PROFL AFFIL & HONORS:** AR Realtors Assn.; Hot Springs Realtors Assn.; IAAO, Cert. Residential & Rural Appraisers; **EDUC:** AR Law School; Am. Bible Inst.; OD Hartfield School of RE Law & RE; Paull Hann RE; Spec. Studies, AR Assessment Co-ordination Div., 1937 - 40; **GRAD EDUC:** LLB; JD; PsyD; M.Psy; NMD, 1941, Law, Psych. & Divinity, AR Law School; John Q. Adams College; Am. Bible Inst.; Lincoln College; **MIL SERV:** US Army, T4; **OTHER ACT & HONORS:** US Commnr. W. Dist. of AR, 1942 - 1943; Garland Cty. Judge of AR, 1947 - 1949; AR Senate, State of AR, 1950 - 1973; AR & ABA (1941 - 1974); AR RE Comm.; AR Ins. Comm.; Am. Assessing Officers; **HOME ADD:** 14 Conway Rd., Hot Springs, AR 71901, (501)624-3039; **BUS ADD:** 209 Orange St., Hot Springs, AR 71901, (501)321-9302.

HURWITZ, Jerome——**B:** Feb. 6, 1929, NY, NY, *Pres.*, Income Prop. Consultants, Inc.; **PRIM RE ACT:** Broker, Consultant, Owner/Investor, Instructor; **SERVICES:** Investment counseling, comml. brokerage, investor; **PREV EMPLOY:** Teacher; **PROFL AFFIL & HONORS:** Long Is. Bd. of Realtors; **EDUC:** BA, 1951, Pol. Sci., Univ. of KY; **GRAD EDUC:** MA, 1953, Soc. Sci., Columbia Univ.; **HOME ADD:** 7 Vanderbilt Pkwy, Dix Hills, NY 11746, (516)549-5381; **BUS ADD:** 275 Broadhollow Rd., Melville, NY 11747, (516)249-8900.

HUSKIN, J. David——**B:** Mar. 11, 1935, Pueblo, CO, *Pres.*, Huskin and Co., Realtors; **PRIM RE ACT:** Broker, Instructor, Syndicator, Consultant, Developer, Owner/Investor; **SERVICES:** Specializes in land acquisition, water resources, investment prop.; **PROFL AFFIL & HONORS:** Denver Bd. of Realtors, CO Bd., NAR, RNMI, Charter member, CCIM, ALDA, Amer. Sales Masters Award, CO Exchangor of the Yr.; **GRAD EDUC:** Bus. Adm., 1957, Advertising, Univ. of Denver; **OTHER ACT & HONORS:** Member, CO State Bd. of Educ., CO Republican Comm.; **HOME ADD:** 5257 S. Boston, Greenwood Village, CO 80111, (303)773-1673; **BUS ADD:** 8000 E. Girard Ave. #305, Denver, CO 80231, (303)695-6577.

HUSTACE, Edward C.——**B:** Aug. 31, 1915, Honolulu, HI, *Gen. Mgr. & Dir.*, Victoria Ward, Ltd.; **PRIM RE ACT:** Broker, Consultant, Appraiser, Developer, Builder, Property Manager; **SERVICES:** RE brokerage, prop. mgmt., appraisal; **PROFL AFFIL & HONORS:** AIREA, IREM, Nat. & Honolulu Chapt., Amer. Chap. of IREF, ULI, NAR, Honolulu Bd. of Realtors, Amer. Right of Way Assn., CPM, MAI, 1963 Pres. of IREM & NAR; **EDUC:** BE, 1938, Educ., Univ. of HI; **GRAD EDUC:** MBA, 1940, Bus. Admin., Harvard Univ.; **EDUC HONORS:** ASUH (student body), Pres. 1936-37; **OTHER ACT & HONORS:** Oahu Ctry. Club, Outrigger Canoe Club; **HOME ADD:** 4715 Aukai Ave., Honolulu, HI 96816, (808)734-8878; **BUS ADD:** 1240 Ala Moana Blvd., Suite 601, Honolulu, HI 96814, (808)531-6444.

HUSTON, Gary W.——**B:** Aug. 25, 1953, Velasco, TX, Grier, Swartzman & Weiner; **PRIM RE ACT:** Attorney; **REP CLIENTS:** Devel., investors and lenders with respect to comml. real estate; **PROFL AFFIL & HONORS:** Amer., MO, Kansas City Bar Assns.; Lawyers' Assn. of KS City; **EDUC:** BA, 1974, Pol. Sci., LA State Univ.; **GRAD EDUC:** JD, 1978, Univ. of VA Law School; **HOME ADD:** 2500 W. 91st St., Leawood, KS 66206, (913)649-2142; **BUS ADD:** 1900 City Center Sq., 1100 Main St., Kansas City, MO 64105, (816)471-6850.

HUSTON, James H.——**B:** Jan. 11, 1954, Laconia, NH, *Lic. RE Broker*, Jim Huston, RE; **PRIM RE ACT:** Broker, Consultant, Builder, Owner/Investor; **SERVICES:** All Aspects of RE; **PREV EMPLOY:** Preferred Props., Inc.; **EDUC:** BS, 1976, Bus. Admin., Univ. of NH; **GRAD EDUC:** MBA, 1985, Mktg., Plymouth State Coll.; **EDUC HONORS:** Cum Laude; **HOME ADD:** Box 12, Moultonboro, NH 03254, (603)476-5909; **BUS ADD:** Box 12, Moultonboro, NH 03254, (603)476-5909.

HUSTON, John M.——**B:** Aug. 29, 1945, Oceanport, NJ, *VP*, T.B.&Z. Realty & Mgmt. Corp., Chicago, IL; **PRIM RE ACT:** Broker, Developer, Property Manager; **SERVICES:** Brokerage, prop. mgmt. & investment in comml. & investment props.; **REP CLIENTS:** Owners/Investors, maj. corps., owner occupants, ins. cos., Insts., investors; **PREV EMPLOY:** Link Programs, Inc., Chicago, 1970-74; major devel. projects, Arthur Anderson & Co., 1968-70, Admin Servs. Div.; **PROFL AFFIL & HONORS:** Pres. Chicago Assn. of Loft Bldgs.; Bd. of Govs.; BOMA; IREM; Chicago RE Bd., CPM; **EDUC:** BS, 1968, Econ. & Bus., Purdue Univ.; **EDUC HONORS:** Hons. Econ. Curriculum; **OTHER ACT & HONORS:** Former Tr. Chicago Lions Rugby Football Club; **HOME ADD:** 606 Glen Ellyn Pl., Glen Ellyn, IL 60137, (312)790-1849; **BUS ADD:** Two N. Riverside Plaza,

Chicago, IL 60606, (312)782-9010.

HUTCHESON, Rex J.——**B:** Feb. 27, 1948, Ft. Worth, TX, *VP*, Republic Bank Dallas, RE Dept.; **PRIM RE ACT:** Banker, Lender; **SERVICES:** Interim const. fin., mort. warehouse fin., other related services; **REP CLIENTS:** Comml. builders/devel., mort. cos., correspondent banks and fin. insts.; **PROFL AFFIL & HONORS:** Robert Morris Assoc., Greater Dallas Planning Council; **EDUC:** BA, 1970, Econ./Govt., Univ. of TX at Austin; **GRAD EDUC:** MBA, 1976, Fin./Applied Econ., The George Washington Univ.; **EDUC HONORS:** Grad. with Honors, Pi Sigma Alpha; **MIL SERV:** USN, Lt. Cmdr., 1970-1976; **OTHER ACT & HONORS:** Amer. Mensa Soc.; **HOME ADD:** 5400 Grantmont Dr., Arlington, TX 76016, (817)429-4945; **BUS ADD:** POB 225961, Dallas, TX 75265, (214)653-5923.

HUTCHINS, Lewis Dee——**B:** Mar. 23, 1944, Fresno, CA, *Pres.*, Citcon Corp.; **PRIM RE ACT:** Broker, Developer, Builder, Owner/Investor; **SERVICES:** Res. & Comml. builder and devel.; **PREV EMPLOY:** VP & Reg. Mgr. for Genstar Pacific Investments, VP Fin. Broadmoor Homes, Mgr. Prudential Ins., Auditor, Arthur Young & Co.; **PROFL AFFIL & HONORS:** AICPA, CA Soc. of CPAs, Member BIA, Home Builders Council, Sales & Mktg. Council, CPA, CA; Gen. Bldg. Contr., CA; RE Broker, CA; Member Beta Alpha Psi, Beta Gamma Sigma, Teaching credential, Dean's Scholar; **EDUC:** BS, 1971, Acctg. & Bus., San Jose State Univ.; **GRAD EDUC:** MBA, 1972, Information Systems, Univ. of So. CA; **EDUC HONORS:** Dean's List, GPA 3.8, GPA 3.7; **MIL SERV:** US Army, E-5, Sgt., Bronze Star, Army Commendation Medal; **OTHER ACT & HONORS:** Phi Kappa Phi, Nat. Hon. Scholastic Soc.; **HOME ADD:** 4763 La Pinta Way, San Jose, CA 95129, (408)247-4860; **BUS TEL:** (408)248-8664.

HUTCHINSON, A.G.——**B:** May 13, 1931, Braintree, MA, *Pres./Treas.*, Hutchinson Co. Realtors; **PRIM RE ACT:** Broker, Consultant, Builder; **REP CLIENTS:** Lending firms, moving cos.; **PROFL AFFIL & HONORS:** NAHB; National Association of Realtors; **EDUC:** BS, 1959, Bus. Teaching, Moorhead State; **MIL SERV:** USN, 3rd Class; **HOME ADD:** 385 8th Ave., S. Fargo, ND 58102, (701)237-5024; **BUS ADD:** 1355 N. P Ave., Box 1515, Fargo, ND 58107, (701)293-1010.

HUTCHINSON, Gary E., CPM——**B:** May 21, 1947, Wash., DC, *Mgr., Wash., DC Office(s)*, Coldwell Banker RE Mgmt. Services; **PRIM RE ACT:** Property Manager; **OTHER RE ACT:** Related consultation and advisory services; **SERVICES:** Total investment mgmt. and related consultation and advisory services; **REP CLIENTS:** Blachridge Investments, Intl. Bank Realty Corp., Carely Capital Development Group, Seven Fifty Joint Venture, CB Capital Mgmt., Providence S&L, misc. local & nat. investors; **PREV EMPLOY:** 12 years of RE Mgmt. experience, (all phases); **PROFL AFFIL & HONORS:** Northern VA Bd. of Realtors, Wash., DC Bd. of Realtors, IREM, AOBA, BOMA, CPM; **EDUC:** Hist. and Educ., Old Dominion Univ.; **MIL SERV:** USMCR; **OTHER ACT & HONORS:** Kappa Alpha Order - Alumni; several published articles in profl. journals; **HOME ADD:** 8835 Windinq Hollow Way, Springfield, VA 22152, (703)644-5454; **BUS ADD:** 2020 K. St., N.W., Suite #340, Wash., DC 20006, (202)457-8565.

HUTCHINSON, Richard——**B:** June 14, 1942, Knoxville, TN, *S.E. Region Real Estate Mgr.*, United Parcel Service; **OTHER RE ACT:** Leasing, buying, selling comml. props. for corporate use and ancillary functions such as appraisal, market studies, tax and lease admin., Legal supervision and devel. for UPS; **PROFL AFFIL & HONORS:** NACORE, former chapter Secretary; **EDUC:** BS, 1964, RE, Univ. of TN; **MIL SERV:** USAF, Capt.; **HOME ADD:** 4598 Westhampton Dr., Tucker, GA 30084, (404)491-1438; **BUS ADD:** 2801 Clearview Pl., Suite 100, Doraville, GA 30340, (404)455-6347.

HUTCHINSON, Robert F.——**B:** June 15, 1912, Lebanon, IN, *Realtor, Architect & Surveyor*, Robert F. Hutchinson & Assocs.; **PRIM RE ACT:** Broker, Engineer, Appraiser, Architect, Developer; **SERVICES:** Surveys, land devel., plans; **EDUC:** BS, 1942, Arch., OH State Univ.; **MIL SERV:** US Air Corps & Engrs.; **OTHER ACT & HONORS:** Hwy. Engr., 11 yrs.; Cty. Surveyor, 12 yrs.; Rotary; Amer. Legion; Elks; Ctry. Club; Masonic Bodies; Architects; RE; **HOME ADD:** 219 Ulen Dr., Lebanon, IN 46052, (317)482-4553; **BUS ADD:** 219 Ulen Dr., Lebanon, IN 46052, (317)482-4553.

HUTCHISON, Jacob A.——**B:** Nov. 19, 1918, Little Rock, AR, *Realtor and VP*, Baner Realty, Inc.; **PRIM RE ACT:** Broker, Instructor; **PREV EMPLOY:** VP, REL Inc. Makers of TROPO Scatter Telecommunications equipment and Radar Command and Control Sets; **EDUC:** 1936-1938, Math, Univ. of CA, Berkeley; **MIL SERV:** USAF, Col., Silver Star, Air Medal, Bronze Star, Three Pres. Citations, Air Force Commendation Medal, Legion of Merit. Served on active duty from 1940 through Jan 1970. Served in the Pac. (68 missions) WWII, Korea as a B-29 Sq. Commander, and in Vietnam as Commander of 1st Combat Support Grp., SAC; **HOME ADD:** 1 Harbourside Dr., Delray Beach, FL 33444, (305)278-8448; **BUS ADD:** 64 N.E. 5th Ave., Delray Beach, FL 33444, (305)276-7401.

HUTCHISON, S. R.——**B:** Oct. 6, 1923, Portsmouth, OH, *Pres.*, Samuel Robert Hutchison, P.C., A Corporation; **PRIM RE ACT:** Consultant, Attorney; **SERVICES:** Western Amer. Mort. Co., State Farm Life Ins. Co., Baltimore Life Ins. Co.; **PREV EMPLOY:** Gen. Counsel Western Amer. Mtg. Co.; Rocky Mtn. Div. Regional Counsel of Standard Oil (IN); Gen. RE Atty., Husky Oil Co.; **PROFL AFFIL & HONORS:** ABA (Real Prop. Sect.); AZ Bar Assn.; **EDUC:** BA, 1947, Econ., OH State Univ. Arts & Sciences; **GRAD EDUC:** JD, 1950, Law, Coll. of Law-OH State Univ.; **MIL SERV:** US Army, 1943-46, Sgt., ATO; **OTHER ACT & HONORS:** Who's Who in the World, Mensa, Who's Who in Commerce, Who's Who in Fin., Who's Who in the West, etc., YMCA Bd., Misc. Bds. of Dirs.; **HOME ADD:** 6617 N. 48th St., Paradise Valley, AZ 85253, (602)959-8907.

HUTENSKY, Allan——**B:** Dec. 24, 1936, Waterbury, CT, *Partner*, Bronson & Hutensky; **PRIM RE ACT:** Developer, Owner/Investor, Property Manager, Syndicator; **PROFL AFFIL & HONORS:** ULI, Intl. Council of Shopping Centers, ABA; **EDUC:** BA, 1958, Govt., Univ. of CT; **GRAD EDUC:** LLB, JD, 1966, Univ. of CT; **OTHER ACT & HONORS:** Zoning Commn. Member, Various Civic Bds.; **HOME ADD:** 35 Old Oak Rd., West Hartford, CT 06117, (203)523-1293; **BUS ADD:** 707 Bloomfield Ave., Bloomfield, CT 06002, (203)522-6262.

HUTMACHER, Gordon——**B:** Jan. 5, 1934, Fort Worth, TX, *Sr. VP*, Brookhollow National Bank; **PRIM RE ACT:** Broker, Banker; **SERVICES:** Comml. & RE lending; **PREV EMPLOY:** Small Bus. Admin.; **EDUC:** BBA, 1969, Mgmt., Univ. of Houston; **MIL SERV:** US Navy, 2nd Class PO; **OTHER ACT & HONORS:** Chandlers Landing Yacht Club; **HOME ADD:** 627 Monte Vista, Dallas, TX 75223, (214)327-5773; **BUS ADD:** 1111 W. Mockingbird, Dallas, TX 75265, (214)631-4500.

HUTZELL, Richard Edward——**B:** Mar. 30, 1935, Washington, DC, *Owner & Pres.*, R.E. Hutzell & Assoc. Mortgage Co. & Donric Real Estate Co., Inc.; **PRIM RE ACT:** Broker, Banker; **OTHER RE ACT:** CPA; **SERVICES:** Comml. RE, Prop. Mgmt., Comml. Leasing, Mort. Broker; **PREV EMPLOY:** Controller, Carl M. Freeman Assoc., Asst. Controller, Shannon & Luchs Co., Washington, DC; **PROFL AFFIL & HONORS:** Mort. Bankers Assn., Nat. RE Bds., CPA; **EDUC:** BCS, 1957, Acctg. & RE Taxation, Strayer Coll.; **GRAD EDUC:** MCS, Benj Franklin Univ.; **HOME ADD:** 8800 Carribean Dr., Ocean City, MD 21842, (301)524-2584; **BUS ADD:** 1810A Phila Ave., Suite C, Ocean City, MD 21842, (301)289-5308.

HYDEN, William U., Jr.——**B:** May 27, 1947, Trion, Chattooga County, GA, *Atty. and Counselor at Law*, Sole Practitioner; **PRIM RE ACT:** Attorney; **SERVICES:** Title exams., curative work, trusts and estates, transfers and loan closings on all types of realty; **REP CLIENTS:** First Fed. S&L Assn. of Summerville, GA, First Natl. Bank of Chattooga Cty. and other firms and indivs. buying, selling or lending on RE; **PROFL AFFIL & HONORS:** State Bar of GA, ABA, Real Prop., Probate and Trust Sec.; **EDUC:** BS, 1970, Pre-Med./Pol. Sci., Univ. of TN, Knoxville; **GRAD EDUC:** JD, 1975, Univ. of GA School of Law; **EDUC HONORS:** Grad. with hon., Grad. cum laude; GA of Law Review Editorial Bd. 1974-75; **HOME ADD:** 250 Simmons St., Trion, GA 30753, (404)734-2846; **BUS ADD:** PO Box 468, 11 E. WA St., Summerville, GA 30747, (404)857-2415.

HYLAND, Kenneth J.——**B:** May 25, 1939, Jersey City, NJ, *Pres.*, Community Management Inc.; **PRIM RE ACT:** Broker, Consultant, Property Manager, Syndicator; **OTHER RE ACT:** Landscape Const.; **SERVICES:** Resort Leasing & Sales; **REP CLIENTS:** Primarily devels.; **PREV EMPLOY:** Habitat Mgmt. Inc.; **PROFL AFFIL & HONORS:** Community Assn. Inst.; IREM, CPM; **EDUC:** Arch. Engr., 1958/62, Arch. Engr., Univ. of Miami, FL; **HOME ADD:** 2242 W. Monterey, Mesa, AZ 85202, (602)839-0240; **BUS ADD:** 325 E. Southern Ave., Suite 5, Tempe, AZ 85282, (602)231-0166.

HYLAND, Mark W.——Hyland Assoc., Inc.; **PRIM RE ACT:** Developer; **BUS ADD:** 45 E. Putnam Ave., Greenwich, CT 06830, (203)661-8700.*

HYLAND, William F.——**B:** Mar. 5, 1917, New Haven, CT, *Owner*, Hyland Assoc.; **PRIM RE ACT:** Developer, Owner/Investor; **OTHER RE ACT:** Mort. Banker, Real Estate Consultant; **SERVICES:** Develop office and indus. bldgs. on lease basis; **REP CLIENTS:** Instnl. investors for comml. prop.; **PREV EMPLOY:** Self employed 35 yrs.; **PROFL AFFIL & HONORS:** MBA; **EDUC:** BA, 1940, Econ., Yale Univ.; **MIL SERV:** USAC, Pilot Maj., French Air Medal; **OTHER**

ACT & HONORS: Yale Club of NY, Riverside Yacht Club; **HOME ADD:** 47 Lafayette Pl., Greenwich, CT 06830; **BUS ADD:** 45 E. Putnam Ave., Greenwich, CT 06830, (203)661-8700.

HYMAN, Leonard J.——B: Nov. 28, 1936, Philadelphia, PA, *Pres., Chrm. of the Bd.*, First Comml. Prop., Inc.; **PRIM RE ACT:** Broker, Developer, Owner/Investor, Property Manager, Syndicator; **SERVICES:** Investments, comml. prop. synd., mobile homes park devel.; **PREV EMPLOY:** Pres. - Mercury Fund, Inc.; **EDUC:** Temple Univ., 1958, Fin. & Mktg.; **MIL SERV:** USAF; **HOME ADD:** 770 Rio Grande Dr., Alpharetta, GA 30201, (404)992-1123; **BUS ADD:** 2063 Main St., Sarasota, FL 33578, (404)992-1123.

IACOVIELLO, Frank——B: Sept. 20, 1947, Boston, MA, *Pres.*, Bay Colony Resources, Inc., Real Prop.; **PRIM RE ACT:** Broker, Consultant, Architect, Developer, Builder, Owner/Investor; **SERVICES:** Project feasibility, mgmt., implementation; **REP CLIENTS:** Resid. & Comml.; **PREV EMPLOY:** Project Mgr., Arch. Designer, RE Broker; **PROFL AFFIL & HONORS:** MA RE Broker; **EDUC:** BS, 1975, Econ., Univ. of MA; **GRAD EDUC:** MArch, 1979, Arch. Design and RE Devel., MA Inst. of Tech.; **HOME ADD:** 1501 La Playa Ave. (6-303), San Diego, CA 92109; **BUS ADD:** 35 Colswell Ave., Beverly, MA 01915, (617)922-0616.

IAN, Joseph M.——*Dir. RE*, Kane-Miller Corp.; **PRIM RE ACT:** Property Manager; **BUS ADD:** 555 White Plains Rd., PO Box 7, Tarrytown, NY 10591, (914)631-6900.*

IANNELLI, Emil L., Esq.——B: Nov. 22, 1937, Philadelphia, PA, *Partner*, Goldman, Isacoff and Iannelli; **PRIM RE ACT:** Attorney, Developer, Instructor, Syndicator, Real Estate Publisher; **SERVICES:** Atty., devel. and synd.; **REP CLIENTS:** RE brokers; instnl. and indiv. investors; **PREV EMPLOY:** Redevel. Authority, City of Philadelphia, 1973-1976; **PROFL AFFIL & HONORS:** Adjunct Faculty DE Law School; **EDUC:** BA, 1960, Psych., LaSalle Coll.; **GRAD EDUC:** JD, 1971, Law, Temple Univ. School of Law; **MIL SERV:** US Army, Capt.; **OTHER ACT & HONORS:** Solicitor Borough of Rockledge; **HOME ADD:** 117 Elm Ave., Rockledge, PA 19111, (215)379-3597; **BUS ADD:** 801 West St. Rd., Feasterville, PA 19047, (215)322-2606.

IANNELLO, Paul——*Prop. Mgr.*, Airport City; **PRIM RE ACT:** Developer; **BUS ADD:** 80 Sugg Rd., Buffalo, NY 14225, (716)632-4445.*

ICHELSON, David——B: May 10, 1937, Montreal, Can, *VP, Gen Mgr.*, Cascade Grp., RE Mktg. Div.; **PRIM RE ACT:** Broker, Developer, Owner/Investor, Property Manager; **SERVICES:** Devel., comml. prop., joint ventures, mgmt.; **REP CLIENTS:** Pension funds, inst. & personal investors; **PREV EMPLOY:** Polaris Realty (Canada) Ltd.; **PROFL AFFIL & HONORS:** Dir. BOMA Calgary; **HOME ADD:** 9204 29th St., SW, Calgary, T2V4R3, AB, Can, (403)281-7211; **BUS ADD:** Suite 300, 715 Fifth Ave., SW, Calgary, T2P2X6, AB, Can, (403)266-9888.

IGER, Mark M.——B: Dec. 14, 1952, Newark, NJ, *In-house Counsel, Sec. of Corp.*, Sage Realty Corp.; **PRIM RE ACT:** Attorney; **PROFL AFFIL & HONORS:** NY Bar Assn.; **EDUC:** AB, 1975, Amer. Studies, CT Coll.; **GRAD EDUC:** JD, 1978, Hofstra Law Sch.; **EDUC HONORS:** Cum Laude; **HOME ADD:** 230 E. 48th St., NY, NY 20017, (212)888-0712; **BUS ADD:** 437 Madison Ave., NY, NY 10022, (212)758-0437.

IGLESK, Thomas R.——B: June 16, 1934, Chicago, IL, *VP Corp. Sec.*, CNA Fin. Corp., CNA Ins. Co., Mort. Loan and RE; **PRIM RE ACT:** Attorney, Lender, Owner/Investor; **EDUC:** BBA, 1955, Fin., Univ. of Notre Dame; **GRAD EDUC:** JD, 1962, Law, De Paul Uni.; **MIL SERV:** US Army; **HOME ADD:** 19110 Pierce Ct., Homewood, IL 60430, (312)798-3425; **BUS ADD:** CWA Plaza., Chicago, IL 60685.

IKEZAWA, Shahin (Sherry) D.——B: Dec. 4, 1930, Iran, *Pres.*, Very Important Properties; **PRIM RE ACT:** Broker, Developer, Owner/Investor, Instructor, Property Manager, Syndicator; **PROFL AFFIL & HONORS:** Member of the Bd. of the Rolling Hills Bd. of Realtors; **EDUC:** B of Arch., 1955, Arch. & Engr., Univ. of MI; B. of Math., 1963, Arch. & Engr., Univ. of MI; **HOME ADD:** 609 Deep Valley Dr., Rolling Hills Estates, CA 90274; **BUS ADD:** 609 Deep Valley Dr., Rolling Hills Estates, CA 90274, (213)377-0333.

ILIFF, George S.——B: June 29, 1945, Pasadena, CA, *Pres.*, Iliff, Thorn & Co., Corp.; **PRIM RE ACT:** Broker; **SERVICES:** Comml. RE brokerage; **REP CLIENTS:** Devel., investors, & users of comml. indus. and multi-family RE; **PREV EMPLOY:** Grubb & Ellis, Sr. VP & S. Rgnl. Mgr.; **PROFL AFFIL & HONORS:** Nat. Assn. of Indus. & Office Parks, Nat. Assn. of Corp. RE Execs., AZ Assn. for Indus. Devel., AZ RE Inst. Pres.; **EDUC:** BS, 1967, Mktg., San Diego Univ.; **OTHER ACT & HONORS:** Phoenix Parks Found. VP., Central Phoenix Redevel. Comm., Fami Serv. Agency Bd. of Dir.; **HOME ADD:** 1001 W. Ecanto Blvd., Phoenix, AZ 85007, (602)252-1432; **BUS ADD:** 2400 N. Central Ave., Suite 300, Phoenix, AZ 85004, (602)253-0300.

ILLING, Joseph R.——B: Apr. 4, 1943, Chicago, IL, *Mgr., Comml. Investment Div.*, Boone and Boone Realty; **PRIM RE ACT:** Consultant, Developer, Owner/Investor, Property Manager, Syndicator; **OTHER RE ACT:** Mgr. Comml. Investment Div.; **PREV EMPLOY:** Dir. Mktg., So. Sound Nat. Bank; **PROFL AFFIL & HONORS:** Realtor; **EDUC:** AB, 1970, Letters & Sci., Univ. of CA, Berkeley; **MIL SERV:** US Army, E-5; **OTHER ACT & HONORS:** Chrmn, WA State Centennial Organizing Comm., Pres., Lacey Intl. Music, Art and Dance Fest.; **HOME ADD:** 6934 Timberlake Dr. SE, Lacey, WA 98503, (206)456-3023; **BUS ADD:** 4535 Lacey Blvd., Lacey, WA 98503, (206)456-8535.

IMANAKA, Mitchell A.——B: Nov. 26, 1954, Honolulu, HI, *Atty.*, Carlsmith & Dwyer; **PRIM RE ACT:** Attorney, Broker; **SERVICES:** Legal; **REP CLIENTS:** Devels., lenders, investors; **PROFL AFFIL & HONORS:** ABA; HI Bar Assn.; **EDUC:** BA, 1976, Sociology, Univ. of HI; **GRAD EDUC:** JD, 1979, Georgetown Univ. Law Ctr.; **EDUC HONORS:** Valedictorian; **OTHER ACT & HONORS:** Phi Beta Kappa, Phi Kappa Phi; **BUS ADD:** Suite 1800 Pioneer Plaza, 900 Fort St., Honolulu, HI 96813, (808)524-8000.

IMPERIALE, Peter——*Director Corporate Development*, AVX; **PRIM RE ACT:** Property Manager; **BUS ADD:** 60 Utter Mill Rd., Great Neck, NY 11021, (516)829-8500.*

INDIEK, Victor H.——B: Nov. 15, 1937, Spearville, KS, *Pres.*, Builders Capital Corp., Div. of Watt Indus., Inc.; **PRIM RE ACT:** Syndicator; **OTHER RE ACT:** SBIC, Bldg. indus. joint venture; **SERVICES:** Joint venture capital; **PREV EMPLOY:** Arthur Andersen & Co., 1961-70, Mgr., Fed. Home Loan Mort. Co., 1970-77, Pres. & CEO; **PROFL AFFIL & HONORS:** Member Bd. of Govs. NASBIC, past pres. VP S. Pac. RASBIC, Member AICPA, CPA; **EDUC:** BA, 1959, Acctg., Univ. of KS; **MIL SERV:** USN, Lt.j.g.; **HOME ADD:** 1166 Las Pulgas Pl., Pac. Palisades, CA 90272, (213)454-8067; **BUS ADD:** 2716 Ocean Park Blvd., PO Box 2114, Santa Monica, CA 90406, (213)450-0779.

INFANTINO, Thomas V.——B: Sept. 5, 1948, Bay Shore, NY, *Atty.*, Law Offices of Thomas V. Infantino, Located in Inverness, Tallahassee and Winter Park, FL; **PRIM RE ACT:** Broker, Attorney, Developer, Owner/Investor, Instructor, Syndicator; **OTHER RE ACT:** Lobbying; **SERVICES:** Legal, devel., brokerage, lobbying, instruction; **REP CLIENTS:** Title Insurance Agent for Chicago Title, Lawyers' Title Guaranty Fund; Sr. Instr. - Farm and Land Inst., NAR; City Atty. - Inverness, FL 1980-1981; Point O'Woods Utilities, Inc.; Oyler Bros. Co., Enslow Homes, Inc., Harvey Builders; REK Group; OWS Group; Philpot Homes, Inc.; Builders; Devels.; Synds; **PREV EMPLOY:** Bert Rodgers Schools of RE - Corp. Counsel; **PROFL AFFIL & HONORS:** ABA, FL Bar, NAR, FL Blue Key; Former Exec. Sec. FL Young Democrats; **EDUC:** BBA, 1970, RE and Urban Land Studies, Univ. of FL; **GRAD EDUC:** JD, 1973, Law, Univ. of FL; **MIL SERV:** USAR, 1st Lt., Honorable Discharge 1978; **BUS ADD:** Main Office: 180 South Knowles Ave. #7, PO Drawer B, Winter Park, FL 32790, (305)644-4673.

ING, Wilbur K.S.——B: Sept. 21, 1941, Honolulu, HI, *REO*, Hawaiian Trust Co., Ltd, Rental Dept.; **PRIM RE ACT:** Property Manager; **PROFL AFFIL & HONORS:** IREM; **EDUC:** BBA, 1966, Univ. of HI; **MIL SERV:** USA, 1st Lt.; **HOME ADD:** 55 S Judd St #2109, Honolulu, HI 96817; **BUS ADD:** PO Box 3170, Honolulu, HI 96802, (415)525-6503.

INGALLS, Barbara O'Donnell——B: July 30, 1955, Denver, CO, *Asst. VP - Corporate Relations*, Van Schaack & Co., Corp. Relations; **OTHER RE ACT:** Public relations/communications; **SERVICES:** Corp. Advertising, Media Relations, Shareholder Relations, Employee Communications; **PROFL AFFIL & HONORS:** Internatl. Assoc. of Bus. Communicators, Dir. & 3rd VP/Treas., 'Grant T. Alley People Award', Van Schaack honor; **EDUC:** BA, 1977, Journ. & Mktg., CO State Univ., Fort Collins; **BUS ADD:** 950 17th St., Suite 1100, Denver, CO 80202, (303)572-5103.

INGEBRITSON, Jack——*Pres.*, Ingebritson Investment Co. Inc.; **PRIM RE ACT:** Broker, Consultant, Developer, Owner/Investor, Syndicator; **SERVICES:** New home sales for builders & devels. of comml. props.; **PROFL AFFIL & HONORS:** Homebuilders Assn. of Central AZ; Sales & Mktg. Council, Phoenix C of C; Solar Energy Inst.; Housing Mag., Advisory Panel 1980-81 NAR; Nat. Assn. of Farm & Land Brokers; Nat. Assn. of Mort. Brokers; **EDUC:** BBA, 1968, Fin. & Investment Mgmt., Northwestern Univ.; **OTHER ACT & HONORS:** Who's Who in the West 1981-82; Who's Who in Fin. & Indus. 1981-82 Marquis Pub.; **HOME ADD:** 1905 E. Medlock, Phoenix, AZ 85016, (602)279-3497; **BUS ADD:** 5301 N. 7th St., Suite 103, Phoenix, AZ 85014, (602)265-1805.

INGEGNI, Albert A., III——**B:** Dec. 30, 1951, Great Barrington, MA, *Sales Mgr.*, Shirl Toolin Bartini Realty Inc.; **PRIM RE ACT:** Broker, Property Manager, Owner/Investor; **PREV EMPLOY:** Bonded Collection Agency, Pittsfield, MA; Mgr. & Devel. of 22 Units in Chicopee and Agawam, MA; **EDUC:** BA, 1974, Eng./Psych., Univ. of Mass Amherst; **OTHER ACT & HONORS:** Planning and Devel. Commn., Chicopee, MA 1979; **HOME ADD:** PO 465, Housatonic, MA 01236, (413)274-6043; **BUS ADD:** Shamrock Bldg., Main St., Housatonic, MA 01236, (413)274-3890.

INGRAHAM, Larry W.——**B:** Aug. 7, 1946, Seattle, WA, *Pres.*, Harmon & Associates Real Estate, Inc.; **PRIM RE ACT:** Broker, Developer, Owner/Investor; **SERVICES:** Acquisitions, site selection, devel. and leasing of office, retail and indus. props.; **REP CLIENTS:** Indiv. investors and synd. investment grps.; **PREV EMPLOY:** 1971-1974 - Yates, Wood & McDonald, Seattle WA Prop. Mgmt. and Leasing; **PROFL AFFIL & HONORS:** Nat. Assn. of Indus. and Office Parks; Intl. Council of Shopping Ctrs.; RNMI, CCIM; Past Officer of Seattle King Cty. Bd. of Realtors, Comml. Investment Div.; **EDUC:** BA, 1968, Bus./Educ., Seattle Pacific Coll.; **MIL SERV:** US Army; 1st Lt., Ranger, Air Born, Bronze Star, Air Medal; **OTHER ACT & HONORS:** Fellow, Seattle Pacific Univ.; Past Member, Seattle Jaycees; **HOME ADD:** 6909 160th SW, Edmonds, WA 98020, (206)743-3392; **BUS ADD:** 11000 Lake City Way, N.E., Seattle, WA 98125, (206)367-5784.

INGRAHAM, Mark J.——*Dir. RE*, St. Regis Paper Co.; **PRIM RE ACT:** Property Manager; **BUS ADD:** 150 East 42nd St., New York, NY 10017, (212)573-6000.*

INGRAHAM, Scott Shane——**B:** Feb. 10, 1954, *Pres.*, The Zane Scott Co., TX; **PRIM RE ACT:** Broker, Consultant, Owner/Investor; **OTHER RE ACT:** Fin., Mort. banking; **SERVICES:** Debt. & Equity Fin. (arranging & consultation); **REP CLIENTS:** Devel., instnl. investors; **PREV EMPLOY:** Philipsborn Co. of TX; Lincoln Fin., Inc.; **EDUC:** BBA, 1976, Fin., Univ. of TX/Austin; **HOME ADD:** 2262 Woodland Springs; **BUS ADD:** 9801 Westheimer, Suite 333, Houston, TX 77042, (713)266-9100.

INGRAM, Darrell——*President*, Petrolite Corp.; **PRIM RE ACT:** Property Manager; **BUS ADD:** 100 N. Broadway, St. Louis, MO 63102, (314)241-8370.*

INGRAM, James W.——**B:** Sep. 3, 1923, Wyoming, IL, *Dir. of Corp. RE*, Kraft, Inc.; **OTHER RE ACT:** Admin. & mgmt. of corp. RE; **PREV EMPLOY:** 37 yrs. with Kraft; **PROFL AFFIL & HONORS:** NACORE; IDRC; ERC; **HOME ADD:** 505 Redondo Dr., Downers Grove, IL, 60516; **BUS ADD:** Kraft Ct., Glenview, IL 60025, (312)998-2430.

INGRAM, Riley E.——**B:** Oct. 1, 1941, Halifax Co., VA, *VP*, Ingram & Houser RE Co.; **PRIM RE ACT:** Broker, Consultant, Appraiser, Developer, Builder, Owner/Investor, Property Manager, Syndicator, Assessor; **SERVICES:** Investment counseling, brokerage, prop. mgmt.; **PROFL AFFIL & HONORS:** Nat. Assn. of Housing and Redevl. Officials; NAR, GRI; CRS; CRB; **MIL SERV:** US Army Reserve, Sgt., Soldier of Yr., 1967; **OTHER ACT & HONORS:** Commnr., Hopewell Redevel. and Housing Auth.; Legion of the Moose; JC's Boss of Yr. Award, 1977; Realtor of Yr. Award, 1978, Southside Bd. of Realtors; **HOME ADD:** 714 Cedar Level Rd., Hopewell, VA 23860, (804)458-2823; **BUS ADD:** 3302 Oaklawn Blvd., Hopewell, VA 23860, (804)458-2823.

INOKON, H. Michael——**B:** Nov. 16, 1945, *Exec. Dir.*, H. M. Inokon & Co., Chartered; **PRIM RE ACT:** Broker, Consultant, Appraiser, Developer, Owner/Investor, Instructor, Property Manager, Syndicator, Real Estate Publisher; **OTHER RE ACT:** Fin. auditor; **SERVICES:** Investment, counseling, valuation, devel. and synd. of comml. props., prop. mgmt., fin. auditing; **REP CLIENTS:** Banks, indiv. or instnl. investors in RE, for investors in US Comml props.; **PROFL AFFIL & HONORS:** AIREA and Counselors, RESSI, AICPA, CPA; **EDUC:** BA & BS, 1973, Bus. & Acctg., Benjamin Franklin Univ.; **GRAD EDUC:** MCS, 1977, Acctg. & Fin. Mgmt., Benjamin Franklin Univ.; PhD, 1980, Acctg. & Fin. Mgmt., Loyola Univ.; **EDUC HONORS:** Benny Award for high scholastic achievements, magna cum laude, magna cum laude; **OTHER ACT & HONORS:** Bd. of Trs., Benjamin Franklin Univ., Adjunct Prof.; **BUS ADD:** 708 Hobbs Dr., Silver Springs, MD 20904, (301)384-1181.

INSCOE, Jim T.——**B:** Feb. 14, 1940, Rocky Mount, NC, *Owner*, Jim Inscoe Agency; **PRIM RE ACT:** Broker, Developer, Property Manager; **SERVICES:** Investment analysis, valuation, mgmt. and sales; **REP CLIENTS:** Numerous local firms and insts. as well as nat. corps.; **PROFL AFFIL & HONORS:** Montgomery Bd. of Realtors; IREM, CPM; Realtor of the Yr., 1980; **EDUC:** BS, 1962, Bus. Admin./Mktg., Univ. of NC; **EDUC HONORS:** Phi Eta Sigma honorary; **OTHER ACT & HONORS:** Montgomery Area C of C; **HOME ADD:** 2180 Woodley Rd., Montgomery, AL 36111, (205)265-7402; **BUS ADD:** 572 S Perry St., Montgomery, AL 36104, (205)263-5713.

INSINGA, James M.——**B:** Aug.20, 1942, NJ, *Pres.*, Rutland Grp. Inc., RE Mgt.; **PRIM RE ACT:** Broker, Developer, Property Manager; **SERVICES:** Property Mgt. Brokerage, Devl. Cost.; **REP CLIENTS:** Investors; **EDUC:** B.A., 1964, Bus.Adm., Moravian Coll.; **GRAD EDUC:** MBA, 1965, Emory Univ.; **HOME ADD:** Meadow Lake Drive, Mendon, VT 05701, (802)755-3812; **BUS ADD:** Box365, Rutland, VT 05701, (802)775-1981.

IRELAND, W.R.——*Mgr., RE Utilization*, Vulcan Materials Co.; **PRIM RE ACT:** Property Manager; **BUS ADD:** PO Box 7497, Birmingham, AL 35253, (205)877-3000.*

IRISH, James H., III——**B:** Oct. 3, 1936, Syracuse, NY, *Owner*, Irish & Assoc.; **PRIM RE ACT:** Broker, Consultant, Appraiser; **SERVICES:** Appraisal of all types of prop., brokerage and counseling concerning investment quality props., potential devel. and reuse; **REP CLIENTS:** Mort. bankers, RE lenders, attys., indiv. owners and investors, govt. agencies, and corps.; **PREV EMPLOY:** Sibley Corp., Mort. Bankers, Rochester, NY; Greene RE Syracuse, NY: Seafirst Mort. Corp., and Washington Mort. Co., Inc. Seattle, WA; **PROFL AFFIL & HONORS:** SREA, Seattle-King Cty. Bd. of Realtors, Inc., SRA; **EDUC:** US Mil. Acad at West Point, RPI, Troy, NY; **OTHER ACT & HONORS:** Chmn. Conservation Bd., Town of Penfield, NY; Senate of Jr. Chamber Intl.; **HOME ADD:** 3248 34th Ave. W, Seattle, WA 98199, (206)283-2008; **BUS ADD:** 3248 34th Ave. W, Seattle, WA 98199, (206)283-2008.

IRISH, Norman S.——**B:** Mar. 7, 1925, Farmington, NH, *Assessor, appraiser*, Town of Jaffrey, NH; **PRIM RE ACT:** Broker, Consultant, Assessor; **SERVICES:** Appraisals, assessments; **REP CLIENTS:** Towns of Jaffrey, Rindge, Dublin, attys.; **PREV EMPLOY:** 10 yrs. R.E. as salesman, apprais., broker.; yrs. selectman, assessor, Farmington; 2 yrs. assessor, Jaffrey; **PROFL AFFIL & HONORS:** IAAO, NHAAO, NARA, Designation CRA; **EDUC:** UNH-IAAO, 1973, Appraisal and the Assessment Process; **EDUC HONORS:** N.H. DRA course, Plymouth State, 1980; **MIL SERV:** USA, Sgt.; **OTHER ACT & HONORS:** Selectman, assessor 4 yrs., Treas., 2 yrs. Budget Comm., 6 yrs., Town of Farmington; Mbr. Bd. of Dir., Bldg. and Loan Assn.; **HOME ADD:** 47 Elm Street, Farmington, NH 03835, (603)755-3759; **BUS ADD:** P.O. Box 386, Jaffrey, NH 03452, (603)532-8322.

IRONS, Eugene J.——**B:** Feb. 2, 1941, Dubuque, IA, *VP*, Masten, Myrabo & Irons, PC; **PRIM RE ACT:** Attorney, Developer, Owner/Investor; **SERVICES:** Legal - Sellers, Purchasers & Fin. Agencies; **REP CLIENTS:** First Amer. Bank, Canton, SD, Farmers Home Admin.; **PREV EMPLOY:** English, Velta & Irons, Attys., Tracy, MN; **PROFL AFFIL & HONORS:** State Bar of SD, MN Bar Assn., ABA (Section of Real Prop., Probate and Trust Law); **EDUC:** BS, 1963, Indust. Admin. (Fin., Acctg. & Govt.), IA State Univ.; **GRAD EDUC:** LLB, 1966, Law, Univ. of MN; **OTHER ACT & HONORS:** City Atty. for Canton and Tea, SD, Deputy States Atty. for Lincoln Cty.; **HOME ADD:** 224 East 2nd St., Canton, SD 57013, (605)987-5892; **BUS ADD:** 108 S. Broadway, Canton, SD 57013, (605)987-4351.

IRVINE, Rixon A.——*VP, RE*, IL Central Gulf RR Co.; **OTHER RE ACT:** Corp. RE mgmt.; **BUS ADD:** 233 N. Michigan Ave., Chicago, IL 60601, (312)565-1600.

IRVING, David M.——*Dir.*, CTD Corp.; **PRIM RE ACT:** Developer; **BUS ADD:** PO Drawer 2400, Daytona Beach, FL 32015, (904)255-7558.*

ISAACSON, Gregg E.——**B:** July 15, 1945, Chicago, IL, *Gen. Counsel*, Quality Homes, Inc; **PRIM RE ACT:** Consultant, Attorney, Developer; **OTHER RE ACT:** Condo. Conversion and Devel. Specialist;

SERVICES: Legal, Mktg., Fin., Community Assn. Operation; **PREV EMPLOY:** Gen. Practice of Law-MN 1974-1979; **PROFL AFFIL & HONORS:** ABA, MN Bar Assn., Community Assns. Inst., Nat. Assn. of Homebuilders; **EDUC:** BA, 1967, Pol. Sci. Psych., St. Olaf Coll., Northfield, MN; **GRAD EDUC:** JD, 1974, William Mitchell Coll. of Law, St. Paul, MN; **OTHER ACT & HONORS:** Dir., MN Symphonic Winds; **HOME ADD:** 5731 Clinton Ave. S., Minneapolis, MN 55419, (612)861-3278; **BUS ADD:** 10700 Hwy. 55, Minneapolis, MN 55441, (612)546-8881.

ISAACSON, Harriett M.——B: Dec. 30, 1933, Tuscaloosa, AL, *Realtor Broker, Pres.*, Isaacson Realty Co., Inc.; **PRIM RE ACT:** Broker; **SERVICES:** RE counseling, sales, props., mgmt.; **PREV EMPLOY:** Branch Mgr. Baker & Billings, RE, Inc.; **PROFL AFFIL & HONORS:** NAR, Dir. of AL Assn. of Realtors, VP Birmingham Area Bd. of Realtors, WCR, GRI, CRS, CRB, Candidate recipient of Realtor of Yr. Award, 1980 at Birmingham Area Bd. of Realtors; **EDUC:** RE, Univ. of AL, Birmingham, Jefferson State Jr. Coll.; **OTHER ACT & HONORS:** Briarwood Presbyterian Church, Campus Crusade for Christ Auxiliary, Former Pres. of PTA & Civic Orgs.; **HOME ADD:** 5114 Split Rail Tr., Birmingham, AL 35244, (205)967-7173; **BUS ADD:** 5108 Oporto-Madrid Blvd., Birmingham, AL 35210, (205)951-2223.

ISAACSON, Steven M.——B: July 26, 1954, Chicago, IL, *Pres.*, S. M. Isaacson Associates; **PRIM RE ACT:** Consultant, Developer, Owner/Investor, Property Manager, Insuror, Syndicator; **SERVICES:** Condo. conversions, prop. mgmt.; **PREV EMPLOY:** Fin. VP, BJF Devel., Inc.; DM Interstate Mgmt., Inc.; Bernstein & Bank, Ltd.; **PROFL AFFIL & HONORS:** AICPA, IL CPA Soc., CPA; **EDUC:** BS, 1976, Acctg., Univ. of IL, Urbana; **GRAD EDUC:** MS, 1978, Taxation, DePaul Univ.; **HOME ADD:** 2217 N. Cleveland, Chicago, IL 60614, (312)327-4221; **BUS ADD:** Suite 200, 109 N. Dearborn, Chicago, IL 60602, (312)372-7700.

ISAKSEN, H. L., Jr.——B: Mar. 9, 1943, Salt Lake City, UT, *Pres.*, AID Assoc. Inc.; **PRIM RE ACT:** Broker, Syndicator, Developer, Property Manager, Owner/Investor; **PROFL AFFIL & HONORS:** IREM, Pres. UT IREM Chap, 1981; **EDUC:** BS, 1971, Fin. Acctg., Brigham Young Univ.; **HOME ADD:** 3610 Doverhill, Salt Lake City, UT 84121, (802)942-6935; **BUS ADD:** 2120 S. 1300 E Ste 303, Salt Lake City, UT 84106.

ISDANER, Lawrence A.——B: June 6, 1934, Philadelphia, PA, *Exec. Partner*, Isdaner & Co. - CPA; **PRIM RE ACT:** Consultant, Owner/Investor; **OTHER RE ACT:** CPA; **SERVICES:** Acctg. and tax serv., investment counseling, evaluation and fin. analysis; **REP CLIENTS:** Various synd. RE entities and investors in comml. props. and residential housing; **PROFL AFFIL & HONORS:** Amer. Inst. of CPA; PA Inst. of CPA; **EDUC:** BS, 1956, Acctg., Wharton School - Univ. of PA; **MIL SERV:** Army; **OTHER ACT & HONORS:** Pres., Golden Slipper Club (1977-78); Trustee, Pop Warner Little Scholars; Bd. of Directors-Society for Jewish Aged; Member of Who's Who in the World; Who's Who in America; Who's Who in Finance and Industry; Bd. of Directors - The Athletic Trauma Research Foundation; **HOME ADD:** 100 Grays Ln., Haverford, PA 19041, (215)896-5460; **BUS ADD:** 100 Presidential Blvd., Bala Cynwyd, PA 19004, (212)839-3422.

ISEMAN, Caryl——B: Apr. 5, 1942, Brooklyn, NY, *RE Broker*, Realty Exec., La Jolla Village Assoc.; **PRIM RE ACT:** Broker, Consultant, Owner/Investor, Instructor, Property Manager, Syndicator; **SERVICES:** RE brokerage, investment sales & consulting; **REP CLIENTS:** Profl. people; **PREV EMPLOY:** Office mgr. of Home Remodeling Co.; **PROFL AFFIL & HONORS:** San Diego Bd. of Realtors; CA Assn. of Realtors; NAR; Small Businesswomen Assn.; WCR; Nat. Notary Assn.; Republican Assn.; Republican Profl. & Bus. Club, 1977 Woman of Achievement for San Diego Cty.; Candidate for CCIM; **OTHER ACT & HONORS:** TIPS (Bus. Club); Member of Church of Religious Sci.; **HOME ADD:** 6171 Rancho Mission Rd., 310, San Diego, CA 92108, (714)280-1170; **BUS ADD:** 8950 Villa La Jolla Dr., La Jolla, CA 92037, (714)455-7850.

ISERI, C. Ernest——*Bd. Chmn.*, Paradise Palisades, Inc.; **PRIM RE ACT:** Engineer, Developer, Builder, Owner/Investor, Property Manager; **BUS ADD:** 38035 US Hwy 101 N., PO Box 117, Manzanita, OR 97130, (503)364-1965.

ISGRO, Joan B.——B: Mar. 11, 1933, Kingston, NY, *Pres.*, Ulster County Realty Inc.; **PRIM RE ACT:** Broker, Appraiser, Property Manager; **SERVICES:** Counseling; prop. mgmt.; appraising; **REP CLIENTS:** Homequity, Transamerica Relocation, Equitable Relocation; **PROFL AFFIL & HONORS:** Past Pres., Ulster Cty. Bd. of Realtors; Pres., MLS of Ulster Cty.; Bd. of Dir., NY State Assn. of Realtors; Bd. of Dir., Nat. Assn. of Realtors, First Female Realtor of Year for Ulster Cty.; Rgnl. VP, Lower Hudson, NYSAR; **OTHER ACT & HONORS:** Member, Bus. Advisory Council UCCC; Deacon, Reformed Church of Comforter, Kingston, NY; Past Pres., Zonta Intl. Kingston Club, Past Pres. Big Sisters of Ulster Cty., VP Ulster Cty. C of C; **HOME ADD:** 2 Garden Court, Saugerties, NY, (914)246-8973; **BUS ADD:** 366 Albany Ave., Kingston, NY 12401, (914)339-3300.

ISHAM, Richard B.——B: Aug. 8, 1939, San Diego, CA, *Pres.*, Richard B. Isham Law Corp.; **PRIM RE ACT:** Attorney; **OTHER RE ACT:** Estate Planning; **SERVICES:** Legal servs.; negotiations, drafting, representation to public agencies; **REP CLIENTS:** Noninstit. investors and devel.; **PREV EMPLOY:** IRS, Estate & Gift Tax Section; **PROFL AFFIL & HONORS:** ABA, CA Bar Assn. Tulare Cty. Bar Assn., Amer. Judicature Soc., Past Pres., Tulare Cty. Bar Assn.; **EDUC:** AB, 1961, Poli. Sci., Occidental Coll.; **GRAD EDUC:** LLB, 1965, Univ. of CA, Berkeley; **OTHER ACT & HONORS:** Visalia City Atty., 1972-1976; **HOME ADD:** 1600 Beverly Dr., Visalia, CA 93277, (209)732-1581; **BUS ADD:** 2929 W. Main St., Suite C, Visalia, CA 93291, (209)733-2257.

ISHAQ, Edward D.——B: Feb. 1, 1947, Mafrak, *Pres.*, E-D-I Real Estate; **PRIM RE ACT:** Broker, Consultant, Engineer, Appraiser, Owner/Investor, Property Manager; **SERVICES:** Comml. brokerage, appraisals, investor, prop. mgmt.; **PROFL AFFIL & HONORS:** MLS, SRS; Westchester Cty. soc. of RE Appraisers; **EDUC:** BS, 1970, Electrical Engrg., NY Inst. of Technology; **OTHER ACT & HONORS:** IEEE; **HOME ADD:** 42 Douglas Ave., Yonkers, NY 10703; **BUS ADD:** 626 McLean Ave., Yonkers, NY 10705, (914)963-4086.

ISING, Dr. Thomas J.——B: Sept. 9, 1939, Luxemburg City, Luxemburg, *Broker-Salesman*, Sheldon F. Good & Co.; **PRIM RE ACT:** Broker, Owner/Investor; **OTHER RE ACT:** Auctioneer; **SERVICES:** Mainly brokerage; **PREV EMPLOY:** Prof. of Econ. Purdue Univ., Loyola Univ.; **PROFL AFFIL & HONORS:** CCIM; **EDUC:** BS, 1961, Physics, MIT; **GRAD EDUC:** PhD, 1971, Econ., Univ. of IL; **HOME ADD:** 19100 Riegel Rd., Homewood, IL 60430, (312)957-0117; **BUS ADD:** 11 N. Wacker Dr., Chicago, IL 60606, (312)346-1500.

ISRAEL, Gary M.——B: July 31, 1944, Somerville, NJ, *Broker/Sales Mgr.*, Shannon & Luchs Co., Sales; **PRIM RE ACT:** Broker, Owner/Investor; **OTHER RE ACT:** Sales Mgr.; **SERVICES:** Resid. & comml. sales; **PROFL AFFIL & HONORS:** Wash. Bd. of Realtors, Montgomery Cty. Bd. of Realtors; **EDUC:** AB, 1967, Hist./Pre Law, George Washington Univ., Ben Franklin Acctg.; **HOME ADD:** 1739 S. St. NW, Washington, DC 20009, (202)265-7743; **BUS ADD:** 2024 P St. NW, Washington, DC 20036, (202)466-8650.

ISRAEL, Paul——*Dir., Appraisal Staff*, U.S. GSA; **PRIM RE ACT:** Broker, Consultant, Appraiser, Banker, Lender, Instructor, Property Manager, Assessor; **SERVICES:** Investment counseling, valuation, mgmt.; **PREV EMPLOY:** Sr. Appraiser, NY Bank for Savings; **PROFL AFFIL & HONORS:** AIREA and Soc. of RE Appraisers; **EDUC:** BS, Bus. Admin., Columbia Univ.; **HOME ADD:** 40 E 9th St., New York, NY 10003; **BUS ADD:** 26 Federal Plaza, New York, NY 10278, (212)264-2612.

ITZEL, John——*Ed.*, California Apt. & Motel Management Assn., Inc., CAMMA News; **PRIM RE ACT:** Real Estate Publisher; **BUS ADD:** 2007 Wilshire Blvd., Los Angeles, CA 90057, (213)483-2321.*

IVERSON, F.K.——*Pres.*, Nvcor Corp.; **PRIM RE ACT:** Property Manager; **BUS ADD:** 4425 Randolph Rd., Charlotte, NC 28211, (704)366-7000.*

IZAGUIRRE, Andrew——*Dir.*, Washington District of Columbia, DC Real Estate Board; **PRIM RE ACT:** Property Manager; **BUS ADD:** 615 A St., N.W., Rm 923, Washington, DC 20001, (202)727-6033.*

JACKMAN, Jerry——B: June 11, 1931, Brigham City, UT, *Sales Mgr.*, Mason-McDuffie Co.; **PRIM RE ACT:** Broker, Consultant, Owner/Investor, Instructor, Property Manager; **PREV EMPLOY:** Sales Mgmt. & VP of Mktg. Nat. Text Book Publishing Firm; **PROFL AFFIL & HONORS:** GRI, CRS; **EDUC:** Elem. & Sec. Educ., 1954, Educ. Admin., Univ. of UT; **EDUC HONORS:** Grad. with Honors; **MIL SERV:** US Army, Sgt.; **HOME ADD:** 12O Gay Ct., Alamo, CA 94507, (415)820-1570; **BUS ADD:** 230 North Hartz Ave., Danville, CA 94526, (415)837-4281.

JACKSON, Bruce G.——B: July 15, 1942, Portland, OR, *Atty. at Law; Owner*, Law Offices of Bruce G. Jackson; **PRIM RE ACT:** Attorney; **SERVICES:** All areas of RE law; **REP CLIENTS:** Assoc. Mgmt. Co.; Bank of HI (comml. mort. conveyancing); "Big G" Construction, Inc.; Bishop Trust Co., Limited (Property Trust, Land Trust documentation); CFP Fin. Services; CIT Fin. Services (HI counsel); CJR Engineering, Inc.; Chattel Leasing, Inc.; Daacon RE Co., Inc.; HI Baptist Academy; **PREV EMPLOY:** US Nat. Bank of OR (comml./RE loans); **PROFL AFFIL & HONORS:** ABA (Real Property Section; Banking & Comml. Law Sections), JD; **EDUC:** BS, 1966, Econ. and Fin., Univ. of OR; **GRAD EDUC:** JD, 1970, Taxation; Real Prop. Law, Boalt Hall, Univ. of CA at Berkeley; **EDUC HONORS:** Cum Laude; **MIL SERV:** US Army, Sgt.; **OTHER ACT & HONORS:** Honolulu Club; Downtown Honolulu Exchange Club; **HOME ADD:** 46-224 Yacht Club St., Kaneohe, HI 96744, (808)235-8056; **BUS ADD:** 190 S. King St., Suite 1132, Honolulu, HI 96813, (808)521-4573.

JACKSON, Clay B.——B: Sept. 21, 1930, Hammond, LA, *VP; Prin. Broker; Sales Mgr.*, Charles R. Hooff, Inc.; **PRIM RE ACT:** Broker; **SERVICES:** Resid. & comml. RE sales; prop. mgmt.; appraisals; **PROFL AFFIL & HONORS:** No. VA Bd. of Realtors; VA Assn. of Realtors; NAR; **EDUC:** BS, 1953, Mil. Engrg., US Military Academy; **GRAD EDUC:** MBA, 1963, Mgmt., George Washington Univ., Washington, DC; **MIL SERV:** USAF, Lt.Col., SS, DFC, Air Medal; **HOME ADD:** 7107 Ft Hunt Rd., Alexandria, VA 22307, (703)660-6678; **BUS ADD:** 1707 Duke St., Alexandria, VA 22314, (703)549-6103.

JACKSON, Earl M.——B: Dec.19, 1949, Richmond, VA, *VP*, Winfree H. Slater, Inc. Realtors, Operations; **PRIM RE ACT:** Broker, Instructor, Property Manager; **OTHER RE ACT:** Resid. Resale Brokerage Office; **SERVICES:** Relocation (Corporate), Gen. Brokerage Services.; **REP CLIENTS:** Third Party Cos. Major Corporate Clients, Indiv. home buyers and sellers; **PROFL AFFIL & HONORS:** NAR, IREM, RNMI, Distinguished Achievers Award 1978 and 1979; **EDUC:** BS, 1976, RE, VA Commonwealth Univ.; **EDUC HONORS:** IREM Scholarship, Herbert U. Nelson Memorial Award; **MIL SERV:** USA, E-4; **OTHER ACT & HONORS:** Cadre of RNMI in Mktg. Mgmt. program; Cadre of VA Assn. of Realtors Inst.; **HOME ADD:** 13621 Hunts Bridge Rd., Midlothian, VA 23113, (804)744-2252; **BUS ADD:** 2737 McRae Rd., Richmond, VA 23235, (804)320-1391.

JACKSON, F. Scott——B: Oct. 13, 1945, Chicago, IL, *Dir.*, Fulop & Hardee; **PRIM RE ACT:** Consultant, Attorney; **SERVICES:** Legal serv. regarding comml. and resid. RE transactions; **REP CLIENTS:** Builders and Devel., Investors, Lenders; **PROFL AFFIL & HONORS:** CA State Bar; ABA; NACORE; **EDUC:** BS, 1967, USAF Academy; **GRAD EDUC:** JD, 1971, Univ. of Denver Coll. of Law; **EDUC HONORS:** Cum Laude; Managing Editor, Denver Law Journal; **MIL SERV:** USAF, Capt., 1967-1971; **OTHER ACT & HONORS:** Pres. Elect, Community Assns. Instit.; Member, Rotary; Several Publications (4 articles in RER, 1 in RELJ); **BUS ADD:** 4041 MacArthur Blvd., 5th Flr., POB 2710, Newport Beach, CA 92660, (714)752-8585.

JACKSON, Guy C., III——B: Aug. 16, 1931, San Antonio, TX, *Pres.*, Cahmbers County Abstract Co., Inc.; **PRIM RE ACT:** Broker, Attorney; **OTHER RE ACT:** Title Insurance Agent; **PREV EMPLOY:** Self 25 yrs.; **PROFL AFFIL & HONORS:** State Bar of TX; TX Land Title Assn.; Amer. Land Title Assn.; TX Assn. of Realtors, JD; **EDUC:** BBA, 1952, TX A&M Coll.; **GRAD EDUC:** JD, 1958, Univ. of TX; **MIL SERV:** US Army; LTC; Service, 1952-1976; Retired (Active & Natl. Guard), Meritorious Service Medal, Army Commendation Medal; **OTHER ACT & HONORS:** County Judge, Chambers Cty., TX 1977-1978; Dir., Trinity River Authority of TX, 1967-1977; Pres., Natl. Guard Assn. of TX; Former Chmn., County Democratic Exec. Comm.; **HOME ADD:** 101 Lynn St., Anahuac, TX 77514, (713)267-3270; **BUS ADD:** 545 Washington Ave., Anahuac, TX 77514, (713)267-6262.

JACKSON, Howard F., Jr.——B: Jan. 2, 1949, Queens, NY, *Exec. VP*, Howard Jackson Assoc., Inc.; **PRIM RE ACT:** Consultant, Appraiser; **OTHER RE ACT:** Computer programmer & systems analyst; **SERVICES:** RE Appraising, RE computer servs.; **REP CLIENTS:** Banks, ins. cos., attys., indus., govt., R&D; **PROFL AFFIL & HONORS:** SREA, NY Acad. of Sci., SRPA, ASA; **EDUC:** BBA, 1971, Econ., Long Island Univ.; **MIL SERV:** ROTC; **HOME ADD:** 116 Stirrup Ln., Levittown, NY 11756, (516)796-8038; **BUS ADD:** 129 Front St., Mineola, NY 11501, (516)248-2844.

JACKSON, James Jay——*Member*, Department of Housing and Urban Development, Fed. Home Loan Bank Board; **PRIM RE ACT:** Lender; **BUS ADD:** 451 Seventh St., S.W., Washington, DC 20410, (202)377-6590.*

JACKSON, Jim——*Ch. of the Board*, ERA; **PRIM RE ACT:** Syndicator; **BUS ADD:** 4900 College Blvd., Shawnee Mission, KS 66201, (913)341-8400.*

JACKSON, John M.——B: Mar. 3, 1945, Dallas, TX, John M. Jackson, Realtor; **PRIM RE ACT:** Broker, Attorney, Developer, Builder, Property Manager, Owner/Investor; **SERVICES:** Counseling, Brokerage & Devel.; **PROFL AFFIL & HONORS:** TX Assoc. Realtors, Dallas Bd. of Realtors, CID Dallas Bd., Nat. Realtors Mktg. Inst., Cert. CCIM; **EDUC:** BBA, 1968, RE, S. Methodist Univ.; **GRAD EDUC:** JD, 1971, RE, Bus. Assoc. & Tax, S. Methodist Univ. Law School; **OTHER ACT & HONORS:** Advisory Bd., Cox School Bus. SMU, Chmn. Bd. Trs., Parents Anonymous, Deacon Park Cities Baptist Church, Member Rotary; **HOME ADD:** 3508 Caruth Blvd., Dallas, TX 75225, (214)369-4746; **BUS ADD:** 3400 Univ. Blvd., Suite 201, Dallas, TX 75205, (214)528-6001.

JACKSON, Mercer H.——*Executive VP*, National Association of RE Investment Trusts; **OTHER RE ACT:** Profl. Assn. Admin.; **BUS ADD:** 1101 17th St. NW Suite 700, Washington, DC 20036, (202)785-8717.*

JACKSON, Mike——*Pres.*, ERA; **PRIM RE ACT:** Syndicator; **BUS ADD:** 4900 College Blvd., Shawnee Mission, KS 66201, (913)341-8400.*

JACKSON, R. Peter——B: June 12, 1944, Palo Alto, CA, *Pres.*, Mariposa RE Corp.; **PRIM RE ACT:** Broker, Consultant, Owner/Investor, Instructor, Property Manager, Syndicator; **OTHER RE ACT:** Devel. of computer servs./progs. for the RE indus.; **SERVICES:** Investment counsel, prop. mgmt. servs., investment brokerage servs. (sales, leasing, exchanging), pvt. offering synds.; **REP CLIENTS:** Indiv. and instit. investors in comml. and resid. props. who need acquisition, mgmt. and sales servs.; **PREV EMPLOY:** Plant Mgr., Lawyers Title Ins. Corp., Santa Barbara Cty. Branch 1969-71; **PROFL AFFIL & HONORS:** Pres., Santa Barbara Bd. of Realtors 1980; Rgnl. VP, CA Assn. of Realtors, 1982; NAR; Nat. Mktg. Inst.; RESSI, Realtor of The Year 1980, Santa Barbara Bd. of Realtors; **EDUC:** BA, 1967, Hist., Univ. of CA Santa Barbara; **OTHER ACT & HONORS:** Santa Barbara C of C; Consultant to CA Time Sharing; Instr., Santa Barbara City Coll. (prop. mgmt.); Author in RE Today: 'Contract Rent, Mkt. Rent and Value', 'All Leverage Isn't Positive', 'A New Form for Calculating Capital Gains Tax and The Minimum Tax'; **HOME ADD:** PO Box 149, Santa Barbara, CA 93102, (805)963-4306; **BUS ADD:** 314 E. Carrillo St., Suite 4, PO 149, Santa Barbara, CA 93102, (805)963-4305.

JACKSON, Randall C.——B: Mar. 21, 1919, Baird, Callahan Cty, TX, *Atty.*, Jackson & Jackson; **PRIM RE ACT:** Attorney; **REP CLIENTS:** Bank of Commerce, Farmers Home Admin., T.S. Lankford & Sons; **PREV EMPLOY:** Dir., First Natl. Bank of Baird; Chmn. , Bd. of Regents, TX Women's Univ., Member State Securities Bd.; **PROFL AFFIL & HONORS:** Bd. Cert., Probate and Estate Planning, State Bar of TX; Member:SW Legal Found., Amer. Judicature Soc., ABA, Abilene Bar Assn. (Pres., 1979-80; Fellow, Amer. Coll. of Probate Law, Who's Who in the South and SW 1955-79; Who's Who in American Law, First and Second Editions; **EDUC:** BBA, 1942, Univ. of TX; **GRAD EDUC:** JD, 1946, Univ. of TX; **MIL SERV:** US Army Air Force, Capt.; **OTHER ACT & HONORS:** Pres.: Texas Hereford Assn., Dir., W. TX Hereford Assn., Concho Hereford Assn., and Sweetwater Hereford Assn., Chmn. State Bd. of Legal Specialization; Pres., Abilene Livestock Assn.; **HOME ADD:** Rte. 2, Box 703, Abilene, TX 79601, (915)529-3232; **BUS ADD:** Suite 210, Bank of Comm. BLdg., PO Box 5006, Abilene, TX 79605, (915)698-9280.

JACKSON, Robert L.——B: Apr. 8, 1945, Jefferson, Iowa, *VP Sec.-Treas.*, Concord Cos., Inc., Concord Dev. Co.; **PRIM RE ACT:** Syndicator, Developer; **SERVICES:** RE investments, dev. services; **REP CLIENTS:** Investors, bus.; **PREV EMPLOY:** VP & Mgr. - The Arizona Bank, 1970-1980; **PROFL AFFIL & HONORS:** Bd. of Realtors, Rotary, Nat. Bd. of Realtors, CCIM Candidate; **EDUC:** BS, 1973, RE & Fin., AZ State Univ.; **OTHER ACT & HONORS:** Chmn., Greater Casa Grande Econ. Dev. Comm. 1978-1980; Rotary; Treas. Casa Grande C of C 1978; VP 1979, 1980; **HOME ADD:** 2256 W Lindner, Mesa, AZ 85202, (602)831-7906; **BUS ADD:** 777 W Southern #211, Mesa, AZ 85202, (602)962-8080.

JACKSON, Robert O.——*Pres.*, Marc Equity Corp., Condo. Conversion Div.; **PRIM RE ACT:** Developer, Owner/Investor; **SERVICES:** Devel. and construction of resid. and comml. prop.; active in condo. conversion projects; **PROFL AFFIL & HONORS:** Gr. Buffalo Bd. of Realtors, Amer. C of C, American Real Estate Exchange, Registered Apt. Mgr.; **EDUC:** Univ. of Buffalo; **BUS ADD:** 2730 Transit Rd., Buffalo, NY 14224, (215)564-6300.

JACKSON, Roscoe D.——**B:** Oct. 31, 1921, Morrilton, AR, *Owner*, R.D. Jackson and Assoc.; **PRIM RE ACT:** Consultant, Appraiser; **SERVICES:** RE appraisals, feasibility studies, consultation; **REP CLIENTS:** Leader Fed. S & L Assn., Metropolitan Fed. S & L Assn., SBA, Commerce Union Bank; **PREV EMPLOY:** VP & Treas., Lovell & Malone, Inc. 1951-67; **PROFL AFFIL & HONORS:** Intl. Right-of-Way Assn., Hendersonville and Nashville C of C; Soc. of RE appraisers; AIREA, SRA, SRPA, MAI, CPA; **MIL SERV:** USAF, Sgt.; **HOME ADD:** 116 Fairways Dr., Hendersonville, TN 37075, (615)824-0250; **BUS ADD:** 1010 J.C. Bradford Bldg., 170 4th Ave., Nashville, TN 37219, (615)255-3584.

JACKSON, Roy——**B:** Jan. 5, 1939, Eldon, MO (Lake of the Ozarks), *Pres.*, Paxton Prop., Inc., Frank Paxton Co.; **PRIM RE ACT:** Developer, Builder, Property Manager; **SERVICES:** Develop & manage investment prop. for parent firm; **EDUC:** BA, 1961, Indus. & Personnel Mgmt., Univ. of MO; **MIL SERV:** US Army, Lt.; **OTHER ACT & HONORS:** NAHB; **BUS ADD:** 9229 Ward Parkway, Kansas City, MO 64114, (816)361-7110.

JACKSON, Steve——*VP Adm.*, Loral Corp.; **PRIM RE ACT:** Property Manager; **BUS ADD:** 600 Third Ave., New York, NY 10016, (212)697-1105.*

JACKSON, Steven L.——**B:** Nov. 9, 1950, Bloomington, IL, *Chief Appraiser/Asst. V.P.*, Gulf Fed. S&L Assn.; **PRIM RE ACT:** Appraiser; **SERVICES:** Research anasis and valuation involving all types of residential and comm'l. prop.; **REP CLIENTS:** Gulf Fed. S&L Assn.; **PREV EMPLOY:** City of Bloomington, IL/HUD; **PROFL AFFIL & HONORS:** SREA: Inst. of Fin. Educ., Mort. Loan Officers Soc., Designation: SRA; **EDUC:** BA, 1972, Soc. Psych./Math., IL Wesleyan Univ., Bloomington; **EDUC HONORS:** Nat. Hon. Soc.; **HOME ADD:** 1218 Twin Palm Dr., Fort Meyers, FL 33907, (813)939-0332; **BUS ADD:** 2301 McGregor Blvd., Fort Meyers, FL 33901, (813)334-2111.

JACOB, Bernard E., Esq.——**B:** Aug. 27, 1932, Baltimore, MD, *Prof. of Law*; **PRIM RE ACT:** Attorney, Instructor; **PREV EMPLOY:** Fried, Frank, Harris, Shriver & Jacobson, NY, part., 1969-1981, Professor of Law, UCLA Law School, Los Angeles, CA, 1964-1968; Gibson, Dunn & Crutcher, L.A. assoc., 1961-1964; clerk, Justice William O. Douglas, 1960-1961; **PROFL AFFIL & HONORS:** Order of the Coif, CA State Bar; ABA Assn. of the Bar of the City of N.Y.; Nassau County Bar Assn.; Amer. Assn. of Legal History; Philosophical Assn.; World Assn. of Lawyers, Participant in PLI and NY Law Journal panels; Dept. Award of Merit, US Commerce Dept., 1968; **EDUC:** BA, 1954, Liberal Arts, St. John's Coll., Annapolis, MD; **GRAD EDUC:** JD, 1960; MA, 1979, Univ. of CA, Berkeley; MA, Philosophy, Graduate Faculty, New School for Soc. Sci.; **HOME ADD:** 502 Park Ave., New York, NY 10022, (212)754-1284; **BUS ADD:** Hofstra Univ. School of Law, Hempstead, NY 11550, (516)560-3278.

JACOB, Robert——*VP Ind. Rel.*, Standard Products Co.; **PRIM RE ACT:** Property Manager; **BUS ADD:** 2130 W. 110 St., Cleveland, OH 44102, (216)281-8300.*

JACOBS, George H.——**B:** Mar. 20, 1952, Syracuse, NY, *Fin. Analyst*, Hartz Mtn. Indus.; **PRIM RE ACT:** Appraiser, Developer, Builder, Owner/Investor; **PREV EMPLOY:** Candeub, Fleissig & Assoc., consultant; H.R. Shapiro, Inc., devel.; New York City, budget analyst; **EDUC:** AB, 1974, Anthro., Rutgers Coll.; **GRAD EDUC:** MCP, 1977, two-thirds completed MBA, Fin. & RE, MCP-Harvard, MBA-Rutgers; **EDUC HONORS:** Phi Beta Kappa; **HOME ADD:** 7 Mayfair Dr., W. Orange, NJ 07052; **BUS ADD:** PO Box 1411, 1 Harmon Plaza, Secaucus, NJ 07094, (201)348-1200.

JACOBS, Harold——**B:** Dec. 11, 1938, Philadelphia, PA, *Partner*, Wolf, Block, Schorr & Solis-Cohen; **PRIM RE ACT:** Attorney; **SERVICES:** Counseling, negotiation, documentation and effecting transactions; **REP CLIENTS:** Devels. of shopping ctrs. and other comml. props., lending inst., investors, landlords and tenants of comml. props.; **PROFL AFFIL & HONORS:** ABA, PA Bar Assn. and Philadelphia Bar Assn.; **EDUC:** BA, 1959, Poli. Sci., Temple Univ.; **GRAD EDUC:** LLB, 1963, Univ. of PA Law School; **EDUC HONORS:** Cum Laude, Law Review; **HOME ADD:** 15 Overbrook Pkwy., Philadelphia, PA 19102, (215)642-4190; **BUS ADD:** 12th Floor, Packard Bldg., Phila., PA 19102, (215)977-2138.

JACOBS, Joseph Charles——**B:** Oct. 6, 1934, Baltimore, MD, *Atty.*; **PRIM RE ACT:** Consultant, Attorney, Developer, Builder, Owner/Investor, Instructor; **SERVICES:** Legal, all phases of development including ownership; **REP CLIENTS:** Dickinson-Heffner, Inc., Baltimore-Washington Mgmt. Co., Inc., Attman Construction Co., Inc., Washington Homes, Inc.; **PREV EMPLOY:** Asst. to the Cty. Exec., Anne Arundel Cty., MD, Asst. Cty. Atty.; **PROFL AFFIL & HONORS:** ABA, MBA; **EDUC:** BA, 1955 & 1961, Econ. and Acctg., Univ. of MD and Johns Hopkins Univ.; **GRAD EDUC:** JD, 1957, Law, Univ. of MD Law School; **MIL SERV:** US Army, E-6; **OTHER ACT & HONORS:** Annapolis Power Squadron, V-P Baltimore Area Council Boy Scouts of Amer.; **HOME ADD:** Po Box 80645, BWIA, Baltimore, MD 21240; **BUS TEL:** (301)859-3335.

JACOBS, Lorraine——**B:** Feb. 19, 1952, Bronx, NY, *Mgr.*, Citibank, N.A., Lower Manhattan Region; **PRIM RE ACT:** Banker, Property Manager; **SERVICES:** Site surveys new branches, prop. mgmt.; **EDUC:** BA, 1973, Pace Univ.; **GRAD EDUC:** MA, 1974, MI State Univ.; **HOME ADD:** 20 Stuyvesant Oval, New York, NY 10009, (212)477-8731; **BUS ADD:** 111 8th Ave., New York, NY 10011, (212)620-1361.

JACOBS, L.W.——*Treasurer*, Aegis Corporation; **PRIM RE ACT:** Property Manager; **BUS ADD:** 256 Catalona Ave., Coral Gables, FL 33134, (305)445-9686.*

JACOBS, Richard L.——**B:** Jan. 16, 1948, Lynn, MA, *Owner/Treas.*, The Yarmouth Co.; **PRIM RE ACT:** Broker, Consultant, Appraiser, Developer, Lender, Owner/Investor; **SERVICES:** Full-serv. comml. and resid. RE devel.; **REP CLIENTS:** Banks, Investors, Corps.; **PREV EMPLOY:** ME Savings Bank, Milton Savings Bank, MA; **PROFL AFFIL & HONORS:** Assoc Member SREA, Member Coll. of RE Profls., CRA; **EDUC:** BS, 1974, Bus. Admin., Salem State Coll., Salem, MA; **GRAD EDUC:** MBA, 1975, Fin., Suffolk Univ., Boston, MA; **MIL SERV:** USA, 1st Lt., Vietnamese Gallantry Cross, Bronze Star; **HOME ADD:** 21 Anderson Ave., Yarmouth, ME 04096, (207)846-9936; **BUS ADD:** 148 Middle St., PO Box 524, Portland, ME 04112, (207)772-6339.

JACOBSEN, Dean A.——**B:** Apr. 3, 1944, Northfield, MN, *Pres.*, Crico Management Corp.; **PRIM RE ACT:** Property Manager; **SERVICES:** Asset & prop. mgmt.; **REP CLIENTS:** Devel. & synd. of multi-family and comml. props.; **PROFL AFFIL & HONORS:** IREM; BOMA; NAA, CPM; **EDUC:** BS, 1966, Bus./Econ., Univ. of MN; **HOME ADD:** 10210 Cedar Pond Dr., Vienna, VA 22180, (703)938-2431; **BUS ADD:** 11300 Rockville Pike, Rockville, MD 20852, (301)770-9170.

JACOBSEN, Heber S.——**B:** Nov. 20, 1945, Salt Lake, UT, *Pres.*, Jacobsen Investment & Jacobsen Brothers Inc.; **PRIM RE ACT:** Developer, Builder, Owner/Investor; **REP CLIENTS:** Mountain States Telephone & Telegraph; Sperry-Univac Div. of Sperry Corp; Kennecott Copper; AT&T; **EDUC:** BS, 1971, Civil. Engrg., Stanford Univ.; **GRAD EDUC:** MS, 1973, Civil Engrg., Stanford Univ.; **BUS ADD:** 62 S. 300 E, Salt Lake City, UT 84111, (801)531-6587.

JACOBSEN, John H.——**B:** Dec. 1, 1942, Chicago, IL, *Investment Broker*, Baird & Warner, Comml./Investment Div.; **PRIM RE ACT:** Broker; **SERVICES:** Brokerage, site selection, valuation serv.; **REP CLIENTS:** Local banks, synd., intl. investors; **PREV EMPLOY:** RE Appraiser; Sr. Prop. Mgr., Continental IL Bank; **PROFL AFFIL & HONORS:** Local RE Bds., Central Assn. of RE Exchangers; Economic Devel. Commn., CPM; Cert. Appraiser; **EDUC:** 1964, Econ., Wright Coll.; 1974, RE Inst.; 1977, Econ., Northwestern Univ.; **HOME ADD:** 3658 N Oak Pk., Chicago, IL 60634; **BUS ADD:** 115 S LaSalle St., Chicago, IL 60603, (312)368-5840.

JACOBSON, Andrew Mark——**B:** Nov. 22, 1953, NY, NY, *Nat. Investment Co.*; **PRIM RE ACT:** Attorney, Developer; **SERVICES:** RE devel. & investment resid.; **PROFL AFFIL & HONORS:** ABA, FL Bar, Palm Beach Cty. Bar Assn., Community Assns. Inst.; **EDUC:** BA, 1975, Poli. Sci., Univ. of Rochester; **GRAD EDUC:** JD, 1978, Univ. of FL Coll.of Law; **EDUC HONORS:** with Honors, with Honors; **OTHER ACT & HONORS:** Govs., PGA Prop. Owners Assn., Inc., Dir. Counterpoint Estates Prop. Owners Assn. Inc.; **HOME ADD:** 10348 Pippin Ln., W. Palm Beach, FL 33411, (305)793-4912; **BUS ADD:** 1675 Plam Beach Lakes Blvd. 900, W. Palm Beach, FL 33401, (305)686-2000.

JACOBSON, Arch K.——**B:** Feb. 1, 1928, Eden, TX, *Pres.*, Mercantile Realty Services Corp.; **PRIM RE ACT:** Banker, Owner/Investor; **SERVICES:** RE investment advice and asset mgmt.; **REP CLIENTS:** Employee benefit pension funds from co's. based primarily in the SW; **PREV EMPLOY:** VP, RE Investment Dept. - The Prudential Ins. Co. of Amer. 1955-1981; **PROFL AFFIL & HONORS:** ULI; **EDUC:** BS, 1949, Agronomy, Texas A&M Univ.; **MIL SERV:** USAF, Capt.; **HOME ADD:** 10214 Epping Lane, Dallas, TX 75229, (214)351-9817; **BUS ADD:** PO Box 225415, Dallas, TX 75265, (214)698-6923.

JACOBSON, Benjamin——**B:** Jan. 24, 1934, Philadelphia, PA, *Pres.*, Benjamin Jacobson Associates, Inc., Indus./comml.; **PRIM RE ACT:** Broker; **SERVICES:** RE Brokerage; **REP CLIENTS:** Indus.; **PROFL**

AFFIL & HONORS: Realtor & SIR, SIR; **EDUC:** 1960, RE, Temple Univ.; **GRAD EDUC:** MBA, 1966, Bus., Drexel Univ.; **MIL SERV:** US Army, Specialist; **HOME ADD:** 7925 Jenkintown Rd., Cheltenham, PA 19012, (215)663-0476; **BUS ADD:** 1616 Walnut St. 1018, Philadelphia, PA 19103, (215)545-8581.

JACOBSON, Bernard——B: Feb. 27, 1930, CT, *Atty.*, Fine Jacovson Block Klein Colan & Simon, P.A.; **PRIM RE ACT:** Attorney, Consultant, Developer, Lender; **SERVICES:** Legal and consultant; **PREV EMPLOY:** Republic Mort. Investors - Pres., 1981; **EDUC:** AB, 1951, Amherst Moll.; **GRAD EDUC:** LL.B., 1954, Columbia Univ.; **BUS ADD:** PO Box 340800, 2401 Douglas Rd, Miami, FL 33134.

JACOBSON, Jack R.——B: Apr. 8, 1930, Bridgeport, CT, *Pres.*, Jack R. Jacobson RE Brokerage; **PRIM RE ACT:** Broker, Consultant, Owner/Investor, Property Manager; **SERVICES:** Prop. mgmt., investment counseling, valuation; **REP CLIENTS:** Indiv. and instnl. investors in comml. RE; **PROFL AFFIL & HONORS:** RE Broker, State of CT, Nat. Assn. of Indep. Fee Appraisers, Sr. Member Intl. Coll. of RE consulting profls., Intl. Inst. of Valuers, Sr. Member; Amer. Mgmt. Assn., Member; **HOME ADD:** PO Box 467, Bridgeport, CT 06601; **BUS ADD:** 2912 Main St. A-13, Bridgeport, CT 06605, (203)334-0790.

JACOBSON, Joel N.——B: Dec. 25, 1946, Perth Amboy, NJ, *Atty. (Part)*, Norris, McLaughlin & Marcus; **PRIM RE ACT:** Attorney; **SERVICES:** Representation in all phases of RE law; **REP CLIENTS:** Lenders, devels., & investors; **PREV EMPLOY:** Fed. Home Loan Bank Bd., Office of Gen. Counsel (1972-75); **PROFL AFFIL & HONORS:** Amer. NJ & Somerset Cty Bar Assns.; **EDUC:** BA, 1968, Univ. of PA; **GRAD EDUC:** JD, 1971, Univ. of PA; **EDUC HONORS:** Cum Laude; **HOME ADD:** 170 Lenape Ln., Berkeley Heights, NJ 07922, (201)464-1450; **BUS ADD:** 1081 Rt 22, PO Box 310, Somerville, NJ 08876, (201)722-0700.

JACOBSON, Richard J.——B: Oct. 1, 1930, Manchester, NH, *VP & Assoc. Gen. Counsel*, Weaver Bros. Inc.; **PRIM RE ACT:** Broker, Consultant, Attorney, Developer, Lender, Instructor, Property Manager; **OTHER RE ACT:** Leasing agent & negotiator; **SERVICES:** Mort. banking, realtor & ins.; **REP CLIENTS:** Metropolitan Life, Riggs Nat. Bank, Jefferson Standard Life, FNMA, Fed. Res. Bd.; **PROFL AFFIL & HONORS:** Intn. Council of Shopping Ctrs., LLB; **EDUC:** AB, 1953, Hist. & Eng., St. Anselm's Coll.; **GRAD EDUC:** LLM, 1957, Law, Real Prop., George Wash. Univ. Law Sch.; **OTHER ACT & HONORS:** USA, Capt.; **HOME ADD:** 4131 Novar Dr., Chantilly, VA 22021, (703)968-7283; **BUS ADD:** 5530 Wisconsin Ave., Wash. DC 20015, (301)986-4263.

JACOBUS, Charles J.——B: Aug. 21, 1947, Ponca City, OK, *VP and Gen. Counsel*, Tenneco Realty, Inc.; **PRIM RE ACT:** Broker, Attorney, Developer, Builder, Owner/Investor, Instructor, Property Manager, Real Estate Publisher; **PROFL AFFIL & HONORS:** ABA; Houston Bar Assn.; Houston Bd. of Realtors; RE Educator's Assn.; State Bar of TX; ABA Comm. on Condo. and Cooperative Housing; Member of the ABA Comm. on RE Legal Practice Methods; Nat. Assn. of Corporate RE Execs.; TX Trial Lawyers Assn.; TX RE Teacher's Assn., Chmn, Houston Chap. 1980; RE Educator's Assn., Charter Member; Member of the ABA Comm. on New Developments in RE Law and Practice, Houston Law Review - Vol. 11, No. 2, "The Condominimum and the Corporation, a Proposal for Texas"; Co-author of "Counseling the Condo. Purchaser", ABA Journal on RE Probate and Trust, Vol. 10, No. 3; Co-author of text, *TX RE Second Edition*, Reston Publishing Co., Reston, VI. Co-authored with Dr. Bruce Harwood; Author of text, *Texas RE Law*, Reston Publishing Co., Reston, VI; Co-author of text, *Real Estate Law*, national in scope, published by Reston Publishing Co. , Reston, VI;. Co-authored with Dr. Donald R. Levi; CRA; Chmn., Bellaire Planning & Zoning Comm. 1976-77; **EDUC:** BS, 1970, Biology, Univ. of Houston; **GRAD EDUC:** JD, 1973, Law, Univ. of Houston; **EDUC HONORS:** Nat. Student Reg.; Who's Who in Amer. Coll. and Univ.; **OTHER ACT & HONORS:** Universal Order of the Knights of the Vine; Les Amis du Vin; Who's Who in Houston; Arbitrator for Better Bus. Bureau; **HOME ADD:** 5223 Pine St., Bellaire, TX 77401, (713)661-3913; **BUS ADD:** PO Box 2511, Houston, TX 77001, (713)757-3422.

JACOBUS, John L.——B: Feb. 16, 1920, Newark, NJ, *Sr. Atty.*, Kraft, Inc. Also VP Phenix-Georgetown, Inc., and Phenix Mgmt. Corp., RE devel. and mgmt. subs. of Kraft, Inc.; **PRIM RE ACT:** Attorney; **PROFL AFFIL & HONORS:** ABA, IL and Chicago Bar Assns., Nat. Assn. of Corporate RE Execs., Employee Relocation Council; **EDUC:** BA in Bus. Admin., 1947, Econ., Rutgers Univ.; **GRAD EDUC:** JD, 1949, Law, Harvard Law School; **EDUC HONORS:** Phi Beta Kappa; High Honors; **MIL SERV:** US Army, 1st Lt.; **HOME ADD:** 3925 N. Triumvera Dr., Unit 3-F, Glenview, IL 60025, (312)299-5736; **BUS ADD:** Kraft Court, Glenview, IL 60025, (312)998-2483.

JACONETTI, Armando E.——B: May 14, 1938, Chicago, IL, *Pres.*, Oak Center Real Estate; **PRIM RE ACT:** Broker, Consultant, Appraiser, Developer, Builder, Owner/Investor, Syndicator; **SERVICES:** Comml. brokerage and devel.; **PROFL AFFIL & HONORS:** Nat. Assn. of Indep. Fee Appraisers, Nat. Assn. of Review Appraisers, CRA; **EDUC:** BS, 1962, Bus., Loyola Univ.; **GRAD EDUC:** 1965, Law, Chicago Kent Coll. of Law; **MIL SERV:** USA, Capt.; **OTHER ACT & HONORS:** Knights of Columbus; Past Pres. Interstate United Props.; **HOME ADD:** 386 Pennsylvania Ave., Glenellyn, IL 60137, (312)858-4308; **BUS ADD:** 17071 W. Hodges Rd., Oakbrook, IL 60181, (312)279-2380.

JAFFE, Arvin J.——B: May 21, 1954, Ft. Knox, KY, *Atty.*, Ballard, Spahr, Andrews & Ingersoll; **PRIM RE ACT:** Attorney; **PROFL AFFIL & HONORS:** Member of FL and PA Bars; **EDUC:** BA, 1976, Intl. Rel., Univ. of PA; London School of Econ.; **GRAD EDUC:** JD, 1979, Univ. of PA Law School; **EDUC HONORS:** Summa Cum Laude; Phi Beta Kappa; **HOME ADD:** 2005 Pine Street, Philadelphia, PA 19103, (215)546-5762; **BUS ADD:** 30 S. 17th St., Philadelphia, PA 19103, (215)564-1800.

JAFFE, Bernard——*Corp. VP & Secy.*, Sun Chemical Corp.; **PRIM RE ACT:** Property Manager; **BUS ADD:** 200 Park Ave., 54th Fl., New York, NY 10017, (212)986-5500.*

JAFFE, Donald S.——B: Apr. 22, 1932, Chicago, IL, *VP*, Arthur Rubloff & Co., Ind. Brokerage Grp.; **PRIM RE ACT:** Broker, Developer; **SERVICES:** Ind. and comml. brokerage to bus. and comml. cos.; **REP CLIENTS:** Ind. and comml. cos., RCA Corp., Internorth Co., Maremont Corp., Federal Express; **PROFL AFFIL & HONORS:** SIR; Assn. of Ind. RE Brokers; Chicago RE Bd.; ABA; Chicago Bar Assn.; **EDUC:** BS, 1953, Chemistry/Physics, Univ. of IL; **GRAD EDUC:** LLB, 1956, Law, Univ. of IL; ML, 1957, Fed. Tax. Law, NY Univ.; **OTHER ACT & HONORS:** Pres., Avoca School P.T.A.; **HOME ADD:** 1247 Sherwood Rd., Glenview, IL 60025, (312)729-3363; **BUS ADD:** 8600 W. Bryn Mawr, Chicago, IL 60631, (312)399-7040.

JAFFE, Richard——B: July 1, 1951, Chicago, IL, *Atty.*, Wickes Cos., Inc.; **PRIM RE ACT:** Attorney; **PREV EMPLOY:** Aldens, Inc.; **PROFL AFFIL & HONORS:** ABA, Chicago Bar Assn., IL Bar Assn.; **EDUC:** BA, 1973, Psych, Univ. of WI, Madison; **GRAD EDUC:** JD, 1976, I.I.T. Chic.-Kent Coll. of Law; **HOME ADD:** 846 W Gunnison, Chicago, IL 60640, (312)878-2310; **BUS ADD:** 2215 Sanders Rd., Northbrook, IL 60062, (312)564-8500.

JAHNS, Jeffrey——B: July 6, 1946, Chicago, IL, *Partner*, Seyfarth, Shaw, Fairweather & Geraldson, Chicago Office; **PRIM RE ACT:** Attorney; **REP CLIENTS:** Devels., builders, investors, lenders; **PROFL AFFIL & HONORS:** Chicago Bar Assn., Arch. Comm. (Chmn. 1978-1981), Urban Affairs Comm. (Chmn. 1978-1979); **EDUC:** AB, 1968, Humanities, Villanova Univ.; **GRAD EDUC:** JD, 1971, Law, Univ. of Chicago; **EDUC HONORS:** Fellow, Ctr. for Urban Studies; **OTHER ACT & HONORS:** Former Bd. Member, Landlords Preservation Council of IL, Chmn., 48th World Zoning Land-Use Advisory Comm. (1978-present); **HOME ADD:** 1339 Catalpa, Chicago, IL 60640, (312)728-0994; **BUS ADD:** 55 E. Monroe St., Suite 4200, Chicago, IL 60603, (312)346-8000.

JAMES, Andy——*Admin.*, Texas, Texas Real Estate Commission; **OTHER RE ACT:** Administrator; **BUS ADD:** PO Box 12188, Capital Station, Austin, TX 78711, (512)459-6544.*

JAMES, Herbert L.——B: Feb. 22, 1923, Spencer, IA, H.L. James & Assoc., Realtor, Appraiser, Mort. Broker, Ins.; **PRIM RE ACT:** Broker, Appraiser; **PROFL AFFIL & HONORS:** Realtor Morg. Broker, Auctioneers, CRB; CRS; SMC; CAS; **OTHER ACT & HONORS:** V. Chmn. Pinellas Co. Housing Auth.; Masons York Rite; Scottish Rite Shrine; Elks; **HOME TEL:** (813)536-6698; **BUS ADD:** 302 W. Bay Dr., Largo, FL 33540, (813)584-7189.

JAMES, John D.——B: Apr. 22, 1941, St. Paul, MN, *Atty.*, Fawell, James and Brooks; **PRIM RE ACT:** Attorney; **SERVICES:** Full RE - zoning; new const., fin.; **REP CLIENTS:** Banks, RE brokers, investors and devels.; **PROFL AFFIL & HONORS:** ABA, IL Bar Assn., DuPage Cty. Bar Assn., Assn. of Trial Lawyers of Amer., IL Trial Lawyers Assn., Fellow., Amer. Acad. of Matrimonial Lawyers; **EDUC:** BA, 1963, Poli. Sci., Valpraiso Univ.; **GRAD EDUC:** JD, 1966, Law, Chicago-Kent Coll. of Law; **HOME ADD:** 209 N. Brainard St., Naperville, IL 60540, (312)961-0296; **BUS ADD:** 101 N. Washington St., P.O. Box 815, Naperville, IL 60540, (312)355-2101.

JAMES, John K.——B: July, 1943, Santa Monica, CA, *Gen. Partner*, Beim & James; **PRIM RE ACT:** Developer, Owner/Investor; **PREV EMPLOY:** Green & Barry Partners; White Weld & Co.; **EDUC:** AB,

1965, Econ., Stanford Univ.; **GRAD EDUC:** MBA, 1970, Fin., Stanford Grad. School of Bus.; **HOME ADD:** Portola Valley, CA 94025; **BUS ADD:** 3000 Sand Hill Rd., Menlo Park, CA 94025.

JAMES, Thomas R.——B: Apr. 21, 1942, Bucks Cty., *Owner*, Elizabeth James "Ctry. RE"; **PRIM RE ACT:** Broker, Instructor, Syndicator, Developer, Owner/Investor; **SERVICES:** RE Counseling; **REP CLIENTS:** Buyers, Sellers, Investors; **PREV EMPLOY:** Part Time Adjunct Prof. (Now); Bucks Cty. Community Coll./Delaware Valley Coll. of Sci. & Agri.; **PROFL AFFIL & HONORS:** Dir. Bucks Cty. Bd. of Realtors; PAR; NAR; CRB; **EDUC:** BA, 1964, Eng., Muhlenberg Coll.; **GRAD EDUC:** 30 Grad. credits, Eng., Educ., Lehigh; **MIL SERV:** US Army; Spec. 4; **BUS ADD:** Box 355, Lanaska, PA 18931, (215)794-7403.

JAMES, Thomas T., III——B: Aug. 16, 1945, Albany, GA, *VP, Indus. Props. Grp.*, Arthur Rubloff & Co.; **PRIM RE ACT:** Broker; **SERVICES:** Indus. Sales & Leasing, Investment Sales; **PREV EMPLOY:** John Hunsinger & Co., 1971-1979; **PROFL AFFIL & HONORS:** Salesman Affiliate SIR; **EDUC:** BBA, 1967, Gen. Bus. Admin., Univ. of GA; **MIL SERV:** USA, Sgt., Bronze Star Republic of Vietnam; **HOME ADD:** 3799 Paces Ferry West, Atlanta, GA 30339, (404)432-9089; **BUS ADD:** 134 Peachtree St. NE, Atlanta, GA 30043, (404)577-5300.

JAMISON, John W., III——B: Sept. 30, 1946, Birmingham, AL, *Pres.*, Capital Resources Corp.; **PRIM RE ACT:** Consultant, Appraiser, Lender, Owner/Investor, Insuror, Syndicator; **OTHER RE ACT:** Income Prop. Mort. Broker; **SERVICES:** Income Prop. Mort. Brokerage, Synd. of income props., investment consulting, valuation and equity fin.; **REP CLIENTS:** RE Mgmt. Cos., RE Investors, RE Devel., Synd. and RE Lenders; **PREV EMPLOY:** VP, Head Income Prop. Div., Collateral Investment Co. 1971-1981; **PROFL AFFIL & HONORS:** Mort. Bankers Assn. of Amer.; Intl. Assn. of Fin. Planners; **EDUC:** BS, 1971, Bus. Admin.-Econ., Univ. of AL in Birmingham, School of Bus.; **GRAD EDUC:** MBA, 1974, Mort. Banking, NW Univ., School of Bus.; **EDUC HONORS:** Dean's List; **OTHER ACT & HONORS:** Member; Episcopal Cathedral Church of the Advent, Riverchase Ctry. Club, Mercedes-Benz Club of Amer., Indus. Task Force in Community Revitalization, Faculty-Workshop on Planning and Fin.-A Health Care Ctr., The School of Public and Allied Health Univ. of AL in Birmingham; **HOME ADD:** 2908 Wisteria Dr., Birmingham, AL 35216, (205)823-6146; **BUS ADD:** 1900 Indian Lake Dr., Birmingham, AL 35244, (205)987-0700.

JAMNICK, William P.——B: Oct. 13, 1940, Poplar Bluff, MO, *Mgr.;Principal*, Weir Manuel Snyder & Ranke, Inc.; **PRIM RE ACT:** Broker; **SERVICES:** Gen. brokerage; **REP CLIENTS:** Homequity; **PROFL AFFIL & HONORS:** Pres. Rochester Bd. of Realtors, 1974; **EDUC:** BA, 1963, Eng., NW Univ., Evanston, IL; **MIL SERV:** USN, Lt., 1963-67, AFEM; **HOME ADD:** 330 W Tienken Rd., Rochester, MI 48063, (313)631-9184; **BUS ADD:** 1205 W Univ., Rochester, MI 48063, (313)651-3500.

JANNEN, Kenneth R.——B: June 25, 1949, Pt. Jefferson, NY, *Assoc. Rgnl. Counsel*, First American Title Insurance Co.; **PRIM RE ACT:** Attorney; **SERVICES:** Title Ins., Underwriting; **PROFL AFFIL & HONORS:** ABA; Broward Cty. Bar Assn., Member of the NY and FL Bars; **EDUC:** BA, 1971, Soc. Sci., Dowling Coll., Oakdale NY; **GRAD EDUC:** JD, 1975, New York Law School; **BUS ADD:** 7520 NW Fifth St., Plantation, FL 33317, (305)587-5860.

JANOVER, Robert H.——B: Aug. 17, 1930, New York, NY, *Lawyer; Head of Own Office*, Law Offices of Robert H. Janover; **PRIM RE ACT:** Attorney; **SERVICES:** Lawyer; **PREV EMPLOY:** Admitted to Bar: NY (1957); DC (1966); MI (1973); US Supreme Court (1962); **PROFL AFFIL & HONORS:** VChmn. (1976-78) and Chmn. (1978-81) of Comm. on Synd. and Comml. Transactions in RE, Real Property Law Section, State Bar of MI; **EDUC:** BA, 1972, Princeton Univ. Also attended Univ. of Vienna (diploma, 1956); **GRAD EDUC:** JD, 1957, Harvard Law School; **MIL SERV:** US Army, 1952-1954; **OTHER ACT & HONORS:** Consultant and Legislative Atty. U.S. Dept. of Health, Education and Welfare (1965-66), Many bar assn. memberships, Dir., Civic Searchlight, Inc.; Pres. and Dir., Oakland Citizens League; **HOME ADD:** 685 Ardmoor Dr., Birmingham, MI 48010, (313)646-0426; **BUS ADD:** 1970 City National Bank Bldg., Detroit, MI 48226, (313)962-2250.

JANZ, James R.——B: Nov. 24, 1948, Hammond, IN, Pettit & Martin; **PRIM RE ACT:** Attorney; **SERVICES:** Legal; **REP CLIENTS:** Devel., synd., landlords and tenants, lenders; **PROFL AFFIL & HONORS:** San Francisco, CA and Amer. Bar Assns., ASCE, Amer. Planning Assn., Profl. Engr. - NY; Beta Gamma Sigma; **EDUC:** BSCE, 1970, Purdue Univ.; **GRAD EDUC:** MS in Urban Planning, 1974, Columbia Univ., Grad. School of Architecture and Urban Planning; JD-MBA, 1979, Univ. of Chicago; **OTHER ACT & HONORS:** Bd. of Dirs. of San Francisco Hearing & Speech Center, Squaw Valley Creative Arts Soc.; **HOME ADD:** 176 Idora Ave., San Francisco, CA 94127; **BUS ADD:** 600 Montgomery St., San Francisco, CA 94111, (415)434-4000.

JARNAGIN, Bruce A.——B: Nov. 20, 1951, Dayton, OH, *Pres.*, River Props. Inc.; **PRIM RE ACT:** Consultant, Developer, Builder, Owner/Investor; **SERVICES:** Total devel. packages in resid. subdivs., total of 350 units present under devel. & constr., some comml. devel.; **PROFL AFFIL & HONORS:** NE FL Bldrs Assn., Member C of C; **HOME ADD:** 1786 Mandarin Estates Dr., Jacksonville, FL 32216; **BUS ADD:** 5541 Bowden Rd., Jacksonville, FL 32216, (904)733-2450.

JARVIS, Dorothy——B: May 3, 1934, Waterloo, IA, *Pres.*, Jarvis and Assoc.; **PRIM RE ACT:** Broker, Owner/Investor; **SERVICES:** sales and lease of commercial investment prop.; **PROFL AFFIL & HONORS:** RESSI, Denver Bd. of Realtors, Comml. Edu. Com., CCIM, Chmn., CCIM, Speakers Bureau for CO and WY; **EDUC:** BA, 1955, Psych, Stanford Univ.; **OTHER ACT & HONORS:** Charter mbr. of Denver Businesswomen's Roundtable, Denver City of Hope, Stanford Alumni Assoc.; **HOME ADD:** 7981 S. Adams Way, Littleton, CO 80122, (303)773-6983; **BUS ADD:** Metro Broker Offices, 5031 S. Ulster Pky, Suite 200, Denver, CO 80237, (303)740-8668.

JARVIS, Ronald D.——B: Sept. 25, 1942, Salt Lake City, UT, *Pres.*, Jarvis Investment Corp.; **PRIM RE ACT:** Broker, Instructor, Consultant, Developer, Property Manager, Real Estate Publisher; **OTHER RE ACT:** Investment Counselor, Exchange Counselor, Mort. Broker; **SERVICES:** Investment Counseling, Exchange Counseling, Mort. Investing, Equity Participation; **REP CLIENTS:** Private Investors, Corp., Pension & Retirement Funds, Dev., Lenders & R.E. Brokers; **PROFL AFFIL & HONORS:** RNMI, (Interex), (CBC), Trustee-Commonwealth Trust, Articles Published Natl., Guest Lecture-Univ. of Wash., Sr. Listee-Who's Who in Creative R.E., Past Pres. Puget Sound Exchangors.; **OTHER ACT & HONORS:** Rotary Intl., Lic. Comml. Pilot; **HOME TEL:** (206)852-1031; **BUS ADD:** 404 W. Titus Bldg, Kent, WA 98031, (206)852-3910.

JASON-WHITE, Donald L.——B: Oct. 26, 1937, St. Louis, MO, *Pres. & CEO*, The Colchis Corp., Jason-White Assocs.; **PRIM RE ACT:** Broker, Consultant, Developer, Owner/Investor, Property Manager, Syndicator; **SERVICES:** Devel. & synd. of comml. props., prop. advisory, mort. brokering; **REP CLIENTS:** Pvt. investors, for. pension funds, prop. bonds, cos., RE owners and comml. prop. devel.; **PREV EMPLOY:** Briscoe Co./Ft. Worth, TX (1970-1974) Sr. VP of RE Mgmt. Consulting Div.; **PROFL AFFIL & HONORS:** Amer. Mgmt. Assn.; NAR; Amer. Psychological Assn.; **EDUC:** BA, 1962, Psych., CA State Univ. - Los Angeles; **GRAD EDUC:** MS, 1964, Psycho., Indust. Psychol., CA State Univ. - LA; MBA/Bus. Admin., 1975, Fin. & Urban Mgmt., Pepperdine Univ. - Los Angeles; **EDUC HONORS:** Cum Laude; **MIL SERV:** US Army, Res.; E-3. Active Duty: 1956-1957; Active Res.: 1957-1959; Standby: 1959-1964; **OTHER ACT & HONORS:** Past Year's Coor., Jr. Achievement Programs (Ft. Worth, TX); **HOME ADD:** 4832 Vista DeOro Ave., Los Angeles, CA 90043, (213)296-3253; **BUS ADD:** 9701 Wilshire Blvd., Suite 730, Beverly Hills, CA 90212.

JAY, Richard A.——B: July 9, 1953, Denver, CO, *VP First Interstate Bank of Casper, N.A. RE Fin.*; **PRIM RE ACT:** Appraiser, Banker, Lender; **SERVICES:** Mort. Banking; **REP CLIENTS:** Life Cos., Govt. Agencies, Other Investors; **EDUC:** BA, 1975, Mgmt., Univ. of Denver; **GRAD EDUC:** MBA, 1979, Fin, Harvard Bus. School; **EDUC HONORS:** Magna Cum Laude; **HOME ADD:** 1601 S. Nebraska, Casper, WY 82601, (307)235-3596; **BUS ADD:** PO Box 40, Casper, WY 82602, (307)235-4307.

JAYE, Carroll B.——B: Mar 14, 1947, Henderson, NC, *VP*, McGrath Mgmt., Inc.; **PRIM RE ACT:** Broker, Consultant, Property Manager; **PREV EMPLOY:** VP, Grace Properties, Inc.; **PROFL AFFIL & HONORS:** CPM, Pres., Central FL chap., IREM, Off., VP Central FL Multi-Housing Assn., Member Better Business Comm., C of C, Nat. Apt. Assn., BOMA; **EDUC:** AA, 1968, Bus., E. NM Univ.; **HOME ADD:** 320 Sandspur Rd., Maitland, FL 32751; **BUS ADD:** 1850 Lee Rd. Suite 133, Winter Park, FL 32789.

JAYSON, Joseph M.——B: Aug. 16, 1938, Buffalo, NY, *Pres*, J.M. Jayson & Co., Inc.; **PRIM RE ACT:** Broker, Property Manager, Syndicator; **PREV EMPLOY:** Realmark Prop.Mgmt.; Westmoreland Capital Corp.; US Energy Corp.; Oilmark Corp.; **PROFL AFFIL & HONORS:** IREM, CPM; **EDUC:** BS, 1961, Educ., IN Univ.; **GRAD EDUC:** MSEd., 1964, Univ. of Buffalo; **HOME ADD:** 21 Westmoreland Rd., Amherst, NY 14226, (716)836-7198; **BUS ADD:** 680 Statler Bldg., Buffalo, NY 14202, (716)854-6767.

JEANNEL, Charles——**B:** May 12, 1945, Nice, France, *Owner*; **PRIM RE ACT:** Consultant, Architect, Developer, Owner/Investor; **SERVICES:** RE devel., design, investments; **REP CLIENTS:** Investors; **PREV EMPLOY:** Self employed for 10 yrs., Sr. Partner in Courtois & Thiersent, Arch., in Paris, France, 1971-76; **PROFL AFFIL & HONORS:** French Inst. of Arch., Paris; **EDUC:** 1962, Philosophy, Paris; **GRAD EDUC:** 1971, Arch., Univ. of Beaux-Arts, Paris; **MIL SERV:** French Air Force, Sport Inst., 1971; **OTHER ACT & HONORS:** French Amer. C of C, Los Angeles; **HOME ADD:** 1707 Viewmont Dr., Los Angeles, CA 90069, (213)659-7224; **BUS ADD:** 1707 Viewmont Dr., Los Angeles, CA 90069, (213)659-3863.

JEFSEN, John I.——**B:** Apr. 7, 1937, CA, *VP and Gen. Counsel*, Ponderosa Homes; **PRIM RE ACT:** Broker, Attorney, Developer; **PROFL AFFIL & HONORS:** ABA, CA Bar Assn., Natl. Assn. of Realtors, CA Assn. of Realtors, Order of Coif; **EDUC:** AB, 1959, Econ., Univ. of CA, Berkeley; **GRAD EDUC:** JD, 1964, Law, Hastings School of Law; **EDUC HONORS:** Order of Coif, Thurston Honor Soc.; **MIL SERV:** USN; **BUS ADD:** 2082 Bus. Ctr. Dr., Irvine, CA 92715, (714)975-1678.

JELORMINE, Michael S.——**B:** Aug. 25, 1947, Bridgeport, CT, *CPA*, Michael S. Jelormine, Heher, & Co. PC; **OTHER RE ACT:** CPA; **SERVICES:** Fin. planning and modeling projections-fin. statements; **REP CLIENTS:** Land devel., res, comml., devel. and const., condo. devel.; **PREV EMPLOY:** Sr. Auditor Price- Waterhouse & Co.; **PROFL AFFIL & HONORS:** AICPA, CSCPA, CPA; **EDUC:** BA, 1972, Acctg., Univ. of Bridgeport; **EDUC HONORS:** Beta Gamma Sigma, Summa Cum Laude; **MIL SERV:** USA, Sp 5; **HOME ADD:** 93 Emerson Dr., Stratford, CT 06497; **BUS ADD:** 160 Hawley Ln. 200, Trumball, CT 06611, (203)377-6041.

JELTES, Charles J.——**B:** Apr. 3, 1946, East Grand Rapids, MI, *Prop. Mgr.*, Practical Mgmt. Co., Mgmt. Dept.; **PRIM RE ACT:** Property Manager; **SERVICES:** Prop. Mgmt.; **REP CLIENTS:** For Resid. Apts. & Props. managed & owned by the Practical Grp. of Cos.; **PREV EMPLOY:** Ann Arbor Trust Co. Trust Div., RE Dept. 1975-1978; **PROFL AFFIL & HONORS:** Lic. RE Salesperson, State of MI 1975; **EDUC:** AB, 1972, Hist., Psych., Univ. of MI, Dearborn, MI; **OTHER ACT & HONORS:** USA, SP5, 1969-1971; **HOME ADD:** 18753-2 Innsbrook Dr., Northville, MI 48167, (313)348-9068; **BUS ADD:** 21790 Coolidge Highway, Oak Park, MI 48237, (313)548-4800.

JEMISON, Frank Z., Jr.——**B:** July 22, 1948, Memphis, TN, *Pres.*, Alco Properties, Incorporated; **PRIM RE ACT:** Broker, Consultant, Developer, Owner/Investor, Property Manager, Syndicator; **SERVICES:** Indiv. investment counseling; synd. formation for the devel. of income prop.; prop. servs. provided for var. private owners as well as n-profit owners, spec. in subsidized housing; **PREV EMPLOY:** VP of Amcon Intl. 1971-75; **PROFL AFFIL & HONORS:** Memphis Bd. of Realtors, Adv. Council; Nat. Council for Managing Agents; **EDUC:** BSE, 1970, Stat. Decision Making Theories, Princeton Univ.; **GRAD EDUC:** Completion of Units I & II, 1980-81, Small Co. Mgmt. Program; **EDUC HONORS:** w. honors; **OTHER ACT & HONORS:** Chmn. of the Center City Comm., 1978-81; Pres. of Commitment Memphis, 1981; Leadership Memphis, 1980; **HOME ADD:** 931 S Cox, Memphis, TN 38104, (901)278-9583; **BUS ADD:** Suite 200, Commerce Title Bldg., 12 S Main, Memphis, TN 38103, (901)526-1211.

JEMISON, W. D., Jr.——**B:** July 3, 1918, *Owner*, W. D. Jemison, Jr., Realtor; **PRIM RE ACT:** Broker, Consultant, Developer, Owner/Investor; **OTHER RE ACT:** CCIM candidate having completed 5 of the required educ. courses.; **SERVICES:** Comml. investment RE. Buy and sell RE portfolio; **REP CLIENTS:** Investors in RE; **PROFL AFFIL & HONORS:** Member Memphis RE Bd., GRI, Candidacy CCIM; **EDUC:** BS Bus. Admin., 1940, Investment RE and some resid. brokerage, MS State Univ.; **MIL SERV:** Signal Corp, Major; **OTHER ACT & HONORS:** Pres. Home Builders Assn.; 1953. Memphis & Shelby Cty. Planning Commn. - 1957-1960; VP Memphis Bd. of Realtors 1980; Dir. Memphis Bd. of Realtors 1981; **HOME ADD:** 47 Avon, Memphis, TN 38117, (901)685-6056; **BUS ADD:** 200 Commerce Title Bldg., Memphis, TN 38103, (901)526-1211.

JENKINS, Bill——*Ed.*, Business Extension Bureau, Western Real Estate News; **PRIM RE ACT:** Real Estate Publisher; **BUS ADD:** 3057 17th St., San Francisco, CA 94110, (415)861-7200.*

JENKINS, L. Howard, III——**B:** May 26, 1948, Richmond, VA, *Dir. of RE*, SPB & Assoc., Inc.; **PRIM RE ACT:** Developer; **PREV EMPLOY:** Prud. Ins. Co., RE Investment Div.; **PROFL AFFIL & HONORS:** ICSC, RE Broker, State of VA; **EDUC:** BS, 1970, Bus. Admin., Furman Univ.; **GRAD EDUC:** MBA, 1975, Fin., Old Dominion Univ.; **HOME ADD:** 1731 Windingridge Dr., Richmond, VA 23233; **BUS ADD:** PO Box 491, Midlothia, VA 23113, (804)794-2188.

JENKINS, Leon H.——**B:** Feb. 4, 1925, Bowling Green, KY, *VP*, National State Bank of Boulder, Mort. Loan; **PRIM RE ACT:** Banker, Lender; **SERVICES:** Const. and permanent fin.; **REP CLIENTS:** Contractors, realtors and indivs.; **PREV EMPLOY:** Valley Natl. Bank of AZ; Branch Mgr.-Flagstaff, AZ, 14 yrs.; **PROFL AFFIL & HONORS:** Assoc. member Boulder Bd. Realtors; **MIL SERV:** US Army, Sgt.; **HOME ADD:** 1930 Kalmia Ave., Boulder, CO 80302, (303)443-0394; **BUS ADD:** 1242 Pearl St., Boulder, CO 80306, (303)442-0351.

JENKINS, Michael A.——**B:** Feb. 1, 1942, Dallas, TX, *Pres.*, Leisure and Recreation Concepts, Inc. (LARC); **PRIM RE ACT:** Consultant; **SERVICES:** Const. supervision, mktg., advertising, operational procedures, site selection, feasibility studies, planning, design, mgmt., operation and layout, special promotions and events; **PROFL AFFIL & HONORS:** Amer. Inst. of Arch.; Amer. Recreational Equip. Assn.; Amusement Park Club of Amer.; Intl. Assn. of Amusement Parks and Attractions (IAAPA); Intl. Assn. of Fairs and Expositions; Outdoor Amusement Bus. Assn.; TX Recreation and Park Soc.; Urban Land Inst., 1964 Central TX Showman's Assn. Award for Outstanding Contributions to the Theater and Amusement Indus. in the S.W.; 1964 Baylor Library Fund Award for Producing and Directing The Bob Hope Show and Raising –52,380.00; 1969 N.S. Alexander Award for the Finest Program Appearance on a Subject Dealing with Amusement Parks or Piers at the IAAPA Convention; 1974 N.S. Alexander Award for the Finest Program Appearance on a Subject Dealing with Amusement Parks or Piers at the IAAPA Convention; 1980 Fred W. Sweepstakes Award for the Most Meritorious Device, Equipment or Supply Exhibit Displayed at the IAAPA Convention; **EDUC:** 1963, Theater/Bus./Journalism, Baylor Univ., Waco, TX; **MIL SERV:** US Army Engrs., (Reserve); **OTHER ACT & HONORS:** Dallas Theater Ctr. Past Member Bd. of Dir.; State Fair of TX; Pres. Task Force; Shakespeare Festival of Dallas Bd. of Tr. (Founding Member); **HOME ADD:** 1805 Burr Oak, Arlington, TX 76012, (817)461-4755; **BUS ADD:** 2151 Ft. Worth Ave., Dallas, TX 75211, (214)942-4474.

JENKINS, Michael W.——**B:** June 2, 1947, Hollywood, CA, *VP, Investment Sales*, Cushman & Wakefield, Inc., Investment Sales; **PRIM RE ACT:** Broker, Consultant; **SERVICES:** Identification, evaluation & mktg. of maj. income props., nationwide; arrange joint ventures & project financings; **REP CLIENTS:** Maj. domestic & for. investors; **PREV EMPLOY:** Nat. Dir., Investment Sales, Cushman & Wakefield (1979-81); Dir. RE Fin., Dillingham Corp., 1973-79; **PROFL AFFIL & HONORS:** Intl. Council of Shopping Ctrs.; Nat. Assn. of Indus. & Office Parks (NAIOP); Young Mens Real Estate Assoc.; **EDUC:** 1970, Econ., UCLA; **GRAD EDUC:** MBA, 1971, Corp. Fin, UCLA; **HOME ADD:** 8 Rainbow Dr., Riverside, CT 06878; **BUS ADD:** 1166 Ave. of the Americas, NY, NY 10036, (212)841-7504.

JENKINS, Robert N.——**B:** May 28, 1951, NJ, *Associate*, Eastdil Realty Inc.; **PRIM RE ACT:** Broker, Syndicator; **REP CLIENTS:** Devel. & investors; **PREV EMPLOY:** Trammell Crow Co. (RE Devel.) 1973-78; **EDUC:** BA, 1973, Eng., CO Coll.; **GRAD EDUC:** MBA, 1980, Fin., RE fin., Columbia Univ. Sch. of Bus.; **HOME ADD:** 322 W. 57th St., New York, NY 10019, (212)977-3226; **BUS ADD:** 40 W. 57th St., New York, NY 10019, (212)397-2700.

JENKS, William T.——**B:** July 14, 1911, Savanna, IL, *RE Appraiser/Consultant*, William T. Jenks; **PRIM RE ACT:** Consultant, Appraiser; **SERVICES:** RE appraisal reports and consultants reports; **REP CLIENTS:** Fed. Govt., State of IL, Local Govt., Fin. Cos., Corps., Attys. and Indivs.; **PROFL AFFIL & HONORS:** Amer. Soc. of Rural Appraisers; Soc. of RE Appraisers; Lic. Broker in the State of IL, Acting Assessor in Winnebago Cty., IL; Chmn. of the Bd. of Review of Winnebago Cty., IL; Tech. Advisor, Dept. of Transportation, State of IL; Pres. of Local Chap. of Soc. of RE Appraisers; Dir. of Local Chap. of Soc. of RE Appraisers; **EDUC:** 1932, Cornell Coll./Loyola Univ.; **OTHER ACT & HONORS:** Chmn. of Winnebago Cty. Bd. of Review, 1967-1968; Rockford Township Assessor, 1954-1957; Tech. Advisor, IL Dept. of Transporation, 1961-1965; Who's Who in the Midwest; Commodore of Abbey Yacht Club, Fontana, WI; Thunderock Gun Club; Rockford Skeet Club. Southern Lakes Trap and Skeet Club, Inc., Lake Geneva, Wis.; **HOME ADD:** 1710 Council Crest Dr., Rockford, IL 61107, (815)399-6731; **BUS ADD:** Suite 818, 206 W. State St., Rockford, IL 61101, (815)963-5143.

JENNERICH, Arthur——**B:** Sept. 24, 1945, Brooklyn, NY, *Exec. VP*, Flack & Kurtz Energy Management Corp.; **PRIM RE ACT:** Consultant, Engineer, Instructor, Property Manager; **OTHER RE ACT:** Energy Mgr.; **SERVICES:** Complete energy servs. from audits to contracting; **REP CLIENTS:** John Hancock, AMFAC Hotels, Prudential Ins. RE many RE management firms; **PREV EMPLOY:** RE mgmt. & lic. engrg. exper.; **PROFL AFFIL & HONORS:** Nat. Assn. of Power Engrs., BOMA Intl.; **EDUC:** 1965, Air Conditioning, Heating & Refrigeration Technol., NY State Tech. Coll.; **OTHER**

ACT & HONORS: Amateur automobile racing; **HOME ADD:** 17 Michelle Ave., Old Bridge, NJ 08879, (201)727-9282; **BUS ADD:** 475 Fifth Ave., New York, NY 10017, (212)532-9600.

JENNINGS, James M.——**B:** Oct. 28, 1924, Tulsa, OK, *Pres.*, James M. Jennings Associates, Co.; **PRIM RE ACT:** Consultant, Regulator, Instructor, Owner/Investor; **OTHER RE ACT:** Active RE Salesperson Lic.; **SERVICES:** Mkt. and Feasibility Analyses, Planning & Devel. Programs, & Location Studies; **REP CLIENTS:** Scott Paper Co., Gen. Devel. Corp., Redman Indus., Maj. Utility Cos., Banks Plus S&L Assns.; **PREV EMPLOY:** Battelle Memorial Inst. 1959-1965; Univ. of Pittsburgh, 1956-1959, other univs., US Dept of Interior & United Nations; **PROFL AFFIL & HONORS:** Natl. State & Local Bds. of Realtors; Amer. Planning Assn. Amer. Soc. of Consulting Planners; Natl. Assn. Bus. Econs.; Amer. Econ. Devel. Council, OH Devel. Assn., Cert. Indus. Devel. & Fellow Member, Amer. Econ. Devel Council, Member-Amer. Inst. of Cert. Planners; **EDUC:** AA, 1949, Geography, George Washington Univ., Washington, D.C.; BA, 1950, Geography, George Washington Univ., Washington, D.C.; **GRAD EDUC:** MA, 1955, Econ., Geography, Univ. of NC; PHD Candidate, 1953-1956, Syracuse Univ.; **MIL SERV:** USA, 1943-1945, S/Sgt.; **OTHER ACT & HONORS:** Chmn. Upper Arlington Planning Commn., Nature Conservancy, OH Farm Bureau Fed., Past Pres. of OH Devel. Assn., Past Pres. of OH Planning Conf., Pres. of OH Planning Found., Exec. Sec. of Nat. Industrial Zoning Comm.; **HOME ADD:** 1858 Chatfield Rd., Columbus, OH 43221, (614)488-9001; **BUS ADD:** 1357 W. Lane Ave., Columbus, OH 43221, (614)488-2643.

JENNINGS, Joseph, Jr.——*Exec. VP Oper.*, Mount Vernon Mills; **PRIM RE ACT:** Property Manager; **BUS ADD:** Daniel Bldg., Greenville, SC 29602, (803)233-4151.*

JENNINGS, Samuel K.——**B:** Boone County, IA, *Pres.*, ERA-The Real Estate Company; **PRIM RE ACT:** Broker, Developer, Owner/Investor, Syndicator; **SERVICES:** Gen. RE serv.; **PROFL AFFIL & HONORS:** CRS; Nat. Realtors Assn.; RESSI; **MIL SERV:** US Army; Capt.; Bronze Star; **HOME ADD:** 510 W Amador, Las Cruces, NM 88005, (505)524-7326; **BUS ADD:** PO Drawer ERA, Las Cruces, NM 88004, (505)523-8611.

JENNINGS, William G.——**B:** Aug. 10, 1928, Evanston, IL, *Chmn.*, Quinlan and Tyson, Inc.; **PRIM RE ACT:** Broker, Syndicator, Property Manager, Engineer, Banker, Owner/Investor, Insuror; **PROFL AFFIL & HONORS:** IREM, RESSI, ASME, CPM, SRS; **EDUC:** BSME, 1951, Eng. and Bus., Cornell Univ.; **GRAD EDUC:** MBA, 1955, Fin., Harvard; **EDUC HONORS:** Distinction, Honor Soc., Distinction; **MIL SERV:** USAF, 1st Lt.; **OTHER ACT & HONORS:** Union League Club; **HOME ADD:** 508 Brier St., Kenilworth, IL 60043, (312)256-1461; **BUS ADD:** 1569 Sherman Ave., Evanston, IL 60204, (312)864-2606.

JENNISON, Gary A.——*Principal*, Corcoran, Mullins, Jennison, Inc.; **PRIM RE ACT:** Developer, Builder, Property Manager; **SERVICES:** Devel., Construct, Mge. Apts. & Condos. & Comml.; **PROFL AFFIL & HONORS:** NAHB; Rental Housing Assoc., AICPA; Mass Soc. of CPA's, CPA; VP Homebuilders of Greater Boston; **EDUC:** BS, Acctg., Bentley Coll.; **GRAD EDUC:** BSBA, Univ. of MA; **MIL SERV:** US Army; **BUS ADD:** 1776 Heritage Dr., Quincy, MA 02171, (617)328-3100.

JENNRICH, Arthur——**B:** Sept. 3, 1922, Eagan, MN, *Pres.*, J&F Enterprises Inc.; **PRIM RE ACT:** Developer, Owner/Investor; **SERVICES:** 2 1/2 Lots Listed with a realtor; **EDUC:** 1936, Rosemount, MN High Sch.; **HOME ADD:** 26140 Cambodia Ave., Farmington, MN 55024, (612)463-8302; **BUS ADD:** 26140 Cambodia Ave., Farmington, MN 55024, (612)463-8302.

JENSEN, Michael M.——**B:** Nov. 2, 1940, Centralia, IL, *Mgr. RE Div., Sec. of Corp*, Musser Fiss Inc. and Fawn Lake Ranch Co., RE; **PRIM RE ACT:** Broker, Property Manager, Syndicator; **SERVICES:** Valuation, prop. mgmt., synd., investment counseling; **PROFL AFFIL & HONORS:** Denver Bd. of Realtors, IREM, CPM; **EDUC:** BA, 1962, Econ., Westminster Coll.; **MIL SERV:** USN, LT., Vietnam, Expeditionary Medal, 1965; **HOME ADD:** 8476 E. Otero Ln., Englewood, CO 80112, (303)741-3898; **BUS ADD:** 90 Madison St. #603, Denver, CO 80206, (303)355-7327.

JENSEN, Paul C.——**B:** Mar. 28, 1930, NY, NY, *Prop. Mgr.*, Environmental Industries, Inc.; **PRIM RE ACT:** Consultant, Appraiser, Instructor, Property Manager; **OTHER RE ACT:** Assoc. Broker; **SERVICES:** Prop. Mgmt.; **REP CLIENTS:** Apt. complexes, shopping ctrs., mobile home parks, hotels; **PREV EMPLOY:** Hotel Mgr., Hospital Bus. Mgr.; **PROFL AFFIL & HONORS:** CPM, ARM, TAA, GCAA, NAA, TAR, VP-GCAA, Director-TAA; **EDUC:** Acctg., Law, RE, Bus., Houston Univ.; **HOME ADD:** 2 Quintana Ct., Galveston, TX 77551, (713)740-1381; **BUS ADD:** 6904 Lasker Dr., Galveston, TX 77551, (713)744-3684.

JENSEN, Paul M.——**B:** Sept. 23, 1944, Salt Lake City, UT, *Pres.*, Oro Financial, Inc.; **PRIM RE ACT:** Broker, Developer, Syndicator; **SERVICES:** Brokerage in comml. & raw land; investment counsel, partnerships in investment prop.; **REP CLIENTS:** Local, nat. & offshore clients (in-house language capabilities in French, Spanish, Italian, German & Chinese); **PREV EMPLOY:** Pres., Home Bldg. & Land Devel. Firm, 1972-1978; **EDUC:** BA, 1970, Univ. of UT; **GRAD EDUC:** 1971, Mgmt./Lang., Amer. Inst. of Foreign Trade; **EDUC HONORS:** Magna Cum Laude; **MIL SERV:** US Army; **HOME ADD:** 1012 E. 3rd St., Mesa, AZ 85203, (602)834-3899; **BUS ADD:** 1901 E. University #400, Mesa, AZ 85203, (602)833-4021.

JENSEN, Robert L.——**B:** July 12, 1920, Kingsburg, CA, *Pres.*, Robert L. Jensen & Associates, Comml. RE, Mgmt., Sales, Leasing; **PRIM RE ACT:** Broker, Owner/Investor, Property Manager; **SERVICES:** Prop. - Mgmt., Leasing, Maintenance; **REP CLIENTS:** Banks, RE Investors; **PREV EMPLOY:** Bus. Admin., Acctg.; **PROFL AFFIL & HONORS:** IREM, Fresno Realty Bd., CPM; **EDUC:** BS, Fin. & Acctg., Univ. of So. CA, School of Bus.; **EDUC HONORS:** Blue Key; **MIL SERV:** USCG, Res.; Lt. j.g.; **OTHER ACT & HONORS:** Mayor, Selma CA City Council 1954; **HOME ADD:** 6294 E. Lyell, Fresno, CA 93727; **BUS ADD:** 1060 Fulton Mall, Suite 1416, Fresno, CA 93721, (209)233-4551.

JENSEN, Ronald R.——**B:** Nov. 22, 1926, Boise, ID, *VP - Prop. Mgmt.*, Broadbent Development Company, Inc.; **PRIM RE ACT:** Developer, Property Manager; **PREV EMPLOY:** Chazan Const. Co., Buckeye Realty and Mgmt. Co.; **PROFL AFFIL & HONORS:** Inst. of RE Mgmt.; BOMA; ASME, CPM; **EDUC:** BS, 1956, Bus. Admin. & Aeronautics, San Jose Univ., San Jose, CA; **EDUC HONORS:** Dept. Hon. in Aeronautics; **MIL SERV:** US Army, T/5, USAF, 1st; **OTHER ACT & HONORS:** Hillerest Ctry. Club; **HOME ADD:** 6450 Granada Ln., Meridian, ID 83642, (208)939-6450; **BUS ADD:** 5410 Kendall St., Boise, ID 83706, (208)345-5161.

JENT, Jim T.——**B:** May 14, 1935, Pittsburgh, KS, *Realty Mgmt. & Acquisition Spec.*, US Postal Service, Rgn. Headquarters, RE & Bldg. Div.; **PRIM RE ACT:** Broker, Appraiser, Property Manager; **OTHER RE ACT:** Advertising and awarding new constr. contracts; **SERVICES:** Manage leased props., evaluate bids and award constr. for new facilities, feasibility and analysis; **REP CLIENTS:** US Govt., Postal Service; **PREV EMPLOY:** US Corps of Engrs., 1971-73; **PROFL AFFIL & HONORS:** Sr. Member Nat. Assn. of Review Apprasers; Nat. Assn. of Corp. RE Execs.; Assn. Fed. Appraisers, CRA; **EDUC:** 1958, Law, Psych, RE (Maj.), OK Central State Univ.; **MIL SERV:** USA, Adj. Gen., 1953-55; **OTHER ACT & HONORS:** Pres. of USPS Chapt., 146 Fed. Mgrs. Assn.; USPS Cert. of Appreciation for Exceptional Performance; **HOME ADD:** 1983 S. Hidden Hills Pkwy., Stone Mountain, GA 30088, (404)981-7605; **BUS ADD:** 2245 Perimeter Pk. Dr., Suite 17, Atlanta, GA 30341, (404)221-5243.

JERSIN, Wayne N.——**B:** Jan. 21, 1938, Baltimore, MD, *Atty. at Law*; **PRIM RE ACT:** Attorney; **SERVICES:** RE closings and title ins. sales & services, gen. practice of law; **REP CLIENTS:** Mort. lenders, S&L assns.; agents for Chicago Title Ins. Co. & Commonwealth Land Title Co.; **PREV EMPLOY:** Mgr. and Atty. for Chicago Title Ins. Co. for Montgomery Cty., MD (1979-1981); **PROFL AFFIL & HONORS:** MD State Bar Assn., Montgomery Cty. Bar Assn.; **EDUC:** 1959, Univ. of MD School of Bus. Admin.; **GRAD EDUC:** JD, 1966, Law, Univ. of Baltimore; **OTHER ACT & HONORS:** Rockville, MD City Bd. of Appeals, 1974-1977; Dir. Rockville City C of C 1981; Gaithersburg, MD C of C; Vestry of Christ Episcopal Church Rockville, MD 1979-1980; **HOME ADD:** 17505 Timberleigh Way, Woodbine, MD 21797, (301)854-6526; **BUS ADD:** Suite 600, 51 Monroe St., Rockville, MD 20850, (301)762-7900.

JERUS, George R., P.E.——**B:** June 10, 1926, Brooklyn, NY, *VP*, Meyer, Strong & Jones, P.C.; **PRIM RE ACT:** Consultant; **SERVICES:** Consulting engrg.-mechanical, electrical, fire protection, vert. trans.; **REP CLIENTS:** Metropolitan Life Ins. Co., Equitable Life Assurance, Chase Manhattan Bank, Mfrs. Hanover Trust, Irving Trust, Galbreath; **PREV EMPLOY:** None - Presently Associate Prof. of Mgmt. at St. John's Univ. in addition to Meyer, Strong & Jones, P.C.; **PROFL AFFIL & HONORS:** Member Soc. of Fire Protection Engrs., Bd. Member Amer. Nat. Stnds. Inst., Amer. Soc. Mechanical Engrs., Licensed in NY State and others, Hon. Chi Epsilon & Beta; **EDUC:** BCE, 1954, Civil & Sanitary, Brooklyn Polytechnic Inst.; **GRAD EDUC:** MCE & Adv. Eng. Econ., 1960, Civil - Sanitary - Eng. Econ. Systems, Brooklyn Polytechnic Inst. (Polytechnic Inst. of NY); MBA, 1977, St. John's Univ.; **EDUC HONORS:** Chi Epsilon, Beta Gamma Sigma; **MIL SERV:** USN, 1943-46, Aer MI/C; **OTHER ACT & HONORS:** Member, License Bd. of City of NY; **HOME ADD:** 241-35

148th Rd., Rosedale, NY 11422, (212)341-1036; **BUS ADD:** 230 Park Ave., New York, NY 10169, (212)599-4660.

JESPERSON, Daryl L.——**B:** Sept. 11, 1947, Richardton, ND, *VP - Operations*, RE/MAX of America, Inc.; **OTHER RE ACT:** Franchising; **SERVICES:** Mgmt. counseling on devel. of successful RE offices; **REP CLIENTS:** Current successful broker/owners or Promising newcomers to RE office ownership; **PREV EMPLOY:** Major oil company mktg. rep.; **PROFL AFFIL & HONORS:** CO CRB Chap./Nat. Assn. of Realtors/CO Assn. of Realtors; **EDUC:** BA, 1969, Bus. Admin. (expanded major) and Psych., Adams State Coll.; **MIL SERV:** USN, Lt.; **HOME ADD:** 5952 S Emporia Cir., Englewood, CO 80111, (303)779-5697; **BUS ADD:** 5251 S. Quebec, Englewood, CO 80111, (303)770-5531.

JESSE, Joan——*Pres.*, Diversified Real Estate Services of Wisconsin, Inc.; **PRIM RE ACT:** Broker, Consultant, Owner/Investor, Syndicator; **OTHER RE ACT:** Partnership mgmt.; **PROFL AFFIL & HONORS:** RESSI, Intl. Assn. of Fin. Planners; **OTHER ACT & HONORS:** RESSI (Past Pres. St. of WI); **HOME ADD:** 157 N. 123rd, Wauwatosa, WI 53226, (414)257-0512; **BUS ADD:** 13000 W. Bluemound Rd., Elm Grove, WI 53122, (414)784-9290.

JESSEN, Howard——*Plng. Dir.*, Ceco Corp.; **PRIM RE ACT:** Property Manager; **BUS ADD:** 1400 Kensington Rd., Oak Brook, IL 60521, (312)242-2000.*

JESSOP, Marilyn——**B:** Mar. 17, 1953, *Sec. of Hickman Land Title Co. & VP of Rich Land Title Co.*, Hickman Land Title Co., Richland Title Co.; **PRIM RE ACT:** Insuror; **OTHER RE ACT:** Title ins. and abstracting; **PROFL AFFIL & HONORS:** UT Land Title Assn.; Amer. Land Title Assn.; Northern UT Home Bldrs. Assn.; **GRAD EDUC:** BS, 1975, Major in Fin. with a minor in Econ., UT State Univ.; **HOME ADD:** Logan, UT; **BUS ADD:** 112 N. Main St., Logan, UT 84321, (801)752-0582.

JETER, Dr. Dwain——*VP Corp. Dev.*, International Multifoods Corp.; **PRIM RE ACT:** Property Manager; **BUS ADD:** 1200 Multifoods Bldg., Minneapolis, MN 55402.*

JEWELL, Keith Dover——**B:** Nov. 29, 1934, Fresno, CA, *VP, Hutton RE Servs., Inc.*, E.F. Hutton & Co., Inc.; **PRIM RE ACT:** Syndicator, Banker; **SERVICES:** Prop. acquisition, nat. synd., sales and mgmt. of ltd. partnerships, includes conventional and subsidized RE, public and pvt. offerings; **PREV EMPLOY:** Former Special Asst. to the Chmn. of the Bd., E.F. Hutton & Co. Founder and Managing Dir., Asian & Euro-American Capital Corp.(Thailand)Ltd.; **PROFL AFFIL & HONORS:** Sr. Analyst, NY Soc. of Security Analysts; **EDUC:** BA, 1956, Poli. Sci., Univ. of CA at Berkeley; **GRAD EDUC:** JD, 1964, Harvard Law School; **EDUC HONORS:** Phi Sigma Alpha (poli. sci. hon.), Joffre Medal; **MIL SERV:** USN, Lt., Qualified in submarines, China Service Medal; **OTHER ACT & HONORS:** Dir., The Deafness Research Found., NY; **HOME ADD:** 535 E. 86th St. #7-E, New York, NY 10028, (212)734-3961; **BUS ADD:** One Battery Park Pl., New York, NY 10004, (212)742-2712.

JEWELL, Mary E.——**B:** Aug. 28, 1938, Danville, KY, *Multi Family Housing Rep.*, US Department of HUD, Housing Production Div. of Indianapolis Area Office; **PRIM RE ACT:** Broker, Consultant, Appraiser, Developer, Lender, Regulator, Instructor, Insuror; **OTHER RE ACT:** Research, mkt. analyst; **SERVICES:** Tech. assistance, expediting, training, public/pvt. liason; **REP CLIENTS:** Mort. lenders, attys., devels., sponsors, owners, public admins.; **PREV EMPLOY:** 1967-75 Mgmt. of (2) leading brokerage/devel., appraising (RE) firms; Tech. assistance advisor w/quasi govt. agency 1975-77; **PROFL AFFIL & HONORS:** National, state & local associations of Realtors; Nat. Assn. Femal Exec.; Soc. Fed. Labor Relations Profl., Realtor, IN RE Broker; Realtor; **EDUC:** Bus., Math, RE & Const. Tech., Public Admin., Western Reserve Univ., Purdue Univ.; **OTHER ACT & HONORS:** Life Member N.A.A.C.P.; Parent Advisory Comm., Washington Township School System; **HOME ADD:** 2280 W. 66th St., Indianapolis, IN 42620, (317)255-6987; **BUS ADD:** 151 N. Delaware St., Indianapolis, IN 46260, (317)269-2765.

JEWELL, Michael L.——**B:** Nov.28, 1944, Ann Arbor, MI, *Partner*, Real Estate Dimensions; **PRIM RE ACT:** Broker, Instructor; **OTHER RE ACT:** Sr. instr., RNMI, Mktg. mgmt. courses, educational consultant; **SERVICES:** Resid. sales and investing; **PREV EMPLOY:** Rgnl. VP and Dir. of Training, Stan Wiley, Inc., Realtors, 1977-79, Univ. of MI, Asst. Dir., Ext. Serv. Statewide RE Prog. 1974-77; **PROFL AFFIL & HONORS:** RNMI, NAR, CRS, CRB; **EDUC:** 1967, bus. admin., Wittenberg Univ.; **MIL SERV:** US Army, S/Sgt.; **HOME ADD:** 12712 NW 20th Ave., Vancouver, WA 98665, (206)573-6716; **BUS ADD:** 2700 NE Andresen Rd., Vancouver, WA 98661, (206)696-0571.

JEWETT, D.J.——*VP Oper.*, Sperry & Hutchinson Co.; **PRIM RE ACT:** Property Manager; **BUS ADD:** 330 Madison Ave., New York, NY 10017, (212)983-2000.*

JOACHIM, Louis Frantz——**B:** Jan. 5, 1942, Haiti, WI, *Pres.*, Dorchester Props. Corp.; **PRIM RE ACT:** Broker, Consultant, Developer, Owner/Investor, Property Manager; **OTHER RE ACT:** Investments servs. for indivs., govts., investment counseling; **SERVICES:** Investment counseling to instnl. investors, devel. indivs. for. investors, govts.; **PREV EMPLOY:** Peck & Sharp & Co., Inc.; **PROFL AFFIL & HONORS:** RE Bd. of NY, Rotary Club of NY (Rotary Intl.); **EDUC:** 1967, Intl. Law, Crane Sch. of Bus. Admin. (Haiti), Law Sch. of Haiti; **GRAD EDUC:** 1980, Southland MBA, Southland Univ.; **OTHER ACT & HONORS:** Chmn. World Comm. Affairs Rotary Intnl.; **HOME ADD:** 20 Beekman Pl., New York, NY 10022, (212)223-0004; **BUS ADD:** 521 Fifth Ave., New York, NY 10175, (212)953-9040.

JODY, Boris——Standard Motor Products; **PRIM RE ACT:** Property Manager; **BUS ADD:** 37-18 Northern Blvd., Long Island City, NY 11101, (212)392-0200.*

JOFFE, Martin Lee——**B:** Jan. 19, 1933, NYC, NY, *Pres.*, Martin Lee Joffe Assocs., Inc.; **PRIM RE ACT:** Broker, Owner/Investor; **SERVICES:** Sales of investment props.; **PREV EMPLOY:** Elliot W. Dann Co.; **PROFL AFFIL & HONORS:** RE Bd. of NY; Member, Sales Brokers Comm.; **EDUC:** BA, 1956, Bard Coll.; **HOME ADD:** 300 Cent. Park W., New York, NY 10024, (212)595-2079; **BUS ADD:** 488 Madison Ave., New York, NY 10022, (212)888-0698.

JOHANSEN, Michael C.——**B:** Jan. 5, 1945, Greenville, SC, *Atty.*, Emmet, Marvin & Martin; **PRIM RE ACT:** Attorney; **SERVICES:** Legal representation; **REP CLIENTS:** Instit. lenders and instit. and indiv. engaged in all aspects of RE; **PROFL AFFIL & HONORS:** ABA, NY State and NJ Bar Assns., MBAA; **EDUC:** BA, 1966, Manhattan Coll.; **GRAD EDUC:** JD, 1970, Georgetown University, Law Center; LLM, 1977, Taxation, NYU, Law School; **HOME ADD:** 12 Crestview Ave., Madison, NJ 07940; **BUS ADD:** 48 Wall St., NY, NY 10005, (212)422-2974.

JOHANSON, Robert——*VP*, Farmland Industries, Inc.; **PRIM RE ACT:** Property Manager; **BUS ADD:** 3315 N. Oak Trafficway, Kansas City, MO 64116, (816)459-6000.*

JOHNSON, Alvin G.——**B:** Sept. 4, 1925, Austin, MN, *Pres.*, The Colorado Real Estate Co.; **PRIM RE ACT:** Consultant, Developer, Owner/Investor, Syndicator; **SERVICES:** Investment and site selection, counseling, devel. & synd. of comml. props., indus devel.; **REP CLIENTS:** TX Instruments, lenders, Instnl. investors; **PREV EMPLOY:** VP Maytag Electronics, Pres. Electro-Comm. Inc.; **PROFL AFFIL & HONORS:** Nat. Assn. of Electronic Engrs., Nat. Assn. of Indus. Devels.; **MIL SERV:** USAF, M/Sgt.; **HOME ADD:** 4615 Bella Dr., Colorado Springs, CO 80918, (303)598-8123; **BUS ADD:** Suite 101, Holly Sugar Bldg., Colorado Springs, CO 80903, (303)471-2700.

JOHNSON, Andrew P., III——**B:** Oct. 10, 1951, Carrizo Springs, TX, *Atty.*, Rowe & Young; **PRIM RE ACT:** Attorney; **SERVICES:** All legal servs. re: devel., water districts, comml. transaction & synds., & for. investment; **PROFL AFFIL & HONORS:** Houston Bar Assn.; ABA; State Bar of TX; ABA & State Real Prop. & Natural Resources & Tax Sects.; **EDUC:** BA, 1974, Intl. Affairs, George Washington Univ., Also Univ. of TX At Austin & Univ. of Salamanca, Spain; **GRAD EDUC:** JD, 1977, So. Methodist Univ.; **HOME ADD:** 5635 DeSoto Dr. No. 1028, Houston, TX 77091, (713)683-0577; **BUS ADD:** Suite 1680, 2727 Allen Pkwy,, Houston, TX 77019, (713)522-6391.

JOHNSON, Basil D.——**B:** July 2, 1927, Pittsburgh, PA, *Pres.*, Colony Management Co.; **PRIM RE ACT:** Owner/Investor, Property Manager; **SERVICES:** Prop. mgmt. and rental; **PROFL AFFIL & HONORS:** Engrg. Soc. of Detroit, Apt. Assn., Registered Prof. Engr.-MI Lic. Marine Chief Engr.; **EDUC:** BS Marine Engrg., 1947, MBA-Fin. and Acctg., Univ. of Detroit; BS Mech. Engr., 1955, MBA-Fin. and Acctg.-Univ. of Detroit; **MIL SERV:** USN, Lt.; **BUS ADD:** PO Box 36475, Detroit, MI 48236, (313)885-3726.

JOHNSON, Bruce B.——**B:** Jan. 31, 1946, Minneapolis, MN, *Partner*, Fairfield and Woods; **PRIM RE ACT:** Attorney; **SERVICES:** Real prop. law representing clients in acquisitions, devel., synd., fin. and sales in all types of RE; **REP CLIENTS:** Large banks, ins. cos., RE devel. cos., synd. and brokerage cos., landlords and tenants; **PREV EMPLOY:** Law Clerk for Justice Donald E. Kelley, Dep. Chief Justice of the CO Supreme Court, 1970-1971; **PROFL AFFIL & HONORS:** CO Bar Assn.; Denver Bar Asn.; ABA, Chmn. ABA Special Comm. on HUD Law, 1980 to present; **EDUC:** BS, 1967, Psych., Cornell Coll.; **GRAD EDUC:** JD, 1970, Univ. of Denver; **EDUC HONORS:** Amer.

Jurisprudence Prizes for Excellence in Taxation, Constitutional Law and Adm. Law; **MIL SERV:** Reserves; **OTHER ACT & HONORS:** Rotary Club of Denver, Bd. of Dir. of Denver Boys, Inc.; **HOME ADD:** 5161 Redwood Dr., Littleton, CO 80123, (303)798-4607; **BUS ADD:** 950 Seventeenth St., Suite 1600, Denver, CO 80202, (303)534-6135.

JOHNSON, Burten C.——B: July 19, 1949, MT, *Investment Officer/RE*, UT State Retirement Office, RE; **PRIM RE ACT:** Broker, Owner/Investor, Property Manager; **SERVICES:** Advise retirement Bd. on RE decisions; **EDUC:** 1971, PE, Sci., Math, S UT State Coll.; **HOME ADD:** 3072 Finlandia Ct., Sandy, UT 84092; **BUS ADD:** 540 E 20050, Salt Lake City, UT 84102, (801)355-3884.

JOHNSON, C.A., II——B: Apr. 19, 1926, Mankato, MN, *Part.*, Rolling Hills Realty; **PRIM RE ACT:** Broker, Attorney; **PREV EMPLOY:** Johnson & Moonan Law Firm, 600 So. 2nd St., Mankato, MN 56001; **PROFL AFFIL & HONORS:** MN Bar Assn., ABA, MN & Amer. Trial Lawyers Assn., Amer. Arbitration Assn.; **EDUC:** BS, 1949, Law, Univ. of MN; **GRAD EDUC:** JD, 1950, Univ. of MN; **MIL SERV:** USN, Pharmacist 2nd class; **HOME ADD:** 130 Crocus Pl., Mankato, MN 56001, (507)345-3671; **BUS ADD:** 600 S. 2nd St., Mankato, MN 56001, (507)387-4002.

JOHNSON, Charles R.——B: Oct. 25, 1954, Columbus, OH, Ball and Galloway Indus. Devel., Amalgamated Bldg. Co.; **PRIM RE ACT:** Developer, Builder; **OTHER RE ACT:** Realtors, indus. devel., gen. contractors, devel. and sale of indus. sites; **SERVICES:** Gen. contractors of distribution/warehouse ctrs., mfrg. plants, plant expansions; **REP CLIENTS:** Nat., rgnl. and local companies desiring new or expanded plant facilities in the Central OH area; **PROFL AFFIL & HONORS:** NAR; OH Assn. of Realtors; Urban Land Inst., GRI; **EDUC:** BA/BS, 1980, RE/Urban Land Econ., OH State Univ.; **HOME ADD:** 2134 Coventry Rd., Columbus, OH 43221, (614)488-8070; **BUS ADD:** 6660 Doubletree Ave., Columbus, OH 43229, (614)888-8283.

JOHNSON, Clifford R.——B: Mar. 23, 1920, Minneapolis, MN, *Pres.*, Clifford R. Johnson & Associates, Inc.; **PRIM RE ACT:** Appraiser, Instructor; **SERVICES:** Comml., indus. and resid. appraising; **REP CLIENTS:** Nursing homes, apt. houses, comml. bldgs., indus. plants, shopping ctrs., etc.; **PROFL AFFIL & HONORS:** AIREA; Soc. of RE Appraisers; Past Chmn. of Chap. Appraisal Review Comm.; Chmn. of the Chap. Educ. Comm. 1977, 1978 and 1979; Member of AIREA, Nat. Comprehensive Exam. Comm.; 1980 Chmn. of AIREA Chap. Educ. Comm.; 1981 Chmn. of AIREA Bus. Mgmt. Comm., MAI; SREA; Past Pres. and Sec.-Treas. of Minneapolis Chap.; Nat. Gov. for State of MN, 1969, 1970 and 1971; Minneapolis Bd. of Realtors; Nat. Assn. of RE Bds.; MN Assn. of Realtors; Amer. Right-of-Way Assn. profl. designation: SR/WA; Profl. Recog. Award; Faculty member, Ext. Div. evening classes of the Dept. of Conf. and Inst., Univ. of MN, since 1964; 1978-1982 Coordinator of Appraisal Courses, Univ. of MN; Instructor of appraising income producing props. for the MN Assessors Assn's Assessors Accreditation Program 1965-1975; Instructor of RE econ. for the BOMA, 1974 & 1978; Lecturer at State Conf. for the MN Assn. of Realtors, MN Assessors Assn., MN Apt. Owners Assn., Minneapolis Home Builders Assn., and the Amer. Right-of-Way Assn.; Lecturer at meetings of MAI and SREA MN Chap.; **OTHER ACT & HONORS:** Published Articles: The RE Appraiser, published by the Soc. of RE Appraisers; Right-of-Way Magazine, published by the Amer. Right-of-Way Assn.; Appraisal Journal, published by the Amer. Inst. of RE Appraisers; **BUS ADD:** 5353 Wayzata Blvd., Suite 212, Minneapolis, MN 55416, (612)546-1338.

JOHNSON, Don——*Dir. Fac.*, Gates Learjet Corp.; **PRIM RE ACT:** Property Manager; **BUS ADD:** PO Box 7707, Wichita, KS 67277, (316)946-2000.*

JOHNSON, Donald E.——B: Aug. 22, 1929, Decatur, IL, *Manager, Real Estate*, E.I. Dupont De Nemours and Co., RE Div.; **PRIM RE ACT:** Developer, Property Manager; **SERVICES:** Land devel. and provision of non-plant facilities, offices and warehouses for Dupont Co.; **PREV EMPLOY:** DuPont RE since 1956, var. positions, devel. of RE since 1973; **PROFL AFFIL & HONORS:** ULI, IOPC, Exec. Grp.; **EDUC:** BS, 1951, Bus. Admin., Univ. of IL, Champaign, IL; **GRAD EDUC:** MBA, 1956, RE, IN Univ., Bloomington, IN; **MIL SERV:** USN, Lt., 1951-54; **OTHER ACT & HONORS:** Chmn. New Castle Cty. Bd. of Ethics; **HOME ADD:** 1109 Artwin Rd., Chatman, Wilmington, DE 19803, (302)478-3367; **BUS ADD:** 1007 Market St., Wilmington, DE 19898, (302)774-4012.

JOHNSON, Donald M.——B: Oct. 26, 1924, Rupert, ID, *Broker*, Johnson & Smith, Realtors; **PRIM RE ACT:** Broker, Consultant, Instructor; **SERVICES:** Marketing, exchanging, consulting, counseling, Ag. and investment prop.; **REP CLIENTS:** Indiv. and Corp. investors and users of agricultural & investment prop.; **PREV EMPLOY:** Prof. memberships EPM, Nampa Bd. of Realtors, Idaho Assn. of Relators, NAR, Farm & Land Instit., RE Securities & Synd. Instit.; **PROFL AFFIL & HONORS:** Accredited Farm & Land Member (AFLM); **OTHER ACT & HONORS:** Nampa C of C, Nat. Sr. Instr. for Farm & Land Instit., specializing in marketing, exchanging, tax and unusual fin.; **HOME ADD:** 907 S. Powerline Rd., PO Box 542, Nampa, ID 83651, (208)466-6491; **BUS ADD:** 222 3rd Ave. S., PO Box 542, Nampa, ID 83651, (208)467-4456.

JOHNSON, Donald R.——B: Sept. 17, 1948, Bluefield, WV, *Sr. Asst. Gen. Counsel*, The Pittston Coal Group; **PRIM RE ACT:** Attorney, Regulator; **SERVICES:** Attorney, coal and oil and gas law, lobbyist; **PREV EMPLOY:** Atty., Hudgins, Coulling, Brewster and Morhous, Bluefield, WV, 1975-1978, Atty.; Ganas and Natkin, Lexington, VA, 1973-1975; **PROFL AFFIL & HONORS:** ABA; VA State Bar; WV State Bar; VA Bar Assn.; VA Trial Lawyers Assn.; Environmental Law Inst., Admitted to practice law in VA & WV; Exec. Comm., Comml. Transaction Litigation Commn. of VA State Bar, Bus. Sect; **EDUC:** BA, 1970, Poli. Sci. and Soc., VA Polytechnic Inst. and State Univ.; **GRAD EDUC:** JD, 1973, Law, Washington and Lee Univ. School of Law; **EDUC HONORS:** Cum Laude; **OTHER ACT & HONORS:** VA Oil and Gas Assn.; **HOME ADD:** 170 Larwood Ln., Bristol, VA 24201, (703)466-3863; **BUS ADD:** PO Box 4000, Lebanon, VA 24266, (703)889-4000.

JOHNSON, Earle B., Jr.——B: July 25, 1941, DeLand, FL, *Investment Analyst*, State Farm Mutual Automobile Insurance Co., Investment Dept., RE; **PRIM RE ACT:** Property Manager, Owner/Investor; **PROFL AFFIL & HONORS:** BOMA, Nat. Assn. of Indus. and Office Parks; **EDUC:** BA & BBA, 1963 & 1966, Econ., Mgmt., Emory Univ.; SMU; **GRAD EDUC:** MBA, 1972, Fin., Bradley Univ.; **OTHER ACT & HONORS:** IIA, Outstanding Young Men of Amer.; **HOME ADD:** 1205 Valentine Dr., Normal, IL 61761, (309)452-1381; **BUS ADD:** 1 State Farm Pl., Bloomington, IL 61701, (309)662-6606.

JOHNSON, Edward C.——B: Nov. 9, 1928 Jackson, MI, *Part.*, Johnson, Auld & Valentine; **PRIM RE ACT:** Attorney; **SERVICES:** RE Securities; **REP CLIENTS:** City Nat. Bank of Detroit Trust Div., Donovan Assoc. Inc., First of Michigan/Schmidt Prop.; **PROFL AFFIL & HONORS:** ABA State Bar of MI, RESSI, Past Pres. RESSI Chap. I, MI; **EDUC:** AB, 1960, Princeton Univ.; **GRAD EDUC:** JD, 1963, Univ. of MI Law School; **HOME ADD:** 500 Washington Rd., Grosse Pointe, MI 48230; **BUS ADD:** 2145 First Nat. Bldg., Detroit, MI 48226, (313)961-4700.

JOHNSON, Elliott A.——B: Feb. 21, 1907, Soldier, IA, *Pres.*, Johnson & Milligan, P.C. (Attys.); **PRIM RE ACT:** Attorney, Syndicator, Owner/Investor; **PROFL AFFIL & HONORS:** various Bar Assns.; **EDUC:** Ph.D., 1927, Univ. of Chicago; **GRAD EDUC:** LLB, 1930 & 1937, JD, U. of Chicago, 1930, So. TX College of Law 1937; **OTHER ACT & HONORS:** Councilman at Large, Houston, 1945-7, Houston Ctry Club, Houston Club, Kiwanis, Masonic Lodge, Shriners.; **HOME ADD:** 2020 Buffalo Speedway 1303, Houston, TX 77098, (713)622-2579; **BUS ADD:** 2200 S. Post Oak Blvd. Suite 707, Houston, TX 77056.

JOHNSON, Eugene——*Dir.*, Iowa Real Estate Commission; **PRIM RE ACT:** Property Manager; **BUS ADD:** 1223 E. Court, Des Moines, IA 50319, (515)281-3183.*

JOHNSON, Fred M.——B: Apr. 24, 1941, Erie, PA, *Owner/Broker*, Benchmark Realty Inc.; **PRIM RE ACT:** Broker, Consultant, Owner/Investor, Syndicator; **SERVICES:** Investor or user consultation concerning RE; synd. of resid. or comml. prop.; **PROFL AFFIL & HONORS:** RNMI, FL RE Exchangers, NAR, FL Assn. of Realtors, RE Securities and Synd., GRI, CRS; **MIL SERV:** US Army Security Agency, Sp 5, 1963-1967; **OTHER ACT & HONORS:** Deacon, First Baptist Church of Elfers; **HOME ADD:** P.O. Box 326, Elfers, FL 33531, (813)849-5855; **BUS ADD:** 2710 U.S. 19 S., New Port Richey, FL 33552, (813)842-9284.

JOHNSON, Gene——B: July 23, 1930, Tacoma, WA, *Pres.*, G.J. Property Services, Inc. AMO; **PRIM RE ACT:** Broker, Consultant, Owner/Investor, Property Manager; **SERVICES:** Investment counseling, problem prop. workout, asset mgmt. & prop. mgmt. of comml., apt. & office bldgs., Rehab. and leasing of office bldgs.; **REP CLIENTS:** Brokers, devels. & instnl. investors in office bldgs. Indiv. & broker investors in apts.; **PREV EMPLOY:** VP and member of Bd. of Dirs. of William Walters Co., Los Angeles, CA for twelve yrs.; **PROFL AFFIL & HONORS:** IREM, CPM; **EDUC:** BA, 1957, Bus. Mgmt./Econ., Univ. of Puget Sound; **EDUC HONORS:** Indep. Study; **MIL SERV:** USN, ET 3rd; **OTHER ACT & HONORS:** Orange Cty. and Long Beach and Southern Ctys. Apt. Assns.; **HOME ADD:** 515 Flint Ave., Long Beach, CA 90814, (213)498-3160; **BUS ADD:** 4201 Long Beach Blvd., Suite 410, Long Beach, CA 90807, (213)595-6661.

JOHNSON, Greg C.——B: Mar. 12, 1948, San Jose, CA, *Exec. VP*, Richards-Woodbury Mort. Corp.; **PRIM RE ACT:** Consultant, Developer, Lender, Owner/Investor, Syndicator; **SERVICES:** Mort. banking and devel.; **PREV EMPLOY:** Pres., Granite Mort. Corp.; **PROFL AFFIL & HONORS:** UT Mort. Bankers Assn.; **EDUC:** BA, 1972, Econ. and Social Sci., Boise State Univ., Boise ID; **GRAD EDUC:** MBA, 1974, RE Fin., Brigham Young Univ., Provo, UT; **EDUC HONORS:** Cum Laude; **HOME ADD:** 2684 Hillsden Dr., Salt Lake City, UT 84117, (801)277-4590; **BUS ADD:** 115 East South Temple, Salt Lake City, UT 84111, (801)364-6114.

JOHNSON, Helen——B: June 7, 1905, Carvallis, MT, *Broker, Pres.*, Helen Johnson RE, Inc.; **PRIM RE ACT:** Broker, Owner/Investor; **SERVICES:** Sales in res. land, comml. consultant; **PROFL AFFIL & HONORS:** Local, state & Nat. Bds. of Realtors,FU, RMI; **EDUC:** BA, 1927, Inst. Mgmt., Home Ec., Univ. of MT; **EDUC HONORS:** Mortor Bd. Pres. of AWS; Assn. of Women Students; **OTHER ACT & HONORS:** State Rep. 2 yrs., 1961-63; Masons Org.; PEO; Have served on many state boards; Health & MSU; Local Hosp. Bd.; Salvation Army; presently presidential elector; **HOME ADD:** 619 S Willson, Bozeman, MT 59715, (406)586-2232; **BUS ADD:** PO Box 1067, 416 N. 7th, Bozeman, MT 59715, (406)586-5472.

JOHNSON, Hewitt B.——B: Oct. 6, 1919, Harrisonburg, LA, *Atty.*, Johnson, Johnson & Johnson; **PRIM RE ACT:** Broker, Attorney; **SERVICES:** Atty. & RE Broker; **EDUC:** AB, 1940, Sci./Eng., LSU; **GRAD EDUC:** JD, 1948, Tulane Univ.; **MIL SERV:** USN, Sr. Lt., Pacific Theater Ribbon; **OTHER ACT & HONORS:** Temporary Appt. Judge, 4th Dist., Court of LA; **HOME ADD:** 2303 Briarmoor St., Monroe, LA 71201, (318)388-0915; **BUS ADD:** 1011 S. Grand St., Monroe, LA 71201.

JOHNSON, J. Allen——B: Feb. 21, 1925, Montreal, Quebec, *Pres.*, Johnson Assoc., Inc.; **PRIM RE ACT:** Broker, Instructor, Consultant, Property Manager; **PROFL AFFIL & HONORS:** CCIM; **EDUC:** Reed Coll.; **HOME ADD:** 1255 Nuuanu, Apt. 3101, Honolulu, HI 96813; **BUS ADD:** 700 Bishop St., Suite 1900, Honolulu, HI 96813, (808)521-8711.

JOHNSON, James A.——B: Apr. 4, 1948, Chicago, IL, *VP*, Stewart Title Guaranty Corp.; **PRIM RE ACT:** Attorney; **OTHER RE ACT:** Agent (closer); **PROFL AFFIL & HONORS:** Houston Bar Assn., TX Bar Assn., ABA; **EDUC:** AA & BA, 1972, 1974, Poli. Sci., Univ. of South; **GRAD EDUC:** JD, 1978, Univ. of Houston School of Law; **MIL SERV:** US Army, Capt., Bronze Star; **HOME ADD:** 2831 Triway, Houston, TX 77043, (713)460-4019; **BUS ADD:** 1100 Milan Bldg., Suite 1500, Houston, TX 77002, (713)651-0810.

JOHNSON, Jeffrey Scott——B: Aug. 12, 1952, Minneapolis, MN, *Atty.*, Barna, Guzy, Merrill, Hynes & Giancola, LTD., RE/Banking; **PRIM RE ACT:** Attorney, Owner/Investor; **SERVICES:** RE and Banking law; **REP CLIENTS:** Lending insts.., RE cos., Brokers, sales indivs., and the general public; **PROFL AFFIL & HONORS:** ABA, Anoka Bar Assn., Hennepin Cty. Bar Assn., MN State Real Prop. Sec., Hennepin Cty. Bar Eminent Domain Comm.; MN. Real Property Exchangers; **EDUC:** AB, 1975, Medieval Russian Hist., Univ. of MN; **GRAD EDUC:** JD, 1978, Hamline Univ. School of Law; **HOME ADD:** 2201 Girard Ave. S., Minneapolis, MN 55411, (612)377-0452; **BUS ADD:** 3700 Central Ave. N.E., Minneapolis, MN 55421, (612)788-1644.

JOHNSON, Jerry——B: Nov. 8, 1949, Roanoke, AL, *Assoc. Broker*, Daniel Realty & Ins. Agency Inc.; **PRIM RE ACT:** Broker; **SERVICES:** Sales of RE homes; **PROFL AFFIL & HONORS:** W. GA Homebuilders Assn.; Troup Cty. Bd. of Realtors, GRI; CRS; **EDUC:** 1971, Mktg., Univ. of GA; **OTHER ACT & HONORS:** LaGrange Jaycees; Kiwanis of LaGrange; Loyd Presbyterian Church; **HOME ADD:** 108 Oakdale Dr., LaGrange, GA 30240, (404)882-5680; **BUS ADD:** 207 Ridley Ave., LaGrange, GA 30241, (404)882-1840.

JOHNSON, Jerry D.——B: Sept. 25, 1942, Clovis, NM, *Appraiser*, First Federal Savings & Loan Assn. of Clovis; **PRIM RE ACT:** Appraiser; **SERVICES:** RE appraisals; **REP CLIENTS:** Lenders, Vet. Admin., US Dept. of Housing and Urban Devel.; **PREV EMPLOY:** Self employed bldg. contract from 1967-1973; **PROFL AFFIL & HONORS:** SREA, Chap. 115 Pres., 1980-1982, SRPA; **HOME ADD:** 3725 Sam Snead, Clovis, NM 88101, (505)762-0688; **BUS ADD:** 801 Pile St., Clovis, NM 88101, (505)762-4417.

JOHNSON, John——*Adm. VP*, Economics Laboratory, Inc.; **PRIM RE ACT:** Property Manager; **BUS ADD:** 370 Wabasha, St. Paul, MN 55102, (612)293-2233.*

JOHNSON, John E.——B: Nov. 8, 1942, Whittier, CA, *Pres.*, Vestcap Corp./Vestcap Securities Corp.; **PRIM RE ACT:** Broker, Syndicator, Property Manager, Owner/Investor; **OTHER RE ACT:** Securities Broker/Dealer; **SERVICES:** Synd. of Multi Family Residential and Comml. Prop., Prop. Mgmt., Securities Underwriting; **REP CLIENTS:** Project Mgmt. Aerospace Industry 1964 - 1980; **PROFL AFFIL & HONORS:** Active Member RESSI, NASD Registered Prin.; **EDUC:** BS, 1964, Mathematics/Physics, CA Poly. Univ. - San Luis Obispo; **HOME ADD:** 1195 Dove Meadow, Solvang, CA 93463, (805)688-2650; **BUS ADD:** 1693 Mission Dr., Solvang, CA 93463, (805)688-3647.

JOHNSON, John E.——B: Apr. 30, 1949, Tremonton, UT, *Exec. Dir.*, Ambrose / Farber Co.; **PRIM RE ACT:** Developer, Property Manager; **OTHER RE ACT:** Comml. Leasing; **SERVICES:** Prop. Mgmt, Comml. Leasing, Developm.; **PROFL AFFIL & HONORS:** BOMA, ICSC, Cert. Shopping Ctr. Mgr.; **EDUC:** BS, 1975, Communication/Bus., Brigham Young Univ.; **HOME ADD:** 4427 South Zinnia, Morrison, CO 80465, (303)979-7282; **BUS ADD:** 650 17th St., Denver, CO 80465, (303)534-8736.

JOHNSON, Ken, MAI——B: Apr. 12, 1921, Duluth, MN, *Owner*, St. Cloud Appraisal Service; **PRIM RE ACT:** Appraiser; **SERVICES:** Appraisal, investment analysis; **REP CLIENTS:** Lenders, instnl., govt.; **PROFL AFFIL & HONORS:** MAI; AIREA; SRPA; Soc. of RE Appraisers; **EDUC:** BA, 1949, Social Sci.; **MIL SERV:** USMG; T/Sgt.; **OTHER ACT & HONORS:** City Assessor, St. Cloud, 7 years; Bd. of Realtors; C of C, St. Cloud; **HOME ADD:** Apt. 206, 1225 Maine Prairie Rd., St. Cloud, MN 56301, (612)252-9367; **BUS ADD:** Ste. 106, Roosevelt Office Park, St. Cloud, MN 56301, (612)253-4488.

JOHNSON, Lee C.——B: Sept. 26, 1931, San Diego, CA, *Pres.*, Lee C. Johnson Co.; **PRIM RE ACT:** Consultant, Appraiser; **SERVICES:** RE Valuation, Court Testimony; **REP CLIENTS:** Fortune 500 Corps., Govt. agencies; **PROFL AFFIL & HONORS:** (past chapt. pres.) SREA, Amer. Right of Way Assn., AIREA (MAI), Prof. Recognition Award, AIREA; **EDUC:** BA, 1953, Poli. Sci. Econ., San Diego State Univ.; **HOME ADD:** 5822 Lomond Dr., San Diego, CA 92020; **BUS ADD:** 8321 Lemon Ave., La Mesa, CA 92041, (714)462-4350.

JOHNSON, Marshall J.——B: May 24, 1925, OH, *President*, Property Factors Inc.; **PRIM RE ACT:** Broker, Consultant, Owner/Investor, Syndicator; **OTHER RE ACT:** Specializing in full services, legal, marketing, packaging, brokerage; **SERVICES:** NASD, SEC licenses in consultation in house; **REP CLIENTS:** Investors, Commercial, Industrial, Multi-family residential; **PREV EMPLOY:** General Contractor, Management Consultant, Financial & loan packaging; **PROFL AFFIL & HONORS:** Nat. Assoc. of Realtors, OR Assn. of Realtors, Washington Cty. Bd. of Realtors; **MIL SERV:** US Army; **HOME ADD:** 2212 "B" St., Forest Grove, OR 97116, (503)357-6218; **BUS ADD:** 2075 S.W. 1st Ave., Portland Center Plaza Suite 2N, Portland, OR 97201, (503)223-4050.

JOHNSON, Martin D.——B: Aug. 20, 1950, Davenport, IA, *Sales person*, Mel Foster Commercial-Industrial Co.; **PRIM RE ACT:** Broker, Owner/Investor, Property Manager; **SERVICES:** Comml./Indus. brokerage, mgmt. broker, prop. mgr.; **REP CLIENTS:** Northwestern Mutual Life, Rand McNally, Bankers Life of Chicago and other local and regional comml.-indus. firms; **PREV EMPLOY:** Grubb & Ellis Commercial Brokerage Co., Phoenix, AZ; **PROFL AFFIL & HONORS:** NAR, Assn. of MBA's; **EDUC:** AB, 1972, Chemistry, Augustana Coll., Rock Island, IL; **GRAD EDUC:** MBA, 1975, Fin. and Mgmt., Northern IL Univ., Dekalb, IL; **HOME ADD:** 3219 - 14th St., Rock Island, IL 61201, (309)788-3833; **BUS ADD:** Third & Brady Streets, Davenport, IA 52801, (319)324-1081.

JOHNSON, Mary M.——B: Nov. 24, 1953, Omaha, NE, *RE Appraiser, VP*, Ed Pierce Appraisals, Resid. & Comml. Appraisals; **PRIM RE ACT:** Developer; **SERVICES:** Resid., comml. & indus. appraising for all purposes; **REP CLIENTS:** Credit unions, banks, fed. agencies, law firms, acctg. firms; **PROFL AFFIL & HONORS:** Member of Nat. Assn. of Independent Fee Appraisers; Member of Nat. Assn. of Revier Appraisers, Sr. Member Cert. Review Appraisers; Candidate Member IFA (Ind. Fee Appraisers); **HOME ADD:** 1952 E Carson Dr., Tempe, AZ 85282, (602)831-1943; **BUS ADD:** 55E Thomas Rd., 207, Phoenix, AZ 85012, (602)265-5291.

JOHNSON, Nile K.——B: Dec. 1, 1939, NE, *Atty.*, Johnson & Mock, Atty's at Law; **PRIM RE ACT:** Broker, Attorney, Developer, Owner/Investor, Property Manager; **OTHER RE ACT:** Title ins. sales - reg. abstractor; **SERVICES:** Atty., title ins., brokering, devel. resid. and comml. props., prop. mgmt.; **REP CLIENTS:** Indivs.; **PROFL AFFIL & HONORS:** ABA, NE Bar Assn., NE Land Title Assn.; **EDUC:** BS, 1962, Bus. Admin. & Bus. Organ., Univ. of NE; **GRAD EDUC:** Law, 1969, Univ. of NE; **MIL SERV:** US Navy, Lt.; **OTHER**

ACT & HONORS: Masons, Amer. Legion, State Planning Comm. on Adult Basic Educ.; **HOME ADD:** 310 Baronage Cir., Blair, NE 68008, (402)426-4774; **BUS ADD:** 1904 South St., Blair, NE 68008, (402)426-9626.

JOHNSON, Orwin, Jr.——B: Nov. 17, 1938, Mitchell, SD, *Owner/Broker*, Hegg Realtors, Inc., Farm Land Div.; **PRIM RE ACT:** Broker, Consultant, Property Manager; **SERVICES:** Consulting, comml. sales mgmt. custodial trusts, appraising, land sales; **REP CLIENTS:** Investors, Farm & Ranch Operators; **PREV EMPLOY:** Owned/operated Mobile Home Park, Rick Realty; **PROFL AFFIL & HONORS:** Sioux Falls/SD Bd. of Realtors, FLI, CCIM Candidate; **EDUC:** BA, 1960, Bus. Admin., Univ. of SD; **OTHER ACT & HONORS:** Shrine, Masons, Sioux Falls Bd. of Appeals, Bldg. Codes; **HOME ADD:** 6301 Cheyenne Dr., Sioux Falls, SD 57106, (605)338-6562; **BUS ADD:** 2804 E. 26th St., Sioux Falls, SD 57103, (605)336-2100.

JOHNSON, Paul A.——B: Mar. 29, 1933, Bendnel Butte, ND, *Broker*, Senter Realty, Comml.; **PRIM RE ACT:** Broker, Instructor, Syndicator, Property Manager, Owner/Investor; **SERVICES:** Brokerage, synd., counseling; **PROFL AFFIL & HONORS:** NAR; RNMI, CCIM; **EDUC:** BBA, 1955, Merch./Sales, Univ. of MN; **GRAD EDUC:** MBA, 1973, Mgmt., Univ. of OK; **MIL SERV:** USAF, Lt. Col.; **OTHER ACT & HONORS:** Abilene C of C; VP, Bd. of Dirs., Abilene Civic Ctr.; Bd. of Dirs., March of Dimes; Bd. of Dirs, Community Action Prog.; VP, RE Teachers Assn.; Bd. of Dir, United Way; **HOME ADD:** 2826 S 40th, Abilene, TX 79604, (915)698-2310; **BUS ADD:** POB 3438, Abilene, TX 79604, (915)676-5725.

JOHNSON, Paul G.——B: Aug. 19, 1942, Staten Island, NY, *Pres.*, Burke, Hansen, & Homan, Inc.; **PRIM RE ACT:** Consultant, Appraiser; **SERVICES:** Reg. RE valuation and non-valuation studies; **REP CLIENTS:** Corps., attys., accts.; **PROFL AFFIL & HONORS:** AIREA, MAI, GRI; **EDUC:** 1964, Econ., Lafayette Coll., Easton, PA; **MIL SERV:** USA, Lt., Army Commendation Medal; **OTHER ACT & HONORS:** Valley Forward, Chmn. Planning Comm.; **HOME ADD:** 4841 E Calle Tuberia, Phoenix, AZ 85018, (602)840-2292; **BUS ADD:** Valley Bank Ctr., Suite 1900, Phoenix, AZ 85073, (602)257-1451.

JOHNSON, Paul S.——B: Feb. 17, 1950, Minneapolis, MN, *Pres. & Owner*, Appraisal Valuation Analysts, Inc.; **PRIM RE ACT:** Appraiser, Instructor, Consultant; **SERVICES:** RE appraisals and consultations; **REP CLIENTS:** Govt., fin. inst., related professions and indiv.; **PROFL AFFIL & HONORS:** Nat. Assn. of Indep. Fee Appraisers; NAR; NARA, Sr. Appraiser, Realtor, 'Nat. Man of Yr.' for Nat. Assn. of Ind. Fee Appraisers; **EDUC:** 1972, Sociology/Ethics, St. Norbert Coll.; **OTHER ACT & HONORS:** Teacher of RE Valuation throughout the US for the NAIFA, Hobby: Aviation; **HOME ADD:** 3235 Pierce St. N.E., Minneapolis, MN 55418, (612)788-2858; **BUS ADD:** 2841 Johnson St. N.E., Minneapolis, MN 55418, (612)781-3141.

JOHNSON, Pearl——*Ed.-Mng. Ed.*, Record Publishing Co., The Commercial Record; **PRIM RE ACT:** Real Estate Publisher; **BUS ADD:** 750 Old Main St., Box 689, Rocky Hill, CT 06067, (203)563-3796.*

JOHNSON, Peter R.——B: Jan. 21, 1947, NY, NY, *RE Fin. Officer*, Coldwell Banker, RE Fin. Servs.; **PRIM RE ACT:** Broker, Consultant, Appraiser; **OTHER RE ACT:** Mort. Banker; **SERVICES:** Debt and equity fin. for comml. RE; **REP CLIENTS:** Devels. and instnl. lenders or investors; **PREV EMPLOY:** Gen. Electric Credit Corp. 1968-78; **PROFL AFFIL & HONORS:** AZ Mort. Bankers Assn., RE Sales License; **EDUC:** AB, 1968, Philosophy, Princeton Univ.; **HOME ADD:** 1043 E. Northern, Phoenix, AZ 85020, (602)944-0752; **BUS ADD:** 2346 N. Central, Phoenix, AZ 85004, (602)262-5586.

JOHNSON, Philip M.——B: Jan. 19, 1931, Twin Falls, ID, Philip M. Johnson, MAI: RE Appraiser & Consultant; **PRIM RE ACT:** Appraiser, Consultant; **SERVICES:** RE appraisals, consultations; **PREV EMPLOY:** Dir. of Community Planning & Devel.; Dir. of Operations/Chief Underwriter, FL Area Office, HUD; **PROFL AFFIL & HONORS:** MAI Desig., AIREA, Chmn., Chapt. Educ. Programs Comm., AIREA, Profl. Recognition Award, 1979; Regional Dir. of Education; **EDUC:** BA, 1953, ID State Univ.; **GRAD EDUC:** LLB, 1964, Blackstone School of Law, Chicago; MBA, 1975, RE & Urban Affairs, Univ. of N. FL; **MIL SERV:** US Army; 1953-55, Lt.; **OTHER ACT & HONORS:** Palms Presbyterian Church; Lions Club, Mason, Shriner, Rho Epsilon RE Frat.; **BUS ADD:** 3345 Eunice Rd., Jacksonville Bch., FL 32250, (904)249-7795.

JOHNSON, Phillip L.——B: June 22, 1949, East St. Louis, IL, *Pres.*, Kenneth J. Johnson Agency, Inc., Comml.-Indus.; **PRIM RE ACT:** Broker, Consultant, Appraiser, Developer, Owner/Investor; **SERVICES:** Profl. appraising & consulting serv. for indus. prop.; **PROFL AFFIL & HONORS:** NAR; IL Assn. of Realtors; Belleville Bd. of Realtors; IL Realtors Inst.; SIR, GRI; **HOME ADD:** 1111 N Charles, Belleville, IL 62221, (618)235-4865; **BUS ADD:** 505 S Illinois St., Belleville, IL 62221, (618)277-0505.

JOHNSON, R. Bruce——B: Dec. 14, 1941, Salina, KS, *Pres.*, Intown Properties, Inc. (IPI); **PRIM RE ACT:** Broker, Consultant, Developer, Owner/Investor, Property Manager, Syndicator; **SERVICES:** Sale of Condo. Projects, Comml. Investment Props., Resid. Resales (DC), Ctry.; **REP CLIENTS:** Estates & Mountain Prop. (VA) Synd. of Historic Prop./Partnerships Individual Investors, Lenders, Condo. Devels.; **PREV EMPLOY:** HUD 1965-1966; **PROFL AFFIL & HONORS:** Member, NAR, WA Bd. of Realtors, Victorian Soc.; Consultant, "Main Street Project" Nat. Trust for Hist. Preservation; **EDUC:** BA, 1964, Hist., Wheaton College, IL; **GRAD EDUC:** JD, 1976, RE & Tax, Catholic Univ. School of Law; **EDUC HONORS:** Pi Gamma Mu; **HOME ADD:** 1861 Newton St., NW, Washington, DC 20010, (202)332-7716; **BUS ADD:** 1318 14th St., NW, Washington, DC 20005, (202)667-8300.

JOHNSON, R. Grant——B: Apr. 12, 1930, Pittsburgh, PA, R. Grant Johnson; **PRIM RE ACT:** Appraiser, Developer, Property Manager, Owner/Investor; **SERVICES:** Valuation-single family residences; **REP CLIENTS:** Equitable Reloc.-Exec. Reloc., Tranamer. Reloc., Allstate Fin., Uniroyal, Cities Service, Eastern Airlines, etc.; **PREV EMPLOY:** HUD 1956-70; **PROFL AFFIL & HONORS:** SREA(SRA); **EDUC:** BS, 1957, Econ., Thiel Coll.; **MIL SERV:** USA, S/Sgt., 1952-54; **HOME ADD:** 2618 Gulfstream Ln., Ft. Lauderdale, FL 33312, (305)581-0412; **BUS ADD:** 2408 Davie Blvd., Ft. Lauderdale, FL 33312, (305)583-2058.

JOHNSON, Randall C.——B: Feb. 12, 1949, Tulsa, OK, *Pres.*, Arvida Mortgage Company; **PRIM RE ACT:** Lender; **SERVICES:** Mort. Banking Co.; **REP CLIENTS:** Builders, Devels., Realtors, Indivs.; **PREV EMPLOY:** VP Baker Mort. Co., Regl. Mgr. GE Credit Corp.; **PROFL AFFIL & HONORS:** Bd. of Governors MBA of FL, Trustee Mortgage Bankers of FL Political Action Comm., Internal Mgmt. Comm. MBAA, Assoc. Member SREA; **EDUC:** BA, 1971, Econ., Univ. of Miami; **EDUC HONORS:** Dean's List; **OTHER ACT & HONORS:** Pinellas County Comm. of 100; **HOME ADD:** 5 Eastwood Ln., Belleair, FL 33516, (813)586-3216; **BUS ADD:** 1307 U.S. Highway 19 S., P O Box 6515, Clearwater, FL 33518, (813)535-1482.

JOHNSON, Reverdy——B: Aug. 24, 1937, New York, NY, *Partner*, Pettit & Martin; **PRIM RE ACT:** Attorney; **SERVICES:** Legal Servs. in all areas of RE acquisition, devel. and fin.; **REP CLIENTS:** Devels. and investors in office, retail and hotel props.; **PROFL AFFIL & HONORS:** ULI, Comml. and Retail Devel. Council Exec. Council; Lambda Alpha; **EDUC:** AB, 1960, Hist., Harvard Coll.; **GRAD EDUC:** BLB, 1963, Harvard Law School; **EDUC HONORS:** Cum Laude; **MIL SERV:** US Army Reserve, 1st Lt.; **OTHER ACT & HONORS:** Dir., Found. for San Francisco's Arch. Heritage; **HOME ADD:** 2503 Broadway, San Francisco, CA 94115; **BUS ADD:** 600 Montgomery St., San Francisco, CA 94111, (415)434-4000.

JOHNSON, Rex——*Dir. Ind. Sales & Leasing*, Mitchell Energy & Development Corp.; **PRIM RE ACT:** Property Manager; **BUS ADD:** 2201 Timberlock, Woodland, TX 77380, (713)363-5500.*

JOHNSON, Richard D.——B: Apr. 30, 1908, Tyler, NM, *Broker*, Zuber-Janiga, Inc., Real Estate Brokers; **PRIM RE ACT:** Broker, Appraiser; **OTHER RE ACT:** Certified Appraiser, NAIFA and Natl. Assn. Review App.; **SERVICES:** Appraising & review appraising; **REP CLIENTS:** Barnett Bank of Highlands Cty.; Sparesbankengt Oslo, Norway, Rep. Mort. Ins. Co., Tampa, FL, review appls., Univ. of Miami, Coral Gables, FL, Town of Lake Placid, Zumerteg Estate Appraisal, Attorney Andrew Jackson; **PREV EMPLOY:** The Cavender Corp., Realtors; **PROFL AFFIL & HONORS:** Nat. Assn. of Independent Fee Appraisers, Nat. Assn. of Review Appraisers; Lake Placid Bd. of Realtors, IFA, CRA (Sr. Member), Realtor; **EDUC:** BARCH, 1928-29, Arch. Engrg., Univ. of MN; **OTHER ACT & HONORS:** Elks Club; Lions Club; **HOME ADD:** P O Box 1257, Lake Placid, FL 33852, (813)465-4800; **BUS ADD:** Rt. 1 Box 37A, Lake Placid, NY 33852, (813)463-5151.

JOHNSON, Robert——*VP, Secy. & Legal Counsel*, Danly Machine Corp.; **PRIM RE ACT:** Attorney, Property Manager; **BUS ADD:** 2100 S. Laramie Ave., Cicero, IL 60650, (312)242-1800.*

JOHNSON, Robert G.——*Exec. Dir.*, National Assn. of Review Appraisers; **OTHER RE ACT:** RE Assn.; **BUS ADD:** Suite 410 Midwest Federal Bldg., St. Paul, MN 55101, (612)227-6696.

JOHNSON, Robert M.——B: Aug. 20, 1942, Thomas, OK, *Shareholder - Dir.*, Crowe & Dunlevy, a professional corporation; **PRIM RE ACT:** Attorney; **SERVICES:** Comml. RE & RE fin. practice; **REP CLIENTS:** Lenders and devel.; **PROFL AFFIL & HONORS:** OK and ABA; ABA RE Fin. Comm., Martindale AV rating; **EDUC:** BS, 1964, Mktg., OK State Univ.; **GRAD EDUC:** JD, 1967, Law, Univ. of OK; **EDUC HONORS:** Who's Who Among Students in Amer. Coll. and Univ., 1963-1964; Dean's Honor Roll, Order of the Coif; Editor, OK Law Review; Phi Delta Phi Nat. Cert. of Merit; **MIL SERV:** US Army, Capt.; Distinguished Grad.; AG School; **OTHER ACT & HONORS:** Dir., Found. for Sr. Citizens; Dir., Pellow Petroleum, Inc.; Dir., YMCA Camp Classen; Visitng Lecturer, RE Fin., Univ. of OK, Coll. of Law; Occasional Lecturer, RE and Banking Groups; **HOME ADD:** 1511 Guilford Ln., Oklahoma City, OK 73120, (405)848-5178; **BUS ADD:** 1800 Mid-America Tower, 20 Broadway, Oklahoma City, OK 73102, (405)235-7724.

JOHNSON, Robert R.J.——B: Dec. 7, 1917, Milwaukee, WI, *COB*, Better Homes Realty, Inc.; **PRIM RE ACT:** Broker, Instructor, Consultant, Owner/Investor; **OTHER RE ACT:** Exchanging; **SERVICES:** Investment counseling, instr., brokerage, investment RE; **REP CLIENTS:** Comml. & Indus.; **PROFL AFFIL & HONORS:** Realtor of the Yr. in 1971 of Milwaukee Bd of Realtors, GRI, WI Realtors Assn., CCIM; **EDUC:** BS, 1938, Educ. Math., Univ. of WI, Milwaukee; **OTHER ACT & HONORS:** Chmn., RE Advisory Comm., Waukresha Cty. Tech. Inst., Omincron Tau Rho (Old Time Realtor); **HOME ADD:** N87 W15465 Kings Hwy, Milwaukee Falls, WI 53051, (414)251-8651; **BUS ADD:** 13620 W Capitol Dr., Brookfield, WI 53005, (414)783-6311.

JOHNSON, Roger——B: Aug. 27, 1939, Lebanon, OH, *Pres.*, Roger Johnson Realty, Inc.; **PRIM RE ACT:** Broker, Appraiser; **SERVICES:** RE brokerage, appraisals; **REP CLIENTS:** Homequity, John Deere Corp., Executrans, Inc.; **PROFL AFFIL & HONORS:** Amer. Assn. of Cert. Appraisers, NAR, OAR, GRI; CAR; **EDUC:** 1973, OH State Univ.; **MIL SERV:** US Navy; **OTHER ACT & HONORS:** 1975, Pres. of Warren Cty. Bd. of Realtors; 1973, Sales Assoc. of Yr., Warren Cty.; 1976, Nominee for Realtor of Yr., OH; **HOME ADD:** 3117 Oregonia Rd., Lebanon, OH 45036, (513)932-3924; **BUS ADD:** 202 E. Warren St., Lebanon, OH 45036, (513)932-4071.

JOHNSON, Roland F.——*Mgr. of RE*, Eaton Corp.; **PRIM RE ACT:** Property Manager; **BUS ADD:** 100 Erieview Plaza, Cleveland, OH 44114, (216)523-5000.*

JOHNSON, Ronald D.——B: July 25, 1948, Pendleton, OR, *VP and Mgr.*, First State Bank of Oregon, Mort. Banking Grp.; **PRIM RE ACT:** Banker; **SERVICES:** RE credit and mort. banking servs.; **PREV EMPLOY:** Asst. VP, Securities-Intermountain, Inc., Portland, OR - Jan. 1971-May 1975; **PROFL AFFIL & HONORS:** Bd. of Regents and fac. of the Nat. School of RE Fin. sponsored by the Amer. Bankers Assn. in conjunction with the OH State Univ.; VP and Dir. of the OR Mort. Bankers Assn.; past Chmn. of the Portland Metropolitan Loan Review Comm.; past Chmn. of the RE Lending Comm. of the OR Bankers Assn.; past Chmn. of various comm. for the Homebuilders Assn. of Metropolitan Portland; lecturer in RE Fin. at Portland State Univ.; member of the Clackamas County, OR, Econ. Devel. Comm.; member of the Univ. Club, Portland, OR; **EDUC:** BS, 1970, Fin., Univ. of WA, Seattle, WA; **MIL SERV:** US Army Reserve, SSG; **HOME ADD:** 12405 SW Foothill Dr., Portland, OR 97225; **BUS ADD:** 10888 SE Main St., PO Box 22352, Milwaukie, OR 97222, (503)653-3386.

JOHNSON, Theodore Karl——B: Oct. 23, 1951, Miami, FL, *Accountant/Broker*, S.R.I.; Society of Real Estate Investors, Inc.; T.K. Johnson & Assoc., Inc.; **PRIM RE ACT:** Broker, Consultant, Instructor; **OTHER RE ACT:** Accountant, specialize in RE Exchanges; **SERVICES:** Invest. consulting, comml. brokerage, buyer brokering, exchange, fin. structuring of RE acquisitions & liquidations; **REP CLIENTS:** Buyers of income props., sellers in RE exchanges; **PREV EMPLOY:** Haskins & Sells, CPA's, Miami, FL, 1974-75; **PROFL AFFIL & HONORS:** Academy Network of Exchangers; FL RE Exchangers; Intl. Assn. of Fin. Planners; **EDUC:** BS, 1974, Acctg./Fin., FL State Univ., Talahassee, FL; **OTHER ACT & HONORS:** Founder & Pres. of Progressive Investors of FL, A Miami RE Investment Club with 350 active members. Teach two day seminar on Creative Real Fin. and Investment Analysis, Acquisition, & Liquidation Techniques of RE; Listed in 1982 Who's Who in "Creative" RE; **HOME ADD:** 1040 N.E. 160 Street, North Miami Beach, FL 33162, (305)947-2548; **BUS ADD:** 2727 East Oakland Park Blvd., Suite 204, Fort Lauderdale, FL 33306, (305)563-9755.

JOHNSON, Walter G.——B: Aug. 16, 1949, Toledo, OH, *Asst. Treas., Long Term Investments & RE Fin.*, Kmart Corp.; **PRIM RE ACT:** Consultant, Lender, Owner/Investor, Property Manager; **OTHER RE ACT:** Arrange fin. for Kmart RE holdings and invest mort. portfolio of life ins. subsidiary; **SERVICES:** Construction & Long Term. Fin., Sale-leasback fin.; **REP CLIENTS:** Comml. devel., equity synd., work with major investment and comml. banks; **EDUC:** BBA, 1971, Fin., OH Univ.; **GRAD EDUC:** MBA, 1981, Fin., Wayne State Univ.; **OTHER ACT & HONORS:** Birmingham Jaycees; **HOME ADD:** 3338 Greenwood, Auburn Hts., MI 48057, (313)852-6566; **BUS ADD:** 3100 W. Big Beaver, Troy, MI 48084, (313)643-1776.

JOHNSON, Wayne C.——B: Jun 3, 1937, Iron Mtn., MI, *Assessor*, City of Ann Arbor; **PRIM RE ACT:** Consultant, Assessor; **PROFL AFFIL & HONORS:** IAAO; SREA; MAA; NCRAAO; NARA, CAE; SRA; CRA; MI State Assessor's Bd. Level IV; **EDUC:** BS, 1967, Educ., Eastern MI Univ.; **OTHER ACT & HONORS:** Deputy Assessor, 1964-1968; Assessor, 1968 to present, City of Ann Arbor; Past Pres. International Assn. of Assessing Officers; Past/ Pres. MI Assessors Assn.; **HOME ADD:** 1815 Ivywood, Ann Arbor, MI 48103, (313)663-7063; **BUS ADD:** City Hall, 100 N. Fifth Ave., POB 8647, Ann Arbor, MI 48107, (313)994-2663.

JOHNSON, Wayne L.——B: Sep. 17, 1928, CA, *Partner*, Northwest RE Systems; **PRIM RE ACT:** Syndicator, Consultant, Developer, Builder, Property Manager, Owner/Investor; **OTHER RE ACT:** Synd.; **SERVICES:** Packaging, mktg. synd., fin., devel.; **REP CLIENTS:** Comml. multi-family & shopping ctrs.; **PROFL AFFIL & HONORS:** NAHB, RESSI, RAMS, Tr George Fox Coll., Member –40,000,000 Club; **EDUC:** BA, 1949, Bus. Admin & Acct.; **MIL SERV:** USA, Capt.; **HOME ADD:** 731 Foothill Dr., Eugene, OR 97405, (503)484-9786; **BUS ADD:** 1342 High St., Suite 2, Eugene, OR 97401, (503)344-1491.

JOHNSTON, David——B: Sept. 9, 1944, Corpus Christi, TX, *Sr. VP*, Jagger Assoc., Inc.; **PRIM RE ACT:** Developer; **SERVICES:** Apt., Office, Condo & Land Devel.; **PREV EMPLOY:** VP Lomas & Nettleton Fin. Corp.; **EDUC:** BA, 1967, Psych., Univ. of AZ; **GRAD EDUC:** MBA, 1973, RE & Fin., So. Methodist Univ.; **EDUC HONORS:** Gen. Resident Scholarship, Glaze Award RE, Dallas Fin. Execs. Award in Fin.; **MIL SERV:** USAF, Capt., 1967-72, Vietnam Cross of Gallentry, Air Medal, DFC, AF Commendation Medal; **HOME ADD:** 4831 Twin Valley Dr., Austin, TX 78731, (512)452-1426; **BUS ADD:** 1201 Spyglass Dr., Austin, TX 78746, (512)327-2900.

JOHNSTON, Frank Z.——B: Sept. 16, 1937, St. Louis, MO, *Pres., Owner*, Johnston Group Inc.; **PRIM RE ACT:** Broker, Consultant, Developer, Builder, Owner/Investor, Instructor, Syndicator; **SERVICES:** Devel. and synd. of comml. props.; **REP CLIENTS:** Higher income indivs., pension plans and lending institutions; **PREV EMPLOY:** Hallcraft Devel. 1964-74, Mitchell Devel. of the S.W. 1974-1975, Gerald D. Hines Interests 1975-79; **PROFL AFFIL & HONORS:** Bd. of Dirs. of Comml. Indus. & Instit. Council of NAHB; Greater Houston Builders Assn.; Sales & Mktg. Execs. of Houston; RE Sec. & Synd. Inst., Greater Houston Builders Assn. PRISM Award, Sales & Mktg. Execs. D.S.A. Award; **EDUC:** BS Bus. Admin., 1959, St. Louis Univ.; **MIL SERV:** US Army, 1962-64, Sgt. E-5, Army Commendation Medal; **OTHER ACT & HONORS:** Houston Exec. Club; Intl. Assn. of Fin. Planners; **HOME ADD:** 274 Litchfield Ln., Houston, TX 77024, (713)464-1362; **BUS ADD:** 2077 S. Gessner, Suite 125, Houston, TX 77063, (713)784-7914.

JOHNSTON, Gary L.——B: Jan. 20, 1946, Bad Axe, MI, *Pres.*, Johnston Investment Real Estate; **PRIM RE ACT:** Broker, Consultant, Syndicator; **SERVICES:** RE acquisitions, apts., office bldgs.; **PROFL AFFIL & HONORS:** NAR; MO Assn. of Realtors; Kansas City Bd. of Realtors; RESSI; RNMI; Intl. Assn. of Fin. Planners, CCIM; **EDUC:** BS, 1977, Bus./Hist., William JewelL Coll., Liberty, MO; **OTHER ACT & HONORS:** Kansas City Rugby/Football Club; **HOME ADD:** 10418 Belinder Rd., Leawood, KS 66206, (913)648-3920; **BUS ADD:** Two Crown Ctr., Suite 250, Kansas City, MO 64108, (816)842-5688.

JOHNSTON, James L.——B: Feb. 21, 1946, London, England, *Nat. Mgr. RE Servs.*, Canada Permanent Trust Co./Realtor; **PRIM RE ACT:** Broker; **OTHER RE ACT:** RE Franchisor, Relocation Home Purchase Co.; **REP CLIENTS:** Relocation clients include Johns-Manville, Xerox (Can), IBM (CAN), CAN Pac., Ford Motor Co. (CAN); **PREV EMPLOY:** Marathon Realty Asst. to VP 1973-75; **PROFL AFFIL & HONORS:** ON RE Assoc., CAN Prop. Mgrs. Assn.; **EDUC:** BA, 1968, Econ., Math., Queens Univ.; **GRAD EDUC:** MA & MBA, 1969 & 1970, labour econ. & Fin. and RE, Queens Univ. and Univ. of BC; **EDUC HONORS:** Honors, J. Walter Thompson Scholarship; **HOME ADD:** 1106 Streambank Dr., Mississauga, L5H3Z1, ON, Canada, (416)274-1221; **BUS ADD:** 145 Front St. E., Toronto, M5A1E3, Ontario, Canada, (416)362-7341.

JOHNSTON, James R.——B: Apr. 27, 1942, Pearisburg, VA, *Part owner*, Hallmond Properties, Inc., Appraising; **PRIM RE ACT:** Consultant, Appraiser, Owner/Investor; **SERVICES:** Comml. appraisals, investment consulting; **REP CLIENTS:** Banks, investors, attys., etc.; **PROFL AFFIL & HONORS:** AIREA, Soc. of RE Appraisers, MAI, SRPA; **EDUC:** BS, 1964, Agricultural Econ., VA Polytechnic Inst.; **EDUC HONORS:** Pres. of Agricultural Econ. Club; **MIL SERV:** USNG, Sgt.; **OTHER ACT & HONORS:** Currently President of AIREA 56 (American Institute of Real Estate Appraisers); **HOME ADD:** 303 Quail Meadows Dr., Forest, VA 24551, (804)525-3036; **BUS ADD:** 3713 Old Forest Rd., Lynchburg, VA 24501, (804)384-9610.

JOHNSTON, Jay S.——B: Feb. 7, 1950, Dallas, TX, *Dept. Mgr. of Prop. Mgmt. and Comml. Sales Div.*, American Real Estate Corp., Prop. mgmt. and comml. sales; **PRIM RE ACT:** Broker, Consultant, Property Manager, Owner/Investor, Syndicator; **SERVICES:** Comml. brokerage, prop. mgmt., synd. of comml. props., investment counseling, indiv. and instnl. investors in comml. props.; **PREV EMPLOY:** Self employed, sales and mgmt.; **PROFL AFFIL & HONORS:** IREM, Austin TX and Natl. Bd. of Realtors, Mgmt., Assn. RESSI, CPM; **EDUC:** BBA, 1972-74, Mktg., Mgmt., Univ. of TX at Austin; **EDUC HONORS:** Member of Kappa Frat., Member of TX Cowboys; **HOME ADD:** 3404 Glenview Ave, Austin, TX 78703, (512)452-3270; **BUS ADD:** 1300 Guadalupe #200, Austin, TX 78701, (512)477-1312.

JOHNSTON, John A.——B: Nov. 16, 1944, Pittsburgh, PA, *VP*, Mellon-Stuart Realty Co.; **PRIM RE ACT:** Consultant, Developer, Owner/Investor; **SERVICES:** Comml./resid. devel., investment & consultation; **PREV EMPLOY:** Oliver Realty Inc., 1977-1979; The Alton Co., Inc., 1973-1977; **PROFL AFFIL & HONORS:** ULI; BOMA; **EDUC:** AB, 1968, Econ./Geography, Colgate Univ.; **GRAD EDUC:** MBA, 1971, Fin./RE, Wharton School; **EDUC HONORS:** Dir. Honor List; **HOME ADD:** 5507 Dunmoyle St., Pittsburgh, PA 15217, (412)681-4867; **BUS ADD:** Three Station Square, Pittsburgh, PA 15219, (412)323-4747.

JOHNSTON, John Sikes——B: Mar. 15, 1937, Charlotte, NC, *Pres., V Chmn.*, Marsh Realty Co., Marsh Assoc.; **PRIM RE ACT:** Broker, Attorney, Developer, Builder, Lender, Owner/Investor, Property Manager; **SERVICES:** FHA/VA-GNMA originator, bLdr., devel., mgr., owner, various R.E.; **PROFL AFFIL & HONORS:** Member & Former Dir., Charlotte Apts. Assn.; Homebuilder Assn. of Charlotte, Atty. of Law; Realtor; **EDUC:** BA, 1959, Econ., Davidson Coll.; **GRAD EDUC:** JD, 1964, Univ. of NC; **EDUC HONORS:** Honors 1964; **MIL SERV:** USA intelligence, 1st lt., 1959-61; **OTHER ACT & HONORS:** Former chmn., Greater Carolinas Chap.; Amer. Red Cross; Chmn., Bd. of Tr., Coker Coll.; Elder, Covenant Presbyterian Church; **HOME ADD:** 2619 Beverwyck Rd., Charlotte, NC 28211, (704)366-5140; **BUS ADD:** 2448 Park Rd., Charlotte, NC 28204, (704)376-0281.

JOHNSTON, Phillip K.——B: Aug. 19, 1952, Camp LeJune, NC, *Appraiser*, Johnston & Assoc.; **PRIM RE ACT:** Appraiser; **PREV EMPLOY:** - Chateau Investments, Inc. - Land Devel. Co.; Harold A. Scott & Assoc.; **PROFL AFFIL & HONORS:** RM to the AIREA; **EDUC:** BBA, 1975, RE, IN Univ.; **HOME ADD:** 3201 S. Albright Rd., Kokomo, IN 46902, (317)453-3557; **BUS ADD:** 105 W. Sycamore, Suite 516, Kokomo, IN 46901, (317)457-3774.

JOHNSTON, Richard J.——B: Dec. 4, 1949, Spanglar, PA, *Assoc. Broker*, John Rawlings Real Estate, Inc.; **PRIM RE ACT:** Broker, Consultant, Appraiser, Owner/Investor, Property Manager; **SERVICES:** Sales, appraisals, prop. mgmt.; **REP CLIENTS:** Atty., lenders, investors; **PROFL AFFIL & HONORS:** NAR, Assoc. Member - Soc. of RE Appraisers, Candidate - AIREA; **MIL SERV:** USMC, L/Cpl.; **OTHER ACT & HONORS:** P.E.R. Elks; **HOME ADD:** 110 Aldrich Ave., Altoona, PA 16602, (814)946-3058; **BUS ADD:** 1111 12th Ave., Altoona, PA 16601, (814)944-2543.

JOHNSTON, Robert K.——B: July 27, 1920, Indpls., IN, *VP & Dept. Head*, First Security Nat. Bank & Trust Co.; **PRIM RE ACT:** Banker, Lender; **OTHER RE ACT:** Head Bank's Mort. Banking Operation; **SERVICES:** Mort. Lending - Direct & Indirect; **PREV EMPLOY:** Mort. Corp. CEO, Second Officer Comml Bank; **PROFL AFFIL & HONORS:** Dir. Lex. Mort. Bankers, Mort. Bankers Assn. of Amer., RE Bds.; **EDUC:** Grad. Cert., 1948-1956, RE Finance, Indiana Univ.; **GRAD EDUC:** Grad. Cert., 1961, Mort. Banking, Northwestern Univ.; **MIL SERV:** USA, T/5, Various Decorations; **OTHER ACT & HONORS:** Presby. Church, Little League, Masonic Lodge, Scottish Rite, Shrine, P.T.A., Kentucky Colonel; **HOME ADD:** 3336 Carriage Ln., Lexington, KY 40502, (606)272-4413; **BUS ADD:** One First Security Plaza, Lexington, KY 40507, (606)231-2432.

JOHNSTON, Robert M.——B: Nov. 7, 1924, Indianapolis, IN, *Owner*, Johnston & Assocs.; **PRIM RE ACT:** Broker, Consultant, Appraiser, Developer, Lender, Builder, Syndicator; **OTHER RE ACT:** Work between for. investors & domestic borrowers; **SERVICES:** Short term 2nd morts.-interim fin.; **REP CLIENTS:** Dunkelwald Finanz Gesellschaft; **PREV EMPLOY:** Same for 20 years - Also Pres. of Bomert Const. Co., Inc. 20 yrs.; **PROFL AFFIL & HONORS:** NAR; **EDUC:** AB, 1948, Econ. & Psych., Kalamazoo Coll.; **EDUC HONORS:** Honors in Econ.; Phi Kappa Delta in Debate; **MIL SERV:** US Army Air Corps, USAF, 1st Lt.; **OTHER ACT & HONORS:** Past Local Pres. Rotary Club & Jaycees; Council of Young Exec. WSWA; **HOME ADD:** 1752 Utica Pike, Jeffersonville, IN 47130, (812)282-5555; **BUS ADD:** PO Box 384, Jeffersonville, IN 47130, (812)282-5555.

JOHNSTON, Rod P.——B: Aug. 23, 1913, Dayton, WA, *Pres.*, Johnston & Co., Inc.; **PRIM RE ACT:** Appraiser; **OTHER RE ACT:** RE investment analyst/advisor; **REP CLIENTS:** Indiv., corps., utility co's., lenders; **PREV EMPLOY:** Bank of Amer. (appraisal dept.) 1946-48; FHA (Chief appraiser & chief underwriter), 1948-59; **PROFL AFFIL & HONORS:** AIREA; Soc. of RE Appraisers; Educare; Amer. R/W Assn., MAI, SREA; **EDUC:** AB, 1937, Law, Univ. of ID; **MIL SERV:** USN; Lt.; Pacific Medal; **OTHER ACT & HONORS:** C of C (Metro. planning); **HOME ADD:** 1225 N Wilson, Boise, ID 83706, (208)343-2373; **BUS ADD:** 3316 Americana Terr., PO Box 7085, Boise, ID 83707, (208)345-4830.

JOHNSTON, Thomas A.——*Assoc.*, Tom LaCava and Assoc.; **PRIM RE ACT:** Developer; **BUS ADD:** PO Box 31, 23846 Sunnymead Blvd., Sunnymead, CA 92388, (714)653-3115.*

JOHNSTON, W. James——B: Apr. 18, 1942, Twin Falls, ID, *Pres.*, Remy-Johnston Real Estate Co., Inc.; **PRIM RE ACT:** Broker, Consultant, Owner/Investor, Instructor, Property Manager; **SERVICES:** Closing office, escrow serv., prop. mgmt.; **PREV EMPLOY:** Owner Mountain State Title Co.; **PROFL AFFIL & HONORS:** RNMI, CRS, CRB, GRI; **EDUC:** BS (Ed), 1965, Psych., Speech, Soc. Sci., Univ. of ID, Moscow, ID; **GRAD EDUC:** MRE, 1968, Educ., Admin., Brigham Young Univ., Provo, UT; **EDUC HONORS:** Distinguished Grad., Student Body Pres.; **OTHER ACT & HONORS:** Pres., Tendoy Area Council of Boy Scouts of Amer.; Nat. Bd. BSA; 1980 Realtor of the Year Pocatello Bd. of Realtors; 1981 Two Million Dollar Club for Residential Sales; Pocatello C of C; Bd. of Dirs. United Campaign; Pres. Jo Pac Associates; Pres. Sunny-Jim Investors; **HOME ADD:** 2126 Pole Line Rd., Pocatello, ID 83201, (208)232-2069; **BUS ADD:** PO Box 938, 1400 N Arthur, Pocatello, ID 83204, (208)234-0550.

JOHNSTONE, Richard O.——B: Dec. 31, 1929, Oak Park, IL, *Trust RE Officer*, Fulton Bank, Trust; **PRIM RE ACT:** Banker; **SERVICES:** Mgmt. - maintenance - sale; **REP CLIENTS:** Estates - trusts - guardianships - investment mgmt. agreements; **PREV EMPLOY:** RE Sales; **PROFL AFFIL & HONORS:** ASA, GRI Broker (PA); **EDUC:** BS, 1962, Physics, Penn State Univ.; **MIL SERV:** US Navy, LCDR (Ret.); **OTHER ACT & HONORS:** Comm. Man - Rapho Twp. Union Sq. 8 yrs., Pres. Lancaster Cty. Conservancy, Lanc. Co. Park Bd.; **HOME ADD:** RD4, Manheim, PA 17545; **BUS ADD:** 1 Penn Sq., Lancaster, PA 17604, (717)291-2561.

JOLLY, Edward A.——B: July 8, 1951, Klamath Falls, OR, *Mgr. Jackson Cty.*, Transamerica Title Insurance Co.; **OTHER RE ACT:** Title Insurance and Escrow; **SERVICES:** Closing and insurance of RE transactions; **REP CLIENTS:** Brokers, salespersons, lenders, attys., surveyers and appraisers; **PROFL AFFIL & HONORS:** Homebuilders Assn., Realty Bd., Comml. Investors and Devels., Educ. Chmn., Homebuilders Assn.; **EDUC:** BA, 1974, Psych., Oral Roberts Univ.; **EDUC HONORS:** Who's Who in Amer. Univ. and Colls.; **OTHER ACT & HONORS:** US Tennis Assn.; BMW Car Club of Amer.; **HOME ADD:** 2509 Stonebrook, Medford, OR 97501, (503)770-5298; **BUS ADD:** 245 S. Grape, Medford, OR 97501, (503)779-7660.

JOLLY, Jerry D.——B: Dec. 29, 1934, Fresno, CA, *CPA*; **PRIM RE ACT:** Consultant, Property Manager; **OTHER RE ACT:** CPA; **SERVICES:** Consultation on tax and econ. impact of RE transactions, **PREV EMPLOY:** Nat. CPA firm; **PROFL AFFIL & HONORS:** CA Inst. of CPA's, AICPA, CPA; **EDUC:** BS, 1957, acctg., Pacific Union Coll.; **GRAD EDUC:** MBA, 1976, tax, Golden Gate Univ.; **EDUC HONORS:** Who's Who Among Coll. & Univ. 1957; **MIL SERV:** US Army; **HOME ADD:** 20050 Fifth St. W, Souoma, CA 95476, (707)996-2775; **BUS ADD:** 75 Andrieux, Souoma, CA 95476, (707)938-0202.

JONAS, Anderson——B: May 8, 1950, Los Angeles, CA, *Owner*, Anderson L. Jonas, Atty. at Law; **PRIM RE ACT:** Consultant, Attorney, Developer, Owner/Investor, Property Manager, Syndicator; **OTHER RE ACT:** Building designer; **SERVICES:** Legal, arch., supervision, investing; **REP CLIENTS:** US Customs, Western Air Lines, Many Airlines and Trucking Firms; **PREV EMPLOY:** Indus. Mgmt. Systems, Metaphase Inc.; All self owned employment; **PROFL AFFIL & HONORS:** ABA; CBA; LACBA; **EDUC:** BS, 1972, Arch., School of Arch., Univ. of So. CA; **GRAD EDUC:** JD, 1977, Law, Loyola Univ.; **EDUC HONORS:** Dean's List, Dean's List; **HOME ADD:** 1206 Lexington Rd., Beverly Hills, CA 90210, (213)271-1361; **BUS ADD:** 125 E. Sunset Blvd. #500, Los Angeles, CA 90012, (213)680-0373.

JONAS, Harry, Jr.——B: Oct. 6, 1943, Richmond, VA, *Pres.*, Hank Jonas Realty Corp.; **PRIM RE ACT:** Owner/Investor; **OTHER RE ACT:** Conversion; **PROFL AFFIL & HONORS:** NAR; **EDUC:** BA, 1966, Econ., Univ. So. CA; **MIL SERV:** USN, Lt.; **OTHER ACT & HONORS:** City Athletic Club (NY), Shelter Is. Yacht Club, Palm Beach Sailing Club; **HOME ADD:** 1 Breakers Row, Palm Beach, FL 33480, (305)655-3628; **BUS ADD:** 8200 E Jefferson Ave., Detroit, MI 48214, (313)822-2400.

JONES, Dr. B.J.——B: Sept. 28, 1920, Iowa City, IA, *Pres./Bd. Chairman & Corp. Atty.; CEO & Founder*, Executive and Developer Consultants, Inc.; **PRIM RE ACT:** Broker, Consultant, Attorney, Appraiser, Banker, Developer, Lender, Owner/Investor, Property Manager, Real Estate Publisher; **OTHER RE ACT:** Labor Law; **SERVICES:** Exec. & condo. devel.; **REP CLIENTS:** Chase Manhattan Bank, NYC; NY Life Ins. Co.; City Nat. Bank Inc.; David Rockefeller & Peter Bezansar; **PREV EMPLOY:** Own labor law consulting firm, 35 yrs.; **PROFL AFFIL & HONORS:** Nat. Labor Relations Bd. & Ind. Relations Natl. Bd. of Directors, PhD in labor law; **EDUC:** BSC, 1942, Bus. Labor Law, Univ. of IA; **GRAD EDUC:** LLB/JD/LLD, 1946, UCLA; PhD, Univ. of Miami; **MIL SERV:** US Air Corps, Maj. (Reserve) & Retd.; **OTHER ACT & HONORS:** Pres. of Frat., Phi Delta Theta; Grand Knight of Knights and Kiwanis also Lions & Rotary Pres.; **HOME ADD:** 715 N. Van Buren St., Suite 2-B, Iowa City, IA 52240; **BUS ADD:** 715 N. Van Buren St., Suite 1-A, Iowa City, IA 52240, (319)338-5031.

JONES, Chuck——B: Feb. 14, 1939, Detroit, MI, *Pres./Founder*, Interface Lion Gate Devel.; **PRIM RE ACT:** Consultant, Architect, Developer, Builder, Owner/Investor; **OTHER RE ACT:** Merchandizing consultant, interiors, const. mgmt.; **SERVICES:** Arch., constr., interiors, comml., condo, luxury housing; **REP CLIENTS:** Devel., builders in estates, banks, profl. orgs.; **PREV EMPLOY:** Environmental System Indus., Albert C. Martin; **PROFL AFFIL & HONORS:** Urban Planning Inst., Assn. of AIA Student Chapts., Nat. Pres. of Student AIA, 1961; **EDUC:** BArch, 1965, Arch., Planning, Univ. of AZ; **MIL SERV:** US Air Nat. Guard & USAF Res., Tech. Sgt., Airman of yr.; **OTHER ACT & HONORS:** Phi Gamma Delta; **HOME ADD:** Bloomfield Dr., Los Angeles, CA 90027, (213)766-2753; **BUS ADD:** 2000 Hyperion Ave., Los Angeles, CA 90027, (213)668-0771.

JONES, Clifford——*VP Resources*, Todd Shipyards; **PRIM RE ACT:** Property Manager; **BUS ADD:** 1 State St. Plaza, New York, NY 10004, (212)688-4700.*

JONES, E. Carl——B: Feb. 17, 1921, Atlanta, LA, *Head, Dept. of Fin.*, Mississippi State Univ.; **PRIM RE ACT:** Consultant, Owner/Investor, Instructor; **OTHER RE ACT:** Administrator, Research; **SERVICES:** Consultant to MS RE Commn. and MS Assn. of Realtors; **PREV EMPLOY:** Head of Univ. Depts. of Fin. and RE and Ins.; **PROFL AFFIL & HONORS:** Fin. Mgmt. Assn., RE Educators Assn., MS Assn of Realtors, NAR, Southern Fin. Assn.; **EDUC:** BS, 1941, Agriculture Sci., Univ. of SW LA; **GRAD EDUC:** MS, 1947, Agricultural Econ., Econ., LA State Univ.; PhD, 1962, Agricultural Econ., Econ., LA State Univ.; **MIL SERV:** US Army, Cpl.; **HOME ADD:** 36 Colonial Cir., Starkville, MS 39759, (601)323-1775; **BUS ADD:** Fin., Ins. and RE, Drawer DF, Mississippi State, MS 39762.

JONES, Fred C.——B: July 18, 1917, Bellaire, OH, *VP and Title Officer*, Midland Title Security Inc.; **PRIM RE ACT:** Attorney; **OTHER RE ACT:** RE Title Ins.; **PROFL AFFIL & HONORS:** OH State Bar Assn.; Lorain Cty. Bar Assn.; **EDUC:** AB, 1939, Poli. Sci./Hist., Hiram Coll.; **GRAD EDUC:** LLB, 1942, Law, Western Reserve Univ. School of Law; **MIL SERV:** USAAC; Capt.; 1942-1945; **HOME ADD:** 200 Longford Ave., Elyria, OH 44035, (216)365-3292; **BUS ADD:** 119 East Avenue, Elyria, OH 44036, (216)323-3361.

JONES, Gainer B., Jr.——B: July 16, 1946, Houston, TX, *Sr. VP*, Western Bank, RE Dept.; **PRIM RE ACT:** Banker, Lender; **SERVICES:** Interim lending; **REP CLIENTS:** Devel. of comml. and resid. prop., mort. cos.; **PREV EMPLOY:** Bank of the Southwest; **PROFL AFFIL & HONORS:** Greater Houston Builders Assn.; **EDUC:** BA, 1968, Hist., VA Mil. Inst.; **GRAD EDUC:** MBA, 1971, Fin., Univ. of TX; **MIL SERV:** US Army, 2nd. Lt.; **HOME ADD:** 6031 Floyd, Houston, TX 77007, (713)869-4159; **BUS ADD:** 5433 Westheimer, Houston, TX 77056, (713)622-7500.

JONES, Gerald G.——B: Jan. 27, 1953, Bakersfield, CA, Self-Employed; **PRIM RE ACT:** Consultant, Owner/Investor, Property Manager, Syndicator; **SERVICES:** Investment Counseling, Prop. Mgmt.; **REP CLIENTS:** Investors in Resid. & Comml. Prop.; **PROFL AFFIL & HONORS:** CA Soc. of CPA's; **EDUC:** BS, 1975, Acctg., CA State Univ., Northridge, CA; **BUS ADD:** 1905 Margo Lane, Bakersfield, CA 93308, (805)399-5121.

JONES, Harrison H.——B: Apr. 30, 1924, Louisville, KY, *Sr. VP*, Commonwealth Land Title Ins. Co., Regional Mgr.; **PRIM RE ACT:** Insuror; **OTHER RE ACT:** Title ins.; **SERVICES:** Ins. of RE interests; **PROFL AFFIL & HONORS:** ALTA, KY Bar Assn.; **EDUC:** Pre-Law, Centre Coll.; **GRAD EDUC:** LLB, 1949, Univ. of Louisville, Louisville, KY; **MIL SERV:** USA, Sgt.; **OTHER ACT & HONORS:** Rotary; **HOME ADD:** 3407 Flinthaven Rd., Louisville, KY 40222, (502)425-4694; **BUS ADD:** 223 South St., PO Box 35180, Louisville, KY 40232, (502)584-0211.

JONES, J. Howard——B: July 6, 1924, Pocahontas, IA, *Owner*, Prop. Sales & RE Appraisal Co.; **PRIM RE ACT:** Broker, Consultant, Appraiser; **REP CLIENTS:** Mort. lenders, indiv. investors & govt. agencies; **PREV EMPLOY:** Owner-prop. sales & RE appraisal co. for 31 yrs.; **PROFL AFFIL & HONORS:** Realtor; SRA-Sr. Resid. Appraiser; Soc. of RE Appraisers; ASA-Sr. Member; ASA; **GRAD EDUC:** BA, 1950, Amer. Hist., Coll. of St. Thomas; **MIL SERV:** USMC; Cpl., 1942-1946; **OTHER ACT & HONORS:** Pres.-St. Paul Rifle & Pistol Club, Inc.; **HOME ADD:** 22 N. Kent at Summit Ave., St. Paul, MN 55102, (612)225-0043; **BUS ADD:** 22 No. Kent St., St. Paul, MN 55102, (612)225-1018.

JONES, J. Michael——B: July 16, 1941, Hutchinson, KS, *Pres.*, Harold Jones RE Corp.; **PRIM RE ACT:** Broker, Consultant, Appraiser, Developer, Builder, Owner/Investor, Instructor, Property Manager, Syndicator; **SERVICES:** Resid./comml. sales, investment counseling, devel. of comml. prop.; **REP CLIENTS:** Lenders; indiv. investors in comml./resid. props.; several banks in area; Homequity/ Homerica; Bank of St. Louis; **PROFL AFFIL & HONORS:** NAR; RNMI; OK Assn. of Realtors; OK City Bd. of Realtors, GRI, 1970; CRB, 1970; CRS, 1979; Realtor of the Yr., 1979; **EDUC:** BS, 1964, Mktg./Econ., OK City Univ.; **GRAD EDUC:** JD, 1968, Law, OK City Univ. Law School; **OTHER ACT & HONORS:** Phi Alpha Delta (Law Frat.); **HOME ADD:** 12604 Arrowhead Terr., Oklahoma City, OK 73120, (405)751-6663; **BUS ADD:** 6301 N. Meridian, Oklahoma City, OK 73112, (405)722-1000.

JONES, Jack R.——B: May 9, 1914, Arlington, VA, *Pres.*, Rucker Enterprises Corp.; **PRIM RE ACT:** Broker, Developer, Owner/Investor; **PREV EMPLOY:** Rucker Realty - 46 yrs.; **MIL SERV:** USA, Ord., 2nd Lt.; **OTHER ACT & HONORS:** Chmn. Bd. Dir. First Fed. S&L Assn., Arlington: Bd. Dir. People's Life Ins. Co., Wash, DC; formerly Bd. Dir. Capital Holding Corp., Louisville, KY: Chmn. Bd. Trustees Fork Union Military Academy: Exec. Comm. Baptist World Alliance; Bd. Dir. & Pres. Classroom for Young Amer., etc., Formerly Pres. Geo. H. Rucker Realty Corp. (still on the Bd.); **HOME ADD:** 4615 N 24th St., Arlington, VA 22207, (703)525-4615; **BUS ADD:** Arlington, VA 22210PO Box 1300, (703)841-7595.

JONES, James G.——B: June 28, 1943, Monterey Park, CA, *Partner*, Knapp, Grossman & Marsh; **PRIM RE ACT:** Attorney; **SERVICES:** Legal advice, transaction negotiation; **PROFL AFFIL & HONORS:** ABA; Los Angeles Cty. Bar Assn.; Real Property Law Sect.; CA Realtors Assn. Legal Panel Member; **EDUC:** BA, 1965, Bus. Admin., Occidental Coll.; **GRAD EDUC:** JD, 1968, Bus. Law, Hastings Coll. of Law (Univ. of CA); **EDUC HONORS:** Law Journal; Jamison Foundation Scholarship recipient; **BUS ADD:** 707 Wilshire Blvd., Suite 1800, Los Angeles, CA 90017, (213)627-8471.

JONES, James Hall——B: May 3, 1933, Murray, KY, *Pres.*, Development Team Associates, Inc.; **PRIM RE ACT:** Owner/Investor, Broker, Architect, Developer, Builder; **SERVICES:** Design, devel., construction, investments; **REP CLIENTS:** Super Circle Markets; **PREV EMPLOY:** Pres. BBA Land Co./Pres. ATA Architects; Pres. James Hall Inves-Devel. & Investments; **PROFL AFFIL & HONORS:** AIA; Amer. Arbitration Assn.; **EDUC:** BS Arch, 1957, Univ. of Cincinnati; **HOME ADD:** 70 Huntington Place, Colorado Springs, CO 80907, (303)576-7948; **BUS ADD:** 750 E. Hwy. 24, Suite 40 (P.O. Box 5), Woodland Park, CO 80863, (303)687-3021.

JONES, James R.——B: July 19, 1952, Portsmouth, VA, *Pres./Owner*, James R. Jones Builder, Inc.; **PRIM RE ACT:** Developer, Builder, Owner/Investor; **PROFL AFFIL & HONORS:** Homebuilder's Assn. of Southside, VA; **HOME ADD:** Fairview Farm, Rt.1, Box 175-D,

Disputanta, VA 23842, (804)861-2517; **BUS ADD:** PO Box 1402, Hopewell, VA, (804)861-2517.

JONES, J.G.——B: Oct. 7, 1951, Bethesda, MD, *Pres.*, Comml. Devel. Grp. Ltd.; **PRIM RE ACT:** Developer, Owner/Investor, Syndicator; **PROFL AFFIL & HONORS:** Pres., Cold Chapt. Natl. Assn. of Indus. & Office Parks, C of C; **HOME ADD:** 2626 E. 4th Ave., Denver, CO 80206; **BUS ADD:** 1350 17th St. #450, Denver, CO 80202, (303)892-0563.

JONES, Jim C.——B: Jan. 25, 1931, Joplin, MO, *Pres.*, Jones & Co., Realtors; **PRIM RE ACT:** Broker, Syndicator, Developer, Builder, Property Manager, Lender, Owner/Investor; **PROFL AFFIL & HONORS:** RNMI, NAR, MO R.E. Assn., GRI, CRS, CRB; **MIL SERV:** US Army,Cpl.; **OTHER ACT & HONORS:** MO C of C, Bd. of Exec. Comm., Past Pres. Springfield C of C; Past Pres. Unity Church, currently Chmn. of MO C of C, currently Pres. of RELO/Inter-City Relocation Serv., Springfield Realtor of the Year in 1973; **HOME ADD:** 3538 Blueridge, Springfield, MO 65804, (417)881-5058; **BUS ADD:** 1555 S. Glenstones, Springfield, MO 65804, (417)885-8000.

JONES, Kenneth K.——B: May 4, 1922, Portland, OR, *Owner*, Kenneth K. Jones, Inc.; **PRIM RE ACT:** Broker, Consultant, Owner/Investor, Property Manager; **SERVICES:** Major office bldg. mgmt., comml. brokerage, office leasing; **REP CLIENTS:** Mgr. and exclusive agent for San Diego Fed. Bldg., San Diego (24 stories); **PREV EMPLOY:** Haas & Haynie Corp., Grubb & Ellis Comml. Brokerage Co., Carter Co.; **PROFL AFFIL & HONORS:** BOMA (Pres., San Diego 1979); San Diegans, Inc.; San Diego Bd. of Realtors; Intl. RE Fed. (Amer. Chap); Delegate to IREF Conventions in 1972, 1975, 1976 (London, Paris and San Francisco), RPA, BOMI; **EDUC:** BA, 1943, Bus., Stanford Univ.; **MIL SERV:** US Army, Capt., Bronze Star (2), WWII and Korean War; **OTHER ACT & HONORS:** Navy League of San Diego, Citizens Council; San Diego City College Coronado Yacht Club; **HOME ADD:** 1429 1st St., Coronado, CA 92118, (714)435-8191; **BUS ADD:** 600 B St., San Diego, CA 92101, (714)234-3321.

JONES, Lawrence Donald——B: Apr. 24, 1931, Columbus, OH, *Chmn Urban Land Econ. Div.*, Univ. of BC, Faculty of Commerce; **PRIM RE ACT:** Instructor; **OTHER RE ACT:** Prof.; **SERVICES:** Acad. profl. seminar instr., consulting; **PREV EMPLOY:** Wharton School, Univ. of PA, Grad. School of Bus., IN Univ., Securities & Exchange Comm.; **PROFL AFFIL & HONORS:** Amer. Econ. Assn., Amer. RE & Urban Econs. Assn., Amer. Fin. Assn.; **EDUC:** BA, 1953, Math., OH State Univ.; **GRAD EDUC:** MA, 1954, Econ., OH State Univ.; PhD, 1959, Econ., Harvard Univ.; **EDUC HONORS:** Cum Laude, Phi Beta Kappa; **HOME ADD:** 3484 W 21st Ave., Vancouver, V65 1E7, BC, Can., (604)733-6425; **BUS ADD:** Faculty of Commerce, Univ. of BC, Vancouver, BC, Can., (604)228-5541.

JONES, Linda N.——B: Sept. 17, 1939, Bonham, TX, *Pres.*, Century 21-Arbor Homes, Inc.; **PRIM RE ACT:** Broker, Consultant, Owner/Investor; **SERVICES:** Resid. and investment counseling, appraising, RE sales; **PROFL AFFIL & HONORS:** Ann Arbor Bd. of Realtors, MI Assn. of Realtors, NAR, REPAC, WCR, Dir. Century-21 of MI, CRS (Certified Residential Specialist) Brokers Council; GRI, (RE Alumni of MI); **EDUC:** Certificate, 1968-72, RE, Univ. of MI; **HOME ADD:** 4345 Crestline, Ann Arbor, MI 48103, (313)426-3390; **BUS ADD:** 1829 W Stadium Blvd., Ann Arbor, MI 48103, (313)995-0244.

JONES, Louie A.——B: Nov. 2, 1941, Washington, IA, *Pres.*, El Paseo Realty, Inc.; **PRIM RE ACT:** Broker, Syndicator, Consultant; **PROFL AFFIL & HONORS:** RNMI, GRI, CRS, CRB; **EDUC:** BA, 1967, Bus. Admin., Parsons Coll.; **MIL SERV:** US Army, LT.; **HOME ADD:** 44691 Monaco Cir., Palm Desert, CA 92260, (714)346-4484; **BUS ADD:** 73350 El Paseo 205, Palm Desert, CA 92260, (714)346-0579.

JONES, Lynn W., II——B: Sept. 30, 1929, Loma Linda, CA, *Sr. VP*, California Association of Realtors; **OTHER RE ACT:** Assn. Exec.; **SERVICES:** Govt. relations, legal servs educ., public relations; **PROFL AFFIL & HONORS:** Amer. Soc. of Assn. Execs., CA Labor and Bus. Council, Amer. Mgmt. Assns., CA C of C; **EDUC:** BS, 1952, Bus. Admin., UCLA; **GRAD EDUC:** MBA, 1961, Univ. of So. CA; **EDUC HONORS:** With Honors; **MIL SERV:** US Army; 1st. Lt.; **OTHER ACT & HONORS:** CA C of C; **HOME ADD:** 23011 Brenford St., Woodland Hills, CA 91364, (213)346-7975; **BUS ADD:** 525 South Virgil Ave., Los Angeles, CA 90020, (213)739-8200.

JONES, Michael F.——B: May 5, 1948, Chicago, IL, *Atty.*, Fabian & Clendenin; **PRIM RE ACT:** Attorney; **SERVICES:** Legal counseling and representation of devels., lenders, bldrs. and investors; **PREV EMPLOY:** Partner, Rosenberg, Savner and Unikel, Chicago, IL; **PROFL AFFIL & HONORS:** ABA; **EDUC:** AB, 1970, Econ., Middlebury Coll.; **GRAD EDUC:** JD, 1973, Law, Univ. of Chicago Law School; **EDUC HONORS:** Hon. in Econ.; **OTHER ACT & HONORS:** Author, 'Office Condos.: Devel. Opportunities, Mktg. and Structuring', ABA Real Prop. Prob. & Trust L. Journ., (Fall 1981); 'Drafting the Installment Contract, '62 Chicago Bar Record 97 (1980); 'Drafting the Installment Contract, Using Purchase Money Mort., and Problems Relating to Due on Sale Clauses'; **HOME ADD:** 299 Center St., Salt Lake City, UT 84103, (801)533-9110; **BUS ADD:** 800 Continental Bank Bldg., Salt Lake City, UT 84101, (801)531-8900.

JONES, Michael J.——B: July 1944, NY, NY, *Lic. RE & Mort. Broker/Investor. FL & NY*, Michael J. Jones; **PRIM RE ACT:** Broker, Consultant, Appraiser, Owner/Investor, Syndicator, Property Manager; **OTHER RE ACT:** Financier; Specializes in Select Investment Properties, Real Estate and Mortgage Brokerage, Consultant etc; International Financier; Acquisition of Agricultural & Mineral Resources; **REP CLIENTS:** Intl. & foreign govts., major synds., Wall St. Firms., prominent indiv., national firms, corps.; **PREV EMPLOY:** Douglas L. Elliman & Co. NY, NY(comml, midtown prime), US Govt. Multi Family Appraiser & Underwriter, US Govt. Leasehold Acquisition & Contract Negotiator; **PROFL AFFIL & HONORS:** RESSI, Member Foreign Policy Assn. NY & DC; **EDUC:** BBA, Aldelphi Univ.; **OTHER ACT & HONORS:** Three time grad. of NY Univ. RE and Mort. Inst., RE Analysis and Appraisal, RE Fin., RE Prop. Mgmt.; Author, "The Legal, Fin. and Practical Aspects of Buying and Owning an Island"; Co-founder and first Pres., NY Univ. RE and Mort. Inst. Alumni Assn.; Co-founder and member of the Bd. of Dir, The NY State Chap., RESSI, NAR, FL State Chap. RE, Spec. Advisor, The Intl. Inst. of RE Studies; Spec. Advisor Warren Gorham & Lamont Publishers, Nat. Dir. of *Who's Who in RE*; Contrib. Editor, RE Weekly Publishers, Largest Weekly RE Publ. in US; **BUS ADD:** 5890 NW 64th Ave., Tamarac, FL 33319, (305)726-0900.

JONES, Mikeal R.——B: Aug. 24, 1951, Boone, NC, *Dist. Mgr.*, Westinghouse Credit Corp., RE Fin.; **PRIM RE ACT:** Lender; **OTHER RE ACT:** Equity Participant; **SERVICES:** Construction, Interim Fin. & Standbys; **PREV EMPLOY:** Mort. Loan Mgr., RE Div., Life of VA, Richmond, VA 1976-1980; **PROFL AFFIL & HONORS:** MBA; **EDUC:** BS, 1973, Bus. Admin., The Citadel, Charleston, SC; **GRAD EDUC:** MBA, 1977, RE and Urban Land Devel., VA Commonwealth Univ.; **HOME ADD:** 91 Karland Dr. NW, Atlanta, GA 30305, (404)237-9652; **BUS ADD:** 5780 Peachtree Dunwoody Rd., Suite 405, Atlanta, GA 30342, (404)252-9871.

JONES, Owen J., Jr.——B: June 25, 1941, Anchorage, AK, *Mgr. US Operations*, Wall and Redekop Corp. Vancouver, British Columbia (Head Office), US Operations; **PRIM RE ACT:** Developer; **SERVICES:** Devel. of Condos., sub. and comml. office bldgs.; **PREV EMPLOY:** RE Appraiser & Consultant - 7 yrs.; Mort. Banker - 7 yrs.; RE Research Corp. (San Francisco) 1974-1976; **PROFL AFFIL & HONORS:** M.A.I. Member Amer. Inst. of RE Appraisers; S.R.P.A. Member, Soc. of RE Appraisers; **EDUC:** BS, 1965, Econ./Psych., Univ. of OR; **GRAD EDUC:** MUP, 1974, Urban Econ., Univ. of WA; **OTHER ACT & HONORS:** Guest Speaker - Seattle - King Cty. Bd. of Realtors; NW Ctr. for Profl. Educ.; Univ. of WA; **HOME ADD:** 14427 SE 47th Pl, Bellevue, WA 98006, (206)747-6316; **BUS ADD:** 520-112th Ave., Bellevue, WA 98002, (206)453-8925.

JONES, Patricia M.——B: July 25, 1925, San Francisco, CA, *Pres.*, Jones Appraisal Service; **PRIM RE ACT:** Appraiser, Consultant, Broker, Instructor; **SERVICES:** Real prop. evaluation, investment counseling, RE brokerage; **REP CLIENTS:** Banks, lending insts., tax & estate attys. relocation cos., govt. agencies, and indivs.; **PREV EMPLOY:** 1965-71 Jack Conway, Inc. (broker, mort. officer, office manager); 1971-78 R.P. Jones Realtors (owner/mgr.); 1976-present Jones Appraisal Serv.; **PROFL AFFIL & HONORS:** MA Bd. of RE Appraisers, NAR, WCR, Intl. Org. of RE Appraisers, Appraisal designations, MRA, ICA; Realtor Nat. Hon. Soc., Omega Tau Rho; **EDUC:** 1943-45, Hist. & Eng., Barnard Coll.; 1976-81, Amer. Inst. RE Appraisal courses, Curry Coll.; **HOME ADD:** 24 Buttonwood Ln., PO Box 44, N. Scituate, MA 02060, (617)545-0663; **BUS ADD:** 24 Buttonwood Ln., PO Box 44, N. Scituate, MA 02060, (617)545-0663.

JONES, Reg. C.——B: Nov. 30, 1902, Los Angeles, CA, *Owner Broker*, Rod's Realtors of Yuma, Inc.; **PRIM RE ACT:** Broker; **SERVICES:** Farms, land, & comml., resid.; **PREV EMPLOY:** Bldg. contractor, farmer, cattle feeder; **PROFL AFFIL & HONORS:** FLI & Yuma Exchangors; **OTHER ACT & HONORS:** CA Lic. Engrg. Contractor, EE and Bldg. Engr.; **HOME ADD:** Rt 1 Box 11 1/2 M, Somerton, AZ 85350, (602)627-8131; **BUS ADD:** 543 East 32nd St., Yuma, AZ 85364, (602)726-5817.

JONES, Richard Alvin——**B:** May 7, 1928, Baltimore, MD, *Pres./Broker*, Skyview Realty Co.; **PRIM RE ACT:** Broker, Engineer, Developer, Builder, Owner/Investor; **SERVICES:** Devel. of resid./comml. props; **PREV EMPLOY:** Engr.-Bendix Corp.; **MIL SERV:** USAF, Sgt.; **HOME ADD:** 1045 Doyle Rd., Street, MD 21154, (301)836-1602; **BUS ADD:** 3538 Prospect Rd., Street, MD 21154, (301)879-6305.

JONES, Richard B.——**B:** Oct. 1, 1944, Little Rock, AR, *Sr. Comml. Appraiser*, Shelby Cty. Assessor's Office; **PRIM RE ACT:** Appraiser, Assessor; **PREV EMPLOY:** Memphis Title Co., Abstract Clerk, 1965-66; Shelby Cty. Assessor's Office, 1966-67; Clerk Abstract Dept., 1967-68; Staff Appraiser, Resid., 1978 to present; Staff Appraiser-Comml.; **PROFL AFFIL & HONORS:** SREA, Intl. Assn. of Assessing Officerrs, TN Assn. of Assessing Officers, SRA, SRPA, Cert. Assessment Eval., TN Cert. Assessor; **EDUC:** 1966-68, Univ. of TN; **OTHER ACT & HONORS:** Boy Scouts, Cubmaster, Disciples of Christ Church, Deacon; **HOME ADD:** 7025 E Foxhill Dr., Memphis, TN 58134, (901)372-2446; **BUS ADD:** 160 Mid America Mall, Memphis, TN 38103, (901)528-3217.

JONES, Richard B.——**B:** Mar. 18, 1950, Newburyport, MA, *Atty.*; **PRIM RE ACT:** Attorney, Developer; **SERVICES:** Devel. (including fin. strategies) resid./comml. prop. and provide legal expertise regarding the same; **PREV EMPLOY:** Clerk, Supreme Ct. of OH; **PROFL AFFIL & HONORS:** MA Bar Assn.; ULI; **EDUC:** BA, 1972, Holy Cross; **GRAD EDUC:** MA, 1973, Tufts Univ.; JD, 1977, Suffolk Law School; **EDUC HONORS:** Moot Court Award; **OTHER ACT & HONORS:** City Solicitor, Jan. 1978 to present; **HOME ADD:** 283 High St., Newburyport, MA 01950, (617)462-8382; **BUS ADD:** PO Box 190, Newburyport, MA 01950, (617)462-8365.

JONES, Richard C., Jr.——**B:** Nov. 2, 1953, Oak Park, IL, *Assoc.*, Schwartz & Freeman; **PRIM RE ACT:** Attorney; **SERVICES:** Atty. for devels, investors and lenders; **PREV EMPLOY:** Chicago Title and Trust Co.; **PROFL AFFIL & HONORS:** ABA; IL Bar Assn.; Chicago Bar Assn.; **EDUC:** BA, 1975, Philosophy, Econ., Vanderbilt Univ., Nashville, TN; **GRAD EDUC:** JD, 1979, The John Marshall Law School; **HOME ADD:** 711 E. Euclid Ave., Arlington Heights, IL 60004, (312)255-7909; **BUS ADD:** 401 N. Michigan Ave., Chicago, IL 60611, (312)222-0800.

JONES, Richard C.——**B:** Oct. 20, 1928, Oak Park, IL, *Atty.*, Sachnoff, Schrager, Jones, Weaver & Rubenstein, Ltd.; **PRIM RE ACT:** Attorney, Owner/Investor, Instructor; **PREV EMPLOY:** Chicago Title & Trust Co., 1947-1964; **PROFL AFFIL & HONORS:** Chicago Bar Assn.; IL Bar Assn.; ABA; Amer. Land Title Assn.; **EDUC:** PhB, 1960, Pre-Law, DePaul Univ.; **GRAD EDUC:** JD, 1963, Law, DePaul Univ.; **MIL SERV:** US Army; Cpl.; Korea, Combat Inf Badge, Bronze Star; **OTHER ACT & HONORS:** Oak Park Kiwanis Past Pres., Chmn., Real Prop. Comm., Chicago Bar Assn. 1980-81; **HOME ADD:** 1044 Forest Ave., River Forest, IL 60305, (312)771-6464; **BUS ADD:** One IBM Plaza, Chicago, IL 60611Suite 700, (312)222-5660.

JONES, Richard E.——**B:** Apr. 9, 1949, San Diego, CA, *Tax Mgr.*, Ernst & Whinney; **OTHER RE ACT:** Tax consultant - CPA; **SERVICES:** Tax planning re: synd. and devel.; **REP CLIENTS:** Synd., devel., wealthy indiv.; **PROFL AFFIL & HONORS:** AICPA's of CPAs, CA CPA Soc., Nat. Assn. of Accts., CPA; **EDUC:** BS, 1971, Bus. - Acctg., Univ. of CA at Berkeley; **EDUC HONORS:** Wiggins E. Creed Memorial Scholarship; **MIL SERV:** USAF Academy, Cadet; **HOME ADD:** 6498 Mojave Dr., San Jose, CA 95120, (408)268-2059; **BUS ADD:** 99 Almaden Blvd. #950, San Jose, CA 95113, (408)287-6010.

JONES, Richard R.——**B:** Oct. 12, 1950, Baltimore, MD, *VP/Mktg.*, Nottingham Properties, Inc.; **PRIM RE ACT:** Broker, Developer, Property Manager; **SERVICES:** RE brokerage, land devel. processing & const., bus. & resid. prop. mgmt.; **REP CLIENTS:** The Rouse Co.; Pulte Home Corp.; The Ryland Grp.; Weyerhaeuser RE Co.; **PROFL AFFIL & HONORS:** Home Builders Assn. of MD-Baltimore County Chap. (Pres.); Baltimore County C of C; Nat. Assn. of Indus. & Office Parks; Greater Baltimore Bd. of Realtors, Outstanding Young Member Baltimore County C of C (1978); Towson's Most Distinguished Indiv. - Jaycees (1981); **EDUC:** BA, 1973, Eng., Univ. of NC; **EDUC HONORS:** Cum Laude/Eng. & Phi Beta Kappa; **OTHER ACT & HONORS:** Baltimore Museum of Art (VChmn. Affiliates Group); **HOME ADD:** 533 Park Ave., Towson, MD 21204; **BUS ADD:** 100 W. Pennsylvania Ave., Towson, MD 21204, (301)825-0545.

JONES, Robert Bruce——**B:** July 17, 1904, Macon, GA, *Member*, Jones & Foster, PA; **PRIM RE ACT:** Attorney, Owner/Investor; **SERVICES:** All facts of RE practice; **PREV EMPLOY:** Jones, Park & Johnston - Johnston & Jones, Macon, GA; Earnest & Lewis; Bureau of Intl. Rev., Chief Counsels Office, Pittsburgh, PA; Earnest, Lewis, Smith & Jones; Jones, Adams, Paine & Foster; Jones, Paine & Foster; Jones & Foster, W. Palm Beach, FL; **EDUC:** AB, 1924, Hist., Univ. of GA; **GRAD EDUC:** LLB, 1927, Mercer Univ., Macon, GA; **EDUC HONORS:** Cum Laude; **MIL SERV:** US Army - 28 yrs., Col., Silver Star, Five Campaign Stars; **OTHER ACT & HONORS:** Cty. Atty. Palm Beach Cty, FL; **HOME ADD:** 455 Worth Ave., Palm Beach, FL 33480, (305)655-7276; **BUS ADD:** 601 N. Flagler Ct. Dr. P O Drawer 'E', W. Palm Beach, FL 33402, (305)659-3000.

JONES, Robert C. (Bob)——**B:** Nov. 12, 1920, San Antonio, TX, *Owner- Pres.*, Bob Jones Realty, Inc.; **PRIM RE ACT:** Broker, Appraiser, Property Manager, Insuror; **PROFL AFFIL & HONORS:** NAR, FIABCI, CRB; **EDUC:** BS, Bus. Fin., TX A & M; **MIL SERV:** USAF, Lt. Col. (Ret.); **OTHER ACT & HONORS:** Member TX RE Comm., 6 yrs., Cty. Council, 6 yrs., San Antonio, TX; **HOME ADD:** 3711 Twisted Oak, San Antonio, TX 78217, (512)656-2530; **BUS ADD:** 420 Jackson Keller Rd., San Antonio, Tx 78210, (512)344-2341.

JONES, Ronald S.——**B:** Aug. 1, 1950, Paris, IL, *Pres.*, RJ Investments; **PRIM RE ACT:** Attorney, Developer, Owner/Investor, Syndicator; **EDUC:** BS, 1973, Communications, Univ. of IL; **GRAD EDUC:** JD, 1980, Denver Univ.; **HOME ADD:** Box 3349, Winter Park, CO 80482; **BUS ADD:** Box 3349, Winter Park, CO 80482, (303)726-8033.

JONES, Roy Farrington——**B:** Feb. 28, 1925, San Francisco, CA, *Owner*, Farrington Jones & Son; **PRIM RE ACT:** Broker, Consultant, Appraiser; **OTHER RE ACT:** Taught RE Appraisal & Coll. of Marin 1968-1974; **SERVICES:** Valuation and Counseling Serv.; **REP CLIENTS:** Indivs., Atty., Govtl. Agencies, Transfer Corps. etc.; **PREV EMPLOY:** After discharge from USN in 1946 went into the family bus.; **PROFL AFFIL & HONORS:** SREA; NARA; Intl. Inst. of Valuers; Marin Cty. Bd. of Realtors, SRA, CRA, SCV; **EDUC:** Attended Coll. of Marin 1942 and 1946; **MIL SERV:** USN, HA1/c; **OTHER ACT & HONORS:** Ross Town Councilman 1962-1978; Local Agency Formation Comnr. 1970-1978; Chmn. 1975-78; Marin Cty. Tax Assmt. Appeals Bd., 1978 to date; Hearing Officer Tax Assmt. Appeals Bd. since 1980; Life Member Marin Cty. Hist. Assn.; Hon. Member Moya del Pino Library; **HOME ADD:** PO Box 364, Ross, CA 94957, (415)454-0656; **BUS ADD:** 224 Sir Francis Drake Blvd., San Anselmo, CA 94960, (415)453-6691.

JONES, Sam——**B:** Dec. 23, 1927, Washougal, WA, *Assoc. Broker - Sales Trainer*, Whitfield-Bernhardt Realtors; **PRIM RE ACT:** Broker, Appraiser, Builder, Instructor; **SERVICES:** Sales - training - appraising; **REP CLIENTS:** Investors - devels.; **PREV EMPLOY:** Auto Dealer; **PROFL AFFIL & HONORS:** Nat. Assn. of RE Appraisers, Vancouver-Clark Cty. Bd. of Realtors, WA Assn. of Realtors, CREA; **EDUC:** BS, Bus., Vancouver Bus. Coll.; **MIL SERV:** US Army; Sgt., WWII Victory Medal; **OTHER ACT & HONORS:** Rotary, Salvation Army, WA Children's Home, Memorial Hosp. Bd. of Dir.; **HOME ADD:** 9721 N.W. 9th Ave., Vancouver, WA 98665, (206)574-1961; **BUS ADD:** PO Box 1338, Vancouver, WA 98666, (206)694-6565.

JONES, Stephen A.——**B:** Aug. 1, 1951, Wilmington, DE, *VP, Bus. Devel.*, Kenneth Parker Assoc.; **OTHER RE ACT:** Interior arch., Bus. Devel.; **SERVICES:** Renovation, space plng., interior design; **REP CLIENTS:** ARCO; Johnson & Johnson; FMC; duPont; SOHIO; INA Corp.; Smith Kline; Price Waterhouse; **PROFL AFFIL & HONORS:** NACORE; BOMA; **EDUC:** BA, 1973, Econ., Johns Hopkins Univ.; **BUS ADD:** The Granary, 411 N 20th St., Philadelphia, PA 19130, (215)561-7700.

JONES, Talova Lane——**B:** Dec. 27, 1925, Henryetta, OK, *Sales Mgr.*, Abide, Inc., Realtors, Resid.; **OTHER RE ACT:** Speaker, author; **SERVICES:** Residential counseling; educ. & training; speaker; **PROFL AFFIL & HONORS:** OK Assn. of Realtors; NAR; RNMI; Women's Council of Realtors, GRI, CRB, Mgr. Realtor of the Yr. 1975; **EDUC:** Drama, Creative Writing, Bus. Law, Muskogee Jr. Coll.; Baldwin Wallace Coll.; Fairleigh Dickinson Univ. and Central State Univ.; **OTHER ACT & HONORS:** Edmond C of C; Republican Women's Club, Order of E. Star; Epsilon Sigma Alpha; United Methodist Church Trustee; **HOME ADD:** 2112 Tall Oaks Trail, Edmond, OK 73043, (405)341-6729; **BUS ADD:** 163 S.E. 33rd St., Edmond, OK 73034, (405)348-2115.

JONES, Thomas F.——**B:** Sept. 14, 1950, Sanford, FL, *Partner*, Jackson - Shaw Company; **PRIM RE ACT:** Developer, Builder, Owner/Investor; **SERVICES:** Indus. and office devel. & leasing, build-to-suit gen. contractor; **REP CLIENTS:** 1st Nat. Bank in Dallas, Equitable Life, Mercantile Bank, TX Amer. Bank, Security Pacific Capital, First Dallas Capital Corp.; **PREV EMPLOY:** VP, First Nat. Bank in Dallas, VP, First Dallas Capital Corp., 1978-1981; **PROFL AFFIL &**

HONORS: BOMA, FL RE Broker, FL Mort. Broker; **EDUC:** BS, 1972, Bus. Admin., FL State Univ.; **OTHER ACT & HONORS:** Bent Tree Ctry. Club; **HOME ADD:** 6329 Prestonshire Ln., Dallas, TX 75225; **BUS ADD:** 8220 Elmbrook Suite 100, Dallas, TX 75247, (214)688-1166.

JONES, Verna N.——B: July 14, 1931, Bakersfield, CA, *Broker-Salesman*, Metroplex, Inc.,- Realtors, Comml.-Investment; **PRIM RE ACT:** Broker; **SERVICES:** Investment counseling, brokering comml. props.; **PROFL AFFIL & HONORS:** RNMI Comml. Investment Member, Soc. RE Appraisers, FL Assn. of Realtors, Provisional Member Inst. of Certified Fin. Planners; **EDUC:** RE, Univ. of FL; **OTHER ACT & HONORS:** Mediator-Citizens Dispute Settlement Program & Juvenile Alternative Servs. Program; **HOME ADD:** 6NW 27 Terr., Gainesville, FL 32607, (904)376-6426; **BUS ADD:** 5200 W. Newberry Rd., Bldg. C, Gainesville, FL 32607, (904)373-3583.

JONES, Virginia Hewitt——B: Dec. 20, 1932, Jackson, MS, Virginia Jones, Realtor; **PRIM RE ACT:** Broker, Owner/Investor, Property Manager; **OTHER RE ACT:** Sales, Leasing, Exchanging of Comml. Industrial & Investment; **PREV EMPLOY:** Trust Dept. of First Nat. Bank, Accountant & Agent for gen. ins. agency (4 yrs.); **PROFL AFFIL & HONORS:** NAR; WCR; First Ladies Civilian Bd.; Served as Sec.-Treas. of Jackson Bd.; Chmn. of Pvt. Prop. Week; Credential Comm. for the past 5 yrs., CCIM; **EDUC:** BA, 1954, Econ., Millsaps Coll.; **HOME ADD:** 949 Morningside (A14), Jackson, MS 39202, (601)355-7917; **BUS ADD:** POB 1672, Jackson, MS 39205, (601)355-7917.

JONES, Walter I.——B: Apr. 17, 1915, Chicago, IL, *Pres.-Owner*, Walter I. Jones & Assoc., Mgmt. Div.; **PRIM RE ACT:** Broker, Consultant, Builder, Property Manager, Insuror; **PROFL AFFIL & HONORS:** IREM; Chicago RE Bd.; FL RE Bd., VP, FL Chap. #36, IREM; **GRAD EDUC:** 1935, Legal Bus. Law, DePaul Univ.; **HOME ADD:** 8573 NW 2nd St., Coral Springs, FL 33065, (305)753-4045; **BUS ADD:** 122 N. Ocean Blvd., Pompano Beach, FL 33062, (305)942-1484.

JONES, Wayne W.——*Owner*, Tri-Phase Co.; **PRIM RE ACT:** Appraiser; **SERVICES:** Comml. & indus. appraisals and bus. valuations; **PREV EMPLOY:** Pres. Chemical Fertilizer Co., Flexiliner Corp.; **PROFL AFFIL & HONORS:** Indus. Comml. Appraiser IFAS, Sr. Level Member of Nat. Assn. of Indep. Fee Appraisers; **EDUC:** BA, Chem., Univ. of CA at Berkeley; **BUS ADD:** 2975 Huntington Dr., Suite 201, San Marino, CA 91108, (213)681-2208.

JONES, William P.——B: Aug. 5, 1949, Baltimore, MD, *Partner*, Whalen Properties; **PRIM RE ACT:** Broker, Consultant, Developer, Owner/Investor, Property Manager, Syndicator; **SERVICES:** Devel. & Synd. of Comml. Projects, consultant to local govt.; **REP CLIENTS:** Investors in comml. prop., local non-profit devel. co.; **PREV EMPLOY:** Bake R. Watts & Co., NYSE & NASD Member 1975-1979; Equitable Trust Co. 1972-1975; **PROFL AFFIL & HONORS:** Pres. and Owner at NASD member firm, William P. Jones and Assoc., Inc. Bd. member Mid-Atlantic Certified Development Co.; **EDUC:** BS, 1971, Bus. Admin., Loyola Coll.; **HOME ADD:** 922 E. 37th St., Baltimore, MD 21218, (301)243-0685; **BUS ADD:** 8455 Baltimore National Pike, Suite E, Ellicott City, MD 21043, (301)461-1666.

JONES, William W., Jr.——*Partner*, Dowling, Sanders, Dukes, Novit & Svalina, P.A., RE Sect.; **PRIM RE ACT:** Attorney; **SERVICES:** Comml. RE Closings; Comml. RE Devel., Acquisitions and Sales; Utility Coordination; **BUS ADD:** PO Drw. 5706, Hilton Head Island, SC 29938, (803)785-4251.

JONKMAN, John——B: Jan. 5, 1950, Netherlands, *Owner*, Northwest Properties; **PRIM RE ACT:** Owner/Investor; **SERVICES:** Resid. rental; **PROFL AFFIL & HONORS:** Lake Park Owners Assn., Pres.; Apt. Assn. of UT; **EDUC:** 1975, Computer Sci./Engrg., Univ. of UT; **GRAD EDUC:** M.Engrg. Admin., 1976, Mgmt., Univ. of UT; **OTHER ACT & HONORS:** Toastmasters Intl.; **HOME ADD:** 1236 Hunt Rd., Salt Lake City, UT 84117, (801)268-6182; **BUS ADD:** 1236 Hunt Rd., Salt Lake City, UT 84117, (801)322-7000.

JONTZ, Dennis E.——B: Feb. 25, 1948, Kewanee, IL, *Atty. at Law*, Civerolo, Hansen & Wolf, P.A.; **PRIM RE ACT:** Attorney; **SERVICES:** Legal Counsel; **REP CLIENTS:** Western Bank; **PREV EMPLOY:** USAF; **PROFL AFFIL & HONORS:** ABA; **EDUC:** BA, 1970, Econ., Drake Univ.; **GRAD EDUC:** MBA, JD, 1973, 1974, Drake Univ.; **MIL SERV:** USAF, Capt., Meritorious Serv. Medal; **HOME ADD:** 8316 Yeager NE, Albuquerque, MN 87109, (505)821-5211; **BUS ADD:** 219 Central Ave., SW, Suite 400, Albuquerque, NM 87103, (505)842-8255.

JORDAN, E. Robert——B: Feb. 22, 1924, Eastbrook, ME, *VP*, Bar Harbor Banking and Trust Co.; **PRIM RE ACT:** Banker; **PREV EMPLOY:** Assessor, Town of Bar Harbor, ME 1976-78; **PROFL AFFIL & HONORS:** Hancock/Washington Cty. Realtors Assn.; **OTHER ACT & HONORS:** Mayor, City of Ellsworth, ME 1962-66; **HOME ADD:** 19 Wayman Ln., Bar Harbor, ME 04609, (207)288-5132; **BUS ADD:** PO Box 400, 82 Main St., Bar Harbor, ME 04609, (207)288-3314.

JORDAN, J.C.——B: Aug. 18, 1929, Burlington, NC, *Exec. VP*, Michael Saunders & Co., Gen. Mgr.; **PRIM RE ACT:** Broker, Consultant, Appraiser, Lender; **REP CLIENTS:** Resid., Retirees/Comml., Devel.; **PREV EMPLOY:** VP, Cameron Brown Co.; Asst. Dir., NC Housing Corp.; Pres., Coastal Mort. Co.; **PROFL AFFIL & HONORS:** Soc. of RE Appraisers; SRA; Sarasota Bd. of Realtors, NC HBA Distinguished Service Award; **EDUC:** BC, Mktg. and Adv., Univ. of NC; **EDUC HONORS:** Dean's List; **HOME ADD:** 1983 Mid Ocean Circle, Sarasota, FL 33579, (813)921-2603; **BUS ADD:** 61 S. Blvd. of Presidents, Sarasota, FL 33577, (813)388-4447.

JORDAN, John C.——B: Oct. 25, 1930, PA, *Pres./Gen. Mgr.*, Fairlane Devel. Corp./Capitol Investors, Ltd.; **PRIM RE ACT:** Consultant, Developer, Property Manager; **SERVICES:** Devel. and mgmt. of conventional family apt. dwellings and ES Hud Section 8 elderly hi and mid-rises; **PREV EMPLOY:** Dept. of HUD, Dir. of Renewal Asst.; Office of Econ. Opportunity, Special Asst. to the Dir.; Whittaker Community Devel. Corp., VP to Govtl. Housing; **PROFL AFFIL & HONORS:** Member, AOBA, Selected by US Sec. of Commerce John Conners as a member of Nat. Advisory Comm. on Econ. Devel.; **EDUC:** Commerce/Acctg., Grove City Coll.; USMC (Hawk) Missiles School; Mellon Nat. Bank Correspondents Banking School; **MIL SERV:** USMC, Maj.; **OTHER ACT & HONORS:** Mayor, City of New Castle, PA; Chmn., PA Republican State Comm.; Dir., First Seneca Bank; Recipient of 1962 Man of the Yr. Award; Jaycees, Past Nat. Dir. and Outstanding Local Pres. in PA; Chmn., Multiple Sclerosis Dir.; **HOME ADD:** 6517 Dearborn Dr., Falls Church, VA 22044, (703)256-9842; **BUS ADD:** 5203 8th Rd., S., Arlington, VA 22204, (703)379-0101.

JORDAN, Kevin Lynn——B: Oct. 29, 1953, Tulsa, OK, *Exec. VP, Gen. Counsel*; **PRIM RE ACT:** Attorney, Syndicator, Developer; **SERVICES:** Personal corp. services, in charge of $10,000,000 public SEC offering, development investments.; **REP CLIENTS:** Synd., Dev., Brokerage, Mgmt. Leasing; **PREV EMPLOY:** Murray Props., Dallas, Public Synd. of RE (Shearson - Murray Funds) Fourth Natl. Bank - Tulsa; **PROFL AFFIL & HONORS:** OK & Amer. Bar, RESSI; **EDUC:** BS, 1977, Bus., OK State Univ.; **GRAD EDUC:** JD, 1979, RE, Tax, Securities, Tulsa Univ.; MS, 1980, RE, So. Methodist Univ.; **EDUC HONORS:** Outstanding Grad., OSU, 1975; **HOME ADD:** 5547 E. 7th, Tulsa, OK 74112, (918)492-1700; **BUS ADD:** 5314 S. Yale, Suite 600, Tulsa, OK 74135, (918)492-1700.

JORDAN, Neal H.——B: Apr. 1, 1939, Haverhill, MA, *Sec. and Gen. Counsel*, FIP Corporation, Legal Dept.; **PRIM RE ACT:** Attorney, Developer, Builder, Owner/Investor, Property Manager, Syndicator; **SERVICES:** Designers, builders, devel. synd. and prop. mgrs. of comml. and indus.; **REP CLIENTS:** Numerous leading indus. and Fortune 1000 Co's.; **PREV EMPLOY:** Private practice of law and devel. 1967-1980; **PROFL AFFIL & HONORS:** ABA; CT Bar Assn.; Forum on Construction Industry; ABA Section of RE, Atty. at Law; **EDUC:** BA, 1964, Poli. Sci., Hist. and Philosophy, Univ. of CT; **GRAD EDUC:** JD, 1967, Law, Univ. of CT School of Law; **EDUC HONORS:** Poli. Sci. Honors; **MIL SERV:** USAF, Sgt; **OTHER ACT & HONORS:** Past Pres., Exchange Club of Windsor, CT; **HOME ADD:** PO Box 331, Simsbury, CT 06070, (203)658-9589; **BUS ADD:** Farmington Indus. Park, Spring Ln., PO Box 354, Farmington, CT 06032, (203)677-1361.

JORDAN, Patrick C.——B: Dec. 8, 1944, Spartansburg, SC, *Sr. VP*, Ben Franklin Fed. S&L Assn.; **PRIM RE ACT:** Appraiser, Developer, Lender, Builder, Property Manager; **SERVICES:** Pres. Williamette Factors, Inc., Devel. & Constr.; **PREV EMPLOY:** BFSL since Coll.; **PROFL AFFIL & HONORS:** AIREA/MAI, Soc. of RE Appraisers; **EDUC:** BS, 1967, Law, Univ. of OR, Sch. of Law; **GRAD EDUC:** MBA, 1971, Portland State Univ.; **OTHER ACT & HONORS:** City of Portland Design Review Comm., 1979-; **HOME ADD:** 31695 Country View Ln., Wilsonville, OR 97070; **BUS ADD:** Suite 1900, 1 Columbia, Portland, OR 97258, (503)248-1215.

JORDAN, Robert K.——B: Dec. 20, 1948, Newark, NJ, *Atty at Law*, Stroock & Stroock & Lavan, Miami Office; **PRIM RE ACT:** Attorney; **SERVICES:** Legal; **REP CLIENTS:** Lenders, instnl. & private, devels & comml. props., investors & mgrs.; **PREV EMPLOY:** Cypen & Nevins, Attys. at Law; **PROFL AFFIL & HONORS:** The FL Bar Assn., ABA, F&D Bar, So. District, FL; **EDUC:** BBA, 1971, Acctg.,

Univ. of Miami; **GRAD EDUC:** JD, 1974, Comml., Univ. of Miami; **EDUC HONORS:** Cum Laude, Phi Kappa Phi, Dean's List, Beta Alpha Pis, Omicron Delta Kappa; **OTHER ACT & HONORS:** Downtown Miami Bus. Assn.; **HOME ADD:** 10480 S.W. 122 St., Miami, FL 33176, (305)255-0725; **BUS ADD:** Suite 2200, 100 N. Biscayne Blvd., Miami, FL 33132, (305)358-9900.

JORDAN, William W.——*VP, RE - Rgnl. Dir.*, Volume Shoe Corp., RE; **OTHER RE ACT:** Site Selector of Shoe Stores; **PROFL AFFIL & HONORS:** NACORE, ICSC; **BUS ADD:** 431 E. Government St., Pensacola, FL 32501, (904)432-8484.

JORDON, James A.——**B:** Pittsburgh, PA, *Pres.*, Finance Insurance Realty Intl.; **PRIM RE ACT:** Broker, Consultant, Attorney; **OTHER RE ACT:** Fin. Broker; **SERVICES:** Financing, consulting, legal, ins. RE, brokerage; **REP CLIENTS:** Indiv., buyers, sellers, devels., investors for primarily comml. and indus. props.; **PREV EMPLOY:** RE Atty.; **PROFL AFFIL & HONORS:** PA Bar; US Tax Court; US District Court of W. PA and MA, Lic. RE and ins. broker, Commonwealth of MA; **EDUC:** BBA, 1947, Univ. of Pittsburgh; MLITT, 1948, Univ. of Pittsburgh; **GRAD EDUC:** JD, 1961, Law, Duquesne Univ.; **MIL SERV:** US Paratroops; **OTHER ACT & HONORS:** Elected to Pittsburgh City Council (1960-66); *Who's Who in US, East, South, Fin. & Indus. World*; **HOME ADD:** 790 Boylston St., Boston, MA 02199, (617)536-4464; **BUS ADD:** 4760 Prudential Tower, Boston, MA 02199, (617)267-9232.

JORRIE, Robert William——**B:** Oct. 30, 1939, San Antonio, TX, Robert Jorrie, PC; **PRIM RE ACT:** Broker, Consultant, Engineer, Attorney, Developer, Builder, Owner/Investor, Instructor, Property Manager, Syndicator; **SERVICES:** Devel., synd.,prop. mgmt. investment counseling; **REP CLIENTS:** Brokers, devels, synds., owners & Investors, primarily indiv.; **PREV EMPLOY:** 10 yrs. Heavy Retailing & RE Devel.; **PROFL AFFIL & HONORS:** ABA, TX Bar Assn., Fed. Bar Assn., San Antonio Bar Assn., Adjunct Prof. of Tax Law, St. Mary's Univ. Law School; **EDUC:** BS, 1962, Aero Space Engineering, TX Univ., Austin; **GRAD EDUC:** JD, 1974, St. Mary's Univ. Law School, San Antonio; LLM, 1975, Tax Law, NY Univ. Law School; **HOME ADD:** 2519 Old Brook Ln., San Antonio, TX 78230, (512)344-2224; **BUS ADD:** 711 Navarro 410, San Antonio, TX 78205, (512)226-8383.

JOSELOW, Robert B.——**B:** May 14, 1944, NY, NY, Federal National Mortgage Association; **PRIM RE ACT:** Attorney, Lender; **SERVICES:** Secondary market for mort.; specialty in condo., PUD's, co-ops, multifam. housing fin.; **PREV EMPLOY:** Law firm of Krooth & Altman; **PROFL AFFIL & HONORS:** Licensed to practice law in Wash. DC Member ABA; Fed. Bar Assn., DC Bar Assn.; **EDUC:** 1966, Eng., NYU; **GRAD EDUC:** JD, 1969, George Washington Univ. Sch. of Law; **EDUC HONORS:** Cum Laude; **OTHER ACT & HONORS:** Grad. Sch. of Mort. Banking; Publications: Washington Post & RE Review Articles; **HOME ADD:** 3612 Yuma St NY, Washington, DC 20008, (202)966-1103; **BUS ADD:** 3900 Wisconsin Ave. NW, Washington, DC 20016, (202)537-6789.

JOSEPH, Peter C.——**B:** May 25, 1941, Wausau, WI, *Profl. Engrg., Broker, Pres.*, P.C. Joseph & Assoc. SC; **PRIM RE ACT:** Broker, Consultant, Engineer, Appraiser, Owner/Investor; **SERVICES:** Constr. Engrg., Appraisers, Surveys, consultation; **REP CLIENTS:** Constr.; **PROFL AFFIL & HONORS:** ASHRAE, NSPE, WSPE, Reg. Profl. Bus. States of WI, Licensed RE Broker, State of WI; **EDUC:** BSME, 1964, Engrg., Univ. of WI, WI Sch. of RE; **EDUC HONORS:** Pi Tau Sigma, Hon. Mech. Engrg. Frat; **HOME ADD:** 3023 Nick Ave., Mosinee, WI 54455, (715)359-5482; **BUS ADD:** 3023 Nick Ave., Mosinee, WI 54455, (715)359-5482.

JOSEPHS, Bennett M.——**B:** July 24, 1925, NYC, NY, *Pres. & Dir.*, Kranzler Realty, Inc.; **PRIM RE ACT:** Broker, Consultant, Appraiser, Owner/Investor, Instructor, Property Manager; **OTHER RE ACT:** Relocation Counselor; **SERVICES:** Fin.; prop. availability locally and at remote areas; **REP CLIENTS:** Transamerica Relocation Services; Equitable Relocation Services; Abbot Laboratories; **PROFL AFFIL & HONORS:** LI Bd. of Realtors, Bd. Officer Sec., Ch. Profl. Standards Comm 3+ years; NY State Assn. Realtors, Dir., 1973 to present 1981, Sr. Member Appraisal Div., LI Bd. of Realtors, Relocation Specialist & Counselor; **EDUC:** BS, 1949, Mgmt. & Indus. Relations; Mktg., New York Univ.; BA, Clemson Univ., Shriveman Univ. (England); **MIL SERV:** US Army; 1943-1946; Corporal, ETO - 2 Battle Stars; **OTHER ACT & HONORS:** NY Univ. Club 1952-1969; **HOME ADD:** 691 Seaman Ave., Baldwin, NY 11510, (516)223-2330; **BUS ADD:** 1875 Grand Ave., Baldwin, NY 11510, (516)223-4440.

JOSEPHS, Julian A.——**B:** Sept. 14, 1950, Chicago, IL, *Pres.*, Julian Josephs Co.; **OTHER RE ACT:** RE Advisor; **SERVICES:** Advisory serv.; **REP CLIENTS:** European devels. pension funds and investors; **PREV EMPLOY:** Intl. Investment Coordinator for Romanek Golub & Co. Chicago, 1977-1980; Intl. Client Coordinator for Hampton & Sons, Paris, France, 1974-1977; Negotiator for Jones Lang Wootton, Brussels, Belgium, 1973-1974; **PROFL AFFIL & HONORS:** Royal Inst. of Chartered Surveyors, Student Member; Nat. Assn. of Indus. & Office Parks; Washington RE Grp.; British Inst. of Mgmt.; Inst. of Mktg.; Washington Board of Realtors; **EDUC:** BA, 1969-1973, Mktg., Middlesex Poly., London, England; **GRAD EDUC:** MBA, 19776-1977, RE mgmt., tri-lingual, INSEAD, Fontainbleu, France; **EDUC HONORS:** Honors; **HOME ADD:** 4845 V Street NW, Washington, DC 20007, (202)342-9146; **BUS ADD:** 2000 L St. NW, Suite 200, Washington, DC 10036, (202)887-5693.

JOST, Lawrence J.——**B:** Oct. 9, 1944, Alma, WI, *Partner*, Quarles & Brady; **PRIM RE ACT:** Attorney; **PREV EMPLOY:** Law Cler, Hon. Myron L. Gordon, US Dist. Ct., Eastern Dist. of WI 1969-1970; **PROFL AFFIL & HONORS:** ABA, WI Bar Assn., Milwaukee Bar Assn., Milwaukee Young Lawyers Assn., Amer. Immigration Lawyers Assn.; **EDUC:** BSCE, 1968, Constr., Indus., Univ. of WI - Madison; **GRAD EDUC:** JD, 1969, Univ. of WI - Madison Law School; **EDUC HONORS:** Law Review; **OTHER ACT & HONORS:** Pres.-Elect Visiting Nurse Assn. of Milwaukee 1981-1982, Bd. of Dirs., WI Heritages, Inc.; **BUS ADD:** 780 N. Water St., Milwaukee, WI 53202, (414)277-5000.

JOWETT, David A.——**B:** July 10, 1942, Sanford, ME, *VP*, First Union Nat. Bank of NC, Gen. Mort. Loans; **PRIM RE ACT:** Banker; **OTHER RE ACT:** Problem RE; **SERVICES:** Const. lending; **EDUC:** BA, 1964, Math., Univ. of ME; **GRAD EDUC:** MBA, 1977, Auburn Univ.; **MIL SERV:** USA, Capt., Bronze Star Medal; **OTHER ACT & HONORS:** Delta Kappa Sigma, Nat. Legal Frat; **HOME ADD:** 309 Water Oak Ln., Matthews, NC 28105, (704)847-7176; **BUS ADD:** 301 S Tryon St., Charlotte, NC 28288, (704)374-6992.

JOYCE, John M.——**B:** Jan., 1951, Rochester, NY, *VP*, Treco Prop. Servs. Inc., Comml.; **OTHER RE ACT:** Comml. Prop. Mgmt. & Leasing; **SERVICES:** Prop. Mgmt., Leasing; **PREV EMPLOY:** VP Balcor Prop. Mgmt., VP Lifetime Communities; **EDUC:** BS, 1973, Jacksonville Univ.; **HOME ADD:** 9252 San Jose, 2801, Jacksonville, FL 32203; **BUS ADD:** 1325 San Marco Blvd., Jacksonville, FL 32207, (904)396-1600.

JOYNER, C. Dan——**B:** Aug. 6, 1937, Greenville, SC, *Pres.*, C. Dan Joyner & Co., Inc.; **PRIM RE ACT:** Broker, Appraiser, Developer, Property Manager, Insuror; **OTHER RE ACT:** Broker-in-charge; **SERVICES:** Resid., comml., valuation, prop. mgmt.; **REP CLIENTS:** Lenders and indiv. investors in comml. prop.; **PREV EMPLOY:** REC Dan Joyner & Co., 1964; **PROFL AFFIL & HONORS:** Mktg. Inst.; CRS; Relocation Council; AACA, GRI; CRS-Amega Tau Rho; SC State Realtor of the Year; Greenville Realtor of the Year; Pres. SC Assn. of Realtors; Pres. Greenville Bd. of Realtors; **EDUC:** BA, 1959, Bus. Admin., Furman Univ., Greenville, SC; **EDUC HONORS:** Pres. of Student Body, Outstanding Student of the Year 1959, Who's Who; **MIL SERV:** USA Intelligence, Lt., Distinguished Military; **OTHER ACT & HONORS:** Pres. of the Greater Greenville C of C; Past Pres. of SC Assn. of Realtors; Nat. Dir. of Nat. Assn. of Realtors; SC REALTOR of the Yr.; Greenville REALTOR of the Yr.; Trustee Furman Univ.; **HOME ADD:** 2015 Cleveland St. Ext., Greenville, SC, (803)288-6677; **BUS ADD:** 745 N Pleasantburg Dr., Greenville, SC 19606.

JOYNER, Crawley F., III——**B:** April 5, 1934, Richmond, VA, *Pres.*, Joyner and Co., Realtors; **PRIM RE ACT:** Broker, Syndicator, Developer; **SERVICES:** Brokerage of commercial, invest. prop., site acquisition; **REP CLIENTS:** Investors and devs.; **PROFL AFFIL & HONORS:** RESSI, NAIOP, Pres. Bd. of Realtors, Pres. VA CCIM Chapter; CCIM; CRB; **EDUC:** BA, 1956, French, Univ. of VA; **MIL SERV:** USN, Lt. J9; **HOME ADD:** 9804 St. Julians Lane, Richmond, VA 23233, (804)741-3816; **BUS ADD:** 2727 Enterprise Pkwy., Richmond, VA 23229, (804)270-9440.

JOYNES, Richard——**B:** May 18, 1949, London, *Pres.*, Hunter & Parnters, Inc.; **PRIM RE ACT:** Consultant, Developer; **SERVICES:** Project mgmt., cost control, fin. consulting; **REP CLIENTS:** Citibank, NY Bank for Savings; **PROFL AFFIL & HONORS:** Fellow of Royal Instn. of Chartered Surveyors, FRICS; **EDUC:** England; **HOME ADD:** 322 W 57th St., New York, NY 10019, (212)977-4578; **BUS ADD:** 1775 Broadway, New York, NY 10019, (212)581-0410.

JUDD, L. Coleman (L. C. Judd)——**B:** July 14, 1912, Cleveland, OH, *Pres.*, L. C. Judd & Co., Inc.; **PRIM RE ACT:** Broker; **PROFL AFFIL & HONORS:** Ft. Lauderdale Area Bd. of Realtors, FL Assn. of Realtors, Nat. Assn. of Realtors, Soc. of Indus. Realtors, FL & Natl. Inst. of Farm Brokers, Hon. degree - Beta Gamma Sigma from Univ. of FL; **MIL SERV:** Army Air Force, Warrant Officer; **OTHER ACT &**

HONORS: Dir. & Chmn. of the Landmark Banking Corp. Bd. & also Dir. & Chmn. of the Landmark First Natl. Bank of Fort Lauderdale, FL; **HOME ADD:** 1301 East Lake Dr., Fort Lauderdale, FL 33316, (305)525-3536; **BUS ADD:** 2230 S. E. 17th St., Ft. Lauderdale, FL 33316, (305)525-3151.

JUDELSON, Robert A.——**B:** 1939, *VChmn.*, The Balcor Co.; **PRIM RE ACT:** Syndicator, Owner/Investor, Property Manager; **SERVICES:** Location, acquisition & disposition of RE investments for Balcor. Also, prop. mgmt. responsibilities; **PREV EMPLOY:** Founder of JMB Realty Corp.; Gen Partner of Carlyle 71 and Carlyle 72; Pres. of Judelson & Assoc.; **PROFL AFFIL & HONORS:** Nat. Assn. of Review Appraisers; **BUS ADD:** Plaza Six Building, Ste. 308, 350 West Camino Gardens Blvd., Boca Raton, FL 33432, (305)368-4700.

JUDGE, James R.——**B:** Mar. 19, 1948, Milwaukee, WI, *Atty.*; **PRIM RE ACT:** Attorney; **SERVICES:** RE advice/litigation; **REP CLIENTS:** Lenders, indiv. and instnl. investors; **PROFL AFFIL & HONORS:** ABA - Member of Real Property, Probate & Trust Sect.; HI State Bar Assn., Pres., Maui Bar Assn.; **EDUC:** BBA, 1970, RE, Univ. of HI; **GRAD EDUC:** JD, 1973, Hastings Coll. of the Law; **OTHER ACT & HONORS:** Judge, per diem, Second Circuit Court, State of HI - 1973 to present, Dir., Friends of the Main Symphony, Hold State of HI RE Broker License; **HOME ADD:** Kula, Maui, HI; **BUS ADD:** P.O. Box 1268, Wailuku, Maui, HI 96793, (808)242-4955.

JUDKINS, David M.——**B:** Mar. 3, 1939, Lakewood, OH, *RE Mgr.*, Weyerhaeuser Co.; **PRIM RE ACT:** Property Manager; **OTHER RE ACT:** Corp. RE acquisitons & disposal; **PREV EMPLOY:** Mortgage Banking 1965-68; **PROFL AFFIL & HONORS:** SIR; NACORE; **EDUC:** Wharton School of Fin. & Commerce, Univ. of PA; **MIL SERV:** USMC, Res.; Capt.; **HOME ADD:** 14216 N.E. 1st Lane, Bellevue, WA 98007, (206)641-0494; **BUS ADD:** Tacoma, WA 98477, (206)924-2151.

JUDY, Henry L.——*Exec VP/Genl. Counsel*, Department of Housing and Urban Development, Fed. Home Loan Mortgage Corp.; **PRIM RE ACT:** Lender; **BUS ADD:** 451 Seventh St., S.W., Washington, DC 20410, (202)789-4734.*

JUELL, Bruce C.——**B:** Feb. 1, 1934, Minneapolis, MN, *Prin.*, Bruce Juell & Co.; **PRIM RE ACT:** Banker; **SERVICES:** RE investment, synd., merger & acquisition, corp. & project fin.; **REP CLIENTS:** Corp., instit. and indiv. RE investors; **PREV EMPLOY:** Chmn., Great Southwest Corp. 1970-80; Partner Victor Palmieri/Bruce Juell & Co.; VP Builders Resources Corp.; Dir. of Planning, Prop. Research Corp.; McKinsey & Co.; **PROFL AFFIL & HONORS:** ULI; Young Pres. Org., UCLA Sch. of Arch. & Urban Planning, Deans Council; **EDUC:** B. Engrg., 1955, Mech. Engrg., Univ. of S. CA; **GRAD EDUC:** MBA, 1963, Mktg. & Planning, Univ. of S. CA; **EDUC HONORS:** NROTC Scholarship, Beta Gamma Sigma; **MIL SERV:** USN, Lt., Pilot; **OTHER ACT & HONORS:** Newcomen Soc.; Bd. of Dir., Olson Farms, Inc.; AMCAP Mutual fund, RayPak, Inc.; Founder: USC MBA Alumni Org.; **HOME ADD:** 1425 Via Zumaya, Palos Verdes Est., CA 90274, (213)541-7330; **BUS ADD:** 1 Wilshire Bldg., Ste. 2314, Los Angeles, CA 90017, (213)485-8904.

JUERGENS, Richard K., Jr.——**B:** July 26, 1941, Chicago, IL, *Pres.*, Frank S. Phillips Mortgage Corp.; **PRIM RE ACT:** Broker, Appraiser, Banker, Developer, Lender, Owner/Investor, Property Manager, Insuror; **REP CLIENTS:** New England Life, Midland Mutual, Berkshire Life, Continental Amer.; **PREV EMPLOY:** Pac. Mutual Life, Nat. Life of VT, Harris Trust and Savings Bank; **PROFL AFFIL & HONORS:** MBA; **EDUC:** BS, Indus. Econ., 1963, Bus. Admin., Purdue Univ., W. Lafayette, IN; **MIL SERV:** US Army, SP-5; **OTHER ACT & HONORS:** Sr. Warden, Holy Cross Church, Dunn Loring, VA; Treas. St. Celia's Church, Northbrook, IL; Kiwanis; **HOME ADD:** 7701 Bridle Path Ln., McLean, VA 22102, (703)821-8729; **BUS ADD:** 6106 MacArthur Blvd., Bethesda, MD 20816, (301)229-9000.

JUERLING, John H.——**B:** Richmond, IN, *Pres.*, V.H. Juerling & Sons, Inc.; **PRIM RE ACT:** Consultant, Developer, Builder, Engineer, Owner/Investor; **OTHER RE ACT:** Design & Build Constr.; **REP CLIENTS:** Richmond Castings, Faith United Lutheran Church, Koons Appliances, Central States Bank; **PREV EMPLOY:** USNR, Civil Engr. Corp.; **PROFL AFFIL & HONORS:** Assoc. Gen. Contr.; **EDUC:** BS, 1957, Civil Engr.; **MIL SERV:** USNR, Lt. j.g.; **OTHER ACT & HONORS:** Civil Defense Ops Office (3 yrs.), Bd. Dirs. Yokefellow Inst., Richmond Civic Theater, Green Acres (Retarded Ctr.), Kiwanis; **HOME ADD:** 2186 Minneman, Richmond, IN 47374, (317)962-1293; **BUS ADD:** 1229 S. 8th St., Richmond, IN 47374, (317)935-2282.

JULIN, Joseph R.——*Prof. of Law and Dean-Emeritus*, Univ. of FL Coll. of Law; **OTHER RE ACT:** Prof. of Law; **BUS ADD:** Univ. of FL Coll. of Law, Gainesville, FL 32611, (904)392-2211.

JUNEAU, Roland B.——**B:** Apr. 7, 1937, New Orleans, LA, *Asst. VP, Resid. Branch Coord.*, Carruth Mort. Corp., Mellow Nat. Mort. Grp.; **PRIM RE ACT:** Lender; **SERVICES:** Resid. Mort. loans; **REP CLIENTS:** FNMA, GNMA, FHLMC, FHA, VA, var. investors; **PREV EMPLOY:** Security Hampstead Assn., S&L Comml. Bank & Trust Co.; **PROFL AFFIL & HONORS:** Mort. Bankers Assn., Realtor; **EDUC:** BBA, 1959, Acctg., Tulane Univ.; **HOME TEL:** (504)454-3198; **BUS ADD:** PO Box 53334, New Orleans, LA 70153.

JUNG, Kristine A.——**B:** Feb. 1, 1950, Chicago, IL, *Sec./Treas. & Branch Office Mgr.*, Century 21 John Jung Real Estate, Inc.; **PRIM RE ACT:** Broker, Developer, Owner/Investor; **OTHER RE ACT:** Relocation; **PROFL AFFIL & HONORS:** NAR, IL Assn. of Realtors, McHenry Co. Bd. of Realtors, WCR, FLI; **EDUC:** BA, 1972, Philisophy & Literature, Mundelein Coll.; **OTHER ACT & HONORS:** Dir., McHenry Cty. Bd. of Realtors; **HOME ADD:** 327 W. Prairie #2, Marengo, IL 60152, (815)568-8908; **BUS ADD:** 229 South State St., Marengo, IL 60152, (815)568-8908.

JUNGBACKER, J. Peter——**B:** Aug. 26, 1952, Manitowoc, WI, *Gen. Part.*, Century Capital Grp.; **PRIM RE ACT:** Attorney, Syndicator, Developer, Property Manager, Owner/Investor; **PROFL AFFIL & HONORS:** ULI, ABA, WI Bar Assoc.; **EDUC:** BA, 1974, Econ., Univ. of WI - Madison; **GRAD EDUC:** MS RE Urban Econ., 1976, MBA Fin. 1977, JD, 1979, Univ. of WI; **HOME ADD:** 1432 W NY, Oshkosh, WI 54901, (414)426-3467; **BUS ADD:** 222 Pearl Ave., Oshkosh, WI 54901, (414)426-1404.

JUNGEN, Richard E.——**B:** Dept. 21, 1947, Clinton, IA, *Pres.*, Space Mgmt., Inc.; **PRIM RE ACT:** Broker, Syndicator, Developer, Property Manager, Owner/Investor; **PREV EMPLOY:** Part. in interior design and const. mgmt. co. for 7 yrs.; **PROFL AFFIL & HONORS:** Local, State & Natl. Bd. of Realtors, RESSI, IREM and BOMA, 1980 Outstanding Young Salesman by Milwaukee Jaycees; **OTHER ACT & HONORS:** Sales & Mktg. Execs. of Mil., Milw. Athletic Club, BOD-Joy, Inc.; Pres. Council-Concordia Coll., Milw., WI; **HOME ADD:** 2623 N. Lake Dr., Milwaukee, WI 53211, (414)963-1943; **BUS ADD:** 7709 W. Lisbon Ave., Milwaukee, WI 53222, (414)445-2600.

JURRIES, James——**B:** July 27, 1941, Grand Rapids, MI, *Pres.*, Woodland Realty, Inc.; **PRIM RE ACT:** Broker, Developer, Builder, Owner/Investor, Syndicator; **PREV EMPLOY:** Comml. Loan Officer - Bank; **EDUC:** BA, 1964, Econ., Hope Coll.; **GRAD EDUC:** MBA, 1965, Fin., Univ. of MI; **MIL SERV:** IL Air Nat. Guard; **HOME ADD:** 444 Brecado Ct., Holland, MI 49423, (616)335-8888; **BUS ADD:** 603 E. 16th St., Holland, MI 49423, (616)396-5211.

JUST, Charles C.——**B:** Oct. 28, 1949, Idaho Falls, ID, *Atty. and VP, First Amer. Title Co.*, Just, Combo & Daw, Attys. at Law; **PRIM RE ACT:** Consultant, Attorney, Owner/Investor, Instructor; **OTHER RE ACT:** Title ins.; **SERVICES:** All areas of RE law; **REP CLIENTS:** RE brokers, lenders, builders and devel.; **PROFL AFFIL & HONORS:** ID State Bar Assn.; Idaho Falls Bd. of Realtors; Cert. Instr.; ID RE Commn., ID Land Title Assn., Pres. 1981-82; **EDUC:** BA, 1972, Univ. of ID; **GRAD EDUC:** JD, 1975, Univ. of ID; **OTHER ACT & HONORS:** Asst. Prosec. Atty., Bonneville Cty., 1980; **HOME ADD:** 217 N. Lloyd Cir., Idaho Falls, ID 83402, (208)524-3219; **BUS ADD:** 452 D Street, P O Box 1057, Idaho Falls, ID 83402, (208)529-1054.

JUSTICE, Albert N.——**B:** May 29, 1938, Hellier, KY, *Pres.*, Justice Corp.; **PRIM RE ACT:** Broker, Consultant, Developer, Instructor, Property Manager; **SERVICES:** Devel., leasing, mgmt., brokerage, consulting for comml. office bldgs. throughout FL; **REP CLIENTS:** Instnl. investors or lenders in comml. props.; **PROFL AFFIL & HONORS:** IREM, Amer. Soc. of RE Counselors, NAR, RMNI, CPM, CRE; **EDUC:** BA, 1959, Eng., Univ. of VA; **MIL SERV:** USAF, 1st Lt. - 1960; **OTHER ACT & HONORS:** Clearwater Yacht Club, Belleview Biltmore Ctry. Club, Useppa Is. Club; Boca Grande Club; Pres. Richmond, VA Bd. of Realtors 1972; Pres., IREM 1975; VChmn., Comm. of 100, Pinellas Cty., FL; **HOME ADD:** 3040 Hibiscus Dr. W, Belleair Beach, FL 33535, (813)595-2640; **BUS ADD:** 1307 U. S. Highway 19, S. Clearwater, FL 33516, (813)535-4651.

JUSTIS, Robert Y., Jr.——**B:** Sept. 21, 1943, Joplin, MO, *Dir. of Indus. Devel.*, State of VT, Econ. Devel. Dept.; **OTHER RE ACT:** Govt. Official; **SERVICES:** Mfg. sites, econ. data, community profiles, plant fin., employee training; **REP CLIENTS:** IBM, Digital Equipment Corp., Mitel Corp., G.E. Co., Simmonds Precision Corp. Bombardier Corp., Emhart Corp., VT American Corp., Colt Indus., Inc., AMP Inc.; **PREV EMPLOY:** Mgr., VT Indus. Devel. Authority; **PROFL**

AFFIL & HONORS: Amer. Econ. Devel. Council, NE Indus. Devel. Assn.; **EDUC:** AB, 1965, Econ., Dartmouth Coll.; **GRAD EDUC:** MBA, 1968, Corp. Fin., Univ. of PA; **MIL SERV:** US Army Res., E-6; **HOME ADD:** 30 Hubbard St., Montpelier, VT 05602, (802)229-4518; **BUS ADD:** Pavilion Bldg., Montpelier, VT 05602, (802)828-3221.

KAAS, Lester——*Corp. VP*, Certainteed Products Corp.; **PRIM RE ACT:** Property Manager; **BUS ADD:** PO Box 860, Valley Forge, PA 19482, (215)687-5000.*

KABACOFF, Lester E.——**B:** Jan. 29, 1913, NY, NY, *Managing Partner*, International Rivercenter; **PRIM RE ACT:** Broker, Attorney, Developer, Owner/Investor; **PREV EMPLOY:** Atty. Garey, Desvernine, Kissaum, 1937-1946; Wall St., NY; **EDUC:** BA, 1934, Lib. Arts/Pol. Sci., Univ. of PA; **GRAD EDUC:** LLB, 1937, Law, Univ. of PA; **EDUC HONORS:** Assoc. Tr.; **MIL SERV:** US Army; Capt.; **HOME ADD:** 111 Bellaire Dr., New Orleans, LA 70124, (504)482-8947; **BUS ADD:** 1404 Intl. Trade Mart Bldg., New Orleans, LA 70130, (504)581-1942.

KABOT, Ronald H.——**B:** Dec. 1, 1937, Newark, NJ, *Pres./Sr. VP*, International Mortgage Co./Kaufman and Broad, Inc.; **PRIM RE ACT:** Banker, Developer, Lender, Builder, Insuror; **SERVICES:** Permanent fin. for housing, loan origination and servicing; **PREV EMPLOY:** Deloitte, Haskins & Sells, Nat. Cert. Public Acctg. Firm; **PROFL AFFIL & HONORS:** 1963 Recipient of John F. Forbes Gold Medal Award; **EDUC:** AB, Dartmouth Coll.; **GRAD EDUC:** MBA, Bus. Admin., Amos Tuck School; **MIL SERV:** USN; **BUS ADD:** 3000 Ocean Park Blvd. 3000, Santa Monica, CA 90405, (213)450-6455.

KADISON, Douglas B.——**B:** Mar. 5, 1947, Newark, NJ, *VP*, Investors, Inc., Comml.; **PRIM RE ACT:** Broker, Consultant, Developer, Owner/Investor; **SERVICES:** Mort. banking services, purchase, devel. & ownership; **REP CLIENTS:** Major instl. lenders on comml. income prop. and indiv. devel./owners; **PREV EMPLOY:** EVP Froling-Kadison & Co., 1975-1978; Jersey Mort. Co., 1973-1975; Blau Mort. Co., 1971-1973; **PROFL AFFIL & HONORS:** MBA, Austin Apartment Assn.; **EDUC:** BBA, 1970, Fin./Acctg./Econ., Univ. of WI, Madison; **GRAD EDUC:** Fin., NYU; **OTHER ACT & HONORS:** C of C; Treas. JCCA of Austin; Heritage Soc. of Austin; Univ. of WI Alumni Assn., Amer. Numismatic Assn., Lauguna Gloria; **HOME ADD:** 8603 Alverstone Way, Austin, TX 78759, (512)346-0777; **BUS ADD:** Travis Bank & Trust Bldg., POB 4219, Austin, TX 78765, (512)451-5791.

KAGAN, David H.——**B:** Apr. 13, 1943, Everett, MA, *Pres.*, Devel. Resources Corp., Sub. of Munigle Corp.; **PRIM RE ACT:** Developer, Owner/Investor, Property Manager, Syndicator; **SERVICES:** Project mgmt., project approvals, fin., mktg., prop. mgmt.; **REP CLIENTS:** land owners, fin. insts., ins. co., pvt. investor; **PROFL AFFIL & HONORS:** RESSI, Amer. Planning Assn., Amer. Inst. of Planners; **EDUC:** BA, 1966, Hist., The Johns Hopkins Univ.; **GRAD EDUC:** MBA, 1972, Urban Planning, Univ. of Hartford; **EDUC HONORS:** John C. Lincoln Fellow; **OTHER ACT & HONORS:** Bd. of Advisors YMCA; **HOME ADD:** Farmington, CT 06032; **BUS ADD:** 55 Airport Rd., Hartford, CT 06114, (203)522-3511.

KAHLER, R. Jan——**B:** Nov. 20, 1947, Lima, OH, *Co-owner, Dir., Officer*, Kahler-Bellows, Inc.; **PRIM RE ACT:** Developer, Builder, Owner/Investor; **SERVICES:** RE Devel.-Specialty Condos., Mobile Home Park Ownership; **REP CLIENTS:** Guarantee S&L; **PREV EMPLOY:** Martin Marietta Corp., Orlando, FL; **PROFL AFFIL & HONORS:** Member-Contractors and Builders Assn. of Pinellas Cty., Outstanding Community Serv. Award, 1979, Clearwater-Dunedin Bd. of Realtors; **EDUC:** BBA, 1970, Bus. Admin., GA Inst. of Tech.; **OTHER ACT & HONORS:** V Chmn., Planning & Zoning Bd. Indian Rocks Beach; Chmn., Bd. of Appeals, Indian Rocks Beach, 1980-81; 1978-80 IRB; 1981 Commr., Pres.-Tax Paying Prop. Owners Assn.; IRB, 1977-1981; Dir., Indian Rocks Area, Hist. Soc. - AOPA 1975-1981; **BUS ADD:** 2499 East Bay Dr., Suite 203, Largo, FL 33541, (813)536-2774.

KAHN, B. Franklin——**B:** Feb. 4, 1925, Washington, DC, *Pres. of the Trs.*, Washington Real Estate Investment Trust; **PRIM RE ACT:** Consultant, Owner/Investor, Instructor; **PROFL AFFIL & HONORS:** Instructor, 35 yrs., Wharton School of Fin.; **EDUC:** BS, 1946, Econ./Fin., Wharton School of Fin.; **HOME ADD:** 5215 Edgemoore Ln., Bethesda, MD 20814; **BUS ADD:** 4936 Fairmont Ave., Bethesda, MD 20816, (301)652-4300.

KAHN, Charles, Jr.——**B:** July 6, 1924, Philadelphia, PA, *Owner*, Kahn & Co.; **PRIM RE ACT:** Broker, Consultant, Appraiser, Developer, Owner/Investor, Property Manager, Insuror; **PROFL AFFIL & HONORS:** Amer. Soc. of Appraisers; Acc. Mgmt. Org.; IREM; NAR, CPM; Soc.of Indep. Fee Appraisers; **EDUC:** BS, 1947, Econ., Franklin & Marshall Coll.; **MIL SERV:** USMC, Cpl., AmiTheatre of Operations; Good Conduct Medal; **OTHER ACT & HONORS:** Abington Twp. Zoning Hearing Bd. - Chmn. 18 years; PA Assn. of Realtors - Pres. - 1980; Philadelphia Bd. of Realtors - Pres. 1977; Beneficial Savings Bank - Bd. Member & Exec. Comm.; **HOME ADD:** 1147 Rydal Rd., Rydal, PA 19046, (215)576-6169; **BUS ADD:** 1516 Locust St., Philadelphia, PA 19102, (215)735-9800.

KAHN, Sanders A.——**B:** Jan 20, 1919, NY, NY, *Pres.*, Sanders A. Kahn Assoc., Inc.; **PRIM RE ACT:** Real Estate Publisher; **OTHER RE ACT:** Writer; **SERVICES:** Sale, leasing, consultation, brokerage, shopping ctrs., office bldgs., indus. parks, and bank branch locations; **REP CLIENTS:** Maj. corps., fin. insts., govts investors, pension funds; **PREV EMPLOY:** Mgr. RE planning, Port Auth.. of NY NJ., concurrent with bus. exp., adjunct prof. in charge of RE courses, City Coll. and Bernard Baruch Coll., CUNY; **PROFL AFFIL & HONORS:** Amer. Soc. of RE Counselors; Soc. of RE Appraisers; Fellow Amer. Soc. of Appraisers; Fellow Soc. of Valuers & Auctioneers; (GRT; BRIT); Citizens Housing and Planning Council of NY (Dir); NJ Planning Assn. (Dir), Recipient of George. L. Schmutz Award from the Amer. Inst. of RE Appraisers; Sanders A Kahn RE Scholarship Program; Bernard Baruch Coll.; 1980 Man of the Yr.; Soc. of RE Appraisers; NY Chapt.; **EDUC:** BBA, 1947, RE, CCNY; **GRAD EDUC:** MBA, 1949, RE, Grad. Sch. of Bus. Admin. of NYO; PhD, 1962, Econ, & Land Econ., Grad. Sch. of Bus. Admin. of NYU; **MIL SERV:** USA, Air Force, Cpl., ETO; **HOME ADD:** 428 Green Hill Rd., Smoke Rise, Kinnelon, NJ 07705; **BUS ADD:** 341 Madison Ave., NY, NY 10017, (212)687-3363.

KAHN, Steven M.——**B:** Apr. 14, 1946, Columbus, OH, *Part.*, Wears Kahn McMenamy & Co.; **PRIM RE ACT:** Broker, Consultant, Developer, Property Manager, Owner/Investor; **SERVICES:** Brokerage (sales & leasing), Prop. Mgmt., Partnership Formations; **REP CLIENTS:** Investment Partnerships; Bank Investment & Trust Depts.; **PROFL AFFIL & HONORS:** IREM, GRI; CPM; Columbus Bd. of Realtors; **EDUC:** 1970, OH State Univ.; **OTHER ACT & HONORS:** Athletic Club of Columbus; Tr., German Village Soc.; Listed in Who's Who in Fin. & Indus., 1980; **HOME ADD:** 165 E Deshler Ave., Columbus, OH 43206, (614)443-7317; **BUS ADD:** 81 S Fifth St., Columbus, OH 43215, (614)228-6321.

KAHT, Joseph Edward——**B:** Feb. 4, 1928, Brooklyn, NY, *Sr. VP & Gen. Counsel*, Dry Dock Savings Bank; **PRIM RE ACT:** Attorney, Banker; **PREV EMPLOY:** Asst. Atty., Dewey, Ballantine, Bushby, Palmer & Wood, NYC; **PROFL AFFIL & HONORS:** ABA; NY State Bar Assn.; Cty. Lawyers Assn., Member of NY & Dist. of Columbia Bars; **EDUC:** St. Francis Coll.; **GRAD EDUC:** 1952, NY Law Sch.; **HOME ADD:** 3309 Milburn Ave., Baldwin Harbor, NY 11510, (516)868-9657; **BUS ADD:** 742 Lexington Ave., NY, NY 10022, (212)644-6143.

KAILIAN, Aram H.——**B:** Oct. 23, 1949, Philadelphia, PA, *Princ./Arch. VP, Princ.*, Kailian Assocs. Architecture/Planning, Advent Ltd., Amber-Sun Partnership Development Co.; **PRIM RE ACT:** Architect, Developer, Builder; **OTHER RE ACT:** Solar Consultant; **SERVICES:** Design & Planning; Design-Build; Devel.; Const.; **REP CLIENTS:** Toll Bros. Inc., Adwin Realty, Roach Bros., Joseph Cutler & Sons Inc., Urban Engrs., Hachik Bleach, Megeurian Corp., Suburban Builders, Hovsons Inc., Sports Factory Inc., Vic Hoffman Inc., Rabena Assocs.; **PREV EMPLOY:** H.A. Kuljian Arch/Engrs (1970-1974), Urban Engrs (1974-1978), William F. Lotz Inc. Des/Engrs/Construct 1978-1980); **PROFL AFFIL & HONORS:** AIA; Pa Soc. Archs., Intl. Solar Energy Soc., Natl. Hist. Trust, Const. Spec. Inst., Urban Plan Inst., NCARB Cert., Reg. Arch. PA, NJ, NY, Amer. Arc. Assn., Natl. Acad. Conciliators; **EDUC:** B.S. Arch., 1973, Fine Arts/Arch./Planning, Tyler Sch. of Fine Arts/Temple Univ.; **GRAD EDUC:** Grad. Studies-Human Geography, Temple Univ.; **OTHER ACT & HONORS:** Mem. Bd. Dir.-Armenian Assembly, Wash. DC., Armenian Sisters Acad., Phila. PA; Mem.-Democratic Nationalities Council, Wash., D.C., Natl. Republican Heritage Grps. Council, Wash. D.C., *Who's Who in the East*, *Personalities of America*, *Directory of Distinguished Americans*, *Community Leaders of America*, *Two Thousand Notable Americans*, *Personalities of the East*, *World Leaders*; **HOME ADD:** 2249 Menlo Ave., Glenside, PA 19038, (215)887-0873; **BUS ADD:** 2032 Sansom St., Philadelphia, PA 19103, (215)972-0532.

KAILO, Norman——**B:** June 11, 1924, NY, NY, *Sales Mgr.*, Soldoveri Agency, RE; **PRIM RE ACT:** Broker, Appraiser, Owner/Investor, Instructor; **OTHER RE ACT:** Counseling; author; **SERVICES:** Sales, appraisals, relocation; **REP CLIENTS:** Indiv., lenders, maj. corps.; **PREV EMPLOY:** Inst. Prof. Sch. of Bus.; (RE Dir, Profl. Inst. of N NJ; Adjunct Faculty William Patterson Coll. (RE); **PROFL AFFIL & HONORS:** Dir NAR; Dir. NJ Assn. of Realtors; Dir. All Points Relocation Serv. (Intl.); Member RNMI, GRI; CRS; **MIL SERV:** USAF; 1942-45; Sgt.; India/China/Taiwan; **OTHER ACT & HONORS:** Past Pres. NJ Assn. of Realtors; Chmn. Energy Comm.; NAR, Rec. Pres. Citation 1980 for cooperating Dept. of Energy Training Program for Realtors; **HOME ADD:** 613 Alps Rd., Wayne, NJ 07470, (201)696-0542; **BUS ADD:** 247 Union Blvd., PO Box 127, Totowa Bor., NJ 07511, (201)942-2200.

KAISER, Anton J., Esq.——**B:** May 6, 1929, College Point, Queens, NY, Anton J. Kaiser, P.C.; **PRIM RE ACT:** Attorney; **SERVICES:** RE-Mort. Practice; **REP CLIENTS:** European Amer. Bank & Trust; **PREV EMPLOY:** 20 yrs. Lending Officer in Franklin Nat. Bank Mort. Dept., 4 yrs. with European Amer. Bank; **PROFL AFFIL & HONORS:** Nassau Ct. Bar Assn., NY State Bar Assn.; **GRAD EDUC:** LLB, 1951, Law, St. John's Univ., Brooklyn, NY; **OTHER ACT & HONORS:** Kiwanis Intl. (1971-72 Gov. of NY Dist.); Presently Tr. of Kiwanis Intl.; **HOME ADD:** 37 Acme Ave., Bellpage, NY 11714; **BUS ADD:** European American Bank Bldg., 925 Hempstead Tpke., Franklin Square, NY 11010, (516)683-5674.

KAISER, Walter——**B:** July 19, 1933, Chicago, IL, *Exec. VP*, Home Builders of America, Inc.; **PRIM RE ACT:** Engineer, Developer, Builder, Owner/Investor; **EDUC:** BS, 1956, ME, Northwestern Univ.; **HOME ADD:** 180 E. Pearson Apt. 5502, Chicago, IL 60611; **BUS ADD:** 1320 W. Fullerton Ave., Chicago, IL 60614, (312)929-9220.

KALABANY, Stephen——**B:** Aug. 14, 1939, South Bend, IN, *VP Gen. Mgr.*, The Koll Co., Asset Mgt. Div.; **PRIM RE ACT:** Developer, Property Manager; **PREV EMPLOY:** 1973-1980 Coldwell Banker - VP Dir. of Operations for Capital Mgmt. Serv.; **PROFL AFFIL & HONORS:** IREM, NAIOP, CPM; **EDUC:** BS, 1963, Econ., Purdue Univ.; **MIL SERV:** USN (1963-1967), Lt.; **HOME ADD:** 18112 Pamela Pl., Villa Park, CA 92667, (714)988-2889; **BUS ADD:** 4490 Von Karman, Newport Beach, CA 92660, (714)833-3030.

KALAVITY, Louis——**B:** Jan. 24, 1932, Akron, OH, *Atty. - RE Broker*; **PRIM RE ACT:** Broker, Attorney, Owner/Investor; **PROFL AFFIL & HONORS:** ABA; OH Bar Assn.; Akron Bar Assn.; Condemnation Law Comm., ABA; **EDUC:** BA, 1958, Univ. of Chicago; **GRAD EDUC:** JD, 1968, RE, Univ. of Akron, Coll. of Law; **MIL SERV:** USAF, S/Sgt.; **HOME ADD:** Fairlawn, OH; **BUS ADD:** Kalavity Square, 60 E. Market St., Akron, OH 44308, (216)376-4444.

KALBITZER, Jane C.——*Mgr.*, Fox & Lazo Realtors; **PRIM RE ACT:** Broker; **PREV EMPLOY:** 1978-1979, Dickinson Inc.; 1975-1978, John Giantonio RE, Mgr.; 1970-1975, Hayes Co.; **PROFL AFFIL & HONORS:** NAREB; Chester Cty. Bd. of Realtors; PA Assn. of Realtors, Million Dollar Club, 1971-1974; Chester Cty. Bd. of Realtors, 1979 & 1980; Fox & Lazo Sales Leader Exton Office, 1980; Instr., Evening Div., RE, Immaculate Coll.; Past VP and Dir., Realtor Assoc. Div., Chester Cty. Bd. of Realtors; **OTHER ACT & HONORS:** W. Whiteland Republican Club; Woman's Club of Downingtown; **HOME ADD:** POB 147, Downingtown, PA 19335; **BUS ADD:** 315 E. Lancaster Ave., Exton, PA 19341, (215)363-2100.

KALIKER, Thomas J.——**B:** Mar. 19, 1943, Ft. Wayne, IN, *VP*, Chemical Mortgage Co.; **PRIM RE ACT:** Appraiser; **SERVICES:** RE valuations and evaluations; **PROFL AFFIL & HONORS:** Realtor, MAI, SREA; **EDUC:** BS, 1967, Chem., OH State Univ.; **GRAD EDUC:** MBA, 1971, Bus., Univ. of W FL; **HOME ADD:** 5047 New Haven Dr., Columbus, OH 43220, (614)451-7106; **BUS ADD:** 101 E Town St., Columbus, OH 43215, (614)460-3228.

KALIKOW, Edward M.——**B:** Feb. 3, 1954, NYC, NY, *VP*, Kaled Management Corp.; **PRIM RE ACT:** Attorney, Developer, Builder, Owner/Investor, Property Manager; **PROFL AFFIL & HONORS:** Assn. Builders & Owners of Gr. NY, Registered Apt. Mgr. (RAM) with the NAHB; **EDUC:** BS, 1975, RE, Syracuse Univ.; **GRAD EDUC:** JD, 1978, Law, Hofstra Univ. School of Law; **EDUC HONORS:** Grad. Magna Cum Laude - Member Beta Gamma Sigma (Business Honorary); **HOME ADD:** 269-25T Grand Central Pkwy., Floral Park, NY 11005, (212)225-0792; **BUS ADD:** 95-25 Queens Blvd., Rego Park, NY 11374, (212)896-4800.

KALLAS, J. Kenneth——**B:** Oct. 11, 1932, Chicago, IL, *Asst. VP - Mgr. RE Div.*, Life and Casualty Ins. Co. of TN; **PRIM RE ACT:** Property Manager; **SERVICES:** Leasing, Mgmt., Devel., Rehab. of Co. owned Props.; **PREV EMPLOY:** Dobson & Johnson Inc., Redman Inc.; Power Regulator Co., DeSoto Inc., GTE; **PROFL AFFIL & HONORS:** IREM, BOMA; **EDUC:** BSC, 1955, Econ., Loyola Univ. - Chicago; **EDUC HONORS:** Econ. Key 1955, Wall St. Journal Award Fin. 1955; **MIL SERV:** USA, SP-4; **OTHER ACT & HONORS:** Pres. of Bd. - Nashville Child Center; **HOME ADD:** 216 Churchill Pl., Franklin, TN 37064, (615)794-9685; **BUS ADD:** L and C Tower, Nashville, TN 37219, (615)244-9300.

KALLOF, Fred, Jr.——**B:** July 26, 1957, Phoenix, AZ, *RE Appraiser*, Executive Investor Realty; **PRIM RE ACT:** Broker, Consultant, Appraiser; **SERVICES:** Investment Analysis, appraisal, consultation; **REP CLIENTS:** various Nat. clients, devels., Attys., Lenders; **PREV EMPLOY:** Burke, Hansen & Homan; ALRASOR Realty; Appraisers/Consultants; **PROFL AFFIL & HONORS:** AIREA; Soc. of RE Appraisers; **EDUC:** RE, AZ State Univ./Baylor Univ.; **BUS ADD:** PO Box 2376, Phoenix, AZ 85002, (602)254-7264.

KALMAN, George——*Mgr. Energy & fac.*, S.P.S. Technologies, Inc.; **PRIM RE ACT:** Property Manager; **BUS ADD:** Benson East, Jenkintown, PA 19046, (215)572-3000.*

KALRA, Madan G.——**B:** Sept. 5, 1940, *Arch.*, M. W. Kellogg, CED Arch.; **PRIM RE ACT:** Architect, Owner/Investor; **PROFL AFFIL & HONORS:** Constr. Specifications Inst. AIA; **EDUC:** BArch, 1965, Sch. of Planning & Arch.; **GRAD EDUC:** MArch, 1974, Pratt Inst., NY; **HOME ADD:** 15302 Bonita Springs Drive, Houston, TX 77083, (713)933-4219; **BUS ADD:** 3 Greenway Plaza E., Houston, TX 77046, (713)960-4156.

KAMMERAAD, Kenneth——*Dir. Corp. Fac. Plng. & Secy.*, Johnson Controls Inc.; **PRIM RE ACT:** Property Manager; **BUS ADD:** 5757 N. Greenbay Ave., Glendale, WI 53209, (414)228-1200.*

KAMMINGA, Fred J.——**B:** Apr. 2, 1944, Grand Rapids, MI, *Pres.*, Markland Dev., Inc.; **PRIM RE ACT:** Broker, Syndicator, Consultant, Developer, Property Manager, Owner/Investor; **SERVICES:** Site acquisition, land devel., mort., fin., const. & prop. mgmt.; **PROFL AFFIL & HONORS:** NACORE, ICSC, NAR, Grand Rapids RE Bd., Kalamazoo RE Bd, and Holland Bd. of Realtors; **HOME ADD:** 2600 Shadowbrook Dr., Grand Rapids, MI 49506, (616)942-0457; **BUS ADD:** 3250 28th St., S.E., Grand Rapids, MI 49508, (616)942-0240.

KAMP, Arthur J.——**B:** July 22, 1945, Rochester, NY, *Atty.*, Diamonstein, Drucker & Kamp; **PRIM RE ACT:** Attorney; **SERVICES:** Concept consultation, fin. negot., legal representation in devel. condos., condo. conversions, townhouse for sale, indus. revenue bond financing, synd.; **REP CLIENTS:** Comml. & resid. devel., synd., prop. mgrs.; **PROFL AFFIL & HONORS:** ABA; VA State Bar; Newport News Bar Assn.; **EDUC:** BA, 1968, Eng., SUNY at Buffalo; **GRAD EDUC:** JD, 1970, SUNY at Buffalo; **MIL SERV:** USAF; First Lt.; **OTHER ACT & HONORS:** Newport News Rotary Club; Chmn., Bd. of Dirs. for Hidewood Presbyterian Pre-School; Past Treas., Newport News Democratic Party; **HOME ADD:** 11 Woolridge Pl., Newport News, VA 23601, (804)599-6041; **BUS ADD:** 103 28th St., POB 324, Newport News, VA 23607, (804)245-2836.

KAMP, Carl O., Jr.——*Pres.*, Federal Home Loan Bank of Atlanta; **PRIM RE ACT:** Banker; **BUS ADD:** PO Box 56527, Atlanta, GA 30343, (404)522-2450.*

KAMPE, Otto H.——**B:** Nov. 20, 1933, Philadelphia, PA, *Pres.*, Rapid Appraisals, Inc.; **PRIM RE ACT:** Appraiser; **SERVICES:** Appraising Real Prop.; **REP CLIENTS:** VA, Fortune Fed. S & L, Sun Bank; **PREV EMPLOY:** Assoc. with Phillip Pickens, MAI, FL; **PROFL AFFIL & HONORS:** Member, ASA, Assoc. with Soc. of RE Appraisers candidate for MAI designation with AIREA, NAR; **EDUC:** BA, 1972, Bus. Admin., Univ. of NE, Omaha; **GRAD EDUC:** MBA, 1975, RE and Urban Land Studies, Univ. of FL; **MIL SERV:** USAF, Maj., Bronze Star, air medals, etc.; **HOME ADD:** 2204 NW 21 Pl., Gainesville, FL 32605, (904)373-8312; **BUS ADD:** 2204 NW 21st Pl., Gainesville, FL 32605, (904)373-8312.

KANDA, Tad T.——**B:** Feb. 22, 1920, Hakalau, HI, *VP*, National Mortgage and Finance Company, Ltd., Prop. Mgmt. Dept.; **PRIM RE ACT:** Property Manager; **SERVICES:** Prop. mgmt. - comml., indus., condos., apts.; **PROFL AFFIL & HONORS:** IREM, HI Assn. of Realtors, CPM; **MIL SERV:** Infantry, Cpl., Purple Heart, Bronze Star; **HOME ADD:** 1430 Wilder Ave., Apt. No. 305, Honolulu, HI 96822, (808)941-4997; **BUS ADD:** 1165 Bethel St., Honolulu, HI 96813, (808)536-7077.

KANE, Gary Paul——**B:** Feb. 4, 1943, San Francisco, CA, *Exec. Dir.*, North Carolina Housing Finance Agency; **PRIM RE ACT:** Attorney, Lender, Owner/Investor; **SERVICES:** Fin. single family & multi-family housing; **PREV EMPLOY:** Nat. Assn. of Homebuilders

1977-80; CA Housing Fin. Agency 1975-76; Dept. of Housing and Urban Devel. 1973-75; **PROFL AFFIL & HONORS:** CA, DC and Amer. Bar Assns.; **EDUC:** AB, 1963, Econ., Statistics, Univ. of CA at Berkeley; **GRAD EDUC:** JD, 1966, Law, Boalt Hall, Univ. of CA at Berkeley; **HOME ADD:** 1122 Queensferry Rd., Cary, NC 27511, (919)467-2436; **BUS ADD:** PO Box 27687, Raleigh, NC 27611.

KANE, George——*Treas. & Secy.*, Mickelberry Corp.; **PRIM RE ACT:** Property Manager; **BUS ADD:** 405 Park Ave., New York, NY 10022, (212)832-0303.*

KANE, Nancy T.——*Apartment Marketing Supervisor*, Morton G. Thalhimer, Inc., Resid. Leasing and Prop. Mgmt.; **PRIM RE ACT:** Broker, Consultant, Property Manager; **SERVICES:** Apt., condo. mgmt.; **PROFL AFFIL & HONORS:** IREM; Bd. of Realtors; Women's Council; Richmond Apt. Council; **BUS ADD:** F & M Ctr., 12th and Main Sts., Richmond, VA 23277, (804)648-5881.

KANE, Robert J.——*Sr. VP*, Omark Industries, Inc.; **PRIM RE ACT:** Property Manager; **BUS ADD:** 2100 SE Milport Rd., Portland, OR 97222, (503)653-8881.*

KANELLOS, James L.——**B:** Jan. 16, 1935, Columbia, SC, *VP - Mktg.*, Hooker/Barnes, Comml. Div.; **PRIM RE ACT:** Broker, Developer; **SERVICES:** Devel. of comml. props.; **REP CLIENTS:** Major tenants for shopping ctrs., office and indus. props.; **PROFL AFFIL & HONORS:** ICSC, NAIOP, GIDA; **EDUC:** BBA, 1959, Retailing/Mktg., Univ. of SC; **MIL SERV:** US Army, SP4; **OTHER ACT & HONORS:** Southern Ctr. for Intl. Studies; **HOME ADD:** 2272 Dartford Dr., Atlanta, GA 30338, (404)455-0986; **BUS ADD:** 2175 Parklake Dr., NE, Suite 250, Atlanta, GA 30345, (404)939-8780.

KANEMOTO, Ken——**B:** Feb. 19, 1945, Longmont, CO, *Broker*, Title Realty; **PRIM RE ACT:** Broker; **SERVICES:** Comml., Investment Brokerage & counseling; **PROFL AFFIL & HONORS:** CCIM; **EDUC:** 1969, Aerospace Engrg., Bus., Univ. of CO; **HOME ADD:** 14 Burlington, CO 80501, (303)772-5233; **BUS ADD:** 203 S. Main, Longmont, CA, (303)772-1310.

KANESHIRO, George M.——**B:** Feb. 14, 1941, Honolulu, HI, *Pres.*, George & Associates, GMK, Inc.; **PRIM RE ACT:** Broker, Consultant, Developer, Owner/Investor, Property Manager, Syndicator; **SERVICES:** Brokerage, investment counseling, devel. & synd. and prop. mgmt.; **REP CLIENTS:** Indivs.; **PROFL AFFIL & HONORS:** RNMI, RESSI, HCCIMC, HI Bd. of Realtors, HI Assn. Realtors; **EDUC:** BBA, 1964, Mktg. and Mgmt., Univ. of HI; **MIL SERV:** US Army, 1 Lt., Army Commendation Award; **HOME ADD:** 1459 Ala Puumalu St., Honolulu, HI 96818, (808)833-2933; **BUS ADD:** 1055 Kalo Place Suite 100, Honolulu, HI 96826, (808)942-9411.

KANNER, Theodore I.——**B:** Sept. 20, 1918, Bronx, NY, *Deputy Gen. Counsel*, The City of NY, Dept. of Ports and Terminals; **PRIM RE ACT:** Attorney, Regulator, Property Manager; **SERVICES:** Legal, prop. mgmt., leasing; **EDUC:** BS, 1939, Pol. Sci., Pre-Law, Brooklyn Law School; **GRAD EDUC:** LLB, 1946, Law; **EDUC HONORS:** Bar Admission, 1947; **MIL SERV:** USN, SK (D) 2C; **HOME ADD:** 125 Gates Ave., Montclair, NJ 07042, (201)744-4310; **BUS ADD:** Battery-Maritime Bldg., NY, NY 10004, (212)248-8041.

KANTER, Jay A.——**B:** Apr. 5, 1942, San Antonio, TX, *Pres.*, Kanter Co.; **PRIM RE ACT:** Broker, Syndicator, Consultant, Property Manager; **OTHER RE ACT:** Applies only to comml. and investment props.; **SERVICES:** Brokerage, mgmt., interior remodel., synd., inv. counsel; **PREV EMPLOY:** Hexter Title and Abstract, Escrow Officer; Raymond D. Nasher Co., Shopping Ctr., Office, Resid. Devel.; Louis J. Hexter, Resid. Devel. Irving Klein Co., Synd. and Mgmt.; **PROFL AFFIL & HONORS:** Gtr. Dallas Bd. of Realtors, Int. Council of Shopping Ctrs.; BOMA, CCIM Candidate; **EDUC:** BBA, 1964, R.E. and Ins., Univ. of TX at Austin; **GRAD EDUC:** Post Grad. Studies in R.E., 1966-68, S. Methodist Univ.; **EDUC HONORS:** Exec. Asst. Student Body Pres. 1962; Interfrat. Council, 1961-64; **MIL SERV:** USA, 1964-70, Sgt.; **OTHER ACT & HONORS:** City of Dallas Bd. of Equalization (2 terms); BOD Shearith Israel Synagogue; Membership Comm. of Dallas C of C; BOD of Amer. Jewish Congress; **BUS ADD:** 8616 N.W. Plaza, Dallas, TX 75225, (214)691-7233.

KANTOFF, Sheldon L.——**B:** Aug. 12, 1936, Chicago, IL, *VP*, Draper & Kramer, Inc.; **PRIM RE ACT:** Broker, Engineer, Attorney, Developer, Builder; **REP CLIENTS:** Dearborn Park Corp.; **PREV EMPLOY:** VP, Urban Investment & Devel. Corp.; **PROFL AFFIL & HONORS:** ABA, ULI, Multifamily Housing Assn., S. Loop Planning Bd., Chicago, Member Chi Epsilon Civil Engrg. Frat.; **EDUC:** BCE, 1957, Structures, IL Inst. of Tech.; **GRAD EDUC:** JD, 1964, Loyola Univ. School of Law; **MIL SERV:** USAF, Capt.; **HOME ADD:** 226 Valley View, Wilmette, IL 60091, (312)256-5412; **BUS ADD:** 407 S. Dearborn Rm 1000, Chicago, IL 60605, (312)663-5170.

KAPANKA, Richard A.——**B:** Dec. 11, 1946, Port Huron, MI, *Counsel*, CT General Life Ins. Co., Investment; **PRIM RE ACT:** Attorney; **PREV EMPLOY:** Robinson, Robinson & Cole, Hartford, CT; **PROFL AFFIL & HONORS:** ABA, CT and Hartford Cty. Bar Assns.; **EDUC:** BS, 1969, Poli. Sci., Econ., MI State Univ.; **GRAD EDUC:** JD, 1973, Law, Univ. of MI Law School; **EDUC HONORS:** Cum Laude; **OTHER ACT & HONORS:** Inland-Wetlands Commn., Town of Canton, 1978 to Present; **HOME ADD:** 42 Dyer Ave., Collinsville, CT 06022, (203)693-0695; **BUS ADD:** Hartford, CT 06152, (203)726-6921.

KAPLAN, Ira G.——**B:** Aug. 31, 1942, Brooklyn, NY, *VP-Fin.*, Collins Development Corp.; **PRIM RE ACT:** Developer, Builder; **SERVICES:** RE fin., acctg., ins., etc.; **PREV EMPLOY:** Chief Fin. Officer, Urban Devel. Corp., Sr. Accountant, S.D. Leidesdant & Co.; **PROFL AFFIL & HONORS:** AICPA, NY State Soc. of CPA's, CPA, NY; **EDUC:** BS, 1964, Acctg., CUNY; **HOME ADD:** 39 Denise Pl., Stamford, CT 06905, (203)329-2421; **BUS ADD:** 43 Lindstrom Rd., Stamford, CT 06905, (203)357-0123.

KAPLAN, Irving M.J.——*VP & Secy.*, Copperweld Corp.; **PRIM RE ACT:** Property Manager; **BUS ADD:** Two Oliver Plaza, Pittsburgh, PA 15222, (412)263-3205.*

KAPLAN, James——**B:** Aug 22, 1950, Chicago, IL, *Pres.*, James Kaplan Cos., Inc.; **PRIM RE ACT:** Property Manager; **SERVICES:** Comml. Prop. Mgmt., Leasing, Consultant; **REP CLIENTS:** Ins. Cos., Mort. Bankers, Instl. holders of RE; **PROFL AFFIL & HONORS:** IREM, Intl. Council of Shopping Ctrs., Chicago RE Bd., CPM (Candidate), CSM; **EDUC:** BA, 1972, Fin. Mgmg., Econ., Univ. of IL; **BUS ADD:** 1750 N Clark St., Chicago, IL 60614, (312)664-3300.

KAPLAN, Jay M.——**B:** May 22, 1944, NY, *Sr. VP/Acquisitons and Sales*, Consolidated Capital; **PRIM RE ACT:** Developer, Lender, Owner/Investor, Property Manager, Syndicator; **SERVICES:** Acquisitions, Sales, Lending, Mgmt.; **PROFL AFFIL & HONORS:** Instr., Univ. of CA, CA RE Broker, CRA; **EDUC:** BS, 1966, Psych, Tufts Univ.; **GRAD EDUC:** MBA, 1968, Mktg., Univ. of Chicago; **EDUC HONORS:** Econ. Honor Soc.; **MIL SERV:** USMC, PFC; **OTHER ACT & HONORS:** Bd. of Dirs., Amer. Cancer Soc., Marin; **BUS ADD:** 1900 Powell St., Emeryville, CA 94608, (415)652-7171.

KAPLAN, Michael——**B:** Mar. 3, 1942, New York, NY, *Pres.*, Kaplan Realty Co., Inc.; **PRIM RE ACT:** Broker; **SERVICES:** Office bldg. specialists; **PROFL AFFIL & HONORS:** Nat. Assn. of Office and Indus. Parks (NAIOP); **EDUC:** BS, 1963, Bus./Acctg., Lehigh Univ.; **MIL SERV:** U.S. Army, 1st Lt.; **HOME ADD:** Box 446, Bedminster, NJ 07921, (201)234-0892; **BUS ADD:** 115 Morristown Rd., Bernardsville, NJ 07924, (201)766-7166.

KAPLAN, William——**B:** Nov. 12, 1938, Cleveland, OH, *Pres.*, William Kaplan Co.; **PRIM RE ACT:** Broker, Consultant, Attorney, Appraiser, Owner/Investor; **SERVICES:** Investment counseling, urban prop. valuation, devel., brokerage of indus. & comml. prop., feasibility studies; **REP CLIENTS:** Instnl. investors, flr. & domestic; devel. and indiv. investors; **PROFL AFFIL & HONORS:** Nat. Assn. of RE Brokers; ABA; OH Bar, Assoc. of the Yr., Cleveland Area Bd. of Realtors, 1970; **EDUC:** BBA, 1961, RE, OH State Univ.; **GRAD EDUC:** JD, 1965, Law, The Cleveland Marshall Law School of Cleveland State Univ.; **OTHER ACT & HONORS:** Tr., Cleveland Area Bd. of Realtors, 1968, 1970, 1971; RE Consultant to the City of Cleveland, 1978-1981; Amer. Inst. of Bus. Mgmt., Pres.; **HOME ADD:** 2663 Cranlyn Rd., Shaker Hts., OH 44122, (216)831-5109; **BUS ADD:** Tower East Bldg., Shaker Hts., OH 44122, (216)991-4666.

KAPPLIN, Dr. Steven D.——**B:** Mar. 22, 1942, Little Rock, AR, *Asst. Prof. of Fin.*, University of South Florida, Coll. of Bus.; **PRIM RE ACT:** Broker, Consultant, Instructor; **SERVICES:** Teaching, training, consulting, research; **REP CLIENTS:** Brokers, investors, grant agencies; **PREV EMPLOY:** GA State Univ. 1971-73; Sangamon State Univ. 1973-75; **PROFL AFFIL & HONORS:** Fin. Mgmt. Assn., Amer. RE & Urban Econs. Assn., Soc. of RE Appraisers; **EDUC:** BA, 1970, English, GA State Univ., Atlanta, GA; **GRAD EDUC:** PhD, 1979, RE and Urban Affairs, GA State Univ.; **EDUC HONORS:** Dissertation Awarded Second Prize by Lincoln Land Inst., 1981; **MIL SERV:** Army, E4; **HOME ADD:** 1711 Moffat Ave., Tampa, FL 33617, (813)985-5611; **BUS ADD:** Dept. of Fin., Tampa, FL 33620, (813)974-2081.

KARABELL, David I.——**B:** Apr. 11, 1939, Phila., PA, *Part.*, O'Sullivan Wolff Karabell; **PRIM RE ACT:** Attorney; **PROFL AFFIL & HONORS:** NY State Bar Assn., NYC Bar Assn., RESSI; **EDUC:** BA, 1961, Eng., Temple Univ.; **GRAD EDUC:** LLB, 1967,

NYU Law; **MIL SERV:** USMCR; **HOME ADD:** 45 E 82 St., New York, NY 10028, (212)238-4892; **BUS ADD:** 280 Park Ave., New York, NY 10017, (212)661-3600.

KARABELNIKOFF, Don G.——B: Aug. 9, 1948, Anchorage, AK, *RE Counselor*, Karabelnikoff & Assoc.; **PRIM RE ACT:** Consultant, Appraiser; **OTHER RE ACT:** Development manager acquisition services; **SERVICES:** Advisory or agency services in acquiring, operating or liquidating RE assets; **REP CLIENTS:** Devel. & investors dealing with substantial props., local and state govt. agencies; **PREV EMPLOY:** Borough-City Devel., Carr-Gottstein Props., State Dept. of Highways; **PROFL AFFIL & HONORS:** Numerous RE organizations; **EDUC:** BS, 1971, Mktg./Mgmt., AK Methodist Univ.; **OTHER ACT & HONORS:** Planning Comm. For Anchorage 1976-79, Member, Aircraft Owners & Pilots Assn.; **HOME ADD:** 9601 Copper Dr., Anchorage, AK 99503, (907)333-4419; **BUS ADD:** 2509 Eide St., Suite 6, Anchorage, AK 99503, (907)338-1500.

KARAN, David——B: Mar. 2, 1948, New Kensington, PA, *Atty. at Law*, Kaplan, Strangis and Kaplan, P.A.; **PRIM RE ACT:** Attorney; **REP CLIENTS:** Republic Airlines, Inc., Lone Star Industries, Can-American Realty Corp.; **PREV EMPLOY:** Asst. Prof., OH State Univ. Coll. of Law, 1975-1978; taught in the areas of RE law and RE finance; **PROFL AFFIL & HONORS:** Hennepin Cty., MN State Bar Assn., ABA; **EDUC:** BA, 1970, Pre-Law, Wash. and Jefferson Coll., and PA State Univ.; **GRAD EDUC:** JD, 1973, Bus. Law, Univ. of MN; **EDUC HONORS:** Cum Laude, Magna Cum Laude, Order of the Coif, Member, MN Law Review, Dir., Univ. of MN Legal Aid Clinic, Member, Univ. of MN Law Council; **OTHER ACT & HONORS:** Recipient, Professor of the Year Award, OH State Univ. Coll. of Law, 1978; **HOME ADD:** 4608 Emerson Ave. South, Minneapolis, MN 55409; **BUS ADD:** 555 Pillsbury Ctr., Minneapolis, MN 55402, (612)375-1138.

KARAS, Steven Lawrence——B: Oct. 11, 1951, Detroit, MI, *Leasing Dir.*, Ramco-Gershenson, Inc.; **PRIM RE ACT:** Developer; **SERVICES:** Shopping ctr. devel.; **REP CLIENTS:** Full range of shopping ctr. tenants; **PREV EMPLOY:** RE Mgr., The Kroger Co., 1973-1978; **PROFL AFFIL & HONORS:** ICSC; Detroit Board of Realtors; **EDUC:** BA, 1973, Mktg., MI State Univ.; **GRAD EDUC:** MBA, 1980, Fin., Wayne State Univ.; **HOME ADD:** 5340 Fox Ridge Dr., W. Bloomfield, MI 48033, (313)661-4529; **BUS ADD:** Suite 201, 31313 Northwestern Hwy., Farmington Hills, MI 48018, (313)851-8300.

KARCH, Samuel——*PH Engineer*, General Instrument Corp.; **PRIM RE ACT:** Property Manager; **BUS ADD:** 1775 Broadway, New York, NY 10019, (212)974-8700.*

KAREM, Michael G.——B: Oct. 29, 1946, Louisville, KY, *Dep. Asst. Sec. - Multi-family Housing Programs*, HUD; **PRIM RE ACT:** Attorney, Builder; **PREV EMPLOY:** Hollenbach, Belilies, Bakes & Karem, Louisuille, KY; **PROFL AFFIL & HONORS:** KY Bar Assn., US Supreme Court; **EDUC:** BA, 1969, Hist., Western KY Univ.; **GRAD EDUC:** JD, 1972, Law, Univ. of Louisville, Louisville, KY; **OTHER ACT & HONORS:** Pres. Reagan's Transition Team (HUD), 1980; **HOME ADD:** 14508 Triple Crown Place, Gaithersburg, MD, (301)963-4855; **BUS ADD:** 451 Seventh St. SW, Washington, DC 20410, (202)755-6495.

KARL, Peter A., III——B: Nov. 17, 1953, Utica, NY, *CPA/Tax Atty.*, Pellegrino and Karl; **PRIM RE ACT:** Attorney; **SERVICES:** Tax advice & fin.; **PROFL AFFIL & HONORS:** Atty./CPA; **EDUC:** BBA, 1975, Pre Law/Acctg., Notre Dame; **GRAD EDUC:** JD, 1978, Albany Law School; MBA, 1979, RPI; **HOME ADD:** Winship Rd., New Hartford, NY 13413, (315)735-4934; **BUS ADD:** 1602 Sunset Ave., Utica, NY 13502, (315)733-0417.

KARLIN, L. Scott——B: Aug. 28, 1948, Brooklyn, NY, *Atty. & Real Estate Broker*; **PRIM RE ACT:** Attorney; **SERVICES:** Real Estate Litigation, Synd., Partnerships., creative fin., exch., comml. leases, Broker Commission Disputes; **PROFL AFFIL & HONORS:** CA Bar, RE Sect.; Orange Cty. Bar, RE Sect.; Amer. Bar Real Prop., Intl. Law Sect.; **EDUC:** BA, 1969, Phil., UCLA; **GRAD EDUC:** MA, 1976, Phil., Univ. of CA, Irvine; JD, 1979, Law, Loyola Law School; **EDUC HONORS:** Magna Cum Laude grad., Cum Laude, Thomas More Law Soc., Intl. Law Rev., Amer. Jurisprudence Award; **OTHER ACT & HONORS:** Pres. Walnut Sq. Homeowners Assn.; **BUS ADD:** 13522 Newport Ave., Ste. 202, Tustin, CA 92680, (714)731-3283.

KARLTON, John S.——B: Aug. 1, 1929, NY, NY, *Pres.*, J.S. Karlton Co.; **PRIM RE ACT:** Owner/Investor, Syndicator; **SERVICES:** Appraiser dept., prop. mgmt.; **EDUC:** BS, 1950, Acctg., Long Island Univ.; **GRAD EDUC:** MBA, 1955, Bus., RE, NY Univ.; **MIL SERV:** US Army, Sgt., Korea; **BUS ADD:** 100N Biscayne Blvd., Miami, FL 33132.

KARMALI, Mansur——B: Dec. 25, 1937, Kenya, Africa, *Pres.*, Pottery & Garden Supply Co.; **PRIM RE ACT:** Broker, Developer, Owner/Investor, Syndicator; **SERVICES:** investor, promoter, Fin. Serv.; **EDUC:** BS, BBA, 1959, London Univ.; **OTHER ACT & HONORS:** Rotary Club; **HOME ADD:** 15905 SE 43rd St., Bellevue, WA 98006, (206)747-0576; **BUS ADD:** 15905 SE 43rd. St., Belleview, WA 98006, (206)822-1666.

KARNES, David——*Exec. Asst.*, Department of Housing and Urban Development, Ofc. of Secy./Under Secy.; **PRIM RE ACT:** Lender; **BUS ADD:** 451 Seventh St., S.W., Washington, DC 20410, (202)755-7123.*

KARP, Harvey——*Pres.*, Monogram Industries, Inc.; **PRIM RE ACT:** Property Manager; **BUS ADD:** 100 Wilshire Blvd., Santa Monica, CA 90401, (213)451-8151.*

KARP, Jane Hausman——B: NY, *Pres.*, JHK Investments; **PRIM RE ACT:** Developer, Owner/Investor; **EDUC:** BA, 1964, Adelphi Univ.; **HOME ADD:** 455 E. 57th St., New York, NY 10022, (212)888-0370; **BUS ADD:** 455 East 57th St., New York, NY 10022, (212)888-0270.

KARP, Kenneth N.——B: Sept. 25, 1935, Toronto, ON, *Partner in charge of RE*, Goodman & Goodman; **PRIM RE ACT:** Attorney, Developer; **REP CLIENTS:** The Cadillac Fairview Corp., Ltd.; The Georgion Building Corp.; **PROFL AFFIL & HONORS:** Can. Bar Assn., Can. Tax Found., LLB QC; **EDUC:** 1957, Pol. Sci. & Econ., Univ. of Toronto; LLB, 1960, Law School of Univ. of Toronto; **HOME ADD:** 3 Chieftain Cres., Willowdale, Ont., Can.; **BUS ADD:** 20 Queen St. W., Suite 3000, Toronto, Ont, Canada.

KARPE, Robert W.——*Govt. Natl. Mortgage Assn. Pres.*, Department of Housing and Urban Development, Ofc. of Secy./Under Secy.; **PRIM RE ACT:** Lender; **BUS ADD:** 451 Seventh St., S.W., Washington, DC 20410, (202)755-5926.*

KARPEL, Philip F.——B: July 3, 1942, New Haven, CT, *Atty.*, Dzialo, Pickett & Allen, PC; **PRIM RE ACT:** Attorney; **SERVICES:** Legal; **PREV EMPLOY:** Law Clerk for Justice Elmor Ryan of CT Supreme Ct.; **PROFL AFFIL & HONORS:** ABA; CT Bar Assn., Member of CT Bar Assn. House of Delegates; Member of CT Conference of Realtors and Lawyers; Member of Exec. Comm. of Real Prop. Sect. of CT Bar Assn.; **EDUC:** BS, 1964, History/Poli. Sci., Holy Cross Coll.; **GRAD EDUC:** LLB, 1967, Law, Univ. of CT School of Law; **EDUC HONORS:** Member/Associate Editor of Bd. of Law Review; **HOME ADD:** 63 Meadowood Dr., Middletown, CT 06457, (203)347-8752; **BUS ADD:** 55 High St., PO Box 661, Middleton, CT 06457, (203)346-8676.

KARR, Jean B.——B: Oct. 26, 1940, Oak Park, IL, *Pres./Fee Appraiser*, Karr & Associates, Inc.; **PRIM RE ACT:** Broker, Appraiser; **SERVICES:** Full RE servs.; **REP CLIENTS:** As fee appraiser, FHA, Relocation Servs., Fin. Inst.; **PREV EMPLOY:** VP, River Forest State B&T Co., River Forest, IL, 1960-1977; **PROFL AFFIL & HONORS:** NAR; AR Realtors Assn.; Rogers Bd. of Realtors; Nat. Assn. of Ind. Fee Appraisers; Nat. Assn. of RE Appraisers; **EDUC:** Manhattanville Coll.; Econ., Barat Coll.; **OTHER ACT & HONORS:** League of Women Voters, Treas.; **HOME ADD:** Rt. 6, Box 44, Rogers, AR 72756; **BUS ADD:** Rt. 6, Box 44, Rogers, AR 72756, (501)636-9349.

KARTALIS, Sam G.——B: Mar. 29, 1937, Sharon, PA, *Executive VP*, Henry S. Miller Co., Comml./ Retail; **OTHER RE ACT:** Brokerage/Mgr., mktg., admin., development, investments; **SERVICES:** Prop. leasing, sales; synd. of comml. prop; prop. mgmt.; devel.of shopping ctrs., warehouses, offices, apts.; const. mgmt.; consulting, REIT; prop. acquisiton; **REP CLIENTS:** Retail comml. and inst. clients/investors in comml. props.; **PREV EMPLOY:** Westinghouse Electric; General Motors Corp.; **PROFL AFFIL & HONORS:** TX RE Broker, CCIM CAndidate, ICSC, NASD Securities Salesman, ULI, RE Instr. Brookhaven Coll.; **EDUC:** 8A, 1959, Math./engrg., PA State Univ.; **GRAD EDUC:** MBA Candidate, Math./engrg., Rutgers Univ., Monmouth Coll., Univ. of Pittsburgh, Univ. of Dallas; **MIL SERV:** US Navy, Lt.; Destroyer Duty; **OTHER ACT & HONORS:** Instructor of Comml. RE, Brookhaven Coll., Dallas, TX; **HOME ADD:** 6921 Clearhaven Dr., Dallas, TX 75248, (214)386-4835; **BUS ADD:** 2001 Bryan Tower 30 fl., Dallas, TX 75201, (214)748-9171.

KARTH, Frank J.——B: Nov. 20, 1943, Milwaukee, WI, *Rgnl. VP*, Mutual of New York, RE and Mort. Investment; **PRIM RE ACT:** Lender, Owner/Investor; **PROFL AFFIL & HONORS:** Member, AIREA; **EDUC:** BS, 1967, RE, Econ., Univ. of WI; **MIL SERV:** USMC; **HOME TEL:** (312)530-0481; **BUS ADD:** One East Wacker, Chicago, IL 60601, (312)644-6560.

KARTSOTIS, C.——B: Jan. 25, 1932, Bethlehem, PA, *Broker, Mgr.*, John W. Moneghan Realtors; **PRIM RE ACT:** Broker, Appraiser, Property Manager; **PROFL AFFIL & HONORS:** Allentown Lehigh Cty Bd. of Realtors, Bethlehem Bd. of Realtors, PA Realtors Par Excellent Award; **EDUC:** BS, 1952, PA State Univ.; **MIL SERV:** USA, Pfc., Letter of Commendation from General for invention; **OTHER ACT & HONORS:** Whitehall Township Planning Comm., Free & Accepted Masonic Lodge Stanley Goodwin, Bethlehem, PA, AHEPA Lodge, Allentown, PA, St. Nicholas Greek Orthodox Church, Bethlehem, PA; **HOME ADD:** 4020 Hamilton St., Allentown, PA 18104, (215)395-5654; **BUS ADD:** Rte. 222, Rd 1, Wescosville, PA 18106, (215)398-1776.

KARTY, Rudy——B: Jan. 12, 1912, Burwell, NE, *Broker Owner*, Karty/Realtors; **PRIM RE ACT:** Broker; **PROFL AFFIL & HONORS:** NRA, CAR, CRB, GRI; **EDUC:** BA, 1947, French, UCLA; **GRAD EDUC:** MA, 1951, French, UCLA; **MIL SERV:** USAF; **HOME ADD:** 2063 Dewberry Ct., Westlake Village, CA 91361; **BUS ADD:** 32129 Lindero Cyn. 110, Westlake Village, CA 91361, (213)889-5300.

KARVEL, Dr. George R.——B: Dec. 8, 1941, Rochester, MN, *Prof. and Holder of MN Chair in RE*, St. Cloud State Univ., Coll. of Bus.; **PRIM RE ACT:** Consultant, Owner/Investor, Instructor; **OTHER RE ACT:** Author; **SERVICES:** Litigation consultant, RE Anti Trust, Educ. consultant; **REP CLIENTS:** NAR, Mpls. Bd. of Realtors, MN Assn. of Realtors, Gaston Snow & Ely Bartlett - Boston, Reuben & Proctor, Chicago; Lukins Annis Shrine, Etc. - Spokane, Robins, Zelle, Larson & Kaplan, Minneapolis; **PREV EMPLOY:** Southern IL Univ., Univ. of WI - LaCross, Univ. of CO; **PROFL AFFIL & HONORS:** AREUEA, Realtor, Honor Socs.: Phi Kappa Phi, Beta Alpha Psi; **EDUC:** BS, 1969, Fin., RE, Univ. of CO; **GRAD EDUC:** MS & DBA, 1971 & 1978, Acctg., Fin., Econ., Univ. of CO; **EDUC HONORS:** Wall St. Journal Award in Fin., 1969, Past Presidents Manuscript Award, NAA - 1973 & MBA Post Doctoral Fellowship - 1981; **MIL SERV:** US Army, PFC, American Defense Serv. Medal; **OTHER ACT & HONORS:** Co-author RE Principles & Practices, 6th Ed.; authored numerous articles published in profl. journals; RE Educ. Advisory Panel, St. of MN Dept. of Commerce, 1980-81; **HOME ADD:** 19 Halliday Rd., St. Cloud, MN 56301; **BUS ADD:** St. Cloud, MN 56301, (612)255-3067.

KASH, Lawrence S.——B: Sept. 23, 1941, Perry Cty., KY, *Pres.*, Rotan Mosle Realty Investments, Inc.; **PRIM RE ACT:** Broker, Consultant, Developer, Syndicator; **SERVICES:** Limited partnership interests in real estate projects; **PREV EMPLOY:** Sr. VP, Mitchell Energy and Devel. Corp., 1972-1976; James W. Rouse & Co., Inc., Asst. VP, 1969-1972; **PROFL AFFIL & HONORS:** FL Bar Assn.; **EDUC:** AB, 1964, Pol. Sci., Bucknell Univ.; **GRAD EDUC:** JD, 1967, George Washington Univ. Law School; **EDUC HONORS:** Grad. Fellow, 1968-1969; **MIL SERV:** U.S. Army, Lt.; **OTHER ACT & HONORS:** Pres., Houston Golf Assn.; **HOME ADD:** 2613 S Wildwind Cir., The Woodlands, TX 77380, (713)367-2285; **BUS ADD:** 1700 S Tower, Pennzoil Place, Houston, TX 77002, (713)236-3370.

KASLIK, Michael S.——B: Feb. 18, 1949, Grosse Pointe, MI, Private Practice; **PRIM RE ACT:** Broker, Owner/Investor, Property Manager; **OTHER RE ACT:** CPA Investment Counselor; **SERVICES:** Financial analysis and the structuring of new investments, major acquisitions & dispositions of property; **PREV EMPLOY:** CPA with Arthur Young & Company; **PROFL AFFIL & HONORS:** Amer. Inst. of CPA; MI Inst. of Certified Accountants; a Licensed MI RE Broker; **EDUC:** BBA, 1971, Acctg., Univ. of MI; **EDUC HONORS:** Beta Alpha Psi (Accounting Honorary); **OTHER ACT & HONORS:** Univ. of MI Club of Ann Arbor; Ferrari Owners Club of Amer.; **HOME ADD:** 1123 Vesper, Ann Arbor, MI 48103, (313)662-2919; **BUS ADD:** Ann Arbor, MI 48104, (313)995-4455.

KASPER, Benjamin——B: Oct. 19, 1915, Jersey City, NJ, *Pres.*, Ben Kasper Real Estate Inc.; **PRIM RE ACT:** Broker, Consultant, Appraiser, Developer, Lender, Builder, Owner/Investor, Property Manager, Syndicator; **MIL SERV:** Field Artillery, Sgt.; **OTHER ACT & HONORS:** Suffolk Cty. RE Bd.; **HOME ADD:** 45 Aberdeen Rd., Hauppauge, NY 11787, (516)265-2480; **BUS ADD:** 325 Nesconset Hwy., Hauppauge, NY 11788, (516)724-2244.

KASPER, Thomas A.——B: Apr. 17, 1953, Philadelphia, PA, *Vice President*, Salomon Brothers, Investment Banking; **OTHER RE ACT:** Investment Banker; **SERVICES:** Structuring of RE Securities; **REP CLIENTS:** Major Corps. and Fin. Instns.; **EDUC:** BA, 1975, Econs., St. Lawrence Univ., Canton, NY; **GRAD EDUC:** MBA, 1977, Fin., Acctg. and Statistics, Univ. of Chicago; **EDUC HONORS:** Magna Cum Laude, Phi Beta Kappa; **HOME ADD:** 422 State St., Brooklyn, NY 11217, (212)522-1186; **BUS ADD:** One New York Plaza, New York, NY 10004, (212)747-3388.

KASS, Benny L.——B: Aug. 20, 1936, Chicago, IL, *Partner*, Kass & Skalet; **PRIM RE ACT:** Attorney; **SERVICES:** Gen. practice; **REP CLIENTS:** Devel., tenant organizations, sellers & buyers of resid. RE; **PROFL AFFIL & HONORS:** Commr., Nat. Conference on Uniform St. Laws; **EDUC:** BS, 1957, Journalism, Northwestern Univ.; **GRAD EDUC:** LLB, LLM, 1960, 1967, Law, George Washington Law School, Univ. of MI Law School; **MIL SERV:** USAF, 1st Lt.; **HOME ADD:** 4860 Linnean Ave. NW, Washington, DC 20008, (202)966-4860; **BUS ADD:** 1528 18th St. NW, Washington, DC 20036, (202)797-2300.

KASS, Franklin E.——B: Aug. 31, 1943, Columbus, OH, *Managing Partner*, Continental Props.; **PRIM RE ACT:** Developer, Owner/Investor, Property Manager; **PREV EMPLOY:** Chmn. of the Bd., Continental Office Furniture & Supply Corp.; **PROFL AFFIL & HONORS:** Natl. Assn. of Indus. and Office Parks, Member Young Presidents Org.; **EDUC:** BS, 1965, Fin. and RE, OH State Univ.; **EDUC HONORS:** Phi Eta Sigma -Financial Honorary; **OTHER ACT & HONORS:** OH Commodore, 1/PO; **HOME ADD:** 98 N. Drexel, Columbus, OH 43209, (614)253-2759; **BUS ADD:** 10170 Morse Rd., Columbus, OH 43229, (614)846-5010.

KASS, Stephen Brent——B: Dec. 2, 1946, Ellenville, NY, *Exec. VP*, Harmet Associates, Inc.; **PRIM RE ACT:** Consultant, Appraiser, Syndicator; **SERVICES:** Gen. mgmt. consulting, packaging for synd., pro-forma analysis, corp. & project valuations, corp. acquisitions & mergers; **REP CLIENTS:** First City Fin., Vancouver, Markborough Props. Limited, Toronto, Diversified Mort. Investors, FL, Monarch Homes, Houston, L.B. Nelson Corp., CA; **PROFL AFFIL & HONORS:** Harvard Bus. School Alumni Assn.; Harvard Bus. School Assn. of So. CA; **EDUC:** BA, 1970, Creative Writing/Eng. Lit., Univ. of NE; **GRAD EDUC:** MBA, 1975, Gen. Mgmt., Harvard Bus. School; JD, 1973, Gen. Law Curriculum, CA Western School of Law; **EDUC HONORS:** Dean's List, Fellowship Recipient, Dean's Award; **HOME ADD:** 8211 Lookout Mountain Ave., Los Angeles, CA 90046, (213)654-9633; **BUS ADD:** 16000 Ventura Blvd., Suite 908, Encino, CA 91436, (213)906-2200.

KASSELL, Burton R.——B: Nov. 11, 1937, NY, NY, *Pres.*, Pico Alexander Capital Corp.; **PRIM RE ACT:** Owner/Investor, Syndicator; **PROFL AFFIL & HONORS:** RESSI; **EDUC:** BBA, 1958, Bus., Baruch Coll.; **BUS ADD:** 1700 Broadway, New York, NY 10019, (212)362-8000.

KASSIS, Gregory——B: Oct. 2, 1947, Sacramento, CA, *Owner*, Bus. Mgmt. Servs.; **PRIM RE ACT:** Consultant, Property Manager; **EDUC:** 1969, Fin., Univ. of Santa Clara; **BUS ADD:** 530 Blackwood St., Sacramento, CA 95815, (916)442-0120.

KASSNER, Milton——B: Nov. 8, 1926, Boston, MA, *Mgr. of Planning & Engrg.*, The Stop and Shop Cos., Inc.; **PRIM RE ACT:** Engineer; **SERVICES:** Planning and engrg. for retail chain; **PROFL AFFIL & HONORS:** Amer. Soc. of Civil Engrs.; Nat. Assn. of Profl. Engrs.; **EDUC:** BS, 1951, Civil Engrg., Northeastern Univ.; **MIL SERV:** US Army, 1944-1946, Pvt.; **HOME ADD:** 11 Lawrence Rd., Brookline, MA 02146, (617)277-3122; **BUS ADD:** POB 369, Boston, MA 02101, (617)463-4441.

KATELL, Gerald L.——B: Jan. 29, 1941, NY, NY, *Pres.*, W & K Co.; **PRIM RE ACT:** Developer, Builder, Owner/Investor; **SERVICES:** Devel. of over 1,500,000 sq. ft. of indus. and office bldgs. in office/indus. parks in past 5 yrs.; **REP CLIENTS:** Great Western S & L Assn., Wang, Arrow Electronics, Pertec Computer Corp., Prime Computer, Oasis Petroleum Corp., Raytheon, Teledyne, Burroughs; **PREV EMPLOY:** Pres., Parking Structures Intl., Mgr. RE Devel., Simpson Timber Co., Pres., Farwest Capital Co.; **PROFL AFFIL & HONORS:** Young Pres. Org., Nat. Assn. Indus. and Office Parks, Amer. Soc. of Civil Engrs.; **EDUC:** BS, 1962, CE, MA Inst. of Tech.; **GRAD EDUC:** MBA, 1964, Mgmt. sci., Stanford Univ. Grad. Sch. of Bus.; **EDUC HONORS:** Tau Beta Pi, Sigma Xi, Chi Epsilon, Dean's List 8 semesters, Grad. in top 10%, Grad. 3rd in class of 196; **OTHER ACT & HONORS:** Regency Club, Jack Kramer Club, Dir., The Meister Co.; **BUS ADD:** 2716 Ocean Park Blvd. Box 2114, Santa Monica, CA 90406, (213)450-0779.

KATSANIS, James A.——B: Nov. 16, 1931, Cincinnati, OH, *Atty.*, Katsanis, Eilers and Haill; **PRIM RE ACT:** Attorney; **SERVICES:** RE & Probate & Trusts; **PROFL AFFIL & HONORS:** OH & Cincinnati Bar Assn.; TX Bar Assn.; **EDUC:** AB, 1953, Am. Hist., Pol. Sci., Univ. of Cincinnati; **GRAD EDUC:** JD, 1955, Law, Univ. of Cincinnati; **MIL SERV:** USAF, Lt. Cdr.; **HOME ADD:** 5280 Ivy Farm Ln., Cincinnati, OH 45243, (513)561-7387; **BUS ADD:** 2004 Dubois Tower, 511 Walnut St., Cincinnati, OH 45202, (513)421-5340.

KATSAROS, Basil S.——B: May 5, 1947, Denver, CO., *Owner*, Katasaros & Assocs.; **PRIM RE ACT:** Appraiser, Consultant; **SERVICES:** Comml. & Resid. Appraising; **PROFL AFFIL & HONORS:** Soc. of RE Appraisers, AIREA, SRPA, MAI; **GRAD EDUC:** BA, 1969, Poli. Sci., Univ. of CO; **HOME ADD:** 6696 Zang St., Arvada, CO 80004, (303)423-1217; **BUS ADD:** 650 Grant St., Denver, CO 80203, (303)839-1002.

KATSKEE, Melvin R.——B: Nov. 19, 1945, Omaha, NE, *Second VP & Gen. Atty.*, The Omaha National Bank, Legal Dept.; **PRIM RE ACT:** Attorney; **PROFL AFFIL & HONORS:** NE State Bar Assn., ABA; **EDUC:** AB, 1967, Hist., Eng., Philosophy, Creighton Univ.; **GRAD EDUC:** JD, 1970, Gen. Legal Educ. Course, Northwestern Univ (1967-1968), Univ. of NE (1968-1970); **EDUC HONORS:** Cum Laude; **OTHER ACT & HONORS:** Author of numerous articles; *Who's Who in Amer. Law*; *Who's Who in NE*; *Outstanding Young Men of Amer.* (1974); **HOME ADD:** 5617 Erskine St., Omaha, NE 68104, (402)556-6892; **BUS ADD:** 17th & Farnam St., Omaha, NE 68102, (402)348-7907.

KATZ, Aron B.——B: Feb. 15, 1936, NY City, *Pres.*, American Midwest Securities, Inc. & The Katz Group, Inc.; **PRIM RE ACT:** Attorney, Developer; **SERVICES:** Devel. and synd. servs. to other devels.; **REP CLIENTS:** Alltex Const., Inc.; Summers Investments, Inc., Dallas, TX; Harlon Group, Tamarac, FL; Duke, Inc., San Antonio, TX; **PREV EMPLOY:** Partner, Proskauer, Rose, Goetz & Mendelsohn 1960-75; **PROFL AFFIL & HONORS:** NY Bar; CO Bar; US Supreme Court; **EDUC:** BA, 1957, Philosophy, Colgate Univ.; **GRAD EDUC:** JD, 1960, Law, Yale Law School; **HOME ADD:** 388 Alder Ln., Boulder, CO 80302, (303)443-6942; **BUS ADD:** 1035 Pearl St. 5th Fl., Boulder, CO 80302, (303)449-7780.

KATZ, Barry S.——B: Dec. 25, 1942, Chicago, IL, *Pres.*, Omnibus Real Estate, Inc.; **PRIM RE ACT:** Consultant, Instructor, Property Manager; **PROFL AFFIL & HONORS:** NAR, CREB, IAR, IREM, CPM; Mgr. of the Year 1976; Acad. of Authors; Pres., Chicago Chap., 1979; **EDUC:** BS in Urban Land Economics, 1965, RE - Urban Land Econ., Univ. of IL; **MIL SERV:** US Army, 1965-1971, Capt., Army Commendation Medal; **HOME ADD:** 2807 Lexington Lane, Highland Park, IL 60035, (312)432-2868; **BUS ADD:** 4801 W. Peterson Ave., Ste. 209, Chicago, IL 60646, (312)725-1600.

KATZ, Daniel B.——B: Aug. 17, 1945, *Pres.*, Melville Realty Co., Inc.; **OTHER RE ACT:** Retail RE, Site Selection; **PROFL AFFIL & HONORS:** Intl. Council of Shopping Ctrs.; NACORE; NY RE Bd.; **EDUC:** BA, 1967, PA State Univ.; **BUS ADD:** 3000 Westchester Ave., Harrison, NY 10528, (914)253-8000.

KATZ, Dean Z.——B: Apr. 24, 1946, Chicago, IL, *Pres.*, The Katz Mgmt. Group, Inc.; **PRIM RE ACT:** Owner/Investor, Consultant, Broker; **SERVICES:** Total operations mgmt. for passive and actively involved clientele; **REP CLIENTS:** Pvt. investors, synds. and instl. owners of large apt. communities throughout the US; **PREV EMPLOY:** VP-Allen Assn., 1977-78; VP-LaSalle partners, Inc., 1972-76; **PROFL AFFIL & HONORS:** Nat. Apt. Assn., Columbus Apt. Assn., Nat. Apt. Council; **EDUC:** BSBA, 1969, Fin., RE, Roosevelt Univ.; **GRAD EDUC:** Certificate in RE, 1971, Roosevelt Univ.; **EDUC HONORS:** Assoc. Prof. of RE; **MIL SERV:** US Army, Spec. E-5, 1969-75; **OTHER ACT & HONORS:** YMCA North, Bd. of Mgmt.; Museum of Art, Columbus Symphony Orchestra; Columbus Apt. Assn., Bd. of Trs.; **BUS ADD:** 150 E. Wilson Bridge Rd., Worthington, OH 43085, (614)885-2400.

KATZ, Donald H.——B: May 16, 1942, Boston, MA, Law Offices of Donald H. Katz; **PRIM RE ACT:** Attorney; **SERVICES:** Legal servs. for indivs. and entities involved in devel. and ownership and mgmt. of comml. investment props.; **REP CLIENTS:** Owners, investors, lenders, mgrs. and devels. of rental housing and other comml. props.; **PREV EMPLOY:** Fanger & Birnbaum, 101 Tremont St., Boston, MA; Bernkopf, Goodman & Houghton, Boston, MA; **PROFL AFFIL & HONORS:** MA Conveyancers Assn., Amer. Trial Lawyers Assn., MA Trial Lawyers Assn., Greater Boston RE Bd. - Rental Housing Assn., ABA, MA Bar Assn., Boston Bar Assn.; **EDUC:** BS in BA, 1963, Bus. Admin., Boston Univ., Boston, MA; **GRAD EDUC:** JD, 1965, Law, Boston Univ., Boston, MA; **MIL SERV:** US Army, 1965-1967, Military Police Corps.; **HOME ADD:** 35 Dunster Rd., Sudbury, MA 01776, (617)443-3226; **BUS ADD:** Ten Post Office Sq., Boston, MA 02109, (617)482-4884.

KATZ, Edward——B: July 5, 1933, Brooklyn, NY, *Partner*, Downtown Realty Co.; **PRIM RE ACT:** Broker, Owner/Investor; **SERVICES:** Parking consultant & loft bldg. consultant; **PREV EMPLOY:** Pres. of The Katz Parking System, Inc.; **PROFL AFFIL & HONORS:** Metropolitan Realty Club; Nat. Parking Assn.; **EDUC:** BA, 1956, Econ., Hobart Coll.; **HOME ADD:** 27 Windmill Cir., Stamford, CT 06903, (203)322-3598; **BUS ADD:** 132 Nassau St., New York, NY 10038, (212)889-4444.

KATZ, Dr. Frederick——B: Aug. 7, 1923, Europe, *Pres.*, Dr. Frederick Katz & Assoc. Agency, Inc., F.A.F. Realty Corp.; **PRIM RE ACT:** Broker, Consultant, Engineer, Appraiser, Owner/Investor, Property Manager; **SERVICES:** Consultant, broker and appraiser for dental, medical & profl. practices; **PROFL AFFIL & HONORS:** NY & Manhasset Bd. of RE, ACS, BOMA, FACEB; **EDUC:** BS Engrg., 1949, Mining, Bldg. & Maintenance, Engrg., Bucharest Univ. & Poly. Inst., Bucharest, Roumania; **GRAD EDUC:** MS Engrg., MBA, PhD, 1949, 1959, 1972, Econ., Appraisal, Establishment of Health Related Facilities, NY Univ.; **EDUC HONORS:** Magna Cum Laude, Fleming Medal for Sci. 1972, First Natl. Award, 1972; **MIL SERV:** Israel, Paratrooper, Lt. Col., 1949 Independence, 1956 Suez, 1967 6 Day War; **OTHER ACT & HONORS:** NY Acad. of Sci.; **HOME ADD:** 96-08 70th Ave., Forest Hills, NY 11375; **BUS ADD:** 42-27 Union St., Flushing, NY 11355, (212)445-9797.

KATZ, Lawrence S.——B: Feb. 22, 1912, Milwaukee, WI, *VP*, First Bank - Milwaukee, RE; **PRIM RE ACT:** Consultant, Banker, Lender, Instructor; **PREV EMPLOY:** WI Dir. FHA; **PROFL AFFIL & HONORS:** Pres. WI Mort. Bankers Assn.; **GRAD EDUC:** JD, 1934, Law, Marquette Univ.; **OTHER ACT & HONORS:** Atty., WI Indus. Commn. 1936-46; Chmn. WI Housing Fin. Authority 1973-76; **HOME ADD:** 4647 N. Lake Dr., Milwaukee, WI 53202, (414)964-1522; **BUS ADD:** 201-W Wisconsin Ave., Milwaukee, WI 53202, (414)278-5996.

KATZ, M. Marvin——B: May 12, 1953, Laredo, TX, *Part.*, De Lange, Huldspeth, Pitman & Kitz; **PRIM RE ACT:** Attorney, Owner/Investor; **REP CLIENTS:** Devels., investors & lenders in connection with resid. & comml. props.; **PROFL AFFIL & HONORS:** Member City of Houston Planning Comm., Houston RE Lawyers Council, Chmn Fed. Courts Admission Comm., S. Sist. of TX Former Adjunct Prof. of Law, Univ. of Houston, Amer. Coll. of RE Lawyers; **EDUC:** BBA, 1954, TX A&M Univ.; **GRAD EDUC:** JD, 1959, Univ. of TX; **EDUC HONORS:** Articles Editor, TX Law Review, Order of the Coif; **MIL SERV:** USAF, Capt.; **HOME ADD:** 5714 Jackwood, Houston, TX, (713)871-9898; **HOME TEL:** (713)774-9877; **BUS ADD:** 11 Greenway Plaza, 2800 Summit Tower, Houston, TX 77046.

KATZ, Marshall——*Pres.*, Papercraft Corp.; **PRIM RE ACT:** Property Manager; **BUS ADD:** Papercraft Park, Pittsburgh, PA 15238, (412)362-8000.*

KATZ, Richard J.——B: Oct. 14, 1941, Pittsburgh, PA, *Pres.*, R.J. Katz & Co.; **PRIM RE ACT:** Broker, Consultant, Developer, Property Manager; **SERVICES:** Specialize in purchasing large props. for clients on fee basis, Industrial RE for corporate use; **REP CLIENTS:** Westinghouse Credit Corp., Gould RE Trust (ASE), Gen. Motors Corp., Trusthouse Forte, Equitable Life Assurance, Greyhound Corp., Storage Technology Corp.; **PREV EMPLOY:** Keyes Co., VP; **PROFL AFFIL & HONORS:** NAR; Realtors Nat. Mktg. Inst.; SIR, CCIM; SIR; **EDUC:** BBA, 1963, Mktg./Fin., Univ. of Pittsburgh; **GRAD EDUC:** 1973, Devel. of Comml. Props., Univ. of Miami; **EDUC HONORS:** Dean's List; **MIL SERV:** US Air. Nat. Guard; **HOME ADD:** 13155 Old Cutler Rd., Miami, FL 33156, (305)665-6850; **BUS ADD:** 255 Alhambra Cir., Suite 715, Coral Gables, FL 33134, (305)443-8802.

KAUFFMAN, David B.——B: Apr. 14, 1940, Philadelphia, PA, *RE Officer*, First Federal Savings and Loan Assn. of PA; **PRIM RE ACT:** Broker, Consultant, Banker, Property Manager; **SERVICES:** Problem loan supervision, service corp. coordination and secondary market underwriting; **PROFL AFFIL & HONORS:** Philadelphia Bd. of Realtors, RE Broker; **EDUC:** BA, 1962, Art Hist., Brown Univ.; **GRAD EDUC:** Fin Arts, Harvard Univ.; **EDUC HONORS:** Cum Laude with Honors in Art Hist.; **MIL SERV:** US Army Reserves; **OTHER ACT & HONORS:** Brown Univ. Club of Philadelphia, Officer and Bd. of Dir., Faculty of the Main Line School Night; Brown Univ. Assoc. Alumni Bd. of Dirs.; **HOME ADD:** 1524 Willowbrook Lane, Villanova, PA 19085, (215)525-2220; **BUS ADD:** Castor and Cottman Avenues, Philadelphia, PA 19111, (215)722-2000.

KAUFFMAN, Kenneth D.——B: Dec. 21, 1935, Noble Cty., IN, *Atty. at Law*, Beaman & Kauffman; **PRIM RE ACT:** Broker, Engineer, Attorney; **SERVICES:** RE Fin. and Investment Counselling; **REP CLIENTS:** Indiv., corps., realtors; **PREV EMPLOY:** IN State Highway Commn.; Gen. Telephone Co. of IN; **PROFL AFFIL & HONORS:** ABA; IN State Bar Assn.; Grant Cty. Bar Assn., State Bar Assn.; Amer. Soc. of Civ. Engrs.; **EDUC:** BSCE, 1961, IN Inst. of Tech., Ft. Wayne, IN; **GRAD EDUC:** JD, 1971, Law, IN Univ., Indianapolis, IN; **EDUC HONORS:** Cum Laude; **MIL SERV:** USN; 1954-56, E-4 (SKG-3); **HOME ADD:** 3211 Wildwood Dr., Marion, IN 46952, (317)662-7062; **BUS ADD:** Box 628, 120 E. 4th St., Marion, IN

46952, (317)662-6655.

KAUFMAN, Alan Jay——**B:** Mar. 15, 1948, Detroit, MI, *Sr. Partner*, Kaufman & Friedman, P.C.; **PRIM RE ACT:** Attorney; **SERVICES:** Legal; **REP CLIENTS:** Maj. Corps., local corps., indiv. and inst., including banks and ins. cos.; **PROFL AFFIL & HONORS:** Detroit, Oakland, MI and Amer. Bar Assns., Tax and R.E, Member Amer. Arbitration, serving on the panel for comml. disputes and R.E.; **EDUC:** BA, 1970, Fin. and Acctg., R.E., MI State Univ.; **GRAD EDUC:** JD, 1973, Bus. Tax, Univ. of Notre Dame; **EDUC HONORS:** High Honors in Tax; **OTHER ACT & HONORS:** V. Counsel of Rep. of Panama, 1975 to present; **HOME TEL:** (313)851-3392; **BUS ADD:** 400 Amer. Ctr., 27777 Franklin Rd., Southfield, MI 48034, (313)353-7550.

KAUFMAN, Eric P.——**B:** Nov. 27, 1948, Hartford, CT, *Part.*, Coordinated RE Services, Grp., The Mgmt Co.; **PRIM RE ACT:** Broker, Syndicator, Consultant, Property Manager; **OTHER RE ACT:** Dev. Consult, Asset Mgr.; **SERVICES:** RE Analysis, Dev. & Synd. Consulting, Investment Analysis, Prop. Mgmt.; **PROFL AFFIL & HONORS:** Pres. CT Chap. RESSI, IREM, Member BOMA, CPM; **EDUC:** BS, 1971, Intl. Bus. Mgmt., Boston Univ.; **MIL SERV:** USA, SP-4; **HOME ADD:** 11-C Talcott Forest Rd., Farmington, CT 06032, (203)678-9484; **BUS ADD:** P.O. Box 333, 5 Beechwood Rd., Farmington, CT 06032, (203)673-6331.

KAUFMAN, John Augustus——**B:** Sept. 3, 1936, Brunswick, GA, *Exec. VP*, Parker-Kaufman, Realtors & Insurors; **PRIM RE ACT:** Broker, Appraiser, Property Manager, Insuror; **SERVICES:** Full Service RE and Ins.; **REP CLIENTS:** Banks, S&L, Attys., Accountants, Corps., Indus.; **PROFL AFFIL & HONORS:** RM-AIREA, SRA; CPM; CRB; GRI; State of GA, Realtor of the Yr., 1969; Past Pres. GA Assn. Realtors - 1970; **EDUC:** AB, 1958, Econ., Mercer Univ., GA; **EDUC HONORS:** Blue Key; **MIL SERV:** US Army, QM Capt.; **OTHER ACT & HONORS:** Jaycees; C of C (Past Pres.); Rotary (Past Pres.); Amer. Cancer Soc. (Past Pres.); Chmn., Bd. of Tr., Brunswick Coll. Foundation; **HOME ADD:** Cottage 278, 33rd St., Sea Island, GA 31561, (912)638-3520; **BUS ADD:** 513 Gloucester St., POB 1797, Brunswick, GA 31521, (912)265-7711.

KAUFMAN, Lewis A.——**B:** Apr. 12, 1926, Pittsburgh, PA, *Pres.*, Lewis A. Kaufman Co., Realtors; **PRIM RE ACT:** Broker, Consultant, Developer, Builder, Owner/Investor, Property Manager, Syndicator; **SERVICES:** All; **PROFL AFFIL & HONORS:** Gr. Pittsburgh Bd. of Realtors, PA Realtors Assn., NAR, RNMA; **EDUC:** BA, 1950-51, Univ. of Pittsburgh; **MIL SERV:** USN, CPO; **OTHER ACT & HONORS:** Country Club - Dir.; Guest Lecturer Univ. of Pittsburgh; Lecturer, Many RE Seminars; **HOME ADD:** 2936 Beechwood Blvd., Pittsburgh, PA 15217, (412)521-6725; **BUS ADD:** 3203 Maryland Ave., N. Versailles, PA 15137, (412)243-2704.

KAUFMAN, Milton——**B:** NY, NY, *VP - Dir. of Mgmt.*, Swig, Weiler and Arnow Mgmt. Co., Inc.; **PRIM RE ACT:** Broker, Engineer; **OTHER RE ACT:** Management; **PREV EMPLOY:** Shubert Theaters, Mgmt.; **PROFL AFFIL & HONORS:** Assn. of Energy Engrs.; Lic. Profl. Engr., CA; Bd. of Dirs., Ave. of Amer. NY Assn.; RE Bd. of NY; **EDUC:** BSME, 1944, Engrg., OK State Univ.; **EDUC HONORS:** Hon. Engrg. Soc., Pi Tau Sigma; **MIL SERV:** USNR, Lt.j.g.; **HOME ADD:** 53 Shelter Ln., Roslyn Heights, NY 11577, (516)484-2081; **BUS ADD:** 1114 Ave. of Amer., NY, NY 10036, (212)869-9700.

KAUFMAN, Stuart——**B:** Feb. 28, 1944, Brooklyn, NY, *Sr. Assoc.*, Howard P. Hoffman Associates, Security Pacific Fin. Services Div. of Security Pacific Bank; **PRIM RE ACT:** Consultant, Developer; **SERVICES:** Packaging, devel., mktg., dispositon, etc. of corp. RE; **REP CLIENTS:** Corp. owners of surplus RE, The Stroh Companies, Security Pacific Bank; **PREV EMPLOY:** Dir. of Environmental Affairs and Environmental Counsel, Gulf & Western Industries Natural Resources Group, 1978-1980; Amer. Electric Power, 1974-1978; Pvt. Law Practice, 1971-1974; US Army Corps of Engrs., 1968-1970; **PROFL AFFIL & HONORS:** ABA, NY, DC and VA Bar Assns.; **EDUC:** BA, 1965, Hist., NYU; **GRAD EDUC:** JD,, 1968, Law, George Wash. Univ.; LLM, 1969, Natural Resources, George Wash. Univ.; **EDUC HONORS:** Deans List, US Army Corps. of Engrs.; **HOME ADD:** 118 Baker Hill Rd., Great Neck, NY 11023, (516)487-2063; **BUS ADD:** 100 Park Ave., NY, NY 10017, (212)883-0533.

KAUFMANN, Louis W., Jr.——**B:** June 7, 1941, Staten Island, NY, *Dir., Asset Mgmt. Div.*; **PRIM RE ACT:** Broker, Consultant, Property Manager; **SERVICES:** Sales, leasing and prop. mgmt. for resid., comml. and indus. prop.; **PROFL AFFIL & HONORS:** CPM, IREM, BOMA, Atlanta Bd. of Realtors; **EDUC:** BA, 1963, Poli. Sci., Wash. & Lee Univ.; **MIL SERV:** US Army, 1st Lt., ACM Intell.; **HOME ADD:** 125 Pine Lake Dr., Atlanta, GA 30327, (404)252-7659; **BUS ADD:** 1164 Spring St., Atlanta, GA 30309RE Professionals, Inc., (404)525-0440.

KAVAL, James A.——**B:** Sept. 7, 1939, Cleveland, OH, *Pres.; VP*, Cragin, Lang, Fres.& Smythe Securities, Inc.; **PRIM RE ACT:** Broker, Consultant, Owner/Investor, Syndicator; **SERVICES:** Investment RE brokerage, RE synd.; **PROFL AFFIL & HONORS:** Nat. Assn. of Securities Dealers, Inc.; Nat. Synd. Forum; RESSI; **EDUC:** BS, 1961, Chem. Engrg., Univ. of Notre Dame; **GRAD EDUC:** MBA, 1963, Stanford Univ.; **HOME ADD:** 10207 Lake Shore Blvd., Bratenahl, OH 44108, (216)249-2963; **BUS ADD:** 1801 E 9th St., Room 1200, Cleveland, OH 44114, (216)696-6050.

KAVANAGH, James L.——**B:** Mar. 17, 1916, Bay City, MI, *Pres.*, Kavanagh Co., PC; **PRIM RE ACT:** Broker, Consultant, Appraiser; **SERVICES:** RE investment counseling, appraisals; **REP CLIENTS:** Argonaut Realty Div., GM; Peoples Nat. Bank & Trust; MI Nat. Bank; 2nd Nat. Bank & Trust; DNR; HUD, etc.; **PREV EMPLOY:** Self-employed for 36 years; **PROFL AFFIL & HONORS:** Nat. Assn. of Re Appraisers; Comm. Apr. Assn., Chmn., Comm. to review bldg. codes; member of last local charter revision commn.; **EDUC:** BFA, 1939, Notre Dame Univ., Univ. of MI; **GRAD EDUC:** RE Evaluation; Constr., Univ. of MI; **EDUC HONORS:** Member Rams of Univ. of MI; **MIL SERV:** CMP, M/Sgt.; **OTHER ACT & HONORS:** Elks Lodge 88; **HOME ADD:** 802 S Warner, Bay City, MI 48706; **BUS ADD:** 802 S Warner Ave., Bay City, MI 48706, (517)893-1051.

KAVOUNAS, Edmond A.——**B:** Dec. 14, 1940, NY, NY, Sullivan, Smith & Kavounas; **PRIM RE ACT:** Owner/Investor, Broker; **PREV EMPLOY:** Mobil Land Devel. Corp., a subsidiary of Mobil Corp.; **PROFL AFFIL & HONORS:** Member of the Bar of the State of NY; Member of the CA State Bar; Member of the Assn. of the Bar of the City of NY; Member of the ABA; ULI, Atty.; **EDUC:** 1961, Hist., Cornell Univ.; **GRAD EDUC:** LLB, 1965, Fordham Law Sch.; **HOME ADD:** 99 Birch Ln., Greenwich, CT 06830, (203)661-3681; **BUS ADD:** 11th Fl. 505 Park Ave., NY, NY 10022, (212)750-4826.

KAWAMOTO, Edwin H.——**B:** Feb. 1, 1943, Honolulu, Hawaii, *Exec. VP & Counsel*, Adams Property Management Company; **PRIM RE ACT:** Broker, Consultant, Attorney, Appraiser, Property Manager, Syndicator; **SERVICES:** RE consulting, prop. mgmt., synd.; **REP CLIENTS:** Cal REIT and private partnerships; **PREV EMPLOY:** RE Consultant for Larry Smith & Co. 1969-1973, Appraiser for Hanford-Freund & Co. 1967-1969; **PROFL AFFIL & HONORS:** ABA, CA State Bar Assn., San Francisco, Bar Assn., and HI Bar Assn., CRA; **EDUC:** BBA, 1965, Acctg. and Bus. Econs., Univ. of HI, Honolulu; **GRAD EDUC:** MBA & JD, 1968 and 1973, RE & Urban Econ. (MBA program), Real Prop. & Tax (JD program), Univ. of CA Graduate School of Bus. Admin. (Berkeley); and Univ. of CA School of Law (Davis); **EDUC HONORS:** Magna Cum Laude, Bd. of Regents Scholarship, Phi Kappa Phi, Pi Sigma Epsilon; **HOME ADD:** 6062 Fairlane Dr., Oakland, CA 94611, (415)654-4696; **BUS ADD:** 601 Montgomery St., Suite 800, San Francisco, CA 94111, (415)433-1800.

KAY, Alan C.——**B:** July 5, 1932, Honolulu, HI, *Part., Pres., Alan C. Kay Atty. at Law, A Law Corp.*, Case, Kay & Lynch; **OTHER RE ACT:** RE; **SERVICES:** Legal-fin., loan documentation, prop. acquisitions, devel., leasing, gen. RE and bus. law; **REP CLIENTS:** GECC Fin. Corp., Bank of HI, First Hawaiian Bank, Molokai Ranch Ltd., Standard Oil of CA, Del Monte Corp., Hawaiian Electric Co., Ltd., Waitec Devel., Inc., MA Mutual Life Ins., Co.; **PROFL AFFIL & HONORS:** HI State & ABA; Amer. Arbitration Assn. Panel of Arbitrators, Dir. Bank of HI & Bancorp HI, Inc.; **EDUC:** BA, 1957, Hist., Princeton Univ.; **GRAD EDUC:** LLB, 1960, Law, Boalt Hall, Univ. of CA at Berkeley; **MIL SERV:** USMC, Cpl.; **OTHER ACT & HONORS:** Pres. & Trustee of Hawaiian Mission Childrens Soc.; Dir. of Fellowship Christian Athletes; Dir. of Good News Mission, HI State Prison; Community Associations; **HOME ADD:** 1990 Judd Hillside Rd., Honolulu, HI 96822, (808)941-8565; **BUS ADD:** PO Box 494, Honolulu, HI 96809, (808)547-5400.

KAY, Bruce A.——**B:** Sept. 19, 1950, Plattsburgh, NY, *Vice President*, Central Fidelity Bank, N.A., Construction Loan Division; **PRIM RE ACT:** Banker; **OTHER RE ACT:** Const. Lending; **SERVICES:** Construction Loan Origination, Underwriting and servicing; **REP CLIENTS:** Income property developers and land developers; **PROFL AFFIL & HONORS:** Mort. Bankers Assn., Amer. Bankers Assn.; Home Builders Assn.; Richmond Bd. of Realtors, Grad. School of Mort. Banking; Treasurer and Dir. of Home Builders Assn. of Richmond.; **EDUC:** AB, 1972, Econ., Colgate Univ.; **GRAD EDUC:** MC, 1976, Banking and Fin., Univ. of Richmond; **EDUC HONORS:** Departmental honors in Econ.; Member Econ. Honor Soc.; **OTHER ACT & HONORS:** West End Civitan Club of Richmond - Past Pres.; Eagle Scout; **HOME ADD:** 9605 Goneway Dr., Richmond, VA 23233, (804)270-4475; **BUS ADD:** PO Box 27602, Richmond, VA 23261,

(804)782-4236.

KAY, Jack R.——**B:** Mar. 15, 1948, *Corporate Dir., RE*, Susquenna Broadcasting Co.; **PRIM RE ACT:** Consultant, Developer, Regulator; **PREV EMPLOY:** City Plann. Commn. - Philadelphia; **PROFL AFFIL & HONORS:** Amer. Soc. of Plann. Officials, NAHRO, ASPA - Outstand. Achievement, Outstand. Young Men of America - 1980; **EDUC:** BA, 1970, Poli. Sci.; **GRAD EDUC:** MPA, 1972, Admin.; **OTHER ACT & HONORS:** VChrmn., Plann. Commn.; **HOME ADD:** 922 McKenzie St., York, PA 17403, (717)843-3145; **BUS ADD:** 140 E. Market St., York, PA 17403, (717)848-5500.

KAY, Richard R.——**B:** Aug. 27, 1919, Charleston, WV, *Dir. of Gen. Serv.., Asst. VP of 3 RE subs.*, Blue Cross of W PA, Gen. Serv.; **PRIM RE ACT:** Property Manager, Owner/Investor; **SERVICES:** Prop. Mgmt., Const. supervision, Space planning, Purchasing, Manage 7 corp.-owned prop. in Pittsburgh plus rental prop. in Erie, Altoona, Johnstown, and Butler, PA; **PREV EMPLOY:** (33 yrs. with Blue Cross); **PROFL AFFIL & HONORS:** Pres. - BOMA of Pittsburgh 1979-81, Chmn.-Pittsburgh/Allegheny Corp. for Energy Recovery 1981, "Real Prop. Administrator", BOMA Intl. "Cert. Admin. Mgr.", Adminis. Mgmt. Soc.; **EDUC:** BA, 1941, Eng. Comp. and Journalism (minor in Econ.), Univ. of Pittsburgh; **GRAD EDUC:** Master in Letters, 1949, Personnel Mgmt., Univ. of Pittsburgh; **EDUC HONORS:** Phi Eta Sigma (Nat. Freshman Scholastic Hon.) Omicron Delta Kappa (Nat. Activities Hon.); **MIL SERV:** USAF, 1st Lt.; **OTHER ACT & HONORS:** Member, Amer. Mgmt. Assn. Gen. and Admin. Serv. Council, 1969 to present; **HOME ADD:** 230 Lucille St., Glenshaw, PA 15116, (412)486-9399; **BUS ADD:** One Smithfield St., Pittsburgh, PA 15222, (412)255-7340.

KAYE, Joel M.——**B:** Dec. 12, 1953, Mt. Vernon, NY, *Partner*, Kaye & Effron, PC; **PRIM RE ACT:** Attorney; **SERVICES:** Gen. legal servs.; **PROFL AFFIL & HONORS:** Member, NE Land Title Assn., Sect. of real prop. probate and trust law, ABA; **EDUC:** BA, 1974, literature, American Univ.; **GRAD EDUC:** JD, 1977, Univ. of CT; **EDUC HONORS:** Grad. with Honors; **OTHER ACT & HONORS:** Member, Greenwich Rep. Town Meeting 1976-78, 1979-81; **HOME ADD:** 30 Riverside Ln., Riverside, CT 06878, (203)637-2288; **BUS ADD:** 165 W Putnam Ave., Greenwich, CT 06836, (203)622-1160.

KAYSSERIAN, Michael M.——**B:** Feb. 12, 1928, Detroit, MI, *Pres.*, B.H.K. Enterprises; **PRIM RE ACT:** Developer, Builder, Owner/Investor, Property Manager, Syndicator; **SERVICES:** Investment counseling, devel. and synd. of prop., prop. mgmt.; **REP CLIENTS:** Investors; **EDUC:** BBA, 1950, Engrg. Econ./Mktg., Univ. of Detroit; **GRAD EDUC:** MBA, 1957, Econ., Univ. of Detroit; **MIL SERV:** US Army, 2nd Lt.; **HOME ADD:** 1387 Three Mile, Grosse Pointe Park, MI 48230, (313)882-5159; **BUS ADD:** 1387 Three Mile, Grosse Pointe, MI 48230, (313)882-5159.

KEARNES, Selden S.——*VP & Secy.*, Southern Industries Corp.; **PRIM RE ACT:** Property Manager; **BUS ADD:** PO Box 1685, Mobile, AL 36601, (205)438-3531.*

KEARNEY, John E.——**B:** Sept. 27, 1939, St. Petersburg, FL, *Pres./Chmn.*, J.K. Financial; **PRIM RE ACT:** Consultant, Developer, Owner/Investor, Property Manager, Syndicator; **SERVICES:** Consultant/Joint Venture Partner; **REP CLIENTS:** Fin. Instns., Devels.; **PROFL AFFIL & HONORS:** AICPA, FICPA; **EDUC:** BS/BA, 1962, Acctg., Univ. of FL; **EDUC HONORS:** Deans List, Beta Alpha Psi Hon. Acctg. Frat.; **OTHER ACT & HONORS:** C of C, Comm. of 100, St. Petersburg Progress, Suncoasters; **HOME ADD:** One Beach Dr., St. Petersburg, FL 33701; **BUS ADD:** One Plaza, Suite #1500, St. Petersburg, FL 33701, (813)823-7234.

KEATING, Edwin L.——**B:** June 10, 1931, NY, NY, *Sr. VP*, The Pep'e Co.; **PRIM RE ACT:** Broker; **SERVICES:** Comml. broker, investment props.; **EDUC:** BBA, 1954, Fin., Boston Coll.; **MIL SERV:** US Army, Sgt.; **HOME ADD:** 181 N. Ridge St., Port Chester, NY 10573, (914)939-0018; **BUS ADD:** 670 White Plains Rd., Scarsdale, NY 10583, (914)472-5700.

KEATING, John S., Jr.——**B:** Apr. 25, 1932, Waterbury, CT, *Pres.*, J.S. Keating Properties, Inc.; **PRIM RE ACT:** Developer, Broker; **EDUC:** BS, 1954, Liberal Arts, Northwestern Univ.; **MIL SERV:** USN, Lt.; **HOME ADD:** 5 W. County Line Rd., Barrington, IL 60010, (312)381-1500; **BUS ADD:** 5 W. County Line Rd., Barrington, IL 60010, (312)382-3339.

KEATINGE, Robert——**B:** Apr. 22, 1948, Berkeley, CA, *Atty.*, Richard E. Young; **PRIM RE ACT:** Attorney; **SERVICES:** Legal; **REP CLIENTS:** Devels., brokers and investors; **PROFL AFFIL & HONORS:** ABA, CO Bar Assn.; **EDUC:** BA, 1970, Poli. Sci., Univ. of CO; **GRAD EDUC:** JD, 1973/LLM, 1981, Law/Taxation, Univ. of Denver (Law School/Grad. Tax Program); **EDUC HONORS:** Law Week Award (1974); **OTHER ACT & HONORS:** Lecturer in Law - Univ. of Denver.; **BUS ADD:** 1020 15th St., Ste. 42C, Denver, CO 80202, (303)892-1690.

KECK, William F.——**B:** Aug. 15, 1939, Aurora, IL, *Internal Auditor*, Draper & Kramer, Inc.; **PRIM RE ACT:** Broker, Developer, Property Manager, Insuror, Syndicator; **OTHER RE ACT:** Mort. Banker; **SERVICES:** Prop. mgmt., mort. banking, sales, leasing, mgm devel. and synd. of resid. and comml. props.; **REP CLIENTS:** Lenders and indiv. or instnl. investors in resid. and comml. props.; **PROFL AFFIL & HONORS:** AICPA; IL CPA Soc.; Amer. Acctg. Assn.; **EDUC:** BBA, 1961, Mgmt., Univ. of Notre Dame; **GRAD EDUC:** MS, 1968, Accountancy, No. IL Univ.; **OTHER ACT & HONORS:** Village of Sugar Grove, Bd. of Trs., 1965-1969 and 1971-1975; Sugar Grove Lions Club; Dominic Club; Corcoran for Congress Comm., Treas.; **HOME ADD:** Box 281 Maple Ave., Sugar Grove, IL 60554, (312)466-4660; **BUS ADD:** 33 W. Monroe St., Chicago, IL 60603, (312)346-8600.

KEEFE, Kenneth M., Jr.——**B:** Nov. 18, 1941, Jacksonville, FL, *Shareholder/Chmn., RE Dept.*, Mahoney Hadlow & Adams, P.A.; **PRIM RE ACT:** Attorney; **SERVICES:** Legal service in RE area of the law; **REP CLIENTS:** Major lenders (banks, ins. cos. and pension funds) and RE devel.; **PROFL AFFIL & HONORS:** FL Bar; ABA; Jacksonville Bar Assn.; Section of Real Prop. and Probate; **EDUC:** BA, 1964, Hist./Philosophy, Univ. of VA; **GRAD EDUC:** LLB, 1967, Univ. of VA; **EDUC HONORS:** Grad. with Honors; **MIL SERV:** US Army, Capt.; **OTHER ACT & HONORS:** Member, FL Condo. & Cooperative Advisory Council, 1979; Author and speaker at FL Continuing Legal Educ. Programs; **HOME ADD:** 2970 St. Johns Ave., Unit 6-F, Jacksonville, FL 32205, (904)384-5216; **BUS ADD:** 100 N. Laura St., POB 4099, Jacksonville, FL 32201, (904)354-1100.

KEEFE, Paul T.——**B:** Oct. 9, 1943, Boston, MA, *Partner*, The Appraisers Collaborative; **PRIM RE ACT:** Appraiser; **SERVICES:** RE Appraisal Services; **REP CLIENTS:** Fin. Inst., Municipal Govts., various private clients; **PREV EMPLOY:** Chief Assessor, City of Attleboro, MA 1978-1980; Appraisal Officer, Citizens Savings Bank, Providence, RI 1975-1978; **PROFL AFFIL & HONORS:** SREA; MA Bd. of RE Appraisers, SRA; MRA; **EDUC:** BS, 1966, Pharmacy, MA Coll. of Pharmacy; **OTHER ACT & HONORS:** Member, Bd. of Assessors, Sharon, MA 1976-1981, Chmn., 1978-1979; **HOME ADD:** 14 Mountain St., Sharon, MA 02067, (617)784-5536; **BUS ADD:** 925 Washington St., Dorchester, MA 02124, (617)265-0401.

KEEFE, Robert L.——**B:** Oct. 9, 1943, Casper, WY, *Pres.*, Brokerage House One Inc.; **PRIM RE ACT:** Broker, Developer, Builder, Owner/Investor, Property Manager; **SERVICES:** Investment Analysis; **PREV EMPLOY:** Mktg. officer & Loan officer, Guaranty Fed. S & L; **PROFL AFFIL & HONORS:** NAR - HUD Commn.; **EDUC:** BS, Arts & Sci., 1970, Sociology Anthropology, Univ. of WY; **GRAD EDUC:** MBus, 1973, Univ. Portland State; **MIL SERV:** USN, Survival Instr.; **OTHER ACT & HONORS:** 12 different Bds. of different orgs. & Cos.; **HOME ADD:** 4020 S. Oak, Deer Run, WY 82601, (307)234-5507; **BUS ADD:** 606 S. David, Casper, WY 82601, (307)234-3573.

KEEL, Phillip J.——**B:** Mar. 16, 1942, Chicago, IL; **PRIM RE ACT:** Consultant, Developer, Builder, Property Manager, Owner/Investor; **PROFL AFFIL & HONORS:** IREM, DuPage Bd. of RE; **EDUC:** BA, 1964, Bus. & Econ., Furman Univ.; **MIL SERV:** USN, Lt. JG; **OTHER ACT & HONORS:** Hinsdale Comm. House Council; **HOME ADD:** 19 N Prospect, Clarendon Hills, IL 60514, (312)323-8797.

KEELER, Jack C.——**B:** Apr. 20, 1923, San Rafael, CA, *Owner*, Jack Keeler Co.; **PRIM RE ACT:** Broker, Consultant, Appraiser, Developer; **PROFL AFFIL & HONORS:** SREA, MAI; **MIL SERV:** US Army, Air Corps., Capt., 5 medals, 1942-45; **HOME ADD:** 17 Willotta Rd., Suisun, CA 94585, (707)864-0609; **BUS ADD:** 1327 Texas St., Fairfield, CA 94533, (707)425-2909.

KEELING, John M.——**B:** Nov. 1, 1946, Kirkland, WA, *Partner*, Laventhol & Horwath, RE Consulting Grp.; **PRIM RE ACT:** Consultant; **SERVICES:** Mkt. and fin. feasibility studies, fin. programming; **REP CLIENTS:** Century Devel. Corp., Friendswood Devel. Co., Cadillac Fairview, The Woodlands Devel. Corp., Wolff Morgan & Co.; **PREV EMPLOY:** Marriott Hotels; **PROFL AFFIL & HONORS:** Intl. Council of Shopping Ctrs., ULI, AICPA, TX Hotel & Motel Assn., CPA; **EDUC:** BA, 1970, Hist., Univ. of CA; **GRAD EDUC:** MBA, 1974, MI State Univ.; **EDUC HONORS:** Cum Laude; **MIL SERV:** USMC, Cpl., Navy Commendation with Combat 'V', 1967-1969; **HOME ADD:** 19306 Leewood Ct., Humble, TX 77338, (713)852-7645; **BUS ADD:** 333 Clay St., Suite 1100, Houston, TX 77002, (713)658-1071.

KEELTY, Kevin C.——**B:** Sept. 19, 1945, Baltimore, *VP-Financial Services*, Commerical Credit Development Corp.; **PRIM RE ACT:** Developer, Lender; **SERVICES:** Responsible for the production of short to intermediate term loans for portfolio; **PREV EMPLOY:** 1973-75, MD National Corp; 1968-73 Equitable Bancorporation; **PROFL AFFIL & HONORS:** MD MBA; MBA; Baltimore Econ. Soc. ; Former Dir. Home Builders Assn. of MD; **EDUC:** BS, 1968, Poli. Sci., Loyola Coll.; **GRAD EDUC:** MBA, 1972, Geo. Wash. Univ.; **OTHER ACT & HONORS:** Tr., Calvert Hall Coll.; **HOME ADD:** 20 Tullycross Ct., Timonium, MD 21093, (301)252-6424; **BUS ADD:** 300 St. Paul Place, Baltimore, MD 21202, (301)332-3504.

KEENAN, John M.——**B:** Mar. 8, 1944, Chicago, IL, *Pres.*, John M. Keenan & Assoc., Inc.; **PRIM RE ACT:** Broker, Instructor, Syndicator, Consultant, Developer, Property Manager, Owner/Investor; **SERVICES:** Investment counseling, prop. valuation, asset mgmt.; **PREV EMPLOY:** VP, Dir. of Mgmt., Arthur Goldner & Assoc., Inc. (1977-81); VP, Gen. Mgr., David L. Pattie RE, Inc. (1973-77); **PROFL AFFIL & HONORS:** IREM, Sr. VP and Dir. Multi-Family Housing Assoc. of IL; Chicago RE Bd., N Side RE Bd.; **EDUC:** BBA, 1970, Econ. and Fin., Chicago, N Park Coll., IL; **HOME ADD:** 5912 N Talman, Chicago, IL 60659, (312)784-5648; **BUS ADD:** 1723 Howard, Suite 203, Evanston, IL 60202, (312)864-0100.

KEENAN, Joseph J.——**B:** Mar. 8, 1945, Charleston, SC, *Partner*, Keenan & Hewitt, Comml. Investment RE; **PRIM RE ACT:** Broker, Consultant, Appraiser, Developer, Property Manager, Syndicator; **SERVICES:** Comml. investment sales, investment counseling, devel., synd., prop. mgmt.; **REP CLIENTS:** Indiv. and corp., users, investors; **PROFL AFFIL & HONORS:** Pres., S.C. CCIM Chapt.; Bd. of Dir., Charleston Comml. Investment Prop. Council, CCIM; **EDUC:** 1967, Bus. Admin., The Citadel; **MIL SERV:** US Army; 1st Lt.; **HOME ADD:** 33 Gibbes St., Charleston, SC 29401, (803)577-3504; **BUS ADD:** POB 492, Charleston, SC 29402, (803)577-2550.

KEENAN, Thomas H.——**B:** Jan. 25, 1949, Chicago, IL, *SE Reg. Mgr.*, Mobile Home Communities, Inc.; **PRIM RE ACT:** Developer, Property Manager; **OTHER RE ACT:** Mobile Home Sales (new and used), Mgmt. & sales training; **SERVICES:** Prop. mgmt., sales, dealer for manuf. homes etc.; **PREV EMPLOY:** Prop. Mgmt., Forest City Enterprises, Cleveland, OH; Apt. & Condo. & Housing Specialist for Elderly; **PROFL AFFIL & HONORS:** IREM, Clearwater-Largo-Dunedin Bd of Realtors, CPM, VP Planned Comm. Chap. of FL Manufactured Housing Assn., FL RE Sales Lic.; **EDUC:** BS, 1971, Bus. Admin. Mktg., Mgmt., John Carroll Univ., OH; **GRAD EDUC:** MBA in process, Gen. Mgmt, John Carroll Univ., OH; **MIL SERV:** US Army, E-5; **OTHER ACT & HONORS:** Golf Comm. Sec./Treas. Countryside CC; **HOME ADD:** 3269 Hude Park Dr, Clearwater, FL 33519, (813)785-2634; **BUS ADD:** 1321 US 19 S, Ste. 506, Clearwater, FL 33516, (813)536-0471.

KEENE, Gerald H.——**B:** Sept. 27, 1930, Auburn, ME, *Owner*, Keene Realty; **PRIM RE ACT:** Broker, Appraiser, Developer, Builder, Property Manager, Owner/Investor; **PREV EMPLOY:** Self employed restaurant owner; **PROFL AFFIL & HONORS:** Natl. Realtors, Androscoggin Valley Realtors; **EDUC:** R.E., 1965, Univ. of ME, Portland; 1962, Weaver School of R.E.; **MIL SERV:** USN, PO, Korean 48-52; **OTHER ACT & HONORS:** UCT, VFW; **HOME ADD:** 203 Winter St., Auburn, ME 04210, (207)783-1392; **BUS ADD:** 203 Winter St., Auburn, ME 04210, (207)783-1392.

KEENE, Mark J.——**B:** Oct. 3, 1952, Seattle, WA, *Investments, Land Dept.*, McAuley Oil Co., Land Dept.; **PRIM RE ACT:** Developer, Owner/Investor, Syndicator; **SERVICES:** Represents McAuley Oil Co. in the investment field; **PROFL AFFIL & HONORS:** RE salesperson, lic. in the state of CA; **HOME ADD:** 10414 Casanes Ave., Downey, CA 90241; **BUS ADD:** P O Box 176, 8881 Los Coyotes Dr., Buena Park, CA 90621, (714)522-6242.

KEEPPER, John H.——**B:** Oct. 17, 1938, Waukegan, IL, *Investment Specialist*, Coldwell Banker Commercial Real Estate Services; **PRIM RE ACT:** Broker, Consultant, Instructor; **SERVICES:** Investment property, brokerage; **REP CLIENTS:** Corporate and institutional investors; **PREV EMPLOY:** III Chap. 14 CCIM; RE Investment Mktg. Council, Central Assn. RE Exchangors; **PROFL AFFIL & HONORS:** CCIM, GRI; **EDUC:** BA, 1961, Math., Lake Forest Coll.; **MIL SERV:** USN, Lt., Viet Nam; **BUS ADD:** 200 E. Randolph, Suite 6509, Chicago, IL 60601, (312)861-7800.

KEESLER, W.F.——**B:** May 23, 1900, NY, *Owner*; **PRIM RE ACT:** Consultant, Banker; **PREV EMPLOY:** The First Natl. Bank of Boston; **PROFL AFFIL & HONORS:** CPA; MAI; **GRAD EDUC:** 1924, Bentley Coll.; **OTHER ACT & HONORS:** Bd. of RE Commnrs., City of Boston, 1938-1965; Past Master of Lodge; **HOME ADD:** 342 Beacon St., Boston, MA 02116, (617)536-0948; **BUS ADD:** 50 Federal St., Boston, MA 02136, (617)542-5245.

KEGEL, Joanne I.——**B:** Oct. 31, 1930, Little Falls, MN, *Realtor*, Eberhardt; **PRIM RE ACT:** Owner/Investor; **PROFL AFFIL & HONORS:** MN Realtors; **EDUC:** BA, 1966, Fin., Marquette Univ.; **HOME ADD:** 1530 E. Minnehaha Pkwy., Minneapolis, MN 55450, (612)729-3010; **BUS ADD:** 66th & York Ave. S., Edina, MN 55410.

KEHR, Robert L.——**B:** May 1, 1944, Los Angeles, CA, *Principal*, Kehr, Siegel & DeMeter, PC; **PRIM RE ACT:** Attorney; **SERVICES:** RE law and related bus. and tax counseling; **REP CLIENTS:** Prop. owners; comml. tenants; brokers; and others involved in RE devel. and operation; **PROFL AFFIL & HONORS:** ABA (Sec. on Real Prop., Probate & Trust Law); CA Bar Assn. (Secs. on Real Prop. and Bus. Law); and Los Angeles Cty., LA Cty. Mcpl. Ct. Judge Pro Tem (1979-); LA Cty. Bar Atty. Fee Arbitrator (1980-); and LA Cty. Bar Ethics Comm. (1981-); **EDUC:** Cornell Univ., 1966; 1969, Columbia Law School; **OTHER ACT & HONORS:** "The Application of Green v. Superior Ct. to Non-Resid. Realty," 1 Los Angeles Lawyer 30 (1979); "Lease Assignments: The Landlord's Consent," 55 Cal.S.B.J. 108 (1980); "The Assignability of Comml. Leases," 9 RE L.J.197 (1981); and "The Changing of Lease Assignments," RE Review, Vol. 11, No. 2, p. 24 (1981); **BUS ADD:** 1875 Century Park East, Suite 1760, Los Angeles, CA 90067, (213)552-9681.

KEIM, Earl G., Jr.——**B:** Feb. 26, 1927, Dearborn, MI, *Pres.*, Earl Keim Realty, Inc.; **PRIM RE ACT:** Broker, Consultant, Instructor; **SERVICES:** Brokerage operations, 80 offices in MI; Warranty Corp., Training Co., Advertising agency, resid., comml. and time-share; **REP CLIENTS:** Maj. Detroit corps., most relocation cos.; **PREV EMPLOY:** Earl Keim Realty since 1958; **PROFL AFFIL & HONORS:** Past Local Bd. of Realtors pres. (twice), Past Pres. 1972 MI Assn. of Realtors, Co-Founder of Metropolitan Detroit Council of Realtors Bds., GRI, RAM; **EDUC:** BS, 1952, Univ. of MI; **MIL SERV:** US Army, Sgt., 1946-48; **OTHER ACT & HONORS:** Pres. Dearborn YMCA, Realtor of the Year Dearborn 1965-66; **HOME ADD:** 30285 Hickory Ln., Franklin, MI 48025, (313)626-4154; **BUS ADD:** 26250 Northwestern Hwy., Southfield, MI 48076, (313)352-3750.*

KEIR, Walter——**B:** July 9, 1916, IA, *Bldg. Mgr.*, Badgerow Bldg. Partners; **PRIM RE ACT:** Property Manager; **PREV EMPLOY:** City Mgmt.; **PROFL AFFIL & HONORS:** Soc. of RPA; **EDUC:** Drake Univ.; **MIL SERV:** US Army, Inf. (4 yrs.), Sgt.; **OTHER ACT & HONORS:** Cty. Auditor, Sac Cty., 4 1/2 yrs.; Asst. City mgr., Sioux City, IA & Skokie, IL; 13 yrs. City Clerk & Dir. of Utilities, Sac City, IA; SAE; Shrine; **HOME ADD:** 3243 Grandview, Sioux City, IA 51104, (712)258-0725; **BUS ADD:** 414 Badgerow Bldg., Sioux City, IA 51101, (712)255-1697.

KEISER, Gordon C.——**B:** Mar. 10, 1935, Detroit, MI, *VP, RE*, Midas International Corp., Midas Realty Corp.; **PRIM RE ACT:** Developer, Builder; **PREV EMPLOY:** Shell Oil Co. 1959-69; **PROFL AFFIL & HONORS:** ICSC; NACORE; **EDUC:** BA, 1958, Econ., MI State Univ.; **EDUC HONORS:** Cum Laude; **MIL SERV:** USMC; Cpl.; **HOME ADD:** 628 Lakeside Circle Dr., Wheeling, IL 60090, (312)398-7826; **BUS ADD:** 222 S. Riverside Plaza, Chicago, IL 60606, (312)648-5600.

KEITH, Harold——*Dir.*, Department of Housing and Urban Development, Publications & Info. Division; **PRIM RE ACT:** Lender; **BUS ADD:** 451 Seventh St., S.W., Washington, DC 20410, (202)426-1891.*

KEITH, John A.——**B:** Dec. 5, 1921, Pasadena, CA, *Pres.*, Keith Realty, Inc.; **PRIM RE ACT:** Broker, Owner/Investor, Property Manager; **SERVICES:** Gen. RE Brokerage; **PROFL AFFIL & HONORS:** Yuma Bd. of Realtors, AAR, NAR, Am. Agron. Soc., Soil Science Soc. of Amer., GRI; **EDUC:** AA & AS, 1942 & 1948, Chemistry, Bus. Admin., Univ. of Redlands, Riverside Jr. Coll.; **GRAD EDUC:** MS, 1952, Soil & Water Chem., Univ. of AZ; **MIL SERV:** US Army; **OTHER ACT & HONORS:** Toastmasters; **HOME ADD:** 250 W. Catalina Dr., Yuma, AZ 85364, (602)344-3434; **BUS ADD:** 250 W. Catalina Dr., Yuma, AZ 85364, (602)344-3434.

KEITH, John P.——*Pres.*, Regional Plan. Assn; **OTHER RE ACT:** Planning; **BUS ADD:** 235 E. 45th St., New York, NY 10017, (212)682-7750.*

KELEDJIAN, E. James——**B:** Nov. 25, 1942, Detroit, MI, *Sr. VP*, VMS Realty, Inc.; **PRIM RE ACT:** Owner/Investor, Syndicator; **SERVICES:** Acquisition, Prop. Mgmt., Synd.; **PREV EMPLOY:** The Robert A. McNeil Corp. 1977-1981; Regional VP; **PROFL AFFIL & HONORS:** ICSC, Assoc. Member; Dir., RESSI Chap. of IL Dir., Mort. Bankers Assn. of IL; Member RE Broker, State of IL; Dir., Multi-Family Housing Assn. of IL; **EDUC:** BS, 1966, Eastern MI Univ.; **GRAD EDUC:** MUP, 1969, Wayne State Univ., Detroit, MI;

MIL SERV: USMC, 1963-1968, Cpl.; **HOME ADD:** 741 Woodhollow, Buffalo Grove, IL 62515, (312)537-7263; **BUS ADD:** 69 W. Washington, Chicago, IL 60602, (312)263-3636.

KELEHER, Peter D.——B: Sept. 4, 1935, NYC, NY, *Pres.*, Land Invest. Dynamics, Ltd. & Peter D. Keleher & Assocs.; **PRIM RE ACT:** Broker, Syndicator, Consultant, Property Manager, Owner/Investor; **OTHER RE ACT:** Buyer's Broker; **SERVICES:** Exchanging, computerized acctg., tax prep., investment analysis; **REP CLIENTS:** Individual investors; **PREV EMPLOY:** Former Owner, Public Acctg. Firm; **PROFL AFFIL & HONORS:** RNMI; FLI; CCIM candidate; AFLM candidate; Who's Who in Creative RE - 1981; FL RE Exchangers Assn.; WI Exchangers Club; MI Assn. Realtors, Exchange Div.; **EDUC:** AB, 1957, Eng./Psych., Rutgers Univ.; **GRAD EDUC:** Bus./Personnel, Loyola Univ., Chicago; **MIL SERV:** USNR; Capt., 3 decorations; **OTHER ACT & HONORS:** Precinct Committeeman - 8 yrs.; Reserve Officers Assn.; Naval Reserve Assn.; Who's Who of Midwest Consultants.; **HOME ADD:** 1536 Towhee Ln., Naperville, IL 60565, (312)420-8171; **BUS ADD:** 6 S. 235 Steeple Run, Suite 12B, Naperville, IL 60540, (312)355-4949.

KELEMEN, Robert C.——B: Jan. 16, 1945, Charleston, WV, *Dir. of Devel.*, City of Parkersburg; **PRIM RE ACT:** Consultant, Developer, Property Manager; **OTHER RE ACT:** Planner; **SERVICES:** Total devel. servs.; **REP CLIENTS:** Public City of Parkersburg; **PREV EMPLOY:** 11 yrs. of planning and devel. work for more than 12 govts.; **PROFL AFFIL & HONORS:** AMA, NARA, ASA; **EDUC:** BA, 1966, Bus. Admin., Glenville State Coll.; **GRAD EDUC:** 1971, Urban & Rgnl. Planning, UNC; **MIL SERV:** US Army; 1st Lt., ACM, GCM; **OTHER ACT & HONORS:** First Pbys. Church, Cty. Bd. of Health, Municipal Planning Comm.; **HOME ADD:** 1610 Princeton St., Parkersburg, WV 26101, (304)428-7325; **BUS ADD:** 1 Govt. Sq., Parkersburg, WV 26101, (304)424-8415.

KELIGIAN, David Leo——B: Apr. 10, 1956, Los Angeles, CA, Peat Marwick, Mitchell & Co. CPA's, Intl. Tax Staff; **PRIM RE ACT:** Consultant, Attorney, Syndicator; **OTHER RE ACT:** Intl. tax practitioner, CPA firm; **SERVICES:** Tax planning, CPA firm, ind. legal practice spec. in RE synd. & consultation; **PROFL AFFIL & HONORS:** Beverly Hills Bar Assn., Los Angeles Cty. Bar Assn.; **EDUC:** BS, 1977, Acctg., Univ. of S. CA; **GRAD EDUC:** JD, 1980, Law, RE, Univ. of So. CA; **EDUC HONORS:** Magna Cum Laude, Dean's List, Dean's List; **HOME ADD:** 18164 Chardon Cir., Encino, CA 91316, (213)705-4505; **BUS ADD:** 2029 Century Park E, Suite 2900, Los Angeles, CA 90067, (213)553-1250.

KELL, Lawrence A.——B: June 17, 1938, Kansas City, KS, *Sr. VP*, Ostendorf-Morris Co., Appraisal/Consulting; **PRIM RE ACT:** Broker, Consultant, Appraiser; **SERVICES:** Prop. valuations, investment analysis, feasibility studies, acquisition, merger and disposition RE valuations; **REP CLIENTS:** Maj. corps., banks, lenders, RE investment trusts; **PREV EMPLOY:** The Prudential Ins. Co., RE Investment Dept.; **PROFL AFFIL & HONORS:** Amer. Soc. of RE Counselors; Amer. Soc. of Appraisers; CABOR; NAR, CRE; **EDUC:** BA, 1962, Math., Psych., Park Coll.; **GRAD EDUC:** MBA, 1966, Bus., Univ. of MO; **EDUC HONORS:** Cum Laude; **MIL SERV:** US Army, Spec. 5; **HOME ADD:** 28905 Osborn Rd., Bay Village, OH 44140, (216)871-9181; **BUS ADD:** 1100 Superior Ave., Cleveland, OH 44114, (216)861-7200.

KELLA, Bee——*Pres.*, Drowned Meadow Real Estate; **PRIM RE ACT:** Broker, Consultant, Appraiser, Developer, Builder, Owner/Investor, Property Manager; **SERVICES:** All phases of RE, full serv.; **PREV EMPLOY:** Realtor in Pt. Jefferson area for 20 yrs.; **PROFL AFFIL & HONORS:** NY State Bd. of Realtors; Long Is. Bd. of Realtors; Multiple Listing Service of Long Is., Past Officer MLS Bd.; **OTHER ACT & HONORS:** New England River Basin Commn. (apptd. by Gov.); Stony Brook Council, 7th Term; Pres., Greater Pt. Jefferson C of C; St. George Ctry. Club; Harbor Hills Ctry. Club; 1981, Head Parking Comm., Pt. Jefferson; Zoning Comm.; 1979, Long Is. Tourism Comm.; Honors from Suffolk Cty. Boy Scouts, Maithe Hospital and Cancer Soc. of SC; First woman pres. of Suffolk Cty. C of C; Past trustee, Stony Brook Found.; Letter of Appreciation from US Navy for services rendered; **HOME ADD:** 1023 Main St., Pt. Jefferson, NY 11777; **BUS ADD:** 1031 Main St., Pt. Jefferson, NY 11777, (516)473-7646.

KELLAM, Richard B., Tr.——B: Feb. 28, 1950, Norfolk, VA, *Pres.*, Richard Kellam Assoc.; **PRIM RE ACT:** Broker, Consultant, Appraiser, Developer, Builder, Owner/Investor, Property Manager; **OTHER RE ACT:** Leasing; **REP CLIENTS:** Lenders & indiv. or instnl. investors in comml. props.; **EDUC:** RE & Fin., Univ. of Richmond; **BUS ADD:** 213 Linkhorn Dr., Virginia Bch., VA 23451, (804)425-9400.

KELLAWAY, William——*Mgr. Branch Bldgs.*, NABISCO, Inc.; **PRIM RE ACT:** Property Manager; **BUS ADD:** East Hanover, NJ 07936, (201)884-0500.*

KELLEHER, D. William——B: Sept. 25, 1931, Westerly, RI, *Pres.*, Eastern Savings & Loan; **PRIM RE ACT:** Banker; **PROFL AFFIL & HONORS:** Chmn. CT S&L League; **GRAD EDUC:** 1953, Econ., Providence Coll.; **OTHER ACT & HONORS:** Dir. Easter Seal SE Ct.; Treas. Amer. Cancer Soc., Dir. Treas. Thames River Devel. Corp.; **HOME ADD:** 7 Thomas Ave., Norwich, CT 06360, (203)887-7425; **BUS ADD:** 257 Main St., Norwich, CT 06360, (203)889-7381.

KELLEN, A.L.——*Mng. Partner*, Pan American Industrial Group; **PRIM RE ACT:** Developer; **BUS ADD:** 6088 Gateway East, Ste C, El Paso, TX 79905, (915)779-3509.*

KELLER, Brian R.——B: Oct. 27, 1945, Telford, PA, *Pres.*, Keller Investment Properties, Inc.; **PRIM RE ACT:** Owner/Investor; **REP CLIENTS:** Buy solely for own account; **EDUC:** BS, 1967, Mktg., PA State Univ.; **EDUC HONORS:** Coll. of Bus. Admin. Honors Program; **OTHER ACT & HONORS:** FL Manufactured Housing Assn. & Gr. Tampa Bay C of C; **HOME ADD:** 1917 Arrowhead Dr., NE, St. Petersburg, FL 33703, (813)525-6622; **BUS ADD:** 9790 66th St. N, Pinellas Park, FL 33565, (813)544-8111.

KELLER, G. Lawrence——*Sr. VP, Law & Corp. Dev.*, Coleman Co., Inc.; **PRIM RE ACT:** Property Manager; **BUS ADD:** 250 N. St.Francis Ave, Wichita, KS 67202, (316)261-3418.*

KELLER, George H., IV——B: Aug. 12, 1947, NY, NY, *Partner*, Jones Lang Wootton, Downtown, NY; **PRIM RE ACT:** Consultant, Property Manager; **PREV EMPLOY:** Charles F. Noyes Co., Inc. (NY, NY); **PROFL AFFIL & HONORS:** YMREA, REBNY; **EDUC:** BS, 1969, Mktg, Villanova Univ.; **HOME ADD:** 28 W. 89th, New York, NY 10024, (212)668-0983; **BUS ADD:** 5 Hanover Sq., New York, NY 10004, (212)482-8210.

KELLER, John E., Jr.——B: Dec. 1, 1948, Blue Is., IL, *VP*, Jack Keller, Inc., Realtors; **PRIM RE ACT:** Broker, Instructor, Property Manager; **OTHER RE ACT:** Wheelchair Accessible Home Spec.; **SERVICES:** Mktg. of wheelchair accessible homes, modifications to able-bodied, homes to create wheelchair accessibility, investment counseling; **REP CLIENTS:** Gen resid. RE Brokerage; **PREV EMPLOY:** US Govt.; **PROFL AFFIL & HONORS:** Clearwater-Largo-Dunedin Bd. of Realtors, Gulf Bch. Seminole Bd. of Realtors, NAR, FL Assn. Realtors; **EDUC:** BA, 1971, Pol. Sci., IN Univ.; **GRAD EDUC:** US Hist. & Urban Devel., Purdue Univ. Grad. Sch., IN Univ. Grad. Sch.; **OTHER ACT & HONORS:** Air Force Assn., Amer. Defense Preparedness Assn., Acad. of Pol. Sci.; **HOME ADD:** PO Box 1708, Largo, FL 33540, (813)586-1497; **BUS ADD:** 2440 W Bay Dr., Largo, FL 33540, (813)586-1497.

KELLER, Kevin E.——B: Aug. 30, 1954, Detroit, MI, RE/MAX; **PRIM RE ACT:** Broker, Syndicator, Consultant, Developer, Property Manager; **PREV EMPLOY:** Dir. of Prop. Mgmt.-Schaefer Props., San Diego, CA; RE Dept. - McLellan Indus., San Francisco, CA - Acquisitions Mgr.; Valley Realty, Asst. Mgr.; **PROFL AFFIL & HONORS:** NAR, CAR, San Mateo Cty. Devel. Council; **OTHER ACT & HONORS:** San Mateo Cty. Hist. Soc., San Francisco Symphony Member; **HOME ADD:** 334 Hobart, San Mateo, CA 94402, (415)348-8241; **BUS ADD:** 1035 Hillsdale Blvd., Foster City, CA 94404, (415)574-9111.

KELLER, Patrick Erle——B: June 5, 1947, Los Angeles, CA, *Chief Appraiser*, Patrick E. Keller & Assocs.; **PRIM RE ACT:** Appraiser, Property Manager; **SERVICES:** RE appraisal and consulting - mgmt.; **PROFL AFFIL & HONORS:** Aplha Appraisal Assn. of Canada, Amer. Assn. of Cert. Appraisers, Amer. Soc. of RE Specialists, Amer. Soc. of Appraisers, CA Assn. of RE Bds., Hawthorne C of C, Inst. of Real Prop. Analysts, Intl. Inst. of Valuers, Intl. Org. of RE Appraisers, Intl. Soc. of RE Econ., Los Angeles-Inglewood Bd. of Realtors, Nat. Assn. of Cert. Real Prop. Appraisers, Nat. Assn. of Indep. Fee Appraisers, Nat. Assn. of RE Appraisers, Nat. Assn. of RE Bds., Nat. Assn. of Review Appraisers, Nat. Soc. of RE Appraisers, Soc. of RE Appraisers, Southbay Area C of C, CRA, CAS, IFAS, ICA, CRPA, DRA, MBA, REPA, DREA, PHD, CREA; **EDUC:** BS, 1971, Fin. & Acctg., CA State Univ.; **GRAD EDUC:** MBA, 1973, Fin. & RE, Pac. NW Univ.; **OTHER ACT & HONORS:** 1978 & 1980 Treasurer, Rep. Cenn. Comm. LA CN. & 1981 City Clerk - Hawthorne; Boy Scouts of Amer.; YMCA; Red Cross; C of C; We-Tip; Boys Club; & Bus. Men's Club; **HOME ADD:** 4734 W Broadway, Hawthorne, CA 90250, (213)973-1979; **BUS ADD:** 4734 W. Broadway, Hawthorne, CA 90250, (213)973-1978.

KELLER, Robert A.——**B:** Mar. 27, 1942, Watervliet, MI, T.R.C. Realty, Comml., Investment; **PRIM RE ACT:** Broker, Builder, Owner/Investor; **OTHER RE ACT:** Exchanging-RE; **PROFL AFFIL & HONORS:** Nat. Assn. of Realtors, MI Assn. of Realtors, Grand Rapids RE Bd., CCIM, GRI; **EDUC:** BS, 1964, Aviation, Western MI Univ.; **MIL SERV:** US Army, Capt., Distinguished Flying Cross, 31 Air Medals; **HOME ADD:** 2685 60th SE, Kentwood, MI 49508, (616)698-6077; **BUS ADD:** 2685-60th SE, Kentwood, MI 49508, (616)698-7768.

KELLER, Robert O.——**B:** May 8, 1943, Springfield, IL, *Part.*, Keller & Anderson; **PRIM RE ACT:** Attorney; **SERVICES:** Residential, farm and comml. transactions; **REP CLIENTS:** S&L Assn.; farmers, investors, resid. sales & purchases; **PROFL AFFIL & HONORS:** Champaign Cty., IL, ABA; Midwest Estate Planning Council; **EDUC:** BS, 1967, Acctg., Murray State Univ.; **GRAD EDUC:** JD, 1970, Univ. of KY; **EDUC HONORS:** Dean's List; **HOME ADD:** 4002 Farhills Dr., Champaign, IL 61820, (217)352-9341; **BUS ADD:** Box 1750, 30 Main St., Champaign, IL 61820, (217)352-9371.

KELLEY, Blaine, Jr.——**B:** Jan. 26, 1929, Charlotte, NC, *Pres. & Chmn.*, The Landmarks Group; **PRIM RE ACT:** Developer; **SERVICES:** Land, design, construction, fin., marketing, managing; **REP CLIENTS:** IBM Corp., S. Central Bell, Tampa Electric, Laing Properties, Mutual of NY, etc.; **PREV EMPLOY:** Marthame Sanders & Co., General contractors; **PROFL AFFIL & HONORS:** Urban Land Instit., Nat. Assn. of Indus. & Office Parks, Nat. Assn. RE Exec., etc.; **EDUC:** BS, 1951, Econ., Davidson Coll.; **MIL SERV:** US Army, Lt.; **HOME ADD:** 400 Glen Arden Dr. NW, Atlanta, GA 30305, (404)266-1695; **BUS ADD:** 880 Johnson Ferry Road NE, Atlanta, GA 30342, (404)252-6490.

KELLEY, Larry K.——**B:** Aug. 20, 1942, Waco, TX, *Pres.*, Larry Kelley Realty, Inc.; **PRIM RE ACT:** Broker, Consultant, Developer, Property Manager, Owner/Investor; **SERVICES:** Specialize in income-producing comml. RE; **PROFL AFFIL & HONORS:** Pres., OK CCIM Chap. (1981), CCIM; **HOME ADD:** 3136 E. 83rd, Tulsa, OK 74136, (918)481-0950; **BUS ADD:** 7030 S. Yale, Suite 100, Tulsa, OK 74177, (918)494-2690.

KELLMAN, Jeffrey A.——**B:** May 21, 1951, Chicago, IL, *VP*, Edward E. Kellman & Co.; **PRIM RE ACT:** Broker, Consultant, Developer, Owner/Investor; **SERVICES:** Brokerage, devel., investor and consultant; **REP CLIENTS:** Major public and private corps.; **PREV EMPLOY:** Edward E. Kellman & Co. since 1973; **PROFL AFFIL & HONORS:** Assn. of Indus. RE Brokers, IL CPA Foundation, CPA; **EDUC:** BS, 1973, Fin., Univ. of IL, Grad. with honors, James Scholar; **GRAD EDUC:** MBA, 1976, Fin./Acctg., Univ. of Chicago; MS, 1980, Taxation, DePaul Univ.; **EDUC HONORS:** CPA, State of IL; **OTHER ACT & HONORS:** Member IL CPA Soc., RE Comm. 1980-1981; **HOME ADD:** 2912 N. Commonwealth, Chicago, IL 60646, (312)935-6407; **BUS ADD:** 5901 N. Cicero, Suite 201, Chicago, IL 60646, (312)286-3200.

KELLOGG, M. B.——**B:** Dec. 25, 1927, Globe, AZ, *Pres.*, MK Real Estate Associates, Inc.; **PRIM RE ACT:** Broker, Consultant, Owner/Investor, Property Manager; **OTHER RE ACT:** RE Investment Counseling; **SERVICES:** Consulting, investment counseling, RE brokerage, prop. mgmt. RE exchange specialist; **REP CLIENTS:** Investors and users of agricultural, resid. income, comml., indust. props. Particularly those needing 1031 Exchanges. (Inc. farmers, attys., accountant, Title Co. mgrs., other RE Brokers, etc.); **PREV EMPLOY:** Investment Counselor, J. Henry Helser & Co. 1963 - 1965, Owner-devel. Mobile Home Park, Motel, apts., various comml. & indus. props.; **PROFL AFFIL & HONORS:** RNMI, NAR, CA Assn. of Realtors, CCIM; **EDUC:** AA, Merced Coll., 1969, sociology, archeology, Univ. of CA Investment Courses, RE Courses; Continuing Educ. courses in RE fin., law, taxes, specialties, exchanges, etc.; **OTHER ACT & HONORS:** Eastern Star, Emblem Club, Pres., Merced Coll. Found.; Merced Evergreen Park Endowment Care Fund Tr.; **HOME ADD:** 2240 E. Yosemite Parkway, Merced, CA 95340, (209)383-3267; **BUS ADD:** PO Box 2185, 760 W. 20th St., Merced, CA 95340, (209)723-8821.

KELLOGG, Ralph M.——**B:** Dec. 13, 1895, Wolcott, CT, *Prin.*, Ralph Kellogg Agency; **PRIM RE ACT:** Broker, Appraiser; **PREV EMPLOY:** Owner, Inter-City Hdw. Co., Norwalk, CT; Owner Welch's Adv. Co., Westport, CT; **PROFL AFFIL & HONORS:** Norwalk Bd. of Realtors; Nat. Inst. of RE Brokers; Nat. Assn. of Ind. Appraisers, IFA (Ind. Fee Appraisers); **EDUC:** BSE, 1918, Univ. of CT; **GRAD EDUC:** BS, 1964, RE Appraiser 1 and 2, Univ. of PA, Wharton Sch. of Fin. Commerce; **MIL SERV:** USN, Res.; Ens.; **OTHER ACT & HONORS:** Norwalk Planning Comm., 10 yrs; Pres., Norwalk C of C; Pres., Norwalk Bd. of Realtors; Dir., CT Assn. of RE Bds.; Pres., Rotary Club, Norwalk Parking Auth.; Chmn. Norwalk Merchants Assn.; Masonic Lodge; **HOME ADD:** 4 Camelot Dr., Norwalk, CT, (203)842-8024; **BUS ADD:** 4 Camelot Dr., Norwalk, CT 06850, (203)847-8024.

KELLY, Charles S.——**B:** Feb. 15, 1920, Lapeer, MI, *VP & Mgr.*, Bateman Investment & Commercial Co.; **PRIM RE ACT:** Broker, Consultant, Appraiser, Owner/Investor, Syndicator; **SERVICES:** Investment counseling, comml. & indus. prop. sales; **PROFL AFFIL & HONORS:** North Oakland Co. Bd. of Realtors; FL RE Exchangors, CCIM, Realtors Nat. Mktg. Inst.; **EDUC:** 1939, MI State Univ.; **MIL SERV:** USN, PO, European & Pacific WW II; **OTHER ACT & HONORS:** Elks, Trout Unltd.; Pres. of MI Assn. of Realtors Exchange Div. 1974; Pres. of CCIM Chapter 8 1978; **HOME ADD:** 3126 Francesca, Drayton Plains, MI 48020, (313)673-5857; **BUS ADD:** 371-A So. Telegraph Rd., PO Box 868, Pontiac, MI 48056.

KELLY, Deborah Kaye——**B:** May 2, 1957, Dayton, OH, *Leasing Representative*, The Beerman Realty Co.; **OTHER RE ACT:** Leasing representative; **PROFL AFFIL & HONORS:** NAIOP, Moraine Bus. Assn.; **EDUC:** BS, 1979, Mktg., Bowling Green State Univ.; **HOME ADD:** 3770 Eileen Road, Kettering, OH 45429, (513)296-1233; **BUS ADD:** 11 West Monument, Dayton, OH 45402, (513)222-1285.

KELLY, Donald P.——*Pres.*, Esmark; **PRIM RE ACT:** Property Manager; **BUS ADD:** 55 East Monroe St., Chicago, IL 60603, (312)431-3600.*

KELLY, Gerald——**B:** Mar. 25, 1947, San Francisco, CA, *Partner*, O'Keefe & Lalanne, CPA's; **PRIM RE ACT:** Consultant, Owner/Investor; **OTHER RE ACT:** RE Acctg. & Tax Consultant; **SERVICES:** Tax Planning and Acctg. Systems; **REP CLIENTS:** RE Sales and Mgmt. Cos., indiv. and grp. investors; **PROFL AFFIL & HONORS:** AICPA, CA Soc. of CPA, CPA; **EDUC:** BS, 1971, Acctg., Golden Gate Univ., San Fransicso; **EDUC HONORS:** Summa Cum Laude; **MIL SERV:** USA, Sgt., Army Commendation; **OTHER ACT & HONORS:** Bus. and Acctg., Teacher - Undergrad. Div.; **HOME ADD:** 1266 Glacier Ave., Pacifica, CA 94044, (415)359-2274; **BUS ADD:** 3130 La Selva, San Mateo, CA 94403, (415)341-7758.

KELLY, Gerald E.——**B:** June 1, 1942, *Exec. VP*, Greater Buffalo Devel. Found.; **OTHER RE ACT:** Civic initiator and advisor for urban devel. projects; **PREV EMPLOY:** NY State Urban Devel. Corp. W. Rgnl. Office, Rochester, Erie, Niagara Area Office, Buffalo, Feb. 1969 to Aug. 1972; Project Assoc., W. NY Area, 1969; Project Coordinator for Niagara Falls, 1969-1970; Project Coordinator for Niagara Cty., 1971-1972; US Dept. of Housing and Urban Devel., Philadelphia Rgnl. Office (Region II), July 1965 to Jan. 1969; Urban Intern, 1965; Renewal Rep. in N.E. PA anthracite region, 1966; Head of Processing, Renewal Assist. Div., 1967; Renewal Rep. for Washington, DC area, 1968; **PROFL AFFIL & HONORS:** ULI, Exec. Group Member; Intl. Downtown Exec. Assn.; Council on Urban Econ. Devel.; Nat. Trust for Hist. Preservation; **EDUC:** BA, 1964, Amer. Govt., Pomona Coll.; **GRAD EDUC:** Master Public Admin., 1965, Urban Studies, Maxwell School of Citizenship & Public Affairs; **HOME ADD:** 759 Bird Ave., Buffalo, NY 14209; **BUS ADD:** 1306 Rand Bldg., Buffalo, NY 14203, (716)856-2708.

KELLY, James F.——**B:** Apr. 11, 1919, Minneapolis, MN, *VP-Brokerage*, Robert Boblett Associates, Inc., Brokerage, Indus. RE; **PRIM RE ACT:** Broker; **PREV EMPLOY:** David C. Cell Investment Co., Sr. VP & Dir., Mort., Sales, Ins., Dept. Head; **PROFL AFFIL & HONORS:** Greater Minneapolis Area Bd. of Realtors; MN Assn. of Realtors, NAR, GRI; CRS; Past Pres., Greater Minneapolis Bd. of Realtors, Credit Union Pres., Dir. of MN Assn.; Distinguished Serv. Award; MN Assn. of Realtors, 1980; Realtor of the year 1980, MN Assn. of Realtors; Chmn., Exec. Comm., Greater Minneapolis Bd. of Realtors; **EDUC:** Pre Law, St. Thomas Coll. and Univ. of MN; **MIL SERV:** USN; 1941- 45, AMM 2/C; **OTHER ACT & HONORS:** Dir. & Big Brother for 35 yrs. of Big Brothers, Inc.; 20 yr. member US Power Squadron; Charter Member of Univ. of MN Alumni Club; Life Member of Univ. of MN Alumni Assn.; Alumni of St. John's Univ.; **HOME ADD:** 2221 Penn Ave. S., Minneapolis, MN 55405, (612)374-1728; **BUS ADD:** 1007 First Bank Place West, Minneapolis, MN 55405, (612)333-6515.

KELLY, James O., III——**B:** Jan. 27, 1934, Waco, TX, *Chmn. of the Bd. and Gen. Counsel*, San Jacinto Savings Assn.; **PRIM RE ACT:** Attorney, Developer, Builder, Property Manager, Banker, Lender; **PROFL AFFIL & HONORS:** ABA; State Bar of TX; Houston Bar Assn.; **EDUC:** BBA, 1956, Fin., The Univ. of TX, Austin; **GRAD EDUC:** JD, 1961, RE, Univ. of Houston, TX; **EDUC HONORS:** Distinguished Mil. Grad.; Pres., Sr. Class, School of Bus., Alpha Delta Sigma; Distinguished Alumnus 1975, Coll. of Bus., Pres., Student Bar Assn.; **MIL SERV:** US Army, Capt.; **HOME ADD:** 5922 Old Lodge Drive, Houston, TX 77066, (713)444-5354; **BUS ADD:** PO Box 35700,

Houston, TX 77096, (713)661-7000.

KELLY, James R.——B: Sept. 16, 1948, Trinidad, CO, *Pres.*, Bus. Investments Services, Inc.; **PRIM RE ACT:** Consultant, Developer, Builder, Owner/Investor; **REP CLIENTS:** Baskin-Robbins Ice Cream Co., Dunkin' Donuts of Amer., Inc.; **EDUC:** BA, 1969, Math., Frostburg State Coll.; **GRAD EDUC:** MBA/PhD, 1974, Bus. Admin./Math., MD Univ.; **EDUC HONORS:** Magna Cum Laude; **HOME ADD:** 1338 Howard Rd., Glen Burnie, MD 21061, (301)768-8022; **BUS ADD:** 1338 Howard Rd., Glen Burnie, MD 21061, (301)768-8022.

KELLY, John M., PE——B: Jan. 3, 1946, New York, NY, *Mgr., Facility Servs., Tunnels, Bridges, and Terminals*, Port Authority of NY and NJ; **PRIM RE ACT:** Consultant, Engineer, Developer, Owner/Investor, Property Manager; **SERVICES:** Coordination of varied develop. interests; Operations Planning; Security and MTCE Plng., Eval.; Labor Rel.; State-of-Art Tech. Svcs.; Ops. Staff Trng.; **REP CLIENTS:** Port Authority Midtown Bus Terminal; George Washington Bridge & Bus Station; Lincoln Tunnel; Holland Tunnel; Goethals Bridge; Bayonne Bridge; Outerbridge Crossing; Port Authority New York Truck Terminal; **PROFL AFFIL & HONORS:** Amer. Soc. of Civil Engrs.; NJ Motor Truck Assn.; Intl. Bridge, Tunnels Turnpike Assn., Lic. Profl. Engr. (NY State & NJ State); **EDUC:** BCE, 1967, Structural/Found.Design, Manhattan Coll.; **GRAD EDUC:** MSCE, 1970, Transportation Planning, Newark Coll. of Engrg.; MBA, 1972, Gen. Mgmt., Fordham Univ.; **OTHER ACT & HONORS:** Borough Engr./Boro of Spotswood, NJ/1975-76; **HOME ADD:** 16 Cheyenne Dr., Parlin, NJ 08859, (201)727-5832; **BUS ADD:** New York, NY 100481 World Trade Center, Suite 71S, (212)466-7580.

KELLY, Mary Dianne——*Pres.*, Kelly Mgmt. Associates, Inc.; **PRIM RE ACT:** Consultant, Developer, Instructor, Property Manager; **PREV EMPLOY:** Dir. of Field Mgmt., Boston Housing Auth.; Admin. Clinton Housing Auth.; Winn Mgmt. - Gen. Mgr.; **PROFL AFFIL & HONORS:** IREM; Chmn. of PR of IREM, CPM; **EDUC:** BS, Bus. Admin., Boston Univ.; **OTHER ACT & HONORS:** NAHRO; CHPA; IREM; **BUS ADD:** 378 North St., Boston, MA 02113, (617)723-4227.

KELLY, Robert H.——B: July 14, 1921, Hamilton, OH, *Sr. VP*, Duffy Real Estate Co., Gallery of Homes; **PRIM RE ACT:** Broker, Consultant, Instructor; **SERVICES:** Sales, appraisals, counseling on feasibilities; **REP CLIENTS:** Fortune 500 companies on personnel relocation; **PREV EMPLOY:** Sr. VP, Cline Realtors 1965-1975; **PROFL AFFIL & HONORS:** NAR, RNMI, CRB, CRS, Adjunct Instr. RE, Univ. of Cincinnati, OH Realtor-Instructor of the Year 1979; **EDUC:** AS, 1956, Retail Merchandising, Univ. of Cincinnati; **EDUC HONORS:** Delta Mu Delta honorary frat. - Alpha Sigma Lambda; **MIL SERV:** USAF, Sgt. 1942-1946; **HOME ADD:** 7042 Woodsedge Dr., Cincinnati, OH 45230, (513)232-2345; **BUS ADD:** 1225 Burney Lane, Cincinnati, OH 45230, (513)232-8870.

KELLY, Timothy Charles——B: Nov. 29, 1946, Toronto, ON, Can., *VP, Gen. Counsel & Sec.*, Nu-West Florida, Inc.; **PRIM RE ACT:** Attorney, Insuror, Syndicator; **PREV EMPLOY:** 1974-77 Assoc. Aird & Berlis Toronto; 1977-78 Partner Kelly & Kelly, Toronto; 1978-81 Gen. Counsel, Headway Corp., Ltd., Thunder Bay; **PROFL AFFIL & HONORS:** Law Soc. of Upper Can., Can. Bar Assn., BA, LLB; **EDUC:** BA, 1969, Pol. Sci. & Econ., Univ. of Toronto; **GRAD EDUC:** LLB, 1972, Law, Univ. of Toronto; **EDUC HONORS:** With honors; **OTHER ACT & HONORS:** Assorted Golf Clubs; **HOME ADD:** 8258 Shadow Wood Blvd., Coral Springs, FL 33065, (305)753-8813; **BUS ADD:** 8751 West Broward Blvd., Plantation, FL 33324, (305)472-8008.

KELMAN, Harold——*Ed.*, Real Estate Forum, Inc., Real Estate Forum; **PRIM RE ACT:** Real Estate Publisher; **BUS ADD:** 30 E. 42nd St., New York, NY 10017, (212)682-6987.*

KELTY, Stephen M.——B: Aug. 23, 1945, Lansing, MI, *Corp. Counsel*, Aladdin Industries, Inc., Aladdin Resources, Inc.; **PRIM RE ACT:** Attorney, Developer, Owner/Investor, Property Manager; **SERVICES:** sell land and devel. & lease & manage office park bldgs.; **REP CLIENTS:** IBM, Xerox, Jack Daniel's, Whirlpool Corp., Fireman's Fund, Travellers, Prudential; **PREV EMPLOY:** Lifemark, Inc., 1978, Pvt. Law Practice, 1975-77; Zachary & Segraves PA, 1973-76; **PROFL AFFIL & HONORS:** ABA, GA Bar Assn., TN Bar Assn., Designated RE Atty., GA; **EDUC:** AB, 1967, Pol. Sci., Dickinson Coll., Carlisle, PA; **GRAD EDUC:** JD, 1973, Bus., Tax Law, Emory Univ. Sch. of Law, Atlanta, GA; **EDUC HONORS:** ROTC Scholarship Cadet, Winner 1972 Moot Ct. Comp., Law Review, 1972; **MIL SERV:** US Army; **OTHER ACT & HONORS:** Kiwanis; **HOME ADD:** 1109 Nichol Ln., Nashville, TN 37205, (615)287-6895; **BUS ADD:** One Vantage Way, Suite 100, Nashville, TN 37228, (615)748-3009.

KELZER, Robert A.——B: Oct. 17, 1950, Minneapolis, MN, *Pres.*, R-Systems, Inc.; **PRIM RE ACT:** Broker, Developer; **SERVICES:** Devel., mktg., sales; **PROFL AFFIL & HONORS:** Two boards; **EDUC:** BA, 1972, Adv., USF; **HOME ADD:** 925 Monticello Blvd., (813)526-8008; **BUS ADD:** POB 7087, St. Petersburg, FL 33734, (813)526-8008.

KEMBEL, Robert D.——B: Nov. 17, 1943, Los Angeles, CA, *Owner*, R.D. Kembel & Assoc.; **PRIM RE ACT:** Syndicator, Developer, Owner/Investor; **OTHER RE ACT:** Project. Mgmt.; **SERVICES:** RE Appraisals; **REP CLIENTS:** Mort. Co., Govt., Banks Relocation, Attys., Pvt. Indiv.; **PROFL AFFIL & HONORS:** Affiliate Member MT Bd. of Realtors, Member of the Amer. Instit. of RE Appraisers (MAI); **EDUC:** BS, 1969, RE and Fin., Univ. of MT; **MIL SERV:** US Army, Spec 4; **OTHER ACT & HONORS:** AOPA & SPA (Airplane Owner Pilot Assn.), (Seaplane Pilots Assn.); **HOME ADD:** 530 Grove, Missoula, MT 59801, (406)549-0101; **BUS ADD:** 910 Kensington, Missoula, MT 59801, (406)549-6151.

KEMP, Gail M.——B: June 7, 1953, N.Y., *Atty. at Law*, Marvin, Kennedy, Reese, Shields and Hirsch; **PRIM RE ACT:** Attorney; **SERVICES:** Lease transactions, title exam., contract, zoning, and dev.; **PROFL AFFIL & HONORS:** Amer. CT and New Canaan Bar Assn.; **EDUC:** BA, 1974, Poli Sci., State Univ. of N.Y.; **GRAD EDUC:** JD, 1978, Univ. of San Diego; **EDUC HONORS:** graduated with honors; **BUS ADD:** 34 Elm St. P.O. Box 1147, New Canaan, CT 06840, (203)966-1618.

KEMPER, A. Claude——B: Aug. 5, 1933, Belgium, *VP*, Citibank, N.A., Intl. Servs. Div.; **PRIM RE ACT:** Consultant, Banker; **OTHER RE ACT:** Investment advice and RE Mktg.; **SERVICES:** Investment advice to wealthy for. indivs. and corps. seeking US RE investments requiring in excess of 5 million dollars of equity; **REP CLIENTS:** Wealthy indivs. from all over the world and for. const. cos.; **PREV EMPLOY:** Headed up Citibank's RE acquisitions and mgmt. dept. for Trust Clients; **PROFL AFFIL & HONORS:** ULI; **EDUC:** BS in Commerce, 1958, Bus., Yale Univ. & Univ. of VA; **MIL SERV:** US Army, M/Sgt.; **HOME ADD:** Box AC, Huntington, New York 11743, (516)549-1708; **BUS ADD:** 153 E. 53rd St., New York, NY 10043, (212)559-9084.

KEMPER, Hugh T.——B: Apr. 4, 1943, Albany, NY, *VP & Head of RE Dept.*, Morgan Guaranty Trust Co. of NY, Banking Div.; **OTHER RE ACT:** Construction Lending; **PROFL AFFIL & HONORS:** RE Bd. of NY; **EDUC:** 1965, Harvard Coll.; **EDUC HONORS:** Cum Laude; **HOME ADD:** 57 S. Dr., Plandome, NY 11030, (516)627-6711; **BUS ADD:** 23 Wall St., New York, NY 10015, (212)483-3931.

KEMPER, Robert E.——B: Nov. 12, 1944, Massillon, OH, *VP*, Wyoming Indus. Devel. Corp.; **PRIM RE ACT:** Developer, Lender, Owner/Investor, Property Manager; **SERVICES:** Investment analysis, valuation, prop. negotiator, lease negotiator, project financing, prop. mgmt., mkt. analysis; **PREV EMPLOY:** Econ. planning; **PROFL AFFIL & HONORS:** WY Chamber, Soc. of Amer. Forresters, Dir. of Indus. Dist., VP Capital Corp., of WY (SBIC); **EDUC:** BS, 1968, Forest Mgmt., VA Poly. Inst.; **GRAD EDUC:** MS, 1974, Forest Sci., UT St.; **EDUC HONORS:** Xi Sigma Pi; **MIL SERV:** Army Engr., Capt., DMG, 1968-72; **HOME ADD:** 1035 Cardiff, Casper, WY 82601, (307)234-1292; **BUS ADD:** Box 612, Casper, WY 82602, (307)234-5351.

KEMPTON, George——*Pres.*, Kysor Industrial Corp.; **PRIM RE ACT:** Property Manager; **BUS ADD:** One Madison Ave., Cadillac, MI 49601, (616)775-4646.*

KENDALL, Gerald R.——B: July 10, 1935, Winnipeg, Can., *Gen. Mgr.*, Dominion Constr. Co., Ltd., Midwest; **PRIM RE ACT:** Engineer, Developer, Builder; **SERVICES:** Design, constr., fin., land assembly; **REP CLIENTS:** Can. Safeway Ltd., Gen. Motors., Can. Motorways, Ltd.; **PREV EMPLOY:** 14 yrs. as a consulting engrg.; **PROFL AFFIL & HONORS:** NE Soc. of Profl. Engrs., Assn. of Profl. Engrs. of Manitoba; **EDUC:** BS, 1957, Mech. Engrg., Univ. of Manitoba; **MIL SERV:** US Army, Pvt.; **OTHER ACT & HONORS:** Council Member, Winnipeg C of C; **HOME ADD:** 155 Victoria Cresc., Winnipeg, R2M 1X6, Manitoba, Canada, (204)256-0270; **BUS ADD:** 701-310 Broadway Ave., Winnipeg, R3C 056, Manitoba, Canada, (204)942-3371.

KENDALL, Lawrence M.——B: June 12, 1946, Emporia, KS, *Pres./Broker*, The Group, Inc., Real Estate Assoc.; **PRIM RE ACT:** Broker, Developer, Owner/Investor, Property Manager, Syndicator; **SERVICES:** Brokerage, investment counseling, devel. and synd. of comml. props.; **REP CLIENTS:** Investors in comml. props., builders and devels.; **PROFL AFFIL & HONORS:** NAR; RESSI, RNMI, 1980 Realtor of the Year, Ft. Collins Bd. of Realtors; Dir., Ft. Collins

Bd. of Realtors; **EDUC:** Bus. Admin., 1969, Mktg., KS State Univ.; **GRAD EDUC:** MBA, 1972, Mgmt., KS State Univ.; **EDUC HONORS:** Dean's List, Dean's List; **MIL SERV:** US Army, 1969-1972, Capt., Army Commendation Medal; **HOME ADD:** 807 Warren Landing, Ft. Collins, CO 80525, (303)223-0349; **BUS ADD:** 425 W. Mulberry, Ft. Collins, CO 80521, (303)493-0700.

KENISON, Robert S.——*Assoc. Genl. Cnsl.*, Department of Housing and Urban Development, Ofc. of Assisted Housing & Comm. Dev.; **PRIM RE ACT:** Lender; **BUS ADD:** 451 Seventh St., S.W., Washington, DC 20410, (202)426-5212.*

KENNEDY, Henry, Jr.——**B:** Apr. 15, 1916, Chatham, VA, *Owner*, Davidson Realty Co.; **PRIM RE ACT:** Broker, Owner/Investor, Property Manager; **PROFL AFFIL & HONORS:** Thomasville Bd. of Realtors, GRI; **OTHER ACT & HONORS:** Pres., Thomasville Bd. of Realtors, 1968-1969; **HOME ADD:** POB 10, Thomasville, NC 27360, (919)476-7871; **BUS ADD:** POB 10, Thomasville, NC 27360, (919)476-6665.

KENNEDY, John C.——**B:** Nov. 23, 1942, Huntington, IN, *Owner - Broker*, Kennedy Realtors; **PRIM RE ACT:** Broker, Appraiser, Owner/Investor, Property Manager; **SERVICES:** RE brokerage, appraisals, prop. mgmt., auctions; **REP CLIENTS:** appraisal serv. to: Transamerica, Merrill Lynch, Employee Transfer, Home Equity, Executrans; **PREV EMPLOY:** Mgr., Larry F. Wells Realty 1972-75; **PROFL AFFIL & HONORS:** IN Assn. of Realtors, NAR, RNMI, GRI, CRS, CRB, Realtor of the Year 1976, 1979-80 Bd. Pres.; **EDUC:** 1971, Bus. Admin., Anthro., Ball State Univ.; **MIL SERV:** USN, HN; **OTHER ACT & HONORS:** City Council 1976-80 (Pres. 78-80); Kiwanis (Pres.), Elks, F.O.P.; Salvation Army Advisory Bd.; **HOME ADD:** 865 Warren St., Huntington, IN 46750, (219)356-6252; **BUS ADD:** 231 W. Park Dr., Huntington, IN 46750, (219)356-0333.

KENNEDY, John P.——*Assoc. Gen. Counsel*, Department of Housing and Urban Development, Ofc. of Program Enforcement; **PRIM RE ACT:** Lender; **BUS ADD:** 451 Seventh St., S.W., Washington, DC 20410, (202)755-6999.*

KENNEDY, Paul I.——**B:** Oct. 29, 1943, Toronto, ON, CAN, *Sr. VP*, Nu-West Development Corp., Urban/Office Div.; **PRIM RE ACT:** Developer; **SERVICES:** Devel. of Comml. Props.; **PREV EMPLOY:** 1978-79 Gen. Mgr., Houston Centre, Houston, TX; 1974-78 VP, Urban Devel. Grp., Cadillac Fairview Corp.; VP CAN Sq. Corp.; 1971-74 Dir. Const. Owners Assn. of AB; **EDUC:** BA, 1966, Pol./Sci., Univ. of Toronto; **GRAD EDUC:** MBA, 1970, Econ. & Pol. Sci., Harvard Univ.; **HOME ADD:** 645 Woodbridge Way, Sherwood Pk., AB, CAN, (403)464-3969; **BUS ADD:** 9405-50 St., Edmonton, Alberta, CAN, (403)468-2900.

KENNEDY, Ray D.——**B:** Dec. 15, 1937, Jacksboro, TN, *Sr. Assessment Systems Coord.*, Office of the Comptroller, State of TN, Prop. Assessments; **PRIM RE ACT:** Consultant, Appraiser, Assessor; **OTHER RE ACT:** Statistician; **SERVICES:** Valuation, instruction, research and devel.; **PREV EMPLOY:** Appraiser, Columbus-Muscogee Cty., GA 1964-1972; **PROFL AFFIL & HONORS:** SREA, NARA, SRA, CRA, TCA; **MIL SERV:** US Army, Sgt. 1955-1958; **OTHER ACT & HONORS:** Pres., Columbus, GA Chap. of SREA, 1969-1970; **HOME ADD:** 104 Shady Dr., Hendersonville, TN 37075, (615)824-6858; **BUS ADD:** Suite 1400, James K. Polk State Office Bldg., 505 Deaderick St., Nashville, TN 37219, (615)741-2837.

KENNEDY, Thomas R.——**B:** Oct. 29, 1939, Brooklyn, NY, *Part., Dir. of Fin.*, The Pyramid Cos. & Affiliates; **PRIM RE ACT:** Developer, Builder, Owner/Investor; **OTHER RE ACT:** Company's program activity is regional type shopping centers and office buildings; arrange all project financings; market analysis; **SERVICES:** Ctr. Devel., mgmt. Also devels. office bldgs.; **REP CLIENTS:** All affiliated Pyramid entities; **PREV EMPLOY:** Assoc, James D. Landauer Assocs., Inc. (1971-72), Tr. Cabot, Cabot & Forbes Co. (1974-76), Part. Phoenix Props. Grp. (1976-80); **EDUC:** BS, 1961, Bldg. Sci., Rensselaer Poly. Inst.; **GRAD EDUC:** MBA, 1970, Harvard Grad. Sch. of Bus. Admin; **MIL SERV:** USN, Lt., Sec. of Navy Medal; **HOME ADD:** 34 Jarvis Dr., Manlius, NY 13104, (315)682-7310; **BUS ADD:** 5795 Widewaters Pkwy, Dewitt, NY 13214, (315)445-0429.

KENNEDY, Wallace W.——**B:** Nov. 22, 1934, Century, FL, *Pres.*, Kennedy and Melvin, Professional Association; **PRIM RE ACT:** Attorney, Owner/Investor, Instructor; **SERVICES:** Legal Representation; **REP CLIENTS:** Bds. of Realtors, condo. devels. and converters, devels. and operators of hotels and other comml. props.; **PROFL AFFIL & HONORS:** Member, ABA, The FL Bar, Broward Bar Assn., Recipient of FL Assn. of Realtors Testimonial of Appreciation, 1979; **EDUC:** BA, 1962, Poli. Sci., Univ. of FL; **GRAD EDUC:** LLB, 1964, Law, Univ. of FL; **MIL SERV:** USMC; Maj.; **OTHER ACT & HONORS:** Charter Member and Pres., Diversified Businessmen's Assn., *Who's Who in Florida*; **HOME ADD:** 4221 NE 25th Ave., Ft. Lauderdale, FL 33308, (305)564-7261; **BUS ADD:** 2929 E. Commercial Blvd., Ste. 402, Ft. Lauderdale, FL 33308, (305)776-0660.

KENNEDY, Wayne P.——**B:** Aug. 7, 1930, Oakland, CA, *Dir. Office of Right-of-Way*, Federal Highway Admin.; **PRIM RE ACT:** Regulator; **OTHER RE ACT:** RE Admin.; **SERVICES:** Oversight for all rights-of-way acquired on federally-aided hwys.; **REP CLIENTS:** All 50 states, PR, Guam, Amer. Samoa, and the N. Marianas; **PREV EMPLOY:** Multi-Fami Appraiser for the FHA, 1961-63; Staff Appraiser for the US Army Corps of Engineers, 1957-61; **PROFL AFFIL & HONORS:** Amer. Soc. of Appraisers; Assn. of Govt. Appraisers; Intl. Right-of-Way Assn.; Nat. Assn. of Review Appraisers, ASA, SGA, SRWA, CRA; **EDUC:** BA, 1957, Bus. Admin., San Jose State; **GRAD EDUC:** MS, 1960, Bus. Admin. Maj. in RE, San Jose State; **MIL SERV:** USAF, 1st Lt.; **HOME ADD:** 1746 Lockerbie Ln., Vienna, VA 22180, (703)255-3875; **BUS ADD:** 400 7th St. SW, Washington, DC 20590, (202)426-0342.

KENNELLY, Thomas A.——**B:** Mar. 19, 1933, Torrington, WY, *Pres.*, Kennelly Mort. and Investment, Inc.; **PRIM RE ACT:** Broker, Instructor, Consultant, Appraiser, Lender; **SERVICES:** Mort. banking, comml. only, appraising, joint venturing, devel. consultant; **REP CLIENTS:** State Farm, National Fidelity Life, Western Life, St. Paul Life, Midland Life, ERC Corp., Fidelity Bankers Life, Centennial Life, Amer. Defender Life; **PREV EMPLOY:** VP The Kissell Co., Springfield, OH; **PROFL AFFIL & HONORS:** MBAA, AZ MBA, NARA, Established the Phoenix Comml. Mort. Bankers Assn., Mbr. Alpha Kappa Psi; **EDUC:** BS, 1955, Fin., Univ. of WY and Univ. of Denver; **GRAD EDUC:** Grad. Studies in Fin., 1956, Fin., Univ. of Denver; **OTHER ACT & HONORS:** Bishop Church of Jesus Christ of Latter Day Saints; guest lecturer in fin., AZ State Univ. past 10 yrs.; **HOME ADD:** 7521 E. Edgemont Ave., Scottsdale, AZ 85257; **BUS ADD:** 4841 N. Scottsdale Rd., Scottsdale, AZ 85257, (602)947-4285.

KENNERDELL, Judith Ann——**B:** May 6, 1947, Natrona Heights, PA, *Landscape Arch./Planner*, Hexagon Associates, Limited; **OTHER RE ACT:** Landscape Arch./Planner; **SERVICES:** Site planning & design, zoning & subdiv. code analysis & evaluation, expert testimony, landscape design, arch. design & working drawings, & comml. inter. design, corp. and/or indiv. devel. of all sizes interested in comml. and resid. devel.; **PREV EMPLOY:** M. Robert Fentorn, Pgh., PA and Richard E. Martin, AIA, Philadelphia, PA; **EDUC:** BS, 1969, Landscape Arch./Planning, The PA State Univ.; **OTHER ACT & HONORS:** Nat. Assn. of Women in Construction; **HOME ADD:** 885 N. Easton Rd., 11B2, Glenside, PA 19038; **BUS ADD:** 102 Greenwood Ave., Wyncote, PA 19095, (215)572-6111.

KENNEY, Robert T.——**B:** Apr. 6, 1935, Belmont, MA, *Pres.*, Urban Consulting Associates of Boston, Inc.; **PRIM RE ACT:** Consultant; **OTHER RE ACT:** Urban Fin. Assistance; **SERVICES:** Public Funding, Mcpl. Mgmt., Devel. Planning & Mgmt.; **PREV EMPLOY:** Boston Redevel. Authority for six years Dir.; **PROFL AFFIL & HONORS:** ULI, AIREA, Nat. Assn. of Housing & Redevel., CUED, Greater Boston RE Bd.; **EDUC:** BSBA, 1956, Econ., Boston Coll.; **GRAD EDUC:** MBA, 1961, Fin. Mgmt., Harvard Grad. Bus. School; **EDUC HONORS:** Cum Laude; **MIL SERV:** USN; **OTHER ACT & HONORS:** Bd. of Dirs., Boston Center for the Arts; Treas., Metropolitan Center; Bd. of Dirs., Workingmen's Co-op Bank; Editorial Advisory Bd., Housing & Community Devel. Reporter; **HOME ADD:** 36 Haviland St., Wollaston, MA 02170, (617)742-6640; **BUS ADD:** 150 Causeway St., Boston, MA 02114, (617)742-6640.

KENNEY, Thomas P.——**B:** May 20, 1928, Rochester, NY, *VP*, Draper & Kramer of GA, Inc.; **PRIM RE ACT:** Property Manager; **PROFL AFFIL & HONORS:** IREM, Dekalb Bd. Realtors; **EDUC:** BS, 1954, Accounting, Univ. of IL; **MIL SERV:** US Army, M/Sgt.; **HOME ADD:** 3651 Winview Ct., Tucker, GA 30084, (404)938-8078; **BUS ADD:** 3301 Buckeye Rd. NE, Suite 309, Atlanta, GA 30341.

KENNEY, William J., Jr.——**B:** Mar. 9, 1949, Huntington Park, CA, *Dir. of Leasing*, John S. Griffith & Co.; **PRIM RE ACT:** Developer; **PROFL AFFIL & HONORS:** Dir. CA Bus. Props. Assn.; Assoc. Member Intl. Council of Shopping Ctrs., CA RE Broker's Lic.; **EDUC:** BA, 1970, Econ., Fin., CA State Univ., Fullerton; **EDUC HONORS:** Econ. 4.0 GPA, Bus. Admin. (Fin.) 3.5 GPA; **OTHER ACT & HONORS:** Guest Lecturer Orange Coast Coll., Saddleback Coll., Santa Ana Jr. Coll., Certs. of Appreciation for Service, Kiwanis Intl., Hemet C of C, Newport Harbor/Costa Mesa Bd. of Realtors; **HOME ADD:** 611 Aldean Pl., Newport Bch., CA 92663, (714)631-2160; **BUS ADD:** 3200 Bristol St., Suite 660, Costa Mesa, CA 92626, (714)979-2230.

KENNISON, Michael S.——B: Feb. 5, 1953, Los Angeles, CA, *Dir. of Acquisitions*, AMSTRD Associates; **PRIM RE ACT:** Owner/Investor, Syndicator; **REP CLIENTS:** Pvt. investors and investment cos.; **PROFL AFFIL & HONORS:** SBA, Fin. and RE; **EDUC:** BA, 1976, Hist./Econs.. Univ. of So. IL; **GRAD EDUC:** MBA, Fin. and RE, UCLA; **EDUC HONORS:** Professionals Scholar; **HOME ADD:** 1568 Manning Ave. 4, Los Angeles, CA 90024, (213)475-7852; **BUS ADD:** 1801 Century Park E., Suite 730, Los Angeles, CA 90067, (213)552-4900.

KENNY, Charles——B: July 29, 1928, Boston, MA, *Managing Partner*, C. W. Whittier & Bro.; **PRIM RE ACT:** Broker, Consultant, Appraiser, Property Manager; **SERVICES:** Variety RE services in indus. and comml. field with particular emphasis on office bldgs.; **PROFL AFFIL & HONORS:** ASREC; CRE; AIREA; MAI; SIR, SIR; **EDUC:** BA, 1950, Harvard Coll.; **OTHER ACT & HONORS:** Trustee, Union Warren Savings Bank; Dir., Mass SPCA; **HOME ADD:** 86 Philip St., Medfield, MA 02052, (617)359-4457; **BUS ADD:** One Federal St., Boston, MA 02110, (617)482-6000.

KENNY, John——*Director Mgmt. Serv.*, Seagram, Joseph E. & Sons, Inc.; **PRIM RE ACT:** Property Manager; **BUS ADD:** 800 Third Ave., New York, NY 10022, (212)572-7000.*

KENNY, Mark V.——B: Apr. 26, 1948, Baltimore, MD, *Pres.*, Sierra-Pacific Capital Co., Inc.; **PRIM RE ACT:** Owner/Investor; **OTHER RE ACT:** CPA; **SERVICES:** Public synd. and devel. of comml. props., consulting, investment counseling; **REP CLIENTS:** Indiv. and inst. investors, devel., public synd.; **PREV EMPLOY:** Asst. to Pres., Univer. Grp. Inc., 1978-1979; Controller/Treasurer, Centennial Grp., Inc., 1977-1978; **PROFL AFFIL & HONORS:** Member AICPA; Intl. Assn. of Fin. Planners, CPA; **EDUC:** BA, 1971, Bus. Admin./Fin., CA State Univ. at Fullerton; **GRAD EDUC:** MBA, 1977, Fin./RE, CA State Univ. at Long Beach; **OTHER ACT & HONORS:** *Who's Who in Orange Cty.*, 1980 Edition; **HOME ADD:** 26422 Pebble Creek, El Toro, CA 92630; **BUS ADD:** 5140 Birch St., Third Floor, Newport Beach, CA 92660, (714)975-0191.

KENT, Alfred——*Dir. RE*, Millipore Corp.; **PRIM RE ACT:** Property Manager; **BUS ADD:** 80 Ashby Rd., Bedford, MA 01730, (617)275-9200.*

KENT, John Paul——B: Nov. 10, 1956, Houston, TX, *VP*, Kent Enterprises; **PRIM RE ACT:** Broker, Consultant, Developer, Builder, Property Manager; **SERVICES:** Land devel., const., re sales; **EDUC:** BS, 1978, Econ., Willamette Univ.; **EDUC HONORS:** John Booth Scholar, Athlete Award; **HOME ADD:** 910 Second St., Gilroy, CA 95020, (408)842-5429; **BUS ADD:** 7949 A Wren Ave., Gilroy, CA 95020, (408)847-1551.

KENT, Jon——B: Feb. 26, 1945, NY, NY, *Asst. Gen. Counsel*, General RE Corp.; **PRIM RE ACT:** Attorney; **OTHER RE ACT:** Assemblage, devel., const.; **PROFL AFFIL & HONORS:** MA, NY and CT Bars; **EDUC:** AB, 1966, Brown Univ.; **GRAD EDUC:** JD, 1969, Boston Univ. Law School; **HOME ADD:** 5 Highwood Ln., Westport, CT 06880, (203)227-2572; **BUS ADD:** 600 Steamboat Rd., Greenwich, CT 06830, (203)622-4528.

KENT, Roy N.——*VP*, Fidelity Mutual Life, Mort. & RE; **PRIM RE ACT:** Developer, Builder; **OTHER RE ACT:** Investor; **SERVICES:** Mort. Lending, Joint Ventures, Equities; **REP CLIENTS:** Maj. Dev. Throughout USA; **BUS ADD:** Fidelity Mutual Life Bldg., So. PA Sq., Philadelphia, PA 19101, (215)977-8261.

KENT, Thomas James——B: Jan. 2, 1930, NY, NY, *Dir. RE*, Stauffer Chemical Co.; **OTHER RE ACT:** Corp. Office & Warehouse Leasing; **PROFL AFFIL & HONORS:** SIR (Assoc. Member), ASME (Member), Assoc. for Systems Mgmt. (Member), Amer. Assoc. of Cost Engineers (Member); **EDUC:** B. Mech. Engineering, 1950, N Y Univ.; **GRAD EDUC:** MME, MBA, (RE & Mgmt.), 1952, 1956, 1978, NY Univ. and Golden Gate Univ.; **MIL SERV:** US Army, Signal Corp., Capt.; **OTHER ACT & HONORS:** Golden Gate Univ. Advisory Comm. for RE Curriculum; **HOME ADD:** 2676 Cedro Lane, Walnut Creek, CA 94598, (415)937-3626; **BUS ADD:** 636 CA ST., P.O. Box 3050, San Francisco, CA 94119, (415)544-9221.

KENT, Wendel G.——B: Oct. 27, 1931, Golden City, MO, *Owner*, Colorado Land Co.; **PRIM RE ACT:** Broker, Developer; **SERVICES:** Land brokerage and devel.; **PROFL AFFIL & HONORS:** Realtor; **EDUC:** BS, 1958, Agriculture, Univ. of MO; **MIL SERV:** US Army, Cpl.; **OTHER ACT & HONORS:** Castle Rock Planning Comm.; **HOME ADD:** 48 Oak Ridge Dr., Box 950, Castle Rock, CO 80104, (303)688-9556; **BUS ADD:** 513 Wilcox St., Castle Rock, CO 80104, (303)688-3158.

KENYON, Archibald B., Jr.——B: Aug. 22, 1927, Wakefield, RI, *Atty.*, Kenyon & Aukerman; **PRIM RE ACT:** Attorney, Developer; **OTHER RE ACT:** Title Ins.; **SERVICES:** Legal and Title Ins.; **PREV EMPLOY:** Town Solicitor for Towns of S Kingstown and Richmond; **PROFL AFFIL & HONORS:** Amer. and RI Bar Assns.; **EDUC:** BS, 1950, Econ. and Acctg., Univ. of RI I; **GRAD EDUC:** LLB, 1953, Georgetown Univ. Law; **EDUC HONORS:** Phi Kappa Phi; **MIL SERV:** USN, Seaman 1C; **HOME ADD:** 89 Pine Hill Rd., Wakefield, RI 02879, (401)783-5486; **BUS ADD:** 51 Tower Hill Rd., Wakefield, RI 02879, (401)789-0217.

KEPNER, P. Leslie——B: Sept. 13, 1927, Princeton, IL, Dickerson Realtors Inc.; **PRIM RE ACT:** Broker, Consultant, Appraiser, Developer, Builder; **SERVICES:** Resid. RE Sales (New construction, existing homes); **PROFL AFFIL & HONORS:** Rockford Bd. of Realtors; IL Assn. Realtors; NAR; RELO, GRI; CRS; CRB; **MIL SERV:** USN, Fireman, 1945-1947; **OTHER ACT & HONORS:** Chmn., Profl. Standards Comm., Rockford Bd. of Realtors, 1978 to 1982; Sec., Rockford Bd. of Realtors; Member & Chmn. Elect, Profl. Standards Comm. IL Assn. Realtors; **HOME ADD:** 1605 Brownwood Dr., Rockford, IL 61107, (815)968-4260; **BUS ADD:** 631 N. Longwood, Rockford, IL 61107, (815)965-4225.

KEPPLER, William——*VP Tech. Oper.*, Schering-Plough Corp.; **PRIM RE ACT:** Property Manager; **BUS ADD:** Galloping Hill Rd., Kenilworth, NJ 07033, (201)931-2000.*

KERFOOT, Roy L.——B: Apr. 16, 1923, Boston, KY, *Owner-Broker*, Roy L. Kerfoot Realtor; **PRIM RE ACT:** Broker, Appraiser, Builder, Property Manager, Assessor, Insuror; **PREV EMPLOY:** Asst. Controller Acctg.; **PROFL AFFIL & HONORS:** Louisville Bd. of Realtors, LaGrange C. of C., CRPA, GRI; **EDUC:** Acctg., R.E. Ins., U. of Louisville, Ky.; **MIL SERV:** USAF 1943-1945, S/Sgt., Air Medal, Active Duty Europe with 6 Battle Stars; **OTHER ACT & HONORS:** Masonic - Blue Lodge, Scottish Rite, Shrine Filson Club, LaGrange Kiwanis Club, Past Pres.; **HOME ADD:** 1300 Yager Ln., LaGrange, KY 40031, (502)222-9265; **BUS ADD:** 1300 Yager Ln., LaGrange, KY 40031, (502)222-9847.

KERLEY, Jack D.——B: May 13, 1934, WV, *Pres.*, Kerley & Assoc., Inc.; **PRIM RE ACT:** Broker, Consultant, Property Manager; **OTHER RE ACT:** Mgmt. & Brokerage; **SERVICES:** Sales, leasing, consultation, mgmt.; **PROFL AFFIL & HONORS:** BOMA, IREM, C of C, CPM, RPA; **MIL SERV:** USAF, Lt. Col.; **HOME ADD:** 1142 Hampton Way, Atlanta, GA 30324, (404)325-4657; **BUS ADD:** 1015 Hurt Bldg., Atlanta, GA 30303, (404)522-4960.

KERMANI, Fereidoun——B: July 25, 1944, Tehran, Iran, *Pres.*, K.F.N. Development Co.; **PRIM RE ACT:** Consultant, Appraiser, Architect, Developer, Builder, Owner/Investor, Syndicator; **SERVICES:** Investment, planning, archit. consultant; builder; synd. of resid. prop.; **PREV EMPLOY:** Partner and Head of Planning Dept. of an Arch. Planning Consultant; **PROFL AFFIL & HONORS:** APA, ITE, Associate Member AIA; **EDUC:** High School Diploma, 1956-1962, Mathematics, Alborz High School, Tehran; **GRAD EDUC:** M.Arch, MA, URB, DES, DIP Transp. Des., 1962-1972, Resid. Devel., Tehran Univ., Manchester Univ. (UK), Liverpool Univ. (UK); **HOME ADD:** 26516 Basswood Ave., Rancho Palos Verdes, CA 90274, (213)378-5042; **BUS ADD:** 415 N. Broadway, Suite 1-D, Redondo Beach, CA 90277, (213)372-1918.

KERN, Robert F.——B: Aug. 16, 1933, St. Louis, MO, *Pres.*, Kern & Padgett Management Co., Inc.; **PRIM RE ACT:** Developer, Owner/Investor; **PREV EMPLOY:** Exec. FP, Cousins Props., Atlanta, GA; Exec. VP, Vantage Cos., Dallas, TX; **PROFL AFFIL & HONORS:** Cobb C of C, Exec. Dir.; Nat. Assn. of Indus. and Office Parks; **EDUC:** BA, 1955, Pol. Sci., Miami Univ., Oxford, OH; **MIL SERV:** USAF, Capt.; **HOME ADD:** 3190 Lemons Ridge, Atlanta, GA 30339, (404)432-7144; **BUS ADD:** 120 Interstate N. Pkwy. E., Suite 150, Atlanta, GA 30339, (404)955-8880.

KERR, Donald C.——B: May 11, 1921, Montreal, Que., *VP*, Canada Permanent Trust Co., RE Services; **PRIM RE ACT:** Broker, Appraiser, Banker, Lender; **OTHER RE ACT:** Franchisor Corp. Relocation; **SERVICES:** Buying & selling resid., invest., comml. & indus. RE; mort. lending; banking services; **REP CLIENTS:** Corp. Relocation - Bell Can., IBM, Xerox; **PREV EMPLOY:** Builder Devel., Self Employed; **PROFL AFFIL & HONORS:** Appraisal Institute; Urban Devel. Institute; Fellow, RE Inst.; Member, Assoc. of Ont. Land Econ., FRI; RPA; OLE; **EDUC:** Univ. of Toronto; **MIL SERV:** Signal Corps, Maj., MID, CD; **OTHER ACT & HONORS:** Alderman/Controller - Borough of Etobicoke, 15 yrs.; **HOME ADD:** 97 Wimbleton Rd., Islington, M9A3S4, Ont., Can., (416)231-8233; **BUS ADD:** 145 Front St. E., Toronto, M5A1E3, Ontario, Canada, (416)362-7341.

KERR, Ivan S.——**B:** Aug. 26, 1935, Minneapolis, MN, *Exec. V.P., Comml. Div.*, Northland Mort. Co., Comml. Div.; **PRIM RE ACT:** Banker; **SERVICES:** Mort. banking, joint venture fin., equity fin.; **PREV EMPLOY:** Comml. Div. Mgr., Mort. Assoc., Inc.; **PROFL AFFIL & HONORS:** MBAA, NAIOP, MBA of MN, ICSC; **EDUC:** Lib. Arts, Univ. of MN; **MIL SERV:** US Army; **HOME ADD:** 5704 DeVille Dr., Edina,, MN 55436, (612)933-5387; **BUS ADD:** 6600 France Ave. S., Suite 570, Minneapolis, MN 55435, (612)925-7736.

KERR, John W., Jr.——**B:** July 30, 1937, Ft. Monroe, VA, *Tax Partner*, Goodman & Co., CPA's; **PRIM RE ACT:** Instructor; **OTHER RE ACT:** CPA; **SERVICES:** Instructor in taxation; acctg.; **PROFL AFFIL & HONORS:** AICPA, VA Soc. of CPA's, ABA, VA Bar Assn., CPA (VA & FL), Member VA State Bd. of Acctg., 1978 Tidewater Bus. person of Yr. Award; **EDUC:** BBA, 1960, Acctg. & Econ., Old Dominion Univ.; **GRAD EDUC:** JD, 1965, Law, George Washington Univ. Law Sch.; **EDUC HONORS:** 1981 Ourstanding Acctg. Alumni Award; **OTHER ACT & HONORS:** Tidewater Estate Planning Council, Kiwanis Club of Norfolk; **HOME ADD:** 1160 Revere Pt. Rd., Virginia Beach, VA 23455, (804)460-0139; **BUS ADD:** 500 Plume St. E, 700 Bank of VA Bldg., Norfolk, VA 23510, (804)622-6366.

KERR, Jon A.——**B:** Feb. 11, 1943, Great Falls, MT, *Atty.*, Jon A. Kerr, Attorney at Law; **PRIM RE ACT:** Attorney; **SERVICES:** Gen. legal work & litigation in fed. courts and before fed. agencies, primarily HUD, registrations and exemptions under Interstate Land Sales Full Disclosure Act; construction, contract claims litigation against US; direct mail marketing law; **PROFL AFFIL & HONORS:** ABA; DC, VA and CO Bar Assns.; **EDUC:** BA, 1964, Eng., Univ. of VA; **GRAD EDUC:** JD, 1967, Washington & Lee Univ.; **EDUC HONORS:** Cum Laude; **MIL SERV:** US Army, Cpt. 1967-1971; **HOME ADD:** 10810 Hunter Station Rd., Vienna, VA 22180, (703)620-9360; **BUS ADD:** 4 east Loudoun St., Leesburg, VA 22075, (703)777-9191.

KERR, Keith H.——**B:** Jan. 14, 1931, Kentfield, CA, *RE Broker*, Scandia Realty, Inc.; **PRIM RE ACT:** Broker, Instructor, Syndicator, Owner/Investor; **SERVICES:** Investment Counseling, Resid. and Comml. Sales; **PREV EMPLOY:** Prof. of Bus., City Coll. of San Francisco (full-time faculty since 1969); **EDUC:** BA, 1956, Pol. Sci., Univ. of CA, Berkeley; **GRAD EDUC:** MA, 1967, Pol. Sci., San Fran. State Univ.; **MIL SERV:** US Army, Sp4; **OTHER ACT & HONORS:** Col. Military Intelligence, USAR; VP, Canon Kip Comm. House, San Fran., Past Pres. - San Fran. Higher Educ. Assn.; **HOME ADD:** 1903 Baker St., San Francisco, CA 94115, (415)563-5876; **BUS ADD:** 765 Monterey Blvd., San Francisco, CA 94127, (415)586-7400.

KERR, Stuart R.——**B:** Feb. 23, 1932, Brooklyn, NY, *Pres.*, Kerr Realty Appraisal Co.; **PRIM RE ACT:** Instructor, Consultant, Appraiser; **SERVICES:** RE appraisal, consulting, and instr.; **REP CLIENTS:** Merrill Lynch Relocation Service, Homequity, Employee Transfer Co.; **PREV EMPLOY:** RE Brokerage since 1956; **PROFL AFFIL & HONORS:** Counselor Mbr. NAIFA, Realtor, Nat. Treas. NAIFA, Nat. Bd. of Dir. NAIFA since 1972; **EDUC:** Bus. and Lib. Arts, 1953, Columbia Coll., Columbia Univ.; **MIL SERV:** USN, Lt., European Occupation Medal, National Service Medal; **OTHER ACT & HONORS:** Past Master Temple Lodge No. 173 F and AM; **HOME ADD:** Salisbury Point, South Nyack, NY 10960, (212)914-1357; **BUS ADD:** PO Box 122, No. 2 Railroad Ave., Montvale, NJ 07645, (201)391-8687.

KERR, W. Bruce——**B:** Mar. 9, 1948, Stillwater, OK, *VP*, Oklahoma Christian College Investment Corp.; **PRIM RE ACT:** Developer, Owner/Investor, Property Manager; **PROFL AFFIL & HONORS:** OK Bar Assn., ABA, OK Cty. Bar Assn., Phi Delta Phi; **EDUC:** BA, 1969, Mgmt., Econ., OK Christian Coll.; **GRAD EDUC:** JD, 1979, OK City Univ.; **EDUC HONORS:** Cum Laude; **HOME ADD:** 2920 Smiling Hill Blvd., Edmond, OK 73034, (405)478-2631; **BUS ADD:** Rt. 1 Box 141, Oklahoma City, OK 73111, (405)478-1661.

KERR, Whitney E.——**B:** May 2, 1934, Kansas City, MO, *Prin.*, Jones & Co., Realtors & Mortgage Bankers; **PRIM RE ACT:** Broker, Consultant, Appraiser, Developer, Owner/Investor, Property Manager; **SERVICES:** Mr. Kerr specializes in counseling on site aquisitions, land use and solutions for problem prop. involving indiv., corp., banks and attys. handling problem situations; land use along interstate highways and solving transitional problems in declining urban areas; **PROFL AFFIL & HONORS:** Member of MO Bar and Kansas City Bar Assns.; Dir. and past VP of the RE Bd. of Kansas City; Past Dir. of the MO RE Assn.; Past Pres. of the W MO-KS Chapt., Soc. of Indus. Realtors, RNMI-Former member of the Bd. of Gov.; CCIM designation; Past VP and Dir. of the C of C of Kansas City; Member of the Amer. Soc. of RE Counselors; **GRAD EDUC:** AB, Princeton Univ., 1956; LLB & JD, 1959, Univ. of MO at Kansas City; **MIL SERV:** USAF, Capt. Res., Judge Adv. Gen. Office; **OTHER ACT & HONORS:** Dir. and member of Exec. Comm. of the Kansas City Corp. for Indus. Devel.; Jr. Warden and Vestryman, Grace & Holy Trinity Episcopal Cathedral; Dir. and Exec. Comm. Member, St. Lude Hospital; Past Pres. Kansas City Museum; **HOME ADD:** 704 E 47th St., Kansas City, MO 64110, (816)561-0032; **BUS ADD:** 1200 Brookfield Bldg., 101 W 11th St., Kansas City, MO 64105, (816)842-5711.

KERR, William A.——**B:** Jan. 6, 1942, Los Angeles, *Pres.*, William A. Kerr A Profl. Corp.; **PRIM RE ACT:** Attorney; **SERVICES:** All Fields of RE Law; **PROFL AFFIL & HONORS:** State Bar of CA; Real Prop. Sec. of State Bar, Los Angeles Cty. Bar Assn.; Santa Monica Bay Dist. Bar Assn., ABA; **EDUC:** BS, 1964, Bus. Admin., UCLA; **GRAD EDUC:** JD, 1967, UCLA; **HOME ADD:** 20966 Pacific Coast Hwy., Malibu, CA 90; **BUS ADD:** 2120 Wilshire Blvd., 4th Floor, Santa Monica, CA 90403, (213)453-5473.

KERSH, Jack R.——**B:** Oct. 4, 1922, Jackson, MS, *Owner & Mgr.*, Kersh Realty; **PRIM RE ACT:** Broker, Appraiser, Developer, Owner/Investor; **PROFL AFFIL & HONORS:** Natl. State & Local Assns. of Realtors; FLI; Nat. Assn. of RE Appraisers; Natl. Auctioneers Assn.; **EDUC:** 1944, USMM; Weaver School of RE/Jim Graham School of Auctioneering; **MIL SERV:** USN; Lt.; **OTHER ACT & HONORS:** Rotary Club and Masonic Lodge; **HOME ADD:** PO Box 506, Heidelberg, MS 39439; **BUS ADD:** PO Box 506, Heidelberg, MS 39439, (601)787-3481.

KERSTEN, Larry C.——**B:** May 27, Wausau, WI, *Dir. of Project Purchasing*, Holiday Inns, Inc.; **PRIM RE ACT:** Broker; **SERVICES:** Purchasing; **PROFL AFFIL & HONORS:** Realtor, Broker Lic. in IL, IN, TN; **EDUC:** BBA, 1962, Mgmt. Engineer, Loyola Univ.; **GRAD EDUC:** GEO-MBA, 1966, Hotel & Rest. Admin., Cornell Univ.; **MIL SERV:** US Army, 1st Lt.; **OTHER ACT & HONORS:** Notary Public; **HOME ADD:** 2340 Kempton Dr., Germantown, TN 38138, (901)755-0522; **BUS ADD:** 3796 Lamar Ave., Memphis, TN 38195, (901)369-7469.

KERSTETTER, Ralph A., Esq.——**B:** Nov. 1, 1948, Philadelphia, PA, *Atty. at Law*, Lillick McHose & Charles, RE and Bus.; **PRIM RE ACT:** Attorney; **SERVICES:** Legal Advice; **REP CLIENTS:** Corp. and instnl. RE owners, investors, devels., and lenders, including banks, employee trusts and for. clients; **PREV EMPLOY:** Tax accountant, Ernst & Whinney, San Francisco & Oakland,CA 1977-79; **PROFL AFFIL & HONORS:** ABA; State Bar of CA; San Francisco Bar Assn.; **EDUC:** BA, 1976, Fin., Univ. of S. FL; **GRAD EDUC:** JD, 1979, Law, Boalt Hall School of Law, Univ. of CA at Berkeley; **EDUC HONORS:** Summa Cum Laude; Dean's Award for Academic Excellence; **MIL SERV:** US Navy, PO 2nd cl.; **HOME ADD:** 1174 Dolores St., San Francisco, CA 94110, (415)824-4276; **BUS ADD:** 2 Embarcadero Ctr., Suite 2600, San Francisco, CA 94111, (415)421-4600.

KERZNER, Paul——**B:** Nov. 3, 1950, Brooklyn, NY, *Coordinator Special Projects*, Consolidated Edison Co. of NY, Brooklyn Div.; **PRIM RE ACT:** Broker, Consultant, Attorney, Appraiser, Developer, Syndicator; **SERVICES:** Housing rehabilitation, arch. design serv., cooperative housing, neighborhood promotion, Legal consultation; **PROFL AFFIL & HONORS:** NY State Bar Assn.; NY Cty. Bar Assn.; **EDUC:** BA, 1972, Amer. Hist., Fordham Univ.; **GRAD EDUC:** JD, 1975, Law, Brooklyn Law School; **EDUC HONORS:** Magna Cum Laude, Moot Court Honor Soc.; **OTHER ACT & HONORS:** Pres., Ridgewood Prop. Owners & Civic Assn.; Pres., Greater Ridgewood Restoration Corp.; Bd. of Dirs., NYC Brownstone Revival Comm.; Bd. of Dirs., Bklyn Brownstone Conf.; V. Chmn., NYC Queens Comm. Bd. #5; Member of the Legal firm, Castoria, Ferrara & Kerzner; **HOME ADD:** 58-41 69 Ave., Ridgewood, NY 11385, (212)381-3366; **BUS ADD:** 30 Flatbush Ave., Brooklyn, NY 11217, (212)834-3556.

KESLAR, William A.——**B:** Nov. 18, 1951, Zanesville, OH, *Contract Mgr.*, The Bunce Corp., Interiors; **PRIM RE ACT:** Consultant, Architect, Developer, Builder, Owner/Investor; **SERVICES:** staffing/operations consulting, space planning, design, const., furnishing; **REP CLIENTS:** corporate/profl. office tenants, fin. insts.; **PROFL AFFIL & HONORS:** BOMA; **EDUC:** AB, 1973, Philosophy, Princeton Univ.; **GRAD EDUC:** MBA cand., 1983, Mktg., Washington Univ.; **OTHER ACT & HONORS:** Dir., Skinker, DeBalivreve Community Council; **HOME ADD:** 6185 Kingsbury, St. Louis, MO 63112, (314)863-3649; **BUS ADD:** 1266 Andas, St. Louis, MO 63132, (314)997-0300.

KESSLER, A.D., PhD——*Chairman*, International Exchangors Association; **OTHER RE ACT:** Profl. Assn. Admin.; **BUS ADD:** Box 2446, Heucatia, CA 92024, (714)438-2446.*

KESSLER, Jan——*Mgr. Facilities*, Shaklee Corp.; **PRIM RE ACT:** Property Manager; **BUS ADD:** 444 Market St., San Francisco, CA 94111, (415)954-3000.*

KESSLER, Neil S.——B: Oct. 15, 1947, Kansas City, MO, *Atty.*, Cohen, Abeloff & Staples, PC; **PRIM RE ACT:** Attorney; **PROFL AFFIL & HONORS:** VA Bar Assn., VA State Bar, ABA, Richmond Bar Assn., V. Chmn. RE Sect. of Richmond Bar Assn.; Sec. Const. Law Sect. of VA State Bar; **EDUC:** BA, 1969, Washington & Lee Univ.; **GRAD EDUC:** JD, 1973, George Washington Univ.; **EDUC HONORS:** Cum Laude, 'Honors'; **HOME ADD:** 7904 Hungary Springs Ct., Richmond, VA 23228, (804)270-9427; **BUS ADD:** 207 W. Franklin St., Richmond, VA 23220, (804)649-2341.

KESSLER, Richard S.——B: Apr. 22, 1928, Russell, KS, *Owner*, R. S. Kessler & Assoc., RE Appraisal Services; **PRIM RE ACT:** Consultant, Appraiser; **SERVICES:** Comm'l, Indus., Royal, Residential Appraisals; **REP CLIENTS:** Corp. Engr., FAA, Dept. of Transportation, Texaco, Phillips Pet. Co., Getty Refining, Mort. Brokers, Investors, Trusts, etc.; **PREV EMPLOY:** Chief Appraiser, KS Dept. Transp.; **PROFL AFFIL & HONORS:** AIREA, MAI, SRPA, ASA; **EDUC:** BS Econ. & Bus. Adm., 1951, Fort Hays State Univ., Hays, KS; **MIL SERV:** US Army Corps of Engrs., Sgt., WW II Amer. Defense, Good Conduct; **HOME ADD:** 210 Willo Esque., Wichita, KS 67209, (316)942-0817; **BUS ADD:** 830 N. Main, Wichita, KS 67209, (316)267-1047.

KESSLER, Sandford J.——B: May 9, 1951, Youngstown, PA, *Salesman*, Lackey Realty; **PRIM RE ACT:** Owner/Investor; **SERVICES:** Fin. Counseling, Prop. Mgr.; **PREV EMPLOY:** Pritchard Realtor, Meadville, PA 16327; **EDUC:** Mechanical Engrg., 1972, Univ. of Cincinnati; **HOME ADD:** 4175 Lockwood Blvd., Youngstown, OH 44512, (216)788-0346; **BUS ADD:** 302 McClure Rd., Youngstown, OH 44512, (216)758-9701.

KESSLER, Steven P.——B: Mar. 7, 1942, Brooklyn, NY, Lauer & Kessler; **PRIM RE ACT:** Attorney; **SERVICES:** Legal; **REP CLIENTS:** Devels., lenders and synds., as well as indiv. and instnl. investors and owners of comml. and resid. prop.; **EDUC:** BA, 1963, Philosophy, Dartmouth Coll.; **GRAD EDUC:** LLB, 1966, Columbia Law School; **EDUC HONORS:** Cum Laude; **HOME ADD:** 1070 Park Ave., New York, NY 10028; **BUS ADD:** Two Dag Hammerskjold Plaza, New York, NY 10017, (212)371-3710.

KETCHUM, R. Kevin——B: Jan. 9, 1952, Glendale, CA, *Dir. of RE*, Thomas Properties; **PRIM RE ACT:** Developer, Owner/Investor, Property Manager; **SERVICES:** RE Portfolio Mgmt. Devel. of Income Props.; **REP CLIENTS:** Indiv. Investors in Income Props.; **PREV EMPLOY:** Gen. VP, Balboa Const. 1976-1979; **PROFL AFFIL & HONORS:** San Fernando Valley Indus. League; **EDUC:** BA, 1975, Psych.; **EDUC HONORS:** Dean's List; **OTHER ACT & HONORS:** Oak Park Civic Assn.; **HOME ADD:** Agoura, CA 91301; **BUS ADD:** PO Box 92151, Los Angeles, CA 90009.

KETTENMANN, Kurt——B: Feb. 15, 1926, Cleveland, OH, *VP/Div. Head*, Bankers Trust Co., Mort. Banking Div.; **PRIM RE ACT:** Banker; **SERVICES:** Warehousing lines of credit; **PREV EMPLOY:** Citibank; White Weld & Co.; Merrill, Lynch-Hubbard; **PROFL AFFIL & HONORS:** ABA, Housing and RE Fin. Exec. Comm.; Advisory Comm., NYU Mort. Inst.; MBA of Amer.; MBA of NY; RE Square Club, Sr. Member, Columbia Soc. of RE Appraisers; **EDUC:** Mech. Engrg., Pratt Inst.; **MIL SERV:** USAF, Cadet; **OTHER ACT & HONORS:** Past Pres., Pascack Hills Lions Club; Past Comdr., Peter Minuit Amer. Legion Post; **HOME ADD:** 8 Chadwick Rd., Hillsdale, NJ 07642, (201)666-3581; **BUS ADD:** 280 Park Ave., NYC, NY 10015, (212)850-3050.

KETTLES, L. Christopher——B: July 17, 1945, Dalton, GA, *Controller*, Lincoln Prop. Co.; **PRIM RE ACT:** Developer, Builder, Property Manager; **PREV EMPLOY:** Cousins Mort. and Equity Invest., Atlanta, Ga, Controller; Coopers & Lybrand, Audit Mgr.; **PROFL AFFIL & HONORS:** AICPA, CPA; **EDUC:** BBA, 1971, Acctg., GA State Univ.; **GRAD EDUC:** MPA, 1974, Acctg., GA State Univ.; **EDUC HONORS:** Beta Gamma Sigma, Beta Alpha Psi; **MIL SERV.** US Army, 1st Lt., 1966-1969; **HOME ADD:** 7642 A E. 49th St. S., Tulsa, OK 74145, (918)663-9422; **BUS ADD:** 2431 E. 61st St., Suite 800, Tulsa, OK 74105, (918)743-3133.

KEUSDER, Walter W.——B: Aug. 17, 1924, Los Angeles, CA, *Pres.*, Keusder Enterprises; **PRIM RE ACT:** Developer, Builder; **PROFL AFFIL & HONORS:** Bldg. Indus. Assn. of S. CA (Past Pres.), CA Bldg. Indus. (Treas. 1981-VP, 1982); **EDUC:** BS, 1949, CE, Univ. of S. CA; **EDUC HONORS:** Chi Epsilon Engrg. Hon. Soc.; **HOME ADD:** 2021 Yacht Vindex, Newport Bch., CA 92660, (714)644-0648; **BUS ADD:** 1100 Quail St., Ste 210, Newport Bch., CA 92660, (714)752-2393.

KEUSEY, Edwin M.——B: Jan. 8, 1935, New York City, NY, *Owner*, Edwin M. Keusey; **PRIM RE ACT:** Broker, Attorney, Appraiser, Owner/Investor, Property Manager, Syndicator; **PROFL AFFIL & HONORS:** NAR; NY State Assn. of Realtors; Long Island Bd. of Realtors; RELO; Amer. Bar Assn.; Nassau Cty. Lawyers Assn., GRI; **EDUC:** BA, 1956, Econ., Colgate Univ.; **GRAD EDUC:** LLB, 1961, St. John's Univ. School of Law; **MIL SERV:** US Army; Cpl.; **OTHER ACT & HONORS:** Mineola, Garden City Rotary Club; Garden City Country Club; **HOME ADD:** 277 New Hyde Park Rd., Garden City, NY 11530, (516)488-4583; **BUS ADD:** 745 Franklin Ave., Garden City, NY 11530, (516)747-1300.

KEVENIDES, Herve A.——B: Apr. 14, 1938, Paris, France, *VP - Dir. RE Econs. & Market Research*, Chemical Bank, RE; **PRIM RE ACT:** Banker, Instructor; **PREV EMPLOY:** Chase Manhattan Bank, VP & Mgr., Econs. & Market Research Div., RE Fin. Dept.; **PROFL AFFIL & HONORS:** Amer. Econ. Assn.; Nat. Assn. of Bus. Econs., "Who's Who in the East", 1973-74 Edition; **EDUC:** BS, 1963, Economics, Seton Hall Univ.; **GRAD EDUC:** MBA, 1965, Econs., NY Univ.; **EDUC HONORS:** Cum Laude and First in Econs., with Distinction; **MIL SERV:** US Army; Sgt.; **OTHER ACT & HONORS:** 1972 to present, NY City Civil Service Commission; 1975 to present, Economic Devel. Comm., Township of Middletown, NJ; **HOME ADD:** 7 Bay Hill Rd., Leonardo, NJ 07737, (201)291-2136; **BUS ADD:** 633 Third Ave., New York, NY 10017, (212)878-7777.

KEYES, William H.——B: Jan. 17, 1928, Sidney, OH, *VP and Atty.*, Abstract Co. of St. Joseph County, Inc.; **PRIM RE ACT:** Attorney, Insuror; **SERVICES:** Title ins. for RE; **PREV EMPLOY:** Practicing Atty.; Sec. and Corporate Counsel: National Homes Corp.; **PROFL AFFIL & HONORS:** Member: In State Bar Assn. and St. Joseph Cty. Bar Assn.; **EDUC:** BS, 1950, Mgmt., IN Univ. School of Bus.; **GRAD EDUC:** LLB, 1952, Law, IN Univ. School of Law; **OTHER ACT & HONORS:** South Bend Rotary Club; Biography in *Who's Who in Amer. Law*, 1st and 2nd Editions; **HOME ADD:** 1203 Helmen Dr., South Bend, IN 46615; **BUS ADD:** 210 J.M.S. Bldg., South Bend, IN 46601, (219)232-5845.

KEYLES, Sidney Alan——B: Sept. 7, 1944, Brooklyn, NY, *Atty.*, Aetna Life & Casualty, Law Dept.; **PRIM RE ACT:** Attorney, Lender; **OTHER RE ACT:** Mgr. of RE Investment Subsection of Law Dept.; **SERVICES:** Lawyer for Fin. Instit. Engaged in Lending and Acquiring Comml. RE; **PROFL AFFIL & HONORS:** ABA; CT Bar; Assn. of Life Insurance Counsel; Amer. Land Title Assn.; **EDUC:** BA, 1966, Hist., NY Univ.; **GRAD EDUC:** JD, 1969, Law, Columbia Univ. School of Law; **HOME ADD:** 25 Stage Coach Ln., Newington, CT 06111, (203)667-1179; **BUS ADD:** One Civic Ctr. Plaza, P.O. Box 1414, Hartford, CT 06143, (203)273-2383.

KEYS, Carol Frances——B: Nov. 23, 1952, Miami, FL, *Atty.*, Carol Frances Keys, Atty. at Law; **PRIM RE ACT:** Attorney; **OTHER RE ACT:** Title co.; **SERVICES:** RE & mort. closings, title ins.; **PREV EMPLOY:** Keys & Keys Attys. at Law, Coopers & Lybrand; **PROFL AFFIL & HONORS:** ABA, FL Bar Assn., Lawyers Title Guaranty Fund, Chicago Title, Real Prop. Law; **EDUC:** BS, 1973, Acctg., Univ. of FL; **GRAD EDUC:** Advanced Bachelor of Acctg./JD/LLM, Taxation, Univ. of FL, Cumberland School of Law, Univ. of Miami Law; **HOME ADD:** 12550 Palm Rd., N. Miami, FL 33181, (305)891-2462; **BUS ADD:** 1911 N.E. 172 St., N. Miami Beach, FL 33162, (305)944-3600.

KEYS, Howard D.——*Secy.*, Stokely-Van Camp; **PRIM RE ACT:** Property Manager; **BUS ADD:** 941 N. Meridian St., Indianapolis, IN 46206, (317)631-2551.*

KHALIL, Noel F.——B: Nov. 21, 1950, New York, NY, *VP Mgr.*, US Home Corp./New Jersey Land Div.; **PRIM RE ACT:** Consultant, Developer; **PREV EMPLOY:** Student-Law; **PROFL AFFIL & HONORS:** Nat. Assn. of Home Builders; **EDUC:** BS, 1973, Urban Hist., Univ. of Rochester; **GRAD EDUC:** JD, 1978, Law, FL State Univ.; **EDUC HONORS:** Grad. with Distinction; **HOME ADD:** 22 Hinsdale Ln., Willingboro, NJ 08046, (609)871-2378; **BUS ADD:** 306 Fellowship Rd., Mt. Laurel, NJ 08054, (609)778-8100.

KHEEL, Thomas H.——B: May 6, 1948, Rochester, NY, *Pres.*, T.H. Kheel Props.; **PRIM RE ACT:** Owner/Investor; **EDUC:** AB, 1971, Hist., Cornell Univ.; **EDUC HONORS:** Deans list, Regents Scholarship; **HOME ADD:** 155 Ludlowville Rd., Lansing, NY 14882, (607)533-7261; **BUS ADD:** 155 Ludlowville Rd., Lansing, NY 14882, (607)533-7261.

KHURANA, Lalit K.——B: Feb. 6, 1949, India, *Project Mgr.*, Roybal Realty, Devel. Div.; **PRIM RE ACT:** Developer; **OTHER RE ACT:** RE investment and sales; **SERVICES:** Investment counseling, packaging & devel. of resid. props.; **PREV EMPLOY:** Bus. consultant with Price, Waterhouse & Co., 1975-1979; **EDUC:** BS, 1970, ME, B.I.T.S., India; **GRAD EDUC:** MS, 1971, Indus. Engrg., Univ. of CA, Berkeley; **HOME ADD:** 465 N. Pierre Rd., Walnut, CA 91789, (714)598-8288; **BUS ADD:** 4601 Santa Anita Ave., El Monte, CA 91731, (213)579-5055.

KIBBE, James W.——B: Oct. 5, 1926, Bound Brook, NJ, *VP/Sales Mgr., Comml. Sales and Leasing*, Weaver Bros. Inc., Comml. Sales & Leasing; **PRIM RE ACT:** Broker, Consultant, Appraiser, Owner/Investor, Instructor, Assessor; **SERVICES:** Consulting, brokerage of investment, comml. and indus. props.; **REP CLIENTS:** Devels. pvt. and instnl. investors, local and natl. corps. and pvt. indivs., for. investors; **PREV EMPLOY:** June 1955 to 1957, Eig & McKeever, RE Salesman Aug. 1957 to present - Weaver Bros., Inc. RE Salesman, Sales Mgr. & VP; **PROFL AFFIL & HONORS:** Washington Bd. of Realtors; NAR; Soc. of Ind. Realtors, Life Member,Million Dollar Sales Club; Life Member , Million Dollar Leasing Club; **EDUC:** BS, 1951, Univ. of MD; **MIL SERV:** USN; **OTHER ACT & HONORS:** Sandy Spring Lions Club; Recipient of numerous Awards from Profl., Civic, and Pvt. Orgs.; **HOME ADD:** 1000 Ashland Dr., Ashton, MD 20861, (301)924-4463; **BUS ADD:** 5530 Wisconsin Ave., Chevy Chase, MD 20815, (301)986-4208.

KIELGASS, Dennis A.——B: Mar. 25, 1951, Phoenix, AZ, *Mgr.*, JMB Property Management Corp., Western Rgn.; **PRIM RE ACT:** Property Manager; **OTHER RE ACT:** Supervision of Phoenix area prop. mgrs.; **PREV EMPLOY:** Arlen Realty Mgmt. Inc. 1974 to 1979 CBL and Assoc. 1979 to 1981; **PROFL AFFIL & HONORS:** NAR, AZ Multi-Housing Assn., CPM; **EDUC:** BS, 1973, Personel and operations mgmt., Univ. of MD, Munich campus and AZ State Univ.; **HOME ADD:** 1695 S Ash,, Mesa, AZ 85202, (602)831-9021; **BUS ADD:** 2101 E. Camelback Rd., Phoenix, AZ 85016, (602)955-6850.

KIELY, Dan R.——B: Jan. 2, 1944, Ft. Still, OR, *Pres.*, DeRand Equity, Group, Inc.; **PRIM RE ACT:** Syndicator, Consultant, Appraiser, Developer, Property Manager, Lender, Owner/Investor; **PREV EMPLOY:** Atty., Holme Roberts & Owen, Denver, CO; **PROFL AFFIL & HONORS:** ABA, ICSC, IREM, Bar. Assn., VA Bar Assn., DC Bar Assn., Natl. Bd. of Realtors, NARA, CPM, CRA; **EDUC:** BA, 1966, Psych., Univ. of CO; **GRAD EDUC:** JD, 1969, So. Univ.; **EDUC HONORS:** Class Pres., 1962-63, 1964-65, *Who's Who in Amer. Colls. & Univs. (1965-66)*; **MIL SERV:** US Army JAGC, Capt., Legion of Merit, Natl. Defense Serv. Medal; **OTHER ACT & HONORS:** Bd. of Dir., Chesterbrook Swim & Tennis Club, Outstanding Young Men of Amer. (1980), Natl. Jaycees, Voting Member of Natl. Assn. of RE Investment Trusts; **HOME ADD:** 1911 Virginia Ave., McLean, VA 22101, (703)241-1188; **BUS ADD:** 2201 Wilson Blvd., 300, Arlington, VA 22201.

KIELY, James L.——B: June 9, 1936, Peru, IL, *Pres.*, Lakeview Properties of Arizona, Inc., Subs. of Lakeview Properties, Ltd.; **PRIM RE ACT:** Developer; **SERVICES:** Devel. Office, Indus., & Shopping Ctrs.; **PREV EMPLOY:** Coldwell Banker, Eaton Intl. Corp.; **PROFL AFFIL & HONORS:** ULI; Intl. Council of Shopping Ctrs.; AZ Assn. of Indus. Devel.; **EDUC:** BA, 1958, Univ. of NE; **MIL SERV:** USA, Capt., 1958-1961; **HOME ADD:** 2228 W. Northern Ave., Phoenix, AZ 85021, (602)943-5965; **BUS ADD:** 141 E Palm Ln., Phoenix, AZ 85004, (602)864-0449.

KIELY, Yvonne C.——B: Nov. 8, 1952, Newark, NJ, *Asst. Mgr.-RE*, NJ Bell Telephone Co.; **OTHER RE ACT:** Corp. RE; **SERVICES:** Leasing and purchasing of RE for Corp. needs; **PREV EMPLOY:** The Boyle Co., NJ; **PROFL AFFIL & HONORS:** Amer. RE & Urban Econ. Assn.; **EDUC:** BA, 1974, Eng., Upsala Coll.; BS, 1977, Acctg., Upsala Coll.; **GRAD EDUC:** MBA, 1979, Fin. & RE, Rutgers Univ. Grad, School of Bus.; **EDUC HONORS:** Magna Cum Laude; **HOME TEL:** (201)964-7422; **BUS ADD:** 650 Park Ave., E. Orange, NJ 07017, (201)675-9226.

KIESER, Richard J.——B: Sept. 1, 1946, Philadelphia, PA, *Asst. VP*, Utah Mortgage Loan Corp., Denver branch office; **PRIM RE ACT:** Lender; **SERVICES:** Mort. lending; **PROFL AFFIL & HONORS:** MBAA; Home Builders Assn.; **EDUC:** BS, 1973, Pol. Sci., UT State Univ. & Northwestern Univ. School of Mort. Banking; **HOME ADD:** 9452 Brentwood St., Broomfield, CO 80020, (303)424-4504; **BUS ADD:** 3025 S. Parker Rd., Aurora, CO 80014, (303)695-7750.

KIEVER, Paul K.——B: Oct. 10, 1946, New Brunswick, NJ, *Gen. Counsel - RE*, Crown Amer. Corp., RE; **PRIM RE ACT:** Attorney; **SERVICES:** Legal; **PREV EMPLOY:** Edward J. DeBartolo Corp. Youngstown, OH; **PROFL AFFIL & HONORS:** ABA, PA, OH Bar Assns., Intl. Council of Shoppings Ctrs., Admitted to Supreme Cts of PA & OH; **EDUC:** BA, 1969, Poli. Sci., Univ. of Pittsburgh Pittsburgh, PA; **GRAD EDUC:** JD, 1972, Law, Case Western Reserve Law School Cleveland OH; **MIL SERV:** US Army, Capt.; **OTHER ACT & HONORS:** Instr. of RE Law - Univ. of Pittsburgh; **HOME ADD:** 146 Daisy St., Johnstown, PA 15905, (814)255-3087; **BUS ADD:** 131 Market St., Johnstown, PA 15907, (814)536-4441.

KILCHRIST, Rubie G.——B: July 28, 1917, Lafayette, LA, *Pres.*, Rubie Kilchrist RE, Inc.; **PRIM RE ACT:** Broker, Consultant, Appraiser, Developer, Owner/Investor, Property Manager; **PROFL AFFIL & HONORS:** Farm & land inst., LA Realtors Assn., Intl. Platform Assn., Historical WA Assn., Outstanding Woman of Lafayette by BPW; 1974 LaFayette Bd. of Realtors, Realtor of the Yr.; 1981 LA State Realtor of the Yr.; 1973 Pres. LA Chap. of FLI; Bd. of Dir. of LRA (5 yrs); Local Bd. of Realtors (2 terms as Tres.); 2 terms as VP, 1 term as pres.; GRI; **OTHER ACT & HONORS:** PTA, Deanery Council, Catholic Dauthers of Amer., Heart Fund, United Givers Fund, Mothers March of Dimes, Bishop's Serv. Appeal, League of Women Voters, Bus. & Profl. Women; **HOME ADD:** 605 Colonial Dr., Lafayette, LA 70501, (318)235-8013; **BUS ADD:** 1313 LaFayette, LaFayette, LA 70501, (318)232-0556.

KILE, J.D.——B: Aug. 12, 1922, Berwick, PA, *Broker*, ERA J.D. Kile & Co.; **PRIM RE ACT:** Broker, Consultant, Appraiser, Banker, Developer, Property Manager; **OTHER RE ACT:** Review Appraiser; **PROFL AFFIL & HONORS:** NAREA; Nat. Assn. of Review Appraisers; Consultant for First Eastern Bank; N.A. of Wilkes Barre, PA branch banks; Central Susquehanna Valley Bd. of Realtors; Nat. & PA Bd. of Realtors; Bd. of Dir. First Eastern Bank, Berwick, PA; **MIL SERV:** USN, 1st Class Petty Officer, 13 Campaigns in S. Pacific WW II; **OTHER ACT & HONORS:** Berwick C of C; Sgt. Luzerne Cty. Sheriff's Dept. Mounted Search & Rescue Team; Nat. Assn. of Search & Rescue; Nat. Ski Patrol; **HOME ADD:** RD 3, Berwick, PA 18603, (717)752-3045; **BUS ADD:** 363 Market St., Berwick, PA 18603, (717)759-2216.

KILE, R. Clayton——B: June 1, 1950, Berwick, PA, *Assoc. Broker/Mgr.*, ERA J.D. Kile & Co.; **PRIM RE ACT:** Broker, Appraiser, Property Manager, Insuror; **SERVICES:** Resid., comml., farm sales, mgmt., appraisals; **PROFL AFFIL & HONORS:** Nat. Assn. of RE Appraisers, Susq. Valley Bd. of Realtors, Nat. Assn. Bd. of Realtors; **OTHER ACT & HONORS:** Kiwanis, Irem Temple; **HOME ADD:** R.D. #3, Box 3785, Berwick, PA 18603, (717)759-2630; **BUS ADD:** 363 Market St., Berwick, PA 18603, (717)759-2216.

KILER, Mike G., Jr.——B: Feb. 12, 1949, Ft. Worth, TX, *Mktg. Mgr., Logic & Applied Systems*, Lennox Indus. Inc., Corp. Hdqtrs.; **PRIM RE ACT:** Consultant, Engineer; **OTHER RE ACT:** Marketer of heating/air cond. equip., energy use simulation studies, economic evaluation of building energy systems, energy mgmt. control system studies, system (HVAC) design consultation, market planning (bldg. and systems); **REP CLIENTS:** Devels., lenders, arch., engrg., bldg. mgrs., mfrs.; **PREV EMPLOY:** 1971-79 Energy simulation and systems design consultant, 1979-present Mktg. Mgr. for Applied Systems and LOGIC (computer aided bldg. design system); **PROFL AFFIL & HONORS:** Amer. Soc. of Heating Refrigeration & Air Cond. Engrs., TX Soc. of Profl. Engrs., BOMA; **EDUC:** BA, 1971, System Design, Univ. of TX; **GRAD EDUC:** MBA candidate, 1982, Mktg. & RE Fin., So. Methodist Univ.; **OTHER ACT & HONORS:** US Yacht Racing Union, Speaker at 2nd Intl. Conf. on Energy Use Mgmt., 1979; Article 'Comml. Bldg. Systems, A Look Ahead' published by Pergamon Press in 'Changing Energy Use Futures' Article (untiled as yet) scheduled for Nov. issue *Specifying Engrg.* magazine. Speaker for 2 seminars on computer simulations at Univ. of WI, Co-inventor in patent application for computer directed robot compliance device; **HOME ADD:** 804 Village Green, Rockwall, TX 75087, (214)722-9198; **BUS ADD:** PO Box 400450, Dallas, TX 75240, (214)783-5405.

KILGORE, Roger V.——B: Nov. 14, 1946, Walker Co., AL, *Pres.*, Kilgore Development Corp., Kilgore Investments & Securities; **PRIM RE ACT:** Broker, Developer, Builder, Syndicator; **PREV EMPLOY:** Still Owner & Chmn. of the Bd. of C & H Constructors Inc., a mechanical contracting firm; **PROFL AFFIL & HONORS:** Birmingham Bd. of Realtors, RESSI, Assoc. Builders & Contractors, Real Prop. Adm.; **EDUC:** Elec. Engrg., 1969, Computer Circuitry Design, UI Elecs. Inst., KY; Univ. of AL; **MIL SERV:** USN, E5; **OTHER ACT & HONORS:** Pres. of the AL Chap. of Assoc. Builders & Contractors; Member Amer. Soc. of Air Conditioning, Refrigeration, Heating Engrs., SEC, DPP Securities License; **HOME ADD:** 4519 Pine Mtn. Rd., Mountain Brook, AL 35213, (205)871-9059; **BUS ADD:** 2937 7th Ave. S., Suite 212, Birmingham, AL 35233, (205)323-1104.

KILLEN, Richard D.——B: June 18, 1947, Toledo, OH, *Mgr. R.E. & Facilities*, Questor Corp.; **PRIM RE ACT:** Property Manager, Engineer, Owner/Investor; **SERVICES:** Negotiation for purchase, sale & leasing of R.E.; Site selection, const.; **PREV EMPLOY:** Questor 15 yrs.; **EDUC:** BSIE, 1972, Univ. of Toledo; **HOME ADD:** 2401 Wildwood Blvd., Toledo, OH 43614; **BUS ADD:** 1 John Goerlich Sq.,

Toledo, OH 43691.

KILLIAN, Richard——*President*, Bethom Corp.; **PRIM RE ACT:** Syndicator; **BUS ADD:** 675 Ygnacio Valley Rd., Suite A202, Walnut Creek, CA 94596, (415)937-9001.*

KILLINS, Thomas H.——B: May 13, 1949, Ann Arbor, MI, *VP*, James Nielander Associates, Inc.; **PRIM RE ACT:** Broker, Owner/Investor, Property Manager; **SERVICES:** Prop. mgmt., mktg., investment; **REP CLIENTS:** The Penn Mutual Life Ins. Co.; Citizens and So. National Bank; M & T Bank; **PROFL AFFIL & HONORS:** IREM; NAR; FL Assn. of Realtors, CPM; Realtor; Lic. Mort. Broker; **EDUC:** BS, 1971, Mgmt./Fin., IN Univ. School of Bus.; **EDUC HONORS:** Dean's List; **HOME ADD:** Ft. Lauderdale, FL; **BUS ADD:** 6451 N. Federal Hwy., Suite 1217, Ft. Lauderdale, FL 33308, (305)772-0950.

KILPATRICK, G. Malcolm——B: Jan. 5, 1941, Greensboro, NC, *VP, Also Pres. Patrick Ventures Inc., Consultant (Investments, Development and Finance)*, Piedmont Development Co., Devel., Joint Ventures & Finance; **PRIM RE ACT:** Broker, Consultant, Appraiser, Developer, Owner/Investor; **SERVICES:** Joint ventures, devel., fin. and coordinating with contractor of multi-family props. and investment and devel. counseling; **REP CLIENTS:** Indiv. and instl. investors and devels.; syndicators; **PREV EMPLOY:** VP Comml. Loan Dept. of Lge. Mort. Banker and subsequently for a RE Investment Trust; **PROFL AFFIL & HONORS:** Atlanta Bd. of Realtors, Apartment Owners and Managers Assn., Homebuilders Assn., Atlanta Bd. of Realtors Million Dollar Club; **EDUC:** BS, 1963, Bus. Admin., Univ. of NC (Chapel Hill, NC); **MIL SERV:** USN, Lt.; **HOME ADD:** 115 Seville Chase, Atlanta, GA 30328, (404)396-7552; **BUS ADD:** 1706 Northeast Expwy., Atlanta, GA 30329, (404)634-6692.

KIM, Sarah——B: Oct. 1, 1938, Seoul, Korea, *Pres.*, JKK Enterprises, Inc.; **PRIM RE ACT:** Owner/Investor; **PREV EMPLOY:** Realtor, Lexington, MA 1973-77; Owner - House of Kim, Inc., 1974-79; Treas. Supertek, Lexington, MA & Los Angeles, CA, 1975 to present; **EDUC:** BA, 1961, Ihwa Women's Univ., Oberlin Coll.; **GRAD EDUC:** MEd, 1973, Rehab. Admin., Northeastern Univ., Boston, MA; **OTHER ACT & HONORS:** AAUW, Republican Party, Methodist Church, Author of var. magazine articles; **HOME ADD:** 1670 Carla Ridge, Beverly Hills, CA 90210, (213)271-4295; **BUS ADD:** 2320 Cotner Ave., Los Angeles, CA 90064, (213)477-1481.

KIMBALL, John H., Jr.——B: Sept. 22, 1943, Melrose, MA, *Owner*, Kimball & Kimball; **PRIM RE ACT:** Attorney, Instructor; **SERVICES:** Full range of representation relative to all RE devel. and sales matters; **PREV EMPLOY:** IRS, Estate Tax Div.; **PROFL AFFIL & HONORS:** ABA, MA Bar Assn., Boston Bar Assn., MA Conveyancers, Eastern Middlesex Bd. of Realtors, New England Land Title Assn.; **EDUC:** AB, 1966, Social Relations, Harvard Coll.; **GRAD EDUC:** JD, 1969, Boston Univ.; **OTHER ACT & HONORS:** Past Pres. and Dir., Member, Lynnfield Rotary Club, Dir., Lynnfield Scholarship Found.; **HOME ADD:** 618 Main St., Lynnfield, MA 01940, (617)334-4015; **BUS ADD:** 590A Main St., Lynnfield, MA 01940, (617)245-1012.

KIMBALL, Paul C., Jr.——B: June 5, 1943, Detroit, MI, *Atty.*, Spindell, Kemp & Kimmons; **PRIM RE ACT:** Attorney; **SERVICES:** Legal services & counseling; **REP CLIENTS:** Indiv investors, devels., condo. converters, synds.; **PROFL AFFIL & HONORS:** ABA, Sect. on Real Prop., Probate & Trust Law; Chicago Bar Assn.; IL State Bar Assn.; **EDUC:** BA, 1965, Hist., Williams Coll., Dean's List; **GRAD EDUC:** LLB, 1968, Northwestern Univ., School of Law; **MIL SERV:** US Army Res.; Sgt.; **HOME ADD:** 550 E. Spruce, Lake Forest, IL 60045, (312)234-7607; **BUS ADD:** Suite 4005, 135 So. La Salle St., Chicago, IL 60603, (312)372-2900.

KIMBALL, Paul H.——B: Feb. 3, 1929, USA, *Dir., Corporate RE*, Combustion Engineering, Inc., Corporate; **OTHER RE ACT:** Corporate RE; **SERVICES:** Asset mgmt., intl. valuations & negotiations; **PREV EMPLOY:** 25 years with Combustion Engrg.; **PROFL AFFIL & HONORS:** Indus. Devel. Research Council; Nat. Assn. of Corporate RE Execs.; Nat. Assn. of Review Appraisers; AMA; **EDUC:** BS, 1961, Mgmt. & Bus., Univ. of TN; **EDUC HONORS:** Pi Gamma Mu; **HOME ADD:** 2 Chestnut Hill Rd., Simsbury, CT 06070, (203)658-6708; **BUS ADD:** 1000 Prospect Hill Rd., Windsor, CT 06095, (203)688-1911.

KIMBLE, Carol——B: Jan 18, 1942, Seattle, WA, *Marketing and Sales, Owner*, Kimble and Associates; **OTHER RE ACT:** Marketing for Developers; Realtor; **REP CLIENTS:** Developers/Builders; **PREV EMPLOY:** Director of Projects Marketing - Mike McCormack Realtors; **PROFL AFFIL & HONORS:** Bd. of Dir., Building Industry Assn. of HI, Bd. of Dir., Housing Coalition, Honolulu Bd. of Realtors, Nat. Assn. of Realtors; National Homebuilders-Sales and Marketing; **EDUC:** BA, 1964, Education, Univ. of AZ; **GRAD EDUC:** 5th Year, 1966, Educ., Univ. of WA; **OTHER ACT & HONORS:** Hawaiian Humane Society; **HOME ADD:** 500 Lunalilo Home Rd., #18G, Honolulu, HI 96825, (808)946-6153; **BUS ADD:** 1778 Ala Moana Blvd. #1203, Honolulu, HI 96815, (808)536-2116.

KIMEL, Donald H.——B: July 1, 1929, Winston-Salem, NC, *Pres.*, Professional Investors Group, Inc.; **PRIM RE ACT:** Owner/Investor, Syndicator; **OTHER RE ACT:** Securities Broker/Dealer; **PROFL AFFIL & HONORS:** RESSI; St. Petersburg, FL Bd. of Realtors; NASD; **EDUC:** Univ. of NC; **MIL SERV:** US Army; **HOME ADD:** 7665 Sun Island Dr., S., St. Petersburg, FL 33707; **BUS ADD:** 5959 Central Ave., St. Petersburg, FL 33710, (813)384-9330.

KIMPTON, William J.——B: Dec. 19, 1946, Ann Arbor, MI, *Pres.*, Case, Kimpton, Tragos & Burke, P.A.; **PRIM RE ACT:** Attorney; **SERVICES:** Closing, title insurance; **REP CLIENTS:** Indiv. and corp. investors in private and comml. props.; **PROFL AFFIL & HONORS:** Clearwater and FL Bar Assn., The FL Bar, Pinellas Cty. Trial Lawyers Assn., Chmn. of Pinellas RE Law Council, Field Atty. for Lawyers Title Guaranty; **EDUC:** 1969, E. MI Univ., Duke Univ.; **GRAD EDUC:** JD, 1972; **MIL SERV:** USAR, Capt.; **HOME ADD:** 265 Bayside Dr., Clearwater Beach, FL 33515, (813)443-6386; **BUS ADD:** 487 Mandalay Ave., Clearwater Beach, FL 33515, (813)461-1976.

KIMURA, Ty H.——B: Feb. 27, 1944, Honolulu, HI, *Pres.*, Ty H. Kimura Corporation, Ty Prop. Consultants, Appraisal Analysts & consultants; **PRIM RE ACT:** Broker, Consultant, Appraiser, Developer, Owner/Investor, Property Manager, Syndicator; **SERVICES:** Appraising, consulting, devel., leasing, managing, mktg., and synd. various types of RE; **REP CLIENTS:** Lenders and indiv. or instnl. investors, profl. designations RECP, ICA, CRA, Cert. Appraiser Sr., SRA, CBC, GRI; **PROFL AFFIL & HONORS:** SREA, Inst. of Cert. Bus. Counselors, Intl. Exchangors Assn., The Investment Group Realtors, RNMI, RESSI, NAR, Hawaii Assn. of Realtors, NARA, Intl. Coll. of RE Consulting Profls., Intl. Org. of RE Appraisers, Amer. Assn. of RE Appraisers, Recipient of The Investment Group Realtors "Counselor of the Year "Award 1978, Sr. Listing in *Who's Who in Creative RE 1979-82*; **EDUC:** BA, 1967, 72, Psych., computer programming & data processing, RE, Univ. of HI, Capitol Radio Engrg. Inst.; **EDUC HONORS:** Distinguished Military Grad.; **MIL SERV:** US Army 1967-73, Capt., Bronze star w/V Device, Air Medal w/2 OLC, Joint serv. commendation medal, Natl. Devense Serv. Medal, Vietnam Serv. Medal w/3 bronze stars, RVN Cross of Gallantry w/bronze star, RVN Medal of Honor 1st Class, RVN Campaign medal; **OTHER ACT & HONORS:** Sec./ Intl. Org. of RE Appraisers, 1981; Pres. The Investment Group Realtors 1981; Sec./ SREA Honolulu Chapt. No 67 1981-82; Dir. HI Assn of Realtors 1981; Dir. Honolulu Bd. of Realtors 1981-82; **HOME ADD:** 811 16th Ave., Honolulu, HI 96816, (808)732-2332; **BUS ADD:** 1560 Kanunu St. 420, Honolulu, HI 96814, (808)947-1010.

KINCAID, Walter G.——B: Mar. 11, 1940, Utica, NY, *Asst. Dir.*, Connecticut Mutual Life Insurance Co., Agents Fin.; **PRIM RE ACT:** Insuror; **OTHER RE ACT:** Field Office Leasing; **PREV EMPLOY:** Newport Assoc., Hartford, CT; Comml. RE; **PROFL AFFIL & HONORS:** BOMA; NACORE; **EDUC:** BA, 1964, Math., Parsons Coll.; **HOME ADD:** 240 S. Main St., W. Hartford, CT 06107, (203)561-1963; **BUS ADD:** 140 Garden St., Hartford, CT 06115, (203)727-6500.

KINDER, JoAnn M.——B: Sept. 7, 1936, Davenport, IA, *Partner*, Kinder Realty; **PRIM RE ACT:** Broker, Consultant, Appraiser, Owner/Investor; **SERVICES:** RE mktg.; **PREV EMPLOY:** Legal sec.; **PROFL AFFIL & HONORS:** Member: Local, State and Nat. Bd. of Realtors; Women's Council of Realtors; Yorktown and Muncie C of C; Amer. Business Women's Assn.; 1981 Woman of the Yr.; **EDUC:** 1976, RE, Ball State Univ., Muncie; **HOME ADD:** 14 Hellis Dr., Muncie, IN 47304, (317)282-9415; **BUS ADD:** 6116 Kilgore Ave., Muncie, IN 47304, (317)282-5986.

KINDIG, Malcolm L.——B: July 21, 1928, Peoria, IL, *Pres.*, Home S&L Assn. of Alton; **PRIM RE ACT:** Lender; **SERVICES:** Savings investments, home imp. loans, auto loans, 'Now' checking accts.; **PREV EMPLOY:** IL Fed. S&L; MO Savings Assn.; Lincoln-Douglas S&L Assn.; **PROFL AFFIL & HONORS:** Past Pres. Alton Godfrey Rotary Club; US League of Sugs Assns.; IL S&L League, Grad. diploma, Amer. S&L Inst.; **EDUC:** BS, 1951, Bus. Admin., Shurtleff Coll., Alton, IL; **MIL SERV:** US Army, Corp., Bronze Star; **OTHER ACT & HONORS:** Sec. Bd. of Educ., Alton Sch. Dist. 11; **HOME ADD:** 685 Douglas Pl., Alton, IL 62002, (618)462-9622; **BUS ADD:** 2410 State St., PO Box 160, Alton, IL 62002, (618)466-7700.

KINDRED, F. D.——B: Apr. 26, 1920, Bardstown, KY, *Pres., Kindred Homes, Inc., Sec.-Treas., First Group Realty, Inc.*, Kindred Homes, Inc., Comml. (First Group); **PRIM RE ACT:** Broker, Developer, Builder; **SERVICES:** Brokerage, land devel., constr.; **PROFL AFFIL & HONORS:** Nat. Assn. of Homebuilders, NAR, RESSI; **EDUC:** AB, 1943, Econ., Univ. of KY; **MIL SERV:** USN, Lt. SG; **OTHER ACT & HONORS:** 2 times Pres. Homebuilders Assn. of Lexington, 1982 Pres. Lexington Bd. of Realtors; **HOME ADD:** 629 Teakwood Dr., Lexington, KY 40502, (606)266-5272; **BUS ADD:** 357 Waller Ave., Lexington, KY 40504, (606)252-1712.

KING, Bert M.——B: Oct. 11, 1948, New York, NY, *Asst. VP*, Milton Abrams Assocs.; **PRIM RE ACT:** Consultant, Lender; **SERVICES:** Mort. banker, RE consultants; **REP CLIENTS:** Devels., local govts., state govts., non profit groups, RE resid. RE rentals, co-ops, condo.; **PREV EMPLOY:** US Dept. of Housing & Urban Devel, MD Community Devel. Admin.; **PROFL AFFIL & HONORS:** Amer. Planning Assn., Nat. Trust for Hist. Preservation, Mort. Bankers Assn.; **EDUC:** BA, 1970, Poli. Sci., Amer. Univ.; **GRAD EDUC:** 1976, Urban Planning, Univ. of PA; **HOME ADD:** 2102 Hanover St., Silver Spring, MD 10910, (301)589-0134; **BUS ADD:** 1025 Conn. Ave. N.W., Ste. 711, Washington, DC 20036, (202)296-0238.

KING, Carl L.——B: Mar. 18, 1917, Chicago, IL, *Pres.- Mgr.*, Quality Mort. & Investment Co.; **PRIM RE ACT:** Broker; **OTHER RE ACT:** Mort. Broker; **PROFL AFFIL & HONORS:** NAR, CAR, San Fernando Valley Bd. of Realtors; **EDUC:** BS, 1946, Acctg., Univ. of CA - Berkeley; **HOME ADD:** 18847 Killoch Way, Northridge, CA 91326, (213)368-1952; **BUS ADD:** 17100 Ventura Blvd. - Suite 222 or PO Box 331, Ensino, CA 91316, (213)986-8770.

KING, Floyd F., Jr.——B: Mar. 4, 1924, Orient, NY, *Owner*, Floyd F. King Jr.; **PRIM RE ACT:** Broker, Consultant, Appraiser, Developer, Owner/Investor, Property Manager; **SERVICES:** Devel., advice, appraisal, and mgmt.; **REP CLIENTS:** Principally resid. prop.; **PREV EMPLOY:** Self employed 25 yrs.; **PROFL AFFIL & HONORS:** Suffolk Cty. RE Bd.; **OTHER ACT & HONORS:** C of C, Dir.; **HOME ADD:** 525 King St., Orient, NY 11957, (516)323-2413; **BUS ADD:** 22420 Main Rd., Orient, NY 11957, (516)323-2570.

KING, Francis——*Secy.*, GF Business Equipment, Inc.; **PRIM RE ACT:** Property Manager; **BUS ADD:** 229 E. Dennick Ave., Youngstown, OH 44501, (216)746-7271.*

KING, Francis J.——B: Feb. 13, 1935, Brooklyn, NY, *Reg. VP*, Marshall & Stevens Inc.; **PRIM RE ACT:** Consultant; **SERVICES:** Profl. valuations; **REP CLIENTS:** Patents, licences, franchises, secret formulae trademarks, goodwill agreements, rights, subscription lists, building, indus. comml. & resid. sites; **PREV EMPLOY:** The Amer. Appraisal Co.; **PROFL AFFIL & HONORS:** NACORE, Assn. for Corp. Growth; **EDUC:** BS, 1959, Civil Engrg., Univ. of Houston; **GRAD EDUC:** MBA, 1963, Fin. & Mktg., Hofstra Univ.; **EDUC HONORS:** Amer. Soc. of Civil Engrs. Student Award, Mu Gamma Tau & Spec. Honors; **MIL SERV:** US Army, 1st Lt.; **HOME ADD:** 107 Browns Rd., Lloyd Harbor, NY 11743, (516)549-0119; **BUS ADD:** 71 Broadway, New York, NY 10006, (212)425-4300.

KING, Hart M.——*Mgr. Mfg. Fac.*, FMC Corp.; **PRIM RE ACT:** Property Manager; **BUS ADD:** 200 East Randolph Dr., Chicago, IL 60601, (312)861-6000.*

KING, John J.——B: Sept. 17, 1948, Aberdeen, SD, *Asst. VP and Sr. Asst. Counsel*, The Bank of California, Legal; **PRIM RE ACT:** Attorney; **PREV EMPLOY:** The Colwell Co., Mort. Bankers; **EDUC:** BA, 1970, Hist., AZ State Univ.; **GRAD EDUC:** JD, 1973, UCLA; **EDUC HONORS:** Dean's List; **BUS ADD:** 400 California St., Bank of CA, San Francisco, CA 94104, (415)765-3245.

KING, Michael Stephen——B: July 8, 1949, Vero Veach, FL, *Owner, King and Co., Pres. IAC*, King and Co., Investment Administrators Corp. of the San Joaquin; **PRIM RE ACT:** Consultant, Syndicator; **OTHER RE ACT:** RE Taxation,delayed exchanges; **SERVICES:** Tax and RE acctg., exchange accomodator; **REP CLIENTS:** Investors, investment brokers. paralegal in exchange and taxation; **PREV EMPLOY:** Drummond, Bates, CPA's San Diego; **PROFL AFFIL & HONORS:** Nat. Assn. of Accountants; **EDUC:** Acctg., Taxation, San Diego State Univ.; **EDUC HONORS:** Deans List; **HOME ADD:** 1594 Lincoln St., Clovis, CA 93612, (209)298-2971; **BUS ADD:** 3170 N. Chestnut St. #103, Fresno, CA 93703, (209)252-7214.

KING, Neil J.——B: Sept. 23, 1929, Chicago, IL, *Pres.*, Armond D. King, Inc.; **PRIM RE ACT:** Broker, Consultant, Appraiser, Banker, Developer, Owner/Investor, Insuror; **REP CLIENTS:** 1st Natl. Bank of Chicago, Continental Bank, Banks, Municipalities, Devels., Schools, Attys.; **PROFL AFFIL & HONORS:** 1976 Pres. of Amer. Soc. of RE Counselors; Soc. of RE Appraisers; North Shore RE Bd. (1961 Pres.); Lambda Alpha, CRE, SRPA; **EDUC:** BS, 1951, Indus. Admin., Yale Univ.; **MIL SERV:** USN, Lt., 3 Battle Stars, Korea; **OTHER ACT & HONORS:** Winnetka Plan Commn.; Dir.: First Natl. Bank of Skokie; Skokie Valley Comm. Hospital; Adventurers Club of Chicago; **HOME ADD:** 711 Oak St., Winnetka, IL 60093, (312)446-1994; **BUS ADD:** PO Box 588, Skokie, IL 60077, (312)673-1234.

KING, Richard W.——*Sr. VP & Mort. Officer*, College Point Savings Bank; **PRIM RE ACT:** Banker, Lender; **SERVICES:** Mort. Fin.; **PROFL AFFIL & HONORS:** Nat. Assn. Mutual Savings Banks Comm. for Mort. Investments; Assoc. Member SRA; Faculty Member Nat. Assoc. of Mutual Savings Banks; **BUS ADD:** 210-15 No. Blvd., Bayside, NY 11361, (212)423-3500.

KING, Russell——B: Mar. 3, 1921, Montreal, Que., Can., *VP Loans & Investments*, Globe Realty Ltd., Loans & Investments Div.; **PRIM RE ACT:** Consultant, Developer, Banker, Lender, Owner/Investor; **SERVICES:** A wholly-owned RE subs. of The Royal Bank of Can.; **REP CLIENTS:** The Royal Bank of Can. & their clients; **PREV EMPLOY:** Mgr. Spec. Proj., RE Resources, The Royal Bank of Can.; **PROFL AFFIL & HONORS:** RE Bd. Can, RE Assn., IREF, NHARO, Nat. Assn. of Housing & Redev. Officials; **EDUC:** Commerce, 1947, Fin., Concordia Univ.; **MIL SERV:** RCAF (Royal Can. AF), Flying Officer; **OTHER ACT & HONORS:** Alderman (elected) City of St. Lambert, 1950-55; **HOME ADD:** 300 Lansdowne, Apt. 51, Westmount, H3Z 2L4, Que., Can., (514)932-3446; **BUS ADD:** PO Box 6001, Montreal, H3C 3A9, Que., Can., (514)874-8110.

KING, Stanley A.——*Corp. Risk Mgr.*, Kellogg Co.; **PRIM RE ACT:** Property Manager; **BUS ADD:** 235 Porter St., Battle Creek, MI 49016, (616)966-2765.*

KING, William John——B: Mar. 23, 1947, Philadelphia, PA, *VP*, Century Partners (Acquisition/Sales Affiliate of Fox & Carskadon Financial Corp.); **PRIM RE ACT:** Syndicator, Owner/Investor; **SERVICES:** Special projects and private placement program; **REP CLIENTS:** Fox and Carskadon Fin. Corp. and its related public limited partnerships and private placements; **PROFL AFFIL & HONORS:** VP, Seattle-King County Housing Assn.; **EDUC:** BA, 1969, Govt. and Intl. Relations, Carleton Coll., Northfield, MN; **GRAD EDUC:** MUP, 1978, Research Methods, Land Use, Arch., Univ. of Washington, Seattle, WA; MPPM, Fin. and Acctg., Yale School of Organization & Mgmt., New Haven, CT; **EDUC HONORS:** Cum Laude, Yale School of Org. & Mgmt. Fellowship, HEW Public Service Fellowship; **HOME ADD:** 4024 23rd St., San Francisco, CA 94114, (415)282-6972; **BUS ADD:** 2755 Campus Dr., San Mateo, CA 94403, (415)574-3333.

KINGSBURY, Marvin R.——B: July 28, 1922, Detroit, MI, *Sole Proprietor (Semi-retired)*, Real Estate Professionals; **PRIM RE ACT:** Broker, Consultant, Appraiser, Builder, Property Manager; **SERVICES:** Gen. RE admin. for past 33 yrs. in SE MI; Profl. appraising, consultation, brokerage, mgmt.; **REP CLIENTS:** Fin. inst., bus. firms, indiv.; **PROFL AFFIL & HONORS:** Sr. Member of Soc. of RE Appraisers, SRA; **OTHER ACT & HONORS:** Member of Parish Liturgical Commn., Eucharistic Minister & Lector; **HOME ADD:** 920 Drexel, Dearborn, MI 48128, (313)274-7295; **BUS ADD:** 920 Drexel, Dearborn, MI 48128, (313)561-8813.

KINGSFORD, Leonard O.——B: May 22, 1918, Grace, ID, *Atty.*, Leonard O. Kingsford; **PRIM RE ACT:** Attorney; **OTHER RE ACT:** Title Insurance, through Caribou Title Co.; **SERVICES:** Title examination and opinions, closing serv., escrows; **REP CLIENTS:** Farmers Home Admin., local banks and realtors; **PREV EMPLOY:** Title Examiner, The Title Ins. Co., Boise, ID, 1956; Title Examiner, Bannock Title Co., 1956-1959, Pocatello, ID; Sec.-Treas., Caribou Title Co., 1959 to date; **PROFL AFFIL & HONORS:** ID State Bar Assn., ABA, ID Land Title Assn.; **EDUC:** BS(Bus.), 1941, Acctg., Univ. of ID; **GRAD EDUC:** JD, 1948, Law, Univ. of ID; **EDUC HONORS:** Phi Alpha Delta, honorary law frat.; **MIL SERV:** US Army, Maj.; **OTHER ACT & HONORS:** Prosecuting Atty., Madison Cty., ID 1950-52; Lions Club, Soda Springs C of C; **HOME ADD:** 271 East 1st North, Soda Springs, ID, (208)547-3890; **BUS ADD:** 160 South Main St., P O Box 915, Soda Springs, ID 83276, (208)547-4321.

KINGSTON, G. Allan——B: May 19, 1935, San Francisco, CA, *Rgnl. Mgr.*, Tecon Realty Corp.; **PRIM RE ACT:** Developer; **PREV EMPLOY:** Pres. & Gen Mgr., World Team Tennis Teams 1975-1978; HHFA, 1963-1965; Exec. Dir., Fresno Redevel. Agency, 1968-1970; Dep. & Dir., Oakland Redevel. Agency, 1965-1968; Real Estate Development Management; Honolulu, Hawaii (V.P./Gen. Mgr., The Hawaiian Company; Mgr., Urban Division, Oceanic Properties; Exec. V.P., The Esplonade) 1970-1975; **EDUC:** AB, 1958, Poli. Sci., Univ. of CA at Berkeley; **MIL SERV:** USN; LCDR. (Retd.); **HOME ADD:**

4551 Conchita Way, Tarzana, CA 91356, (213)343-6665; **BUS ADD:** 2029 Century Park E., Suite 2790, Los Angeles, CA 90067, (213)557-0219.

KINISH, Rita——B: June 5, 1937, Phila., PA, *Pres.*, Kinish D'Ejaculate; **PRIM RE ACT:** Consultant, Owner/Investor; **EDUC:** 1959, Chestnut Hill Coll.; **OTHER ACT & HONORS:** Pres. PWP, B'nai Brith; **HOME ADD:** PO Box 2741, Philadelphia, PA 19120; **BUS ADD:** PO Box 2741, Philadelphia, PA 19120.

KINNARD, William N., Jr.——B: Sept. 12, 1926, Philadelphia, PA, *Prof. Emeritus, Fin. & RE*, Univ. of CT, RE Ctr.; **PRIM RE ACT:** Consultant, Engineer, Instructor; **SERVICES:** Valuation, appraisal review, investment analysis, counseling; **REP CLIENTS:** Maj. indus. comml. firms on prop. tax appeals, Life ins. cos., public utilities; **PREV EMPLOY:** Univ. of PA 1948-50, Wesleyan Univ. CT 1950-54, Dir. Urban Redev., Middletown CT, 1954-55; **PROFL AFFIL & HONORS:** Amer. Inst. RE Appraisers, Soc. RE Appraisers, Amer. Soc. Appraisers, Amer. Soc. RE Counselors, Inst. Prop. Taxation, SREA, MAI, CRE, ASA, CMI, Beta Gamma Sigma, Beta Gamma Sigma Distinguished Scholar, 1979-80, Outstanding Educators of Amer.; **EDUC:** BA, 1947, Econ., Swarthmore Coll.; **GRAD EDUC:** MBA, 1949, Fin., Univ. of PA; PhD, 1956, Fin. and Econ., Univ. of PA; **EDUC HONORS:** Acad. Honors, T.H. Dudley Perkins Scholar, Univ. Scholar, Harrison Fellow, Pi Gamma Mu; **OTHER ACT & HONORS:** Pres., Amer. RE and Urban Econ. Assn. 1968; **HOME ADD:** 61 Birchwood Heights Rd., Storrs, CT 06268, (203)429-9102; **BUS ADD:** Storrs, CT 06268, (203)486-3227.

KINNEY, Robert L.——B: Apr. 21, 1938, Everett, WA, *VP & Dir.*, Merrill Lynch, Hubbard, Inc., Mgr. - Instl. Asset Mgmt. Group; **OTHER RE ACT:** Investment Mgr./Pension Funds; **SERVICES:** Purchase RE assets for pension funds & manage portfolio; **REP CLIENTS:** Westinghouse, Atlantic-Richfield Co., Borg-Warner Corp., Northern IL Gas Co., City of Detroit; **PREV EMPLOY:** Lomes & Nettleton Financial Corp., Del E. Webb Corp.; **EDUC:** BBA, 1960, Bus. Admin., Univ. of HI; **EDUC HONORS:** BBA with Honors; **HOME ADD:** Stage Rd., Halifax, VT 05358, (802)368-7034; **BUS ADD:** Two Broadway, Suite 2315, New York, NY 10004, (212)908-8438.

KINNEY, Robert R.——B: Nov. 22, 1915, Bellefontaine, OH, *Commr. of Tax Equalization*, State of OH, Dept. of Tax Equalization; **OTHER RE ACT:** State tax admin.; **SERVICES:** supervise local real prop. tax assessment and admin.; **PROFL AFFIL & HONORS:** AIREA; Intl. Assn. of Assessing Officers, MAI; **EDUC:** BSci, 1940, Agric. Econ.; **MIL SERV:** Signal Army Corp. 1st Lt.; **HOME ADD:** 150 E Beechwold Blvd., Columbus, OH 43214, (614)268-5565; **BUS ADD:** 21st Fl., 30 E Broad St., Columbus, OH 43215, (614)466-5744.

KINSELLA, Thomas E.——B: June 25, 1947, Rochester, NY, *Pres.*, Rochester Leeway Corp., Subs. of Rochester Savings Bank; **PRIM RE ACT:** Broker, Developer; **OTHER RE ACT:** Joint Ventures; **SERVICES:** Diversified RE Investment Co.; **PREV EMPLOY:** Corporate Sec. HWD Serv. Corp., Wholly owned Subs. of First Federal S&L Assn. of Rochester; **PROFL AFFIL & HONORS:** Vice Chmn. - Monroe Cty. Housing commn.; Dir., Citizens Tax League of Rochester and Monroe Cty., Inc.; **EDUC:** BS, 1969, Mgmt., Univ. of Dayton, Dayton, OH; **GRAD EDUC:** MBA, 1972, Mgmt., SUNY at Buffalo; **MIL SERV:** US Army; **HOME ADD:** 68 Woodlawn, Rochester, NY 14607, (716)473-6543; **BUS ADD:** 40 Franklin St., Rochester, NY 14604, (716)263-6874.

KINSER, Wayne——B: Sept. 14, 1933, Athens, TN, *Pres.*, Peppertree Resorts Ltd.; **PRIM RE ACT:** Developer, Owner/Investor, Syndicator; **OTHER RE ACT:** Developer, owner operator of interval ownership resorts; **EDUC:** BS, 1955, Bus., Wake Forest Univ.; **BUS ADD:** 28 Heritage Dr., Asheville, NC 28806, (704)254-8991.

KINYON, Betty C.——B: June 13, 1943, VA, *Pres.*, Sun Belt Intl. Realty Corp., Inc.; **PRIM RE ACT:** Broker, Consultant, Owner/Investor; **SERVICES:** Resid. Comml. Devl. Mgmt. Time-Share Exchangers; **REP CLIENTS:** Orlando, Intl. Resort Club; **PREV EMPLOY:** Resid. RE and Retail Buying Career; **PROFL AFFIL & HONORS:** NAR, Orlando Winter Park BD of Realtors, FL RE Exchange, Orlando RE Exchange, Academy of RE GA RE Exchange, RESSI, Interex, C.I.D SC RE Exchange.; **EDUC:** BS, 1966, General Bus. Admin., Univ. of TN; **OTHER ACT & HONORS:** Million Dollar Producer every yr. in RE; **HOME ADD:** 1045 Camelot Way, Casselberry, FL 32707, (305)695-3549; **BUS ADD:** 431 E. Central Blvd., Orlando, FL 32801, (305)425-6330.

KINZLER, Andrew——B: May 16, 1942, NYC, NY, *Part.*, Kinzler & Ritter/Land Planning; **PRIM RE ACT:** Architect, Instructor, Consultant, Developer, Owner/Investor; **OTHER RE ACT:** Land Planner; **SERVICES:** Devel. Feasibility, Master Planning, Site Planning Environmental Assessment, Econ. Analyses, Graphics; **REP CLIENTS:** Coral Ridge Prop. (Westinghouse), The Allan-Deane Corp. (Johns-Manville)Houdaille Indus., Inc. (HCMI Division) Inland Steel Co. (Instud Div.) K. S. Sweet Assoc., US Land Resources, Inc.; **PREV EMPLOY:** RSWA, INC., Land Planners, Phila. PA '68-'76; **PROFL AFFIL & HONORS:** ULI, ASLA, APA, Hon. Award/ American Consulting Engineers Council 1980; Merit Award/AIA WA Chapter 1981; **EDUC:** BA, 1964, Arch., Univ. of PA; **GRAD EDUC:** Arch/LA (M.L.A.), 1966, 1968, Univ. of PA (both grad. degrees); **EDUC HONORS:** Maj. Hon.; **OTHER ACT & HONORS:** Registered Landscape Arch in SC, Metropolitan Policy Club, Nat. Trust Historic Preservation, Asst. Prof./Dept. of Arch./Drexel Univ., Dir. of the Dupont Grp., RE Investments, WA, DC, Dir. of US Land Resources, RE Dev., WA, DC; **HOME ADD:** 1908 Panama St., Philadelphia, PA 19103, (215)732-3557; **BUS ADD:** 1704 Walnut St., Philadelphia, PA 19103, (215)546-5446.

KIPPER, Richard N.——B: Apr. 28, 1940, Los Angeles, CA, *Partner*, Laventhol & Horwath, CPA's, Tax; **PRIM RE ACT:** Consultant; **OTHER RE ACT:** Tax partner in nat. CPA firm; **SERVICES:** Tax planning, preparation of tax projections; **REP CLIENTS:** Bateman, Eichler, Hill, Richards Realty Services, Inc.; Amer. Capital Investors, Inc.; Pacific Mgmt. Group, Inc.; DeAnza Corp.; Nat. Partnerships Investment Corp.; **PROFL AFFIL & HONORS:** AICPA; CA Soc. of CPA's; ABA; RESSI; Coalition for Low and Moderate Income; Rural Builders Council of CA, MBA; JD; CPA; **EDUC:** MS, 1962, Bus. Admin., UCLA; **GRAD EDUC:** MBA, 1963, Acctg., UCLA; JD, 1967, Law, UCLA; **MIL SERV:** US Army, Sgt.; **OTHER ACT & HONORS:** Award of Appreciation, City of Hope, 1978; **BUS ADD:** 3700 Wilshire Blvd., Los Angeles, CA 90010, (213)381-5393.

KIRBY, James J.——B: Feb. 10, 1946, Chicago, IL, *Pres.*, Lakewoods Realty & Mort. Corp.; **PRIM RE ACT:** Syndicator, Developer, Regulator, Property Manager, Owner/Investor; **OTHER RE ACT:** Advisor to Brauvin RE, Fund I (–10,000,000) Registered Offering; **REP CLIENTS:** Various Major Banks, Personal Securities, Firms and Public Fund.; **PREV EMPLOY:** Hawthorn Realty Group 1968-1979; **EDUC:** AB, 1968, Hist. Phil., Georgetown Univ.; **HOME ADD:** 501 W. Grant Place, Chicago, IL 60614, (312)248-5003; **BUS ADD:** 11 S. LaSalle St., Chicago, IL 60603, (312)782-1600.

KIRBY, Ronald P.——B: Jan. 29, 1939, Rochester, NY, *Pres.*, Almist, Inc.; **PRIM RE ACT:** Developer; **OTHER RE ACT:** Volunteer Pres. of Community Assn. Inst.; **PROFL AFFIL & HONORS:** CAI, NAHB, AOBA, CDA; **EDUC:** Bus. Admin. & Acctg., Univ. of MD; **MIL SERV:** USAF, S/Sgt., 1956-65; **OTHER ACT & HONORS:** Bd. of Dirs., AOBA & CDA Bd. of Trs. & Exec. Comm. CAI 1981-82 Pres.; **HOME ADD:** 9514 Hunt Sq. Court, Springfield, VA 22152, (703)455-9821; **BUS ADD:** 2801 Park Center, Alexandria, VA 22302, (703)671-3134.

KIRCHOFF, George——B: Nov. 12, 1938, Eugene, OR, *Partner*, Brownfield Ltd., Developers; **PRIM RE ACT:** Broker, Consultant, Appraiser, Developer, Lender, Builder, Owner/Investor, Instructor, Syndicator; **SERVICES:** Income Prop. Devel., Seminars, Appraisal; **REP CLIENTS:** Lenders and Indiv. or inst. investors in resid. income prop.; **PREV EMPLOY:** Capital S&L Assn Sr. VP, Loans, 1970-1979; **PROFL AFFIL & HONORS:** AIREA, Sr. Member, (C.R.A.); NARA; MAI (candidate); **EDUC:** B.C.S, 1960, Mktg., Seattle Univ.; **EDUC HONORS:** Student of Year 1960, Amer. Mktg. Assn.; **MIL SERV:** US Army, Sgt., 1960-1962; **OTHER ACT & HONORS:** Member of the Bd., Security Savings, Kent, WA; Instructor, RE Fin., Ft. Steilacoom, Community Coll.; **HOME ADD:** 3701 N. Shore Blvd., Tacoma, WA 98422, (206)927-9394; **BUS ADD:** 10107 S. Tacoma Way, Tacoma, WA 98499, (206)581-2553.

KIRDANI, H.——B: Jan. 8, 1931, Cairo, Egypt, *Investment Counselor*, International Investment Concepts, Investments & Exchanges; **OTHER RE ACT:** International Trade; **SERVICES:** RE Counseling, Mktg., 1031 Tax-Deferred Exchanges; **PROFL AFFIL & HONORS:** Nat. Council of Exchangers (NCE), Interex, Long Beach Exchange Counselors; **EDUC:** BA, 1956, Econ., Pol. & Soc. Sci., Amer. Univ. at Cairo (AUC); **HOME ADD:** 120 E. Louise St., Long Beach, CA 90805, (213)428-1987; **BUS ADD:** PO Box 5185, Long Beach, CA 90805, (213)428-1987.

KIREHOFF, N.A.——*VP Ind. Devel.*, St. Louis - San Francisco Railway Co.; **PRIM RE ACT:** Developer; **BUS ADD:** 906 Olive St., St. Louis, MO 63101, (314)342-8455.*

KIRK, Ballard H. T.——B: Apr. 1, 1929, Williamsport, PA, *Pres.*, Kirk & Associates, Inc.; **PRIM RE ACT:** Consultant, Architect, Developer, Builder, Syndicator; **SERVICES:** Arch. & dev. consulting; planning; arch.; dev.; bldg.; **REP CLIENTS:** The Klingbeil Co.; General

Investment & Dev. Co.; Amer. Housing Guild; Sigma Continental Corp.; Provident United Corp.; **PROFL AFFIL & HONORS:** AIA; OH Bd. of Bldg. Standards, 1974-79; OH Bd. of Examiners of Arch., 1973-1978, 1978-1983; Nat. Council of Arch. Registration Bds., Sec. 1979-1981, VP, 1981-1982; **EDUC:** BArch., 1959, School of Arch.; OH St. Univ.; **HOME ADD:** 2459 Tremont Rd., Columbus, OH 43221, (614)486-7241; **BUS ADD:** 2130 Arlington Ave., Columbus, OH 43221, (614)486-6783.

KIRK, Judd——B: Apr. 29, 1945, Salt Lake City, UT, *Partner*, Davis Wright Todd Riese & Jones; **PRIM RE ACT:** Attorney; **PROFL AFFIL & HONORS:** Amer. Coll. of RE Lawyers; Past Chmn., Real Prop., Probate & Trust Section of WA State Bar Assn.; Lecturer for Practicing Law Instit.; **EDUC:** BA, 1967, Fin., Univ. of WA; **GRAD EDUC:** JD, 1970, Harvard Law School; **EDUC HONORS:** Cum Laude; **OTHER ACT & HONORS:** Bd. of Tr., Epiphany School; **HOME ADD:** 3802 47th NE, Seattle, WA 98105, (206)525-7931; **BUS ADD:** 4200 Seattle First Nat. Bank Bldg., Seattle, WA 98154, (206)622-3150.

KIRKLAND, James A., Jr.——*Reg. RE Dir.*, Winchell Div., Denny's Inc., Southwest, Mountain States, Mid-States; **PRIM RE ACT:** Attorney, Developer; **SERVICES:** Purchase, sell, lease, lease terminate Winchell retail locations; **BUS ADD:** 1178 W. Pioneer Parkway, Arlington, TX 76013, (817)261-3601.

KIRKOFF, J.B.——*Dir. Corp. Dev. & Secy.*, Park-Ohio Industries, Inc.; **PRIM RE ACT:** Property Manager; **BUS ADD:** 20600 Chagrin Blvd., 600 Tower East, Cleveland, OH 44122, (216)991-9700.*

KIRKPATRICK, Michael L.——B: Jan. 4, 1940, IL, *VP*, Halkirk Companies; **PRIM RE ACT:** Broker, Consultant, Developer, Builder, Owner/Investor, Property Manager; **SERVICES:** Complete RE Services, Counseling, Synd., Devel., Sales Mgmt.; **REP CLIENTS:** Indiv., Pension Plans, Corp. Investors; **PROFL AFFIL & HONORS:** RESSI, NRBA, Local Historic Societies, Owners & Mgrs. Assn., etc.; **EDUC:** BS Bus. Admin., Adv. Credits MBA, 1961, Gen. Bus. and RE, Murray State Univ.; **MIL SERV:** US Army, 1st Lt.; **BUS ADD:** 2625 Cumberland Pkwy., Suite 480, Atlanta, GA 30339, (404)432-2244.

KIRKSEY, John M.——B: Sept. 29, 1946, Denton, TX, *Pres.*, Kirksey Assocs. Architects and Kirksey Devel. Servs.; **PRIM RE ACT:** Architect, Developer, Builder, Owner/Investor; **SERVICES:** Arch. firm: full servs.; Devel. firm: as owners - site selection, fin., const. supervision, leasing and prop. mgmt. of finished product; completed 16 bldgs. in Houston, TX totaling over –50 MM; **PREV EMPLOY:** Neuhaus & Taylor, CRS; **PROFL AFFIL & HONORS:** Amer. Inst. of Arch.; TX Soc. of Arch.; Houston Chap. AIA, Past Member Exec. Comm., Past Sec.; Houston C of C; LA Soc. of Arch.; CO Soc. of Arch.; NCARB; Co-Founder, The Beautification of Richmond Ave. Comm.; Charter The Beautification of Woodway Group; Rice Design Alliance; S. Main Assn.; Sponsor/Contrib., Clean Houston; Sponsor/Contrib., Soc. for the Performing Arts; BOMA; Devel. of Houston Club, Inc.; Nat. Trust for Historic Preservation Bd., of Dirs.; TX Commerce Bank, Richmond/Sage; **EDUC:** BArch., 1970, Univ. of TX, Austin; **EDUC HONORS:** High Hon.; **HOME ADD:** 2247 Stanmore Dr., Houston, TX 77019; **BUS ADD:** 4299 San Felipe, Suite 300, Houston, TX 77027, (713)960-9444.

KIRSCH, H. Bruce——B: July 18, 1948, New York, NY, *Princ.*, Harley, Little Assoc.; **PRIM RE ACT:** Consultant, Appraiser, Instructor; **SERVICES:** RE research, devel. of hospitality and foodservice props., operational analysis; **REP CLIENTS:** Indiv. and instnl. investors, govt. agencies and lenders; **PREV EMPLOY:** Helmsley-Spear Hospitality Services, Inc. 1974-1980; **PROFL AFFIL & HONORS:** Cornell Soc. of Hotelmen, RE Bd. Mgmt. of NY, Amer. Hotel & Motel Assn., Soc. of Foodservice Mgmt.; **EDUC:** BS, Hotel Admin., Cornell Univ.; **GRAD EDUC:** Course work towards MBA, Fin., Pace Univ.; **HOME ADD:** 3690 Oceanside Rd. East, Oceanside, NY 11572, (516)764-4352; **BUS ADD:** 170 Hamilton Ave., White Plains, NY 10601, (914)428-6116.

KIRSCHNER, Gerald M.——B: July 18, 1937, Detroit, MI, *Pres.*, Kirschner Hutton Shevin, PC; **PRIM RE ACT:** Consultant, Owner/Investor; **OTHER RE ACT:** CPA; **SERVICES:** Projections, tax planning & consulting, reviewing, auditing; **REP CLIENTS:** synd. devel., builders, mgrs. and owners of shopping ctrs., apt. complexes and office bldgs.; **PREV EMPLOY:** Touche Ross & Co., Hirsch and Kirschner; **PROFL AFFIL & HONORS:** AICPA, MI Assn. of CPA, CPA; **EDUC:** BA, 1958, Acctg., MI State Univ.; **HOME ADD:** 4462 Ramsgate Ln., Bloomfield Hills, MI 48013, (313)626-1414; **BUS ADD:** 30200 Telegraph Rd., 237, Birmingham, MI 48010, (313)642-8616.

KIRTLAND, George W.——B: Oct. 6, 1921, Chicago, IL, *VP, Real Estate*, Jo-Ann Enterprises, Inc.; **PRIM RE ACT:** Broker, Developer; **OTHER RE ACT:** Retail RE locations, 121 units; **SERVICES:** Planning expansion, negotiating leases, construction of units, franchising; **REP CLIENTS:** Franchisees; **PREV EMPLOY:** 12 yrs. with maj. shopping ctr. devel. leasing; 25 yrs. gen mgr. dept. stores; **PROFL AFFIL & HONORS:** Intl. Council of Shopping Ctrs.; **EDUC:** Jr. Coll., 1940, Mgmt. Course II, Intl. Council Shopping Ctrs., others studies at Univ. of GA, Rutgers Univ., Duquesne Univ. Extension RE; **MIL SERV:** US Army Air Force, Sgt. 1940-42; **OTHER ACT & HONORS:** 32 deg. Mason, Shriner; **HOME ADD:** 1591 Springfield Ave., New Providence, NJ 07974, (201)464-7609; **BUS ADD:** 657 Line Rd., PO Box 336, Aberdeen, NJ 07747.

KIRWAN, Ernest E.——B: Dec. 26, 1928, Providence, RI, *Arch.*, Keyes Assoc., Arch. & Planning; **PRIM RE ACT:** Architect; **OTHER RE ACT:** Planner; **SERVICES:** Master planning, environmental analysis, bldg. design, engrg. space planning; **REP CLIENTS:** Industr., comml. banking, health care, & RE devel. orgs.; **PREV EMPLOY:** Prin. Urban Designer, City of Providence, RI; **PROFL AFFIL & HONORS:** Boston Soc. of Archs., Amer. Inst. of Arch.; **EDUC:** BS, 1956, Arch., RI Sch. of Design; **GRAD EDUC:** MArch, 1954, Arch., MIT; **EDUC HONORS:** Edward Langley Scholarship (AIA), Skidmore, Owings & Merrill Travelling Scholarship; **MIL SERV:** USAFR, 1st Lt.; **OTHER ACT & HONORS:** Exec Comm., Harvard Sq. Neighborhood Assn., Tr. RI Sch. of Design; **HOME ADD:** 2 Kenway St., Cambridge, MA 02138, (617)491-0166; **BUS ADD:** 267 Moody St., Waltham, MA 02154.

KISER, Jack D.——B: Oct. 26, 1942, Carter Co., KY, *Atty.*; **PRIM RE ACT:** Broker, Consultant, Attorney, Owner/Investor, Property Manager; **SERVICES:** All phases of legal councel RE; **PROFL AFFIL & HONORS:** ABA, KY Bar Assn.; **EDUC:** BS, 1968, Hist., Univ. of KY; **GRAD EDUC:** JD, 1972, Univ. of KY Law School; **EDUC HONORS:** Dean's List; **MIL SERV:** US Army, Sgt.; **HOME ADD:** 129 McDowell Rd., Lexington, KY 40502, (606)269-4167; **BUS ADD:** 400 E. Vine St. Suite 209, Lexington, KY 40507, (606)254-7392.

KISHI, Louise N.——B: Jan. 29, 1923, Aln, TX, *Owner Pres.*, Louise N. Kishi Assoc., Inc., d/b/a Red Carpet Realty; **PRIM RE ACT:** Consultant, Owner/Investor, Property Manager; **OTHER RE ACT:** Owner, broker, 1974-80; **PREV EMPLOY:** RE salesperson, Ft. Lauderdale, FL, 1958-62 (4 yrs.); Taught high school English & Bus. for 11 and half yrs.; **PROFL AFFIL & HONORS:** CRB applicant; CCIM applicant; Member RESSI; First woman Pres. of Coffee-Geneva Bd. of Realtors, 1976 and 1977; Member Bd. of Dir. of C of C in Enterprise, 1979; **EDUC:** BBA, 1944, Comml. teaching, Univ. of TX, Austin; **OTHER ACT & HONORS:** First United Methodist Church; Registrar for John Coffee Chapt. of DAR; Enterprise Music Club; Coffee Cty. Arts Alliance; Ft. Rucker ADTA Ladies; Officer's Wives Club; **HOME ADD:** 202 Northside Dr., Enterprise, AL 36330, (205)347-8707; **BUS ADD:** Rt. #3., Box 413, PO Box 1252, Enterprise, AL 36331, (205)347-2287.

KISIEL, Mark M.——*Pres.*, Leggat McCall & Werner Ventures; **PRIM RE ACT:** Developer; **BUS ADD:** 60 State St., Boston, MA 02109, (617)367-1177.*

KISKER, George——*Mgr. RE Dept.*, Proctor & Gamble Co.; **PRIM RE ACT:** Property Manager; **BUS ADD:** PO Box 599, Cincinnati, OH 45201, (513)562-1100.*

KISNER, Daniel R.——B: Mar. 22, 1946, Cleveland, OH, *Div. Council*, Ponderosa Homes, Santa Clara; **PRIM RE ACT:** Broker, Attorney; **PREV EMPLOY:** Aminoil USA, Inc.; **PROFL AFFIL & HONORS:** ABA;Cal Bar Assn.; **EDUC:** B.E.E., 1969, Cleveland State Univ.; **GRAD EDUC:** JD, 1975, Pepperdine Univ.; **EDUC HONORS:** Tau Beta Pi, ETA Kappa Nu Hon. Frats, Cum Laude Law Review, Corpus Juris Secundum, Amjurawards; **HOME ADD:** 47375 Galindo Dr., Fremont, CA 94539; **BUS ADD:** 3080 Olcott St., Santa Clara, CA 95051, (408)727-4500.

KISSEL, Katherine V.——B: Aug 15, 1915, Burlington, WI, *Owner, Broker*, Katherine V. Kisell RE; **PRIM RE ACT:** Broker, Owner/Investor; **PREV EMPLOY:** Baird & Warner, Glenview, IL, 8 yrs., Own firm 10 yrs.; **PROFL AFFIL & HONORS:** GRI, CRB; **EDUC:** 1938, Journl., Univ. of WI; **GRAD EDUC:** MBA, 1942, Mktg., Commerce, Northwestern Univ.; **OTHER ACT & HONORS:** Northfield Township High School Dist. 225, 7 yrs., Pres. League of Women Voters of Glenview; **HOME ADD:** 1739 de l'Ogier Dr., Gel Dr., Glenview, IL 60025, (312)724-0948; **BUS ADD:** 1247 Waukegan Rd., Glenview, IL 60025, (312)998-9121.

KISSINGER, Michael J.——B: Apr. 29, 1947, San Francisco, CA, *Atty.*, Construction Law Office; **PRIM RE ACT:** Consultant, Attorney, Developer, Instructor; **SERVICES:** Const. RE litigation; **EDUC:** BS, 1971, Bus. Admin., Univ. of San Francisco; **GRAD EDUC:** 1976, Law, Univ. of San Francisco; **MIL SERV:** US Army, Sgt.; **BUS ADD:** 1231 Market St., Penthouse Suite, San Francisco, CA 94103, (415)552-9495.

KISSMAN, Nadra D.——B: Dec. 2, 1934, St. Joseph, MI, *Owner/ Broker*, Nadra K. Real Estate; **PRIM RE ACT:** Broker, Appraiser, Owner/Investor; **OTHER RE ACT:** Exclusive Agents for Timber Lane Estates; **SERVICES:** Listing & selling resid. prop., second home prop., lakefront & lake access; **REP CLIENTS:** Indiv. from the S. Bend and Chicago Areas interested in Lake MI or Lake MI access prop. for weekend and vacation us; **PREV EMPLOY:** Assoc. Broker, Lakeshore Realty, New Buffalo, MI; **PROFL AFFIL & HONORS:** Member Harbor Cty. Council; Berrien Cty. Econ. Devel. Corp.; Building Trades Advisory Comm. for W. Berrien Cty. Vocational Educ. Consortium; State of MI Notary Public; Member SW MI Bd. of Realtors; Multiple Listing System of Southwestern MI; MI Assn. of Realtors; Nat. Assn. of Realtors, Member of SW MI Million Dollar Club; **EDUC:** Sociology/Psychology, Lake MI Coll., Univ. of MI - RE Curriculum; Ho Holloway RE School - Gen. RE; South Bend Coll. of Commerce - Bus.; **OTHER ACT & HONORS:** New Buffalo Service League (Past Pres. & Life Member); New Buffalo PTA (Past Pres.); New Buffalo Bicentenial Comm. 1975-76; Author & Researcher of *The New Buffalo Story*; New Buffalo Blossomtime Chairperson (Past Co-Chairperson); **HOME ADD:** R #1, Box 304, Union Pier, MI 49129, (616)469-1365; **BUS ADD:** R #2, Box 795K, Red Arrow Highway, New Buffalo, MI 49117, (616)469-2090.

KISTLER, Hazel M.——B: Dec. 9, 1928, NC, *Broker/Owner*, A-1 Realty; **PRIM RE ACT:** Broker, Appraiser, Developer, Property Manager, Owner/Investor; **OTHER RE ACT:** Farm and Land Inst. Academy of RE Exchangors; **SERVICES:** Sales, Mgt., Counseling, Exchanging, Investing; **PREV EMPLOY:** Fin. Const.; **PROFL AFFIL & HONORS:** GRI, Candidate for AFLM in Dothan Brd. of Realtors, BPW Personel Devel. Award, 1971; **EDUC:** BS Mktg. & Bus. Admin., 1971, Mktg., Troy State Univ.; **GRAD EDUC:** RE GRI Candidate for AFLM, Farms & Land & Comml., NA Realtors & AL Assn. of Realtors; **EDUC HONORS:** Cum Laude; **OTHER ACT & HONORS:** C of C of Dothan, First United Methodist Church, Bus. & Professional Women's League; **HOME ADD:** 1501 Seminole St, Dothan, AL 36303, (205)792-5802; **BUS ADD:** P.O. Drawer 7147, Dothan, AL 36302, (205)792-5802.

KITCHEN, E. Joseph——B: Dec. 24, 1944, Kadiz, KY, *Asst. VP*, Gaylord State Bank; **PRIM RE ACT:** Banker; **OTHER RE ACT:** Head RE mort. dept.; **SERVICES:** RE fin.; **PREV EMPLOY:** MI Nat. Bank., 11 yrs., RE Fin. & Prop. Mgmt.; **PROFL AFFIL & HONORS:** N Central Home Builders Assn., Bd. Member & Treas., Water Wonderland Bd. of Realtors; MI Bankers Assn. (Mort. Review Comm. 1980-1983), Chmn., Fin. Review Comm. for N. Central Home Builders Assn.; **EDUC:** Mott Comm. Coll.; **MIL SERV:** USMC, Cpl., Good Conduct; **OTHER ACT & HONORS:** Eagles; **HOME ADD:** RT 6, 2519 Manorwood Dr., Gaylord, MI 49735, (517)732-3737; **BUS ADD:** PO Box 600, Gaylord, MI 49735, (517)732-2411.

KITCHIN, John J.——B: Mar. 23, 1933, Kansas City, MO, *Part.*, Swanson, Midgley, Gangwere, Clarke & Kitchin; **PRIM RE ACT:** Attorney; **SERVICES:** Legal; **REP CLIENTS:** Fairmont Foods Co., Pizza Hut of Amer., Inc.; **PREV EMPLOY:** In firm since 1961; **PROFL AFFIL & HONORS:** ABA, Kansas City Bar Assn. & Lawyers Assn. of Kansas City; **EDUC:** BA, 1954, Phil., Indus. Relations, Rockhurst Coll., Kansas City, MO; **GRAD EDUC:** JD, 1957, St. Louis Univ.; **EDUC HONORS:** Alpha Sigma Nu Hon. Soc., Order of Woolsock, Law Review Staff, Cum Laude; **MIL SERV:** USAF, Capt.; **OTHER ACT & HONORS:** Chmn. Kansas City Liquor Commn., 1972-75; Serra Club of Kansas City, MO, Pres. 1979-80; **HOME ADD:** 11548 Baltimore, Kansas City, MO 64114, (816)942-5089; **BUS ADD:** 1500 Commerce Bank Bldg., 922 Walnut, Kansas City, MO 64106, (816)842-9692.

KITE, Richard L.——B: Jan. 26, 1934, Chicago, IL, *Pres.*, Kite Development Corp.; **PRIM RE ACT:** Broker, Consultant, Attorney, Developer, Owner/Investor, Property Manager, Syndicator; **SERVICES:** Developing RE projects, construction, acquisition and syndication; **PREV EMPLOY:** Corp. law & RE practice, 1960-1964; **PROFL AFFIL & HONORS:** ICSC, Young President's Org., Lic. RE Broker; **EDUC:** BA, 1955, Acctg., UCLA; **GRAD EDUC:** JD, LLB, 1958, Law, UCLA School of Law; **EDUC HONORS:** Grad. with Highest Honors; Phi Beta Kappa, Grad. 1st in Class; Order of the Coif; **MIL SERV:** USAF Res., Airman 1st Class, 1959-1964; **OTHER ACT & HONORS:** Corp. Member of Milwaukee Children's Hosp., Bd. of Dir. of the Ballet Foundation of Milwaukee Inc.; **HOME ADD:** 251 W. Nokomis Ct., Milwaukee, WI 53217, (414)352-1218; **BUS ADD:** 324 E. Wisconsin Ave., Suite 1010, Milwaukee, WI 53202, (414)289-0990.

KITTLESON, John Alden——B: May 24, 1932, Mayville, ND, *RE Broker*, Realty World - Kittleson; **PRIM RE ACT:** Broker; **SERVICES:** Gen. RE brokerage, spec. single family; **PROFL AFFIL & HONORS:** Bemidji Bd. of Realtors; MN Assn. of Realtors; NAR, CRB; **EDUC:** BA, 1955, Bemidji State Univ.; **MIL SERV:** USN; **OTHER ACT & HONORS:** Elks; Lions Club; 1st Lutheran Church; **HOME ADD:** Rt. 8, Box 474, Bemidji, MN 56601, (218)751-3955; **BUS ADD:** 1425 Hwy. #2 West, Bemidji, MN 56601, (218)751-2511.

KITTRELL, John R.——B: Aug. 3, 1938, Paris, TX, *Pres.*, Kittrell Properties; **PRIM RE ACT:** Broker, Consultant, Developer, Instructor, Syndicator; **PROFL AFFIL & HONORS:** SIR; **EDUC:** BBA, 1960, R.E. and Fin., Univ. of TX at Austin; **EDUC HONORS:** With honors; **MIL SERV:** US Army, 1st Lt.; **OTHER ACT & HONORS:** Chmn. Advisory Council-School of Bus. & Admin., St. Mary's Univ. 1975-76; UTSA Coll. of Bus. Advisory Council; **HOME ADD:** 102 Sheffield Pl., San Antonio, TX 78213, (512)344-0224; **BUS ADD:** 909 NE Loop 410, 528, San Antonio, TX 78209, (512)822-8890.

KLAFTER, Mark H.——B: June 28, 1910, Youngstown, OH, *VP*, Burke, Hansen, Homan & Klafter; **PRIM RE ACT:** Consultant, Appraiser, Owner/Investor; **SERVICES:** Valuation and counseling RE all phases of RE investment; **PROFL AFFIL & HONORS:** AIREA; Soc. of RE Appraisers; SREA, Amer. Soc. of RE Counselors; Amer Right of Way Assoc., MAI, SREA, CRE, SR/WA; **EDUC:** AB, 1933, Econ., Adelbert Coll., Western Reserve Univ.; **HOME ADD:** 6985 E. Calle Dorado, Tucson, AZ 85715; **BUS ADD:** 6245 E. Broadway, Ste. 690, Tucson, AZ 85711, (602)790-8555.

KLAMAN, Saul B.——*Pres.*, Natl. Assn. of Mutual Savings Banks; **PRIM RE ACT:** Banker; **BUS ADD:** 200 Park Ave., New York, NY 10017, (212)973-5432.*

KLAMEN, Marvin——B: Mar. 12, 1931, St. Louis, MO, *Partner*, Klamen & Danna; **PRIM RE ACT:** Attorney; **PROFL AFFIL & HONORS:** St. Louis & St. Louis Cty. Bar; MO Bar Assn.; ABA; numerous comm. appointments; **EDUC:** BA, 1953, Eng. Lit. & Psych., Washington Univ.; **GRAD EDUC:** LLB, 1955, Law, Washington Univ.; **EDUC HONORS:** Scholarship; **MIL SERV:** USAF; Capt.; **OTHER ACT & HONORS:** Bd. of Dir. Univ. School Dist.; Member Planning & Zoning Commn., Richmond Heights; **HOME ADD:** 7 Ridgetop, Richmond Heights, MO 63117, (314)994-1529; **BUS ADD:** 7820 Marykind, Clayton, MO 63105, (312)726-1000.

KLARICH, Richard M.——B: Nov. 11, 1940, Chicago, IL, *Gen. Mgr., RE Div.*, Arvey Corp.; **PRIM RE ACT:** Developer, Owner/Investor, Property Manager; **REP CLIENTS:** All in house for Arvey Corp.; **PREV EMPLOY:** Gen. Mgr. of Klarich Const. Co., Chicago based comml./indus. designers-builders and devels.; **PROFL AFFIL & HONORS:** NACORE; **EDUC:** BArch, 1962, Univ. of Notre Dame; **HOME ADD:** 10321 S. Hoyne Ave., Chicago, IL 60643, (312)238-9731; **BUS ADD:** 3450 N. Kimball Ave., Chicago, IL 60618, (312)463-0030.

KLASS, Richard L.——B: Jan. 6, 1946, Columbus, OH, *Pres.*, Magna Group Inc.; **PRIM RE ACT:** Developer, Builder; **PREV EMPLOY:** Dept. of Housing and Urban Devel. 1975-1976, Carl M. Freeman Assoc. Inc. 1972-1974; **PROFL AFFIL & HONORS:** Natl. Assn. of Homebuilders, No. VA Homebuilders Assn.; **EDUC:** BS, 1968, Aeronautical and Astronautical Engrg., MIT; **GRAD EDUC:** MS, 1972, Fin., Univ. of So. CA; MBA, 1974, Aerospace Engrg., Fin., Harvard Bus. School; **OTHER ACT & HONORS:** Harvard Bus. School Club, MIT Club Dir. and head of area Alumni Fund; **BUS ADD:** 11015 W. Ave., Kensington, MD 20895, (301)942-7490.

KLASSEN, Charles R.——B: Oct. 23, 1927, Los Angeles, CA, *Pres.*, Charles R. Klassen, Inc.; **PRIM RE ACT:** Developer, Builder; **PREV EMPLOY:** Self-employed since 1955; **PROFL AFFIL & HONORS:** Member of the Kern Cty. Builders; CA State Builders Exchange (dir. 1975-77); Bd. of Dirs. Greater Bksfld. C of C (1980-82); **MIL SERV:** US Army, Engrs., **OTHER ACT & HONORS:** Kern Cty. Shrine Club Pres. 1975; Chmn. Potato Bowl of the Shrine 1977-; YMCA Dir. 1970-78; Salvation Army Dir. 1968-75; YWCA Advisory Bd.; **HOME ADD:** 2730 21st St., Bakersfield, CA 93301; **BUS ADD:** 104 Lake St., Bakersfield, CA 93305, (805)327-4034.

KLATSKIN, Charles——B: Nov. 5, 1934, Brooklyn, NY, *Pres.*, Charles Klatskin Co., Inc.; **PRIM RE ACT:** Broker, Consultant, Appraiser, Developer, Builder, Owner/Investor, Instructor, Property Manager; **REP CLIENTS:** Beatrice Foods, Xerox Corp., Standard Brands, Automatic Data Processing, Norton Simon Inc., Sanyo, US Pioneer Electronics Corp.; **PREV EMPLOY:** VP & Mgr. NY Indus. Div. of Brown, Harris, Stevens; **PROFL AFFIL & HONORS:** Inc. RE

Brokers Assn.; Soc. of Indus. Realtors; Nat. Assn. of Indus. & Office Parks; Intl. Coll. of RE Consulting Profls.; S. Bergen Cty. Bd. of Realtors; Central Bergen Cty. Bd. of Realtors, Past Pres. of the NJ Chapter of S.I.R.; Currently Dist. VP of that Org.; Gov. Byrne Early Warning Task Force; **EDUC:** BS, Pharmacy, RE; BS, 1959, Econ. & RE, Wharton School of Fin. & Commerce Univ. of PA, 1959; **GRAD EDUC:** BS, 1956, Pharmacy, Temple Univ.; **OTHER ACT & HONORS:** VP and Bldg. Chmn. for the Jewish Community Ctr. on the Palisades; Member of UJF; JWB Young Leadership Award; Expert Witness to the Supreme Court of Bergen Cty.; **HOME ADD:** 18 Thatcher Rd., Tenafly, NJ 07670, (201)567-5655; **BUS ADD:** 400 Hollister Rd., Teterboro, NJ 07608, (201)288-5700.

KLAUS, John B.——**B:** July 23, 1939, Chicago, IL, *Shopping Ctr. Mgr.*, Old Capitol Center Partners; **OTHER RE ACT:** Mall Manager; **REP CLIENTS:** Retail tenants; **PREV EMPLOY:** Dir. of Urban Renewal, City of Iowa City; **EDUC:** BA, 1962, Philosophy, Loyola of Chicago; **GRAD EDUC:** MA, 1968, Urban Studies, Loyola; **MIL SERV:** US Marine Corp., 1st Lt.; **HOME ADD:** 909 Maplewood Ln., Iowa City, IA 52240, (319)354-3150; **BUS ADD:** 201 S. Clinton, Iowa City, IA 52240, (319)338-7858.

KLEE, John P.——**B:** Apr. 26, 1941, Pittsburgh, PA, *Counsel*, Dravo Corp.; **PRIM RE ACT:** Broker, Attorney; **PROFL AFFIL & HONORS:** ABA; PA Bar Assn.; Allegheny Cty. Bar Assn.; **EDUC:** BA, 1963, Hist., Washington & Jefferson Coll.; **GRAD EDUC:** JD, 1967, Univ. of Pittsburgh, School of Law; **EDUC HONORS:** Phi Alpha Theta; **HOME ADD:** 604 Pitcairn Pl., Pittsburgh, PA 15232, (412)682-7128; **BUS ADD:** One Oliver Plaza, Pittsburgh, PA 15222, (412)566-3428.

KLEEMAN, Jack W.——*Exec. VP*, Realtors National Marketing Institute; **OTHER RE ACT:** Profl. Assn. Admin.; **BUS ADD:** 430 N. Michigan Ave., Chicago, IL 60611, (312)440-8000.*

KLEID, Richard M.——**B:** Apr. 13, 1932, NY, NY, *E. Rgnl. Atty.*, JC Penney Co. Inc., RE Dept.; **PRIM RE ACT:** Attorney; **PROFL AFFIL & HONORS:** Allegheny Cty. Bar Assn., Lecturer-ICSC Law Conferences, Writer-Shopping Ctr. World; **EDUC:** AB, 1953, Eng., Columbia Univ.; **GRAD EDUC:** JD, 1955, Columbia; LLM, 1964, Tax., NYU; **EDUC HONORS:** Deans List; **MIL SERV:** US Army, PFC; **OTHER ACT & HONORS:** Pres., Upper St. Clair Sch. Bd. 1979; **HOME ADD:** 1884 Tilton Dr., Pittsburgh, PA 15241, (412)221-2255; **BUS ADD:** 799 Castle Shannon Blvd., Pittsburgh, PA 15234, (412)531-9940.

KLEIMAN, Irving——**B:** July 31, 1925, NYC, NY, *VP Prop.*, Olympia & York Props.; **PRIM RE ACT:** Broker, Developer, Builder, Owner/Investor, Property Manager; **PREV EMPLOY:** Metro Radial Devel. Corp., Corbetta Enterprises, Inc.; **EDUC:** BS, 1949, Bus. Admin., NY Univ.; **GRAD EDUC:** MA, 1950, Bus. Admin., NY Univ.; **EDUC HONORS:** Cum Laude; **MIL SERV:** USN, SKV 2/C; **HOME ADD:** 110 Riverside Dr., New York, NY 10024, (212)724-7840; **BUS ADD:** 245 Park Ave., New York, NY 10067, (212)850-9626.

KLEIMAN, Macklen——**B:** Aug. 15, 1913, Boston, MA, *Pres.*, Lynn Screw Corp.; **PRIM RE ACT:** Consultant, Property Manager, Engineer, Owner/Investor; **PREV EMPLOY:** Beaver Enterprises, Inc. - Treasurer; **EDUC:** BS EE, 1935, MIT; **MIL SERV:** BOD, Civilian Eng.; **OTHER ACT & HONORS:** Rotary, Masons; **HOME ADD:** 1 Coolidge Rd., Marblehead, MA 01945, (617)631-5374; **BUS ADD:** 14 Mt. Vernon St., Lynn, MA 01901, (617)593-5819.

KLEIN, Allan Eric——**B:** Jan. 28, 1948, London, England, *Dir. of Prop. Mgmt.*, Mayer Management Inc.; **PRIM RE ACT:** Consultant, Property Manager; **SERVICES:** Energy consumption surveys & property management; **PREV EMPLOY:** Ring Bros. Management Co., 1972-1973; Mariani-Buss & Assoc., 1974-1979; **PROFL AFFIL & HONORS:** IREM, CPM candidate; CA RE Lic.; **EDUC:** AA, 1967, CA State Univ. at Los Angeles; BS, 1970, Mktg./Ad./Public Relations, CA State Univ. at Los Angeles; **EDUC HONORS:** First Recipient of the Robert Renberg Scholastic Achievement Award, 1969; Dean's List, 1969; **MIL SERV:** US Army; Sp. E-5, 1969-1974; **HOME ADD:** 4748 Columbus Ave., Sherman Oaks, CA 91403, (213)990-1800; **BUS ADD:** 9171 Wilshire Blvd., Beverly Hills, CA 90210, (213)927-3341.

KLEIN, Ervin——**B:** Mar. 25, 1949, Louisville, KY, *Part.*, McAdam & Klein; **PRIM RE ACT:** Attorney, Owner/Investor; **SERVICES:** All legal services relating to R.E.; **PREV EMPLOY:** City of Lousiville Real Prop. Tax Collector 1976-78; City of Louisville Dept. of Bldg. and Housing Hearing Officer 1974-77; Land Surveyor, Schimpeler-Corradino Assoc. 1967-73; Const. Engr., Blount Bros. Const. Co. 1973-74; **PROFL AFFIL & HONORS:** ABA; KBA; LBA Probate & R.E. & Taxation Div., KBA Cont. Legal Educ. Award, 1981; **EDUC:** BA, 1972, Hist., Louisville; **GRAD EDUC:** JD, 1975, Law, Louisville; **OTHER ACT & HONORS:** VP, YMCA Bd. of Mgrs.; Pres., Community Coordinated Child Care; **HOME ADD:** 1909 Dorothy Ave., Louisville, KY 40205, (502)459-5769; **BUS ADD:** 1495 Starks Bldg., 445 Fourth Ave., Louisville, KY 40202, (502)584-7255.

KLEIN, Fred W.——**B:** Mar. 9, 1946, Somers Point, NJ, *Partner*, Trammell Crow Co.; **PRIM RE ACT:** Developer, Builder, Owner/Investor; **PROFL AFFIL & HONORS:** Soc. of Indus. Realtors; **EDUC:** BSIE, 1968, Engrg., Lehigh Univ.; **GRAD EDUC:** MBA, 1973, Fin., Wharton School, Univ. of PA; **EDUC HONORS:** Grad. with highest honors, Grad. with highest honors; **MIL SERV:** USN, Lt.; **HOME ADD:** 1915 Trillium Ln., Charlotte, NC 28211, (704)364-2462; **BUS ADD:** 1505 So. Nat. Ctr., 200 So. Coll. St., Charlotte, NC 28202, (704)376-5910.

KLEIN, Harris——**B:** Jan. 7, 1949, Seattle, WA, *Sr. Leasing Consultant*, Wallace & Wheeler, Inc., Comml.; **PRIM RE ACT:** Broker, Consultant; **OTHER RE ACT:** Leasing Consultant; **SERVICES:** RE Investment Analyst; **EDUC:** BBA, 1971, RE and Fin., Univ. of WA; **OTHER ACT & HONORS:** Certificate in RE; **HOME ADD:** 520 9th Ave., Kirkland, WA 98033, (206)822-1980; **BUS ADD:** 924 Bellevue Way N.E., Bellevue, WA 98004, (206)454-6550.

KLEIN, Larry R.——**B:** Jan. 29, 1949, Orchard Park, NY, *VP; Operations*, Justice Corp.; **PRIM RE ACT:** Broker, Consultant, Developer, Property Manager, Owner/Investor; **SERVICES:** Comml. Dev., Consulting, Office Bldg. Prop. Mgmt., Comml. Sales & Leasing; **REP CLIENTS:** Instnl. Investors in Comml. Prop.; **PROFL AFFIL & HONORS:** IREM, Amer. Mgmt. Assn.; Board of Realtors; **EDUC:** BS, 1972, Mgmt., Univ. of Wisc.; **GRAD EDUC:** MA, 1977, Mgmt., Pepperdine Univ.; **MIL SERV:** USN, Lt. Natl. Defense, Vietnam Service, Navy Achievement Award; **OTHER ACT & HONORS:** Sigma Alpha Epsilon, Tampa C of C, Big Brothers of Amer., Comm. of 100, Merchants Assn; **HOME ADD:** 1260 Abbey Cresent Lane,, Clearwater, FL 33519, (813)797-1372; **BUS ADD:** Arbor Shoreline Office Ctr, 1307 US 2950., Clearwater, FL 33516, (813)535-4651.

KLEIN, Lewis D.——**B:** Dec. 30, 1923, Akron, OH, *Registered Architect*, Lewis D. Klein, Architect; **PRIM RE ACT:** Architect, Developer, Owner/Investor; **SERVICES:** Complete planning, design, build on various types of projects; **PROFL AFFIL & HONORS:** Amer. Instit. of Architect, Architects Soc. of OH, Construction Specifications Instit., Nat. Instit. Office & Ind. Parks; **EDUC:** BArch, 1949, Carnegie Mellon Univ., Pittsburgh, PA; **MIL SERV:** US Army Signal Corp.; **HOME ADD:** 3700 Judy Lane, Dayton, OH 45405; **BUS ADD:** 1508 N. Main St., Dayton, OH 45405, (513)277-9331.

KLEIN, M. Mark——**B:** Dec. 30, 1934, Cambridge, MA, *Partner, Law Firm*, Wasserman & Salter; **OTHER RE ACT:** Private Practice; **SERVICES:** Legal service to persons interested in RE transactions; issue title ins. policies; **PROFL AFFIL & HONORS:** Boston Bar Assn.; MA Bar Assn.; MA Conveyancer's Assn.; **EDUC:** BA, 1956, Sociology, Harvard Coll.; **GRAD EDUC:** JD, 1959, Univ. of MI Law School; **EDUC HONORS:** Cum Laude; **OTHER ACT & HONORS:** Sec. of Noddle's Is. Lodge, AF & AM; Past Pres., Temple B'Nai Moshe Brotherhood; Past Pres., Temple Emanuel PTA; **HOME ADD:** 35 Wiswall Rd., Newton Centre, MA 02159, (617)332-1121; **BUS ADD:** 31 Milk St., Boston, MA 02109, (617)956-1700.

KLEIN, Robert A.——**B:** July 28, 1944, Newark, NJ, *Partner*, Finley, Kumble, Wagner, Heine, Underberg & Casey; **PRIM RE ACT:** Attorney; **SERVICES:** RE Synd. and Fin., Condo.; **REP CLIENTS:** Synd., Broker-Dealers, Devels., Condo. Converters; **PROFL AFFIL & HONORS:** Member ABA, MD and DC Bar Assns.; **EDUC:** BA, 1966, Hist., Poli. Sci., Rutgers Univ.; **GRAD EDUC:** JD, 1969, Georgetown; LLM, 1972, Taxation, George Washington; **HOME ADD:** 11109 Stackhouse Ct., Potomac, MD 20854, (301)983-0076; **BUS ADD:** 1120 Connecticut Ave., NW, Washington, DC 20036, (202)857-4000.

KLEIN, Robert M.——**B:** June 19, 1953, Louisville, KY, *Atty.*, Gittleman, Charney & Barber; **PRIM RE ACT:** Attorney; **SERVICES:** all legal serv. regarding RE; **REP CLIENTS:** New Directions, Inc. Non-profit landlord, devel. and land trust; close-corporate clients; **PROFL AFFIL & HONORS:** ABA, Louisville Bar Assn., KY Bar Assn.; **EDUC:** BS Econ., 1975, Pol. Sci., Wharton School, Univ. of PA; **GRAD EDUC:** JD, 1978, Univ. of Louisville School of Law; **OTHER ACT & HONORS:** The Third Century; Univ. of Louisville Assoc.; **BUS ADD:** 800 Marion E. Taylor Bldg., Louisville, KY 40202, (502)585-2100.

KLEIN, Robert N., II——**B:** Aug. 15, 1945, Jacksonville, FL, *Managing Partner*, Bernard Klein Financial Group; **PRIM RE ACT:** Developer; **OTHER RE ACT:** Financial Consultant; **SERVICES:** Rehab. and devel. of apts.; multi-family, comml. and profl. office projects, finacial consulting; **PREV EMPLOY:** Paine, Webber, Jackson & Curtis, Inc.,

VP, 1976-1977; RE & Urban Devel., 1973-1976; OGO Assoc. of No. CA, 1972-1973; ESK Land Co., 1967 to present; **EDUC:** BA, 1967, Hist., Stanford Univ.; **GRAD EDUC:** JD, 1971, Law, Stanford Law School; **EDUC HONORS:** Honors in Hist.; **HOME ADD:** 2890 Huntington Blvd. #168, Fresno, CA 93721; **BUS ADD:** 2115 Kern Street, Fresno, CA 93721, (209)441-7901.

KLEIN, Robert N.——B: Apr. 24, 1916, Cincinnati, OH, *Pres.*, Robert Klein and Assoc.; **PRIM RE ACT:** Broker, Developer; **REP CLIENTS:** Indus. Corps.; **PREV EMPLOY:** First Chief Admin. officer, City of Fresno 1958-63; City Mgr. Santa Cruz, CA 1952-58; City Mgr. Mont. Pk. 1950-58; Asst. City Mgr. San Jose, CA 1948-50; SIR; **PROFL AFFIL & HONORS:** SIR Review Appraisers Assn. of Amer., CCIM; **EDUC:** AB, 1938, UCLA; **GRAD EDUC:** MS, 1941, USC; **MIL SERV:** USN, Lt. Cmdr.; **OTHER ACT & HONORS:** Honorary Life Member Santa Cruz C of C; Former consultant on devel. CA Hwy. Comm.; **HOME ADD:** 1440 W. Robinwood Ln., Fresno, CA 93711, (209)439-6785; **BUS ADD:** 108 W. Shaw, Fresno, CA 93704, (209)226-5222.

KLEIN, Stephen B.——B: Sept. 17, 1940, Philadelphia, PA, *Pres.*, Financo Realty Co.; **OTHER RE ACT:** Private investment firm in resid. and comml. RE; **EDUC:** BS, PA State Univ.; **GRAD EDUC:** Temple Univ. School of Law; NY Univ. Grad. School of Law; **HOME ADD:** 1150 Penllyn Pike, Blue Bell, PA 19422; **BUS ADD:** 1700 Market St., Suite 1240, Philadelphia, PA 19103, (215)568-7991.

KLEINSMITH, Mark John——B: Apr. 11, 1951, Davenport, IA, *Pres., Owner*, Marmel Cos.; **PRIM RE ACT:** Developer, Builder, Owner/Investor, Property Manager; **SERVICES:** Act as managing partner for devel. of comml. RE and prop. mgmt. for our own accounts; **REP CLIENTS:** Clients include indiv. investors, and instn. as both gen. and ltd. partners; **PREV EMPLOY:** Indus. Sales Consultant with Coldwell Banker, Denver from 1975 to 1980 at which time present co. was started; **EDUC:** BS Gen. Studies, 1975, Chemistry, Biology, Physics, Univ. of AZ, Tucson; **EDUC HONORS:** Presidents Award (for perfect grades) Summa Cum Laude, Phi Kappa Phi; **HOME ADD:** 455 Dahlia St., Denver, CO 80220; **BUS ADD:** 8200 E. Pacific Place, Suite 401, Denver, CO 80231, (303)695-8343.

KLEMOVEC, Lucie L.——B: Aug. 27, 1925, K.C. MO, *Owner, Broker*, Modern Realty; **PRIM RE ACT:** Broker, Appraiser, Property Manager; **PREV EMPLOY:** 25 yrs. mort. lending; **HOME ADD:** 3815 Bell, Kansas City, MO 64111; **BUS ADD:** 3815 Bell, Kansas City, MO 64111, (816)561-5411.

KLEPACKI, Hank——*Fac. Mgr.*, Kellwood, Co.; **PRIM RE ACT:** Property Manager; **BUS ADD:** PO Box 14374, St. Louis, MO 63178, (314)576-3100.*

KLEPPER, Martin——B: Sept. 23, 1947, NY, NY, *Esq.*, Lane and Edson, PC; **PRIM RE ACT:** Consultant, Attorney; **SERVICES:** Securities, tax and fin. for RE, energy conservation and alternative energy projects; **PROFL AFFIL & HONORS:** ABA; Chmn. of Energy Law Comm. of the Real Prop., Probate and Trust Sect.; **EDUC:** BS, 1969, Fin./Pol. Sci., Univ. of PA, Wharton School; **GRAD EDUC:** JD, 1973, Rutgers Law School; **EDUC HONORS:** Dean's List, Grad. in top 20% of class, Articles Editor, Rutgers Law Review; **OTHER ACT & HONORS:** Advisory Bd. of Nat. Community Energy Mgmt. Ctr.; Contributing Editor for the RE Review; **HOME ADD:** 9305 Orchard Brook Dr., Potomac, MD 20854, (301)279-5733; **BUS ADD:** 1800 M St. N.W., Suite 400, Washington, DC 20036, (202)457-6800.

KLIMAN, Albert——*Dir.*, Department of Housing and Urban Development, Budget; **PRIM RE ACT:** Lender; **BUS ADD:** 451 Seventh St., S.W., Washington, DC 20410, (202)755-7296.*

KLINE, Jack M.——B: Apr. 9, 1923, Indianapolis, IN, *Div 1 Prop. Mgr.*, Gene Glick Mgmt. Corp.; **PRIM RE ACT:** Property Manager, Owner/Investor; **OTHER RE ACT:** Manage 7500 Co. built and owned apt. units in 39 projects; **PREV EMPLOY:** None, with this co. 31 yrs.; **PROFL AFFIL & HONORS:** Apt. Assn. of IN Inc., IREM, CPM; **MIL SERV:** USAF, Sgt., 3 European Theater Battle Stars; **OTHER ACT & HONORS:** Past Pres. Apt. Assn. of IN Inc. 1972; **HOME ADD:** 715 Spring Mill Lane, Indianapolis, IN 46260, (317)255-7345; **BUS ADD:** 9102 N. Meridian St., Indianapolis, IN 46240, (317)844-7741.

KLINE, Morton S.——B: Apr. 1, 1912, Trenton, NJ, *Pres.*, H.S. Kline & Co., Inc.; **PRIM RE ACT:** Broker, Appraiser, Property Manager, Owner/Investor; **PREV EMPLOY:** H.S. Kline & Co., Inc.; **PROFL AFFIL & HONORS:** SRA, CPM-CRA, Natl. State and Local Bd. Realtors, Dir. Emeritus Mercer Cty. Bd. Realtors; Realtor of the Yr.; Past Pres. SRA, CPM & NJ Bd. Realtors, Mercer Co. Bd. Realtors; **EDUC:** Trenton High School, 1933, Various RE Courses and Seminars; **OTHER ACT & HONORS:** Former Member of Lawrence Township Zoning Bd.; Elks - All Masonic Bodies; Citizens Rifle & Revolver Club; Crescent Temple Yacht Club; Cedar Mar Yacht Club; **HOME ADD:** 102 Roxboro Rd., Lawrenceville, NJ 08648, (609)882-4443; **BUS ADD:** 156 W. State St., Trenton, NJ 08608, (609)392-4153.

KLINE, William R.——B: May 29, 1930, Gary, IN, *VP and Sales Mgr.*, Baird & Warner, Inc., Residential; **PRIM RE ACT:** Broker; **SERVICES:** Residential RE Office Sales Mgmt.; **PROFL AFFIL & HONORS:** Greater S. Suburban Bd. of Realtors; RPAC; Capitol Club; CRB; CRS, Two Million Dollar Club; Lifetime Member - Million Dollar Club; **EDUC:** CRB from RNMI, 1980; CRS, 1977; **GRAD EDUC:** Grad. Realtors Inst.(GRI), 1976; IL Brokers Lic., 1970; IL RE Salesman Lic., 1964; **HOME ADD:** 18600 Golfview Dr., Hazel Crest, IL 60429, (312)798-5954; **BUS ADD:** 2333 Flossmoor Rd., Flossmoor, IL 60422, (312)798-1855.

KLINGER, Bruce K.——B: Jan 20, 1947, Auburn, PA, *VP*, First Columbia Mgmt. Inc.; **PRIM RE ACT:** Broker, Syndicator, Consultant, Developer, Property Manager; **SERVICES:** Full Range of Synd. & Mgmt. Serv.; **PREV EMPLOY:** Nat. Corp. for Housing Partnerships; **PROFL AFFIL & HONORS:** NAR, IREM, BOMA, ARM Instr., CPM; **EDUC:** BA, 1971, Bus. Admin., Antrim Coll.; **GRAD EDUC:** MS, 1973, RE & Urban Dev. Planning, Amer. Univ.; **EDUC HONORS:** Dean's List; **OTHER ACT & HONORS:** Rho Epsilon; **HOME ADD:** 401 Fireside Dr., Richardson, TX 75081, (214)644-2827; **BUS ADD:** 9441 LBJ Freeway, Suite 504, Dallas, TX 75243, (214)669-2211.

KLINGER, Phillip D.——B: Dec. 8, 1942, Cedar Rapids, IA, *Pres.*, Klinger, Robinson & McCuskey, A Profl. Corp.; **PRIM RE ACT:** Attorney; **SERVICES:** Legal counsel for RE devels., brokers and comml. land loans; **REP CLIENTS:** Devels., contractors, brokers, prop. mgrs.; **PREV EMPLOY:** Asst. Linn Cty. Atty. 1968 - 1974; Council to Linn Cty. Bldg. Dept.; Linn Cty. Zoning Commn.; Linn Cty. Bd. of Adjustment & Linn Cty. Bd. of Suprs.; **PROFL AFFIL & HONORS:** IA State Bar Assn.; Linn Cty. Bar Assn.; **EDUC:** BBA, 1964, Mktg., Univ. of IA; **GRAD EDUC:** JD, 1968, Univ. of IA; **HOME ADD:** 3012 Adirondack Dr., NE, Cedar Rapids, IA 52402, (319)366-1610; **BUS ADD:** 401 Old Marion Rd. NE, Cedar Rapids, IA 52402, (319)395-7400.

KLINK, James J.——B: May 7, 1931, Detroit, MI, *Partner and Chmn. of the RE Indus. Serv. Grp.*, Price Waterhouse & Co., RE Indus. Serv. Grp.; **OTHER RE ACT:** CPA; **SERVICES:** Acctg., auditing, tax and mgmt. advisory services; **PROFL AFFIL & HONORS:** Amer. Inst. of CPA's; RE Accounting Comm.; Fin. Acctg. Standards Bd.; Task Force on Specialized Principles for the RE Industry; NY State Soc. of CPA's, Past Chmn. of RE Acctg. Comm.; **EDUC:** BS, 1953, Acctg., Univ. of Notre Dame; **GRAD EDUC:** JD, 1960, Law, Wayne State Univ. Law School; **MIL SERV:** US Army, 1953-1955; **OTHER ACT & HONORS:** Nat. Assn. of RE Investment Trusts, Acctg. Comm.; Nat. Assn. of RE Co., Acctg. Comm.; RESSI, Taxation Comm.; Author of the book "Real Estate Accounting & Reporting - A Guide for Developers, Investors and Lenders" and numerous other publications; **HOME ADD:** 2 Stratford Ln., Ho-Ho-Kus, NJ 07423, (201)445-2588; **BUS ADD:** 153 E. 53rd St., NY, NY 10022, (212)371-2000.

KLINKENSTEIN, Bill——B: July 29, 1946, Pittsburgh, PA, *Acct. Exec.*, Merrill Lynch, Pierce, Fenner & Smith; **PRIM RE ACT:** Syndicator; **OTHER RE ACT:** Fin. planning, GNMA Pools; **REP CLIENTS:** J & B Income Props., Merrill Lynch Hubbard; **PREV EMPLOY:** Arlen Realty Mgmt., Inc.; **PROFL AFFIL & HONORS:** Amer. Stock Exchange Club; **EDUC:** BA, 1969, Sociology, Tulane Univ.; **GRAD EDUC:** MBA, 1971, Mktg., Acctg., Tulane Univ.; **HOME ADD:** PO Box 9963, Bakersfield, CA 93389, (805)397-4258; **BUS ADD:** 5558 California Ave., Bakersfield, CA 93309, (805)325-0714.

KLISTON, Theodore S.——B: Jan. 14, 1913, Utica, NY, *President (Realty Growth Corp.); Professor (FL Atlantic Univ.*; **PRIM RE ACT:** Lender, Owner/Investor, Instructor; **PREV EMPLOY:** Vice Pres., Kratter Corp. 1959-1961; Pres., Todd Industries, Inc., 1962-1969; **PROFL AFFIL & HONORS:** Fin. Analysts Assn., PhD, Fin. and Econ.; **EDUC:** BBA, 1933, Banking, Branch School, City Univ. of NY; **GRAD EDUC:** MBA, 1936, Fin., Amer. Univ.; PhD, 1939, Econ., Amer. Univ.; **EDUC HONORS:** Board Club of NY Scholarship and Award; **OTHER ACT & HONORS:** Dir. in a number of other companies; **BUS ADD:** 21000 Highland Lakes Blvd., North Miami Beach, FL 33179, (305)932-6273.

KLOCK, Joseph P.——B: Sept. 18, 1926, Philadelphia, PA, *Pres.*, The Klock Co., Realtors; **PRIM RE ACT:** Consultant, Instructor, Broker; **OTHER RE ACT:** Lecturer; **REP CLIENTS:** Merrill Lynch, Employee Transfer Corp., Homequity, Equitable Relocation Serv.;

PREV EMPLOY: Pres. Poquessing Corp., Philadelphia, PA; **PROFL AFFIL & HONORS:** RNMI, NAR, Intl. RE Federation, Cert. RE Mgmt. Broker, Cert. Resid. Specialist; **MIL SERV:** USMC, Pvt.; **OTHER ACT & HONORS:** V. Chmn. Philadelphia City Planning Comm.; PA Realtor of the Year, 1965; Merrill Lynch Relocation Mgmt. Exec. Advisory Bd.; **HOME ADD:** 1227 So. Alhambra Circ., Coral Gables, FL 33146, (305)666-1049; **BUS ADD:** 1507 Sunset Dr., Coral Gables, FL 33143, (305)661-1839.

KLOCKERS, Darwin K.——**B:** Jan. 20, 1944, Chicago, IL, *VP Props. & Const.*, National Car Rental System, Inc.; **PRIM RE ACT:** Attorney, Owner/Investor; **OTHER RE ACT:** Bldg. Design; **PROFL AFFIL & HONORS:** Nat. Assn. of Corporate RE Execs. - Bd. of Dirs.; Hennepin Cty. Bar Assn.; MN Bar Assn.; **EDUC:** BA, 1966, Poli. Sci., Macalester Coll.; **GRAD EDUC:** JD, 1969, Law, Univ. of MN; **EDUC HONORS:** Law Review - 1 yr.; **HOME ADD:** 6830 Wash. St. NE, Fridley, MN 55432, (612)571-7623; **BUS ADD:** 7700 France Ave. So., Edina, MN 55435, (612)893-6249.

KLOECKNER, Vincent W.——**B:** Feb. 11, 1928, Albers, IL, *Owner*, J. Vassen, Prof. Corp.; **PRIM RE ACT:** Owner/Investor, Instructor; **OTHER RE ACT:** Tax Consultant; **SERVICES:** Tax audits, appeal & litigation; **REP CLIENTS:** Anyone needing repres. before IRS; **PREV EMPLOY:** IRS-1956-1979; **EDUC:** BS in Comm. & Fin., 1956, Acctg., St. Louis Univ. Sch. of Comm. & Fin.; **MIL SERV:** US Army, Cpl.; **OTHER ACT & HONORS:** St. Louis Univ. Alumni, Counsel; **HOME ADD:** 6353 Murdoch, St. Louis, MO 63109, (314)481-1113; **BUS ADD:** 1801 N Belt West, Belleville, IL 62223.

KLONICK, Allan S.——**B:** Nov. 27, 1920, Rochester, NY, *Pres.*, Allan Klonick and Sons, Inc.; **PRIM RE ACT:** Broker, Appraiser, Assessor; **SERVICES:** Appraisal and Lic. RE Broker NY State and Comm. of MA; **PROFL AFFIL & HONORS:** Realtor - RE Bd. of Rochester, NY; NY State Realtors Assn; NAR; SIR, International Right of Way Assn.; SR/WA; Cert. Assessor State of NY; Member RE Bd. of Rochester Quarter Century Club; **MIL SERV:** USAF, Capt.; **OTHER ACT & HONORS:** (Present) Assessor (6 years), Town of Middlesex, Yates Cty. NY; Member Emeritus Amer. Ornithologists Union; Fellow Rochester Museum and Sci. Ctr.; Fellow Rochester Academy of Sci.; Member Amer. Bird Assn.; The Nature Conservatory; **HOME ADD:** 111 Rowland Parkway, Rochester, NY 14610, (716)473-2996; **BUS ADD:** 923 Sibley Tower, Rochester, NY 10888, (716)546-7420.

KLONOSKI, Michael Joseph——**B:** Nov. 9, 1946, Saginaw, MI, *VP Indus. Grp.*, Midwest Realty Exchange; **PRIM RE ACT:** Broker, Consultant, Developer, Owner/Investor, Property Manager, Syndicator; **SERVICES:** Acquisition and/or disposition of bus. RE via brokerage or devel.; **REP CLIENTS:** Corps. or indivs. interested in office & indus. realty, instns. or indivs. investing in same; **PREV EMPLOY:** Indus. Devel. Dept., C&O/B&O Railroads; **PROFL AFFIL & HONORS:** Assn. of Indus. RE Brokers; IL Devel. Council; Pres., Lake MI Chap., Nat. Assn. of Office & Indus. Parks; **EDUC:** BS, 1969, Econ./Urban Planning, AZ State Univ.; **HOME ADD:** 847 Jackson, River Forest, IL 60305, (312)771-6244; **BUS ADD:** Two Illinois Center, Chicago, IL 60601, (312)856-0080.

KLOPPENBURG, Richard L.——**B:** Mar. 22, 1941, Twin Falls, ID, *Pres.*, Keystone-Pacific Dev. Corp.; **PRIM RE ACT:** Consultant, Developer, Owner/Investor, Syndicator; **EDUC:** BS, 1964, Bus. Fin./Mktg., Univ. of ID; **MIL SERV:** US Army, Capt., 11 Air Medals; **HOME ADD:** 15404 N.E. 6th Pl., Bellevue, WA 98007, (206)747-2144; **BUS ADD:** 15404 N.E. 6th Pl., Bellevue, WA 98007, (206)747-2144.

KLOSKA, Ronald F.——*Pres.*, Skyline Corp.; **PRIM RE ACT:** Property Manager; **BUS ADD:** 2520 By-Pass Rd., Elkhart, IN 46514, (219)294-6521.*

KLOTSCHE, Charles——**B:** Jan. 30, 1941, Milwaukee, WI, *Pres.*, First Equity Corp.; **PRIM RE ACT:** Developer, Real Estate Publisher; **SERVICES:** Devel. and synd.; **PREV EMPLOY:** Pres., Western Equities Corp. 1965-1974; **PROFL AFFIL & HONORS:** Natl. Assoc. of Gen. Contractors, NAR, ULI, Author: "RE & Investing, A Practical Guide to Wealth Bldg. Secrets", Prentice Hall, Inc.; **EDUC:** BA, 1960, Econ., Boston Coll.; **GRAD EDUC:** MBA, 1968, RE Fin., Univ. of WI; **MIL SERV:** USMC, Lt., 1961-1963; **OTHER ACT & HONORS:** Bd. of Dirs., NM Special Olympics; Bd. of Dirs., Santa Fe Assn. for Retarded Citizens; **HOME ADD:** 624 E. Alameda, Santa Fe, NM 87501, (505)988-4537; **BUS ADD:** 236 Montezuma St., Santa Fe, NM 87501, (505)988-9217.

KLUDJIAN, Armen G.——**B:** May 20, 1941, Lowell, MA, Mt. Vernon Realty/ Armen G. Kludjian RE; **PRIM RE ACT:** Broker, Appraiser, Owner/Investor; **SERVICES:** Brokering, rentals, appraising (resid. & Comml.) devel., investor; **PREV EMPLOY:** Self employed; **EDUC:** BA, 1975, Educ., Suffolk Univ.; **GRAD EDUC:** MEd., 1976, Educ., Univ. of Lowell; **EDUC HONORS:** Cum Laude; **MIL SERV:** USCG 1966-1972; **HOME TEL:** (617)458-9666; **BUS ADD:** 16 Lombard St., Lowell, MA 01854, (617)458-9666.

KLUTNICK, James J.——**B:** Oct. 27, 1946, Springfield, IL, *Owner*, Keystone Investment; **PRIM RE ACT:** Consultant, Owner/Investor; **SERVICES:** Investment Counseling; **PREV EMPLOY:** Controller, Sinclair Paint Co., Div. of Insilco Corp.; Arthur Andersen & Co.; **PROFL AFFIL & HONORS:** AICPA, CA Soc. of CPA, Amer. Mgmt. Assn.; **EDUC:** BA, 1968, Acctg./Fin., St. Ambrose Coll.; **BUS ADD:** 17582 Berlark Cr., Huntington Beach, CA 92649, (714)846-7345.

KNABUSCH, C.T.——*Pres.*, La-Z-Boy Chair Co.; **PRIM RE ACT:** Property Manager; **BUS ADD:** 1284 N. Telegraph, Monroe, MI 48161, (313)242-1444.*

KNAPE, Edward J., Sr.——**B:** Jan. 19, 1925, Ruskin, NE, *Pres.*, Altoona Appraisal Services; **PRIM RE ACT:** Appraiser; **SERVICES:** RE appraisal & sales; **PREV EMPLOY:** (1961-1973) Fed. Housing Admin., Des Moines Insuring Office - Staff Appraiser 1961-1973; **PROFL AFFIL & HONORS:** Amer. Assn. of Cert. Appraisers, Nat. Assn. of Review Appraisers, Cert. Appraiser & CRA; **OTHER ACT & HONORS:** RE appraiser since 1952; **HOME ADD:** 10856 NE Glenn Dr., Mitchellville, IA 50169, (515)967-7661; **BUS ADD:** 103 8th St. SE, Altoona, IA 50009, (515)967-4544.

KNAPEK, Henry J.——*Pres.*, Vantage Cos.; **PRIM RE ACT:** Developer; **BUS ADD:** 4635 Southwest Freeway, Houston, TX 77027, (713)626-7770.*

KNAPP, John J.——*Gen. Counsel*, Department of Housing and Urban Development, Ofc. of Gen. Counsel; **PRIM RE ACT:** Lender; **BUS ADD:** 451 Seventh St., S.W., Washington, DC 20410, (202)755-7244.*

KNAUER, Leonard——*Pres.*, Knauer Realtcorp.; **PRIM RE ACT:** Broker, Syndicator, Consultant, Property Manager; **PROFL AFFIL & HONORS:** SIR, NAR, IREBA; **EDUC:** BS/BA, 1959, Econ. Fin., Muhlenberg Coll.; **BUS ADD:** 350 Grove St., P.O. Box 6864, Bridgewater, NJ 08807, (210)526-7600.

KNEAFSEY, Thomas——**B:** Feb. 16, 1938, Chicago, IL, *Partner*, Charles Dunn Co., Metropolitan Holding Co.; **PRIM RE ACT:** Broker, Consultant, Appraiser, Developer, Syndicator; **SERVICES:** Brokerage Investment Counseling, Valuation & Sund. of Comml. Indus. Projects; **REP CLIENTS:** Pension Funds, Firms & Indivs.; **PREV EMPLOY:** County Assessor's Office & Banking; **PROFL AFFIL & HONORS:** AIREA, Inter. Council of Shopping Ctrs., MAI; **EDUC:** BS, 1961, RE/Fin., Marquette Univ.; **MIL SERV:** US Army; **HOME ADD:** 325 S. Lucerne Blvd., Los Angeles, CA 90020, (213)931-7461; **BUS ADD:** 1200 Wilshire Blvd., Los Angeles, CA 90017, (213)481-1800.

KNEPPER, Eugene Arthur——**B:** Oct. 8, 1926, Sioux Falls, SD, *Owner*, R.E. Investment Planning Assoc., Controlling Gen. Part., Various LTD Partnerships; **PRIM RE ACT:** Broker, Syndicator, Property Manager, Owner/Investor; **SERVICES:** Investment Counseling Synd. of Comml. and Apt. Props. Prop. Mgmt, Tax Deferred Exchanges, Creative Financing, Accredited Instr. of R.E. Commn.; **REP CLIENTS:** Indiv. and Grp. Investors, Indiv. Grp. and Instnl. Prop. Owners; **PREV EMPLOY:** Public accounting and auditing, corp. accounting (including asst. controller of fire and casualty insuror).; **PROFL AFFIL & HONORS:** RESSI; NAR; Nat. Assn. of Accountants; Comml. Investment Div. of IA; Assn. of Realtors 1973 & 1980; Pres., Comml. Investment of IA Assn. of Realtors; S.J. Storm Acctg. Manuscript Award 1975-76.; **EDUC:** BA, 1951, Acctg., Drake Univ., Des Moines, IA; **MIL SERV:** USN; 1945-46, S 1st Class; **OTHER ACT & HONORS:** BD member & VP, E. IA Exec. Club; Patron and Bd. Member - Cedar Rapids Symphony; Member, Int. Platform Assn.; Fellow, IBA (Intl. Biographical Assn.); **HOME ADD:** 283 Tomahawk Trail S.E., Cedar Rapids, IA 52403, (319)364-0810; **BUS ADD:** 1808 Tower, Cedar Rapids, IA 52401, (319)366-7691.

KNIAZ, Lorna——**B:** Nov. 23, 1939, WI, *Atty.*, Kniaz Law Offices; **PRIM RE ACT:** Attorney; **SERVICES:** Closings, feasibility, bus. applicability; **PROFL AFFIL & HONORS:** ABA, WI Bar Assn., Dane Cty. Bar Assn., Probate, Prop. sect. & multiple others; **EDUC:** BA, 1975, Amer. Instns., hist., Univ of WI; **GRAD EDUC:** JD, 1978, Univ. of WI; **EDUC HONORS:** Motarboard, Cum Laude; **BUS ADD:** 131 W Wilson #903, Madison, WI 53703, (608)257-2232.

KNICKMAN, Robert L.——**B:** Sept. 1, 1948, Jamaica, NY, *Partner*, Knickman Associates; **PRIM RE ACT:** Broker, Consultant, Appraiser, Owner/Investor, Property Manager, Syndicator; **SERVICES:** Prop. Mgmt., Investment Counseling, Synd.; **PREV EMPLOY:** George W. Hickey, RE Appraiser; **PROFL AFFIL & HONORS:** NY State

SREA; NY State Assn. of Realtors; LI Bd. of Realtors, GRI; **EDUC:** BA, 1975, Hist. & Pol. Sci., Adelphi Univ.; **GRAD EDUC:** working on MBA, 1984, Fin. & Econ., Adelphi Univ.; **HOME ADD:** 43 Locust St., Garden City, NY 11530, (516)746-4922; **BUS ADD:** 195 Willis Ave., Mineola, NY 11501, (516)294-9720.

KNIGHT, Bob——B: Aug. 3, 1944, Santa Ana, CA, *Pres.*, Star Enterprises, RE; **PRIM RE ACT:** Owner/Investor; **SERVICES:** Inv. Counsel., devel. resid. & mgmt.; **REP CLIENTS:** Lenders & indiv.; **EDUC:** BS, 1968, Psych., Univ. Bridgeport; **GRAD EDUC:** MS ED, 1971, Education, Richmond Coll.; **BUS ADD:** 185 Clinton Ave., Staton Island, NY 10301, (212)448-8420.

KNIGHT, James T.——B: Mar. 14, 1935, Athena, OR, *Own.-Mgr.*, Richland Colonial Apts.; **PRIM RE ACT:** Engineer, Owner/Investor, Property Manager; **SERVICES:** Res. Rent. (Apts.); **PROFL AFFIL & HONORS:** Amer. Inst. of Chem. Engr., Cert. ARM; **EDUC:** BS - ChE, 1958, Chem. Engrg., OR State Coll.; **GRAD EDUC:** MS, 1963, Chem. Engrg., Univ. of WA; **HOME ADD:** Box 1329, Richland, WA 99352, (509)627-1126.

KNIGHT, Loretta E.——B: Nov. 30, 1933, New York City, NY, *Pres.*, Gateway Realty, Inc.; **PRIM RE ACT:** Broker, Appraiser, Owner/Investor, Property Manager; **SERVICES:** Resid. RE, Prop. Mgmt.; **REP CLIENTS:** Local; **PREV EMPLOY:** Asst. Prop. Mgt., Gilpin Van Trump, Wilmington, DE; **PROFL AFFIL & HONORS:** Nat. Assn. of Realtors; WV Assn. of Realtors; Parkesburg/Wood County Bd. of Realtors; Member Institute of RE Management; Altnusa Club of Parkersburg, GRI, CPM; **EDUC:** Associate, 1952, Bus., Univ. of CT; **OTHER ACT & HONORS:** Pres.-Parkersburg/Wood Cty. Bd. of Realtors; Sec.-St. Paul Lutheran Church (2 yrs.) 1977-78; Bd. of Dir.-WV Assn. of Realtors 1978-present; **HOME ADD:** 1515 36th St., Parkersburg, WV 26104, (304)464-5686; **BUS ADD:** 1515 3rd St., Parkersburg, WV 26104, (304)485-3896.

KNIGHT, Robert E.——B: Mar. 12, 1941, Austin, TX, *Pres.*, Knight RE Corp.; **PRIM RE ACT:** Broker, Attorney, Consultant, Developer, Property Manager, Owner/Investor; **SERVICES:** Site Loc., Site Evals., Feasibility Anal.; **REP CLIENTS:** Nat. Chains, Local & Reg. Inst.; **PREV EMPLOY:** Columbia Broadcasting System; **PROFL AFFIL & HONORS:** TX Bar Assn., Austin Bd. of Realtors, Austin Assn. of Builders, Urban Land Inst.; **EDUC:** BA, 1964, Hist., Univ. of TX; **GRAD EDUC:** LLB, MBA, 1966, 1968, Univ. of TX - School of Law, Univ. of VA. - Grad. School Bus. Admin.; **OTHER ACT & HONORS:** Dir. Austin Heritage Soc., Elizabeth Ney Museum; **HOME ADD:** 3216 Cherry Ln., Austin, TX 78703, (512)472-7944; **BUS ADD:** 307 East 2nd, Austin, TX 78701, (512)472-1800.

KNIGHT, T.K.——B: May 6, 1933, NC, *Pres.*, T.K. Knight, Inc.; **PRIM RE ACT:** Broker, Developer, Owner/Investor, Property Manager, Syndicator; **REP CLIENTS:** Builders, devels., pension plans, Life Cos., banks, indiv. investors; **PROFL AFFIL & HONORS:** MBA, Bd. Realtors, C of C, Profl. Mort. Grp.; **EDUC:** BS, 1955, Univ. of SC; **MIL SERV:** USAF, Capt., Res., 1955-58; **HOME ADD:** 5701 Mariner, Tampa, FL 33679; **BUS ADD:** 3212 W. Kennedy Blvd., Tampa, FL 33609, (813)872-9327.

KNIGHT, William L.——B: Sept. 12, 1938, NY, *Pres.*, Knight Enterprises, Inc., Corporate; **PRIM RE ACT:** Broker, Developer, Builder; **PROFL AFFIL & HONORS:** FABA; Urban Land Devel.; Nat. Assn. of Corp. RE Execs.; ICSC; Nat. Assn. of Indus. and Office Parks; **EDUC:** BS, 1959, Bus. Admin., Babson Coll.; **OTHER ACT & HONORS:** Recipient Nat. Environmental Award, 1970; **HOME ADD:** 3049 N.E. 8th Ave., Boca Raton, FL 33431, (305)392-3362; **BUS ADD:** 7000 W. Camino Real, #200, Boca Raton, FL 33433, (305)395-9200.

KNIPE, William B., Jr.——B: July 27, 1923, Emmett, ID, *Pres.*, Robison Realty, Inc., W. B. Knipe and Assoc.; **PRIM RE ACT:** Broker, Syndicator, Consultant, Appraiser, Property Manager; **OTHER RE ACT:** Specializing in large row crop farms and cattle ranches; **SERVICES:** Investment Counseling, Valuation, Farm and Ranch Mgmt., Farm and Ranch Acquisitions, Synd. & Mktg.; **REP CLIENTS:** Banks, Ins. Cos., Venture Capital Cos., Landing Insts., Corps., and Indiv. Investors; **PREV EMPLOY:** Managing Partners, Knipe-Shaw Ranches, 1962 - 1976; Gen. Mgr., The Sawtooth Co., Constr. Equip. Distrib., 1951 - 1962; **PROFL AFFIL & HONORS:** AFLM; CRA; CRS; GRI; SCV; **EDUC:** BS, 1977, Bus./RE, CA Western Univ.; **GRAD EDUC:** MBA, 1979, CA Western Univ.; **MIL SERV:** USAF, Sgt.; **OTHER ACT & HONORS:** Phi Delta Theta Soc. Frat.; BPOE (Elks); Nat. Cattleman's Assn. (Charter Member); Amer. Security Council, Advisory Bd.; Assn. of MBA Exec; Mountain States Legal Found. Designated member, Amer. Soc. of Agricultural Consultants; **HOME ADD:** PO Box 986, Boise, ID 83701, (208)344-0128; **BUS ADD:** 200 N. Third St., Suite 204, Imperial Plaza, Boise, ID 83702, (208)345-3163.

KNISKERN, Joseph Warren——B: July 7, 1951, Coral Gables, FL, *Assoc.*, Smathers & Thompson, RE; **PRIM RE ACT:** Attorney, Consultant; **SERVICES:** All Legal and Consulting Servs.; **REP CLIENTS:** Lenders and Devels. of Large Comml. and Resid. Prop.; **PROFL AFFIL & HONORS:** ABA FL Bar and Dade Cty. Bar Assns., member, Lawyers Title Guaranty Fund; **EDUC:** BS/BA, 1973, Bus./RE, Univ. of FL; **GRAD EDUC:** JD, 1976, Gen., Univ. of FL; **EDUC HONORS:** Grad. Cum Laude; **OTHER ACT & HONORS:** Chmn. Bd. of Trs. of Miami-Gables Church of Christ; **HOME ADD:** Unit 430, 7985 S. 86th St., Miami, FL 33143, (305)279-0609; **BUS ADD:** 1301 Alfred I. Dupont Bldg., 169 E. Flagler St., Miami, FL 33131, (305)379-6523.

KNOBLAUCH, Joel P.——B: May 30, 1955, Reading, PA, Murry & Sidney Knoblauch, Inc., Shopping Centers; **PRIM RE ACT:** Broker, Property Manager; **SERVICES:** Rehab. of shopping centers, full serv., org., sale, lease, devel., and mgmt.; investment counseling; **REP CLIENTS:** Pvt. and instnl. investors; **PROFL AFFIL & HONORS:** Nat., PA and Greater Reading Assn. of Realtors; Reading Housing & Nghbrhd. Devel. Corp.; **EDUC:** AB, 1977, Economics, Harvard Univ.; **EDUC HONORS:** Cum Laude; Pres., Harvard Student Econ. Assn.; Publisher, Harvard Undergraduate Econ. Journal; **HOME ADD:** 1517 Hill Rd., Reading, PA 19602, (215)375-3918; **BUS ADD:** 619 Walnut St., Reading, PA 19601, (215)376-4821.

KNOCHENHAUER, Theo. G.——*VP, Mktg.*, T.G.K. Construction Co., Inc.; **PRIM RE ACT:** Broker, Builder; **OTHER RE ACT:** Mort. Broker; **REP CLIENTS:** Motorola, G.E., Howard Johnsons, Penney's, State of AZ, St. Josephs Hosp., Sperry Rand, James Stewart Co., City of Phoenix, Maricopa Cty.; **PROFL AFFIL & HONORS:** AZ St. Indus. Comm., Phoenix Bd. of Realtors; **BUS ADD:** 12809 N. 15th. Ave., Phoenix, AZ 85029, (602)866-0299.

KNODELL, C.W.——*Fin. VP, Secy. & Treas.*, Williamette Industries, Inc.; **PRIM RE ACT:** Property Manager; **BUS ADD:** 1300 S.W. Fifth Ave., Ste. 3800, Portland, OR 97201, (503)227-5585.*

KNODL, James J.——Pinnacle Investments; **PRIM RE ACT:** Broker, Consultant, Owner/Investor, Instructor, Syndicator; **OTHER RE ACT:** Exchangor; **SERVICES:** Counsellor in all comml. and investment RE, taxation and exchanging; **PROFL AFFIL & HONORS:** WI Realtors Assn.; NAR; Milwaukee and Waukesha Bds. of Realtors; WI Exchange Club; Milwaukee Traders Club, Instructor, GRI; **OTHER ACT & HONORS:** Treas., WI Exchange Club; **BUS ADD:** 13950 W. Capitol Dr., Brookfield, WI 53005, (414)781-0052.

KNOEDEL, Patricia Kelley——B: Feb. 4, 1954, Davenport, IA, *Atty.*, Beving, Swanson & Forrest, P.C.; **PRIM RE ACT:** Attorney; **SERVICES:** Examinations of abstracts of title, preparation of legal documents pertaining to RE transactions, negotiations on RE transactions; **PROFL AFFIL & HONORS:** Polk Cty. & IA Bar Assn., ABA, ABA Div. of Real Prop., Probate & Trust Law; **EDUC:** BA, 1975, Pol. Sci., Journalism, Psychology, Univ. of IA, IA City, IA; **GRAD EDUC:** JD, 1978, Tax, Probate, RE, Univ. of IA; **EDUC HONORS:** Phi Beta Kappa, Mortarboard Kappa Tau Alpha, Alpha Lambda Delta, Dean's List, Finkbine Student, Degree with Honors; **OTHER ACT & HONORS:** Soroptomists; **HOME ADD:** 7412 Canterbury Rd., Urbandale, IA 50322, (515)278-2179; **BUS ADD:** 626 E. Locust, Des Moines, IA 50309, (515)288-6572.

KNOELL, Joseph——*VP and Gen. Mgr.*, Hugh Knoell & Sons; **PRIM RE ACT:** Broker, Developer, Builder; **SERVICES:** Multi-family and single-family small to medium comml. devel./investment; **PREV EMPLOY:** Knoell & Sons, Inc. since 1946; **PROFL AFFIL & HONORS:** Nat. Assn. of Home Builders, BBB, C of C, NAR, Hugh F. Knoell, Pres. - Nat. Dir. of Nat. Assn. of Home Builders, Life Dir. of Home Builders Assn. of Central AZ; **OTHER ACT & HONORS:** Hugh F. Knoell - AZ Dept. of RE Advisory Bd. 8 years; **BUS ADD:** 3520 East McDowell Rd., Phoenix, AZ 85008, (602)244-1199.

KNOLL, E. Joseph——B: June 5, 1939, NE City, NE, *Partner, Law Firm*, Krooth & Altman; **PRIM RE ACT:** Attorney; **OTHER RE ACT:** Comml. RE, Housing Law, Practice before HUD; Other; **PROFL AFFIL & HONORS:** ABA, DC and NE Bar Assns.; **EDUC:** BS, 1961, Bus. Admin., Univ. of NE; **GRAD EDUC:** LLB, 1964, Georgetown Univ. Law Ctr.; **HOME ADD:** 5120 39th Street, N.W., Washington, DC 20016; **BUS ADD:** 2101 L Street, N.W., Washington, DC 20037, (202)393-6300.

KNOLLER, Herman——B: Aug. 28, 1921, New York, NY, *Controller*, National Birchwood Corp. & Affiliated Companies; **PRIM RE ACT:** Developer, Builder, Owner/Investor, Property Manager; **PROFL AFFIL & HONORS:** NY CPA Soc.; Amer. Arbitration Assn., CPA;

EDUC: BBA, 1943, Acctg., CCNY; **GRAD EDUC:** MBA, 1950, Taxation, New York Univ.; **MIL SERV:** US Army, Sgt.; **HOME ADD:** 134 Bengeyfield Dr., E. Williston, NY 11596; **BUS ADD:** 410 E. Jericho Tpk., Mineola, NY 11501.

KNORR, Gerard K.——B: June 23, 1939, Sioux Falls, SD, *VP, Gen. Counsel and Sec.*, St. Paul Title Insurance Corp., Home Office; **PRIM RE ACT:** Attorney, Insuror; **SERVICES:** Title Insurer; **PROFL AFFIL & HONORS:** ABA, ALTA, CA LTA; **EDUC:** BS, 1966, Bus. Admin., Augustana Coll., Sioux Falls, SD; **GRAD EDUC:** JD, 1969, Law, Univ. of SD, Vermillion, SD; **MIL SERV:** USN, 3rd. Class petty officer; **HOME ADD:** 5512 Garden Dr., Woodbury, MN 55125, (612)458-0659; **BUS ADD:** 1900 American Natl. Bank Bldg., St. Paul, MN 55101, (612)221-9555.

KNOTT, John Edwin——B: July 23, 1938, Morristown, NJ, *Exec. VP*, Whitesell Const. Inc.; **PRIM RE ACT:** Syndicator, Developer, Builder, Owner/Investor; **SERVICES:** Build, sell or lease indus. props.; **PREV EMPLOY:** 15 yrs. exp. in indus., comml. mort. banking; **PROFL AFFIL & HONORS:** Camden Cty, NJ & Natl. Bd. of Realtors; **EDUC:** Acctg., Still attending Rutgers Univ.; **OTHER ACT & HONORS:** Bd. of Trs. Camden Cty. YWCA; **HOME ADD:** 132 Farmington Rd., Cherry Hill, NJ 08034; **BUS ADD:** 1819 Underwood Blvd., Delran, NJ 08075, (609)829-2600.

KNOTT, Joseph M.——B: Sept. 18, 1918, Baltimore, MD, *Salesman*, Parker Frames & Co., Inc.; **PRIM RE ACT:** Broker, Appraiser; **SERVICES:** Indus. & comml. RE - lease, sell, to developers, users; **REP CLIENTS:** Bendix Corp., GM, GE, Owens IL, Dorsey Corp.; **PREV EMPLOY:** Indus. Realty Co., Inc., Hearn & Knott, Inc. (partner), VP of Henry A. Knott, Inc.; **PROFL AFFIL & HONORS:** Active membership, SIR, Associate Broker member of NAR, Gr. Baltimore Bd. of Realtors, SIR; **EDUC:** AB, 1940, Social Sci. & Language, Loyola Coll.; **OTHER ACT & HONORS:** Past Pres. of Towson Kiwanis Club; Pres. of Sierra Club of Baltimore; Past Pres. of Ancient Order of Hibernians Div. 12; Sec. of Hibernians Soc. of Baltimore; Bd. Member of The Boys Home Soc.; **HOME ADD:** 204 Westway, Baltimore, MD 21212, (301)435-9225; **BUS ADD:** SunLife Building, 20 S. Charles St., Baltimore, MD 21201, (301)727-2284.

KNOWER, Stewart B.——B: June 3, 1934, Birmingham, AL, *Pres., Chmn.*, King & Cornwall, Inc.; **PRIM RE ACT:** Broker, Consultant, Owner/Investor, Property Manager; **SERVICES:** Brokerage of farms, estates, comml. & indus. land; **REP CLIENTS:** Domestic & for. indiv. & corps.; **PROFL AFFIL & HONORS:** Realtors; **EDUC:** BA, 1956, Art/Arch./Arch., Princeton Univ.; **HOME ADD:** Box 336, Leesburg, VA 22075, (703)777-7844; **BUS ADD:** 32 N. King St., Leesburg, VA 22075, (703)777-2503.

KNOWLES, William R.——B: May 19, 1920, Decatur, IL, *Pres.*, ERA-Knowles Realty Corp.; **PRIM RE ACT:** Broker, Consultant, Appraiser; **SERVICES:** Brokerage and prop. mgmt. on comml. & resid. RE; **PROFL AFFIL & HONORS:** Chicago RE Bd., Fox Valley Bd. of Realtors, Electronic Realty Assocs., Inc., NAR, CCIM, NAR; **EDUC:** BS, 1943, Fin. and Law, School of Law, Univ. of So. CA; **MIL SERV:** Infantry, Sgt., 5 Battle Stars, Bronze Star; **OTHER ACT & HONORS:** Dir., Geneva C of C, Fin. Execs. Inst.; **HOME ADD:** 1101 Fargo Blvd., Geneva, IL 60134; **BUS ADD:** 227 South Third St., Geneva, IL 60134, (312)232-6202.

KNOWLTON, Craig F.——B: May 2, 1941, Seattle, WA, *Pres. - Broker*, Edgewood Realty, Inc.; **PRIM RE ACT:** Broker, Consultant; **SERVICES:** Work with clients on investment portfolios; **PROFL AFFIL & HONORS:** Tacoma-Pierce Cty. Bd. of Realtors; IREF; Puget Sound Exchangors; Intl. Exchangors Assn., CCIM; **EDUC:** BS, 1965, Psych., Statistics, Western WA State Univ., Bellingham, WA; **MIL SERV:** USAR, E-5; **OTHER ACT & HONORS:** Puyallup Valley C of C; **HOME ADD:** 13303 Monta Vista Dr. NE, Sumner, WA 98390, (206)863-3457; **BUS ADD:** 5905 N Meridian, Puyallup, WA 98371, (206)927-5900.

KNOX, Robert D.——B: May 30, 1924, Jamestown, ND, *Pres.*, Robert D. Knox. Assoc., Inc.; **PRIM RE ACT:** Broker, Syndicator, Developer, Property Manager; **EDUC:** BA, 1948, Econ., MI State Univ.; **MIL SERV:** US Army, PFC, 1943-46; **OTHER ACT & HONORS:** Housing & Urban Renewal Dir., Detroit, 8 yrs.; **HOME ADD:** 8100 E Jefferson, Apt. #607D, Detroit, MI 48214, (313)331-4113; **BUS ADD:** 8100 E Jefferson, Detroit, MI 48214, (313)823-3600.

KNUDSON, John A.——*Secy. & Treasurer*, Stepan Chemical Co.; **PRIM RE ACT:** Property Manager; **BUS ADD:** Edens & Winnetka, Northfield, IL 60093, (312)446-2500.*

KNUTSEN, Morris A.——B: Nov. 22, 1946, Los Angeles, CA, *Pres.*, M.A. Knutsen Inc.; **PRIM RE ACT:** Consultant, Developer, Builder, Owner/Investor; **PROFL AFFIL & HONORS:** Merit Award IA Inst. of Arch. 1976; Community Reward Des Moines Arch. Council 1980; **EDUC:** AB, 1968, Hist., Univ. MN; **HOME ADD:** 103 SW 51st St., Des Moines, IA 50312, (515)274-0572; **BUS ADD:** PO Box 65095, 504 Maple St., W. Des Moines, IA 50265, (515)279-9075.

KNUTSON, William A.——B: Feb. 8, 1938, San Diego, CA, *President*, Knutson, Burley & Reese, Ltd.; **PRIM RE ACT:** Property Manager; **SERVICES:** Physical and fiscal mgmt. of prop.; **REP CLIENTS:** Condo. assns. and comml. bldg. owners; **PREV EMPLOY:** First Hawaiian Bank, Honolulu, HI; **PROFL AFFIL & HONORS:** Hawaii Chapter IREM; Kona Bd. of Realtors; CPM; **MIL SERV:** U.S. Army, Medical Discharge; **OTHER ACT & HONORS:** Kona Coast C of C; Central Kona Union Church, Trustee; **HOME ADD:** 75-5812 Kini Loop, Kailua-Kona, HI 96740, (808)329-1919; **BUS ADD:** 75-5722 Kuakini Hwy., Suite 216A, Kailua-Kona, HI 96740, (808)329-8555.

KOBLENTZ, Arnold E.——B: Apr. 5, 1923, Cleveland, OH, *Pres.*, Costa Camino RE Co.; **PRIM RE ACT:** Broker, Consultant, Owner/Investor, Syndicator; **SERVICES:** Investment counseling, synd., and mktg. of comml.-investment RE; **REP CLIENTS:** Private investors; **PROFL AFFIL & HONORS:** NAR, CA Assn. of Realtors, RNMI, RESSI, So. CA CCIM Chap., and the Nat. Council of Exchangors, GRI, CRS; **EDUC:** Western Reserve Univ.; **GRAD EDUC:** Service interrupted-did not grad., Bus. Admin.; **MIL SERV:** USAF, Sgt.; **OTHER ACT & HONORS:** Past Pres. of S. CA Chapter of CCIM, Runner-up Award from CA Assn. of Realtors 1974-"Best Exchange"; **HOME ADD:** P O Box 647, Rancho Santa Fe, CA 92067, (714)756-1370; **BUS ADD:** 140 Marine View Dr., Suite 204, Solana Beach, CA 92075, (714)755-5177.

KOCH, Carl G.——B: May 26, 1916, Seattle, WA, *Chmn. of the Bd.*, Karr, Tuttle, Koch, Campbell, Mawer & Morrow, Inc., A Prof. Service Corp.; **PRIM RE ACT:** Attorney, Owner/Investor; **SERVICES:** Advice, preparation of documents, tax planning; **PROFL AFFIL & HONORS:** Seattle Estate Planning Council, Amer. Arbitration Assn., Amer. Judicature Soc., WA and Amer. Bar Assn.; **EDUC:** BA, 1938, Univ. of WA; **GRAD EDUC:** JD, 1940; **MIL SERV:** US Army, 1st Lt.; **OTHER ACT & HONORS:** Judge Protem, King Cty. WA Superior Ct.; Coll. Club, Glendale Cty. Club; Tamarisk Cty. Club, Rancho Mirage, CA; **HOME ADD:** 6034 Lake Shore Dr. S., Seattle, WA 98101, (206)725-2122; **BUS ADD:** 1111 3rd Ave., Suite 2500, Seattle, WA 98101, (206)223-1313.

KOCH, James H.——*Ed.*, Aquarian Advertising Assoc. Inc., Country Property News; **PRIM RE ACT:** Real Estate Publisher; **BUS ADD:** 1020 Park Ave., New York, NY 10028, (212)988-1720.*

KOCH, June——*Dpty Under Secy./Intergovernmental Relations*, Department of Housing and Urban Development, Ofc. of the Secy./Under Secy.; **PRIM RE ACT:** Lender; **BUS ADD:** 451 Seventh St., S.W., Washington, DC 20410, (202)755-6480.*

KOCH, Richard——B: Sept. 7, 1941, Newark, NJ, *Sr. RE Rep.*, Dorman & Wilson of NJ, Inc.; **PRIM RE ACT:** Banker, Lender; **OTHER RE ACT:** Mort. Banker; **SERVICES:** Mort. Underwriting; **REP CLIENTS:** Aetna Life & Casualty, INA Capital Advisors, Inc.; **PREV EMPLOY:** Pres., Leone Mort. Corp.; **PROFL AFFIL & HONORS:** NAIOP, NY RE Bd.; **EDUC:** BS, 1963, Ind. Mgmt., Univ. of Rochester; **GRAD EDUC:** MBA, 1965, Fin., Univ. of Chicago; **HOME ADD:** 28 Lancaster Ave., Maplewood, NJ 07040, (201)763-2787; **BUS ADD:** 120 Littleton Rd., Parsippany, NJ 07054, (201)263-1322.

KOCH, William P.——B: Mar. 22, 1948, Davenport, IA, William P. Koch, CPA; **OTHER RE ACT:** CPA; **SERVICES:** Acctg., tax prep. & consultation, fin. stmts.; **PREV EMPLOY:** Big Eight & local CPA firms.; **PROFL AFFIL & HONORS:** CA Soc. of CPA's, E. Bay Chap. member of Taxation Comm.; **EDUC:** BA, 1970, Acctg., St. Ambrose Coll.; **GRAD EDUC:** MBA, 1981, Taxation, Golden Gate Univ.; **HOME ADD:** PO Box 96, Concord, CA 94522; **BUS ADD:** 1911 San Miguel, Walnut Creek, CA 94596, (415)944-5993.

KOCHEL, Kenneth D.——B: Aug. 21, 1928, Lancaster, PA, *Owner*, The Fulton Tavern & The Fulton Apartments; **PRIM RE ACT:** Owner/Investor; **PREV EMPLOY:** Research Acct. of Hercules Powder Co.-Wilmington, Delaware; **EDUC:** High School (12 yrs.), 1946, Bus., McCaskey High School; **GRAD EDUC:** BA, 1956, Accountant-Bus.-Minor Hist., Franklin & Marshall Coll.; **EDUC HONORS:** Nat. Honor Soc., Honor Soc. Pi Gamma Mu (Science Frat. Nat. Honorary Soc.); **MIL SERV:** US Army, Sgt. 1951-52, Bronze Star; **OTHER ACT & HONORS:** Masonic Lodge; Shrine; Elks; Tall Cedars; Amer. Legion; Cosmopolitan Club; **HOME ADD:** 729 E

Orange St., Lancaster, PA 17602, (717)392-2716; **BUS ADD:** 637 N Plum St., Lancaster, PA 17602, (717)392-9349.

KOE, Jan E.——B: July 14, 1950, Chicago, IL, *Prop. Mgr.*, Romenek-Golub & Co., Comml., Mgmt.; **PRIM RE ACT:** Property Manager; **OTHER RE ACT:** Ins. broker, Real Prop. administrator; **PROFL AFFIL & HONORS:** Sec.-Tr. of Chicago Suburban Bldb. Owners & Mgrs. Assoc., VP of Metropolitan Mgrs. Assoc., Real Prop. Admin., Ins. Broker, RE Broker, Energy Conservation Achievement Award, Greater Chicago "Use Energy Wisely"; **EDUC:** BA, 1974, Bud. Admin & Psych., Luther Coll., Decorah, IA; **MIL SERV:** USAF, Tech. Sgt.; **HOME ADD:** 197 Smethwick, Elk Grove Village, IL 60007, (312)364-7307; **BUS ADD:** 444 N Mich. Ave., Suite 1930, Chicago, IL 60611, (312)440-8828.

KOEHLER, Charles, Jr.——*VP*, The Louisiana Land and Exploration Co.; **PRIM RE ACT:** Property Manager; **BUS ADD:** PO Box 60350, New Orleans, LA 70160, (504)566-6500.*

KOEHLER, Stephen K.——B: Sept. 7, 1944, Davenport, IA, *Pres.*, Stephen K. Koehler Co.; **PRIM RE ACT:** Developer, Owner/Investor, Property Manager; **SERVICES:** Devel. comml. office bldgs. for lease; **REP CLIENTS:** Fin. instns., ins. firms, nat. sales fimrs, law firms, acctg. firms and other gen. office users; **PREV EMPLOY:** Cabot, Cabot & Forbes, 1973-76 Project Mgr., Comml. Div.; **PROFL AFFIL & HONORS:** Nat. Assn. of Indus. and Office Parks; **EDUC:** BS, 1966, Navigation & Cargo, Marine Trans., US Merchant Marine Acad.; BS, Building Const., 1970, Univ. of WA; **GRAD EDUC:** MBA, 1973, RE & Fin., Harvard Grad. School of Bus. Admin.; **EDUC HONORS:** Superintendents Cup for Character Officers club award, VP, Bldg. Const. Hon. Soc., Second Yr. Academic Honors, VP of RE Club; **MIL SERV:** USN, Res.; Lt.; **OTHER ACT & HONORS:** VP Bd. of Govs., Seattle Prep. 1981; **HOME ADD:** 6806 96th Ave. SE, Mercer Island, WA 98040, (206)232-7163; **BUS ADD:** 10800 NE 8th, Bellevue, WA 98004, (206)454-0490.

KOEHLER, Thilo B.——B: Sept. 28, 1943, Goettingen, Germany, *EVP*, Mayntz Corp.; **PRIM RE ACT:** Consultant, Syndicator; **SERVICES:** Search, synd., fin. and mgmt. of real prop.; **REP CLIENTS:** German investors; **PREV EMPLOY:** Tax Lawyer, State of Bavaria, West Germany, Mayntz Firms in Berlin, West Germany; **PROFL AFFIL & HONORS:** Doctor of Jurisprudence, Munich, West Germany; **EDUC:** Final examination, Gymnasium, 1963, Albert Einstein Gymnasium, Munich, West Germany; **GRAD EDUC:** 2 Legal Examinations, 1968, 1973, Univ. of Munich, Law School; **HOME ADD:** 12 Katlas Ct., Novato, CA 94947, (415)897-1579; **BUS ADD:** 600 Montgomery, San Francisco, CA 94111, (415)956-2244.

KOELKER, Donald R.——B: July 27, 1934, Cumberland, MD, *Pres.*, Vestco, Inc.; **PRIM RE ACT:** Broker, Instructor, Syndicator, Developer, Owner/Investor; **PREV EMPLOY:** Legal Research; **PROFL AFFIL & HONORS:** RESSI, NAR, FLI; **EDUC:** BA, 1962, Educ., Columbia Union Coll.; **GRAD EDUC:** LLB, 1970, Univ. of Baltimore; **MIL SERV:** USAF; Sgt.; **OTHER ACT & HONORS:** Civitan, Jaycees; **HOME ADD:** 738 Santa Fe, Ormond Beach., FL 32074, (904)672-5495; **BUS ADD:** 1127 Ridgewood Ave., Holly Hill, FL 32017, (904)258-7434.

KOENIG, Charles A.——B: Jan. 11, 1954, Cleveland, OH, *Tax Specialist*, Coopers & Lybrand; **OTHER RE ACT:** Reorganizations; Estate Planning; Tax Shelters; **SERVICES:** Devel. and analysis of synd. offerings; **REP CLIENTS:** Devels./contractors, synds., investment bankers; **PREV EMPLOY:** Smith & Tobin, Attorneys-at-Law (1976-77); **PROFL AFFIL & HONORS:** ABA; **EDUC:** BS, 1975, Fin. and Acctg., OH State Univ.; **GRAD EDUC:** MBA, 1978, Tax, OH State Univ.; JD, 1978, Tax, OH State Univ.; **EDUC HONORS:** Cum Laude, President's Scholarship Recognition; **BUS ADD:** 100 East Broad St., Columbus, OH 43215, (614)221-7471.

KOENITZER, Robert L.——B: Dec. 4, 1933, Manhattan, KS, *Pres./Owner*, Redwood Empire Appraisal; **PRIM RE ACT:** Appraiser; **SERVICES:** RE Appraisal, Consultant, Right of Way Agent; **PREV EMPLOY:** Redwood Empire S&L, 1961-1970; **PROFL AFFIL & HONORS:** SREA; Intl. Right of Way Assn., SRA; SR/WA; CRA; **EDUC:** BA, 1957, Econ., UC at Davis; **MIL SERV:** US Army, 1st Lt. (1957 - 1959); **OTHER ACT & HONORS:** Bd. of Tr., Main/Sonoma Mosquito Abatement Dist. (1971 - 1979); City of Petaluma Planning Commn., (1967 - 1970); City of Petaluma Parks & Rec. Comm. (1964 - 1967, 1979 - present); Sonoma Cty. Tax Appeals Bd. (1976 - present); **HOME ADD:** 311 Keller St., Petaluma, CA 94952, (707)763-1130; **BUS ADD:** Petaluma, CA 94952199 Petaluma Blvd., (707)763-2772.

KOEPKE, Robert L.——B: Dec. 4, 1936, Berwyn, IL, *Prof. and Dir. of Area Devel.*, Southern Illinois University at Edwardsville; **PRIM RE ACT:** Consultant, Instructor; **PROFL AFFIL & HONORS:** ULI, Amer. Econ. Devel. Council, Amer. Planning Assn., Cert. Indus. Devel.; **EDUC:** 1958, Geo., So. IL Univ at Carbondale; **GRAD EDUC:** PhD, 1966, Univ. of IL; **HOME ADD:** 620 Montclaire, Edwardsville, IL 62025, (618)656-8336; **BUS ADD:** Edwardsville, IL 62026, (618)692-3668.

KOHEN, David M.——B: Jan. 26, 1951, NYC, *VP*, Winthrop Fin. Co., Inc., Gov. assisted housing; **PRIM RE ACT:** Attorney, Syndicator; **SERVICES:** Equity synd., gap fin.; **REP CLIENTS:** Numerous builders and devel. across the country; **PREV EMPLOY:** Atty., Tax Dept., Piper & Marbury, Baltimore, MD; **PROFL AFFIL & HONORS:** ABA, Comm. on RE Tax Problems, Subcomm. on synd.; **EDUC:** BA, BS in Econ., 1972, Soc., Fin., Wharton School of Fin. and Commerce of the Univ. of PA; **GRAD EDUC:** JD, LLM, 1975, 1976, SUNY at Buffalo, NYU School of Law, Bernard & Pauline Lasker Graduate Fellowship; **EDUC HONORS:** Fin. Honor Program; **OTHER ACT & HONORS:** Admitted to practice law in NY, PA, MD, MA; **HOME ADD:** 121 Rachel Rd., Newton Ctr., MA 02159, (617)527-8082; **BUS ADD:** 225 Franklin St., Boston, MA 02110, (617)482-6200.

KOHL, Timothy O.——B: Mar. 15, 1942, Hartford, WI, *Atty.*, Oscar Mayer & Co. Inc.; **PRIM RE ACT:** Attorney, Property Manager; **PREV EMPLOY:** Chicago Title & Trust Co.; **PROFL AFFIL & HONORS:** State Bar of WI; **EDUC:** BS, 1964, Pol. Sci., Univ. of WI-Milwaukee; **GRAD EDUC:** JD, 1967, Law, Univ. of WI Law School; **OTHER ACT & HONORS:** BOD-Amer. Players Theatre; **HOME ADD:** 2110 Bascom St., Madison, WI 53705, (608)238-7068; **BUS ADD:** 910 Mayer Ave., Madison, WI 53704, (608)241-6864.

KOHLER, Dale F.——B: Jan. 15, 1921, York Cty., PA, *Chmn. of the Bd.*, BASCO Assoc.; **PRIM RE ACT:** Consultant, Architect; **SERVICES:** Site selction, plans & specifications, fin.; **REP CLIENTS:** Indus., comml., municipal bldgs.; **PROFL AFFIL & HONORS:** Nat. Council of Arch. Registration Bd., Soc. for Mktg. Profl. Serv., Amer. Mil. Engrs., SRA; **MIL SERV:** USAF, Cadet; **OTHER ACT & HONORS:** 1981-1982 Chmn., United Way Campaign; Nat. Trust for Historic Preservation; **HOME ADD:** 176 E. Springettsbury Ave., York, PA 17403, (717)843-5612; **BUS ADD:** 611 W Market St., York, PA 17405, (717)843-3854.

KOHLER, Karl E.——B: Oct. 26, 1932, Washington, DC, *Prin./Pres.*, Karl E. Kohler Assoc., Architects, Devel. & Prop. Mgmt.; **PRIM RE ACT:** Architect, Developer, Owner/Investor, Property Manager; **SERVICES:** Arch. design, devel., prop. mgmt.; **PROFL AFFIL & HONORS:** AIA, No. VA Builders Assn., Nat. Council of Arch. Registration Bds., Vienna Bldg. Beautification Award, Fairfax Cty. Bldg. Beautification Award; **EDUC:** BS Building Design, 1954, Arch., VA Polytechnic Inst. & State Univ.; **GRAD EDUC:** MS Arch., 1957, Arch, VA Polytechnic Inst. & State Univ.; **MIL SERV:** Army Engr., 1st Lt.; **OTHER ACT & HONORS:** Lodge Creek Yacht Club, Windmill Point Y.C.; **HOME ADD:** 8205 Woodland Ave., Annandale, VA 22003, (703)280-2590; **BUS ADD:** 301 Maple Ave. W, Vienna, VA 22180, (703)281-0301.

KOHLHEPP, Daniel B.——B: July 17, 1947, DuBois, PA, *Owner*, Kohlhepp Company; **PRIM RE ACT:** Broker, Consultant, Appraiser, Developer, Instructor, Owner/Investor; **SERVICES:** Investment counseling, valuation, brokerage of comml. RE; **REP CLIENTS:** Ins. cos.; devel.; indiv. investors; **PREV EMPLOY:** Univ. of OK; **PROFL AFFIL & HONORS:** Soc. of RE Appraisers, Realtors, Amer. RE and Urban Econ. Assn.; Fin. Mgmt. Assn., SRPA; **EDUC:** BS, RE, PA State Univ.; **GRAD EDUC:** MBA, 1971, Ins., PA State Univ.; PhD, 1974, RE, OH State Univ.; **HOME ADD:** 7013 N. Roff Ave., Oklahoma City, OK 73116, (405)843-4842; **BUS ADD:** 3217 N.W. 63rd St., Oklahoma City, OK 73116, (405)842-8825.

KOHN, Arnold J.——B: May 4, 1940, New York City, NY, *Partner*, Sacks & Kohn, Chartered; **PRIM RE ACT:** Attorney; **SERVICES:** Legal representation; **REP CLIENTS:** Owners, developers, lenders and investors in comml. RE; **PREV EMPLOY:** Partner: Arent, Fox, Kintner, Plotkin & Kahn, Wash., DC; **PROFL AFFIL & HONORS:** Member, DC, MD and NY Bars; ABA; Amer. Coll. of RE Lawyers; **EDUC:** BA, 1962, Hist., Duke Univ., Pi Sigma; **GRAD EDUC:** JD, 1964, 1965, Law, Tax Law, Duke Univ. LLM, New York Univ.; **MIL SERV:** USNR, Lt.; **HOME ADD:** 7711 Ivymount Terrace, Potomac, MD 20854; **BUS ADD:** 1707 L St. NW, Washington, DC 20036, (202)223-8601.

KOHN, Richard Fredrick——B: Dec. 28, 1933, Chicago, IL, *Sr. Counsel*, The Abacus Group; **PRIM RE ACT:** Attorney, Lender; **OTHER RE ACT:** Mort. banking; **SERVICES:** Mort. banking and direct lending; **PREV EMPLOY:** Enforcement Atty., Region V, US Environmental Protection Agency; Gen. Counsel, Shur-Chem Industries; Sr. Counsel, The Abacus Group; **PROFL AFFIL & HONORS:**

ABA; Chicago Bar Assn.; Chicago Mort. Attys. Assn.; **EDUC:** AB, 1955, Econ., Univ. of MI; **GRAD EDUC:** JD, 1957, Law, Univ. of MI Law School; **EDUC HONORS:** With Honors and Distinction; **MIL SERV:** USAFR, Capt.; **HOME ADD:** 681 Smoke Tree Rd., Deerfield, IL 60015, (312)945-6555; **BUS ADD:** 10 S. LaSalle St., Room 200, Chicago, IL 60603, (312)346-9172.

KOHUT, William——B: Nov. 14, 1938, Bethlehem, PA, *VP - RE & Store Construction, also Pres. Sherwin Williams Devel. Corp.*, The Sherwin Williams Company; **PRIM RE ACT:** Engineer, Developer; **OTHER RE ACT:** Corp. RE; **PROFL AFFIL & HONORS:** NACORE, ICSC, SIR; **EDUC:** BS ChE, 1960, Lehigh Univ.; **GRAD EDUC:** MBA, 1967, Duquesne Univ.; **MIL SERV:** US Army; **HOME ADD:** 31312 Roberta Dr., Bay Village, OH 44140, (216)871-4258; **BUS ADD:** 101 Prospect Ave., Cleveland, OH 44115, (216)566-2428.

KOINES, Niles P.——B: Aug. 31, 1932, Newton, MA, *Gen. Counsel*, Beneficial Standard Properties, Inc.; **PRIM RE ACT:** Attorney; **PREV EMPLOY:** Asst. Gen. Counsel, Pacific Mutual Life Ins. Co., Newport Beach, CA; **PROFL AFFIL & HONORS:** Los Angeles County Bar Assn., Fin. Lawyers Conference, Orange Cty. Bar Assn., *Who's Who in Amer. Law*; **EDUC:** 1954, Hist., Yale Univ.; **GRAD EDUC:** 1957, Harvard Law School; **EDUC HONORS:** Dean's List; **MIL SERV:** US Army; **HOME ADD:** 18022 Weston Pl, Tustin, CA 92680, (714)832-4756; **BUS ADD:** 3700 Wilshire Blvd., Los Angeles, CA 90010, (213)381-8416.

KOKALIS, Soter George, PhD——B: Jan. 29, 1936, East Chicago, IL, *Assoc. Prof. of Chemistry*, William Rainey Harper Coll., Engrg.-Math-Physical Sci.; **PRIM RE ACT:** Consultant, Owner/Investor, Instructor, Property Manager; **SERVICES:** Educ. the profl. to the benefits of realty ownership. I have aided MD, lawyers and teachers; **PREV EMPLOY:** Owner-mgr. farm props. in WI; **PROFL AFFIL & HONORS:** Amer. Chemical Soc.; **EDUC:** BS, 1958, Purdue Univ., Lafayette, IN; **GRAD EDUC:** PhD, 1962, Inorganic Chemistry, Univ. of IL-Champaign/Urbana; **EDUC HONORS:** Walter M. Miller Scholar, Graduate with honors, Ethyl Corp Fellow; DuPont Teaching Fellow; **OTHER ACT & HONORS:** Schaumburg, IL Masonic Lodge; **HOME ADD:** Suite # 102, 522 E. Algonquin Rd., Schaumburg, IL 60195, (312)397-2963; **BUS ADD:** Roselle & Algonquin Rds., Palatine, IL 60067, (312)397-3000.

KOLB, Nathaniel Key——B: Aug. 17, 1933, Sherman, TX, *Pres.*, Omniplan Architects; **PRIM RE ACT:** Architect; **PROFL AFFIL & HONORS:** AIA, TX Soc. of Archs., Coll. of Fellows, AIA; **EDUC:** B.Arch, 1957, TX A&M Univ.; **GRAD EDUC:** M. of Arch., 1960, Univ. of PA; **OTHER ACT & HONORS:** Urban Design Task Force, 1974-present; Chmn, 1980 to 1981; Hist. Landmark Comm., 1977 to present; Save Open Space Bd. of Dir.; Neighborhood Conservation Alliance; TX Land Assembly; Urban Affairs Comm. Dallas C of C, Environ. Quality Comm; City of Dallas; **HOME ADD:** 4402 Rawlins, Dallas, TX 75219, (214)521-7656; **BUS ADD:** 1700 Republic Nat. Bank Tower, Dallas, TX 75201, (214)742-1261.

KOLLAER, Jim C.——B: Jan. 5, 1943, Amarillo, TX, *Pres. and Advisory Board Member*, Henry S. Miller, Co., Houston; **PRIM RE ACT:** Broker, Consultant, Architect, Instructor, Property Manager; **SERVICES:** Brokerage, devel., consultant, mgmt., comml. RE; **REP CLIENTS:** Major Corps., Developers, RE Investors for Instns.; **PREV EMPLOY:** VP & Dir. of Mktg., Caudill Rowlett Scott Inc., Houston; **PROFL AFFIL & HONORS:** Houston Bd. of Realtors; TX Assn of Realtors; NAR; NACORE; SMPS; Hou. Chapt. AIA; TX Sec. of Archs. AIA; Steering Comm., Comml. Council, NACORE, Young Arch. of Yr. Dallas, 1974; **EDUC:** LSU, 1969, Arch., TX Tech, Amarillo Coll.; **EDUC HONORS:** Dean's List, Coll. Award, Natl. VP Student Chapt. AIA; **OTHER ACT & HONORS:** Intl. Bus. Comm., Houston C of C; **HOME ADD:** 2907 Conway, Houston, TX 77025, (713)667-6652; **BUS ADD:** 3000 Post Oak Blvd. Suite 1750, Houston, TX 77056, (713)626-8880.

KOLODNER, Bernard B.——B: Oct. 19, 1945, Philadelphia, PA, Fox, Rothschild, O'Brien & Frankel; **PRIM RE ACT:** Attorney; **PROFL AFFIL & HONORS:** ABA; Philadelphia, Montgomery Cty. & PA Bar Assns., JD; **EDUC:** BS, 1967, Elec. Engrg., Univ. of PA; **GRAD EDUC:** JD, 1971, Univ. of PA; **EDUC HONORS:** Cum Laude; **HOME ADD:** 1767 Meadow Glen Dr., Lansdale, PA 19446, (215)855-6501; **BUS ADD:** 2000 Market St., 10th Fl., Philadelphia, PA 19103, (215)299-2062.

KOLODNY, Jeffrey E.——B: Aug. 14, 1949, Chicago, IL, *Pres.*, Hallmark & Johnson Properties, Ltd.; **PRIM RE ACT:** Broker, Consultant, Owner/Investor, Property Manager, Syndicator; **SERVICES:** Prop. mgmt., sales, synds., consulting; **REP CLIENTS:** Attys., admin. of estates, private investors; **PROFL AFFIL & HONORS:** IREM, RESSI, Chicago RE Bd., NAR, Multi-Family Housing of IL, CPM; **EDUC:** BA, 1971, Psych., Northwestern Univ.; **EDUC HONORS:** Dean's List; **BUS ADD:** 2800 W. Peterson Ave., Chicago, IL 60659, (312)465-8000.

KOLOM, Alfred J.——B: June 14, 1946, Chicago, IL, *Part.*, Howard Brinkmann & Kolom; **PRIM RE ACT:** Attorney, Property Manager; **PROFL AFFIL & HONORS:** IL Bar Assn., ABA, Member IL State Bar Assn., Comm. Estate Planning, Probate & Trust; **EDUC:** BA, Liberal Arts, Univ. of Notre Dame; **GRAD EDUC:** JD, 1973, Memphis State Univ.; **MIL SERV:** US Army; **HOME ADD:** 704 N 'G' St., Monmouth, IL 61462, (309)734-4129; **BUS ADD:** 92 Public Sq., Courthouse Side, Monmouth, IL 61462, (309)734-2149.

KOLPIEN, James K.——B: May 7, 1927, Lakewood, OH, *Mgr., Space Planning*, The Ohio Bell Telephone Co., RE Mgmt.; **PRIM RE ACT:** Engineer, Property Manager; **OTHER RE ACT:** Planning, design/construct, buy, sell & lease; **PROFL AFFIL & HONORS:** Amer. Soc. of Civil Engrs. (Member); Cleveland Engr. Soc. (Member); **EDUC:** BCE, 1952, Structural, The Ohio State Univ.; **GRAD EDUC:** Misc. RE Courses, Cleveland State Univ., Cuyahoga Com. Coll., Dyke Coll.; **MIL SERV:** US Army, Capt., Corps of Engr.; **OTHER ACT & HONORS:** Republican Precinct Committeeman (4 Yrs.); YMCA (Member-Board of Mgrs.); Boy Scouts of Amer. (Explorer Advisor; Merit Badge Counselor); **HOME ADD:** 811 Richmar Dr., Westlake, OH 44145, (216)871-4229; **BUS ADD:** Rm. 1900, 1300 E. 9th St., Cleveland, OH 44114, (216)822-8543.

KOLTZ, Leo——B: Feb. 13, 1922, Stevens Point, WI, *VP*, Baird & Warner, Inc., Shopping Center; **PRIM RE ACT:** Broker, Developer, Property Manager; **REP CLIENTS:** GREIT Realty Trust, Paine Weber Prop. Inc., NW Fed. Savings & Loan Assoc. of Chicago, Hinsdale Fed. Savings & Loan Assoc., Bayswater Realty, First City Prop. Corp., Lincoln Natl. Life; **PREV EMPLOY:** Natl. Tea Co., RE Div.; **PROFL AFFIL & HONORS:** ICSC, IREM, Guest lecturer at ICSC seminars & educ. schools; CPM; **EDUC:** BA, Bus., 1949, Mktg. Major, Mgmt. Minor, OK Univ., Norman, OK; **MIL SERV:** USN, Ens.; **OTHER ACT & HONORS:** Published articles on shopping center rehabilitation, remodeling and recycling; **HOME ADD:** 5 Oakbrook Club Dr., Oakbrook, IL 60521, (312)530-2989; **BUS ADD:** 115 S. La Salle St., Chicago, IL 60603, (312)368-5858.

KOMITO, Donald H.——B: July 30, 1935, Ft. Wayne, IN, *Owner*, Consulting Engineer; **PRIM RE ACT:** Consultant, Engineer, Builder; **SERVICES:** Consulting engrg. and constr. mgmt.; **PROFL AFFIL & HONORS:** Amer. Soc. of Civil Engrs. - Member Chmn. Subcomm. of Constr. Mgmt., Pres. Cape Coral Contractors Licensing Bd., Profl. Engr. - FL, IN, Lic. Contr. - FL; **EDUC:** BS Geo., 1960, Geophysics, IN Univ.; **GRAD EDUC:** BS Civil Engrg., 1961, Structural Engrg., IN Inst. of Tech.; **EDUC HONORS:** Dean's List 4 times; **HOME ADD:** RR5 12 Bonaire Cir., Ft. Myers, FL 33908, (813)481-1325; **BUS ADD:** RR5 12 Bonaire Cir., Ft. Myers, FL 33908, (813)481-1325.

KOMMER, Robert Joel——B: Sept. 8, 1940, NY, NY, *VP*, HLR, Inc.; **PRIM RE ACT:** Developer, Builder; **PROFL AFFIL & HONORS:** FL Atlantic Builders Assn., Nat. Assn. of Home Bldrs.; **EDUC:** BBA, 1962, Acctg., Adelphi Univ.; **HOME ADD:** 4361 Sugar Pine Dr., Boca Raton, FL 33431, (305)994-1091; **BUS ADD:** 6701 N University Dr., Tamarac, FL 33431, (305)722-1620.

KONINGISOR, James——*Dir. Fac.*, GCA Corp.; **PRIM RE ACT:** Property Manager; **BUS ADD:** Burlington Rd., Bedford, MA 01730, (617)275-9000.*

KONOVER, Michael——B: Apr. 28, 1952, Hartford, CT, *Dir. of Operations*, Konover & Assoc.; **PRIM RE ACT:** Developer, Builder, Property Manager, Owner/Investor; **SERVICES:** Full Range of Dev. Activities; **PROFL AFFIL & HONORS:** ICSC; **EDUC:** BA, 1975, Amer. Econ., Wesleyan Univ., Middletown, CT; **BUS ADD:** 8 Shawmet Rd., W Hartford, CT 06117, (203)232-4545.

KONTRABECKI, John T.——B: Sept. 13, 1951, Buffalo, NY, Berg & Berg Indus. Devels.; **PRIM RE ACT:** Broker, Consultant, Attorney, Developer, Owner/Investor, Property Manager; **OTHER RE ACT:** Devel. of Office and Indus. Parks; **SERVICES:** RE Devel.; **REP CLIENTS:** IBM, AMDAHL, Four Phase Systems, Fairchild Semiconductor; **PREV EMPLOY:** Wells Fargo Bank (1979-80); Lord, Bissell & Brook (Attys.) (1976-79); Richard Ellis, Inc. (1980-81); **PROFL AFFIL & HONORS:** CA & IL Licensed Atty. & broker; **EDUC:** AB, 1973, Amer. Studies, Cornell Univ.; **GRAD EDUC:** MBA, 1976, Fin., Cornell Univ.; JD, 1976, Corp. Law, Cornell Univ.; **BUS ADD:** 10062 Miller Ave., Suite 104, Cupertino, CA 95014, (408)725-0700.

KOON, Charles——*VP Corp. Dev.*, American Maize Products; **PRIM RE ACT:** Property Manager; **BUS ADD:** 41 Harbor Plaza Dr., Stanford, CT 06904, (203)356-9000.*

KOON, Richard——**B:** July 14, 1946, CO, *VP & Mgr.*, Crocker National Bank, Const. Finance; **PRIM RE ACT:** Appraiser, Banker, Lender; **SERVICES:** Interim const. lending tracts & com; **REP CLIENTS:** Numerous; **PREV EMPLOY:** VP Bank of Amer.; **PROFL AFFIL & HONORS:** CMBA; **EDUC:** 1967, Math., Mt. San Antonio Jr. Coll.; **GRAD EDUC:** 1969, Econ., Whittier Coll.; **OTHER ACT & HONORS:** Staff appraisers rating, private pilots lic., RE sales lic.; **HOME ADD:** 18210 Crystal Dr., Morgan Hill, CA 95037, (408)779-1722; **BUS ADD:** 1475 S. Bascom, Ste. 101, Campbell, CA 95008, (408)998-3767.

KOOP, Howard A.——**B:** Sept. 13, 1934, Melrose Park, IL, *Pres.*, Koop-McKinney Grp., Inc.; **PRIM RE ACT:** Developer, Builder, Owner/Investor, Syndicator; **SERVICES:** Investment counseling, const., devel. & synd. of comml., and indus. props.; **REP CLIENTS:** Indivs., lenders and instnl. investors in comml. & indus. props.; **PREV EMPLOY:** Pres., KPK Corp.; **EDUC:** I.I.T., Northwestern Univ.; **MIL SERV:** US Army; 1953-1955, Cpl.; **OTHER ACT & HONORS:** Pres. Dist. 34 School Bd. 8 yrs.; Chmn. of Bldg. Comm. & Elder of Church; **HOME ADD:** 52 Aintree Rd., St. Charles, IL 60174; **BUS ADD:** 103 E. Wilson, Batavia, IL 60510, (312)879-0200.

KOOPER, Howard M.——**B:** Oct. 17, 1939, *Pres.*, Howard M. Kooper Investments, Inc.; **PRIM RE ACT:** Broker, Syndicator, Developer, Property Manager, Owner/Investor; **PREV EMPLOY:** Overland - Wolf, Inc.; VP/Pres., Kooper Investments; **PROFL AFFIL & HONORS:** NAR; IREM, CPM; **EDUC:** BS, 1962, Bus. Admin., Univ. NE, Lincoln; **GRAD EDUC:** Creighton Univ., Law School; **OTHER ACT & HONORS:** Tr., Children's Memorial Hospital; Tr., Beth El Synagogue; **HOME ADD:** 9917 Broadmoor Dr., Omaha, NE 68114, (402)397-4197; **BUS ADD:** 7389 Pacific St., Omaha, NE 68114, (402)392-1800.

KOORSE, Sidney——**B:** Mar. 2, 1914, Newark, NJ, *Owner*, Sidney H. Koorse; **PRIM RE ACT:** Broker, Instructor, Consultant, Property Manager; **OTHER RE ACT:** Specialize in mgmt. of Sr. Citizen Housing Dev.; **SERVICES:** Prop. Mgmt.; Counciling; Mgmt. of Investment Prop.; **PROFL AFFIL & HONORS:** NAR, NJ Assn. of Realtors, IREM, NJ Realtor of Yr. 1968, NJ Prop. Mgr. of Yr. 1975, Past Pres.: NJ Assn. of Realtors, Past Regional VP of IREM, GRI, CPM; **EDUC:** PhB, 1935, Teaching, Muhlenberg Coll.; **EDUC HONORS:** Class Treas., Pres. of School Chap. of Nat. Frat.; **MIL SERV:** US Army, S/Sgt.; **OTHER ACT & HONORS:** Hist. Dist. Commnr. - Jersey City, NJ 1970-1973, Phi Epsilon Pi Frat. - Pinehurst Golf & Country Club; **HOME ADD:** 61 Sandy Hill Rd., Westfield, NJ 07090, (201)232-4740; **BUS ADD:** 141 South Ave. PO Box 67, Fanwood, NJ 07023, (201)322-4272.

KOOYMAN, Michael——*VP*, Emerson Electric Co.; **PRIM RE ACT:** Property Manager; **BUS ADD:** PO Box 4100-8000W Florissant, St. Louis, MO 63136, (314)553-2000.*

KOPFF, Gary J.——**B:** May 18, 1945, Denver, CO, *Sr. VP*, North American Developments, NV; **PRIM RE ACT:** Consultant; **PREV EMPLOY:** Laventhol & Horwath, 1980-1981; McKinsey & Co., Inc., 1974-1980; Special Asst. to Sec. of US Dept. HUD, 1968-1974; **PROFL AFFIL & HONORS:** ULI; RESSI; NACORE; **EDUC:** BS, 1967, Admin. Sci., Yale Coll.; **GRAD EDUC:** MBA, 1971, Cornell Grad. Sch. of Bus. Admin.; **EDUC HONORS:** Magna Cum Laude; **HOME ADD:** 2939 Newark St., N.W., Washington, DC 20008, (202)363-0073; **BUS ADD:** 734 15th St., NW, Ste. 401, Washington, DC 20005, (301)585-8200.

KOPIETZ, Richard J.——**B:** Jan. 11, 1931, Detroit, MI, *Home Office Bldg. Mgr. Automobile*, Auto Club of MI, Main Office; **PRIM RE ACT:** Property Manager; **PROFL AFFIL & HONORS:** BOMA of Detroit, Assoc. Member of Intl. Assn. of Chiefs of Police, Member of Energy Info. Tech. Review Grp., Dept. of Commerce, State of MI, Past Pres. of BOMA Detroit, also Detroit Bldg. Superintendants Assn., recipient of Ins. Acctg. Statistical Assn. award for Emergency/Disaster Recovery Presentation; **EDUC:** Bldg., 1964, Gen. Bldg. courses - Admin., Maint. & Const., Univ. of MI Ext. Serv.; **GRAD EDUC:** RPA, 1980, BOMA; **MIL SERV:** US Army, Cpl.; **OTHER ACT & HONORS:** US Power Squadron; **HOME ADD:** 11194 Charles Dr., Warren, MI 48093, (313)264-6977; **BUS ADD:** Auto Club Dr., Dearborn, MI 48126, (313)336-1550.

KORAN, Arley J.——**B:** Mar. 24, 1928, Cleveland, OH, *Arch.*, Arley J. Koran, Inc., Architects; **PRIM RE ACT:** Architect; **PROFL AFFIL & HONORS:** AIA, Amer. Arbitration Assn., Nat. Cert. from the Nat. Council of Arch. Bd. (NCARB); Exhibition of School Arch. Cert. from the Amer. Assn. of Admin. & the Amer. Instit. of Arch.; Recognition Cert. from the Arts Council of Bergin Cty. & the Arch. League of Northern New Jersey; **EDUC:** BArch, 1959, Arch./Art History, Western Reserve Univ.; **GRAD EDUC:** Additional study at Baldin Wallace College & OH Univ.; **EDUC HONORS:** Alpha Rho Chi Medal; **MIL SERV:** US Army, Service throughout Europe, 1950-52; **HOME ADD:** 13003 Hathaway Dr., Silver Spring, MD 20906, (301)949-7581; **BUS ADD:** 2311 Univ. Blvd., West, Silver Spring, MD 20902, (301)933-1154.

KORB, Irving——*Pres.*, Korb Co. Real Estate Constultants; **PRIM RE ACT:** Consultant, Developer, Owner/Investor; **SERVICES:** Consultation, negotiation, expert witness & arbitration serv. to intl. clientele; **REP CLIENTS:** Indiv. & corp. decision makers, CPA's, attys. and fin. advisors; **PROFL AFFIL & HONORS:** Amer. Soc. of RE Counselors (CRE), SIR, IREM (CPM), Nat. Mktg. Inst. (CCIM), Hon. Life Dir. Oakland Bd. of Realtors, Hon. Life Dir. CA Assn. of Realtors.; **MIL SERV:** USAF, 1st Lt.; **BUS ADD:** One Kaiser Plaza, Oakland, CA 94612, (415)832-1000.

KORDOPATIS, Nicholas G.——**B:** Nov. 6, 1936, Reading, PA, *VP*, Union Bank and Trust Co. of E. PA, Mort.; **PRIM RE ACT:** Banker; **PROFL AFFIL & HONORS:** Bethlehem Bd. of Realtors, Inc.; Leheigh Valley Home Bldrs. Assn., Treas.; **EDUC:** Banking, Amer. Inst. of Banking; Banking, School of Banking of NY State Bankers Assn.; Banking, PA State Univ. Ctr.; Banking, Nat. Mort. School, OH State Univ.; **MIL SERV:** USNR, USAR, PANG, 2nd Lt.; **OTHER ACT & HONORS:** Pres., C of C, Bethlehem; 1970, Young Man of Yr.; 1977, Commendation, Senate of PA; **HOME ADD:** 1925 Main St., Bethlehem, PA 18017, (215)865-1370; **BUS ADD:** 65 E. Elizabeth Ave., Bethlehem, PA 18018, (215)861-1727.

KORINKE, Walter M.——**B:** Apr. 16, 1942, Houghton, MI, *Rgnl. VP of RE Investment*, Mutual of New York, RE; **PRIM RE ACT:** Lender, Owner/Investor; **PREV EMPLOY:** Mass Mutual Life, Erie Cty. Savings; **PROFL AFFIL & HONORS:** ICSC, BAMA; **EDUC:** BS, 1966, Econ. & Ind. Geography, Memphis State Univ.; **GRAD EDUC:** RE, Misc.; **HOME ADD:** 12546 Northampton Ct., Saratoga, CA 95070; **BUS ADD:** 2988 Campus Dr., Suite 340, San Mateo, CA 94403, (415)573-0442.

KORKOW, Donald C.——**B:** Jan. 5, 1944, Pierre, SD, *Owner*, Korkow and Associates, Inc.; **PRIM RE ACT:** Broker, Consultant, Appraiser, Property Manager; **SERVICES:** Farm/ranch RE; **PREV EMPLOY:** Pres. of Fed. Land Bank, Pierre, SD, (1966-1976); **PROFL AFFIL & HONORS:** Amer. Soc. of Farm Mgrs. and Rural Appraisers and Farm and Land Inst.; **EDUC:** BS, Econ., SD State Univ., Brookings, SD; **MIL SERV:** SD Nat. Guard, Capt.; **HOME ADD:** 122 W. Broadway, Pierre, SD 57501, (605)224-8497; **BUS ADD:** P O Box 939, 110 W. MO, Pierre, SD 57501, (605)224-O441.

KORNBLATT, David——**B:** June 30, 1927, Baltimore, MD, *Chmn.*, David Kornblatt Associates, Inc.; **PRIM RE ACT:** Broker, Consultant, Developer, Property Manager; **SERVICES:** RE - comml./indust. brokerage, consultant, mgr.; **REP CLIENTS:** First Nat. Bank of MD; IBM; USF&G; Time, Inc.; Alexander & Alexander; GE; **PROFL AFFIL & HONORS:** SIR; Amer. Soc. of RE Counselors (CRE); AACA, SIR; CRE; AACA; **EDUC:** BS, 1950, Bus. Admin., Univ. of MD; **MIL SERV:** USCG; Cox, Alaskan Tour '45 '46; **OTHER ACT & HONORS:** Comm: Baltimore Econ. Devel. '61-'65; MD Savings & Loan Comm. '66-'70; Gr. Baltimore Comm. - Dir. '79-'81; **HOME ADD:** 3512 Old Court Rd., Pikesville, MD 21208, (301)484-4564; **BUS ADD:** 25 So. Charles St., Baltimore, MD 21201, (301)539-4316.

KORNBLAU, Barry M.——**B:** June 5, 1949, Richmond, VA, *VP*, Realty Indus., Inc.; **PRIM RE ACT:** Broker, Developer, Owner/Investor, Instructor, Property Manager, Syndicator; **PROFL AFFIL & HONORS:** IREM, NAHB, AOMA, NAR, RESSI, CPM, RAM; **EDUC:** BA, 1971, Pol. Sci.(Public Admin.), Old Dominion Univ.; **OTHER ACT & HONORS:** Old Dominion Univ. Intercoll. Found. Dir.; Past Pres.-Richmond Apt. Council; **HOME ADD:** 910 Beveridge Rd., Richmond, VA 23226, (804)288-5808; **BUS ADD:** PO Box 7218, Richmond, VA 23221, (804)359-9391.

KORNBLUM, Eugene Harold——**B:** June 15, 1945, Atlanta, GA, *Dir. of Operations*, Prop. Services, Inc., Multi-Family; **PRIM RE ACT:** Broker, Instructor, Consultant, Property Manager, Owner/Investor; **SERVICES:** Fee Mgmt., Brokerage, Consultation, Investment and Dev.; **REP CLIENTS:** First Natl. Bank of Chicago, Mellon Bank, Prudential Ins. Co., Dain Corp.; **PREV EMPLOY:** Security Mgmt. Co. 1969 - 1975 Mandarin Prop. Mgmt. 1975 - 1979; **PROFL AFFIL & HONORS:** IREM, Jacksonville Apt. Council, Bd. of Realtors, CPM, FL R.E. Broker; **EDUC:** BA, 1967, Liberal Arts, Univ. of GA; **OTHER ACT & HONORS:** VP Jacksonville Jewish Ctr., Bd. Member Jewish Family Serv., Teacher Jacksonville Jewish Ctr.,

Member Brierwood Athletic Assn.; **HOME ADD:** 2419 Saragossa Ave., Jacksonville, FL 32217, (904)737-6127; **BUS ADD:** 815 S. Main St., Jacksonville, FL 32207, (904)396-1782.

KORNHEISER, Martin H.——B: May 3, 1940, New York, NY, *VP*, First American Title Insurance Co.; **PRIM RE ACT:** Attorney, Insuror; **SERVICES:** Title Insurance; **REP CLIENTS:** Lenders Investors Atty. Brokers Resid. & Comml.; **PREV EMPLOY:** Chicago Title Ins. Co., Title Officer; Edison S&L Assn., Closing Atty.; Kimco Devel. Corp-House Counsel; **PROFL AFFIL & HONORS:** NY State Bar Assn., NJ Land Title Assn.; **EDUC:** BA, 1962, Hist. & Govt., Adelphi Univ.; **GRAD EDUC:** LLB, 1965, Brooklyn Law School; **EDUC HONORS:** *Who's Who American Colls.*; **BUS ADD:** 170 Broadway, New York, NY 10038, (212)962-2780.

KORNMEIER, Richard——B: Apr. 28, 1946, Providence, RI, *Exec. VP*, Stiles Construction; **PRIM RE ACT:** Consultant, Developer, Builder, Owner/Investor, Property Manager; **OTHER RE ACT:** CPA, specialty RE; **SERVICES:** Acquisition, build, fin., lease, manage; **REP CLIENTS:** Bekins Moving, Burnham Moving, IBM, Motorola, Pantry Pride, Xerox, Leigh Products, Hamilton Au Net, SCM; **PREV EMPLOY:** Wilson Fancher & Co., 1977; Price Waterhouse; **PROFL AFFIL & HONORS:** Advisory Council Small Bus. Admin.; Pres., Oakland Park/Wilton Manors C of C; Bd. of Govs., Barry Coll.; Treas., Exec. Council of Nova Univ.; VP, Oakland Park Hist. Soc.; Tr., Oakland Park Pension Bd.; Member, Ft. Lauderdale C of C; Nat. Assn. of Accountants; So. FL Mfrs. Assn.; Broward Indus. Bd.; Sales & Mktg. Execs.; Intl. Delta Sigma Pi and Beta Alpha Psi; AICPA; FL Inst. of CPA's, State of FL, CPA; Coll. level instr.; RE salesman; **EDUC:** BA, 1969, Mgmt./Econ., FL State Univ.; **GRAD EDUC:** Masters of Acctg., 1970, Acctg., FL State Univ.; **EDUC HONORS:** Honors Program; **OTHER ACT & HONORS:** Nat. Conf. of Christians and Jews; Citizens Advisory Bd. Metropolitan Planning Org.; numerous antique car orgs. and clubs; Delegate, Whitehouse Conf. on Small Bus.; Price Waterhouse grad. fellowship; Wall St. Journal award for econ.; outstanding contributions to educ. efforts; Broward Cty. Hist. Commn.; Oakland Park civic involvement; Member, Broward Community Coll. Advisory Bd.; Sunday School asst. dir.; Author of numerous articles on mgmt., taxation, const., RE and antique automobiles; currently negotiation with Prentice Hall to author a book on mgmt. in the Const. Indus.; past editor of "Intl. Antique Automobile Journal"; **HOME ADD:** 4311 N.W. 19th Ave., Ft. Lauderdale, FL; **BUS ADD:** 6400 N. Andrews, Ft. Lauderdale, FL 33309, (305)771-4900.

KOROM, Steve——B: Mar. 22, 1935, Hungary, *Pres., Broker*, All Points West Realty & Builders Inc.(c-21); **PRIM RE ACT:** Broker, Instructor, Consultant, Appraiser, Builder, Property Manager, Owner/Investor; **SERVICES:** Sales, Prop. mgmt., investments counceling, const., modular home sales, synd., of investment & comml. props., valuations, mobile home sales; **PREV EMPLOY:** New Homes Sales Custom Builder Sales from prints & ideas 1973-78; **PROFL AFFIL & HONORS:** OAR, NAR, CABOR, GRI, CRS; **EDUC:** Cert. in R.E., 1974, Cuyahoga Community Coll.; **MIL SERV:** USN, Med. Research; **HOME ADD:** 17609 Fallingwater, Strongsville, OH 44136, (216)238-5396; **BUS ADD:** 15076 Pearl Rd., Strongsville, OH 44136, (216)238-1000.

KORPACZ, Peter F.——B: Oct. 25, 1942, NYC, NY, *Pres.*, Peter F. Korpacz & Associates, Inc.; **PRIM RE ACT:** Consultant, Appraiser; **SERVICES:** Objective, unbiased and imaginative RE advice and counsel to those engaged in evaluating, buying, selling, leasing, fin. or devel. RE; **REP CLIENTS:** Insurance companies, banks, investors, pension funds, law firms, investment bankers, stock brokers; **PREV EMPLOY:** Landauer Associates, Inc., 1971-1977; **PROFL AFFIL & HONORS:** AIREA, MAI; **EDUC:** BA, 1967, Hist., St. John's Univ.; **HOME ADD:** 31 Bluff Cir., Hauppauge, NY 11788, (516)265-4131; **BUS ADD:** 122 E. 42nd St., Suite 1700, NY, NY 10168, (212)370-9750.

KORTIER, Richard G.——B: May 31, 1921, Toledo, OH, *Pres.*, Broadview Mgmt. Corp.; **PRIM RE ACT:** Broker, Consultant, Builder, Property Manager, Lender, Owner/Investor; **OTHER RE ACT:** Const. Mgmt.; **PROFL AFFIL & HONORS:** IREM; BOMA; NAR; Cleveland Area Bd. Of Realtors; **EDUC:** BBA, Acctg./Ins., Univ. of Toledo; **MIL SERV:** US Army, Lt.; **HOME ADD:** 12550 Lake Ave., Lakewood, OH 44107, (216)521-4360; **BUS ADD:** 6000 Rockside Woods Blvd., Cleveland, OH 44131, (216)447-1900.

KORY, Peter——B: July 29, 1931, Berlin, Germany, *Pres*, KBS Devel. Assoc. Inc.; **PRIM RE ACT:** Developer; **SERVICES:** Devel. mgmt.; **PREV EMPLOY:** John W. Galbreath & Co.; NY State UDC City of Cincinnati; **PROFL AFFIL & HONORS:** ULI, NAHRO, Hon AIA 1975; **EDUC:** BS, 1953, Arch., CCNY; **MIL SERV:** US Army, Pvt., Commendation; **HOME ADD:** Shore Dr., RFD 4, Brewster, NY 10509, (212)674-2966; **BUS ADD:** 330 W. 42nd St., NY, NY 10036, (212)594-8415.

KOSEIAN, John C.——B: Sept. 25, 1925, NYC, NY, *Owner*, Enfield Realty Assoc.; **PRIM RE ACT:** Broker, Appraiser, Builder, Property Manager, Lender, Owner/Investor, Insuror; **OTHER RE ACT:** Remodeler; **MIL SERV:** US Army;; Sgt., Bronze Star, Purple Heart, Combat Infantry Badge; **OTHER ACT & HONORS:** Enfield Republican Town Chmn. 1970-74, Morning Star Lodge, #28 Warehouse Point, CT; Justice of the Peace; Notary Public; **HOME ADD:** 8 Quaker Ln., Enfield, CT 06082, (203)745-1466; **BUS ADD:** 95 N. Rd., Warehouse Point, E Windsor, CT 06085, (203)623-8247.

KOSENE, Gerald A.——B: Dec. 6, 1943, Indianapolis, IN, *Pres.*, Kosene & Kosene Development Co., Inc.; **PRIM RE ACT:** Broker, Developer, Builder, Owner/Investor, Property Manager, Syndicator; **SERVICES:** Devel. and owners of shopping ctrs. & office bldgs.; **PREV EMPLOY:** Dir. of Leasing & Devel. Sandor Dev. Co. 1972-1977; **PROFL AFFIL & HONORS:** Intl. Council of Shopping Ctrs.; CSM; **EDUC:** 1966, Bus., IN Univ.; **OTHER ACT & HONORS:** Nora Community Council Service Award 1981; Traders Point Hunt Club; Zionsville Optimist Club; Indianapolis Child Abuse Program; Stanley K. Lacey Leadership Series 1981; **HOME ADD:** 6814 W. 96th St., Zionsville, IN 46077, (317)873-5556; **BUS ADD:** 3390 W. 86th St., Indianapolis, IN 46268, (317)872-0131.

KOSKE, Keith——*Dir.*, Colorado, Colorado Real Estate Commission; **BUS ADD:** 1776 Logan, Denver, CO 80203, (303)866-2633.*

KOSKE, Otis F.——B: Pulcifer, WI, *Dir. of RE*, Wisconsin Electric Power Co.; **PRIM RE ACT:** Broker, Property Manager; **OTHER RE ACT:** Dir. of elec. utility RE dept., Right of Way Mgr.; **PROFL AFFIL & HONORS:** Beta Alpha Psi, Profl. Acctg. Frat.; Milwaukee Bd. of Realtors; WI Utilities Assn.; Intl. Right of Way Assn. (SR/WA), Recipient of IR/WA Frank C. Balfor Right of Way Prof. of the Year Award for 1980; IR/WA Badger Chap. 17 Right of Way, Profl. of the Year, 1973, 79 & 80; **EDUC:** BBA, 1950, Acctg., Univ. of WI; **MIL SERV:** US Army 1941-46; US Army Res. 1946-64, Maj.; **OTHER ACT & HONORS:** Res. Officers Assn.; RE Advisory Comm. Milwaukee Area Tech. Coll.; Electrical Lic. & Examining Comm., C/Glendale; Milwaukee Assn. of Commerce; The Maer. Legion; Century Club; The Martin Club; Treas. of St. John's Lutheran Church; **HOME ADD:** 7755 N. Chadwick Rd., Glendale, WI 53217, (414)352-5485; **BUS ADD:** 231 W. Michigan St., Milwaukee, WI 53201, (414)277-2713.

KOSKINEN, Carl——*VP Engr.*, Sun Electric Corp.; **PRIM RE ACT:** Property Manager; **BUS ADD:** 6323 Avondale Ave., Chicago, IL 60631, (312)631-6000.*

KOSKINEN, John A.——B: June 30, 1939, Cleveland, OH, *Pres.*, Victor Palmieri & Co., Inc. (Asset Mgmt. firm); **OTHER RE ACT:** Mgr. of asset portfolios; **SERVICES:** All direct mgmt. servs.; **PREV EMPLOY:** Law clerk to Chief Judge, US Court of Appeals, Wash., 1965-66; Atty. with Gibson, Dunn & Crutcher, LA, 1966-67; Spec. Asst. & Dep. Exec. Dir. Nat. Advisory Comm. on Civil Disorders (Kerner Comm), Wash. 1967-68; Legislative Asst. to Mayor John Lindsay of NYC, Wash. 1968-69; Admin. Asst. of Sen. Abraham Ribicoff of CT, 1969-73; VP, Victor Palmieri & Co., Inc., 1973-77; Pres. & CEO, 1977-79' Pres. & CEO, 1979-present; **PROFL AFFIL & HONORS:** Member Pres. Mgmt. & Improvement Council, 1979-80; Vice Chmn. Bd. of Dir. Nat. Captioning Inst., State Bars of CA & CT; RE Broker, CA, PA, DC, NC; **EDUC:** BA, 1961, Physics, Duke Univ.; **GRAD EDUC:** LLB, 1964, Yale Law School & Cambridge Univ., 1964-65; **EDUC HONORS:** Phi Beta Kappa, 1960, Magna Cum Laude, Order of the Coif, (1964), Cum Laude; **OTHER ACT & HONORS:** Member Exec. Comm. Duke Univ. Gen. Alumni Assoc., 1977-present; Pres. Duke Univ. Gen. Alumni Assoc., 1980-81, Member Duke Univ. Bd. of Visitors, Inst. of Poli. Sci. & Pub. Affairs, 1981; Member, Yale Law Sch. Alumni Assn. Exec. Comm., 1971-76; **HOME ADD:** 1846 Redwood Terr., NW, Washington, DC 20012, (202)723-4020; **BUS ADD:** 2021 K St., NW, Suite 700, Washington, DC 20006, (202)223-8690.

KOSSIS, James——B: Pittsburgh, PA, *Pres.*, Meyers Mgmt.; **PRIM RE ACT:** Broker, Consultant, Appraiser, Owner/Investor, Property Manager, Syndicator; **PROFL AFFIL & HONORS:** Pittsburgh Bd. of Realtors, IREM Independent Appraisers; **EDUC:** 3 1/2 yrs. Bus. Admin., RE Bus. Admin., Univ. of WI; **MIL SERV:** US Army Reserves, Pvt.; **HOME ADD:** 3315 Scathelocke Rd., Pittsburgh, PA 15235, (412)823-5096; **BUS ADD:** 1823 Pen Ave., Pittsburgh, PA 15221, (412)243-7120.

KOSSMAN, Paul——B: Mar. 13, 1926, Canonsburg, PA, *Owner/Pres.*, Kossman Development Co.; **PRIM RE ACT:** Architect, Developer, Builder, Owner/Investor, Property Manager; **SERVICES:** Design, construct & manage office & retail complexes; **REP CLIENTS:** Westinghouse; J.C. Penney; Dresser Industries; US Air; St. Regis Paper; K-Mart; Thrift Drug; Giant Eagle; Minnesota Fabrics; **EDUC:** BA, 1949, Arch. Engrg., PA State Univ.; **EDUC HONORS:** Zigma Tau; **MIL SERV:** USN, Electronic Tech. Mate, 3rd Class PO; **HOME ADD:** 1073 Dorset Rd., Pittsburgh, PA 15213, (412)621-4024; **BUS ADD:** Seven Parkway Ctr., Suite 860, 835 Greentree Rd., Pittsburgh, PA 15220.

KOSTER, Thomas L.——**B:** Grand Rapids, MI, *Pres.*, Realvesco Props.; **PRIM RE ACT:** Broker, Developer, Syndicator; **SERVICES:** Investment & comml. prop. brokerage, synd. indus.; **PROFL AFFIL & HONORS:** CCIM; **HOME TEL:** (616)455-0327; **BUS ADD:** 2627 E Beltline SE, Grand Rapids, MI 49506, (616)942-6470.

KOSTOSKY, Thomas J.——**B:** Mar. 3, 1954, Pittsburgh, PA, Gove Associates, Inc.; **PRIM RE ACT:** Consultant, Engineer, Architect, Developer; **SERVICES:** Site selection, mort. packaging, all technical & design services; **REP CLIENTS:** Indiv. devels, investment groups; **PROFL AFFIL & HONORS:** NAHB, MSPO, MALA, MSPO Design Award, 1977; **EDUC:** BS Landscape Arch., 1976, Environmental Design/Planning/Mktg., MI State Univ.; **HOME ADD:** 202 E. Riverside, Williamston, MI 48995, (517)655-3271; **BUS ADD:** 2224 E. MI Ave. St. 200, Lansing, MI 48912, (517)485-0555.

KOSTYRKA, R.J.——*Mgr. RE*, Kaiser Aluminum & Chemical Corp.; **PRIM RE ACT:** Property Manager; **BUS ADD:** 300 Lakeside Dr., Oakland, CA 94643, (415)271-3467.*

KOTLEN, Arnold S.——**B:** Apr. 28, 1947, Providence, RI, *Architect*; **PRIM RE ACT:** Architect; **SERVICES:** Architectural; **PREV EMPLOY:** NY City, Dept. of City Planning; **EDUC:** B.Arch., 1970, Arch., Pratt Institute; **HOME ADD:** 510 7th St., Brooklyn, NY 11215, (212)499-6811; **BUS ADD:** 510 7th St., Brooklyn, NY 11215, (212)499-6811.

KOTTEL, Deborah J.——**B:** June 15, 1952, IN, *Atty.*, Kottel, Janikowski & Light; **PRIM RE ACT:** Attorney, Developer, Owner/Investor, Syndicator; **SERVICES:** Legal counseling, devel. and synd. of comml. prop.; **REP CLIENTS:** Comml. devels.; **PROFL AFFIL & HONORS:** Chicago Bar Assn., IL State Bar Assn., ABA; **EDUC:** BS, 1974, Psych., Loyola Univ. of Chicago; **GRAD EDUC:** JD, 1978, Law, DePaul Coll. of Law; **EDUC HONORS:** Law Review, Editor; **OTHER ACT & HONORS:** W.O.M.A.N. (Women Owners, Mgrs., Administrators Networking); **HOME ADD:** 412 N. Humphrey, Oak Park, IL 60302, (312)386-5293; **BUS ADD:** 1 N. LaSalle, 45th Floor, Chicago, IL 60602, (312)853-0800.

KOUTNIK, L. James——**B:** June 20, 1921, Ft. Dodge, IA, *Pres.*, Western Realty Co., Inc. & Western Appraisal & Investment Co.; **PRIM RE ACT:** Broker, Instructor, Consultant, Appraiser, Property Manager, Owner/Investor; **PREV EMPLOY:** RE Rel.; **PROFL AFFIL & HONORS:** NAR, SREA, CRB, CRS, SRA, ARA, GRI; **EDUC:** GS, 1947, Bus. Econ., Univ. of ID; **MIL SERV:** USAF, Lt. Col.; **OTHER ACT & HONORS:** Member ID RE Comn. Rotary, Elks, Shriner, Toastmasters, Amer. Legion; **HOME ADD:** 710 N. Wash., Rt. 1, Twin Falls, ID 83301, (208)733-1505; **BUS ADD:** Box 365, Twin Falls, ID 83301, (208)733-2365.

KOVACH, Jerry——**B:** Feb. 2, 1944, Pittsburgh, PA, *Prin.*, The J. Kovach Group, Inc.; **PRIM RE ACT:** Consultant; **OTHER RE ACT:** Exec. search; **SERVICES:** Profl. recruiting exclusively for the RE indus.; **REP CLIENTS:** RE devel., owners, investors, mgr., financiers; **PROFL AFFIL & HONORS:** NAIOP, Intl. Council of Shopping Ctrs., NAR; **EDUC:** BS, 1966, Math., IN Univ.; **MIL SERV:** USMC, E-4; **HOME ADD:** 102 Bradberry Dr., Monroeville, PA 15146, (412)373-1612; **BUS ADD:** 400 Penn Ctr. Blvd., Suite 303, Pittsburgh, PA 15235, (412)823-5890.

KOVACH, Richard A.——**B:** Apr. 5, 1948, Indiana, PA, *Part.*, Kovach & Kovach Attys.; **PRIM RE ACT:** Attorney, Owner/Investor, Insuror; **SERVICES:** Legal & title ins., investment counseling; **REP CLIENTS:** Lenders, grp. & indiv. investors, RE brokers, land title underwriters; **PROFL AFFIL & HONORS:** Amer. Land Title, ABA, PA Bar Assn.; **EDUC:** BA, 1970, Econ., Soc. Sci., Univ. of Pittsburgh; **GRAD EDUC:** JD, 1973, Bus. & Taxation, Univ. of Pittsburgh Sch. of Law; **OTHER ACT & HONORS:** Rotary, Knights of Columbus, Advisor & Dir. Mater Amoris Montessori Sch., Washington DC; **HOME ADD:** RD 7, Box 304, Greensburg, PA 15601, (412)834-9280; **BUS ADD:** Terry Way & Rte. 981, Latrobe, PA 15650, (412)537-5535.

KOVACH, William J.——**B:** May 26, 1925, Homestead, PA, *Broker/Owner*, Berkshire Realty; **PRIM RE ACT:** Broker, Appraiser, Property Manager, Insuror; **SERVICES:** Resid., comml., indus. props., help private indiv. find bus. and manage props screen tenants; **EDUC:** 1959, RE courses, Weaver School of RE; 1967, fin., appraising, fundamentals, Univ. of Pittsburgh; **MIL SERV:** Merchant marine, Chief PO, Atl., Pac. Medit. War Zones, 1943-46; **OTHER ACT & HONORS:** Notary public, Republican Comm. 12 yrs., Pres. local civic assn. 1 yr., Moose, Public relations, photographer for PA Sports Hall of Fame Pittsburgh Chapter 12 yrs., Sports editor & feature writer & photo. 6 yrs., Suburban Newspaper, AAU Official, Allegheny Mountain Assn.; **HOME ADD:** 4750 Liberty Ave., Pittsburgh, PA 15224, (412)682-2992; **BUS ADD:** 4750 Liberty Ave., Pittsburgh, PA 15224, (412)682-2992.

KOVATCH, Paul R.——**B:** Feb. 6, 1949, McKeesport, PA, *Owner*, National Rentals; **PRIM RE ACT:** Consultant, Owner/Investor, Instructor, Property Manager; **OTHER RE ACT:** Finder's servs., educ. servs.; **SERVICES:** Mgmt. and fin. consulting - problem props. - advice for beginners; **PREV EMPLOY:** Owner and operator 9 years; **PROFL AFFIL & HONORS:** Apt. Assn., Amer. Mgmt. Assn., MBA; **EDUC:** AA RE/Mgmt./Electronics, 1974, Mgmt., Barstow Coll. and Barston Coll.; BA Psych./Religion, 1978, Mgmt., Chapman Coll.; Johns Hopkins Univ.; **GRAD EDUC:** MBA, in progress, Mgmt., Golden Gate Univ.; **MIL SERV:** USAF, S/Sgt.; **OTHER ACT & HONORS:** Nasa Meritorious Effort Accommodations, FCC 1st Class Radiotelephone Lic. - Christian Bus., CA Community Coll. Faculty; **HOME ADD:** 3012 Garbett St., McKeesport, PA 15132, (412)673-6783; **BUS ADD:** Box 324, Barstow, CA 92311, (714)256-2231.

KOWAL, Walter C.——**B:** June 27, 1935, Detroit, MI, *Dir. of RE*, Foodmaker, Inc., Continental Restaurant Systems; Ralston Purina Co.; **PRIM RE ACT:** Developer, Owner/Investor, Property Manager; **SERVICES:** Budgeting, admin., market analysis, site selection; negotiations; **REP CLIENTS:** Owners, investors, devels., brokers; **PREV EMPLOY:** Regional RE mgr. - Shell Oil; **PROFL AFFIL & HONORS:** NACRE, Amer. Mgmt. Assn., Delta Sigma Pi; ICSC; **EDUC:** BS, 1960, Mktg., Univ. of Detroit; **MIL SERV:** US Army, 1954-1956; **OTHER ACT & HONORS:** Recreation Comm. Chmn. 1977-1979; I Care Organization; Focus Hope; **HOME ADD:** 32760 Friar Tuck, Birmingham, MI 48010, (313)646-0462; **BUS ADD:** 29508 Southfield, Suite 200, Southfield, MI 48076, (313)559-9380.

KOWALCZYK, V Scott——*Investment Rep.*, Ackerman & Co., Investment Div.; **PRIM RE ACT:** Broker; **OTHER RE ACT:** Synd., prop mgr.; **SERVICES:** Investment counseling; **REP CLIENTS:** Foreign pension funds; **PROFL AFFIL & HONORS:** RESSI (NAR), Outstanding Young Men of Amer, 1974, 1977; **EDUC:** BA, 1970, Phil., Wittenberg Univ.; **GRAD EDUC:** MBA, 1980, Fin. and RE, Harvard Bus. School; **EDUC HONORS:** Dean's List; **HOME ADD:** 138 LeBrun Rd., NW, Atlanta, GA 30342, (404)261-2540; **BUS ADD:** 3340 Peachtree Rd., NE, Atlanta, GA 30026, (404)262-7171.

KOZA, John W.——**B:** Apr. 2, 1941, Boston, MA, *VP*, FMR Prop. Inc.; **PRIM RE ACT:** Broker, Developer, Property Manager; **OTHER RE ACT:** Corp. RE Mgr.; **SERVICES:** Dev. & Mgmt. of comml. props.; **REP CLIENTS:** Instnl. investors in comml. props.; **PROFL AFFIL & HONORS:** Dir. Boston Chap. BOMA, CPM; **EDUC:** BS, 1962, Econ., Boston Coll.; **GRAD EDUC:** MBA, 1968, Fin., Boston Coll.; **MIL SERV:** US Army, 1st Lt.; **OTHER ACT & HONORS:** Dir. Learning & Cognitive Dev. Ctr., Member Kennedy Hospital Assoc., Past Pres., Boston Chapter, Society for Advancement of Management; **HOME ADD:** 253 Pleasant St., Millis, MA 02054, (617)376-2144; **BUS ADD:** 7 Water St., Boston, MA 02109, (617)726-0370.

KOZLOWSKI, Dennis——*Chief Fin. Officer*, Ludlow Corp.; **PRIM RE ACT:** Property Manager; **BUS ADD:** 145 Rosemary St., Needham Height, MA 02194, (617)444-4900.*

KRACKOW, Stuart E.——**B:** June 8, 1931, NYC, *VP, Dir., Office Support Services*, Young & Rubicam, Inc., NY; **PRIM RE ACT:** Property Manager, Owner/Investor; **SERVICES:** Internal & external support for all residents; **PROFL AFFIL & HONORS:** BOMA, AMA; **MIL SERV:** USN, AF-2; **OTHER ACT & HONORS:** Aircraft Owners & Pilots Assn., Private Pilot; **HOME ADD:** 5 Bates Rd., Great Neck, NY 11020, (516)482-0906; **BUS ADD:** 285 Madison Ave., NY, NY 10017, (212)953-2196.

KRAEMER, Richard C.——**B:** July 15, 1943, Rochester, NY, *Exec. VP*, Universal Development Corp.; **PRIM RE ACT:** Developer, Builder; **SERVICES:** Resid. devel. & homebuilding; **EDUC:** BS, 1965, Chemistry, Coll. of Wm. & Mary; **GRAD EDUC:** MBA, 1972, Mktg./Fin., Harvard Bus. School; **HOME ADD:** 8236 Pecan Grove Cir., Tempe, AZ 85284; **BUS ADD:** 3110 S Rural Rd., Tempe, AZ 85282, (601)829-8822.

KRAFSUR, Howard G.——**B:** May 6, 1922, Boston, MA, *Partner*, Bennett & Kahnweiler Assoc.; **PRIM RE ACT:** Broker, Consultant, Developer, Owner/Investor; **SERVICES:** Devel. of Indus. & Office Parks, counseling to major corps.; **REP CLIENTS:** Maj. corps., instnl. investors; **PREV EMPLOY:** Landau & Perlaman 1947-57; **PROFL AFFIL & HONORS:** Society of Industrial Realtors; American Society of Real Estate Counselors; Industrial Development Research Council; NAIOP; **EDUC:** BA, 1943, Brown Univ.; **MIL SERV:** USN, Lt.; **HOME ADD:** 36 Bridlewood Rd., Northbrook, IL 60062, (312)272-3453; **BUS ADD:** 9700 W Bryn Mawr Ave., Rosemont, IL 60018, (312)671-7911.

KRAFT, Geraldine (Geri) M.——**B:** Jan. 28, 1947, Portland, OR, *Assoc. Broker*, Macaulay, Nicolls, Maitland Inc., Subsidiary of MNM & Co., Ltd.; **PRIM RE ACT:** Broker, Consultant; **SERVICES:** Sales & leasing of comml. prop., facilities location consultation; **REP CLIENTS:** Motarola; Merrill Lynch etc., private & corp. investors, devels., landlords and tenants; **PREV EMPLOY:** Principal-Kraft & Bulsa Comml. Brokerage Co., office bldg. specialist; Cushman & Wakefield; also 5 yrs.-Coldwell Banker Comml. Brokerage Co.; **PROFL AFFIL & HONORS:** BOMA; Seattle Downtown Devel. Assn.; Bldg. Comm., YWCA Seattle, First Woman hired nat. in comm. RE sales by Coldwell Banker & Co.; **EDUC:** BS, 1970, Marketing, Port. State Univ.; **EDUC HONORS:** Nat. Mktg. Assn. Honorarium, AIBSEC Trainee, Copenhagen, Denmark; **OTHER ACT & HONORS:** YWCA Bd. guest lecturer, Women's Univ. Club Investment Seminar; guest speaker, YWCA Successful Women Speak Out; guest speaker Environment Protection Agency NAFE; **HOME ADD:** 1528-46th SW, Seattle, WA 98116, (206)935-0856; **BUS ADD:** 800 5th Ave. Seafirst Fifth Ave. Plaza #3900, Seattle, WA 98104, (206)223-0866.

KRAFT, Jeffrey J.——**B:** Feb. 27, 1950, Lyndhurst, OH, *VP*, Fidelity Union Bank, Corp. Bank; **PRIM RE ACT:** Consultant, Banker, Lender; **SERVICES:** Investment counseling, short and medium-term fin.; **REP CLIENTS:** Indiv. and instit. investors/purchasers of comml. & indus. prop.; **PREV EMPLOY:** Marine Midland Bank, N.A. (NYC) 1973-1980; **PROFL AFFIL & HONORS:** Bank Credit Associates of NY; **EDUC:** BA, 1972, Eng. and Psych., Duke Univ. (Durham, NC); **GRAD EDUC:** MBA, 1980, Mgmt., NY Univ.; **EDUC HONORS:** Dean's List, Grad. with Distinction; Elected Member of Beta Gamma Sigma; **OTHER ACT & HONORS:** Crestview Club Corp. (Tennis & Swim Club); **HOME ADD:** 27 George Rd., New Providence, NJ 07974, (201)665-0590; **BUS ADD:** 765 Broad St., Newark, NJ 07101, (201)430-4476.

KRALICEK, Robert——*Exec. VP*, Motel Brokers Association of America; **OTHER RE ACT:** Profl. Assn. Admin.; **BUS ADD:** 10920 Ambassador Dr., Kansas City, MO 64153, (816)891-7070.*

KRAMER, Donald A.——**B:** Nov. 3, 1942, Trenton, NJ, *VP and Sr. Mort. Officer*, The Nat. State Bank, Mort. Dept.; **PRIM RE ACT:** Banker; **SERVICES:** Comml. and consumer mort. lending, includ1ng const. lending; **REP CLIENTS:** Maj. rgnl. devel.; **PREV EMPLOY:** CIT Financial; **PROFL AFFIL & HONORS:** Soc. of RE Appraisers; MBAA; Mort. Comm., NJ Bankers; **EDUC:** BS, 1972, Bus. Admin., Fin. and Commerce, Rider Coll.; **GRAD EDUC:** 1976, Banking, Stonier Grad. School of Banking, Rutgers Univ.; **EDUC HONORS:** Dean's List; **MIL SERV:** US Army, Spec. E4, Foreign Service Medal, Sharp Shooter; **OTHER ACT & HONORS:** Hamilton Township Bd. of Educ., Pres., 1976-1980; Numerous civic and fraternal Orgs.; Outstanding Young Man of America 1976; **HOME ADD:** 59 Acres Dr., Hamilton Square, NJ 08690; **BUS ADD:** 214 Smith St., PO Box 1316, Perth Amboy, NJ 08861, (201)324-1400.

KRAMER, Donald W.——**B:** Nov. 14, 1938, Philadelphia, PA, *Partner*, Montgomery, McCracken, Walker & Rhoads, RE; **PRIM RE ACT:** Attorney; **SERVICES:** Legal services; **PREV EMPLOY:** Deputy Devel. Coordinator and Asst. to the Mayor, City of Philadelphia; **PROFL AFFIL & HONORS:** Amer., PA and Philadelphia Bar Assns.; Mayor's Sci. and Tech. Council; Amer. Soc. for Public Admin.; **EDUC:** AB, 1960, Public and Intl. Affairs, Princeton Univ., Woodrow Wilson; **GRAD EDUC:** LLB, 1964, Harvard Law School; **EDUC HONORS:** Grad. with Honors; **OTHER ACT & HONORS:** Deputy Devel. Coord., 1968-1970; Asst. to the Mayor of Philadelphia, 1970-1972; Co-publisher, Delaware Valley Agenda, the magazine for nonprofit enterprise; Dir., Octavia Hill Assn.; **HOME ADD:** 2408 Golf Rd., Philadelphia, PA 19131, (215)879-8418; **BUS ADD:** Three Parkway, 20th Fl., Philadelphia, PA 19102, (215)563-0650.

KRAMER, John R.——**B:** May 11, 1939, Pittsburgh, PA, *Pres.*, Carey, Kramer, Crouse & Associates, Inc.; **OTHER RE ACT:** RE fin./mort. banking; **SERVICES:** Debt & equity fin. for maj. real estate ventures; **REP CLIENTS:** Maj. instl. investors: Aetna Life & Casualty, CT Gen., Mutual Benefit Life, State Farm Life, Equitable Life of IA, Commonwealth of PA Sch. Employees Retirement Fund, Dollar Savings Bank of Pittsburgh; **PREV EMPLOY:** Pres., Century RE Fin., Pittsburgh, PA; Sr. VP, James W. Rouse & Co., Columbia, MD; Indus. Engr., US Steel Corp., Pittsburgh, PA; **PROFL AFFIL & HONORS:** Mort. Bankers Assn. of Pittsburgh; Intl. Council of Shopping Ctrs.; **EDUC:** BS, 1961, Bus./Indus. Engrg., Bus. Sch.; **MIL SERV:** USCG, Radioman; **OTHER ACT & HONORS:** The PA Soc.; Former Chmn., Greater Pittsburgh Housing Council; Former Pres., Mort. Bankers Assn. of Pittsburgh; **HOME ADD:** 135 Wilmar Dr., Pittsburgh, PA 15238, (412)963-7947; **BUS ADD:** 730 Grant Bldg., Pittsburgh, PA 15219, (412)281-8714.

KRAMER, Keith M.——**B:** Nov. 8, 1949, Boonville, MO, *Pres.*, Keith M. Kramer RE; **PRIM RE ACT:** Broker, Consultant, Developer, Instructor, Owner/Investor, Syndicator; **SERVICES:** Brokerage investment counseling, site selection, market and feasibility analysis, devel. and synd. of comml. RE; **REP CLIENTS:** Major Corps., fin. instit., indiv. and instit. investors in income producing prop.; **PREV EMPLOY:** Bank Bldg. and Equipment Corp., City of St. Louis Plan Commn.; **PROFL AFFIL & HONORS:** Home Builders Assn.; **EDUC:** AB, 1972, Poli. Sci. - Urban Politics, Univ. of MO; **GRAD EDUC:** MA, 1976, Urban Affairs - Urban Econ., Wash. Univ. - St. Louis; **EDUC HONORS:** Curators Award; **HOME ADD:** 8796 Fern Glen Drive, St. Louis, MO 63126; **BUS ADD:** 1221 Locust St., Suite 201, St. Louis, MO 63103, (314)621-2311.

KRAMER, Klaus——*Dir. Corp. Const. & Plng.*, ROLM Corp.; **PRIM RE ACT:** Property Manager; **BUS ADD:** 4900 Old Ironside Dr., Santa Clara, CA 95050, (408)988-2900.*

KRAMER, Russell P., Jr.——**B:** Apr. 30, 1940, Washington, DC, *CPA*; **PRIM RE ACT:** Broker, Consultant, Owner/Investor, Syndicator; **SERVICES:** Broker, synd. of investment prop., tax planning and investment counseling; **REP CLIENTS:** Indiv. and corp. investors; **PREV EMPLOY:** The Klingbeil Co., VP, Synd.; Pulte Corp., Controller; **PROFL AFFIL & HONORS:** RE Broker; **EDUC:** BS, 1963, Acctg., Univ. of Denver; **OTHER ACT & HONORS:** CPA; **HOME ADD:** 3812 E. Briarwood Ave., Littleton, CO 80122, (303)771-0726; **BUS ADD:** 10395 W. Colfax Ave., Suite 315, Lakewood, CO 80215, (303)234-0600.

KRANZ, Lloyd R.——**B:** Apr. 15, 1940, Williamsport, PA, *VP*, True-Kranz RE, Inc., Comml., Investment, Land; **PRIM RE ACT:** Broker, Developer, Owner/Investor; **SERVICES:** Sub-div., devel. of comml. & resid. prop., sales of investment, comml., indus. RE; **PREV EMPLOY:** The Burlington Free Press, 1965-76, Newspaper Advt. Dir., Adv. Mgr, Classified Adv. Mgr., 1965-76, Adv. Sales Rep. 1958-65, at Williamsport Sun Gazette Co.; **PROFL AFFIL & HONORS:** RNMI; **MIL SERV:** USAR, Sgt. E-5; **OTHER ACT & HONORS:** S Burlington Kiwanis Club, Past Pres., School COB, Dir. Burlington Boys Club, C of C, various fund drives, Medical Ctr. Hosp. Assn.; **HOME ADD:** 23 Scotsdale Rd., S Burlington, VT 05401, (802)863-4805; **BUS ADD:** 217 S Union St., Burlington, VT 05401, (802)658-6288.

KRANZDORF, Norman M.——**B:** Sept. 28, 1930, Hanover, PA, *Pres.*, Kranzco Realty, Inc.; **PRIM RE ACT:** Broker, Consultant, Developer, Owner/Investor; **PREV EMPLOY:** Pres. of Amterre Devel., Inc.; **PROFL AFFIL & HONORS:** Intl. Council of Shopping Ctrs.; PA Bar Assn.; New Amer. Network; **EDUC:** BA, 1952, Eng., Dickinson Coll.; **GRAD EDUC:** LLB, 1955, Corp., Univ. of PA Law School; **HOME ADD:** 340 Sprague Rd., Narberth, PA 19072; **BUS ADD:** 115 Cynwyd Rd., Bala Cynwyd, PA 19004, (215)668-9200.

KRASNER, Sanford——**B:** Sept. 29, 1920, Newark, NJ, *Pres.*, Krasner & Co.; **PRIM RE ACT:** Broker, Consultant, Appraiser, Owner/Investor, Property Manager; **REP CLIENTS:** State of NJ, Numerous Municipalities, Corporations, Banks, Savings & Loans, Individuals; **PROFL AFFIL & HONORS:** Past Pres. RE Bd. of Newark, Past Pres. NJ Chap. AIREA, Past VP NJ Chap. IREM, Pauel Member Amer. Arbitration Fund, CPM, MAI; **EDUC:** BS, Bus. Admin., 1934, Bus., LeHigh Univ.; **MIL SERV:** US Army, Capt.; **HOME ADD:** 89 Lowell Ave., W. Orange, NJ 07052, (201)731-5636; **BUS ADD:** 60 Park Pl., Newark, NJ 07102, (201)622-1570.

KRASNOFF, Eric——*Dir. Adm.*, Pall Corp.; **PRIM RE ACT:** Property Manager; **BUS ADD:** 30 Sea Cliff Ave., Glen Cove, NY 11542, (516)671-4000.*

KRASNOW, William D.——*Mgr. RE Aquisition*, Digital Equipment Corp.; **PRIM RE ACT:** Property Manager; **BUS ADD:** 200 Baker Ave., W. Concord, MA 01742, (617)897-5111.*

KRATOVIL, Robert——**B:** May 21, 1910, Oshkosh, WI, *Prof.*, John Marshall Law School, RE Transactions; **PRIM RE ACT:** Instructor; **OTHER RE ACT:** Author; **PREV EMPLOY:** Chief Title Officer: Chicago Title & Trust Co.; Gen. Counsel, Chicago Title Ins. Co.;

GRAD EDUC: JD, 1933; **EDUC HONORS:** Pi Gamma Mu; Lambda Alpha (honor frats.); **OTHER ACT & HONORS:** Author of: *RE Law* (7th Ed. 1979) (with Raymond J. Werner), *Modern Mortgage Law & Practice* (2nd Ed., 1981) (with Raymond J. Werner), *Modern RE Documentation* (1975), *Buying, Owning & Selling a Home in the 1980s* (with Ruth Kratovil); All published by Prentice-Hall; numerous articles in legal periodicals; **HOME ADD:** 2772 Garrison Ave., Evanston, IL 60201, (312)869-0772; **BUS ADD:** 315 So. Plymouth Ct., Chicago, IL 60604, (312)427-2737.

KRATZ, Donald W.——**B:** Sept. 4, 1943, Lansdale, PA, *Partner*, Kratz Associates, Resid.; **PRIM RE ACT:** Broker, Consultant, Appraiser, Instructor, Property Manager; **SERVICES:** Resid. resales, new const. appraisals, consulting, investments; **PREV EMPLOY:** Dir., Schlicher Kratz Inst. of RE; Instr., Penn State Univ.; **PROFL AFFIL & HONORS:** No. PA Bd. of Realtors; PA Assn. Realtors; NAR; RNMI, GRI; CRS; CRB; **EDUC:** 1964-65, Bus. Admin., Univ. of HI; **MIL SERV:** US Army, Sgt. E-5, Air Medal, 1962-1965; **OTHER ACT & HONORS:** Para Legal Cert., Penn State; Outstanding Young Man of Amer., 1975 & 1980; **HOME ADD:** 630 Conestoga Ln., Lansdale, PA 19446, (215)855-1066; **BUS ADD:** POB 131, Sunneyforce Sq., Lansdale, PA 19446, (215)368-6106.

KRATZ, Kent P.——**B:** Apr. 28, 1923, Sidney, NE, *Area Counsel*, HUD; **PRIM RE ACT:** Attorney, Owner/Investor; **PREV EMPLOY:** VP, Nat. Bank of Commerce; Private Law Practice; and Gen. Atty., Cudahy Packing Co.; **PROFL AFFIL & HONORS:** NE & Amer. Bar Assns., ABA; **EDUC:** AB, 1947, Pol. Sci. & Eng., Univ. of NE; **GRAD EDUC:** JD, 1950, Univ. of NE; **MIL SERV:** US Army, Capt., Bronze Star; **HOME ADD:** 12041 Douglas St., Omaha, NE 68154, (402)334-1451; **BUS ADD:** Univac Bldg., 7100 W Center Rd., Omaha, NE 68106, (402)221-9316.

KRAUS, Harold C.——**B:** May 12, 1935, Brooklyn, NY, *Pres.*, West Ledge Corp./The Performance Org.; **PRIM RE ACT:** Developer, Builder, Owner/Investor, Property Manager; **SERVICES:** Devel. planning, prop. mgr., const. mgmt.; **REP CLIENTS:** Fortune 500 cos.; **PROFL AFFIL & HONORS:** BSCA, BOMA; **EDUC:** BA, 1957, Geology, Colgate Univ.; **GRAD EDUC:** MBA, 1966, Bus., Univ. of CT; **EDUC HONORS:** Cum Laude; **MIL SERV:** USAF; **OTHER ACT & HONORS:** Young Pres. Org., BOD, Hartford Symphony; **HOME ADD:** P O Box 127, W. Hartford, CT 06107; **BUS ADD:** 11 School St., E. Granby, CT 06026, (203)653-7217.

KRAUS, Richard W.——**B:** Oct. 18, 1953, Baltimore, MD, *Owner and Pres.*, Kraus & Stolzenberg; **PRIM RE ACT:** Consultant, Developer; **SERVICES:** Devel., fin., leasing and managing of RE props.; shopping ctrs., malls, office bldgs. and specialty projects; **PREV EMPLOY:** RE Mgr. for the A&P Food Co.; Devel. of shopping ctrs., malls and office bldgs. for PENSCO, the Devel. Co. for Frank S. Phillips, Inc.; **PROFL AFFIL & HONORS:** NACORE; **EDUC:** BA, 1976, Mktg., Loyola Coll.; **GRAD EDUC:** MBA, Mktg./Fin., Loyola Coll.; **EDUC HONORS:** Dean's List; **OTHER ACT & HONORS:** Authoring a RE Book "The Art of Comml. RE Leasing" to be published in 1982 by I.B.P., a subs. of Prentice Hall; **BUS ADD:** 865 Coachway, Annapolis, MD 21401, (301)841-5182.

KRAUS, Ted——**B:** May 13, 1945, NJ, *Pres.*, Ted Kraus & Co.; **PRIM RE ACT:** Consultant, Real Estate Publisher; **OTHER RE ACT:** Publisher of Retail Vacancy Reporter; **SERVICES:** Retail RE consultant & troubleshooter; **REP CLIENTS:** Homart Devel., Lila Nay's Good Time Emporium, Mangels Rt. 18 Intl. Mkt., Zeeman Mfg. Brentwood Property; **PREV EMPLOY:** Arlen Shopping Ctrs.; Ups N Downs, Proving Ground; Hit or Miss; United Skates Roller Skating; **PROFL AFFIL & HONORS:** Nat. Assn. of Corp. RE Execs.; Intl. Council of Shopping Centers; **EDUC:** BS, 1967, Bus., Bloomfield Coll.; **HOME ADD:** 999 Hidden Lake Dr. #8D, N. Brunswick, NJ 08902, (201)821-6175; **BUS ADD:** 999 Hidden Lake Dr. #8D, N. Brunswick, NJ 08902, (201)821-7840.

KRAUSE, David H.——**B:** Mar. 23, 1945, Kalamazoo, MI; **PRIM RE ACT:** Consultant, Appraiser, Developer; **SERVICES:** RE Valuation & Investment Consultation; **PROFL AFFIL & HONORS:** AIREA, Soc. of RE Appraisers, MAI, SRPA; **EDUC:** BS, 1967, MI State Univ.; **GRAD EDUC:** MS, 1970, MI State Univ.; **MIL SERV:** US Army Artillery, 2nd Lt.; **HOME ADD:** 231 Beal St., E. Lansing, MI 48823, (517)351-6088; **BUS ADD:** 1710 E. Michigan Ave., Lansing, MI 48912.

KRAUSE, Edwin L.——**B:** Oct. 17, 1922, Genoa City, WI, *Pres.*, Allied Realty Co.; **PRIM RE ACT:** Broker, Consultant, Appraiser, Developer, Instructor, Property Manager; **OTHER RE ACT:** Expert Witness; **PROFL AFFIL & HONORS:** Greater Mason City Bd. of Realtors & Multiple Listing Exch. IA Assn. of Realtors, NAR, IREM, CPM, GRI, Cert. VA Appraiser, Condemnation Appraiser, City of Mason City; **EDUC:** BA, 1946, Bus. Admin., Alumni Award Winner, Grinnell Coll.; **GRAD EDUC:** 1947-1948, Acctg., State Univ. of IA; **MIL SERV:** USN, Commanding Officer, USS 271 1st, Lt (j.g.), WW II Pacific Theatre; **OTHER ACT & HONORS:** Dir. & Sec., All Veterans Social Ctr. of Clear Lake, IA which owns C.L. Golf & Ctry. Club; Land Baron, Owns Land in all 50 states, Dir., NAR 1978-1979-1980; 2nd longest tenure, Exec. Comm., IA Assn. of Realtors; Longest Service, Bd. of Dirs., Greater Mason City Bd. of Realtors, Only Honorary Life Member, Crystal Lake, IL Athletics Boosters; **HOME ADD:** 200 Fairway Dr., Shorewood Hills, Clear Lake, IA 50428, (515)357-4706; **BUS ADD:** One Allied Alley, 1530 S. Federal Ave., Mason City, IA 50401, (515)423-0314.

KRAUSE, George F.——*VP Fin. & Treas.*, International Rectifier Corp.; **PRIM RE ACT:** Property Manager; **BUS ADD:** 9220 Sunset Blvd., Los Angeles, CA 90069, (213)278-3100.*

KREIDER, Daniel J.——**B:** Apr. 8, 1927, Lebanon, PA, *Broker-Realtor-Pres. of Corp.*, Penn Ave. Real Estate, Inc.; **PRIM RE ACT:** Broker, Appraiser, Builder, Owner/Investor, Property Manager; **SERVICES:** Listing & selling of RE, appraisals, builder of new homes; **REP CLIENTS:** ALCOA, Bethlehem Steel Corp., Rhom & Hass Co., Executrans, Inc., Transamerica Relocation Service, Inc., Relocation Realty Service Corp.; **PREV EMPLOY:** Building construction, building material salesman; **PROFL AFFIL & HONORS:** Lebanon Cty. Bd. of Realtors, Inc.; Lebanon Cty. MLS Serv.; PA Assn. of Realtors; NAR; PA Bldrs. Assn.; Lebanon Cty. Bldrs. Assn.; Lebanon Cty. C of C Assn., Past Pres. Lebanon Cty. Bd. of Realtors Inc.; **GRAD EDUC:** 1945, Attended Lebanon Bus. Coll., completed six Continuing Educ. Courses in RE with PA State Univ.; **MIL SERV:** US Army 1950-1952, Cpl., Korean Serv.; **OTHER ACT & HONORS:** Served as Chmn. of Cleona Zoning Bd.; Free & Accepted Masons of PA Lodge 226; Scottish Rite of Harrisburg; AAONMS Zembo Temple, Harrisburg, PA; **HOME ADD:** 1 E. Penn Ave., Cleona, PA 17042, (717)273-8894; **BUS ADD:** 1 E. Penn Ave., Cleona, PA 17042, (717)273-8894.

KREIMER, A. Jonathan——**B:** Feb. 22, 1953, Pittsburgh, PA, *Sr. RE Analyst*, Penn Mutual Life Ins. Co.; **PRIM RE ACT:** Owner/Investor; **PREV EMPLOY:** Waldbaum, Rockower & Co., CPA's, Philadelphia, PA; **PROFL AFFIL & HONORS:** Amer. Inst. of CPA's; PA Inst. of CPA's, CPA; **EDUC:** BS, 1975, Psych. Measurement, Univ. of Pittsburgh; **GRAD EDUC:** MBA, 1978, Acctg., Temple Univ.; **EDUC HONORS:** Dept. Honors; **HOME ADD:** 78-8 Van Buren Rd., Voorhees, NJ 08043, (609)772-9017; **BUS ADD:** Independence Sq., Philadelphia, PA 19172, (215)629-0600.

KREINZ, Robert L.——**B:** June 10, 1934, Beloit, WI, *Pres.*, Rowland Securities Corp.; **PRIM RE ACT:** Broker, Syndicator; **OTHER RE ACT:** RE Ltd. Partnership; **PROFL AFFIL & HONORS:** Nat. Bd. of Realtors, RESSI, Intl. Assn. of Fin. Planners; **EDUC:** BA, 1956, Beloit Coll.; **HOME ADD:** 212 S. East Ave., Waukesha, WI 53186, (414)542-0342; **BUS ADD:** 12970 W. Bluemound Rd., Elm Grove, WI 53122.

KREISER, Frank D.——**B:** Sept. 20, 1930, Minneapolis, MN, *Pres.*, Frank Kreiser RE Inc., 1966; **PRIM RE ACT:** Broker, Developer, Property Manager, Owner/Investor, Insuror; **SERVICES:** Corp. Reloc., Residential Sales & Mktg.; **REP CLIENTS:** Corp. Transferees, Home Sellers, Home Builders; **PROFL AFFIL & HONORS:** NAR, RNMI, ERC, Minneapolis Bd. Realtors, CRS & CRB & Cert. Residential Broker; **EDUC:** U of MN; **MIL SERV:** US Army, Korea; **OTHER ACT & HONORS:** Founder-Chmn. of Bd.Translo Atlanta, GA 1976-1981, Decathlon Athletic Club, Outward Bound; **HOME ADD:** Edina, MN, (612)920-1053; **BUS ADD:** 5036 France Ave. S, Minneapolis, MN 55410, (612)920-1091.

KRELL, William A.——**B:** July 1, 1948, Chicago, IL, *Pres.*, The Krell Co.; **PRIM RE ACT:** Broker, Consultant; **PREV EMPLOY:** Hotel/restaurant devel. mgmt. & consulting; **PROFL AFFIL & HONORS:** RNMI; Natl., State & Local Realtors Inst. Cert.; RESSI, GRI; CCIM; CBC; **EDUC:** BSBA, 1970, Mgmt. & Fin., School of Hotel & Rest. Mgmt.; Univ. of Denver; **OTHER ACT & HONORS:** W Towne Optimist Club, Past Pres.; W. Branch YMCA, Past Pres.; **HOME ADD:** 6893 Midtown Rd., Madison, WI 53711, (608)845-9846; **BUS ADD:** 6893 Midtown Rd., Madison, WI 53711, (608)845-9847.

KRESBACH, Michael L.——**B:** June 10, 1950, Pensacola, FL, *Pres.*, Realty South; **PRIM RE ACT:** Broker, Consultant, Developer, Builder, Owner/Investor; **SERVICES:** Complete brokerage serv., investment counseling; **PREV EMPLOY:** SE Realty and Investment Prop., Inc. 1975-1980; **PROFL AFFIL & HONORS:** NAR, Talahassee Builders Assn.; Tallahassee Hist. Soc. and Preservation Bd.; **EDUC:** BS, 1973, Mgmt./RE, FL State Univ.; **GRAD EDUC:** 1974, Multi-family Devel./Planning Urban Rgnl. Planning, FL State Univ.;

EDUC HONORS: Dean's List, Cum Laude; **OTHER ACT & HONORS:** Little Bros. of Amer.; SAE Alumni, Pres. Club; **HOME ADD:** 5441 Sybil Ct., Bradfordville, FL 32308, (904)893-4004; **BUS ADD:** P.O. Box 4111, Tallahassee, FL 32303, (904)386-5301.

KRESGE, Walter——*Ed.*, NY State Society of Real Estate Appraisers, Appraisal Digest; **PRIM RE ACT:** Real Estate Publisher; **BUS ADD:** Executive Park Tower, Western Ave. at Fuller Rd., Albany, NY 12203, (518)482-4485.*

KRESIN, Bruce——*Urban Land Dev.*, Getty Oil Co.; **PRIM RE ACT:** Property Manager; **BUS ADD:** PO Box 54050, Los Angeles, CA 90054, (805)399-4456.*

KRETCHMAR, John F.——**B:** July 20, 1948, Chicago, IL, *Sales Dir.*, Habitat Co., Condo. Div.; **PRIM RE ACT:** Broker, Consultant, Developer; **SERVICES:** Condo. sales & mktg.; **REP CLIENTS:** American Invsco; First Condo. Co. (Sandburg Village 2700 units); **PREV EMPLOY:** Carl Sandburg Village, largest condo. conversion in USA; Amer. Invsco Realty, developing 2020 Lincoln Park W. to condo.; **PROFL AFFIL & HONORS:** Chicago RE Bd.; RESSI; **EDUC:** 1975, Acctg./Mgmt., Roosevelt Univ., Chicago; **GRAD EDUC:** MBA, 1976, Acctg./Mgmt., Roosevelt Univ., Chicago; **MIL SERV:** USN; Lt.; Purple Heart; **OTHER ACT & HONORS:** 400 E. Randolph Condo. Assn.; **HOME ADD:** PO Box 153, Argo, IL 60501, (312)284-1530; **BUS ADD:** 2020 N. Lincoln Park W., Chicago, IL 60614, (312)525-2020.

KRETSCH, J.A.——**B:** May 10, 1935, WI, *Owner*, J.A. Kretsch & Co.; **OTHER RE ACT:** Mort. Broker; **SERVICES:** Indus. & Comml. brokerage; **PREV EMPLOY:** IBM, Mobil Oil; **EDUC:** BS, 1962, Lakeland Coll., Plymouth, WI; **MIL SERV:** USAF, Sgt., 55-59; **HOME ADD:** 15 Essex Ct., Alamo, CA 94507, (415)838-9412; **BUS ADD:** 1 Maritime Plaza, Suite 1300, San Francisco, CA 94111, (415)986-7986.

KRETZSCHMAR, Angelina——**B:** July 19, 1946, San Antonio, TX, *Owner*, Kretzschmar Properties; **PRIM RE ACT:** Owner/Investor, Property Manager; **SERVICES:** Rental homes and duplexes; **PROFL AFFIL & HONORS:** San Antonio Apt. Assn., TX Apt. Assn., Nat. Apt. Assn., Assn. of Govt. Accts., Amer. Soc. of Mil. Comptrollers; **EDUC:** BBA, 1974, Personnel Mgmt., St. Mary's Univ., San Antonio; **EDUC HONORS:** Cum Laude; **OTHER ACT & HONORS:** Prince of Peace Lutheran Church, San Antonio; **HOME ADD:** 6314 Meadow Grove, San Antonio, TX 78239, (512)653-4205; **BUS ADD:** 6314 Meadow Grove, San Antonio, TX 78239, (512)653-4205.

KREVLIN, Sol——**B:** Feb. 23, 1928, Port Chester, NY, *Sr. VP*, Coldwell Banke/Commercial RE Services, Comml. RE; **PRIM RE ACT:** Broker; **SERVICES:** Leasing, Sales, & Consulting; **PREV EMPLOY:** Sutton & Towne Inc.; **PROFL AFFIL & HONORS:** RE Bd. of NY; **EDUC:** BS in Bus. Admin., 1949, Bus. Admin., Syracu Univ.; **OTHER ACT & HONORS:** Sacia, Quaker Ridge Golf Club; **HOME ADD:** 1023 Old White Plains Rd., (914)698-9140; **BUS ADD:** 1600 Summer St., Stamford, CT 06905, (203)329-7900.

KRIEGER, Jean——**B:** Nov. 5, 1941, Columbus, OH, *VP*, M/I Schottenstein Co.; **OTHER RE ACT:** CPA; **SERVICES:** Acctg., Tax Planning, Gen. Bus. Advisor; **PREV EMPLOY:** Deloitte, Haskins & Sells - Concentrated in Taxes and RE; **PROFL AFFIL & HONORS:** AICPA, OH Soc. CPA's, Amer. Soc. of Women Accountants and Amer. Woman's Soc. CPA's, CPA; **EDUC:** BS Bus. Admin., 1963, Acctg., Capital Univ.; **EDUC HONORS:** Tau Pi Phi Honorary Bus. Soc.; **OTHER ACT & HONORS:** Currently Bd. Member of OH Soc. of CPAs and Treas. for Amer. Soc. of Women Accountants; **HOME ADD:** 3963 Fairlington Dr., Columbus, OH 43220, (614)451-8615; **BUS ADD:** 1855 E. Dublin-Granville Rd., Columbus, OH 43229, (614)436-5600.

KRIEGER, Robert S.——**B:** Dec. 16, 1947, NYC, NY, *VP*, Berman & Brickell, Inc.; An affiliate of Lehman Bros. Kuhn Loeb Inc., Leasing, Comml. & Retail; **PRIM RE ACT:** Broker; **PROFL AFFIL & HONORS:** RE Bd. of NY, Inc., Young Men's RE Assn.; **EDUC:** BS/BA, 1970, Investments, Babson Coll., Wellesley, MA; **GRAD EDUC:** MBA, 1971, Acctg., Babson Coll., Wellesley, MA; **EDUC HONORS:** Cum Laude; **HOME ADD:** 333 E 79th St., New York, NY 10021, (212)744-9352; **BUS ADD:** 1251 Avenue of the Americas, New York, NY 10020, (212)541-4337.

KRIEGSFELD, Lee J.——**B:** Feb. 23, 1949, Rochester, NY, *Exec. Dir.*, St. Clair Cty. Housing Auth.; **PRIM RE ACT:** Broker, Instructor, Developer, Property Manager; **SERVICES:** Prop. Mgmt., dev. rehab. and fin.; **PREV EMPLOY:** Material Systems Corp. Pittsburgh Housing Auth. and City of Cleveland; **PROFL AFFIL & HONORS:** NAHRO, IREM, CPM, Grad. School of Mort. Banking; **EDUC:** BA, 1970, Urban & Environmental Studies, Case Western Reserve; **GRAD EDUC:** M of Public Admin, 1972, Univ. of Pittsburgh; **OTHER ACT & HONORS:** Instr., Belleville Area Coll.; **HOME ADD:** 15 Kenwood, Belleville, IL 62221; **BUS ADD:** 100 N 48th St, Belleville, IL 62223, (618)277-3290.

KRIGEL, A. Arnold——**B:** Mar 6, 1936, NY, NY, *Dir. Facilities Admin.*, Ogden Corp.; **PRIM RE ACT:** Architect, Consultant, Appraiser, Developer, Builder, Owner/Investor; **OTHER RE ACT:** Responsible for all the RE and Facility acquisitions and RE disposition for the corp.; **PREV EMPLOY:** Xerox Corp., (1972-1977); IBM Corp. (1969-1972); **PROFL AFFIL & HONORS:** AIA, NACORE, IDRC (Dir. 1979-1981); **EDUC:** BArch, 1962, Carnegie Mellon Univ.; **MIL SERV:** USN; **HOME ADD:** 5 Lakeview Ave. E., Peekskill, NY 10566, (914)737-1724; **BUS ADD:** 277 Park Ave., NY, NY 10017, (212)572-4086.

KRIGER, Alvin H.——**B:** Oct. 10, 1942, Memphis, TN, *Gen. Partner*, Source Capital, a Ltd. Partnership; **PRIM RE ACT:** Syndicator; **PREV EMPLOY:** Partner - Law Firm, Weiss, Stevee, Berzowski & Kriger, 1973-1981; **PROFL AFFIL & HONORS:** ABA; RESSI; WI Bar Assn., JD, LLM (in taxation); **EDUC:** BS, 1964, Philosophy, Univ. of WI; **GRAD EDUC:** JD, 1967, Univ. of WI; LLM, 1968, Taxation, NYU; **EDUC HONORS:** Dean's List; **HOME ADD:** 8455 N. Fielding Rd., Milwaukee, WI 53217, (414)351-0766; **BUS ADD:** 735 N. Water St., Suite 921, Milwaukee, WI 53202, (414)272-7700.

KRIPPAEHNE, William W., Jr.——**B:** Feb 27, 1951, Portland, OR, *Sr. Vice President & Branch Manager*, Cushman & Wakefield of Washington, Inc.; **PRIM RE ACT:** Broker, Consultant, Appraiser, Property Manager; **REP CLIENTS:** Prudential Life Insurance, Daon, Quadrant Corp., Cadillac Fairview; **PREV EMPLOY:** Sr. VP & General Manager, The Gilley Co., A subsidiary of Cushman & Wakefield; **PROFL AFFIL & HONORS:** SIR, NAIOP, BOMA; **EDUC:** Bus./Pol. Sci., 1973, Fin. & Constitutional Law, Religion, Geology, OR State Univ.; **GRAD EDUC:** MBA, 1975, Fin. & Marketing, OR State Univ.; **EDUC HONORS:** Grad. with honors; **HOME ADD:** 4502 NE #38, Seattle, WA 98105, (206)524-9636; **BUS ADD:** 720 Olive Way, Suite 500, Seattle, WA 98101, (206)682-0666.

KRISTIAN, Stanley——*Owner*, Stanley Kristian RE Nation-wide & Store Mart Realty; **PRIM RE ACT:** Broker, Consultant, Owner/Investor, Property Manager, Syndicator; **SERVICES:** Investment Props. Land & Sites Planning Consultants, Mort., Feasibility Studies, Appraisals Store Leasing, Prop. Mgmt., Leasing Office & Indus. Space; **BUS ADD:** 2 Nelson Ave., Hicksville, NY 11801, (516)822-8359.

KRISTOL, Daniel M.——**B:** July 7, 1936, Wilmington, DE, *Dir.*, Prickett, Jones, Elliott, Kristol & Schnee, P.A.; **PRIM RE ACT:** Attorney; **SERVICES:** legal counsel for builders, devels, investors and borrowers; **REP CLIENTS:** DE State Housing Authority; Homequity, Inc.; Ernest DiSabatino & Sons, Inc.; Bellevue Holding Co.; Petrillo Brothers, Inc.; and other contractors, const. mgrs., devels., investors, brokers, and prop. mgrs. for both resid. and comml. RE; **PREV EMPLOY:** Asst. City Solicitor (Wilmington, DE 1968-70; **PROFL AFFIL & HONORS:** ABA, DE Bar Assn.; **EDUC:** BA, 1958, Eng., Univ. of PA; **GRAD EDUC:** LLB, 1961, Univ. of PA; **MIL SERV:** US Army Res., DE Nat. Guard; **HOME ADD:** 815 Augusta Rd., Wilmington, DE 19807, (302)655-7084; **BUS ADD:** 1310 King St., PO 1328, Wilmington, DE 19899, (302)658-5102.

KRITZ, Michael H.——**B:** Apr. 27, 1945, Fulton, MO, *Pres.*, The Triton Co., RE Inc.; **PRIM RE ACT:** Broker, Owner/Investor, Property Manager, Syndicator; **SERVICES:** Comml. prop., brokerage mgmt., synd.; **REP CLIENTS:** Indiv., partnership & Instnl. investors; **PREV EMPLOY:** Pres., 1976-80 Hardin Inc., Prop. Mgmt. firm; **PROFL AFFIL & HONORS:** IREM, Dallas Apt. Assn., TX Apt. Assn., NAA, RESSI, CPM; **EDUC:** BS, 1967, Geology, Math., Physics, Western IL Univ.; **GRAD EDUC:** MS (23 hrs. toward), Geophysics, Univ. of AZ; **MIL SERV:** US Army, 1st Lt.; **HOME ADD:** 6131 Glendora, Dallas, TX 75230, (214)696-1518; **BUS ADD:** 11300 N Central, Dallas, TX 75243, (214)387-9200.

KROM, David B.——**B:** Apr. 25, 1931, Marshfield, WI, *Partner*, Krom & Schmidt, Attorneys at Law; **PRIM RE ACT:** Attorney; **SERVICES:** Legal; **REP CLIENTS:** Indiv. sellers and buyers, devel., realtors, indiv. lessors and lessees; **PREV EMPLOY:** Deputy County Atty., Condemnations; **PROFL AFFIL & HONORS:** OR State Bar; State Bar of AZ; ABA; OR Trial Lawyers Assn.; **EDUC:** BS, 1961, Pol. Sci., Univ. of WI; **GRAD EDUC:** JD, 1965, Law, Univ. of AZ; LLM, 1971, Intl. Law, So. Methodist Univ.; **EDUC HONORS:** Senior Honors, Dean's List, Law Review; **MIL SERV:** U.S. Army, Cpl., 1952-1954; **OTHER ACT & HONORS:** Lincoln City C of C; Kiwanis; Bd. of Dir., Roads End Improvement Assn., SRA Course 101; **HOME ADD:** POB 65, Lincoln City, OR 97367, (503)994-5875; **BUS**

ADD: 2137 N.W. Hwy. 101, Suite B, POB 10, Lincoln City, OR 97367, (503)994-9188.

KROMELOW, Michael B.——**B:** Mar. 29, 1951, Chicago, IL, Jones, Lang, Wootton, Investment; **PRIM RE ACT:** Consultant; **SERVICES:** Investment, project devel., mgmt., leasing & appraisal; **REP CLIENTS:** Pension funds, ins. cos., indiv., prop. devel. from UK, US, Europe and Far East in US and Canadian RE; **PREV EMPLOY:** Mutual of NY, 1976-1980; Wells Fargo Realty Advisors, 1980; Hunter Realty Trust 1973-1975 (Boston); **EDUC:** BS, 1972, Advertising/Journalism, Univ. of WI; **GRAD EDUC:** 1979, NYU, RE Inst.; **HOME ADD:** 8940 Wonderland Ave., Los Angeles, CA 90046; **BUS ADD:** 523 W. Sixth St., Suite 220, Los Angeles, CA 90014, (213)624-2800.

KRONE, Norman B.——**B:** Sept. 13, 1938, Memphis, TN, *Sr. VP*, Walgreen Co., Physical Resources; **PRIM RE ACT:** Attorney, Developer, Builder, Owner/Investor; **OTHER RE ACT:** Corp. mgmt.; **PREV EMPLOY:** Montgomery Ward Property Corp., 1967-75; **PROFL AFFIL & HONORS:** ICSC Small Ctr. Devels. Comm.; Member, Bd. of Govs. of Metro. Housing & Planning Council of Chicago; Member of Advisory Bd. of Shopping Ctr. World Magazine; Past Tr. ICSC Retailing Advisory Comm., ICSC Tenant's Comm. Chmn. -1977-78, BCA 1976 Affirmative Action Award; Featured Speaker, 1977 SPECS; **GRAD EDUC:** LLB, 1964, Stetson Univ. Coll. of Law; **EDUC HONORS:** Editor Law School Publication; **OTHER ACT & HONORS:** Acting Municipal Judge, Tampa, FL, 1964-67; Elgin Ctry Club; Member Bd. of Dirs. Myers Indus.; **HOME ADD:** 6 N. 622 Fair Oaks Dr., St. Charles, IL 60174, (312)584-4256; **BUS ADD:** 200 Wilmot Rd., Deerfield, IL 60015, (312)948-5000.

KRONER, Gary——**B:** Nov. 6, 1940, Green Bay, WI, *Broker Assoc.*, RE/Max of Boulder; **PRIM RE ACT:** Broker, Consultant, Owner/Investor; **SERVICES:** Resid. Mkt. Evaluations, Mktg. & Consulting; **PROFL AFFIL & HONORS:** GRI, CRS, RESSI, Recipient of RE/Max "100% Club" award; **EDUC:** BSEE, 1965, Univ. of WI-Madison; **HOME ADD:** 2202 Kalmia Ave., Boulder, CO 80302, (303)443-3000; **BUS ADD:** 1810-30th St., Boulder, CO 80301, (303)449-7000.

KRUEGER, Donald A.——**B:** July 6, 1928, West Union, IA, *V.P.*, Banco Mort. Co., Resid. Fin.; **OTHER RE ACT:** Mort. banking; **SERVICES:** Branch mgr., admin. at Dubuque and all areas of res. fin., Rochester, MN; **PREV EMPLOY:** Contract Dept., Sunray D-X Oil Co.; **PROFL AFFIL & HONORS:** MBA, SREA, R.E. Broker State of IA; **EDUC:** 1952, Liberal Arts, Edu., Wartburg Coll., Waverly, IA; **MIL SERV:** USN, PO 3rd , Korean Conflict; **OTHER ACT & HONORS:** Community Housing Resource Bd., Rochester, MN, Instructor for Principles of R.E. GRI-1, Continuing Edu. and Ext. for MN; **HOME ADD:** 710 29 St. N.W., Rochester, MN 55901, (507)282-4386; **BUS ADD:** 1530 Hwy. #52, P.O. Box 6610, Rochester, MN 55903, (507)289-0768.

KRUER, Patrick——**B:** Mar. 3, 1945, Hart, MI, *Managing Partner*, Patrick Devel. Co.; **PRIM RE ACT:** Consultant, Developer, Lender, Builder, Owner/Investor, Property Manager, Syndicator; **SERVICES:** Investment counseling, resid. & comml. devel. and joint ventures; **PROFL AFFIL & HONORS:** Member of Bd. of Dir. of the Fed. Home Loan Bank of San Francisco, VChmn. of the CA Housing Fin. Agency, Housing Commnr. City of San Diego, 1978 Builder of the Year for Meritorious Serv. by Home Buyers Guide Magazine 1979 HOW Award by the San Diego & CA Home Owners Council; **OTHER ACT & HONORS:** Member of the Bd. San Diego Symphony & Natural Hist. Museum; **HOME ADD:** 3311 Ocean Front Walk, San Diego, CA 92109; **BUS ADD:** 2643 4th Ave., San Diego, CA 92109, (714)231-3637.

KRUK, Richard——*VP, Gen. Counsel & Secy.*, Joslyn Mfg. & Supply Co.; **PRIM RE ACT:** Attorney; **BUS ADD:** 2 North Riverside Plaza, Chicago, IL 60606, (312)454-2900.*

KRULL, Dana L.——**B:** Sept. 22, 1944, Goshen, IN, *Pres.*, Dana L. Krull, Inc.; **OTHER RE ACT:** CPA; **SERVICES:** Tax & Accounting Consultation; **REP CLIENTS:** Small investors in the Resid. Rental Market; **PROFL AFFIL & HONORS:** Amer. Inst. of CPA's and Indiana Assn. of CPA's; **EDUC:** BS, 1966, Bus. Admin., Manchester Coll.; **HOME ADD:** 502 S. 1st, Pierceton, IN 46562, (219)594-2002; **BUS ADD:** St. Rd. #13, South Pierceton, IN 46562, (219)594-2002.

KRUMSICK, Herbert J.——**B:** May 30, 1943, Pittsburg, KS, *Sales Mgr.*, J.P. Weigand & Sons, Realtors, Comml. Indus. Div.; **PRIM RE ACT:** Broker, Instructor, Owner/Investor; **PROFL AFFIL & HONORS:** SIR, AMA, NAIOP, Salesman of the yr.(WMBOR), Past Pres. (CCIM), Nat. Seminar Chmn.(SIR); CCIM; **GRAD EDUC:** BBA, 1965, Wichita State Univ.; **OTHER ACT & HONORS:** BOD-Wichita YMCA 1971 to present; BOD Century Club WSU 1973-present; BOD Letterman's Club WSU 1973 to present; **HOME ADD:** 8702 Stoneridge, Wichita, KS 67206, (316)685-4436; **BUS ADD:** 150 N. Market St., Wichita, KS 67202, (316)262-6404.

KRUPKA, Robert J.——**B:** Aug. 15, 1942, Ft. Sill, OK, *RE Rep.*, Fabri-Centers of Amer.; **OTHER RE ACT:** Retailer; **PREV EMPLOY:** Sherwin-Williams Co., Reg. RE Mgr.; **PROFL AFFIL & HONORS:** Intl. Council of Shopping Ctrs.; **EDUC:** BBA, 1972, Mktg., Econ., Cleveland State Univ.; **EDUC HONORS:** Dean's List.; **MIL SERV:** US Air Nat. Guard, SP-5; **HOME ADD:** 12661 N. Star Dr., N. Royalton, OH 44133; **BUS ADD:** 23550 Commerce Park Rd., Beachwood, OH 44122, (216)464-2500.

KRUPNIK, Vee M.——*Asst. Sales VP*, Baird & Warner Inc., Comml. Investment Div.; **PRIM RE ACT:** Broker, Consultant, Owner/Investor, Instructor, Insuror, Syndicator; **OTHER RE ACT:** Lecturer; **SERVICES:** Comml. investment sales, sales of businesses, investment counseling, tax-deferred exchanges; **REP CLIENTS:** Lenders and indiv. or instl. investors in comml. props.; **PREV EMPLOY:** Weis, Voisin, Cannon (Members of the NY Stock Exchange) (Stock Broker); **PROFL AFFIL & HONORS:** IL RE Chapt. of Cert. Comml. Investment Members, CCIM, RESSI, ICSC, FIABCI, CPA RE; **EDUC:** BS, 1956, Acctg., Northwestern Univ.; **OTHER ACT & HONORS:** Dir., Chicago RE Bd.; Pres., Chicago RE Bd., Comml/Investment MLS; VP, IL Chap. of CCIM; **HOME ADD:** 5757 N Sheridan Rd., Chicago, IL 60660, (312)561-6565; **BUS ADD:** 115 S LaSalle St., 1700, Chicago, IL 60603, (312)368-5771.

KRUSE, John J.——**B:** Mar. 31, 1946, Casa Grande, AZ; **PRIM RE ACT:** Developer, Builder, Owner/Investor; **SERVICES:** Hotel ownership devel.; resort condo. devel. comml./indus. construction; **PREV EMPLOY:** Asst. Professor of Law, Univ. of SC Law School 1975-77; **EDUC:** BA, 1968, English Lit., Harvard Coll.; **GRAD EDUC:** JD, 1972, Harvard Law School, Cum Laude; **EDUC HONORS:** Cum Laude; **MIL SERV:** US Army Res.; Sp 4; **HOME ADD:** 225 Shoreline Dr., Columbia, SC 29210, (813)781-0690; **BUS ADD:** 1821 Pickens St., Columbia, SC 29201, (803)252-9500.

KRUSZEWSKI, Stanley——**B:** May 22, 1943, CT; **PRIM RE ACT:** Consultant, Developer, Owner/Investor, Syndicator; **SERVICES:** Re-hab and re-cycling; primarily resid.; **PREV EMPLOY:** Acquisitions and Devel. Mgmt.; Synd.; 10 yrs. in RE incldg. Gen. Inv. & Dev. Co., Boston; **EDUC:** BS, 1965, Engrg., US Coast Guard Academy; **GRAD EDUC:** MBA, 1971, Stanford Univ.; **MIL SERV:** USCG, Lcdr.; **BUS ADD:** 302 Winchester St., Newton Highlands, MA 02161, (617)965-5455.

KRUTTSCHNITT, Theodore H.——**B:** Jan. 14, 1943, San Mateo, CA, *Chmn. of the Bd.*, California Innkeepers; **PRIM RE ACT:** Owner/Investor; **SERVICES:** Purchase & operate for our own account hotels & motor hotels; **PREV EMPLOY:** President, Western Investment Realty; **PROFL AFFIL & HONORS:** Dir., CA Hotel & Motel Assn.; **EDUC:** BS, 1964, Acctg., Univ. of CA, Berkeley; **GRAD EDUC:** MBA, 1966, Fin., Harvard Bus. School; **EDUC HONORS:** Beta Alpha Psi; **OTHER ACT & HONORS:** Pres., Burlingame Rotary Club; **HOME ADD:** 130 Country Club Dr., Hillsborough, CA 94010; **BUS ADD:** 400 Primrose Rd., Suite 200, Burlingame, CA 94010, (415)348-7400.

KRYZANOWSKI, Richard——*Secy.*, Crown Cork & Seal; **PRIM RE ACT:** Property Manager; **BUS ADD:** 9300 Ashton Rd., Philadelphia, PA 19136, (215)698-5100.*

KUBESH, Kenneth——**B:** Sept. 25, 1942, Glendive, MT, *Pres.*, Kubesh Prop., Inc.; **PRIM RE ACT:** Broker, Developer, Owner/Investor; **PROFL AFFIL & HONORS:** Pres. Gateway Bd. of Realtors; Nat. Mktg. Assn.; FLI; **EDUC:** BS, 1966, Agric. Sci., MT State Univ.; **MIL SERV:** US Army, 1967-69, Sp 5; **HOME ADD:** P.O. Box 887, Glendive, MT 59330, (406)365-2023; **BUS ADD:** 322 S. Merrill Ave., Glendive, MT 59330, (406)365-5201.

KUBLY, Roger——**B:** July 19, 1950, Madison, WI, *Prop. Mgr.*, Management Specialists; **PRIM RE ACT:** Broker, Owner/Investor, Property Manager; **PROFL AFFIL & HONORS:** Realtor, CAM; **EDUC:** 1978, Univ. of WI, Madison; **MIL SERV:** US Army, Sp. 4; **HOME ADD:** 15 Mondale Ct., Madison, WI 53705, (608)238-0455; **BUS ADD:** 801 S. Gammon Rd., Madison, WI 53719, (608)271-2000.

KUEHL, Cliff W.——**B:** July 26, 1924, Milwaukee, WI, *Partner/General Manager*, CEBA Appraisal Associates; **PRIM RE ACT:** Appraiser, Assessor; **SERVICES:** Appraisals/valuations all prop., real & personal; **REP CLIENTS:** Comml., instnl., indus., pvt.; **PROFL AFFIL & HONORS:** Amer. Soc. Appraisers, Amer. Assn. of Cert. Appraisers, Nat. Assn. Independent Fee Appraisers, Intl. Inst. of Valuers, Intl. Org. of RE Appraisers, Nat. Assn. of Review Appraisers, Inst. of Bus.

Appraisers, Const. Specifications Inst., Federation of Cert. Appraisers; **MIL SERV:** Navy, SMCS, 15 various decorations; **OTHER ACT & HONORS:** Cert. Appraiser Assessor - State of WI; Various Fraternal Orders, DAV-FRA.; **HOME ADD:** 3445 Hollywood Lane, Brookfield, WI 53005, (414)781-1588; **BUS ADD:** POB 10154, Milwaukee, WI 53210, (414)781-1888.

KUEHNLE, Kenton L.——B: Nov. 10, 1945, Chicago, IL, *Atty.-at-Law*, Scott, Walker & Kuehnle; **PRIM RE ACT:** Attorney; **REP CLIENTS:** Ted Hobson (Condo. Converter); Primeland Properties; The Kissell Co.; **PREV EMPLOY:** Dunbar, Kienzle & Murphey, 1970-1977; Loveland, Collard, Clapham & Scott, Partner, 1977-1980; **PROFL AFFIL & HONORS:** Columbus Bar Assn., Real Prop. Comm., Chmn., 1976-1978; OH Bar Assn., Real Prop. Comm., Bd. of Gov., 1979-1982, Lecturer on title aspects of new condo. law for Amer. Land Title Assn.; Author of article in Capital Univ. Law Review on Condo. Law 'Condo. Revision in OH: A Nightmare for Devel. and the Courts' Vol. 9, Number 2; **EDUC:** BA, 1967, Pol. Sci., Augustana Coll.; **GRAD EDUC:** JD, 1970, Duke School of Law; **EDUC HONORS:** Law Review; **OTHER ACT & HONORS:** Jaycees, JCI Senator 30826; Ambassador 876; **HOME ADD:** 11325 Big Plain-Circleville Pike, Orient, OH 43146, (614)877-9501; **BUS ADD:** 50 W. Broad St., 35th Floor, Columbus, OH 43215, (614)469-1700.

KUEHNLE, Walter R.——B: June 3, 1902, Chicago, IL, *Pres.*, Walter R. Kuehnle & Co.; **PRIM RE ACT:** Consultant, Appraiser; **SERVICES:** RE valuation & consultation for all purposes; **PROFL AFFIL & HONORS:** AIREA, Chicago RE Bd., NAR, SREA, ASA, Realtor Emeritus, NAR, Gold Medal, Mexican Inst. of Valuation A.C., World Medal of Honor, FIABCI; **BUS ADD:** 36 S. State St., Chicago, IL 60603, (312)332-4000.

KUGLER, Mark William——B: Dec. 13, 1949, Washington, DC, *Lawyer/Partner*, Wheeler & Korpeck; **PRIM RE ACT:** Consultant, Attorney, Owner/Investor, Property Manager, Syndicator; **SERVICES:** Legal representation concerning all aspects of RE; **REP CLIENTS:** Suburban Trust Co.; Nat. Permanent Fed. S & L Assn.; Loyola Fed. S & L Assn.; N.A.S.A. Fed. Credit Union; Bus. Publishers, Inc.; Tretter Enterprises; The Washington Corp.; **PROFL AFFIL & HONORS:** Montgomery Cty. Bar Assn., MD State Bar Assn., ABA; **EDUC:** BS, 1971, Bus. Admin., Econ., Univ. of MD; **GRAD EDUC:** JD, 1974, Law, Univ. of Baltimore; **EDUC HONORS:** Heuisler Honor Soc., Cum Laude; **OTHER ACT & HONORS:** Nat. Capital Trap and Skeet Club, Amer. Rivers Conservation Council, EAA (Experimental Aviation Assn.); **HOME ADD:** 4006 Hillwood Ct., Beltsville, ND 20705, (301)937-8749; **BUS ADD:** 930 Bonifant St., Silver Spring, MD 20910, (301)588-6290.

KUHN, F. Stuart——B: July 31, 1928, Dubuque, IA, *Owner*, F. Stuart Kuhn, RE Investments; **PRIM RE ACT:** Broker, Consultant, Developer, Owner/Investor, Syndicator; **PREV EMPLOY:** Dillingham Corp.; BankAmerica Realty Services, Inc.; Urban Investment and Devel. Co.; **EDUC:** BA, 1950, Econ., Hist., Pol. Sci., Yale Univ.; **GRAD EDUC:** MBA, 1952, Fin. RE, Stanford Univ.; **EDUC HONORS:** Cum Laude; **MIL SERV:** USN Res.; Capt.; **OTHER ACT & HONORS:** Dir., San Francisco Boys Club; **HOME ADD:** 377 Madrone Ave., Larkspur, CA 94939, (415)924-7785; **BUS ADD:** 221 Pine St., Suite 502, San Francisco, CA 94104, (415)781-2363.

KUHN, John F., Sr.——B: May 1, 1924, Homestead, FL, *RE Broker*; **PRIM RE ACT:** Broker, Consultant, Developer, Owner/Investor, Syndicator; **MIL SERV:** USN; **OTHER ACT & HONORS:** Masonic Lodge; Mahi Shrine; Silver Palm Methodist Church; **HOME ADD:** POB 4244, Princeton, FL 33032, (305)247-1906; **BUS ADD:** 420 S. Dixie Hwy., Suite 3-14, Coral Gables, FL 33146, (305)667-4151.

KUHRAU, Edward W.——B: Apr. 19, 1935, Caney, KS, *Partner*, Perkins, Coie, Stone, Olsen & Williams; **PRIM RE ACT:** Attorney; **SERVICES:** Legal services related to acquisition, devel., and fin. of RE; **REP CLIENTS:** Bank of Amer.; Mercantile Bank of Canada; NY Life Ins. Co.; The Prudential Ins. Co.; Bank of British Columbia; Cadillac Fairview/C.H.G. Joint Ventures; Pacific Cascade Corp.; McCann Development Corp.; Pioneer Nat. Title Ins. Co.; Alaska Title Guaranty Co.; **PROFL AFFIL & HONORS:** Member: WA State Bar Assn.; AK Bar Assn.; CA State Bar Assn.; Real Prop. Probate & Trust Sects. and Bus. and Banking Law Sects. of ABA, WABA & KCBA; Intl. Council of Shopping Ctrs., Editor-in-Chief, WA Real Property Desk Book; **EDUC:** BA, 1960, Eng., Univ. of TX; **GRAD EDUC:** JD, 1965, Univ. of So. CA School of Law; **EDUC HONORS:** Order of Coif; Note and Comment Editor, South. CA Law Review; **BUS ADD:** 1900 Washington Bldg., Seattle, WA 98101, (206)682-8770.

KUIPER, John——*Secy. & Treas.*, Dutch Boy Co.; **PRIM RE ACT:** Property Manager; **BUS ADD:** 430 W. 23rd St., Holland, MI 49423, (616)392-9402.*

KULICK, Joel——B: July 5, 1948, Philadelphia, PA, *Pres.*, Joel D. Kulick Co.; **PRIM RE ACT:** Broker, Consultant, Appraiser, Owner/Investor; **SERVICES:** RE appraising, counseling, and investment brokerage; **REP CLIENTS:** Attys., governmental agencies, mortgage & insurance cos., railroads, banks, misc. Corp.; **PREV EMPLOY:** First PA Bank N.A., Jackson Cross Co., Anthony J. Stagliano, Commonwealth Land Title Insurance Comp., Peoples Bond and Mortgage Co.; **PROFL AFFIL & HONORS:** RESSI, AIREA, IREF, NACORE, AIREA, MAI, SRPA, PA RE Broker; **EDUC:** BS, 1969, RE & Insurance, Penn State Univ.; **HOME ADD:** 8 Powers Place, Dresher, PA 19025, (215)886-9779; **BUS ADD:** Benson-East, Suite 212, Jenkintown, PA 19046, (215)572-1008.

KULIK, Joseph Michael——B: Sept. 17, 1957, Pittsburgh, PA, *Assoc.*, Peter J. King, Esquire; **PRIM RE ACT:** Attorney, Owner/Investor; **SERVICES:** Legal services, etc.; **REP CLIENTS:** Kocs Crane and Marine, Inc; firm has represented municipal units (govt. units) in sales/purchases of prop.; firm was former trial counsel for Lawyers Title Ins. Corp.; **PREV EMPLOY:** Former Pres., Polish Amer. Assocs.; **PROFL AFFIL & HONORS:** ABA; Nat. and PA School Bd. Assn., Detroit Renaissance Award for work in festival promotion; **EDUC:** BS, 1978, Pol. Sci./Sociology, Duquesne Univ.; **GRAD EDUC:** JD, 1981, Duquesne Univ. Sch. of Law; **EDUC HONORS:** Summa Cum Laude, *Who's Who in Amer. Coll. & Univ.*, Phi Kappa Phi, Mortarboard, Outstanding Sr. Award, Law Review; **OTHER ACT & HONORS:** School Dir., Montour Sch. Dist., 1977 to present; Former Chmn. of the Bd., Polish Amer. Assocs.; Member, Pkwy. W. Area Tech. Sch. Joint Comm., 1977 to present; Outstanding Young Men of Amer. Award; Intl. Youth in Achievement Award; **HOME ADD:** 121 Lorish Rd., McKees Rocks, PA 15136, (412)771-7147; **BUS ADD:** 700 Fifth Ave., 2nd Floor, Pittsburgh, PA 15219, (412)391-1200.

KULLA, Sylvia——B: Feb. 14, 1918, Philadelphia, PA, *Treasurer*, Jerome Belson Assoc., Inc.; **PRIM RE ACT:** Broker, Consultant, Property Manager; **OTHER RE ACT:** Fiscal Officer; **PROFL AFFIL & HONORS:** Nat. Leased Housing Assn.; Nat. Assn. Home Builders; NAR; Nat. Ctr. for Housing Mgmt.; RE Bd. of NY, CPM, RAM; **EDUC:** Acctg., Temple Univ.; **MIL SERV:** US Army, Maj.; **HOME ADD:** 35 Park Ave., New York, NY 10016, (212)684-7592; **BUS ADD:** 39 Broadway, New York, NY 10006, (212)269-5958.

KULOK, William A.——*Pres.*, New York Management Center, Inc.; **OTHER RE ACT:** Educator; **SERVICES:** Devel. educ. programs for the RE profl.; **REP CLIENTS:** The Wharton School, New York Univ.; **BUS ADD:** 360 Lexington Ave., New York, NY 10017, (212)953-7272.

KUNIANSKY, David——M.K. Construction Co.; **PRIM RE ACT:** Developer; **BUS ADD:** 1011 Collier Rd. NW, Atlanta, GA 30318, (404)355-6000.*

KUNICK, Alan D.——B: Mar. 31, 1954, Bismarck, ND, *Apprais.*, Gate City S&L Assn.; **PRIM RE ACT:** Appraiser; **OTHER RE ACT:** const. Insp.; **SERVICES:** Appraisals; **PROFL AFFIL & HONORS:** Assoc. Member Soc. of RE Apprais.; **EDUC:** BA, 1976, Bus. Admin., Mayville State Coll.; **HOME ADD:** 1548 Oakland Dr., Bismark, ND 58501, (701)258-3375; **BUS ADD:** 304 Rosser Ave., Bismark, ND 58501, (701)223-3450.

KUNSTADT, Herbert——B: July 31, 1931, Vienna, Austria, *Pres.*, Kunstadt Assoc., P.C.; **PRIM RE ACT:** Consultant, Engineer, Owner/Investor; **SERVICES:** Consulting engrg.; **REP CLIENTS:** Devels., bldrs., synds., archs.; **PREV EMPLOY:** SYSKA & Hennessy, Inc., Cosentini Assoc., Falotico, Inc.; **PROFL AFFIL & HONORS:** NSPE, ASHRAE, AEE, New York Academy of Sci., A-soc. Prof. Pratt Inst.; Pres. NY Assn. of Energy Engrs.; Chrmn. consultants council for energy conservation; **EDUC:** MME, 1954, Tech. Univ. of Vienna, Austria; **GRAD EDUC:** PhD, 1972, Energy Master Planning and Cogeneration, Univ of Vienna, Austria; **EDUC HONORS:** 1st in class of 80; **MIL SERV:** Corps. of Eng., Lt.; **OTHER ACT & HONORS:** *Who's Who in the world*; *in fin. & indus.*; *in the east*; registered profl. engr. in NY, NJ, CA, MA, PA, TX, FL, CT, Wash. DC; **HOME ADD:** 870 Fifth Ave., New York, NY 10021, (212)628-7643; **BUS ADD:** 415 Lexington Ave., New York, NY 10017, (212)697-7775.

KUNSTADT, Michael E.——B: Oct. 5, 1947, Chicago, IL, *Sr. Realty Mgmt. and Acquisition Specialist*, US Postal Service, RE Div., Central Region; **PRIM RE ACT:** Appraiser, Property Manager; **SERVICES:** Leasing, acquisition, valuation and mgmt. of postal facilities; **PREV EMPLOY:** Army Corps of Engrs.; IL Dept. of Trans.; **PROFL AFFIL & HONORS:** IL State RE Broker; Member of the Inst. for the Cert. of Engrg. Technicians; **EDUC:** BA, 1969, Pol. Sci., Psych., Univ. of IL, Chicago; **MIL SERV:** US Army, Sgt.; **HOME ADD:** 321 Fifth St., Downers Grove, IL 60515; **BUS ADD:** 433 W. Van Buren St., Chicago, IL 60699, (312)886-5064.

KUPFERER, John R.——*Exec. VP*, Natl. Assn. of Home Manufacturers; **OTHER RE ACT:** Profl. Assn. Admin.; **BUS ADD:** 6521 Arlington Blvd., Falls Church, VA 22042, (703)533-9606.*

KUPPER, Emily——**B:** Aug. 22, 1923, Peking, China, *Pres.*, Guide Points Realty Co., Inc.; **PRIM RE ACT:** Broker; **OTHER RE ACT:** Pres. Connect Inc. Relocation Grp., Real Estate Sales; **SERVICES:** RE Sales, Appraisals, counseling; **REP CLIENTS:** Amer. Can, Phillips Chemicals, Chesebrough Pond; **PROFL AFFIL & HONORS:** Greenwich Bd. of Realtors, NAR, CT Bd. of Realtors, WCR, FLI, Realtor, GRI, CRS; **EDUC:** AB, 1945, Eng., Art, French, Meredith Coll.; **GRAD EDUC:** Study, 1946, Adv. Design, Pratt Inst.; **HOME ADD:** 2 Merry Ln., Greenwich, CT 06830, (203)869-2847; **BUS ADD:** 403 E. Putnam Ave., Cos Cob, CT 06807, (203)661-5960.

KURETSKY, William H.——**B:** May 24, 1939, St. Paul, MN, *Spec. Asst., Atty. Gen.*, Atty. General's Office for the State of MN, MN Housing Fin. Agency; **PRIM RE ACT:** Engineer, Attorney; **SERVICES:** Provide all legal servs. for MN Housing Fin. Agency; **PREV EMPLOY:** Private practice representing RE devels., constr. co., banking insts. & small businesses; **PROFL AFFIL & HONORS:** MN State Bar Assn.; Hennepin Cty. Bar Assn., JD Cum Laude; **EDUC:** BME, 1961, Mech. Engrg., Univ. of MN; **GRAD EDUC:** MME, 1967, Heat Transfer & Fluid Dynamics, Univ. of MN; **EDUC HONORS:** Magna Cum Laude, Tau Beta Pi, Pi Tau Sigma, Summa Cum Laude; **HOME ADD:** 5244 Beachside Dr., Minnetonka, MN 55343, (612)938-2766; **BUS ADD:** Suite 200, Nalpak Bldg., 333 Sibley, St. Paul, MN 55101, (612)296-9806.

KURRAS, J. Fred——**B:** Aug. 16, 1938, Long Island,NY, *MAI/SRPA*, J. Fred Kurras R.E. Appraisals; **PRIM RE ACT:** Consultant, Appraiser; **SERVICES:** R.E. Appraisals/Investment Consultations; **PROFL AFFIL & HONORS:** Lake County Bd. of Realtors, AIREA,SREA, Published author, Prof. journals; **EDUC:** BS in Engrg., 1961, The Citadel, Military Coll. of S.C.; **MIL SERV:** USAF, Maj.; **OTHER ACT & HONORS:** Mason, Reserve Officers' Assn.; **HOME ADD:** 152 E. Lake Joanna Dr., Eustis, FL 32726; **BUS ADD:** 209 W. Alfred St., Tavares, FL 32778, (904)343-8102.

KURSH, Steven R.——**B:** Nov. 24, 1953, Wilmington, DE, *Asst. Prof. of Bus.*, Northeastern Univ., Fin.; **PRIM RE ACT:** Consultant, Instructor, Developer; **OTHER RE ACT:** Research; **SERVICES:** Investment counseling, seminar teaching, research on impact of Macro trends, in particular, energy and monetary policy on RE; **PREV EMPLOY:** Univ. of PA; Office of Majority Leader, US Ho. of Rep., US Congress; **PROFL AFFIL & HONORS:** Amer. RE and Urban Econ. Assn., Amer. Fin. Assn., and Amer. Econ. Assn.; Financial Mgmt. Assn.; **EDUC:** BA, 1975, Pol. Sci.-Econ., Boston Coll.; **GRAD EDUC:** AM, Univ. of PA; PhD, 1982, Finance/Planning, Univ. of PA; **EDUC HONORS:** Scholar of the Coll/ Magna Cum Laude; **HOME ADD:** 252 Commonwealth Ave., Boston, MA 02116, (617)266-6711; **BUS ADD:** 319 Hayden Hall, Boston, MA 02115, (617)437-8540.

KURTZ, Bernward Ulrich——**B:** Oct. 30, 1936, Neustadt/Weinstrasse, W. Germany, *Exec. VP and Dir.*, The Eggers Group, P.C., Architects and Planners; **PRIM RE ACT:** Architect; **SERVICES:** All arch. and planning services, interior design; **REP CLIENTS:** Air Products and Chemicals, Inc.; St. Regis Paper Co.; Rudin Mgmt. Co., Inc.; Pepsico, Inc.; Prudential Ins. Co.; Metropolitan Life Ins. Co.; Ford Motor Co.; **PROFL AFFIL & HONORS:** AIA; NY State Assn. of Arch.; The Arch. League of NY; Nat. Council of Arch. Registration Bds.; **EDUC:** 1957, Arch./Engrg., Bauschule Kaieserslautern, W. Germany; **OTHER ACT & HONORS:** The Union League, The Murray Hill Assn., New Jersey Business Magazine, Good Neighbor Award, 1970 BASJ Wyandotte Corp. and 1971, American Hoechst Corp., L.I. Association of Commerce & Industry, Honor Award, 1972 Security Nat. Bank HQ Assoc. Industries of Mass., Ecologue Flag Award, 1975 Wm. Underwood Co. Corporate Hdqtrs, Assoc. Landscape Contractors of Mass., Inc., Henry David Thoreau Grand Award, 1975, Pennsylvania Power & Light Co., Award for Excellence in Mgmt. of Electrical Energy Resources, 1978 Air Products & Chemicals, Inc. Corporate Headquarters, Amer. Consulting Engrg. Council, Honor Award for Engrg. Excellence in Energy Conservation, 1978 Air Products & Chemicals, Inc. Corporate Headquarters, Eastern New York Chap. Amer. Concrete Inst. Annual Award 1980, St. Regis Paper Co. Office Building, Concrete Industry Bd., Inc. of NY Special Award 1980, St. Regis Paper Co. Office Bldg., Special Citation by Reliance Devel. Award for Distinguished Arch., 1981, 560 Lexington Ave., New York, NY, Bard Award, 1981, 560 Lexington Ave., New York, NY; **HOME ADD:** 160 E 38 St., New York, NY 10016, (212)697-0219; **BUS ADD:** 2 Park Ave., New York, NY 10016, (212)725-2100.

KURTZ, Kenneth C.——**B:** June 8, 1931, Milwaukee, WI, *VP Dev.*, Steele Dev. Corp.; **PRIM RE ACT:** Architect, Developer, Owner/Investor; **SERVICES:** Dev. & Arch.; **PREV EMPLOY:** Orput Assoc., Inc. VP Mgr/Mktg.; **PROFL AFFIL & HONORS:** AIA, BOMA; **EDUC:** BArch, 1955, Arch. Engr., Univ. of IL; **MIL SERV:** US Army Engrs., 1st Lt.; **OTHER ACT & HONORS:** Rotary, church, YMCA, etc.; **HOME ADD:** 8429 Kenyon Ave., Wauwatosa, WI 53226; **BUS ADD:** 200 Exec. Dr., Brookfield, WI 53005, (414)784-5611.

KURTZ, L.S., Jr.——**B:** Feb. 23, 1934, Toledo, OH, *Sr. VP and Atty.*, Burr, Pease & Kurtz, A Professional Corp.; **PRIM RE ACT:** Attorney, Owner/Investor; **SERVICES:** Legal serv.; **REP CLIENTS:** AK Bank of Commerce, Rainier Mort., Union Oil Co. of CA; **PREV EMPLOY:** Counsel, AK State Housing Authority, 1963-1964; **PROFL AFFIL & HONORS:** ABA; AK Bar Assn.; Anchorage Bar Assn.; Amer. Judicial Soc., AK Bar Assn., Bd. of Gov., 1970-1974; Pres., 1973-1974; **EDUC:** AB, 1956, Econ., Princeton Univ.; **GRAD EDUC:** LLB, 1959, Bus./Public Entity Law, Stanford Univ.; **EDUC HONORS:** Cum Laude, Managing Editor, Stanford Law Review; **OTHER ACT & HONORS:** AK Code Revision Commn., 1979; **BUS ADD:** 810 N St., Anchorage, AK 99501, (907)279-2411.

KURZ, Christopher W.——*VP*, Alex Brown Realty, Inc.; **PRIM RE ACT:** Syndicator, Consultant, Appraiser, Developer, Owner/Investor; **OTHER RE ACT:** Mortgage Banker; **PREV EMPLOY:** The Rouse Co., 1971-75; Maryland Natl. Bank, 1975-77; H.G. Smithy Co. 1977-81; **PROFL AFFIL & HONORS:** ULI, MBA, Home Builders Assn.; **EDUC:** BA, 1969, Pol. Sci., U. of PA; **GRAD EDUC:** MBA, 1971, Wharton; **EDUC HONORS:** Dean's List; **OTHER ACT & HONORS:** Treas. U. Penn. Alumni Club of Balt.; **BUS ADD:** 7 N. Calvert St., Baltimore, MD 21202, (301)727-4083.

KURZMAN, H. Michael——**B:** Apr. 4, 1939, San Francisco, CA, *Exec. VP*, The Lurie Co.; **OTHER RE ACT:** Office building operations, acquisitions & development; **SERVICES:** Own and operate office bldgs. - Chicago, San Francisco; **REP CLIENTS:** Bank of Amer., Amer. Nat. Bank & Trust of Chicago, Central Nat. Bank of Chicago, Midwest Stock Exchange, Kemper Financial Servs.; **PREV EMPLOY:** Continental Serv. Co.; **PROFL AFFIL & HONORS:** Bldg. Mgrs. Assn., Chicago - Dir.; **EDUC:** 1961, RE, Univ. of CA; **HOME ADD:** 2800 Lake Shore Dr., Chicago, IL 60657; **BUS ADD:** 120 S. LaSalle, Chicago, IL 60603, (312)984-1700.

KUSHNER, John E.——**B:** Apr. 22, 1949, Montreal, Can., *VP/Dir.*, Latter & Blum, Inc./Realtors, Office Bldg. Division; **PRIM RE ACT:** Broker; **PROFL AFFIL & HONORS:** Bd., First City Bank, Waugespack, Pratt Award; **EDUC:** BA, Mktg./Psychology, Univ. of Miami; **HOME ADD:** 5828 Sylvia Drive, New Orleans, LA 70124, (504)482-5828; **BUS ADD:** 916 Gravier St., New Orleans, LA 70112, (504)525-4775.

KUSIC, Daniel T.——**B:** May 25, 1946, Steubenville, OH, *Shareholder*, Fergeson, Skipper, Shaw & Kusic, P.A.; **PRIM RE ACT:** Attorney; **SERVICES:** Real Estate Legal Services; **REP CLIENTS:** Justice Builders, Inc.; Stoker Corp.; SPG, Inc.; **PREV EMPLOY:** Assistant Vice President, DMG, Inc. (formerly Diversified Mortgage Investors) NYSE; General Counsel, First Capital Financial Corp.; **PROFL AFFIL & HONORS:** Amer. Bar Assn.; FL Bar Assn.; **EDUC:** BSBA, 1968, Fin., WV Univ.; **GRAD EDUC:** JD, 1972, Real Property, Univ. of Miami; **EDUC HONORS:** School of Bus. Staff Asst.; Co-founder, Chapter of Society of Advancement of Management, Chief Judge, Honor Council, Bar & Gavel Society; **MIL SERV:** US Army; Lt.; **HOME ADD:** 1432 Westbrook Dr., Sarasota, FL 33581, (813)922-7111; **BUS ADD:** 1390 Main St., Suite 828, Sarasota, FL 33577, (813)957-1900.

KUSKA, Lee——*Mgr. of Plant Engr.*, Warner Electric Brake & Clutch Co.; **PRIM RE ACT:** Property Manager; **BUS ADD:** 449 Garden St., South Beloit, IL 61080, (815)389-3771.*

KUSNET, Jack——**B:** Aug. 12, 1916, New York, NY, *Sr. RE Editor*, Warren, Gorham & Lamont, Inc.; **PRIM RE ACT:** Real Estate Publisher; **PREV EMPLOY:** Inst. for Bus. Planning, Managing Editor & Sr. RE Editor; **PROFL AFFIL & HONORS:** Numerous publications; Arnold Encyclopedia of RE (Jt. Author); Modern RE Acquisition & Disposition Forms; RE Law Digest; Air Rights, The 3rd Dimension, Member, NY Bar; **EDUC:** BS, 1937, CCNY; **GRAD EDUC:** LLB, 1939, Brooklyn Law School of St. Lawrence Univ.; **HOME ADD:** 11 Riverside Dr., New York, NY 10023, (212)496-7742; **BUS ADD:** 1633 Broadway, New York, NY 10019, (212)977-7409.

KUTCHINS, Allen Ira——**B:** Oct. 6, 1948, Chicago, IL, *CPA*, Kutchins, Berg & Co., A Professional Corporation; **OTHER RE ACT:** CPA; **SERVICES:** Acctg. and fin. and tax planning; **REP CLIENTS:** RE devel. and condo. converters; **PROFL AFFIL & HONORS:** Amer. Inst. of CPA's; IL Soc. of CPA's; **EDUC:** BBA, 1970, Acctg., Loyola Univ., Chicago, IL; **GRAD EDUC:** MST, 1973, Taxation, DePaul Univ.; **HOME ADD:** 610 Pheasant Lane, Deerfield, IL 60015,

(312)541-4050; **BUS ADD:** 255 Revere Dr., Suite 120, Northbrook, IL 60062, (312)291-9600.

KUTCHINS, Bryan A.——B: Oct. 27, 1943, Lansing, MI, *VP & Gen. Counsel*, Beztak Co.; **PRIM RE ACT:** Attorney, Developer, Syndicator; **SERVICES:** Gen. legal counsel, acquisition, Synd. negotiations, mkt. analys, devel. of multifamily units, shopping ctrs, offices; **REP CLIENTS:** Devel. and synd. of comml. and multifamily props.; **PREV EMPLOY:** Comml. banking - 8 yrs., corp. law practice-1 yr., Trial Law Practice-2 yrs., RE Devel.-3 yrs.; **PROFL AFFIL & HONORS:** Natl. Assn. of Corp. RE Execs., RESSI, MI & FL Bar Assn.; **EDUC:** Bus. Admin., 1965, Acctg. Mgmt., MI State Univ.; **GRAD EDUC:** JD, 1972, Law, Wayne State Univ.; **OTHER ACT & HONORS:** Capt. Coll. Fencing Team; **HOME ADD:** 45369 Dunbarton Dr., Novi, MI 48369, (313)352-7432; **BUS ADD:** 23999 W. 10 Mile, Southfield, MI 48034.

KUTRIEB, Ronald E.——B: May 13, 1942, Canton, OH, *Pres.*, Transar Mgmt. Corp.; **PRIM RE ACT:** Broker, Syndicator, Consultant, Owner/Investor; **SERVICES:** Investment advisory co. including RE investment, mgmt. and brokerage activities for selected clients; **REP CLIENTS:** Middle Eastern and European investors in US; **PREV EMPLOY:** Tr., Pres. and CEO of Realty Income Trust 1969-1980; **PROFL AFFIL & HONORS:** Bd. of Gov. (NAREIT); past VP. also.; **EDUC:** BA, 1964, Econ., Colgate Univ.; **GRAD EDUC:** MBA, 1969, Bus. Admin., Harvard Bus. School; **EDUC HONORS:** Franklin G. Brehmer Scholar, Pres. - Inter Club Council, New Programs Award; **HOME ADD:** 97 Highland Ave., Warwick, RI 02886, (401)884-0292; **BUS ADD:** 12 James St., Providence, RI 02901, (401)331-7220.

KYHOS, Thomas Flynn——B: May 13, 1947, Cheverly, MD, *Prin.*, The Equity Group, Ltd.; **OTHER RE ACT:** Investment bankers; **SERVICES:** Fin. servs.; **REP CLIENTS:** Giant Food, Inc.; Safeway Stores, Inc.; **PREV EMPLOY:** Tax Specialist, Laventhol & Horwath; **PROFL AFFIL & HONORS:** RE Grp., DC Bar Assn.; MD Bar Assn.; AICPA; **EDUC:** BA, 1969, Econ/Acctg., DePaul Univ.; **GRAD EDUC:** JD, 1973, Tax, Catholic Univ. of Amer./Columbus School of Law; **MIL SERV:** US Army; **OTHER ACT & HONORS:** Intercollegiate Official; The Univ. Club; Tred Avon Yacht Club; **HOME ADD:** 5714 Massachusetts Ave., Bethesda, MD 20816, (301)320-4474; **BUS ADD:** 3524 K St., N.W., Washington, DC 20007, (202)337-7227.

KYLE, Robert C.——B: Jan. 6, 1935, Cleveland, OH, *Pres.*, Real Estate Education Company; **PRIM RE ACT:** Real Estate Publisher; **SERVICES:** Educational products; **REP CLIENTS:** All major firms and educational orgs.; **PROFL AFFIL & HONORS:** Pres., RE Educators Assn.; Dir., Grubb & Ellis Co.; RE Advisory Comm. Univ. of Denver, CO; Dir., IL Assn of RE Educators; **EDUC:** BS, 1957, Bus., Univ. of CO; **GRAD EDUC:** MA, 1959, Educ. Psych., Case Western Reserve Univ.; MBA, 1963, Bus. Admin., Harvard Univ.; DBA, 1966, Bus. Admin., Harvard Univ.; **EDUC HONORS:** Sumalia, with Distinction; **MIL SERV:** Air Force; **HOME ADD:** 935 Private Rd., Winnetka, IL 60093, (312)446-6534; **BUS ADD:** 500 N Dearborn St., Chicago, IL 60610, (312)836-4400.

KYLE, Steve——B: Jan. 13, 1951, OK City, OK, *Pres.*, Steve Kyle Enterprizes; **PRIM RE ACT:** Builder, Owner/Investor; **OTHER RE ACT:** RE Salesman; **SERVICES:** Remodeler; **PROFL AFFIL & HONORS:** Central OK Home Bld's. Assn., Bldr. Member; **EDUC:** Gen.Bus., Central State Univ.; **OTHER ACT & HONORS:** Member, Piedmont Town Council 2 yrs. NRA, Bass, Wild Life Federation; **HOME ADD:** Rte 1, Box 80-A, Edmond, OK 73034; **BUS ADD:** Rte.1 Box 80-A, Edmond, OK 73034, (405)373-1917.

LABORDE, Joseph M.——*Corp. RE*, Ethyl Corp.; **PRIM RE ACT:** Property Manager; **BUS ADD:** Ethyl Tower, Baton Rouge, LA 70801, (504)388-7358.*

LABOVITZ, Joel——B: June 3, 1928, *Owner*, Labovitz Enterprises; **PRIM RE ACT:** Consultant, Developer, Banker, Lender, Owner/Investor, Syndicator; **PREV EMPLOY:** Pres. and CEO of Maurices Inc. a 270 store chain of women's and men's apparel; **HOME ADD:** 4750 London Rd., Duluth, MN 55804, (218)525-1255; **BUS ADD:** Lake Superior Plaza, Suite 200, Duluth, MN 55802, (218)727-7765.

LABRIE, Adrien A., Jr.——B: Feb. 2, 1949, Nashua, NH, *VP*, Labrie Const. Co.,Inc., Labrie Realty; **PRIM RE ACT:** Broker, Consultant, Appraiser, Developer, Builder, Property Manager, Owner/Investor; **SERVICES:** Comml. Inv. Counseling & Cost Appraisals; **REP CLIENTS:** Varco-Pruden Bldg. Sys. & Comml. Bldgs., Maisons d'Autrefois du Québec Inc. and Log Homes; **PREV EMPLOY:** ANA Realty Trust, Consulting Part.; **PROFL AFFIL & HONORS:** Past VP of Merrimack C of C, Bd. of Dirs. 2 yrs. with C of C, Membership Comm. for 2 yrs.; **EDUC:** Assoc. Deg., 1969, Mktg. and Bus. Mgmt., Bryant & Stratton Jr. Coll.; **GRAD EDUC:** Non-degree courses, 1972-1980, RE and Land, Merrimack Valley Branch - Univ. of NH, Notre Dame Coll., Manchester, NH; **MIL SERV:** USMC, E-5, 6 yrs Service Star; **OTHER ACT & HONORS:** JP, NH; Notary Public, NH; Amer. Legion, Merrimack; YMCA; BPOE Elks 720; Amherst Tennis Club; Off the Wall Racquet Club; **HOME ADD:** 17 Dena Ave., 03054, Merrimack, NH, (603)882-3009; **BUS ADD:** DW Hwy., PO Box 850, Merrimack, NH 03054, (603)424-9977.

LABRIE, James A.——B: July 26, 1935, Concord, NH, *Broker*, Century 21 Ocean Realty; **PRIM RE ACT:** Broker, Consultant, Developer, Builder, Property Manager, Owner/Investor; **SERVICES:** Complete RE consulting & mktg.; **PREV EMPLOY:** Mktg. mgr for Diamond Intl. Corp., Eastern Retail Div.; **PROFL AFFIL & HONORS:** Seacoast Bd. of Realtors, Century 21 Investment Soc., Seacoast MLS, York County MLS, York Cty. Bd. of Realtors, Portsmouth Rotary; **EDUC:** BA, 1958, Bus. Admin., St. Anselm Coll.; **OTHER ACT & HONORS:** Past Commodore Portsmouth Yacht Club; **HOME ADD:** 1451 Ocean Blvd., Rye, NH 03870, (603)431-6945; **BUS ADD:** 2069 Lafayette Rd., PO Box 4250, Portsmouth, NH 03801, (603)436-2100.

LABRIE, Wallace A.——B: Apr. 19, 1927, Redmond, WA, *Assoc. Broker*, Westmark Prop., Inc., Comml.; **PRIM RE ACT:** Syndicator, Consultant, Appraiser, Insuror; **OTHER RE ACT:** Bus. & Comml Props.; **PROFL AFFIL & HONORS:** RESSI; Local Bd. of Realtors, Cert. RE Appraiser; Cert. Bus. Counselor; **MIL SERV:** USN, Lt.; **OTHER ACT & HONORS:** Pres. of Bd. of Tr., Lakewood Hospital; Gen. - Securities Broker Dealer in State of WA; **HOME ADD:** 8703 Wildwood Ave., SW, Tacoma, WA 98498, (206)584-3623; **BUS ADD:** 3815-100 St. SW, Suite 2A, Tacoma, WA 98499, (206)582-5352.

LABROSSE, Luc R.——B: Mar. 23, 1939, Central Falls, RI; **PRIM RE ACT:** Attorney; **OTHER RE ACT:** Specializing in title ins.; **SERVICES:** State Counsel, issuer of Title Ins., Title Searchers; **REP CLIENTS:** All major Title Cos. in the NE and Cos. that specialize in moving execs. etc.; **PREV EMPLOY:** Pres. and Mgr. of Hope Title Agency, Inc.; **PROFL AFFIL & HONORS:** New England Title Assn., RI Bar and Fed. Bar; **GRAD EDUC:** LLB, 1965; **OTHER ACT & HONORS:** City Solicitor, Le Foyer, Recipient of the Eagle of The Cross Award; **HOME ADD:** 93 Bagley St., Central Falls, RI 02863; **BUS ADD:** 914 Lonsdale Ave., Central Falls, RI 02863, (401)722-6335.

LACAILLE, Georgeann——*Dir. Adm.*, Envirodyne Industries; **PRIM RE ACT:** Property Manager; **BUS ADD:** 222 West Adams St., Chicago, IL 60606, (312)822-0030.*

LACHMAN, M. Leanne——B: March 16, 1943, Vancouver, BC, Canada, *Pres.*, RE Research Corp.; **PRIM RE ACT:** Consultant; **SERVICES:** Investment advisory services and portfolio appraisal; **REP CLIENTS:** Fortune 1000 Firms, RE Devels., Fed., State and Local Govts.; **PROFL AFFIL & HONORS:** Lambda Alpha, Chicago Fin. Exchange; **EDUC:** BA, 1964, Eng., Univ. of So. CA; **OTHER ACT & HONORS:** Econ. Club of Chicago; Chicago Network; **BUS ADD:** 72 W. Adams St., Chicago, IL 60603, (312)346-5885.

LACY, Craig W.——B: Mar. 6, 1949, Yokohama, Japan, *VP*, RE Loan Dept.; **PRIM RE ACT:** Developer, Banker, Lender, Owner/Investor; **REP CLIENTS:** Numerous Builders in S CA; **PREV EMPLOY:** Pres. of Craig W. Lacy & Co. (RE Dev. and Investments); A.V.D. of Amer. City Bank, LA - RE Loans; **PROFL AFFIL & HONORS:** Homebuilders Council of Orange Cty., Builder Industry, Assoc., S CA Mtg. Bankers Assn.; **EDUC:** BS, 1971, Fin. RE & Accounting, IN Univ., School of Bus.; **MIL SERV:** USAR, Capt.; **HOME ADD:** 30902 Cypress Pl., Laguna Niguel, CA 92677, (714)831-6628; **BUS ADD:** 695 Town Center Dr., Costa Mesa, CA 92626.

LACY, James T.——B: Jan. 15, 1938, Kansas City, MO, *Pres.*, Lacy & Co.; **PRIM RE ACT:** Developer, Owner/Investor; **OTHER RE ACT:** Realtor; **SERVICES:** Build to suit for Nat. office tenants; **REP CLIENTS:** Travelers, USF&G, St. Paul, Liberty Mutual; **PREV EMPLOY:** 1960-1969, Terrydale Devel. Corp.; 1969-1981, Ted Greene Co., Pres., Office Bldg. Devels. & Owners; **PROFL AFFIL & HONORS:** RE Bd. of Kansas City; Past Pres. of Kansas City Chap. of Bldg. Owners and Mgrs. Assn.; Planning Commn., City of Mission

Hills, KS; RESSI; **EDUC:** BA, 1960, Bus./Liberal Arts, Westminster Coll.; **EDUC HONORS:** Distinguished Military Grad., Omicron Delta Kappa, *Who's Who*; **MIL SERV:** Infantry, 1st Lt., 1960-1961; **OTHER ACT & HONORS:** Chmn., Mark Twain Plaza Bank, Kansas City; Tr., St. Luke's Hospital, Kansas City; Dir., Heart of Amer. Council, BSA; **HOME ADD:** 2000 Drury Ln., Shawnee Mission, KS 66208; **BUS ADD:** 4901 Main St., Kansas City, MO 64112, (816)531-7000.

LACY, Jerrill L.——B: Sept. 20, 1947, Celina, OH, *Mktg. & Fin. Dir.*, Brumbaugh Const., Inc.; **PRIM RE ACT:** Broker, Developer, Builder, Owner/Investor, Property Manager, Syndicator; **SERVICES:** Packaging, mktg., and fin. projects; **PROFL AFFIL & HONORS:** RE, Securities and Synd. Inst., NAR, GRI; **EDUC:** BA, 1969, Bus. Admin., OH No. Univ.; **GRAD EDUC:** M.Ed., 1975, Wright St. Univ.; **HOME ADD:** 704 Pat Dr., Selma, OH 45822, (419)586-2687; **BUS ADD:** 101 S. Lablond St., Selma, OH 45822, (419)586-6390.

LACY, Robert P.——B: July 31, 1950, Denver, CO, *Sr. Prop. Mgr.*, Daon Corp.; **PRIM RE ACT:** Property Manager; **SERVICES:** Diversified RE Devel.; **PREV EMPLOY:** Ankirk Devel. corp.; **PROFL AFFIL & HONORS:** IREM, CPM; **EDUC:** BA, 1973, Bus. Admin., Acctg., CA State Univ.; **BUS ADD:** 3200 Park Center Drive, Costa Mesa, CA 92626, (714)641-6666.

LACY, W.——*RE Mgr.*, Utotem, Inc.; **PRIM RE ACT:** Property Manager; **BUS ADD:** 5200 West Loop South, Bellaire, TX 77401, (713)667-7501.*

LADD, Wilfred A.——*Mgr. Bldg. & Office Services*, Inland Steel Co.; **PRIM RE ACT:** Property Manager; **BUS ADD:** 30 W. Monroe St., Chicago, IL 60603, (312)346-0300.*

LADERMAN, Harvey R.——B: Apr. 13, 1934, Los Angeles, CA, *Pres.*, Laderman Corp.; **PRIM RE ACT:** Developer, Owner/Investor, Syndicator; **SERVICES:** Devel. of mobile home parks, housing, business parks, indus. park, comml. & office projects, provides equity and mortgage financing; **EDUC:** BA, 1956, Econ., Stanford Univ.; **GRAD EDUC:** MBA, 1958, Bus. Admin., Stanford Univ.; **MIL SERV:** US Army, 1st Lt., 1958-1961; **OTHER ACT & HONORS:** Bd. of Holy Family Services; Parish Council at St. Martin of Tours; Bel Air Bay Club; **HOME ADD:** 705 S. Westgate Ave., Los Angeles, CA 90049, (213)472-8624; **BUS ADD:** 9701 Wilshire Blvd., Beverly Hills, CA 90212, (213)273-2483.

LADIPO, Jerry G.——B: Feb. 16, 1947, Ibadan, Nigeria, *Pres.*, Total Equity Mgmt. Corp.; **PRIM RE ACT:** Broker, Developer, Owner/Investor, Property Manager; **SERVICES:** 85% of our portfolio is prop. mgmt.; **PROFL AFFIL & HONORS:** IREM, Apt. Owners and Mgrs. Assn.; **EDUC:** BS, 1971, Quantitative Analysis-Chemistry, Central State Univ., OH; **GRAD EDUC:** MSA, 1974, Quantitative and Behavorial Mgmt., Univ. of Houston, TX; **EDUC HONORS:** Cum Laude Deans List, Lubrizol Award, Pres. Award, Cum Laude, First Grad. with MSA degree from Coll. of Bus. Univ. of Houston; **OTHER ACT & HONORS:** Notary Public, Atlanta Bus. League, Neighborhood Planning Unit (Atlanta) Dir. Collection of Life and Heritage, Kappa Alpha Psi; **HOME ADD:** 2232 Belvedere Ave. SW, Atlanta, GA 30311, (404)758-6275; **BUS ADD:** 57 Forsyth St., Suite 311, Atlanta, GA 30303, (404)523-2842.

LADNER, Dale——B: Sept. 19, 1950, Houston, TX, *Pres.*, The Omni Group, Assoc. with Omni Construction Inc.; **PRIM RE ACT:** Developer, Owner/Investor, Property Manager, Syndicator; **SERVICES:** Planning, devel. and synd. of comml. props.; **PROFL AFFIL & HONORS:** Intl. council of shopping ctrs., BOMA; **EDUC:** BA, 1974, mgmt., TX Christian Univ.; **HOME ADD:** 2433 Medford Ct., West Ft. Worth, TX 76109, (817)927-8567; **BUS ADD:** PO Box 12187, Ft. Worth, TX 76116, (817)731-2301.

LAFATA, John M.——B: Apr. 16, 1934, Detroit, MI, *Pres.*, John M. LaFata Ltd.; **PRIM RE ACT:** Broker, Instructor, Syndicator, Consultant, Developer, Builder, Property Manager; **OTHER RE ACT:** Arch. Designer, Land Planner; **SERVICES:** Full serv. - land org., Investor sale, design const.; sale and leasing - prop., mgmt.; **PREV EMPLOY:** Dykema, Gossett, Spencer, Goodnow & Trigg law firm, Para-Legal RE; **PROFL AFFIL & HONORS:** NAR, RESSI, NAHB, Securities Agent, Builder, RE Broker; **MIL SERV:** US Army, M/Sgt.; **OTHER ACT & HONORS:** Warren Beautification Commn., Nat. Forestry Assn., Nat. Rifle Assn., Detroit Sportsman Congress; **HOME ADD:** 54604 Iroquois, Utica, MI 48087, (313)781-2151; **BUS ADD:** 27440 Hoover Rd., Warren, MI 48093, (313)754-5830.

LAFLAMME, Earl A., Jr.——B: Dec. 21, 1929, Brattleboro, VT, *Pres.*, Allyn & O'Donnell, Realtors; **PRIM RE ACT:** Broker, Instructor, Consultant, Appraiser, Property Manager, Owner/Investor; **SERVICES:** Taxes & investment counseling, indus. expert; **REP CLIENTS:** Indus. & commercial investors, site rep.; **PREV EMPLOY:** USN; **PROFL AFFIL & HONORS:** NAR, Mass. Assn. of Realtors, RNMI, Pres. MAR Assn. (1978), MA Realtor of Year (1976), Nat. Dir. (1976-1984) Member of Omega Tau Rho, Dean of GRI Inst.; **EDUC:** BA, 1953, Accounting, Univ. of MA; **MIL SERV:** USN, Lt. Cmdr.; **OTHER ACT & HONORS:** Pres. Holyoke C of C (1972-1974); Chmn. Red Cross; Chmn. Salvation Army; Dir. Taxpayers Assn.; Dir. Holyoke Inc.; Incorporator People's Savings Bank; Amer. Legion Post 353; Holyoke Elks; **HOME ADD:** 240 West Madison Ave., Holyoke, MA 01040, (413)534-5233; **BUS ADD:** 346 High St., Holyoke, MA 01040, (413)536-6409.

LAFLAMME, Robert G.——B: July 2, 1939, New Bedford, MA, *Pres.*, Target Engineering, Inc.; **PRIM RE ACT:** Engineer, Builder; **OTHER RE ACT:** Mgmt., estimating; **SERVICES:** Design, build, gen. const., contracting, estimating mgmt. on site & off; **EDUC:** AA, 1968, Civil, Arch. Engrg., Wentworth Inst.; **EDUC HONORS:** WHH Honor; **MIL SERV:** USAF, A1C, Sgt., Letter of Favorable Communication; **OTHER ACT & HONORS:** Ctry. Club of New Bedford; **HOME ADD:** 1038 American Legion Hwy., Box 428, Westport, MA 02790, (617)636-5524; **BUS ADD:** 1038 American Legion Hwy., PO Box 428, Westport, MA 02790, (617)636-5524.

LAFLEUR, Edmond J.——B: May 8, 1938, Taunton, MA, *Gen. Mgr.*, Professional Real Estate Associates; **PRIM RE ACT:** Broker, Instructor, Consultant, Developer; **SERVICES:** Complete Mktg. Program, Sales Training, Data Processing; **REP CLIENTS:** 10+ Profl. RE Offices on Cape Cod; **PREV EMPLOY:** Resort Devel.; **PROFL AFFIL & HONORS:** NAR, MA Assn. of Realtors, Cape Cod Bd. of Realtors; **EDUC:** AA, 1964, Bus. Admin., Cape Cod Community Coll.; **MIL SERV:** US Army; **OTHER ACT & HONORS:** Planning Bd. 7 yrs., RE Text Book Critic; **HOME ADD:** 80 Old Colony Rd., Hyannis, MA 02601, (617)775-5270; **BUS ADD:** 250 Barnstable Rd., Hyannis, MA 02601, (617)775-2821.

LAGERBAUER, L. J.——B: Dec. 18, 1940, Minneapolis, MN, *Exec. VP*, Landmark Communities Inc.; **PRIM RE ACT:** Developer; **PROFL AFFIL & HONORS:** AICPA, CPA (CA); **EDUC:** 1962, Math./Soc., Univ. of MN; **GRAD EDUC:** Acctg., Univ. of NV; **MIL SERV:** US Navy, Lt., various decorations; **HOME ADD:** 5900 Moss Bank Dr., Rancho Palos Verdes, CA 90274, (213)373-7987; **BUS ADD:** 9595 Wilshire Blvd., Ste. 301, Beverly Hills, CA 90212.

LAGHI, Louis C.——B: Jan. 21, 1935, Norristown, PA, *Pres./Owner*, Marian, Inc., Realtors; **PRIM RE ACT:** Broker, Appraiser; **SERVICES:** Appraisal for Estates; **PROFL AFFIL & HONORS:** NH Bd. of Realtors, Local Bd., CRB, GRI; **MIL SERV:** US Army; PFC; **OTHER ACT & HONORS:** Treasurer of Local School Bd.; Member, Pres., Local Bd. of Parent Club; Chmn. of Church Council; **HOME ADD:** 6600 Mango Ave. S, St. Petersburg, FL 33707, (813)347-1850; **BUS ADD:** 720 Pasadena Ave. S, St. Petersburg, FL 33707, (813)381-5555.

LAIRD, Robert W., Jr.——*Broker, Owner*, Century 21, The Laird Agency; **PRIM RE ACT:** Broker, Appraiser, Property Manager; **SERVICES:** RE Rentals, Prop. mgmt., appraising; **REP CLIENTS:** Appraisal clients have included Exxon Co., US Small Bus. Admin., S. Railway, Bank and Fin. Cos.; **PROFL AFFIL & HONORS:** Aiken Bd. of Realtors; **EDUC:** BS, 1941, Econ., Commerce, Univ. of SC; **MIL SERV:** USNR, Comdr., Bronze Star; **OTHER ACT & HONORS:** Aiken Chapt., Ret. Officers Assn., (Past Pres.); **BUS ADD:** 217 Park Ave., SE, Aiken, SC 29801.

LAISERIN, Jerry Albert——B: Oct. 19, 1944, Atlanta, GA, *Pres.*, Exponential Systems Corp.; **PRIM RE ACT:** Architect, Appraiser, Developer, Builder; **OTHER RE ACT:** Planner, accountant; **SERVICES:** Devel., const., design, planning & zoning, code compliance, feasibility analysis, fin. & tax planning, mkt. research, sales training & promotion; **REP CLIENTS:** Princeton B&T, First Nat. Bank of Princeton, State of NJ, Princeton Univ., RCA Labs., US Postal Serv., USN, AT&T, Bell Labs., Western Electric, Peterson's Guides, Phila. Insulated Wire, Nassau S&L Assn., Palmer Square, Inc.; **PREV EMPLOY:** Hellmuth, Obata & Kassabaum (HOK); Princeton Design & Devel. Corp.; **PROFL AFFIL & HONORS:** AIA, ULI, NCARB, AIA, CPA, Lic. Prof. planner; **EDUC:** BA, 1966, Hist., Brandeis Univ.; **GRAD EDUC:** MArch., 1971, Princeton Univ.; MBA, 1974, NYU; **EDUC HONORS:** With Distinction, Beta Gamma Sigma; **BUS ADD:** 398 Clarksville Rd., Princeton Junction, NJ 08550, (609)799-2135.

LAITILA, Edward E.——B: June 19, 1935, Houghton, MI, *Assoc. Prof.*, Univ. of Hawaii, Coll. of Bus. Admin.; **PRIM RE ACT:** Consultant, Instructor; **SERVICES:** RE educ., research & consulting; **REP CLIENTS:** Govt., fin. instns., attys.; **PREV EMPLOY:** Assoc. Fellow, Battelle Memorial Inst. Columbus, OH, Instr., Univ. of IL,

Urbana; **PROFL AFFIL & HONORS:** Amer. RE and Urban Econ. Assn., Amer. Econ. Assn., Honors Graduate, UCLA, Ford Found. Fellow.; **EDUC:** BS, 1960, Const. Mgmt., UCLA; **GRAD EDUC:** MBA, 1961, RE and Urban Econ., UCLA; DBA, 1970, Urban & Rgnl. Econ., IN Univ.; **EDUC HONORS:** Univ. Honors; **MIL SERV:** US Army; E-5; **OTHER ACT & HONORS:** Member, Condo. Owners Assn., Bd. of Dirs. Former Pres. Coll. Housing Fund.; **HOME ADD:** PO Box 27214, Honolulu, HI 96827, (808)955-7422; **BUS ADD:** 2404 Maile Way, Honolulu, HI 96822, (808)948-7284.

LAKE, Jack S.——B: Oct. 1, 1936, Salt Lake City, UT, *Owner*, Lake Devel. Grp., Inc.; **PRIM RE ACT:** Consultant, Developer; **PREV EMPLOY:** Western Fin. Corp.; **EDUC:** BS, 1960, Mgmt. & Econ., Univ. of UT; **GRAD EDUC:** MBA, 1962, Fin., Univ. of UT; **MIL SERV:** US Army, Inf., Capt.; **OTHER ACT & HONORS:** Hospital Bd. of Dir. - Valley Lutheran; VP Exploring, Roosevelt Council, Boy Scouts of Amer.; **HOME ADD:** 5410 E. Camelhill Rd., Phoenix, AZ 85018, (602)952-0623; **BUS ADD:** 6901 E. Broadway Rd., Phoenix, AZ 85208.

LALLY, Gary W.——B: Jan. 27, 1947, Minneapolis, MN, *Dir. of Comml. Indus. Sales & Devel.*, Portfolio Development; **PRIM RE ACT:** Broker, Consultant, Developer, Owner/Investor; **OTHER RE ACT:** Investment consultant; **SERVICES:** Investment Consultant & Sales, Developer; **REP CLIENTS:** Indiv., Corp. & Instnl. Investors and Ower Users of Comml., Indus. & Investment Props.; **PREV EMPLOY:** Owner of own retail bus. for 10 yrs.; **PROFL AFFIL & HONORS:** Realtor Nat. Mktg. Council; Minneapolis, State & Nat. Bd. of Realtors, Realtor; GRI; Realty World Salesperson of the Month Upper Midwest Region (2 times); CCIM Candidate; **EDUC:** BA, 1969, Pol. Sci./Philosophy, Univ. of MN; **OTHER ACT & HONORS:** Pres., Bloomington Devel. Council; Bloomington Planning Commnr.; Bloomington C of C; Area Devel. Council; Fund Raising Chmn., State Senator Wm. Belanger; **HOME ADD:** 8650 Penn Ave. S., Bloomington, MN 55431, (612)884-5877; **BUS ADD:** 1301 E. 79th St., Bloomington, MN 55420, (612)854-0732.

LAM, Man Ching——B: Aug. 19, 1935, China, *Pres.*, West - East Design, Development & Associates; **PRIM RE ACT:** Broker, Consultant, Architect, Developer, Owner/Investor; **SERVICES:** Arch., planning, RE investment & devel.; **PREV EMPLOY:** Associated with prominent arch. here & overseas for the past 15 years; **PROFL AFFIL & HONORS:** AIA, Housing Design (low-cost housing in 1959); **EDUC:** BS, Arch. Design & Engrg., Cheng Kung Univ., Tainan Taiwan; **GRAD EDUC:** MArch., Washington Univ., St. Louis, MO; **EDUC HONORS:** Honor degree in design; **HOME ADD:** 3907 Catamarca Dr., San Diego, CA 92124; **BUS ADD:** 8361 Vickers St., Suite 200, San Diego, CA 92111, (714)565-8484.

LAMB, Larry E.——B: Apr. 21, 1937, Charlottesville, VA, *Pres.*, Nathaniel Greene Dev. Corp.; **PRIM RE ACT:** Developer, Builder, Property Manager, Owner/Investor; **EDUC:** BS, 1966, Bus. Econ, Univ of VA, Sch. of Comm.; **MIL SERV:** US Army, S/Sgt.; **HOME ADD:** Standardsville, VA 22973; **BUS ADD:** Court Square Bldg, Standardsville, VA 22973, (804)985-7504.

LAMBERT, Ernest——B: Aug. 3, 1940, Woonsocket, RI, *Owner*, Lambert & Lambert Library of Homes; **PRIM RE ACT:** Broker, Insuror; **OTHER RE ACT:** FL sales, land & condos & resid.; **SERVICES:** RE ins.; **PREV EMPLOY:** Sales supervisor; **PROFL AFFIL & HONORS:** NAR, Nat. Realty Relocation Assn., RI State Wide MLS; **GRAD EDUC:** Resid Sales, Ins., FL Sales; **OTHER ACT & HONORS:** Little League Mgr., Blackstone Valley C of C, Gr. Woonsocket C of C; **HOME ADD:** 55 Westwood Dr., Cumberland, RI 02864, (401)333-0339; **BUS ADD:** 1555 Mendon Rd., Cumberland, RI 02864, (401)333-1919.

LAMBERT, Joe——*Mgr. RE Dept.*, Cannon Mills Co.; **PRIM RE ACT:** Property Manager; **BUS ADD:** PO Box 107, Main St., Kannapolis, NC 28081, (104)933-1221.*

LAMBERT, Lee F.——B: May 18, 1936, Antwerp, Belgium, *Regional IC & L Supv., Que.*, Royal Trust, Indus., Comml. & Investment; **PRIM RE ACT:** Broker; **SERVICES:** Supervision of all IC & L RE Activities in Que.; **REP CLIENTS:** Pvt., inst. lenders & investors; **PREV EMPLOY:** Mgr., Investment Div., Royal Tr. Le Permanent; **PROFL AFFIL & HONORS:** CREA Montreal RE Bd., Can. Club., Italian, French, German, Montreal C of C, MTCI; **EDUC:** Fin., Econ., RE Investment Analysis, Wharton, HEC Montreal; **GRAD EDUC:** 1957, Bus. Adm., Intl. Fin., Univ. Brussels; **OTHER ACT & HONORS:** Key City of Miami & Scroll of Friendship; **HOME ADD:** 23 Paul De Maricourt, Ste. Julie, J0L2S0, Que, Canada, (514)649-4699; **BUS ADD:** 630 Dorchester W., Montreal, H3B1S6, Que, Canada, (514)876-7678.

LAMBERT, Richard L.——B: Nov. 20, 1941, Detroit, MI, *Pres.*, L.P.R. Land Company & Collins & Associates; **PRIM RE ACT:** Consultant, Developer, Builder, Owner/Investor, Property Manager, Syndicator; **SERVICES:** Devel. of RE projects for owners, clients & internal ownership. Consultant to RE owners; **REP CLIENTS:** Finishish Centers, Standard Federal Savings of Detroit; **PREV EMPLOY:** Arthur Young & Co., CPAs; **PROFL AFFIL & HONORS:** Amer. Inst. of CPAs, CPA; **EDUC:** BS, 1967, Acctg., Wayne St. Univ.; **GRAD EDUC:** MS, 1969, Fin., Wayne St. Univ.; **HOME ADD:** 44 Depetris Way, Grosse Pointe Farms, MI 48236, (313)884-3802; **BUS ADD:** Suite 2720, 400 Renaissance Ctr., Detroit, MI 48243, (313)644-8973.

LAMBERT, Thomas C.——B: July 23, 1942, New York City, NY, *Atty.*; **PRIM RE ACT:** Attorney; **SERVICES:** Specialize in RE litigation; **PREV EMPLOY:** Dreyer and Traub; Finley, Kumble et al.; **PROFL AFFIL & HONORS:** NY State and Amer. Bar Assns.; **EDUC:** BA, 1964, Philosophy, Univ. of WI; **GRAD EDUC:** JD, 1968, NYU School of Law; **EDUC HONORS:** Phi Eta Sigma; **HOME ADD:** 130 E 18th St., New York, NY 10003, (212)254-7258; **BUS ADD:** 18 E 48th St., New York, NY 10017, (212)371-8787.

LAMERTON, Robert E.——B: Apr. 16, 1944, Phila, PA, *Pres.*, Pinebrook Devel. Co.; **PRIM RE ACT:** Broker, Consultant, Developer, Property Manager; **SERVICES:** Devel. & mgmt. of office & indus. park props.; **PROFL AFFIL & HONORS:** Nat. Assn. of Indus. & Office Pks., Member of Bd. of Dirs & Exec. Comm.; **EDUC:** AB, 1966, Pol. Sci., Princeton Univ.; **GRAD EDUC:** MBA, 1968, Ins., Wheaton Sch., Univ. of PA; **HOME ADD:** 650 E. Gravers Ln., Wyndmoor, PA 19118, (215)233-5250; **BUS ADD:** Suite 230, Dublin Mall, 177 Wilton Rd., Blue Bels, PA 19422, (215)643-0232.

LAMMERSEN, William Barry——B: Dec. 31, 1940, Los Angeles, CA, *VP*, Charlton Consolidated Cos., Inc., Mktg., Acquisition; **PRIM RE ACT:** Broker, Consultant, Developer, Owner/Investor, Syndicator; **SERVICES:** Devel., consulting, acquisiton, synd. of investment props.; **PREV EMPLOY:** VP/Mktg. Dir., Investment Props., Coldwell Banker & Co., 1974-1981; **PROFL AFFIL & HONORS:** Colorado Springs Bd. of Realtors, NAR; **EDUC:** BA, 1973, Poli. Sci., Bus./Fin., Univ. of CO; **MIL SERV:** US Army; Sgt.; 1964-1966; **OTHER ACT & HONORS:** Ctry. Club of CO; **HOME ADD:** 50 Briarcrest Place, Colorado Springs, CO 80906, (303)576-7176; **BUS ADD:** 300 Holly Sugar Bldg., Colorado Springs, CO 80903, (303)630-1600.

LAMMONS, Aubrey O.——B: Feb. 14, 1933, Hartford, AL, *Part.*, Lammons, Bell & Sneed; **PRIM RE ACT:** Attorney; **SERVICES:** Gen. Legal Services pertaining to Acquisition, Sale, Land Mgmt., Fin. of RE; **PROFL AFFIL & HONORS:** ABA, AL State Bar Assn., Huntsville - Madison Cty. Bar Assn., AL Trial Lawyers Assn.; **EDUC:** BS, 1958, Bus. Admin., Univ. of AL; **GRAD EDUC:** JD, 1961, Univ. of AL, School of Law; **MIL SERV:** USAF S/Sgt.; **OTHER ACT & HONORS:** Asst. US Atty., N. Dist. of AL; DA Pro-tem, Madison Cty., AL; Huntsville - Madison Cty. C of C; Mason (32 day), Shrine; Planning Commnr., City of Huntsville 1964-72; **HOME ADD:** 2712 Westminster Way, Huntsville, AL 35801, (205)881-7178; **BUS ADD:** 132 W. Holmes Ave., Huntsville, AL 35801, (205)533-2410.

LAMOREAUX, William——B: Jan. 18, 1944, Brooklyn, NY, *V.P./Gen. Mgr.*, Merrill Lynch Realty/Chris Coile, Inc., Baltimore Div.; **PRIM RE ACT:** Broker, Instructor, Owner/Investor; **OTHER RE ACT:** Multi office responsibility, Regional Mgr./VP; **PROFL AFFIL & HONORS:** AA County Bd. of Realtors, NAR, CRB; **EDUC:** BA, 1966, Psych. Soc., Univ. of MD, Coll. Park, MD; **MIL SERV:** US Army 1966-69, 1 Lt.; **HOME ADD:** 806 Oak Grove Cir., Severna Park, MD 21146, (301)647-7291; **BUS ADD:** 565 Benfield Rd., Severna Park, MD 21146, (301)647-8030.

LAMOS, Adrian C., Jr.——B: Mar. 28, 1951, Brooklyn, NY, *VP*, Century 21 Professional Realty, Inc.; **PRIM RE ACT:** Broker, Consultant, Owner/Investor; **SERVICES:** Fin. Consulting, RE Investment; **PREV EMPLOY:** Vista Coll. & UC Berkeley Extension Instr.; **PROFL AFFIL & HONORS:** Oakland Bd. of Realtors; Century 21 Investment Soc.; **EDUC:** BA, 1972, Bus., Franklin & Marshall Coll.; **GRAD EDUC:** DIRE, 1974, RE, NYU/RE Instit.; **EDUC HONORS:** Black Pyramid Sr. Honor Soc.; **OTHER ACT & HONORS:** Nat. Wildlife Fed.; Grand St. Boys Club; San Antonio Health Ctr.; **HOME ADD:** POB 1118, Alameda, CA 94501, (415)536-1972; **BUS ADD:** 4050 Foothill Blvd., Oakland, CA 94601, (415)533-1700.

LAMPE, John F.——B: March 6, 1945, Wauwatosa, WI, *Atty. at Law, Pres., Gen. Part.*, C.L. Ltd., H.I.S. Ltd.; **PRIM RE ACT:** Attorney, Syndicator; **REP CLIENTS:** Pvt. investors; **PREV EMPLOY:** Hinshaw, Culbertson, Moelmann, Hoban, and Fuller, Joslyn and Green, P.C.; **PROFL AFFIL & HONORS:** Marquis *Who's Who* Pub.

Bd., Bd. of Dir. Wise Law Alumni Assn., 1970-71, Mbr. of IL State Bar, Editor Genl. Practice Sec. Newsletter, 1976-78; **EDUC:** BA, 1967, Hist., Coll. of William and Mary; **GRAD EDUC:** JD, 1970, Law, Univ. of WI; **MIL SERV:** USMC, Maj.; **OTHER ACT & HONORS:** Past. Pres. McHenry Jaycees Bd. of Dir. McHenry C of C, Past Chmn. Amer. Cancer Dr., Lynn Martin for Congress, Fin. Comm.; **HOME ADD:** 9213 High Meadow Ln., Woodstock, IL 60098, (815)338-8677; **BUS ADD:** 3424 W. Elm St., McHenry, IL 60050.

LANA, Edward C.——B: Dec. 3, 1925, Flagler, CO, *VP & Sr. Appraiser*, Western Fed. Savings; **PRIM RE ACT:** Instructor, Consultant, Appraiser, Developer, Builder, Property Manager, Lender, Owner/Investor; **SERVICES:** RE Investing, Consulting & Appraising; **REP CLIENTS:** Investors & Lenders; **PREV EMPLOY:** 24 yrs. in present position; **PROFL AFFIL & HONORS:** MAI, SRPA, Past Pres. CO MAI Chap. #22 & Past Pres. Denver Chap. #9 - SREA's; **EDUC:** Sr. Status, 1982, RE, CO Univ.; **MIL SERV:** US Army, Cpl.; **OTHER ACT & HONORS:** Dir. of Numerous Orgs.; **HOME ADD:** 3797 S Josmine St., Denver, CO 80237, (303)758-0803; **BUS ADD:** 200 Univ. Blvd., Denver, CO 80206, (303)370-1212.

LANCE, James W.——B: July 26, 1943, Little Rock, AR, *Pres.*, AR Fin. Serv., Inc.; **PRIM RE ACT:** Consultant, Attorney, Lender, Syndicator; **SERVICES:** RE lending, feasibility analysis and synd.; **REP CLIENTS:** Co. is owned by 44 S&L in AR and represents another 75 S&L and banks in the S. and SW; **EDUC:** BS/BA, Acctg., Univ. of AR at Fayetteville; **GRAD EDUC:** JD, School of Law, Univ. of AR; **MIL SERV:** US Army, 1st Lt., Defense Atomic Support Agency, Cett. of Achievement; **OTHER ACT & HONORS:** *Who's Who in Fin. and Indus.*; **HOME ADD:** 10 Heritage Park Cir., N. Little Rock, AR 72116, (501)753-8301; **BUS ADD:** 300 Spring Bldg. Suite 800, Little Rock, AR 72201, (501)376-9997.

LANCY, John S.——B: Jan. 22, 1945, E. St. Louis, IL, *Pres.*, Lancy, Scult & Ryan, A Professional Association; **PRIM RE ACT:** Attorney; **SERVICES:** Legal serv. in RE, tax analysis and partnership formation; **REP CLIENTS:** Trammell Crow Co., Park West Devel. Co., Leo Eisenberg & Assoc., Bellamah Devel. Corp., Roth Devel. Corp., United Devel., Inc. and others involved in RE lending, devel. and investment; **PREV EMPLOY:** Judicial Clerk, US Ct. of Appeals (Ninth Circuit); Streich, Lang, Weeks & Cardon (Phoenix, AZ); **PROFL AFFIL & HONORS:** State Bar of AZ; State Bar of CA; ABA, Comm. on RE Tax Problems, Who's Who in Amer. Law (Marquis-2nd Ed.); **EDUC:** BS, 1966, Acctg., AZ State Univ.; **GRAD EDUC:** MS, 1968, Acctg., AZ State Univ.; JD, 1970, Law, AZ State Univ.; **EDUC HONORS:** Magna Cum Laude; **BUS ADD:** 3003 N. Central Ave., 26th Floor, Phoenix, AZ 85012, (602)266-4747.

LANDECK, John H.——B: Mar. 2, 1920, Evanston, IL, *Gen. Partner*, Northern Illinois Appraisal Serv.; **PRIM RE ACT:** Broker, Consultant, Appraiser; **SERVICES:** RE appraising and consulting; **REP CLIENTS:** Lending instns., relocation servs., attys., indivs., and devels.; **PROFL AFFIL & HONORS:** Cert. Appraiser - Sr. (CA-S), Amer. Assn. of Cert. Appraisers; **EDUC:** BS E.E., 1942, Electronics and Mech. Engr., IL Inst. of Tech.; **MIL SERV:** US Navy, Ensign; **OTHER ACT & HONORS:** Register of Profl. Engr., State of IL; **HOME ADD:** 2219 W. Langdon Place, Hoffman Estates, IL 60195, (312)885-0024; **BUS ADD:** 2219 W. Langdon Place, Hoffman Estates, IL 60195, (312)885-0024.

LANDERS, Jeffrey A.——B: Sept. 14, 1955, New York, NY, *Leasing Coordinator*, Merrill, Lynch, Pierce, Fenner & Smith, Inc., Locations, Dept., 50th Fl.; **OTHER RE ACT:** Comml. leasing; **SERVICES:** In-house site selection, lease negotiations; **PREV EMPLOY:** Shearson, Loeb, Rhoades, Inc.; Metro. Life Ins. Co.; **PROFL AFFIL & HONORS:** NACORE; **EDUC:** BA, 1979, Psych., Columbia Univ.; **EDUC HONORS:** Dean's List; **HOME ADD:** 43-30 44th St., Long Island City, NY 11104, (212)784-3578; **BUS ADD:** 165 Broadway, 1 Liberty Plaza, New York, NY 10080, (212)637-5230.

LANDESS, Fred S.——B: Jan. 27, 1933, Memphis, TN, *Part.*, McGuire, Woods & Battle, Charlottesville; **PRIM RE ACT:** Attorney; **SERVICES:** Gen. legal; **REP CLIENTS:** Charlottesville-Albermarle Bd. of Realtors; **PROFL AFFIL & HONORS:** Charlottesville-Albemarle, VA & Amer. Bar Assns.; Assoc. Member Charlottesville-Albemarle Bd. of Realtors, Former Chmn. RE Comm. for VA Bar Assn.; **EDUC:** BA, 1955, Pol. Sci., Wake Forest 1951-53; Geo. Wash. Univ., 1953-55; **GRAD EDUC:** LLB, 1958, Univ. of VA; **EDUC HONORS:** Editorial Bd. VA Law Review; **OTHER ACT & HONORS:** Sec. Charlottesville Bd. of Zoning Appeals, 1965-67; **HOME ADD:** 806 Gilliams Mountain Rd., Charlottesville, VA 22901, (804)293-9384; **BUS ADD:** PO Box 1191, Charlottesville, VA 22902, (804)977-2500.

LANDIS, Martin——B: New York, NY, *Chairman*, Oak Partners; **PRIM RE ACT:** Consultant, Developer, Owner/Investor; **OTHER RE ACT:** Administrator/Developer; **HOME ADD:** 3494 Red Rose Dr., Encino, CA 91436, (213)990-9898; **BUS ADD:** 3494 Red Rose Dr., Encino, CA 91436, (213)990-9898.

LANDMEIER, Allen L.——B: Nov. 24, 1942, Elmhurst, IL, *Lawyer*, Smith & Landmeier, P.C.; **PRIM RE ACT:** Attorney; **SERVICES:** Legal; **PROFL AFFIL & HONORS:** IL State Bar Assn. (State Tax Sect. Council), ABA and Kane County Bar Assn.; **EDUC:** BSEE, 1964, Valparaiso Univ.; **GRAD EDUC:** J.D., 1967, Valparaiso Univ.; **EDUC HONORS:** Tau Beta Pi (Engrg. Hon.) & Alph Pi (Sr. Mens Honorary), Law Review Notes Editor; **MIL SERV:** USNR, Lieut.; **OTHER ACT & HONORS:** City Atty. St. Charles, IL 1977, St. Marks Lutheran Church, Chmn Bd. of Dir. 1977 - 1978; **HOME ADD:** 513 South 13th St., St. Charles, IL 60174, (312)584-8988; **BUS ADD:** 15 North Second St., Geneva, IL 60134, (312)232-2880.

LANDOW, Nathan——B: Oct. 22, 1932, Orange, NJ, *Owner*, Landow & Co.; **PRIM RE ACT:** Developer, Builder, Owner/Investor, Property Manager; **BUS ADD:** 4710 Bethesda Ave., Bethesda, MD 20814, (301)657-4600.

LANDRY, Brian F.——B: March 22, 1948, Boston, MA, *Managing Dir.*, Smith Barney Realty Serv.; **PRIM RE ACT:** Broker, Syndicator, Consultant; **REP CLIENTS:** Nat. prominent dev., corp., domestic and offshore invest.; **PREV EMPLOY:** VP Soc. for Savings, 1978-80, Asst. VP Chase Manhattan Bank, 1974-78; **EDUC:** AB, 1970, Amer. Hist., Harvard Coll.; **GRAD EDUC:** MBA, 1974, Fin, Tuck School, Dartmouth Coll.; **EDUC HONORS:** Cum Laude; **HOME ADD:** 353 E. 83rd St., New York, NY 10028, (212)535-0985; **BUS ADD:** 1345 Ave. of the Americas, New York, NY 10028, (212)399-3382.

LANDRY, Charles A.——B: Dec. 5, 1953, Crowley, LA, *Partner/Stock Holder*, Gary and Field, A Professional Corp.; **PRIM RE ACT:** Attorney; **SERVICES:** Legal representation; **REP CLIENTS:** Bank and S&L; **EDUC:** BA, 1975, Bus., LA State Univ.; **GRAD EDUC:** JD, 1977, Estate Planning, LA State Univ.; **EDUC HONORS:** Phi Kappa Phi; **HOME ADD:** 6341 Jefferson Hwy., Baton Rouge, LA; **BUS ADD:** Suite 302, 5420 Corporate Blvd., Baton Rouge, LA 70808, (504)923-3570.

LANE, Arthur——*Dir. Emp. Rel.*, UMC Industries, Inc.; **PRIM RE ACT:** Property Manager; **BUS ADD:** High Ridge Park, Stamford, CT 06904, (203)329-6000.*

LANE, Bruce S.——B: May 15, 1932, New London, CT, *President*, Lane and Edson, PC, Attys. at Law; **PRIM RE ACT:** Attorney; **SERVICES:** General practice with emphasis on federal tax matters, corp. and securities law, real estate, housing and urban affairs.; **REP CLIENTS:** Investment bankers, lending institutions, equity capital corps., public and pvt. ltd. partnerships, foreign pension funds and other investors in US RE, developers, trade assns., businesses and corps.; **PREV EMPLOY:** VP and Gen Counsel, Nat. Corp. for Housing Partnerships , 1969 - 1970; Sec. and Asst. Gen. Counsel, Corp. and Tax Matters, Communications Satellite Corp., 1965 -1969; Tax Atty., Dinsmore, Shohl, Barrett, Coates & Deupree, Cincinnati, OH, 1961 -1965;Sr. Trial Atty., Tax Division, US Dept of Justice, 1959-1961; Assoc., Squire, Sanders, & Dempsey, Cleveland, OH, 1955-1959; **PROFL AFFIL & HONORS:** Member, Amer. Law Inst.; ABA: Member, ABA Special Comm. on Housing and Urban Devel. Law, 1970-1974; Member, Sect. of Taxation (Chmn., Comm. on Ct. Procedure, 1968-1969); Amer. Coll. of RE Lawyers, Member of Bd. of Govs.; **EDUC:** AB, 1952, Harvard Coll.; **GRAD EDUC:** JD, 1955, Harvard Law School; **EDUC HONORS:** Magna Cum Laude, Phi Betta Kappa; **OTHER ACT & HONORS:** Incorporator, Dir. and Past Pres. of the DC Inst. of Mental Hygiene; Past Chmn. of the Citizens' Comm. of Sect. 5 of the Village of Chevy Chase, MD; Member, Montgomery Cty. Hist. Preservation Commn.; **HOME ADD:** 3711 Thornapple St., Chevy Chase, MD 20815, (301)656-3827; **BUS ADD:** Suite 400 S., 1800 M St., N.W., Washington, DC 20036, (202)457-6800.

LANE, Daniel P.——B: Sept. 4, 1938, Syracuse, NY, *VP*, Appraisers and Planners, Inc.; **PRIM RE ACT:** Consultant, Appraiser; **SERVICES:** Appraisal, RE Investment and Tax Counseling; **REP CLIENTS:** Corps., Investors, Lending Instns., Law Firms, Govt. Agencies, Devels. & Owners of Comml. and Indust. RE; **PREV EMPLOY:** Sr. Appraiser, Stone & Webster Appraisal Corp.; RE Officer, NY State Urban Devel. Corp.; **PROFL AFFIL & HONORS:** AIREA; ASA; SREA; Intl. Right of Way Assn.; IIV; RE Bd. of NY; **EDUC:** BA, 1965, Lib. Arts/Econ., State Univ. of NY at Oswego; **GRAD EDUC:** Grad. Studies, 1970 - 1972, Pub. Admin., City Univ., Baruch Coll.; **EDUC HONORS:** Member, Lambda Alpha, Land Econ. Frat.; **MIL SERV:** US Army; Spec. - 5, Good Conduct Medal; Third Infantry

NCO Academy; **OTHER ACT & HONORS:** Metrop. Museum of Art; Eagle Scout; **HOME ADD:** 110 Riverside Dr., New York, NY 10024, (212)595-6061; **BUS ADD:** 500 Fifth Ave., New York, NY 10024, (212)221-8300.

LANE, Edward E., Jr.——B: July 19, 1945, Richmond, VA, *Pres.*, Windsor Properties Inc.; **PRIM RE ACT:** Broker, Attorney; **SERVICES:** Sale of larger Apt. Props. (100+ Units) in VA & NC & other Southeastern States to investors; **REP CLIENTS:** Large public funds, medium sized pvt. placements, synds., sales over $30,000,000 in 1981; **PREV EMPLOY:** Apt. & Condo. Devel.; **PROFL AFFIL & HONORS:** ABA, VA Bar Assn., NAR, Richmond Bd. of Realtors; **EDUC:** BA, 1967, Econ., Univ. of VA; **GRAD EDUC:** JD, 1970, Law, Univ. of VA; MBA, 1976, Bus., V.C.U.; **EDUC HONORS:** Deans List, Top 5% of Class; **OTHER ACT & HONORS:** Currently working part time on a Master of Law in Taxation at William and Mary Law School(to be completed June, 1983); **BUS ADD:** Ste 1604, 700 Bldg., Richmond, VA 23219, (804)780-1312.

LANE, Edwin Green——B: July 29, 1942, Nashville, TN, *Prin.*, Lane & Associates; **PRIM RE ACT:** Consultant; **SERVICES:** Bus. and real prop. consultants; **REP CLIENTS:** Indivs. and corps. with real prop. interests; **PREV EMPLOY:** Pres., Farmer Enterprises; Rgnl. Dir. of RE, Volume Shoe Corp. (Div. of May Dept. Store Co.); Nat. Dir RE, Jerrico, Inc.; **PROFL AFFIL & HONORS:** Intl. Council of Shopping Ctrs.; Nat. Assn. of Corp. RE Execs.; Amer. Arbitration Assn., Lic. RE Broker, GA, KY, TN, NC, SC; **EDUC:** BA, 1964, Mktg./Advtg./Bus., Univ. of GA; **OTHER ACT & HONORS:** Member, Amer. Contract Bridge League; **HOME ADD:** 312 Henry Clay Blvd., Lexington, KY 40502, (606)266-4175; **BUS ADD:** 2670 Wilhite Dr., Lexington, KY 40503, (606)278-9427.

LANE, Franklin K., III——B: Jan. 30, 1924, Los Angeles, CA, *Atty.-at-Law*, Self-employed; **PRIM RE ACT:** Broker, Consultant, Attorney, Developer, Owner/Investor; **REP CLIENTS:** The Kissell Co.; George Elkins Co.; numerous mort., escrow and RE cos., and RE devels.; **PROFL AFFIL & HONORS:** Real Prop. Sec. of L.A. Cty. Bar Assn.; **EDUC:** BS, 1947, Chemistry, Univ. of VA; **GRAD EDUC:** LLB, 1949, Taxation, Univ. of VA; **MIL SERV:** US Navy, Lieut.; **OTHER ACT & HONORS:** Various civic and cultural organizations; **HOME ADD:** 1745 Selby Ave., Los Angeles, CA 90024, (213)474-7722; **BUS ADD:** 10100 Santa Monica Blvd. (25th floor), Los Angeles, CA 90067, (213)879-2535.

LANE, James P.——B: Sept. 18, 1926, Los Angeles, CA, *RE Consultant*; **PRIM RE ACT:** Consultant; **SERVICES:** Problem solving - procedure advice; **REP CLIENTS:** Corporate RE depts.; **PREV EMPLOY:** V.P. Levitt Multi-housing - Div. of Levitt & Sons (ITT) Admin. Planning; V.P. Valley Forge Corp. (Motel Div., Prop. Mgmt., Mobil Park Devel.); Project Coordinator DEVCOA- Div. of W.R. Grace, Comml. Devel.; **PROFL AFFIL & HONORS:** NACORE (Presently Atlanta Chap. Pres.); **EDUC:** BS, 1950, Econ., Univ. of VA; **GRAD EDUC:** MBA, 1975, Bus., GA Tech; **MIL SERV:** USNR-R, Lt.j.g.; **HOME ADD:** 2683 Leslie Dr., Atlanta, GA 30345, (404)939-2572; **BUS ADD:** 1925 Century Blvd., Suite 4, Atlanta, GA 30345, (404)325-7999.

LANE, John Marshall——B: Oct. 31, 1910, New Haven, CT, *Atty.*; **PRIM RE ACT:** Broker, Attorney; **OTHER RE ACT:** Estate planning; **SERVICES:** Investment, financial, taxation, legal, title; **PROFL AFFIL & HONORS:** ABA; MA Bar Assn.; Boston Bar Assn.; Barnstable Cty. Bar Assn.; ABA Sections, Probate, Real Property, Taxation, Chmn., MA Bar Assns., Probate Comm. Estate & Gift Tax Comm., 1968-1978; Member, Probate Council MBA, 1978 - term ends 1983; co-author MA Estate Tax (joint MA-Boston Bar Comm.); **EDUC:** BA, 1935, Pol. Sci./pre-Med., Univ. Pacific; **GRAD EDUC:** JD, 1940, Law, Geo. Wash. Univ.; BSc, 1937, Med., Geo. Wash. Univ.; **MIL SERV:** USN, Lt., WW II; **OTHER ACT & HONORS:** Pres., Barnstable Cty. Bar Assn., 1975-1976; **HOME ADD:** 528 Main St., Dennisport, MA 02639, (617)394-4105; **BUS ADD:** 530 Main St., Box 86, Dennisport, MA 02639, (617)398-3371.

LANE, John W., Jr.——B: Sept. 1, 1933, Pittsfield, ME, *Pres.*, The Lane Assoc.; **PRIM RE ACT:** Broker, Instructor, Consultant, Appraiser, Owner/Investor; **OTHER RE ACT:** Health care exec.; **SERVICES:** Feasibility; **REP CLIENTS:** Investors participating in partial interests; **PREV EMPLOY:** RE since 1959; **PROFL AFFIL & HONORS:** S. Kennebec Valley Bd. of Realtors, Omega Tau Rho, Nat. RE Honor Soc., Maine Realtor of Yr., 1975, GRI, CRS; **EDUC:** BA, 1956, Bus. Admin., Econ., Univ. of ME, Orono; **MIL SERV:** USNR, Lt. j.g., 1956-59; **OTHER ACT & HONORS:** Member Amer. Coll. of Nursing Home Admins., Member Pres. 'Devel. Council' Univ. of ME, Orono, 3rd term; Distinguished Service Award 1974; Jack Orino Memorial Award; JCI Senator; **HOME ADD:** Lookout Point E, Winthrop, ME 04343, (207)395-4729; **BUS ADD:** 8 Green St., Augusta, ME 04330, (207)622-6221.

LANE, Joseph, Jr.——*Partner*, The Evans Partnership; **PRIM RE ACT:** Developer; **BUS ADD:** 745 Fifth Ave., New York, NY 10022, (212)755-0443.*

LANE, Landon B.——*Sr. VP*, Lane Co., Inc.; **PRIM RE ACT:** Property Manager; **BUS ADD:** PO Box 151, Altavista, VA 24517, (804)369-5641.*

LANE, Lucien B.——B: July 22, 1947, Baltimore, MD, *Mgr. Prop. Mgmt. Dept.*, Sharp - Boylston Co.; **PRIM RE ACT:** Property Manager; **SERVICES:** Full service prop. mgmt.; **PREV EMPLOY:** Comml. Sales Mgr. Askew Realty; Gen. Mgr. Diego, Prime Comml. Prop. (Ft. Lauderdale); **PROFL AFFIL & HONORS:** IREM, Atlanta Bd. of Realtors, CPM; **EDUC:** BA, 1970, Eng. Lit., The Citadel, The Military Coll. of SC; **GRAD EDUC:** MBA, 1975, RE, GA State Univ.; **MIL SERV:** US Army, 1st Lt.; **HOME ADD:** 2489 Bayard St., E. Point, GA 30344, (404)767-1809; **BUS ADD:** 66 Luckie St., 7th Fl., Atlanta, GA 30303, (404)522-2929.

LANE, Michael——*VP, Secy. & Cont.*, Laclede Steel Co.; **PRIM RE ACT:** Property Manager; **BUS ADD:** Equitable Bldg., 10 Broadway, St. Louis, MO 63102, (314)425-1400.*

LANE, Robert D., Jr.——B: Apr. 10, 1952, New York, NY, Fox, Rothschild, O'Brien & Frankel; **PRIM RE ACT:** Attorney; **SERVICES:** Comml. RE Transactions and Litigation; **REP CLIENTS:** Devel., Lenders, Synd., Brokers, Condo., Public & Pvt. Bus.; **PREV EMPLOY:** Law Clerk, Hon. Harry A. Takiff, Phila. Court of Common Pleas 1977-1978; **PROFL AFFIL & HONORS:** ABA; PA B.A., Committee on Condo., Phila. Bar Assn., Comm. on Condemnations & Appraisals, Phila. Volunteer Lawyers for the Arts.; **EDUC:** BA, 1973, English Lit. Honors Program, Brown Univ.; **GRAD EDUC:** JD, 1977, Law, Univ. of PA; **EDUC HONORS:** Founder and Editor, Brown/RISD Literary-arts Magazine, Arthur Littleton Fellowship, Moot Court Bd.; **OTHER ACT & HONORS:** Citizens Crime Comm. of Phila; Instructor, RE Law, Manor Jr. Coll.; **BUS ADD:** 10th Floor, 2000 Market St., Philadelphia, PA 19103, (215)299-2142.

LANE, Robert H.——B: Apr. 3, 1940, Boston, MA, *Pres.*, Boston Development Associates, Inc.; **PRIM RE ACT:** Consultant, Developer, Builder, Owner/Investor, Property Manager; **SERVICES:** Devel., Gen. Contracting, Mgmt., Consulting; **REP CLIENTS:** Retail Chains for all of the services listed; **PREV EMPLOY:** Star Market (Division of Jewel Co.)-1964-1965; Zayre Corp. 1966-1969; **PROFL AFFIL & HONORS:** ICSC; **EDUC:** BA, 1962, Pol. Sci. and Econ., Brown Univ.; **GRAD EDUC:** MBA, 1964, Fin., Grad. School of Bus., Columbia Univ.; **OTHER ACT & HONORS:** Bd. of Dir. of *For Spacious Skies*; **HOME ADD:** 168 Point Rd., Marion, MA 02738, (617)748-1045; **BUS ADD:** 233 Needham St., Newton, MA 02164, (617)964-1760.

LANE, Robert K.——*Pres.*, R. Kingsbury Lane, Inc.; **PRIM RE ACT:** Attorney, Developer, Builder, Owner/Investor; **PREV EMPLOY:** James W. Rouse, Inc. Mort. Bankers; **EDUC:** 1966, Hist., Univ. of CA at Berkeley; **GRAD EDUC:** JD, 1969, Loyola School of Law; **MIL SERV:** US Army Intelligence, 1st Lt.; **HOME ADD:** 8 Sotelo, Piedmont, CA 94611; **BUS ADD:** 125 - 12th St., Ste. 102, Oakland, CA 94607, (415)465-1933.

LANE, Tom R.——B: Dec. 15, 1928, McKinney, TX, *Owner*, Lane Real Estate Appraisers; **PRIM RE ACT:** Appraiser; **REP CLIENTS:** Banks, savings & loan assns., govt. agencies, attys.; **PREV EMPLOY:** Self-employed since 1950; **PROFL AFFIL & HONORS:** Soc. of RE Appraisers; Intl. Right of Way Assn.; Bd. of Realtors, SRA; SR/WA; **EDUC:** BBA, 1950, Bus., N TX State Univ.; **HOME ADD:** 1731 Bonner St., McKinney, TX 75069, (214)542-4765; **BUS ADD:** 1414 S Tennessee St., McKinney, TX 75669, (214)542-0168.

LANE, William M.——B: Sept. 15, 1935, Columbus, OH, *Partner*, Lane, Alton & Horst; **PRIM RE ACT:** Attorney; **PROFL AFFIL & HONORS:** Columbus, OH Bar Assns., and ABA; **EDUC:** BA, 1957, English, Amherst Coll.; **GRAD EDUC:** JD, 1960, Law, Univ. of MI Law Sch.; **EDUC HONORS:** The Rotary Club of Columbus, Inc., Administrative Law Representatives Bd. of Advisors Childhood League, Inc., Exec. Comm., Amer. Cancer Soc., OH Div., Inc.; **HOME ADD:** 2350 Brentwood Rd., Columbus, OH 43209, (614)252-4123; **BUS ADD:** 155 E. Broad St., 16th Flr., Columbus, OH 43215, (614)228-6885.

LANER, Harlan S.——B: July 12, 1928, Kansas City, MO, The Laner Co.; **PRIM RE ACT:** Consultant, Developer, Owner/Investor, Property Manager, Syndicator; **SERVICES:** Site location, leasing, fin., bldg. comm. property; **REP CLIENTS:** Grocery, drug, general merch.

retailers; **PROFL AFFIL & HONORS:** Landscape Award, State of FL, Comml. Prop., 1976; **EDUC:** BS, 1949, Univ. of MO, School of Bus.; **GRAD EDUC:** MBA, 1969, Bus., Univ. of MO at Kansas City; **MIL SERV:** US Army, Sgt.; **OTHER ACT & HONORS:** C of C, Palm Beach, FL; Bd. of Dir. Bus. School, Univ. of MD at Kansas City; also associated with H. Laner & Assoc., 11C Westgate Lane, Boynton Beach, FL 33436; **BUS ADD:** 5315 W. 95 Terr. 210, Shawnee Mission, KS 66207.

LANG, Judith A.——B: July 1, 1942, Red Wing, MN, *Pres.*, The RE School; **PRIM RE ACT:** Broker, Consultant, Owner/Investor, Instructor, Real Estate Publisher; **PREV EMPLOY:** 1977-1979, Dir. of Instr., Amer. RE Schools, Inc.; 1975-1977, Sr. Instr., Amer. RE Schools, Inc.; 1971-1975, RE Salesperson, Jambor Realtors; 1969-1971, RE Salesperson, Spring Co.; **HOME ADD:** 2088 Randolph, St. Paul, MN 55105, (612)698-1241; **BUS ADD:** 7101 York Ave. S., Edina, MN 55435, (612)698-1241.

LANG, Nancy E.——B: Oct. 23, 1938, Rich Landtown, PA, *Pres.*, Hometrend North, Inc.; **PRIM RE ACT:** Broker, Consultant, Developer, Builder, Owner/Investor, Instructor, Syndicator; **SERVICES:** Lang Assoc. - Comml. & Resid. Brokerage; Hometrend North, Inc. - RE Regional Franchise; **PREV EMPLOY:** Broker, Hickok & Boardman, Inc. (1961-69); **PROFL AFFIL & HONORS:** NAR; RNMI; VT Assn. of Realtors (Past Pres.); Northwestern VT Bd. of Realtors (Past Pres.), Realtor of the Year (1974) Northwestern VT Bd. of Realtors; GRI; CRB; CRS; 1980; **EDUC:** 1955-57, Civil Engrg.; **OTHER ACT & HONORS:** Past Member: Medical Ctr. Assn. Bd. of Trustees, Essex Planning Bd. Chittenden Trust Co., Advisory Bd., Univ. Health Ctr. Bd. of Trustees; Gr. Burl. Indust. Corp. (1st VP); VT Sm. Bus. Devel. Ctr. (Sec./Treas.); Lake Champlain Regional C of C (Past Dir.); VT State C of C (Past Dir); **HOME ADD:** 43 Upper Main St., Essex Jct., VT 05452, (802)878-5720; **BUS ADD:** 360 Main St., Burlington, VT 05401, (802)864-0541.

LANG, Richard F.——B: Apr. 27, 1944, New York, NY, *VP & Mort. Admin.*, Inst. Securities Corp.; **PRIM RE ACT:** Consultant, Appraiser, Banker, Lender, Owner/Investor, Property Manager; **SERVICES:** All mort. loan operations & serv., includes sec. mktg.; **REP CLIENTS:** Savings banks & pension funds; **PREV EMPLOY:** Appraiser NY Life Ins. Co., Comml. RE loans, Marine Midland Banks, Inc.; **PROFL AFFIL & HONORS:** NYS Soc. of RE Appraisers; **EDUC:** AAS, 1968, Acctg., City Univ. of NY; BS, 1972, Fin., Mktg., City Univ. of NY; **MIL SERV:** US Army, Sgt.; **OTHER ACT & HONORS:** Various Local Charities and Civil Assns.; Seminar Speaker Conventional Secondary Market Operations; **BUS ADD:** 200 Park Ave., New York, NY 10166, (212)949-9738.

LANG, Tom H.——B: May 26, 1929, Cleveland, OH, *Owner*, Tom H. Lang & Co.; **PRIM RE ACT:** Broker, Consultant, Developer, Owner/Investor; **SERVICES:** Complete indus. and office bldg. broker; **REP CLIENTS:** AGE, Consulting & Devel. many of Fortune 500; **PREV EMPLOY:** Founding partner (Ragin, Lang, Free & Smythe, Inc.) (originally founded 1867 and restructured 1965); **PROFL AFFIL & HONORS:** SIR, ASREC, ULI, local, state & national associations of realtors, Past president (1976) S.I.R., member executive officer Cleveland area bldg. realtors; **EDUC:** BS, 1951, Econ. - Bus. - Polit. Sci., Univ. of MI; **MIL SERV:** USNR, Non-Com Officer; **OTHER ACT & HONORS:** Ex. Council Boy Scouts, Brd M.S. and many others; **HOME ADD:** 2781 Chesterton Rd., Shaker Heights, OH 44122, (216)321-6404; **BUS ADD:** 30195 Chagrin Blvd., Suite 200, Cleveland, OH 44124, (216)292-6777.

LANGE, Angelika C.——B: Feb. 17, 1947, Germany, *Partner*, Hollrah, Lange & Thoma; **PRIM RE ACT:** Attorney; **SERVICES:** Drafting of comml. RE and const. contracts, formation of partnerships, corporations and other bus. entities.; **REP CLIENTS:** For. comml. investors; **PROFL AFFIL & HONORS:** ABA, RE Sect.; TX Bar Assn.; Houston Bar Assn.; **EDUC:** BA, 1972, Languages, Univ. of Houston; **GRAD EDUC:** JD, 1975, Law, Bates Coll. of Law, Univ. of Houston; **OTHER ACT & HONORS:** Task Force Chmn. Houston C of C; German-Amer. C of C; VChmn.-Young Execs. of Houston World Trade Assn.; Dir.-Houston Young lawyers Assn.; **HOME ADD:** 8433 Merlin, Houston, TX 77055, (713)932-1607; **BUS ADD:** Twelve Greenway Plaza, Suite 1200, Houston, TX 77046, (713)961-1212.

LANGE, Ed——B: Jan. 31, 1920, Chicago, IL, *Pres.*, E.G. L. Enterprises, Inc.; **PRIM RE ACT:** Consultant, Developer, Builder, Property Manager, Lender, Owner/Investor; **PROFL AFFIL & HONORS:** AIA Creative Visualations; **EDUC:** AA, BA, 1941, Design Criteria & Mass Moulding, ILL; **HOME ADD:** 700 Robinson Rd., Topanga, CA 90290; **BUS ADD:** 5436 Fernwood Ave., Los Angeles, CA 90027, (213)465-7121.

LANGE, Sylvin R.——*San Joaquin County Economic Development Assn.*; **PRIM RE ACT:** Property Manager, Developer; **BUS ADD:** 709 N. Center, Ste 2A, Stockton, CA 95202, (209)465-5931.*

LANGENDOEN, Gary——B: Sept. 4, 1945, *Sr. VP*, Pacifica Real Property Investments, Corp.; **PRIM RE ACT:** Consultant, Developer, Owner/Investor, Property Manager, Syndicator; **SERVICES:** Synd/pf apts. in sunbelt states; **REP CLIENTS:** Joint venture lenders, instnl. investors, stock brokerage houses, for comml. prop.; **PREV EMPLOY:** Wilshire Mort. Corp., 1978-81; **PROFL AFFIL & HONORS:** IREM, RESSI, CPM; IREM L.A. Chapter President; IREM Academy of Authors; **EDUC:** BBA, 1967, Bus. Admin., Univ. of TX; **GRAD EDUC:** MBA, 1976, Bus. Admin., Pepperdine Univ.; **EDUC HONORS:** Honors; **MIL SERV:** USN, Lt., Vietnam; **HOME ADD:** 12720 Burbank Blvd., #329, N Hollywood, CA 91607, (213)506-6245; **BUS ADD:** 16055 Ventura Blvd., Suite 400, Encino, CA 91436, (213)986-4005.

LANGERUD, Don——B: Aug. 26, 1951, Rolla, ND, *Pres.*, Town & Country RE, Inc.; **PRIM RE ACT:** Broker, Owner/Investor, Property Manager, Syndicator; **SERVICES:** Resid. Re-Sale, Devel., Synd. of devel. of prop. mgmt.; **REP CLIENTS:** Comml. Prop., indiv. investors, gen. public, comml. and bus. opportunities re-sale; **PREV EMPLOY:** VP (Sales Mgr.) Severson RE Grand Forks, ND 1975-1980; **PROFL AFFIL & HONORS:** Grand Forks Bd. of Realtors, ND Bd. of Realtors, NAR, GRI, 1981 Realtor of the year-Grand Forks Bd. of Realtors; **EDUC:** 1968-1971, Mktg. and Mgmt., Devils Lake Region Jr. Coll.; Mktg. and Mgmt., 1974, Univ. of ND; **MIL SERV:** USAF, E-4, Sgt.; **OTHER ACT & HONORS:** Optimist Club, YMCA, Elks Lodge #255, C of C - all of Grand Forks, and RNMI; **HOME ADD:** 4120 Walnut St., Grand Forks, ND 58201, (701)772-5280; **BUS ADD:** 1306 10th Ave. S., Grand Forks, ND 58201, (701)746-8477.

LANGLEY, Arlington R.——B: Apr. 26, 1915, New York, NY, *Owner*, LL Management Co.; **PRIM RE ACT:** Broker, Consultant, Instructor, Property Manager; **SERVICES:** Prop. mgmt., RE consultant; **REP CLIENTS:** Devel. builders, investors; **PREV EMPLOY:** RE Broker since 1951; **PROFL AFFIL & HONORS:** IREM, CPM; **EDUC:** BA, 1951, Bus. admin., RE, Ins., Univ. of CA, Berkeley, San Jose Univ.; **MIL SERV:** Artillery, Col., Soldiers Medal, 3 Bronze Stars, others; **OTHER ACT & HONORS:** Rotary Club; **HOME ADD:** PO Box 292, Capitola, CA 95010, (408)476-2115; **BUS ADD:** 523 Capitola Ave. Suite B, Capitola, CA 95010, (408)476-2115.

LANGLEY, John W.——B: Nov. 3, 1935, Hollywood, CA, *Broker*, Commerce Properties, Inc.; **PRIM RE ACT:** Broker, Developer, Owner/Investor, Instructor, Syndicator; **SERVICES:** Comml. & Investment Brokerage; Devel.; Construction; **REP CLIENTS:** Lenders & Indiv. or Institut. Investors or users of Comml. Prop.; **PREV EMPLOY:** Box Elder Cty. Bank, Brigham City, UT 1961-1968, Bank of UT, Ogden, UT 1957-1961; **PROFL AFFIL & HONORS:** RNMI, Chmn. UT RE Educ. Found., GRI, CRB, CRS; **EDUC:** AA, 1960, Acctg., Weber State Coll.; **MIL SERV:** USMC, Cpl.; **HOME ADD:** 780 E Nancy Dr., S Ogden, UT 84403, (801)479-3817; **BUS ADD:** 780 E. Nancy Dr., South Ogden, UT 84403, (801)479-3322.

LANGSON, Jack M.——Investment Building Group; **PRIM RE ACT:** Developer; **BUS ADD:** 515 South Flower St. Ste. 970, Los Angeles, CA 90071, (213)613-1000.*

LANGSTON, William E.——B: Aug. 8, 1931, NC, *Corp. Sec.*, Snyder-Langston, Inc.; **PRIM RE ACT:** Consultant, Banker, Developer, Builder; **SERVICES:** Construction consultation, gen. contractor; **REP CLIENTS:** Ford Motor Co., The Irvine Co., Montgomery-Ward; **PROFL AFFIL & HONORS:** AGCA; **OTHER ACT & HONORS:** Commnr., Orange Cty. Airport Land Use Comm.; Big Canyon Ctry. Club; Back Bay Club; **HOME ADD:** 18 Oakcrest Ln., Newport Beach, CA 92660, (714)640-5133; **BUS ADD:** 17962 Cowan, Irvine, CA 92714, (714)557-7533.

LANIER, Randolph H.——B: Aug. 26, 1949, Owensboro, KY, *Partner (Attorney)*, Balch, Bingham, Baker, Hawthorne, Williams & Ward; **PRIM RE ACT:** Attorney; **SERVICES:** Legal consultation and advice, RE purchase, sale and mgmt. of RE props. (comml.); **REP CLIENTS:** Lenders, devels. and indiv. or institutional investors in comml. RE; **PREV EMPLOY:** Law Clerk, US District Court for N.D. of AL (Judge James H. Hancock) (1974-75); **PROFL AFFIL & HONORS:** ABA, AL Bar Assn., Birmingham Bar Assn.; **EDUC:** BS, 1971, Bus. Admin., Univ. of AL; **GRAD EDUC:** JD, 1974, Vanderbilt Univ. School of Law; **MIL SERV:** USAR, Capt.; **HOME ADD:** 301 Dexter Ave., Birmingham, AL 35213, (205)870-8382; **BUS ADD:** 600 N. 18th St., Birmingham, AL 35203, (205)251-8100.

LANIER, Thomas——*VP Fin. & Treas.*, Salem Carpet Mills, Inc.; **PRIM RE ACT:** Property Manager; **BUS ADD:** I-40 at Linville Rd., PO Box 12429, Winston-Salem, NC 27107, (919)727-1200.*

LANNING, J. Clair——**B:** March 23, 1913, Hastings, NE, *CPM*, J. Clair Lanning; **PRIM RE ACT:** Consultant, Property Manager, Owner/Investor; **SERVICES:** Condo. Consulting, Prop. Mgr., Arbitrage; **REP CLIENTS:** Condo Assoc., Lenders, Owners of Prop.; **PREV EMPLOY:** 1972-73 Natl. Center for Housing Mgmt., US Govt., Comml. Facilities, 1944-45, Manhattan Project 1943; **PROFL AFFIL & HONORS:** IREM, Realtor, Mgr. of Yr. (1973), IREM Fl W. Coast Chapt., Author of Best Magazine Article, FL Realtor (1976); **EDUC:** Attended Univ. of NE, 1930-33, Bus. Admin./Architecture, Univ. of NE; **MIL SERV:** US Army, Non-Com; **OTHER ACT & HONORS:** St. Petersburg, FL, Chrm. of City Housing Commn, 1969; Mem. of Planning Bd., 1975-76, Past Pres. of Kiwanis, Shrine, Rod & Gun Club; **HOME ADD:** 6144 10th Ave. So., Gulfport, FL 33707, (813)347-2809; **BUS ADD:** P.O. Box 11515, St. Petersburg, FL 33733, (813)823-2518.

LANNING, Robert E.——**B:** Sept. 30, 1932, Rochester, NY, *Owner*, Robert E. Lanning, Appraisals and Consultations; **PRIM RE ACT:** Broker, Consultant, Appraiser; **SERVICES:** Appraisals, Consultations; **REP CLIENTS:** Citibank, Bankers Trust, Chemical Bank, FNMA, GMIG, FHYA, VA, Northfield S.B., Ninth Fed. S&L Assn., East River S.R., DIMC S.B. etc.; **PROFL AFFIL & HONORS:** SIBOR, MAI, SREA; **EDUC:** BA, 1954, Lib. Arts., Univ. of Rochester; **HOME ADD:** 70 Youmalt Ave., Staten Is., NY 10312, (212)984-1356; **BUS ADD:** 26 Bay St., Staten Is., NY 10301, (212)727-2100.

LANNOYE, Lee D.——**B:** Oct. 23, 1937, Wenatchee, WA, *Pres.*, BA Mortgage of Washington; **PRIM RE ACT:** Broker, Banker; **OTHER RE ACT:** Mort. banker; **SERVICES:** RE investment counseling; **PREV EMPLOY:** VP, BankAmerica Realty Services, Inc., 1974-1978; Self-employed RE developer 1969-1973; Mgr. Income Prop. Loans, United CA Mort., 1962-1969; **PROFL AFFIL & HONORS:** ULI, Mort. Bankers Assn., NAIOP; ICSC; **EDUC:** BA, 1959, Fin., Univ. of WA; **MIL SERV:** US Army, Pvt.; **HOME ADD:** 7363 Champagne Pt. Rd., Kirkland, WA 98033; **BUS ADD:** 11058 Main St., Suite 235, Bellevue, WA 98004, (206)451-8120.

LANSFORD, Raymond W.——**B:** Sept. 25, 1920, Linn, MO, *Prof. of Fin.*, Univ. of Missouri-Columbia, College of Bus. & Public Admin.; **PRIM RE ACT:** Consultant, Appraiser; **OTHER RE ACT:** Professor of Fin.; **SERVICES:** Consultant, appraiser and lecturer; **PREV EMPLOY:** Broker for 30 yrs.; **PROFL AFFIL & HONORS:** MO Assn. of Realtors; NIREB; Fin. Mgmt. Assn., MO Realtor of the Yr., 1976; **EDUC:** BBA, 1946, Bus., Southwest MO State Univ.; **GRAD EDUC:** MS, 1947, Mktg./Fin., Northwestern Univ.; PhD, 1954, Mktg./Fin., NYU; **MIL SERV:** USAF; 1st Lt.; Air Medal and Clusters; **OTHER ACT & HONORS:** VP, Kiwanis Intl., 1981-1982; **HOME ADD:** 115 W. Ridgeley Rd., Columbia, MO 65201, (314)442-6943; **BUS ADD:** 11 Middlebush Hall, UMB, Columbia, MO 65211, (314)882-6681.

LANSING, Glenn V.——**B:** Aug. 25, 1919, Lembi Co., ID, *Pres.*, Bullier & Bullier of Washington Inc.; **PRIM RE ACT:** Broker, Consultant; **SERVICES:** Comml. & Indus. Brokerage; **PROFL AFFIL & HONORS:** SIR; Seattle King Co. Bd. of Realtors; **EDUC:** BS, 1950, Geology, Univ. of WA; **EDUC HONORS:** Sigma Gamma Epsilon; **MIL SERV:** US Navy; **HOME ADD:** 16521 NE 1st Pl., Bellevue, WA 98008, (206)747-9989; **BUS ADD:** One Union Sq., Seattle, WA 98101, (206)223-1171.

LANSINGER, John P.——**B:** Aug. 23, 1936, Baltimore, MD, *Project Mgr.*, Transcontinental Properties; **PRIM RE ACT:** Developer; **SERVICES:** Fully devel. bus. parks Baltimore, MD area; **PREV EMPLOY:** Mgr., Industrial Dev. Penn Central Railroad; **PROFL AFFIL & HONORS:** SIR; NAIOP; **EDUC:** RE and Trans., Univ. of Baltimore/Johns Hopkins Univ.; **OTHER ACT & HONORS:** Anne Arundel Trade Council; Howard County C of C; Pres., Archbishop Keough High School Bd.; **HOME ADD:** 947 Circle Dr., Baltimore, MD 21227, (301)247-2725; **BUS ADD:** Beltway Profl. Bldg., Suite 360, 1900 Sulphur Spring Rd., Baltimore, MD 21227, (301)242-8811.

LANY, Enrique——*President*, Polychrome International; **PRIM RE ACT:** Property Manager; **BUS ADD:** One the Hudson, Yonkers, NY 10702, (914)965-8800.*

LAP, Ha Hoc——**B:** June 10, 1923, Viet Nam, *Broker - Realtor*, Happy Homes Realty; **PRIM RE ACT:** Broker, Consultant; **SERVICES:** RE investment and mgmt.; **PREV EMPLOY:** V-Chmn./Bd. of Dirs., Trung Viet Bank - Vietnam (1969-1975); Publisher/Editor *Saigon Roundup Weekly* Magazine; **PROFL AFFIL & HONORS:** CA Assn. Realtors and NAR; **EDUC:** 1959-1961, Law School, Saigon; 1977-1978, RE, Chabot Coll., Hayward; **OTHER ACT & HONORS:** The Vietnamese Assn. of Friendship and Mutual Assistance - San Francisco; The Vietnamese C of C in Amer.; The American Univ. Alumni Association/AUAA; **HOME ADD:** 25386 Uvas Ct., Hayward, CA 94542, (415)886-4612; **BUS ADD:** 25386 Uvas Court, Hayward, CA 94542, (415)886-6591.

LAPIER, Terrence W.——**B:** Feb. 3, 1954, Plattsburgh, NY, *VP*, Dominion Corporation, RE Investment Banking; **PRIM RE ACT:** Broker, Consultant, Banker, Developer, Lender, Owner/Investor; **OTHER RE ACT:** RE Investment Banking Serv.; **SERVICES:** RE Investment Banking, consulting, arrange land devel. and joint ventures; **REP CLIENTS:** Major pension funds, devel., ins. cos., and domestic and foreign pvt. investors; **PREV EMPLOY:** Union Bank - 1980-81; Security Pacific Corp. 1978-1980; **PROFL AFFIL & HONORS:** Intl. Council of Shopping Ctrs., ULI, Los Angeles World Affairs Council; Republican Committee; **EDUC:** BA, 1977, Bus./Gvt., Syracuse Univ.; **GRAD EDUC:** D.R.P., 1981, Exec. Program in the Devel. of Real Prop., Harvard Univ., Grad. School of Bus./Grad. Sch. of Design; University of VA, Graduate School of Architecture; **EDUC HONORS:** Dean's List/Univ. Scholar; **OTHER ACT & HONORS:** Pres. Syracuse Univ. Alumni Assn., Syracuse Univ., Devel. Council; **BUS ADD:** POB 2786, Fairfax, VA 22031, (703)385-3100.

LAPIN, David A.——**B:** Jan. 13, 1952, St. Louis, MO, *Atty.*, Pacht, Ross, Warne, Bernhard & Sears, Inc.; **PRIM RE ACT:** Attorney, Developer, Owner/Investor, Syndicator; **SERVICES:** All aspects of RE Law; **PROFL AFFIL & HONORS:** CA Bar Assn., Los Angeles Bar Assn., Beverly Hills Bar Assn., CA Broker; **EDUC:** BA, 1974, Public Affairs, Claremont McKenna Coll.; **GRAD EDUC:** JD, 1975, Columbia Law School; **EDUC HONORS:** Summa Cum Laude; **HOME ADD:** 406 N Oakhurst Dr., Beverly Hills, CA 90210; **BUS ADD:** 1800 Ave. of the Stars, #500, Los Angeles, CA 90067, (213)277-1000.

LAPINE, Kenneth M.——**B:** Jan. 30, 1942, Cleveland, OH, *Partner*, Parks, Eisele, Bates & Wilsman; **PRIM RE ACT:** Attorney, Owner/Investor, Instructor, Property Manager, Syndicator; **SERVICES:** Specialist in RE law and banking law; **REP CLIENTS:** Northland Plaza Associates, Ltd.; Cardinal Fed. S & L Assn.; Superior Savings Assn.; **PREV EMPLOY:** VP, Sec. & Chief Counsel for Shaker Savings Assn. 1971-78; Partner, Cavitch, Familo & Durkin Co., LPA 1978--1980; **PROFL AFFIL & HONORS:** ABA, OH Bar Assn.; Cleveland Bar Assn.; Nat. S & L League - Assoc. Member; **EDUC:** AB, 1964, Govt., Dartmouth Coll.; **GRAD EDUC:** JD, 1967, Univ. of MI Law School; **OTHER ACT & HONORS:** Pres., Bd. of Trustees of Big Brothers/Big Sisters of Greater Cleveland; Dartmouth Alumni Assn. of Greater Cleveland; Author: Consumer Credit Volumes to Banking Law (multi-volume treatise published in 1981 by Matthew Bender & Co.); **HOME ADD:** 3685 Lytle Road, Shaker Heights, OH 44122, (216)921-1795; **BUS ADD:** 1100 Iluminating Bldg., Cleveland, OH 44113, (216)241-2840.

LAPOINTE, Merle L., CA-R——**B:** Nov. 8, 1935, Omro, WI, *Owner*, La Pointe & Co.; **PRIM RE ACT:** Broker, Instructor, Appraiser, Property Manager, Insuror; **SERVICES:** Appraising (valuation), Prop. Mgr., Inst. of RE Courses; **REP CLIENTS:** Attys., 2nd Mort. Lenders; **PREV EMPLOY:** US Mil.; **PROFL AFFIL & HONORS:** AIREA, AACA, RESSI, AACA; **EDUC:** BS, 1978, Bus. Admin., Cameron Univ., Lawton, OK 73505; **MIL SERV:** US Army, Warrant Officer, Bronze Star; **OTHER ACT & HONORS:** Veterans of Foreign Wars, Lawton C of C (Ambassador); **HOME ADD:** 106 NW 14th St., Lawton, OK 73501, (405)355-7922; **BUS ADD:** 106 NW 14th St., Lawton, OK 73501, (405)248-3444.

LAPORTE, Robert P., Jr.——**B:** Apr. 3, 1947, Lowell, MA, *VP*, Foster Appraiser & Consulting Co., Inc.; **PRIM RE ACT:** Consultant, Appraiser; **SERVICES:** RE Appraising & Consulting; **REP CLIENTS:** Dev. Indus., Attys. Investors, Accountants, Fed., State & Local Gov'ts.; **PROFL AFFIL & HONORS:** AIREA; SREA; 1980 Outstanding Young Man of the Yr. Award; **EDUC:** BA, Urban Studies, St. Anselm Coll.; **MIL SERV:** US Army, Spec. 4, Bronze Star, Army Commendation, Good Conduct, Nat. Defense; Vietnam Camp; **OTHER ACT & HONORS:** Pres. Leominster Rotary Club; **HOME ADD:** 795 Fisher Rd., Fitchburg, MA 01420, (617)343-7040; **BUS ADD:** 337 Lunenburg St., Fitchburg, MA 01420, (617)343-6946.

LAPRES, Ann——*Pres.*, Realty World - Ann Lapres Realtors; **PRIM RE ACT:** Broker; **OTHER RE ACT:** Cert. Appraiser; **SERVICES:** Sales, Appraisals, Rentals; **PROFL AFFIL & HONORS:** CRB, GRI, IFA, CRA, CREA; **OTHER ACT & HONORS:** Sec. NJ Chap. CRB; Sec. Bergen Cty. Chap. IFA; **HOME ADD:** 404 Bromley Place, Wyckoff, NJ 07481, (201)891-6440; **BUS ADD:** 283 Franklin Ave., Wyckoff, NJ 07481, (201)891-6440.

LAPUMA, Anthony P., Jr.——**B:** Nov. 11, 1951, Cambridge, MA, *Pres.*, A. LaPuma Corp.; **PRIM RE ACT:** Developer, Builder, Owner/Investor; **PROFL AFFIL & HONORS:** NAHB; **EDUC:** BS, 1973, Bus. Admin., Boston Coll.; **EDUC HONORS:** Cum Laude; **OTHER ACT & HONORS:** Braintree Planning Bd., 1 yr.; **HOME ADD:** 135 Old Country Way, Braintree, MA 02184, (617)848-4514; **BUS ADD:** 135 Old Country Way, Braintree, MA 02184, (617)848-4514.

LAPWING, Thomas W.——**B:** June 11, 1929, Brooklyn, NY, *Pres.*, Investment Property Consultants, Inc.; **PRIM RE ACT:** Consultant; **SERVICES:** Act as prin. agent in making acquisitions, divestitutes and arranging fin. including joint ventures, investment counseling; **REP CLIENTS:** Indiv. and instnl. investors in income prop. and nat. hotel cos.; **PREV EMPLOY:** VP in charge of RE Investment, MA Mutual Life Co.; **PROFL AFFIL & HONORS:** Past Member, Fin. Comm., Soc. Indus. Realtors, Lic. Broker in GA; **EDUC:** BA, 1950, Econ., NY Univ.; **GRAD EDUC:** MBA, 1959, RE/Fin., So. Methodist Univ. Grad. School of Bus.; **MIL SERV:** U.S. Air Force, 1st Lt. Pilot; **OTHER ACT & HONORS:** VP, River Chase Civic Assn.; Pres., River Chase Homeowners Assn.; **HOME ADD:** 5990 River Chase Cir., Atlanta, GA 30328, (404)955-1733; **BUS ADD:** 5990 River Chase Cir., Atlanta, GA 30328, (404)955-0543.

LAPWORTH, George R.——**B:** Aug. 23, 1942, Chestnut Hill, PA, *Pres.*, Century 21 Lapworth & Vecchiolli, Admin. Div.; **PRIM RE ACT:** Broker, Consultant, Appraiser, Owner/Investor, Property Manager, Syndicator; **SERVICES:** Consulting, appraising, resid. and comml. sales; **PROFL AFFIL & HONORS:** NAR; NMI; PA Assn. of Realtors; NA Land Title Assn.; E. Montgomery Cty. Bd. of Realtors; Lic. RE Broker in NJ; Lic. Title Officer in PA, GRI and CRB; **MIL SERV:** U.S. Army; **HOME ADD:** 1074 Hemlock Dr., Blue Bell, PA 19422, (215)646-5422; **BUS ADD:** 2923 Cheltenham Ave., Philadelphia,, PA 19150, (215)828-4005.

LARDINOIS, Vincent H.——**B:** Apr. 15, 1937, Door Cty., WI, *Broker Assoc. Gen. Mgr.*, ERA Investors Realty; **PRIM RE ACT:** Broker; **SERVICES:** RE; **PREV EMPLOY:** ERA Colkan Co-owner VP Co., NAK ERA; **PROFL AFFIL & HONORS:** CO Springs Bd. of Realtors, RNMI, 1976 Realtors Yr. Co., GRI Instr. GRI, CRS, CRB; **OTHER ACT & HONORS:** Pres. Patrick Henry PTO, Divine Redeemer Parish Council Past Comm. Chmn., Cub Scouts; **HOME ADD:** 1770 Kimberly Place, CO Springs, CO 80915, (303)596-1500; **BUS ADD:** 21 N. Union Blvd., Colorado Springs, CO 80909, (303)471-3333.

LARENO, Richard R.——*Pres.*, Richard R. LaRena & Co.; **PRIM RE ACT:** Developer; **BUS ADD:** 1325 Wiley Rd., Ste. #160, Schaumburg, IL 60195, (312)885-9600.*

LARKIN, James——*Mgr. Properties*, Sealed Power Corp.; **PRIM RE ACT:** Property Manager; **BUS ADD:** 100 Terrace Plaza, Muskegon, MI 49443, (616)724-5011.*

LARRICK, Donald R.——**B:** Apr. 6, 1951, Denver, CO, *Pres.*, Larrick Development Co.; **PRIM RE ACT:** Syndicator, Consultant, Developer, Owner/Investor; **SERVICES:** Devel. serv., investment and valuation counseling, devel. and synd. of raw land and comml. props., office park devel.; **REP CLIENTS:** Regional and natl. instl. investors seeking the above services, local investors, regional and natl. user clients; **PREV EMPLOY:** VP of Continental Investment Services, Inc. (Subsidiary of Frederick Ross Co.); **PROFL AFFIL & HONORS:** Treas. of CO Chap. of RESSI; NAR; NAIOP; **EDUC:** BA, 1973, Fin., R.E., CO State Univ.; **GRAD EDUC:** MS Program, 1974, Urban land econ., fin., appraisal, computer application to R.E., Univ. of WI; **OTHER ACT & HONORS:** Masons; Bd. of Advisors of Sigma Phi Epsilon, CO Gamma;, Denver C of C, Task forces - City Ctr. Rejuvenation, Foreign Trade Directory; **HOME ADD:** 457 Elm St., Denver, CO 80202, (303)355-5668; **BUS ADD:** 1805 S. Bellaire, Denver, CO 80222, (303)691-0113.

LARSEN, Kurt L.——**B:** July 22, 1944, Logan, UT, *VP*, Westam Corp.; **PRIM RE ACT:** Consultant, Developer; **SERVICES:** Mktg., prop. mgmt., RE devel., consulting, construction mgmt.; **REP CLIENTS:** Golden Corral Corp.; **PREV EMPLOY:** VP of Devel., Busch Corp.; Pres., Wasatch Front Investments; **PROFL AFFIL & HONORS:** Member ICSC; Chmn. Legislative and Public Affairs, UT Chap.; NAIOP; **EDUC:** BS, 1968, Personnel and Econ., UT State Univ.; **GRAD EDUC:** MPA, 1976, Urban City Planning, Admin., Ball State Univ.; **MIL SERV:** US Army, Capt., Bronze Star, Meritorious Service Medal, Army Commendation Medal; **HOME ADD:** 8514 S. Escalante Dr., Sandy, UT 84092, (801)942-6300; **BUS ADD:** 200 South 47 West, American Plaza III, Suite 600, Salt Lake City, UT 84101, (801)322-1034.

LARSEN, Richard A.——**B:** June 16, 1942, Kansas City, MO, *VP, Regnl. Mgr.*, Norris, Beggs & Simpson; **PRIM RE ACT:** Broker, Property Manager; **OTHER RE ACT:** Finance, Joint Ventures; **SERVICES:** Indus. , comml., investment brokerage, Mort. Fin.; **REP CLIENTS:** All maj. devel., Large & small users, all maj. investors, Lenders; **PREV EMPLOY:** S&L, Maj. indus. devel.; **PROFL AFFIL & HONORS:** Soc. of Indus. Realtors, Intl. Council of Shopping Ctrs., Nat. Assn. of Indus. & Office Parks, SIR; **EDUC:** BS, 1964, Bus. Admin., mktg., UCLA; **MIL SERV:** USAFR; **HOME ADD:** 10 Greenwood Ct., Orinda, CA 94563, (415)254-5203; **BUS ADD:** 243 Kearny, San Francisco, CA 94108, (415)362-5660.

LARSEN, Richard L.——**B:** Apr. 16, 1934, Jackson, MS, *Pres.*, Richard Larsen & Assoc., Inc.; **PRIM RE ACT:** Consultant, Property Manager; **SERVICES:** Consultant to devel., owners, cities, counties, etc. in dealing with local and Fed. Gov. including fundings source review; **REP CLIENTS:** Devel. (public and private) and municipalities; **PREV EMPLOY:** City Mgr. for 16 yrs. and pvt. consultant of New City Devel. and Local Govt. admin.; **PROFL AFFIL & HONORS:** Int. City Mgmt. Assn.; Aff. with Louis C. Kramp, Assoc., Wash, DC - Consul., 1976 UT Admin. of the Yr.; Citizen Award; Bur. of Rec.; numerous ICMA awards and honors; **EDUC:** BA, 1959, Econ. and Bus., Acctg., Stat., Poli. Sci., Westminster Coll., Fulton, MO; **GRAD EDUC:** Public Admin. grad. studies, Univ. of KS, Lawrence, KS 1959-1961; **MIL SERV:** USCG, P.O./2nd Class; **OTHER ACT & HONORS:** City Manager 1963-1979 in four cities - Munising, MI, Sault St. Marie, MI, Ogden, UT, Billings, MT; Bd. of Dir. Billings, YMCA, MT; Bd. of Dir. Rimrock Foundation, Billings, MT; **HOME ADD:** 1733 Parkhill Dr., Billings, MT 59102, (406)259-4236; **BUS ADD:** 1733 Parkhill Dr., Billings, MT 59102, (406)248-4252.

LARSON, Lennart V.——**B:** June 1, 1913, Sweden, *Prof. of Law*, Southern Methodist Univ., School of Law; **PRIM RE ACT:** Attorney, Instructor; **PROFL AFFIL & HONORS:** TX, NM, MI, WA, Dallas Bars; ABA; Member of Real Prop., Probate & Trusts Sect. of ABA and TX Bar, Amer. Coll. of Probate Counsel; **EDUC:** BS, 1933, Mat., Chemistry, Univ. of WA (Seattle); **GRAD EDUC:** JD, 1936, 1942, Gen. Labor Law, Univ. of WA (Seattle), Order of Coif; **EDUC HONORS:** Magna Cum Laude; Phi Beta Kappa; **OTHER ACT & HONORS:** Public Member, Reg. War Labor Bd., Dallas, TX, 1942-1944; DAC Cty. Club, Dallas, TX; **HOME ADD:** 7608 Southwestern Blvd., Dallas, TX 75225, (214)361-2519; **BUS ADD:** Dallas, TX 75275, (214)692-2634.

LARSON, Lori S.——**B:** Jan. 31, 1954, Richmond,VA, *VP*, CRI, Inc./CRICO Mgmt. Corp.; **PRIM RE ACT:** Developer, Instructor, Syndicator, Consultant, Property Manager; **SERVICES:** Asset and Prop. mgmt., Investment Counseling, Synd. of multi-family and comml. prop.; **REP CLIENTS:** Devels., mgmt. cos., and investors; **PREV EMPLOY:** Dir. of Mgmt.-TN, HDA; **PROFL AFFIL & HONORS:** Institute of RE Mgmt., Amer. Assn. of Housing Educators, Natl. Leased Housing Assn., Council of State Housing Agencies, CPM; **EDUC:** BA, 1974, Housing, VA Poly. Inst. and Univ.; **GRAD EDUC:** MBA, 1980, Fin. and Inv., George Wash. Univ.; **EDUC HONORS:** Danforth Award-Outstanding Coll. Fr., Phi Upsilon Omicron-Natl. Honorary Society, Beta Gamma Sigma, Nat. Bus. Hon. Soc.; **HOME ADD:** 4423 Walsh St., Chevy Chase, MD 20815, (301)654-4562; **BUS ADD:** 11300 Rockville Pike, Rockville, MD 20852, (301)468-9200.

LARSON, Robert C.——*Pres.*, Robert Larson Assoc., Inc.; **PRIM RE ACT:** Developer, Builder; **SERVICES:** Gen. Contractor; **EDUC:** BA, 1960, Univ. of CA at Los Angeles; **MIL SERV:** US Army, Lt.; **BUS ADD:** PO Box 990, Rancho Santa Fe, CA 92067, (714)756-1128.

LARSON, Steve H.——**B:** Dec. 4, 1948, Mason City, IA, *Pres.*, Quest Corp.; **PRIM RE ACT:** Broker, Banker, Owner/Investor, Property Manager, Syndicator; **PROFL AFFIL & HONORS:** Realtor; **EDUC:** BA, 1970, Bus. Admin., Coe Coll.; **MIL SERV:** US Army, Lt.; **HOME ADD:** 9323 Mohawk Ln., Leawood, KS 66206, (913)648-4436; **BUS ADD:** 701 Westport Rd., Kansas City, MO 64111, (816)756-2026.

LARUE, Clifford G.——**B:** Feb. 15, 1946, Philadelphia, PA, *Pres.*, Zygus Corp., Prop. Mgmt. Services; **PRIM RE ACT:** Property Manager; **SERVICES:** Prop. mgmt. leasing, devel. and sales of comml. and condo. props.; **REP CLIENTS:** The Green Cos., Trego, Sisler/Baal, Inc., Condo. Assns. throughout S. FL; **PREV EMPLOY:** Investment Mgr., The Prudential Insurance Co. of Amer. 1971-79; VP, NCNB Corp.; VP, Headway Corp.; **PROFL AFFIL & HONORS:** CPM (IREM); Assoc. Member SREA; CAI Member of the community Assns. Inst.; Chmn., Membership Comm., Chap. 19 IREM; **EDUC:** BS, 1968, Mgmt., FL Atlantic Unic., Boca Raton, FL; **GRAD EDUC:** MSM, 1975, RE & Fin., Rollins Coll., Winter Pk., FL; **EDUC HONORS:** Cum Laude; **MIL SERV:** US Navy, Lt. (O-3); **OTHER ACT & HONORS:** Coral Gables Bd. of Realtors; **HOME ADD:** 9820 SW 157th Terr., Miami, FL 33157, (305)251-6341; **BUS ADD:** 17637

S. Dixie Hwy., Miami, FL 33157, (305)252-0631.

LASERWA, Bruce——B: Dec. 10, 1948, Los Angeles, CA, *Indus. Mgr.*, Pac. Telephone Co.; **PRIM RE ACT:** Consultant; **OTHER RE ACT:** Consultation in communication information transfer with specialized training in RE (Assoc. & Brokers, Prop. Mgmt., Escrow, etc.); **SERVICES:** Consulting, planning & implementing communications services/systems internally and externally from an applications orientation; **PROFL AFFIL & HONORS:** San Fernando Valley Bd. of Realtors; **BUS ADD:** 611 Wilshire Blvd., Suite 201, Los Angeles, CA 90017, (213)975-5830.

LASKIN, Dennis A.——B: Sept. 3, 1943, Charleston, WV, *Pres.*, Laskin Development, Inc.; **PRIM RE ACT:** Broker, Attorney, Developer, Builder; **SERVICES:** Gen. brokerage, devel. and const. of resid. and comml. bldgs.; **EDUC:** BA, 1964, OH State Univ.; **GRAD EDUC:** LLB, JD, 1967, George Washington Univ. School of Law; **OTHER ACT & HONORS:** Sales of resid. homes const., $15,000,000 1980; **HOME ADD:** 4580 Indian Rock Terr., Washington, DC 20007; **BUS ADD:** 9000 Old Georgetown Rd., Bethesda, MD 20814, (301)530-8780.

LASKO, Warren A.——*Exec.VP*, Department of Housing and Urban Development, Government Nat'l. Mortgage Assoc.; **PRIM RE ACT:** Lender; **BUS ADD:** 451 Seventh St., S.W., Washington, DC 20410, (202)755-5926.*

LASON, John P.——B: June 19, 1942, New York, NY, *Pres.*, Lason & Assoc., Inc.; **PRIM RE ACT:** Broker, Consultant, Appraiser, Developer, Owner/Investor, Syndicator; **SERVICES:** Mkt. feasibility for devel. entering new mkts., land search; **REP CLIENTS:** Comml. devel., investors; **PREV EMPLOY:** Meridian Valley Realty; **PROFL AFFIL & HONORS:** RESSI; **EDUC:** BA, 1963, Biochemistry, Yale; **EDUC HONORS:** Dean's List, Ranking Scholar; **MIL SERV:** US Army, 1st Lt. 1965-1968; **HOME ADD:** 1816 B S. 330th, Federal Way, WA 98003, (206)838-3475; **BUS ADD:** 22030 7th Ave. #3, Des Moines, WA 98188, (206)824-1110.

LASSER, John O.——*Pres.*, John O. Lasser Associates Inc.; **PRIM RE ACT:** Consultant, Appraiser; **SERVICES:** RE consulting and appraising; **REP CLIENTS:** AT&T, Exxon, Jersey Central Power & Light Co., State of NJ, pvt. clients; **PROFL AFFIL & HONORS:** AIREA; Amer. Soc. of RE Counselors, MAI; CRE; **EDUC:** BA, 1952, Yale Univ.; **MIL SERV:** USN, Lt.j.g.; **BUS ADD:** Gateway One, Newark, NJ 07102, (201)622-7149.

LASSETTER, James G.——B: Sept. 13, 1916, Villa Rica, GA, *Pres.*, Tallahassee Realty Co.; **PRIM RE ACT:** Broker, Consultant, Appraiser, Owner/Investor; **SERVICES:** RE sales and RE appraisals; Specialize in the sale of large acreage for farming, timber and devel. and in comml. & exchanging; **REP CLIENTS:** Buckeye Cellulose, Bartlesville Bank of Tulsa, MD Nat. Bank, Anheuser Busch, Ford Motor Co., Brunswick Co.; **PREV EMPLOY:** US Govt., Soil Conservation Serv. prior to RE in 1951; RE since 1951; **PROFL AFFIL & HONORS:** Tallahassee Bd. of Realtors (Pres. 1964), FL Assn. of Realtors (Dist. VP in 1962 and 1965), Soc. of Indep. Fee Appraisers, Member Nat. Assn. of Review Appraisers, State and Nat. Member of Farm and Land Brokers; **EDUC:** BS, 1940, Agriculture Engr., Univ. of GA; **GRAD EDUC:** BSAE, 1940; **EDUC HONORS:** Phi Kappa Phi; **OTHER ACT & HONORS:** East Hill Baptist Church; Member Million Dollar Club; Tallahassee Bd. of Realtors; **HOME ADD:** P O Box 1333, Tallahassee, FL 32302, (904)926-7327; **BUS ADD:** 1349 E. LaFayette St., PO Box 1333, Tallahassee, FL 32302, (904)878-2145.

LASSETTER, Maggie S.——B: Feb. 25, 1922, Villa Rica, GA, *VP*, Tallahassee Realty Co.; **PRIM RE ACT:** Broker, Consultant, Appraiser, Instructor; **SERVICES:** Selling and appraising RE & instr. in RE law; **PREV EMPLOY:** RE Broker since 1953; **PROFL AFFIL & HONORS:** Tallahassee Bd. of Realtors Pres. 1970, FL Assn. of Realtors VP 1971, NAR, Women's Council of NAR, Omega Tau Rho, *Who's Who in Fin. and Indus.*; **EDUC:** Psych. and Educ., W. GA and Tallahassee Community Coll.; **OTHER ACT & HONORS:** FL RE Commn. 1976-79, V. Chmn. - 1978, Chmn. 1979; Member: Tallahassee Million Dollar Club - Bd. of Realtors; **HOME ADD:** P O Box 1333, Tallahassee, FL 32302, (904)926-7327; **BUS ADD:** 1349 E. Lafayette St., P O Box 1333, Tallahassee, FL 32303, (904)878-2145.

LASTINGER, William R.——B: Mar. 19, 1937, Pensacola, FL, *Bldg. Mgr. (office)*, Ar. Title Bldg.; **PRIM RE ACT:** Property Manager; **PREV EMPLOY:** Ins., Bus. & Estate Planning; **PROFL AFFIL & HONORS:** BOMA; **MIL SERV:** US Army 7/59-6/61, PFC; **OTHER ACT & HONORS:** Rotary, Asst. Scoutmaster; **HOME ADD:** 1816 W. Avalon, Phoenix, AZ 85015, (602)252-3324; **BUS ADD:** 111 W. Monroe, Suite 919, Phoenix, AZ 85003, (602)253-3000.

LATHLAEN, Robert F.——B: May 25, 1925, Philadelphia, PA, *Pres.*, W.J. Barney Corp.; **PRIM RE ACT:** Engineer, Developer, Builder; **PROFL AFFIL & HONORS:** Nat. AGC, (Dir. 1974-Present); Gen. Bldg. Contractors, NY State, PE; **EDUC:** BS, 1945, Civil Engrg., Drexel Univ.; **GRAD EDUC:** MS, 1946, Civil Engrg., MIT; **EDUC HONORS:** Lambda Chi Alpha, Tau Beta Pi, Phi Kappa Phi; **BUS ADD:** 360 Lexington Ave., New York, NY 10017, (212)972-0720.

LATHROP, Donald B., Jr.——B: Dec. 10, 1956, Arlington, VA, *VP*, Continental Bank; **PRIM RE ACT:** Appraiser, Banker, Lender, Owner/Investor; **SERVICES:** Comml. and resid. RE lending; **PREV EMPLOY:** Community Bank of Lafourche, Galliano, LA; American Bank & Trust Co., Houma, LA; **PROFL AFFIL & HONORS:** Amer. Inst. of Banking; Regional Dir., Bank Admin. Inst. So. Central Chap., Outstanding Young Man of Amer., 1980; **EDUC:** Fin., LA Tech. Univ.; **OTHER ACT & HONORS:** Sec./Treas., So. Lafourche Jaycees; **HOME ADD:** Apt. 278, Metarie, LA 700014817 York St., (504)887-3386; **BUS ADD:** PO Box 8090, Metairie, LA 70002, (504)885-1855.

LATIMER, James D.——B: Dec. 27, 1941, Richmond, VA, *N. FL RE Mgr.*, Jack Eckerd Corp., Eckerd Drugs; **OTHER RE ACT:** Site selection & lease negotiation; **PREV EMPLOY:** Winchell's Donut House, Pizza Hut & Burger King; **EDUC:** BA, 1964, RE & Urban Land Studies, Univ. of FL; **MIL SERV:** USN, Lt.; **HOME ADD:** 2900 Cove Cay Dr., Unit 7E, Clearwater, FL 33520, (813)536-8904; **BUS ADD:** PO Box 4689, Clearwater, FL 33518, (813)397-7461.

LATNER, Albert J.——B: Apr. 25, 1927, Hamilton, Ont. Can., *Pres. and CEO*, Greenwin; **PRIM RE ACT:** Developer, Builder, Property Manager; **OTHER ACT & HONORS:** Dir. of the Mt. Sinai Hospital; Past Pres. of Tel Aviv Univ.; Dir. of Toronto Sun; Dir. of Consumer's Distributing; Dir. of Unicorp; **HOME ADD:** Trillium Woods Farm, RR 2, King, L0G1K0, Ont., Can., (416)859-3956; **BUS ADD:** 111 Davisville Ave., Toronto, M4S1G6, Ont., Can..

LATSHAW, Robert E., Jr.——B: Dec. 10, 1944, Milwaukee, WI, *Pres.*, Latshaw Commercial Properties, Latshaw Mgmt. Co.; Latshaw & Co.; **PRIM RE ACT:** Broker, Developer, Owner/Investor, Property Manager, Syndicator; **OTHER RE ACT:** Exchanging; **SERVICES:** Sales, leasing, exchanging, synd., mgmt.; **PREV EMPLOY:** Johns Hopkins; Broadway Mgmt. Corp.; **PROFL AFFIL & HONORS:** Pres. 1981-1982 Greater Baltimore Bd. of Realtors; RNMI; RESSI; Greater Baltimore Committee, CCIM; **EDUC:** BS-Fin., 1968, Corporate Investment, Johns Hopkins Univ.; **OTHER ACT & HONORS:** MD House of Delegates 1970-1974; MD C of C 1981; Greater Baltimore REALTOR of the YR., 1981; MD REALTOR of the YR., 1981; Assoc. Bldrs. & Contr's. Outstanding Legislator, 1972; Outstanding Young men of Amer., 1973; **HOME ADD:** 334 Broadmoor Rd., Baltimore, MD 21212, (301)323-9777; **BUS ADD:** 600 E. Joppa Rd., Baltimore, MD 21204, (301)296-6000.

LATTIMORE, William, Jr.——B: May 25, 1954, Sacannah, GA, *Pres.*, Oglethorpe Devel. Assoc.; **PRIM RE ACT:** Developer; **PROFL AFFIL & HONORS:** GA Savannah Home Builders Assn., Bd. of Dirs.; Savannah Bd. of Realtors; Savannah Ayer C of C; Young Realtors; ULI; GA Land Devel. Assn.; **EDUC:** BBA, 1975, RE, Univ. of GA; **OTHER ACT & HONORS:** St. John's Episcopal Church; Savannah Yacht Club; Savannah Inn & Ctry. Club; Savannah YMCA (Bd.); **HOME ADD:** 107 N Milard Ct., Savannah, GA 31410, (912)897-3365; **BUS ADD:** PO Box 3936, Savannah, GA 31404, (912)897-1222.

LAU, Donald K.W.——B: Feb. 15, 1942, Honolulu, HI, *VP*, First Fed. S&L Assn. of HI, Comml. & Constr. Loan Dept.; **OTHER RE ACT:** Financing; **SERVICES:** Constr. & comml. loans; **REP CLIENTS:** Devel. Realtors & indiv.; **PROFL AFFIL & HONORS:** Mort. Lenders of HI, Soc. of RE Appraisers, NARA, Honolulu Bd. of Realtors, GRI, CRA; **EDUC:** BBA, 1966, Banking & Fin., Univ. of HI; **OTHER ACT & HONORS:** Hawaiian Lodge 21 F&AM, BPOE Lodge 616, Building Indus. Assn., Aloha Temple (Shriners); **HOME ADD:** 645 Kuliouou Pl., Honolulu, HI 96821; **BUS ADD:** 851 Fort St. Mall, PO Box 3346, Honolulu, HI 96801, (808)531-9418.

LAU, George K.H.——B: Dec. 4, 1940, Honolulu, HI, *Pres.*, George K.H. Lau & Assoc., Inc.; **PRIM RE ACT:** Consultant, Appraiser, Property Manager; **SERVICES:** RE counseling, brokerage, valuations; **REP CLIENTS:** Shidler Investment Co., J.C. Reynolds Co., Dura Contractors, Dillingham Land Corp., City Bank, Smith Devel Corp, Transamercia Corp, Times Supermarkets, State of Hawaii; **PROFL AFFIL & HONORS:** Amer.Soc. of Appraisers, Nat. Assn. of Review Appraisers, IREM, Amer. Coll. of RE Consulting Profls., ASA, CRA, CPM, RECP; **EDUC:** BBA, 1962, Econ., Univ. of HI; **MIL SERV:** USAF, S/Sgt.; **HOME ADD:** 619 Kuliouou Pl., Honolulu, HI 96821, (808)396-9066; **BUS ADD:** 225 Queen St, Suite 17-F, Honolulu, HI 96813, (808)536-8651.

LAUBER, Evelyn Gremli——B: July 8, 1917, Sarasota, FL, *Pres. Owner*, Erwin Gremli RE, Inc.; **PRIM RE ACT:** Broker, Consultant, Property Manager; **OTHER RE ACT:** Gen. RE servs.; **REP CLIENTS:** Gen. public; **PROFL AFFIL & HONORS:** FL Assn. of Realtors; NAR; RNMI; WCR, GRI, CRS, CRB; **EDUC:** Attended Julliard, Music, Profl.; **OTHER ACT & HONORS:** Women of Yr.; Sarasota Chap., Order of Eastern Star, Womens Council 1971; **HOME ADD:** 230 Scott Ave., Sarasota, FL 33580, (813)355-4837; **BUS ADD:** 1535 Second St., Sarasota, FL 33577, (813)366-9606.

LAUER, Harold J.——B: March 16, 1943, Jefferson City, MO, *Broker, Owner*, Lauer & Assoc., Realtors; **PRIM RE ACT:** Broker, Appraiser, Property Manager; **SERVICES:** Six Cty. appraisal work, Fiscal prop. mgr.; **REP CLIENTS:** Merrill; **PREV EMPLOY:** First licensed state of IA 1964, active in RE bus. since 1967; **PROFL AFFIL & HONORS:** AIREA, RNMI, Candidate RM Desig.; **OTHER ACT & HONORS:** Pres. Burlington Bd. of Realtors 1976 & 1977; VP IA Assn. of Realtors 1978, 1979, 1980, IAR Dir. 1981; **HOME ADD:** 1925 Highland St, Burlington, IA 52601, (319)752-8824; **BUS ADD:** 1417 Mt. Pleasant St., PO Box 82, Burlington, IA 52601, (319)752-4308.

LAUNER, Deborah——*Ed.*, Warren, Gorham & Lamont, Inc., Condominium Report; **PRIM RE ACT:** Real Estate Publisher; **BUS ADD:** 210 South St., Boston, MA 02111, (617)423-2020.*

LAURETANO, Ralph J.——B: Sept. 25, 1938, Malden, MA, *Pres.*, University Title, Inc.; **OTHER RE ACT:** Title ins. agent; **SERVICES:** Ins. comml. and resid. prop.; **REP CLIENTS:** Indiv. and instnl. lenders in real prop. sales/purchases; **PREV EMPLOY:** Exec. VP, Southern Title & Abstract Co.; **PROFL AFFIL & HONORS:** Pres., Land Title Assn. of Broward Cty.; **MIL SERV:** USN, Second Class Petty Officer; **OTHER ACT & HONORS:** Davie/Cooper City Chamber; Charter Member Davie Rotary Club; Charter Member Land Title Assn. of Broward Cty.; Miramar/Pembroke Pines C of C; Intl. Fellowship of Flying Rotarians; Broward Cty. Sheriff's Posse; **HOME ADD:** 14741 SW 69 St., Ft. Lauderdale, FL 33330; **BUS ADD:** 269 N. University Dr., Pembroke Pines, FL 33024, (305)963-0530.

LAURICH, Eugene J.——B: July 24, 1953, Jersey City, NJ, *Atty.*, Vaux, Howard & Laurich, P.A., RE; **PRIM RE ACT:** Attorney; **SERVICES:** Represent largest resid. home builder on Hilton Head; **REP CLIENTS:** Austin Construction & Devel. Co., Inc.; Palmetto Homes of Hilton Head Island, Inc.; Indiv.; **PREV EMPLOY:** Associated with Law Offices of J. Ray Westmoreland; **PROFL AFFIL & HONORS:** ABA, Beaufort Cty. Bar Assn., Hilton Head Bar; **EDUC:** BA, 1975, Eng. & Phil., Univ. of Notre Dame; **GRAD EDUC:** JD, 1978, Tax, RE, Univ. of SC; **EDUC HONORS:** Dean's List; **OTHER ACT & HONORS:** Jaycees, K of C; **HOME ADD:** 18 Misty Cove Lane, Hilton Head Island, SC 29938, (803)785-4244; **BUS ADD:** 7 Pope Ave. Mall, Hilton Head Island, SC 29928, (803)785-2169.

LAURITZEN, Anna M.——B: Jan. 14, 1923, Belleville, IL, *Member Will Cty. Bd. of Review/self-employed Atty.*; **PRIM RE ACT:** Attorney; **OTHER RE ACT:** Bd. of Review (tax assessments); **SERVICES:** Conduct hearing on complaints regarding tax valuations for RE taxes; **PREV EMPLOY:** Title Ins. Co., title examiner and RE tax title officer; **PROFL AFFIL & HONORS:** IL State Bar Assn., ABA; **EDUC:** 1969, Educ., N. IL Univ.; **GRAD EDUC:** 1976, John Marshall Law School; **OTHER ACT & HONORS:** Joliet Bus. & Profl. Women; Bd. of Dirs., Joliet Jr. Coll. Alumni Assn.; **HOME ADD:** 201 Fairview Dr., Manhattan, IL 60442, (815)478-3092; **BUS ADD:** 81 N. Chicago St., Joliet, IL 60431, (815)726-2478.

LAURITZEN, James Lawrence——B: Dec. 30, 1943, Oakland, CA, *VP, RE Fin. Div. Head*, Bank of Newport, RE Fin.; **PRIM RE ACT:** Consultant, Appraiser, Banker, Developer, Lender, Owner/Investor; **SERVICES:** RE loans, lines of credit, participations, etc.; **REP CLIENTS:** J.B.S. Devel. Corp., S.A. Katz Corp., Samuel Wachs & Assoc., McClellan, Cruz & Gaylord, US Housing Corp., Urbatec, Inc., Plaza Builders, Beneficial Standard Props., R.J.B. Unlimited, Chazan Const. Co., Woodview Props., Subbiordo and Assoc., Inc., SBE Corp., San Roque, Inc., KEK Ltd.; **PREV EMPLOY:** CA Fed. Savings, US Life Savings; Imperial Saving; Warner Bros. Studios; **PROFL AFFIL & HONORS:** Bldg. Indus. Assn.; LA Jr. Chamber; MBAA; **EDUC:** 1973, Bus. Admin./RE Fin., CA State Univ.; **GRAD EDUC:** 1976, RE Fin., UCLA; **MIL SERV:** USAF, S/Sgt., Expert Markmanship, Good Conduct, Outstanding Unit; **OTHER ACT & HONORS:** US Golf Assn.; **BUS ADD:** Pacific Coast Hwy. and Avocado, Newport Beach, CA 92660, (714)760-6000.

LAUSE, Michael F.——B: Aug. 3, 1948, Washington, MO, *Atty.*, Thompson & Mitchell; **PRIM RE ACT:** Attorney; **PREV EMPLOY:** Been with firm since 1973, grad. law sch.; **PROFL AFFIL & HONORS:** ABA, RE Sect., MO Bar, Metro. St. Louis Bar (Prop. Sect.); **EDUC:** AB, 1970, Pol. Sci., Benedictine Coll., Atchinson, KS; **GRAD EDUC:** JD, 1973, Univ. of IL; **EDUC HONORS:** Magna Cum Laude, *Who's Who Amer. Coll.*, Sr. Class Pres., Order of Coif, Law Review, Notes & Comments Editor; Cum Laude; **HOME ADD:** 24 Foxboro, Ladue, MO 63124, (314)994-1245; **BUS ADD:** One Mercantile Ctr., St. Louis, MO 63101, (314)231-7676.

LAUTERBACH, W.E.——B: Dec. 3, 1949, Frankfurt, Germany, *Chief Exec.*, Galt Corp.; **PRIM RE ACT:** Broker, Developer, Builder, Owner/Investor, Syndicator; **REP CLIENTS:** Lenders, indiv. and inst. investors, resid. and comml. buyers; **PROFL AFFIL & HONORS:** HAB, NAHB, Reg. Profl. Builder; **EDUC:** 1972, Fin., Bus. Admin.; **MIL SERV:** USMC, Purple Heart; **BUS ADD:** 16950 Dallas Pkwy., Ste 105, Dallas, TX 75248, (214)931-0256.

LAUX, Donnell H.——B: Feb. 7, 1948, Dallas, TX, *Partner*, Chamberlain, Hrdlicka, White, Johnson & Williams; **PRIM RE ACT:** Attorney; **SERVICES:** Legal Rep.; **REP CLIENTS:** Indivs. and bus. assns.; investing and devel.; **PROFL AFFIL & HONORS:** State Bar of TX, Houston Bar Assn., Houston Young Lawyers Assn., JD; **EDUC:** BBA, 1970, Mktg.; Quantitative Analysis, So. Methodist Univ.; **GRAD EDUC:** JD, 1974, Univ. of Houston; **EDUC HONORS:** Beta Gamma Sigma, Order of the Barons; Caldwell Award; **MIL SERV:** TX National Guard, Sgt., 1970-1976; **HOME ADD:** 3464 Locke Ln., Houston, TX 77027, (713)627-7765; **BUS ADD:** 28th Floor 1100 Milam, Houston, TX 77002, (713)658-1818.

LAVELLE, Joseph M.——B: Nov. 6, 1939, Charleston, SC, *Broker-in-Charge*, Southern Commercial Brokers; **PRIM RE ACT:** Broker; **SERVICES:** Exclusive Bus. Brokerage; **EDUC:** BS, 1961, EE, Clemson Univ.; **GRAD EDUC:** Masters, 1969, Bus. Admin., Roosevelt Univ., Chicago, IL; **MIL SERV:** USAF, Capt.; **OTHER ACT & HONORS:** VP Cr. Union, School Bd.; **HOME ADD:** 1428 Barbara St., Mt. Pleasant, SC, (803)884-2396; **BUS ADD:** 5639 Attaway Ave., No. Chas., SC 29406, (803)744-1616.

LAVIN, James W.——B: Dec. 2, 1945, Worcester, MA, *Pres.*, South Bayshore Management Inc.; **PRIM RE ACT:** Broker, Consultant, Property Manager; **OTHER RE ACT:** CPA; **SERVICES:** RE Mgmt. and fin. servs.; **REP CLIENTS:** Indivs. and corp. investors in comml. props.; **PREV EMPLOY:** Controller Grossman Indus. Props., Inc., 1975-80; Supervisor Laventhol Horwath, 1971-75; **PROFL AFFIL & HONORS:** MA Soc. of CPA's. AICPA; **EDUC:** BS, 1967, Acctg., Stonehill Coll.; **HOME ADD:** 9 Minuteman Rd., Hingham, MA 02043, (617)749-1236; **BUS ADD:** 142 Union St., Braintree, MA 02184, (617)848-1960.

LAVINE, Richard A.——B: Jan. 14, 1935, Chicago, IL, *Partner*, Irwin Pomerantz and Associates, CPA's; **OTHER RE ACT:** CPA; **SERVICES:** Tax planning and compliance; **REP CLIENTS:** Synd., gen. partners, owners; **PROFL AFFIL & HONORS:** AICPA, CA Soc. of CPA's, CPA; **EDUC:** BA, 1957, Acctg., UCLA; **HOME ADD:** 23251 Bigler St., Woodland Hills, CA 91364; **BUS ADD:** 7700 Sunset Blvd., Suite 205, Los Angeles, CA 90046, (213)874-0201.

LAVINE, Thomas——B: Sept. 16, 1945, Los Angeles, CA, *Pres.-Dir.*, GMG Capital Enterprises, Inc.; **PRIM RE ACT:** Consultant, Developer, Owner/Investor; **SERVICES:** Investment & Exchange Consulting, Devel. and Synd. of Comml. and Resid. Props.; **REP CLIENTS:** Indivs., & Instnl.. Investors; **EDUC:** BS, 1967, Fin., USC; **GRAD EDUC:** MBA, 1969, Fin., UCLA; **BUS ADD:** 9301 Wilshire Blvd., Los Angeles, CA 90024, (213)550-3959.

LAW, James G.——B: Apr. 28, 1944, Tacoma, WA, *Corp. Mgr. Land and Facilities*, Hewlett-Packard, Corporate; **PRIM RE ACT:** Consultant, Engineer, Developer, Property Manager; **SERVICES:** Site selection, land negotiations, sale/lease back, project mgmt.; **PREV EMPLOY:** Project Engineer/Mgr. for Facilities in U.S., So. Amer., S.E. Asia, Europe, Australia, So. Africa ULI; **PROFL AFFIL & HONORS:** Indus. Devel. Research Council, Bd. of Dir., IDRC, Richard Muther Scholarship Award; **EDUC:** BS Engin., 1966, Civil/Building Construction, Univ. of WA; **GRAD EDUC:** MSCE, MBA, 1969, 1975, Construction Mgmt. Long Range Planning, San Jose State Univ., Pacific Lutheran Univ.; **OTHER ACT & HONORS:** Bd. of Dir. Skywood Assn., WA Athletic Club; **HOME ADD:** 50 Ranch Road, Woodside, CA 94062, (415)851-1832; **BUS ADD:** 3000 Hanover St., Palo Alto, CA 94304, (415)857-4760.

LAW, Jay L.——*Pres.*, World-Wide Distributors Inc., Bus. Serv. Div.; **PRIM RE ACT:** Consultant, Developer, Lender, Owner/Investor, Property Manager, Syndicator; **SERVICES:** Investment counseling, devel. & synd. of comml. props., lending, prop. mgmt. & investor; **REP CLIENTS:** indiv. & instnl investors; **PREV EMPLOY:** Prin. officer of related bus. serv. & sales corp. with offices in 32 cities; **PROFL AFFIL & HONORS:** Several; **HOME ADD:** 7841 Island, Anchorage, AK

99504; **BUS ADD:** PO Box 2735, Anchorage, AK 99510, (907)333-5015.

LAWHORN, Jess S.——**B:** Jan. 20, 1933, Cincinnati, OH, *Sr. VP*, Southeast Banks, Credit Policy; **PRIM RE ACT:** Appraiser, Banker, Lender; **PREV EMPLOY:** Sr. VP Southeast Mortgage Co., Pres. - SEMCO Services Reg. RE Broker; **PROFL AFFIL & HONORS:** Soc. of RE Appraisers, Mort. Bankers Assn. of Amer., FL, Miami, Realtor, SRA, CMB, Distinguished Mort. Banker - FL, Past Pres.: MBA of FL, Greater Miami Chap. Soc. of RE Appraisers; **EDUC:** BBA, 1953, Mktg. & Econ., Univ. of Miami, FL; **MIL SERV:** USAF, 1st Lt.; **OTHER ACT & HONORS:** Rotary, FL Bankers Assn.; **HOME ADD:** 500 Perugia Ave., Coral Gables, FL 33146, (305)667-1794; **BUS ADD:** 100 S. Biscayne Blvd., Miami, FL 33131, (305)577-3520.

LAWING, Alvin L., Jr.——**B:** Nov. 25, 1933, Maiden, NC, *Pres., CEO Dir.*, Major Realty Corp.; **PRIM RE ACT:** Developer, Owner/Investor; **SERVICES:** Joint ventures, planning; **PREV EMPLOY:** Hardee's Food Systems, Inc. Fin. VP & Treas.; **PROFL AFFIL & HONORS:** AICPA, NC Assn. of CPA's, FL Inst. of CPA's; **EDUC:** BBA, 1956, Acctg., Wake Forest Univ.; **MIL SERV:** US Army, E-6 Sgt.; **OTHER ACT & HONORS:** Orlando C of C; **HOME ADD:** 5141 Cypress Creek Dr., Orlando, FL 32805, (305)351-3883; **BUS ADD:** 5750 Major Blvd., Suite 500, Orlando, FL 32805, (305)351-1111.

LAWINGER, Ernest J.——**B:** Feb. 24, 1935, Dodgeville, WI, *Sr. VP*, Valuation Research Corp.; **PRIM RE ACT:** Consultant, Appraiser, Owner/Investor; **OTHER RE ACT:** Review of appraisals and feasibility studies; **SERVICES:** Valuation of props. & related bus.; **PROFL AFFIL & HONORS:** Fellow Fin. Analysts Feds., Sr. Member Amer. Soc. of Appraisers, Sr. Cert. Valuer Intl. Inst. of Valuers, Author of various articles; **EDUC:** BBA, 1960, Fin. & Econ., Univ. of Notre Dame; **MIL SERV:** US Army, Sgt.; **HOME ADD:** 8300 N Indian Oak Pkwy, Fox Point, WI 53217, (414)352-6390; **BUS ADD:** 250 E WI Ave., Milwaukee, WI 53202, (414)271-8662.

LAWLER, Frank——**B:** Dec. 20, 1922, Atlanta, GA, *Pres.*, Frank Lawler Realty, Inc.; **PRIM RE ACT:** Broker, Owner/Investor, Property Manager; **PREV EMPLOY:** Pres., Riggs Mgmt. Co., 1973-1979; VP, Allen & Rocks, Inc., 1954-1972; **PROFL AFFIL & HONORS:** Member, Prop. Mgmt. Assn.; **EDUC:** B.Comml. Sci., 1954, Acctg., Strayer Coll. of Accountacy; **EDUC HONORS:** Sr. Class Pres., Valedictorian; **MIL SERV:** US Army/AF, Sgt.; **HOME ADD:** 5905 Folkstone Rd., Bethesda, MD 20817, (301)530-2330; **BUS ADD:** 5905 Folkstone Rd., Bethesda, MD 20817, (301)530-2330.

LAWLER, J. Klein——**B:** May 10, 1948, Westport, CT, *VP*, Gladstone Assoc.; **PRIM RE ACT:** Consultant; **OTHER RE ACT:** Dev. Pckg.; **SERVICES:** Mkt. analysis, fin. feasibility, portfolio dev.; **EDUC:** BS, 1971, Urb. Pl., Mich. Univ.; **GRAD EDUC:** MCP, 1973, RE Dev., Fin. & Urb. Econ., Harvard Univ.; **EDUC HONORS:** Mellon Fellowship; **OTHER ACT & HONORS:** Adviser, Nat'l. Trust for Historic Pres., 1977-1980; **HOME ADD:** 5300 Marw Dr., Bethesda, MD 20016, (301)229-6506; **BUS ADD:** 2030 M St., N.W., Wash., DC 20036, (202)293-9000.

LAWLESS, Harris E.——**B:** Feb. 28, 1919, Union County, SD, *Chmn. of the Bd. and Pres.*, Harris Lawless & Associates; **PRIM RE ACT:** Broker, Consultant, Instructor, Syndicator, Real Estate Publisher; **OTHER RE ACT:** Editor - RE Securities Journal; **PROFL AFFIL & HONORS:** RESSI, NAR, SRS; **EDUC:** BS, 1954, Bus., Coll. of the Pacific; **GRAD EDUC:** MBA, 1956, Bus., Harvard Bus. School; **EDUC HONORS:** Phi Kappa Phi; **MIL SERV:** USAF, Maj., Air Medals (6); **OTHER ACT & HONORS:** Pres., RESSI, 1976; **HOME ADD:** Sausalito, CA; **BUS ADD:** P.O. Box 1366, Sausalito, CA 94966, (415)332-2980.

LAWLOR, John M., Jr.——*VP*, Cabot, Cabot & Forbes; **PRIM RE ACT:** Developer; **BUS ADD:** 440 E. Swedesford Rd., Wayne, PA 19087, (215)964-8700.*

LAWN, Ronald Keith——**B:** June 8, 1952, Long Branch, NJ, *Atty.*, Ronald K. Lawn, Atty; **PRIM RE ACT:** Attorney; **SERVICES:** Real prop., probate & civil litigation & appellate; **REP CLIENTS:** Lenders, indiv. purchasers & investors, First Carolina Props., Community Volunteer Services; **PREV EMPLOY:** CA Ct. of Appeals - The FL Bar; **PROFL AFFIL & HONORS:** ABA (Real Property Probate & Trusts Div.), SC Bar Real Prop. and Probate Division, SC Trial Lawyers Assn., ABA (Bus. Law Div.), Member of both SC and FL Bars; **EDUC:** BA, 1975, Sociology, Eckerd Coll.; **GRAD EDUC:** JD, 1979, Real Property, Probate & Trusts, Litigation & Appellate Procedure, Southwestern Univ.; **EDUC HONORS:** Honor Student & Dean's List, Phi Theta Kappa, Top 15%; **OTHER ACT & HONORS:** Member Civitan, United Way; **HOME ADD:** 17-8 Dolphin Dr., Myrtle Beach, SC 29577, (803)272-7223; **BUS ADD:** P O Box 7516, Myrtle Beach, SC 29577, (803)448-8405.

LAWRENCE, Cuyler——**B:** June 13, 1950, Austin, TX, *Exec. VP*, Sentry Prop. Mgmt., Inc.; **PRIM RE ACT:** Property Manager; **SERVICES:** Mgmt., leasing, and consulting for income prop.; **REP CLIENTS:** Equity trusts, banks, partnerships and indiv.; **PROFL AFFIL & HONORS:** ICSC, IREM, CPM, Past Pres. IREM Chap. 90 (West Texas); **EDUC:** BBA, 1972, Marketing, TX Tech. Univ.; **GRAD EDUC:** MBA, 1973, Mktg. & RE, S. Methodist Univ.; **OTHER ACT & HONORS:** Rotary Intl.; **HOME ADD:** 4506-11th, Lubbock, TX 79416, (806)792-5002; **BUS ADD:** 2005 Broadway, Lubbock, TX 79401, (806)762-8775.

LAWRENCE, Norman L., Jr.——**B:** May 12, 1947, Kingston, Jamaica, *Asst. VP*, The First National Bank of Chicago, RE Asset Mgmt.; **PRIM RE ACT:** Banker, Owner/Investor, Property Manager; **OTHER RE ACT:** RE work-out's; **PREV EMPLOY:** Citibank, N.A.; **EDUC:** BA, 1974, Liberal Arts, Columbia Univ.; **GRAD EDUC:** MBA, 1975, Fin./Mktg., Columbia Univ.; **HOME ADD:** 611 W. Oakdale Ave., Chicago, IL 60657, (312)327-5451; **BUS ADD:** 1 First Nat. Plaza, Chicago, IL 60670, (312)732-5379.

LAWRENCE, Peter Hutchinson——**B:** Sept. 18, 1943, Monroe, LA, *Atty.*, Avco Community Devel., Inc., Rancho Bernardo; **PRIM RE ACT:** Broker, Attorney, Developer, Instructor; **PREV EMPLOY:** Assoc. Counsel, Mission Viejo Co.; **PROFL AFFIL & HONORS:** ABA, State Bar of CA; San Diego Cty. Bar Assn., Bldg. Contractors Assn., Home Builders Assn., Atty.; **EDUC:** BA, 1965, Econ., Washington & Lee Univ.; **GRAD EDUC:** JD, 1973, Laws, Univ. of San Diego; **MIL SERV:** USNR, Lt.; **HOME ADD:** 2954 Lawrence St., San Diego, CA 92106, (714)222-4443; **BUS ADD:** 16770 W. Bernardo Dr., San Diego, CA 92127, (714)277-2132.

LAWRENCE, Thomas B.——**B:** July 8, 1943, Richmond, VA, *Pres.*, Equity Associates, Inc.; **PRIM RE ACT:** Consultant, Developer, Owner/Investor, Property Manager, Syndicator; **OTHER RE ACT:** Mort. Broker; **SERVICES:** Investment Counseling, Valuation, Devel., Mort. Brokerage, Synd. of Comml. Prop., Prop. Mgmt.; **REP CLIENTS:** Indiv. and Inst. investors in comml. props.; **PREV EMPLOY:** Heindl-Evans, Inc.; Gen. Contractors; **PROFL AFFIL & HONORS:** Nat. Assn. of Indus. Office Parks and Assn. of Gen. Contractors; **EDUC:** BS, 1965, Econ./Mktg., VA Commonwealth Univ.; **GRAD EDUC:** M. of Commerce, 1967, Fin., Univ. of Richmond; **MIL SERV:** US Army, Capt., Bronze Star; **OTHER ACT & HONORS:** Bd. of Dir., VA Commonwealth Univ. Alumni Assn; **HOME ADD:** 2016 Park Ave., Richmond, VA 23220, (804)264-5058; **BUS ADD:** 5601 Staples Mill Rd., Richmond, VA 23228, (804)264-5058.

LAWRENCE, William B.——**B:** April 4, 1940, Dallas, TX, *Sr. VP/Dir. of Acquisitions*, Century Partners; **PRIM RE ACT:** Consultant, Owner/Investor, Property Manager, Banker; **OTHER RE ACT:** Acquisitions; **SERVICES:** Locating, evaluating and closing of approx. 200 million in RE annually supervise staff of 17 prof. acquisition personnel; **REP CLIENTS:** Fox & Carskadon Fin. Corp; Montgomery REalty Corp.; Various Corps. that are owners of Real props. valued at over 50 million, lenders and indiv. or inst. investors in comml props.; **PREV EMPLOY:** RE Dept. Equitable Life Assurance Soc. of NY employed there form 1966- 77; Rgnl. RE Mgr.-Acquisitions for Western US Operating out of their regional office in San Francisco; **EDUC:** BS, 1965, Fin. & Mktg., Univ. of KS; **MIL SERV:** US Army, 1962-64, 1st Lt.; **HOME ADD:** 2527 Hastings Dr., Belmont, CA 94002, (415)595-0994; **BUS ADD:** 2755 Campus Dr., San Mateo, CA 94403, (415)574-9133.

LAWSON, Edward A.——**B:** May 8, 1950, San Francisco, CA, *Atty.*, Lawson & Peebles; **PRIM RE ACT:** Attorney; **REP CLIENTS:** Bald Mtn. Props., Nelson Realty, Inc.; OLH Devel. Co.; Ritzau Contractors & Engrs., Trail Creek Co. Realtors; WoodRiver Building Supply Co.; **PREV EMPLOY:** Tobin & Tobin Attys. at Law, San Francisco, CA; **PROFL AFFIL & HONORS:** Member, CA and ID State Bar Assns., ABA; **EDUC:** BA, 1972, Pol. Sci., Univ. of San Francisco; **GRAD EDUC:** JD, 1975, Law, Univ. of CA at Hastings; **EDUC HONORS:** Alpha Sigma Nu, Research Ed., Hastings Constitutional Law Quarterly; **OTHER ACT & HONORS:** Instructor, Hastings College of Law; **HOME ADD:** PO Box 2312, Ketchum, ID 83340, (208)726-5657; **BUS ADD:** 319 Walnut Ave., PO Box 297, Ketchum, ID 83340, (208)726-5657.

LAWTHER, Pamela C.——**B:** Sep. 11, 1946, Bethlehem, PA, *VP*, Drexel Burnham Lambert Realty, Inc.; **PRIM RE ACT:** Broker; **OTHER RE ACT:** NASD Broker/Dealer, Equity Fin. for both Synd. & Devel.; **PREV EMPLOY:** VP, Moseley Assoc., The Tax Shelter Investment Div. of Moseley, Hallgarten, Estabrook & Weeden, Inc., 1977-80; **PROFL AFFIL & HONORS:** RESSI, NLHA; **EDUC:** BA,

1968, Hist., Univ. of DE, Newark, DE; **EDUC HONORS:** Dean's List; **HOME ADD:** 21 Corcoran Rd., Burlington, MA 01803, (617)273-2769; **BUS ADD:** 1 Federal St., 34th Floor, Boston, MA 02110, (617)482-3600.

LAY, Richard E.——B: Nov. 22, 1955, Athens, TN, *Pres. and Gen. Mgr.*, Lay Realty Co., Inc.; **PRIM RE ACT:** Broker, Developer; **SERVICES:** Residential Brokerage, New Homes Devel.; **PROFL AFFIL & HONORS:** RNMI (CRB, CRS); FLI, RESSI, 1980 Membership Chmn. Award from NAR - Medium State; **EDUC:** BA, 1978, Math. and Eng., TN Wesleyan Coll.; **EDUC HONORS:** Cum Laude; **OTHER ACT & HONORS:** Athens Kiwanis Club, Athens Council of Serv. Org. (Chmn. 1981); **HOME ADD:** 1113 Woodward Ave., Athens, TN 37303, (615)745-4400; **BUS ADD:** 105 Park Ave., PO Box 461, Athens, TN 37303, (615)745-4100.

LAYCOCK, Thomas B., II——B: Sept. 23, 1926, Indianapolis, IN, *Pres.*, Graves, Inc. (Construction Development) - Laycock Properties, Inc. (Prop. Mgmt.), Graves Architects, Inc. (Architectural Services); **PRIM RE ACT:** Architect, Developer, Builder, Owner/Investor, Property Manager; **PROFL AFFIL & HONORS:** NAHB, AIA, CSI, NAA; **EDUC:** BS, 1948, Arch. Engrg.; **MIL SERV:** USNR (1944-1952), LT; **OTHER ACT & HONORS:** Admin. Bldg. Council of IN 1971-1979 (Chrmn. 1978); **HOME ADD:** 3836 Cranbrook Dr., Indianapolis, IN 46240, (317)849-4893; **BUS ADD:** 3010 E. 56th St., P.O. Box 20463, Indianapolis, IN 46220, (317)257-4103.

LAYLAND, David N.——B: Nov. 11, 1945, Chicago, IL, *Controller*, CMD Real Estate Group; **PRIM RE ACT:** Broker, Developer, Builder, Owner/Investor, Property Manager; **SERVICES:** Full serv. RE devel.; **REP CLIENTS:** The Prudential Ins. Co. of Amer.; **PREV EMPLOY:** The Prudential Ins. Co. of Amer., RE Investment Dept., 1975-1981; **PROFL AFFIL & HONORS:** AICPA, Jrs. CPA Soc.; **EDUC:** Roosevelt Univ., 1970, Acctg., Walter E. Heller Coll. of Bus. Admin.; **HOME ADD:** 431 Grant Pl., Chicago, IL 60614, (312)929-0089; **BUS ADD:** One 1st National Plaza, Suite 4950, Chicago, IL 60603, (312)726-2232.

LAYNE, B.J.——B: Nov. 18, 1933, Norfolk, VA, *Sr. Part.*, Layne & Brill P.A., Attys. at Law; **PRIM RE ACT:** Attorney, Banker; **EDUC:** BA, 1954, Bus., Univ. of VA; **GRAD EDUC:** LLB, 1957, Comml. Law, Boston Univ., Law School; **MIL SERV:** USM; US Army; Sgt.; **OTHER ACT & HONORS:** Numerous Legal & Banking Orgs.; **HOME ADD:** 1865 79th St. Causeway, Miami Beach, FL 33139, (305)865-0956; **BUS ADD:** 21 S.E. 1st Ave., Miami, FL 33131, (305)358-0888.

LAYTIN, William M.——B: Feb. 10, 1947, Fort Smith, AR, *VP Gen. Counsel*, Amer. Insvsco Realty, Inc.; Homemarketing of America, Inc.; **PRIM RE ACT:** Attorney; **PROFL AFFIL & HONORS:** IL State Bar Assn. Chicago Bar Assn., ABA; **EDUC:** BA, 1969, Hist., Poli. Sci., Univ. of IL; **GRAD EDUC:** JD, 1972, Univ. of OK; **EDUC HONORS:** Dean's List, Dean's List; **HOME ADD:** 806 E. Burr Oak Dr., Arlington Hts., IL 60004, (312)259-2807; **BUS ADD:** Suite 500, 120 S. LaSalle St., Chicago, IL 60603, (312)621-4065.

LAZAR, Ron——B: May 1, 1932, NY, *Partner VP*, Schacker Realty; **PRIM RE ACT:** Broker, Developer, Owner/Investor, Property Manager, Syndicator; **SERVICES:** Indus., office and comml. RE brokerage and prop. mgmt.; **PREV EMPLOY:** Northwest Ind. Mktg. VP; **EDUC:** AB, 1953, Dartmouth Coll.; **GRAD EDUC:** MBA, 1954, Amos Tuck Sch.; **MIL SERV:** USNR, Lt.; **OTHER ACT & HONORS:** Pres. Head Agents Assn., Dartmouth Coll. Alumni Fund; **HOME ADD:** 37 Hill Ln., Roslyn Hts., NY 11577, (516)621-8703; **BUS ADD:** 401 Broad Hollow Rd., Melville, NY 11747, (516)293-3700.

LAZARUS, Howard J.——B: June 19, 1948, Queens, NY, *Partner*, Trubin, Sillcocks, Edelman & Knapp; **PRIM RE ACT:** Attorney; **REP CLIENTS:** Devel, indiv. and instl. investors, and lenders; **PROFL AFFIL & HONORS:** NY State Bar Assn., Real Prop. Law Section, **EDUC:** 1970, Indus. & Labor Relations, Cornell Univ.; **GRAD EDUC:** JD, 1973, Law, Boston Coll. Law School; **EDUC HONORS:** Editor of Law Review; **BUS ADD:** 375 Park Ave., New York, NY 10152, (212)759-5400.

LAZARUS, Jerry——*Pres.*, Jerry Lazarus Assoc.; **PRIM RE ACT:** Developer, Builder, Owner/Investor; **PROFL AFFIL & HONORS:** Lic. RE Broker, CW Post Coll. Man of the year. in RE; Hon. Member, Roslyn Hist. Soc.; **HOME ADD:** Old Westbury, NY 11568; **BUS ADD:** 6901 Jericho Tpke., Syosset, NY 11791, (516)364-2000.

LAZERUS, Gilbert——B: June 24, 1912, New York, NY, *Part., Atty.*, Stroock, Stroock & Lavan, RE Dept.; **PRIM RE ACT:** Attorney; **PROFL AFFIL & HONORS:** Dir. The Title Guarantee Co.; **EDUC:** PhD, 1931, Econ., Yale Univ.; **GRAD EDUC:** JD, 1934, Columbia Law Sch.; **HOME ADD:** 1175 York Ave., New York, NY 10021, (212)838-0153; **BUS ADD:** 61 Broadway, New York, NY 10006, (212)425-5200.

LAZRUS, Jonathan E.——B: Feb. 24, 1934, New York, NY, *CEO & Partner*, Lazrus Associates; **PRIM RE ACT:** Developer, Lender, Property Manager; **SERVICES:** Ownership, operation, leasing, fin., and devel.; **PREV EMPLOY:** VP Sovereign Watch Co. Subsidiary of Benrus Watch Co., Inc., 1955-1958; **PROFL AFFIL & HONORS:** Tr. of Jewish Memorial Hospital, Dir. RE Bd. of NY; **EDUC:** New Lincoln High School, 1953; **OTHER ACT & HONORS:** Harmonie Club of NY, Quaker Ridge Golf Club; **HOME ADD:** 535 E. 86th St., New York, NY 10028, (212)988-1115; **BUS ADD:** 1776 Broadway, New York, NY 10019, (212)245-2355.

LEACH, J. Frank——*President*, Arcata National Corp.; **PRIM RE ACT:** Property Manager; **BUS ADD:** 2750 Sand Hill Rd., Menlo Park, CA 94025, (415)854-5222.*

LEADBETTER, Bruce——B: Sept. 4, 1938, Hugo, CO, *Pres.*, Post Co.; **PRIM RE ACT:** Owner/Investor; **PREV EMPLOY:** Investment Corp. (1966-1969); Summit Props. Kona-Post Corp; Aspen-Post Corp.; Dir. Levitz Furniture Co. 1974; **PROFL AFFIL & HONORS:** Amer. Assn. of Small Bus.; Pres. N. AZ Bd. of Realtors 1961-1965; Nat. Assn. of Indep. Businessmen, Outstanding businessman of AZ 1972; Govs. Hon. Citizen TX (1966); Man of Year, Dallas 1965; **OTHER ACT & HONORS:** Phoenix Ctry. Club; Tres Vidas Ctry. Club; Dir. Salvation Army; **HOME ADD:** 7855 Meadow Park, Dallas, TX 75234; **BUS ADD:** 4633 N. Central Expressway, Suite 215, Dallas, TX 75205, (214)528-3270.

LEARY, John H.——B: Nov. 29, 1950, Philadelphia, PA, *Dir., Mgmt. Advisory Services*, Laventhol & Horwath; **PRIM RE ACT:** Consultant; **SERVICES:** Market studies and fin. projections; **PROFL AFFIL & HONORS:** Detroit Bd. of Realtors; MI Lodging Assn.; MI Restaurant Assn., Visiting Faculty Member, MI State Univ.; **EDUC:** BA, 1972, Eng., LaSalle Coll.; **GRAD EDUC:** MBA, 1975, Hotel & Restaurant Mgmt., MI State Univ.; **EDUC HONORS:** Cum Laude, Beta Gamma Sigma; **HOME ADD:** 312 Chesterfield, Birmingham, MI 48009, (313)644-0650; **BUS ADD:** 26400 Lahser Rd., Suite 200, Southfield, MI 48034, (313)354-6000.

LEARY, Theodore M., Jr.——B: Feb. 18, 1945, Beverly, MA, *VP-Acquisitions*, Lehndorff Mgt. (USA) LTD., INC.; **PRIM RE ACT:** Broker, Consultant, Property Manager, Owner/Investor; **SERVICES:** Purchase & Manage assets for European clients; **PREV EMPLOY:** VP,Victor Palmieri & Co., Inc.; **PROFL AFFIL & HONORS:** ULI, DC Bar; **EDUC:** BA, 1966, Hist., Harvard Coll.; **GRAD EDUC:** JD, 1969, George Washington Univ. Law School; **EDUC HONORS:** Cum Laude, Cum Laude; **HOME ADD:** 5630 Spreading Oak Dr., Los Angeles,, CA 90068, (213)469-0400; **BUS ADD:** 609 South Grand Ave. Suite 501, Los Angeles,, CA 90017, (213)489-4670.

LEAVENGOOD, John B.——B: Nov. 28, 1943, Des Moines, IA, *Mgr., (Prop. Mgmt. Div.); Mgr., (Commerical Div.)*, Stanbrough Realtors; **PRIM RE ACT:** Broker, Instructor, Property Manager; **SERVICES:** Fee mgmt. of income props., comml. sales; **REP CLIENTS:** Ltd. partnerships, doctors, attys. etc.; **PROFL AFFIL & HONORS:** IREM, IA Assn. of Realtors, Greater Des Moines Bd. of Realtors, CPM, IA Chap. Mgr. of the Year Award 1978; IREM Nat. Gov. Council 1980, 81 & 82; **EDUC:** BS, 1966, Physics & math, Univ. of N. IA; **HOME ADD:** 4216 SE 3rd, Des Moines, IA 50315, (515)285-0960; **BUS ADD:** 3111 Douglas Ave., Des Moines, IA 50310, (515)271-1100.

LEAVITT, K. Michael——B: May 26, 1946, San Francisco, CA, *Partner*, Bell, Leavitt & Grenn, Chartered; **PRIM RE ACT:** Attorney; **SERVICES:** Legal servs. in real prop. and related fields; **REP CLIENTS:** Investors, devel., contractors, brokers, engrs., prop. mgrs., lenders; **PREV EMPLOY:** RE Dept., Hughes Tool Co.; Rgnl. Counsel's Office, IRS, Appraisers Asst.; **PROFL AFFIL & HONORS:** NV Devel. Authority; Greater Las Vegas C of C; Clark Cty. and NV State Bar Assns., Lecturer at profl. seminars; **EDUC:** BS, 1968, Bus. Admin., Acctg., Univ. of So. CA; **GRAD EDUC:** JD, 1972, Univ. of So. CA; **EDUC HONORS:** Cum Laude, Order of the Coif; **HOME ADD:** 5575 Fire Is. Dr., Las Vegas, NV 89120, (702)382-5111; **BUS ADD:** 601 E. Bridger Ave., Las Vegas, NV 89101.

LEBENSOLD, Linda R.——B: Nov. 24, 1944, New York, NY, *Asst. Gen. Counsel*, The Mutual Life Insurance Company of New York; **PRIM RE ACT:** Attorney; **PROFL AFFIL & HONORS:** Real Prop. Sec. of ABA, ALTA, Assn. of Life Insurance Counsels; **EDUC:** AB, 1965, Govt., Barnard Coll.; **GRAD EDUC:** LLB, 1968, Columbia Univ. School of Law; **EDUC HONORS:** Cum Laude; **OTHER ACT & HONORS:** Pres. and Dir., River Point Towers Cooperative, Inc.

1976-present; **HOME ADD:** 555 Kappock St., Riverdale, NY 10463, (212)884-3816; **BUS ADD:** 1740 Broadway, New York, NY 10019, (212)708-2262.

LEBOVITZ, Charles B.——**B:** Feb. 1, 1937, Chattanooga, TN, *Pres. & CEO*, CBL & Associates, Inc.; **OTHER RE ACT:** Shopping Center Development, Manager/Owner; **SERVICES:** Devel. & Mgmt. of Shopping Ctrs. including rgnl. malls and strip shopping ctrs. on a nation-wide basis; **PREV EMPLOY:** Pres., Arlen Shopping Centers Co.; **PROFL AFFIL & HONORS:** Intl. Council of Shopping Ctrs.; Licensed RE Broker, TN & GA, TN State Dir. for Intl. Council of Shopping Ctrs.; **EDUC:** BA, 1959, Vanderbilt Univ.; **MIL SERV:** USN, Lt.j.g.; **OTHER ACT & HONORS:** Rotary Club; Past Pres., B'Nai Zion Congregation; Past Pres., McCallie Sch. Alumni Council; Tr., McCallie Sch.; Dir., Brooks Stores, Inc.; **HOME ADD:** 2920 Brownwood Dr., Chattanooga, TN 37415, (615)698-7166; **BUS ADD:** One Northgate Park, Chattanooga, TN 37415, (615)877-1151.

LEBRO, Theodore P.——**B:** Feb. 12, 1910, Fulton, NY, *Owner*, Lebro Real Estate D.B.A.; **PRIM RE ACT:** Broker, Consultant, Appraiser, Owner/Investor, Instructor, Property Manager, Insuror, Assessor; **REP CLIENTS:** Columbia Banking Savings & Loan Assn.; **PROFL AFFIL & HONORS:** Oswego Cty. Bd. of Realtors, NY Bd. of Realtors National Bd., CPM, IAO, SRA, CRA; **EDUC:** BS, 1954, Syracuse Univ. School of Mgmt.; **GRAD EDUC:** Orchard Lake Coll.; **EDUC HONORS:** Alumni Honary Degree; **OTHER ACT & HONORS:** Dir. of Real Prop., Oswego Co.; Dir. of Lee Memorial Hosp.; C.Y.O.; Heart Fund; St. Michaels Soc.; American Legion; V.F.W., Polish Legion; **HOME ADD:** RD 2, Box 111, Phoenix, NY 13135, (315)593-7979; **BUS ADD:** 316 West 1st. St., Fulton, NY 13069, (315)592-5363.

LEBUS, L. Martin——*Sr. VP Treas.*, Tonka Corp.; **PRIM RE ACT:** Property Manager; **BUS ADD:** 4144 Shoreline Blvd., PO Box 445, Spring Park, MN 55384, (612)475-9500.*

LECKEY, Merrick W.——**B:** Mar. 4, 1943, San Francisco, CA, *Pres.*, Intl. Innkeepers, Inc.; **PRIM RE ACT:** Owner/Investor, Property Manager, Syndicator; **SERVICES:** Hotel mgt. & distressed prop. workouts; **PROFL AFFIL & HONORS:** Amer. Hotel & Motel Assn., CA Hotel & Motel Assn., CPA; **EDUC:** BA, 1966, Hotel Admin., Washington State Univ.; **GRAD EDUC:** MBA, 1968, Fin. & Instit. Mgt., MI State Univ.; **EDUC HONORS:** Honor Roll, Outstanding Graduated Student - 1968; **HOME ADD:** 31901 National Park, Laguna Niguel, CA 92677; **BUS ADD:** 1205 N. Pacific Coast Highway, Laguna Beach, CA 92651, (714)497-4855.

LECKLIDER, Robert W.——**B:** Nov. 22, 1922, Greenville, OH, *Architect*, Lecklider/Jay, Architects; **PRIM RE ACT:** Architect; **SERVICES:** Architectural Servs.; **PROFL AFFIL & HONORS:** AIA, CSI; **EDUC:** B. Arch, 1950, Indus. Comml. & Instl., Miami Univ.; **EDUC HONORS:** Edward M. Berry Award, 1949; **MIL SERV:** Corp. of Engrs., Sgt.; **OTHER ACT & HONORS:** Kettering Planning Comm. 1968-72, Miami Valley Regional Planning Comm. 1969-71; **HOME ADD:** 704 Brubaker Dr., Kettering, OH 45429, (513)298-2774; **BUS ADD:** 110 E. Second St., Dayton, OH 45402, (513)222-1117.

LECRAW, David S.——**B:** Dec. 30, 1947, Westport, CT, *Pres.*, The LeCraw Co.; **PRIM RE ACT:** Broker, Consultant, Owner/Investor, Property Manager; **SERVICES:** Sales, leasing, mgmt. of comml. RE; **REP CLIENTS:** Several German investment funds and numerous Amer. investors and developers; **PREV EMPLOY:** VP, Mktg., The Myrick Co.; **PROFL AFFIL & HONORS:** GA Indus. Devels. Assn., Nat. Assn. of Office & Indus. Parks; **EDUC:** BBA, 1973, RE, GA State Univ.; **GRAD EDUC:** MBA, 1980, Fin., GA State Univ.; **EDUC HONORS:** Pres. Rho Epsilon 1972, Kirkland RE Scholarship 1972; **MIL SERV:** US Army, Sgt., Bronze Star; Republic of Vietnam Gallantry Cross; **OTHER ACT & HONORS:** Bd. of Dirs., Boy Scouts of Amer., Atlanta Area Council 1977; Guest Lecturer at GA Inst. of Tech. and GA State Univ.; **HOME ADD:** 4173 Glen Meadow Dr., Norcross, GA 30092, (404)447-6131; **BUS ADD:** 3169 Holcomb Bridge Rd., Suite 135, Norcross, GA 30071, (404)447-5111.

LEDBETTER, Bureon E., Jr.——**B:** Jan. 10, 1953, Tallassee, AL, *Gen. Counsel and Dir. of Leasing*, Chick-fil-A, Inc.; **PRIM RE ACT:** Attorney; **OTHER RE ACT:** Retail Leasing; **EDUC:** BA, 1975, Auburn Univ.; **GRAD EDUC:** JD, 1979, Cumberland School of Law; **HOME ADD:** 3110 Lakeridge Dr., Marietta, GA 30067, (404)953-0137; **BUS ADD:** 801 VA Ave., Hapeville, GA 30354, (404)765-8000.

LEDBETTER, Norman M.——**B:** Aug. 9, 1955, OK City, OK, *Dept. Mgr.*, Tedmon & Associates, Inc., Local Stocks; **PRIM RE ACT:** Owner/Investor, Property Manager, Insuror, Syndicator; **SERVICES:** Investment counseling, synd., devel.; **REP CLIENTS:** Indiv. and institl. investors in comml. and agric. prop.; **PREV EMPLOY:** Ledbetter Props., Inc., Market Research, Acquisitions; **EDUC:** BA, 1977, Geography, Colgate Univ.; **GRAD EDUC:** MBA, 1979, Fin., Univ. of WA; **EDUC HONORS:** Dean's List; **HOME TEL:** (206)632-5038; **BUS ADD:** 2015 152nd N.E., Redmond, WA 98052, (206)643-5000.

LEDBETTER, Patricia——**B:** Sept. 25, 1931, Newton, IA, *Sr. VP*, National Bank of Alaska, Corporate Headquarters; **PRIM RE ACT:** Banker, Lender; **SERVICES:** Comml. Banking; **PROFL AFFIL & HONORS:** AK Mort. Bankers, Anchorage Mort. and Profl. Women, Nat. Assn. of Bank Women Officers; **EDUC:** Mort. Banking School 1977; **HOME ADD:** 2617 Shepherdia Dr., Anchorage, AK 99504; **BUS ADD:** Pouch 7-025, Anchorage, AK 99510, (907)276-1132.

LEDBETTER, Robert Harbin, Sr.——**B:** Sept. 24, 1935, Rome, GA, *Pres.*, Ledbetter Brothers, Inc.; **PRIM RE ACT:** Developer, Owner/Investor, Property Manager; **SERVICES:** RE Mgmt.; **PROFL AFFIL & HONORS:** VP, Dir. Ledbetter Bros. Inc. 1960-70; Pres., Dir. 1970- ; VP Dir. LBI Quarries, Inc., Ledbetter Trucks, Inc.; Dir. Echota Realty Co., Shorter Realty Co.; GA Highway Contractors Assn. (Dir. Mem. Exec. Comm. 1st VP, GA Asphalt Pavement Assn. (Dir. 1965-70 , Mem. Exec. Comm., Past Pres.); **EDUC:** BA, 1958, GA Instit. of Tech.; **MIL SERV:** USN 1958-60, Lt.; **OTHER ACT & HONORS:** Sigma Alpha Epsilon, Presbyn. Clubs, Coosa Cty. Club, Bd. Dir. Boys Club of Rome, S.A.R.; **HOME ADD:** 1121 Kingston Rd., Rome, GA 30161, (404)291-6863; **BUS ADD:** PO Box 1067, 2 West Sec. Ave., Rome, GA 30161, (404)291-7283.

LEDBETTER, Scott P.——**B:** Apr. 17, 1942, South Bend, IN, *Owner*, S.P. Ledbetter, Realtor; **PRIM RE ACT:** Broker, Owner/Investor; **SERVICES:** Income Prop. Investments; **PREV EMPLOY:** Pres. of Cook Investment Props., Inc. 1969-1976; **PROFL AFFIL & HONORS:** Lambda Alpha Land Inst., Mid-American Chap.; Memphis C of C; Leadership Memphis; **EDUC:** BS, 1965, ME, Cornell Univ.; **GRAD EDUC:** MBA, 1967, Corporate Fin., Cornell Univ.; **OTHER ACT & HONORS:** Memphis Ctry. Club; Chmn. of Memphis Arts Council; Pres. of Bd. of Memphis; Museum of Natural & Cultural Hist.; Tr. of the Hutchison School; and Member Bd. of Dirs. of Boys Club of Memphis; **HOME ADD:** 395 Goodwyn, Memphis, TN 38111, (901)458-8257; **BUS ADD:** P.O. Box 17276, Memphis, TN 38117, (901)761-3490.

LEDBETTER, Thomas D.——**B:** Oct. 6, 1937, Pryor, OK, *Atty.*, Ledbetter & Associates, Ltd.; **PRIM RE ACT:** Attorney, Syndicator; **OTHER RE ACT:** Title Insurance Agent; **SERVICES:** Counseling and legal services on lease, purchase, devel., operation, fin. and sale of real prop. interest; **REP CLIENTS:** Purchasers and lenders of resid., comml. and indus. props.; **PROFL AFFIL & HONORS:** AR and ABA, AR and Amer. Trial Lawyers Assns., AR and Amer. Land Title Assns., Pres. Attys' Title Guaranty Fund, Inc. of AR; **EDUC:** BA, Math: Univ. of Denver, 1964, Aeronautical Engrg.; Minor in Secondary Educ.;, Univ. of OK and Univ. of Denver; **GRAD EDUC:** JD, 1967, Gen. school, Univ. of AR at Fayetteville, AR; **EDUC HONORS:** Educ. and Frat.; **MIL SERV:** USAFR, Enlisted; **OTHER ACT & HONORS:** Asst. Prosecuting Atty.: 1967-69, 70-74; City Atty.: 1970-74; Episcopal Church, Boy Scouts of Amer., Lions Club; **HOME ADD:** 1107 Circle Dr., Harrison, AR 72601, (501)741-2882; **BUS ADD:** 301 E. Nicholson, PO Box 637, Harrison, AR 72601, (501)743-1207.

LEDGARD, Bert L., Jr.——**B:** July 15, 1933, Flushing, NY, *Atty.*, Wilkes & Artis, Chartered; **PRIM RE ACT:** Attorney, Instructor; **OTHER RE ACT:** Adjunct Prof. of Real Prop. Law; **SERVICES:** RE fin., RE devel. and synd., RE counseling, zoning, planning and municipal law; **REP CLIENTS:** Various major ins. cos., mort. bankers., educ. instit., agencies of the U.S. and public intl. org. with respect to the fin. and devel. of comml. and investment prop.; **PROFL AFFIL & HONORS:** ABA; Bar Assn. of the DC; **EDUC:** BS, 1955, Soc. Sci., Georgetown Univ.; **GRAD EDUC:** LLB, 1959, Taxation, Georgetown Univ.; LLM, 1962, Taxation, Georgetown Univ.; **EDUC HONORS:** Cum Laude; **MIL SERV:** U.S. Army, Lt., 1955-1957; **OTHER ACT & HONORS:** Law Clerk, U.S. Court of Appeals for DC, 1959; Law Clerk, U.S. Dist. Court for DC, 1960; **HOME ADD:** 3014 Dent Pl., N.W., Apt. 4E, Wash., DC 20007, (202)333-6447; **BUS ADD:** 1666 K St., N.W., Suite 600, Wash., DC 20006, (202)457-7846.

LEE, Adelbert W.——**B:** Dec. 27, 1901, *RE Appraiser*, Adelbert W Lee & Son; **PRIM RE ACT:** Appraiser; **REP CLIENTS:** Banks & ins. cos., US Fed. Govt. Agencies, DC State Agencies, Cty. Auth., Public Utilities; **PREV EMPLOY:** Have conducted my own bus. since 1922; **PROFL AFFIL & HONORS:** Past Nat. Sec. ASA, Capitol Hill Club, Amer. Right of Way Assn.; **OTHER ACT & HONORS:** VP, Bd. of Educ., 1945-48, Capitol Hill Lions Club, Kiwanis Club, Selective Serv. Bd.; **HOME ADD:** 9500 Michael Dr., Clinton, MD 20735; **BUS ADD:**

9016 Clinton St., Box 307, Clinton, MD 20735, (301)868-3700.

LEE, Carol Mon——**B:** July 20, 1947, MA, *VP and Dir. of Land Trust Services*, American Trust Co. of Hawaii, Inc.; **PRIM RE ACT:** Attorney, Instructor; **OTHER RE ACT:** Admin., client service; **SERVICES:** Educate community on uses of land trusts, admin. land trusts and other types of personal trusts, structure land trusts; **REP CLIENTS:** Nat. and foreign investors, devel. and home owners; **PREV EMPLOY:** Asst. Prof. of Law, Univ. of HI Sch. of Law; Assoc. Atty. in private practice, Gibson & Palmer, Los Angeles, CA; **PROFL AFFIL & HONORS:** CA Bar; HI Bar; HI Real Estate License; NY Teaching Credential; **EDUC:** BA, 1965, Art Hist., Barnard Coll./Columbia Univ.; **GRAD EDUC:** MA, 1970, Art, Columbia Univ.; JD, 1974, Law, Univ. of CA, Hastings Coll.; **OTHER ACT & HONORS:** HI Women Lawyers, Past Pres.; Fed. State Tax Inst., Member, Bd. of Dir.; HI Bd. of Bar Examiners, Member; Univ. of HI School of Law, Law Review Advisory Bd.; **HOME ADD:** 1221 Victoria St. 1402, Honolulu, HI 96814, (808)537-6493; **BUS ADD:** 841 Bishop St. 1203, Honolulu, HI 96813, (808)521-6543.

LEE, Donald——**B:** Aug. 17, 1927, CT, *Indiv. Owner*, Don Lee, Realtor; **PRIM RE ACT:** Broker, Appraiser; **PROFL AFFIL & HONORS:** NAR, NYSAR, DCBOFR, F&L, IOFF&LB, NYSS of REA, MLS of DC Inc., GRI, CRS, CRB; **MIL SERV:** US Navy, Y1C; **OTHER ACT & HONORS:** BPOE, Kiwanis; **BUS ADD:** Rt 82 Box 430, Dutchess Cty., NY 12533, (914)221-2081.

LEE, Everett M.——**B:** Nov. 1, 1933, St. Clair, MO, *Mgr. of Area Devel.*, Missouri Public Service CO., Community Services; **PRIM RE ACT:** Developer; **PROFL AFFIL & HONORS:** MO Indus. Devel. Council, Amer. Econ. Devel. Council, S. Indus. Devel. Council; **EDUC:** BA, 1959, Indus. arts, Lincoln Univ.; **BUS ADD:** 10700 E. 350 Hwy., Kansas City, MO 64138, (816)737-9345.

LEE, Guy A.——**B:** Sep. 2, 1922, NYC, *Dir. Corp. Services*, Washington Park Bldg., Inc.; **PRIM RE ACT:** Property Manager, Insuror; **SERVICES:** Facilities Mgmt., Purchasing, Risk Mgmt.; **PROFL AFFIL & HONORS:** BOMA - Greater NY - Bd. Member and Officer(Ass't. Sec.), RPA; **EDUC:** BBA, Mgmt., St. Johns Univ.; **EDUC HONORS:** 3.0 Ave.; **MIL SERV:** USA, CE, T/5 1942-45; **OTHER ACT & HONORS:** Officer W. Orange Republican Club, Advisory Bd. Newark YMCA, Advisory Bd. W. Orange Cable TV; **HOME ADD:** 58 Seaman Rd., W. Orange, NJ 07052, (201)736-2248; **BUS ADD:** 33 Washington St., Newark, NJ 07102, (201)456-2391.

LEE, Jack H.——**B:** Feb. 5, 1915, Milwaukee, WI; **PRIM RE ACT:** Broker, Consultant, Attorney, Owner/Investor, Instructor; **REP CLIENTS:** Nat. retail, fin. insts., investors; **PROFL AFFIL & HONORS:** WI Bar Assn.; Nat. Assn. of Realtors; RNMI, CCIM; **EDUC:** BA, 1936, Econ., Univ. of WI; **GRAD EDUC:** JD, 1939, Law of RE, Univ. of WI, School of Law; **EDUC HONORS:** Artus, Nat. Hon. Econ. Soc., Pres., 1937; **MIL SERV:** FBI, Special Agent, 1940-1946; **HOME ADD:** 3395 Heatheridge Ln., Reno, NV 89509, (702)329-2112; **BUS ADD:** 3395 Heatheridge Ln., Reno, NV 89509, (702)329-2112.

LEE, James P.——**B:** May 25, 1943, Chicago, IL, *RE Dir., Northern Terr.*, Montgomery Ward & Co., Inc., Corp. Devel.; **OTHER RE ACT:** Retail dept. store RE; **REP CLIENTS:** Employer; **PROFL AFFIL & HONORS:** ICSC; **EDUC:** BA, 1965, Psych, De Paul Univ., Chicago, IL; **EDUC HONORS:** IL State Scholarship Recipient; **MIL SERV:** IL Nat. Guard, Spec. 4th class; **HOME ADD:** 465 Dominion Dr., Wood Dale, IL 60191, (312)766-9131; **BUS ADD:** One Montgomery Ward Plaza, Chicago, IL 60671, (312)467-3684.

LEE, John Jin——**B:** Oct. 20, 1948, Chicago, IL, *VP and Managing Sr. Counsel*, Wells Fargo Bank, N.A., Legal Dept.; **PRIM RE ACT:** Attorney; **SERVICES:** Legal Serv.; **REP CLIENTS:** Wells Fargo Bank, N.A.; **PREV EMPLOY:** Manatt, Phelps & Rothenberg, Los Angeles, CA-Assoc. Atty. (1976-1977); **PROFL AFFIL & HONORS:** ABA; CA State Bar Assn.; Bar Assn. of San Francisco; Asian Amer. Bar Assn.; Asian Bus. League; **EDUC:** BA, 1971, Physics/Math., Rice Univ.; **GRAD EDUC:** JD, MBA, 1975, Law School-Bus., Bus. Sch.-Fin. & Acctg., Stanford Law Sch. & Stanford Univ. Grad. Sch. of Bus.; **EDUC HONORS:** Magna Cum Laude, Phi Beta Kappa, Sigma Pi Sigma, Pres. Honor Roll, Wiess Coll. Fellow, Stanford Law Review (Editor), Stanford Journal of Intl. Studies (Editor & Book Review Editor); **HOME ADD:** 116 Galewood Cir., San Francisco, CA 94131; **BUS ADD:** 415 Sansome St., San Francisco, CA 94111, (415)396-2310.

LEE, Lawrence M.——**B:** Nov. 26, 1944, Laurel, MS, *Regional Dir. & Asst. VP*, Lincoln National Life Ins. Co., Southwestern Regional Mortgage Loan Office; **PRIM RE ACT:** Lender; **SERVICES:** Loans and joint ventures in the West and Southwestern part of the US; **PREV EMPLOY:** US Naval Officer, 1968 to 1971, Lincoln Nat. Life Ins. Co. from 1973 to present; **PROFL AFFIL & HONORS:** Young Mortgage Bankers, Dallas; **EDUC:** BBA, 1968, Fin., Univ. of TX, School of Bus.; **GRAD EDUC:** MBA, Fin., Old Dominion Univ.; **EDUC HONORS:** Dean's List; Scholastic Scholarship; Speech Scholarship; **MIL SERV:** US Navy, Lcdr.; **HOME ADD:** 209 Turpin Dr., Lewisville, TX 75067, (214)221-4134; **BUS ADD:** 12200 Ford Rd., Ste. 136, Dallas, TX 75234, (214)247-6494.

LEE, R. Randy, Esq.——**B:** Nov. 20, 1942, Chicago, *Atty.-At-Law*, R. Randy Lee, Esq.; **PRIM RE ACT:** Attorney, Syndicator, Developer, Builder; **SERVICES:** Legal, Devel./Investment Counseling, Prop. Synd.; **REP CLIENTS:** NYC Builders Assn., City Home Ownership Corp; Charter Abstract Co., Ltd.; Intercounty Morts. Corp.; **PROFL AFFIL & HONORS:** ABA, NY State Bar Assn., NAHRO, AVREA, ULI, NYCBA, NAHB; **EDUC:** NY Univ., 1965, RE/Econ./Fin., SCAF; **GRAD EDUC:** JD, 1969, Brooklyn Law School; **EDUC HONORS:** JD; **OTHER ACT & HONORS:** MENSA, VP., Jewish Community Ctr., S.I.; Dir NYCBA & NYSBA; **HOME ADD:** 86 Merrick Ave., Staten Is., NY 10301, (212)981-9767; **BUS ADD:** 3461 Richmond Ave., Staten Is., NY 10312, (212)948-2300.

LEE, Randolph E., Jr.——**B:** July 16, 1953, Colorado Springs, CO, *Tax Supervisor*, Laventhol & Horwath; **OTHER RE ACT:** Accountant, tax analysis; **SERVICES:** Fin. projections & tax advice; **REP CLIENTS:** Indiv. & partnerships involved primarily in devel., acquisition, renovation & synd. of comml. prop.; **PREV EMPLOY:** Deloitte Haskins & Sells; **PROFL AFFIL & HONORS:** AICPA, VA Soc. of CPA's, DC Inst. of CPA's, No. VA Soc. of CPA; **EDUC:** BS in Commerce, 1975, Acctg., Univ. of VA; **GRAD EDUC:** MBA, 1978, Fin. & Acctg., George Mason Univ.; **EDUC HONORS:** Dean's List, US Army Special Scholarship, NMSQT Scholarship, Dean's List; **HOME ADD:** 1726 Preston Rd., Alexandria, VA 22302, (703)820-2514; **BUS ADD:** 8630 Fenton St., Suite 800, Silver Spring, MD 20910, (301)585-8200.

LEE, Robert E.——**B:** Apr. 21, 1927, Woodhaven, NY, *Partner*, S.M. & D.E. Meeker; **PRIM RE ACT:** Attorney; **SERVICES:** Legal; **REP CLIENTS:** The Williamsburgh Savings Bank, One Hanson Pl., Brooklyn, NY; **PROFL AFFIL & HONORS:** ABA, NY State Bar Assn., Exec Comm. Real Prop. Law Sect., Savings Bank Attys., Brooklyn, NY; **EDUC:** BBA, 1950, Fin., St. Johns Univ.; **GRAD EDUC:** LLB, 1952, St. John's Univ.; JD, 1963, St. John's Univ.; **MIL SERV:** USN, AMM3/c; **OTHER ACT & HONORS:** Title Advisory Bd., Security Title Co.; **HOME ADD:** 30 Hofstra Dr., Plainview, NY 11803, (516)692-5370; **BUS ADD:** One Hanson Pl., Brooklyn, NY 11243, (212)783-3340.

LEE, Soloman——**B:** Sept. 18, 1948, Canton, China, *Sr. Assoc.*, Marcus & Millichap, Inc.; **PRIM RE ACT:** Broker, Consultant, Instructor; **OTHER RE ACT:** Portfolio mgmt.; **SERVICES:** Represent clients in sale/purchase of income props. over $2 million per transaction; **REP CLIENTS:** Far Eastern investors; **PREV EMPLOY:** Touche Ross & Co., CPA's, Specialized in RE and Fin. Instns.; **PROFL AFFIL & HONORS:** AICPA, CA Soc. of CPA's, RE Broker and Cert. CPA; **EDUC:** BA, 1974, Acctg., San Francisco State Univ.; **GRAD EDUC:** MBA, 1976, Fin. and Intl. Bus., Univ. of CA, Berkeley; **EDUC HONORS:** Beta Alpha Psi Nat. Council Award, Piccaro and Lerman Award, Nat. Accountant Assn. Past Pres. Memorial Award, Magna Cum Laude, Beta Gamma Sigma; **OTHER ACT & HONORS:** Bd. of Dirs., CRDC Maintenance Training Corp., a non-profit org.; **HOME ADD:** 3159 Kirby Lane, Walnut Creek, CA 94598, (415)932-6526; **BUS ADD:** 875 Battery St., San Francisco, CA 94111, (415)391-9220.

LEE, Theodore B.——**B:** Dec. 28, 1932, Stockton, CA, *Pres.*, NDS Investment Co.; **PRIM RE ACT:** Consultant, Attorney, Developer, Owner/Investor, Property Manager; **PROFL AFFIL & HONORS:** ULI, ICSC, ABA, CA State Bar, HI Bar Assn.; **EDUC:** AB, 1954, Soc. Relations; **GRAD EDUC:** MBA, 1966, RE & City Planning; **MIL SERV:** US Army, PFC; **HOME ADD:** 837 Mason St., San Francisco, CA 94108, (415)928-0100; **BUS ADD:** 44 Montgomery St., 1350, San Francisco, CA 94104, (415)956-7700.

LEECH, Joyce——**B:** Aug. 1, 1940, Tupelo, MS, *Broker/Owner*, Leech RE; **PRIM RE ACT:** Broker, Property Manager; **PROFL AFFIL & HONORS:** Dir.-Jackson Bd. of Realtors-Jackson Women's Council of Realtors - Jackson Multiple Listing Service; **HOME ADD:** Rte. 1, Box 174-C, Jackson, MS 39212, (601)372-7863; **BUS ADD:** 2815 Suncrest Dr., Jackson, MS 39212, (601)373-7462.

LEED, John R.——**B:** Nov. 20, 1951, Council Bluffs, IA, *Atty. at Law*, John R. Leed Law Office; **PRIM RE ACT:** Attorney; **SERVICES:** Gen. Practice; **PROFL AFFIL & HONORS:** ABA, IA State Bar Assn., Pottawattamie Cty. Bar Assn.; **EDUC:** BA, 1974, Eng., The Colorado Coll.; **GRAD EDUC:** JD, 1977, Creighton Univ., Omaha, NE; **EDUC HONORS:** Distinction in Eng., Creighton Univ. Law School Moot Ct.

Bd.; **OTHER ACT & HONORS:** Optimists Club, Pottawattamie Cty. Red Cross Dir., Amer. Angus Assn., Masons; **HOME ADD:** Schueman Apt., Oakland, IA 51560, (712)482-3359; **BUS ADD:** 118 N. Main St., Oakland, IA 51560, (712)482-3441.

LEEDER, Stuart L.——**B:** Jan. 24, 1943, NYC, NY, *VP - Financial Services*, Lincoln Property Co. N.C. Inc.; **PRIM RE ACT:** Developer, Builder, Owner/Investor, Property Manager, Syndicator; **SERVICES:** Tax shelter partnerships - synd. placement forecast models, tax advice, acctg.; **REP CLIENTS:** Gen. partners in RE devels.; **PREV EMPLOY:** Prop. Serv. Co.; **PROFL AFFIL & HONORS:** RESSI; **EDUC:** BA, 1964, Mathematics, Harpur Coll. - S.U.N.Y.; **GRAD EDUC:** MBA, 1967, 1967, Fin./Econ., Columbia Univ. Graduate School of Bus.; **OTHER ACT & HONORS:** Peace Corps Vol. - Niger, Africa 1967-69; **HOME ADD:** 55 Golden Oak Dr., Portola Valley, CA 94025; **BUS ADD:** 553 Pilgrim Dr., Foster City, CA 94404, (415)349-7602.

LEEDS, A. Hobart——**B:** Jult 7, 1929, Yonkers, NY, *VP - Devel.*, AIRCOA; **PRIM RE ACT:** Developer, Owner/Investor; **PROFL AFFIL & HONORS:** AHMA, HRA; **EDUC:** BS, BA, 1952, Hotel Mgmt., Univ. of Denver; **HOME ADD:** 740 Bald Eagle Dr., Naples, FL 33942, (813)262-4768; **BUS ADD:** 4995 Airport Rd. N, Naples, FL 33942, (813)261-5777.

LEEDY, Carleton C., Jr.——**B:** Aug. 1, 1943, Hartford, CT, *Sr. VP*, Forest City Dillon, Inc.; **PRIM RE ACT:** Developer, Builder, Owner/Investor; **OTHER RE ACT:** Manufactured Housing Producer; **SERVICES:** Acquisition, devel. & operation of income prop. & housing devel.; **PREV EMPLOY:** Larwin Grp., Prop. Research Corp.; **PROFL AFFIL & HONORS:** Dir. - Nat. Housing Conf., Member - ULI, NAHRO; **BUS ADD:** 11611 San Vicente Blvd. #740, Los Angeles, CA 90049.

LEENSTRA, Cal——**B:** Aug. 6, 1937, Lynden, WA, *Pres.*, Kelstrup Inc. Realtors; **PRIM RE ACT:** Broker, Instructor, Syndicator, Consultant, Developer, Owner/Investor; **SERVICES:** Invest. counseling, mktg. comml. RE; **REP CLIENTS:** Indiv. investors & partnerships in sale & requisition of comml. prop.; **PREV EMPLOY:** Mgr. SCM Corp., Operations for State of AZ 1966-68; Sales Mgr. SCM Corp. Seattle, 1964-66; Mktg. Mgr. EW Hall Office Equip. Co., Seattle 1961-63; **PROFL AFFIL & HONORS:** RESSI, RNMI, Wash. Assoc. Realtors (Dir. 1969 to present), Bd. Gov. Wash RE Educ. Foundation, 1973-74, Pres. CCIM 1980; Named realtor of Yr. 1972, CCIM, CRS, GRI; **EDUC:** BA, 1962, RE & Fin., Univ. of WA; **OTHER ACT & HONORS:** Chmn. City Bellingham Bd. Zoning Adjustment 1975, V. Chmn. 1974; Member 1969-75 Mayor's Advisory Council 1977. BOD Mt. Baker Ski Patrol, Bellingham Yacht Club, Bellingham Lions Club - Advisory Council Homebuilders Assn., 1980-81, Exec. Bd. HBA 1979, Washington Pilots Assoc.; **HOME ADD:** 1802 Lakeside, Bellingham, WA 98225, (206)734-8250; **BUS ADD:** 315 Lakeway Dr., Bellingham, WA 98225, (206)734-6050.

LEEPSON, Peter L.——**B:** July 2, 1941, New York, NY; **PRIM RE ACT:** Attorney; **SERVICES:** Practice of law in both NY and CT, specializing in comml. and indus. RE; **PREV EMPLOY:** Partner - Leepson, Rubman & Ross, 230 Park Ave., NY, NY, 10017; **PROFL AFFIL & HONORS:** Governor of National Realty Club, Member of Real Property, Cooperative & Condominimum and Estate Planning Section of New York State Bar Assn. and Member of Real Property, Condominium, Zoning and Estate Planning Sections of CT Bar Assn.; **EDUC:** BA, 1963, Soc., Brandeis Univ.; **GRAD EDUC:** Doctor of Law, 1966, Fordham Law School; **EDUC HONORS:** Dean's List, Amer. Jurisprudence Award in Estate Planning; **OTHER ACT & HONORS:** Gov. of Birchwood Ctry. Club, Westport, CT 06880; **HOME ADD:** 1 Nutmeg Lane, Westport, CT 06880, (203)226-0427; **BUS ADD:** 59 Wilton Rd., Westport, CT 06880.

LEFFEL, Charles——*President*, Sunbeam Corp.; **PRIM RE ACT:** Property Manager; **BUS ADD:** 2001 So. York Rd., Oakbrook, IL 60521, (312)654-1900.*

LEFFELMAN, Dean J.——**B:** June 23, 1953, Amboy, IL, *Atty.*, Matthews, Dean, Eichmeier, Simantz & Hem, P.C.; **PRIM RE ACT:** Consultant, Attorney, Syndicator; **OTHER RE ACT:** Involved in synd. of comml. & Resid. RE; **PREV EMPLOY:** Consultant, Fiscal Controls Trust; Tax Specialist, Alexander Grant & Co.; **PROFL AFFIL & HONORS:** Member: Amer., IL, Kane County & Chicago Bar Assns.; Member: RE & Fed. Tax Comm. of Chicago Bar Assn., Published: "Avoiding Recognition of Income on Dept Cancellation", *The Tax Advisor*, February, 1980; **EDUC:** BS, 1976, Acctg. & Fin., Northern IL Univ.; **GRAD EDUC:** JD, 1979, John Marshall Law School; **EDUC HONORS:** Law Review; Order of John Marshall; **OTHER ACT & HONORS:** K of C; **HOME ADD:** 1295 Marshall Blvd., Aurora, IL 60606; **BUS ADD:** 1851 W. Galena Blvd., P.O. Box 1304, Aurora, IL 60507, (312)892-7021.

LEFKOWITZ, Jerome L.——**B:** Mar. 15, 1935, NY, NY, *CPA*, Laventhol & Horwath; **PRIM RE ACT:** Real Estate Publisher; **OTHER RE ACT:** CPA - Auditor; **SERVICES:** Evaluation of RE Investment; Consultant; **REP CLIENTS:** Partner, Large RE Audits; **PROFL AFFIL & HONORS:** AICPA; RI CPA Soc.; MA CPA Soc.; RI Builders Assn.; **EDUC:** BBA, 1957, Acctg., Univ. of MA; **MIL SERV:** US Army; **HOME ADD:** 160 Sweetbriar Dr., Cranston, RI 02920, (401)944-0113; **BUS ADD:** 140 Westminster St., Providence, RI 02920, (401)421-4800.

LEGANZA, Leonard F.——*Exec. VP Fin.*, Scovill Manufacturing Co.; **PRIM RE ACT:** Property Manager; **BUS ADD:** Scoville Plaza, Waterbury, CT 06720, (203)757-6061.*

LEGG, William J.——**B:** Aug. 20, 1925, Enid, OK, *Atty.*, Andrews Davis Legg Bixler Milsten & Murrah, Inc.; **PRIM RE ACT:** Attorney; **SERVICES:** Legal rep., all phases; **REP CLIENTS:** Adams James Foor & Co.; Air FL, Inc.; OK Assn. of Realtors Inc.; Weaver Exploration Co.; NJ Natural Gas Co., etc.; **PROFL AFFIL & HONORS:** Admitted to US Supreme Ct. & OK Bar; Member of ABA, OK & OK Cty. Bar Assns.; **EDUC:** BBA, 1946, Bus. Admin., Univ. of TX at Austin; **GRAD EDUC:** JD, 1954, Law, Univ. of Tulsa; **EDUC HONORS:** USN Coll. Programs, Scholastic Award (highest GPA), Phi Beta Gamma; **MIL SERV:** USNR Lt.j.g., WWII, 1943-1946; **OTHER ACT & HONORS:** OK State Energy Advisory Council; Who's Who in America; Who's Who in the World; Published articles; Adjunct Prof., OCU Law School; Speaker at Profl. Seminars; **HOME ADD:** 3017 Brush Creek Rd., Oklahoma City, OK 73120, (405)755-2901; **BUS ADD:** 1600 Midland Ctr., Oklahoma City, OK 73102, (405)272-9241.

LEGRAND, Ritch——**B:** Feb. 13, 1950, Fargo, ND, *MAI, SRPA*, Glenn LeGrand-Realtor; **PRIM RE ACT:** Consultant, Appraiser; **SERVICES:** Comml. & indus. appraisals, Ct. Testimony, investment consultation, feasibility studies; **REP CLIENTS:** GM Corp., US Postal Serv., 1st Natl. Bank, Chicago; **PREV EMPLOY:** City of Denver, CO (1973-75); **PROFL AFFIL & HONORS:** Bd. of Govs., SREA (1981-83), AIREA, Instr. IA Assn. of Realtors; **EDUC:** BS, 1972, Bus. Admin, Econ., Univ. of SD. Also Univ. of CO & KS; **OTHER ACT & HONORS:** Chmn. City of Sioux City Central City Exec. Comm. 1978-79, C of C, Downtown Bd. Council, 1980; **HOME ADD:** 3133 Morrison, Sioux City, IA 51104, (712)255-7038; **BUS ADD:** 401 11th St., Sioux City, IA 51105, (712)277-1070.

LEGUM, Leslie——**B:** Dec. 23, 1911, Norfolk, VA, *Gen. Partner*, Parkway Industrial Ctr.; **PRIM RE ACT:** Developer, Builder, Property Manager; **SERVICES:** Devel., const., leasing, mgmt.; **REP CLIENTS:** G.M.; Int. Paper; Champion Paper; Armour; Mercedes Benz; Hewlett Packard; Motorola; Hamilton Aunet; Ford Aerospace, Intel; Scott Paper; MN Honeywell, etc.; **PREV EMPLOY:** Pres., Park Cir. Motor Co.; **PROFL AFFIL & HONORS:** Nat. Assn. of Indus. & Office Parks; **EDUC:** BS, 1933, Mgmt./Mktg., William & Mary; **GRAD EDUC:** Diploma, 1939, Mktg./Mgmt., Chevrolet Grad. Sch. of Mktg. & Mgmt./Johns Hopkins Univ.; **OTHER ACT & HONORS:** Economic Dev. Committee, Greater Baltimore Committee; Washington-Baltimore Devel. Committee; **HOME ADD:** 7111 Park Heights Ave., Baltimore, MD 21215, (301)764-0110; **BUS ADD:** 7223 Parkway Dr., Hanover, MD 21076, (301)796-4446.

LEHMAN, Paul E.——**B:** Aug. 13, 1931, Chambersburg, PA, *Pres.*, Pelco Realty, Inc., Paul E. Lehman, Inc.; **PRIM RE ACT:** Developer, Builder, Owner/Investor; **SERVICES:** Design/build contractors - devels. of Sunset Comml. & Indus. Park and Culbertson Comml. & Indus. Park; **PREV EMPLOY:** Self employed for 30 years; **PROFL AFFIL & HONORS:** Treas. PA Assn. Builders & Contractors, Member, Metal Bldg. Dealers Assn., Master Builder of the Year 1976 - Star Mfg. Co.; **MIL SERV:** US Army, Cpl.; **OTHER ACT & HONORS:** Greene Township Lions Club, Bd. of Trs., Huntington Coll., Huntington, IN; **HOME ADD:** 5800 Cumberland Hwy., Chambersburg, PA 17201, (717)264-2265; **BUS ADD:** 5800 Cumberland Hwy., Chambersburg, PA 17201, (717)264-2265.

LEHNER, Paul M.——**B:** Dec. 5, 1941, Mishawaka, IN, *Exec. VP*, Tipton Lakes Co., Inc.; **PRIM RE ACT:** Developer, Property Manager; **PREV EMPLOY:** Haskins & Sells (1968); Irwin Management Co. (1969-1981); **PROFL AFFIL & HONORS:** Nat. Assn. of Homebuilders; Intl. Council of Shopping Ctrs.; Columbus Bd. of Realtors (Affiliate Member), Pres., Tipton Lakes Community Assn., Inc.; **EDUC:** BBA, 1963, Acctg., Univ. of Notre Dame; **GRAD EDUC:** MBA, 1969, Gen. Bus., Harvard; **EDUC HONORS:** NROTC Reg. Scholarship, Chicago Tribune Mil. Leadership Award, Haskins & Sells Award, Dean's List, Summa Cum Laude, Blue Cir. Honor Soc., Student Senate, Hamilton Award, Grad. with Distinction, Harvard Fellowship; **MIL SERV:** USN, Lt., 1963-1967; **OTHER ACT &**

HONORS: Nashville, IN, Bd. of Tr. (1977-1981); Pres., 1976-1977, Bd. of Zoning Appeals, Brown Co.; VP, Brown Co., Plan Commn.; VP, St. Agnes Parish Council; Region XI Devel. Commn.; Who's Who in the Midwest; **HOME ADD:** 2265 W. Carr Hill Rd., Columbus, IN 47201, (812)372-0784; **BUS ADD:** 235 Washington St., Columbus, IN 47201, (812)378-3331.

LEHRER, Dr. Kenneth Eugene——B: Apr. 17, 1946, NYC, NY, *Dir. of Fin.*, Allison/Walker Interests; **PRIM RE ACT:** Consultant, Developer, Owner/Investor; **PREV EMPLOY:** Affiliated Capital Corp., Coventry Devel. Corp., Bankers Trust Co.; **PROFL AFFIL & HONORS:** Houston Assn. of Bus. Econ., Amer. RE & Urban Econ Assn., American Inst. of Planners, TX RE Lic. salesman; **EDUC:** BS, 1967, Corp. Fin., NY Univ.; **GRAD EDUC:** MA/MBA/Doct. of Public Admin, 1972/1969/1980, Corp. Banking, Urban Econ., NY Univ.; **EDUC HONORS:** Former Dir. of NY Univ. Alumni Fed., Pres. Cornerstone Municipal Utility Dist.; **OTHER ACT & HONORS:** Nat. Steeple Chase & Hunt Assn., US Polo Assn., American Horse Shows Assn., Rolls-Royce Owners Assn.; **HOME ADD:** 5555 Del Monte Dr., 802, Houston, TX 77056, (713)626-8184; **BUS ADD:** 9898 Bissonet Blvd., Ste. 600, Houston, TX 77036, (713)981-9898.

LEHRER, Paul——B: June 17, 1949, NJ, *Pres.*, Stiles-Lehrer Co., Realtors; **PRIM RE ACT:** Broker, Developer; **SERVICES:** Indus. and office brokerage and devel.; **REP CLIENTS:** Indivs. and devel. cos. solely involved in SE FL; **PROFL AFFIL & HONORS:** Natl. Assn. of Indus. and Office Parks; NAR; FL Indus. Devel. Council; Broward Indus. Board; **EDUC:** 1971, Indus. Mgmt., Bus., Univ. of Hartford; **OTHER ACT & HONORS:** Natl. Conf. of Christians and Jews; **HOME ADD:** 2343 NE 28th St., Lighthouse Point, FL 33064, (305)943-5285; **BUS ADD:** 6400 N. Andrews Ave., Ft. Lauderdale, FL 33309, (309)776-7000.

LEIBSLE, Robert C.——B: May 15, 1946, Los Angeles, CA, *Atty. at Law*, Godfrey, Pfeil & Neshek, SC; **PRIM RE ACT:** Attorney; **SERVICES:** RE & devel. counseling, inc. condo. devel.; **REP CLIENTS:** Lenders and indiv. devels. of comml. and resid. props.; **PROFL AFFIL & HONORS:** Walworth Cty. Bar Assn., ABA, State Bar of WI, Amer. Judicature Soc., WI Acad. of Trial Lawyers; **EDUC:** BS, 1968, Educ., Northern IL Univ.; **GRAD EDUC:** JD, 1972, Law, Marquette Univ., Milwaukee, WI; **EDUC HONORS:** Dean's List; **MIL SERV:** USA, Capt.; **HOME ADD:** 429 Edgewood, Elkhorn, WI 53121, (414)723-4468; **BUS ADD:** 11 N Wisconsin St., Elkhorn, WI 53121, (414)723-3220.

LEIBSOHN, Ronald——B: Nov. 17, 1940, Los Angeles, CA, *Pres., Sole Owner*, Leibsohn & Co.; **PRIM RE ACT:** Broker, Developer, Owner/Investor, Property Manager; **SERVICES:** Largest comml., indus. brokers in maj. suburban area of Seattle; **REP CLIENTS:** Maj. bldg. owners, lenders, investors; **PROFL AFFIL & HONORS:** NAR; **BUS ADD:** 600 108th NE, Bellevue, WA 98004, (206)455-1777.

LEICHT, Steven M.——B: Sept. 8, 1949, NY, NY, *Tax Consultant*, Stuart Becker CPA PC, Tax; **PRIM RE ACT:** Attorney; **OTHER RE ACT:** Acct.; Tax Shelters; **PREV EMPLOY:** Arthur Anderson & Co., Tax Mgr.; **PROFL AFFIL & HONORS:** NY State Bar Assn., NY State CPA, AICPA; **EDUC:** BS, 1971, Fin., Acctg., PA State Univ.; **GRAD EDUC:** JD, 1974, Tax Law, Buffalo Law Sch.; LLM, 1978, Tax, NYU Law Sch.; **HOME ADD:** 158 Broadview Terr., Paramus, NJ 07652, (201)265-6467; **BUS ADD:** 645 Fifth Ave., NYC, NY 10022, (212)758-3340.

LEIFERMAN, Harold W.——B: July 17, 1926, SD, *VP*, Northwestern National Life Insurance Co., Mort. Loan; **PRIM RE ACT:** Lender, Owner/Investor; **REP CLIENTS:** Developers, brokers, mort. bankers, builders; **PROFL AFFIL & HONORS:** MBA; NAIOP; **EDUC:** BBA, 1949, Univ. of MN; **MIL SERV:** USN; **HOME ADD:** 14151 Green View Ct., Eden Prairie, MN 55344, (612)937-9129; **BUS ADD:** 20 S. Washington, Minneapolis, MN 55440, (612)372-5407.

LEIGH, Samuel——B: Mar. 5, 1923, New York, NY, *Pres.*, Leigh Realty Co., Inc.; **PRIM RE ACT:** Broker, Consultant, Property Manager, Owner/Investor; **SERVICES:** Locate, study, recommend and manage income producing RE; **REP CLIENTS:** Maj. nationwide pension funds; **PREV EMPLOY:** Exec. VP, Martin E. Segal Co., Inc. - Consultants and Actuarys for Pension Funds 1952-1970; **GRAD EDUC:** LLB, 1948, NY Univ. Law School; **MIL SERV:** USAF, Sgt. WW II; **OTHER ACT & HONORS:** Various Natl. and Local RE Bds., Occasional Lecturer NY Univ. Law School, Cornell Univ., Rutgers Univ.; **HOME ADD:** 9801 Collins Ave. P.H. 17, Bar Harbour, FL 33154; **BUS ADD:** 26 Pond Rd., Great Neck, NY 11024, (516)466-4220.

LEIGH, Thomas G.——*Sr. VP & CEO*, O'Hare Intl. Bank, NA; **PRIM RE ACT:** Appraiser, Banker, Lender; **SERVICES:** Const. loans for local comml. projects; **BUS ADD:** 8501 W Higgins Rd., Chicago, IL 60631, (312)693-5555.

LEISHMAN, R.W.——*Director Corp. Fac.*, Sanders Assoc., Inc.; **PRIM RE ACT:** Property Manager; **BUS ADD:** Daniel Webster Hgwy, Nashua, NH 03060, (603)885-2132.*

LEKAS, Ernest Peter——B: Nov. 3, 1934, Portland, OR, *Assoc. Broker*, Norris, Beggs & Simpson; **PRIM RE ACT:** Broker; **SERVICES:** Full service comml. & industrial RE; **PROFL AFFIL & HONORS:** NARAB, BOMA, IREM, CPM; **EDUC:** Univ. of Portland; Portland State Univ.; **MIL SERV:** US Army, Sp-4, 1957-1959; **HOME ADD:** 3105 SW 116th, Beaverton, OR 97005, (503)646-3437; **BUS ADD:** 720 SW Washington St., Portland, OR 97205, (503)223-7181.

LEKISCH, Peter A.——B: Jan. 7, 1941, Midland, TX, *Atty.*, Hoge & Lakisch; **PRIM RE ACT:** Attorney; **SERVICES:** Document prep., consultation and litigation; **REP CLIENTS:** Area, Inc. Realtors, Dynamic Realty, Inc.; **PROFL AFFIL & HONORS:** AK Bar Assn., Anchorage Bar Assn., CA Bar Assn., ABA, Chmn of RE Sect. of the AK Bar Assn.; **EDUC:** BA, 1963, Govt. & Phil., OH Wesleyan Univ.; **GRAD EDUC:** JD, 1967, Univ. of TX, Austin, TX; **OTHER ACT & HONORS:** Speaker at Bar Assn. Continuing Legal Educ. Programs Involving RE; **HOME ADD:** 1403 P St., Anchorage, AK 99501, (907)279-3180; **BUS ADD:** 437 E St., Suite 500, Anchorage, AK 99501, (907)276-1726.

LELAND, David C.——B: May 9, 1939, Somerville, NJ, *Pres.*, Leland & Hobson Economics Consultants, Consulting Devel. Econ.; **PRIM RE ACT:** Consultant, Developer; **OTHER RE ACT:** Development Economics; **SERVICES:** Mkt. studies, feasibility analysis, loan packages; **REP CLIENTS:** Daon Corp., Oxford Devel., Carma Devel., Marathon Devel., Standard Ins., Farmers Ins., HUD, SOM, CH2M-Hill; **PREV EMPLOY:** Pres., The Leland Company; CH2M-Hill; **PROFL AFFIL & HONORS:** AIA, Amer. RE Econ. Assn.; **EDUC:** Urban Geography, 1962, Urban Econ./Urban Planning, Portland State Univ., Portland, OR; **MIL SERV:** US Army, S/Sgt. 1962-65; **OTHER ACT & HONORS:** Salem, OR Renewal Design Bd.; Portland Transportation Corridor Advisory Bd.; Chmn., Budget Task Force, City of Portland; **HOME ADD:** 3030 SW Gardenview Ave, Portland, OR 97225, (503)297-5169; **BUS ADD:** 9400 SW Barnes Rd., Suite 140, Portland, OR 97225, (503)297-5501.

LE MASTER, Harry A.——B: June 26, 1946, Portsmouth, OH, *VP/Customer Services*, Peoples Banking and Trust Co.; **PRIM RE ACT:** Appraiser, Banker, Lender; **OTHER RE ACT:** Coll. Instructor; **SERVICES:** Appraisals; Investment Counseling Seminars; **REP CLIENTS:** Employee Transfer Corp.; **EDUC:** BA, 1975, Acctg. and Psych., Marietta Coll.; **HOME ADD:** 309 W. Jefferson Ave., McConnelsville, OH 43756, (614)962-6233; **BUS ADD:** PO Box 666, Marietta, OH 45750, (614)373-3155.

LEMLE, L. Craig——B: Nov. 25, 1952, New York City, NY, *VP*, Julien J. Studley, Inc., Comml. Leasing; **PRIM RE ACT:** Broker, Consultant; **SERVICES:** Tenant rep., consultation; **REP CLIENTS:** Law firms, trade assns., corporations; **PREV EMPLOY:** 1973-75 Charles F. Noyes Co., Inc., New York, NY; **PROFL AFFIL & HONORS:** WA Bd. of Realtors; NAR, 1980 Special Merit Award; WA Bd. of Realtors; **EDUC:** BS, 1974, Mgmt., Lehigh Univ.; **OTHER ACT & HONORS:** Dir., WA Lehigh Alumni Club; **HOME ADD:** 9 Leonard Ct., Rockville, MD 20850, (301)424-1435; **BUS ADD:** 810 1333 New Hampshire Ave., NW, Washington, DC 20036, (202)296-6360.

LEMMON, J.H.——B: June 28, 1937, MO, *VP RE*, Giant Food Stores, Inc.; **PRIM RE ACT:** Developer, Property Manager; **OTHER RE ACT:** Retail leasing rep.; **PREV EMPLOY:** Jewel Cos., Inc.; **PROFL AFFIL & HONORS:** Intl. Council of Shopping Ctrs.; **EDUC:** BS, 1964, Mktg., SW MO State Univ.; **GRAD EDUC:** RE, NW Univ., Chicago; **MIL SERV:** USA, SP-4; **OTHER ACT & HONORS:** C of C; **HOME ADD:** 245 Glendale St., Carlisle, PA 17013, (717)243 3948; **BUS ADD:** PO Box 249, Carlisle, PA 17013, (717)249-1424.

LEMONS, J. Stephen——B: Jan. 6, 1943, Colfax WA, *Pres.*, Lemons & Associates Mortgage Co.; **PRIM RE ACT:** Lender; **SERVICES:** Complete RE lending, from small 2nd mort. to large CT lending; **REP CLIENTS:** Small home owners to very large RE devel.; **PREV EMPLOY:** Treasurer, Hexcel Corp., Partner, CPA Firm; **PROFL AFFIL & HONORS:** Beta Gamma Sigma, Mort. Bankers Assn.; **EDUC:** BS, 1968, Fin. RE, George Washington Univ., Univ. of NV; **GRAD EDUC:** MBA, 1969, Fin., Univ. of NV; **EDUC HONORS:** Dean's List, Outstanding Fin. Major, High G.P.A. for Grad Class, Beta Gamma Sigma; **OTHER ACT & HONORS:** Sigma Nu, Guest

Lecturer, Univ. of NV, Kiwanis; **HOME ADD:** 4245 Christy Way, Reno, NV 89509, (702)329-7031; **BUS ADD:** 437 S. Sierra St., Reno, NV 89501, (702)322-7765.

LENAZ, Gerald——B: Feb. 3, 1942, New York, NY, *VP*, RPPW, Inc.; **PRIM RE ACT:** Architect; **SERVICES:** Land planning, mkt. & econ. studies; site planning; building recycling; energy design; **REP CLIENTS:** Corporate RE orgs., pvt. builders, devels. of resid., comml., & indus. props.; **PREV EMPLOY:** Urban Devel. Corporation, NY; **PROFL AFFIL & HONORS:** AIA, AICPA, Amer. Soc. of Consulting Planners, NJACP, Registered Architect, NY, NJ & PA; Profl. Planner, NJ; **EDUC:** BArch, 1963, Architecture, RE Devel., RPI, Troy, NY; **GRAD EDUC:** MSCP, 1967, Community/City Development, Pratt Inst., Brooklyn, NY; **EDUC HONORS:** Alcoa Scholarship-Arch., Dean's List; **MIL SERV:** US Army, Capt., Army Commendation Medal; **OTHER ACT & HONORS:** Elks Club, VP Rensselaer Alumni Assn.; **HOME ADD:** 75 Woods Way, Princeton, NJ 08540, (609)448-4294; **BUS ADD:** 621 Alexander Rd., Princeton, NJ 08540, (609)452-2520.

LENCZYCKI, Wayne A.——B: Nov. 28, 1946, Chicago, IL, *Pres.*, Wayne A. Lenczycki, Ltd.; **PRIM RE ACT:** Broker, Attorney, Owner/Investor; **SERVICES:** Atty.; **REP CLIENTS:** Contractors, corps., private investors; **PROFL AFFIL & HONORS:** ABA, IL State Bar Assn., Nat. Assn. of Related Title Insurers, South Suburban Bar Assn., Attys. Title Guaranty Fund, Inc.; **EDUC:** BS, 1970, Indus. Admin., Univ. of IL; **GRAD EDUC:** JD, 1975, DePaul Univ.; **OTHER ACT & HONORS:** Lecturer, Attys Title Guaranty Fund, Inc., Bus. Law Thornton Community Coll.; Dir. South Suburban Bar Assn.; **HOME ADD:** 322 Mallette, Thornton, IL 60476, (312)877-8961; **BUS ADD:** 900 E 162nd St., South Holland, IL 60473, (312)333-0707.

LENGEN, John J.——B: May 6, 1933, Bridgeport, CT, *Transportation Rights of Way Div. Chief of Appraisals*, State of CT-DOT, Appraisal Div. Office of Rights of Way; **PRIM RE ACT:** Instructor, Appraiser; **SERVICES:** Condemnation appraising; **REP CLIENTS:** State of CT; **PREV EMPLOY:** 1959-63-RE Mgr. Remington Electric Shaver, Sperry Rand Corp; **PROFL AFFIL & HONORS:** AGA; SRA, ASA; **EDUC:** BSS-Econ., 1956, Bus., Fairfield Univ.; **MIL SERV:** USN; **HOME ADD:** 62 Westerly Terr., Rocky Hill, CT 06067, (203)563-4569; **BUS ADD:** 24 Wolcott Hall Rd., Wethersfield, CT 06709, (203)566-3013.

LENNHOFF, David C.——B: Nov. 15, 1946, Panama Canal Zone, *VP*, RE Appraisal Services, Inc.; **PRIM RE ACT:** Consultant, Appraiser; **SERVICES:** RE Appraisal; **REP CLIENTS:** Lenders, Attys., Indus., etc.; **PREV EMPLOY:** Construction Loan Officer, Standard Fed. S&L Assn.; **PROFL AFFIL & HONORS:** Amer. Inst. RE Appraisers, Soc. of RE Appraisers, RM, SRA; **EDUC:** BA, 1969, English Lit., Univ. of Kentucky; **MIL SERV:** US Army, 1st Lt., CIB, BS, AM, VCBS; **HOME ADD:** 16521 Montecrest Ln., Gaithersburg, MD 20877,, (301)926-7323; **BUS ADD:** 481 N Frederick Ave., Gaithersburg, MD 20760, (301)948-1327.

LENNON, Lawrence B.——B: Dec. 7, 1940, Oneida, NY, *Atty.-partner*, FitzPatrick, Bennett, Trombley & Lennon; **PRIM RE ACT:** Broker, Attorney, Owner/Investor, Property Manager; **OTHER RE ACT:** Acquisitions; **SERVICES:** All aspects of contract negotiation, sales, title review, leasing, managing, searching for investment props., including comml., rural, timber; **REP CLIENTS:** Indiv. clients & investors, physicians, mfrs.; **PROFL AFFIL & HONORS:** ABA; NY State Bar Assn.; Clinton Cty. Bar Assn.; **EDUC:** AB, 1962, Social Sci., Liberal Arts, Union Coll., Schenectady, NY; **GRAD EDUC:** LLB, JD, 1965, Law-real prop., tax, comml, litigation, Albany Law School; **MIL SERV:** USN (JAGC); LCDR; Presid. Unit citation, 21st Naval Construction Regiment (seabees); **OTHER ACT & HONORS:** 1st Asst. Dist. Atty., Clinton Cty. 1974- 81; Tr, Plattsburgh & Clinton Cty. C of C; Trustee, Plattsburgh Public Library; BPOE Lodge 621; Clinton Lodge 155 F & AM; Noble, Oriental Temple; 32 Degree Scottish Rite Mason; SPEBSQUA; **HOME ADD:** 22 Lynde St., Plattsburgh, NY 12901, (518)563-3258; **BUS ADD:** PO Box 1009, 48 Court St., Plattsburgh, NY 12901, (518)561-4400.

LENROW, Jay Laurence——B: Mar. 29, 1951, Hackensack, NJ, *Asst. Atty. Gen.*, Office of the Attorney General of MD, Consumer Protection Div.; **PRIM RE ACT:** Attorney; **PREV EMPLOY:** Assoc., Venable, Baetjer & Howard, Baltimore, MD; **PROFL AFFIL & HONORS:** Member of MD & DC Bars; **EDUC:** BA, 1973, Intl. Relations, Johns Hopkins Univ.; **GRAD EDUC:** JD, 1977, Amer. Univ.; **EDUC HONORS:** Nat. Pol. Sci. Hon. Frat., Dean's Fellow; Articles Editor, Law Review; **OTHER ACT & HONORS:** Member, Campaign Cabinet, Assoc. Jewish Charities & Welfare Fund, Inc.; **HOME ADD:** 204 E. Churchill St., Baltimore, MD 21230, (301)659-9368; **BUS ADD:** 26 S. Calvert St., Baltimore, MD 21202, (301)659-4250.

LENTFER, Richard H.——B: Apr. 19, 1936, Chicago, IL, *Pres.*, Rich RE, Inc.; **PRIM RE ACT:** Broker, Appraiser, Developer, Builder, Property Manager; **SERVICES:** RE sales and RE mgmt., appraisals; **REP CLIENTS:** Indiv., investor groups, synds.; **PROFL AFFIL & HONORS:** S.W. Suburban Bd. of Realtors; Joliet-Will Cty. Bd. of Realtors; RNMI; FLI; IL Assn. of Realtors, Cert. RE Salesman; Cert. RE Broker; GRI; Realtor of the Yr., 1975; **EDUC:** AA, 1956, Bus., Thornton Community Coll.; **MIL SERV:** US Army Engrs.; Spec. 5th Class; **OTHER ACT & HONORS:** Orland Park Rotary, Past Pres.; Orland Park C of C, Past Pres.; Palos Heights C of C, Past Pres.; S.W. Suburban Bd. of Realtors, Past Pres.; Dist. #11 Credit Union, Founding Pres.; **BUS ADD:** 14340 LaGrange Rd., Orland Park, IL 60462, (312)349-0833.

LENZA, Anthony A.——B: May 25, 1944, Staten Island, NY; **PRIM RE ACT:** Attorney; **PREV EMPLOY:** IRS; **EDUC:** BS, 1966, Hist., St. Peter's Coll.; **GRAD EDUC:** JD, 1971, Law, New York Law; LLM, 1975, Tax, NYU; **EDUC HONORS:** Law Review; **BUS ADD:** Suite 501, 30 Bay St., Staten Island, NY 10301, (212)727-7100.

LENZINI, Michael, Jr.——B: Oct. 6, 1946, Walsenburg, CO, *Owner*, Lenzini & Co.; **PRIM RE ACT:** Broker, Consultant, Appraiser, Instructor, Owner/Investor, Syndicator; **OTHER RE ACT:** Bus. broker & consultant-acquisitions, mergers, divestitures, bus. valuations, negotiations; **SERVICES:** Brokerage, investment counseling, consulting; **REP CLIENTS:** Indiv. & corp. owners and buyers of bus., attys., accountants and other profls. for business valuations, indiv. and corp. investors in comml. and investment RE; **PREV EMPLOY:** Branch mgr. of RE co., investment adviser with nat. co.; **PROFL AFFIL & HONORS:** Realtor, local, CO & Nat., Member, Amer. Arbitration Assn.(various offices with local, state and nat. 1 & 2 groups), Amer. Soc. of Appraisers, Cert. Bus. Counselor, Rgnl. delegate White House Conference on Small Business; **EDUC:** BA, 1968, Univ. of CO, Boulder; **OTHER ACT & HONORS:** CO Assn. of Commerce & Indus. (small bus. council); Lakewood C of C; **HOME ADD:** 761 Park Ln., Lakewood, CO 80215, (303)237-6098; **BUS ADD:** 55 Wadsworth Blvd., Lakewood, CO 80226, (303)233-3533.

LEONARD, Joe H.——B: Mar. 17, 1919, Davidson Cty., NC, *Atty.*, Joe H. Leonard; **PRIM RE ACT:** Attorney; **SERVICES:** Gen. Civil and Criminal Practice in State and Fed. Cts.; Probate, RE, Family, Ins. and Corp. Law; **REP CLIENTS:** Coble Dairy Prod. Coop., Inc.; Gen. Transmission Supplies, Inc.; Lexington State Bank; Kepley-Frank Hardwood Co., Inc.; P&H Const. Co., Inc.; G&E Auction and Sales, Inc.; Quality Wholesale Meats, Inc.; **PROFL AFFIL & HONORS:** Davidson Cty., 22nd Judicial Dist., NC and Amer. Bar Assns.; The NC State Bar; NC Acad. of Trial Lawyers; **EDUC:** AB, 1940, Wake Forest Coll.; **GRAD EDUC:** JD, 1947, Univ. of NC; **OTHER ACT & HONORS:** Judge, Davidson Cty. Ct., 1956-1960; Chmn., Davidson Cty. Bd. of Elections, 1950-1952; **HOME ADD:** Country Club Dr., Lexington, NC 27292, (704)246-6115; **BUS ADD:** 113 W. Center St., Lexington, NC 27292, (704)249-9156.

LEONARD, Keith D.——B: July 23, 1941, Montreal, Quebec, *Pres.*, K. D. Leonard & Associates, Inc.; **PRIM RE ACT:** Appraiser; **SERVICES:** RE consulting & appraiser; ct. witness; **REP CLIENTS:** Major banks, lending instns., devels., indus. orgs., hotel chains, etc.; **PROFL AFFIL & HONORS:** RE Inst. of Canada, BOMA, Inst. of RE Valuators (Int. Inst. of Valuers), Appraisal Inst. of Canada, Soc. of RE Appraisers, AIREA - Corporation Des Evaluateurs Agrees Du Quebec, BSc, AACI, FRI, SCV, MAI, SREA, EA; **EDUC:** BS, 1966, Mathematics, Physics, Econ., Concordia Univ., Montreal; **OTHER ACT & HONORS:** Assoc. Prof. McGill Univ., Montreal; **HOME ADD:** 80 Pentland Place, Ottawa, K2K1V8, Ontario, (613)592-2844; **BUS ADD:** 245 Victoria Ave., Suite 801, Montreal, H3Z2M6, Quebec, Canada, (514)931-5873.

LEONARD, William Michael——B: May 25, 1953, Santa Monica, CA, *Atty. at Law*, Meserve, Mumper & Hughes; **PRIM RE ACT:** Attorney; **SERVICES:** Tax counseling, pertaining to the devel. & synd. of RE; **PROFL AFFIL & HONORS:** State Bar of CA; Los Angeles Cty. Bar Assn.; ABA; **EDUC:** BA, 1975, Hist., Univ. of CA at Los Angeles; **GRAD EDUC:** JD, 1978, Loyola School of Law; **EDUC HONORS:** Cum Laude, Dean's List 4 years, Dean's Honor List; **OTHER ACT & HONORS:** Bel Air Bay Club; **HOME ADD:** 8160 Manitoba St., #103, Playa del Rey, CA 90291, (213)821-6540; **BUS ADD:** 333 S Hope St., 35th Floor, Los Angeles, CA 90071, (213)620-0300.

LEONHARDT, Alec F.——B: Dec. 19, 1917, New Orleans, LA, *Pres.*, Enterprise Constr. Corp.; **PRIM RE ACT:** Engineer, Builder; **OTHER RE ACT:** General Contractor; **SERVICES:** Constr.; **PREV EMPLOY:** Soverign Const. Co. Ltd.; Titan Groupe Inc.; **EDUC:** BS, 1941, Engrg., MIT; **MIL SERV:** USN Res., LtC; **OTHER ACT & HONORS:** NY Yacht Club, Gibson Island Club, Carolina Yacht Club,

Off Soundings Club, Norton Yacht Club; **HOME ADD:** 37 Tory Hole Rd., Darien, CT 06820, (203)655-3318; **BUS ADD:** PO Box 3316, Noroton, CT 06820, (203)655-3318.

LEONHART, C.J.——*Pres.*, The G M Horton Corp.; **PRIM RE ACT:** Broker, Developer, Property Manager, Syndicator; **SERVICES:** Apt. & shopping ctr. devel.; **REP CLIENTS:** Mgmt. & brokerage; **BUS ADD:** 2100 N Central, Phoenix, AZ 85004, (602)258-0700.

LEONI, Ronald J.——**B:** Mar. 5, 1949, Chicago,IL, *Bldg. Mgr.*, Centre Properties Ltd., Prop. Mgmt.; **PRIM RE ACT:** Property Manager; **SERVICES:** All maintenance and operational support; leasing-tenant; **REP CLIENTS:** Tenants; **PROFL AFFIL & HONORS:** IREM, Chicago Bd. of Realtors, CPM; **EDUC:** BS, 1975, Intl. Bus., N. IL Univ., DeKalb, IL; **EDUC HONORS:** Natl. Honor Soc.; **MIL SERV:** USAF, Sgt., AF Commendation; **HOME ADD:** 319 Lorraine, Glen Ellyn, IL 60137, (312)858-3122; **BUS ADD:** 180 N. LaSalle St., Chicago, IL 60601, (312)346-7858.

LEPLASTRIER, Geoffrey Ross——**B:** July 28, 1946, Townsville, Australia, *VP/Div. Mgr.*, The Housing Group, Southern California; **PRIM RE ACT:** Architect, Developer, Builder; **PREV EMPLOY:** VP - Operations - Bixby Ranch Co.; Long Beach, CA 1976-1980; **PROFL AFFIL & HONORS:** AIA, Royal Australian Instit. of Architects, AIA, ARAIA, NCARB; **EDUC:** BArch., 1972, N.S.W. Inst. of Tech. (Sidney, Australia); **GRAD EDUC:** MArch. (Harvard Univ.), 1975; MCP (MIT), 1975; **OTHER ACT & HONORS:** Tr., Leukemia Soc. of Amer. (Tri-Cty. Chap.); **BUS ADD:** 18831 Bardeen Ave., Irvine, CA 92715, (714)752-1660.

LEQUIEU, Reginald R.——**B:** Oct. 25, 1945, Wasco, CA, *Pres./Broker*, LeQuieu & LeQuieu, Inc., Agriculture; **PRIM RE ACT:** Broker, Consultant, Developer, Owner/Investor; **SERVICES:** Farm & ranch sales & exchange brokerage; **PREV EMPLOY:** Special Agent US Army Intelligence 1969-1972; **PROFL AFFIL & HONORS:** FLI; NAR; Nat. Fed. of Indep. Bus.; Klamath City & Nat. C of C, GRI; Realtor of the Year - Klamath Bd. of Realtors 1981; **EDUC:** BS, 1968, Social Sci., Criminology, So. OR State Coll.; **MIL SERV:** US Army, Special Agent, Special Commendation Medal; **OTHER ACT & HONORS:** Klamath Cty. Comprehensive Land Use Master Plan Task Force Commn. 1980-1981; **HOME ADD:** 4426 Anderson, Klamath Falls, OR 97601, (503)884-2830; **BUS ADD:** 6408 S. 6th St., Klamath Falls, OR 97601, (503)882-4469.

LERMAN, David——**B:** Jan. 30, 1951, Vineland, NJ, *Foreman & Dyess*; **PRIM RE ACT:** Attorney, Consultant, Owner/Investor, Syndicator, Developer; **SERVICES:** Legal; investment counseling; syn.; **EDUC:** AB, 1972, Govt., Harvard Coll.; **GRAD EDUC:** JD, 1975, Georgetown Univ. Law Center; **EDUC HONORS:** AB, Cum Laude; Harvard College Scholar; **BUS ADD:** First International Plaza - 42nd Floor, Houston, TX 77002.

LERMAN, Terry A.——**B:** July 11, 1946, Pittsburgh, PA, *Pres.*, First Capital Corp.; **PRIM RE ACT:** Consultant, Attorney, Syndicator; **SERVICES:** Synd. of resid. & comml. props., investment counseling, valuation & devel.; **REP CLIENTS:** Indivs. & instnl investors & devel. of multi-family housing & comml. prop.; **PREV EMPLOY:** Security Pacific Inc., 1976-77; Babb investments Inc., 1974-76; Urban Redevel. Auth. of Pittsburgh, 1973-80; **PROFL AFFIL & HONORS:** Coalition for low & moderate income housing; RE Securities Synd. Instit. Amer. Allegheney Cty & PA Bar Assn.; **EDUC:** BS, 1968, Chem. & Math., Univ. of Pittsburgh; **GRAD EDUC:** JD, 1971, Law, Duquesne School of Law; **EDUC HONORS:** Sullivan Award, 1968, US Law Week Award; **OTHER ACT & HONORS:** Downtown Club of Pittsburgh; **HOME ADD:** 1412 Barnsdale St., Pittsburgh, PA 15217, (412)521-5800; **BUS ADD:** 1350 Old Freeport Rd., Suite 3A, Pittsburgh, PA 15238, (412)963-1320.

LERNER, Lawrence——**B:** Sept. 21, 1923, NY, NY, *Chmn. of the Bd./Pres.*, Environetics International, Inc.; **OTHER RE ACT:** Interior arch., const. mgmt. space planning, interior design, arch., const. mgmt., computer graphics, space acctg., mgmt., **REP CLIENTS:** Sears, Amer. Can, Blue Cross & Blue Shield, Coopers & Lybrand, Digital Equipment, Gulf Oil Corp., IBM, Nabisco, Amerada Hess, Doyle, Dane, Bernbach, Federated Dept. Stores, Fed. Reserve Bank, Gilman Paper Co., Hanes Corp., Otis Elevator, Swiss Bank Corp., Seiko Time Corp., TRW; **EDUC:** BA, 1948, Indus. Design, Brooklyn Coll.; **MIL SERV:** US Army, 2 Lt.; **OTHER ACT & HONORS:** Chief Exec. Forum, World Bus. Council; **HOME ADD:** 10749 William Tell Dr., Orlando, FL 32809; **BUS ADD:** 600 Madison Ave., NY, NY 10022, (212)759-3830.

LERNER, Martin L.——**B:** May 29, 1950, Milwaukee WI, *Atty. at Law*, Lerner & Veit, PC; **PRIM RE ACT:** Attorney; **SERVICES:** RE Law; **REP CLIENTS:** RE brokers, synd., investors; **PROFL AFFIL & HONORS:** State Bar of CA, State Bar of WI, Real prop. law sect., ABA, ABA, section of real prop, probate and trust law; **EDUC:** BA, 1972, Univ. of WI; **GRAD EDUC:** JD, 1976, Univ. of WI; **OTHER ACT & HONORS:** 1979 to present Hearing Officer, S.F. Resid. rent, Arbitration Bd.; **BUS ADD:** 425 California St., #303, San Francisco, CA 94104, (415)781-4000.

LERVICK, Timothy D.——**B:** Dec. 23, 1953, Crosby, ND, *Atty. at Law*, Lundberg, Conmy, Nodland Lucas & Schulz, P.C.; **PRIM RE ACT:** Attorney; **SERVICES:** All legal matters relating to RE; **PREV EMPLOY:** Trust Officer, First Tr. Co. of ND, (1978-1981); Bismarck, ND, Prop. Mgmt., Dept. of HUD, 1972-73; **PROFL AFFIL & HONORS:** State Bar Assn. of ND, ABA, Real Prop. Probate, & Trust Law Sects.; **EDUC:** BS, 1975, Bus. Econ., ND State Univ.; **GRAD EDUC:** JD, 1978, Law, Univ. of ND; **HOME ADD:** 523 N 1st St., Bismarck, ND 58501, (701)222-1192; **BUS ADD:** 425 N 5th St., Box 1398, Bismarck, ND 58502, (701)223-4022.

LESAR, Hiram H.——**B:** May 8, 1912, Thebes, IL, *Distinguished Serv. Prof.*, S. IL Univ., Sch. of Law; **PRIM RE ACT:** Attorney, Instructor; **OTHER RE ACT:** Arbitrator; **PROFL AFFIL & HONORS:** Amer. Fed., IL, MO, Metropolitan St. Louis Bar Assns., Amer. Law Inst., Amer. Arbritration Assn., Amer. Judicature Soc., Pres. Award, MO Bar, 1968; **EDUC:** AB, 1934, Hist. and law, Univ. of IL; **GRAD EDUC:** JD, 1936, Univ. of IL; JSD, 1938, Estates and Trusts, Yale; **EDUC HONORS:** With honors; **MIL SERV:** USN, Lt. Cmdr.; **HOME ADD:** 11 Hillcrest Dr., Carbondale, IL 62901; **BUS ADD:** Lesar Law Bldg., S. IL Univ., Carbondale, IL 62901, (618)536-7711.

LESHER, Raymond A.——**B:** May 7, 1928, Jamaica, *Pres.*, Lesher & Co. Ltd.; **PRIM RE ACT:** Consultant, Appraiser; **SERVICES:** R.E. Counseling and Appraisal; **REP CLIENTS:** Fin. Instns., Trust Cos., Maj. Corps., U.S. Agencies; **PROFL AFFIL & HONORS:** AIREA, ASREC, SREA, IAAO(1961), NARA(1976), Appraiser of the Year Award-SREA(1975), Prof. Recognition Award,-AIREA(1976-81), Educ. Cert. Award-AIREA(1981), Omega Tau Rho Award-NAR(1980), MAI, CRE, CAE, CRA; **MIL SERV:** USNR, WW II; **OTHER ACT & HONORS:** Pres. Honolulu Chapt. AIREA (1974)(1981) Pres. Honolulu Chapt. SREA (1975), Member Governing Council AIREA(1979-80), Vice Gov. Pacific Region SREA (1974-79) Member Natl. Appraisal Review Comm. AIREA(1976-80) Chmn. S.W. Regional Conference (Honolulu) AIREA (1977) Chmn. Natl. Convention Comm. (Honolulu) AIREA (1978), Chmn. Natl. Meetings and Conferences Subcomm. AIREA (1981), Chmn. Pan Pacific Division AIREA (1981), Member Intl. Relations Comm. (Natl. Appointment) (1981), Member and/or Chmn. over the past few yrs. of the following Comm. of the Honolulu Chapt. AIREA, Admissions, Educ., Ethics, Member Amer. Arb. Assn.- Comml. Panel (1981); **HOME ADD:** 406 Dune Cir., Kailua, Oahu, HI 96734, (808)262-4935; **BUS ADD:** Grosvenor Ctr., 733 Bishop St., Suite 1616, Honolulu, HI 96813, (808)524-1511.

LESHOWITZ, Edward——**B:** Apr. 12, 1915, NY City, *Partner*, Cali Associates; **PRIM RE ACT:** Consultant, Developer, Builder, Owner/Investor, Property Manager; **SERVICES:** Const., devel., mgmt. office bldgs. and multi-family resid.; **PREV EMPLOY:** Const. 32 yrs.; **PROFL AFFIL & HONORS:** NJ & Nat. - NAIOP - NAHB, NJ Home Builders Apt. House Council of NJ, C of C, Union Cty. C of C, 6 times winner of NJ 'New Good Neighbor' award; NAHB Nat. Merit Award for best comml. bldg.; **EDUC:** BA, 1936, Soc. Studies, NJ State Coll., Montclair; **EDUC HONORS:** Cum Laude; **MIL SERV:** US Army, Sgt., ETO-5, Battle Stars; **HOME ADD:** 66 Blanchard Rd., S. Orange, NJ 07079, (201)763-3685; **BUS ADD:** 11 Commerce Dr., Cranford, NJ 07016, (201)272-8000.

LESLEY, Dan——**B:** Jan. 30, 1944, Phoenix, AZ, *Owner*, Dan Lesley & Associates; **PRIM RE ACT:** Broker, Developer, Owner/Investor, Property Manager, Syndicator; **SERVICES:** Complete evaluation of clients investment & tax needs; **PROFL AFFIL & HONORS:** CCIM, CFP, Newport Harbor - Costa Mesa Bd. of Realtors, CCIM, Chap. So. CA; **EDUC:** BS Bus. Pre Law, 1966, Gen. Bus., AZ State Univ.; **MIL SERV:** USMC, Cpl.; **OTHER ACT & HONORS:** Newport Beach C of C; **HOME ADD:** 10220 Olympic Ct., Fountain Valley, CA 92708, (714)963-8128; **BUS ADD:** 1000 Quail St., Suite 155, Newport Beach, CA 92660, (714)833-7630.

LESLIE, Beatrice S.——**B:** May 24, 1927, Jefferson Cty., KY, *VP*, Warren G. Harding, Inc., Commercial RE & Prop. Mgmt.; **PRIM RE ACT:** Broker, Consultant, Developer, Builder, Owner/Investor, Property Manager, Syndicator, Real Estate Publisher; **SERVICES:** Investment consulting, Feasiblility studies-RE sales-mgmt. surveys; RE Exchanging; **PREV EMPLOY:** Owner-Pres. St. Matthews Co., Inc.; **PROFL AFFIL & HONORS:** NAR, KY Bd. of Realtors, FL Bd. of Realtors, Womens Council, IREM, Acad. Network; BOMA, CPM; **OTHER ACT & HONORS:** St. Matthews Womens Club, Brooklawn

Children's Home Tr.; **HOME ADD:** 721 Tarawitt Dr., Longboat Key, FL 33548, (813)383-6587; **BUS ADD:** 46 N. Washington Blvd., Sarasota, FL 33577.

LESLIE, J. Millard——**B:** July 11, 1922, Brownsville, NE, *Broker*, Newberg Realty Inc.; **PRIM RE ACT:** Broker, Property Manager; **SERVICES:** Sales, investments, mgmt.; **REP CLIENTS:** Lenders, indivs.; **PREV EMPLOY:** 26 years teaching in public schools; **PROFL AFFIL & HONORS:** NAR, OR Assn. of Realtors, Yamhill Cty. Bd. of Realtors, OR Educ. Assn. 26 yrs., GRI; **EDUC:** BMus, 1947, Music, Willamette Univ.; BA, 1948, Math, Portland State Coll., Univ. of ID, OR Coll. of Educ.; **MIL SERV:** USN, Lt. j.g.; **OTHER ACT & HONORS:** Christian Church; **HOME ADD:** 220A Ilafern Lane, Dundee, OR 97115, (503)538-2761; **BUS ADD:** 1805 Portland Rd., P O Box 498, Newberg, OR 97132, (503)538-3188.

LESSENBERRY, Robert A.——**B:** May 7, 1926, Glasgow, KY, *Pres.*, Lessenberry Building Ctr., Inc.; **PRIM RE ACT:** Broker, Developer, Builder, Owner/Investor; **EDUC:** BA, 1950, Bus., Centre Coll. of KY; **MIL SERV:** US Army, Capt., Expert Infantry Badge, Bronze Star w/Cluster; **HOME ADD:** 913 S. Green, Glasgow, KY 42141, (502)651-3117; **BUS ADD:** 1010 W. Main St., Glasgow, KY 42141, (502)651-8862.

LESSER, Elliot A.——**B:** Mar. 6, 1945, Bronx, NY, *Audit Partner/Dir. of RE*, Laventhol & Horwath, NY Office; **OTHER RE ACT:** CPA; **SERVICES:** Structuring of RE transactions, counseling, acctg. and auditing; **PROFL AFFIL & HONORS:** RESSI; AICPA; **EDUC:** BS, 1966, Acctg., Univ. of Bridgeport; **HOME ADD:** 15 Rolling Way, New Rochelle, NY 10804, (914)235-2035; **BUS ADD:** 919 Third Ave., NY, NY 10022, (212)980-3100.

LETO, David D.——**B:** May 15, 1941, Brooklyn, NY, *Mgr., Admin. Servs.*, ITT-Community Development Corp., Admin.; **PRIM RE ACT:** Broker, Attorney, Architect, Developer, Regulator, Builder, Owner/Investor, Property Manager; **OTHER RE ACT:** Total community planning and devel.; **PREV EMPLOY:** Claims Supervisor, Liberty Mutual Ins. Co.; **PROFL AFFIL & HONORS:** Amer. Mgmt. Assn., Bldg. Operator's Mgmt. Assn., Nat. Bd. of Realtors; **EDUC:** BA, 1962, Pol. Sci., Queens Coll. of the Univ. of the City of NY; **MIL SERV:** USN, Comdr., American Defense Ribbon; **OTHER ACT & HONORS:** Naval Res. Assn.; **HOME ADD:** PO Box 1544, Palm Coast, FL 32037, (904)445-2485; **BUS ADD:** Executive Offices, Palm Coast, FL 32051, (904)445-5000.

LEUCK, Frank——**B:** Apr. 3, 1929, Baker, OR, VFJ Enterprises - Prop. Mgmt. Services, Rainbow Homes, Inc.; **PRIM RE ACT:** Developer, Builder, Owner/Investor, Property Manager; **OTHER RE ACT:** All weather solar heat & hot water distributor; **SERVICES:** Rentals, prop. mgmt., consulting, constr., multi-family, single family; **PREV EMPLOY:** Chmn. Music Dept. SW OR Community Coll.; **PROFL AFFIL & HONORS:** Natl. Assn. of Home Builders; Multi-Family Housing Council OR; **EDUC:** 1951, Music Educ., Lewis & Clark Univ., Portland, OR; **GRAD EDUC:** 1961, Music Admin., Eastman School of Music; **MIL SERV:** USA, Cpl.; **OTHER ACT & HONORS:** Coos Bay Planning Commn./ 8 yrs., Port of Coos Bay Commn./ 2 yrs.; 1160 AF of Musicians, Music Educators Natl. Assn.; **HOME ADD:** 1925 Newmark, Coos Bay, OR 97420, (503)888-4411; **BUS ADD:** 1925 Newmark, Coos Bay, OR 97420, (503)888-4411.

LEVENSTEIN, Robert——**B:** Aug. 13, 1926, NY, NY, *Pres.*, Olympia/Roberts Co.; **PRIM RE ACT:** Developer, Builder; **PREV EMPLOY:** Pres.-Kaufman & Broad, Inc., Pres.-Philips Indus., Inc.; **PROFL AFFIL & HONORS:** CA Housing Task Force; CA Public Investment Task Force; **EDUC:** 1948, Math & Physics, St. Lawrence Univ.; **MIL SERV:** USN; **HOME TEL:** (213)472-0844; **BUS ADD:** 4640 Admiralty Way, Suite 531, Marina del Rey, CA 90291, (213)822-7665.

LEVESQUE, Ronald A.——**B:** May 14, 1948, Fall River, MA, *VP, Operations*, MBT Constr. Corp.; **PRIM RE ACT:** Developer, Builder, Owner/Investor, Property Manager; **SERVICES:** Constr. devel.; **REP CLIENTS:** Condos & rehab. work, generally for investor; **EDUC:** BS, 1980, Fin. & Acctg., Johnson & Wales; **MIL SERV:** USAF; S/Sgt.; A commendation medal; **HOME ADD:** 105 Lisa Terr., Portsmouth, RI 02871, (401)683-2731; **BUS ADD:** 124 Aquioneck Ave., Middletown, RI 02840, (401)847-2620.

LEVEY, Kenneth E.——**B:** June 15, 1935, Waltham, MA, *Superintendent*, Boston Gas Co., Customer Activities; **PRIM RE ACT:** Broker, Consultant, Property Manager; **REP CLIENTS:** Knox Mountain Landowners Assoc., Highlanders Realty Trust, Boldt Family Trust; **PREV EMPLOY:** Apt. Gallarys Inc., Indep. Banker, Boldt Family Trust, Indep. Broker; **PROFL AFFIL & HONORS:** MA RE Broker 123817, Cert. Consumer Credit Exec.; **EDUC:** 1979, Bus. Admin., Northeastern Univ., Lee Inst. of RE; BA, 1976, Indus. Relations, New England Sch. of RE, Northeastern Univ.; **OTHER ACT & HONORS:** Soc. of Cert. Consumer Credit Exec., New England Assn. of Credit Exec., Past Treas., N. Shore Consumer Credit Assn., Treas. Knox Mt. Landowners Assn., Pres. Highlanders Realty Trust; **HOME ADD:** 17 Pine St., Natick, MA 01760, (617)655-0764; **BUS ADD:** 1 Beacon St., Boston, MA 02108, (617)742-8400.

LEVEY, Lewis A.——**B:** Feb. 20, 1942, St. Louis, MO, *Managing Partner*, Paragon Group, Inc.; **PRIM RE ACT:** Broker, Developer, Builder, Owner/Investor, Property Manager; **SERVICES:** Investment, devel., mgmt.; **REP CLIENTS:** Pvt. investors and instl. lenders, joint venture partners; **PROFL AFFIL & HONORS:** Nat. Assn. of Home Builders; Inst. of RE Mgmt.; Nat. Multi-Housing Council; Intl. Council of Shopping Ctrs., Member, Inst. of Resid. Mktg.; Reg. Apt. Mgr.; Lifetime Member, Sales and Mktg. Council; **EDUC:** BS, 1964, Univ. of WI; **GRAD EDUC:** MBA, 1967, Mktg./Corp. Fin., Washington Univ.; **HOME ADD:** 505 N. Spoede Rd., St. Louis, MO 63141, (314)567-1607; **BUS ADD:** 12312 Olive Blvd., Suite 93, St. Louis, MO 63141, (314)878-1660.

LEVI, Donald R.——**B:** Mar. 7, 1941, Stockton, MO, *Prof. of RE & Holder, KS Chair of RE & Land Use Econ.*, Wichita State Univ.; **PRIM RE ACT:** Broker, Attorney, Owner/Investor, Instructor; **PREV EMPLOY:** Assoc. Dir., TX RE Research Ctr.; Prof. of RE, TX A&M Univ.; **PROFL AFFIL & HONORS:** AREUEA; ULI; NARA; NAR; State Bars of TX & MO, JD; PhD; CRA; GRI; **EDUC:** BS, 1964, Univ. of MO; **GRAD EDUC:** JD, 1974, Washington State Univ.; PhD, 1966, Univ. of MO; **EDUC HONORS:** Cum Laude, Omicron Delta Kappa; **HOME ADD:** 1408 Deer Trail, Derby, KS 67037; **BUS ADD:** Campus Box 88, Wichita, KS 67208, (316)689-3219.

LEVI, James H.——**B:** Oct. 28, 1939, Boston, MA, *Pres.*, Oppenheimer Properties, Inc.; **PRIM RE ACT:** Broker, Consultant, Owner/Investor, Syndicator; **EDUC:** BA, 1961, Harvard Coll.; **GRAD EDUC:** MBA, 1964, Harvard Bus. School; **MIL SERV:** USN, Ens.; **HOME ADD:** 85 Larchmont Ave., Larchmont, NY 10538, (914)834-1963; **BUS ADD:** One New York Plaza, New York, NY 10004, (212)825-8180.

LEVIEN, Kenneth D.——**B:** Feb. 23, 1952, NYC, NY, *VP*, Levien, Rich & Co., PC; **PRIM RE ACT:** Consultant, Engineer, Architect, Developer, Builder, Owner/Investor; **OTHER RE ACT:** Constı. mgr.; **REP CLIENTS:** Bank of NY, US Life Realty; **PREV EMPLOY:** Self employed Arch.; **PROFL AFFIL & HONORS:** AIA, NCARB, Reg. Arch.; **EDUC:** BA, 1974, Arch., Washington Univ., St. Louis, MO; **GRAD EDUC:** M Arch, 1976, Arch., Washington Univ., St. Louis, MO; **HOME ADD:** 33 W. 75th St., New York, NY 10023; **BUS ADD:** 305 E. 46th St., New York, NY 10017, (212)832-0450; **BUS TEL:** (212)799-7865.

LEVIN, Allan E.——**B:** Sept. 27, 1925, Minneapolis, MN, *Pres.*, Allan E. Levin & Associates, Ltd.; **PRIM RE ACT:** Engineer, Attorney; **SERVICES:** Legal, planning, devel.; **PROFL AFFIL & HONORS:** 1972-1973 Nat. Assn. Home Builders, Nat. Dir., Chicago Bar Assn.; **EDUC:** B Aero Engrg., 1948, Univ. of MN; **GRAD EDUC:** BS/Law, JD, 1957, 1959, William Mitchell Coll. of Law; **MIL SERV:** USAF, Capt., Presidential Unit Citation; **HOME ADD:** 3600 N. Lakeshore Dr., Chicago, IL 60613; **BUS ADD:** 1 N LaSalle Suite 1700, Chicago, IL 60602, (312)782-7776.

LEVIN, Charles R.——**B:** Dec. 14, 1945, Cambridge, MA, *Atty.*, Gorman, Voss, Brodbine & Gorman; **PRIM RE ACT:** Consultant, Attorney, Developer, Instructor, Property Manager; **SERVICES:** Site selection, devel. & fin. analysis, lease draft & neg., legal services for entire project; **REP CLIENTS:** Hanslin Devel. Co., Grossman Co., NE Life; **PREV EMPLOY:** Asst. VP Field Housing, New England Life, Responsible for site location for 180 field offices throughout US; **PROFL AFFIL & HONORS:** ABA, MBA, Boston Bar Assn., Gr. Boston RE Bd., NE Realty Lodge; **EDUC:** 1967, Econ., Math., Colby Coll.; **GRAD EDUC:** JD, 1973, Suffolk Univ. Law Sch.; **MIL SERV:** Nat. Guard, Spec. 5; **HOME ADD:** 95 Tower Ave., Needham, MA 02194, (617)444-5683; **BUS ADD:** 27 School St., Ste 502, Boston, MA 02108, (617)523-5271.

LEVIN, Jeffrey H.——**B:** July 28, 1952, Boston, MA, , Jeffrey H. Levin; **PRIM RE ACT:** Attorney; **OTHER RE ACT:** RE broker; **SERVICES:** All aspects of resid. & Comml. RE; **REP CLIENTS:** Mutual Bank for Savings, formerly Suffolk Franklin Savings Bank; **PREV EMPLOY:** Assoc. at Bove, Katz and Charmoy Barron & Stadfeld; **PROFL AFFIL & HONORS:** FL & MA Bars, ABA, MA and Boston Bar Assn., MA Conveyaners Assn.; **EDUC:** BA, 1974, Poli. Sci., Univ. of MA, Amherst; **GRAD EDUC:** JD, 1977, Western New England Coll.; 1982, LLM (taxation) Boston University Law School; **EDUC HONORS:** Magna Cum Laude; **BUS ADD:** 15 Court Sq., Boston, MA 02108, (617)367-2220.

LEVIN, Jonah D.——B: July 25, 1945, Philadelphia, PA, *Atty. At-Law*; **PRIM RE ACT:** Attorney; **SERVICES:** Legal; **REP CLIENTS:** Mort., Bankers, Lenders; **PROFL AFFIL & HONORS:** Philadelphia, PA Bar Assns., ABA, Vice Chmn.-ABA Probate & Real Prop. Sect. - Comm. on Creditors Rights in RE Fin.; **EDUC:** Drexel BS, 1968, Bus. - Fin. & Acctg., Drexel Univ.; **GRAD EDUC:** JD, 1972, Law, Univ. of Toledo Coll. of Law; **EDUC HONORS:** Jurisprudence Award in Estates; **OTHER ACT & HONORS:** Bd. Member - Planned Parenthood of SE, PA; **HOME ADD:** 4046 MacNiff Dr., Lafayette Hill, PA 19444, (215)828-5310; **BUS ADD:** 536 Swede St., Norristown, PA 19401, (215)279-6440.

LEVIN, Paul Mason——B: July 27, 1953, Wash., DC, *VP*, Habitex Construction Corp.; **PRIM RE ACT:** Broker, Developer, Builder, Owner/Investor; **SERVICES:** Devel. of resid. & comml. props.; **PREV EMPLOY:** Health Facilities Devel. Assoc.; **PROFL AFFIL & HONORS:** N. VA Buildiers Assn.; Fairfax Cty. C of C; **EDUC:** AB, 1976, Gen. Studies, Univ. of MD; **OTHER ACT & HONORS:** United Jewish Appeal, Young Leadership Affiliate; **HOME ADD:** 1717 Crestview Dr., Potomac, MD 20854, (301)251-1470; **BUS ADD:** 6525 Belcrest Rd. 200, Hyattsville, MD 20782, (301)779-4800.

LEVIN, Richard David——B: June 11, 1945, Phila., PA, *Dir.*, Levin, Spiller & Goldlust, P.A.; **PRIM RE ACT:** Attorney, Owner/Investor; **SERVICES:** Legal Serv. RE: Synd., Fin., Acquisition, Leasing; **PROFL AFFIL & HONORS:** ABA, Delaware Bar Assn., Fed. Bar Assn.; **EDUC:** BA, 1967, Hist., Univ. of DE, Newark, DE; **GRAD EDUC:** JD, 1970, Georgetown Univ. Law Ctr., Washington, DC; **OTHER ACT & HONORS:** Asst. US Atty. - DE 1970-1973; Attended Grad. RE Law Courses Temple Univ. Law School, Law Firm Does Tax and Securities Law; **HOME ADD:** 3204 Romilly Rd., Wilmington, DE 19810, (302)478-6994; **BUS ADD:** 913 Market Tower, PO Box 2094, Wilmington, DE 19899, (302)575-0500.

LEVIN, Stuart S.——B: Jan. 6, 1950, Pittsburgh, PA, *VP & Sr. Assoc. Title Counsel*, Pioneer National Title Ins. Co.; **PRIM RE ACT:** Attorney; **PROFL AFFIL & HONORS:** ABA, VA State Bar; **EDUC:** PA State Univ., 1971, Gen. Arts & Sciences; **GRAD EDUC:** The Amer. Univ., 1975, Law, Washington College of Law; **HOME ADD:** 1626 19th St., NW, Washington, DC 20009, (202)483-2303; **BUS ADD:** 1129 20th St., NW, Washington, DC 20036, (202)466-6990.

LEVINE, Arthur Stephen——B: Mar. 22, 1941, Toronto, Ont. Can, *Investment Mgr.*, Genstar Devel. Inc., Genstar Investment Housing/Genstar Corp.; **OTHER RE ACT:** Gen. Mgmt., Operations, Land Devel., Acquistion; **SERVICES:** Oversee on behalf of Genstar, all S. CA operations of Broadmoor Homes; **PREV EMPLOY:** Genstar/Broadmoor Homes Northern mgr. of operations, Mgr. of land acquit-s. & devel.; **PROFL AFFIL & HONORS:** OR Assn. of Arch., Royal Arch. Inst. of Canada, Award of Merit, Can. Housing Devel. Council, 1974; **EDUC:** BA, 1963, Pol. Sci. & Econ., Univ. of Toronto; **GRAD EDUC:** BArch, 1970, Dalhousie/NS Tech.; **OTHER ACT & HONORS:** Bd. of Dir., Youth Serv. Assn of Newport Beach, Univ. Athletic Club; **HOME ADD:** 303 Marguerite Ave., Apt. D, Corona Del Mar, CA 92625, (714)675-9636; **BUS ADD:** 25241 Paseo de Alicia, Suite 220, Laguna Hills, CA 92653, (714)951-2866.

LEVINE, Barton P.——B: Sept. 2, 1948, NY, NY, *Atty./Bldr./Devel.*, Levine Organization, Inc.; **PRIM RE ACT:** Attorney, Developer, Builder, Owner/Investor; **PROFL AFFIL & HONORS:** NY Bar Assn.; FL Bar Assn.; **EDUC:** BS, 1970, Acctg./Govt., NY Univ., School of Commerce; **GRAD EDUC:** JD, 1972, Law, St. John's Law School; **EDUC HONORS:** Dean's List, 1969, Law Review; **MIL SERV:** USAR; **HOME ADD:** Iroquais Trail, Harrison, NY 10528; **BUS ADD:** 111 Great Neck Rd., Great Neck, NY 11021, (516)482-5450.

LEVINE, Bernard H.——B: June 29, 1925, Eau Claire, WI, *Prop.*, Levine Realty; **PRIM RE ACT:** Broker, Consultant, Owner/Investor; **PROFL AFFIL & HONORS:** NARA; Nat. Assn. of Corp. RE Exec.; NAR; **EDUC:** 1947, Bus. Admin., Univ. of WI; **MIL SERV:** USN, Lt.; **HOME ADD:** 1031 Weston Ave., Wausau, WI 54401, (715)845-5778; **BUS ADD:** POB 1205, Wausau, WI 54401, (715)359-7002.

LEVINE, Ellen H.——B: Feb. 20, 1948, Denver, CO, *Realtor*, Levine, Ltd., Realtors; **PRIM RE ACT:** Broker; **SERVICES:** Sales; **PROFL AFFIL & HONORS:** NAR, Women's Council, etc.; **EDUC:** Attended U. of CO; **OTHER ACT & HONORS:** Office in Civic Groups; **HOME ADD:** 180 So. Dahlia, Denver, CO 80222, (303)321-1786; **BUS ADD:** 1129 Cherokee, Denver, CO 80204, (303)893-8200.

LEVINE, Gary H.——B: Nov. 3, 1951, Denver, CO, *Atty.*, Robinson, Waters, O'Dorisio & Rapson, P.C.; **PRIM RE ACT:** Attorney; **SERVICES:** Contracts, negotiation, consultation; **PREV EMPLOY:** Levine & Pitler, PC, Attys. at Law, 1150 Delaware St., Denver, CO 80204; **PROFL AFFIL & HONORS:** ABA; Bldr. Bar Assn.; Denver Bar Assn.; CO Bar Assn., CPA, CO RE Salesman; **EDUC:** BS (Bus. & Admin.), 1974, Acctg., Univ. of CO; **GRAD EDUC:** JD, 1977, Univ. of CO; **EDUC HONORS:** President's List 1971; **MIL SERV:** US Army Nat. Guard, Sp 4, 1969-1975; **HOME ADD:** 2650 9th St. #202, Boulder, CO 80302, (303)447-9749; **BUS ADD:** 1640 Grant St., Denver, CO 80203, (303)830-8000.

LEVINE, Kent Jay——B: June 1, 1948, Denver, CO, Levine, Ltd., Realtors; **PRIM RE ACT:** Broker, Attorney, Instructor, Real Estate Publisher; **REP CLIENTS:** RE Brokerage Co.; **PREV EMPLOY:** VP RE Unlimited, Inc., Levine, Pittler & Westerfeld Co. RE Co. VP, Burnham Van Service, Mile Hi Enterprises, Dukes Food Producers; **PROFL AFFIL & HONORS:** ABA, CO Bar Assn., Denver Bar Assn., CO Assn. Realtors; **EDUC:** BA, 1970, Bus. Admin., Western State Coll.; **GRAD EDUC:** JD, 1973, Law (RE, Comml.), Drake Univ. Law Sch.; **EDUC HONORS:** Dean's List, JD with Honors, Amer. Jurisprudence Award; **BUS ADD:** 1150 Delaware St., Denver, CO 80204, (303)892-5891.

LEVINE, Lawrence A.——B: Jan. 30, 1945, NY, NY, *Gen. Pmrtner*, Country Lakes Associates Ltd.; **PRIM RE ACT:** Developer, Builder, Owner/Investor, Property Manager; **PROFL AFFIL & HONORS:** Builders Assn. S. FL; NAHB; **EDUC:** BS, 1965, Acctg., NYU; **GRAD EDUC:** Doctor of Law, 1968, Fordham Univ.; **EDUC HONORS:** Bruce Futhey Memorial Award in Govt. Acctg.; Beta Alpha Psi, Comments Editor, Law Review, 1967-1978; **MIL SERV:** USAR; **HOME ADD:** 8841 S. Lake Dasha Dr., Plantation, FL 33324, (305)472-2442; **BUS ADD:** 7132 McNab Rd., Tamarac, FL 33319, (305)721-4201.

LEVINE, Marc S.——B: Feb. 24, 1941, Meriden, CT, *Pres.*, Dwelling Development Corp.; Levine & Cohen, Atty.; **PRIM RE ACT:** Developer, Attorney; **SERVICES:** Devel. of multi-family housing, both govt. assisted and conventional; Representation of RE devels., shopping ctrs., housing, motels; **REP CLIENTS:** Simon Konover and Assocs., West Hartford CT; **PREV EMPLOY:** Atty., Lessner, Rottner, Karp & Plepler, P.C., Manchester, CT 1967-1972; **PROFL AFFIL & HONORS:** ABA; CT; Hartford Cty.; Bar Assns.; Nat. Leased Housing Assns.; **EDUC:** BA, 1963, Eng. Literature, Brown Univ.; **GRAD EDUC:** JD, 1966, Law, Georgetown Univ. Law Center; **EDUC HONORS:** Assoc. Editor, Law Journal; **OTHER ACT & HONORS:** Bds. of Dirs., Hartford Jewish Federation; Hartford Jewish Community Center; Tumblebrook Country Club; Recipient, Young Leadership award of Hartford Jewish Fed. 1977; **BUS ADD:** 8 Shawmet Rd., West Hartford, CT 06117, (203)232-4831.

LEVINE, Mark——B: May 4, 1943, Denver, CO, *Pres.*, Levine Ltd., Realtors, Comml.; **PRIM RE ACT:** Broker, Consultant, Attorney, Appraiser, Developer, Lender, Owner/Investor, Instructor, Property Manager, Insuror, Syndicator, Real Estate Publisher; **SERVICES:** Same as primary RE activities; **REP CLIENTS:** All sites; **PREV EMPLOY:** 1968 to date, Private law practice, Levine and Pitler, PC; 1968-1970, Arthur Young & Co., CPA's - Tax Div, Cty. Ct. Practice; 1967, State Ct. Practice, Prosecutor's Office, DA Clerkship; 1966-1968, Goldsmith & Carter, Attys. - Law Clerk; 1963, RE Sales and Devel.; **PROFL AFFIL & HONORS:** NAR; ABA; NASH; RESSI; RNMI; NIREB; Nat. Assn. of Home Builders; IREM; FLI; CO Soc. of CPA's; CO Bar Assn., CCIM; CRS; CRB; GRI CA-C; SRS; Sr. Prof., RESSI Div.; CCIM-RNMI Super Session Inst. and Faculty, CCIM; Univ. of CO, RE Instr., Cont. Ed., 5 & 10 yr. award; VP and Pres., RESSI, CO Chap.; Tr., RESSI; RESSI Nat. Comm.; RESSI Rgnl. VP and Gov.; RNMI Course Comm. CI-103; Designationetc.; Member of Profession Lia. Real Prop. Practitioners Comm., ABA; Univ. of Denver Comms., e.g., Promotions & Tenure, Evaluation, Library, Tax Inst., SBA/JD, etc.; Univ. of Denver Speakers' Bureau; Pres., CO Chap. on RESSI; Rgnl. Govs., RESSI; Annual Tax Inst. Comm., Univ. of Denver; Univ. of Denver Rho Epsilon Faculty Advisor - trips to NAR; Dir., CO Assn. Realtors; RESSI, Chmn. of Rgnl. VP; **EDUC:** BS, Bus., CO State Univ.; **GRAD EDUC:** JD, Univ. of Denver School of Law; LLM, Tax Law, NYU School of Law; PhD, Century Univ.; **EDUC HONORS:** Magna Cum Laude; **OTHER ACT & HONORS:** Numerous publications in the field of RE; **HOME ADD:** 1150 Delaware, Denver, CO 80204, (303)892-5891; **BUS ADD:** 1129 Cherokee, Denver, CO 80204, (303)893-8200.

LEVINE, Melvin F.——B: Aug. 16, 1924, Boston, MA, *Pres.*, Melvin F. Levine & Associates, Inc.; **PRIM RE ACT:** Consultant; **SERVICES:** Devel. feasibility studies; **REP CLIENTS:** Public devel. agencies; private devels.; **PREV EMPLOY:** The Rouse Co. and The Amer. City Corp. 1970-1981; **PROFL AFFIL & HONORS:** Amer. Inst. of Cert. Planners, Charter Member; Amer. Planning Assn.; Lambda Alpha, Honorary Land Econ. Frat.; NAHRO; **EDUC:** BS, 1944, Mech. Engrg., Northeastern Univ.; **GRAD EDUC:** MCP, 1956, Urban Planning, MIT; **HOME ADD:** 5619 Open Sky, Columbia, MD 21044, (301)596-6905; **BUS ADD:** 5619 Open Sky, Columbia, MD 21044,

(301)730-4726.

LEVINE, Robert C.——**B:** Apr. 9, 1951, Jersey City, NJ, *Atty.*; **PRIM RE ACT:** Attorney; **SERVICES:** Legal services, RE partnerships, contractors, title work, estate planning and taxation; **REP CLIENTS:** Corp. limited partnerships and indiv., both investors and contractors in real prop. and synd.; **PREV EMPLOY:** Belding & Chelius, Corp. Plaza, Newport Beach, CA 1977-79; **PROFL AFFIL & HONORS:** ABA, sect. of Real Propl; sect. of Taxation, CA Bar Assn., NH Bar Assn., Sect. of Real Prop.; **EDUC:** BA, 1974, Zoology & Philosophy; **GRAD EDUC:** JD, 1978, Tax, Pepperdine Univ., School of Law; **OTHER ACT & HONORS:** Legal Counsel NH Jaycees; **HOME ADD:** Old Governor's Rd., Brookfield, NH 03872, (603)522-3021; **BUS ADD:** 17 Madbury Rd., Durham, NH 03824, (603)868-7034.

LEVINE, Stanley E.——**B:** Jan. 5, 1948, Middletown, NY, *Corp. Asst. VP, Branch Mgr.*, Commonwealth Land Title Ins. Co.; **OTHER RE ACT:** Title Insurance; **PREV EMPLOY:** TPS Abstract Corp.; **PROFL AFFIL & HONORS:** NY State Land Title Assn., Chmn.-Land Surveying Comm.; **EDUC:** BA, 1970, Poli. Sci., Harpur Coll.-State Univ. of NY at Binghampton; **HOME ADD:** 32A Pequot Ave., Port Washington, NY 11050, (516)883-0782; **BUS ADD:** 370 Old Country Rd., Garden City, NY 11530, (516)742-7474.

LEVINE, Stu——**B:** Feb. 18, 1942, Denver, CO, *Broker/Owner*, Orchard Realty; **PRIM RE ACT:** Broker, Instructor, Consultant; **SERVICES:** Investment Counseling, Exchanging, Tax; **PROFL AFFIL & HONORS:** CCIM; **EDUC:** BS, 1978, Aerospace Science, Metropolitan State Coll.; **EDUC HONORS:** Magna Cum Laude; **MIL SERV:** USN; TD-3; **HOME ADD:** 7818 E. Long Pl., Englewood, CO 80112, (303)773-1978; **BUS ADD:** 67-1 S. Emporia St., Englewood, CO 80112, (303)773-1009.

LEVINE, Walter M.——**B:** Nov. 23, 1946, NY, *Regional VP*, Equity Programs Investment Corp., Realty; **PRIM RE ACT:** Lender, Owner/Investor, Syndicator; **OTHER RE ACT:** Builder model home purchase/leaseback; **SERVICES:** Resid. RE investment, builder fin.; **REP CLIENTS:** U.S. Homes, Ryan, Ryland, Pulte, NuWest, 80% of PB's top 500 homebuilders; **PREV EMPLOY:** Boise Cascade; Nat. Homes Corp.; Alsco Anaconda Aluminum Inc.; **PROFL AFFIL & HONORS:** NAHB; SME; AMA; **EDUC:** BS, 1968, Mktg., CCNY, Baruch Coll., VCU; **EDUC HONORS:** NY State Regents Coll. Scholarship, 4 yrs.; **MIL SERV:** USMCR, S/S; **HOME ADD:** 2687 N Ocean Blvd., Boca Raton, FL 33431; **BUS ADD:** One N Ocean Blvd., Suite 12, Boca Raton, FL 33432, (305)395-4459.

LEVITT, William M.——**B:** Mar. 9, 1933, Detroit, MI, *Sr. VP*, Carl Rosman & Co.; **PRIM RE ACT:** Broker; **SERVICES:** Comml./Indus. Brokers, only; **PROFL AFFIL & HONORS:** NAR, State & Local Bds., Active Member, SIR; **EDUC:** BA, 1954, Bus. Admin., Wayne State Univ.; **HOME ADD:** 3000 Chewton Cross Rd., Birmingham, MI 48010, (313)647-2433; **BUS ADD:** 26555 Evergreen Rd., Suite 717, Southfield, MI 48076, (313)353-2100.

LEVY, Alan D.——**B:** July 19, 1938, St. Louis, MO, *Exec. VP & Dir.*, Tishman West Management Corp.; **PRIM RE ACT:** Broker, Consultant, Developer, Owner/Investor, Property Manager, Syndicator; **SERVICES:** Devel., mgmt. & leasing of comml. RE; **REP CLIENTS:** Indus. & instnl. lenders & investors and private parties of comml. RE; **PROFL AFFIL & HONORS:** ULI, BOMA, IREM, ICSC, Various RE Bds., CPM; **EDUC:** 1960, RE, Wash. Univ. - St. Louis; **MIL SERV:** US Army; **OTHER ACT & HONORS:** Co-Founder & Honorary Dir. - NJ - BOMA; Former Dir. - BOMA of Los Angeles; **HOME ADD:** 541 Loring Ave., Los Angeles, CA 90024, (213)470-3464; **BUS ADD:** 10960 Wilshire Blvd., Los Angeles, CA 90024, (213)477-1919.

LEVY, Arthur C.——**B:** May 19, 1918, Jamaica, NY, *Pres.*, Arthur C. Levy Co. Inc.; **PRIM -RE ACT:** Broker, Consultant; **SERVICES:** Sales, leasing, indus./comml. RE; **REP CLIENTS:** Investors, users, indus. comml. prop.; **GRAD EDUC:** MBA, 1952, Hamilton State Univ.; **MIL SERV:** US Army; S/Sgt.; Bronze Star, Purple Heart, Pres. Citation, 1941-1945; **OTHER ACT & HONORS:** Dir., Nassau Cty. Police Res. Assn.; Dir., L.I. Conference Christians and Jews; **HOME ADD:** 34 Pearsall Ave., Glen Cove, NY 11542; **BUS ADD:** 333 Jericho Tpk., Jericho, NY 11753, (516)822-3800.

LEVY, David——*VP & Secy.*, National Service Industries, Inc.; **PRIM RE ACT:** Property Manager; **BUS ADD:** 1180 Peachtree St. NE, Atlanta, GA 30309, (404)892-2400.*

LEVY, Fred J.——**B:** June 3, 1946, Chicago, IL, *VP*, The Sack Realty Co., Inc.; **PRIM RE ACT:** Broker, Attorney, Developer, Syndicator; **PROFL AFFIL & HONORS:** ISBA; **EDUC:** BA, 1968, Pol. Sci., Econ., Univ. of IL; **GRAD EDUC:** JD, 1971, Law, DePaul Univ.; **HOME ADD:** 320 Oakdale, Chicago, IL 60657, (312)935-9288; **BUS ADD:** 1459 E. Hyde Park Blvd., Chicago, IL 60615, (312)684-8900.

LEVY, Gerald M.——**B:** May 13, 1939, Camden, NJ, *VP & District Head*, Chemical Bank, RE Div.; **PRIM RE ACT:** Banker, Lender; **OTHER RE ACT:** Arbitrator, Consultant, Appraiser, Instructor; **SERVICES:** Primarily RE fin. and comm. banking services; also valuation, consulting and arbitration; **PREV EMPLOY:** Sr. VP, Merritt & Harris, Inc., 1967-1977; Appraiser & Dir. of RE Studies, Alexander Summer Co., 1963-1967; Administrative Assist., Urban Redevel. Agency, 1962-1963; **PROFL AFFIL & HONORS:** Member, AIREA; Nat. Panel Amer. Arbitration Assn.; Sr. Real Prop. Appraiser, SREA; Sr. Member, ASA; Profl. Member, Amer. RE & Urban Econ. Assn.; **EDUC:** BA, 1961, Hist., Columbia Univ.; **GRAD EDUC:** MA, 1962, Social Sci., Harvard Univ.; **OTHER ACT & HONORS:** Served as Civilian Participant, Nat. Security Seminar, US Army War Coll.; Guest Lecturer on RE, Wharton School of Univ. of PA; Amos Tuck School of Bus. Admin. at Dartmouth Coll.; Columbia Univ. Grad. School of Bus.; RE and Mort. Inst. of NYU; Urban Redevel. Program at Rutgers Univ.; Urban Affairs Program at CT Coll.; US Dept. of Housing and Urban Devel.; Articles on RE in trade, govt. and institl. publications; Drafted official 'RE Valuation Arbitration Rules' of the Amer. Arbitration Assn.; **HOME ADD:** 29 Bronson Ave., Scarsdale, NY 10583, (914)723-5462; **BUS ADD:** 633 Third Ave., New York, NY 10017, (212)878-7728.

LEVY, James L.——**B:** Apr. 26, 1939, NY, NY, *Pres.*, Appraisers and Planners, Inc.; **PRIM RE ACT:** Broker, Consultant, Appraiser; **REP CLIENTS:** Leading Banks, Atty. & Corps.; **PROFL AFFIL & HONORS:** Amer. Soc. of Appraisers, Columbia Soc., IFAS; **EDUC:** BA, 1961, Econ., Rollins Coll.; **MIL SERV:** US Army, SP-4; **HOME ADD:** 416 Ridgeway, White Plains, NY 10605, (914)428-7810; **BUS ADD:** 500 5th Ave., New York, NY 10036, (212)221-8300.

LEVY, John S.——**B:** Jan 16, 1941, Detroit, MI, *Pres.*, Levy Investment Corp.; **PRIM RE ACT:** Broker, Consultant, Attorney, Developer, Owner/Investor, Instructor, Syndicator; **SERVICES:** Acquisitions for equity partners; **PREV EMPLOY:** Creation & presentation of 24 hour lecture series on RE investment; **EDUC:** BA, 1964, Univ. of MI; **GRAD EDUC:** JD, 1968, 1968, Wayne State Univ. Law School; **BUS ADD:** 6643 E. Caballo Dr., Paradise Valley, AZ 85253, (602)991-9898.

LEVY, Jules E.——**B:** May 13, 1939, Brooklyn, NY, Hofheimer Gartlir Gottlieb & Gross; **PRIM RE ACT:** Attorney, Owner/Investor; **PROFL AFFIL & HONORS:** Builders Inst. of Westchester Cty.; **EDUC:** BBA, 1961, Public Acctg., City Coll. of NY; **GRAD EDUC:** JD & LLM, 1964 & 1970, LLM (Taxation), Cornell Law School - NY Univ. Law School; **HOME ADD:** 100 Plainview Rd., Woodbury, NY 11797, (516)367-4189; **BUS ADD:** 469 Fifth Ave., New York, NY 10017, (212)725-0400.

LEVY, Lawrence F.——**B:** Feb. 1, 1944, St. Louis, MO, *Pres.*, The Levy Org.; **PRIM RE ACT:** Developer, Consultant, Owner/Investor; **EDUC:** BS/BA, 1966, Mktg., Northwestern Univ.; **GRAD EDUC:** MBA, 1967, Mktg., Northwestern Univ.; **BUS ADD:** 840 N. MI Ave., Chicago, IL 60611, (312)280-2750.

LEVY, Michael R.——**B:** May 17, 1946, Dallas, TX, *Pres.*, Mediatex Communications Corp.; **PRIM RE ACT:** Owner/Investor; **PROFL AFFIL & HONORS:** Young Pres. Org., Member of Bd. of Dirs. of Magazine Publishers Assn.; **EDUC:** BS, Econ., 1968, Fin., RE, Wharton Sch. of Fin. and Commerce, Univ. of PA, Philadelphia; **GRAD EDUC:** JD, 1972, Univ. of TX Law Sch.; **OTHER ACT & HONORS:** Headliners Club of Austin; **BUS ADD:** PO Box 1569, Austin, TX 78767, (512)476-7085.

LEVY, Philip D.——**B:** Aug. 8, 1930, Syracuse, NY, *Treas.*, Becker, Card & Levy, P.C.; **PRIM RE ACT:** Attorney, Owner/Investor; **SERVICES:** Investment Counseling, Title Certification; **PROFL AFFIL & HONORS:** ABA, NY Bar Assoc., Broome Cty. Bar Assoc., Estate Planning Council, So. NY; **EDUC:** AB, 1952, Pol. Sci., Syracuse Univ.; **GRAD EDUC:** JD, 1958, Univ. of WI; **MIL SERV:** USN, HN; **OTHER ACT & HONORS:** Village Atty., Endicott, NY 1967-79, Kiwanis of Endicott, Past Pres., Dir. Broome Cty. Bar Assn.; **HOME ADD:** 1220 Hartwick La., Binghamton, NY 13903, (607)724-5604; **BUS ADD:** 141 Wash. Ave., Endicott, NY 13760, (607)754-0106.

LEVY, Roger——**B:** Sep. 4, 1920, Saverne, France, *VP*, Y.A.N. Management Corp.; **PRIM RE ACT:** Broker, Consultant, Instructor, Property Manager; **OTHER RE ACT:** Investment Analyst & Consultant; **SERVICES:** Investment counseling, prop. mgmt., mgmt. planning; **PREV EMPLOY:** J.I. Kislak Management Corp. Newark NJ 1957-1969; **PROFL AFFIL & HONORS:** Hoboken Bd. of Realtors, NJ Chap. No. 1, IREM (VP), CPM, Realtor Community

Service Award (1978) NJ Assn. of Realtors; **MIL SERV:** US Army Mil. Intell., 1942-1945, M/Sgt.; **HOME ADD:** 52 Kossuth Pl., Wayne, NJ 07470, (201)696-6429; **BUS ADD:** P.O. Box M-82, Hoboken, NJ 07030, (201)659-2993.

LEVYN, Thomas S.——**B:** Apr. 2, 1949, Los Angeles, CA, *Part.*, Agapay & Levyn, PC; **PRIM RE ACT:** Attorney; **REP CLIENTS:** Mort. bankers, maj. devels., synds., prop. mgrs.; **PROFL AFFIL & HONORS:** LA Cty. Beverly Hills Bar Assns., Land Use Subcomm. of Real Prop. of LA Cty Bar Assn.; **EDUC:** BS, 1971, Univ. of S CA; **GRAD EDUC:** JD, 1974, Univ. of S CA; **BUS ADD:** 10801 Natl. Blvd., Suite 405, Los Angeles, CA 90064, (213)470-1700.

LEWAND, Kevin O.——**B:** Mar. 31, 1938, Toledo, OH, *Atty.*, Lewand and Graves; **PRIM RE ACT:** Attorney, Owner/Investor, Syndicator; **SERVICES:** Synd. of comml. props.; **EDUC:** BA, 1961, Hist./Acctg., Univ. of Toledo; **GRAD EDUC:** JD, 1966, Securities Law, Loyola Law School of Los Angeles; **EDUC HONORS:** Dean's Honors/Pres. of Legal Frat.; **MIL SERV:** US Army, Capt.; **HOME ADD:** 12132 Singingwood, Santa Ana, CA 92705; **BUS ADD:** 2100 N. Main St., Santa Ana, CA 92701, (714)547-7551.

LEWIS, A. Barton——**B:** Aug. 4, 1925, Philadephia, PA, *Pres.*, A. Barton Lewis & Co., Inc.; **OTHER RE ACT:** RE Fin.; **SERVICES:** Ins., Appraisal, Consultant; **PROFL AFFIL & HONORS:** Philadephia Bd. of Realtors; NAR; Fin. Analysts Assn.; **EDUC:** BCE, 1946, Univ. of DE; **GRAD EDUC:** MBA, 1947, Wharton School, Univ. of PA; **OTHER ACT & HONORS:** Racquet Club; Bd. of Dir., SE PA Chap. Amer. Red Cross; Chmn., U.S. Comm. for Oceans; **HOME ADD:** 257 Hothorpe Ln., Villanova, PA 19085, (215)964-1557; **BUS ADD:** 1908 Two Girard Plaza, Philadephia, PA 19102, (215)563-3520.

LEWIS, Austin L.——**B:** Oct. 11, 1940, Dallas, TX, *Pres.*, Austin L. Lewis Co.; **PRIM RE ACT:** Consultant, Owner/Investor, Property Manager; **SERVICES:** Devel. of corp. RE facilities, speculative office bldgs., and office parks; **PREV EMPLOY:** One Main Place; **PROFL AFFIL & HONORS:** BOMA, TX RE Assn., Dallas Bd. of Realtors, NAR, Office Leasing Man of Year 1971; **EDUC:** BBA, 1963, Fin., TX Tech. Univ.; **OTHER ACT & HONORS:** Chmn., Small Bus. Council, Dallas C of C, Leadership Dallas Grad. 1975; **HOME ADD:** 10122 Church Rd., Dallas, TX 75238, (214)348-0888; **BUS ADD:** 7515 Greenville Ave., Suite 700, Dallas, TX 75231, (214)361-0937.

LEWIS, Barnet M.——**B:** May 10, 1950, Tucson, AZ, *Mgr.*, Comml. Properties Unlimited; **PRIM RE ACT:** Broker, Consultant, Owner/Investor, Property Manager; **SERVICES:** Brokerage and leasing of comml., investment & bus. prop. and investment counseling; **REP CLIENTS:** Local professional and business people; several groups of investors; **PREV EMPLOY:** Cedarview Mgmt., 1971-1973; Properties Unlimited, 1973-1978; **PROFL AFFIL & HONORS:** NAR; NMI; Bloomington Bd. of Realtors; Metropolitan Indianapolis Bd. (Comml. Div.), GRI; RAM (Registered Apt. Mgmt.); Nat. Assn. of Home Builders; **EDUC:** BS, 1972, Bus./Educ., IN Univ.; **OTHER ACT & HONORS:** City of Bloomington, Housing Quality Appeals Bd., 1976 to present; Bd. of Dir. of Big Brothers/Big Sisters; Rotary Club; **HOME ADD:** 837 Sheridan Rd., Bloomington, IN 47401, (812)339-7845; **BUS ADD:** 431 1/2 S. College Ave., Bloomington, IN 47401, (812)334-8827.

LEWIS, Bertram——**B:** Jan. 13, 1955, NY, *Pres.*, Sybedon Corp.; **PRIM RE ACT:** Broker, Consultant, Syndicator; **PREV EMPLOY:** Sonnenblick Goldman Corp., NY, NY; **PROFL AFFIL & HONORS:** RE Bd. of NY; **EDUC:** Cornell Univ., 1956, Econ.; **GRAD EDUC:** 1958, Fin., Columbia Univ.; **MIL SERV:** US Army, Sgt.; **HOME ADD:** 10 Paddington Rd., Scarsdale, NY 10583, (214)723-0627; **BUS ADD:** 1211 Ave. of the Americas, NY, NY 10036, (212)354-5756.

LEWIS, Charles D.——**B:** Nov. 24, 1933, Pasadena, CA, *Sr. RE Officer*, Title Insurance and Trust Co., Trust Dept.; **PRIM RE ACT:** Broker, Consultant, Appraiser, Property Manager; **SERVICES:** Appraisal, prop. mgmt., sale of RE; **REP CLIENTS:** Various estates, private trusts, corp. title holding accts.; **PREV EMPLOY:** Mort. Brokerage, Gen. RE Sales; **PROFL AFFIL & HONORS:** Member SRA, IARA CA Bankers Grp., S.R.A.; **EDUC:** BS, 1955, Bus Admin. Personnel Admin., Univ. of So. CA; **OTHER ACT & HONORS:** Bd. of Trustees First Baptist Church; **HOME ADD:** 470 Fairview, Arcadia, CA 91006, (213)447-8929; **BUS ADD:** 700 Wilshire Blvd., Los Angeles, CA 90017, (213)614-7371.

LEWIS, David A., Jr.——**B:** Feb. 14, 1950, Pittsburgh, PA, *VP, Loan Admin.*, Security Savings & Loan Assn., Loan Div.; **PRIM RE ACT:** Banker, Lender; **SERVICES:** Loans to devel. for purposes of constr. and takeout commitments, secondary mkt. activities; **REP CLIENTS:** Builders, devels., buyers and seller in the secondary mkt.; **PREV EMPLOY:** Mellon Bank N.D., Banking Officer, 6 yrs.; First Nat. Bank of SJ, Atlantic City, NJ, Mort. officer, 3 yrs.; **EDUC:** BA, 1972, Pol. Sci., Allegheny Coll., Meadville, PA; **OTHER ACT & HONORS:** Past. Pres. Alpha Chi Rho Bldg. Comm., Member of VISA, Allegheny Coll. Outreach Program; **HOME ADD:** Turnersville, NJ; **BUS ADD:** 818 Landis Ave., Vineland, NJ 08360, (609)691-2400.

LEWIS, David R.——**B:** Dec. 11, 1940, Bulawayo, Rhodesia, *Pres.*, Oxford Development Services Corp.; **PRIM RE ACT:** Developer, Builder, Owner/Investor, Property Manager; **SERVICES:** Design, devel., fin., const., mgmt.; **REP CLIENTS:** Partnerships sponsored by my firm; **PREV EMPLOY:** Sheraton Design & Development Corp., ITT; **PROFL AFFIL & HONORS:** Member of the Inst. of Civil Engrs. (Great Britain), Member of Assn. of Profl. Engrs., ON, Can.; **EDUC:** BS, 1961, Civil Engrg., Univ. of Cape Town; **GRAD EDUC:** M of Engr., 1963, Structural Engrg., Nova Scotia Tech. Coll.; **HOME ADD:** Annapolis, MD 21401; **BUS ADD:** 4351 Garden City Dr. Suite 300, Landover, MD 20785, (301)459-8700.

LEWIS, Edward——*Mgr. RE*, Motorola, Inc., Communications Div.; **PRIM RE ACT:** Property Manager; **BUS ADD:** 1303 E. Algonquin Rd., Schaumburg, Il 60196, (312)397-5000.*

LEWIS, Glenn W.——**B:** June 27, 1934, San Angelo, TX, *Atty.*, Logan, Lewis, Symes & Keeling (Law Firm); **PRIM RE ACT:** Attorney, Owner/Investor; **SERVICES:** Legal Services; **REP CLIENTS:** Central Nat. Bank of San Angelo, TX; First TX Savings Assn.; **PROFL AFFIL & HONORS:** State Bar of TX (RE Sect.) RE Specialization Adv. Comm. - 1980; ABA (RE & probate sect.), The Green Cty. Bar Assn., Fellow, TX Bar Found.; **EDUC:** BA, 1957, Govt., TX Univ.; **GRAD EDUC:** JD, 1958, Univ. of TX; **EDUC HONORS:** With honors; **MIL SERV:** USAF; **HOME ADD:** 2633 Vista Del Arroyo, San Angelo, TX 76901, (915)949-4373; **BUS ADD:** 602 Central National Bank Bldg., San Angelo, TX 76903, (915)655-8176.

LEWIS, H. Wendell——**B:** Jan. 18, 1928, Columbus, GA, *Owner*, Lewis Realtors; **PRIM RE ACT:** Broker, Property Manager; **SERVICES:** RE Sales; **REP CLIENTS:** Equitable Relocation - Homequity - Merrill Lynch; **PROFL AFFIL & HONORS:** NAR, CRB - CRS Member Omega TAU RHU; **OTHER ACT & HONORS:** Pres. Rotary Club E. Columbus 1965-1966, Pres. Columbus Bd. of Realtors 1962, Pres. GA Chap. of CRB 1976 1977; **HOME ADD:** Apt. L1 Windsor Village Apts., Columbus, Ga 31904, (404)563-8222; **BUS ADD:** PO Box 5287, Columbus, GA 31906, (404)324-3466.

LEWIS, Heydon Z.——**B:** July 11, 1935, Fayetteville, AR, *Pres.*, Thermo Scan Engineering, Inc.; **PRIM RE ACT:** Broker, Engineer, Banker, Owner/Investor, Property Manager; **SERVICES:** Engrg. & Mgmt. servs. in roof problems and energy conservation; **PROFL AFFIL & HONORS:** IEEE, ACEC, ASHRAE, NSPE, AIPE; **EDUC:** BSEE, 1958, Elec. Engr., Univ. of AR; **GRAD EDUC:** MS & PhD, 1960 & 1969, Elec. Engrg., Univ. of IL & Univ. of CO; **EDUC HONORS:** High Honors; **MIL SERV:** US Army, 1st. Lt.; **OTHER ACT & HONORS:** Nat. Ski Patrol, Mt. Rescue Assn., AOPA; **HOME ADD:** 7880 S. Ogden Way, Littleton, CO 80122, (303)795-6858; **BUS ADD:** Box 2327, Littleton, CO 80161, (303)795-1611.

LEWIS, J. Alan——**B:** Aug. 21, 1951, Warner & Smith; **PRIM RE ACT:** Attorney; **SERVICES:** Closing, Title Exam., Synd.; **REP CLIENTS:** United Peoples S&L, Fairfield Communities, Inc., Sparks Regional Med. Ctr., Whirlpool Fed. Credit Union, Amer. Investors Mort. Co.; **PROFL AFFIL & HONORS:** ABA; Sec. Real Prop. & Probate Law, AR Bar Assn.; **EDUC:** BA, 1973, Westminster Coll.; **GRAD EDUC:** JD, 1977, Tax/Comml., Univ. of AR School of Law; **OTHER ACT & HONORS:** Ft. Smith Planning Commn. (1980-); **HOME ADD:** 21 Vista Blvd., Fort Smith, AR 72901, (501)782-5642; **BUS ADD:** PO Box 1626, 214 North Sixth, Fort Smith, AR 72901, (501)782-6041.

LEWIS, James A.——**B:** Nov. 7, 1944, San Jose, CA, *Gen. Mgr.*, H-J-K Enterprises, Prop. Mgmt.; **PRIM RE ACT:** Syndicator, Consultant, Property Manager, Owner/Investor; **SERVICES:** Prop. Mgmt. for apts., office bldgs. & indust. bldgs, investment counseling, partnerships & property mgmt. for limited partnerships, testimentory and Inter Vivos Trusts and Indiv. clients; **PREV EMPLOY:** Sr Prop. Mgr., CA RE Mgmt. Corp., 1969-72; **PROFL AFFIL & HONORS:** Tri-Cty Apt. Assn., Fin. Planning Forum, RESSI; **EDUC:** BS, 1966, Bus. Mgmt., San Jose State Univ.; **GRAD EDUC:** MBA, 1969, Bus. Admin., San Jose State Univ.; **EDUC HONORS:** Meritorous Service Award, Who's Who of Students in Colls. & Univs.; **MIL SERV:** USAF, T/Sgt., Airman of the Month; **HOME ADD:** 315 Oak Court, Menlo Park, CA 94025, (415)326-6931; **BUS ADD:** 489 Middlefield Rd., Palo Alto, CA 94301, (415)326-5121.

LEWIS, James C.——B: Feb. 4, 1922, Jefferson Cty., AL, *Pres.*, Jim Lewis Realty Sales Co.; **PRIM RE ACT:** Developer, Builder, Owner/Investor; **SERVICES:** Devel. build office bldgs. apts., shopping center condos. housing; **PREV EMPLOY:** Started bus. upon grad. from coll.; **EDUC:** BSME, 1948, ME, Univ. of AL; **MIL SERV:** USAF Pilot, Capt.; **OTHER ACT & HONORS:** Past Pres., Birmingham Assn. of Home Builders; Tr. Cumberland Coll., TN; Bank Dir. City Nat. Bank; Past Pres. AL Homebuilders Assn.; Also affil with: Southland Bank Corp. (Dir.); **HOME ADD:** 3040 Weatherton Dr., Birmingham, AL 35223, (205)967-1968; **BUS ADD:** 2101 Magnolia Ave., Suite 501, Birmingham, AL 35205, (205)324-9559.

LEWIS, Jeff D.——B: Mar. 23, 1945, Wichita Falls, TX, *Pres.*, S.B.G. Inc.; **PRIM RE ACT:** Syndicator, Developer, Builder, Property Manager; **EDUC:** BS, 1972, Econ., Univ. of NV at Las Vegas; **GRAD EDUC:** MBA, 1974, Fin., Stanford Univ.; **EDUC HONORS:** Dean's List; **MIL SERV:** USA, 1st Lt.; **BUS ADD:** 366 Cambridge Ave., Palo Alto, CA 94306, (415)327-3353.

LEWIS, Jerry L.——B: Feb. 24, 1941, Portland, OR, *Pres.*, Cal-Pacific Development Corp.; **PRIM RE ACT:** Consultant, Developer, Owner/ Investor, Syndicator; **SERVICES:** Comml., retail, & resid. devel. servs.; **REP CLIENTS:** Inst. and large pvt. investors; **PREV EMPLOY:** Coldwell, Banker & Co.; **PROFL AFFIL & HONORS:** Salesman of the Yr. Award, 1972, Coldwell, Banker & Co.; **EDUC:** 1963, Acct./Bus. Statistics, Univ. of OR; **EDUC HONORS:** Kemper Ins. Scholar; **OTHER ACT & HONORS:** Chmn. of Bd., Valley Christian School; Member, CA Pistachio Growers Assn.; Founder, Comml. Bank of San Francisco; Pres., Triadic Oil Corp.; Dir., Profl. Lease Mgmt., Inc.; **HOME ADD:** 18 Mt. Diablo Cir., San Rafael, CA 94903, (415)479-5927; **BUS ADD:** 433 California St., San Francisco, CA 94104, (415)479-5927.

LEWIS, Jimmie C.——B: Nov. 20, 1947, Eunice, LA, *Dir.*, Lewis & Assoc., Realtors; **PRIM RE ACT:** Broker, Consultant, Owner/Investor, Instructor, Property Manager; **OTHER RE ACT:** Relocation mgmt..; **SERVICES:** Resid., comml. & investment brokerage; relocation mgmt.; **REP CLIENTS:** Third party relocation firms; builders; indivs., corp. & indus.; **PREV EMPLOY:** Instr., Div. of Continuing Educ., LA State Univ.; **PROFL AFFIL & HONORS:** Sales & Mktg. Exec. (SME) - Pres. 1980; RNMI; NAR, First recipient of the W. Max Moore Award for brokerage mgmt., NAR; GRI; **EDUC:** BS, 1969, Soc. Studies, LA State Univ.; **HOME ADD:** 8878 Tiger Bend Rd., Baton Rouge, LA 70816, (504)292-1049; **BUS ADD:** 5200 Corporate Blvd., Suite B, Baton Rouge, LA 70808, (504)927-1450.

LEWIS, John O.——B: Nov. 20, 1935, Quanah, TX, *Pres.*, The Lewis Co.; **PRIM RE ACT:** Broker, Consultant, Developer, Owner/Investor, Property Manager; **SERVICES:** RE brokerage, consulting, appraisals, devel. consulting., prop. mgmt.; **REP CLIENTS:** RCA Corp., Hughes Corp.; Superior Indus.; IBM; Coco Cola Los Angeles; American Standard Corporation; **PREV EMPLOY:** Exec. VP, W. US Indus.; Dir., Indus. Consulting, Cushman & Wakefield; VP, Partner, Dir., Indus. Sales, The Seeley Co.; **PROFL AFFIL & HONORS:** Soc. of Indus. Realtors; Los Angeles Realty Bd.; CA RE Assn.Amer. Soc. of RE Counselors, Recipient of Fred W. Marlowe Award, 1970; **EDUC:** AB, 1958, Econ., Univ. of CA, Santa Barbara; **MIL SERV:** USN; Lt.; **OTHER ACT & HONORS:** Founder, Montessori Children's Ctr., Pasadena; RE Rep., Los Angeles Council Boy Scouts of Amer.; **HOME ADD:** 800 W. 1st, Los Angeles, CA 96012, (213)629-3919; **BUS ADD:** 619 S. Olive St., Ste. 400, Los Angeles, CA 90014, (213)629-2264.

LEWIS, L.R.——B: Aug. 8, 1931, Moundsville, WV, *Pres.*, Lewis Contracting & Design; **PRIM RE ACT:** Consultant, Developer, Builder, Engineer, Owner/Investor; **OTHER RE ACT:** B.O.C.A. Inspector; **PREV EMPLOY:** FHA, Col. Gas System, Amer. Electric Power; **EDUC:** Eng., 1951, WV Univ.; **OTHER ACT & HONORS:** Also associated with Great Western Systems Inc. & American Shelter Co. Inc.; **HOME ADD:** 1503 6th St., Moundsville, WV 26041, (304)845-3144; **BUS ADD:** PO Box 76, Moundsville, WV 26041, (304)845-8652.

LEWIS, Mary Alexis——B: Jan. 19, 1951, San Francisco, CA, *VP*, Fenix, Inc.; **PRIM RE ACT:** Consultant, Developer, Owner/Investor; **SERVICES:** Devel. comml. RE for own acct. and for land-owner clients; annual volume - –12,000,000; **REP CLIENTS:** William Vieser, First City Investments, misc. others; **PREV EMPLOY:** Operations Coordinator, First City Investments (Comml. RE Devel.); Admin. Asst., Narod Development; Previously Ins. Field; **PROFL AFFIL & HONORS:** NAIOP; ICSC; **EDUC:** Various courses in const. mgmt. and const. methods; **HOME ADD:** 12523 N.E. 154th, Woodinville, WA 98072, (206)488-4520; **BUS ADD:** PO Box 2363, Kirkland, WA 98033, (206)881-9388.

LEWIS, N. Richard——B: Aug. 3, 1925, New York, NY, *Pres.*, Lewis & Assoc.; **PRIM RE ACT:** Consultant; **SERVICES:** Mktg., advertising, public rels.; **REP CLIENTS:** Home S&L Assn.; Grubb & Ellis; Ashphalt Roofing Mfrs. Assn.; Robert Charles Lesser & Co.; **PROFL AFFIL & HONORS:** Bldg. Indus. Assn. of CA;Public Relations Soc. of Amer.; Nat. Assn. of RE Editors; Soc. for Mktg. Profl. Serv.; **EDUC:** BS, 1950, Journalism, OH Univ.; **MIL SERV:** US Army; 1st Lt., Bronze Star; **OTHER ACT & HONORS:** Jonathan Club; Los Angeles Press Club; Sigma Delta Chi; **HOME ADD:** 9260 Cordell Dr., Los Angeles, CA 90069, (213)276-7467; **BUS ADD:** 801 N La Brea Ave., Los Angeles, CA 90038, (213)936-7212.

LEWIS, Neil D.——B: July 21, 1934, Milbank, SD, *Pres.*, International Mergers and Acquisitions, Inc., World Headquarters; **PRIM RE ACT:** Broker, Consultant, Banker, Lender, Owner/Investor, Syndicator; **OTHER RE ACT:** Franchisor; **SERVICES:** Primarily in larger mergers and acquisitions; **PREV EMPLOY:** Always an indep. broker/consultant since the early 1950s until I founded Intl. Mergers & Acquisitions in 1970; **HOME ADD:** 1602 Boulder, Rapid City, SD 57701, (605)343-8337; **BUS ADD:** 2040 W. Main St., Suite 306, Rapid City, SD 57701, (605)348-5442.

LEWIS, Paul J.——B: Feb. 15, 1955, Pittsburgh, PA, *Project Mgr.*, Specialty Consultants, Inc., RE; **OTHER RE ACT:** Exec. search exclusively in the RE indus.; **SERVICES:** Identification, eval. and placement of middle and upper mgmt. RE profls.; **REP CLIENTS:** Devel. brokerage, investments, prop. mgmt., Lincoln Props., Fifield Palmer Co., R&B Enterprises, Citibank; **PREV EMPLOY:** Prop. Mgmt.; **PROFL AFFIL & HONORS:** RE Securities and Synd. Inst-; **EDUC:** BS, 1977, Bio., Chem., Slippery Rock State Coll.; **EDUC HONORS:** Dean's List., 3 yrs.; **OTHER ACT & HONORS:** Knights of Columbus; **HOME ADD:** 1521 Woodstream Dr., Glenshaw, PA 15116, (412)487-6949; **BUS ADD:** Suite 2710, Gateway Towers, Pittsburgh, PA 15222, (412)355-8200.

LEWIS, Philson J.——B: Dec. 10, 1949, Trinidad, WI, *VP*, Robert W. Jones & Assoc., Inc., Appr. & Devel.; **PRIM RE ACT:** Instructor, Consultant, Appraiser, Developer; **SERVICES:** Appraisal, planning, studies, mgmt. & devel.; **REP CLIENTS:** Lending Insts., Gov. Agencies, and private clients; **PREV EMPLOY:** Jones & Darby, Inc., Appraiser; **EDUC:** BS/BA, 1974, Math & Econ., Tougaloo Coll.; **GRAD EDUC:** MBA/MUP, 1976, Fin. & Urban Planning, Columbia & NY Univ.; **EDUC HONORS:** Magna Cum Laude, Who's Who Among Amer. Univ. & Coll.; **OTHER ACT & HONORS:** Outstanding Young Man of Amer., 1977, Nat. Alumni Bd. of Dirs., Tougaloo Coll.; **HOME ADD:** 230-36 130th Ave., Laurenton, NY 11413, (212)527-0415; **BUS ADD:** 84 Fifth Ave., NY, NY 10011, (212)929-5318.

LEWIS, Ralph M.——B: Nov. 9, 1919, Johnstown, PA, *COB*, Lewis Homes; **PRIM RE ACT:** Broker, Attorney, Developer, Builder, Property Manager, Owner/Investor; **PREV EMPLOY:** COB, Republic Sales Co.; COB, Lewis Bldg. Co.; **PROFL AFFIL & HONORS:** CPA: State of CA Bar Assn., Distinguished Service Award, NAHB: Builder of the Year award, Bldg. Assoc. of S. CA; Lifetime Dir., CA Bldg. Industry Assoc.; **EDUC:** BS, 1941, Acctg., UCLA; **GRAD EDUC:** Bus. Admin., USC; **EDUC HONORS:** Composed own law study course and passed CA Bar Exam. 1947-52; **OTHER ACT & HONORS:** Pres., Bd. of Educ., Citrus Community Coll. Dist. CA Cmn. on Housing and Community Devel. Partner, Foothill Investment Co.; Western Props.: Republic Mgmt. Corp. Dir. and V.P. Kimmel Enterprises; Bd. of Dir. Gen. Tel. CA; **HOME ADD:** 2120 Vallejo Way, P.O. Box 670, Upland, CA 91786, (714)985-6975; **BUS ADD:** 1156 N. Mt. Ave.,P.O. Box 670, Upland, CA 91786, (714)985-0971.

LEWIS, Richard C.——B: Apr. 11, 1942, New York, NY, *Partner*, Shorenstein & Lewis; **PRIM RE ACT:** Attorney; **SERVICES:** All legal servs. regarding acquisition and sale of realty.; **PROFL AFFIL & HONORS:** ABA, Florida, and Dade Cty. Bar Assns. Real Prop., Probate & Trust Sect., ABA; Greater Miami Estate Planning Council; **EDUC:** AB, 1962, Hist., Dartmouth Coll.; **GRAD EDUC:** JD and LLM (Taxation), 1965 and 1966, Univ. of Miami Law School and NYU Grad. Law School; **HOME ADD:** 14565 S.W. 75 Avenue, Miami, FL 33158, (305)255-7955; **BUS ADD:** 407 Lincoln Rd., 9L, Miami Beach, FL 33139, (305)531-1131.

LEWIS, Robert P.——B: July 12, 1924, Yakima, WA, *Partner*, Cook-Lewis; **PRIM RE ACT:** Developer, Builder, Owner/Investor, Property Manager, Syndicator; **PROFL AFFIL & HONORS:** Yakima Construction Fed.; **EDUC:** BS, 1948, Univ. of WA; **MIL SERV:** USAF, Lt. 1942-1945; **HOME ADD:** 5306 Bitterroot Way, Yakima, WA 98908; **BUS ADD:** Box 1393, Yakima, WA 98907, (509)248-4851.

LEWIS, Stephen E.——**B:** Dec. 21, 1946, Rockaway, NY, *Editor/Assoc. Publisher*, National RE Investor; **PRIM RE ACT:** Real Estate Publisher; **SERVICES:** News of industry trends, major deals, area market studies; **PROFL AFFIL & HONORS:** Nat. Assn. of RE Editors, Participated in study on future of comml. RE; writing awards; **EDUC:** AB, 1969, Eng., Colgate Univ.; **OTHER ACT & HONORS:** VP, Temple Emanu-El of Greater Atlanta; **HOME ADD:** 215 Tawneywood Way, Alpharetta, GA 30201, (404)475-1826; **BUS ADD:** 6285 Barfield Rd., Atlanta, GA 30328, (404)256-9800.

LEWIS, Thomas E.——**B:** Aug. 12, 1945, St. Louis, MO, *Pres. & Chief Operating Officer, Dir.*, Avatar Holdings, Inc.; **PRIM RE ACT:** Developer, Builder, Owner/Investor; **OTHER RE ACT:** Utilities, Title Insurance and Cable TV; **PREV EMPLOY:** Tom Lewis & Assoc., Inc.; **PROFL AFFIL & HONORS:** ULI; ICSC; ABA; GA Bar Assn.; Young Pres. Org.; **EDUC:** BA, 1967, Econ., SMU; **GRAD EDUC:** JD, 1970, Emory Univ.; **EDUC HONORS:** Dean's List, Law Review; **MIL SERV:** USAR, Spec. 4; **HOME ADD:** 10200 Old Cutter Rd., Coral Gables, FL 33156, (305)665-8736; **BUS ADD:** 201 Alhambra Cir., Coral Gables, FL 33134, (305)442-7000.

LEWIS, W. Eugene——**B:** Dec. 23, 1928, Danville, VA, *Part.*, Calvert, Lewis & Smith; **PRIM RE ACT:** Architect; **PROFL AFFIL & HONORS:** AIA; **EDUC:** AA, 1947, Bldg. Constr., Mars Hill; **GRAD EDUC:** MS, 1952, Arch., V.P.I. & S.U.; **HOME ADD:** 326 Oakwood Circle, Danville, VA 24541, (804)793-9103; **BUS ADD:** 753 Main St., Danville, VA 24541, (804)793-9445.

LEWIS, Will J.——**B:** May 15, 1921, *Dir.*, State of WA, Dept. of Gen. Admin., Div. of RE; **PRIM RE ACT:** Broker, Consultant, Appraiser, Architect, Developer, Property Manager; **OTHER RE ACT:** Indus. Mgmt.; **SERVICES:** Negotiate leases for office space for state agencies in privately owned bldgs.; provide layout plans and specifications for alteration and remodeling of leased space; acquire RE sites for state agencies; **REP CLIENTS:** All State Agencies of the State of WA; **PREV EMPLOY:** Curtis Middlebrook & Co., Seattle, 1947-1952; Continental, Inc., Seattle, 1952-1956; Guy Stevens, Inc. & Irving N. Peeples & Assoc., 1956-1963; **PROFL AFFIL & HONORS:** Member, Nat. Assn. of RE Bds.; IREM; Amer. Right of Way Assn.; BOMA, 1977-1978 Member of the Nat. Comm. on Govt. Bldgs.; Past Member, Nat. Assn. of Corp. RE Execs.; Assoc. Member, Olympia RE Bd.; Nat. Assn. of Review Appraisers, CPM; CRA; **EDUC:** BA, 1947, Mgmt., Univ. of WA; **MIL SERV:** USN, Lt.j.g.; **HOME ADD:** 1900 Lakemoore Pl., Olympia, WA 98502, (206)943-0478; **BUS ADD:** 207 Gen. Admin. Bldg., Mail Stop AX-22, Olympia, WA 98504, (206)753-7429.

LEWKOWITZ, Burt——**B:** Nov. 1, 1921, Phoenix, AZ, *Exec. VP*, AZ Assn. of Realtors; **PRIM RE ACT:** Broker, Developer, Owner/Investor, Instructor, Syndicator, Real Estate Publisher; **OTHER RE ACT:** Asociation Exec.; **PREV EMPLOY:** Attorney, Consultant; **EDUC:** AB, 1943, Government & Econ., Harvard Univ.; **GRAD EDUC:** JD, 1948, Law, Univ. of AZ; **MIL SERV:** USNR, Lt., Silver (2), Bronze; **OTHER ACT & HONORS:** ASAE; Pres. AZ SAE; Member, Real Estate Institute, AZ State Univ.; Member, Public Policy Institute, AZ State Univ. Member, Real Estate Education Advisory Bd., State of AZ; **HOME ADD:** 5164 N. 76th Pl., Scottscale, AZ, (602)945-6677; **BUS ADD:** 4414 N. 19th Ave., Phoenix, AZ 85015, (602)248-7787.

LEWMAN, Harry——**B:** Oct. 23, 1919, Louisville, KY, *Owner*, The Harry Lewman Co.; **PRIM RE ACT:** Broker, Consultant, Appraiser, Owner/Investor, Property Manager; **PROFL AFFIL & HONORS:** Member, Amer. Inst. of RE Appraisers(MAI); Designated Sr. RE Analyst(SREA); Member Nat. Assn. of Realtors(NAR); Member, Louisville Bd. of Realtors: Certified Property Mgr. (CPM); Member, Amer. Right of Way Assn.; Member, KY Chap. Rural Appraisers and Farm Mgrs.; MAI-SREA; **EDUC:** BS, 1943, Econ., Univ. of VA; **GRAD EDUC:** MS, 1971, Community Devel., Univ. of Louisville; **MIL SERV:** USN, Lt.; **HOME ADD:** 101 Wampum Rd., Louisville, KY 40207, (502)895-8184; **BUS ADD:** 3211 Kemmons Dr., Louisville, KY 40218, (502)456 1020.

LEX, Richard A.——**B:** Aug. 14, 1938, Bethlehem, PA, *VP*, Citibank, N.A., RE Indus. Div.; **PRIM RE ACT:** Consultant; **SERVICES:** Appraisals, feasibility studies, constr. loan mgmt.; **REP CLIENTS:** Citibank and maj. USA and for. devels.; **PREV EMPLOY:** RE Consultant with Jackson-Cross Co., Philadelphia, PA; **PROFL AFFIL & HONORS:** AIREA, SREA, Nat. Assn. of RE Bd., MAI, SRPA, Realtor; **EDUC:** AA, 1966, RE, Los Angeles Valley Coll., UCLA; **HOME ADD:** 118 Bruce Rd., Washington Crossing, PA 18977, (215)493-6007; **BUS ADD:** 399 Park Ave., NY, NY 10043, (212)559-0701.

LEXA, Joseph J.——**B:** Oct. 20, 1955, *Gen. Counsel*, Magna Properties, Inc., a subs. of Bankers Life & Casualty Co.; **PRIM RE ACT:** Attorney; **SERVICES:** Gen. legal servs.; **REP CLIENTS:** In-house counsel; **PREV EMPLOY:** Assoc. Atty., Coleman, Leonard, Morrison, Ft. Lauderdale, FL; **PROFL AFFIL & HONORS:** FL Bar; Broward Cty. Bar Assn., Young Lawyers Sect.; **EDUC:** BA, 1977, Law, Wake Forest Univ.; **GRAD EDUC:** JD, 1979, Law, Univ. of SC; **EDUC HONORS:** Cum Laude; **HOME ADD:** 720 Bayshore Dr. #604, Ft. Lauderdale, FL 33304; **BUS ADD:** POB 2249, 1301 W. Copans Rd., Pompano Beach, FL 33061, (305)971-9100.

LEYNSE, Waldo H.——**B:** Aug. 10, 1923, Peking, China, *Pres.*, Rancho Raymundo Inc., Greendyk Investments Inc.; **PRIM RE ACT:** Broker, Owner/Investor, Developer, Syndicator; **OTHER RE ACT:** Devel. of rural subdivisions; **SERVICES:** Land devel., synd., investor; **REP CLIENTS:** Builders and indivs., investors in comml. props.; **PROFL AFFIL & HONORS:** CCIM; NAR; GRI; **EDUC:** BA, 1947, Econ., Ponoma Coll.; **GRAD EDUC:** 1948, Bus. Admin., Stanford Univ., Grad. School of Bus. Admin.; **MIL SERV:** US Army; Capt.; 1942-1946; 50-51; **OTHER ACT & HONORS:** Advisor, Univ. of CA at Santa Cruze on RE courses; **HOME ADD:** 297 Selby Lane, Atherton, CA 94025, (415)364-1348; **BUS ADD:** 2600 El Camino Real, Palo Alto, CA 94306, (415)857-1111.

LHOTKA, Betty K., CRB——**B:** Dec. 16, 1935, Macon, GA, *VP*, Century 21, The Omnimark Grp., Inc.; **PRIM RE ACT:** Broker, Owner/Investor; **PREV EMPLOY:** Const. co., legal sec.; banking & Finance; **PROFL AFFIL & HONORS:** NAR; St. Petersburg Bd. of Realtors; **EDUC:** Wesleyan Coll., Macon GA; **OTHER ACT & HONORS:** Sec. of Local Easter Seals Soc.; Bd. of Dirs. of "Neighborly Sr. Services"; Amer. Bus. Women's Assn.; Boss of the Yr. 1981; Order of Eastern Star; RNMI; CRB; **HOME ADD:** 8922 St. Andrews Dr., Seminole, FL 33543, (813)393-0380; **BUS ADD:** 1901 Tyrone Blvd., St. Petersburg, FL 33710, (813)344-5713.

LIASKOS, Michael P.——**B:** June 30, 1921, NY, NY, *Pres.*, 266-Third Ave. Corp.; **PRIM RE ACT:** Owner/Investor; **MIL SERV:** Maritime, Warrant-fleet, 1943-46, Pacific , Indian, Atlantic, Mediterannean; **OTHER ACT & HONORS:** Pres. Lions Club , Englewood Cliffs, NJ; **HOME ADD:** 2457 Camner St., Fort Lee, NJ 07024, (201)944-4380; **BUS ADD:** 266 Third Ave., NY, NY 10010, (212)473-9753.

LIBBY, Bruce A.——**B:** Apr. 25, 1939, Portland, ME, *Dir., RE Investment Operations*, Massachusetts Mutual Life Insurance Co., RE Investment; **PRIM RE ACT:** Lender, Owner/Investor; **SERVICES:** Lending US & Can.; **REP CLIENTS:** Builders and devels.; **PREV EMPLOY:** ME Hwy. Commn. 1964-68; **PROFL AFFIL & HONORS:** MBAA; Income Prop. Comm.; AIREA, IREM, Instr. Univ. of MA; **EDUC:** Bus. Admin., 1961, Mgmt., Univ. of ME; **GRAD EDUC:** JD, 1964, Law, Univ. of ME School of Law; **HOME ADD:** 339 South Rd., Hampden, MA 01036, (413)566-3654; **BUS ADD:** 1295 State St., Springfield, MA 01101, (413)788-8411.

LIBBY, Howard A.——**B:** Oct. 8, 1943, *Atty.*; **PRIM RE ACT:** Developer, Consultant, Attorney, Owner/Investor, Property Manager; **GRAD EDUC:** JD, Georgetown Univ. School of Law; **HOME ADD:** 3899 N. Stafford St., Arlington, VA 22207; **BUS ADD:** 2005 L St., N.W., Wash., DC 20036, (202)466-6000.

LIBBY, John E.——*SIR, Manager RE & Prop. Development*, Agway Inc.; **PRIM RE ACT:** Property Manager; **BUS ADD:** Box 4933, Syracuse, NY 13221, (315)477-6187.*

LIBERIS, Charles S.——**B:** Mar. 31, 1942, Pensacola, FL, *Pres.*, Charles S. Liberis, P.A.; **PRIM RE ACT:** Attorney, Developer; **PROFL AFFIL & HONORS:** ABA; FL Bar Assn.; Nat. Assn. of Homebuilders; **GRAD EDUC:** JD, 1967, Stetson Univ.; **HOME ADD:** 1900 Scenic Hwy., Unit 601, Pensacola, FL 32501, (904)432-4845; **BUS ADD:** 421 North Palafox St., Pensacola, FL 32501, (904)438-9647.

LIBICKI, Henry——*VP Operations*, Nordson; **PRIM RE ACT:** Property Manager; **BUS ADD:** 555 Jackson St., Amherst, OH 44001, (216)988-9411.*

LIBMAN, Isidore M.——**B:** Jan. 5, 1903, Russia, *Pres.*, Ninety Two State St., Inc.; **PRIM RE ACT:** Consultant, Developer, Property Manager, Owner/Investor; **SERVICES:** RE Mgmt.; **PROFL AFFIL & HONORS:** Greater Boston RE Bd. and BOMA; **GRAD EDUC:** LLB, 1927, Suffolk Univ.; **HOME ADD:** 33 Pond Ave., Brookline, MA 02146, (617)566-6223; **BUS ADD:** 100-110 State St., Boston, MA 02109, (617)523-5580.

LICHAUCO, Marcial P., Jr.——**B:** May 17, 1950, Philippines, *VP*, Edgewood Investments Inc.; **PRIM RE ACT:** Consultant, Owner/Investor, Property Manager, Syndicator; **SERVICES:** Comml. prop.

acquisition mgmt.; investment consulting, portfolio mgmt.; **REP CLIENTS:** For. based indiv. and instnl. investors, primarily Asian based; **PREV EMPLOY:** Sycip Gorres Velayo & Co., CPA's; **EDUC:** BA, BS, 1973, Econ., Engrg., Stanford Univ.; **GRAD EDUC:** MBA, 1975, Fin., Acctg., Stanford Univ.; **HOME ADD:** 2640 Kiowa Ct., Walnut Creek, CA 94598; **BUS ADD:** 153 Kearny St. #201, San Francisco, CA 94108, (415)956-8787.

LICHENSTEIN, Robert Maurice, Sr.——B: May 18, 1927, Hoboken, NJ, *Pres.*, Lichenstein and Associates Inc.; **PRIM RE ACT:** Broker, Owner/Investor; **OTHER RE ACT:** Arrange Joint Ventures; **SERVICES:** Match investors with Appropriate Devels.; **REP CLIENTS:** Builders and Devels.; **PROFL AFFIL & HONORS:** TX Assn. of Realtors, Houston Bd. of Realtors; **EDUC:** BA, 1948, Psychology, Princeton Univ.; **MIL SERV:** USAAF, Sgt., Victory Medal, Occupation Medal, Air Force Intelligence; **OTHER ACT & HONORS:** Tres., Bergen Cty. Young Republican NJ, VP NY Rugby Football Club; **HOME ADD:** 3706 Robinhood, Houston, TX 77005; **BUS ADD:** 1405 S. Post Oak Rd., Suite 208, Houston, TX 77056, (713)965-0392.

LICHT, Martin C.——B: Sept. 21, 1941, NY, *Atty. at Law*, Herzfeld & Rubin, PC; **PRIM RE ACT:** Attorney; **SERVICES:** Evaluation of RE investments, devel. & synd. of comml. & resid. props., representation of lenders & borrowers; **REP CLIENTS:** Mast Prop. Investors, Inc., Arthur L. Dann & Assoc., Inc., Richard B. Duckett, Richard L Pinto, Quay Assoc., RE Synds.; **PROFL AFFIL & HONORS:** ABA, NY State Bar Assn., Assn. of Bar of the City of NY; **HOME ADD:** 16 Soundview Dr., Eastchester, NY 10709; **BUS ADD:** 40 Wall St., NY, NY 10005, (212)344-0680.

LICHT, Nathan——B: June 24, 1918, Manhattan, NY, *Pres.*, Lane Realty; **PRIM RE ACT:** Broker, Builder, Owner/Investor, Property Manager; **SERVICES:** Complete RE serv. - all areas, resid. comml., indus.; **PROFL AFFIL & HONORS:** Nat. Assn. RE Bds., Nat. Assn. of Home Builders, RE Bd. of NY, Jamaica RE Bd., LIBI, Long Is. RE Bd.; **MIL SERV:** Ordinance, 1st Lt.; **BUS ADD:** 112-45 Queens Blvd., Forest Hills, NY 11375, (212)268-3500.

LICHTENFELS, J. Reid——B: June 15, 1948, Chicago, IL, *Atty. - RE Broker*, J. Reid Lichtenfels, PC; **PRIM RE ACT:** Broker, Attorney; **SERVICES:** Legal representation and consultation, including contract negotiations.; **REP CLIENTS:** Brokers, Devel., Indiv., Lenders, Corp. Investors and Owners; **PROFL AFFIL & HONORS:** CO Bar Assn., Denver Bar Assn.; **EDUC:** BA, 1970, Eng. Lit., Univ. of Notre Dame; **GRAD EDUC:** JD, 1974, Univ. of Denver, Coll. of Law; **HOME ADD:** 8692 East Doane Pl., Denver, CO 80231, (303)751-3498; **BUS ADD:** 650 So. Cherry St., Suite 810, Denver, CO 80222, (303)399-7002.

LICHTENSTEIN, Stephen F.——*VP & Secy.*, Lenox, Inc.; **PRIM RE ACT:** Property Manager; **BUS ADD:** 3190 Princeton Pike, Lawrenceville, NJ 08648, (609)896-2800.*

LICHTER, Stuart——B: Feb. 7, 1949, NYC, NY, *Pres.*, Quadrelle Realty Services, Inc.; **PRIM RE ACT:** Developer, Owner/Investor, Property Manager, Syndicator; **PREV EMPLOY:** NY Life; Marine Midland Realty; Credit Corp.; **PROFL AFFIL & HONORS:** MAI, Candidate; **EDUC:** BA, 1969, Econ., Hunter Coll.; **BUS ADD:** Two East Ave., Larchmont, NY 10538, (914)834-2600.

LICHTIGMAN, Charles S.——B: Oct. 9, 1941, NY, NY, *Pres.*, Republic Funding Corp. of FL; **PRIM RE ACT:** Broker, Builder, Developer, Owner/Investor, Property Manager; **SERVICES:** Comml. brokerage, retail site selection prop. mgmt. resld. & comml. devel.; **REP CLIENTS:** Builders, retailers, foreign & domestic investors; **PREV EMPLOY:** VP ITT Comm. Devel. Corp., 1972-77; **EDUC:** AB, 1962, Univ. of MI; **GRAD EDUC:** LLB, 1966, Yale Law Sch.; **MIL SERV:** USA; **OTHER ACT & HONORS:** Bd. of Dir., US Investment Mgmt. Corp.; Republic Funding Corp. (NY); Charles Wayne Co.; **HOME ADD:** 22 Riverridge Tr., Ormond Bch., FL 32074, (904)672-6529; **BUS ADD:** 201 E Pine St., Orlando, FL 32074, (305)425-5544.

LICKEL, George R.——B: Mar. 5, 1931, Altoona, PA, *Appraisal Off. and Cf. Appraiser*, Nat. City Bank, RE Loans; **PRIM RE ACT:** Appraiser; **SERVICES:** Appraise all comml. industl. prop. and manage resid. staff; **PREV EMPLOY:** Equitable Life Assurance Soc., Resid. Loan Appraiser, Cole Layer Trumble Co., Mass appraisal firm, Staff appraiser; **PROFL AFFIL & HONORS:** SREA; **EDUC:** BE, 1953, Geog. and Soc. Stds., Shippensburg State Teachers Coll., PA; **HOME ADD:** 8206 Fenway Dr., Parma, OH 44129, (216)845-0175; **BUS ADD:** 1900 E. Ninth St., Cleveland, OH 44114, (216)575-2125.

LIEB, L. Robert——B: July 15, 1941, Jersey City, NJ, *Partner*, Lieb, Samnick & Lukashok; **PRIM RE ACT:** Attorney, Developer, Owner/Investor, Syndicator; **SERVICES:** Legal & devel. principals; **REP CLIENTS:** Lending instit., devel. & converters; **EDUC:** BA, 1962, Pol. Sci., Univ. of Buffalo; **GRAD EDUC:** LLB, 1965, NYU; **EDUC HONORS:** Regents Scholar, Dean's List; **MIL SERV:** USAF, 1st Lt.; **OTHER ACT & HONORS:** Chmn., Bd. of Dir., Mt. Washington Hotel Co., Mountain Devel. Co., Inc.; **HOME ADD:** 2 Tabor Court, Livingston, NJ 07039, (201)994-3258; **BUS ADD:** 1133 Ave. of the Americas, NY, NY 10036, (212)391-1260.

LIEBCHEN, Carolyn——B: Oct. 27, 1939, Vanderburgh County, IN, *Pres./Treas.*, CENTURY 21 Carolyn Liebchen Realty, Inc.; **PRIM RE ACT:** Broker; **SERVICES:** Listing and selling residential and comml. RE; **PROFL AFFIL & HONORS:** Nat. State & Local Bd. of Realtors, Multiple Listing, GRI, CRS & CRB; **HOME ADD:** 5204 Winding Way, Evansville, IN 47711, (812)477-7001; **BUS ADD:** 1000 First Ave., Evansville, IN 47710, (812)464-3988.

LIEBERMAN, Bruce R.——B: Sept. 16, 1940, Brooklyn, NY, *Pres.*, Lieberman Cos.; **PRIM RE ACT:** Consultant, Developer, Owner/Investor, Insuror, Property Manager, Syndicator; **SERVICES:** Valuation, acquisition and mgmt. of income prop.; some synd.; **REP CLIENTS:** Indiv. and instnl. investment in income prop.; **PROFL AFFIL & HONORS:** NY Supreme Ct. (1965); US Circuit Ct. of Appeals (1966); Tax Court of the US (1968); Supreme Ct. of the US (1970); ABA (1967); RE Bd. of NY (1965); Young Men's RE Assn. of NY (1965); IREM (1968); Apt. Owners and Mgrs. Assn. of Amer.; Nat. Apt. Assn. (1977); Apt. Council of OK (1976), CPM; "Man of the Year" 1971, New York Council for Civic Affairs; "Civic Achievements Award" 1973, NY Urban Affairs Council; NJ BOMA, Pres. 1972; NJ Builder's Assn. (1970); NJ Apt. House Council (1971), Chmn. 1973-1974, Co-Chmn. 1974-1975; Fort Lee Prop. Owner's Assn. (1972), Founder 1970, Pres./Dir. 1970-1975; NJ Builders Assn. (1970), Dir. 1972-1975; **EDUC:** BS Bus. Admin., 1962, Acctg., Bucknell Univ.; **GRAD EDUC:** LLB, 1964, Tax Law, NY Univ. School of Law; **EDUC HONORS:** Dean's List; **OTHER ACT & HONORS:** Youngmen's RE Assn. of NY; US Circuit Ct. of Appeals; **HOME ADD:** 199 West Shore Rd., Great Neck, NY 11024, (516)482-6625; **BUS ADD:** 554 Middle Neck Rd., Great Neck, NY 11023, (516)466-6565.

LIEBERMAN, Harold G.——B: June 26, 1927, St. Louis, MO, *Chmn.*, Lieberman Corp. 1959; **PRIM RE ACT:** Developer, Builder, Owner/Investor, Property Manager, Insuror, Syndicator; **PROFL AFFIL & HONORS:** Natl. Assn. of Home Builders, NAREB, IREM, BOMA; **EDUC:** BS-Bus. Admin., 1949, Fin. and Mktg., Washington Univ., St. Louis, MO; **MIL SERV:** USAF, 2nd Lt.; **OTHER ACT & HONORS:** Westwood Ctry. Club, St. Louis, MO; Pres. of the Jewish Ctr. For Aged in St. Louis, MO 1965-1973; Dir. of Jewish Hospital of St. Louis 1971-1973; **HOME ADD:** 809 S. Warson Rd., St. Louis, MO 63124; **BUS ADD:** 11970 Borman Dr., Suite 222, St. Louis, MO 63141, (314)878-4111.

LIEBETRAU, Theodore Lambert——B: July 5, 1925, Freeport, IL, *RE Appraiser*, Indep. Fee Agent; **PRIM RE ACT:** Appraiser; **SERVICES:** Appraisals of comml., indus., resid., and special use props.; **REP CLIENTS:** Comml. and Indus.; banks, cos., and indivs., resid. relocation cos., (Southwest Bell Telephone, Reynolds Metals, Merrill Lynch Relocation Mgmt., Inc.) fee appraiser for Veterans Admin.; **PREV EMPLOY:** Assoc. Givens Realty, Thomas Givens; SREA, 1965-1970; City of Corpus Christi Appraiser and Right-of-Way Agent 1970-1972; **PROFL AFFIL & HONORS:** Soc. of RE Appraisers, SRA; **EDUC:** BS, 1951, Geology, Univ. of OK; **MIL SERV:** USAF, 1943-1945, S/Sgt., Air Medal; **HOME ADD:** 521 Cunningham, Corpus Christi, TX 78411, (512)853-4673; **BUS ADD:** 521 Cunningham, Corpus Christi, TX 78411, (512)853-4673.

LIEBMAN, Lawrence M.——B: Sept. 13, 1930, New Haven, CT, *Pres.*, Liebman, Rashba, Goldblatt and Greenstein, P.C.; **PRIM RE ACT:** Attorney, Banker, Developer, Owner/Investor, Syndicator; **SERVICES:** Legal serv., investment counseling, devel. & synd. of resid. and comml. props.; **REP CLIENTS:** Lenders, indiv. investors in resid. & comml. prop.; **PROFL AFFIL & HONORS:** New Haven Cty. Bar Assn.; CT Bar Assn.; ABA; RESSI; **EDUC:** BS, 1952, Mktg., Univ. of CT; **GRAD EDUC:** LLB, 1955, Boston Univ.; **HOME ADD:** 49 Tumblebrook Rd., Woodbridge, CT 06525, (203)397-2170; **BUS ADD:** 2405 Whitney Ave., Hamden, CT 06518, (203)288-6293.

LIEBSCHER, Dr. V.K. Chris——B: Jan. 30, 1925, Munich, West Germany, *Univ. Prof./Pres., Profl. Service Co.*, Governors State University/Universal Realty-Consultants, Econ./Mktg./RE; **PRIM RE ACT:** Broker, Consultant, Engineer, Appraiser, Developer, Owner/Investor, Instructor, Property Manager, Insuror, Syndicator; **OTHER RE ACT:** Fin. Counselor & Mediator, Econ. Forecaster & Consultant; **SERVICES:** Investment Counseling, Valuation, Engrg. Feasibility, Econ. Feasibility, Fin. Mediation, Insurance Counseling, Planning & Deve., Synd.; **REP CLIENTS:** Corp. users: Bus.-Prod., Distr., Ret., Institl. Lenders, Comml. & Indiv. Investors; **PREV EMPLOY:** Project Engr.

Constr.: Hydro-Electric Facilities, Ship Locks, Production Plants, Hwys. & Bridges; Econ. Consultant State of IL; Village Park Forest South; Consult. Corresp. to var. Instit. Lenders; Grad. Bus. - MBA Faculty; Appraisal Instr.; **PROFL AFFIL & HONORS:** Gr. South Suburb Bd. of Realtors; RAIR; Am. Econ. Assoc.; NAR; Intern. Bus. & Fin. Consults.; Am. Assoc. Univ. Professors; NEUEA, RE Ed. Assoc., Prof. Engrs., Doctorate Econ., Reg. Profl. Engr., Outstanding Educ. of America Award 75 Licenses: Engrg., RE, Insurance; **EDUC:** BS, 1953, Heavy Construction; Engr. Admin., Concrete-Steel-Wood Engr. Design; Project Site Mgmt., Staatsbauschule Munich, West Germany; **GRAD EDUC:** MS, Bus.; Doct. Phil. Econ., 1971; 1972, Bus.: Behavioral Organization; Econ.; Econ. Devel.: Nat. and Urban, Southern IL Univ., Carbondale, IL; **EDUC HONORS:** Beta Gamma Sigma; Omicron Delta Epsilon; Dissertation Fellow SIU 1971/72; **OTHER ACT & HONORS:** Member, Bd. of Appeals: Village of Richton Park, IL 1973-81; Biographicals: Who's Who in Intl. Higher Educ., Men of Achievement-Cambridge, England; Who's Who in the Midwest 1982; **HOME ADD:** 22610 Lakeshore Dr., Richton Park, IL 60471, (312)748-0609; **BUS ADD:** 4557 "C" W. 211th, Matteson, IL 60443, (312)748-3330.

LIEF, Inez——B: Sept. 19, 1926, Newark, NJ, *Mgr. Prop. Mgmt. Dept.*, Weichert Co. Realtors, Prop. Mgmt.; **PRIM RE ACT:** Broker, Consultant, Property Manager; **REP CLIENTS:** Corp., indivs., office; **PREV EMPLOY:** Self-employed - 3 offices; **PROFL AFFIL & HONORS:** Nat. Assn. Female Execs.; Morris Cty. Bd. of Realtors; NJAR; NAR; Nat. Mktg. Inst., GRI; CRS; CRB; Harry L. Schwarz Award, 1975; Who's Who American Women 1981; Morris Cty. Bd. of Realtors; Who's Who in RE 1982; Who's Who in NJ 1975; **OTHER ACT & HONORS:** Commissioner of the Superior Ct. of NJ on Condemnation Proceedings; Pres., Morris Cty. Bd. of Realtors 1981-1982; **HOME ADD:** 15 Humphrey Rd., Convent Station, NJ 07961, (201)538-8785; **BUS ADD:** 6 Dumont Pl., Morristown, NJ 07960, (201)267-7777.

LIEK, James E.——B: Apr. 26, 1926, Cedar Rapids, IA, *Pres.*, BRAVO Realty Services, Inc.; **PRIM RE ACT:** Broker, Consultant, Appraiser, Instructor, Owner/Investor, Property Manager; **SERVICES:** All RE servs.; **REP CLIENTS:** Banks, REITS, other lenders, synd., attys., pvt. owners, govt. agencies; **PREV EMPLOY:** VP, First WI National Bank of Milwaukee, Exec. VP, Instnl. investors trust; **PROFL AFFIL & HONORS:** Dir., Boynton Beach/Ocean Ridge Bd. of Realtors; Charter Member, Natl. Assn. Review Appraisers, SRPA, Soc. of RE Appraisers; Past Pres. Milwaukee Wis. Chapter; **EDUC:** BA, 1950, Econ. and Poli. Sci., Univ. of IA; **GRAD EDUC:** MA, 1952, Econ., public admin., for. affairs, Univ. of IA; **MIL SERV:** USN, 1944-46, S 1/c; **HOME ADD:** 1310 SW 25th Way, Boynton Beach, FL 33435, (305)734-7441; **BUS ADD:** 10236 Cedar Point Blvd., Boynton Beach, FL 33437, (305)737-5260.

LIEN, Della——B: Apr. 20, 1927, MA, *Part.*, Intl. RE Network, Lucas Realty; **PRIM RE ACT:** Broker, Syndicator, Property Manager, Owner/Investor; **PROFL AFFIL & HONORS:** Palos Verdes, Rolling Hills, Torrance, South Bay & Long Beach Bd. of Realtors, Women's Council of Realtors; **OTHER ACT & HONORS:** Palos Verdes Golf Club, Little Co. of Mary Hospital Auxiliary; **HOME ADD:** 3629 Via La. Selva, Palos Verdes Estates, CA 90274, (213)375-3843; **BUS ADD:** 421 Via Chico, Palos Verdes Estates, CA 90274, (213)378-1218.

LIENHARD, Garry D.——B: Sept. 7, 1945, Silverton, OR, *RE Appraiser & Property Appraiser*, Self employed and Clatsop County, Assessor's Office; **PRIM RE ACT:** Appraiser, Instructor, Assessor; **SERVICES:** RE Appraisals on resid. and small tract acreage; **REP CLIENTS:** Attys., Banks, Thrifts, Indivs.; **PREV EMPLOY:** Locator for a title ins. co., previously an appraiser with another assessor's office; **PROFL AFFIL & HONORS:** Soc. of RE Appraisers, SRA; **EDUC:** BS, 1969, Bus. Admin./Mktg. Mgmt., OR State Univ.; **OTHER ACT & HONORS:** Astoria Oregon Lions Club; **HOME ADD:** 1343 9th St., POB 855, Astoria, OR 97103, (503)325-8460; **BUS ADD:** 690 Taybin Rd., N.W., Salem, OR 97304.

LIE-NIELSEN, John——B: Mar. 16, 1935, Boston, MA, *Chmn. of the Bd.*, Johnstown Amer. Contr.; **PRIM RE ACT:** Broker, Developer, Lender, Builder, Owner/Investor, Property Manager, Syndicator; **SERVICES:** Manage Apts., convert and build condos., syndication; **PREV EMPLOY:** Personnel Dir. & Hosp. Admin. for Langley Porter Neuropsychiatric Inst. from 1966-72; VP Acquisitions for Consolidated Capital from 1972-75; **PROFL AFFIL & HONORS:** Johnstown Amer. is member of AOMA, IREM, Johnstown Props. & Lane Co. have 'Accredited Mgmt. Org' title (AMO) from IREM; **EDUC:** BA, 1958, Econ., Emory Univ.; **EDUC HONORS:** Phi Beta Kappa; **MIL SERV:** USMC Res., Cpl.; **BUS ADD:** 5775-A Peachtree Duwy Rd., Atlanta, GA 30342, (404)252-8780.

LIESSMANN, Ohland W.——B: May 7, 1927, Watertown, WI, *VP*, The American Appraisal Co., RE; **PRIM RE ACT:** Consultant, Appraiser; **SERVICES:** Valuation; Eval.; Counseling for real property; Enterprises; machinery and equipment; Intangibles; **REP CLIENTS:** Indiv. or Inst. investors or lenders in comml. or indus. prop. and/or enterprises; **PROFL AFFIL & HONORS:** AIREA (MAI), (ASA), Amer. Right of Way Assn. (SR/WA), MAI Prof. Recognition Award 1977-79, 1980-82; **EDUC:** BA, 1949, Econ., Carroll Coll., Waukesha, WI; **GRAD EDUC:** MBA, 1950, Mgmt., Univ. of Denver; **MIL SERV:** USN; Lt. J.G.; **HOME ADD:** 735 E. Wabash Ave., Waukesha, WI 53186, (414)544-4939; **BUS ADD:** 525 E. Michigan St., Milwaukee, WI 53201, (414)271-7240.

LIFSHUTZ, Bernard L.——B: Oct. 2, 1926, San Antonio, TX, *Pres.*, Texas Home Improvement, Inc.; **PRIM RE ACT:** Developer, Builder, Owner/Investor, Property Manager; **SERVICES:** Devel., const., investing, prop. mgmt.; **PROFL AFFIL & HONORS:** Bd. of Bank of San Antonio; Underwriting Member of Lloyd's of London; **EDUC:** BS, 1946, Econ., Wharton School, Univ. of PA; **GRAD EDUC:** MBA, 1947, Harvard Bus. School; **MIL SERV:** USN, Lt.; **HOME ADD:** 780 Terrell Rd., San Antonio, TX 78209, (512)822-1964; **BUS ADD:** 215 N. Flores St., San Antonio, TX 78205, (512)226-6221.

LIFTIN, Muriel Zeitlin——B: New York, NY, *Atty.*, Self employed; **PRIM RE ACT:** Attorney; **SERVICES:** Legal; **REP CLIENTS:** Indiv. Homeowners or buyers, corp. RE; **PROFL AFFIL & HONORS:** Chicago Bar Assn.; IL Bar Assn.; FL Bar Assn.; ABA; North Sub. Bar Assn., Amer. Chem. Soc.; **EDUC:** BA, Chem., Brooklyn Coll.; **GRAD EDUC:** MS, Chem., State Univ. of IA; MA, Perf. Arts, NE IL State Univ.; JD, 1976, Law, John Marshall; **EDUC HONORS:** Order of John Marshall, Honors; **HOME ADD:** 224 Brown Ave., Evanston, IL 60202; **BUS ADD:** 2632 W.Devon Ave., Chicago, IL 60645, (312)262-2333.

LIFTIN, Sidney J.——B: Jan. 3, 1909, NY, NY; **PRIM RE ACT:** Attorney, Property Manager, Owner/Investor; **EDUC:** AB, 1929, Govt., C.C. OF NY; **GRAD EDUC:** LLD, 1932, Genl., Harvard Law School; **EDUC HONORS:** Legal Aid Bureau; **MIL SERV:** USA, PFC, GCM; **HOME ADD:** 134-11 Newport Ave., Rockaway Pk., NY 11694, (212)634-7008; **BUS ADD:** 134 11 Newport Ave., Rockaway Pk., NY 11694, (212)634-6662.

LIGHT, Kenneth——*Sr. VP Adm.*, Allied Products Corp.; **PRIM RE ACT:** Property Manager; **BUS ADD:** 10 South Riverside Plaza, Chicago, IL 60606, (312)454-1020.*

LIGHTBODY, Jack S.——B: July 29, 1940, St. Louis, MO, *VP, RE Investment Dept.*, The Prudential Ins. Co., RE Investment Dept.; **PRIM RE ACT:** Developer, Property Manager; **SERVICES:** Coordinator RE Devel. activities of Prudential; **PREV EMPLOY:** VP Ogden Devel. Co.; V.P. J.A. Jones Construction Co.; **PROFL AFFIL & HONORS:** CPM (of IREM), Nat. Assn. of RE Appraisers, NARA; **EDUC:** BS, 1964, Fin., Mktg. & Econ., CA State Univ. at LA; **GRAD EDUC:** 1962, RE Fin., Univ. of CA at LA; **MIL SERV:** USN, 1960-64; Submarines; **HOME ADD:** 63 Union Hill Rd., Madison, NJ 07940; **BUS ADD:** 20 Prudential Plaza, Newark, NJ 07101, (201)877-7552.

LIGON, Jeffrey Lynn——B: Dec. 19, 1953, Richmond, VA, *RE Officer*, First & Merchant's Nat. Bank, Trust; **PRIM RE ACT:** Property Manager, Banker; **SERVICES:** Buy, sell, lease & mgmt. of Trust props.; **PROFL AFFIL & HONORS:** IREM, Richmond Bd. of Realtors, CPM; **EDUC:** BS, 1976, Bus. Admin, RE & Urban Land Dev., VA Commonwealth Univ.; **EDUC HONORS:** Hon. Award; **HOME ADD:** 22 Lexington Rd., Richmond, VA 23226, (804)359-0144; **BUS ADD:** 12th & Main St., PO Box 26903, Richmond, VA 23261, (804)788-2188.

LILES, Paul——*Pres.*, Radnor Realty Serv., Inc., Financial Consulting, Investments; **PRIM RE ACT:** Consultant, Appraiser, Developer; **SERVICES:** RE devel., appraisal, consulting and syndication; **PREV EMPLOY:** NY Life Ins. Co. (Investment Officer); **PROFL AFFIL & HONORS:** AIREA; Amer. Soc. of Appraisers; Nat. Assn. of Review Appraisers; BOMA; RE Bd. of NY; ULI; Amer. Arbitration Assn.; RESSI; Soc. of Real Prop. Admins.; NASD, MAI, ASA, CRA, RPA, SRPA; **EDUC:** BBA, Baruch Coll.; **BUS ADD:** 100E 42nd St., 25th Floor, New York, NY 10017.

LILJENQUIST, Newell Lavon——B: Feb. 14, 1911, *Owner*, Tuskatella Shopping Center; **PRIM RE ACT:** Developer, Owner/Investor, Property Manager; **SERVICES:** Ownership & devel. of office complexes & shopping ctrs.; **PROFL AFFIL & HONORS:** UT Bar Assn.; **GRAD EDUC:** LLD, 1936, Univ. of UT; **MIL SERV:** USAF, 2nd Lt.; **HOME ADD:** 1400 E. Katella Ave., Orange, CA 92667, (214)997-8000; **BUS ADD:** PO Box 5544, Orange, CA 92667,

(714)639-1013.

LILLARD, John S.——**B:** May 31, 1930, Cincinnati, OH, *Pres.*, JMB Instl. Reality Corp; **OTHER RE ACT:** Investment Mgmt.; **SERVICES:** Mgrs. Trust for Pension Funds; **REP CLIENTS:** Large Corporate Retirement Funds; **PREV EMPLOY:** Investment Counselor with Scudder Stevens & Clark 1955-79, General Partner, Member of Bd. of Dirs.; **EDUC:** BA, 1952, Eng. Lit., Univ. of VA; **GRAD EDUC:** MBA, 1961, Bus. Admin., Xavier Univ. (Cinncinnati); **MIL SERV:** USN,Lt.(j.g.); **OTHER ACT & HONORS:** Tavern Club, Trustee of Chicago Symphony, Ravinia Festival, past pres. Cinn. Soc. of Fin. Analysts, past pres. of Cinn. Symphony Orch., Dir. Mathers Fund, Strylar Corp., Civtas Corp., Gateway Option Income Fund; **HOME ADD:** 1300 N. Waukegan Rd., Lake Forrest,, IL 60045, (312)295-2098; **BUS ADD:** 875 N. Michigan Ave. Suite 3900, Chicago, IL 60611, (312)440-5042.

LILLICRAPP, Charles J., Jr.——**B:** July 13, 1939, Darby, PA, *Owner, Operator*, Geary Mortgage Service Co.; **OTHER RE ACT:** Mort. loans, savings investment broker; **SERVICES:** Originate and service S&L investment accounts for fin. sources; **REP CLIENTS:** S&L, 2nd mort., lenders, comml. lenders, pvt. lenders; **PROFL AFFIL & HONORS:** CRA; Cert. Mort. Underwriter; RE Broker; **EDUC:** BS, 1970, Bus. Admin., St. Joseph's Univ.; **MIL SERV:** US Army; Spec. 4, 1957-1959; **OTHER ACT & HONORS:** Councilman, Morton Borough, 4 yrs.; Rotary; Univ. of PA, Wharton School of Bus.; **HOME ADD:** 114 Locust Rd., Morton, PA 19070, (215)544-5893; **BUS ADD:** 1404 Bywood Ave., Upper Darby, PA 19082, (215)352-4604.

LILLICROP, John——*Pres.*, Wynn's International Inc.; **PRIM RE ACT:** Property Manager; **BUS ADD:** PO Box 4370, Fullerton, CA 92634, (714)992-2000.*

LILLY, Lauren C.——**B:** June 1, 1953, Alamogordo, NM, *Prop. Mgmt. Product Specialist*, Timberline Systems, Inc.; **PRIM RE ACT:** Consultant, Instructor; **SERVICES:** Info. mgmt. consultant, computer acctg.; **REP CLIENTS:** C.W. Whittier & Bros., Boston; Jack A. Benaroya, Seattle, WA; Podolski & Assoc., Chicago; Hignell & Hignell, Chico, CA; **EDUC:** BS, 1975, Math., Northwest Nazarene Coll.; **GRAD EDUC:** MA, 1977, Math. Statistics, WA State Univ.; **EDUC HONORS:** Magna Cum Laude, Phi Kappa Lambda Honor Soc., Cum Laude; **HOME ADD:** 3670 SW 108th, Beaverton, OR 97005, (503)643-7092; **BUS ADD:** 10550 SW Allen Blvd., Beaverton, OR 97075, (503)643-9461.

LILLYDAHL, Earl D.——**B:** June 10, 1930, Milwaukee, WI, *VP, RE*, First WI Mort. Co.; **PRIM RE ACT:** Broker, Attorney, Consultant, Developer, Builder, Property Manager, Lender, Owner/Investor; **SERVICES:** Devel. Sales & Mgmt. of income props., land, condos, and workout props.; **PREV EMPLOY:** VP RE Mort. Assoc. Inc., Dir. Sec. & Counsel Lillydahl Realty Corp., & Commonwealth Land Corp.; **PROFL AFFIL & HONORS:** WI Bar Assn., Nat. Assn Realtors, WI Realtors Assn., Milw. Bd. of Realtors, Inst. of RE Mgt., Nat. Review Appraisers, WI Mort. Bankers, WI Mgr. of yr 1970, IREM, Past Pres. WI IREM, Dir. of Milw Bd. of Realtors; **EDUC:** BA, 1952, Govt., Hist., Soc., Cornell Univ.; **GRAD EDUC:** LLB, 1957, Univ. of WI; **MIL SERV:** USN, Lt. j.g.; **OTHER ACT & HONORS:** Milw. Public Schools RE Educ. Comm., Bldg. Comm. of Milw. School of Engrg.; **HOME ADD:** 1629 E. Blackthorne Pl., Milwaukee, WI 53211, (414)332-2333; **BUS ADD:** 777E WI Ave., Milwaukee, WI 53202, (414)765-4844.

LIMA, Salvatore A.——**B:** Feb. 6, 1937, San Francisco, CA, *Part.*, Hunt, Gram & Lima, Attys.; **PRIM RE ACT:** Attorney, Instructor, Owner/Investor; **REP CLIENTS:** Synds. of RE Prop. Limited Partnerships, Buyers and Sellers of RE Prop.; **PREV EMPLOY:** CPA; **PROFL AFFIL & HONORS:** State Bar of CA, ABA; **EDUC:** BBA Golden Gate Univ., 1964, Accounting/Bus. Admin.; **GRAD EDUC:** J.D., LLM., Tax, 1968, 1971, Univ. of San Fran. School of Law, NY Univ.; **OTHER ACT & HONORS:** RE Broker, Pres. Student Bar Assn. (1968), Moot Court (1968); **HOME ADD:** 37 El Camono Dr., Corte Madera, CA 94925, (415)924-3200; **BUS ADD:** 1 Market Plaza, Spear Tower, Ste. 2210, San Francisco, CA 94105, (415)777-0300.

LIMEHOUSE, Harry Bancroft, Jr.——**B:** Dec. 3, 1938, Charleston, SC, *Pres.*, Limehouse Properties; **PRIM RE ACT:** Broker, Consultant, Developer, Owner/Investor, Property Manager, Syndicator; **SERVICES:** Synd., consulting, devel., investing; **PREV EMPLOY:** Republican Nat. Comm. Campaign Dir., 1969-71; White House staff, 1969, Prudential Ins. Co., Dir. Mgr., 1962-70; **PROFL AFFIL & HONORS:** Home Builders Assn., Dir., 1972; Comml. Investment & Props. Council; Pres. Ressi, Carolinas, CCIM Designate; **EDUC:** 1960, Bus. Admin., The Citadel, The Mil. Coll. of SC, Charleston; **EDUC HONORS:** Dean's List; **OTHER ACT & HONORS:** Charleston Tennis Club, Hibernian Soc.; **HOME ADD:** Airy Hall Plantation, Green Pond, SC 29446, (803)844-8420; **BUS ADD:** 8 Cumberland St., Charleston, SC 29401, (803)577-6242.

LINANE, William E.——**B:** Apr. 15, 1928, Chicago, IL, *Pres.*, Linane & Co., Inc.; **PRIM RE ACT:** Broker, Developer, Syndicator; **SERVICES:** Nationwide Specialists in the Brokerage and Devel. of Distribution Facilities.; **PROFL AFFIL & HONORS:** NAR, IL Assn. of Realtors, Chicago RE Board and Assn. of Indus. RE Brokers, Assn. of Indus. RE Brokers (Dir); **EDUC:** BS, 1952, Bus. Adm., Major in Transp. Mgmt., Northwestern University; **GRAD EDUC:** MBA, 1964, Econ., Univ. of Chicago; **HOME ADD:** 5310 N. Chester Ave., Chicago, IL 60656, (312)693-3222; **BUS ADD:** 9801 W. Higgins Rd., Rosemont, IL 60018, (312)692-5650.

LINBURN, Michael R.——**B:** Aug. 27, 1933, New York, NY, *VP*, The Balcor Co.; **PRIM RE ACT:** Syndicator; **OTHER RE ACT:** Mktg. (wholesaling); **SERVICES:** Mktg. of RE snyds.; **REP CLIENTS:** Most major NY stock exchange firms; **PREV EMPLOY:** Oppenheimer Prop., Inc.; Shearson Hammill & Co., Inc.; **PROFL AFFIL & HONORS:** Former Gov. of RESSI; **EDUC:** BS, 1954, Indus. Admin., Yale Univ.; **GRAD EDUC:** MBA, 1959, Fin., Harvard Bus. School; **EDUC HONORS:** Tau Beta Pi; **MIL SERV:** USA, 1st Lt.; **OTHER ACT & HONORS:** Yale Club of NY City, Skating Club of NY City. Harvard Club of Boston; **HOME ADD:** 1125 Park Ave., Apt. 10A, New York, NY 10028, (212)860-2409; **BUS ADD:** 122 E. 42d St., 17th Floor, New York, NY 10068, (212)986-9090.

LINCOLN, Walter Stephen, II——**B:** Nov. 19, 1932, Chicago, IL, *Asst. VP, Mgr. Design Serv.*, Urban Investment & Development Co.; **PRIM RE ACT:** Architect, Developer, Builder; **REP CLIENTS:** Our own projects; Water Tower Place, Chicago; Copley Place, Boston; City Place, Hartford; One Logan Sq., Philadelphia; First City Tower, Houston; Energy Center I, II & III, Denver; 333 W. Wacker, Chicago; **PREV EMPLOY:** Metropolitan Structures 1973-79, New Community Enterprises 1970-1973; **PROFL AFFIL & HONORS:** AIA Corp.; Lambda Alpha; Ely Chap., Chicago; **EDUC:** AB, 1954, Harvard Coll.; **GRAD EDUC:** MArch., 1961, Harvard Univ.; **EDUC HONORS:** Cum Laude; **MIL SERV:** US Army (C.E.), Sgt., 1954-56; **HOME ADD:** 415 Washington, Glencoe, IL 60022, (312)835-0354; **BUS ADD:** 845 N MI, Chicago, IL 60611, (312)440-3446.

LIND, H. Robert——**B:** Jan. 17, 1944, Boston, MA, *Pres.*, Lind, Larraguibel & Co., Inc.; **PRIM RE ACT:** Consultant; **OTHER RE ACT:** Intl. bus. consult. and invest. banker; **SERVICES:** Money mgmt., intl. bus. consult., RE invest. service; **REP CLIENTS:** Lat. Amer. clients; **PREV EMPLOY:** Chemical Bank, Allied Bank Intl. - VP; **PROFL AFFIL & HONORS:** Pan Amer. Soc. - other bank memberships; **EDUC:** BA Latin Amer. Affairs, 1968, Univ. of PA; **GRAD EDUC:** LaSalle Univ. - RE, 1971, LaSalle Univ. - Chicago, IL; **EDUC HONORS:** Universidad de las Americas, Mexico - Sr. yr. 1st Semester; **OTHER ACT & HONORS:** Pres. Elect - Puerto Rico C of C in the U.S.; **HOME ADD:** 26 Ferris Hill Rd., New Canaan, CT 06840, (203)966-7460; **BUS ADD:** 630 Fifth Ave. at Rockefeller Center, New York, NY 10020.

LINDBERG, Craig J.——**B:** May 7, 1948, Fargo, ND, *Dir. of RE Mgmt.*, W. Lyman Case & Co.; **PRIM RE ACT:** Broker, Consultant, Appraiser, Property Manager; **SERVICES:** Prop. mgmt., leasing, brokerage, consulting; **REP CLIENTS:** Prudential Life Insurance Co., Greit, Red Roof Inns, Planned Communities, Schottenstein Investment Co.; **PROFL AFFIL & HONORS:** IREM, Intl. Council of Shopping Ctrs. BOMA, NAR, OAR; **EDUC:** BBA, 1970, Fin., OH Univ.; **MIL SERV:** US Army, Spec. 5; **OTHER ACT & HONORS:** OH Univ. Alumni Assn., Columbus C of C; **HOME ADD:** 219 Waterford Dr., Dublin, OH 43017, (614)889-8359; **BUS ADD:** 23 N. Fourth St., Columbus, OH 43215, (614)228-5484.

LINDBERG, Dexter Clayton——**B:** May 12, 1938, Edmonton, CAN, *VP*, Genstar Devel. Inc., Land & Housing; **PRIM RE ACT:** Developer, Builder, Property Manager; **SERVICES:** Devel. of land, income prop., and housing; **PREV EMPLOY:** Controller, Tr., Corp. Sec. & Corp. Prop. Mgr., with predecessor companies; **PROFL AFFIL & HONORS:** Soc. of Mgmt. Accountants, Appraisal Inst. of Can.; International Institute of Valuers, RIA; **EDUC:** 1966, Acctg., Univ. of Alberta Extension Branch, Soc. of Mgmt. Accountants; **HOME ADD:** 2368 Lariat Ln., Walnut Creek, CA 94596, (415)934-0119; **BUS ADD:** Suite 3900, Four Embarcadero Ctr., San Francisco, CA 94111, (415)986-7200.

LINDBERG, Steven C.——**B:** Oct. 20, 1955, Melrose Park, IL, *Atty.*, Self-employed; **PRIM RE ACT:** Attorney; **SERVICES:** Mort. foreclosures, RE closing, fin. transactions; **REP CLIENTS:** Unity Savings Assn.; Harriscorp Fin., Inc.; Citicorp Person to Person to Person Fin. Ctr., Inc.; Citicorp Homeowners Inc.; Citicorp Acceptance Corp.; **PROFL AFFIL & HONORS:** IL State Bar; FL State Bar;

Chicago Bar Assn.; Comml. Law League; Amer. Trial Lawyers Assn.; ABA; **EDUC:** BA, 1976, Pol. Sci./Criminal Justice, Univ. of IL; **GRAD EDUC:** JD, 1980, The John Marshall Law School; **EDUC HONORS:** Grad. with Univ. Honors; **HOME ADD:** 215 Franklin Ave., River Forest, IL 60305, (312)366-5862; **BUS ADD:** 53 W. Jackson Blvd., Suite 1250, Chicago, IL 60604, (312)663-5316.

LINDEMAN, J. Bruce——B: June 17, 1941, Wash., DC, *H. Clyde Buchanan Professor of RE*, University of AR at Little Rock, Coll. of Bus. Admin.; **PRIM RE ACT:** Broker, Consultant, Instructor, Real Estate Publisher; **OTHER RE ACT:** RE Computer Applications; **SERVICES:** Consulting, market studies, office and firm management, microcomputer programming for RE bus., prop. analysis; **REP CLIENTS:** Devels., planning firms, brokerage firms; **PREV EMPLOY:** Assoc. Prof. of RE & Urban Affairs, GA State Univ., 1967-1975; **PROFL AFFIL & HONORS:** AREUEA, Realtor-Assoc., Phi Beta Kappa, a number of profl. awards; **EDUC:** BA Cum Laude, 1964, Econs., Syracuse Univ.; **GRAD EDUC:** PhD, 1968, Econs., Land Use, Duke Univ.; **EDUC HONORS:** Phi Beta Kappa, Woodrow Wilson Honorary Fellow; **HOME ADD:** 1724 S. Fillmore, Little Rock, AR 72204, (501)666-2069; **BUS ADD:** 33rd & Univ., Little Rock, AR 72204, (501)569-3354.

LINDENAU, Judith Wood——B: May 22, 1941, Zanesville, OH, *Exec. VP*, Traverse City Bd. of Realtors; **OTHER RE ACT:** RE Assn., Mgr.; **SERVICES:** Multiple Listing, Educ., Consumer Protection; **PROFL AFFIL & HONORS:** Amer. Soc. of Assn. Execs.; MI Soc. of Assn. Exec.; MI. Exec. Officers Council (Pres.), GRI; **EDUC:** BA, 1963, Eng., Music, Baldwin-Wallace Coll., Borea, OH; **GRAD EDUC:** MA, 1964, Eng., Univ. of SD; **EDUC HONORS:** Who's Who in Colls. and Univs., Teaching Fellow; **OTHER ACT & HONORS:** Township Supervisor, 2 yrs., City Planning Commn. 3 yrs., Unitarian-Universalist Fellowship (Pres.) Acad. of Amer. Poets; **BUS ADD:** 852 Garfield Ave., Traverse City, MI 49684, (616)947-2050.

LINDENBERG, Donald L.——B: Jan. 23, 1927, NY; **PRIM RE ACT:** Broker, Consultant, Developer, Lender, Owner/Investor, Syndicator; **HOME ADD:** PO Box 486, Geneva, IL 60134; **BUS ADD:** 300 W. Wash. St., Chicago, IL 60606, (312)641-3300.

LINDER, Dale A.——B: July 19, 1947, NY, NY, *Assoc.*, Choate, Hall & Stewart; **PRIM RE ACT:** Attorney; **PROFL AFFIL & HONORS:** MA Bar Assn.; Boston Bar Assn.; MA Conveyancers Assn.; **EDUC:** 1975, NY Univ.; **GRAD EDUC:** 1979, Boston Univ. Law Sch.; **EDUC HONORS:** Cum Laude; **OTHER ACT & HONORS:** Justice of the Peace, Marshfield, VT 1975-79; **HOME ADD:** 40 Commonwealth Ave., Boston, MA 02116, (617)247-2212; **BUS ADD:** 60 State St., Boston, MA 02116, (617)227-5020.

LINDHOLM, Albert——*Pres.*, Vermont Land and Development, Inc.; **PRIM RE ACT:** Developer; **EDUC:** BSME, 1956, Univ. of VT; **BUS ADD:** POB 63, Jericho, VT 05465.

LINDLEY, Jonathan——*Exec. VP*, Natl. Savings and Loan League; **PRIM RE ACT:** Banker; **BUS ADD:** 1101 15th St., NW, Washington, DC 20005, (202)331-0270.*

LINDQUIST, Warren T.——*New Comm. Devel. Corp. Gen. Mgr.*, Department of Housing and Urban Development, Ofc. of Secy./Under Secy; **PRIM RE ACT:** Lender; **BUS ADD:** 451 Seventh St., S.W., Washington, DC 20410, (202)755-7920.*

LINDSEY, Curtis L.——B: June 12, 1925, W. Helena, AR, *Chief, Cost Evaluation Branch*, Dept. of HUD, Housing; **PRIM RE ACT:** Appraiser; **OTHER RE ACT:** Mort. Ins.; **SERVICES:** RE Appraising; **REP CLIENTS:** Lenders, Investors, and Indivs.; **PREV EMPLOY:** Self employed, RE Appraising, Const.; **PROFL AFFIL & HONORS:** SREA & NARA, Who's Who in Finance and Industry, 1979-80 Ed., SRA, Outstanding Performance Award (HUD); **EDUC:** BA, 1974, Econ.-Bus. Admin., Park Coll., Kansas City, MO; **MIL SERV:** USA, SFC, Bronze Star Medal Combat Inf. Badge; **OTHER ACT & HONORS:** VFW; **HOME ADD:** 7115 Caenen, Shawnee, KS 66216, (913)268-7691; **BUS ADD:** 1103 Grand Ave., Prof. Bldg., Kansas City, MO 64106.

LINDSHIELD, Dennis——B: Feb. 15, 1942, L.A., CA, *Pres.*, Western Land Inc.; **PRIM RE ACT:** Broker, Syndicator, Developer, Owner/Investor; **PREV EMPLOY:** Eric Petterson Broker 1979-80; **EDUC:** BA, 1963, Acctg., Univ. of Redlands; **GRAD EDUC:** MBA, 1965, MBA-RE, USC; **BUS ADD:** PO Box 2456, Escondido, CA 92025, (714)747-3434.

LINDSTROM, Rodney B.——B: June 19, 1948, New Rockford, ND, *Sec.*, Surety Title Co.; **PRIM RE ACT:** Broker, Property Manager, Insuror; **OTHER RE ACT:** Abstracter; **EDUC:** BA, 1971, Acctg., Minot State Coll.; **MIL SERV:** ND Nat. Guard, E-6, 1970-76; **OTHER ACT & HONORS:** Amer. Legion, Kiwanis, Eagles, Volunteer Fire Dept. Chief, Volunteer Ambulance Squad; **HOME ADD:** 604 2nd Ave. N, New Rockford, ND, (701)947-5396; **BUS ADD:** Box 551 523 Central Ave., New Rockford, ND 58356, (701)947-2446.

LINDWALL, Gregory B.——B: Nov. 23, 1942, Minneapolis, MN, *Sr. Assoc. Counsel*, St. Paul Title Insurance Corp.; **PRIM RE ACT:** Attorney; **PREV EMPLOY:** Examiner of Titles of Anoka Cty., MN (1973-1978); **PROFL AFFIL & HONORS:** MN State Bar Assn.; Real Prop. Sect. of MSBA; **EDUC:** BS, 1968, Econ. and Pol. Sci., Mankato State Coll., Mankato, MN; **GRAD EDUC:** JD, 1971, Univ. of MN Law School, Minneapolis, MN; **HOME ADD:** 5711 West 235th St., Farmington, MN 55024, (612)463-4399; **BUS ADD:** 1900 American National Bank Bldg., St. Paul, MN 55101, (612)221-9591.

LINEWEAVER, Wilford——*Pres.*, Unifi, Inc.; **PRIM RE ACT:** Property Manager; **BUS ADD:** PO Box 21368, Greensboro, NC 27420, (919)294-4410.*

LINIGER, David——B: Sept. 25, 1945, Marion, IN, *Chmn. of the Bd.*, RE/MAX of Amer., Inc.; **PRIM RE ACT:** Broker, Consultant, Owner/Investor, Instructor, Syndicator; **SERVICES:** RE franchising; **PROFL AFFIL & HONORS:** NAR; CO Assn. of Realtors; RESSI, Broker; CRB; **MIL SERV:** USAF, Staff Sgt.; **HOME ADD:** 10266 E. Fair Place, Englewood, CO 80110, (303)779-0915; **BUS ADD:** 5251 S. Quebec, Englewood, CO 80111, (303)770-5531.

LINK, Dennis——B: Oct. 4, 1946, Pittsburgh, PA, *Pres.*, Leaf Enterprises, Inc.; **PRIM RE ACT:** Consultant, Appraiser, Developer, Builder, Owner/Investor, Property Manager, Syndicator; **SERVICES:** Prop. mgmt., consultation, synd., devel.; **REP CLIENTS:** US Dept. of HUD,, City of Pittsburgh, various corp. & Inst. Devels.; **PREV EMPLOY:** Dept. of HUD (1977-1980); **PROFL AFFIL & HONORS:** Los Angeles Planning Commn., AID Council on Intl. Devel., N.E. Rgnl. Devel. Comm.; **EDUC:** BA, Econ., 1968, UCLA; **GRAD EDUC:** MBA, 1970, Mktg./Mgmt., Harvard Bus. Sch.; **EDUC HONORS:** Magna Cum Laude, Sloan Honors; **MIL SERV:** USA, Adj. Gen., Capt., DMG, DFC; **HOME ADD:** 109 Rama Rd., Beaver Falls, PA 15010, (412)842-8283; **BUS ADD:** 109 Rama Rd., Beaver Falls, PA 15010, (412)843-8283.

LINQUIST, Lee R.——*Mort. Loan Officer*, The Security National Bank of Sioux City, Iowa, Real Estate Dept.; **PRIM RE ACT:** Banker; **SERVICES:** Resid. mort., const. loans, & interim fin.; **REP CLIENTS:** Indiv. or comml. borrowers on a local level; **PROFL AFFIL & HONORS:** Amer. Bankers Assn.; Mort. Bankers Assn., Grad., Nat. School of RE Fin. OH State Univ.; **EDUC:** BS, 1974, Bus. Admin. & Econ., Morningside Coll.; **BUS ADD:** P.O. Box 147, Sioux City, IA 51101, (712)277-6532.

LINTZ, Robert H.——B: Dec. 6, 1927, Santa Barbara, CA, *Pres.*, Sterling Homes Corp.; **PRIM RE ACT:** Developer, Builder, Property Manager; **HOME ADD:** 2412 Mesa Dr., Santa Ana, CA 92707, (714)646-6850; **BUS ADD:** 19752 MacArthur Blvd., Suite 250, Irvine, CA 92715, (714)752-8200.

LINVILLE, George——B: Mar. 3, 1929, Live Oak, FL, *Sr. Pres.*, George M. Linville Corp.; **PRIM RE ACT:** Broker; **PROFL AFFIL & HONORS:** Advisory Bd., 1972-1980, Nat. Alliance of Businessmen of Jacksonville; Pres., 1977, Jacksonville Bd. of Realtors, 1981, Chmn. of Diamond Pin and Leadership Devel. Comms.; MLS of Jacksonville, Inc., 1969, Pres. and Chmn. of the Bd. of Gov.; FL Assn. of Realtors: 1981, Nominating and Profl. Standards Comm., 1980, VP and Dir., 1979, Dir., 1978, Dir., 1977, Dir., 1975, Chmn., Special Bicentennial Comm., 1971, Chmn., Public Relations for Annual Convention, 1969, Chmn., Realtor Public Relations Comm., 1968, Dir., 1965, Dir., 1965, Chmn., Educ. Comm. Member, 1962-1967, 1965, Dean of the Educ. Inst., 1965-1981, Founder, Member, Realtor Speaker's Bureau, 1964, Dir., 1972, Top Mgmt. Award from Sales and Mktg. Execs. of Jacksonville, FL; Jaycees Presid. Award of Honor, 1975; Charter Life Member Beaches Area Hist. Soc., Jacksonville Beach; **OTHER ACT & HONORS:** Pres., Chmn. of the Bd. and Founder, Amer. Bicentennial Commn. of Jacksonville, FL, Inc., 1972-1981; Past Member, FL Methodist Conf., Bicentennial Task Force; Founding Pres., Jacksonville Univ. Nat. Parents Assn., 1975-1977; Life Member, Past Dir. and Chmn. of Naval Affairs Comm., Jacksonville Council Navy League of the US, 1977-1981; Dir., Camp Fire Girls, 1973-1975; Greater Jacksonville Taxpayer's Assn., 1968-1971, VP, Govt. Relations, 1966-1971, Dir., 1969 - , Chmn., Cross FL Barge Canal Comm.; **BUS ADD:** 6842 St. Augustine Rd., Jacksonville, FL 32217.

LIPAWSKY, Edward J.——*Pres.*, Dentsply International Inc.; **PRIM RE ACT:** Property Manager; **BUS ADD:** 570 W. College Ave., York, PA 17404, (717)845-7511.*

LIPHART, George von——**B:** Aug. 9, 1946, NY, NY, *Exec. VP*, The Stearns Co.; **PRIM RE ACT:** Developer, Owner/Investor; **SERVICES:** Acquisition and devel. of comml. and indus. props. for direct ownership and in joint venture with other devel.; **REP CLIENTS:** Devel.; funds and instit. investors; **PREV EMPLOY:** VP, Acquisitions Unit, RE Investment Mgmt. Dept., Citibank; **PROFL AFFIL & HONORS:** ULI, NAIOP, Soc. of Indus. Realtors, ICSC; **EDUC:** AB, 1967, His., Harvard; **GRAD EDUC:** MBA, 1969, Bus. Admin., Harvard Grad. School; **EDUC HONORS:** Cum Laude; **HOME ADD:** 2866 Jackson St., San Francisco, CA 94115, (415)921-6367; **BUS ADD:** 505 Sansome St., S.F., CA 94111, (415)398-2643.

LIPMAN, Barry R.——**B:** Dec. 10, 1948, Brooklyn, NY, *Atty.*, Goldfarb & Lipman; **PRIM RE ACT:** Attorney; **SERVICES:** Representation before fed., state and local govts.; subdivision and dept. of RE applications; **REP CLIENTS:** Devel.; subdivs; invesotrs; lender; **PROFL AFFIL & HONORS:** Member of the CA and FL Bars, Juris Doctor, RE Broker; **EDUC:** BS, 1970, Fin., Econ., Univ. of PA; **GRAD EDUC:** JD, 1975, Hastings Coll. of Law; **HOME ADD:** 1820 Vallejo St., PH2, San Francisco, CA 94123, (415)441-2071; **BUS ADD:** La Salle Bldg., 9th & Washington St., Oakland, CA 94607, (415)839-6336.

LIPMAN, H.L.——**B:** Oct. 4, 1939, Boston, MA, *Owner*, Hilliard Lipman & Associates; **PRIM RE ACT:** Consultant, Appraiser; **SERVICES:** RE valuation & consultation; **REP CLIENTS:** Lenders, devel., attys. & indiv.; **PREV EMPLOY:** Philip E. Klein & Assoc., Partner, 1966-1972; Coldwell Banker, VP; **PROFL AFFIL & HONORS:** Member, Amer. Inst. of RE Appraisers; Intl. Right of Way Assn.; Member, ULI, MAI; Licensed RE Broker, State of CA; **EDUC:** AB, 1961, Hist./Poli. Sci., Bethany Coll.; **MIL SERV:** USN, Lt., Cuban & Viet. Expeditionary Medals, Sec. of Navy Unit Commen. Ribbon; **OTHER ACT & HONORS:** Young Friends of the San Diego Symphony; San Diego C of C; Past Pres., San Diego Chap., Amer. Inst. of RE Appraisers; **HOME ADD:** 1411 Seventh St., Coronado, CA 92118, (714)435-9361; **BUS ADD:** 319 Elm St., San Diego, CA 92101, (714)232-2801.

LIPNER, Jonathan——**B:** Apr. 13, 1953, Philadelphia, PA; **PRIM RE ACT:** Consultant, Owner/Investor; **EDUC:** BS, 1976, Acctg., Philadelphia Coll. of Textiles & Sci.; **HOME ADD:** PO Box 337, Bala Cynwyd, PA; **BUS ADD:** PO Box 337, Bala Cynwyd, PA 19004, (215)755-7112.

LIPNIK, Alvin P.——**B:** Oct. 1, 1929, Detroit, MI, *VP & Counsel*, Great Lakes Fed. S & L Assn.; **PRIM RE ACT:** Attorney, Lender; **SERVICES:** Total legal services to S & L Assn. including advice, negotiations, litigation, drafting documentation, etc.; **PREV EMPLOY:** VP Homewood Bldg. Co., Columbus OH; **PROFL AFFIL & HONORS:** State Bar of MI, Washtenaw Cty. Bar Assn., Member MI S & L League Atty's Comm (Past Chmn), R. Prop. Law Sec., MI St Bar; **EDUC:** BA, 1951, Econ., Univ. of MI; **GRAD EDUC:** LLB, 1954, Univ. of MI Law Sch.; **MIL SERV:** USN, Lt.; **OTHER ACT & HONORS:** Member Assessors Bd of Review, Ann Arbor, MI 1972&1975 (Past Chmn.); **HOME ADD:** 2610 Page Ct, Ann Arbor, MI 48104, (313)971-9373; **BUS ADD:** 401 E Liberty St, PO Box 8600, Ann Arbor, MI 48107, (313)769-8300.

LIPSCOMB, Sharon——**B:** Oct. 6, 1936, Bellingham, WA, *Owner-Broker*, Realty World - Lipscomb Realty; **PRIM RE ACT:** Broker, Consultant, Owner/Investor; **SERVICES:** Investment counciling; resid., land & comml. sales; **PROFL AFFIL & HONORS:** Whatcom Co. Bd. of Realtors; WA Assn. of Realtors; NAR; CCIM, CCIM; **EDUC:** BA, 1958, Educ., Biology, French, Principia Coll., Elsah, IL; **OTHER ACT & HONORS:** P.E.O.; **HOME ADD:** 1915 Eldridge, Bellingham, WA 98225, (206)676-9991; **BUS ADD:** 2900 Meridian, Bellingham, WA 98225, (206)734-6349.

LIPSHUTZ, Hal A.——**B:** Apr. 12, 1956, Chicago, IL, *Atty.*, McCoy & Morris; **PRIM RE ACT:** Attorney; **SERVICES:** Gen. RE practice and consultant; **REP CLIENTS:** S&L Assns., comml. investors, resid. investors, RE brokers; **PREV EMPLOY:** RE appraiser & salesman; **PROFL AFFIL & HONORS:** ABA; IL Bar Assn.; Nat. Assn. of Realtors, No. Side RE Bd.; Legislative & Tax Comm.; **EDUC:** BA, 1977, RE, Univ. of IL; **GRAD EDUC:** JD, 1980, Prop. Law, IL Inst. of Tech., Chicago Kent Coll. of Law; **EDUC HONORS:** Dean's List; **HOME ADD:** 2150 Valencia, Northbrook, IL, (312)291-1142; **BUS ADD:** 32 W Randolph, Suite 1014, Chicago, IL 60601, (312)372-4390.

LIPSICK, David M.——**B:** Mar. 17, 1951, Miami Beach, FL, *Pres.*, Lee Mgmt. Inc., Realtors; **PRIM RE ACT:** Broker, Syndicator, Developer, Property Manager, Owner/Investor; **SERVICES:** Prop. Mgmt., Comml. Leasing; Devel.; **REP CLIENTS:** Private Investors (intl. & domestic) FHA/HUD; **PROFL AFFIL & HONORS:** Miami Bd. Realtors; IREM; RESSI; **EDUC:** Mass Comm., Univ. FL; **OTHER ACT & HONORS:** Grievance Comm. Member - 11th Judicial Dist. - FL Bar; Franchise rights to Prime - PM - for Dade, Broward, Palm Beach Counties; Nationwide Property Management Network; **BUS ADD:** 13201 NE 16th Ave., N. Miami, FL 33181, (305)895-6930.

LIPSON, Jay H.——**B:** Sept. 27, 1920, Philadelphia, PA, *Realtor Appraiser*, Jay H. Lipson, Realtors; **PRIM RE ACT:** Broker, Appraiser, Instructor, Property Manager, Insuror; **PROFL AFFIL & HONORS:** Del. Cty. Bd/ of Realtors, PA Assn. of Realtors, Nat. Assoc. of RE Bd., SREA, AIREA, NARA, SRA, RM, CRA, AACA; **EDUC:** BS, 1950, RE Appraising, Temple Univ.; **GRAD EDUC:** Teacher, 1973-77, RE Inst., Temple Univ.; **EDUC HONORS:** Magna Cum Laude, Beta Gamma Sigma (Nat. Bus. Hon. Soc), Pi Gamma Mu (Nat. Soc. Serv. Hon. Soc.); **MIL SERV:** USA, Sgt., 3 Battle Stars, 5 Campaign Ribbons; **OTHER ACT & HONORS:** Pres W Philadelphia RE Bd., 1969, VP Philadelphia Bd. of Realtors, Temple Univ. Bd. of Mgrs. (VP), Pres Civic Assoc. Lynnewood, Pres. of 3 fraternal orgs.; **HOME ADD:** 1614 Rose Glen Rd., Upper Darby, PA 19083, (215)446-4687; **BUS ADD:** 8919 W Chester Pike, Upper Darby, PA 19082, (215)449-2600.

LIPSTEIN, Michael——**B:** June 8, 1936, NY, *Principal*, Michael Lipstein Realty and Construction; **PRIM RE ACT:** Consultant, Developer, Builder, Owner/Investor; **OTHER RE ACT:** Co-op princ.; **SERVICES:** Investments counseling, devel. of resid., retail and comml. props., workout of institutional foreclosed props.; **REP CLIENTS:** NY Tele. Co.; Whitlock Corp., NY; Bernland Corp., NY; Chacofi, Buenos Aires; **PREV EMPLOY:** Self-employed; **PROFL AFFIL & HONORS:** RE Bd. of NY, Young Men's RE Association; **EDUC:** BS, 1960, Arch. Engrg., Pratt; **GRAD EDUC:** Bernard Baruch, 1962, RE, CCNY; **MIL SERV:** US Army; Artilary; **OTHER ACT & HONORS:** B'nai B'rith; U.J.A. Federation; **HOME ADD:** 48 Potters Ln., Kings Point, NY; **BUS ADD:** 136 East 56th, New York, NY 10022, (212)688-5600.

LIPTMAN, Allen——*President*, Amalgamated Sugar Co.; **PRIM RE ACT:** Property Manager; **BUS ADD:** PO 1520, Odgen, VT 84402, (801)399-3431.*

LISLE, Robert W.——**B:** Aug. 18, 1927, Butler, MO, *VP*, The Prudential Ins. Co. of Amer., RE Investment Dept.; **PRIM RE ACT:** Consultant, Appraiser, Developer, Lender, Owner/Investor; **PREV EMPLOY:** 30 yrs. exp.; **PROFL AFFIL & HONORS:** AIREA; NACORE; ICSC; MBA; Amer. Motel & Hotel Assn.; Nat. Exec. Comm. of Nat. Inst. of Bldg. Sciences; **EDUC:** BS, 1950, Pub. Admin., Univ. of MO; **GRAD EDUC:** Exec. Mgmt., 1972, Columbia Univ., Grad. School of Bus.; **EDUC HONORS:** Citation of Merit Award, Alumni Assn.; **MIL SERV:** US, Inf., S/Sgt.; **HOME ADD:** 73 Kensington Rd., Basking Ridge, NJ 07920, (201)766-4830; **BUS ADD:** 20 Prudential Plaza, Newark, NJ 07101, (201)877-7550.

LISS, Jeffrey G.——**B:** Apr. 30, 1943, Chicago, IL, *Counsel*, Mangum, Beeler, Schad & Diamond; **PRIM RE ACT:** Attorney; **SERVICES:** Legal serv. in connection with RE transactions; **PROFL AFFIL & HONORS:** ABA; IL State Bar; Chicago Bar; **EDUC:** AB, 1965, Pol. Sci., Brown Univ.; **GRAD EDUC:** JD, 1968, Harvard Law School; LLM, 1981, Taxation, DePaul Coll. of Law; **OTHER ACT & HONORS:** Dir., Assoc. Alumni Brown Univ.; Council, RE Sect. ISBA; **HOME ADD:** 2812 Manor Dr., Northbrook, IL 60062, (312)564-2382; **BUS ADD:** 208 S. LaSalle St., Chicago, IL 60604, (312)726-8950.

LISS, Michael R.——**B:** July 22, 1955, Libertyville, IL, *Legal counsel*, John F. Amico & Coorp.; **PRIM RE ACT:** Attorney, Insuror; **SERVICES:** Legal counsel, ins. Procurement; **REP CLIENTS:** The Hair Performers Franchise System; **PROFL AFFIL & HONORS:** ABA; IL State Bar Assn.; Chicago Bar Assn.; **EDUC:** AB, 1977, Psych. & Phil., Univ. of IL, Champaign; **GRAD EDUC:** JD, 1980, Loyola Univ. of Chicago, Sch. of Law; **HOME ADD:** 611 W Barry Ave., Apt. 3W, Chicago, IL 60657, (312)477-7409; **BUS ADD:** 7327 W 90th St., Bridgeview, IL 60455, (312)430-2552.

LIST, Martin——*Pres.*, ML Properties, Inc.; **PRIM RE ACT:** Developer, Owner/Investor; **SERVICES:** Devel., owner/investor, land - banking; **EDUC:** BS, 1956, Columbia Univ.; **GRAD EDUC:** Doctoral, 1961; **BUS ADD:** Suite 407, 351 Hospital Rd., Newport Beach, CA 92663, (714)642-0864.

LITEPLO, Donald N.——B: Feb. 10, 1937, Radway, Alberta, Can, *Gen. Mgr.*, Donald N. Liteplo & Assocs. Ltd.; **PRIM RE ACT:** Broker, Consultant, Appraiser, Instructor; **SERVICES:** Investment Analysis, Real Prop. Valuation, Negotiation, Workshops; **REP CLIENTS:** Lenders, Corporate Investors & Devels.; **PREV EMPLOY:** Assoc. Prof. Univ. of Alberta, Responsible for RE Extension Program 1967-1970; **PROFL AFFIL & HONORS:** Soc. of RE Appraisers, Appraisal Inst. of CAN, Sr. RE Analyst, Accredited Appraiser Can. Inst.; **EDUC:** BA, 1960, Commerce, Univ. of Alberta; **GRAD EDUC:** MBA, 1972, Fin., Univ. of Alberta; **HOME ADD:** 3616-113A St., Edmonton, T6J1L4, Alberta, CAN, (403)435-2270; **BUS ADD:** 305 Strathcona Centre, Edmonton, T6E1X2, Alberta, CAN, (403)439-3242.

LITEWITZ, Robert——B: Nov. 14, 1919, *Developer*; **PRIM RE ACT:** Developer, Property Manager; **SERVICES:** Devel. shopping ctr., apartments, office bldgs.; **EDUC:** BA, 1938, Univ. of PA; **GRAD EDUC:** DDS, 1941, Univ. of IL; **HOME ADD:** 5189 Alton Rd., Miami Beach, FL 3314O, (305)866-7435; **BUS ADD:** 11469 SW 40 St., Miami, FL 33165, (305)552-5775.

LITKA, Michael P.——B: Nov. 22, 1930, Chicago, IL, *Professor*, U of Akron, College of Business Administration; **PRIM RE ACT:** Attorney, Owner/Investor, Instructor, Real Estate Publisher; **SERVICES:** Teaching and publishing; **PROFL AFFIL & HONORS:** Amer. Bus. Law Assn., Professor; **EDUC:** BA, 1953, Grinnell Coll.; **GRAD EDUC:** MA, JD, 1958, Univ. of IA; **HOME ADD:** 2370 Beechmour Dr., North Canton, OH 44720, (216)494-5311; **BUS ADD:** Akron, OH 44304, (216)375-7302.

LITOWITZ, Budd——B: Feb. 21, 1950, Miami Beach, FL, *Pres.*, Howitz, Fundora, Gen. Contractors, Lic. RE Broker; **PRIM RE ACT:** Broker, Consultant, Developer, Property Manager; **OTHER RE ACT:** Investment counseling, acquisitions advisor, brokerage specializing in shopping ctrs., prop. mgmt., const., leasing, gen. contracting; **REP CLIENTS:** Mgr. for inst. owners of comml. props., exclusive advisor for acquisition of income producing props., S. Amer. funds, contr. specializing in comml. renovation, alteration & new constrc. shopping ctr. devel. & brokerage; **PROFL AFFIL & HONORS:** ICSC; FL Gen. Contractor; Miami Bd. of Realtors; Legislative Comm. Member; **EDUC:** BS, 1971, Operations Research/Econ./City Planning, Cornell Univ., Coll. of Engrg.; **EDUC HONORS:** Dean's List; **HOME ADD:** 12001 S.W. 97 St., Miami, FL, (305)595-6814; **BUS ADD:** 11475 SW 40th St., Miami, FL 33165, (305)553-8581.

LITT, Robert D.——B: Oct. 3, 1930, Brooklyn, NY, *CEO*, Assoc. Capital Mgmt. Corp.; **PRIM RE ACT:** Syndicator, Consultant, Property Manager, Owner/Investor; **OTHER RE ACT:** Chief Exec. of Co., Handle also detailed Pre- Acquisition Reports for Owners; **SERVICES:** Mgmt., Pre- Acquisiton, Rehabiltiation, Full Line Mgmt. Service; **REP CLIENTS:** Numerous Ltd. Part.; **PREV EMPLOY:** VP Danac RE Investment Corp. Bethseda MD; Past Dir. of Prop. Mgmt. VGB Prop. Wash. DC; Dir. RE of Planning Research Corp.; **PROFL AFFIL & HONORS:** Past Assoc. Member AIA, Founding Member of Soc. of REAL Prop. Admin.; **EDUC:** Assoc. in Applied Sci., 1955, Engrg.-Arch., NY State Univ; **MIL SERV:** US Army; Cpl., Korean Service Medal, United Nations Medal; **OTHER ACT & HONORS:** Past Pres., Woodhollow, CT Town House Assn.; **HOME ADD:** 1100 E. Berkley, Richardson, TX 75081, (214)644-6155; **BUS ADD:** Park Forest Plaza, Suite 300-3530 Forest Lane, Dallas, TX 75234, (214)351-1035.

LITTELL, Jeffrey D.——B: June 23, 1954, Lansing, MI, *Asset Mgr.*, Westfield Development Co., Indus.; **PRIM RE ACT:** Developer; **OTHER RE ACT:** Devel., asset mgmt.; **PREV EMPLOY:** Norris, Beggs & Simpson, Los Angeles Office; **PROFL AFFIL & HONORS:** NAIOP; **EDUC:** BS, 1976, Acctg., Univ. of S. CA; **EDUC HONORS:** Student Serv. Award; **HOME ADD:** 1662 Bimini Pl., Costa Mesa, CA 92626; **BUS ADD:** 17802 Skypark Cir., Suite 104, Irvine, CA 92714, (714)979-3900.

LITTIN, Obee O'Brien——B: Oct. 24, 1928, NY, NY, *Pres.*, Littin, Inc.; **PRIM RE ACT:** Broker, Consultant, Owner/Investor, Property Manager; **SERVICES:** Gen. resid. and comml. RE brokerage; **PREV EMPLOY:** Formerly VP Sales for Reuter's Inc. Realtors, 1976-77; Realtor Assoc. H.A. Gill & Son. Realtors, 1972-76; Beckey Owne Props., 1971-72; Dorothy K. Winston, Realtors, 1971; **PROFL AFFIL & HONORS:** NAR, Washington Bd. of Realtors, Montgomery Cty. Bd. of Realtors, Chmn Leg. Comm., Washington Bd. of Realtors, Outstanding Contribution Award of Recognition, Republican Nat. Comm., 1970, Pres. Metropolitan Fed. Rep. Women's Club, 1967-68, NY, NY; **EDUC:** BA, 1948, Lib. Arts., Psych., Umiv. Coll., Cork, Ireland; **GRAD EDUC:** Studies, 1951, Psych., Fordham Univ., NY, NY; **OTHER ACT & HONORS:** Elected Member Republican Central Comm., Washington DC, AFTRA, Catholic Actor's Guild, Nat. Fed. of Republican Women, Congressional Ctry. Club, Nat. Assn. of TV Arts & Sci.; **HOME ADD:** 5105 Duvail Dr., Bethesda, MD 20816, (301)229-8225; **BUS ADD:** 4545 42nd St., NW, Washington, DC 20016, (202)686-6810.

LITTLE, Carol Cordl——B: July 6, 1945, Memphis, TN, *Pres.*, Security Pacific Development, Inc.; **PRIM RE ACT:** Consultant, Developer, Syndicator; **SERVICES:** Full-serv. devel. of conventional and FHA multi-family props.; consultant for fin. and synd. devels.; prop. and land owners; **PREV EMPLOY:** Security Pacific, Inc., VP Devel. 1978-1981, UMIC Housing Devel Corp., Devel. Mgr. 1975-1978, New South Investment Corp., 1973-1975, Consultant to Housing Corp. of Diocese of Memphis, 1975-1978; **EDUC:** Memphis State Univ., 1978, Hist.; **HOME ADD:** 2920-74th Ave. SE, Mercer Island, WA 98040, (206)232-7867; **BUS ADD:** 2030 First Ave., Seattle, WA 98121, (206)623-3851.

LITTLE, Ford D., Jr.——B: Jan. 17, 1925, Commerce, GA, *Pres.*, Select I Yost & Little Realty & Ins. Co.; **PRIM RE ACT:** Broker, Appraiser, Owner/Investor, Property Manager, Insuror; **SERVICES:** Brokerage, resid. & comml., appraising, mgmt.; **REP CLIENTS:** Indiv., Third Party Relocation Firms; **PROFL AFFIL & HONORS:** NAR, NC Assn. of Realtors, Greensboro Bd. of Realtors, Independent Fee Appraisers, Nat. Assn. of Independent Ins. Agents, IFA; **EDUC:** BS, 1948, Econ., Bus., Davidson Coll.; **MIL SERV:** US Army Tank Corps., S/Sgt., European Theatre, 2 stars, Combat Infantry Badge; **OTHER ACT & HONORS:** V Chmn. Greensboro Zoning Comm., 6 yrs.; Greensboro Kiwanis Club, Pres. 1972; Greensboro Jr. C of C; Greensboro Realtor of Yr., 1960; Treas. & VP of NC Assn. of Realtors; **HOME ADD:** 2108 Carlisle Rd., Greensboro, NC 27408, (919)273-7653; **BUS ADD:** 113 N Green St., PO Box 1198, Greensboro, NC 27402, (919)272-0151.

LITTLE, Jack M.——B: Feb. 1, 1922, Mt. Clemens, MI, *Pres. of Myglo Corp., Exec. VP of Blanco Investments & Land, Ltd.*; **PRIM RE ACT:** Developer, Owner/Investor, Property Manager, Syndicator; **OTHER RE ACT:** Const. mgmt.; **PREV EMPLOY:** Aerojet-General Corp., Digital Logic Corp., Central Computer Corp., Own Public Acct. Practice; **PROFL AFFIL & HONORS:** Amer. Soc. of Ins. Mgmt., Inst. of Internal Auditors, Soc. of CA Accountants, P.A. (Public Accountant); **EDUC:** BS (FL Southern Coll.), 1952, Acctg., Cleary Coll. (1941-1943) FL So. Coll. (1952); **EDUC HONORS:** Graduate of the Year - 1942 (Cleary Coll.); **MIL SERV:** USAF, 1043-53, Capt., Air Medal & 4 Oakleaf Clusters; **OTHER ACT & HONORS:** VP, Rescue Elementary School Bd. - 1965-1966, Christian Bus. Men's Comm., Gold Medal Club of Athletes-in-Action, Masonic Lodge; **HOME ADD:** 712 E. Riverdale, Orange, CA 92665, (714)637-6438; **BUS ADD:** P O Box 1, East Irvine, CA 92650(both), (714)770-9661.

LITTLE, Justin F.——B: May 24, 1949, Mount Holly, NJ, *Assoc. Dir. of Community Devel.*, City of Wilmington, Devel. Programs; **PRIM RE ACT:** Developer, Lender; **OTHER RE ACT:** Gov. Redev.; **SERVICES:** Rehabilitation Fin. (resid.), Fixed asset fin., (Comml. and Indus.); **REP CLIENTS:** Low-and-moderate income homeowners, Housing devel., Businesses with deals <$500,000; **PREV EMPLOY:** NC RE Broker; **PROFL AFFIL & HONORS:** NC Community Devel. Assoc., Amer. Planning Assoc.; **EDUC:** BA, 1971, Amer. Studies, Amherst Coll.; **GRAD EDUC:** Masters City Planning, 1975, Harvard Univ.; **EDUC HONORS:** Magna cum Laude, Phi Beta Kappa; **OTHER ACT & HONORS:** Cape Fear Farmer's Mktg. Assoc.; **HOME ADD:** 1820 Chestnut, Wilmington, NC 28405, (919)762-0520; **BUS ADD:** PO Box 1810, Wilmington, NC 28405, (919)763-3931.

LITTLEFIELD, Douglas C.——B: Nov. 19, 1945, Hackensack, NJ, *Pres.*, Littlefield Real Estate, Inc.; **PRIM RE ACT:** Broker, Consultant, Developer, Owner/Investor, Syndicator; **SERVICES:** Complete RE brokerage, feasibility studies, consultant mktg. and permit acquisitions; **REP CLIENTS:** Intl. indivs. and corp. clients; **PREV EMPLOY:** IT&T, Planning and Scheduling Analyst; **PROFL AFFIL & HONORS:** Nat., VT and N.W. VT Bds. of Realtors, Electronic Realty Assocs., Inc., Member - Governmental Affairs Comm.; **OTHER ACT & HONORS:** Tax Assessor - Jericho, VT 1976-1979, Lions Club, Advisor - BSA, Ethan Allen Club, Duck Unlimited; **HOME ADD:** Box 430, Jericho, VT 05465, (802)899-3361; **BUS ADD:** Radisson Hotel, Burlington, VT 05401, (802)864-0033.

LITTLEJOHN, Jean C.——B: May 22, 1917, Columbus, OH, *Sr. Admin. Officer*, Chemical Mort. Co.; **PRIM RE ACT:** Appraiser; **OTHER RE ACT:** Underwriter; **SERVICES:** Underwriter for Residential Loans - Review of Appraisals, and Credit Package; **PROFL AFFIL & HONORS:** MBA, SREA, Pres. - Local Chap., SREA, Several Who's Who - Publications; **OTHER ACT & HONORS:** Past Pres. Altrusa Club of Columbus; **HOME ADD:** 4270 Chaucer La., Columbus, OH 43220, (614)457-8754; **BUS ADD:** 101 E Town St., Columbus, OH 43215, (614)460-3227.

LITTLEWOOD, Donald G.——**B:** Sep. 20, 1937;, Bryn Mawr, PA, *Managing Consultant*, Littlewood, Westhead & Co.; **PRIM RE ACT:** Broker, Consultant, Appraiser, Banker, Property Manager; **SERVICES:** Mort. lending consultant to fin. instns.; mort. brokering; **REP CLIENTS:** Comml. banks, thrifts, RE devels.; **PROFL AFFIL & HONORS:** MBAA, Philadelphia Mort. Bankers; **EDUC:** BA, 1958, Econ., PA State Univ.; **MIL SERV:** US Army; **BUS ADD:** 175 Strafford Ave., Wayne, PA 19087, (215)687-6129.

LITTON, Claude J.——**B:** Feb. 6, 1935, Giessen, Germany, *Exec. V.P.*, Manhattan Prop. Co.; **PRIM RE ACT:** Broker, Attorney, Property Manager, Owner/Investor; **PREV EMPLOY:** Irving Trust Co., 1971-78; **PROFL AFFIL & HONORS:** Staten Is. Bar Assn., BOMA of Greater NY, RE Bd. of NY, Panelist, Amer. Arbitration Assn.; **EDUC:** BS, 1956, Mgmt., NYU; **GRAD EDUC:** JD, 1969, Law, Brooklyn Law School; **EDUC HONORS:** Admitted to NY Bar Assn, Dec.1969; **MIL SERV:** USAF, Capt. multi-engine pilot; **BUS ADD:** 295 5th Ave., New York, NY 10016, (212)685-0530.

LITUCHY, Harold——**B:** Feb. 15, 1926, New York, NY, *Pres.*, Halandia Construction Co.; **PRIM RE ACT:** Developer, Builder, Owner/Investor, Property Manager, Syndicator; **PROFL AFFIL & HONORS:** NYSARHO, Nat. Assn. of Housing and Redevel., Long Island Builders Assn., Lic. RE Broker, Cert. as Registered Apt. Mgr.; **EDUC:** BBA, 1949, Bus. Admin., Adelphi Univ.; **MIL SERV:** USN, WWII; **HOME ADD:** 167 Vermont Ave., Oceanside, NY 11572, (516)764-7515; **BUS ADD:** 3115 S. Long Beach Rd., Oceanside, NY 11572, (516)766-3732.

LIVELY, Gail L.——*Dir.*, Department of Housing and Urban Development, Training; **PRIM RE ACT:** Lender; **BUS ADD:** 451 Seventh St., S.W., Washington, DC 20410, (202)755-7113.*

LIVETT, Robert L.——**B:** Aug. 4, 1919, IL, *Dir. of RE*, Oshman Sporting Goods, Inc., RE; **PRIM RE ACT:** Broker, Consultant, Appraiser; **PREV EMPLOY:** VP McDonalds, Reg. Dir. RE Howard Johnson Co.; **PROFL AFFIL & HONORS:** Nat. Assn. of Review Appraisers; Intl. Coll. of RE Consulting Profls., NACORE, CRA; **HOME ADD:** 4014 Cedar Forest Dr., Kingwood, TX 77339, (714)358-0098; **BUS ADD:** 2302 Maxwell Ln., Houston, TX 77023, (713)928-3171.

LIVINGSTON, Bruce M.——*Pres.*, Woodward Governor Co.; **PRIM RE ACT:** Property Manager; **BUS ADD:** 5001 N. Second St., Rockford, IL 61101, (815)877-7441.*

LIVINGSTON, Craig Raymond——**B:** May 17, 1953, Teaneck, NJ, *Architect*, Craig Livingston and Assocs.; **PRIM RE ACT:** Architect, Developer, Builder; **SERVICES:** Design-build, const. mgmt.; **PREV EMPLOY:** I.M. Pei and Partners, Architect; Skidmore, Owings and Merrill, Architect; Edward Durell Stone Assocs., Architect.; **PROFL AFFIL & HONORS:** NY Soc. of Architects, Registered Architect, NY; Who's Who in the East; **EDUC:** BArch, 1976, Architecture, Pratt Inst. School of Arch.; **OTHER ACT & HONORS:** Consultant to Rockland Cty. Legislature; Member of Selection Comm. for Rockland Cty. Jail; **HOME ADD:** 55 Washburns Lane, Stony Point, NY 10980, (914)429-9303; **BUS ADD:** 55 Washburns Lane, Stony Point, NY 10980, (914)429-8303.

LIVINGSTON, David——**B:** June 9, 1949, Great Falls, MT, *Atty.*, Amer. Heart Assn., Counsel for Nat. Planned Giving; **PRIM RE ACT:** Attorney; **OTHER RE ACT:** Estate planning; **SERVICES:** Counseling in aspects of estate planning, esp. regarding charitable gift arrangements; **PREV EMPLOY:** Phillips Petroleum Co.; **EDUC:** BA, 1971, Soc. & His., E. TX State Univ.; **GRAD EDUC:** JD, 1977, Univ. of TX; MA, 1972, Mod. Amer./Black Hist. & Guidance Counseling, E. TX Univ.; **EDUC HONORS:** Alphi Chi, Dean's List, Grad. teaching fellowship; **MIL SERV:** USAF, Lt.; **HOME ADD:** 3333 Blackburn, The Terraces 212, Dallas, TX 75204; **BUS ADD:** 7320 Greenville Ave., Dallas, TX 75231, (214)750-5393.

LIVINGSTON, Edgar——**B:** Aug. 27, 1922, NY, NY, *VP*, Aspen Gardens Housing Corp.; **PRIM RE ACT:** Broker, Builder; **OTHER ACT & HONORS:** Hofstra Univ. Advisory Bd., Past Pres., VP Brookville Taxpayers Assoc.; **HOME ADD:** Woodland Rd., Old Brookville, NY 11545, (516)671-3450; **BUS TEL:** 12)426-1350.

LIVINGSTON, Frank H.——**B:** Aug. 25, 1935, Chicago, IL, *Sr. VP*, Draper and Kramer, Inc.; **PRIM RE ACT:** Property Manager; **SERVICES:** Resid. & Comml. Prop. Mgmt.; **REP CLIENTS:** Indiv. owners, banks, ins. cos., RE investment trusts, pension funds; **PROFL AFFIL & HONORS:** IREM, Chicago RE Bd., Nat. Assn. of RE Investment Trusts, Community Assns. Inst., Apt. BOMA of IL, CPM; **EDUC:** BS, 1957, Bus., Univ. of NC; **OTHER ACT & HONORS:** Highland Park Plan Commn.; **BUS ADD:** 33 W. Monroe St., Chicago, IL 60603, (312)346-8600.

LLANES, Ginger Akuna——**B:** Sept. 13, 1951, Honolulu, HI, *Principal Broker*, Llanes Realty & Management; **PRIM RE ACT:** Broker, Consultant, Owner/Investor, Property Manager, Syndicator; **OTHER RE ACT:** Exchangor; **REP CLIENTS:** Individual investors, Kona Bd. of Realtors, Hawaii Exchangors; **PROFL AFFIL & HONORS:** GRI; **EDUC:** BA, 1972, Psychology, CA State Univ.; **EDUC HONORS:** Cum Laude, Phi Kappa Phi; **OTHER ACT & HONORS:** Amer. Bus. Women's Assn.; Toastmasters; Kona Chamber of Commerce; **HOME ADD:** 745104 Palihiold Pl., Kailua-Kona, MI 96740, (808)329-1208; **BUS ADD:** PO Box 68, Kailua-Kona, HI 96740, (808)329-1208.

LLEWELLYN, Leonard F.——**B:** Oct. 13, 1933, Harlowton, MT, *Pres.*, Marco Beach Realty, Inc.; **PRIM RE ACT:** Broker, Consultant, Appraiser, Developer; **SERVICES:** Gen. RE, investment counseling, valuation, condo. devel. consultants; **REP CLIENTS:** Instl. investors from Europe and Can. in PUD's and condo. devel.; **PREV EMPLOY:** Broker and Franchised Dealer, Deltona Corp. (NYSE) in VA, DC, MD, NC, 1964-1974; **PROFL AFFIL & HONORS:** FIABCI; Nat. Assn. Salesmasters; Life Member of RPAC Intl. Institute of Valuers, Sr. Certified Valuer, Pres., Marco Island Area Bd. of Realtors; **EDUC:** 1955, EE, Eastern MT Coll. of Educ.; **MIL SERV:** USMC, Capt., Air Medal w/6 stars and several other medals; flew 156 combat missions in Vietnam; **OTHER ACT & HONORS:** Dir., 1st Nat. Bank of Naples; Dir., Collier Cty. Conservancy; Tr./Dir., Naples Hospital; Pres.-Elect, Marco Island C of C; Who's Who in Aviation; **HOME ADD:** 174 S. Collier Blvd., PH-E, Princess del Mar, Marco Island, FL 33937, (813)394-7959; **BUS ADD:** 207 N. Collier Blvd., Marco Island, FL 33937, (813)394-2505.

LLOYD, Brent L.——**B:** Nov. 4, 1947, Arlington, VA, *VP*, Winthrop Securities; **PRIM RE ACT:** Syndicator; **OTHER RE ACT:** Investor; **SERVICES:** Thru subsidiaries, Angeles Corp. provides fin. servs. and mgmt. of investment products and engages in various RE activites. FDI acts as gen. partner of several RE ltd. partnerships; **REP CLIENTS:** Leading nat. and rgnl. securities brokerage firms; **PREV EMPLOY:** VP, First Diversified Investments, Inc., Assoc. Dir., Nat. Corp. For Housing Part./NHP RE Securities, Inc. 1977-1981; **PROFL AFFIL & HONORS:** RE Securities and Synd. Inst., Intl. Assn. of Fin. Planners; **EDUC:** BS, 1969, Univ. of TN; **GRAD EDUC:** M.Ed.; MLA, 1971; 1972, Univ. of VA; Johns Hopkins Univ.; **EDUC HONORS:** Dean's List; **HOME ADD:** 5731 Waters Edge Landing Ct., Burke, VA 22015; **BUS ADD:** 603-05 King St., Alexandria, VA 22314, (703)548-0863.

LLOYD, Dennis W., CRB——**B:** July 1, 1939, Roseburg, OR, *Owner-Broker*, Evergreen Land Inc.; **PRIM RE ACT:** Broker, Consultant, Developer, Builder; **PROFL AFFIL & HONORS:** Realtor, RNMI, FLI, CRS; CBC; GRI; **MIL SERV:** US Navy Reserves, AEC-Ret., 1957-80; **OTHER ACT & HONORS:** Rotary; **HOME ADD:** 1011 NW Stavlite Pl., Grants Pass, OR 97526, (503)479-5655; **BUS ADD:** 505 NE 7th St., Grants Pass, OR 97526, (503)479-5555.

LLOYD, Frank——**B:** Dec. 3, 1939, Kansas City, MO, F.L. Contracting; **PRIM RE ACT:** Builder, Owner/Investor; **HOME ADD:** 3343 Agnes, Kansas City, MO 64128, (816)861-4144; **BUS ADD:** 2225 Olive 2nd Floor, Kansas City, MO 64127, (816)231-4163.

LLOYD, Jim——*Executive Search*, Inexco Oil; **PRIM RE ACT:** Property Manager; **BUS ADD:** 1100 Milam Bldg., Ste. 1900, Houston, TX 77002, (713)651-3300.*

LLOYD, Robert J.——**B:** Oct. 19, 1918, Jamestown, ND, *Deputy Asst. Sec. for Public Housing & Indian Housing - HUD*, Housing & Urban Devel.; **OTHER RE ACT:** Govt.; **PREV EMPLOY:** Lloyd Co's. Inc., Mankato, MN; **EDUC:** 1940, Bus., Univ. of MN; **MIL SERV:** US Navy, Lt. Comdr., 2 DFC, 5 Air Medals; **HOME ADD:** Rt. 6 Box 45, Mankato, MN 56001, (507)625-4945; **BUS ADD:** Dept. of HUD, Washington, DC, (202)755-6522.

LLOYD, Robert M.——**B:** Mar. 21, 1945, Lockport, NY, Sheppard, Mullin, Richter & Hampton; **PRIM RE ACT:** Attorney, Owner/Investor; **SERVICES:** Representation of lenders and investors; **REP CLIENTS:** Major banks and other inst. lenders; **PROFL AFFIL & HONORS:** Chmn., RE Fin., subsection, LA Cty Bar, 1980-81; Assn. of RE Attys.; **EDUC:** BS, 1967, Aerospace Engrg., Princeton Univ.; **GRAD EDUC:** JD, 1975, Law, Univ. of MI; **EDUC HONORS:** Cum Laude, Magna Cum Laude; **MIL SERV:** USMC, Capt.; **OTHER ACT & HONORS:** Instr., UCLA Extension; **HOME ADD:** 370 Cherry Dr., Pasadena, CA 91105, (213)258-6449; **BUS ADD:** 48th Fl., 333 S. Hope St., Los Angeles, CA 90071, (213)620-1780.

LLOYD, Ross J.——**B:** Jan. 27, 1943, Reading, PA, *Contributing Editor*, Warren, Gorham & Lamont, Inc.; **OTHER RE ACT:** Writer; **SERVICES:** author of all articles appearing in "RE Law Report";

PREV EMPLOY: Condo. Admin., Commonwealth of VA (1974-76); Agreement Negotiator, US Dept. of HUD, (1976-79); **EDUC:** BS, 1964, Biology, Albright Coll., Reading, PA; **GRAD EDUC:** JD, 1974, Law, Marshall-Wythe School of Law, Coll. of Wm. & Mary, Williamsburg, VA; **EDUC HONORS:** Law Review, St. George Tucker Soc.; **MIL SERV:** USMC, Capt., Navy Commendation Medal, Vietnamese Cross of Gallantry; Purple Heart; **HOME ADD:** 272 Walnut St., Brookline, MA 02146, (617)277-7317; **BUS ADD:** 203 Turnpike St., North Andover, MA 01845, (617)687-4170.

LOBAN, Michael L.——B: Dec. 20, 1944, Bridgeport, CT, *VP*, Graham Intl. Inc., RE; **PRIM RE ACT:** Broker, Attorney, Syndicator, Consultant, Developer, Owner/Investor; **OTHER RE ACT:** Developer; **SERVICES:** Investment counseling; Dev. of Comml. Prop.; **REP CLIENTS:** Individual and Institutional Investors; **PREV EMPLOY:** Crocker Nat. Bank - VP and Mgr. of RE Investments for Pension Funds (1978-1979); Wells Fargo Realty Advisors - VP (1973-1978); **PROFL AFFIL & HONORS:** DC Bar Assn., ABA, NARA, ULI; **EDUC:** BA, 1966, Econ., Boston Coll.; **GRAD EDUC:** JD, 1969, Law, Georgetown Law Ctr.; **EDUC HONORS:** Cum Laude; **HOME ADD:** 13759 Nogales St., Del Mar, CA 92014, (714)481-2114; **BUS ADD:** 2121 Palomar Airport Rd., Carlsbad, CA 92008, (714)438-1545.

LOCH, Bruce C.——B: Feb. 6, 1944, Allentown, PA, *Partner*, Loch & Wells Equity; **PRIM RE ACT:** Developer; **SERVICES:** Purchase, Zone, Package, Promote & Develop. Multi Family Sites; **PREV EMPLOY:** Licensed CPA and Partner in local CPA since 1971; **PROFL AFFIL & HONORS:** Amer. & PA Inst. of CPA's; Lehigh Valley Homebuilders Assn., CPA; **EDUC:** BA, 1967, Acctg./Fin., Drexel Univ.; **OTHER ACT & HONORS:** Member, Mayor's Task Force on Physical Devel., Member, City's Ad Hoc Comm. on Comprehensive Zoning Changes.; **HOME ADD:** 1881 Greenwood Rd., Allentown, PA 18103, (215)435-5833; **BUS ADD:** 1045 N 17th St., Allentown, PA 18104, (215)434-9641.

LOCKARD, Dale——*Manager Fac. Services*, AMP, Inc.; **PRIM RE ACT:** Property Manager; **BUS ADD:** 5000 Paxton St., Box 3608, Harrisburg, PA 17105, (717)564-0100.*

LOCKARD, William A.——B: Aug. 29, 1920, LA, *Owner*, Lockard Realty, Gen. RE; **PRIM RE ACT:** Broker, Assessor, Syndicator; **PREV EMPLOY:** RE, 25 yrs.; **EDUC:** Journalism/Acctg., LA State Univ.; Univ. of WY; **HOME ADD:** 1130 Devonshire Dr., Encinitas, CA 92024, (714)753-3074; **BUS ADD:** 560 E. Valley Pkwy., Suite 208, Escondido, CA 92025, (714)743-6365.

LOCKE, Michael P.——B: July 11, 1920, CA, *Pres.*, Locke Land Services, Inc.; **PRIM RE ACT:** Consultant, Appraiser; **SERVICES:** Real prop., appraisals, expert testimony; **REP CLIENTS:** US Postal Service, City of Long Beach, General Motors, Metro. Water District of S CA; **PREV EMPLOY:** Land Dept., S CA Gas Co.; **PROFL AFFIL & HONORS:** Soc. of RE Appraisers; Amer. Soc. of Appraisers; Natl. Assn. of Review Appraisers, SRA, ASA (Urban Realty), CRA; **EDUC:** BS, 1941, Engrg., CA Maritime Acad.; **MIL SERV:** USNR, Lt.; **OTHER ACT & HONORS:** Comml. arbitrator, Amer. Arbitration Assn. since l958; **BUS ADD:** 6754 Paramount Blvd., Long Beach, CA 90805, (213)634-2612.

LOCKEY, Melbourne D.——*Pres.*, Lockey Investment Co.; **PRIM RE ACT:** Broker, Developer; **PREV EMPLOY:** Lockey Investment Co.; **PROFL AFFIL & HONORS:** RNMI; NIR; NAR; IREBA, CCIM; **EDUC:** BA/AA, Mgmt., St. Mary's Coll./Coll. of San Mateo; **BUS ADD:** 1524 Perersen Ave., San Jose, CA 95129, (408)257-8119.

LOCKHART, Thomas A.——B: Apr. 5, 1928, Mecklenburg Cty., NC, *Pres.*, Cansler Lockhart Parker & Young, P.A.; **PRIM RE ACT:** Attorney; **SERVICES:** Title examinations, closing atty. for indus., comml. and resid. transactions; **REP CLIENTS:** Metropolitan Life Ins. Co.; Pboenix Mutual Life Ins. Co.; Pilot Life Ins. Co.; Charlotte Liberty Mututal Ins. Co.; indiv. purchasers and investors; **PROFL AFFIL & HONORS:** Assn. of Life Ins. Counsel; ABA; NC State Bar; NC Bar Assn.; **EDUC:** AB, 1949, Univ. of NC at Chapel Hill; **GRAD EDUC:** JD, 1951; **MIL SERV:** US Army, 1st Lt., Bronze Star; **HOME ADD:** 801 Ardsley Rd., Charlotte, NC 28207, (704)333-1035; **BUS ADD:** 1010 City Nat. Ctr., Charlotte, NC 28202, (704)372-1282.

LOCKWOOD, Samuel A.——*Nat'l. RE Mgr.*, United Parcel Service; **PRIM RE ACT:** Property Manager; **BUS ADD:** 51 Weaver St., Greenwich Office Park 5, Greenwich, CT 06830, (203)622-6000.*

LOCKWOOD, William R.——B: Mar. 24, 1944, Lafayette, LA, *Owner*, Lockwood and Associates; **PRIM RE ACT:** Broker, Consultant, Owner/Investor, Property Manager; **OTHER RE ACT:** Tax Analysis; **SERVICES:** Sales, Mgmt. for Clients Income Tax Preparation and Analysis; **PROFL AFFIL & HONORS:** Natl. Assn. of Income Tax Practitioners, Associated Brokers Listing Exchange, Gtr. Lansing C of C; **EDUC:** BA, 1966, Poli. Sci./Econs., Univ. of MI; **HOME ADD:** 2671 Greencliff, E Lansing, MI 48823, (517)332-0540; **BUS ADD:** 5918 Marsh Rd., Haslett, MI 48840, (517)339-2580.

LOEDDING, James A.——B: Aug. 26, 1931, NY, NY, *Owner*, James Loedding Co.; **PRIM RE ACT:** Broker, Consultant; **SERVICES:** Maj. investment prop., brokerage and consulting; **REP CLIENTS:** Indiv. and inst. investors, and major investment prop. owners; **PREV EMPLOY:** Stapleton Assoc., Ltd.; Cushman & Wakefield (Los Angeles); Crown Center Corp. (Kansas City); Ritchie & Ritchie (San Francisco); **PROFL AFFIL & HONORS:** NAR, RE Broker, Licensed CA and HI; **EDUC:** BS, 1953, Engrg., US Military Acad., West Point, NY; **GRAD EDUC:** JD, 1968, Law, Golden Gate Coll. Sch. of Law, San Francisco; **MIL SERV:** US Army, 1st Lt.; **HOME ADD:** 700 Richards St., Apt. 2603, Honolulu, HI 96813; **BUS ADD:** 700 Richards St. #2603, Honolulu, HI 96813, (808)521-1721.

LOEVIN, Robert H.——B: Dec. 12, 1934, NY, NY, *Pres.*, Amer. Capital Corp.; **PRIM RE ACT:** Attorney, Developer, Builder; **OTHER RE ACT:** Mktg. and Sale of RE; **SERVICES:** Dev. of Shelter Communities; **PREV EMPLOY:** VP for Mktg., F & R Builders 1976-1980; **EDUC:** BA, 1955, History, Econ., Univ. Coll. of NY Univ.; **GRAD EDUC:** LLB, 1959, NY Univ. School of Law; **MIL SERV:** US Army, 2nd Lt.; **OTHER ACT & HONORS:** Asst. Atty. Gen. NY 1959-1963, 1st Deputy of Comm. of Licenses NYC 1967-1968 Asst/Dep. Administer of Econ. Dev. Cty. of NY 1969-1970 Member NY and FL Bar; **HOME ADD:** 900 Boy Dr., Miami Beach, FL 33141, (305)864-4737; **BUS ADD:** 5555 Biscayne Blvd., Miami, FL 33137, (305)754-5555.

LOEWENTHAL, Marc S.——B: Feb. 15, 1949, Newark, NJ, *Atty.*, Kadish & Krantz Co., LPA; **PRIM RE ACT:** Attorney; **REP CLIENTS:** Equity Planning Cor.; CIDCO Investment Services, Inc.; **PREV EMPLOY:** Ameritrust Co., in-house counsel; **PROFL AFFIL & HONORS:** ABA; Cleveland Bar Assn.; OH State Bar Assn.; **EDUC:** AB, 1971, Govt., Franklin and Marshall Coll.; **GRAD EDUC:** JD, 1974, Law, Case Western Reserve Univ.; **HOME ADD:** 19619 Sussex Rd., Shaker Heights, OH 44122, (216)991-1279; **BUS ADD:** 2112 E. Ohio Bldg., Cleveland, OH 44114, (216)696-3030.

LOEWY, Steven A.——B: Dec. 21, 1952, NYC, NY, *Atty.*, Constable, Alexander, Danker & Skeer; **PRIM RE ACT:** Consultant, Attorney; **REP CLIENTS:** Comml. investors, devel.; **PROFL AFFIL & HONORS:** ABA (Real Prop. Sect.); MD Bar Assn. (Real Prop. Sect.); **EDUC:** BA, 1974, Philosophy, Washington Univ.; **GRAD EDUC:** JD, 1979, Benjamin Cardozo School of Law (Yeshiva Univ); **EDUC HONORS:** Dean's List; **OTHER ACT & HONORS:** Chmn., Baltimore Jewish Comm. on Law and Public Affairs; **HOME ADD:** 7108 Boxford Road, Baltimore, MD 21215, (301)764-8094; **BUS ADD:** 1000 Maryland Trust Building, Baltimore, MD 21202, (301)539-3474.

LOFTIN, William H.——B: July 24, 1928, Troutman, NC, *Pres.*, Loftin RE, Inc.; **PRIM RE ACT:** Broker, Developer, Builder, Owner/Investor, Property Manager; **SERVICES:** Turn-key; **PREV EMPLOY:** Realtor for past twenty yrs.; **PROFL AFFIL & HONORS:** SIR, NAR, Lakeland Bd. of Realtors, Polk Co. Builders Assn.; **EDUC:** Mars Hill Coll., Appalachian State Univ. (NC); **MIL SERV:** USMC, Cpl.; **OTHER ACT & HONORS:** Mayor, City of Lakeland 1963; C of C; various civic clubs, Past Pres. Lakeland Bd. of Realtors; **HOME ADD:** 5905 Oakmont Lane, Lakeland, FL 33803, (813)646-6995; **BUS ADD:** 202 Lake Miriam Dr., Lakeland, FL 33803, (813)644-6651.

LOFTIS, Ronald W., Jr.——B: Oct. 18, 1952, Fayetteville, NC, *VP, Prop. Mgmt.*, Landura Corp.; **PRIM RE ACT:** Broker, Developer, Property Manager, Syndicator; **SERVICES:** Devel./mgmt. multi-family housing; **EDUC:** BA, 1974, Hist., Wake Forest Univ.; **GRAD EDUC:** MBA, 1976, Fin., Babcock Grad. School of Mgmt.; **EDUC HONORS:** Omicron Delta Kappa; **HOME ADD:** 5064 Eastwin Dr., Winston-Salem, NC 27104, (919)765-5394; **BUS ADD:** P.O. Box 1401, Winston-Salem, NC 27102, (919)722-3344.

LOFTUS, Tom M.——*Exec. VP*, Vantage Companies; **PRIM RE ACT:** Developer; **BUS ADD:** 13895 Industrial Park Blvd., Plymouth, MN 55441, (612)559-5500.*

LOHMANN, Thomas R.——B: Nov. 21, 1952, *Asst. VP*, Dain Bosworth, Inc., Public Finance Dept.; **PRIM RE ACT:** Syndicator; **OTHER RE ACT:** Investment Banking; **SERVICES:** Full serv. investment banking in 20 Midwestern states; **REP CLIENTS:** Dayton-Hudson Corp., Cargill Inc., Supervalu Stores, Amer. Hoist & Derrick, Ball Corp.; **PROFL AFFIL & HONORS:** NAIOP; Bd. of Dirs., MN Indus. Devel. Assn.; **EDUC:** St. Thomas Coll., Bus. Admin.; **BUS ADD:** 100 Dain Tower, Minneapolis, MN 55402, (612)371-2896.

LOHRMAN, John J.——*Pres. & Chief Officer*, Russell, Birdsall, & Ward, Inc.; **PRIM RE ACT:** Property Manager; **BUS ADD:** 8100 Tyler Blvd., Mentor, OH 44060, (216)255-1500.*

LOMAGA, A.W.——**B:** Dec. 27, 1941, Europe, *VP Land Devel.*, Guaranty Properties Ltd., Subsidiary of Traders Group; **PRIM RE ACT:** Developer; **OTHER RE ACT:** Devel.; **SERVICES:** Land devel. in CAN and US; **PREV EMPLOY:** Bramalea Ltd. 1975-80; Consolidated Bldg. 1972-75; Municipal Govt. 1969-72; Provincial Govt. 1968; **EDUC:** BASc., 1968, Civil Engrg., Univ. of Toronto; **GRAD EDUC:** MASc., 1969, Civil Engrg., Environmental Planning, Univ. of Toronto; **OTHER ACT & HONORS:** Dir. of Ukranian Businessmen's Assn.; **HOME ADD:** 18 Robaldon Rd., Islington, Ont., CAN, (416)245-7996; **BUS ADD:** 625 Church St., Toronto, Ont., CAN, (416)925-1461.

LOMAX, Henry C.——**B:** Mar. 20, 1935, *Sr. Partner*, Kennedy, Covington, Lobdell & Hickman, RE; **PRIM RE ACT:** Consultant, Attorney, Developer, Owner/Investor, Syndicator; **SERVICES:** Synd. of props., multi-family housing devel., consultant to number of RE devels.; **REP CLIENTS:** Indiv. and instnl. devels. in comml. RE; **PROFL AFFIL & HONORS:** NC Bar Assn., ABA; **EDUC:** AB, 1957, Univ. of NC at Chapel Hill; **GRAD EDUC:** LLB, 1958, Univ. of NC at Chapel Hill; **EDUC HONORS:** Order of the Coif; **HOME ADD:** Route 2, Box 574-D, Huntersville, NC 28078, (704)892-1757; **BUS ADD:** 3300 NCNB Plaza, Charlotte, NC 28280, (704)377-6000.

LOMBARD, James M.——**B:** June 11, 1938, London, Eng., *Consultant*, Self-employed; **PRIM RE ACT:** Consultant, Property Manager, Banker, Owner/Investor; **PREV EMPLOY:** VP, Mohegan Land Co., Tampa, FL; **EDUC:** AB, 1961, Gov., Harvard Coll.; **GRAD EDUC:** Harvard Bus. School & Boston Univ. Law School; **MIL SERV:** US Army, Res.; 1st Lt.; **OTHER ACT & HONORS:** Chmn., Boston Arena Authority, Comm. of MA, 1966 - 1976; Chmn., Venice - Nokomis B&T, Venice, FL; **HOME ADD:** River Rd., Lower Waterford, VT 05848; **BUS ADD:** 61 S Washington Dr., Sarasota, FL 33577, (813)388-1978.

LOMBARD, John W.——**B:** Aug 3, 1955, Waterbury, CT, *Partner*, L&M Investments; **PRIM RE ACT:** Consultant, Developer, Owner/Investor, Property Manager, Syndicator; **SERVICES:** RE Mgmt., devel. & synd. of comml. prop., condo conversions consultant; **HOME ADD:** PO Box 7014, Prospect, CT 06712, (203)758-6614; **BUS ADD:** Lombard Dr., Prospect, CT 06712, (203)756-8391.

LOMBARDO, John J.——**B:** July 9, 1944, Cleveland, OH, *Sec. & Chief Counsel*, Guardian Title Ins. Co.; **PRIM RE ACT:** Engineer, Insuror; **OTHER RE ACT:** Legal Matters; **SERVICES:** Title Ins., Legal Representation; **REP CLIENTS:** Devels., Lenders, Synds.; **PREV EMPLOY:** 1966-72, Right of Way Engrg. Supv., OH Dept. of Transportation; 1972-74, Asst. Gen. Counsel Devel. Diversified (Nat. RE Devel.); 1974-79, Acting Chief Counsel Shaker Savings Assn.; **PROFL AFFIL & HONORS:** Member: OH Bar Assn., Cleveland Bar Assn., FL Bar Assn., ABA; **EDUC:** BS, 1966, Civil Engrg., Carnegie Mellon Univ.; **GRAD EDUC:** JD, 1971, Law, Cleveland State Univ., Cleveland Marshall Coll. of Law; **EDUC HONORS:** Dean's List, Summa Cum Laude; 3rd in class of 134; Wall St. Journal Award; ABA Law Student Div. Silver Key Award; Amer. Jurisprudence Awards for wills, comml. law, domestic relations; Publication: *Eminent Domain Date of Valuation in OH*; **OTHER ACT & HONORS:** Guest Lecturer Cleveland State Univ., Cleveland Marshall Coll. of Law; RE Title Ins. Winning Team Moot Court Competition ABA LSD 6th Circuit 1971; **HOME ADD:** 2604 Charney Rd., University Hts., OH 44118, (216)371-4138; **BUS ADD:** 1348 Standard Bldg., Cleveland, OH 44113, (216)861-5225.

LONDEREE, Dr. Joseph W.——*Dir. Corp. Plng.*, Lancaster Colony Corp.; **PRIM RE ACT:** Property Manager; **BUS ADD:** 37 W. Broad St., Columbus, OH 43215, (614)224-7141.*

LONG, Alvin W.——**B:** Oct. 9, 1923, Steubenville, OH, *Chmn. of the Bd. and Pres.*, Chicago Title and Trust Co.; **OTHER RE ACT:** Title Insurance and Fin. Services; **SERVICES:** Title insurance, escrow, land trust, conventional trust, mutual funds, homeowners insurance, employee relocation services; **PREV EMPLOY:** Employed Chicago Title and Trust 1945; **EDUC:** JD, 1949, Law, John Marshall Law School; **GRAD EDUC:** MBA, 1955, Univ. of Chicago; **EDUC HONORS:** Honorary LLD 1977; **MIL SERV:** USAAF, Lt.; **HOME ADD:** 1110 Lake Shore Dr., Chicago, IL 60611, (312)787-3441; **BUS ADD:** 111 W. Washington St., Chicago, IL 60602, (312)630-2684.

LONG, Bud.——**B:** Sept. 13, 1947, NYC, *Pres.*, Civic Ctr. Sq. Inc.; **PRIM RE ACT:** Consultant, Developer, Builder, Owner/Investor, Property Manager; **SERVICES:** RE devels., comml. & indus. const.; **PREV EMPLOY:** Past and current managing assoc. of John Tutclian Investments; **PROFL AFFIL & HONORS:** RE Devel. & Consultant; **OTHER ACT & HONORS:** 1976 & 1979 Central Bus. Dist Adv. Comm., City of Fresno; Chmn. Mortwest Sch. System, Sch. Bd.; **HOME ADD:** 546 E Harvard, Fresno, CA 93721, (209)227-6676; **BUS ADD:** 900 Civic Ctr. Sq., 906 N St., Fresno, CA 93721, (209)485-4700.

LONG, Henry A., Jr.——**B:** Jan. 8, 1936, Fort Deposit, AL, *Sr. VP & Trust Officer*, The First National Bank of Birmingham, Trust Div. - Natural Resources Dept.; **PRIM RE ACT:** Consultant, Appraiser, Banker, Property Manager; **SERVICES:** Appraisal and mgmt. of all types of rural prop.; **REP CLIENTS:** Numerous corps. and indiv.; **PREV EMPLOY:** The Federal Land Bank of New Orleans (1963-1967); **PROFL AFFIL & HONORS:** AIREA, Amer. Soc. of Farm Mgrs. & Rural Appraisers, MAI, Accredited Rural Appraiser (ARA), Accredited Farm Manager (AFM); **EDUC:** Agciculture, 1958, Animal Sci., Auburn Univ.; **EDUC HONORS:** Graduated with high honor, distinguished mil grad Phi Kappa Phi; **MIL SERV:** USAF, 1st Lt.; **OTHER ACT & HONORS:** Dir., AL Forestry Assn., Member Advisory Comm. Auburn Univ. School of Forestry, Affiliate Member B'ham Bd. of Realttrict Vice President American Society of Farm Mgrs. & Rural Appraisers-1981-1984, President ALA Chapter AIREA 1982; **HOME ADD:** 2281 S. Sherrlyn Drive, Birmingham, AL 35226, (205)822-7406; **BUS ADD:** P.O. Box 11426, Birmingham, AL 35202, (205)326-5443.

LONG, Henry Arlington——**B:** May 18, 1937, Arlington Cty., VA, *Pres.*, The Henry A. Long Company; **PRIM RE ACT:** Broker, Consultant, Developer, Owner/Investor, Property Manager, Syndicator; **SERVICES:** Devel. & synd. of comml. props., investment counseling, prop. mgmt.; **PREV EMPLOY:** Industrial & comml. RE sales, VA and Wash., DC, 1965-1968; Co-owner Long & Foster RE, Inc., Fairfax, VA, 1968-1979; **PROFL AFFIL & HONORS:** NAR; NAHB; RNMI; RESSI; Pi Delta Epsilon, CCIM; Disting. Service Award N. VA Bd. of Realtors, 1972 & 1973; **EDUC:** BS, 1959, Bus. Admin., VA Polytechnic Inst.; **EDUC HONORS:** Award for Military Merit, Chicago Tribune, 1959; **MIL SERV:** USAF, Pilot/SAC, Capt., 1959-1965; **OTHER ACT & HONORS:** Vestry, Truro Episcopal Church, 1981-1984; Jaycees; Kiwanis (Dir. Fairfax Chapter 1970-71); **HOME ADD:** 11214 Country Pl., Oakton, VA 22124, (703)620-2048; **BUS ADD:** 4085 University Dr., Fairfax, VA 22030, (703)385-0450.

LONG, Oliver Denier, Esq.——**B:** Dec. 13, 1951, Paris, France, *Partner*, Long, Shaw, and Long, PA; **PRIM RE ACT:** Broker, Attorney; **SERVICES:** Legal serv. involving RE; **PROFL AFFIL & HONORS:** ABA, MD State Bar Assn., Montgomery Cty. Bar Assn., Phi Delta Phi Intl. Legal Fraternity; **EDUC:** BA, 1973, Human Devel., Univ. of Chicago; **GRAD EDUC:** JD, 1976, The Nat. Law Ctr., George Washington Univ.; **HOME ADD:** The Riviera of Chevy Chase Condo., 4242 East West Hwy., Chevy Chase, MD 20815, (301)654-8372; **BUS ADD:** 850 Air Rights Bldg. W., 7315 WI Ave., Bethesda, MD 20814, (301)652-6280.

LONG, Pauline W. (Winnie)——**B:** July 10, 1942, Glendale, CA, *Broker*, Long Realty & Investments, Inc.; **PRIM RE ACT:** Broker, Consultant, Owner/Investor, Property Manager, Syndicator; **SERVICES:** RE Brokerage, Prop. Mgmt.; **REP CLIENTS:** Ronald A. Kolar, Synd. Prop. Mgmt.; Andre Dutch, Synd.; Donald W. Little, Mort. Broker Synd.; **PREV EMPLOY:** Century 21; Investment Mgr.; **PROFL AFFIL & HONORS:** RESSI, Top Resid. Sales C-21, 1979; Top Investment Sales C-21, 1980; **EDUC:** Bus., Long Beach State; **OTHER ACT & HONORS:** Arch. Comm., Florence Ave. Foursquare Church; **HOME ADD:** 8663 Muller, Downey, CA 90241, (213)869-1800; **BUS ADD:** 10535 Paramount Blvd., Downey, CA 90241, (213)928-1306.

LONG, Robert J.——**B:** May 19, 1947, Villa Rica, GA, *Chmn of the Bd.*, Trans/Mark Intnl., Realex Corp.; **PRIM RE ACT:** Broker, Consultant, Developer, Owner/Investor, Instructor, Syndicator, Real Estate Publisher; **OTHER RE ACT:** Relocation serv. & indus. telecommunications; **SERVICES:** Telecommunications, consulting, brokerage & investment portfolio mgmt.; **REP CLIENTS:** Phipps Land Corp., Zadelhoff & Assoc. Ltd., Chase Manhattan, Southern Fed., Standard Fed. & Numerous RE Brokerages; **PREV EMPLOY:** R.J. Long & Assoc. Inc.; **PROFL AFFIL & HONORS:** ICSC, RNMI, NARB, Licensed RE Broker & Securities Dealer; **EDUC:** BBA, 1970, Bus. Psych. & Communications, RE, Univ. of GA; **OTHER ACT & HONORS:** United Way Co-Chmn.; **HOME ADD:** 225 Franklin Rd., Atlanta, GA 30342; **BUS ADD:** 1800 Century Blvd., Suite 1850, Atlanta, GA 30345, (404)252-7596.

LONG, Roy H., II——**B:** Apr. 11, 1955, Tucson, AZ, *Comml. Devel.*, Roy H. Long Realty Co.; **PRIM RE ACT:** Developer, Owner/Investor, Syndicator; **SERVICES:** Synd. for acquisition & Devel.; **PROFL AFFIL & HONORS:** RNMI Tucson Bd. of Realtors, CCIM Candidate; **EDUC:** Univ. of OR, Univ. of AZ; **HOME ADD:** 2222 E.

2nd St., Tucson, AZ 85719, (602)795-2568; **BUS ADD:** 3950 N. Oracle, Tuscon, AZ 85705, (602)888-8973.

LONG, Wm. G.——**B:** May 28, 1916, Weiser, ID, *Pres.*, W.G. Long Corp.; **PRIM RE ACT:** Engineer, Developer, Builder, Owner/Investor, Syndicator; **SERVICES:** We buy large parcels of land & subdivide into user size parcels which we then sell to the public (anything from ten acres down to 6000 lot size); **PREV EMPLOY:** Pres. & Owner, Four Seasons Homes in Orange Cty.; Pres., Modular Cores; Pres., Indust. Housing Inc.; **PROFL AFFIL & HONORS:** BIA; VP, Base Community Council of March AF Base, Gen. Bldg. Contractors Lic, BI - C44-SC35; **OTHER ACT & HONORS:** Pres. & VP, Perris Valley C of C; Pres., Perris Rotary Club; Member, Canyon Crest Ctry. Club; **HOME ADD:** 366 Citrus, Perris, CA 92320, (714)657-2777; **BUS ADD:** 2900 N. Perris Blvd., Perris, CA 92370, (714)657-1017.

LONGGREAT, Dara——Calhoun County Economic Development Council; **PRIM RE ACT:** Developer; **BUS ADD:** PO Box 1087, Anniston, AL 36202, (205)237-3539.*

LONGINAKER, Jay W.——**B:** Jan. 14, 1953, Shenandoah, IA, *Partner*, Eaton, Eaton & Longinaker; **PRIM RE ACT:** Attorney, Owner/Investor, Property Manager; **OTHER RE ACT:** Farm Mgr.; **SERVICES:** RE transactions, structured farms managed, legal & tax advice, RE litigation; **REP CLIENTS:** Randolph State Bank, L & L Land Co., Loewe Farms, Inc., Hold RE; **PREV EMPLOY:** Irrigation Law Specialist, IA Natural Resources Council 1977; **PROFL AFFIL & HONORS:** ABA (Real Prop., Probate & Trust Sect.), IA Bar Assn., ATLA, ATLI; **EDUC:** BA, 1974, Geography, Drake Univ.; **GRAD EDUC:** JD, 1978, Univ. of IA, Coll. of Law; **EDUC HONORS:** Magna cum laude, Grad. with honors; **HOME ADD:** RR No. 1, Randolph, IA 51649, (712)625-4441; **BUS ADD:** 416 Clay St., Sidney, IA 51652, (712)374-2641.

LONGOBARDO, Richard G.——**B:** Jan. 25, 1947, Chicago, IL, *Pres.*, Associated Realty Brokers; **PRIM RE ACT:** Broker, Consultant, Developer, Syndicator; **SERVICES:** Investment Brokerage -Synd. throughout CA; **PREV EMPLOY:** VP Ernest Auerbach Co., Santa Monica, CA; **PROFL AFFIL & HONORS:** NAR; CA Assn. of Realtors; Pasadena Bd. of Realtors; IREM; RE Synd. and Securities Inst., CPM, RE Broker; **EDUC:** BS, 1070, Fin. Mktg., Univ. of So. CA; **GRAD EDUC:** RE, UCLA; **MIL SERV:** US Army, E-6; **BUS ADD:** 3838 E. Foothill Blvd., Pasadena, CA 91107, (213)796-3166.

LOOME, James Michael——**B:** Nov. 3, 1942, Albany, NY, *Real Estate Broker/Attorney*, Jim Loome Investments; **PRIM RE ACT:** Broker, Attorney, Instructor, Developer, Owner/Investor, Syndicator; **SERVICES:** RE Brokerage; Ltd. Partnership Investment; Condo. Devel.; **REP CLIENTS:** Buyer's Broker, for Improved and unimproved props. synd. for devel. and build-out of resid. and comml.; **PROFL AFFIL & HONORS:** CA Bar; San Diego Cty. Bar Assn., Broker; Atty. at Law; Lic. Instr. Community Coll. System; **EDUC:** 1966, Naval Sci., U.S. Naval Acad.; **GRAD EDUC:** JD, 1980, Western State Law Sch.; **MIL SERV:** USN, LCDR, Navy Commendation; **OTHER ACT & HONORS:** Cdr. U.S. Naval Res.; **HOME ADD:** 1209 Hueneme St., San Diego, CA 92110, (714)233-3138; **BUS ADD:** 1850 Fifth Ave., San Diego, CA 92101, (714)233-3138.

LOONEY, Stuart W.——**B:** Dec. 19, 1947, *VP, Fin.*, Capretto & Clark, Inc.; **PRIM RE ACT:** Consultant, Lender, Property Manager; **OTHER RE ACT:** Tax and fin. specialist; EDP applications; Brokerage; **SERVICES:** Inv. counseling, data processing defel., RE taxation; **REP CLIENTS:** Comml. and indiv. and multifamily investors; **PREV EMPLOY:** Tax Specialist, Deloitte Haskins & Sells, CPA's; **PROFL AFFIL & HONORS:** WA State Soc. of CPA's; **EDUC:** 1975, Acctg. and Fin., Univ. of WA; **MIL SERV:** US Army, Capt., Aviation; **BUS ADD:** 2200 Westlake Ave., Seattle, WA 98121, (206)623-7300.

LOPATIN, Lawrence H.——**B:** Sept. 20, 1925, Detroit, MI, *Pres.*, LoPatin & Co.; **PRIM RE ACT:** Broker, Developer, Owner/Investor, Instructor, Property Manager, Syndicator; **SERVICES:** Devel. & synd. of comml. props.; **REP CLIENTS:** Kroger, K-Mart, Sears; **PROFL AFFIL & HONORS:** ULI, Amer. Planning Assn., MI Soc. of Planning Officials; **EDUC:** Poli. Sci.; **GRAD EDUC:** JD, 1950, Law, Wayne State Univ.; **MIL SERV:** USN, 1943-1946, PO; **OTHER ACT & HONORS:** Chmn. Southfield Planning Commn.; **HOME ADD:** 28545 River Crest Dr., Southfield, MI 48034, (313)353-9437; **BUS ADD:** 3000 Town Center, Suite 1000, Southfield, MI 48075, (313)352-4747.

LOPATKA, Arthur J., Jr.——**B:** July 3, 1951, Chicago, IL, *Prop. Mgr.*, Midas International, Midas Realty Corp.; **PRIM RE ACT:** Attorney, Property Manager; **OTHER RE ACT:** Investment Analyst, Site Selection; **PREV EMPLOY:** Site Selection/Mkt. Analyst & RE Atty. for Midas; **PROFL AFFIL & HONORS:** ABA & others; **EDUC:** BA, 1973, Pol. Sci., DePaul Univ.; **GRAD EDUC:** JD, 1976, Law, DePaul Univ.; **EDUC HONORS:** Grad. with honors; **OTHER ACT & HONORS:** Pres., Chicago Beer Soc.; **BUS ADD:** 222 South Riverside Plaza, Chicago, IL 60606, (312)648-5613.

LOPEZ, Daniel——**B:** Oct. 23, 1946, Argentina, *Pres.*, Lopez Development Co.; **PRIM RE ACT:** Developer, Property Manager, Assessor, Banker; **OTHER RE ACT:** Condo. conversions & hist. restorations.; **SERVICES:** Investment counseling, valuation devel. & synd. of comml. props. & prop. mgmt.; **REP CLIENTS:** Indiv. & trust funds; **PREV EMPLOY:** Pres. of Vaufin, Inc., fin co. in Argentina; **EDUC:** BS/BA, 1965, Mktg., Nat. Univ. of LaPlata, Argentina; **GRAD EDUC:** BS/BA, 1968, Mktg., Nat. Univ. of LaPlata, Argentina; **HOME ADD:** 310 Hampton Ct., Lexington, KY; **BUS ADD:** 175 Malabu Dr., Lexington, KY 40503, (606)278-0457.

LOPEZ, David T.——**B:** July 17, 1939, Laredo, TX, *Atty. at Law*, David T. Lopez & Assoc., Attys.; **PRIM RE ACT:** Attorney; **SERVICES:** Legal Servs.; **PROFL AFFIL & HONORS:** ABA, TX Bar Assn., Intl. Bar Assn. (Bus. Law Sect.), Inter-Amer. Bar Assn.; **EDUC:** B of Journ., 1962, Journalism, Econ., Univ. of TX, Austin, TX; **GRAD EDUC:** JD, 1971, S. TX Coll. of Law; **EDUC HONORS:** Editor *TX Ranger*, Man. Ed. *Daily Texan*, Sigma Delta Chi, Cum Laude, Order of Lytae, Law Review, Phi Alpha Delta; **MIL SERV:** Army Res.; **OTHER ACT & HONORS:** Houston, TX Bd. of Educ., 1972-75, Numerous civic, social & pol. orgs.; **HOME ADD:** 12343 Honeywood Trail, Houston, TX 77077, (713)497-5410; **BUS ADD:** 3935 Westheimer, Suite 202, Houston, TX 77027, (713)965-9240.

LORAH, Richard J., Sr.——**B:** Aug. 19, 1915, Reading, PA, *Owner*; **PRIM RE ACT:** Broker, Appraiser; **SERVICES:** Broker of sales, re appraisals for relocatees; **REP CLIENTS:** Firestone Co., Homequity Inc., Philco-Ford Corp., Bethlehem Steel Corp., Abbotts Laboratories, Gen. Electric Co.; Equitable Relocation Service; Merrill Lynch Relocation Mgt., Inc.; **PREV EMPLOY:** Jackson-Cross Co., 1976-1980; PA Dept. of Transportation, 1960-1976; **PROFL AFFIL & HONORS:** Amer. Soc. of Appraisers, Pres. 1972; Soc. of RE Appraisers; Amer. Right of Way Assn., ASA; SRA; SR/WA; **EDUC:** 1953, Bus. Admin./Gov. Admin., Alexander Hamilton Inst./Univ. of PA/Univ. of CT; **OTHER ACT & HONORS:** BPO Elks (PER); **HOME ADD:** 84 Cedar St., Pottstown, PA 19464, (215)326-5347; **BUS ADD:** 84 Cedar St., Pottstown, PA 19464, (215)326-5347.

LORBACHER, Rodney A.——**B:** Jan. 27, 1945, Raleigh, NC, *Pres.*, Johnson & Lorbacher, Inc.; **PRIM RE ACT:** Broker, Appraiser, Developer; **OTHER RE ACT:** Investments; **SERVICES:** RE Appraising, Devel., Fin. & Sales; **REP CLIENTS:** Lenders, indiv. & inst. investors in all areas of RE; **PREV EMPLOY:** Landmark RE Inc. (partner) 1972-74; **PROFL AFFIL & HONORS:** Intl. Inst. of Valuers; Nat. Assn. of Review Appraisers, SCV, Intl. Assn. of Valuers, CRA NARA, Sr. Member in both; **EDUC:** AB, 1967, Acctg. & Econ., E Carolina Univ.; **MIL SERV:** US Army, SP-5; **OTHER ACT & HONORS:** Exchanger Club of Gr. Raleigh, Bd. of Dir.; **HOME ADD:** 306 Pell St., Raleigh, NC 27604, (919)833-3509; **BUS ADD:** PO Box 30483, Raleigh, NC 27604, (919)833-3509.

LORD, Leonard A.——**B:** Nov. 29, 1935, Concord, NH, *Broker/Owner*, Landmark Assoc. RE; **PRIM RE ACT:** Broker; **SERVICES:** RE listing, sales, rental, prop. mgmt., appraisals; **REP CLIENTS:** Homequity, Inc.; **PREV EMPLOY:** Sales Mgr., Fischer Agency, Dover, NH (1962-1978); VP/DIR/Sales Mgr., Kendall RE, Inc., Dover, NH (1979-1980); **PROFL AFFIL & HONORS:** NAR; NH Assn. of Realtors; Strafford Cty. Bd. of Realtors, Strafford Cty. Realtor of the Yr., 1968 and 1981; Pres., NH Assn. of Realtors; Served as official of Strafford Cty. Bd. of Realtors; Dir., Tri-State Realtors Inst.; Dir., NW Realtors Educ. Foundation; Served on various local, State and Nat. Realtors Comm's.; **EDUC:** 1960, Univ. of NH; **MIL SERV:** USMC; **OTHER ACT & HONORS:** Dover Kiwanis Club; Somersworth Rotary Club (past pres.); Corporator of Seacoast Savings Bank of Dover, NH; **HOME ADD:** 3 Lily Pond Rd., Somersworth, NH 03878, (603)742-3957; **BUS ADD:** 50 Chestnut St., Dover, NH 03820, (603)749-0055.

LORD, Terry R.——**B:** July 13, 1942, Waxahache, TX, *Atty.*, Lord and Lord; **PRIM RE ACT:** Attorney, Owner/Investor; **SERVICES:** Legal Representation; **REP CLIENTS:** Indiv. buyers & sellers; **PROFL AFFIL & HONORS:** State Bar of TX, Houston Bar Assn.; **EDUC:** BA, 1963, Hist., S.M.U.; **GRAD EDUC:** JD, 1966, Law, Univ. of TX School of Law; **MIL SERV:** US Army, 1966-1969, 1Lt, JSCM; **HOME ADD:** 3002 Plumb, Houston, TX 77005, (713)664-6740; **BUS ADD:** 5619 Morningside, Houston, TX 77005, (713)526-1423.

LORDI, Robert A., S.R.A.——**B:** July 10, 1950, East Orange, NJ, *2nd V.P., Sr. Appraisal Off.*, Fidelity Union Bank, R.E.; **PRIM RE ACT:** Consultant, Appraiser, Property Manager, Banker; **SERVICES:** Appraisal, mgmt.; **PROFL AFFIL & HONORS:** SREA, Sec. North Jersey Chptr. No. 37; SRA; **EDUC:** BS, 1973, Bus. Adm, Monmouth Coll, W. Long Branch, NJ; **HOME ADD:** 981 Redwood Pl., Union, NJ 07083, (201)964-0589; **BUS ADD:** 765 Broad St., Newark, NJ 07101, (201)430-4245.

LORE, Kurt W.——**B:** July 21, 1914, Brooklyn, *Part.*, Thacher, Proffit & Wood, RE; **PRIM RE ACT:** Attorney; **REP CLIENTS:** Chemical Bank, Seamen's Bank, Amer. Sav. Bank; **PROFL AFFIL & HONORS:** NYC Bar Assn., NYC, NY, ABA; **EDUC:** BA, 1936, Econ., Brooklyn Coll.; **GRAD EDUC:** LLB, 1939, Columbia Law School; **MIL SERV:** US Army, 1st Lt., Bronze Star; **HOME ADD:** 10 Plaza St., Brooklyn, NY 11238, (212)638-3773; **BUS ADD:** 40 Wall St., NY, NY 10005, (212)483-5938.

LORENZEN, Paul——**B:** Sept. 21, 1947, Sayre, PA, *Broker*, Jenkins & Martin Mgmt. Corp.; **PRIM RE ACT:** Broker, Instructor, Syndicator, Consultant, Owner/Investor; **SERVICES:** Consulting, Analysis & Brokerage of Comml. Investment RE; **PROFL AFFIL & HONORS:** NAR; CAR; RNMI; FLI; RESSI, CCIM; **EDUC:** AB, 1970, Psych., Pasadena Coll.; **GRAD EDUC:** MBA, RE, Columbia Pacific Univ.; **HOME ADD:** 3707 Windflower Cir., Colorado Springs, CO 80907, (303)598-6086; **BUS ADD:** 722 S Tejon St., Colorado Springs, CO 80903, (303)634-5552.

LOREY, Patricia S.——**B:** Oct. 1, 1946, Washington, DC, *Partner*, Land Sales/Asset Mgmt.; **PRIM RE ACT:** Broker, Consultant, Appraiser, Owner/Investor; **OTHER RE ACT:** RE Journalism; **SERVICES:** RE Brokerage, Investment Counseling, Valuation, Feasibility Analysis and Free-Lance Writing; **REP CLIENTS:** Instit. and indiv. investors, corp. RE depts., builder/dev. of comml. and indus. prop.; **PREV EMPLOY:** Gulf-Reston, Inc. (New Town Development of Planned Cities) Dulles Indus. Aerospace Park; **PROFL AFFIL & HONORS:** Natl. Bd. of Realtors; VA Bd. of Realtors; N. VA Bd. of Realtors; Natl. Assn. of Indep. Fee Appaisers; Natl. Appraisers Instit., G.R.I. (Graduate of Realtors Inst.), S.I.A. (Sr. Investment Analyst-Nat. Appraisers Inst.); **EDUC:** AA, 1978, Bus. Admin., Coll. of William & Mary, N. VA Community Coll., George Mason Univ.; **EDUC HONORS:** Cum Laude-NVCC, Bus. Honor Soc.-Geo. Mason Univ.; **OTHER ACT & HONORS:** Committee for Dulles Church (Bd. of Dir., Past Secretary, Council on Ministries of United Meth. Past Treasurer) in Herndon, VA; **HOME ADD:** 918 Rolling Holly Dr., Great Falls, VA 22066, (703)430-9090; **BUS ADD:** Suite 7; 11250 Roger Bacon Dr., Reston, VA 22070, (703)471-1881.

LOREY, Ruan M.——**B:** July 20, 1945, Washington, DC, *Owner/Partner*, Land Sales/Asset Mgmt.; **PRIM RE ACT:** Broker, Developer, Owner/Investor, Instructor; **SERVICES:** Brokerage, appraisals, feasibility studies; **REP CLIENTS:** Mobil Land Corp., Reston VA; Centennial Devel. Corp.; **PREV EMPLOY:** Southland Corp. (7-11 Stores), RE Rep.; Levitt & Sons. Inc., Rgnl. Mgr., RE; Larwin Grp., Dir. RE Atlantic Rgn.; **PROFL AFFIL & HONORS:** VA Assn. of Realtors; RNMI, CCIM designation; **EDUC:** AB, 1969, Bus. Admin.; **OTHER ACT & HONORS:** RE Faculty, N VA Bd. of Realtors; Arlington Cty. Distributive Educ. Serv.; **HOME ADD:** 918 Rolling Hol Dr., Great Falls, VA 22066, (703)430-9090; **BUS ADD:** Suite 7, 11250 Roger Bacon Dr., Reston, VA 22090, (703)471-1881.

LOSEY, Pat——**B:** Mar. 21, 1939, Dallas, TX, *Owner*, Pat Losey Realtors/Appraisers; **PRIM RE ACT:** Broker, Consultant, Appraiser, Owner/Investor; **SERVICES:** Comml./investment brokerage, appraisals, counseling; **PROFL AFFIL & HONORS:** AIREA; MAI; Bd. of Dir., Dallas Chap., MAI (1981-83); VChmn., CID, 1981; Gr. Dallas Bd. of Realtors; NAR; TX Assn. of Realtors, MAI, Outstanding Young Women of America, 1970; **EDUC:** So. Methodist Univ.; **OTHER ACT & HONORS:** 1976 1st woman in TX to receive the MAI designation, 1st woman to be elected to Comml./Invest. Div., Gr. Dallas Bd. of Realtors; **HOME ADD:** 4551 Westway Ave., Dallas, TX 75205, (214)526-5552; **BUS ADD:** 4551 Westway Ave., Dallas, TX 75205, (214)526-1810.

LOTHMAN, Carl D.——**B:** Mar 4, 1955, Denver, CO, *Atty.*, Cook, Murphy, Biesanz & Kenney (law firm); **PRIM RE ACT:** Attorney; **SERVICES:** Legal serv. in connection with leasing, sale or purchase; **PROFL AFFIL & HONORS:** ABA (Member, ABA section of Real Prop., Probate and Trust Law), MO Bar Assn., Bar Assn. of Metropolitan St. Louis; **EDUC:** BA, 1976, Econ., Univ. of MO; **GRAD EDUC:** JD, 1979, Univ. of MO - Columbia; **EDUC HONORS:** Honors; **HOME ADD:** 875 Victoria Pl., Glendale, MO 63122, (314)821-7316; **BUS ADD:** 10 S. Brentwood, Suite 201, Clayton, MO 63105, (314)727-4222.

LOTTY, John F.——**B:** Nov. 7, 1945, Bridgeport, CT, *Rgnl. VP*, Merrill Lynch Relocation Management; **PRIM RE ACT:** Consultant, Appraiser; **SERVICES:** Home purchase, rental mgmt., homefinding, relocation consulting; **REP CLIENTS:** Major US Corps. - Mostly Fortune 1000; **PREV EMPLOY:** Mutual of NY, Homequity, Inc.; **PROFL AFFIL & HONORS:** Nat. Assn. Review Appraisers, NAt. Assn. Indep. Fee Appraisers, CRA, IFA; **EDUC:** BS, 1967, Mktg., Univ. of CT; **MIL SERV:** US Army, S/Sgt.; **OTHER ACT & HONORS:** Danbury Athletic Youth Org., Advisor; Also Hold Brokers Licenses in states of CT, MA & ME; **HOME ADD:** 8 Heritage Dr., Danbury, CT 06810, (203)792-6637; **BUS ADD:** 4 Corporate Park Dr., White Plains, NY 10604, (914)694-8484.

LOTZE, Keith A.——**B:** Jan. 26, 1931, Colville, WA, *Pres.*, American West Realty, Inc.; **PRIM RE ACT:** Broker, Developer, Property Manager; **SERVICES:** Brokerage, devel., mgmt.; **PROFL AFFIL & HONORS:** Spokane Bd. of Realtors, WA Assn. of Realtors, NAR; **EDUC:** BME, 1953, WA State Univ.; **MIL SERV:** US Army, Cpl.; **OTHER ACT & HONORS:** Tr., Spokane Area Devel. Council; **HOME ADD:** E. 915 Rockwood Blvd., Spokane, WA 99203, (509)534-5474; **BUS ADD:** W. 901 Broadway St., Spokane, WA 99201, (509)328-3866.

LOUDERMILK, Michael——**B:** Aug. 3, 1940, Ft. Worth, TX, *Owner/Pres.*, Loudermilk Investments; **PRIM RE ACT:** Broker, Consultant, Developer, Syndicator; **SERVICES:** Land synd.; & comml. devel., mgmt. and leasing; **PROFL AFFIL & HONORS:** NAR, RESSI; **EDUC:** 1962, Poli. Sci., Govt., and Hist., TX Christian Univ.; **OTHER ACT & HONORS:** NV Devel. Authority; Sustaining Member Republican Party; **HOME ADD:** 3803 Monument, Las Vegas, NV 89121, (702)451-8474; **BUS ADD:** 3803 Monument St., Las Vegas, NV 89121, (702)451-8474.

LOUETTE, Glenn A.——**B:** Oct. 28, 1954, Greensboro, NC, *Sole Proprietor*, Glenn A. Lovette, CPA; **PRIM RE ACT:** Consultant; **OTHER RE ACT:** CPA; **SERVICES:** Tax consultation, investment analysis; **REP CLIENTS:** Stuard Ford Inc., and many local RE firms such as J.D. CA-NEAL and Sons, Johnson & Thomas, Inc.; **PREV EMPLOY:** 4 years exper. with Straub & Dalch, CPA's; Local and Nat. Public Acctg. firms tax depts.; Ernst and Whinney; **PROFL AFFIL & HONORS:** Member of the VA Soc. of CPA's and AICPA, CPA; **EDUC:** BS in Bus. Admin., 1977, Acctg., Univ. of Richmond; **GRAD EDUC:** Master of Taxation, 1981, Indiv. & Corporate Tax, VA Commonwealth Univ. (enrolled in); **EDUC HONORS:** Dean's List; **HOME ADD:** 2412 East Loop, #820 North, PO Box 18400, Ft. Worth, TX 76118, (817)284-5235; **BUS ADD:** PO Box 18460, Ft. Worth, TX 76110, (817)284-5235.

LOUGHLIN, Joseph F.——**B:** Aug. 22, 1922, Brooklyn, NY, *Assessor*, Town of Riverhead; **PRIM RE ACT:** Broker, Appraiser; **SERVICES:** RE Brokerage, Resid. Appraisal; **PREV EMPLOY:** Dir. of Sales, Leisure Tech., Inc. & Levitt & Sons; **PROFL AFFIL & HONORS:** NY State Assessors Assn., Cited 1971-72, NAHB for profl. leadership; **EDUC:** BS, 1948, Econ., Niagara Univ. of NY; **EDUC HONORS:** Cum Laude; **MIL SERV:** US Army, 1943-45, Cpt.; **OTHER ACT & HONORS:** Assessor, Town of Riverhead, 1977-81, Past Pres. Wading River C of C; **HOME ADD:** RR1, Box 582A, Cliff Rd., Wading River, NY 11792; **BUS ADD:** 200 Howell Ave., Riverhead, NY 11901, (516)727-3200.

LOUGHLIN, Richard J.——*Pres./CEO*, Century 21 Real Estate Corp.; **OTHER RE ACT:** Franchising; **SERVICES:** Various RE services through 7500 indep. owned offices; training and other programs through 33 rgnl. offices; **BUS ADD:** 18872 MacArthur Blvd., Irvine, CA 92715, (714)752-7521.

LOUGHRIDGE, John Halsted, Jr.——**B:** Oct. 30, 1945, Chestnut Hill, PA, *VP and Counsel*, The Wachovia Corp.; **PRIM RE ACT:** Attorney, Banker; **SERVICES:** Legal and fin. advice and counsel; **PREV EMPLOY:** Wachovia Mort. Co., Div. Head, responsible for const. lending and RE devel.; **PROFL AFFIL & HONORS:** ABA; NC Bar Assn.; NC State Bar; **EDUC:** AB, 1967, Econ., Davidson Coll.; **GRAD EDUC:** JD, 1970, Corporate Law, Wake Forest Univ., School of Law; **MIL SERV:** US Army, Judge Advocate General's Corps., Capt.; **OTHER ACT & HONORS:** The Union League of Philadelphia; First Presbyterian Church of Winston-Salem; **HOME ADD:** 615 Arbor Rd., Winston-Salem, NC 27104, (919)723-4360; **BUS ADD:** The Wachovia Bldg., Winston-Salem, NC 27101, (919)748-6375.

LOUKAS, Anthony G.——**B:** June 15, 1945, Corinth, Greece, *Owner*, The Loukas Co.; **PRIM RE ACT:** Broker, Consultant, Developer, Owner/Investor, Property Manager, Syndicator; **OTHER RE ACT:** Condo. converter; **SERVICES:** Investment brokerage, synd. investment prop. mgt. of multi-unit RE & comml. prop.; **REP CLIENTS:** Condo. Assns., RE Investors, Comml. Prop owners & partnerships;

PREV EMPLOY: Amer. Invsco Realty Inc., VP Investment Brokerage; **PROFL AFFIL & HONORS:** Chicago RE Bd., Admissions Comml. Member, RE Securities & Synd. Inst., Silver Chalice Award, Amer. Invsco Realty Inc., 1976-77, Top Performance Investment Brokerage Nationally; **EDUC:** 1968, Educ., Univ. of WI; **OTHER ACT & HONORS:** St. Andrew Greek Orthodox Church, Lehman Courts Racquetball Club, Capt., 1966, Univ. of WI Football Team; **BUS ADD:** 664 N. Michigan Ave., Chicago, IL 60611, (312)337-0214.

LOVALLO, Michael Daniel——B: Sept. 10, 1926, Torrington, CT, *Princ. (Proprietor)*, MDL Architect; **PRIM RE ACT:** Consultant, Architect; **SERVICES:** All Basic Arch. Serv.; **PREV EMPLOY:** Chief Arch., Holley, Kenney, Schott; Div. of Babcock Contractors, Inc.; **PROFL AFFIL & HONORS:** WV Soc. of Arch. - Past Pres. 1981, Amer. Inst. of Arch., WV Counciltative Council of NIBS current Pres., AIA, NCARB Certification; **GRAD EDUC:** Hartford Tech. Inst., Hartford St. Tech. Inst., Yale Univ.; **MIL SERV:** USMC, PFC 1945-1946, Pacific Duty, Good Conduct; **OTHER ACT & HONORS:** B.P.O. Elks, C of C, Past Pres. Torrington CT Jaycees, Past VP Suncrest Kiwanis, Morgantown, WV, Past Chmn. Jobs for Veterans Task Force Morgantown, WV; **HOME ADD:** Route 1, Box 37B, Shady Spring, WV 25918, (304)763-3861; **BUS ADD:** 1928 Harper Rd., Beckley, WV 25801, (304)255-4190.

LOVE, Donald N.——B: 1938, Newark, NJ, *Pres.*, Clover Fin. Corp.; **PRIM RE ACT:** Developer, Lender, Owner/Investor, Property Manager, Syndicator; **SERVICES:** Acquisition, Fin. & Synd. of multi-family & comml. props., prop. mgt.; **REP CLIENTS:** Indiv. and corp. investors in income producing props.; **PROFL AFFIL & HONORS:** RESSI; IAFP; NARA; **EDUC:** BS, 1959, Bus. Admin./ Fin., Temple Univ.; **BUS ADD:** 23 W Park Ave., Merchantville, NJ 08109, (609)662-1116.

LOVE, O. Goode——B: Aug. 26, 1920, South Hill, VA, *Broker*, Love Realty; **PRIM RE ACT:** Broker, Consultant, Developer, Syndicator; **SERVICES:** Gen. bus. of RE with emphasis on investment counseling, devel. & synd. of comml. props. & apts.; **REP CLIENTS:** Lenders & indiv. or instn investors in RE; **PREV EMPLOY:** Many yrs. of exp. in personal & bus. fin. planning, tax planning, & estate analysis; **PROFL AFFIL & HONORS:** NAR, CLU & GRI; **EDUC:** BS, 1949, Bus. & Econ., Univ. of VA; **GRAD EDUC:** Chartered Life Underwriter, 1955, Amer. Coll. of Life Underwriters; Grad. of Realtors Inst. of VA, 1976, Univ. of VA; **MIL SERV:** USAF, Lt. Col.; **HOME ADD:** 237 Huntington Village, Charlottesville, VA 22901, (804)293-3527; **BUS ADD:** PO Box 7345, Charlottesville, VA 22906, (804)973-1361.

LOVE, Robert T.——B: Sept. 10, 1938, Indianapolis, IN, *Pres.*, CPA Realty Inc.; **PRIM RE ACT:** Broker, Consultant, Owner/Investor, Property Manager, Syndicator; **SERVICES:** Prop. mgmt. (apts., office bldgs. & shopping ctrs.); **PREV EMPLOY:** VP, Castle Park Systems Inc., 1968-1973 (land devel. & consulting firm); **PROFL AFFIL & HONORS:** Inst. of RE Mgmt.; DeKalb Cty. Bd. of Realtors; Apt. Owners & Mgrs. Assn., CPM; Pres., Atlanta Chap. IREM; CPA Realty Inc. (an accredited mgmt. organization); **EDUC:** BA, 1964, Pol. Sci., Univ. of Miami; **GRAD EDUC:** MBA, 1968, Mktg., GA State Univ.; **HOME ADD:** 5099 Golfbrook Dr., Stone Mountain, GA 30088, (404)469-2851; **BUS ADD:** 2951 Flowers Rd. S., Suite 220, Atlanta, GA 30341, (404)457-4395.

LOVE, Terrence L.——B: Feb. 6, 1937, Covington, VA, *Chmn. of the Bd. and Broker*, Land Development Analysts and First Land Collaborative, Inc.; **PRIM RE ACT:** Broker, Consultant, Appraiser, Architect, Owner/Investor; **OTHER RE ACT:** Assoc. Professor, GA Tech.; **SERVICES:** Consu. Appraiser and broker; **REP CLIENTS:** Maj. devels., lending inst., attys. in SE; **PREV EMPLOY:** GA State Univ.; Adley Assoc.; Planning Consultants Aeck Assoc.; Art Arch.; **PROFL AFFIL & HONORS:** AIREA; Amer. Inst. of Cert. Planners; Soc. of RE Appraisers; Nat. Council of Arch. Review Bds.; AIA, MAI, AIA, AICP, SRPA, NCARB; **EDUC:** BArch, 1961, VA Tech.; **GRAD EDUC:** MBA, 1969, RE and Urban Affairs, GA State Univ.; PhD, 1970, RE and Urban Affairs, GA State Univ.; **MIL SERV:** US Army, PFC; **OTHER ACT & HONORS:** Elder, Peachtree Presbyterian Church; **HOME ADD:** 521 Peachtree Battle Ave., NW, Atlanta, GA 30305, (404)351-9035; **BUS ADD:** Suite 310 N., 521 Peachtree Battle Ave., Atlanta, GA 30305.

LOVE, Timothy——B: Sept. 7, 1955, Los Angeles, CA, *VP*, Tarantello & Company; **PRIM RE ACT:** Consultant, Appraiser, Instructor; **SERVICES:** Appraisals, Feasibility Studies, Investment Analysis, Mkt. Studies; **REP CLIENTS:** Devels., Fin. Instns., Public Agencies, Investors, Profl. Firms, Maj. Cos.; **PROFL AFFIL & HONORS:** Soc. of RE Appraisers, Amer. RE and Urban Econ. Assn.; **EDUC:** BS/Bus. Admin., 1977, RE.Fin., Univ. of S CA; **GRAD EDUC:** MBA, 1979, RE & Urban Land Economics, Univ. of S CA; **EDUC HONORS:** Cum Laude; **OTHER ACT & HONORS:** Beta Gamma Sigma, Alpha Kappa Psi, Lecturer at CA State Univ., Long Beach since Fall 1980; Classes: RE Fin., RE Investment Analysis & Taxation; **HOME ADD:** 18461 Linden St., Fountain Valley, CA 92708, (714)968-8100; **BUS ADD:** 3931 MacArthur Blvd., Suite 102, Newport Beach, CA 92660, (714)833-2650.

LOVE, William B.——B: Oct. 17, 1927, Tulsa, OK, *Pres.*, Skyland Agency, Inc.; **PRIM RE ACT:** Broker, Appraiser, Property Manager; **SERVICES:** Inv. Counseling, Prop. Mgmt., valuation; **REP CLIENTS:** Indiv. and lending inst.; **PROFL AFFIL & HONORS:** MAI, SRPA, GRI, Past Pres., Four Corners Bd. of Realtors, Charter Member of the NM Roadrunner Chap. of the Amer. Right of Way Assoc.; **EDUC:** BS, 1951, Acctg., Univ. of CO; **MIL SERV:** US Army, Cpl.; **HOME ADD:** 210 W. Downey, Cortez, CO 81321, (303)565-8578; **BUS ADD:** 216 West Montezuma, Cortez, CO 81321, (303)565-8552.

LOVELACE, Gary S.——B: Mar. 14, 1946, Atlanta, GA, *Pres.*, Coronado Props., Inc.; **PRIM RE ACT:** Broker, Developer, Owner/Investor, Syndicator; **SERVICES:** RE investment and devel.; **REP CLIENTS:** Canadian investment firms, chain supermarkets: Safeway, Lucky; various investment groups with 50K and above; **PREV EMPLOY:** RE appraiser; comml.indus. brokerage; **PROFL AFFIL & HONORS:** RNMI, RESSI; **EDUC:** BBA, 1969, Acctg. and Mgmt., Western MI Univ.; **GRAD EDUC:** MBA, 1971, Mgmt. & Computers, Western MI Univ.; **EDUC HONORS:** Sigma Phi Kappa, Grad. top 10%; **OTHER ACT & HONORS:** Bd. of Dirs., Tucson Pre-release Ctr., Spirit Filled Son of God; **HOME ADD:** 8122 N. Bayou, Tucson, AZ 85741, (602)744-1176; **BUS ADD:** 7355 N. Oracle, Suite 205, Tucson, AZ 85704, (602)742-4101.

LOVELAND, McKay M.——B: June 25, 1923, Garden City, UT, *Pres.*, Century 21, Inland, Inc., RE Broker & Contractor; **PRIM RE ACT:** Broker, Developer, Builder, Owner/Investor, Property Manager, Insuror; **SERVICES:** Complete RE brokerage; **REP CLIENTS:** Indiv. and instl. investors; **PROFL AFFIL & HONORS:** Nat. Assn. of RE Bds.; CRB, State of UT, GRI; CRB; Candidate for VIP (Century 21 designation); **EDUC:** 1942, UT State Univ.; **MIL SERV:** US Army; Combat Engr., Pvt.; 1944-1945; **OTHER ACT & HONORS:** Zoning and Planning Bd. of Alpine; **HOME ADD:** 1035 N. Grove Dr., Alpine, UT 84003, (801)756-7152; **BUS ADD:** 320 E. 3900 S., Salt Lake City, UT 84107, (801)262-3316.

LOVELESS, Rodney L.——B: Oct. 18, 1925, Seattle, WA, *Pres.*, Woodland Properties, Inc.; Mirrormont Services Inc.; Northwest Tree Farms Inc.; Northshore Marine Inc.; **PRIM RE ACT:** Broker, Developer, Builder, Owner/Investor, Property Manager, Syndicator; **OTHER RE ACT:** Water system operator; **SERVICES:** Water system operation, road building, prop. mgmt., land devel., RE sales; **PROFL AFFIL & HONORS:** Masterbuilders Assn.; **EDUC:** BA, 1949, Psych. and Bus. Admin., Univ. of WA; **GRAD EDUC:** 1 yr. towards MBA, 1950, Corp. Fin., Univ. of WA; **MIL SERV:** US Army; Inf.; **OTHER ACT & HONORS:** Tr., Ames Lake Water Assn.; **HOME ADD:** 13127 66th Pl.NE, Kirkland, WA 98033, (206)823-1339; **BUS ADD:** 6147 NE Bothell Way, Seattle, WA 98155, (206)362-2066.

LOVELESS, Roland A.——*Mgr.*, Gtr. Shreveport Econ. Devel. Foundation; **PRIM RE ACT:** Developer; **BUS ADD:** PO Box 20074, 529 Corckett St., Shreveport, LA 71120, (317)226-8521.*

LOVELL, John T.——B: Jan. 20, 1944, Winnsboro, LA, *Sr. Sales Assoc.*, Marcus & Millichap, Inc., Dallas-Ft. Worth Rgnl. Office; **PRIM RE ACT:** Broker; **OTHER RE ACT:** Tax advisor in re acquisitions & dispositions; **SERVICES:** Brokerage of income props. (apts., office bldgs, retail ctrs.) and tax advice; **REP CLIENTS:** Synd. and pvt. indiv., devel.; **PREV EMPLOY:** Fin. analyst and mgr., bus. devel., Rockwell Intl. Corp., 1973-1979; **PROFL AFFIL & HONORS:** TX Soc. of CPA's, Licensed RE Broker, TX; Licensed CPA, TX; **EDUC:** BS, 1966, Mgmt., Univ. of NC; **GRAD EDUC:** MBA, 1971, Fin./Acctg., Univ. of TX; **EDUC HONORS:** Dean's List, Dean's Award of Acad. Excellence, Phi Kappa Phi (4.0 GPA); **MIL SERV:** USMC; Maj.; Navy Commendation Medal; **HOME ADD:** 1519 Creekside Dr., Richardson, TX 75081, (214)231-3074; **BUS ADD:** 12201 Merit Dr., Suite 270, Dallas, TX 75251, (214)980-4800.

LOVETT, Blake——*President*, Valley Industries, Inc.; **PRIM RE ACT:** Property Manager; **BUS ADD:** 2 South Front St., Memphis, TN 38103, (901)526-5941.*

LOW, Melvin R.——B: Mar. 6, 1931, Waltham, MA, *VP*, Portsmouth Trust Co.; **PRIM RE ACT:** Banker; **EDUC:** BS, 1957, Univ. of NH; **GRAD EDUC:** Grad. School of Savings Banking, 1971; **MIL SERV:** US Army, Sgt., 1952 Korea; **OTHER ACT & HONORS:** Dirs.: NH SPCA, Wentworth Home; **HOME ADD:** 650 Washington Rd., Rye, NH 03870, (603)964-8066.

LOWDEN, William M.——B: Feb. 15, 1949, Indianapolis, IN, *President*, Trail Realty Inc.; **PRIM RE ACT:** Broker, Developer, Owner/Investor, Property Manager, Syndicator; **SERVICES:** General Brokerage, Investments; **PROFL AFFIL & HONORS:** Realtors, FLI; **EDUC:** Hist. Pol. Sci., 1971, Univ. MT; **OTHER ACT & HONORS:** Trout Unlimited, Ducks Unlimited; **HOME ADD:** 2707 Mount, Missoula, MT 59801, (406)549-0862; **BUS ADD:** 3207 Brooks St., PO Box 9017, Missoula, MT 59801, (406)549-6161.

LOWDER, Fred H.——B: Sept. 30, 1933, TX, Lowder Investment Co.; **OTHER RE ACT:** Investor; **EDUC:** 1955, Acctg., Midwestern State Univ.; **MIL SERV:** US Army, Sgt.; **OTHER ACT & HONORS:** Pres. NACS; Pres. TRGA; **HOME ADD:** 109 Pembroke Ln., Wichita Falls, TX 76301, (817)723-1093; **BUS ADD:** 109 Pembroke Ln., Wichita Falls, TX 76301, (817)723-4221.

LOWE, Johnnie R.——B: Dec. 23, 1934, Houston, TX, *Owner-Pres.*, Manvel Devel. Co., Inc.; **PRIM RE ACT:** Broker, Developer, Lender, Owner/Investor, Insuror; **SERVICES:** Appraisals, mktg. prop. for public sale, lender; **REP CLIENTS:** Public; **PREV EMPLOY:** Aetna Ins., 25 yrs.; **PROFL AFFIL & HONORS:** Alvin/Manvel C of C, Dir. Citizens B&T of Manvel, TX; **EDUC:** BS, 1958, Econ., Univ. of Houston; **HOME ADD:** Route 1, Box 78, Manvel, TX 77578, (713)489-8177; **BUS ADD:** PO Box 498, Manvel, TX 77578, (713)489-9444.

LOWE, Robert J.——B: Jan. 20, 1940, Kansas City, MO, *Pres.*, Lowe Devel. Corp., Lowe Assoc., Inc.; **PRIM RE ACT:** Developer, Builder, Owner/Investor, Property Manager; **OTHER RE ACT:** RE Asset Mgmt.; **SERVICES:** Full serv. project mgmt. to instnl. and pvt. RE investors; unique background in problem project mgmt.; **PROFL AFFIL & HONORS:** ULI, Lambda Alpha Frat., Young Pres. Org.; **EDUC:** BA, 1962, Econ., Claremont McKenna Coll.; **GRAD EDUC:** MBA, 1964, Fin., Stanford Grad. School of Bus.; **EDUC HONORS:** Cum Laude, H.B. Erhart Fellowship; **OTHER ACT & HONORS:** Member, Econ. and Efficiency Commn., Los Angeles Cty.; Tr., Claremont McKenna Coll.; **BUS ADD:** 11611 San Vicente Blvd., 860, Los Angeles, CA 90049, (213)820-6661.

LOWE, Ronald E.——B: Sept. 7, 1947, Milwaukee, WI, Brown & Bain, P.A.; **PRIM RE ACT:** Attorney; **SERVICES:** Legal counsel; **REP CLIENTS:** Universal Development Corp., E. Allen Group of Companies, Ltd. and Spencer Development Corp.; **PROFL AFFIL & HONORS:** Maricopa Cty. Bar Assn.; ABA; State Bar of AZ; **EDUC:** BA, 1969, Pol. Sci., Brandeis Univ.; **GRAD EDUC:** JD, 1973, Harvard Law Sch.; **EDUC HONORS:** Magna Cum Laude, Cum Laude; **OTHER ACT & HONORS:** Adjunct Instr., AZ State Univ. 1979; Author of *Bailouts: Their Role in Corporate Planning* and *The Arizona Alien Land Law: Its Meaning and Constitutional Validity*; **HOME ADD:** 5816 N. Casa Blanca, Paradise Valley, AZ 85253, (602)991-1507; **BUS ADD:** 222 N. Central, PO Box 400, Phoenix, AZ 85001, (602)257-8777.

LOWE, Steven F.——B: Mar. 8, 1947, *VP*, Clark Fin. Corp., Fin. & Divestitures; **PRIM RE ACT:** Consultant, Developer, Owner/Investor, Property Manager, Syndicator; **SERVICES:** Investment consulting, pvt. ltd. parts., devel., mgmt.; **REP CLIENTS:** High income indivs., corps., pension plans; **PROFL AFFIL & HONORS:** Intl Council of Shopping Ctrs., CSM; **EDUC:** BA, 1971, Econ. & German, Univ. of UT; **GRAD EDUC:** MBA, 1973, Fin. & RE, Harvard Univ.; **EDUC HONORS:** Cum Laude; **HOME ADD:** 919 S 2200 E, Salt Lake City, UT 84108, (801)582-4228; **BUS ADD:** 4535 S 2300 E, Salt Lake City, UT 84117, (801)278-4633.

LOWELL, Jack——B: Sept. 2, 1943, Waltham, MA, *VP, Resid. Mgr., Broker*, Coldwell Banker Commerical Real Estate Services Inc.; **PRIM RE ACT:** Broker, Consultant, Property Manager; **SERVICES:** Sales & leasing of comml. prop.; **REP CLIENTS:** Major devel., Fortune 500 Cos. and indiv. owners; **PREV EMPLOY:** Love Companies, St. Louis, 1969-1973; CC&F Land Trust, 1973-1976; Grove Isle Ltd., 1977-1978; **PROFL AFFIL & HONORS:** NAIOP; ICSC; Miami Bd. of Realtors; **EDUC:** AB, 1965, Eng., Harvard Coll.; **MIL SERV:** USNR, Lt.; **OTHER ACT & HONORS:** Pres., Zoological Soc. of FL; Pres., Coconut Grove C of C, 1978-1979; **HOME ADD:** 3535 Hiawatha St., Miami, FL 33133, (305)854-7512; **BUS ADD:** 1201 Brickell Ave., Suite 721, Miami, FL 33131, (305)374-1000.

LOWEN, Richard N.——B: May 14, 1945, New York, NY, *Shareholder*, Buchalter, Nemer, Fields, Chrystie & Younger; **PRIM RE ACT:** Attorney; **SERVICES:** Gen. rep.; **REP CLIENTS:** Barclays-American Bus. Credit, Inc.; Occidental Life Ins. Co.; Bank of the West; Transamerican Credit Corp.; DeAnza Corp.; Gen. Electric; **PROFL AFFIL & HONORS:** Resort Timeshare Council, Amer. Land Devel. Assn.; NY State Bar Assn.; ABA; Los Angeles Cty. Bar Assn.; Mort. Banker Assn.; **EDUC:** BS, 1967, Acctg., Univ. of RI; **GRAD EDUC:** JD, 1970, Law, Univ. of MI; **EDUC HONORS:** Nat. Econ. Honor Soc., Acctg. Honors, with honors; **MIL SERV:** US Army; 1st Lt.; **HOME ADD:** 4043 Coldstream Terr., Tarzana, CA 91356, (213)343-5657; **BUS ADD:** 700 S. Flower St., Ste. 700, Los Angeles, CA 90017, (213)626-6700.

LOWENSTINE, Marilyn T.——B: Apr. 12, 1931, Gary IN, *Owner/Lowenstine RE*, Lowenstine RE; **PRIM RE ACT:** Broker; **SERVICES:** Listing & selling prop., prop. mgmt., appr. inv. prop.; **PREV EMPLOY:** Local RE Cos., Mgmt. positions, training positions; **PROFL AFFIL & HONORS:** Natl., State & local Bd. of Realtors, Women's Council of Realtors, CRS & CRB, VP, IN Chap. WCR; Pres. WCR; Past chmn. Ed. Comm., Pub. Comm., Mbrshp. Comm. Miltiple Listing Serv. Comm for the Valparaiso Bd. of Realtors; **EDUC:** Attended Valparaiso Univ.; **OTHER ACT & HONORS:** C of C, Culver Mother's Assoc./ Bd. of Dirs., RNMI, Amer. Cancer Soc./ Crusade Chrmn., RPAC, United Way vol. wk., Heart Assoc. vol. wk.; **HOME ADD:** 511 Long Lake La., Valparaiso, IN 46383, (219)464-1611; **BUS ADD:** 606 Morgan Blvd., Valparaiso, IN 46383, (219)464-1007.

LOWER, Louis G., II——B: July 3, 1945, New York, NY, *VP*, Allstate Insurance Co., RE Venture Capital, Oil & Gas; **PRIM RE ACT:** Developer, Owner/Investor; **EDUC:** BA, 1967, Amer. Studies, Yale Univ.; **GRAD EDUC:** MBA, 1970, Fin., Harvard Bus. School; **MIL SERV:** US Army Res.; **HOME ADD:** Wilmette, IL; **BUS ADD:** Allstate Plaza, Northbrook, IL 60091, (312)291-6619.

LOWRY, Albert J., PhD——B: Apr. 14, 1927, Thunder Bay, Ontario, Canada, *Dir.*, Education Advancement Inst.; **PRIM RE ACT:** Instructor; **OTHER RE ACT:** Author; **SERVICES:** Seminars on RE investing; **PROFL AFFIL & HONORS:** CBC; CPM; IREM; **GRAD EDUC:** Masters, 1975, RE, Coll. of RE, San Antonio; PhD, 1975, Bus. Admin., CA Western; **OTHER ACT & HONORS:** Listed in both Who's Who in Creative RE & Who's Who in Hard Money Economics; Network Academy of Exchangors Hall of Fame; IREM Academy of Authors; **HOME ADD:** 50 Washington St., Reno, NV 89503; **BUS ADD:** 500 Washington St., Reno, NV 89503, (702)322-1923.

LOWRY, Edward F.——B: Sept. 24, 1925, Dayton, OH, *Pres.*, E.F. Lowry & Co.; **PRIM RE ACT:** Broker, Developer, Owner/Investor, Property Manager; **REP CLIENTS:** I have represented various Supermarket Chains; **PREV EMPLOY:** None, I have been doing this same work for over 20 yrs.; **PROFL AFFIL & HONORS:** Dayton Area Bd. of Realtors, OH and Natl. Bd. of Realtors member of I.C.S.C., Won an Award of Merit for subdiv. Devels. for 1956 by the Natl. Inst. of Realtors Brokers of the Natl. Assn. of RE Bds.; **EDUC:** BS, 1947, Univ. of Dayton, Miami Univ., Univ. of Cincinnati, Univ. of Kentucky (army specialized training program) Northwestern Univ., MI State Univ.; **MIL SERV:** US Army, Lt., Good Conduct Medal; **HOME TEL:** (513)274-1451; **BUS ADD:** 211 Folsom Dr., Dayton, OH 45405, (513)274-1451.

LOWY, Allan N.——B: June 19, 1949, NYC, NY, *Sr. VP*, Lesny Development Co.; **PRIM RE ACT:** Developer, Builder; **SERVICES:** Land devel., const., sales and mktg., prop. mgmt., synd.; **PREV EMPLOY:** Beverly Hills Fed. S & L Assoc. 1967-73; **PROFL AFFIL & HONORS:** Bldg. Industry Assn.; Sales & Mktg. Council; Assn. of HUD Mgrs.; LA Cty. Bar Assn. (Real Prop.); State Bar of CA (Real Prop.), Atty. at Law, RE Broker; **EDUC:** BA, 1971, Poli. Sci./econ., Univ. of CA, L.A.; **GRAD EDUC:** JD, 1974, Loyola Univ. of Los Angeles School of Law; **EDUC HONORS:** Dept. Honors; **BUS ADD:** 8200 Wilshire Blvd., Box 5526, Beverly Hills, CA 90210, (213)653-7117.

LOWY, Rudolph J.——B: Apr. 30,, Belgium, *Pres.*, Lesny Development Co.; **PRIM RE ACT:** Engineer, Developer, Builder, Owner/Investor, Property Manager; **PROFL AFFIL & HONORS:** Pres., Bldg. Indus. Assn., L.A. Chap.; **EDUC:** BS, 1969, Engrg., Univ. of CA at Los Angeles; **GRAD EDUC:** MBA, 1971, UCLA; **EDUC HONORS:** Cum Laude; **BUS ADD:** POB 5526, Beverly Hills, CA 90210, (213)653-7117.

LOZYNIAK, Andrew——*Pres.*, Dynamics Corp. of America; **PRIM RE ACT:** Property Manager; **BUS ADD:** 475 Steamboat Rd., Greenwich, CT 06830, (203)869-3211.*

LUBE, Beth——B: Sept. 10, 1943, Washington, GA, *Assoc. Broker*, Key Real Estate; **PRIM RE ACT:** Broker, Owner/Investor, Instructor; **PROFL AFFIL & HONORS:** GRI; Omaha Bd. of Realtors; Women's Council of Realtors, Salesman of the Year 1978, 79, 80 & 81; **EDUC:** BS, 1965, Math., Univ. of GA; **HOME ADD:** 809 Galway Circ., Papillion, NE 68046, (402)592-4478; **BUS ADD:** 11531 S. 36th St., Omaha, NE 68123, (402)292-2200.

LUBELL, Harold——*Partner*, Robinson, Silverman, Pearle, Aaronsohn & Berman; **PRIM RE ACT:** Attorney; **SERVICES:** RE law including acquisition, development, mortgage financing (co-operatives & condos) & joint ventures; **PROFL AFFIL & HONORS:** ABA, NY Bar Assn., Amer. Land Title Assn., Adjunct Asst. Prof. at NYU, Former contributing ed. to Real Estate Review (over 20 articles); **EDUC:** BA, 1953, NYU; **GRAD EDUC:** LLB, 1956, NYU; **OTHER ACT & HONORS:** Former Asst. Attorney General of RE Financing Bureau, State of NY; **BUS ADD:** 230 Park Ave., New York, NY 10169, (212)687-0400.

LUBIN, Ruth M.——**B:** Mar. 6, 1931, Camden, NJ, *Bd. Dir.*, Award Realty; **PRIM RE ACT:** Broker; **OTHER RE ACT:** Salesman; **PREV EMPLOY:** Greyhound Exposition Services; Sec.-Treas. of United Audio Visual Corp; VP of United Audio Visual Corp.; WCR; Open Line Magazine; **OTHER ACT & HONORS:** NAVA, AOPA; **HOME ADD:** 3000 Lantern Lane, Las Vegas, NV 89107, (702)870-1872; **BUS ADD:** 801 S. Rancho Rd. B-2, Las Vegas, NV 89106, (702)385-7400.

LUBOW, Howard——**B:** Aug. 13, 1927, NYC, NY, *Pres.*, Lubow Realty Co.; **PRIM RE ACT:** Broker, Consultant, Attorney, Instructor; **SERVICES:** Resid. sales, comml. sales & leasing, counseling, legal servs.; **REP CLIENTS:** Corps. & indivs.; **PREV EMPLOY:** Beerman Realty Co., George P. Huffman, Inc., John L. Stotter & Herb Simon, Realtors; **PROFL AFFIL & HONORS:** Dir. Nat. Assn. of Realtors, Tr., VP OH Assn. of Realtors; Exec. Comm. OH Assn. of Realtors; Gov. Realtors NMI; Dir. 1982-Pres. Elect Dayton Area Bd. of Realtors, Cert. Resid. Broker; Cert. Resid Spec., Dayton Area Bd. of Realtors Realtor of the Year 1979, VA Broker of the Yr., 1977; **EDUC:** BS, 1951, OH State Univ.; **GRAD EDUC:** JD, 1971, Salmon P. Chase Coll. of Law; **MIL SERV:** US Army, T-5, WWII Victory Medal, Good Conduct Medal, European Campaign Medal; **OTHER ACT & HONORS:** Member Planning Allocations & Research Council for United Way of Dayton, OH; Past Pres. of Dayton Area Bd. of Realtors Fed. Credit Union; Past. Bd. Member and Treas. of Council for Retarded Citizens, Montgomery Cty., OH; **HOME ADD:** 6257 Freeport Dr., Dayton, OH 45415, (513)890-6441; **BUS ADD:** 2128 E Whipp Rd., Dayton, OH 45440, (513)435-2511.

LUBRANO, Timothy J.——**B:** Mar. 28, 1954, Detroit, MI, *FL State Counsel*, US LIFE Title Insurance Co. of NY; **PRIM RE ACT:** Consultant, Attorney, Insuror; **SERVICES:** Title insurance; **PREV EMPLOY:** Law Office of Dennis Fontaine, 740 S FL Ave., Lakeland, FL; **PROFL AFFIL & HONORS:** FL Bar; ABA, Atty.; **EDUC:** BA, 1976, Bus./Acctg., Univ. of S FL; **GRAD EDUC:** JD, 1978, Law (RE), Nova Law Ctr.; **HOME ADD:** 6909 Silver Run Dr., Tampa, FL 33617, (813)989-0830; **BUS ADD:** 7402 N 56th St., Suite 820, Tampa, FL 33617, (813)985-6165.

LUCARELLI, Joseph P.——**B:** Dec. 27, 1936, USA, *Pres.*, Lucarelli Constr. Co.; **PRIM RE ACT:** Broker, Developer, Owner/Investor; **PROFL AFFIL & HONORS:** CPM, RAM, NJ Home Bldrs, Aptmt House Coun. Dir.; **EDUC:** BS, 1959, Fin, Lehigh Univ.; **BUS ADD:** 6600 Boulevard E, W New York, NJ 07093, (201)861-3600.

LUCAS, Michael J., Jr.——**B:** Aug. 17, 1948, Geneva, IL, *Pres.*, Professional RE Serv.; **PRIM RE ACT:** Broker; **SERVICES:** Brokerage, Investment Analysis; Consulting; Prop. Mgmt.; **REP CLIENTS:** The Travelers Ins. Co.; Northwestern Mutual Life Ins. Co.; Duval Fed. S&L Assn.; **PROFL AFFIL & HONORS:** CPM; IREM, Nat. & Local Levels; Candidate CCIM; RNMI, Jacksonville Bd. of Realtors; NAR; **EDUC:** BA, 1971, Poli. Sci./Bus., Univ. of FL, Gainesville, FL; **MIL SERV:** USNR, YN-3; **HOME ADD:** 3464 Beauclerc Rd., Jacksonville, FL 32217, (904)737-5285; **BUS ADD:** 3015 Hartley Rd., Suite 1, Jacksonville, FL 32217, (904)268-8493.

LUCAS, Roy G.——**B:** Nov. 16, 1929, New York, NY, *VP*, James E. Hanson, Inc.; **PRIM RE ACT:** Broker, Consultant; **SERVICES:** Brokerage, indus., comml. props.; **PROFL AFFIL & HONORS:** Treas., IREBA (NY Metro. Area); SIR, Salesman Affiliate; **EDUC:** BS, 1951, Chem. Engrg., NYU Coll. of Engrg.; **GRAD EDUC:** MBA, 1958, Columbia Univ. Grad. School of Bus.; **EDUC HONORS:** Tau Beta Pi, **MIL SERV:** U.S. Coast Guard, Lt.; **OTHER ACT & HONORS:** Chmn., Hockey Program, Ringwood, 1981; **HOME ADD:** 351 Cupsaw Dr., Ringwood, NJ 07456, (201)962-6451; **BUS ADD:** 235 Moore St., Hackensack, NJ 07601.

LUCENO, Samuel F.——**B:** Feb. 3, 1945, Coaldale, PA, *Owner*, Samuel F. Luceno, Realtor; **PRIM RE ACT:** Broker, Consultant, Appraiser, Developer, Lender, Owner/Investor; **OTHER RE ACT:** Loan broker; **SERVICES:** General Brokerage, investment counseling, appraisals, fin., portfolio mgmt., tax deferred exchanges & foreclosure prevention; **REP CLIENTS:** Lenders and indiv. or inst. investors in comml. and investment props. Appraisals for indivs., relocation agencies & govt. agencies. fin. for indivs. & insts., appraisals for fin. inst.; **PROFL AFFIL & HONORS:** NAR; PA Assn. of Realtors; Local Bds.; PA RE Exchange; Metropolitan Philadelphia RE Exchange; Multiple Listing Service; **MIL SERV:** USN, AQF-3; **OTHER ACT & HONORS:** Sons of Italy; Advisor to local lending insts. Review appraiser for Schuylkill Cty. Cts.; Pres., Terrace Devel. Corp.; CSM of Amer. Frat. of RE Appraisers; **HOME ADD:** 608 Luceno Blvd., Spring Mt. Terrace, McAdoo, PA 18237, (717)929-2212; **BUS ADD:** 603 N. Broad St., West Hazleton, PA 18201, (717)459-1419.

LUCK, James S.——**B:** Feb. 12, 1949, Boston, MA, Barnes, Morris and Pardoe, Inc., Comml./Investment Sales; **PRIM RE ACT:** Broker, Consultant, Owner/Investor; **SERVICES:** Investment and comml. sales, counseling pension; **REP CLIENTS:** Devels./investors, major corps. from US and Foreign Countries; **PROFL AFFIL & HONORS:** Metropolitan Washington Bd. of Trade; Washington Bd. of Realtors; **EDUC:** BS, 1972, Mktg. and Fin., Coll. of Bus. Admin., Boston Univ.; **GRAD EDUC:** MBA, 1976, Babson Coll.; **BUS ADD:** 919 18th St., NW, Washington, DC 20006, (202)463-8200.

LUCK, Richard S.——**B:** Aug. 29, 1944, Brooklyn, NY, *Owner*, Luck Realty; **PRIM RE ACT:** Broker, Owner/Investor; **PREV EMPLOY:** Morgan, Altemus & Barrs C.P.A. Now merged with Touche, Ross, C.P.A.; **PROFL AFFIL & HONORS:** Miami Bd. of Realtors, Kendall - Perrine Bd. of Realtors, Realtor; **EDUC:** BBA, 1969, Acctg., Univ. of Miami; **MIL SERV:** US Army Reserve, E-4, Honorable Discharge, 1974; **HOME ADD:** 9904 SW 133 Court, Miami, FL 33186, (305)387-3611; **BUS ADD:** 11543 N. Kendall Dr., Miami, FL 33176, (305)271-4444.

LUCKEY, R.V.——**B:** Mar. 20, 1924, North Star, MI, *Pres.*, Robert V. Luckey Appraisal Assoc.; **PRIM RE ACT:** Broker, Consultant, Appraiser, Developer, Owner/Investor, Property Manager; **OTHER RE ACT:** Pres. of Home Serv., Inc. (sole Corp.); **SERVICES:** Cert. inventories; comml. and resid. appraisals; **REP CLIENTS:** Central Bank of Wichita; 1st Natl. Bank of Bartlesville, OK; Brown Forman Distillers Corp.; W.R. Grace & Co.; Employee Transfer Corp.; Martin Marietta; Procter & Gamble; Brunswick Corp.; McDonald's Corp.; **PREV EMPLOY:** Self-employed 35 yrs. Prior in USAF; **PROFL AFFIL & HONORS:** Nat. Assn. of Review Appraisers; Nat. Assn. of Indep. Fee Appraisers; Intl. Right of Way Assn.; **EDUC:** Equivalent 3 1/2 yrs., 1946-51, Liberal Arts and Geology, Wichita State Univ.; Appraisal Seminars KS State Univ.; **MIL SERV:** USAF, SSgt., Flight Engr., Rhur-Rhine plus usual European theater; **OTHER ACT & HONORS:** 32nd Degree Mason and Shrine; DAV; VFW; **HOME ADD:** 3939 S. Hydraulic, Wichita, KS 67216, (316)267-9797; **BUS ADD:** 3939 South Hydraulic, Wichita, KS 67216, (316)522-0881.

LUCKSINGER, Michael J.——**B:** Apr. 25, 1952, Austin, TX, *Partner*, Hutto & Lucksinger; **PRIM RE ACT:** Attorney; **OTHER RE ACT:** Co-owner title ins. agency; **SERVICES:** Gen. law office practice with concentration in RE, tax and general business law; **REP CLIENTS:** Gen. public and small bus.; **PROFL AFFIL & HONORS:** ABA; State Bar of TX; TX Land Title Assn., Approved atty. - Chicago Title Ins. Co. - Lawyer's Title Ins. Corp. - US Tax Ct.; **EDUC:** BBA, 1974, Acctg., St. Edwards Univ., Austin, TX; **GRAD EDUC:** JD, 1977, Law, Univ. of TX School of Law, Austin, TX; **EDUC HONORS:** Magna Cum Laude; Alpha Chi honor Soc.; Delta Mu Delta bus. honor frat.; Acctg. excellence award - TX Soc. of CPA's; **OTHER ACT & HONORS:** Dir., Llano Cty. C of C; Dir., Llano Lions Club; VP, Llano Agri-Bus. Assn.; **HOME ADD:** Parkview Acres, PO Box 224, Llano, TX 78643, (915)247-5493; **BUS ADD:** 103 E. Main, PO Box 506, Llano, TX 78643, (915)247-4149.

LUDEMANN, Robert F.——*Gen. Mgr. RE*, The Continental Group; **PRIM RE ACT:** Property Manager; **BUS ADD:** 633 Third Ave., New York, NY 10017, (212)551-7735.*

LUDOVICI, Philip F.——**B:** Nov. 18, 1929, Philadelphia, PA, *Pres.*, Action RE; **PRIM RE ACT:** Broker, Consultant, Attorney, Owner/Investor, Instructor, Property Manager; **SERVICES:** Advancement counseling regarding comml. prop. & prop. mgmt.; **PROFL AFFIL & HONORS:** ABA, FL Bar Assn., NAR, Judge, 1965-70, Civitan Club of S. Dade; **EDUC:** AB, 1956, Econ., Univ. of Miami; **GRAD EDUC:** JD, 1959, RE, Univ. of Miami; **EDUC HONORS:** Iron Arrow, Bar & Gavel; **MIL SERV:** US Army; **HOME ADD:** 7601 SW 122nd St., Miami, FL 33156, (305)238-0428; **BUS ADD:** 704 Perrine Ave., Miami, FL 33157, (305)235-8720.

LUDWIG, Lloyd, Jr.——**B:** Feb. 21, 1944, Ridgewood, NJ, *VP*, National Bank of N. America, RE Div.; **PRIM RE ACT:** Banker, Lender; **PREV EMPLOY:** United Jersey Mortgage Co.; **PROFL AFFIL & HONORS:** RE Bd. of NY; **EDUC:** BA, 1966, Amer. Civilization, Hillsdale Coll., Hillsdale, MI; **GRAD EDUC:** 1971-73, Nat. Sch. of RE, OH State; **MIL SERV:** USMC, Capt. 1966-69;

HOME ADD: 434 George St., Ridgewood, NJ 07450, (201)445-7615; **BUS ADD:** 44 Wall St., NY, NY 10005, (212)623-2930.

LUDWIG, L.T.——**B:** Nov. 27, 1937, Miami, FL, *Dir., Sr. VP*, Fin. Serv. Corp., Fin. Serv. Realty Corp.-Pres.; **PRIM RE ACT:** Broker, Instructor, Syndicator, Consultant, Owner/Investor; **PREV EMPLOY:** 1968-79 Barton and Ludwig Realtors; **PROFL AFFIL & HONORS:** CCIM (past pres. GA Chapter), NAREB, GA Assn. Realtors, NIREB, GA Chapter, CCIM; GRI; **EDUC:** BBA, 1964, RE, Econ. and Fin., GA State Univ.; **EDUC HONORS:** Pres., Beta Gamma Sigma Honor Soc.; **MIL SERV:** US Army, 1957-59,E-5; **OTHER ACT & HONORS:** Lecturer 1977-78-Grad. School of Atlanta Univ., 1980-81-Grad. School of Bus.-Emory Univ.; **HOME ADD:** 140 Pruitt Dr., Alpharetta, GA 30201, (404)475-0661; **BUS ADD:** Suite 1900, 250 Piedmont Ave, N.E., Atlanta, GA 30365, (404)659-1234.

LUHNOW, Fred V., Jr.——**B:** Sept. 26, 1929, Dallas, TX, *Owner*, Fred Luhnow, Jr., Custom Builder; **PRIM RE ACT:** Builder, Owner/Investor; **SERVICES:** New home constr.; **PROFL AFFIL & HONORS:** Home & Apt. Builders Assn. of Metro. Dallas; **EDUC:** BS, 1950, EE, So. Methodist Univ.; **HOME ADD:** 4107 Holland Ave., Dallas, TX 75219, (214)528-8848; **BUS ADD:** 4107 Holland Ave., Dallas, TX 75219, (214)528-8848.

LUIGS, A. Melvin, Jr.——**B:** Feb. 2, 1953, Paducah, KY, *Gen. Mgr.*, Plumley Rubber Co.; **PRIM RE ACT:** Consultant, Owner/Investor; **EDUC:** AM, 1976, Murray State Univ.; **GRAD EDUC:** 1978, Fin., Acctg., Murray State Univ.; **EDUC HONORS:** Grad. Cum Laude; **HOME ADD:** 206 Lankford Dr., Paris, TN 38242, (901)642-8313; **BUS ADD:** PO Box 278, Belzoni, MS 39038, (601)247-4940.

LUK, King S.——**B:** Sept. 1, 1932, Canton, China, *Pres.*, King S. Luk & Assoc., Inc.; **PRIM RE ACT:** Consultant, Engineer, Developer, Owner/Investor; **SERVICES:** RE Devel. Consulting & Constr. Mgmt.; **REP CLIENTS:** Hollyview Dev. Co., Glenview Dev. Co., Huntington Dev. Co.; **PREV EMPLOY:** Consulting Engr. Since 1957, in charge of many major public and pvt. projects in West Coast; **PROFL AFFIL & HONORS:** Member, Structural Engr. Assn. of So. CA, Fellow, Amer. Soc. of Civil Engrs., Prof. of Engrg. CA, State Univ., Los Angeles, PhD with Distinction UCLA, Twice Receipient of Natl. Sci. Foundation Fellowship & other Research Grants; **EDUC:** BS, 1957, Engrg., CA State Univ., Los Angeles; **GRAD EDUC:** MCE, 1960, Structural Engrg., Univ. of So. CA; PhD, 1971, Structures, Dynamics & Soil Mechanics, UCLA; **OTHER ACT & HONORS:** Commn., CA State Seismic Safety Commn., Corp. Officers & Dir. for other major Corps; Chi-Epilson (Highest Honor Civil Engrg. Frat.); **HOME ADD:** 5525 Huntington Dr., Los Angeles, CA 90032; **BUS ADD:** 5525 Huntington Dr., Los Angeles, CA 90032, (213)222-2008.

LUKASHOK, Alvin——**B:** Dec. 20, 1921, New York, NY, *Managing Partner*, Ephraim Associates; **PRIM RE ACT:** Broker, Engineer, Developer, Owner/Investor; **PROFL AFFIL & HONORS:** IEEE; **EDUC:** BS, 1950, Const., MIT; AB, 1943, Columbia Coll.; **MIL SERV:** Infantry, S/Sgt.; **HOME ADD:** 300 E. 74 St., New York, NY 10021; **BUS ADD:** 81 Centre Ave., New Rochelle, NY 10802, (914)576-1515.

LUKE, Henry——**B:** Jan. 4, Newton, MS, *Pres.*, Plantec Corporation; **PRIM RE ACT:** Consultant; **SERVICES:** Market research, fin. feasibility services & strategic planning; **REP CLIENTS:** Devels., builders, savings & loans, & investment bankers, comml. banks, comml. prop. owners, foreign investors; **PREV EMPLOY:** TN Valley Authority 1961-65; **PROFL AFFIL & HONORS:** APA, Nat. Soc. of Profl. Engrs., Realtor in the state of FL, AREUEA Assn.; **EDUC:** BS, 1959, Civil Engrg., MS State Univ.; **GRAD EDUC:** MS, 1965, Civil Engrg., Univ. of TN; **EDUC HONORS:** Phi Kappa Phi & Chi Epsilon; **OTHER ACT & HONORS:** Member of FL Governor's Econ. Advisory Council 1980-1982; **HOME ADD:** 345 Greencastle Dr., Jacksonville, FL 32211, (904)725-5998; **BUS ADD:** P O Box 52507, Jacksonville, FL 32201, (904)396-2011.

LUKE, Vernon B.——**B:** Mar. 26, 1941, Honolulu, HI, *Chmn. of Bd.*, Central Pacific Development Corp.; **PRIM RE ACT:** Broker, Developer; **SERVICES:** CEO, Consultant in RE Devel.; **REP CLIENTS:** As a Devel. Co. - 37 clients; As Indiv. - 14 clients; **PROFL AFFIL & HONORS:** Honolulu Bd. of Realtors; REL Devel. Assoc., GRI; RE Broker; Mort. Broker; Ins. Agent (all lines); **EDUC:** 1964, Personnel & Ind. Rel., RE, Univ. of HI; **OTHER ACT & HONORS:** Kaneohe Yacht Club, Plaza Club; **HOME ADD:** 329 Hamakua Dr., Kaizua, Oahu, HI 96734, (808)261-0234; **BUS ADD:** 900 Fort St., Suite 1200, Honolulu, HI 96813, (808)524-8505.

LUKE, Warren K.K.——**B:** May 22, 1944, Honolulu, HI, *Pres.*, Indus. Investors Inc.; **PRIM RE ACT:** Owner/Investor; **EDUC:** BSBA, 1966, Fin., Babson Inst. of Bus. Admin.; **GRAD EDUC:** MBA, 1970, Fin./RE, Harvard Grad. School of Bus. Admin.; **BUS ADD:** 84 N. King St., Honolulu, HI 96817, (808)521-3626.

LUM, Albert B.——**B:** Dec. 25, 1941, Vicksburg, MS, *Pres.*, Al Lum Properties, Inc.; **PRIM RE ACT:** Broker, Consultant, Developer, Builder, Owner/Investor, Property Manager, Syndicator; **PREV EMPLOY:** Shindler-Cummins; **PROFL AFFIL & HONORS:** Houston Bd. of Realtors Million Dollar Club; Soc. of Indus. Realtors; TX Assn. of Realtors; Greater Houston Builders Assn.; Nat. Assn. of Home Builders; Amer. Inst. of CPA's, Prism Award recipient, Greater Houston Builders Assn.; **EDUC:** BBA, 1963, Acctg., Univ. of MS; **GRAD EDUC:** MBA, 1965, Acctg., Univ. of TX; **EDUC HONORS:** Phi Beta Lambda; Sigma Alpha Epsilon; Delta Sigma Pi; Beta Gamma Sigma, CPA, TX & MS - 1966; Highest score on 1964 exam in MS; **MIL SERV:** US Army, 1st Lt.; **HOME ADD:** 9 Westlane, Houston, TX 77019, (713)621-5331; **BUS ADD:** 1010 Lamar, Suite 350, Houston, TX 77002, (713)654-2121.

LUM, Richard M.C.——**B:** Nov. 19, 1925, Honolulu, HI, *Pres.*, Richard M.C. Lum, Atty. at Law, A Law Corp.; **PRIM RE ACT:** Attorney; **SERVICES:** RE and estate counseling, valuation, devel. of resid. condo., prop mgmt., consultant on HI land title problems; **REP CLIENTS:** Indiv. and investors of real props.; **PREV EMPLOY:** Deputy Atty. Gen., Territory of HI 1955-56; Asst., Right of Way Agent, Territorial Hwy. Dept. 1957-58; Asst. Right of Way Agent, Dept. of Trans. State of HI 1958-59; Deputy Atty. Gen. State of HI 1960; Instructor, Dept. of Education, Territory of HI, 1955-57; Instructor in Principles of RE Univ. of HI, 1958-1960; **PROFL AFFIL & HONORS:** ABA; Amer, Judicature Soc.; HI State Bar Assn.; Intl. Right of Way Assn.; affilitate member, Soc. of RE Appraisers, Fellow Amer. Coll. of Probate Counsels, 1981; **EDUC:** BA, 1949, Bus. and Econ., Univ. of HI; **GRAD EDUC:** LLB, 1953, Hastings Coll of the Law, Univ. of CA, S.F.; **MIL SERV:** US Army; T/4; **OTHER ACT & HONORS:** Commr., Rent Control Commn. City and Cty. of Honolulu, 1954-55; Dist. Judge (per diem) First Circuit State of HI 1975-date; Pres. Kiwanis Club of Ala Moana, 1971-72; Sec. Amer. Right of Way Assn. Chap. 30, 1959-60; Tr., Kiwanis Club of HI Loa 1976-81; **HOME ADD:** 5294 Poola St., Honolulu, HI 96821, (808)373-2697; **BUS ADD:** 705 City Bank Bldg., 810 Richard St., Honolulu, HI 96813, (808)537-5955.

LUMAN, R. Lynn——*Admin.*, Nevada, Nevada RE Div.; **PRIM RE ACT:** Property Manager; **BUS ADD:** 201 So. Fall St., Carson City, NV 89710, (702)885-4280.*

LUMP, F.A.——*SIR, RE Mgr.*, Scott Paper Co.; **PRIM RE ACT:** Property Manager; **BUS ADD:** Scott Plaza One, Philadelphia, PA 19113, (215)521-5000.*

LUND, William S.——**B:** June 5, 1931, Colton, CA, *Part.*, Watson, Eberling & Lund; **PRIM RE ACT:** Consultant, Developer, Builder; **PREV EMPLOY:** Exec. VP, Econ. Research Assocs. 1960-72; Chmn. of Bd. & CEO, CA Inst. of the Arts 1972-75; Chmn. of Bd., Terramics, Inc. 1972-pres.; **PROFL AFFIL & HONORS:** ULI, Nat. Assn. of Review Appraisers; **EDUC:** BS, 1956, Geology, Stanford Univ.; **MIL SERV:** USN, A1C; **OTHER ACT & HONORS:** Nat. Park Found. Trustee; Dir. First Los Angeles Bank; Transamer. Realty; Investors, Terramics, Inc.; Sunterra Props., Inc.; Big Brothers of Greater Los Angeles; Trusteee, Occidental Coll., Marlborough School Found.; Art Center Coll. of Design; Orange Cty. Music Center; **HOME ADD:** 1317 Bayside Dr., Corona Del Mar, CA 92625; **BUS ADD:** 900 Cagney Ln., Newport Beach, CA 92663, (714)645-2016.

LUNDBERG, Nils A.——**B:** July 20, 1911, Yonkers, NY, *Counselor (1977-Present); Pres. (1969-76); Partner (1952-69)*, Brooks, Harvey & Co., Inc.; **PRIM RE ACT:** Broker, Consultant; **OTHER RE ACT:** RE fin. and counseling; RE investment counseling; **SERVICES:** Mort. financing/investment counseling/sales - nat. & intl.; **REP CLIENTS:** Maj. instnl. lenders; corporate and indiv. investors, devels., builders, etc.; **PREV EMPLOY:** Charles G. Keller & Co., (RE investments) 1934-52) (Partner); **PROFL AFFIL & HONORS:** RE Bd. of NY; NAR; Fifth Avenue Assn. Intnl. Cols. of RE RAT Pack, Former Gov., RE Bd. of NY; Former Dir., Realty Found. of NY; Dir., NY World's Fair Corp. 1964-65; Dir, Burns Intl. Security Servs. Member, Comm. of Separate Accounts, Equitable Life Assurance Soc.; **EDUC:** BA, 1933, Lit., Univ. of MI; **OTHER ACT & HONORS:** Univ. Club; Presidents Club, Univ. of MI; Sleepy Hollow Country Club; Blind Brook Country Club; National Golf Links of America; Ekwanok Country Club; Surf Club; Indian Creek Country Club; Univ. of MI Club of NY; **HOME ADD:** 14 Ridgecrest Rd., Briarcliff Manor, NY 10510, (914)941-2887; **BUS ADD:** 1251 Ave. of the Americas, New York, NY 10020, (212)974-2511.

LUNDBERG, William——*Treasurer*, Apache Corp.; **PRIM RE ACT:** Property Manager; **BUS ADD:** Foshay Tower, Minneapolis, MN 55402, (612)332-7222.*

LUNDEEN, Howard K.——**B:** Mar 5, 1948, San Bernadino, CA, *Pres.*, HKL Prop.; **PRIM RE ACT:** Broker, Syndicator, Developer, Property Manager; **SERVICES:** Investment counseling, gen. brokerage, dev. & synd. of comml. props., prop. mgmt.; **REP CLIENTS:** Lenders & indivs., or insts. investors in comml. RE; **PREV EMPLOY:** Prop Mgmt Dir for the Trammell Crow Co., Dallas, TX, 1973-80; **PROFL AFFIL & HONORS:** BOMA, IREM, CPM Candidate; **EDUC:** 1971, Soc., Brigham Young Univ.; **GRAD EDUC:** MBA, 1973, Fin., Brigham Young Univ.; **HOME ADD:** 1123 Grassmere, Richardson, TX 75080, (214)783-7579; **BUS ADD:** 13140 Colt Rd., Suite 207, Dallas, TX 75240, (214)231-2258.

LUNDGREN, Richard J.——**B:** Dec. 13, 1940, New York, NY, *VP*, Hunneman Investment Mgmt. Corp.; **PRIM RE ACT:** Architect, Builder, Syndicator; **SERVICES:** Acquisition, Financing and Mgmt. of Office Bldgs.; **REP CLIENTS:** Office Bldg. Owners, Investors and Lenders; **PREV EMPLOY:** Hilgenhurst Assoc., Boston, MA (1972-1977); **PROFL AFFIL & HONORS:** Greater Boston RE Bd., IREM, BOMA, RESSI, APA; **EDUC:** BS, 1964, Bus. Admin., Rensselaer Polytechnic Inst., Troy, NY; **GRAD EDUC:** MS, 1968, City Planning, Pratt Inst., Brooklyn, NY; **MIL SERV:** USCG, Specialist 4; **OTHER ACT & HONORS:** Project Dir., Boston Redev. Authority (1969-72); Nat. Trust for Historic Preservation; Soc. for the Preservation of New England Antiquities; Piedmont Environmental Council; **HOME ADD:** 48 Center St., Dover, MA 02030, (617)785-1533; **BUS ADD:** One Winthrop Sq., Boston, MA 02110, (617)426-4260.

LUNDQUIST, C. David——**B:** Feb. 20, 1935, Plainwell, MI, *Atty.*; **PRIM RE ACT:** Attorney; **SERVICES:** Complete legal serv. for RE Transactions; **REP CLIENTS:** Lic. Brokers; Income Prop. Owners; Devels.; Several Church-related Grps. Involving RE Transactions; **PROFL AFFIL & HONORS:** ABA and RE Sec.; MI Bar Assn. and RE Section; **EDUC:** BA, 1957, Pol. Sci., Univ. of MI; **GRAD EDUC:** LLB, 1960, Law, Duke Univ.; **EDUC HONORS:** Estate Planning Award; **OTHER ACT & HONORS:** Kiwanis Intl.; **HOME ADD:** 2336 Bronson Blvd., Kalamazoo, MI 49008, (616)381-5700; **BUS ADD:** 508 ISB Bldg., Kalamazoo, MI 49007, (616)342-9811.

LUNDSTROM, James E.——**B:** Oct. 13, 1936, Fargo, ND, *Pres.*, Team Builders; **PRIM RE ACT:** Developer, Builder; **SERVICES:** Sales/Dev./Build; **PREV EMPLOY:** Dynamic Homes, Det. Lakes, MN; **PROFL AFFIL & HONORS:** NAHB/H.O.W. Program; **EDUC:** 93 Credits, 1958, Mechanical Engineering, NDSU; **MIL SERV:** ROTC; **OTHER ACT & HONORS:** Elks, IC's, Pres. Dilworth Lutheran Church Council; **HOME ADD:** 502 NE 5th, Dilworth, MN 56529, (218)287-2222; **BUS ADD:** Box 3132, Fargo, ND 58102.

LUNDSTROM, John E.——**B:** Apr. 8, 1929, Aurora, IL, *Pres.*, Lundstrom Realty, Inc.; **PRIM RE ACT:** Broker, Consultant, Appraiser, Builder, Owner/Investor; **SERVICES:** RE listings and sales, appraising; **REP CLIENTS:** indiv., Vets. Admn., lenders, corps., attys., relocation cos.; **PROFL AFFIL & HONORS:** NAREA, NAREC, NARA, AACA (Sr. Design), Homebuilders Assn. of IA, Greater Des Moines Bd. of Realtors, IA Assn. of Realtors, State Legislative Comm., Cert. RE Cons. Amer. Coll. of RE Cons., Chmn. of the Legislative Comm. for the Greater Des Moines Bd. of Realtors, 2nd VP of the Greater Des Moines Bd. of Realtors 1981, Realtor of the Year, 1979; Des Moines Bd. of Realtors; **MIL SERV:** US Army, Cpl.; **OTHER ACT & HONORS:** 12 yrs. served on the Ankeny, IA Sch. bd., presently serving 4 yrs. on the Ankeny City Council; 1st United Methodist Church, Lions Club, Amer. Legion; **HOME ADD:** 514 NW Cindy Ln., Ankeny, IA 50021, (515)964-0242; **BUS ADD:** 104 E. 1st. St., Ankeny, IA 50021, (515)964-1114.

LUNDY, Raymond E.——**B:** Apr. 28, 1927, Seattle, WA, *Trust Officer and Mgr. Prop. Mgmt. Dept.*, Peoples National Bank, Trust RE; **PRIM RE ACT:** Property Manager; **OTHER RE ACT:** Trust officer; **PROFL AFFIL & HONORS:** BOMA, IREM, CPM; **EDUC:** BA, 1952, Ins., acctg., Univ. of WA; **MIL SERV:** USN, SFC; **OTHER ACT & HONORS:** 32 Mason, Shriner; **HOME ADD:** 9028 23rd NW, Seattle, WA 98117, (206)784-4378; **BUS ADD:** 1414 4th Ave., Seattle, WA 98111, (206)344-4570.

LUNSFORD, Walter B.——**B:** Nov. 18, 1952, Hamilton, OH, *Broker/Owner*, The Assn. of RE and Insurance, Resid. sales, Prop. Mgmt.; **PRIM RE ACT:** Broker, Property Manager, Insuror; **OTHER RE ACT:** Resid. sales specialist; **SERVICES:** Resid. sales, spec. in creative fin., prop. mgmt., builder & ins. sales relating to home ownership; **REP CLIENTS:** Resid. homeowners, investors; **PREV EMPLOY:** Staff mgmt. & consultant for sixth largest Amer. Corp., 1975-77; **PROFL AFFIL & HONORS:** Hamilton-Fairfield, OH, & Nat. member of Assn. of Realtors, Profl. of yr., 1979, Hamilton-Fairfield Bd. of Realtors, Profl. of yr., 1980, OH Assn. of Realtors, Profl. of Yr., 1981 OH Assn. of Realtors; **EDUC:** AA, 1973, Mgmt., fin., Maimi Univ., OH; BA, 1975, Mgmt., fin., Miami Univ., OH; **HOME ADD:** 5975 Allison Ave., Hamilton, OH 45011, (513)896-1173; **BUS ADD:** 780 Nilles Rd., Suite. C, Fairfield, OH 45014, (513)829-0220.

LUNSFORD, William J.——**B:** Oct. 3, 1944, New York, NY, *VP, Mgr. of Investments*, Van Schaack & Co., Mort. Loan; **PRIM RE ACT:** Developer, Lender, Owner/Investor, Insuror; **OTHER RE ACT:** Realtor, Resid. & Comml., Leasing; **SERVICES:** Sales, leasing, lending, investments, ins.; **REP CLIENTS:** Medium-large RE devels. operating in the Denver Metropolitan area; **PREV EMPLOY:** Chase Manhattan Bank, 1971-1975; United Bank of Denver, 1975-1980; **PROFL AFFIL & HONORS:** Dir., CO Mort. Bankers Assn.; MBAA; Homebuilders Assn.; **EDUC:** AB, 1966, Econ., Dartmouth Coll.; **MIL SERV:** USCG, Lt. j.g., 1966-1969; **OTHER ACT & HONORS:** Tr., Denver Botanic Gardens; **HOME ADD:** 537 Concord, Boulder, CO 80302; **BUS ADD:** 950 17th St., Denver, CO 80202, (303)572-5350.

LUNT, Jack——**B:** Oct 19, 1944, Hartford, CT, *Sr. Partner (Dir.)*, Jones, Waldo, Holbrook & McDonough; **PRIM RE ACT:** Attorney; **SERVICES:** Acquisition, devel. of fin. of RE devel.; **REP CLIENTS:** Amer. Stores Co. (Prop. Devel. for Country's 7th Largest Retailer - Skuggs Cos., Inc., Alpha Beta Co., Various Local, Rgnl. and for. Lending Instns.; **PROFL AFFIL & HONORS:** UT State Bar Assn., ABA (including real prop. sec.); **EDUC:** BS, 1966, Poli. Sci., Univ. of UT; **GRAD EDUC:** JD, 1969, Law, Univ. of UT; **EDUC HONORS:** Magna Cum Laude; **OTHER ACT & HONORS:** Univ. Club; **BUS ADD:** 800 Walker Bldg., Salt Lake City, UT 84111.

LUPO, Robert N.——**B:** June 11, 1946, Newton, MA, *Atty.*, Lupo and Lupo; **PRIM RE ACT:** Broker, Consultant, Attorney, Appraiser, Developer, Owner/Investor, Property Manager; **SERVICES:** Fin. consultation with respect to RE acquisition with legal and tax overview; **PREV EMPLOY:** Cambridge Rent Control Bd.; **EDUC:** BS, 1968, Fin., Boston Coll.; **GRAD EDUC:** JD, 1972, Law, Suffolk Univ. Law School; **EDUC HONORS:** Magna Cum Laude, Upper 25 percent; **MIL SERV:** US Army, Sp. 5; **OTHER ACT & HONORS:** Jaycees; Rotary; Knights of Columbus; **HOME ADD:** 7 Worth Cir., Newton, MA 02158, (617)964-6809; **BUS ADD:** 313 Washington St., Newton, MA 02158, (617)893-7888.

LURIE, David L.——**B:** Dec. 15, 1934, Great Neck, NY, *Pres.*, Century 21, Adlman-Lurie Realty; **PRIM RE ACT:** Broker, Appraiser, Developer, Builder, Owner/Investor, Property Manager; **SERVICES:** Design & build office, multiple dwellings & single family homes; **PROFL AFFIL & HONORS:** Cert. Sr. Appraiser, AACA; Sec., Great Neck RE Bd.; Member, RE Bd. of NY, Cert. Appraiser, Sr.; **EDUC:** BS, 1956, Rider Coll.; **OTHER ACT & HONORS:** USCG; Comdr.; **HOME ADD:** 320 E. Shore Rd., Great Neck, NY 11023, (516)487-5882; **BUS ADD:** 643 Middle Neck Rd., Great Neck, NY 11023, (516)482-3200.

LURIE, Paul M.——**B:** Apr. 9, 1941, Chicago, IL, *Prin.*, Fohrman, Lurie, Sklar & Simon, Ltd.; **PRIM RE ACT:** Attorney; **SERVICES:** Legal services including negotiations and structuring; **REP CLIENTS:** Sellers and buyers in RE, lenders and syndicators, architects and engineers whose clients are engaged in RE construction; **PROFL AFFIL & HONORS:** Real Prop. Law Comm., ABA, RESSI, Chicago Mort. Attys. Assoc., Chmn., Land Dev. and Construction Comm.; Chicago Bar Assn.; **EDUC:** BA, 1962, Hist., Poli. Sci., Econ., Univ. of MI; **GRAD EDUC:** J.D., 1965, Univ. of MI Law School; **OTHER ACT & HONORS:** Adjunct Prof. Univ. of IL at Chicago, Coll. of Arch. Courses on RE and Const.; **HOME ADD:** 641 Sheridan Sq., Evanston, IL 60202; **BUS ADD:** 180 N. Michigan Ave., Chicago, IL 60601, (312)641-5252.

LURTSEMA, Hal B.——**B:** June 19, 1945, Los Angeles, CA, *Pres.*, Lurtsema-Patrick Fin. Co.; **PRIM RE ACT:** Syndicator, Developer, Builder; **SERVICES:** Joint venture capital, synd. & all types of devel. projects, devel.; **PROFL AFFIL & HONORS:** CAR, NAR, GAR Synd. Div., Natl. Bldr. Award, Amer. Wood Council; **EDUC:** BA, 1967, Bus., Univ. of the Pacific; **EDUC HONORS:** Varsity Football, Hon. Mention all Amer.; **HOME ADD:** 6002 Portsmouth, Stockton, CA 95209, (209)951-1785; **BUS ADD:** 5713 W Pershing, Stockton, CA 95207, (209)951-7191.

LUSHING, Jonathon——*Sr. Vice Pres. Plng. & Control*, Bangor Punta Corp.; **PRIM RE ACT:** Property Manager; **BUS ADD:** Greenwich Plaza, Greenich, CT 06830, (203)622-8100.*

LUSK, John D.——*COB and CEO*, John D. Lusk & Son; **PRIM RE ACT:** Developer; **PROFL AFFIL & HONORS:** Past Pres., Bldg. Contractors' Assn. of Los Angeles; Dir., Home Bldrs. Assn.; W. Tr., ICSC; Tr., Mead Housing Trust; Builder of the Yr., Bldg. Contractors' Assn. of Los Angeles; **EDUC:** Univ. of S. Cal.; **OTHER ACT & HONORS:** Life Tr., Claremont Mens Coll.; **BUS ADD:** 17550 Gillette, Irvine, CA 92713, (714)557-8220.

LUSSA, Ray——**B:** Oct. 23, 1943, Chicago, IL, *Owner/Broker*, Ray Lussa & Assocs., Inc.; **PRIM RE ACT:** Broker, Owner/Investor, Property Manager; **SERVICES:** Condo. mgmt., new subdiv. sales; **PROFL AFFIL & HONORS:** Bldg. Contractor Assn., San Diego Bd. of Realtor, NAR and CA Bd. of Realtor, Community Assocs. Inst.; **EDUC:** AA, 1967, Acctg., San Diego City Coll.; BS, 1969, Mktg., San Diego State Univ., Western State College of Law; **MIL SERV:** USAF; **HOME ADD:** 8834 Capcano Rd., San Diego, CA 92126, (714)271-1847; **BUS ADD:** 9373 Mera Misa Blvd., San Diego, CA 92126, (714)695-1600.

LUSTGARTEN, Stephen F.——**B:** Aug. 26, 1949, New York, NY, *VP*, Blake Construction Co., Inc., RE; **PRIM RE ACT:** Broker, Developer, Builder, Owner/Investor, Property Manager; **SERVICES:** Devel., const., brokerage, prop. mgmt.; **REP CLIENTS:** Maj. corps., assns., law firms; **PROFL AFFIL & HONORS:** Wash. Bd. of Realtors; Wash. Bd. of Trade, Life Member Wash. Bd. of Realtors; One Million Dollar Leasing Club; **EDUC:** BBA, 1971, Fin., George Washington Univ.; **HOME ADD:** 1430 Fallsmead Way, Potomac, MD 20854, (301)424-2126; **BUS ADD:** 1120 CT Ave., NW, Washington, DC 20036, (202)828-9000.

LUTCHANSKY, Herman——**B:** Jan. 23, 1925, Detroit, MI, *Pres.*, King Midas Real Estate Corp.; **PRIM RE ACT:** Broker, Consultant, Owner/Investor, Instructor, Property Manager, Syndicator, Real Estate Publisher; **OTHER RE ACT:** Instr. in CA Con. Educ. Program; **PREV EMPLOY:** 27 years bus. experience (wholesale food bus., Detroit & San Diego); **PROFL AFFIL & HONORS:** San Diego Bd. of Realtors, Problem Solver, GRI, Gold Card Carrier, Several Exchange Groups, RESSI, Notary Public, GRI, Lifetime Teaching Cert. Adult Community Colleges; Author and Publisher of *The Real World of RE Investing*; CA Community Colleges Lifetime Cert.; **EDUC:** Took 2 yrs. Law School (Western State Univ. Coll. of Law); Had to drop out because of medical problem; **MIL SERV:** USN, FC 2/C, Good Conduct Medal, Several Battlefield Campaign Ribbons with Stars; **OTHER ACT & HONORS:** 32nd Degree Mason & Shriner; **HOME ADD:** 2428 Amity St., San Diego, CA 92109, (714)272-8171; **BUS ADD:** 950 Hotel Circle, North, Suite "G", San Diego, CA 92108, (714)296-0118.

LUTEN, William C.——**B:** Sept. 30, 1942, Quincy, FL, *Pres. and Owner*, Luten Properties, Inc.; **PRIM RE ACT:** Broker, Consultant, Developer, Owner/Investor, Syndicator; **SERVICES:** Sale and/or devel. of comml. RE and raw land; **PREV EMPLOY:** British Petroleum, Wash., DC; Rgnl. RE Mgr.; VP Orlando Metro Devel., Orlando, FL; **PROFL AFFIL & HONORS:** NAR, FL Assn. of Realtors; Clearwater-Largo-Dunedin Bd. of Realtors; CCIM, Certified Comml. Investment Member; Interstate Motel Brokers Assn., CCIM, Cert. Comml. Investment Member; **EDUC:** BS, 1965, Insurance and RE, Bus. and Admin., FL State Univ.; **MIL SERV:** USMC, Sgt.; **OTHER ACT & HONORS:** Member, Bd. of Dirs., Clearwater-Largo-Dunedin Bd. of Realtors; Member, Clearwater Bd. of Appeals on Signs; **HOME ADD:** 904 Wellington Dr., Clearwater, FL 33516, (813)447-8829; **BUS ADD:** 615 S. Missouri Ave., Suite B, Clearwater, FL 33516, (813)446-4280.

LUTES, Kendall H.——**B:** Sept. 19, 1926, Lexington, KY, *Pres.*, Kendall H. Lutes Company, Ltd.; **PRIM RE ACT:** Developer, Owner/Investor, Consultant; **SERVICES:** RE Development Management, Investment Banking Counseling; Joint Ventures; **REP CLIENTS:** Ford Found., Gerald D. Hines Interest, Realty Mort. & Investors of Pac. Indiv. RE Owners, Instl. Client in Comml. RE Devel., Office Bldg., Shopping Centers, Hotel, Retail Stores; Condo. Resort Prop.; **PREV EMPLOY:** Pres., Kidder Peabody Realty Corp., 10 Hanover Sq., New York, NY 10005; **PROFL AFFIL & HONORS:** RE Bd. of NY, Honolulu Bd. of Realtors, Urban Land Institute, ULI; Practing Law Institute; **EDUC:** 1950, Econ., Univ. of Ky; **MIL SERV:** USN, Boatswain 1st Class; **HOME ADD:** 795 Sutter St., San Francisco, CA 94109, (415)441-7976; **BUS ADD:** 970 N. Kalaheo Ave., Kailua, HI 96734, (808)254-1505.

LUTZ, Arthur A.——**B:** Apr. 26, 1937, Portland, OR, *Pres.*, Lutz Service Corp.; **PRIM RE ACT:** Broker, Developer, Builder, Owner/Investor, Property Manager, Syndicator; **SERVICES:** Largest full serv. RE co. in OR; **PROFL AFFIL & HONORS:** CRB, NAR; **EDUC:** BA, 1959, Lib. Arts., Univ. of OR; **MIL SERV:** USAF, 1959-62, Capt.; **OTHER ACT & HONORS:** Advisory Bd. St. Vincent Hospital, Bd. of Dir. Boys and Girls Aid Soc.; **HOME ADD:** 5120 SW Hewett, Portland, OR 97221, (513)297-4600; **BUS ADD:** 8925 SW Beauerton Hillsdale Hwy., Portland, OR 97225, (503)247-4521.

LUTZ, W. Kent——**B:** May 20, 1946, Pottsville, PA, *Project Mgr., Peripheral Land Devel.*, Jacobs, Visconsi, & Jacobs Co.; **PRIM RE ACT:** Owner/Investor, Developer, Property Manager; **OTHER RE ACT:** Shopping center development, comml. land development; **SERVICES:** Comml. land devel., prop. mgmt.; **REP CLIENTS:** Comml. devels., restaurants, investors, both indiv. & instnl., retail & department stores; **PREV EMPLOY:** Investment banking and corporate RE; **PROFL AFFIL & HONORS:** Intl. Council of Shopping Ctrs.; Nat. Assn. of Corp. RE Execs; BOMA; Soc. of RE Appraisers, Associate, GRI; **EDUC:** BS, 1969, Mktg., Miami Univ.; BS, 1979, RE, Univ. of Cincinnati; **GRAD EDUC:** MBA, 1982, Fin., Xavier Univ.; **OTHER ACT & HONORS:** Cincinnati Rotary Club; Cincinnati Club; Cincinatti C of C; **HOME ADD:** 8188 Capitol Dr., Cincinnati, OH 45244, (513)474-3210; **BUS ADD:** 4412 Aicholtz Rd., Cincinnati, OH 45245, (513)752-3033.

LUXEN, John W.——**B:** Aug. 14, 1946, Des Moines, IA, *VP, Fin.*, The Young Companies; **PRIM RE ACT:** Developer; **OTHER RE ACT:** Chief Fin. Officer; **SERVICES:** Office bldgs., housing, apts.; **PREV EMPLOY:** Hunt Intl. Resources (Great Western Cities), 1972-79; **PROFL AFFIL & HONORS:** RE Fin. Exec. Assn.; TX/Dallas Soc. of CPA's, CPA; **EDUC:** BSBA, 1968, Acctg., Drake Univ.; **MIL SERV:** US Army, E-5; **HOME ADD:** 9537 Highland View Dr., Dallas, TX 75238, (214)349-7588; **BUS ADD:** 8131 LBJ Frwy, Suite 875, Dallas, TX 75251, (214)669-0400.

LYDA, Harold——*Ed.*, ATCOM, Inc., Real Estate Insider Newsletter; **PRIM RE ACT:** Real Estate Publisher; **BUS ADD:** 2315 Broadway, NY, NY 10024, (212)873-3760.*

LYDECKER, Gerrit——**B:** Oct. 28, 1929, Maywood, NJ, *Pres.*, Moodna Development Co., Inc.; **PRIM RE ACT:** Developer, Builder, Owner/Investor; **OTHER RE ACT:** Land Devel. and Investor; **EDUC:** ME, 1951, Mech. Engrg., Stevens Inst. of Tech.; **GRAD EDUC:** MS, 1966, Indus. Mgmt., Mass. Inst. of Tech.; **EDUC HONORS:** Sloan Fellow; **MIL SERV:** USNR, Aviator, LCDR; **OTHER ACT & HONORS:** Also affiliated with North American Homes, Inc.; **HOME ADD:** 33 Sweet Briar Rd., Stamford, CT 06905, (203)322-9719; **BUS ADD:** 832 Bedford St., Stanford, CT 06901, (203)348-2273.

LYLE, John Kennett Christopher——**B:** Mar. 4, 1940, Calgary, Can., *Pres.*, Lyle Real Estate Ltd.; **PRIM RE ACT:** Broker, Consultant, Owner/Investor; **SERVICES:** All brokerage, resid. & comml. investment; **REP CLIENTS:** Investors and users of RE located in Calgary, Alberta or near; **PREV EMPLOY:** The Royal Trust Co.; 1966-1976; Alberta RE Area Manager; **PROFL AFFIL & HONORS:** The RE Inst. of Can.; The Calgary RE Bd., Pres. 1981, FRI, BA; **EDUC:** BA, 1963, Mktg. Sales Mgmt., Univ. of Western Ontario; **OTHER ACT & HONORS:** Pres. Calgary RE Bd. 1981 (sales 1981 approximately one billion five hundred million dollars); Assoc. Dir. Calgary Stampeder Football Club; Currently included in the Canadian Who's Who 1981 Edition; **HOME ADD:** 3408 8A St. SW, Calgary, Canada T2T 3B2, (403)243-2246; **BUS ADD:** 8413 Elbow Dr. SW, Calgary, T2V 1K8, Alberta, Canada, (403)253-2626.

LYNCH, Darrel D.——**B:** Feb. 6, 1937, Ft. Smith, AR, *Gen. Mgr.*, Patsy S. Lynch RE; **PRIM RE ACT:** Broker; **SERVICES:** Brokerage of comml., indus., & resid. RE; **PROFL AFFIL & HONORS:** NAR, IEEE, Reg. Profl. Engr.; **EDUC:** BS, 1969, EE, Univ. of NH; **GRAD EDUC:** MS, 1970, EE, Univ. of NJ; **EDUC HONORS:** Cum Laude; **MIL SERV:** USAF, Lt. Col., Bronze Star Medal; **OTHER ACT & HONORS:** Air Force Assn., The Ret. Officers Assn.; **HOME ADD:** PO Box 930, Durham, NH 03824, (603)868-7372; **BUS ADD:** Pettee Brook Offices, Durham, NH 03824, (603)868-5777.

LYNCH, Dennis J.——**B:** Aug. 28, 1940, Cleveland, OH, *Pres.*, Meeks & Lynch, Inc.; **PRIM RE ACT:** Broker, Syndicator, Consultant, Appraiser, Property Manager, Owner/Investor; **SERVICES:** Mktg. of Comml. & Resid. Props., Appraising Prop. Mgmt. Synds.; **REP CLIENTS:** Gen. Public, Corps. and Third Party Cos. in the Mkt. of Resid. and Comml. Props., Investors in the Acquisition, Mktg. or Holding of RE Involving Synds.; **PROFL AFFIL & HONORS:** NAR; RESSI; **HOME ADD:** 1175 Creekwood Ln., Westlake, OH 44145, (216)871-2979; **BUS ADD:** 650 Dover Ctr. Rd., Bay Village, OH 44140, (216)835-3200.

LYNCH, Edwin Williams, Jr.——**B:** Dec. 11, 1952, Alexandria, VA, *General Partner*, Lynch Limited Partnership, Elmdale Limited Partnership, MTW Limited Partnership; **PRIM RE ACT:** Developer, Owner/Investor; **SERVICES:** Comml./indus. rental space; **EDUC:**

BA, 1975, Pol. Sci., Occidental Coll.; **EDUC HONORS:** Coro Found. Fellowship in Public Affairs, 1975-1976; **HOME ADD:** 7901 Treeside Ct., Springfield, VA 22152; **BUS ADD:** POB 607, Springfield, VA 22150.

LYNCH, Michael——*VP Fin.*, Mirro Corp.; **PRIM RE ACT:** Property Manager; **BUS ADD:** 1512 Washington St., PO Box 409, Manitowac, WI 54220, (414)684-4421.*

LYNCH, Michael E.——**B:** Apr. 5, 1951, Boston, MA, *VP Comml. Leasing*, Great America Company; **PRIM RE ACT:** Broker, Architect, Regulator, Consultant, Developer, Property Manager; **OTHER RE ACT:** Devel. of Comml. Props.; **SERVICES:** Mgmt. of facilities nationwide (USA) and overseas; **PREV EMPLOY:** Honeywell; **PROFL AFFIL & HONORS:** Mass Salesman, TX Broker, AMA; **EDUC:** BA, 1975, Bus., School of Mgmt., Boston Coll.; **GRAD EDUC:** MBA, Pres., Exec Training Program Honeywell, Harvard; **HOME ADD:** 11500 Braesview, San Antonio, TX 78213, (512)492-5152; **BUS ADD:** 4204 Gardendale Suite 303, San Antonio, TX 78284, (512)690-0300.

LYNCH, Robert Francis——**B:** Apr. 19, 1941, San Francisco, CA, *First VP & Rgnl. Mgr.*, Coldwell Banker, RE Fin.; **PRIM RE ACT:** Broker; **OTHER RE ACT:** Fin.; **SERVICES:** Comml. & Resid. brokerage, fin., capital mgt., etc.; **REP CLIENTS:** Lenders & instnl. investors in comml. props.; **PREV EMPLOY:** Blyth & Co., Corp. Fin.; **PROFL AFFIL & HONORS:** MBAA; Harvard Bus. Sch. Club of No. CA, Lic. RE Broker, State of CA; **EDUC:** BS, 1963, Phil., Bus., Univ. of San Francisco; **GRAD EDUC:** MBA, 1968, Mktg., Fin., Harvard Grad. Sch. of Bus. Admin.; **EDUC HONORS:** Cum Laude; **MIL SERV:** US Army, 1st Lt., Expert's Infantryman's Badge; **HOME ADD:** 121 Lake Merced Hill, San Francisco, CA 94132; **BUS ADD:** One Embarcadero Ctr., San Francisco, CA 94111, (415)772-0423.

LYNCH, Robert J.——**B:** Oct. 30, 1926, Lancaster, PA, *VP*, Lomas & Nettleton Co.; **PRIM RE ACT:** Lender; **PREV EMPLOY:** Lomas & Nettleton, 19 yrs at same co.; **PROFL AFFIL & HONORS:** MBA, ECO RE Bd., Lancaster, Lebanon, Reading, Allentown; **EDUC:** BS, 1951, Bus. Admin., Rider Coll., Trenton, NJ; **EDUC HONORS:** Dean's List; **MIL SERV:** US Army, 1944-46, 1st Lt., Several decorations; **OTHER ACT & HONORS:** Lancaster Human Realtion, 1980-82, Boys Club, Elks, Outstanding Young Men of PA, 1951, Outstanding Young Man of Lancaster, 1958; **HOME ADD:** 607 E. Roseville Rd., Lancaster, PA 17601, (717)569-5296; **BUS ADD:** 1794 Oregon Pk., Lancaster, PA 17601, (717)569-5388.

LYNCH, William W., Jr.——**B:** Aug. 26, 1936, Dallas, TX, *Pres.*, Insurance Building Corp.; *Pres.*, Argus Realty Corp.; *VP/Dir.*, Lynch Properties Corp.; *Dir.*, Broadmoor Properties, Inc.; *Partner*, Encino Co.; **PRIM RE ACT:** Broker, Developer, Owner/Investor, Property Manager; **SERVICES:** Devel. of office bldgs., shopping ctrs. and resid. housing; **EDUC:** BSEE, 1959, Electronics & EE, Univ. of AZ; **GRAD EDUC:** MBA, 1962, Fin. and Acctg., Stanford Univ.; **EDUC HONORS:** Tau Beta Pi, Blue Key, Pi Mu Epsilon, Who's Who in Amer. Coll.; **MIL SERV:** US Army; Capt.; **OTHER ACT & HONORS:** Who's Who in the South and SW; Dir., NM Electric Service Co., Hobbs Gas Co.; **HOME ADD:** P.O. Box 25105, Dallas, TX 75225; **BUS ADD:** 8333 Douglas Ave., Suite 550, Dallas, TX 75225, (214)363-7407.

LYNE, Kerry R.——**B:** Jan. 17, 1930, Chestnut Hill, MA, *Part.*, Sullivan & Worcester; **PRIM RE ACT:** Attorney; **SERVICES:** Full range of RE law practice; **REP CLIENTS:** Lenders, indiv. & instnl. investors, condo devels., office park devel., indus. revenue bond issuers, synd. & corp. RE; **PREV EMPLOY:** 1970-76 Gen. Counsel & Sr. VP of First Nat. Stores Inc., resp. included RE & constr. activities for over 400 stores; 1960-70 Part. in law firm of Lyne, Woodworth & Evarts, spec. in RE law; **PROFL AFFIL & HONORS:** ABA, Boston Bar Assn., Gr. Boston RE Bd.; **EDUC:** AB, 1952, Eng. Lit., Harvard Coll.; **GRAD EDUC:** LLB, 1957, Harvard Law Sch.; **MIL SERV:** USN, LTJG; **HOME ADD:** 131 Glen Rd., Wellesley Hills, MA 02181, (617)235-8988; **BUS ADD:** 100 Federal St., Boston, MA 02110, 17)338-2800.

LYNN, James C.——**B:** Nov. 17, 1947, New York, NY, *Pres.*, James Lynn & Assocs.; **PRIM RE ACT:** Consultant, Developer; **SERVICES:** Investment counseling, adaptive re-use, fin. packaging; **REP CLIENTS:** Corps., instns., maj. builders; **PREV EMPLOY:** Lehman Bros. Kuhn Loeb - Hoffman Assocs; **EDUC:** BS, 1969, Civil Engrg., Columbia Univ.; **GRAD EDUC:** MRP, 1971, Urban Econ., Univ. of NC; **EDUC HONORS:** Tau Beta Pi, Hud Fellow; **OTHER ACT & HONORS:** Nat. Trust for Historic Preservation; **HOME ADD:** 220 E. 49th St., New York, NY 10017, (212)688-5792; **BUS ADD:** 757 Third Ave., 12th Floor, New York, NY 10017, (212)688-0035.

LYNN, Paul A.——**B:** Mar. 13, 1953, Chicago, IL, *Pres.*, Paul A. Lynn & Assoc., Inc.; **PRIM RE ACT:** Broker, Consultant, Developer, Owner/Investor; **OTHER RE ACT:** Office leasing specialist; **SERVICES:** Office prop. leasing, sales and consulting; **REP CLIENTS:** Tenant and user rep., with some devels. rep., principle; **PROFL AFFIL & HONORS:** NAR; Houston Bd. of Realtors; RNMI; **EDUC:** BA, 1973, Pol. Sci., Econ., Gen. Bus., Drake Univ.; **OTHER ACT & HONORS:** Houston C of C; Aviation Comm.; Forum Club; Houston Grand Opera Advisory Bd.; **HOME ADD:** 3123 Las Palmas, Houston, TX 77027, (713)961-7655; **BUS ADD:** PO Box 27701, Dept. 411, Houston, TX 77227, (713)840-0011.

LYON, Constantine G.——**B:** Feb. 24, 1936, Durham Cty., NC, *Asst. Treas. & Mgr. of Mortgage Loans*, North Carolina Mutual Life Insurance Co.; **PRIM RE ACT:** Lender; **SERVICES:** Mortgage loans (RE first liens); **EDUC:** BS, 1958, Bus. Educ., NC Central Univ.; **GRAD EDUC:** MS, 1972, Bus. Educ., NC Central Univ.; **OTHER ACT & HONORS:** Zafa Court 41; **HOME ADD:** 6106 Yellowstone Dr., Durham, NC 27713, (919)544-7444; **BUS ADD:** 411 W. Chapel Hill St., Durham, NC 27701.

LYON, Rexford L.——**B:** Aug. 25, 1942, Binghamton, NY, Seobel & Lyon, A Professional Corp.; **PRIM RE ACT:** Attorney; **SERVICES:** Legal serv. to purchasers, sellers, synds., converters; **REP CLIENTS:** Various purchasers, sellers, and synd. of income producing prop., condo. conversion corp.; **PROFL AFFIL & HONORS:** ABA (Sect. of Real Prop. Probate and Trust Law); NJ Bar Assn.; Essex Cty. Bar Assn.; Morris Cty. Bar Assn.; **EDUC:** 1964, Psych. and Anthropology, Univ. of AZ; **GRAD EDUC:** 1967, Law, Rutgers Univ.; **EDUC HONORS:** Psi Chi, Hon. Frat., with Honors; **HOME ADD:** 96 Mt. Harmony Rd., Bernardsville, NJ 07924, (201)766-6252; **BUS ADD:** 83 Hanover Rd., Florham Park, NJ 07932, (201)966-1550.

LYON, William Jake——**B:** Feb. 11, 1936, Buffalo, TX, *Pres.*, William J. Lyon and Assoc., Inc.; **PRIM RE ACT:** Consultant, Appraiser; **SERVICES:** Real Estate appraisals, consultation; **REP CLIENTS:** Lenders, indiv., and inst. investors; **PREV EMPLOY:** TX Hwy. Dept.; **PROFL AFFIL & HONORS:** SREA; **EDUC:** BBA, 1958, Fin., TX A&M Univ.; **MIL SERV:** US Army, Capt.; **OTHER ACT & HONORS:** VP Beaumont Chapter SREA; **HOME ADD:** Rt. 9, Lufkin, TX 75901, (713)632-6234; **BUS ADD:** P.O. Box 708, Lufkin, TX 75901, (713)632-7763.

LYONS, John H.——**B:** Jan. 6, 1920, Toronto, Can., *Co-ordinator, Bus. & Commerce*, George Brown Coll., Bus. & Commerce; **PRIM RE ACT:** Consultant, Owner/Investor, Property Manager; **SERVICES:** Counselor and contributor for Hume Publishing Co.; **PREV EMPLOY:** Prop. Mgr. 2000+ Rental Units, Greenwin Prop. Mgmt.; Toronto Mktg. Mgr.; 1500+ Condo Apts., Belmont Prop. Mgmt.; **PROFL AFFIL & HONORS:** Member of Educ. Comm., HUDAC; Member of Educ. Comm.,Toronto Home Builders Assn.; Member of Educ. Comm.,ON Bldg. Officials Assn.; Member of Educ. Comm., ON Mort. Brokers Assn.; **MIL SERV:** Royal Can. Air Force; **OTHER ACT & HONORS:** Masonic Order; **HOME ADD:** 11 King St. W, Millbrook, L0A 1G0, ON, Can., (705)932-2095; **BUS ADD:** PO Box 1015, Station 'B', Toronto, M5T 2T9, ON, CAN, (416)967-1212.

LYONS, John M.——**B:** May 29, 1950, Methuen, MA, *Sr. Examining Atty.*, Chicago Title Insurance Co.; **PRIM RE ACT:** Attorney, Insuror; **SERVICES:** Legal Research and Title Ins. Underwriting; **PREV EMPLOY:** Law Clerk; Glassie, Pewett, Beebe & Shanks, Washington, DC 1975-1976; Legal Asst., Virginia Mortgage & Investment Co. 1975; **PROFL AFFIL & HONORS:** US Supreme Ct. Bar; VA State Bar; District of Columbia Bar; Arlington Cty. Bar Assn.; ABA-Sect. of Real Prop., Probate and Trust Law; **EDUC:** BA, 1972, Hist., Boston Coll.; **GRAD EDUC:** JD, 1975, RE and Land Devel. Law, The Nat. Law Center of the George Washington Univ.; **EDUC HONORS:** Grad. Cum Laude in the Honors Program; **OTHER ACT & HONORS:** Big Brothers of the Nat. Capital Area, Washington, DC; **HOME ADD:** 706 N Wayne St., #201, Arlington, VA 22201, (703)527-3352; **BUS ADD:** 2039 Wilson Blvd., Arlington, VA 22201, (703)525-5959.

LYONS, Michael J.——B: Apr. 17, 1945, NJ, *V.P.*, Merrill Lynch Realty; **PRIM RE ACT:** Broker; **PREV EMPLOY:** Sales Assoc. Chris Coile & Assoc., Inc. 2.5 Million Dollar Agent 1975-1967-1973; Teacher, Coach, High School; **PROFL AFFIL & HONORS:** NAR, Anne Arundel Co. Bd. of Realtors, CRB; Who's Who in MD 1975; Certified Residential-Broker; Million Dollar Agent '75; 2 Million Dollar Agent '75; **EDUC:** BS, 1967, Econ., Mt. St. Mary's Coll., Emmitsburg, MD; **OTHER ACT & HONORS:** Past Membership, Saefern Saddle & Yacht Club and Berrywood Community Assn.; Also Affiliated with Chris Coile, Inc.; **HOME ADD:** 659 Shore Rd., Sevenna Park, MD 21146, (301)647-5864; **BUS ADD:** 3905 Mountain Rd., Pasadena, MD 21122, (301)437-1700.

MAAS, Norman B.——B: Apr 8, 1933, Seattle, WA, *Sr. Part.*, Maas & Lantz, P.S.; **PRIM RE ACT:** Attorney, Instructor, Appraiser, Developer, Owner/Investor; **SERVICES:** Legal consultations, escrow, appraisals, rezones; **PREV EMPLOY:** Pres. and G.M. of northwest's largest private mtg co., 5 yrs. Pres. and G.M. of const. firm bldg. apts., houses & comm'l., as well as subdiv. and remodels. Member Wash State Bar.; **PROFL AFFIL & HONORS:** Former Pres. of WA chap., Nat. Home Improvement council. Former member of mtg. bankers group, RE Agent's lic in 1954. RE Broker's lic. in 1958. Securities Broker 1960. Securities Agent 1957; **EDUC:** BA, 1974, Econ., Univ. of Wash.; **GRAD EDUC:** J.D., 1976, Univ. of Puget Sound; **EDUC HONORS:** No. 1 in RE Transactions course; **MIL SERV:** USNR 1951-1959, hon. discharge; **HOME ADD:** P.O. Box 1, Kenmore, WA 98028; **BUS ADD:** 6555 N.E. 181st St., P.O. Box 366, Kenmore, WA 98028, 06)485-8575.

MAAS, William——*Fac. Manager*, Avery International; **PRIM RE ACT:** Property Manager; **BUS ADD:** 415 Huntington Dr., San Marino, LA 91108, (213)682-2812.*

MABEE, Nancy C.——B: Nov. 23, 1946, Boston, MA, *Exec. Mktg. Dir.*, Action Comm. of Fifty; **PRIM RE ACT:** Developer; **OTHER RE ACT:** Econ. Devel.; **SERVICES:** Indus. Devel.; **PROFL AFFIL & HONORS:** Indus. Devel. Council of ME N.E. Ind. Devel. Council; **EDUC:** BA, 1968, Univ. of ME; **GRAD EDUC:** MBA, currently, Univ. of ME; **HOME ADD:** 28 Fern St., Bangor, ME 04401, (207)942-5329; **BUS ADD:** 151 Broadway, Bangor, ME 04401, (207)947-3535.

MACADAM, Gordon L.——*Mgr. Corp. RE*, R.R. Donnelley & Sons Co.; **PRIM RE ACT:** Property Manager; **BUS ADD:** 2223 Martin Luther King Dr., Chicago, IL 60616, (312)326-8000.*

MCADOO, Ralph W.——B: July 24, 1924, Runnells, IA, *Pres.*, Mid-Iowa Savings & Loan; **PRIM RE ACT:** Lender; **EDUC:** BSC, 1949, Bus., Univ. of IA; **MIL SERV:** USN, Lt.; **HOME ADD:** 1101 S. 14th Ave. W., Newton, IA 50208, (515)792-2456; **BUS ADD:** Box 687, Newton, IA 50208, (515)792-6236.

MCANALLY, Joseph——*Dir. Purchasing*, H.B. Fuller Co.; **PRIM RE ACT:** Property Manager; **BUS ADD:** 2400 Kasota Ave., St. Paul, MN 55108, (612)645-3401.*

MCANDREWS, James P.——B: May 11, 1929, Carbondale, PA, *Atty., part.*, Thompson, Hine & Flory, RE Area; **OTHER RE ACT:** Real Estate law; **SERVICES:** Gen. RE Legal Servs.; **REP CLIENTS:** Ins. cos., banks, S&L assns., devels., retailers & investors; **PREV EMPLOY:** Teachers Ins. & Annuity Assn., NYC, Counsel Investment Law Dept.; Emigrant Savings Bank., NYC, Law Dept., Atty.; **PROFL AFFIL & HONORS:** ABA; OH State Bar Assn.; Bar Assn. of Greater Cleveland (Chmn Real Prop. Sec. 1980-81); Amer. Coll. of RE Lawyers; Amer. Land Title Assn., (Past Chmn. Lenders Counsel Grp.), ULI; Mort. Bankers Assn.; Intl. Council of Shopping Ctr.; Fellow of the Amer. Bar Found.; OH Land Title Assn.; Nat. Assn. of Corp. RE Execs. Delta Theta Phi Law Frat.; **EDUC:** BS, 1949, Acctg., Univ. of Scranton, Scranton, PA; **GRAD EDUC:** LLB, 1952, Law, Fordham Univ. Sch. of Law, NYC; RE Inst. Cert., NY Univ.; **MIL SERV:** USAF; 1st Lt.; **OTHER ACT & HONORS:** Rotary Intl.; Listed in Who's Who in Amer. Law; Who's Who in the Mid-West.; Lawyers Register by Specs. & Fields of Law; and Who's Who in Fin. & Indus.; My articles: "Air Rights, For Sale or Lease" published by Intnl. Council of Shopping Ctrs.; "Operating Agreements, Control Within the Shopping Ctr. Complex" published in Real Property Probate & Trust Journal, ABA; **HOME ADD:** 2971 Litchfield Rd., Shaker Heights, OH 44120, (216)991-9143; **BUS ADD:** 1100 Nat. City Bank Bldg., Cleveland, OH 44114, (216)566-5500.

MCANLY, L.D., Jr.——*Dir. Distr. Serv.*, The Maytag Co.; **PRIM RE ACT:** Property Manager; **BUS ADD:** 403 W. Fourth St. North, Newton, IA 50208, (515)792-7000.*

MCARDLE, Montrose P., IV——*Owner*, McArdle Dev. Co.; **PRIM RE ACT:** Developer, Builder, Owner/Investor, Property Manager; **PREV EMPLOY:** Asst. Prof., Mgmt./Mktg., Thomas Coll., Waterville, ME, 7 yrs.; **EDUC:** 1960, Econ., Boston Coll.; **GRAD EDUC:** MBA, 1962, Babson Inst.; MED, 1963, Harvard Univ.; MPsy., 1968, Univ. of ME; **MIL SERV:** US Army, Capt., MSC; **BUS ADD:** 1481 Arkansas St., Gulf Breeze, FL 32561.

MCARTHUR, Cameron D.——B: Nov. 23, 1934, Santa Barbara, CA, *VP, Prop. Mgmt.*, Jay Prop. Sys. Inc., A Member of Jacobs Engin. Grp., Inc.; **PRIM RE ACT:** Developer, Property Manager; **SERVICES:** Comml. RE mgmt., Resid. RE Mgmt., Comml. Parking Lot Mgmt., RE Devel. and RE Brokerage; **PREV EMPLOY:** Wilshire Prop. Realty Co. 1977-78; VP Standard Mgmt. Co. 1973-77; **PROFL AFFIL & HONORS:** Cand. Mem. for RPA; **EDUC:** BA, 1959, UCLA; **MIL SERV:** USMCR; **OTHER ACT & HONORS:** Bd. of Dirs. LA Chap., BOMA; Bd. of Dirs., Pasadena C of C; Tournament of Roses; **HOME ADD:** 1435 Wellington Ave., Pasadena, CA 91103; **BUS ADD:** 251 S. Lake Ave., Pasadena, CA 91101, (213)449-2171.

MCARTHUR, Charles H.——B: Aug. 30, 1923, Phoenix, AZ, *VP*, Julien J. Studley, Inc.; **PRIM RE ACT:** Broker, Consultant; **SERVICES:** Consultant to major cos. and devels. re office space & office bldgs. Tenant rep. in lease negotiations for office space; **EDUC:** BA, 1950, Liberal Arts/Eng., Cornell Univ.; **MIL SERV:** Pilot - USNR, Lt. j.g.; **OTHER ACT & HONORS:** The Houston Club; **HOME ADD:** 1208 Fountainview Dr., Houston, TX 77057, (713)780-0007; **BUS ADD:** 5433 Westheimer, Suite 1010, Houston, TX 77056, (713)622-9000.

MACARTHUR, William H.——B: May 7, 1941, Boston, MA, *Pres.*, Transar Capital Corp.; **PRIM RE ACT:** Broker, Attorney, Banker, Owner/Investor; **REP CLIENTS:** Specialize in handling investment on behalf of foreign high-net worth indiv. and foreign instns.; includes purchase and sale of prop. and devel.; frequently will invest own funds alongside; **PREV EMPLOY:** Amer. Express Intl. Banking Corp.; Patterson Belknap & Webb, NY (Law); Anderson & Rabinowitz, Tokyo (Law); **PROFL AFFIL & HONORS:** NY Bar Assn.; **EDUC:** BA, 1963, Hist., Yale Univ.; **GRAD EDUC:** 1967, Columbia Law School; **EDUC HONORS:** Dean's List, Dean's List; **HOME ADD:** 311 E. 51st St., New York, NY; **BUS ADD:** 430 Park Ave., New York, NY 10022, (212)832-7120.

MCATEE, Patrick O.——B: Oct. 15, 1954, Peoria, IL, *RE Appraiser*, McAtee Appraisal Serv.; **PRIM RE ACT:** Appraiser; **SERVICES:** RE appraisals, all types, any reason; **REP CLIENTS:** Homequity, Equitable Relocation, Employee Transfer Corp.; **PROFL AFFIL & HONORS:** Assoc. Member Peoria Bd. of Realtors, SREA, SRA; **OTHER ACT & HONORS:** Grader of single fam. narrative demonstration reports for SREA; **HOME ADD:** 2223 W. Callender, W. Peoria, IL 61604, (309)674-4777; **BUS ADD:** 2223 W. Callender, W. Peoria, IL 61604, (309)674-4777.

MCATEER, Paul Murray——B: July 2, 1948, London Ontario, Can., *Gen. Counsel and Sec.*, Carma Ltd.; **OTHER RE ACT:** land Devel.; **PREV EMPLOY:** Francana Oil & Gas Ltd.; Qualico Devel. Ltd.; **PROFL AFFIL & HONORS:** Bar Assns. Manitoba, Alberta & BC, Call to the Bd. Man. (77), B.C. (79) Alberta (81); **EDUC:** BASc (Civil Engr.), 1974, Univ. of Ottawa; **GRAD EDUC:** LLB, 1976, Common Law, Univ. of Ottawa; **HOME ADD:** 201 4th Ave. NE, Calgary, T2E 0J2, Alberta, (403)239-6684; **BUS ADD:** 6715 8th St. NE, Calgary, T2E7H7, Alberta, CN, (403)275-5555.

MCAULEY, Michael Freeman——B: June 11, 1938, Moline, IL, *Sr. VP, Exec. Investment Grp.*, Henry S. Miller Co., Exec. Investments; **PRIM RE ACT:** Broker, Consultant, Owner/Investor, Property Manager, Syndicator; **PREV EMPLOY:** 3-M Co., 1961-1971; **PROFL AFFIL & HONORS:** NAR; RESSI; GDBR; RNMI; **EDUC:** BA, 1960, Psych./Sociology, State Univ. of IA; **HOME ADD:** 1300 Chippewa, Richardson, TX 75080, (214)783-1700; **BUS ADD:** 2001 Bryan Tower, 30th Floor, Dallas, TX 75201, (214)748-9171.

MCAULIFF, William J., Jr.——*Executive Vice President*, American Hand Title Association; **OTHER RE ACT:** Profl. Assn. Admin.; **BUS ADD:** 1828L St. NW, Suite 705, Washington, DC 20036, (202)296-3671.*

MACBETH, William G.——**B:** Nov. 20, 1928, Lubbock, TX, *RE Broker*, W.G. Macbeth, Realtor; **PRIM RE ACT:** Broker; **OTHER RE ACT:** Investor; **SERVICES:** RE counseling, exchanging; **PREV EMPLOY:** Controller for Yellowstone Park Co.; **PROFL AFFIL & HONORS:** Yuma Bd. of Realtors; Yuma RE Exchangors; Soc. of Exchange Counselors, CCIM; **OTHER ACT & HONORS:** Tr., AZ 4-H Found.; **HOME ADD:** 2725 Ave. A, Yuma, AZ 85364, (602)726-8997; **BUS ADD:** POB 5359, Yuma, AZ 85364, (602)726-0843.

MCBRAYER, John H.——**B:** Apr. 28, 1914, Shelby, NC, *Owner*, John H. McBrayer, Realty; **PRIM RE ACT:** Broker; **MIL SERV:** US Army, CWS, Lt.; **HOME ADD:** 721 W Warren St., Shelby, NC 28150, (704)487-4256; **BUS ADD:** 102 W Marion St., Shelby, NC 23150, (704)487-4343.

MCBREARITY, Frank B., Jr.——**B:** July 17, 1942, NY, NY, *Sr. VP and Gen. Mgr.*, Landauer Associates, Inc.; **PRIM RE ACT:** Broker, Consultant, Appraiser; **SERVICES:** Counseling, investment feasibility, mkt. research studies, acquisition and disposition serv.; **PREV EMPLOY:** Landauer Assoc.-Atlanta, GA; McBrearity & Co., Inc. Atlanta, GA; Hammer, Siler, George Assoc., Atlanta, GA; **PROFL AFFIL & HONORS:** ULI, BOMA, NAR, W. Palm Beach Bd. of Realtors; **EDUC:** BS, 1964, Electric Engr., Villanova Univ.; **GRAD EDUC:** MBA, 1966, Univ. of Chicago; **HOME ADD:** 236 Sudbury Dr., Atlantis, FL 33462, (305)439-4274; **BUS ADD:** 1675 Palm Beach Lakes Blvd., W. Palm Beach, FL 33401, (305)689-8111.

MCBRIDE, Carl——**B:** July 13, 1918, Minneapolis, MN, *VP*, Richfield State Agency, Inc.; **PRIM RE ACT:** Consultant, Developer, Property Manager; **SERVICES:** Office space; **REP CLIENTS:** Bank, Atty., CPA & Drs.; **PREV EMPLOY:** Sales & Mgmt.; **PROFL AFFIL & HONORS:** BOMA, PTA; **OTHER ACT & HONORS:** Township clerk; **HOME ADD:** Annandale, MN 55302, (612)274-8627; **BUS ADD:** 6625 Lyndale Ave. So., Richfield, MN 55423, (612)861-7355.

MCBRIDE, Dennis——**B:** Apr. 28, 1940, Akron, OH, *Sr. Appraiser*, Tri-County Appraisal Serv.; **PRIM RE ACT:** Broker, Appraiser; **SERVICES:** Appraisals, Feasibility Studies, Component Cost Breakdown; **REP CLIENTS:** S&L's, Banks, Mort. Co., Indiv. Investors; **PREV EMPLOY:** Santa Barbara S&L Assn., Kings County Assessors Office; **PROFL AFFIL & HONORS:** SREA, Intl. Inst. of Valuers, SRA; **EDUC:** BS, 1974, RE, Urban Land Econ., Fresno State Univ.; **MIL SERV:** US Army, PFC; **HOME ADD:** 25021 Southport St., Laguna Hills, CA 92653, (714)586-5016; **BUS ADD:** PO Box 4025, Santa Ana, CA 92702.

MACBRIDE, Dexter P.——*Exec. VP*, American Society of Appraisers; **PRIM RE ACT:** Banker; **BUS ADD:** Dulles Intl. Airport, PO Box 17265, Washington, DC 20041.*

MCBRIDE, Gardner S.——*Executive Vice President*, Building Owners & Managers Association International; **OTHER RE ACT:** Profl. Assn. Admin.; **BUS ADD:** 1221 Massachusetts Ave. NW, Washington, DC 20005, (202)638-2929.*

MCBRIDE, J. Nevins, Jr.——**B:** Mar. 6, 1942, Paterson, NJ, *Partner*, Great Pacific Group, Inc.; **PRIM RE ACT:** Developer, Builder, Owner/Investor, Property Manager, Insuror, Syndicator; **OTHER RE ACT:** Hotel acquisition, devel. & mgmt. of own projects and for other owners/invesors; **REP CLIENTS:** Great Pac. Hotels; Great Pacific Mgmt. Co. - prop. mgmt.; CA Fin. Assoc. - mort. brokerage; CA Devels. Ins. Co. - const. bonding; **PREV EMPLOY:** Devel., mort. broker, in NYC area, 1964-1974; **EDUC:** BSBA, 1964, Georgetown Univ.; **BUS ADD:** 4875 North Harbor Dr., San Diego, CA 92106, (714)226-0451.

MCBRIDE, John Daniel, Jr.——**B:** Sep. 12, 1944, New Orleans, LA, *Metropolitan Buildings Property Manager*, Santa Fe Land Improvement Co.; **PRIM RE ACT:** Property Manager; **SERVICES:** Office and shopping ctr. prop. mgmt.; **REP CLIENTS:** Santa Fe Land Improvement Company; The Atchison, Topeka, and Santa Fe Railway Company (Divisions of Santa Fe Industries, Inc.);Santa Fe Realty Development, Inc.; **PREV EMPLOY:** Angwin Apartment Management Company; **PROFL AFFIL & HONORS:** IREM; Bldg. Owners and Mgrs. Assns.; Greater Dallas Assn. of Realtors, CPM; RPA Candidate; **EDUC:** Bus. Admin., 1974, RE, CA State Univ., Northridge; **MIL SERV:** USN, PO, Vietnam Service Medal; Vietnam Campaign Medal; Navy Unit Citation; National Service Medal; **HOME ADD:** 2710 Belaire Ct., Arlington, TX 76013, (817)265-5917; **BUS ADD:** 2900 Turtle Creek Plaza, Suite 520, Dallas, TX 75219, (214)522-8068.

MCBRIDE, Philip J.——**B:** Dec. 30, 1942, Minneapolis, MN, *Pres.*, McBride and Company; **PRIM RE ACT:** Broker, Consultant, Developer, Lender, Builder, Owner/Investor, Property Manager, Syndicator; **SERVICES:** Portfolio mgmt. for personal and selected clients including devel., leasing, mktg.; **PREV EMPLOY:** Van Schaack & Co., 1968-70, Denver, CO; **PROFL AFFIL & HONORS:** Denver Bd. of Realtors, RNMI, ULI, CCIM, Bd. of Dirs. - Denver Bd. of Realtors; **EDUC:** BA, 1965, Philosophy - Humanities, Univ. of MN; **MIL SERV:** US Army, SSgt.; **OTHER ACT & HONORS:** Denver Building Code Revision Commn., Denver Handicapped Code Requirements; Instructor, CI Div., RNMI; **HOME ADD:** 1044 Olive St., Denver, CO 80220, (303)321-3738; **BUS ADD:** 235 Fillmore St., Denver, CO 80206, (303)321-3334.

MCBRIDE, Robert David——**B:** Jan. 5, 1942, Evansville,IN, *Sr. Resid. Appraiser*, McBride, Appraiser Consultant; **PRIM RE ACT:** Consultant, Appraiser, Owner/Investor; **SERVICES:** Appraisals - Consultant; **REP CLIENTS:** Lenders-Investors-Gov.-Indiv.; **PREV EMPLOY:** Sales-Sales Mgr.-Tax Consultant-Staff Appraiser; **PROFL AFFIL & HONORS:** NAR-NAIFA-SREA; **MIL SERV:** USMC; **OTHER ACT & HONORS:** Masonic Lodge, Scottish Rite, Shriner, Member Hadi Temple Dir.'s Staff, Sec. Tre. Shrine Luncheon Club; **HOME ADD:** 707 Reis Ave., Evansville, IN 47711, (812)422-3301; **BUS ADD:** 707 Reis Ave., Evansville, IN 47711, (812)422-3301.

MCCABE, Barry——**B:** Oct. 13, 1940, Los Angeles, CA, *Assoc. Gen. Counsel*, DeAnza Corp.; **PRIM RE ACT:** Broker, Consultant, Attorney, Syndicator; **SERVICES:** Devel., const., synd., of comml. and resid. prop.; **REP CLIENTS:** Indiv. & instnl. investors; **PROFL AFFIL & HONORS:** ABA; Comm. on Const. Indus.; Beverly Hills Bar Assn. Comm. on RE & Comm. on Taxation; **EDUC:** BA, 1963, Philosophy & Psych., Catholic Univ. of Amer., Washington, DC; **GRAD EDUC:** MA, 1967, Psychology, Catholic Univ. of Amer.; JD, 1977, Law, Univ. of So. CA, Los Angeles; **HOME ADD:** 1757 N. Orange Grove Ave., Hollywood, CA 90046; **BUS ADD:** 9171 Wilshire Blvd., Beverly Hills, CA 90210, (213)550-1111.

MCCABE, Brooks F., Jr.——**B:** Jan. 19, 1949, Charleston, WV, *Pres.*, McCabe & Henley Props., Inc.; **PRIM RE ACT:** Broker, Consultant, Developer, Owner/Investor, Property Manager, Syndicator; **PREV EMPLOY:** Spec. Asst. to WV Gov. & acted as Gov's Housing Coordinator and Dir. of Disaster Recovery Office; **PROFL AFFIL & HONORS:** APA, NAR, RESSI, RNMI, Amer. Inst. Cert. Planners; CCIM; **EDUC:** BA, 1970, Mgmt., Engrg., Univ. of VT; **GRAD EDUC:** MEd, 1972, Univ. of VT; EdD, 1975, Univ. of VT; **EDUC HONORS:** Sr. Class Hon., Pres. of Student Body, Pres. of Phi Delta Theta Frat., WV Univ. Found. Predoctoral Fellowship; **MIL SERV:** Capt.; **OTHER ACT & HONORS:** Member Bd. of Dir. of Charleston Exchange Club, Member Univ. of VT Bd. of Tr., Member Bd. of Dir. Charleston Community Council.; **HOME ADD:** 1251 Edgewood Dr., Charleston, WV 25305, (304)342-1961; **BUS ADD:** 19 Summers St., PO Box 3708, Charleston, WV 25335, (304)342-4415.

MCCABE, Carol——*Genl. Counsel*, Department of Housing and Urban Development, Neighborhood Reinvestment Corp.; **PRIM RE ACT:** Lender; **BUS ADD:** 451 Seventh St., S.W., Washington, DC 20410, (202)377-6076.*

MCCABE, Francis J., Jr.——**B:** Apr. 8, 1924, Providence, RI, *Owner*, F.J. McCabe & Son, Realtors; **PRIM RE ACT:** Broker, Consultant, Appraiser, Regulator, Instructor; **SERVICES:** Brokerage; appraisals; consultant; property tax consultant; **REP CLIENTS:** Fed., state & local govt.; several banks; maj. corps.; estates; lawyers; bus.; homeowners; etc.; **PREV EMPLOY:** Bd. of Assessment Review & City Assessor 15 years, Warwick, R.I.; Instr. in RE & Appraising 20 years at Johnson & Wales Coll., Providence, RI; **PROFL AFFIL & HONORS:** Past Dir., NAR; Past Pres. of RI and Kent Cty. & Washington Cty. Bd. of Realtors; etc., Cert. Sr. Appraiser-Consultant (AACA), Omega Tau Rho (NAR honor), Realtor of the Year for RI & local bd. (3 times); **EDUC:** BS, 1944, Bus. Admin., Holy Cross Coll.; Also attended Univ. of RI; Boston Coll; many other seminars in RE, appraising and assessing; **MIL SERV:** USNR, 1942-46, Lt. j.g., Pac. & Atl. Area Medals & Victory Medal, **OTHER ACT & HONORS:** City Assessor 1960-72; RI RE Commn. 1976 - Still serving; Amer. Fed. of Musicians; Tr., St. Catherine's Church; Knights of Columbus; etc.; **HOME ADD:** 346 Potters Ave., Warwick, RI 02886, (401)737-7651; **BUS ADD:** 3220 Post Rd., Warwick, RI 02886, (401)737-5400.

MCCABE, James F., Jr.——**B:** July 21, 1938, New York, NY, *Dir. Reg. Appraisal Staff*, US Gen. Servs. Admin., Public Bldg. Serv., Region 9; **PRIM RE ACT:** Consultant, Appraiser; **PREV EMPLOY:** Savings Banking, Sales Leasing and Mort. Brokerage, Dir., Appraisal Staff, Region 2, NY; **PROFL AFFIL & HONORS:** Rho Epsilon, RE Frat., Amer. Soc. of Appraisers, SREA, NARA, Lic. RE Broker, SRA, ASA, CRA, CSA; **EDUC:** BS, 1961, RE, NY Univ.; **MIL SERV:** US Army;

Sgt.; **HOME ADD:** 257 San Filipe Way, Novato, CA 94947, (415)892-8530; **BUS ADD:** 525 Market St., San Francisco, CA 94105, (415)974-9121.

MCCABE, John F., Jr.——B: Mar. 15, 1947, Washington, DC, *Shareholder*, Wilkes & Artis, Chartered; **PRIM RE ACT:** Attorney; **SERVICES:** Legal; **REP CLIENTS:** Somerset Assocs.; W.C. & A.N. Miller Devel. Co.; Kettler Brothers, Inc.; Montgomery Village Found, Inc.; **PROFL AFFIL & HONORS:** DC Bar; Bar Assn. of the Dist. of Columbia; Prince George's, Montgomery, and MD State Bar Assns.; The Barristers; CAI; ABA; **EDUC:** AB, 1969, English, Coll. of Arts & Sciences Georgetown Univ.; **GRAD EDUC:** JD, 1972, Georgetown Univ. Law Center; **EDUC HONORS:** Cum Laude, Phi Beta Kappa; **OTHER ACT & HONORS:** Rockville C of C; Montgomery Cty. C of C; **HOME ADD:** 5913 Woodacres Dr., Bethesda, MD 20816, (301)229-7639; **BUS ADD:** Suite 1407, 51 Monroe St., Rockville, MD 20850, (301)279-7900.

MCCABE, Joseph T., Jr.——B: Mar. 12, 1949, NJ, *VP*, US Trust Co. of NY, Specialized Lending; **PRIM RE ACT:** Lender; **SERVICES:** Construction and acquisition fin., partnership fin.; **REP CLIENTS:** Major devel - nat. and reg.; **PREV EMPLOY:** Investment synd., US Trust; **PROFL AFFIL & HONORS:** MBA; **EDUC:** BA, 1971, Philosophy, Yale Univ.; **EDUC HONORS:** Cum Laude; **HOME ADD:** 77 Bleecker St., New York, NY 10012, (212)473-2847; **BUS ADD:** 45 Wall St., New York, NY 10005, (212)425-4500.

MCCABE, Michael J.——*Sales Mgr.*, Pacific Freeport Group; **PRIM RE ACT:** Developer; **BUS ADD:** 901 E. Glendale Ave., Sparks, NV 89431.*

MCCAFFERY, Edward J.——*RE Mgr.*, General Electric Realty Corp.; **PRIM RE ACT:** Property Manager; **BUS ADD:** One River Rd., Schenectady, NY 12345, (518)385-4410.*

MCCAIN, Charlie R.——B: Nov. 12, 1931, Roby, TX, *Owner*, Charlie McCain - Appraiser, Consultant; **PRIM RE ACT:** Broker, Consultant, Appraiser, Owner/Investor, Property Manager; **SERVICES:** All types of RE appraisals and consultation; comml. sales; **REP CLIENTS:** Numerous lending instns., attys. and firms involved in acquisition, condemnation or disposition of real prop. rights; **PREV EMPLOY:** TVA, Chattanooga, TN, 1964-69; Wortman & Mann, Jackson, MS, 1970-71; Self employed, 1972-present; **PROFL AFFIL & HONORS:** AIREA, Soc. of RE Appraisers, Amer. Soc. of Farm Mgrs. & Rural Appraisers, Intl. R/W Assn., NAR, MAI, SRPA, SR/WA; **EDUC:** BS, 1963, Agricultural Econ. and Gen. Statistics, LA State Univ.; **MIL SERV:** US Army, SFC, Br. Star/4 clusters; **HOME ADD:** P O Box 335, Newllano, LA 71461-0335, (318)238-9102; **BUS ADD:** Hwy. 1211, P O Box 616, Leesville, LA 71446, (318)238-9006.

MCCAIN, David W.——B: Oct. 30, 1933, Buffalo, NY, *VP*, Koger Props. Inc.; **PRIM RE ACT:** Developer, Builder, Property Manager; **SERVICES:** Devel., constr. mgr., suburban office pks; **PROFL AFFIL & HONORS:** Lic. RE Broker, St. of FL; **EDUC:** BS, 1955, Lib. Arts., Wash. & Lee Univ.; **GRAD EDUC:** MBA, 1966, Fin., Harvard Grad. Sch. of Bus.; **EDUC HONORS:** Cum Laude; **MIL SERV:** USNR, Lt.; **HOME ADD:** 4118 Leeward Point, Jacksonville, FL 32225, (904)642-2935; **BUS ADD:** 3986 Blvd. Ctr. Dr., Jacksonville, FL 32207, (904)396-4811.

MCCAIN, Michael B.——*Exec. Fir.*, Tuscaloosa Industrial Development Authority; **PRIM RE ACT:** Property Manager; **BUS ADD:** PO Box 2667, Tuscaloosa, AL 35903, (205)349-1414.*

MCCALLIE, Thomas H., III——B: Apr. 10, 1942, Ft. Oglethorpe, GA, *Partner*, Harris, Moon, Bell & McCallie; **PRIM RE ACT:** Attorney; **REP CLIENTS:** Title Co.; purchasers, sellers and lenders of resid. or comml. prop. materialmen; **PROFL AFFIL & HONORS:** Chattanooga Bar Assn.; ABA (Member Section Real Prop., Probate & Trust Law, Corp. Banking and Bus. Law); Chattanooga Estate Planning Council; **EDUC:** Engrg./Acctg., Univ. of TN, Knoxville; **GRAD EDUC:** JD, 1966, Univ. of TN Law Sch., Knoxville; **EDUC HONORS:** Awards - Admin. Law, Bankruptcy Law, Moot Court Outstanding Lawyer; **MIL SERV:** US Naval Res., Lt.; **OTHER ACT & HONORS:** Kiwanis Club, Advisory Bds. Salvation Army, Covenant Coll.; Speaker, Adv. RE Seminar; TN Bar Assn.; **HOME ADD:** 614 Sunset Road, W., Lookout Mountain, TN 37350, (615)821-0766; **BUS ADD:** 1217 First Tennessee Bldg., Chattanooga, TN 37402, (615)266-6461.

MCCALLUM, Robert——*VP Engineering*, Courier Corp.; **PRIM RE ACT:** Property Manager; **BUS ADD:** 165 Jackson St., Lowell, MA 01852, (617)458-6351.*

MCCANN, William A.——B: Oct. 7, 1937, Chicago, IL, *Pres.*, Wm. A. McCann & Assoc., Inc.; **PRIM RE ACT:** Consultant, Appraiser; **SERVICES:** RE appraising and consulting; expert testimony, condemnation, zoning, taxes, etc.; **REP CLIENTS:** Major law firms, banks, pension funds, govt. agencies, utility cos., devel., investors; **PREV EMPLOY:** S & L, Loan Officer; Field Supervisor for Nat. Appraisal Co.; **PROFL AFFIL & HONORS:** AIREA; Soc. of RE Appraisers; Chicago RE Bd.; Nat. Assn. of RE Bds., MAI, SRPA; Lambda Alpha RE Frat.; **EDUC:** ABA, 1966, RE, Central RE Inst., Central Jr. Coll.; AIREA; Soc. of RE Appraisers; **OTHER ACT & HONORS:** Chairman, IL S & L Advisory Bd., 1974-75 Guest Speaker; AIREA, Soc. of RE Appraisers, Amer. ROW Assn., Chicago RE Bd.; **BUS ADD:** 180 N. LaSalle St., Chicago, IL 60601, (312)372-0943.

MCCARTHY, Adair Bernard——B: Oct. 5, 1931, San Francisco, CA, *Sr. VP, The Innisfree Cos.*, Pres., Innisfree Mktg. Assoc.; **PRIM RE ACT:** Broker, Developer, Owner/Investor; **SERVICES:** Responsible for Co. Mktg., Land Acquisition and Sale of Product; Project Mgr.; **REP CLIENTS:** Indiv. or Instnl. Investors and Land Owners; other devels.; **PREV EMPLOY:** McCarthy RE Co.; **PROFL AFFIL & HONORS:** NAR, CA Assn. of Realtors, Sales and Mktg. Council of NO. CA, Bldg. Indus. Assoc. of No. CA, Amer. Land Devels. Assn., GRI; **EDUC:** BA, 1956, Acctg./Bus. Admin., San Jose State Univ.; **EDUC HONORS:** Cum Laude; **MIL SERV:** USN, PO; **HOME ADD:** 79 Greenwood Way, Mill Valley, CA 94941, (415)383-5095; **BUS ADD:** 2656 Bridgeway, Sausalito, CA 94965, (415)332-6250.

MCCARTHY, Douglas——*Asst. VP*, Capital Manufacturing Co.; **PRIM RE ACT:** Property Manager; **BUS ADD:** PO Box 262, Woburn, MA 01801, (617)933-7979.*

MCCARTHY, Fred. R., Jr.——B: Nov. 17, 1924, Red Bay, Franklin Co., AL, *Consultant*, Sears Auth. Catalog Sales Merchant, Catalog Sales; **PRIM RE ACT:** Developer, Builder, Owner/Investor; **SERVICES:** Purchase, sub-divide, & devel. props.; **REP CLIENTS:** McCarthy Enterprises, Inc.; **PREV EMPLOY:** Indep. Ins. Agency.; **PROFL AFFIL & HONORS:** Public Housing Admin. 1950-present, Chmn. Red Bay Housing Auth., Ex. Chmn SCS Franklin Co.; **EDUC:** BS, 1949, Bio., Samford (Howard) Coll., Birmingham, AL; **GRAD EDUC:** 1950-51, Econ., Univ MS; **MIL SERV:** USNR; PHM 1st Class, Pres. Unit. Cit. 6th Marine Div.; **OTHER ACT & HONORS:** Red Bay Housing Authority, Chmn., 9 yrs. service; Various state & nat. orgs. through above, VFW, Amer. Legion, Civitan Club, Soil Conservation Co., Comm.; **HOME ADD:** Route 3, Box 617, Red Bay, AL 35582, (205)356-4488; **BUS ADD:** PO Drawer 536, Red Bay, Franklin Co., AL 35582, (601)454-7672.

MCCARTHY, John A.——*Dir. RE*, Standard Brands, Inc.; **PRIM RE ACT:** Property Manager; **BUS ADD:** 625 Madison Ave., New York, NY 10022, (212)759-4400.*

MCCARTHY, Luke V., Esq.——B: Nov. 11, 1946, Algona, IA, *Pres., Bd. of Dirs.*, August Financial Corp.; **PRIM RE ACT:** Consultant, Attorney, Developer, Owner/Investor, Syndicator; **OTHER RE ACT:** CPA; **SERVICES:** Synd. of RE partnerships for investors, including public; **PREV EMPLOY:** RE and Tax Atty. with Maj. San Francisco Law Firm; Tax Specialist with CPA firm; **PROFL AFFIL & HONORS:** ABA, CA CPA Soc., RESSI, IAFP; **EDUC:** BS, 1970, Acctg. and Fin., CA Polytechnic Univ., Pomona, CA; **GRAD EDUC:** JD, 1974, Law, Univ. of Santa Clara, CA; **EDUC HONORS:** Grad. with Honors; **MIL SERV:** US Army, Sgt., E-5; **HOME ADD:** 1155 Winston Ave., San Marino, CA 91108; **BUS ADD:** 4401 Atlantic Ave., Suite 400, Long Beach, CA 90807, (213)428-1211.

MCCARTHY, R. Michael——*Pres.*, Chippewa County Economic Devel. Corp.; **PRIM RE ACT:** Developer; **BUS ADD:** Bldg. 127, Chippewa Cty, Int'l. Airport, Kincheloe, MI 49788, (906)495-5631.*

MCCARTHY, Sean E.——*Exec. VP-Counsel*, California Land Title Assn.; **PRIM RE ACT:** Attorney, Insuror; **BUS ADD:** 1024 Tenth St., Sacramento, CA 95814.

MCCARTIN, Gary L.——B: July 14, 1954, New Allway IN, *Dir. of RE*, Chi-Chi's Inc.; **OTHER RE ACT:** Site Selector; **SERVICES:** Purchase, Lease, Acquisition of RE Sites; **PREV EMPLOY:** Burger Chef Systems Inc.; Taco Bell Inc.; **PROFL AFFIL & HONORS:** ICSC, NACORE, Indianapolis Bd. of Realtors; **EDUC:** BS, 1977, RE, IN Univ.; **HOME ADD:** 731 Yorkwood Pl., Louisville, KY 40223, (502)244-9410; **BUS ADD:** 1939 Goldsmith Ln., Louisville, KY 40232, (502)459-4646.

MCCARTNEY, Robert C.——B: May 3, 1934, *Partner*, Eckert, Seamans, Cherin & Mellott; **PRIM RE ACT:** Attorney, Owner/Investor; **SERVICES:** Legal Services; **REP CLIENTS:** Ryan Homes, Inc., Holleran Serv., Inc., Wilmar Prop. Limited Partnership I;

Education Management Corp.; **PROFL AFFIL & HONORS:** ABA, PA and Allegheny Cty. Bar Assns.; **EDUC:** 1956, Woodrow Wilson School of Public & Intl. Affairs, Princeton Univ.; **GRAD EDUC:** Harvard Univ., 1959, Law, Harvard Law School; **EDUC HONORS:** High Honors, Honors; **HOME ADD:** 9843 Woodland Rd. N., Pittsburgh, PA 15237, (412)366-0959; **BUS ADD:** 42nd Fl., US Steel Bldg., 600 Grant St.,, Pittsburgh, PA 15219, (412)566-6025.

MCCARTNEY, Ronnie Gladen——B: Sept. 5, 1942, Waco,TX, *Owner - Mgr.*, Ron McCartney; **PRIM RE ACT:** Developer, Lender, Builder, Owner/Investor, Property Manager; **SERVICES:** Suburban devel.; bldg., managing, selling & fin. of these properties; **REP CLIENTS:** Lenders & indivs. of surburban props.; **PREV EMPLOY:** Bldg. trades - electrical, structural, Sales Rep. - Fed. Pac.; **PROFL AFFIL & HONORS:** Heart of TX Builders' Assn., Home Onwers Warranty Bd. Member, Electrical Local Union, Waco Bd. of Realtors; **EDUC:** BBA, 1970, RE and Mktg., Baylor Univ.; **OTHER ACT & HONORS:** TX Hist. Soc.; **HOME ADD:** 4308 Guthrie Circle, Waco, TX 76710, (817)776-5296; **BUS ADD:** Rt. 5, Box 324, Waco, TX 76705, (817)829-1524.

MCCARTY, Arlon R.——B: Mar. 19, 1925, Kalamazoo, MI, *Mgr., Land Acquisition*, Florida Power & Light Co., Land Management; **PRIM RE ACT:** Broker, Owner/Investor, Property Manager; **OTHER RE ACT:** Land & Right of Way Acquisition; **SERVICES:** Land Acquisition & Mgmt.; **REP CLIENTS:** Employer; **PROFL AFFIL & HONORS:** Amer. Right of Way Assn.; **EDUC:** BSBA, 1951, Mktg., FL State Univ.; **MIL SERV:** USAF, Pvt.; **HOME ADD:** 9 Maryann Terr., Ormond Beach, FL 32074, (904)672-6175; **BUS ADD:** PO Box 529100, Miami, FL 33152, (305)552-3899.

MCCARVER, Barbara B.——B: Apr. 4, 1920, Austin, TX, *Pres.*, McCarver Co., Inc., Realtors; **PRIM RE ACT:** Broker; **SERVICES:** Gen. RE Brokerage Bus.; **PROFL AFFIL & HONORS:** Intl. Fed. of RE Brokers; Houston Bd. of Realtors; Women's Council of NAR; ABWA; NAR; TX Assn. of Realtors, Past Pres. Bd. of Realtors 1977; "Realtor of Yr.", 1980; **OTHER ACT & HONORS:** Clear Lake City Presbyterian Church, Houston, TX; Dir. NAR; TX Assn. of Realtors and Houston Bd. of Realtors, Tr. of Realty Breakfast Club, "99 Club", TAR; **HOME ADD:** 16339 Craighurst St., Houston, TX 77059, (713)488-8336; **BUS ADD:** 2150 Bay Area Blvd., Houston, TX 77058, (713)486-4800.

MCCARVER, W.F.——B: Apr. 10, 1925, Corsicana, TX, *VP*, Foster Mortgage Corp.; **PRIM RE ACT:** Broker, Consultant, Appraiser, Banker, Lender; **SERVICES:** Mort. banking functions including consulting; **REP CLIENTS:** Instnl. lenders; **PREV EMPLOY:** Owner, Pioneer Mort. Co.; **PROFL AFFIL & HONORS:** RE Brokers Lic.; **EDUC:** BBA, 1952, Univ. of TX; 1952, Mort. Banking, Northwestern Univ.; **MIL SERV:** USN, RM1C, Unit Citation; **OTHER ACT & HONORS:** Ridglea Ctry. Club; **HOME ADD:** 6304 Malvey, Ft. Worth, TX 76116, (817)731-4487; **BUS ADD:** 1101 Summit, Ft. Worth, TX 76101, (817)335-5441.

MCCAULEY, James G.——B: Aug. 15, 1935, NYC, NY, *VP/Dir. of Appraisals*, Helmsley Spear, Inc., Mktg.; **PRIM RE ACT:** Appraiser; **SERVICES:** RE Appraisal and consultation; **REP CLIENTS:** Maj. firms, lending instns., attys., synds., fin. advisors and indivs.; **PREV EMPLOY:** VP Mort. Officer, Mahhattan Life Ins. Co.; **PROFL AFFIL & HONORS:** AIREA, SREA, Westchester Cty. Soc. of RE Appraisers, (Pres. 1977), MAI, SRPA; **EDUC:** BA, 1960, Bus. Admin., St. Michael's Coll., VT; **MIL SERV:** US Army, Cpl.; **HOME ADD:** 5 Valley Stream Rd. W, Larchmont, NY 10538, (914)834-4719; **BUS ADD:** 60 E. 42nd St., 55th Fl., NY, NY 10065, (212)880-0507.

MCCLAIN, Joseph E.——B: Oct. 8, 1931, Cabin Creek, WV, *Rgn. RE Mgr.*, United Parcel Service, Inc., Midwest and North-Central regions; **PRIM RE ACT:** Consultant, Appraiser, Developer, Owner/Investor, Regulator, Property Manager, Real Estate Publisher; **EDUC:** BS, 1953, Secondary educ., W. VA Inst. Tech., US Navy Line Sch., Monterey, CA; **MIL SERV:** USN, 1953-64, Lt.; **HOME ADD:** 713 S. Humphrey, Oak Park, IL 60304, (312)383-2648; **BUS ADD:** 1400 S. Jefferson St., Chicago, IL 60607, (312)942-7637.

MCCLAREN, Mike E.——B: Apr. 10, 1946, Kansas City, MO, *Exec. Dir.-RE*, Murfin Drilling Co.; **PRIM RE ACT:** Developer, Builder, Owner/Investor, Property Manager; **PREV EMPLOY:** Arbor Homes, Inc., Pres.; VP/Gen. Mgr. 1st National Bank of Memphis, RE; Kaiser/Aetna Devel. Mgr., FL, Paul T. Pholy, Sr. Market Analyst; Jack P. Deboer Mgr. Market Research; **PROFL AFFIL & HONORS:** NAIOR, NHB, BOMA; **EDUC:** BBA, 1970, Econ. and Mktg., Wichita State Univ.; **HOME ADD:** 5 Briar Ln., Towanda, KS 67144, (316)778-1900; **BUS ADD:** 612 Union Center Bldg., Wichita, KS 67202, (316)267-3241.

MCCLARTY, Willis R.——B: Aug. 20, 1930, Kalispell, MT, *Architect*, The McClarty Associates; **PRIM RE ACT:** Consultant, Architect; **SERVICES:** Design of multifamily, medical & comml. projects in the states of WA, OR, ID, AK, AZ, TX, CO, HI, CA; **REP CLIENTS:** Indiv. owners and developers; **EDUC:** BArch., 1954, Univ. of WA; **MIL SERV:** USAF, Capt.; **HOME ADD:** 2026 182 N.E., Redmond, WA 98052, (206)747-5239; **BUS ADD:** 11061 N.E. 2nd St., Suite 105, Bellevue, WA 98004, (206)454-9779.

MCCLATCHY, Walter A., Jr.——B: May 6, 1950, Bryn Mawr, PA, *Atty.*, Law Offices of Walter A. McClatchy, Jr.; **PRIM RE ACT:** Attorney, Owner/Investor; **OTHER RE ACT:** Approved Atty. for Title Ins.; **SERVICES:** Legal advice, document prep., title ins. & investment counseling; **PROFL AFFIL & HONORS:** ABA Litigation; RE and Probate Divs., Nat. Comm. of ABA - Litigation Sect. of Pleadings, Pre-Trial Motions and Trial of Bus. Torts, Approved Atty. for Title Insurance for IVT and US Life Title Ins. Co. of NY; Chicago Title Atty. for GNMA; **EDUC:** BA, 1972, Acctg./Pol. Sci., Villanova Univ.; **GRAD EDUC:** JD, 1976, Tax and RE Law, John Marshall Law School, Various Courses of Amer. Inst. of RE Appraisal; **EDUC HONORS:** Law Review; **OTHER ACT & HONORS:** State Legal Counsel; PA Jaycees, 1980-1981; **HOME ADD:** 170 Willowburn Rd., Villanova, PA 19085, (215)525-2906; **BUS ADD:** 6454 Market St., Upper Darby, PA 19082, (215)352-1030.

MCCLEAN, Robert J.——B: Oct. 20, 1938, New York, NY, *VP Regnl. Prop. Mgr.*, Cushman & Wakefield, Inc., Northeastern Rgn.; **PRIM RE ACT:** Property Manager; **SERVICES:** Full prop. mgmt. servs. and prop. mgmt. consulting; **REP CLIENTS:** IBM; Sears Roebuck; Champion Intl.; LaSalle Nat. Bank; Chase Manhattan Bank; Schroeder Trust; Daon Corp.; Amer. Motors Realty Corp.; **PROFL AFFIL & HONORS:** Inst. of RE Mgmt., BOMA - RE Bd., NYC; **EDUC:** ME, Air Conditioning Sys. Design, Nassau Coll. - Voorhees Tech. Inst.; **MIL SERV:** USN; Avia. Elect. Instr. 2 P-1; **HOME ADD:** PO Box 593, Hampton Bays, NY 11946, (212)721-2036; **BUS ADD:** 1166 Ave. of the Americas, New York, NY 10036, (212)841-7641.

MCCLELLAN, W.M.——B: Oct. 10, 1939, Stamford, TX, *Pres.*, McClellan Massey Inc.; **PRIM RE ACT:** Broker, Consultant, Appraiser, Instructor; **SERVICES:** Appraisal and Consultation, Southern and Western US; **PROFL AFFIL & HONORS:** AIREA; Soc. of RE Appraisers; Realtor; Amer. Right of Way Assn., MAI; Member, AIREA; **EDUC:** BBA, 1963, Petroleum Land Mgmt., OK Univ.; **MIL SERV:** US Army, 1st Lt.; **OTHER ACT & HONORS:** Published articles for The Appraisal Journal; **HOME ADD:** 1801 Longbranch Ct., Arlington, TX 76012, (817)265-5979; **BUS ADD:** 4509 N. Central, POB 12602, Dallas, TX 75225, (214)559-2150.

MCCLELLAND, Arthur D.——B: July 9, 1935, Monroe, MI, *Sec. VP*, New York Life, RE and Mort. Loan; **PRIM RE ACT:** Lender, Owner/Investor; **SERVICES:** Loans, joint ventures & equities; **REP CLIENTS:** Devels. of comml. props., usually through mort. bankers; **PREV EMPLOY:** The Prudential 1963-1968; **EDUC:** BA, 1957, Eng., Hiram Coll., Hiram, OH; **HOME ADD:** 226 Cedar Heights Rd., Stamford, CT 06905, (203)322-6387; **BUS ADD:** 51 Madison Ave., New York, NY 10010, (212)576-6393.

MCCLELLAND, Lou——B: Sept. 2, 1947, Topeka, KS, *Research Assoc.*, University of CO at Boulder, Inst. of Behavioral Sci.; **PRIM RE ACT:** Consultant; **OTHER RE ACT:** Research; **SERVICES:** Research and advising on energy efficiency and metering in multi-family props.; **REP CLIENTS:** US Dept. of Energy, state and local govts., private owners; **PROFL AFFIL & HONORS:** Nat. Apt. Assn.; **EDUC:** BA, 1969, Psych., Mathematics, Univ. of KS; **GRAD EDUC:** PhD, 1974, Social Psych., Univ. of MI; **EDUC HONORS:** Phi Beta Kappa, Summa Cum Laude; **HOME ADD:** 3846 Lakebriar Dr., Boulder, CO 80302, (303)443-5125; **BUS ADD:** Campus Box 468, Univ. of CO, Boulder, CO 80309, (303)492-6746.

MCCLELLAND, W. Craig——*Sr. VP*, Hammermill Paper Co.; **PRIM RE ACT:** Property Manager; **BUS ADD:** 1540 East Lake Rd., PO Box 1440, Erie, PA 16533.*

MCCLELLAND, William H.——B: Dec. 19, 1944, Denver, CO, *Pres./Broker*, Cabin Country, Inc.; **PRIM RE ACT:** Broker, Appraiser, Developer, Owner/Investor; **SERVICES:** Devel. and sale of mountain ranch props. in No. CO; **PROFL AFFIL & HONORS:** FLI, RNMI, NAR, CRB; **EDUC:** BA, 1967, Econ., Univ. of AZ; **MIL SERV:** US Army, Capt., Army Commendation Medal; **OTHER ACT & HONORS:** Lambda Chi Alpha Frat., BPO Elks; **HOME ADD:** 1515 S. Shields St., Ft. Collins, CO 80526, (303)224-2455; **BUS ADD:** 312 E. Mulberry, Ft. Collins, CO 80524, (303)482-5263.

MCCLENAGHAN, Charles——*Superintendent*, Ohio, Ohio Div. of Real Estate; **PRIM RE ACT:** Property Manager; **BUS ADD:** 2 Nationwide Plaza, Columbus, OH 43215, (614)466-4100.*

MCCLENDON, Janet S.——**B:** Feb. 6, 1948, Kenwood,CA, *Pres.*, Underinvest,Inc.; **PRIM RE ACT:** Instructor, Syndicator, Consultant, Owner/Investor; **OTHER RE ACT:** Systems Analyst Computer Applications to RE; **SERVICES:** Consultation on investment in RE; **PREV EMPLOY:** Comshare, Inc.; **EDUC:** BA, 1970, Econ., Harvard; **GRAD EDUC:** MA MBA, 1972:1975, Computer sci. Mgmt., Stanford, Harvard Bus. School; **EDUC HONORS:** Summa cum laude; **OTHER ACT & HONORS:** Pres. Univ. Profl. Women; column in Ann Arbor News; **HOME ADD:** 1109 S. Forest Apt. #1A, Ann Arbor, MI 48104; **BUS ADD:** 1109 S. Forest Apt. #1A, Ann Arbor, MI 48104, (313)996-0766.

MCCLINTON, Mr., Jr.——**B:** June 25, 1938, Muskogee, OK, *Pres.*, Devel. Mgmt. Ass. Ltd.; **PRIM RE ACT:** Syndicator, Consultant, Developer, Property Manager, Insuror; **OTHER RE ACT:** Investment Banking, Ins. brokerage, devel., synd. of comml. and multi-family prop.; **REP CLIENTS:** Brokers, dealers, lender indivs. in comml., multi-family and indus. props.; **PREV EMPLOY:** Exec. V.P. Swope Park Natl. Bank; Dir. Special Projects, Dept. of Commerce; **PROFL AFFIL & HONORS:** NASD, NHB intl. Assoc. Fin. Planners, Young Man of Amer. C of C, Congressman Warren Mitchell Capital Access Award; **EDUC:** BS, 1961, Bus.-Educ., Univ. of KS; **GRAD EDUC:** MBPA, 1975, Bus. & Mgmt., Central MI Univ.; **EDUC HONORS:** All Amer.; **MIL SERV:** US Army, NON/COM; **OTHER ACT & HONORS:** Sr. Exec. Serv. Dept. of Commerce; **HOME ADD:** 10224 Locust, K.C., MO, (202)484-3123; **BUS ADD:** 520 N. St. S.W., Wash., DC 20024, (202)463-7383.

MCCLOSKEY, Anthony——*Pres.*, Occidental Petroleum Corp., Occidental Land, Inc.; **PRIM RE ACT:** Property Manager; **BUS ADD:** 10889 Wilshire Blvd., Los Angeles, CA 90024, (714)957-7801.*

MCCLOSKEY, Richard E.——**B:** Aug. 1, 1944, Pittsburgh, PA, *Owner*, R.E. McCloskey & Assoc.; **PRIM RE ACT:** Instructor, Consultant, Appraiser, Owner/Investor; **SERVICES:** Appraisal and consulting services on all types of R.E. including resid., comml. and indus., special purpose props., recreational props., etc.; **REP CLIENTS:** First and second mort. lenders, employee transfer cos., Fed. Housing Admin., various cities and towns, U.S. Postal Service, various realtors and attys., major devels. and investors; **PREV EMPLOY:** Staff appraiser, First Fed. S&L Assn. of Valparaiso, IN 1973-1976; **PROFL AFFIL & HONORS:** Member, AIREA , SREA, Amer. R.E. and Urban Econ. Assn.; Realtor (S. Bend/Mishawaka Bd. of Realtors), MAI, SRPA; **EDUC:** AB, 1967, Modern Languages, Univ. of Notre Dame; **GRAD EDUC:** MS, 1972, Systems Mgmt., Univ. of S. CA; **MIL SERV:** USAF, Capt.; **HOME ADD:** 1621 Arcadia Ave., S. Bend, IN 46635, (219)287-7859; **BUS ADD:** P.O. Box 6173, S. Bend, IN 46660, (616)683-4504.

MCCLUNE, James C.——**B:** Sept. 18, 1920, Doon On, Can., *Pres.*, Crown Center Redevelopment Corp., Gen. & Adm.; **PRIM RE ACT:** Developer, Property Manager; **OTHER RE ACT:** RE devel. co. of Hallmark Cards. Devels. of an 85 acre urban renewal project in downtown Kansas City.; **PREV EMPLOY:** Sr. VP, Devel. and Operations, Dayton Hudson Props.; **PROFL AFFIL & HONORS:** Past Pres., Intl. Council of Shopping Centers, CSM; **EDUC:** Bus. Admin., 1951, Univ. of Detroit; **MIL SERV:** US Army; USAF; S/Sgt.; **HOME ADD:** 1200 Huntington Rd., Kansas City, MO 64113, (816)523-9255; **BUS ADD:** 2440 Pershing Road, Suite 500, Kansas City, MO 64108.

MCCLURE, Charles A., III——**B:** Oct. 17, 1946, Abilene, TX, *Pres.*, Frances McClure, Inc.; **PRIM RE ACT:** Broker, Consultant, Developer, Owner/Investor, Instructor, Property Manager; **PROFL AFFIL & HONORS:** Pres., Abilene Bd. of Realtors, Inc.; Dir., TX Assn. of Realtors; Fed. Dist. Coordinator, 17th Congrl. Dist.; NAR; Chmn., Pol. Affairs Comm., TX Assn. of Realtors, CRB; **EDUC:** BBA, 1969, Admin. Mgmt./Fin., TX Tech. Univ.; **GRAD EDUC:** MBA, 1971, Econ., Hardin-Simmons Univ.; **OTHER ACT & HONORS:** Member, Church of the Heavenly Rest; Abilene Jaycees; Abilene C of C; **HOME ADD:** 26 Glen Abbey, Abilene, TX 79606, (915)698-3210; **BUS ADD:** 3157 S. 27th, Abilene, TX 79605, (915)698-3211.

MCCLURE, J. Kelly——*Investment Broker*, J. Kelly McClure; **PRIM RE ACT:** Broker; **SERVICES:** Broker large investment props.; **REP CLIENTS:** Foreign investors, pension funds, synd., devel.; **PREV EMPLOY:** Mktg. devel., investor specialist with Coldwell Banker; **BUS ADD:** 4 Embarcadero Ctr., Suite 1980, San Francisco, CA 94111, (415)331-1660.

MCCLURE, Roger J.——**B:** Nov. 22, 1943, Cleveland, OH, *Owner*, Roger J. McClure Law Offices; **PRIM RE ACT:** Attorney, Broker, Banker, Owner/Investor; **OTHER RE ACT:** RE Lecturer; **SERVICES:** Legal advice, prop. investments located; **REP CLIENTS:** RE investors and lenders; **PREV EMPLOY:** Staff Atty. Bur. of Competition, Fed. Trade Comm., 1972-77; **PROFL AFFIL & HONORS:** ABA, Real Prop. Probate & Tr. Sect-, Wash. Bd. of Realtors; **EDUC:** BA, 1963, Intl. Studies, OH State Univ.; **GRAD EDUC:** MA, 1977, Northwestern Univ.; JD, 1972, OH State Univ.; **EDUC HONORS:** Grad. Deg., Cum Laude, Member Bd. of Editors, Law Review; **MIL SERV:** US Army; 1st Lt., Bronze Star; **OTHER ACT & HONORS:** Chmn. Antitrust Trade Regulation & Consumers Affairs Sect., DC Bar, 1981-82; Who's Who in Creative Real Estate; **HOME ADD:** 219 Rock Creek Church Rd. NW, Wash. DC 20011, (202)723-2740; **BUS ADD:** 1800 CT Ave., NW, Suite 201, Washington, DC 20009, (202)387-8000.

MCCLURG, William B.——**B:** Nov. 24, 1930, Homer, NY, Corning Glass Works, Mfg. Services; **PRIM RE ACT:** Property Manager; **SERVICES:** Corp. prop. mgmt.; **PROFL AFFIL & HONORS:** NACORE, NYS Broker; **EDUC:** Glass Techno., 1952, NYS Coll. of Ceramics, Alfred Univ.; **EDUC HONORS:** Cum Laude; **MIL SERV:** USNR, Lt.; **HOME ADD:** 34 Downing St., Big Flats, NY 14814, (607)562-3216; **BUS ADD:** Corning Glass Works, M.P. Bldg. 8-4, Corning, NY 14830, (607)974-7838.

MCCOLLUM, James H.——**B:** Sept. 24, 1948, Bethesda, MD, *VP*, Bankston & McCollum; **PRIM RE ACT:** Attorney; **PROFL AFFIL & HONORS:** ABA, Real Prop. Probate & Trust Div. TX State Bar, Real Prop. Probate & Trust Div.; **EDUC:** BA, 1970, Govt., Univ. of TX; **GRAD EDUC:** JD, 1976, RE, Univ. of TX; **MIL SERV:** USAF, 1st Lt.; **HOME ADD:** SRA Box 78-L, Anchorage, AK 99507; **BUS ADD:** 601 W. 5th Ave., Suite 601, Anchorage, AK 99501, (907)276-1711.

MCCOLLUM, William J.——**B:** Jan. 6, 1942, Garden City, NY, *VP/Area Research*, , Batus Retail Division; **OTHER RE ACT:** Retailer; **SERVICES:** Build retail store; **PREV EMPLOY:** Larry Smith & Co., 1966-72; **PROFL AFFIL & HONORS:** ULI; General Growth Dev. Corp. 1972-1981; **EDUC:** BA, 1963, Econ., OH Wesleyan Univ.; **MIL SERV:** US Army, S/Sgt.; **HOME ADD:** 17 Salem Ln., Port Washington, NY 11050, (515)225-0620; **BUS ADD:** 1275 Ave. of the Americas, New York, NY 10001, (212)290-5521.

MCCOMB, James B.——**B:** Apr. 25, 1938, Rochester, MN, *Prin.*, James B. McComb & Assoc.; **PRIM RE ACT:** Consultant; **OTHER RE ACT:** Econ. Consulting; **SERVICES:** Mkt. research, fin. feasibility, fin. packaging; **REP CLIENTS:** Dayton Hudson Corp., Oxford Devel. Grp. Ltd., Radisson Hotel Corp., Carlson Props., Twentieth Century Fox, RE Co.; **PREV EMPLOY:** Dayton Hudson Corp.; **EDUC:** BS, 1961, Econ., Fin., Acctg., Macalester Coll.; **HOME ADD:** 2701 E. Lake of the Isles Pkwy., Minneapolis, MN 55408, (612)872-7581; **BUS ADD:** 830 TCF Tower, 121 S. Eighth St., Minneapolis, MN 55402, (612)338-9014.

MCCOMBS, Donald D.——**B:** Jan. 26, 1922, Eureka, MI, *CEO Pres.*, McCombs Corp.; **PRIM RE ACT:** Syndicator; **SERVICES:** Complete synd.-mktg, negotiations, prop. mgmt. & Gen. partners activities; **REP CLIENTS:** Stock brokerage through-out western US; **MIL SERV:** US Army Air Corps., 1st Lt.; **OTHER ACT & HONORS:** Who's Who-Bus. Fin.-CA; **HOME ADD:** 30462 Paseo del Valle, Laguna Niguel, CA 92677, (714)495-4647; **BUS ADD:** 2392 Morse, Irvine, CA 92714, (714)957-1901.

MCCOMIC, R. Barry——**B:** Nov. 6, 1939, Selmer, TN, *Pres. & CEO*, Avco Community Devels., Inc.; **PRIM RE ACT:** Builder; **OTHER RE ACT:** New Town Devel.; **REP CLIENTS:** Town of Rancho Bernardo, CA; Leguna Niguel; **PROFL AFFIL & HONORS:** BCA, NAHB, ABC, Member of TN Bar, NY Bar, CA Bar; **EDUC:** BS, 1961, Union Univ.; **GRAD EDUC:** LLB, 1964, Tulane Univ., Postgrad. in Law (Ford Found. grantee; **EDUC HONORS:** Frederick Ebert Found. fellow, Univ. Freilburg (W. Ger.), 1964-65, Acad. Law, 1965, Tulane Order of the Coif, Thomas Dewey Nelson Award, Recipient Human Relations Award, Amer. Jewish Committee, 1981; **OTHER ACT & HONORS:** Mem. Chancellor's Assn., Univ. CA, San Diego; Pres. Club, USD; Bd. Dirs. Contemporary Art Museum of San Diego; Children's Hospital & Health Ctr; San Diego Symphony Orchestra Assn.; San Diego Econ. Devel. Corp.; W Behavioral Sci. Inst.; Mem City Club of San Diego, San Diego Yacht Club; **HOME ADD:** 2676 Caminito Tom Morris, La Jolla, CA 92037, (714)454-8340; **BUS ADD:** 16770 W Bernardo Dr., San Diego, CA 92127, (714)487-1011.

MACCONAUGHA, Donald G.——**B:** Apr. 24, 1930, Dearborn, MI, *Pres.*, Red Fir Ltd.; **PRIM RE ACT:** Broker, Consultant, Developer, Property Manager; **SERVICES:** Prop. mgmt. and consulting primarily to merchandise marts and trade centers, comm. and resid.; **REP CLIENTS:** condo. mgmt. owners and devel. of trade centers, condo.

bds.; **PROFL AFFIL & HONORS:** IREM, NAR, BOMA, The Engrs. Club of San Francisco, CPM; **EDUC:** Civil Engrg., Akron Univ., Akron, OH; **MIL SERV:** US Army, Corps of Engrs., Capt., 1948-56; **HOME ADD:** 170 Lk. Arrowhead, Waleska, GA 30183, (404)479-9875; **BUS ADD:** 228 Spring St. N.W., Atlanta, GA 30303, (404)522-2220.

MCCONNELL, John A.——**B:** Nov. 11, 1917, Abingdon, VA, *Owner*, McConnell & Co., Realtors; **PRIM RE ACT:** Broker, Appraiser; **PREV EMPLOY:** Thomas J. Majjey Co., Realtors 1951-1956, VP and Sales Mgr.; **PROFL AFFIL & HONORS:** NAR, VA Assn. of Realtors Richmond Bd. of Realtors, Richmond MLS, VP Richmond MLS, GRI, CRS CRA; **EDUC:** AA, 1940, Lees McRae Coll., Banner Elk, H.C. Univ. of VA 1940-1941; Night School, 1959-1960, Univ. of Richmond; **EDUC HONORS:** Pres. Studen Body, Lees Murae Coll. 1939-1940, Univ. of VA-Pre Law; **MIL SERV:** US Air Corps, 1941-1948, Capt., DFC Air Medal-with Clusters; **OTHER ACT & HONORS:** Chief Judge-Voting Precient Democratic Party 10 yrs. Rep. Del. West Richmond Rotary Club, 1981 Conf. Amer. Legion Post 84, West Richmond Bus. Mens Assn. Channel Choir, Grace Covenant Presbyterian Church, 28 yrs.; Trustee - Realtors Institute, 18 yrs.; Asst. Dean, Member of Faculty, Realtors Institute; **HOME ADD:** 1004 Westham Pkwy, Richmond, VA 23229, (804)282-4965; **BUS ADD:** 1004 Westham Pkwy, Richmond, VA 23229, (804)282-4965.

MCCORKLE, Jack E.——**B:** Oct. 12, 1923, Kelso, WA, *Assoc. Broker*, Preston Q. Hale & Assoc.; **PRIM RE ACT:** Broker, Consultant, Owner/Investor; **PROFL AFFIL & HONORS:** Member SIR; **EDUC:** BA, 1946, Social Sci., Stanford Univ.; **MIL SERV:** US Navy; **HOME ADD:** 1000 Dartmouth Dr., Reno, NV 89509, (702)322-6330; **BUS ADD:** 1885 S. Arlington Ave., 12+205, Reno, NV 89509, (702)329-4000.

MCCORKY, W. Bradley——**B:** Mar. 19, 1937, Philadelphia, PA, *VP, Sr. Loan Officer*, Dartmouth Savings Bank; **PRIM RE ACT:** Appraiser, Banker, Lender; **PROFL AFFIL & HONORS:** NARA; SREA; Intl. Coll. of RE Consulting Profl.; **EDUC:** BA, 1959, Math & econ., Bowdoin Coll.; **MIL SERV:** US Army; Capt.; 1960-62; **OTHER ACT & HONORS:** Treas. and Tr. Montshire Museum; **HOME ADD:** 10 Parkway, Hanover, NH 03755; **BUS ADD:** 40 S. Main St., Hanover, NH 03755, (603)643-3310.

MCCORMACK, Wm.——*Corp. Counsel*, Geo. A. Hormel Co.; **PRIM RE ACT:** Attorney, Property Manager; **BUS ADD:** PO Box 800, Austin, MN 55912, (507)437-5611.*

MCCORMICK, Albert M.——**B:** Sept. 7, 1949, Wilkes-Barre PA, *Dir. of RE*, Redevelopment Authority of Luzerne Cty., PA, Land Acquisition and Disposition; **PRIM RE ACT:** Consultant, Regulator, Instructor, Property Manager; **OTHER RE ACT:** Chief Negotiator for Purchase of RE for the 2nd Largest Redevel. Authority in PA, 9 yrs. experience; **SERVICES:** Provide Land for Resid., Comml. & Indus., Devel.; **REP CLIENTS:** Indus., Mfgr., Co., Home Builders & Multi Housing Devels., Small Bus.; **EDUC:** BS, 1972, Govt., Public Admin.; **OTHER ACT & HONORS:** Notary Public, Lic. RE Salesman; **HOME ADD:** 575 Warren Ave., Kingston, PA 18704; **BUS ADD:** 272 Pierce St., Kingston, PA 18704, (717)288-4340.

MCCORMICK, John E.——**B:** Sept. 1, 1951, Darby, PA, Hillcrest Homes; **PRIM RE ACT:** Broker, Instructor, Insuror; **SERVICES:** FuLl serv. resid. & comml. props. and ins.; **PROFL AFFIL & HONORS:** Greater Boston RE Bd.; Homes for Living Network; Indep. Ins. Agents; **EDUC:** BS, 1973, Fin./Acctg. Mgmt., Mount St. Mary's Coll.; **OTHER ACT & HONORS:** Notary Public Comm. of MA; Medfield Lions Club, 3rd VP; Greater Boston RE Bd. Education Comm.; **HOME ADD:** 32 Granite St., Medfield, MA 02052, (617)359-7608; **BUS ADD:** 687 Highland Ave., Needham, MA 02194, (617)444-2002.

MCCORMICK, Joseph P.——**B:** Oct. 3, 1950, Minneapolis, MN, *Pres.*, J. Patrick Inc.; **PRIM RE ACT:** Broker, Consultant, Developer, Builder, Owner/Investor, Property Manager, Syndicator; **SERVICES:** Devel. & synd. of comml. prop./prop. mgmt.; **PROFL AFFIL & HONORS:** NAR, RE Securities and Synd. Inst.; **EDUC:** BA, 1976, Econ., Poli. Sci., Univ. of MN; **GRAD EDUC:** Hamline Law School, 1982, Law, Hamline Univ.; **MIL SERV:** US Army, E-5; **HOME ADD:** 3631 Glenhurst Ave., Minneapolis, MN 55416, (612)922-6082; **BUS ADD:** 1422 W. Lake St., Minneapolis, MN 55408, (612)827-5409.

MCCOUN, Phillip M.——**B:** Sept. 9, 1945, Indianapolis, IN, *Pres.*, McCoun & Assoc. Inc.; **PRIM RE ACT:** Broker; **SERVICES:** Resid. RE Investment counseling, Valuation corp. relocation; **REP CLIENTS:** Major corps., var. of indus., Dow Chemical Co., Eli Lilly & Co., Sears & Roebuck, Amax Coal, Marathon Oil, US Govt.; **PROFL AFFIL & HONORS:** GRI, CRS, Candidate for Cert. Resid Broker; **EDUC:** BS, 1967, Bus., IN Univ.; **HOME ADD:** 7901 Teelway, Indianapolis, IN 46256, (317)842-4840; **BUS ADD:** 5524 E. 82nd St., Indianapolis, IN 46250, (317)842-5744.

MCCOWNAUGHEY, George——*Prop. Mgr.*, Trico Products Corp.; **PRIM RE ACT:** Property Manager; **BUS ADD:** 817 Washington St., Buffalo, NY 14203, (716)852-5700.*

MCCOY, Robert L.——**B:** May 18, 1928, Baltimore, MD, *VP*, Charles A. Skirven, Inc.; **PRIM RE ACT:** Broker, Owner/Investor; **OTHER RE ACT:** Gen. Brokerage; **SERVICES:** Gen. Brokerage, Consulting, Appraising; **REP CLIENTS:** Central MD Homebuyers & Sellers, Investors in RE; **PREV EMPLOY:** Mgr. of Resid. Land Sales, Howard Research & Devel. Corp., The Rouse Co., Devels. of Planned City of Columbia, MD, 1970; **PROFL AFFIL & HONORS:** RNMI; Educ. adjunct of the NAR, Pres. Howard Cty. Md. Bd. of Realtors 1963-64; Howard Cty. Bd. Realtor of the Yr. - 1976; CRB; **EDUC:** BA, 1949, Econ., Pol. Sci., Hist., Math., Swarthmore Coll., PA; **GRAD EDUC:** MBA, 1951, Indus. Mgmt. & Personnel Admin., Wharton School of Fin. & Commerce, Univ. of PA, Phila.; **EDUC HONORS:** Grad. with Hon.; **HOME ADD:** 514 N Chapelgate Ln., Baltimore, MD 21229, (301)788-7788; **BUS ADD:** 115 Teachers Bldg., Columbia, MD 21044, (301)730-7373.

MCCRACKEN, Lloyd——**B:** Sept. 25, 1932, Jonesboro, AR, *Pres.*, United Financial Services of United Federal S&L Assn.; **PRIM RE ACT:** Consultant, Appraiser; **REP CLIENTS:** AR Fin. Servs.; City of Jonesboro; Jonesboro Downtown Improvement Dist.; St. Bernards Rgnl. Medical Ctr.; AR State Univ.; Nat. Mort. Co.; Citizens Bank of Jonesboro; Bank of OK; Relocation Realty; FMC Corp.; Dupont Corp.; General Electric; IBM; Reynolds Aluminum Co.; Derby Oil Co.; Midas Realty Corp.; **PREV EMPLOY:** Fed. S&L Assn., Jonesboro, AR, 1978; Fee Appraiser for Citizens Fed. S&L Assn., Jonesboro, AR, 1965-1978; Approved Vet. Admin. Fee Appraiser, 1967 to date; Approved FHA Fee Appraiser, 1966 to date; Approved Underwriter, Appraiser, Prop. Inspector, FHA Coinsurance Program, 1979 to date; **PROFL AFFIL & HONORS:** Pres., N.E. AR Chap., 1978-1980; S.E. Rgnl. Gov., (AL, AR, LA, MS, TN), 1979; AR State Dir., 1980; Nat. Publications Comm., 1978-1982, Chmn., 1981; Nat. Dir., 1980-1983; Nat. Assn. of Indep. Fee Appraisers, Man of the Yr., 1980, SRA, Member of the Soc. of RE Appraisers; IFAS of the Nat. Assn. of Indep. Fee Appraisers; **EDUC:** AA, 1974, SUNY; **OTHER ACT & HONORS:** Member, Bd. of Dir., Craighead Cty. Hist. Soc.; Pres., Craighead Cty. Hist. Soc., 1978; Editor, Craighead Cty. Hist. Quarterly, 1975-1977; **HOME ADD:** 605 Elm, Jonesboro, AR 72401, (501)935-2816; **BUS ADD:** 533 W. Washington, PO Drawer 1060, Jonesboro, AR 72401, (501)935-1710.

MCCRARY, Oscar W., Jr.——**B:** Oct. 24, 1948, Detroit, MI, *Project Mgr., Housing Div.*, National Urban League; **PRIM RE ACT:** Consultant; **OTHER RE ACT:** Research, Training; **SERVICES:** Training packages & research; **PROFL AFFIL & HONORS:** Amer. Soc. of Planning Officials; **EDUC:** AB, 1971, Pol. Sci., Wayne State Univ.; **GRAD EDUC:** Masters, 1973, Housing/Comm. & Econ. Devel., MIT; **EDUC HONORS:** Urban FelLow, HUD Minority Internship Program; **HOME ADD:** 400 Central Park W, Apt. 18V, New York, NY 10023, (212)864-6813; **BUS ADD:** 500 E 62nd St., New York, NY 10021, (212)310-9124.

MACCRATE, John, Jr.——**B:** Aug. 23, 1916, Brooklyn, NY, *Pres.*, MacCrate Associates, Inc.; **PRIM RE ACT:** Broker, Consultant, Appraiser, Instructor, Insuror; **OTHER RE ACT:** Member of Bank Advisory Bd.; **SERVICES:** Spec. in Long Island RE; **REP CLIENTS:** Bankers Trust Co., European Amer. Bank, Chemical Bank, Morgan Guaranty Trust Co., US Trust Co., Merrill Lynch Reloc. Management, NY Tel. Co.; **PROFL AFFIL & HONORS:** Soc. of RE Appraisers, AIREA, Amer. Soc. of Appraisers Urban, Nat. Assn. of Review Appraisers, SRPA, MAI, ASA, CRA; **EDUC:** AB; **GRAD EDUC:** BA, 1938, Columbia Coll.; **HOME ADD:** PO Box 310, Sea Cliff, NY 11579, (516)676-1430; **BUS ADD:** 212 Sea Cliff Ave., PO Box 310, Sea Cliff, NY 11579, (516)676-1430.

MCCRAY, Joe Richard——**B:** Nov. 12, 1928, Bucksport, SC, *Pres.*, Joe R. McCray Enterprises, Inc.; **PRIM RE ACT:** Broker, Syndicator, Consultant, Property Manager, Owner/Investor; **SERVICES:** Resid. & comml. sales, counseling synd. of comml. props. and prop. mgmt.; **REP CLIENTS:** Homeowners & investors; **PREV EMPLOY:** US Army 1946-72; **PROFL AFFIL & HONORS:** NAR, RNMI, Wash. DC & Prince George's Cty. Bd. of Realtors, DC C of C, Better Bus. Bur.; **MIL SERV:** US Army, Lt. Col., Legion of Merit w/Oak Leaf Cluster, Army Commendation Medal, Natl. Defense Serv. Medal, Armed Forces Reserve Medal, Army of Occupation Medal, Korean Serv. Medal, UN Serv. Medal, Rep. of Korea Pres. Unit Citation, Vietnam Serv. Medal, Vietnam Campaign Medal; **OTHER ACT & HONORS:** Comm. Chmn, DC Baptist Convention; Tr. Greater SE

Community Hosptal Found., Inc.; Life Fellow, Kiwanis Intl.; Life Member Capital Dist. Found., Kiwanis Intl.; Member Kiwanis Club of Eastern Branch; **HOME ADD:** 3926 Alabama Ave., SE, Washington, DC 20020, (202)575-3903; **BUS ADD:** 1315 Pennsylvania Ave., SE, Washington, DC 20003, (202)546-2100.

MCCREADY, Richard F.——B: Mar. 14, 1905, Easton, MD, *Pres.*, Winchester Federal Savings and Loan Association; **PRIM RE ACT:** Broker, Insuror; **OTHER RE ACT:** S & L Assn.; **SERVICES:** Certificates of Deposits, Savings and home loans; **EDUC:** BA, 1927, KY Wesleyan Coll.; **HOME ADD:** 1108 W. Lexington Ave., Winchester, KY 40391; **BUS ADD:** 57 South Main St., Winchester, KY 40391, (606)744-2940.

MCCUARG, Donald——*Pres.*, Commonwealth Oil Refining Co.; **PRIM RE ACT:** Property Manager; **BUS ADD:** 8626 Tesoro Dr., San Antonio, TX 78217, (512)828-8444.*

MCCUE, Daniel——B: Mar. 20, 1937, San Antonio, TX, *Pres.*, Crossroads Abstract & Title Co.; **OTHER RE ACT:** Land Title Work; **SERVICES:** Title insurance and abstracting; **PROFL AFFIL & HONORS:** Amer. Land Title Assn.; TX Land Title Assn.; AHBA; TX Assn. of Realtors; Victoria Bd. of Realtors; Victoria Home Builders Assn.; **EDUC:** BBA, 1960, Mgmt., Univ. of Houston; **GRAD EDUC:** 1976, Mgmt., Univ. of Houston, Victoria Campus; **OTHER ACT & HONORS:** Exchange Club of TX; Victoria Jaycees; Victoria Livestock Show; **HOME ADD:** Hanselman Rd., Victoria, TX, (512)578-0452; **BUS ADD:** P.O. Box 2449, 104 S. Main St., Victoria, TX 77902, (512)573-5268.

MCCULLOCH, Robert P.——B: Sept. 2, 1928, Newark, NJ, *Pres.*, McCulloch Realtors; **PRIM RE ACT:** Broker, Syndicator, Appraiser, Developer, Property Manager, Insuror; **REP CLIENTS:** Homequity, Merrill Lynch, Exxon, Executrans; **PREV EMPLOY:** Sales manager, UniRoyal; **PROFL AFFIL & HONORS:** Danbury Bd. of Realtors, Newtown Bd. of Realtors, CRB, Cert. Resid. Broker, (CRB), Realtor of the yr, 1974 & 1977; **EDUC:** BS, 1955, Bus. Mgmt., Fairleigh Dickinson Univ.; **GRAD EDUC:** Major cert. RE, Univ. of CT; **MIL SERV:** USN/US Army, Cpl., 1946-52; **OTHER ACT & HONORS:** JP 12 yrs., Dir. C of C, Newtown, CT; **HOME ADD:** Smoke Rise Ridge, Newtown, CT, (203)426-9606; **BUS ADD:** 38 Church Hill Rd., Newtown, CT 06470, (203)426-5200.

MCCULLOUGH, Chester C.——B: Mar. 18, 1917, Chicago, IL, *Sr. VP*, Chicago Title Ins. Co.; **OTHER RE ACT:** Title Ins.; **SERVICES:** Title ins., abstracts, escrows, closings; **REP CLIENTS:** Lenders on and owners of real prop.; **PREV EMPLOY:** Chicago Title and Trust Co., 1939-1963; **PROFL AFFIL & HONORS:** IL Sate Bar Assn., Chicago Assn. of Commerce & Indus., Amer. Land Title Assn. (Past Governor), ALT; **EDUC:** BA, 1939, Econ., Beloit Coll.; **GRAD EDUC:** MBA, LLB, JD, 1953, Bus. Admin., Law, Univ. of Chicago; **EDUC HONORS:** Phi Beta Kappa, Beta Gamma Sigma; **MIL SERV:** US Army; Infantry, Capt.; Army Commendation Medal, and Seven Serv. and Campaign Awards; **OTHER ACT & HONORS:** Presbyterian Church, Deacon, Elder; **HOME ADD:** 314 Forest Ave., River Forest, IL 60305, (312)366-5821; **BUS ADD:** 111 W. Washington St., Chicago, IL 60602, (312)630-2577.

MCCULLOUGH, Douglas Arthur——B: Sept. 23, 1951, Madeste, CA, *Pres.*, McCullough-Grilliot Realtors, Inc.; **PRIM RE ACT:** Broker, Builder; **SERVICES:** Selling resid. props. - buyers and sellers; **PREV EMPLOY:** VP, Century 21 Clowers Realty; **PROFL AFFIL & HONORS:** NAR; **EDUC:** BA, 3yrs., Bus. Mgmt., Univ. of AL; **HOME TEL:** (205)883-9491; **BUS ADD:** 2515 S. Parkway, Huntsville, AL 35801, (205)539-8114.

MCCULLOUGH, Graham——B: Dec. 6, 1935, Clouis, NM, *Atty.*, McCullough, Murray & McCullough; **PRIM RE ACT:** Attorney; **PROFL AFFIL & HONORS:** Past Pres., Cameron Cty. Bar; Member State Bar, ABA, RE Probate and Trust Council; RE Specialization Comm., State Bar of TX; **EDUC:** Hist., Univ. of TX Law School; **GRAD EDUC:** JD, 1958, Univ. of TX Law School; **EDUC HONORS:** Rotary Fellowship - Univ. of Sydney; **MIL SERV:** Army, Capt.; **OTHER ACT & HONORS:** Past Pres. Rotary, Rio Grande Title Co. & Past Chmn. of Bd.; **HOME ADD:** 917 E Taylor, Harlingen, TX 78550, (512)423-3379; **BUS ADD:** P.O. Box 2244, Harlingen, TX 78550, (512)423-1234.

MCCURDY, Dennis O.——B: Sept. 22, 1944, Parkersburg, WV, *Pres.*, Realty Investments Corp. of Amer.; **PRIM RE ACT:** Broker, Consultant, Appraiser, Lender, Owner/Investor, Property Manager, Syndicator; **SERVICES:** Comml. investment synd., resid. brokerage, real estate investment planning, mort. brokerage, appraisal servs.; **REP CLIENTS:** Pension plans, indiv. (med. profession), and inst. investors in comml. props., indiv. in resid. investments, lender appraisals, and owner occupied resid. clients by referral only; **PREV EMPLOY:** Levitt & Sons; Artery Org.; Universal Funding; **PROFL AFFIL & HONORS:** Pres., Realty Investments Mort. Corp.; Pres., PCL-Realty Investment Corp.; Pres., Realty Investments Corp. (VA); VP, Realty Preservation, Inc., RE Broker, MD, VA, DC; **EDUC:** BS, 1967, RE/Econ./Psych., Fairmont State Coll.; **EDUC HONORS:** Dean's Lists, Bus. Honorary; **HOME ADD:** 4109 Dresden St., Kensington, MD 20895, (301)949-8064; **BUS ADD:** 3702 Perry Ave., Kensington, MD 20895, (301)933-1551.

MCDANIEL, Donald C.——B: Apr. 2, 1932, Los Angeles, CA, *Atty. at Law*, Crawford, Scott, McDaniel & DaVanzo, Atty.; **PRIM RE ACT:** Attorney, Owner/Investor; **SERVICES:** Comml. and Indus. Leases; Acquisition and/or Sales of Real Prop.; **REP CLIENTS:** Watson Indus. Prop.; **PROFL AFFIL & HONORS:** ABA; State Bar of CA, Los Angeles Cty. Bar Assn.; **EDUC:** AB, 1954, Econ. and Acctg., Stanford Univ.; **GRAD EDUC:** LLB and JD, 1961, Univ. of CA at Los Angeles; **EDUC HONORS:** Grad. Cum Laude, Amer. Jurisprudence Award for receiving highest grade in Comml. Law and Trust; **MIL SERV:** USAF, Capt.; **OTHER ACT & HONORS:** Republican Central Comm. 60th Assembly Dist. and 38th Congrl. Dist. (1962-1980); **HOME ADD:** 547 Ocampo Dr., Pacific Palisades, CA 90272, (213)454-2600; **BUS ADD:** 606 S. Broadway, Suite 200, Santa Monica, CA 90401, (213)451-1555.

MCDANIEL, Hugh——B: Jan. 23, 1940, Englewood, NJ, *Pres.*, The McDaniel Company, Realtors, Mktg., Mgmt., Investment; **PRIM RE ACT:** Broker, Owner/Investor, Property Manager; **SERVICES:** Mktg., mgmt., investment; **PREV EMPLOY:** Naval officer, Rank: Commander; **PROFL AFFIL & HONORS:** San Diego Bd. of Realtors, CA Assn. of Realtors, NAR, RNMI, CRB (Mgr.), CRS (Cert. Resid. Specialist), GRI, and RECI; **EDUC:** BA, 1962, Hist. and Eng., TX A&M Univ.; **GRAD EDUC:** Advanced Certificate in RE, 1975, RE, Univ. of CA Extension - San Diego; **EDUC HONORS:** Fin. Chmn., Sixth Student Conference on Nat. Affairs, Student Assistantship in Dept. of History and Govt.; **MIL SERV:** USN, CDR, Combat Action Ribbon, Navy Unit Commendation, Combat Patrol Pin, Vietnam Service Medal w/two silver stars; **OTHER ACT & HONORS:** US Naval Inst., Naval Reserve Assn. (Life Member), San Diego Yacht Club, Texas A&M Club of San Diego Cty. (Pres. 1976, 1980, 1981); **HOME ADD:** P O Box 22104, San Diego, CA 92122; **BUS ADD:** P O Box 22104, San Diego, CA 92122, (714)296-3015.

MCDANIEL, Robert E.——B: Dec. 11, 1927, Floyd Cty., *Pres.*, McDaniel Constr. & Devel. Co.; **PRIM RE ACT:** Consultant, Developer, Builder, Owner/Investor; **SERVICES:** Land devel. & resid. constr.; **PREV EMPLOY:** Pres. of US Steel Homes Div., 1972-75; **PROFL AFFIL & HONORS:** Nat. Assn. of Home Builders, Nat. Fed. of Ind. Bus., Consultative Council of Nat. Inst. of Bldb. Soc., Life Dir. of OH Home Builders Assn. & Nat. Assn. of Home Builders; **EDUC:** BS, 1950, Indus. Mgmt., Univ. of KY; **MIL SERV:** US Army, 1945-46, Sgt.; **HOME ADD:** 900 W Whipp Td., Dayton, OH 45459; **BUS ADD:** 900 W Whipp Rd., Dayton, OH 45459, (513)434-6958.

MCDANIEL, Robert Tate——B: Feb. 24, 1945, Lewisburg, TN, *Pres.*, Appraisal Consultants Co. Inc.; **PRIM RE ACT:** Appraiser; **SERVICES:** RE Appraisals - prop. tax consultants; **PROFL AFFIL & HONORS:** Member AIREA - SREA, MAI, SRPA, CAE; **EDUC:** BS, 1966, Indus. Mgmt., Middle TN State Univ.; **HOME ADD:** 6775 Holt Rd., Nashville, TN 37211, (615)833-2141; **BUS ADD:** P O Box 724, Brentwood, TN 37027, (615)833-5441.

MCDANIEL, Sara——B: Mar. 11, 1949, Borger, TX, *Pres.*, McDaniel & Tate; **OTHER RE ACT:** Public relations; **SERVICES:** Public Relations, Advertising, Mktg. for R.E. clients; **REP CLIENTS:** Fuller Comml. Brokerage, Lincoln Prop. Co., Bolin Devel. Corp., Atlantic Devel. Co., (devel., brokerage houses); **PREV EMPLOY:** Sr. Acct. Exec., A.R. Busse & Assoc.; **PROFL AFFIL & HONORS:** Public relations soc. of Amer.; **EDUC:** BA, 1971, Eng., Fine Arts, Rice Univ.; **OTHER ACT & HONORS:** Bd. of Dir., DePelchin Faith Home; **HOME ADD:** 1628 W. Main, Houston, TX 77006; **BUS ADD:** 1110 Lovett, Suite 209, Houston, TX 77006, (713)526-2292.

MCDANNEL, Donald W.——B: June 13, 1928, Aurora, NE, *Owner*, McDannel Realty Co.; **PRIM RE ACT:** Broker, Consultant, Appraiser, Instructor, Insuror; **SERVICES:** Prop. mgmt., sales & loans; **REP CLIENTS:** Lenders, investors and attys. in comml. agric. and ranch props., Pittsburgh Plate Glass Co., Pfister Hybrid Co., Farmers Union NE State Exch., Schlitz Brewing Co., Holiday Inns of Amer., Inc., Humble Oil Co., Abbott Labs., W.R. Grace Co.; **PREV EMPLOY:** Loan Asst., 1950-51, Farmer State Bank; **PROFL AFFIL & HONORS:** ULI, RNMI, MAI, Member AIREA; **EDUC:** Univ. of NE, Coll. of Agric.; **MIL SERV:** US Army, Pvt.; **HOME ADD:** 2123 W. Division St., Grand Island, NE 68801; **BUS ADD:** 1521 W 2nd St., PO Box 1182, Grand Island, NE 68802, (308)382-1482.

MCDERMOTT, Dr. Cecil——B: Aug. 19, 1935, Parkin, AR, *Prof., Hendrix Coll.*, Appraisal Consultant Central AR Appraisal Serv.; **PRIM RE ACT:** Appraiser; **OTHER RE ACT:** Instructor in Mathematics; **REP CLIENTS:** FHA, First Fed. S&L of Little Rock, First Fed. S&L of Morrilton, Conway, Russellville; Various transfer firms, lawyers; **PREV EMPLOY:** 1959-1965, AR Dept. of Educ.; 1965-1967, Auburn Univ.; 1967-1981, Hendrix Coll., Conway, AR; **PROFL AFFIL & HONORS:** NAIFA; IFA Designation; Math. Assn. of Amer.; Amer. Math. Soc.; Nat. Council of Teachers of Math., IFA Designation; Nat. Assn. of Independent Fee Appraisers; **EDUC:** BS, 1957, Math., Univ. of AR, Fayetteville; **GRAD EDUC:** MS, 1962, Statistics, Purdue Univ.; PhD, 1967, Math., Auburn Univ.; **EDUC HONORS:** Student Senate, Pres. of Dorm Council, Phi Delta Kappa, Phi Gamma Phi, Pi Mu Epsilon; **MIL SERV:** U.S. Army, ROTC, 2 yrs.; **OTHER ACT & HONORS:** AR Atheletic Intercollegiate Conf., Pres.; **HOME ADD:** 1204 Hunter, Conway, AR 72032, (501)329-6157; **BUS ADD:** 1204 Hunter, Conway, AR 72032, (501)329-6157.

MCDERMOTT, James P.——B: Feb 26, 1942, Chicago, IL, *VP*, Dominick's Finer Foods, Inc.; **PRIM RE ACT:** Broker, Developer, Builder, Owner/Investor, Property Manager; **OTHER RE ACT:** Corp. RE; **SERVICES:** Retail tenant, prop. mgmt., comml. devel.; **PREV EMPLOY:** RE Mgr. - Jewel Food Stores, Nat. Dir. RE Admin. & Group Dir. - Great Atlantic & Pacific Tea Co.; **PROFL AFFIL & HONORS:** RE Broker - IL; **EDUC:** BS, Hist., Loyola Univ. - Chicago; **MIL SERV:** USNR, LT-03; **BUS ADD:** 333 Northwest Ave., Northlake, IL 60164, (312)562-1000.

MCDERMOTT, R.G.——*VP Fin. & Treas.*, Longview Fibre Corp.; **PRIM RE ACT:** Property Manager; **BUS ADD:** PO Box 639, Longview, WA 98632, (206)425-1550.*

MCDERMOTT, Ruth E.——B: Aug. 30, 1931, Boston, MA, *Gen. Mgr.*, Ruth E. McDermott RE; **PRIM RE ACT:** Broker, Consultant, Appraiser; **OTHER RE ACT:** Resid. sales, appraising, consulting and timeshare sales; **SERVICES:** Notary, consulting, appraising, selling rentals; **PROFL AFFIL & HONORS:** NAR, MA Assn. of Realtors, Greater Boston Assn. of Realtors, Gr. Boston MLS, Quincy & S. Shore Bd. of Realtors, Realtors Comml. investment div., Women's council of realtors, RELO-Intercity relocation service, FL RE Exchange, 1977 Pres. Womens council of realtors, VP GREB 1978, Dir. of GREB 75, 76, 77, 78, 79, 80, Dir. MA Assn. of Realtors 76, 77, 78, 79, GRI designation & CRB Designation, numerous certificates of appreciation; **EDUC:** 2 yrs., Bus. & office mgmt., Hickox Bus. School; **OTHER ACT & HONORS:** Cert. of Appreciation from March of Dimes-Town Chairman 4 yrs., Wollaston Golf Club, Quincy Neighborhood Club; **HOME ADD:** 148 Ridgewood Rd., Milton, MA 02186; **BUS ADD:** 558 Adams St., Milton, MA 02186, (617)698-0250.

MACDONALD, David J.——B: July 3, 1939, San Francisco, CA, *Owner*, David J. Macdonald RE; **PRIM RE ACT:** Broker, Appraiser, Developer, Lender, Builder, Owner/Investor, Property Manager, Syndicator; **SERVICES:** Total; **PREV EMPLOY:** PhD work at Varian Assoc., 1961-74, current founding dir. of Bay Area Bank; **PROFL AFFIL & HONORS:** San Jose, Los Altos, Sunnyvale, Belmont, San Carlos, Redwood City Bd. of Realtors, Sequoia Club; **EDUC:** RE, Bus., Coll. of San Mateo; **MIL SERV:** US Army, Spec. 4; **HOME ADD:** 1600 Laurel St., San Carlos, CA 94070, (415)592-1467; **BUS ADD:** 1600 Laurel St., San Carlos, CA 94070, (415)592-1104.

MACDONALD, Ian A.——B: June 11, 1934, MI, *VP*, Honofed Devel. Corp.; **PRIM RE ACT:** Broker, Consultant, Attorney, Developer; **SERVICES:** Devel. mgmt., equity fin.; **REP CLIENTS:** Builders, contrs. devels. & investors; **PROFL AFFIL & HONORS:** ABA, HI Bar Assn., NAR, Nat. Assn. of Homebuilders, HI Devel. Assn.; Building Indus. Assn. of HI; Honolulu Bd. of Realtors; **EDUC:** BS, 1956, Engrg., Univ. of MI; **GRAD EDUC:** JD, 1968, Law, Detroit Coll. of Law; **EDUC HONORS:** Evans Scholar, Five scholarship awards; **MIL SERV:** US Army; SP-3, 1957-59; **OTHER ACT & HONORS:** Asst. Prosecuting Atty., Oakland Cty. MI, 1969-71; Bd. of Advisors, Salvation Army; Church Elder; **HOME ADD:** 1712 Halekoa Dr., Honolulu, HI 96821, (808)737-0039; **BUS ADD:** 182 Merchant St., Honolulu, HI 96813, (808)546-8587

MCDONALD, J. Michael——B: Apr. 24, 1942, Menominee, MI, *Pres.*, Northstar Development Co.; **PRIM RE ACT:** Builder; **SERVICES:** Home bldg.; realty; **PREV EMPLOY:** CHG Intl., Inc., Tacoma; Arlen Realty & Devel. Co., NYC; Christiana Cos., Santa Monica; Kenneth Leventhal & Co., CPA's, Los Angeles; **PROFL AFFIL & HONORS:** AICPA; CA Soc. of CPAs; WA Soc. of CPAs' Nat. Assn. of Home Builders; Seattle Master Builders; NAR; Seattle Bd. of Realtors, CPA; GEN Contractor; RE Broker; **EDUC:** BS-Bus., 1968, Acctg., CA State Univ. Los Angeles; **HOME ADD:** 3619 Nassau NE, Tacoma, WA 98422, (206)927-6923; **BUS ADD:** PO Box 3169, Federal Way, WA 98003, (206)952-3200.

MCDONALD, Jack——B: Nov. 16, 1944, Springfield, OH, *Pres. & CEO*, ACRE Realty Inc.; **PRIM RE ACT:** Broker, Instructor, Consultant, Developer, Property Manager, Owner/Investor; **OTHER RE ACT:** Condo. conversion; **SERVICES:** Condo. Conversion Consulting to Prop. Owners', Prop. mgmt., RE analysis, Homeowner Assoc. consulting; **REP CLIENTS:** Prop. Owners (residential) Homeowner Assoc.; **PREV EMPLOY:** V.P., Amer. Invsco Inc. 1972-1976; **PROFL AFFIL & HONORS:** NAR, Chicago RE Bd., IREM, Capitol Club Member - Chicago RE Bd., Condo. Comm. Chicago RE Bd., CPM, Instr. (RE) Chicago RE School and Triton Coll. Author of several RE articles; **EDUC:** PhB, 1970, Hist., Northwestern Univ., Evanston, IL; **MIL SERV:** US Army (1970-72), E-7 (SFC), ARCOM; **OTHER ACT & HONORS:** Jaycees; **HOME ADD:** 921 N. LaSalle, Chicago, IL 60610, (312)280-1680; **BUS ADD:** 1216 N. LaSalle, Chicago, IL 60610, (312)649-0300.

MCDONALD, Jack W.——B: Oct. 27, 1931, Frankfort, NY, *Broker*, Hines & McDonald Realtors, Inc.; **PRIM RE ACT:** Broker, Consultant, Developer; **SERVICES:** RE brokerage, prop. mgmt. consulting; **REP CLIENTS:** Equitable Relocation, Homequity, Employee Transfer Corp. Farmers Bank & Capital Trust Co.; **PROFL AFFIL & HONORS:** ULI; Amer. RE and Urban Econ. Assn.; RE Educators Assn.; RE Leaders of Amer.; RNMI; RELO, Realtor of the Yr., 1968; **EDUC:** 1955, Educ., Univ. of KY; **MIL SERV:** USN, Lt.j.g.; **HOME ADD:** 318 Parkwood Pl., Frankfort, KY 40601, (502)875-3887; **BUS ADD:** 903 Louisville Rd., Frankfort, KY 40601, (502)223-2173.

MCDONALD, John C., Jr.——B: Sept. 4, 1927, Charlotte, NC, *Pres.*, McDonald Realty, Co.; **PRIM RE ACT:** Broker, Consultant, Appraiser, Owner/Investor, Instructor, Property Manager; **SERVICES:** Broker, appraiser, consultant, instr., prop. mgr.; **REP CLIENTS:** Attys., investors, user owners, instns.; **PREV EMPLOY:** Gen. Electric Supply Corp., Territorial Mgr., 1950-53; **PROFL AFFIL & HONORS:** AIREA, SREA, NAR, MLS, CLE, MAI, SRA, SRPA, Realtor; **EDUC:** BS, 1950, Bus., Davidson Coll.; **MIL SERV:** USN, Seaman 2nd., 1945-46; **OTHER ACT & HONORS:** Trinity Presbyterian Church; Olde Providence Racquet Club; Charlotte Ctry Club.; Charlotte City Club; Charlotte Appraiser's Mkt. Data Assn.; Nat. Ranked Tennis Player; **HOME ADD:** 3131 Providence Rd., Charlotte, NC 28211, (704)366-1695; **BUS ADD:** PO Box 6158, 110 Perrin Pl., Charlotte, NC 28207, (704)375-4441.

MACDONALD, John H.——*Treas.*, Esterline Corp.; **PRIM RE ACT:** Property Manager; **BUS ADD:** CBT Plaza, 1120 Post Rd., Darien, CT 06820, (203)655-7651.*

MCDONALD, Joseph F.——B: Sept. 8, 1916, Reno, NV, *Pres.*, Joe McDonald & Assoc.; **PRIM RE ACT:** Attorney, Consultant, Developer, Property Manager, Owner/Investor; **PREV EMPLOY:** Staff Member US Sens. McCarran, Bible, Cannon - Wash., DC; **PROFL AFFIL & HONORS:** IREM, Realtors, Nat. Dir., NAHB; **EDUC:** BA, 1941, Journ., Univ. of NV - Reno; **GRAD EDUC:** LLB, 1953, Amer. Univ. Wash. DC; **HOME ADD:** 1830 Palisade Dr., Reno, NV 89509, (702)323-0874; **BUS ADD:** 75 Bank St. #3, Sparks, NV 89431, (702)331-1126.

MACDONALD, Kirkpatrick——B: Oct. 21, 1940, San Francisco, CA, *Managing Partner*, MacDonald & Cie; **PRIM RE ACT:** Owner/Investor, Broker, Banker, Developer, Property Manager; **SERVICES:** Principal and fiduciary representing substantial W. European investors; **EDUC:** BS, 1962, Engrg., Yale Univ.; **GRAD EDUC:** MA, 1964, Politics, Philosophy & Econ., Oxford Univ.; further studies, Univ. of Geneva, 64-67; **BUS ADD:** 114 West 78th St., New York, NY 10024, (212)580-7990.

MACDONALD, Leona I.——B: July 6, 1925, Alma, MI, *Pres.*, Century 21 Lee-Mac Realty, Inc.; **PRIM RE ACT:** Broker, Appraiser, Consultant; **SERVICES:** Resid., farms, investment, comml.; **PROFL AFFIL & HONORS:** Gratiat, Isabella Bd. of Realtors, MI Assn. of Realtors, NAR, GRI, RAM, CRS, CRB; **OTHER ACT & HONORS:** Past Pres., Bd. of Realtors; Realtor of the Year 1980, Bd. of Realtors; **HOME ADD:** 7710 N. Alger Rd., Alma, MI 48801, (517)463-3937; **BUS ADD:** 220 N. State St., Alma, MI 48801, (517)463-6085.

MCDONALD, Robert J.——B: May 25, 1936, Minneapolis, MN, *VP Comml. Dept.*, Sunbelt West, Inc., Realtors; **PRIM RE ACT:** Broker, Consultant, Owner/Investor, Property Manager, Syndicator; **OTHER RE ACT:** Sales comml., indus. & resid.; **PREV EMPLOY:** N.L. McDonald Co., Realtors, Minneapolis 1961-81, Morehouse- McDonald Realty Minneapolis 1968-73, Tucson Realty & Trust Tucson, AZ, 1973-76, AZ Homesteds Realty, Tucson, AZ 1976-79; **PROFL AFFIL & HONORS:** Realtor, GRI; **EDUC:** AA, 1958, Univ. of Minnesota; **MIL SERV:** US Army; Sp. 4, 1959-61; **HOME ADD:** 7110 N. Pampa Pl., Tucson, AZ 85704, (602)297-5777; **BUS ADD:** 925 W. Prince Rd.,

Tucson, AZ 85705, (602)887-4200.

MCDONALD, Rose——*Dir.*, Inst. for Devel. of Sales Potential, Inc.; **PRIM RE ACT:** Broker; **OTHER RE ACT:** Dir. of RE Educ.; **SERVICES:** Pre-licensing classes, also for broker's classes; **PREV EMPLOY:** Broker Starck Realtors (concurrent); **PROFL AFFIL & HONORS:** AIREE, AAUW, AREE, N Suburban Bd. of Realtors Educ. Comm., WCR; **EDUC:** BA, 1947, Ed. Lang., Rosary Coll.; **GRAD EDUC:** MALS, 1970, Library Admin., Rosary Coll. Sch. of Library Sci.; **EDUC HONORS:** Honor Roll, IL State Scholarship; **HOME ADD:** 298 S Cir., Palatine, IL 60067, (312)397-3856; **BUS ADD:** 235 N NW Hwy., Palatine, IL 60067, (312)358-0744.

MCDONALD, Samuel James, Jr.——**B:** May 18, 1914, Boston, MA, *Pres.*, S.J. McDonald, Realtors; **PRIM RE ACT:** Broker, Consultant, Appraiser, Instructor; **SERVICES:** All phases of resid. RE, catering especially to the transferred exec. family; **REP CLIENTS:** GTE, Polaroid, Phillips ECG; **PROFL AFFIL & HONORS:** MA Realtor of the Year 1972; Pres., MA Assn. of Realtors 1976 and Nat. Dir.; **EDUC:** BA, 1938, Bus., Brown Univ.; **GRAD EDUC:** 1958, Mktg., Syracuse Univ.; **OTHER ACT & HONORS:** Amer. Nat. Red Cross - Chap. Chmn.; Past Pres., Boston Brown Club and Fairfield Cty. Brown Club; Weston Golf Club; **HOME ADD:** 15 Pinecroft Rd., Weston, MA 02193, (617)894-2230; **BUS ADD:** 45 Colpitts Rd., Weston, MA 02193, (617)894-1423.

MCDONALD, Wm. A.——**B:** Nov. 1, 1944, Defuniak Sigs, FL; **OTHER RE ACT:** Applied to take the CA Bar Exam; **SERVICES:** RE, Intl. tax planning; **REP CLIENTS:** Hasegawa Komuten (USA) Inc., The Petty Corp., Rex Realty, ADM Corp.; MEPC; **PREV EMPLOY:** Tax Mgr. Coopers & Lybrand; **PROFL AFFIL & HONORS:** AICPA, CA Soc. of CPA, HI Soc. of CPA, FL Soc. of CPA's; **EDUC:** BS, Acctg., FL State Univ.; **GRAD EDUC:** MBA, 1977, Bus., Pepperdine Univ.; JD, 1981, Southland Univ.; **MIL SERV:** USMCR, Cpl.; **OTHER ACT & HONORS:** Treas. of Student Budget, FSU, Dir. Sudden Infant Death Found., Program Chmn., Unity Pre School; **HOME ADD:** 4715 Moa St., Honolulu, HI 96816, (808)734-5131; **BUS ADD:** Suite 702C, 820 Mililani St., Honolulu, HI 96816, (808)523-9065.

MCDONNELL, David K.——**B:** Oct. 31, 1950, Detroit, MI, *Atty.*, Barris, Sott, Denn & Driker; **PRIM RE ACT:** Attorney, Appraiser; **SERVICES:** Legal servs. and counseling; **REP CLIENTS:** Lenders and investors; **PREV EMPLOY:** Edward J. McDonnell Appraisal Co.; **PROFL AFFIL & HONORS:** MI State Bar; Amer. and Detroit Bar Assns.; Soc. of RE Appraisers; MI Assessor's Assn., SRA; **EDUC:** B.Gen. Studies, 1973, Univ. of MI; **GRAD EDUC:** JD, 1977, Univ. of MI Law Sch.; **EDUC HONORS:** Magna Cum Laude; **HOME ADD:** 2219 Ferncliff, Royal Oak, MI 48073, (313)541-1875; **BUS ADD:** 2100 First Fed. Bldg., Detroit, MI 48226, (313)965-9725.

MCDONNELL, Edward P.——**B:** Sept. 12, 1946, NY, *Prop. Investment Specialist*, Edward P. & Gail S. McDonnell; **PRIM RE ACT:** Consultant, Developer, Lender, Owner/Investor, Property Manager; **SERVICES:** Investment counseling, financing, prop. mgmt.; **REP CLIENTS:** Non profl. indiv. investors; **MIL SERV:** US Army, Pvt. E1, Nat. Defense Sec. Medal; **OTHER ACT & HONORS:** Past Pres., Logger's Run Civic Assn.; **HOME ADD:** 11107 Woodset La., Boca Raton, FL 33433, (305)482-9808; **BUS ADD:** 11107 Woodset La., Boca Raton, FL 33433, (305)482-9808.

MCDONNELL, Michael James——**B:** June 21, 1949, Evanston, IL, *Pres.*, AGS Fin. Corp.; **PRIM RE ACT:** Consultant, Appraiser, Owner/Investor, Syndicator; **SERVICES:** Investment advisory, synd. of large comml. and resid. props., asset mgmt. & part. admin.; **REP CLIENTS:** Indiv. investors, pension funds, maj. devels.; **PREV EMPLOY:** Fox & Carskadon Fin. (and affil.) 1977-80; Liquid Air, Inc., 1974-77; **PROFL AFFIL & HONORS:** RESSI, Amer. Econ. Assn., Lic. CA RE Broker; **EDUC:** BSBA, 1972, Double maj. Fin & Econ., Aquinas Coll., Grand Rapids, MI; **GRAD EDUC:** MA, 1974, Econ, Urban Econ., W. MI Univ.; MBA, 1974, Fin., W MI Univ.; **MIL SERV:** US Army, Intelligence, 1968-70; **HOME ADD:** 151 Briar Ln., San Mateo, CA 94403, (415)349-9807; **BUS ADD:** 177 Bovet Rd., Suite 575, San Mateo, CA 94402, (415)570-7100.

MCDONOUGH, Douglas J.——**B:** May 24, 1939, Chicago, IL, *VP, Comm.*, Amer. Inst. of RE Appraisers; **PRIM RE ACT:** Real Estate Publisher; **OTHER RE ACT:** Profl. assn.; **SERVICES:** Periodicals and texts for RE appraisers; **PREV EMPLOY:** Dir. of Mktg. RNMI; Dir. of Publishing IREM; **PROFL AFFIL & HONORS:** NAREE, Publ Rel. Soc. of Amer., Amer. Soc. of Assn. Execs; **EDUC:** IL Inst. of Tech.; **HOME ADD:** 18442 Gottschalk, Homewood, IL 60430; **BUS ADD:** 430 N Michigan Ave., Chicago, IL 60611, (312)440-8129.

MCDONOUGH, Lawrence J.——**B:** Aug. 6, 1931, Woodridge, NJ, *Pres.*, L. McDonough Realty; **PRIM RE ACT:** Broker; **PROFL AFFIL & HONORS:** N Hudson Bd. of Realtors, NJ CID, RNMI, Realty MLS Inc., 3T CPM Past Pres. RMLS, Past Pres. N Hudson Bd. of Realtors, 1978, State Dir., 1979, NJAR Exec. Comm., 1980; **EDUC:** BS, Bus. Mgmt., Fairleigh Dickinson Univ.; **MIL SERV:** USN, RMSN, 1953-55; **OTHER ACT & HONORS:** Selected Realtor of Yr., 1978; Active sportsman competes in ski races, tennis tournaments, bowling tournaments and pitches softball in league; **HOME ADD:** 1115 27nd St., N Bergen, NJ 07047, (201)348-1915; **BUS ADD:** 1115 27nd St., N Bergen, NJ 07047, (201)866-9141.

MCDORMAN, Max——**B:** July 15, 1922, Greene Cty., OH, *Pres.*, Max McDorman, Inc., Realtors; **PRIM RE ACT:** Broker; **SERVICES:** Complete RE brokerage of all categories and appraisal services; **REP CLIENTS:** The Kissell Co.; BancOhio Nat. Bank; Merrill-Lynch; **PREV EMPLOY:** Broker for 30 yrs.; assoc. with The Kissell Co., Realtors and Mort. Bankers from 1948 to 1960 and have been self employed since that time; **PROFL AFFIL & HONORS:** SRA member of SREA; Springfield, OH Bd. of Realtors, SRA; **MIL SERV:** USN; Lt.j.g.; 1942-1945; **OTHER ACT & HONORS:** C of C, Springfield, OH; **HOME ADD:** 2504 Red Coach Dr., Springfield, OH 45503, (513)399-5385; **BUS TEL:** (513)322-2222.

MCDOUGALD, Ronald J.——**B:** Mar. 5, 1939, Houston, TX, *Part.*, Bove, Katz & Charmoy; **PRIM RE ACT:** Attorney, Syndicator, Consultant; **SERVICES:** Deal structuring and netotiation; synd.; tax shelters; MIFA and other financings; document prep.; tax, legal and inv. counseling - comm. or residential. Comml. leases; const. contracts; tax and legal opinions; dispute negotiation and arbitration; **REP CLIENTS:** Indiv. and comml. inv., users, builders, lenders, synd.; **PROFL AFFIL & HONORS:** Member of MA Bar; also, MA C.P.A.; **EDUC:** BA, 1961, Lib. Arts, Dartmouth Coll.; **GRAD EDUC:** LLB, 1967, Law, Harvard Law School; LLM, 1965, Taxation, Boston Univ. Sch. of Law, Grad. Tax Program.; **EDUC HONORS:** Phi Beta Kappa, Magna Cum Laude; **HOME ADD:** Lincoln Rd., Lincoln, MA 01773, (617)259-0883; **BUS ADD:** 11 Beacon St., Ste. 1010, Boston, MA 02108, (617)367-1212.

MCDOWELL, Derek P.——**B:** Sept. 8, 1951, Wash, DC, *Atty.*, Bedford Stuyvesant Restoration Corp., 1973, Legal Dept.; **PRIM RE ACT:** Broker, Consultant, Attorney, Owner/Investor, Property Manager, Insuror; **SERVICES:** Legal counsel, constr. contracts of deveLs., owner/mgrs. of comml./resid., risk mgmt. owners, contractors; **REP CLIENTS:** Corp., indiv. owners of comml. & resid. props., ltd. partnerships and joint venturers; **PROFL AFFIL & HONORS:** Member of Bar State of NY, US Dist. Court, So. & E. Dists.; **EDUC:** AB, 1973, Econ., Pol. Sci., Phil., Princeton Univ., Woodrow Wilson Sch. of Public & Intl. Affairs; **GRAD EDUC:** JD, 1977, Rutgers Sch. of Law; **EDUC HONORS:** Poole Memorial Prize; **HOME ADD:** 7 Arlington Pl., Brooklyn, NY 11266, (212)622-7045; **BUS ADD:** 1368 Fulton St., Brooklyn, NY 11216, (212)636-3343.

MCDOWELL, Scott D., Esq.——**B:** Jan. 9, 1949, Cleveland, OH, *Partner, Gen. Counsel*, Miller & McDowell, P.C.; Centric Corp.; **PRIM RE ACT:** Attorney, Developer, Builder, Owner/Investor; **SERVICES:** Legal; **REP CLIENTS:** Lenders, Realtors, Gen. Contractors, Sub-contractors, Suppliers; **PROFL AFFIL & HONORS:** ABA; CO Bar Assn.; Denver Bar Assn., First Judicial Bar Assn., Assn. of Trial Lawyers; CO Trial Lawyers Assn., Assn. of Gen. Counsel; **EDUC:** BA, 1971, Poli. Sci. & English, Wittenberg Univ.; **GRAD EDUC:** JD, 1974, Law, Cleveland Marshall School of Law, Cleveland State Univ.; **OTHER ACT & HONORS:** Assn. of Gen. Contractors, Member, Subcontract Drafting Subcomm.; **HOME ADD:** 1755 Glen Dale Dr., Lakewood, CO 80215; **BUS ADD:** 6595 W. 14th Ave., Suite 200, Lakewood, CO 80214, (303)232-8819.

MCELFRESH, Donald C.——**B:** Dec. 1, 1931, Chicago, IL, *Dir. of Design and Construction*, Texas Plaza Partners; **PRIM RE ACT:** Developer; **SERVICES:** Devel. mgmt.; **REP CLIENTS:** Tecon Realty Corp. (Two Co's. part of TSI Holdings, Inc.); latest project is Marriott Pavilion Hotel, St. Louis, MO - renovation of existing hotel plus new 320 rm. tower and garage; **PREV EMPLOY:** T.Y. Lin (Conrad Assoc.) 1962-1972; G.D. Hines Interest, 1972-1975; Devel. Serv., 1975-1980; Tecon Realty Corp., 1980; **PROFL AFFIL & HONORS:** Nat. Parking Assn., Reg. Struct. Eng., IL; Reg. Profl. Engr., TX, OH; Parking Consultants Council; Nat. Pkg. Assn.; **EDUC:** BArch., 1958, Arch. Engrg., Univ. of IL; **GRAD EDUC:** MS, 1959, Struc. Engrg., Univ. of IL; **EDUC HONORS:** Class Honors, Upper 10%; **MIL SERV:** USN, FT/2, Korea, United Nations, China Serv., Korean Unit Citation for Task Force 95, 1949-1953; **HOME ADD:** 6560 Shady Brook Ln., Apt. 4145, Dallas, TX 75206, (214)987-9745; **BUS ADD:** Suite 660, 8222 Douglas, Dallas, TX 75225, (214)373-6600.

MCELYEA, J. Richard——**B:** Aug. 6, 1930, Palo Alto, CA, *Sr. VP*, Econ. Research Assoc.; **PRIM RE ACT:** Consultant; **SERVICES:** Market Analysis, Fin. Analysis, Fiscal Impact, Redevelopment, etc.; **REP CLIENTS:** Rouse Corp., Marriott, Southern Pacific, City of San Francisco, San Jose, Arvida, Major Corps. in RE Cities, Counties, Instit.; **PREV EMPLOY:** Booz, Allen & Hamilton, Pres., Devel. Research Div.; **PROFL AFFIL & HONORS:** Trustee, Urban Land Instit. ALDA, Travel Research Assn.; **EDUC:** BA, 1952, Econ., Stanford Univ.; **GRAD EDUC:** MBA, 1954, Marketing, Fin., Stanford Grad. Bus. School; **HOME ADD:** 566 E. Crescent Dr., Palo Alto, CA 94301, (415)324-8488; **BUS ADD:** 680 Beach St., Suite 370, San Francisco, CA 94109, (415)775-3170.

MCENERY, John T.——**B:** Apr. 25, 1942, Evanston, IL, *Part.*, MAC-VAR Assoc.; **PRIM RE ACT:** Developer; **SERVICES:** Rehab. of Older Bldgs. into Condominium or Rental, Brokerage & Prop. Mgmt.; **PREV EMPLOY:** Mort. with Baird & Warner, Inc. Chicago, IL 1970-1976 Appraisal & Prop. Mgmt.; **PROFL AFFIL & HONORS:** IREM; **EDUC:** BA, 1964, Bus. Admin., Finance, St. Mary's Coll., Winona MN; **MIL SERV:** USN 1964-1968, Lt.; **HOME ADD:** 2220 N. Halsted St., Chicago, IL 60614, (312)528-1357; **BUS ADD:** 2220 N. Halsted St., Chicago, IL 60614, (312)528-1357.

MCEVERS, Robert——*Acting Chief Officer*, Reading Industries, Inc.; **PRIM RE ACT:** Property Manager; **BUS ADD:** PO Box 126, Reading, PA 19603, (215)371-7800.*

MCFADDEN, George V.——**B:** July 1,1922, Wheeling, WV, *Pres.*, George V. McFadden Co. Inc.; **PRIM RE ACT:** Broker, Property Manager, Owner/Investor; **PREV EMPLOY:** Same over 25 yrs.; **PROFL AFFIL & HONORS:** CPM Realtor; **HOME ADD:** James Island, Charleston, SC 29412; **BUS ADD:** 1452 Burning Tree Rd., Charleston, SC 29412, (803)795-4519.

MCFARLAND, Henry D.——**B:** Aug. 11, 1941, Bremerton, WA, *Broker*, United Properties, Investment; **PRIM RE ACT:** Broker, Consultant, Owner/Investor, Syndicator; **SERVICES:** RE counseling, supervision; **REP CLIENTS:** Judge, school principal, plumber, photographer, nurse, carpenter; **PREV EMPLOY:** Legal Clerk; **PROFL AFFIL & HONORS:** Exchange Club, North Bay Investment Counselors, Sec.-Treas., NBIC; **EDUC:** BA, 1965, Journalism, Ambassador Coll.; **MIL SERV:** US Navy, Yeoman; **HOME ADD:** 629 Monroe St., Santa Rosa, CA 95404, (707)546-3547; **BUS ADD:** 1209 College Ave., Santa Rosa, CA 95404, (707)526-6777.

MCFAUL, Donivan——**B:** Aug. 21, 1941, TX-Kaufman Cty., *Pres.*, Delta Trading Corp. & D.D. McFaul, Inc.; **PRIM RE ACT:** Broker, Developer, Owner/Investor, Syndicator; **EDUC:** BBA, 1964, Acctg., Baylor Univ.; **OTHER ACT & HONORS:** St. John's Episcopal Church, Park Cities Rotary Club, St. Simon's Child Care Bd.; **BUS ADD:** Suite 110, 9550 Forest Ln., Dallas, TX 75243.

MCFERRIN, Michael W.——**B:** June 29, 1945, Waco, TX, *Pres./Owner*, Pacific Equity Investment Corp. and, Pacific Management Group Inc.; **PRIM RE ACT:** Broker, Owner/Investor, Syndicator; **OTHER RE ACT:** Broker/Dealer Asset Mgr./CPA; **SERVICES:** Synd., Acquisition, Mktg., Asset Mgr.; **REP CLIENTS:** Developers, Investors, Broker Dealers; **PREV EMPLOY:** Arthur Anderson & Co., Kaufman's Broad; **PROFL AFFIL & HONORS:** RESSI, NLHA, Advisory Bd. Housing Devel. Reporter, AICPA, CPA, Broker/Dealer; **EDUC:** BBA, 1968, Acctg., Baylor Univ.; **MIL SERV:** US Army Res., E-5; **HOME ADD:** 19220 Dearborn St., Northridge, CA 91324, (213)349-0431; **BUS ADD:** 5855 Topanga Canyon, Woodland Hill, CA 91367.

MCGARR, Paul——*Treas.*, Guilford Mills, Inc.; **PRIM RE ACT:** Property Manager; **BUS ADD:** 4925 West Market, Greensboro, NC 27402, (919)292-7550.*

MCGARRY, John T.——**B:** Aug. 19,1939, Chicago, IL, *Pres.*, John T. McGarry Ltd. & K & G. Bldg. Mgmt. Inc.; **PRIM RE ACT:** Broker, Consultant, Attorney, Developer, Builder, Owner/Investor, Property Manager; **SERVICES:** Atty. Devel. & Rehab. Rental Mgmt.; **REP CLIENTS:** Indiv. investors; **PREV EMPLOY:** Asst. Public Defender of Cook Cty. Asst. State's Atty.; **PROFL AFFIL & HONORS:** ABA CBA, ISBA, NAIFA, S&L IL Comm., Bd. member; **EDUC:** BS, 1962, Hist., Siena Coll., Albany, NY; **GRAD EDUC:** JD, 1965, Condemnation & RE, John Marshall Law School; **HOME ADD:** 20800 Alexander St., Olympia Fields, IL 60461, (312)747-9034; **BUS ADD:** 1609 E. 53rd St., Chicago, IL 60615, (312)288-2758.

MCGEE, Jack P.——**B:** Jan. 16, 1952, Atlanta, GA, *Owner*, Real Estate Appraisal Service; **PRIM RE ACT:** Consultant, Appraiser, Property Manager; **SERVICES:** RE appraisals; **REP CLIENTS:** Savings & loan, bd. of realtors, home builders, attys., relocation services, etc.; **PREV EMPLOY:** First Shelter Serv. Corp., Brunswick, GA; **PROFL AFFIL & HONORS:** Bd. of Realtors, Candidate with AIREA, HBA of GA; **EDUC:** BBA, 1974, RE & Urban Devel, Univ. of GA & Middle GA Coll.; **OTHER ACT & HONORS:** US Jaycees; **HOME ADD:** PO Box 525, St. Simons, GA 31522, (912)638-9555; **BUS ADD:** PO Box 525, St. Simons Island, GA 31522, (912)638-9555.

MCGEE, Walter T.——**B:** July 4, 1943, New York, NY, *Pres.*, Walter T. McGee, Inc.; McGee, Collins & Associates, Inc.; **PRIM RE ACT:** Broker, Consultant, Developer, Owner/Investor, Property Manager, Syndicator; **OTHER RE ACT:** Marketing mgmt., timeshare mgmt.; **SERVICES:** RE investment advisory services; **REP CLIENTS:** Indiv. and corp. investor groups, interested in RE devel. and invesmtnet; **PREV EMPLOY:** Exec. VP, RE Devel. Co. 1975-1979; **PROFL AFFIL & HONORS:** NAR; RESSI; **EDUC:** BS, 1966, Fin. & Acctg., Univ. of MD; **GRAD EDUC:** Grad. Certificate, 1974, Health Care Admin., OH State Univ., School of Allied Medical Profs.; **OTHER ACT & HONORS:** Vero Kiwanis Club; **HOME ADD:** 560 Acacca Rd., Vero Beach, FL 32960, (305)231-2109; **BUS ADD:** 1025 Flamevine Ln., Suite 6, Vero Beach, FL 32960, (305)231-4100.

MCGILL, Douglas F.I.——**B:** Feb. 19, 1941, Warren, OH, *Pres.*, McGill Corp., The Real Estate Co.; **PRIM RE ACT:** Broker, Consultant, Developer, Builder, Owner/Investor, Property Manager, Syndicator; **OTHER RE ACT:** Condo. Converter; **SERVICES:** Sales, mgmt., mktg., programs designed, mkt. analysis; **REP CLIENTS:** Sheraton Hotels, Ling Tempco Vought, Energy Fuels (Getty Oil), Merritt Knitting Kills, Transamerica Corp.; **PREV EMPLOY:** SD Broker for Resort Props., Formerly Gen. Mgr. for Terry Peak Devel. Corp. (1970-1979); **PROFL AFFIL & HONORS:** Member NW CO Bd. of Realtors, CO Assn. of Realtors and NAR; **EDUC:** 1960-1968, Eng. & Bus. Admin., Univ. of NC, Chapel Hill; **OTHER ACT & HONORS:** Pres. Country Green Devel. Corp., General Partner Steamboat Hotels, Pine Grove Assoc., Twenty Mile Ranch, Steamboat Town Apts Partnership; **HOME ADD:** 30205 Country Green Rd., Box 773058, Steamboat Springs, CO 80477, (303)879-1719; **BUS ADD:** PO Box 773058, Steamboat Springs, CO 80477, (303)879-2345.

MCGILL, Maurice——*VP & Treas.*, Iowa Beef Processors, Inc.; **PRIM RE ACT:** Property Manager; **BUS ADD:** PO Box 515, Dakota City, NE 68731, (402)494-2061.*

MCGILL, Peter R., Jr.——**B:** May 22, 1941, Baltimore, MD, *Pres.*, The McGill Co.; **PRIM RE ACT:** Consultant, Developer, Owner/Investor; **PROFL AFFIL & HONORS:** Intl. Council of Shopping Ctrs., ULI; **EDUC:** BS, 1963, Psych., Univ. of VA; **MIL SERV:** US Coast Guard Res.; **HOME ADD:** 202 Paddington Rd., Baltimore, MD 21212, (301)377-2124; **BUS ADD:** 6229 N. Charles St., Baltimore, MD 21212, (301)377-2124.

MCGILL, Scott——**B:** Apr. 3, 1951, Indianapolis, IN, *Pres.*, Graves & McGill, P.C.; **PRIM RE ACT:** Broker, Attorney, Owner/Investor; **SERVICES:** Counsel to numerous builders, devels., lenders, arch. & realtors; **PREV EMPLOY:** Sharp & Black, P.C., 1977-80; **PROFL AFFIL & HONORS:** Amer., CO, NW CO & Routt Cty. Bar Assns.; **EDUC:** BA, 1973, Econ., Amherst Coll.; **GRAD EDUC:** JD, 1977, Univ. of ME; **BUS ADD:** Box 772810, Steamboat Springs, CO 80477, (303)879-6200.

MCGILLIN, William Gregory——**B:** Mar. 23, 1950, Los Angeles, CA, *VP*, Nelson & McCarty, P.S.; **PRIM RE ACT:** Attorney; **REP CLIENTS:** Partners Fin. Inc., Chicago Title Ins. Co., Jerald E. Scofield, The Scofield Corp.; **PREV EMPLOY:** Instrc. City Coll., Dupont Campus; **PROFL AFFIL & HONORS:** WA State Bar Assn., Bus. Banking & RE Sects.; ABA Legal Econ Sect.; WSTLA; ATLA; SKCBA; EKCBA; Past Member of Bd. of Trs. and Comm. on Continuing Legal Educ.; **EDUC:** BA, 1972, Pol. Sic., Intl. Affairs, Univ. of CA, Riverside Campus; **GRAD EDUC:** JD, 1974, Comml. Law & RE, Univ. of Puget Sound, Sch. of Law; **EDUC HONORS:** Cum Laude; **HOME ADD:** 4029 145th NE, Bellevue, WA 98007; **BUS ADD:** 10800 NE 8th St., 710 ONB Plaza, Bellevue, WA 98004, (206)454-2344.

MCGINNIS, Claude A.——**B:** Sept. 5, 1929, Atlanta, GA, *Pres.*, McGinnis Realty, Inc.; **PRIM RE ACT:** Broker, Developer, Syndicator; **SERVICES:** Sale and leasing of comml. and investment prop., synd. of investment prop.; **PROFL AFFIL & HONORS:** Atlanta Bd. of Realtors; RESSI, Gov.; **EDUC:** BS, 1951, Chemical Engrg., GA Inst. of Tech.; **GRAD EDUC:** MBA, 1961, Econ/Fin., Xavier Univ., Cincinnati, OH; **MIL SERV:** Chemical Corps., 1st Lt., Bronze Star, Pres. Unit Citation, Korean Pres. Unit Citation; **HOME ADD:** 1565 Moores Mill Rd., Atlanta, GA 30327, (404)351-2029; **BUS ADD:** 2022 Powers Ferry Rd., Suite 180, Atlanta, GA 30339, (404)955-3808.

MCGINNIS, R. J.——**B:** July 21, 1948, Panama, *VP*, Hudgins RE; **PRIM RE ACT:** Broker, Syndicator, Developer, Property Manager, Owner/Investor; **PROFL AFFIL & HONORS:** NAR, RNMI, RESSI, CRB, Cert. Comml. Investment Member Candidate; Designation Programs of NAR; **EDUC:** BS Chem. Engrg., 1970, Engrg., VPI, Blackburg VA; **HOME ADD:** 403 34th St., VA Beach, VA 23451, (804)422-6437; **BUS ADD:** 3701 Pacific Ave., VA Beach, VA 23451, (804)428-0046.

MCGINTY, Milton, Jr.——**B:** July 6, 1946, Houston, TX, *Pres. and Chmn. of the Bd.*, City Associates, Inc.; **PRIM RE ACT:** Broker, Architect, Developer; **SERVICES:** Brokerage, devel. mgmt., analysis; **REP CLIENTS:** Sawyer Office Investors; Fairgrounds Investors; 5300 Memorial Investors Ltd.; instnl. and private investors; **PROFL AFFIL & HONORS:** NAR; Houston Bd. of Realtors; TX Assn. of Realtors; Amer. Mgmt. Assn.; **EDUC:** BA, 1970, Arch., Rice Univ.; **GRAD EDUC:** MArch, 1973, Rice Univ.; MBA, 1980, FL Atlantic Univ.; **EDUC HONORS:** 1970 Pres. Honor Roll; **OTHER ACT & HONORS:** Member, Kiwanis Club of Houston; Member AIA; **BUS ADD:** 601 Sawyer 5th Floor, Houston, TX 77007, (713)880-2880.

MCGINTY, Rush——**B:** July 30, 1939, Lubbock, TX, *Pres.*, Rush McGinty Real Estate, Inc.; **PRIM RE ACT:** Broker, Consultant, Developer, Builder, Owner/Investor, Syndicator; **SERVICES:** Wide range of counseling & brokerage; **REP CLIENTS:** Lawyers, banks & builders; **PROFL AFFIL & HONORS:** CID member Austin Bd., RESSI, TX RE Exchangors, FLI, CCIM candidate; **EDUC:** BS, 1962, Hist. - Chemistry, TX A&M Univ.; **GRAD EDUC:** Law, Univ. of TX; **EDUC HONORS:** VP MSC Council, Outstanding Cadet in Regiment 1958, Dean of Delta Theta Phi - Most Court Winner; **OTHER ACT & HONORS:** Exec. Asst. to Speaker of Texas House - 4 years; Officer on Bd. of Realtors; Also assoc. with Cimarron Realty Inc. (Pres.) 701 Shiloh Rd. Tyler, TX 75703; **HOME ADD:** 1204 West 29th, Austin, TX 78701, (512)477-4797; **BUS ADD:** 1501 West Ave., Austin, TX 78701, (512)477-3077.

MCGIVNEY, James H.——**B:** Apr. 25, 1947, Brooklyn, NY, *Atty.*, Gibney, Anthony & Flaherty, Head RE Dept.; **PRIM RE ACT:** Attorney; **REP CLIENTS:** Comml. Landlords and Tenants; **EDUC:** BA, 1968, Eng. & Pol. Sci.; **GRAD EDUC:** JD, LLM, 1972, 1978, 1979, NYU; **HOME ADD:** 1523 Argyle Rd., Wantagh, NY 11793, (914)785-2652; **BUS ADD:** 420 Lexington Ave., NY, NY 10170, (914)986-3800.

MCGLONE, James J.——**B:** June 17, 1933, Phila., PA, *VP - Regl. Mgr.*, Fox & Lazo Realtors Inc., S NJ - Resid.; **PRIM RE ACT:** Broker, Instructor; **OTHER RE ACT:** Lecturer - TV Talk Show; **SERVICES:** Resid. RE Sales; **PROFL AFFIL & HONORS:** RELA, Burlington Cty. Bd. of Realtors, NAR Bds., CRB, NJARB Million Dollar Club 1972; **MIL SERV:** US Army, 1953-1956, German Occupation Natl. Defense; **OTHER ACT & HONORS:** Certificate of Appreciation Phila. Bulletin Home Buyers Clinic; **HOME ADD:** 241 Heritage Rd., Cherry Hill, NJ 08034, (609)428-8287; **BUS ADD:** 2101 Rte. 70 E, Cherry Hill, NJ 08003, (609)424-2800.

MCGLYNN, D. Jerry——**B:** July 6, 1938, St. Louis, *Atty. at Law*; **PRIM RE ACT:** Attorney, Consultant; **SERVICES:** Legal and Consulting Serv.; **REP CLIENTS:** Dev., Contractors, Realtors, and other Consultants; **PREV EMPLOY:** Banker, Dir. of Housing Dev. Corp.; **PROFL AFFIL & HONORS:** ABA, CA Bar Assn., Maniu Co. Bar Assn., Assn. of MBA Exec.; **EDUC:** BBA, 1960, Fin., Univ. of Notre Dame; **GRAD EDUC:** MBA (JD), 1972, 1974, Bus. Planning/Bus. & RE, Univ. of Notre Dame; **OTHER ACT & HONORS:** Univ. of Notre Dame Nat. Alumni Bd. Dir.; **HOME ADD:** 825 Las Gallinns Ave., #204, San Rafael, CA 94903, (415)499-8030; **BUS ADD:** 880 Las Gallinns Ave., Suite B, San Rafael, CA 94093, (415)472-6868.

MCGLYNN, Joseph M.——**B:** Jan. 15, 1937, Detroit, MI, *Pres.*, Joseph M. McGlynn, PC; **PRIM RE ACT:** Attorney, Consultant; **SERVICES:** Representing and assisting clients in evaluating, purchasing, managing and selling real prop.; **REP CLIENTS:** Several medium size corporate clients and many indivs., partners and joint ventures; **PREV EMPLOY:** Sales, Frank J. McGlynn RE Detroit 1954-1961; **PROFL AFFIL & HONORS:** ABA; State Bar of MI; Oakland Cty. Bar Assn.; Detroit Bar Assn.; RE Sects. of ABA and State Bar of MI; Fin. and Estate Planning Council of Detroit; Oakland Cty. Estate Planning Council; **EDUC:** BS, 1958, Acctg., Univ. of Detroit; **GRAD EDUC:** JD, 1960, Law, Univ. of Detroit; **EDUC HONORS:** Cum Laude; Beta Gamma Sigma (Profl. Hon. Soc.); Alpha Sigma Nu (Jesuit Hon. Soc.), First Prize, ASCAP, Nathan Burkan Memorial Competition; Class Officer; Editor, Univ. of Detroit Law Journal; **MIL SERV:** USAR, SFC, 1960-1966; **HOME ADD:** 2251 Park Ridge Dr., Bloomfield Hills, MI 48013; **BUS ADD:** 500 Northland Towers E., Southfield, MI 48075.

MCGOFF, James J.——**B:** July 2, 1917, Barre, VT, *Partner*, McGoff Assoc., Appraisal; **PRIM RE ACT:** Consultant, Appraiser; **SERVICES:** Market Value reports, counseling on RE; **REP CLIENTS:** Banks, attys., buyers, sellers, fed., state and municipal agencies; **PREV EMPLOY:** VP, Meredith & Grew, Inc., 125 High St., Boston; US Govt.; **PROFL AFFIL & HONORS:** AIREA, SREA, Boston RE Bd., MAI; **EDUC:** BS, 1941, Forestry, Civil Engrg., Univ. of NH; **MIL SERV:** Capt. US Army (Retd.); USA 1941-45, Air Medal with 6 Clusters; MA National Guard 1945-1961; **HOME ADD:** 11 Appletree Ln., Andover, MA 01810, (617)475-8185; **BUS ADD:** Musgrove Bldg., 2 Elm Sq., Andover, MA 01810, (617)475-2102.

MCGOLDRICK, Richard J.——*Pres.*, Commercial Properties, Inc.; **PRIM RE ACT:** Broker, Developer, Owner/Investor, Property Manager, Syndicator; **SERVICES:** Devel., investment packaging, prop. mgmt., brokerage; **PROFL AFFIL & HONORS:** Greater Portland C of C, Port of Portland Devel. Comm.; **EDUC:** Econ., Boston Coll.; **GRAD EDUC:** Labor Relations, Univ. of IL; **EDUC HONORS:** Dean's List; **MIL SERV:** US Army; **BUS ADD:** 53 Exchange St., Portland, ME 04101, (207)774-1885.

MCGONIGAL, William M.——**B:** June 27, 1928, St. Paul, MN, *Dir. of Sales, Mktg. & Mgmt.*, Community Management; **PRIM RE ACT:** Broker, Consultant, Developer, Builder, Instructor, Property Manager, Syndicator; **OTHER RE ACT:** Condo. and coop conversions; **SERVICES:** Sales, mktg. mgmt. of apts., condos., coops, townhouses; prop. devel.; specializing in condo. conversions; **PROFL AFFIL & HONORS:** Member, Inst. of Resid. Mktg.; Community Assn. Inst.; NAHB, NAHB, Sales and Mktg. Council, NAHB, Marketing Man of the Yr., 1975; NAHB, Idea of the Yr., 1974 and 1980; NAHB-MIRM; **EDUC:** BA, 1952, Sociology/Hist./Bus., Coll. of St. Thomas; **EDUC HONORS:** Arnold Soc.; **MIL SERV:** USAF, 1st Lt.; **OTHER ACT & HONORS:** C of C; Brooklyn Hist. Soc.; **HOME ADD:** 4806 Howe Ln., Minneapolis, MN 55429, (612)533-7348; **BUS ADD:** 6400 Flying Cloud Dr., Minneapolis, MN 55344, (612)781-3184.

MCGOUGH, Bobby C.——**B:** Nov. 10, 1921, Lake City, AR, *Prof. & RE Chairholder*, AR State Univ., Coll. of Bus.; **PRIM RE ACT:** Broker, Consultant, Appraiser, Owner/Investor, Instructor; **SERVICES:** Indep. appraising; **REP CLIENTS:** Frisco RR, Burlington Northern RR, Bell Telephone, GM RE; **PREV EMPLOY:** Univ. of FL, Central & Southern FL Flood Control, Univ. of AZ, Jonesboro Urban Renewal, E. AR Planning & Devel. Dist.; **PROFL AFFIL & HONORS:** SREA, SRA, IFA, CRA, PhD (RE); **EDUC:** BS, 1948, Bus., AR State Univ.; **GRAD EDUC:** MBA, 1951, RE, Syracuse Univ., Syracuse, NY; PhD, 1962, RE, Univ. of FL, Gainesville, FL; **EDUC HONORS:** Who's Who in Amer., Who's Who in RE; **MIL SERV:** USAF, Ltc., Purple Heart, Air Medal & Cluster, Good Conduct; **OTHER ACT & HONORS:** S Econ. Assn., Amer. Financial Assn.; **HOME ADD:** Rt. 1, Box 24, Jonesboro, AR 72401, (501)935-8555; **BUS ADD:** Coll. of Bus., ASU, Box 1530, State Univ., AR 72467, (501)972-3416.

MCGOUGH, Robert J.——*President*, Apartment Owners & Managers Assoc. of America; **PRIM RE ACT:** Real Estate Publisher; **OTHER RE ACT:** Profl. Assn. Admin.; **PROFL AFFIL & HONORS:** Ed., Apt. Owners & Mngrs. Assoc. of America, Who's Who in Multi-Family Housing; **BUS ADD:** 65 Cherry Ave., Watertown, CT 06795, (203)274-2589.*

MCGOVERN, E. Tom——**B:** Sept. 11, 1923, Racine, WI, *Pres., Chmn.*, Thomas Equities Corp.; **PRIM RE ACT:** Syndicator, Developer, Builder, Property Manager, Owner/Investor; **SERVICES:** Resort Timeshare Mgmt.; **REP CLIENTS:** Tierra Verde Is. Resort; **PREV EMPLOY:** Have owned Maj. Comml. Brokerage and prop. Mgmt. Firms; **PROFL AFFIL & HONORS:** IREM, RESSI, National Syndication Forum, NAHB, CPM; former Nat. Dir., NAHB, Successful Completion of 1st RESSI courses for D.P.P. Salesman & Principal; **EDUC:** Mktg., Univ. of WI; **MIL SERV:** USAF, Capt.; **OTHER ACT & HONORS:** Treas. & Lifetime Hon. Dir., Tierra Verde Yacht Club; Tr., Canterbury School, St. Petersburg, FL; **HOME ADD:** 5110 62nd Ave., St. Petersburg, FL 33715, (813)864-1479; **BUS ADD:** 200 Madonna Blvd., St. Petersburg, FL 33715, (813)867-1181.

MCGOWAN, J. Joseph——**B:** July 16, 1936, Newburgh, NY, *Part.*, McCabe & Mack; **PRIM RE ACT:** Attorney; **SERVICES:** Full legal; **REP CLIENTS:** Lending instns. & investors re. comml. agricultural & resid. props.; **EDUC:** BS, 1958, Econ., Georgetown Univ.; **GRAD EDUC:** JD, 1961, Law, Harvard Univ.; **EDUC HONORS:** Cum Laude; **MIL SERV:** US Army, Capt., 1962-63, Commendation Medal; **OTHER ACT & HONORS:** Tr. Mount St. Mary Coll., Dir. Mid-Hudson Civic Ctr.; **HOME ADD:** 4 Ferris Ln., Poughkeepsie, NY 12601, (914)471-8517; **BUS ADD:** 42 Catherine St., PO Box 509, Poughkeepsie, NY 12602, (914)452-2800.

MCGOWIN, Gerald Anthony——B: June 2, 1943, Fort Worth, TX, *Treas., Controller and Chief Financial Officer*, Norris, Beggs & Simpson; **PRIM RE ACT:** Broker, Developer, Lender, Property Manager; **SERVICES:** Sales, leasing, prop. mgmt., mort. banking, devel.; **REP CLIENTS:** Fin. inst.; **PREV EMPLOY:** Touche Ross & Co.; **PROFL AFFIL & HONORS:** AICPA, CA Soc. of CPA's, CPA; **EDUC:** BA, 1965, Hist., Stanford Univ.; **GRAD EDUC:** MBA, 1970, Acctg. & Fin., Stanford Univ.; **MIL SERV:** US Army, Capt.; **HOME ADD:** 100 Sutherland Dr., Atherton, CA 94025; **BUS ADD:** 243 Kearny St., San Francisco, CA 94108, (415)362-5660.

MCGRATH, John W.——B: Oct. 22, 1929, New York, NY, *VP Devel.*, Associated Inns and Restaurants Co. of America; **PRIM RE ACT:** Broker, Attorney, Developer; **OTHER RE ACT:** AIRCOA develops, acquires and manages hotel props. for its own and the accounts of others; **PREV EMPLOY:** Ford Found. - RE Investment Officer 1977-79; Rock Resorts, Dir. Resort Land Devel.; Sea Pines Plantation Co., Exec. VP; **PROFL AFFIL & HONORS:** NY Bar Assn.; ULI, NY RE Bd.; **EDUC:** BA, 1951, Econ., Amherst Coll.; **GRAD EDUC:** LLB, 1954, Law, Yale Law School; **EDUC HONORS:** Magna Cum Laude, Phi Beta Kappa, Law Journal; **MIL SERV:** USN, SN; **OTHER ACT & HONORS:** Yale Club of NY; **HOME ADD:** 2770 S. Elmira 33, Denver, CO 80231, (303)695-9133; **BUS ADD:** 4552 S. Quebec, Denver, CO 80237, (303)779-1219.

MCGRATH, Michael P.——B: Mar. 3, 1943, Boston, MA, *Tax Dir.*, Cabot, Cabot & Forbes Co.; **PRIM RE ACT:** Developer, Builder, Property Manager; **PREV EMPLOY:** Public Acctg., 1970-1974; IRS, 1967-1970; **PROFL AFFIL & HONORS:** CPA; **EDUC:** BS, 1967, Acctg., Bentley Coll.; **GRAD EDUC:** MS, 1977, Taxation, Bentley Coll.; **HOME ADD:** 30 Oakland Cir., Wellesley Hills, MA 02181; **BUS ADD:** 60 State St., Boston, MA 02109, (617)742-7600.

MCGRATTY, Christopher F.——B: Jan. 14, 1943, Brooklyn, NY, *Pres.*, Tishman Realty Corporation; **PRIM RE ACT:** Owner/Investor; **PREV EMPLOY:** VP, Eastdil Realty; VP and Dir. RE Investment Banking, Div., Merrill Lynch Hubbard, Inc.; **PROFL AFFIL & HONORS:** ULI, Young Mort. Bankers Assn., Intl. Council of Shopping Centers, MBAA, RE Bd. of NY, NY Mort. Bankers Assn.; **EDUC:** BS, 1964, Econ., Coll. of the Holy Cross; **HOME ADD:** 200 E. 62nd St., New York, NY 10021; **BUS ADD:** 666 Fifth Avenue, New York, NY 10103, (212)399-3664.

MACGREGOR, Gordon——B: July 1, 1944, New York City, NY, *Sales Mgr.*, Bridge Street Real Estate and Investment Co.; **PRIM RE ACT:** Broker, Consultant, Developer, Owner/Investor, Syndicator; **SERVICES:** Full serv. brokerage, including comml. opportunities and devel.; **PROFL AFFIL & HONORS:** Vail Bd. of Realtors, RESSI; **EDUC:** BA, 1968, Poli. Sci., Econ.,, Lake Forest Coll.; **MIL SERV:** USMCR, Pvt 1st Class; **HOME ADD:** PO Box 1722, Vail, CO 81658, (303)476-0773; **BUS ADD:** 286 Bridge St., Vail, CO 81657, (303)476-2212.

MCGREGOR, LeGrande N.——B: Mar. 18, 1946, Preston, ID, *Exec. VP*, Western Securities Co.; **PRIM RE ACT:** Broker, Developer; **OTHER RE ACT:** Mort. Banking; **SERVICES:** Comml. & resid. mort. investment synd., joint ventures, brokerage; **REP CLIENTS:** Life ins. cos., S&L's, devels., brokers, pension cos.; **PREV EMPLOY:** Realty Income Trust, First PA Mort. Tr., Equitable Life Assurance of US; **PROFL AFFIL & HONORS:** RESSI, MBA, Nat. Assn. of Home Builders, RE broker in sev. states., Alpha Kappa Psi, Distinguished Serv. Award, Novicks, Creative Financing Award; **EDUC:** BSBA, 1970, Gen. Bus. & Econ., ID State Univ.; **EDUC HONORS:** Econ. Hon. Frat.; **HOME ADD:** 12740 Harney St., Omaha, NE 68154, (402)334-2588; **BUS ADD:** 5060 Dodge St., Omaha, NE 68132, (402)558-2800.

MACGREGOR, Valerie——B: Jan. 30, 1949, Detroit, MI, Macgregor Realty Co.; **PRIM RE ACT:** Broker, Consultant, Builder, Owner/Investor, Property Manager, Syndicator; **PROFL AFFIL & HONORS:** Flint RE Exchangers, MI Assn. of Realtors Exchange Div., Flint Bd. Educ. Comm., GRI - Candidate for CCIM; **HOME ADD:** 8300 Jordon Rd., Grand Blanc, MI 48439, (313)636-2020; **BUS ADD:** 536 Perry Rd., Grand Blanc, MI 48439, (313)695-4550.

MCGRUDER, James P.——B: Mar. 11, 1926, Los Angeles, CA, *Rgnl. Counsel*, Prudential Ins. Co., RE Investment Dept.; **PRIM RE ACT:** Attorney; **SERVICES:** Legal servs. re: RE transactions; **PREV EMPLOY:** City Atty's. office - Denver, CO, Asst. US Atty. - Dist. of CO; **PROFL AFFIL & HONORS:** CA Bar, CO Bar; **EDUC:** 1950-52, Regis Coll. - Denver, CO; **GRAD EDUC:** JD, 1953, Law, Univ. of Denver, Denver, CO; **MIL SERV:** USMC, 1943-1946; **HOME ADD:** 10036 Shoshone Ave., Northridge, CA 91325, (213)886-7143; **BUS ADD:** 2049 Century Park E., Suite 2550, Los Angeles, CA 90067, (213)277-1400.

MCGUIRE, Edward D., Jr.——B: Apr. 11, 1948, Waynesboro, VA, *Staff Atty. & Assistant Corp. Secretary*, Peoples Drug Stores, Inc.; **PRIM RE ACT:** Attorney, Property Manager; **SERVICES:** Lease negotiation & analysis, prep. of legal documents for all types of comml. RE transactions (devel., const., leasing and prop. mgmt.), RE litigation, and acquistions; **REP CLIENTS:** Owners, lenders, title ins. cos., contractors and tenants of comml. props.; **PREV EMPLOY:** 1980-81 - Amtrak RE Dept. (Sr. Contracts Officer), Washington, DC; 1978-80 - Mark Winkler Mgmt., Inc., Alexandria, VA (Gen. Counsel & Comml. Prop. Mgr.); 1973-78 - Law Offices of Wilkes & Artis, Chartered, Washington, DC (Assoc.); **PROFL AFFIL & HONORS:** ABA; VA State Bar; DC Bar; VA Bar Assn.; VA Trial Lawyers Assn.; Assn. of Trial Lawyers of Amer.; **EDUC:** BS, 1970, Commerce, Major - Bus. Mgmt.; Minor - Econ., Univ. of VA; **GRAD EDUC:** JD, 1973, Law, Marshall-Wythe School of Law, Coll. of William and Mary; **EDUC HONORS:** Dean's List; University Scholarship, Goodman Scholarship; **MIL SERV:** VA Army, National Guard, JAG, 1973-81, Capt.; **OTHER ACT & HONORS:** N. VA Dist. Bd. of VA Student Aid Found.; Pres. of Bd. of Dirs. of New Hope Found., Inc.; Class Agent-Univ. of VA Fund; Class Agent- William and Mary Law School Fund; **HOME ADD:** 18A W. Chapman St., Alexandria, VA 22301, (703)836-3172; **BUS ADD:** 6315 Bren Mar Dr., Alexandria, VA 22312, (703)750-6791.

MCGUIRE, Kevin——B: Aug. 11, 1946, Lowell, MA, *Second VP*, John Hancock Mutual Life Insurance Co., Mort. & RE Dept.; **OTHER RE ACT:** Portfolio Mgr., Equity RE acct.; **SERVICES:** Acquisition of Prop. and Mgmt. of prop. for equity RE separate acct.; **REP CLIENTS:** Qualified pension plans; **PROFL AFFIL & HONORS:** NAIOP, ICSC; **EDUC:** AB, 1968, Econ., Boston Coll.; **GRAD EDUC:** MBA, 1974, Fin., Babson Coll.; **MIL SERV:** US Army Res.; **HOME ADD:** 16 Vine Brook Rd., Lexington, MA 02173; **BUS ADD:** John Hancock Pl., PO Box 111, Boston, MA 02117, (617)421-2081.

MCGUIRE, Mary C., Esq.——B: Jan. 28, 1954, Jersey City, NJ, *Mgr. of RE Planning and Dev.*, Pepperidge Farm, Inc., RE; **PRIM RE ACT:** Attorney, Property Manager; **SERVICES:** Drafting and negotiation of RE Contracts and Leases, representation of client at zoning hearings; **REP CLIENTS:** Pepperidge Farm, Inc. and its subs., i.e. Godiva Chocolatier, Inc. and Lexington Gardens, Inc.; **PREV EMPLOY:** Atty. - Blazzard, Grodd & Hasenauer (Law Firm) 1978-1981; **PROFL AFFIL & HONORS:** ABA, CT Bar Assn., Westport Bar Assn., NACORE; **EDUC:** BA, 1975, Eng., Coll. of the Holy Cross, Worcester, MA; **GRAD EDUC:** JD, 1978, Law, W. New England Coll. of Law, Springfield, MA; **EDUC HONORS:** Dean's List; **HOME ADD:** 125 Weston Rd., Westport, CT 06880; **BUS ADD:** 542 Westport Ave, Norwalk, CT 06856, (203)846-7281.

MCGUIRE, R. C., Jr.——B: Jan. 9, 1931, Paducah, KY, *Owner*, Mickey McGuire, Realtor; **PRIM RE ACT:** Broker, Consultant, Appraiser, Banker, Developer, Builder, Owner/Investor, Instructor, Property Manager; **SERVICES:** Rentals, Appraising, Prop. Mgmt.; **REP CLIENTS:** Equitable Relocation Serv., S. Central Bell, Sears, ICGRR, Willamette Paper Mill, Executrans, TX Commerce Bank; **PREV EMPLOY:** Area Mgr. for HUD 1974-77; Area Mgr. for HUD 1981-82; Area Mgr. for VA 1981; **PROFL AFFIL & HONORS:** KY C of C, Paducah Area C of C, NAR, KY Assn. of Realtors, Paducah Bd. of Realtors, IREM, CPM, GRI, CRS; **EDUC:** BS, 1953, Murray State Univ., Murray, KY; **OTHER ACT & HONORS:** KY Gen. Assembly 1958-59; Elks; Masons; Past Pres. Paducah Bd. of Realtors, 1975; **HOME ADD:** 125 Lakeview Dr., Paducah, KY 42001, (502)554-1736; **BUS ADD:** PO Box 3058, Paducah, KY 42001, (502)442-8223.

MCGUIRE, William B.——B: June 17, 1944, Charlotte, NC, *Pres.*, McGuire Properties, Inc.; **PRIM RE ACT:** Broker, Developer, Owner/Investor, Property Manager, Syndicator; **SERVICES:** Mgmt., devel., brokerage; **PROFL AFFIL & HONORS:** Bd. of Dir., Charlotte Apt. Assn.; Bd. of Realtors; NC Income Prop. Assn., Lic. RE Broker, Ins. Broker, Stock Broker; **EDUC:** BArch., 1966, Econ./Bus., Davidson Coll.; **GRAD EDUC:** MBA, 1970, Urban Land Devel., Harvard Univ. Bus. School; **EDUC HONORS:** ODK;ODE, Baker Scholar, Love Fellow, Grad. with High Distinction; **MIL SERV:** US Army, Lt., Bronze Star; **OTHER ACT & HONORS:** Indus. Revenue Bond Auth. for Mecklenburg Cty.; Pres., Neighborhood Med. Clinic; Elder, Myers Park Presbyterian Church; **BUS ADD:** 139 S. Tryon St., Suite 501, Charlotte, NC 28202, (704)334-7383.

MCGURK, Helen M.——B: Phila., PA, *Asst. VP*, Binswanger Mgmt. Corp.; **PRIM RE ACT:** Property Manager; **SERVICES:** Prep. of Leases and Servicing of Tenant Problems; **PROFL AFFIL & HONORS:** BOMA - Phila. Bd. of Realtors; **EDUC:** Comml. - Office Space Leasing, Temple Univ.; **GRAD EDUC:** RE Law; **HOME ADD:** 1900 JFK Blvd., Philadelphia, PA 19103; **BUS ADD:** 1845 Walnut St., Philadelphia, PA 19103, (215)448-6000.

MACHAT, Sydney L.——**B:** June 18, 1939, Philadelphia, PA, *Pres.*, Machat Realty Inc.; **PRIM RE ACT:** Broker, Developer, Owner/Investor, Instructor; **PROFL AFFIL & HONORS:** NAR; MD Assn. of Realtors; RNMI; RESSI, CRB; Pres., Greater Hagerstown Bd. of Realtors; Dir. & Educ. Comm. Chmn., MD Assn. of Realtors; **EDUC:** AB, 1962, Dickinson Coll.; **GRAD EDUC:** MBA, RE, Amer. Univ.; **EDUC HONORS:** NAR, RNMI, Moore Trophy, Hon. Ment. (Mgt. Award, 1979); **MIL SERV:** VP, Ruritan, Torch Club; **HOME ADD:** Box 247, Keedysville, MD 21756, (301)432-8859; **BUS ADD:** 9 S. Main St., Boonsboro, MD 21713, (301)432-5454.

MACHULAK, Edward——**B:** July 14, 1926, Milw., WI, *Pres.*, Commerce Group Corp.; **PRIM RE ACT:** Broker, Instructor, Owner/Investor, Property Manager; **PROFL AFFIL & HONORS:** Milwaukee Bd. of Realtors, WI Bd. of Realtors, Natl. Assn. of Review Appraisers, Chmmn. SBA Natl. Small Bus. Investment Cos. Advisory Council, 1973-74, Advisory Member 1972; **EDUC:** 1949, Acctg., RE, Univ. of WI, various seminars throughout past 30 yrs.; **MIL SERV:** USA, 1945-46, Cpl.; **OTHER ACT & HONORS:** Past Honors: State of WI Council of Small Bus. Invest. Co., Chmn.; President's Council Marmion Mil. Acad., Advisory Bd. Member LeMane Acad., Spencerian Coll. Chmn; **HOME ADD:** 903 W. Green Tree Rd., River Hills, WI 53217, (414)352-9555; **BUS ADD:** 6001 N 91st St., Milwaukee, WI 53225, (414)462-5310.

MCILVAIN, Alan Max——**B:** Feb. 7, 1947, Enid, OK, *Atty.*; **PRIM RE ACT:** Attorney, Owner/Investor; **PROFL AFFIL & HONORS:** ABA, OK Bar Assn., Stephens Cty. Bar Assn.; **EDUC:** BS, 1971, Hist., OK State Univ.; **GRAD EDUC:** JD, 1980, Univ. of OK; **MIL SERV:** USA, 1966-68; **BUS ADD:** PO Box 387, Kingfisher, OK 73750, (405)375-5771.

MCINTOSH, Dr. Willard——**B:** Apr. 8, 1955, Dayton, OH, *Instructor; Ph.D. Cand.*, Univ. of SC; **PRIM RE ACT:** Instructor; **SERVICES:** Also involved in consulting and counseling work; Investment Analysis & Valuation; **REP CLIENTS:** Arthur Rubloff & Co., Central Trust Mort. Co., Republic Nat. Bank of Dallas, Etc.; **PREV EMPLOY:** Arthur Rubloff & Co., Eastern KY Univ., and Morehead State Univ.; **PROFL AFFIL & HONORS:** AIREA; SREA; ULI; NAR; NAA; NAHB; NARA; AREUEA; REEA; Rho Epsilon, etc., CRA - RECP, Grad. of the School of Mort. Banking Herbert U. Nelson Memorial Scholarship, Natl. Assn. of Realtors; **EDUC:** BS, 1977, Bus. Educ., Eastern KY Univ.; **GRAD EDUC:** MBA, 1979, RE, Eastern KY Univ.; **EDUC HONORS:** Pi Omega Pi - Bus. Ed. Honorary Frat., Herbert U. Nelson Memorial Scholarship, NAR; **OTHER ACT & HONORS:** VP, Morehead Bd. of Realtors 1979-1980; Demolay; **HOME ADD:** 1600 Longcreek Dr. Apt. 270, Columbia, SC 29210, (803)798-7263; **BUS ADD:** Univ. of SC, Columbia, SC 29208, (606)777-7035.

MACINTYRE, David William——**B:** Apr. 2, 1940, Detroit, MI, *Paradise Valley Mgr.*, Ed Post Realty, Owned by Berg Corp., American Stock Exchange; **PRIM RE ACT:** Broker; **SERVICES:** Resid. sales; **REP CLIENTS:** Manage one of largest most profitable resid. RE offices in the nation; **PREV EMPLOY:** Dir. of Educ., AZ State RE dept. 1974-1975; **PROFL AFFIL & HONORS:** Phoenix and Scottsdale Bd. of Realtors, State, Nat., RNMI, GRI, CRB, Realtor Associate of the Year 1976; **EDUC:** BS and AA, 1972, RE major, AZ State Univ.; **MIL SERV:** USN, with Honor; **OTHER ACT & HONORS:** Foothills Tennis & Swim Club Paradise Valley; **HOME ADD:** 9315 Morning Glory Rd., Paradise Valley, AZ 85253, (602)998-4771; **BUS ADD:** 14602 North Tatum, Phoenix, AZ 85032, (602)867-2000.

MCINTYRE, Donald F.X.——**B:** Mar. 9, 1928, Bryn Mawr, PA, *Rgnl. Const. Safety Inspector*, U.S. Govt., GSA/Frederick Properties, Inc.; **PRIM RE ACT:** Engineer, Developer, Owner/Investor, Instructor, Property Manager; **OTHER RE ACT:** Hist. Dist. Restorations; **PREV EMPLOY:** Chief VA Heating and Refrigeration Plant and Steam Distribution Complex, 1974-1981; **PROFL AFFIL & HONORS:** Hon. Mech. Engrg. Soc.; Pi Tau Sigma; **EDUC:** AB, 1951, Sci. Educ., Univ. of MD; **GRAD EDUC:** BS, 1957, Mech. Engrg./Const., NM State; **EDUC HONORS:** Honor Soc.; **MIL SERV:** USAF, 1st Lt., Medical Serv. Corp., Commendations; **OTHER ACT & HONORS:** Univ. of MD, Grad. Program in Bus. & Econ., 1979; **HOME ADD:** 9507 Edgeley Rd., Bethesda, MD 20814, (301)530-0001; **BUS ADD:** 9507 Edgeley Rd., Bethesda, MD 20814, (301)530-0001.

MCINTYRE, H. Neil——**B:** May 24, 1940, Pontiac, MI, *Second VP*, Advance Mort. Corp., Gen. Partner of Advance Mort. Co. Ltd., Customer Serv./Servicing; **PRIM RE ACT:** Lender, Insuror; **SERVICES:** Provide customer serv. to approximately 170,000 loans; **PREV EMPLOY:** 8 yrs. at Liberty Mutual Ins. Co.; **PROFL AFFIL & HONORS:** MBAA; **EDUC:** BS in Bus. Admin., 1962, Mktg., Acctg., E. MI Univ.; **OTHER ACT & HONORS:** Councilman-City of Brighton-Chmn. of Planning Commission, Past Pres. Local Baseball Recreation Program, Road Study Commn., And Past Pres. of ZBA; **HOME ADD:** 835 Nelson, Brighton, MI 48116, (313)229-2396; **BUS ADD:** P.O. Box 146, Detroit, MI 48232, (313)424-2497.

MCINTYRE, J. William——**B:** Jan. 30, 1920, Six Mile Run, PA, *Owner*, J. William McIntyre, Atty. at Law; **PRIM RE ACT:** Attorney; **SERVICES:** Drafting deeds, mort., leases, contracts and the gen. practice of RE law; **REP CLIENTS:** The First Nat. Bank of Saxton, Saxton, PA 16678; Bedford Branch, Altoona Fed. S&L Assn., 100 W. Pitt St., Bedford, PA; **PROFL AFFIL & HONORS:** Bedford Cty. Bar Assn.; PA Bar Assn.; ABA; **EDUC:** AB, 1941, Hist./Pre-Law, Franklin and Marshall Coll.; **GRAD EDUC:** JD, 1948, Law, Univ. of PA Law School; **EDUC HONORS:** Honors in Hist.; **MIL SERV:** Anti-Aircraft, 1st Lt., Artillery; **OTHER ACT & HONORS:** Bedford Masonic Lodge No. 320; Bedford Chapter No. 255; Altoona Consistry; Jaffa Shrine; Bedford Elks; Bedford Legion Post No. 113; **HOME ADD:** Orchard Heights, RD 5, PO Box 45, Bedford, PA 15522, (814)623-5822; **BUS ADD:** 117-1/2 S. Juliana St., POB 45, Bedford, PA 15522, (814)623-8318.

MACK, David A.——**B:** March 3, 1948, Bridgeport, CT, *Partner*, Curtiss & Crandon; **PRIM RE ACT:** Broker, Developer, Builder, Owner/Investor, Syndicator; **SERVICES:** Brokerage, leasing, devel. & bldg.; **PROFL AFFIL & HONORS:** BOMA; NAR; Nat. Assn. of Home Builders, CCIM Candidate; **EDUC:** BS, 1970, Psych./Zoology, Univ. of CT; **HOME ADD:** 6 Old Dairy Rd., Trumbull, CT 06611, (203)377-0357; **BUS ADD:** 1676 Huntington Tpke, Trumbull, CT 06611, (203)378-6606.

MACK, Dennis——*Secy.*, D.H.J. Industries, Inc.; **PRIM RE ACT:** Property Manager; **BUS ADD:** 1040 Avenue of the Americas, New York, NY 10018, (212)944-4500.*

MACK, Francis Wayne——**B:** Nov. 18, 1936, Columbia, SC, *Pres.*, Wayne Homes, Inc.; **PRIM RE ACT:** Broker, Appraiser, Developer, Builder, Owner/Investor; **OTHER RE ACT:** Home design, certain bldg. systems; **SERVICES:** Fin., qualifying, application for Fed. programs, computer cost controls; **REP CLIENTS:** Single & multi-family; **PROFL AFFIL & HONORS:** Nat. Assn. Home Builders, Nat. Single Family Housing Comm.; **EDUC:** BS, 1959, Educ. & Econ., Clemson Univ.; **EDUC HONORS:** With honors; **MIL SERV:** USAF, ROTC, Lt.; **OTHER ACT & HONORS:** Inter American Advisory Council, San Jose, Costa Rica; Assoc. CATIE, Turrialba, Costa Rica, Central Amer.; **HOME ADD:** 418 5th Ave. W., Hendersonville, NC 28739, (704)693-0880; **BUS ADD:** 418 5th Ave. W., Hendersonville, NC 28739, (704)693-8221.

MCKAIG, Michael D.——**B:** May 27, 1946, Oakland, CA, *Acquisitions Dir.*, Gen. Western Co.; **PRIM RE ACT:** Consultant, Syndicator; **SERVICES:** Devel. & investment consultant, devel. & synd. of comml. prop.; **REP CLIENTS:** Indiv. investors; **PREV EMPLOY:** NW Mutual Life - RE Dept. 78-81, Practicing Architect 70-75; **PROFL AFFIL & HONORS:** Soc. for Historic Preservation, Bay Area Mort. Assn., Registered Architect, CA; **EDUC:** BArch, 1970, Univ. of CA Berkeley; **GRAD EDUC:** MBA, 1977, RE & Fin., Univ. of CA, Berkeley; **OTHER ACT & HONORS:** Bd. member CITYWEST Inc.; **HOME ADD:** 5442 Shafter Ave., Oakland, CA 94618, (415)653-1228; **BUS ADD:** 235 Montgomery St. #1656, San Francisco, CA 94104, (415)391-6010.

MCKAY, John P.——**B:** Nov. 15, 1917, Everett, MA, *Pres. Century 21 McKay-Nealis Realtors*; **PRIM RE ACT:** Broker, Consultant, Appraiser, Developer, Builder, Instructor, Property Manager, Owner/Investor, Insuror; **SERVICES:** Custom bldg, relocation of comml, indus. and resid. props.; **PROFL AFFIL & HONORS:** NW Suburbs Bd. of Realtors, Past Pres., Past State Dist. VP, GRI; **MIL SERV:** U.S. Navy, BMIC, Pac. & Eur. Medals, 3rd Fleet Citation; **OTHER ACT & HONORS:** Elks; VFW; K of C; Itasca CC; Tamarak CC; Bristol Oaks CC; **HOME ADD:** 205 W. Dulles Rd., Des Plaines, IL 60016, (312)827-8988; **BUS ADD:** 1818 E.N.W. Hwy., Arlington Hts., IL 60004, (312)255-3535.

MACKAY, M. Randy——**B:** Mar. 24, 1950, Madison, WI, *Owner*, Mackay Realty & Investments; **PRIM RE ACT:** Broker, Consultant, Owner/Investor, Instructor, Property Manager; **SERVICES:** Investment & exchange counseling, private offering synd., sales; **REP CLIENTS:** Middle and upper income investors; **PROFL AFFIL & HONORS:** Rho Epsilon, CAR, NAR, RECI, NAA, CAA, TCAA, RECI; **EDUC:** AA, 1977, Bus. Admin., West Valley Coll.; **GRAD EDUC:** BS, 1978, Bus. Admin., San Jose State Univ.; **EDUC HONORS:** 1977/78 RE Student of the Yr., AIREA Award; **MIL SERV:** USN, 2nd class petty officer; **OTHER ACT & HONORS:** YMCA, CYSA, Quito Little League; **HOME ADD:** 1475 Ginden Ct., Campbell, CA 95008, (408)866-1959; **BUS ADD:** 250 E Hamilton Ave., Ste. C, Campbell, CA 95008, (408)866-7200.

MACKAY, Malcolm——*RE Mgr.*, White Motor Corp.; **PRIM RE ACT:** Property Manager; **OTHER RE ACT:** Property Manager; **BUS ADD:** 842 E. 79th St., Cleveland, OH 44101, (216)431-2000.*

MCKAY, William T.——*Pres.*, International Business Parks, Inc.; **PRIM RE ACT:** Developer; **BUS ADD:** 2001 Fortune Dr., San Jose, CA 95131, (408)263-7171.*

MACKE, Elmer H.——**B:** Mar. 24, 1930, Ft. Wayne, IN, *Pres. & Owner*, Macke Development Corp.; **PRIM RE ACT:** Broker, Developer, Builder, Owner/Investor; **SERVICES:** Devel. & mktg. of single & multi-family units.; **REP CLIENTS:** Builders & indiv. investors; **PROFL AFFIL & HONORS:** Ft. Wayne Bd. of Realtors, Ft. Wayne Home Builders Assoc.; **EDUC:** BS Bus. Admin., 1957, Mktg., IN Univ.; **MIL SERV:** USAF, SSgt.; **HOME ADD:** 1407 Traders Crossing, Ft. Wayne, IN 46825, (219)637-5797; **BUS ADD:** 1407 Traders Crossing, Fort Wayne, IN 46825, (219)637-3111.

MCKEEVER, Patrick C.——**B:** Mar. 17, 1938, Washington, DC, *Partner*, Miles & Stockbridge; **PRIM RE ACT:** Consultant, Attorney; **SERVICES:** Consultation and advice, document preparation, loan closings, RE litigation; **REP CLIENTS:** Prudential Ins. Co. of Amer.; US Home Corp.; Pulte Home Corp.; Steed Mort. Co.; Carl M. Freeman Assocs.; **PROFL AFFIL & HONORS:** ABA; MD State Bar Assn.; Montgomery Cty. Bar Assn.; MBA of Metro. Wash.; Nat. Assn. of Home Builders; Community Assns. Inst.; **EDUC:** BA, 1960, Philosophy/Eng., Universite de Fribourg, Switzerland/Georgetown Univ.; **GRAD EDUC:** JD, 1963, Georgetown Univ. Law Ctr.; **EDUC HONORS:** Managing Editor, Georgetown Law Journal; **HOME ADD:** One Tanager Court, Potomac, MD 20854, (301)340-3099; **BUS ADD:** 342 Hungerford Court, Rockville, MD 20850, (301)762-1600.

MCKELLAR, Donald M., III——**B:** Feb. 3, 1941, NY City, *VP*, McKellar & Co.; **PRIM RE ACT:** Broker, Engineer, Property Manager; **SERVICES:** Investments, synds., devel. & prop. mgmt.; **REP CLIENTS:** Indiv. and instnl. investors in comml. props.; **PREV EMPLOY:** William Walters Co. 1977-1981; **PROFL AFFIL & HONORS:** IREM; RNMI; Western Soc. of Engrs., CPM; **EDUC:** BSEE, 1965, EE, Chicago Inst. of Technol.; **GRAD EDUC:** Bus., Northwestern Univ.; **OTHER ACT & HONORS:** AZ Marathon Soc.; Bd. Member, AZ Multi-Housing Assn.; **HOME ADD:** 8206 N. 33rd Ln., Phoenix, AZ 85021, (602)973-2655; **BUS ADD:** 8206 N. 33rd Ln., Phoenix, AZ 85021, (602)973-2655.

MCKENNA, Harold C.——**B:** July 1, 1939, Pittsfield, MA, *Chmn.*, Boston Mortgage Co., Inc.; **PRIM RE ACT:** Broker, Consultant; **OTHER RE ACT:** Mort. Banker; **SERVICES:** RE Fin., Sales, Consulting; **PREV EMPLOY:** Cabot, Cabot & Forbes, 1971-75; **PROFL AFFIL & HONORS:** ULI, MBA; **EDUC:** BBA, 1961, Fin. & Acctg., Univ. of Notre Dame; **MIL SERV:** USCG, Lt.; **BUS ADD:** 1 Faneuil Hall Marketplace, Boston, MA 02109, (617)227-2022.

MCKENNA, Judith Schmitz——**B:** Oct. 11, 1948, Cedar Rapids, IA, *Dir., Mktg. Communications*, The Norwood Group, Inc.; **PRIM RE ACT:** Consultant, Real Estate Publisher; **OTHER RE ACT:** Advertising, public relations, mktg. consultant, Publisher - monthly newsletter (The Norwood Report); **SERVICES:** Advertising & public relations counseling & builders, devel., own firm; **REP CLIENTS:** Own firm plus devels. of single & multi-family housing; time share devels.; **PREV EMPLOY:** Berges RE, Salem, NH; Dir. of Adv. & Public Relations, St. Petersburg Times & Evening Indep.; Deck House, Inc.; **PROFL AFFIL & HONORS:** Bus. & Profl. Advertising Assn.; NH Ad Club; Mktg. Comm., Inter-community Relocation; **EDUC:** BA, 1970, Psych., Univ. of S. FL; **GRAD EDUC:** MS, 1982, Public Communications, Boston Univ., School of Public Communications; **EDUC HONORS:** Dean's List; **OTHER ACT & HONORS:** VP, Public Realtions, Manchester NH YWCA; **HOME ADD:** RFD 1, Lawrence Rd., S. Weare, NH, (603)529-2286; **BUS ADD:** 116 S. River Rd., Bedford, NH 03102, (603)668-7000.

MCKENNA, Quentin C.——*Pres.*, Kennametal, Inc.; **PRIM RE ACT:** Property Manager; **BUS ADD:** PO Box 231, Latrobe, PA 15650, (412)537-3311.*

MCKENZIE, H.E.——**B:** May 5, 1921, Berlin, PA, *Pres.*, Financial Structures, Inc.; **PRIM RE ACT:** Broker, Consultant, Architect, Developer, Builder, Owner/Investor; **SERVICES:** Design, build, devel., fin.; **PREV EMPLOY:** Marsh Realty Co., Charlotte, NC; **PROFL AFFIL & HONORS:** NC Bd. of Realtors; GA Bd. of Realtors; ASME; ASPE; **EDUC:** BSME & CE, 1939, Civil & Mech. Engrg., VA Poly. Inst., Blackburg, VA; **GRAD EDUC:** MSCE, 1941, Engrg., MIT; **MIL SERV:** US Army; Lt. Col.; Silver Star; Bronze Medal; Purple Heart; **HOME ADD:** Fairfax, Mansfield, GA 30255, (404)786-8109; **BUS ADD:** 2990 Brandywine Rd., Atlanta, GA 30341, (404)458-2165.

MACKENZIE, K. Bruce——**B:** Sept. 19, 1942, Chicago, IL, *VP*, Nu-West Inc., Comml./Indus. Div.; **PRIM RE ACT:** Developer, Owner/Investor; **SERVICES:** Devel. office and indus. projects; **PREV EMPLOY:** Sr. VP, Greenbaum, O'Brien & Co., Chicago, IL - Mort. Banking; **PROFL AFFIL & HONORS:** NAIOP; IL Mort. Bankers Assn., Past; **EDUC:** BA, 1964, Bus. Admin., MI State Univ.; **OTHER ACT & HONORS:** Church Treas.; Fund-Raising Comm. for Maryville Home for Youth, Des Plaines, IL; **HOME ADD:** 5959 S. Akron Cir., Englewood, CO 80111, (303)741-2079; **BUS ADD:** 3035 S. Parker Rd., Aurora, CO 80014, (303)696-1777.

MACKENZIE, Roderick L.——**B:** May 9, 1946, Placerville, CA, *Atty. at Law*, MacKenzie & Brody; **PRIM RE ACT:** Attorney; **PROFL AFFIL & HONORS:** ABA; Sacramento Cty. Bar Assn.; CA State Bar Assn.; Sacramento Estate Planning Council, CLU; **EDUC:** BA, 1969, Hist./Soc. Sci., Univ. of MT, Missoula, MT; **GRAD EDUC:** MBA, 1978, Bus./Taxation, Golden Gate Univ., San Francisco, CA; JD, 1978, Law, McGeorge School of Law; **MIL SERV:** USMC, Cpl.; **HOME ADD:** 2016 D St., Sacramento, CA 95814; **BUS ADD:** 721 Ninth St., Suite 200, Sacramento, CA 95814, (916)448-6436.

MCKENZIE-SMITH, Robert H.——**B:** Aug. 11, 1942, Wichita Falls, TX, *CEO*, The Americana Group of Companies; **PRIM RE ACT:** Broker, Consultant, Developer, Owner/Investor, Instructor, Property Manager, Syndicator; **SERVICES:** Investment counseling, devel., synd., mgmt., mort. lending; **PREV EMPLOY:** Regular US Army, 1961-1981; **PROFL AFFIL & HONORS:** RE Securities and Synd. Inst.; Realtor's Nat. Mktg. Inst., CCIM, SRS; **EDUC:** BA, 1971, Pol. Sci., Park Coll.; **GRAD EDUC:** MS, 1976, Mgmt., Naval War Coll., Newport, RI; **EDUC HONORS:** Magna Cum Laude; **MIL SERV:** US Army, Ltc., Silver Star, Purple Heart, Bronze Star w/V, 3 OLC; **OTHER ACT & HONORS:** Chmn., Investigational Review Comm., Dallas Eye Found.; **HOME ADD:** 919 Jungle Dr., Duncanville, TX 75116, (214)298-0370; **BUS ADD:** 1701 N. Hampton Rd., DeSoto, TX 75115, (214)296-7000.

MCKEW, Walter Martin——**B:** July 17, 1948, NY, NY, *Gen. Counsel*, Terteling Marketing, Inc.; **PRIM RE ACT:** Attorney, Developer, Syndicator; **OTHER RE ACT:** Mort. fin.; **SERVICES:** Legal counsel to TMI, and all Terteling Co. Entities; **REP CLIENTS:** Terteling Co., Eagle Aircraft, Geolinear Inc., Western Equipment Co., Western States Equipment; **PREV EMPLOY:** Asst. Gen. Counsel, Nat. Corp. for Housing Partnerships, 1980-81; Dir. of Fin., Cardinal Indus. 1979-1980; **PROFL AFFIL & HONORS:** ABA; Member OH, ID Bar Assn.; **EDUC:** BA, 1969, Govt. & Intl. Relations, Univ. of Notre Dame; **GRAD EDUC:** JD, 1972, Law, Univ. of Cincinnati; **OTHER ACT & HONORS:** City Atty., Numerous OH Cites, 1974-1979; **HOME ADD:** 5566 Kercliffe Ct., Boise, ID 83704, (208)377-2036; **BUS ADD:** 1755 Westgate Dr., P.O. Box 4127, Boise, ID 83704, (208)376-6700.

MACKEY, Maurice F.——*Partner*, Callahan, Calwell and Laudeman; **PRIM RE ACT:** Attorney; **SERVICES:** Legal representation in counseling and in litigation involving real prop.; **REP CLIENTS:** Lenders and instnl. investors in comml. prop., title ins. cos. in litigation; **BUS ADD:** 210 E. Redwood St., Baltimore, MD 21202, (301)539-6841.

MCKIM, Dennis R.——**B:** Mar. 15, 1945, Kansas City, MO, *VP - Cty. Mgr.*, California World Title Co.; **PRIM RE ACT:** Instructor, Insuror; **OTHER RE ACT:** Conduct lectures & seminars on legal aspects of RE; **SERVICES:** Title ins. and escrow servs.; **REP CLIENTS:** Devels., RE agents, lenders, and escrow cos.; **PREV EMPLOY:** Title Ins. and Trust Co., 1968-1973; **PROFL AFFIL & HONORS:** Assoc. Builders & Contractors, Builders and Contractors Assn., CA Land Title Assn.; **EDUC:** BS, 1968, Personnel and Indus. Relations, Northern AZ Univ.; **OTHER ACT & HONORS:** Pi Sigma Epsilon, Sigma Chi, Kiwanis, Community Coll. Teaching Credential - RE; **HOME ADD:** 13479 Black Hills Rd., San Diego, CA 92129, (714)484-1108; **BUS ADD:** 8304 Clairemont Mesa Blvd., San Diego, CA 92111, (714)278-4171.

MCKINLEY, David B.——**B:** March 28, 1947, Wheeling, WV, *Pres.*, Wheeling Homes of WV; **PRIM RE ACT:** Builder, Engineer; **SERVICES:** Design-build single family dwellings, renov. bldgs. to apts.; **PREV EMPLOY:** VP Jarvis, Downing and Emch-Wheeling; **PROFL AFFIL & HONORS:** ASCE, NSPE, WVSPE, Outstanding Young Engr. for 1976 in WV, WVSPE; **EDUC:** BSCE, 1969, Civil Engrg., Mgmt., Purdue Univ.; **OTHER ACT & HONORS:** Delegate from Third Dist. in Ho. of Del. of WV legsl.; Rotary BDOE No. 28; Exec. Comm. of Nat. Trail Council; BSA; C of C; Tr. of OH Valley Med. Center, Vestry of St. Matthew, Symposiarch Order of Engrg.; Advisory Bd. of Jefferson Cty. Tech. Inst. and Belmont Cty. Tech Coll.; Wheeling Zoning Bd. of Appeals; Regnl. Planning Council.; **HOME ADD:** 33 Walnut Ave., Wheeling, WV 26003, (304)233-4443; **BUS ADD:** P.O. Box 6879, Wheeling, WV 26003, (304)233-0140.

MCKINLEY, Douglas R.——**B:** Jan. 3, 1948, Taylorsville, MS, *Atty. & Broker*, Capricorn, Inc., 8 Central MS Realty; **PRIM RE ACT:** Broker, Attorney, Lender, Owner/Investor; **EDUC:** BS, Chem., Bio., M.T. (A.S.C.P.); **GRAD EDUC:** JD, 1973, Jackson School of Law; **EDUC HONORS:** Cum Laude Grad.; **HOME ADD:** PO Box 6226, Pearl, MS 39208, (601)825-5128; **BUS ADD:** PO Box 6231, Pearl, MS 39208, (601)939-3913.

MCKINLEY, Michael R.——**B:** Oct. 21, 1951, Lansing, MI, *Atty.*, Wotitzky, Wotitzky, Mandell, Batsel & Wilkins; **PRIM RE ACT:** Attorney; **SERVICES:** Admin. & govtl. law, RE transactions, corp., zoning and land use matters; **REP CLIENTS:** General Devel. Corp., Freedom Savings & Loan Assn.; Charlotte Cty. Abstract & Title Co., School Bd. of Charlotte Cty., Fishermen's Village, Ltd., Emerald Pointe, Ltd.; **PREV EMPLOY:** Asst. General Counsel, Broward Cty., FL, 1979-1980; Asst. Cty. Atty., Charlotte Cty., FL, 1980-1981; **PROFL AFFIL & HONORS:** FL Bar, 1979; Exec. Council of FL Bar, General Practice Section; Member of Real Property & Probate Section, Amer. and Charlotte County Bar Associations; **EDUC:** AB, 1973, Eng., Dartmouth Coll.; **GRAD EDUC:** JD, 1978, Law, Univ. of FL Law Center; **EDUC HONORS:** Dean's List, Honors Program, Citation for Excellence in Eng. Comp.; **HOME ADD:** 4410 Deltona Dr., Punta Gorda, FL 33950, (813)639-1745; **BUS ADD:** 201 W. Marion Ave., Punta Gorda, FL 33950, (813)639-2171.

MCKINLEY, Robert J.——**B:** Nov. 25, 1947, Pittsburgh, PA, *Gen. Contr.*, R.J McKinley Co.; **PRIM RE ACT:** Engineer, Architect, Builder; **SERVICES:** Western NY area; **PREV EMPLOY:** Red Wing Co.; **PROFL AFFIL & HONORS:** Seawalls Designing Hon.; **OTHER ACT & HONORS:** Amer. Soc. of Metals; Profl. Ideals on Bldg. for Better Amer.; **HOME ADD:** Van Buren Pt., Dunkirk, NY 14048, (716)672-4553; **BUS ADD:** Van Buren Pt., Dunkirk, NY 14048, (716)672-4553.

MCKINNEY, Dr. David C.——**B:** May 16, 1944, McCook, NE, *Pres.*, American Community Development Corp.; **PRIM RE ACT:** Broker, Consultant, Developer, Builder, Owner/Investor, Property Manager; **OTHER RE ACT:** City Planner, Econ., Designer; **SERVICES:** Devel. mgmt., site and bldg. design, construction mgmt., mktg., Prop. mgmt., financial analysis; **REP CLIENTS:** Govt. agencies, devel., prop. owners, investors, synd., lending inst.; **PREV EMPLOY:** RE Research Corp., 1967-1970; Office of the Mayor, City of Chicago, 1970-1973; Turner Const. Co., 1973-1976; Oxford Devel. Corp., 1976-1979; **PROFL AFFIL & HONORS:** Nat. Assn. of Homebuilders; Amer. Planning Assn.; Amer. Inst. of Cert. Planners; Builders Assn. of Greater Indianapolis, AICP; **EDUC:** B.Arch., 1967, Arch., IL Inst. of Tech.; **GRAD EDUC:** MSC & RP, 1968, IL Inst. of Tech.; PhD C & RP, 1976, IL Inst. of Tech.; **OTHER ACT & HONORS:** Soccer Assn. for Youth; **HOME ADD:** 4018 Gamay Lane, Indianapolis, IN 46254, (317)299-9197; **BUS ADD:** 7344 Lakeside Dr., Indianapolis, IN 46278, (317)298-8824.

MCKINNEY, James R.——**B:** Dec. 13, 1946, Evansville, IN, *Dir., Leasing & Devel.*, Regency Prop. Mgmt.; **PRIM RE ACT:** Developer, Owner/Investor; **PREV EMPLOY:** Advance Mort. Corp. - Detroit, MI, 1972-1977, Asst. VP; **PROFL AFFIL & HONORS:** Intl. Council of Shopping Ctrs.; **EDUC:** BS, 1972, Acctg., IN Univ., School of Bus.; **GRAD EDUC:** 1974, RE/Fin., IN Univ., Bus.; **EDUC HONORS:** Honorary Bus. Frat.; **OTHER ACT & HONORS:** Evansville Ctry. Club, Evansville Petroleum Club, Pres. Elect, Evansville Philharmonic, Pres., Evansville Civic Theatre, VP, Conrad Baker Found.; **HOME ADD:** 141 Hartin Dr., Evansville, IN 47711, (812)422-0569; **BUS ADD:** 5011 Washington Ave., PO Box 5189, Evansville, IN 47715, (812)477-8893.

MCKINNEY, Joseph F.——*President*, Tyler Corp; **PRIM RE ACT:** Property Manager; **BUS ADD:** 3100 Southland Centre, Dallas, TX 75201, (214)747-8251.*

MCKINNEY, Russell R.——**B:** Sept. 26, 1942, Visalia, CA, *Sr. Partner*, McKinney, Enes and Wainwright; **PRIM RE ACT:** Consultant, Attorney, Developer, Owner/Investor, Syndicator; **SERVICES:** Legal services and advice; **REP CLIENTS:** Northern CA Devel. Co., Inc., Marlin Realty, Vis-Cal Investment Corp., Marin Enterprises, Inc.; **PROFL AFFIL & HONORS:** Bd. of Govs. CA Trial Lawyers Assn., Amer. Trial Lawyers, Amer. Jud. Soc., Pres. Tulane Cty. Trial Lawyers Assn. 1971-1973, Frequent lecturer at legal seminars of CTLA, ATLA, Dive-Med Intl.; **EDUC:** BA, 1964, Polit. Sci., Econs., Stanford Univ.; **GRAD EDUC:** JD, 1967, Hastings Coll.; **EDUC HONORS:** Pres., Delta Kappa Epsilon; **MIL SERV:** USNR, Lt.; **OTHER ACT & HONORS:** Judge Pro Tempore Visalia Municipal Court, Tulare Cty. Superior Court; Rotary Club Intl.; **HOME ADD:** 509 Gilmer Ct., Visalia, CA 93277 93277; **BUS ADD:** 220 S. Mooney Blvd., Visalia, CA 93277, (209)732-3471.

MCKINSTRY, Frederick H.——**B:** Jan. 8, 1918, Savannah, GA, *Pres.*, Frederick H. McKinstry, Inc.; **PRIM RE ACT:** Broker, Syndicator, Consultant, Appraiser; **OTHER RE ACT:** Securities & invest. consultants; **SERVICES:** All services incidental to comml./invest RE; **REP CLIENTS:** Property Trust of Amer./Trigon, John R. Schatzman, Contr.; **PREV EMPLOY:** City Alderman, 6 yrs., Mayor Pro-Tem, 4 yrs.; **PROFL AFFIL & HONORS:** NAR, CCIM; **EDUC:** BS, 1939, Gen. Bus., Univ. of IL; **MIL SERV:** US Army, Maj., Pearl Harbor; **OTHER ACT & HONORS:** Alderman, City of El Paso, 6 yrs, Mayor Pro-tem, 4 yrs.; **HOME ADD:** 724 Green Cove Dr., El Paso, TX 79932, (915)584-2844; **BUS ADD:** 5862 Cromo Dr., El Paso, TX 79912, (915)581-1141.

MACKINTOSH, Earl M., III——**B:** Oct. 10, 1949, Washington, DC, *Pres./Broker*, Mackintosh, Inc., Realtors; **PRIM RE ACT:** Broker, Consultant, Developer, Property Manager; **SERVICES:** RE sales, residential, comml., etc.; **PREV EMPLOY:** Pres., Mackintosh Dev. Corp.; Exper. in resid. & comml. const.; **PROFL AFFIL & HONORS:** CRS; GRI; Candidate AFLM; CRB Designation, Realtor of Yr., Frederick Cty. Bd. of Realtors, 1980; **EDUC:** BS, 1972, Bus., High Point Coll., NC; **HOME ADD:** 1005 Buckeystown Pike, Adamstown, MD 21710, (301)663-0533; **BUS ADD:** 262 W Patrick St., Frederick, MD 21701, (301)662-0155.

MCKITRICK, Michael J.——**B:** May 12, 1948, Marion, IN, *Part.*, Morganstern, Drumm, Soraghan, Synder, Stockenberg & McKitrick; **PRIM RE ACT:** Attorney; **SERVICES:** Legal servs.; **REP CLIENTS:** Devels., RE brokers, constr. cos & contractors; **PROFL AFFIL & HONORS:** RE Comm. of Metro. Bar Assn. of St. Louis, Real Prop., Probate & Trust Sect. ABA; **EDUC:** BA, 1970, Pol. Sci., N. IL Univ.; **GRAD EDUC:** JD, 1973, Univ. of IA; **EDUC HONORS:** Member Bd. of Editors, IA Law Review; **MIL SERV:** US Army, 1st Lt.; **OTHER ACT & HONORS:** Member Profl. Advisory Bd., St. Louis; Assn. for Retarded Children; **HOME ADD:** 8907 Ulysses Ct., St. Louis, MO 63123, (314)842-4850; **BUS ADD:** 7733 Forsyth Blvd., Suite 2162, Clayton, MO 63105, (314)725-7100.

MCKNIGHT, D.L.——**B:** Dec. 13, 1946, Ronceuerte, WV, *Pres.*, McKnight Assoc. - Realty Advisors, Inc.; **PRIM RE ACT:** Broker, Consultant, Appraiser; **SERVICES:** Limited brokerage; all types of econ., feasibility & market studies in addition to comml. RE appraising; **REP CLIENTS:** Bank of VA; Bankers Tr. of NY; Harvey Lindsay & Co.; USN; Chesapeake S&L; Seaboard S&L; **PROFL AFFIL & HONORS:** AIREA; SREA; ULI; VA Assn. of Realtors; NAR, MAI, SRPA; **EDUC:** BSBA, 1970, Fin., WV Univ.; **MIL SERV:** USA, E-5, Bronze Star & Air Medal; **HOME ADD:** 1008 Windsor Rd., Virginia Beach, VA 23451, (804)422-8581; **BUS ADD:** 210 Laskin Rd., Suite 5, F & M Bldg., Virginia Beach, VA 23451, (804)422-5403.

MCKOOL, Richard J.——*Exec. VP*, National Homes Corp., National Homes Const. Co.; **PRIM RE ACT:** Property Manager; **BUS ADD:** Earl Ave. & Wallace St., Lafayette, IN 47903, (317)448-2000.*

MCLAIN, Maurice Clayton——**B:** Sept. 22, 1929, Hillsboro, TX, *Sr. VP & Gen.Counsel*, USLIFE RE Services Corp., Legal Dept.; **PRIM RE ACT:** Attorney; **SERVICES:** Legal Services for comml. mort. loan investments; **PREV EMPLOY:** Fed. Nat. Mort. Assn.; **PROFL AFFIL & HONORS:** Member of Dallas, TX, Amer. & Fed. Bar Assn.; Amer. Judicature Soc.; Amer. Coll. of RE Lawyers; Attorneys; RE Fin. Exec. Assn.; Phi Delta Phi, Chmn. of the RE Spec. Advisory Comm. to the Bd. of Legal Spec. of the State Bar of TX; **EDUC:** BA, 1950, Math., No. TX State Univ.; **GRAD EDUC:** JD, 1962, S Methodist Univ.; **MIL SERV:** USN, Res.; CT-3; **OTHER ACT & HONORS:** Dallas Scottish Soc.; English Speaking Union; Son of Amer. Rev.; **HOME ADD:** 3908 Royal Ln., Dallas, TX 75229, (214)257-6984; **BUS ADD:** 6500 Harry Hines Blvd., PO Box 35266, Dallas, TX 75235, (214)357-1861.

MCLANE, Gregory A.——**B:** July 15, 1950, Dallas, TX, *Devel. Dir.*, Williams Realty Corp.; **PRIM RE ACT:** Developer; **SERVICES:** Devel. larged mixed use projects for our own acct.; **PREV EMPLOY:** Trammell Crow Co.; **EDUC:** BS, 1972, Math, Principia Coll.; **GRAD EDUC:** MBA, 1975, RE, So. Methodist Univ.; **EDUC HONORS:** Scholastic Honors; **OTHER ACT & HONORS:** Bd., Tulsa Boys Home; **BUS ADD:** POB 2400, Tulsa, OK 74101, (918)588-2815.

MCLARNON, W.Brian——**B:** Dec. 6, 1924, Belfast, Ireland, *Dir.*, Smith Kline Corp., Corp. Facilities Planning; **OTHER RE ACT:** Facilities planning & const.; **EDUC:** BS, 1950, Bio. & Chem., Villanova Univ.; **MIL SERV:** RAF; **HOME ADD:** 1047 King of Prussia Rd., Radnor, PA 19087, (215)688-6264; **BUS ADD:** 1 Franklin Plaza, Phila., PA 19101, (215)854-4232.

MACLAUCHLAN, Donald John, Jr.——B: Mar. 2, 1935, Staten Is., NY; **PRIM RE ACT:** Broker; **PREV EMPLOY:** CT Gen. Life Ins. Co. (1957-1960); James Reuse & Co. (1960-1962); Nat. Homes Corp. (1966-1975); Criterion Group (1975-present); **PROFL AFFIL & HONORS:** Lafayette Bd. of Realtors; Greater Lafayette Chamber of Commerce, Dir. Bd. of Dirs., Tip Cty. Apt. Owners Assn. (1977-present) Pres. 1980; Dir. Apartment Assn. of IN (1980-present); **EDUC:** BA, 1957, Harvard Univ.; **EDUC HONORS:** Magna Cum Laude; **OTHER ACT & HONORS:** Romwell Foxhounds Lafayette Cty.; Bd. of Dirs. Lafayette Concerned Citizens for Better Housing (1969-1970); Elder, Central Presbyterian Church, Lafayette 1971-present; Gen. Council Presbytery Wabash Valley 1976-1918; **HOME ADD:** 1704 Ocala Ct., Lafayette, IN 47905.

MCLAUGHLIN, Frank——B: Sept. 23, 1941, Philadelphia, PA, *Exec Officer*, McLaughlin, Realtors; **PRIM RE ACT:** Broker, Appraiser, Owner/Investor, Property Manager, Syndicator; **SERVICES:** Primarily RE brokerage, mgmt. and devel. through synd.; **PREV EMPLOY:** Past Dir. of NAR; Past. Pres. of VI State Bd. of Realtors; **PROFL AFFIL & HONORS:** GRI; CRB; CRA; **EDUC:** Lib. Arts School, Temple Univ.; **MIL SERV:** US Army; Spec.; 5th class; **OTHER ACT & HONORS:** Pres. Rotary II St. Thomas; Dir. C of C; VP VI Council, Boy Scouts of Amer.; **HOME ADD:** 37-36 Estate Pearl, PO Box 3692, St. Thomas, VI 00801, (809)774-6917; **BUS ADD:** 14B Norre Gade, PO Box 3692, St. Thomas, VI 00801, (801)774-6780.

MCLAUGHLIN, James Daniel——B: Oct. 2, 1947, Spokane, WA, *Pres.*, James D. McLaughlin A.I.A. Architect Chartered; **PRIM RE ACT:** Architect; **SERVICES:** Arch., land planning and devel.; **REP CLIENTS:** Indiv. or instl. investors in pvt. and comml. arch. and devel.; **PREV EMPLOY:** Project Arch., Neil M. Wright Arch., 1971-1974; Project Arch., McMillen & Hayes Arch., 1974-1975; J.D. McLaughlin AIA Arch. Chtd., 1975-Pres.; **PROFL AFFIL & HONORS:** AIA; Nat. Council of Arch. Reg. Bds.; Nat. Home Builders Assn., ID State Amer. Inst. of Arch., Award for Excellence in Arch.; **EDUC:** BArch., 1971, Arch., Univ. of ID; **MIL SERV:** US Army, 1st Lt.; **OTHER ACT & HONORS:** Ketchum Planning and Zoning Commn. Chmn.; Rotary Club; Who's Who in the West; **HOME TEL:** (208)726-9637; **BUS ADD:** POB 479, Sun Valley, ID 83353, (208)726-9392.

MCLAUGHLIN, Nathaniel L.——B: Dec. 16, 1930, Las Cruces, NM, *Real Appraiser and Consultant*, N.L. McLaughlin, Real Appraiser & Consultant; **PRIM RE ACT:** Consultant, Appraiser; **SERVICES:** Appraisals for Sale, Purchase, Lending, Insurance and Allocation of Purchase Price for tax purposes; **REP CLIENTS:** Major Corps., Banks, S&L Assns. & Redev. Agencies; **PROFL AFFIL & HONORS:** SRPA SREA; **EDUC:** Bus., Univ. of So. CA; **MIL SERV:** USAF, M/Sgt.; **HOME ADD:** 5539 Buffalo Ave., Van Nuys, CA 91401, (213)780-1051; **BUS ADD:** 5539 Buffalo Ave., Van Nuys, CA 91401, (213)780-1051.

MCLAUGHLIN, Stephen Frank——B: Apr. 10, 1945, St. Louis, MO, *Sr. Devel. Counsel*, Holiday Ins, Inc.; **PRIM RE ACT:** Attorney, Developer, Owner/Investor; **SERVICES:** Legal counsel RE acquisition, mgmt., fin., ownership (including joint ventures), and disposition of co. owned and/or managed props.; **PREV EMPLOY:** Partner, Troutman, Sanders, Lockerman & Ashmore, Atlanta, GA (1972-1978); Partner, Meals & McLaughlin, 1978-1981; **PROFL AFFIL & HONORS:** ABA, State Bar of GA, Who's Who in Amer. Law, First Ed. 1979; Chmn. Supplying Legal Servs. Comm., State Bar of Georgia, 1974-1980; **EDUC:** BA, 1967, Econ., Univ. of OR Honors Coll.; BS, 1967, Mktg., Ins. & Transportation, Univ. of OR School of Bus. Admin.; **GRAD EDUC:** JD, 1972, Law, Duke Univ.; LLM (Taxation), 1977, Emory Univ.; **EDUC HONORS:** Phi Eta Sigma & Phi Beta Kappa, Natl. Scholastic Hon., Editorial Bd., Duke Law Journal, Order of the Coif; **MIL SERV:** USA, SP4, 1969-1970, NDSM, ARCOM, Good Conduct Medal; **OTHER ACT & HONORS:** Selected "Outstanding Atlantans" 1st Ed., 1979; **HOME ADD:** 409-1 S. Perkins, Memphis, TN 38117, (901)767-0673; **BUS ADD:** 3742 Lamar Ave., Memphis, TN 38195, (901)362-4624.

MCLAURY, Hugh C.——*Mgr.*, Burlington Area Devel. Corp., **PRIM RE ACT:** Developer; **BUS ADD:** PO Box 1024, Burlington, IA 52601, (319)752-2320.*

MACLEAN, H. Grant——B: June 13, 1945, CO, *Dir., Comml. RE*, Davis Enterprises; **PRIM RE ACT:** Developer, Builder, Owner/Investor, Property Manager; **OTHER RE ACT:** Shopping ctr., office bldg, owner-devels.; **PROFL AFFIL & HONORS:** ICSC, OH Bd. of Realtors; **EDUC:** BS, 1969, Agriculture, Univ. of AZ; **GRAD EDUC:** Bus. Law & RE, Univ. of AZ; **MIL SERV:** SIG, 1st Lt.; **HOME ADD:** 1833 Harwitch Rd., Columbus, OH 43221, (614)486-4219; **BUS ADD:** 5929 Karl Rd., Columbus, OH 43229, (614)888-1616.

MCLEAN, John William, Jr.——B: Oct. 2, 1936, Cleveland, OH, *VP*, Continental Wingate Co., Inc., GA - SE; **PRIM RE ACT:** Broker, Attorney, Developer, Builder, Owner/Investor; **SERVICES:** Devel., mgmt., synd., const.; **PREV EMPLOY:** Dir. of Devel., VA Housing Devel. Authority; **PROFL AFFIL & HONORS:** Home Builders; **EDUC:** Emory Univ.; **GRAD EDUC:** LLD, 1960, Law, Woodrow Wilson Coll. of Law; **HOME ADD:** 4610 Holliston Rd., Atlanta, GA 30360, (404)451-2410; **BUS ADD:** 5775 Peachtree - Dunwoody Rd., Building E, Suite 200, Atlanta, GA 30342, (404)255-6944.

MCLEAN, Kenneth E.——B: Nov. 1, 1950, Opelika, AL, *Gen. Mgr.*, Robert B. Aikens & Assocs., Inc., Panama City Mall; **PRIM RE ACT:** Property Manager; **SERVICES:** Mgmt., Leasing, Constr. Mgmt.; **PREV EMPLOY:** Over 10 yrs. in Shopping Ctr. Mgmt., Mktg., Devel.; **PROFL AFFIL & HONORS:** ISCS, CSM, CMD; **EDUC:** BBA, 1972, Personnel Mgmt., Indus. Relations, Auburn Univ.; **HOME ADD:** 218 Harvard Blvd., Lynn Haven, FL 32444, (904)265-9229; **BUS ADD:** 2150 Cove Blvd., Panama City, FL 32405, (904)785-9587.

MCLEAN, Norman——B: Apr. 26, 1917, Marquette, MI, *Atty. at Law*, McLean & McCarthy; **PRIM RE ACT:** Attorney, Owner/Investor; **SERVICES:** Title opinions and conveyances, etc.; devel. and rental of comml. props.; **REP CLIENTS:** Houghton Nat. Bank, local RE brokers; **PREV EMPLOY:** Continental IL National Bank & Trust Co.; **PROFL AFFIL & HONORS:** MI Bar Assn., ABA, Copper Cty. Bar Assn., Amer. Judicature Soc., MI Assn. of the Professions; **EDUC:** BA, 1937, No. MI Univ.; **GRAD EDUC:** LLB, 1947, Chicago-Kent Coll. of Law; **MIL SERV:** USNR, Lt.s.g.; **HOME ADD:** US 41, Chassell, MI 49916, (906)523-4070; **BUS ADD:** 706 Shelden Ave., PO Box 65, Houghton, MI 49931, (906)482-5340.

MCLEAN, W.E. "Bud"——B: June 18, 1928, Tulsa, OK, *Mgr.*, Kerr-McGee Corp., Mgmt. Div.; **PRIM RE ACT:** Appraiser, Developer, Property Manager; **OTHER RE ACT:** All phases of RE W Kerr-McGee Corp. & Subs.; **PROFL AFFIL & HONORS:** (NACORE), (NARA); **EDUC:** BS, OK State Univ.; **MIL SERV:** USAF, 1st Lt.; **OTHER ACT & HONORS:** Bd. of Dir. - Basic Mgmt., Inc., Henderson, NV; **HOME ADD:** 6604 N St. Cla1r, Oklahoma City, OK 73125, (405)843-6914; **BUS ADD:** Kerr-McGee Ctr., Oklahoma City, OK 73125, (405)270-2511.

MCLEMORE, Gilbert Carmichael, Jr.——B: Dec. 15, 1942, Savannah, GA, *Partner*, Fending, McLemore, Taylor & Whitworth; **PRIM RE ACT:** Attorney; **SERVICES:** Legal; **REP CLIENTS:** First Fed. S&L Assn., First Nat. Bank of Brunswick (trust dept. counsel), Island Ltd. (devel. of retreat village shopping ctr.), The First Nat. Bank of Boston; **PREV EMPLOY:** With present firm for 11 yrs.; **PROFL AFFIL & HONORS:** ABA, State Bar of GA(former comm. chmn. in Younger Lawyers Sect.); Brunswick Bar Assn.(former Pres., vp & treas.), Pres. Brunswick Golden Isles Estate Planning Council; **EDUC:** BA, 1965, Pol. Sci., Univ. of NC at Chapel Hill; **GRAD EDUC:** JD, 1970, Univ. of GA; **EDUC HONORS:** Moot Ct. Bd.; Member, Student Editorial Bd., GA State Bar Journal 1969-70; **MIL SERV:** USNR, Lt.; **OTHER ACT & HONORS:** Bd. of Glynn Cty. Red Cross; **HOME ADD:** 545 Old Plantation Rd., Jekyll Island, GA 31520, (912)635-2619; **BUS ADD:** Box 1996, Brunswick, GA 31521, (912)264-4126.

MCLENNAN, Robert G., Jr.——B: Aug. 13, 1943, Chicago, IL, *Pres., Devel.*, McLennan & Thebault, Inc.; **PRIM RE ACT:** Consultant, Developer, Builder, Syndicator; **SERVICES:** Devel., gen. contractor, synd., consultant; **PREV EMPLOY:** Standard Oil Co., Gen. Counsel Staff; **PROFL AFFIL & HONORS:** ABA, IL Bar Assn., Chicago Bar Assn., NAR; **EDUC:** AB, 1965, Econ., Cornell Coll.; **GRAD EDUC:** JD, 1968, Law, Univ. of IL, Coll. of Law; **EDUC HONORS:** Law Review; **HOME ADD:** 2042 Brandon Rd., Glenview, IL 60068, (312)998-5787; **BUS ADD:** 1771 Commerce Dr., Suite 104, Elk Grove Village, IL 60007, (312)228-6700.

MCLONG, Dale——*Secretary*, Ameron Inc.; **PRIM RE ACT:** Property Manager; **BUS ADD:** 4700 Ramona Blvd., PO 3000, Monterey Park, CA 91754, (213)268-4111.*

MCMACKIN, John J.——B: June 6, 1908, NY, NY, *Consultant, Facilities Planning/Site Search, also Lic. RE Broker*, J.J. McMackin; **PRIM RE ACT:** Broker, Consultant, Appraiser, Property Manager, Engineer; **OTHER RE ACT:** Former Project Coord. - Facilities Planning and Site Search for Kidde Constructors, Inc.; **REP CLIENTS:** Many-Confidential; **PREV EMPLOY:** VP, Operations, unit of Amer. Express Co., VP Operations, Chain of Tidewater Terminals, Consultant Fac. Plan; **PROFL AFFIL & HONORS:** Sr. Member, Columbia SREA, Charter Member, Defense Trans. Assn.; **OTHER ACT & HONORS:** Past Dist. Dep., Knights of Columbus; **HOME ADD:** 82 S. Kensington Ave., Rockville Centre, NY 11570; **BUS ADD:** 526 Route 25-A, St. James, NY 11780, (516)584-5858.

MCMACKIN, Raymond F.——B: Oct. 5, 1926, NYC, *Pres.*, Ray Mc Mackin Associates, Inc., Comml.-Indus.-Land; **PRIM RE ACT:** Broker, Consultant, Appraiser, Owner/Investor, Property Manager; **SERVICES:** Comml. and home sales, appraisals, land; **REP CLIENTS:** Suffolk Cty., Town of Smithtown, NY Telephone Co., Grumman Aircraft, US Navy, etc.; **PROFL AFFIL & HONORS:** MLS, LIBOR, NY State Bd. of Realtors, Natl. Bd. of Realtors; **EDUC:** Bus. Admin., 1952; **HOME ADD:** 1 Thompson Hill Rd., St. James, NY 11780, (516)862-6960; **BUS ADD:** 1 Thompson Hill Rd., St. James, NY 11780, (516)584-6400.

MCMAHAN, John——B: Aug. 4, 1937, San Antonio, TX, *Pres.*, John McMahan Assoc., Inc.; **OTHER RE ACT:** RE investment adv.; **SERVICES:** Reg. RE Asset Mgmt.; **REP CLIENTS:** Pension funds, for. investors, corp. fin. instns., govt. agencies; **PREV EMPLOY:** Found., pres. Devel. Research Assoc.; **PROFL AFFIL & HONORS:** ULI, Amer. Econ. Assn., AIP, Lambda Alpha, AREUEA, NARA, Royal Town Planning Inst. (UK); **EDUC:** AB, 1959, Econ., Univ. of S CA; **GRAD EDUC:** MBA, 1961, Fin., Harvard Univ.; **EDUC HONORS:** Cum Laude; **HOME ADD:** 3865 Clay St., San Francisco, CA 94118, (415)668-0962; **BUS ADD:** 201 California St., Ste. 400, San Francisco, CA 94111, (415)433-7770.

MCMAHAN, John A.——B: Sept. 7, 1916, Boise City, OK, *Co-owner, Mgr.*, John A. McMahan & Assocs.; **PRIM RE ACT:** Broker, Consultant, Attorney, Developer, Property Manager, Syndicator; **OTHER RE ACT:** Mort. broker; **SERVICES:** RE sales, leases, acquisitions, mgmt., devel., fin.; **PREV EMPLOY:** Mgr. RE Devel. Cos., Mort. Banking firms., Formerly practicing atty.; **PROFL AFFIL & HONORS:** Local & Natl. RE Bd. of Realtors; **EDUC:** BA, 1936, Econ., Fin., Pre-Law, Univ. of OK; **GRAD EDUC:** LLB/JD, 1939, Law, emphasis on RE Law, Univ. of OK; **EDUC HONORS:** Dean's Honor Roll, Phi Eta Sigma; **OTHER ACT & HONORS:** Cty. Atty. Cimarron Cty, OK, 1940-42, Justice of Peace, 1959, Wichita, KS, AOPA, C of C, Ind. Business Men's Org., OX-5; **HOME ADD:** 5849 E. Hummingbird Ln., Scottsdale, AZ 85253, (602)948-9651; **BUS ADD:** 5849 E. Hummingbird Ln., Scottsdale, AZ 85253, (602)948-9851.

MCMAHAN, W. Edwin——B: Aug. 13, 1944, Asheville, NC, *Pres.*, Little - McMahan Properties, Inc.; **PRIM RE ACT:** Broker, Consultant, Developer, Owner/Investor, Property Manager; **PREV EMPLOY:** 1967-69 Dist. Mort. Loan Supv., Jefferson Standard Life; 1969-74 Sr. VP Carolina Nat. Mort. Co. (sub. of C & S Bank of SC); **PROFL AFFIL & HONORS:** Mort. Banker of Year, NC & SC 1972; **EDUC:** BS, 1966, Econ., Univ. of NC at Chapel Hill; **MIL SERV:** USAR, Spec. 4, 1966-72; **OTHER ACT & HONORS:** Pres. Income Prop. Assn. of DC 1971; **HOME ADD:** 3007 Clarendon Rd., Charlotte, NC 28211, (704)366-7196; **BUS ADD:** 4000 Park Rd., Charlotte, NC 28209, (704)523-8661.

MCMAHON, Brian Neill——B: Aug. 21, 1952, Newark, OH, *Atty.*, Wendy's International, Inc.; **PRIM RE ACT:** Consultant, Attorney; **PREV EMPLOY:** Riley, Ucker & Lavinsky 1978-80; **PROFL AFFIL & HONORS:** ABA, OH Bar Assn., Columbus Bar Assn.; **EDUC:** BA, 1974, Hist., OH State univ.; **GRAD EDUC:** JD, 1978, Capital Univ.; **HOME ADD:** 355 St. Andrews Ct., Dublin, OH 43017, (614)764-1541; **BUS ADD:** 4288 W Dublin Granville Rd., Dublin, OH 43017, (614)764-3471.

MCMAHON, Douglas——B: Nov. 18, 1950, Cleveland, OH, *Asst. RE Counsel; Asst. Secretary*, Fed. Stores Realty, Inc.; **PRIM RE ACT:** Attorney; **PREV EMPLOY:** Atty., Forest City Enterprises, Inc.; **PROFL AFFIL & HONORS:** Amer.; OH and Cincinnati Bar Assns., ICSC; **EDUC:** BA, 1972, Biology, Middlebury Coll.; **GRAD EDUC:** JD, 1976, Law, Case Western Reserve Univ. School of Law; **HOME ADD:** 3016 Marshall Ave., Cincinnati, OH 45220, (513)961-7986; **BUS ADD:** 7 West Seventh St., Cincinnati, OH 45202, (513)579-7020.

MCMANUS, Hank——B: Boston, MA, Samalot Real Estate; **PRIM RE ACT:** Broker, Consultant, Developer, Owner/Investor; **EDUC:** BA, 1965, Phil., St. Alphonsus Coll.; **GRAD EDUC:** MSW, 1971, Soc. Serv., Fordham Univ.; **OTHER ACT & HONORS:** Regnl. Rep., US Sec. of Trans. 1979-80; Pres. Bd. of Trs., Baptist Medical Ctr., NY; **HOME ADD:** 35 Prospect Park, Brooklyn, NY 11215, (212)638-0094; **BUS ADD:** 18 E. 41st St., NY, NY 10017.

MCMANUS, James——*Dir.*, NY, New York Dept. of State, Div. of Licensing; **PRIM RE ACT:** 145; **BUS ADD:** 162 Washington Ave., Albany, NY 12231, (518)484-4664.*

MCMANUS, Jerry A.——B: May 15, 1934, Kansas City, MO, *VP, Fin.*, E. P. Wilbur & Co.; **PRIM RE ACT:** Owner/Investor; **SERVICES:** Acquisition, ownership and mgmt. of RE for instns. and indiv. investors; **PREV EMPLOY:** Arthur Young & Co., CPAs (1957-1963); Aikman Corp. (1963-1969); Fiduciary Trust Co. of NY (1969-1970); Main Hurdman & Cranstoun (1970-1980); **PROFL AFFIL & HONORS:** AICPA; NY State Soc. of CPA; Nat. Assn. of Accountants; NUAC, CPA; **EDUC:** BSBA, 1956, Washington Univ., St. Louis, MO; **GRAD EDUC:** MS, 1957, Columbia Univ., Grad. School of Bus.; **MIL SERV:** US Army, Res.; Capt.; **HOME ADD:** 2401 Redding Rd., Fairfield, CT 06430; **BUS ADD:** 368 Center St., Southport, CT 06490, (203)255-3434.

MCMENAMY, William C., Jr.——B: Oct. 5, 1940, Columbus, OH, *Partner*, Wears, Kahn, McMenamy & Co.; **PRIM RE ACT:** Broker, Consultant, Developer, Owner/Investor, Syndicator, Property Manager; **SERVICES:** Devel., prop. mgmt., sales and leasing; **REP CLIENTS:** Bank Trust Depts., Corps., and Indivs. Investors; **PROFL AFFIL & HONORS:** SIR, NAR, OH & Colubus Bd. of Realtors, Columbus Mort. Bankers Assn., IREM; **EDUC:** BS, 1962, Mktg., OH State Univ.; **GRAD EDUC:** MBA, 1966, RE, Xavier Univ.; **OTHER ACT & HONORS:** Bd. of Dirs. Columbus, Bd. of Realtors, OH Assn. of Realtors, Creative Living, Salvation Army, Columbus Jr. Theatre of the Arts, Columbus Ctry. Club, City Club of Columbus, Past Bd. Member, Edler, Deacon, Christ Lutheran Church; **HOME ADD:** 275 Ashbourne Pl., Columbus, OH 43209, (614)253-6300; **BUS ADD:** 81 S. Fifth St., Columbus, OH 43215, (614)228-6321.

MCMILLAN, Thomas L.——B: Oct. 25, 1942, Minneapolis, MN, *Pres.*, Monticello Realty Corp.; **PRIM RE ACT:** Broker, Developer, Owner/Investor, Property Manager; **PROFL AFFIL & HONORS:** NAR, ULI, IL Assn. of Realtors; **EDUC:** BA, 1965, Poli. Sci., Univ. of CO; **GRAD EDUC:** MA, 1966, Poli. Sci., Univ. of WA; PhD, 1970, Poli. Sci., Univ. of KS; **EDUC HONORS:** With honors; **MIL SERV:** US Army Reserve, Sp4; **HOME ADD:** 1940 Clover Rd., Northbrook, IL 60062, (312)291-1533; **BUS ADD:** 300 W. Washington, Chicago, IL 60606, (312)236-6300.

MCMILLIN, Terry J.——B: June 12, 1937, Ames, IA, *Dir., FL Division*, General Development Corp. of FL, Housing; **PRIM RE ACT:** Broker, Consultant, Builder, Owner/Investor, Instructor, Insuror; **OTHER RE ACT:** Nat. Motivator and Trainer (Personal Growth); **SERVICES:** RE investment counseling, sales training, motivation; **REP CLIENTS:** OH Bell Telephone, Intl. Distillers Inc., Greater MI Prop. Mgmt. Inc.; **PREV EMPLOY:** Psycho-Dynamics: Nat. speaker and lecturer, personal growth, motivation, directed goal orientation, expanded conscious awareness; **PROFL AFFIL & HONORS:** MI Prop. Mgmt. Assn.; Nat. Speakers Forum; RE Ethics Comm., Wayne Cty., Recipient of the G.L. Goldinger Human Resources Award, 1979; **EDUC:** BBA, 1960, Acctg./Econ./Hist., Bowling Green State Univ.; **GRAD EDUC:** CPA Prep., 1962, Walsh Inst.; **OTHER ACT & HONORS:** Aircraft Owners and Pilots Assn.; Bd. of Dirs. of the Unified Churches MI; **HOME ADD:** 8046 Macomb, Grosse Ile, MI 48138, (313)675-6916; **BUS ADD:** 26600 Southfield, Lathrup Village, MI 48076, (313)552-9200.

MCMULLAN, David M.——B: Nov. 28, 1938, Newton, MS, *Partner*, Low & McMullan; **PRIM RE ACT:** Attorney; **PREV EMPLOY:** Watkins, Pyle, Ludlam Winter & Stennis Attys.; **PROFL AFFIL & HONORS:** MS State Bar; ABA; Jackson Home Builders Assn.; **EDUC:** BA, 1960, History, Millsaps Coll.; **GRAD EDUC:** LLB, 1963, Univ. of VA; **HOME ADD:** 971 Morningside, Jackson, MS 39202, (601)355-4162; **BUS ADD:** 1212 Capital Towers, P.O. Box 22966, Jackson, MS 39205, (601)948-0700.

MCMURPHY, Edward——*Mgr. RE Operations*, Marion Corp.; **PRIM RE ACT:** Property Manager; **BUS ADD:** One Marion Ave., Daphne, AL 36526, (205)626-3300.*

MCNABB, Charlie L.——B: July 24, 1923, Los Angeles, CA, *Pres. - Owner*, McNabb Appraisers and Consultants; **PRIM RE ACT:** Broker, Consultant, Appraiser, Developer, Owner/Investor, Property Manager; **OTHER RE ACT:** Public Acctg.; **SERVICES:** Valuation & investment counseling, RE and going concern, RE Broker, Gen. Bldg. contractor, public acctg.; **REP CLIENTS:** Banks, S&L assns., ins. cos., corps., and indivs., attys. and govt. agencies; **PREV EMPLOY:** Prior to 1969: Exec. VP, Managing Officer, Dir., Community S&L Assn.; **PROFL AFFIL & HONORS:** Lambda Alpha (Honorary Profl. Land Econ. Fraternity), AIREA (MAI Designation), Soc. of RE Appraisers (SRPA Designation), Pasadena Bd. of Realtors, Intl. Inst. of Valuers (SCV Designation), CA Assn. of Realtors, Nat. Assn. of Realtors; **EDUC:** Bachelor of Bus. Admin., 1947, Higher Accountancy, Woodbury Coll.; **EDUC HONORS:** (Honorary Academic Fraternity); **MIL SERV:** USN, Petty Officer First Class, Purple Heart, Good Conduct; **OTHER ACT & HONORS:** CA Licenses: General Building Contractor, Cement and Masonry Contractor, Solar Contractor, Real Estate Broker, Public Accountant; Past Pres., Los Angeles Chap. No. 1 Soc. of RE Appraisers, Past Pres. and Past Governing Councilor So. CA Chap. No. 5 AIREA; **HOME ADD:** 536 No. Old Ranch Rd., Arcadia,

CA 91006, (213)446-7834; **BUS ADD:** 61 So. Lake Ave., Ste. Six, Pasadena, CA 91101, (213)449-0206.

MCNAIR, Russell A., Jr.——**B:** Dec. 2, 1934, Detroit, MI, *Part.*, Dickinson, Wright, Moon, VanDusen & Freeman; **PRIM RE ACT:** Attorney; **SERVICES:** Legal servs; **REP CLIENTS:** Inst. RE lenders & investors in comml. props.; **PROFL AFFIL & HONORS:** ABA; MI & Detroit Bar Assns.; Amer. Law Inst.; **EDUC:** AB, 1956, Econ., Princeton Univ.; **GRAD EDUC:** JD, 1960, Univ. of MI Law Sch.; **EDUC HONORS:** Cum Laude; **OTHER ACT & HONORS:** Tr. Children's Home in Detroit; Member Detroit Foreign Relations Council; Adjunct Prof. Univ. of Detroit Sch. of Law, 1968-72; **HOME ADD:** 308 Touraine Rd., Grosse Pointe Farms, MI 48236, (313)886-0228; **BUS ADD:** 800 First Nat. Bldg., Detroit, MI 48226, (313)223-3500.

MCNALLY, H. Charles——**B:** Mar. 4, 1925, Staten Island, NY, *Pres.*, Lanid Corp.; **PRIM RE ACT:** Consultant, Developer, Builder, Owner/Investor, Property Manager; **PROFL AFFIL & HONORS:** HBA, Homebuilders Assn. of Morris & Somerset Ctys., NAIOP, Morris Cty. C of C, Apt. House Council of US; **HOME ADD:** 335 Old Army Rd., Basking Ridge, NJ 07920, (201)766-1448; **BUS ADD:** 300 Lanidex Plaza, Parsippany, NJ 07054, (201)386-5800.

MCNALLY, Mike D.——**B:** Fresno, CA, *Owner*, Architectural Drafting; **PRIM RE ACT:** Architect; **OTHER RE ACT:** Custom Resid. Design & Devel.; **PREV EMPLOY:** James P. Lockett, Inc. Architect 1971-77; Warren Thompson, Architect, 1970-71; **EDUC:** AS, 1971, Arch., Fresno City Coll.; **MIL SERV:** USANG, Sp5; **OTHER ACT & HONORS:** Arch. Review Bd. 5 yrs., Pacific Grove; Pacific Grove C of C Pres.; City Housing Appeals Bd.; **BUS ADD:** 207 16th St. Suite 202, Pacific Grove, CA 93950, (408)375-1022.

MCNAMARA, Paul S.——**B:** Sept. 7, 1943, Bridgeport, CT, *Part.*, Donnelly & McNamara; **PRIM RE ACT:** Attorney; **SERVICES:** Planning, Zoning; Devel./Bldr. Rep.; **REP CLIENTS:** BRT Corp; Ridgefield Savings Bank (lender); Union Trust Co. (lender); Equitable Life Relocation; **PROFL AFFIL & HONORS:** CT Bar Assn.; ABA; **EDUC:** BS, 1966, Fin., Amer. Univ.; **GRAD EDUC:** JD, 1969, Univ. of ME, School of Law; **OTHER ACT & HONORS:** Bd. of Dir, Ridgefield Family Y; Bd. of Dir., Ridgefield Library; Bd. of Dir., Ridgefield Boy's Club; Incorporator of Ridgefield Savings Bank; Assoc. Bd. of Dir. Union Trust Co.; **HOME ADD:** 9 Doubleday Lane, Ridgefield, CT 06877, (203)438-9718; **BUS ADD:** 27 Governor St., Ridgefield, CT 06877, (203)438-6534.

MCNEIL, J. William——**B:** Jan. 1, 1917, Pittsburgh, PA, *Mgr.*, Bernhard Realty Sales Co.; **PRIM RE ACT:** Broker, Developer, Builder, Instructor; **PROFL AFFIL & HONORS:** Greater Pittsburgh Bd. of Realtors; PA Assn. of Realtors; NAR; RNMI; **EDUC:** BS, 1938, Waynesburg Coll., Waynesburg, PA; **OTHER ACT & HONORS:** Pres., Bellevue Community Devel. Corp.; Pres., Revest, Inc.; **HOME ADD:** 135 Drood Ln., Pittsburgh, PA 15237, (412)366-1396; **BUS ADD:** 690 Lincoln Ave., Pittsburgh, PA 15202, (412)761-1300.

MCNEIL, Robert A.——**B:** July 6, 1920, San Francisco, CA, *Chmn.*, The Robert A. McNeil Corp.; **PRIM RE ACT:** Broker, Syndicator, Property Manager, Lender; **EDUC:** BA, 1942, Stanford Univ.; **GRAD EDUC:** LLB, 1948, Stanford Law School; **MIL SERV:** USA, 1st Lt.; **HOME ADD:** 229 Polhemus, Atherton, CA 94025; **BUS ADD:** 2855 Campus Dr., San Mateo, CA 94403, (415)572-0660.

MCNEIRNEY, James A.——*Dep. Exec. Dir.*, Department of Housing and Urban Development, Neighborhood Reinvestment Corp.; **PRIM RE ACT:** Lender; **BUS ADD:** 451 Seventh St., S.W., Washington, DC 20410, (202)377-6376.*

MCNITT, Joseph E.——**B:** Oct. 19, 1929, Chicago, IL, *Dir.*, Pope, Ballard, Shepard & Fowle, Ltd.; **PRIM RE ACT:** Attorney; **SERVICES:** RE & Finance Law; **PROFL AFFIL & HONORS:** ABA, IL State Bar Assn.; **EDUC:** BA, 1951, Econ., Univ. of Notre Dame; **GRAD EDUC:** JD, 1954, Law, Northwestern Univ. School of Law; **EDUC HONORS:** Magna Cum Laude; **MIL SERV:** US Army, SP-3; **OTHER ACT & HONORS:** Vice Chmn., Comm. on RE Fin., Real Prop. Section, ABA; **HOME ADD:** 2217 N. Fremont St., Chicago, IL 60614; **BUS ADD:** 69 W. Washington St., Chicago, IL 60602.

MCNULTY, Charles S.——**B:** Aug. 10, 1914, Roanoke, VA, *RE Consultant*, Progress Rush Co.; **PRIM RE ACT:** Broker, Consultant, Appraiser, Developer, Builder, Owner/Investor, Instructor, Assessor; **SERVICES:** Sales & appraisals of comml. prop.; **REP CLIENTS:** Shell Oil, Humana Inc., FNEB, United BA Bank, Natural Bridge VA, J.M. Turner Const. Co.; **PREV EMPLOY:** Assessor, City of Roanoke, 1966-1976; Retired at 62 yrs.; **PROFL AFFIL & HONORS:** AIREA; Retired from SREA & IAAO in 1979, MAI (Retired SRPA & CAE); **EDUC:** BS, 1973, Urban & Surburban Planning, Univ. No. CO; **EDUC HONORS:** 1st Place Essay Award, 1968 (St. Louis - IAAO) Published; **MIL SERV:** USAR, Lt., Soldiers Medal, Purple Heart, 3 Battle Stars; **OTHER ACT & HONORS:** Help, Inc., Pres., 1968-1969; DAV, Life Member; **HOME ADD:** 2722 Fawn Rd. S.W., Roanoke, VA 24015, (703)774-5371; **BUS ADD:** 2502 Broadway S.W., Roanoke, VA 24014, (703)345-1081.

MCNULTY, Peter J.——**B:** June 19, 1951, Evanston, IL, *Atty.*, Hopkins & Sutter; **PRIM RE ACT:** Attorney; **SERVICES:** Condo. - from assembling the prop. to final sales of units; **REP CLIENTS:** Indiv.; **PROFL AFFIL & HONORS:** ABA; Il State Bar Assn.; Chicago Bar Assn.; The FL Bar; CPA; **EDUC:** BSBA, 1973, Acctg., Georgetown Univ.; **GRAD EDUC:** JD, 1976, Taxation, Georgetown Univ. Law Ctr.; **BUS ADD:** One First Nat. Plaza, Suite 5200, Chicago, IL 60603, (312)558-6768.

MCNUTT, Jack R.——*VP Mort. Loans*, Provident Life & Accident Ins. Co., Mort. Loan Dept.; **PRIM RE ACT:** Lender; **BUS ADD:** Fountain Sq., Chattanooga, TN 37402, (615)755-1564.

MCPARTLAND, Charles J.——**B:** Aug. 9, 1931, New York, NY, *Pres.*, Indepro Corp.; **PRIM RE ACT:** Syndicator; **PREV EMPLOY:** Nat. RE Mgt. 20 years United Parcel Serv., Greenwich, CT; **EDUC:** BBA, 1961, Fin., Baruch School, City Coll. of NY (Evening); **GRAD EDUC:** Courses RE, 1961-1964, RE, Baruch School, City Coll. of NY (Evening); **MIL SERV:** US Army; Sgt., Signal Corps; **HOME ADD:** 701 Weatherstone Dr., Paoli, PA 19301, (215)647-4686; **BUS ADD:** 3520 Silverside Rd., Suite 27, Wilmington, DE 19810, (302)478-8780.

MCPHERSON, Donald P., III——**B:** Aug. 9, 1941, Baltimore, MD, *Partner*, Piper & Marbury, RE Devel., Tax-exempt securities; **PRIM RE ACT:** Attorney; **SERVICES:** Legal advice and preparation of documents; **PROFL AFFIL & HONORS:** ABA, MD State Bar Assn.; **EDUC:** AB, 1963, Phil. of Sci., Princeton Univ.; **GRAD EDUC:** LLB, 1966, Law, Columbia Univ.; **EDUC HONORS:** Cum Laude; **BUS ADD:** 1100 Charles Center S., 36 S. Charles St., Baltimore, MD 21201, (301)539-2530.

MCPHERSON, Mrs. Marilyn D.——**B:** Nov.6,1941, Mayfield,KY, *RE Sales Agent*, Weigl Realty, Residential sales and investment sales; **PRIM RE ACT:** Consultant; **OTHER RE ACT:** RE Sales (Residential and Investment); **SERVICES:** Information & services regarding investing; **PREV EMPLOY:** Fed. Reserve Bank-Securities Dept., Market Clerk, H&R Block (tax consultant), Seidman & Seidman, CPA's; **EDUC:** Home Ec. Acctg., RE, Murray State Univ., Memphis State Univ., Univ.of TN, Belhaven Coll.; **HOME ADD:** 17 Thornhill Cove, Brandon, MS 39042, (601)825-4397; **BUS ADD:** 440 Bounds Street, Jackson, MS 39206, (601)982-8426.

MCPHERSON, Robert E.——**B:** Oct. 23, 1925, Wheeling, WV, *Appraiser-Auctioneer*, Real Estate Auction Service; **PRIM RE ACT:** Appraiser, Assessor; **OTHER RE ACT:** RE Salesman and Auctioneer; **SERVICES:** Appraisal and RE Sales by the Auction Method; **PROFL AFFIL & HONORS:** Nat. Assn. of Indep. Fee Appraisers, AZ Auctioneers Assn., Nat. Assn. of Indep. Fee Appraisers approved by State of AZ to assess prop.; **EDUC:** Bus., 1976, RE, Glendale Community Coll., Glendale, AZ; **MIL SERV:** USAF; T/Sgt.; **HOME ADD:** 2051 W. Citrus Way, Phoenix, AZ 85015, (602)249-2343; **BUS ADD:** 2051 W. Citrus Way, Phoenix, AZ 85015, (602)249-2343.

MCPHILLIPS, George F.——**B:** Mar. 10, 1925, NY, NY, *VP-RE & Construction*, First National Supermarkets, Inc.; **OTHER RE ACT:** Corp. Officer of RE; **PREV EMPLOY:** Supermarkets General Corp. 1963-77; VP RE and Construction; **PROFL AFFIL & HONORS:** ICSC, NACORE; **EDUC:** BS, 1949, Bus. Admin., Syracuse Univ.; **MIL SERV:** USAF, 1943-45, T/Sgt., Air Medal & Clusters; **OTHER ACT & HONORS:** Former condemnation Commissioner-Bergen Co., NJ; Former Trustee- Elmira Coll. 1973-1979; **HOME ADD:** 103 Woodside Dr., Longmeadow, MA 01106, (413)567-6790; **BUS ADD:** 1 Myrtle St., Hartford, CT 06105, (203)727-9511.

MCQUAILLAN, Jeremiah E.——*President*, Barnes Group Inc.; **PRIM RE ACT:** Property Manager; **BUS ADD:** 123 Main Street, Briston, CT 06010, (203)583-7070.*

MACQUEEN, Virginia——**B:** Jan. 16, 1916, Portland, ME, *Pres.*, MacQueen Realty Co., Inc.; **PRIM RE ACT:** Broker, Consultant, Appraiser, Owner/Investor, Syndicator; **SERVICES:** Gen. RE - Nat. & Intl.; **REP CLIENTS:** Coverage - specifically sale, leasing and devel. of motels/hotels; **PREV EMPLOY:** Firm established 1945; **PROFL AFFIL & HONORS:** RE Bds. - Rochester; NY; NY State Assn. and NAR; NY State Soc. of Resid. Appraisers Chap. 99; Realtors 25 Year Club; Intl. Society of Realtors FIABCI; Member Motel Brokers Assn.

of Amer. and Life Member of RE Bd. of Rochester since 1974; **GRAD EDUC:** Courses, 1963, 1970, Appraising, Cornell Univ., NYU; **OTHER ACT & HONORS:** Who's Who Amer. Women, Who's Who in the East, Omega Tau Rho, featured in "Top of Professions" Gannett News, 1976; **HOME ADD:** 233 Overbrook Rd., Rochester, NY 14618, (716)385-4149; **BUS ADD:** 55 Canterbury Rd., Rochester, NY 14607, (716)473-0670.

MCQUEENEY, Charles T.——B: Jan. 20, 1946, New Haven, CT, *VP*, W.J. Barney Realty Corp.; **PRIM RE ACT:** Appraiser, Developer, Builder, Owner/Investor, Property Manager, Syndicator; **SERVICES:** Devel., const., synd. & mgmt. of income prop.; **REP CLIENTS:** Major comml. and indus. firms; major hopsitals; **PREV EMPLOY:** Devel. Mgr., W.J. Megin, Inc.; **PROFL AFFIL & HONORS:** Candidate, Appraisal Inst.; Lic. RE Broker and Broker/Dealer of RE Securities, Selected as Young Profl. of the Yr. by Bldg. Design & Const. magazine for innovative techniques used to develop and finance an office bldg.; **EDUC:** BA, 1969, Psych./Bus. Admin., Harvard Univ.; **EDUC HONORS:** Magna Cum Laude; **OTHER ACT & HONORS:** Harvard Club of So. CT; Harvard Varsity Club; **HOME ADD:** 66 Buell St., Hamden, CT 06518, (203)288-9515; **BUS ADD:** 360 Lexington Ave., NY, NY 10017, (212)972-0720.

MCRAE, Colin L.——B: June 28, 1943, Queens, NY, *VP Prop. Mgmt.*, J. Emil Anderson & Son, Inc.; **PRIM RE ACT:** Architect, Developer, Property Manager, Builder, Owner/Investor, Insuror; **EDUC:** BS, 1967, Econ./Poli. Sci., Univ. of IL; **MIL SERV:** USA, 1967-69, Sgt.; **OTHER ACT & HONORS:** Village trustee 75-77; Mayor 77-81, Mayor 81(term ends 85); Chmn. Central Cty. Radio Network; Lake Cty. Community Devel. 77-present; Commnr., Lake Cty. Econ. Devel. Commnr. 1977-81; Lake Cty. 208 Water Quality Commn.; VP Lake Cty. Municipal League; **HOME ADD:** 225 Edgemont, Mundelein, IL 60060, (312)566-1044; **BUS ADD:** 1400 E. Touhy Ave, Des Plaines, IL 60018, (312)297-7710.

MCRAE, Hamilton E., III——B: Oct. 29, 1937, Midland, TX, *Partner*, Jennings, Strouss & Salmon; **PRIM RE ACT:** Consultant, Attorney, Owner/Investor; **OTHER RE ACT:** Pres. of and own 50% interest in RE brokerage co.; **SERVICES:** RE and comml. practice; **REP CLIENTS:** Various nat. and local; **PREV EMPLOY:** Electronics Officer USAF, Assoc. Jennings, Strouss & Salmon; **PROFL AFFIL & HONORS:** ABA; AZ State Bar Assn.; Mericopa Cty. Bar Assn., Atty., JD; **EDUC:** BSEE, 1961, EE, Univ. of AZ, Tucson, AZ; **GRAD EDUC:** JD, 1967, RE and Comml. Law, Univ. of AZ, Tucson, AZ; **MIL SERV:** USAF; Lt.; Various Decorations; **OTHER ACT & HONORS:** Amer. Inst. of Mining Engrs.; Phoenix Exec. Club; Continental Ctry. Club; Elks Club; AZ Club; Phoenix Ctry. Club; **HOME ADD:** 8101 N. 47th St., Paradise Valley, AZ, (602)991-0601; **BUS ADD:** 111 West Monroe, Phoenix, AZ 85003, (602)258-5873.

MCRAE, James W.——B: Nov. 4, 1939, Atlanta, GA, *Pres.*, McRae & Holloway, P.C.; **PRIM RE ACT:** Consultant, Attorney, Instructor; **SERVICES:** Legal rep. of comml. RE devel. and investors; **REP CLIENTS:** RE devel., domestic and foreign investors, synd., instl. investors and lenders; **PREV EMPLOY:** Troutman, Sanders, Lockerman & Ashmore, Atlanta, GA 1967-1981; Nall, Miller, Cadenhead & Dennis, Atlanta, GA 1963-1967; **PROFL AFFIL & HONORS:** Atlanta, GA, Amer. & Intl. Bar Assn., Lawyers Club, Chmn., Real Prop. Section, State Bar of GA, Chmn., Real Prop. Section, Atlanta Bar Assn.; **EDUC:** BA, 1961, Eng., Emory Univ.; **GRAD EDUC:** JD, 1964, Emory Univ., Lamar School of Law; **HOME ADD:** 2026 Castleway Lane N.E., Atlanta, GA 30345, (404)325-9574; **BUS ADD:** Suite 210, Eight Piedmont Ctr., Atlanta, GA 30305, (404)261-0500.

MCRAE, Kenneth G.——B: Nov. 13, 1951, Stillwater, OK, *VP*, Pulaski Mortgage Co., Comml. and Insured Project Loans; **PRIM RE ACT:** Lender; **OTHER RE ACT:** Mort. banker; **SERVICES:** Financing provided for comml. & insured projects; **REP CLIENTS:** Developers, RE brokers, builders, housing authorities; **PREV EMPLOY:** Pulaski Bank & Trust Co. VP 1974-1980, Little Rock, AR; **PROFL AFFIL & HONORS:** Member MBAA Insured Project Comm.; **EDUC:** BA in Bus. & Econ., 1974, Econ., Bus., and Acctg., Hendrix Coll., Cunway, AR; **GRAD EDUC:** Grad. Degree in Banking, 1980 from So. Methodist Univ. Comml. Banking, Income Property Finance, Athens, GA. Insured Project Lending, Kansas City, MO; **BUS ADD:** P O Box 7200, Little Rock, AR 72217, (501)661-7854.

MCRAE, William H.——B: June 1, 1937, Dallas, TX, *Partner*, May, Herridge, & McRae; **PRIM RE ACT:** Broker, Attorney, Owner/Investor; **SERVICES:** Legal services, brokerage; **PROFL AFFIL & HONORS:** TX Bar Assn.; Dallas Bar Assn.; TX RE Broker; **EDUC:** BA, 1959, Poli. Sci., So. Methodist Univ.; **GRAD EDUC:** JD, 1962, Tax/Prop., So. Methodist Univ.; **EDUC HONORS:** Phi Beta Kappa, Magna Cum Laude, Order of the Woolsack, Cum Laude; **HOME ADD:** 4565 Belclaire Ave., Dallas, TX 75205, (214)528-0416; **BUS ADD:** One Main Place, Suite 2950, Dallas, TX 75250, (214)742-9411.

MACRUS, A.——B: May 18, 1928, NYC, NY, Tudor Gate Dev. & Bldgs.; **PRIM RE ACT:** Broker, Attorney, Developer, Builder; **PREV EMPLOY:** 30 yrs. Builder & Devel., Homes, Apts., Office Bldgs., Shopping Ctrs., Apt. Bldgs., & Town Houses; **PROFL AFFIL & HONORS:** Const. Official NJ; **EDUC:** LLB, 1949, Syracuse Univ.; **GRAD EDUC:** Fordam Law School; **MIL SERV:** USA, Capt.; **OTHER ACT & HONORS:** Const. Official Borough of Englewood Cliffs, BOCA; **BUS ADD:** PO Box 1111, Englewood, NJ 07632, (201)567-4446.

MCSWAIN, Charles——B: July 30, 1950, Tampa, FL, *Mgr.*, Tampa Indus. Park; **PRIM RE ACT:** Developer; **SERVICES:** Prop. mgmt. and mktg.; **PREV EMPLOY:** Oglethorpe Power Corp., Sr. Econ. Devel. Officer, Atlanta, GA; **PROFL AFFIL & HONORS:** NAIOP, AEDC, CID, AEDC; **EDUC:** BA, 1972, Univ. of So. FL; **HOME ADD:** 4501 Dale Ave., Tampa, FL 33609, (813)879-8038; **BUS ADD:** Box 420, Tampa, FL 33601, (813)228-7777.

MCSWAIN, S.R.——*Mgr. Corp. Fac.*, Dresser Industries, Inc.; **PRIM RE ACT:** Property Manager; **BUS ADD:** 1505 Elm St., Dallas, TX 75201, (214)746-6000.*

MCSWEENEY, John J.——B: May 27, 1943, Boston, MA, *RE Mgr.*, The Stop & Shop Co. Inc., Stop & Shop Super Mkts.; **PRIM RE ACT:** Developer, Property Manager, Assessor; **OTHER RE ACT:** Manage and Direct RE Acquisition; **PROFL AFFIL & HONORS:** MA Assessing Officers; **EDUC:** BS, 1965, Mktg. and Advertising, Northeastern Univ.; **GRAD EDUC:** MBA, 1966, Gen. Bus., Univ. of MA - Amherst; **OTHER ACT & HONORS:** Conservation Commn., Lexington, 1975-1977, Town Meeting Member - Lexington, Assessor 1977, Lexington Minuteman; **HOME ADD:** 503 Concord Ave., Lexington, MA 02173, (617)861-9019; **BUS ADD:** PO Box 369, Boston, MA 02101, (617)463-4232.

MACTAGGART, Sandy A.——B: Mar. 11, 1928, Glasgow, Scotland, *Pres. & Managing Dir.*, Maclab Enterprises Ltd.; **PRIM RE ACT:** Developer, Owner/Investor, Property Manager; **SERVICES:** Resid. & Comml. investment devel. and mgmt.; **REP CLIENTS:** For our own account only; **EDUC:** AB, 1950, Arch., Harvard Univ.; **GRAD EDUC:** MBA, 1952, Bus. & Math., Harvard Bus. Sch.; **EDUC HONORS:** Cum Laude; **MIL SERV:** Fleet Air Arm, Lt.; **OTHER ACT & HONORS:** Dir. in community affairs; **HOME ADD:** PO Box 3160, Edmonton, Alberta, Canada, (403)434-2435; **BUS ADD:** PO Box 3160, Edmonton, Alberta, Canada, (403)420-6666.

MCTIGHE, Michael J.——B: Sept. 6, 1935, NYC, *Managing Partner*, Rancho Bernardo Jt. Venture; **PRIM RE ACT:** Consultant, Banker, Developer, Owner/Investor, Property Manager; **PREV EMPLOY:** Citibank, NA 1964-79; Established const. & devel. loan programs in Hong Kong, Guam, etc. prior joining RE Indus. Div. in NY in 1976 as VP; **EDUC:** AB, 1957, Phil., Princeton Univ.; **GRAD EDUC:** BFT, 1964, Fin., Amer. Grad. School of Intl. Mgmt.; **EDUC HONORS:** Honors; **MIL SERV:** USMC, 1st. Lt.; **HOME ADD:** 72 Quail Close, Irvington, NY 10533, (914)591-7654; **BUS ADD:** 72 Quail Close, Irvington-on-Hudson, NY 10533, (914)591-7654.

MCVAY, Tom D.——B: July 15, 1946, Columbus, OH, *Managing Partner*, American Property and Mortgage; **PRIM RE ACT:** Owner/Investor; **OTHER RE ACT:** Underwriter; **PREV EMPLOY:** Mellon Nat. Mort. Co. of OH; **PROFL AFFIL & HONORS:** Candidate affiliation with AIREA; **EDUC:** 1968, Fin., AIREA Schools at Vilanova, Univ. of Tampa and Chicago; **OTHER ACT & HONORS:** Owner, Tom McVay & Co. - RE Appraising and Fin.; **HOME ADD:** 2762 Shady Ridge Dr., Columbus, OH 43229, (614)890-1233; **BUS ADD:** 500 W. Wilson Bridge Rd., Suite 220, Worthington, OH 43085, (614)436-4957.

MCVETY, William F.——B: Aug. 20, 1914, Piqua, OH, *Pres. - Exec. VP*, Premier Investment Corp. - Park Ridge, Inc.; **PRIM RE ACT:** Broker, Developer, Builder; **PREV EMPLOY:** 1940-1945 - Tool & Die Shop; **PROFL AFFIL & HONORS:** Miami Co. Realtors; OH Assn. of Realtors; Nat. Assn. of RE; Miami Co. Bldrs.; OH Bldrs.; **OTHER ACT & HONORS:** Kiwanis - 35 years; Elks; Eagles - 34 years, Past pres. Miami Cty. Bd. of Realtors, Member Piqua C of C, Member Piqua Ctry Club, Member Westminster Presbyterian Church; **HOME ADD:** 507 N Parkway Dr., Piqua, OH 45356, (513)773-4408; **BUS ADD:** 222 W. Ash St., Piqua, OH 45356, (513)773-8215.

MCWHORTER, David R.——B: Aug. 15, 1959, Fresno, CA, *Retail/Comml. Salesman*, Coldwell Banker Commercial Real Estate Services; **PRIM RE ACT:** Broker; **SERVICES:** Sales & leasing of comml.-retail RE in San Joaquin Valley; **REP CLIENTS:** Major retail chains and indiv. or inst. investors in comml./retail props.; **PREV**

EMPLOY: Res. income & inv. prop. salesman 1978-1980; **PROFL AFFIL & HONORS:** Member Intl. Council of Shopping Centers, Realtor Assn.; **OTHER ACT & HONORS:** Futures Comm. O.K. Nazarene Church, BKF, CA; Believed to be youngest comm. salesman in Coldwell Banker's History (CB founded 1906) at age 21; **HOME ADD:** 5501 Midsummer Dr., Bakersfield, CA 93308, (805)393-2290; **BUS ADD:** 1510 E. Shaw Ave., Suite 103, Fresno, CA 93710, (209)226-4321.

MCWILLIAMS, Mike C.——B: Nov. 10, 1948, Dallas, TX, *Partner*, Moore & Peterson; **PRIM RE ACT:** Attorney; **SERVICES:** Legal representation; **REP CLIENTS:** Interim and permanent RE Lenders, Devels. of office, shopping center, apt. and condo. projects; **PROFL AFFIL & HONORS:** State Bar of TX, Dallas Bar Assn., ABA; **EDUC:** BBA, 1969, Fin., Univ. of TX, Austin; **GRAD EDUC:** JD, 1973, Univ. of TX at Austin; **EDUC HONORS:** Graduation with Honors, Beta Gamma Sigma; **HOME ADD:** 7139 Currin Dr., Dallas, TX 75230, (214)692-1823; **BUS ADD:** 2400 One Dallas Centre, Dallas, TX 75201, (214)651-1721.

MCWILLIAMS, Peter D.——B: Sept. 15, 1929, Can, *Pres.*, Santana Mgmt. Corp.; **PRIM RE ACT:** Broker, Consultant, Appraiser, Developer, Builder, Owner/Investor, Syndicator; **SERVICES:** Appraising, Counseling & Synd. Devel. of Comml. Indus. & Resid. Props.; **REP CLIENTS:** Devels./Investors in Resid., Comml. and Indus. Props.; **PREV EMPLOY:** Progressive Contracting Ltd 1974-1979; **PROFL AFFIL & HONORS:** SREA, Appraisals Instit. of Canada; **EDUC:** 1971-1974, RE Appraisal, BC Instit. of Technol.; **GRAD EDUC:** RE, 1967-1971, RE Law, Fin. & Practices, Univ. of BC; **MIL SERV:** Royal Can. Air Force, NCO; **OTHER ACT & HONORS:** J-G 52 Flying Club, Newport Beach Power Squadron; **HOME ADD:** 2237 N. Westwood Blvd., Santa Ana, CA 92706, (714)547-4990; **BUS ADD:** 17802 Irvine Blvd., Suite 103, Tustin, CA 92630, (714)730-0590.

MCWILLIAMS, Richard L.——B: Apr. 21, 1937, Platteville WI, *Owner*, Poolside Apts.; **PRIM RE ACT:** Developer, Property Manager, Owner/Investor; **MIL SERV:** USA, 2nd Lt.; **OTHER ACT & HONORS:** Councilman City of Platteville 4 yrs., Pres. Platteville area Devel. Corp.; **HOME TEL:** (608)348-8057; **BUS ADD:** 45 S. Chestnut St., Platteville, WI 53818, (608)348-3156.

MADACEY, John R.——B: May 26, 1932, Peoria, IL, *Owner-Broker*, Madacey & Associates, Comml. & Investment RE; **PRIM RE ACT:** Broker, Consultant, Appraiser, Developer, Owner/Investor, Instructor, Property Manager, Syndicator; **OTHER RE ACT:** Counselor; **SERVICES:** RE brokerage, investment counseling, land devel. instr. for MAR in Comml. RE; instr. for Univ. of MI in Comml. RE; **PREV EMPLOY:** MI State Hwy. Dept., Rd. Design Engr. 1957-1962; **PROFL AFFIL & HONORS:** MAR, NAR, RNMI, RAM, RESSI, VP of District 9 MAR, RAM, GRI, CCIM, U.P. Realtor of the Yr. 1980; Past Pres. U.P. Bd. for 2 terms; **EDUC:** 1951, Coll. Prep, Hawkeye Boy's State, DuBuque IA; **GRAD EDUC:** 4 yrs., Resid. Building, Sch. of Forestry, MI State Univ.; **HOME ADD:** 353 W. Crescent, Marquette, MI 49855, (906)226-7776; **BUS ADD:** 816 N. Third St., Marquette, MI 49855, (906)228-9093.

MADDEN, John E.——*Ind. Rel. & Off. Mgr.*, White Consolidated Industries; **PRIM RE ACT:** Property Manager; **BUS ADD:** 11770 Berea Rd., Cleveland, OH 44111, (216)252-3700.*

MADDOX, Cone——B: Sept. 11, 1936, Atlanta, GA, *Chmn.*, Dargan, Whitington & Conner, Inc.; **PRIM RE ACT:** Broker, Consultant, Appraiser, Developer, Owner/Investor, Property Manager, Syndicator; **PROFL AFFIL & HONORS:** IREM; Nat. Assn. of RE Appraisers; Intl. Inst. of Valuers, CRA; CPM; CREA; Sr. Cert. Valuer; **EDUC:** BBA, 1958, RE/Ins., Univ. of GA; **GRAD EDUC:** Emory Univ. Law School; **HOME ADD:** 163 Mt. Pauk Rd., Roswell, GA 30075; **BUS ADD:** 5715 Buford Hwy. N.E., Atlanta, GA 30340, (404)993-1198.

MADDOX, Jim——B: Aug. 1, 1948, Fresno, CA, *Pres.*, Maddox & Co., Realtors/Jim Maddox Inc., Builder; **PRIM RE ACT:** Broker, Developer, Builder, Owner/Investor, Property Manager, Syndicator; **OTHER RE ACT:** Restoration hist. prop.; **SERVICES:** Brokerage, prop. mgmt., devel., building; **PROFL AFFIL & HONORS:** NM Realtors Assn.; **EDUC:** BS, 1972, Pol. Sci., Univ. of NM; **HOME ADD:** 715 Gold SE, Albuquerque, NM 87107, (505)843-9230; **BUS ADD:** 6400 Uptown Blvd. N.E., Suite 351, W. Albuquerque, NM 87110, (505)881-0400.

MADISON, Mike——*Professor of Law*, Fordham Univ., School of Law; **PRIM RE ACT:** Attorney; **OTHER RE ACT:** Law Professor, writer, author, practitioner; **SERVICES:** Professor of 1st year property & RE financing; **PROFL AFFIL & HONORS:** NY Bar, VA Bar, Tax Court, Real Property Section of ABA, Author of numerous articles for Law Reviews and Journal of RE Taxation, also co-author, Madison & Dwyer "The Law of RE Financing" WG&L, 1981; Works in progress: "Casebook on RE Financing", Little, Brown; Treatise on Comml. Leasing for WG&L; **EDUC:** BA, 1963, George Washington Univ.; **GRAD EDUC:** JD/LLm, 1966, 1971, Taxation, Harvard/NYU; **EDUC HONORS:** Summa Cum Laude and Phi Beta Kappa (1962); **BUS ADD:** 140 W. 62nd St., New York, NY 10023, (212)841-5343.

MADSEN, Don——B: Nov. 14, 1943, Oklahoma City, OK, *Arch.*, Trammell Crow Co.; **PRIM RE ACT:** Architect, Developer, Builder, Owner/Investor; **SERVICES:** Design, build, spec. builder, devel.; **REP CLIENTS:** Polaroid; GE; Warner Electric Atlantic; AMP, Inc.; Xerox; Amer. Olean; etc.; **PROFL AFFIL & HONORS:** NAIOP; NCARB; **EDUC:** B.Arch., 1969, Arch., CA Poly SLO; **BUS ADD:** 2001 Bryan St., Suite 3200, Dallas, TX 75201, (214)742-2000.

MAEHL, Gary O.——B: May 3, 1928, Milwaukee, WI, *Owner*, Allied Appraisal Servs.; **PRIM RE ACT:** Appraiser; **SERVICES:** Appraisals for market value and ins. value; **REP CLIENTS:** Banks, mort. lenders, trust cos., ins. cos.; **PREV EMPLOY:** Amer. Appraisal Co., 1954-72; **PROFL AFFIL & HONORS:** ASA, SREA, AIREA; **EDUC:** BBA, 1952, Fin., Univ. of WI; **MIL SERV:** USA, E-5; **OTHER ACT & HONORS:** ASA; **HOME ADD:** 3210 SE 10th St., Pompano Bch., FL 33062, (305)943-6623; **BUS ADD:** 900 E. Atlantic Blvd., Pompano Bch., FL 33060, (305)782-3130.

MAESTRE, Ed——B: Aug. 23, 1944, Colombia, SA, *Pres.*, Hispanic Management & Financial Corp.; **PRIM RE ACT:** Broker, Consultant, Property Manager; **OTHER RE ACT:** Mort. Broker; **SERVICES:** Fin. Counselling, Prop. Mgmt., Selling; **REP CLIENTS:** Apt. Owners and Prospective investors for apts.; **PREV EMPLOY:** Risk and Fin. Mgmt., Panamer. Ins. Agcy.; **PROFL AFFIL & HONORS:** Amer. Econ. Assn., Amer. Mgmt. Assn., Bd of Realtors, Amer. Assn. Mort. Brokers; **EDUC:** BBA, 1968, Econ., MS State Univ.; **GRAD EDUC:** MBA, 1976, Econ., MS State Univ.; **HOME ADD:** 2255-A Lindmont Cr., Altanta, GA 30324, (404)262-2534; **BUS ADD:** 2172 Park Terr., Suite 3, College Park, GA 30337, (404)736-1036.

MAFFEO, A. Fred——B: Mar. 22, 1928, Fair Haven, NJ, *Owner*, A. Fred Maffeo Assoc.; **PRIM RE ACT:** Broker, Consultant, Appraiser, Instructor, Assessor; **SERVICES:** Broker, fee appraiser; **REP CLIENTS:** Dept. of Trans., State of NJ, Merrill Lynch, Dupont, Midlantic, Lenders & Investers, Comml. & resid. props.; **PROFL AFFIL & HONORS:** AIREA, SREA, MAI, SRPA, CTA; **EDUC:** AA, 1949, Bus.; **MIL SERV:** USA, Cpl.; **OTHER ACT & HONORS:** Tax Assessor Boro. of Red Bank; **HOME ADD:** 19 Morford Pl., Red Bank, NJ 07701; **BUS ADD:** 569 River Rd., Fair Haven, NJ 07701, (201)741-9333.

MAFFETT, Mack D.——B: July 20, 1936, Mercer Cty., OH, *Counsel*, The Mutual Benefit Life Insurance Co., Farm Investment Div.; **PRIM RE ACT:** Lender; **SERVICES:** Counsel to nat. lender to manage its portfolio, lender has loans and other vehicles throughout the US; **PREV EMPLOY:** Legal rep. for S&L Assn.; **PROFL AFFIL & HONORS:** ABA - RE and Probate Sect.; IA State Bar Assn.; Story Cty. Bar Assn. (Past Pres.); **EDUC:** 1958, Muskingum Coll., New Concord OH; **GRAD EDUC:** LLB, 1960, Univ. of Cincinnati, Coll. of Law; **OTHER ACT & HONORS:** Kiwanis (Past Pres.), Ames-ISU Tennis Club (Past Pres.), Northminster Presby. Church (Elder); **HOME ADD:** 2705 Northwood Dr., Ames, IA 50010, (515)233-2790; **BUS ADD:** PO Box 570, 500 Fifth St., Ames, IA 50010, (515)232-7310.

MAGA, Joseph L., Jr.——B: Apr. 30, 1943, CA, *Shareholder*, Windes & McClaughry Accountancy Corp.; **PRIM RE ACT:** Consultant, Owner/Investor; **OTHER RE ACT:** CPA; **SERVICES:** Tax and fin. planning; **REP CLIENTS:** Synd. and investors in resid., indus. & comml. props.; **PROFL AFFIL & HONORS:** AICPA's, CA Soc. of CPA's; **EDUC:** BA, 1969, Acctg., CA State Univ. at Fullerton; **GRAD EDUC:** MBA, 1981, Taxation, Golden Gate Univ.; **MIL SERV:** US Army, 1965-67, Spec., Army Commendation Medal; **HOME ADD:** 9521 Newfame, Fountain Valley, CA 92708; **BUS ADD:** 611 Anton, Suite 730, PO Box 6750, Costa Mesa, CA 92626, (714)641-1299.

MAGEE, William F.——B: Mar. 2, 1934, Houston, TX, *Pres.*, Gulf Houston Corp.; **PRIM RE ACT:** Broker, Developer, Builder, Owner/Investor, Property Manager, Insuror, Syndicator; **SERVICES:** Design-build services and construction mgmt. with complete in-house arch., engrg., and construction capabilities; **PREV EMPLOY:** Managing Partner, W.T. Magee & Son - RE, Mort. Banking Insurance 1958-1972; **EDUC:** BS, 1968, Mgmt., Fin., Insurance, Southern Methodist U., Univ. of Houston; **MIL SERV:** US Army, E-5 Sgt.; **OTHER ACT & HONORS:** Houston Lodge 1189 AF & AM, Houston, Consistory, Scottish Rite 328, Arabia Temple Shrine; **HOME ADD:** 8323 Partlow, Houston, TX 77040, (713)466-8794; **BUS ADD:** 4530-G, West 34th St., Houston, TX 77092.

MAGEE, William J.——**B:** Oct. 15, 1916, NY City, NY, *Exec. VP*, Cohoes Indus. Terminal, Inc.; **PRIM RE ACT:** Broker, Consultant, Appraiser, Property Manager; **SERVICES:** Complete RE Mgmt.-Indus.-Apts.., Investment Feasibility Services, Appraisers; **REP CLIENTS:** City of Cohoes, NY State, Bauies, Investment Groups, and Private Investors; **PREV EMPLOY:** VP of Construction Firms-Comml., Instnl. and Public Construction Projects; **PROFL AFFIL & HONORS:** Lic. NY State RE Broker; **EDUC:** 1943, Methods Engrg.; **OTHER ACT & HONORS:** Bd. Chmn. Cohoes Model Cities, Program Cohoes Indust. Devel. Commnr., Bd. Member Cohoes Community Ctr., Found. Pres. Cohoes Commerce & Indus. Assn.; **HOME ADD:** 43 Brookwood Dr., Latham, NY 12110, (518)785-5241; **BUS ADD:** 100 N. Mohawk St., Cohoes, NY 12047, (518)237-5000.

MAGGIO, Roger H.——**B:** Feb. 3, 1946, NJ, *Pres.*, Summa Group, Ltd.; **PRIM RE ACT:** Syndicator; **SERVICES:** Structuring, devel. and placement via private ltd. partnership, synd. of comml. props.; **EDUC:** 1965-1966, Liberal Arts, PA State Univ.; 1975-1977, Liberal Arts, Fordham Univ.; **HOME ADD:** 21 Madison Ave., Rochelle Park, NJ 07662; **BUS ADD:** 140 Sylvan Ave., PO Box 1054, Englewood Cliffs, NJ 07632, (201)947-6330.

MAGILL, Douglas E.——**B:** Dec. 28, 1944, Walla Walla, WA, *Chief Operating Officer*, Magill Yerman and Company, Better Homes and Gardens; **PRIM RE ACT:** Broker, Consultant, Developer, Builder, Instructor, Syndicator; **SERVICES:** Resid. and comml. sales & synd., subdiv. and condo. devel., sales, synd. and consultation; **PROFL AFFIL & HONORS:** NAR, HBAM, RNMI, Sales & Mktg. Council of Home Builders Assn., GRI, CRS, CRB; **EDUC:** BA, 1967, Math, Econ., Colgate Univ.; **MIL SERV:** US Army, Sp5, BSM w/OLC; **HOME ADD:** 101 Beech Bark Ln., Towson, MD 21204, (301)321-1110; **BUS ADD:** 118 W Pennsylvania Ave., Baltimore, MD 21204, (301)828-4700.

MAGNAN, Jacques——**B:** Oct. 10, 1947, Quebec, Can, *Assoc.*, Poulin, Dussault, Magnan & Assoc.; **PRIM RE ACT:** Appraiser, Assessor, Insuror; **SERVICES:** Investment counselor, valuation; **REP CLIENTS:** Investment corp., lenders & inst.; **PREV EMPLOY:** Quebec Dept. of Public Works, 1977-78; **PROFL AFFIL & HONORS:** La Corporation des evaluateurs agrees du Quebec, La Corp. des adminstrateurs agees du Quebec, Appraisal Inst. of Can., EA, ADm. A, AACI; **GRAD EDUC:** L SC Adm., 1973, Admin., Univ Laval; **HOME ADD:** 1231 Defoe, Ste-Foy, G2E 4H4, Can, (418)683-2777; **BUS ADD:** 1015 Ave Du Parc, G1S-2W4, Quebec, Can, (418)683-2777.

MAGNONI, Peter H.——**B:** Jan. 21, 1940, LaSalle, IL, *Pres.*, Midwest Mgmt. Inc.; **PRIM RE ACT:** Property Manager; **SERVICES:** Prop. Mgmt.; **REP CLIENTS:** 3000 plus units; **PREV EMPLOY:** Consultant Health Car Prof. for 7 yrs. and fin. VP of Chicago State Univ.; **EDUC:** BS, 1962, Bus. Admin., No. IL Univ.; **GRAD EDUC:** MS, 1964, Bus. Admin., No. IL Univ.; Doctorate, 1969, No. IL Univ.; **HOME ADD:** RR 2, Box 73, Waterloo, WI 53594, (414)648-3331; **BUS ADD:** 111 North Pinkney, Madison, WI 53703, (608)251-9000.

MAGNUSON, John W.——**B:** Aug. 21, 1940, Seattle, WA, *CPM Pres.*, Magnuson Mgmt., Inc., Accredited Managment Organization; **PRIM RE ACT:** Broker, Instructor, Consultant, Property Manager, Owner/Investor; **SERVICES:** Asset/prop. mgmt.; investment RE; consulting; feasibility studies; **REP CLIENTS:** Accountants, atty., synd., investors; **PREV EMPLOY:** Former VP/Gen. Mgr. MDS, Inc., Seattle, WA; **PROFL AFFIL & HONORS:** IREM: WA Assoc. Realtors; HBA; WA Coalition Affordable Housing; C of C-Tacoma and Lakewood; Fife Rotary; Downtown Better Bus. Bureau, Pres. West WA IREM Chap. 27 - 1981; **EDUC:** BA, 1963, Poli. Sci. - Govt. Econ., Univ. of WA; **EDUC HONORS:** Sr. Honorary Org. *FIR TREE*; **MIL SERV:** USAF, Capt., Air Medal; **OTHER ACT & HONORS:** C of C, Rotary; **HOME ADD:** 10317 Interlaaken Dr. SW, Tacoma, WA 98498, (206)581-4900; **BUS ADD:** 10107 South Tacoma Way, PO Box 99479, Tacoma, WA 98499, (206)581-4900.

MAGNUSON, Paul E.——**B:** Dec. 17, 1952, Chicago, IL, *VP*, DiVall RE Investment Corp.; **PRIM RE ACT:** Syndicator; **OTHER RE ACT:** Condo Conversion; **SERVICES:** Devel., direct brokerage of comml. and apt. props., and prop. mgmt.; **REP CLIENTS:** Private investors seeking tax shelter and capital appreciation, smaller pension funds; **PROFL AFFIL & HONORS:** Natl. Synd. Forum Member of RESSI, Realtor; **EDUC:** BBA, 1977, RE and Fin., Univ. of WI; **HOME ADD:** 4521 Deerwood Dr., Madison, WI 53716, (608)221-9734; **BUS ADD:** 111 N. Pinckney St., Madison, WI 53716, (608)251-5559.

MAGOWAN, James L.——**B:** June 22, 1940, NY, *Exec. Dir.*, State of AK, Dept. of Commerce and Econ. Devel., RE Commn.; **PRIM RE ACT:** Regulator; **SERVICES:** Regulation - licensing and enforcement - public assistance; **REP CLIENTS:** Public and licensees; **PREV EMPLOY:** Founder/Partner, RE Brokerage; Founder/Partner, RE Lic. Prep. School, Education; **PROFL AFFIL & HONORS:** Nat. Assn. of Lic. Law Officials Dir.; **EDUC:** BS, 1962, Wildlife Mgmt., Forestry, State Univ. of NY, Coll. of Forestry; **GRAD EDUC:** MEd, 1964, Secondary Edu., Admin., Univ. of Pittsburgh, Syracuse Univ.; **EDUC HONORS:** Ford Found., Teaching Intern; Fort Found., Teaching Scholarship; Experienced Teacher Fellow; **OTHER ACT & HONORS:** NDEA Education Admin. Fellow; 2nd Lt. Civil Air Patrol, Alaska Wing; Aircraft Owners & Pilots Assn.; **HOME ADD:** SRA Box 1420X, Anchorage, AK 99502, (907)345-3298; **BUS ADD:** 620 E. 10th Ave., Rm. 203, Anchorage, AK 99501, (907)272-5508.

MAHAFFEY, Charles Olin, Jr.——**B:** July 19, 1953, Winston-Salem, NC, *RE Mgr.*, Lance, Inc.; **PRIM RE ACT:** Developer, Property Manager; **SERVICES:** Acquisition and devel. of warehouses for co. distribution system, i.e., acquiring land, site design, gen. contracting, and lease negotiation for leased warehouses and rgnl. fin. offices; **PREV EMPLOY:** Altamaha GA Southern Area Planning & Devel. Commn., 1975-1976; Western Piedmont Council of Govts., 1976-1978; Lance, Inc. - Present; **PROFL AFFIL & HONORS:** NC RE Broker; **EDUC:** BS, 1975, Site Planning, E Carolina Univ.; **OTHER ACT & HONORS:** Kappa Sigma Frat.; **HOME ADD:** 1213 Norland Rd., Charlotte, NC 28205, (704)568-2631; **BUS ADD:** POB 32368, Charlotte, NC 28232, (704)554-1421.

MAHAFFEY, Thomas, Jr.——**B:** Feb. 23, 1910, Marion, IN, *Partner*; **PRIM RE ACT:** Developer, Builder, Property Manager; **SERVICES:** Owner & devel. of various apt. complexes; **REP CLIENTS:** Carlton Towers, Carlton Arms & Coquina Kay Arms in St. Petersburg, Carlton Arms, Lake Magdalene Arms of Tampa FL, Carlton Arms, Bradenton FL, Lake Castleton Arms & Westlake Arms of Indianapolis, IN; **PROFL AFFIL & HONORS:** Tr. and Lifetime Dir. of the Nat. Apt. House Assn.; **EDUC:** BCS, 1933, Fin., Notre Dame Univ.; **OTHER ACT & HONORS:** Treas. of Republican Party for the State of IN, Co Chmn. Fin. Comm. Republican Party State of FL; **HOME ADD:** 3242 A 67th Terr. S., St. Petersburg, FL 33712, (813)867-2350; **BUS ADD:** 5000 Coquina Key Dr. SE, St. Petersburg, FL 33705, (813)894-1888.

MAHAN, Paul D.——**B:** May 7, 1930, Cheney, KS, *VP, Treas., CPA*, Canevari Timber Co., Inc.; **PRIM RE ACT:** Consultant, Developer, Owner/Investor; **OTHER RE ACT:** CPA; **SERVICES:** Investment counseling, devel. of comml. props.; **REP CLIENTS:** Indiv. investors in comml. props.; **PREV EMPLOY:** Fox & Co., CPA's; **PROFL AFFIL & HONORS:** AICPA; CA & KS Soc. of CPA's; Alpha Kappa Psi., CPA; **EDUC:** BS, 1958, Acctg. & Taxation, Univ. of Wichita State; **MIL SERV:** USN, DK2; **OTHER ACT & HONORS:** Town Hall; Ingomar Club; Wichita State Univ. Alumni Assn., Bd. of Dir.; Tr. to Bloomfield Found.; **HOME ADD:** 403 Penny Ln., Fortuna, CA 95540, (707)725-5051; **BUS ADD:** 200 Dinsmore Dr., PO Box 686, Fortuna, CA 95540, (707)725-5114.

MAHANEY, Patrick D.——**B:** Nov. 17, 1930, Buffalo, NY, *Mgr., Prop.*, Sea-Land Service, Inc.; **PRIM RE ACT:** Owner/Investor, Property Manager; **SERVICES:** Negotiate leases, mgmt. corp. prop.; **PROFL AFFIL & HONORS:** NACORE, Terminal Prop. Exchange; **EDUC:** BS, 1955, Marine Transp, Kings Point; **GRAD EDUC:** Acctg., NY Univ. Grad. School; **MIL SERV:** USN, LT; **HOME ADD:** 459 Island Rd., Ramsey, NJ 07446, (201)327-8429; **BUS ADD:** PO Box 1050, Elizabeth, NJ 07207, (201)558-6608.

MAHANNA, Simon A., Jr.——**B:** Sept. 14, 1948, St. Louis, MO, *Pres.*, Professional Builders of St. Louis, Inc.; **PRIM RE ACT:** Developer, Builder, Owner/Investor, Syndicator; **PROFL AFFIL & HONORS:** ASCE; NSPE; ASHI, PE in MD, IL and CA; **EDUC:** BSCE, 1970, Const. Mgmt., Univ. of MO; **GRAD EDUC:** MS, 1975, Civil Engrg., Univ. of MO; Dr. of Engrg., Bus./Civil Engrg., Univ. of MO; **EDUC HONORS:** Cum Laude, Magna Cum Laude, Magna Cum Laude; **MIL SERV:** US Army, 1st Lt.; **HOME ADD:** 9006 Middlewood Ct., Sunset Hills, MO 63127; **BUS ADD:** Woodsmill Tower Office Center, 14323 South Forty Outer, Chesterfield, MD 63017, (314)878-0086.

MAHER, James A.——**B:** Dec. 9, 1942, W. Palm Beach, FL, *CPA - Controller*, P.T. Green Const. Co., Inc.; Town and Country Homes, Inc., Fin. and Control; **PRIM RE ACT:** Broker, Consultant, Developer, Builder, Property Manager, Owner/Investor; **OTHER RE ACT:** Primary CPA - Fin. Mgr. Fin.; **SERVICES:** Controller - Devel. and Const. Cos.; **PREV EMPLOY:** CPA; **PROFL AFFIL & HONORS:** FL CPA, AICPA, FL Inst. of CPA, Community Awards for Serv.; **EDUC:** BS, 1964, Acctg., Bus. Admin., FL State Univ., Tallahassee, FL; **GRAD EDUC:** CPA - CPE Educ., Various; **OTHER ACT & HONORS:** Various Clubs and Assns.; **HOME ADD:** 48 Sky Lake Dr., Hendersonville, NC 28739, (704)891-8037; **BUS ADD:** 220 S. Main St., PO Box 1776, Hendersonville, NC 28739, (704)692-0583.

MAHER, Jerard F.——**B:** Nov. 8, 1945, NJ, *Gen. Partner*, Gallagher Maher Assoc.; **PRIM RE ACT:** Consultant, Attorney, Owner/Investor, Property Manager, Syndicator; **SERVICES:** RE Investment advice, devel. and synd. of RE; **REP CLIENTS:** Indiv. and instnl. investors; Broker Dealer security firms; **PREV EMPLOY:** Gen. Counsel, Fed. Bus. Ctrs., Edison NJ; **EDUC:** AB, 1967, Georgetown Univ., Washington, DC; **GRAD EDUC:** JD, 1971, Fordham Univ. Law School, NY, NY; **MIL SERV:** NJ Nat. Guard, Sgt.; **HOME ADD:** RD1 Box 89-B, Far Hills, NJ 07931, (201)234-2575; **BUS ADD:** 999 Mt. Kemble Ave., Morristown, NJ 07960, (201)766-7703.

MAHER, Thomas F.——**B:** St. Louis, MO, *Owner*, Thomas F. Maher Co.; **PRIM RE ACT:** Broker, Consultant, Developer; **SERVICES:** Brokerage, Developing, Consulting - investment RE; **PROFL AFFIL & HONORS:** MAI; CCIM; **EDUC:** BA, 1953, Univ. of MO; **MIL SERV:** USN, Lt.j.g.; **HOME ADD:** E. 1430 Overbluff Rd., Spokane, WA 99203, (509)535-8680; **BUS ADD:** Seafirst Financial Center, Suite 1260, Spokane, WA 99201, (509)838-5604.

MAHON, James F.——**B:** Aug. 22, 1922, NJ, *Asst. Mgr., Area Devel.*, Public Serv. Electric & Gas Co.; **PRIM RE ACT:** Consultant; **SERVICES:** Site searches & econ. studies; **PROFL AFFIL & HONORS:** IREBA, (NYC), NJ Ind. Devel. Assn., NE Ind. Devel. Assn., Com. Ind. Inv. Brokers of SJ, Nat. Assn. of Indus. & Office Parks, Nat. Soc. of Profl. Engrs.; **EDUC:** BS, 1943, Physics, St. Peters Coll., Jersey City, NJ; **GRAD EDUC:** ME, 1948, St. Inst. of Tech., Hoboken, NJ; **MIL SERV:** USAF, 1st Lt., Air Medal, POW; **OTHER ACT & HONORS:** SJ Soc. of PE (Past Pres.), Dir. Joint Burlington Econ. Devel. Corp.; **HOME ADD:** 265 Kings Hwy W, Haddonfield, NJ 08033, (609)428-9388; **BUS ADD:** 418 Federal St. cCamden, NJ 08101, (609)365-7411.

MAHONEY, John J.——**B:** May 8, 1943, Columbus, OH, *Partner*, Mahoney & Zentz; **PRIM RE ACT:** Attorney; **OTHER RE ACT:** Title Ins.; Pres., Attorney's Title Corp.; **SERVICES:** Gen. RE, condo. conversion, settlements; **PROFL AFFIL & HONORS:** ABA; DC Bar Assn.; DC Builders Assn.; DC Land Title Assn.; **EDUC:** BA, 1966, Philosophy, Providence Coll.; **GRAD EDUC:** MA, 1970, Psych., St. Stephens Coll.; JD, 1973, Law, Catholic Univ.; **HOME ADD:** 412 A St.S.E., Washington, DC 20003, (202)547-0008; **BUS ADD:** 310 6th St. S.E., Washington, DC 20003, (202)547-8989.

MAHONEY, L. James——**B:** Dec. 16, 1953, *VP*, The Zane Scott Co.; **PRIM RE ACT:** Broker, Consultant, Owner/Investor; **OTHER RE ACT:** RE fin., mort. banking; **SERVICES:** Debt & equity fin. (arranging & consultation); **REP CLIENTS:** Devels., instnl. investors; **PREV EMPLOY:** Philipsborn Co. of TX; First City Bank, Austin; **EDUC:** BBA, 1976, Fin., Univ. of TX at Austin; **HOME ADD:** 1220 Harvard, Houston, TX 77008; **BUS ADD:** 9801 Westheimer, Ste. 333, Houston, TX 77042, (713)266-9100.

MAHONEY, Lucille Scott——**B:** Jan. 11, 1925, Pittsburgh, PA, *Pres./Broker*, Scott-Mahoney Real Estate, Inc.; **PRIM RE ACT:** Broker, Appraiser, Instructor; **OTHER RE ACT:** Mort. negotiator, securing approvals for land devel., Comml. & resid. Salesperson; **SERVICES:** Sales, leases, resid., comml. & indus.; **PREV EMPLOY:** Merrill-Lynch Realty-Hammill Quinlan, Stroschein Rd., Monroeville, PA 15146; **PROFL AFFIL & HONORS:** PAR, NAR, Grtr Pittsburgh Bd. of Realtors, Notary Gallery of Homes, West PA Multilist, Better Bus. Bur., Statewide CI&I MLS, Broker; **EDUC:** 1959-60, RE, Univ. of Pittsburgh, PA; **GRAD EDUC:** 1972, RE, Barry Coll., N. Miami, FL; **HOME ADD:** 1228 Old Concord Rd., Monroeville, PA 15146, (412)373-1275; **BUS ADD:** 3936 Monroeville Blvd., Monroeville, PA 15146, (412)373-8870.

MAHONEY, Patrick D.——**B:** Nov. 14, 1930, Buffalo, NY, *Mgr., Prop.*, Sea-Land Serv., Inc., Subs. of R.J. Reynolds Industries; **OTHER RE ACT:** Corporate RE Mgr.; **SERVICES:** Lease & Sublease Negotiations; **PREV EMPLOY:** Prop. Rep., Port Authority; **PROFL AFFIL & HONORS:** NACORE, IREBA, Terminal Prop. Exchange; **EDUC:** BS, 1955, Transportation, King's Point; **MIL SERV:** USNR, Lt.; **OTHER ACT & HONORS:** Recipient Exec. Dir. Award, Port Authority of NY & NJ; **HOME ADD:** 459 Island Rd., 02446, Ramsey, NJ, (201)327-8429; **BUS ADD:** PO Box 1050, Elizabeth, NJ 07207, (201)558-6608.

MAHONEY, Robert W.——**B:** Oct. 7, 1944, Big Spring, TX, *Part.*, M & W Investments; **OTHER RE ACT:** Outdoor advertising, invest. counseling, prop. mgmt., resid. land devel., comml. income props. devel.; **REP CLIENTS:** Indiv. & inst. investors; **PREV EMPLOY:** Continental Natl. Bank, Fort Worth, TX, First City Nat. Bank, Arlington, TX; **EDUC:** BBA, 1967, Banking, Fin. & RE, N TX State Univ.; **OTHER ACT & HONORS:** Past pres. Prof. Bus. Men's Club, Young Men for Arlington, Boy Scouts of Amer., Jr. Achievement, Jaycees; **HOME ADD:** 3906 Shady Creek Dr., Arlington, TX 76013, (817)277-5097; **BUS ADD:** 1211 S. Bowen Rd., Suite 212, Arlington, TX 76013, (817)460-6600.

MAHOOD, Willard S.——**B:** Aug. 1, 1942, Wilmington, DE, *Investment Sales*, Coldwell Banker Comml. RE Servs.; **PRIM RE ACT:** Broker; **SERVICES:** Comml. Investment Sales; **REP CLIENTS:** Maj. Fin. Instns.; **PREV EMPLOY:** Bankers Trust Co. 1970-81; **EDUC:** BA, 1964, Sociology/Anthropology, Univ. of VA; **GRAD EDUC:** MBA, 1970, Intl. Fin., Univ. of Chicago; **MIL SERV:** USN, Lt. Comdr., Navy Commendation; **HOME ADD:** 20 W. 77th St., New York, NY 10024, (212)595-0299; **BUS ADD:** 600 Third Ave., New York, NY 10016, (212)867-5900.

MAHR, F. Sanford——**B:** Mar. 6, 1949, Buffalo, NY, *Pres.*, Mahr Realty and Devel. Co.; **PRIM RE ACT:** Broker, Consultant, Developer, Owner/Investor, Property Manager, Syndicator; **SERVICES:** Comml. and indus. sales and leasing, prop. mgmt., fin. and synd., investment counseling, private sector bus. investors and indus., instnl. prop. owners and investors; **PROFL AFFIL & HONORS:** Greater Buffalo Bd. of Realtors Lic. RE Broker NY, Lic. RE Broker MA, Affiliated in Dallas, TX, CCIM candidate; **EDUC:** 1975, Bus. Mgmt. & Fin., Canisius Coll. and State Univ. of NY at Buffalo; **OTHER ACT & HONORS:** Bd. of Dir. Fed. Credit Unions; **BUS ADD:** 534 Delaware Ave., Buffalo, NY 14202, (716)833-1000.

MAIDMAN, Richard H.——**B:** Nov. 17, 1933, New York, NY; **PRIM RE ACT:** Attorney, Consultant, Developer, Owner/Investor; **PREV EMPLOY:** Dir. The Central Foundry Co., Mem. NY Stock Exchange, Holt Ala. 1963-71; Dir. Microbiol Scis. Inc., Member Boston Stock Exchange, Providence, RI, 1971- ; Sec. 1971- , pres. MBS Equities, Inc., NYC, 1975- ; Gen. Partner, Barcelona Hotel Ltd., Miami Bch. FL, 1975- ; Assoc., firm Saxe, Bacon & O'Shea, NYC, 1962-64; Partner, Weiner, Maidman & Goldman, NYC, 1964-67; pvt. practice law NYC FL, 1968- ; Of Counsel Shwal, Thompson & Boch, NYC and Geneva, Switzerland, 1976- ; Gen. Counsel, NY Young Republican Club, 1969; Chmn. Bd. Met. Rep. Club, NYC 1969-70; **PROFL AFFIL & HONORS:** RE Bd. of NY; ABA; NY Bar Assn.; FL Bar Assn.; Bar City of NY; Bankruptcy Lawyers Assn. of NYC, Contributed articles to profl. journals, Legislative Counsel; **EDUC:** BA, 1955, Williams Coll.; **GRAD EDUC:** JD, 1959, Yale Univ.; Postgrad, 1977, NY Univ. Grad. Sch. of Law; 1960, NY Univ. Grad. School of Bus.; 1960, NYU Grad. School of Bus.; **HOME ADD:** 300 East 56th St., New York, NY 10022; **BUS ADD:** 485 Madison Ave., New York, NY 10022, (212)755-0500.

MAIER, Richard N.——**B:** Aug. 23, 1949, Pittsburgh, PA, *Pres.*, Green Mark Corps., A subsidiary of Gerlad D. Hines Interests; **PRIM RE ACT:** Developer, Builder, Owner/Investor; **PREV EMPLOY:** Mellon Bank, N.A., Albee Homes, Inc., Allegheny Cty. Housing Auth.; **PROFL AFFIL & HONORS:** Greater Houston Builders Assn., Houston C of C, Reg. RE Broker; **EDUC:** BS, 1971, Poli. Sci. & Philos., Univ. of Pitt.; **GRAD EDUC:** Duquesne Univ. RE School; **HOME ADD:** 2229 Mimosa, No. 8, Houston, TX 77019; **BUS ADD:** 6220 Westpark, Suite 225, Houston, TX 77057, (713)780-1130.

MAIER, Walter——**B:** Aug. 17, 1906, Austria, *Owner*, Maier-Perlin; **PRIM RE ACT:** Developer, Builder, Owner/Investor, Property Manager; **PREV EMPLOY:** Exec. VP, Foster Oil, Inc., Texaco Dist.; **GRAD EDUC:** Dr. of Pol. Sci., 1929, Univ. of Innsbruck, Austria; **MIL SERV:** Military Govt., Pvt.; **HOME ADD:** 11559 Sunset Blvd., Los Angeles, CA 90049, (213)879-0149; **BUS TEL:** (213)386-1816.

MAIER, Walter A.——**B:** Dec. 7, 1925, Jacksonville, FL, *Dist. Right of Way Consultant*, FL Dept. of Transportation, 4th Dist.; **PRIM RE ACT:** Broker, Instructor, Consultant, Appraiser, Owner/Investor; **SERVICES:** Counseling, Consultant, Valuation, Eminent Domain Evaluation; **PREV EMPLOY:** Title & Trust Co. of FL (1946-1957), FL State Road Dept. (1957-1971), FL State Dept. of Trans. (1971-present); **PROFL AFFIL & HONORS:** NARA, SREA, Intl. R/W Assn., SR/WA; CRA; SRA; Past Pres. & Intl. Dir., Intl. R/W Assn.; **MIL SERV:** USN, 1942-45; **HOME ADD:** 1000 River Reach Dr., Apt.409, Ft. Lauderdale, FL 33315, (305)524-5612; **BUS ADD:** 780 SW 24th St., Ft. Lauderdale, FL 33315, (305)467-4432.

MAIHOCK, Donald J.——*Mgr. Corp. Fac. Plng.*, North American Philips Co.; **PRIM RE ACT:** Property Manager; **BUS ADD:** 100 East 42nd St., New York, NY 10017, (212)697-3600.*

MAIKRANZ, Larry W.——**B:** Dec. 29, 1948, Evansville, IN, *Pres.*, Maikranz Auction Ins. & RE; **PRIM RE ACT:** Broker, Appraiser, Insuror; **OTHER RE ACT:** Auctioneer; **SERVICES:** Gen. Ins.; RE Brokerage; **REP CLIENTS:** Inst., Dir. Credit Union & S&L's; **PROFL AFFIL & HONORS:** NAR; IN Assn. Realtors; NAIFA; IN Auctioneer Assn.; Nat. Auctioneers Assn.; **EDUC:** BS, 1972, Bus. Admin. Mktg., Univ. of Evansville; **GRAD EDUC:** 1975, Auctioneering, RE, IN Coll. of Auctioneering, Univ. Evansville; **MIL SERV:**

USA, 1st Lt.; **OTHER ACT & HONORS:** Appraisal Inst. Univ. of Evansville; **HOME ADD:** 1710 Division St., Evansville, IN 47714, (812)479-3835; **BUS ADD:** 1710 Division St., Evansville, IN 47714, (812)422-1101.

MAIN, Gail——**B:** July 23, 1945, St. Louis, MO, *Pres.*, RE/MAX of Americs, Inc.; **PRIM RE ACT:** Broker; **SERVICES:** RE franchising; **PROFL AFFIL & HONORS:** NAR, CO Assn. of Realtors, Broker, CRB; **EDUC:** BS, 1968, Mktg., S. IL Univ.; **HOME ADD:** 10266 E. Fair Pl., Englewood, CO 8011O, (303)779-0915; **BUS ADD:** 5251 S. Quebec, Englewood, CO 80110, (303)770-5531.

MAIOCCHI, Christine T.——**B:** Dec. 24, 1949, New York, NY, *Mgr. of RE*, G. K. Technologies Inc.; **PRIM RE ACT:** Broker, Attorney, Regulator; **OTHER RE ACT:** Indust. & Comml. RE; **SERVICES:** All site information, lease negotiation, office const. necessary for office relocation; **REP CLIENTS:** All sub. of GK Technologies; **PREV EMPLOY:** Getty Oil Co., The Home Ins. Co., Paine Webber; **PROFL AFFIL & HONORS:** ABA & NY State Bar Assn., RE Section Nat. Assn. of Corporate RE Execs., NY Chap. VP & Sec.; **EDUC:** BA, 1971, Urban Studies/Pol. Sci., Fordham Univ.; **GRAD EDUC:** MA, 1972, Fordham Univ.; JD, 1974, RE/Labor Law, Fordham Univ. Law School; **EDUC HONORS:** Participation in accelerated BA/MA Program, Awarded NYS Legislative Internship, Student Clerk for the Fed. Ct., Southern District; **HOME ADD:** 84 Clinton Ave., Dobbs Ferry, NY 10522, (914)693-0014; **BUS ADD:** 500 West Putnam Ave., Greenwich, CT 06830, (212)437-6129.

MAJEWSKI, Edward J.——**B:** Mar. 9, 1927, New York, *Dir., RE and Mort. Investments*, New York State Employees Retirement System, Cash Mgmt. and Investments; **PRIM RE ACT:** Lender; **PREV EMPLOY:** Sr. VP - Greenwich Savings Bank Mort. Dept.; **PROFL AFFIL & HONORS:** NY RE Bd., Mort. Bankers Assn. of NY, Long Is. Appraisal Soc., Columbia Appraisal Soc., Mort. Inst. of NY; **EDUC:** BS, 1948, Psych., Fordham Univ.; **MIL SERV:** US Naval Res.; **OTHER ACT & HONORS:** US Power Squadrons - South Shore Squadron; **HOME ADD:** 201 Anchorage Dr., West Islip, NY 11795, (516)661-8359; **BUS ADD:** 270 Broadway, Suite 2300, New York, NY 10007, (212)587-5027.

MAJOR, Steve——**B:** June 13, 1930, Chicago, IL, *Pres.*, Major Financial Corp.; **PRIM RE ACT:** Broker, Consultant, Appraiser, Owner/Investor, Property Manager; **OTHER RE ACT:** Mort. Broker; **SERVICES:** Fin. Consultant, Comml. Sale & Mort. Brokerage/ Mgmt.; **REP CLIENTS:** Nalac, Allianz, Hauser Holding Co., C & C Dev. - Mutual of NY; **PREV EMPLOY:** Sr. VP Northland Mort. Co. Mort. Supervisor Elas; **PROFL AFFIL & HONORS:** AIREA, Soc. of RE Appraisers - Natl. Assn. of Review Appraisers, MAI, SRA, CRA; **EDUC:** 1948-1954, Econ., NW Univ., U. of WI, LaSalle Extension Univ.; **MIL SERV:** US Natl. Guard, Sgt. Maj.; **OTHER ACT & HONORS:** Mason-Shriner; **HOME ADD:** 4705 N. Shore Dr., Mound, MN 55364, (612)472-1698; **BUS ADD:** 7920 Cedar Ave., Bloomington, MN 55420.

MAKENS, Hugh H.——**B:** Feb. 22, 1939, *Atty.*, Warner, Norcross & Judd; **PRIM RE ACT:** Attorney; **SERVICES:** Devel., synd., condo., legal servs.; **PREV EMPLOY:** 1972-1978, Corp. & Securities Bureau MI Dept. of Commerce, Dir.; 1966-1972, US Securities & Exchange Commn., Detroit Branch, Trial Atty.; 1964-1966, US Army Electronics Command, Ft. Monmouth, NJ, Sec. Trial Counsel; **PROFL AFFIL & HONORS:** MI Bar Assn.; IL Bar Assn.; ABA; Fed. Bar Assn.; Central Securities Admin. Council, Past Pres., 1975-1976; US Securities & Exchange Commn., Report Coordinating Grp., 1973-1976; Commodity Futures Trading Commn., Advisory Comm. on State Jurisdiction and Responsibilities, 1977-1978; Atty. Gen. Advisory Comm. on Rules to Implement the MI Consumer Protection Act, 1977-1978; Atty. Gen. Mcpl. Fin. Advisory Comm., 1977-1978; Gov. Advisory Commn. on Admin. Law, 1977; N. Amer. Securities Admin. Assn., Franchise Law Advisory Comm., 1980 -, Recipient of Gov. Award for Distinguished Public Employee, 1976; Marquis' Who's Who in Govt.; N. Amer. Securities Admin., Past Pres. 1976-1977, Past Chmn., Uniform Require. Comm., Past VChmn., ALI-ABA Proposed Fed. Code Comm., Past Member - RE Ltd. Partnership Comm., Oil & Gas Comm., and CFTC Liaison Comm.; Fed. Bar Assn., Detroit Chap., Treas., Sec., VP; MI Bar Assn., Council Member, Admin. Law Sect., 1977-1979; Council Member, Corp., Fin. and Bus. Law Sect., 1980-; Council Member, Antitrust Law Sect., 1979-; **EDUC:** BS, 1961, Acctg./Econ., MI Technol. Univ.; **GRAD EDUC:** JD, 1964, Law, Northwestern Univ. School of Law; **EDUC HONORS:** Who's Who in Amer. Colls. and Univs., 1961; Cum Laude, Dean's List; **MIL SERV:** US Army, Capt.; **OTHER ACT & HONORS:** Dir., Corp. & Securities Bureau, State of MI; **HOME ADD:** 7555 Aspenwood, S.E., Grand Rapids, MI 49508, (616)942-9426; **BUS ADD:** 900 Old Kent Bldg., One Vandenberg Ctr., Grand Rapids, MI 49503, (616)459-6121.

MALAKER, A. Deane——**B:** Apr. 9, 1932, Aurora, IL, *VP*, Chicago Title Ins., Co., MI; **PRIM RE ACT:** Attorney, Property Manager; **SERVICES:** Title insurance and related svcs.; **PROFL AFFIL & HONORS:** IN Bar Assn.; State Bar of MI; **EDUC:** BS, 1958, Bus., IN Univ. School of Law; **GRAD EDUC:** LLB, 1960; **HOME ADD:** 3261 Roxbury Dr., Troy, MI 48084; **BUS ADD:** 4000 Town Ctr., Suite 980, Southfield, MI 48075, (313)352-4545.

MALAND, Robert A.——**B:** Oct. 2, 1940, Story City, IA, *Pres. and Dir.*, Maland Management Consultants, Ltd.; **PRIM RE ACT:** Consultant, Banker, Lender, Syndicator; **OTHER RE ACT:** Find investors and/or lenders; **SERVICES:** Represent investors/owners in devel., acquiring or divesting comml./bus. - form synd. to do same; **PROFL AFFIL & HONORS:** Intl. Soc. of Fin., Soc. of Mgmt. Consultants, Cert. Fin. Planner; **EDUC:** BS, 1976, Econ., Univ. of WI, Whitewater; **GRAD EDUC:** MBA, 1977, Mgrl./Econ., Univ. of WI; **MIL SERV:** USAF, 1961-1976, Mjr., Joint Serv. Commendation, Pentagon; **OTHER ACT & HONORS:** Amer. Entrepreneurs Assn., Intl. Entrepreneurs Assn., Intl. Assn. of Bus. & Fin. Consultants, WI Independent Bus. Toastmasters Intl., C of C, Downtown Bus. Assn., Outstanding Young Man - 1980, Dist. Toastmaster of the Year - 1980; **HOME ADD:** 427 Parkview Terrace, Marshfield, WI 54449, (715)387-3310; **BUS ADD:** 455 S. Knowles Ave., New Richmond, WI 54017, (715)246-3223.

MALASKY, Donald C.——**B:** July 16, 1936, Pittsburgh, PA, *Partner*, M&S Investment Co.; **PRIM RE ACT:** Developer, Owner/Investor, Property Manager; **PREV EMPLOY:** Gen. Mgr. - B&I Management - Youngstown, OH; **EDUC:** BS in Econ., 1958, RE and Fin., Univ. of PA, Wharton School of Fin. & Commerce; **OTHER ACT & HONORS:** Pres. of ARM, Ltd. 100 Lakeview Dr., Royal Palm Beach, FL 33411; Condominium Developers, State of FL; **HOME ADD:** 21031 Arms Dr., Girard, OH 44420, (216)759-0320; **BUS ADD:** 469 W. Market St., Warren, OH 44481, (216)399-1879.

MALIN, Thaw——**B:** Apr. 8, 1917, Philadelphia, PA, *Mgr., Farm & land Div.*, Holmes Agency; **PRIM RE ACT:** Broker, Consultant, Appraiser; **SERVICES:** Land, urban and rural, horse farms, special projects, appraising, consulting, counselling, exchanging, marketing; **PREV EMPLOY:** Thaw Malin Assoc., Realtor; **PROFL AFFIL & HONORS:** Natl. accredited member FLI, CT, NJ, NY, PA Chap's.; PA RE Exchangers; ULI; Regl. Assoc. Horse Farms of America; American Farmland Trust, Omega Tau Rho, Honor Soc., NAR; Farm and Land Realtor of the yr. 1979; **EDUC:** BA, 1939, Arch., Yale Univ., Kent School, Kent CT; **EDUC HONORS:** Cum Laude Soc.; **MIL SERV:** Mil. Intellignece, WW II and Korean War; **OTHER ACT & HONORS:** Chmn. S. Central Dist., Republican Comm. Morris Cty.; **HOME ADD:** 7 Glen Gary Dr., Mendham, NJ 07945, (201)543-7155; **BUS ADD:** PO Box 428, Mendham, NJ 07945, (201)543-4371.

MALLENDR, William H.——*VP*, Talley Industries, Inc.; **PRIM RE ACT:** Property Manager; **BUS ADD:** PO Box 849, Mesa, AZ 85201, (602)898-2200.*

MALLIN, John R.——**B:** July 28, 1950, Woonsocket, RI, *Atty.*, Updike, Kelly and Spellacy, P.C.; **PRIM RE ACT:** Attorney; **SERVICES:** All serv. incident to resid. and comml. acquisitions and devel.; **REP CLIENTS:** Lenders, indiv. and corp. prop. owners and mgrs. including Hartford Fire Ins. Co., J.C. Penny Co., CT B & T CO., Hartford Nat.Bank, Dimeo Const. Co., The Wm. B. Martin Co.; **PROFL AFFIL & HONORS:** CT Bar Assn., ABA; **EDUC:** BA, 1972, Philosophy, Providence Coll.; **GRAD EDUC:** JD, 1975, Harvard Law School; **EDUC HONORS:** Summa Cum Laude; **OTHER ACT & HONORS:** Jaycees, Past VP & Tr. Wethersfield; **HOME ADD:** 100 Wildwood Rd., Wethersfield, CT 06109, (203)563-1908; **BUS ADD:** 1 Constitution Pl., Hartford, CT 06103, (203)547-1120.

MALLIS, Charles H.S.——**B:** Oct. 31, 1950, Miami, FL, *Mgr.*, Citicorp, Intl. Fin. Instit.; **PRIM RE ACT:** Banker; **SERVICES:** Intl. Funding; **REP CLIENTS:** Fin. Instit. from Switzerland; **EDUC:** BS, 1972, Aerospace Engrg./Computer Sci., GA Tech.; **GRAD EDUC:** MBA, 1979, Fin./RE, Univ. of UT; **EDUC HONORS:** With Honors, Sigma Gamma Tau; **MIL SERV:** USAF, Capt., Meritorious Service Medal; **HOME ADD:** 400 E 71st St., Apt. 21A, New York, NY 10021, (212)288-1628; **BUS ADD:** 111 Wall St., NY, NY 10017, (212)288-1628.

MALLORY, Richard——**B:** July 3, 1945, Rapid City, SD, *Sr. Partner*, Allen, Matkins, Leck, Gamble & Mallory; **PRIM RE ACT:** Attorney; **SERVICES:** Legal advice relative to acquisition, fin., devel. and mktg. of comml. and indus. RE; **REP CLIENTS:** Devels. and instnl. lenders and comml. and indus. real prop. projects; **PROFL AFFIL & HONORS:** Lecturer, Continuing Educ. of the Bar for programs involving leasing, mktg. and fin. of real prop.; **EDUC:** BS, 1966, fin. and RE, Univ. of CA; **GRAD EDUC:** JD, 1969, Corp.and RE Law, Stanford Law School; **EDUC HONORS:** Phi Kappa Phi, Beta

Gamma Sigma; **HOME ADD:** 3536 Twin Lake Ridge, Westlake Vill., CA 91361, (213)991-4761; **BUS ADD:** 707 Wilshire Blvd. 54th Fl., L.A., CA 90017, (213)620-0777.

MALLOT, Jerry M.——B: Dec. 31, 1947, Parsons, KS, *Sr. VP*, Wichita Area Chamber of Commerce; **OTHER RE ACT:** Econ. devel.; **PROFL AFFIL & HONORS:** Nat. Assn. of Corp. RE, Amer. Econ. Devel. Council, SIDC, IDRC, KS Indus. Devel. Assn., CID, Silver Stirrup Award (KS); **EDUC:** BBA, 1970, Econ., Wichita State Univ.; **GRAD EDUC:** MA, 1978, Econ., Wichita State Univ.; **MIL SERV:** US Army, Capt.; **OTHER ACT & HONORS:** YMCA, Crestview Ctry. Club, AISEC, District Export Council, Dept. of Comm.; **HOME ADD:** 218 North Broadview, Wichita, KS 67208, (316)682-4050; **BUS ADD:** 350 West Douglas, Wichita, KS 67202, (316)265-7771.

MALNOR, Robert J.——B: Jan. 29, 1924, Moran, MI, *VP*, State Wide Real Estate of Escanaba, MI, Comml.; **PRIM RE ACT:** Broker, Consultant, Instructor, Syndicator; **OTHER RE ACT:** Sales; **SERVICES:** Listing & selling assistance to other brokers; **REP CLIENTS:** 80+ franchised state wide RE offices in MI and WI; **PREV EMPLOY:** Salesman, Sears Roebuck, Pitney Bowes; **PROFL AFFIL & HONORS:** VP Bd. & Nat. Bd. of Realtors; CCIM Chap. of MI, GRI; CCIM; **MIL SERV:** US Army Inf., Sgt., 2 Bronze Stars; **OTHER ACT & HONORS:** Past Pres., Gladstone C of C; **HOME ADD:** 1125 Minn. Ave., Gladstone, MI 49837, (906)428-9757; **BUS ADD:** 2209 Ludington St., Escanaba, MI 49837, (906)786-1308.

MALONE, David J., Jr.——B: Feb. 12, 1943, Mayfield, KY, *VP RE*, Hospital Corp. of Amer.; **PRIM RE ACT:** Broker, Syndicator, Developer, Property Manager; **SERVICES:** Site selection; dev. of medical office buildings; **EDUC:** BA, 1965, Hist., Vanderbilt Univ.; **GRAD EDUC:** MA, 1967, Hist, Vanderbilt Univ.; **MIL SERV:** USAF; Sgt.; **HOME ADD:** 909 Lakemont Dr, Nashville, TN 37220, (615)373-0334; **BUS ADD:** 1 Park Plaza, Nashville, TN 37220, (615)327-9551.

MALONE, James——*Pres.*, Facet Enterprises, Inc.; **PRIM RE ACT:** Property Manager; **BUS ADD:** 7030 S. Yale Ave., Tulsa, OK 74177, (918)492-1800.*

MALONE, Thomas J.——B: Mar. 3, 1925, St. Louis, MO, *Pres.*, Comml. Realty Sold, Inc., BAREB Bus. Brokerage; **PRIM RE ACT:** Broker, Consultant; **OTHER RE ACT:** Bus. Brokerage, Comml. & Indus. RE; **SERVICES:** Nat. service to buyers and sellers; **PREV EMPLOY:** Founding Pres. at Realty Programming Corp. (Homes for Living) in 1962; Founding Pres. of Interstate Referral Service (Realty USA) in 1972; **PROFL AFFIL & HONORS:** Amer. Entrepreneur Assn., Listed in Who's Who in MO, 1974 Issue; **MIL SERV:** USN, RM 3/c, Asiatic Pacific Ribbon w/4 Battle Stars; Philippine Liberation Ribbon w/2 Battle Stars; **HOME ADD:** Rt. 1, Box 236, Warrenton, MO 63383, (314)456-4020; **BUS ADD:** 13422 Clayton Rd., St. Louis, MO 63131, (314)576-6822.

MALONEY, John T.——B: Feb. 12, 1936, *Pres.*, J.T. Maloney & Associates Ltd.; **PRIM RE ACT:** Broker, Consultant, Developer, Owner/Investor, Property Manager; **OTHER RE ACT:** RE Exchanging; **SERVICES:** Investment counseling, confidential site acquisitions, all types of comml. leasing, consulting and negotiating, national accounts, corp. and small bus., as well as indiv. owners and investors; **PROFL AFFIL & HONORS:** MI Assn. of Realtors Exchange Div.; **EDUC:** BBA, 1958, Acctg., General Motors Inst.; **GRAD EDUC:** Numerous courses and seminars; **OTHER ACT & HONORS:** Flint Rotary; Past Bd. Member of Flint Sales & Mktg. Exec.; **HOME ADD:** 404 N. McKinley Rd., Flushing, MI 48433, (313)659-5531; **BUS ADD:** 1810 Genesee Towers, Flint, MI 48502, (313)232-7409.

MALONEY, Vincent J.——*Dir., RE*, Colt Industries, Inc.; **PRIM RE ACT:** Property Manager; **BUS ADD:** 430 Park Ave., New York, NY 10022, (212)940-0400.*

MALONEY, William——B: Jan. 26, 1930, Paterson, NJ, Trans American Development; **PRIM RE ACT:** Consultant, Developer, Builder, Owner/Investor, Property Manager, Syndicator; **SERVICES:** Complete energy, ecological and economic; **HOME ADD:** 32 Dover St., Paterson, NJ 07501, (201)881-7171; **BUS ADD:** 261 Marshall St., Paterson, NJ 07503, (201)881-7070.

MALOTT, James S.——B: June 3, 1940, Palo Alto, CA, *Prin.*, James Malott & Assoc., Architects & Developers; **PRIM RE ACT:** Architect, Developer, Builder, Owner/Investor, Property Manager, Syndicator; **OTHER RE ACT:** Gen. partner, several ltd. partnerships, hotels, apts., offices; **SERVICES:** Architecture, devel., prop. mgmt., const.; **PREV EMPLOY:** Sert Jackson & Assoc., Architects, 1968-1970; Hertzka & Knowles, Architects, 1970-1971; **PROFL AFFIL & HONORS:** NCARB Certificate; Arch. Lic. in CA, MA, AZ, IA, MISL Design Awards; **EDUC:** BA, 1962, Arch./Sculpture, Stanford Univ.; **GRAD EDUC:** MA, 1966, Sculpture, Univ. of DE; MArch., 1969, Harvard Grad. School of Design; **EDUC HONORS:** Various Sculpture Prizes; **MIL SERV:** USN; Lt.; 1962-1966; **OTHER ACT & HONORS:** Bohemian Club; San Francisco Planning & Urban Research (SPUR); Chmn., Bd. of Adjustments & Review (Design Review) Tiburon, CA; **HOME ADD:** 1 Sutter St., Ste. 501, San Francisco, CA 94104, (415)981-6556; **BUS ADD:** 1 Sutter St., Ste. 501, San Francisco, CA 94104, (415)981-6556.

MALOY, Carol——B: Oct. 19, 1954, NY, *Assoc.*, Donaldson, Lufkin & Jenrette, Inc., DLJ RE, Inc.; **PRIM RE ACT:** Broker, Consultant; **EDUC:** AB, 1976, Psych., Mt. Holyoke Coll.; **GRAD EDUC:** MBA, 1981, Fin., Mktg., Columbia Univ. Grad. School of Bus.; **EDUC HONORS:** Cum Laude; **HOME ADD:** 1641 Third Ave., New York, NY 10028; **BUS ADD:** 140 Broadway, New York, NY 10005, (212)747-9742.

MALZO, Joseph, Jr.——B: Sept. 7, 1943, NY, *Asst. VP*, Citicorp. Real Estate Inc.; **PRIM RE ACT:** Consultant, Appraiser, Banker, Lender; **SERVICES:** Fin.; **REP CLIENTS:** Devel.; **PROFL AFFIL & HONORS:** Soc. of RE Appraisers; Mort. Bankers Assn.; NY RE Bd., SRPA; **EDUC:** BBA, 1964, RE/Fin., Univ. of Miami; **OTHER ACT & HONORS:** NY State Assessment Review Bd.; **HOME ADD:** 22 Allen Rd. RD 2, Peekskill, NY 10566, (914)737-3565; **BUS ADD:** 399 Park Ave., NY, NY 10043, (212)559-5447.

MANAK, John Robert——B: Dec. 30, 1939, Weehawken, NJ, *Mgr., Area Devel.*, Consolidated Edison Co. of NY, Inc., Div. Operations Central Staff; **PRIM RE ACT:** Consultant; **SERVICES:** Assist mfrs. to relocate or expand their bus., includes area studies, RE location, street closing, fin. and govt. coordination; **PROFL AFFIL & HONORS:** SIR, Edison Electic Inst., Edison Engrg. Soc.; **EDUC:** BBA, 1965, Mktg., Psych., Pace Coll.; **GRAD EDUC:** MBA, 1972, Mktg. Mgmt., Pace Coll.; **EDUC HONORS:** Dean's List; **OTHER ACT & HONORS:** Member Bd. of Dirs. - Pace Univ., Lubin Grad. School of Bus. Alumni Assn.; **HOME ADD:** 26 Nicholson Dr., Chatham Township, NJ 07928, (201)635-5706; **BUS ADD:** 4 Irving Pl., New York, NY 10003, (212)460-4153.

MANCHEE, William L.——B: Aug. 22, 1947, Ventura, CA, *Attorney*; **PRIM RE ACT:** Attorney, Owner/Investor; **OTHER RE ACT:** Rep. many planned unit devel. Assn.; **SERVICES:** Closing, planning and joint venture syndications, etc.; **REP CLIENTS:** Raldon Corp., Broadway Village Residents Assn., PM Life Ins. Co.; **PROFL AFFIL & HONORS:** ABA, State Bar of TX, Dallas Estate Planning Bar Assn., C of C; **EDUC:** BA, 1965, Poli Sci, Econ,, UCLA; **GRAD EDUC:** JD, 1975, Law, SMU; **HOME ADD:** 2725 Teakwood Ln, Plano, TX 75075; **BUS ADD:** 13601 Preston Rd., #718W, Dallas, TX 75240, (214)233-2485.

MANDEL, Bruce Ansel——B: Mar 16., 1952, Minneapolis, MN, *Partner*, West Side Investment Co.; **PRIM RE ACT:** Consultant, Developer, Builder, Owner/Investor, Property Manager, Syndicator; **PREV EMPLOY:** Intervest Mgmt. Co.; I.M.C.; **PROFL AFFIL & HONORS:** Lawyer - JD 1977, Southwestern Univ.; **EDUC:** BS, 1974, Poli. Sci. & Bus., UCLA, Southwestern Univ. - School of Law; **GRAD EDUC:** JD, 1977, RE & Bus. Law, Southwestern; **HOME ADD:** 10980 Ohio Ave., Los Angeles, CA 90024, (213)478-5466; **BUS ADD:** 36 Washington St., Marina del Rey, CA 90291, (213)392-8525.

MANDEL, Newton W.——B: Aug. 27, 1926, NY,NY, *VP and Gen. Counsel*, Zimton Capital Corp.; **PRIM RE ACT:** Attorney, Developer, Owner/Investor, Syndicator; **SERVICES:** Devel. of new bldgs., rehab. and synd. of varied RE; **REP CLIENTS:** Investors and synd. of shopping ctrs., office bldgs. and resid. props.; **PREV EMPLOY:** Madison Sq. Garden Corp.; Gulf & Western Realty Corp.; **PROFL AFFIL & HONORS:** RESSI, ABA Tax Section, Real Prop. Problems Comm., ABA Corp. Sect. (State Regulation of Security ABA); **EDUC:** BS, 1948, Textile Chemist, NC State Univ.; **GRAD EDUC:** JD, 1951, Law, NY Law School; **EDUC HONORS:** Pi Kappa Delta; **MIL SERV:** USNR, Lt.; **HOME ADD:** 2846 Beltagh Ave., Bellmore, NY 11710, (516)221-8899; **BUS ADD:** 155 E. 55th St., NY, NY 10022, (212)758-2900.

MANDELL, Mark P.——B: July 5, 1950, Chicago, IL, *Pres.*, Mark P. Mandell, A.P.C.; **PRIM RE ACT:** Broker, Attorney, Owner/Investor, Syndicator; **SERVICES:** RE Law; **PROFL AFFIL & HONORS:** CA Bar Assn., San Diego Cty. Bar Assn.; **EDUC:** BA, 1972, Psychology, Univ. of WI; **GRAD EDUC:** JD, 1977, Law, CA Western School of Law; **EDUC HONORS:** Cum Laude; **BUS ADD:** 8950 Villa La Jolla Dr., Suite 2171, La Jolla, CA 92037, (714)452-5050.

MANGAN, Paul C.——B: Lynn, MA, *Realtor*, Mangan & Associate Realtors; **PRIM RE ACT:** Broker, Consultant, Instructor, Property Manager; **OTHER RE ACT:** Exchanges; **SERVICES:** Full Brokerage Service; **REP CLIENTS:** Indiv. Investors, Attys.; **PROFL AFFIL & HONORS:** NAR; CAR; NCE; OC Exchangors; Rancho Los Cerritos Bd. of Realtors, Realtor of the Year 1980; VP, Rancho Los Cerritos Bd. of Realtors; **GRAD EDUC:** Cerritos Coll., RE; **MIL SERV:** USMC, Sgt. E-5; **OTHER ACT & HONORS:** Commr L.A. Cty. Community Devel.; Cerritos C of C; Kiwanis; Jaycees; **HOME ADD:** 18725 Alfred Ave., Cerritos, CA 90701, (213)865-4405; **BUS ADD:** 13205 South St., Cherritos, CA 90701, (213)924-8837.

MANGU, John, Jr.——B: Nov. 4, 1925, Akron, OH, *VP, RE and Prop.; Asst. Sec.*, Ryder Truck Lines Inc.; **PRIM RE ACT:** Engineer; **OTHER RE ACT:** Corporate RE; **SERVICES:** Leasing, purchase land & bldg., arch. drwys.; **PROFL AFFIL & HONORS:** Fellow, Amer. Soc. Civil Engrs.; Member, Nat. Soc. of Prof. Engrs., Reg. PE and Land Surveyor; **EDUC:** BS, 1950, Civil Engrg., Univ. of Akron, OH; **MIL SERV:** U.S. Army, 1944-1946; **OTHER ACT & HONORS:** Terminal Props. Exchange; **HOME ADD:** 3857 Musket Trail, Jacksonville, FL 32211, (904)744-3317; **BUS ADD:** POB 2408, Jacksonville, FL 32203, (904)353-3111.

MANGUM, Cary R.——B: Jan. 19, 1926, TN, *Pres.*, Heritage House Health & Survival Products Inc., RE Div.: Mangum Realtors; **PRIM RE ACT:** Broker, Consultant, Instructor, Property Manager; **OTHER RE ACT:** Tax Deferred Exchanges; **SERVICES:** Investment/ comml./land brokerage, consulting, tax deferred exchanges; **REP CLIENTS:** Indiv. investors and cos.; **PREV EMPLOY:** Sr. VP and Gen. Mgr. of a title ins. and escrow co. in CA; **PROFL AFFIL & HONORS:** NAR, CA Assn. Realtors, Sacramento Bd. of Realtors, CCIM; **EDUC:** Naval Sci., Univ. of CA, Berkeley; **GRAD EDUC:** JD, 1951, Law, SW Univ.; **MIL SERV:** USNR; **OTHER ACT & HONORS:** ARE, NHF, NNFA; **HOME ADD:** 5542 Wildwood Way, Citrus Hts., CA 95610, (916)966-2292; **BUS ADD:** 5374 Sunrise Blvd., Fair Oaks, CA 95628, (916)966-2291.

MANKIN, Roxanne——B: Nov. 26, 1943, Berkeley, CA, *Pres.*, The Roxanne Mankin Co., Inc.; **PRIM RE ACT:** Broker, Owner/Investor, Property Manager, Instructor, Syndicator; **SERVICES:** Investment consultation, synd., joint venture, brokerage; **REP CLIENTS:** Domestic and for. indivs., grps. and corps.; **PREV EMPLOY:** Marcus & Millichap, 1977-81; **PROFL AFFIL & HONORS:** CA RE Assn.; Nat. Realtor's Mktg. Assn.; **EDUC:** BA, 1965, Humanities Field Major, Univ. of CA, Berkeley; **GRAD EDUC:** MBA Candidate, 1981, Gen. Fin. Mgmt., Pepperdine Univ.; **OTHER ACT & HONORS:** Commonwealth Club; NOW; Women's Forum West; Dir., Threshold Found., (non-profit high tech. housing corp.); **BUS ADD:** 1701A Octabia St., San Francisco, CA 94109, (415)346-4755.

MANLEY, James L.——B: Sept. 5, 1934, Fairmont, W.VA, *Pres.*, Century 21-Manley Assoc., Inc.; **PRIM RE ACT:** Broker, Consultant, Appraiser, Owner/Investor, Instructor; **SERVICES:** Investment Counseling Comml. and Resid. Sales, Valuation and Prop. Mgmt.; **REP CLIENTS:** Southland Corp.; **PREV EMPLOY:** Acct. Exec.-ITT Co.; **PROFL AFFIL & HONORS:** Charlottesville Albemarle Bd. of Realtors, VA Assn. of Realtors, NAR, C.R.S., C.R.B., G.R.I.; **EDUC:** BS, Bus. Admin., 1957, Mgmt., WV Univ.; **EDUC HONORS:** Bus. Honorary Soc.; **HOME ADD:** 30 Georgetown Green, Charlottesville, VA 22905, (804)973-7014; **BUS ADD:** 1709 Emmet St., P.O. Box 5765, Charlottesville, VA 22905, (804)977-7300.

MANN, Jack I.——B: Feb. 12, 1949, Linz, Austria, *Exec. VP & Gen. Counsel*, Adma Co., Inc.; **PRIM RE ACT:** Broker, Consultant, Attorney, Developer, Builder, Owner/Investor, Property Manager, Syndicator; **PREV EMPLOY:** RE Atty.; **PROFL AFFIL & HONORS:** ICSC, ABA; **EDUC:** BBA, 1971, bus. admin., fin., Univ. of CA; **GRAD EDUC:** JD, 1974, Univ. of San Diego; **EDUC HONORS:** Grad. with highest honors, Summa cum laude 1st in class; **HOME ADD:** 1831 Hacienda Dr., El Cajon, CA 92020; **BUS ADD:** 4398 Bonita Rd., Bonita, CA 92002, (714)475-9330.

MANN, James M.——B: Apr. 21, 1946, Chicago, IL, *Pres.*, Joseph J. Duffy Co.; **PRIM RE ACT:** Developer, Builder, Owner/Investor; **EDUC:** BSCE, 1969, Marquette Univ.; **GRAD EDUC:** MBA, 1975, Fin., Loyola Univ.; **EDUC HONORS:** Magna Cum Laude; **BUS ADD:** 4994 N Euston Ave., Chicago, IL 60630, (312)777-6700.

MANNING, Fred W.——B: Aug. 15, 1924, Youngstown, OH, *VP*, F.W. Woolworth Co., RE Dept.; **PRIM RE ACT:** Owner/Investor; **EDUC:** BS, 1948, Bus. Admin., Youngstown State Univ.; **GRAD EDUC:** LLB, 1951, Western Reserve Univ.; **MIL SERV:** USAF, 2nd Lt.; **HOME ADD:** 77 Huron Dr., Chatham, NJ 07928; **BUS ADD:** 233 Broadway, NYC, NY 10279, (216)553-2034.

MANNING, Kenneth——*Pres. RE Div.*, W.R. Grace & Co.; **PRIM RE ACT:** Property Manager; **BUS ADD:** 1114 Avenue of the Americas, New York, NY 10036, (212)764-5555.*

MANNING, Richard J.——B: June 10, 1945, Woodburn, OR, *RE Appraiser*, Dick Manning Co.; **PRIM RE ACT:** Consultant, Appraiser, Builder, Owner/Investor; **SERVICES:** RE appraiser; **REP CLIENTS:** Lenders, fed. and state agencies, corp. relocation cos.; **PREV EMPLOY:** Self-employed appraiser since 1970; **PROFL AFFIL & HONORS:** Sr. Member Amer. Soc. of Appraisers; Sr. Member Nat. Assn. Indep. Fee Appraisers; OR Realtor; **EDUC:** 1969, RE, Chemeketa Community Coll.; **MIL SERV:** USAF 1963-1967, Sgt.; **HOME ADD:** 6777 Fenwick Ct. N, Salem, OR 97303, (503)390-4565; **BUS ADD:** 1020 Shipping St. NE, Salem, OR 97303, (503)364-5179.

MANNING, William H.——B: June 24, 1930, Del Rio, TX, *Owner*, William H. Manning; **PRIM RE ACT:** Consultant, Appraiser; **SERVICES:** Investment analysis and appraisals on major urban and rural income producing props.; **REP CLIENTS:** Major domestic and foreign investors, both instnl. and priv.entities; bank trust depts.; maj. corp. owners; **PREV EMPLOY:** Dist. Mgr. of RE Investments and Mort. Loans, The NW Mutual Life Ins. Co. 1958-1971; Reg. Mgr. of RE Investments and Mort. Loans, The Lincoln Nat. Life Ins. Co. 1971-1973; Analyst and appraiser, RE Research Corp. 1973-1975; Self-employed 1975-present; **PROFL AFFIL & HONORS:** The Amer. Soc. of Farm Mgrs. and Rural Appraisers; AIREA (MAI), Professional Recognition Award of the AIREA; **EDUC:** BS, 1951, Agri., TX Tech. Univ.; **GRAD EDUC:** MEd., 1958, Agri., TX Tech. Univ., Lubbock, TX; **EDUC HONORS:** Alpha Zeta Honor Frat.; **MIL SERV:** USN 1953-1957, Lt. (jg), Carrier Pilot, China Service Medal; **OTHER ACT & HONORS:** Lions Club. Intl.; **HOME ADD:** 24 Villa Casita, Plano, TX 75074, (214)422-4769; **BUS ADD:** PO Box 31481, Citizens Bank Ctr., Suite 500, Dallas, TX 75231, (214)238-9615.

MANNING, William R.——B: Dec. 31, 1938, Birmingham, AL, *Sr. VP & COO*, Van Schaack & Co., Mort. Banking Div.; **PRIM RE ACT:** Lender; **SERVICES:** Res., comml. & agri. lending; **PREV EMPLOY:** Churchill Mort. Corp.-Atlanta; **PROFL AFFIL & HONORS:** Member Nat. MRA, CO MBA, Nat. HBA, CRA, CMB; **EDUC:** BA Bus. Admin., 1960, Mktg., Auburn Univ.; **GRAD EDUC:** LLB, 1975, Contracts- Law, LaSalle Univ.; **MIL SERV:** USAF, 1st Lt.; **OTHER ACT & HONORS:** Denver Athletic Club; **HOME ADD:** 15455 E. Monmouth Pl., Aurora, CO 80015; **BUS ADD:** 950 17th St. # 1200, Denver, CO 80202, (303)572-5301.

MANNY, Gary J.——B: July 10, 1945, Ft. Worth, TX, *Owner*, Gary J. Manny, Atty. at Law; **PRIM RE ACT:** Consultant, Attorney, Builder, Owner/Investor; **SERVICES:** RE Law, Title Ins., RE Closings; **REP CLIENTS:** Investors, Banks, RE Brokers; **PROFL AFFIL & HONORS:** Ft. Worth RE Bd., ABA, TX & Ft. Worth Bar Assn.; **EDUC:** BA, 1967, Hist.-Govt., TX Christian Univ., Ft. Worth; **GRAD EDUC:** JD, 1975, Gen. Law, So. Methodist Univ., Dallas; **EDUC HONORS:** Magna Cum Laude, Order of the Coif; **MIL SERV:** USN, Lt.; **OTHER ACT & HONORS:** Univ. Area Kiwanis Club; **HOME ADD:** 2313 Mistletoe Dr., Ft. Worth, TX 76110, (817)923-5405; **BUS ADD:** 3719 S. Univ. Dr., PO Box 11445, Ft. Worth, TX 76109, (817)924-3211.

MANOS, Alexander A.M.——B: Feb. 5, 1929, Greensburg, PA, *Realtor*, Brown Realtors; **PRIM RE ACT:** Broker, Owner/Investor, Syndicator; **SERVICES:** Full serv. in resale RE field, synd. & devel. of resid. & comml. prop., valuation; **REP CLIENTS:** Buyers & sellers of resid. prop., indiv.; **PREV EMPLOY:** US & Can. Mktg. Mgr., Scott Paper Co.; **PROFL AFFIL & HONORS:** NAR, CA Assn. of Realtors, Covejo Valley Bd. Realtors, Intl. RE Fed., Intl. Inst. of Valuers, RESSI, CRB, CRS, GRI, SCV, Pres. 1982 Conejo Valley Bd. of Realtors; **EDUC:** BA, 1950, Bus., Lake Forest Coll., IL; **MIL SERV:** USAF, OSI Agent; **OTHER ACT & HONORS:** St. Patricks Episcopal Church, Conejo Future Found., Salesman of Year 1976, 77, 78, 80, 81; **HOME ADD:** 2075 Calle Yucca, Thousand Oaks, CA 91360, (805)498-6363; **BUS ADD:** 883 S Westlake Blvd., Westlake Village, CA 91361, (805)495-1048.

MANSON, Dean A.——B: Nov. 3, 1939, Toledo, OH, *Counsel*, Multiple Southwest Investment Corp.; **PRIM RE ACT:** Consultant, Attorney, Owner/Investor, Instructor; **OTHER RE ACT:** Workout Specialist; **SERVICES:** Fin. consulting, counsel; **REP CLIENTS:** Fin. inst., synd., builders; **PREV EMPLOY:** Prof. of RE, S. Methodist Univ.; **PROFL AFFIL & HONORS:** ALDA, ULI, Fed. Bar Assn., Amer. Econ. Assn., Amer. Fin. Assn., Practicing Law Inst., Nicholas Salgo Distinguished Teaching Award 1975; **EDUC:** BBA, 1962, Mktg., fin., prelaw, Univ. of Toledo, OH; **GRAD EDUC:** JD, 1966, RE and fin., Univ. of Toledo; **EDUC HONORS:** Louisville Title RE Excellence Award; **OTHER ACT & HONORS:** Asst. Dir. of Law, City of Toledo, 1966-68, Chandlers Landing Yacht Club, Nat. Yacht

Racing Union, Nat. Defenders Assn., Outstanding Young Men in Amer. 1965; **HOME ADD:** 11318 Drummond Dr., Dallas, TX 75228, (213)681-5364; **BUS ADD:** Box 2684, Dallas, TX 75221, (214)681-5364.

MANSON, R. Hunter——B: Dec. 12, 1941, Honolulu, HI, Browder, Russell, Morris & Butcher, P.C.; **PRIM RE ACT:** Attorney; **PROFL AFFIL & HONORS:** Member, Bd. of Governors, RE Section, VA State Bar Assn.; Member, RE Comm., VA Bar Assn.; Member, ABA; Subcommittee on Condo and Corporate Housing; Listed among Municipal Bond Attys. of the US in the Bond Buyers Dir. of Municipal Bond Dealers of the US, Member, Condo Advisory Comm., VA RE Comm.; **EDUC:** BA, 1963, English, Washington & Lee Univ.; **GRAD EDUC:** LLB later converted to JD, 1969, Washington & Lee Univ.; **EDUC HONORS:** Scholarship; **MIL SERV:** US Army, Capt., Aviator; **HOME ADD:** 706 Spottswood Rd., Richmond, VA 23229, (804)282-0027; **BUS ADD:** 1200 Ross Bldg., Richmond, VA 23219, (804)771-9314.

MANTEI, Richard C.——B: Apr. 21, 1942, Appleton, WI, *Stock Holder & Dir.*, Investment Services, Inc.; **PRIM RE ACT:** Broker, Developer, Owner/Investor; **PROFL AFFIL & HONORS:** Member of RNMI, Named Realtor of the year, Madison, WI, 1976; CCIM; **EDUC:** BS, 1964, Econ., Univ. of WI-Stevens Point; **HOME ADD:** 10 Dunraven Ct., Madison, WI 53705, (608)833-8337; **BUS ADD:** 217 S Hamilton, Suite 500, Madison, WI 53703, (608)251-3111.

MANUKAS, Nick D.——B: May 5, 1940, Trenton, NJ, *Pres.*, The Bayberry Agency; **PRIM RE ACT:** Broker, Consultant, Appraiser, Owner/Investor; **SERVICES:** Comml. Prop., land and investment prop brokerage; **REP CLIENTS:** Indiv. investors and users of above type props.; **PROFL AFFIL & HONORS:** NJ Assn. of Realtors (Dir.), Comml. Investment Div. (Dir.), FLI, Pres. NJ Chapt., 13, CRS, GRI, CAS; **MIL SERV:** USCG; **OTHER ACT & HONORS:** AHEPA, Member Bd. of Dirs. of Anchor House; **HOME ADD:** 47 Redwood Ave., Trenton, NJ 08610, (609)888-0772; **BUS ADD:** 1200 Whitehorse Mercerville Rd., Trenton, NJ 08619, (609)585-0600.

MANZULLI, Michael F.——B: Feb. 1, 1941, NYC, *Atty.*, Lahr, Dillon, Manzulli & Kelley, P.C.; **PRIM RE ACT:** Attorney; **SERVICES:** Bank counsel and RE advisor to indiv. or instnl. investors in comml. and resid. prop.; **REP CLIENTS:** Lenders and indiv. and instnl. investors in comml. and resid. prop.; **PREV EMPLOY:** Assoc. Counsel, Emigrant Savings Bank; **PROFL AFFIL & HONORS:** NY State Bar Assn.; Richmond Cty. Bar Assn., Dir., Richmond Cty. Bar Assn.; **EDUC:** BS, 1962, Niagara Univ.; **GRAD EDUC:** LLB, 1965, St. John's Univ. School of Law; **OTHER ACT & HONORS:** Rotary Intl., Staten Is. Div.; YMCA, Staten Is. Branch, Member of Bd. of Dir.; **HOME ADD:** 711 Pelton Ave., Staten Island, NY 10310, (212)273-4213; **BUS ADD:** 207 Taylor St., Staten Island, NY 10310, (212)447-8841.

MAPLE, Michael L.——B: Oct. 22, 1946, Columbus, IN, *Partner*, Maple & Stinson Attorneys; **PRIM RE ACT:** Consultant, Attorney, Developer, Syndicator; **SERVICES:** Full serv. RE atty.; **REP CLIENTS:** Banks, title cos., mort. bankers, devels., builders, engrs., promoters, investors, First Nat. Bank of Louisville, Citizens Fidelity Bank & Trust, Commonwealth Land Title, Security Title, United KY Bank, Liberty National Bank; **PROFL AFFIL & HONORS:** ABA; CAI; KY Bar; Louisville Bar; **EDUC:** AB, 1969, Govt., Eng., Phil., Western KY Univ.; **GRAD EDUC:** JD, 1974, Univ.of Louisville; **MIL SERV:** US Army, E-4; **OTHER ACT & HONORS:** Chmn., KY Bar RE Comm., Member LA Bar RE Comm.; **HOME TEL:** (502)423-0111; **BUS ADD:** 200 7th 100, Louisville, KY 40202, (502)585-3979.

MAPPIN, Richard——*Exec. Dir.*, Allegany County Economic Devel. Co.; **PRIM RE ACT:** Developer; **BUS ADD:** 2100 Bedford St., Cumberland, MD 21502, (301)777-5968.*

MAPSTONE, Grace A.——B: Sept. 19,1934, Pittston, PA, *Realtor*, Dolphin Bay Realty, Inc; **PRIM RE ACT:** Broker, Consultant; **OTHER RE ACT:** Mobile Homes with lots (Sales); **SERVICES:** All phases; **PROFL AFFIL & HONORS:** NAR; State Assoc. Pres. of Bd. of Realtors; GRI, Member of Women's Council of Realtors.; **OTHER ACT & HONORS:** Catholic Women's Council, Isabella; **HOME ADD:** 330 Belvedere Ct., Punta Gorda, FL 33950, (813)639-4942; **BUS ADD:** 777 S. Ind. Ave., Englewood, FL 33533, (813)474-0535.

MARBLE, Roland D.——B: May 12, 1920, Greenville, MS, *Atty.*, Wells, Wells, Marble & Hurst; **PRIM RE ACT:** Attorney; **SERVICES:** Closing various agri. bus. and comml. loans; **REP CLIENTS:** Ins. cos. and other comml. investors; **PROFL AFFIL & HONORS:** ABA; Fed. of Ins. Counsel; **EDUC:** BA, 1946, Hist./Eng., MS Coll.; **GRAD EDUC:** JD, 1948, Law, Univ. of MS; **EDUC HONORS:** Grad. with Special Distinction, Grad. with Distinction, Editor of MS Law Journal; **MIL SERV:** US Army, Capt., 1940-1945; **OTHER ACT & HONORS:** Nat. Vice Comdr. of Amer. Legion; Intl. VP of Civitan Intl.; **HOME ADD:** 4065 Eastwood Dr., Jackson, MS 39211, (601)982-3622; **BUS ADD:** 200 Lamar Life Bldg., POB 131, Jackson, MS 39205, (601)355-8321.

MARCECA, Robert K.——B: Dec. 1, 1943, NY, *Pres.*, E. Thirtieth Street Realty Co.; **PRIM RE ACT:** Developer, Builder, Owner/Investor, Property Manager; **OTHER RE ACT:** Tax sheltering; **EDUC:** 1961, Univ. of Bridgeport, Harvard Bus. School; **HOME ADD:** 240 E. 58th St., New York, NY 10022, (212)758-9300; **BUS ADD:** 314 E. 53rd St., New York, NY 10022, (212)486-1150.

MARCHAND, Arturo Jose——B: Jan. 22, 1948, British Honduras, *Prop. Mgr.*, Bank of America, Administrative Facilities Dept.; **PRIM RE ACT:** Property Manager; **SERVICES:** Manage the Bank's Computer Ctr. & Bankamericard Ctr., and the RE Loan Service Center; **PROFL AFFIL & HONORS:** BOMA & IREM, CPM (candidate); **EDUC:** Assoc. of Applied Sci., 1970, Bus. Admin., Pace Univ.; **HOME ADD:** 499 Woodbluff, Duarte, CA 91010, (213)357-8672; **BUS ADD:** 1000 W. Temple St., Los Angeles, CA 90012, (213)683-4498.

MARCHAND, James E.——B: Sept. 18, 1931, Haubstadt, IN, *Partner*, Fine, Hatfield, Sparrenberger & Fine; **PRIM RE ACT:** Attorney; **SERVICES:** Represent all types of clients in RE transactions, purchases, sales, morts., leases, title work, rezoning, oil, gas, coal and other minerals, subdiv., condo., etc.; **REP CLIENTS:** Permanent Fed. S & L Assn.; Citizens Nat. Bank; Old Nat. Bank in Evansville; Mead, Johnson & Co., Stagg Indus. Devel. Co., Inc.; Factory Devel. Co., Inc.; **PROFL AFFIL & HONORS:** Evansville Bar Assn. (Title Standards Comm.); IN Bar Assn.; ABA, RE Sect.; Phi Delta Phi, legal frat., Past Pres. Evansville Estate Planning Council; **EDUC:** AB, 1953, Govt., Econ., IN Univ. Bloomington; **GRAD EDUC:** JD, 1958, Law, IN Univ. Law School, Bloomington; **MIL SERV:** US Army; Armor, 1st Lt.; **OTHER ACT & HONORS:** Dir. and Counsel Evansville Goodwill Indus., Inc.; Past Area Gov. Toastmasters Intl.; Co-author of pamphlet, 'Legal Aspects of Suggestion Systems'; **HOME ADD:** 7019 Old State Rd., Evansville, IN 47710, (812)867-5795; **BUS ADD:** 1600 Old National Bank Bldg., PO Box 779, Evansville, IN 47708, (812)425-3592.

MARCHANT, Robert G.——B: Sept. 30, 1933, Hamilton, Ontario, Can, *VP, Major Loans, Comml./Indus.*, Coast Federal S & L Assn., Loan Production; **PRIM RE ACT:** Developer, Lender; **SERVICES:** Const. & perm. fin./joint venture/redevel.; **REP CLIENTS:** Major devel., CA & out-of-state mort. brokers, fin. instns.; **PREV EMPLOY:** 11 yrs. with Coast Federal, 5 yrs. with Lytton S & L, Los Angeles (S & L) 2 yrs, Tishman Realty & Const.; **PROFL AFFIL & HONORS:** Western Mobile Home Assn. Mfg. Housing Inst.; **EDUC:** BS, 1957, Bus. Admin, Hotel Admin.; **HOME ADD:** 736 Tufts Ave., Burbank, CA 91504, (213)846-3490; **BUS ADD:** 855 S. Hill St., Los Angeles, CA 90015, (213)624-2110.

MARCHITELLI, Richard——B: Aug. 11, 1947, NYC, NY, *Pres.*, Richard Marchitelli, Inc.; **PRIM RE ACT:** Broker, Instructor, Consultant, Appraiser, Developer, Owner/Investor; **SERVICES:** Investment analysis, valuation reports, feasibility studies, consultation involving indiv. RE problems and advice in making RE decisions; **REP CLIENTS:** Lenders, instnl. & private investors, corps., and govt.; **PROFL AFFIL & HONORS:** AIREA, SREA, MAI, SRPA; **EDUC:** BA, 1969, Govt., Belmont Abbey Coll., NC; **EDUC HONORS:** Who's Who in Amer. Univs. & Colls. (1968-69), Dean's List; **HOME ADD:** 72 Pamoqua Ln., W Islip, NY 11795, (516)669-4712; **BUS ADD:** 400 W Main St., Babylon, NY 11702, (516)587-7510.

MARCUS, Alan P.——B: May 15, 1925, New York, NY, *Pres.*, Tudor Gate Developers & Builders; **PRIM RE ACT:** Broker, Attorney, Developer, Builder, Owner/Investor, Property Manager; **PROFL AFFIL & HONORS:** NJ Home Bldrs. Assoc., NAHB Assoc., Bergen-Passaic Bldg. Official Assoc.; **EDUC:** BA, 1945; **GRAD EDUC:** LLB, 1949, Fordham Law School; **MIL SERV:** US Army, 1st LT; **OTHER ACT & HONORS:** 1970 1981 Construction Official State of NJ, Bldg. Sub Code Official State of NJ, Bldg. Inspector State of NJ; **HOME ADD:** 26 Jane Dr., Englewood Cliffs, NJ 07632; **BUS ADD:** 601 Palisade Ave. (P.O. Box 1111), Englewood Cliffs, NJ 07632, (201)567-4446.

MARCUS, David——*Mgr. Corp. Bldg. Eng. & Const.*, Cincinnati Milacron Co.; **PRIM RE ACT:** Property Manager; **BUS ADD:** 4701 Marburg Ave., Cincinnati, OH 45209, (518)841-8100.*

MARCUS, Jerry Lee——B: Nov. 13, 1924, NYC, *Sr. VP*, Sonnenblick - Goldman Corp.; **PRIM RE ACT:** Broker; **EDUC:** 1941-42, Engrg. School (Aero), Univ. of AL; **MIL SERV:** Air Corps, Flight Officer;

OTHER ACT & HONORS: 1977 Winner RE Bd. of NY Manhattan Deal of the year Award; **HOME ADD:** 400 E. 56th St., Apt. 24L, New York, NY 10022, (212)753-8772; **BUS ADD:** 1251 Ave. of Americas, New York, NY 10020, (212)541-4321.

MARCUS, Walter F.——**B:** Feb. 5, 1921, Buffalo, NY, *Pres.*, Hansen Appraisal Service, Inc.; **PRIM RE ACT:** Broker, Appraiser; **SERVICES:** All phases of RE appraisals, feasibility studies, etc.; **REP CLIENTS:** All fin. instns., lawyers, investors & corp. bus.; **PREV EMPLOY:** 30 yrs. with Hansen Appraisal; **PROFL AFFIL & HONORS:** Member AIREA, Soc. of RE Appraisers, Local & Nat. RE Bds., MAI, SRPA, 1981 LW Ellwood Award, NY State Appraiser of Yr., Panel of Arbitrators, Amer. Assn. of Arbitrators; **MIL SERV:** US Air Corp., S/Sgt.; **HOME ADD:** 66 Wickham Dr., Williamsville, NY 19221, (716)632-0020; **BUS ADD:** 560 Delaware Ave., Buffalo, NY 14202.

MARCUSSEN, Steven E.——**B:** June 10, 1956, Philadelphia, PA, *Sr. Assoc.*, C. Thomas Ruppert & Assoc.; **PRIM RE ACT:** Broker; **SERVICES:** Spec. in leasing high grade retail/whole props. in the Beverly Hills, W. Hollywood areas. Providing acquisition & devel. consultation regarding retail props.; **PROFL AFFIL & HONORS:** Los Angeles Bd. of Realtors, Beverly Hills Bd. of Realtors, CA Assn. of Realtors; **EDUC:** BS, 1978, Fin. RE, Univ. of S. CA; **EDUC HONORS:** Dean's List; **OTHER ACT & HONORS:** USC Commerce Assocs.; **BUS ADD:** 319 S. Robertson Blvd., Beverly Hills, CA 90211, (213)659-4460.

MARDER, Harry——**B:** Oct. 1942, Phila., PA, *Harry Marder Assoc. Inc.*, Anchor Realty; **PRIM RE ACT:** Broker, Appraiser, Property Manager, Owner/Investor; **REP CLIENTS:** Transamerica Credit CA, Manuf. Hanover Credit NY, Other Banks & Credit Unions, Phila. Elec. Co. Relocation Div. Appraiser; **PREV EMPLOY:** Clover Realty Co. Cornwell Hgts. PA; **PROFL AFFIL & HONORS:** ASA Cert. Appraiser, ASA CAR; **EDUC:** BA, 1975, RE, Temple U.; **MIL SERV:** US Army; **OTHER ACT & HONORS:** Notary Public Phila. & Montgomery Cty. since 1970; **HOME ADD:** 7909 Ronaele Dr., Elkins Park, PA 19117, (215)635-6085; **BUS ADD:** 613 W Cheltenham Ave., Melrose Park, PA 19126, (215)782-8740.

MARDO, Guy——*RE Mgr.*, Dow Jones & Co., Inc.; **PRIM RE ACT:** Property Manager; **BUS ADD:** 22 Cortland St., New York, NY 10007, (212)285-5000.*

MARES, Robert——*Dir. RE*, Dart Industries, Inc.; **PRIM RE ACT:** Property Manager; **BUS ADD:** PO Box 3157, Terminal Annex, Los Angeles, CA 90051, (312)498-8000.*

MARETZ, Fred R.——**B:** Mar 26, 1924, New Haven, CT, *Partner*, Levey, Miller, Maretz, Realtors; **PRIM RE ACT:** Broker, Syndicator, Consultant, Property Manager, Owner/Investor; **SERVICES:** Full range of R.E. activity; **PROFL AFFIL & HONORS:** NAR, RMNI, CCIM; **EDUC:** BS, 1948, Bus. Adm., Univ. of CT; **MIL SERV:** USA, Capt.; **OTHER ACT & HONORS:** Comm. on Equal Opportunity, City of New Haven; Capital Projects Comm., City of New Haven; CT Development Commission; Bd. of Directors, Hospital of St. Raphael Foundation; **HOME ADD:** 5 Whittier Rd., New Haven, CT 06515, (203)397-3140; **BUS ADD:** 1308 Whalley Ave., New Haven, CT 06515, (203)389-5377.

MARGID, Leonard——**B:** May 13, 1927, NY, *Atty.*, Otterbourg, Steindler, Houston & Rosen, P.C., Corp.-RE; **PRIM RE ACT:** Attorney; **SERVICES:** All phases of RE including synd., condo. and co-op conversions, sale and leasebacks, buying & selling of RE; **PREV EMPLOY:** Proskauer, Rose, Goetz & Mendensohn, 1951-1958; **PROFL AFFIL & HONORS:** Member NYC Bar Assn.; Past Member of Municipal Affairs Comm.; Family Law Comm.; Member of Amer. Bar Assn., Sections of Corp., Banking and Bus. Law and Real Prop., Probate and Trust Law; Member of NYU Law Alumni Assn., Fund Raising Comm., Past Pres. and Treas. of Law Alumni Class; **EDUC:** BA, 1949, Pol. Sci./Econ., Univ. of IA; **GRAD EDUC:** JD, 1951, NYU; **EDUC HONORS:** Law Review; **MIL SERV:** US Army; **OTHER ACT & HONORS:** Past Member, City Club and its Housing and Planning Comm.; Past Member, Exec. Bd. of Henry Street Settlement and its Mental Hygiene Advisory Comm.; Past Member, Bd. of Tr. of Riverdale Neighborhood House and Chmn. of its Expansion Comm.; Past Member, Dist. Advisory Comm. of Citizens' Comm. for an Effective Constitution; Past Member, Anti-Proverty Comm. of Citizens' Comm. for A Better NY; Current Member, Local Community Planning Bd. by appointment of Borough Pres. of Bronx Cty. and VChmn. of Land Use Comm.; Visiting Prof., Univ. of San Diego Law School, teaching business planning Spring 1980; Presently Adj. Prof. of Law, Univ. of Bridgeport, teaching business planning; **HOME ADD:** 4455 Douglas Ave., Bronx, NY 10471, (212)543-0723; **BUS ADD:** 230 Park Ave., New York, NY 10169, (212)661-9100.

MARGOLIS, Jonathan S.——**B:** Dec. 28, 1955, NY, NY, *Assoc.*, Fried, Frank, Marris, Shriver & Jacobson, RE; **PRIM RE ACT:** Attorney; **SERVICES:** Legal rep. for all types of participants in the RE Bus.; **PROFL AFFIL & HONORS:** ABA; NYC and NY Bar Assns.; **EDUC:** BA, 1976, Pol. Sci./Econ., Columbia Coll.; **GRAD EDUC:** JD, 1979, Columbia Law School; **EDUC HONORS:** Dean's List, Stone Scholar; **HOME ADD:** 10 W. 86th St., New York, NY 10024, (212)877-8411; **BUS ADD:** One New York Plaza, New York, NY 10004, (212)820-8103.

MARGOLIS, Sidney——*VP*, United Merchants & Manufacturers, Inc.; **PRIM RE ACT:** Property Manager; **BUS ADD:** 1407 Broadway, New York, NY 10018, (212)930-3900.*

MARGRABE, William——**B:** Dec. 17, 1948, Frederick, MD, *Asst. Prof.*, George Washington University, School of Govt. and Bus. Admin.; **PRIM RE ACT:** Consultant, Instructor; **SERVICES:** Computerized models of investment and fin.; **REP CLIENTS:** Alcoa Props., Inc.; **PREV EMPLOY:** Lecturer, The Wharton School, Univ. of PA; **PROFL AFFIL & HONORS:** Amer. RE & Urban Econ. Assn., Amer. Educ. Assn.; **EDUC:** BA, 1970, Econ., Johns Hopkins Univ.; **GRAD EDUC:** PhD, 1978, Econ., Univ. of Chicago; **EDUC HONORS:** Gen. Honors, Phi Beta Kappa; **HOME ADD:** 7005 Wake Forest Dr., College Pk., MD 20740, (301)927-4741; **BUS ADD:** 710 21st St., N.W., Washington, DC 20052, (202)676-8342.

MARIOTTI, Mark——*Consultant*, Future Management Systems; **PRIM RE ACT:** Consultant, Banker, Owner/Investor, Insuror; **SERVICES:** Computer Systems & consulting services; **REP CLIENTS:** Large Banks & S & L; **BUS ADD:** 825 Civic Ctr., Van Nuys, CA 91408, (213)997-8100.

MARITSAS, Paul D.——**B:** Nov. 24, 1932, Sacramento, CA, *Pres.*, Valley International, Inc.; **PRIM RE ACT:** Consultant, Appraiser, Developer, Regulator, Builder, Owner/Investor, Instructor, Property Manager; **SERVICES:** Planning, construction, valuation, consulting, mgmt.; **REP CLIENTS:** Salt Lake Cty., Arrow Indus. etc.; **PREV EMPLOY:** UT Hwy. Dept.; Dir. SL County Real Estate Dept.; RE Broker & Appraiser; **PROFL AFFIL & HONORS:** SREA, NARA, ASA, Amer. Arbitration Assn., SRPAM CRA, ASA; **EDUC:** 1954, Coll. of the Pacific; **EDUC HONORS:** Gov. Reg. 8 ASA; Nat. Alliance of Bus. Men (Job Training of Disadvantaged); **OTHER ACT & HONORS:** Kappa Sigma Kappa Frat., Boy Scout Ldr., Choir Dir. - Greek Orthodox Church, Western Boys Baseball League Dir., Hillview PTA, Bicentennial Music Comm.; **HOME ADD:** 1158 East 4500 South, Salt Lake City, UT 84117, (801)262-3789; **BUS ADD:** 740 South 300 West, Salt Lake City, UT 84101, (801)532-1717.

MARK, Henry Allen——**B:** May 16, 1909, Brooklyn, NY, *Of Counsel*, Cadwalader, Wickersham & Taft; **PRIM RE ACT:** Attorney; **SERVICES:** Legal advice and drafting; **REP CLIENTS:** Bowery Savings Bank, Manhattan Savings Bank, NY Life Ins. Co., Macmillan Co., NY Bank for Savings; **PREV EMPLOY:** Partner, Cadwalader, Wickersham & Taft, 1953-1977; **PROFL AFFIL & HONORS:** ABA, NY State, CT, Litchfield Cty. Bar Assns., Assn. of the Bar of City of NY; **EDUC:** BA, 1932, Latin, Williams Coll.; **GRAD EDUC:** JD, 1935, Cornell Univ. Law School; **EDUC HONORS:** Phi Beta Kappa, Cum Laude; **OTHER ACT & HONORS:** Village of Garden City, NY - Tr., 1961-1965, Mayor, 1965-1967, Member NY Advisory Bd., Chicago Title Ins. Co., 1968-1979, Chmn. of Washington, CT Planning Commn., 1979-; **HOME ADD:** The Green, Washington, CT 06793, (203)868-2517; **BUS ADD:** One Wall St., New York, NY 10005, (212)785-1000.

MARK, Stephen S.——**B:** Jan. 2, 1945, Oklahoma City, OK, *VP, Gen. Counsel*, Valley View Holdings, Inc., Legal and RE; **PRIM RE ACT:** Attorney; **SERVICES:** Oversee investment and devel.; **PREV EMPLOY:** Partner, Dallas law firm, Johnson, Swanson & Barbee; **PROFL AFFIL & HONORS:** ABA; Dallas Bar Assn.; **EDUC:** AB, 1967, Amer. Civilization, Williams Coll.; **GRAD EDUC:** JD, 1972, Univ. of TX School of Law; **EDUC HONORS:** Degree with Hon., Assoc. Editor, TX Law Review, Order of the Coif, Degree with Hon.; **MIL SERV:** USN; Lt.j.g.; Combat Action Ribbon; **OTHER ACT & HONORS:** Co-author, "Special Problems of Unregistered RE Securities,"; UCLA Law Review, Aug., 1975; **HOME ADD:** 6005 Swiss Ave., Dallas, TX 75214, (214)824-7139; **BUS ADD:** 4100 First National Bank Building, Dallas, TX 75202, (214)741-1000.

MARKOFF, Gary M.——**B:** Mar. 25, 1949, Providence, RI, *Atty.*, Singer, Stoneman & Kurland; **PRIM RE ACT:** Consultant, Attorney, Developer, Owner/Investor, Syndicator; **SERVICES:** Fin. consulting, tax advice, legal advice; **REP CLIENTS:** RE devel., banks; **PREV EMPLOY:** Tax accountant for Arthur Anderson & Co., Boston, MA; **PROFL AFFIL & HONORS:** ABA; Amer. Lawyer's Assn.; MBA; BBA; MA Broker; MA CPA; RI Bar; MA & RI all courts; MA Fed.

Dist Ct.; 1st Circuit Court of Appeals; US Tax Court, VP New England Investors and Legal Council thereof; **EDUC:** BA, 1971, Econ., Oberlin Coll.; **GRAD EDUC:** MBA, 1973, Fin., Cornell Univ.; JD, 1977, BC; **EDUC HONORS:** Dean's List; **OTHER ACT & HONORS:** Co-Chairperson with wife of Couples Forum, Combined Jewish Philanthropies; **HOME ADD:** 39 Woodside Ave., Wellesley, MA 02121, (617)235-9196; **BUS ADD:** 70 Federal St., Boston, MA 02110, (617)542-8461.

MARKOFF, Ronald C.——B: Mar. 25, 1949, Providence, RI, *Atty.*, Ronald C. Markoff; **PRIM RE ACT:** Attorney; **SERVICES:** RE transactions; title examinations; **PROFL AFFIL & HONORS:** RI Bar Assn., ABA; **EDUC:** AB, 1971, Classics, Brown Univ.; **GRAD EDUC:** JD, 1975, Classics, Boston Coll; 1971, A.M. Classics, Brown Univ.; 1971-72, Amos Tuck School of Bus. Admin., Dartmouth Coll.; **EDUC HONORS:** Phi Beta Kappa, Magna Cum Laude; **HOME ADD:** 11 Fireside Dr., Barrington, RI, (401)245-0305; **BUS ADD:** 72 S. Main St., Providence, RI 02903, (401)272-9330.

MARKS, Anthony David.——B: Sept. 13, 1942, London, England, *Mgr. Prop. Mgmt. Dept.*, Pemberton Realty Corp.; **PRIM RE ACT:** Broker, Consultant, Property Manager; **SERVICES:** RE brokerage, mgmt. & consulting; **PREV EMPLOY:** Prop mgr., Montreal Trust Co., Vancouver; **EDUC:** BA, 1966, Pol. Sci., Soc. of Law, Univ. of B.C.; **EDUC HONORS:** Grad. with Honors; **OTHER ACT & HONORS:** Author 'Understanding Condos & Coops., A Comprehensive Handbook' (313 pages), Currently working on a time-sharing supplement; **HOME ADD:** 303-4683 Arbutus St., Vancouver, BC, Canada, (604)263-2039; **BUS ADD:** 744 W Hastings St., Vancouncer, BC, Canada, (604)684-9172.

MARKS, F. Morales——B: Sept. 27, 1955, NYC, NY, *Associate Atty.*, Content, Stewart, Tatusko & Patterson, Chartered; **PRIM RE ACT:** Attorney; **PROFL AFFIL & HONORS:** Fed. Bar. Assn., ABA, member of NY and DC Bar; admitted before EDNY & SDNY; **EDUC:** BA, 1976, Poli. Sci., Barnard Coll.; **GRAD EDUC:** JD, 1979, Columbia Univ. School of Law; **EDUC HONORS:** Dean's List, Regents Scholar, Davison Forman Scholar, Honors in Poli. Sci.; **HOME ADD:** 1110 Fidler Ln. #1515, Silver Spring, MD 20910, (301)587-1379; **BUS ADD:** 1225 19th St. N.W., Suite 600, Washington, DC 20036, (202)887-1000.

MARKS, Kenneth L.——B: Aug. 8, 1945, Wash., DC, *VP*, Carey Winston Co., Indus. Sales & Leasing; **PRIM RE ACT:** Broker, Developer, Owner/Investor; **SERVICES:** Indus. leasing, indus. sales, indus. devel., consultation with devels.; **REP CLIENTS:** Private devels., life ins. & pension fund investors; **PROFL AFFIL & HONORS:** Assoc. Realtor WA Bd. of Realtors, SIR, Nat. Assn. of Office & Indus. Parks, Million Dollar Sales Club, Million Dollar Leasing Club; **EDUC:** BS, 1967, Bus. Admin. & Mgmt., Boston Univ.; **MIL SERV:** USMC, L/Cpl.; **OTHER ACT & HONORS:** Member of MODAC (Mayors Overall Econ. Devel. Advisory Comm.); **HOME ADD:** 3415 Cummings Ln., Chevy Chase, MD 20815, (301)986-9414; **BUS ADD:** 4350 E. W. Hwy, Bethesda, MD 20814, (301)656-4212.

MARKS, Lloyd C.——B: Oct. 30, 1916, OH, *Broker/Realtor*, Marks Properties Realtors; **PRIM RE ACT:** Broker, Consultant, Appraiser, Developer, Property Manager; **PREV EMPLOY:** Engr. at IBM, San Jose; Beckman Palo Alto, Auto Sales Owner of Bus.; Owner Metal Mfg. Firm; **EDUC:** AA, Engrg., Kent State, Ursinus, San Jose SU, UCLA; **GRAD EDUC:** BA, 1955, Engrg., W Valley Coll.; Bus. Acctg., CA Berkeley; **EDUC HONORS:** RE/Bus.; **MIL SERV:** USAF, Capt., Multi eng. pilot, Air Force Medal, Purple Heart, Pres. Citation; **OTHER ACT & HONORS:** TROA (Ret. Officers), DAV; **HOME ADD:** 13784 Camino Rico, Saratoga, CA 95670, (408)867-0537; **BUS ADD:** 1251 Kentwood Ave., San Jose, CA 95129, (408)253-3640.

MARKUS, Andrew Joshua——B: Nov. 24, 1948, Akron, OH, *Atty.*, Barron, Lehman, Cardenas & Picken, P.A.; **PRIM RE ACT:** Attorney; **SERVICES:** Counseling, Negotiation, Documentation of RE transactions; **PREV EMPLOY:** Mahoney, Hadlow & Adams 1976 to 1979; **PROFL AFFIL & HONORS:** Member: FL & Wash. DC Bars; ABA, (Sections of Corp. Banking and Bus. Law, Intl. Law and Real Prop., Probate and Trust Law); FL Bar - Real Prop., Probate and Trust Law Sect.-Intl. Prop.; Estate and Trust Law Comm.; Condo. and Cooperative Comm.; Construction Law Comm.; Intl. Law Comm., Specialization in Real Prop. Law; **EDUC:** BA, 1970, Eng., Duke Univ.; **GRAD EDUC:** JD, 1973, Law, Univ. of FL Law School; **EDUC HONORS:** Cum Laude, Phi Kappa Phi, Order of the Coif, Honorary Univ. of FL Law Ctr. Scholarship; **OTHER ACT & HONORS:** LLM 1974 Vrije Universiteit Brussel (Intl. and Comparative Law), Magna Cum Laude; **HOME ADD:** 7516 S.W. 58th Ave., Miami, FL 33143, (305)665-2665; **BUS ADD:** 888 Brickell Ave., Suite 200, Miami, FL 33131, (305)374-4747.

MARLOWE, Earl S.——B: Feb. 9, 1938, Williamsburg, KY, *Broker*, Century 21 Murray - Marlowe Realty Inc.; **PRIM RE ACT:** Broker, Appraiser, Owner/Investor, Instructor, Property Manager; **SERVICES:** Resid., comml., sales & appraising; **PREV EMPLOY:** RE, 1968; **PROFL AFFIL & HONORS:** Nat. Assn. of RE Appraisers; **EDUC:** BS, Bus., Sinclair & Carlsbad Coll.; **GRAD EDUC:** Bus., SMI; **MIL SERV:** USMC, Pfc., Good Conduct; **HOME ADD:** 5461 Shedwick Dr., Dayton, OH 45426, (513)890-5400; **BUS ADD:** 8200 N. Main St., Dayton, OH 45415, (513)890-8600.

MARMIS, Cary——B: Jan. 17, 1942, Dubuque, IA, *Pres.*, Empire West Companies Inc.; **PRIM RE ACT:** Consultant, Developer, Builder, Owner/Investor, Property Manager; **SERVICES:** Apt. Builder/Devel.; **PROFL AFFIL & HONORS:** 1974, Outstanding Young Men of Amer.; 1979, Exec. of the Yr., Nat. Secretaries Assn., Tucson, AZ; **EDUC:** BS, 1965, Univ. of IL; **GRAD EDUC:** MS, 1966, Univ. of MI; **MIL SERV:** USAF, Capt. (Fighter Pilot), Distinguished Flying Cross, Air Medal w/9 OLC; **OTHER ACT & HONORS:** AZ Theater Co.; Selective Serv. Bd.; Tucson Jewish Community Council; **HOME ADD:** 2455 E. Miraval Primero, Tucson, AZ 85718, (602)299-0234; **BUS ADD:** 5656 E. Grant Rd., Ste. 100, Tucson, AZ 85712, (602)886-4000.

MAROON, G. Tyson——B: Nov. 4, 1929, New York, NY, *Sr. VP*, Cushman & Wakefield, Inc., Headquarters Office; **PRIM RE ACT:** Broker, Consultant; **SERVICES:** Help define customer's objectives and requirements for office or warehouse facilities on a national basis; Locate and negotiate these facitities as needed; **REP CLIENTS:** Fortune 500, major service organ. and intl. clients; **PROFL AFFIL & HONORS:** RE Bd. of NY, Rotary Club of NY, Optimist Club of NY; **EDUC:** BS, 1952, Mgmt. & Mktg., Fordham Univ.; **OTHER ACT & HONORS:** Mendham, NJ - Mayor's Fin. Comm.; **HOME ADD:** Cherry Lane RFD 1, Mendham, NJ 07945, (201)543-7070; **BUS ADD:** 1166 Ave. of the Amer., New York, NY 10036, (212)841-7531.

MAROVITZ, James L.——B: Feb. 21, 1939, Chicago, IL, *Partner*, Sidley & Austin; **PRIM RE ACT:** Attorney; **REP CLIENTS:** Shopping center devels., lenders, comml. lessors and lessees and office devels.; **PROFL AFFIL & HONORS:** ABA, IL State Bar Assn., Chicago Bar Assn.; **EDUC:** BS, 1960, Bus. Admin., Northwestern Univ.; **GRAD EDUC:** JD, 1963, Law, Northwestern Univ.; **EDUC HONORS:** Order of the Coif; **HOME ADD:** 1443 Dartmouth Lane, Deerfield, IL 60015, (312)945-6659; **BUS ADD:** One First National Plaza, Suite 4800, Chicago, IL 60603, (312)853-7617.

MARQUARDT, Christel E.——B: Chicago, IL, *Atty.*, Cosgrove, Webb & Oman; **PRIM RE ACT:** Attorney; **PROFL AFFIL & HONORS:** KS Bar Assn., ABA, Topeka Bar Assn., KS Trial Lawyers Assn., Secr.-Treas. KS Bar Assn., Bd. of Editors, KTLA Journal; Chmn. of KS Bar Assn.; Corp. Bus. and Banking Sect.; **EDUC:** BS Ed, 1971, Education, MO Western, St. Joseph, MO; **GRAD EDUC:** JD, 1974, Law, Washburn Univ., School of Law; **EDUC HONORS:** Managing Editor Washburn Law Journal, Mobee Scholar, Grad. With honors; **OTHER ACT & HONORS:** YWCA Fund; Who's Who in Amer. Women; Mayors Comm. on status of Women; Topeka & KS Women's Poli. Caucus Republican Comm. Woman & Ward Capt., Phi Kappa Phi; **HOME ADD:** 3121 Briarwood Circle, Topeka, KS 66611, (913)266-4590; **BUS ADD:** Suite 1100, First Natl. Bank Tower, Topeka, KS 66603, (913)235-9511.

MARQUARDT, Vern A.——B: July 5, 1922, Dixon, SD, *Pres.*, Commercial National Bank of L'Anse; **PRIM RE ACT:** Banker; **PROFL AFFIL & HONORS:** Member of Fed. Reserve Bank Bd., Minneapolis, MN; **EDUC:** 1948, Gustavus Adolphus Coll.; **GRAD EDUC:** 1961, School of Banking, Madison, WI; **MIL SERV:** USN, Lt.j.g.; **OTHER ACT & HONORS:** Treas., W. Upper Peninsula Planning & Devel. Rgn.; Bayview Shrine Club (Ahmed Temple), L'Anse, MI; L'Anse Lions Club; **HOME ADD:** 218 W. Eastern, L'Anse, MI 49946, (906)524-6230; **BUS ADD:** 1 E. Broad St., L'Anse, MI 49946, (906)524-6172.

MARQUIS, George L.——B: Sept. 11, 1918, Oakland, CA, *Principal*, George L. Marquis Real Estate Appraisal Consultant; **PRIM RE ACT:** Broker, Consultant, Appraiser; **SERVICES:** RE, counseling, valuation & appraisal review; **REP CLIENTS:** Lenders, indivs., public & govt. agencies; **PREV EMPLOY:** Loans Guarantee Div. V.A. & FHA, 1946-1957, RE Spec. & Chief Appraiser, Dept. of the Navy, 1957-1980; **PROFL AFFIL & HONORS:** Sr. Member, American Soc. of Appraisers; Sr. Member, Intl. Right of Way Assn., Natl. Assn. of Review Appraisers - Cert. Member of the Intl. College of RE Consulting Profls.; Member Nat'l. Bd. of Realtors; Sr. Member, Assn. of Govt. Appraisers, ASA, SR/WA, AGA, CRA, RECP, Cert. Review Appraiser; **EDUC:** BA, 1942, Educ., Univ. of CA, Berkeley; **MIL SERV:** US Army, 1st Lt., Purple Heart (2), Bronze Star, Combat Infantry Badge; **OTHER ACT & HONORS:** Pres., San Francisco

Chap. Amer. Soc. of Appraisers (1980-1981); **HOME ADD:** 83 Nevada St., Redwood City, CA 94062, (415)368-4834; **BUS ADD:** 83 Nevada St., Redwood City, CA 94062, (415)368-4834.

MARRON, Edward W., Jr.——B: Jan. 29, 1945, NYC, NY, *VP*, Bankers Trust Co., Const. Lending Div./RE Banking Grp.; **PRIM RE ACT:** Banker; **SERVICES:** Const. loans and interim RE Fin.; **PROFL AFFIL & HONORS:** Young Men's RE Assn. of NY; **EDUC:** BS, 1967, Engineering, Wharton School of Fin. and Commerce, Univ. of PA; **HOME ADD:** 22 Winding Trial, 07430, Mahway, NJ; **BUS ADD:** 280 Park Ave., NYC, NY 10017, (212)850-3047.

MARRS, Edward J.——B: Apr. 28, 1923, Salem, MA, *Dir. - RE & Indus. Devel.*, Boston & ME Corp.; **PRIM RE ACT:** Property Manager; **PROFL AFFIL & HONORS:** Amer. Railway Devel. Assn., MA Econ. Devel. Council, Northeastern Indus. Devel. Counicl; **EDUC:** BBA, 1949, Mgt., Boston Univ.; **MIL SERV:** USN; **HOME ADD:** 3 Hamilton St., Salem, MA 01970, (617)744-1493; **BUS ADD:** Iron Horse Park, No. Billerica, MA 01862, (617)663-9300.

MARSELE, Peter R.——B: Aug. 12, 1924, Waterbury, CT, *RE Appraiser & Assessor*, Town of Bloomfield; **PRIM RE ACT:** Consultant, Appraiser, Assessor; **SERVICES:** RE Appraising; **REP CLIENTS:** Govt. agencies; mcpl., state & fed. banks; attys.; public utilities; **PROFL AFFIL & HONORS:** Soc. of RE Appraisers; Intl. Assn. of Assessing Officers; Amer. Rights of Way, SRA; CCMA; Cert. Assessment Evaluator; **OTHER ACT & HONORS:** Assessor, Bloomfield, CT 30 yrs.; Self-employed RE Appraiser 37 yrs.; **HOME ADD:** 2 Cyrus Ln., Bloomfield, CT 06002, (203)242-1051; **BUS ADD:** Town Hall, Bloomfield, CT 06002, (203)243-8971.

MARSH, Daniel A., Jr.——B: July 18, 1941, Chicago, IL, *Sr. Partner*, Forsberg, Marsh, Wenzel and Kerwin; **PRIM RE ACT:** Broker, Attorney, Owner/Investor, Instructor; **SERVICES:** Legal services, counseling devel.; **PREV EMPLOY:** RE Mgr. and Asst. to RE VP, Nat. Tea Co., Chicago, IL, 1965-1970; **PROFL AFFIL & HONORS:** ABA; Chicago Bar Assn.; IL State Bar Assn.; **EDUC:** BBA, 1964, Mktg., Loyola Univ., Chicago; **GRAD EDUC:** JD, 1971, John Marshall Law School, Chicago; **MIL SERV:** US Army, E-4; **OTHER ACT & HONORS:** Pres., John Marshall Law School Alumni Assn., 1981; Tr., Morris Animal Found.; Adjunct Prof., John Marshall Law School, Chicago - Courses Real Prop. and Land Use Control; **HOME ADD:** 653 W. Wrightwood, Chicago, IL 60614, (312)528-8897; **BUS ADD:** 135 S. LaSalle St., Chicago, IL 60614, (312)782-1403.

MARSH, Dexter H., Jr.——B: March 30, 1931, Newton, MA, *VP*, Meredith & Grew Inc.; **PRIM RE ACT:** Broker, Consultant, Appraiser; **PREV EMPLOY:** 27 Yr. with Meredith & Grew; **PROFL AFFIL & HONORS:** Soc. of Indus. & Realtors, N.E. Chap. Pres. 1972; **EDUC:** Univ. NH, Boston Univ.; **MIL SERV:** USA, Cpl.; **OTHER ACT & HONORS:** Needham Housing Auth.(Chmn. 1977), MA Maternity & Foundling Hospital (dir.), Needham YMCA (dir.); **HOME ADD:** 304 Country Way, Needham, MA 02192, (617)444-8555; **BUS ADD:** 125 High St., Boston, MA 02110, (617)482-5330.

MARSH, R.——B: Jan. 30, 1937, Chicago, IL, *Pres.*, Marsh & Assoc.; **PRIM RE ACT:** Broker, Architect, Consultant, Appraiser, Builder, Property Manager, Lender, Owner/Investor, Insuror; **SERVICES:** Above; **PREV EMPLOY:** Arthur Rubloff & Co. 1966-1975; **PROFL AFFIL & HONORS:** RESSI; **EDUC:** BS, 1958, Const./RE Fin., MI State Univ.; **GRAD EDUC:** MBA, 1964, Bus., Northwestern Univ.; **EDUC HONORS:** Summa Cum Laude, Magna Cum Laude; **MIL SERV:** USAF, 1st Lt.; **OTHER ACT & HONORS:** Bd. of Advisors ISS Co.; **BUS ADD:** 11 Wimbledon Rd., Lake Bluff, IL 60044, (312)234-9168.

MARSH, William D.——B: Aug 29, 1947, Detroit, MI, *Pres.*, Renaissance Investment Co., Inc.; **PRIM RE ACT:** Broker, Developer, Property Manager, Owner/Investor; **SERVICES:** Sales, exchanges, mgmt. of comml. investment props.; **PREV EMPLOY:** B. F. Chamberlain Co., R.E. Sales 1970; **PROFL AFFIL & HONORS:** Detroit Bd. of Realtors, The Academy of Real Estate, MI Realtors Exchange Div. (MARED), FL Real Estate Exchange(FREE), CCIM, CPM; **EDUC:** BBA, 1969, Real Estate Law, W. MI Univ.; **EDUC HONORS:** Cum Laude; **OTHER ACT & HONORS:** The Detroit Club; **HOME ADD:** 7102 Woodbank Dr., Birmingham, MI 48025, (313)626-0081; **BUS ADD:** 4470 Second Blvd., Detroit, MI 48201, (313)833-1540.

MARSHALL, Carol M.——B: Aug. 27, 1935, Cincinnati, OH, Public & Private Consultants, Inc.; **PRIM RE ACT:** Attorney, Developer, Owner/Investor; **SERVICES:** Comml. & indus. devel.; **PREV EMPLOY:** Leg. Asst. to Sen. C. Percy, Sen. R. Griffin, Cong. Robert Jaft, Cong William Stanton; Asst. Dir. OEO for Cong Rels, Vista & OPD; **EDUC:** BA, 1960, Pol. Sci., George Washington Univ.; **GRAD EDUC:** JD, 1975, Univ. of CA, Berkeley; **OTHER ACT & HONORS:** Asst. Dir., OEO; Dir. Vista; Bd. of Govs.; Opportunity Funding Corp., Wash.,DC; **HOME ADD:** 1645 Timberhill Rd., Santa Rosa, CA 94501; **BUS ADD:** 225 10th Ave., San Francisco, CA 94118, (415)387-7122.

MARSHALL, Donald L.——*VP*, Wyman-Gordon Co.; **PRIM RE ACT:** Property Manager; **BUS ADD:** 105 Madison St., Worcester, MA 01613, (617)756-5111.*

MARSHALL, E. David——B: Dec. 18, 1943, Dallas, TX, *VP of Operations*, S & S Properties, Inc.; **PRIM RE ACT:** Broker, Appraiser, Developer, Property Manager, Syndicator; **SERVICES:** Prop. Mgmt., Synd., Devel., Appraisal; **REP CLIENTS:** Indiv. investors in multifamily and comml. props.; **PREV EMPLOY:** Henry S. Miller Housing Corp., VP 1975-79; **PROFL AFFIL & HONORS:** Instit. of RE Mgmt. & NAR; Dir. Houston Apt. Assn. & TX Apt. Assn., Cert. Prop. Mgr.; **EDUC:** Pol. Sci., 1968, Pre-Law, E. TX State Univ., Commerce, TX; **GRAD EDUC:** MBA, 1977, RE, So. Methodist Univ., Dallas, TX; **MIL SERV:** USMC, Sgt.; **OTHER ACT & HONORS:** Dir. Houston Apt. Assn. & TX Apt. Assn.; **HOME ADD:** 9403 Fondren Rd., Houston, TX 77074, (713)981-5083; **BUS ADD:** 11,100 S. Wilcrest, Houston, TX 77099, (713)495-9523.

MARSHALL, Marvin G.——B: July 4, 1937, Linn Cty., KS, *VP*, Farb Investments; **PRIM RE ACT:** Developer; **REP CLIENTS:** Major Nat. and Intl. Corp.; **PREV EMPLOY:** Crown Ctr. Redevelopment Corp.; **PROFL AFFIL & HONORS:** ULI, Recipient of Mktg. Exec. of the Year Award 1974; **EDUC:** KS City Univ.; **GRAD EDUC:** So. Methodist Univ.; **MIL SERV:** US Army 1954; **OTHER ACT & HONORS:** Nat. Trust for Hist. Preservation; **HOME ADD:** 1927 North Blvd., Houston, TX 77002, (713)654-4444; **BUS ADD:** 5444 Westhiemer, Ste. 400, Houston, TX 77056, (713)840-7333.

MARSHALL, Richard K.——B: Sept. 3, 1948, Great Bend, KS, *Principal*, Denton Harper Marshall, Inc.; **PRIM RE ACT:** Consultant, Owner/Investor; **OTHER RE ACT:** Land Planner, Landscape Arch.; **SERVICES:** Consulting Land Planning, Site Design Landscape Arch.; **REP CLIENTS:** Public Agencies, Dev.; **PREV EMPLOY:** Other Consulting Firms 1971-1975; **PROFL AFFIL & HONORS:** Amer. Soc. of Landscape Arch.; **EDUC:** B of Landscape Arch., 1971, KS State Univ.; **HOME ADD:** 819 St. Paul St., Denver, CO 80206, (303)388-3745; **BUS ADD:** 1756 Blake St., Denver, CO 80202, (303)892-5566.

MARSHALL, W. Thomas, Jr.——B: July 28, 1949, VA, *Pres.*, Marshall Appraisals, Inc.; **PRIM RE ACT:** Consultant, Syndicator; **SERVICES:** Sponsor synd., consult with devels.; **REP CLIENTS:** Pensions, trusts, indivs.; **PROFL AFFIL & HONORS:** AIREA; Soc. of RE Appraisers, MAI, SRPA; **EDUC:** BS, 1973, Fin., Troy State Univ.; **MIL SERV:** US Army, CW2, Bronze Star, 2 Distinguished Service Medals, Air Medals; **OTHER ACT & HONORS:** Instr. of FL License Law Update, SREA, AIREA; **HOME ADD:** 3186 Hyde Park Pl., Pensacola, FL 32503; **BUS ADD:** 124 W. Romana St., PO Box 1882, Pensacola, FL 32589, (904)434-6783.

MARSILJE, E.H.——B: Nov. 7, 1942, Holland, MI, *Mgr. - Gen.*, Title Office, Western MI; **PRIM RE ACT:** Owner/Investor; **OTHER RE ACT:** Title Insurance; **SERVICES:** Aid in RE transaction; **PROFL AFFIL & HONORS:** ALTA; MLTA; AICPA; MACPA, CPA; **EDUC:** BA, 1964, Bus., Hope College; **GRAD EDUC:** MBA, 1965, Acctg., Univ. of MI; **OTHER ACT & HONORS:** Township Planning Commn.; **HOME ADD:** 1493 S. Shore Dr., Holland, MI 49423, (616)335-3800; **BUS ADD:** 226 River Ave., POB 1119-C, Holland, MI 49423, (616)396-2303.

MARSTERS, Frank H., III——B: Aug. 14, 1949, Erie, PA, *Pres.*, Marsters Company; **PRIM RE ACT:** Consultant, Builder, Owner/Investor; **SERVICES:** Resid. Bldg. Light Comm.-Bldg./Remodeling; **PROFL AFFIL & HONORS:** Nat. Assn. Home Builders, TX Assn. of Home Builders; Greater Houston Builders Assn., GHBA-Remodelers Council-Bd. of Dir.; GHBA-Membership Comm.; GHBA-Consumer Affairs Comm.; GHBA-Life Spike; Spike Club Comm.; **OTHER ACT & HONORS:** Life Member NRA; Life Member Houston Livestock Show & Rodeo; Member USGA; Ft. Bend Assn. for Retarded Citizens; Life Member TX Rifle Assn.; Member Bayou Rifles; **HOME ADD:** 2911 Glenn Lakes, Missouri City, TX 77459, (713)437-7202; **BUS ADD:** Quail Valley Business Park, 1306 FM 1092 #404, Missouri City, TX 77459, (713)499-5506.

MARSTON, W. Emmett——B: Nov. 11, 1928, Birmingham, AL, *Partner*, Martin, Tate, Morrow & Marston; **PRIM RE ACT:** Attorney, Instructor; **SERVICES:** Closing Atty. for comml. & resid. prop. trial atty. for comml. and resid. loans; **REP CLIENTS:** National insurance cos., banks, reits and other instnl. investors in comml. prop.; **PREV**

EMPLOY: Law Clerk to Judge Edwin R. Holmes, United States Ct. of Appeals for the 5th Circuit (1953-1955); **PROFL AFFIL & HONORS:** ABA, TN Bar Assn., Memphis & Shelby Cty. Bar Assn.; MS Bar Assn., Amer. Coll. of Mort. Attys.; Pres. Memphis & Shelby Cty. Bar Assn.; Standing Committee on Membership ABA; Bd. of Govs., TN Bar Assn.; **EDUC:** BBA, 1952, Acctg., Money & Banking, Univ. of MS, Univ. of TN; **GRAD EDUC:** LLB with Distinction, 1953, Law, Univ. of MS; **EDUC HONORS:** Beta Gamma Sigma, Phi Delta Phi Award for Outstanding Sr.; **MIL SERV:** US Army, Lt. Korea; **OTHER ACT & HONORS:** Pres. Law Alumni, Univ. of MS; VChmn. Lamar Order, Univ. of MS; **HOME ADD:** Memphis, TN; **BUS ADD:** 705 Union Planters National Bank Bldg., Memphis, TN 38103, (901)525-5881.

MARTELL, James G.——B: May 6, 1952, Ashland, WI, *Dir., RE Div., VP*, The Madsen Corp.; **PRIM RE ACT:** Broker, Consultant, Appraiser, Developer, Lender, Builder, Owner/Investor, Property Manager, Syndicator; **SERVICES:** All aspects of the total RE process; **REP CLIENTS:** Indivs., corps., instnl. pension funds; **PREV EMPLOY:** S&L indus. 1974-1978; **PROFL AFFIL & HONORS:** Soc. of RE Appraisers; CCIM; Local, State Natl. Bd. of Realtors; **EDUC:** BBA, 1974, Fin. & Inv. Banking - Urban Land Econs., Univ. of WI; **HOME ADD:** 7605 Westchester, Middleton, WI, (608)836-7838; **BUS ADD:** 502 Atlas Ave., Madison, WI 53714, (608)221-3432.

MARTENS, Barry J.——B: June 11, 1941, Chicago, IL, *Owner/Proprietor*, Development Enterprises; **PRIM RE ACT:** Consultant, Developer, Builder, Owner/Investor, Property Manager; **SERVICES:** Total Shopping Center Devel. from Beginning to Final Ownership; **REP CLIENTS:** Also Land Devel. and Consulting for Retailers and Other Devels. Props. Mgmt. and Equity Synd.; **PREV EMPLOY:** Dir. of RE, Fabri-Centers of Amer. 1969-1972 Dir. of Leasing, Feast & Feist 1966-1969; **PROFL AFFIL & HONORS:** Intl. Council of Shopping Centers, Nat. Assn. of Homebuilders, CSM; **EDUC:** Bus. Admin., 1962, RE, Univ. of Denver, Scholarship-Nat. Assn. of Home Builders; **GRAD EDUC:** Bus., 1964, Fin., Univ. of Denver; **HOME ADD:** 9094 S Normandy Lane, Dayton, OH 45459, (513)885-7050; **BUS ADD:** 5450 Far Hills Ave., Suite 207, Dayton, OH 45429, (513)434-7665.

MARTENS, Dr. Frank H.——B: Mar. 25, 1915, MA, *Pres.*, RE Inst. of FL, Inc.; **PRIM RE ACT:** Broker, Consultant, Appraiser, Owner/Investor, Instructor, Property Manager; **SERVICES:** RE consultant & educator; **PROFL AFFIL & HONORS:** Ft. Lauderdale Bd. of Realtors, FL Assn. of Realtors, NAR, GRI, CRS, CRA, CRB, CPN, CCIM, AFIM; **EDUC:** AIB, 1952, Law & Bus., Norheastern Univ.; BBA, 1953, RE, Univ. of FL; **GRAD EDUC:** MA, 1955, RE, Univ. of FL; DBA, 1973, RE, Univ. of FL; **MIL SERV:** USN; **BUS ADD:** Suite 12-B, 1151 N Atlantic Blvd., Ft. Lauderdale, FL 33304, (305)565-9293.

MARTENS, Steven J.——B: Oct. 13, 1953, Wichita, KS, *VP and Gen. Mgr. of RE Div.*, The Martens Co.; **PRIM RE ACT:** Broker, Consultant, Appraiser, Developer, Property Manager, Owner/Investor; **SERVICES:** Full Service RE Co.; **PROFL AFFIL & HONORS:** IREM; NAR, Adjunct Prof. of RE Friends Univ., Wichita, KS; **EDUC:** B.G.S., 1975, Univ. of KS; **OTHER ACT & HONORS:** Metro. Area Planning Comn.; **BUS ADD:** PO Box 486, Wichita, KS 67201, (316)262-0000.

MARTENSEN, Robert L.——B: Jan. 1, 1947, Painesville, OH, *Partner*, Martensen, Wong & Co.; **PRIM RE ACT:** Owner/Investor, Syndicator; **REP CLIENTS:** Indiv. and instnl. investors; **EDUC:** BA, 1969, Arch. Sci., Harvard Coll.; **GRAD EDUC:** MD, 1974, Dartmouth Medical School; **EDUC HONORS:** Cum Laude; **BUS ADD:** 1818 Union St., San Francisco, CA 94118, (415)563-3490.

MARTIN, Bill G.——B: Feb. 25, 1930, Centre, AL, *Pres.*, Martin Realty Inc.; **PRIM RE ACT:** Broker; **SERVICES:** Brokerage (listing & selling); **PROFL AFFIL & HONORS:** RESSI, CRB, CRS, GRI; **EDUC:** BS Ind. Mgmt., 1957, Georgia Tech.; **EDUC HONORS:** Phi Kappa Phi; **MIL SERV:** USN, Lt.(JG), Korean Air Medal; **HOME ADD:** 166 Azalea Dr., Gadsden, AL 35901, (205)546-0752; **BUS ADD:** PO Box 1456, Gadsden, AL 35902, (205)547-4943.

MARTIN, Charles E.——B: Aug. 5, 1920, Chicago, IL, *Chmn of Bd.*, Financial Facilities Grp.; **PRIM RE ACT:** Syndicator, Developer, Owner/Investor; **SERVICES:** Entrepreneurial Fin.; **EDUC:** BA, 1942, Cornell Univ.; **GRAD EDUC:** MBA, 1949, Fin., Harvard Univ., Grad. Sch. of Bus. Admin.; **EDUC HONORS:** Magna Cum Laude, With distinction; **MIL SERV:** USA Air Corp., Lt. Col., DFC, 6 air medals, 4 Bronze stars, silver star, others; **OTHER ACT & HONORS:** N. Amer. Yacht Racing Union, Natl. Republican Comm., Who's Who in the World; **BUS ADD:** 1707 Steward St., Santa Monica, CA 90404, (213)829-9076.

MARTIN, Charles Tyler, Jr.——B: Dec. 26, 1949, Burnett, TX, *Dir.; Partner*, Stephenson Props.; Stone Acre Co.; **PRIM RE ACT:** Broker, Consultant, Developer, Owner/Investor, Property Manager, Syndicator; **SERVICES:** Investment counseling, synd., devel., & brokerage of comml. RE; **REP CLIENTS:** US & foreign indivs. & insts.; **PREV EMPLOY:** Pres. HBF Prop. Mgmt., 1971-80, Gerald D. Hines Interests, 1972-77; **PROFL AFFIL & HONORS:** IREM, Denver Bd. of Realtors, NAR, CO Assn. of Realtors, BOMA, Cert. Prop. Mgr., RE Broker (CO); **EDUC:** BA, 1972, Mgmt., engrg., Univ. of TX; **EDUC HONORS:** Silver Spurs, Men's Hon. Soc.; **OTHER ACT & HONORS:** Jaycees, Junior Achievement, Amer. Cancer Soc.; **HOME ADD:** 8751 E Mineral Cir., Englewood, CO 80112, (303)771-9114; **BUS ADD:** 899 Logan, Denver, CO 80203, (303)837-1700.

MARTIN, Dick——B: Jan. 24, 1933, Chicago, IL, *Co-Owner, Mgr.*, Red Carpet Michael Shinn & Assoc., RE Investment Div.; **PRIM RE ACT:** Broker, Instructor, Syndicator, Consultant, Owner/Investor; **OTHER RE ACT:** Resid., Comml., Investment, Prop. Mgmt.; **PREV EMPLOY:** Sr. Operations Control Analyst in Aerospace Business; **PROFL AFFIL & HONORS:** RESSI, NAR; **EDUC:** BS, 1960, Mktg., Univ. of San Diego; **EDUC HONORS:** Member MENSA; **MIL SERV:** USA, Cpl.; **HOME ADD:** Box 31393, Aurora, CO 80041, (303)696-0448; **BUS ADD:** 6630 E. Hampden, Denver, CO 80224, (303)759-2100.

MARTIN, Don——*VP Fin. Admin. & Treas.*, Martin Processing Inc.; **PRIM RE ACT:** Property Manager; **BUS ADD:** PO Box 5068, Martinsville, VA 24112, (703)629-1711.*

MARTIN, Donald O.——*VP, Leasing*, Hart Schaffner & Marx; **PRIM RE ACT:** Property Manager; **BUS ADD:** 101 N. Wacker Dr., Chicago, IL 60606, (312)372-6300.*

MARTIN, Douglas F.——B: Dec. 10, 1949, Pittsburgh, PA, *Mgr.*, Price Waterhouse, Mgmt. Advisory Servs.; **PRIM RE ACT:** Consultant; **SERVICES:** Forecasting, project feasibility studies, manual and computerized acctg. systems; **REP CLIENTS:** Tompkins Devel. Co., Trend Mgmt., Tampa Fin. Ctr., First Fed. Mort., Land/Tech., WG Developement Co.; **PROFL AFFIL & HONORS:** Assn. of Accountants, FL Inst. of CPAs; **EDUC:** BS, 1972, Bus. Admin. & Econ., Washington and Lee Univ.; **EDUC HONORS:** Honor Roll, Dean's List; **OTHER ACT & HONORS:** Tampa Bay Museum; **HOME ADD:** 106 Adriatic Ave., Tampa, FL, 33606, (813)253-2347; **BUS ADD:** PO Box 2640, Tampa, FL 33601, (813)223-7577.

MARTIN, Eugene S.——B: March 25, 1925, Portland, ME, *Pres. & Treas.*, Gene Martin Associates, RE; **PRIM RE ACT:** Broker, Developer, Owner/Investor, Property Manager; **SERVICES:** Specializing in selected comml. props.; **PREV EMPLOY:** Community and Indus. Park Devel.; **PROFL AFFIL & HONORS:** NAR, ME Assn. of Realtors, Portland Bd. of Realtors, Past Pres., Indus. Devel. Council of ME; **EDUC:** 1948, Mktg., Univ. of PA (Wharton School); **OTHER ACT & HONORS:** Member City of Portland Bd. of Appeals, Portland Rotary Club (Past Pres.), Portland Ctry. Club, Cumberland Club (Past Pres.); **HOME ADD:** 340 Eastern Promenade Apt. #218, Portland, ME 04101, (207)772-5858; **BUS ADD:** 553 Congress St., P.O. Box 4100 Sta. A, Portland, ME 04101, (207)772-5800.

MARTIN, F. Lewis, Jr.——B: Oct. 19, 1926, Dublin, GA, *Pres.*, Albany Pools, Inc.; **PRIM RE ACT:** Broker, Developer, Owner/Investor, Property Manager, Syndicator; **SERVICES:** Devel., synd., sales of comml. props.; **MIL SERV:** USAAF, 1943-45; **OTHER ACT & HONORS:** Masons, Shriners, Past Pres. Albany Boy's Clubs, Porterfield Mem. Methodist Church; **HOME ADD:** 2100 Lullwater Rd., Albany, GA 31707, (912)436-1361; **BUS ADD:** PO Box 52, Albany, GA 31702, (912)883-2345.

MARTIN, Harry, Jr.——B: June 3, 1944, Bloomington, IL, *Pres.*, H. Martin Const. Co. Inc.; **PRIM RE ACT:** Builder, Property Manager; **MIL SERV:** USA, E-4, 1966-68 GCM; **OTHER ACT & HONORS:** Life Member Amvets, VFW, KC's, Outstanding Local VP-Rantoul Jaycees; **HOME ADD:** 707 Oakcrest, Rantoul, IL 61866, (217)892-8002; **BUS ADD:** 670 N. Ohio, Rantoul, IL 61866, (217)893-4089.

MARTIN, J. Roy, III——B: June 8, 1943, Fayetteville, NC, *VP Const. and Devel.*, The Brandermill Grp.; **PRIM RE ACT:** Developer, Builder, Owner/Investor; **PREV EMPLOY:** Sea Pines, Terry Const. Co.; **PROFL AFFIL & HONORS:** ULI; **EDUC:** 1965, Indus. Mgmt., Clemson Univ.; **GRAD EDUC:** MEd, 1968, Hist., Clemson Univ.; **OTHER ACT & HONORS:** Little League Coaching, Active in Church; **HOME ADD:** 13411 Woodbriar Ridge, Midlothian, VA 23113, (804)744-1732; **BUS ADD:** P.O. Box 287, Midlothian, VA 23113, (804)744-1000.

MARTIN, J. Steven——B: Oct. 20, 1954, Evansville, IN, *Pres.*, Pleasant View Mgmt. Corp.; **PRIM RE ACT:** Broker, Consultant, Developer, Owner/Investor, Property Manager, Syndicator; **SERVICES:** Prop. mgmt. devel. of RE, comml. & investment sales, investment groups, consulting; **PROFL AFFIL & HONORS:** NAR; IREM; RESSI; NAA, CPM, Broker; **EDUC:** BBA, 1976, Mktg., Univ. of Evansville; **OTHER ACT & HONORS:** Kiwanis; **HOME ADD:** 202 Van Buren St., Huntingburg, IN 47542, (812)683-3524; **BUS ADD:** 409 Van Buren St., Huntingburg, IN 47542, (812)683-4258.

MARTIN, James A.——B: Oct. 6, 1945, Columbus, OH, *Dir. Prop. & Facility Mgmt.*, Donaldson Co., Inc., Corp. Staff; **PRIM RE ACT:** Consultant, Engineer, Appraiser, Architect, Builder, Property Manager; **SERVICES:** Corp. staff assistance and control in all RE & const.; **PREV EMPLOY:** Gen. Supt. Bldg. Projects, N. States Power Co., MN; **PROFL AFFIL & HONORS:** NACORE, SORPA, MN Soc. of Profl. Engrs.; IORC, Reg. Profl. Engr. RPA; **EDUC:** B. Mech. Engrg., 1968, HVAC Indus. Engrg., Univ. of MN, Inst. of Tech.; **OTHER ACT & HONORS:** Dakota Cty. Assn. of Retarded Citizens, Bloomington C of C; **HOME ADD:** 7886 131st St., Apple Valley, MN; **BUS ADD:** 1400 W 94th St., Bloomington, MN 55431, (612)887-3103.

MARTIN, James W.——B: Dec. 20, 1949, Turlock, CA, *Atty.*, James W. Martin, PA; **PRIM RE ACT:** Attorney, Owner/Investor; **OTHER RE ACT:** Title ins.; **SERVICES:** Atty. for buyers, sellers and contractors; title ins. atty./agent for Lawyers Title Ins. Co., Richmond, VA; **REP CLIENTS:** Represent brokers and dealers; instructor on corp. law at St. Pete Jr. Coll.; Author and publisher of LOM's Corp. System Manual; upcoming RE manual; **PREV EMPLOY:** Brickley & Martin, Attys. at Law; Gen. Counsel to Presbytery of United Pres. Church and its landholdings and HUD projects; **PROFL AFFIL & HONORS:** FL Bar Assn. (Chmn. Econ. Comm., Real Prop. Sect.; Secretary, Law Office Mgmt. Sect.; Member Corps. Sect.); ABA Sects. of Real Prop.; Mgmt. Law, Econ.); St. Pete Bar Assn.; Dir. & Secretary of Commerce Club of Pinellas Cty., AmJur Book Award in Real Prop., Stetson Law School 1971; St. Pete C of C Outstanding Contribution to Community, Salvador Dali Inst. & Museum; FL Bar Designation in Real Prop. Law; approved atty. for Lawyers Title Ins. Corp.; **EDUC:** BS, 1971, Mathematics, Computers, Stetson Univ.; **GRAD EDUC:** JD, 1974, Law, Stetson Univ. Coll. of Law; **EDUC HONORS:** Kappa Mu Epsilon Math Hon.; Computer lab assistant, AmJur Book Award in Real Prop. Law; Freshman Scholarship; Pres. Intl. Law Soc.; **OTHER ACT & HONORS:** Sec., Dir., Gen. Counsel to Salvador Dali Inst. and Museum; Leadership St. Pete alumni; former Dir., Stetson Univ. Alumni Assn.; Rotary Club of St. Pete; St. Pete C of C; Commerce Club of Pinellas Cty.; **BUS ADD:** Suite 1008, One Plaza Place, St. Petersburg, FL 33701, (813)821-0904.

MARTIN, John (Jack) C.——B: March 27, 1937, Warwick, RI, *Pres.*, The Ross Org., Inc., Ross RE, Inc.; **PRIM RE ACT:** Broker, Developer, Builder, Insuror; **PREV EMPLOY:** Chmn. Bd. of Cty. Commners., Orange Cty., FL 8 yrs.; **PROFL AFFIL & HONORS:** Orlando/WP Bd. of Realtors, GAMA, LVA; **EDUC:** Orlando Jr. Coll., Orlando, FL; **GRAD EDUC:** Univ. of FL; **OTHER ACT & HONORS:** Orange Cty. Commnr., COB of Comm.; COB E. Central FL Regl. Emergency Medical Serv.; Chmn./Orange Cty. 911 Emergency Tele. System Advisory Bd., Chmn., Nat. Conf. of Local Officials Regl. VI, Nat. Assn. of Cities.; **HOME ADD:** 5032 Denis Court, Orlando, FL 32807, (305)857-3481; **BUS ADD:** 4640 S. Orange Blossom Tr., Orlando, FL 32809, (305)851-5510.

MARTIN, Joseph H.——B: Sep. 7, 1932, Trenton, NJ, *Pres.*, Joseph H. Martin Appraisal & RE Co.; **PRIM RE ACT:** Broker, Consultant, Appraiser; **SERVICES:** Valuation, Consultation; **REP CLIENTS:** Princeton Univ., RCA, US Steel, IRS, US Postal Serv.; **PROFL AFFIL & HONORS:** AIREA, SREA, ASA, Inst. of Cert. Valuers; **EDUC:** BS, 1961, RE & Ins., Rider Coll.; **MIL SERV:** USAF, S/Sgt.; **OTHER ACT & HONORS:** Tax Assor, Lawrence Township, 1960-70, RE Educators Assn., Amer. Assn. of Univ. Professors; **HOME ADD:** 2700 Princeton Pike, Lawrenceville, NJ 08648, (609)882-0224; **BUS ADD:** 3131 Princeton Pike, Lawrenceville, NJ 08648, (609)896-2245.

MARTIN, Joseph H.——B: May 23, 1944, Columbus, GA, *Gen. Mgr.*, Plaza Las Americas, Inc.; **PRIM RE ACT:** Consultant, Developer, Owner/Investor, Property Manager; **SERVICES:** Shopping Ctr. Ownership, Devel. Mgmt. & Consulting; **PREV EMPLOY:** Plant Mgr. & Asst. to the Pres., Baster/Travenol Lab., Carolina, PR; **PROFL AFFIL & HONORS:** ICSC, BOMA, Coll. of Engrs. & Surveyors. of PR, PR C of C, Profl. Engr. (PE), Cert. Shopping Ctr., Mgr. (CSM); **EDUC:** BS, 1967, Indus. Engrg., Coll. of Agriculture & Mechanical Arts, PR; **MIL SERV:** USA, Lt., Silver Star w/OLC, Bronze Star V, Bronze Star M w/OLC, Army Comm. Medal, Purple Heart w/OLC; **HOME ADD:** GPO Box 3036, San Juan 00936, PR; **BUS ADD:** GPO Box 3268, San Juan 00936, Puerto Rico, (809)767-1501.

MARTIN, Kurt S.——B: Feb. 20, 1947, Seattle, WA, *VP, Resident Mgr.*, Coldwell Banker Comml. RE Services; **PRIM RE ACT:** Broker; **OTHER RE ACT:** Resdient Mgr. of Stamford and White Plains offices; **PROFL AFFIL & HONORS:** NAR; Intl. Council of Shopping Ctrs.; Nat. Assn. of Indus. & Office Parks; **EDUC:** BA, 1968, Intl. Relations, Stanford Univ.; **GRAD EDUC:** MBA, 1977, Fin., Univ. of Santa Clara; **MIL SERV:** USN, Lt., Air Medal; **HOME ADD:** 507 E. Grauers Ln., Wyndmoor, PA 19118; **BUS ADD:** 1600 Summer St., Stamford, CT 06905, (203)329-7900.

MARTIN, LaDoris——B: June 26, 1933, Oklahoma City, OK, *VP Mktg.*, Bruti-Velchek, Ltd.; **PRIM RE ACT:** Broker, Developer, Builder, Owner/Investor; **OTHER RE ACT:** Resid. Sales; **SERVICES:** Resid., comml. sales, reloc., prop., mgmt., investment counseling, devel., builder; **REP CLIENTS:** Referral Mktg., Inc., Employee Transfer Corp., Homequity; **PROFL AFFIL & HONORS:** RNMI, Greater S Suburban Bd. of Realtors, GRI, CRS, CRB; **HOME ADD:** 18645 Center, Homewood, IL 60430, (312)799-7261; **BUS ADD:** 233 W. Joe Orr Rd., Chicago Heights, IL 60411, (312)756-4700.

MARTIN, Larry——B: Nov. 28, 1939, Columbia, TN, *Chmn*, The Keystone Grp., Inc.; **PRIM RE ACT:** Consultant, Developer, Property Manager, Syndicator; **OTHER RE ACT:** Downtown Redev. & Reuse; **SERVICES:** Consulting devel., feasibility, project mgmt., planning; **REP CLIENTS:** Harbor E, Inc., Hist. Capital Hotel, Ltd., State of AR, Hot Springs Devel. Found., Southside, Ltd.; **PREV EMPLOY:** Dir. of Planning & Devel. Cromwell, Neyland, Trumper, Levy & Gatchell, A/E; Exec. Dir. Petaluma Downtown Assn.; **PROFL AFFIL & HONORS:** Hot Springs Planning Comm.; **EDUC:** BA, 1963, Physics, Hendrix Coll.; **MIL SERV:** USA, Res.; **OTHER ACT & HONORS:** Chmn. Garland Cty. Heart Fund; **BUS ADD:** 402-H ABT Tower, Hot Springs, AR 71901, (501)623-7332.

MARTIN, Lawrence G.——B: Sept. 9, 1938, Toledo, OH, *VP - RE*, Bankers Life and Casualty Company; **PRIM RE ACT:** Broker, Attorney, Developer, Lender, Owner/Investor, Property Manager; **SERVICES:** Responsible for RE and mort. investment portfolio; **PREV EMPLOY:** VP, RE CNA Insurance Cos., 1975-1978; **PROFL AFFIL & HONORS:** Chicago RE Bd., IL State Bar Assn., JD; **EDUC:** BA, 1960, Hist., Univ. of Notre Dame; **GRAD EDUC:** MA, 1963, Hist., Northwestern Univ.; JD, 1966, Law, Univ. of Chicago; Post-Grad. work - Oxford Univ., 1978-1979; **EDUC HONORS:** Cum Laude, Woodrow Wilson Fellowship; **MIL SERV:** USMC; 2nd Lt., 1960-1961; **OTHER ACT & HONORS:** Dir., Center for Amer. Archaeology; Dir., Hist. Pullman Found.; Dir., Duncan YMCA (Chicago); **HOME ADD:** 1332 Sunview Lane, Winnetka, IL 60093, (312)446-2191; **BUS ADD:** 1000 Sunset Ridge Rd., Northbrook, IL 60062, (312)498-1500.

MARTIN, Margaret C.——B: Dec. 10, 1909, IA, *Cert. Resid. Broker*, Martin Realty; **PRIM RE ACT:** Broker, Appraiser, Instructor; **SERVICES:** Gen. RE sales, resid. appraising; **PROFL AFFIL & HONORS:** Springfield Bd. of Realtors; MAR; NAR; RNMI; Asoc., Soc. RE Appraisers, GRI; CRB; Realtor of the Yr., Springfield Bd. of Realtors; **EDUC:** BS, 1931, Biology, MO ValLey Coll.; BS, 1963, Bus. Admin., Drury Coll.; **OTHER ACT & HONORS:** Soroptimist, Intl.; **HOME ADD:** 2365 S. Cedarbrook, Springfield, MO 65804, (417)887-3884; **BUS ADD:** 306 E. Pershing, Springfield, MO 65806, (417)862-6677.

MARTIN, Patrick A.——B: Apr. 25, 1950, Green Bay, WI, *VP*, The Abacus Group, Abacus Realty Advisors, Inc.; **PRIM RE ACT:** Consultant, Lender; **OTHER RE ACT:** Asset Mgmt.; **SERVICES:** Investment counseling & asset mgmt., RE lending; **REP CLIENTS:** Pension funds and instnl. investors; **PREV EMPLOY:** Banking Dept., The Northern Trust Co., Chicago, IL 1974-1976; **PROFL AFFIL & HONORS:** IL Soc. of CPA, CPA; **EDUC:** AB, 1972, Econ., Dartmouth Coll.; **GRAD EDUC:** MBA, 1974, Amos Tuck School; **HOME ADD:** 1350 N. Astor St., Chicago, IL 60610, (312)642-9225; **BUS ADD:** 115 S. LaSalle St., Chicago, IL 60603, (312)346-9172.

MARTIN, Paul E.——B: Feb. 5, 1928, Atchison, KS, *Partner*, Chamberlain, Hadlicka, White, Johnson & Williams; **PRIM RE ACT:** Attorney; **PREV EMPLOY:** Fulbright & Jaworski, Partner 18 yrs; **PROFL AFFIL & HONORS:** ABA, Houston Bar Assn., State Bar of TX, (sect. of real prop. probate & trust law and taxation of ABA), Houston estate & fin. forum (pres. 1965- 66); Houston Bus. & Estate Planning Council, Admitted US Supreme Ct. of TX 1956; Supreme Ct. of PA 1957; Instr. in Estate Planning, Univ. of Houston, Fellow Amer. Coll. of Probate Counsel; **EDUC:** BBA, 1955, Bus., Baylor Univ.; **GRAD EDUC:** LLB, 1956, Baylor Univ.; LLM, 1957, Harvard Univ.; **MIL SERV:** USN, Lt. Comdr.; **OTHER ACT & HONORS:** Tr. Mem. Hospital System, Tr. Baylor Univ.; Pres. Baylor Univ. Devel. Council 1973-74; Chmn. of Deacons, W. Memorial Baptist Church; Co-Author, *How to Live and Die with TX Probate*; **HOME ADD:** 3604

Meadow Lake, Houston, TX 77027, (713)622-6100; **BUS ADD:** 28th Fl. 1100 Milam St., Houston, TX 77002, (713)658-1818.

MARTIN, Peter H.——B: Apr. 11, 1926, Tientsin, China, *Sr. Appraiser*, Union Bank, RE; **PRIM RE ACT:** Consultant, Appraiser; **SERVICES:** RE Appraisal, income tax prep.; **REP CLIENTS:** Union Bank, various indivs., small partnerships and corps.; **PREV EMPLOY:** RE Acctg. with Union Bank; **PROFL AFFIL & HONORS:** Candidate for membership in AIREA, Enrolled to practice before the IRS; **EDUC:** BA, 1948, psych., Occidental Coll.; **MIL SERV:** USN, Ens.; **HOME ADD:** 400 S Flower St. #167, Orange, CA 92668, (714)978-2446; **BUS ADD:** 3505 Hart Ave., Rosemead, CA 91770, (213)687-5070.

MARTIN, Ralph H.——B: Mar. 3, 1930, Buffalo, NY, *Pres.*, Wm. L. Kunkel & Co.; **PRIM RE ACT:** Broker, Developer, Property Manager, Syndicator; **PREV EMPLOY:** General Mills; Dun & Bradstreet; **PROFL AFFIL & HONORS:** Past Pres., Northwest Suburban Bd. of Realtors; Past Pres., IL Assn. of Realtors; Dir., NAR, GRI, IL; **EDUC:** BS, 1957, Mktg./Sales, IN Univ.; Cert. in RE, Central YMCA, REI; **MIL SERV:** US Army; Cpl.; **OTHER ACT & HONORS:** Alderman, City of Des Plaines, 1963-1967; Dir., First Nat. Bank of Des Plaines; Past Pres., Des Plaines Assn. of Commerce & Industry, 1979; **HOME ADD:** 745 Marcella Rd., Des Plaines, IL 60016, (312)827-2275; **BUS ADD:** 734 Lee St., Des Plaines, IL 60016, (312)298-5055.

MARTIN, Robert B., Jr.——B: July 12, 1944, Akron, OH, *Part./Head of Tax Dept.*, Meserve, Mumper & Hughes; **PRIM RE ACT:** Attorney, Instructor; **SERVICES:** Tax and legal advise on RE synds.; **PROFL AFFIL & HONORS:** CA State Bar; ABA; Intl. Assn. Fin. Planners, RESSI; **EDUC:** BA, 1966, Kent State Univ.; **GRAD EDUC:** JD, 1969, Univ. of S. CA; **HOME ADD:** 99 Annandale Rd., Pasadena, CA 91105, (213)793-9742; **BUS ADD:** 333 S. Hope, 35th Floor, Los Angeles, CA 90071, (213)620-0300.

MARTIN, Robert C., Jr.——B: June 2, 1943, Savannah, GA, *Pres.*, Marshall & Martin, Inc.; **PRIM RE ACT:** Broker, Developer, Property Manager, Syndicator; **PROFL AFFIL & HONORS:** NAR, NAHB, Charter Active Life Member Savannah Bd. of Realtors - Million Dollar Club; **EDUC:** Bus. Admin., Armstrong State Coll.; **HOME ADD:** 43 Hemingway Circle, Savannah, GA 31411, (912)352-9683; **BUS ADD:** 401 East 40th St., Savannah, GA 31401, (912)234-2576.

MARTIN, Robert P.——B: Nov. 17, 1947, New Orleans, LA, *Pres., Partner*, R & D Martin Realty Inc.; **PRIM RE ACT:** Broker, Consultant, Appraiser; **SERVICES:** Investment counseling, valuation (comml., indus., timber, recreation); sales of recreation, timber and rural props.; **REP CLIENTS:** TransAmerica; LA Pacific Lumber; So. Pacific Land Co.; U.S. Dept. of Agriculture; CA Dept. of Wildlife; Various Lenders and Corps., Attys.; etc.; **PREV EMPLOY:** Right of Way Agent (CA Dept. of Transportation); RE Analyst; Santa Clara Valley Water Conservation and Flood Control Dist.; **PROFL AFFIL & HONORS:** AIREA; SRA; Shasta Cty. Bd. of Realtors; NAR; CA Assn. of Realtors, Sr. Resid. Member of the Soc. of RE Appraisers; Sr. Resid. Member of the AIREA; **EDUC:** BA, 1969, Econ. Geography, CA State Univ.; **OTHER ACT & HONORS:** Asst. Chief, Whitmore Volunteer Fire Dept.; Ethics Comm., Shasta Co. Bd. of Realtors; **HOME ADD:** Star Rte. Box AK, Whitmore, CA 96099, (916)472-3714; **BUS ADD:** 1538 West St., Redding, CA 96099, (916)472-3024.

MARTIN, Stephen J.——B: Mar. 23, 1948, Michigan City, IN, *Director, RE Certification Program*, Indiana University; **PRIM RE ACT:** Consultant, Instructor, Real Estate Publisher; **OTHER RE ACT:** Auction; **SERVICES:** Auction consultation, comml. brokerage, valuation and instruction; **REP CLIENTS:** Financial instns., intl. corps., and educational instns., Fed. state and local govts.; **PREV EMPLOY:** Private consultant; **PROFL AFFIL & HONORS:** Inst. for RE Inst.; RE Educ. Assn.; Consultant to AIREA; Consultant to Nat. Auctioneers Assn.; IN RE Educ. Assn.; Editorial Review Bd., RE Review, NARA, CREI, CRA, Outstanding Young Man of Amer. 1981; **EDUC:** BS, 1970, mgmt., mktg., IN Univ.; **GRAD EDUC:** MBA/JD, In progress, IN Univ.; **OTHER ACT & HONORS:** IN Soc. of Chicago; IN Univ. Varsity Club; IN Univ. Alumni Assn.; Rotary Intl.; **HOME ADD:** 2001 E. Hillside Dr. Ten Stier Pk., Bloomington, IN 47401, (812)336-8788; **BUS ADD:** IMU 445, Bloomington, IN 47405, (812)333-2299.

MARTIN, Thomas——*Pres.*, Texas Industries, Inc.; **PRIM RE ACT:** Property Manager; **BUS ADD:** 8100 Carpenter Freeway, Dallas, TX 75247, (214)630-8600.*

MARTIN, Vernon A.——*Pres. & Treas.*, Vernon A. Martin, Inc.; **PRIM RE ACT:** Broker, Instructor, Consultant, Appraiser, Developer, Builder, Owner/Investor; **SERVICES:** Gen. Brokerage; **REP CLIENTS:** 10 offices - Bldg. and other corp.; **BUS ADD:** NE Office Park, Rte. 1, Topsfield, MA 01983, (617)887-2371.

MARTIN, Vincent F., Jr.——B: Oct. 20, 1941, Waterbury, CT, *Exec. VP-Gen. Mgr.*, Coldwell Banker, Capital Mgmt. Serv.; **PRIM RE ACT:** Consultant, Developer, Owner/Investor; **OTHER RE ACT:** Investment Mgr.; **SERVICES:** Investment Mgr. and Advisor for Institutional Investors; **REP CLIENTS:** Major Corporate Pension Funds; **PREV EMPLOY:** Peat Marwick, Mitchell & Co.; **PROFL AFFIL & HONORS:** ULI-Intl. Found. of Employee Benefit Plans, Cert. Sr. Review Appraiser; **EDUC:** BS, 1963, Acctg., Boston Coll.; **GRAD EDUC:** 1968, Fin., Harvard Grad. School of Bus. Admin.; **EDUC HONORS:** Cum Laude-Beta Gamma Sigma-Honors Program and Council, MBA with Distinction; **MIL SERV:** US Army, 1st Lt.; **OTHER ACT & HONORS:** Los Angeles Athletic Club-Mountaingate Country Club; **HOME ADD:** 12307 3rd Helena Dr., Los Angeles, CA 90049, (213)472-2890; **BUS ADD:** 533 Fremont Ave.-5th Floor, Los Angeles, CA 90071, (213)613-3491.

MARTIN, Wayne Mallott——B: Jan. 9, 1950, Chicago, IL, *VP*, Inland Real Estate Corporation-1977 to present, Sales; **PRIM RE ACT:** Broker, Consultant, Attorney, Lender, Owner/Investor; **SERVICES:** Counseling-RE: Sales, Purchasing, Legal and Financing; **PREV EMPLOY:** Clyde Fed. S&L - 1972-1975; Amer. Nat. Bank, 1976-1977; **PROFL AFFIL & HONORS:** Chicago Bar Assn.; ABA; IL State Bar Assn.; Northwest RE Bd., Biographical inclusions in Who's Who in the Midwest, Who's Who in Fin. and Indus. and Personalities of Amer.; **EDUC:** BS, 1972, Pre-Medicine, Drake Univ.; **GRAD EDUC:** JD, 1977, Law, DePaul Univ. Law School; **OTHER ACT & HONORS:** Pres.-Golfview Commons Townhouse Owners Assn. - 1979-Present; **HOME ADD:** 219 Golfview Terr., Palatine, IL 60067, (312)934-4382; **BUS ADD:** 829 E. Dundee Rd., Palatine, IL 60067, (312)991-8604.

MARTINSON, Stanley E.——B: Sept. 11, 1935, Clatskanie, OR, *Atty. at Law*, Bullivant, Wright, Leedy, Johnson, Pendergrass & Hoffman; **PRIM RE ACT:** Attorney; **SERVICES:** Legal services; **REP CLIENTS:** Devels., builders, brokers, investors, owners, mgrs.; **PROFL AFFIL & HONORS:** Sect. of Real Prop., Probate and Trust Law of the ABA; RE and Land Use Sect. of the OR State Bar, Past Chmn. OR State Bar, Comms. on Automated Legal Research and Legal Assts.; **EDUC:** BS, 1957, Pol. Sci., Lewis & Clark Coll., Portland, OR; **GRAD EDUC:** JD, 1970, Northwestern School of Law of Lewis and Clark Coll.; **MIL SERV:** US Army; Sgt.; **OTHER ACT & HONORS:** Past Chmn. City Club of Portland—Comm. on Bus. and Labor; **HOME ADD:** 12615 S.W. Bowmont St., Portland, OR 97225, (503)644-9078; **BUS ADD:** 1000 Willamette Center, 121 S.W. Salmon St., Portland, OR 97204, (503)228-6351.

MARVIN, Daniel——B: Oct. 10, 1933, Detroit, MI, *Pres., Chmn. of the Bd.*, Ithaca Landmarks Ltd.; **PRIM RE ACT:** Broker, Consultant, Developer; **OTHER RE ACT:** Bus. & Fin. Consultation and Hist. Preservation Consultation; **SERVICES:** Listing, sales & devel. of comml. & indus. prop., leasing of comml. prop. and bus. fin. consultation to "troubled" cos., co-brokerage of props. across the country; **REP CLIENTS:** Buyers, sellers, tenants and ongoing bus.; **PREV EMPLOY:** Comml. Loan Officer and Bus. Devel. Officer, First Bank & Trust Co., Ithaca, NY (1974/75); **PROFL AFFIL & HONORS:** Intl. Council of Shopping Ctrs.; **MIL SERV:** US Army, Lt. Col.; **OTHER ACT & HONORS:** Masonic - Jeanne D'Arc No. 5, Grand Lodge of France, Rouen, Chmn., Ithaca Street Railway - Ad-Hoc Comm., Chmn., Bdman. House Preservation Project, Past Sec., Tompkins Cty. Art Council; **HOME ADD:** 12 McLallen St., Trumansburg, NY 14886, (607)387-5802; **BUS ADD:** P O Box 202, Trumansburg, NY 14886, (607)387-5742.

MARVIN, Wilbur——B: Apr. 8, 1921, Jamaica, NY, *Pres.*, Commercial Properties Development Corp.; **PRIM RE ACT:** Developer, Owner/Investor; **PROFL AFFIL & HONORS:** Intl. Council of Shopping Ctrs. (State Dir. LA, MS, 3 yrs.; ICSC Bd. of Trus. - 3 yrs.), CSM; **EDUC:** Harvard Univ., 1941, Econ.; **MIL SERV:** USNR, Lt. Cmdr., Purple Heart; **OTHER ACT & HONORS:** City Club, Camelot, Bocage Racquet Club, Baton Rouge, LA; Harvard Club, New Orleans, LA; Rock Tennis Club, San Juan, PR, Navy League, **HOME ADD:** 1127 Longwood Dr., Baton Rouge, LA 70806, (504)343-3079; **BUS ADD:** 1762 Dallas Dr., Baton Rouge, LA 70806, (504)924-7206.

MARX, Max C.——B: Mar. 20, 1953, Bogalusa, LA, *Corp. Counsel*, Saxon Industries, Inc., Legal Dept.; Corp. Hdqtrs.; **PRIM RE ACT:** Attorney; **SERVICES:** Leases & tax certiorari; **PROFL AFFIL & HONORS:** Assn. of the Bar of Cty. of NY; NY State Bar Assn.; Assn. Henri Capitant; LA Bar Assn.; NY Bar and LA Bar Admissions; **EDUC:** BA, 1975, Phil., LA State Univ., Baton Rouge, LA; **GRAD EDUC:** JD, 1978, Law, LA State Univ.; M.Phil, 1981, Phil., Columbia Univ., NY, NY; **EDUC HONORS:** Mu Sigma Rho, Phi Kappa Phi,

Moot Court Bd.; Teaching Asst. in Trial and Appellate Advocacy, President's Fellowship; **OTHER ACT & HONORS:** Amer. Philosophical Assn.; **HOME ADD:** 977 Woodbury Rd., Highland Mills, NY 10930, (914)928-2969; **BUS ADD:** 1230 Ave. of the Americas, NY, NY 10020, (212)246-9500.

MARZOCCO, Leonard J.——**B:** Dec. 17, 1942, Brooklym, NY, *Dir. of Leasing & Devel.*; **PRIM RE ACT:** Developer, Builder, Owner/Investor, Property Manager; **SERVICES:** Recycling reg. shopping ctrs., leasing, master planning, reconstruction; **REP CLIENTS:** Maj. shopping ctrs.; **PROFL AFFIL & HONORS:** ICSC; **EDUC:** BSME, 1964, Polytechnic Inst. of NY; **MIL SERV:** US Army, 1st Lt.; **HOME ADD:** 913 Park Ave., Huntington, NY 11743, (516)549-8086; **BUS ADD:** 358B Mid Island Plaza, The Plaza at Mid Island, Hicksville, NY 11802, (516)935-9700.

MASERITZ, Guy B.——**B:** June 5, 1937, Baltimore, MD, *Atty.*, Sole Practitioner; **PRIM RE ACT:** Attorney; **SERVICES:** Contract law, secs. law, and tax law; **REP CLIENTS:** Devels., gen. partners, and mgmt.; **PREV EMPLOY:** U. S. Securities & Exchange Commn. (1966-1970); American Life Insurance Assn. (1971-74); U. S. Dept. of Justice - Antitrust (1974-1978); **PROFL AFFIL & HONORS:** MD Bar Assn.; ABA; Howard Cty. Bar Assn., Recipient of Justice Dept. Awards for Outstanding Performance and Spec. Achievement (1976, 1977); Marquis' Who's Who in Amer. Law; **EDUC:** BA, 1959, Poli. Sci., Johns Hopkins Univ.; **GRAD EDUC:** MA and LLB, 1961 & 1966, Econ. and Law, Johns Hopkins Univ. and Univ. of MD; **EDUC HONORS:** Omicron Delta Kappa, Pi Sigma Alpha, Law Review Editorial Bd.; **MIL SERV:** US Army; **OTHER ACT & HONORS:** Chief, Legislative Unit, Antitrust Div., U. S. Dept. of Justice (1977-78), Bd. of Dirs., Howard Co. C of C, Author of various articles and publications; **HOME ADD:** 10510 Green Mt. Cir., Columbia, MD 21044, (301)730-7227; **BUS ADD:** 2000 Century Plaza - Suite 125, Columbia, MD 21044, (301)997-9400.

MASLIN, Harvey L.——**B:** Oct. 22, 1939, Chicago, IL, *Sr. VP & Gen. Counsel; Mgr. Intl. Dept.*, Western Temporary Services, Inc. & Affiliated co's.; **PRIM RE ACT:** Attorney, Owner/Investor, Property Manager; **SERVICES:** Investment counseling, valuation, devel., legal & prop. mgmt.; **PREV EMPLOY:** Partner, law firm of Maslin, Rotundo & Maslin, 1966-67; **PROFL AFFIL & HONORS:** ABA; AZ Bar Assn.; CA Bar Assn.; Phi Alpha Delta; **EDUC:** BS, 1961, Bus. and Public Admin., Univ. of AZ; **GRAD EDUC:** JD, 1964, Law, Univ. of AZ; **EDUC HONORS:** William Khoeler Award, Univ. of AZ, 1960; **OTHER ACT & HONORS:** Republican Club of CA; Commonwealth Club; World Trade Club; John Muir Associates; Who's Who in CA; Who's Who in the West; Who's Who in Indus. & Commerce; Who's Who in American Law; **HOME ADD:** 611 Creekmore Cr., Walnut Creek, CA 94598, (415)933-7167; **BUS ADD:** World Headquarters Bldg., 101 Howard St., San Francisco, CA 94105, (415)981-8480.

MASON, Carroll A.——**B:** Aug. 14, 1935, Portsmouth, VA, *Pres.*, Mand Ent.; **PRIM RE ACT:** Consultant, Developer, Owner/Investor; **SERVICES:** Counseling, devel., packaging; **PREV EMPLOY:** Structural engr., Norfolk, Naval Shipyard, Asst. City Mgr., Portsmouth, VA, Exec. Dir. Ports. Red. & Hous. Auth., Dir. VA FHA, Area Dir. Richmond Area Office, HUD; **PROFL AFFIL & HONORS:** ICMA NAHRO; **EDUC:** BS, Civil engrg., VMI; **GRAD EDUC:** MPA, Public admin., Nova Univ.; **HOME ADD:** 12611 Easthampton Dr., Midlothian, VA 23113, (804)794-8446; **BUS ADD:** 1108 701 E Franklin St., Richmond, VA 23219, (804)643-7261.

MASON, Frank H.——**B:** Jan. 27, 1943, Dallas, TX, *Reg. Mgr.*, Public Storage Mgmt. Inc., Southeastern Region; **PRIM RE ACT:** Consultant, Property Manager; **SERVICES:** Prop. mgmt., consulting for mini-warehouses; **REP CLIENTS:** Lenders, indiv. or inst. investors or owners of mini-warehouses; **PREV EMPLOY:** Capital Devel. Corp., 1972-77; **PROFL AFFIL & HONORS:** NARA; Intl. Coll. of RE Consulting Profls.; Intl. Inst. of Valuers; Inst. of Bus. Appraisers; Amer. Inst. of Mgmt., CRA; RE Consulting; Prof.; Sr. Cert. Appraiser; **EDUC:** 1965, Russell Sage Coll.; **OTHER ACT & HONORS:** Who's Who in the West, 16th ed.; Who's Who in Comm. Serv., Anaheim Police Officers Hon. Assn.; **HOME ADD:** 7060 Roundtable Ct., Smyrna, GA 30080, (404)436-9881; **BUS ADD:** 1905 Powers Ferry Rd., Suite 100, Marietta, GA 30067, (404)952-4040.

MASON, Glenn E.——*Mng. Broker*, Mason Realty Service; **PRIM RE ACT:** Developer; **BUS ADD:** 4429 Brook Dr., Jackson, MS 39206, (601)366-7254.*

MASON, Joel——**B:** June 19, 1938, NYC, *Partner*, Mason Raich & Co., Hotels & Motels; **PRIM RE ACT:** Developer, Owner/Investor, Syndicator; **REP CLIENTS:** Holiday Inn, Ramada Inn, Quality Inn, own and operate. We are consultants to banks and fin. instns regarding troubled props. in hospitality field. We acquire for our own portfolio; **EDUC:** CPA, 1960, Acctg., NY Univ. Sch. of Commerce, Accounts & Fin.; **EDUC HONORS:** Statistic Hon. Soc.; **OTHER ACT & HONORS:** Mill River Club, Brookville, NY; **HOME ADD:** 70 Village Hill Dr., Dix Hills, NY 11746, (516)499-5625; **BUS ADD:** 60 Cuttermill Rd., Great Neck, NY 11021, (516)466-8800.

MASON, Thomas A.——**B:** May 4, 1936, Cleveland, OH, *Partner*, Thompson, Hine & Flory; **PRIM RE ACT:** Attorney; **SERVICES:** Legal; **REP CLIENTS:** Lenders and Indiv. or instnl. investors in comml. prop.; **PROFL AFFIL & HONORS:** ABA, OH State Bar Assn., Cleveland Bar Assn., Cleveland Mort. Bankers Assn., Member of Lenders Council of Amer. Land Title Assn.; **EDUC:** BA, 1958, Econ., Kenyon Coll.; **GRAD EDUC:** LLB, 1961, Case-Western Reserve Univ.; **EDUC HONORS:** Cum Laude; **MIL SERV:** US Marines, Capt., 1962-65, Distinguished Serv. Award; **HOME ADD:** 23375 Duffield Rd., Shaker Hts., OH 44122, (216)283-2443; **BUS ADD:** 1100 National City Bank Bldg., Cleveland, OH 44114, (216)566-5519.

MASON, Thomas G.——**B:** June 17, 1936, Ft. Atkinson, WI, *Owner*, Mason & Co.; **PRIM RE ACT:** Broker, Appraiser, Property Manager, Owner/Investor, Insuror; **SERVICES:** RE Sales, RE Mgmt., Insurance; **PROFL AFFIL & HONORS:** IREM; NAA; TAA; TAR; NAR, CPM; **EDUC:** BBA, 1958, RE & Fin., Univ. of WI, Madison; **OTHER ACT & HONORS:** City of Harlingen, Bd. of Adjustments; Capitol Improvements Bd.; Bd. of Equalization; Harlingen C of C; **HOME ADD:** 101 Wildwood, Harlingen, TX 78550, (512)423-5143; **BUS ADD:** 522 E Harrison, Harlingen, TX 78550, (512)423-6166.

MASSACHI, Benjamin——**B:** July 29, 1941, Iran, *Owner*, Sunny Realty; **PRIM RE ACT:** Broker, Engineer, Owner/Investor, Property Manager, Syndicator; **REP CLIENTS:** Private Indivs.; **PREV EMPLOY:** 8 years exper. in RE in NY, NC; **PROFL AFFIL & HONORS:** NAR & State & Local Chap., Amer. Soc. of ME; **EDUC:** BS, 1962, Civil Engrg., Abadan Inst. of Tech.; **GRAD EDUC:** MSE, 1967, 1973, MBA, ME, Fin., City Univ. of NY, Univ. of Rochester; **HOME ADD:** 417 Bass Lane, Matthews, NC 28105, (704)847-0527; **BUS ADD:** PO Box 233, Matthews, NC 28105, (704)847-3258.

MASSEY, Gary E.——**B:** Nov. 3, 1946, Lakeland, FL, *Partner*, Massey, Alper & Walden P.A.; **PRIM RE ACT:** Attorney, Developer, Owner/Investor; **SERVICES:** Closings for RE, title ins., devel condo & synd.; **REP CLIENTS:** Indian Ridge Patio Homes, Inc.; Spring Pines Devel. Corp.; Chelsea Title & Abstract Co.; Headlands, Inc.; Delco Inc.; Pinnacle Prop. Inc.; Cameo Prop. Inc.; Ricara Inc.; **PROFL AFFIL & HONORS:** Home Builders Assn., Mid-FL; FL Bar, Real Prop. Sect.; Dir. Seminole Bd. of Realtors and Attys; Advisory Bd. Comml. Bank, Altamonte Springs; Arbitrator with the Amer. Arbitration Assn.; **EDUC:** BSBA, 1968, Bus. Admin., Univ. of FL; **GRAD EDUC:** JD, 1971, Univ. of FL; **EDUC HONORS:** Grad. with Honors; **OTHER ACT & HONORS:** City atty. Winter Springs, 1975-78; City Atty. Lake Mary, FL, 1975-; Chmn. 18th curcuit Judicial Nominating Comm.; **HOME ADD:** 715 Tuscawilla Tr., Winter Springs, FL 32708, (305)678-2213; **BUS ADD:** 355 E Semoran Blvd., Altamonte Springs, FL 32701, (305)834-8111.

MASSEY, J. Alvin——**B:** Jan. 13, 1948, Hagerstown, MD, *Pres.*, Massey RE Ltd.; **PRIM RE ACT:** Broker, Consultant, Developer, Owner/Investor; **SERVICES:** Devel. & synd. comml. & investment counseling; **REP CLIENTS:** Investor joint venture with landowners; **PROFL AFFIL & HONORS:** MD and WV Chap. CCIM, MD & WV FLI, Past Pres. WV FLI; **EDUC:** BS, 1970, Bus. Admin., Towson State Univ.; **HOME ADD:** Rt. 3 Box 227, Williamsport, MD 21795, (301)223-6386; **BUS ADD:** Rt. 3 Box 227, Williamsport, MD 21795, (301)223-6386.

MASSIE, James Corban——**B:** Apr. 22, 1941, Washington, DC, *Part.*, LaCapra & Massie; **PRIM RE ACT:** Attorney, Owner/Investor, Insuror; **OTHER RE ACT:** Lobbyist; **REP CLIENTS:** Alliance of Amer. Ins., Church Mutual Ins. Co.; **PROFL AFFIL & HONORS:** FL Bar, Tallahassee Bar, ABA; **EDUC:** BA, 1964, Pol. Sci. & Econ., Miami Univ., OH; **GRAD EDUC:** JD, 1974, FL State Univ.; **EDUC HONORS:** Dean's List, Law Review, Freshman Moot Ct. Hon. Winner; **MIL SERV:** USA, Sgt.; **HOME ADD:** 211 Mill Branch Rd., Tallahassee, FL 32312, (904)893-2639; **BUS ADD:** PO Box 10137, Suite 712, Barnett Bank Bldg., Tallahassee, FL 32302, (904)222-8021.

MASTERMAN, John S.——**B:** Mar. 24, 1949, Los Angeles, CA, Ashwill - Burke & Co.; **PRIM RE ACT:** Broker, Developer, Builder, Syndicator; **PREV EMPLOY:** Construction; **PROFL AFFIL & HONORS:** Assn. of S. Bay Brokers (San Jose area); **EDUC:** BS, 1971, World trade & econ., St. Marys Coll., Moraga, CA; **OTHER ACT & HONORS:** Big Brothers of Amer.; **HOME ADD:** 15626 Zayante Rd., Los Gatos, CA 95030, (408)353-3912; **BUS ADD:** 2200 Laurelwood Rd., Santa Clara, CA 95050, (408)496-1000.

MASTERSON, James W.——B: Nov. 3, 1917, Milton, WI, *Realtor - Owner*, Jim Masterson Assocs.; **PRIM RE ACT:** Broker, Consultant, Appraiser, Owner/Investor, Property Manager, Insuror; **PREV EMPLOY:** US Army, 1941-1945, Instructor - Univ. of WI 1945-1950; Account Exec., Foote, Cone, Belding Adver. Agency Chicago, 1950-53; **PROFL AFFIL & HONORS:** SRA - CRS - GRI; **EDUC:** BS, 1941, Univ. of WI; **GRAD EDUC:** BS, 1942, Speech & Eng., Albert Hall - London, England - 1945; **MIL SERV:** US Army Infantry, Corp., Purple Heart with cluster; **OTHER ACT & HONORS:** Grand Counselor of WI United Comml. Travelers 1979-80; **HOME ADD:** 5116 E. Milwaukee St., R-1, Janesville, WI 53545, (608)754-5736; **BUS ADD:** 121 South Jackson St., Suite #1, PO Box 110, Janesville, WI 53545, (608)752-9011.

MASTIN, R. Fred——B: Jul. 20, 1920, Elkin, NC, *Owner and Sec. & Treasurer*, Foothills Realty & Auction, Inc.; **PRIM RE ACT:** Broker, Appraiser, Insuror; **EDUC:** 1977, Surry Cty. Community Coll.; 1959, LaSalle Ext. Univ.; **EDUC HONORS:** Outstanding Sales Performance: Ins. Cos. (Salesmanships); **OTHER ACT & HONORS:** Mason, York Rite; Shriner; **HOME ADD:** 125 James St., Elkin, NC 28621; **BUS ADD:** 125 James St., Elkin, NC 28621, (919)835-1339.

MATANKY, Eugene——*Pres.*, Eugene Matanky & Assoc. Inc.; **PRIM RE ACT:** Broker, Syndicator, Consultant, Appraiser, Developer, Property Manager, Owner/Investor, Insuror, Real Estate Publisher; **SERVICES:** Mort. financings, mgmt, condo conversions; **REP CLIENTS:** City of Chicago, Lincoln Natl. Bank, IBM; **PROFL AFFIL & HONORS:** NAR, AMO, IL Assoc. of Realtors, GRI, CPM, CCIM, SRS, CRS, CRB, only Realtor in US to have earned all 6 designations; **EDUC:** AA, 1941, Herzl Jr. Coll., Chicago; BS, MS, 1943-55, NW Univ.; **HOME ADD:** 2950 W. Pratt, Chicago, IL 60645; **BUS ADD:** 5250 N. Broadway, Chicago, IL 60640, (312)334-0010.

MATARAZZO, Anthony P.——B: May 13, 1947, Somerville, MA, *Gen Mgr.*, Matarazzo RE; **PRIM RE ACT:** Broker, Consultant, Appraiser, Builder, Property Manager, Owner/Investor; **SERVICES:** Appraisals, const., sales, rentals, devel.; **REP CLIENTS:** Attys., lenders, reloc. firms, V.A. and Sen. public practice; **PROFL AFFIL & HONORS:** Dir. SREA, Dir. S. NH MLS, Sr. Member IREA, Intl. Cert. Appraiser, Local State & Natl. Membership in Bds. of Realtors, NAHB, MLS Highest no. of sales, listing, and highest percentage of submitted listings for member, 1980; Who's Who in the East, Bus. & Fin. 1980-81; **EDUC:** BBA, 1969, Personnel Mgmt., Indus. Relations, Univ. of Miami; **GRAD EDUC:** Acctg., NH Coll.; **EDUC HONORS:** Cited by Dean of B.S., for founding the first 'Bus. Week for Univ. of Miami'; **OTHER ACT & HONORS:** Univ. of Miami Alumni Assn.; **HOME ADD:** 530 Broad St., Nashua, NH 03063, (603)882-1582; **BUS ADD:** 25 Main St., Nashua, NH 03060, (603)883-0136.

MATESICH, Joy——*RE Mgr.*, H.J. Heinz Co.; **PRIM RE ACT:** Property Manager; **BUS ADD:** PO Box 57, Pittsburgh, PA 15230, (412)237-5003.*

MATHIAS, Ray Kermit——B: July 15, 1914, Cheviot, OH, Mathias Real Estate; **PRIM RE ACT:** Broker, Consultant, Appraiser, Builder, Owner/Investor; **SERVICES:** Evaluation RE; **REP CLIENTS:** Lending instns., attys., city, cty., and fed. agencies; **PREV EMPLOY:** Former builder-devel., self-employed, always affiliated with RE activities; **PROFL AFFIL & HONORS:** Soc. of RE Appraisers, Nat. Assn. of Review Appraisers, SRA, CRA; **EDUC:** BBA, 1936, Acctg., Fin. & Banking, Miami Univ., Oxford, OH; **EDUC HONORS:** Delta Sigma Pi, Bus. Profl. Soc.; **MIL SERV:** USNR, 3rd c PO; **HOME ADD:** 3017 Daytona Ave., Cincinnati, OH 45211, (513)661-3322; **BUS ADD:** 3128 Harrison Ave., Cincinnati, OH 45211, (513)661-3322.

MATINHO, Al——B: Apr. 30, 1945, Portugal, Realty Assoc. Execs./DMI Const. Inc.; **PRIM RE ACT:** Broker, Syndicator, Developer, Builder, Property Manager, Owner/Investor; **SERVICES:** Mgmt., Devel., Synd.; **PREV EMPLOY:** Bldg. Contr.; **PROFL AFFIL & HONORS:** RESSI, Various certs. and achievement awards; CCIM; **EDUC:** RE Dev./Bus, AMA Community Coll. AZ; **MIL SERV:** USAF, Sgt.; **OTHER ACT & HONORS:** Toastmasters, Bd. AZ. Apt. Assn.; **HOME ADD:** 2637 N. Plumer Ave., Tucson, AZ 85716, (602)326-6211; **BUS ADD:** 2545 E. Ft. Lowell Rd., Tucson, AZ 85716, (602)323-7661.

MATSEN, Glenn——B: Aug. 11, 1956, Eureka, CA, *VP*, Freeman-Matsen Ins.; **PRIM RE ACT:** Owner/Investor, Insuror; **EDUC:** Bus. Admin., 1979, Oral Roberts Univ.; **HOME ADD:** 2360 Home Dr., Eureka, CA 95501, (707)443-8484; **BUS ADD:** PO Box 122, Eureka, CA 95501, (707)443-4958.

MATSEN, Jeffrey R.——B: Nov. 24, 1939, Salt Lake City, UT, *Partner*, Davidson & Matsen; **PRIM RE ACT:** Broker, Attorney, Instructor; **OTHER RE ACT:** Cert. Tax Specialist by CA State Bar; **SERVICES:** Legal, Tax & Synd. Counseling; **REP CLIENTS:** Security Pac. Nat. Bank; Edwards Theatre Circuit; Kimtruss Corp.; Lumsdaine Const.; Frost Spence Trinen; Self Enterprises, Inc.; Ekotech, Inc.; **PROFL AFFIL & HONORS:** RESSI, Prof. of Law, Western State Univ. Coll. of Law, Fullerton, CA; Instr., Golden Gate Univ., Program of Adv. Taxation, Los Angeles, CA; **EDUC:** BA, 1964, Brigham Young Univ.; **GRAD EDUC:** JD, 1967, UCLA School of Law; **EDUC HONORS:** Cum Laude, Order of the Coif; **MIL SERV:** USMC, Capt., Navy Commendation Medal; **BUS ADD:** 4000 MacArthur Blvd., Suite 600, Newport Beach, CA 92660, (714)752-6426.

MATTHEWS, C. David.——B: June 15, 1946, Anniston, AL, *Pres.*, David Matthews Assoc.; **PRIM RE ACT:** Consultant, Appraiser; **SERVICES:** Appraisals, market analysis, feasibility studies, computer analysis of investment props.; **REP CLIENTS:** Fed., state, and local govt. agencies, maj. corps., investors, attys. and lenders; **PREV EMPLOY:** IL Asst. Assessor, 1969-71; IL Hwy Dept., appraiser, 1971-73; Appraiser & Dir. of counseling, Norman Benedict Assoc. (CT); 1973-76; Dir. of Appraising & Counciling, Citizens Realty & Ins. (IN), 1976-80; **PROFL AFFIL & HONORS:** AIREA, Bd. of Dir.; SREA, Past Chapt. Pres.; Nat., state and local Bd. of Realtors (local Bd. of Dir.); RE Educ. Assn., MAI, SRPA appraisal designations; **EDUC:** BS, 1968, RE, Univ. of TN; **EDUC HONORS:** Dean's List; **OTHER ACT & HONORS:** Leadership Evansville (Comm. Chmn); Evansville C of C (Comm. Chmn); Adjunct faculty member Univ. of Evansville, 1978-81; Univ. of CT, 1974-76; **HOME ADD:** 430 S Boeke Rd., Evansville, IN 47714, (812)477-8037; **BUS ADD:** 711 Southern Securities Bldg., Evansville, IN 47708, (812)428-6000.

MATTHEWS, Drew I.——B: May 24, Rockaway NJ, *V.P.*, W.W.L. Dev. Inc.; **PRIM RE ACT:** Broker, Architect, Syndicator, Developer, Builder, Property Manager, Owner/Investor; **SERVICES:** All services Synd., Devel., Real Prop. Mgmt.; **REP CLIENTS:** Owners, Investors; **PREV EMPLOY:** USMC 1951-1972; **PROFL AFFIL & HONORS:** NAOIP; **EDUC:** AB, 1951, Arch., Dartmouth Coll.; **MIL SERV:** USMC, Lt. Col., several decorations; **OTHER ACT & HONORS:** Soc. Amer. Mil. Engrs., Lions Intl.; **HOME ADD:** 1232 Elizabeth Ave., Naperville, IL 60540, (312)357-2540; **BUS ADD:** 3033 Ogden Ave., Naperville, IL 60540, (312)357-5115.

MATTHEWS, G. Grippe——B: Jan 25, 1943, Indianapolis, IN, *Reg. VP*, Robert A. McNeil Corp., IN; **PRIM RE ACT:** Syndicator, Property Manager, Owner/Investor; **SERVICES:** Synd., acquisition & mgmt.; **REP CLIENTS:** Private investors; **PREV EMPLOY:** Dir. Prop Mgmt. Edward Rose of Ind., 1979-81; Area Mgr. Johnstown Prop., Atlanta GA, 1978-79; Dir. Prop Mgmt., Oxford Dev. Corp, 1972-77; **PROFL AFFIL & HONORS:** Bd. of Dir., Apt. Assn. of IN; Apt. Assn.; Metropolitan Indianapolis Bd. of Realtors; IN, RE Broker, IREM; **EDUC:** BA, 1965, Eng., & Psych., Wabash Coll., Crawfordsville, IN; **GRAD EDUC:** 1968, RE, Mort Lending, RE Mgmt., RE, Law., IN Univ Law School, IREM, CPM; **EDUC HONORS:** Academic Scholarship Jr. Yr., Dean's List, Sr. Yr.; **OTHER ACT & HONORS:** World Vision, Child Sponsor; **HOME ADD:** 1165 Maxwell Ln., Zionsville, IN 46077, (317)873-6826; **BUS ADD:** 9240 N Meridian, Suite 380, Indianapolis, IN 46260, (317)848-1575.

MATTHEWS, Joe F., Jr.——B: Apr. 21, 1919, Durham, ME, *Owner*, Joe F. Matthews & Son; **PRIM RE ACT:** Broker, Appraiser, Developer, Lender, Builder, Owner/Investor; **PREV EMPLOY:** Brown's Auto Supply, Salesman 1944-49; Miller Brudson 49-54 Salesman; **PROFL AFFIL & HONORS:** Lions Club-NC RE Lic. Bd.; NC Auctioneer Bd. member; Rotary; **HOME ADD:** Rt. 2, Brisbane Dr., Farms of New Hope Estate, Chapel Hill, NC, 27514, (919)929-8747; **BUS ADD:** 4420 Boxboro Dr., Durham, ME 27704, (919)477-7395.

MATTICK, Thomas C.——*VP Fin. Treas. & Secy.*, Mark Controls Corp.; **PRIM RE ACT:** Property Manager; **BUS ADD:** 1900 Dempster St., Evanston, IL 60204.*

MATTIS, Taylor——B: Dec. 12, 1937, AL, *Profr. of Law*, So. IL Univ. School of Law; **PRIM RE ACT:** Instructor; **SERVICES:** Teaching first year property, RE fin., and devel. and future interests; **PREV EMPLOY:** Assoc. with law firm of Saunders, Curtis, Ginestra & Gore, Fort Lauderdale, FL; former member of Lawyers' Title Guaranty Fund; **PROFL AFFIL & HONORS:** ABA, Real Property, Probate and Trust Sect.; IL State Bar Assn.; The FL Bar; Amer. Judicature Soc.; **EDUC:** BA Hist., 1960, Hist., Univ. of AL; **GRAD EDUC:** JD, 1963, Law, Univ. of Miami, Coral Gables, FL; **EDUC HONORS:** Phi Beta Kappa, Wig and Robe; Univ. of Miami Law Review; Roger Sorino Award for Outstanding Law Graduate; **OTHER ACT & HONORS:** LLM degree, Yale Univ., 1969; **HOME ADD:** Route 1, Box 396, Carbondale, IL 62901, (618)549-8253; **BUS ADD:** So. IL Univ. School of Law, Carbondale, IL 62901, (618)536-7711.

MATTISON, William——B: July 11, 1935, Troy, NY, *Pres. - Planning Consultant*, Design Consortium Inc., Corp. Design & PLanning; **PRIM RE ACT:** Broker, Architect, Instructor, Consultant, Appraiser, Developer, Builder, Property Manager, Engineer, Lender, Owner/Investor; **OTHER RE ACT:** Investment counseling, Feasibility studies, Design & Const. of Comml. & Residential Prop., Prop. Mgmt.; **REP CLIENTS:** Lenders, Indiv., Corp. & Instnl. Users & Invest.; **PREV EMPLOY:** Assoc. - Dir. Corp. Planning & Design - Walker/Girad. Inc. 1971-1974; Asst. Pres. - JFN Assoc. 1971-1965, Arch. Pres. Designer - Edward Durell Stone, Assoc. 1962-1965; **PROFL AFFIL & HONORS:** Pres.- Realtor-Assoc., Pres. - Neighborhood Assoc. of Taxpayers, Affiliations/Memberships NJ & Nat. RE Assn., Am. Inst. of Arch., AIA; **EDUC:** BID, 1958, Indus. Design, Pratt Inst.; **GRAD EDUC:** MA - PhD, 1965, Arch. RE & Brokerage Law - Econ., NYU - R.I.T. - Academie De La Grande Chaumiere; **EDUC HONORS:** Hon. Grad., Tuition Scholarship, Jr. Class Pres., Magna Cum Laude; **MIL SERV:** USA - Artillery, Capt., Scabbard & Blade Soc.; **OTHER ACT & HONORS:** YMCA, Notary Public (NJ), Coll. Inst.; **HOME ADD:** 133 Grove St., Montclair, NJ, (201)783-5058; **BUS ADD:** 8 Douglas Rd., Glen Ridge, NJ 07028, (201)748-1452.

MATTONE, Joseph M.——B: Sept. 15, 1931, Brooklyn, NY, *Pres.*, Joseph M. Mattone, Mattone Grp. Ltd.; **PRIM RE ACT:** Consultant, Attorney, Developer, Owner/Investor, Syndicator; **SERVICES:** Legal & related fin., evaluation & fin. of substantial RE; **REP CLIENTS:** Joint venture with subs. of maj. savings banks and comml. inst. in NY area, represents Citibank Queens Co., closings and foreclosures; **PREV EMPLOY:** Self employed atty. & devel., fin. consultant for past 25 yrs., former assoc. counsel - NY Senate Authority 1965-67; **PROFL AFFIL & HONORS:** NYS & Amer. Bar Assns., Queens Cty. Builders Assn. Settlement Housing Fund, SJU Council, Columbia Soc. of RE Appraisers, Columbian Lawyers, Equestrian Order of The Holy Sepulchre of Jerusalem, CO of Queens Cty.; **EDUC:** BA, 1953, Hist,. Govt., & Psych., St. Johns Univ.; **GRAD EDUC:** JD, St. Johns Univ.; Various Certificates for attending post grad. seminars & PLI courses; Appraising RE, Columbia; **OTHER ACT & HONORS:** Guest lecturer on co-op & condo. conversions - various seminars hosted by Citibank; **HOME ADD:** 37-20 Regatta Pl., Douglaston, NY 11363; **BUS ADD:** 159-18 N.Blvd., Flushing, NY 11358, (212)961-8880.

MATTSON, B.O.——*RE Mgr.*, Caterpillar Tractor Co.; **PRIM RE ACT:** Property Manager; **BUS ADD:** 100 NE Adam St., Peoria, IL 61629, (309)675-4131.*

MATTSON, Charles W.——B: May 18, 1940, Cadott, WI, *Atty.*; **PRIM RE ACT:** Attorney; **OTHER RE ACT:** Bus. Law Inst.; **SERVICES:** Title examinations, RE Probate matters; **PROFL AFFIL & HONORS:** MN Bar Assn., ABA, ABA Sections: Corp., Banking, & Bus. Law; Real Prop., Probate & Trusts; **EDUC:** BS, 1962, Math. and Physics-Maj., Minor, respec., Univ. of WI at Eau Claire; **GRAD EDUC:** MA, 1966, Math., Univ. of MN; JD, 1975, Law, Hamline Univ. School of Law; **EDUC HONORS:** Summa Cum Laude - Highest G.P.A.; **HOME ADD:** 1766 Bruce Ave., St. Paul, MN 55113, (612)633-6044; **BUS ADD:** 10267 Univ. Ave., N.E., Blaine, MN 55434, (612)786-1360.

MATYAS, Eugene J.——B: July 19, 1933, Hazleton, PA, *Pres.*, F.D. Rich Realty; **PRIM RE ACT:** Engineer, Developer, Builder; **OTHER RE ACT:** Comml. leasing & sales; **PROFL AFFIL & HONORS:** Arbitrator, AAA; Nat. Soc. of Prof. Engrs.; ASCE; CT Soc. of Prof. Engrs.; Soc. of Amer. Mil. Engrs.; ACI; **EDUC:** BSCE, 1955, Civil Engrg., PA State Univ.; **MIL SERV:** US Navy, Lt.; **HOME ADD:** 108 Marshall Ridge Rd., New Cannan, CT 06840; **BUS ADD:** One Landmark Sq., Stamford, CT 06901, (302)359-4440.

MATZ, Kevin D.——B: Sept. 6, 1947, Evergreen Park, IL, *Atty.*, Jenks & Hentzel; **PRIM RE ACT:** Attorney; **PROFL AFFIL & HONORS:** ABA; IL Bar Assn.; Chicago Bar Assn.; **EDUC:** BA, 1972, Mass Communications, Univ. of Miami; **GRAD EDUC:** JD, 1979, John Marshall Law School; **HOME ADD:** 4410 Joliet Ave., Lyons, IL 60534; **BUS ADD:** 7941 Ogden Ave., Lyons, IL 60534, (312)442-6244.

MAURIN, James E.——B: Jan. 23, 1948, Baton Rouge, LA, *VP*, Maurin-Ogden, Inc.; **PRIM RE ACT:** Developer, Owner/Investor; **SERVICES:** Acquisition, devel., mgmt. of shopping ctrs.; **PROFL AFFIL & HONORS:** Intl. Council of Shopping Centers; AICPA, CPA; CMA; Reg. Engr.; **EDUC:** BSME, 1970, Mech./Aerospace Engrg., LA State Univ., Baton Rouge; **GRAD EDUC:** MBA, 1972, Fin., Tulane Univ.; **EDUC HONORS:** Omicron Delta Kappa, Tau Beta Pi, Outstanding Grad. Award, Beta Gamma Sigma; **MIL SERV:** USAF, Capt.; **OTHER ACT & HONORS:** The Boston Club, New Orleans; **HOME ADD:** Rte. 2, Box G-42, Hammond, LA 70401, (504)345-0138; **BUS ADD:** 1518 Martens Dr., Hammond, LA 70401, (504)542-0372.

MAURY, Deane——B: Feb. 16, 1930, Wash., DC, *VP & Sec.*, Stuart and Maury, Inc.; **PRIM RE ACT:** Broker, Appraiser, Insuror; **SERVICES:** Residential Sales, Leasing and Prop. Mgmt., Regional Appraising; **PROFL AFFIL & HONORS:** MAI (RM); **GRAD EDUC:** 1947; **MIL SERV:** USMC, Sgt.; **OTHER ACT & HONORS:** WA Bd. of Tr., Montgomery Bd. of Realtors, DC Bd. of Realtors, Staff Appraiser Montgomery Cty. Register of Wills, Licensed RE Broker DC. MD. VA; **HOME ADD:** 4101 Fordham Rd., Washington, DC 20016, (202)966-1962; **BUS ADD:** 5010 Wisc. Ave. NW, Washington, DC 20016, (202)244-1000.

MAVEC, Bruce V.——B: May 14, 1950, Cleveland, OH, *Pres.*, Royal American Mgmt. Corp.; **PRIM RE ACT:** Developer; **PROFL AFFIL & HONORS:** IREM; **EDUC:** AB, 1972, Religion, Kenyon Coll.; **OTHER ACT & HONORS:** Bd. of Tr., Cleve. Inst. of Music; Cleve. Playhouse; Young Audiences of Cleve.; Euclid Devel. Corp.; Chmn., Kenyon Coll. Athletic Complex Fund Drive; Editorial Advisory Council, Kenyon Review; **BUS ADD:** 27181 Euclid Ave., Euclid, OH 44132, (216)289-0600.

MAWSON, James E.——B: Sept. 9, 1935, Detroit, MI, *Sr. VP*, The Lambrecht Co.; **PRIM RE ACT:** Consultant, Appraiser, Instructor; **SERVICES:** RE Consulting; **REP CLIENTS:** Inst. investors and maj. corps.; **PROFL AFFIL & HONORS:** Amer. Soc. of RE Counselors; AIREA; Inst. of Prop. Taxation; Amer. Inst. of Corp. Asset Mgmt.; Natl. Assn. of Corp. RE Exec., CRE; MAI; CMI; FCA; **EDUC:** BS, 1958, Bus. Admin. and Econ., Wayne State Univ.; **GRAD EDUC:** 1964, RE, Univ. of Mi; **HOME ADD:** 195 Longford Dr., Rochester, MI; **BUS ADD:** 3300 City Natl. Bank Bldg., Detroit, MI 48226, (313)964-4522.

MAXEY, David W.——B: May 17, 1934, Scranton, PA, *Partner (In charge of RE Dept.)*, Drinker, Biddle & Rath, I.C.; **PRIM RE ACT:** Attorney; **REP CLIENTS:** Major lenders, devels. and for. investors; **PROFL AFFIL & HONORS:** Philadelphia; PA; ABA; Intl. Council of Shopping Centers; **EDUC:** 1956, Harvard Univ.; **GRAD EDUC:** 1960, Harvard Law School; **HOME ADD:** 700 Woodleave Rd., Bryn Mawr, PA 19010, (215)527-2694; **BUS ADD:** 1100 Philadelphia Natl. Bank Bldg., Philadelphia, PA 19107.

MAXFIELD, Robert C.——*Pres.*, Lawyers Appraisal Service, Inc.; **PRIM RE ACT:** Appraiser; **SERVICES:** Gen. Appraisal, Real Prop. for Lenders and the Legal Profession; **PROFL AFFIL & HONORS:** Sr. Member and Past Pres., San Francisco Bay Area Chap. Amer. Soc. of Appraisers; Sr. Member Nat. Assn. of Review Appraisers, ASA, CRA; **BUS ADD:** 3661 Grand Ave., Oakland, CA 94610, (415)835-5410.

MAXIM, John A., Jr.——*Assoc. Gen. Counsel*, Department of Housing and Urban Development, Ofc. of Insured Housing & Finance; **PRIM RE ACT:** Lender; **BUS ADD:** 451 Seventh St., S.W., Washington, DC 20410, (202)755-6274.*

MAXSON, Mary Ann Sowul——B: July 28, 1952, Detroit, MI, *Tax Acct.*, Advanced Management Services; **PRIM RE ACT:** Consultant; **SERVICES:** Advise clients on tax effects of RE transactions; **PROFL AFFIL & HONORS:** AMA Alpha Gamma Sigma, Lifetime member; Chi Pi Alpha (Golden Gate Univ. Acctg. Soc.); **EDUC:** BS, 1981, Acctg., Golden Gate Univ., San Francisco, CA; AA, 1979, Acctg., De Anza Coll., Cupertino CA; Cert. of Proficiency, 1978, Taxation, De Anza Coll.; **HOME ADD:** 154 Bristol Blvd., San Leandro, CA 94577, (415)562-6115; **BUS ADD:** 304 E. 14th St., San Leandro, CA 94577, (415)632-2711.

MAXWELL, Glenn M.——B: Mar. 17, 1923, OR, *Pres.*, Alpine RE, Inc.; **PRIM RE ACT:** Broker, Consultant, Appraiser, Builder, Owner/Investor; **SERVICES:** Gen. RE Brokerage, Exchanging, Counseling; **REP CLIENTS:** Appraised for Transamer. Corp. & Merrill Lynch; **PREV EMPLOY:** Owner-Hardware Bus.; **PROFL AFFIL & HONORS:** RNMI, NAR, CAR, CRB; **MIL SERV:** USAF, Capt., DFC, 5 Air Medals; **OTHER ACT & HONORS:** Elks, Bd. of Advisors, Butte Coll. 2 yrs.; **HOME ADD:** PO Box 457, Paradise, CA 95969, (916)877-5371; **BUS ADD:** 6349 Skyway, Paradise, CA 95969, (916)877-4424.

MAXWELL, Richard——B: Aug. 22, 1933, Johnstown, PA, *Pres.*, Maxwell Assoc., Inc.; **PRIM RE ACT:** Broker, Developer, Owner/Investor, Instructor, Property Manager, Syndicator; **REP CLIENTS:** Owner/investors comml. & indus. props.; **PROFL AFFIL & HONORS:** NC & Greensboro Bd. of Realtors, GRI; **EDUC:** BSCE, 1955, Civil Engrg., Duke Univ.; **MIL SERV:** USAF, Capt.; **OTHER ACT & HONORS:** Chmn. Guilford Cty. Bd. of Commrs.; **HOME ADD:** 803 Woodland Dr., Greensboro, NC 27408, (919)272-9954; **BUS ADD:** 127 N. Greene St., Greensboro, NC 27401, (919)373-0995.

MAXWELL, W. Michael——**B:** Aug. 25, 1952, Lake Chars, LA, *Owner, Partner*, Calhoun & Maxwell; **PRIM RE ACT:** Appraiser; **SERVICES:** RE Appraisals; **PROFL AFFIL & HONORS:** AIREA, SREA, MAI, SRPA; **EDUC:** BBA, 1974, RE, Fin., Univ. of Miami; **OTHER ACT & HONORS:** Kiwanis; **HOME ADD:** 6384 Morgan La Fee Ln., Ft. Myers, FL 33908; **BUS ADD:** 2069 First St., Suite 302, Ft. Meyers, FL 33907, (813)332-7767.

MAY, Darwin D.——**B:** Jan. 9, 1945, St. Louis, MO, *VP*, Merchants Nat. Bank & Trust of Indianapolis, RE Dept.; **PRIM RE ACT:** Banker, Lender; **SERVICES:** Interim constr. loans; **PREV EMPLOY:** Mgr. resid Mort. loan Dept., Merchants Nat. Bank of Indianapolis; **PROFL AFFIL & HONORS:** Metro Indianapolis Bd. of Realtors, Mort. Bankers Assn., Indianapolis, Lic. RE Broker, State of IN; **EDUC:** BS, 1968, Bus. Mgmt., S. IL Univ.; **HOME ADD:** 6235 Forest View Dr., Indianapolis, IN 46260, (317)253-4001; **BUS ADD:** One Merchants Plaza, Suite 828E, Indianapolis, IN 46255, (317)267-7946.

MAY, Laurence T., Jr.——**B:** Mar. 31, 1946, Waltham, MA, *Pres.*, Quick & Fayre, Ltd.; **PRIM RE ACT:** Broker, Consultant, Developer, Builder, Owner/Investor; **OTHER RE ACT:** Rehab. contractors; **SERVICES:** Investment counseling, brokerage, prop. mgmt., builder/rehab.; **PROFL AFFIL & HONORS:** Const. Specifications Inst. NAHB; **EDUC:** AB, 1972, Hist., Harvard Coll.; **MIL SERV:** US Navy; **OTHER ACT & HONORS:** Cambridge Community Econ. Devel. Corp.; Southside Neighbors CDC, Amer. Orchid Soc.; **HOME ADD:** 203 Clark St., Cambridge, MA 02139, (617)661-9779; **BUS ADD:** 203 Clark St., Cambridge, MA 02139, (617)491-8108.

MAY, Stephen——**B:** 1931, Rochester, NY, *Asst. Sec. for Legislation & Congressional Relations*, US Dept. of HUD; **OTHER RE ACT:** Congressional liaison; **SERVICES:** Devels. legislation and provides servs. to congress concerning programs & activities of HUD Dept. Principal advisor to Sec. of Hud; **PREV EMPLOY:** Exec. Asst. to Rep. & Sen. Kenneth B. Keating (1955-1964); Member of Law Firm Branch, Turner & Wise; **PROFL AFFIL & HONORS:** Travelled widely and written and spoken extensively on urban problems, election reforms and govt. politics; **EDUC:** BA, Wesleyan Univ.; **GRAD EDUC:** LLB, Georgetown Univ.; **EDUC HONORS:** Phi Beta Kappa; **OTHER ACT & HONORS:** Mayor of Rochester NY (1970-1974); City Councilman at Large 1966-1974; Commnr. & Chmn., NY State Bd. of Elections (1975-79) Former Chmn. of Bd. Empire State Report; Bd. Member Inst. for Mediation & Conflict Resolution; VP NY State Conf. of Mayors; State Crime Control Planning Bd., Police Foundation; **BUS ADD:** Hud Bldg. 451 7th St. SW, Washington, DC 20410.

MAY, Tom——*Managing Owner*, Tom May & Assoc.; **PRIM RE ACT:** Consultant, Appraiser, Syndicator; **OTHER RE ACT:** Personal Fin. Planner; Investment Advisor; Portfolio Manager; **SERVICES:** Capital and tax planning, portfolio asset mgmt., trustee or conservator, investment worth valuations, investment prop. and personal resid. brokerage; **REP CLIENTS:** Trusts and estates, educ. and charitable instns., foreign investors, indivs.; **PREV EMPLOY:** Indep. Fin. Advisor since 1952; Resource Mgmt. Consultant, State of CA, 1952-67, 1971; **PROFL AFFIL & HONORS:** RNMI, RESSI, PDI, Profl. Designation in Investment, CRS, GRI; **EDUC:** BA, 1950, Nat. Sci., Stanford Univ.; **GRAD EDUC:** PDI, 1979, Mgmt. & Bus., Univ. of CA; **EDUC HONORS:** Research Assoc., Hoover Inst. and Library; **MIL SERV:** OSS, 1943; **OTHER ACT & HONORS:** Var. elective and appointive local pol. offices, 1956-79; Regl. Planning Comm., 1957-60; Sec. Monterey Cty. Estate Planning Council, 1955-61; Univ. of CA Adv. Comm. on RE Educ., 1977-80; **HOME TEL:** (408)625-3000; **BUS ADD:** PO Box 715, Carmel, CA 93921, (408)625-3000.

MAYER, Albert J., III——**B:** May 23, 1939, Cincinnati, OH, *Pres.*, Theodore Mayer & Bro. Realtor; **PRIM RE ACT:** Broker, Consultant, Appraiser, Developer, Builder, Instructor, Property Manager, Syndicator; **PROFL AFFIL & HONORS:** Cincinnati, OH, Nat. Assn. of Realtors, RNMI, AIREA, IREM, GRI, CRB, CRS, CRA, R.M. Pres. Cincinnati Bd. 1971, Ohio & Cincinnati Realtor of the Year 1973; **EDUC:** BA, 1961, Hist., Trinity Coll., Hartford, CT; **MIL SERV:** US Army, S/Sgt.; **OTHER ACT & HONORS:** Tennis Patrons of Cincinnati, Citizens School Comm., Trinity College Alumni, Big Brothers of Cincinnati; **HOME ADD:** 8568 Wyoming Club Dr., Cincinnati, OH 45215, (513)821-4441; **BUS ADD:** 36 E. 4th St., Cincinnati, OH 45202, (513)621-0921.

MAYER, Andrew——**B:** June 19, 1941, San Francisco, CA, *Pres.*, Andrew Mayer Inc.; **PRIM RE ACT:** Broker, Consultant, Developer, Property Manager, Syndicator; **SERVICES:** Synd. & mgmt. of older 'strip' ctrs., fin. consulting, re fin. (structure); **REP CLIENTS:** The Shamrock Grp., San Francisco based - fin. mgmt. firm, negotiate acquisitions and dispositions of real prop.; **PROFL AFFIL & HONORS:** ICSC; AMREX; **HOME ADD:** 1950 Tasso, Palo Alto, CA 94301, (415)328-5989; **BUS ADD:** 151 Lytton Ave., Palo Alto, CA 94301, (415)328-3073.

MAYER, Martin C.——**B:** Nov. 3, 1935, Newark, NJ, *Gen. Partner/Owner*, The Mayer Cos.; **PRIM RE ACT:** Consultant, Developer, Builder, Owner/Investor, Property Manager, Syndicator; **OTHER RE ACT:** Land assemblies for investment; **PREV EMPLOY:** Owner-Builder since 1965, Practice Law prior to 1965; **PROFL AFFIL & HONORS:** NJ Bar; Natl. Assn. of Indus. & Office Parks; **EDUC:** AB, 1956, Columbia Coll.; **GRAD EDUC:** LLB, 1959, Columbia Law School; **BUS ADD:** 127 E. Mount Pleasant Ave., Livingston, NJ 07039, (201)994-1060.

MAYER, Roger——*RE Mgr.*, Metro-Goldwyn Mayer Film; **PRIM RE ACT:** Property Manager; **BUS ADD:** 10202 W. Washington Blvd., Culver City, CA 90230, (213)836-3000.*

MAYER, Theodore A.——**B:** Oct. 21, 1940, Cincinnati, OH, *Pres.*, Mayer Properties; **PRIM RE ACT:** Developer, Owner/Investor, Property Manager, Syndicator; **SERVICES:** Investment & prop. mgmt. & devel.; **REP CLIENTS:** Ryland Group, Gradison Co.; **PROFL AFFIL & HONORS:** IREM, CPM; **EDUC:** BS, 1962, RE, IN Univ.; **MIL SERV:** USCG; **OTHER ACT & HONORS:** Past Pres. Cincinnati Jr. C of C and Cincinnati Chap. IREM; **HOME ADD:** 990 St. Paul, Cincinnati, OH 45206, (513)221-8080; **BUS ADD:** 2825 Burnet Ave., Cincinnati, OH 45219, (513)751-3000.

MAYES, Alan D.——**B:** June 13, 1946, *Dir. of Leasing*, Amer. Greetings Corp.; **OTHER RE ACT:** Retail leasing; **PROFL AFFIL & HONORS:** ICSC; **EDUC:** BA, 1968, Psych., Univ. of NC; **HOME ADD:** 351 Pinewood Dr., Bay Village, OH 44140, (216)871-5947; **BUS ADD:** 10500 American Rd., Cleveland, OH 44144, (216)252-7300.

MAYES, Gilford H., Jr.——**B:** Dec. 23, 1927, Kellogg, ID, *Rocky Mountain States Counsel*, Lawyers Title Insurance Corp.; **PRIM RE ACT:** Insuror; **SERVICES:** Title Ins.; **PROFL AFFIL & HONORS:** CO Bar Assn.; St. Bar of MI; VA St. Bar; WA St. Bar Assn.; **EDUC:** BA, 1950, Pol. Sci., Univ. of ID; **GRAD EDUC:** JD, 1953, Univ. of MI; **MIL SERV:** USAF, 1955-1957, 1st Lt.; **HOME ADD:** 3255 S. Parker Rd., Aurora, CO 80014, (303)751-7358; **BUS ADD:** 5660 S. Syracuse Cir., Suite 412, Englewood, CO 80111, (303)773-6061.

MAYFIELD, Robert G.——**B:** June 16, 1946, Salina, KS, *VP*, Bellamah Devel. Corp.; **PRIM RE ACT:** Broker, Consultant, Developer, Owner/Investor, Property Manager; **SERVICES:** Devel. and mgmt. of shopping ctrs., office bldgs., apts., mobile home parks; provide devel. serv. on fee basis to investor clients; brokerage; **REP CLIENTS:** Fin. insts., land owners, insts. investors; **PROFL AFFIL & HONORS:** International Council of Shopping Centers, Certified Shopping Center Manager; **EDUC:** BA, 1978, English, Univ. of CO; **MIL SERV:** US Army, Sp. 5; **HOME ADD:** 2844 North 76th Place, Scottsdale, AZ 85257, (602)994-3837; **BUS ADD:** 6900 Indian School Rd., Scottsdale, AZ 85253, (602)941-3488.

MAYNARD, Carl K.——**B:** Dec. 19, 1934, Pittsfield, MA, *Sr. VP*, HMG Property Investors, Inc.; **PRIM RE ACT:** Owner/Investor; **SERVICES:** Advisor to a REIT; **PREV EMPLOY:** RE Consultant - 5 yrs.; Pres. Westminster Properties (INB) - 5 yrs.; Investment Officer - New England Life; **EDUC:** BSEE, 1956, Engrg., Union Coll.; **OTHER ACT & HONORS:** Eastern Yacht Club; **HOME ADD:** 5737 Riviera Dr., Coral Gables, FL 33146, (305)665-9756; **BUS ADD:** 2701 S. Bayshore Dr., Coconut Grove, FL 33133, (301)854-6803.

MAYNARD, Hugh M.——*Atty.*, Leonard, Street and Deinard; **PRIM RE ACT:** Attorney; **SERVICES:** Negotiation and closing of RE transations; title examination and title clearance; subdivision devel.; title registration proceedings; comml. leasing; RE fin. including indus. devel. revenue bonds; multiparcel land assembly and devel.; **BUS ADD:** 510 Marquette Ave., Minneapolis, MN 55402, (612)339-1200.

MAYNARD, Jo Helen——**B:** Aug. 23, 1935, TX, *Pres.*, Market America, Inc.; **PRIM RE ACT:** Broker, Owner/Investor, Property Manager; **SERVICES:** Acquisition oriented brokerage co. representing partnerships with ownerships in apt. units and numerous comml. bldgs. and shopping ctrs. Mgmt. of props. one of our servs.; **REP CLIENTS:** Robert W. Pulley & Assocs., Delco Devels., Ltd., Fong Holdings, Ltd.; **PROFL AFFIL & HONORS:** NAR, Seattle C of C; **HOME ADD:** 88 Virginia, Unit #20, Seattle, WA 98121, (206)587-0485; **BUS ADD:** 2033 Sixth Ave., Suite 707, Seattle, WA 98121, (206)624-5054.

MAYNARD, W. Douglas——**B:** Aug. 11, 1931, Lakeland, FL, *VP - Partner*, Carl Storey Co.; **PRIM RE ACT:** Broker, Owner/Investor; **SERVICES:** RE Brokerage (Comml. - Indust. - Investment); **PROFL AFFIL & HONORS:** Nashville Bd. of Realtors, TN, Assn. of Realtors, NAR; **EDUC:** AB, 1953, Econ., Boston Univ.; **MIL SERV:** US Army, SP3; **HOME ADD:** 6013 Ashland Dr, Nashville, TN 37215, (615)373-

3671; **BUS ADD:** 13th Floor, Third Nat. Bank Bldg, Nashville, TN 37219, (615)244-7560.

MAYO, Jacque L.——**B:** Mar. 21, 1931, Seattle, WA, *Pres., Owner*, River Rim Development, Inc.; **PRIM RE ACT:** Developer, Owner/Investor; **OTHER RE ACT:** Investor, owner, devel., mktg., Dentistry; **PROFL AFFIL & HONORS:** Acad. of Gen Dentistry, DDS, FAGD; **EDUC:** Dentistry, Univ. of WA; **GRAD EDUC:** DDS, 1956, Univ. of WA; **MIL SERV:** USN, Cmdr.; **HOME ADD:** 527 NW 196th Pl., Seattle, WA 98177, (206)546-3312; **BUS ADD:** P.O. Box 60065, Richmond Beach, WA 98160, (206)524-0824.

MAYO, Walter H.——**B:** Oct. 30, 1936, St. Paul, MN, Clark, Mayo & Gilligan; **PRIM RE ACT:** Attorney; **REP CLIENTS:** Lenders, devels., and indiv. or instnl. investors in resid. and comml. prop. devel. projects; **PROFL AFFIL & HONORS:** ABA; CT and Hartford Bar Assns.; **EDUC:** AB, 1958, Eng., Princeton Univ.; **GRAD EDUC:** LLB, 1961, Harvard Law School; **EDUC HONORS:** Cum Laude; **MIL SERV:** USAF, Capt.; **HOME ADD:** 373 Main St., Wethersfield, CT 06109, (203)563-2470; **BUS ADD:** 60 Washington St., Hartford, CT 06106, (203)247-3297.

MAYS, Ben——**B:** Feb. 19, 1945, Mt. Vernon, TX, *Asst. VP, RE*; **PRIM RE ACT:** Consultant, Property Manager, Lender, Owner/Investor; **SERVICES:** Investment analysis, valuation, leasing, sales, mktg., rehabilitation, prop. mgmt. and all phases of RE fin.; **PREV EMPLOY:** CT Bank & Trust Realty Co.; General Electric Credit Corp.; **PROFL AFFIL & HONORS:** NAR; IREM; Mort. Bankers Assn., MBA; CPM; **EDUC:** BBA, 1970, Mgmt. and Econ., ETSU; **GRAD EDUC:** MBA, 1972, Fin. and RE, Univ. of MA; **EDUC HONORS:** Alpha Zeta Honor Soc., Beta Gama Sigma, Honor Soc.; **MIL SERV:** USMC; Capt.; **HOME ADD:** 9 Columbia Ct., Rockville, MD 20850, (301)762-4807; **BUS ADD:** 51 Louisiana Ave. NW, Washington, DC 20001, (200)628-4506.

MAYS, Jeffrey D.——**B:** May 4, 1952, New Orleans, LA, *Partner*, Mays RE; **PRIM RE ACT:** Broker; **PROFL AFFIL & HONORS:** Quincy Bd. of Realtors; **EDUC:** BA, 1974, Hist., Northwestern Univ.; **OTHER ACT & HONORS:** IL State Representative, 48th Dist., 1981, Quincy C of C; **HOME ADD:** 14 Spring Lake, Quincy, IL 62301, (217)222-3985; **BUS ADD:** 920 Vermont, Box 7, Quincy, IL 62301, (217)224-5588.

MAYS, Richard A.——**B:** May 4, 1940, Wooster, OH, *Mgr. RE*, Elgin, Joliet and Eastern Railway Co.; **PRIM RE ACT:** Broker, Property Manager; **PREV EMPLOY:** Cent. Nat. Bank of Cleveland; **PROFL AFFIL & HONORS:** Amer. Railway Devel. Assn., Nat. Assn. Corp. RE Execs., IL RE Broker; **EDUC:** BS, 1963, Bus. Admin., Kent State Univ., Kent, OH; **MIL SERV:** USMC, Cpl.; **OTHER ACT & HONORS:** Naperville C of C, Grad., Amer. Instit. of Banking, 1964; **HOME ADD:** 36 W. Bailey Rd., Naperville, IL 60565, (312)355-0171; **BUS ADD:** P O Box 880, Joliet, IL 60434, (815)740-6643.

MAYS, W. Gene——*Sr. VP*, Continental Development Corp.; **PRIM RE ACT:** Developer; **BUS ADD:** 215 Fremont St., San Francisco, CA 94105, (415)495-8181.*

MAZZOTTI, Richard R.——**B:** Dec. 8, 1937, Taylorville, IL; **PRIM RE ACT:** Broker, Owner/Investor; **PROFL AFFIL & HONORS:** Nat. Assn. Realtors; RESSI; Realtors Nat. Mktg. Inst., GRI, CCIM, SRS; **EDUC:** BS, 1961, Duke Univ.; St. Louis Coll. of Pharmacy; **HOME ADD:** 1203 Roosevelt Rd., Taylorville, IL 62568, (217)824-3617; **BUS ADD:** 1203 Roosevelt Rd., Taylorville, IL 62568, (217)824-6612.

MEAD, Dale C.——**B:** Dec. 3, 1955, Castro Valley, CA, *Atty.*, Mead & Wells; **PRIM RE ACT:** Attorney; **SERVICES:** LL/Tenant disputes (rent control, evictions); RE contract litigation; appeals (all areas); **REP CLIENTS:** Prop. mgmt. firms & apt. owners; **PROFL AFFIL & HONORS:** ABA, Christian Legal Soc.; **EDUC:** BA, 1976, Philosophy, Westmont Coll.; **GRAD EDUC:** JD, 1979, Law, Golden Gate Univ., School of Law; **EDUC HONORS:** Cum Laude, Phi Sigma Tau; **HOME ADD:** 20370 Santa Cruz Hwy., Los Gatos, CA 95030, (408)353-4288; **BUS ADD:** Fidelity Savings Bldg., Suite 3,, 15879 Los Gatos Blvd., Los Gatos, CA 95030, (408)358-3734.

MEADE, James Monroe——**B:** April 26, 1932, NY, NY, *Partner, Atty.*, Giles, Hedrick & Robinson P.A.; **PRIM RE ACT:** Attorney; **PROFL AFFIL & HONORS:** FL Bar; Orange Cty. Bar; ABA; **EDUC:** 1955, Pol. Sci., Univ. of FL; **GRAD EDUC:** JD, 1958; **EDUC HONORS:** ODK; **MIL SERV:** USN, 1948-1952, European Occupation Medal, Korean Service Medal, Good Conduct Medal; **OTHER ACT & HONORS:** Admitted U.S. Supreme Court; FL Public Serv.; All Fed. & State Courts; **HOME ADD:** 1006 Sweetwater Blvd. S, Longwood, FL, (305)869-0862; **BUS ADD:** 109 E Church St., Orlando, FL 32750, (305)425-3591.

MEADOR, Thomas E.——**B:** July 19. 1947, Hempstead, NY, *VP*, Balcor Mortgage Advisors; **PRIM RE ACT:** Lender; **SERVICES:** First Mort. and Wrap Around Fin.; **REP CLIENTS:** Devels., synd., owners of comml. RE; **PREV EMPLOY:** Harris Bank, Chicago, IL; **EDUC:** AB, 1969, Econ. & Math., IN Univ.; **GRAD EDUC:** MBA, 1971, Fin., IN Univ.; **EDUC HONORS:** Econ. Hon.; **MIL SERV:** US Army-Fin. Corps.; Capt.; **HOME ADD:** 1660 N Lasalle #2401, Chicago, IL 60614, (312)266-8723; **BUS ADD:** 10024 Skokie Boulevard, Skokie, IL 60077, (312)677-2900.

MEADOWS, Dan S.——**B:** Jan. 3, 1947, Watertown, SD, *Gen. Mgr.*, Creative Realty & Inv. Inc., Re-Sale; **PRIM RE ACT:** Broker, Instructor, Syndicator, Consultant, Property Manager, Owner/Investor; **SERVICES:** Land Synd., Investment Prop., Sun Belt Investment Counseling; **REP CLIENTS:** Large and Small Investors; **PREV EMPLOY:** 10 yrs. exp. in RE Mkt., Phoenix, AZ; **PROFL AFFIL & HONORS:** Phx. Bd. of Realtors, Scottsdale Bd. of Realtors, Outstanding contribution to Growth and Prosperity - 1980; **EDUC:** BS, 1968, Acctg., Dakota State Coll.; **GRAD EDUC:** MBA, 1971, Mktg., Univ. of SD; **EDUC HONORS:** All Amer. Small Coll. Football Team, Thesis accepted by Harvard School of Bus. for Case Study; **MIL SERV:** USA, E-5, High Pro-Park Leadership Award; **OTHER ACT & HONORS:** Optimist Club of Phoenix, NW Community Church; **HOME ADD:** 2002 E Vista Ave., Phx., AZ 85020, (602)997-2782; **BUS ADD:** 8611 N Black Canyon Hwy., S-100, Phx., AZ 85021, (602)995-7399.

MEADOWS, Glenn H.——*Pres.*, McNeil Corp.; **PRIM RE ACT:** Property Manager; **BUS ADD:** 666 W. Market St., Akron, OH 44303.*

MEAGHER, William——*Mgr. RE*, Dow Chemical Co.; **PRIM RE ACT:** Property Manager; **BUS ADD:** 2030 Building, Midland, MI 48640, (517)636-1000.*

MEAGHER, William D., II——**B:** Sept. 10, 1950, PA, *Atty.*, Hite & Hite; **PRIM RE ACT:** Attorney, Syndicator; **OTHER RE ACT:** Title Insurance; **SERVICES:** Title Insurance, Closing, Oil and Gas Synd., Leases; **REP CLIENTS:** The Fed. Land Bank of Louisville, KY; Cols. Prod. Credit Assn.; BancOhio; Park Nat. Bank; Cty. Savings Assn.; Ind. Oil & Gas Drillers; Producers; **PROFL AFFIL & HONORS:** OH Bar Assn.; ABA; **EDUC:** BA, 1972, Eng., Case Western Reserve; **GRAD EDUC:** MA, 1972, Linguistics, Case Western Reserve Univ.; JD, 1975, Prop./Secured Transactions, Case Western Reserve Univ.; **EDUC HONORS:** IGS; **OTHER ACT & HONORS:** Solicitor, St. Louisville, 3 yrs.; **BUS ADD:** 26 S Main St., Utica, OH 43080, (614)892-3993.

MEANEY, Robert——*Dir. Plant Engr.*, Warnaco; **PRIM RE ACT:** Property Manager; **BUS ADD:** 350 Lafayette St., Bridgeport, CT 06602, (203)579-8272.*

MEANS, Al, Jr.——**B:** Aug. 20, 1941, Atlanta, GA, *Pres.*, Means & McGinnis Realtors; **PRIM RE ACT:** Broker; **SERVICES:** Comml., indus. & investment propls; sales, exchanges and site acquisitions; **REP CLIENTS:** Local and Rgnl. Comml. and Indus. Devel.; Builders; Fin. Instn.; Nat. and Local Indus. & Mfg. Concerns; Local, Rgnl., Nat. and For. Investors; **PROFL AFFIL & HONORS:** Atlanta Bd. of Realtors, RMNI Life Member Million Dollar Club, CCIM; **EDUC:** BBA, 1964, Fin., Univ. of GA; **OTHER ACT & HONORS:** Church, Social and a variety of Civic Orgs.; **HOME ADD:** 3930 E Brookhaven Dr., N.E., Atlanta, GA 30339, (404)261-2352; **BUS ADD:** 2022 Powers Ferry Rd., Suite 180, Atlanta, GA 30339, (404)955-3808.

MEANS, James D.——**B:** Nov. 23, 1949, Buffalo, NY, *Super. of Prop. Mgmt.*, Nat. Life Ins. Co., Investment Dept.; **PRIM RE ACT:** Developer, Property Manager, Owner/Investor; **PREV EMPLOY:** Sr. Prop. Mgr., The Pioneer-Pyramid Grp., Syracuse, NY; **PROFL AFFIL & HONORS:** Intl. Council of Shopping Ctrs., IREM, BOMA, Cert. Shopping Ctr. Mgr., CPM; **EDUC:** BS,Indus. Mgmt., 1971, Bus. Admin.,Engrg., Clarkson Coll., Potsdam, NY; **HOME ADD:** Ridgewood Ter., Barre,, VT 05641, (802)476-6445; **BUS ADD:** National Life Dr., Montpelier, VT 05602, (802)229-3757.

MEANS, Scott A.——**B:** Nov. 7, 1951, Iowa City, IA, *VP*, The Means Agency, Inc.; **PRIM RE ACT:** Broker, Appraiser, Property Manager; **SERVICES:** Mktg., appraisal & prop. mgmt.; **PROFL AFFIL & HONORS:** Amer. Assn. of Cert. Appraisers; Nat. Assn. of Realtors, Realtor; Cert. Sr. Appraiser; **EDUC:** BA, 1974, Social Work/Sociology, Univ. of IA; **OTHER ACT & HONORS:** Past Pres., Iowa City Jaycees; Iowa City C of C; Boy Scouts of Amer.; Recipient, 1981 Outstanding Young Men of Amer. Award; **HOME ADD:** 2010 E. Court St., Iowa City, IA 52240, (319)354-3648; **BUS ADD:** POB 508,

Iowa City, IA 52244, (319)338-1109.

MEANS, William V., II——B: Apr. 28, 1938, Jacksonville, FL, *Mgr. Mandarin Sales/Asst. VP*, Stockton, Whately, Davin & Co. Realtors, Resid. RE; **PRIM RE ACT:** Broker, Owner/Investor, Instructor; **OTHER RE ACT:** Mort. broker; **SERVICES:** Full serv. co.; **PROFL AFFIL & HONORS:** Pres., Jacksonville Bd. of Realtors, CRB; CRS; GRI; Realtor of the Yr., 1979; **EDUC:** Resid. RE Sales, FL So. Coll.; Journalism, FL So. Coll.; **MIL SERV:** USN; **OTHER ACT & HONORS:** Past Pres./Life Member, W. Duval Jaycees; **HOME ADD:** 1928 Morningside Dr., Jacksonville, FL 32205, (904)389-8316; **BUS ADD:** 9872 San Jose Blvd., Jacksonville, FL 32217, (904)268-2200.

MECKSTROTH, John R.——B: Mar. 18, 1931, Cincinnati, OH, *Atty.*, Meckstroth, Schwierling & Monnie; **PRIM RE ACT:** Attorney; **SERVICES:** Synd., consultation, RE closing, owner/builder/seller consultation as to sale; **REP CLIENTS:** The Ryland Group, Cardinal Federal Savings & Loan, Barnhorn Realty, Blue Ash Savings & Loan, First National Bank of Louisville, and The Kanter Corp.; **PROFL AFFIL & HONORS:** ABA, OH and Cincinnati Bar Assns.; Cincinnati Bd. of Realtors; OH-Cincinnati Title Insurance Assns.; Cincinnati Mort. Bankers; **EDUC:** BA, 1953, Xavier Univ., Cincinnati, OH; **GRAD EDUC:** JD, 1956, Law, Coll. of Law, Univ. of Cincinnati; **OTHER ACT & HONORS:** Member OH St. Bd. of Educ., 1965 to present, Pres. 1973-74; Law Dir. of Green Township Bd. of Tr. Hamilton Cty., OH 1964/1972; **HOME ADD:** 7319 Thompson Rd., Cincinnati, OH 45247, (513)385-1805; **BUS ADD:** 8 West Ninth St., Friedlander Bldg., Cincinnati, OH 45202, (513)241-5556.

MEDANSKY, Earl T.——B: Sept. 3, 1935, Chicago, IL, *Principal and a Founding S/H*, Rotman, Medansky & Elovitz, Ltd.; **PRIM RE ACT:** Consultant, Attorney, Developer, Owner/Investor, Syndicator; **REP CLIENTS:** Indiv. and corp. devels. - synd. investors; **PROFL AFFIL & HONORS:** ISBA, CBA, CREB, ITA - (RE Comm.) (Condo Comm.) (Mtg. Comm.) CBA; **EDUC:** Fin., Econ., DePaul; **GRAD EDUC:** JD, 1960; **OTHER ACT & HONORS:** City of Chicago Rehab. Supervisor, Dept. of Urban Renewal 1961-63, Past Master AF & AM, 32 - Shrine; **HOME ADD:** 9240 Nashville, Morton Grove, IL 60053, (312)965-5292; **BUS ADD:** 180 North LaSalle St., Chicago, IL 60601, (301)236-2202.

MEDCRAF, James Howard——B: Oct. 14, 1948, Syracuse, NY, *Atty. at Law*; **PRIM RE ACT:** Attorney, Owner/Investor; **PROFL AFFIL & HONORS:** Onondaga Cty., NY State Bar Assns.; Onondaga Title Assn.; ABA; **EDUC:** BA, 1970, Pol. Sci., Syracuse Univ. - Maxwell School of Citizenship & Public Affairs; **GRAD EDUC:** JD, 1973, Rutgers Univ. School of Law; **EDUC HONORS:** Cum Laude; **OTHER ACT & HONORS:** Bd. of Tr., Onendaga Yacht Club; **HOME ADD:** 777 Ostrom Ave., Syracuse, NY 13210, (315)471-4300; **BUS ADD:** 305 Gridley Bldg., Syracuse, NY 13202, (315)478-3587.

MEDICI, Donald——*Dpty Admin.*, Rhode Island, RI Real Estate Division; **PRIM RE ACT:** Property Manager; **BUS ADD:** 100 N. Main St., Providence, RI 02903, (401)277-2255.*

MEDINGER, Alan P.——B: May 18, 1936, Baltimore, MD, *VP - Treas.*, McCormick Properties, Inc.; **PRIM RE ACT:** Developer; **SERVICES:** RE devel. and const.; **REP CLIENTS:** Westinghouse, W. Electric, Gen. Instrument, PHH, Farm Credit Banks; **PROFL AFFIL & HONORS:** MD Assn. of CPA's, CPA; **EDUC:** BA, 1958, Acctg./Econ., Johns Hopkins Univ.; **EDUC HONORS:** Haskins & Sells Award; **HOME ADD:** 1023 Hart Rd., Towson, MD 21204, (301)823-1953; **BUS ADD:** 11011 McCormick Rd., Hunt VaLley, MD 21031, (301)667-7764.

MEDVECKY, Thomas E.——B: Apr. 22, 1937, Bridgeport, CT, *Atty.*, Law Office of T.E. Medvecky; **PRIM RE ACT:** Attorney; **SERVICES:** Document preparation, title searches, counseling and title closings; **REP CLIENTS:** owners, investors and lenders; **PROFL AFFIL & HONORS:** Danbury CT Bar Assn.; CT Bar Assn.; ABA; Section of Real Prop. Probate and Trust Law of ABA; **EDUC:** AB, 1959, Econ. and Govt., Bowdoin Coll., Brunswick, ME; **GRAD EDUC:** LLB, 1962, St John's Univ., Brooklyn, NY; **EDUC HONORS:** Deans List, Recipient Amer. Jurisprudence Prize; **MIL SERV:** US Army, E-6; **OTHER ACT & HONORS:** Asst. Town Council in Bethel, CT 1963-67; Assoc. Dir. State Natl. Bank of CT; **HOME ADD:** Redding, CT 06875; **BUS ADD:** 99 Greenwood Ave., Bethel, CT 06801, (203)744-6200.

MEEKCOMS, Leon D.——B: Jan. 4, 1949, London, England, *Director, Prop. Acquisition*, Western Capital Corp.; **PRIM RE ACT:** Broker, Consultant, Owner/Investor, Instructor, Syndicator; **SERVICES:** Investment counseling, income prop. brokerage, buyer's ageny; **REP CLIENTS:** Synd., foregn investors; **PREV EMPLOY:** Co-owner, RE Trainers, Inc.; Regional Training Dir., Century 21 RE, OR Region; **PROFL AFFIL & HONORS:** Portland Bd., OR Assn. & NAR; RESSI; **EDUC:** BS, 1971, Psych., Econ., Univ. of OR; **OTHER ACT & HONORS:** Optimists; Jaycees; C of C; **HOME ADD:** 12 St. Helens Cir., Lake Oswego, OR 97034, (503)635-8989; **BUS ADD:** 1221 SW Yamhill, Suite 304, Portland, OR 97205, (503)225-0338.

MEEKER, David Olan, Jr.——*Exec. VP*, Amer. Institute of Architects; **PRIM RE ACT:** Architect; **BUS ADD:** 1735 New York Ave., NW, Washington, DC 20006, (202)785-7300.*

MEENGS, Dirck Z.——*Prin.*, Meengs Assoc.; **PRIM RE ACT:** Broker, Consultant, Developer, Property Manager; **SERVICES:** Facility location, planning, site selection, econ. comm devel., prop. mgmt.; **REP CLIENTS:** High tech. mfrg., state econ. devel. agencies, hosp. indus.; **PREV EMPLOY:** VP GSC Corp., VP & Treas. Macco Corp., Mgr. Corp RE, Pertec Computer Corp.; **PROFL AFFIL & HONORS:** Broker, CA; **EDUC:** BA, 1954, Econ., The College of Wooster (OH); **GRAD EDUC:** MBA, 1956, Fin., Harvard Grad. Sch. of Bus. Admin.; **BUS ADD:** 8211 Owensmouth Ave., 107, Conoga Park, CA 91304, (213)346-1752.

MEER, Gerald L.——*RE Broker*; **PRIM RE ACT:** Broker; **PREV EMPLOY:** Ambrose/Farber Co.; **PROFL AFFIL & HONORS:** IREM; CO RE Broker, CPM; **EDUC:** BS, Fin./Econ./Banking, Univ. of Denver; **BUS ADD:** 160 S Monaco Pkwy., Denver, CO 80224, (303)321-0347.

MEGERT, Russell A.——B: Nov. 19, 1925, Topeka, KS, *Arch. & Engr.*, Shiver-Megert & Assoc.; **PRIM RE ACT:** Engineer, Architect, Owner/Investor; **PROFL AFFIL & HONORS:** AIA, TSA, CSI; **EDUC:** BArch, 1951, TX Tech. Univ., Lubbock, TX; **MIL SERV:** USN, Eng. Man; **OTHER ACT & HONORS:** Lions; **HOME ADD:** 1522 Kentucky, Amarillo, TX 79102, (806)355-7120; **BUS ADD:** 102 E. 9th St., Suite 200, Amarillo, TX 79101, (806)372-5662.

MEHRER, Richard L.——B: Sept. 6, 1945, Oakland, CA, *Broker, VP*, Baldwin & Assoc. Realty, Inc.; **PRIM RE ACT:** Broker, Syndicator, Consultant, Appraiser, Developer; **SERVICES:** Counseling; Tax planning; Synd. Feasibility analysis; **PREV EMPLOY:** Bellingham Comp. Plan Consultant; **PROFL AFFIL & HONORS:** RESSI, NAR, GRI; **EDUC:** Econ./Psych., 1967, Banking/Counseling, WA State; **GRAD EDUC:** MA Psych., MS Econ., 1969 & 1970, Univ. of So. CA; **OTHER ACT & HONORS:** Intnl. Kiwanas; Bd. of Dirs., Los Angeles Boys Clubs; **HOME ADD:** 1506 SW Montgomery, Portland, OR, (503)223-8200; **BUS ADD:** 352 B Avenue, Lake Oswego, OR 97034, (503)635-9301.

MEIGS, Walter R.——B: Sep. 7, 1948, Macon, GA, *Gen. Counsel & Asst. Corp. Sec.*, AL Dry Dock & Shop Bldg. Co., Exec.; **PRIM RE ACT:** Attorney, Property Manager; **SERVICES:** Counsel to corp in Mobile, AL; **REP CLIENTS:** Responsible for legal and practical mgmt. aspects of corp. RE ownership; **PREV EMPLOY:** Assoc. Hubbard, Waldrop & Jenkins, Tuscaloosa, AL, 1974-75; **PROFL AFFIL & HONORS:** AL State Bar, ABA, RE, Probate & Estate Sect.; **EDUC:** AB, 1970, Hist., Birmingham Coll., AL; **GRAD EDUC:** JD, 1973, Law, Univ. of AL, School of Law; **EDUC HONORS:** Dean's List, Pres. frat. council, Pres. Lambda Chi Alpha, John A. Campbell Moot Court Comp.; **OTHER ACT & HONORS:** Amer. Lawyer Assn., AL & So. Hist. Assn., Kiwanis Club of Mobile, AL; **HOME ADD:** 3505 Springwood Dr. E., Mobile, AL 36608, (205)343-5755; **BUS ADD:** PO Box 1507, Mobile, AL 36633, (205)690-7021.

MEINTS, Paul A.——B: Mar. 11, 1947, Quincy, IL, *Atty.*, Austermiller & Meints; **PRIM RE ACT:** Consultant, Attorney, Owner/Investor, Instructor, Real Estate Publisher; **SERVICES:** Legal with emphasis upon the taxation of RE transactions; **PROFL AFFIL & HONORS:** Active on ABA Sects. of Taxation and RE, Probate & Trust; **EDUC:** BBA, 1969, Bus. Fin., W. IL Univ.; **GRAD EDUC:** JD, 1974, Practice limited to taxation and RE transactions, Valparaiso Univ. School of Law; **EDUC HONORS:** Outstanding student in a couple of classes; Dean's List; **MIL SERV:** US Army; Spec. 5; Viet Nam; **OTHER ACT & HONORS:** Bd. of Dirs. for McLean Cty. Mental Health Assn.; Have written several short articles, and write regularly for local RE Newsletter; **HOME ADD:** 2206 East Pierce, Bloomington, IL 61701, (309)663-5846; **BUS ADD:** 108 S.W. Arch, Atlanta, IL 61723, (217)648-2277.

MEISEL, Elliott——B: Sept. 20, 1946, New York City, NY, *Partner*, Brill & Meisel; **OTHER RE ACT:** Legal Rep.; **SERVICES:** Legal counsel; investment analysis & packaging; **REP CLIENTS:** Loft converters; co-op & condo converters; syndicators; commercial & residential owners; **PREV EMPLOY:** Paul, Weiss, Rifkind, Wharton & Garrison 1974-1978; Marshall, Bratter, Greene, Allison & Tucker 1971-73; **PROFL AFFIL & HONORS:** Amer. Bar Assn.; Assn. Bar of NYC; Coop Housing Lawyers Group; **EDUC:** 1968, Cornell Univ.;

GRAD EDUC: 1971, Yale Univ. Law School; **EDUC HONORS:** Law Journal; **HOME ADD:** 585 West End Ave., New York City, NY 10024, (212)787-4429; **BUS ADD:** 532 Madison Ave., New NY 10022, (212)753-5599.

MEISLER, Paul Steven——**B:** Apr. 8, 1955, Houston, TX, *Pres.*, Paul S. Meisler Props./The Paul S. Meisler Cos.; **PRIM RE ACT:** Broker, Developer, Property Manager, Owner/Investor, Lender, Real Estate Publisher; **PROFL AFFIL & HONORS:** Realtor/Apt. Assn./Locator Assn./NFIB/BBB & Chamber, Past Pres.-Texas Assn. Apt. Loc. Serv./Apt. Assn. Bd. Member; **EDUC:** BBA, 1976, Fin. and RE, Univ. of TX, Austin; **EDUC HONORS:** 3.2 overall Avg.; **HOME ADD:** 1821 Westlakehighs Dr. #127, Austin, TX 78746, (512)327-3260; **BUS ADD:** 1920 E. Riverside Dr.(Main), Austin, TX 78741, (512)443-2212.

MEISNER, Robert M.——**B:** Oct. 30, 1944, Detroit, MI, *Pres.*, Robert M. Meisner, P.C.; **PRIM RE ACT:** Attorney; **OTHER RE ACT:** Columnist. Detroit News; **REP CLIENTS:** United Condo. Owners of MI; Environmental Energies, Inc.; The Other Utility Co.; Pebble Creek Assn. of Co-owners; Oakbrook Condo. Assn.; Pontiac Assn. of School Administrators; Durbin Co.; Realtors; New Center Devel. Partnership; Versailles Place Condo. Assn.; **PROFL AFFIL & HONORS:** ABA; State Bar of MI; Community Assns. Inst.; Amer. Arbitration Assn.; Oakland Cty. Bar Assn.; Detroit Bar Assn., Phi Kappa Phi Honor Soc.; **EDUC:** BA, 1966, Pol. Sci., Univ. of MI; **GRAD EDUC:** JD, 1969, Univ. of MI Law School; **EDUC HONORS:** Phi Kappa Phi; **OTHER ACT & HONORS:** Univ. of MI Victors Club; Univ. of MI Pres. Club; **HOME ADD:** 3631 Tyrconnel Trail, W. Bloomfield, MI 48033, (313)851-8485; **BUS ADD:** 30200 Telegraph Rd., Ste. 467, Birmingham, MI 48010, (313)644-4433.

MELANIPHY, F.J.——**B:** Apr. 6, 1937, Chicago, IL, *Pres.*, Site Location Specialists; **PRIM RE ACT:** Broker, Consultant, Appraiser, Owner/Investor, Instructor, Property Manager; **OTHER RE ACT:** Contract negotiators; **SERVICES:** Comml. RE Brokerage, consulting, market analyses, prop. mgmt.; **REP CLIENTS:** Nat., intl. & local Co's & indiv. seeking new locations or surplus prop disposition, comml. prop. owners/investors, multi- unit operators; **PREV EMPLOY:** Melaniphy & Assoc., Inc. 1972-77; **PROFL AFFIL & HONORS:** Nat. Assn. of Corp. RE Exec.; NAR; Alpha Eta Rho, Special Award for Consulting Servs-USAF; **EDUC:** BS, 1960, Aeronautical Engrg., Univ. of IL; **GRAD EDUC:** MSBA, 1972, Econ., mgmt. sci., US Intl. Univ.; **EDUC HONORS:** Summa Cum Laude; **OTHER ACT & HONORS:** Boy Scouts of Amer., Aircraft Owners and Pilots Assn., Experimental Aircraft Assn.; **HOME ADD:** 307 N. Derbyshire Ln., Arlington Hts., IL 60004, (312)398-8478; **BUS ADD:** 1818 E. Northwest Hwy., Arlington Hts., IL 60004, (312)394-0550.

MELANIPHY, John C., Jr.——**B:** Jan. 30, 1936, Chicago, IL, *Pres.*, Melaniphy & Assoc., Inc.; **PRIM RE ACT:** Consultant; **SERVICES:** RE consultants, mkt. analysts, urbanologists & economists; **REP CLIENTS:** City of Chicago, Dept. of Planning; International Multifoods, MN; Forest City Enterprises, Madigan's, Chicago; Marriott Corp., Wash., DC; Gimbel Bros., NY; Continental IL Nat. Bank, Chicago; Jewel Co., Chicago; **PREV EMPLOY:** VP, Kentucky Fried Chicken Corp.; Sr. VP, RE Research Corp.; **PROFL AFFIL & HONORS:** Amer. Soc. of RE Counselors; Nat. Council of Shopping Ctrs.; Lambda Alpha; ULI, Amer. Soc. of RE Counselors; **EDUC:** 1957, Acctg., Univ. of IL, Coll. of Commerce; **GRAD EDUC:** Exec. Program, Univ. of Chicago; **MIL SERV:** Army, E-2; **HOME ADD:** 6293 N. Louise, Chicago, IL 60646, (312)775-7584; **BUS ADD:** One North LaSalle, Chicago, IL 60602, (312)726-1212.

MELCER, Duane Scott——**B:** Jan. 29, 1942, Brooklyn, NY, *EVO*, Kaufman Leasing Co., Kaufman Mgmt. Co.; **PRIM RE ACT:** Broker, Consultant, Property Manager, Syndicator; **SERVICES:** Leasing, sales, consulting, full serv. RE; **REP CLIENTS:** Major indus. and comml. cos.; **PROFL AFFIL & HONORS:** REBNY, IREBA, NYSAR; **EDUC:** BBA, 1973, Bus. mgmt., Community Coll. of NY; **MIL SERV:** USAR, 1961-67; **HOME ADD:** 480 Halstead Ave., Harrison, NY 10528, (914)835-2297; **BUS ADD:** 450 7th Ave., NYC, NY 10023, (212)563-6252.

MELCHIOR, Frank A.——**B:** Oct. 7, 1928, Germany, *VP & Assoc. Eastern Reg. Counsel*, First Amer. Title Ins. Co.; **PRIM RE ACT:** Attorney, Instructor, Insuror; **SERVICES:** Title ins., legal representation, educ.; **PREV EMPLOY:** Chicago Title Ins. Co.; **PROFL AFFIL & HONORS:** ABA, PA & NJ Bar Assns.; **EDUC:** 1951, Pol. Sci., Econ., Roosevelt Univ.; **GRAD EDUC:** JD, 1963, Law, Chicago Kent Coll. of Law/IIT; **OTHER ACT & HONORS:** Former Member PA Joint State Govt. Advisory Comm. on Condos. in PA; **HOME ADD:** 103 Duffy Dr., Allendale, NJ 07401, (201)327-2838; **BUS ADD:** 170 Broadway, NY, NY 10038, (212)962-2761.

MELI, Anthony P., Jr.——**B:** Oct. 29, 1944, Hoboken, NJ, *VP*, Howard Savings Bank; **PRIM RE ACT:** Banker, Lender; **SERVICES:** Permanent and const. mort. fin. for resid. and comml. RE; **PROFL AFFIL & HONORS:** Trustee, Mort. Bankers Assn., Educ. Found., Honor Grad. NAMSB Grad. School of Savings Banking; **EDUC:** AB, 1967, Econ., St. Peters CoLl.; **GRAD EDUC:** MBA, 1975, Fin., Rutgers Univ.; **MIL SERV:** USA, Capt.; **HOME ADD:** 3 Rand Rd., Montville, NJ 07105; **BUS ADD:** 200 S Orange Ave., Livingston, NJ 07039, (201)533-7721.

MELICK, John M.——*Dir. Pers. Admin.*, Crompton Co., Inc.; **PRIM RE ACT:** Property Manager; **BUS ADD:** 11 W. 49th St., New York, NY 10018, (212)398-9900.*

MELIKIAN, Robert A.——**B:** May 21, 1946, Philadelphia, PA, *VP*, International Resource Management, Inc.; **PRIM RE ACT:** Broker, Developer, Owner/Investor; **SERVICES:** Acquisitions, devels., investment type props.; **REP CLIENTS:** House; **PROFL AFFIL & HONORS:** Univ. of PA RE Soc.; **EDUC:** BS, 1969, Mgmt., St. Joseph's Coll. - Univ. of PA - Wharton School - RE 1971; **GRAD EDUC:** MBA, 1980, Mktg., St. Joseph's Univ.; **OTHER ACT & HONORS:** Courses - Amer. Instit. RE Appraisers toward MAI; **HOME ADD:** 1222 Gladwyne Dr., Gladwyne, PA 19035, (215)649-5739; **BUS ADD:** PO Box 361, (Union Hill Rd.), West Conshohocken, PA 19428, (215)825-7430.

MELILL, Jack C.——**B:** Feb. 15, 1931, Chicago IL, *Broker & Pres.*, John T. Dunney Co., Inc.; **PRIM RE ACT:** Broker, Instructor, Consultant, Developer, Property Manager, Owner/Investor, Real Estate Publisher; **OTHER RE ACT:** Columnist Local Newspaper, Consultant City and School Councils; **SERVICES:** RE Residentials/ Comml. Consultant; **REP CLIENTS:** Cty. and school officials, planners/ developers; **PREV EMPLOY:** Instr. (Head) Evergreen RE School, Adult Edu. Dir. M.I. School Dist. 400 1965-1970, Public Relations Dir.; **PROFL AFFIL & HONORS:** NRAB, WAB Seatle King County Bd., Phi Delta Kappa, Sigma Delta (Hon. Frat.); **EDUC:** BA, 1956, Psych., Hist., Univ. IL; **GRAD EDUC:** MS ED. Admin., 1966, Admin., Journ., Econ.,, Univ. of WA; **EDUC HONORS:** Athletic Letter Swimming 2 yrs., Editor & Publisher Coll. Magazine, Hon. Educ. Frat. Hon. Jour. Frat.; **MIL SERV:** 11th Airbourne, Corporal/Lt. JG; Con., Korean Conflict 1952-1954, Proganda Corp. Marksman; **OTHER ACT & HONORS:** Brd. Member, Mercer Island Youth Services 1978-1981, Amer. Alpine Club, Natl. Ski Patrol, Trustee Alpental Ski Patrol, Park Ranger Mt. Ranier 1956-1967; **HOME ADD:** 7446 92nd St., Mercer Island, WA 98040, (206)232-8936; **BUS ADD:** 8114 SE 28th St., Mercer Island, WA 98040, (206)232-2700.

MELLING, George D., Jr.——**B:** Mar. 31, 1941, Detroit, MI, *Atty.*, Fabian & Clendenin; **PRIM RE ACT:** Attorney; **OTHER RE ACT:** Legal counseling and representation in all areas of RE including acquisitions, zoning, devel., leasing and secured lending; **PROFL AFFIL & HONORS:** ABA; **EDUC:** BS, 1963, Mech. Engrg., Univ. of CO; **GRAD EDUC:** JD, 1966, Law, Univ. of MI; **EDUC HONORS:** Tau Beta Pi, Cum Laude; **OTHER ACT & HONORS:** Member, Salt Lake Cty. Planning Commn. 1977-80, Chmn. 1978-79; **HOME ADD:** 2218 Berkeley St., Salt Lake City, UT 84109, (801)485-1327; **BUS ADD:** 800 Continental Bank Bldg., Salt Lake City, UT 84101, (801)531-8900.

MELSON, Bill——**B:** Dec. 26, 1940, Artesia, NM, *VP*, Hendry Investments; **PRIM RE ACT:** Instructor, Consultant, Property Manager, Real Estate Publisher; **REP CLIENTS:** We plan, construct, lease and manage our own devel.; **PREV EMPLOY:** Dir. of Multi-Family Operations Baker-Crow Co., Dallas, TX; **PROFL AFFIL & HONORS:** Bd. Member for San Antonio Apt. Assoc. TX Apt. Assn., CPM Designation, VP San Antonio IREM Charter; **EDUC:** BA, 1963, Communications, Abilene Christian Univ.; **MIL SERV:** USN; Lt., Air Intelligence Officer; **HOME ADD:** 705 AZ Ash, San Antonio, TX 78232, (512)494-5486; **BUS ADD:** 8700 Crown Hill Blvd., San Antonio, TX 78209, (512)824-2322.

MELSON, Joseph N., Jr.——**B:** June 23, 1937, Wilmington, DE; **PRIM RE ACT:** Broker, Consultant, Appraiser, Owner/Investor, Instructor; **SERVICES:** Appraising and consulting; **PREV EMPLOY:** Dept. of Housing and Urban Devel. 1962-1973; **PROFL AFFIL & HONORS:** MAI, SRPA; **EDUC:** BS, 1965, Bus. Admin., Univ. of DE; **MIL SERV:** US Army, E-5; **HOME ADD:** 108 Old Point Rd., Fairfax, Wilmington, DE 19803, (302)654-9629; **BUS ADD:** 108 Old Point Rd., Fairfax, Wilmington, DE 19803, (302)654-9629.

MELTON, James——**B:** May 7, 1912, Dillon, MT, *Pres.*, James O. Melton & Assoc.; **PRIM RE ACT:** Broker, Consultant; **OTHER RE ACT:** Supply equity capital; **PREV EMPLOY:** 30 yrs. in mktg., 17 yrs. in RE; **EDUC:** BA, 1935, Hist., Econ., Phys. Educ., Educ., Econ.,

Univ. of MT; **GRAD EDUC:** EdM, 1941, Econ., Univ. of S. CA; **EDUC HONORS:** Phi Delta Kappa; **HOME ADD:** 4122 Druid Lane, Dallas, TX 75205, (214)521-5698; **BUS ADD:** Ste. 721, Cotton Exchange Bldg., 608 N. St. Paul, Dallas, TX 75201, (214)744-0118.

MELTON, Robert Witcher——B: Sept. 20, 1926, Rutherfordton, NC, *Pres.*, Melton Company, Realtors; **PRIM RE ACT:** Broker, Consultant, Developer; **SERVICES:** Investment counseling, single agency, and exchanging; **REP CLIENTS:** Indivs. and instnl. investors that buy, sell, or exchange comml. and investment props.; **PROFL AFFIL & HONORS:** Soc. RE Appraisers; NAR, Sr. Member, Intl. Right Way; Sr. listing "Who's Who in Creative RE"; SRA; CRB; CRS; **EDUC:** BA, 1949, Bus. Admin., Duke Univ.; **MIL SERV:** USN; PO, 1945-1946; **OTHER ACT & HONORS:** Member, City Council, Brevard, 1960-1964; Tr., Transylvania Community Hospital; Bd. of Advisors, Daniel Boone Council Boy Scouts; Dir., Brevard Bd., First Citizens Bank and Trust Co.; Faculty Member, NC Realtors' Inst., Chapel Hill, NC; **HOME ADD:** 210 Maple St., Brevard, NC 28712, (704)883-9262; **BUS ADD:** 300 N. Broad St., PO Box 787, Brevard, NC 28712, (704)884-4300.

MELZER, Robert M.——B: Jan. 28, 1941, NY, *Pres.*, Property Capital Trust; **PRIM RE ACT:** Owner/Investor; **SERVICES:** Equity investment vehicle designed primarily for instnl. tax exempt investors; **REP CLIENTS:** Corp. pension funds, univ. endowments, and tax exempt found.; **PROFL AFFIL & HONORS:** ICSC, SIR; **EDUC:** BA, 1961, Econ., Cornell Univ.; **GRAD EDUC:** MBA, 1969, Harvard Bus. School; **MIL SERV:** US Army, 1st Lt.; **BUS ADD:** 200 Clarendon St., Boston, MA 02116, (617)536-8600.

MENDELSON, Laurans A.——B: July 7, 1938, NY, *Chmn.*, The Four Ambassadors; **PRIM RE ACT:** Developer; **SERVICES:** Condo. sales; **PROFL AFFIL & HONORS:** AICPA, FL Inst. of CPA's; NY State Soc. of CPA's; Dir., Intl. Bank of Miami, N.A.; **EDUC:** AB, 1960, Econ., Columbia Coll., NY; **GRAD EDUC:** MBA, 1961, Acctg. and Fin., Columbia Univ., Grad. School of Bus.; **MIL SERV:** US Army, Sgt.; **OTHER ACT & HONORS:** Greater Miami Opera Assn., Bd. of Patrons; **BUS ADD:** 825 Bayshore Dr., Suite 1643, Miami, FL 33131, (305)374-1744.

MENDENHALL, E. Hirst——B: Mar. 21, 1919, Winchester, IN, *COB*, Boone Realty Corp.; **PRIM RE ACT:** Broker, Appraiser, Lender, Real Estate Publisher; **REP CLIENTS:** Prop. Mgmt: Numerous large and small apt. owners, Shopping Ctr. Owner-Mgrs.; **PREV EMPLOY:** In own business since 1949; **PROFL AFFIL & HONORS:** NAR; RNMI; Columbia Bd. of Realtors, MO Assn. of Realtors, CRB, GRI; **EDUC:** BA, Journ., Univ. of MO; **GRAD EDUC:** 1941; **MIL SERV:** USA Air Corp, Lt., Distinguished Flying Cross, Air Medal with 11 Oak Leave Clusters; **OTHER ACT & HONORS:** Past Pres., Columbia Kiwanis Club, Pachyderm Club of Boone Cty., Commodore, Lake of the Ozarks Yachting Assn., Welfare Commn., Boone County, MO; **HOME ADD:** 705 Eastlake Dr., Columbia, MO 65201, (314)445-2273; **BUS ADD:** 1 Broadway Bldg., Columbia, MO 65201, (314)449-3101.

MENDENHALL, Ed.——B: June 24, 1909, Greensboro, NC, *Sr. Partner*, Mendenhall-Moore, Realtors; **PRIM RE ACT:** Broker, Consultant, Appraiser, Property Manager; **PROFL AFFIL & HONORS:** SIR; Amer. Soc. of RE Counselors; IREM; Pres. NC Assn. of Realtors 1938; Pres. NAR 1964; Pres. RNMI, 1949; Professional Designations: CRE, CPM; **EDUC:** BS in Commerce, 1930, Personnel Mgmt., Univ. of NC at Chapel Hill; **GRAD EDUC:** LLD, 1966, High Point Coll., High Point, NC; **OTHER ACT & HONORS:** Rotary Club of High Point, String & Splinter Club; **HOME ADD:** 1003 Parkwood Cir., High Point, NC 27260, (919)883-1197; **BUS ADD:** 201 Church Ave., Box 2288, High Point, NC 27261.

MENDIK, Bernard H.——B: May 24, 1929, Glasgow, Scotland, *Pres.*, Mendik Realty Co., Inc.; **PRIM RE ACT:** Developer, Builder, Owner/Investor, Attorney; **EDUC:** BA, 1955, Bus. Admin., CCNY; **GRAD EDUC:** LLB, 1958, NY Law School; **EDUC HONORS:** Editor, Law Review; **HOME ADD:** 209 East 72nd St., New York, NY 10017; **BUS ADD:** 330 Madison Ave., New York, NY 10017, (212)557-1100.

MENDIOLA, Helen E.——B: Oct. 20, 1958, Houston, TX, *Pres.*, Mendiola Investments, Inc., Prop. Devel. and RE Investments; **PRIM RE ACT:** Broker, Consultant, Owner/Investor; **SERVICES:** Consulting, feasibility studies, fin., sales, land planning, devel., estates, mktg.; **REP CLIENTS:** Indiv., corp., lenders and instnl. clients for RE investments and/or investment bldg.; **PROFL AFFIL & HONORS:** Pasadena Bd. of Realtors; TX Assn. of Realtors; Realtors Nat. Mktg. Inst.; TX RE Mktg. & Exchange Assn., Inc.; Gulf Coast Rgnl. Prop. Exchangors; Women's Council of Realtors; NAR, CRB; **EDUC:** Coll. of the Mainland; **OTHER ACT & HONORS:** Clear Lake Area C of C; Clear Lake Area Convention & Visitors Bureau; Houston Livestock Show & Rodeo; Lunar Rendezvous Festival, Advisory RE Council - College of the Mainland; **HOME ADD:** 2113 Willow Wisp, Seabrook, TX 77586, (713)474-3803; **BUS ADD:** PO Box 58373, Houston, TX 77058, (713)486-1900.

MENICUCCI, John A.——B: Mar. 6, 1952, Albuquerque, NM, *Prop. Mgr.*, Berger Briggs RE & Ins. Inc.; **PRIM RE ACT:** Property Manager; **SERVICES:** Full Serv. RE Office; **PROFL AFFIL & HONORS:** IREM, CPM; **EDUC:** BA, 1974, Soc. & Anthrop., Univ. of NM; **GRAD EDUC:** MBA, 1979, Fin., Univ. of NM, Robert O. Anderson School of Mgmt.; **EDUC HONORS:** Phi Beta Kappa, Phi Beta Kappa; **HOME ADD:** 2907 Rhode Island NE, Albuquerque, NM 87110, (505)292-2688; **BUS ADD:** 215 Third St. SW, PO Drawer K, Albuquerque, NM 87102, (505)247-0444.

MENNELL, Robert L.——B: Mar. 5, 1934, Boston, MA, *Prof. of Law*, Hamline University School of Law; **PRIM RE ACT:** Attorney, Instructor; **SERVICES:** Teach RE law to law students; **PREV EMPLOY:** Notre Dame Law School; Southwestern Univ.; **EDUC:** BA, 1955, Hist., UCLA; **GRAD EDUC:** JD, 1962, Law, Harvard Law School; **EDUC HONORS:** Dean's List, AA with Honorable Mention; **MIL SERV:** US Army; **HOME ADD:** 75 Mid Oaks Lane, Roseville, MN 55113; **BUS ADD:** 1536 Hewitt Ave., St. Paul, MN 55104, (612)641-2071.

MENNER, A. Keith——B: May 6, 1952, Jasper, IN, *Apartment Specialist*, Coldwell - Banker Serv., Comml. RE; **OTHER RE ACT:** Investment Prop. Brokerage; **SERVICES:** Asst. prop. owers & investors in analysis, mktg., acquiring comml. & multi-family resid., income prop.; **PROFL AFFIL & HONORS:** NAR, Metro, Indianapolis Bd. of Realtors; **EDUC:** BS, 1974, Bus., Fin. & Acctg., IN Univ., Bloomington, IN; **HOME ADD:** 1311-B Racquet Club Dr., Indianapolis, IN 46260, (317)844-8431; **BUS ADD:** Merchants Plaza, Ste 1470S, Indianapolis, IN 46204, (317)269-1054.

MENOWITZ, Frederick A.——B: NYC, NY, *VP*, Menowitz Management Corp. - Reliance Properties, Inc.; **PRIM RE ACT:** Attorney, Builder, Owner/Investor; **SERVICES:** Builder/Investor Comml. & Multiple Dwelling Resid.; **PROFL AFFIL & HONORS:** ABA; NY Bar Assn.; Queens C of C; **EDUC:** BA, 1957, Hist., Univ. of VA; **GRAD EDUC:** JD, 1960, RE Prop. & Taxation, Univ. of VA; **OTHER ACT & HONORS:** Assoc. Tr. N. Shore Hosp., Manhasset, NY; **HOME ADD:** Dock Ln., Kings Pt., NY 11024; **BUS ADD:** 91-31 Queens Blvd., Elmhurst, NY 11373, (212)457-2400.

MENTZER, Jeanne M.——*Dir. of Training*, U.S. Brokers Inc. and Westdale "L" Cos.; **PRIM RE ACT:** Broker, Consultant, Owner/Investor, Instructor, Property Manager; **OTHER RE ACT:** Serving on Gov. Adv. Bd.; **SERVICES:** Preparation of RE Lic. Exam - Basics for success in the RE bus.; **REP CLIENTS:** Brokers, salespeople, gen. public; **PREV EMPLOY:** School Teacher K-12, RE Sales; **PROFL AFFIL & HONORS:** NAR, MI Assn. of Realtors, Greater Lansing Bd. of Realtors, Lansing C of C; **EDUC:** BS, 1955, Sec. Edu. in Sci., Purdue Univ.; **GRAD EDUC:** MS, 1972, Elem. Ed. - Lang. Arts and Math, Purdue Univ.; **HOME ADD:** 4204 Michelle Cir., Lansing, MI 48917, (517)323-9444; **BUS ADD:** 4600 W. Saginaw, Lansing, MI 48917, (517)323-4382.

MERCHANT, John F.——B: Feb. 2, 1933, Greenwich, CT, *Partner*, Merchant & Rosenblum; **PRIM RE ACT:** Attorney; **OTHER RE ACT:** Savings Bank Dir.; **SERVICES:** Represent prop. mgmt. firm and bank; **REP CLIENTS:** Hayco Mgmt. Co., Peoples Savings Bank; Aetna Casualty & Surety; **PREV EMPLOY:** Deputy Commnr., CT Dept. of Communuty Affairs, Consultant - Morris B. Fleissig & Assocs.; **PROFL AFFIL & HONORS:** CT, Bridgeport and ABA; **EDUC:** BA, 1955, Socio./Hist., VA Union University; **GRAD EDUC:** JD, 1958, The Law School, Univ. of VA; **MIL SERV:** USNR, LCDR; **HOME ADD:** 69 Parkway, Fairfield, CT 06430, (203)255-6643; **BUS ADD:** 51 Bank St., Stamford, CT 06901, (203)327-5548.

MERCIER, Pierre-Paul——B: June 4, 1934, Montreal, Quebec; **PRIM RE ACT:** Consultant, Lender, Owner/Investor, Property Manager; **SERVICES:** Investment counseling, prop. mgmt.; **PROFL AFFIL & HONORS:** Order of Chartered Accts. of Quebec, C.A.; **EDUC:** BA, Commerce & Acctg., Univ. of Montreal; **HOME ADD:** 252 du Dauphine, St. Lambert, J4S1N5, Quebec, CAN, (514)671-1455; **BUS ADD:** 252 du Dauphine, St. Lambert, J4S1N5, Quebec, CAN, (514)671-1455.

MERCOLA, Vincent E.——B: Apr. 23, 1917, Chicago, IL, *Prop. Mgr.*, City of Los Angeles, Gen. Servs; **PRIM RE ACT:** Property Manager; **PROFL AFFIL & HONORS:** Intl. Council of Shopping Ctrs.; **EDUC:** BA, 1949, Liberal Arts, Univ. of MI; **MIL SERV:** Mil Int., 2-D, Lt.; **HOME ADD:** 15910 Jarupa Ave., Fontana, CA 92335, (714)822-1611;

BUS ADD: 200 N Main St., Rm. 800, Los Angeles, CA 90012.

MEREDITH, Allen K.——**B:** Mar. 27, 1950, Schenectady, NY, *Partner*, Trammell Crow Co.; **PRIM RE ACT:** Developer; **PREV EMPLOY:** Corporate Finance; **EDUC:** BA, 1972, Econ., Stanford Univ.; **GRAD EDUC:** MBA, 1976, Gen., Harvard Bus. School; **EDUC HONORS:** Econ. honors; **HOME TEL:** (404)261-5264; **BUS ADD:** C205 Barfield Rd. #200, Atlanta, GA 30328, (404)256-5780.

MEREDITH, Timothy E.——**B:** May 11, 1952, Easton, MD, *Atty.*, Corbin, Heller & Warfield, Chartered; **PRIM RE ACT:** Attorney; **SERVICES:** Litigation (at all levels of courts); gen. legal counseling; **REP CLIENTS:** Merrill Lynch Realty/Chris Coile, Inc.; Broadneck Devel. Corp.; Fred Pritt Bldg. Co., Inc.; **PREV EMPLOY:** Law Clerk, Hon. Marvin H. Smith, Court of Appeals of MD; **PROFL AFFIL & HONORS:** ABA; MD State Bar Assn. (member, Appellate Practice Comm); Anne Arundel Cty. Bar Assn.; **EDUC:** BA, 1974, Econ., Western MD Coll; **GRAD EDUC:** JD, 1977, Duke Univ.; **EDUC HONORS:** Cum Laude; **OTHER ACT & HONORS:** V.Chmn. Four Rivers District, Baltimore Area Council, Boy Scouts of Amer.; **HOME ADD:** 287 Oak Court, Severna Park, MD 21146, (301)544-2735; **BUS ADD:** 4 Evergreen Rd., Severna Park, MD 21146, (301)544-0314.

MERIN, Kenneth S.——**B:** 1950, New York City, NY, *VP*, Baker Merin Associates, Inc.; **PRIM RE ACT:** Broker, Consultant, Developer; **SERVICES:** Anything relating to office bldg. devel. & leasing; **REP CLIENTS:** TRW, Travelers Ins., Shell Oil, Mutual of Omaha; **PREV EMPLOY:** Sutton & Towne Suburban, Inc. (Long Is. Office); **PROFL AFFIL & HONORS:** Amer. Arbitration Assn., RE Bd. of NY; **EDUC:** 1973, Univ. of PA; **MIL SERV:** USCG, Seaman, Nat. Serv. Medal; **BUS ADD:** 80 Main St., W Orange, NJ 07052, (201)678-0200.

MERLO, Andrew E.——**B:** June 19, 1942, Jersey City, NJ, *Dir., Nat. Bus. Devel.*, A.E. Merlo Associates; **PRIM RE ACT:** Broker, Consultant, Developer, Builder, Owner/Investor; **REP CLIENTS:** Gen. Tire, Sony, RADICE Corp., Robert Trent Jones, Inc., St. Michael Clothes; **PROFL AFFIL & HONORS:** Nat. Assn. of Corp. RE Execs.; Intl. Council of Shopping Ctrs.,; IREBA; **EDUC:** 1964, Arch./RE, Miami Univ.; **GRAD EDUC:** 1968, Urban Land Econ., NY Univ.; **OTHER ACT & HONORS:** Who's Who in Fin. & Indus. (22nd Ed.); Bd. of Dirs., Creative Music Found. Woodstock, NY; Bd. of Dirs., Found. for Innervision Mahwah, NY; **HOME ADD:** 314 19th St., Union City, NJ 07087, (201)863-6676; **BUS ADD:** 314 19th St., Union City, NJ 07087, (201)863-6676.

MERRILL, Rick——**B:** Apr. 30, 1951, Newark, NJ, *Owner*, Merrill Land Co.; **PRIM RE ACT:** Broker, Consultant, Appraiser, Developer, Owner/Investor, Syndicator; **OTHER RE ACT:** Exchangor; **SERVICES:** Devel., consultation & supervision-sales, exchanges, mktg., appraisals, and cash flow analysis; **PREV EMPLOY:** Land surveyor's asst., Vista Volunteer; **PROFL AFFIL & HONORS:** VP Hendersonville Bd. of Realtors, Dir. Hendersonville MLS, Member of Henderson Cty. Commissioners Blue Ribbon Comm. on Growth; **EDUC:** Engeg., Cornell Univ.; **OTHER ACT & HONORS:** Kiwanis Club of Hendersonville, Elks Club; **HOME ADD:** Rt. 1 Box 347, Zirconia, NC 28780, (704)692-0906; **BUS ADD:** 228 N Church St., Hendersonville, NC 28739, (704)693-6556.

MERRILL, William Blakemore, II——**B:** Apr. 27, 1944, Boston, MA, *RE Investment Officer*, John Hancock Mutual Life Insurance Co., Equity Real Estate Dept.; **PRIM RE ACT:** Consultant, Appraiser, Developer, Lender, Owner/Investor, Property Manager; **OTHER RE ACT:** Acquisition Specialist; **PREV EMPLOY:** The Codman Co.; R.M. Bradley & Co., Inc.; **PROFL AFFIL & HONORS:** IREM, BOMA, CPM, RPA Candidate; **EDUC:** BS, 1970, Sociology, Psych., Univ. of Denver; **MIL SERV:** USNR; **HOME ADD:** 94 Harbor Ave., Marblehead Neck, MA 01945, (617)631-6715; **BUS ADD:** PO Box 111, Boston, MA 02117, (617)421-2249.

MERRILL, William H., Jr.——**B:** Apr. 11, 1942, Indianapolis, IN, *Gen. Counsel/VP & Gen. Counsel*, Everett I. Brown Co., Landeco, Inc.; **PRIM RE ACT:** Consultant, Attorney, Owner/Investor; **PREV EMPLOY:** Trust Officer, Merchants Nat. Bank & Tr. Co. of Indianapolis, 1965-69; **PROFL AFFIL & HONORS:** Indianapolis Bar Assn., IN State Bar Assn., ABA, Amer. Judicature Soc.; **EDUC:** BS, 1965, Bus. Admin., Butler Univ.; **GRAD EDUC:** JD, 1967, IN Univ. Sch. of Law; **OTHER ACT & HONORS:** Carmel Plan Comm., Columbia Club, Crooked Stock Golf Club, Who's Who in Amer. Law, Who's Who in the Midwest & Indianapolis City-Wide Beautification Program, 1981; **HOME ADD:** RR 2, Box 339A, Carmel, IN 46032, (317)872-4861; **BUS ADD:** 5500 W. Bradbury Ave., Indianapolis, IN 46241, (317)244-7881.

MERRIMAN, Robert L.C.——**B:** 1929, MO, Merriman Real Estate Co.; **PRIM RE ACT:** Broker, Consultant, Developer, Owner/Investor; **SERVICES:** RE Assembly Prop. revaluation consultation; **EDUC:** SW MO State Univ., Drury Coll.; **OTHER ACT & HONORS:** Bus. and Profl. Orgs.; **HOME ADD:** 3160 Wilshire Dr., Springfield, MO 65804, (417)883-3281; **BUS ADD:** 2420 S Campbell Ave., Springfield, MO 65807, (417)883-3226.

MERRITT, William J.W., P.C.——**B:** Dec. 18, 1947, Riverside, CT, *Atty. at Law*, Merritt, Hicks, Solari & Thompson; **PRIM RE ACT:** Attorney; **SERVICES:** Taxation, (Corp. & Indiv.); Estate Planning; Corp.; **PROFL AFFIL & HONORS:** IN Bar Assn., GA Bar Assn.; **EDUC:** AB-Princeton Univ., 1970, Econ. & Pol. Sci., Princeton's Woodrow Wilson Sch. of Public & Intl. Affairs; **GRAD EDUC:** JD, MBA-Univ. of VA, 1974, Taxation, Coll. for Fin. Planning in Denver, CO-Cerf. Fin. Planner; LLM, 1980, Emory Univ.; **MIL SERV:** US Marine Res., 2nd Lt. (1970); **HOME ADD:** 198 Hidden Lake Ct., Marietta, GA 30067, (404)977-0540; **BUS ADD:** 550 River Edge One, 5500 Interstate N Pkwy., Atlanta, GA 30328, (404)952-6550.

MERRYMAN, Robert H.——**B:** May 9, 1923, WA, *Broker - Owner*, Tarbuck Realty Realtors; **PRIM RE ACT:** Broker, Consultant, Developer, Owner/Investor, Property Manager, Syndicator; **PREV EMPLOY:** Self-employed mfg. rep. in bldg. materials; **PROFL AFFIL & HONORS:** RESSI; RNMI; Seattle-King Co., Bd. of Realtors; WA Assn. of Realtors; NAR, CCIM (Cert. Comml. Investment Member); **EDUC:** BBA, 1948, Mktg., Univ. of WA; **MIL SERV:** USN, Lt.j.g.; **OTHER ACT & HONORS:** Seattle Coll. Club; Tres. of the Bd., Shorewood Osteopathic Hosp.; **HOME ADD:** 3527 SW 170th, Seattle, WA 98166, (206)243-8783; **BUS ADD:** 15401 1st Ave. S, Seattle, WA 98148, (206)244-8550.

MERSEREAU, Wallace D.——**B:** Mar. 7, 1931, Los Angeles, CA, *Dir. of Prop.*, Port of Oakland; **PRIM RE ACT:** Developer, Property Manager; **PREV EMPLOY:** S.F. Bay Area Rapid Transit, 1964-73, Dir; CA Dept. of Transp., 1953-64; **PROFL AFFIL & HONORS:** AIREA, SIR, NAIOP, ULI, Amer. R/W Assn., MAI; **EDUC:** BS, 1953, Fin., Univ. of S. CA; **MIL SERV:** USN, Lt., 1953-55; **HOME ADD:** 338 Avila Rd., San Mateo, CA 94402, (415)341-3021; **BUS ADD:** 66 Jack London Sq., Oakland, CA 94607, (415)444-3188.

MERTZ, Michael F., Jr.——**B:** May 17, 1931, Weston, WV, *Broker/Pres.*, Mertz Realty, Inc.; **PRIM RE ACT:** Broker, Consultant, Appraiser, Owner/Investor, Instructor, Property Manager; **OTHER RE ACT:** Coal, oil and gas broker/titles/mapping/appraisal; **SERVICES:** Right of Way Acquisition, titles, mapping, appraisal, coal, oil & gas leasing; **REP CLIENTS:** AT&T, Atlantic Richfield, Colonial Pipeline, Public Serv. Electric & Gas., Interstate Energy, Diversified Energy Servs, MI/WI Pipeline Co., OH Bell Tel., TX Eastern Gas Transmission Corp., C.E. Beck, Inc., Grafton Coal Co., Bitner Fuel Co., Bitner Mining Co.; **PROFL AFFIL & HONORS:** WV Assn. of Realtors, NAR, Sr. Member Intl. Right of Way Assn., Sr. Member IFAS designation, Nat. Assn. of Ind. Fee Appraisers, GRI, Past Pres. Clarksberg Bd. of Realtors, Past Pres. Weston Bd. of Realtors, Past Pres. (State Dir.) Nat. Assn. of Ind. Fee Appraisers for WV; **EDUC:** BS, 1955, Eng., Sci. & Agric., WV Univ., Morgantown WV; **GRAD EDUC:** GRI, 1975, Parkersburg Comm. Coll.; **EDUC HONORS:** Names to Marquis Who's Who in S & SW, Who's Who in Fin. & Indus., Candidate for MAI Designation, AIREA; **MIL SERV:** USA Armor, Capt. Degree of 'Tanker', US Army Armor Sch., Fort Knox, KY; **OTHER ACT & HONORS:** Cert. Surveyor, WV Dept. of Nat. Resources, 1968; Alpha Gamma Rho., Alumni Sec., Member WVU Livestock Judging Team, Chicago, 1954; **HOME ADD:** 236 E 1st St., PO Box 587, Weston, WV 26452, (304)269-4343; **BUS ADD:** 236 E 1st St., PO Box 587, Weston, WV 26452, (304)269-4343.

MESENBOURG, Michael J.——**B:** June 4, 1947, Milwaukee, WI, Corrigan Properties Inc.; **PRIM RE ACT:** Developer, Owner/Investor, Property Manager; **PREV EMPLOY:** Draper & Kramer Inc. 1975-1980; **PROFL AFFIL & HONORS:** Intl. Council of Shopping Ctrs. Bd. of Realtors, CSM; **EDUC:** BA, 1969, Urban Affairs, Univ. of WI-Milwaukee, Sr. Honors; **GRAD EDUC:** MSArch, 1974, Arch., Univ. of WI-Milwaukee; **HOME ADD:** 1581 Goodes Glen, Hubertus, WI 53033; **BUS ADD:** 5900 N Port Washington Rd., Suite 114, Milwaukee, WI 53217, (414)332-8136.

MESIROW, M. Marvin——**B:** July 3, 1933, Chicago, IL, *Pres.*, Great Western Cities, Inc.; **OTHER RE ACT:** Land Dev.; **PREV EMPLOY:** Arthur Andersen & Co., Padre Island Dev. Co.; **PROFL AFFIL & HONORS:** ALDA; AICPA; CA Soc. of CPA;s, CPA Atty.; **EDUC:** BS, 1961, Bus. Adm. Acctg., UCLA; **GRAD EDUC:** JD, 1969, Law, Loyola Univ. at Los Angeles; **MIL SERV:** USAF, Sgt., 1951-1955; **HOME ADD:** 10444 Canoga Ave., Chatsworth, CA 91311, (213)700-1349; **BUS ADD:** 4605 Lankershim Bldv., Suite 600, N Hollywood, CA 91602, (213)985-9000.

MESJAK, Theodore C.——*Mgr., RE Investment*, The Northwestern Mutual Life Insurance Co., RE investment dept.; **PRIM RE ACT:** Lender, Owner/Investor; **SERVICES:** Analyze large RE projects for investment, structure financing, RE portfolio mgmt.; **PROFL AFFIL & HONORS:** IL Mort. Bankers Assn., Chicago Assn. of Commerce & Indus.; **EDUC:** BS, 1960, Bus. Admin., Univ. of MN; **GRAD EDUC:** MBA, 1976, Univ. of Chicago Grad. Sch. of Bus.; **EDUC HONORS:** Beta Gamma Sigma Key for Scholastic Excellence; **MIL SERV:** USN, Lt.; **HOME ADD:** 3840 Downers Dr., Downers Grove, IL 60515, (312)852-0783; **BUS ADD:** 100 S. Wacker Dr. #834, Chicago, IL 60606, (312)372-5380.

MESSENKOPF, Eugene J.——**B:** Jan. 26, 1928, NYC, *Pres., CEO*, Donaldson, Lufkin and Jenrette, Real Estate; **PRIM RE ACT:** Broker, Syndicator, Consultant, Developer, Builder, Property Manager; **PREV EMPLOY:** Peat, Marwick, Mitchell, The Amer. Tobacco Co.; **PROFL AFFIL & HONORS:** Fin. Execs. Inst., AICPA, Bonnie Briar Ctry. Club; **EDUC:** BBA, 1950, Acctg., Iona Coll.; **GRAD EDUC:** MBA, 1956, Corp. Fin., NY Univ.; **EDUC HONORS:** Awarded Br. Loftus award for meritorious achievement in bus.; **MIL SERV:** USA, M/Sgt., Combat Inf. Badge; **HOME ADD:** 54 Park Rd., Scarsdale, NY 10583, (914)725-2588; **BUS ADD:** 140 Broadway, NY, NY 10005, (212)747-9733.

MESSICK, Harold M.——**B:** Nov. 13, 1933, Winston-Salem, NC, *Pres.*, Marathon Associates, Inc.; **PRIM RE ACT:** Appraiser, Developer; **SERVICES:** Appraisals, Feasibility Studies, Land Devel.; **REP CLIENTS:** Home Fed. S&L, Ins. Cos., Relocation Cos., Other Banks and S&L; **PREV EMPLOY:** Architect; **PROFL AFFIL & HONORS:** ASREA, Chicago, IL Local Chap. 153, SRA, SRPA; **EDUC:** AS, 1962, Arch. Engrg., GA Tech. (Engrg. Extension Div. -So. Tech.); **MIL SERV:** USA, sp-3, European Theatre; **OTHER ACT & HONORS:** Elder Friendly Ave. Church of Christ; Past Member Greensboro Jaycees, Chmn. of the Bd. Greensboro Sertoma Club 1981-1982; Assoc. member Greensboro-High Point Home Builders Assn.; **HOME ADD:** 4812 Fox Chase Rd., Greensboro, NC 27410, (919)292-2449; **BUS ADD:** 1702 Battleground Ave., Greensboro, NC 27408, (919)272-0209.

MESSICK, John A.——**B:** Oct. 8, 1934, Spencer, NC, *VP and Gen. Mgr.*, Bald Head Island Corp.; **PRIM RE ACT:** Broker; **OTHER RE ACT:** Resid. resort devel.; **SERVICES:** Devel. and sale of lots & villas - operation of hotel, golf course and other resort facilities; **EDUC:** BBA, 1957, E. Carolina Univ.; **MIL SERV:** USA; **HOME ADD:** 1936 Hawthorne Rd., Wilmington, NC 28403, (919)762-8274; **BUS ADD:** 704 E. Moore St., Southport, NC 28461, (919)457-6763.

MESSING, Terry F.——**B:** Dec. 10, 1923, Columbus, NE, *Pres., Owner*, Terry Messing Realtors; **PRIM RE ACT:** Broker, Developer, Builder, Property Manager; **OTHER RE ACT:** Affiliations etc., Presently serving on KS RE Commn.; **SERVICES:** Comp. RE & Bldg., prop. mgmt.; **PROFL AFFIL & HONORS:** Local RE Bd., Kansas Assn. Realtors, NAR, Past Bd. Pres., local, Realtor of the Yr.; Former VP, KS Assn. Realtors; Local and KS Pres. of AHB; NAHB; **MIL SERV:** USAF, 1st Lt., POW; **HOME ADD:** 608 Eldorado, Hutchinson, KS 67501, (316)662-4265; **BUS ADD:** 1011 N. Main, Hutchinson, KS 67501, (316)662-2336.

METCALF, George C.——**B:** Jan 30, 1932, Greenfield, IL, *Owner*, Century 21 Metcalf Agency; **PRIM RE ACT:** Broker, Appraiser, Property Manager, Owner/Investor, Insuror; **SERVICES:** RE & Ins. Bus.; **PREV EMPLOY:** Ins. & RE Bus. since 1957; **PROFL AFFIL & HONORS:** NAR & State Assn. IL, Past Pres. Edws-Collinsville Bd. of Realtors, Presently on Bd. of Dirs., (Edws-Collinsville Bd. of R); **EDUC:** BS, 1954, Bus. (Ins. & RE), Bradley Univ.; **MIL SERV:** USAF; Maj. (USAFR) Retd.; **OTHER ACT & HONORS:** Edwardsville Rotary Club; Moose Lodge; **HOME ADD:** 1009 St. Louis St., Edwardsville, IL 62025, (618)656-5014; **BUS ADD:** 112 N. Main St., EdwardsvilLe, IL 62025, (618)656-5178.

MEYER, Conrad, IV——**B:** Jan. 27, 1945, New Orleans, LA, *Atty.*, Baldwin & Haspel; **OTHER RE ACT:** Banking law and mortgage lending; **PROFL AFFIL & HONORS:** LA State & New Orleans Bar Assns., ABA, Amer. Coll. of Mort. Attys.; **EDUC:** BA, 1966, Lib. Arts., Tulane Univ.; **GRAD EDUC:** JD, 1969, Tulane Univ.; **EDUC HONORS:** Tulane Law Review; **OTHER ACT & HONORS:** Past pres. Whitney Hghts Improv. Assn.; **BUS ADD:** Suite 2411, 225 Baronne St., New Orleans, LA 70112, (504)581-1711.

MEYER, David R.——**B:** Oct. 11, 1947, Sedalia, MO, *VP*, Meyer Brothers Building Co.; **PRIM RE ACT:** Broker, Developer, Builder; **SERVICES:** Comml. & indus. RE, devel. & const.; **PROFL AFFIL & HONORS:** NAR; RNMI; **EDUC:** BSBA, 1969, Bus. Mgmt., Central MO State Univ.; **MIL SERV:** US Army, E-4; **HOME ADD:** 1510 S. 19th St., Blue Springs, MO 64015, (816)229-6864; **BUS ADD:** 604 S. Industrial Dr., POB 846, Blue Springs, MO 64015, (816)228-5516.

MEYER, Edward J.——**B:** July 2, 1931, Queens, NY, *Pres.*, J. Gordon Carr & Assoc., P.C. Architects/Planners; **PRIM RE ACT:** Consultant, Architect; **SERVICES:** Bldg. analysis, planning & design of comml. bldgs., offices, lease education; **REP CLIENTS:** Corporate Headquarters, space planning & design as well as planning & design of comml. instnl. bldgs.; **PREV EMPLOY:** Edwin H. Cordes AIA-Arch/; **PROFL AFFIL & HONORS:** AIA, NY Bldg. Congress, NCARB, BOMA NY, BOMA Intl., Amer. Arbit. Assn., NY Assn. of Archs.; **EDUC:** BA, 1959, Arch., Pratt Inst.; **MIL SERV:** USMC, Sgt., Service Medal, Good Conduct; **OTHER ACT & HONORS:** C of C of U.S.; **HOME ADD:** 24 Saratoga St., Commack, NY 11725, (516)499-5246; **BUS ADD:** 80 West 40th St., NY, NY 10018, (212)221-0600.

MEYER, Edwin C.——**B:** Mar. 5, 1920, Los Angeles, CA, *Owner*, Meyer Appraisal Co., Comml. & Indus. Spec.; **PRIM RE ACT:** Appraiser; **SERVICES:** Appraisals, consultation, synd., loans; **REP CLIENTS:** Have recently served IBM, Beatrice Foods, Roadway Trucking Co.; **PREV EMPLOY:** Chief Appraiser-Sequoia Mort. Co., Chief Appraiser-Bank of The West; **PROFL AFFIL & HONORS:** AIREA, Soc. of RE Appraisers, Realtor Bd. Member San Jose RE Bd., MAI; SRPA; **EDUC:** BA, 1951, Bus. Admin.;RE Appraisals, Whittier Coll.; **MIL SERV:** USN, AMMF 2/c; **HOME ADD:** 6936 Chiala Ln., San Jose, CA 95129, (408)252-5045; **BUS ADD:** 6936 Chiala Ln., San Jose, CA 95129, (408)252-5045.

MEYER, F. Weller——**B:** Dec. 15, 1942, Washington, DC, *Managing Dir.*, Mortgage Systems Corp.; **PRIM RE ACT:** Consultant; **SERVICES:** Consulting Resid. Mort. Fin. Origination, Sale & Serv.; **REP CLIENTS:** Comml. banks, Mort. bankers, S&Ls, Credit Unions, Trade Assns. & Educ. Instns.; **PREV EMPLOY:** MBAA; **PROFL AFFIL & HONORS:** MBAA; **EDUC:** Bus. Admin., 1967, Econ. Fin., Univ. of MD; **MIL SERV:** USA, 1st Lt., Combat Infantry Badge, Bronze Star Medal 'V' 2 Oak Leaf Clusters, Air Medal, Purple Heart, Good Conduct Medal, Nat. Defense Serv. Medal, Vietnam Campaign Medal, Vietnam Service Medal; **OTHER ACT & HONORS:** NW Optimist Club of WA, Congressional Ctry. Club and Green Acres Gun Club; **HOME ADD:** 16006 Jerald Rd., Laurel, MD 20707, (301)490-8624; **BUS ADD:** 4813 Bethesda Ave., Bethesda, MD 20814, (301)654-4310.

MEYER, Harry G.——**B:** June 23, 1945, Buffalo, NY, *Partner*, Hodgson, Russ, Andrews, Woods & Goodyear; **PRIM RE ACT:** Attorney; **REP CLIENTS:** Como Mall Assocs., Transitown Plaza Assocs., Western NY Indus. Park Inc., Clarence Research Park Inc., (Industrial Park); **PROFL AFFIL & HONORS:** Erie Cty., NY State and ABA; **EDUC:** BA, 1967, Hist. and Econ., Yale Univ.; **GRAD EDUC:** LLB, 1970, Yale Univ.; **EDUC HONORS:** Phi Beta Kappa, Magna Cum Laude; **HOME ADD:** 96 Morningside Ln., Williamsville, NY 14221, (716)632-8659; **BUS ADD:** 1800 One M & T Plaza, Buffalo, NY 14203, (716)856-4000.

MEYER, Larry E.——**B:** June 24, 1939, Mattoon, IL, *Broker-owner*, Heart of Amer., Realtors; **PRIM RE ACT:** Broker, Appraiser; **SERVICES:** Resid. & comml. sales, investment counseling, appraising; **PROFL AFFIL & HONORS:** IL Assn. of Realtors, NAR; **EDUC:** BS, 1962, Phys. Ed., So. IL Univ., Carbondale, IL; **GRAD EDUC:** MS, 1962, Phys. Educ., So. IL Univ.; Dr. of Educ., 1969, Phys. of Exercise, Univ. of MO, Columbia; **EDUC HONORS:** Dean's List for Acad. Achievement 7 times, Dean's List for Acad. Achievement 3 Times, Dean's List for Academic Achievement 4 Times; **HOME ADD:** 108 S Bellemont Rd., Bloomington, IL 61701, (309)662-4771; **BUS ADD:** 2301 E Washington, Bloomington, IL 61701, (309)662-1327.

MEYER, Michael P.——**B:** Aug. 9, 1938, New York, *Sales & Mktg. Mgr.*, Robert Bruce Realty, Inc.; **PRIM RE ACT:** Broker; **SERVICES:** Resid. Brokerage, Corp. Relocation, New Constr.; **PROFL AFFIL & HONORS:** NAR, PAR, RMSI, GRI; **EDUC:** BS, 1960, Econ., Mt. St. Mary's; **GRAD EDUC:** MBA, 1973, Bus. Mgmt., Mktg., Pace Univ.; **MIL SERV:** USN, Lt. 1961-1965; **HOME ADD:** 325 Caswallen Dr., West Chester, PA 19380, (215)692-6351; **BUS ADD:** 1223 West Chester Pike, West Chester, PA 19380, (215)353-6200.

MEYER, Shirley——**B:** Dec. 15, 1934, Washington County,IL, *Prop. Mgr.-Pres.*, Goss Prop. Mgr., Inc.; **PRIM RE ACT:** Property Manager; **PROFL AFFIL & HONORS:** Egyptian Bd. of Realtors, Inst. of RE Mgt.; **EDUC:** Attended IL Univ. and John Logan Coll.; **OTHER ACT & HONORS:** Member of Fair Housing Bd. of Carbondale, IL; **HOME ADD:** 810 S. Oakland, Carbondale, IL 62901, (618)549-3849; **BUS ADD:** Westown Mall, Carbondale, IL 62901, (618)549-2621.

MEYER, Theodore James——**B:** Aug. 20, 1948, Des Moines, IA, *Partner*, Oppenheimer, Wolff, Foster, Shepard & Donnelly; **PRIM RE ACT:** Attorney; **OTHER RE ACT:** RE; **SERVICES:** General RE -

related legal services; **REP CLIENTS:** Control Data Corp.; **PROFL AFFIL & HONORS:** Ramsey County, MN and ABA; **EDUC:** BS, 1970, Distributed Studies, IA State Univ.; **GRAD EDUC:** JD, 1973, Harvard Law School; **EDUC HONORS:** With Distinction; **HOME ADD:** 1710 St. Mary's Ave., Falcon Heights, MN 55113, (612)644-2914; **BUS ADD:** 1700 First National Bank Bldg., St. Paul, MN 55101, (612)227-7271.

MEYERS, Bertram H.——B: Apr. 8, 1935, Washington, DC, *Dir. of Leasing & House Counsel*, Carrollton Enterprises; **PRIM RE ACT:** Attorney, Property Manager; **OTHER RE ACT:** Leasing; **SERVICES:** Lease procurement negotiations and drafting mgmt.; **PREV EMPLOY:** C.D. Hylton Enterprises, Woodbridge, VA; **PROFL AFFIL & HONORS:** Intl. Council of Shopping Centers., Apt. and Office Bldg. Assn., ABA, DC Bar Assn., Prince George's Community Coll. Faculty; Who's Who in Maryland 1975; **EDUC:** 1957, Amer. Univ.; **GRAD EDUC:** 1960, WA Coll. of Law, Amer. Univ.; **MIL SERV:** USCG; **OTHER ACT & HONORS:** Counsel, Charlestown Village 1974; Chmn., Rules & Regulations Comm., Westbridge Condo. 1981; **HOME ADD:** 6100 Westchester Park Dr. Apr. #1104, College Park, MD 20740, (301)441-8383; **BUS ADD:** 11700 Beltsville Dr., PO Box 826, Beltsville, MD 20705, (301)572-7800.

MEYERS, Larry W.——B: May 30, 1937, Memphis, TN, *Pres.*, Meyers Realty/Better Homes & Gardens; **PRIM RE ACT:** Broker, Appraiser, Developer, Owner/Investor; **SERVICES:** Resid. & comml. RE mktg.; **REP CLIENTS:** Homequity, Equitable, Merrill Lynch, Bank of St. Louis, Reynolds Metals; **PROFL AFFIL & HONORS:** NAR, RNMI, Soc. of RE Appraisers, GRI, SRA, Pres. AR Realtors Assn.; **EDUC:** BSChE, 1959, Chemical Engrg., Univ. of AR; **MIL SERV:** USA - Infantry, Capt.; **OTHER ACT & HONORS:** Garland Co., Industrial Devel. Corp.; **HOME ADD:** 200 E Vista Dr., Hot Springs, AR 71913, (501)262-2574; **BUS ADD:** 3999 Central Ave., Hot Springs, AR 71913, (501)624-5622.

MEYERS, William, II——B: Mar. 23, 1938, Philadelphia, PA, *Chmn. of the Bd.*, Meyers & D'Aleo Inc., Architects & Planners; **PRIM RE ACT:** Consultant, Architect, Developer, Owner/Investor; **OTHER RE ACT:** Planner; **SERVICES:** Arch., planning, feasibility, & land use & zoning studies; **REP CLIENTS:** Devel., corp., local & state govts., partnerships, investors, owners, tenants, renovators; **PROFL AFFIL & HONORS:** National Trust for Hist. Preservation; Victorian Soc.; Soc. for the Preservation of MD Antiquities, Urban Design Award, AIA Honor Award, P/A Award; **EDUC:** BS Arch., 1962, Arch., Univ. of Cincinnati; **EDUC HONORS:** Metro Honor Society, Scarab Arch. Hon. Frat.; **OTHER ACT & HONORS:** On several Bd. of Dir.; **HOME ADD:** 1400 W. Joppa Rd., Baltimore, MD 21204, (301)321-6822; **BUS ADD:** 108 Water St., Baltimore, MD 21202, (301)752-7848.

MEYERSON, Stanley P.——B: Apr. 13, 1916, Spartansburg, SC, *Part.*, Westmoreland, Hall McGee & Warner & Oxford; **PRIM RE ACT:** Attorney; **SERVICES:** All legal including tax aspects; **REP CLIENTS:** Lenders, devels. & synd.; **PREV EMPLOY:** Part. Hatcher, Meyerson, Oxford & Irvin, Atlanta, GA; **PROFL AFFIL & HONORS:** Amer. Coll. of Mort. Attys., NY, SC & GA Bars, ABA, State Bar of GA, Atlanta Lawyers Club, Atlanta & GA Bar Assn. Chmn., Tax Comm., Who's Who in Amer. Law; **EDUC:** BA, 1937, Duke Univ., GA Tech.; **GRAD EDUC:** JD, 1939, Tax & Real Prop., Duke Univ.; **MIL SERV:** USN, 1943-46, Lt. Cmdr., World War II, Four Battle Stars, Pacific; **OTHER ACT & HONORS:** Kiwanis; **HOME ADD:** 975 Nawench Dr., NW, Atlanta, GA 30327, (404)355-5923; **BUS ADD:** 2800 Tower Pl., Atlanta, GA 30026, (404)231-1935.

MEZERA, Gerald T.——B: May 5, 1943, Cleveland, OH, *Mgr. RE*, Post Oak Develpment Enterprises, Ltd.; **PRIM RE ACT:** Developer, Property Manager; **SERVICES:** Townhomes, Apts., Offices; **PREV EMPLOY:** Patrick Realty & Assoc, Atlanta, GA; **PROFL AFFIL & HONORS:** Natl. Assn. of Corp. RE Execs., CRA; **EDUC:** BA, 1965, Mgmt., MI State Univ.; **GRAD EDUC:** MBA, 1969, Bus., Univ. of MI; **MIL SERV:** US Army, E-5, Award of Merit; **OTHER ACT & HONORS:** Phi Kappa Theta; **HOME ADD:** 9718 Braesmont St., Houston, TX 77096, (713)721-0142; **BUS ADD:** 5909 W. Loop S., Houston, TX 77401, (713)665-2444.

MICEK, John J.——B: Sept. 23, 1952, Omaha, NE, *Corp. Counsel*, Armanino Farms of CA; **PRIM RE ACT:** Attorney; **EDUC:** BA, 1974, Hist., Univ. of Santa Clara; **GRAD EDUC:** JD, Univ. of San Francisco Sch. of Law; **EDUC HONORS:** Editor, Law Review; **HOME ADD:** 600 Pacheco, San Francisco, CA 94116, (415)756-9367; **BUS ADD:** 1945 Carroll Ave., San Francisco, CA 94124, (415)467-3500.

MICHAEL, Jerome J.——B: Sept. 19, 1928, *Prin.*, Jerome Michael & Assoc.; **PRIM RE ACT:** Consultant; **SERVICES:** Market research, income producing props., investment synd., shopping ctr. mgmt. & leasing consulting; **PREV EMPLOY:** Larry Smith & Co., 1961-73, VP RE market research & investment counsulting; **PROFL AFFIL & HONORS:** ULI, Intl. Council of Shopping Ctrs.; **EDUC:** BA, 1955, Econ., George Washington Univ., DC., Charles Univ., Prague; **GRAD EDUC:** MBA, 1959, Fin., Geo. Washington Univ.; **OTHER ACT & HONORS:** Alpha Kappa Psi, Beta Mo Chap. (Pres).; **HOME ADD:** 16670 Emory Ln., Rockville, MD 20853, (301)774-7094; **BUS ADD:** 7315 Wisconsin Ave., Suite 609E, Bethesda, MD 20814, (301)652-7487.

MICHAEL, Kenneth H.——B: June 1, 1938, Winchester, VA, *Pres.*, Kenneth H. Michael Cos., Inc.; **SERVICES:** Comml. & indus. leasing & mgmt., appraising, synd., arch., etc.; **REP CLIENTS:** Indiv. & instnl. investors in comml. & indus. props.; **PROFL AFFIL & HONORS:** Member - IREM, Pres. - Prince George's Cty. Bd. of Realtors; **EDUC:** BS, Univ. MD; **MIL SERV:** USAF; **OTHER ACT & HONORS:** Chmn., Sal. Army - Wash., DC, Advisory Comm. & Prince George's Cty. Advisory Bd.; **HOME ADD:** 3920 Calverton Dr., Hyattsville, MD 20782, (301)927-4434; **BUS ADD:** 4701 Lydell Rd., Cheverly, MD 20781, (301)341-1166.

MICHALAK, Craig L.——B: Oct. 23, 1947, Milwaukee, WI, *Assoc. Broker*, CLM, Inc., Assoc. with Kidder Mathews & Segner Inc., Commercial and Industrial Real Estate; **PRIM RE ACT:** Broker, Consultant, Developer, Owner/Investor, Instructor, Property Manager, Syndicator; **OTHER RE ACT:** Expert witness, joint venturer, exchanges; **SERVICES:** Full comml. and investment brokerage servs., acquisition mgmt., leasing, valuation and sales of comml. props., develop income producing props., create partnership entities, joint venturer and investor through Kidder, Mathews & Segner Inc.; **REP CLIENTS:** Pension funds and other instnl. investors in comml. props., private investors, contrs. and other devels., consultant to other comml. RE brokerage firms and bus. consultant firms. Expert witness for law and acctg. firms; **PREV EMPLOY:** Over a decade of mgmt., mgmt. consulting and sales experience. Previously held faculty position at Univ. of CA, Speaker at several profl. conferences; **PROFL AFFIL & HONORS:** Realtor, RNMI, Past Member Bd. of Dirs. Radford & Co., Candidate CCIM; **EDUC:** AB, 1969, Psych., Univ.of CA, Santa Cruz; **GRAD EDUC:** MBA, 1971, Bus. Admin., Mgmt., UCLA; **EDUC HONORS:** Robert Hoover Scholarship, CA State Scholarship, Clinton Swanson Memorial Scholarship, Nat. Sci. Found. Inst. Fellowship, MBA Comprehensive Exam Rating, Superior; **OTHER ACT & HONORS:** Speaker on Comml. RE. 1980 Seattle-King Cty. Bd. of Realtors Annual Convention, Keynote Speaker, 1979 AAUA Nat. Conf.; **HOME ADD:** 11000 NE 39th Pl., Bellevue, WA 98004, (206)827-1930; **BUS ADD:** 550 S. Michigan Ave., Seattle, WA 98108.

MICHALS, Stephen A.——B: Nov. 18, 1954, Minneapolis, MN, *Office Leasing*, Neal A. Perlich Realty; **PRIM RE ACT:** Broker, Property Manager; **OTHER RE ACT:** Office & indus. leasing; **SERVICES:** Devel., counseling of office & ind. parks; **REP CLIENTS:** Instns., owners; **PREV EMPLOY:** Eberhardt Co.; **PROFL AFFIL & HONORS:** Nat. Assn. Indus. Office Parks; **EDUC:** BS, 1977, Bus., RE, Fin., Univ.of MN; **HOME ADD:** 2304 Rivendell Ln., Minnetonka, MN 55343, (612)546-2582; **BUS ADD:** 12300 Wayzata Blvd., Minnetonka, MN 55343, (612)546-2500.

MICHEEL, Richard J.——B: Dec. 18, 1938, Philadelphia, PA, *Pres.*, Investment Corporation of America; **PRIM RE ACT:** Appraiser, Lender, Owner/Investor; **REP CLIENTS:** Leedy Mort. Co., Inc.; Abstract Corp. of America; Jefferson Bank; Philadelphia Mortgage Trust; **PROFL AFFIL & HONORS:** Voting Member, National Assn. of RE Investment Trusts; Assoc. Member, ASA; Sr. Member, Nat. Assn. of Cert. Mort. Bankers; Amer. Assn. of Cert. Appraisers; NARA; **EDUC:** 1961, Bus. Admin., Fin., Econ., Bus. Law, LaSalle Coll.; **MIL SERV:** US Army; Specialist; **OTHER ACT & HONORS:** Dir., Jefferson Bank; Philadelphia Mort. Trust; Leedy Mortgage Co.; **BUS ADD:** One Decker Square, Bala Cynwyd, PA 19004, (215)839-3610.

MICHEL, James C.——B: July 16, 1936, Milford Ctr., OH, *Pres.*, James C. Michel- Associates Inc.; **PRIM RE ACT:** Broker, Appraiser, Instructor, Property Manager, Owner/Investor; **PROFL AFFIL & HONORS:** NAR, Independant Fee Appraisers, Farm and Land Brokers, IFA; **EDUC:** BS, 1958, Fin., OSU; **EDUC HONORS:** Alpha Kappa Psi-Honorary; **OTHER ACT & HONORS:** Chmn. Union Cty. Building Standards Committee, 1975 to present, Union Twp., Union Cty. Central Comm., Rep.; **HOME ADD:** 4 Pleasant St., Milford Ctr., OH 43045, (513)349-5851; **BUS ADD:** 873 E 5th, Marysville, OH 43040, (513)642-3015.

MICHELS, Hugh C., Jr.——B: Mar. 17, 1932, Evanston, IL, *Pres./Owner*, Hugh C. Michels & Co.; **PRIM RE ACT:** Broker, Appraiser, Developer, Property Manager; **PREV EMPLOY:** Franklin Savings Assn., Chicago Eye, Ear, Nose & Throat Hosp., M&M Parking Co., Old Colonial Ins. Agency Inc., United S&L Assn., North Shore Hotels Corp., Pres./Developer/Owner, d/b/a Sheraton-North Shore Inn, 933 Skokie Blvd., Northbrook, IL 60062 - (312)498-6500; Mallers

Building, Ltd., Pres./Owner/Managing Agent, 5 South Wabash Ave., Chicago, IL 60603 - (312)346-6168; Loop Center Building, Pres./ Owner/Managing Agent, 105 West Madison Street, Chicago, IL 60602 - (312)346-7766; Was Pres. of: Franklin Savings and Loan Assn.; Chicago Eye, Ear, Nose & Throat Hospital; M & M Parking Co.; Old Colonial Insurance Agency, Inc.; **OTHER ACT & HONORS:** Exmoor Ctry. Club, Mid-Day Club, Univ. Club, TWA Ambassadors Club, United Airlines Admiral Club, The Ocean Club of FL; **HOME ADD:** 473 Sheridan Rd., Winnetka, IL 60093; **BUS ADD:** 105 W. Madison St., Chicago, IL 60602, (312)346-7766.

MICHELSON, Bruce V.——B: Sept. 11, 1941, St. Louis, MO, *Pres.*, Michelson Org.; **PRIM RE ACT:** Broker, Syndicator, Developer, Property Manager, Owner/Investor; **EDUC:** BS, 1963, R.E. & Fin./ Econ., Wharton School of Fin, Univ. of PA; **MIL SERV:** USA, 1st Lt.; **BUS ADD:** 7745 Carondelet Ave., St. Louis, MI 63105, (314)862-7080.

MICHETTI, Mark——B: Nov. 3, 1947, Sewickley, PA, *Pres.*, Cardinal Design & Constr. Inc.; **PRIM RE ACT:** Broker, Consultant, Appraiser, Developer, Builder, Owner/Investor; **OTHER RE ACT:** Gen. Cont.; **PREV EMPLOY:** Cullmark Builders, Inc., Pres. 1977-79; **PROFL AFFIL & HONORS:** Nat. Assn. Home Builders; **EDUC:** RE, Econ., Const., Kent State Univ.; **MIL SERV:** USN, E-5, Natl. Serv.; **OTHER ACT & HONORS:** Notary Public, Farm Bur., Buckeye Sheriff's Assn.; **HOME ADD:** Box 2, Fowler, OH 44418, (216)637-1610; **BUS ADD:** 3612 Youngstown Kingsville Rd., Cortland, OH 44410.

MICKELSON, Ralph R.——B: Aug. 15, 1927, Chicago, IL, *Atty.*, Rudnick & Wolfe; **PRIM RE ACT:** Attorney, Developer, Owner/ Investor; **EDUC:** BS, 1951, Econ./Acctg., DePaul Univ.; **GRAD EDUC:** JD, 1954, Law, DePaul Univ.; **HOME ADD:** 1172 Green Bay Rd., Highland Park, IL 60035, (312)433-1331; **BUS ADD:** 30 N. LaSalle St., Suite 2900, Chicago, IL 60602, (312)368-4077.

MICLAU, Daniel C.——B: Apr. 17, 1943, Chicago, IL, *Atty., Pres.*, Fremont Bldg. Co.; **PRIM RE ACT:** Appraiser, Attorney, Developer, Owner/Investor, Property Manager; **OTHER RE ACT:** Realtor; **SERVICES:** Legal, mgmt. for rep. clients; **REP CLIENTS:** Potter Village Shopping Ctr., 200 West Apts., Albert Apts., Theodore Miclau; **PROFL AFFIL & HONORS:** OH Bar Assn.; Cuyohoga Cty. Bar Assn.; Cleveland Bar Assn.; Apt. & Homeowners Assn.; Cleveland Area Bd. of Realtors; **EDUC:** BA, 1965, For. Serv. Affairs, Pol. Sci., Hist., Georgetown Univ., Washington, DC; **GRAD EDUC:** JD, 1970, Bus. Law, Case Western Res. Univ., Cleveland, OH; **MIL SERV:** USA, 1st Lt.; **OTHER ACT & HONORS:** Council Pres., St. Mary's Romanian Orthodox Church, Cleveland, OH; Former Pres. Amer. Romanian Orthodox Youth; Chmn. Berea Area Montessori Assn.; **HOME ADD:** 7699 Aldersyde Dr., Middleburg Heights, OH 44130, (216)243-8226; **BUS ADD:** 20201 Lorain Rd., Suite 117, Fairview Park, OH 44126, (216)333-4431.

MIDDELBERG, Hans A.——B: Dec. 3, 1940, Osnabruck, W. Germany, *Chmn.*, Helikon Corp., RE Div.; **PRIM RE ACT:** Consultant, Engineer, Owner/Investor, Syndicator; **SERVICES:** Synd., consultation, RE brokerage to overseas investors; **PROFL AFFIL & HONORS:** Council of Arch., W. Germany; Synd., Counselors, W. Germany; RE Bd. W. Germany; **GRAD EDUC:** Arch. & Engrg., 1963, Staatl. Ingenieur Schule, Hildesheim, W. Germany; **EDUC HONORS:** Summa Cum Laude; **MIL SERV:** Pioneers, W. German Army, 2nd Lt.; **HOME ADD:** 94 Betsy Brown Circ., Port Chester, NY 10573, (914)937-3431; **BUS ADD:** 111 Brook St., Scarsdale, NY 10583, (914)723-2757.

MIDDELSTEADT, Bernice——B: CA, *Realtor*, Properties Unlimited; **PRIM RE ACT:** Broker, Consultant, Owner/Investor, Property Manager; **OTHER RE ACT:** Comml. investments and exchanging of investment props.—no territorial limits; **PREV EMPLOY:** RE Broker for 30 years; **PROFL AFFIL & HONORS:** S.F. Bd. of Realtors, State and Nat. C of C, S.F., CA, GRI; CRS; CBC; RECI; **EDUC:** City Coll., San Francisco; **HOME ADD:** 1810 Eighth Ave., San Francisco, CA 94122, (415)681-7210; **BUS ADD:** 360 W. Portal Ave., San Francisco, CA 94127, (415)661-7000.

MIDDENDORF, Garland——*Partner*, Wolf Lake Industrial Centers; **PRIM RE ACT:** Developer; **BUS ADD:** PO Box 565, Hammond, IN 46320, (219)937-4300.*

MIDDLETON, Earl M.——B: Feb. 18, 1919, Orangeburg, SC, *Owner*, The Middleton Agency; **PRIM RE ACT:** Broker, Appraiser, Insuror; **SERVICES:** RE - Sales, rental mgmt. & appraisals; Ins. - Prop. & Casualty, Life & Health; **REP CLIENTS:** Area Broker - HUO & VA; **PROFL AFFIL & HONORS:** C&S Bank Advisory Bd.; BSA - Silver Beaver Recipient; **EDUC:** BA, 1942, Claflin Coll.; **MIL SERV:** USAF, Lt.; **OTHER ACT & HONORS:** State Legislator, 1975 to present; Trinity United Methodist Church; **BUS ADD:** PO Drawer 1305, Orangeburg, SC 29115, (803)534-8152.

MIDDLETON, Ernest F., III——B: Mar. 20, 1948, Charleston, SC, *Broker in Charge*, Beachwalker Properties, Inc.; **PRIM RE ACT:** Broker, Property Manager; **SERVICES:** Sales and prop. mgmt.; **REP CLIENTS:** Specializing in Charleston's Resort Is., Kiawah, Seabrook, Bohicket Marina Village and Isle of Palms Beach and Racquet Club; **PREV EMPLOY:** Kiawah Island Co., Asst. Prop. Mgr.; **EDUC:** BS, 1971, Bus. Admin., The Citadel; **HOME ADD:** 19 Charlton Lane, Charleston, SC 29407, (803)556-0188; **BUS ADD:** 5 Beachwalker Office Park, Kiawah Island, Johns Island, SC 29455, (803)768-9111.

MIDDLETON, Ernest F., Jr.——B: Aug. 5, 1923, Savannah, GA, *Pres.*, Carolina Southeast Corp./E.F. Middleton Corp.; **PRIM RE ACT:** Broker, Consultant, Appraiser, Developer, Instructor, Property Manager; **SERVICES:** Investment counseling, asset mgmt., problem solving, acquisitions, exchange counseling, broker guidance, RE computer application cons; **PREV EMPLOY:** Heavily involved in ownership of RE Cos. since 1946; Lic. broker in three states; Bd.of Dirs., Public RE Corp.; **PROFL AFFIL & HONORS:** Member Amer. Soc. RE Counselors of NAR; Amer. Soc. of RE Counselors of NAR; Member of Bd. of Dir. of publicly owned RE firm; Consultant to the Bd. of Dirs. of Save Charleston Found.; Consultant to the Coastal Boys Council; Consultant Corporate and Indiv. Investors; Founder of SC Mktg. and Exchange Council; Founder of Low Ctry. Exchangors; Chmn. of Ethics Comm. of SC Chap. RESSI; Chmn. of the Ethics Comm. of the SC Mktg. and Exchange Council; Bd. of Dirs. of Comml. and Investment Broker Council; Chmn. of the Educ. Comm. Charleston Chap. of Soc. of RE Appraisers; Member of the Advisory Comm. of the SC Tech. Coll. System, Counselor RE; Coll. level Lecturer of Sect. 1031 Exchanges and on RE Fin. and Analysis; **EDUC:** BS, USAF Command & Staff Coll.; **MIL SERV:** USAF, Lt. Col. (Ret.), Bronze Star, DFC, AM, AF Com. Combat Service WWII, Korea, Vietnam, Command Pilot, Missile Main. O., Missile Launch O., Missile Cmdr.; **OTHER ACT & HONORS:** Current listee at Senior Status in "Who's Who in Creative RE"; Current listee in "Who's Who in SC"; **HOME ADD:** 9 Sand Alley, Kiawah Island, SC 29455; **BUS ADD:** Peoples Bldg., 18 Broad St., P.O. Box 315, Charleston, SC 29402, (803)722-1964.

MIFSUD, Paul Charles——B: Jan 25, 1947, New York City, NY, *Exec. VP*, George S. Voinovich, Inc.; **PRIM RE ACT:** Consultant, Architect, Developer, Property Manager; **OTHER RE ACT:** Construction mgr.; **SERVICES:** Arch., engrg., urban planning, prop. & construction mgt.; **REP CLIENTS:** Municipalities, hosps., educ. instits., corp. entities; **PREV EMPLOY:** VP, Union Commerce Bank Cleveland, OH (1972-1981); **PROFL AFFIL & HONORS:** Amer. Bankers Assn., Amer. Mgmt. Assn., Bank Admin. Inst., Admin. Mgmt. Soc., Outstanding Young Man of Amer. (by US Jaycees in 1978, 1979, & 1981); **EDUC:** BBA, 1970, Profl. Mgmt., Angelo State Univ., San Angelo, TX; **GRAD EDUC:** MBA, 1975, Profl. Mgmt./Org. Behavior, Case Western Reserve Univ.; **EDUC HONORS:** 3rd in Class, Elected to Beta Gamma Sigma; **MIL SERV:** USAF, S/Sgt., Natl. Defense, Good Conduct, Selected AECP-Airman Education & Commissioning Program; **OTHER ACT & HONORS:** Councilman at Lge., Bd. of Income Tax Review, Chrmn. - Reagan-Bush Comm., Berea Rotary Club, Rep. to Berea C of C, Berea Historical Soc., Citizens League of Gr. Cleveland, Private Indus. Council; **HOME ADD:** 674 Merrimak Dr., Berea, OH 44017, (216)826-1074; **BUS ADD:** 1224 Huron Rd. Mall, Cleveland, OH 44115, (216)621-9200.

MIHALIK, Frank M.——B: Feb. 20, 1929, Aliquippa, PA, *Pres.*, Comml. Realty Marketing, Inc.; **PRIM RE ACT:** Broker, Consultant, Appraiser, Developer; **OTHER RE ACT:** Site and mktg. analyst; **SERVICES:** Site and mktg. analysis, locations, leasing; **REP CLIENTS:** Red Lobster Inns, McDonald's, Arby's, Burger King, Pizza Hut, Taco Bell, Steak-n-Ale, US Steel Corp., Skylight Inns, Jiffy Lube, Holiday Inns; **PREV EMPLOY:** VP RE, Penn Intl., Inc.; PR Dir., Union Switch & Signal Div. of Westinghouse Air Brake; Metro Goldwyn Mayer; **PROFL AFFIL & HONORS:** Amer. Mgmt. Assn.; Nat. Assn. of Corporate RE Execs.; Intl. Council of Shopping Ctrs.; Nat. Assn. of Review Appraisers, CRA; **EDUC:** AB, 1949, Poli. Sci. and Hist., Duquesne Univ. and Univ. of WI; **MIL SERV:** Navy, Lt. (jg); **OTHER ACT & HONORS:** Intl. Platform Assn., Knights of Columbus; **BUS ADD:** Suite 1-A, Law & Commerce Bldg., 2490 Mosside Blvd., Monroeville, PA 15146, (412)372-6610.

MIKELL, J. Thomas——B: Apr. 29, 1941, Beaufort, SC, *Atty.*, Harvey, Battey and Mikell, P.A.; **PRIM RE ACT:** Attorney; **SERVICES:** Representation of developers, contractors, owners assns. & lenders; **REP CLIENTS:** Fripp Island Co., Inc., Fripp Is. Service Corp., First Carolina Bank, C & S National Bank, Distant Is. Co., Bankers Trust of S.C.; Harbor Island Development Co.; C & C Investors; First Community Credit Union individuals and investors of real prop.;

PREV EMPLOY: First Nat. Bank of SC, 1964-1969; **PROFL AFFIL & HONORS:** ABA; SC Bar; Nat. Assn. of Home Builders; Beaufort Cty. Bd. of Realtors; Amer. Land Development Inst.; **EDUC:** BA, 1964, Hist., The Citadel; **GRAD EDUC:** JD, 1972, Law, Univ. of SC; **EDUC HONORS:** Francis Marion Cup; **HOME ADD:** P. O. Box 1107, Beaufort, SC 29902, (803)524-8788; **BUS ADD:** POB 1107, 1001 Craven St., Beaufort, SC 29902, (803)524-3109.

MIKES, James R.——**B:** Feb. 26, 1948, Champaign, IL, *Partner*, Rudnick & Wolfe, Tampa, FL & Chicago, IL; **PRIM RE ACT:** Attorney; **SERVICES:** Legal servs. to nat. and intl. RE devels., lenders, investors, contractors, synds.; **EDUC:** BS, 1970, RE, Fin., AZ State Univ.; **GRAD EDUC:** JD/MBA, 1973, Acctg./Fin./Law, Univ. of Chicago; **MIL SERV:** US Army Res., Capt.; **OTHER ACT & HONORS:** Other bus. address: 201 E. Kennedy Blvd., Tampa FL 33602; **HOME ADD:** 4322 Carrollwood Vill. Dr., Tampa, FL 33624, (813)962-2667; **BUS ADD:** 30 N. LaSalle St., Chicago, IL 60602, (312)368-4027.

MIKO, Richard S.——**B:** Apr. 15, 1947, Milwaukee, WI, *VP*, RE Education Co., Special Accounts; **PRIM RE ACT:** Real Estate Publisher; **SERVICES:** Devel. and prod. of RE training programs and custom RE publishing products; **REP CLIENTS:** Major Films and Networks: Gallery of Homes, Relo, Coldwell Banker, Grubb & Ellis, Better Homes and Gardens, NAR, FLI, etc.; **PROFL AFFIL & HONORS:** RE Educators Assn.; **EDUC:** BA, 1969, English, Univ. of WI, Madison; **GRAD EDUC:** M.Div., 1972, McCormick Theological Seminary; MA, 1976, Mgmt., Webster Coll.; **HOME ADD:** 27 W 154 Canary Rd., Lombard, IL 60148, (312)627-4059; **BUS ADD:** 500 N Dearborn, Chicago, IL 60610, (312)836-4400.

MILAZZO, Salvator, III——**B:** Nov. 16, 1941, Brooklyn, NY, *Asst. VP*, Citibank, NA, Domestic Corp. RE (30-FL); **PRIM RE ACT:** Broker, Consultant, Appraiser, Developer, Property Manager, Banker, Lender, Owner/Investor, Insuror; **SERVICES:** Full RE Serv. for Corp. & Corp. Clinets; **REP CLIENTS:** Atlantic Richfield, Swedish Consulate, Harper & Row Publishers, Bank of Amer., Morris & McVeigh Esqs., Ruther Ford Family; **PROFL AFFIL & HONORS:** FIABCI, NACORE, CPM, Soc. of RE Appraiser NYS, CRA, Lic RE & Ins. Broker, NY, Intl. Inst. of Valuers; **EDUC:** Hofstra Univ., 3 yrs., Pol. Sci., Pre-Law, Specialized Courses in RE; **OTHER ACT & HONORS:** Citibank outstanding volunteer award 1978, Dyker Community Block Assn. Man of the Yr. 1979, NYC Police Dept.'s Certificate of recognition 1979, Mayor of City of New York Certificate of Appreciation 1978, CORP68-Founder Past Pres., Dyker Community Block Assn. Bd. of Dir., Bay Ridge Forum, Bay Ridge Civic Improvement, Advisory Bd., The Entertainers - Advisory Bd., Knights of Columbus - Recorder/Bd. of Dir., Reclaimer Community Bay Co. - Treas.; **HOME ADD:** 419 100th St., Brooklyn, NY 10029, (212)833-6360; **BUS ADD:** One Citicorp. Center, 153 E 53rd St., NYC, NY 10043, (212)559-1898.

MILEAF, Howard——*Tax Dir. & Secy.*, Keene Corp.; **PRIM RE ACT:** Property Manager; **BUS ADD:** 200 Park Ave., New York, NY 10166, (212)557-1900.*

MILES, Don——**B:** May 5, 1920, Spokane, WA, *Sr. Partner*, Miles, Way & Caldart; **PRIM RE ACT:** Attorney; **SERVICES:** Trans Amer. Title Ins. Co. (local counsel et al.); **PREV EMPLOY:** 20 yrs. general counsel Capital S&L Assn.; Former Asst. Prof. of WA State Univ.; **PROFL AFFIL & HONORS:** ABA, WA State Bar Assn.; Trial Lawyers of Amer., WA State; **EDUC:** BA, 1942, Pol. Sci., WA State Univ.; **GRAD EDUC:** JD, 1948, Univ. of WA; **EDUC HONORS:** Phi Alpha Delta; **MIL SERV:** US Army; Lt.; ETO; 3 battle stars; **OTHER ACT & HONORS:** Asst. Atty. Gen, State of WA, 1953-56; State Rep. of WA, 1963-65; Chmn. of Bd. of Freeholders Thurston Cty.; Gov. Pacific NW Kiwanis Intl.; **HOME ADD:** 3230 French Ln., NW, Olympia, WA 98502, (206)866-0618; **BUS ADD:** 10 Ranier Bank Bldg., Olympia, WA 98401, (206)943-7713.

MILES, Jerold L.——**B:** Aug. 4, 1936, Rocky Ford, CO, *Partner*, Finley, Kumble, Wagner, Heine, Underberg & Manley; **OTHER RE ACT:** Const. and Devel.; **EDUC:** BS, Bus., Univ. CO; **GRAD EDUC:** JD, Univ. CA at Los Angeles; **HOME ADD:** 11323 Dona Lola Dr., Studio City, CA 91604, (213)656-0767; **BUS ADD:** 9100 Wilshire Blvd., 10th Floor, E. Tower, Beverly Hills, CA 90212, (213)557-0111.

MILES, Zane Stanley——**B:** Jan. 30, 1935, Eagle City, OK, *Atty.*, Law Offices of Zane Stanley Miles; **PRIM RE ACT:** Consultant, Attorney; **PROFL AFFIL & HONORS:** NV, Elko, OK, Amer. Bar Assns., Amer. & NV Trial Lawyers; Real Prop. Sect. ABA; **GRAD EDUC:** JD, 1977, Law, Univ. of Pacific's McGeorge Sch. of Law; **MIL SERV:** USAF, S/Sgt.; **OTHER ACT & HONORS:** Elko Cty. GOP Central Comm., Chmn 1980-pres. NV State GOP Central Comm., Exec. Comm. Elko C of C, Dir. 1979-pres.; **HOME ADD:** 907 Hillside Dr., PO Box 1607, Elko, NV 89801, (702)738-3303; **BUS ADD:** 687 Sixth St., PO Box 1607, Elko, NV 89801, (702)738-3139.

MILGRAM, A. S.——**B:** Sept. 25, 1936, Venezuela, *Exec. VP*, Bella Co.; **PRIM RE ACT:** Builder; **SERVICES:** Gen. const. serv.; **REP CLIENTS:** Mobil Oil Corp., Texaco Inc., E. I. DuPont de Nemoues & Co., TX Commerce Bankshares, Inc., PPG Indus., Inc., Gulf Oil Corp., B. F. Goodrich Co.; **PREV EMPLOY:** Project Engr., U. S. Steel Corp.; **PROFL AFFIL & HONORS:** ASCE, ASTM, ACI, Chi Epsilon, ASPE, Who's Who in the S and SW; **EDUC:** BSCE, 1957, Civil Engrg., Univ. of TX; **GRAD EDUC:** Advanced Mgmt., 1959, Mgmt., Central Univ. of Venezuela; **EDUC HONORS:** Chi Epsilon, Dean's Honor Roll; **OTHER ACT & HONORS:** Chmn., Bd. of Tax Equalization, Beaumont, TX 5 yrs., Beaumont C of C; **HOME ADD:** 680 Heritage W., Beaumont, TX 77706, (713)866-5224; **BUS ADD:** P O Box 5421, Beaumont, TX 77706, (713)838-6484.

MILLAR, David G.——**B:** Mar. 27, 1943, St. Louis, MO, *Part.*, Millar, Schaefer & Hoffmann; **PRIM RE ACT:** Attorney; **REP CLIENTS:** Roosevelt Fed. S&L Assn.; Carl G. Stifel Realty Co.; **PROFL AFFIL & HONORS:** ABA, MO Bar; CA Bar; **EDUC:** AB with Distinction, 1963, Hist., Stanford Univ.; **GRAD EDUC:** JD, 1966, NYU Law School; **EDUC HONORS:** Order of the Coif; Law Review; **MIL SERV:** USA, 1st Lt., Army Commendation Medal; **BUS ADD:** 818 Olive St., Suite 430, St. Louis, MO 63101, (314)621-0983.

MILLARD, Neal S.——**B:** June 6, 1947, Dallas, TX, *Partner*, Morrison & Foerster; **PRIM RE ACT:** Attorney; **SERVICES:** Legal counseling in all aspects of RE law; **REP CLIENTS:** Major lending inst. and devel. investing in all types of RE; **PROFL AFFIL & HONORS:** Chmn., Gen. RE Practice Subsection, Los Angeles Cty. Bar Assn.; Member, RE Fin. Section; ABA; **EDUC:** BA, 1969, Sociology, UCLA; **GRAD EDUC:** JD, 1972, Law, Univ. of Chicago; **EDUC HONORS:** Phi Beta Kappa and Pi Gamma Mu, Cum Laude, Phi Kappa Phi; **MIL SERV:** US Army, Capt.; **OTHER ACT & HONORS:** Member, Bd. of Dirs., Univ. of Chicago Law Alumni Assn. of So. CA; **BUS ADD:** One Bunker Hill Bldg., 601 W. 5th St., 5th Floor, Los Angeles, CA 90017, (213)626-3800.

MILLARD, T.E.——**B:** May 3, 1945, Ada, OK, Millard & Olson, PC; **PRIM RE ACT:** Attorney; **REP CLIENTS:** Instnl. lenders and devels.; **PROFL AFFIL & HONORS:** TX, Amer. & Dallas Bar Assns.; **EDUC:** BBA, 1967, So. Methodist Univ.; **GRAD EDUC:** JD, 1969, So. Methodist Univ.; **HOME ADD:** 4548 Arcady Ave., Dallas, TX 75205, (214)528-4324; **BUS ADD:** The Hartford Bldg., 13th Fl., 400 N. St. Paul St., Dallas, TX 75201, (214)747-8862.

MILLE, Dennis G.——**B:** Aug. 6, 1947, Cleveland, OH, *Atty. at Law*, Sharratt, Willmann, James & Mille; **PRIM RE ACT:** Attorney, Owner/Investor, Syndicator; **SERVICES:** Contract drafting; lease agreements; **REP CLIENTS:** ERA- Chandler Realty; priv. indiv.; **PROFL AFFIL & HONORS:** ABA-Real prop. section; OH Bar Assn.; OH Trial Lawyers Assn.; Amer. Trial Lawyers Assn.; **EDUC:** BA, 1969, Pol. Sci.-Econ., Capital Univ.; **GRAD EDUC:** JD, 1972, Capital Univ. Law Sch.; **EDUC HONORS:** Cum Laude, Law Review; **MIL SERV:** USAF, Capt., AF Commendation, Medal w/2OLC, 1972-pres. (res.); **OTHER ACT & HONORS:** Jaycees; Capital Univ. Assn., Middleburg Hts. C of C; **HOME ADD:** 16395 Parklawn Ave., Middleburg Gts., OH 44130, (216)845-5020; **BUS ADD:** 6837 Pearl Rd., Cleveland, OH 44130, (216)845-5020.

MILLER, Alan Benjamin——**B:** Feb. 25, 1944, Chicago, IL, *Gen. Counsel*, The Abacus Grp.; **PRIM RE ACT:** Attorney; **SERVICES:** All areas of RE & fin. law, including RE securities; **PREV EMPLOY:** Friedman & Koven, Borg-Warner Corp., Aldens, Inc.; **PROFL AFFIL & HONORS:** Chicago Bar Assn., 1968-present; Real Prop. Law Comm. (1980-present), IL State Bar Assn. (1969-present), ABA (1968-present), Sect. of Corp. Banking & Bus. Law & Sect. of Real Prop., Probate & Tr. Law; **EDUC:** AB, 1965, Univ. of IL, Champaign, IL; **GRAD EDUC:** MBA, 1976, Univ. of Chicago; JD, 1968, Northwestern Univ. Sch. of Law; **MIL SERV:** USAR, Cpt., JAGC, 1968-75; **OTHER ACT & HONORS:** Dir. Bd. of Jewish Educ. of Metro. Chicago; **HOME ADD:** 179 Roger Williams, Highland Park, IL 60035, (312)433-2058; **BUS ADD:** 10 S. LaSalle St., Chicago, IL 60603, (312)346-9172.

MILLER, Albert M.——*Dep. Dir.*, Department of Housing and Urban Development, Finance & Accounting; **PRIM RE ACT:** Lender; **BUS ADD:** 451 Seventh St., S.W., Washington, DC 20410, (202)755-6310.*

MILLER, Arthur——*Mgr. RE Plng.*, Rochester & Pittsburgh Coal Co.; **PRIM RE ACT:** Property Manager; **BUS ADD:** 655 Church, Indiana, PA 15701, (412)349-5800.*

MILLER, Barbara Shaw——**B:** Oct. 31, 1933, Passaic, NJ, *VP/Chief Appraiser*, Southwest Savings & Loan Assn., Appraisal Div.; **PRIM RE ACT:** Consultant, Appraiser, Developer, Lender, Builder, Owner/Investor, Instructor, Property Manager, Syndicator, Real Estate Publisher; **OTHER RE ACT:** Active mostly in offshore investment counseling and appraising; **PREV EMPLOY:** Formerly with Western Savings & Loan Assn., VP and Mgr. of the dept.; **PROFL AFFIL & HONORS:** SRA/SRPA; Intl. Assn. of Valuers; Soc. of RE Appraisers, SRA; SRPA; Published author - Prentice Hall, 'RE Appraisers Kit', Jan. 1981; **EDUC:** NYU School of Retailing; Katharine Gibbs School; **OTHER ACT & HONORS:** Past Pres., Chapter 68 Soc. of RE Appraisers; Member, Intl. Assn. of Assessing Officers; Zonta; AZ Biltmore Racquet and Golf Club; **HOME ADD:** 5319 N. 26th St., Phoenix, AZ 85016, (602)955-5575; **BUS ADD:** 3101 N. Central Ave., Phoenix, AZ 85012, (602)241-4425.

MILLER, Callix E.——*VP Fac.*, Clark Equipment Co.; **PRIM RE ACT:** Property Manager; **BUS ADD:** Circle Dr., Buchanon, MI 49107, (616)697-8000.*

MILLER, Carl T.——**B:** Apr. 17, 1932, Alesia, MD, *VP*, Rockefeller Ctr. Mgmt. Corp., Operations; **PRIM RE ACT:** Consultant, Property Manager; **SERVICES:** Prop. Mgmt. Cons.; **REP CLIENTS:** Owners of comml. props.; **PREV EMPLOY:** Mgr., Gen. Serv. Dept. Christian Sci. Ctr, Boston, MA 1969-73; **PROFL AFFIL & HONORS:** BOMA, NYC; **EDUC:** BS, 1954, Naut. Sci., USMMA; **MIL SERV:** USNR, Lt. 1955-57; **HOME ADD:** 95 Highland Rd., Scarsdale, NY 10583; **BUS ADD:** 1230 Ave. of the Americas, NY, NY 10020, (212)489-4460.

MILLER, Cassie——**B:** May 15, 1919, Cleveland, OH, *Broker/Owner*, Cassie's Realty; **PRIM RE ACT:** Broker, Instructor; **PREV EMPLOY:** RE 18 yrs.; **PROFL AFFIL & HONORS:** Cir. CO Springs Bd. of Realtors, GRI, CRS, CRB; **MIL SERV:** USMC, Sgt.; **OTHER ACT & HONORS:** Election Judge - Precinct Comm. Woman; Lic. & Cert. RE Instr.; **BUS ADD:** 16 Circle 'C' Rd., Fountain, CO 80817, (303)382-7474.

MILLER, Charles J.——**B:** Jan. 5, 1924, Barbourville, NY, *Pres.*, Miller, Good & Danerl, P.C.; **PRIM RE ACT:** Attorney; **SERVICES:** Prop. acquisition, leasing, sales and foreclosures; **REP CLIENTS:** Investors in comml. props.; **PREV EMPLOY:** Dep. Atty. Gen., State of CA; **PROFL AFFIL & HONORS:** ABA; CA State Bar; Sacramento Cty. Bar Assn., Arbitrator, Sacramento Superior Ct.; **EDUC:** AB, 1949, Econ., Princeton Univ.; **GRAD EDUC:** JD, 1952, Law, Stanford Univ.; **EDUC HONORS:** Phi Beta Kappa, Magna Cum Laude; **HOME ADD:** 3200 Kadena Dr., Sacramento, CA 95825, (916)483-1805; **BUS ADD:** 3620 American River Dr., Suite 224, Sacramento, CA 95825, (916)486-8955.

MILLER, Dale——**B:** May 20, 1941, Cashmere, WA, *Corporate VP and Project Mgr.*, The Phoenix Group; **OTHER RE ACT:** Planning, design & mgmt.; **SERVICES:** Program Planning, Land Use Planning, Landscape and Bldg. Design, Project Mgmt., & Prop. Mgmt.; **REP CLIENTS:** Cities of Chehalis, Everett & Seattle; Ctys. of King & Snokomish; State of WA; Devels. Phoenix Development, 403 Associates, Bellwood Corp. & Cascade Devels., Owners of small comml. props. and homeowners; **PREV EMPLOY:** Dir. of the Mt. Baker Housing Rehab Program 1975-78; Dir. of Housing Policy for Seattle 1973-75; Dir. of the Environmental Works 1970-73; Member of Townhouse Design Team-MIT 1968-70; **PROFL AFFIL & HONORS:** Member, Amer. Planning Assn., Assoc. Member of AIA, Environmental Design Award 1970 from Seattle/King Cty. Bd. of Realtors; **EDUC:** BA, 1964, Pol. Sci. & Hist., Univ. of Puget Sound; **GRAD EDUC:** MArch, 1970, Urban Design, Univ. of WA; **MIL SERV:** US Army, E4; **OTHER ACT & HONORS:** Pres., Madrona Neighborhood Devel. Assn., VP NW owner Builder Center; Publications & Housing Program Management Handbook, 1978 & 1980; Home Repair and Improvement Pamphlet Series, 1976; **HOME ADD:** 1537 38th Ave., Seattle, WA, (206)329-8557; **BUS ADD:** 1139 34th Ave., Seattle, WA 98122, (206)324-3060.

MILLER, Daniel A.——**B:** Sept. 19, 1943, Redland, CA, *Pres. of D.M. Props., Inc.*, D.M. Properties, Inc.; **PRIM RE ACT:** Syndicator, Consultant, Attorney, Instructor; **SERVICES:** RE acquisition, mgmt. servs. for wealthy indivs.; **PREV EMPLOY:** Partner in law firm of Miller and Stern; **PROFL AFFIL & HONORS:** Los Angeles Cty. Bar Assn.; CA Assn. of Realtors, Synd. Div., Author of numerous articles on ltd. partnerships and synds.; **EDUC:** BS Bus. Admin., 1965, Acctg., Univ. of CA at Los Angeles; **GRAD EDUC:** JD, 1968, Law, Univ. of CA at Los Angeles; **EDUC HONORS:** Honors Grad., Order of Coif, Law Review; **OTHER ACT & HONORS:** Author: How to Invest in RE Syndicates, 1978; **HOME ADD:** 10525 Rocca Pl., Los Angeles, CA 90024, (213)475-0494; **BUS ADD:** 10850 Wilshire Blvd., Sixth Floor, Los Angeles, CA 90024, (213)475-0494.

MILLER, David——**B:** May 31, 1935, Elmhurst, IL, *Salesman*, J.W. Reedy; **OTHER RE ACT:** Salesman; **PREV EMPLOY:** Broker/Owner; Sales Mgr.; **PROFL AFFIL & HONORS:** Dupage Bd. of Realtors; IL Assn.; NAR, GRI; CRS; CRB; **EDUC:** BA, 1962, Pol. Sci./Law, Univ. of IL; **MIL SERV:** USMC, Sgt., 1953-1956; **OTHER ACT & HONORS:** Rotary; **HOME ADD:** 246 W Collen Dr., Lombard, IL 60148, (312)620-0337; **BUS ADD:** 1136 S Main, Lombard, IL 60148, (312)629-0016.

MILLER, D.K.——*RE Dept.*, National Distillers & Chemical Corp.; **PRIM RE ACT:** Property Manager; **BUS ADD:** 99 Park Ave., New York, NY 10016, (212)949-5700.*

MILLER, Dub W.C.——**B:** Dec. 31, 1905, Brownwood, TX, *Part.*, Bolanz & Miller, Comml.; **PRIM RE ACT:** Broker, Consultant, Appraiser; **SERVICES:** Sales, leases and appraisal of comml. prop. and land; **PROFL AFFIL & HONORS:** SIR, Easterwood Cup, Realtor outstanding service 1954; CCIM, CPM; **EDUC:** BA, 1927, Govt., 1930, So. Methodist Univ.; **GRAD EDUC:** JD, So. Methodist Univ.; **MIL SERV:** USMC; **OTHER ACT & HONORS:** City Council of Dallas 1953-59, School Bd., 1940-50, Bd. of Trustees, Austin Coll., Bd., TX Presbyterian Foundation; **HOME ADD:** 5810 Lakehurst Ave., Dallas, TX 75230, (214)363-3562; **BUS ADD:** One Lee Park W-401, 3303 Lee Pkwy., Dallas, TX 75219, (214)522-6040.

MILLER, Eric R.——**B:** May 19, 1947, Louisville, KY, *Pres.*, Miller Investment & Devel., Co. Ltd.; **PRIM RE ACT:** Syndicator, Consultant, Developer, Builder, Owner/Investor; **SERVICES:** Prop. Devel., constr. analysis, feasibility study; **PREV EMPLOY:** Burk & Assoc., Engrs. & Planners, New Orleans, LA; **PROFL AFFIL & HONORS:** RE Sec. & Synd. Inst.; **EDUC:** BA, 1971, Govt., So. IL Univ., Carbondale, IL; **GRAD EDUC:** MA, 1972, Pol. Sci., St. Louis Univ., St. Louis, MO; **MIL SERV:** USA, PFC, Vietnam Service Medal; **OTHER ACT & HONORS:** Advisory Bd. to New Orleans Energy Cons. Comm., Irish Channel Improvement Assoc.; **HOME ADD:** 615 Exhibition Blvd., New Orleans, LA 70118, (504)895-6456; **BUS ADD:** 615 Exhibition Blvd., New Orleans, LA 70118, (504)895-6456.

MILLER, Forrest W., Jr.——**B:** May 15, 1931, Omaha, NE, *VP*, The Lomas & Nettleton Co., Comml. Div.; **OTHER RE ACT:** RE investment bankers; **SERVICES:** Fin., joint ventures, sales; **REP CLIENTS:** Too numerous to list; **PREV EMPLOY:** The Carlson Cos., VP - RE, DeLoitre, Haskins & Sells; **PROFL AFFIL & HONORS:** IL Mort. Bankers, MN Mort. Bankers, MBAA, Nat. Assn. of Indus. & Office Parks; **EDUC:** BBA, 1957, Acctg.-Econ., Univ. of MN; **MIL SERV:** USAF, SSgt.; **OTHER ACT & HONORS:** Masonic Lodge - PMC Order of Demolay; **HOME ADD:** 7201 York Ave. S., #502, Edina, MN 55435, (612)835-6752; **BUS ADD:** 300 Shelard Plaza N, Suite 560, Minneapolis, MN 55426, (612)545-8844.

MILLER, Garry L.——**B:** Sept. 10, 1950, KY, *RE Broker & Co-Owner*, Center Relaty, Inc.; **PRIM RE ACT:** Broker, Consultant, Appraiser, Owner/Investor, Insuror; **SERVICES:** All types of RE; **PROFL AFFIL & HONORS:** NAR; IN Assn. of Realtors; Koscuisko Bd. of Realtors; Nat. & Ind. CRB Chaps., CRB; **EDUC:** 1968, Warsaw; **OTHER ACT & HONORS:** Warsaw Masonic Lodge; Fort Wayne Valley Scottish Rite 32nd Degree Mason - Warsaw Elk Lodge #802; IN Auction Assn. - Auctioneer; **HOME ADD:** R#3, Warsaw, IN 46580, (219)267-7753; **BUS ADD:** 2304 E. Center St., Warsaw, IN 46580, (219)267-5513.

MILLER, Gerald——**B:** Jan. 8, 1935, Parsons, KS, *Chmn. & Pres.*, Con./Steel Corp.; **PRIM RE ACT:** Developer, Builder, Owner/Investor; **SERVICES:** Indus. & Office Devel., Construction, Leasing; **REP CLIENTS:** From GM to Multiple Indust. & Office Users; **PREV EMPLOY:** Founder & CEO of C/S Corp. & Subsidiaries-June 1963; **PROFL AFFIL & HONORS:** Exec. Comm. Dayton Devel. Council, Dir. First Nat. Bank of Dayton, Young Presidents Organiz.; **EDUC:** BCE, 1957, CE, Univ. of Dayton; **OTHER ACT & HONORS:** Dir., Goodwill Industries of Dayton; Also Assoc. w/Mid-States Devel. Co.; **HOME ADD:** 646 E Sr. 73, Springboro, OH 45066; **BUS ADD:** PO Box 744, Dayton, OH 45401, (513)293-0900.

MILLER, Henry S., Jr.——**B:** Oct. 16, 1914, Dallas, TX, Henry S. Miller Co.; **PRIM RE ACT:** Broker; **PREV EMPLOY:** 1931-1938, Life Underwriter for Bankers Life Co. of Des Moines; 1938-1942, Henry S. Miller Co.; 1942-1945, US Army 1946-present, Henry S. Miller Co., Chmn. of the Bd.; **PROFL AFFIL & HONORS:** Tr., Lomas & Nettleton Mort. Investors; Member and Past Pres., Greater Dallas Bd. of Realtors and TX Assn. of Realtors; Member and Past Exec. Comm. member and Dir., NAR; Member of Bd. of Govs., Amer. Soc. of RE Counselors; Member and Past VP, IREM; Member of Bd. of Govs. and Past Chmn. of Comml. Prop. Comm., RNMI; Member, Soc. of Indus. Realtors and Past Pres. of Dallas Chap.; Member and former Tr., ULI; Member and former Tr., Intl. Council of Shopping Ctrs.; Member and former Pres. of N. TX Chap., Amer. Inst. of RE Appraisers; Member of Nat. Assn. of RE Investment Funds, IREF; **EDUC:** BS, Commerce, So. Methodist Univ.; **MIL SERV:** US Army Res., 2nd Lt., Maj.; **OTHER ACT & HONORS:** Dir. and Founding Pres., Dallas Civic Opera Co.; Hon. Chmn. of the Bd., Dallas Symphony Assn., Inc.; Dir., Dallas Ballet; Dir., Dallas Hist. Soc. and TACA; Member of Bd. of Dirs., Amer. Symphony Orchestra League; Dir., TX Arts Alliance; 1979 Jas. K. Wilson Silver Cup Award for Outstanding Contribution to the Fine Arts; Dir., Central Bus. Dist. Assn. and Greater Dallas Planning Council; Tr., So. Methodist Univ. and TX Scottish Rite Hospital for Crippled Children; Member and Past Pres., Dallas Rotary Club; Dir., Metro. Dallas YMCA; Past Pres., So. Methodist Univ. Alumni Assn.; Scottish Rite Mason, 33rd degree; Insp. Gen. Honorary; Recipient of the 1978 Distinguished Alumnus Award of So. Methodist Univ., "Distinguished Salesperson of Dallas Award", 1981, "Outstanding Business Leader Award" Northwood Institute, 1982; **BUS ADD:** 2001 Bryan Tower, 30th Floor, Dallas, TX 75201, (214)748-9171.

MILLER, Herbert——**B:** July 17, 1922, Philadelphia, PA, *Pres.*, Herbert Miller Enterprises, Inc.; **PRIM RE ACT:** Developer, Builder, Owner/Investor; **PROFL AFFIL & HONORS:** Home Builders Assn., Philadelphia Builders Assn., Phila. Advisory Comm. Landmarks, Bd. Member Various Corporate Entities; Mayor's Committee on the Historic Preservation City of Philadelphia, Arch. Design Awards (House & Home Nat.), Intl. Joseph Herzog Award Citation; Justice Louis D. Brandeis Distinguished Service Award; **OTHER ACT & HONORS:** Art Alliance, Squires At Rium, NYC, Pinnacle; **HOME ADD:** 1901 Walnut St., Phila., PA 19103, (215)563-0881; **BUS ADD:** 1630 Locust Street, Philadelphia, PA 19103, (215)546-1444.

MILLER, Howard C.——**B:** Oct. 22, 1923, Brooklyn, NY, *Sr. VP*, Queens Cty. Savings Bank, Mort.; **PRIM RE ACT:** Banker; **PROFL AFFIL & HONORS:** MBA, CRA, CMU, NAMSB, MTGE Comm.; **EDUC:** Northwestern U.; **MIL SERV:** USMC, Sgt.; **BUS ADD:** 38-25 Main St., Flushing, NY 11354, (212)359-6400.

MILLER, Howard M.——*Executive Vice President*, Real Estate Securities & Syndication Institute; **OTHER RE ACT:** Profl. Assn. Admin.; **BUS ADD:** 430 N. Michigan Ave., Chicago, IL 60611, (312)440-8183.*

MILLER, Jack——*Mgr. Real Property & Investment*, General Dynamics Corp.; **PRIM RE ACT:** Property Manager; **BUS ADD:** Pierre Laclede Center, St. Louis, MO 63105, (314)889-8200.*

MILLER, Jack M.——**B:** Dec. 20, 1930, Salem, OR, *Pres.*, Rockwood Development Corporation; **PRIM RE ACT:** Broker, Developer, Builder, Owner/Investor, Property Manager, Syndicator; **SERVICES:** Full mgmt. services for ltd. partnerships in which we are the gen. partner; **PROFL AFFIL & HONORS:** OR State Bar; NAR; IREM; RESSI, CPM; Lic. RE Broker; Past Pres. OR Young Republicans; **EDUC:** BA, 1953, Econ., Bus. Admin., Willamette Univ.; **GRAD EDUC:** JD, 1956, Law, Willamette Univ. Coll. of Law; **MIL SERV:** USMC; **HOME ADD:** 3275 Crestview Dr., Salem, OR 97302, (503)364-9683; **BUS ADD:** 161 High St., SE, Suite 122, PO Box 230, Salem, OR 97308, (503)364-5500.

MILLER, James M.——**B:** Nov. 23, 1937, Parsons, KS, *Managing Partner*, Mid-States Development Co.; **PRIM RE ACT:** Developer, Owner/Investor, Property Manager; **PROFL AFFIL & HONORS:** Nat. Pres., 1981, Nat. Assn. of Indus. and Office Parks; **EDUC:** BS, 1959, Acctg., Univ. of Dayton; **GRAD EDUC:** MBA, 1967, Univ. of Dayton; **MIL SERV:** US Air Force; **HOME ADD:** 1490 W. Alex-Bell Rd., Dayton, OH 45459, (513)433-1513; **BUS ADD:** P.O. Box 744, Dayton, OH 45401, (513)293-0900.

MILLER, John E.——**B:** July 18, 1942, Youngstown, OH, *Mgr., Indus. Mktg. and Area Devel.*, Consolidated Natural Gas Service Co., Inc.; **PRIM RE ACT:** Broker, Consultant, Developer, Owner/Investor; **SERVICES:** Site location assistance, demographic analysis, project fin.; **REP CLIENTS:** Mfg. firms; **PROFL AFFIL & HONORS:** Amer. Econ. Devel. Council, Northeastern Indus. Devels. Assn., Amer. Gas Assn. Hall of Flame; **EDUC:** BS, 1964, Mgmt. Sci., Case Inst. of Tech.; **GRAD EDUC:** MBA, 1970, Mktg., Case Western Reserve Univ.; **HOME ADD:** 429 Barry Dr., Pittsburgh, PA 15237, (412)366-8498; **BUS ADD:** 4 Gateway Ctr., Pittsburgh, PA 15222, (412)227-1136.

MILLER, Julianne——**B:** Nov. 19, 1939, Oxford, CT, *S.E. RE Mgr.*, Jewel Companies, Inc., Jewel T. Discount Grocery; **PRIM RE ACT:** Broker; **OTHER RE ACT:** Site Acquisiton, Leasing, Const. Estimator; **PROFL AFFIL & HONORS:** NAR, IREM, Orlando, Winter Park Bd. of Realtors, Pres. Central FL Chap. IREM, CPM; **EDUC:** Univ. of CT; **OTHER ACT & HONORS:** Better Bus. Bureau - Orlando C of C, Central FL Commn. Status of Women 1978; **HOME ADD:** 3521 Conway Gardens Rd., Orlando, FL 32806, (305)859-7621; **BUS ADD:** 4353 Edgewater Dr., Orlando, FL 32804, (305)299-8305.

MILLER, Ken R.——**B:** June 7, 1938, Cashmere, WA, *Pres.*, Miller Building Enterprises, Inc.; **PRIM RE ACT:** Developer, Builder, Owner/Investor; **SERVICES:** Resid. RE Dev. & Sales, Investment; **PREV EMPLOY:** Have been in land devel., residential const. & investment since beginning high school/college era; **PROFL AFFIL & HONORS:** NAHB; **EDUC:** BA, 1961, Bus./Econ., Univ. of Puget Sound; **HOME ADD:** 4520 S Orchard St., Tacoma, WA 98466, (206)475-2633; **BUS ADD:** 4520 S Orchard St., Tacoma, WA 98466, (206)474-1001.

MILLER, Kenneth M.——**B:** Sept. 10, 1941, Los Angeles, CA, *Atty.*, Buchman, Kass, Morgan & Miller Profl. Corp.; **OTHER RE ACT:** Litigation; **PROFL AFFIL & HONORS:** CA Bar Assn., Amer. Bar Assn., CA Trial Lawyer's Assn., Recognition of experience as a Trial Lawyer by the CA Trial Lawyer's Assn.; **EDUC:** AB, 1963, UCLA; **GRAD EDUC:** JD, 1966, law, Univ. of CA-Berkeley; **HOME ADD:** 868 Paramount Rd., Oakland, CA 94610, (415)836-0666; **BUS ADD:** 1939 Harrison St., Suite 300, Oakland, CA 94612, (415)465-1093.

MILLER, Kirk——**B:** Dec. 15, 1942, High River, Alb., Can., *Pres.*, Hood Miller Props., Inc.; **PRIM RE ACT:** Architect, Developer; **SERVICES:** Condo Devel.; Medical Office Bldgs.; **PREV EMPLOY:** Kaiser Aetna RE; **PROFL AFFIL & HONORS:** ULI, AIA, AIA; **EDUC:** BA, 1965, Pol. Sci., Univ. of Alberta; **GRAD EDUC:** MArch., 1971, RE Devel., Univ. of CA at Berkeley; **MIL SERV:** Can. Army, Capt.; **HOME ADD:** 44 Macondray Ln., 6E, San Francisco, CA 94133, (415)771-7788; **BUS ADD:** 2051 Leavenworth St., San Francisco, CA 94133, (415)771-7770.

MILLER, Laurel L.——**B:** Oct. 2, 1949, Casper, WY, *Pres.*, Brokerage House Two Realty, Inc.; **PRIM RE ACT:** Broker, Owner/Investor; **SERVICES:** Resid. & comml. RE sales, prop. mgmt., corp. moves, referral services mktg., RE; **PREV EMPLOY:** 5 yrs. in RE; **PROFL AFFIL & HONORS:** NAR, FLI, RNMI; CCIM candidate, Pres. Casper Bd. of Realtors; **EDUC:** Med. Technology & Microbiology, 1972 & 1973, Univ. of CO & Univ. of WY; **EDUC HONORS:** Mortar Bd.; **OTHER ACT & HONORS:** Advisory Bd. Small Bus. Admin., Advisory Bd. KTWO TV & Radio; **HOME ADD:** 3940 S. Oak, Casper, WY 82601, (307)266-4543; **BUS ADD:** 1814 E. 2nd, Suite 111, Casper, WY 82601, (307)265-2266.

MILLER, Lawrence J.——**B:** June 6, 1952, Newark, NJ, *Atty.*, Lawrence J. Miller, Atty. at Law; **PRIM RE ACT:** Attorney; **SERVICES:** Devel. & Condo. Law; **PROFL AFFIL & HONORS:** ABA (Real Prop., Probate, and Trust Law Sect.) GA State Bar Assn., FL Bar (Condo & Cooperative Comm. of Real Prop. - Probate & Trust Law Sect.), Palm Beach Cty. (Probate & Guard. Proced. Comm.), Broward Bar Assn. (Ethics Comm. 79-80); **EDUC:** BA, 1974, Amer. Studies, Lehigh Univ.; **GRAD EDUC:** JD, 1977, Law, Emory Univ.; **EDUC HONORS:** Summa Cum Laude, Omicron Delta Kappa, Phi Alpha Theta, Undergrad Merit Award, The Order of Barristers; **OTHER ACT & HONORS:** VP - Profl. Forum of Boca Raton, VP - Lehigh Alumni Club of S. FL, Boca Raton C of C (Legislative Affairs, and Econ. Devel.); **HOME ADD:** 4931 Acorn Dr., Boca Raton, FL 33432, (305)994-8565; **BUS ADD:** 1300 N. Federal Hwy., Suite 208, Boca Raton, FL 33432, (305)392-1405.

MILLER, Lowell W.——**B:** Mar. 16, 1931, Rockingham Co., VA, *Pres.*, Hess & Miller Inc.; **PRIM RE ACT:** Broker, Appraiser, Property Manager; **SERVICES:** RE sales, appraisals, prop. mgmt.; **PROFL AFFIL & HONORS:** Nat. Assn. of Realtors, VA Assn. of Realtors (Past VP), Harrisonburg-Rockingham Bd. of Realtors (Past Pres.); **EDUC:** BA, 1952, Bus. Admin. and Econ., Bridgewater Coll.; **GRAD EDUC:** One yr. of work in Econ., Univ. of VA; **EDUC HONORS:** Magna Cum Laude; **OTHER ACT & HONORS:** Treasurer, Bridgewater Home & Retirement Village, Director of Friendship Industries; **HOME ADD:** 1052 S Dogwood Dr., Harrisonburg, VA 22801, (703)434-2592; **BUS ADD:** 234 E Market St., Harrisonburg, VA 22801, (703)434-7383.

MILLER, Mark E.——**B:** Mar. 31, 1951, *VP*, Rockwood Development Corp.; **PRIM RE ACT:** Developer, Owner/Investor, Property Manager, Syndicator; **SERVICES:** Tax structured investments, income structured investments; **REP CLIENTS:** Indivs., pension funds; **PROFL AFFIL & HONORS:** OR Assn. of Realtors, RESSI; **EDUC:** AB, 1973, Econ., Dartmouth Coll.; **GRAD EDUC:** MBA, 1975, Bus., Stanford Grad. School of Bus.; **EDUC HONORS:** Phi Beta Kappa, Magna Cum Laude; **BUS ADD:** PO Box 230, 161 High St. SE, Salem, OR 97308, (503)364-5500.

MILLER, Mark W.——B: Oct. 18, 1951, Tulia, TX, *Pres.*, Televise, Inc.; **PRIM RE ACT:** Broker, Owner/Investor, Property Manager; **OTHER RE ACT:** Video tape production serv.; **SERVICES:** Video taping of RE for listing, selling, ins.; **REP CLIENTS:** Wimberley Land Co., Inc.; Rehmet Prop.; Univ. of TX; **PREV EMPLOY:** Jim McCrocklin and Assoc.; Pran Audio-Visual, Inc.; **PROFL AFFIL & HONORS:** San Marcos, TX and Nat. Bd. of Realtors, Lic. RE Broker in TX; **EDUC:** BS, 1976, TV Prod./Middle E. Studies, School of Communications, Austin; **HOME ADD:** Rt. 2, Box 74, Wimberley, TX 78676, (512)847-9698; **BUS ADD:** POB 371, Wimberley, TX 78676, (512)847-9191.

MILLER, Merwyn J.——B: Aug. 30, 1947, Beverly Hills, CA, *Atty.*, Law Offices of Merwyn J. Miller; **PRIM RE ACT:** Attorney, Syndicator; **SERVICES:** RE related matters including synds., contracts, lease options, consultation, litigation; **REP CLIENTS:** Synds., brokers, investors; **PREV EMPLOY:** RE Broker, RE Instr., RE Text Author; **PROFL AFFIL & HONORS:** ABA, ABA Real Prop., Probate, and Trust Section; San Diego Bar Assn.; CA Bar Assn.; Phi Delta Phi Legal Frat., Lifetime Community Coll. Teaching Certificate; Admitted to practice-all CA Courts, U.S. Supreme Court, Fed. Dist. Court for Southern & Central Dists. of CA; **EDUC:** BA, 1970, Psych., Univ. of CA, Los Angeles; **GRAD EDUC:** JD, 1974, CA Western School of Law; **OTHER ACT & HONORS:** Tau Epsilon Phi Frat.; **HOME ADD:** 219 Chapalita Dr., Encinitas, CA 92024, (714)753-0295; **BUS ADD:** 191 Calle Magdalena, Suite 270, Encinitas, CA 92024, (714)436-8832.

MILLER, Michael B.——B: Apr. 23, 1942, Houston, TX, *Div. Pres.*, First Federal S & L of Little Rock, Hot Springs S & L; **PRIM RE ACT:** Developer, Banker, Lender; **SERVICES:** Checking, investment accts., mort. loans, RE devel.; **PREV EMPLOY:** First Boston Co.; Union Natl. Bank of Little Rock; Merrill Lynch; **EDUC:** BA, 1965, Math, Univ. of AR; **GRAD EDUC:** MBA, 1969, Econ., Univ. of AR; **EDUC HONORS:** Omicron Delta Kappa, Beta Gamma Sigma; **MIL SERV:** US Army; 1st Lt.; **HOME ADD:** 111 Saxony Circle, Hot Springs, AR 71901, (501)624-9119; **BUS ADD:** PO Box 1200, Quadhita & Grand, Hot Springs, AR 71901, (501)624-4694.

MILLER, Michael B.——B: Jan. 26, 1953, Pasadena, CA, *Atty.*, Michael B. Miller Atty. and Counselor at Law; **PRIM RE ACT:** Attorney, Consultant; **PREV EMPLOY:** Lobbyist; **PROFL AFFIL & HONORS:** State Bar of CA, ABA; **EDUC:** AB cum laude AA, 1975-78, Hist. - RE, Univ. of So. CA - Fullerton Coll.; **GRAD EDUC:** J.D., Western State; **EDUC HONORS:** Phi Alpha Theta; **OTHER ACT & HONORS:** Kiwannis; **HOME ADD:** Arcadia, CA; **BUS ADD:** 5926 Temple City Blvd. Ste D, P.O. Box 428, Temp City, CA 91780, (213)285-2295.

MILLER, Michael Paul——B: Dec. 20, 1938, NY, *V.P. R.E.*, Toys R Us, Inc.; **PRIM RE ACT:** Appraiser, Developer, Builder, Property Manager, Owner/Investor; **OTHER RE ACT:** Retail R.E. Exec.; **SERVICES:** Legal R.E., const., arch.; **PROFL AFFIL & HONORS:** SREA, ICSC; CSA; **EDUC:** BBA, Bus., Hofstra Univ.; **MIL SERV:** US Army; MP; **OTHER ACT & HONORS:** V.P. Bd. of Ed.; **HOME ADD:** 29 Springhill Rd., Randolph, NJ 07869, (201)895-4663; **BUS ADD:** 395 W. Passaic St., Rochelle Pk, NJ 07662, (201)845-9322.

MILLER, Monte G.——B: Apr. 18, 1927, Ft. Wayne, IN, *RE Broker*, Roth & Wehrly, Inc., Realtors, Resid.; **PRIM RE ACT:** Broker, Consultant, Appraiser, Builder, Owner/Investor, Instructor, Property Manager, Insuror; **SERVICES:** Resid. investment counseling, instnl. appraising, new const.; **REP CLIENTS:** Indiv., investors, thrift instns., attys.; **PREV EMPLOY:** Pres. of RE firm for 21 yrs.; **PROFL AFFIL & HONORS:** NAR, RNMI, CRB, GRI, Realtor of Year 1969; **MIL SERV:** USN, PO, Pac. Theater; **OTHER ACT & HONORS:** Emmanueal Lutheran Church; **HOME ADD:** 3705 Stone Creek Run, Ft. Wayne, IN 46804, (210)432-3760; **BUS ADD:** 7331 W. Jefferson St., Ft. Wayne, IN 46804, (219)432-0531.

MILLER, Murray H.——B: Apr. 20, 1932, Montreal, Can., *Pres.*, Murray H. Miller Mgmt. Corp.; **PRIM RE ACT:** Developer; **OTHER RE ACT:** Devel. of apt. houses, office bldgs, shopping ctrs.; **EDUC:** BS, 1954, Bus. Admin. and RE, Lehigh Univ.; **MIL SERV:** USAF; Capt.; **HOME ADD:** Tibbits Ln., Sands Point, NY 11050, (516)883-3391; **BUS ADD:** 143 Old Country Rd., Carle Place, NY 11514, (516)741-8440.

MILLER, Nita——B: Apr. 4, 1920, Cleaburne, TX, *Broker/Owner*, Nita Miller & Assoc., Inc., Red Carpet; **PRIM RE ACT:** Broker, Instructor, Consultant, Owner/Investor; **PREV EMPLOY:** Assoc. with Earl Page RE (1964), Cooper RE (1966-69), Bud Archer RE (1969-73), Opened office under Red Carpet Franchise in 1975 with one agent. Now largest office in Irving with 37 agents.; **PROFL AFFIL & HONORS:** Gov. Women's Council of Realtors; Pres. Irving Bd. of Realtors, CRB/GRI. Top 10 in Nation, 1980, Red Carpet Corp., 2nd in TX 1980, Red Carpet Corp.; **EDUC:** Massey RE Coll., N. Lake Coll.; **OTHER ACT & HONORS:** Irving C of C, Member Altrusa Club, Advisory Bd. for N. Lake Coll.; **HOME ADD:** 400 Irongate, Irving, TX 75060; **BUS ADD:** 2015 W. Airport Frwy, Irving, TX 75062, (214)255-7186.

MILLER, Paul D.——B: Aug. 22, 1949, Frankfurt, Germany, *RE Appraiser*, County Bank of Santa Cruz; **PRIM RE ACT:** Appraiser; **SERVICES:** Appraisal of all types of RE; **PREV EMPLOY:** County of Santa Clara, CA - Assessor's Office, 1973-1976; **PROFL AFFIL & HONORS:** Sr. Member, ASA; Assoc. Member, SREA; Candidate, AIREA, ASA, Sr. Member; **EDUC:** BS, 1972, RE, San Jose State Univ.; **OTHER ACT & HONORS:** Lic. RE Broker, State of CA; Pres., San Jose Chap., Amer. Soc. of Appraisers, 1981-1982; **HOME ADD:** 8750 Glen Arbor Rd., Ben Lomond, CA 95005, (408)336-5766; **BUS ADD:** 25 River St., Santa Cruz, CA 95060, (408)423-8200.

MILLER, Raymond W.——B: Oct. 30, 1942, Detroit, MI, *Pres.*, Raymond W. Miller Associates; **PRIM RE ACT:** Developer; **PREV EMPLOY:** Cabot, Cabot & Forbes Co.; **EDUC:** BS, 1965, Mech. Engrg., Northwestern Univ.; **GRAD EDUC:** MS, 1967, Aeronautic Sci., Univ. of CA, Berkeley; MBA, 1969, Harvard Bus.; **HOME ADD:** 21 Estabrook Rd., Swamscott, MA 01907; **BUS ADD:** Sixty State St., Boston, MA 02109, (617)720-2100.

MILLER, Richard C., Jr.——B: Sep. 8, 1953, St. Charles, LA, *Lawyer*, Barbetta & Miller, P.C.; **PRIM RE ACT:** Attorney; **SERVICES:** Legal servs., all aspects of RE law, land use planning & environmental law; **PROFL AFFIL & HONORS:** ABA, NYSBA, Saratoga Co. Bar Assn., APA, NYSBA Land Use Control Comm., NYSBA Sec. on Real Prop., ABA Section on Real Prop., Probated Trust Law, ABA Section on Urban, State & Local Govt. Law; **EDUC:** BS, 1975, Indus. & Labor Relations, Cornell Univ.; **GRAD EDUC:** JD, 1978, Albany Law School; **EDUC HONORS:** Quill & Dagger Sr. Hon. Soc.; **OTHER ACT & HONORS:** Asst. Town Atty., Clifton Park, NY; **HOME ADD:** 1743 Rt. 9, Clifton Park, NY 12065, (518)371-0332; **BUS ADD:** PO Box 438, Rt. 9, Clifton Park, NY 12065, (518)371-2352.

MILLER, Richard E.C., Jr.——B: Mar. 18, 1945, Alexandria, LA, *VP*, Mortgage and Trust, Inc.; **PRIM RE ACT:** Broker, Consultant, Appraiser, Developer, Lender; **SERVICES:** Fin. and sales of comml. props., consulting, appraising; **REP CLIENTS:** Instnl. investors including life ins. companies, mutual savings banks, pension funds; **PREV EMPLOY:** Mortgage Banque, Inc. (Houston, TX); Fannin Bank (Houston, TX); **PROFL AFFIL & HONORS:** Mort. Bankers Assn.; **EDUC:** BA, 1968, Liberal Arts, LA State Univ.; **GRAD EDUC:** MBA, 1971, Fin./RE, LA State Univ.; **MIL SERV:** Army Nat. Guard; Capt., 1968-74; **HOME ADD:** 2011 Milford, Houston, TX 77098, (713)523-1228; **BUS ADD:** P.O. Box 2885, Houston, TX 77001, (713)525-8270.

MILLER, Richard I.——B: Oct. 7, 1944, Pittsburgh, PA, *Gen. Counsel*, Oxford Development Co.; **OTHER RE ACT:** Legal services in connection with RE devel.; **SERVICES:** Overall supervision & coordination of all legal servs. relative to RE. fin., devel., leasing, operations & litigation; **PREV EMPLOY:** Pvt. practice, Rothman, Gordon, Foreman, Groudine, Pittsburgh, PA; **PROFL AFFIL & HONORS:** Allegheny Cty Bar Assn., PA Bar Assn., Intl. Council of Shopping Ctrs.; **EDUC:** BS, 1967, Bio., Univ. of Pittsburgh; **GRAD EDUC:** JD, 1970, Duquense Univ. Sch. of Law; **EDUC HONORS:** Law Review; **OTHER ACT & HONORS:** Nat. Ski Patrol; **HOME ADD:** 6522 Darlington Rd., Pittsburgh, PA 15217, (412)521-0971; **BUS ADD:** 300 Monroeville Mall, Pittsburgh, PA 15146, (412)243-4800.

MILLER, Richard T.——B: Sept. 2, 1932, Detroit, MI, *Pres.*, Miller-Christensen Real Estate, Inc.; **PRIM RE ACT:** Broker, Consultant, Appraiser, Developer, Owner/Investor, Property Manager, Syndicator; **OTHER RE ACT:** Exchanger; **SERVICES:** Full RE serv.; **PROFL AFFIL & HONORS:** NAR; MI Assn. of Realtors; Farm & Land Institute; MI Assn. of RE Exchangors; Home Builders Assn., Grad. Realtors Inst.; **MIL SERV:** US Army, Corporal; **HOME ADD:** 5107 Foxcroft, Midland, MI 48640, (517)835-9965; **BUS ADD:** 2200 N. Saginaw Rd., Midland, MI 48640, (517)631-3410.

MILLER, Robert G.——B: Feb. 7, 1918, Nevada, MO, *Bldg. Mgr.*, El Paso Natural Gas Bldg. Co.; **PRIM RE ACT:** Broker, Consultant, Property Manager; **SERVICES:** Bldg. Mgmt, operations, leasing & alterations; **REP CLIENTS:** Bldg. owners; **PREV EMPLOY:** Natl. Council Boy Scouts of Amer., Bldg. Mgr. Tulsa, OK 1956-70, Ogden Devel. Corp., Resident Mgr & Project Dir., El Paso, TX 1970-72; **PROFL AFFIL & HONORS:** Tulsa, OK Planning Comm., BOMA, SW BOMA, TX Assn. of Bldg. Owners & Mgrs., Cert. Real Prop. Admin. by BOMA, Past Pres. of Tulsa Assn. of BOMA & Southwest

Conf. BOMA; **EDUC:** BS, 1954, Mgmt., Tulsa Univ., OK; **GRAD EDUC:** 1 yr. grad. work, 1965, Mgmt, Tulsa Univ., Tulsa, OK; **MIL SERV:** USAF, 1943-46, S/Sgt., Air Medal, Pacific Theater; **OTHER ACT & HONORS:** Elks Lodge 1747, Farmington, NM, Chmn Adv. Bd. Farmington Salvation Army, Pres. Parish Council, St. Mary's Church, Farmington, NM; **HOME ADD:** 2712 E. 30th, Farmington, NM 87401, (505)327-5522; **BUS ADD:** 3535 30th, P.O. Box 990, Farmington, NM 87401, (505)327-5531.

MILLER, Robert T.——**B:** Nov. 10, 1918, Delta, AL, Miller & Sweat; **PRIM RE ACT:** Attorney; **SERVICES:** Title exam closings, title ins., all RE related inquiries; **REP CLIENTS:** United First Fed. S&L, loans for indivs.; **PREV EMPLOY:** Practice of law, Feb., 1949 to date; **EDUC:** AA, 1947, Univ. of FL; **GRAD EDUC:** LLB, Law, Univ. of FL; **MIL SERV:** USAF, Capt.; **OTHER ACT & HONORS:** City Atty., Lakeland, 1959-61; City Civil Serv. & Pension Bd.; **HOME ADD:** 623 Easton Dr., Lakeland, FL 33802, (813)686-1704; **BUS ADD:** 3rd Fl., United First Fed. Bldg., Lakeland, FL 33802, (813)688-7038.

MILLER, Ronald A.——*Manager RE Services*, Bausch & Lomb, Inc.; **PRIM RE ACT:** Property Manager; **BUS ADD:** One Lincoln First Square, Rochester, NY 14601, (716)338-6000.*

MILLER, Ronald J.——**B:** July 7, 1943, Marshalltown, IA, *Partner*, Pred and Miller; **PRIM RE ACT:** Broker, Attorney, Owner/Investor, Syndicator; **SERVICES:** RE acquisition, sale, synd., including securities offerings; **REP CLIENTS:** Synd. and devel., RE brokers; **PROFL AFFIL & HONORS:** Denver and CO Bar Assns.; CO Assn. of Realtors; **EDUC:** BA, 1965, Poli. Sci., Simpson Coll.; **GRAD EDUC:** 1968, Univ. of Denver Coll. of Law; **EDUC HONORS:** Barborka Trophy, Magna Cum Laude; fellowships; First in class; **HOME ADD:** 1935 Monaco Pkwy., Denver, CO 80220, (303)388-0221; **BUS ADD:** 469 South Cherry St., Suite 200, Denver, CO 80222, (303)320-1146.

MILLER, Samuel M.——*VP, Treas. & Contr.*, Manhattan Industries, Inc.; **PRIM RE ACT:** Property Manager; **BUS ADD:** 1271 Avenue of the Americas, New York, NY 10020, (212)265-3700.*

MILLER, Seth A.——**B:** Feb. 27, 1952, Cleveland, OH, *Pres.*, Aegis Prop. Serv. Corp.; **PRIM RE ACT:** Broker, Consultant; **SERVICES:** Leasing & Sales of Comml. Prop.; **REP CLIENTS:** United Jewish Appeal., Health Ins. Plan of NY; Amer. Express Co.; **PREV EMPLOY:** Williams RE Co. Inc.; **PROFL AFFIL & HONORS:** Young Mens RE Assn. of NY; NACORE; **EDUC:** BA, 1973, Psych., NYU; **GRAD EDUC:** MBA, 1974, Fin., NYU; **HOME ADD:** 60 Sutton Place S, New York, NY 10017; **BUS ADD:** 574 Fifth Ave., New York, NY 10017, (212)944-5999.

MILLER, Stan——**B:** Jan. 24, 1950, Hot Springs, AR, Miller, Jones & Goldman; **PRIM RE ACT:** Attorney, Developer, Owner/Investor, Syndicator; **SERVICES:** Agent for Amer. Title and Insured Title; **REP CLIENTS:** RESCOM Realty Devel. Co., Inc., Harbor E., Inc.; Point Lookout Condos.; **PROFL AFFIL & HONORS:** ABA, AR Bar Assn., Garland Cty. Bar Assn.; **EDUC:** BA, 1972, AR Tech. Univ.; **GRAD EDUC:** JD, 1976, Vanderbilt Univ.; **OTHER ACT & HONORS:** Chmn. Garland Cty. Public Facilities Housing Bd.; AR Commerative Commn.; AR Hsit. Preservation; **HOME ADD:** 600 Higdon Ferry Apt. 501, Hot Springs, AR 71901, (501)321-9698; **BUS ADD:** PO Box 1440, Grand Nat. Bank Building, Hot Springs, AR 71910, (501)321-1931.

MILLER, Steven——**B:** Aug. 4, 1942, Dallas, TX, *Sr. VP*, Oppenheimer Properties, Inc.; **PRIM RE ACT:** Consultant, Owner/Investor, Instructor, Syndicator; **PREV EMPLOY:** Exec. VP - Lawrence Miller Co. Realtors; Pres. - Steven Miller Co. Realtors; **PROFL AFFIL & HONORS:** Pres. RESSI, 1978; Member NAR Exec. Comm. 1979-1980; **EDUC:** BBA, 1965, RE, So. Methodist Univ.; **MIL SERV:** TX Air Nat. Guard, S/Sgt.; **OTHER ACT & HONORS:** NAR, RESSI; **HOME ADD:** 145 Lockwood Rd., Riverside, CT 06878, (203)637-2713; **BUS ADD:** One New York Plaza, New York, NY 10004, (212)825-8287.

MILLER, Tanfield C.——**B:** Jan. 25, 1947, Phila., PA, *Sr. Part.*, T.C. Miller Co.; **PRIM RE ACT:** Property Manager; **SERVICES:** Acct. mgmt. of synd. of comml. & resid. props.; **REP CLIENTS:** Foreign & domestic indiv. investors; **PREV EMPLOY:** Price Waterhouse Co., NY; **PROFL AFFIL & HONORS:** FL Inst. of CPA's, NY Soc. of CPA's, Amer. Inst. of CPA's; **EDUC:** BA, 1967, Hist., Pol. Sci., ND State Univ.; **GRAD EDUC:** MBA, 1974, Fin. & Acctg., Univ. of PA, Wharton School of Fin.; **OTHER ACT & HONORS:** Tr. NOSU Devel. Found. FL Oaks, School Mental Health Assoc., Dir. Schagrini, Inc. (OTC); **HOME ADD:** 425 Royal Plaza Dr., Ft Lauderdale, FL 33301; **BUS ADD:** 1012 E Broward Blvd., Ft. Lauderdale, FL 33301, (205)462-8282.

MILLER, Thomas L.——**B:** Feb. 16, 1936, Buffalo, NY, *Exec. VP*, Realty World - Realty 1; **PRIM RE ACT:** Broker, Instructor, Appraiser; **PROFL AFFIL & HONORS:** NAR; NY State Assn. Realtors; NY State SREA; Nat. Mktg. & Inst.; Buffalo Bd. of Realtors, CRB, CRS, GRI, Past Pres. - Buffalo Bd. Realtors (1980); **MIL SERV:** USA, Specialist 3rd Class, Nat. Defense; **HOME ADD:** 4801 Glenwood Dr., Clarence, NY 14221, (716)632-3615; **BUS ADD:** 716 Niagara Falls Blvd., N. Tonawanda, NY 14120, (716)694-5800.

MILLER, William R.——**B:** Apr. 20, 1923, Chester, NY, *VP*, Douglas Elliman-Gibbons & Ives Inc.; **PRIM RE ACT:** Broker, Consultant, Owner/Investor, Property Manager; **PROFL AFFIL & HONORS:** RE Bd. of NY, IREM, CPM; **EDUC:** BS, 1950, Acctg., Fordham Univ.; **MIL SERV:** USNR, Lt.; **OTHER ACT & HONORS:** Univ. Club, NY, NY; Rockaway Hunting Club, Cedarhurst, NY; St. Nicholas Soc.; Mayflower Descendants; Soc. of Colonial Wars; **HOME ADD:** Deer Track Ln., Valley Cottage, NY 10989, (914)268-3256; **BUS ADD:** 575 Madison Ave., NY, NY 10022, (212)832-5505.

MILLIKAN, James R.——**B:** Jan. 15, 1950, Beaumont, TX, *Pres.*, The Millikan Co's.; **PRIM RE ACT:** Broker, Consultant, Property Manager; **SERVICES:** Investment, renovation, operations consultant; **REP CLIENTS:** Sun Life Group of Amer. etc., investors & instns. active in RE lending specializing in coord. of mgmt. programs for instn. not oriented toward the RE field; **PREV EMPLOY:** Dir. of Prop., Sun Life Group of Amer.; **PROFL AFFIL & HONORS:** BOMA; **EDUC:** BA, 1968, Music, Univ. of Houston; **MIL SERV:** US Army Res.; Sgt.; E-6; **OTHER ACT & HONORS:** Bd. of Dir., St. Judes House (Alcoholic Reform); Pres. - St. Lukes Economic Developement Corp. (Ctr. for Devel. of Inner City Employment Opportunites & Reform); **HOME ADD:** 2506 LeHaven Dr., Tucker, GA 30084, (404)493-9416; **BUS ADD:** 3390 Peachtree Rd. NE, Atlanta, GA 30326, (404)458-6295.

MILLISON, Stuart——**B:** Aug. 13, 1937, Baltimore, MD, *Pres.*, Millison, Inc.; **PRIM RE ACT:** Appraiser, Developer, Builder, Owner/Investor; **SERVICES:** Appraisal and valuation services related to real prop. damages; devel. and const. of rehabilitated resid. and comml. prop. with participation; **REP CLIENTS:** Indiv. and comml. owners and investors; **EDUC:** BA, 1959, Bus., Univ. of MD; **HOME ADD:** Harper House, Village of Cross Keys, Baltimore, MD 21210, (301)435-4711; **BUS ADD:** 6821 Reisterstown Rd., Baltimore, MD 21215, (301)358-4711.

MILLKEY, John M.——**B:** Feb. 4, 1945, Atlanta, GA, *Atty.*, Ledbetter, Millkey & Siegel; **PRIM RE ACT:** Attorney; **SERVICES:** All legal services including synd., tax planning, etc. in connection with ownership, acquisition & sales of RE; **PROFL AFFIL & HONORS:** Real Prop. Sect. of State Bar of GA; **EDUC:** BA, 1967, Yale College; **GRAD EDUC:** JD, 1972, Columbia Univ., School of Law; **HOME ADD:** 2878 Ridgemore Rd., N.W., Atlanta, GA 30318, (404)351-7142; **BUS ADD:** Suite 801, Harris Tower, 233 Peachtree St., N.E., Atlanta, GA 30303, (404)659-1410.

MILLNER, N. Wayne——**B:** Oct. 2, 1930, Baltimore, MD, *Sales Agent*, Merrill Lynch Realty/Chris Coile, Inc., Comml. Investment; **PRIM RE ACT:** Broker, Owner/Investor, Property Manager; **PREV EMPLOY:** Sales and mktg. mgmt. positions with Black & Decker Mfg. Co., Towson, MD; Am. Chain Div. of Am. Chain and Cable Corp. subsidiary of Babcock Intl., York, PA; **PROFL AFFIL & HONORS:** Past Officer and Dir. of Sales and Mktg. Execs., Candidate for CCIM; **EDUC:** BS, 1953, Bus. Mgmt., Univ. of Baltimore; **MIL SERV:** USCG, Bosns. mate 3rd, Expert 45 cal. pistol; **OTHER ACT & HONORS:** Past Pres., Havenwood Invest. Club; **HOME ADD:** Apt. 303, 2308 Chetwood Circ., Timonium, MD 21093, (301)252-1835; **BUS ADD:** 517 Benfield Rd., Severna Park, MD 21146, (301)647-5830.

MILLS, Elli M.A.——**B:** Sept. 6, 1943, Brooklyn, NY, *Pres.*, The Mills Development Group, Inc.; **PRIM RE ACT:** Broker, Developer; **SERVICES:** Devel. condos., land devel., RE broker, prop. mgmt.; **PREV EMPLOY:** Dir., Office of Asset Valuation, US Railway Assn.; **PROFL AFFIL & HONORS:** Member, NY, DC, and FL Bars; Lic. RE Broker, NY, DC, FL; **EDUC:** AB, 1966, Poli., Brandeis Univ.; **GRAD EDUC:** JD, 1969, NYU, School of Law; MBA, 1971, Harvard Bus. School; **OTHER ACT & HONORS:** Bd. of Dirs., Tampa Bay Harvard Bus. School Club; Bd. of Dirs., Jewish Federation of Pinellas Cty.; **HOME ADD:** 1520 Gulf Blvd., Belleair Shore, FL 33535; **BUS ADD:** 801 W. Bay Dr., Suite 800, Largo, FL 33540, (813)585-4727.

MILLS, Greg——**B:** July 20, 1954, Los Angeles, CA, *Sales Assoc.*, Zugsmith & Associates, Inc., Office Div.; **PRIM RE ACT:** Broker, Consultant, Owner/Investor; **SERVICES:** Mktg., sales and leasing of office bldgs.; **REP CLIENTS:** Office bldg. devel. and investors; **PREV EMPLOY:** Escrow Co., 1978; **EDUC:** BS, 1977, Bus./Fin., San Diego State Univ.; **HOME ADD:** 5720 Owensmouth Ave. 124, Woodland

Hills, CA 91367, (213)703-1072; **BUS ADD:** 12711 Ventura Blvd. #230, Studio City, CA 91604, (213)760-1211.

MILLS, Howard D., Jr.——*Pres.*, Mills Heights, Inc., Indus. Park; **PRIM RE ACT:** Consultant, Developer, Builder, Owner/Investor, Property Manager; **OTHER RE ACT:** Builder & operator of 300+ acre indus. park; RE sales; **SERVICES:** Building to suit leasing & all needed services; Also subdivisions 200 single family homes & lots; **EDUC:** 1942; **OTHER ACT & HONORS:** Committee man 20 yrs., NYS Econ. Devel. Bd. Member, Kiwanis, Elks; **HOME ADD:** 426 Silver Lake Rd., Middletown, NY 10940, (914)692-4477; **BUS ADD:** 426 Silver Lake Rd., Middletown, NY 10940, (914)692-4476.

MILLS, Stephen C.——**B:** Feb. 6, 1948, Monmouth, IL, *Pres.*, Bear Realty Inc.; **PRIM RE ACT:** Broker, Instructor, Consultant, Appraiser, Developer, Property Manager, Owner/Investor; **SERVICES:** Investment Counseling, Brokerage, Devel., Exchanging, Agricultural & Comml. Investment; **REP CLIENTS:** Indiv. and/or Instnl. investors in comml. and agricultural props.; **PROFL AFFIL & HONORS:** CCIM of NAR, Dir., WI Exchange Club; Cert. RE Instr.; GRI; CRS; SREA; FLI; **EDUC:** BS, 1971, Admin., W. IL Univ.; **HOME ADD:** POB 128, Salem, IL 53168, (414)843-2317; **BUS ADD:** Rte. 2, Box 39, Salem, WI 53168, (414)843-2317.

MILNER, Harold W.——**B:** Nov. 11, 1934, Salt Lake City, UT, *Pres. & CEO*, Americana Hotels Corporation (Formerly Pick Hotels Corp.); **PRIM RE ACT:** Developer, Owner/Investor, Property Manager; **PREV EMPLOY:** Pres., Hotel Investors (an REIT) 1970-1975; Treas., Marriott Corp., 1967-1970; **PROFL AFFIL & HONORS:** Member, Indus. Advisory Council, Amer. Hotel & Motel Assn.; **EDUC:** BS, 1960, ME, Univ. of UT; **GRAD EDUC:** MBA, 1962, Harvard Grad. School of Bus. Admin.; **MIL SERV:** US Army, 1st Lt.; **OTHER ACT & HONORS:** Trustee: Property Capital Trust (on REIT), Boston, MA; **HOME ADD:** 474 Butler Dr., Lake Forest, IL 60045, (312)234-5581; **BUS ADD:** 532 S. Michigan Ave., Chicago, IL 60605, (312)435-8920.

MILSTEIN, Paul——*Pres.*, United Brands Co.; **PRIM RE ACT:** Property Manager; **BUS ADD:** 1271 Ave. of the Americas, 42nd Fl., New York, NY 10020, (212)397-4000.*

MILTENBERGER, Frederick D.——**B:** Feb. 1, 1933, Muncie, IN, Miltenberger Assoc.; **PRIM RE ACT:** Consultant, Instructor; **SERVICES:** RE Valuation, mkt analysis, gen. consultant; **REP CLIENTS:** Lenders, corps. and indiv.; **PROFL AFFIL & HONORS:** AIREA, Inst. for RE Instruction, MAI, CREI; **EDUC:** BS, 1954, RE, IN Univ.; **GRAD EDUC:** MBA, 1957, RE, IN Univ.; **MIL SERV:** US Army, SP-3; **OTHER ACT & HONORS:** Instr. of Fin., Ball State Univ., Adjunct lecturer in RE, RE Certification Program, School of Continuing Educ., IN Univ.; **HOME ADD:** 2505 W. Queensbury Rd., Muncie, IN 47304, (317)282-4741; **BUS ADD:** 116 N. Walnut St., Muncie, IN 47305, (317)288-9979.

MILWEE, Frank——*Secretary & Assistant Treasurer*, National Realty Committee; **OTHER RE ACT:** Profl. Assn. Admin.; **BUS ADD:** 2033 M. Street NW, Washington, DC 20036, (202)785-0808.*

MIMNA, Curtis John——**B:** Dec. 7, 1943, Colorado Springs, CO, *VP*, DRG Financial Corp., Land Fin. & Sales; **PRIM RE ACT:** Broker, Banker, Developer, Lender; **OTHER RE ACT:** Land devel. fin. & project sales for medium to large land devel. tracts; **REP CLIENTS:** Nu-West, Deltona, Cadillac Fairview Leisure Technology, Alpert Corp., L.B. Nelson, William Lyons; **PREV EMPLOY:** Comml./Indus. RE Sales, Appraisal, Mktg., Feasibility Studies; **PROFL AFFIL & HONORS:** Washington Bd. of Realtors; Lic. Broker in MD, VA, DC; **EDUC:** BS, 1965, Econ/Bus./Fin., VA Polytechnic Inst.; **GRAD EDUC:** MBA, 1971, Fin., George Washington Univ.; **HOME ADD:** 2000 N St., NW 722, Washington, DC 20006, (202)293-2511; **BUS ADD:** 1909 K St. N.W., Suite 200, Washington, DC 20006, (202)833-3680.

MIMNING, Gary C.——**B:** July 19, 1949, Myrtle Point, OR, *Pres.*, Cole-Pacific Corp.; **PRIM RE ACT:** Broker, Syndicator, Developer; **SERVICES:** Invmt. brokerage, dev. and synd. of apt. and comml. props.; **REP CLIENTS:** Prof. Profit sharing trusts; **PROFL AFFIL & HONORS:** RESSI, Realtors, Inv. RE Sch.; **EDUC:** Pol. Sci., 1973, Intl. Aff., Univ. of OR; **OTHER ACT & HONORS:** Young Rep.; **HOME ADD:** 8380 SW Power Ct., Portland, OR 97225, (503)292-3813; **BUS ADD:** 8380 SW Power Ct., Portland, OR 97225, (503)292-2786.

MINAHAN, Neal Edward——**B:** Sept. 19, 1944, Boston, MA, *Staff Counsel*, Raytheon Co.; **PRIM RE ACT:** Attorney; **SERVICES:** Legal servs., corp. acquisitions & leases; **PROFL AFFIL & HONORS:** ABA (Real Prop. Probate & Trust Sect.) Boston Bar Assn., Amer. Judicature Soc.; **EDUC:** BS, 1966, Bus., Boston Coll.; **GRAD EDUC:** JD, 1969, Law, Boston Coll. Law School; **EDUC HONORS:** Cum Laude; **HOME ADD:** 15 Morton St., Needham, MA 02194, (617)444-4748; **BUS ADD:** 141 Spring St., Lexington, MA 02173, (617)862-6600.

MINCHEN, Meyer A.——**B:** June 8, 1923, Houston, TX, *Co-owner*, Minchen Mort. Co., Minchen Investments; **PRIM RE ACT:** Broker, Consultant, Owner/Investor; **OTHER RE ACT:** Comml. bldg. morts.; **SERVICES:** Long term morts.; **EDUC:** 1946, Univ. of TX; **MIL SERV:** USN, Capt., Air Medal with a Gold Star and an Oak Leaf Cluster in lieu of additional awards of the Air Medal, Meritorious Service Medal, Navy Commendation Medal, 8 lesser medals for Humane Action, Occupation Medal with Berlin Airlift Device, Victory Medal, Nat. Defense Medal with bronze star, two Reserve participation medals and two theater medals; **OTHER ACT & HONORS:** Served as Asst. Exec. Dir. of Pres., Prop. Review Bd., Asst. Exec Sec. of Fed. Prop. Council, Exec. Office of the Pres., Wash. DC, Amer. Red Cross, Houston Chapt.; Community Welfare Planning Assn.; United Fund of Houston, Museum of Nat. History; Houston C of C; Mayor's Advisory Comm., Houston; Houston Civil Defense; Amer. Soc. for Oceanography; Naval Aviation Museum, Pensacola, FL; Naval Inst., Annapolis, MD; Navy League of the US; Res. Officers Assn.; Naval Res. Assn.; Air Force Assn.; Amateur Radio Operator; Amer. Radio Relay League; Awarded Cert. of Merit by Amer. Red Cross for saving a man's life; Hon. Doctor of Laws Degree from Mexican Acad. for Intl. Law in Mexico, DF; **HOME ADD:** 1753 North Blvd., Houston, TX 77098, (713)528-6967; **BUS ADD:** 4635 SW Fwy, Houston, TX 77027, (713)622-6161.

MINDICH, Mel Leigh——**B:** Nov. 25, 1942, New York, NY, *Pres.*, Mindich Developers Inc.; **PRIM RE ACT:** Developer, Builder, Owner/Investor; **PROFL AFFIL & HONORS:** American Arbitration Assn., Nat. Assn. of Home Builders; **EDUC:** BSCE, 1963, Civil Engrg., Lafayette Coll.; **BUS ADD:** 51 Park Rd., Scarsdale, NY 10583.

MINER, Christopher A.——**B:** Feb. 26, 1952, Palo Alto, CA, *Partner/Appraiser*, Miner & Silverstein Appraisal Co.; **PRIM RE ACT:** Consultant, Appraiser, Instructor; **SERVICES:** RE appraisal, consultation, special studies, and expert testimony; **REP CLIENTS:** State and municipal govts., buyers, sellers, lenders, investors, bus., attys., and relocation companies; **PREV EMPLOY:** Staff Appraiser, John F. Rowlson MAI-SREA; RE Broker & Partner, Miner Agency; Instr., Advanced Appraisal Courses; **PROFL AFFIL & HONORS:** Member, New London Bd. of Realtors; Assoc. Member, Soc. of RE Appraisers; Adjunct Faculty Member, Univ. of CT; Dir. CT Assn. of Realtors, GRI; Realtor; **EDUC:** BS, Physics/Math, So. CT State Coll.; **EDUC HONORS:** VP, Senior Class; Who's Who Among Students in Amer. Coll. & Univ.; **OTHER ACT & HONORS:** Dir. & Treas., William Billings Inst. of Amer. Music; **HOME ADD:** 13 Highland Dr., Waterford, CT 06385, (203)443-4638; **BUS ADD:** 322 Captains Walk, New London, CT 06320, (203)443-8405.

MINER, Martin P.——**B:** Dec. 9, 1941, NY, Hyman & Miner; **PRIM RE ACT:** Attorney; **PREV EMPLOY:** Sec. 1965-68, VP an Counsel 1968-1972 Granreal Corp.; **PROFL AFFIL & HONORS:** ABA, NYSBA; **EDUC:** AB, 1962, Muhlenberg Coll.; **GRAD EDUC:** LLB, 1965, Columbia Law School; **OTHER ACT & HONORS:** Chmn. Bd. of Zoning & Appeals, Village of Great Neck Plaza (1979-80); **HOME ADD:** 203 W 8th St., New York, NY 10024, (212)799-3798; **BUS ADD:** 148 East 78 St., New York, NY 10021, (212)737-0400.

MINIK, Frank——**B:** Feb. 19, 1941, Vandergrift, PA, *Sr. VP & Gen. Mgr.*, Indus. Prop. Group, Arthur Rubloff & Co.; **PRIM RE ACT:** Broker; **PREV EMPLOY:** Teacher, St. Laurence High School; **PROFL AFFIL & HONORS:** Assn. of Indus. RE Brokers of Chicago, Chicago RE Bd., Chicago Assn. of Commerce & Industry; **GRAD EDUC:** BA, 1963, Soc., Notre Dame; **HOME ADD:** 9655 S. Harding, Evergreen Pk, IL 60642, (312)425-3907; **BUS ADD:** 8600 W. Bryn Mawr Ave., Chicago, IL 60631, (312)399-7007.

MINK, Lawrence B.——**B:** Oct 26, 1943, Orange, NJ, *Counsel*, Clapp & Eisenberg, P.C.; **PRIM RE ACT:** Attorney, Consultant; **SERVICES:** Legal Counsel & Rep.; **REP CLIENTS:** Lenders, devels, users of comml. & indus. props., condo. co-op & tract devels., rep. of borrowers, lenders & govtl. agency in indus. devel bond transactions; **PROFL AFFIL & HONORS:** MBA of NJ, Amer. Arbitration Assn., GRI Faculty; **EDUC:** AB, 1965, Govt., Columbia Univ.; **GRAD EDUC:** LLB, 1968, Columbia Univ., School of Law; **EDUC HONORS:** Cum Laude; **HOME ADD:** 19 Sheridan Ave., W. Orange, NJ 07052, (201)325-0154; **BUS ADD:** 80 Park Plaza, Newark, NJ 07102, (201)642-3900.

MINKIN, Rodney T.——**B:** Oct. 5, 1935, Kansas City, MO, *Pres.*, Minkin Real Estate Company; **PRIM RE ACT:** Broker; **SERVICES:** Brokerage of comml. and indus. RE; **PROFL AFFIL & HONORS:**

SIR, CPA; **EDUC:** 1957, NY Univ., Wichita State Univ.; **MIL SERV:** US Naval Reserve; **HOME ADD:** 8965 Linden Lane, Prairie Village, KS 66207, (913)648-7625; **BUS ADD:** 911 Main St., Kansas City, MO 64105, (816)474-1010.

MINOIA, Nicholas W.——**B:** June 17, 1955, Binghamton, NY, Capital Income Properties, Comml. Investment; **PRIM RE ACT:** Broker, Consultant, Owner/Investor; **SERVICES:** Specializing in the Sale & Purchase of large income producing props.; **PREV EMPLOY:** Contractor; **PROFL AFFIL & HONORS:** NAR, State Assn. of Realtors, CID (Comml. Investment Div., of the State Assn., GRI; **MIL SERV:** USAF, AIC; **HOME ADD:** 648 State St., Binghamton, NY 13901, (607)724-2378; **BUS ADD:** 648 State St., Binghamton, NY 13901, (607)772-6211.

MINOR, John Christopher——**B:** Oct. 20, 1942, Hobbs, NM, *Atty.*, Minor, Yeck & Beeson, PC, Attys.; **PRIM RE ACT:** Attorney, Owner/Investor, Instructor; **SERVICES:** Legal; **REP CLIENTS:** Nat. Security Bank; Lincoln Cty. Bd. of Realtors; Pioneer Nat. Title Ins. Co. (Local counsel); Family Fed. S&L Assn. (Local counsel); numerous devels. and RE brokers; City of Newport; Port of Newport; **PROFL AFFIL & HONORS:** ABA; OR State Bar Assn., Past Member, Comm. on Real Prop. Law; Present Member, Realtors Joint Comm.; Lincoln Cty. Bar Assn., Past Pres.; Lincoln Cty. Bd. of Realtors; OR Assn. of Realtors; Lincoln Cty. Counsel, 1975-1977; Amer. Assn. of Hospital Attys.; Chmn., OR State Bar Profl. Resp. Comm., Lincoln-Benton Counties; Newport City Atty., 1975-; Inst. of Municipal Law Officers; Port Atty., Port of Newport 1975-; Admitted to practice; U.S. Supreme Court; U.S.C.C.A. (9th Cir.); U.S. Tax Court; **EDUC:** BS, 1965, Physics/Philosophy, Univ. of Santa Clara/ Willamette Univ.; **GRAD EDUC:** JD, 1967, Law, Willamette Univ.; **OTHER ACT & HONORS:** Deputy Dist. Atty., Lincoln Cty., 1968-1969; Mcpl. Judge, Newport, 1972-1973; Newport Rotary Club, Pres.; Bd. of Dir., Nat. Security Bank; Lincoln Cty. Red Cross, Pres., 1972; **HOME ADD:** 517 S.W. Minnie St., Newport, OR 97365, (503)265-2076; **BUS ADD:** 236 W. Olive St., POB 510, Newport, OR 97365, (503)265-8888.

MINSKOFF, Henry H.——**B:** May 27, 1911, NYC, NY, *Pres.*, Sam Minskoff & Sons; **PRIM RE ACT:** Property Manager, Appraiser; **OTHER RE ACT:** RE investments; **PROFL AFFIL & HONORS:** Bd. of Gov. of RE Bd. of NY, Dir. of Sterling Nat. Bank, Adv. Council of NYU, RE Inst., Dir. & Chmn. of Gemco Nat. Inc., MAI; **EDUC:** BS, 1934, Bus. Admin., Lehigh Univ.; **OTHER ACT & HONORS:** City Athletic Club, Fenway Golf Club, Palm Beach Ctry. Club; **HOME ADD:** 710 Park Ave., New York, NY 10021; **BUS ADD:** 1350 Ave. of the Amers., New York, NY 10019, (212)765-9700.

MINTER, David A.——**B:** Aug. 5, 1944, Eden, NC, *Dir. of Project Devel.*, J.N. Pease Assoc.; **PRIM RE ACT:** Consultant, Engineer, Architect; **SERVICES:** Arch., Engr., Planning, Interior Design; **PROFL AFFIL & HONORS:** Nat. Assn. of Indus. & Office Parks; SIDC; AIA; SMPS; Nat. Soc. of PE; AFS; **EDUC:** 1966, Arch. Engrg./Engrg. Tech., VA Commonwealth Univ./Univ. of WI; **OTHER ACT & HONORS:** VP, SMPA; Pres., AFS Loudoun Chap.; Bd. Member, Fairfax City Chamber; Loudoun Cty. C of C; **HOME ADD:** Rt. 1, Box 456, Hamilton, VA 22068, (703)338-4020; **BUS ADD:** 2925 East Independence Blvd., Charlotte, NC 28205, (704)376-6423.

MINTO, Robert W., Jr.——**B:** Apr. 13, 1947, Kirkland, WA, *Prin.*, Worden, Thane & Haines, P.C.; **PRIM RE ACT:** Consultant, Attorney; **SERVICES:** Interstate land RE sales and RE Securities registrations (state & fed.,)devel. feasibility consulting and document preparation, RE tax and investment evaluation; **REP CLIENTS:** Devel., RE brokers, attys. (consultations), RE profl. assns.; **PROFL AFFIL & HONORS:** State Bar of MT (section on Real Prop.) ABA (section on Real Prop., Trusts and Probate, comm. on interstate land sales regulation), Phi Delta Phi; **EDUC:** BBA, 1969, Bus. and Fin., Univ. of WA; **GRAD EDUC:** JD, 1973, Law, Univ. of MT; **EDUC HONORS:** B.N.A. Award (1973); **OTHER ACT & HONORS:** Missoula Lions Club (Pres.) 1981-1982, Bd. of Dir., Missoula Planned Parenthood 1973-1976; **HOME ADD:** 912 Parkview Way, Missoula, MT 59803, (406)543-8854; **BUS ADD:** 3203 Russell St.,PO Box 4747, Missoula, MT 59806, (406)721-3400.

MINTZ, Frederick W.——**B:** June 1, 1933, Los Angeles, CA, *Dir., Estate Planning Servs.*, Fuller Theological Seminary; **PRIM RE ACT:** Consultant, Developer, Builder, Owner/Investor, Property Manager; **EDUC:** MS, 1972, Mgmt. Sci., Pac. Christian College; **GRAD EDUC:** MS, 1972, Computer Systems, West Coast Univ.; **MIL SERV:** USN; **BUS ADD:** 135 N. Oakland Ave., Pasadena, CA 91101, (213)449-1745.

MINTZ, Lewis R.——**B:** March 20, 1922, Springfield, OH, *Prin.*, Lewis R. Mintz Assoc.; **PRIM RE ACT:** Broker, Appraiser; **SERVICES:** Resid., Comml. and Indus. Appraisals; **REP CLIENTS:** Homequity, Inc.; Merril Lynch Relocation; Potere, Inc.; **PROFL AFFIL & HONORS:** NAIFA, NAR, CAR, GRI; IFA designation; **EDUC:** BBA, 1944, Acctg., Univ. of MI; **MIL SERV:** USN, Lt. (j.g.); **OTHER ACT & HONORS:** Kiwanis; **HOME ADD:** May Dr., Norwalk, CT 06850, (203)847-3824; **BUS ADD:** 213 Wanbury Rd., Wilton, CT 06897, (203)762-3555.

MIOT, Sanford B.——**B:** Dec. 22, 1938, New York, NY, *Pres.*, Arvida Southern; **PRIM RE ACT:** Developer, Builder; **PREV EMPLOY:** Levitt and Son; **PROFL AFFIL & HONORS:** Builders Assn. of S. FL, Nat. Home Builders Assn., FL Home Builders Assn., Amer. Mgmt. Assn.; **EDUC:** BS, 1960, Poli. Phil., City Coll. of NY; BE, 1965, Civil Engrg., City Coll. of NY; **GRAD EDUC:** ME, 1967, Engrg., City Coll. of NY; **MIL SERV:** USAF, A2c; **OTHER ACT & HONORS:** Israel Bond Drive, United Way, C of C, Builder's Assn. of S. FL, Amer. Mgmt. Assn., FHBA Govt. Affairs; **BUS ADD:** 9400 S. Dadeland Blvd.-Penthouse, Miami, FL 33156, (305)667-1124.

MIRABELLA, Frank J.——**B:** Jan. 3, 1921, Rochester, NY, *Realtor*, Frank J. Mirabella; **PRIM RE ACT:** Broker, Appraiser, Builder, Insuror; **PROFL AFFIL & HONORS:** RE Bd. of Rochester; Rochester Home Builders, 1961; Rochester C of C, 1954; **OTHER ACT & HONORS:** Romulus Club; Pres., Holy Name, 1958; **HOME ADD:** 44 Overbrook Ave., Rochester, NY 14609, (716)288-9128; **BUS ADD:** 44 Overbrook Ave., Rochester, NY 14609, (716)482-1459.

MIRAFZALI, Hamid——**B:** Feb. 18, 1956, Persia, *Pres.*, Foreman-Mirafzali Ent.; **PRIM RE ACT:** Consultant, Developer, Owner/Investor, Property Manager, Syndicator; **SERVICES:** Investment counseling & research; **REP CLIENTS:** Lenders and indiv. or prof. investors in comml. props.; **PREV EMPLOY:** Jackson Comm. Coll. Instr.; Data Processing Mgmt. Assn.; Amer. Entrepeneur Assns.; **EDUC:** 1979, Computer Sci., Mgmt., econ., Albion Coll.; **GRAD EDUC:** Computer Sci., 1981, Computer prog. in the field of Bus. & Fin., Control Data Inst. of Detroit; **EDUC HONORS:** Honor Grad.; **OTHER ACT & HONORS:** Amer. Red Cross; **HOME ADD:** 307 N. Park Ave., Jackson, MI 49201, (517)787-3758; **BUS ADD:** 5517 Vermont, Jackson, MI 49201, (517)787-2839.

MIRKIL, John M.——**B:** Oct. 22, 1925, Bryn Mawr, PA, *Proprietor*, Mirkil & Co.; **PRIM RE ACT:** Broker, Consultant; **PROFL AFFIL & HONORS:** Soc. of RE Counselors; Soc. of Indus. Realtors; RNMI; Intl. RE Federation; Intl. Council of Shopping Ctrs., Past Pres., Philadelphia Bd. of Realtors and Philadelphia Chap. SIR; **EDUC:** BS, 1950, Fin., Wharton School Univ. of PA; **MIL SERV:** USMC, Capt.; **HOME ADD:** 2 Hopeton Ln., Villanova, PA 19085; **BUS ADD:** 1521 Locust St., Philadelphia, PA 19102, (215)545-1100.

MIRRER, William——*Dir. of Taxes*, Gleason Works; **PRIM RE ACT:** Property Manager; **BUS ADD:** 1000 University Ave., Rochester, NY 14692, (716)473-1000.*

MIRZA, Nathan A.——**B:** Dec. 12, 1932, Indiana, *Mgr. RE Dept., Central Region*, The Amer. Appraisal Co.; **PRIM RE ACT:** Appraiser; **SERVICES:** RE Appraisal; **REP CLIENTS:** Corps., Insurance Cos., Devels., Banks, and Indivs.; **PREV EMPLOY:** UOP Realty Devel. Co., VP Land Devel. 1972-1980; **PROFL AFFIL & HONORS:** Member: Amer. Inst. of RE Appraisers, MAI; **EDUC:** BS, 1959, Bus. Admin., RE Admin., Indiana Univ.; **MIL SERV:** USA, Cpl.; **OTHER ACT & HONORS:** Member Univ. WI RE Alumni; **HOME ADD:** 5501 Carriage Way Dr., Rolling Meadows, IL 60008, (312)392-9348; **BUS ADD:** One Crossroads of Commerce, Suite 201, Rolling Meadows, IL 60008, (312)255-6550.

MISCEVIC, D. Mark N.——**B:** May 28, 1947, LaSalle, IL, *Pres.*, Americana Group, Realtors/Better Homes & Gardens, Adm. Offices; **PRIM RE ACT:** Broker, Consultant, Appraiser, Developer, Lender, Owner/Investor, Instructor, Property Manager; **SERVICES:** Res., Comml., Indus., Land, Leasing, Prop. Mgmt., Relocation, Mort. Lending, RE Licensing; **REP CLIENTS:** Individ. Corps. Lenders, Cts.; **PREV EMPLOY:** Sr. VP Jack Matthews & Co., Realtors, Administrator/VP RE Sch. of NV; **PROFL AFFIL & HONORS:** Las Vegas Bd. of Realtors, NV Assn. of Realtors, NAR, RS Instr. & Councelor for RNMI, Grad. Realtors Inst., CRS, Cert. RE Broker Mgr.; **EDUC:** BA, 1969, Engl./Chem., Univ. of WI; **OTHER ACT & HONORS:** 1980 Pres. Las Vegas Bd. of Realtors; 1981 Rgnl. VP of NV Assn. of Realtors, 1981 Pres., Humane Soc. of So. NV; 1981 Pres. of Georgetown Assn.; 1981 Pres. of Fairview Assn.; **HOME ADD:** 2986 Bel Air Dr., Las Vegas, NV 89109, (702)731-5858; **BUS ADD:** 3790 S. Paradise Rd., Suite 100, Las Vegas, NV 89109, (702)798-7777.

MISCEVIC, Tobias C.——B: June 4, 1951, Spring Valley, IL, *Admin./Dir.*, Americana Sch. of RE, Div. of Consolidated Americana Corp.; **PRIM RE ACT:** Instructor; **SERVICES:** Salesmen, broker, continuing educ. courses; **EDUC:** BA, 1974, Pol. Sci., Univ. of WI, Milwaukee; **OTHER ACT & HONORS:** 1982 Pres. NV Assn. of Private Schools; **HOME ADD:** 485 Naples Dr., Las Vegas, NV 89109, (702)735-8513; **BUS ADD:** 2917 W Wash. Ave., Suite 7, Las Vegas, NV 89107, (702)647-3557.

MITCHELL, Allan R.——B: Jan. 10, 1933, NY, *Staff VP, RE*, RCA Corp.; **PRIM RE ACT:** Broker, Attorney; **OTHER RE ACT:** Gen. resp. for all corp. RE matters; **PREV EMPLOY:** VP, Prop., The Hertz Corp.; **PROFL AFFIL & HONORS:** NY State Bar Assn.; **EDUC:** BS, 1955, Accounting, Lehigh Univ.; **GRAD EDUC:** JD, 1960, NY Univ. School of Law; **MIL SERV:** US Army, 1st Lt.; **OTHER ACT & HONORS:** Asst. Cty. Atty., Nassau Cty., 1963; **HOME ADD:** 1 Mitchell Dr., Kings Point, NY 11024, (516)466-5598; **BUS ADD:** 30 Rockefeller Plaza, NY, NY 10020, (212)621-6182.

MITCHELL, Bruce——*Mgr. RE*, Cities Service Co.; **PRIM RE ACT:** Property Manager; **BUS ADD:** Box 300, Tulsa, OK 74102, (918)561-2211.*

MITCHELL, Frank E.——B: Apr. 9, 1905, Philadelphia, PA, *Owner*, C.J. Mitchell Co.; **PRIM RE ACT:** Broker, Appraiser; **PROFL AFFIL & HONORS:** Philadelphia Bd. of Realtors; PA Assn. of Realtors; NAR; Intl. Right of Way Assn.; SIR (Retd. Member Status); **EDUC:** Wharton Evening School, Univ. of PA; **OTHER ACT & HONORS:** Chmn, Upper Moreland Twp. Zoning Bd. 1962-66; Assessor, Montgomery Cty. Bd. of Assessment 1966-72; **HOME ADD:** 722 Ellis Rd., Willow Grove, PA 19090, (215)659-2863; **BUS ADD:** 2047 Locust St., Philadelphia, PA 19103, (215)567-0445.

MITCHELL, Grant E.——B: Jan. 3, 1937, Oneonta, NY, *Asst. Gen. Counsel for New Communities*, HUD; **PRIM RE ACT:** Attorney; **SERVICES:** Legal advice RE: Fed. New Communities program; **REP CLIENTS:** New Community Devel. Corp.; **PROFL AFFIL & HONORS:** DC Bar Assn.; **EDUC:** BS, 1958, SUNY; **GRAD EDUC:** MA, 1961, Eng., Univ. of FL; JD, 1964, Law, Tulane Univ.; **HOME ADD:** 2604 Baywood Ct., Silver Spring, MD 20906; **BUS ADD:** 451 7th St., SW, Washington, DC 20410, (202)755-6550.

MITCHELL, James R.——B: May 22, 1951, High Point, NC, *Partner*, Boyd & Hassell, Realtors; **PRIM RE ACT:** Broker, Consultant, Appraiser, Builder, Property Manager; **SERVICES:** Prop. Mgt. & Indus. Devel.; **PROFL AFFIL & HONORS:** IREM,ULI Realtors, CPM; **EDUC:** BS-BA, 1973, Bus., Appalachian State Univ.; **HOME ADD:** 1744 4th St. CT N.E., Hickory, NC 28601, (704)327-9274; **BUS ADD:** 127 1st Ave. N.E., Hickory, NC 28601, (704)322-1005.

MITCHELL, Jim——*Ed.*, Communication Channels, Inc., Southwest Real Estate News; **PRIM RE ACT:** Real Estate Publisher; **BUS ADD:** 6285 Barfield Rd., Atlanta, GA 30328, (214)348-0739.*

MITCHELL, John Eric——B: Dec. 1, 1951, Boston, MA, *Pres., Realtor*, FL E. Coast Assoc.; **PRIM RE ACT:** Broker, Syndicator, Property Manager, Owner/Investor; **SERVICES:** Comml. R.E.; **PREV EMPLOY:** Demarco and Sons, Inc., Johnson and Johnson Realty Inc.; **PROFL AFFIL & HONORS:** RESSI, NAR, Boca Raton Bd. of Realtors, GRI, MBA; **EDUC:** BS, 1972, Fin., Miami U, Oxford, OH; **OTHER ACT & HONORS:** Boca Raton Hotel and Club, Boca Raton, FL, Towers Club, Ftl., Real Estate Instructor; **HOME ADD:** P.O. Box 297, Boca Raton, FL 33432, (305)997-6588; **BUS ADD:** 301 Crawford Blvd., Ste. 103, Boca Raton, FL 33432, (305)368-6600.

MITCHELL, Kenneth Lee——B: Apr. 7, 1931, Pittsburgh, PA, *VP*, Dwyer, Curlett & Co.; **PRIM RE ACT:** Broker, Appraiser, Banker, Developer, Lender, Owner/Investor, Insuror; **SERVICES:** Mort. bankers for 16 major life ins. co's.; **REP CLIENTS:** Many major CA devel., and prominent and well-known investors and borrowers; **PROFL AFFIL & HONORS:** CA MBA; So. CA Mort. Bankers Assn., ICSC; **EDUC:** BA, 1950, Santa Monica City Coll.; **GRAD EDUC:** BS, 1957, Bus. Admin.; Fin., Major-Bus., Minor, Univ. of So. CA; **MIL SERV:** USN; AB2, Korean War; **OTHER ACT & HONORS:** Chmn., RHE Planning Comm. - 7 yrs.; Charity Organizations; Sigma Phi Epsilon, Nat. Frat.; USC Chap.; USC Bus. Assn.; **HOME ADD:** 1 Peartree Ln., Rolling Hills Estates, CA 90274, (213)541-9435; **BUS ADD:** 6336 Wilshire Blvd., Los Angeles, CA 90048, (213)653-8300.

MITCHELL, N. Edmund——*Pres.*, Mitchell Realty Co., Comml.; **PRIM RE ACT:** Broker, Owner/Investor; **REP CLIENTS:** Principally chain stores; **BUS ADD:** Empire State Bldg., Suite 5620, New York, NY 10023, (212)695-1640.

MITCHELL, Norman S.——B: Dec. 2, 1942, Minneapolis, MN, *VP, Dist. Mgr.*, Grubb and Ellis Commercial Brokerage Co.; **PRIM RE ACT:** Broker, Consultant, Appraiser, Property Manager, Insuror; **SERVICES:** Leasing & sales agent for all types of comml. props., including appraisal, brokerage, ins. and prop. mgmt.; **REP CLIENTS:** Users, investors and devels.; **PREV EMPLOY:** Coldwell Banker Comml. RE Servs.; **EDUC:** BA, 1964, Hist., RE, Univ. of So. CA; **OTHER ACT & HONORS:** Advisory Bds., St. Luke Hospital, Pasadena, and CA Museum of Sci. and Indus. Bd. of Trustees; Flintridge Prep. School; **BUS ADD:** 1126 Wilshire Blvd., Los Angeles, CA 90017, (213)481-2350.

MITCHELL, Ralph——B: Sept. 30, 1912, Greensburg, KY, *Partner*, Mitchell & Riggs; **PRIM RE ACT:** Attorney, Owner/Investor; **REP CLIENTS:** Commonwealth Land Title Ins. Co., Farmers & Traders Bank, Equitable Life Ins. Co.; **EDUC:** AB, 1933, Centre Coll.; **GRAD EDUC:** LLB, 1940, Univ. of Louisville, Harvard Law School; **MIL SERV:** USMC Res., Sgt.; **OTHER ACT & HONORS:** Shelby Cty. Judge, 1952-64, KY State Rep. Shelby & Henry Ctys. 1968-71; **HOME ADD:** Rte. 6, Haven Hill, Shelbyville, KY 40065, (502)633-1376; **BUS ADD:** Box 367, Fed. Land Bank Bldg., Shelbyville, KY 40067, (502)633-2012.

MITCHELL, Robert L.——B: Sept. 24, 1921, OK, *VP*, Placer S&L Assn., RE; **PRIM RE ACT:** Appraiser, Developer, Owner/Investor; **OTHER RE ACT:** Project Mgr., Single family & town home projects; **SERVICES:** Branch offices leasing/purchase; subdivision, land & devel.; **PREV EMPLOY:** Chief Appraiser; **PROFL AFFIL & HONORS:** SRA;SREA, Past Pres., Sacramento Chap. SREA; **MIL SERV:** USN (1942 - 1948), 1st Class P.O.; **OTHER ACT & HONORS:** Local Cty. Rezoning Comm.; Exchange Club; VFS; Masons; **HOME ADD:** 110 Colonial Dr., Auburn, CA 95603, (916)885-9398; **BUS ADD:** 949 Lincoln Way, Auburn, CA 95603, (916)823-7777.

MITCHELL, Ryland L., III——B: May 15, 1943, Baltimore, MD, *Partner*, Lipman, Frizzell & Mitchell; **PRIM RE ACT:** Consultant, Appraiser; **SERVICES:** RE Appraising and Consulting; **REP CLIENTS:** Accountants, Attorneys, Life Ins. Co., Banks, S & L; **PREV EMPLOY:** Assoc. Appraiser, McCurdy-Lipman 1970-1977; **PROFL AFFIL & HONORS:** AIREA, Soc. of RE Appraisers, MAI & SRPA; **EDUC:** BS, 1965, Mgmt., Univ. of Richmond, VA; **MIL SERV:** US Army, Lt. 1966-1968; **HOME ADD:** 1234 Pinecrest Cir., Silver Spring, MD 20910, (301)585-4009; **BUS ADD:** 1316 Fenwick Lane, Suite 1307, Silver Spring, MD 20910, (301)565-3380.

MITCHELL, Stuart B.——B: Oct. 5, 1946, New Eagle, PA, *Counselor at Law*, Stuart B. Mitchell, Counselor at Law; **PRIM RE ACT:** Consultant, Attorney, Owner/Investor, Syndicator; **PROFL AFFIL & HONORS:** RESSI, ABA, VA State Bar, US Tax Ct. Bar Member; US Supreme Ct. Bar Member; **EDUC:** BA, 1967, Psych., Asbury Coll.; **GRAD EDUC:** JD, 1977, Intl. School of Law, George Mason Univ. Law School; **MIL SERV:** USCG, Lt. 1969-1974; **BUS ADD:** 803 W. Broad St., Suite 240, Falls Church, VA 22046, (703)241-3770.

MITCHELL, Thomas——*Executive Vice President*, Society of Real Estate Appraisers; **OTHER RE ACT:** Profl. Assn. Admin.; **BUS ADD:** 645 N. Michigan, Chicago, IL 60611, (312)346-7422.*

MITCHELL, Thomas G.——B: July 2, 1944, Cincinnati, OH, *Pres.*, Mitchell & Co. RE, Inc., CRI Props.; **PRIM RE ACT:** Broker, Developer, Owner/Investor, Property Manager, Syndicator; **SERVICES:** Brokerage, devel., prop. mgmt.; **REP CLIENTS:** Planning Research Corp., LSI Logic Corp., Data Systems Design, Inc., Racal-Vadic, Inc., King Bearing Corp., Qume Corp.; **PREV EMPLOY:** Norris, Beggs & Simpson, Brokers (1976-77); **PROFL AFFIL & HONORS:** Assn. of South Bay Brokers (Pol. Affairs Comm.), Citizens for Housing & Econ. Stability; **EDUC:** BBA, 1967, Mktg. & Fin., Univ. of Cincinnati; **GRAD EDUC:** Univ. of Cinn., & Santa Clara Univ. Grad Schools; **EDUC HONORS:** Dean's List, Pres. Amer. Mktg. Assn.; **HOME ADD:** 777 Hollenbeck Ave., 23T, Sunnyvale, CA 94087, (408)738-2630; **BUS ADD:** 2075 Bering Dr., Suite A, San Jose, CA 95131, (408)998-8400.

MITCHELL, Todd J.——B: Nov. 18, 1943, Milwaukee, WI, *Atty.*, Mitchell & Norman S.C.; **PRIM RE ACT:** Attorney, Developer, Owner/Investor; **PREV EMPLOY:** Trust Officer; **PROFL AFFIL & HONORS:** WI Bar Assn.; ABA; Milw. Bar Assn.; Milw. Estate Planning Council; **EDUC:** BA, 1965, Econ., Lawrence Univ.; **GRAD EDUC:** JJD, 1968, Law, Univ. of WI; **EDUC HONORS:** Honors in Indep. Studies; **HOME ADD:** 2951 N. Marietta, Milwaukee, WI 53211, (414)332-7260; **BUS ADD:** 2631 N. Downer, Milwaukee, WI 53211, (414)962-8300.

MITLIN, Ira G.——B: May 18, 1922, NYC, NY, *VP, Operations*, Whittner & Co.; **PRIM RE ACT:** Property Manager; **OTHER RE ACT:** Admin. of RE Div., prop. mgmt., leasing; **REP CLIENTS:** Profl. services - attys., accts., banks, stock brokers, med.; **PREV EMPLOY:** Broadway Mgmt. Corp. - VP of Operations, Click-Brooklyn Navy Yard - Dir. of RE; **PROFL AFFIL & HONORS:** SME, Comm. of 100, C of C; Nat. Assn. of Corporate RE Engrs.; **GRAD EDUC:** Bus. Admin., 1942, NY Univ., School of Bus. Admin., NY City; **MIL SERV:** USAF, Sgt.; **HOME ADD:** 1101 80th St. Court S., St. Petersburg, FL 33707, (813)381-9100; **BUS ADD:** 5999 Central Ave., St. Petersburg, FL 33710, (813)384-3000.

MITNICK, Philip——B: May 21, 1953, Brooklyn, NY, *Sr. Assoc.*, Steven Winter Assoc.; **PRIM RE ACT:** Consultant, Architect; **SERVICES:** Energy audits; life cycle cost analysis; inspection reports; feasibility studies; design; rehab.; conversion; **REP CLIENTS:** Helmsley Spear; Korean Evangelical Church; Dept. of HUD; Dept. of Energy; Blimpie Indus.; Coward Shoes; Cobble Hill Assn.; Gramercy Lofts; Monsanto, Inc.; **PROFL AFFIL & HONORS:** BOCA; ASTM; ASHRAE; **EDUC:** BArch./BS, Arch., Pratt Inst., GWU; **HOME ADD:** 333 E. 30th St., New York, NY 10016; **BUS ADD:** 6100 Empire State Bldg., New York, NY 10001, (212)564-5800.

MITNICK, Searle E.——B: Mar. 8, 1946, Baltimore, MD, *Member of firm*, Kaplan, Heyman, Greenberg, Engelman & Belgrad, P.A.; **PRIM RE ACT:** Attorney; **SERVICES:** Legal; **PROFL AFFIL & HONORS:** RE Sec. of Amer. & MD Bar Assns.; **EDUC:** BS, 1966, Pol. Sci., Loyola Coll., Baltimore, MD; **GRAD EDUC:** JD, 1969, Law, Univ. of PA Law School; **EDUC HONORS:** Dean's List.; **OTHER ACT & HONORS:** Law Clerk, Court of Appeals of MD, 1969-70; **HOME ADD:** 2629 Rockwood Ave., Baltimore, MD 21215, (301)466-7527; **BUS ADD:** 10th Fl., Sun Life Bldg., 20 S. Charles St., Baltimore, MD 21201, (301)539-6967.

MITTELMAN, David——*Treas.*, Williamhouse-Regency, Inc.; **PRIM RE ACT:** Property Manager; **BUS ADD:** 28 W. 23 St., New York, NY 10010, (212)691-2000.*

MIULLI, Robert V.——B: Apr. 25, 1947, Chicago, IL, Cumberland Northwest, Inc.; **PRIM RE ACT:** Architect, Developer; **OTHER RE ACT:** Project Mgmt.; **PREV EMPLOY:** City of Los Angeles 1971-77; BE & C Engrs. Inc. 1977-79; **PROFL AFFIL & HONORS:** Amer. Inst. of Archs., NCARB Certificate Holder; **EDUC:** BS, 1974, Arch., Univ. of So. CA; **GRAD EDUC:** March/MBA, 1976, Arch. & Bus. Admin., Univ. of IL Urbana Champaign; **MIL SERV:** USA, Sp5, Ar. Com.; **OTHER ACT & HONORS:** USC & U of I Alumni Assns.; **HOME ADD:** 12505 SE 215 Place, Kent, WA 98031, (206)631-4233; **BUS ADD:** PO Box 306, Bellevue, WA 98009, (206)454-6393.

MIXON, Marvin W.——B: Nov. 21, 1943, Cordele, GA, *Atty.*, Perry, Walters, Lippitt & Custer; **PRIM RE ACT:** Attorney; **SERVICES:** Title exams., loan closing, sale closing; **EDUC:** BA, 1965, Pre-law, Mercer Univ.; **GRAD EDUC:** JD, 1967, Law, Mercer Univ.; **MIL SERV:** US Army, Lt.; **HOME ADD:** 1904 Chatham Dr., Albany, GA 31707, (912)436-0224; **BUS ADD:** 409 N. Jackson St., PO Box 527, Albany, GA 31703, (912)432-7438.

MIXON, Todd——B: Feb. 9, 1949, Indianola, MS, *VP*, First Mississippi National Bank; **PRIM RE ACT:** Banker, Lender; **SERVICES:** Const. lending; **PROFL AFFIL & HONORS:** Homebuilders Assn.; **EDUC:** BS, 1971, Banking & Fin., Univ. of So. MS; **HOME ADD:** 103 Bookwood Lane, Hattiesburg, MS 39401; **BUS ADD:** P O Box 1231, Hattiesburg, MS 39401, (601)545-5219.

MIYAMOTO, Theodore T.——B: Mar. 15, 1951, Honolulu, HI, T T Miyamoto; **PRIM RE ACT:** Broker, Attorney; **PREV EMPLOY:** Clerk-Bailiff 1st Circuit Ct. Honolulu 9/79-3/80, Legal Aid for Small Claims in San Francisco (Internship) 1/79-6/79; **PROFL AFFIL & HONORS:** ABA, HI Bar Assn.; **EDUC:** BA, 1974, Psych.-Econ., Stanford Univ.; **GRAD EDUC:** MBA, 1976, Fin./Acctg., Univ. of CA, Berkeley; JD, 1979, Tax & Bus. Law, Golden Gate Univ.; **EDUC HONORS:** Masters Thesis in Mktg.; **HOME ADD:** 675 Hakaka Pl., Honolulu, HI 96816, (808)737-9277; **BUS ADD:** 733 Bishop St. +1550, Honolulu, HI 96813, (808)523-7736.

MIYOSHI, David M.——B: Jan. 2, 1944, Overton, NV, *Atty. at Law*, Morgan, Lewis and Bockius; **PRIM RE ACT:** Attorney; **SERVICES:** RE fin., consultation, negotiation and representation of documentation, investment analysis and consultation; **PREV EMPLOY:** Mori and Ota Law Office; **PROFL AFFIL & HONORS:** ABA; CA Bar Assn.; CA Broker; Los Angeles/Beverly Hills Listing Bd. Member, Atty. at Law; RE Broker; **EDUC:** BS, 1966, Fin./Mktg., Univ. of So. CA; **GRAD EDUC:** JD, 1973, Corp. Law, Univ. of CA; MBA, 1978, RE Fin., Harvard Univ.; **EDUC HONORS:** Dean's List, Beta Gamma Sigma Hon. Soc.; **MIL SERV:** USMC, Capt. Naval Commendation Medal; **OTHER ACT & HONORS:** Los Angeles Jr. C of C; Private Pilot; **HOME ADD:** 4307 Newton St., Torrance, CA 90505, (213)378-4797; **BUS ADD:** 611 W. 6th St., Los Angeles, CA 90017, (213)612-2522.

MIZE, David W.——B: May 17, 1946, Topeka, KS, *VP, Gen. Mgr.*, English Realty, Inc.; **PRIM RE ACT:** Broker, Consultant, Developer, Builder, Lender, Owner/Investor; **SERVICES:** Above - New and used home sales; **PREV EMPLOY:** Coll. and Serv. USA; **PROFL AFFIL & HONORS:** Nat. Assn. of Realtors, KS Assn. of Realtors, Independent Brokers Assn., Wichita Bd. of Realtors, RNMI, CRB; **EDUC:** BA, 1968, Econ., Washburn Univ., Topeka, KS; **MIL SERV:** USA, S/Sgt., 3 bronze stars with 2 oak leaf clusters, air medal, purple heart, serv. Rep. of Vietnam; **OTHER ACT & HONORS:** KS Jaycees, Derby C of C, Sales & Mktg. Execs. of Wichita; **HOME ADD:** 937 Marguerite Pkwy.,, Derby, KS 67037, (316)788-2770; **BUS ADD:** 200 E. Madison, Derby, KS 67037, (316)788-1523.

MIZE, Franklin H.——*Corp. Atty.*, Jantzen, Inc.; **PRIM RE ACT:** Attorney, Property Manager; **BUS ADD:** PO Box 3001, Portland, OR 97208, (503)238-5000.*

MIZRACHI, Joseph——B: June 25, 1945, Jerusalem. Israel, *Pres.*, Midwest Planning & Fin. Grp. Inc.; **PRIM RE ACT:** Consultant, Owner/Investor, Insuror, Syndicator; **SERVICES:** Investment Planning, Insur. Planning; **PREV EMPLOY:** Mgr. of Agency for Baulcers Life (Iowa); **PROFL AFFIL & HONORS:** CLU, Realtor Am. Prop. Mgmt., Assn., NALU, Estate Planners Council, MDRT, CLU, MFS; **EDUC:** BA, 1967, Econ. & Poli. Sci., Hebrew Univ., Jerusalem, Israel; **GRAD EDUC:** MBA, 1970, Fin. & Acctg., Hebrew Univ.; MA(MES), 1978, Fin. Services, Amer. Coll., Bryn Manor, PA; **EDUC HONORS:** Deans List; **HOME ADD:** 1046 Clifton Hills Ave., Cincinnati, OH 45220, (513)281-1772; **BUS ADD:** 355 Carew Tower, 441 Vine St., Cincinnati, OH 45202, (513)579-0101.

MLETSCHNIG, Peter F.——B: May 20, 1941, Springfield, MA, *Realtor*, Shore & Country Real Estate; **PRIM RE ACT:** Broker, Appraiser, Property Manager; **SERVICES:** Sales, rentals, appraisal of resid., land, comml.; **PROFL AFFIL & HONORS:** NAR, CT Bd. of Realtor, CRS, GRI; **EDUC:** BS, 1964, Fin., RE, Babson Coll., New York Univ.; **GRAD EDUC:** MBA, 1965, Fin., Babson Coll.; **MIL SERV:** CTARNG, Cpt., since 1965; **HOME ADD:** Old Lyme, CT 06371; **BUS ADD:** P O Box 69, So. Lyme, CT 06376, (203)434-1695.

MLYNARYK, Peter——*Pres.*, Peter Mlynaryk and Assocs.; **PRIM RE ACT:** Consultant, Appraiser, Developer, Owner/Investor, Instructor; **SERVICES:** Econ. and fin. feasibility studies, valuation, devel.; **REP CLIENTS:** Devels., investors, lenders income producing prop.; **PROFL AFFIL & HONORS:** ULI, NARA; **EDUC:** BS, 2963, Electrical Engrg., MA Inst. of Tech.; **GRAD EDUC:** MBA (1966) DBA (1971), Fin., RE, Urban Econ., Univ. of So. CA; **HOME ADD:** 4524 Sherington Ct., Cypress, CA 90630, (714)527-2843; **BUS ADD:** 4524 Sherington Ct., Cypress, CA 90630, (714)527-2843.

MOECKEL, William G., Jr.——B: June 11, 1946, Wilmington, DE, *Sr. Prin.*, Laventhol & Horwath, Atlanta Office, Mgmt. Advisory Services Div.; **PRIM RE ACT:** Consultant; **SERVICES:** Econ. feasibility analysis, valuation, strategic devel. planning; **REP CLIENTS:** Devels., lenders, investors and owners of comm. RE ventures; **PREV EMPLOY:** Mktg. Consultant, Mitchell Marketing, 1973-1975; Holiday Inns, Inc, Development & Acquisitions, 1975-1978; **PROFL AFFIL & HONORS:** Central Atlanta Progress; Atlanta Convention & Visitors Bureau; GA Hospitality & Travel Assn.; Atlanta C of C; **EDUC:** BS, 1972, Cornell Univ.; **EDUC HONORS:** Dean's List; Hon. Soc.; **MIL SERV:** Military Intelligence, 1966-1969, Republic of Vietnam; **BUS ADD:** 225 Peachtree St., Ste. 2300, Atlanta, GA 30303, (404)581-0100.

MOELLER, L. C., Dr.——B: Dec. 14, 1941, Elgin, IL, *Broker*, RX Realty, Inc.; **PRIM RE ACT:** Broker, Consultant, Appraiser, Owner/Investor; **OTHER RE ACT:** Tax Shelters & Exchange; **SERVICES:** Tax Shelter consulting & Brokerage, Paper Brokerage, Primarily Inv. Single Fam. Res.; **REP CLIENTS:** 50% Bracket Prof.; **PREV EMPLOY:** Prof. at OR State Univ., Tech. Dir.-Bio Solar Research & Dev. Corp.; **PROFL AFFIL & HONORS:** Realtor, FLI, SREA Assoc., Phi Delta Kappa, Epsilon Pi Tau, Soc. of Automotive Engineers; **EDUC:** BS, 1964, Indus Tech., Iowa State Univ.-Ames; **GRAD EDUC:** MA & PHD, 1971&1980, PHD Mgmt. & Statistical Research, Iowa State (MA-Chapman Coll.); **EDUC HONORS:** PDK Grimmel Award for Outstanding Research 1980; **MIL SERV:** USAF, Capt., Rated Pilot: Air Medal, Presidential Unit Citation, Vietnam Service Medal, etc.; **OTHER ACT & HONORS:** Porche Club of Amer., Int'l Arabian Horse Assn.; **HOME ADD:** 31150 Kay St., Lebanon, OR 97321; **BUS ADD:** 31150 Kay St., Lebanon, OR 97355.

MOEN, Richard S.——**B:** Mar. 1, 1927, LaCrosse, WI, *Pres.*, Moen, Sheehan, Meyer & Henke, Ltd.; **PRIM RE ACT:** Attorney; **SERVICES:** Devel. & Legal; **REP CLIENTS:** First Bank (N.A.); Burlington Northern, Inc.; Sunmark Indus.; Pepsi Cola Bottling Co.; Dahl Props., Inc.; **PROFL AFFIL & HONORS:** ABA; WI State Bar; Fellow, Amer. Coll. of Probate Counsel; **EDUC:** BS, 1950, Chem., Bradley Univ.; **GRAD EDUC:** LLB, 1953, Univ. of WI, Madison; **MIL SERV:** USN; **OTHER ACT & HONORS:** LaCrosse Redevel. Auth., 1962-1976; **HOME ADD:** 2917 Farnam St., LaCrosse, WI 54601, (608)788-6577; **BUS ADD:** 402 First Bank Bldg., PO Box 786, LaCrosse, WI 54601, (608)784-8310.

MOFFETT, H. Thomas——**B:** May 9, 1947, Easton, PA, *Dir. of Tax Services*, Laventhol & Horwath; **PRIM RE ACT:** Consultant; **OTHER RE ACT:** CPA; **SERVICES:** Syndication and transaction structuring; partnership taxation consulting; **REP CLIENTS:** Syndicators, devels. and RE investors; **PROFL AFFIL & HONORS:** CA Society of CPA's; **EDUC:** BS, 1970, Bus./Acctg., Univ. of CA; **BUS ADD:** 50 California St., Ste. 2450, San Francisco, CA 94111, (415)989-0110.

MOFFITT, Mark Howard——**B:** July 21, 1954, Dragerton, UT, *Dir. of Acquisitions*, Kenman Corp.; **PRIM RE ACT:** Broker, Consultant, Appraiser, Owner/Investor, Syndicator; **SERVICES:** Consulting, Appraisals, Brokerage; **PREV EMPLOY:** Comml. Brokerage, 1979-1980, VP Houston Operations - RE Synd. & Brokerage, 1980-1981; **PROFL AFFIL & HONORS:** Lic. RE Broker, TX & UT, Outstanding Young Men of Amer., 1980; **EDUC:** BA, 1979, Fin./Acctg., Univ. of UT; **EDUC HONORS:** Magna Cum Laude, Dean's Honor Roll - Coll. of Bus., Skull & Bones Honorary, Cert. of RE, Mortar Bd. Honorary; **OTHER ACT & HONORS:** Houston Tennis Umpires Assn.; US Tennis Assn.; **HOME ADD:** 3926 Feramorz Dr., Salt Lake City, UT 84117, (801)272-0105; **BUS ADD:** Beneficial Life Tower, Ste. 850, 36 S State St., Salt Lake City, UT 84111, (801)363-6170.

MOGHADAM, Hamid R.——**B:** Aug. 26, 1956, Tehran, Iran, *Associate*, John McMahan Assoc., Fin. Advisory & Devel. Servs.; **PRIM RE ACT:** Consultant, Owner/Investor; **SERVICES:** Asset mgmt.; **PROFL AFFIL & HONORS:** SPUR; San Francisco Forward; **EDUC:** SB, 1977, Civil Engrg., MIT; **GRAD EDUC:** SM, 1978, Const. Mgmt., MIT; MBA, 1980, Bus. Admin., Stanford Univ.; **EDUC HONORS:** Chi Epsilon, Sigma Xi; **BUS ADD:** 201 California St., Suite 400, San Francisco, CA 94111, (415)433-7770.

MOHAR, Gregory J.——**B:** Nov. 14, 1928, Harrisburg, PA, *VP*, Bennett, Coleman, Grant & Assoc. Inc., Prop. Asset Mgmt.; **PRIM RE ACT:** Broker, Instructor, Consultant, Property Manager, Engineer; **OTHER RE ACT:** Cert. Energy Auditor (State of FL); **SERVICES:** Total Prop/Assets Mgmt. - Apt. Condo, Shopping Ctrs., Warehouses, Office Bldgs., Theme Park Mgmt. & Facilities Admin.; **REP CLIENTS:** Synds., Insts., Investors, Court Appointed Rec., Expert Witness, RE Investment Trusts, etc.; **PREV EMPLOY:** Anheuser Busch (Facilities Mgmt.), Project Engr., Program Mgr., Gen. Mgr. (Tampa Busch Gardens for Anheuser-Busch); **PROFL AFFIL & HONORS:** Pres. W. Coast Chap. (1977); IREM, CPM, Energy/Auditor (State of FL), Gov. Energy Office, BOMA, Expert Witness; **EDUC:** Engrg. and Bus. Mgmt., Univ of S Fl (Continuing Programs); **MIL SERV:** USNR, 1946-48, 1948-54; **OTHER ACT & HONORS:** FL Apt. Assn., DAR St. Patrick's School Bd.; **HOME ADD:** 4401 Prescott St., Tampa, FL 33616, (813)839-2590; **BUS ADD:** Suite 208, 1805 N. Westshore Blvd., Tampa, FL 33616, (813)877-8216.

MOHLER, Robert L.——**B:** Sept. 12, 1922, Lebanon, PA, *RE Sales*, Warnock Realty Co, Comml. & Investment; **PRIM RE ACT:** Broker, Appraiser, Owner/Investor; **OTHER RE ACT:** Comml. and investment; **PROFL AFFIL & HONORS:** RNMI, NAR, CCIM; **EDUC:** BA, 1951, Math, Univ. of CO; **GRAD EDUC:** MA, 1955, Ed. Admin, Univ. of N CO; **MIL SERV:** USA, Cpl.; **HOME ADD:** 1611 Dotsero, Loveland, CO 80537, (303)667-8333; **BUS ADD:** 525 Cleveland Ave, Loveland, CO 80537, (303)667-2510.

MOHUN, J. Brook, Jr.——**B:** June 25, 1926, San Francisco, CA, *Broker*, The Brooke Co.; **PRIM RE ACT:** Broker, Consultant; **OTHER RE ACT:** Exchanger; **SERVICES:** Land, Ranches, lots; **PREV EMPLOY:** Boise Cascade 1969; **PROFL AFFIL & HONORS:** Sacramento RE Exchange Group, Exchangers, Central Valley Exchangers; **EDUC:** AA, 1950, San Mateo Jr. Coll.; **MIL SERV:** USN; WWII; **HOME ADD:** 4914 N. Thesta, Fresno, CA 93726, (209)229-4190; **BUS ADD:** Chandler Airport, Ste. F, 510 W. Kearney Blvd., Fresno, CA 93706, (209)441-1327.

MOISTER, Peter Corbin——**B:** Mar. 25, 1946, Atlanta, GA, *Principal*, Morgan Stanley & Co., Inc., Brooks Harvey & Co., Inc./Morstan Development Company, Inc.; **PRIM RE ACT:** Broker, Owner/Investor, Developer; **SERVICES:** Comml. prop. sales and fin. brokerage, investment and devel.; **PROFL AFFIL & HONORS:** RE Bd. of NY, ULI; **EDUC:** BA, 1964, Econ., Univ. of NC, Chapel Hill; **GRAD EDUC:** MBA, 1973, Corp. Fin., Columbia Univ. Grad. School of Bus. Admin.; **MIL SERV:** US Army, 1st Lt.; **HOME ADD:** 1225 Park Ave., New York, NY 10028; **BUS ADD:** 1633 Broadway, New York, NY 10019, (212)974-2510.

MOLE, Tom——*Mgr. RE*, Quaker Oats Co.; **PRIM RE ACT:** Property Manager; **BUS ADD:** 345 Merchandise Mart Plaza, Chicago, IL 60654, (312)222-6820.*

MOLENAAR, James E.——**B:** Feb. 24, 1937, Hammond, IN, *Atty.*, Molenaar & Vlasek, Ltd.; **PRIM RE ACT:** Attorney; **REP CLIENTS:** Codelco, Inc., First Fed. S&L Assn. of Lansing, Van Der Noord Builders, other devels.; **PROFL AFFIL & HONORS:** ABA, IL Bar Assn., S. Suburban Bar Assn., Past Pres. S. Suburban Bar Assn.; **EDUC:** AB, 1959, Pol. Sci., Econ., Univ. of IL; **GRAD EDUC:** LLB, 1964, Univ. of IL; **EDUC HONORS:** Depart. Distinction, Lib. Arts & Sci., Hon. in Pol. Sci.; **MIL SERV:** USA, 1st Lt.; **OTHER ACT & HONORS:** Tr. Village of Lansing, 1977-81, Rotary Club of Lansing; **HOME ADD:** 18908 Louise Dr., Lansing, IL 60438, (312)474-7473; **BUS ADD:** 3546 Ridge Rd., Lansing, IL 60438, (312)895-2800.

MOLINARO, C. Joseph——**B:** June 8, 1922, Winchester, MA, *Pres.*, C. Joseph Molinaro & Assoc., Inc.; **PRIM RE ACT:** Broker, Consultant; **SERVICES:** Motel specialist - 25 yrs.; **REP CLIENTS:** Motel operators, owners; **PREV EMPLOY:** Frequent writer on Hospitality Industry in Major Hospitality Periodicals - Synd. & Investor; **PROFL AFFIL & HONORS:** Motel Brokers Assn. of Amer., Pres., 1974, Hospitality Investment Seminar for past 3 yrs.; **EDUC:** BBA, 1944, Mergers & Consolidations, Boston Univ.; **GRAD EDUC:** 1947-48, Fin., George Washington Univ.; **EDUC HONORS:** Dean's List 1942-43, Cum Laude; **MIL SERV:** USN, Lt. JG; **OTHER ACT & HONORS:** Pres., Bay Bridge Authority; Active in Boys Clubs; **HOME ADD:** R-4 Box 273, Eastin, MD 21601, (301)822-5557; **BUS ADD:** 8401 Connecticut Ave., Chevy Chase, MD 20815, (301)951-0995.

MOLINE, Jack D.——**B:** Sept. 26, 1924, Grand Rapids, MI, *Pres.*, Cape Kennedy Realty, Inc.; **PRIM RE ACT:** Broker, Consultant, Engineer, Developer, Builder, Owner/Investor, Property Manager, Assessor; **SERVICES:** Investment counseling; **PREV EMPLOY:** Engr. with Aerospace Corp.; **PROFL AFFIL & HONORS:** Cape Kennedy Area Bd. of Realtors; FL RE Exchangers; NAR; RNMI; FAMB, GRI; CCIM; FL Exhanger of the Year 1979; **GRAD EDUC:** BEE, 1948, Electrical Engrg., Univ. of MI; **MIL SERV:** US Army; Cpl.; **OTHER ACT & HONORS:** City Commissioner, Cocoa Beach 1963-1965; **HOME ADD:** 517 Naish Ave., Cocoa Beach, FL 32931; **BUS ADD:** 6619 No. Atlantic Ave., Cape Canaveral, FL 32920, (305)783-5150.

MOLL, Burkhard E. "Hardy"——**B:** Jan. 15, 1949, Germany, *Pres.*, Hardy Moll Realty, Inc.; **PRIM RE ACT:** Broker, Syndicator, Developer, Builder, Property Manager, Owner/Investor; **SERVICES:** Aquisition & disposition of residential & income RE & loans; income tax structuring, exchanges; synd. for dev. & income & tax structuring; **REP CLIENTS:** Indiv. & Relocation Cos.; **PROFL AFFIL & HONORS:** GAR, NAR, RESSI, RNMI, CAR Prop. Mgmt. Div., GRI, GRS, Bd. Past Pres.; **MIL SERV:** USN, E-4; **OTHER ACT & HONORS:** Oxnard; Port Hueneme; Ventura C of C; **HOME ADD:** 3833 Thacher Rd., Ojai, CA 93023, (805)646-7828; **BUS ADD:** 511 W Channel Islands Blvd., Port Hueneme, CA 93041, (805)985-9878.

MOLL, Jerome R.——**B:** Dec. 14, 1949, Effingham, KS, *Coordinator, RE Indus. Team*, Main Hurdman; **OTHER RE ACT:** Acct.; **SERVICES:** Fin. projections, consulting, acctg. and auditing serv., tax planning and prep., RE synd., investors, operators; **PROFL AFFIL & HONORS:** AICPA; KS Soc. of CPA's, Internal Auditors, CPA; **EDUC:** BA, 1971, Acctg., KS State Univ.; **GRAD EDUC:** MS, 1972, Acctg., KS State Univ.; **HOME ADD:** 3655 W. 13th, Apt. 9T, Wichita, KS 67203, (316)942-1541; **BUS ADD:** 401 E. Douglas, Suite 300, Wichita, KS 67202, (316)267-7231.

MOLLARD, W. Ross——*Partner*, United Dominion Capital, Comml. Investment & Devel.; **PRIM RE ACT:** Developer, Owner/Investor; **PREV EMPLOY:** Canadian Devel. and Law Practice, RE; **PROFL AFFIL & HONORS:** ULI, Atty.; **EDUC:** BA, 1958, Commerce, Notre Dame Univ.; **GRAD EDUC:** LLB, 1962, Commercial, Dalhonie Univ.; **EDUC HONORS:** Eng.; **OTHER ACT & HONORS:** CAN Bar Assn.; **BUS ADD:** 2081 Business Ctr. Dr., Suite 245, Irvine, CA 92715, (714)955-1833.

MOLLICA, Anthony F.——**B:** Aug. 9, 1932, Franklin Cty., OH, *Pres.*, Assoc. Consultants & Appraisers, Inc.; **PRIM RE ACT:** Consultant, Appraiser; **SERVICES:** Appraisal serv., appraisal of stock & bus. valuations.; **PREV EMPLOY:** Self-employed; **PROFL AFFIL & HONORS:** AIREA, Sr. Member, ASA, Past Pres. of ASA, Columbus

Chapter, Professional Recognition Award, AIREA; MAI; **HOME ADD:** 2077 Mackenzie, Columbus, OH 43220, (614)459-1110; **BUS ADD:** 5151 Reed Rd., Columbus, OH 43220, (614)267-6361.

MOLLING, Charles F.——**B:** Jan. 5, 1940, Grafton, WI, *Partner*, Boatright and Boatright; **PRIM RE ACT:** Attorney; **SERVICES:** Legal Servs. in connection with RE and business matters; **REP CLIENTS:** RE investors, comml. and resid. selers and purchasers, banks, condo. devels. and assns.; **PREV EMPLOY:** Assoc. Counsel, Pioneer Nat. Title Insurance Co., 1976-1977; **PROFL AFFIL & HONORS:** ABA, CO Bar Assn., Denver Bar Assn., and First Judicial District Bar Assn., Admitted to practice in the states of CO and IL and in federal courts in CO, Northern Dist. of IL, 7th & 10th circuits and US Ct. of Claims; **EDUC:** BA, 1973, Hist., Marquette Univ. and Univ. of MO, St. Louis; **GRAD EDUC:** JD, 1977, Law, Loyola Univ. of Chicago; **EDUC HONORS:** Dean's List, Magna Cum Laude; **MIL SERV:** USMC, Cpl.; **HOME ADD:** 1050 Cedar St., Broomfield, CO 80020, (303)466-6006; **BUS ADD:** 4315 Wadsworth Blvd., Wheat Ridge, CO 80033, (303)423-7131.

MOLTER, Fred W.——**B:** Oct. 13, 1937, San Antonio, TX, *VP, Comml. Loans*, Bexar Cty. Savings, Devel. Div.; **PRIM RE ACT:** Broker, Consultant, Appraiser, Developer, Lender, Owner/Investor; **SERVICES:** Gen. loans, devel. loans, joint ventures, valuation consulting; **PREV EMPLOY:** Tobin Aerial Surveys, San Antonio, TX; **PROFL AFFIL & HONORS:** San Antonio Builders Assn., SA Apt. Assn., Soc. of RE Appraisers, Realtor San Antonio, TX; **EDUC:** BA, 1961, Geo., Bus., St. Mary's Univ.; **MIL SERV:** USA; **HOME ADD:** 4403 Desert View, San Antonio, TX 78217, (512)655-2852; **BUS ADD:** PO Box 23280 San Antonio, TX 78223, (512)532-3136.

MOLZULSKI, Kenneth S.——**B:** May 6, 1952, Cleveland, OH, *Project Mgr.*, Gerald D. Hines Interests; **PRIM RE ACT:** Developer, Owner/Investor; **PREV EMPLOY:** RE Lending, Comml. Banking; **EDUC:** BCE, 1975, Constr. Mgmt. & Structures, Univ. of Cincinnati; **GRAD EDUC:** MBA, 1978, Fin., RE, Harvard Bus. School; **EDUC HONORS:** ODK; **HOME ADD:** 7018 Westlake, Dallas, TX 75214, (214)321-4090; **BUS ADD:** 5501 LBJ Freeway, Ste. 1000, Dallas, TX 75240, (214)934-3600.

MONAGHAN, Red——*Owner*, Red Monaghan Co. Realtors; **PRIM RE ACT:** Developer; **BUS ADD:** Grand Floor Plaza Towers, Springfield, MO 65804, (417)887-2826.*

MONAHAN, Denis C.——**B:** July 18, 1949, Cheverly, MD, Mager and Monahan; **PRIM RE ACT:** Broker, Attorney; **OTHER RE ACT:** Legal Serv.; **SERVICES:** RE Brokerage; **PROFL AFFIL & HONORS:** ABA; Sections on Real Prop., Forum Comm. on Const. Law, MI State Bar; **EDUC:** BA, 1971, Bus. Admin., MI State Univ.; **GRAD EDUC:** JD, 1974, Wayne State Univ.; **EDUC HONORS:** With Honors; **OTHER ACT & HONORS:** Lic. RE Broker-MI; **HOME ADD:** 2070 Pembroke, Birmingham, MI 48008, (313)649-6591; **BUS ADD:** 2000 First Nat. Bldg., Detroit, MI 48226, (313)965-3282.

MONASEBIAN, Dennis M.——**B:** Feb. 25, 1953, New York City, *Asst. VP*, Sybedon Corp.; **PRIM RE ACT:** Broker; **OTHER RE ACT:** Comprehensive debt and equity funding work; **SERVICES:** Evaluation, structuring and implementation of fin. plans; **PREV EMPLOY:** RE Appraiser, Empire Savings Bank, New York; **PROFL AFFIL & HONORS:** Young Mort. Bankers Assn.; **EDUC:** BA, 1974, Hist. and Poli. Sci., Washington Univ., St. Louis, MO; **GRAD EDUC:** MBA, 1979, Fin., Pace Univ., NYC; **HOME ADD:** 442 West 57th St., New York, NY 10019, (212)581-9514; **BUS ADD:** 1211 Ave. of the Americas, New York, NY 10036, (212)354-5756.

MONNIE, Terrance R.——**B:** Apr. 18, 1944, Meadville, PA, *Atty./Partner*, Meckstroth, Schwierlins & Monnie; **PRIM RE ACT:** Attorney, Builder, Owner/Investor, Instructor, Syndicator; **SERVICES:** Legal to numerous S & L Assn.; **REP CLIENTS:** Banks, devels., builders, realtors specialize in condo.; **PREV EMPLOY:** Instr.: RE Law/Fin., Univ. of Cincinnati, Evening Coll. 1978-present; **EDUC:** BA, 1966, Pol. Sci., PA State Univ.; **GRAD EDUC:** JD, 1974, Law, Salmon P. Chase Coll. of Law, No. KY State Univ.; **MIL SERV:** US Army, 1st Lt., Bronze Star; **BUS ADD:** 8 West 9th St., Cincinnati, OH 45202, (513)241-5556.

MONROE, Michael J.——**B:** June 24, 1942, Buffalo, NY, Monroe Wilson and Collins; **PRIM RE ACT:** Attorney; **REP CLIENTS:** Tucson Bd. of Realtors, US Homes Fin. Corp., BA Mort. Co.; **PROFL AFFIL & HONORS:** ABA, AZ Bar Assn., Pima Cty. Bar Assn.; **EDUC:** BS, 1964, Bus. Fin., Univ. of AZ; **GRAD EDUC:** JD, 1967, Law, Univ. of AZ; **MIL SERV:** US Army, Sgt.; **OTHER ACT & HONORS:** PER; BPO Elks; Past Pres. Businessmen's Assn. of Tucson; Bd. of Dirs. Catholic Community Servs. of Southern AZ; **HOME ADD:** 2132 E. Blacklidge, Tucson AZ 85719, (602)327-0736; **BUS ADD:** Suite 1002 Home Fed. Tower, Tucson, AZ 85701, (602)792-9220.

MONROIG, Antonio——**B:** 1944, San Juan, PR, *Asst. Sec. for Fair Housing and Equal Opportunity*, US Dept. of HUD, Fair Housing & Equal Opportunity; **PRIM RE ACT:** Attorney, Regulator; **SERVICES:** Assures fair housing for all citizens throughout the country and ensures that HUD-assisted programs are administered without discrimination, based on race, sex color or nat. origin. Assures equal employment opportunity within Dept. and in local agencies founded by HUD; **PREV EMPLOY:** Special Asst. to Mayor of San Juan (1977); Deputy Dir. of San Juan Legal Servs. (1973-1975); Trial Atty. Land Affairs Div. of Dept. of Justice; Administrator, Municipal Services Admin., San Juan, PR Jan. 1977 to Mar. 1981; **EDUC:** BS, 1965, Univ. of PR; **GRAD EDUC:** JD, 1968, Catholic Univ. of PR; **BUS ADD:** HUD Bldg. 451 7th St., Washington, DC 20410.

MONTANARI, Fred P.——**B:** May 25, 1921, Ridgefield, CT, *Pres.*, Keeler and Durant, Inc.; **PRIM RE ACT:** Broker, Consultant, Appraiser, Builder, Property Manager; **PREV EMPLOY:** 1940-1941, Clerk/Assessor's Off./Ridgefield; 1946-1958, Aircraft Research and Devel. Projects with Continental Inc. and Doman Helicopters Inc.; 1958-1960, Fred P. Montanari RE and Ins. Agency, Proprietor and Mgr.; 1961 to date, Pres. of Keeler and Durant, Inc.; **PROFL AFFIL & HONORS:** Chmn., Multiple Listing Comm.; Cert. Resid. Broker; Member, Past Pres. and Dir., Ridgefield Bd. of Realtors, Greater Danbury Bd. of Realtors, CT Assn. of RE Bds., CT Comml. Investment Div., Farm and Land Brokers; Member, Nat. Assn. of RE Bds and Nat. Inst. of RE Bds.; Assoc. Member, Amer. Soc. of Appraisers; Nat. Assn. of Prof. Counselors; **EDUC:** Assoc., 1942, Engrg., Univ. of Santa Clara; Shorts Bus. Sch. & Spartan Sch. of Aeronautics; **MIL SERV:** 11th Armored Div.; Patton's 3rd Army; 56th Army Engrs.; **OTHER ACT & HONORS:** Ridgefield Bd. of Selectmen, 1967-1979; Justice of the Peace, 1971 to present; Member and Chmn., Zoning Bd. of Appeals, 1953-1961; Member and Chmn., Various School Bldg. Comms., Secondary School Study Comms., Dir. of Town Bldg. Comms., 1961 to present; Member and Past Chmn., Republican Town Comm.; Past Member and Dir., Ridgefield Kiwanis Club; Member, Comdr. VFW, Marquette Council, Knights of Columbus and Italian Mutual Aid Soc.; Member and Dir., Ridgefield C of C; Member, 11th Armored Div. Assn.; **HOME ADD:** 99 Barry Ave., Ridgefield, CT 06877, (203)438-2745; **BUS ADD:** 360 Main St., Ridgefield, CT 06877, (203)438-2608.

MONTELEONE, Mike——**B:** May 23, 1945, Buffalo, NY, *Pres.*, Monteleone & Assocs. Inc. Realtors; **PRIM RE ACT:** Broker, Consultant, Appraiser, Instructor; **PROFL AFFIL & HONORS:** RE Certificate Inst. Bd. Dirs. Sherman Oaks Homeowners Assn.; **EDUC:** AA, 1970, Bus. & Law, Pierce Coll.; **OTHER ACT & HONORS:** Sherman Oaks Homeowners Assn.; **HOME ADD:** Sherman Oaks, CA, (213)995-0844; **BUS ADD:** 14235 Ventura Blvd., Sherman Oaks, CA 91423, (213)995-0844.

MONTEMARANO, Joseph——**B:** June 6, 1932, Brooklyn, NY, *Owner*, Montemarano Assocs., Private practice; **PRIM RE ACT:** Consultant, Engineer, Appraiser, Owner/Investor; **SERVICES:** Consulting engrs., planners, cost consultant, forensic engrg.; **REP CLIENTS:** Municipalities, indiv., instns. & comml.; **PREV EMPLOY:** Borough Pres. of Queens, Bd. of Educ., Civil Engr.; **PROFL AFFIL & HONORS:** Nat. Soc. of P.E.; ASCE; Columbia Soc. of RE; ASA; Amer. Assoc. of Cost Engrs.; Amer. Academy of Environmental Engrs., Profl. Engr.; NY, NJ, MA, CT, Cert. Cost Engr.; Nat., Diplomate, Amer. Academy of Environmental Engrs.; **EDUC:** BS-CE, 1958, CE, NYU; AA, Science-Structural, SUNY; **OTHER ACT & HONORS:** Former Commnr., Nassau Cty. Planning Bd.; Former Commnr. of Appraising, NY State Supreme Court; Order Sons of Italy in America, NY State Pres.; **HOME ADD:** 247 Guildford Ct., West Hempstead, NY 11552, (516)483-4368; **BUS ADD:** 1040 Hempstead Tpk., Franklin Square, NY 11010, (516)328-1125.

MONTEVERDE, John P., Jr.——**B:** Oct. 23, 1945, Pittsburgh, PA, *Pres.*, Monteverde Corp.; **PRIM RE ACT:** Consultant, Owner/Investor, Syndicator; **OTHER RE ACT:** Investment RE; **SERVICES:** Acquisition of lge. investment props.; **REP CLIENTS:** For inst. investors; **PREV EMPLOY:** The Baker Cos., Stamford, CT; **EDUC:** BS, Bus., Univ. of Pittsburgh; **GRAD EDUC:** RE & Corp. Fin., 1964-1966; **MIL SERV:** USAR, SP-4, 1966-1972; **HOME ADD:** 800 Eleventh St., Oakmont, PA 15139, (412)828-1067; **BUS ADD:** Suite 204 RIDC Plaza, Pittsburgh, PA 15238, (412)963-7555.

MONTGOMERY, Michael B.——**B:** Sept. 12, 1936, Santa Barbara, CA, M.B. Montgomery Properties, Inc.; **PRIM RE ACT:** Attorney, Developer, Owner/Investor; **OTHER RE ACT:** Community Redevel. Law Counsel; **SERVICES:** Consultation, negotiation and coordination of prop. devel. within community redevel. projects; **PREV EMPLOY:** State of CA, Community Redevel. Agencies of Monterey Park,

Irwindale, Huntington Park; **PROFL AFFIL & HONORS:** State Bar of CA, admitted to practice before US Supreme Court; **EDUC:** BS, 1960, Fin., RE, UCLA; **GRAD EDUC:** JD, 1963, USC; **MIL SERV:** US Navy; Engs.; US Army, Sgt.; **OTHER ACT & HONORS:** Mayor, City of S. Pasadena; Member, CRA S. Pasadena; Former State Chmn., CA Rep. Party; **HOME ADD:** 2033 Monterey Rd., S. Pasadena, CA 91030, (213)682-1333; **BUS ADD:** 2460 Huntington Dr., San Marino, CA 91108, (213)285-9711.

MONTGOMERY, William D.——B: Aug. 15, 1944, Toccoa, GA, *Partner*, Johnson & Montgomery; **PRIM RE ACT:** Attorney; **SERVICES:** Comml. RE, Atty., both devel. and lender rep.; **REP CLIENTS:** Morstan Devel. Co., Inc., Dunwoody Devel. Co., Inc., Tarton Corp., Larry Morris & Assoc., Peachtree Fed. S&L, Amer. Fletcher Nat. Bank and Amer. Fletcher Mort. Co.; **PREV EMPLOY:** Formerly partner, Gambrell & Mobley, GA; **EDUC:** BA, 1966, eng., Emory Univ.; **GRAD EDUC:** JD, 1970, Univ. of GA; **EDUC HONORS:** Articles editor, GA Law Review, Justice, Honor Ct., Cum Laude; **HOME ADD:** 208 Rumson Rd. NE, Atlanta, GA 30305, (404)266-1370; **BUS ADD:** 2200 Century Pkwy NE, Atlanta, GA 30345, (404)321-5640.

MONTOURI, Warren K.——B: June 6, 1929, Washington, DC, *VP*, Shannon & Luchs Co.; **PRIM RE ACT:** Broker, Consultant, Appraiser, Banker, Developer, Owner/Investor; **PROFL AFFIL & HONORS:** MAI; Member IREA; SRPA; SREA; Former Member Bd. of Equalization and Review, DC Govt. Dir.; DC Nat. Bank; Dir. Westwood Mgmt. Corp.; Dir. Amer. AIREA, DC Chapt.; **EDUC:** BS, 1954, Fin., Housing & Urban Devel., Amer. Univ., Washington, DC; **OTHER ACT & HONORS:** Dir. Audubon Naturalist Soc.; **HOME ADD:** 8801 Bradley Blvd., Potomac, MD 20854, (301)365-1935; **BUS ADD:** One Farragut Sq. S, Suite 600, Washington DC 20006, (202)659-7186.

MONTZ, Andre S.——B: July 26, 1940, New Orleans, LA, *Pres.*, Montz Mort. & Investment Inc.; **PRIM RE ACT:** Consultant, Appraiser, Developer; **SERVICES:** Income prop. analysis, appraisal and fin.; **REP CLIENTS:** Lenders, devels., instns. investors, and users of income prod. props.; **PROFL AFFIL & HONORS:** MBAA; Past Chmn., Young Men's Activity Comm. of the LA Mort. Bankers Assn.; Formerly a Candidate for membership in the AIREA; Bd. of Govs. of the LA Mort. Bankers Assn. for three years; Past Pres., New Orleans Mort. Bankers Assn.; Affiliate Member, New Orleans and Jefferson Bds. of Realtors; Author of "Real Estate-Finance Review," a monthly column in *The Jefferson Democrat*; Formerly an Approved Fed. Nat. Mort. Assn. Single Family Loan Underwriter, and Auditor; Advisory Dir., First City Bank, New Orleans, Mort. Banker; **EDUC:** AB, 1964, Bus. Admin., Econ., SE LA Univ.; **OTHER ACT & HONORS:** Advisory Dir., First City Bank, 935 Common St., N.O. LA 70112; Past. Dir. - LA Mort. Bankers Assn.; Past Pres. - New Orleans MBA; **HOME ADD:** 1148 Beverly Garden Dr., Metairie, LA 70002, (504)837-6761; **BUS ADD:** 3925 I-10 Service Rd., Metairie, LA 70002, (504)456-2357.

MONTZ, Lawrence J.——B: Aug. 25, 1949, New Orleans, LA, *Comml. Mgr.*, Central Appraisal Bureau, Inc.; **PRIM RE ACT:** Consultant, Appraiser, Builder; **OTHER RE ACT:** RE Agent; **SERVICES:** RE investment, consulting, valuation, evaluation, bus. valuation; **REP CLIENTS:** Various S&L, mort. cos., banks, attys. and indiv.; **PREV EMPLOY:** Pres., Montz and Montz Contractors, Inc. (Resid. Constr.); **PROFL AFFIL & HONORS:** Sr. Cert. Valuer of the Intl. Inst. of Valuers; MAI Candidate of AIREA; Assoc. Member, SREA, SCV; Sr. Cert. Valuer of IIV; **EDUC:** BS, 1972, Econ., Nicholls State Univ.; **OTHER ACT & HONORS:** Pres., Mu Zeta Alumni Chapt. of Tau Kappa Epsilon Intl. Frat.; **HOME ADD:** 7511 E. Oak Ridge Ct., New Orleans, LA 70128, (504)245-0111; **BUS ADD:** 348 Baronne, New Orleans, LA 70112, (504)581-9282.

MOODY, Errold F., Jr.——B: Jan. 16, 1944, Worcester, MA, *Owner*, E. F. Moody & Assoc.; **PRIM RE ACT:** Broker, Consultant, Appraiser, Instructor; **SERVICES:** Consulting, feasibility studies, brokerage, appraisals; **REP CLIENTS:** Corps., private indivs., attys., CPA; **PREV EMPLOY:** Major RE devel. cos. 1969-1976; **PROFL AFFIL & HONORS:** Realtor, B-1 Contractor, Lic. Securities Broker, Coll. Instructor in RE Investments, RE Econ., Syndications, Securities; **EDUC:** BS, 1966, Civil Engineering, Worcester Polytechnic Inst.; **GRAD EDUC:** LLB - Law, 1974, LaSalle; MBA, 1977, Univ. Beverly Hills; PhD - RE, 1979, Univ. B.H.; **HOME ADD:** 1200 Park Newport #403, Newport Beach, CA 92660, (714)644-0821; **BUS ADD:** 3816 Bristol St., Ste. M, Santa Ana, CA 92704, (714)720-0269.

MOODY, Jack W.——B: July 18, 1922, Ft. Worth, TX, *VP*, Bank of the Southwest, Bldg. Mgmt.; **PRIM RE ACT:** Property Manager; **PREV EMPLOY:** Bldg. Mgr., Shell Bldg., Houston, TX, 15 yrs., 1955-1969; **PROFL AFFIL & HONORS:** RPA-BOMI; Intl. BOMA; SWC BOMA; TX State BOMA; BOMA Houston, Real Prop. Administrator; **EDUC:** BA, 1947, Bus. Admin., Rice Inst.; **MIL SERV:** Air Corps, 1st Lt., Finance Officer; **OTHER ACT & HONORS:** Arabia Temple; Summit Club; **HOME ADD:** 8818 Haverstock, Houston, TX 77031, (713)777-1920; **BUS ADD:** 1330 Bank of the Southwest Bldg., Houston, TX 77002, (713)751-6597.

MOOK, Wesley, L.——B: June 16, 1939, Plainfield, NJ, *Exec. Off.*, Bennington Cooperative Savings and Loan Assoc.; **PRIM RE ACT:** Instructor, Consultant, Banker, Lender, Owner/Investor; **SERVICES:** Resid., comml., and 2nd home lending invest. counseling; **PREV EMPLOY:** U.S. Dept. of Af. Farmers Home Admin. Cty. Super.; **PROFL AFFIL & HONORS:** Dir. Fed. Savings League, Pres. VT League of S&L; **EDUC:** BS, 1966, Agri. and Econ. Mktg., Univ. of VT; **EDUC HONORS:** Alpha Zata, Agri. Honor. Soc.; **MIL SERV:** USN, PO 2nd class; **OTHER ACT & HONORS:** Town rep. Brattleboro, VT, 1971-75, VP 204 Depot St. Boys Home, Dir. Rotary Club, VP Downtown Living Corp.; **HOME ADD:** 208 Washington Ave., Bennington, VT 05201, (802)442-5028; **BUS ADD:** PO Box 28, 155 North St., Bennington, VT 05021.

MOON, Dr. David A.——B: Aug. 21, 1956, Washington, DC, *Pres., Chief Exec.*, Teledyne, Inc. c/o US Govt., Los Angeles, CA; **PRIM RE ACT:** Consultant, Engineer, Architect, Developer, Owner/Investor, Instructor, Property Manager, Insuror; **OTHER RE ACT:** Mgmt. labor relations policies; **REP CLIENTS:** Amer. Mgmt. Assn., Soc. of Mfg. Engrs., NSBA, IMS, etc.; **PREV EMPLOY:** Indus., US Dept. of Labor 1972-present; **PROFL AFFIL & HONORS:** Nat. Small Bus. Assn.; Intl. Money Brokers Assn.; MBAA; **EDUC:** 1970-1973, Diplomacy, MIT, Univ. of CA, MSU; **HOME ADD:** 8525 DeSoto Ave., Canoga Park, CA 91304, (213)822-3679; **BUS ADD:** 1901 Ave. of the Stars, Los Angeles, CA 90067, (213)277-3311.

MOON, Richard W.——B: June 26, 1944, Wash., DC, *Partner*, Satin, Tenenbaum, Eichler & Zimmerman; **OTHER RE ACT:** CPA; **SERVICES:** Audits, reviews and complications, MAS, public offering asst., & tax serv.; **REP CLIENTS:** Devel., contractors, indiv., investors, foreign & domestic, synd. & escrow cos.; **PREV EMPLOY:** RE Broker 1970-72; **PROFL AFFIL & HONORS:** AICPA; CA Soc. of CPA's; RE Committee, LA Chap. of CPA's, CPA; **EDUC:** BS, 1973, Bus. Admin., Acctg., CA State Polytechnic Univ.- Pomona; **GRAD EDUC:** MBA, 1981, RE, Fin., Univ. of S CA; **EDUC HONORS:** Deans List; **MIL SERV:** US Army; Spec. 5th Class, Vietnam Service Medal, Vietnam Combat Medal, Good Conduct Medal, Parachutist Badge; **HOME ADD:** 5670 W. 62nd St., Los Angeles, CA 90056, (213)641-7012; **BUS ADD:** 2049 Century Park E., 3700, Los Angeles, CA 90067, (213)553-1040.

MOONEY, G. Austin——B: Sept. 23, 1944, New York, NY, *VP, Grp. Head*, National Bank of North America, RE Loan Div.; **PRIM RE ACT:** Banker, Lender; **SERVICES:** Const. Loans; **PREV EMPLOY:** Marine Midland Bank; **EDUC:** BS, 1968, Bus. Admin., Wagner Coll.; **HOME TEL:** (516)367-3172; **BUS ADD:** 44 Wall St., New York, NY 10005, (212)623-2907.

MOORE, Alfred——B: May 28, 1912, Hattiesburg, MS, *COB and CEO*, First Magnolia Fed. S&L Assn.; **PRIM RE ACT:** Attorney, Banker; **SERVICES:** Fin.; **PROFL AFFIL & HONORS:** Ins. of Fin. Educ., Intl. Bar Assn., ABA, MS State Bar Assn., MS Bar Foundation, S. Central MS Bar Assn., Newcomen Society of N. Amer., Amer. Judicature Soc., US League of Savings Assn., Bd. of Dir., 1968-71 and 1974-77; Fed. Home Loan Bank Bd. of Dir., 1973-74; MS S & L League, Pres. 1964-1965; USM Foundation Bd. of Dir., S. Western S&L Conf. Dir., 1965-1967; Gov. Staff 1964-68 and 1972-76; **EDUC:** BA, 1934, Hist., Univ. of S. MS; **GRAD EDUC:** JD, 1936, Univ. of MS; **MIL SERV:** USN, Lt.; **OTHER ACT & HONORS:** Prosecuting Atty., Cty. of Hattiesburg, 1938-41 and 1947-49; Judge, Cty. of Hattiesburg, 1941-42; Cty. Atty., 1949-53. Hattiesburg C of C, Rotary Club, Elks Club, USM Alumni Assn., UM Alumni Assn., Hattiesburg Civic Assn., Owner of KY Colonels, Soc. War of 1812, MS Folklore Soc., Phi Alpha Delta, Pi Kappa Alpha, Phi Kappa Phi, MS Econ. Council and Hattiesburg Ctry. Club; **HOME ADD:** 2312 Carriage Rd., Hattiesburg, MS 39401, (601)545-2050; **BUS ADD:** PO Box 1858, Hattiesburg, MS 39401, (601)545-4722.

MOORE, Charles A., Jr.——B: Sept. 23, 1931, Washington, DC, *Pres.*, Republic Real Estate Appraisal Corp.; **PRIM RE ACT:** Consultant, Appraiser; **SERVICES:** RE appraising & counseling; **REP CLIENTS:** Attys., accountants, investors, lenders, devels., corps., and govt. agencies; **PROFL AFFIL & HONORS:** Amer. Assn. of Univ. Prof.; Amer. Soc. of Appraisers; Intl. Assn. of Assessing Officers; FIABI; Intl. Right of Way Assn.; Nat. Assn. of Indep. Fee Appraisers; Nat. Assn. of RE Appraisers; NAR; Nat. Assn. of Review Appraisers; Nat. Trust for Hist. Preservation; N. VA Bd. of Realtors; RE Educators Assn.; The Amer. RE and Urban Econ. Assn.; The Inc. Soc. of Valuers &

Auctioneers (United Kingdom); ULI; VA Assn. of Assessing Officers; VA Assn. of Realtors, ASA; FSVA; IFAS; CRA; CREA; Lambda Alpha Land Econ. Honorary; **EDUC:** BS, 1955, RE, Univ. of MD; **GRAD EDUC:** Grad. Cert., RE & Urban Devel., American Univ.; **EDUC HONORS:** Rho Epsilon Nat. RE Frat.; **MIL SERV:** USAF, Capt.; **OTHER ACT & HONORS:** Bd. of Advisors, The Salvation Army, Fairfax Cty. Corps; Adjunct Faculty, Univ. of VA, 1977-1981; RE Appraisal, George Mason Univ., 1978-1981; Tr., Philadelphia Mort. Trust, 1979-1981; **HOME ADD:** 6905 Lupine Ln., McLean, VA 22101, (703)356-3560; **BUS ADD:** 8027 Leesburg Pike, Suite 300, Tysons Corner, VA 22180, (703)893-2700.

MOORE, Clara L.——B: Aug. 29, 1925, Orlando, FL; **PRIM RE ACT:** Owner/Investor, Property Manager; **PREV EMPLOY:** Language, Speech and Hearing Pathologist, Escambia Cty. P-S; **EDUC:** BS, 1966, Educ., FL State Univ.; **GRAD EDUC:** MS, 1974, Speech, FL State Univ., Tallahassee, FL; **HOME ADD:** 401 N.U. St., Pensacola, FL 32505, (904)433-0924; **BUS ADD:** 401 North U St., Pensacola, FL 32505, (904)433-0924.

MOORE, Collice C.——B: Aug. 19, 1939, Warren Cty., NC, *Partner*, Moore & Sauter; **PRIM RE ACT:** Broker, Consultant, Appraiser, Developer, Owner/Investor; **SERVICES:** RE valuations & consultation; **REP CLIENTS:** Banks, attys., instns., dept. of transportation; **PREV EMPLOY:** Port Authority for State of NC; **PROFL AFFIL & HONORS:** Realtor, Soc. of Review Appraisers, MAI; SRA; **EDUC:** BS, 1961, NC State Univ. in Raleigh; **HOME ADD:** 202 Chippendale Dr., Greenville, NC 27834, (919)752-3367; **BUS ADD:** POB 7123, Greenville, NC 27834, (919)752-1010.

MOORE, Cornell L.——B: Sept. 18, 1939, Tignall, GA, *Pres.*, Lease Moore Equipment, Inc.; **PRIM RE ACT:** Attorney, Developer, Lender, Builder, Owner/Investor, Instructor; **SERVICES:** Realty Fin. & investments; **REP CLIENTS:** Granada Royale Hometels, Red Owl Stores; **PREV EMPLOY:** Asst. VP NW Nat. Bank; Exec. VP Shelter Mort. Co.; Pres. Leverette, Weekes & Co., Inc.; **PROFL AFFIL & HONORS:** Hennepin Cty. Bar Assn., MN Bar Assn., NBA; **EDUC:** AB, 1961, Sociology, VA Union Univ.; **GRAD EDUC:** JD, 1964, Law, Howard Univ. Law School; **HOME ADD:** 2727 Dean Parkway, Minneapolis, MN 55416, (812)920-0074; **BUS ADD:** 5100 Gamble Dr., Minneapolis, MN 55416, (612)546-8989.

MOORE, Doug——*VP Mktg.*, Tampax, Inc.; **PRIM RE ACT:** Property Manager; **BUS ADD:** 5 Dakota Drive, Lake Success, NY 11040, (516)437-8800.*

MOORE, Doyle——*Mgr.*, Southwestern Public Service; **PRIM RE ACT:** Developer; **BUS ADD:** Box 1261, Amarillo, TX 79170, (806)378-2121.*

MOORE, Eugene L.——B: June 6, 1946, Cincinnati, OH, *Pres.*, Trend Management, Inc./E.P. Wilbur & Co., Inc.; **PRIM RE ACT:** Broker, Owner/Investor, Instructor, Property Manager; **SERVICES:** Prop. mgmt., investment; **PREV EMPLOY:** Younkman, Roch & Assocs.; **PROFL AFFIL & HONORS:** Inst. of RE Mgmt.; Bldg. Owners and Mgrs. Assn.; Nat. Apartment Assn., CPM; **EDUC:** BA, 1973, Acctg., Univ. of So. FL; AA, Data Processing, St. Petersburg Jr. Coll.; **EDUC HONORS:** Phi Theta Kappa; **MIL SERV:** USN, Amn.; **OTHER ACT & HONORS:** Member, Masonic Lodge & Scottish Rite; Past Member, Nat. Apt. Mgmt. Accreditation Bd.; Past RE Instr., St. Petersburg Jr. Coll.; Past Sec. Chapt. 44, IREM as well as Comm. Chmn.; **HOME ADD:** RFD 5, Hanover Rd., Newtown, CT 06470, (203)426-5582; **BUS ADD:** 368 Center St., Southport, CT 06490, (203)254-1333.

MOORE, Harvin C., Jr.——B: Aug. 24, 1937, Houston, TX, *Pres.*, Village Devel., Inc.; **PRIM RE ACT:** Attorney, Developer, Builder, Owner/Investor, Property Manager; **SERVICES:** Land Devel., Project Devel.; **PREV EMPLOY:** Partner, Bracewell and Patterson, Attys. at Law, 1968-1974; **PROFL AFFIL & HONORS:** Houston Bar Assn., ABA; **EDUC:** BA, 1959, Liberal Arts, Ria Univ.; **GRAD EDUC:** LLB, 1963, Law, Univ. of TX; **HOME ADD:** 1912 Larchmont, Houston, TX 77019, (713)621-5248; **BUS ADD:** 7001 Corporate Dr., Suite 301, Houston, TX 77036, (713)777-0114.

MOORE, James C.——B: Aug. 27, 1949, Lubbock, TX, *Pres.*, James C. Moore Investments; **PRIM RE ACT:** Broker, Attorney, Developer, Builder, Owner/Investor; **OTHER RE ACT:** negotiations; raising equities; **PREV EMPLOY:** Atty.: Ross, Griggs & Harrison; Pres.: Northpark Corp.; Pres.: W. Houston Plaza Corp.; VP/Mktg.: Holmes Investments, Inc.; **PROFL AFFIL & HONORS:** Texas Bar Assn.; Houston Bar Assn.; Federal Bar; **EDUC:** BS, 1974, Hist. & Pol. Sci., Stephen F. Austin Univ.; **GRAD EDUC:** JD, 1977, Univ. of TX Law Sch.; **EDUC HONORS:** Grad. w/honors (Cum Laude), Chmn. of the honor council; Permanent Class Officer; **MIL SERV:** USAF, S. Sgt.; **HOME ADD:** 3623 Wildwood Ridge, Kingwood, TX 77339, (713)358-5021; **BUS ADD:** 3623 Wildwood Ridge, Kingwood, TX 77339, (713)358-9213.

MOORE, John F.——*Mgr. RE*, Reynolds Metals Co.; **PRIM RE ACT:** Property Manager; **BUS ADD:** Reynolds Metals Bldg., PO Box 27003, Richmond, VA 23261, (804)281-2000.*

MOORE, John J., III——B: Aug. 24, 1945, Medina, OH, *Dir.*, Cardinal Indus. of FL, Inc., Apt. Mgmt.; **PRIM RE ACT:** Instructor, Consultant, Appraiser, Property Manager; **SERVICES:** Investment counseling, Mgmt.; **REP CLIENTS:** Indiv. and investment partnerships and synd. in multifamily apt. devel.; **PREV EMPLOY:** Investment counseling and RE sales and appraisal; **PROFL AFFIL & HONORS:** IREM, NAA; **EDUC:** BS, 1969, Bus. Mgmt., Mktg., Bus. Admin., Ferris State Coll.; **GRAD EDUC:** GRI, 1976, Sinclair Coll.; **MIL SERV:** ASA, SP 5, 1969-71; **OTHER ACT & HONORS:** CPM; **HOME ADD:** 303 E. 19th St., Sanford, FL 32771, (305)323-3157; **BUS ADD:** P. O. Box U, Sanford, FL 32771, (305)323-3157.

MOORE, Judith S.——B: Sept. 24, 1946, Memphis, TN, *Dir. of Relocation Serv., Asst. Sales Mgr.*, Hokanson & Jenks, Inc.; **PRIM RE ACT:** Broker, Instructor, Consultant, Owner/Investor; **OTHER RE ACT:** Dir. of relocation, Corp. contact; **SERVICES:** Home finding, home mktg, corp. contact, RE mgmt., prop. mgmt.; **REP CLIENTS:** N. Trust Bank, Citibank Intl., Signature Fin. Mktg. Inc.; **PREV EMPLOY:** French, Spanish, and Eng. teacher, Sec. and Coll.; **PROFL AFFIL & HONORS:** Chicago, Assn. of Comm. and Ind., RELO, N. Shore Bd. of Realtors, Nat. Assn. of Realtors, Women in Intl. Trade, Nat. Mktg. Inst., Evanston C of C, GRI, Certified RE Brokerage Mgr.; **EDUC:** BA, 1968, French, Spanish, Secondary Ed, Peabody Coll. for Teachers, Nashville, TN; **GRAD EDUC:** Linguistics, Old Dominion Coll., Norfolk, VA; **EDUC HONORS:** Dean's List; **OTHER ACT & HONORS:** Cradle Society, P.E.O.; **HOME ADD:** 1135 Michigan, Evanston, IL 60202, (312)864-6259; **BUS ADD:** 513 Davis St, Evanston, IL 60201, (312)475-1617.

MOORE, L.H.——B: Apr. 3, 1939, Lynchburg, VA, *Pres.*, Moore & Co., RE Service; **PRIM RE ACT:** Broker, Consultant, Property Manager; **SERVICES:** Sales & leasing of comml. & indus. props., resid. & comml. prop. mgmt.; **REP CLIENTS:** Income prop. investors, small and large; **PREV EMPLOY:** 18 yrs. exper. in present fields of endeavor; **PROFL AFFIL & HONORS:** Nat. Assn. of Home Builders; Bd. of Realtors, Registered Apt. Mgr.; GRI; **EDUC:** 1958, VA Polytech. Inst.; 1961, Univ. of VA; **MIL SERV:** USMC, Pfc.; **OTHER ACT & HONORS:** Past Pres., Roanoke Valley Apt. Council; BPO Elks 197; **HOME TEL:** (703)982-2663; **BUS ADD:** 813 Franklin Rd., Suite 103, Roanoke, VA 24016, (703)343-8075.

MOORE, Mechlin D.——*Pres.*, Insurance Information Institute; **PRIM RE ACT:** Insuror; **BUS ADD:** 110 William St., New York, NY 10038, (212)233-7650.*

MOORE, R. Joseph——*Pres.*, Baltimore Fin. Corp.; **OTHER RE ACT:** Morg. Banker; **SERVICES:** Arrange const. & permanent fin.; **REP CLIENTS:** Devel. of office bldgs., indus. bldgs., shopping ctrs., office & indus. condos.; **PREV EMPLOY:** VP & Mgr. Imperial Bank, S.F. 1979-80; VP & Mgr. Union Bank-S.F. 1970-74; **PROFL AFFIL & HONORS:** Mort. Bankers Assn.; Bay Area Mort. Assn., Lic. RE Broker 1967; Lic., Gen. Contractor, 1974; **EDUC:** BS, 1965, Bus. & Indus. Mgmt., San Jose State; Cert. RE, 1968, Univ. of CA; **GRAD EDUC:** Grad. School of Mort. Banking, 1968, Northwestern Univ.; **OTHER ACT & HONORS:** St. Francis Yacht Club; **BUS ADD:** 44 Montgomery St. 515, San Francisco, CA 94104, (415)981-8062.

MOORE, Randall J.——B: July 3, 1943, Los Angeles, CA, *Regl. Mgr.*, Paramount Grp., Inc., W. Region; **PRIM RE ACT:** Broker, Property Manager, Owner/Investor; **SERVICES:** Mgr., Lease 2,500,000 square feet of Comml. Office Bldgs.; **PREV EMPLOY:** Coldwell Banker - 3 yrs., Prop. Mgr. Amer. Realty & Mgt. Co. - 8 yrs.; VP, Prop. Mgmt.; **PROFL AFFIL & HONORS:** BOMA-Dir. & First VP, Los Angeles, IREM & Los Angeles Headquarters City Assn., CPM, Candidate for RPA, Lic. CA RE Broker; **EDUC:** AA, 1966, Bus. Admin., Option in RE, CA State - Los Angeles; **MIL SERV:** CA National Guard, E-6 (Sgt.); **HOME ADD:** 5110 Greencrest Rd., La Canada, CA 91011, (213)790-6909; **BUS ADD:** 624 S. Grand Ave., Suite 1207, Los Angeles, CA 90017, (213)680-4222.

MOORE, Randolph G.——B: Feb. 12, 1939, Honolulu, HI, *Exec. VP*, Oceanic Props., Inc.; **PRIM RE ACT:** Developer, Builder; **EDUC:** BA, 1961, Math., Swarthmore Coll.; **GRAD EDUC:** MBA, 1963, Stanford Univ.; **HOME ADD:** 59-161 Ke Nui Rd., Haleiwa, HI 96712, (808)638-7098; **BUS ADD:** 130 Merchant St., Honolulu, HI 96813, (808)548-4811.

MOORE, Richard D.——B: Nov. 20, 1946, Des Moines, IA, *Pres.*, Vanguard Commercial Managers, Inc.; **PRIM RE ACT:** Broker, Developer, Owner/Investor, Property Manager, Syndicator; **SERVICES:** Land synds., devel., comml. investment synds., brokerage & prop. mgmt.; **REP CLIENTS:** Indiv. investors, joint venture partners; **PREV EMPLOY:** Coldwell Banker Prop. Mgmt. Co., Lincoln Prop. Co., Horizon Corp.; **PROFL AFFIL & HONORS:** IREM, BOMA, CPM; **EDUC:** BS, 1972, Fin., Mktg., N. AZ Univ.; **OTHER ACT & HONORS:** Past Pres. BOMA; **HOME ADD:** 6236 N 16th St. 5, Phoenix, AZ 85016, (602)266-8468; **BUS ADD:** 3014 N Hayden Rd. 109, Scottsdale, AZ 85251, (602)994-1920.

MOORE, Terry——B: Nov. 5, 1935, *COB*, Hathaway, Moore and Assoc.; **PRIM RE ACT:** Consultant, Appraiser, Developer, Property Manager, Syndicator; **OTHER RE ACT:** Comml. & Indus. Sales and Exchanging; **PREV EMPLOY:** GM Corp.; **PROFL AFFIL & HONORS:** NAR Little Rock-N. Little Rock Bd. of Realtors, CCIM; **EDUC:** BS, 1957, Geology, Millsaps Coll.; **HOME ADD:** 4 Wingfield Cr., Little Rock, AR 72205, (501)372-1700; **BUS ADD:** 1210 Worthen Bldg., Little Rock, AR 72205, (501)372-1700.

MOORE, Walter——*RE Dept.*, Tosco Corp.; **PRIM RE ACT:** Property Manager; **BUS ADD:** 10100 Santa Monica Blvd., Ste. 1700, Los Angeles, CA 90067, (213)552-7000.*

MOORE, William C.——B: Nov. 23, 1906, New Rochelle, NY, *Pres.*, International Community Development Assocs.; **PRIM RE ACT:** Attorney, Developer, Owner/Investor; **SERVICES:** Assembling devels. both in US and abroad; **REP CLIENTS:** MD Vestar Inc., Federation of Karnataka C of C and Indus. (M V Krishna Murthy) Bangalore, India; **PREV EMPLOY:** VA Homes (Prefabricated houses) Pres. 1946-55, employed by various housing agencies of US Govt. including resettlement admin. 1930's; **PROFL AFFIL & HONORS:** The D.C. Bar; Soc. For Gen. Systems Research; Gen. Counsel of the World Future Soc. World Peace Through Law Center, Inter-Amer. Bar Assn., Amer. Assn. for the Advancement of Sci.; **EDUC:** BA, 1928, Hist., Yale Univ.; **GRAD EDUC:** JD, 1931, Harvard Univ.; **EDUC HONORS:** Cum laude; Hist. honors; **MIL SERV:** US Army, Pvt. 1st Class; **OTHER ACT & HONORS:** Div. Dir. of Dept. of State, Lend-lease Admin. 1940-46, Reg. Dir. Resettlement Admin. 1934-37 Building new towns govt. acquisition of 4,000,000 Acres; **HOME ADD:** 1434 Kennedy St. NW, Washington, DC 20011; **BUS ADD:** 1819 H St. NW, Washington, DC 20006, (202)293-1456.

MOORE, William J.——B: Aug. 31, 1920, Philadelphia, PA, *Sr. VP*, Fidelity Bond and Mortgage Co.; **OTHER RE ACT:** Mort. banking, resid. and comml., ground devel.; **SERVICES:** Mort. servicing, comml. & resid. mort. origination; **REP CLIENTS:** Instnl. investors, Ins. Cos., Pension Funds, FNMA & GNMA; **PREV EMPLOY:** Prudential Ins. Co. RE & Mort. Investment; **PROFL AFFIL & HONORS:** Mort. Bankers Assn.; **EDUC:** Univ. of PA, 1942, Acctg. and RE, Amer. Soc. of Appr., PA RE Inst.; **MIL SERV:** USAF, 1942-46, Unit Citations, Pacific Medal; **OTHER ACT & HONORS:** Veterans of For. Wars, Knights of Columbus; **HOME ADD:** 11 Purnell Ave., Cinnaminson, NJ 08077, (609)829-7426; **BUS ADD:** SECor. 16th & Walnut Sts., Philadelphia, PA 19102, (215)893-8663.

MOPPERT, Edward J.——B: Nov. 9, 1921, Camden, NJ, *Partner*, Hoffman, Moppert & Angel; **PRIM RE ACT:** Attorney, Owner/Investor, Instructor; **SERVICES:** Closing atty., title examiner, zoning counsel; **REP CLIENTS:** Homequity Inc., Interstate Indus. Parks, Northfield Indus. Park, Lohrman Medical Clinic, PF Realty, Roach-Thomas Realtors, Approved Counsel with All Title Cos. to Exam. Title; **PREV EMPLOY:** Former Cty. Zoning & Counsel; **PROFL AFFIL & HONORS:** Phi Delta Thi; **EDUC:** AB, 1946, Poli. Sci., Duke Univ.; **GRAD EDUC:** JD, 1949, RE & Labor Law, Duke Univ.; **MIL SERV:** US Army Air Force, 1st Lt., 1942-1945 Prisoner of War in Europe, Purple Heart; **HOME ADD:** 13211 Liberty Mills Rd., Fort Wayne, IN 46804, (219)672-2988; **BUS ADD:** 1212 Anthony Wayne Bank Bldg., Fort Wayne, IN 46802, (219)423-3331.

MORAN, Harold J.——B: Feb. 21, 1907, New York, NY, *Sr. Atty, (Ret.)*, Dept. of Law, State of NY, Real Prop. Bur., 1957-77; **OTHER RE ACT:** Title examination and related duties US & Puerto Rican Mort. Loan examiner for Cadwalder, Wickersham & Taft, Esqs., also for 9th Fed. S&L Assn.; **SERVICES:** Examine & approve VA guaranteed & FHA ins. indiv. home loan mort. as independent contractor from 1952 (Cadwalder), from 1971 (9th Fed.); **REP CLIENTS:** State of NY, Cadwalder, Wickersham & Taft, 9th Fed. Provided legal services in State's eminent domain program and other of its acquisitions of RE for public use; **PREV EMPLOY:** Title examiner, Title Guarantee & Tr. Co., 1945-48; Title closer City Title Co., Law Instr. St. John's Univ. Sch. of Commerce, 1956-57, Private law practice from 1934; **PROFL AFFIL & HONORS:** ABA, Past Member Condemnation Law Comm., Amer. Judicature Soc., NY Cty. Lawyers Assn., Past member Membership Comm. Nassau Cty. Bar Assn.; **EDUC:** AB, 1928, Lib. Arts., Holy Cross Coll.; **GRAD EDUC:** LLB, 1932, Fordham Univ. Sch. of Law; JD, 1968; **EDUC HONORS:** Cum Laude; **MIL SERV:** USA, Headquarters 4th Army, Tec 5th Grade; **OTHER ACT & HONORS:** Spec. Deputy Atty. Gen (Election Frauds, NY State), 1973; Amer. Assn. of Retired Persons, Boynton-Leisureville Chapt. 3190, 1st VP 1981; Knight of the Holy Sepulchre 1966; Listed in Who's Who in the East, Who's Who in S. & SW; Who's Who in Fin. & Indus., Who's Who in the World, Appt. Disbursing Agent in Bankruptcy by US Dist. Ct., So. Dist. of NY, 1978; **HOME ADD:** 1509 Alfred Dr., Boynton Beach, FL 33435, (305)734-3205; **BUS ADD:** 277 Hempstead Ave., Malverne, NY 11565, (516)599-5818.

MORAN, John F., Jr.——B: Sept. 8, 1945, New York, NY, *Project Mgr.*, Erikietian Constr. Corp., Almist, Inc.; **PRIM RE ACT:** Developer, Builder; **SERVICES:** Condo devel.; **PREV EMPLOY:** VP Watergate Const. Corp., Alexandria, VA; **PROFL AFFIL & HONORS:** Comm. Assn. Inst.; **MIL SERV:** USMC; Cpl.; **HOME ADD:** 117 E Maple St., Alexandria, VA 22313, (703)548-1325; **BUS ADD:** 2801 Park Ctr. Dr., Suite 201, Alexandria, VA 22313, (703)671-4400.

MORAN, John J.——B: June 4, 1951, Indianapolis, IN, *VP/Gen. Mgr.*, Vantage Co., Vantage Props., Inc.; **PRIM RE ACT:** Developer; **SERVICES:** Comml. & indus. devel.; **REP CLIENTS:** Maj. of the *Fortune* 500 Cos.; **PREV EMPLOY:** RE Broker, F.C. Tucker Co.; Dir. of Mktg., Park 50 TechneCenter; **PROFL AFFIL & HONORS:** Nat. Assn. of Indus. and Office Parks; NAR; Sales & Marketing Execs.; **EDUC:** BS, 1975, Mgmt., IN Univ. School of Bus.; **OTHER ACT & HONORS:** Sigma Alpha Epsilon; Knights of Columbus; **HOME ADD:** 1128 White Pine Ct., Cincinnati, OH 45230, (513)474-4963; **BUS ADD:** 37 Triangle Park Dr., Cincinnati, OH 45246, (513)772-9200.

MORAN, John P.——B: July 29, 1929, Scranton, PA, *Pres.*, Lewis C. Bowers & Sons; **PRIM RE ACT:** Architect, Developer, Builder, Property Manager, Engineer; **SERVICES:** Devel., ownership and mgmt. of indus. and office bldgs.; **REP CLIENTS:** Princeton, NJ; **PREV EMPLOY:** Princeton, Univ.; **EDUC:** BS, 1951, Engrg., Princeton Univ.; **GRAD EDUC:** Attended Columbia Univ.; **MIL SERV:** USN; Officer; **OTHER ACT & HONORS:** Chmn. of the Mercer Cty. Planning Bd., Founding Pres. of the Middlesex-Somerset-Mercer Regional Planning Council; **HOME ADD:** 207 Laurel Cir., Princeton, NJ 08540, (609)921-6900; **BUS ADD:** 341 Nassau St., Princeton, NJ 08540, (609)921-6900.

MORAN, Thomas L.——B: Apr. 26, 1923, IA, *Pres.*, National Auctioneers, Inc.; National, Inc., Realtors; **PRIM RE ACT:** Broker, Consultant, Appraiser, Developer, Builder, Owner/Investor, Property Manager, Syndicator; **SERVICES:** Complete RE brokerage, builder of office bldgs. and small shopping ctrs.; **REP CLIENTS:** Many European clients; **PREV EMPLOY:** Always self-employed; **OTHER ACT & HONORS:** TX Auctioneers Assn., Nat. Auctioneers Assn., Amarillo Bd. of Realtors, Nat. Bd. of Realtors; **HOME ADD:** 2813 James Louis Dr., Amarillo, TX 79110, (806)352-7352; **BUS ADD:** Suite 704, TX Commerce Bank Bldg., Amarillo, TX 79109, (806)355-9415.

MORAZAN, Nancy G.——B: June 2, 1944, Stuttgart, AR, *Asst. VP*, Ambank Mort. Co.; **PRIM RE ACT:** Banker, Lender; **OTHER RE ACT:** Mort. banker; **SERVICES:** Ambank Mort. Co. provides both const. and permanent fin. for single-family, multi-family housing and comml. builders, devels. and indivs.; **PROFL AFFIL & HONORS:** Baton Rouge Mort. Bankers Assn.; LA Mort. Bankers Assn., 1978 Chairperson, Baton Rouge Young Mort. Bankers Comm.; 1979 LA State Chairperson, Young Mort. Bankers Comm.; 1980 Treas. 1981 VP, 1982-Pres., Baton Rouge Mort. Bankers Assn.; **EDUC:** Acctg./Bus., LA State Univ.; **HOME ADD:** 2246 Gen. Taylor Ave., Baton Rouge, LA 70808, (504)769-4142; **BUS ADD:** One Amer. Place, Baton Rouge, LA 70825, (504)346-6082.

MORDECAI, Charles F.——B: Jan. 5, 1920, San Francisco, CA, *Owner*, Charles F. Mordecai; **PRIM RE ACT:** Broker, Consultant, Builder, Property Manager, Owner/Investor; **OTHER RE ACT:** Gen. Bldg. Contractor (B-1); Solar Contractor (C44); **SERVICES:** Gen. Constr., Comml. & Resid. Remodel.; **PREV EMPLOY:** 5 yrs. Broker, 10 yrs. Carpentry (Journeyman & Foreman), 1 yr. Const. Material Sales; **HOME ADD:** 2440 Gower St., Los Angeles, CA 90068; **BUS ADD:** 2440 Gower St., Los Angeles, CA 90068, (213)465-4025.

MOREHOUSE, Leo A., Jr.——B: Mar. 10, 1945, Boston, MA, *Reg. VP*, Fairfield Communities, Inc., Central Region; **PRIM RE ACT:** Developer, Builder, Owner/Investor, Property Manager; **SERVICES:** Devel. & Mgmt./Large Scale Devels.; **PREV EMPLOY:** Gen. Mgr. Harert Equitable Joint Venture (Riverchase) Birmingham, AL; **EDUC:** BS, 1966, Engrg., US Coast Guard Academy; **GRAD EDUC:**

MBA, 1973, Fin., Harvard Bus. School; **MIL SERV:** USCG, LCDR; **HOME ADD:** P.O. Box 1596, Fairfield Glade, TN 38555, (615)484-0027; **BUS ADD:** P.O. Box 1500, Crossville, TN 38555, (615)484-7521.

MORELLI, Fred F.——**B:** Feb. 6, 1921, Trenton, NJ, *Prop. Mgmt. Rep. & Staff Appraiser*, Vet. Admin., Loan & Guaranty; **PRIM RE ACT:** Consultant, Appraiser, Developer, Lender, Regulator, Property Manager, Insuror; **PREV EMPLOY:** NJ Dept. of Transportation, Right of Way Div.; **PROFL AFFIL & HONORS:** SRA; NJ Lic. RE Broker; **EDUC:** BS, 1960, Bus. Admin./RE Appraising, Trenton State, Rider Coll, Farleigh Dickinson; **MIL SERV:** USAAF; Sgt.; ETO; **HOME ADD:** 139 Beech Ave., Trenton, NJ 08610, (609)888-2067; **BUS ADD:** 20 Washington Pl., Newark, NJ 07102, (201)645-6687.

MORELLI, Michael——**B:** June 4, 1935, Italy, *Pres.*, Morelli Investment Co.; **PRIM RE ACT:** Builder, Owner/Investor, Property Manager; **OTHER RE ACT:** Renovations; **SERVICES:** Investments in resid. & comml. props.; **REP CLIENTS:** Indiv. investors & self; **PREV EMPLOY:** US Govt., until 1979; **EDUC:** BA, 1960, Econ., Brooklyn Coll., Brooklyn, NY; **MIL SERV:** USA, PFC; **HOME ADD:** 1306 Woodside Pkwy., Silver Spring, MD 20910, (301)565-0946; **BUS ADD:** 1306 Woodside Pkwy, Silver Spring, MD 20910, (301)565-0946.

MOREY, Emil J.——**B:** Apr. 26, 1923, Danbury, CT, *Pres.*, Morey Associates, Inc. Realtors; **PRIM RE ACT:** Broker, Consultant, Appraiser, Instructor, Syndicator; **SERVICES:** Firm maintains two divs., comml. indusl. and gen. resid. brokerage; **PROFL AFFIL & HONORS:** Greater Danbury Bd. of Realtors, CT Assn., of Realtors, NAR, VChmn. 1981 of urban econ. studies Danbury C of C, Member of Advisory Comm. Ctr. for RE & urban econ. studies at Univ. of CT; **MIL SERV:** USAF, 1946; **OTHER ACT & HONORS:** 1973, CT Realtor of the Year Award, 1976 Pres. CT Assn. of Realtors, Dir. NAR; **HOME ADD:** 12 Fairview Ave., Danbury, CT 06810, (203)743-0909; **BUS ADD:** Lower South st., Danbury, CT 06810, (203)792-0000.

MORFORD, Ted——**B:** Sept. 17, 1928, Nashville, TN, *VP and Rgnl. Mgr.*, Marvin F. Poer and Co., E. Rgn.; **OTHER RE ACT:** Property Tax Consultant, Real Estate Appraiser; **SERVICES:** Designing and implementing a competent ad valorem tax program; **REP CLIENTS:** Leonard Farber Co.-Nat. Corp. for housing, partnerships, Chase Manhattan Bank, United VA Bankshares, Servico Inc., Roses Stores, etc.; **PREV EMPLOY:** Prop. tax mgr., S. territory; Sears Roebuck and Co.; Asst. City Tax Assessor; Nashville, TN; **PROFL AFFIL & HONORS:** Inst. of Prop. Taxation; Intl. Assn. of Assessing Officers-Various State Assessors Orgs., CAE of IAAO, CMI of Inst.Prop. Tax, Cert. Assessment evaluator, Cert. member of the inst.; **EDUC:** BA, 1951, Hist. & Psych., Vanderbilt Univ.; **GRAD EDUC:** LLB, 1958, Law, Nashville Night Law School; **EDUC HONORS:** Outstanding Moot Court Award; **MIL SERV:** USA-Corps. of Engrs., Capt., Korean Serv. Medal (2 combat clusters) Sygman Rhee Unit Citation; **OTHER ACT & HONORS:** Atlanta Apt. Owners & Mgrs. Assn.; Pres. Assn. Council-Member Bd. of Dir. and Exec. Bd.; **HOME ADD:** 2867 Thornbriar Rd. NE, Atlanta, GA 30340, (404)491-0104; **BUS ADD:** 588-2200 Century Pkwy., Atlanta, GA 30345, (404)321-6817.

MORGA, William E.——**B:** Nov. 21, 1933, Dickson, AR, *Atty. at Law*; **PRIM RE ACT:** Attorney; **REP CLIENTS:** Monsanto Devel. Corp., Herrist Devel. Corp.; **PREV EMPLOY:** Engr.; **PROFL AFFIL & HONORS:** ABA, MCBA, SBA, IEEE, Sigma Xi, Kappa Ku Epsilon, Tau Sigma; **EDUC:** BSEE & Math, 1961, Engrg. & Math, CA State; **GRAD EDUC:** MSEE & JD, 1964 & 1976, Engrg. & Law, Moore School of Engrg. & Fordham Law School; **EDUC HONORS:** Tau Sigma, Kappa Nu Epsilon, IEEE, Sigma Xi; **MIL SERV:** US Army; **OTHER ACT & HONORS:** IEEE, Boy Scouts, PADI, YNCI, Church; **HOME ADD:** 6512 E. Turquoise Ave., Scottsdale, AZ 85253, (602)991-4043; **BUS ADD:** Suite 1-E, 8100 E. Indian School Rd., Scottsdale, AZ 85251, (602)949-8885.

MORGAN, Barbara A.——**B:** Dec. 27, 1937, Owenton, KY, *Owner-Broker*, Century 21/Barbara Morgan RE, Inc.; **PRIM RE ACT:** Broker, Consultant, Owner/Investor, Property Manager; **OTHER RE ACT:** Comm. Investments; **SERVICES:** Resid., Comml., Consultant, Prop. Mgmt.; **PROFL AFFIL & HONORS:** National Association of Realtors, KY Assn. of Realtors, Lexington Bd. of Realtors, Women's Council, GRI, CRS; **OTHER ACT & HONORS:** Instructor, Lexington Technical Inst. in Commercial Investment; President, Bluegrass RE Exchangors; Past President Women's Council; Past Secretary, Lexington Bd. of Realtors; **HOME ADD:** 703 Bullock Place, Lexington, KY 40508, (606)255-4597; **BUS ADD:** 139 Walton Ave., Lexington, KY 40508, (606)252-1781.

MORGAN, Charles A.——**B:** March 14, 1950, Evansville, IN, *Atty. at Law*, Smith, Stroud, McClerkin, Dunn & Nutter; **PRIM RE ACT:** Consultant, Attorney; **SERVICES:** Examination of title, preparation of instruments and closing of sales and loans; **REP CLIENTS:** The State First National Bank of Texarkana; Texana Savings & Loan Assn.; **PROFL AFFIL & HONORS:** Amer. Coll. of Mort. Atty., Inc., Bd. of Dir. of Attys.' Title Guaranty Fund, Inc., Natural Resources Sect., and Real Prop. Comm. for AR Bar Assn.; **EDUC:** BBA, 1973, Baylor Univ.; **GRAD EDUC:** JD, 1973, Baylor Univ.; **HOME ADD:** 17 Clay Ave., Texarkana, TX 75503, (214)832-1093; **BUS ADD:** Suite Six, State Line Plaza, Texarkana, AR 75502, (501)773-5651.

MORGAN, Douglas——*Dir. Engr.*, Rorer Group; **PRIM RE ACT:** Property Manager; **BUS ADD:** 500 Virginia Drive, Fort Washington, PA 19034, (215)628-6000.*

MORGAN, Douglas A.——**B:** Aug. 7, 1950, Los Angeles, CA, *CPA*, Arthur Young & Co.; **OTHER RE ACT:** CPA; **SERVICES:** Fin. analysis, project consultation; **REP CLIENTS:** Tomar, Inc., Robert Klein II; **PROFL AFFIL & HONORS:** AI of CPA's, CA Soc. of CPA's; **EDUC:** BS, 1976, Acctg., CA State Univ., Long Beach; **EDUC HONORS:** Presi. List; Dean's List; Cum Laude; **MIL SERV:** USAF, S/Sgt.; **HOME ADD:** 8193 N. San Pablo, Fresno, CA 93711, (209)431-8252; **BUS ADD:** 2030 Fresno St., Fresno, CA 93721, (209)486-8660.

MORGAN, G. Edward——**B:** Oct. 29, 1931, Ipswich, MA, *Controller*, Williamson Cadillas, Treas.; **PRIM RE ACT:** Owner/Investor; **OTHER RE ACT:** Accountant; **SERVICES:** Acctg., auditing, taxes; **PROFL AFFIL & HONORS:** Nat. Assn. of Accountants; **EDUC:** BBA, 1962, acctg., fin., Univ. of Miami, Coral Gables; **EDUC HONORS:** Delta Sigma pi, profl. bus., life member; **MIL SERV:** USAF, S/Sgt., Korean Serv.; **OTHER ACT & HONORS:** Lutheran Church Deacon and Ex Council Member. Masonic lodge, Scottish Rite, Mahi Shrine; **HOME ADD:** 7635 SW 99th Ct., Miami, FL 33173, (305)271-1730; **BUS ADD:** 7250 N. Kendall Dr., Miami, FL 33156, (305)666-1901.

MORGAN, Jack C., Jr.——**B:** Aug. 4, 1948, Palmerton, PA, *Pres.*, J.C. Morgan Co.; **PRIM RE ACT:** Appraiser; **SERVICES:** Comml./Indus. Appraising, Consulting, Feasibility Studies; **REP CLIENTS:** Transportation Depts., Utility Cos., Private Investment Cos., Lending Instns., etc.; **PROFL AFFIL & HONORS:** AIREA, MAI, Realtor of the Yr. 1976 & 1978 (Fairmont, WV); **EDUC:** BA, 1971, Econ., Bethany Coll., WV; **OTHER ACT & HONORS:** C of C; **HOME ADD:** 3600 Broadfield Rd., Charlotte, NC 28211, (704)542-8264; **BUS ADD:** 2320 First Union Plaza, Charlotte, NC 28282, (704)333-3147.

MORGAN, Michael H.——**B:** Feb. 27, 1931, London, England, *Sr. VP & Gen. Mgr.*, Morguard Properties Limited, Portfolio Mgmt.; **OTHER RE ACT:** Portfolio Mgmt.; **PREV EMPLOY:** VP MEPC Canadian Prop. Limited, Toronto, Can; **PROFL AFFIL & HONORS:** FRICS (Fellow Royal Instit. Chartered Surveyors; FRI (Fellow Realtors Instit., Can.) OLE (Ontario Land Economist), FRICS, FRI, OLE; **MIL SERV:** British Army, Lt.; **HOME ADD:** 14 Forest Glen Cres., Toronto, Can., (416)487-7223; **BUS ADD:** 1027 Yonge St., Toronto, Can., (416)964-2811.

MORGAN, Norman R.——**B:** Nov. 23, 1923, St. Louis, MO, *Pres.*, Morgan Enterprises, Inc., Morgan Enterprises Realtors; **PRIM RE ACT:** Broker, Consultant, Appraiser, Developer, Builder, Owner/Investor, Property Manager, Syndicator; **OTHER RE ACT:** Land use planning - site design; **SERVICES:** Governmental Process Work; **REP CLIENTS:** Public & private cities, state, cty. districts; private devels., bldrs., etc.; **PREV EMPLOY:** Private Business Union Oil Co. Distributor 1950-1974; **PROFL AFFIL & HONORS:** Associate Member Amer. Soc. of Re Appraisers; **EDUC:** BS, 1950, Indus. Admin., OR State Univ.; **EDUC HONORS:** Scabord & Blade Military Science; **MIL SERV:** USA 1943-1949, 2nd Lt., Unit Citation, USAF 1948-1953; **OTHER ACT & HONORS:** School Bd. Chmn. 14 Years Total; Lions Club past Pres.; Distinguished Service Award; Junior C of C; Outstanding Comm. Serv.; **HOME ADD:** 495 Carlson Dr., Lebanon, OR 97355, (503)258-5894; **BUS ADD:** 2500 S Main, Lebanon, OR 97355, (503)451-1010.

MORGAN, Travis C.——**B:** Sept. 9, 1929, New Boston, TX, *VP and Sr. Mort. Off.*, Business Men's Assurance Co. of America, Investment Dept.; **PRIM RE ACT:** Lender; **PROFL AFFIL & HONORS:** MBAA, MBA, Greater Kansas City C of C; **EDUC:** BBA, 1952, TX A&M Univ.; **MIL SERV:** USAF, 1st Lt.; **OTHER ACT & HONORS:** Bd. of Dir. Bus. Men's Assurance Co. of America; **HOME ADD:** 14500 W. 79 St., Lenexa, KS 66215, (913)888-0232; **BUS ADD:** PO Box 458, One Penn Valley Park, Kansas City, MO 64108, (816)753-8000.

MORGAN, William T., Jr.——**B:** Nov. 12, 1913, Chicago, IL, *Dir. of RE*, The Terson Company, Inc.; **PRIM RE ACT:** Broker, Consultant, Attorney, Property Manager; **PREV EMPLOY:** Marriott Corp., Consolidated Foods Corp.; **EDUC:** BSL, 1935, Northwestern Univ. School of Law; **GRAD EDUC:** LLD, 1937; **MIL SERV:** Navy,

1942-45, Lt.; **HOME ADD:** 1251 Alvin Ct., Glenview, IL 60025, (312)724-0308; **BUS ADD:** 1251 Alvin Ct., Glenview, IL 60025, (312)724-0308.

MORGANO, Del——**B:** June 5, 1914, Pullman, MI, *Mgr., Facility Planning*, UARCO Inc., Corp. Office; **OTHER RE ACT:** Site Searcher for new facilities; **PREV EMPLOY:** 50 yrs. with UARCO in many capacities; **OTHER ACT & HONORS:** Past Pres. Paris TX Rotary Club; **HOME ADD:** 1516 Churchill Rd., Shaumburg, IL 60195, (312)882-8252; **BUS ADD:** W County Line Rd., Barrington, IL 60010, (312)381-7000.

MORGANSTERN, Gerald H.——**B:** Dec. 19, 1942, New York, NY, *Atty. (Partner)*, Hofheimer Gartlir Gottlieb & Gross; **PRIM RE ACT:** Attorney; **SERVICES:** sales & acquisitions, comml. leasing; **PROFL AFFIL & HONORS:** ABA, NYS Bar Assn., Bar Assn. of City of New York; **EDUC:** BS, 1963, Acctg., Wharton Sch. of the Univ. of PA; **GRAD EDUC:** LLB, 1966, Columbia Univ. Law Sch.; **EDUC HONORS:** Dean's List; **OTHER ACT & HONORS:** Dep. Police Commr., 1979-80; Treas. 1980 to present Village of Hewlett Harbor, Pres. & Bd. of Tr. of the Bridge Inc.; **HOME ADD:** 207 Richards Lane, Hewlett Harbor, NY 11557; **BUS ADD:** 469 Fifth Ave., New York, NY 10017, (212)725-0400.

MORGENSTERN, Arthur B.——**B:** Dec. 19, 1939, Philadelphia, PA, *Gen. Counsel*, Strouse, Greenburg and Co.; **PRIM RE ACT:** Consultant, Attorney, Developer, Owner/Investor, Syndicator; **EDUC:** BS, 1961, Liberal Arts; **GRAD EDUC:** 1964, Villanova Law School; **EDUC HONORS:** Editor, Law Review; **HOME ADD:** 443 Clairemont Rd., Villanova, PA 19085; **BUS ADD:** 1626 Locust St., Philadelphia, PA 19103, (215)985-1100.

MORHOUSE, Sanford W.——**B:** Dec. 13, 1944, Keene Valley, NY, *Partner*, Dewey, Ballantine, Bushby, Palmer & Wood; **PRIM RE ACT:** Attorney; **REP CLIENTS:** Instit. lenders, investors; **PROFL AFFIL & HONORS:** ABA; NY State Bar Assn.; Assn. of the Bar of the City of New York; **EDUC:** BA, 1966, Liberal Arts, Williams Coll.; **GRAD EDUC:** JD, 1969, Columbia Univ. Law School; **EDUC HONORS:** Honors in Hist.; **HOME ADD:** 22 Edgewood Rd., Summit, NJ 07901, (201)273-5189; **BUS ADD:** 140 Broadway, New York, NY 10005, (212)820-1750.

MORI, Dean——**B:** Nov. 2, 1908, PA, *Broker, Pres.*, Rostraver Realty Co.; **PRIM RE ACT:** Broker; **SERVICES:** All RE sales, appraisals, home bldg., land devel.; **PREV EMPLOY:** Self employed since 1932; **PROFL AFFIL & HONORS:** Monongahela Valley Bd. of Realtors, Mon Valley Homebuilders, PA Assn. of Realtors, NAR, Realtor; **HOME ADD:** RD 5, Box 247, Belle Vernon, PA 15012, (412)929-8373; **BUS ADD:** Route 201, Belle Vernon, PA 15012, (412)929-8866.

MORIARTY, John L.——**B:** Feb. 7, 1948, Boston, MA, *Senior RE Investment Officer*, Columbia Univ., Office of Investments; **PRIM RE ACT:** Lender; **PREV EMPLOY:** Tchrs. Insurance and Annuity Assn.; **PROFL AFFIL & HONORS:** Young Mort. Bankers Assn.; **EDUC:** BA, 1970, Econ., Fairfield Univ.; **GRAD EDUC:** MBA, 1977, Fin., St. Johns Univ.; **BUS ADD:** 225 Broadway, New York, NY 10007, (212)227-3300.

MORINER, Robert H.——**B:** Aug. 5, 1940, Sharon, PA, *Asst. Counsel*, Sheraton Corp., Legal Dept.; **OTHER RE ACT:** Rep. of major RE devel. in FL; RE; Corporate; **PREV EMPLOY:** ITT Community Devel. Corp.; Private Practice, 1969-1977, Representation of RE Developers; **PROFL AFFIL & HONORS:** FL Bar; MA Bar; **EDUC:** BA, 1962, Pol. Sci., FL State Univ.; **GRAD EDUC:** JD, 1964, Law, Univ. of FL; **MIL SERV:** USMCR, E-4; **OTHER ACT & HONORS:** Asst. State Atty., FL; Lecturer - FL Bar Continuing Legal Educ. - Subject: Complex RE Transactions; **HOME ADD:** 28 Squirrel Hill Rd., Acton, MA 01720, (617)263-6490; **BUS ADD:** 60 State St., Boston, MA 02109, (617)367-3600.

MORINI, Guillermo R.——*Pres.*, Morini Realty, Inc.; **PRIM RE ACT:** Engineer; **OTHER RE ACT:** Realtor; **SERVICES:** Marketability, plans revision, financing remodeling, sales, advertising and promotional counseling, mort. transmittals, closings, coordination with co-owners assn.; **REP CLIENTS:** Most of the principal devel. and banks; **PROFL AFFIL & HONORS:** San Juan Bd. of Realtors, NAR of PR, Nat. Assn. of Home Bldrs., Home Bldrs. Assn., C of C of PR, SME, Assn. Interamer. de Hombres de Empresa, Assn. Pro-Libre Empresa de PR; **EDUC:** Engrg., Agriculture, Bus. Admin., Appraising, Univ. of Havana- Univ. of DE, Univ. of PR; **HOME ADD:** Tulipan 212 S.F., Rio Piedras, PR 00927; **BUS ADD:** Tulipan 212 San Francisco, Rio Piedras, PR 00927.

MORISSETTE, Mimi——**B:** Nov. 6, 1944, Minneapolis, MN, *Broker, Pres.*, Access Grp., Inc.; **PRIM RE ACT:** Broker, Syndicator, Consultant, Developer, Property Manager, Owner/Investor; **SERVICES:** Land devel., synd., consulting, natl. acquisitions & sales, member New Amer. Pension Fund Network; **REP CLIENTS:** Affiliate offices in New York, Vancouver, London, Seattle & LA; **PREV EMPLOY:** 13 yrs. self; **PROFL AFFIL & HONORS:** RNMI, Campbell Trophy, Comm Transaction of Yr. 1980; CCIM; **EDUC:** 1967, Speech & Eng., OR State Univ.; **HOME ADD:** 3210 SW Dosch Rd., Portland, OR 97201, (503)295-2121; **BUS ADD:** 714 SW 20th Place, Ste. E, Portland, OR 97205.

MORK, G.T.——**B:** June 20, 1943, Minneapolis, MN, *VP*, The First Group of Investment Cos., First Equity Corp.; **PRIM RE ACT:** Lender, Owner/Investor; **SERVICES:** Instnl. equity placement servs.; **REP CLIENTS:** Instnl. investors; **PREV EMPLOY:** Kidder Peabody & Co. ,Inc.; **PROFL AFFIL & HONORS:** ULI, RESSI, Nat. Assn. Office & Indus. Parks, NAIOP Instr.; **EDUC:** BS, 1967, Econ., Fordham Univ.; **GRAD EDUC:** MS, Econ., Fordham Univ. Grad. arts & sci.; **HOME ADD:** 210 W. Grant St., Suite 409, Minneapolis, MN 55403, (612)332-5741; **BUS ADD:** 200 Third Ave. No., Minneapolis, MN 55401, (612)333-3638.

MORLEY, Nicholas H.——**B:** July 11, 1929, Sofia, Bulgaria, *Chmn. of the Bd.*, Interterra, Inc.; **PRIM RE ACT:** Developer; **OTHER RE ACT:** Intl. sales, land banking; **PROFL AFFIL & HONORS:** Who's Who in Amer.; Who's Who in Amer. Politics; **MIL SERV:** Israeli Commandos; **OTHER ACT & HONORS:** FL Repulican Party; 200 Club of Miami; Member, SBA Nat. Advisory Council; Pres. Elector 1980; Former Fin. Chmn., FL Republican, 1980-81; Nat. Conf. Christians and Jews and Member, Metropolitan Dade Cty. Charter Review Commn.; **HOME ADD:** 1420 S. Bayshore Dr., Miami, FL 33145; **BUS ADD:** PO Box 450249, Miami, FL 33145, (305)751-9898.

MORPHEW, Ronald R.——*Pres.*, Federal Home Loan Bank of Indianapolis; **PRIM RE ACT:** Banker; **BUS ADD:** 2900 Indiana Tower, One Indiana Square, Indianapolis, IN 46204, (317)269-5200.*

MORREALE, John M.——**B:** Sept. 4, 1941, Middletown, NY, *Owner*, John M. Morreale-Real Estate; **PRIM RE ACT:** Broker; **SERVICES:** Primary Emphasis on Sale of Props. Suitable for Thoroughbred Horse Breeding Farms; **PROFL AFFIL & HONORS:** Orange Cty., NY Bd. of Realtors, Multiple Listing Serv. of the Orange Cty. Bd. of Realtors; **EDUC:** AA, 1970, Psych., St. Petersburg Jr. Coll.; **EDUC HONORS:** Dean's List; **MIL SERV:** USN, Leading Seaman; **OTHER ACT & HONORS:** Mamakating Conservation Club; Otterkill Golf and Country Club; **HOME ADD:** 105 Sproat St., Middletown, NY 10940, (914)343-4344; **BUS ADD:** 23 South St., Middletown, NY 10940, (914)343-1188.

MORRICE, Bruce A.——**B:** Sept. 26, 1933, MI, *Pres.*, Morrice Financial Corp.; **PRIM RE ACT:** Consultant, Banker, Syndicator; **SERVICES:** Equity and debt fin.; **REP CLIENTS:** Penison Funds, Ins. Co.; **PREV EMPLOY:** Ford Motor Credit; Amer., Nat. and Equitable Life; **PROFL AFFIL & HONORS:** MAI; **EDUC:** BA, MI State Univ.; **BUS ADD:** 920 Two Turtle Creek, Dallas, TX 75219, (214)559-0350.

MORRILL, Denis R.——**B:** Jan. 17, 1939, Kingston, UT, *Atty.*, Prince, Yeates & Geldzahler; **PRIM RE ACT:** Attorney; **OTHER RE ACT:** Law Practice; **SERVICES:** Legal servs.; **REP CLIENTS:** Devels., synds., lenders, brokers; **PROFL AFFIL & HONORS:** UT Bar Assn., ABA, Order of the Coif; **EDUC:** BS, 1965, Univ. of UT; **GRAD EDUC:** JD, 1967, Univ. of UT; **EDUC HONORS:** Order of the Coif; **MIL SERV:** USA, Sp. 4; **HOME ADD:** 6024 S 2200 W, Salt Lake City, UT 84118, (801)969-2334; **BUS ADD:** 424 E 5th S., Salt Lake City, UT 84111, (801)521-3760.

MORRIS, Bill——**B:** Jan. 11, 1950, S. Bend, IN, *Broker, Owner, Partnership*, Accent Properties; **PRIM RE ACT:** Broker, Appraiser, Lender, Instructor, Syndicator; **OTHER RE ACT:** Ski resort props.; **SERVICES:** Repairs, inter city moving, decorating, appraisals, exchange RE devel, building, solar spec.; **REP CLIENTS:** Univ. of CO, Greenwood Commons, Twin Lakes, Starboard Subdiv., Boulder Hts.; **PREV EMPLOY:** Wood Bros., Homes, Painting contr.; **PROFL AFFIL & HONORS:** Summit Cty. Bd. of Realtors, Boulder Bd. of Realtors, CAR, NARA, Boulder C of C; **EDUC:** BS, 1972, Fin., Mktg., IN Univ., Bloomington, IN; **EDUC HONORS:** Grad. with distinction; **HOME ADD:** 827 Deertrail Cir., Boulder, CO 80382, (303)449-2235; **BUS ADD:** 1905 9th St., Boulder, CO 80302, (303)449-2900.

MORRIS, Charles Arthur——**B:** Dec. 9, 1947, Redlands, CA, *Treas.*, MBC Constructors, Ltd., Barnyard Realty, Morris Co.; **PRIM RE ACT:** Broker, Developer, Builder, Owner/Investor, Instructor; **SERV-**

ICES: Gen. Engrg. Contractors, Devel., Gen. Building Contractors, Investment Counseling; **REP CLIENTS:** Devel., Investors, Indiv., Engrs.; **PREV EMPLOY:** Management Consultant, Westernbancorporation; Fin. Planning, Amer. Hospital Supply Corp.; Auditor: Peat, Marwick, Mitchell and Co-Partners (CPA's); **PROFL AFFIL & HONORS:** Valley Investment Group, Lake Elsinore Valley Bd. of Realtors; BIA, State of CA: RE Broker, Gen. Bldg. Contractor, Gen. Engrg. Contractor, Community Coll. Teaching Credential; CCIM Candidate; **EDUC:** BS, 1970, Bus. Mgmt./Acctg., Long Beach State; **GRAD EDUC:** MBA, 1973, Fin./Mktg., CA State Univ., Long Beach; **EDUC HONORS:** Grad. Cum Laude, Pres., Student Housing Council, Grad. Cum Laude; **OTHER ACT & HONORS:** Treas., Lake Elsinore Valley Bd. of Realtors; **BUS ADD:** 15076 Grand Ave., Lake Elsinore, CA 92330, (714)678-1222.

MORRIS, C.T.——B: Oct. 9, 1917, New York, NY, *Dir. of Facilities Planning*, Itek Corp., Corporate; **PRIM RE ACT:** Property Manager; **SERVICES:** Control acquisition, disposition, contruction & mgmt. of corporate RE worldwide; **PROFL AFFIL & HONORS:** Nat. Assn. of Corp. RE Exec.; Nat. Press Club; **EDUC:** Dramatics, Journalism, Public Speaking; **MIL SERV:** USA, Infantry, Lt.Col., Bronze Star, Purple Heart; **OTHER ACT & HONORS:** Member Zoning Bd., Planning Bd., Elected Township Comm.-Princeton, NJ (Lawrence Township) 1954-1961; Member - Actors Equity 1935-1937; **HOME ADD:** 13 Honeysuckle Rd., S. Hamilton, MA 01982, (617)468-4890; **BUS ADD:** 10 Maguire Rd., Lexington, MA 02173, (617)276-2444.

MORRIS, Dorothy E.——B: College Point, NY, *Sr. Partner & Founder*, Morris Real Estate; **PRIM RE ACT:** Broker, Consultant, Appraiser, Instructor; **SERVICES:** RE brokerage, leasing, appraisals, mergers & acquisitions; **PREV EMPLOY:** RE sales, mort., fin. co.; **PROFL AFFIL & HONORS:** New York City RE Bd. (Committees - Community Seminar Series, Grammercy); Assn. of RE Women; Nat. Soc. of Review Appraisers; NY State Soc. of RE Appraisers; Amer. Arbitration Assn., Panel Member, Lic. RE Broker; CRA Sr. Member; **EDUC:** Psychology/RE Law, Hofstra Univ./Westchester Community Coll.; **OTHER ACT & HONORS:** Guest Lecturer, Pace Univ. & IBM; Listed in Who's Who in Amer. Women; **HOME ADD:** 388 Cedar Dr. W., Briarcliff Manor, NY 10510, (914)941-4006; **BUS ADD:** 500 Fifth Ave., New York, NY 10110.

MORRIS, Evon——B: Jan. 18, 1922, Dayton, OH, *Pres./Assoc.*, Morris-Hooveri/Morris & Vasquez; **PRIM RE ACT:** Appraiser, Owner/Investor, Property Manager; **SERVICES:** Analytical valuation & appraisal services, econ. analysis; **REP CLIENTS:** HUD; Hughes Aircraft; Lear-Siegleri; Bralco Metals; **PREV EMPLOY:** Marshall & Stevens; SBA; United Fruit; Tropical Radio; Appraised in Central & S. Amer.; **PROFL AFFIL & HONORS:** Amer. Soc. of Appraisers; Amer. Assn. of Petroleum Land Men; Intl. Soc. of Valuers, Amer. Soc. of Appraisers; AAPL; CVS; **EDUC:** AB, 1946, Econ., OH State Univ.; **HOME ADD:** 10220 Ralph Rd., Beaumont, CA 92223, (714)845-1549; **BUS ADD:** 4731 Topeka Dr., Tarzana, CA 91356.

MORRIS, Kenneth——*Asst. to Pres. & Secy.*, Wolverine World Wide Inc.; **PRIM RE ACT:** Property Manager; **BUS ADD:** 9341 Courtland Dr., Rockford, MI 49351, (616)866-1561.*

MORRIS, Kenneth B.——B: Feb. 12, 1922, Brooklyn, NY, *Sr. Partner*, Morris RE; **PRIM RE ACT:** Broker, Consultant, Engineer, Appraiser, Instructor; **OTHER RE ACT:** City Planning; **SERVICES:** RE Brokerage, appraising, consulting, mergers and acquisitions; **REP CLIENTS:** Maj. corps.; **PREV EMPLOY:** Const. exec., head of own consulting arch., engr. & planning firm; Univ. VP; Pres. of corp. (sponsored housing); Sr. Officer of maj. NY City bank; Chief Engr. & Asst. to Pres. of intl. design & const. firm; **PROFL AFFIL & HONORS:** Amer. Soc. of Appraisers (Sr. Member); Securities Broker, Pres. (2 terms), Chmn. (2 terms) of NYC C of C; Chmn., Security Comm. NY State Savings Bank Assn.; Listed in Who's Who in the World, Who'sWho in Amer., Who's Who in Engrg., Who's Who in Consulting.; P.E., P.P., A.S.A., C.R.A., Realtor; **EDUC:** BCE, 1949, Structural Engrg., Manhattan Coll., Inst. of Design, Hoffberg's Inst.; **GRAD EDUC:** Coll. and Univ. Admin., Univ. of NE; **MIL SERV:** Air Force, Pilot Officer; **HOME ADD:** 388 Cedar Dr., W., Briarcliff Manor, NY 10510, (914)941-4006; **BUS ADD:** 500 Fifth Ave., New York, NY 10110, (212)221-6392.

MORRIS, Leland——B: Aug. 5, 1956, New York, NY, *VP*, Norman M. Morris Corp., Realty; **PRIM RE ACT:** Developer, Owner/Investor, Property Manager, Syndicator; **SERVICES:** Synd. of resid. & comml. props., prop. mgmt. & joint venture equity; **REP CLIENTS:** Indiv. investors - our own account; **PREV EMPLOY:** C. L. Develop., Cincinnati, OH, Asst. VP, 1978-1980; **EDUC:** BS, 1978, Psych. & Mgmt., Eckerd Coll.; **HOME ADD:** 455 Martling Ave., Tarrytown, NY 10591; **BUS ADD:** 6 Corporate Park Dr., White Plains, NY 10604, (914)694-1380.

MORRIS, Max A.——B: Mar. 12, 1941, W. Terre Haute, IN, *Assoc. Owner*, Property Professionals, Commercial and Investment Property; **PRIM RE ACT:** Broker, Consultant, Owner/Investor; **SERVICES:** Comml., indus., and income props.; **PREV EMPLOY:** Allied Brokers Castro Valley; **PROFL AFFIL & HONORS:** Amrex Exchange Grp., Northern CA Chapter of CCIM, Member Commercial & Indus. Bd. of Dirs. Southern Alameda Co. Bd. of Realtors; Castro Valley C of C Bd. of Dir.; **EDUC:** AA, 1977, Bus. Admin., Econ., Mktg., El Camino Coll., Los Angeles; **HOME ADD:** 2524 Marina Blvd., San Leandro, CA 94577, (415)351-6612; **BUS ADD:** 20200 Redwood Rd., Castro Valley, CA 94546, (415)886-2900.

MORRIS, Robert E.——B: Jan. 25, 1925, Waterloo, IA, *Pres., Sec., Treas.*, RE Morris Investments Inc. - RE Morris Co. Inc.; **PRIM RE ACT:** Developer, Builder, Property Manager; **SERVICES:** Same as Primary RE Activities; **REP CLIENTS:** Self; **PREV EMPLOY:** Owner & Mgr. Retail Hardware, Evansdale, IA Sole Owner & Mgr. Town & Ctry. Shopping Ctr. Evansdale, IA; **PROFL AFFIL & HONORS:** IRHA - IA Master Plumbers; Evansdale Devel. Assn., Bd. Dir. United Hardware Dist. Minneapolis MN; **MIL SERV:** USAF, 1st Lt., D.F.C. 1 Oakleaf, Air Medal 3 Oak Leaf; **OTHER ACT & HONORS:** Evansdale School Bd., Col. Confederate Air Force, Elkair Shrine Temple Cedar Rapids IA-Humps Pilots Assn.; **HOME ADD:** 631 Home Acre, Evansdale, IA 50707, (319)234-2201; **BUS ADD:** 3560 Lafayette Rd., Evansdale, IA 50707, (319)233-8449.

MORRIS, William R.——B: July 4, 1922, Champaign, IL, *Chief Devel. Officer/RE*, Nat. Consumer Coop. Bank, Credit & Lending; **PRIM RE ACT:** Broker, Consultant, Appraiser, Developer, Builder, Property Manager; **OTHER RE ACT:** Currently writer of nat. synd. column on housing & comm. devel. programs, not related to employment; **SERVICES:** Loan origination & devel. for housing coops.; Loan Mgmt.; Pilot Co-op Demonstrations; **REP CLIENTS:** Nonprofit housing coop. throughout US; **PREV EMPLOY:** Dir., Urban Liaison, Fed. Nat. Mort. Assn.; Exec. Dir., Nat. Assn. RE Brokers, Inc.; Housing Dir., Nat. Assn. Advancement of Colored People; Owner: Gen. RE Agency; **PROFL AFFIL & HONORS:** Amer. Soc. Profl. Consultants; Sr. Member, Nat. Soc. RE Appraisers; Nat. Assn. RE Brokers (Dir. Member), Realtor of the Yr. (NAREB); HUD Fair Housing Awards (2); CRA Cert. RE Appraiser, Numerous awards from local groups and housing orgs.; **EDUC:** 1951-54, IN Univ.; **MIL SERV:** USAF; Maj.; SS, GC, WWII, Inf. Medals; **OTHER ACT & HONORS:** Bd. Dir., Nat. Housing Conf.; Low Income Housing Coalition; Metro. Action Inst.; Housing Assistance Council, FNMA Adv. Comm., HUD Task Forces; Oper. Breakthrough, Minority Bus.; Fair Housing, FHLBB Alternative Mortgages Adv. Comm.; **HOME ADD:** 1604C Beekman Pl., NW, Washington DC 20009, (202)232-1443; **BUS ADD:** 2001 S St., NW, Washington DC 20009, (202)673-4343.

MORRISETT, H. Dallas——B: Apr. 8, 1937, Muskogee, OK, *Pres. and Chmn.*, The Morrisett Co.; **PRIM RE ACT:** Broker, Consultant, Developer, Owner/Investor, Property Manager; **PREV EMPLOY:** VP & Bd. Member, Williams Realty Corp.; VP & Gen. Mgr., Helmerich & Payne Props., Inc.; **PROFL AFFIL & HONORS:** ICSC, IREM, NACORE, CSC, CPM, Realtor; **EDUC:** BS, 1966, Bus. Mgmt., Univ. of Tulsa; **MIL SERV:** US Army; **HOME ADD:** 2638 S. 90 E. Ave., Tulsa, OK 74129, (918)622-2990; **BUS ADD:** Suite 303, 320 S. Boston Bldg., Tulsa, OK 74103, (918)583-8105.

MORRISON, Rick——B: Sept. 30, 1946, Kalamazoo, MI, Chuck Jaqua, Realtor; **PRIM RE ACT:** Broker, Consultant, Owner/Investor, Property Manager; **OTHER RE ACT:** Rehab.; **SERVICES:** Investment brokerage, rehab., spec. in turnaround props., prop. mgmt.; **REP CLIENTS:** Indiv. investors; **PROFL AFFIL & HONORS:** Kalamazoo Cty. Econ. Expansion Corp., Bd. of Dir.; **EDUC:** BS, 1968, Personnel & Labor Relations, W. MI Univ.; **OTHER ACT & HONORS:** Cty. Commissioner, Kalamazoo, 1979 to pres.; **HOME ADD:** 1444 W. Maple, Kalamazoo, MI 49008, (616)385-4144; **BUS ADD:** 2727 South 11th St., Kalamazoo, MI 49009, (616)375-5470.

MORRISON, Robert Haywood——B: Mar. 27, 1927, Hickory, NC, *Pres.*, Catawba Capital Corp.; **PRIM RE ACT:** Consultant, Lender, Owner/Investor, Instructor, Real Estate Publisher; **SERVICES:** Gen. office services; **REP CLIENTS:** Koppers, Texaco, Standard-Coosa-Thatcher, A. O. Smith, Ametek, Hill Directory, Terminix, Mead Packaging, Royal Worcester; **PREV EMPLOY:** Prof. of Journalism, Winthrop Coll., Chmn. of Bus. Communication, Univ. of KS; **PROFL AFFIL & HONORS:** Sales & Mktg. Execs. Intl., Delta Sigma Pi, Charlotte Comml. Listing Exchange, Chmn., Charlotte Prop. Mgmt. Bureau, Dir., Charlotte Bd. of Realtors; **EDUC:** AB, 1947, Eng./Journalism, Univ. of NC (Chapel Hill); **GRAD EDUC:** MA, 1948, Eng., Univ. of NC (Chapel Hill); **EDUC HONORS:** Grad. with honors, Editor of The Daily Tar Heel; **OTHER ACT & HONORS:** Magistrate, Newton Township 1954-59, Phi Beta Kappa, Rotary Intl., Author of five books on business writing; **HOME ADD:** 1333 Queens

Rd., Charlotte, NC 28207, (704)375-6170; **BUS ADD:** 1373 East Morehead St., Charlotte, NC 28204, (704)333-9645.

MORRISSEY, John Drew——B: Jan. 31, 1937, Boston, MA, *Self employed RE consultant and consulting devel.*; **PRIM RE ACT:** Consultant, Developer; **SERVICES:** Consulting devel., econ. feasibility studies, portfolio analysis, valuation/investment analysis, devel. negotiations; **REP CLIENTS:** Bank of Amer.; Cabot, Cabot & Forbes; Chase Manhattan; Chemical Bank; The First Nat. Bank of Chicago; The Samuel Goldwyn Found.; Security Pacific; Wells Fargo Bank; **PROFL AFFIL & HONORS:** ASCE; Amer. Soc. of RE Counselors; Los Angeles Realty Bd. ULI; **EDUC:** 1959, Civil Engrg., Northeastern Univ.; **GRAD EDUC:** 1964, Fin./Control, Harvard Bus. School; **OTHER ACT & HONORS:** RE Investment Prop., Tr.; Testing Engrs. San Diego, Dir.; **HOME ADD:** 10230 Autumn Leaf Circle, Los Angeles, CA 90024, (213)275-3546; **BUS ADD:** 10960 Wilshire No. 204, Los Angeles, CA 90024, (213)477-4578.

MORSE, Bernard L.——B: Dec. 15, 1936, New York, NY, *VP*, Sybedon Corp.; **PRIM RE ACT:** Broker, Consultant, Lender, Owner/Investor, Syndicator; **PREV EMPLOY:** Edward S. Gordon Co.; **PROFL AFFIL & HONORS:** Past Chmn.-Young Mort. Bankers Assn.; Mort. Bankers Assn. of NY-Westchester Home Bldrs.; **EDUC:** BS, 1959, Econ., Cornell-NYU; **HOME ADD:** 21 Stratton Rd., Scarsdale, NY 10583, (914)723-3014; **BUS ADD:** 1211 Ave. of The Americas, New York, NY 10036, (212)354-5756.

MORSE, Ted——Penta Pacific Properties; **PRIM RE ACT:** Developer; **BUS ADD:** 20850 Leapwood Ave., Ste. A, Carson, CA 90746, (213)537-7900.*

MORSE, Thomas E.——B: Dec. 21, 1931, Los Angeles, CA, *Co-Owner*, Ferncreek Properties, Inc.; **PRIM RE ACT:** Broker, Consultant, Developer, Property Manager, Syndicator; **SERVICES:** Specialist in office, retail and warehouse props.; **REP CLIENTS:** Leasing and managing agents, devel., and leasing brokers for owners of office parks, office bldgs., warehouses and shopping ctrs.; **PREV EMPLOY:** VP & Mgr. of Investment Div. Ryan Elliott & Co., Boston, Mass.; **PROFL AFFIL & HONORS:** Orlando -Winter Park Bd. of Realtors; Boston Bar Assn.; NAR; Nat. Assn. of Review Appraisers; MA & District Ct. Bars; National Assn. Indus. and Office Parks; Indus. Devel. Commn. of Mid-FL, CRA, CCIM; **GRAD EDUC:** JD, 1954, Boston Univ.; MBA, 1965, Boston Univ.; **MIL SERV:** USAF, Capt.; **OTHER ACT & HONORS:** Chmn., Planning Bd. and Chmn., Capital Budget Comm., Cohasset MA; **HOME ADD:** 733 Granville Dr., Winter Park, FL 32789, (305)628-0432; **BUS ADD:** 33 E. Robinson St., Orlando, FL 32801.

MORTIMER, Rory Dixon——B: Jan. 6, 1950, Flint, MI, *Pres.*, Chellis and Mortimer, P.A.; **PRIM RE ACT:** Attorney; **SERVICES:** RE practice, taxation, probate, estate planning, comml., bankruptcy and corps.; **PROFL AFFIL & HONORS:** ABA, SC Bar (Comm. on RE and Probate Practices), Dorchester Cty. Bar Assn. (Treasurer, 1980), Atty.; **EDUC:** BA, 1972, Bus. Admin., MI State Univ.; **GRAD EDUC:** JD, 1978, Bus. Law and Taxation, Detroit Coll. of Law; **OTHER ACT & HONORS:** Commerce Club of Charleston, Pres. (1979); Rotary Club; Atty. for Summerville Bd. of Realtors; **HOME ADD:** 223 Pointer Dr., Summerville, SC 29483, (803)875-4498; **BUS ADD:** 118 E. Richardson Ave., PO Box 430, Summerville, SC 29483, (803)871-7765.

MORTON, Paul D. "Dan"——B: Nov. 23, 1933, Wheatland, WY, *Pres.*, Morton, Smith and Assoc., Inc., Condo. Ctr.; **PRIM RE ACT:** Broker, Instructor, Consultant, Property Manager; **SERVICES:** Mgmt. of Homeowner Assn.; **REP CLIENTS:** US Home; Gen. Electric; Pvt. Investors; **PREV EMPLOY:** Proj. Mgr. of Fed. Housing Admin., Multi-Family Props. in Scottsdale, Tucson and Green Valley, AZ; **PROFL AFFIL & HONORS:** IREM, CPM; **EDUC:** Psych./Soc., AZ State Univ., Tempe, AZ; **MIL SERV:** USAF; E-5, Good Conduct, Presidential Unit Citation; **HOME ADD:** PO Box 18018, Tucson, AZ 85731, (602)886-1265, **BUS ADD:** PO Box 18018, Tucson, AZ 85731, (602)886-1265.

MORTON, Perry W.——B: Oct. 17, 1939, Lincoln, NE; **PRIM RE ACT:** Broker, Consultant, Attorney, Developer, Owner/Investor; **SERVICES:** Fin., Operating, Gen. Mgmt. Consulting; Law; **PREV EMPLOY:** Sr. VP, Bay Fin. Corp. 1973-1980; **PROFL AFFIL & HONORS:** ABA, Tr, Amer. Fletcher Mort. Investors (publicy-owned RE trust), Member, MA & NY Bar; **EDUC:** BA, 1961, Econ., Univ of MI; **GRAD EDUC:** LLB, 1964, Law, Harvard Law School; **MIL SERV:** US Army, Capt.; **HOME ADD:** 17 Indianhead Cir., Marblehead, MA 01945, (617)631-2737; **BUS ADD:** PO Box 53, Marblehead, MA 01945, (617)639-0675.

MORTON, Robert E.——B: Nov. 14, 1925, Rockford, IA, *Pres.*, Realty Investment Co., Inc.; **PRIM RE ACT:** Broker, Syndicator, Consultant, Property Manager, Owner/Investor; **SERVICES:** Synd., Prop. Mgmt, Partnership Admin.; **REP CLIENTS:** Prof. & Bus. Persons of NM; **PREV EMPLOY:** Sandia S & L Assn. - VP 1962-1968; **HOME ADD:** 4616 Hannett Ave., Albuquerque, NM 87110, (505)268-2323; **BUS ADD:** Suite 999 Sandia Savings Bldg.,, Fourth & Gold, Albuquerque, NM 87102, (505)843-9700.

MORTON, Walt——The Haskell Co.; **PRIM RE ACT:** Developer; **BUS ADD:** Haskell Bldg., 720 Gilmore St., Jacksonville, FL 32204, (904)358-1601.*

MOSELEY, David B., Jr.——B: Dec. 16, 1946, Dallas, TX, *Atty.*, Moseley, Jones, Allen and Fuquay; **PRIM RE ACT:** Broker, Attorney, Property Manager, Owner/Investor; **PROFL AFFIL & HONORS:** ABA; State Bar of TX (RE Probate and Trust Sec. Member), Dallas Bar Assn., Dallas Estate Planning Council; **EDUC:** BA, 1969, Religion, Baylor Univ.; **GRAD EDUC:** JD, 1974, Tax., S Methodist Univ.; **MIL SERV:** USAR, Capt., Master Parachutist, Expert Infantryman, Jungle Expert, Pathfinder; **OTHER ACT & HONORS:** Wilshire Baptist Church, Dallas, TX; **HOME ADD:** 7117 Claybrook, Dallas, TX 75231, (214)343-2378; **BUS ADD:** 6060 N Central Expwy., Suite 850, Dallas, TX 75206, (214)369-8596.

MOSELEY, George E.——*Corp. Counsel & Secy.*, Reeves Brothers, Inc.; **PRIM RE ACT:** Property Manager; **BUS ADD:** PO Box 1898, Spurtanburg, SC 29304, (803)576-1210.*

MOSELEY, Morris G.——B: June 1, 1940, Newport News, VA, *Realtor-owned*, Moseley & Co., Realtors; **PRIM RE ACT:** Broker, Consultant, Builder; **SERVICES:** Comml. & resid. sales; **PROFL AFFIL & HONORS:** Hampton Bd. of Realtors; VA Assn. of Realtors; NAR; NMI, GRI; CRS; CRB; Salesman of the Year 1969 & 1972; Realtor Best Exemplifying the Code of Ethics, Local & State Dir.; **MIL SERV:** USMC Res.; **OTHER ACT & HONORS:** Dir. of Warwick Yacht & Ctry. Club; **HOME ADD:** 612 Windemere Rd., Newport News, VA 23602, (804)877-5751; **BUS ADD:** 12472 Warwick Blvd., Newport News, VA 23606, (804)595-2241.

MOSELEY, Ray F., Jr.——B: June 11, 1920, Kansas City, MO, *Pres.*, Moseley & Co.; **PRIM RE ACT:** Broker, Consultant, Developer, Owner/Investor, Property Manager; **SERVICES:** Sale, leasing and managing of RE & sale of businesses; **REP CLIENTS:** Nat. and regl. accounts-Sears, Woolworth, Zales, Kenney, Goodyear, Firestone, Avon and many others; **PROFL AFFIL & HONORS:** RE Bs. of KS City and Nat. RE Bd., Winner of the 1962 Award Inter City-Intl. Transaction Soc. of Indus. Realtors, Nat. Assn. RE Bd. Indus.; **MIL SERV:** USAF, Capt.; **OTHER ACT & HONORS:** Kansas City Club, Kansas City Ctry. Club; **HOME ADD:** 1028 W. 58th St., Kansas City, MO 64114; **BUS ADD:** 7920 Ward Pkwy. #100, Kansas City, MO 64114, (816)842-7765.

MOSELEY, Richard H.——B: Nov. 24, 1929, Kansas City, MO, *Pres.*, Reserve Mort. Corp.; **PRIM RE ACT:** Consultant, Lender; **OTHER RE ACT:** Joint ventures, mort. loans, const. loans, condos., investment in comml. prop.; **PROFL AFFIL & HONORS:** MBAA; RESSI; REALTOR; **EDUC:** BA, 1952, Bus. Mgmt., Wharton School of Fin. - Univ. of PA; **MIL SERV:** USA, 1st Lt.; **OTHER ACT & HONORS:** Bd.: Big Bros. & Sisters of KS City; Bd.: Bishop Spencer Place, Boy Scouts; **HOME ADD:** 2910 W. 66 Terr., Shawnee Mission, KS 66208, (913)432-3430; **BUS ADD:** 800 W. 47th St., Kansas City, MO 64112, (816)753-0221.

MOSELEY, William B.——B: Dec. 28, 1929, Evanston, IL, *First VP, Mktg./Advertising*, Century 21 Real Estate Corporation, Intl. Headquarters; **OTHER RE ACT:** Mktg./Advertising; **EDUC:** BA, 1956, Telecommunications, Minor-Bus. Admin., Univ. of S. CA; **GRAD EDUC:** MBA, 1978, Mgmt., Fairleigh Dickinson Univ.; **MIL SERV:** US Army, 1952-1954, Korea; **HOME ADD:** 1452 Stockbridge Rd., Santa Ana, CA 92705, (714)731-0104; **BUS ADD:** 18872 MacArthur Blvd., Irvine, CA 92715, (714)752-7521.

MOSER, Dean J.——B: Apr. 5, 1942, San Francisco, CA, *Broker*, Esprit Realty Co.; **PRIM RE ACT:** Broker; **OTHER RE ACT:** CPA; **SERVICES:** Tax consultation in RE; **REP CLIENTS:** RE Brokers, investors, synds.; **PREV EMPLOY:** Arthur Andersen & Co.; **PROFL AFFIL & HONORS:** CA Soc. of CPA; Rotary; **EDUC:** BS, 1964, Acctg., Univ. of San Francisco; **GRAD EDUC:** Univ. of San Francisco Law School; **EDUC HONORS:** Golden Gate Univ.; **OTHER ACT & HONORS:** Novato Human Needs Center; Scouts of Amer.; **BUS ADD:** 250 Bel Marin Keys Blvd., Novato, CA 94947, (415)883-6123.

MOSER, Eric——B: Dec. 26, 1925, Washington, DC, *Pres.*, Moser Enterprises, Inc.; **PRIM RE ACT:** Consultant, Developer, Builder, Owner/Investor, Property Manager, Syndicator; **SERVICES:** Conceive, build, devel. and mgr. real income props.; **REP CLIENTS:** Banker's Trust of NY, Lynx Golf Club Corp.; **PREV EMPLOY:** 25 yrs Mosler Safe Co., Reg. Mgr.; **PROFL AFFIL & HONORS:** Pres. 1981 Region 6, Self Service Storage Assn.; **EDUC:** 3 yrs. Bus. Ad. Fin. Math, Univ. of CO; **MIL SERV:** USAAF WW II; **OTHER ACT & HONORS:** 1977 Pres. GA Chpt., Nat. Arthritis Found.; **HOME ADD:** 5267 Glenridge Dr., Atlanta, GA 30342, (404)252-6551; **BUS ADD:** 6820 Roswell Rd., Ste. 2-C, Atlanta, GA 30328, (404)393-3604.

MOSES, Arthur L.——B: Nov. 20, 1948, New York, NY, *Pres.*, Vector Land Group, Inc.; **PRIM RE ACT:** Broker, Developer; **OTHER RE ACT:** Economist; Planner; **SERVICES:** Land devel., project mgmt., feasibility studies, site selection; **REP CLIENTS:** Evaluation and mgmt. of comm. and res. props.; **PREV EMPLOY:** Fingerlakes Commercenter, Inc. (pres.), Indus. devel. 1979-pres.; Radian Intl. Corp (pres.) Econ. analysis and proj. mgmt. 1978-pres.; Radian Ralty Corp. (pres.), Brokerage, 1979-pres.; United Nations 1975-77; **PROFL AFFIL & HONORS:** Bldrs. Assn. of S. FL; Coral Gables Bd. of Realtors; Amer. Econ. Assn.; **EDUC:** AB, 1970, Econ., Franklin and Marshall Coll.; **GRAD EDUC:** MA, 1973, Econ., Duke Univ.; PhD, 1975, Econ., Duke Univ.; **EDUC HONORS:** Deans List 4 yrs. Omicron Delta Epsilon; Pi Gamma Nu; Black Pyramid, Doris Duke Fellow in Slavic and Russian Studies; Equitable Life Assurance Fellow; Grad. Scholar; **MIL SERV:** USARNG, Sgt.; **HOME ADD:** 17103 SW 79 Pl., Miami, FL 33157, (305)233-1343; **BUS ADD:** 2121 Ponce De Leon Blvd., Suite 743, Coral Gables, FL 33134, (305)445-2544.

MOSES, C. Lynn——B: July 21, 1946, ID Falls, ID, *Pres.*, Continental RE Co.; **PRIM RE ACT:** Broker, Consultant, Developer; **SERVICES:** RE Exchanges, investment counsulting on farms, ranches, & income prop., devel. of recreational prop.; **PREV EMPLOY:** Sales mgr., Amer. Realty Corp., 1970-71; **PROFL AFFIL & HONORS:** Farm & land inst., NAR, Exchange Counselors of ID, Dir. ID Assn. of Realtors, Soc. of Exchange Counselors, Most Creative Transaction in the Sate of ID, 1975; **EDUC:** BS, 1970, Mgkt., Econ., Brigham Young Univ.; **OTHER ACT & HONORS:** Driggs State Young Men Pres., The Church of Jesus Christ of Latter Day Saints., Pres. Greater Driggs C of C; **HOME ADD:** 880 N Main, Driggs, ID 83422, (208)354-2969; **BUS ADD:** 130 N. Main, Driggs, ID 83422, (208)354-8111.

MOSHER, Walter W., Jr.——B: Apr. 15, 1934, Hollywood, CA, *Pres.*, Eridon Development Corp.; **PRIM RE ACT:** Developer, Builder, Owner/Investor; **SERVICES:** Res. Devel.; **PREV EMPLOY:** Pres., Precision Dynamics Corp. (concurrent); **PROFL AFFIL & HONORS:** ORSA; IEEE; Sigma Xi; **EDUC:** BS, 1956, Engrg., UCLA; **GRAD EDUC:** MS, 1966, Computer Sci. Tech./Transport Sci., UCLA; PhD, 1971, Applied Math/Computer Tech./Transport Sci.., UCLA; **EDUC HONORS:** PhD with Distinction; **OTHER ACT & HONORS:** Dir., Health Indus. Mfrs. Assn.; **HOME ADD:** 12433 Woodley Ave., Granada Hills, CA 91344, (213)360-8026; **BUS ADD:** 12433 Woodley Ave., Granada Hills, CA 91344, (213)360-8026.

MOSK, Alan C.——B: Sept. 11, 1928, San Diego, CA, *Pres.*, ALCAN Mgmt.; **PRIM RE ACT:** Broker, Developer, Property Manager; **SERVICES:** Real Prop. Mgmt.; **PROFL AFFIL & HONORS:** Assoc. of HUD Managing Agents; **EDUC:** BBA, 1953, Mktg. RE, UCLA; **GRAD EDUC:** MA, 1971, Urban Affairs, Boston Univ.; **HOME ADD:** 29500 Heathercliff Rd., 111, Malibu, CA 90265, (213)457-4809; **BUS ADD:** 1725 The Promenade, Santa Monica, CA 90401, (213)451-1781.

MOSKOF, Howard R.——B: May 19, 1935, New York, NY, *Part.*, Hogan & Hartson; **PRIM RE ACT:** Attorney; **OTHER RE ACT:** Law sch. prof.; **SERVICES:** Gen. RE practice, fin. synd., condemndation; **PREV EMPLOY:** Exec Dir., Pres. Commn. on Urban Housing (Kaiser Commn.); Dep. and Gen. Counsel, DC Redev. Land Agency; Gen. Mgr., Flower Mound New Town; Raymond Nasher Co.; Asst. Gen Counsel; Gen. Dir. New Haven Redev. Agency; Consultant, Ford Found.; **PROFL AFFIL & HONORS:** Pi Sigma Alpha; Phi Delta Phi; DC Bar Assn., RE Comm., ABA; Fed. Bar Assn., Adjunct Prof., Georgetown Law Sch. (Land Devel. Seminar); **EDUC:** AB, 1956, Pol. Sci., Colgate Univ.; **GRAD EDUC:** 1959, Yale Law Sch.; **EDUC HONORS:** Departmental Hons. (Pol. Sci.); **MIL SERV:** USAF; S/Sgt.; **OTHER ACT & HONORS:** Dir. Georgetown Day Sch.; Univ. Club; Dir. Comm. for a Responsible Fed. Budget; Dir. Nat. Ctr. for Preservation Law; **HOME ADD:** 4528 28th St., NW, Washington, DC 20008, (202)244-4629; **BUS ADD:** 815 CT Ave., NW, Washington, DC 20006, (202)331-4722.

MOSKOWITZ, Frank D.——B: Sept. 29, 1922, Tulsa, OK, *Partner*, Moskowitz, Realtors; **PRIM RE ACT:** Broker, Developer, Owner/Investor; **SERVICES:** Primarily comml., indus. brokerage; **PROFL AFFIL & HONORS:** NAR, OK Assn. of Realtors, Realtors Nat. Mktg. Inst., CCIM; **EDUC:** OK Univ.; **MIL SERV:** US Air Force, Cpl., Medical discharge; **OTHER ACT & HONORS:** Tulsa C of C; **HOME ADD:** P O Box 2875, Tulsa, OK 74101, (918)743-1295; **BUS ADD:** 3530 E. 31st, Ste. 100, Tulsa, OK 74135, (918)743-7781.

MOSKOWITZ, Harold L.——B: June 6, 1953, Cincinnati, OH, *Tax Atty.*, Joel Carlins, Ltd.; **PRIM RE ACT:** Attorney; **SERVICES:** Tax and other legal advice including synd. work; **PREV EMPLOY:** Tax Atty. - Gordon, Schlack, Glickson, Gordon & Davidson, P.C., 444 N. Michigan Ave., Chicago, IL 60611; **PROFL AFFIL & HONORS:** ABA (Sections: Taxation & Real Prop., Probate & Estate; Chicago Bar, IL Bar, Baltimore City Bar Assns.; **EDUC:** BA, 1973, Acctg., Loyola Univ. of Baltimore; **GRAD EDUC:** JD, 1977, Tax, Univ. of MD Law; L.L.M. - Taxation, 1978, Tax, Georgetown Natl. Law Ctr.; **EDUC HONORS:** Magna Cum Laude; **HOME ADD:** 2527 W. Lunt Ave., Chicago, IL 60645, (312)764-7187; **BUS ADD:** 180 N. LaSalle, Suite 1810, Chicago, IL 60601, (312)726-9710.

MOSKOWITZ, Rita J.——B: Aug. 31, 1928, Little Rock, AR, *Partner*, Moskowitz, Realtors; **PRIM RE ACT:** Broker, Owner/Investor; **SERVICES:** Primarily comml.,indus. brokerage; **PROFL AFFIL & HONORS:** NAR, RE Securities and Synd. Inst.; OK Assn. of Realtors; Metropolitan Tulsa Bd. of Realtors; **EDUC:** 1945, Radiographic Technology, Univ. of AR Med Sch; **OTHER ACT & HONORS:** 1973 Appointed by Gov. of OK to serve on the OK RE Commn. (first woman so appointed); reappointed by next Gov. to serve another 4 yr. term and serve as Chairperson 3 yrs.; Nat. Writers Club, OK Writers Federation, Tulsa Night Writers; Amer. Registry of Radiologic Technologists; Nat. Council of Jewish Women; Bd. of Dir., OK Assn. of Realtors; Bd. of Dir., First OK Savings; Bd. of Dir., Fenster Art Gallery; Bd. of Dir., Nursing Service, Inc.; **HOME ADD:** P O Box 2875, Tulsa, OK 74101, (918)743-1295; **BUS ADD:** 3530 E 31st, Ste. 100, Tulsa, OK 74135, (918)743-7781.

MOSS, Jerry——B: Feb. 15, 1918, Wheeling, WV, *Pres.*, Jerry Moss & Co.; **PRIM RE ACT:** Developer; **EDUC:** BA, 1940, Univ. of CA, Berkley; **GRAD EDUC:** IA, 1942, Stanford Univ.; **MIL SERV:** QMC,1st Lt.; **HOME ADD:** Rancho Palos Verdes, CA 90274, (213)377-9566; **BUS ADD:** 655 Deep Valley Dr., Palos Verdes Peninsula, CA 90274, (213)377-9566.

MOSS, John P.——B: Dec. 6, 1938, Middletown, OH, *Sr. Part.*, Moss-Bronson Co.; **PRIM RE ACT:** Broker, Owner/Investor; **PROFL AFFIL & HONORS:** NAR, 1972 HBA Man of the Yr. Award; **EDUC:** AB, 1962, Hist. & Poli. Sci., Washburn Univ.; **HOME ADD:** 5536 E. Camelhill Rd., Phoenix, AZ 85016, (602)959-0935; **BUS ADD:** 7127 E. Sahuaro Dr., Ste. 201, Scottsdale, AZ 85254, (602)998-1051.

MOSS, Richard D.——B: Oct. 19, 1942, Springfield, IL, *VP-Branch Mgr.*, Banco Mortgage Co., Income Loan; **PRIM RE ACT:** Appraiser, Banker, Lender; **OTHER RE ACT:** Mort. Banker; **SERVICES:** Originate & service income prop. loans, J-v's; **REP CLIENTS:** MONY; Metropolitan Life; OH Nat. Life; Bankers Life; Teachers Ins. & Amer.; Several Other Life Ins. Cos., Banks, Pension Funds & RE Devel.; **PREV EMPLOY:** Appraiser for RE Research Corp. for 5 yrs.; **OTHER ACT & HONORS:** Other Bus. Address: 907 Walnut St., Des Moines, IA 50309; tel.: (505)244-4100; **HOME ADD:** 527 S. 215th St., Elkhorn, NE 68022, (402)289-3894; **BUS ADD:** 10330 Regency Pkwy. Dr., Omaha, NE 68114, (402)397-7920.

MOTLUCK, William J.——B: July 12, 1952, Chicago, IL, *Pres.*, Century 21 Host - Reichert, Ltd.; **PRIM RE ACT:** Broker, Consultant, Developer, Builder, Instructor, Property Manager, Insuror; **PROFL AFFIL & HONORS:** Greater So. Suburban Bd. of Realtors; IL Assn. of Realtors; NAR; **EDUC:** BA, 1974, Bus. Admin., Lewis Univ.; **HOME ADD:** 424 Sandra Lane, Chicago Heights, IL 60411, (312)755-1121; **BUS ADD:** 191 W. Joe Orr Rd., Chicago Heights, IL 60411, (312)481-3500.

MOTT, Clyde E.——B: Jan. 14, 1924, Jackson, TN, *Exec. VP*, Seattle Hearing & Speech Center, Inc., Mott Rehabilitation Services, Inc.-VP; **PRIM RE ACT:** Owner/Investor; **PREV EMPLOY:** State Dept. of Health-WA; **PROFL AFFIL & HONORS:** Conference of Execs., NRA, Pres. Comm. Employment-Under Johnson & Carter, Gov. Comm. Employment; **EDUC:** BA, 1950, Speech Pathology, MI State Univ.; **GRAD EDUC:** MA, 1962, Admin., CA State Univ.-Northridge; **MIL SERV:** USAF, Capt.; **OTHER ACT & HONORS:** Pres. Nat. Assn. of Execs. 1970-71, Lions Club, Pres. WA State NRA, Rehab. Assn. 1962-63; **HOME ADD:** 22044 99th Place W., Edmonds, WA 98020, (206)775-8866; **BUS ADD:** 22010 66th Arc West, Mountlake Terr., WA 98020, (206)778-3707.

MOTZ, Richard W.——B: Dec. 6, 1929, Rock Is., IL, *Pres.*, Oakwood Realty Co .; **PRIM RE ACT:** Broker, Developer, Owner/Investor, Property Manager, Syndicator; **SERVICES:** Synd. and mgr. of downtown office bldgs.; **REP CLIENTS:** Indiv. investors in comml. props.; **PROFL AFFIL & HONORS:** Rock Is. Cty. Bd. of Realtors, First Recipient of "Realtor of the Yr."Award Made by Rock Is. Cty. Bd. of Realtors in 1973; **EDUC:** BSBA, 1951, RE, Northwestern Univ.; **MIL SERV:** USN, 1953-1956, Lt.; **OTHER ACT & HONORS:** Chmn. Bd. of Tr., 1st Methodist Church, Serv. Council United Way, Past Pres. of: Rock Is. Community Chest, United Appeal of Rock Is. Cty., Rock Is. Bd. of Realtors, Kiwanis, Indep. Ins. Agts., Admin. Bd. 1st Methodist Church; **HOME ADD:** 2547 35th Ave., Rock Is., IL 61201, (309)788-7793; **BUS ADD:** 1800 3rd Ave., Rock Is., IL 61201, (309)794-0161.

MOUREK, Anthony J.——B: Apr. 21, 1943, Chicago, IL, *Sec./Treas.*, A. Mourek and Son, Inc., RE; **PRIM RE ACT:** Broker, Developer, Builder, Owner/Investor, Property Manager; **PROFL AFFIL & HONORS:** Amer. Mgmt. Assn.; **OTHER ACT & HONORS:** Union League Club of Chicago; Chicago Exec. Club; Irish Amer. Cultural Inst.; Czechoslovak Nat. Council; Manuscript Soc.; **BUS ADD:** 970 N. Oaklawn Ave., Elmhurst, IL 60126, (312)279-3770.

MOWBRAY, Kermit——*Pres.*, Federal Home Loan Bank of Topeka; **PRIM RE ACT:** Banker; **BUS ADD:** PO Box 176, Topeka, KS 66601, (913)233-0507.*

MOYER, Richard A.——B: May 17, 1929, Urbana, IL, *Pres.*, Moyer Mortgage Co., Inc. (Subsidiary of Baldwin-United Corp.); **PRIM RE ACT:** Lender; **SERVICES:** Mort. banker - all types of RE loans; **PROFL AFFIL & HONORS:** MBAA; **EDUC:** BS, 1951, Acctg., Miami Univ., Oxford, OH; **HOME ADD:** 531 Belmonte Park N., Apt. 1001, Dayton, OH 45405, (513)224-7268; **BUS ADD:** 811 Third National Bldg., Dayton, OH 45402, (513)223-8109.

MOYER, Stephen R.——B: Mar. 20, 1943, Abington, PA, *Exec Officer*, N. Penn Bd. of Realtors; **PRIM RE ACT:** Broker; **SERVICES:** Service & publish MLS; **REP CLIENTS:** 500 brokers & sales members; **PREV EMPLOY:** 11 yrs. RE Broker & mgmt., 5 yrs. exp. as RE instr., 5 courses Polley Assn.; **PROFL AFFIL & HONORS:** PAR, NAR, GRI, 1978 Realtor Associate of the Yr. (PA); **MIL SERV:** USN, E-5; **HOME ADD:** 27 W 9th St., Lansdale, PA 19446, (255)362-0370; **BUS ADD:** PO Box 252, Lansdale, PA 19446, (215)362-0379.

MOYLAN, Robert J.——*SIR Director RE*, American Can Co.; **PRIM RE ACT:** Property Manager; **BUS ADD:** American Lane, Greenwich, CT 06830, (203)552-2190.*

MOZILO, Ralph S.——B: Jan. 1, 1942, New York, NY, *Sr. VP*, Countrywide Funding Corp.; **PRIM RE ACT:** Lender; **SERVICES:** FHA, Vet Admin and conventional first trust deed loans; **PROFL AFFIL & HONORS:** Amer. Assn. of Mort. Underwriters; Nat. Assn. of Review Appraisers'; Mort. Bankers Assn.; Intrl. Org. of RE Appraisers, CRMU; CRA; CMHA; **EDUC:** BA, 1963, Language/Educ., Iona Coll.; **GRAD EDUC:** 1966, Foreign Language/Educ., Hunter Coll.; **HOME ADD:** 11003 Allegheny St., Sun Valley, CA 91352, (213)768-6164; **BUS ADD:** 3440 Wilshire Blvd., Los Angeles, CA 90010, (213)380-1731.

MROSAK, Stanley M.——B: June 23, 1926, Minneapolis, MN, *Dir. of RE Devel. & Mgmt.*, Soo Line RR Co., Minneapolis; **PRIM RE ACT:** Developer, Owner/Investor, Property Manager; **PROFL AFFIL & HONORS:** SIR; **EDUC:** BS, 1951, Univ. of MN; **MIL SERV:** USMC; Cpl.; 1943-46; **HOME ADD:** 3900 Bassett Creek Dr., Golden Valley, MN 55422, (612)588-9614; **BUS ADD:** Box 530, Minneapolis, MN 55440, (612)332-1261.

MUCCI, Patrick J.——B: May 14, 1947, Albany, NY, *Asst. VP Mort. Mgr.*, Home Savings Bank of Upstate NY; **PRIM RE ACT:** Consultant, Property Manager, Banker, Lender; **SERVICES:** Mort., Banking, Mort. Brokering and Consultants; **PREV EMPLOY:** Heritage Savings Bank, Kingston, NY - 1976-78, Nat. Savings Bank Albany, NY - 1973-76; **PROFL AFFIL & HONORS:** Mort. Bankers Assn. of Amer., Inst. of RE Mgmt. BOMA. SREA, Nat. NARA. NAHB, Assn. of MBA Exec., NAR, CRA; **EDUC:** BS and AAS, 1977-1967, Bus. Admin., Suny at Albany, NY, Hudson Valley CC, Troy, NY; **GRAD EDUC:** MBA, 1979, Mgmt., Falrleigh Dickson Univ.; **MIL SERV:** USAF, S/Sgt., 1969-1972, Nat. Def. Medal, Distinguished Unit Citation of 1 Oak, Leaf, A.F. Good Conduct, Squadron Airman of Month, Base Airman of Month, Nominated for Airman of the Year For USA, Gold Pride Award for Achievement; **OTHER ACT & HONORS:** Sunya Alumni Assn., Fairlegh Dickinson Univ. Alumni Assn., Historic Albany Foundation, Inc., Albany League of Arts; **HOME ADD:** 157 Luther Rd., E. Greenbush, NY 12061, (518)477-4057; **BUS TEL:** (518)445-1561.

MUCHNICK, Saul——B: Apr. 27, 1932, Brooklyn, NY, *Pres.*, Metrohouse Bldrs. & Devels. Inc.; **PRIM RE ACT:** Developer, Builder; **PROFL AFFIL & HONORS:** Long Is. Bldrs. Inst., Homeowner/Warranty Corp.; NY State Soc. of Profl. Engrs.; **EDUC:** BCE, 1952, Poly. INst. of Brooklyn; **GRAD EDUC:** MCE, 1954; **OTHER ACT & HONORS:** Knickerbocker Yacht Club, Shelter Park Tennis Club; **HOME ADD:** 92 Cypress Dr., Woodbury, NY 11797, (516)367-9090; **BUS ADD:** 136 Woodbury Rd., Woodbury, NY 11797, (516)367-3320.

MUCKLESTONE, Robert S.——B: May 15, 1929, Seattle, WA, *Partner*, Perkins, Coie, Stone, Olsen & Williams, Estate Planning; **PRIM RE ACT:** Attorney, Developer, Owner/Investor; **EDUC:** BA, 1953, Univ. of WA; **GRAD EDUC:** JD, 1954, Univ. of WA; **HOME ADD:** 1519 Third Ave. 701, Seattle, WA 98101, (206)583-8491; **BUS ADD:** 1900 Washington Bldg., Seattle, WA 98101, (206)583-8464.

MUDD, John P.——B: Aug. 22, 1932, Wash., DC, *VP - RE and Corp. Counsel*, American Hospital Management Corporation; **PRIM RE ACT:** Attorney, Developer, Builder, Owner/Investor, Property Manager, Syndicator; **PREV EMPLOY:** VP & Corp. Sec., Deltona Corp., 1965-1972; Sec. and Chief Legal Officer, Nat. Community Builders, 1972-1973; VP & Gen. Counsel, Continental Mort. Investors, 1973-1980; **PROFL AFFIL & HONORS:** Member, FL Bar, CA Bar, MD Bar, Wash. DC Bar, FL Bar Assn., CA Bar Assn., MD Bar Assn., DC Bar Assn.; **EDUC:** BS, 1954, Econ., Georgetown Univ.; **GRAD EDUC:** JD, 1956, Georgetown Univ. of Law School; **HOME ADD:** 1211 Hardee Rd., Coral Gables, FL 33146; **BUS ADD:** Suite 201, 11880 Bird Rd., Miami, FL 33175, (305)553-1174.

MUDDIMER, Hazel M.——B: Mar. 9, 1923, Brecksville, OH, *Owner and Broker, Pres.*, Centry 21 Trademark Realty, Inc.; **PRIM RE ACT:** Broker, Syndicator, Consultant, Appraiser, Builder, Owner/Investor; **SERVICES:** Off. also provides prop. mgmt.; **PREV EMPLOY:** Escrow off. for adv. mort. Co., Cleveland, OH office and Pres. and Gen. Contr. for D and H Const. Co.; **PROFL AFFIL & HONORS:** NAR, CRS, CCIM, RESSI, Designations of CRS and GRI; **EDUC:** Certif. School of Banking, 1966, N.W. Univ.; **OTHER ACT & HONORS:** Blossom Womens Comm.; **HOME ADD:** 3506 Shovee Ct., Brunswick, OH 44212, (216)225-6696; **BUS ADD:** 3487 Center Rd., Brunswick, OH 44212, (216)225-0666.

MUELLER, Arthur W.——B: May 17, 1931, NJ, *Sr. VP*, Crocker Mortage Co.; **PRIM RE ACT:** Appraiser, Lender; **OTHER RE ACT:** Construction loans, Fin. RE; **SERVICES:** Fin. of income comml. props.; **REP CLIENTS:** Lenders & pension funds, insurance co., S & L assn.; **PREV EMPLOY:** Sr. VP Amer. Fletcher Nat. Bank; **PROFL AFFIL & HONORS:** Assoc. Member, SRA Mort. Bankers Assn., Econ. Club of Indianapolis; **EDUC:** BA, 1953, Fin., Georgetown Univ.; **MIL SERV:** USN, CDR; **OTHER ACT & HONORS:** Highland Golf Club; **HOME ADD:** 1952 Huckleberry Ct., Indianapolis, IN 46260, (317)872-0598; **BUS ADD:** 20 East 91st, Indianapolis, IN 46260, (317)844-4944.

MUELLER, Werner A.——B: July 21, 1932, New York, NY, *VP - Sales*, Walnut Realty Co., Inc., Comml. Investment/Indus.; **PRIM RE ACT:** Broker, Consultant, Owner/Investor, Instructor; **SERVICES:** Synds., consulting, RE Investments, Brokerage; **REP CLIENTS:** Corporate and indiv. investors in resid., comml. and indus. RE; **PREV EMPLOY:** Educator, Entrepreneur; **PROFL AFFIL & HONORS:** CA Assn. Realtors, NAR, Realty Investment Assn. of Orange Cty., Los Angeles Cty. Bus. Mktg. Assn.; **EDUC:** BS, 1958, Educ., Ithaca Univ., Ithaca, NY; **GRAD EDUC:** MS, 1961, Admin., Hofstra Univ., Hempstead, NY; **MIL SERV:** US Army, S/Sgt., 1952/54; **OTHER ACT & HONORS:** Bd. of Dir. Hacienda Heights Improvement Assn., Bd. of Dir. Foothill Apt. Assn., Los Angeles Cty. Apt. Assn., Los Angeles Cty. Taxpayers Assn., Dir. Investment Div., Realty Bd.; **HOME ADD:** 16083 Mesa Robles Dr., Hacienda Heights, CA 91745, (213)336-2151; **BUS ADD:** 20288 Carrey Ave., Walnut, CA 91789, (714)594-0074.

MUIR, A. Gary——B: May 15, 1932, Pisgah, IA, *Pres.*, A.G. Muir Investment Co.; **PRIM RE ACT:** Broker, Owner/Investor; **SERVICES:** Analysis of existing income producing props. for submission to investors and sale of land for comml. devel.; **REP CLIENTS:** Indiv. and instl. investors in comml. prop.; **PREV EMPLOY:** VP of Cannon Devel. Corp. for 6 yrs. (4th largest multi-family home devel. in the ctry. in 1974); **EDUC:** BS, 1954, Commerce and Fin., Drake Univ., Des Moines, IA; **MIL SERV:** US Army, Sgt., Various decorations; **OTHER ACT & HONORS:** Kiwanis (twice pres.); **HOME ADD:** 11003 Montrose Way, Scottsdale, AZ 85254, (602)948-7702; **BUS ADD:** 6560 N. Scottsdale Rd., Suite E-201, Scottsdale, AZ 85253, (602)998-4200.

MUIR, James H.——**B:** June 23, 1947, Marshfield, WI, *Mgr., Equities*, The Northwestern Mutual Life Insurance Co., Atlanta RE Investment Office; **PRIM RE ACT:** Lender, Property Manager; **SERVICES:** Joint venture & construction loan fin.; **EDUC:** BBA, 1969, RE and Fin., Univ. of WI; **GRAD EDUC:** MBA, 1973, RE, GA State Univ.; **EDUC HONORS:** Honors Grad., SRA Scholarship; **MIL SERV:** U.S. Army, E-5, 1971-1973; **HOME ADD:** 5135 River Pine Ridge, Marietta, GA 30067, (404)971-6995; **BUS ADD:** 219 Perimeter Center Parkway, Suite 460, Atlanta, GA 30346, (404)396-4800.

MUIR, Robert C.——**B:** Mar. 10, 1928, Salt Lake City, UT, *Owner*, Robert Muir Co.; **PRIM RE ACT:** Broker, Developer, Builder, Owner/Investor, Property Manager; **SERVICES:** Devel. and managing hi-rise office bldgs., medical bldgs. and rgnl. shopping centers; **PREV EMPLOY:** Part owner, Inter-Mountain Ins. Agency, Mort. Loan Appraiser for Travelers Ins., Correspondent, Founded Robert Muir Co. in 1959; **PROFL AFFIL & HONORS:** Lakeside Ctry. Club, Magic Castle (Charter Member), Jockey Club, Boca Raton Hotel & Club; **EDUC:** Bus. Admin., Univ. of UT; **MIL SERV:** Sgt., 11th Airborne Div. (WWII), 1st Lt., Air Force Res.; **OTHER ACT & HONORS:** Nat. Design Award (1966), Soc. of Amer. Reg. Arch. for Muir Med. Bldg., Salute to Commerce Award (1971), from Hollywood C of C, for Community Serv. and leadership, Golden Key to City from City of Blaine, MN, 1972, in recognition of Northtown Shopping Ctr.; **HOME ADD:** 4335 Marina City Dr., PH 30 E, Marina Del Rey, CA 90291; **BUS ADD:** 7060 Hollywood Blvd., Los Angeles, CA 90028, (213)464-9111.

MULCAHY, James, III——*VP & Dir. of RE*, Armway Products, Inc.; **PRIM RE ACT:** Broker, Owner/Investor, Property Manager; **BUS ADD:** 42 Blacksmith Dr., Needham, MA 02192, (617)325-4700.

MULCAHY, Michael D.——**B:** May 9, 1947, Detroit, MI, *Partner*, Miller, Canfield, Paddock & Stone; **PRIM RE ACT:** Attorney; **SERVICES:** Legal; **REP CLIENTS:** Manufacturers Hanover Mort. Corp., Equitable Life Assurance Soc. of the US & Detroit Bank & Trust Co.; **PROFL AFFIL & HONORS:** ABA, MI State Bar Assn., Oakland Cty. Bar Assn., Detroit Bar Assn.; **EDUC:** BA, 1969, Poli. Sci., Econ., Wayne State Univ.; **GRAD EDUC:** JD, 1972, Univ. of MI Law School; **EDUC HONORS:** Phi Beta Kappa, Omicron Delta Kappa, Grad. with Distinction, Editor of the MI Law Review 1970-1972; **BUS ADD:** 300 Wabeek Bldg., Birmingham, MI 48012, (313)645-5000.

MULDOON, William D.——**B:** Nov. 5, 1943, Niagara Falls, NY, *Atty.*, William D. Muldoon; **PRIM RE ACT:** Attorney; **SERVICES:** RE closings, contracts, leases, deeds, options; **REP CLIENTS:** Red Lake Cty State Bank, Plummer State Bank, Security State Bank, First Fed. S&L Assn.; **PROFL AFFIL & HONORS:** MN State Bar Assn.; **EDUC:** 1965, Eng., Hist., Univ. of Buffalo; **GRAD EDUC:** 1971, Law, Univ. of ND; **MIL SERV:** USA, E-5; **OTHER ACT & HONORS:** Red Lake Cty. Atty., 1978-; **HOME ADD:** 803 Stevens Ave., Red Lake Falls, MN 56750, (218)253-4134; **BUS ADD:** PO Box 327, Red Lake Falls, MN 56750, (218)253-4321.

MULHERIN, Gregory J.——**B:** Mar. 15, Syracuse, NY, *Pres.*, Century 21 - Gregory Mulherin Realtors, Inc., Comml.; **PRIM RE ACT:** Broker, Consultant, Appraiser, Owner/Investor, Instructor, Property Manager, Syndicator; **OTHER RE ACT:** Investment, Exchanging; **SERVICES:** Resid., Comml., Investment, Exchanging, Mgmt.; **PROFL AFFIL & HONORS:** CCIM; **OTHER ACT & HONORS:** Orange Econ. Devel. Comm., 1966 to present; Past Pres., Orange Rotary Club; Past Pres. - CT Chapter Farm & Land Brokers; Past Pres. CT Assn. Realtors - Comml. Investment Div.; **HOME ADD:** 416 Longmeadow Rd., Orange, CT 06477, (203)795-4831; **BUS ADD:** 222 Boston Post Rd., Orange, CT 06477, (203)795-9791.

MULKEY, J.E.——*SIR Mgr., RE Adm.*, Shell Oil Co.; **PRIM RE ACT:** Property Manager; **BUS ADD:** PO Box 2099, Houston, TX 77001, (713)241-1394.*

MULL, Melvin Henry——**B:** Feb. 9, 1928, Toledo, OH, *VP, Pres.*, VP, Angel, Mull & Assoc., Inc., Pres., Arc/Cor. Inc.; **PRIM RE ACT:** Architect, Developer, Owner/Investor; **OTHER RE ACT:** RE Sales License, OH; **SERVICES:** Project Design, Feasibility Studies; **REP CLIENTS:** Govt., Inst., & Pvt. Investors; **PROFL AFFIL & HONORS:** AIA, Arch. Soc. of OH, Vistula Hist. Commn.; **EDUC:** BS in Arch., 1951, Arch. Design & Engrg., Univ. of Cincinnati; **GRAD EDUC:** C.E.U.S. in Fin., Mgmt.; **EDUC HONORS:** Phi Eta Sigma Tau Kappa Alpha Scarab; **OTHER ACT & HONORS:** OH Bd. of Bldg. Standards 1972-1976, Lucas Cty. Bd. of Mental Healty/The Toledo Club; **BUS ADD:** 3049 Sylvania Ave., Toledo, OH 43613, (419)474-5496.

MULLAN, Velda——**B:** Nov. 30, 1931, Harmon, OK, *Pres.*, All Star Mgmt. Corp., RE Div. (Mgmt); **PRIM RE ACT:** Broker, Instructor, Syndicator, Consultant, Property Manager, Real Estate Publisher; **OTHER RE ACT:** Co. does synd.; **SERVICES:** Purchase prop. for tax purposes. Rehabilitation of prop.; **REP CLIENTS:** Prof. bus. people, Drs., Attys., Staff bldgs., mktg., mgmt. surveys, budgeting, maximizing investment return; **PREV EMPLOY:** RE Mgmt. since 1970, managing apt. houses and office bldgs. from 40 units to 1200 units; **PROFL AFFIL & HONORS:** Affiliate member of Arlington Bd. of Realtors; IREM; Bd. of Dir. Tarrant Cty. Apt. Assn.; Past Second VP of TAA, Past Bd. of Dir. for TX Apt. Assn.; Nat. Apt. Assn., World's Who Who of Women; **EDUC:** CPM, 1976, RE Mgmt, Inst. of RE Mgmt. of NAR; **EDUC HONORS:** CAM through TX Apt. Assn.; **OTHER ACT & HONORS:** Poetry Soc. of TX; **HOME ADD:** 315 Robin Hill Ln, Duncanville, TX 75137, (214)298-9166; **BUS ADD:** 315 Roibn Hill Lane, Duncanville,, TX 75116, (214)821-8700.

MULLANE, John P.——**B:** July 19, 1929, Kansas City, MO, *Pres.*, John P. Mullane Co.; **PRIM RE ACT:** Broker, Syndicator, Consultant, Appraiser, Property Manager, Owner/Investor; **OTHER RE ACT:** R.E. Tax consultant; **SERVICES:** Comml. Sales & leasing, prop. mgmt., site acquisitions, RE counseling, prop. tax consulting, synd. investment RE analysis; **PROFL AFFIL & HONORS:** IREM, NAR, MO Assn. of Realtors, Kansas City, R.E. Bd., IAAO, CPM, Member of Omega Tau RHO; **MIL SERV:** USA; **HOME ADD:** 243 W. 61st St., Kansas, MO 64113, (816)363-1347; **BUS ADD:** 1734 E. 63rd St. Suite 200, Kansas City, MO 64110, (816)361-4448.

MULLEN, Elmer A.——**B:** May 31, 1902, Pittsburgh, PA, *Owner*, Nationwide Appraisal Inst.; **PRIM RE ACT:** Consultant, Appraiser, Developer, Builder, Instructor; **SERVICES:** Consultant, appraising; **REP CLIENTS:** Diplomat Hotel - Presential Towers (Hollywood, FL); The Bank of Miami, FL; **PROFL AFFIL & HONORS:** Nat. Assn. of Indep. Fee Appraisers; Amer. Assn. of Cert. Appraisers; Miami Bd. of Realtors, Nat. Assn. of Indep. Fee Appraisers; Amer. Assn. of Cert. Appraisers; **EDUC:** Duquesne Univ. School of Law; **OTHER ACT & HONORS:** Personalities of the US, 1970 ed.; **HOME ADD:** 11905 N.E. 2nd Ave., C-109, N. Miami, FL 33161, (305)893-9605; **BUS TEL:** (305)893-9605.

MULLEN, Robert J.——**B:** July 16, 1927, Pittsburgh, PA, *Dir., Bldg. Operations & Serv. Dept.*, Gulf Oil; **PRIM RE ACT:** Consultant, Engineer, Appraiser, Architect, Builder, Property Manager; **SERVICES:** Operate & provide all ancillary office servs. at Gulf's world headquarters in Pittsburgh, PA; **REP CLIENTS:** Single tenant bldg. above the 1st floor/corporate entities; **PREV EMPLOY:** Owner/contractor 17 yrs., 1951-68; **PROFL AFFIL & HONORS:** BOMA/Committeeman, Ally Conf. on Community Devel., RPA; **MIL SERV:** USN; P.O. 3rd Cl.; **OTHER ACT & HONORS:** Dir. & Pres. C.I.T. Youth Council; Dir., Downtown Club Pittsburgh; **HOME ADD:** 58 N. Emily St., Pittsburgh, PA 15205, (412)921-1537; **BUS ADD:** Box 1166, Pittsburgh, PA 15130, (412)263-6012.

MULLER, Albert F., Jr.——**B:** Dec. 9, 1936, Temple, TX, *Pres.*, LaBata Land Development Co.; **PRIM RE ACT:** Developer, Builder; **PREV EMPLOY:** Instructor - Middle Mgmt.; **EDUC:** BA, Business, East TX State Univ. & Golden Gate; **GRAD EDUC:** MBA, Golden Gate Coll., CA; **MIL SERV:** USAF, Capt.; **OTHER ACT & HONORS:** Del Mar Water Bd., St. Patricks Men's Club. Am. Heart Assn.; **HOME ADD:** P.O. Box 2929, Laredo, TX 78041, (512)723-1994; **BUS ADD:** P.O. Box 2929, Laredo, TX 78041, (512)723-1994.

MULLER, Henry J.——**B:** July 27, 1919, New York, NY, *Pres.*, Muller & Assoc., Muller Devel. Corp.; **PRIM RE ACT:** Broker, Syndicator, Consultant, Developer, Builder; **SERVICES:** Condo devel., office bldg. devel., comml. devel., gen. contracting; **REP CLIENTS:** First Fed. S&L, Ft. Pierce, FL; **PREV EMPLOY:** Sr. VP, Citicorp, NY; Pres.-Citicorp Realty Consultants, Inc.; **EDUC:** BSME, 1945, Mechanical Engrg., Polytechnic Inst. of NY; **EDUC HONORS:** Tau Beta Pi (Honorary); **HOME ADD:** 1805 Cutlass Cove Dr., Vero Beach, FL 32960, (305)231-5378; **BUS ADD:** Box 3938, Vero Beach, FL 32960, (305)231-4223.

MULLIGAN, James M.——**B:** Oct. 15, 1945, Boston, MA, *Pres.*, Mulligan & Co. PC; **PRIM RE ACT:** Broker, Attorney, Developer, Owner/Investor; **SERVICES:** RE legal servs. primarily comml./office and multi-family resid.; **REP CLIENTS:** Wood Bros. Homes, Urban Renovatons, Inc., Tosco, Otis Cos.; **PREV EMPLOY:** VP for Fin. & Legal Building Group, Ltd., former maj. devel. in Denver metro. area; **PROFL AFFIL & HONORS:** Amer, CO & Denver Bar Assns., Downtown Denver Planning Policy Comm., Comm. Assn. Inst., RE Exec. Council, CO Bar Assn.; **EDUC:** AB, 1967, Eng. Lt. & Journalism, Univ. of MA, Amherst; **GRAD EDUC:** JD, 1974, RE Law, Univ. of Denver Coll. of Law; **OTHER ACT & HONORS:** Historic Denver, Inc., DCPA Sponsor, 1978 Volunteer Award, Lost &

Found, Inc.; **HOME ADD:** 6115 E 6th Ave. Pkwy, Denver, CO 80220, (303)321-7546; **BUS ADD:** 1350 17th St., Suite 360, Denver, CO 80202, (303)572-0600.

MULLIKIN, Kent R.——B: Nov. 28, 1899, Collington, Pr. George's Co., MD, *Retired - Regnl. VP Equitable Life Assurance Soc. of US*, Pres., Port of Annapolis, Inc., RE Preservation in Annapolis, MD, Investment RE & Mort.; **PRIM RE ACT:** Consultant, Appraiser, Property Manager, Owner/Investor, Lender; **OTHER RE ACT:** Historical Preservation; **SERVICES:** Purchased and restored old MD hotel; **PREV EMPLOY:** Regnl. VP Equitable Life 1945-65; Zone Commn. Fed. Housing & Dir. 1939-45; Pres. MD Realty Investment Trust, Inc., Baltimore, MD 1933-1939; **PROFL AFFIL & HONORS:** Lamda Alpha-Land Ec. Soc.;Bd. of Trade, Wash.,DC Bd-Dir. Balt. R; **EDUC:** BS, 1921, Chem., US Infantry Sch., Ft. Benning, CA; **EDUC HONORS:** Class Pres, Penm. Pres. 1921, J.H. Univ.; **MIL SERV:** Chem. Warfare Sen., 1st Lt., Capt. USA Reserves; **OTHER ACT & HONORS:** 3 term MD House Delegates; Chmn., Ways & Means Comm. & Maj. Floor Leader; former Pres., MD Hotel & Motel Assoc.; former Pres., Historic Annapolis; former Pres., Southern MD Society; 1st Chmn., Capitol City Com. Annapolis; 1st Chmn., MD Historical Trust; **HOME ADD:** 13C President Pt. Dr., Annapolis, MD 21403, (301)268-3130; **BUS ADD:** 13C President Pt. Dr., Annapolis, MD 21403, (301)268-3130.

MULLIN, Richard J.——B: Nov. 19, 1932, Syracuse, NY, Richard J. Mullin & Assoc.; **PRIM RE ACT:** Broker, Consultant, Appraiser; **SERVICES:** Consulting & appraisal services; **PROFL AFFIL & HONORS:** Amer. Soc. of RE Counselors, Soc. of RE Appraisers; **EDUC:** BS, 1963, Urban Land Econ., Syracuse Univ.; **HOME ADD:** 6881 Woodchurch Hill Rd., Fayetteville, NY 13066; **BUS ADD:** The Market Pl., Route 92, Manlius, NY, (315)682-9444.

MULLINS, Brian William——B: July 6, 1955, Madison, WI, Moore, Costello & Hart; **PRIM RE ACT:** Attorney, Engineer, Owner/Investor; **SERVICES:** Legal rep. of Owners, Devels., Contractors, Engrs. and Archs. in RE transactions and Cons. Instr; **PREV EMPLOY:** Instr., Legal Aspects of Engrg., Univ. of WI - Madison, 1980; **PROFL AFFIL & HONORS:** Member of MN and WI State Bar Assns.; Member of Nat. Soc. of Prof. Engrs.; **EDUC:** BCE, 1977, Univ. of WI; **GRAD EDUC:** JD, 1980, Univ. of WI; **EDUC HONORS:** Magna cum laude, cum laude; **HOME ADD:** 146 S. Victoria St., St. Paul, MN 55105, (612)227-4565; **BUS ADD:** 1400 Northwestern Nat. Bank Bldg., St. Paul, MN 55101, (612)227-7683.

MULLINS, Howard J.——*Pres.*, Century 21, Queen City; **PRIM RE ACT:** Broker, Consultant, Appraiser, Property Manager, Insuror; **SERVICES:** Insurance and the above etc.; **REP CLIENTS:** Toll Free Natl. 1-800-341-8720 Ext. F659, Maine 1-800-452-8783 Ext. F659; **BUS ADD:** 416 Hammond St., Box 978, Bangor, ME 04401, (207)942-4618.

MULLINS, William L.——B: Jan. 1, 1929, Houston, TX, *Pres. & Dir.*, FBS Mortgage Corp.; **PRIM RE ACT:** Lender; **SERVICES:** Mort. Banking, Const. Lending, Equities; **PREV EMPLOY:** Pres., Tower Mort. Corp. & IDS Mort. Corp.; **PROFL AFFIL & HONORS:** Mort. Bankers Assn. of Amer.; Mort. Bankers Assn. of MN (Past Pres. & Gov.); NACORE; ICSC; NAIOP; BOMA; Pres. Assn. (AMA); **EDUC:** BBA, 1950, Fin., N. TX State Coll.; **GRAD EDUC:** MBA, 1951, Fin., Univ. of TX; **MIL SERV:** USMCR; **OTHER ACT & HONORS:** Sigma Chi; **HOME ADD:** 412 Griffit St., Edina, MN 55343, (612)935-9903; **BUS ADD:** 900 Peavey Bldg., 730 Second Ave., S., Minneapolis, MN 55402, (612)343-5101.

MULRENAN, Tim——B: June 30, 1949, Jersey City, NJ, *Owner, RE Representative*, Tara Development, Pacific Telephone; **PRIM RE ACT:** Broker, Consultant, Developer, Owner/Investor, Property Manager; **SERVICES:** Consultation & Mgmt. & Brokerage; **REP CLIENTS:** Indiv. and corps. in comml. RE; **PREV EMPLOY:** San Val Devel. 1980, CEECO Devel. 1979, Mulrenan Contractors, Inc. 1973-1978; **EDUC:** BA, 1973, Natural Science, Rutgers Univ.; **GRAD EDUC:** MBA, 1970, Fin., RE, Rutgers Univ., **HOME ADD:** 7802 19th Street, Westminster, CA 92683, (714)891-9582; **BUS ADD:** 177 E. Colorado Rm. 938, Pasadena, CA 91105, (213)578-4238.

MULVANEY, Conrad M.——B: Sept. 19, 1938, Chicago, IL, *Rgnl. Counsel*, Federal National Mortgage Assn., Regional Counsel; **PRIM RE ACT:** Attorney; **PROFL AFFIL & HONORS:** Fed. Bar Assn., IL State Bar Assn., ABA, Chicago Bar Assn.; **EDUC:** JD, 1958, Law, DePaul Univ. Law School; **GRAD EDUC:** LLM, 1972, Fin., Loyola Univ.; MBA, 1979, Taxation, John Marshall Law School; **MIL SERV:** US Army; **HOME ADD:** 6 East James Way, Cary, IL 60013, (312)639-3694; **BUS ADD:** 150 S. Wacker Dr., Chicago, IL 60606, (312)641-0740.

MULVANIA, Walter L.——B: Sept. 20, 1905, Rock Port, MO, *Atty. at Law*, Sole Proprietor; **PRIM RE ACT:** Attorney; **SERVICES:** Legal; **REP CLIENTS:** The Bank of Atchison Cty., Farmers Home Admin. Title Examiner for Metropolitan Life Ins. Co., Big Tarkio Drainage Dist., Atchison Cty. Co-operative Assn.; **PROFL AFFIL & HONORS:** MO Bar, ABA, Fellow in Amer. Coll. of Probate Counsel, ABA Real Prop. and Probate Comm., Prop. Law Comm. of MO Bar; Probate & Trust Comm. of Mo. Bar., Former member 1965-71 of Bd. of Govs. of the MO BAr; **EDUC:** AB, 1927, Hist., Soc., William Jewell coll.; **GRAD EDUC:** JD, 1931, Univ. of MO; **MIL SERV:** US Army, Sgt.; **OTHER ACT & HONORS:** Prosecuting Atty. 8 yrs. Atchison Co., MO, Rock Port City Atty. 25 yrs., Fairfax, MO City Atty. 2 yrs., Rotary Club Rock Port, C of C; **HOME ADD:** 400 E. Mill St., Rock Port, MO 64482, (806)744-2936; **BUS ADD:** 213 S. Main St., Rock Port, MO 64482, (816)744-2575.

MUMFORD, Patrick Wayne——B: Oct. 10, 1944, Kinston, NC, *Exec. VP and Gen. Counsel*, Commonwealth Land Title Co. of NC; **OTHER RE ACT:** Title ins.; **SERVICES:** All titLe ins. needs; **PREV EMPLOY:** 1976-1981, VP to Pres., AMIC Title Ins. Co.; 1974-1976, Title Atty./Staff Atty., So. Title Ins. Co.; **PROFL AFFIL & HONORS:** NC State Bar; NC Bar Assn.; TN Bar Assn.; ABA (Real Prop., Trust, Probate Sect.); NC Land Title Assn., Member, NCLTA Special Comms.; **EDUC:** BS, 1966, E. Carolina Univ.; **GRAD EDUC:** JD, 1972, Law, Univ. of TN Coll. of Law; **MIL SERV:** USAF, 1966-1970 Active, 1973-1978 Reserve, Capt./Asst. Staff Judge Advocate, Missile Combat Crew, Commander of Month, Marksmanship, Outstanding Unit Award, Nat. Defense Medal; **OTHER ACT & HONORS:** Phi Alpha Delta Legal Frat.; 1978 Who's Who in S./SW; 1978 Personalities of the South; Member, E. Carolina Univ., Advisory Bd. to Dean, School of Bus.; **HOME ADD:** 8809 Trailing Cedar Dr., Raleigh, NC 27612, (919)782-3628; **BUS ADD:** POB 17966, Raleigh, NC 27619, (919)878-0303.

MUNDY, Bill——B: Mar. 22, 1940, Ellensburg, WA, *Owner & Pres.*, Bill Mundy and Associates, Inc.; **PRIM RE ACT:** Owner/Investor; **SERVICES:** BM&A Inc.: RE econ., mkt. & survey research; MUNDEVCO: RE devel.; **REP CLIENTS:** Public and prv. sector in Pacific NW, AK and HI; **PREV EMPLOY:** Appraiser, Farm Mgr., Doane Agric. Service; RE Analyst, Fenton, Conger & Ballaine; Land Economist, Weyerhaeuser; Inst., Univ. of WA; **PROFL AFFIL & HONORS:** AIREA; ULI; Amer. Mktg. Assn., Member, Bd. of Dir., Member, AIREA; **EDUC:** BS, 1965, Agriculture, WA State Univ.; **GRAD EDUC:** MA, 1971, Urban Econ., Univ. of WA; PhD, 1977, Mktg./Survey Research, Univ. of WA; **EDUC HONORS:** Beta Gamma Sigma; **MIL SERV:** USN, PN2; **HOME ADD:** 3111 37th Ave. S., Seattle, WA 98144, (206)722-3663; **BUS ADD:** 900 Seattle Tower Bldg., Seattle, WA 98101, (206)623-2935.

MUNK, Ralph——B: Feb. 25, 1956, Montreal, Can., *Engr.*, Hy-Ral Construction Inc.; **PRIM RE ACT:** Developer; **OTHER RE ACT:** Project Mgr.; **PREV EMPLOY:** Alcan Engrg. Servs.; **PROFL AFFIL & HONORS:** Que. Order of Engrs., Profl. Engr.; **EDUC:** BEng. Civil, 1978, Structures, McGill Univ.; **GRAD EDUC:** MBA, 1981, Gen. Studies, McGill Univ.; **HOME ADD:** 5970 Freud, Czn. Que., Montreal, Canada, (514)487-1697; **BUS ADD:** 4890 Hotel DeVille, Montreal, H2T2B7, Que., Can., (514)843-5365.

MUNKRES, Ted W.——B: Feb. 23, 1944, San Francisco, CA, *Pres.*, Best & Co. Contractors, Inc.; **PRIM RE ACT:** Broker, Developer, Builder, Owner/Investor, Property Manager; **SERVICES:** RE Acquisition Devel. Sales; **PREV EMPLOY:** Woodmoor Corp. Monument, CO; W. Wood Shores Corp. Trinity, TX; **PROFL AFFIL & HONORS:** NAT, Assn. of Home Builders, City of Baytown; Urban Rehab. Standards Bd.; **EDUC:** Bus., Advertising, Univ. of CA, Haward; **GRAD EDUC:** MBA, Acctg., Univ. of CA, Berkeley; **MIL SERV:** USN, EM 4; **OTHER ACT & HONORS:** Other branch office: 1238 Bookcliff Ave., Grand Junction, CO, 81501 (303)243-9494; **HOME ADD:** 4711 Country Club View, Baytown, TX 77521, (713)424-5940; **BUS ADD:** PO Box 3826, Baytown, TX 77520, (713)427-3000.

MUNSEY, William Ira, Jr.——B: Feb. 10, 1943, Bluefield, WV, *Atty. at Law*; **PRIM RE ACT:** Consultant, Attorney, Instructor; **REP CLIENTS:** Assoc. Prof.: Saint Leo Coll.; **PREV EMPLOY:** Office of the Auditor Gen.; FL Dept. of Legal Affairs; **PROFL AFFIL & HONORS:** ABA (member Real Prop. Sect. of ABA); FL Bar; Bar of the Dist. of Columbia, Former MAI Candidate; **EDUC:** BS, 1965, RE, OH State Univ.; **GRAD EDUC:** MA, 1969, Admin., Stetson Univ.; JD, 1972, Law, TX Univ.; **EDUC HONORS:** Pres. of Grad. Students Assn.; Resid. of Honors House, Phi Delta Phi; **OTHER ACT & HONORS:** Former Asst. Atty. Gen. (1974-1980); FL Hist. Preservation Soc.; **HOME ADD:** 1522 River Dr., M-302, Tampa, FL 33603, (813)234-2841; **BUS ADD:** 1522 River Dr., M-302, Tampa, FL 33603, (813)234-2841.

MUNZER, Stephen I.——**B:** Mar. 15, 1939, New York, NY, *Attorney*, Jomar Properties; **PRIM RE ACT:** Attorney, Owner/Investor, Syndicator; **SERVICES:** Investment counseling, synd. legal services; **PREV EMPLOY:** Partner, Law Firm Fincus, Munzer, Bizar, D'Alessandro & Solomon; **PROFL AFFIL & HONORS:** Assn. of the Bar of the City of New York; NY State Bar Assn.; **EDUC:** AB, 1960, Eng. Lit., Brown Univ.; **GRAD EDUC:** LLD, 1963, Cornell Law School; **EDUC HONORS:** Dean's List; **MIL SERV:** USNR, Lt.; **OTHER ACT & HONORS:** City Atheletic Club; **HOME ADD:** 850 Park Ave., New York, NY 10021; **BUS ADD:** One Citicorp Ctr., Ste. 5502, New York, NY 10022, (212)371-2400.

MURAD, B. Bill——*Atty.*, House of Murad; **PRIM RE ACT:** Broker, Consultant, Attorney, Appraiser, Instructor, Property Manager; **PROFL AFFIL & HONORS:** OH Fed. Bar Assns., ABA; Fed. Dist. Ct.; US Ct. of Military Appeals; US Supreme Ct.; All OH Cts.; Amer. Assn. of Univ. Profs; Inter-Bar Assn. Judicature Soc., Author of various articles, books, booklets; **EDUC:** BA, 1933, OH Univ.; **GRAD EDUC:** LLB, 1938, Cleveland Marshall Law School; LLD, 1955, Kent State Univ., MA; MA, 1963, Trinity Hall; **MIL SERV:** Army, S2, S3; **OTHER ACT & HONORS:** San Diego Educ. Assn.; Civic Activities, Panels, Panel Discussion Grps. (also Radio and TV); Americanism - author, resolution creating Flag Day, June 14th - Past member, Nat. Bd., Bellemy, Pledge of Allegiance and Bellamy Flag Award; **HOME ADD:** Hornblend St., San Diego, CA 92109; **BUS ADD:** 1976 Hornblend St., San Diego, CA 92109, (714)273-7878.

MURAR, E. James——**B:** Oct. 12, 1940, Tarentum, PA, *Pres.*, Recreations Inc.; **PRIM RE ACT:** Broker, Developer, Builder, Owner/Investor; **SERVICES:** Full range devel. including land, primary resid. resort & office indust.; **REP CLIENTS:** Johns Manville Corp., Columbia S&L; Foreign and Individual Investors; **PROFL AFFIL & HONORS:** CA Soc. of CPA's; ULI, Homebuilders Assn.; **EDUC:** BA, 1962, Econ., Dartmouth Coll.; **EDUC HONORS:** Cum Laude - with Highest Distinction in Econ. Major; **OTHER ACT & HONORS:** Bd. of Dirs. - Acme General Corp.; **HOME ADD:** 35 Monaco, Newport Beach, CA 92660, (714)644-0667; **BUS ADD:** 332 Forest Ave., Laguna Beach, CA 92652, (714)497-2415.

MURDOCH, William F., Jr.——**B:** Jan. 22, 1931, Pittsburgh, PA, *Pres.*, Hubbard Real Estate Investments; **PRIM RE ACT:** Owner/-Investor; **PREV EMPLOY:** Pres., Schroder RE Corp.; VP Eastdil Realty; Mgr. Comml. Devel., Columbia, MD-The Rouse Co.; **EDUC:** AB, 1952, Princeton Univ.; **GRAD EDUC:** MBA, 1956, Harvard Bus. School; **MIL SERV:** US Army, 1st Lt., 1952-54; **HOME ADD:** 33 Cleveland Ln., Princeton, NJ 08540; **BUS ADD:** c/o Merrill Lynch Hubbard, Inc., 2 Broadway 23rd Fl, New York, NY 10004, (212)908-8478.

MURFIT, Wallace G.——**B:** June 7, 1946, PA, *RE Devel. Mgr.*, Carl N. Swenson Co., Inc.; **PRIM RE ACT:** Developer, Builder, Owner/Investor; **OTHER RE ACT:** Comml. RE Devel.; **PREV EMPLOY:** 1976-79 Coldwell Banker, Comml. brokerage, 1973-76 Touche Ross & Co., CPA; **PROFL AFFIL & HONORS:** NAIOP, Amer. Inst. CPA's; **EDUC:** BA, 1968, Wesleyan Univ., Middletown, CT.; **GRAD EDUC:** MBA, 1973, Fin., Acctg., Stanford Bus. Sch.; **EDUC HONORS:** Dean's List; **MIL SERV:** USAF, 1968-71, Capt., Pilot; **HOME ADD:** 2339 Branner Dr., Menlo Pk, CA 94025, (408)854-1157; **BUS ADD:** PO 1337, San Jose, CA 95109, (408)287-9550.

MURGO, Rudy M.——**B:** Aug. 31, 1949, Everett, WA, *City Atty.*, City of Pendleton; **PRIM RE ACT:** Attorney; **SERVICES:** Legal; **REP CLIENTS:** City of Pendleton; **PROFL AFFIL & HONORS:** ABA; OR Bar Assn.; Member OR Bar; US Dist. Bar OR; US Supreme Court Bar; **EDUC:** BA, 1971, Poli. Sci./Econ., Univ. of WA; **GRAD EDUC:** JD, 1975, Law, Willamette Univ., Salem, OR; **EDUC HONORS:** Cum Laude grad., Dean's List; various scholarships, Amer. Jurisprudence Award; Col. Robertson Scholarship; **MIL SERV:** US Army; S/Sgt.; **OTHER ACT & HONORS:** DePuty DA-Marion Cty. 1976; Chief Deputy DA-Unatilla Cty. 1976-1980; Rotary; **HOME ADD:** 4509 SW Olson, Pendleton, OR 97801, (503)276-4199; **BUS ADD:** PO Box 190, Pendleton, OR 97801, (503)276-1811.

MURNION, Nickolas C.——**B:** June 22, 1953, Jordan, MT, *Atty.*, Private Practictioner; **PRIM RE ACT:** Attorney; **SERVICES:** Legal servs. assoc. with RE sales and probates of estates; **PREV EMPLOY:** Krutzfeldt and Haker, Attys. at Law, 1977; **PROFL AFFIL & HONORS:** Phi Kappa Delta, ABA, MT Bar Assn., Nat. Dist. Attys. Assn., MT Cty. Atty. Assn.; **EDUC:** BS, 1975, Pre-law, MT State Univ; **GRAD EDUC:** JD, 1978, Univ. of MT School of Law; **OTHER ACT & HONORS:** Garfield Cty. Atty. 1979-present, Garfield Jaycees, Garfield Cty. Comml. Club, BPO Elks, Miles City Lodge No. 537; **HOME ADD:** PO Box 375, Jordan, MT 59337, (406)557-2506; **BUS ADD:** PO Box 375, Jordan, MT 59337, (406)557-2480.

MURO, Michael L.——**B:** July 22, 1940, Yonkers, NY, *Sole Assessor-Dir. of RE*, Town of Cortlandt; **PRIM RE ACT:** Appraiser, Assessor; **PREV EMPLOY:** Fee RE Appraiser; **PROFL AFFIL & HONORS:** AACA, IAAO, , NYSAA, and Westchester Planning Federation, Cert. Appraiser Consultant by AACA; **EDUC:** BA, 1962, Hist. and Poli. Sci., Iona Coll.; **OTHER ACT & HONORS:** Westchester Cty.-Special Advisory Comm. formulating Cty. Housing Policy - 1978, Cty. Task Force on Full Value Assessing 1979-1981; **HOME ADD:** 4 Cleveland Pl., Yonkers, NY 1071O, (914)961-5106; **BUS ADD:** Municipal Bldg., Van Wyck St., Croton-On-Hudson, NY 10520, (914)961-9128.

MURPHEY, Julian C.——**B:** July 24, 1937, Louisville, KY, *VP*, Murphey, Taylor & Ellis, Inc.; **PRIM RE ACT:** Broker, Developer, Property Manager; **SERVICES:** Sale, lease and devel. of income producing prop.; **REP CLIENTS:** Indiv. or instnl. investors; **PROFL AFFIL & HONORS:** RNMI; IREM, Cert. Comml. Investment Member of RNMI (CCIM) Cert. Prop. Mgr. (CPM) IREM: Omega Tau Rho; **MIL SERV:** USA, 1st Lt.; **OTHER ACT & HONORS:** Lecturer for RNMI on comm. - investment prop.; **HOME ADD:** 498 Wesleyan Drive, Macon, GA 31210, (912)477-8607; **BUS ADD:** PO Box 4468, Macon, GA 31213, (912)743-2671.

MURPHY, Brian P.——**B:** June 29, 1943, Providence, RI, *Atty.*, Repetti, Murphy & Evans, P.C.; **PRIM RE ACT:** Attorney; **REP CLIENTS:** Lenders; **PREV EMPLOY:** Ragan & Mason, Washington, DC 1969-1974; **PROFL AFFIL & HONORS:** Dist. of Columbia and MD Bars; Guest Lecturer, Urban Ventures School; **EDUC:** AB, 1965, Govt., Georgetown Univ.; **GRAD EDUC:** JD, 1968, Catholic Univ. of Amer.; **MIL SERV:** US Naval Res., JAGC, Lt.; **HOME ADD:** 5207 Chandler St., Bethesda, MD 20814, (301)530-3623; **BUS ADD:** 1010 Wisconsin Ave. NW, Washington, DC 20007, (202)333-8040.

MURPHY, Charles J.——*VPO*, The Westport Co.; **PRIM RE ACT:** Developer; **BUS ADD:** 275 Broadhollow Rd., Melville, NY 11747, (516)752-9085.*

MURPHY, Daniel M.——**B:** Feb. 12, 1936, New York, NY, *VP, Forward Planning*, Kaufman & Broad, NJ; **PRIM RE ACT:** Consultant, Engineer, Attorney, Developer, Builder; **OTHER RE ACT:** Land acquisition, zoning & subdiv.; **PREV EMPLOY:** Part., Lincoln Prop. Co., VP Landauer Assoc.; **PROFL AFFIL & HONORS:** NY Fed. Bar Assn., Profl. Engrg. (NY, NJ), Profl. Planner (NJ); **EDUC:** B. Civil Engrg., 1957, Manhattan Coll.; **GRAD EDUC:** LLB(JD), 1964, Law, St. John's Univ.; **HOME ADD:** 13 Sunrise Cir., Holmdel, NJ 07733, (201)739-0283; **BUS ADD:** 100 Craig Rd., Freehold, NJ 07728, (201)780-1800.

MURPHY, Edward B.——**B:** Apr. 3, 1908, Buffalo, NY, *Atty.*, Self; **PRIM RE ACT:** Attorney; **SERVICES:** Legal, contracts, morts., closings, deeds, etc.; **PROFL AFFIL & HONORS:** ABA; NY State & Erie Cty. Bar Assns.; **GRAD EDUC:** LLB, 1927, RE, Estates, Corps., Municipal, Univ. of Buffalo; **OTHER ACT & HONORS:** Co-Author of Erie Cty. Charter; Buffalo C of C; Past Pres.: (A) Buffalo-Niagara Frontier Bus. Mens Assn.; (B) United Taxpayers League of Buffalo & Erie Cty.; (C) Riverside Lions; (D) Riverside Bus. Mens Assn.; and of Buffalo Athletic Club; **HOME ADD:** 150 Carpenter Ave., Tonawanda, NY 14223, (716)833-3568; **BUS ADD:** 1010 Western Bldg., Buffalo, NY 14202, (716)852-7773.

MURPHY, Edward J.——*Assoc. Gen. Counsel*, Department of Housing and Urban Development, Ofc. of Legislation & Regulations; **PRIM RE ACT:** Lender; **BUS ADD:** 451 Seventh St., S.W., Washington, DC 20410, (202)755-7093.*

MURPHY, George M.——**B:** June 18, 1946, Dallas, TX, *Broker/Partner*, Parks Jones Realtors, Resid. Sales/Prop. Mgmt.; **PRIM RE ACT:** Broker, Property Manager; **SERVICES:** Resid. Listing/Sales, Single and Multi Family Prop. Mgmt.; **PROFL AFFIL & HONORS:** Lawton Bd. of Realtors, OK Assn. of Realtors, NAR, CRB, GRI; **MIL SERV:** USAR, 1st. Lt., Bronze Star with V; **HOME ADD:** 301 Ridgwview Way, Lawton, OK 73505, (405)357-4827; **BUS ADD:** 1705 Cache Rd., Lawton, OK 73501, (405)357-8300.

MURPHY, Gerald D.——*Pres.*, Early California Inds., Inc.; **PRIM RE ACT:** Property Manager; **BUS ADD:** 10960 Wilshire Blvd., Los Angeles, CA 90024, (213)879-1480.*

MURPHY, Harold B.——**B:** Sept. 6, 1923, Oakland, CA, *Pres.*, Murco Development Inc. & Murco Management Inc.; **PRIM RE ACT:** Developer, Builder, Property Manager; **SERVICES:** Devel. & Build Comml. & Indus. Projects for our own account and manage said projects; **EDUC:** BS, 1948, Bus. Admin., Univ. of San Francisco; **MIL SERV:** USAF, 1st Lt., Pilot; **HOME ADD:** 41777 Murphy Pl., Fremont, CA 94538; **BUS ADD:** 39111 Paseo Padre Pkwy., Fremont, CA 94538, (415)791-2345.

MURPHY, James——*Pres. Retail Store*, Phillips-Van Heusen; **PRIM RE ACT:** Property Manager; **BUS ADD:** 1290 Ave. of the Americas, New York, NY 10019, (212)541-5200.*

MURPHY, James M.——**B:** Nov. 4, 1947, E. Elmhurst, Long Island, NY, *Second VP and Port Folio Mgr.*, Union Mutual Life Insurance Corp., Investment; **PRIM RE ACT:** Lender, Owner/Investor, Instructor, Property Manager; **REP CLIENTS:** Devel., Builders; **PREV EMPLOY:** MA Mutual Life Ins. Co.; **PROFL AFFIL & HONORS:** Member-Intl. Council of Shopping Ctrs., Mort. Bankers Assn. of America, Urban Land Inst.; **EDUC:** BA, 1970, Econ., Univ. of MA; **GRAD EDUC:** MBA, 1973, Fin., Univ. of MA; **OTHER ACT & HONORS:** VP of Bd. of Dir. Ferry Village Neighborhood Housing Serv., Advisor to Jr. Achievement; **HOME ADD:** 16 Ctry. Charm Rd., Cumberland, ME 04021; **BUS ADD:** 2211 Congress St., Portland, ME 04112, (207)780-2270.

MURPHY, Joseph W.——**B:** Dec. 7, 1921, Sedolia, MO, *Pres.*, Welsh & Assoc., Inc.; **PRIM RE ACT:** Broker, Appraiser, Builder, Owner/Investor, Property Manager; **SERVICES:** Investment counseling, valuation, prop. mgmt., sales; **REP CLIENTS:** Indiv., lenders; **PROFL AFFIL & HONORS:** Nat. Assn. of Realtors; State & Local, NAR Dir.; CO Realtor of Year 1979, Greeley Bd. Realtor of the Year 1971, CAR Dir.; **EDUC:** BS (Bus. Admin.), 1949, Acctg., Fin., Personnel Mgmt., Univ. of CO; **MIL SERV:** US Army Engr.; S/Sgt.; E.T.O. 1942 (Sept.) 1945 (Dec.), 4 Battle Stars; **OTHER ACT & HONORS:** Mayor Protem City of Greeley 1979-81; City Council 1974-81; St. Mary's Catholic Church; Rotary; American Legion; Elks; Greeley Country Club; Legionaire of the Yr. 1970; Knights of Columbus 4 Degree; **HOME ADD:** 1930 - 12 St., Greeley, CO 80631, (303)352-4968; **BUS ADD:** Box 879, Greeley, CO 80632, (303)352-3833.

MURPHY, Michael Terrence——**B:** July 25, 1946, Riverside, CA, *Partner*, Rosenberg Law Firm; **PRIM RE ACT:** Attorney, Instructor; **SERVICES:** Legal services re: transfers, encumbrancing and investment counseling and title work; **REP CLIENTS:** Devel., comml. lenders and brokers; **PREV EMPLOY:** Lic. CA RE Broker and Assoc. Prof., NM State Univ. at Carlsbad, NM; **PROFL AFFIL & HONORS:** CA Bar Assn; NM Bar Assn.; ABA, Sect. on Real Prop., Probate and Trust; **EDUC:** BS, 1973, RE Fin., CA State Univ. at Long Beach; **GRAD EDUC:** JD, 1976, Law, Pepperdine Univ. School of Law; **EDUC HONORS:** Bus. Editor, Pepperdine Law Review; **MIL SERV:** USAF; **HOME ADD:** POB 1257, Carlsbad, NM 88220, (505)885-9353; **BUS ADD:** Cabeza de Vaca Bldg., 314 W. Mermod St., POB 1597, Carlsbad, NM 88220, (505)885-4163.

MURPHY, Neil——**B:** Jan. 10, 1948, Boston, MA, *President*, Creative Real Estate, Inc.; **PRIM RE ACT:** Broker, Consultant, Owner/Investor, Syndicator; **OTHER RE ACT:** Specialist in Equity Sharing; **SERVICES:** Computer Analysis of Real Estate Investments; Single Family Homes; **PROFL AFFIL & HONORS:** Candidate for the CCIM Designation, Senior Listing - Who's Who in Creative Real Estate; **EDUC:** BS, 1969, Physics, Rensselaer Polytechnic Inst.; **GRAD EDUC:** MS, 1973, Oceanography, Univ. of NC at Chapel Hill; MA, 1973, Physics, Wake Forest Univ.; **OTHER ACT & HONORS:** Toastmasters; **HOME ADD:** 620 3rd St. NE, Washington, DC 20002; **BUS ADD:** 620 3rd St. N.E., Washington, DC 20002, (202)543-7342.

MURPHY, Stephen C.——**B:** May 28, 1947, Kansas City, MO, *Partner*, Cook, Murphy & Kenney; **PRIM RE ACT:** Attorney; **REP CLIENTS:** RE Bd. of Metropolitan St. Louis; Bomar RE Co.; Laurene Davis, Inc.; D.S. Anderson Co.; **PROFL AFFIL & HONORS:** ABA; MO & St. Louis Bar Assns.; **EDUC:** AB, 1969, Eng., Duke Univ.; **GRAD EDUC:** JD, 1974, Law, Washington Univ.; **HOME ADD:** 41 Thorncliff Ln., Kirkwood, MO 63122, (314)965-1940; **BUS ADD:** 10 S. Brentwood Blvd., Room 201, Clayton, MO 63105, (314)727-4222.

MURPHY, Thomas——*Asst. Treasurer*, The Pillsbury Company; **PRIM RE ACT:** Property Manager; **BUS ADD:** 608 2nd Ave. South, Pillsbury Bldg., Minneapolis, MN 55402, (612)330-4966.*

MURPHY, Thomas Michael——**B:** Feb. 25, 1921, *Supervisor*, General Motors, Truck & Coach; **PRIM RE ACT:** Engineer; **PREV EMPLOY:** Western Electric Co.; **PROFL AFFIL & HONORS:** Phil Kapata Kapata; **EDUC:** Queens Vocational High School; **GRAD EDUC:** 1938, NY Univ.; **MIL SERV:** US Army, Cpl.; **HOME ADD:** 72 Decker Ave., Staten Island, NY 10303, (212)727-3575; **BUS ADD:** 6O1 West 57th St., New York, NY 10019, (212)727-3575.

MURPHY, W. Michael——**B:** Oct. 28, 1945, San Jose, CA, *Sr. VP and Director of Acquisitions*, Montgomery Realty Investors; **OTHER RE ACT:** Hotel investor; **SERVICES:** Acquisition of hotels through joint ventures on behalf of public limited partnerships; **PREV EMPLOY:** Holiday Inns, Inc., Memphis, TN as Regional Dir. of Devel.; **EDUC:** BA, 1967, Eng., Memphis State Univ.; **GRAD EDUC:** MA, 1969, Eng., Univ. of IA; **HOME ADD:** 725 Magnolia, Menlo Park, CA 94025, (415)321-8471; **BUS ADD:** 2655 Campus Dr., Suite 250, San Mateo, CA 94403, (415)572-7111.

MURPHY, Walter L.——**B:** Oct. 1 1939, KC, *Pres.*, Walter Murphy Inc.; **PRIM RE ACT:** Broker; **PROFL AFFIL & HONORS:** CCIM, CPM; **EDUC:** Arch., 1964, KS State Univ.; **HOME ADD:** 4105 Delmar Dr., Prairie Vill., KS City, MO 64111, (813)432-2729; **BUS ADD:** 3929 Broadway, KS City, MO 64111, (816)931-4949.

MURRAY, Carl——*Dir. Acq.*, Lear Siegler; **PRIM RE ACT:** Property Manager; **BUS ADD:** 2850 Ocean Park Blvd., PO Box 2158, Santa Monica, CA 90406, (213)391-7210.*

MURRAY, F. Alden, Jr.——**B:** March 27, 1926, Washington, DC, *Pres.*, Alden, Inc.; **PRIM RE ACT:** Broker, Consultant, Appraiser, Owner/Investor, Syndicator; **OTHER RE ACT:** Mort. Broker; **SERVICES:** Income producing sales, appraising, counseling & fin.; **PROFL AFFIL & HONORS:** Washington DC Bd. of Realtors; Dir., Columbia First Fed. S & L; Advisory Dir., Columbia RE Title Ins. Co., Sr. Member, Amer. Soc. of Appraisers; Sr. Member (CRA), Nat. Assn. of Review Appraisers; Sr. Member (SCV), Intl. Inst. of Valuers (Zurich, Switzerland); **EDUC:** BBA, 1950, Commerce, Washington & Lee Univ.; **MIL SERV:** USNR, ETM 3/c; **OTHER ACT & HONORS:** Columbia Country Club; Univ. Club of Washington; **HOME ADD:** 4982 Sentinel Dr., Bethesda, MD 20816, (301)320-3216; **BUS ADD:** 4801 Montgomery Ln., Bethesda, MD 20814, (301)657-2960.

MURRAY, George——*Dir., Construction*, US Tobacco Co.; **PRIM RE ACT:** Property Manager; **BUS ADD:** 100 W. Putnam Ave., Greenwich, CT 06830, (203)661-1100.*

MURRAY, Joseph C.——**B:** Oct. 17, 1919, *VP*, Shannon & Luchs Co., Apt. & Community Mgmt.; **PRIM RE ACT:** Consultant, Instructor, Property Manager; **PROFL AFFIL & HONORS:** Prop. Mgrs. Assn.; Inst. of RE Mgmt. (Nat. Assn. of Realtors); Washington DC Bd. of Realtors; Nat. Housing Conference; Apt. & Office Bldg. Assn., Cert. Prop. Mgr.; Member, Academy of Authors, IREM; Realtor of the Yr., Wash. DC Bd. of Realtors; J. Wallace Paletou Award, IREM; **MIL SERV:** US Army, SSgt., Bronze Star; **HOME ADD:** 11813 Greenleaf Ave., Potomac, MD 20854, (301)762-3370; **BUS ADD:** 900 17th St., N.W., Washington, DC 20006, (202)659-7117.

MURRAY, Michael J.——**B:** Aug. 15, 1948, Madison, WI, *Dir.*, Univ. of WI, La Crosse, Bureau of Bus. and Econ. Research; **PRIM RE ACT:** Broker, Consultant, Appraiser, Instructor; **OTHER RE ACT:** Mkt. Research; **SERVICES:** Mkt., feasibility studies, valuation, investment seminars, counseling, computer programming, model bldg.; **REP CLIENTS:** Lenders, RE devels., investors; **PREV EMPLOY:** Premack Research Assocs. - Mkt., Feasibility Studies, Ball St. Univ. RE, Finance Courses; **PROFL AFFIL & HONORS:** Nat. Assn. of Bus. Econ., Amer. Fin. Assn.; **EDUC:** BA, 1970, Econs./Fin., Univ. of So. FL; **GRAD EDUC:** MA, PhD, 1973, 1975, Econs./Fin., Univ. of Notre Dame; **HOME ADD:** 523 Troy St., Onalaska, WI 54650, (608)783-6758; **BUS ADD:** 1725 State St., La Crosse, WI 54601, (608)785-8647.

MURRAY, Norbert T.——**B:** June 6, 1936, Chicago, IL, *Pres.*, Murray Enterprises, Inc.; **PRIM RE ACT:** Consultant, Developer, Builder, Owner/Investor, Property Manager, Syndicator; **GRAD EDUC:** BS, 1959, Mgmt., DePaul Univ., Chicago, IL; **MIL SERV:** US Naval Res., 3rd Class; **HOME ADD:** 422 Schaeffer Dr., Clare, MI 48617, (517)386-2653; **BUS ADD:** 1480 W. Center Rd., Unit 1, Essexville, MI 48732, (517)892-3579.

MURRAY, Sean E.——**B:** Sept. 3, 1949, Edmonton, Alb., Can., *Exec. Asst.*, Maclab Enterprises Ltd.; **PRIM RE ACT:** Developer, Property Manager; **PROFL AFFIL & HONORS:** Soc. of Mgmt. Accountants of Alberta; **EDUC:** BA, 1971, Sociology/Psych., Univ. of Alberta; **HOME ADD:** 10519 17 Ave., Edmonton, T6J5C2, Alb., Can., (403)436-0721; **BUS ADD:** POB 3160, Edmonton, T5J2G7, Alb., Can., (403)420-6666.

MUSCARELLE, Jos. L.——**B:** Nov. 24, 1903, New York, NY, *Chmn. of the Bd.*, Jos. L. Muscarelle, Inc.; **PRIM RE ACT:** Banker, Developer, Builder, Owner/Investor, Property Manager; **GRAD EDUC:** Fairleigh Dickinson Univ., Teaneck NJ; **EDUC HONORS:** Hon. LLD; **OTHER ACT & HONORS:** Dir., Natl. Community Bank; Tr. Columbus Hosp. Newark, NJ; Tr., Bergen Cty. Laborers' Welfare & Pension Funds, Hackensack, NJ; **HOME ADD:** 300 Fairmount Ave., Hackensack, NJ 07601, (201)487-2368; **BUS ADD:** Essex St. & Route 17, Maywood, NJ 07607, (201)845-8100.

MUSCARNERA, Sam——*House Counsel*, Fedders Corp.; **PRIM RE ACT:** Attorney, Property Manager; **BUS ADD:** Woodbridge Ave., Edison, NJ 08817, (201)549-7200.*

MUSCILLO, Alfonso——**B:** May 4, 1931, NY, *Pres.*, Muscillo Agency/Muscillo Appraisal Assoc.; **PRIM RE ACT:** Broker, Consultant, Appraiser, Developer, Builder, Property Manager; **PREV EMPLOY:** 25 yrs. Self Employed; **EDUC:** BS, RE, NYU; **GRAD EDUC:** Educ., C.W. Post; **MIL SERV:** USA, Cpl.; **HOME ADD:** 20 Weaver Dr., Apt. 6a, Massapequa, NY 11758; **BUS ADD:** 5368 Merric Rd., Massapequa, NY 11758.

MUSKAT, Marc L.——**B:** June 10, 1946, Chicago, *Sr. VP*, Quinlan and Tyson R.E. Investment Advisors, Inc.; **PRIM RE ACT:** Broker, Attorney, Instructor, Syndicator, Consultant; **OTHER RE ACT:** CPA, Lic. Securities Princ.; **SERVICES:** Consult. synd.; **PREV EMPLOY:** Public acctg. firms; **PROFL AFFIL & HONORS:** ABA, AICPA, RESSI, SRS; **EDUC:** BSBA, 1968, Acctg., Univ. of Denver; **GRAD EDUC:** MS,JD, 1971, Taxes, DePaul Univ.(MS), Northwestern Univ.(JD); **EDUC HONORS:** Beta Alpha Psi; **BUS ADD:** 707 Lake Cook Rd. Suite 200, Deerfield, IL 60015, (312)498-6600.

MUSTACCHIO, Diana L.——**B:** Mar. 29, 1943, Canton, OH, *Corp. Sec.*, Security Savings Mortgage Corp., Secondary Market, Investor Sales; **OTHER RE ACT:** Mort. Banker, Corp. Sec.; **SERVICES:** Fin. for home mort., RE devel., fin. consulting; **REP CLIENTS:** Lenders and instnl. investors; **PROFL AFFIL & HONORS:** Canton - Women's Council in RE; **HOME ADD:** 120 Ingram S.W., Canton, OH 44710, (216)453-0919; **BUS ADD:** 5686 Dressler Rd. N.W., N. Canton, OH 44720, (216)494-8000.

MYERS, Brevard S.——**B:** Mar. 12, 1923, Charlotte, NC, *Pres.*, Myers & Chapman, Inc.; **PRIM RE ACT:** Developer, Builder, Owner/Investor; **SERVICES:** Comml. and Indus. Bldgs.; **REP CLIENTS:** NCNB, NCR, Southern Rhy., Hartford Ins. Co., Coca Cola Consolidated, Gen. Electric Supply Co.; **EDUC:** BS, 1945, Engrg., VA Military Instit.; **GRAD EDUC:** MBA, 1950, Harvard Bus. School; **MIL SERV:** USAF, Lt. 1943-46; **OTHER ACT & HONORS:** Charlotte City Council - 1958-60; COB, Mercy Hospital 76 to present, Central Piedmont Indus. Pres. 64-65; Johnson C. Smith Univ., Bd. of Visitors, Mutual S&L Assn., Board 1956-Present; **HOME ADD:** 2746 Hampton Ave., Charlotte, NC 28207, (704)332-3394; **BUS ADD:** PO Box 4163, Charlotte, NC 28204, (704)372-4230.

MYERS, Bruce E.——**B:** Jan. 10, 1943, Portsmouth, VA, *Atty. at Law*, Bruce Edward Myers; **PRIM RE ACT:** Attorney; **OTHER RE ACT:** Oil & Gas; **SERVICES:** All matters relating to RE practice; **REP CLIENTS:** RE Transactions; **PROFL AFFIL & HONORS:** ABA, TN Bar Assn., ATLA, TNTLA; **EDUC:** BS, 1966, Acctg., Univ. of TN, Knoxville; **GRAD EDUC:** JD, 1970, Univ. of TN; **MIL SERV:** US Army, SP4; **OTHER ACT & HONORS:** Gen. Sessions, Probate, & Juvenile Judge 1974-1981; **HOME ADD:** 304 4th St., Livingston, TN 38570, (615)823-5594; **BUS ADD:** 213 N. Church St., Livingston, TN 38570, (615)823-1298.

MYERS, Carl——**B:** July 4, 1943, NM, *Pres.*, Future Homes of AR; **PRIM RE ACT:** Builder; **SERVICES:** Planning, construction, sales; **PROFL AFFIL & HONORS:** NAHB, Ft. Smith Bd. Realtors; **EDUC:** Psych., 1969, San Diego State Univ.; **GRAD EDUC:** MA, 1972, Sociology, US Intl. Univ.; **EDUC HONORS:** Deans List; **HOME ADD:** 10116 Jenny Lind, PO Box 5649, Ft. Smith, AR 72913; **BUS ADD:** PO Box 1962, Ft. Smith, AR 72902, (501)646-0407.

MYERS, Dale W.——**B:** Aug. 23, 1938, Tacoma, WA, *Pres.*, Pacific West Properties, Inc.; **PRIM RE ACT:** Broker, Owner/Investor, Property Manager, Syndicator; **SERVICES:** RE brokerage, prop. mgmt., investment counseling; **PROFL AFFIL & HONORS:** NAR; WA Assn. of Realtors; Seattle-King Cty. Bd. of Realtors, GRI; CRB; **MIL SERV:** US Army, Pfc; **HOME ADD:** 17101 156th Ave. S.E., Renton, WA 98055, (206)228-0717; **BUS ADD:** 14410 S.E. Petrovitsky Rd., Suite 200, Renton, WA 98055, (206)271-5300.

MYERS, Daniel W., II——**B:** Mar. 21, 1931, Camden, NJ, *Atty. (Partner)*, Myers, Matteo, Rabil & Norcross; **PRIM RE ACT:** Attorney; **SERVICES:** Legal Services; **REP CLIENTS:** Land Owners, Devels. and Lending Instit.; **PROFL AFFIL & HONORS:** ABA; JN NJ State Bar Assn.; Camden Cty. Bar Assn.; VA State Bar, Atty. at Law; **EDUC:** BS, 1952, Econ., Univ. of VA; **GRAD EDUC:** LLB, 1957, Taxation, Univ. of VA; **EDUC HONORS:** Beta Gamma Sigma; **MIL SERV:** USA, Transp. Corp., 1st Lt. 1952-1954; **HOME ADD:** 325 Rhoads Ave., Haddonfield, NJ 08033, (609)429-4849; **BUS ADD:** Suite 800, 2201 Route 38, Cherry Hill, NJ 08034, (609)667-7272.

MYERS, Darrold D.——**B:** June 26, 1931, Whittier, CA, *Mgr. - Facilities Planning Div.*, County of Orange, CA, Facilities Planning Div.; **PRIM RE ACT:** Broker, Instructor, Consultant, Appraiser, Property Manager; **OTHER RE ACT:** Facilities Planner; **SERVICES:** Tech. College RE Courses, Consult; **PROFL AFFIL & HONORS:** IREM, Interntl. Right of Way Assoc. (IRWA), CPM; **EDUC:** BA, 1966, Bus. Admin, Acctg., Spec., CA State Univ. at Long Beach; **EDUC HONORS:** Cum Laude; **HOME ADD:** 13752 Sanderstead Rd, Santa Ana, CA 92705, (714)838-2297; **BUS ADD:** 628 No. Sycamore, Santa Ana, CA 92701, (714)834-7468.

MYERS, George C., Jr.——**B:** Mar. 20, 1955, Orleans, France, *Exec. Group Controller*, Boyer Realty, Boyer Realty Mgmt.; **PRIM RE ACT:** Consultant, Property Manager, Owner/Investor; **OTHER RE ACT:** Investment Group Controller; **SERVICES:** Mgmt. of Investment Prop.; **PROFL AFFIL & HONORS:** Realtor Assoc. New London Bd. of Realtors; **EDUC:** BA, 1978, Philosophy, St. Michaels Coll, Winooski, VT; **HOME ADD:** 50 Old Colony Rd., No. Stonington, CT 06359, (203)535-3424; **BUS ADD:** 391 Long Hill Rd., Groton, CT 06340, (203)445-8168.

MYERS, Jacqueline——*Prep. & Sales Mgr.*, Fairmount Co./Realtors & Developers; **PRIM RE ACT:** Developer; **BUS ADD:** 3101 Mercier St., Ste 420, Kansas City, MO 64111, (816)531-6043.*

MYERS, John A.——**B:** Dec. 29, 1946, Wilmington, DE, *Atty.*, Johnson & Lanphere PC; **PRIM RE ACT:** Attorney; **SERVICES:** Representative of RE Devels. and RE Lenders - zoning work; **PREV EMPLOY:** Deputy City Atty., City of Albuquerque Head Real Prop. Sect.; **PROFL AFFIL & HONORS:** ABA, Real Prop. Sect., Alburquerque Bar Assn., NM State Bar; Amer Right of Way Assn., Outstanding Young Men of America - 1981; **EDUC:** BE, 1968, Mech. Engrg., Vanderbilt Univ.; **GRAD EDUC:** JD, 1974, Law, Univ. of NM; LLM, 1975, Law, Prop. Law Concentration, Harvard Univ.; **EDUC HONORS:** Summa Cum Laude, Honor thesis; **MIL SERV:** USN, Lt.; **HOME ADD:** 5719 Hannett NE, Albuquerque, NM 87110, (505)256-9115; **BUS ADD:** 200 W. 6400 Uptown Blvd., Albuquerque, NM 81110, (505)881-3333.

MYERS, Robert L.——**B:** Jan. 21, 1954, Dallas, TX, *Partner/Office Leasing Broker*, Joe Gallini & Co.; **PRIM RE ACT:** Broker, Owner/Investor; **SERVICES:** Land sales, office leasing, bldg. sales; **PREV EMPLOY:** IBM Office Products Div., Dallas, TX; **PROFL AFFIL & HONORS:** Comml. Investment Div., Greater Dallas Bd. of Realtors; **EDUC:** BS, 1977, Mktg., Univ. of TX; **HOME ADD:** 4217 Camden Ave., Dallas, TX 75206, (214)823-8952; **BUS ADD:** 8235 Douglas, Suite 217, Dallas, TX 75225, (214)696-5506.

MYERS, Russell C.——**B:** Mar. 24, 1927, Cincinnati, OH, *Pres.*, Glaser & Myers and Assoc., Inc.; **PRIM RE ACT:** Architect; **SERVICES:** Arch. & Engrg. Profl. Servs., Master Planning, Interior Design; **REP CLIENTS:** State and local govtl. bodies, univs., local school districts, fin. instns., multi-housing devels., comml. and indus. clients, zoos, religious orgs.; **PROFL AFFIL & HONORS:** AIA, Arch. Soc. of OH, Amer. Registered Archs.; **EDUC:** BS, Arch., Univ. of Cincinnati; **EDUC HONORS:** Magna Cum Laude; **OTHER ACT & HONORS:** Rotary; Tr. of Family Service, Deaconess Hospital, Beech Acres Orphans Home, Bell Home for the Sightless; Univ. of Cincinnati Found.; **HOME ADD:** 9250 Given Road, Indian Hill, OH 45243; **BUS ADD:** 2753 Erie Ave., Cincinnati, OH 45208, (513)871-9111.

MYERS, Wallace Haslett——**B:** Nov. 21, 1929, Worcester, MA, *Atty. at Law*; **PRIM RE ACT:** Broker, Attorney, Owner/Investor; **SERVICES:** Legal servs. primarily, also broker servs.; **PREV EMPLOY:** Atty., Grp. Law Staff, State Mutual of Amer., 1963-1967; Assoc., Atty. Frank Howard, 1957-1962; **PROFL AFFIL & HONORS:** Worcester Cty. Bar Assn.; MBA; **EDUC:** AB, 1951, Chemistry, Clark Univ.; **GRAD EDUC:** JD, 1954, Law, Harvard Law School; LLM, 1962, Taxation, Boston Univ. School of Law; **MIL SERV:** US Army, Spec. 3, 1955-1957; **HOME ADD:** 78 1/2 Elm St., Worcester, MA 01609, (617)754-2922; **BUS ADD:** 78 1/2 Elm St., Worcester, MA 01609, (617)752-0855.

MYLES, Ronald L.——**B:** Mar. 9, 1941, Tulsa, OK, *Partner*, Harlan and Myles Co.; **PRIM RE ACT:** Broker, Consultant, Developer, Owner/Investor, Instructor; **SERVICES:** Brokerage, consulting and devel. for indivs., bus. and instns. in comml. RE; **REP CLIENTS:** S&L cos., railroad cos., devels. and indivs.; **PREV EMPLOY:** Nine years in comml. RE brokerage and devel.; 3-1/2 yrs. as a Certified Public Accountant; **PROFL AFFIL & HONORS:** NAR, RNMI, CO Assn. of Realtors, Denver Bd. of Realtors, AICPA, CO Soc. of CPA's, CCIM, CPA, GRI; **EDUC:** BBA, 1963, Bus. Stats. & Econ., Univ. of OK; **GRAD EDUC:** MS, 1965, Bus. Statistics & Econ., Univ. of OK; **MIL SERV:** USAF, Capt.; **OTHER ACT & HONORS:** Denver C of C; **HOME ADD:** 5026 West Lake Place, Littleton, CO 80123, (303)798-

1963; **BUS ADD:** 1777 S. Harrison St., Suite P-305, Denver, CO 80210, (303)753-9988.

NADEAU, James A.——**B:** Nov. 6, 1945, Dunedin, FL, *Atty.*, Hamblett & Kerrigan Professional Assoc.; **PRIM RE ACT:** Attorney; **SERVICES:** Legal representation - all areas of RE law; **PREV EMPLOY:** Janelle, Nadeau & Jette; **PROFL AFFIL & HONORS:** NH Bar Assn.; ABA; **EDUC:** BA, 1967, Math., Boston Univ.; **GRAD EDUC:** JD, 1970, Harvard Law Sch.; **EDUC HONORS:** Phi Beta Kappa, Summa Cum Laude; **OTHER ACT & HONORS:** Bd. of Education, Nashua, NH, 1970-1973; **HOME ADD:** 286 Lake St., Nashua, NH 03061, (603)883-7395; **BUS ADD:** 4 Water St., POB 868X, Nashua, NH 03061, (603)883-5501.

NAGAN, Harold R.——*Mng. Partner*, Investment Partnerships; **PRIM RE ACT:** Developer; **BUS ADD:** 280-17th St., Ste. A, Oakland, CA 94612, (415)444-8661.*

NAGAN, Michael P.——**B:** Mar. 30, 1943, Appleton, WI, *Municipal Facilities Admin.*, City of Seattle, Dept. of Admin. Serv.; **PRIM RE ACT:** Architect, Builder, Property Manager, Engineer; **SERVICES:** Buy, build, lease, renovate, maintain & manage city facilities; **REP CLIENTS:** Other city agencies; **PROFL AFFIL & HONORS:** BOMA Seattle; BOMA Intl.; **EDUC:** BA, 1965, Econ., Univ. of WI; **GRAD EDUC:** MA, 1966, Pol. Sci., Univ. of WI; **HOME ADD:** 2666-51st SW, Seattle, WA 98116, (206)935-3225; **BUS ADD:** 400 Yesler Bldg., Seattle, WA 98104, (206)625-2185.

NAGEL, Bob E.——**B:** June 30, 1932, Memphis, TN, *Pres.*, Nagel & Co.; **PRIM RE ACT:** Broker, Consultant, Developer, Owner/Investor, Syndicator; **SERVICES:** Any involved with land acquisition, Devel., selling improved prop.; **REP CLIENTS:** Mainly large local and natl. devels. of office, indus., multi-family or single family land. Also, purchasers of improved props.; **PREV EMPLOY:** 18 yrs. in brokerage and devel. bus. in Atlanta GA; **EDUC:** BS Textile Engrg., 1954, Engrg., Auburn Univ.; **EDUC HONORS:** Phi Psi Honorary Textile Frat.; **MIL SERV:** USAF, 1st Lt.; **HOME ADD:** 2844 Glade Springs Dr. NE, Atlanta, GA 30345, (404)325-8066; **BUS ADD:** Suite 312,, Oaktree Plaza, 3845 N. Druid Hills Rd., Decatur, GA 30033, (404)321-2927.

NAGEL, John R.——*Pres.*, Carlson Properties, Inc.; **PRIM RE ACT:** Developer; **BUS ADD:** 12805 State Hwy. 55, Plymouth, MN 55441, (612)540-5541.*

NAGLE, Gary J.——**B:** June 13, 1952, Huntington, NY, *Atty.*, Scott, Royce, Harris & Bryan, P.A.; **PRIM RE ACT:** Attorney; **SERVICES:** Legal servs.; **REP CLIENTS:** Indiv. buyers and sellers of resid. and comml. props.; **PROFL AFFIL & HONORS:** FL Bar Assn.; Palm Beach Cty. Bar Assn.; **EDUC:** 1973, Journalism, Univ. of TX; **GRAD EDUC:** JD, 1977, Law, OH No. Univ.; **OTHER ACT & HONORS:** Palm Beach Kiwanis Club; **HOME ADD:** 811 Claremore Dr., W. Palm Beach, FL 33401, (305)832-4661; **BUS ADD:** 450 Royal Palm Way, Palm Beach, FL 33480, (305)655-8433.

NAHIGAN, Edward A.——**B:** Jul. 25, 1924, Los Angeles, CA, *Pres.*, Redhill Realty & Patrician Devel. Co.; **PRIM RE ACT:** Broker, Developer, Builder, Owner/Investor, Instructor, Property Manager, Syndicator; **GRAD EDUC:** Pepperdine Univ., 1948; **OTHER ACT & HONORS:** Christian Bus. Men's Comm.; Big Canyon Ctry. Club; Balboa Bay Club; Newport Beach Tennis Club; Satchel Club (Support Grp. for W. Medical Ctr.); **HOME ADD:** 12122 Theta Rd., Santa Ana, CA 92705, (714)544-2363; **BUS ADD:** 18002 Irvine Bldg., Ste. 110, Tustin, CA 92680, (714)544-2175.

NAHIGIAN, Ann Lawrence——**B:** Sept. 27, 1944, Burns, OR, *Pres.*, Nahigian Investment Co.; **PRIM RE ACT:** Owner/Investor, Property Manager, Syndicator; **EDUC:** BA, 1974, Art Hist., NY Univ.; **EDUC HONORS:** Magna Cum Laude; **BUS ADD:** 3151 Maple Dr., NE, Suite 206, Atlanta, GA 30305, (404)233-7302.

NAHL, Michael C.——*Group VP, Corp.*, Albany Intl. Corp.; **PRIM RE ACT:** Consultant, Owner/Investor, Property Manager, Syndicator; **BUS ADD:** POB 1907, Albany, NY 12201.

NAHON, Santos M.——**B:** Jan. 19, 1923, Argentina, *VP, Comptroller*, Cooper Realty Co.; **PRIM RE ACT:** Property Manager; **PREV EMPLOY:** VP in a Bank in Europe; **PROFL AFFIL & HONORS:** IREM; Home Builders Apt. Council, Apt. Council or Yr., 1974; CPM; **EDUC:** 1944, French School; **OTHER ACT & HONORS:** Baron Hirsch Congregation; Baron Hirsch Men's Club; B'nai B'rith; **HOME ADD:** 5282 Meadowcrest Cove, Memphis, TN 38117, (901)682-3675; **BUS ADD:** 1407 Union Ave., Ste. 400, Memphis, TN 38104, (901)725-9631.

NAIMAN, Marvin I.——**B:** June 21, 1931, Denver, CO, *Pres.*, The Sherman Agency, Inc.; **PRIM RE ACT:** Broker, Instructor, Syndicator, Consultant, Property Manager, Lender, Owner/Investor; **OTHER RE ACT:** Handle problem prop.; **PROFL AFFIL & HONORS:** Soc. of Exchange Counselors and CCIM designations; **MIL SERV:** USAF, A/IC; **HOME ADD:** 6690 E. Exposition Ave., Denver, CO 80224, (303)355-2688; **BUS ADD:** 820 16th St., Denver, CO 80224, (303)572-8778.

NAIMOWITZ, H.H.——**B:** Apr. 27, 1937, Telaviv, Israel, *Principal*, Rubinstein & Naimowitz; **PRIM RE ACT:** Consultant, Engineer; **SERVICES:** Consulting mechanical & electical engrg.; **REP CLIENTS:** Arch., devels. & owners of RE, govt. agencies; **PREV EMPLOY:** Combustion Engrg. Inc., 1962-1968; M.W. Kellogg Co. 1968-1970; Syska & Hennessey, 1970-1972; Caretsky & Assoc. 1972-1975; **PROFL AFFIL & HONORS:** Member, Amer. Soc. of Heating, Refrigeration & Air Conditioning Engrs.; NY State Assn. of Environmental Profls; **EDUC:** BS, 1962, NY Univ., Coll. of Engrg.; **GRAD EDUC:** MS (ME), 1968, Rensselaer Polytechnic Inst.; PhD, presently enrolled, Engrg., NYU; **OTHER ACT & HONORS:** Lic. Profl. Engr., States of: NY, NJ, FL, WI; **HOME ADD:** 319 E. 24th St., New York, NY 10010, (212)689-6376; **BUS ADD:** 25 E. 26th St., New York, NY 10010, (212)685-5530.

NAKAMOTO, Keith——**B:** May 22, 1948, Chicago, IL, *Tax Mgr.*, Coopers & Lybrand; **OTHER RE ACT:** CPA; **SERVICES:** Tax planning and compliance; **REP CLIENTS:** Public and pvt. synd.; **PROFL AFFIL & HONORS:** AICPA, IL Soc. of CPA's, RESSI; **EDUC:** BBA, 1970, Acctg., Northwestern Univ.; **GRAD EDUC:** MBA, 1971, Fin., Northwestern Univ.; **EDUC HONORS:** Beta Gamma Sigma, Beta Alpha Psi; **HOME ADD:** 640 W. Aldine Ave., Chicago, IL 60657; **BUS ADD:** 222 S. Riverside Plaza, Chicago, IL 60606, (312)559-5500.

NAKAMURA, Edward H.——**B:** July 12, 1934, Lihue, Kauai, HI, *Asst. Area Devel. Mgr.*, Kamehameha Schools/Bishop Estate, Neighbor Islands; **PRIM RE ACT:** Owner/Investor, Property Manager; **PROFL AFFIL & HONORS:** ICSC, IREM, CPM; **EDUC:** BBA, 1961, Personnel Indus. Relations, Univ. of Hawaii; **MIL SERV:** US Army, Sgt. 1954-1957; **HOME ADD:** 46-227 Aeloa St., Kaneohe, HI 96744, (808)235-8524; **BUS ADD:** Po Box 3466, Honolulu, HI 96801, (808)523-6200.

NALEN, Paul A.——*Owner*; **PRIM RE ACT:** Consultant, Engineer; **PREV EMPLOY:** VP Mutual Benefit Life Ins.; **EDUC:** BS, 1921, PA State Univ.; **MIL SERV:** USN; **BUS ADD:** 51 Upper Montclair Plaza Upper Montclair, NJ 07043, (201)783-9633.

NANCE, Joseph Hanover——**B:** June 18, 1952, Bryan, TX, *Asst. VP and Trust Officer*, First Nat. Bank of Odessa, Trust Div.; **PRIM RE ACT:** Banker, Lender, Owner/Investor, Property Manager; **OTHER RE ACT:** Trustee; **SERVICES:** Trust Services, Prop. Mgmt., Investment Counseling, Estate Planning, Income Tax Planning; **PREV EMPLOY:** First City Nat. Bank of San Angelo, Trust Officer; First Nat. Bank of Bryan, TX, Trust Officer; **PROFL AFFIL & HONORS:** TX Bar Assn.; ABA; Amer. Inst. of Banking; Midland Bus. and Estate Council; **EDUC:** BBA, 1974, Fin., TX A&M Univ.; **GRAD EDUC:** JD, 1977, Trial Law, Baylor School of Law; **OTHER ACT & HONORS:** Lions Club; Episcopal Church; **HOME ADD:** PO Box 7798, Odessa, TX 79760, (915)362-6839; **BUS ADD:** PO Box 4798, Odessa, TX 79760, (915)332-7311.

NANOS, H. Gerald——**B:** Jan. 22, 1948, New Orleans, LA, *Asst. VP*, The Philadelphia Saving Fund Society, Income Prop. Loan Dept.; **PRIM RE ACT:** Lender; **EDUC:** BS, 1970, Econ., Susquehanna Univ.; **GRAD EDUC:** MBA, 1976, Fin./RE, Rutgers Univ.; **BUS ADD:** 12 S. 12th St., Philadelphia, PA 19107, (215)629-2657.

NAPOLETAN, Joseph A.——**B:** Aug. 3, 1921, Schenectady, NY, *Owner*, Joseph A. Napoletan, Realtor; **PRIM RE ACT:** Broker, Appraiser, Builder, Owner/Investor, Property Manager; **PREV EMPLOY:** Superintendent Steel Fabrication; **PROFL AFFIL & HONORS:** NAR, RNMI, FL Assn. of Realtors, GRI, CRS; **EDUC:** BS, 1951, Acctg., Bus. Admin., Albany Bus. Coll., Sch. of Bus. Admin.; **MIL SERV:** US Navy, SP; **OTHER ACT & HONORS:** Bd. Member 7 yrs., Pres. Lakeland Bd. of Realtors, 1977, BPO Elks, Amer. Bd. Legion, Knights of Columbus, 3rd & 4th degree; **HOME ADD:** 1433 Ellison Ln., Lakeland, FL 33801; **BUS ADD:** 1416 S. FL Ave.,

Lakeland, FL 33802, (813)683-7505; **BUS TEL:** (813)682-5655.

NAPOLI, Robert Alexander——**B:** Jan. 14, 1940, Chicago, IL, *Pres.*, Allied Appraisal Co.; **PRIM RE ACT:** Broker, Consultant, Appraiser; **SERVICES:** Consultation, Appraisals; **REP CLIENTS:** Banks, S & L's, Attys. & Devels.; **PROFL AFFIL & HONORS:** AIREA, NARA, Intl. Inst. of Valuers, SRA, CRA, Sr. Cert. Valuer; **EDUC:** BA, 1963, Poli. Sci, Hist. Econ., Loyola Univ. of Chicago; **EDUC HONORS:** Dr. of Literary Letters from Ryodoraku Research Inst.; **HOME ADD:** 4241 Franklin, W. Springs, IL 60558, (312)246-7728; **BUS ADD:** 111 W. Wash., Chicago, IL 60602, (312)368-8619.

NASH, Diane G.——**B:** Mar. 11, 1937, NY, *Asst. Gen. Mgr.*, Merrill Lynch Realty Barrows Co.; **PRIM RE ACT:** Broker; **PREV EMPLOY:** Dir. New Homes/Condo. Div., Merrill Lynch Realty Barrows; **PROFL AFFIL & HONORS:** CRB; **EDUC:** BSEd, 1958, Elementary Educ., Hofstra Univ.; **EDUC HONORS:** Who's Who in Amer. Univ. & Colls.; **HOME ADD:** 5 Merrywood, Simsbury, CT 06070, (203)658-0530; **BUS ADD:** 54 Elm St., Hartford, CT 06106, (203)525-5010.

NASH, Richard——**B:** May 27, 1952, Chicago, IL, *Pres.*, Nash Realty & Richard Nash and Associates; **PRIM RE ACT:** Broker, Consultant, Owner/Investor; **SERVICES:** Brokerage and consulting for govt. fin. devel.; **REP CLIENTS:** Pvt. partnerships; **PREV EMPLOY:** Loan Officer, IL Housing Dept. Authority; **PROFL AFFIL & HONORS:** Realtor, NAR; **EDUC:** AB, 1974, Econ./Urban Studies, Yale Univ.; **GRAD EDUC:** MBA, 1979, Univ. of Chicago; **EDUC HONORS:** Cum Laude; **HOME ADD:** 1249 Richmond Ln., Wilmette, IL 60091, (312)251-5134; **BUS ADD:** 618 Davis St., Evanston, IL 60201, (312)869-2500.

NASHNER, Richard——**B:** Mar. 3, 1949, Oceanside, NY, *Dir. of Bus. Planning*, Kiawah Island Co.; **PRIM RE ACT:** Developer; **OTHER RE ACT:** Resort operator; **PREV EMPLOY:** ITT Community Devel. Corp. 1976-1979; **EDUC:** BArch., 1972, Arch., Univ. of VA; **GRAD EDUC:** MBA, 1974, Univ. of VA; **HOME ADD:** 814 N. Channel Ct., Charleston, SC 29412, (803)795-9324; **BUS ADD:** P O Box 12910, Charleston, SC 29412, (803)768-2121.

NASKY, H. Gregory——**B:** June 9, 1942, Titusville, PA, *Atty.*, Vargas & Bartlett, Las Vegas, Nevada Office; **PRIM RE ACT:** Attorney; **REP CLIENTS:** Various life insurance cos., banks and REIT's as lenders for comml. devel.; **PROFL AFFIL & HONORS:** ABA, Member of RE Fin. Comm. of Real Prop., Probate & Trust Sect.; NV State Liaison to Corp. Laws Comm. of Corp., Banking & Bus. Sect.; State Bar of NV - Chmn. of Las Vegas Panel of Fee Dispute Comm.; PA State Bar; **EDUC:** BA, 1964, English, St. Bonaventure Univ.; **GRAD EDUC:** JD, 1967, Notre Dame; **MIL SERV:** U.S. Army JAGC, Capt., Bronze Star, Army Commendation Medals, Vietnam Service Medals; **OTHER ACT & HONORS:** NV Resort Assn. Legal Comm.; **BUS ADD:** 300 S. Fourth St., Suite 500, Las Vegas, NV 89101, (702)385-4700.

NASSIF, George P.——**B:** Jan. 24, 1947, Wheeling, WV, *Pres.*, Management Systems Corporation; **PRIM RE ACT:** Consultant, Property Manager; **PROFL AFFIL & HONORS:** Greater Dallas Bd. of Realtors, Dallas Apt. Assn., BOMA, IREM, Bd. of DIrs., Dallas Apt. Assn.; **EDUC:** BS, 1971, Mgmt., Univ. of Dayton; **GRAD EDUC:** MBA, 1977, Acctg., North TX State Univ.; **EDUC HONORS:** "Planning for the '70's", Outstanding Scholarship; **OTHER ACT & HONORS:** Treas., P.T.A.; **HOME ADD:** 433 Fieldwood Dr., Richardson, TX 75081, (214)238-9876; **BUS ADD:** 7001 Fair Oaks, Suite 529, Dallas, TX 75231, (214)692-8891.

NASUTI, Dana N.——**B:** Apr. 1, 1940, Washington, DC, *Pres.*, Prop. Promotions; **PRIM RE ACT:** Consultant; **SERVICES:** Mktg., advertising and prop. promotion; **REP CLIENTS:** Warner-Lambert, Coldwell Banker Comml. RE Services Philadelphia Office, New America Network, INA, Urban Investment & Devel., Chicago; **PREV EMPLOY:** Dir. of RE, Nat. Freight, Inc.; Dir. of Mktg., Reed & Stambaugh Co.; Dir. of Mktg., Binswanger Co.; **EDUC:** BA, 1963, Electronic Media, Univ. of MD; **MIL SERV:** USAF, Capt., AFCM, A.F. Outstanding Unit Award; **HOME ADD:** 642 Guilford Rd., Cherry Hill, NJ 08003, (609)424-3432; **BUS ADD:** 642 Guilford Rd., Cherry Hill, NJ 08003, (609)424-6822.

NATHANSON, Marilyn Elise——**B:** Jan. 6, 1953, Chicago, IL, *Counsel*, Federal Home Loan Mortgage Corp.; **PRIM RE ACT:** Attorney; **SERVICES:** Legal advice to the corp. in RE areas; **PROFL AFFIL & HONORS:** ABA; MO Bar Assn.; **EDUC:** BA, 1974, Psych./Sociology, WA Univ.; **GRAD EDUC:** JD, 1977, Law, WA Univ. Law School; **EDUC HONORS:** Asst. Editor of Law Review; **HOME ADD:** 2825 S. Columbus St., Arlington, VA 22206, (703)931-1344; **BUS ADD:** 1776 G St., N.W., Washington, DC 20013, (202)789-4604.

NAUGHTON, Gary Langdon——**B:** July 9, 1940, NY, *VP*, Loeb Partners Realty (Previously Loeb Rhoades, Hornblower Realty); **OTHER RE ACT:** RE acquisitions/investment advisor; **SERVICES:** Prop. acquisition, sales, fin., mgmt. advisory and consulting services for domestic and overseas clients.; **REP CLIENTS:** Domestic and overseas indiv., instnl. and pension fund clients; **PROFL AFFIL & HONORS:** RE Bd. of NY, Mort. Brokers Assn. of NY, Licensed RE Broker, NY; **EDUC:** BS, 1962, Bus. Admin., Gettysburg Coll.; **MIL SERV:** Army, CPL 1961-62; **OTHER ACT & HONORS:** Phi Delta Theta Frat.; **HOME ADD:** 244 Mamaroneck Rd., Scarsdale, NY 10583, (914)472-6963; **BUS ADD:** 521 Fifth Ave., New York, NY 10017, (212)883-0371.

NAUROCKI, Gloria——*Ed.*, Institute of Real Estate Mgmt., Journal of Property Management; **PRIM RE ACT:** Real Estate Publisher; **BUS ADD:** 430 N. Michigan Ave, Chicago, IL 60611, (312)440-8600.*

NAY, Ward H.——*SIR VP Eng.*, Upjohn Co., The; **PRIM RE ACT:** Property Manager; **BUS ADD:** 7171 Portage Rd., Kalamazoo, MI 49001, (616)323-4000.*

NAYE, John R.——**B:** July 7, 1945, Philadelphia, PA, *Pres.*, Envestrek; **PRIM RE ACT:** Broker, Instructor, Syndicator, Consultant, Developer, Property Manager, Owner/Investor; **SERVICES:** Dev. & synd. of investment prop.; Fin. planning in RE; **REP CLIENTS:** Private investors; **PREV EMPLOY:** Exec. VP, Vistar Fin., Inc. 1974-79, Marina Del Rey, CA; **PROFL AFFIL & HONORS:** NAR, Guest Lecturer at USC Grad. School of Bus.; **EDUC:** BS, 1966, US Naval Academy; **GRAD EDUC:** MBA, 1974, Entrepreneurship, USC; **EDUC HONORS:** Grad. with Honors (top 7% of class), Elected to Beta Gamma Sigma (Nat. Hon. Frat. of MBA's); **MIL SERV:** USN 1966-72, Lt., Naval Aviator carrier qualified; **OTHER ACT & HONORS:** US Ski Writers Assn. (Press), Past Chmn., USC Bus., Entrepreneur Alumni; **HOME ADD:** 8215 SE 59th St., Mercer Island, WA 98040, (206)236-0815; **BUS ADD:** PO Box 747, Mercer Island, WA 98040, (206)232-5808.

NAYLOR, Pleas C., Jr.——*Pres.*, Naylor Realty Inc.; **PRIM RE ACT:** Broker, Developer, Owner/Investor, Property Manager; **PROFL AFFIL & HONORS:** Tr., S.W. Research Inst.; Soc. of Indus. Realtors; Accredited Farm & Land Broker of the Farm & Land Inst.; CPM of the Inst. of RE Mgmt.; FIABCI; TX Assn. of Realtors; San Antonio Bd. of Realtors, Honorary LLD, Univ. of TX at San Antonio, 1969; Realtor of the Yr., TX Assn. of Realtors and San Antonio Bd. of Realtors; Member of Masonic Orders; **OTHER ACT & HONORS:** Governors Council of Advisors; Elected to City Council of San Antonio 1971-1973; Professional Accomplishments can be found listed in: "Men of Achievement", "Who's Who in the Southwest", "Southwest Texans", "Notable Americans" and other reference publications; **BUS ADD:** 7475 Callaghan Rd., Suite 200, San Antonio, TX 78229, (512)341-9191.

NEAL, James Edward——**B:** July 29, 1937, Charlestown, WV, *CEO*, Westminster Trading Co., Inc.; **PRIM RE ACT:** Attorney, Syndicator; **SERVICES:** Dev., synd. & mgmt. of suburban office bldgs., indus RE; **REP CLIENTS:** Non-Instnl. Investors; **PREV EMPLOY:** City of Long Beach 1965-67; Private Law Practice; **PROFL AFFIL & HONORS:** RESSI; Real Prop. sections of ABA and CA State Bar; CA State Lic. Contractors Assn., Judge Pro Tempore; **EDUC:** BS, 1961, Mktg., CA State Univ. at Long Beach; **GRAD EDUC:** JD, 1964, Law, Univ. of CA, Hastings School of Law; GRI; **MIL SERV:** US Army, Res; Sgt; 1955; **OTHER ACT & HONORS:** Past Officer/Dir. Kiwanis; Boys Club; C of C; Who's Who 1976-1981; **HOME ADD:** 12632 Gilbert Dt., Garden Grove, CA 92641, (714)534-3629; **BUS ADD:** Liberty Bldg., 8231 Westminster Ave., Westminster, CA 92683, (714)898-0565.

NEAL, John A.——**B:** Sept. 25, 1932, NC, *Partner*, Robertson, Neal & Co., Inc.; **OTHER RE ACT:** CPA; **SERVICES:** Acctg., mgmt. & tax planning; **PROFL AFFIL & HONORS:** AICPA, NC Assn, CPA; **EDUC:** BS, 1969, Acctg., Guilford Coll.; **GRAD EDUC:** MBA, 1974, Bus., Univ. of NC at Greensboro; **MIL SERV:** US Army, SP-4; **HOME ADD:** Route 1, Box 133, Pleasant Garden, NC 27313, (919)674-3406; **BUS ADD:** 440 W. Market St., Greensboro, NC 27402, (919)379-9932.

NEAL, Kenneth A.——**B:** Apr. 7, 1943, Sault Ste. Marie, MI, *Pres.*, *Dir.*, Homac, Inc.; **PRIM RE ACT:** Developer, Owner/Investor; **PREV EMPLOY:** Atty. in Pvt. Practice; **PROFL AFFIL & HONORS:** MI & FL Bar Assns.; **EDUC:** BA, 1965, Econ., Albion Coll.; **GRAD EDUC:** JD, 1969, Wayne Univ. Law School; **EDUC HONORS:** Magna Cum Laude; **HOME ADD:** 1967 Fairway St., Birmingham, MI 48009, (313)642-5113; **BUS ADD:** 400 Renaissance Ctr., Ste. 1150, Detroit, MI 48243, (313)259-3620.

NEAL, Patrick——B: Mar. 4, 1949, Des Moines, IA, *Pres.*, Neal Communities; **PRIM RE ACT:** Developer, Owner/Investor; **SERVICES:** RE brokerage, ins., devel., prop. mgmt., RE investments; **PROFL AFFIL & HONORS:** NIREB, NAHB, local and state bd. of realtors, State Senator; **EDUC:** BS, 1971, fin., Wharton's School of Fin., Univ. of PA; **MIL SERV:** US Army, 2nd Lt.; **OTHER ACT & HONORS:** FL House of Reps. 1975-78, Tr., Univ. of S. FL, Tr., New Coll. Found., Dir., SE Bank of Sarasota; **HOME ADD:** 3701 Cortez Rd. W., Bradenton, FL 33507, (813)756-0677; **BUS ADD:** Box 500, Long Boat, FL 33548, (813)756-0677.

NEAL, Raymond R. "Ray"——B: Jan. 5, 1922, Mesa, AZ, *Owner*, Neal Management Co.; **PRIM RE ACT:** Property Manager; **SERVICES:** Mgmt., Consulting on Taxes & Acquisitions; **REP CLIENTS:** All Pvt. Investor/Operators; **PREV EMPLOY:** Const. Industry 1945-1956, Devel.-Const.-Mgmt. 1957-1967, Prop. Mgmt. Supervisor/Dept. Head of Tucson Realty & Trust Co. 1967-1974, Self-Employed 1974 to date; **PROFL AFFIL & HONORS:** IREM, CPM; **MIL SERV:** US Army Air Corps, S./Sgt. Pilot; **OTHER ACT & HONORS:** Past Pres. Mountain Rescue Assn., Bd. of Dir. Tucson Fund Raising Review Bd., Profl. Standards Comm. (1981-84) Tucson Bd. of Realtors; **BUS ADD:** 4560 E Broadway, S-7, Tuscon, AZ 85711, (602)795-7536.

NEALE, Richard E.——B: July 22, 1939, Omaha, NE, *Broker/Owner, Pres.*, Colonial RE and Investments, Inc.; **PRIM RE ACT:** Broker, Syndicator, Builder, Owner/Investor; **PREV EMPLOY:** Teacher and School Admin., 14 yrs.; **PROFL AFFIL & HONORS:** Loveland, CO NAR, RESSI, Chmn. of Prof. Standards Comm.; **EDUC:** BS in Educ., 1961, Hist., Peru State Coll., Peru, NE; **GRAD EDUC:** MEd., 1964, Guidance and Counseling, Univ. of WY; **EDUC HONORS:** Who's Who in Amer. Coll. and Univ., 1961; **HOME ADD:** 2006 W. 23rd St., Loveland, CO 80537, (303)677-5264; **BUS ADD:** 1130 Lincoln Ave., Loveland, CO 80537.

NEEL, Joe C.——B: Aug. 16, 1937, Sallisaw, OK, *Joe C. Neel Company*; **PRIM RE ACT:** Broker; **SERVICES:** RE brokerage of income producing props.; **PREV EMPLOY:** Henry S. Miller Co.; Baptist Foundation of TX; **PROFL AFFIL & HONORS:** NAR, TX Assn. of Realtors, Dallas Bd. of Realtors, CCIM, GRI; **EDUC:** BS, 1959, Engrg./Physics, Univ. of Tulsa; **GRAD EDUC:** MS, 1962, Solid State Physics, So. Methodist Univ.; **HOME ADD:** 548 Valley Trail Rte. 4, Rockwall, TX 75087, (214)226-2156; **BUS ADD:** Plaza of the Americas, 2202 South Tower, Lock Box 202, Dallas, TX 75201, (214)748-8300.

NEELON, David E.——B: Sept. 27, 1941, Waltham, MA, *VP*, Neelon Cos.; **PRIM RE ACT:** Broker, Developer, Property Manager, Owner/Investor; **SERVICES:** Indus. RE Brokerage, Dev., Investment Mgmt.; **PROFL AFFIL & HONORS:** SIR, IREM, CPM; **EDUC:** BS, 1963, Bus. Admin., Econ. & Transp., Northwestern Univ., Evanston, IL; **OTHER ACT & HONORS:** Smaller Bus. Assn. of New England; **HOME ADD:** 23 Meriam St., Lexington, MA 02173, (617)861-0692; **BUS ADD:** 255 Bear Hill Rd., Waltham, MA 02254, (617)890-4610.

NEELY, Jack——*Chrmn.*, KY Real Estate Commission; **PRIM RE ACT:** Property Manager; **BUS ADD:** 100 E. Libery, Ste. 204, Louisville, KY 40202, (502)588-4462.*

NEELY, Thomas H.——B: Aug. 4, 1941, Hampton, VA, *Pres.*, Thomas H. Neely, Inc.; **PRIM RE ACT:** Broker, Owner/Investor; **SERVICES:** Comml. brokerage only. Specializing in representation of the end beneficiary through lease and/or purchase of RE in the downtown Washington, DC & No. VA Areas; **PREV EMPLOY:** Comml. RE bus. in the Washington, DC metropolitan area for 10 yrs.; **EDUC:** BA, 1966, Hist., Univ. of MD.; **HOME ADD:** 11004 Warwickshire Dr., Great Falls, VA 22066, (703)430-7111; **BUS ADD:** 7777 Leesburg Pike, Suite 400, Falls Church, VA 22043, (703)893-1770.

NEFF, Cecil L.——B: May 16, 1908, Delta, CO, *Owner*, Cecil L. Neff, Realtor; **PRIM RE ACT:** Broker, Consultant, Appraiser, Owner/Investor; **PROFL AFFIL & HONORS:** Columbus Bd. of Realtors, OH & Nat. Bd. of Realtors; AIREA; Soc. of RE Appraisers; Columbus Comml. Investment, Indus. Realtors Grp., MAI; SREA; **EDUC:** Franklin Univ.; **OTHER ACT & HONORS:** Ambassadors Club; Shrine; Masonic Orders; **HOME ADD:** 2589 Sherwin Rd., Upper Arlington, OH 43221, (614)486-3388; **BUS ADD:** 828 S. High St., Columbus, OH 43206, (614)444-7833.

NEFF, Edward R.——B: Mar. 4, 1943, Youngstown, OH, *Pres. & Dir.*, Amerifirst Mortgage Corp., A Wholly Owned Subsidiary of Amerifirst Fed.; **PRIM RE ACT:** Broker, Banker, Lender; **SERVICES:** Resid. origination, second mortgages, bldrs., RE brokers, developers; **PROFL AFFIL & HONORS:** MBA, Nat.; MBA, FL; MBA, Miami; **EDUC:** BA, 1966, Psych., Bowling Green State Univ.; **MIL SERV:** US Army; 1966-1968, E-5; **OTHER ACT & HONORS:** Boy Scouts of Amer.; Bd. of Dir., Amerifirst Devel. Corp.; Bd. of Advisors, Crittenden Fin., Inc.; **HOME ADD:** 11445 SW 110 Lane, Miami, FL 33176, (305)595-1679; **BUS ADD:** 13701 N. Kendall Dr., Miami, FL 33186, (305)387-5085.

NEILL, M.D.——B: Dec. 31, 1928, AR, *Pres.*, Interstate Motel Brokers USA; **PRIM RE ACT:** Broker, Instructor, Syndicator, Consultant, Owner/Investor; **SERVICES:** Investment RE Brokerage with Spec. in Hotels, Motels and Motor Inns; **REP CLIENTS:** Attys., CPA Firms and Instl. Investors; **PROFL AFFIL & HONORS:** RESSI, REEA, Realtor, IMBUSA Multi-Million Dollar Club Award 1980; **EDUC:** BA, 1966, RE, Univ. of OK; **OTHER ACT & HONORS:** BBB, CC; **HOME ADD:** 4504 N. 56th St., Phoenix, AZ 85018, (602)941-0404; **BUS ADD:** 7050 Third Ave., Scottsdale, AZ 85251, (602)945-6363.

NEIMAN, Cary L.——B: Mar. 3, 1947, Houston, TX, *Pres.*, Hawthorn Realty Grp.; **PRIM RE ACT:** Developer, Property Manager, Owner/Investor; **SERVICES:** All devel. and condo. conversion serv.; **REP CLIENTS:** IBM; Nalco Chemical; Alexander & Alexander; Dominick's Finer Foods; Gen. Motors; **PROFL AFFIL & HONORS:** Chicago RE Bd., ICSC, NACORE; **EDUC:** BS, 1968, Engineering & Applied Sci., Yale Univ.; **BUS ADD:** 8 E. Huron, Chicago, IL 60611, (312)266-8100.

NEIN, Sam N.——B: 1943, *Realtor*, Nein & Co.; **PRIM RE ACT:** Broker, Developer, Owner/Investor; **PROFL AFFIL & HONORS:** CRB; CRS; GRI; **EDUC:** BA, 1966, Bus. Admin./Econ., Hastings Coll.; AS, 1962, Spec. Tech., Thaddeus Stevens State School of Tech.; **OTHER ACT & HONORS:** Outstanding Young Man of Boulder, 1975; Univ. of CO, Distinguished Instr. Award, 1979; **BUS ADD:** 777 29th St., Suite 105, Dur Plaza Bldg., Boulder, CO 80303, (303)499-3000.

NEINAS, Bob——B: Feb. 25, 1940, Marshfield, WI, *Sr. Partner in Charge of Devel.*, Carroll, McPeak, Bolesky & Neinas; **PRIM RE ACT:** Attorney; **OTHER RE ACT:** RE Law; **SERVICES:** Practice limited to RE Law; primarily condo. devel. & buyers; **REP CLIENTS:** Power Corp. (Laurentians; Princess Del Mar, The Prince, Duchess and Dorchester Condos.); and The Charter Club of Naples Bay, Inc. (Interval Ownership Condo.); **PROFL AFFIL & HONORS:** RE Section of FL Bar; FL Bar; Collier Cty. Bar Assn.; Collier Cty. RE Attys., Inc., Rated 'AV' in Martindale Hubbell Law Directory; **EDUC:** BBA, 1962, Bus., Univ. of WI; **GRAD EDUC:** LLB, 1965, Fin./Law, Univ. of WI Law School; **EDUC HONORS:** Top 10% of Class; **OTHER ACT & HONORS:** Cty. Atty., Collier Cty., FL in 1972; Pres., Collier Cty. Bar Assn. in 1972; **HOME ADD:** 75 Broad Ave. S, Naples, FL 33940, (813)261-7281; **BUS ADD:** 1169 8th St. S, Naples, FL 33940, (813)261-8915.

NEISH, David MacGregor——B: Aug. 19, 1919, Kensington, PEI, Can., *Pres.*, David MacGregor Neish Real Estate; **PRIM RE ACT:** Broker, Consultant, Appraiser, Builder; **OTHER RE ACT:** Author; **SERVICES:** Realtor, appraiser, counselor, builder of New England homes in –250,000 - –300,000 range; **REP CLIENTS:** Many of the major employee relocation co's. in USA & Can.; also Northern Telecom, Bell Can., Digital, Merrill Lynch, etc.; **PREV EMPLOY:** Realtor, Ottawa area for 20 yrs.; **PROFL AFFIL & HONORS:** NAR; Design. Sr. Resid. Appraiser by Soc. of RE Appraisers and Sr. Member by Nat. Assn. of Indep. Fee Appraisers (USA); Desig. Accredited Appraiser by Appraisal Inst. of Can.; Fellow of RE Inst. of Can., CRS; CRB; **EDUC:** King's Collegiate School, Windsor, NS, Can.; **MIL SERV:** Black Watch, Royal Highland Reg. of Can., Infantry Officer (WW II), eight serive and campaign medals; **BUS ADD:** 2028 Prince of Wales Dr., Ottawa, K2E7M2, Ont., Can., (613)224-9770.

NEKRITZ, Barry B.——B: Dec. 16, 1938, Chicago, IL, *Partner*, Aaron, Schimberg, Hess, Rusnak, Deutsch & Gilbert; **PRIM RE ACT:** Attorney, Owner/Investor; **SERVICES:** Legal services; **PROFL AFFIL & HONORS:** ABA; IL Bar Assn.; Chicago Bar Assn.; FL Bar Assn.; **EDUC:** BA, 1959, Pol. Sci., Univ. of IL; **GRAD EDUC:** LLB, 1962, Law, Univ. of IL; **MIL SERV:** U.S. Army, MSgt.; **OTHER ACT & HONORS:** Trustee, Village of Northbrook, 1973-1981; Member, miscellaneous charities and civic bds. and comm.; **HOME ADD:** 1111 Buttonwood Ln., Northbrook, IL 60062, (312)498-4940; **BUS ADD:** 3400 Xerox Centre, 55 W. Monroe St., Chicago, IL 60603, (312)726-5700.

NELABOVIGE, Joseph M.A.——B: Nov. 13, 1940, Hamburg, PA, *Atty.*, Law Offices of Joseph M.A. Nelabovige, Inc.; **PRIM RE ACT:** Consultant; **REP CLIENTS:** Local agent & approved counsel for Lawyers Title Ins. Co., we also represent as general counsel over 20 fed. credit unions; **PROFL AFFIL & HONORS:** Berks. Cty. Bar Assn., PA Bar Assn., Phi Alpha Delta Law Frat., JD; **EDUC:** BS, 1962, Pharmacy, Fordham Univ.; **GRAD EDUC:** JD, 1965, Univ. of MD

Sch. of Law; **EDUC HONORS:** Distinguished Serv. Medal, A.H. Robbins Plaque & Gavel, A.Ph.A. Serv. Cert.; **MIL SERV:** USA, Res., S/Sgt., Good Conduct Medal; **HOME ADD:** 7 South 4th St., Hamburg, PA 19526, (215)562-3802; **BUS ADD:** 5 South 4th St., Hamburg, PA 19526, (215)562-3801.

NELL, Donald F.——**B:** Apr. 3, 1923, Livingston,MT, *RE Consultant*; **PRIM RE ACT:** Instructor, Syndicator, Consultant, Developer; **PREV EMPLOY:** 30 yrs. Self-Employed; **PROFL AFFIL & HONORS:** SRA; **BUS ADD:** PO Box 577, Bozeman, MT 59715, (406)586-0266.

NELLANS, Larry W.——**B:** June 12, 1941, Warsaw, IN, *Pres.*, Red Carpet of Mid-America; and Larry Nellans, Inc., Realtor; **PRIM RE ACT:** Broker, Consultant, Appraiser, Developer, Owner/Investor, Property Manager; **OTHER RE ACT:** RE franchising; **SERVICES:** Full serv. RE; **PREV EMPLOY:** In RE bus. since 1963; **PROFL AFFIL & HONORS:** NAR, IN Assn. of Realtors, Kosciusko Cty. Assn. of Realtors, RNMI, REPAC, CCIM, CRB, CRS; **EDUC:** BS in Bus. Admin., 1963, RE Admin., IN Univ.; **OTHER ACT & HONORS:** 1976 IN Realtor of the Year; **HOME ADD:** 1712 Willow Lane, Warsaw, IN 46580, (219)269-1230; **BUS ADD:** 301 North Lake St., Warsaw, IN 46580, (919)269-1265.

NELSON, Brian R.——**B:** Mar. 30, 1950, WI, *Pres.*, Asset Devel. Servs. Inc.; **PRIM RE ACT:** Consultant, Developer, Owner/Investor, Property Manager, Syndicator; **SERVICES:** Investment Advice; Comml. and Resid. RE; **REP CLIENTS:** Small & med. size cos. and their pension & profit sharing funds; high income indivs.; small investor grps.; **PREV EMPLOY:** VP, Gen. Mgr. Prop. Div., Regan Cos., Inc. Mpls; **PROFL AFFIL & HONORS:** CPM; RESSI; NASD; **EDUC:** BA, 1972, RE, Econ., Univ. of WI, Madison; **HOME ADD:** 2400 Bryant Ave. S., Minneapolis, MN 55405, (612)822-6297; **BUS ADD:** 10 S. 5th St., Suite 909, Minneapolis, MN 55402, (612)340-0488.

NELSON, Clark R.——**B:** Aug. 16, 1948, Wichita, KS, *Atty.*, Kahrs, Nelson, Fanning, Hita & Kellogg; **PRIM RE ACT:** Attorney, Owner/Investor; **SERVICES:** Legal, fin. analysis; **REP CLIENTS:** Hahner, Foreman & Harness, Gen. Contractors, Conco, Inc. Jim Smith Realty, Inc, Dale Lucas & Assoc., Bus. Systems Inc., Finn Distributing Co., Inc., Finn Leasing & Fin. Inc., Assoc, Druggists, Inc., 10 Main Partnership, Land Office Co, Darrell Leason and Assoc., Realtors Midway Oil, Inc., Gateway Outdoor Advertising, Inc. Investors, Comml. Realtors, Devels., Lenders; **PREV EMPLOY:** Acctg. Instr.; **PROFL AFFIL & HONORS:** ABA, KS Bar Assn., Member of Real Prop., Probate & Trust Sect. of ABA & KS Bar Assn., Wichita Bar Assn., Pres. Wichita Lawyers Club, JD; **EDUC:** BA, 1970, Acctg., Wichita State Univ.; **GRAD EDUC:** JD, 1973, Washburn Univ.; **EDUC HONORS:** Cum Laude, Deans list, Washburn Law Review, Co-ments Editor; **OTHER ACT & HONORS:** Lions Club, Beta Theta Pi; **HOME ADD:** 6919 E. 14th, Wichita, KS 67206, (316)685-6604; **BUS ADD:** 200 W. Douglas 630, Wichita, KS 67203, (316)265-7761.

NELSON, David Robert——**B:** May 16, 1942, Detroit, MI, *Pres.*, The Nelson GRP. Inc.; **PRIM RE ACT:** Developer, Owner/Investor; **SERVICES:** Project Mgmt., Const. Mgmt.; **PREV EMPLOY:** Asst. VP of Land Sales at the Taubman Co. Inc.; **PROFL AFFIL & HONORS:** ULI, RESSI, Builders Assn., Exec. Council Member of Urban Devel./Mixed Use Council at ULI; **EDUC:** BA, 1965, Design, Univ. of MI; **GRAD EDUC:** JD, 1968, Wayne State Univ. Law School; **OTHER ACT & HONORS:** Lectured at Univ. of MI Law School, lectured before various groups at ULI, Authored numerous articles on R.E.; **HOME ADD:** 27681 Wellington Rd., Farmington Hills, MI 48018, (313)855-2329; **BUS ADD:** 3270 W, Big Beaver Rd., Suite 143, Troy, MI 48084, (313)649-2350.

NELSON, Gary L.——**B:** July 8, 1949, Phoenix, AZ, *VP*, Roadrunner Estatês Corp.; **PRIM RE ACT:** Engineer, Developer, Regulator, Builder, Syndicator; **PREV EMPLOY:** Del E. Webb, Project Engr.; **PROFL AFFIL & HONORS:** Nat. Homebuilders Assn., Bus. Comm.; **EDUC:** BS, 1971, Bus. Mgmt., Engrg., AZ State Univ., Sam Officer; **OTHER ACT & HONORS:** Central Homebuilder Assn. of AZ, Bus. Exec. Commn., Nat. Homebuilder Assn.; **HOME ADD:** 7431 E Wethersfield Rd., Scottsdale, AZ 85254; **BUS ADD:** 7339 E Acoma 7, Scottsdale, AZ 85260, (602)998-4444.

NELSON, James——*RE Mgr.*, Raychem Corp.; **PRIM RE ACT:** Property Manager; **BUS ADD:** 300 Constitution Dr., Menlo Park, CA 94025, (415)361-2410.*

NELSON, Jeffrey Alan——**B:** Mar. 19, 1952, Toledo, OH, *Atty.*, Boggs, Boggs & Boggs. Co., LPA; **PRIM RE ACT:** Attorney; **SERVICES:** Legal servs. in the areas of RE sales, purchases, litigation, creative fin., leases, and options; **REP CLIENTS:** Homeowners, buyers, sellers, investors, and comml. & resid. landlords; **PREV EMPLOY:** Assoc. Planner, OH, Dept. of Econ. & Comm. Devel., Land Use Bur.; **PROFL AFFIL & HONORS:** ABA (Sect. of Real Prop., Probate & Trust Law), OH State Bar Assn., State Bar of MI, Toledo Bar Assn. (Comm. for Lawyers and Realtors), Wood Co. Bar Assn.; **EDUC:** BA, 1974, Econ. & Urban Studies, Denison Univ., Granville, OH; **GRAD EDUC:** JD, 1978, Univ. of MI Law Sch.; **EDUC HONORS:** Grad. summa cum laude, Member Phi Beta Kappa, Omicron Delta Epsilon (Econ. Hon.); **OTHER ACT & HONORS:** Authored 1974 publication by OH Dept. of Econ. & Comm. Devel., *Local Land Use Regulations in OH, Their Extent and Effectiveness*, 1974; **HOME ADD:** 879 Brookfield Ln., Perrysburg, OH 43551, (419)874-7123; **BUS ADD:** 413 Michigan St., Toledo, OH 43624, (419)243-5117.

NELSON, Jeffrey L.——**B:** Dec. 29, 1939, Jamestown, NY, *Pres., Indiv., Gen. Partner*, Jeffrey L. Nelson Development & Management, Inc., Sinclairville Housing Ltd. Partnership; **PRIM RE ACT:** Broker, Consultant, Appraiser, Developer, Builder, Owner/Investor, Property Manager, Syndicator; **SERVICES:** Investor counseling, devel. of rental props., prop. mgmt.; **REP CLIENTS:** Investors in bus., comml. and resid. RE; **PREV EMPLOY:** Naetzker, Thorsell, & Dove, Arch. (1963-1969); Deputy Dir. of Devel. for Urban Renewal, Jamestown, NY (1970-1974); Community Develop. Consultant (1974-1978); **PROFL AFFIL & HONORS:** NAR, RESSI, Community Housing Resource Bd., Guest Panelist HUD Econ. Devel. Seminar (June, 1980); **EDUC:** AA, 1969, Engrg., Bus., Jamestown Community Coll.; **OTHER ACT & HONORS:** Viking Temple; Lakewood Rod & Gun Club; Council Member; Sunday Sch. Superintendent at First Lutheran Church; **HOME ADD:** 90 Howard St., Jamestown, NY 14701, (716)487-0347; **BUS ADD:** 90 Howard St., Jamestown, NY 14701, (716)487-0337.

NELSON, John M., IV——**B:** Apr. 21, 1945, Baltimore, MD, *Exec. VP and Managing Dir.*, Winthrop Financial Co., Inc.; **PRIM RE ACT:** Owner/Investor, Syndicator; **SERVICES:** Investment analysis, consulting; **REP CLIENTS:** Builder-developer corps. (IBM, Safeway, K-Mart, GA Power, Wang Labs); **PROFL AFFIL & HONORS:** Bus. Assoc. Club; Harvard Club; Yale Club; **EDUC:** BBA, 1967, Hist., Yale Univ.; **GRAD EDUC:** MBA, 1972, Harvard Univ.; **EDUC HONORS:** Cum Laude; **MIL SERV:** USN; Lt.; **HOME ADD:** 9 Stratford Rd., Winchester, MA; **BUS ADD:** 225 Franklin St., Boston, MA 02110, (617)482-6200.

NELSON, Kathleen M.——**B:** Oct. 5, 1945, Washington, DC, *Second VP*, Teachers Insurance and Annuity Assn. of Amer., Mort. and RE; **PRIM RE ACT:** Lender; **PROFL AFFIL & HONORS:** Mort. Bankers Assn. - Member of Income Prop. Comm. of the MBA, The RE Bd. of NY, Cardinal's Comm. of the Laity - RE Comm.; **EDUC:** BS, 1968, RE, IN Univ.; **HOME ADD:** 109 Bay St., E. Atlantic Beach, NY 11561, (516)431-6455; **BUS ADD:** 730 Third Ave., New York, NY 10017, (212)490-9000.

NELSON, Kenneth E.——**B:** Dec. 27, 1950, Kenosha, WI, *Broker*, James T. Barry Co., Inc.; **PRIM RE ACT:** Broker, Consultant, Owner/Investor, Syndicator; **OTHER RE ACT:** CPA; **SERVICES:** Brokerage of investment prop., financing advice, limited partnerships, grp. trusts; **PREV EMPLOY:** Peat, Marwick, Mitchell & Co. 1976-79; **PROFL AFFIL & HONORS:** WI Inst. of CPA's, Largest RE sale in WI hist.; Second largest partnership offering in WI; **EDUC:** BBA, 1974, Acctg., Univ. of WI; **GRAD EDUC:** MBA, 1976, Fin., Univ. of WI; **EDUC HONORS:** Beta Gamma Sigma, Beta Alpha Psi; **HOME ADD:** 1918 E. Jaris St., Shorewood, WI 53211, (414)962-0263; **BUS ADD:** 735 North Water St., Milwaukee, WI 53202, (414)271-1870.

NELSON, L. Bruce——**B:** Aug. 6, 1946, Minneapolis, MN, *Part.*, Sherman & Howard; **PRIM RE ACT:** Attorney; **SERVICES:** Gen. RE representation; **REP CLIENTS:** Gen. Elec. Credit Corp.; First Nat. Bank of Chicago; Equity Mort. Investors; Instnl. and indiv. lenders and devels.; **PROFL AFFIL & HONORS:** ABA; CO Bar Assoc.; **EDUC:** AB, 1968, Govt./Econ., Hamilton Coll.; **GRAD EDUC:** JD, 1971, Univ. of CO; **EDUC HONORS:** Storke Scholar; Order of the Coif; **HOME ADD:** 909 S. Josephine, Denver, CO 80210, (303)733-7604; **BUS ADD:** 2900 First of Denver Plaza, Denver, CO 80202, (303)893-2900.

NELSON, Larry E.——**B:** June 10, 1944, Santa Monica, CA, *Owner, President*, L.E. Nelson Co., Inc.; **PRIM RE ACT:** Developer, Builder, Owner/Investor; **PREV EMPLOY:** Investment Builders Corp., Irvine; Alex Robertson Co., Irvine; **PROFL AFFIL & HONORS:** The Lincoln Club of Orange Cty.; Univ. of Redlands Alumni Org.; **EDUC:** BA, 1966, Bus. Admin., Univ. of Redlands; **EDUC HONORS:** Honor Roll; **MIL SERV:** USNR, Lt.; **OTHER ACT & HONORS:** Who's Who in CA; **HOME ADD:** 11632 Vista Mar, Santa Ana, CA, (714)731-8246; **BUS ADD:** 23101 Moulton Parkway, Suite 210, Laguna Hills, CA 92653, (714)951-7791.

NELSON, Lem V.——B: Nov. 6, 1921, Concordia, KS, *Sr. VP*, Far West Federal Savings, RE Operations; **PRIM RE ACT:** Consultant, Banker, Architect, Developer, Lender, Builder, Owner/Investor, Property Manager, Syndicator; **PROFL AFFIL & HONORS:** ULI; Nat. Assn. of Home Builders; **EDUC:** Arch., USC; **MIL SERV:** US Army; **HOME ADD:** 11110 SW Collina, Portland, OR 97219, (503)636-5700; **BUS ADD:** 421 SW 6th, Portland, OR 97204, (503)224-4444.

NELSON, Mary——B: Jan. 10, 1925, Shreveport, LA, *Pres.*, Century 21 Mary Nelson, Realtors; **PRIM RE ACT:** Broker, Instructor, Owner/Investor; **SERVICES:** Sales, Mgmt., Counseling; **PROFL AFFIL & HONORS:** DeKalb, GA Assn. of Realtors, NAR, Women's Council of Realtors, RNMI, Realtor of the Yr., DeKalb Bd. of Realtors, CA Assn. of Realtors; **OTHER ACT & HONORS:** Church, civic club, garden clubs, Metro Atlanta Century 21 Council, Pres. or Past Pres. of: DeKalb Bd. of Realtors, Metro Listing Serv., Women's Council of Realtors (GA); NAR Gov. of Women's Council, Dir. GAR, Dean GA. Realtors' Inst., GAR Ins. Tr.; **HOME ADD:** 2689 Parkview Dr., NE, Atlanta, GA 30345, (404)325-4621; **BUS ADD:** 2171 Northlake Pkwy, Suite 120, Tucker, GA 30084, (404)939-8447.

NELSON, Oren F.——B: May 23, 1925, Whitmore Lake, MI, *Realtor, Owner/Mgr.*, Nelson's Real Estate; **PRIM RE ACT:** Broker, Appraiser, Banker, Owner/Investor, Insuror; **PREV EMPLOY:** Realtor over 25 yrs.; **PROFL AFFIL & HONORS:** GRI, RAM, CRB, CRS, CCIM candidate; **MIL SERV:** USN, Radioman, Several decorations; **OTHER ACT & HONORS:** Advisory Bd. Ann Arbor Bank & Trust Co.; First and Present Chmn. Econ. Devel. Corp.; VFW; Ann Arbor Bd. of Realtors; Livingston Cty. Bd. of Realtors; **HOME ADD:** 581 East Shore Dr., Whitmore Lake, MI 48189, (313)449-2506; **BUS ADD:** 9163 Main St., PO Box 665, Whitmore Lake, MI 48189, (313)449-4466.

NELSON, Ronald W., Esq.——B: Apr. 11, 1944, San Francisco, CA, *Atty. at Law*, Lillick McHose & Charles, RE Grp.; **PRIM RE ACT:** Attorney; **SERVICES:** Advice regarding all RE matters with emphasis on large RE devels./acquisitions and for. investors; **PROFL AFFIL & HONORS:** ABA; CA Bar Assn.; San Francisco Bar Assoc.; **EDUC:** AB, 1971, E. Asian Hist., Univ. of CA, Berkeley; **GRAD EDUC:** JD, 1975, Law, Univ. of CA, Hastings Coll. of the Law; **EDUC HONORS:** Phi Beta Kappa, Order of the Coif; **MIL SERV:** USAF, 1963-68; **BUS ADD:** 2 Embarcadero Ctr., Suite 2600, San Francisco, CA 94111, (415)421-4600.

NELSON, Scott A.——B: Aug. 22, 1952, Fargo, ND, *VP*, GM Ent., Inc.; **PRIM RE ACT:** Consultant, Developer, Builder, Owner/Investor, Property Manager; **OTHER RE ACT:** Tax Advisor; CPA; Prop. Mgmt.; **SERVICES:** Prop mgmt. comml. & resid. devel.; **PREV EMPLOY:** McGladrey Hendreckson & Co., CPA's, Partner; **PROFL AFFIL & HONORS:** AICPA, NAHB, CPA; **EDUC:** BA, 1974, Acctg., Moorhead State Univ.; **EDUC HONORS:** Magna Cum Laude; **OTHER ACT & HONORS:** Bd. of Dir. NDSU YMCA, Bd. of Dir. Red River Valley Hospice; **HOME ADD:** 1819 S 19th St., Fargo, ND 58103, (701)237-9399; **BUS ADD:** 55 S 27th St., Fargo, ND 58103, (701)293-3005.

NELSON, Stephen C.——B: Mar, 15, 1942, Ogden, IA, Moyer & Bergman; **PRIM RE ACT:** Attorney, Developer, Owner/Investor; **REP CLIENTS:** Lenders, contractors, devels., investors, prop. mgrs., and RE firms; **PROFL AFFIL & HONORS:** Linn Cty. Bar Assn., The IA State Bar Assn. and ABA; **EDUC:** BS, 1964, Indus. Engrg., IA State Univ., Ames, IA; **GRAD EDUC:** JD, 1967, Law, Univ. of IA; **EDUC HONORS:** Tau Beta Pi; **OTHER ACT & HONORS:** Chmn. of The IA State Bar Assn. Legal Forms Comm., 1976; Contributed to the RE Practice Manual of The IA State Bar Assn.; **HOME ADD:** 2516 Amber Dr. N.E., Cedar Rapids, IA 52402, (319)393-7744; **BUS ADD:** 2720 First Ave. N.E., Third Floor, P O Box 1943, Cedar Rapids, IA 52406, (319)366-7331.

NELSON, Wilfrid D.——B: Sept. 16, 1941, Minneapolis, KS, *Sr. Atty.*, Brown & Root, Inc., Legal Dept.; **PRIM RE ACT:** Attorney; **SERVICES:** Perform legal serv. for RE trans. of Brown & Root, one of the world's largest engrg.-const. co.; **PREV EMPLOY:** Law firms, Seattle, WA; **PROFL AFFIL & HONORS:** ABA, WA Bar Assn., TX Bar Assn.; **EDUC:** BS, 1963, Acctg. & Commerce, KS State Univ.; **GRAD EDUC:** JD, LLB, 1968, Law, Univ. of TX, School of Law; **MIL SERV:** USAF & USA, E-3; **HOME ADD:** 3604 Amherst, Houston, TX 77005, (713)668-1342; **BUS ADD:** PO Box 2002, Houston, TX 77001, (713)676-3307.

NELSON, William E.——B: July 16, 1926, Los Angeles, CA; **PRIM RE ACT:** Consultant, Attorney, Developer, Property Manager; **PROFL AFFIL & HONORS:** ABA; CA Bar; Los Angeles Bar; San Diego Bar; Lamda Alpha; ULI; **EDUC:** 1949, Eng., George Pepperdine; **GRAD EDUC:** JD, 1951, Loyola Univ., School of Law; **MIL SERV:** USN, FC 2nd, Pac. Medal 2 stars; **OTHER ACT & HONORS:** Tr., La Jolla Town Council, Pres. San Diegan's; **HOME ADD:** 8457 Paseo Del Ocaso, La Jolla, CA 92037, (714)459-6727; **BUS ADD:** 1020 Prospect St., La Jolla, CA 92037, (714)454-5086.

NEMOEDE, Albert H.——B: Mar. 31, 1916, Chicago, IL, *Owner*; **PRIM RE ACT:** Architect; **SERVICES:** Arch. practice; **EDUC:** BArch, 1941, Arch., Univ. of IL; **MIL SERV:** USN; CB's; CPO; **OTHER ACT & HONORS:** Prof. Wright Branch, City of Chicago Colls.; **HOME ADD:** 600 Warren Terr., Hinsdale, IL 60521, (312)325-4277; **BUS ADD:** P.O. Box N 4921 Forest Ave., Downers Grove, IL 60515, (312)969-4100.

NEPTUNE, C.A.——*VP Corp Dev.*, Rubbermaid, Inc.; **PRIM RE ACT:** Property Manager; **BUS ADD:** 1147 Akron Rd., Wooster, OH 44690, (216)264-6464.*

NESTER, Ronald L.——B: Nov. 2, 1946, Martinsville, VA, *VP*, Holywell Corp.; **PRIM RE ACT:** Consultant, Attorney, Developer, Regulator, Owner/Investor, Property Manager, Syndicator; **SERVICES:** All aspects of comml. devel. from fin. to constr.; **REP CLIENTS:** Holywell Corp. portfolio; **PREV EMPLOY:** Atty. at law, VA & DC; **PROFL AFFIL & HONORS:** VA & DC Bar Assns.; **EDUC:** BA, 1972, Hist., Univ. of VA; **GRAD EDUC:** JD, 1975, Law, Univ. of VA; **EDUC HONORS:** Phi Beta Kappa, Grad. with distinction; **MIL SERV:** USA, Sgt., Bronze Star; **OTHER ACT & HONORS:** Lecturer, Univ. of Miami Sch. of Arch.; **HOME ADD:** 132 Wentworth St., Chas., SC 29401, (803)577-9364; **BUS ADD:** 1300 N. 17th St., Suite 500, Arlington, VA 22209, (703)522-3330.

NESTOR, Brenda——B: Palm Beach, FL, *Pres.*, Brenda Nestor Assoc., Inc.; **PRIM RE ACT:** Broker, Consultant, Developer, Property Manager, Owner/Investor; **PROFL AFFIL & HONORS:** Realtor Bds./RESSI; **EDUC:** RE & Ins., U of MI; **OTHER ACT & HONORS:** Cricket Club & 1800 Club; **HOME ADD:** 6917 Collins Ave., Miami Beach, FL 33141, (305)866-7771; **BUS ADD:** 6917 Collins Ave. #1611, Miami Beach, FL 33141, (305)866-7771.

NEUER, Fred S.——B: Jan. 21, 1946, York, PA, *VP*, KNK Partnership; **PRIM RE ACT:** Developer, Owner/Investor; **PROFL AFFIL & HONORS:** Emporia Builders Assn.; **EDUC:** BS, 1967, Chem., Mount St. Marys, MD; **GRAD EDUC:** MD, 1971, Univ. of NC; **EDUC HONORS:** Radiology Bd. Cert.; **MIL SERV:** USAF, Capt., United Nations; **OTHER ACT & HONORS:** Bd. of Dir., Lions Club Intl.; **BUS ADD:** 1517 Berkeley Rd., Emporia, KS 66801, (316)343-6097.

NEUMANN, Mark——B: Aug. 7, 1952, Miami Beach, FL, *Prop. Evaluation Specialist*, Dade County Property Appraiser, Econ. Analysis; **PRIM RE ACT:** Appraiser, Assessor; **SERVICES:** Analysis of income producing props.; **PROFL AFFIL & HONORS:** Nat. Assn. of Review Appraisers, Intl. Assn. of Assessing Officers; Nat. Assn. of Independent Fee Appraisers, CRA; CFE; **EDUC:** BBA, 1974, RE, FL Intl. Univ.; **HOME ADD:** 12130 NE Miami Ct., No. Miami, FL 33161, (305)685-5534; **BUS ADD:** 140 W. Flagler St. 8A, Miami, FL 33138.

NEUNER, Charles——*VP Plng. & Bus. Dev.*, Potlach Corp.; **PRIM RE ACT:** Property Manager; **BUS ADD:** PO Box 3591, San Francisco, CA 94119, (415)981-5980.*

NEUSTADT, Paul——B: July 6, 1931, Bronx, NY, *VP and Sr. Counsel*, Security Title and Guaranty Co.; **PRIM RE ACT:** Consultant, Attorney; **SERVICES:** Consultant on Title Problems, Presides at Meetings of Bd. of Counsel, Advisory Bds. for Security Title; **PREV EMPLOY:** VP and Branch Mgr.-The Title Guarantee Co.; **PROFL AFFIL & HONORS:** NY State Bar Assn.; **EDUC:** BA, 1952, Govt., Hist., NY Univ.; **GRAD EDUC:** MA, 1956, Educ., Columbia Teachers Coll.; LLB, 1955, Law, Harvard Law School; **EDUC HONORS:** Phi Delta Kappa, Educ. Hon. Soc.; **OTHER ACT & HONORS:** Chmn., Housing Bd. of Appeals; Dobbs Ferry NY-1980-date; Pres. Zoning Bd. of Appeals Greenburgh Hebrew Center, Dobbs Ferry, 1976-1979; Pres., Beacon Hill Estates Housing Coop-1971-1973; V Chmn.-Comm. on Title and Transfer-NY State Bar Assn.; **HOME ADD:** 15 Manor House Dr., Dobbs Ferry, NY 10522, (914)693-3829; **BUS ADD:** 300 East 40th St., New York, NY 10016.

NEUWIRTH, Frederick——*VP RE & Construction*, American Broadcasting Co.; **PRIM RE ACT:** Property Manager; **BUS ADD:** 1330 Ave. of the Americas, New York, NY 10019, (212)887-7777.*

NEVIASER, Daniel H.——B: Oct. 14, 1922, Wash., DC, *Pres.*, Neviaser Investment; **PRIM RE ACT:** Broker, Developer, Engineer, Owner/Investor; **OTHER RE ACT:** Hotels & Comml.; **PROFL AFFIL & HONORS:** Madison Bd. of Realtors, Member - WI Currie

Commn. on RE; **EDUC:** BS ME, Univ. of MD; **MIL SERV:** USA, 11th Airborne Paratroopers, 1st Lt.; **HOME ADD:** 7221 Colony Dr., Madison, WI 53717, (608)833-4463; **BUS ADD:** 25 W Main St., Suite 465, Madison, WI 53703, (608)257-3777.

NEVIUS, William A.——B: May 17, 1932, Lancaster, KY, *VP/Treas.*, Paul Semonin Co.; **PRIM RE ACT:** Consultant; **OTHER RE ACT:** Accountant; **PREV EMPLOY:** CPA, Coopers & Lybrand, 1958-1972; **PROFL AFFIL & HONORS:** AICPA; KY Soc. of CPA's, CPA; **EDUC:** AB, 1958, Acctg., Centre Coll.; **MIL SERV:** USAF, Sgt., 1951-1955; **HOME ADD:** 3611 Fallen Timber Dr., Louisville, KY 40222, (502)425-0627; **BUS ADD:** 4812 US Hwy. 42, Louisville, KY 40222, (502)426-1650.

NEW, Manfred E. "Fritz"——B: Dec. 20, 1935, Chicago, IL, *Managing Partner*, Baldwin Harris Co.; **PRIM RE ACT:** Consultant, Developer, Builder, Property Manager; **REP CLIENTS:** approx. 300 tenants in all existing bldgs.; **PREV EMPLOY:** VP & Dir. Fidelity Union Life Ins. Co. 1964-70; **PROFL AFFIL & HONORS:** Pres. BOMA, IREM Cand.; **EDUC:** 1957, Ripon Coll., Ripon, WI; **MIL SERV:** US Army, 1st Lt.; **OTHER ACT & HONORS:** United Cerebral Palsy Assn., Dir.; **HOME ADD:** 4126 Shenandoah, Dallas, TX 75205, (214)526-8203; **BUS ADD:** 12200 Ford Rd., Suite 280, Dallas, TX 75234, (214)243-1371.

NEWBERRY, Terry V.——B: Feb. 22, 1947, Beaumont, TX, *Atty.*, Eikenburg & Stiles; **PRIM RE ACT:** Attorney; **SERVICES:** Concentration in RE Law; **PREV EMPLOY:** Coldwell, Banker & Co.; **PROFL AFFIL & HONORS:** ABA, State Bar of TX, Houston Bar Assn., Phi Delta Phi; **EDUC:** BS, 1968, Educ., Lamar Univ.; **GRAD EDUC:** MEd, 1969, Educ., Lamar Univ.; JD, 1978, Law, Univ. of Houston; **EDUC HONORS:** Phi Kappa Phi; **HOME ADD:** 775 Worthshire, Houston, TX 77008, (713)862-5704; **BUS ADD:** 1st City National Bank Bldg. Ste. 608, Houston, TX 77002, (713)652-2144.

NEWBERY, Donald A.——B: Sept. 29, 1934, Newark, NJ, *Mgr. Facilities Devel.*, Eastern Airlines, Facilities; **PRIM RE ACT:** Engineer, Builder, Owner/Investor; **SERVICES:** Planning, design, const., contract admin.; **PREV EMPLOY:** Bell Telephone Laboratories; **PROFL AFFIL & HONORS:** PE - FL; **EDUC:** BSME, 1961, ME, Newark Coll. of Engrg.; **GRAD EDUC:** MS, 1966, Engrg. Mgmt., Newark Coll. of Engrg.; **EDUC HONORS:** Nat. ME Honor Soc.; **MIL SERV:** USN, AG2, 1953-1957; **HOME ADD:** 8240 SW 164 Terr., Miami, FL 33157, (305)235-7899; **BUS ADD:** Miami International Airport, Miami, FL 33148, (305)873-6538.

NEWELL, David R.——B: June 1, 1940, Ft. Worth, TX, *Gen. Partner*, Newell and Newell Business Park; **PRIM RE ACT:** Developer, Builder, Owner/Investor, Property Manager; **OTHER RE ACT:** Fin. Analyst; **SERVICES:** Devel. 369 acres in Metroplex as garden bus. park; **PREV EMPLOY:** Asst. Prof. of Fin. at Univ. of MD, Asst. Treas. for Jack P. DeBoer in Wichita, KS, Exec. VP at Reynolds, Smith & Hills of Jacksonville, FL; **PROFL AFFIL & HONORS:** Nat. Assn. of Indus. & Office Parks, Amer. Fin. Assn., the Amer. Soc. for Fin. Analysts, Asst. Dir. of Ft. Worth Bank & Trust, Bd. of Dirs. of Ft. Worth C of C; **EDUC:** BBA, 1966, Bus. Admin., Univ. of TX, Arlington; **GRAD EDUC:** MBA, 1967, Fin., Univ. of Houston; MA, 1967, Econ., Univ. of Houston; **EDUC HONORS:** Outstanding Student in Bus. Admin., Fin. Analyst Fellowship; **MIL SERV:** USN, E-5, Amer. Spirit of Honor Medal; **HOME ADD:** 4017 Inwood, Ft. Worth, TX 76109, (817)923-3429; **BUS ADD:** 2501 Gravel Dr., Ft. Worth, TX 76118, (817)284-5555.

NEWELL, Stewart P.——B: Oct. 10, 1946, Chicago, Illinois, *Pres.*, The Newheight Grp.; **PRIM RE ACT:** Broker, Developer, Property Manager, Owner/Investor; **SERVICES:** Dev., leasing & Prop. Mgmt.; **PREV EMPLOY:** Şamuel Gary, Oil Producer (1974-77), Treas.; **PROFL AFFIL & HONORS:** AICPA, Member of CO Soc. of CPA's, Recipient of Downtown Denver, Inc. Award, 1981; **EDUC:** AB, 1968, Econ., Bowdoin Coll., Brunswick, ME; **GRAD EDUC:** MBA, 1969, Fin. & Acctg., Rutgers Univ., Newark, NJ; **EDUC HONORS:** Beta Gamma Sigma (Hon. Bus. Frat.); **OTHER ACT & HONORS:** Bd. Member Historic Denver, Denver Central YMCA, Leadership Denver Assn.; **HOME ADD:** 1201 Williams 15C, Denver, CO 80218; **BUS ADD:** 1665 Grant St., Denver, CO 80203, (303)861-1887.

NEWIROW, Andrew——*Dir. Ind. Rel.*, Great Northern Nekoosa Corp.; **PRIM RE ACT:** Property Manager; **BUS ADD:** 75 Prospect St., Stamford, CT 06901, (203)359-4000.*

NEWMAN, Bruce A.——B: Oct. 9, 1943, Muskogee, OK, *Atty.*, Mansour, Newman & Thomas PC; **PRIM RE ACT:** Attorney; **REP CLIENTS:** RE brokers & devel.; indiv. sellers & purchasers of RE with focus on comml. and land devel.; **PROFL AFFIL & HONORS:** ABA; MI Bar Assn.; Escrow Agent, US Farm Home Loan Admin.; **EDUC:** AB, 1966, Soc. Sci, Eng., Phil., Univ. of Detroit; **GRAD EDUC:** Law, 1969-1979, Tax Law, Univ. of Detroit; George Wash. Univ.; **EDUC HONORS:** With distinction; Nat. Sociological Honor toc., Amer. Jurisprudence Award; Staff Writer (in brief); **MIL SERV:** US Army; 1970-1971, 1st Lt., Foreign Service Korea, Letter of Commendation; **OTHER ACT & HONORS:** Chmn., Genesee Co. Bd. of Canvassors 1973-1979; Chmn., 7th Congressional Dist. Dem Comm.; Co-Author, Amer. Law Source Book for the Classroom Teacher; Amer. Bar Assn. 1981; **HOME ADD:** 471 Boutell Dr., Grand Blanc, MI 48507; **BUS ADD:** 1000 Beach St., Flint, MI 48502, (313)232-4186.

NEWMAN, Clifton——B: Nov. 7, 1951, SC, *Atty.*, Belcher & Newman; **PRIM RE ACT:** Attorney, Owner/Investor; **PROFL AFFIL & HONORS:** ABA; OH Bar; SC Bar; **EDUC:** 1973, Pol. Studies, Cleveland State Univ.; **GRAD EDUC:** 1976, Law, Cleveland State Univ.; **OTHER ACT & HONORS:** Second Office: PO Box 263, Greeleyville, SC 29056; **HOME ADD:** PO Box 292, Greeleyville, SC, (803)426-2449; **BUS ADD:** One Public Sq., 305, Cleveland, OH 44113, (216)696-5888.

NEWMAN, Herbert C.——*Secretary-Treasurer*, National Association of Real Estate Apprasisers; **OTHER RE ACT:** Profl. Assn. Admin.; **BUS ADD:** 853 Broadway, New York, NY 10003, (212)673-2300.*

NEWMAN, Jerold D.——*Pres.*, RE Investments of WI; **PRIM RE ACT:** Broker, Syndicator, Developer, Owner/Investor; **REP CLIENTS:** Univ. Park Estates, Heritage Farm, Imperial Estate Subdiv.; **PREV EMPLOY:** Newman Ins. & Realty Inc.; **PROFL AFFIL & HONORS:** CLU, CFP; **EDUC:** BBA, 1960, RE, Ins., Univ. WI; **EDUC HONORS:** Ins. Scholarship, Sr. Yr. Tuition School; **BUS ADD:** 101 Broadview Dr., Green Bay, WI 54301, (414)337-0101.

NEWMAN, Karel——B: Feb. 5, 1928, Prague, Czechoslovakia, *Broker*, Newman Realtors, Pres.; **PRIM RE ACT:** Broker, Developer, Lender, Owner/Investor, Property Manager, Syndicator; **SERVICES:** RE; **PROFL AFFIL & HONORS:** Contra Costa Bd. of Realtors; C.A.R.-N.A.R., GRI - Cert. in RE Univ. of CA; **EDUC:** BS, Chemistry, Univ. of Prague, Czechoslovakia; **HOME ADD:** 875 Ridge Dr., Concord, CA 94518; **BUS ADD:** 2979 Ygnacio Valley Rd., Walnut Creek, CA 94598.

NEWMAN, Lawrence R.——B: Oct. 9, 1945, Elgin, IL, *Mgr. Underwriting Servs.*, Westinghouse Credit Corp., RE Fin.; **PRIM RE ACT:** Lender; **SERVICES:** Short term lending of all types; **PREV EMPLOY:** Prudential Ins. Co.; **EDUC:** BA, 1967, Pol. Sci., Lawrence Univ.; **GRAD EDUC:** MBA, 1973, Fin., NY Univ.; **MIL SERV:** USAF; Capt.; **HOME TEL:** (412)761-1015; **BUS ADD:** 3 Gateway Ctr., Pittsburgh, PA 15222, (412)255-3300.

NEWMAN, Norman R.——B: Dec. 16, 1934, Indianapolis, IN, *Atty.*, Dann Pecar Newman Talesnick & Kleiman, P.C.; **PRIM RE ACT:** Attorney; **SERVICES:** Legal serv. in connection with all types of RE transactions; **REP CLIENTS:** Devel., lenders, contractors; **PROFL AFFIL & HONORS:** ABA (including Probate, Real Prop. and Trust Sect. and Corporate, Banking and Bus. Law Sect.), IN St. Bar Assn. and Indianapolis Bar Assn., Lecturer on Comml. RE Transactions, Indiana Continuing Legal Educ. Forum 1979-80. Panelist, Intl. Council of Shopping Ctrs. Law Conference, 1980; **EDUC:** AB, 1957, Pol. Sci., IN Univ.; **GRAD EDUC:** LLB, 1960, Law, IN Univ.; **EDUC HONORS:** Cum Laude; Order of Coif; **OTHER ACT & HONORS:** Deputy Prosecuting Atty., Marion Cty., IN 1963-67; Pres., Broadmoor Ctry. Club, Indianapolis, IN; Bd. of Governors, Jewish Welfare Federation, Indianapolis, IN; VP, Jewish Community Relations Council and recipient of David M. Cook Memorial Award; VP, Jewish Educational Association, Indianapolis, IN; **HOME ADD:** 7990 N. Meridian St., Indianapolis, IN 46260, (317)255-4372; **BUS ADD:** 1600 Market Square Ctr., Indianapolis, IN 46204, (317)632-3232.

NEWMAN, Philip——*Mgr. Mfg.*, Glenmore Distillers; **PRIM RE ACT:** Property Manager; **BUS ADD:** 500 W. Jefferson St., Citizens Plaza, Louisville, KY 40202, (502)589-0130.*

NEWMAN, Robert A.——B: Jan. 19, 1932, Portsmouth, OH, *Exec. VP*, Scioto Econ. Devel. Corp.; **PRIM RE ACT:** Consultant, Developer, Lender, Builder, Owner/Investor; **OTHER RE ACT:** Designer, Planner, Financing; **SERVICES:** Environmental design, bus. devel. fin.; **REP CLIENTS:** Devels., indus. firms, entrepreneurs; **PREV EMPLOY:** Owner Bob Newman & Assoc. Planners/Designers; **PROFL AFFIL & HONORS:** Amer. Inst. Building Designers, Nat. Council for Urban Devel., ULI, Amer. Soc. of Landscape Arch., Amer. Soc. Interior Designers, Design Awards, Food Service Magazine & Amer. Inst. of Building Designers; **EDUC:** 1949-53, Arch. Design, Univ. of Cincinnati; **MIL SERV:** USA, Nat. Sec. Agency; **OTHER ACT & HONORS:** Past Pres. Portsmouth Home Builders, Young Man of Yr., 1964; **HOME ADD:** 4425 Hickory Ln., Portsmouth, OH; **BUS**

ADD: Suite 1-2, Cty Courthouse, PO Drawer 1606, Portsmouth, OH 45662, (614)354-7779.

NEWMAN, Robert E.——**B:** Feb. 4, 1922, Elizabeth, NJ, *Pres.*, Robert E. Newman Bldg. Co., Inc.; **PRIM RE ACT:** Broker, Syndicator, Consultant, Appraiser, Developer, Builder, Property Manager, Insuror; **OTHER RE ACT:** Also serve on the Bd. of Dir., Central Jersey Bank and Trust Co.; **PROFL AFFIL & HONORS:** NAR, SREA; **EDUC:** BS, 1946, Econ., Franklin and Marshall Coll., Lancaster, PA; **MIL SERV:** USN, Warrant Off., North Atlantic Ribbon; **HOME ADD:** 260 Prospect St., Westfield, NJ 07090, (201)232-6068; **BUS ADD:** 185 Elm St., Westfield, NJ 07091, (201)232-5800.

NEWMAN, Robert M.——*Dir. RE*, Martin Marietta Corp.; **PRIM RE ACT:** Property Manager; **BUS ADD:** 6801 Rockledge Dr., Bethesda, MD 20034, (301)897-6000.*

NEWQUIST, Daniel——*Ed.*, Commerce Clearing House, Estate Planning Review; **PRIM RE ACT:** Real Estate Publisher; **BUS ADD:** 4025 West Peterson Ave., Chicago, IL 60646, (312)583-8500.*

NEWSOME, Larry D.——**B:** May 13, 1956, Pikeville, KY, *Asst. VP, Mort. Loans*, Pikeville Nat. Bank; **PRIM RE ACT:** Appraiser, Lender, Owner/Investor; **SERVICES:** Provide all levels of mort. fin., counseling; **REP CLIENTS:** Consumers., i.e., potential homeowners investors, office leasing counseling; **PREV EMPLOY:** Lexington Appraisal Co., Lexington, KY, Resid. Prop. Appraiser; **PROFL AFFIL & HONORS:** MBAA, Soc. of RE Appraisers, SREA, SREA designated appraiser, CRA, KY RE Salesman; **EDUC:** BBA, 1978, Mktg., RE, Eastern KY Univ.; **GRAD EDUC:** MBA, 1979, RE Fin., Eastern KY Univ.; **EDUC HONORS:** Rho Epsilon Nat. Real Frat., 1978-79, RE Fin. Prize, Sigma Tau Pi, Hon. Bus. Frat., 3.75 GPA on 4.00; **OTHER ACT & HONORS:** Hon. KY Col. Member Big Sandy Bd. of Realtors, Member East KY Home Builders Assn.; **HOME ADD:** Rt. 3, Box 413A, Pikeville, KY 41501, (606)432-0980; **BUS ADD:** PO Box 712, Piteville, KY 41501, (606)432-1414.

NEWSON, Darryl Charles——**B:** May 11, 1953, Phila, PA, *Pres./C.E.O.*, Continental Companies; **PRIM RE ACT:** Consultant, Appraiser, Developer, Builder, Lender, Owner/Investor, Property Manager; **OTHER RE ACT:** Loan packaging and presentation; **SERVICES:** RE Mgmt. Devel., Bldg., Mort. Loans; **PREV EMPLOY:** W.T. Syphax Management Company, Syphax Enterprises, EBAS Equitable Life Assurance Soc.; **PROFL AFFIL & HONORS:** Apt. Office Bldg. Assn., Nat. Assn. RE Brokers; Prop. Mgmt. Assn.; **GRAD EDUC:** MBA Candidate, in progress, Bus. Admin., Journalism, RE, DC Teachers Coll., American Univ.; **OTHER ACT & HONORS:** IREM; **HOME ADD:** 10517 Indigo Lane, Fairfax, VA 22032, (703)250-4814; **BUS ADD:** 2812 Pennsylvania Ave., N.W., Washington, DC 20007, (202)978-4913.

NEWSON, Edward——**B:** May 2, 1937, Eudora, AR, *Broker*, Tanden Co. & Assoc.; **PRIM RE ACT:** Broker, Instructor, Lender; **PREV EMPLOY:** Dept. of HUD, 1969-75; Veteran Admin. Ctr.; **PROFL AFFIL & HONORS:** IFA, Amer. Assn. of Cert. Appraisers; **EDUC:** Wichita Business Coll.; **MIL SERV:** USMCR, Pfc; **HOME ADD:** 827 N. Green, Wichita, KS, (316)683-5017; **BUS ADD:** 642-44 N. Grove, Wichita, KS 67214.

NEWTON, James W.——**B:** Apr. 19, 1925, Cross Cut, TX, *Owner*, J.W. Newton, Appraisals and Consultations; **PRIM RE ACT:** Broker, Appraiser, Owner/Investor, Instructor, Property Manager; **OTHER RE ACT:** Investment studies, Rural props.; **SERVICES:** Appraisals, consultant; **REP CLIENTS:** Indiv., banks, attys., investment firms; **PREV EMPLOY:** PCA, bank, Texas General Land Office, Ins. Co. Mort. Loan Rep.; **PROFL AFFIL & HONORS:** Amer. Soc. Farm Mgrs. & Rural Appraisers, Soc. of RE Appraisers, Accredited Rural Appraiser, SRA; **EDUC:** BS, 1949, Agricultural Ed., TX A & M Univ.; **MIL SERV:** USN, AMM 3/C; **OTHER ACT & HONORS:** Lubbock Ag. Club, Lubbock A & M Club; **HOME ADD:** 6123 Nashville Ave., Lubbock, TX 79413, (806)795-2723; **BUS ADD:** 3403 73rd St., Lubbock, TX 79423, (806)799-5240.

NEWTON, Joseph——**B:** Dec. 13, 1944, Antioch, CA, *Prof., RE Education*, Bakersfield Coll., Bus. Ed.; **PRIM RE ACT:** Broker, Developer, Builder, Instructor; **SERVICES:** Coordinator of RE Education, 1971 - present; **PREV EMPLOY:** RE Broker, 1971 - present; **PROFL AFFIL & HONORS:** CA Assn. Realtors; NAR; **EDUC:** BA, 1966, RE/Mgmt., Fresno State Univ.; **GRAD EDUC:** MBA, 1968, Mktg./Mgmt., Fresno State Univ.; **HOME ADD:** 4500 Panorama Dr., Bakersfield, CA 93306, (805)871-7160; **BUS ADD:** 1801 Panorama Dr., Bakersfield, CA 93305, (805)395-4272.

NEWTON, Richard——*Corp. Dir. RE Admin. & Services*, Sperry Corp.; **PRIM RE ACT:** Property Manager; **BUS ADD:** Avenue of the Americas, New York, NY 10019, (212)484-4444.*

NEYHART, Ron——**B:** Apr. 6, 1956, PA, *Appraiser*, American Appraisal, RE Div.; **PRIM RE ACT:** Consultant, Appraiser; **REP CLIENTS:** GTE, Gen. Elec., W.R. Grace, Citizen & Southern Bank, Diamond Shamrock, etc.; **PREV EMPLOY:** Investment Banker With J.D. Hanauer; **EDUC:** BS, 1978, Fin., RE, FL State Univ.; **HOME ADD:** 2183 Palmyra Dr., Marietta, GA 30067, (404)953-4734; **BUS ADD:** 1819 Peachtree Rd., Atlanta, GA 30304, (404)352-2167.

NEZAMUDDIN, Mohammed——**B:** Apr. 7, 1953, Calcutta, India, *Technical Dir.*, Midco Products Co.; **PRIM RE ACT:** Owner/Investor; **SERVICES:** Resid. Rental Prop. Investment Prop.; **PROFL AFFIL & HONORS:** Amer. Inst. of Aeronautics and Astronautics, Amer. Chem. Soc.; **EDUC:** Physics, Math, 1973, Calcutta Univ.; **GRAD EDUC:** BS, 1977, Aerospace Engr., St. Louis Univ.; **EDUC HONORS:** Distinction; **HOME ADD:** 4216 Iowa, St. Louis, MO 63111, (314)481-8392; **BUS ADD:** 11697 Fairgrove Indus. Blvd., Maryland Height, St. Louis Cty, MO 63043, (314)567-1710.

NEZIN, Len——**B:** June 10, 1927, New York, NY, *Pres.*, Nezin Assoc.; **PRIM RE ACT:** Consultant, Appraiser, Developer, Owner/Investor, Property Manager, Syndicator; **OTHER RE ACT:** For. Prop., Canary Islands, Spain; **SERVICES:** Trades, Workouts, Fin., Tax, Legal Assistance for the Small Investor; **EDUC:** BS, 1949, NYU; **GRAD EDUC:** MA, 1953, Columbia Univ.; **EDUC HONORS:** Emily Lowe Award - Artist; **MIL SERV:** US Naval Res., S 1/c, WWII Medals of Good Conduct, European-Pacific Theatre; **HOME ADD:** 487 Guy Lombardo Ave., Freeport, NY 11520, (516)378-7313; **BUS ADD:** 487 Guy Lombardo Ave., Freeport, NY 11520, (516)378-7313.

NG, Thien Koan——**B:** Mar. 14, 1045, India, Thien Koan Ng, Attorney; **PRIM RE ACT:** Broker, Attorney, Developer, Owner/Investor, Syndicator; **PREV EMPLOY:** Partner, Caldwell & Toms, Attys., L.A. CA, Mgr. - Arthur Young & Co., CPA, L.A., CA, Superviser - Tonche Ross & Co., NYC & L.A., CA; **PROFL AFFIL & HONORS:** ABA, CA State Bar, AICPA, CA CPA Soc., Broker - CA; **EDUC:** BBA, 1965, Bus., Golden Gate Univ. - San Francisco, CA; **GRAD EDUC:** MBA, 1967, JD (Law), 1968, Fin., Golden Gate Univ., San Francisco, CA; LLM, 1969, George Washington Univ., Wash., DC - Taxation; PhD Candidate, 1969-1971, NY Univ. - Fin.; **HOME ADD:** 972 Linda Vista Ave., Pasadena, CA 91103, (213)795-9052; **BUS ADD:** 3660 Wilshire Blvd., Penthouse G, Los Angeles, CA 91103, (213)487-0882.

NIBLETT, John E.——**B:** May 18, 1933, Christopher, IL, *Owner*, John Niblett Real Estate Appraising; **PRIM RE ACT:** Broker, Consultant, Appraiser, Owner/Investor; **SERVICES:** Valuation Consultant, Gen. Brokerage; **PREV EMPLOY:** Dept. of Housing and Urban Devel.; **PROFL AFFIL & HONORS:** American Soc. of Appraisers, Soc. of Real Estate Appraisers, Nat. Assn. of Review Appraisers, Nat. Assn. of RE Brokers, ASA, SRA, CRA; **MIL SERV:** USN, Amn., Serv. Medal Good Conduct Medal; **HOME ADD:** 6646 N Winchester Ave., Fresno, CA 93704, (209)432-3232; **BUS ADD:** 6646 N Winchester Ave., Fresno, CA 93704, (209)432-3232.

NICHOLAS, Frederick M.——**B:** May 30, 1920, New York, NY, *Pres.*, The Hapsmith Company; **PRIM RE ACT:** Developer, Owner/Investor; **PROFL AFFIL & HONORS:** ICSC, Beverly Hills, Los Angeles Cty. and CA Bar Assns., Citizen of the Year 1978 Beverly Hills Realty Board; Distinguished Serv. Award, 1974, Beverly Hills Bar Assn.; **EDUC:** BA, 1947, Journalism, USC; **GRAD EDUC:** JD, 1952, USC; **MIL SERV:** US Army 1941-46, Capt., Bronze Star; **OTHER ACT & HONORS:** Chmn., CA Public Broadcasting Commn. 1976, Maple Ctr. (1977-79); **HOME ADD:** 880 Loma Vista Dr., Beverly Hills, CA 90210, (213)275-2802; **BUS ADD:** 9454 Wilshire Blvd., Beverly Hills, CA 90212, (213)271-5176.

NICHOLAS, Nick——**B:** June 18, 1953, Dallas, TX, Nicholas Realty Co.; **PRIM RE ACT:** Broker, Consultant, Developer; **SERVICES:** Comml., investment brokerage and consulting; **PROFL AFFIL & HONORS:** Member Gr. Dallas Bd/ of Realtors, TX Assn. of Realtors, NAR; **EDUC:** 1975, N TX State Univ.; **HOME ADD:** 5527 W Amherst, Dallas, TX 75209, (214)357-5990; **BUS ADD:** 5319 N Central Exp., Suite 202, Dallas, TX 75205, (214)363-8511.

NICHOLLS, Richard B.——*Dir.*, Arizona, Arizona Dept. of Real Estate; **PRIM RE ACT:** Property Manager; **BUS ADD:** State Capital, 1700 W. Washington St., Phoenix, AZ 85007, (602)255-4900.*

NICHOLS, Geoffrey H.——**B:** Sept. 21, 1941, Haverhill, MA, *Partner*, Woodstock Properties; **PRIM RE ACT:** Broker, Consultant, Appraiser, Developer, Owner/Investor, Property Manager, Syndicator; **PROFL**

AFFIL & HONORS: GRI; **EDUC:** BA, 1964, Middlebury Coll.; **OTHER ACT & HONORS:** Commnr. Off. Research Planning Comm.; Dir., CT River Valley Watershed Council; **HOME ADD:** Pomfret, VT, (802)457-2260; **BUS ADD:** 61 Central St., Woodstock, VT 03091, (802)457-1322.

NICHOLS, Hal E.——B: Nov. 5, 1926, Tunica, MS, Nichols RE; **PRIM RE ACT:** Broker, Instructor, Consultant, Property Manager, Owner/Investor; **SERVICES:** Sales, Valuation, Mgmt., Site Location; **PROFL AFFIL & HONORS:** NAR; ARK Realtors Assn., Realtors Nat. Mktg. Assn., Nat. Assn. of Review Appraisers; **EDUC:** BBA, 1950, Econ., Univ. of MS; **MIL SERV:** USA; **OTHER ACT & HONORS:** Pres. Kiwanis Club 1969/Dir. United Fund Bd. of Adjustment-Chmn./Dir. Ark Realtors Assn. 1974, 1975, 1976; **HOME ADD:** 101 Oak Ridge, Helena, AR 72342, (501)338-3765; **BUS ADD:** 315 Helena Nat. Bank Bldg., Helena, AR 72342, (501)338-3437.

NICHOLS, John——*Pres.*, Illinois Tool Works, Inc.; **PRIM RE ACT:** Property Manager; **BUS ADD:** 8501 West Higgins Rd., Chicago, IL 60631, (312)693-3040.*

NICHOLS, Richard M.——B: Mar. 11, 1954, Charleston, SC, *Assoc.*, Chellis and Mortimer, P.A.; **PRIM RE ACT:** Attorney; **SERVICES:** RE Practice, taxation, probate, estate planning, comml. bankruptcy and corps.; **PROFL AFFIL & HONORS:** ABA, SC Bar; Dorchester Cty. Bar Assn., AICPA, SC Assn. of CPA's, Atty; CPA; **EDUC:** BS, 1976, Bus. Admin., Acctg. and Econ., Coll. of Charleston; JD, 1981, Bus. Law and Taxation, Univ. of SC; **EDUC HONORS:** (Magna Cum Laude), Outstanding Scholar Award (Bus. Admin./Econ. Dept.); **HOME ADD:** 19 Avondale Ave., Charleston, SC 29407, (803)766-7567; **BUS ADD:** 118 E. Richardson Ave., PO Box 430, Summerville, SC 29483, (803)871-7765.

NICHOLS, Robert John——B: Oct. 7, 1949, Erie, PA, *Partner*, Boyd & Parks; **PRIM RE ACT:** Attorney, Instructor; **SERVICES:** Gen. Counsel to trade assn.; instr. of seminars; General Pratice of Law; **REP CLIENTS:** Metro Tulsa Bd. of Realtors; OK Assn. of Realtors; OK Real Estate Comm.; legal counsel to RE devel., builders, lenders, consumers and realtors; **PREV EMPLOY:** Staff Legal counsel to Metro Tulsa Bd. of Realtors 1975-1977; **PROFL AFFIL & HONORS:** Tulsa Cty. Bar Assn.; OK Bar Assn.; Tulsa Land Use Lawyers Assn. Pres. 1981; OK Trial Lawyers Assn.; RE Editor of semi-monthly publication--The Advocate; **EDUC:** BS, 1971, Ecology, Syracuse Univ.; **GRAD EDUC:** JD, 1974, Law, Univ. of Tulsa; **HOME ADD:** 2410 W. Quincy Circle, Broken Arrow, OK 74012, (918)258-8972; **BUS ADD:** 800 Granston Bldg., 111 W. Fifth St., Tulsa, OK 74103, (918)582-3222.

NICHOLS, Stephen R.——B: Sept. 10, 1940, Kansas City, MO, *Pres.*, Premier Props. Corp.; **PRIM RE ACT:** Developer, Owner/Investor; **PREV EMPLOY:** VP First Nat. Bank of Chicago, Chmn. RE Research Corp., Sr. VP Amer. Invesco Corp.; **PROFL AFFIL & HONORS:** ULI, Chicago, RE Bd.; **EDUC:** BA, 1963, Hist. & Econ., Simpson Coll.; **GRAD EDUC:** MS, 1967, Fin., Univ. of IL; **EDUC HONORS:** Omicron Delta Epsilon; **HOME ADD:** 2500 Lakeview, Chicago, IL 60614, (312)248-8218; **BUS ADD:** 400 N. State, Chicago, IL 60610, (312)670-2525.

NICHOLS, William H., II——*KMA RE Mgr.*, The Kroger Co., Mid Atlantic Mktg. Area; **OTHER RE ACT:** RE Mgr.; **SERVICES:** Site election, leasing; **REP CLIENTS:** Acquisition of prop. for co. ownership and lease admin. for 112 stores mid atl. mktg. area (parts of VA, WV, TN, NC, OH, KY); **BUS ADD:** Box 1078, Salem, VA 24153, (703)387-5250.

NICHOLS, Wm. Frederick——B: Feb. 6, 1914, Oklahoma City, OK, *VP and Sr. Appraiser*, Liberty Mortgage Co., Comml. Loans; **PRIM RE ACT:** Broker, Consultant, Appraiser; **OTHER RE ACT:** Loan Officer; **SERVICES:** Comml. loan origination and serv.; **REP CLIENTS:** We are correspondents for 102 investors and serv. a portfolio in the amount of $548,000,000.00, consisting of 15,000 customer accounts; **PREV EMPLOY:** VP Doric Corp.; **PROFL AFFIL & HONORS:** OK RE Commn. (lic. broker); Nat. Assn. of Fee Appraisers; OK Mort. Bankers Assn.; **EDUC:** Attended Oklahoma City Univ. (45 Hours); **MIL SERV:** US Air Corp., WW II; 45th Infantry Div., M/Sgt., Bronze Star Medal, Korea; **HOME ADD:** 3016 Finchley Lane, Oklahoma City, OK 73120, (405)842-4971; **BUS ADD:** 100 Broadway, P.O. Box 25757, Oklahoma City, OK 73125, (405)231-6640.

NICHOLSON, Don——*Vice President Fin. & Tre.*, Artic Enterprises; **PRIM RE ACT:** Property Manager; **BUS ADD:** 800 S. Brooks, PO Box 635, Thief River Falls, IN 56701, (218)681-1147.*

NICHOLSON, James R.——B: Feb. 7, 1945, Morristown, TN, *Pres.*, J.R. Nicholson & Co.; **PRIM RE ACT:** Broker, Consultant, Developer, Owner/Investor, Property Manager; **SERVICES:** Prop. Mgmt. (Comml. - Indus.) Brokerage; Consulting; **REP CLIENTS:** NY Life Ins.; Litton Ind.; NCNB; First Union Nat. Bank; **PREV EMPLOY:** VP Percivals, Inc.; **PROFL AFFIL & HONORS:** IREM, BOMA, NC Assn. of Realtors, CPM; Past Pres. IREM Chap. 40; Sec./Treas. BOMA Carolina, Virginia; **EDUC:** Central Piedmont Comm. College & UNCC; **HOME ADD:** 8742 Lorraine Dr., Matthews, NC 28105; **BUS ADD:** PO Box 35031, Charlotte, NC 28235, (704)374-0655.

NICHOLSON, Kerry L.——B: Nov. 22, 1947, Davenport, IA, *Rgnl. VP & Mgr., Portland Office*, Wells Fargo Realty Advisors; **PRIM RE ACT:** Lender, Owner/Investor; **SERVICES:** Large RE const. loans; joint ventures; purchase of RE equities; **REP CLIENTS:** Harsh Investment Corp.; Robert Randall Co., Mercury Devel.; Thunderbird/Red Lion Inns; Hines Interests, Urban Investment, CBL, Mel Simon, May Co., Koll Co.; **PREV EMPLOY:** First Natl. Bank of Chicago 1973-78; **PROFL AFFIL & HONORS:** C of C, Portland, CPA; **EDUC:** AB, 1970, Pol. Sci., Univ. of CA, Berkeley; **GRAD EDUC:** MBA, 1976, Fin./Acctg., Univ. of Chicago; **EDUC HONORS:** Phi Beta Kappa; **BUS ADD:** 111 SW Columbia St., Suite 350, Portland, OR 97201, (503)241-2791.

NICHOLSON, Paul——*VP Mfg.*, Mohawk Rubber Co.; **PRIM RE ACT:** Property Manager; **BUS ADD:** 50 Executive Parkway, Hudson, OH 44236, (216)650-1111.*

NICKERSON, Adams H.——B: Feb. 9, 1924, NJ, *Pres.*, Adams H. Nickerson Corp.; **PRIM RE ACT:** Developer, Owner/Investor, Syndicator; **SERVICES:** Supervision of investments including reports and tax services; **REP CLIENTS:** pvt. indivs.; **PROFL AFFIL & HONORS:** NY RE Bd.; **EDUC:** BA, 1946, Amer. Hist., Harvard Univ.; **HOME ADD:** 130 E. 94th St., New York, NY 10028, (212)369-1044; **BUS ADD:** 342 Madison Ave., New York, NY 10173, (212)490-7470.

NICKERSON, Joseph T.——B: Oct. 16, 1946, Abington, PA, *Pres.*, The Nickerson Corp.; **PRIM RE ACT:** Broker, Developer, Builder, Owner/Investor, Property Manager, Syndicator; **PROFL AFFIL & HONORS:** NAR; BOMA; **OTHER ACT & HONORS:** Rotary Intl.; **HOME ADD:** 11 Effingham Rd., Morrisville, PA 19067, (215)295-7759; **BUS ADD:** Riverview Plaza, Suite 202, Yardley, PA 19067, (215)493-8550.

NIEBUHR, Fred J.——B: Mar. 7, 1926, New York, NY, *Pres.*, Exec. Realty; **PRIM RE ACT:** Broker, Consultant, Developer, Instructor, Property Manager, Owner/Investor, Insuror; **SERVICES:** Indus. & comml. RE; **PREV EMPLOY:** Island Realty Exec. VP 1958-1979; **PROFL AFFIL & HONORS:** Long Island Bd. of Realtors, SIR; **MIL SERV:** USN; **OTHER ACT & HONORS:** VChmn. of Bd. RE Inst. at C.W. Post Coll.; **HOME ADD:** 42 Woodlake Dr. E, Woodbury, NY 11797, (516)364-8167; **BUS ADD:** 125 Jericho Tnpk., Jericho, NY 11753, (516)333-6000.

NIEDERGANG, Murray A.——B: Jan. 7, 1926, New York, NY, *Partner*, Blum, Haimoff, Gersen, Lipson, Slavin & Garley; **PRIM RE ACT:** Attorney, Owner/Investor, Instructor; **OTHER RE ACT:** Negotiator; **SERVICES:** RE lawyer - all phases; **REP CLIENTS:** Co-op and condo. converters, lessors and lessees of comml. and indus. prop., buyers and sellers of all types of RE, investment groups, etc.; **PROFL AFFIL & HONORS:** Local, State and ABA; **EDUC:** BS, 1948, Poli. Sci., Columbia; **GRAD EDUC:** LLB, 1951, Harvard Law School; **MIL SERV:** US Army, Cpl., Bronze Star/Valor; **HOME ADD:** 140 Riverside Dr., New York, NY 10024, (212)362-7102; **BUS ADD:** 270 Madison Ave., New York, NY 10016, (212)683-6383.

NIELSEN, Laura A.——B: Nov. 28, 1956, Omaha, NE, *Broker-Assoc.*, CBS RE Co.; **PRIM RE ACT:** Broker, Syndicator, Appraiser, Developer, Owner/Investor; **SERVICES:** RE Sales, Appraisals, Dev. & Synd., Prop. Mgmt.; **REP CLIENTS:** Home Buyers, Investors, Builders, Prop. Owners; **PREV EMPLOY:** RE Sales; **PROFL AFFIL & HONORS:** Omaha Bd. of Realtors, NAR, BE Realtors Assn., RESSI, Amer. Bus. Women's Assn., GRI, CRSI; **OTHER ACT & HONORS:** Omaha Sports Club; Appointment to Zoning Bd. of Appeals; **HOME ADD:** 640 North 152nd Cir., Omaha, NE 68154, (402)493-5153; **BUS ADD:** 9202 W Dodge Rd. #107, Omaha, NE 68114, (402)391-8300.

NIELSEN, Wallace D.——B: May 7, 1925, Milwaukee, WI, *Pres.*, Nielsen Realty, Inc.; **PRIM RE ACT:** Broker, Lender, Owner/Investor; **OTHER RE ACT:** Exchangor; **SERVICES:** We buy, sell, exchange comml., investment and recreational props. worldwide; **REP CLIENTS:** Trusts; Syndicators; **PROFL AFFIL & HONORS:** NAR, WI Exchange Club, Milwaukee Traders Club, CCIM WI Chapter,

CCIM, (Charter Member); SCV; **EDUC:** BA, U. of Toledo; U. of WI; **EDUC HONORS:** Instructor Marquette U. (Exchange & Taxation); **MIL SERV:** US Air Force, WW II Pilot; **OTHER ACT & HONORS:** Milwaukee Athletic Club; **HOME ADD:** 1740 Arrowhead Ct., Elm Grove, WI 53122, (414)786-6855; **BUS ADD:** 4225 W. North Ave., Milwaukee, WI 53208, (414)445-1303.

NIERENBERG, Norman M.——B: Feb. 16, 1943, Bronx, NY, *VP, Investment Div.*, PYMS-SUCHMAN RE co. P-S Securities, Inc.; **PRIM RE ACT:** Broker, Syndicator, Consultant, Developer, Property Manager, Owner/Investor; **SERVICES:** Creative Dev. of Comml. & Indust. Prop., Private RE Synd. & Placements; **REP CLIENTS:** Med., Prof., & Bus. Exec., Pension Funds; **PREV EMPLOY:** General Mills; Zayre Corp.; **PROFL AFFIL & HONORS:** Nat. Assn. of Securities Dealers, RESSI, NAR; **EDUC:** BS, 1966, Bus. Mgnt., Econ., Educ., Long Island Univ.; **HOME ADD:** 11604 S. W. 98th Pl., Miami, FL 33176, (305)251-5224; **BUS ADD:** 9205 S. Dixie Hwy., Miami, FL 33156, (305)667-6461.

NIERMAN, James S.——B: Nov. 7, 1949, Chicago, IL, *Pres.*, Nierman and Associates, Ltd.; **PRIM RE ACT:** Broker, Developer, Owner/Investor; **SERVICES:** Mktg. and acquisition of large comml. investment prop.; **REP CLIENTS:** Indiv. and instnl. investors and prop. owners; **PREV EMPLOY:** Arthur Rubloff and Co. (4 years); First National Bank of Chicago; **PROFL AFFIL & HONORS:** NAR, IL Assn. of Realtors, Chicago RE Bd., WI RE ALumni Assn., CCIM; **EDUC:** BBA, 1972, Mktg. and Fin., Univ. of WI (at Madison); **GRAD EDUC:** MBA, 1974, RE and Fin., Univ. of WI at Madison; **EDUC HONORS:** Henry Vilas Fellowship Award; **OTHER ACT & HONORS:** Dir., Chicago Youth Centers; Standard Club of Chicago; **HOME ADD:** 2020 Lincoln Park W., Chicago, IL 60614, (312)327-3363; **BUS ADD:** Suite 2300 Xerox Centre, 55 W. Monroe, Chicago, IL 60603, (312)346-0061.

NIGHTINGALE, Robert S., Jr.——B: June 19, 1947, San Diego, CA, *Pres.*, Nightingale Properties, Inc.; **PRIM RE ACT:** Broker, Developer; **SERVICES:** Devel. of comml. props. in So. CA; **REP CLIENTS:** Neighborhood serv. ctrs., fin./office bldgs.; **PREV EMPLOY:** C.W. Clark, Inc. - co-founder and VP; **PROFL AFFIL & HONORS:** Intl. Council of Shopping Ctr. Devel.; Soc. of Indus. Realtors; Save our Heritage Organization; Hist. Preservation Soc.; Nat. Tr. For Hist. Preservation; **EDUC:** BA, 1973, Conservation Geography, RE, Urban Planning, San Diego State Univ.; **EDUC HONORS:** Who's Who in Amer. Coll. and Univ., Assoc. Students Council, Member ASB Fin. Comm.; **MIL SERV:** US Army; Sp-5 1976-1978, Army Commendation Medal; **OTHER ACT & HONORS:** C of C, Bd. of Dir., YMCA, Sierra Club, Zoological Soc.; **HOME ADD:** 2555 Caminito Muirfield, LaJolla, CA 92037, (714)459-3945; **BUS ADD:** 111 Elm St., Ste. 201, San Diego, CA 92101, (714)235-8822.

NIKITINE, André V.——B: June 8, 1937, Liege, Belgium, *Pres.*, Commercial Centers Management Co.; **PRIM RE ACT:** Owner/Investor, Property Manager; **SERVICES:** Consulting in Latin Amer.; **PREV EMPLOY:** IBEC, Dir. Fin., Supermarket Div.; **PROFL AFFIL & HONORS:** ICSC, ULI; **EDUC:** BA, 1958, Econ., Harvard Univ.; **GRAD EDUC:** MBA, Bus., Harvard Bus. School; **EDUC HONORS:** Dean's List; **OTHER ACT & HONORS:** Presbyterian Hospital, Tr. & Dir.; **HOME ADD:** 2305 Laurel St., San Juan, Pr 00913, (809)726-1962; **BUS ADD:** G.P.O. Box 2983, San Juan, PR 00936, (809)765-3288.

NIKOLAS, Thomas D.——B: June 18, 1943, Aberdeen, SD, *Mgr. Tax & Prop. Dept.*, Farmers Union Central Exchange, Inc.; **PRIM RE ACT:** Property Manager, Insuror; **EDUC:** BA, 1967, Pol. Sci. & Econ., Univ. of OK; **MIL SERV:** USA, 1964-71, Res., Sgt.; **HOME ADD:** 1414 Sophia, Maplewood, MN 55109, (612)777-0134; **BUS ADD:** PO Box 43089, St. Paul, MN 55164, (612)451-5077.

NILAND, William F., Jr.——B: Apr. 3, 1942, Medford, MA, *Pres.*, Niland and Co., Realtors and Execu-System, Realtors; **PRIM RE ACT:** Broker, Consultant, Appraiser, Property Manager; **SERVICES:** Brokerage of comml. and indus. prop. north of Boston; **PREV EMPLOY:** Former VP and Partner of Hunneman and Co.; **PROFL AFFIL & HONORS:** NAR; MA Assn. of Realtors; Greater Salem Bd. of Realtors; Greater Salem Bd., Comml. Indus. Investment Div.; North Shore Econ. Council; **EDUC:** BS, 1973, Mgmt., Suffolk Univ.; **GRAD EDUC:** Post Grad. Cert., 1980, RE, Univ. of TN; **HOME ADD:** 244 Ipswich Rd., Topsfield, MA 01983, (617)887-6074; **BUS ADD:** 2 Enon St., Beverly, MA 01923, (617)922-7084.

NILES, John——B: Jun. 22, 1937, Boston, MA, *Pres.*, North Coast Properties, Inc.; **OTHER RE ACT:** RE Investment & Devel.; **SERVICES:** Devel., RE Tax Abatement Counseling; **PREV EMPLOY:** Pvt. RE Law Practice 1963-80; **PROFL AFFIL & HONORS:** Member MA Bar; Greater Boston RE Bd.; **EDUC:** AB, 1959, Harvard Coll.; **GRAD EDUC:** JD, 1963, Harvard Law Sch.; **EDUC HONORS:** Cum laude, Cum laude; **MIL SERV:** USA Res., Capt.; **HOME ADD:** 4 Alton Ct., Brookline, MA 02146, (617)232-1303; **BUS ADD:** 28 State St., Boston, MA 02109, (617)742-8610.

NILGES, David C.——*VP, Dir.*, The T. W. Grogan Co.; **PRIM RE ACT:** Broker, Instructor, Consultant, Property Manager, Lender, Real Estate Publisher; **SERVICES:** Mgmt., feasibility, rehabilitation, brokerage, mort.; **REP CLIENTS:** Mfrs. Life Ins. Co., Toronto, Can., Mutual Benefit Life Ins. Co., Newark, NJ, Prudential Ins. Co., Metropolitan Life Ins. Co., The Travelers Ins. Co.; **PREV EMPLOY:** Shelter Resources Corp.-VP and Dir. of RE; **PROFL AFFIL & HONORS:** Regional VP IREM Chmn. Pub. Div., Faculty Member; Ohio Realtor., Realtors Omega Tau Rho, 1974; Mgr. of the Yr., 1979, Cleveland, OH; **EDUC:** BSS, Hist., Bus., John Carroll Univ., Cleveland, OH; **MIL SERV:** USA, 1st Lt.; **OTHER ACT & HONORS:** Dept. of Continuing Educ., Cuyahoga Community Coll., Housing Mgmt. Advisory Comm.; **HOME ADD:** 25145 Lake Rd., Bay Village, OH 44140, (216)835-1603; **BUS ADD:** 640 Hanna Bldg., Cleveland, OH 44115, (216)241-5080.

NILGES, Jan A.——B: Sept. 21, 1946, Lorain, OH, *VP*, Gulfstream Bank N.A., Dept. Head Comml. RE Lending; **PRIM RE ACT:** Banker; **SERVICES:** Const. fin. & comml. mort. lending; **REP CLIENTS:** Devels. of comml./medical/indus. and high rise multi-family projects; **PROFL AFFIL & HONORS:** FL Atlantic Builders Assn.; **EDUC:** BBA, 1973, Mktg./Mgmt., FL Atlantic Univ.; **GRAD EDUC:** MPA, 1976, Bus./Public Admin., FL Atlantic Univ.; **MIL SERV:** US Air Force, Sgt.; **HOME ADD:** 1126 SW 13th St., Boca Raton, FL 33432, (305)391-1230; **BUS ADD:** 150 East Palmetto Park Rd., Boca Raton, FL 33432, (305)997-1141.

NILSSON, Gunnar P.——B: 1945, *Sr. VP - Acquisitions*, The Balcor Co.; **PRIM RE ACT:** Owner/Investor; **SERVICES:** Involved in acquisition of RE investments for Balcor Co.; **PREV EMPLOY:** Asst. VP of RE Dept. - First Nat. Bank of Chicago (1974-1976); **GRAD EDUC:** MBA, IN Univ. Grad. School of Bus.; **BUS ADD:** Balcor Bldg., 10024 Skokie Blvd., Skokie, IL 60077, (312)677-2900.

NISHBALL, Robert L.——B: Jan. 20, 1933, Bridgeport, CT, *CPA*, Nishball, Srebnick, Zaluda & Carp, P.C.; **PRIM RE ACT:** Consultant; **SERVICES:** Evaluation of fin. viability of projects and asst. with fin. presentations; **REP CLIENTS:** Devels., synds., investors and those using RE to secure fin.; **EDUC:** BSE, 1954, Econ., Wharton School, Univ. of PA; **BUS ADD:** 144 Golden Hill St., Bridgeport, CT 06604, (203)333-2321.

NISHIUWATOKO, Tetsu——B: Sept. 20, 1941, Kagoshima, Japan, *Chief Rep.*, Kajima Corp. p., NY Representative Office; **PRIM RE ACT:** Developer, Builder, Owner/Investor; **PREV EMPLOY:** 1964-68 Staff of Intl. Div. Kajima Corp. Tokyo 1971-73 Kajima Corp. Rep. in Okinawa; **PROFL AFFIL & HONORS:** The RE Bd. of NY; Japan Econ. Inst. of Amer. (aka: US-Japan Trade Council); The Japanese C of C of NY, Inc.; Japan Soc., Inc., Member of the Bd., Kajima Devel. Corp.; **EDUC:** BA, 1964, Econ., Takushoku Univ.; **GRAD EDUC:** 1971-72, Intl. Inst. for Studies & Training (Trade Univ.); **HOME ADD:** 3 Horizon Rd. Apt. 1011, Fort Lee, NJ 07024, (201)224-9101; **BUS ADD:** Park Ave. Plaza, 55 E. 52nd St. 24th Floor, New York, NY 10055, (212)355-4571.

NISLEY, Frank, Jr.——B: Sept. 2, 1918, Grand Junction, CO, *Pres. & major stockholder*, Mountain Realty Sales & Development and Frank Nisley Jr & Associates; **PRIM RE ACT:** Broker, Consultant, Appraiser, Developer; **SERVICES:** RE sales, devel., consulting, appraisals; **REP CLIENTS:** Indivs., attys., govt. agencies; **PREV EMPLOY:** Firm started in 1946 - prior to this US Navy; **PROFL AFFIL & HONORS:** NAR, CO Assn. of Realtors, ARA, AIREA and CO Chap., Amer. Soc. of Farm Mgrs. and Rural Appraisers and CO Chapter, C of C, ARA, MAI, CRA, Pres. IDI of C of C; **EDUC:** BS, 1938, Mesa Coll.; **OTHER ACT & HONORS:** Author of several articles for appraisal publications; **HOME ADD:** 2119 Kadesh, Grand Junction, CO 81503, (303)243-0762; **BUS ADD:** Box 446, Grand Junction, CO 81501, (303)242-8063.

NITTI, Thomas Anthony——B: July 12, 1952, NJ, *Attorney*, Condon & Condon; **PRIM RE ACT:** Attorney; **REP CLIENTS:** Tax and legal services regarding RE, estate planning; **PROFL AFFIL & HONORS:** Real Prop Law Sect.; Taxation Sect.; Estate Planning, Trusts and Probate Sect. of CA St. Bar Assn; Assn of RE Attys.; Santa Monica Bar Assn.; **EDUC:** BA, 1974, Poli. Sci., UCLA; **GRAD EDUC:** JD, 1977, UCLA Law School; **EDUC HONORS:** Cum Laude with Dept. Highest Honors; **BUS ADD:** 632 Arizona Ave., Santa Monica, CA 90401, (213)393-0701.

NITZKORSKI, Douglas W.——B: Sept. 21, 1951, Moorhead, MN, *Pres.*, Appraisal Services Inc.; **PRIM RE ACT:** Consultant, Appraiser; **SERVICES:** RE appraisals, consultation; **REP CLIENTS:** Corp. Instit. Govtl.; **PROFL AFFIL & HONORS:** Cert. Review Appraiser; Cand. for MAI, AIREA; Assoc. Member of Bd. of Realtors; **EDUC:** BS, 1980, Bus./Econ./Fin., Moorhead State Univ., Moorhead, MN; **MIL SERV:** US Army, Sgt.; **HOME ADD:** 1401 18th Ave. S., Moorhead, MN 56560, (218)236-0676; **BUS ADD:** 1330 Gateway Dr., PO Box 1821, Fargo, ND 58107, (701)235-1189.

NIX, John P.——B: May 10, 1942, Greenville, AL, *Owner*, The John Nix Co.; **PRIM RE ACT:** Developer, Builder, Owner/Investor, Property Manager, Syndicator; **EDUC:** BS, 1964, GA Tech.; **OTHER ACT & HONORS:** The Pres. Club. of AL; **HOME ADD:** 5132 Kirkwall Ln., Birmingham, AL 35243, (205)967-3169; **BUS ADD:** 200 Century Pk. S., Suite 126, Birmingham, AL 35226, (205)979-5670.

NIXON, Don L.——B: Jan. 3, 1918, Ann Arbor, MI, *Pres.*, Don L. Nixon, Realtor; **PRIM RE ACT:** Broker, Developer, Owner/Investor; **SERVICES:** Indus., comml., acreage, office-research site location; **PROFL AFFIL & HONORS:** Detroit Bd. of Realtors; MI Assn. of Realtors; NAR; SIR; **EDUC:** AB, 1940, Econ., Univ. of MI; **MIL SERV:** USN, Lt.; **HOME ADD:** 830 St. Clair Ave., Grosse Pointe, MI 48230, (313)882-6386; **BUS ADD:** 830 St. Clair Ave., Grosse Pointe, MI 48230, (313)885-7990.

NIXON, R.P.—— *VP, Secy. & Treas.*, Franklin Electric Co., Inc.; **PRIM RE ACT:** Property Manager; **BUS ADD:** 400 E. Spring St., Bluffton, IN 46714, (219)824-2900.*

NIXON, S. Reed——B: May 30, 1926, Los Angeles, CA, *Pres.*, Marco Enterprises; **PRIM RE ACT:** Broker, Consultant, Developer, Builder, Engineer, Owner/Investor; **REP CLIENTS:** Builders, Consultants, Lending Instns., Investors; **PREV EMPLOY:** Consultant, Maj. Inds.; **PROFL AFFIL & HONORS:** Kiwanis; **EDUC:** Elec. Engrg., 1946, CA Inst. of Tech.; **GRAD EDUC:** Nuclear Engrg., 1955, Oak Ridge School of Reactor Tech.; **EDUC HONORS:** Honor Standing, Tau Beta Pi, Who's Who Amer. Colls. & Univ., upper 10% of Class; **MIL SERV:** USN, Ens.; **HOME ADD:** 1065 E. 260 So., Orem, UT 84057, (801)225-9444; **BUS ADD:** 1160 S. State St., 240, Orem, UT 84057, (801)225-0991.

NIZIOL, Edward——B: May 24, 1941, Flint, MI, *Sr. Partner*, The Investor's Real Estate Development Group; **PRIM RE ACT:** Broker, Developer, Owner/Investor, Syndicator; **SERVICES:** Brokerage, mktg. of condos.; **PREV EMPLOY:** Self employed, electronics design and manufacture; Author/Publisher of Seven Motivational Books; **EDUC:** AS, 1961, Space/Military Elec., DeVry Tech. Inst.; **HOME ADD:** 5445 N. Sheridan Rd., Chicago, IL 60640, (312)263-7119; **BUS ADD:** 134 N. LaSalle, Suite 204, Chicago, IL 60602.

NOAKES, D.T.——B: June 13, 1946, New Rochelle, NY, *Pres.*, Capital Homes, Inc., Subsidiary of Nat. Corp. for Housing Partnerships; **PRIM RE ACT:** Developer, Builder; **PREV EMPLOY:** Center Homes Corp., Dallas, TX; **PROFL AFFIL & HONORS:** NAHB; **EDUC:** AB, 1969, Liberal Arts, PA State Univ.; **GRAD EDUC:** MBA, not complete, Fin., DePaul Univ.; **HOME ADD:** 9009 Edgepark Rd., Vienna, VA 22180, (703)734-0355; **BUS ADD:** Suite 200, 6500 Rock Spring Dr., Bethesda, MD 20817, (301)897-9200.

NOBIL, James H.——B: June 7, 1930, Akron, OH, *Pres.*, TMI Realty, Inc.; **PRIM RE ACT:** Broker, Syndicator, Consultant, Property Manager, Owner/Investor; **SERVICES:** Prop. Mgmt. & Investment Consulting; **REP CLIENTS:** Indiv. & Instl. Investors; **PREV EMPLOY:** Chmn., Summit Prop.; **PROFL AFFIL & HONORS:** IREM; **EDUC:** BA, 1952, Econ., Yale Unlv.; **GRAD EDUC:** MBA, 1954, RE & Land Econ., NYU; **MIL SERV:** USA, SP4; **HOME ADD:** 807 NE 35 St., Boca Raton, FL 33431, (305)368-1611; **BUS ADD:** Suite 204, 200 N Federal Hwy., Boca Raton, FL 33432, (305)395-9320.

NODVIN, Joseph J.——B: Nov. 8, 1944, Savannah, GA, *Pres.*, RE Showcase, Div. of Minali, Inc.; **PRIM RE ACT:** Broker, Consultant, Developer, Builder, Owner/Investor, Property Manager, Syndicator; **SERVICES:** Brokerage, mgmt., devel. & bldg. resid. & comml.; **REP CLIENTS:** Purchasers, investors & joint-venturers; **PREV EMPLOY:** S.E. and S.W. Reg. prop. supervisor for Arlen Realty, responsible for apts., shopping ctrs. & office bldgs.; **PROFL AFFIL & HONORS:** Assn. of GA RE Exchangers, Rho Epsilon Profl. RE Fraternity, Pres. Brokerage Award: Qualified 1972-1980 Life Member; **EDUC:** BBA, 1966, RE and Fin., GA State Univ.; **EDUC HONORS:** Dean's List; Pres. of Fraternity (P.C.); **OTHER ACT & HONORS:** Appointed to Cty. panel that wrote fee-simple townhouse ordinance, numerous civic & religious organ.; **HOME ADD:** 4818 Coach Lane, Dunwoody, GA 30338, (404)396-8056; **BUS ADD:** 4470 Chamblee-Dunwoody Rd., Suite 355, PO Box 888632, Atlanta, GA 30338, (404)457-6351.

NOE, James A.——B: June 3, 1938, Indianapolis, IN, *Chief Fin. Officer*, McBail Co.; **PRIM RE ACT:** Developer, Builder, Property Manager; **PREV EMPLOY:** VP Wells Fargo Bank, RE Indus. Group 1976-1980; **PROFL AFFIL & HONORS:** ICSC; BIA; **EDUC:** BA, 1960, Econ., Purdue Univ.; **GRAD EDUC:** MBA, 1979, RE, Golden Gate Univ.; **EDUC HONORS:** Grad. of Northwestern School of Mort. Banking, 1979; **MIL SERV:** USN; Lt.j.g.; 1960-1964; **HOME ADD:** 210 San Carlos Ave., Piedmont, CA 94611, (415)658-0787; **BUS ADD:** 3732 Mt. Diablo Blvd., Suite 390, Lafayette, CA 94549, (415)284-4900.

NOE, James T.C.——B: July 30, 1932, Whittier, CA, *Counsel*, Beneficial Standard Properties, Inc.; **PRIM RE ACT:** Attorney; **PREV EMPLOY:** Counsel, Beneficial Standard Mort. Co.; **PROFL AFFIL & HONORS:** CA Bar; Real Property Sect., Los Angeles Cty. Bar Assn.; Fin. Lawyers of Los Angeles; **EDUC:** BA, 1954, Liberal Arts, UCLA; **GRAD EDUC:** JD, 1973, Loyola Univ. School of Law; **EDUC HONORS:** Law Review; **MIL SERV:** USAF, Capt.; **HOME ADD:** 3004 Allenton Ave., Hacienda Hts., CA 91745, (213)333-8926; **BUS ADD:** 3700 Wilshire Blvd., Suite 210, Los Angeles, CA 90010, (213)381-8276.

NOFFSINGER, Hugh G., Jr.——B: Oct. 4, 1907, Chase City, VA, *Chmn.*, Noffsinger, Inc.; **PRIM RE ACT:** Broker, Consultant, Appraiser, Insuror, Syndicator; **REP CLIENTS:** Appraisals - Chase Manhattan Bank; Bank of NC; Equitable (Relocation Div.); & most of the 3rd party relocation firms; **PREV EMPLOY:** N.W. Ayer & Son, Philadelphia, VA Intermont Coll.; **PROFL AFFIL & HONORS:** NAR; NC Assn. of Realtors; Wilmington NC Bd. of Realtors; Former Dir., Dominion National Bank, Bristol, VA; Chmn., Governing Bd., C. and I. Div.; Wilmington Bd. of Realtors Amer. Soc. of Appraisers; NC Assn. of Realtors; Served on Comml. and Indus. Devel. Comm., Educ. Comm., External Affairs Comm., Wilmington, NC Bd. of Realtors; One of the original group org. MLS (resid.) Chmn. and one of original organizers, C. and I. Div., and org. of Computer MLS; Active in speaking at seminars, specialty Comml. and Indus. brokerage, computer analysis of RE investments; Speaker at Charter meeting Charlotte, NC C. and I. Div.; Member, Wilmington Comm. of 100; Member NC Indus. Devels. Assn.; Member Carolina Yacht Club, Cape Fear Ctry. Club; Former Lions Club (Old Monarch award); Exec. Club of Wilmington, NC Tr., Member, Prop. Mgmt. Div., NC Assn. of Realtors, GRI; **EDUC:** AB, 1928, Univ. of Richmond; **GRAD EDUC:** MBA, 1930, Bus., Harvard Bus. School; **MIL SERV:** US Naval Res., Lt. Comdr.; **OTHER ACT & HONORS:** American Society of Appraisers, Associate member, Cardina Yacht Club; Cape Fear Ctry. Club; Deacon First Baptist Church, Wilmington, NC; **HOME ADD:** Country Club Rd., Wilmington, NC 28403; **BUS ADD:** Box 3626, Wilmington, NC 28406, (919)791-6094.

NOLAN, Agnes——B: Aug. 6, 1931, New York, *Pres.*, Whitbread-Nolan, Inc.; **PRIM RE ACT:** Broker; **SERVICES:** Sell investment comml., resid. prop.; lease comml. prop.; **PROFL AFFIL & HONORS:** RE Bd. of NY; **EDUC:** BA, 1952, Trinity Coll.; **GRAD EDUC:** LLB, 1955, Columbia Law School; **HOME ADD:** 271 Central Park West, (212)787-2964; **BUS ADD:** 600 Madison Ave., New York, NY 10022, (212)750-0400.

NOLAN, Barbara Ann——B: June 30, 1943, TN, *Pres.*, J.J. Nolan Realty, Farm Div.; **PRIM RE ACT:** Broker, Consultant, Appraiser, Property Manager; **SERVICES:** Sale of farmland, investment counseling, farm appraisals; **REP CLIENTS:** Farmers and investors concerning farm land; **PROFL AFFIL & HONORS:** S. Central IA RE Bd.; Broker Member, IA Farm and Land Inst.; Realtor; Several Appraisal Soc., Realtor; CRA; Amer. Assn. Cert. Appraisers; CRPA; SCV; **EDUC:** Rural Appraising, Univ. of AR; **HOME ADD:** 1200 S. Ridge Rd., Osceola, IA 50213, (515)342-4374; **BUS ADD:** 114 E. McLane, Osceola, IA 50213, (515)342-6502.

NOLAN, B.J.—— *Adv. Dir.*, American Industrial Real Estate Assn., A.I.R. Journal; **PRIM RE ACT:** Real Estate Publisher; **BUS ADD:** 5670 Wilshire Blvd., Los Angeles, CA 90036, (213)933-5749.*

NOLAN, John M.——B: June 21, 1948, Conway, AR, *Dir./Shareholder*, Winstead, McGuire, Sechrest & Minick, RE; **PRIM RE ACT:** Attorney; **SERVICES:** Work in all phases of RE activity; **REP CLIENTS:** Permanent interim lenders, brokers, devels., archs., prop. mgmt. firms, synds., and gen. RE investors, both domestic and for.; **PROFL AFFIL & HONORS:** Member: ABA, State Bar of TX, Dallas Bar Assn., Scribes; **EDUC:** BA, 1970, Modern European Hist., Univ. of TX; **GRAD EDUC:** JD & LLM, 1973 & 1976, Univ. of TX & George Washington Univ.; **EDUC HONORS:** Phi Alpha Theta; **MIL SERV:** US Army, Capt.; **HOME ADD:** 7320 Syracuse, Dallas, TX 75214, (214)349-3593; **BUS ADD:** 1700 Mercantile Dallas Bldg., Dallas, TX 75201, (214)742-1700.

NOLEN, Michael——B: Nov. 27, 1946, Philadelphia, PA, *VP*, Nolen Cos.; **PRIM RE ACT:** Broker, Consultant, Developer, Builder; **PROFL AFFIL & HONORS:** Nat. Home Builders Assn., PA Builders Assn., Home Builders of SE PA, BOCA; **EDUC:** BS, 1970, Mktg.; **BUS ADD:** 4 E Germantown Pike, Plymouth Meeting, PA 19462, (215)825-3435.

NOLL, Jerome R.——B: Dec 14, 1949, Effingham,KS, *Audit Mgr. - CPA*, Main Hurdman; **OTHER RE ACT:** Accountant; **SERVICES:** Fin. Projections, Audit and Acctg. Ser. Tax Planning and Preparation; **PROFL AFFIL & HONORS:** Amer. Soc. CPA's, KS Soc. of CPA's, Internal Auditors, Nat. Assoc. Accountants, Coordinator of Wichita, KS Main Hurdman & Cranston RE and Const. team; **EDUC:** BS Acctg., 1971, Acctg., KS State Univ.; **GRAD EDUC:** MBA, 1972, Acctg., KS State Univ.; **HOME ADD:** 3655 W. 13th, Apt.9T, Wichita, KS 67203, (316)942-1541; **BUS ADD:** 401 E. Douglas, Suite 300, Wichita, KS 67202, (316)267-7231.

NOONAN, John R.——B: May 19, 1946, Medford, MA, *VP of Operations*, The Village at Smugglers Notch (4 season ski resort); **PRIM RE ACT:** Engineer, Developer, Builder, Property Manager; **SERVICES:** Resort Mgmt., Devel. and Const.; **PREV EMPLOY:** Stanmar, Prop. Mgr. Owner-Resort Bldr., Design Bldr.; Beacon Corp., Prop. Mgr., Resort Bldr., Design Bldr.; Lazard Freres, Owner/Devel.; Franchi Const. Co., Bldr., Owner; **PROFL AFFIL & HONORS:** Member ULI; Bd. of Dir. of Lamoille Cty. Devel. Council; Tr. of the Old Town Hall, Jeffersonville, VT; **EDUC:** BS, 1969, Civil and Sanitary Engrg., NE Univ.; **OTHER ACT & HONORS:** Member Nashawtuc Ctry. Club, Concord, MA; Bd. Member and Treas. of Cambridge Rgnl. Health Ctr.; **HOME ADD:** RR 1, Jeffersonville, VT 05464, (802)644-5797; **BUS ADD:** Rte. 108, Jeffersonville, VT 05464, (802)644-8851.

NOONAN, Patrick F.——B: Dec. 2, 1942, St. Petersburg, FL, *Pres.*, Conservation Resources Inc.; **PRIM RE ACT:** Broker, Appraiser, Instructor, Owner/Investor; **OTHER RE ACT:** Advisor; **REP CLIENTS:** Non-Profit Orgs., Investors, Corps.; **PREV EMPLOY:** Pres., The Nature Conservancy, 1973-1980; **PROFL AFFIL & HONORS:** Sr. Member, Amer. Soc. of Appraisers; Member, Amer. Inst. of Certified Planners; Consultant, The Nature Conservancy, Who's Who in America, 1975-1982; Amer. Motors Convervation Award, 1974; Horace Albright Conservation Medd, 1976.; **EDUC:** BA, 1965, Bus. Admin., Gettysburg Coll.; **GRAD EDUC:** Master's, 1967, City & Rgnl. Planning, Catholic Univ.; MBA, 1971, American Univ.; **OTHER ACT & HONORS:** Tr., Gettysburg College; Tr., Student Conservation Assn.; Chmn., Advisory Bd. Amer. Farm Land Trust; Bd. of Advisors, Duke Univ., School of Forestry; Bd. of Advisors, Sec. of Interior's Appalachian Trail Advisory Council; **HOME ADD:** 11901 Glen Mill Rd., Potomoc, MD 20854; **BUS ADD:** POB 34606, Washington, DC 20034, (301)424-6276.

NORBERG, Douglas E.——B: Oct. 26, 1940, Los Angeles, CA, *Exec. VP*, Wright Runstad & Company; **PRIM RE ACT:** Developer; **SERVICES:** Investment bldr., investments, development management; **REP CLIENTS:** Major fin. insts., equity investors, major office users; **PREV EMPLOY:** Community Television of So. CA, KCET Channel 28, Los Angeles, Sr. VP; **PROFL AFFIL & HONORS:** Fin. Execs. Inst. (Sec. & Dir.-Seattle Chap.; ULI, Urban Design and Mixed Use Council; AICPA; WA & CA Socs. of CPA's; **EDUC:** BBA, 1962, CO Coll., CO Springs; **MIL SERV:** US Army, Lt.; **OTHER ACT & HONORS:** Downtown Seattle Devel. Assn.; City Club; Seattle Ctr. Found.; Seattle Bd. of Govs.; **BUS ADD:** 1111 3rd Ave., Suite 3200, Seattle, WA 98101, (206)447-9000.

NORDBLOM, Rodger P.——B: July, 5, 1927, Quincy, MA, *Pres.*, Nordblom Co.; **PRIM RE ACT:** Broker, Consultant, Developer, Property Manager; **PROFL AFFIL & HONORS:** SIR, Greater Boston RE Bd., Natl. Pres., Soc. of Indus. Realtors 1977; **EDUC:** BA, 1950, Econ., Harvard Coll.; **MIL SERV:** USN, Seaman, 1945-1946; **OTHER ACT & HONORS:** Tr. N.E. Medical Ctr., Emerson Hospital Young Presidents Org., Chief Execs. Forum, Bd. of Overseers, Boys Club of Boston Inc.; **HOME ADD:** 200 Barnes Hill Rd., Concord, MA 01742, (617)369-2515; **BUS ADD:** 50 Congress St., Boston, MA 02109, (617)482-7000.

NORDGREN, Paul E.——B: Aug. 30, 1910, Wilmette, IL, *Owner*, Nordgren Realty Associates; **PRIM RE ACT:** Broker, Consultant, Owner/Investor, Property Manager; **OTHER RE ACT:** Site finder for fast food industry and others seeking multiple sites; **REP CLIENTS:** McDonalds, Dennys, Pizza Hut, K-Mart devels.; **PREV EMPLOY:** Managed & sold RE for former Chicago Northshore & Milwaukee Ry 1952-1967; **PROFL AFFIL & HONORS:** Chicago & Lk. Cty. RE Bds., Assn. of Indus. RE Brokers; **OTHER ACT & HONORS:** Medinah Temple AAONS (Shriner); C of C; **HOME ADD:** 405 Glen Flora, Waukegan, IL 60085, (312)336-3574; **BUS ADD:** 509 N. Green Bay Rd., Waukegan, IL 60085, (312)662-4497.

NOREM, LeRoy K.——B: Jan. 20, 1922, Westbrook, MN, *Assoc. Broker*, Merrill Lynch Realty Chris Coile, Inc., Comm'l./Investment Div.; **PRIM RE ACT:** Broker, Syndicator, Consultant, Appraiser; **SERVICES:** Investment Counseling, Synd. of investment prop., Income and dev. prop. appraisal, Mkt. and feasibility analysis and studies; **REP CLIENTS:** Individuals, investment grps., Instit., Lenders, Formation of grps. for synd.; **PREV EMPLOY:** Mgmt. consultant (Fin.); **PROFL AFFIL & HONORS:** RESSI; SREA; RNMI; Intl. Exchangers Assn.; **EDUC:** BS, 1971, Hospital Admin., Strayer Coll.; **GRAD EDUC:** MA, 1973, Public Admin., Univ. of No. CO; **EDUC HONORS:** Highest Honors; **MIL SERV:** USA, Lt. Col., Bronze Star, Air Medal, Army Commendation Medal, (several others), 1940 to 1967; **HOME ADD:** 4221 Isbell St., Silver Spring, MD 20906, (301)933-8996; **BUS ADD:** 6410 Rockledge Dr., Bethesda, MD 20034, (301)897-5000.

NORMAN, Billy H.——B: Aug. 3, 1947, Sterling, CO, *RE Broker*, Billy Norman Realty; **PRIM RE ACT:** Broker, Owner/Investor, Instructor, Property Manager, Syndicator; **OTHER RE ACT:** Specialize in lakefront recreational prop.; **SERVICES:** RE brokerage and prop. mgmt., instr. for prop. mgmt. school every 3 months in Anchorage, AK; **PREV EMPLOY:** The Apt. Co., Anchorage, AK, owner/broker managed 600 apt. units, 70 locations, also marketed these units for sale; **PROFL AFFIL & HONORS:** Nat. Assn. of Realtors, Multiple Listing Serv., Selected for Outstanding Young Men of Amer. in 1978; **EDUC:** two years, Soc. Sci. and Bus., Black Hills State Univ.; **MIL SERV:** US Army, E-4, 23 Combat Air Medals; **OTHER ACT & HONORS:** US Jaycees (State Officer 3 years), Moose Club, Big Lake Lions Club, AK State Officer Quarter 1978; **HOME ADD:** Box 17299, S. Big Lake Shore, Big Lake, AK 99687, (907)892-6680; **BUS ADD:** Box 17299 Fisher's Y, Big Lake, AK 99687, (907)892-6111.

NORMAN, Richard——B: Apr. 1, 1925, Jersey City, NJ, *Pres.*, All-Amer. Realty Co., Inc.; **PRIM RE ACT:** Broker, Consultant, Developer, Builder, Property Manager, Engineer; **OTHER RE ACT:** All Above in Realm of 2nd Home and Time-Share Dev.; **SERVICES:** Complete Mktg. Studies-Mgmt. Engrg. Joint venture in that category; **PROFL AFFIL & HONORS:** Member of Alda Bd. Pres. 1978-1980, (1972-to present, Member), Pres. Pulda 1973, Member Passaic Cty Bd. of Realtors; **EDUC:** BA, 1948, Univ. of Miami,FL; **MIL SERV:** USA; **OTHER ACT & HONORS:** Pres. Voc Bd. of Educ. Bergen Cty. 1976, Member NJ Youth Correction Comm.-Bd. of Trustees 1976, Asst. Nat. Dir. Biddy Basketball; **HOME ADD:** 868 Perry Lane, Teaneck, NJ 07660, (201)833-1464; **BUS ADD:** 155 Willowbrook Blvd., Wayne, NJ 07470, (201)785-3400.

NORMAN, Thomas Edmund——B: Mar. 20, 1944, Charlotte, NC, *Pres.*, Lat Purser & Associates, Inc.; **PRIM RE ACT:** Broker, Developer, Builder, Owner/Investor, Instructor; **SERVICES:** Mort. banking, appraisal, devel., mgmt.; **REP CLIENTS:** Winn Dixie, CT Mutual, Life & Casualty, Liberty Life, Food Town, Eckerds Roses, Revco, Rite Aid, Harris Teeter, Sky City Food World, lenders, investors and retailers involved in comml. prop.; **PREV EMPLOY:** McDevitt & Street Co.; Chemical Bank; **PROFL AFFIL & HONORS:** MBA; NC Income Prop. Assn.; Mort. Bankers Assn. of the Carolinas; Charlotte Bd. of Realtors; NC Assn. of Realtors; NAR; Intl. Council of Shopping Ctrs.; **EDUC:** BBA, 1966, Bus. Admin., Wake Forest Univ.; **GRAD EDUC:** MBA, 1970, Fin./Investment, NY Univ.; **MIL SERV:** US Army Spec. Forces, 2nd Lt., Parachutists Badge, Nat. Defense; **OTHER ACT & HONORS:** Charlotte City Club; Charlotte Ctry. Club; Chmn. of Bd., Charlotte Summer Pops; Bd. of Dirs., Open House Counseling Serv.; Chmn., Mecklenburg Cty., Dept. of Social Serv.; **HOME ADD:** 3821 Sedagwood Cir., Charlotte, NC 28211, (704)366-8999; **BUS ADD:** POB 18067, 919 Norland Rd., Charlotte, NC 28205, (704)537-9583.

NORMANDEAN, Pierre——B: May 1, 1946, Montreal, Can., *Pres.*, Immo-Constil Lte; **OTHER RE ACT:** Researcher; **SERVICES:** Feasibility study, researcher on special topics prof. at Univ. & in-house com. programs; **REP CLIENTS:** Hydro-Que., Can. Central Mort., Pvt. Investors; **PREV EMPLOY:** Cai ai De Depot, et Placement appraising for mort. purpose; **PROFL AFFIL & HONORS:** MBA of Que., Project Mgmt. Inst., MBA, Real Consultant; **EDUC:** BA, 1967, Geog., Urban Devel., Rgnl. Devel., Univ. of M.; **GRAD EDUC:** M Geog., 1972, Ecole Des Hautes Etudes Comml., Montreal; MBA, 1973, Fin., Mktg., RE, Ecole Des Hautes Etudes Comml., Montreal; **EDUC HONORS:** Geography; **HOME ADD:** 2086 Montarville, St. Bruno, J3V 3V7, Que., Can., (541)653-8492; **BUS ADD:** 2086 Montarville, St. Bruno, J3V 3V7, Que., Can., (514)282-4261.

NORRIS, G. Kennon——B: Apr. 16, 1929, Kearney, NE, *Pres.*, Spencer Realty, Inc./Better Homes & Gardens; **PRIM RE ACT:** Broker, Consultant, Appraiser, Builder, Owner/Investor, Property

Manager; **PROFL AFFIL & HONORS:** NAR, GRI, CRS, CRB; **GRAD EDUC:** BA in Education, 1950, Bus., Kearney State Coll.; **MIL SERV:** US Army 1951-1953; **OTHER ACT & HONORS:** Pres. YMCA, Pres. Spencer Golf & Ctry. Club; **HOME ADD:** 2101 W. 11th, Spencer, IA 51301, (712)262-2965; **BUS ADD:** 1801 Hwy. Blvd., Spencer, IA 51301, (712)262-1066.

NORTON, David——*Dir. Fac.*, Teradyne, Inc.; **PRIM RE ACT:** Property Manager; **BUS ADD:** 183 Essex St., Boston, MA 02111, (617)482-2700.*

NORTON, Peter E.——B: May 27, 1932, Oak Park, Chicago, IL, *Pres.*, Peter Norton & Assoc. Ltd.; **PRIM RE ACT:** Broker, Appraiser, Owner/Investor; **OTHER RE ACT:** Specialty, Motel & Comml. Sales & Bus. Ops.; **SERVICES:** IL Rep. for Nationwide Motel Brokers; **PREV EMPLOY:** Contract Admin., GTE Automatic Electric, 1963-64; Resid. Brokerage, 1965-74; Added Comml. in 1975; Motels in 1978; **PROFL AFFIL & HONORS:** Leyden Bd. of Realtors, W Suburban Bd. of Realtors; NW Suburban Bd. of Realtors, MAP MLS; Nat. Assn. of RE Appraisers, IAR, NAR; **GRAD EDUC:** MBA, 1963, Prod. Mgmt., Operations Research, Grad. Sch. of Bus., Univ. of Chicago; **OTHER ACT & HONORS:** Chmn. Northlake Plan Comm., 1965-74; **HOME ADD:** 325 Armitage, Northlake, IL 60164, (312)562-1441; **BUS ADD:** 114 E. North Ave., Northlake, IL 60164, (312)562-0822.

NORTON, Warner D.——B: May 14, 1936, NY, *Legal Counsel*, Helmsley-Spear Inc.; **PRIM RE ACT:** Attorney; **PREV EMPLOY:** Investors Funding Corp.; **PROFL AFFIL & HONORS:** NY Bar Assn.; **EDUC:** Accounting, Queens Coll.; **GRAD EDUC:** Brooklyn Law, 1966; **MIL SERV:** USMC; **HOME ADD:** 36 Bowler Rd., E. Rockaway, NY 11518, (516)599-1357; **BUS ADD:** 60 E 42nd St., New York, NY 10165, (212)687-6400.

NORVELL, Jerry T., Jr.——B: April 22, 1936, Morganton, NC, *Pres.*, The Norvell Co.; **PRIM RE ACT:** Broker, Appraiser, Developer, Builder, Property Manager, Insuror; **PROFL AFFIL & HONORS:** RAMI, CCIM; **EDUC:** BA, 1958, Davidson Coll.; **HOME ADD:** 115 Rockview Ln., Morganton, NC 28655, (704)437-7407; **BUS ADD:** P.O. Drawer 1419, One Northsq., Morganton, NC 28655.

NORVILLE, Robert J.——B: Jan. 9, 1936, Chicago, IL, *Mgr., RE & Facilities*, Justin Indus., Inc.; **OTHER RE ACT:** Corp. RE mgmt.; **SERVICES:** Acquisition, disposition, prop. mgmt., use analysis of RE assets; **PREV EMPLOY:** USAF (Retired) Program Mgr., Air Crew Training Devices Acquisition; **PROFL AFFIL & HONORS:** NACORE; **EDUC:** BBA, 1978, RE, Univ. of TX at Arlington; **EDUC HONORS:** with High Honors; **MIL SERV:** USAF; m/Sgt.; Meritorious Serv. Medal, AF Commendation Medal(s); **OTHER ACT & HONORS:** Elected to Beta Gamma Sigma, Nat. Honor Frat.; **HOME ADD:** 3708 Danbury Dr., Arlington, TX 76016, (817)457-5525; **BUS ADD:** Box 425, Ft. Worth, TX 76101, (817)336-5125.

NORWOOD, Jim E.——B: Dallas, TX, *Pres.*, Empire Prop., Realtors; **PRIM RE ACT:** Broker; **SERVICES:** Realtor sales & leasing; **PROFL AFFIL & HONORS:** Greater Dallas Bd. of Realtors; NAR; Dallas Home & Apt. Builders Assn.; TX Realtors Assn.; NAHB; Dallas C of C, Dir., Greater Dallas Bd. of Realtors; TX By-Laws Comm.; **EDUC:** BS, Hardin-Simmons Univ., Abilene, TX; B. Div. New Orleans Baptist Seminary; M. Div. New Orleans Baptist Seminary; D. Laws (honorary) Burton Coll., CO; **GRAD EDUC:** Comml., investment, devel. prop.; **EDUC HONORS:** Written up in Who's Who in South and Southwest, 1976-1977; **HOME ADD:** 5757 Trail Meadow Dr., Dallas, TX 75219, (214)369-9000; **BUS ADD:** 3131 Turtle Creek Blvd., Dallas, TX 75219, (214)522-1000.

NORWOOD, Roy G., Jr.——B: Feb. 11, 1945, Dallas, TX, *RE Devel., Project Mgr.*, Norwood Interests, RE Devel.; **PRIM RE ACT:** Broker, Consultant, Property Manager, Developer; **OTHER RE ACT:** Financing Specialist; **SERVICES:** RE Devel.; leasing; project mgmt.; gen. brokerage; consulting; acquisition; fin. and feasibility studies; **REP CLIENTS:** Lenders and indiv. or instnl. investors in comml. props. and major office, shopping ctr., indus. tenants and multi-family resid. tenants; **PREV EMPLOY:** Pres., Unit Mgmt. Corp.; VP, Gen. Mgr. of the Prop. Mgmt. Div. of West Shell Realtors; VP of the Henry S. Miller Co.; **PROFL AFFIL & HONORS:** IREM; BOMA; CPM-IREM; RPA-BOMA; NAt. Ethics; AMO & memberships comm.; VP Bd. of Dir., Local Chap., Real Prop. Admin. (RPA), BOMA; Local Chap. VP & Bd. of Dir.; Founding meber - SORPA; **EDUC:** BBA, 1969, RE and Mktg., Southern Methodist Univ.; **EDUC HONORS:** Student Senate, Deans List, Tennis, scholarship; **OTHER ACT & HONORS:** Beta Theta Pi, Mustang Club, SMU Alumni Club; **HOME ADD:** 6307 Marquita, Dallas, TX 75214, (214)745-1988; **BUS ADD:** 6307 Marquita Ave., Dallas, TX 75214, (214)745-1988.

NOSEWORTHY, Frederick N.——B: June 25, 1942, Laconia, NH, *Managing Partner*, Monterra Real Estate; **PRIM RE ACT:** Consultant, Broker, Developer, Syndicator; **OTHER RE ACT:** Land Devel.; **SERVICES:** All RE related; **PROFL AFFIL & HONORS:** Past Pres., Monterey Peninsula C of C, Certified Fin. Planner; **EDUC:** BA Econ., 1965, Middlebury Coll.; **MIL SERV:** US Army, 1st Lt., Silver Star, Vietnamese Cross of Gallantry, Bronze Star, Purple Heart; **OTHER ACT & HONORS:** Pres., Del Monte Forest Prop. Owners (Pebble Beach); **HOME ADD:** Box 396, Pebble Beach, CA 93953; **BUS ADD:** 2999 Monterey Salinas Hwy., Monterey, CA 93940, (408)375-4170.

NOTEWARE, James D.——B: June 4, 1952, Stockton, CA, *Natl Dir.*, Laventhol & Horwath, RE Advisory Services; **PRIM RE ACT:** Consultant; **SERVICES:** RE devel. & fin. counseling; **REP CLIENTS:** Devels., fin. instns., govt. agencies, indus. corps.; **PREV EMPLOY:** Booz Allen, Hamilton; **PROFL AFFIL & HONORS:** Urban Land Inst.; **EDUC:** BS, 1974, Civil Engrg., Stanford Univ.; **GRAD EDUC:** MBA, 1976, Fin., Wharton Sch., Univ. of PA; **HOME ADD:** 3729 Jocelyn St., NW, Washington, DC 20015, (202)966-8190; **BUS ADD:** 1845 Walnut St., 19th Fl., Philadelphia, PA 19103, (215)299-1600.

NOTHNAGLE, Raymond A.——*Chairman of the Board*, Gallery of Homes; **PRIM RE ACT:** Syndicator; **BUS ADD:** 1001 International Blvd., Atlanta, GA 30354, (404)768-2460.*

NOURSE, Peter W.——B: Apr. 6, 1930, Los Angeles, CA, *Owner*, Nourse Devel. Co.; **PRIM RE ACT:** Broker, Developer, Builder, Owner/Investor, Property Manager; **EDUC:** BS, 1953, Bus. Admin., Univ. of CA, Berkeley; **MIL SERV:** USA, Artillery, 1st. Lt.; **OTHER ACT & HONORS:** 1971 Home Buyers Magazine Award for Outstanding Achievement in the field of Home Building in CA; **BUS ADD:** 901 Dover Dr., Suite 110, Newport Beach, CA 92660, (714)645-7800.

NOVACK, Kenneth M.——B: Jan. 12, 1946, Richmond, VA, *Pres.*, Summit Properties, Inc.; **PRIM RE ACT:** Developer, Owner/Investor; **SERVICES:** Investment counseling, devel. & synd. of comml. props., prop. mgmt.; **REP CLIENTS:** Indiv. and inst. investors in comml. props.; **PREV EMPLOY:** Pres., Schnitzer Investment Corp.; **EDUC:** BA, 1967, Econ., Claremont Men's Coll.; **GRAD EDUC:** JD, 1970, USC; **EDUC HONORS:** Cum Laude, Orders of the Coif; **HOME ADD:** 3303 SW Sherwood Pl., Portland, OR 97201, (503)222-3959; **BUS ADD:** 111 SW Columbia St., Suite 1000, Portland, OR 97201, (503)220-0580.

NOVAK, James M.——B: Mar. 28, 1951, Clearfield, PA, *Atty.*, Lynch, Kabala & Geeseman; **PRIM RE ACT:** Attorney; **SERVICES:** Negotiation, settlement, spec. fin. such as via indus. devel. auth.; **PROFL AFFIL & HONORS:** ABA, PA, Allegheny Cty. Bar Assns., Sect. of Real Prop., Probate & Trust; **EDUC:** BA, 1973, Math., St. Vincent Coll., Latrobe, PA; **GRAD EDUC:** MA, 1975, Math., Boston Coll.; JD, 1978, Law, Duquesne Univ.; **EDUC HONORS:** Summa Cum Laude, Award for excellsence in math., Fellowship; **HOME ADD:** 173 McIntyre Rd., Pittsburgh, PA 15237; **BUS ADD:** 700 Commonwealth Bldg., 316 Fourth Ave., Pittsburgh, PA 15222, (412)397-1334.

NOVAK, John P.——B: Aug. 6, 1949, New York, NY, *Counsel*, US Life Title Ins. Co. of NY; **PRIM RE ACT:** Attorney, Insuror; **SERVICES:** Title ins., asst. to RE atty.; **REP CLIENTS:** All members of the Suffolk Cty. Bar, lending instns.; **PREV EMPLOY:** Bank Counsel for Union Savings Bank w/law firm of Pelletreau & Pelletreau of Patchogue, NY; **PROFL AFFIL & HONORS:** NY State Bar Assn., Suffolk Cty. Bar Assn., ABA; **EDUC:** BS, 1971, Bus. mgmt., acctg. & econ., Univ. of Dayton, OH; **GRAD EDUC:** JD, 1974, Suffolk Univ. Law School, Boston, MA; **HOME ADD:** 16 Palmer Ter., Sag Harbor, NY 11963, (516)725-2794; **BUS ADD:** 127 W. Main St., Riverhead, NY 11901, (516)727-4140.

NOVICK, Steven E.——B: Mar. 30, 1945, Denver, CO, *Pres.*, IPFR Publishing, Inc.; **PRIM RE ACT:** Broker, Developer, Owner/Investor, Syndicator, Real Estate Publisher; **EDUC:** BA, 1967, Wesleyan Univ., CT; **BUS ADD:** 111 John St., New York, NY 10038, (212)233-7360.

NOVIT, Herbert L.——B: Apr. 9, 1937, Anderson, SC, *Partner*, Dowling, Sanders, Dukes, Novit & Svalina, P.A., Hilton Head Is., SC; **PRIM RE ACT:** Attorney; **SERVICES:** Full representation of purchasers, sellers and devel. and fin. inst.; **PREV EMPLOY:** US Gen. Acctg. Office; **PROFL AFFIL & HONORS:** Member, Beaufort Cty., SC, Amer. Bar Assns., Chmn., RE Practices Section of SC Bar Assn., 1980-1981; **EDUC:** BS, 1959, Acctg., Univ. of SC; **GRAD EDUC:** JD, 1963, Univ. of SC, School of Law; **MIL SERV:** USN, Lt.j.g.; **HOME ADD:** 22 Plantation Dr., Sea Pines Plantation, Hilton Head Is., SC 29928, (803)671-6428; **BUS ADD:** PO Drawer 5706, Hilton Head Is.,

SC 29938, (803)785-4251.

NOWELL, Samuel G.——B: July 20, 1930, Altoona, PA, *VP*, Summit Associates Inc.; **PRIM RE ACT:** Developer, Builder, Owner/Investor, Property Manager; **SERVICES:** Design/Build Lease Office, Indust.; **REP CLIENTS:** Gen. Cable, Revere Copper & Brass, Wilson Sporting Goods, Masonite Corp., Litton Indust., Centel, Bell Labs, Control Data, NJ Bell, Linden Chemical & Plastics; **PREV EMPLOY:** VP - Jos. L. Muscarelle, Inc. Maywood, NJ; **PROFL AFFIL & HONORS:** IREBA; NAIOP; NACORE; **EDUC:** BS, 1953, Civil Engr., Franklin/Marshall, Penn. State Univ.; **EDUC HONORS:** Lion's Paw Honor Soc.; **MIL SERV:** USA, Pvt.; **HOME ADD:** 17 Park Ln., Fair Haven, NJ 07701, (201)747-5502; **BUS ADD:** Raritan Plaza II, Raritan Ctr., Edison, NJ 08837, (201)225-2900.

NUEY, Vernita——B: Mar. 4, 1952, Chicago, IL, *RE Broker and Atty.*, Vernita Nuey, Esq.; **PRIM RE ACT:** Broker, Consultant, Attorney, Property Manager; **REP CLIENTS:** Managing agent, res. and comml. tenants, investment and fin. of RE deals, representation on legal problems involved with the mgmt. and maintenance of these props.; **PROFL AFFIL & HONORS:** ABA, NBA, Phi Alpha Delta, NYSBA, Harlem RE Bd.; **EDUC:** 1971, Intl. Studies & Hist., Univ. of CA; **GRAD EDUC:** LLB, 1974, Howard Univ. School of Law, Wash., DC; **BUS ADD:** 2090 7th Ave., 110, New York, NY 10027, (212)864-5232.

NUGENT, James G.——B: Jan. 23, 1953, Chicago, IL, *RE Rep.*, Marriott Corp., Restaurant; **PRIM RE ACT:** Developer; **SERVICES:** Mkt. Analysis, Site Selection, Lease Negotiation, Site Plan and Variance Rep.; **PREV EMPLOY:** RE Rep.-Midas Realty Corp.; Accountant I - Standard Oil Co. (IN); **PROFL AFFIL & HONORS:** AICPA, Soc. of CPA's, NACORE, NJ Fed. of Planning Officials; **EDUC:** BBA, 1975, Acctg., W IL Univ.; **HOME ADD:** 2003 Coral Way, Wall, NJ 07719, (201)681-7221; **BUS ADD:** 625 From Rd., Paramus, NJ 07652, (201)262-1000.

NULL, Gary G.——B: June 25, 1950, Lakehurst, NJ, *Partner*, Hughes & Hill; **PRIM RE ACT:** Attorney; **SERVICES:** Legal Counsel for Acquisition, Devel., Fin., Disposition of Property; **REP CLIENTS:** Mercantile Nat. Bank at Dallas; TX, Amer. Bank, Dallas N; Merrill Lynch/Comm. Real Estate; **PROFL AFFIL & HONORS:** ABA, State Bar of TX, Dallas Co. Bar; **EDUC:** AB, 1972, Econ., Dartmouth Coll.; **GRAD EDUC:** JD, 1975, Harvard Law School; **EDUC HONORS:** Summa Cum Laude, Phi Beta Kappa, Cum Laude; **HOME ADD:** Churchill Way, Dallas, TX 75230; **BUS ADD:** 1000 Mercantile Dallas Bldg., Dallas, TX 75201, (214)651-0477.

NUSBAUM, Charles G.——B: June 2, 1926, Norfolk, VA, *Indus. Broker*, Charles G. Nusbaum, Realtor; **PRIM RE ACT:** Broker, Engineer, Property Manager; **OTHER RE ACT:** Indus. Realtor, Marine Engr.; **SERVICES:** Sales/leasing, indus. props. & land; **PROFL AFFIL & HONORS:** SRA, SREA; Pres., Tidewater Chapter 117, for 1970-71 and 1971-72; SIR Designation, Pres. VA Chapter 1977; CPM of IREM of the NAREB, Pres. 1977 VA - Tidewater Chapter No. 39; Member of Tidewater Bd. of Realtors; **EDUC:** BS, 1946, Engineer-Marine, US Merchant Marine Academy; BS, 1949, Commerce, Univ. of VA; **MIL SERV:** USN Res. Retd., Lt.; **HOME ADD:** 1342 Buckingham Ave., Norfolk, VA 23508, (804)423-6644; **BUS ADD:** 1220 United VA Bank Bldg., Norfolk, VA 23510, (804)622-1688.

NUSBAUM, Robert E.——B: Mar. 28, 1927, Springfield, IL, *Owner*, Nusbaum and Assocs.; **PRIM RE ACT:** Broker, Consultant, Appraiser, Owner/Investor, Property Manager, Syndicator; **SERVICES:** Comml. RE, synd., prop. mgmt., appraisals; **PROFL AFFIL & HONORS:** NAR, RESSI, Nat. Assn. of Home Builders; **EDUC:** BS, 1950, Bus. Admin., Bradley Univ.; **MIL SERV:** USAF, SGt.; **OTHER ACT & HONORS:** City of Danville Zoning Comm., Chmn.; **HOME ADD:** 65 Country Club Dr., Danville, IL 61832, (217)446-6940; **BUS ADD:** 65 Country Club Dr., Danville, IL 61832, (217)446-6940.

NUSS, Carol A.——B: May 7, 1951, Cleveland, OH, *Dist. VP & Co-Owner*, Redhill Realty, Tustin, Irvine, Newport/Lido, CA; **OTHER RE ACT:** Broker; **SERVICES:** Resid. new homes div., comml. indus.; **PROFL AFFIL & HONORS:** Member of Irvine Bd. of Realtors, East Orange Cty. Bd. of Realtors, E. Orange Cty. Investment Div., Network Dir for Nat. Assn. of Female Execs; **HOME ADD:** 690 Ranchroad, Orange, CA 92669, (714)855-9299; **BUS ADD:** 18002 Irvine Blvd., Tustin, CA 92680, (714)544-4900.

NUSSBAUM, Paul A.——B: July 8, 1947, Brooklyn, NY, *Sr. RE Partner*, Schulte Roth & Zabel; **PRIM RE ACT:** Attorney; **PROFL AFFIL & HONORS:** ABA (Real Prop. Sec.), NY State Bar Assn. (Real Prop. Sec.), NY County Lawyers (Banking Comm.), Adjunct Asst. Prof. of RE Law at NY Univ.; **EDUC:** BA, 1967, Poli. Sci., SUNY, Buffalo, NY; **GRAD EDUC:** JD, 1971, Georgetown Univ. Law School; **MIL SERV:** USAR, Lt.; **OTHER ACT & HONORS:** Planning Bd. Town of No. Salem 1975-1977; **HOME ADD:** 5001 Iselin Ave., Riverdale, NY 10471; **BUS ADD:** 460 Park Ave., New York, NY 10022, (212)758-0404.

NUSSMEIER, Donald K.——B: Nov. 21, 1938, Evansville, IN, *Dir. of Fin.*, Oak Hill Investment Corp.; **PRIM RE ACT:** Developer, Builder, Owner/Investor, Property Manager; **SERVICES:** Devel., construction, mktg. and feasibility, site selection; **REP CLIENTS:** Several nat. retail and food outlets; **PREV EMPLOY:** CPA 15 yrs., investment RE broker 3 yrs., Cushman & Wakefield; **PROFL AFFIL & HONORS:** Amer. Inst. of CPA's, OR Soc. of CPA's, Portland (OR) Bd. of Realtors, OR Assoc. of Realtors, NAR, RNMI OR CCIM Chap., 1982 Pres.-OR CCIM Chap.; **EDUC:** BS - Bus. Admin., 1962, Acctg., Wayne State Univ.; **HOME ADD:** 1493 S.W. 66th Ave., Portland, OR 97206, (503)297-7312; **BUS ADD:** 7941 SE Johnson Creek Blvd., Portland, OR 97206, (503)777-4861.

NUTER, John E.——*Dir. Prop.*, Zenith Radio; **PRIM RE ACT:** Property Manager; **BUS ADD:** 1900 No. Austin Ave., Chicago, IL 60639, (312)745-2000.*

NUTI, Maria——*Dir. Corp. RE*, MacMillan; **PRIM RE ACT:** Property Manager; **BUS ADD:** 866 Third Ave., New York, NY 10022, (212)935-3160.*

NUTTLE, Daniel E.——B: June 20, 1936, Flint, MI, *Exec. VP*, R.J. Den Herder Assoc. Inc.; **PRIM RE ACT:** Broker, Appraiser, Insuror, Instructor; **SERVICES:** Resid. relocation, comml. & indus. brokerage; **REP CLIENTS:** Consumers Power Co., Aeroquip Corp.; **PROFL AFFIL & HONORS:** NAR, MAR, Jackson Bd. of Realtors, RNMI, CRB, CRS, GRI; **EDUC:** BBA, 1960, Personnel, Psych, W. MI Univ.; **MIL SERV:** MI Air Nat. Guard, AIC; **OTHER ACT & HONORS:** Pres. Jackson Local Devel. Corp.; **HOME ADD:** 806 S. Webster, Jackson, MI 49203, (517)782-1171; **BUS ADD:** 760 W. Franklin, Jackson, MI 49203, (517)787-7711.

NUTTLE, John C.——B: Apr. 16, 1922, Baltimore, *Pres.*, The Jacole Co.; **PRIM RE ACT:** Broker, Consultant, Developer; **PREV EMPLOY:** Investors Mgmt. Group, Inc., The Rouse Co.; **EDUC:** BEE, 1942, Mech. Engrg., Johns Hopkins Univ.; **EDUC HONORS:** Omicron Delta Kappa; **MIL SERV:** US Army, Col., Bronze Star, American and SW Pacific Theater Ribbons; **HOME ADD:** 2721 Caves Rd., Owings Mills, MD 21117, (301)363-6739; **BUS ADD:** PO Box 580, Brooklandville, MD 21022, (301)363-6739.

NYENHVIS, Jack——*Mgr. Corp. Prop.*, Jostens, Inc.; **PRIM RE ACT:** Property Manager; **BUS ADD:** 5501 Norman Center Dr., Minneapolis, MN 55437, (612)830-3300.*

NYKIEL, Frank——*Pres.*, Chromalloy American Corp.; **PRIM RE ACT:** Property Manager; **BUS ADD:** 120 South Central St., St. Louis, MI 63105, (314)726-9200.*

NYMARK, Richard M.——B: Ju 22, 1949, Montevideo, Uruguay, *Partner*, Nebyn Peterson Assoc.; **PRIM RE ACT:** Consultant; **OTHER RE ACT:** Mktg., research, planning servs.; **SERVICES:** Creating and implementing mktg. solutions for RE; **REP CLIENTS:** Corp. and fin. inst. nationwide; **PREV EMPLOY:** Lehman Bros., Kuhn Loeb, RE Div. of Howard P. Hoffman Assoc.; **PROFL AFFIL & HONORS:** RE Bd. of NY, Amer. Planning Assoc.; **EDUC:** BArch., 1975, Arch., NYC Coll.; **GRAD EDUC:** 1977, Urban Planning, & RE, CCNY & NYU; **MIL SERV:** USA, Sgt., 1967-70, Paratrooper; **HOME ADD:** 248 E. 58th St., New York, NY 10022, (212)753-6637; **BUS ADD:** 15 E. 40th St., New York, NY 10016, (212)684-0086.

NYREN, Dennis R.——B: May 4, 1950, N. Franklin, MA, *Asst. VP*, The Abacus Grp.; **OTHER RE ACT:** Mortgage banker; **SERVICES:** Acquisition loans open end construction loans, condo. conversions, permanent mort., joint ventures, presales, indus. revenue bonds; **REP CLIENTS:** Devels., brokers, condo. Converters, investors, comml. props. only; **PREV EMPLOY:** The Abacus Grp. 4 yrs.; **PROFL AFFIL & HONORS:** Jr. RE Bd.; IMBA; **EDUC:** BA, 1972, Econs., Lake Forest Coll.; **GRAD EDUC:** MBA, 1974, Fin. & Acctg., Univ. of Chicago; **EDUC HONORS:** Irving T. Young Scholar, Dean's List; **OTHER ACT & HONORS:** Lake Forest Bd. of Alumni Gov's Fundraising Chmn. Recipient of Edwin L. Gilroy Award; **HOME ADD:** 411 Sunset Ln., Glencoe, IL 60022, (312)835-0456; **BUS ADD:** 10 S. LaSalle St., Chicago, IL 60603, (312)346-9172.

NYSTROM, John A.——B: April 8, 1944, San Francisco, CA, *Pres. (CEO)*, Growth Equities Corp.; **PRIM RE ACT:** Broker, Consultant, Appraiser, Developer, Lender, Owner/Investor, Property Manager, Syndicator; **SERVICES:** Comml. brokerage - mort. banking - synd.; **REP CLIENTS:** Bank of America Realty Trust, Great Western

Savings & Loan, Del Chase, Ted Thomas, General Western Co.; **PREV EMPLOY:** Systech Fin. Corp., a Dillingham Co. - previous CPA experience; **PROFL AFFIL & HONORS:** Realtor, MBA; **EDUC:** BS, 1966, Acctg., Univ. of CA Berkeley; **GRAD EDUC:** MBA, 1973, RE, Univ. of CA Berkeley; **EDUC HONORS:** Beta Gamma Sigma; **MIL SERV:** US Army, Sgt.; **OTHER ACT & HONORS:** Commonwealth Club, Diablo Ctry. Club; **HOME ADD:** 1811 Calle Arroyo PO Box 335, Diablo, CA 94528, (415)820-4919; **BUS ADD:** 36 Quail Ct., Walnut Creek, CA 94596, (415)937-1900.

NYSTROM, Robert——*VP Mfg.*, Loctite Corp.; **PRIM RE ACT:** Property Manager; **BUS ADD:** 705 N. Mountain Rd., Newington, CT 06111, (203)278-1280.*

NYSTROM, Steven G.——**B:** Nov. 7, 1941, Rockford, IL, *Sr. VP*, Hartford National Bank and Trust Co., RE Div.; **PRIM RE ACT:** Banker, Lender; **SERVICES:** Const. loans, long term mort. loans, home morts., secondary mktg.; **REP CLIENTS:** RE devels.; comml. (non RE) clients of Hartford Nat. Bank, instnl. investors; **PREV EMPLOY:** First Nat. Bank of Chicago; **EDUC:** BA, 1963, NW Univ.; **GRAD EDUC:** MBA, 1972, Univ. of Chicago; **OTHER ACT & HONORS:** Dir., Second VP of Corp. for Indep. Living, Hartford, CT; **HOME ADD:** 7 Somerset Lane, Simsbury, CT 06070, (203)658-6463; **BUS ADD:** 777 Main St., Hartford, CT 06115, (203)728-2804.

OAKS, Gilbert E., Jr.——**B:** July 16, 1944, Monterey, CA, *Pres.*, OMA Intnl.; **PRIM RE ACT:** Attorney, Architect, Syndicator, Developer, Consultant, Property Manager, Banker, Owner/Investor; **OTHER RE ACT:** Advisor; **SERVICES:** Mort. banking, investment/fin. counseling, devel. & synd. of comml. props. & prop. mgmt., Tax Shelters; **REP CLIENTS:** Maj. corps., indiv., lenders or instnl. investors in comml. props.; **PREV EMPLOY:** US Atomic Energy Commission; **PROFL AFFIL & HONORS:** MBAA, Intl. Financiers Soc., Intl. Assn. of Bus. & Fin. Consultants; Int'l. Assn. of Financial Planners, Cert. Intl. Financier; **EDUC:** BSEE, BSME, 1966, Elec., Mech., Arch. Engrg., Findlay Engrg. Coll., Univ. of MO; **GRAD EDUC:** MS, 1974, Intl. Fin., Frotsburg State Coll.; PhD, 1981, Mgmt., Amer. Western Univ., Intl. Fin.; **EDUC HONORS:** Magna Cum Laude, Grad. Degree; **OTHER ACT & HONORS:** Dist Commnr. of Boy Scouts of Amer.; **HOME ADD:** 3030 Nassau Dr., Brookfield, WI 53005; **BUS ADD:** PO Box 234, Elm Grove, WI 53122, (414)785-0151.

OBERLE, Edwin F.——**B:** Feb. 13, 1941, Grand Rapids, MI, *VP RE*, Victory Markets, Inc.; **PRIM RE ACT:** Consultant, Attorney, Developer, Builder, Owner/Investor, Property Manager; **PREV EMPLOY:** Dir. of RE Law, Midwest Group, The Great Atlantic & Pacific Tea Co., Montvale, NJ; RE Rep., Ford Motor Co., Dealership RE Office, Dearborn, MI; **PROFL AFFIL & HONORS:** Member of MI State Bar, IL State Bar, NY State Bar; **EDUC:** BA, 1962, St. Mary's Univ., Baltimore, MD; **GRAD EDUC:** JD, 1965, Univ. of Detroit Law School; **MIL SERV:** US Army; Sgt.; **HOME ADD:** Randall Ave., Norwich, NY 13815; **BUS ADD:** 54 E. Main St., Norwich, NY 13815, (607)335-4812.

OBERT, R. Paul——*Corp. Counsel*, CF Industries, Inc.; **PRIM RE ACT:** Property Manager; **BUS ADD:** Salem Lake Drive, Long Grove, IL 60047, (312)438-9500.*

OBLEY, Ross P.——**B:** Dec. 22, 1928, West Newton, PA, *Pres.*, Coral Ridge-Collier Props., Incs., A subsidiary of Westinghouse Electric Corp.; **PRIM RE ACT:** Engineer, Banker, Developer, Builder, Owner/Investor; **OTHER RE ACT:** Land devel., ecologist; **SERVICES:** Devel. and sale of resid. and comml. props.; **REP CLIENTS:** Condo devels., home builders and upscale resid. purchasers of apts. ($200,000 and up) and homes ($350,000 and up); **PREV EMPLOY:** 30 years with various divs. and subsidiaries of Westinghouse; **PROFL AFFIL & HONORS:** Bd. of Dirs.; Citizens National Bank; (Investment; Trust; Bus. Devel. Comms.); Econ. Devel. Commn.; Trustee; U.L.I.; Exec. Member; Fed. Policy Council, Engr.; **EDUC:** BS, 1951, Engrg., Univ. of Pittsburgh; **GRAD EDUC:** MBA, 1958, The Amer. Univ.; **MIL SERV:** USCG, Lt.; **OTHER ACT & HONORS:** Pres.; The Club at Pelican Bay; 4-H Found.; Bd. of Dir. Collier Cty. Conservancy; Trustee; Rotary Intl.;; **HOME ADD:** 6554 Ridgewood Dr., Naples, FL 33940, (813)597-1586; **BUS ADD:** 5801 Pelican Bay Blvd., Naples, FL 33940, (813)597-6061.

OBLOY, Stanley J.——**B:** Sept. 4, 1947, Cleveland, OH, *VP RE and Const.*, The Richman Brothers Co.; **PRIM RE ACT:** Attorney, Property Manager; **OTHER RE ACT:** Retail expansion and const.; **PREV EMPLOY:** The Nobil Shoe Co., VP RE and Counsel; **PROFL AFFIL & HONORS:** ABA; Intl. Council of Shopping Ctrs.; **EDUC:** BA, 1969, Pol. Sci., Math., OH State Univ.; **GRAD EDUC:** JD, 1972, RE and Bus. Law, Univ. of Toledo Coll. of Law; **BUS ADD:** 1600 E. 55th St., Cleveland, OH 44103, (216)431-0200.

OBNINSKY, Victor Peter——**B:** Oct. 12, 1944, San Rafael, CA, *Pres.*, The Mahoney Company, Co.; **PRIM RE ACT:** Attorney, Developer, Owner/Investor, Property Manager; **SERVICES:** Legal services; **REP CLIENTS:** RE devels./synds.; realtors; investors in RE; bldg. contractors; **PROFL AFFIL & HONORS:** State Bar of CA, ABA, Marin Cty. Bar Assn., Who's Who in Creative RE; **EDUC:** BA, 1966, Hist.; Econ., Columbia Univ.; **GRAD EDUC:** JD, 1969, Law, Univ. of CA, Hastings Coll. of the Law; **EDUC HONORS:** Wilkinson Award Nominee, 1966; **OTHER ACT & HONORS:** Richardson Bay Sanitary Dist., 1973-75; Commonwealth Club of CA; Intl. Hospitality Ctr.; Who's Who in CA, 1981 Edition; **BUS ADD:** 100 Galli Dr., Novato, CA 94947, (415)883-3211.

OBREGON, Conrad J.——**B:** Oct. 23, 1936, Chicago, IL, *Deputy Counsel*, New York State Housing Finance Agency, Law; **PRIM RE ACT:** Attorney; **SERVICES:** Legal services; **PREV EMPLOY:** Asst. Gen. Counsel, Dir. of Project Mgmt., Area Housing Dir., NY City Housing and Devel. Admin., 1966-1977; **PROFL AFFIL & HONORS:** NY City Lawyers Assn.; Rgnl. Plan Assn.; **EDUC:** BS, 1958, Sociology, Fordham Coll.; **GRAD EDUC:** JD, 1963, Law, NYU Law Sch.; MPA, 1967, Housing & Urban Renewal, NYU Grad. Sch. of Public Admin.; **MIL SERV:** Army Res., Transportation, Col., Army Commendation Medal; **OTHER ACT & HONORS:** Nat. Model Railroad Assn.; **HOME ADD:** 1448 E. 26th St., Brooklyn, NY 11210, (212)338-3275; **BUS ADD:** 3 Park Ave., New York, NY 10016, (212)686-9700.

O'BRIEN, B. Wells——**B:** Aug. 28, 1930, Omaha, NE, *Shareholder*, Woodburn, Wedge, Blakey and Jeppson; **PRIM RE ACT:** Attorney; **PREV EMPLOY:** General Counsel, McCulloch Props., Inc.; **PROFL AFFIL & HONORS:** ABA, State Bar Assn of NV, State Bar Assn. of AZ and CA; **GRAD EDUC:** LLB, 1956, Law Degree, Univ. of NE and Univ. of AZ; **MIL SERV:** USN, Seaman; **HOME ADD:** 2000 Holcomb Ln., Reno, NV 89511, (702)852-9251; **BUS ADD:** One East First St., Suite 1600, Reno, NV 89505, (702)329-6131.

O'BRIEN, Bob——*Mgr. Corp. facilities*, Graco, Inc.; **PRIM RE ACT:** Property Manager, Engineer, Owner/Investor; **PREV EMPLOY:** Control Data Corp.-10 yrs., The Trane Co.-5 yrs.; **PROFL AFFIL & HONORS:** IDRC; **EDUC:** BSEE, 1962, Univ. of WI; **BUS ADD:** 88 11th Ave. NE, Minneapolis, MN 55440.

O'BRIEN, Daniel M.——**B:** Nov. 24, 1951, *Treas.*, Summer & Co.; **PRIM RE ACT:** Developer, Property Manager; **REP CLIENTS:** Builder/Dev.; **PREV EMPLOY:** Ernst & Whitney, Tax Supr.; **PROFL AFFIL & HONORS:** NAA, OSCPA, AICPA, BIA, CPA; **EDUC:** BA, 1973, Econ., OH State Univ.; **GRAD EDUC:** MBA, 1976, Fin., OH State Univ.; **BUS ADD:** 870 Michigan Ave., Columbus, OH 43215, (614)224-8191.

O'BRIEN, John M.——**B:** Sept. 6, 1947, NY, *Partner*, Sickels/O'Brien Development Group; **PRIM RE ACT:** Developer; **SERVICES:** Indus. park devel. and research park devel.; **REP CLIENTS:** Imed Corp., Daon Corp. Sub-4, Inc.; **PREV EMPLOY:** Coldwell Banker Comml. RE Servs., 4 yrs.; **PROFL AFFIL & HONORS:** Nat. Assn. of Indus. & Office Parks, Pres. - San Diego Chap.; Member, Amer. Inst. of Plant Engrs.; **EDUC:** Naval Engrg., 1969, Poli./Econ., US Naval Acad.; **MIL SERV:** USN, Lt.; **HOME ADD:** 2741 Bayside Walk, San Diego, CA 92109, (714)488-6565; **BUS ADD:** 326 Broadway, Suite 800, San Diego, CA 92101, (714)231-3515.

O'BRIEN, John R.——**B:** Oct. 10 1943, Omaha, NE, *Atty. at law*, Gray & O'Brien; **PRIM RE ACT:** Attorney; **SERVICES:** Legal; **PREV EMPLOY:** Spridgen, Barrett, Archor, Luckhardt, Anderson, James & Ziegler, partner, RE specialty; **PROFL AFFIL & HONORS:** ABA; CA Bar Assn. (RE Sect.); Sonoma Cty. Bar Assn., Who's Who in CA; **EDUC:** BA, 1965, Econ., Creighton Univ., Omaha, NE 1962-1965; Regis Coll. Denver, 1961-1962; **GRAD EDUC:** JD, 1968, Law, Hastings Coll. of Law, San Francisco, CA; **EDUC HONORS:** Dean's List, Thurston Honor Soc.; Order of the Coif; Law Journal; **MIL SERV:** US Army JAGC; Capt.; **OTHER ACT & HONORS:** Dir., Sonoma Wildlife Rehab. Ctr.; Legacy Chmn. Amer. Cancer Soc., Sonoma Cty. Unit; **HOME ADD:** 5105 Monte Verde Dr., Santa Rosa, CA 95405, (707)539-1283; **BUS ADD:** P.O. Box 1852, 100 E. St., Santa Rosa, CA 95402.

O'BRIEN, Joseph F.——**B:** May 5, 1942, Manchester, NH, *Pres.*, OLH Devel. Co.; **PRIM RE ACT:** Engineer, Architect, Developer, Builder, Owner/Investor; **SERVICES:** Design (Arch. & Engr.), build, devel. condos., apts., office; **PREV EMPLOY:** Devel. (NV & ID) 1976 to present, own firm; RE Broker (NV) 1974-1976; **PROFL AFFIL & HONORS:** ASCE; NSPE; NV and CA registered Civil Engr.; **EDUC:** BS, 1966, Math., CA State Coll., Hayward; BS, 1971, Civil Engrg., Univ. of NV, Reno; **EDUC HONORS:** Grad. with Honors; **HOME ADD:** POB 1617, Sun Valley, ID 83353, (208)726-7514; **BUS ADD:** POB 1764, Sun Valley, ID 83353, (208)726-9102.

O'BRIEN, Michael C., Jr.——**B:** May 5, 1928, Brooklyn, NY, *Pres.*, M.C. O'Brien, Inc.; **PRIM RE ACT:** Broker, Consultant, Appraiser; **SERVICES:** Indus. RE brokerage, all types of appraisal services, large comml., indus. & fin. counseling; **REP CLIENTS:** Pfizer, Con Edison, Anheuser Busch, Comml. & Savings Banks; **PROFL AFFIL & HONORS:** AIREA; SIR; Amer. Soc. of RE Counselors, CRE; MAI; SIR; **EDUC:** BBA, 1949, Holy Cross Coll.; **MIL SERV:** USN, Lt.j.g., PVC; **OTHER ACT & HONORS:** Tr., Lincoln Savings Bank; VP, Brooklyn C of C; **HOME ADD:** 35 Nassau Blvd., Garden City, NY 11530, (516)294-9742; **BUS ADD:** 3832 Kings Highway, Brooklyn, NY 11234, (212)252-9191.

O'BRIEN, Richard H.——**B:** Oct. 4, 1931, Brooklyn, NY, *Pres.*, First American Title Insurance Company of New York; **OTHER RE ACT:** Title Insurance; **SERVICES:** Provide buyers & lenders with title ins. policies; **REP CLIENTS:** Brokers, bankers, attys. & builders; **PROFL AFFIL & HONORS:** Amer. Land Title Assn., NY Title Assn., Member, Long Is. Assn. of Bus. & Commerce, Mort. Bankers Assn., Listed in Who's Who, Hofstra Alumni Assn.; **EDUC:** BS - Fin., 1958, RE and Fin., Hofstra Univ.; **MIL SERV:** US Army, Cpl.; **OTHER ACT & HONORS:** Dwight D. Eisenhower Award for Public Serv., Garden City Ctry. Club, Dir. YMCA, Tr. Leukemia Soc. of L.I., Lions, Elks, Tamadachi Frat.; **HOME ADD:** 115 Stone Hurst La., Dix Hills, NY 11746; **BUS ADD:** 1050 Franklin Ave., Garden City, NY 11530, (516)742-7500.

O'BRIEN, Thomas F.——**B:** Sept. 9, 1948, IA City, IA, *Sales Mgr.*, Coldwell Banker Co., Comml. RE Servs.; **PRIM RE ACT:** Broker; **SERVICES:** Office, Industrial, retail, investment prop. sales & leasing brokerage; **EDUC:** BS, 1971, Naval Engrg. & Pol. Sci., US Naval Acad.; **GRAD EDUC:** Diploma Program in RE, 1980, RE Analysis & Appraisal, NY Univ.; **MIL SERV:** USN, Lt., 1971-76; **BUS ADD:** 50 Staniford St., Boston, MA 02114, (617)367-7600.

O'BRIEN, William B.——*VP Adm. & Secy.*, Robintech, Inc.; **PRIM RE ACT:** Property Manager; **BUS ADD:** PO Box 2342, Fort Worth, TX 76113, (817)336-7323.*

O'BRIEN, William J.——*Pres.*, Continental Copper & Steel Industries; **PRIM RE ACT:** Property Manager; **BUS ADD:** 12 Commerce Dr., Cranford, NJ 07016, (201)272-3850.*

O'CALLAGHAN, R.J. Patrick——**B:** Aug. 8, 1924, Minneapolis, MN, *RE Consultant*, REI Management Group Inc.; **PRIM RE ACT:** Broker, Consultant, Instructor; **SERVICES:** Buyer's agent, comml. & investment prop.; farm and ranch; **PREV EMPLOY:** Atty. at Law 30 yrs.; Primary Practice in RE; Lic. RE Broker since 1952; **PROFL AFFIL & HONORS:** Realtor Pueblo Bd. of Realtors; FLI; FIABCI; ABA, Realtor of the Yr., 1981; SCV; **EDUC:** BA, 1949, Drake Univ.; **GRAD EDUC:** LLB, 1951, Law, Univ. of Denver Law School; JD, 1951, Law, Univ. of Denver Law School; **MIL SERV:** USN, QM 2nd, 1943-1946; **OTHER ACT & HONORS:** Past Exalted Ruler BPO Elks; 10 Yr. Award Univ. of CO Distinguished Instr., Continuing Educ. RE; Other bus. address: Suite 600, 3300 E. First Ave. Denver, CO 80206; **HOME ADD:** 300 W. Abriendo, Pueblo, CO 81004, (303)544-1910; **BUS ADD:** 510 United Bank Bldg., Pueblo, CO 81003, (303)545-4112.

O'CALLAGHAN, William L., Jr.——**B:** Aug. 6, 1941, Atlanta, GA, *Atty.*, O'Callaghan, Saunders & Stumm, P.A.; **PRIM RE ACT:** Attorney; **SERVICES:** Legal; **REP CLIENTS:** Synd., devel., inst. investors; **PROFL AFFIL & HONORS:** Amer., State of GA and Local Bar Assns.; **EDUC:** BBA, 1963, Univ. of GA; **GRAD EDUC:** JD, 1965, Univ. of GA; LLM, 1968, Taxation, Georgetown Univ.; **EDUC HONORS:** Beta Gamma sigma, Phi Kappa Phi, Pi Sigma Alpha, Phi Beta Kappa, Cum Laude; Sylvanus Morris Order of Juris Prudence; **MIL SERV:** US Army, Capt., Nat. Def. Serv. Award; Army commendation medal; **OTHER ACT & HONORS:** Optimist & Rotary Club; Sandy Springs C of C; Mort. Bankers Assn. of GA; **HOME ADD:** 351 Green Oak Ridge, Marietta, GA 30067, (404)973-9077; **BUS ADD:** 6201 Powers Ferry Rd. 330, Atlanta, GA 30339, (404)953-3300.

OCONE, Louis M.——**B:** Oct. 9, 1939, Jersey City, NJ, *VP*, US Realty Operations, Info. Center; **OTHER RE ACT:** Accountant; **SERVICES:** Acctg., fin. analysis and info.; **PREV EMPLOY:** Deloitte Haskins & Sells; **PROFL AFFIL & HONORS:** AICPA, NY Soc. of CPA's, CPA; **EDUC:** BS, 1961, Acctg., St. Peters Coll.; **MIL SERV:** Army, infantry, 1st Lt.; **BUS ADD:** 1285 Ave. of the Americas, New York, NY 10019, (212)554-3585.

O'CONNELL, Anthony Wayne——**B:** Aug. 4, 1907, Norwich CT, *Sr. Part.*, Anthony Wayne O'Connell Agency, RE Appraising & Consulting; **PRIM RE ACT:** Broker, Consultant, Appraiser; **SERVICES:** RE Appraiser and Consultant; **REP CLIENTS:** CT Bank & Trust Co.; VA;. Conn. Dept. of Transportation; FAA; HUD; CT Commnr. of Public Works; Various Redevel. Agencies and many others; **PREV EMPLOY:** Founder of the Anthony Wayne O'Connell Agency; **PROFL AFFIL & HONORS:** Sen. Member-Amer. Soc. of Appraisers; Sen. Member-Nat. Assn. of Review Appraisers; Sen. Member-Intl. Inst. of Valuers; Cert. RE Consultant; Sr. Govt. Appraiser, Member Omega Taio Rho, Past Pres. CT Assn. of RE Bds., Past Dir. of NAREB; **EDUC:** Studied law in the law firm of Shields & Shields, 1928-1932; **OTHER ACT & HONORS:** Mayor of Norwich-1938-1940; State Senator-1935-1937; Judge Norwich City Court-1935-1937; State Rep., 1933-1935; various frat. org.; **HOME ADD:** 340 Harland Rd., Norwich, CT 06360, (203)887-0948; **BUS ADD:** 40 Main St., Norwich, CT 06360, (203)889-8449.

O'CONNELL, James Joseph——**B:** Sept. 18, 1941, Scranton, PA, *Facilities Specialist*, General Electric, Information Serv. Co.; **PRIM RE ACT:** Property Manager; **SERVICES:** Property Mgmt.; **EDUC:** BS, 1963, Math., Fordham Univ., NY; **GRAD EDUC:** MS, 1966, Math./Educ., Fordham Univ.; M.Div., 1972, Theology, Woodstock Coll., NY; **OTHER ACT & HONORS:** Past Advisor Jr. Achievement Program, Wash., DC; **HOME ADD:** 9122 Bobwhite Cir., Gaithersburg, MD 20879, (301)869-5783; **BUS ADD:** 401 North Washington St., Rockville, MD 20850, (301)340-4259.

O'CONNELL, Sam——**B:** July 15, 1920, Indianapolis, IN, *Formerly District Sales Mgr.*, Baird & Warner, Inc., Resid. sales, North Shore of Chicago; **PRIM RE ACT:** Broker; **SERVICES:** Resid. sales; **REP CLIENTS:** Middle mgmt. and top execs., Chicago-based and nat. corps.; **PREV EMPLOY:** Nine years advertising & publishing. Formerly Managing Editor, *Buildings Magazine*, Stamats Publishing, Cedar Rapids, IA; **PROFL AFFIL & HONORS:** Member, past Pres., No. Shore Bd. of Realtors, Member, Chicago RE Bd., GRI, CRS, CRB, Realtors Nat. Mktg. Inst.; **EDUC:** AB, 1947, English (journalism), DePauw Univ.; **MIL SERV:** USCG, 1942-1945 (WWII); **HOME ADD:** 1717 Northfield Sq., Northfield, IL 60093, (312)446-0079; **BUS ADD:** 576 Lincoln Ave., Winnetka, IL 60093, (312)446-1855.

O'CONNER, James V.——**B:** Oct. 21, 1931, Yakima, WA, *Pres.*, O'Conner Law Corp., PS; **PRIM RE ACT:** Broker, Attorney, Instructor; **OTHER RE ACT:** CPA, RE Taxation; **SERVICES:** Legal & acctg. servs.; Investments advice; **REP CLIENTS:** Investors, RE brokers; **PROFL AFFIL & HONORS:** ABA, WA Bar Assn., AICPA, WA Soc. of CPA's, NAR, Seattle King Cty. Bd. of Realtors; **EDUC:** BA, 1955, Acctg., Univ. of WA; **GRAD EDUC:** JD, 1958, Law, Univ. of WA; **EDUC HONORS:** Beta Alpha Psi, Acctg. Hon., Law Review Editorial Bd.; **HOME ADD:** 6310 52nd Ave. S, Seattle, WA 98118, (206)723-6819; **BUS ADD:** 1900 S. Perget Dr., Renton, WA 98055, (206)271-3250.

O'CONNOR, James F.——**B:** Nov. 7, 1932, New Bedford, MA, *Pres.*, O'Connor RE Assoc., Inc.; **PRIM RE ACT:** Consultant, Appraiser, Instructor; **SERVICES:** RE appraisals, consultation, and analysis; **REP CLIENTS:** Indivs., corps., local, state and fed. agencies, public utilities; **PROFL AFFIL & HONORS:** SREA, Sr. Member ASA; **EDUC:** BS, 1954, Educ., Math. & Sci., North Adams State Coll.; **GRAD EDUC:** MEd, 1956, Sec. Educ., Bridgewater State Coll.; **EDUC HONORS:** Honor Soc.; **OTHER ACT & HONORS:** Former inst., RE Appraisal, Univ. of MA, W. New England Coll., and Springfield Tech. Comm. Coll.; **HOME ADD:** 189 Sackett Rd., Westfield, MA 01085, (413)562-4041; **BUS ADD:** 14 Franklin St., PO Box 1211, Westfield, MA 01086, (413)562-5096.

O'CONNOR, James J., III——**B:** Sept. 25, 1947, St. Louis, MO, *VP*, Nooney Co., Partnership Fin.; **PRIM RE ACT:** Developer, Property Manager, Syndicator; **PREV EMPLOY:** VP, Corp. Fin., Sifel, Nicolaus & Co., Inc., 1970-1977 (Investment Banker); **PROFL AFFIL & HONORS:** Nat. Synd. Forum; RESSI; **EDUC:** BSBA, 1970, Fin., St. Louis Univ.; **HOME ADD:** 7945 Park Dr., St. Louis, MO 63117, (314)645-5087; **BUS ADD:** 7701 Forsyth, St. Louis, MO 63105, (314)863-7700.

O'CONNOR, Jerome P.——**B:** Feb. 10, 1932, Chicago, IL, *Pres.*, J. P. O'Connor & Company; **PRIM RE ACT:** Developer, Builder, Owner/Investor, Property Manager; **SERVICES:** Devel., sales, mgmt. of multi-family housing and land; **PREV EMPLOY:** Dell Corporation, Northbrook, IL, 1964-75; **EDUC:** BCE, 1953, CE, Univ. of Notre Dame; **GRAD EDUC:** MBA, 1959, Bus. Admin., Northwestern Univ.; **EDUC HONORS:** Cum Laude; **MIL SERV:** Navy Civil Engineer Corp, Lt. Jg.; **HOME ADD:** 1710 Forest Ave., Wilmette, IL 60091, (312)251-1461; **BUS ADD:** 1000 Skokie Blvd., Wilmette, IL 60091, (312)256-0750.

O'CONNOR, Larry——**B:** July 7, 1948, MA, *Pres./Treas.*, Native Sun Company, Inc.; **PRIM RE ACT:** Appraiser, Developer, Builder, Owner/Investor, Property Manager; **OTHER RE ACT:** Specialize in Solar Properties; **SERVICES:** Site evaluations, planning, mktg.; **REP CLIENTS:** Homeowners, small bus. people, RE offices, lenders; **PREV EMPLOY:** O'Connor Devel. Corp.; **PROFL AFFIL & HONORS:** New England Solar Energy Assn., 1978 Passive Solar Design Award from HUD; **EDUC:** BA, 1971, Hist. - Amer. Civ., Univ. of PA; **BUS ADD:** 368 Chesterfield Rd., Leeds, MA 01053, (413)584-7099.

O'CONNOR, Llani——**B:** Chicago, IL, *VP-Publishing*, Realtors National Marketing Institute of the National Association of Realtors, Publishing; **PRIM RE ACT:** Real Estate Publisher; **SERVICES:** Training Programs-Audio Visual; Books; Magazines; **PREV EMPLOY:** Mgmt. Editor-*Institutions* Magazine; **PROFL AFFIL & HONORS:** Assn. of Amer. Publishers, Inc., Soc. of Nat. Assn. Publications; **EDUC:** BS-Mktg., 1965, Bus. Admin., IN State Univ.; **HOME ADD:** 336 Wellington, Chicago, Il 60657; **BUS ADD:** 430 N Michigan Ave., Chicago, IL 60611, (312)670-3520.

O'CONNOR, Otis L.——**B:** July 6, 1935, Charleston, WV, *Part.*, Steptoe & Johnson; **PRIM RE ACT:** Attorney; **OTHER RE ACT:** Examination; **SERVICES:** Title exams., title ins.; **REP CLIENTS:** City Nat. Bank of Charleston, Chicago Title Ins. Co.; **PROFL AFFIL & HONORS:** Kanawha & WV Bar Assns.; **EDUC:** BA, 1957, Public Affairs, Woodrow Wilson Sch. of Public Intl. Affairs, Princeton Univ.; **GRAD EDUC:** JD, 1963, Harvard Law Sch.; MBA, 1979, WV Coll. of Grad. Studies; **MIL SERV:** USN, 1957-60, Commander, US Naval Res.; **OTHER ACT & HONORS:** Charleston City Councilman, 1971-75; Bd. of Dir. Girl Scout Council; Bd. of Dir. Boy Scout Council; Pres. of Daymark, Inc. (Youth Runaway Home); **HOME ADD:** 890 Chester Rd., Charleston, WV 25302, (304)342-6248; **BUS ADD:** 608 Kanawha Valley Bldg., Charleston, WV 25301, (304)342-2191.

O'CONNOR, Patrick M.——**B:** Oct. 24, 1946, Springfield, MA, *Supr. RE Dept.*, Lucas Cty Auditor's Office; **PRIM RE ACT:** Instructor, Appraiser, Assessor; **OTHER RE ACT:** Specialty - Computer Assisted Mass Appraisal Systems; **PREV EMPLOY:** Cuyahoga Cty OH 1973 to 1979; **PROFL AFFIL & HONORS:** SREA, IAAO, ASA & NAIFA; **EDUC:** BS, 1968, Pol. Sci., Xavier Univ. - Cinn., OH; **MIL SERV:** USA, 1st. Lt., Bronze Star; **OTHER ACT & HONORS:** Publication: "Profile II; A Mgmt. Aid in the Assessor's Office"; **HOME ADD:** 6170 Larchway Ct., Toledo, OH 43613, (419)474-2596; **BUS ADD:** Lucas County Courthouse, Toledo, OH 43624, (419)259-8992.

O'CONNOR, Thomas J.——*Dir.*, Department of Housing and Urban Development, Procurement & Contracts; **PRIM RE ACT:** Lender; **BUS ADD:** 451 Seventh St., S.W., Washington, DC 20410, (202)755-5290.*

O'DEA, Michael J.——**B:** Oct. 16, 1914, Louisville, KY, *Pres.*, Michael J. O'Dea Co.; **PRIM RE ACT:** Broker, Consultant, Appraiser, Property Manager; **SERVICES:** Gen. RE Brokerage, Comm'l., Indus., Resid. Sales, Mgmt. Appraising and Consultant; **REP CLIENTS:** Represent number of both local and nat. clients; **PROFL AFFIL & HONORS:** Louisville Bd. of Realtors; KY Bd. of Realtors; NAR; Past Pres. of Local & State; Past Dir. & VP Nat., Past VP, Broker's Inst. now RNMI; Past Pres., Chap. IFA Appraisers - now member of NAIFA; Member of CRPA, NAA, SCV, IIV; **EDUC:** 1937, Acctg., Univ. of Louisville; **MIL SERV:** USN, CPO, Seebee Batt., Unit 6, Guadal Canal Invasion, Pres. Citation, 1954 - 1962; **OTHER ACT & HONORS:** Civic Serv., Chmn., 8 yrs., Urban Renewal Commn.; Taught RE courses at U. of Louisville on part-time basis; Catholic - served on Bd. of Tr. Catherine Spalding Coll., Louisville; **HOME ADD:** 9817 Marksfield Rd., Louisville, KY 40222, (502)425-0924; **BUS ADD:** 1335 Bardstown Rd., Louisville, KY 40204, (502)459-6000.

ODELL, Mark C.——**B:** Dec. 17, 1943, San Mateo, CA, *Pres.*, Commonwealth Pacific, Inc.; **PRIM RE ACT:** Syndicator; **PROFL AFFIL & HONORS:** RESSI; **EDUC:** BS, 1967, Fin., Univ. of OR; **HOME ADD:** 3102 W. Laurelhurst Dr., Seattle, WA 98105, (206)523-6886; **BUS ADD:** Seafirst Fifth Ave. Plaza, 36th Floor, Seattle, WA 98104, (206)624-6868.

ODELL, Melvin——**B:** Jan. 5, 1942, Roeland Park, KS, *Owner-Mgr.*, Odell Props.; **PRIM RE ACT:** Broker, Developer, Builder, Owner/Investor, Property Manager; **PROFL AFFIL & HONORS:** IREM; RESSI; Realtors Nat. Mkt., Cert. Prop. Mgr. - Candidate for CCM; **HOME ADD:** 3040 S. 11th Pl., Kansas City, KS 66103, (913)262-0391; **BUS ADD:** 3040 Suntree Plaza, Kansas City, KS 66103, (913)432-3117.

ODOM, F. Perry——**B:** Jan. 3, 1932, Jacksonville, FL, *Partner*, Ervin, Varn, Jacobs, Odom & Kitchen; **PRIM RE ACT:** Attorney; **SERVICES:** Contract negotiations, drafting, and all phases of rep. including title opinions and title ins. RE closing of resid. or comml. loans; **REP CLIENTS:** W. Devel. & Investment Corp., Littleton, CO; FL Credit Union League, Tallahassee, FL; MD Nat. Bank, Baltimore, MD; First Nat. Bank of MD, Baltimore, MD; MD Realty Trust, Tallahassee, FL; The Commonwealth Corp., Tallahassee, FL; **PREV EMPLOY:** Prudential Ins. Co. 1954-61; **PROFL AFFIL & HONORS:** Member, The FL Bar; Chmn. of Comm. on Credit Unions, Corp., Banking, and Business Law Section; Member, ABA, Member of Comm. on Credit Unions, Corp., Banking and Bus. Law Section, Phi Kappa Phi, Order of the Coif; **EDUC:** BS, 1952, Math. and Statistics, FL State Univ.; **GRAD EDUC:** JD, 1963, Gen. Practice, Univ. of FL; **HOME ADD:** 3014 Windsor Way, Tallahassee, FL 32312, (904)385-3624; **BUS ADD:** 305 S. Gadsden St., P.O. Box 1170, Tallahassee, FL 32302, (904)224-9135.

O'DONNELL, Donald L.——**B:** Dec. 10, 1925, Cincinnati, OH, *Pres.*, Casom, Inc.; **PRIM RE ACT:** Broker, Appraiser, Owner/Investor, Property Manager, Syndicator; **PROFL AFFIL & HONORS:** IREM; RESSI; NAR; OH Assn. of Realtors; Cincinnati Bd. of Realtors, CPM; **EDUC:** 1947, Science, Univ. of Cincinnati, Univ. of Notre Dame; **MIL SERV:** USN, Res.;Sgt.;1945; **HOME ADD:** 3312 Mowbray Ln., Cincinnati, OH 45226, (513)321-1216; **BUS ADD:** 1811 Losantiville Rd., Cincinnati, OH 45237, (513)631-0021.

O'DONNELL, William——*VP Adm.*, St. Joseph Mineral Corp.; **PRIM RE ACT:** Property Manager; **BUS ADD:** 250 Park Ave., New York, NY 10017, (212)953-5000.*

O'DRISCOLL, Richelle——*Ed.*, State of Nevada - Real Estate Division, Open House; **PRIM RE ACT:** Real Estate Publisher; **BUS ADD:** 201 S. Fall St., Carson City, NV 89710, (702)885-4280.*

OEFINGER, Robert E.——**B:** Nov. 9, 1944, San Antonia, TX, *Gen. Mgr.*, Prop. Mgmt. Systems, San Antonio; **PRIM RE ACT:** Broker, Consultant, Property Manager; **SERVICES:** Prop. Mgmt.; Office Leasing; Assistence in devel. of comml. prop-; **PREV EMPLOY:** Vantage Cos. - 1971-77; **PROFL AFFIL & HONORS:** TX RE Broker; **EDUC:** BBA, 1966, Mgmt., Univ. of TX; **GRAD EDUC:** MBA, 1967, Mktg., Univ. of Houston; **HOME ADD:** 422 Tower, San Antonio, TX 78232, (512)494-5653; **BUS ADD:** 84 NE Loop 410, Suite 149E, San Antonio, TX 78216, (512)341-1344.

OESTERREICH, G.T.——*Mgr. Empl. Rel.*, Conoco, Inc.; **PRIM RE ACT:** Property Manager; **BUS ADD:** High Ridge Park, Stamford, CT 06904, (203)329-2300.*

O'FARRELL, Lucy S.——**B:** Dec. 25, 1918, Warren County, GA, *VP*, Clover ReaLty Co., Mgr./Broker - Sandy Springs Office; **PRIM RE ACT:** Broker, Instructor, Owner/Investor; **SERVICES:** RE Sales, Listings, Eval., Energy Audits, Reloc. Serv., Notary Public; **REP CLIENTS:** Homeowners, Transferees, Apt. occupants, investors, builders & dev.; **PREV EMPLOY:** Merritt & McKenzie Ins. Agency, Office Mgr. & Lic. Ins. Agent - 1941-1971; **PROFL AFFIL & HONORS:** NAR, GA Assn. of Realtors, Atlanta Bd. of Realtors, Womens Council Realtors, Atlanta Assn. of Ins., GRI Designation Women CRB; **EDUC:** 1936-1937, Educ., GA State Coll. for Women, Milledgeville, GA; **OTHER ACT & HONORS:** Nat. Assn. of Parliamentarians, GA Assn. of Parliamentarians - Dogwood Unit, GA, Toastmasters Intl. Criterion Toastmasters Club & Sandy Springs Toastmasters Club; Nat. Assn. of Female Exec., Sandy Springs C of C, Atlanta, GA; **HOME ADD:** 7264 Selkirk Dr., NW, Atlanta, GA 30328, (404)393-1396; **BUS ADD:** 257 Mt. Vernon Hwy., NE, Atlanta, GA 30328, (404)255-6122.

O'GARA, Robert M.——**B:** Apr. 2, 1939, Lincoln, NE, *Atty.*, Marti, Dalton, Bruckner, O'Gara & Keating, P.C.; **PRIM RE ACT:** Attorney; **PROFL AFFIL & HONORS:** Lincoln Title Comm., Lincoln Bar Assn.; **EDUC:** AB, 1961, Pol. Sci., Benedictine Coll.; **GRAD EDUC:** JD, 1964, Law, Univ. of NE Coll. of Law; **HOME ADD:** 2115 Heather Ln., Lincoln, NE 68512, (402)423-6663; **BUS ADD:** 530 S. 13th, Suite A, Lincoln, NE 68508, (402)475-8230.

OGDEN, John——B: Oct. 23, 1916, Milwaukee, WI, *Pres.*, Ogden & Co., Inc.; **PRIM RE ACT:** Broker, Developer, Owner/Investor, Property Manager, Insuror; **SERVICES:** Listing & Selling of Resid. Prop.; Listing & Seller of Comml. Prop., Prop. Mgmt., Leasing of Comml. Space; **PROFL AFFIL & HONORS:** Inst. of RE Mgmt.; Natl. Assn. of Realtors, Milwaukee Bd. of Realtors, Member of Relo, Wisconsin Realtors Assn., Certified Prop. Mgr., Licensed RE Broker, Past Pres. of Milwaukee Bd. of Realtors, Realtor of the Yr.-1974; **EDUC:** BS, 1939, Hotel Admin., Cornell Univ.; **MIL SERV:** US Army Air Force, Capt.; **OTHER ACT & HONORS:** Gr. Milwaukee Comm.; Metropolitan Milwaukee Assn. of Commerce; Better Bus. Bureau; Citizen's Governmental Research Bureau; Bd. of Dir. American Cancer Society; Milwaukee Div.; **HOME ADD:** 7707 N Merrie Ln., Fox Point, WI 53217, (414)352-8998; **BUS ADD:** 1234 N Propsect Ave., Milwaukee, WI 53202, (414)276-5385.

OGDEN, Roger Houston——B: June 14, 1946, Denver, CO, *Pres.*, Maurin-Ogden, Inc.; Exec. office; **PRIM RE ACT:** Developer, Owner/Investor, Property Manager; **SERVICES:** Acquisition, devel. & mgmt. of income-producing props.; **REP CLIENTS:** K-Mart, TGY Family Ctrs., Delchamps Foodstore, Kroger Foodstores, K & B Drugs, Eckerd Drugs, Morse Shoe, Inc., Shoe Corp. of Amer., Radio Shack, Hallmark, Piccadilly Cafeteria; **PREV EMPLOY:** Atty. Lemle, Kelleher, Kohlmeyer & Matthews (Corp. litigation); **PROFL AFFIL & HONORS:** Intl. Council of Shopping Ctrs., ULI, LA Assn. of Bus. & Ind., ABA; LA Bar Assn.; **EDUC:** BS, 1968, Bus. Admin., pre-law, LA State Univ., Baton Rouge; **GRAD EDUC:** JD, 1971, Tulane Univ. Sch. of Law; **EDUC HONORS:** Grad. 2nd in class of Bus. Admin, Rotary Intnl. Fellowship for grad study at Univ. of London Sch. of Econ., Phi Kappa Phi, Omicron Delta Kappa, Who's Who, Student Body Pres., Grad. Order of the Coif, Nat. Moot Court, Tulane Law Review; **MIL SERV:** Army, Lt.; **OTHER ACT & HONORS:** Chmn. New Orleans Clean City Comm.; LA Preservation Resource Ctre.; Contemporary Arts. Ctr.; New Orleans Museum of Art; Metro. Area Crime Comm.; Metro. Area Comm.; Friends of the Zoo; Friends of the Cabildo; LA Landmarks Soc.; LA Hist. Soc.; LA State Univ. Varsity Club; LA State Univ. Assn. of Past Student Body Pres.; La State Univ Found. Member; Operations Hq. of Maurin-Ogden located at 1518 Martens Dr., Hammond, LA 70401, (504)542-0372; **HOME ADD:** 460 Broadway St., New Orleans, LA 70118, (504)866-2846; **BUS ADD:** 460 Broadway St., New Orleans, LA 70118, (504)861-8186.

OGLESBY, R. Schaefer——B: Sept. 30, 1940, Lynchburg, VA, *Pres.*, RE Investment Consultants, Inc.; **PRIM RE ACT:** Broker, Owner/Investor, Property Manager, Syndicator; **PREV EMPLOY:** State Dir. Diran Corp., RE Analysis; **PROFL AFFIL & HONORS:** RNMI CCIM Chapter; RESSI VA Chapter, Past Pres. Lynchburg Bd. of Realtors, Pres. VA Chapter RESSI, Dir. VA Assn. of Realtors; **EDUC:** BS, 1962, Bus. Admin., FL State Univ.; **OTHER ACT & HONORS:** Lynchburg C of C, Past Dir. Lynchburg Rotary Club; **HOME ADD:** 2309 Heron Hill Pl., Lynchburg, VA 24503, (804)384-6616; **BUS ADD:** 1401 Lakeside Dr., Lynchburg, VA 24501, (804)528-3333.

OGLETREE, Joyce B.——B: May 20, 1937, Walton Cty, *Pres.*, Number One Realty, Inc.; **PRIM RE ACT:** Broker, Builder; **PROFL AFFIL & HONORS:** Life Time Member Million Dollar Club; CRB; SRI; **EDUC:** MKTG, 1969, Univ. of GA; **OTHER ACT & HONORS:** Amer. Bus. Woman of the Yr.; **HOME ADD:** 1244 Pirkle Rd., Norcross, GA 30093, (404)921-1049; **BUS ADD:** 662 N. Indian Creek Dr., Clarkston, GA 30021, (404)294-7190.

OGOREK, James J.——B: Apr. 24, 1945, Chicago, IL, *VP, Finance and Operations*, Gould Florida, Inc.; **OTHER RE ACT:** Land Devel.; **SERVICES:** Financial Management/Real Estate Development; **PREV EMPLOY:** Ernst & Whinney, Certified Public Accountants; **PROFL AFFIL & HONORS:** FL Inst. of CPA's; IL Inst. of CPA's; AICPA, CPA; **EDUC:** BS, 1967, Acctg., Commerce, Univ. of IL; **EDUC HONORS:** Cum Laude; **MIL SERV:** US Army, Lt., Army Commendation Medal; **OTHER ACT & HONORS:** CPA; Member AICPA Real Estate Committee; **HOME ADD:** 12706 Headwater Circle, Wellington, FL 33411, (305)793-3316; **BUS ADD:** 12230 Forest Hill Blvd., West Palm Beach, FL 33411, (305)793-5100.

OHLIG, Rick——*VP Leasing*, McCormick & Co., Inc.; **PRIM RE ACT:** Property Manager; **BUS ADD:** 11011 McCormick Rd., Hunt Valley, MD 21031, (301)667-7700.*

OHLMAN, James P.——B: Nov. 13, 1938, Grand Rapids, MI, *Pres.*, HMF, Inc.; **PRIM RE ACT:** Broker, Appraiser, Developer, Lender, Owner/Investor, Property Manager; **SERVICES:** Mort. lending, RE asset mgmt., devel., mort. brokerage; **REP CLIENTS:** Lenders, Devels., RE Investors; **PREV EMPLOY:** Travelers Ins. Co., Kassler & Co. Continental Advisors Inc., Pres. Western Portfolio Mgmt., Inc. San Francisco; **PROFL AFFIL & HONORS:** NAHB, Broker, CA; **EDUC:** BBA, 1960, Fin., Econ., Speech, Western MI Univ.; **MIL SERV:** USN, Lt., 1960-1964; **OTHER ACT & HONORS:** Fellowship of Christian Athletes; **HOME ADD:** 107 Kailuana Lp., Kailua, HI 96734, (808)261-7795; **BUS ADD:** 841 Bishop St., Honolulu, HI 96813, (808)526-0611.

OHS, Larry D.——B: Sept.1, 1954, Sioux City, IA, *Atty. at Law*; **PRIM RE ACT:** Attorney, Instructor; **SERVICES:** Legal Advice to purchasers, sellers, lessors, lessees of resid. and comml. props.; **REP CLIENTS:** RE brokers and title cos.; **PREV EMPLOY:** Branch counsel, Security Land Title Co., Legal Counsel , Lincoln Title Agency, Inc.; **PROFL AFFIL & HONORS:** ABA, ABA Sect. on Real Prop., Probate and Trust Law, NE State Bar Assn., NSBA Sect. of Real Prop. and Probate Law, Lincoln Bar Assn., NE Realtors Assn. , Lincoln Bd. of Realtors; **EDUC:** BS, 1976, Philosophy, NE Wesleyan Univ.; **GRAD EDUC:** JD, 1979, Univ. of NE; **EDUC HONORS:** Who's Who Among Students in Amer. Univ. and Coll., Blue Key Natl. Honor Frat., Deans List, Four yr. Tru. Scholarship; **OTHER ACT & HONORS:** Lincoln Jaycees, Lincoln, Lancaster Cty., Genealogy Soc., Attending Univ of NE, MBA Program; **HOME ADD:** 2760 S 37th St., Lincoln, NE 68506, (402)488-9697; **BUS ADD:** 1039 K St., Lincoln, NE 68508, (402)475-1993.

O'KEEFE, William——*Dir. of RE*, General Motors Corp., RE & Prop. Mgmt.; **PRIM RE ACT:** Property Manager; **BUS ADD:** 3304 West Grand Blvd., Detroit, MI 48202, (313)556-2712.*

OKENICA, Kathleen——*Asst. Exec. Dir.*, New Jersey Housing Finance Agency; **PRIM RE ACT:** Developer, Syndicator, Regulator; **OTHER RE ACT:** Construction; **PREV EMPLOY:** Project Mgr., Div. of Housing, NJ Dept. of Community Affairs; **PROFL AFFIL & HONORS:** NJ Bar Assn.; DC Bar Assn.; ABA; **EDUC:** AB, 1971, Govt., Douglass Coll., Rutgers Univ., New Brunswick, NJ; **GRAD EDUC:** JD, 1976, Rutgers Law Sch., Newark, NJ; **EDUC HONORS:** Dean's List; **HOME ADD:** 321 Wood Mill Dr., Cranbury, NJ 08512; **BUS ADD:** 3625 Quakerbridge Rd., Trenton, NJ 08625, (609)890-8900.

OKIN, Edward J.——B: May 14, 1943, Hackensack, NJ, *Dir. Corp. RE*, Carrier Corp. (wholly award Subs. of United Technologies Corp.); **PRIM RE ACT:** Instructor, Consultant, Appraiser, Property Manager; **OTHER RE ACT:** Intl. RE; **SERVICES:** All Lease, Buy, & Build Serv. for Carrier Corp. Worldwide; **PROFL AFFIL & HONORS:** Past Member Bd. of Dir. Nacore; IDRC, Intl. RE Federation (FIABCI), Bd. of Govs. Inst. of Asset Mgmt.; **EDUC:** BA, 1967, Soc. Sci., Shimer Coll., Mt. Carroll, IL; **GRAD EDUC:** NYU RE Inst. - grad. approved, 1976, RE Appraisal; **MIL SERV:** USAR, Spc. 4; **OTHER ACT & HONORS:** Fraternal order of Masons; Former member Prime, Raters Financial Club of NY; **HOME ADD:** 4822 Candy Lane, Manlius, NY 13104, (315)682-6190; **BUS ADD:** PO Box 4800 Currier Tower, Syracuse, NY 13221.

OKIN, Robert——*Exec. VP Oper.*, Faberge, Inc.; **PRIM RE ACT:** Property Manager; **BUS ADD:** 1345 Avenue of the Americas, New York, NY 10019, (212)581-3500.*

OKINGA, Sam——B: Nov. 26, 1926, Honolulu, HI, *Chmn. of the Bd.*, State S & L Assn., Hawaii Div.; **PRIM RE ACT:** Lender; **PREV EMPLOY:** 27 yrs. at State Savings in increasingly important mgmt. positions.; **PROFL AFFIL & HONORS:** Member MBA, Member NACMB, Member US League of Savings Assns., Capital Stock Comm. and Political Liaison Comm.; **EDUC:** BA, 1949, Maj. Bus., Min. Econ., Univ. of HI; **OTHER ACT & HONORS:** Member Pacific Club, Member Plaza Club; **HOME ADD:** 2980 Laukoa PL, Honolulu, HI 96813; **BUS ADD:** 180 So. King St., Honolulu, HI 96813, (808)523-3111.

OKKEMA, Matthew——*Treas.*, Gerber Products Co.; **PRIM RE ACT:** Property Manager; **BUS ADD:** 445 State St., Freemond, MI 49412, (616)928-2000.*

OKREPKIE, Ralph G.——B: Oct. 19, 1925, Newark Valley, NY, *Sr. Consultant*, Okrepkie Associates; **PRIM RE ACT:** Broker, Consultant, Engineer, Appraiser; **OTHER RE ACT:** Feasibility studies; **SERVICES:** Appraise comml./indus. prop., cost approach and mach./equip. depreciation studies, consultant and expert witness; **REP CLIENTS:** Many major firms through U.S.A.; **PREV EMPLOY:** Civil Engr., USAF; Industrial Engr., Sikorsky Aircraft; Avco R&D; IBM; Todd Shipyards; Perkin-Elmer; Remington Electric; **PROFL AFFIL & HONORS:** Amer. Soc. of Appraisers; Intl./Amer. Right of Way Soc.; Fellow, Soc. of Valuers & Auctioneers, London, England, Sr. ASA; Fellow FSVA; Lt. Col., USAF (Ret.); 1979 & 1981, ASA Appreciation Award; ASA NY State Dir., 1978-1982; ASA Sec. NY Chap., 1982; ASA Intl. Bd. of Examiners, 1978-1982; Who's Who in the East, 1979 & 1982; **EDUC:** AA, 1949, Bus. Admin., Fairleigh Dickinson; BS, 1951, Indus. Mgmt./Engrg., Syracuse Univ./Univ. of Bridgeport/Northeastern; **MIL SERV:** USN/USAF; WT 3/c/Lt. Col.; All theaters and Dept. of Defense Meritorious Serv. Medal; **OTHER ACT & HONORS:** Candidate for Mayor, Trumbull 1971; 1978-1981, Pres., AF Assn., NYC; 1978-1982, Commander, Military Order of Foreign Wars of NJ; **HOME ADD:** 93 Canterbury Ln., Trumbull, CT 06611, (203)268-6403; **BUS ADD:** 93 Canterbury Ln., Trumbull, CT 06611, (203)268-6403.

OLAND, Mark——**B:** Oct. 25, 1947, Brooklyn, NY, *Part.*, Schatz & Schatz, Ribicoff & Kotkin; **PRIM RE ACT:** Attorney; **REP CLIENTS:** Hartford Fed. S&L Assoc., T&M Bldg. Co., Inc., Avonridge, Inc., Alan Temkin Assocs., Farmington Woods Master Assoc., Inc., Cromwell Hills Assoc., Lakeridge Assoc., and Lakeridge Tax District & other lenders and instnl. investors in resid., comml. & indus. props; **PROFL AFFIL & HONORS:** Member Exec. Comm., Real Prop. Sect., Condo Cooperatives & Homeowner Assocs. of Sect. of Real Prop. Probate & Trust Law, ABA; **EDUC:** 1969, Hist. & Pol. Sci, Univ. of VT, School of Liberal Arts; **GRAD EDUC:** 1972, Columbia Univ., School of Law; **HOME ADD:** 5 Cadbury Trun, Avon, CT 06001, (203)673-9749; **BUS ADD:** One Fin. Plaza, Hartford, CT 06103, (203)522-3234.

OLDRIDGE, Evelyn——*Ed. - Adv. Dir.*, Stamats Publishing Co., National Roster of Realtors; **PRIM RE ACT:** Real Estate Publisher; **BUS ADD:** 427 6th Ave., S.E., Cedar Rapids, IA 52406, (319)364-6032.*

O'LEARY, Tommie (Mrs.)——**B:** Oct. 12, 1934, El Paso, TX, Bonded Realty, Inc., Better Homes & Gardens; **PRIM RE ACT:** Broker, Instructor, Developer, Builder, Owner/Investor, Insuror; **PROFL AFFIL & HONORS:** NAR, TAR El Paso Bd. of Realtors, RNMI, CRB; **EDUC:** RE/Bus. Law/Theology/Music, TX Tech. Univ., SW Bible Coll.; **HOME ADD:** 4308 Park Hill, El Paso, TX 79912; **BUS ADD:** 7400 Viscount, El Paso, TX 79925, (915)779-7777.

O'LEIGH, Thomas——*Sr. VP*, O'Hare Intl. Bank; **PRIM RE ACT:** Appraiser, Banker, Lender; **SERVICES:** Const. and local permanent morts.; **REP CLIENTS:** N.W. Metropolitan Chicago and Suburban Area; **PROFL AFFIL & HONORS:** SRA; MBA; **EDUC:** Univ. of IL; **GRAD EDUC:** MS, Econ., Grad. School of Banking/Nat. Mort. School; **BUS ADD:** 8501 W. Higgins Rd., Chicago, IL 60631.

OLENICOFF, Igor M.——**B:** Sept. 20, 1943, Russia, *Pres.*, Olen Properties Corp.; **PRIM RE ACT:** Developer, Builder, Owner/Investor, Property Manager; **SERVICES:** Devel., construction & mgmt. of comml . & indust. props.; **REP CLIENTS:** Devel. prop. for own acct., retain ownership & mgmt. primarily in So. CA; **PREV EMPLOY:** VP, Dunn Properties; Sr. Consultant, Touche, Ross & Co.; VP, Motown Records; VP, Gemini Pacific; **EDUC:** BS, 1964, Engrg. & Fin., USC; **GRAD EDUC:** MS & MBA, 1965 & 1966, Quantitative Analysis & Acctg., USC; **BUS ADD:** 17991 Cowan, Irvine, CA 92714, (714)546-5750.

OLESKER, Sara L.——**B:** Oct. 3, 1942, Chicago, IL, *VP, Mktg.*, The Childs/Dreyfus Group, Inc.; **PRIM RE ACT:** Consultant, Instructor; **OTHER RE ACT:** Design Consultant; **SERVICES:** Concept, design & implementation of interior merchandising of apts.; **REP CLIENTS:** Model homes and public areas for the shelter industry; **PROFL AFFIL & HONORS:** Home Builders Assn. of Metropolitan Dallas; Sales and Mktg. Council of Phoenix, Nat. Sales and Mktg. Council; Nat. Assn. of Home Builders; **EDUC:** BFA, 1964, Studio Art/Art Hist./Bus., IN Univ.; **GRAD EDUC:** Post Grad. Work in Grad. School, 1965/1968/1969, Design, Inst. of Design/IL Inst. of Tech.; **OTHER ACT & HONORS:** Pres., Chicago Chamber Music Soc., 1978-1979; Treas., Mother's Aid of Chicago Lying-In Hospital, 1974-1976; **HOME ADD:** 444 W. Webster, Chicago, IL 60614, (312)549-5815; **BUS ADD:** Suite 3700, 919 N. Michigan Ave., Chicago, IL 60611, (312)642-3200.

OLESON, H. James——**B:** May 24, 1934, Lemmon, SD, *Atty.*, Oleson Law Firm; **PRIM RE ACT:** Attorney; **SERVICES:** All servs. that can be furnished by an atty.; **PROFL AFFIL & HONORS:** MT Bar Assn., Lawyers-Pilots Bar Assn., admitted to practice before the US Dist. Ct. of MT and the 9th Cir. Ct. of Appeals in San Francisco; **EDUC:** Civil Engrg., 1956, SD State at Brookings; **MIL SERV:** USN, Lt. j.g.; **OTHER ACT & HONORS:** Cty. Atty., Flathead Cty., MT from 1967-75; **HOME ADD:** 1300 Foys Lake Rd., Kalispell, MT 59901, (406)755-5823; **BUS ADD:** PO Box 1057, Kalispell, MT 59901, (406)755-5063.

OLIVA, Raymond S.——**B:** Aug. 5, 1935, McDonald, Ohio, *VP*, Town & Country Prop. Inc.; **PRIM RE ACT:** Broker, Instructor, Consultant, Real Estate Publisher; **PREV EMPLOY:** GTI, VTD, VTN; **PROFL AFFIL & HONORS:** N VA Bd. of Realtors (Arbitration Comm.), N VA Distributive Educ./Adult Classes in RE, CRB, CRS, GRI; **MIL SERV:** USN, Fire Control Tech. S.N.; **HOME ADD:** 1510 Hardwood Ln., McLean, VA 22101, (703)241-1106; **BUS ADD:** 8313 Arlington Blvd., Fairfax, VA 22031, (703)698-4907.

OLIVER, Hal——**B:** Apr. 9, 1923, Walla Walla, WA, *Pres.*, Homeland Properties, Inc.; **PRIM RE ACT:** Broker, Consultant, Appraiser, Owner/Investor; **SERVICES:** RE Buyer Broker, RE Seller Broker, RE Exchanges (1031), Nat. Comml./Investment Computer Network Rep. (FLI-Datanet); **REP CLIENTS:** Buyers and sellers or exchangers of real property; **PROFL AFFIL & HONORS:** NAR; FLI; Nat. Assn. of RE Appraisers; Intl. Exchangers Assn.; **EDUC:** Mech. Engr., WA State Univ.; **MIL SERV:** USAF, 1st Lt., Combat Medals; **OTHER ACT & HONORS:** Cty. Civil Serv. Bd., 8 yrs.; BPOE; Exchange Club; **HOME ADD:** P.O. Box 534, Walla Walla, WA 99362, (509)525-8149; **BUS ADD:** POB 534, Walla Walla, WA 99362, (509)529-3990.

OLIVER, James F., Sr.——**B:** Nov. 9, 1914, Elkhart, IN, *Pres.*, Acme Group of Nevada, Inc.; **PRIM RE ACT:** Broker, Consultant, Developer, Lender, Builder, Owner/Investor, Property Manager, Syndicator; **OTHER RE ACT:** Joint Venturer, Intl. Fin.; **SERVICES:** Complete RE & Investment Services; **PREV EMPLOY:** Owner, The Oliver Agency; Marketing, RE & Public Relations, So. CA, 20 yrs.; **PROFL AFFIL & HONORS:** Las Vegas, NV State & Nat. Bds. of Realtors; RE Securities & Synd. Instit., Realtor; White House Pres. Citations; **EDUC:** AB, 1933, IN; **GRAD EDUC:** 1969, Lumbleau RE School; **MIL SERV:** U.S. Army, Lt., Bronze Star (3), Purple Heart, Combat Inf. Badge, Citations; **OTHER ACT & HONORS:** Member, Bd. of Dir. of Six Corps; Founder, Intl. Fin. Consultants Instit. of NV; U.S. Nat. Solo Flute Champion, 1932; **HOME ADD:** 5640 Rio Vista Rd., Las Vegas, NV 89130, (702)645-3857; **BUS ADD:** 5640 Rio Vista Rd., Las Vegas, NV 89130, (702)645-0135.

OLIVER, Luther E.——**B:** Sept. 21, 1949, St. Louis, MO, *Pres.*, Oliver Realty, Inc.; **PRIM RE ACT:** Consultant, Owner/Investor, Property Manager, Syndicator; **SERVICES:** Investment counseling, valuation, devel. and synd. of props., prop. mgmt.; **PREV EMPLOY:** Lipton Realty, 800 Chestnut, St. Louis, MO; **PROFL AFFIL & HONORS:** IREM; RESSI; NAR; HBA; NASO; SEC; NASO; SEC, CPM, RAM; **EDUC:** BS, 1971, Chemistry, Univ. of MO - St. Louis; **MIL SERV:** US Army; Lt.; **OTHER ACT & HONORS:** Dir., Mark Twain Bank, Harvester; Rgnl. VP, Region 10 of IREM; **HOME ADD:** 1294 White Rd., Chesterfield, MO 63017, (314)469-1730; **BUS ADD:** 760 Office Pkwy., Suite 82, Creve Coeur, MO 63141, (314)576-1610.

OLIVER, William Taylor——**B:** Aug. 11, 1952, Morgantown, WV, *Gen. Mgr.*, The John R. Oliver Co. Inc.; **PRIM RE ACT:** Broker, Developer, Builder; **EDUC:** BA, 1974, Botany, Taylor Univ.; **GRAD EDUC:** SM, 1977, Biol., Ball State Univ.; **EDUC HONORS:** Who's Who in Amer. Colls. & Univs., Cum Laude; **HOME ADD:** RT 5, Box 2, Hagerstown, MD 21740, (301)797-3186; **BUS ADD:** Rt. 5, Box 2, Hagerstown, MD 21740.

OLIVIERI, Henry J., Jr.——**B:** Aug. 1, 1951, Chicago, IL, *Atty. at Law*; **PRIM RE ACT:** Broker, Consultant, Attorney, Appraiser, Banker, Developer, Instructor; **SERVICES:** Contracts, closings, leasing, litigation and condo. conversions; **REP CLIENTS:** Indiv. and investors in gen. RE ownership matters, including litigation; **PREV EMPLOY:** Legal counsel to IL Joint Condo. Study Commn.; **PROFL AFFIL & HONORS:** Chicago Bar Assn., IL State Bar Assn., Dir. of East Side B&T of Chicago; **EDUC:** BS, 1973, RE Fin. & Urban Econ., Univ. of IL at Urbana-Champaign; **GRAD EDUC:** MS, 1974, Fin., Univ. of IL at Urbana-Cbampaign; JD, 1977, St. Louis Univ.; **EDUC HONORS:** Outstanding Sr., Dept. of RE Fin., Outstanding Grad. Scholar, Dept. of RE; **OTHER ACT & HONORS:** Chief Counsel to the Majority Leader of IL Ho. of Rep.; **HOME ADD:** 1524 N Dearborn Pkwy., Chicago, IL 60610, (312)944-6298; **BUS ADD:** 111 W Washington St., Ste 1755, Chicago, IL 60602, (312)781-0008.

OLSEN, Bradley A.——**B:** Nov. 5, 1948, Elgin, IL, *Sr. VP & Mgr.*, Richard Ellis, Inc.; **PRIM RE ACT:** Consultant; **OTHER RE ACT:** RE Investor; **SERVICES:** RE investment counseling to instnl. investors; **REP CLIENTS:** Pension and profit-sharing plans, ins. cos. and maj. corps.; **PREV EMPLOY:** J. Smil Anderson & Son, Inc. (1975-1980); Hopkins & Sutter (1974-1975); **PROFL AFFIL & HONORS:** ABA; IL State Bar Assn., Lic. RE Broker IL; **EDUC:** AB, 1970, Public and Intl. Affairs, Princeton Univ.; **GRAD EDUC:** JD, 1974, Harvard Law School; **EDUC HONORS:** Cum Laude; **HOME ADD:** 427 Lenox, Oak Park, IL 60302, (312)848-6604; **BUS ADD:** Suite 6545, 200 E. Randolph Dr., Chicago, IL 60601, (312)861-1105.

OLSEN, Gary K.——**B:** May 26, 1938, Titusville, PA, *Pres.*, Homestead Properties of Front Royal, Inc.; **PRIM RE ACT:** Broker, Consultant, Appraiser, Owner/Investor, Instructor, Property Manager; **SERVICES:** Gen. brokerage, subdiv. mgmt.; **REP CLIENTS:** 2 dozen prop. owners' assns.; **PROFL AFFIL & HONORS:** Dir., Prop. Owners Assns. of VA; Rotary Intl.; **EDUC:** BS Econ., 1961, Intl., Haverford Coll.; **MIL SERV:** USAF, Maj.; **OTHER ACT & HONORS:** Amer. Legion; **HOME ADD:** 505 S. Royal Ave., Front Royal, VA 22630, (703)635-7158; **BUS ADD:** 505 S. Royal Ave., Front Royal, VA 22630, (703)635-7157.

OLSEN, G.J.——*Prop. & Fac. Admin.*, McDonnell Douglas Co.; **PRIM RE ACT:** Property Manager; **BUS ADD:** PO Box 416, St. Louis, MO 63166, (314)232-0232.*

OLSEN, Raymond S.——*Executive Vice President*, National Apartment Association; **OTHER RE ACT:** Profl. Assn. Admin.; **BUS ADD:** 1825 K St. NW, Ste. 604, Washington, DC 20006, (202)785-5111.*

OLSEN, Richard——*Comptroller*, Towle Manufacturing Co.; **PRIM RE ACT:** Property Manager; **BUS ADD:** 260 Merrimac St., Newburyport, MA 01950, (617)462-7111.*

OLSON, Carl Re.——**B:** Sep. 13, 1947, San Antonio, TX, *Pres.*, Carl Olson, Inc.; **PRIM RE ACT:** Broker, Owner/Investor, Syndicator; **PROFL AFFIL & HONORS:** San Antonio Bd. of Realtors, GRI, CCIM; **EDUC:** BA Bus., 1970, Bus. Fin., Univ. of TX (Austin); **HOME ADD:** 8202 Countryside Dr., San Antonio, TX 78209, (512)824-2577; **BUS ADD:** 1100 NE Loop 410 Suite 650, San Antonio, TX 78209, (512)828-1622.

OLSON, John F.——**B:** Dec. 24, 1939, Santa Monica, CA, *Part.*, Gibson, Dunn & Crutcher; **PRIM RE ACT:** Attorney; **SERVICES:** Gen. legal services; **REP CLIENTS:** Lender and owner-dev. with respect to RE devel.; design, const. and const. mgmt. firms in negotiation of intl. contracts and in intl. claims matters; **PROFL AFFIL & HONORS:** ABA; D.C. Bar; State Bar of CA; Amer. Soc. of Intl. Law; Fed. Bar Assn., Member, ABA Coordinating Group on Regulatory Reform, ABA Real Prop. Probate and Trust Law Sect.; ABA Fed. Securities Law Comm.; ABA Foreign Claims Comm.(V. Chmn) and Intl. Law Section frequent author and lecturer; Comml. Arbitrators Panel; Amer. Arbitrators Assn.; **EDUC:** AB (with highest honors), 1961, Poli. Sci., Univ. of CA, Berkeley; **GRAD EDUC:** LLB, 1964, Harvard Law School; **EDUC HONORS:** Phi Beta Kappa, Order of the Golden Bear, Cum Laude; **HOME ADD:** 3719 Bradley Lane, Chevy Chase, MD 20015; **BUS ADD:** 1776 G St. N.W., Wash., DC 20006, (202)789-8522.

OLSON, Rodger L.——**B:** Oct. 28, 1933, Knox, CO, *Owner*, Olson Apts. & Olson Electric; **PRIM RE ACT:** Developer, Builder, Owner/Investor, Property Manager; **SERVICES:** Gen. contr., prop. mgmt., rental & condos; **REP CLIENTS:** Lois M. Olson & Family; **PREV EMPLOY:** Ins. adjustor, 1955-66; Electrician, 1951-53; US Army, 1953-55; Self employed 1966-81; **MIL SERV:** USA, Sgt., Korean, CIC; **OTHER ACT & HONORS:** Fire Dist. Tr., Ambulance Tr., Mayor, Lions Pres., Church Lay Leader, PTA Pres. (1962-72); **HOME ADD:** 521 Mathew St., Box A, Oneida, IL 61467, (309)493-3612; **BUS ADD:** Contr. & Devel., Box 4, Oneida, IL 61457, (309)483-3612.

OLSON, Victor D.——**B:** Nov. 1, 1924, Des Moines, IA, *Pres.*, Vic Olson Realty Investment Inc.; **PRIM RE ACT:** Broker; **SERVICES:** Synd., sale/lease backs, investment counseling, investment prop.; **REP CLIENTS:** Indiv. or instl. investors, income prop.; **PREV EMPLOY:** VP, C. Brewer, RE Companies; **PROFL AFFIL & HONORS:** NAR; RNMI; HI Assn. of Realtors; Honolulu Bd. of Realtors, GRI; CCIM; **EDUC:** The Citadel, Charleston, SC; San Diego State Coll.; Univ. of HI; **MIL SERV:** USN, Lt.j.g., Aviator; **HOME ADD:** 1407 Pueo St., Honolulu, HI 96816, (808)737-5668; **BUS ADD:** 700 Bishop St., Suite 1900, Honolulu, HI 96813, (808)521-8711.

O'MALLEY, Robert Eugene——**B:** Feb. 27, 1940, Chicago, IL, *Owner*, R.E. O'Malley Assoc.; **PRIM RE ACT:** Broker, Consultant, Developer, Builder, Instructor, Property Manager, Syndicator; **OTHER RE ACT:** CPA; **SERVICES:** Fin. planning, investment counseling; **REP CLIENTS:** Indiv., corporate & instnl. investors; **PREV EMPLOY:** Price Waterhouse & Co., 1967-69, Sr. Tax Advisor; **PROFL AFFIL & HONORS:** AICPA, IL Soc. of CPA's, NASD, Reg. Rep.; **EDUC:** BBA, 1962, Acctg., fin., Loyola Univ., Chicago; **GRAD EDUC:** CPA, 1969; **OTHER ACT & HONORS:** Var. religious & charitable orgs., Blackhawk Area Council of Boy Scouts; **HOME ADD:** 1312 Old Dominion Rd., Naperville, IL 60540; **BUS ADD:** 710 E Ogden Ave., Naperville, IL 60540, (312)369-6511.

OMAN, Roy Erik——**B:** Sept. 17, 1938, Englewood, NJ, *Special Asst. to VP for Mort. Programs*, Fed. Natl. Mortg. Assn. (FNMA), Mort. Programs; **PRIM RE ACT:** Attorney, Real Estate Publisher; **PREV EMPLOY:** Counsel, Foreign Claims Settlement Commn. U.S.; Sr. Counsel, Fed. Natl. Mort. Assn. (9 yrs.); **PROFL AFFIL & HONORS:** DC Bar; WV Bar, Tax Ct.; Claims; Military Apprais.; Fed. Bar; CAI; **EDUC:** BA, 1960, Pol. Sci., WV Univ.; **GRAD EDUC:** LLB, 1963, WV Univ., Coll. of Law; **HOME ADD:** 1800 R St. N.W., Washington, DC 20009; **BUS ADD:** 3900 WI Ave., N.W., Washington, DC 20016, (202)537-7408.

O'NEAL, Patricia Conyers——**B:** Apr. 24, 1955, Chicago, IL, *Land Trust Officer*, Sears Bank and Trust Co., Trust Div.; **PRIM RE ACT:** Banker; **SERVICES:** Land Trust Serv.; **REP CLIENTS:** Indiv. and comml. prop. investors; **PROFL AFFIL & HONORS:** IL Land Trust Council, RE Sales Lic.; **EDUC:** BBA, 1976, Mktg., Chicago State Univ.; **EDUC HONORS:** Dean's List; **OTHER ACT & HONORS:** Chicago Assn. of Commerce and Ind. Panelist Speaker; **HOME ADD:** 637 E. 84th St., Chicago, IL 60619, (312)994-0604; **BUS ADD:** 233 S. Wacker Dr., Chicago, IL 60606, (312)876-4413.

O'NEIL, Daniel R.——**B:** Aug. 14, 1947, Columbus, OH, *VP*, Century 21 C.R., O'Neil & Co.; **PRIM RE ACT:** Broker, Appraiser, Owner/Investor, Property Manager, Syndicator; **SERVICES:** Complete resid. RE serv.; **REP CLIENTS:** Indus. Nucleonics; Chemical Abstract; OH State Univ.; Battelle Inst.; **PREV EMPLOY:** Tax Agent, State of OH; **PROFL AFFIL & HONORS:** CPM, IREM; **EDUC:** BA, 1970, Bus. Admin., OH Dominican Coll.; **MIL SERV:** OH Army Guard; E-5, Good Conduct; **OTHER ACT & HONORS:** VP, 1981, NE Realtors Assn.; **HOME ADD:** 1736 Alpine Dr., Columbus, OH 43229, (614)890-0555; **BUS ADD:** 3151 N High St., Columbus, OH 43202, (614)261-6767.

O'NEIL, Peggy——*Pers. Mgr.*, Telex Corp.; **PRIM RE ACT:** Property Manager; **BUS ADD:** 6422 E. 41st. St., Tulsa, OK 74135, (918)627-2333.*

O'NEIL, Thomas——*Dir. Corp. Dev.*, Signode Corp.; **PRIM RE ACT:** Property Manager; **BUS ADD:** 3600 W. Lake Ave., Glenview, IL 60025, (312)724-6100.*

O'NEILL, Francis Edward——**B:** Kansas City, MO, *Owner*, O'Neill & Assoc.; **PRIM RE ACT:** Owner/Investor; **EDUC:** AB, 1933, Econ., Rockhurst Coll.; **GRAD EDUC:** MD, 1935-39, Univ. of KS; **MIL SERV:** USA, Major, S. Pac., etc.; **HOME ADD:** 2207 Briarwood, San Antonio, TX 78820, (512)822-5432; **BUS ADD:** 125 Metropolitan Bldg., San Antonio, TX 78820, (512)223-5543.

O'NEILL, Jamie——**B:** June 24, 1926, Okla. City, OK, *Pres.*, Jamie O'Neill, Inc., Realtors; **PRIM RE ACT:** Broker, Instructor, Appraiser, Property Manager; **OTHER RE ACT:** Residential & Comml.; **PROFL AFFIL & HONORS:** NAR, RNMI, Women's Council of Realtors, Omega Tau Rho 1961 - OK City and State of OK Realtor of the Yr. 1961; CRB; GRI; **HOME ADD:** 3710 NW 46th St., Okla. City, OK 73112, (405)943-3668; **BUS ADD:** 4335 N.W. 50th St., OK City, OK 73112, (405)943-3361.

O'NEILL, John J.——*Pres.*, Southgate Development Co; **PRIM RE ACT:** Developer; **BUS ADD:** Southgate Shopping Ctr., Newark, OH 43055, (614)522-2151.*

O'NEILL, John T.——**B:** May 3, 1924, IL, *Exec. VP*, Apt. and Office Bldg. Assn. of Metro Wash. DC; **PRIM RE ACT:** Regulator, Consultant, Property Manager, Owner/Investor; **OTHER RE ACT:** Trade Assn. Exec., Writer, Lecturer, Lobbyist; **SERVICES:** Lobbyist, Educator, Speaker, Editor; **REP CLIENTS:** Apt. and Office Bldg. Owners, Developers, Agents and Prop. Mgrs.; **EDUC:** BA, 1950, Bus., RE, Univ. of CA; **MIL SERV:** USMC, Cpl., WWII; **BUS ADD:** 1511 K. St. NW, Washington, DC 20005, (202)293-3995.

O'NEILL, Thomas E.——**B:** Dec. 6, 1916, Nashua, NH, *Atty.*, Clancy & O'Neill, P.A.; **PRIM RE ACT:** Attorney; **SERVICES:** Conveyancing, title examination, title insurance; **EDUC:** BS, 1939, Holy Cross Coll.; **GRAD EDUC:** LLB, 1948, Boston Univ. Law School; **MIL SERV:** US Army, Capt.; **HOME ADD:** 34 Raymond St., Nashua, NH 03060, (603)883-5915; **BUS ADD:** 53 E. Pearl St., Nashua, NH 03060, (603)883-3379.

O'NEILL, Timothy J.——**B:** Mar. 13, 1944, Detroit, MI, *Pres.*, O'Neill Developments, Inc.; **PRIM RE ACT:** Developer, Builder, Owner/Investor, Property Manager; **SERVICES:** Devel. of offices, shopping centers, and warehouses; **EDUC:** BBA, 1966, Org./Mgmt., Univ. of Notre Dame; **GRAD EDUC:** MBA, 1967, Fin., Univ. of NC; **EDUC HONORS:** Cum Laude; **HOME ADD:** 4161 Thunderbird Dr., Marietta, GA 30067; **BUS ADD:** Suite 101, 1400 Marietta Pkwy., Marietta, GA 30067, (404)422-4281.

OPAS, David M, Sr.——**B:** Nov. 22, 1929, Chicago, IL, *CEO*, Loomis Savings & Loan Assn.; **PRIM RE ACT:** Broker, Consultant, Appraiser, Developer, Lender, Builder, Insuror; **PREV EMPLOY:** 21

yrs. at Loomis Savings; **PROFL AFFIL & HONORS:** S/W RE Bd., S/W Suburban Builders Assn., US Savings & Loan League, IL S&L League, Chicago Area Council of S&L (Dir.), Past Pres. of S&L League, IFA, CRA, Sr. Loan Underwriter; **GRAD EDUC:** DePaul Univ. (2yrs.), Grad. S&L Exec. School; **MIL SERV:** USN, 1948-1952, 1st Class PO, Korean Camp, Unit Commendations; **OTHER ACT & HONORS:** VFW, MOOSE, ELKS; **HOME ADD:** 9125 S. Keeler, Oak Lawn, IL 60453, (312)423-5032; **BUS ADD:** 6350 W. 63rd St., Chicago, IL 60638, (312)586-8600.

OPITZ, Kenneth D.——B: Sept. 3, 1918, La Crosse, WI, *Pres.*, Opitz Realty, Inc.; **PRIM RE ACT:** Broker, Consultant, Appraiser, Developer, Builder, Owner/Investor, Instructor, Property Manager, Syndicator; **PROFL AFFIL & HONORS:** Nat. Assn. of RE Brokers, WI Assn. of RE Brokers, Dir., 1966-69; Gr. Madison Bd. of Realtors, Inc., Pres. 1965, Dir. & VP, 1964; Chmn. MLS, 1969; Chmn. Madison Home Show Comm., 1966; **EDUC:** RE & Fin. Appraisal I & II of AIREA, Univ. of WI, Madison; **GRAD EDUC:** BBA, 1949, Univ. of WI, Madison; MBA, 1949, Univ. of WI, Madison; **MIL SERV:** USA, Lt.; **OTHER ACT & HONORS:** Dir. Madison C of C, Bd. of Review Chmn. Downtown Devel. Comm., Chmn. of 'Design for Tomorrow' Comm., City of Madison Chmn. Working Comm., Equal Opportunits Comm., Dir. Henry Vilas Zoological Soc., State of WI Dept. of Local Affairs and Dev., Gen Exec Facility, Steering Comm.; **HOME ADD:** 202 Ozark Tr., Madison, WI 55703, (608)233-5981; **BUS ADD:** 502 N. Eau Claire Ave., Madison, WI 53705, (608)257-0111.

OPPEGARD, Paul R.——B: Jan. 28, 1924, Wadena, MN, *Attorney (Associate)*, Gunhus, Grinnell, Jeffries, Klinger, Vinje & Swenson; **PRIM RE ACT:** Attorney; **SERVICES:** Legal Services-Sales of Real Prop.; **REP CLIENTS:** Twin Valley State Bank, Clay Cty. State Bank, Amer. State Bank of Erskine; **PROFL AFFIL & HONORS:** MN State Bar Assn.; **EDUC:** BA, 1976, Poli. Sci., Hist., Bus. Admin., Concordia Coll., Moorhead, MN; **GRAD EDUC:** JD, 1980, Tax and Corps., Wm. Mitchell Coll. of Law; **EDUC HONORS:** Summa Cum Laude; **OTHER ACT & HONORS:** Jaycees; **HOME ADD:** 3254 16th Ave. S., Fargo, ND 58105, (701)232-4997; **BUS ADD:** 512 Center Ave., Moorhead, MN 56560, (218)236-6462.

OPPENHEIMER, Arthur F.——B: May 27, 1946, Boise, ID, *Pres.*, Oppenheimer Devel. Corp.; **PRIM RE ACT:** Developer; **SERVICES:** All devel. serv.; **EDUC:** Hist., 1967-68, Univ. of ID; Sorbonne Univ. of Paris, Paris, France; **GRAD EDUC:** MBA, 1972, Gen. Corp. Mgmt with emphasis on fin. mgmt., Harvard Grad. Sch. of Bus. Admin.; **MIL SERV:** US Army, M-4; **OTHER ACT & HONORS:** Boise Public Library Bd. Chmn. 73-74, 1980-81; Harvard Club. of NY; Arid Club of Boise; Beta Theta Pi; Alpha Kappa Psi; Young Pres. Org.; 'Outstanding Young Man of the Year Boise' & 'Outstanding Young Man of the Year, ID; **HOME ADD:** 1009 Warm Springs Ave., Boise, ID 83702, (208)345-3213; **BUS ADD:** 999 Main St., Dr. O, Boise, ID 83702, (208)343-4883.

OPPER, Ralph E.——B: June 19, 1934, Grand Rapids, MI, *Pres.*, OMNI Real Estate, Inc.; **PRIM RE ACT:** Broker, Appraiser, Owner/Investor; **SERVICES:** Investment, Resid. (MLS), Relo. Services, Marketing, Appraising & Closing Transactions; **REP CLIENTS:** Indiv. & group investors, Corp. & small bus. investing & relocating, Families in resid. sales; **PREV EMPLOY:** RE Business since 1962, self-employed since 1969 in RE; **PROFL AFFIL & HONORS:** MAR, Greater Lansing Bd. of Realtors, Nat. Realty Relocation Assoc., NAR, NIREB, REALTOR, GRI, RAM, CCIM, Pres. Million Dollar Club; **GRAD EDUC:** Certificate, 1969, RE, Univ. of MI, Ann Arbor; **MIL SERV:** Army, Pvt. 1/c, Honor Student; **OTHER ACT & HONORS:** East Lansing Trinity Church, Greater Lansing Youth for Christ; **HOME ADD:** 2711 Libbie Dr., Lansing, MI 48917, (517)322-0777; **BUS ADD:** 500 N. Homer St., Lansing, MI 48912, (517)351-3500.

ORBE, Felix A.——B: Dec. 12, 1946, Brooklyn, NY, *Mgr.*, Metropolitan Life Ins. Co., RE Investments; **PRIM RE ACT:** Owner/Investor; **SERVICES:** Investment in comml. RE; **PROFL AFFIL & HONORS:** NAIOP; ICSS; Greater Boston Bd. of Realtors; **EDUC:** CCNY, 1968, Econ., Baruch Sch. of Bus. Admin., Dist. Mil. Grad.; **GRAD EDUC:** 1975, Corp. Fin., NYU, Grad. Bus. Sch.; **MIL SERV:** Special Forces, Capt.; Bronze Star with V Device, Sr. Paracbutist, Ranger, Air Medal; **HOME ADD:** 10 Penni Ln., Andover, MA 01810, (617)681-0502; **BUS ADD:** 300 Unicorn Park Dr., Woburn, MA 01801, (617)938-0160.

ORDWAY, Philip E.——B: Jan. 13, 1948, Battle Creek, MI, *Pres.*, Ordway Development Company, Inc.; **PRIM RE ACT:** Broker, Consultant, Developer; **SERVICES:** Full devel. mgmt. serv. for out of town owners; **PREV EMPLOY:** VP RE Devel. for Beaver Creek (new destination ski resort near Vail); VP Hilton Head Plantation Co., Hilton Head Isl., SC; **PROFL AFFIL & HONORS:** Recreation Devel. Council, ULI, Reg. Broker, State of CO; **EDUC:** AB, 1971, Econ., Harvard Univ.; **GRAD EDUC:** MBA, 1973, Mktg. & fin., Harvard Bus. Sch.; **EDUC HONORS:** Cum Laude; **HOME ADD:** PO Box 1881, Vail, CO 81658; **BUS ADD:** PO Box 1881, Vail, CO 81658, (303)926-3550.

O'REARDON, Francis——*Corp. Secy.*, Conrac Corp.; **PRIM RE ACT:** Property Manager; **BUS ADD:** Three Landmark Sq., Stamford, CT 06901, (203)348-2100.*

O'REILLY, Mel Brian——B: Aug. 5, 1947, New York, NY, *Atty., Pres.*, O'Reilly & Huckstep P.C.; **PRIM RE ACT:** Attorney, Developer, Owner/Investor; **REP CLIENTS:** Navajo Ctr.; Sierra Devel. & Co.; Revel, Inc.; **PROFL AFFIL & HONORS:** State Bar, NM; Lincoln City Bar Assn.; ABA; **EDUC:** BA, 1968, Pol. Sci., Gabriel Richard Inst.; **GRAD EDUC:** JD, 1971, Univ. of NM; **EDUC HONORS:** Who's Who in Amer. Coll. & Univ.; **OTHER ACT & HONORS:** Dir., Security Bank, Ruidoso; C of C; Sertoma - Soccer Assn., Dir.; **HOME ADD:** Box 2295, Ruidoso, NM 88345, (505)257-7614; **BUS ADD:** Box 2295, Ruidoso, NM 88345, (505)257-5035.

ORENDORFF, James M.——B: Oct. 24, 1938, Monterey Park, CA, *Lawyer*; **PRIM RE ACT:** Attorney; **SERVICES:** Lawyer for gen. bus. & corp., RE fin. & urban devel. matters; **PREV EMPLOY:** G.C., The Colwell Co., 1972-1975; G.C., Western Mort. Corp., 1975-1979; **PROFL AFFIL & HONORS:** CA Bar Assn.; L.A. Cty. Bar Assn.; ABA; **EDUC:** BS, 1960, Bus. Admin., Fresno State Coll.; **GRAD EDUC:** JD, 1963, Law, Boalt Hall, Univ. of CA; **EDUC HONORS:** Dean's List, Blue Key, High Honors; **MIL SERV:** USNR, Lt. Com.; **HOME TEL:** (213)799-7427; **BUS ADD:** 3600 Wilshire Blvd. - 1902, Los Angeles, CA 90010, (213)386-4251.

ORENSTEIN, Paul I.——B: Dec. 20, 1943, Toronto, Can., *Pres.*, Financial Placements Ltd.; **PRIM RE ACT:** Broker, Banker, Lender, Owner/Investor, Property Manager, Syndicator; **SERVICES:** Mort. bankers; **REP CLIENTS:** RE Devel. requiring interim & permanent fin.; **PROFL AFFIL & HONORS:** Ont. Mort. Brokers Assn., Can. Inst. of Chartered Accountants; **EDUC:** B. Commerce, 1966, Econ. & Acctg., Univ. of Toronto; **GRAD EDUC:** MBA, 1971, Fin., Wharton Grad. Sch. of Bus., Univ. of PA; **EDUC HONORS:** Director's List.; **OTHER ACT & HONORS:** Honor's List, Can. Inst. of Chartered Accountants Final Exams.; **HOME ADD:** 3 Sydnor Rd., Willowdale, M2M2Z9, Ont, (416)226-4721; **BUS ADD:** 80 Richmond St., W, Suite 1905, Toronto, M5H2A4, Ont., Can., (416)366-2795.

ORGAIN, E. Stewart, Jr.——B: Feb. 19, 1942, Durham, NC, *VP, Sales Mgr.*, Allenton Realty and Ins. Co.; **PRIM RE ACT:** Broker, Consultant, Appraiser, Developer, Property Manager, Insuror, Syndicator; **PROFL AFFIL & HONORS:** Durham Bd. of Realtors, NC Assn. of Realtors, NAR, Sales and Mktg. of Durham, GRI, CRB; **EDUC:** BA, 1965, Hist., Univ. of NC; **HOME ADD:** 3304 Devon Rd., Durham, NC 27707, (919)489-4886; **BUS ADD:** 119 Orange St., P.O. Box 731, Durham, NC 27702, (919)683-1410.

ORLANDO, Rocco A.——B: Feb. 4, 1925, Erie, PA, *Realtor-Broker-Owner*, R.A. Orlando, Realtor; **PRIM RE ACT:** Broker, Appraiser, Developer, Owner/Investor, Syndicator; **OTHER RE ACT:** Complete RE Serv.; **PROFL AFFIL & HONORS:** Greater Erie Bd. of Realtors, PA Assn. of Realtors; NAR; Member of Nat. Assn. of RE Appraisers; Member, Intl. Coll. of RE Consulting Profls.; **MIL SERV:** USMC, 1943-1946, Sgt.; **HOME ADD:** 3220 Auburn St., Erie, PA 16508, (814)864-4578; **BUS ADD:** 700 Peach St., Erie, PA 16501, (814)455-7535.

ORLEANS, Marvin——B: June 1, 1919, Philadelphia, PA, *Chmn. of the Bd.*, FPA Corp.; **PRIM RE ACT:** Architect, Developer, Builder, Owner/Investor, Property Manager; **PROFL AFFIL & HONORS:** World Bus. Council, Chief Execs. Forum; **GRAD EDUC:** Drexel Univ.; **MIL SERV:** USAF, Capt.; DFC, Air Medal w/5 OLC; **OTHER ACT & HONORS:** 1973 Top Mgmt. Award presented by Sales and Mktg. Execus. of Broward Cty. (FL); 1979 Man of the Yr. by RE Sales Dirs. of FL; **BUS ADD:** 2507 Philmont Ave., Huntingdon Valley, PA 19006, (215)676-2400.

ORLOFF, Allen D.——B: Dec. 27, 1917, New York, NY, *Pres.*, ADO Associates, Inc.; **PRIM RE ACT:** Broker, Appraiser, Lender, Owner/Investor, Property Manager; **SERVICES:** Consulting, appraising, lender; **REP CLIENTS:** Brown-Forman, Inc.; Reputlic Nat. Bank of Dallas; **PROFL AFFIL & HONORS:** AIREA; IREM; ASA, MAI, CPM, ASA, GRI; **EDUC:** BBA, 1948, Acctg., City Coll. of NY; **HOME ADD:** 1936 So. Ocean Dr., Hallandale, FL 33009, (305)457-7593; **BUS ADD:** 1936 So. Ocean Dr., Hallandale, FL 33009, (305)457-7593.

ORMSBY, Michael C.——**B:** Jan. 6, 1957, Spokane, WA, *Atty.*, Lukins, Annis, Shine, McKay, Van Marter & Rein, P.S.; **PRIM RE ACT:** Attorney; **EDUC:** BA, 1979, Poli. Sci., Personnel Mgmt. & Acctg.-minor, Gonzaga Univ.; **GRAD EDUC:** JD, 1981, Gonzaga Univ.; **EDUC HONORS:** Magna Cum Laude; **OTHER ACT & HONORS:** Spokane School Dist. Bd. of Dir. 1975-Pres.; Spokane City Planning Com.; **HOME ADD:** E. 404 Augusta, Spokane, WA 99207, (509)326-4865; **BUS ADD:** 1600 Washington Trust Fin. Ctr., Spokane, WA 99204, (509)455-9555.

ORPUT, Alden——**B:** 1931, Rockford, IL, *Pres.*, Steele Development Orput Corp.; **PRIM RE ACT:** Architect, Developer, Builder, Owner/Investor, Property Manager, Syndicator; **SERVICES:** Design, prop. mgmt., land mgmt.; **REP CLIENTS:** Devel. analysis, const. mgmt. for indus., shopping ctrs., condo.; subsidized housing, office bldgs.; **PROFL AFFIL & HONORS:** AIA; Intl. Council of Shopping Ctrs.; ULI, Design Awards, AIA, No. IL Chap. Special Design Citations, Amer. Assn. School Admin.; **EDUC:** B.Arch., 1955, Arch./Engrg., Univ. of IL; **GRAD EDUC:** 1981, Smaller Co. Mgmt. Program, Harvard Bus. Sch.; **EDUC HONORS:** Univ. Honors, Gargoyle, Tau Beta Phi; **MIL SERV:** Corps of Engrs., 1st Lt.; **OTHER ACT & HONORS:** Rockford Park Dist., VP & Sec.; AIA, No. IL Chap.; Pres., IL Council, AIA, VP & Sec.; Union League Club; Council on For. Relations; **HOME ADD:** 295 E. Vine Ave., Lake Forest, IL 60045; **BUS ADD:** 1639 N. Alpine Rd., Rockford, IL 61107, (815)226-7122.

ORR, Marj——**B:** Dec. 4, 1921, Childress, TX, *CRB*, Orr R.E.; **PRIM RE ACT:** Broker, Appraiser, Property Manager, Owner/Investor; **PROFL AFFIL & HONORS:** RNMI, NAR, Local Bd. of Realtors; Dir. Kingsville C of C, V.P. OF the Kingsville Bd. of Realtors; CRB; **EDUC:** Bus. Coll in San Diego, CA/Courses at A&I-TX; **OTHER ACT & HONORS:** Tr. for the First Methodist Church, Kingsville, TX; Kingsville Bd. of Realtors--First Woman Pres. 1969; First woman C of C Chrmn.- 1980; **HOME ADD:** 421 E. King, Kingsville, TX 78363, (512)592-9311; **BUS ADD:** 421 E. King, Kingsville, TX 78363, (512)592-9311.

ORTEGA, Manuel E.——**B:** Jan. 4, 1948, Torrion, Mexico, *Pres.*, Omega Phi Props. & MO Investments Inc.; **PRIM RE ACT:** Consultant, Engineer, Architect, Developer, Builder, Owner/Investor, Property Manager, Syndicator; **SERVICES:** RE investments, devel., const. & mgmt.; **REP CLIENTS:** Private investors; **PREV EMPLOY:** US Dept. of the Army, Engrg. Dept.; **PROFL AFFIL & HONORS:** Amer. Soc. of Civil Engrs.; **EDUC:** BS, 1971, Civil Engrg., Univ. of TX at El Paso; **HOME ADD:** 6713 Morningside Cir., El Paso, TX 79904, (915)562-6713; **BUS ADD:** 914 Octavia St., El Paso, TX 79902, (915)532-6663.

ORWICK, Kenneth J.——**B:** Nov. 4, 1940, Twin Falls, ID, *Sr. VP*, Securities-Intermountain, Inc., Comml. Loan div., Mgr.; **PRIM RE ACT:** Banker, Lender; **SERVICES:** Const., mort. banker for take-outs, J.V.'s, equities; **PROFL AFFIL & HONORS:** Mort. Bankers Assn., Intl. Council of Shopping Ctrs.; **EDUC:** BA, 1970, Pre-Law, Poli. Sci., Portland State Univ.; **MIL SERV:** US Army, Spec. 4, 1959-62; **HOME ADD:** 12511 NE Siskiyou, Portland, OR 97230, (503)255-6949; **BUS ADD:** 1336 E. Burnside, Portland, OR 97214, (503)231-3429.

ORWOLL, Kimball G.——**B:** July 20, 1954, Minneapolis, MN, *Assoc.*, Petersen & Stepehnson; **PRIM RE ACT:** Attorney; **SERVICES:** All forms of legal representation; **PROFL AFFIL & HONORS:** ABA, MN Bar Assn., Olmsted Cty. Bar Assn., Amer. Judicature Soc.; **EDUC:** BA, 1976, Poli. Sci., St. Olaf Coll., Northfield, MN; **GRAD EDUC:** JD, 1980, Hamline Univ. Sch. of Law, St., Paul, MN; **EDUC HONORS:** Deans List; **HOME TEL:** (507)288-8808; **BUS ADD:** 108 7th Ave. SW, Rochester, MN 55901, (507)285-1216.

OSBORN, Frank K.——*Pres.*, Osborn-Miller Appraisers, Inc.; **PRIM RE ACT:** Consultant, Appraiser; **SERVICES:** RE Appraisers & consulting; **PREV EMPLOY:** Mort. & Investment Dept., Prudential Ins. Co., 1947-58; **PROFL AFFIL & HONORS:** AIREA, MAI; **EDUC:** BBA, Bus. Admin, Univ. of FL; **MIL SERV:** USA, 1942-45, Capt., Air Medal; **OTHER ACT & HONORS:** Tax Assessor, Duval Cty, FL., 1960-62; **HOME ADD:** 2101 Sweet Briar Ln., Jacksonville, FL 32217, (904)737-2047; **BUS ADD:** 131 E Bay St., Jacksonville, FL 32202, (904)355-7531.

OSBORN, John S., Jr.——**B:** Jan. 14, 1926, Louisville, KY, *Partner*, Wyatt, Tarrant & Combs; **PRIM RE ACT:** Attorney; **SERVICES:** Atty. for lenders, investors, devels.; **REP CLIENTS:** The Equitable Life Assurance Soc. of the U.S.; Aetna Life Ins. Co.; Baldwin United Mort. Co.; Commonwealth Land Title Ins. Co.; **PREV EMPLOY:** Formerly, Exec. VP and Gen. Counsel of Louisville Title Ins. Co. 1954-1972; **PROFL AFFIL & HONORS:** KY Bar Assn.; Louisville Bar Assn.; ABA; Amer. Land Title Assn/, Fellow, Amer. Bar Found.; **GRAD EDUC:** LLB, 1949, Univ. of Louisville School of Law; **MIL SERV:** US Army, Capt. 1952-1954; **OTHER ACT & HONORS:** Rotary Club; **HOME ADD:** 815 Circle Hill Rd., Louisville, KY 40207, (502)896-9828; **BUS ADD:** 28th Floor, Citizons Plaza, Louisville, KY 40202, (502)589-5235.

OSBORNE, Earl——**B:** Mar. 29, 1933, Casa Grande, AZ, *RE Assoc.*, United Realty, Comml. & Investment; **PRIM RE ACT:** Consultant, Developer, Builder, Owner/Investor, Instructor, Property Manager; **SERVICES:** Mobile home park analysis spec.; **PREV EMPLOY:** Electronic Realty Assoc.; **PROFL AFFIL & HONORS:** NAR, MLS; **EDUC:** BS, 1955, Bus., Investments; **GRAD EDUC:** MA, 1960, Physics & Math., AZ State Univ.; **OTHER ACT & HONORS:** AZ Sci. Teachers Assn. Pres.; Pres. Educ. Assn., RE VP; **HOME ADD:** 1144 N. Walnut Dr., Casa Grande, AZ 85222; **BUS ADD:** 118E Florence Blve., Casa Grande, AZ 83222, (602)836-7758.

OSBORNE, Gerold F.——**B:** Dec. 24, 1932, Falls City, NE, *Project Dir.*, Pershing Square Redevel. Corp.; **PRIM RE ACT:** Broker, Developer, Property Manager; **OTHER RE ACT:** VP Trizec Western Inc.; **SERVICES:** Office & Retail space; **PROFL AFFIL & HONORS:** RE Bd. of KS City, MO, Broker; **EDUC:** BS, 1959, Univ. of KS; **EDUC HONORS:** Physics Honor Soc.; **MIL SERV:** USN, S02; **HOME ADD:** 2100 E. 125th St., Kansas City, MO 64146, (816)942-2261; **BUS ADD:** 2301 Main St., Suite 670, Kansas City, MO 64108, (816)474-4575.

OSBORNE, Larry W.——**B:** May 11, 1939, San Pedro, CA, *Pres.*, Osborne Real Estate Inc.; **PRIM RE ACT:** Broker, Consultant; **PROFL AFFIL & HONORS:** CRS; GRI; **EDUC:** BA, 1961, Math., San Jose State Univ.; **OTHER ACT & HONORS:** Bd. of Dirs., Founders Title Grp.; Trustee, Valley Memorial Hospital; **HOME ADD:** 1159 Kottinger Dr., Pleasanton, CA 94566, (415)846-7368; **BUS ADD:** 699 Peters Ave., Suite A, Pleasanton, CA 94566, (415)462-6880.

OSGOOD, Warren D.——**B:** July 22, 1947, Montebello, CA, *Broker*, Osgood Realty; **PRIM RE ACT:** Broker, Consultant, Owner/Investor; **PREV EMPLOY:** 4 Yrs. Sales Mgr. Golden West Realty, 5 Yrs. Midwest Realty; **PROFL AFFIL & HONORS:** 3 Yrs. Million Dollar Club, Salesman of the Yr. Finalist, CRB, CRS, GRI; **MIL SERV:** USA, Sgt.E5; **OTHER ACT & HONORS:** UT Orchid Soc., SPEBSQSA; **HOME ADD:** 5998 Burrell St., Salt Lake City, UT 84118, (801)966-3316; **BUS ADD:** 241 E. 3900 South, Salt Lake City, UT 84107, (801)262-8800.

OSHINS, Harvey B.——**B:** July 4, 1939, New York, NY, *Exec. VP*, National Realty & Development Corp.; **PRIM RE ACT:** Attorney, Developer, Owner/Investor, Property Manager; **PROFL AFFIL & HONORS:** ABA, NY St. Bar Assn.; Intl. Council of Shopping Ctrs.; Nat. Assn. of Indus. and Office Parks; **EDUC:** AB, 1961, Econ., Syracuse Univ.; **GRAD EDUC:** JD, 1963, NY Univ. School of Law; **MIL SERV:** US Army National Guard; **BUS ADD:** 80 Field Point Rd., Greenwich, CT 06830, (203)622-0220.

OSINSKI, Henry J.——**B:** Sept. 9, 1911, Buffalo, NY, *Pres.*, Henry J. Osinski & Assoc., Inc.; **PRIM RE ACT:** Broker, Consultant, Banker, Syndicator; **SERVICES:** Bus. & Fin. Consulting; **PREV EMPLOY:** VP, Manufacturers and Traders Trust Co.; **EDUC:** BS, 1935, Social and Community Affairs, Banking, RE Invest., Canisius Coll, Fordham Univ., Univ. of Buffalo, Amer. Inst. of Banking, Bryant & Stratton Coll.; **GRAD EDUC:** Dr. of Human Letters; **EDUC HONORS:** Hon. Degree Danisus Coll., Knight of St. Gregory, Pope Paul VI, Pi Gamma (Honor Frat.); **MIL SERV:** Conf., Christian and Jews; **OTHER ACT & HONORS:** Who's Who in East, Catholic Who's Who, Who's Who Leading Bus. In Amer.; Amer. Bankers Assn.; **HOME ADD:** 175 Parkside, Buffalo, NY 14214; **BUS ADD:** 175 Parkside Ave., Buffalo, NY 14214.

OSIO, Salvatore P.——**B:** Feb. 22, 1938, Los Angeles, CA, *Chmn. of Bd.*, City Investors, Inc.; **PRIM RE ACT:** Developer, **OTHER RE ACT:** Const. & Fin.; **SERVICES:** Joint venture mgmt.; **REP CLIENTS:** Instnl. Investors; **PROFL AFFIL & HONORS:** CA State Bar; **EDUC:** BS, 1959, Fin., Univ. of So.CA; **GRAD EDUC:** JD, LLB, 1962, Law, USC; **MIL SERV:** USAF; **OTHER ACT & HONORS:** Exec. Office, 853 Camino del Mar, Del Mar, CA, 92014; **HOME ADD:** PO Box 2486, Rancho Santa Fe, CA 92067, (714)756-3724; **BUS ADD:** 1700 Ocean Ave., Santa Monica, CA 90401, (714)481-1141.

OSMAN, David L.——*Asst. VP*, University Properties Corp.; **PRIM RE ACT:** Developer; **BUS ADD:** 666 E. Ocean Blvd., Long Beach, CA 90802, (213)432-7423.*

OSMYCKI, Daniel A.——B: Nov. 26, 1931, Detroit, MI, *Owner/Broker*, Daniel A. Osmycki, Realtor; **PRIM RE ACT:** Broker, Consultant, Appraiser; **OTHER RE ACT:** RE securities agent; **SERVICES:** Buy, sell, lease, appraise, comml. RE exclusively; sell synd. interest; **REP CLIENTS:** Local and nat.; **PREV EMPLOY:** Self employed since 1961 as owner/broker, mort. broker/banker; mort. investment co., RE investment co.; **PROFL AFFIL & HONORS:** Macomb Cty. Bd. of Realtors, MI Assn. of Realtors; RE Securities & Synd. Inst.; Nat. Assn. of Realtors; Amer. Assn. of Cert. Appraisers; Intl. Inst. of Valuers; GRI; RAM; CA-S; SCV; **EDUC:** BCS, 1954, Acctg., Detroit Bus. Univ.; BBA, 1973, Acctg., Detroit Inst. of Tech.; **MIL SERV:** USN, YN2, 1948-1952; **OTHER ACT & HONORS:** Former Commodore & Current Dir., Clinton River Boat Club; Founder of the Ctr. for Intl. Security Studies of the Amer. Security Council Educ. Found.; Former Flotilla V Comdr., US Coast Guard Auxiliary; Prior candidate for "Who's Who of Michigan Businessmen"; **HOME ADD:** 1228 Burlington Dr., Mt. Clemens, MI 48043, (313)465-0904; **BUS ADD:** 9 S. Gratiot, Suite 108, Mt. Clemens, MI 48043, (313)469-2252.

OSNOS, David M.——B: Jan. 10, 1932, Detroit, MI, *Sr. Part.*, Arent, Fox, Kintner, Plotkin & Kahn; **PRIM RE ACT:** Attorney; **SERVICES:** Legal serv. covering all aspects of RE transactions; **REP CLIENTS:** Dev., contractors, lenders, synd., investors, prop. mgrs., leasing agents; **EDUC:** BAWy1953, Eng. Lit., Harvard Univ.; **GRAD EDUC:** JD, 1956, Fed. Tax., Harvard Law School, Cum Laude; **EDUC HONORS:** Summa cum Laude; **HOME ADD:** 6606 Rivercrest Ct., Bethesda, MD 20816, (301)229-0372; **BUS ADD:** 1815 H St., NW, Washington, DC 20006, (202)857-6150.

OSSIG, Hanns——B: Oct. 2, 1930, Breslau, Germany, *VP Prop. Mgr.*, Valley Fed. S&L Assn., Prop. Mgmt. Dept.; **PRIM RE ACT:** Property Manager; **SERVICES:** Mgmt. of all physical facilities, liaison between Valley Fed. Savings Exec. Mgmt. and architects, engineers, devel., brokers, etc.; **PREV EMPLOY:** N/A; **PROFL AFFIL & HONORS:** BOMA/Los Angeles - Dir. Nat. Assn. of Power Engineers - Past State Pres.; **EDUC:** Educated in Germany; **OTHER ACT & HONORS:** Mid-Valley Y.M.C.A. - Van Nuys; **HOME ADD:** 15144 Burbank Blvd. 207, Van Nuys, CA 91408, (213)786-0562; **BUS ADD:** 6842 Van Nuys Blvd., Van Nuys, CA 91405, (213)902-3703.

OSTENDORF, George J.——B: Oct. 21, 1944, Chicago, IL, *Second VP*, Continental Illinois National Bank, Continental IL Mort.; **PRIM RE ACT:** Banker, Lender; **SERVICES:** Single family mort. loans on large resid. devel.; **REP CLIENTS:** Maj. condo. conversion devel., single family tract builders; **PROFL AFFIL & HONORS:** IL mort. bankers assn.; **EDUC:** BS, 1966, Fin., De Paul Univ.; **GRAD EDUC:** MBA, 1970, Fin., De Paul Univ.; **EDUC HONORS:** Who's Who in Amer Coll. 1966; **HOME ADD:** 506 E. Marshall, Arlington Heights, IL 60004, (312)398-5873; **BUS ADD:** 231 S. LaSalle, Chicago, IL 60693.

OSTERHOUT, Clark N.——B: July 2, 1952, Lodi, CA, *Indus. and Investment Spec.*, Coldwell Banker Commercial RE Services, Inc.; **PRIM RE ACT:** Broker; **SERVICES:** Sales & Leasing of Indus. Projects and Indus. Devel. Consultation; **REP CLIENTS:** The Koll Co., Precision Castparts Corp., Trammel Crow Co., Triangle Pacific Corp., US National Bank, Cumberland Realty Group, Ltd.; **PROFL AFFIL & HONORS:** NAR, OR Assn. of Realtors, Portland Bd. of Realtors; **EDUC:** BS, 1976, Gen. Sci. Studies, Portland State Univ.; **HOME ADD:** 13400 SW Bay Meadows Ct., Beaverton, OR 97005, (503)641-5903; **BUS ADD:** 1300 SW Fifth Ave., Suite 2600, Portland, OR 97201, (503)221-1900.

OSTERLING, Michael J.——B: July 7, 1953, Lafayette, IN, *Branch Mgr.*, Lomas & Nettelton Co.; **PRIM RE ACT:** Broker, Banker, Lender; **SERVICES:** FHA, VA, Conv. single family & 2-4 family lending; **REP CLIENTS:** Resid. Brokers, appraisers and builders; **PROFL AFFIL & HONORS:** MBA, Metro Indianapolis Bd. of Realtors; **EDUC:** BS, 1975, Bio. & Chem., Purdue Univ.; **HOME ADD:** 5317 Broadway, Indianapolis, IN 46220, (317)255-6075; **BUS ADD:** 6100 N. Keystone Ave., Suite 318, Indianapolis, IN 46220, (317)257-8818.

OSTLER, David S.——B: June 17, 1931, Nephi, UT, *Pres.*, The Bus. Brokerage; **PRIM RE ACT:** Broker, Owner/Investor; **SERVICES:** Indus. & Comml. RE Brokerage, Corp. Sales & Acquisitions; **EDUC:** AB, 1956, Mktg., Brigham Young Univ.; **GRAD EDUC:** MBA, 1958, Gen. Admin., Harvard Grad. School of Bus. Admin.; **EDUC HONORS:** Phi Kappa Phi; **MIL SERV:** US Army, S.F.C., Korean Service Ribbon; **HOME ADD:** 2666 Hillsden Dr., Holladay, UT 84117, (801)278-9038; **BUS ADD:** 722 E 900 So., Salt Lake City, UT 84105, (801)532-1188.

OSTLING, Lar Eric——B: Jan. 25, 1947, Bloomington, IL, *Atty.*, Citizens Savings and Loan; **PRIM RE ACT:** Attorney, Lender, Owner/Investor, Insuror, Property Manager, Instructor; **PREV EMPLOY:** State Farm Ins. Companies, Country Companies, Ins. Companies; **PROFL AFFIL & HONORS:** ABA, IBA, McLean Co. Bar; **EDUC:** BS, 1969, Psych., socl, spec. educ., IL State Univ.; **GRAD EDUC:** JD, 1974, Bus. and ins. law, KS Univ.; **EDUC HONORS:** Dean's list, Pres. 3rd yr. class; **MIL SERV:** US Marines, Sgt.; **HOME ADD:** Box 612, Normal, IL 61761, (309)726-1878; **BUS ADD:** 301 Broadway, Normal, IL 61761, (309)452-1102.

OSTRANDER, Fred——B: Apr. 23, 1926, Berkeley, CA, *Exec. VP*, Twin Pines Fed. Sav. & Loan Assn.; **PRIM RE ACT:** Appraiser, Lender; **PROFL AFFIL & HONORS:** Soc. of RE Appraisers, Bay Area Mort. Assn., Sr. Real Prop. Appraiser; **EDUC:** BA, 1948, Hist., Univ. of CA, Berkeley; **MIL SERV:** US Merchant Marines, 1944-46, Cadet Midshipman; **OTHER ACT & HONORS:** Berkeley Commons Club; **HOME ADD:** 2741 Woolsey St., Berkeley, CA 94705, (415)652-0546; **BUS ADD:** 2905 Telegraph Ave., Berkeley, CA 94705, (415)848-7923.

OTIS, James, Jr.——B: July 8, 1931, Chicago, IL, *Chmn. CEO*, Otis Assoc., Inc.; **PRIM RE ACT:** Architect; **SERVICES:** Land planners, architects, devel.; **REP CLIENTS:** Allstate Ins. Co., GBC, Combined Ins. Co., Occidental Petro Co.; **PROFL AFFIL & HONORS:** AIA, ARA, NCARB, Chicago C of C, Ten Outstanding Young Men in Chicago for achievements in arch., AIA and Chicago C of C Bldg. Award; **EDUC:** AB, 1953, Arch., Princeton Univ.; **GRAD EDUC:** MBA, Chicago Univ. Bus. School; **EDUC HONORS:** Cum Laude; **MIL SERV:** USN, Lt.; **OTHER ACT & HONORS:** Chmn. Northbrook Arch. Control Bd., Chicago Economics Clb., Comml. Club Chgo., Chgo C of C, Brookfield Zoo and Shedd Aquarium Gov. Mbr.; **BUS ADD:** 899 Skokie Blvd., Northbrook, IL 60062, (312)272-4310.

OTT, Lawrence L.——B: Oct. 27, 1913, Dansville, NY, *Att. & VP*, Monroe Abstract & Title Corp.; **PRIM RE ACT:** Consultant, Attorney; **SERVICES:** RE - estates & title ins.; **PROFL AFFIL & HONORS:** NY State Bar Assn., Amer. Land Title Assn., NY Land Title Assn.; **EDUC:** Pre-Law, Niagara Univ.; **GRAD EDUC:** LLB, 1040, Fordham; **MIL SERV:** USA, Warrant Officer; **HOME ADD:** 256 Bradley Blvd., Schenectady, NY 12304, (518)372-6538; **BUS ADD:** 608 State St., Schenectady, NY 12305, (518)374-8438.

OTTEAU, Jeffrey G.——B: Oct. 16, 1953, E. Orange, NJ, *Real Prop. Appraisal Consultant*, Jeffrey G. Otteau Appraisal Co.; **PRIM RE ACT:** Consultant, Appraiser; **OTHER RE ACT:** Consultant to the relocation mgmt. indus.; **SERVICES:** RE appraising & consulting; relocation mgmt. consulting; **REP CLIENTS:** Bank of OK, Dun & Bradstreet Corp., Bell Telephone Co., GM Corp., Prudential; **PROFL AFFIL & HONORS:** NAIFA; **EDUC:** Farleigh Dickinson Univ.; Upsala Coll.; Monmouth Coll.; Prof. School of Bus.; **HOME ADD:** 12 Dobson Rd., E. Brunswick, NJ 08816; **BUS ADD:** POB 655, E. Brunswick, NJ 08816, (201)238-2550.

OUJESKY, Buddy——B: Ju 27, 1936, Ft. Worth, TX, *RE Mgr.*, Winn-Dixie TX, Inc., Ft. Worth; **PRIM RE ACT:** Property Manager; **SERVICES:** Site selection, lease negotiation, store remodeling; **REP CLIENTS:** Corp. work only; **PREV EMPLOY:** Kimbell, Inc. (4 yrs. before acquisition by Winn-Dixie); Mobil Oil Corp. (10.5 yrs.); **PROFL AFFIL & HONORS:** ICSC, NACORE; **EDUC:** BBA, 1958, Mktg., Bus. Law, Univ. of OK; **EDUC HONORS:** Big Eight Guard 1957; Big Eight Scholastic Team 1958; **MIL SERV:** USA, Capt.; **OTHER ACT & HONORS:** MO Valley Conf. Football Official, SW Football Official's Assn.; **HOME ADD:** 324 Mayfair, Hurst, TX 76053, (817)282-4018; **BUS ADD:** PO Box 1540, Ft. Worth, TX 76101, (817)921-1100.

OUTLAW, Larry A.——B: Jan. 28, 1944, Goldsboro, NC, *Educ. Dir.*, North Carolina Real Estate Licensing Board; **PRIM RE ACT:** Broker, Attorney, Regulator; **OTHER RE ACT:** RE Educator; **SERVICES:** Supervise RE educ. activities of the NC RE Licensing Bd.; **PREV EMPLOY:** Educ. Admin. - Inst.; **PROFL AFFIL & HONORS:** NC State Bar; RE Educators Assn.; NC RE Educators Assn.; Consultant to Educ. Testing Serv. on RE licensing examinations; Nat. Assn. of RE License Law Officals; **EDUC:** BA, 1965, Hist., Davidson Coll.; **GRAD EDUC:** JD, 1968, Law, Univ. of NC; **MIL SERV:** US Army, Capt., 1969-1972; **HOME ADD:** 4223-1 Avent Ferry Rd., Raleigh, NC 27606, (919)851-5211; **BUS ADD:** PO Box 17100, Raleigh, NC 27619, (919)872-3450.

OVERBERG, Robert A.——B: Sept. 6, 1928, Cincinnati, OH, *Pres.*, Mohawk Realty Co.; **PRIM RE ACT:** Broker, Consultant, Architect, Developer, Builder, Owner/Investor, Instructor, Property Manager, Syndicator; **PREV EMPLOY:** Founded Mohawk Realty Co., 1953; **PROFL AFFIL & HONORS:** Homebuilders Assn.; Bd. of Realtors; Amer. Assn. of Cert. Appraisers; RESSI; Nat. Assn. of Homebuilders & Realtors, GRI, CAC; **EDUC:** AB, 1951, Eng./Math./Sci., Univ. of Cincinnati; **GRAD EDUC:** ABS, 1969, Comm./RE, Univ. of

Cincinnati; **EDUC HONORS:** High Honors; **MIL SERV:** US Navy Air, Cadet; **OTHER ACT & HONORS:** Montgomery Bus. Club; **HOME ADD:** 7701 Glenover Dr., Cincinnati, OH 45236, (513)891-6861; **BUS ADD:** 9464 Montgomery Rd., Cincinnati, OH 45242.

OVERMAN, Edwin S.——*Pres.*, Insurance Institute of Amer.; **PRIM RE ACT:** Insuror; **BUS ADD:** PO Box 314, Malvern, PA 19355, (215)644-2100.*

OVERMAN, Mary Jayne——**B:** Sept. 28, 1945, Oakland, CA, *Asst. VP*, R & B Comml. Mgmt.; **PRIM RE ACT:** Developer, Property Manager; **SERVICES:** Hi rise, low rise, combo, corp. parks; **REP CLIENTS:** Own properties; **PROFL AFFIL & HONORS:** CPM, Newport Harbor Bd. of Realtors, O.C. Apt. Assn., Pres. IREM Orange County, Instructor ARM Course; **HOME ADD:** 21062 Indigo Cir., Huntington Beach, CA 92646, (714)963-4001; **BUS ADD:** 2222 Corinth Ave., Los Angeles, CA 90064, (213)478-1021.

OVERMEYER, Paul——*Manager Fac. Engr.*, Bandag Inc.; **PRIM RE ACT:** Property Manager; **BUS ADD:** Bandag Center, Muscatire, IA 52761, (319)262-1400.*

OVERSTREET, Homer, Jr.——**B:** Apr. 8, 1937, Atlanta, GA, *RE Appraiser*, Hughes & Overstreet, RE Appraisers, Single Family Branch; **PRIM RE ACT:** Appraiser; **SERVICES:** Appraisal; **REP CLIENTS:** Decatur Fed. S & L; Fin. Amer., B.A. Bus. Credit (Bank of Amer.); Equitable Relocation Serv.; **PREV EMPLOY:** HUD/FHA; First Fed. S & L Atlanta; **PROFL AFFIL & HONORS:** Soc. of RE Appraisers; AIREA, SRA & RM Designations; **EDUC:** Emory Univ., GA State Univ. Dept. of Bus. Educ.; **MIL SERV:** US Army; **OTHER ACT & HONORS:** Gwinnett C of C; Published Article in Mobility Magazine 1981; **HOME ADD:** 6146 Flowery Branch Rd., Auburn, GA 30203, (404)945-6656; **BUS ADD:** 235 E. Ponce de Leon Ave., Suite 307, Decatur, GA 30203, (404)373-8947.

OVERSTREET, Reading, Jr.——**B:** Nov. 24, 1950, Phoenix, AZ, *VP/Property Sales*, Consolidated Capital 1980-.; **PRIM RE ACT:** Syndicator, Owner/Investor, Developer; **PREV EMPLOY:** DLA Props. Inc., Pres. 1979-1980; Ramada Inns, Inc., Dir. of Devel. 1976-1979; **EDUC:** BA, 1972, Govt., Hist., Univ. of AZ; **BUS ADD:** 360 Campbell Centre I, Dallas, TX 75206, (214)987-2222.

OWEN, Douglas——**B:** Aug. 1, 1945, Maquoketa, IA, *VP*, Ins. Planning Serv.; **PRIM RE ACT:** Consultant, Builder, Lender, Owner/Investor, Insuror; **OTHER RE ACT:** Estate & fin. planning; **SERVICES:** Consultation, tax reports, investment reports; **PREV EMPLOY:** Amer. Natl. Bank of Kekalb, IL; **MIL SERV:** USN, E-5; **OTHER ACT & HONORS:** Jaycees, Rotary; **HOME ADD:** 404 E. Angus Ct., Maquoketa, IA 52060, (319)652-5848; **BUS ADD:** 123 S. 2nd, Box 777, Maquoketa, IA 52060, (319)652-2556.

OWEN, Park H., III——**B:** Feb. 19, 1949, Nashville, TN, *VP & Branch Mgr.*, TVB Mortgage Corp. (1976-); **PRIM RE ACT:** Consultant, Appraiser, Property Manager; **OTHER RE ACT:** Mort. banker; **SERVICES:** Mort. and equity fin., appraisals, investment consultant, & prop. mgmt.; **REP CLIENTS:** Lenders, indivs. or instits. investors in comml. & indus. prop.; **PREV EMPLOY:** Commerce Union Bank, Nashville, TN 1972-1976; Comml. Banking Officer; **PROFL AFFIL & HONORS:** Louisville C of C; Mort. Bankers Assn. of Louisville; Louisville Apt. Assn.; **EDUC:** BA, 1971, Psych. & Econ., Univ. of NC at Chapel Hill; **OTHER ACT & HONORS:** Nat. Ski Patrol System, Inc.; **HOME ADD:** 1300 Everett Ave., Louisville, KY 40204, (502)451-5636; **BUS ADD:** Suite 211, 312 Fourth Ave., Louisville, KY 40202, (502)589-1100.

OWENS, A.R., Jr.——*VP & Treas.*, Norris Industries; **PRIM RE ACT:** Property Manager; **BUS ADD:** One Golden Shore, Long Beach, CA 90802, (213)435-6676.*

OWENS, Dawson——**B:** Oct. 17, 1926, Albany, GA, *Part./Pres.*, Owens E. Ownes (Allen-Owens Co., Inc.), RE, Appraisals-Consults.; **PRIM RE ACT:** Broker, Consultant, Appraiser; **SERVICES:** RE Cert. Appraiser Consultant; **REP CLIENTS:** Exxon, GM, IBM, Proctor & Gamble, Ford Motor Co., S. Bell, Howard Johnson Motels; **PROFL AFFIL & HONORS:** GA Bd, Realtors, NAR, NARA, Alvin Cotes Annual Award/GA. Bd. of Realtors, outstanding sales.; **EDUC:** BS, 1950, Psych & Bus., Univ. of GA; **EDUC HONORS:** Pres. ATO, Demosthenian, Who's Who; **MIL SERV:** USA, Sgt., Several; **OTHER ACT & HONORS:** City of Albany Chmn OB Zoning Appeals, Cty & Cty Appraiser & Arbitor, COB of Tax Eqqualzers, Chmn Minimum Housing Authority, Past Pres. Kiwanis; **HOME ADD:** 5411 Old Dawson Rd., Albany, GA 31707, (912)435-4060; **BUS ADD:** Slappey Blvd., P.O. Box A, Albany, GA 31702, (912)432-0557.

OWENS, Gary L.——*Exec. Dir.*, Industrial Devel. Council of Sioux City; **PRIM RE ACT:** Developer; **BUS ADD:** 101 Pierce St., Sioux City, IA 51101, (712)258-7577.*

OWENS, Stephen L.——**B:** Sept. 11, 1948, Plymouth, NC, *VP Comml. Props.*, Swire Props. Inc.; **PRIM RE ACT:** Developer, Owner/Investor, Property Manager; **PREV EMPLOY:** Trizec Southern Ltd.; Cameron Brown Co.; **EDUC:** BS, 1970, Fin./RE Analysis, East Carolina Univ./Univ. of PA & Univ. of GA; **HOME ADD:** 1208 Lisbon Ave., Coral Gables, FL 33134, (305)447-1161; **BUS ADD:** 777 Brickell Ave., Ste 504, Miami, FL 33134, (305)341-3877.

OWENS, Thomas R.——**B:** Sept. 6, 1944, Utica, NY, *Gen. Counsel*, Pacific Union Co.; **PRIM RE ACT:** Attorney, Developer, Builder, Owner/Investor; **SERVICES:** Gen. counsel and related prin. to the co.; **PREV EMPLOY:** Partner, Goldfarb & Owens, 1971-1980; **PROFL AFFIL & HONORS:** CA Bar Assn., ABA, Author: Cooperative Conversions in California (1979), Contributor: San Francisco Chronicle RE Sect.; **EDUC:** BA, 1966, Eng. Lit., Univ. of PA Law School; **EDUC HONORS:** Keedy Cup Winner, Am. Jur. Awards; **OTHER ACT & HONORS:** Also Treas., Land Exec. Assn.; **HOME ADD:** 1816 Lyon St., San Francisco, CA 94115; **BUS ADD:** 3640 Buchanan, San Francisco, CA 94123, (415)929-7100.

OWENS, William Harold——**B:** Mar. 5, 1916, Somerset, KY, *Owner*, Danville Realty Co.; **PRIM RE ACT:** Broker, Appraiser, Developer, Insuror; **PROFL AFFIL & HONORS:** KY RE Assn., Nat. RE Assn., SRWA, Nat. Assn. of RE Appraisers; Dir. and VP of the KY RE Assn.; **EDUC:** BS, 1938, Commerce, Eastern KY Univ.; **HOME ADD:** 467 Boone Trail, Danville, KY 40422, (606)236-5598; **BUS ADD:** 110 North Second St., Danville, KY 40422, (606)236-5494.

OWENS, William S.——**B:** Jan. 4, 1931, Greensburg, PA, *Chief of Operations*, Montgomery Cty., MD, Dept. of Housing & Comm. Devel.; **PRIM RE ACT:** Appraiser, Regulator; **OTHER RE ACT:** Prop. acquisition & disposition; **SERVICES:** Admin. of mod. priced housing programs & devel.; **PREV EMPLOY:** Ind. profl. appraiser; **PROFL AFFIL & HONORS:** NARA; Intl. Right of Way Assn.; Intl. Inst. of Valuers, CRA, SR/WA, SCV; **EDUC:** BS, 1959, Bus. Admin., Univ. of Baltimore; **MIL SERV:** USA, Sgt., Korean Campaign Ribbon with 5 clusters, UN Ribbon; **HOME ADD:** 170 Talbott St., Apt. 201, Rockville, MD 20852, (301)279-9340; **BUS ADD:** 100 Maryland Ave., Rockville, MD 20850, (301)279-1254.

OWINGS, Theodore R.——**B:** Dec. 8, 1921, Union, NE, *Pres.*, Trocorp, Inc.; **PRIM RE ACT:** Broker, Developer, Builder; **PREV EMPLOY:** Asst. City Mgr. and Dir. of Fin. for ten years, Culver City, CA 92330; **PROFL AFFIL & HONORS:** CA Bldrs. Assn.; **EDUC:** BS, 1948, USC School of Public Admin.; **GRAD EDUC:** Law School, 1955; **MIL SERV:** USAF, Lt. Col., several; **OTHER ACT & HONORS:** Former Asst. Dir. of the Nat. Park Service; **HOME ADD:** 1221 W. Coast Hwy, 402, Newport Beach, CA 92663, (714)254-4824; **BUS ADD:** 1221 W.Coast Hwy., Newport Beach, CA 92663, (714)631-7506.

OWINGS, Thomas G.——**B:** Aug. 31, 1944, Birmingham, AL, *VP*, Jo-NI R.E. Co., Inc., Const.; **PRIM RE ACT:** Consultant, Appraiser, Developer, Builder, Property Manager; **SERVICES:** R.E. sales, const. consultation; **EDUC:** BS, 1968, Bio., Livingston Univ.; **GRAD EDUC:** MEd, 1969, Sec. Ed., Livingston Univ.; PhD, 1972, Higher Ed./ Admin., Univ. of AL; **EDUC HONORS:** Phi Delta Kappa, Natl. Ed. Hon.; **MIL SERV:** USAF; S/Sgt.; **OTHER ACT & HONORS:** Councilman, City of Brent, AL 1980 - present; Commander, Bibb Co., Civil Air Patrol; Mason; Shriner; Pres., S.E. Community Coll.; Research Assn. 1980-81; Bibb Cty. Democratic Exec. Comm., 1978-present; **HOME ADD:** 105 Wilson St., Brent, AL 35034, (205)926-7753; **BUS ADD:** 128 Nicholson Ave., Centreville, AL 35042, (205)926-9211.

OZELIS, Casey——*Mgr. Mfg.*, Wallace Business Forms; **PRIM RE ACT:** Property Manager; **BUS ADD:** 4600 Roosevelt Rd., Hillside, IL 60162, (312)449-8600.*

PACE, A. Brooks——**B:** Dec. 1, 1942, St. George, UT, *Pres.*, The Dammeron Corp.; **PRIM RE ACT:** Developer, Builder, Owner/Investor, Property Manager; **OTHER RE ACT:** Land Devel.; **SERVICES:** Devel., build and manage comml., prof. and res. projects; **PROFL AFFIL & HONORS:** Heritage foundation award of merit for

Ancestor square; **EDUC:** BS, 1966, Banking & Fin., Univ. of UT; **MIL SERV:** US Army/Spec. Forces, Capt.; **HOME ADD:** Dammeron Valley, UT 84722, (801)628-1626; **BUS ADD:** 151 N. Main St., St. George, UT 84770, (801)673-9798.

PACE, James G.——B: Jan. 8, 1912, Shelbyville, KY, *Pres.*, Miami Industrial, Inc. Realtors, Pace & Associates, Realtors; **PRIM RE ACT:** Broker, Attorney, Appraiser, Developer, Builder; **SERVICES:** Large acreage, vacant indus. and comml.; **PROFL AFFIL & HONORS:** FL State Bar, FL & intl. Realtors Assns., NAR, Pres. Aviation Chap., Nat. FLI; **EDUC:** LLB, 1934, Jefferson School of Law, Univ. of Louisville; **GRAD EDUC:** JD, 1969, Univ. of Louisville; **MIL SERV:** US Army, Sgt., For. Serv. (1941-1945); **HOME ADD:** 15200 NE Biscayne Blvd., N. Miami Beach, FL, (305)949-9155; **BUS ADD:** 15180 Biscayne Blvd., N. Miami Beach, FL 33160, (305)949-4113.

PACHTER, Milton H.——B: Dec. 5, 1929, Brooklyn, NY, *Chief, Litigation Div.*, The Port Auth. of NY & NJ, Law Dept.; **PRIM RE ACT:** Attorney, Owner/Investor; **OTHER RE ACT:** Adj. Prof. RE, NY Univ.; **PREV EMPLOY:** Touche, Niven, Bailey & Smart (CPA's); **PROFL AFFIL & HONORS:** ABA, NY State Bar Assn., Assn. of the Bar of the City of NY, NY Cty. Lawyers, NY Condemnation Conference (Former Pres.); Nat. Assn. of Accountants, NY Univ. Sch. of Cont. Educ., Award for Teaching Excellence, Exec. Dir. Unit Citation (Port Auth.); **EDUC:** BBA, 1952, Acctg., CCNY; **GRAD EDUC:** JD, 1956, NY Univ., Sch. of Law; LLM, 1957, NY Univ. Sch. of Law; SJD, 1966, NY Law Sch.; **MIL SERV:** USA Res., JAGC, Col., Meritorious Serv. Medal, Army Commendation Medal; Korean Service Medal, United Nations Service Medal; **HOME ADD:** 4 Washington Sq. Village, New York, NY 10012; **BUS ADD:** One World Trade Ctr., Suite 66SE, New York, NY 10048, (212)466-8762.

PACK, Andre J.——B: Feb. 23, 1947, Esglingen, Germany, *Projects Mgr.*, SCS Engineers, Planning Div.; **OTHER RE ACT:** Urban Development Specialist; **SERVICES:** Devel. feasibility studies, prop. mgmt planning, mgmt. information systems; **REP CLIENTS:** Devel., RE brokerages, prop. mgrs., builders; **PREV EMPLOY:** Univ. of WA, Dept. of Urban Planning, 1976-78; State of CA 1969-74; CA State Univ., Northridge, 1974-76; **PROFL AFFIL & HONORS:** Amer. Planning Assn., ULI, Amer. RE & Urban Econ. Assn.; **EDUC:** BA, 1969, Eng., Poli. Sci., Econ., Loyola Univ. of Los Angeles; **GRAD EDUC:** MA, 1972, Urban Devel., environmental mgmt., UCLA; **HOME ADD:** 2715 185th Ave. NE, Redmond, WA 98052, (206)883-9927; **BUS ADD:** 1008 140th Ave., NE, Bellevue, WA 98005, (206)643-5800.

PACKER, Mark B.——B: Sept. 18, 1944, Philadelphia, PA, *Atty. at Law*, Nelle & Packer; **PRIM RE ACT:** Consultant, Attorney, Owner/Investor, Property Manager; **SERVICES:** Advise clients on RE and other investments; **PROFL AFFIL & HONORS:** Member of WA State and MA Bars; ABA sections on real prop., trust and probate; corp., banking and bus., Member Bellingham Planning Commn. 1975 (Chmn. 1977-1981); **EDUC:** BA, 1965, Amer. Hist. and Lit., Harvard Coll.; **GRAD EDUC:** LLB, 1968, Land use planning, environment law, local government law, Harvard Law School; **EDUC HONORS:** Magna Cum Laude; **OTHER ACT & HONORS:** Pres., Congregation Beth Israel, Bellingham, WA; Chmn., Bellingham UJA Campaign; Biography in 1980-1981 and 1982-1983 Editions of Who's Who in the West; **HOME ADD:** 208 South Forest, Bellingham, WA 98225, (206)676-0516; **BUS ADD:** 805 Dupont St., Suite 2, Bellingham, WA 98225, (206)734-3870.

PADGETT, Douglas J.——B: Apr. 29, 1947, Macon, GA, Merrill Lynch Realty; **PRIM RE ACT:** Broker; **OTHER RE ACT:** Comml. & Retail Prop.; **SERVICES:** Arrange sale, pre-sale, & joint ventures; **REP CLIENTS:** Many instns.; **PREV EMPLOY:** Mort. Broker; **PROFL AFFIL & HONORS:** Intl. Council of Shopping Ctrs., Nat. Assn. of Indus. and Office Parks; **EDUC:** BBA, Mgmt., GA Southern Coll.; **HOME ADD:** Atlanta, GA; **BUS ADD:** 233 Peachtree St. N.E., Ste. 300, Atlanta, GA 30303, (404)658-5358.

PADIA, Russell F.——B: Jan. 6, 1933, Los Angeles, CA, *Pres.*, Sunset Pacific; **PRIM RE ACT:** Developer, Builder; **EDUC:** BS, 1959, Indus. Eng., USC; **GRAD EDUC:** MS, 1965, Indus. Engr., USC; **EDUC HONORS:** Tau Beta Pi - Nat. Eng. Honor Soc., Alpha Pi Mu Nat. Ind. Eng. Honor Soc. Cum Laude; **MIL SERV:** USA, Cpl; **BUS ADD:** 17701 Mitcell Ave. N., Irvine, CA 92714, (714)966-0651.

PADILLA, Diane——*Ed.*, B.D.A. News Inc., Builder, Developer, Apt. Owner News; **PRIM RE ACT:** Real Estate Publisher; **BUS ADD:** 440 So. Anaheim Blvd., Anaheim, CA 92805, (714)956-2680.*

PAESANI, Judith B.——B: Oct. 8, 1933, Wheeling, WV, *Asst. Dir.*, Center for Real Estate and Urban Economic Studies, Univ. of CT; **PRIM RE ACT:** Consultant, Real Estate Publisher; **OTHER RE ACT:** Educ.; **SERVICES:** Reference and Resource coordination, bibliographic servs.; **PROFL AFFIL & HONORS:** RE Educators Assn., Rgnl. VP; **EDUC:** BA, 1955, Gen. Bus. and Eng., West Liberty State Coll., W. Liberty, WV; **GRAD EDUC:** MA, 1977, Higher, Tech., Adult Educ., Univ. of CT, Storrs, CT; **EDUC HONORS:** Cum Laude, Who's Who in Amer. Coll. and Univ., Alpha Phi Sigma, Scholastic Frat.; **OTHER ACT & HONORS:** Tolland Country 4-H Club Program, League of Women Voters; **HOME ADD:** 16 Sawmill Brook Ln., Willimantic, CT 06226, (203)423-7883; **BUS ADD:** U-41RE, The Univ. of CT, Storrs, CT 06268, (203)486-3227.

PAFFHAUSEN, James V.——B: Aug. 3, 1925, Grand Rapids, MI, *Pres.*, Presidio Capital Corp.; **PRIM RE ACT:** Broker, Syndicator; **OTHER RE ACT:** Morg. banking; **SERVICES:** Arranging 1st mort. on income props. from -500,000 up, also joint ventures, equity sales, constr. loans, etc.; **PREV EMPLOY:** Pres. Metro. Fin. Corp.; Exec. VP A.H. Gruetzmacher & Co., Inc.; **EDUC:** Bus. Admin., Pre-law, MI State Normal, DePaul Univ., Univ. CA, Los Angeles; **MIL SERV:** USA, M/Sgt.; **HOME ADD:** 5850 Sagebrush Rd., La Jolla, CA 92037, (714)459-0437; **BUS ADD:** 8950 Villa La Jolla Dr., Suite 2150, La Jolla, CA 92037.

PAFFROTH, Harold——*Dir. Fac.*, Hazeltime Corp.; **PRIM RE ACT:** Property Manager; **BUS ADD:** Cuba Hill Rd., Greenlawn, NY 11740, (516)261-7000.*

PAGE, Charles M.——B: Mar. 3, 1946, Baltimore, MD, *RE Apprasser*, City of Alexandria, Office of Housing; **PRIM RE ACT:** Appraiser; **SERVICES:** Appraise props. for City of Alexandria; **PREV EMPLOY:** Sr. RE Appraiser, Alex. City's Assessment Office; Staff Appraiser, R.H. Jones & Assoc., Inc.; Staff Appraiser, Alex. Redev. & Housing Auth.; **PROFL AFFIL & HONORS:** Assoc. Member, Soc. of RE Appraisers; **EDUC:** BS, 1968, Math, Chemistry, Engr., NC State Univ.; **MIL SERV:** USA, 1st. Lt. 1968-1972; **HOME ADD:** 2905 Old Dominion Blvd., Alexandria, VA 22305, (703)549-0870; **BUS ADD:** City Hall PO Box 178, Alexandria, VA 22313, (703)838-4622.

PAGE, Melvin E., Jr.——B: June 11, 1918, Ann Arbor, MI, *Atty.-at-Law*, Melvin E. Page, Jr., Attorney; **PRIM RE ACT:** Attorney, Regulator; **SERVICES:** All services; **PROFL AFFIL & HONORS:** ABA, FL, St. Petersburg Bar Assns., RE Sect.; **EDUC:** BA, 1948, Bus. Admin., Babson Inst. of Bus. Admin.; **GRAD EDUC:** JD, 1957, Law, Stetson Univ. Coll. of Law; **MIL SERV:** US Army AC, 1st Lt.; **HOME ADD:** 2307 Pass-a-Grille Way, St. Petersburg Beach, FL 33706, (813)360-6481; **BUS ADD:** 915 Tyrone Blvd. North, St. Petersburg, FL 33710, (813)345-1027.

PAGLIARI, Joseph L., Jr.——B: Feb. 13, 1957, Chicago, IL, *Consultant*, Laventhol & Horwath, Mgmt. Advisory Servs.; **PRIM RE ACT:** Consultant; **SERVICES:** Investment analysis, deal structuring, valuation and market studies; **REP CLIENTS:** Sydn., devels., lenders, investment bankers and mort. bankers; **PROFL AFFIL & HONORS:** IL MBA; IL CPA Soc.; Fin. Mgmt. Assn., CPA; **EDUC:** BS, 1979, Investment & Banking, Univ. of IL, Urbana/Champaign; **GRAD EDUC:** MBA, 1982, Fin., De Paul Univ.; **HOME ADD:** 555 Graceland, 505, Des Plaines, IL 60016, (312)635-6287; **BUS ADD:** 111 E Wacker Dr., Chicago, IL 60601, (312)644-4570.

PAHL, David R.——B: Aug. 22, 1948, Buffalo, NY, *Pres.*, R. David Pahl & Co., Inc.; **PRIM RE ACT:** Broker, Consultant, Developer; **OTHER RE ACT:** Mort. broker/banker; **SERVICES:** Devel. consulting; arranging & negotiating debt & equity fin. for income prop.; Sales and Sale-leaseback negotiations; arranging tax-exempt debt placements; **REP CLIENTS:** Foreign and domestic, devel. and instns. engaged in the construction, acquisition, or refin. of income prop.; **PREV EMPLOY:** 1972-74, Condo. Marketing & Devel., 1974-76 Econ. Consultant, Harbridge House Inc., 1976-78 Devel. Fin., United Community Devel. Inc.; **EDUC:** BS, 1970, operations research, Cornell Univ.; **GRAD EDUC:** 2 yrs. PhD, Urban Studies, fin., MIT, Grad. School of Bus., Boston Univ.; **EDUC HONORS:** Honors, Tau Beta Pi Hon. Soc., Phi Kappa Phi, Grad. School Honorary; **HOME ADD:** 21 Sheafe St., Chestnut Hill, MA 02167, (617)566-0882; **BUS ADD:** 50 Milk St., Suite 1500, Boston, MA 02109, (617)367-6909.

PAILLE, Richard L.——B: May 9, 1949, Reno, NV, *Pres.; Design Corp.*, Design Realty; **PRIM RE ACT:** Broker; **SERVICES:** Resort prop. mgmt.; **PROFL AFFIL & HONORS:** NAR; Realtors Nat. Mktg. Inst.; NV Assn. of Realtors; CA Assn. of Realtors, Immed. Past Pres., Incline Village Bd. of Realtor; GRI, Realtor of the year 1979; RENPAC, trustee State of NV; **EDUC:** BS, 1973, Educ. Communication/Eng., Univ. of NV; **MIL SERV:** US Air Forst Natl. Guard; E-5; **HOME ADD:** P O Box 7959, Incline Village, NV 89450, (702)831-5553; **BUS ADD:** P O Box 5559, 264 Village Blvd., Incline Village, NV 89450, (702)831-5550.

PAJESKI, Stephen J.——B: Nov, 8, 1933, Auburn, NY, *Prop. Mgmt.*, Eastman Kodak Co., Kodak Park Div. Food Serv.; **PRIM RE ACT:** Instructor, Consultant, Property Manager; **SERVICES:** Prop. Mgmt. in Food Serv. Operations; **REP CLIENTS:** Co. operated employee services; **PREV EMPLOY:** Republic Nat. Bank Bldg. Co., Dallas, TX; **PROFL AFFIL & HONORS:** IREM; RE Bd. of Rochester, NY, CPM; **EDUC:** BS, 1957, Hotel & Restaurant Admin., Cornell Univ.; **GRAD EDUC:** MBA, 1979, Bus. Mgmt., Rochester Inst. of Tech.; **EDUC HONORS:** Ratph Hitz Memorial Scholarship; **OTHER ACT & HONORS:** Bd. of Dirs. of the Assn. for Bd. of Dirs. - Council Club of Rochester, NY; Cornell Univ. Council - Member of the Bd.; Dir. - Council/Soc. of Hotel Mgmt.; **HOME ADD:** 11 Highview Trail, Pittsford, NY 14534, (716)248-2612; **BUS ADD:** 200 Ridge Rd., W Bldg. 28, Rochester, NY 14650, (716)722-2642.

PAKENHAM, John E., Jr.——B: Sept. 16, 1940, New Brunswick, NJ, *Prop.*, Prestige Agency; **PRIM RE ACT:** Broker, Syndicator, Consultant, Appraiser, Property Manager, Owner/Investor; **PROFL AFFIL & HONORS:** IREM, NJAR, AHC, NJBAS, NAR, CPM of Yr. (1979); **HOME ADD:** 18 Hidden Lake Dr., New Brunswick, NJ 08902; **BUS ADD:** 205 Livingston Ave., New Brunswick, NJ 08902, (201)846-6677.

PALADINO, Patrick J.——B: Aug. 17, 1943, Brooklyn, NY, *Controller*, GTE Realty Corp.; **PRIM RE ACT:** Developer, Owner/Investor; **OTHER RE ACT:** Chief Fin. Person; **SERVICES:** Devel., build, construct, lease, mge. all RE holdings for GTE; **PREV EMPLOY:** Harris, Kerr, Forster and Co. 1964-71; GTE Serv. Corp. 1971-74; GTE Information Systems, Inc. 1974-79; **PROFL AFFIL & HONORS:** Inst. of Internal Auditors; NY State Soc. of CPA's, Cert. Int. Auditor and CPA; **EDUC:** BBA, 1965, Acctg., Iona Coll.; **GRAD EDUC:** MBA, 1976, Fin. and Taxation, Univ. of CT; **EDUC HONORS:** Acctg. Honors Soc. 1962 thru 1965; **OTHER ACT & HONORS:** Bd. of Dirs., Northern Little League, Stamford, CT; Cos Cob Revolver and Rifle Club; **HOME ADD:** 44 Calass Ln., North Stamford, CT 06903, (203)322-9069; **BUS ADD:** One Stamford Forum, Stamford, CT 06904, (203)965-3762.

PALCANIS, Gregory F.——B: Apr. 14, 1945, Plainfield, NJ, *Gen. Counsel*, The Empire Savings, Building & Loan Assn., Gen. Counsel; **PRIM RE ACT:** Attorney, Lender, Regulator, Instructor; **SERVICES:** In-house counsel and contributions to CO Continuing Legal Educ. Programs through lectures and articles; **REP CLIENTS:** The Empire Savings, Bldg. and Loan Assn.; **PREV EMPLOY:** The Woodmor Corporation; Columbia S&L Assn.; Security Pacific Mort. Corp.; **PROFL AFFIL & HONORS:** ABA; Real Prop. and Probate Sect. and Corp.; Banking & Bus. Law Sect.; CO & Denver Bar Assns.; Real Prop. & Corporate Bus. Sects.; **EDUC:** BS, 1968, Bus./Mktg., OH State Univ.; **GRAD EDUC:** JD, 1970, Bus., Univ. of Denver, Coll. of Law; **EDUC HONORS:** Law Review; **MIL SERV:** USA, Capt.; **HOME ADD:** 830 York St., Denver, CO 80206, (303)321-7284; **BUS ADD:** 1654 California St., Denver, CO 80202, (303)623-1771.

PALKOWITSH, Marcus S.——B: Oct. 7, 1946, Great Bend, KS, *Owner*, MSP Co.; **PRIM RE ACT:** Developer, Builder, Owner/Investor; **EDUC:** BS, 1968, Econ., Regis Coll.; **HOME ADD:** POB 71, Edwards, CO 81632; **BUS ADD:** Suite 1050, 650 S. Cherry St., Denver, CO 80222, (303)399-9804.

PALLARDY, L.F., Jr.——B: April 23, 1920, Tampa, FL, *Pres.*, Pallardy-Watrous, Inc.; **PRIM RE ACT:** Broker, Appraiser, Builder, Owner/Investor; **OTHER RE ACT:** Builder-Holds State of FL Class A. Contractor's license; **SERVICES:** Primarily appraisals, secondary broker, builder, investor; **REP CLIENTS:** City of Tampa, Hillsborough Cty. Aviation Auth., Schlitz Brewing Co.; **PREV EMPLOY:** 35 years with same corp.; **PROFL AFFIL & HONORS:** Tampa Bd. of Realtors; FL Assn. of Realtors; Amer. Right of Way Assn.; AIREA; Soc. of RE Appraisers; ULI; City of Tampa Park Mgmt. Bd., MAI; SRPA Licensed RE Broker, Class "A" Gen. Contractor; **EDUC:** BS, 1937, Univ. of FL; **MIL SERV:** USNt; Lt. Comdr.; Navy Commendation Ribbon; **OTHER ACT & HONORS:** Univ. Club, Tower Club, Tampa Yacht & Ctry. Club, Krewe of Gasparilla Boca Grande Club, Rotary Club; **HOME ADD:** 104 Ladoga Ave., Tampa, FL 33606, (813)253-0876; **BUS ADD:** 415 South Hyde Park Ave., Tampa, FL 33606, (813)253-0381.

PALM, Henry——B: Jan. 6, 1933, Newark, NJ, *Asst. Sec.*, Travelers Ins. Co., Urban Div. RE Investment; **PRIM RE ACT:** Property Manager, Owner/Investor, Insuror; **PROFL AFFIL & HONORS:** BOMA, IREM, RPA, CPM; **EDUC:** BCE, 1956, Univ. of PA; **MIL SERV:** USN, LCDR; **HOME ADD:** 19 Tanglewood Rd., Farmington, CT 06032, (203)673-5558; **BUS ADD:** 1 Tower Sq., Hartford, CT 06115, (203)277-4972.

PALMER, Alice H.——B: Jan. 27, 1928, Crown Point, IN, *Program Dir.*, Montgomery Coll.; **PRIM RE ACT:** Broker; **OTHER RE ACT:** Program Dir. of RE Programs at Montgomery Coll.; **SERVICES:** Basic RE courses and continuing educ., consumer courses; **PREV EMPLOY:** Assoc. Broker, Long and Foster Realtors, Inc.; Broker and Branch Mgr., A. Menter RE, Inc., Fayetteville, NY; **PROFL AFFIL & HONORS:** MD RE Educators' Assoc., Treas.; Assn. of Part-time Profls.; **EDUC:** BA, 1950, Health/Physical Educ./Biology, Earlham Coll.; **GRAD EDUC:** MEd, 1976, Health Educ., Temple Univ.; **OTHER ACT & HONORS:** Suburban MD Fair Housing; **HOME ADD:** 10537 Wheatley St., Kensington, MD 20895, (301)933-8011; **BUS ADD:** 7815 Woodmont Ave., Bethesda, MD 20814, (301)656-7482.

PALMER, Charles B.——B: Aug. 29, 1942, Lynn, MA, *Sec./Treas.*, Archaeonics Corp.; **PRIM RE ACT:** Consultant, Developer, Builder, Owner/Investor, Syndicator; **OTHER RE ACT:** Devel. building systems; **SERVICES:** Design, build; **PROFL AFFIL & HONORS:** Intl. Assn. for Housing Sciences; NAHB; **EDUC:** BS, 1965, Bus. Admin., Stetson; **BUS ADD:** 524 W. Miller St., Orlando, FL 32805, (305)422-0830.

PALMER, E. Marshall——*Asst. Secy.*, Stevens, J.P. & Co.; **PRIM RE ACT:** Property Manager; **BUS ADD:** 1185 Avenue of the Americas, New York, NY 10036, (212)930-2000.*

PALMER, Jeffrey E.——B: July 5, 1953, LA, *VP*, Moir Devco; **PRIM RE ACT:** Developer; **PREV EMPLOY:** VP, Kaufman & Broad, Asset Mgmt. Div.; **EDUC:** BA, 1975, Econ., Univ. of CA, LA; **GRAD EDUC:** MBA, 1977, Fin., Wharton Sch.; **EDUC HONORS:** Summa Cum Laude, Phi Beta Kappa, Grad. with Distinction; **BUS ADD:** 9595 Wilshire Blvd., Beverly Hills, CA 90212, (213)273-7300.

PALMER, Marvin H.——B: Dec. 19, 1945, Memphis, TN, *Co-owner*, Palmer Brothers, Inc.; **PRIM RE ACT:** Broker, Consultant, Appraiser, Owner/Investor, Instructor, Property Manager, Insuror; **REP CLIENTS:** Mort. lenders, attys., corps. banks, govt., insts., and private indivs.; **PREV EMPLOY:** with Palmer Brothers, Inc. since 1969; **PROFL AFFIL & HONORS:** IREM, SREA, AIREA (candidate), NAR, Memphis Bd. of Realtors' Million Dollar Sales Club (1980), Cert. Prop. Mgr., Sr. Resid. Appraiser; **EDUC:** BA, 1967, Eng., Bus., Vanderbilt Univ.; **GRAD EDUC:** Cert. in RE, 1970-1978, Univ. of TN/Memphis State Univ.; **EDUC HONORS:** Student Court, Residence Halls Council; **MIL SERV:** USN, Lt.; **HOME ADD:** 6430 Kirby Ridge Cove, Memphis, TN 38119, (901)767-3039; **BUS ADD:** 841 S. Cooper, Memphis, TN 38104, (901)726-1674.

PALMER, Michael C.——B: Jan. 6, 1949, Long Beach, CA, *Partner*, Parks, Adams and Palmer; **OTHER RE ACT:** CPA; **SERVICES:** Acctg. & tax; **REP CLIENTS:** Synd, devel., builders, brokers, arch., owners & investors; **PROFL AFFIL & HONORS:** AICPA; CA Soc. of CPA's, CPA; **EDUC:** BS, 1972, Acctg., USC; **GRAD EDUC:** MBT, 1975, Tax, USC; **HOME ADD:** Northridge, CA, (213)368-6540; **BUS ADD:** 400 S. Beverly, Beverly Hills, CA 90212, (213)551-2700.

PALMER, Perry F.——B: Aug. 21, 1951, Iowa City, IA, *VP*, Waggott Merrill Inc.; **PRIM RE ACT:** Broker, Developer, Owner/Investor, Property Manager, Syndicator; **OTHER RE ACT:** Broker/dealer, Securities & Exchange Commn.; **SERVICES:** Synd. & devel. of resid., comml. & indust. props.; **REP CLIENTS:** Indiv. investors & pension plan funds; **PREV EMPLOY:** Deloitte, Haskins & Sells, 1973-79; **PROFL AFFIL & HONORS:** AICPA; CA Soc. of CPAs, Licensed RE Salesman/CA, CPA/CA & AZ; **EDUC:** BS, 1973, Acctg./Fin., IA State Univ.; **GRAD EDUC:** MBA, 1977, Investment Fin., AZ State Univ. Post Graduate Studies - Univ. of CA, Berkeley: RE Law (1980-81); CA State Univ., Long Beach; Corp. Strategy Policy; **EDUC HONORS:** Alpha Kappa Psi; **OTHER ACT & HONORS:** Nat. Co-Chmn., Amer. Inst. of Cooperation; **HOME ADD:** 812 Inverness Way, Sunnyvale, CA 94087, (415)746-3987; **BUS ADD:** 285 Hamilton Ave., Suite 430, Palo Alto, CA 94301.

PALMER, Stephen B.——B: May 27, 1927, Orange, NJ, *Sr. VP*, Alexander Summer Co.; **PRIM RE ACT:** Broker; **PROFL AFFIL & HONORS:** NJ Chap. SIR; Realtor Member, RE Bd. of Newark, Irvington, Hillside; **EDUC:** AB, 1949, Princeton Univ.; **HOME ADD:** 62 Joanna Way, Short Hills, NJ 07078, (201)467-3125; **BUS ADD:** 3 ADP Blvd., Roseland, NJ 07068.

PALMER, William E., Jr.——B: May 14, 1940, Pittsfield, MA, *Owner*, Modern Resid. Serv.; **PRIM RE ACT:** Builder; **OTHER RE ACT:** Home Remodeling & Repair; **SERVICES:** Complete Resid. Bldg.; **PREV EMPLOY:** 20 yrs. building experience; **GRAD EDUC:** AAS, 1960, Electrical Technology, Hudson Valley Community Coll.; **HOME ADD:** Box 203 Bly Hollow Rd., Berlin, NY 12022, (518)658-2696; **BUS ADD:** Box 203 Bly Hollow Rd., Berlin, NY 12022, (518)658-2696.

PALMISANO, Laurence J.——**B:** Mar. 21, 1934, Lawrence, MA, *Pres.*, Cedar Homes Inc.; **PRIM RE ACT:** Consultant, Engineer, Developer, Builder, Owner/Investor, Property Manager, Syndicator; **SERVICES:** Const., const. mgmt., prop. mgmt.; **REP CLIENTS:** Colonial Village Inc.; Washington Park Inc.; Delmont Estates, Inc.; Washington Park Assocs.; **PREV EMPLOY:** Civil Engr., US Army Corps. of Engrs., New England Div., Master Builder Company Cleveland OH, Concrete Design; **PROFL AFFIL & HONORS:** Nat. Assn. of Home Builders, Builder of the Yr., MAHBA, 1972; Local HBA, 1970; **EDUC:** BS, 1957, Civil Engrg., Merrimack Coll.; **MIL SERV:** US Army, Sgt. E-7; **OTHER ACT & HONORS:** Lions Club; C of C; Bons Secours Hospital Guild; Men of Merrimack; **HOME ADD:** 53 Kimball Rd., Methuen, MA 01844, (617)685-1912; **BUS ADD:** 38 Water St., Lawrence, MA 01841, (617)685-1911.

PALOMAROS, Larenzo J.——**B:** Apr. 23, 1951, Havana, Cuba, *Pres.*, Total Realty Inc.; **PRIM RE ACT:** Broker, Instructor, Consultant, Appraiser, Developer, Property Manager; **OTHER RE ACT:** Intl. RE Investments; **PROFL AFFIL & HONORS:** NAR, RNMI, AACA; **EDUC:** BBA, 1972, Mktg, Univ. of Eastern FL; **HOME ADD:** 4890 SW 141 Ave, Miami, FL 33175, (305)261-6436; **BUS ADD:** 5840 W Flagler St., Suite 104, Miami, FL 33144, (305)261-5025.

PANAGAKO, John P.——**B:** Mar. 23, 1944, Hartford, CT, *Pres.*, Interstate Realty Mgmt. Co.; **PRIM RE ACT:** Consultant, Developer, Property Manager, Owner/Investor; **PREV EMPLOY:** Dir. of Dev., Kelly & Picerne, Inc.; **PROFL AFFIL & HONORS:** RESSI; Inst. of RE Mgmt; NAHB, CPM Designation; Registered Apt. Mgr. Designation; Marquis Who's Who in Fin. and Indus.; **EDUC:** BS, 1966, Bus. Admin., Univ. of RI; **MIL SERV:** USAF; 1st Lt.; **HOME ADD:** 14 S Derby Ave, Ventnor, NJ 08406, (609)822-3777; **BUS ADD:** 48 S Main St, Pleasantville, NJ 08232, (609)645-2044.

PANCHOT, Dudley——**B:** Feb. 25, 1930, Yakima, WA, *Lawyer*, Wolfstone, Panchot, Bloch & Kelley; **PRIM RE ACT:** Attorney, Owner/Investor; **SERVICES:** Legal rep. of owners, investors, devels., arch., synds. and realtors; **PROFL AFFIL & HONORS:** ABA, WA State and Seattle King Cty. Bar Assns. (past chmn., tax sect., & state Bar Assn.), Tax and Real Prop., probate and trust law sects. of WA State Bar Assn.; Bd. of Trs. Settle YMCA.; **EDUC:** BA, 1951, Econ., Univ. of Puget Sound and Univ. of WA; **GRAD EDUC:** JD, 1955, Corp. and RE law, Univ. of WA; **EDUC HONORS:** Degree of Honor in Oratory, Phi Kappa Delta Forensic hon., First Place award, Moot appellate Ct. Competition, 1953; **OTHER ACT & HONORS:** Medina City Council-2 yrs.; **HOME ADD:** 1700 90th NE, Bellevue, WA 98004, (206)454-2718; **BUS ADD:** 1117 Norton Bldg., Seattle, WA 98104, (206)682-3840.

PANCOE, Walter——**B:** Oct. 18, 1923, Chicago, IL, *Pres.*, Walart Mgmt. Co; **PRIM RE ACT:** Developer, Builder, Owner/Investor; **SERVICES:** Devel. of Condos. in Ft. Myers Beach, FL; RE interests in Chicago & suburbs & Ft. Wayne, IN; **PROFL AFFIL & HONORS:** Licensed RE Broker, State of IL; **EDUC:** BS, 1947, Mech. Engrg., Univ. of WI; **MIL SERV:** USN, Ens.; **OTHER ACT & HONORS:** Tr., Univ. of WI Student Union, Also Affiliated w/Caper Beach Corp.; **HOME ADD:** 2607 Hydrangeo Pl., Wilmington, NC 28403; **BUS ADD:** 1020 S. Wabash Ave., Chicago, IL 60605, (312)487-8530.

PANERO, Carl Kenyon——**B:** May 7, 1932, New York, NY, *Pres. - Partner*, The Domus Group, Inc. - Tessler and Panero Architects; **PRIM RE ACT:** Consultant, Architect, Developer, Owner/Investor; **OTHER RE ACT:** Project mgmt.; **SERVICES:** Devel., project mgmt., arch.; **REP CLIENTS:** Corp. bldrs., private devels., municipalities; **PREV EMPLOY:** NY State Urban Devel. Corp.-Dir.-Design and Engineering;; Dir. of Disign and Engineering; **PROFL AFFIL & HONORS:** Amer. Arbitration Assn.; NY Soc. of Arch. (Dir. 1982-1985); NY State Assn. of Arch., Lic. Architect NY, RI, MD, NJ, CT; Cert. by NCARB; AIA Award; **EDUC:** BArch., 1958, Arch., Regents Scholarship, Scheur Grant, Pratt Inst.; **MIL SERV:** USA, Cpl. 1954-1956; **HOME ADD:** One Lincoln Plaza, New York, NY 10023, (212)799-8424; **BUS ADD:** 575 8th Ave, New York, NY 10018, (212)947-9870.

PANKOWSKI, Joseph Michael——**B:** Jan. 29, 1942, Cleveland, OH, *Consultant*, Righty Enterprises, Righty Investments; **PRIM RE ACT:** Consultant, Owner/Investor; **SERVICES:** Investment counseling, mktg., mgmt.; **REP CLIENTS:** Indiv. investors and distributors; **PREV EMPLOY:** Counselor, State Supervisor, Div. of Vocational Rehabilitation, State Dept. of Educ. 1965-76; **PROFL AFFIL & HONORS:** Nat. Rehab. Assn., Amer. Soc. for Public Admin., Amer. Soc. for Training & Devel., Chmn., Prime Study Grp., 1981 Inst. of Rehab. Issues; Pres., Tallahassee Chap., Amer. Soc. for Training and devel.; **EDUC:** BA, 1963, Speech, Eng., Journ., Univ. of FL; **GRAD EDUC:** Master of Rehab. Counseling, 1965, Univ. of FL; **EDUC HONORS:** Deans List, Pres., Univ. of FL Rehab. Assn.; **OTHER ACT & HONORS:** Chmn. FL State Univ. Rehab. Counseling Advisory Comm. 1977-81; Experimental Aircraft Assn., Aircraft Owners and Pilots Assn.; **HOME ADD:** 744 DuParc Cir., Tallahassee, FL 32312, (904)385-3432; **BUS ADD:** 744 DuParc Cir., Tallahassee, FL 32312, (904)385-3432.

PANTAZELOS, Peter——*Exec. VP*, Thermo Electron Corp.; **PRIM RE ACT:** Property Manager; **BUS ADD:** 101 First Ave., Waltham, MA 02154, (617)890-8700.*

PAOLINI, A. Joseph——**B:** Feb. 8, 1944, Italy, *Mgr., Facility Planning & RE*, Prime Computer Inc., Corporate Services; **OTHER RE ACT:** RE acquisition; space planning & design; **SERVICES:** Define RE needs; project justification & implement; **REP CLIENTS:** Different Corp. functions - engrg., mfrg., mktg., fin. & admin.; **PREV EMPLOY:** Data General Corp., RE Analyst; **PROFL AFFIL & HONORS:** IDRC, NACORE, BOMA, Bd. of Advisors New England RE Directory; **EDUC:** BBA, 1968, Mgmt., Nichols Coll. of Bus. Admin.; **HOME ADD:** 135 Parker Rd., Framingham, MA 01701, (617)872-3017; **BUS ADD:** 2 California Ave., Framingham, MA 01701, (617)879-2960.

PAPADOPOULOS, Joan——*Mng. Ed. - Circ. Mgr.*, Real Estate Research Corp., Real Estate Report; **PRIM RE ACT:** Real Estate Publisher; **BUS ADD:** 72 W. Adams, Chicago, IL 60603, (312)346-5885.*

PAPARAZZO, Henry J.——**B:** June 14, 1928, New Haven, CT, *Pres.*, Heritage Devel. Grp., Inc.; **PRIM RE ACT:** Developer, Builder, Property Manager, Owner/Investor; **OTHER RE ACT:** Own and operate Sewer & Water Cos., conf. ctr., comml. bldgs., rec. facilities; **SERVICES:** Manage and devel. various RE joint ventures, condo. conversions; **PROFL AFFIL & HONORS:** ULI(Tr.); NAHB, Numerous nat. bldg. and devel. awards; **EDUC:** BS, 1952, Geo., IN Univ.; **HOME ADD:** Route 100, Somers, NY 10589; **BUS ADD:** Admin. Bldg., Heritage Village, Southbury, CT 06488, (203)264-8291.

PAPAS, P.N., II——**B:** Boston, MA, *Pres.*, Centre Assoc.; **PRIM RE ACT:** Broker, Syndicator, Consultant, Appraiser, Developer, Builder, Property Manager; **SERVICES:** RE Sales, Mgmt, constr., custom bldg.; **PREV EMPLOY:** Also Pres. of Capital Return Co., a money broker & mort. investor; **EDUC:** BS, Criminal Justice, minor in Econ., Northeastern Univ., Coll. of Crim. Justice; **MIL SERV:** ARNGUS - Officer; **BUS ADD:** PO Box 253, Dedham, MA 02060, (617)329-4777.

PAPAZICKOS, Chris G.——**B:** Dec. 25, 1930, New Castle, PA, *Sr. VP and Gen. Counsel*, American Title Insurance Co., Corp. Legal Dept.; **PRIM RE ACT:** Insuror; **SERVICES:** Title Insurance; **PROFL AFFIL & HONORS:** ABA; PA Bar Assn.; **EDUC:** BA, 1951, Pol. Sci. and Pre-law, Univ. of MI; **GRAD EDUC:** LLB, 1954, Law, Univ. of MI Law School; **MIL SERV:** US Army; Spec. 2, Good Conduct Medal; **HOME ADD:** 11605 S.W. 98th Place, Miami, FL 33176, (305)253-9050; **BUS ADD:** 1101 Brickell Ave., P.O. Box 01-5002, Miami, FL 33101, (305)374-4300.

PAPELL, Nathan——**B:** Apr. 5, 1931, Bronx, NY, *Pres.*, Federated Business Agencies; **PRIM RE ACT:** Consultant, Owner/Investor; **OTHER RE ACT:** Mergers & Acquisitions - Bus. & Comml. prop., Bus. Broker, RE Broker; **SERVICES:** Bus. brokerage - fin. analysis; **PREV EMPLOY:** 13 years - CPA; 13 years - Bus. and RE Brokerage; **PROFL AFFIL & HONORS:** NY State Soc. of CPA's; **EDUC:** BBA, 1956, Public Acctg. - Sales Mgmt., City Coll. NY; **MIL SERV:** USA, Cpl., Korean Service MedaL with 1 Bronze Service Star; United Nations Service Medal; Merit Unit Commendation - 8th US Army; **BUS ADD:** 1790 Broadway, New York, NY 10019, (212)246-4700.

PAPP, Robert——*VP Pureh.*, Modine Mfg. Co.; **PRIM RE ACT:** Property Manager; **BUS ADD:** 1500 Dekaven Ave., Racine, WI 53401, (414)636-1200.*

PAPPAS, George——*Dir. RE & Construction*, EG & G; **PRIM RE ACT:** Developer, Property Manager; **BUS ADD:** 45 Williams St., Wellesley, MA 02181, (617)237-5100.*

PAQUIN, Gary N.——**B:** Nov. 8, 1940, Chicago, IL, *Pres.*, Sunmark Dev. Corp.; **PRIM RE ACT:** Consultant, Developer, Builder, Property Manager, Owner/Investor; **OTHER RE ACT:** Devel., Builder; **PREV EMPLOY:** Pres., Key Royale Homes, Edmonton, AB, Can (1975-1978); VP, Levitt & Sons, NY, NY (1972-1975); **EDUC:** BS, 1967, Mktg./Fin., N. IL Univ.; **MIL SERV:** USN, AT-2; **OTHER ACT & HONORS:** Coronado Cays Yacht Club; **HOME ADD:** 408 Green Turtle Rd., Coronado, CA 92118, (714)575-1272; **BUS ADD:** 8 Green Turtle Rd., Coronado, CA 92118, (714)575-1272.

PARADIS, Pierre R.——B: Nov. 7, 1938, New Bedford, MA, *Owner*, Whittier & Paradis; **PRIM RE ACT:** Attorney; **SERVICES:** Agreements, title searches, closings, land ct. registrations, deeds, mortgages; **REP CLIENTS:** Chicago Title Ins. Co., St. Anne Credit Union; **PROFL AFFIL & HONORS:** MA Conveyancers Assn., New Bedford Bar Assn., Land Court Title Examiner; **EDUC:** BA, 1960, French, Eng., Bowdoin Coll.; **GRAD EDUC:** JD, 1963, Medico-legal problems, Harvard Law School; **EDUC HONORS:** Cum laude, deans list, James Bowdoin Scholar, Cum laude; **OTHER ACT & HONORS:** New Bedford Visiting Nurse Serv. Profl. Advisory Comm.; **HOME ADD:** 51 Juliette St., N. Dartmouth, MA 02747; **BUS ADD:** 160 William St., New Bedford, MA 02740, (617)992-9505.

PARDILLO, Armando A.——B: Nov. 8, 1924, Moron, Camaguey, Cuba, *Pres.*, Armando Pardillo Law Offices, PA; **PRIM RE ACT:** Attorney; **SERVICES:** Legal Services; **PROFL AFFIL & HONORS:** FL Bar, ABA, Cuban-Amer. Bar Assn.; **MIL SERV:** Cuban Navy, Lt. Sr. Grade; **HOME ADD:** 4753 Alton Rd., Miami, FL 33140, (305)532-8986; **BUS ADD:** 1401 Ponce de Leon Blvd. Ste. 202, Coral Gables, FL 33134, (305)444-0100.

PARDOM, Charles F.——B: Nov. 13, 1934, Flint, MI, *Sr. VP*, The Trerice Mgmt. Co.; **PRIM RE ACT:** Broker, Consultant, Developer, Owner/Investor, Property Manager; **SERVICES:** Comml., indus. RE brokerage, devel. & mgmt.; **REP CLIENTS:** PIC, NY Life, Equitable, Ford Motor, GM; **PREV EMPLOY:** VP Prop. Mgmt. Nat. Bank of Detroit, 1967-81; **PROFL AFFIL & HONORS:** BOMA, IREM, Amer. Bd. of Realtors, Past Pres & Dir. BOMA; **EDUC:** BA, 1959, Bus. Admin., Eastern MI Univ.; **OTHER ACT & HONORS:** Metro. Det. Constrc. User's Council; Engrg. Soc. of Detroit; Bd. of Commerce; **HOME ADD:** 336 McMillan Rd., Grosse Pte. Farms, MI 48236, (313)886-2984; **BUS ADD:** 24245 Northwestern Hwy., Southfield, MI 48075, (313)353-1000.

PARDUE, William Pierce, Jr.——B: May 21, 1931, Orlando, FL, *Pres.*, Pardue, Heid, Church, Smith & Waller, Inc.; **PRIM RE ACT:** Broker, Instructor, Consultant, Appraiser; **OTHER RE ACT:** Mkt. analyst; **SERVICES:** RE appraisals, Mkt. analysis & counseling; **REP CLIENTS:** Investors, lenders, attys., gov. agencies; **PROFL AFFIL & HONORS:** AIREA, ASREC, SREA, Past Pres. FL Chap. 2, AIREA, etc.; **EDUC:** Tulane Univ. & Univ. of the South; **HOME ADD:** 809 Hyde Park Place, Altamonte Springs, FL 32701, (305)831-4354; **BUS ADD:** 1412 W Colonial Dr., Orlando, FL 32804, (305)841-3602.

PARENT, Gerald Brunsell——B: Feb. 25, 1932, South Bend, IN, *Atty.*, Hatch & Parent, A Profl. Corp.; **PRIM RE ACT:** Attorney; **REP CLIENTS:** The Bank of Montecito; **PREV EMPLOY:** State Inheritance Tax Appraiser, 1964 to 1970; **PROFL AFFIL & HONORS:** CA Bar Assn, ABA, Trial Lawyers of Amer. Assn.; **EDUC:** BA, 1954, Pol. Sci., UCLA; **GRAD EDUC:** LLB, 1959, Hastings Coll. of Law; **MIL SERV:** USA, 1st Lt., 1955-56; **OTHER ACT & HONORS:** City airport commr., 1962-70; Dir. 19th Ag. dist. 1981 to-; La Cumbre Ctry Club; Univ. Club; **HOME ADD:** 2301 Santa Barbara St., Santa Barbara, CA 93105, (805)682-3054; **BUS ADD:** 21 East Carrillo St., Santa Barbara, CA 93101, (805)963-1971.

PARISH, J. Michael——B: June 17, 1948, Jackson, TN, *Pres.*, MPM Devel. Corp.; **PRIM RE ACT:** Broker, Consultant, Developer, Owner/Investor, Property Manager, Syndicator; **SERVICES:** RE sales, sale-leasebacks, build-to-suit, turn key devel., synd., comml. & multi-family devel.; **PROFL AFFIL & HONORS:** RESSI; **EDUC:** BS, 1970, Pol. Sci., Univ. of TN, Knoxville; **GRAD EDUC:** MBA, 1976, RE & Urban Devel., Univ. of TN, Knoxville; **MIL SERV:** US Army, 1st. Lt.; **HOME ADD:** 1802 Nantasket Rd., Knoxville, TN 37922; **BUS ADD:** 238 Peters Rd., Suite 302, Knoxville, TN 37923, (615)691-3552.

PARISSE, Alan J.——B: July 31, 1943, Bronx, NY, *Pres.*, Ameribond Prop.; **PRIM RE ACT:** Broker, Instructor, Syndicator, Real Estate Publisher; **SERVICES:** Synd. of Comml. & Resential Prop.; Consulting on Synd., Inst. in Synd. and Direct Participation Program Licensing; **PREV EMPLOY:** Sr. VP Oppenheimer Prop.; **PROFL AFFIL & HONORS:** RESSI, 1st VP (RESSI) - Synd. of Yr. Award (RESSI) 1978, Featured Speaker on Synd. at NAR Annual Convention for 7 consecutive yrs.; **EDUC:** BS, 1965, Bus. Adm., Univ. of Buffalo; **GRAD EDUC:** MBA, 1968, Bus., Univ. of AZ; **EDUC HONORS:** Beta Gamma Syna Hon. Bus. Frat.; **HOME ADD:** 23 Park Ave., New York, NY, (212)889-4953; **BUS ADD:** 500 Park Ave., New York, NY 10022, (212)888-1140.

PARK, Dale E.——B: Mar. 22, 1950, New Castle, PA, *Sec.*, Park Ventures, Inc.; **PRIM RE ACT:** Owner/Investor; **EDUC:** BS, 1973, Acctg., Econ., Youngstown State Univ., Youngstown, OH; **HOME ADD:** 90 W Main St., Glen Rock, NJ 07452, (201)652-4988; **BUS ADD:** 729 Countyline St., New Castle, PA 16101, (201)652-4988.

PARK, Richard E.G.——B: May 22, 1945, Newark, NJ, *VP and Div. Mgr.*, Security Pacific Nat. Bank, Fiduciary Servs. Grp.-RE Mgmt. Div.; **PRIM RE ACT:** Consultant, Appraiser, Banker, Developer, Lender, Owner/Investor, Property Manager; **SERVICES:** Acquisition, evaluations, prop. mgmt., land devel., use analysis, negotiation servs., related fin. servs., investment advice; **REP CLIENTS:** Confidential; **PREV EMPLOY:** Various positions in fin. and investment mgmt. and consulting with Security Pac. Nat. Bank and Fidelcor, Inc. (Philadelphia); **EDUC:** BA, 1967, Pol. Sci., Univ. of PA; **GRAD EDUC:** Law School of the Univ. of GA; Nat. Grad. Trust School, Northwestern Univ.; **EDUC HONORS:** Honors Thesis - Making A Profit in the Large Trust Dept.; **BUS ADD:** Security Pacific Bank, 333 S. Hope St. H40-6, Los Angeles, CA 90051, (213)613-7067.

PARKER, Cortland——*Secretary Treasurer*, Society of Exchange Counselors; **OTHER RE ACT:** Profl. Assn. Admin.; **BUS ADD:** PO Box 41964, Sacramento, CA 95841, (916)920-4031.*

PARKER, James E.——B: Oct. 3, 1933, Tyler, TX, *Pres.*, Par-Mar RE, Inc., Chickasha Millwork and Supply, Parker Paint and Decorating; **PRIM RE ACT:** Broker, Consultant, Developer, Builder, Owner/Investor, Property Manager; **SERVICES:** Land devel., resid. design, resid. & comml. custom cabinetry, interior design, Custom millwork, resid. and comml. bldg.; **PREV EMPLOY:** Plant Mgr., Pet Inc., Chickasha, OK; **PROFL AFFIL & HONORS:** Grady Cty. Bd. of Realtors, OK Assn. of Realtors, NAR, Washita Valley Home Builders Assn., Nat. Assn. of Home Builders, Nat. C of C, Realtor of the Year 1977; **EDUC:** BS, 1956, Agronomy, NM State Univ. Las Cruces, NM; **MIL SERV:** USN, Lt.; **OTHER ACT & HONORS:** City Councilman 1974-76, Mayor 1976-80; Rotary; All Sports Booster Club; Elks; C of C; OK Heritage Assn.; Rotary - Paul Harris Fellow 1981; **HOME ADD:** 219 Willowcreek Rd., Chickasha, OK, (405)224-5433; **BUS ADD:** 3204 S. 4th, Chickasha, OK 73018, (405)224-5444.

PARKER, King, Jr.——B: May 19, 1917, San Francisco, CA, *Pres.*, King Parker, Jr., Inc.; **PRIM RE ACT:** Broker, Consultant, Appraiser, Developer, Instructor, Property Manager, Syndicator; **PROFL AFFIL & HONORS:** NAR; RNMI; Inst. of RE Mgmt., CPM; CCIM; **EDUC:** BS, 1939, Univ. of CA; **MIL SERV:** Royal Air Force; Capt.; **HOME ADD:** 1403 Via Loma, Walnut Creek, CA 94598; **BUS ADD:** 1990 No. CA Blvd., Walnut Creek, CA 95696, (415)938-6900.

PARKER, Mark D.——B: Jan. 29, 1955, Billings, MT, *Atty.*, Kurth Law Firm, P.C.; **PRIM RE ACT:** Attorney, Developer; **OTHER RE ACT:** Pres. of Alkali Creek Land Co.; **SERVICES:** Legal; **REP CLIENTS:** Alkali Creek Land Co.; **PREV EMPLOY:** Alkali Creek Land Co., Dean Realty (a dvi. of Pulte Homes); **PROFL AFFIL & HONORS:** ABA, Member CA Bar Assn.; **EDUC:** BA, 1977, Econ., Univ. of MT; **GRAD EDUC:** JD, 1980, Comml. Law, Univ. of San Diego; **EDUC HONORS:** Honors, Who's Who in Amer. Colls. & Univs., Order of the Barristers, Chmn. of Moot Ct. Bd.; **HOME ADD:** 306 S. 37th St., Billings, MT 59103, (406)248-5309; **BUS ADD:** 350 Securities Bldg., PO Box 2137, Billings, MT 59103, (406)248-1111.

PARKER, Phil——B: July 15, 1940, Miami, AZ, *Broker*, The Buyers Broker; **PRIM RE ACT:** Broker, Consultant, Owner/Investor, Syndicator; **SERVICES:** Representation of buyer's in RE transactions; **PROFL AFFIL & HONORS:** RMNI; RESSI; Phoenix Bd. of Realtors; AZ Chapter CCIM (candidate), CCIM; **EDUC:** AA/BA, 1972, Bus., Phoenix Coll.; **MIL SERV:** Airborne, Mgt. E-5; **HOME ADD:** 4022 W. Loma Ln., Phoenix, AZ 85021, (602)939-1822; **BUS ADD:** 620 M. 2nd St., Phoenix, AZ 85004, (602)252-0233.

PARKER, Vincent L.——B: Nov. 15, 1920, Portsmouth, VA, *Lawyer*, Cooper, Davis, Kilgore, Parker, Leon & Fennell, P.C.; **PRIM RE ACT:** Attorney; **REP CLIENTS:** VA Investment & Mort. Corps., Central Fidelity Bank, Portsmouth Redevel. & Housing Authority; **PROFL AFFIL & HONORS:** ABA, VA Bar Assns., Former Pres. Portsmouth Bar Assn.; Member Exec. Comm. Norfolk-Portsmouth Bar Assn.; Chmn. 4th Dist. Comm. (Disciplinary) of VA State Bar; **GRAD EDUC:** LLB, 1951, U. of VA; **MIL SERV:** USAF, Capt.; **HOME ADD:** 532 North St., Portsmouth, VA 23704, (804)397-1412; **BUS ADD:** Suite 500, Central Fidelity Bank Bldg.,, PO. Drawer 1475, Portsmouth, VA 23705, (804)397-3481.

PARKER, W. Wright——B: May 7, 1919, Brunswick, GA, *Pres.*, Parker-Kaufman, Realtors & Insurors; **PRIM RE ACT:** Broker, Appraiser, Owner/Investor, Insuror; **SERVICES:** All RE servs. & gen. ins. agency; **PREV EMPLOY:** Have been with present co. since 1941 except for 3 years in Army Air Corps; **PROFL AFFIL & HONORS:** AIREA, Soc. of RE Appraisers, MAI, SRPA; **EDUC:** BS in Commerce, 1941, Acctg., Univ. of GA; **EDUC HONORS:** Dean's List; **MIL SERV:** US Army Air Corps, 1st Lt., Europe-Africa Theater of Operations; **OTHER ACT & HONORS:** City Commnr. 1966-1970; Pres. Brunswick-Glynn Cty. C of C; Pres. of Brunswick-Glynn Cty. Bd.

of Realtors and of GA Assn. of Realtors; **HOME ADD:** 303 Union St., Brunswick, GA 31520, (912)265-4865; **BUS ADD:** 513 Gloucester St., Brunswick, GA 31521, (912)265-7711.

PARKINS, Raymond A.——*Pres.*, Raymond A. Parkins & Assoc.; **OTHER RE ACT:** Asset & investment mgmt.; **PREV EMPLOY:** First Natl. Bank of Atlanta; Financial Service Corp. (Sr. VP); **PROFL AFFIL & HONORS:** Cert. Fin. Planner; **EDUC:** BS, Clemsen Univ.; **GRAD EDUC:** MS, G A Tech.; **OTHER ACT & HONORS:** Exec. Officer AIM; BOD Pen Amer. Bank of Orlando, FL; Pres. of the Parkins Cos.: (A) Asset and Investment Mgmt. Inc., (B) The Parkins Investment Securities Corp., (C) The Parkins Natural Resource Investment Corp.; **BUS ADD:** 200 Robinson St., Suite 880, Orlando, FL 32801.

PARKINSON, Steve——**B:** Feb. 22, 1944, Houston, TX, *Prop. Mgr.*, Title Insurance and Trust Co., Trust RE; **PRIM RE ACT:** Broker, Consultant, Appraiser, Owner/Investor, Property Manager; **SERVICES:** Primarily manage prop. held in trust; **PREV EMPLOY:** Merrill Lynch Relocation Mgmt., Inc.; **PROFL AFFIL & HONORS:** CA RE Broker; **EDUC:** BBA, 1981, Bus. Admin., Univ. of La Verne; **HOME ADD:** 354 Avocado #22, Costa Mesa, CA 92627, (714)239-6081; **BUS ADD:** 220 "A" St., San Diego, CA 92101, (714)239-6081.

PARKS, John R.——**B:** July 31, 1952, Rantoul, IL, *Staff Atty.*, Attorneys' Title Guaranty Fund, Inc.; **PRIM RE ACT:** Attorney, Insuror; **OTHER RE ACT:** Author of articles on condos. and morts.; **SERVICES:** Advice and underwriting on title insurance matters; **PREV EMPLOY:** Atty. at Powell, Goldstein, Frazer & Murphy in Atlanta, GA specializing in comml. RE law; **PROFL AFFIL & HONORS:** ABA, IL Bar Assn. and Chicago Bar Assn.; **EDUC:** BS, 1974, Fin., Univ. of Illinois; **GRAD EDUC:** JD - MBA, 1977, Law and Bus., Columbia Univ.; **EDUC HONORS:** Beta Gamma Sigma, Bronze Tablet, Morrey and Nurton Awards, Stone Scholar, Berle Award; **HOME ADD:** 33 Ashley Lane, Champaign, IL 61820, (217)356-4702; **BUS ADD:** PO Box 3036, Champaign, IL 61820, (217)359-2000.

PARLETT, Philip M.——**B:** Mar. 23, 1949, Atlantic City, NJ, *Investment Counselor/Fin. Planner*, Vistar Fin. Inc.; **PRIM RE ACT:** Broker, Syndicator, Property Manager, Owner/Investor; **OTHER RE ACT:** Fin. Planne; Mort. Broker; Investment Counselor; **SERVICES:** Investment counseling, synd. of comml. & resid. props., mort. & RE brokerage, fin. estate planning for indiv. & corp. clients; **PROFL AFFIL & HONORS:** NAR; RESSI; Intl. Assoc. of Fin. Planners; US C of C, Assoc. Realtor of Yr., 1979; RECI, Sr. Recipient; Who's Who in Creative RE; **EDUC:** 1972, Acctg. & Fin., Minor RE, UCLA; **GRAD EDUC:** MBA, 1983, RE, UCLA; **OTHER ACT & HONORS:** Past Pres., Venice Marina Lions Club; Sec. Treas., Venice C of C; Dir., Venice Boys Club, Dir., CA Assn. of Realtors, Past Pres., Pac. Police Boosters Assn., Exec Bd. Member, Grt. Western Council, Boy Scouts of Amer.; **HOME ADD:** 420 Rialto Ave., Venice, CA 90291, (213)399-7458; **BUS ADD:** 13465 Wash. Blvd., Marina Del Rey, CA 90291, (213)822-8733.

PARMENTER, William E.——**B:** Sept. 13, 1927, Providence, RI, *Sr. Member*, Parmenter & Assoc.; **PRIM RE ACT:** Attorney; **OTHER RE ACT:** Agent, Title Ins. Co. of MN; **SERVICES:** Conveyancing, fin. counseling, title ins.; **REP CLIENTS:** Attys.; lenders; brokers; indiv. and inst. investors; condo. devel.; synd.; **PROFL AFFIL & HONORS:** RI Bar Assn.; ABA; Fed. Bar Assn.; **EDUC:** BA, 1950, Liberal Arts, Brown Univ.; **GRAD EDUC:** JD, 1954, Real Prop., Univ. of MI Law Sch.; **EDUC HONORS:** Editor, MI Law Review; **OTHER ACT & HONORS:** Restoration and preservation of colonial bldgs.; **HOME ADD:** 401 Benefit St., Providence, RI 02903, (401)272-4544; **BUS ADD:** 401 Benefit St., PO Box 1653, Providence, RI 02901, (401)272-4544.

PARMET, Donald J.——**B:** Aug. 12, 1931, New York, NY, *Partner*, Parmet & Robbins; **PRIM RE ACT:** Attorney; **REP CLIENTS:** Builders of resid. communities, owners and operators of motels, landlords of comml. prop.; **PROFL AFFIL & HONORS:** NY State Bar Assn.; Nassau Cty. Bar Assn.; NY Cty. Bar Assn.; Bankruptcy Bar Assn.; **EDUC:** AB, 1952, Cornell Univ.; **GRAD EDUC:** JD, 1955, Cornell Law School; **EDUC HONORS:** NY State Scholarship, Cornell St. Scholarship, Sigma Delta Chi, Pi Delta Epsilon, Hon. Soc.; **MIL SERV:** US Army, Lt.; **OTHER ACT & HONORS:** Dir., Federation of Cornell Alumni Clubs, 1982; VP, Cornell Club of LI, 1981-82; Pres., Cornell Club of LI, 1982-; **HOME ADD:** 9 Giffard Way, Melville, NY 11747; **BUS ADD:** 99 Jericho Tpk., Jericho, NY 11753, (516)333-3377.

PARRIS, Joe W.——*Pres.*, Interstate Devel. & Investment Corp.; **PRIM RE ACT:** Broker, Developer, Builder, Owner/Investor; **SERVICES:** Full RE devel. constr. and fin. servs. for comml. & indus. clients; **REP CLIENTS:** Free standing comml., comm. shopping ctrs. and light indus. parks, GA Dept. of Motor Veh., Cormin Foods., Inc., Carl Jr's Restaurant, Mobil, Taco Bell, Western Auto., Del Taco, Invsco, Mexican Restaurant, Kindercare Learning Centers; **PREV EMPLOY:** Interstate Devel. and Investment Corp., Comml. Devel. & Invest. Corp., Parris & Assoc., Lockheed Amercraft Co., Military Serv.; **PROFL AFFIL & HONORS:** Cobb Cty. C of C, Metro Atlanta Home Builders Assn., RE Brokers, Private Pilot, Building Contractor GA, FL, NC, SC; **EDUC:** BBA, RE Mktg., GA State Univ.; **MIL SERV:** USAF; **HOME ADD:** 3518 Nantucket Dr., Marietta, GA 30067, (617)971-7342; **BUS ADD:** 2814 New Spring Rd., Suite 309, Atlanta, GA 30339, (404)433-8586.

PARRISH, Donald R.——**B:** Jan. 10, 1936, Daytona Beach, FL, *VP*, The Seamen's Bank for Savings, Mort.-RE; **PRIM RE ACT:** Engineer, Banker, Lender; **SERVICES:** Const. loans, permanent mort., joint ventures; **PREV EMPLOY:** RE Dept. - Bankers Trust Co.; **PROFL AFFIL & HONORS:** Mort. Bankers Assn. of NY, Registered Profl. Engr. - NY; **EDUC:** BA, 1957, Physics, OH Wesleyan Univ.; **GRAD EDUC:** BS, 1959, CE, MIT; MBA, 1973, Econ., NY Univ. Grad School of Bus. Admin.; **OTHER ACT & HONORS:** Chmn., Croton-on-Hudson Planning Bd. 1977-1981; **HOME ADD:** 135 Old Post Rd. S., Croton-on-Hudson, NY 10520, (914)271-3553; **BUS ADD:** 30 Wall Street, New York, NY 10005, (212)797-5046.

PARRISH, Lowe L., III——**B:** Feb. 25, 1949, Spartanburg, SC, *Pres.*, Realaw Assoc., Inc.; **PRIM RE ACT:** Consultant, Developer, Owner/Investor, Property Manager, Syndicator; **SERVICES:** Investment counseling, devel. & synd. of comml. RE & prop. mgmt.; **REP CLIENTS:** Indiv. inst. investors in comml props.; **EDUC:** BS, 1969, Bio. & Chem., Augusta Coll.; **GRAD EDUC:** MBA, 1973, Pharm., Mktg., Fin., Med. Coll. of GA, Univ. of GA, Georgia State Univ., Old. Dom. Univ.; **MIL SERV:** Army; **HOME ADD:** PO Box 413, Haddonfield, NJ 08033; **BUS ADD:** 24 Louella Ct., Wayne, PA 19087, (215)964-9225.

PARRISH, Michael R.——**B:** Oct. 15, 1947, Fullerton, CA, *Pres.*, Parrish Company, Realtors; **PRIM RE ACT:** Broker; **SERVICES:** Sales, leasing, devel. of comml. indus. and investment RE; **REP CLIENTS:** Builders, devels., doctors, dentists, small oil cos.; **PREV EMPLOY:** Turner Corp., mort. bankers and Rice Realtors; **PROFL AFFIL & HONORS:** NAR, Nat. Assn. of Home Builders, Metropolitan Tulsa Bd. of Realtors, Metro Tulsa Builders Assn.; **EDUC:** BS, 1969, Econ., OK State Univ.; **MIL SERV:** Army-Nat. Gd., Sgt.; **OTHER ACT & HONORS:** Tulsa Bus. Builders, VP, Southside Rotary, Tsa La Gi Yacht Club, Vice Commodore; **HOME ADD:** 7802 E. 79th St., Tulsa, OK 74133, (918)252-4034; **BUS ADD:** 6315 So. Memorial Dr., Tulsa, OK 74133, (918)252-4571.

PARROTT, A. Leonard——**B:** Oct. 12, 1933, New York, NY, *Pres.*, Parrott Real Estate Associates, Inc., Resid.; **PRIM RE ACT:** Broker, Consultant, Appraiser, Developer, Owner/Investor, Instructor, Property Manager; **SERVICES:** Resid. RE Brokerage; **REP CLIENTS:** GE, IBM, GT & E, Homequity; **PREV EMPLOY:** The Fairfield Land & Title Co., VP, 1961-70; **PROFL AFFIL & HONORS:** NAR, CT Assn. of Realtors, Fairfield Bd. of Realtors, CT Chap. Cert. Resid. Brokers, Grad. Realtors Ins. Cert. Resid. Broker Mgrs.; Manager Realtor of The Year 1975; Distinguished Serv. Award, Fairfield Jaycees 1968; **EDUC:** BS, 1959, Mktg., Babson Coll.; **MIL SERV:** US Army, PFC; **OTHER ACT & HONORS:** RTM 1973- 78; Rep. to CT Ctr. for RE & Urban Econ. Studies; Rotary; C of C; Outstanding Young Men of Amer. 1967; Who's Who in RE Marketing Mgmt. 1975-81; Who's Who in RE in Amer. 1981-1982; **HOME ADD:** 1940 Merwins Ln., Fairfield, CT 06430, (203)259-3139; **BUS ADD:** 765 Post Rd., Fairfield, CT 06430, (203)255-6101.

PARSON, E.I.——*Pres.*, Holly Corp.; **PRIM RE ACT:** Property Manager; **BUS ADD:** 2600 Diamond Shamrock Tower, 717 North Harwood St., Dallas, TX 75201, (214)651-0311.*

PARSONS, Bernard——**B:** Aug. 4, 1938, Liverpool, Eng., *Prop. Mgr.*, Globe Realty Management Ltd., Royal Bank Centre; **PRIM RE ACT:** Engineer, Developer, Property Manager; **PREV EMPLOY:** Y & R Prop. Ltd., Devel. Mgrs., 390 Bay St., Toronto; **PROFL AFFIL & HONORS:** SORPA, Real Prop. Administrator; **EDUC:** Structural Engrg., Liverpool Coll. of Bldg.; **GRAD EDUC:** 1960, Inst. of Struct. Engrs., U.K.; **OTHER ACT & HONORS:** Treas., BOMA, Ottawa; **HOME ADD:** 25 Silver Aspen Cres. - Blackburn Hamlet, Ottawa, Ont., Canada, (613)824-0546; **BUS ADD:** 90 Sparks St., Ottawa, K1P5T6, Ont., Can., (613)566-3181.

PARSONS, Charles A., Jr.——**B:** July 16, 1943, Minneapolis, MN, *Atty. at Law*, Moss, Flaherty, Clarkson & Fletcher, a profl. assn.; **PRIM RE ACT:** Attorney; **REP CLIENTS:** lenders, investors; **PROFL AFFIL & HONORS:** Hennepin Cty. Bar Assn.; MN State Bar Assn.; ABA; Legal Advice Clinics, Ltd.; **EDUC:** BBA, 1965, Acctg., Univ. of MN; **GRAD EDUC:** JD, 1972, RE Law, Univ. of MN; **EDUC**

HONORS: Cum Laude; **MIL SERV:** USMC, Capt., N.A.M. w/V; **OTHER ACT & HONORS:** Instr. for various RE education programs; **HOME ADD:** 5146 Knox Ave. S., Minneapolis, MN 55419, (612)922-3361; **BUS ADD:** 1200 Pillsbury Ctr., Minneapolis, MN 55402, (612)339-8551.

PARSONS, Frederick M.——*Mgt., RE and Prop. Taxes*, Morton-Norwich Products, Inc., Corporate; **PRIM RE ACT:** Consultant, Appraiser, Property Manager; **SERVICES:** Buying, selling, and leasing of RE for four divs., including Morton Salt, Morton Chemical, Norwich-Eaton Pharmaceutical and Texize; responsibility for all domestic and Can. prop. taxes, both real & personal; **BUS ADD:** 110 N. Wacker Dr., Chicago, IL 60606, (312)621-5577.

PARSONS, Garrett S.——**B:** Feb. 12, 1948, Mineola, NY, *Pres.*, Chesapeake Investment, Inc.; **PRIM RE ACT:** Broker, Developer, Builder, Owner/Investor, Syndicator; **SERVICES:** Synd., RE brokerage, resid. prop. devel.; **REP CLIENTS:** Foreign investors, lending inst., investors for resid. housing; **PROFL AFFIL & HONORS:** CCIM; RESSI; **EDUC:** BS, 1969, Econ., Univ. of MD; **MIL SERV:** USN, Lt., Aviator Wings, 1969-1972; **HOME ADD:** 5001 Shorekine Way, Oxnard, CA 93030, (805)985-6269; **BUS ADD:** 475 W. Channel Island Blvd., Suite 103, Pt. Hueneme, CA 93041, (805)985-8894.

PARSONS, George M.——**B:** Sept. 7, 1930, Nashville, TN, *Owner*, ABC Properties; **PRIM RE ACT:** Developer, Builder, Owner/Investor; **PREV EMPLOY:** Same 25 years; **PROFL AFFIL & HONORS:** Nat. Apt. Assn. Talk - Landlords of KS, Pres. - Rental Owners of Wichita; **EDUC:** BA, 1956, Bus. Admin., Wichita State Univ.; **OTHER ACT & HONORS:** Housing Commnr.- City of Wichita; **HOME ADD:** 415 Greenwood, Wichita, KS 67211, (316) 262-3731; **BUS ADD:** 415 Greenwood, Wichita, KS 67211, (316)262-3731.

PARTIN, Marcus K.——**B:** June 3, 1953, Portland, OR, *Pres., Board Chairman; V.P. Research and Acqu., Director*, Environmental Research and Development Corp. (ERADCO), Commercial Pacific Brokerage Services Inc.; **PRIM RE ACT:** Broker, Owner/Investor, Syndicator; **SERVICES:** Researched bases land invest. services; **REP CLIENTS:** ERADCO Sponsored Limited partnerships; Key West Dev. Corp.; **PREV EMPLOY:** Environ. Research and Devel. Corp., VP 1976-79; Comml. Pacific Brokerage Services Inc., Pres. 1979-80; **PROFL AFFIL & HONORS:** RESSA; NAR; NASD; **EDUC:** Highline Coll., 1973-74, Bus. Admin. - Mktg., Cent. OR Coll. 1971-72; **GRAD EDUC:** WsNYU, 1979; **EDUC HONORS:** Phi Theta Kappa; **OTHER ACT & HONORS:** Appoint., City of Renton, WA Planning Commn.; **HOME ADD:** 4352 North Camino Real, Tucson AZ 85718, (602)299-5333; **BUS ADD:** 18000 Pacific Highway South, Suite 1115, Seattle, WA 98188, (206)244-0080.

PASCHOW, Joel M.——**B:** Feb. 18, 1943, New York, NY, *Chmn. of Bd.*, American Property Investors; **PRIM RE ACT:** Owner/Investor; **REP CLIENTS:** Major US corp.; **PROFL AFFIL & HONORS:** Past Gov., RE Securities Inst.; **EDUC:** BA, 1964, Govt., Cornell Univ.; **GRAD EDUC:** JD, 1967, Harvard Law School; **OTHER ACT & HONORS:** Tr., Children's Hospital, Long Island Jewish Medical Ctr.; **BUS ADD:** 666 3rd Ave., New York, NY 10017, (212)878-9304.

PASKEY, Ernest L.——**B:** May 19, 1942, Poughkeepsie, NY, *Landscape Arch.*, SKS Assoc.; **PRIM RE ACT:** Consultant, Engineer, Architect; **OTHER RE ACT:** Landscape Arch.; **SERVICES:** Land planning, survey, engrg., arch. design, planting plans; **REP CLIENTS:** Single family subdiv. & multi-famiLy project devel., restaurant & comml. devel., attys. (survey - tape maps - environmental impact assessment); **PREV EMPLOY:** Pvt. practice as consultant since 1966; **PROFL AFFIL & HONORS:** Amer. Soc. of Landscape Arch., Consultant to Rochester Preservation Bd.; **EDUC:** Bach. of Landscape Arch., 1964, Coll. of Forestry, Syracuse Univ.; **GRAD EDUC:** Masters/Instr. Tech., Pursuing, Rochester Inst. of Tech.; **MIL SERV:** U.S. Army, Corps of Engrs., Capt.; **OTHER ACT & HONORS:** Educator, St. Thomas Episcopal Church; Member, Landmark Soc. of Western MY; **HOME ADD:** 246 Glen Ellyn Way, Rochester, NY 14618, (716)275-0468; **BUS ADD:** 47 Steel St., Rochester, NY 14606, (716)458 1330.

PASNER, Edith A.——**B:** June 6, 1927, Vienna, Austria, *Gen. Partner*, E.A.P. Investment Grps.; **PRIM RE ACT:** Broker, Syndicator, Consultant, Developer, Property Manager, Owner/Investor; **OTHER RE ACT:** Comml. & Indus. Brokerage; **SERVICES:** Creating Limited Partnerships; **PREV EMPLOY:** Merchandising, GI Models New York - Buyer - 1945-1952; RE Investment Grps. Hence; **PROFL AFFIL & HONORS:** RESSI, GRI Cont. Edu. Cert.; **EDUC:** 1951, Merchandising, CCNY; **OTHER ACT & HONORS:** Downey Bd. of Realtors, Lecturing, Investment Div.; **HOME ADD:** 9150 E Florence Ave., Downey, CA 90240, (213)773-2300; **BUS ADD:** 7419 E Florence Ave., Downey, CA 90240, (213)927-1487.

PASNIK, Alan——*Circ. Mgr.*, Warren Gorham & Lamont, Inc., Real Estate Law Report; **PRIM RE ACT:** Real Estate Publisher; **BUS ADD:** 210 South St., Boston, MA 02111, (617)423-2020.*

PASQUARELLA, Val, Jr.——**B:** Aug. 10, 1948, Philadelphia, PA, *Pres.*, V.H. Pasquarella Company Realtors; **PRIM RE ACT:** Consultant, Appraiser, Instructor; **OTHER RE ACT:** Educ. Dir.-N Philadelphia Realty Bd.; **SERVICES:** Valuations and investment counseling; **REP CLIENTS:** Prudential Ins. Co.; Merrill Lynch; Homequity; various mort. lenders and investors; **PREV EMPLOY:** RE Instr.-School of Bus. Admin., Temple Univ., Philadelphia, PA 1974-1977; **PROFL AFFIL & HONORS:** Soc. of RE Appraisers, Amer. Soc. of Appraisers, NAR, SRA, ASA; **EDUC:** BS, 1971, Bus. Admin., Philadelphia Coll. of Textiles & Sci.; **MIL SERV:** USN, PO-2; **HOME ADD:** 30 Daffodil Dr., Churchville, PA 18966, (215)357-2149; **BUS ADD:** 9231 Frankford Ave., Philadelphia, PA 19114, (215)332-8700.

PASQUINELLI, Anthony R.——**B:** Sept. 12, 1933, Chicago, IL, *Exec. VP*, Pasquinelli Constr. Co.; **PRIM RE ACT:** Consultant, Developer, Builder, Property Manager, Owner/Investor; **PROFL AFFIL & HONORS:** BD. of Dir. Local HBA, Flossmoor Planning Comm. Member; **EDUC:** BAS, 1955, Acctg. and Econ, Univ. of IL; **MIL SERV:** USA, Sp4; **HOME ADD:** 852 Bruce St, Flossmoor, IL 60422, (312)798-4588; **BUS ADD:** Homewood, IL 60430PO Box 1639, (312)957-9020.

PASS, Mark O.——**B:** Oct. 26, 1942, Seattle, *Co-owner*, Seattle Pacific Comml. Brokerage Co.; **PRIM RE ACT:** Broker, Syndicator, Consultant, Developer; **SERVICES:** Site acquisition (retail/industrial) Mkt. and feasibility studies, investment analysis; **PREV EMPLOY:** Worked for the Fed. Bankruptsy Court Managing Prop.; **PROFL AFFIL & HONORS:** Seattle-King Cty. Bd. of Realtors, RNMI, CCIM; **EDUC:** BA, 1964, Econ. and Fin., Univ. of AZ; **MIL SERV:** USAF, Sgt.; **OTHER ACT & HONORS:** Seattle C of C; **HOME ADD:** 6520-83rd Pl. SE, Mercer Island, WA 98040, (206)232-2135; **BUS ADD:** 1904-3rd Ave., Suite 400, Seattle, WA 98040, (206)682-3100.

PASSMORE, Luther I.——**B:** Mar. 24, 1913, Humbeldt, TN, *RE Analyst*, 2nd Appraiser; **PRIM RE ACT:** Consultant, Appraiser; **SERVICES:** Advising buyers, sellers, lenders of various RE values; **PREV EMPLOY:** State Tax Commnr.; **PROFL AFFIL & HONORS:** AIREA, SREA; **EDUC:** BS, 1947, Coll. of ID; **MIL SERV:** USN, Sp. 1st; **OTHER ACT & HONORS:** Shriner, Elk.; **HOME ADD:** 1601 Dearborn, Caldwell, ID 83605, (208)459-2034; **BUS ADD:** 1601 Dearborn, Caldwell, ID 83605, (208)459-2034.

PASSOLT, James C., Jr.——**B:** Apr. 23, 1944, Minneapolis, MN, *RE Mgr.*, United Parcel Service, Pacific Rgn.; **PRIM RE ACT:** Attorney, Property Manager; **OTHER RE ACT:** Site acquisition, lease & contract negotiation, lease admin. and prop. mgmt. over nine state area; **PREV EMPLOY:** Asst. to Pres., Seldin Devel. & Mgmt. Co., Omaha, NE 1972-1973; **PROFL AFFIL & HONORS:** NE Bar Assn. (1972-75); NACORE (1977-); **EDUC:** BBA, 1969, Bus. Mgmt., TX Wesleyan Coll., Fort Worth, TX; **GRAD EDUC:** JD, 1972, School of Law, Univ. of SD, Vermillion S.D.; **EDUC HONORS:** Phi Beta Lambda (Pres. 1969); Young Republicans (Pres. 1969) Dean's List 3 years; **MIL SERV:** NE Air Nat. Guard, 1965-72, Tech. Sgt.; **OTHER ACT & HONORS:** Masons; Shrine; Saddleback Valley Stamp Club; Bd. of Dir. of Douglas Sarpy Cty. (NE) Heart Assn. (1972-77); Exec. Comm. of S. CA NACORE Chap. (1981-82); **HOME ADD:** 25055 Costeau, Laguna Hills, CA 92653, (714)951-3449; **BUS ADD:** 12822 Garden Grove Blvd., Garden Grove, CA 92643, (714)999-6431.

PATCHEL, Robert——*RE Mgr.*, Robin Industries, Inc.; **PRIM RE ACT:** Property Manager; **BUS ADD:** 101 East Avenue, North Tonawanda, NY 14120, (716)796-6600.*

PATCHIN, Peter J.——**B:** Mar. 13, 1934, Minneapolis, MN, *Pres.*, Peter J. Patchin & Assoc., Inc.; **PRIM RE ACT:** Appraiser; **SERVICES:** Valuation of comml. & indus. RE; **REP CLIENTS:** Gen. Mills, Inc., Cargill, Inc., K-Mart, Inc., 3-M Corp., Pillsbury Co.; **PREV EMPLOY:** Patchin Appraisals, Inc., VP, 1961-81; **PROFL AFFIL & HONORS:** Member AIREA; Amer. Soc. of Appraisers; Inst. of Bus. Appraisers, MAI, ASA, CBA; **EDUC:** BS, 1956, KS State Univ.; **EDUC HONORS:** With Hons., Phi Kappa Phi; **MIL SERV:** USA, 1957-59; **OTHER ACT & HONORS:** City Council, Prior Lake, MN, 1972-76; **HOME ADD:** 5428 CanodyCove Tr., Prior Lake, MN 55372, (612)447-3852; **BUS ADD:** 12700 Nicollet Ave., Burnsville, MN 55337, (612)894-2070.

PATE, Douglas M.——**B:** Dec. 26, 1924, Austin, TX, *Mgr. Asset Mgmt.*, Conoco, Inc.; **PRIM RE ACT:** Property Manager; **OTHER RE ACT:** Eval., Acquiring & Disposal of RE; **PROFL AFFIL & HONORS:**

NACORE, NARA; **EDUC:** BBA, 1950, Accounting, TX Univ.; **MIL SERV:** USAF, 1st Lt., Several decorations; **HOME ADD:** 6231 Bayou Bridge, Houston, TX 77096, (713)772-1382; **BUS ADD:** PO Box 2197, Houston, TX 77001, (713)965-1619.

PATERSON, Andrew A.——**B:** Mar. 2, 1943, Arlington, MA, *Partner*, Cross Wrock Miller & Vieson; **PRIM RE ACT:** Attorney; **SERVICES:** Legal; **REP CLIENTS:** Lenders, contractors, devel., and owners of comml. and indus. RE; **PROFL AFFIL & HONORS:** Real Prop. Sect., MI State Bar Assn.; Forum Comm. on const.; ABA; Faculty Member, Nat. Const. Inst., ABA; **EDUC:** BS, 1966, Math., Univ. of MI; **GRAD EDUC:** JD, 1969, Univ. of IL, Coll. of Law; **BUS ADD:** 400 Renaissance Center, Suite 1900, Detroit, MI 48243, (313)259-1144.

PATINOS, Gloria H.——**B:** Nov. 10, 1926, Lancaster, PA, *Mgr. of Branch Office*, First United Realtors, Mgmt.; **PRIM RE ACT:** Broker; **SERVICES:** Listing, selling, resid.; **REP CLIENTS:** Resid. primarily and comml.; **PREV EMPLOY:** Educ. in Greece (eng., soc. studies), Anglo Amer. School and Quito, Equador, S. Amer., Athens, Greece; **EDUC:** BS, 1947, Eng. and Soc. Studies, Millersville Coll.; **GRAD EDUC:** Grad. work for learning disabilities, Natl. Coll. of Education, Evanston, IL; **EDUC HONORS:** Honor Sorority; **OTHER ACT & HONORS:** Bd. member Family Serv. Assn.; **HOME ADD:** 1804 E. Hawthorne Blvd., Wheaton, IL 60187, (312)665-4583; **BUS ADD:** 101 E. Front St., Wheaton, IL 60187, (312)668-3630.

PATRICK, Earl B.——**B:** June 3, 1944, Dallas, TX, *VP*, Jim Stewart Realtors, Inc.; **PRIM RE ACT:** Broker, Developer, Owner/Investor; **SERVICES:** Comml.-Inv., indust./sales, leasing, devel.; **PROFL AFFIL & HONORS:** Waco Bd. of Realtors, TX Assoc. of Realtors, NAR, RNMI, ICSC, N. TX Chap. CCIM, CCIM; **EDUC:** BBA, 1966, Mktg., Baylor Univ.; **OTHER ACT & HONORS:** Dir. Hankamer Sch. of Bus., Baylor Univ.; **HOME ADD:** 8927 Raven, Waco, TX 76710, (817)772-2929; **BUS ADD:** 8320 Hwy. 84 West, PO Box 8050, Waco, TX 76710, (817)776-0000.

PATRICK, Richard M.——**B:** Oct. 20, 1946, Victoria, BC, Can., *Partner*, Lewis Mitchell & Moore (law firm); Tycon Developers (development firm); **PRIM RE ACT:** Attorney, Developer, Owner/Investor; **SERVICES:** Site selection, financing, devel., mktg.; **PREV EMPLOY:** Partner in law firm; **PROFL AFFIL & HONORS:** ABA; VA Bar Assn.; **EDUC:** BA, 1968, Eng., Dartmouth Coll.; **GRAD EDUC:** JD, 1971, Amer. Univ.; **HOME ADD:** 10395 Adel Rd., Oakton, VA 22124; **BUS ADD:** 8320 Old Courthouse Rd., Vienna, VA 22180, (703)790-9200.

PATT, Charles B., Jr.——**B:** June 16, 1915, Swissvale, PA, *Pres.*, Patt, White Co.; **PRIM RE ACT:** Broker, Consultant, Appraiser; **SERVICES:** A full RE service co.; **REP CLIENTS:** Major corps., attys., banks, govt. agencies, US, state, local; **PROFL AFFIL & HONORS:** AIREA; Soc. of RE Appraisers; Nat. Assn. of Review Appraisers; Intl. Right of Way Assn.; Nat. Assn. of Realtors, MAI; SREA; CRA; **EDUC:** AB, 1937, Econ., Penn State Univ.; **MIL SERV:** USN, Lt.j.g.; **OTHER ACT & HONORS:** Allentown Zoning, Hearing Bd., 1956 to 1961; Livingston Club; Leihgh Ctry. Club; Past Pres., Phoebe Apts., Housing for Elderly, a non-profit United Church of Christ Devel.; **HOME ADD:** Devonshire Rd., Allentown, PA 18104, (215)433-5337; **BUS ADD:** 4203 Tilghman St., Allentown, PA 18104, (215)395-2082.

PATTERSON, Bill——*Dir.*, Delaware, Delaware Real Estate Commission; **PRIM RE ACT:** Property Manager; **BUS ADD:** State Capital, Dover, DE 19901, (302)736-4000.*

PATTERSON, Charlene——**B:** Mar. 31, 1947, Orange, CA, *Partner*, Williams, Patterson & Assoc., CPA's; **PRIM RE ACT:** Consultant, Instructor; **OTHER, RE ACT:** CPA; **SERVICES:** Acctg. with emphasis on tax planning and tax return preparation; **PREV EMPLOY:** Teach RE taxation at Saddleback Coll.; **PROFL AFFIL & HONORS:** HI Soc. of CPA's' CA CPA's; AICPA, Pres.-elect Soc. of CA Accountants; **EDUC:** BBA, 1974, Acctg., CA State Univ.-Fullerton; **GRAD EDUC:** MBA, 1980, Taxation, Golden State Univ.; **HOME ADD:** 31781 Via de Linda, San Juan Capistrano, CA 92675, (714)493-0416; **BUS ADD:** 647 Camino de Los Mares, Suite 109, San Clemente, CA 92672, (714)493-8200.

PATTERSON, Douglas J.——**B:** June 13, 1948, Kansas City, MO, *Atty.*, J.C. Nichols Co.; **PRIM RE ACT:** Attorney, Developer, Owner/Investor; **SERVICES:** Legal; **REP CLIENTS:** J.C. Nichols Co. and Self; **PREV EMPLOY:** Gen. Counsel Homebuilders of Kansas City; **PROFL AFFIL & HONORS:** ABA; MO Bar; Kansas City Bar; Home Builders Assn., Order of The Bench - Robe, Univ. of MO; **EDUC:** BA, 1970, Bus. Admin., Univ. of MO; **GRAD EDUC:** 1973, Law, Univ. of MO; **EDUC HONORS:** Law Review Research Ed.; Order of Bench & Robe; **MIL SERV:** MO Nat. Guard; **HOME ADD:** 12111 Madison Court, Kansas City, MO 64145, (816)942-7718; **BUS ADD:** 310 Ward Pkwy., Kansas City, MO 64112, (816)561-3456.

PATTERSON, Jerome C.——**B:** May 26, 1947, Amery WI, *Tax Part.*, Gazzola Wolf Etter & Co.; **PRIM RE ACT:** Consultant, Owner/Investor; **OTHER RE ACT:** CPA's; **SERVICES:** Consultation RE Tax Planning, purchase & sale of partnership interests; **REP CLIENTS:** RE devel., synd., owner/investors; **PREV EMPLOY:** CPA with Arthur Andersen & Co., Minneapolis Office; **PROFL AFFIL & HONORS:** MN Soc. of CPA's., AICPA, Past Pres. S. MN Soc. of CPA's., CPA-1972; **EDUC:** BA, 1969, Poli. Sci./Soc./Math., Mankato State Univ.; **GRAD EDUC:** MBA, 1971, Acctg., Mankato State Univ.; **OTHER ACT & HONORS:** Gov's. appointee to State Bd. of Accountancy (1980); **HOME ADD:** 200 Brace Ave., PO Box 189, Eagle Lake, MN 56024, (507)257-3896; **BUS ADD:** 1120 South Ave., PO Box 1937, N. Mankato, MN 56001.

PATTERSON, John N.——**B:** Oct. 13, 1943, Taylor, TX, *Atty.*, White Koch Kelly & McCarthy, PA; **PRIM RE ACT:** Attorney; **SERVICES:** Legal; **REP CLIENTS:** Lenders and devel. of condo. and subdiv.; lessors of comml. prop.; **PROFL AFFIL & HONORS:** ABA; ULI; Community Assns. Inst.; State Bar of NM; **EDUC:** BA, 1966, Eng., Univ. of VA; **GRAD EDUC:** JD, 1970, Law, Univ. of TX; **EDUC HONORS:** Phi Delta Phi; **OTHER ACT & HONORS:** Dir., Old Santa Fe Assn.; Member, Mayor's Urban Policy Bd.; **HOME ADD:** 2115 Fort Union Dr., Santa Fe, NM 87501, (505)983-3786; **BUS ADD:** 220 Otero St., Box 787, Santa Fe, NM 87501, (505)982-4374.

PATTERSON, Robert M.——**B:** Sept. 10, 1942, Norristown, PA, *VP, Office Development*, Faison Associates; **PRIM RE ACT:** Developer, Owner/Investor; **SERVICES:** Mixed-use devel.; **REP CLIENTS:** Joint venture partners (instnl. & indivs.) in comml. projects, large tenants; **PREV EMPLOY:** Romanek Gloolub & Co. Chicago 1973-1981; IBM 1964-1973; **PROFL AFFIL & HONORS:** NAR; Realtor's NMI, Candidate, CCIM; RNMI; **EDUC:** BA, 1964, Econ., Univ. of Notre Dame; **GRAD EDUC:** MBA, 1978, Univ. of Chicago; **HOME ADD:** 530-E N. Poplar St., Charlotte, NC 28202, (704)333-7888; **BUS ADD:** 122 E. Stonewall, Charlotte, NC 28202, (704)374-1711.

PATTERSON, Roy L.——**B:** May 22, 1949, Long Island, NY, *CPA/Part.*, Cowles, Craig, Silverman & Wooten, CPAs; **PRIM RE ACT:** Consultant; **OTHER RE ACT:** RE tax planning; **SERVICES:** Tax planning, feasibility analysis, pre-acquisition; **REP CLIENTS:** Indiv. & corp. investor market; **PREV EMPLOY:** Non-relative member of existing firm since 1974; **PROFL AFFIL & HONORS:** Amer. Inst. of CPAs, FL Inst. of CPAs; **EDUC:** BS, 1974, Acctg., Univ. of Tampa; **EDUC HONORS:** Spec. Sr. Hons., Alpha Chi Nat. Hon. Soc.; **MIL SERV:** USAF; S Sgt.; **OTHER ACT & HONORS:** Tampa Civitan Club, Tres., BOD; Guest speaker through FICPA, Var. RE tax topics; **HOME ADD:** 4625 Landscape Dr., Tampa, FL 33624, (813)962-8313; **BUS ADD:** Ste. 500, Founders Life Bldg., Tampa, FL 33602, (813)223-1701.

PATTERSON, Thomas Brooks——**B:** Nov. 16, 1952, Indianapolis, IN, *Fin. Officer*, Coldwell Banker/Commercial Real Estate Services, RE Fin.; **PRIM RE ACT:** Broker, Syndicator; **SERVICES:** Investment counseling - secure fin. for comml. RE devel. projects; **REP CLIENTS:** Lenders, pension funds, indivs., and fin. instns.; **PREV EMPLOY:** Trust Co. Bank, Atlanta, GA, 1974-1977; **PROFL AFFIL & HONORS:** Member - Atlanta Bd. of Realtors; **EDUC:** BA, 1974, Bus. Admin./Econ., Vanderbilt Univ.; **GRAD EDUC:** MBA, 1979, Fin./Acctg., Emory Univ.; **HOME ADD:** 828 Longwood Dr., Atlanta, GA 30305, (404)351-8137; **BUS ADD:** Peachtree Center - Cain Tower, Suite 1401, 229 Peachtree St. N.E., Altanta, GA 30043, (404)656-1424.

PATTERSON, Thomas L.——**B:** Mar. 10, 1952, Harrisburg, PA, *Atty.*, Content, Stewart, Tatusko & Patterson, Chartered; **PRIM RE ACT:** Attorney; **SERVICES:** Legal - Comml. RE, Taxation; **REP CLIENTS:** RE devel., synd., indiv., RE investors; **PREV EMPLOY:** Arent, Fox, Kintner, Plotkin & Kahn - law firm, Washington D.C.; **PROFL AFFIL & HONORS:** Amer. Bar Assn. including Sect. on Taxation, Section, Legal Econ., VA State Bar; DC Bar; **EDUC:** AB, 1974, Religion, Bucknell Univ.; **GRAD EDUC:** JD, 1977, Georgetown Univ. Law Ctr.; **EDUC HONORS:** Magna Cum Laude, Georgetown Univ. Law Journal; **HOME ADD:** 4032 Elliott St., Alexandria, VA 22304, (703)379-1403; **BUS ADD:** 1225 19th St., N.W., Washington, DC 20036, (202)887-1000.

PATTON, Orin C.——**B:** Jan. 14, 1933, Miami, FL, *Col., USAF*, Private Investor/Owner; **PRIM RE ACT:** Owner/Investor; **EDUC:** BA, 1954, Univ. FL; **GRAD EDUC:** MS, 1960, Econ. Geography, Univ. of FL; PhD, 1973, Poli. Geography, Univ. of NC; **MIL SERV:** USAF, Col., Meritorious Service Medal w/3 OLC, Air Medal w/15 OLC; **HOME ADD:** 41 Mittman Circ., New Braunfels, TX 78130,

(512)629-2506; **BUS TEL:** (512)629-2506.

PAU, Peter S.——B: Aug. 28, 1953, China, *Pres.*, Peter Pau Co.; **PRIM RE ACT:** Consultant, Developer, Builder, Owner/Investor; **SERVICES:** Devel. of comml. projects, constr. mgmt., investments; **REP CLIENTS:** Corp. and indiv. investors from CA, Can. and Hong Kong; **PREV EMPLOY:** Emkay Devel. and Realty Co., Newport Beach, CA, 1976-1979; **PROFL AFFIL & HONORS:** BOMA, ULI; **EDUC:** BS, 1975, CE, Univ. of CA, Berkeley; **GRAD EDUC:** MS, 1976, Constr. Mgmt., Stanford Univ.; **HOME ADD:** 890 Curling Lane, Boise, ID 83702, (208)343-8882; **BUS ADD:** Suite 103, 10332 Fairview Ave, Boise, ID 83704, (208)376-8826.

PAUL, Bert H., III——B: Jan. 29, 1947, Long Beach, CA, Bert Paul Real Estate Brokerage, Land Planning & Development; **PRIM RE ACT:** Broker, Consultant, Developer, Owner/Investor; **SERVICES:** Comml. brokerage, comml. devel., hist. renovation; **PREV EMPLOY:** MICT Research & Consulting; **PROFL AFFIL & HONORS:** Nat. and local Bd. of Realtors, Nat. Trust for Hist. Preservation, City of Tacoma Landmarks Preservation Commn.; **EDUC:** BS, 1970, Bus. Admin., Univ. of S. CA; **GRAD EDUC:** AA, 1967, Bus. Admin., Menlo Coll.; MBA, 1972, Bus., Mktg., Fin. Acctg., CA State Univ. at Long Beach; **HOME ADD:** 3406 N. 34th St., Tacoma, WA 98402, (206)752-6333; **BUS ADD:** 2100 N. 30th, Tacoma, WA 98403, (206)272-4224.

PAUL, David L.——B: May 1, 1939, New York, NY, *Pres.*, AmMart Realty Corp.; **PRIM RE ACT:** Developer; **PROFL AFFIL & HONORS:** Standard Club and Mid-Amer. Club, Chicago, IL; Tr., Mt. Sinai Medical Ctr., NYC; CUNY; Mt. Sinai Hospital, NYC; Mt. Sinai School Nursing and Neustadter Convanlescent Ctr., NYC Governing Member, Lincoln Ctr. Repertory Theatre, NYC, JD; PhD; **EDUC:** BS, 1961, Econ., Wharton School, Univ. of PA; **GRAD EDUC:** MBA, 1965, Columbia Univ.; JD, 1967, Columbia Univ.; PhD, 1968, Planning, Harvard Univ.; **OTHER ACT & HONORS:** Chmn. of Bd., The Westport Co.; **BUS ADD:** 666 N. Lake Shore Dr., Chicago, IL 60611.

PAUL, Richard S.——B: Nov. 23, 1944, Greenville, NC, *Pres.*, McGee & Paul, Inc.; **PRIM RE ACT:** Broker, Attorney, Owner/Investor, Syndicator; **SERVICES:** Investment & tax shelter advise; RE exchanges; syndic.; **REP CLIENTS:** Indiv. and Corp. engaged in synd. or investors in tax shelters; RE & Escrow Co's.; **PREV EMPLOY:** Criminal Investigator, IRS - 9 yrs.; Pres., Investors Emporium, Inc.; **PROFL AFFIL & HONORS:** CA Trial Lawyers Assn.; Orange Cty. Bar Assn., RE Broker; **EDUC:** BS, 1966, Econ./Fin., E Carolina Univ.; **GRAD EDUC:** MBA, 1969, Fin., E Carolina Univ.; JD, 1979, Western State Univ., Fullerton; **EDUC HONORS:** Scholastic Merit; **MIL SERV:** U.S. Army, Sgt. E-5; **OTHER ACT & HONORS:** Newport Beach Active 20/30 Club; **HOME ADD:** 1094 Katella, Laguna Beach, CA 92651, (714)494-4262; **BUS ADD:** 1301 Dove St., Suite 750, NewPort Beach, CA 92660, (714)752-5454.

PAUL, Vincent P.——B: Dec. 20, 1920, Italy, *Pres.*, Corporate Properties Ltd.; **PRIM RE ACT:** Broker, Developer, Builder, Property Manager, Syndicator; **PROFL AFFIL & HONORS:** Member of Inst. of Chartered Accts. of Ont.; **MIL SERV:** Canadian Army 1942-44; Royal Canadian Air Force 1944-45; **OTHER ACT & HONORS:** Dir., CAN Opera Co.; Dir., St. Joseph Hospital, Toronto; **HOME ADD:** 264 Old Yonge St., Willowdale, M2P1R4, ON, Canada, (416)226-2303; **BUS ADD:** 95 Barber Greene Rd., Suite 300, Don Mills, M3C3E9, ONT, Canada, (416)441-2830.

PAUL, William R.——B: Sept. 22, 1942, Johnstown, PA, *Atty.*, Carlton, Fields, Ward, Emmanuel, Smith & Cutler, P.A.; **PRIM RE ACT:** Attorney; **SERVICES:** Counsel: Securities, partnership, corp., RE and partnership and RE tax law; **REP CLIENTS:** Indiv. and corp. synd., builders, devel., packagers and NASD and SECO broker-dealers; **PREV EMPLOY:** Sr. staff atty. with US Securities & Exchange Commn. and Atty. with Poletti Freidin Prashker Feldman & Gartner and Schulte & McGoldrick (now Schulte Roth & Zabel); **PROFL AFFIL & HONORS:** ABA, Assn. of the Bar of the City of NY, DC Bar and FL Bar; **EDUC:** BS in Econ., 1964, Fin. and Comm., Wharton School of the Univ. of PA; **GRAD EDUC:** JD, 1973, Law, Brooklyn Law School; Georgetown Univ. Law Ctr.; **EDUC HONORS:** Four-year scholarship award, Moot Court Honor Soc.; Nat. Order of Barristers; Nat. Moot Court Team; **OTHER ACT & HONORS:** C of C; Rotary Club, Dir. of Local Homeowners Assn. and member of Arch. Review Comm.; **HOME ADD:** 4104 Stillwater Terrace Cove, Tampa, FL 33624, (813)961-6825; **BUS ADD:** PO Box 3239, Tampa, FL 33601, (813)233-5366.

PAULS, Robert——*President*, Ampco-Pittsburgh Corp.; **PRIM RE ACT:** Property Manager; **BUS ADD:** 700 Porter Bldg., Pittsburgh, PA 15219, (412)456-4400.*

PAULSEN, Harry L.——B: June 27, 1930, Burke, SD, *Regional VP*, First American Title Insurance Company; **OTHER RE ACT:** Title insurance and escrow services; **PROFL AFFIL & HONORS:** NARA - C.R.A., Legislative Comm. Chmn. - Land Title Assn. of CO, Pres. - CO Title Ins. Rating Bureau, Sec.-Treas. - Land Title Assn. of CO, 1978-79 Title Man of the Year - Land Title Assn. of CO; **MIL SERV:** USMC, SSgt.; **OTHER ACT & HONORS:** Comm. work for AMC Cancer Research Ctr. and Nat. Jewish Hosp.; **HOME ADD:** 711 Gilbert St., Castle Rock, CO 80104, (303)688-4310; **BUS ADD:** 1777 South Bellaire, Suite 215, Denver, CO 80222, (303)758-5230.

PAULSEN, Peter H.——B: June 17, 1934, Schlesweg-Holstein, Germany, *Pres.*, Peter Paulsen Co.; **PRIM RE ACT:** Developer, Builder; **OTHER RE ACT:** Office Devel. and Leasing of office bldgs.; **EDUC:** Educated in Germany, Builder & Building Design, Constr., Mgmt.; **OTHER ACT & HONORS:** Tr. and Past Pres. of the Found. for Hope Charitable Organ.; Dir. of CA Bus. Bank; **HOME ADD:** Hillsborough, CA 94010; **BUS ADD:** 4000 Moorpark Ave., Ste. 106, San Jose, CA 95117, (408)984-8400.

PAVETTI, Francis J.——B: Dec. 14, 1931, New Haven, CT, *Atty.*, Law Offices of Francis J. Pavetti; **PRIM RE ACT:** Attorney; **SERVICES:** Legal serv. concerning RE and land use; **PROFL AFFIL & HONORS:** Member CT Bar Assn. Exec. Comm. Planning & Zoning, Member ABA Sect. on RE, Probate & Trusts, Served as law clerk to Hon. J. Joseph Smith, Judge U.S. Court of Appeals for second circuit; **EDUC:** BS, 1953, Bus. Admin., Univ. of CT; **GRAD EDUC:** JD, 1959, Boston Coll. Law School; **EDUC HONORS:** With Honors; Recipient Amer. Juris Prudence Award for Academic Excellence; **MIL SERV:** USAF, 1st Lt.; **OTHER ACT & HONORS:** Town Clerk, Waterford, CT 1970-1978, Tr. & Corp. Secy. - Eugene O'Neill Mem Theater Center Inc.; **HOME ADD:** The Strand, Waterford, CT 06385, (203)443-3564; **BUS ADD:** 83 Huntington St., Court House Sq. Bldg., New London, CT 06320, (203)442-9408.

PAVONE, Louis V.——B: Mar. 18, 1953, Chicago, IL, *Atty. at law*, Provenzano, Serpico, Loss and Pavone; **PRIM RE ACT:** Attorney; **SERVICES:** Legal assistance concerning RE closings, tax advise concerning purchase; **PREV EMPLOY:** IRS; **PROFL AFFIL & HONORS:** IL State Bar Assn.; ABA; Justinian Soc. of Lawyers; Fed. Bar Assn.; Chicago Bar Assn.; **EDUC:** BS, 1975, Mathematics, bus. admin. and acctg., Monmouth Coll.; **GRAD EDUC:** JD, 1978, Taxation, probate, and bus. law, Lewis Univ. of Law now known as Northern Univ. of Law; **EDUC HONORS:** Grad. Summa Cum Laude in acctg. & bus. admin.; **OTHER ACT & HONORS:** VP of IACOB; **HOME ADD:** 321 Dee Court, Bloomingdale, IL 60108; **BUS ADD:** 1440 W. North Ave., Suite 301, Melrose Park, IL 60160, (312)343-9669.

PAXTON, Jay L.——B: Dec. 24, 1947, Ft. Worth, TX, *Partner*, Bianchi & Hoskins; **PRIM RE ACT:** Attorney; **SERVICES:** Legal serv. in fin., conveyancing and subdiv.; **REP CLIENTS:** Monumental corp.; Fireman's Fund Ins. Co.; **EDUC:** BA, 1970, Poli. Sci., Univ. of CA At Berkeley; **GRAD EDUC:** JD, 1973, Law, Boalt Hall, Univ. of CA at Berkeley; **EDUC HONORS:** Honors in Poli. Sci.; **BUS ADD:** 1000 Fourth St., Suite 600, San Rafael, CA 94901, (415)456-6020.

PAYNE, Gordon D.——B: Nov. 28, 1950, Washington D.C., *Product Devel. Div. Mgr., Atty.*, US League of Savings Assns., SAF Systems and Forms; **PRIM RE ACT:** Consultant, Attorney, Regulator; **SERVICES:** Fin. product devel., regulatory consulting and review; **REP CLIENTS:** Savings and Loan Assns., Savings Banks, Comml. Banks, Mort. Bankers, all nationwide; **PREV EMPLOY:** VP, RE Loan Div. Mgr., Gary Wheaton Bank, Wheaton, IL, 1978-1980; **PROFL AFFIL & HONORS:** Chicago DuPage Cty., IL State, Amer. and Fed. Bar Assns.; **EDUC:** AB, 1971, Hist., Franklin & Marshall Coll., Lancaster, PA; **GRAD EDUC:** A.M., 1973, Hist., Rutgers Univ., New Brunswick; J.D., 1979, Law, IIT-Chicago-Kent Coll. of Law, Chicago, IL; **EDUC HONORS:** Phi Alpha Theta Nat. Hist. honor Soc.; **OTHER ACT & HONORS:** Treas., Bd. of Dirs., Hoffman Estates Boys Club, 1975-1976; **HOME ADD:** 8000 Woodglen Ln. 203, Downers Grove, IL 60516; **BUS ADD:** 111 E. Wacker Dr., Chicago, IL 60601, (312)644-3100.

PAYNE, L.D.——B: Aug. 11, 1935, Bullyhill, OK, *RE Assoc.*, Alpine Village Realty; **PRIM RE ACT:** Broker, Consultant, Appraiser, Developer, Owner/Investor; **OTHER RE ACT:** Real Exchange Exchange; **SERVICES:** Sales-Exchangor-Appraisal-Auction; **PREV EMPLOY:** Telephone Co.; **PROFL AFFIL & HONORS:** Natl. Council of Exchangors; **EDUC:** RE, Fullerton CA State Fullerton, CA; **MIL SERV:** USA, Pvt., Natl. Defense; Korea Defense; **HOME ADD:** 1919 Oak Spring Valley St., Rt 92334 Box 475, Wrightwood, CA 92397, (714)249-4629; **BUS ADD:** 1263 Evergreen Rd., Wrightwood, CA 92397, (714)249-3349.

PAYNE, Raymond D., Jr.——**B:** Feb. 21, 1926, Fairmount, GA, *Prop. Mgr.*, C.V. Brown & Bros.; **PRIM RE ACT:** Broker, Property Manager; **OTHER RE ACT:** Filing and presentation of RE tax appeals before local and state tax appeal bds.; **SERVICES:** 30 yrs. exper. gen. sales and mgmt. of office and retail props.; **REP CLIENTS:** Trust Dept. Amer. Bank; Culver Corp.; Stone Ft. Land Co.; Brainerd Profl. Center; Ashland Profl. Center; Belvoir Plaza Shopping Ctr.; **PROFL AFFIL & HONORS:** IREM, BOMA, CPM; **EDUC:** BS in Bus. Admin., 1950, Air Transp., Univ. of TN at Knoxville; **MIL SERV:** USN, Seaman; **OTHER ACT & HONORS:** V-Chmn., Hamilton Cty. Bd. of Equalization 1976-77; Pres., Taxpayers Assn., 1975; Chmn., Beautification & Improvement Comm., Central City Council 1978; **HOME ADD:** 1635 Mary Du Pre Dr., Chattanooga, TN 37402, (615)892-6505; **BUS ADD:** 615 Lindsay St., Suite 320, Chattanooga, TN 37402, (615)265-1656.

PAYNE, Roslyn Braeman——**B:** Apr. 30, 1946, Kansas City, MO, *Sr. VP*, Genstar Mort.; **PRIM RE ACT:** Consultant, Lender, Owner/Investor; **PREV EMPLOY:** Eastdil Realty, Inc. - VP 1970-1981; **PROFL AFFIL & HONORS:** Bay Area Mort. Assn. Pres.; Lambda Alpha; ULI; ICSC; Women's Forum West - Bd. of Dir.; 1st Amer. Title Guaranty Co. - Bd. of Dirs.; **EDUC:** BBA, 1968, Bus., Univ. of MI; **GRAD EDUC:** MBA, 1970, Bus.-Fin., Harvard Bus. School; **EDUC HONORS:** Mortar Bd.; Univ. Activities Ctr. Exec. VP, Chmn., Publications Bd.; Student Govt. Referendum Comm.; **OTHER ACT & HONORS:** Commonwealth Club, Menlo Circus Club, Peninsula Golf & Tennis Club; **HOME ADD:** 3616 Jackson St., San Francisco, CA 94118; **BUS ADD:** 4 Embarcadero, 38th Floor, San Francisco, CA 94111, (415)986-7200.

PAYNE, Silas Owen——**B:** Dec. 28, 1919, Cartersville, GA, *Pres.*, Payne & Thompson, PC; **PRIM RE ACT:** Attorney; **SERVICES:** RE, mort. law, probate, civil litigation, comml. real prop. receiverships, all related RE legal problems; **REP CLIENTS:** Real Estate Counsel to Carpenters Pension Trust Fund, Laborers' Pension Trust Fund, Nationwide Ins. Co., Old Stone Bank, Union Mutual Life Ins. Co., Trust Dept. Crocker Bank, Bank of the West; **PREV EMPLOY:** Loan Guaranty Div., US Veterans Admin, VP and Mgr. of No. Div. of Marble Mort. Co. (now First Interstate Bank); **PROFL AFFIL & HONORS:** Lambda Alpha Intl. Land Econ. Frat., Former Pres. Golden Gate Chapt., ABA, CA State Bar, San Francisco Bar Assn., Lawyers Club of San Francisco, Writer & reviewer on RE subjects for CA real prop. continuing educ. of the Bar publications; **EDUC:** 1939, Bus., North GA Coll., San Francisco Law Sch.; **GRAD EDUC:** JD, 1953, RE subjects, San Francisco Law Sch.; **MIL SERV:** USA, Capt.; **OTHER ACT & HONORS:** Planning Commnr. and Councilman, Menlo Park; **HOME ADD:** 450 Liberty St., 7, San Francisco, CA 94114; **BUS ADD:** 235 Montgomery St., Suite 1530, San Francisco, CA 94104, (415)434-3471.

PAYTON, Michael B.——**B:** Nov. 29, 1947, Slayton, MN, *Mall Mgr.*, Gateway Mall; **PRIM RE ACT:** Property Manager; **PREV EMPLOY:** VP for Prop. Mgmt., First Realty Fargo, ND; **PROFL AFFIL & HONORS:** Member, Bismarck-Mandan Bd. of Realtors; **EDUC:** BA, 1973, Fin., Acctg., & Mgmt., Moorhead State Univ.; **MIL SERV:** US Navy, HM-2; **HOME ADD:** 1724 Heritage Ave., Bismarck, ND 58501, (701)222-8478; **BUS ADD:** 2700 State St., Bismarck, ND 58501, (701)222-8350.

PAZAHANICK, Andrew W.——**B:** Jan. 16, 1952, Athens, AL, *Exec. Dir.*, Southern Tier Economic Growth; **PRIM RE ACT:** Developer, Owner/Investor; **SERVICES:** Fin., site location, devel.; **PROFL AFFIL & HONORS:** NY State Econ. Devel. Council; Amer. Indus. Devel. Council; Nat. Council for Urban Econ. Devel.; **EDUC:** BS, 1973, Social Studies, Mansfield St. Coll.; **GRAD EDUC:** MPA, 1974, Public Admin., Penn St. Univ.; **HOME ADD:** 406 Foster Ave., Elmira, NY 14905, (607)734-0368; **BUS ADD:** 139 W. Gray St., POB 251, Elmira, NY 14902, (607)733-6513.

PEACE, Jack——**B:** July 20, 1951, Princeton, MO, *Atty.*, Stockard, Andereck, Hauck, Sharp and Evans; **PRIM RE ACT:** Attorney; **PROFL AFFIL & HONORS:** ABA, MO Bar; **EDUC:** BS, 1973, Bus. Admin., NW MO State Univ.; **GRAD EDUC:** JD, 1976, Univ. of MO, Kansas City; **EDUC HONORS:** Dean's List; **BUS ADD:** PO Box 549, Trenton, MO 64683, (816)359-2244.

PEACOCK, James S.——**B:** June 15, 1942, Baltimore, MD, *Dir. in charge of Howard Cty., MD, office & RE client serv.*, Stegman & Associates, P.A.; **PRIM RE ACT:** Consultant, Owner/Investor; **OTHER RE ACT:** Public Acctg.; **SERVICES:** Profl. acctg. serv. including mgmt. advisory & income tax; **REP CLIENTS:** Arch., Synd., Devel., Builders, and Investors; **PROFL AFFIL & HONORS:** MD Assn. of CPA, AICPA, Nat. Assn. of Home Builders; **EDUC:** BS, 1965, Acctg., Univ. of MD; **HOME ADD:** 10083 Cabachon Ct., Ellicott City, MD 21043, (301)465-8606; **BUS ADD:** 2000 Century Plaza, Suite 124, Columbia, MD 21044, (301)995-1181.

PEARCE, Lawrence——**B:** Dec. 24, 1943, Indianapolis, IN, *Partner*, Realco Holdings Ltd. (US); **PRIM RE ACT:** Developer, Owner/Investor; **PREV EMPLOY:** Inland Steel Devel. Corp.; **PROFL AFFIL & HONORS:** ULI; **EDUC:** BS, 1966, Purdue Univ.; **GRAD EDUC:** MBA, 1968, Econ./Fin., Univ. of Chicago; **HOME ADD:** 141 Hobart Ave., Summit, NJ 07901, (201)273-5219; **BUS ADD:** 200 Executive Dr., Suite 155, W. Orange, NJ 07052, (201)325-8500.

PEARLSTEIN, Marvin B.——**B:** Sept. 14, 1949, Gary, IN, *Atty.*, Steefel, Levitt & Weiss, A Professional Corp.; **PRIM RE ACT:** Attorney; **SERVICES:** Legal Representation; **REP CLIENTS:** Devel., Lending Instit., Brokers, Property Mgrs.; **PREV EMPLOY:** Clerk - CA Supreme Court Justice; **PROFL AFFIL & HONORS:** Member-CA State Bar, San Francisco Bar Assn., Amer. Bar Assn.; **GRAD EDUC:** AB, 1971, Econ., Wash. Univ. (St. Louis); M.B.A., 1972, Acctg., Organizational Devel., Wash. Univ. (St. Louis); JD, 1977, Boalt Hall School of Law; **EDUC HONORS:** Max A. Hayutin Award; M.B.A. Scholar Award; William S. Krebs Acctg. Award; Beta Gamma Sigma, Editor-in-Chief, CA Law Review, 1976-1977; Order of the Coif; **BUS ADD:** One Embarcadero Ctr., 28th Floor, San Francisco, CA 94111, (415)788-0900.

PEARLSTEIN, Paul D.——**B:** Jan. 3, 1938, Berlin, NH; **PRIM RE ACT:** Attorney; **PROFL AFFIL & HONORS:** VA Bar; DC Bar; US Supreme Ct.; Atty. in private practice, 1968-present (concentration in RE, domestic relations, bankruptcy and civil litigation); Admin. of Const. and Purchasing Activites, Cafritz Co. and affiliated cos., 1966-1968; Atty., US Dept. of HUD, 1964-1966; Chmn., Real Prop. Law Comm. of the Bar Assn. of DC, 1976-1978; Chmn. of the Yr. Award, 1977 and 1978; Chmn., Speakers Bureau of the Bar Assn. of the DC, 1973-1974; Member, Corp. Reorg. & Bankruptcy Comm. of the DC Bar; ABA; Real Prop. and Family Law Sects., WA Bd. of Realtors, The WA, DC Estate Planning Council; Bankruptcy Tr., DC and VA; **EDUC:** BA, 1959, Econ./Latin Amer. Studies, Univ. of PA; **GRAD EDUC:** LLB, 1962, Law, Univ. of VA; **MIL SERV:** US Army Signal Corps, Capt.; **OTHER ACT & HONORS:** Washington Hebrew Congregation, Pres., Brotherhood, 1974-1975; Pres., Young Marrieds, 1969-1970; Member, Bd. of Mgrs., 1969-1975; Jewish Community Council; Inter Group Relations Comm., 1974-present; Pres., Toastmasters Club, US Dept. of HUD, 1966-1967; First Mandolinist, The Takoma Mandoleers, 1972-present; Artile: Realtor Magazine: Oct. 1981 (Intrafamily Financing Techniques); September 1980 (Lease Options); July 1979, (Prop. Div. in Divorce); Aug. 1978, (New DC RE Contract); Jan. 1977, (Title Reg. and Recordation); Contributing book reviewer for the ABA Journal, 1972-present; Speaking: WA Bd. of Realtors; Call For Action, WTOP; GWU Law School; Univ. of MD, WAMU-FM: Amer. Univ.; Banneker Community Club; Nat. Health Care Credit Grp.; Kewanis Club of WA; GWU Grad. Womens Club; DC Nursing Soc. Annual Meeting; **HOME ADD:** 2928 Ellicott St., N.W., Washington, DC 20008; **BUS ADD:** 1730 Rhode Island Ave., N.W. #708, Washington, DC 20036, (202)223-5848.

PEARSON, Edwin L.——**B:** Aug. 6, 1946, Dallas, TX, *Pres.*, Bekland Resources Corp.; **PRIM RE ACT:** Consultant, Engineer, Banker, Developer, Builder, Owner/Investor, Property Manager, Assessor; **SERVICES:** Investment counseling, devel. and synd. of mgmt. and prop.; **PREV EMPLOY:** Exploration Surveys, Inc., Dallas, TX, 1968-1971; The Cty. of Dallas, Engr., 1965-1968; George L. Dahl, Arch. & Engr., 1962-1965; **EDUC:** Cml. Engrg./Bus. Psych., Univ. of TX/No. TX State Univ./E. TX State Univ.; **HOME ADD:** 4709 Spanish Trail, Grand Prairie, TX 75050; **BUS ADD:** 110 W. 7th St., Suite 307, Ft. Worth, TX 76102, (817)870-1251.

PEARSON, Ernest J.——**B:** Dec. 3, 1934, Seattle, WA, *VP, Branch Mgr.*, Cushman & Wakefield of California, Inc.; **PRIM RE ACT:** Broker; **SERVICES:** Indus., comml., investment brokerage, project consulting, mgmt.; **REP CLIENTS:** major corporate users and indus. park devels.; **PREV EMPLOY:** Sales Consultant, Coldwell Banker Comml. Brokerage Co., Oakland CA, 1969-1976; **PROFL AFFIL & HONORS:** Active Member Soc. of Indus. Realtors; Member Nat. Assn. of Indus. & Office Parks, SIR; **EDUC:** 1956, Mktg., Univ. of WA; **OTHER ACT & HONORS:** Bd. Member Lafayette Moraga Youth Assn.; Camping Chmn., Campfire Girls, Contra Costa Council; **HOME ADD:** 75 Las Quebradas Lane, Alamo, CA 94507, (415)838-9648; **BUS ADD:** 1 Kaiser Plaza, Suite 1501, Oakland, CA 94612, (415)763-4900.

PEARSON, John E.——**B:** Aug. 20, 1946, Jamaica, NY, *Partner*, Sage, Gray, Todd & Sims, RE; **PRIM RE ACT:** Attorney; **SERVICES:** Representation of banks on RE loans and RE developers; **REP CLIENTS:** Chem. Bank, The Royal Bank & Trust Company of Can., indiv. investors in comml. & resid. RE; **PREV EMPLOY:** Guaranty Title Insurance Co.; **PROFL AFFIL & HONORS:** Mort. Bankers

Assn.; NY State Bar Assn.; FL Bar Assn.; Assn. of Bar of City of NY; ABA; Dade Cty. Bar Assn.; **EDUC:** BA, 1968, Govt., Manhattan Coll.; **GRAD EDUC:** JD, 1972, Law, St. Johns Law School; **EDUC HONORS:** Law Review; **MIL SERV:** USMCR; **HOME ADD:** 201 Crandon Blvd., Apt. 109, Key Biscayne, FL, (305)361-7898; **BUS ADD:** 777 Brickell Ave., Miami, FL 33131, (305)358-1666.

PEARSON, Paul E.——B: July 11, 1926, Seattle, WA, *Pres.*, Pacific Ind.; **PRIM RE ACT:** Engineer, Developer, Owner/Investor, Builder; **PREV EMPLOY:** Convair; **PROFL AFFIL & HONORS:** Soc. Indus. Engrs.; **EDUC:** BS, 1952, Engrg. & Econ., AZ State Univ.; **EDUC HONORS:** Pres. Phi Sigma Kappa; **HOME ADD:** 8025 Calle Del Cielo, La Jolla, CA 92037, (714)454-5006; **BUS ADD:** 8025 Calle Del Cielo, La Jolla, CA 92037, (714)298-6021.

PEASE, Robert——*Director, RE*, Baxter Travenol Laboratories, Inc.; **PRIM RE ACT:** Property Manager; **BUS ADD:** One Baxter Parkway, Deerfield, IL 60015, (312)948-2000.*

PEAVEY, Roy——B: Nov. 15, 1930, Bennettsville, SC, *Owner*, Roy Peavey & Co.; **PRIM RE ACT:** Broker, Appraiser, Instructor, Property Manager; **SERVICES:** RE Sales, rentals, appraisals, prop. mgmt.; **PROFL AFFIL & HONORS:** NAR, SCAR, Member SC RE Commn., FHA-HUD Appraiser, SC State Hwy. Dept. Appraisal Panel, RE Instr. Tech. Coll.; **MIL SERV:** US Army, 1st Lt.; **OTHER ACT & HONORS:** SC RE Commn.-6th Congressional Dist.; ctry. Club, 1st Baptist Church; **HOME ADD:** 203 Barfield Rd., Darlington, SC 29532, (803)393-3185; **BUS ADD:** 100 Exchange St., PO Box 15, Darlington, SC 29532.

PECK, David C.——*Sr. VP*, Vantage Cos.; **PRIM RE ACT:** Developer; **BUS ADD:** 785 Crossover Ln., Memphis, TN 38117, (901)682-9100.*

PECK, Harold G.——B: Aug. 14, 1938, AL, *Atty.*, Peck & Slusher, Attys., PC; **PRIM RE ACT:** Attorney, Developer, Builder, Owner/Investor; **REP CLIENTS:** RE Devel. & most maj. mort. brokers; **PROFL AFFIL & HONORS:** AL Bar Assn., ABA, Nat. Assn. of Homebuilders, Amer. Judicature Soc.; **EDUC:** 1962, Math., Univ. of N AL; **GRAD EDUC:** 1966, Cumberland Sch. of Law; **OTHER ACT & HONORS:** City Judge, 1967-70; Cititan, C of C; **HOME ADD:** R-1, Jilver, AL 35645, (205)757-1931; **BUS ADD:** 118 W Reeder St., Florence, AL 35670, (205)766-4490.

PECK, John Weld——B: Jan. 29, 1944, Cincinnati, OH, Peck Shaffer & Williams; **PRIM RE ACT:** Attorney; **SERVICES:** Bond counsel, FHA counsel; **PROFL AFFIL & HONORS:** Cincinnati, OH State, Fed. Bar Assns.; ABA; US Dist. Ct. of Appeals (1971); US Dist. Ct., So. Dist of OH (1970); **EDUC:** BS, 1966, Univ. of Miami; **GRAD EDUC:** JD, 1969, Univ. of Cincinnati; **EDUC HONORS:** Phi Delta Phi Frat; **OTHER ACT & HONORS:** Bd. of Trs. Miami Univ.; Chmn. Fed Nominating Commn. of OH; Special Counsel to Atty. Gen. of OH (1971-1978); **BUS ADD:** 2200 First National Bank Center, 425 Walnut St., Cincinnati, OH 45202, (513)621-3394.

PECK, Ronald L.——B: June 13, 1947, Oakland, CA, *Exec. VP*, Brondon Corp.; **PRIM RE ACT:** Consultant, Real Estate Publisher, Owner/Investor, Property Manager, Syndicator; **SERVICES:** Synd., devel., brokerage & mgmt. of income prop. in No. CA; **PREV EMPLOY:** Systech Fin. Corp. 1971-73; CFA, Inc. 1973-75; **PROFL AFFIL & HONORS:** Interex, CA Assn. of Realtors; **EDUC:** BA, 1969, Arch., Univ. of CA, Berkeley; **GRAD EDUC:** MBA, 1971, RE & Fin., Univ. of CA, Berkeley; **EDUC HONORS:** cum laude; **MIL SERV:** US Army Res., 1st Lt.; **HOME ADD:** 259 Gravatt Dr., Berkeley, CA 94705; **BUS ADD:** 111 Broadway, Oakland, CA 94607, (415)834-4900.

PECKHAM, John Munroe, III——B: July 25, 1933, Abington, MA, *Pres./COB*, The Peckham Boston Company; **PRIM RE ACT:** Owner/Investor, Real Estate Publisher; **OTHER RE ACT:** Developer; **PROFL AFFIL & HONORS:** NAR; RNMI; FLI; CCIM; RESSI; IREM; CPM, Pres, MA Assn. Realtors; VP NAR; **EDUC:** AB, 1955, Tufts Univ.; **GRAD EDUC:** 1956, Columbia Law School; **MIL SERV:** LCDR USNR, 1956 - 1962; **OTHER ACT & HONORS:** Syndicated Columnist; Author; MA Realtor of the Year; **HOME ADD:** Chas. River Pk., Boston, MA 02114; **BUS ADD:** Four Longfellow Place, Boston, MA 02114.

PECKRON, Harold S.——B: Apr. 5, 1946, St. Louis, MO, *Atty.*, O'Brien, Char & Peckron, Tax Partner; **PRIM RE ACT:** Consultant, Attorney, Instructor, Syndicator; **SERVICES:** Synd. of Real Prop.; Fin.; **REP CLIENTS:** Hawaii RE Comm.; State Savings; Universal RE Corp; **PREV EMPLOY:** Atty., Advisor, US Tax Court, Wash., DC; Office of Chief Counsel, Treas., Wash., DC; **PROFL AFFIL & HONORS:** ABA Comm., Synd., RE Tax Problems; RESSI; IA, HI Bar Assns.; Fed. Bar Assn., Author of several publications; **EDUC:** BBA, 1970, 1972, Acctg., Acctg., Marquette Univ., Univ. of CHI - Loyola; **GRAD EDUC:** JD, 1976, Drake Univ.; LLM, 1980, Taxation, Georgetown Univ.; **EDUC HONORS:** Top 10%, Beta Gamma Sigma MBA, Top with honors, Member Assoc. Editor The Tax Lawyer; **OTHER ACT & HONORS:** Monthly Tax Column in HI RE Investor; Honolulu C of C; Phi Alpha Delta; Who's Who in Bus. & Indus.; **HOME ADD:** 1062 Hunaki St., Honolulu, HI 96816, (808)732-7041; **BUS ADD:** Penthouse, Hawaii Bldg., Honolulu, HI 96813, (808)526-2646.

PEDDICORD, Thomas——Dorchester Gas Corp.; **PRIM RE ACT:** Property Manager; **BUS ADD:** PO Box 31049, Dallas, TX 75231, (214)750-3500.*

PEDEN, Katherine——*Dir. Ind. Dev.*, General Development Corp.; **PRIM RE ACT:** Developer; **BUS ADD:** 1111 So. Bayshore Dr., Miami, FL 33131, (305)350-1271.*

PEDEN, Ronald K.——B: Jan. 15, 1944, Harper, KS, *Owner*, Peden Properties, Inc.; **PRIM RE ACT:** Broker, Consultant; **SERVICES:** Investment counseling, acquisition serv.; **REP CLIENTS:** Indiv. and instnl. investors in income producing props.; **EDUC:** BS, 1966, EE & Math, Univ. of KS; **GRAD EDUC:** MBA, 1970, Mktg., Wichita State Univ.; **HOME ADD:** 1157 Briarcliff Cir., Wichita, KS 67207, (316)686-1174; **BUS ADD:** 645 Fourth Financial Center, 100 N. Broadway, Wichita, KS 67202, (316)262-2605.

PEDERSON, Ernest A., Jr.——*Dir. Corp. Ind. RE*, General Mills, Inc.; **PRIM RE ACT:** Property Manager; **BUS ADD:** 9200 Wayzata Blvd., PO Box 1113, Minneapolis, MN 55440, (612)540-2445.*

PEDOWITZ, James M.——B: Oct. 29, 1915, Brooklyn, NY, *Partner*, Marshall, Bratter, Greene, Allison & Tucker; **PRIM RE ACT:** Attorney; **SERVICES:** All Phases of Real Prop. Law; **PREV EMPLOY:** First VP & Chief Counsel of the Title Guarantee Co. and Rgnl. Counsel (Eastern US), Pioneer Nat. Title Ins. Co. 1969-1979; **PROFL AFFIL & HONORS:** Bar Assns.: Amer., NY State, Nassau Cty., Assoc. of the Bar of the City of New York, New York City Lawyers: Amer. and NY State Land Title Assns; Amer. Coll. of RE Lawyers; Anglo-Amer. Real Prop. Inst., RE Bd. of NY; **EDUC:** BA, 1935, Econ., Law, NY Univ., WA Square Coll.; **GRAD EDUC:** JD, 1938, NYU, School of Law; **EDUC HONORS:** Univ. Prize Scholarship, 1937; **MIL SERV:** USA, Lt. Col.; **OTHER ACT & HONORS:** Jewish War Veterans; Rufus King Ladge F&AM, Member of Planning Bd. of Inc. Village of East Williston 63-74; **HOME ADD:** 200 Dickson Cir., East Williston, NY 11596, (516)746-4977; **BUS ADD:** 430 Park Ave., New York, NY 10022, (212)421-7200.

PEDRO, Frank A.——B: Jan. 21, 1952, Cambridge, MA, *Prop. Mgr.*, L.E. Smith Management Associates, Inc., Just-A-Start, Cambridge; **PRIM RE ACT:** Consultant, Property Manager; **SERVICES:** Organizational and prop. mgmt.; **PREV EMPLOY:** City of Cambridge, Dept. of Fin., Budget Analyst, 1975-1978; **PROFL AFFIL & HONORS:** IREM, Boston, ARM, 1980; **EDUC:** BA, 1973, Pol. Sci., Salem State Coll.; **GRAD EDUC:** MPA, 1976, Suffolk Univ.; **OTHER ACT & HONORS:** Bd. of Dirs., Cambridge Community Econ. Devel. Comm.; **HOME ADD:** 208 Harvard St., Cambridge, MA, (617)868-7574; **BUS ADD:** 243 Broadway, Cambridge, MA 02139, (617)661-7190.

PEDULLA, Thomas V.——B: Sept. 10, 1933, Somerville, MA, *Regnl. Dfr. Dev. & Dir. Prop. Mgmt.*, Howard Johnson Co.; **PRIM RE ACT:** Broker, Instructor, Consultant, Developer, Property Manager; **OTHER RE ACT:** Franchisor; **SERVICES:** Dev. of Comm'l. Prop. for Hotels and Restaurants; Dispose of Surplus Prop. and Restaurants & Lodging Facilities as Dir. by Sr. Mgmt.; **PREV EMPLOY:** IBM Corp.- Data Processing Div.; **PROFL AFFIL & HONORS:** NACORE, Greater Boston RE Bd., MA Assoc. Realtors; **EDUC:** BS, 1960, Hotel Admin., Cornell Univ.; **EDUC HONORS:** Cum Laude; **MIL SERV:** USAF, S/Sgt.; **OTHER ACT & HONORS:** Cornell Univ. Council, Advisory Council Cornell; School of Bus. & Public Admin.; Eastern Reg. VP Cornell Soc. of Hotelmen; Pres. New England Chap. NACORE, Boy Scouts, Gen. Area Chmn. Cornell Fund; **HOME ADD:** 54 Knight Rd. Ext., Framingham, MA 01701, (617)877-4719; **BUS ADD:** 220 Forbes Rd., Braintree, MA 02184, (617)848-2350.

PEEL, Norman D.——B: Feb. 27, 1943, Los Angeles, CA, *W. Div. Counsel*, Mobil Land Development Corp., W. Div.; **PRIM RE ACT:** Attorney; **PREV EMPLOY:** Gray, Cary, Ames & Frye, Attys. at Law, San Diego, CA 1971-79; **PROFL AFFIL & HONORS:** ABA, State Bar of CA; **EDUC:** BS, 1968, Acctg., Brigham Young Univ., Provo, UT; **GRAD EDUC:** JD, 1971, Law, Stanford Law Sch., Stanford, CA; **EDUC HONORS:** Cum Laude, Law Review; **HOME ADD:** 225 Tim Ct., Danville, CA 94526, (415)837-8625; **BUS ADD:** 1515 Spear St.

Tower, 1 Mkt. Pl., San Francisco, CA 94105, (415)764-1507.

PEETE, Don C.——**B:** Aug 26, 1930, Kansas City, MO, *Pres.*, Don C. Peete & Assoc., Inc.; **PRIM RE ACT:** Consultant, Appraiser, Developer, Lender; **SERVICES:** Appraising, consulting, mort. banking, dev.; **REP CLIENTS:** Brokerage; **PREV EMPLOY:** 18 yrs (1962-80) Sr. VP & Treas. Natl. Fidelity Life Ins. Co., and VP ERC Corp.; **PROFL AFFIL & HONORS:** AIREA, Pres. Kansas City Chapt., 1978; **EDUC:** BS, 1952, Bus. & Personnel Mgmt., Univ. of KS; **EDUC HONORS:** Dean's Honor Roll; **MIL SERV:** USA, Enlisted; **HOME ADD:** 3508 W 71, Prairie Village, KS 66208, (913)362-3304; **BUS ADD:** 7301 Mission Rd., Prairie Village, KS 66208, (913)831-2115.

PEHRSON, Donald——**B:** Jan. 13, 1921, Los Angeles, CA, *Manager - RE*, Rockwell Intl. Corp.; **PRIM RE ACT:** Consultant, Appraiser, Property Manager; **SERVICES:** Acquisition, disposition and Mgmt. of Co. props.; **PROFL AFFIL & HONORS:** AIREA, Lambda Alpha Econ. Frat., Amer. Arbitration Assn., Los Angeles Realty Bd.; **EDUC:** BS-BA, 1942, RE and Transp., USC; **HOME ADD:** 8 Shadow Ln., Rolling Hills Estates, CA 90274, (213)377-7675; **BUS ADD:** 2230 E. Imperial Hwy, El Segundo, CA 90245, (213)647-5492.

PEI, T'ing C.——**B:** Nov. 10, 1944, Princeton, NJ, *Pres.*, PEI Property Development Corp.; **PRIM RE ACT:** Consultant, Developer; **OTHER RE ACT:** Urban planning; **PREV EMPLOY:** Sefrius Corp. (VP and Dir. 1974-81); NY State Urban Devel. Corp. 1971-74; City of NY 1967-71; **PROFL AFFIL & HONORS:** Amer. Inst. of Cert. Planners; Amer. Planning Assn.; ULI; Citizens Housing and Planning Council; Rgnl. Plan Assn.; Arch. League of NY, Who's Who in Fin. and Indus.; Who's Who in the World; 1980 Nat. RE Investor Young Leaders in RE, article; **EDUC:** BA, 1965, Hist., Harvard Univ.; **GRAD EDUC:** MA, 1967, Urban planning, MIT; **OTHER ACT & HONORS:** Harvard Club of Boston; VP, Dir. of Miami World Trade Center, Inc.; Dir., WNCN Listeners Guild, Inc.; **HOME ADD:** 325 E 57th St., New York, NY 10022, (212)421-0551; **BUS ADD:** 600 Madison Ave., New York, NY 10022, (212)593-2820.

PEIFER, Chris A.——**B:** Mar. 31, 1948, Evanston, IL, *VP Fin.*, Wickes Lumber; **PRIM RE ACT:** Builder, Owner/Investor; **PREV EMPLOY:** VP of Operations(Wickes Furniture), Natl. Sales Mgr., (Wickes Furniture); **EDUC:** BA, 1970, Lib. Arts, Denison Univ.; **GRAD EDUC:** MBA, 1972, Fin./Mktg., Northwestern Univ.; **EDUC HONORS:** Deans list, Published Research Work, Deans list; **OTHER ACT & HONORS:** Bd. member child & family services & United Way solicitation exec.; **HOME ADD:** 3289 Delevan Dr., Saginaw, MI 48607, (517)790-0645; **BUS ADD:** 515 N. Wash. Ave., Saginaw, MI 48607, (517)754-9121.

PEINADO, Arnold B., Jr.——**B:** Oct. 22, 1931, El Paso, TX, *Exec. VP*, AVC Devel. Corp.; **PRIM RE ACT:** Engineer, Developer, Builder, Owner/Investor, Syndicator; **OTHER RE ACT:** Joint venture; **SERVICES:** Design, devel. & const. for own acct.; **REP CLIENTS:** Joint venture with indivs., synds. or fin, insts.; **PREV EMPLOY:** AB Peinado & Sons., Consulting Engrs.; Teaching Univ. of TX at El Paso; **PROFL AFFIL & HONORS:** Engr. of the Yr., El Paso Chap. of TX Soc. of PE; **EDUC:** BCE, 1952, Civil Engrg., Johns Hopkins Univ.; **GRAD EDUC:** MS, 1953, Civil Engrg., MIT; **EDUC HONORS:** Honors Grad.; **MIL SERV:** US Army; Cpl.; **OTHER ACT & HONORS:** Pres., El Paso C of C; El Paso Branch of the Fed. Res. Bd.; The MT States Tel & Tel Co. Advisory Bd.; Rotary Club, El Paso Art Museum; **HOME ADD:** 5729 Mira Grande Dr., El Paso, TX 79912, (915)584-0654; **BUS ADD:** 279 Shadow Mountain Dr., Suite CC, El Paso, TX 79912, (915)581-4468.

PEINADO, George A.——**B:** Jan. 22, 1944, El Paso, TX, *VP, Sec., & Treas.*, AVC Development Corp.; **PRIM RE ACT:** Broker, Developer; **PROFL AFFIL & HONORS:** ULI; NAHB; AICPA, CPA; **EDUC:** BBA, 1965, Pol. Sci., Acctg., Univ. TX El Paso, Johns Hopkins Univ.; **EDUC HONORS:** Deans List, (Univ. of TX); **OTHER ACT & HONORS:** Charter Member, El Paso Girls Club; C of C; **HOME ADD:** 5725 Mira Grande, El Paso, TX 79912, (915)581-5128; **BUS ADD:** 5778 Mira Grande, El Paso, TX 79912, (915)581-4468.

PELLER, Sidney L.——**B:** May 16, 1942, NY, Tudor Assoc., Siplo Realty Corp.; **PRIM RE ACT:** Owner/Investor, Property Manager; **EDUC:** BA, NYU; **GRAD EDUC:** MA, Sec. Educ. Econ., Cornell Univ., & Personal Fin. Mgt.; **EDUC HONORS:** Fin. Inst.; **MIL SERV:** USA & Air Force, Cpl.; **HOME ADD:** 11 Overhill Rd., Monsey, NY 10952, (914)312-4677; **BUS ADD:** 11 Overhill Rd., Monsey, NY 10952, (914)352-4677.

PELLET, M.F.——**B:** Dec. 7, 1946, Oak Park, IL, *Pres.*, Fredric Dwight, Inc., Fredric Dwight Assocs.; **PRIM RE ACT:** Consultant, Developer, Lender, Owner/Investor, Syndicator; **SERVICES:** Devel. prop. as owner/investor or syndicator. Give assistance in devel. or synd. to other parties; **EDUC:** 1965-1969, Univ. of IL; **MIL SERV:** U.S. Army, 1st Lt., Viet. Gallantry Cross, Bronze Star, Purple Heart; **BUS ADD:** PO Box 84, Yankton, SD 57078, (605)665-8297.

PELTZ, Alan H.——*Treas.*, Burndy Corp.; **PRIM RE ACT:** Property Manager; **BUS ADD:** Richards Ave., Norwalk, CT 06856, (203)838-4444.*

PENCE, Thomas R.——**B:** Oct. 11, 1952, Cedar Rapids, IA, *Assoc.*, Hines, Pence, Day & Powers; **PRIM RE ACT:** Attorney; **SERVICES:** Rep. of buyers and sellers; closing services; **PROFL AFFIL & HONORS:** Linn Cty. Bar Assn.; IA Bar Assn.; ABA; **EDUC:** BBA, 1974, Fin., Univ. of IA; **GRAD EDUC:** MBA, JD, 1977, Univ. of IA; **EDUC HONORS:** Cum Laude; **OTHER ACT & HONORS:** Pres., Cedar Rapids Jaycees 1980-81; **HOME ADD:** 3000 J. St. S.W., Cedar Rapids, IA 52404, (319)363-8748; **BUS ADD:** 815 Merchants Nat. Bank Bldg., Cedar Rapids, IA 52401, (319)365-0437.

PENDELTON, Kathleen——*Ed.*, Realtors National Marketing Inst., Real Estate Today/Real Estate Perspectives; **PRIM RE ACT:** Real Estate Publisher; **BUS ADD:** 430 N. Michigan Ave., Chicago, IL 60611, (312)420-8540.*

PENDLETON, Lawrence R.——**B:** May 16, 1950, Miami, FL, *Pres.*, The Ernest Jones Co., Realtors-Appraisers-Consultants; **PRIM RE ACT:** Broker, Consultant, Appraiser, Owner/Investor, Instructor, Property Manager; **SERVICES:** Full RE services; **REP CLIENTS:** Lenders & devels. & investors both local & natl.; **PROFL AFFIL & HONORS:** NAIFA; SREA; ASA, IFAS; **EDUC:** 1972, RE & ULS, Univ. of FL; **GRAD EDUC:** MBA, 1976, RE; **OTHER ACT & HONORS:** Past Pres. Miami Chap. of NAIFA; Served on Bd. of Dirs. for 7 yrs.; Miami Shores Kiwanis Club-Bd. of Dirs.; Chmn. of Bd. of N. Dade YMCA; **HOME ADD:** 500 NW 121 St., Miami, FL 33168; **BUS ADD:** 643 Northeast 125 St., N. Miami, FL 33161, (305)893-3464.

PENDLETON, Thomas C., Jr.——**B:** Oct. 5, 1945, Camden, ME, *Pres.*, Pendleton Assoc.; **PRIM RE ACT:** Broker, Consultant, Appraiser, Developer, Property Manager, Syndicator; **OTHER RE ACT:** Bus. broker; **PREV EMPLOY:** City of Brewer, ME Devel. Dir. (1971-74); **PROFL AFFIL & HONORS:** Realtors Nat. Mktg. Inst., NAR; **EDUC:** BS, 1967, Math, Stats., Engr. Physics, Univ. of ME; **GRAD EDUC:** MBA, 1971, Univ. of ME; **HOME ADD:** Orrington, ME; **BUS ADD:** Merrill Ctre., Ste 604, Bangor, ME 04401, (207)945-6434.

PENFIELD, Robert E.——**B:** Dec. 2, 1930, Lemmon, SD, *Owner*, Penfield Auction Realty; **PRIM RE ACT:** Broker, Instructor, Consultant, Appraiser; **OTHER RE ACT:** Auctioneer; **SERVICES:** Merchandising all kinds of R.E. at auction; **REP CLIENTS:** Owners, estate representatives & local & fel. cts.; **PROFL AFFIL & HONORS:** ND, SD, MT, WA Auctioneers Assns., Natl. Auctioneers, Assn. & Realtors, Recipient 1973 Natl. Hall of Fame Auctioneer Award; GRI; **GRAD EDUC:** BS, 1953, Animal Sci., S.D. State Univ.; **MIL SERV:** USA, Sgt., OSM; **OTHER ACT & HONORS:** ND AA Pres. 1962-63-64; Natl. Auctioneer Assn. Pres. 1968-69; Tr. Bowman Church of God; State Bd. of Easter Seals Soc.; **HOME ADD:** Bowman, ND, (701)523-5347; **BUS ADD:** N. Main, Bowman, ND 58623, (701)523-3652.

PENN, Christopher H.——**B:** Apr. 24, 1946, Bronx, NY, *VP*, Chelsea Moore Development Corp., Comml. Devel.; **PRIM RE ACT:** Consultant, Developer, Builder, Owner/Investor, Syndicator; **PROFL AFFIL & HONORS:** ULI, Wash. DC, Intl. Council of Shopping Ctrs., New York, NY, BOMA; **EDUC:** BS, 1969, Univ. of Dayton; **GRAD EDUC:** NY Univ., New York, NY; **OTHER ACT & HONORS:** City Comm, City of Edgewood, KY, 1976-77; Summit Hills Ctry Club; Bankers Club of Cincinnati, OH; State of KY C of C; Urban Devel. Task Force; **HOME ADD:** 3080 Arbor Ln., Edgewood, KY 41017, (606)331-8131; **BUS ADD:** PO Box 46175, 1325 E Kemper Rd., Cincinnati, OH 45246, (513)671-1600.

PENN, Robert——*VP*, Unarco Industries, Inc.; **PRIM RE ACT:** Property Manager; **BUS ADD:** 332 S. Michigan Ave., Chicago, IL 60604, (312)341-1234.*

PENNER, Arlin L.——**B:** Nov. 17, 1945, KS, *Investment Counselor*; **PRIM RE ACT:** Broker, Syndicator, Developer, Owner/Investor; **SERVICES:** Fin. & Estate Planning for investors; **REP CLIENTS:** Lic. in ins., activities of RE; **PREV EMPLOY:** Project Coord. Century 21 Comml. Co., Inc., W. Covina, CA; **PROFL AFFIL & HONORS:** RESSI, Intl. Assn. of Fin. Planners, Top investment salesperson for month - several times; **EDUC:** BA, 1967, Bus./Chem., Tabor Coll., Hillsboro, KS; **MIL SERV:** Alternate service, taught Bio. & Chem. to Zairian nationals in French; **OTHER ACT & HONORS:** Lipidopterist Soc., 12000 W. African Butterfly Collection; **HOME ADD:** 330 Golden Carriage Ln., Pomona, CA 91767, (714)593-0495; **BUS ADD:** 330 Golden Carriage Ln., Pomona, CA 91767, (714)593-0495.

PENNEY, John S., Jr.——B: Aug. 11, 1920, Cincinnati, OH, *Dir., RE*, Warner-Lambert Co.; **PRIM RE ACT:** Consultant, Property Manager; **OTHER RE ACT:** conduct all corp. RE matters; **SERVICES:** acquisition, disposition, leasing, consulting; **REP CLIENTS:** co. operating groups, corp. mgmt.; **PROFL AFFIL & HONORS:** Member & former Dir. of Indus. Devel. Research Council; **EDUC:** BS, 1941, Indus. Admin., Yale Univ. Sheffield Sci. Sch.; **EDUC HONORS:** Tau Beta Pi; **MIL SERV:** US Naval Res., Lt. JG; **OTHER ACT & HONORS:** Millburn NJ Township Comm. 1980-82; **HOME ADD:** 21 Twin Oak Rd., Short Hills, NJ 07078, (201)379-3983; **BUS ADD:** 201 Tabor Rd., Morris Plains, NJ 07950, (201)540-2796.

PENNINGTON, David L.——B: Jan. 25, 1931, Phila., PA, *Pres.*, Harvey, Pennington, Herting & Renneisen Ltd.; **PRIM RE ACT:** Attorney; **SERVICES:** Legal servs. to realtors, buyers, sellers, lessors, & lessees; **REP CLIENTS:** Howard Coffey RE (Broker), Numerous buyers, sellers, lessors & lessees; **PROFL AFFIL & HONORS:** Amer., PA & Phila. Bar Assns.; **EDUC:** 1963, Pre-law, Sch. of Law, NYU; **GRAD EDUC:** LLB, 1956; **EDUC HONORS:** Root Tilden Scholar; **MIL SERV:** USA, Pvt.; **OTHER ACT & HONORS:** Tr. DE Valley Chap. Natl. Hemophilia Found.; **HOME ADD:** 129 Old Gulph Rd., Wynnewood, PA 19096, (215)642-8270; **BUS ADD:** 7 Penn Centre Plaza, Philadelphia, PA 19103, (215)563-4470.

PENNINGTON, Robert E.——B: Sept. 1, 1947, Memphis, TN, *VP Income Prop. Mgr.*, First Union National Bank, Bank RE; **PRIM RE ACT:** Broker, Property Manager; **SERVICES:** Purch. of prop. mgmt. of income producing prop.; **REP CLIENTS:** First Union Corp.; **PREV EMPLOY:** Robt. Pennington Realty, Memphis, TN; **PROFL AFFIL & HONORS:** BOMA, IREM, AIREA, Pres.; RPA & CPM Candidate; **EDUC:** BBA, 1969, Acctg., Mgmt., Memphis State Univ.; **HOME ADD:** 6145 Page Ct., Charlotte, NC 28211, (704)374-6769; **BUS ADD:** 920 First Union Plaza, Charlotte, NC 28288, (704)374-6769.

PENSEL, Edward C.——B: Apr. 10, 1920, Baltimore, MD, *Asst. Prof.*, Dundalk Community Coll.; **PRIM RE ACT:** Broker, Instructor; **SERVICES:** Educ. RE; **PREV EMPLOY:** VP, W. Burton Guy & Co., 11 E. Chase St., Baltimore, MD 21202; **PROFL AFFIL & HONORS:** RE Educ. Assn.; Greater Baltimore Bd. of Realtors; RNMI; **EDUC:** BS, 1942, US Merch. Marine Academy; **HOME ADD:** 228 Ridgeway Rd., Baltimore, MD 21228, (301)747-2642; **BUS ADD:** 7200 Sollers Point Rd., Dundalk, MD 21222, (301)282-6700.

PENSON, Edward I.——B: Feb. 5, 1937, New York, NY; **PRIM RE ACT:** Attorney, Developer, Owner/Investor, Property Manager, Syndicator; **OTHER RE ACT:** Specializing urban development and Hud subsidized or related projects, mgmt.; **PREV EMPLOY:** Member, Demov, Morris, Levin, Shein; Assoc., Dreyer & Traub; **PROFL AFFIL & HONORS:** Member, Advisory Bd., Security Title & Guaranty Co.; Lambda Alpha Frat., Land Econ.; **EDUC:** BS, 1959, Econ., Hofstra Coll.; **GRAD EDUC:** LLB, 1961, Brooklyn Law School; **MIL SERV:** US Army, 1955-57, GCM; **HOME ADD:** 485 East Shore Rd., Kings Pt., NY, (516)466-2348; **BUS ADD:** 111 Great Neck Rd., Great Neck, NY 11021, (212)895-7485.

PENTLER, Harold E.——B: Mar. 8, 1917, Milwaukee, WI, *Pres.*, RE Appraisers, Inc.; **PRIM RE ACT:** Consultant, Appraiser, Developer, Owner/Investor, Property Manager, Insuror; **PROFL AFFIL & HONORS:** NAR, MAI, SRPA (SREA), Realtor; **EDUC:** 1938, Mktg., Univ. of WI Sch. of Commerce; **MIL SERV:** Army Air Corp., 1st Lt., China Ribbon; **OTHER ACT & HONORS:** Realtor of Yr., 1970; Pres. Milwaukee Bd., 1965; Pres. WI Chapt 16 MAI,: Nat. Dir. MAI; **HOME ADD:** 6232 N Berkeley Blvd., Milwaukee, WI 53217, (414)332-3984; **BUS ADD:** 350 W Green Tree Rd., Milwaukee, WI 53217, (414)352-8680.

PEPITONE, James A.——*Pres*, James A. Pepitone, Inc.; Empire State Const. & Devel. Inc.; Blaich RE, Inc.; **PRIM RE ACT:** Broker, Instructor, Syndicator, Consultant, Developer, Builder, Property Manager, Owner/Investor; **PREV EMPLOY:** Cushman & Wakefield, Sackman Gilliland, BTMI; **PROFL AFFIL & HONORS:** LIBOR, IREM (CPM); **EDUC:** BS, Bus. Mgmt.; **GRAD EDUC:** MBA; **BUS ADD:** PO Box 472, Locust Valley, NY 11560, (516)759-2770.

PEPPER, Henry Louis——B: Feb. 3, 1927, New Orleans, LA, *Port RE Coord.*, Bd. of Commissioners of the Port of New Orleans, Indus. and RE; **PRIM RE ACT:** Broker, Property Manager; **SERVICES:** Plan and assist location of marine oriented indus.; Lease and contract mgmt. of Port Lands; **REP CLIENTS:** Exporters, importers, mfrs., distributors; **PREV EMPLOY:** New Orleans Public Belt Railroad, 1949-1967, A terminal railroad for all mainline railroads in port Area; **PROFL AFFIL & HONORS:** SIR; (Associate), Intl. RWY, Agency rep. to New Orleans Planning Advisory Comm.; **EDUC:** 1943, Pre-Med, LA State Univ.; 1944, Engrg., OK A&M; 1944, Areas and Lang., Yale; 1945, Areas and Lang., Univ. of MN; **GRAD EDUC:** 1947, Arts & Scis., LA State Univ.; **MIL SERV:** US Army; Sgt.; Far East interpreter, Hon. etc.; Batt. Comdr. Washington Art.; Lang., Retd.; **OTHER ACT & HONORS:** Various Social & Veteran Organizations (N.O., LA); **HOME ADD:** 5005 Dauphine St., New Orleans, LA 70117, (504)949-8475; **BUS ADD:** PO Box 60046, New Orleans, LA 70160, (504)528-3399.

PERABO, Fred H.——*Mgr. RE Div.*, Ralston-Purina Co.; **PRIM RE ACT:** Property Manager; **BUS ADD:** Checkerboard Square, St. Louis, MO 63188, (314)982-1000.*

PERACCHIO, Peter J.——B: Apr. 3, 1952, New York, NY, *Property Manager*, Grenadier Realty Corp., Starrett Housing Corp.; **PRIM RE ACT:** Property Manager; **OTHER RE ACT:** Rental agent; **SERVICES:** Mgmt. & rental of subsidized housing (Section 236, Section 8, etc.) and market rate housing; **REP CLIENTS:** Prop. owners of HUD supervised subsidized housing; **PROFL AFFIL & HONORS:** Certificate in Bldg. & Prop. Mgmt.; NYU RE Inst. (Candidate); **EDUC:** 1971, Pol. Sci., Earlham Coll.; 1972, Pol. Sci., Columbia Univ.; **GRAD EDUC:** Current, NYU, Inst. of RE; **HOME ADD:** 356 E. 13th St., New York, NY 10003, (212)673-8353; **BUS ADD:** 100 W. 93rd St., New York, NY 10025, (212)865-1877.

PERCIVAL, Robert H.——B: June 5, 1923, Salt Lake City, UT, *Pres.*, Percival's, Inc.; **PRIM RE ACT:** Broker, Consultant, Developer, Property Manager; **SERVICES:** Fee devel. for firms who need a Turnkey package; **REP CLIENTS:** NC Natl. Bank, Kemper Ins. Co., Southern Railway System; **PROFL AFFIL & HONORS:** NAR, IREM, NAIOP, CPM; **EDUC:** BA, 1948, Indus. Engrg., Univ. of Notre Dame; **MIL SERV:** USMC, Lt.; **OTHER ACT & HONORS:** Dir. - Gr. Charlotte C of C & Charlotte Athletic Club; **HOME ADD:** 2816 Wheelock Rd., Charlotte, NC 28211, (704)364-3481; **BUS ADD:** 301 S. McDowell St., Suite 1212, Cameron Brown Bldg., Charlotte, NC 28204, (704)333-1535.

PERCY, Jerry G.——B: Feb. 3, 1949, Sioux City, IA, *Corp. Counsel, VP, Secretary*, Columbia Savings and Loan Association; **PRIM RE ACT:** Attorney, Banker, Developer, Lender, Owner/Investor; **SERVICES:** Gen. legal serv. to fin. inst., including all areas of RE; **REP CLIENTS:** Columbia S&L Assn.; **PREV EMPLOY:** Asst. State Counsel; Asst. Mgr., Transamer. Title Ins. Co.; **PROFL AFFIL & HONORS:** ABA, ABA Real Property, Probate and Trust Law Section, and ABA S&L Counsel Section; CO Bar Assn., CBA RE Section; Denver Bar Assn., various RE Comms., Chmn. Atty's. Committee, S&L League of CO, Instructor, the Inst. for Fin. Education; Lecturer, Cont. Legal Educ. in CO, Inc.; Lecturer, Program for Adv. Prof. Dev.; Lecturer, Intl. Practicum Inst.; and Lecturer to several Bar Assns. and realtor groups., Certified Abstractor; **EDUC:** BS, 1971, Journalism, Univ. of KS; **GRAD EDUC:** JD, 1974, Univ. of Denver, Coll. of Law; **EDUC HONORS:** Contemporary Music Project, Minor: Music Theory; **HOME ADD:** 5681 East Weaver Cir., Englewood, CO 80111, (303)771-4913; **BUS ADD:** Building 14, Denver Tech. Ctr., 5850 DTC Pkwy., Englewood, CO 80111, (303)773-3444.

PEREL, Jonathan Seth——B: Jan. 24, 1950, Richmond, VA, *Pres.*, Gen. Services Corp.; **PRIM RE ACT:** Developer, Builder, Owner/Investor, Property Manager; **EDUC:** BA, 1971, Pol. Sci., Princeton Univ.; **EDUC HONORS:** Univ. Scholar; **MIL SERV:** US Army; Res.; **BUS ADD:** PO Box 8984, Richmond, VA 23225, (804)320-7101.

PERERIA, James P.——*Mgr. Ind. Dev.*, New Orleans East; **PRIM RE ACT:** Developer; **BUS ADD:** PO Box 29188, New Orleans, LA 70189, (504)254-1400.*

PERINI, Bart W.——*VP*, Paramount Development Assoc. Inc.; **PRIM RE ACT:** Developer; **BUS ADD:** 73 Mt.Wayte Ave., Framingham, MA 01701, (617)875-6171.*

PERKINS, Dr. Ed R.——B: June 22, 1938, Austin, TX, *Pres.*, Perkins Enterprises; **PRIM RE ACT:** Consultant, Developer, Builder, Owner/Investor, Property Manager, Syndicator; **SERVICES:** Investment counseling, devel. and synd. of comml. props., prop. mgmt.; **REP CLIENTS:** Wal-Mart; Montgomery Ward; IGA; Super-Valu; P.N. Hirsch; Rite-Aid; Sears; Ashley's (Coast to coast); **PREV EMPLOY:** Coll. VP for Devel., 1970-1973; **PROFL AFFIL & HONORS:** ICSC, Community Leader of Amer.; Outstanding Personalities of the South; Nat. Advisory Council of NFIB; Dist. Gov. of Rotary Intl.; Intl. Scholar; Outstanding Educator of Amer.; **EDUC:** Bachelor's, 1961, Bethel Coll.; **GRAD EDUC:** Master's, 1965, Murray State Univ.; PhD, 1973, Univ. of KY; **OTHER ACT & HONORS:** 1981

Outstanding Alumni Achievement Award, Bethel Coll.; **HOME ADD:** 1036 E. Paris Ave., McKenzie, TN 38201, (901)352-2754; **BUS ADD:** Box 370, McKenzie, TN 38201, (901)352-7189.

PERKINS, Lawrence Bradford——B: Jan. 13, 1943, Chicago, IL, *Partner*, Attia & Perkins; **PRIM RE ACT:** Architect; **SERVICES:** Arch., planning, int. design, RE consulting; **REP CLIENTS:** Major devel., US Govt. agencies, instit., banks, and foreign govts.; **PREV EMPLOY:** Partner & gen. mgr. Eastern Operations Perkins & Will, Managing Partner LlEwelyn-Davies Assoc.; **PROFL AFFIL & HONORS:** AIA, Amer. Planning Assn.; **EDUC:** AB, 1967, Latin Amer. Hist., Cornell Univ.; BArch., 1971, Arch., City Coll. of NY, Cornell Univ.; **GRAD EDUC:** MBA, 1969, Bus., Stanford Univ.; **EDUC HONORS:** Magna Cum Laude, Distinction, Gargoyle; **HOME ADD:** 4 Rectory Ln., Scarsdale, NY 10583, (914)723-8875; **BUS ADD:** 437 Fifth Ave., New York, NY 10016, (212)889-1720.

PERKINS, Richard F.——B: May 9, 1935, *Pres.*, LandVest, Inc.; **PRIM RE ACT:** Broker, Consultant, Appraiser, Developer; **SERVICES:** Land and timber mgmt., estate brokerage; **PREV EMPLOY:** Stanmar Inc.; WR Grace; **PROFL AFFIL & HONORS:** Realtor; **EDUC:** BA, Geology, Dartmouth Coll.; **GRAD EDUC:** MBA, Bus., Dartmouth Coll.; **HOME ADD:** Red Acre Rd., Stow, MA 01775, (617)897-5297; **BUS ADD:** 14 Kilby St., Boston, MA 02109, (617)723-1800.

PERKINS, Steven L.——B: Dec. 19, 1950, Pipestone, MN, *Broker*, Earl Perkins Realty; **PRIM RE ACT:** Broker, Instructor, Property Manager; **SERVICES:** Maj. concentration of farm, home and comml. props.; **REP CLIENTS:** Gen. public and investors, Instr. of RE educ.-Worthington Comm. Coll.; **PROFL AFFIL & HONORS:** Bd. of Realtors (SW MN, MN & Nat.)past member; Bd. of Dir. MN Assn. of Realtors, Past Pres. and VP of SW MN Bd. of Realtors, 1978 Distinguished Serv. Award, 1980 Realtor of the Year MN Assoc. of Realtors; **EDUC:** BA, 1976, Bus. Econ.-Poli. Sci., Macalester Coll. St. Paul, MN; **OTHER ACT & HONORS:** Mayor, City of Pipestone, MN since 4/1977, Commnr. SW MN Rgnl. Devel. Comm., Member Bd. of Dir., League of MN Cities; Pres. MN Balance of State Private Indus. Council; Pres. SW MN Emergency Med. Serv.; **HOME ADD:** 121 3rd Ave. SE, Pipestone, MN 56164, (507)825-4663; **BUS ADD:** 214 NW 2nd St., Pipestone, MN 56164, (507)825-2525.

PERKINS, Thomas G.——B: July 28, 1945, Malden, MA, *Member*, Hopkins & Carley; **PRIM RE ACT:** Attorney; **SERVICES:** Negotiating and Drafting comml. RE leases; **REP CLIENTS:** Landlords and Tenants of Comml. RE including office, indus. and shopping ctr. prop.; **PROFL AFFIL & HONORS:** ABA, Real Prop., Probate and Trust Law Sec.; **EDUC:** BA, 1967, Poli. Sci., Tufts Univ.; **GRAD EDUC:** JD, 1971, The George Washington Univ. Law School; **EDUC HONORS:** With Honors; **HOME ADD:** Los Gatos, CA; **BUS ADD:** Union Bank Bldg. - Suite 1000, 99 Almaden Blvd., San Jose, CA 95113, (408)286-9800.

PERLMAN, John R.——B: Jan. 27, 1956, NY, *Representative*, North Western Mutual Life Ins. Co., R.E. Investment Office - Atlanta; **OTHER RE ACT:** Investor and Fin. Mgr.; **SERVICES:** Supervise the mgmt. of existing portfolio investment in new props., disposal of owned props.; **PROFL AFFIL & HONORS:** Pres., Adams & Co. R.E. Inc., a GA Corp.; involved in the brokerage of and investment in income producing props.; licensed R.E. broker, Candidate for CPM degree; **EDUC:** BBA, 1977, Acctg./Fin., Emory Univ.; **GRAD EDUC:** MBA, 1979, RE Fin./Devel., The Wharton Sch. of the Univ. of PA; **EDUC HONORS:** With Highest Distinction, Teaching Assistantship; **HOME ADD:** 13 Stratford Hall Pl., Atlanta, GA 30342, (404)255-1718; **BUS ADD:** 219 Perimeter Ctry. Pkwy., Suite 460, Atlanta, GA 30346, (404)396-4800.

PERLMUTTER, Alan J.——B: Aug. 26, 1947, St. Louis, MO, *VP*, Paragon Group, Inc.; **PRIM RE ACT:** Broker, Developer; **REP CLIENTS:** Penn Mutual, CT General, Travelers; **PROFL AFFIL & HONORS:** ICSC; BOMA; NAHB; St. Louis Rgnl. Commerce & Growth Assn.; NAIOP; **EDUC:** BA, 1969, Econ., Univ. of WI; **GRAD EDUC:** MBA, 1970, Mktg., Columbia Univ.; **EDUC HONORS:** Deans List; **OTHER ACT & HONORS:** St. Louis Council on World Affairs; **HOME ADD:** 3 Wedgewood Ln., St. Louis, MO 63141, (314)872-8832; **BUS ADD:** 12312 Olive Blvd., St. Louis, MO 63141, (314)878-1660.

PERLSTEIN, Mitchell L.——B: Jan. 4, 1948, New York, NY, *Atty.*, Mitchell L. Perlstein, P.A.; **PRIM RE ACT:** Attorney; **SERVICES:** RE conveyancing and fin., representation of condo. devel. and assns., RE litigation, title insurance; **REP CLIENTS:** Lenders, devels., investors and synds. in real prop. condo. assns.; **PREV EMPLOY:** Asst. Prof. Bus. Law, IL State Univ.; **PROFL AFFIL & HONORS:** ABA; FL Bar Assn.; Community Assns. Instit.; Intl. Assn. of Fin. Planners; **EDUC:** BS, 1969, Banking & Fin., NY Univ.; **GRAD EDUC:** JD, 1972, Law, Wash. Univ., School of Law; **EDUC HONORS:** Sphinx Hon. Soc.; **HOME ADD:** 10363 SW 142 St., Miami, FL 33176; **BUS ADD:** 2000 S. Dixie Hwy, Suite 206, Miami, FL 33133, (305)856-0777.

PERMUT, Barry Michael——B: Mar. 5, 1945, Chicago, IL; **PRIM RE ACT:** Attorney; **REP CLIENTS:** Lenders - Comml. and Resid. Devels.; **PROFL AFFIL & HONORS:** CO Bar, Amer. Bar, Denver Bar Assn.; **EDUC:** 1966, Univ. of IL; **GRAD EDUC:** JD, 1969, Univ. of IL; LLM, 1972, Harvard Univ.; **EDUC HONORS:** Order of Coif; **HOME ADD:** 2071 Albion, Denver, CO 80207, (303)377-9009; **BUS ADD:** 1660 Lincoln St., Denver, CO 80264.

PEROM, Stuart S.——B: Oct. 13, 1931, St. Louis, MO, *Owner/Broker*, The Real Connection; **PRIM RE ACT:** Broker, Consultant, Lender, Syndicator; **SERVICES:** Resid. RE counseling, synd. of resid. & comml. props.; **REP CLIENTS:** Lenders & indiv. investors for secondary loans; **PROFL AFFIL & HONORS:** Realtors Nat. Mktg. Instit., CRS; **OTHER ACT & HONORS:** Soc. of Amer. Magicians (Member); Past Pres., Kiwanis Club - Tarzana, CA; Past Member, L.A. Mayors Citizens Advisory Comm., Listed in Who's Who in Resid. RE , Published by Realtors Nat. Mktg. Instit.; **HOME ADD:** 20141 Allentown Dr., Woodland Hills, CA 91364, (213)716-1252; **BUS ADD:** 5850 Canoga Ave., Suite 400, Woodland Hills, CA 91367, (213)888-0202.

PERRINE, James J.——B: June 1, 1955, New York, NY, *Dir. of Operations*, Harvard Square Management Corp.; **PRIM RE ACT:** Broker, Consultant, Developer, Owner/Investor, Property Manager, Syndicator; **OTHER RE ACT:** Counselor; Mgr.; **SERVICES:** Resid. devel., condo. conversions, investment mgmt.; **PREV EMPLOY:** Staff of Robert F. Huntsman, Atty. at Law; **PROFL AFFIL & HONORS:** MA RE Broker; **EDUC:** BA, 1977, Gvt., Harvard Coll.; **EDUC HONORS:** Dean's List, Ada Howe Kent Found. Scholarship, Cum Laude; **HOME ADD:** 20 Concord Ave., Cambridge, MA 02138; **BUS ADD:** 29 Concord Ave., Cambridge, MA 02138, (617)492-8100.

PERRON, Leo F., Jr.——*Pres.*, Perron and Co., Inc.; **PRIM RE ACT:** Broker, Property Manager, Owner/Investor; **SERVICES:** Buying, selling, investing,and managing comml. RE; **PROFL AFFIL & HONORS:** San Antonio Bd. of Realtors, CCIM; **EDUC:** BBA, 1968, Fin. and Mktg., TX Lutheran Coll.; **HOME ADD:** 2619 Friar Tuck, San Antonio, TX 78209, (512)824-4677; **BUS ADD:** 1100 N.E. Loop 410, Ste. 614, San Antonio, TX 78209, (512)828-6111.

PERRY, A. Fred, Jr.——B: June 19, 1948, WV, *Broker, KS & MO*, Re/Max Overland Park Real Estate, Inc., Comml./Resid. Investment; **PRIM RE ACT:** Broker, Consultant, Appraiser, Developer, Owner/Investor, Instructor, Property Manager, Syndicator, Real Estate Publisher; **OTHER RE ACT:** CPA; **PREV EMPLOY:** Univ. of KS, Instructor Econ.; **PROFL AFFIL & HONORS:** CCIM; CPA; NAIM; Multi-Million Dollar Club, PhD, Econ.; **EDUC:** BS Bus., 1971, Acctg., Eastern IL Univ.; **GRAD EDUC:** MBA, 1973, Bus., Univ. of IL; PhD, 1976, Univ. of KS; **EDUC HONORS:** top 10% of Class, Publisher RE Handbooks, etc.; **MIL SERV:** Nat. Guard, Capt.; 1967-1979, Hon. Disc.; **HOME ADD:** 5668 Marty, Overland Park, KS 66212; **BUS ADD:** 7399 W. 97th, Overland Park, KS 66212, (913)341-3800.

PERRY, Jack R.——B: Mar. 29, 1923, Columbus, OH, *VP Fin.*, Seroyal Brands, Inc.; **PRIM RE ACT:** Consultant, Owner/Investor, Instructor, Property Manager, Insuror; **PREV EMPLOY:** VP RE - 50 CA Bldg. Corp.; **PROFL AFFIL & HONORS:** CPM; Registered Prop. Admin.; CPA, Soc. of RPA's; BOMA; AICPA; Faculty of Golden Gate Univ., San Francisco; Faculty of St. Mary's Coll., Moraga, CA; **EDUC:** BA, 1948, Acctg., OH State Univ.; **GRAD EDUC:** Grad. Work, 1977, RE, Univ. of CA; **MIL SERV:** Infantry, M/Sgt.; **OTHER ACT & HONORS:** Concord C of C; Beta Alpha Psi; Fin. Principal, Nat. Assn. Security Dealers; Lecturer, Amer. Mgt. Assn.; **HOME ADD:** 628 Burton Dr., Lafayette, CA 94549, (415)283-5970; **BUS ADD:** 2615 Stanwell Dr., Concord, CA 94524.

PERRY, Michael G.——B: Mar. 4, 1948, Preston, ID, *Pres.*, Great Basin Investment Co.; **PRIM RE ACT:** Broker, Developer, Property Manager, Syndicator; **SERVICES:** Multi-family synd. & mgmt., condo. conversions; **REP CLIENTS:** RE and non RE profls. investments; **PREV EMPLOY:** Sierra West Investment Co., San Jose, CA; Merritt Mgmt. & Devel. Co., Oakland, CA; **EDUC:** BBA, 1978, Mgmt. and Org., ID State Univ.; **MIL SERV:** USN, YN3, Vietnam Service (2); **BUS ADD:** 1526 Bench Rd., Pocatello, ID 83201, (208)237-3781.

PERRY, Paul E.——B: May 5, 1951, Zanesville, OH, *Atty.*, Cole, Billig, Wear & Perry; **PRIM RE ACT:** Attorney, Instructor; **SERVICES:** RE title & gen. RE law; planning; **REP CLIENTS:** Bacher Intl., Inc.; RE/MAX 100, Inc.; **PREV EMPLOY:** Trinity

Title Co., Columbus, OH; **PROFL AFFIL & HONORS:** Amer., OH, Cincinnati Bar Assns., OH Land Title Assn.; **EDUC:** BA, 1973, Poli. Sci., OH State Univ.; **GRAD EDUC:** JD, 1976, OH State Univ.; **OTHER ACT & HONORS:** Hamilton-Fairfield Jaycees; **HOME ADD:** 4586 Southridge Dr., Batavia, OH 45103, (513)752-3466; **BUS ADD:** 102-E Bacher Sq., Fairfield, OH 45014, (513)868-2221.

PERRY, Peter P.——B: Apr. 30, 1935, Allentown, PA, Peter P. Perry, Esq.; **PRIM RE ACT:** Attorney; **SERVICES:** Legal; **REP CLIENTS:** Devel., sellers, purchasers, indiv. and instns., lenders and investors in all phases of RE; **PROFL AFFIL & HONORS:** ABA, member, sect. on real prop. probate & trust laws, corp. banking & bus. law adjunct member, sect. on taxation and PA Bar Assn.(member, sect. real prop., probate & trust laws, corp. banking & bus. law, tax law),Lehigh Cty. Bar Assn.; **EDUC:** BA, 1957, pre-law, Univ. of PA; **GRAD EDUC:** JD, 1960, Dickinson School of Law, Carlisle, PA; **HOME ADD:** 3040 Fernor St., Allentown, PA 18103, (215)437-4595; **BUS ADD:** 1600 Lehigh Pkwy., E., Allentown, PA 18103, (215)437-4595.

PERRY, Robert——B: June 27, 1929, MA, *Owner*, Amistad Amer.; **PRIM RE ACT:** Consultant, Developer, Owner/Investor, Property Manager, Insuror, Syndicator; **SERVICES:** Interested in consulting/synd. w/equity position; **REP CLIENTS:** Indiv. who needs tax shelters; **HOME ADD:** Hwy. 90W, Box 44, Del Rio, TX 78840, (512)775-7100; **BUS ADD:** Hwy 90W, Box 44, Del Rio, TX 78840, (512)775-6484.

PERRY, Tony——B: Apr. 25, 1931, Chicago Hgts., IL, *Pres.*, Perry Land Co., Inc.; **PRIM RE ACT:** Broker, Instructor, Syndicator, Consultant, Appraiser, Property Manager, Owner/Investor; **SERVICES:** Indus., comm'l., investments, sales & leasing; **REP CLIENTS:** Fed. Paperboard; Gen. Foods; McDonalds; Armstrong World Enterprises; Mobil Chem.; Short Milling; Imperial Int'l. Learning; Scot Lad Foods; Birmingham Bolt; **PREV EMPLOY:** 1 of 3 in State of IL to have attained the dual designations of SIR and CCIM; **PROFL AFFIL & HONORS:** CCIM; SIR, Realtor of Yr., Kankakee Cty., 1978; **EDUC:** BA, 1954, Psych., Univ. of Notre Dame; **EDUC HONORS:** Cum Laude; **MIL SERV:** US Army; CPL.; **OTHER ACT & HONORS:** Great Lakes Devel. Council, Dir.; IL Dept. of Commerce & Community Affairs, Advisory Bd.; Peoples Bank, Kankakee, IL, Dir.; Kankakee Comm. Coll., Faculty; **HOME ADD:** 1399 Guildford Dr., Bourbonnais, IL 60914, (815)932-1531; **BUS ADD:** Box 1615, Kankakee, IL 60901, (815)933-2120.

PERRYMAN, Bruce C.——B: Jan. 28, 1939, Laramie, WY, *VP/Mgr.*, United S&L Assn. of WY; **PRIM RE ACT:** Instructor, Consultant, Lender, Insuror; **SERVICES:** Comml. lending, resid. home lending, all savings functions, share loans, NOW Accts., pay-by-phone, PALP, HIPs, mobile home; **PREV EMPLOY:** Asst. Prof., Bus., Adams St. Coll. of CO (1967-1968); Pres., Mt. Plains, Inc., Glasgow, MT (1971-1977); NYLIC Field Underwriter (1977-1979); **PROFL AFFIL & HONORS:** Nat. Assn. Life Underwriters; USL of S&L, Who's Who in the West, 8th ed.; Who's Who in Fin. & Indus., 22nd ed.; **EDUC:** BA, 1965, Bus. Admin./Mgmt./Mktg., Univ. of WY, Laramie, WY; **GRAD EDUC:** MS, 1966, Mgmt./Educ., Univ. of WY; **EDUC HONORS:** Phi Delta Kappa, WY St. Tchrs. Scholar (1965-1966), Grad. Research & Teaching Asst. (1965-1966); **MIL SERV:** USAF, Sgt., Good Conduct; **OTHER ACT & HONORS:** School Bd. Member, 1981; Econ. Dev. Corp., Bd. one yr., Glasgow, MT (1976); NEA; Masons; Rotary Intl.; Amer. Voc. Assn.; Amer. Mgmt. Assn.; Amer. Assn. School Admin; AACJC; **HOME ADD:** 404 S 18th, Worland, WY 82401, (307)347-6547; **BUS ADD:** Box 227, 15th & Bighorn, Worland, WY 82401, (307)347-3255.

PERRYMAN, J. Edwin——*Mgr., RE Div.*, Aluminum Co. of America; **OTHER RE ACT:** Manage indus. RE for co.; **BUS ADD:** 370 Alcoa Bldg., Pittsburgh, PA 15221, (412)553-4773.

PERSIANO, Patricia A.——B: Mar. 5, 1933, Niles, OH, *VP; Manager*, HGM-Hilltop Realtors, Lyndhurst Office; **PRIM RE ACT:** Broker, Consultant, Owner/Investor, Instructor; **OTHER RE ACT:** RNMI Instr.; **PROFL AFFIL & HONORS:** RNMI; NAR; IREF; OH Assn. of Realtors; Cleveland Area Bd. of Realtors; League of Women Voters, GRI; CRS; CRB; Dale Carnegie Sales Talk Champion Award, 1971; Million Dollar Sales Club, 1970-1979; **EDUC:** BS, 1954, Mech. Engrg., Fenn Coll.; **OTHER ACT & HONORS:** Pres., League of Women Voters of Cuyahoga Cty., 1968-1970; **HOME ADD:** 6442 Foxboro Dr., Mayfield Village, OH 44143, (216)442-1628; **BUS ADD:** 5035 Mayfield Rd., Lyndhurst, OH 44124, (216)382-2000.

PERSIL, Herbert G.——*Dir.*, Department of Housing and Urban Development, Organization & Management Info.; **PRIM RE ACT:** Lender; **BUS ADD:** 451 Seventh St., S.W., Washington, DC 20410, (202)755-5196.*

PERSKY, Jeffrey M.——B: Dec. 25, 1949, Brooklyn, NY, *Exec. VP*, Eric Bram & Co.; **PRIM RE ACT:** Broker, Owner/Investor; **SERVICES:** Office & Indus. Site Location, Fin., Constr., build to suit; **PROFL AFFIL & HONORS:** Indus. RE Brokers Assn.; **EDUC:** BS, 1972, Bus. Admin., Acctg., Univ. of SC; **MIL SERV:** US Army, Sgt.; USAR; **HOME ADD:** 13 Tally Ho Tr., Belle Mead, NJ 08502, (201)359-6886; **BUS ADD:** 77 Milltown Rd., E. Brunswick, NJ 08816, (201)238-3500.

PERSON, Kenneth W.——B: June 1, 1916, *Pres.*, The Preserve of Eden Prairie; **PRIM RE ACT:** Developer; **SERVICES:** Land subdivision, resid. & comml.; **PREV EMPLOY:** MN Gas Co., VP, Bus. Devel.; **EDUC:** BCE, 1938, Univ. of MN; **MIL SERV:** Corps of Engr., Capt.; **HOME ADD:** 4520 Laguna Dr., Edina, MN 55435, (612)922-4547; **BUS ADD:** 11111 Anderson Lakes Pkwy., Eden Prairie, MN 55344, (612)941-2001.

PERUCCI, Thomas Robert——B: Aug. 25, 1948, Riverside, NJ, *Sales Assoc.*, Coldwell Banker & Co., Comml. RE Serv. - WA, DC; **PRIM RE ACT:** Broker; **SERVICES:** Leasing & Sales of Retail & Comml. Props.; **REP CLIENTS:** Devels., Investors & Retail Tanants; **PREV EMPLOY:** Asst. of COB, Westgate Corp.; **PROFL AFFIL & HONORS:** IREM, CPM; **EDUC:** BS, 1970, Indus. Engrg., RPI; **GRAD EDUC:** MBA, 1972, Fin., Northeastern Univ.; **EDUC HONORS:** Grad. Teaching Fellow; **HOME ADD:** 2500E S. Walker Reed Dr., Arlington, VA 22206, (203)671-5755; **BUS ADD:** 2020 K St. NW, Suite 340, Wash., DC 20006, (202)457-5700.

PESCHIO, Thomas D.——B: Sept. 15, 1940, Buffalo, NY, *Pres. and Chmn.*, Peschio & Co.; **PRIM RE ACT:** Broker, Consultant, Developer; **OTHER RE ACT:** Development management, syndicating, due diligence studies, real estate securities consulting; **SERVICES:** Brokerage; leasing; property management; development management; general real estate consulting; analysis of investments, markets, development projects, site location, real estate securities programs and assisted housing projects; administrative facilities planning and analysis; **REP CLIENTS:** Instnl., group and indiv. investors; corp. and bus. real prop. owners and users; the fin. and investment/devel. community, and; other profls.; **PREV EMPLOY:** United Benefit Life Ins. Co., Maenner Co., Mayer Co., Surkamp Co.; **PROFL AFFIL & HONORS:** NAR, RESSI, ASPEC, NE RE Assn., Gr. Omaha C of C, CRE, SRS; Director of NAR, RESSI, NRA C of C; **EDUC:** BS, 1964, Geology, Geog., Philosophy, St. Louis Univ.; **GRAD EDUC:** MBA, 1966, Econ. and Investment Analysis, Washington Univ.; **OTHER ACT & HONORS:** 1978 President of the Omaha Board of Realtors; 1979 Realtor of the Year; Director of NAR, RESSI, C of C, NRA, Urban Housing Foundation, Creator Omaha Housing and Community Development Corporation, Omaha Hearing School, YMCA; Member of Advisory Committees to the City of Omaha, the Mayor of Omaha, the Univ. of NE at Omaha; **HOME ADD:** 3624 South 102 St., Omaha, NE 68124, (402)397-5956; **BUS ADD:** 1016 Douglas-on-the-Mall, Omaha, NE 68102, (402)341-5400.

PESTARINO, F.A.——B: June 26, 1945, San Jose, CA, *Pres.-Chief Exec. Officer*, Fortune Realty and Investment Co. Inc.; **PRIM RE ACT:** Broker, Attorney, Syndicator, Consultant, Developer, Builder, Property Manager, Owner/Investor; **SERVICES:** Investment counseling, dev. construction, mgmt. of multi family and self storage facilities; **REP CLIENTS:** Individual investors; corporate pension plans; **PROFL AFFIL & HONORS:** State Bar of CA, NAR, TX Assn. of Realtors, CA Assn. of Realtors; **EDUC:** 1966, Econ., San Jose State Univ.; **GRAD EDUC:** Law, 1970, Lincoln Univ. Law School, San Jose, CA; **OTHER ACT & HONORS:** Dep. Dist. Atty. - Santa Clara Cty., CA 1972-1974; **BUS ADD:** NE Nat. Bank Tower, Suite 314, Ft. Worth, TX 76118, (817)282-0777.

PESTRAK, Walter——B: Nov. 25, 1913, Monessen, PA, *Owner*, Walter Pestrak & Assoc.; **PRIM RE ACT:** Broker, Appraiser, Insuror; **SERVICES:** RE sales, appraisal servs., ins.; **PREV EMPLOY:** Govt. serv., also as welding engr. private indus., 1936-48, Welding consulting, 1951059, 1969-73; **PROFL AFFIL & HONORS:** NAIFA, NARA, Indep. Ins. Assn.; **EDUC:** RE Appraising, Kent State Univ.; **GRAD EDUC:** ICS, 1936-39, Welding Eng., Electronics, ICS & Natl. Radio Inst.; **EDUC HONORS:** Cited by OH Gen. Assembly 1980, House & Senate for Public Serv.; **OTHER ACT & HONORS:** Was Civility Key Man, during war as Welding Engr., with all ordnance div., Dir. Public Ser. Safety, 1948-51, Mayor 1960-62, Cty. Admin. 1964-69, Cty. Comm., 1973-80; Elks, AARP, P Emp. Retirees, *Who's Who in Govt.*, 1956, *Who's Who in OH*, 1960; **HOME ADD:** 774 Hollywood St. NE, Warren, OH 44483, (216)372-2382; **BUS ADD:** 774 Holwood St. NE, Warren, OH 44483.

PETERMAN, Gordon G.——B: Mar. 27, 1927, IA, *Prof.*, AZ State Univ., Coll. of Engrg. & Applied Sci.; **PRIM RE ACT:** Instructor, Consultant, Engineer; **PREV EMPLOY:** Const. Mgmt.; **PROFL**

AFFIL & HONORS: AACE, ASCE, AIC, PE, CCE; EDUC: BCE, 1949, Univ. of IA; MIL SERV: USN; HOME ADD: 2517 S Forest Ave., Tempe, AZ 85282, (602)967-1981; BUS ADD: AZ State Univ. Coll. of Eng. & Applied Sci., Tempe, AZ 85287, (602)965-3615.

PETERS, Lee A.——**B:** Oct. 9, 1945, Washington, DC, *Pres.*, Construction Support Services, Inc.; **OTHER RE ACT:** Consulting Engr.; Proj. Mgr.; **SERVICES:** Construction review, construction engrg., facilities engrg.; **REP CLIENTS:** Construction lenders, investors, and mfrs.; **PROFL AFFIL & HONORS:** Amer. Soc. of Civil Engrs.; Amer. Soc. of Cost Engrs.; Amer. Arbitration Assn., RE Broker; Profl. Engr.; **EDUC:** BS, 1967, Chemistry, Rose-Hulman Instit. of Tech.; **GRAD EDUC:** MSCE, 1974, Construction Mgmt., School of Civil Engrg., Purdue Univ.; MS, 1975, Organizational Devel., Krannert Grad. School of Mgmt., Purdue Univ.; **MIL SERV:** U.S. Army, Maj., Bronze Star w/OLC, Army Commendation Medal, Humanitarian Service Medal; **OTHER ACT & HONORS:** United Methodist Church; **HOME ADD:** 1845 Weslynn Dr., Indianapolis, IN 46208, (317)257-2568; **BUS ADD:** 1845 Weslynn Dr., Indianapolis, IN 46208.

PETERS, Raymond James.——**B:** Aug. 27, 1946, Buffalo, NY, *VP, RE Loan Production Mgr.*, Home Fed. S&L Assn., S. AZ; **PRIM RE ACT:** Banker, Lender, Insuror; **SERVICES:** Interim & permanent fin. on resid. multi-family & comml. prop. & joint ventures; **REP CLIENTS:** Devels., synds., venture capitalists; **PREV EMPLOY:** SW S&L Assn., Phoenix, AZ, 1974-77; **PROFL AFFIL & HONORS:** S AZ Home Builders Assn.; S AZ Mort. Bankers Assn., Class II FNMA Underwriter; **EDUC:** BA, 1969, Latin Amer. Hist., Harvard Coll.; **EDUC HONORS:** Cum Laude; **OTHER ACT & HONORS:** Exec. VP, Harvard Club of S. AZ; Chmn of Bd. Amer. Red Cross, Tucson Chapt.; **HOME ADD:** 1710 S Olympic Club Dr., Tucson, AZ 85710, (602)296-1325; **BUS ADD:** 32 N Stone Ave., Tucson, AZ 85701, (602)623-7771.

PETERS, Robert E.——**B:** Sept. 3, 1928, Wichita, KS, *Owner*, Mark 8 Inns; **PRIM RE ACT:** Developer, Builder, Owner/Investor, Property Manager, Syndicator; **SERVICES:** Motel Devel.; **PREV EMPLOY:** Mark 8 Inns.; Scotsman 8 Inns; **PROFL AFFIL & HONORS:** NAHB, AMA, KLA; **OTHER ACT & HONORS:** Public Bldg. Commn.; Zoning Commn.; **HOME ADD:** 1106 N Armour, Wichita, KS 67206, (316)683-0935; **BUS ADD:** 1106 N Armour, Wichita, KS 67206, (316)683-8731.

PETERS, Sid——*Executive Vice President*, National Association of Industrial Office Parks; **OTHER RE ACT:** Profl. Assn. Admin.; **BUS ADD:** 1700 N. Moore St., Ste. 1010, Arlington, VA 22209, (703)525-5638.*

PETERSON, Bert——**B:** Sept. 17, 1924, Chicago, IL, *Dir. of Mkt. Devel.*, A-J Contracting Co. Inc.; **OTHER RE ACT:** Const. mgrs. gen. contractors; **REP CLIENTS:** CBS, Citibank, Ebasco Services, General Motors, Standard Brands, McGraw Hill, Arthur Young, etc.; **PREV EMPLOY:** Exec. VP - Fisher & Brother 1961-1979; **PROFL AFFIL & HONORS:** Pres., Admin. Mgmt. Soc., Mayors Comm. for a Better NY, Founder & First Pres. Optimist Club of NY, - Pres. VIP Executives Club, Profl. Mgmt. Citation (Soc. of Advancement of Mgmt. - Merit Award) Adminstrative Mgmt. Soc.; **EDUC:** BA, 1950, Bus. Admin., CCNY; **MIL SERV:** Served with US Army, 1945-1946; **OTHER ACT & HONORS:** Moderated & conducted seminars for Amer. Mgmt. Assn., Commerce & Indus. Assn., Purchasing Agents Assn. Admin. Mgmt. Soc., written numerous articles in profl. publications, Exec. Bd. of the Manhattan Council of the Boy Scouts of America - Rotary Club of NY, RE Bd. of NY, Membership Chmn. - NY Bd. of Trade, Listed in *Who's Who in Fin. & Ind.*, Sales Exec. Club, NYAC; **HOME ADD:** 1920 East 17th St., Brooklyn, NY 11229, (212)339-1809; **BUS ADD:** 470 Park Ave. South, New York, NY 10016, (212)889-9100.

PETERSON, Bonita J.——**B:** Apr. 29, 1950, Lincoln, NE, *Pres.*, Campbell State Bank; **OTHER RE ACT:** Salesperson; **PROFL AFFIL & HONORS:** Mbr. NE Bankers Assn. NE Independent Bankers Assn., Proff. Ins. Agents, Indept. Ins. Agent; **EDUC:** BA, 1972, Drama, Speech Ed., Hastings Coll., Hasting, NE; **EDUC HONORS:** Cum Laude with distinction in drama, speech, *Who's Who at Hasting College*; **HOME ADD:** Campbell, NE 68932, (402)756-8251; **BUS ADD:** Campbell, NE 68932, (402)756-8601.

PETERSON, Dale H.——**B:** Mar. 25, 1937, SD, *Pres.*, First Amer. Homes Corp.; **PRIM RE ACT:** Builder; **PREV EMPLOY:** Grt. Plains Mktg. Co.; **PROFL AFFIL & HONORS:** Minneapolis Home Builders Assn.; **MIL SERV:** USAS, ARC; **OTHER ACT & HONORS:** Elks, C of C; **HOME ADD:** 4230 137th Ct., Savage, MN 55378, (612)894-5658; **BUS ADD:** 4232 137th Ct., Savage, MN 55378, (612)894-5658.

PETERSON, E. Eugene——**B:** Feb. 17, 1945, Upland, CA, *Pres.*, Avante Construction; **PRIM RE ACT:** Builder; **PROFL AFFIL & HONORS:** Nat. Homebuilders Assn.; **EDUC:** BS, 1969, Mgmt., Sacramento State Coll.; **GRAD EDUC:** MS, 1977, Indus. Engrg./Psych./Econ., IA State Univ.; **MIL SERV:** USN, Lt. Cmdr., Meritorious Unit; **BUS ADD:** 9500 500th St., S. West, Suite 101, Sandy, UT 84070, (801)268-6006.

PETERSON, Eric C.——**B:** Dec. 13, 1944, Derby, CT, *Editor*, Indprop Publishing Co., Amer. Indus. Props. Report (Magazine); **PRIM RE ACT:** Real Estate Publisher; **SERVICES:** publish econ. devel. magazine with intl. circulation; **PREV EMPLOY:** Public Affairs Dir., Intl. Council of Shopping Ctrs., Editor Shopping Center World Magazine; **EDUC:** BA, 1967, Hist., Pol. Sci., OH Wesleyan Univ.; **MIL SERV:** US Army, 1968-69, Spec. 5, Commendation Medal; **HOME ADD:** 200 Portland Rd., Highlands, NJ 07732, (201)872-9561; **BUS ADD:** 90 Monmouth St., PO Box 2060, Red Bank, NJ 07701, (201)842-7433.

PETERSON, Henrik T.——*Director RE Services*, American Standard, Inc.; **PRIM RE ACT:** Property Manager; **BUS ADD:** 40 W. 40th St., New York, NY 10018, (212)840-5100.*

PETERSON, James D.——**B:** June 12, 1947, NC, *Pres.*, Peterson Investment Co.; **OTHER RE ACT:** Investment Builder; **PREV EMPLOY:** Wachovia Bank & Trust Co.; **PROFL AFFIL & HONORS:** SIR, CRE; **EDUC:** BS, 1969, Univ. of NC; **GRAD EDUC:** MBA, 1970, Univ. TX at Austin; **MIL SERV:** US Army; **BUS ADD:** 480 Shepherd St., Winston Salem, NC 27103, (919)768-2300.

PETERSON, Joel C.——**B:** May 20, 1947, IA, *Partner & Chief Financial Officer*, Trammell Crow Co.; **PRIM RE ACT:** Developer; **EDUC:** BS, 1971, Brigham Young Univ.; **GRAD EDUC:** MBA, 1973, Harvard Business School; **EDUC HONORS:** Valedictorian, Magna Cum Laude; **BUS ADD:** 2001 Bryan St. 3200, Dallas, TX 75201, (214)742-2000.

PETERSON, Larry——*Mgr. Bldg. Adm.*, Meredith Corp.; **PRIM RE ACT:** Attorney; **BUS ADD:** 1716 Locust St., Des Moines, IA 50336, (515)284-3000.*

PETERSON, Michael A.——**B:** Sept. 12, 1949, Indianapolis, *Controller*, Geupel Demars, Inc.; **PRIM RE ACT:** Consultant, Engineer, Architect, Developer, Builder, Owner/Investor; **SERVICES:** Gen. contractor, constr. mgr.; **REP CLIENTS:** Comml. indus. cos. seeking complete devel. & constr. of plant, office or resid facilities; **PREV EMPLOY:** Ernst & Whinney for 10 years; exper. in constr., mfg., & retail private & publicly owned cos.; **PROFL AFFIL & HONORS:** IACPA, IN CPA Soc.; Nat. Assn. of Accountants; Assoc. Gen. Contractors; **EDUC:** BS, 1971, Acctg. and Bus., Butler Univ.; **OTHER ACT & HONORS:** American Cancer Soc., Econ. Club of Indianapolis; **HOME ADD:** 6640 N. Ewing St., Indianapolis, IN 46220, (317)257-7273; **BUS ADD:** 1919 N. Meridian St., Indianapolis, IN 46202, (317)924-9192.

PETERSON, Ray Douglas——**B:** Dec. 6, 1947, Detroit, MI, *VP*, Lambrecht Realty Co., Comml. Loan Div.; **PRIM RE ACT:** Broker, Consultant, Appraiser; **SERVICES:** Joint venture, mort., equity placement; appraisal; **REP CLIENTS:** Devel., lenders and instnl. investors in comml. prop., pension funds; **PROFL AFFIL & HONORS:** Mort. Bankers Assn. of America, Detroit Bd. of Realtors, Nat. Assn. of Review Appraisers Builders Assn. of MI; NAR; Econ. Club of Detroit; CBMC, CRA, Realtor broker; **EDUC:** 1971, Oakland Univ.; 1975, Notre Dame Univ., Mort. Banking School; **GRAD EDUC:** 1977, MI State Univ.; **EDUC HONORS:** Income Prop. Studies; **HOME ADD:** 2355 N. Pine Center Dr., West Bloomfield, MI 48033, (313)681-7768; **BUS ADD:** 3300 City National Bank Bldg., Detroit, MI 48226, (313)964-4522.

PETERSON, Richard A.——**B:** Dec. 2, 1940, Willmar, MN, *Partner*, Best & Flanagan; **PRIM RE ACT:** Attorney; **SERVICES:** Legal representation in RE activities; **REP CLIENTS:** Instnl. lenders, devels., investors, title ins. cos.; **PREV EMPLOY:** Title Ins. Co. of MN; **PROFL AFFIL & HONORS:** ABA, Real Prop. Sect., MN State Bar Assn. Real Prop. Sect.; **EDUC:** BA, 1962, Humanities, Univ. of MN; **GRAD EDUC:** JD, 1965, Law, Univ. of MN; **EDUC HONORS:** Dean's List; **MIL SERV:** US Army, Capt.; **HOME ADD:** 12345 Arcola Trail North, Stillwater, MN 55082, (612)439-5108; **BUS ADD:** 4040 IDS Center, Minneapolis, MN 55402, (612)339-7121.

PETERSON, Robert H.——*Exec. VP*, Natl. Assn. of Real Estate License Officials; **PRIM RE ACT:** Regulator; **BUS ADD:** 2580 S. 90th St., Omaha, NE 68124.*

PETERSON, Scott P.——**B:** Nov. 2, 1951, Phoenix, AZ, *Atty.*, Yavapai Title Co.; **PRIM RE ACT:** Attorney; **SERVICES:** Escrow, Title Insurance and Trusts; **PREV EMPLOY:** BC Enterprises (Comml. Construction); **PROFL AFFIL & HONORS:** State Bar of AZ, Yavapai Cty. Bar Assn., Amer. Bar Assn., Pi Alpha Delta Law Fraternity; **EDUC:** BA, 1974, Gen. Bus.-Pre Law, Arizona State Univ.; **GRAD EDUC:** JD, 1978, Law, Univ. of AZ; **OTHER ACT & HONORS:** Theta Delta Chi Fraternity; **HOME ADD:** 133 Frontier Dr., Prescott, AZ 86301, (602)778-2799; **BUS ADD:** PO Box 2019, Prescott, AZ 86302, (602)445-2528.

PETRIE, Paul E.——**B:** Jun. 1, 1926, Downers Grove, IL, *Dir., RE Operations*, The Univ. of Chicago, RE Operations; **PRIM RE ACT:** Consultant, Property Manager; **PROFL AFFIL & HONORS:** CPM; **GRAD EDUC:** JD, 1954, John Marshall Law School; **MIL SERV:** US Army, 1944, Pvt.; **HOME ADD:** 5605 S. Dorchester Ave., Chicago, IL 60615, (312)947-9090; **BUS ADD:** 5100 S. Dorchester Ave., Chicago, IL 60615, (312)753-2200.

PETRINI, Joseph A.——**B:** Nov. 27, 1949, Sharon, PA, *Pres.*, Petrini & Assoc., Inc.; **PRIM RE ACT:** Broker, Instructor, Syndicator, Consultant, Appraiser, Property Manager, Owner/Investor; **OTHER RE ACT:** Comml. & investment; **SERVICES:** Mktg., appraisal, investment analysis; **PREV EMPLOY:** Builder; **PROFL AFFIL & HONORS:** RNMI; NAR, PA Assn. of Realtors; CCIM; CRB; CCIM; CRB; Shenangs Valley Bd. of Realtors; CCIM; CRB; CCIM; CRB (Past Pres.); Western PA Council of Realtors; CCIM; CRB; CCIM; CRB; CCIM; CRB; **MIL SERV:** USMC, Cpl., Purple Heart, Vietnam Serv., etc.; **OTHER ACT & HONORS:** Kiwanis, Red Cross (V Chmn.) Mercer Cty. Chap., Past Pres. St. Joseph Church Council; **HOME ADD:** 40 Pinetree Ln., Hermitage, PA 16148, (412)981-4986; **BUS ADD:** 44 Sharpsville Ave., Sharon, PA 16146, (412)981-4567.

PETROCELLI, Frank J., Jr.——*VP & Treas.*, Sterling Drug; **OTHER RE ACT:** VP & Treas.; **BUS ADD:** 90 Park Ave., New York, NY 10016, (212)907-2000.*

PETTIS, Marilyn——**B:** Oct. 28, 1947, Columbus, OH, *Owner/Broker*, Dynamic Realty; **PRIM RE ACT:** Broker, Banker, Owner/Investor; **OTHER RE ACT:** Equity share dir.; **SERVICES:** All aspects; **EDUC:** BA, 1975, Psych., San Jose State Univ.; **EDUC HONORS:** Pi Lambda Theta, Alpha Kapa Delta; **HOME ADD:** 19 Hilldale Ct., Orinda, CA 94563, (415)254-9342; **BUS ADD:** 1530 Parkmoor Ave., San Jose, CA 95128, (408)279-1919.

PETTIT, Joe——**B:** Mar. 7, 1942, Relso, WA, *Project Mgr.*, Kiemle & Hagood Co.; **PRIM RE ACT:** Consultant, Developer, Property Manager; **SERVICES:** Complete packaging & mgmt. of comml. & multifamily resid. projects; **REP CLIENTS:** Churches sponsoring HUD fin. or ins. multifamily props., acqusition & devel. of bank facilities, investment grps. as their needs pertain to income producing real props.; **PROFL AFFIL & HONORS:** Candidate for CPM, CCIM; **EDUC:** BS, 1968, Math, physical sci., WA State Univ.; **GRAD EDUC:** ME, 1973, Education admin., Whitworth Coll.; **HOME ADD:** Lakeside Dr., Liberty Lake, WA 99019, (509)255-6682; **BUS ADD:** 315 Washington Mutual Bldg., Spokane, WA 99204, (509)838-6541.

PETTY, Wayne G.——**B:** July 6, 1947, Salt Lake City, UT, *Atty., Partner, Adjunct Prof. Fin. Dept., Univ. of UT*, Moyle & Draper; **PRIM RE ACT:** Attorney, Instructor; **SERVICES:** Legal servs. assoc. with all aspects of RE, RE devel., mort. lending, synd., condo, contrs., mech. liens, comml. leasing, RE sales & acquisitons; **REP CLIENTS:** Lenders, RE devel. cos., contrs., synds., prop. mgrs., archs., RE devel. brokers, investors; **PREV EMPLOY:** Keith Romney Assoc., Condo Consultants, 1972-74; **EDUC:** BA, 1969, Eng. Lit., Univ. of UT; **GRAD EDUC:** JD, 1972, Univ. of UT Coll. of Law; **EDUC HONORS:** Cum Laude, Beehive Hon. Soc., Skull & Bones Hon., Owl & Key Hon., UT Law Review; **MIL SERV:** USAR, 1966-72, Lt.; **HOME ADD:** 383 'M' St., Salt Lake City, UT 84103, (801)355-6873; **BUS ADD:** 600 Deseret Plaza, No. 15 E First So., Salt Lake City, UT 84111, (801)521-0250.

PETZ, Frederick A.——**B:** March 26, 1950, Detroit, MI, *Partner/VP*, Petz & Povlitz, Attorneys at Law, Mort. Div.; **PRIM RE ACT:** Consultant, Attorney, Lender, Owner/Investor; **SERVICES:** Business entity org., lending consultation, acquisition analysis; **REP CLIENTS:** Investors Mortgage Ins. Co., Edward Rose Const. Co.; **PROFL AFFIL & HONORS:** ABA; MI Bar Assn.; Detroit Bar Assn.; MI and Amer. Mort. Bankers Assn., Former Vice Chmn. Young Mort. Bankers of MI; **EDUC:** 1972, Business and Urban Planning, Xavier Univ.; **GRAD EDUC:** JD, 1976, RE and Bus. Law, Detroit Coll. of Law; **EDUC HONORS:** *Who's Who in Amer. Coll. & Univ.*; Dean's List; Alumni Award for Outstanding Sr., Dean's List; Lawyer's Pub. Co. Constitutional Law Award; **HOME ADD:** 642 Shoreham, Grosse Pointe Woods, MI 48236, (313)886-1647; **BUS ADD:** 17150 Kercheval, Grosse Pointe, MI 48230, (313)886-5553.

PEXA, Ellard——*Exec. Secretary*, American College of RE Consultants; **OTHER RE ACT:** Profl. Assn. Admin.; **BUS ADD:** 305 Foshay Tower, Minneapolis, MN 35402, (612)325-4648.*

PEYTON, Steven D.——**B:** Nov. 15, 1954, Atlanta, GA, *Dir., Mktg. & Sales-Peachtree City Development Corp.*, Pres./Broker-Peachtree City Marketing Group; **PRIM RE ACT:** Broker, Consultant, Developer; **SERVICES:** Resid. Devel. Consultant/Advertising-Mktg.; **REP CLIENTS:** Peachtree City Dev. Sales Numerous Builders-Equitable Life; **PREV EMPLOY:** Pulte Home Corp.; **PROFL AFFIL & HONORS:** MIRM-Homebuilders Assoc. Sales & Mktg. Exec.-NAR; **EDUC:** GA State Univ.; **GRAD EDUC:** GA Inst. of RE/Fortune Inst. of RE, Dale Carnegie Sales & Public Speaking; **OTHER ACT & HONORS:** Former Exec. Dir. N.E. Cobb J.C. #1 JC Club in Nation 1976, Youngest RE Broker in GA (age 21); **HOME ADD:** 604 Doubletrace Ln., Peachtree City, GA 30269, (404)487-7837; **BUS ADD:** Aberdeen Village Ctr., Peachtree City, GA 30269, (404)487-8585.

PEZZUTO, Joseph Louis——**B:** Sept. 26, 1937, Brooklyn, NY, *Prin. RE Appraiser*, State of NY Banking Dept., Appraisal; **PRIM RE ACT:** Consultant, Appraiser; **SERVICES:** Examine mort. portfolios of State chartered banks; **PREV EMPLOY:** City of NY Dept. of RE, 1970-73 (Sr. RE appraiser); **PROFL AFFIL & HONORS:** Soc. of RE Appraisers; Columbia Soc. of Appraisers; Assn. of Govt. Appraisers; CRA, SRA, CSA, AGA, CRA; **EDUC:** BS, 1963, NYU; **GRAD EDUC:** NY Law Sch. (1 yr.); **EDUC HONORS:** 100 percent Scholarship by State of NY; **MIL SERV:** AMEDS; **OTHER ACT & HONORS:** Bd. of Dir. Brooklyn Coll. Alumni Assn.; Pres. Bath Branch Comm. Improvement Assn.; *Who's Who in Bus. & Fin.*, 1979-80; **HOME ADD:** 285 Bay 14th St., Brooklyn, NY 11214, (212)236-4339; **BUS ADD:** 2 World Trade Ctr., New York, NY 10047, (212)488-2340.

PFEFFER, Elvira——**B:** Oct. 22, Austria, *Corp. Treasurer & Corp. Sec.*, Freid-El Corp.; **PRIM RE ACT:** Consultant, Developer, Property Manager, Syndicator; **SERVICES:** Prop. mgmt., valuation, investment counseling, synd.; **PREV EMPLOY:** Amer. Foam Latex Corp. as Corp. Sec. & Treas.; **EDUC:** BA, 1951, Educ., Univ. of Pittsburgh; **HOME ADD:** 6554 Bartlett St., Pittsburgh, PA 15217; **BUS ADD:** 1501 Preble Ave., Pittsburgh, PA 15233, (412)322-1361.

PFEFFER, Murray B.——**B:** Dec. 26, 1926, New York City, *Pres.*, Freidel Corp; **PRIM RE ACT:** Developer, Owner/Investor, Syndicator; **SERVICES:** Evaluation Aquisition & Mgmt. of Investment Props.; **REP CLIENTS:** Services Exclusively for the Account of Freidel Corp.; **PREV EMPLOY:** Amer. Foam Latex Corp. as Exec. VP; **EDUC:** BCE, 1948, Const. - Planning & Structures, Polytechn Inst. of Brooklyn; **HOME ADD:** 6554 Bartlett St., Pittsburgh, PA 15217, (412)421-1074; **BUS ADD:** 1501 Preble Ave., Pittsburgh, PA 15233, (412)322-1363.

PFEIFER, Ted R.——**B:** Nov. 1, 1947, Bluffton, IN, *RE Mgr.*, Walgreen Co., Mid-West, Middle S.; **OTHER RE ACT:** Corp. RE Mgr.; **PREV EMPLOY:** Jack Eckerd Corp., KY Fried Chicken Corp., General Tire & Rubber Co.; **PROFL AFFIL & HONORS:** NACORE, ICSC, IN RE Broker; **EDUC:** 1971, RE Admin., IN Univ.; **BUS ADD:** 200 Wilmot Rd., Deerfield, IL 60015, (312)358-5000.

PFEIL, Jeffrey W.——**B:** Jan. 30, 1946, New York, NY, *Prop. Mgr.*, Stuyvesant Plaza, Inc.; **PRIM RE ACT:** Broker, Property Manager; **PROFL AFFIL & HONORS:** BOMA, Mgrs. Inst. Intl.; **MIL SERV:** US Army, E-5, Vietnam Service; **HOME ADD:** 393A Spore Rd., Delmar, NY 12054, (518)768-2908; **BUS ADD:** Exec. Park, Albany, NY 12203, (518)482-8986.

PFISTER, Jean Paul——*Mgr. Dev.*, Baker Properties; **PRIM RE ACT:** Developer; **BUS ADD:** 316 Cortland Ave., Stamford, CT 06906, (203)348-9293.*

PFISTER, Paul J.——**B:** Sept. 15, 1920, Terre Haute, IN, *Pres.*, Pfister & Co. Inc.; **PRIM RE ACT:** Broker, Syndicator, Consultant, Appraiser, Developer, Builder, Property Manager, Lender, Owner/Investor, Insuror; **SERVICES:** Resid. & Comml./Indus. Brokerage, RE Fin.; **REP CLIENTS:** T.H. Banks, Attys., Chase Natl. Bank, Citizens Natl. Bank of Paris, Pillsbury, Pfizer, CBS, Bemis; **PROFL AFFIL & HONORS:** NAR, SIR, FIABCI, NMI, IL Assn. Realtors; MBAA; Terre Haute Bd. of Realtors; IN Assn. of Realtors, Faculty Advisor IN Univ. School of Bus., Jr. C of C., Man of Year, 1955; **EDUC:** BS, 1947, RE, Acctg., IN Univ. School of Bus.; **EDUC HONORS:** Grad. High Distinction, Phi Beta Gamma; **OTHER ACT & HONORS:** Chmn. Terre Haute C of C, K of C, BPOE; **HOME ADD:** 3047 N. 9th, Terre Haute, IN 47804, (812)466-4646; **BUS ADD:** 711 Ohio St., P.O. Box 988, Terre Haute, IN 47808, (812)232-5083.

PHANEUF, David W.——B: Mar. 17, 1944, Scranton, PA, *VP*, First State Bank; **PRIM RE ACT:** Banker, Lender; **PREV EMPLOY:** 12 yrs. banking, consumer lending; **PROFL AFFIL & HONORS:** Amer. Inst. of Banking; **EDUC:** BA, 1966, Bus. admin., Lackananna Jr. Coll.; **HOME ADD:** 1812 Academy St., Scranton, PA 18504, (717)344-0428; **BUS ADD:** 101 N. Main Ave., Scranton, PA 18504, (717)961-7995.

PHELPS, Anthony D.——B: June 20, 1947, Visalia, CA, *Owner*, RE Unlimited; **PRIM RE ACT:** Broker, Consultant, Developer, Owner/Investor, Property Manager, Syndicator; **SERVICES:** Devel. & synd. of income & comml. props., prop. mgmt., investment counseling; **REP CLIENTS:** Indiv. and/or instnl. investors in income and comml. props; **PREV EMPLOY:** The RE Co., 1975-80, co-owner; **PROFL AFFIL & HONORS:** Natl. Assn. of Realtors, CA Assn. of Realtors, Amer. Mort. Assn., Small Bus. Men Assn., Nat. Inst. of Farm & Land Brokers, Grad Realtor Inst., Realtors Nat. Mktg. Inst. Salesman of yr for 1975, 1976, 1977, Visalia Bd. of Realtors; **EDUC:** BA, Psych; **GRAD EDUC:** 1969, Psych, Bus., San Francisco State Coll., San Francisco, CA; **OTHER ACT & HONORS:** Visalia JC's, Visalia YMCA, Visalia C of C, Visalia Kiwanis Club; **HOME ADD:** 815 W. Kaweah St., Visalia, CA 93277, (209)625-9207; **BUS ADD:** 1441 S. Mooney Blvd., Suite D, Visalia, CA 93277, (209)627-6464.

PHELPS, C. Edward——B: Sept. 29, 1937, Champaign, IL, *VP*, Gate Way Federal Savings and Loan Assn., Loan Admin.; **PRIM RE ACT:** Banker, Lender; **PREV EMPLOY:** Gen. City Savings - Dayton, OH 17 years; **PROFL AFFIL & HONORS:** Amer. Business Men's Assn.; Bd. Member Home Builders Assn. of Cincinnati; **EDUC:** BBA, 1962, Mktg.-Fin., Univ. of Cincinnati; **GRAD EDUC:** 1978, Fin., Grad. School of Bus. - IN Univ.; **OTHER ACT & HONORS:** Bd. - Mgr., Little League Baseball; Soccer Coach, SAY Soccer Assn.; **HOME ADD:** 10726 Escondido Dr., Cincinnati, OH, (513)791-6362; **BUS ADD:** 6070 Montgomery Rd., Cincinnati, OH 45213, (513)631-1515.

PHILIPPS, Edward W.——B: Dec. 19, 1939, New York City, *VP, Mort. Officer*, American Savings Bank; **PRIM RE ACT:** Appraiser, Banker; **SERVICES:** Mort. lending, co-op & condo. conversions; **PROFL AFFIL & HONORS:** AIREA; Mort. Bankers Assn. of NY, MAI, 5191; **EDUC:** Cert., 1969, School of Banking, Amer. Inst. of Banking; **HOME ADD:** 261 Kimball Ave., Yonkers, NY 10704, (914)237-9430; **BUS ADD:** 380 Madison Ave., New York, NY 10017, (212)880-7671.

PHILIPS, W.B., Jr.——B: May 27, 1926, Birmingham, AL, *Pres.*, W.B. Philips & Co.; **OTHER RE ACT:** Mort. Banker; **SERVICES:** Comml. RE fin., both debt and equity; **REP CLIENTS:** Numerous life ins. Co. and savings Inst.; **PROFL AFFIL & HONORS:** MBAA, ICSC, Former Pres., MBA of AL; **EDUC:** BA, 1950, Business, Univ. of AL; **MIL SERV:** US Army, Sgt.; **OTHER ACT & HONORS:** Kiwanis, Vestavia Ctry. Bluc, The Club, Birmingham RE Bd., Elder - Independent Presbyterian Church; Trustee - Presbytery of Birmingham; **HOME ADD:** 4157 Kennesaw Dr., Birmingham, AL 35213, (205)871-6821; **BUS ADD:** 2118 4th Ave. N, Birmingham, AL 35203, (205)322-4472.

PHILLIPS, Arlie E.——B: Dec. 29, 1951, Moorhead, MN, *Part.*, Phillips Investment Assn.; **PRIM RE ACT:** Owner/Investor; **EDUC:** BS, 1973, Elem. Ed., Valley City State Coll., ND; **GRAD EDUC:** Grad. studies in Econ., Univ. of ND, Grand Forks; **HOME ADD:** RR 1, Box 119, Summit, SD 57266; **BUS ADD:** RR 1, Box 119, Summit, SD 57266, (605)947-4159.

PHILLIPS, C. Eugene——B: July 12, 1932, Peoria, IL, Murphy, Robinson, Heckathorn & Phillips; **PRIM RE ACT:** Attorney; **REP CLIENTS:** First Interstate Bank of Kalispell, N.A.; Pacific Power & Light Co.; Northwestern Telephone; **PROFL AFFIL & HONORS:** ABA; MT Bar Assn.; NW MT Bar Assn.; **EDUC:** BS, 1954, Bradley Univ./CO State Univ.; **GRAD EDUC:** LLB, 1965, Univ. of MT; **MIL SERV:** US Army; **OTHER ACT & HONORS:** Dir., Flathead Cty. United Givers; MT Constitution Conv. Comm.; Chmn., Flathead Co. Rep. Central Comm.; C of C, Dir.; C of C, VP; **HOME TEL:** (406)257-8238; **BUS ADD:** One Main Bldg., POB 759, Kalispell, MT 59901, (406)755-6644.

PHILLIPS, Charles J.——B: Jan. 17, 1919, Buffalo, NY, *Partner*, Johnson, Peterson, Tener & Anderson, Attorneys; **PRIM RE ACT:** Attorney; **PROFL AFFIL & HONORS:** Jamestown Bar Assn., NY State Bar Assn.; **EDUC:** BA, 1941, econ., Amherst Coll., MA; **GRAD EDUC:** LLB, 1948, Cornell Law School; **MIL SERV:** US Army, Capt., Infantry; **OTHER ACT & HONORS:** Tr., Presbyterian Homes of Western NY, Elder First Presbyterian Church, Jamestown, Ny, Past Chmn. ,Chautauqua Cty. Chap., Amer. Red Cross; **HOME ADD:** RD 1 Driftwood Rd., Bemus Point, NY 14712, (716)386-6232; **BUS ADD:** Bankers Trust Bldg., Jamestown, NY 14701, (716)664-5210.

PHILLIPS, David C.——B: Apr. 15, 1928, Chicago, IL, *Exec. VP*, First Amer. Realty Co.; **PRIM RE ACT:** Consultant, Developer, Property Manager; **OTHER RE ACT:** Gen. contr.; **SERVICES:** Brokerage, mgmt., consulting, bldg. gen. devel.; **REP CLIENTS:** Equitable Life Assur. Soc. of US, Sweetheart Cup div. of MD Paper Co., Consolidated Freightways; **PROFL AFFIL & HONORS:** IL Soc. of CPA's, CPA; **EDUC:** 1966, Acctg., Northwestern Univ.; **MIL SERV:** US Army, Pvt.; **BUS ADD:** 123 W. Madison St., Chicago, IL 60602, (312)782-2900.

PHILLIPS, Edward B.——B: Oct. 26, 1928, Lewisburg, WV, *President-Broker*, Century 21 - Stuart & Watts, Inc.; **PRIM RE ACT:** Broker, Consultant, Appraiser, Regulator, Builder, Insuror; **SERVICES:** Comml. and resid.; **REP CLIENTS:** Fast food and relocation co's.; **PREV EMPLOY:** Been in this bus. for 27 yrs.; **PROFL AFFIL & HONORS:** Dir., Investment Soc. - Century 21 NY Rgn., GRI; **EDUC:** BS, 1950, Engrg./Bus. Admin., WV Univ.; **MIL SERV:** Signal Corps; **OTHER ACT & HONORS:** Greenbrier Cty. Planning Commn., 1968 -; Rotary; BPOE; Bd. of Realtors; Indep. Ins. Agents Assn.; **HOME ADD:** 140 Rader Rd., Rolling Hills Estates, Lewisburg, WV 24901, (304)645-2520; **BUS ADD:** 112 W. Washington St., Lewisburg, WV 24901, (304)645-1242.

PHILLIPS, Edward N.——B: Feb. 28, 1944, Longview, TX, *Pres. - Chmn.*, DaMarc, Inc.; **PRIM RE ACT:** Broker, Developer, Owner/Investor, Property Manager, Syndicator; **SERVICES:** Brokerage, sale/lease-backs, ltd. partnerships - J.V.s; **PREV EMPLOY:** VP, 1st Federal S & L, Marshall, TX; **EDUC:** BBA, 1968, Banking & Fin., RE Law, No. TX State Univ.; **HOME ADD:** Rt. 9, Box 530A, Longview, TX 75601, (214)757-5400; **BUS ADD:** 101 Woodbine Pl., Ste. V, PO Box 853, Longview, TX 75606, (214)757-2304.

PHILLIPS, E.M,, Jr.——B: Sept. 19, 1930, Assumption,IL, *Partner*, Hill, Barth & King; **OTHER RE ACT:** CPA; **SERVICES:** Acctg., auditing, taxation and mgmt. consulting; **REP CLIENTS:** The Edward J. DeBartolo Corp., Assoc. Contractors, A.P. O'Horo Co.; **PREV EMPLOY:** Peat, Marwick, Mitchell & Co. 1958-1972; **PROFL AFFIL & HONORS:** CPA in AR, FL, IL, NJ, NY, OH and PA; Member of AICPA, OSCPA, PICPA and Amer. Acctg. Assn., Past VP of OSCPA, Chmn. of OSCPA Acctg. and Auditing Inst.; **EDUC:** BS, 1957, Acctg. and Econ., AR State Univ.; **GRAD EDUC:** MS, 1958, Acctg., Univ. of IL; **EDUC HONORS:** Magna Cum Laude, Grad. Asst.; **MIL SERV:** USN 1949-1953, DK2; **OTHER ACT & HONORS:** Boardman Rotary; **HOME ADD:** 430 Ingram Dr., Youngstown, OH 44512, (216)758-5272; **BUS ADD:** 7680 Market St., Youngstown, OH 44512.

PHILLIPS, Ernest Clifford——B: June 14, 1931, Jackson, MS, *Pres.*, Reliable Management Co., Inc.; **PRIM RE ACT:** Broker, Consultant, Attorney, Developer, Owner/Investor, Property Manager, Syndicator; **SERVICES:** Prop. mgmt. devel. rehab.; **REP CLIENTS:** First Nat. Bank of Dallas, Synds. of pvt. investors; **PROFL AFFIL & HONORS:** IREM, TX Apt. Assn., Nat. Apt. Assn., CPM; **EDUC:** BBA, 1953, Bus., Fin. Law, Univ. of MS; **GRAD EDUC:** JD, 1960, Law, Univ. of MS; **MIL SERV:** USAF, Capt.; **OTHER ACT & HONORS:** Pres. Greater Longview Apt. Assn., Bd. of Dir. TX Apt. Assn.; **HOME ADD:** 1602 Willow Oak Dr., Longview, TX 75601, (214)753-1137; **BUS ADD:** Suite 200, The ATRIUM, 119 W. Tyler St., Longview, TX 75601, (214)753-0969.

PHILLIPS, James——*Asst. Dir. Engr. Adm. & Fac. Plng.*, Thomas J. Lipton, Inc.; **PRIM RE ACT:** Property Manager; **BUS ADD:** 800 Sylvan Ave., Englewood Cliffs, NJ 07632, (201)567-8000.*

PHILLIPS, R.J.——*Director RE*, Allegheny International, Inc.; **PRIM RE ACT:** Property Manager; **BUS ADD:** 2 Oliver Plaza, Pittsburgh, PA 15222, (412)562-4000.*

PHILLIPS, Robert W.——B: Dec. 18, 1944, Eureka, KS, *Sales Mgr.*, Dick Edmondson Real Estate; **PRIM RE ACT:** Broker, Developer, Owner/Investor, Property Manager, Syndicator; **SERVICES:** Prop. mgmt. broker; **PROFL AFFIL & HONORS:** Lawrence Bd. of Realtors, KS Assn. of Realtors, NAR, Pres. Lawrence Bd. of Realtors, 1981; **EDUC:** BBA, 1969, Bus., Wichita State Univ.; **EDUC HONORS:** Dean's Honor Roll; **MIL SERV:** US Army, Capt.; **HOME ADD:** 303 Bowstring, Lawrence, KS 66044, (913)842-9953; **BUS ADD:** 846 Illinois, Lawrence, KS 66044, (913)841-8744.

PHILLIPS, Roger Van Dorn——B: Oct. 8, 1937, Philipsburg, PA, *VP & Gen. Mgr., Prop. Mgmt. Ops.*, RE One Comm. Investmt. Inc., Prop. Mgmt. - FL; **PRIM RE ACT:** Broker, Instructor, Consultant, Property Manager; **SERVICES:** Complete prop. mgmt. serv. for all types of income; **REP CLIENTS:** Prudential, Aetna, Disney World; **PREV EMPLOY:** 10 yrs USN, Capt. of USN Ship; **PROFL AFFIL & HONORS:** IREM, Bd. of Realtors; **EDUC:** BAE, 1959, Hist., Univ. of

FL; **GRAD EDUC:** Worked on Masters, Psych, Univ. of FL; **EDUC HONORS:** Pres. Achievement List - Sr. Yr.; **MIL SERV:** USN, Lt.; **OTHER ACT & HONORS:** Diocese of Cent. FL (Episcopal) Bd. of Dir. Vestry, Cath. of St. Luke (Episcopal); **HOME ADD:** 1801 Santa Maria Pl., Orlando, FL 32806, (305)896-3006; **BUS ADD:** 340 N Maitland Ave, Maitland, FL 32751, (305)644-6244.

PHILLIPS, Virginia M.——B: Apr. 2, 1914, Dothan, AL, *Owner/Operator*, Phillips Realty; **PRIM RE ACT:** Broker, Consultant, Developer, Owner/Investor, Appraiser; **SERVICES:** Selling, Finding - Housing, Comml., Land; **PROFL AFFIL & HONORS:** Dothan Bd. of Realtors; AL Assn. of Realtors; NAR; RNMI; Dothan Women's Council of Realtors, Charter Pres.; AL WCR; Nat. WCR, GRI, CRS; **EDUC:** Correspondence, Law Course, LaSalle Univ., Chicago; **OTHER ACT & HONORS:** First Presbyterian Church, Dothan, AL; **HOME ADD:** POB 542, Dothan, AL 36302, (205)792-4390; **BUS ADD:** POB 542, Dothan, AL 36302, (205)792-4390.

PHILLIPS, Wayne——B: July 29, 1947, MD, *Pres.*, Phillips Brothers & Assoc.; **PRIM RE ACT:** Developer, Owner/Investor, Syndicator; **SERVICES:** RE operator of over 400 units, rehab./devel. & synd., seminar instr.; **PREV EMPLOY:** VP of Star Attractions, Bangkok, Thailand, 1967-1970; **PROFL AFFIL & HONORS:** Member, Los Angeles Prop. Owners Assn., Inc.; Prop. Owners Assn. of Baltimore City, Inc.; **EDUC:** BA, 1965, Music, Baltimore City Coll.; **EDUC HONORS:** 1st in Music Class of 477; **OTHER ACT & HONORS:** Member of Los Angeles Musicians Union; Baltimore Musicians Union; Voted 7th best drummer in the Nov. issue of "Downbeat" music poll, Nov. 1979; **HOME ADD:** Towson, MD; **BUS ADD:** 4 East Biddle St., Baltimore, MD 21202, (301)528-1600.

PIANA, Edward R.——B: July 2, 1930, Canton, MA, *Exec VP*, Baybank Forfolk Cty. Trust; **PRIM RE ACT:** Banker, Lender; **PROFL AFFIL & HONORS:** South Shore C of C, Cred. Data of SE MA, Inc., Robert Morris Assoc., MA Bankers Assn., NE Sales Fin. Assn., MA Higher Ed. Corp., New England Education Loan Marketing Corp.; **EDUC:** ABA, 1952, Econ., Northeastern Univ.; **GRAD EDUC:** AMP, 1979, Gen. Mgmt., Harvard Univ.; Rutgers Univ. Stonier Grad. School of Banking; **MIL SERV:** US Army, Sgt., CMB; **OTHER ACT & HONORS:** Ctr. Ind. Fin. Agency Member, Harvard Club, French Library; **HOME ADD:** 87 Independence St., Canton, MA 02021, (617)828-4491; **BUS ADD:** 858 Washington St., Dedham, MA 02026, (617)329-3700.

PIAZZA, Charles——B: Aug. 9, 1952, NY, *VP*, Williams RE Co., Inc.; **PRIM RE ACT:** Broker; **SERVICES:** Leasing, sales, mgmt of comml. prop.; **REP CLIENTS:** Ins. companies, indiv. investors, industrial & comml. office companies; **PREV EMPLOY:** H. Wien Real Estate; **PROFL AFFIL & HONORS:** The RE Bd. of NY, The Young Men's RE Assn. of NY, Nat. Realty Club; **EDUC:** Econ, Pol. Sci., Brooklyn Coll; **GRAD EDUC:** RE, NY Univ.; **HOME ADD:** 2185 Lemoine Ave., Fort Lee, NJ 07024, (201)592-9283; **BUS ADD:** 1700 Broadway, New York, NY 10019, (212)582-8000.

PICCOLO, Michael D.——*Pres.*, Red Carpet Spectrum Realty Co.; **PRIM RE ACT:** Broker, Syndicator, Consultant, Owner/Investor; **SERVICES:** Sale & Listing of Residential RE, including comm. & Investment RE; **PREV EMPLOY:** Mort. Banking & Title Ins.; **PROFL AFFIL & HONORS:** Phila. Bd. of Realtors, RESSI; **BUS ADD:** 2650 S. 16th St., Philadelphia, PA 19145, (215)389-2222.

PICKER, Joel A.——*Mgr.*, Elmwood Development Co.; **PRIM RE ACT:** Developer; **BUS ADD:** 800 Commerce Rd. East, Ste. 100, Elmwood Park, New Orleans, LA 70123, (504)733-1200.*

PICKETT, David R.——B: May 18, 1944, Cabbock, TX, Palace Enterprises; **PRIM RE ACT:** Broker, Instructor, Syndicator, Consultant, Appraiser, Developer, Builder, Engineer, Owner/Investor; **REP CLIENTS:** Numerous Drs., Lawyers, Investors, Several Corps.; **PREV EMPLOY:** Sr. Project Mgr. at Cobe Labs, Sr. Engherut S.T.C.; **PROFL AFFIL & HONORS:** AIIE, SPE, CO Assn. of Realtors, NAR, GRI; **EDUC:** BA, 1971, Econ., Univ. TX at Arlington; **GRAD EDUC:** GRI, 1979, Univ. of CO; **EDUC HONORS:** Deans List, Pres. list, upper 1/3 of class; **HOME ADD:** 1117 Clark St., Fort Collins, CO 80524, (303)224-2732; **BUS ADD:** 1117 Clark St., Fort Collins, CO 80524, (303)224-2731.

PICKETT, James C.——B: Apr. 27, 1924, Louisville, KY, *VP*, CSX Resources; **PRIM RE ACT:** Developer, Property Manager; **PREV EMPLOY:** AVP Seaboard Coastline Industries, AVP L and N Railroad; **PROFL AFFIL & HONORS:** CCIM, NAR, ULI; **MIL SERV:** Air Nat. Guard, B/G, DFC; **HOME ADD:** 1507 Regency Woods Rd., 304, Richmond, VA 23233, (804)782-1493; **BUS ADD:** Suite 350, 8th and Main Bldg., Richmond, VA 23219, (804)782-1493.

PICKETT, James V.——B: Jan. 21, 1942, Dayton, OH, *Pres.*, The Pickett Companies; **PRIM RE ACT:** Broker, Architect, Developer, Builder, Property Manager, Owner/Investor; **PREV EMPLOY:** Founded home bldg. co. in 1965 to develop single family luxury homes; **PROFL AFFIL & HONORS:** ULI, NAHB, Young Pres. Org.; **EDUC:** Univ. of Dayton, 1960-61, 1961-1964, Engin., Univ. of Notre Dame (Arch. and Civ. Engin.); **OTHER ACT & HONORS:** Columbus Area C of C, Trustee; Columbus We're Making it Great, Chmn; Citizens Research, Trustee; Muirfield Village Assn., Trustee; **HOME ADD:** 8483 Torwoodlee Ct, Dublin, OH 43017, (614)889-0022; **BUS ADD:** 555 Metro Place N, Dublin, OH 43017, (614)889-6500.

PICKETTE, T. Robert——B: Aug. 3, 1933, Waltham, MA, *Pres.*, Corcoran Mgmt. Co.; **PRIM RE ACT:** Consultant, Property Manager; **PROFL AFFIL & HONORS:** IREM, CPM, Reg. VP - Region I, IREM; **EDUC:** BS/BA, 1958, Acctg., Boston Coll., Sch. of Mgmt.; **MIL SERV:** US Army, SP3; **OTHER ACT & HONORS:** Greater Boston RE Bd.; **HOME ADD:** 43 Shawmut Rd., Waltham, MA 02154, (617)894-4869; **BUS ADD:** 500 Granite Ave., E. Milton, MA 02186, (617)696-9010.

PIECEWICZ, Walter M.——B: Jan. 27, 1948, Concord, MA, *Atty.*, Boodell, Sears, Sugrue, Giambalvo & Crowley; **PRIM RE ACT:** Consultant, Attorney; **SERVICES:** Tax planning, legal structuring of transactions; **PROFL AFFIL & HONORS:** ABA, Sect. on Taxation (Comm. on Estate and Gift Taxation), Sect. on Real Prop. Probate and Trusts (Comm. on Fed. Tax Aspects of RE Transactions) Chicago Bar Assn. - Fed. Taxation Comm.; **EDUC:** AB, 1970, Econ. and Hist., Colgate Univ.; **GRAD EDUC:** JD, 1973, Law, Columbia Univ.; **EDUC HONORS:** Phi Beta Kappa, Magna Cum Laude; **OTHER ACT & HONORS:** Oak Park Community Planning Bd.; **HOME ADD:** 1103 N. Lombard Ave., Oak Park, IL 60302, (312)386-3933; **BUS ADD:** 69 West Washington St., Ste. 500, Chicago, IL 60602, (312)269-0300.

PIEL, J. Richard——B: May, 8, 1943, Montgomery, AL, *Atty.*, Piel, Bright & Goggans; **PRIM RE ACT:** Broker, Consultant, Attorney, Developer, Lender, Builder, Owner/Investor, Instructor, Property Manager, Syndicator; **SERVICES:** Any and all servs. pertaining to the above checked activities; **PREV EMPLOY:** Atty. Gen. Office, State of AL (Asst. Atty. Gen), 1972-74; Spec. Asst. Atty. Gen., 1974 to date; **PROFL AFFIL & HONORS:** AL Bar Assn.; ABA; Assn. of Trial Lawyers of Amer.; AL Trial Lawyers Assn.; Montgomery Cty. Bar Assn.; Amer. Judicature Soc.; Montgomery Jaycees; Sigma Delta Kappa; Legal Frat.; Nat. Assn. of Home Bldgs.; Gr. Montgomery Home Bldgrs.; AL Home Bldrs.; Pi Kappa Phi Frat.; Title Agent for US Life Title; Miss. Valley Title & Amer. Land Title.; AL Soc. foe Crippled Children & Adults; State Gen. Counsel's & Bd. of Dir., ABA; Chmn. & Sub. of Personal Office Computers; Central AL Rehab Ctr. Bd. of Dirs.; ASCCA, Mongomery Chapt. Treas.; Montgomery Knife & Fork Club, Bd. of Dirs.; **EDUC:** 1961-65, Univ. of AL; **GRAD EDUC:** JD, 1973, Jones Law Sch.; **OTHER ACT & HONORS:** Morningview Baptist Church; **HOME ADD:** 137 Old Field Dr., Montgomery, AL 36117, (205)272-9389; **BUS ADD:** 503 S Court St., Montgomery, AL 36104, (205)834-7872.

PIEL, Theodore F.——*Oper. Mgr., Toledo Properties*, Owens-Illinois Inc.; **PRIM RE ACT:** Property Manager; **BUS ADD:** One Seagate, Toledo, OH 43666, (419)247-5072.

PIENTA, Robert P.——B: June 27, 1946, Peckville, PA, *Asst. VP, Mort. Loan Div. Mgr.*, First Natl. Bank of Toms River, NJ; **PRIM RE ACT:** Banker; **SERVICES:** Comml. and Resid. Mort., Construction and Permanent; **REP CLIENTS:** Bus. and indiv. markets; **PREV EMPLOY:** Colonial First Natl. Bank, Red Bank, NJ; **PROFL AFFIL & HONORS:** Mort. Bankers Assn., Natl. Assn. of Home Builders, NJ Shore Builders Assn., NJ Builders Assn., Ocean Cty. Bd. of Realtors; **EDUC:** BS, 1969, Bus. Admin., Monmouth Coll., W. Long Branch, NJ; **GRAD EDUC:** Mort. Banking, 1979, Northwestern Univ., Grad. School of Mgmt.; **OTHER ACT & HONORS:** Natl. Exchange Club; **HOME ADD:** 153 Castlewall Ave., Elberon, NJ 07740, (201)870-1694; **BUS ADD:** 975 Hooper Ave., Toms River, NJ 08753, (201)244 2800.

PIERCE, Jorganne——B: July 31, 1948, Atchison, KS, *Prin.*, Patton Group, RE Investment Consulting; **PRIM RE ACT:** Consultant, Owner/Investor; **OTHER RE ACT:** Mort. and bus. loan packaging; **SERVICES:** Strategic investment and fin. planning, fin. liaison, transaction mgmt., shopping center devel. specialty; **REP CLIENTS:** Indiv. and instnl. investors in comml. props.; **PREV EMPLOY:** Sr. Analyst, Trigon RE Research Corp.; **PROFL AFFIL & HONORS:** Intl. Council of Shopping Centers, Nat. Assn. of Mort. Brokers, Amer. Inst. of Fin. Planners, Assoc. Fin. Planner; **EDUC:** BA, 1971, Poli. Sci., Barnard Coll.; **GRAD EDUC:** JD, MBA, 1981 (joint degree), JD: Banking law; MBA: RE Investment Analysis, Franklin Univ.; **EDUC**

HONORS: Sidney F. Holdman Award; **OTHER ACT & HONORS:** Amer. Numismatic Assn., Sierra Club; **HOME ADD:** 225-12 137th Ave., Laurelton, NY 11413, (212)527-3131; **BUS ADD:** 595 Fifth Ave., New York, NY 10017, (212)529-3406.

PIERCE, Philip Foster——**B:** Jan. 24, 1930, Royal Oak, MI, *Pres.*, Pierce-Foster & Co.; **PRIM RE ACT:** Consultant, Appraiser, Developer, Owner/Investor, Property Manager; **SERVICES:** Investment analysts, appraisers, mgmt. consultants; **REP CLIENTS:** Indus., govt. and foreign investors; **PROFL AFFIL & HONORS:** Amer. Soc. of Appraisers, Amer. Arbition Assn., AIREA, Fellow - Amer. Soc. Appraisers, MAI, Former Intl. Pres. of Amer. Soc. Appraisers; **EDUC:** BBA, 1957, Bus. Admin. & Econs., Univ. of Detroit; **MIL SERV:** US Army, Lt.; **OTHER ACT & HONORS:** Outstanding Man of Year; C of C; **BUS ADD:** 25801 Harper, St. Clair Shores, MI 48081, (313)776-4810.

PIERCE, Robert Evans——**B:** June 8, 1933, Sioux City, IA, *Owner*, Alta Property Mgmt., Corporate Offices; **PRIM RE ACT:** Owner/Investor, Instructor, Property Manager; **EDUC:** 1964, Engrg./Bus. Fin., Univ. of CA, Long Beach; **MIL SERV:** USM/USAF, E-2/A1C; **HOME ADD:** 23975 Carrillo Dr., Mission Viejo, CA 92691, (714)830-4346; **BUS ADD:** 16721 Hale Ave., 2nd Floor, Irvine, CA 92714, (714)957-8711.

PIERCE, Samuel Riley, Jr.——**B:** Long Island, NY, *Sec. of HUD*, US Dept. of HUD; **PRIM RE ACT:** Attorney, Regulator; **SERVICES:** Administers all programs, functions & authorities of dept. including mort. ins., rental subsidy & neighborhood rehab. programs. Advises Pres. on fair policy & programs concerning housing & community devel.; **PREV EMPLOY:** Sr. Partner Battle, Fowler, Jaffia, Pierce & Keel; Gen. Counsel Dept. of Treas. (1970-1973); Asst. US Atty. for So. Dist. of NY (1953-1955); **PROFL AFFIL & HONORS:** NY State Bar, Author of many legal articles for profl. journals; Dept. of Treas'. highest honor: Alexander Hamilton Award 1973; **EDUC:** BA, 1947, Cornell Univ.; **GRAD EDUC:** JD, 1949, Cornell Univ.; LLM, 1952, Taxation, NY Univ. School of Law; LLD, 1972, NY Univ School of Law; **EDUC HONORS:** Phi Beta Kappa; **MIL SERV:** US Army, Criminal Investigation Div.; **OTHER ACT & HONORS:** NY City Bd. of Educ.; Battery Park City Auth.; Dir. NY World's Fair Corp.; Gov. of Amer. Stock Exchange; Adjunct Prof. NY Univ. Law School; Tr. of Rand Corp, Cornell Univ., Howard Univ.; Tr.: Mt. Holyoke Coll. & Hampton Inst.; Dir.: Gen. Electric Co., First Nat. Bank Boston, Prudential Ins. Co. of Amer.; **BUS ADD:** HUD Bldg., 451 7th St. SW, Washington, DC 20410, (202)755-6417.

PIERI, Kenneth H.——**B:** Mar. 18, 1932, Buffalo, NY, *Pres. of "Peace Bridge Apts., Inc."*; **PRIM RE ACT:** Owner/Investor, Property Manager; **PROFL AFFIL & HONORS:** Registered Apt. Mgr. (RAM); **EDUC:** Bus. Admin., 1963, Univ. of Buffalo; **MIL SERV:** USAF, A/1C; **OTHER ACT & HONORS:** Also assoc. with: Can-Am Properties, Inc. (Pres.); Indus. Funding Corp. (Pres.); Donowill Apts., Ltd. (Pres.); Rent-A-Relic, Inc. (Pres.); **BUS ADD:** 2100 Sheridan Dr., Buffalo, NY 14223, (716)874-6010.

PIERMARINI, James J.——**B:** Feb. 6, 1956, Leominster, MA, Crowley Corporation; **PRIM RE ACT:** Broker, Engineer, Developer, Builder, Owner/Investor, Property Manager, Syndicator; **SERVICES:** Indust. devel., devel. and gen. contractors, prop. mgrs., consultants; **EDUC:** BA Bus. Admin., 1974-1978, BA Acctg. & Fin., Bentley Coll.; **OTHER ACT & HONORS:** Nat. Assn. of Accountants; **HOME ADD:** Fire Rd. #12, Lancaster, MA 01523 01523, (617)534-4022; **BUS ADD:** 25 Mohawk Dr., Leominster, MA 01453, (617)534-6111.

PIERSON, Bruce E.——**B:** Aug. 14, 1945, Salinas, CA, *Part.*, The Phillip L. Moncrief; **PRIM RE ACT:** Broker, Consultant, Appraiser, Developer, Owner/Investor; **SERVICES:** Investment counseling to for. inst. clients, acquisitions; **REP CLIENTS:** Indiv., inst. investors in comml. props. nationwide; **PROFL AFFIL & HONORS:** ULI, Amer. Planning Assn., BOMA, NAHB, ICSC, Cert. of Appreciation, Center City Auth. For Revitalization Projects, City of Salinas, 1975, 1976; **EDUC:** BA, 1968, Fin, RE, Univ. CA, Santa Barbara, CA State Univ., Fullerton; **MIL SERV:** USAR; S/Sgt., Outstanding Trainer Leader, Ft. Ord.; **OTHER ACT & HONORS:** Rotary Intl., Sigma Chi Found., Dir. Young Life of Salinas Valley; **HOME ADD:** 7120 Nada St., Downey, CA 90242, (213)928-7497; **BUS ADD:** 660 Newport Ctr. Dr., Suite 215, Newport Beach, CA 92660, (714)752-5208.

PIERSON, Richard W.——**B:** Sept. 22, 1935, Coeur d'Alene, ID, *Atty., Shareholder*, Thom, Navoni, Pierson, Ryder & Major Inc. P.S.; **PRIM RE ACT:** Attorney; **SERVICES:** Law, RE & Condemnation; **REP CLIENTS:** Kidder, Mathews & Segner Inc. Indus. Brokers; Barbie Lumber Co. and King Cty. Water Dist #111; **PREV EMPLOY:** Law practice since 1963; **PROFL AFFIL & HONORS:** Amer., WA State and King Cty. Bar Assns., JD, Univ. of WA; **EDUC:** BA, 1957, WA State Univ.; **GRAD EDUC:** JD, 1962, RE/Trial, Univ. of Washington; **MIL SERV:** US Army, Artillery, Capt. 1957-1959; **OTHER ACT & HONORS:** King Cty. Deputy Prosecutor, 1963-1965; Washington Council on Crime & Delinquency, Bd. Member, 1968-1980; **HOME ADD:** 2007 19th Ave. E., Seattle, WA 98112, (206)329-5617; **BUS ADD:** 3737 Bank of CA Ctr., Seattle, WA 98164, (206)623-8433.

PIETROWITZ, Richard G.——**B:** Dec. 21, 1937, East Orange, NJ, *VP*, Alexander Summer Co., Appraisal; **PRIM RE ACT:** Appraiser; **SERVICES:** Full RE appraisal services; all types of prop.; **REP CLIENTS:** Municipalities, lenders, prop. owners, lawyers, govt. agencies; **PROFL AFFIL & HONORS:** Soc. of RE Appraisers, Amer. Soc. of Appraisers, Assn. of Govt. Appraisers, SRA-SRPA, ASA Vice Gov., Soc. of RE Apprs. 1979-1981 Dist. 16, NJ Gov., Soc. of RE Appraisers 1982 - Dist. 16, NJ; **MIL SERV:** US Army, Security Agent, Cpl.; **OTHER ACT & HONORS:** Tr./Pres. - Alpine Assn. Inc. of Lake Mohawk, NJ; **HOME ADD:** 197 Alpine Trail, Sparta, NJ 07871, (201)729-9534; **BUS ADD:** 222 Cedar Ln., Teaneck, NJ 07666, (201)836-4500.

PIGNA, Franc Joseph——**B:** June 1, 1954, New York, NY, *Exec. VP*, The Euramsas Group, Inc. (Subs. of Roland International Corp.); **PRIM RE ACT:** Broker, Developer, Builder, Owner/Investor, Syndicator; **OTHER RE ACT:** International RE Marketing Specialist Brokerage of commercial/industrial properties, turnkey devel. projects, overseas synd. of existing projects; **REP CLIENTS:** Foreign multinationals'-Foreign instit. investors and private investors, lenders, in comml./industrial, resid. devel. projects and investments; **PREV EMPLOY:** The Allen Morris Co.-1977-1979 Commercial/Indus. specialists; **PROFL AFFIL & HONORS:** RE Securities and Synd. Inst., Nat. Bd. of Realtors, Internat. RE Fed., Intl. Academy of Bus.; **EDUC:** BBA, 1975, Intl. Marketing, Univ. of Miami; **GRAD EDUC:** MBA, 1977, Intl. Bus.-Fin., The George Wash. Univ.; **EDUC HONORS:** Deans List; **OTHER ACT & HONORS:** Also w/Dade Interamerica, Corp. (VP); **HOME ADD:** 90 Edgewater Dr., Coral Gables, FL 33133, (305)667-2722; **BUS ADD:** 8101 Biscayne Blvd., Miami, FL 33138, (305)758-5681.

PIHLGREN, A.E.——*Owner*; **PRIM RE ACT:** Broker, Appraiser, Owner/Investor, Property Manager, Insuror; **BUS ADD:** 109 W. 5th, Austin, TX 78701.

PIKE, Laurence B.——**B:** Sept. 11 1927, Brattleboro, VT, *Partner*, Simpson Thacher & Bartlett; **PRIM RE ACT:** Attorney; **SERVICES:** Gen. RE practice; **REP CLIENTS:** Comml. bank; **PROFL AFFIL & HONORS:** Amer. NY State and NYC Bar Assn., Admitted NY and Fed. Courts; **EDUC:** BA, 1951, Poli. Sci., Univ. of IA; **GRAD EDUC:** LLB, 1954, Columbia Univ.; **EDUC HONORS:** Phi Beta Kappa; **MIL SERV:** US Navy, PO 2d; **OTHER ACT & HONORS:** Univ. Club; Scarsdale Golf Club; Mayflower Soc.; **HOME ADD:** 26 Tunstall Rd., Scarsdale, NY 10583, (914)472-4218; **BUS ADD:** 350 Park Ave., New York, NY 10022, (212)753-8700.

PILISH, Andre——**B:** Nov. 29, 1921, *VP, Del Realty Inc., Prop. Mgmt. Div.*, Del Realty Inc.; **PRIM RE ACT:** Consultant, Engineer, Property Manager; **OTHER RE ACT:** RE Counseling; **SERVICES:** Appraisal, Aquisition, Operation, Admin., Up-grading & Re-cycling of Investment Props.; **PREV EMPLOY:** Penstar Ltd.; **PROFL AFFIL & HONORS:** Can. Prop. Mgrs. Assn., Civil Engr.; Economist; **GRAD EDUC:** MA, Technical Univ.; Hungary; **HOME ADD:** 10 Mylesview Pl, Willowdale, ONT, Canada, (416)225-6462; **BUS ADD:** Suite 200, 4800 Dufferin St., Downsview, M3H 5S9, ONT, Canada, (416)661-3640.

PILLERS, Charles M.——**B:** Dec. 7, 1927, Kimberly, ID, *Pres. & CEO*, Sage Research Corp.; **PRIM RE ACT:** Broker, Consultant, Appraiser, Developer, Owner/Investor, Instructor, Property Manager, Syndicator, Real Estate Publisher; **OTHER RE ACT:** Tax planning, environmental reports; **SERVICES:** Prin. counseling for fee in RE econ. & taxation, investment planning and operation and computer application to RE; **REP CLIENTS:** Indiv. corps., synds., govt. agencies in RE applications; **PREV EMPLOY:** Former Asst. Prof. RE, San Jose State Univ.; Currently Prof. RE Taxation, West Valley Coll., & RE Econ., San Jose City Coll.; **PROFL AFFIL & HONORS:** Amer. Soc. RE Conselors; NARA; Nat. Assn. Enrolled Agents; local; state & nat. RE Assns.; CA Assn. RE Teachers, CRE; CRA; Enrolled agent, GRI; RECI; **EDUC:** BA, 1972, Urban Land Econ. & Bus., San Jose State Univ.; **EDUC HONORS:** Summa Cum Laude; **MIL SERV:** US Army; SFC, Korean Medal; **OTHER ACT & HONORS:** Past GK K of C; Past Pres. Stevens Creek Blvd. Assoc.; Past. Dir. San Jose RE Bd.; CA Assoc. Realtors, Listed *Who's Who in West*; **BUS ADD:** 3275 Stevens Creek Blvd., San Jose, CA 95117, (408)241-5600.

PINARD, Jean C.——B: Oct. 16, 1935, Trois-Rivieres, Que., Can., *VP*, The Marcil Grp. Ltd.; **PRIM RE ACT:** Broker, Banker, Consultant, Appraiser; **OTHER RE ACT:** Mort. Banker; **SERVICES:** Appraisal, loan servicing, asset mgmt., loan closing, RE; **REP CLIENTS:** Excelsior Life, Dominion Life, Standard Life, Prudential of England Life, Citadel Life, Laurentienne Life, Can. Pacific Pension Fund, Can. Nat. Pension Fund, Imperial Oil Pension Fund, Air Can. Pension Fund, ON Municipal Employee Retirement Fund; **PROFL AFFIL & HONORS:** Mort. Bankers Assn., Intl. Council Shopping Ctr. (IESE), C of C, Chartered Appraiser, Bd. of Trade, B. Comm. Profl. RE Appr.; **GRAD EDUC:** Bach. of Commerce, 1961; **HOME ADD:** 327 Prince Albert Ave., Westmount, H3Z 2X9, Que., Canada, (514)488-3954; **BUS ADD:** Suite 2875, 630 Dorchester Blvd., Montreal, H3B 4H6, Canada, (514)866-3771.

PINDAR, George A.——B: May 19, 1906, Valdosta, GA, *Atty. and RE Author*, Counsel, Gershon, Ruden, Pindar & Olim; **PRIM RE ACT:** Consultant, Attorney; **OTHER RE ACT:** Author of Amer. RE Law (1976); GA RE Law (2nd ed. 1979); GA RE Sales Contracts (2nd ed. 1980); **SERVICES:** Legal problems and litigation involving RE; **PREV EMPLOY:** Former law prof., GA State Univ. and Mercer Univ.; Title sect. of TN Valley Authority, 1940-1944; Title Officer, Lawyers Title Ins. Corp., 1945-1971; **PROFL AFFIL & HONORS:** Member of ABA (RE Sect.); GA State Bar; Atlanta Bar Assn.; **GRAD EDUC:** JD, 1927, Law, Mercer Univ.; **EDUC HONORS:** First Honor Grad., Magna Cum Laude, Highest three yr. average, Faculty Medal; **OTHER ACT & HONORS:** Past Fin. Chmn., N. Atlanta Dist. Boy Scouts of Amer.; Bd. Chmn., The Hambidge Found., 1965-1975; Trustee, GA Industrial Home, 1930-1940; **BUS ADD:** POB 2872, Atlanta, GA 30301, (404)524-4991.

PINES, J.——B: July 9, 1925, Milwaukee, WI, *Owner*; **PRIM RE ACT:** Broker, Developer, Owner/Investor, Property Manager; **PROFL AFFIL & HONORS:** Intl. Council of Shopping Centers, FPZA; **EDUC:** BS, 1950, Chemical Engrg., MIT; **GRAD EDUC:** MBA, 1952, Harvard Bus. School; **HOME ADD:** 2345 Collins Ln., Lakeland, FL 33803, (813)682-2844; **BUS ADD:** Box 392, Winter Haven, FL 33880, (813)299-4455.

PINKERTON, Donald——*Exec. Dir.*, Natl. conference of States on Building Codes & Standards; **PRIM RE ACT:** Regulator; **BUS ADD:** 1970 Chain Bridge Rd., McLean, VA 22102, (703)790-5750.*

PINNER, John G.——B: Dec. 13, 1928, Berlin, Germany, *Asst. Treas.*, Mattel, Inc., Corp. Hdqtrs.; **OTHER RE ACT:** RE Dir. for Mattel, Inc.; **EDUC:** AA, 1949, Bus. Admin., Los Angeles City Coll.; **MIL SERV:** US Army; M/Sgt.; **HOME ADD:** 28911 Scotsview Dr., Rancho Palos Verdes, CA 90274; **BUS ADD:** 5150 Rosecrans Ave., Hawthorne, CA 90250, (213)978-6324.

PINTEL, Paul——B: Jan. 9, 1932, New York, NY, *Partner*, Halpern & Pintel Inc., RE Investment; **PRIM RE ACT:** Broker, Consultant, Developer, Builder, Owner/Investor, Property Manager, Syndicator; **SERVICES:** Investment counseling; **REP CLIENTS:** Private investors, banking inst.; **PREV EMPLOY:** Self-employed; **PROFL AFFIL & HONORS:** AI CPA's, NJ CPA Soc., NY CPA Soc., CPA; **EDUC:** BS, 1953, Acctg., NY Univ.; **MIL SERV:** Fin. Corp., US Army, Pvt.; **OTHER ACT & HONORS:** Grant Admin. Fairlawn, NJ, appointed by Borough Council; **HOME ADD:** 23 Garwood Rd., Fairlawn, NJ 07410, (201)791-7870; **BUS ADD:** 14-25 Plaza Rd., Fairlawn, NJ 07410, (201)791-2221.

PINTO, John V.——B: Oct. 17, 1951, Brooklyn, NY, *Broker*, Executive Realty Services; **PRIM RE ACT:** Broker, Owner/Investor, Property Manager; **SERVICES:** Resid. and investment brokerage; **PROFL AFFIL & HONORS:** Nat. and CA Assns. of Realtors; San Jose, Sunnyvale and Los Gatos/Saratoga Bds. of Realtors; **EDUC:** BA, English, 1973, English Lit./Communications, Hunter Coll. of CUNY; **HOME ADD:** 199 Kimble Ave., Los Gatos, CA 95030, (408)395-4444; **BUS ADD:** 69 E. Hamilton Ave., Campbell, CA 95008, (408)378-7662.

PIPER, Janet——B: Nov. 14, 1948, Oakland, CA, *Co-Owner/Mgr.*, Harris Realty; **PRIM RE ACT:** Broker; **SERVICES:** Resid. & comml. sales/investment counseling; **REP CLIENTS:** Indivs.; **PREV EMPLOY:** Income tax consultant; **PROFL AFFIL & HONORS:** NAR/CA Assn. of Realtor; RNMI, GRI; CRS; CRB; Lifetime Member Million $ Club (Local RE Bd.); **OTHER ACT & HONORS:** Toastmaster's Intl./Soroptimist Intl. (Past Pres. Local Club); Pleas. C of C; **HOME ADD:** 2592 Willowren Way, Pleasanton, CA 94566, (415)462-2272; **BUS ADD:** 3820 Hoppard Rd., Pleasanton, CA 94566, (415)462-3676.

PIPPITT, Charles R.——B: Aug. 19, 1938, Glenwood, IA, *Sales Mgr.*, Dawson & Co., Sales; **PRIM RE ACT:** Broker; **OTHER RE ACT:** Mgr.; **SERVICES:** Resid. & Comml. Sales, Relocation, Prop. Mgmt.; **REP CLIENTS:** Homeowners, Corp. Relocation, Investors, Builders, Devel.; **PROFL AFFIL & HONORS:** Outstanding MLS Member, S. Suburban Bd. of Realtors, 1980; CRB; GRI; **EDUC:** BS, 1970, Bus., Univ. of NE at Omaha; **MIL SERV:** US Army, Major, 3 Bronze Stars, 4 Army Commendation Medals, Air Medal, Combat Infantrymen's Badge, Vietnamese Cross of Gallantry; **OTHER ACT & HONORS:** Lions Club President's Award for Outstanding Leadership 1981; Pres. - Elect South Suburban Bd. of Realtors 1981-82; **HOME ADD:** 5435 S. Camargo Rd., Littleton, CO 80123, (303)798-5149; **BUS ADD:** 609 W. Littleton Blvd., Littleton, CO 80120, (303)795-5511.

PIROG, Joseph M.——B: Sept. 8, 1916, Goshen, NY, *Sr. Appraiser*, James E. Gibbons Assoc.; **PRIM RE ACT:** Appraiser; **SERVICES:** Residential, indus, and comml. appraisals; **PREV EMPLOY:** Regional Appraiser, 1946-1969, Equitable Life Assurance Soc.; **PROFL AFFIL & HONORS:** SREA, Pres. Chap. Nat. Assoc. of Indep. Fee Appraisers, SRPA: IFAS; **MIL SERV:** USN, Y2/C; **OTHER ACT & HONORS:** Pres. L.I. Soc. of RE Appraisers, V.P. Columbia Soc. of RE Appraisers; **HOME ADD:** 241 Oak St., West Hempstead, NY 11552, (516)486-2978; **BUS ADD:** 1100 Franklin Ave., Garden City, NY 11530, (516)747-5000.

PISARETZ, Peter——B: Aug. 16, 1924, Bridgeport, CT; **PRIM RE ACT:** Consultant, Appraiser, Instructor; **REP CLIENTS:** Lenders, Estates, Third Party Cos.; **PROFL AFFIL & HONORS:** Amer. Soc. of Appraisers, ASA; Nat. Assn. of IFA; Nat. Assn. of CRA; **EDUC:** BS, 1956, Acctg., Univ. of Bridgeport; **MIL SERV:** US Army Air Force, Sgt. 1943-46; **OTHER ACT & HONORS:** Bellarmine Father's Club, Fairfield C of C; **HOME ADD:** 265 Westport Rd., Easton, CT 06612, (203)268-9740; **BUS ADD:** PO Box 116, Southport, CT 06490, (203)255-4464.

PISCITELLI, Mark Andrew——B: Sept. 17, 1942, LaSalle, IL, *VP/Gen. Mgr.*, Aswill-Burke & Co., Comml., Indus. Brokerage; **PRIM RE ACT:** Broker; **SERVICES:** Sale & leasing comml. and indus. RE; **PROFL AFFIL & HONORS:** Intl. Council of Shopping Centers; **EDUC:** BS, 1965, DePaul Univ., Chicago, IL; **HOME ADD:** 1078 LeConte Dr., Riverside, CA 92507, (714)686-9979; **BUS ADD:** 2086 S. E St., San Bernardino, CA 92410, (714)825-9922.

PISTOLE, Steven C.——B: Nov. 12, 1941, Los Angeles, CA, *Owner*; **PRIM RE ACT:** Broker, Appraiser, Developer, Builder; **SERVICES:** Appraisal work, consulting, devel.; **REP CLIENTS:** MA Mutual, B of A, Amer. Forest Prods., Lenders in gen. for appraisal work; real prop. devel. for S.F.R.; **PROFL AFFIL & HONORS:** Soc. of RE Appraisers, assoc. member, Bldg. Indus. Assn.; **EDUC:** BA, 1966, Liberal Arts, Econ., CA State at Los Angeles; **GRAD EDUC:** Cert. program, 1968, RE, UCLA; **HOME ADD:** 1760 E. Sierra, Fresno, CA 93710, (209)435-1744; **BUS ADD:** 1760 E. Sierra, Fresno, CA 93710, (209)435-1744.

PITCAITHLEY, Alan L., Esq.——B: July 7, 1948, Oakland, CA, *Atty. At Law*, Pitcaithley & Reina; **PRIM RE ACT:** Attorney, Property Manager, Syndicator; **SERVICES:** Legal-secured real prop. transactions, broker law, synds., land-use, comml. leases; **PROFL AFFIL & HONORS:** San Diego Trial Lawyers Assn., San Diego Cty. Bar Assn., ABA, Sect. Member Real-Prop. in State Bar of CA; **EDUC:** BA Journalism, 1970, U.S. Constitution and Free Press, Univ. of OR; **GRAD EDUC:** JD, 1976, Real Prop. Law, Western State Univ. School of Law; **OTHER ACT & HONORS:** Player-NY Giants Football Team, Edmonton Eskimo Football Team, CFL (NFL); **HOME ADD:** 4877 Jewell St., San Diego, CA 92109, (714)483-4738; **BUS ADD:** 2333 Camino del Rio S., Ste. 110, San Diego, CA 92108, (714)291-5648.

PITCHER, Charles D.——B: Dec. 13, 1934, Danbury, CT, *Pres.*, Charles D. Pitcher Appraisal Co.; **PRIM RE ACT:** Appraiser; **SERVICES:** RE appraising; **REP CLIENTS:** Homequity, Inc., State Nat. Bank of Ct., City Savings Bank, The Baker Cos., Merrill Lynch Relocation Servs.; **PREV EMPLOY:** RE sales; **PROFL AFFIL & HONORS:** Nat. Assn. of Realtors, Inc., Nat. Assn. of Indep. Fee Appraisers, Nat. Assn. of Review Appraisers, IFA, CRA, (Realtor) Nat. Assoc. of Realtors, Awarded "Realtor of the Year in 1976 from Greater Bpt. Bd. of Realtors; **OTHER ACT & HONORS:** Grand Knight, (1971-72) Knights of Columbus #5806; Pres. (1980) Greater Bridgeport Bd. of Realtors, Inc.; Pres. (1980-1981) Local Chap. of the Nat. Assn. of Indep. Fee Appraisers, District Two;(1982) VP, CT Assn. of Realtors, Inc.; **HOME ADD:** 117 Hill Top Dr., Trumbull, CT 06611, (203)378-7665; **BUS ADD:** 1100 Essex Pl., Stratford, CT 06497, (203)375-5236.

PITCHER, Tom——*VP Adm. (RE)*, Wausau Paper Mills; **PRIM RE ACT:** Property Manager; **BUS ADD:** 1 Clark Island, Wausau, WI 54401, (715)675-3361.*

PITLOCK, Lee P.——**B:** Nov. 6, 1947, Chicago, IL, *Mgr.*, Santefort Cowing Realtors, Agricultural Investment; **PRIM RE ACT:** Broker, Consultant, Owner/Investor, Property Manager, Syndicator; **PROFL AFFIL & HONORS:** FLI, NASO, RESSI; **EDUC:** BS, 1969, Journalism, So. IL Univ.; **HOME ADD:** 3506 Ionia, Olympia Fields, IL 60461, (312)481-1924; **BUS ADD:** 900 E. 162nd St., South Holland, IL 60473, (312)333-0600.

PITSTICK, Jerry W.——**B:** Feb. 8, 1941, Dayton, OH, *Pres.*, Gateway Realty & Construction Co., Inc.; **PRIM RE ACT:** Broker, Consultant, Appraiser, Property Manager; **PROFL AFFIL & HONORS:** CCIM, AFLM; SRS; CRS; GRI; CRB; **EDUC:** BS, Fin. Bus. Admin., Univ. of Cincinnati, OH; **GRAD EDUC:** MBA, 1968, Mktg. Mgmt., Univ. of Dayton, Dayton, OH; **EDUC HONORS:** 2nd in the class; Dean's List all 5 years; Sophos Hon. Soc., Grad. 1st in class; **HOME ADD:** 3548 Springdale Dr., Kettering, OH 45419, (513)294-2470; **BUS ADD:** 2176 Hewitt Ave., Dayton, OH 45440, (513)434-6099.

PITT, Theophilus Harper, Jr.——**B:** Apr. 5, 1936, Rocky Mount, NC, *Pres. and CEO*, Home Savings and Loan Assn.; **PRIM RE ACT:** Appraiser, Developer, Lender, Owner/Investor; **SERVICES:** Prop. appraisal, consulting and feasibility study, mort. brokerage and direct lending; **REP CLIENTS:** City of Rocky Mount, NC Dept. of Transportation, Peoples Bank and Trust Co., Spruill, Lane and McCotter, Attys., Wellongate Enterprises; **PREV EMPLOY:** Special Rep., Pilot Life Ins. Co., July 1958 - 1961; **PROFL AFFIL & HONORS:** Dir., Savers Life Ins. Co., Chmn., Bd. of Trustees, NC S&L Academy, Boss of the Year, Rocky Mount Jaycees, 1977; Boss of the Year, Amer. Business Women's Assn., 1978; **EDUC:** BA, 1958, Hist., Univ. of NC; **GRAD EDUC:** 1966, Econ., Fin. and Mgmt. Practices, Univ. of IN Grad. School of S&L; **EDUC HONORS:** Grad. NC; **OTHER ACT & HONORS:** Cert. Review Appraiser; **HOME ADD:** 318 Gravely Dr., Rocky Mount, NC 27801, (919)443-5706; **BUS ADD:** PO Drawer 2088, Rocky Mount, NC 27801, (919)446-0611.

PITTS, William R.——**B:** Boston, MA, *RE Investment Officer*, John Hancock Mutual Life Ins. Co., RE; **PRIM RE ACT:** Owner/Investor, Property Manager; **PROFL AFFIL & HONORS:** Gr. Boston RE Bd.; IREM, CPM; Public Acct.; **EDUC:** BS, 1960, Acctg., Northeastern Univ.; **HOME ADD:** 149 Harris Ave., Needham, MA 02192, (617)444-0841; **BUS ADD:** John Hancock Pl., Boston, MA 02117, (617)421-4071.

PIVKO, Tibor——**B:** Aug. 31, 1921, Bratislava, Czechoslovakia, *Pres.*, Pivko Group, Inc.; **PRIM RE ACT:** Consultant, Owner/Investor; **PREV EMPLOY:** Centro Indus., Caracas, Venezuela; Three Star Const., Montreal, Can.; Marcil Props., Can. & NY; The Pivko Group, Inc.; **PROFL AFFIL & HONORS:** IREF; Lic. Can. RE Salesman; Intl. Council of Shopping Centers; NARA; Nat. Assn. of Indus. & Office Parks; **MIL SERV:** Army, Capt. (Czech.); **HOME ADD:** 417 E. 57th St., New York, NY 10022, (212)223-0298; **BUS ADD:** 10 E. 53rd St., New York, NY 10022, (212)355-4460.

PIZZAGALLI, James——**B:** Nov. 23, 1944, Burlington, VT, *VP*, Pizzagalli Construction Co.; **PRIM RE ACT:** Developer; **SERVICES:** Devel. of Comml. & Indus. Projects; **EDUC:** BS, 1966, Acctg., Univ. of VT; **GRAD EDUC:** JD, 1969, Law, Boston Univ.; **MIL SERV:** VT Air National Guard, Sgt.; **HOME ADD:** 147 DeForest Rd., Burlington, VT 05401, (802)862-7551; **BUS ADD:** 50 Joy Dr., S Burlington, VT 05401, (802)658-4100.

PLACEY, Clayton G.——**B:** Oct. 3, 1924, St. Jounsbury, VT, *Branch Mgr.*, Strout Realty, Inc., Wells River, VT; **PRIM RE ACT:** Broker; **SERVICES:** Sales; **PREV EMPLOY:** Placey's RE; **MIL SERV:** US Army, Pvt.; **OTHER ACT & HONORS:** Chmn. Wells River Area Devel. Grp., 32 Mason, Full Gospel Bus. Fellowship Int., Rotary; **HOME ADD:** Railroad St., Wells River, VT 05081, (802)757-2211; **BUS ADD:** Railroad St., Wells River, VT 05081, (802)757-2211.

PLANEY, James B.——**B:** Oct. 8, 1946, Chicago, IL, *VP*, MRX - Midwest Realty Exchange, Inc.; **PRIM RE ACT:** Broker; **SERVICES:** Brokerage, mgmt., land assembly, devel.; **REP CLIENTS:** Instnl. investors, corporate users mainly in areas of indus. and comml. props.; **PREV EMPLOY:** Central Mfg. District (CMD), 1975-1981; **PROFL AFFIL & HONORS:** SIR; Assn. of Indus. RE Brokers (Chicago); **EDUC:** BS, 1968, Mktg., No. IL Univ.; **MIL SERV:** US Army; Spec. 4, 1968-1970; **HOME ADD:** 1521 Canterbury Ln., Glenview, IL 60025, (312)998-0236; **BUS ADD:** Two Illinois Ctr., Ste. 1621, Chicago, IL 60601, (312)856-0080.

PLASEIED, Badreddin——**B:** Mar. 17, 1938, Rezaieh, Iran, *Pres.*, Haph, Inc.; **PRIM RE ACT:** Architect, Consultant; **SERVICES:** Arch., engrg., devel. const. mgmt.; **REP CLIENTS:** Investors, comml. prop. owners, governmental props.; **PREV EMPLOY:** Project coordinator LBC & W; Victor Smolen and Assoc.; **PROFL AFFIL & HONORS:** Nat. Home Bldrs.; Dir. No. VA Chap.; **EDUC:** BA, 1966, Design, Howard Univ.; **HOME ADD:** 9713 Counsellor Dr., Vienna, VA 22180, (703)281-2884; **BUS ADD:** 133 Park St., NE, Vienna, VA 22180, (703)281-5242.

PLATT, David S.K.——**B:** May 18, 1936, Evanston, IL, *Asst. Atty. Gen.*; **PRIM RE ACT:** Attorney; **SERVICES:** Representing, private clients, State of IL in collecting inheritance taxes; **PREV EMPLOY:** Mayer Brown & Platt, Gen. practice law firm, Personal spec. in RE & RE taxation; **PROFL AFFIL & HONORS:** ABA, ISBA; **EDUC:** BA, 1958, Amer. Hist., Hobart Coll.; **GRAD EDUC:** LLB, 1961, WI Law Sch.; **HOME ADD:** 2525 Orrington, Evanston, IL 60201, (312)328-4795; **BUS ADD:** 160 N La Salle St., Chicago, IL 60602, (312)793-2534.

PLATT, Gordon L.——**B:** Mar. 2, 1928, Indianapolis, IN, *Pres.*, Gordon L. Platt Co.; **PRIM RE ACT:** Broker, Consultant, Attorney, Developer, Lender, Builder, Owner/Investor, Property Manager, Syndicator; **OTHER RE ACT:** Indus. park devel.; **SERVICES:** Fin., comml. fed tax exempt, grant programs; **REP CLIENTS:** State, city & cty. govt. authority, community econ. devel. authority, in OH; **PREV EMPLOY:** U.S. Dept. of Commerce; **PROFL AFFIL & HONORS:** Phi Alpha Delta; Realtor; **EDUC:** BS, 1949, Bus. Admin., IN Univ., Bloomington, IN; **GRAD EDUC:** LLB, 1951, IN Univ. Law School; **EDUC HONORS:** Magna Cum Laude, OH State Univ. Community Econ. Cert. of Achievement; **MIL SERV:** USAF; Lt. Col.; retired; **OTHER ACT & HONORS:** Sigma Alpha Mu; Optimist; Toastmaster; **HOME ADD:** 2651 Yalonda Ct., Beavercreek, OH 45385, (513)426-9955; **BUS ADD:** 237 West Riverview, Dayton, OH 45405, (513)223-3922.

PLATT, Norman——**B:** Feb. 7, 1919, Boston, MA, *Pres.*, Norman Platt Realty Corp. and Frank Moore Realty Inc.; **PRIM RE ACT:** Broker, Appraiser, Builder, Property Manager; **OTHER RE ACT:** Mortgage Broker; **SERVICES:** Investment counseling, prop. mgmt., resid. & comml., appraising; **REP CLIENTS:** Lawyers, accountants, indiv. & corp.; **PROFL AFFIL & HONORS:** Sr. Member, Nat. Soc. of Fee Appraisers; Sr. Member, Amer. Assn. of Cert. Appraisers; Member, Nat. Assn. of Review Appraisers; Realtor Member, Hollywood-S. Broward Bd. of Realtors; Realtor Non-Resident Member, Ft. Lauderdale Bd. of Realtors; Member, FL Assn. of Realtors; Nar; Member, Realtors Nat. Mktg. Inst.; Member, Nat. Inst. of Farm and Land Brokers; Florida Investment Div.; **EDUC:** Northeastern Law School; **MIL SERV:** US Army; T-5, 1944-1946, European African Middle Eastern Theatre Campaign Ribbon Victory Medal; **OTHER ACT & HONORS:** City of Hallandale Unsafe Structures Bd., 1979-1982; **HOME ADD:** 4507 Fillmore St., Hollywood, FL 33021, (305)989-2643; **BUS ADD:** 2450 Hollywood Blvd., Suite 201, Hollywood, FL 33020, (305)920-3500.

PLEASANT, Willard——**B:** June 9, 1916, Angier, NC, *Pres.*, Willard Pleasant Assoc., Inc.; **PRIM RE ACT:** Broker, Appraiser, Developer, Builder, Owner/Investor; **REP CLIENTS:** Al Brown, Al Brown Realty Co., 201 N. 2nd St., Smithfield, NC; **PREV EMPLOY:** Nationwide Ins. Cos., Columbus, OH, 14 yr. sales agent, 15 yrs. dist. sales mgr.; **EDUC:** BS, 1933, Univ. NC; **MIL SERV:** USMCR, Capt.; **HOME ADD:** 408 Seapath Towers, Wrightsville Beach, NC 29480, (919)256-3248; **BUS ADD:** 201 N 2nd St., Smithfield, NC 27577, (919)934-0505.

PLESS, Hubert A., Jr.——**B:** Feb. 8, 1917, Knoxville, TN, *VP*, Wortman & Mann, Inc., RE Serv.; **PRIM RE ACT:** Broker, Consultant, Property Manager, Owner/Investor; **SERVICES:** Investing Consultant, Lease Counseling; **REP CLIENTS:** Political Entities, Individual & Religious Insts.; **PROFL AFFIL & HONORS:** IREM-Realtors-BOMA; **EDUC:** BBA, 1939, Econ., U of TN, Chattanooga; **EDUC HONORS:** Blue Key Hon. Soc.; *Who's Who Amer. U & Coll.*; **MIL SERV:** US Army, Mstr. Sgt.; **OTHER ACT & HONORS:** Kiwanis; **HOME ADD:** 2222 Southwood Rd., Jackson, MS 39211, (601)366-8180; **BUS ADD:** PO Box 2337, Jackson, MS 39205, (601)944-3307.

PLETCHER, Harold D.——**B:** Oct. 11, 1930, Elkhart, IN, *VP*, The First Nat. Bank of Chicago, RE Asset Mgmt. Div.; **PRIM RE ACT:** Broker, Attorney, Banker; **SERVICES:** Acquisition, mgmt., mktg., of RE assets for employer, plus control operating subs.; **PROFL AFFIL & HONORS:** Chicago Mort. Attys.; **EDUC:** BS, 1952, Bus. & Econ., N. Central Coll.; **GRAD EDUC:** JD, 1962, John Marshall Law Sch.; MBA, 1974, Univ. of Chicago; **MIL SERV:** US Army, Special Agent Counter Intelligence Corp.; **OTHER ACT & HONORS:** Member DePage Cty Zoning Bd. of Appeals, 1972-73; VP & Dir. N. Central Coll. Alumni Bd.; **HOME ADD:** 23W637 Hemlock Ln., Naperville, IL 60540, (312)355-9578; **BUS ADD:** One First Natl. Plaza, Chicago, IL 60670, (312)732-6930.

PLISKA, Robert J.——B: Oct. 4, 1947, Detroit, MI, *VP*, Lambrecht Realty Co., Mort.; **PRIM RE ACT:** Broker, Consultant, Appraiser, Developer, Lender, Builder, Owner/Investor, Property Manager, Assessor; **REP CLIENTS:** Instit. or indiv. investors in comml. & resid. props., All types of organizations for appraisal, prop. mgmt., brokerage, consulting, and counseling servs.; **PREV EMPLOY:** Coopers & Lybrand, 1970-1980; **PROFL AFFIL & HONORS:** AICPA's; MI Assn. of CPA's, MBA, CPA; **EDUC:** BS, 1969, Acctg., Univ. of Detroit; **GRAD EDUC:** MBA, 1970, Acctg. & Fin., MI State Univ.; **EDUC HONORS:** Cum Laude, Beta Alpha Psi, Beta Alpha Psi; **OTHER ACT & HONORS:** Builders Assn. of S.E. MI, Univ. of Detroit, Natl. Alumni Bd., Toastmasters Intl.; **HOME ADD:** 26011 Timber Trail, Dearborn Hts., MI 48127, (313)278-8353; **BUS ADD:** 3300 City Natl. Bank Bldg., Detroit, MI 48226, (313)964-4522.

PLOTKIN, Jonathan Dean——B: July 27, 1924, Chicago, IL, *Comml. RE Broker and Consultant*, Sudler & Company, RE Div.; **PRIM RE ACT:** Broker; **SERVICES:** RE Consultation; **PREV EMPLOY:** Commerical Property Mgr. - Boston Safe Deposit & Trust; **PROFL AFFIL & HONORS:** IREM; BOMA; **EDUC:** BA Pol. Sci., 1976, Intl. Relations of Mid-East and Africa, The George Wash. Univ.; **GRAD EDUC:** MBA, 1980, Fin. and Strategic Planning, Northeastern Univ.; **EDUC HONORS:** Grad. Asst.; **OTHER ACT & HONORS:** New Priorities in Amer.; **HOME ADD:** 1519 Hinman, Evanston, IL 60201, (312)869-1395; **BUS ADD:** 875 N. Michigan Ave., Chicago, IL 60201, (312)751-3653.

PLOURDE, Kathryn M.——B: May 28, 1932, Omaha, NE, *VP and Counsel*, Security Land Title Co.; **PRIM RE ACT:** Attorney, Instructor; **OTHER RE ACT:** Title Ins.; **SERVICES:** Title Ins., Abstracts and Opinions, Escrow and Closings; **REP CLIENTS:** Banks, S&L Assns., Day Firms, RE Agents, Mort. Bankers, HUD; **PREV EMPLOY:** Have been in this field for 15 yrs. since grad. from law school; **PROFL AFFIL & HONORS:** NE Bar Assn., Omaha Bar Assn., ABA, Title Standards Comm. of both the Omaha and NE Bar Assn.; **EDUC:** BS Bus. Admin., 1954, Bus. and Mktg., Creighton Univ., Omaha, NE; **GRAD EDUC:** JD Law, 1968, Law, Creighton Univ., Omaha, NE; **OTHER ACT & HONORS:** Altrusa Club of Omaha; Several Bd. of Dir. Appointments; 66 Dancing Club; **HOME ADD:** 12525 Oakair Dr., Omaha, NE 68137, (402)895-4758; **BUS ADD:** Suite 7000 Grain Exchange Bldg., Omaha, NE 68102, (402)346-5410.

PLUNK, Don Royl——B: Mar. 7, 1935, Emory, TX, *Pres.*, Dalcon, Inc.; **PRIM RE ACT:** Consultant, Developer, Builder, Property Manager, Owner/Investor; **SERVICES:** Dev. Consulting, Prop. Mgmt.; **REP CLIENTS:** Woods Bros. Homes, Inc.; Raldon Corp.; Ayrshire Corp.; E-Systems Inc.; Electronic Data Systems Realty; Hunt Prop., Inc.; Santa Anita Consol.; Builders Resources Corp.; International Investment Advisors, Inc.; Henry S. Miller Co.; **PREV EMPLOY:** Sr. VP Raldon Corp. 1970-75; Dir. of Dev., Hunt Prop., 1968-70; Proj. Eng./Municipal Consultant, Henningson Durham & Richardson. 1962-68; **PROFL AFFIL & HONORS:** NH HAB; Dallas HAB; Dallas Bd. of Realtors, Soc. of Eng. Technicians, Div. Pres. - Natl. Dir. - NAHB; **EDUC:** Arch. Engineering, Univ. of TX - Austin - 1952-53; **MIL SERV:** US Army, SF4, Merit Svc., Purp. Ht.; **HOME ADD:** 6518 Clubhouse Cir., Dallas, TX 75240, (214)661-3924; **BUS ADD:** 16901 Dallas Pkwy., Suite 145, Dallas, TX 75248, (214)931-1244.

POAG, G. Dan, Jr.——B: Apr. 4, 1941, Nashville, TN, *Pres.*, Poag and Thomason Devel. Co.; **PRIM RE ACT:** Developer, Owner/Investor; **SERVICES:** Shopping Ctr. Devel. and Ownership; **PROFL AFFIL & HONORS:** CPM, Realtor; **EDUC:** AB, 1963, Eng., Princeton Univ.; **GRAD EDUC:** MBA, 1965, Fin., Emory Univ.; **OTHER ACT & HONORS:** Exec. Comm. Theatre Memphis, Chmn. Schools Comm. Princeton Alumni Assn. of Memphis, Princeton Club of NY; **HOME ADD:** 4275 Gwynne Road, Memphis, TN 38117, (901)685-6518; **BUS ADD:** 4711 Poplar Ave., Suite 210, Memphis, TN 38117, (901)761-2571.

PODLIN, Mark Joseph——B: Sept. 20, 1953, Chicago, IL, *RE Dept. Atty., SE Rgn.*, J.C. Penney Co., Inc., RE Dept.; **PRIM RE ACT:** Attorney; **SERVICES:** Negotiation, drafting and review of const., operation and reciprocal easement agreements, leases, and related comml. RE documents; documentation for store acquisitions and divestment; supervision of litigation; **PREV EMPLOY:** K-Mart Corp., 1975; Bradley, Guthery, Turner and Curry, Charlotte, NC, 1976-1977 - Summers; **PROFL AFFIL & HONORS:** GA State Bar Assn.; Atlanta Bar Assn.; Member of RE Sect. of State Bar and Zoning Survey and Analysis Task Force; Consultant to Springdale Estates Homeowners Assn.; **EDUC:** BFA, 1975, Drama and Theatre, Univ. of GA; **GRAD EDUC:** JD, 1978, Univ. of GA School of Law; **EDUC HONORS:** Summa Cum Laude with Gen. Honors, Univ. Theatre Freshman Scholarship, 1971-1972; Univ. Theatre Serv. Award, 1973, First Prize, 1978, Nathan Burkan Memorial Competition Sponsored by Amer. Soc. of Composers, Authors, and Publishers; **HOME ADD:** 5757 Kimberly Ln., Norcross, GA 30071, (404)449-4990; **BUS ADD:** 715 Peachtree St., N.E., Atlanta, GA 30308, (404)897-5490.

PODOLAK, Steven——B: April 22, 1954, Brooklyn, NY, *Owner*, Black Forest Construction Company; **PRIM RE ACT:** Developer, Builder, Property Manager; **PROFL AFFIL & HONORS:** Eatontown C of C, NJ, NJ Builders Assoc.; NJ Builders Assoc.; Wayne Cty. Builders Assn.; Wayne Cty. C of C; Wayne Cty. Bldrs. Assn.; Nat. Assn. of Home Bldrs. of the US; PA Bldrs. Assn.; Hideout Bldrs. Assn.; **OTHER ACT & HONORS:** Wayne Cty. C of C; **HOME ADD:** Box 371 The Hideout, Lake Ariel, PA 18436, (717)698-9390; **BUS ADD:** Box 371 The Hideout, Lake Ariel, PA 18436.

PODOLSKY, Milton——B: July 1, 1921, Chicago, IL, *Pres.*, Podolsky and Associates, Ltd.; **PRIM RE ACT:** Broker, Consultant, Appraiser, Developer, Property Manager; **PROFL AFFIL & HONORS:** SIR; Intl. RE Federation; Nat. Assn. of RE Bds.; IL C of C; ULI; Nat. Assn. of IN Parks; **EDUC:** DePaul Univ.; **GRAD EDUC:** John Marshall Law School; **BUS ADD:** 9655 Bryn Mawr, Rosemont, IL 60018, (312)671-7600.

PODOLSKY, Steven H.——B: Nov. 13, 1946, Chicago, IL, *Pres.*, Podolsky and Associates, Ltd.; **PRIM RE ACT:** Broker, Consultant, Developer, Owner/Investor, Property Manager, Syndicator; **SERVICES:** Office, indus. and investment brokerage, mgmt., devel. and synd. as well as investment consultation; **REP CLIENTS:** Small and large corp. (users and owners of prop.), pvt. and instnl. investors of office and indus. props.; **PREV EMPLOY:** Arthur Rubloff & Co. 1975-79 (full service, nat. RE firm; **PROFL AFFIL & HONORS:** Soc. of Indus. Realtors; Nat. Assn. of Realtors; IL Assn. of Realtors; Jr. RE Bd. of Chicago (Past Pres.); Assn. of Indus. Chicago Brokers Office Leasing Brokers Assn. (Charter Member) of Chicago (Pres. Elect); Realtors Nat. Mktg. Inst., soc. of Indus. Realtors; **EDUC:** BA, 1969, Bus. Admin., Educ. and Hist., Univ. of WI, Madison; **OTHER ACT & HONORS:** Member, Standard Club of Chicago; Member, Bd. of Dir., Young Men's Jewish Council; Member, Jr. Comm. Highland Park Hospital; **HOME ADD:** 60 Mulberry E. Dr., Deerfield, IL 60015, (312)948-5285; **BUS ADD:** 9655 W. Bryn Mawr Ave., Rosemont, IL 60018, (312)671-7600.

POE, Robert C.——B: Apr. 19, 1938, OK City, OK, *Pres. & CEO*, The Fracorp.; **PRIM RE ACT:** Broker, Consultant, Developer, Builder, Owner/Investor, Syndicator; **SERVICES:** The above servs. for office bldgs., shopping ctrs., apts., condos. & land devel.; **REP CLIENTS:** pension funds, private investors & our own account; **PREV EMPLOY:** Found & princ. owner of Poe Assocs., Inc., an engrg. News Record top 500 consulting engrg. co.; **PROFL AFFIL & HONORS:** OK Soc. of Profl. Engrg.; **EDUC:** BS Mech. Engrg., 1960, Mech., Univ. of OK; **GRAD EDUC:** MS Mech. Engrg., 1961, Stress Analysis, Univ. of Pittsburgh; MS Civil, 1963, Municipal improvements, Univ. of OK; **EDUC HONORS:** Pres. Tau Beta Pi, Pi Tau Sigma, Top ten srs. Leitzeiser Medal for #2 man in Univ.; **MIL SERV:** US Army, Capt., Letter of Commendation; **OTHER ACT & HONORS:** City Comm., Norman, OK, 1964-66, Dir. Blue Cross & Blue Shield of OK, Dir. Frontier Fed. S&L; **HOME ADD:** 4505 E. 68th St., Tulsa, OK 74136; **BUS ADD:** 4505 E 68th St., Tulsa, OK 74136, (918)494-2002.

POETTER, Bruce E.——B: May 18, 1951, Berwyn, IL, *VP and Mgr.*, Coldwell Banker, RE Appraisal Services; **PRIM RE ACT:** Broker, Consultant, Appraiser, Owner/Investor, Instructor; **SERVICES:** RE appraisal & counseling of comml., indus. & resid. props. on a nat. & intl. basis; **REP CLIENTS:** Major corps., lenders, insts. and private indivs. who require RE valuation and evaluation around the world; **PREV EMPLOY:** Formerly the Chief Appraiser for Thorsen Realtors, Chicago, IL; **PROFL AFFIL & HONORS:** SREA, Amer. Inst. of RE Appraisers, SRPA, MAI; **EDUC:** BA, 1974, Major: Bus. Admin.; Minor: Physics & Math., Hope Coll. - Holland, MI; **GRAD EDUC:** Profl. Designations; **EDUC HONORS:** Dean's List; **OTHER ACT & HONORS:** Approved RE Inst. State of IL - Sr. Instr., SREA - RE Broker State of IL; **HOME ADD:** 312 South Sone Ave., La Grange, IL 60525, (312)352-7317; **BUS ADD:** 1900 Spring Rd., Oak Brook, IL 60521, (312)655-7050.

POHORYLES, Louis——B: Mar. 6, 1937, Poland, *Atty.*, Pohoryles, Goldberg, Forester, Staton & Harris, PC; **PRIM RE ACT:** Attorney, Owner/Investor, Real Estate Publisher; **OTHER RE ACT:** Author & lecturer; **REP CLIENTS:** Devels., banks, S&L assns., synds., realtors; **PROFL AFFIL & HONORS:** ABA; DC Bar; MD State Bar Assn.; **EDUC:** BBA, 1959, Public Acctg., CCNY; **GRAD EDUC:** JD, 1963, Law, George Washington Univ. Law School; **EDUC HONORS:** With Honors; **OTHER ACT & HONORS:** Dir., Washington DC Bd. of Realtors; Published: "Real Estate Review," °"Condominium World," "George Washington Law Review"; Lectured: Nat. Assn. of Home Builders; Nat. Assn. of Mort. Bankers; Exec. Enterprises; Apt.

Builder/Devel. Conference & Exposition; Bar Assn. Continuing Legal Educ. Programs; **HOME ADD:** 8809 Church Field Ln., Laurel, MD 20708, (301)953-3020; **BUS ADD:** 1801 K St., NW, Suite 1105, Wash., DC 20006, (202)785-2940.

POIRIER, Joseph L.——**B:** Jan. 24, 1929, Fall River, MA, *Pres.*, The Peartree Grp.; **PRIM RE ACT:** Broker, Consultant, Instructor, Syndicator; **OTHER RE ACT:** Fin. planning; **SERVICES:** Valuation, investment counseling, income prop., synd., sales, fin. and estate planning; **REP CLIENTS:** indivs. and fin. mgrs.; **PREV EMPLOY:** Pres. The Peartree RE Fin. Co., 1980-81, Pres. The Trust Deed Corp., Sr. Loan Officer Amer. Family Mort., 1979-80; Dir. of Mktg. OWA Mort., 1978-79; **PROFL AFFIL & HONORS:** Intl. Assn. of Fin. Planners; **EDUC:** AA, 1981, RE, Santa Ana Coll., Santa Ana, CA; **MIL SERV:** USAF, Sgt.; **OTHER ACT & HONORS:** Toastmasters Intl.; **HOME ADD:** 329 Cameo Ln., Fullerton, CA 92631, (714)528-6073; **BUS ADD:** 1421 Burr St., Los Angeles, CA 90032, (213)227-1026.

POITRAS, Dick——**B:** Dec. 7, 1925, Seattle, WA, *Pres.*, Poitras & Rogers, Inc.; **PRIM RE ACT:** Broker, Consultant, Developer; **PROFL AFFIL & HONORS:** CRB Assoc.; CCIM Assoc.; Seattle King Cty. Bd. of Realtors; Realtors Nat. Mktg. Instit., CRB, CCIM candidate; **EDUC:** Engrg., 1947, Univ. of OK; **MIL SERV:** USN; P.O., V5 - Cadet; **OTHER ACT & HONORS:** Teamsters (Retd.), SPEEA (Retd.), Masons, (Past Master) Scottish Rite, Shriner, Seafair Commodore (Personel officer), Bellevue Kiwanis; **HOME ADD:** 6702 - 139th Ave. NE, Redmond, WA 98052, (206)881-6019; **BUS ADD:** 6702 - NE 139th Ave., Redmond, WA 98052, (206)881-6019.

POLACHEK, Ralph R.——**B:** Oct. 5, 1955, Pittsburgh, PA, *Atty.*, Ash, Bauersfeld, & Burton; **PRIM RE ACT:** Attorney; **SERVICES:** Tax Planning, Fin., Settlements, Titles; **REP CLIENTS:** Agent for Chicago Title Ins. Co., Act as Settlement and Escrow Atty., Represent Purchasers or Sellers; **PROFL AFFIL & HONORS:** ABA (Tax, Real Prop., and Corps. Sects.), MD State Bar Assn., Bar Assn. of DC, Phi Delta Phi Legal Frat.; **EDUC:** BBA, 1976, Fin., Econ., Univ. of Miami; **GRAD EDUC:** JD, 1979, Tax and Bus. Law, Amer. Univ., Wash. Coll. of Law; **EDUC HONORS:** Magna Cum Laude, Beta Gamma Sigma, Phi Kappa Phi; **HOME ADD:** 10616 Radstock Ct., Damascus, MD 20872, (301)253-5127; **BUS ADD:** Suite 505, 4520 East-West Hwy., Bethesda, MD 20814, (301)986-8600.

POLAN, Laurence S.——*Asst. Secy.*, Vista Resources; **PRIM RE ACT:** Property Manager; **BUS ADD:** 350 Fifth Ave., New York, NY 10118, (212)594-1870.*

POLAND, Claude W.——**B:** Nov. 18, 1926, Clark Dale, MS, *VP*, Bank of Mississippi, Loan Div.; **PRIM RE ACT:** Broker, Banker; **PREV EMPLOY:** Bank of MS Mort. Banking Dept.; **PROFL AFFIL & HONORS:** Cer. Comml. Lender. ABA, GRI, CRA; **EDUC:** BBA, 1949, Banking & Fin., Univ. of MS; **GRAD EDUC:** Certificates, 1960, School of Banking of the South, LA State Univ..; **MIL SERV:** USMM, Ensign; **OTHER ACT & HONORS:** Mayor, Townylula, Sigma Chi Soc. Frat.; **HOME ADD:** 2118 Ctry Club Rd., Tupelo, MS 38201, (601)844-4161; **BUS ADD:** 1 Mississippi Plaza, Tupelo, MS 38801, (601)842-6661.

POLEVOY, Martin D.——**B:** Feb. 13, 1943, Suffern, NY, *Part.*, Bachner, Tally & Mantell; **PRIM RE ACT:** Attorney; **REP CLIENTS:** Major owners-dev. of comml. r.e., instl. clients: ins. cos. and banks, RE counsel to several Fortune 500 Companies; **PROFL AFFIL & HONORS:** ABA; Bar of NYC; **EDUC:** BA, 1964, Pol. Sci./Econ., Colgate Univ.; **GRAD EDUC:** LLB, 1967, Univ. of PA Law School; **EDUC HONORS:** Cum Laude; High Honors in Pol. Sci.; **HOME ADD:** 1155 Park Ave., New York, NY; **BUS ADD:** 850 Third Ave., New York, NY 10022, (212)355-1800.

POLITIS, John——**B:** Oct. 4, 1938, New Bedford, MA, *Pres.*, Florida Mortgage & Realty Co.; **PRIM RE ACT:** Broker; **SERVICES:** Synd., joint ventures, equity sales on shopping centers only; **REP CLIENTS:** Pension funds, insurance cos. & Syndicators; **PROFL AFFIL & HONORS:** Intl. Council of Shopping Ctrs., CCIM; **EDUC:** 1965, RE Fin., Rutgers Univ.; **MIL SERV:** US Air Force, Sgt.; **HOME ADD:** 3753 N.W. 20th St., Ft. Lauderdale, FL 33311, (305)485-2437; **BUS ADD:** 4200 N.W. 16th St., Ft. Lauderdale, FL 33313, (305)485-1483.

POLK, James H., III——**B:** Nov. 4, 1942, Cornwell-on-Hudson, NY, *Pres. & CEO*, Property Trust of America; **PRIM RE ACT:** Owner/Investor; **OTHER RE ACT:** RE Investment Trust; **SERVICES:** Investment in medium-sized comml. RE in the SW and western US; **REP CLIENTS:** Approximately 4000 shareholders; **PREV EMPLOY:** 1972-1974: The Leavell Co., El Paso, TX-const. and RE devel.; **PROFL AFFIL & HONORS:** City of El Paso Hist. Landmark Commn.; El Paso Cty. Planning Commn.; Fed. Legislation Comm.-Nat. Assn. of RE Investment Trusts; **EDUC:** BS, 1965, ME, Vanderbilt Univ., Nashville, TN; **GRAD EDUC:** MBA, 1967, Marketing and Mfg./Operations Research, Univ. of VA, Charlottesville, VA; **MIL SERV:** US Army 1967-1969, 1st Lt.; **OTHER ACT & HONORS:** Advisory Bd. of Dirs.-Coll. of Bus. Admin.-Univ. of TX; United Way of El Paso; El Paso C of C; Jr. Achievement of El Paso-Bd. of Dirs.; El Paso Rehab. Center-Bd. of Dirs.; **HOME ADD:** 6012 Pinehurst, El Paso, TX 79912, (915)581-0158; **BUS ADD:** PO Box 9702, El Paso, TX 79987, (915)581-6691.

POLLAK, Mark——**B:** July 16, 1947, Paris, France, *Part.*, Piper & Marbury; **PRIM RE ACT:** Attorney; **SERVICES:** Rep. lenders, devels., public agencies in wide variety of RE and devel. activities; **EDUC:** BA, 1968, Hist., Brooklyn Coll.; **GRAD EDUC:** JD, MCP, 1972, Univ. of PA; **EDUC HONORS:** Cum Laude, Hist. Honors; **HOME ADD:** 315 Thornhill Rd., Baltimore, MD 21201; **BUS ADD:** Suite 1100, Charles Center S, 36 S. Charles St., Baltimore, MD 21201, (301)539-2530.

POLLAN, Stephen M.——**PRIM RE ACT:** Consultant, Attorney, Instructor; **SERVICES:** Debt structuring feasability; **REP CLIENTS:** Amer. Express, Natl. Bank of NA, Marymount Manhattan Coll.; **BUS ADD:** 1095 Park Ave., New York, NY 10028, (212)369-4746.

POLLARD, Forrest J.——**B:** Feb. 6, 1925, KS, *Co-owner, Broker*, DA-LY Realty & Ins. Inc.; **PRIM RE ACT:** Broker, Appraiser, Lender, Insuror; **SERVICES:** Farm/Ranch, Resid., Comml., Sales & Mgmt.; Full Line Ins. Agency; Appraising; Auctioneering; **REP CLIENTS:** City-Rural-Suburban; **PREV EMPLOY:** Personal Ins. Sales & Mgmt. Mutual & United of Ohaha; **PROFL AFFIL & HONORS:** GRI; CRS; CRB; PREB; IIAA; PIA; Past Pres. Grand Island Bd. of Realtors; Current Dist. VP NE Realtors Assn. - Nat. Consumers Fin. Assn.; **MIL SERV:** USN; 1942; **OTHER ACT & HONORS:** Masonic Lodge - Central Nebraska Shrine; Messiah Ev. Lutheran Church (LCA) Council Chairman; **HOME ADD:** 115 W. 23rd, Grand Island, NE 68801, (308)384-2521; **BUS ADD:** 2514 S. Locust St., PO Box 1846, Grand Island, NE 68802, (308)384-1101.

POLLARD, Frank E.——**B:** Oct. 26, 1932, Framingham, MA, *Atty.*, Frank E. Pollard Esq.; **PRIM RE ACT:** Attorney; **REP CLIENTS:** Greater Westfield Bd. of Realtors, Woronoco Savings Bank, Westfield Savings Bank; **PROFL AFFIL & HONORS:** Westfield Bar Assn., MA Bar Assn., Hampden Cty. Bar Assn., ABA; **EDUC:** BA, 1954, Prelaw, Northeastern Univ.; **GRAD EDUC:** JD, 1956, Boston Univ. Law School; **EDUC HONORS:** Hon. Soc. - all years; **OTHER ACT & HONORS:** Westfield C of C; Westfield Kiwanis, Westfield Boys Club Bd. of Dirs., Counsel and Bd. of Dir. Westfield Area Dev. Corp., Counsel Greater Westfield Bd. of Realtor; **HOME ADD:** 73 Glenwood Dr., Westfield, MA 01085, (413)562-6725; **BUS ADD:** 70 Court St., Westfield, MA 01085, (413)568-1476.

POLLARD, John N.——**B:** Aug. 14, 1952, Nashville, TN, *Dist. Sales Mgr.*, Burroughs Corp., BMG; **OTHER RE ACT:** Part-time Sales; Sales Mgmt.; **SERVICES:** Mktg. New Custom Homes; **PROFL AFFIL & HONORS:** AMA; **EDUC:** BBA, Mktg./ RE, SMU; **EDUC HONORS:** Hon.; **HOME ADD:** 2609 Ramblewood Dr., Carrollton, TX 75006; **BUS ADD:** 2609 Ramblewood Dr., Carrollton, TX 75006.

POLLARD, Ronald Terrell——**B:** Dec. 21, 1934, Cuba, TN, *Pres.*, Alpine Western Properties, Inc.; **PRIM RE ACT:** Broker, Consultant, Developer, Builder, Owner/Investor; **PREV EMPLOY:** Cmdr., USN (Naval Aviator) Commanding Officer, Reconnaisance Attack Squadron 14; **PROFL AFFIL & HONORS:** GRI; **EDUC:** BA, 1966, Poli. Sci., Memphis State Coll. - US Naval Postgrad. Sch.; **GRAD EDUC:** MBA, 1977, Gen./RE, Denver Univ.; **MIL SERV:** USN, Cmdr., 1955-1976, many decorations - highest Air Medal w/cluster of four; **HOME ADD:** PO Box 5126, 2800 Alpen Glow Way, Steamboat Village, CO 80499, (303)879-3418; **BUS ADD:** PO Box 5555, 1830 MT Werner Rd., Steamboat Village, CO 80499, (303)879-5100.

POLLARD, Thomas B., Jr.——**B:** July 24, 1933, Nashville, TN, *Partner*, Nexsen, Pruet, Jacobs & Pollard; **PRIM RE ACT:** Attorney; **SERVICES:** Land acquisitions, dispositions, gen. RE financing; **REP CLIENTS:** CT Gen. Life Ins. Co.; Mutual Benefit Life Ins. Co.; Westinghouse Electric Corp.; Bank of Amer., N.A.; First Nat. Bank of SC; The Binswanger Co.; **PROFL AFFIL & HONORS:** State, Cty. and Amer. Bar Assns.; **EDUC:** AB, 1954, Pol. Sci./Eng./Naval Sci. (NROTC), Univ. of SC; **GRAD EDUC:** LLB, 1959, Univ. of SC Law School; **MIL SERV:** USN, 1954-1956, Lt.j.g.; **HOME ADD:** Devils Backbone Rd., Rt. 2, Leesville, SC 29070, (803)799-9168; **BUS ADD:** PO Drawer 2426, Columbia, SC 29202.

POLLARD, Thomas E.——**B:** Dec. 6, 1934, Tenaha, TX, *Gen. Part.*, Delta Props. Ltd.; **PRIM RE ACT:** Broker, Consultant, Developer, Property Manager, Syndicator; **SERVICES:** Comml. & indus. RE, lease, sales, prop. mgmt., bus. sales, synd. & devel.; **REP CLIENTS:** Gould, IBM, Fed. Express, FinanceAmerica; **PREV EMPLOY:** VP & Gen. Mgr. The Levy Org., Rgnl. Mgr. (15 states) for RE, IBM Corp.; **EDUC:** BS, 1956, Sci. & Educ., East TX State Univ.; **GRAD EDUC:** MBA, 1977, Fin., Keller Grad. Sch.; **MIL SERV:** USAF, AZC; **OTHER ACT & HONORS:** Dir. C of C, Dir. B.R.Ryall YMCA; **HOME ADD:** 169 E Longfellow Dr., Wheaton, IL 60187, (312)668-5114; **BUS ADD:** 957 C N. Plum Grove Rd., Schaumburg, IL 60195, (312)843-1919.

POLLER, Jeri A.——B: Nov. 3, 1952, Tampa, FL, *Atty.*, Arvida Corp.; **PRIM RE ACT:** Attorney, Developer; **PROFL AFFIL & HONORS:** FL Bar Assn.; **EDUC:** AB, 1974, Pol. Sci., Boston Univ.; **GRAD EDUC:** JD, 1976, Univ. of FL; **EDUC HONORS:** Cum Laude; **BUS ADD:** POB 100, Boca Raton, FL 33432, (305)395-2000.

POLLIS, John P.——B: June 14, 1927, Boston, MA, *Atty.*, Armstrong, Pollis and Clapp; **PRIM RE ACT:** Attorney; **SERVICES:** All services required in RE related matters; **REP CLIENTS:** Attleborough Savings Bank, Attleboro, MA 02703; BayBank United, N. A., Taunton, MA 02780; **PREV EMPLOY:** Asst. Reg. of Deeds, Bristol Cty., Taunton, MA 02780, from 1953 to 1958; **PROFL AFFIL & HONORS:** ABA; MBA; MA Conveyancers Assn.; New England Land Title Assn.; Bristol Cty. and Fourth Dist. Bar Assns., Judge, Fourth Dist. Court, Bristol Cty., 1974-1977; **EDUC:** AA, 1948, Suffolk Univ.; **GRAD EDUC:** LLB, 1950, Suffolk Univ. Law School, Boston, MA; **EDUC HONORS:** Cum Laude; **MIL SERV:** USN; SM 2C; **OTHER ACT & HONORS:** Former Moderator, Former Town Counsel, Town of North Attleboro; MA RE Broker; Member of Home Builders Assn.; approved Atty. for various title co's.; former Pres. of N. Attleboro C of C; member of Exec. Bd., Annawon Council, Boy Scouts of Amer.; **HOME ADD:** 163 Raymond Hall Dr., N. Attleboro, MA 02760, (617)699-7782; **BUS ADD:** 52 N. Washington St., N. Attleborough, MA 02760, (617)695-3554.

POLLOCK, David S.——B: Dec. 11, 1949, Altoona, PA, *Atty.*, Jubelirer, Pass & Intieri, PC; **PRIM RE ACT:** Attorney; **SERVICES:** legal; **PREV EMPLOY:** Law clerk, Hon. Maurice Louik; **PROFL AFFIL & HONORS:** ABA, ATLA, Pa TLA, PBA, ACBA; **EDUC:** BA, 1970, PA State Univ.; **GRAD EDUC:** JD, 1974, Duquense Univ. Sch. of Law; **EDUC HONORS:** Law Review; **MIL SERV:** US Army Res., Spec. 4; **HOME ADD:** 1204 Malvern Ave., Pittsburgh, PA 15217, (412)681-1949; **BUS ADD:** 219 Ft. Pitt Blvd., Pittsburgh, PA 15222, (412)281-3850.

POLLOCK, Wilson F., Jr.——B: Mar. 22, 1940, Reading, PA, *Prin.*, ADD, Inc.; **PRIM RE ACT:** Architect; **SERVICES:** Arch., Int. design, master planning, adaptive re-use; **REP CLIENTS:** Pvt. devels., banks, ins. cos., high-tech. and other private corps.; **PREV EMPLOY:** Cambridge Seven Assoc., Sert, Jackson & Assoc.; **PROFL AFFIL & HONORS:** Amer. Inst. of Arch., MA Assn. of Arch., Boston Soc. of Arch., Nat. Council of Arch. Reg. Bds. Cert.; **EDUC:** BArch, 1963, PA State Univ.; **GRAD EDUC:** MS, 1968, Columbia Univ.; **OTHER ACT & HONORS:** Bd. of Dir., Newton Comm. Devel. Found; Tr., Jackson Homestead; **HOME ADD:** 52 Nonantum St., Newton, MA 02158, (617)527-2612; **BUS ADD:** 80 Prospect St., Cambridge, MA 02139, (617)661-0165.

POLUNSKY, Allan B.——B: Oct. 3, 1948, San Antonio, Bexar Cty., TX, *Atty. at Law*, Law Offices of Allan B. Polunsky; **PRIM RE ACT:** Attorney, Developer, Owner/Investor, Instructor, Syndicator; **SERVICES:** RE atty., synd., devel., investor; **REP CLIENTS:** RE brokers, title cos., mort. cos., RE investors; **PROFL AFFIL & HONORS:** ABA (Hist. Preservation Law Comm.); State Bar of TX (Sect. of RE, Probate and Trust Law); San Antonio Bar Assn.; **EDUC:** BA, 1971, Pol. Sci., Univ. of TX at Austin; **GRAD EDUC:** JD, 1975, Law, St. Mary's Univ. of San Antonio; **EDUC HONORS:** Pi Sigma Alpha, Nat. Honorary Pol. Sci.; Dean's List, Phi Delta Phi, Nat. Hon. Frat.; Dean's List; **OTHER ACT & HONORS:** VChmn., San Antonio Zoning Commn.; Bd. of Dirs., San Antonio Builder's Assn.; Realtor-Lawyer Comm., TX Assn. of Realtors; Instr. of RE Law, San Antonio Bd. of Realtors; Dir., San Antonio River Auth.; VChmn., San Antonio Local Devel. Co.; Pres., City of San Antonio Indus. Devel. Auth.; **HOME ADD:** 13707 Bluffrock, San Antonio, TX 78216, (512)494-4191; **BUS ADD:** Ste. 310, Mercantile Bank Bldg., San Antonio, TX 78216, (512)349-4488.

POMERANTZ, John L.——*Pres.*, Leslie Fay, Inc.; **PRIM RE ACT:** Property Manager; **BUS ADD:** 1400 Broadway, New York, NY 10018, (212)221-4000.*

POMERANTZ, Marvin——B: May 19, 1934, NY, *Treas.*, Community Serv. Inc., Controller; **PRIM RE ACT:** Consultant; **OTHER RE ACT:** Fin. and audit; **SERVICES:** Prep. of fin. statements, budgets cash flow, projections, audits, etc.; **REP CLIENTS:** Amalgamated Housing Corp., Park Reservoir Housing Corp., United Housing Retirement Fund, United Housing Found., Inc. Mutual Redevel. Houses; **PREV EMPLOY:** IRS, CFA firm; **EDUC:** BS, 1957, Acctg., Brooklyn Coll.; **GRAD EDUC:** NY Univ.; **EDUC HONORS:** Prin. & Practice of RE; **MIL SERV:** US Army; **OTHER ACT & HONORS:** Notary Public, State of NY, Bd. Member of Urban Comm. Insurance Co., & Rochdale Inst.; **HOME ADD:** 2790 West 5th St., Brooklyn, NY 11224, (212)996-5440; **BUS ADD:** 465 Grand St., New York, NY 10002, (212)673-3900.

POMP, Howard——B: Sept. 25, 1938, NY, NY, *Pres.*, First Southern Realty Grp., Inc.; **PRIM RE ACT:** Broker, Consultant, Developer, Builder; **SERVICES:** Consultation, comml., new home subdiv. sales; **PROFL AFFIL & HONORS:** Orlando-Winter Park Bd. of Realtors; Mid-FL Home Builders Assn.; **EDUC:** B.S.A., 1960, Bus. Econs., Univ. of GA; **OTHER ACT & HONORS:** Dir. of Home Owners Warranty Corp. of Mid-FL; **HOME ADD:** 110 Sand Pine Ln., Longwood, FL 32750; **BUS ADD:** 826 N. Irma Ave., Orlando, FL 32803, (305)841-3116.

PONGRACE, Otto W.——B: July 8, 1911, NY, NY, *Plant Location Specialist*, Self-Employed; **PRIM RE ACT:** Broker, Consultant, Engineer, Developer; **PREV EMPLOY:** Dir. of Indus. Devel., Penn Central Trans. Co.; **PROFL AFFIL & HONORS:** Amer. Economic Devel. Council; Engrg. Soc. Detroit, Fellow & Cert. Ind. Dev., AEDC; Lic. Realtor, NY and PA; **EDUC:** BS, 1935, CE, MI State Univ.; **GRAD EDUC:** Const., Devel., Environment, Transportation, Colombia Univ., Wayne Univ., Univ. of MI, OK Univ.; **MIL SERV:** AA Arty., Col., Theatre Ribbons, Amer. PAC; **OTHER ACT & HONORS:** Councilman, City of Grosse Pointe, Lecturer on Indus. Devel. Activities; **HOME ADD:** 629 Rivard Blvd., Grosse Pointe, MI 48230, (313)881-1498; **BUS ADD:** 629 Rivard Blvd., Grosse Pointe, MI 48230, (313)881-1498.

PONS, Albert E.——B: Aug. 21, 1926, New Orleans, LA, *Pres.*, Sun Belt Management Corp.; **PRIM RE ACT:** Broker, Consultant, Developer, Owner/Investor, Instructor, Property Manager, Syndicator; **SERVICES:** Prop. mgmt., brokerage, RE investment counseling, consulting; **REP CLIENTS:** Indiv. and synd. investors in income prop. and condo. assns., court-appointed receiver; **PREV EMPLOY:** Episcopal Ministry, 1949-69; **PROFL AFFIL & HONORS:** Nat. Apt. Assn.; OK Multi-Housing Assn.; Apt. Assn. of Central OK; Greater Oklahoma City Chap. of IREM, CPM; **EDUC:** BA, 1946, Eng., Univ. of the South, Sewanee, TN (previously attended Tulane Univ.); **GRAD EDUC:** MA, 1949, Theology, Univ. of the South, Sewanee, TN; **EDUC HONORS:** Study Grant, St. Austine's Coll., Canterbury, England, 1962-63; **HOME ADD:** 401 N.W. 34th, Oklahoma City, OK 73118, (405)521-1658; **BUS ADD:** 527 N.W. 23rd, P.O. Box 60758, Oklahoma City, OK 73146, (405)521-1078.

PONTIUS, H. Jackson——*Ed.*, Calif. Real Estate Assn., CA Real Estate Assn. Annual Roster; **PRIM RE ACT:** Real Estate Publisher; **BUS ADD:** 505 Shatto Place, Los Angeles, CA 90020, (213)380-7190.*

POOLE, Charles E., Jr.——B: Oct. 23, 1932, Raleigh, NC, *Pres.1976*, Bath & Kitchen Designers, Inc.; **OTHER RE ACT:** Interior remodel & new const.; **SERVICES:** Bath, Kitchen and other design & execution, single & multiple; **REP CLIENTS:** Indiv., architects, bldrs., realtors; **PROFL AFFIL & HONORS:** Amer. Inst. of Kitchen Dealers; FL State Cert. Genl. Contractor; **EDUC:** BS, 1956, Military Art & Engrg., U.S. Military Academy, West Point, NY; **GRAD EDUC:** MA, 1964, German Linguistics, Univ. of Mainz, Germany & Middlebury Coll., VT; **MIL SERV:** US Army 1949-75, Lt. Col.(ret.), Legion of Merit, twice; Bronze star three; Commendation medal, twice; **OTHER ACT & HONORS:** Administrative Bd. 1st United Methodist, Ft. Lauderdale; **HOME ADD:** 4321 NE 28th Ave., Ft.Lauderdale, FL 33308, (305)561-1589; **BUS ADD:** 4711 N. Dixie Hwy., Ft. Lauderdale, FL 33334, (305)772-2221.

POOLE, Dennis K.——B: Nov. 7. 1950, Blackfoot, ID, *Atty.*, Poole, Cannon & Ward; **PRIM RE ACT:** Attorney; **REP CLIENTS:** Devel. of resid. and comml. props.; **PROFL AFFIL & HONORS:** Amer. Bar Assn.; UT State Bar, Salt Lake Cty. Bar; **EDUC:** BBA, 1973, Fin., ID State Univ.; **GRAD EDUC:** JD, 1976, J. Reuben Clark Law School; Brigham Young Univ.; **EDUC HONORS:** Honors, Magna Cum Laude; **HOME ADD:** 503 W 5987 So., Murray, UT 84107, (801)261-3458; **BUS ADD:** 4885 South 900 East, Suite 210, Salt Lake City, UT 84117, (801)263-3344.

POOLE, Harrison——*Treasurer*, Philip Morris; **PRIM RE ACT:** Property Manager; **BUS ADD:** 100 Park Ave., New York, NY 10017, (212)679-1800.*

POOLE, James R.——**B:** May 19, 1941, Englewood, NJ, *Partner*, James R. Poole & Co.; **PRIM RE ACT:** Owner/Investor, Property Manager, Syndicator; **OTHER RE ACT:** Mort. Banker; **PREV EMPLOY:** Pres., Underwood Mort. & Title Co.; **PROFL AFFIL & HONORS:** NAIOP; Chmn. of membership committee NJ Chap., IREBA; MBA of NJ, CMB; **EDUC:** BBA, 1963, Bus./Fin., Fairfield Univ.; **GRAD EDUC:** MBA, 1967, Econ./Fin., Fairleigh Dickinson Univ.; **OTHER ACT & HONORS:** Bd. of Dir., Midland Bank; **HOME ADD:** 279 W. End Ave., Ridgewood, NJ 07450, (201)447-4067; **BUS ADD:** 550 Broad St., Suite 1203, Newark, NJ 07102, (201)623-2424.

POOLE, William T., Jr.——**B:** May 4, 1948, Philadelphia, PA, *RE Dir.*, A.V. Williams Trust, RE; **PRIM RE ACT:** Broker, Consultant, Developer, Property Manager; **SERVICES:** Devel. and mgmt. of income prop., shopping ctrs. & manufactured housing communities; **PREV EMPLOY:** Wachouia Mort. Co.-Mort. banking (income prop. div.) and advisor to Wachouia Realty Investments (REIT); **PROFL AFFIL & HONORS:** ICSC; Bd. of Dir. of MD Manufactured Housing Assn.; RE Broker, MD and NC; **EDUC:** BS, 1970, Commerce, Wash. & Lee Univ.; **GRAD EDUC:** MBA, 1974, RE Fin., Wharton School of Fin., Univ. of PA; **EDUC HONORS:** Deans List, Honor Roll; **MIL SERV:** USNR, Lt.j.g.; **OTHER ACT & HONORS:** Trustee, Towson Presbyterian Church; Other Bus. Tel. (301)574-8666; **HOME ADD:** 518 Dunkirk Rd., Baltimore, MD 21212, (301)377-4063; **BUS ADD:** 1460 Martin Blvd., Baltimore, MD 21220, (301)686-1000.

POPKESS, Alfred W.——**B:** Aug. 30, 1944, Washington, DC, *Atty.-Partner*, Mackenzie Smith Lewis Michell & Hughes; **PRIM RE ACT:** Attorney; **REP CLIENTS:** Bankers Trust Co., of Albany, N.A.; W.J. Camperlino Custom Homes, Inc.; **PROFL AFFIL & HONORS:** ABA, NY State Bar Assn., Onondaga Bar Assn.; **EDUC:** BA, 1966, Econ., OH Wesleyan Univ.; **GRAD EDUC:** JD, 1969, Law, St. Johns Law School; **MIL SERV:** US Army; **OTHER ACT & HONORS:** Advisory Bd. Dirs. Bankers Trust Co. of Albany N.A.; House of Delegates NY State Bar Assn.; Exec. Comm. Young Lawyers Sect. of NY State Bar Assn.; **HOME ADD:** 1944 Amnaste Ln., Marcellus, NY 13108, (315)673-4765; **BUS ADD:** Onon. Savings Bank Bldg., Syracuse, NY 13202, (315)474-7571.

POPKO, Julian S.——**B:** Dec. 20, 1938, *Pres.*, Popko Realty; **PRIM RE ACT:** Broker, Builder, Property Manager, Owner/Investor; **PROFL AFFIL & HONORS:** NH NAR; Rental Housing Assoc. of Springfield; Springfield Home Builders; **MIL SERV:** US Army 1962-1964; **OTHER ACT & HONORS:** Past Pres. of Indian Orchard C of C; Member of Elks, Moose; **HOME ADD:** 30 Meadow St., Indian Orchard, MA 01151, (413)543-1956; **BUS ADD:** 20 Parker St., Springfield, MA 01151, (413)543-5000.

POPPEN, Robert A.——**B:** Jan. 12, 1928, Detroit, MI, *Broker*, Poppen & Assoc.; **PRIM RE ACT:** Broker, Developer, Syndicator; **OTHER RE ACT:** Franchise Site Locator; **SERVICES:** Devel. & synd. of comml. & indus. props.; **REP CLIENTS:** Indiv. investors, franchisees; **PREV EMPLOY:** Mort. Banking 1962-68; **PROFL AFFIL & HONORS:** RESSI, RNMI, CCIM; **EDUC:** BS, 1949, Gen. Sci., Univ. of IA; **GRAD EDUC:** MS, 1951, Fisheries Biology, OH State Univ.; **OTHER ACT & HONORS:** Rotary, Natl. Ski Patrol System; **HOME ADD:** 1908 Carmel Ave., Eugene, OR 97401, (503)343-9669; **BUS ADD:** 1599 Oak St., Eugene, OR 97401, (503)485-0808.

PORRECA, Roland L.——**B:** Feb. 26, 1920, Philadelphia, PA, *Owner*, Roland L. Porreca; **PRIM RE ACT:** Appraiser; **SERVICES:** RE Appraisals; **REP CLIENTS:** Banks, S&L's, City of Philadelphia, Attys., State Hwy. Dept., Gen. Public; **PROFL AFFIL & HONORS:** AIREA; SREA; Amer. Right of Way Assn.; Nat. Assn. of RE Bds., MAI, SRPA, Sr. Member Amer. Right of Way; **EDUC:** BS, 1943, Commerce, Temple Univ.; **MIL SERV:** US Army, Sgt., Five battle stars; **HOME ADD:** 1219 W Wynnewood Rd., Wynnewood, PA 19096; **BUS ADD:** 1732 S Broad St., Philadelphis, PA 19145, (215)465-3635.

PORT, Richard B.——**B:** Sept. 17, 1917, Chicago, *Chmn.*, Rich Port, Realtor; **PRIM RE ACT:** Broker, Consultant, Appraiser; **OTHER RE ACT:** Prop. mgmt. appraising; **SERVICES:** Resid., comml., indus., brokerage; **REP CLIENTS:** All major corps.; **PROFL AFFIL & HONORS:** SREA, RNMI, Realtor of yr. IL; Past Pres. NAR, CRB, CRS, SRA; **EDUC:** BS, 1939, Univ. of IL, St. Norbert Coll.; **MIL SERV:** US Army, Inf., Brig. Gen., 1939-1972; **OTHER ACT & HONORS:** Electoral Coll., Nat. Convention Delegate, State Central Comitteeman, Past Chmn. W. Suburban YMCA, Past Lt. Gov. Kiwanis, Past State Comdr. Military Order World Wars; **HOME ADD:** 801 N. Spring Ave., Lagrange Park, IL 60525, (312)352-5869; **BUS ADD:** 547 S. Lagrange Rd., Lagrange, IL 60525, (312)354-9250.

PORTER, Alan B.——**B:** April 14, 1954, Modesto, CA, *Atty.*, Kerner, Colangelo & Implay; **PRIM RE ACT:** Attorney; **PROFL AFFIL & HONORS:** CA State Bar Assn.; **EDUC:** AB, 1976, Geography, Univ. of CA at Berkeley; **GRAD EDUC:** JD, 1979, Law, Hastings Coll. of Law; **EDUC HONORS:** Summa cum laude, Phi Beta Kappa, Chancellor's Award; **HOME ADD:** 1238 Willard St., San Francisco, CA 94117, (415)681-1273; **BUS ADD:** 114 Sansome St., Suite 500, S.F., CA 94104, (415)986-1520.

PORTER, Clyde E.——**B:** Aug. 5, 1954, San Antonio, TX, *VP Comml., Indus. & Land Devel.*, Cook Realtors; **PRIM RE ACT:** Consultant, Developer, Property Manager, Syndicator; **OTHER RE ACT:** Comml., Indus., Land Devel. & Sales; **SERVICES:** Locating and packaging of comml. & indus., agric. props. for sale; **PROFL AFFIL & HONORS:** Bakersfield C of C, Ambassador; NAR; ULI; CA Assn. of Realtors; Nat. RE Investors; **EDUC:** AA, 1976, Poli. Sci., Econ.; RE Law; Fin., Bakersfield Coll.; **BUS ADD:** 1301 California Ave., Bakersfield, CA 93304, (805)327-1751.

PORTER, Geraldine L.——**B:** Dec. 30, 1921, Okmulgee, OK, *Broker-Assoc.*, L & S Development Corp.; **PRIM RE ACT:** Broker, Builder; **SERVICES:** Specialize in resid. sales; **PREV EMPLOY:** Co-owner, broker and bldg. contractor, Porter Realty & Const. Co. 1970-76; **PROFL AFFIL & HONORS:** Met. Tulsa Bd. of Realtors, RNMI, NAR, Amer. Bus. Women's Assn., GRI, CRB, CRS, Woman of the Yr. in 1976, Hobbs Charter Chapt. Amer. Bus. Women's Assn., *Who's Who of American Women 1977 and 1979*; **OTHER ACT & HONORS:** Faith United Methodist Church; **HOME ADD:** 5946 E. 96th Ct., Tulsa, OK 74136, (918)299-6692; **BUS ADD:** 5215 E. 71st St., Ste. 1000, Tulsa, OK 74136, (918)492-7206.

PORTER, Howard J., Jr.——**B:** Dec. 30, Birmingham, AL, *Pres.*, H. J. Porter & Associates, Inc.; **PRIM RE ACT:** Consultant, Appraiser, Syndicator; **SERVICES:** Appraisals, mkt. research, and analysis; **REP CLIENTS:** Birmingham Trust National Bank, Brookwood Health Services, Colonial Financial Services, US Postal Service; **PREV EMPLOY:** The Hearn Co., RE Appraisers & Consultants, Birmingham, AL; **PROFL AFFIL & HONORS:** AIREA, Soc. of RE Appraisers, Intl. Right of Way Assn., Nat. Assn. of Review Appraisers, Nat. Assn. of Indus. & Office Parks, RESSI, MAI, SRPA, CRA, Young Advisory Council, SREA; **EDUC:** BBA, 1974, Econ. - Fin., Auburn Univ.; **MIL SERV:** Army - Nat. Guard, Sgt.; **OTHER ACT & HONORS:** Bd. of Deacons, Asst. Treas. - South Highland Presbyterian Church, State Chmn. AL SREA Mkt. Data Center, Inc.; **HOME ADD:** 716 Euclid Ave., Birmingham, AL 35213, (205)870-1652; **BUS ADD:** 2117 Magnolia Ave., Suite 102, Birmingham, AL 35205, (205)323-1612.

PORTER, James Gordon, Jr.——**B:** Mar. 6, 1937, Sewickley, PA, *Atty. at Law*; **PRIM RE ACT:** Attorney; **EDUC:** BS, 1962, Indus. mgmt., econ., Wharton, Univ. of PA; **GRAD EDUC:** JD, 1972, Villanova Univ. Sch. of Law; **MIL SERV:** US Army, 1957-59; **HOME ADD:** 120 E. Ashbridge St., West Chester, PA 19380, (215)692-6139; **BUS ADD:** 103 S. High St. Box 381, West Chester, PA 19380, (215)431-2600.

PORTER, Max L.——**B:** Oct. 25, 1942, Hamburg, IA, *Structural Engrg.*, Porter Engineering; **PRIM RE ACT:** Engineer; **SERVICES:** Structural engrg. analysis and design; **PREV EMPLOY:** Prof., Civil Engrg. Dept., IA State Univ.; **PROFL AFFIL & HONORS:** NSPE, ASCE, IES, IABSE, Nat. Young Engr. of Yr. in 1978, *Who's Who in Engrg.*; **EDUC:** BCE, 1965, IA State Univ.; **GRAD EDUC:** MS, 1968, Structural Engrg., IA State Univ.; PhD, 1974, IA State Univ.; **EDUC HONORS:** Chi Epsilon, Sigma Xi, Tau Beta Pi, Sigma Xi; **MIL SERV:** US Army; **HOME ADD:** 3224 Wyman St., Ames, IA 50010, (515)292-3321; **BUS ADD:** 3224 Kingman, Ames, IA 50010, (515) 292-3321.

PORTER, Robert C., III——**B:** Dec. 3, 1954, Cincinnati, OH, *Atty.*, Porter & McKinney; **PRIM RE ACT:** Attorney; **SERVICES:** Legal; **REP CLIENTS:** Paul Homes, Inc.; **PROFL AFFIL & HONORS:** Cincinnati Bar Assn., OH Bar Assn., ABA; **EDUC:** AB, 1976, Econ. and Poli. Sci., Univ. of MI; **GRAD EDUC:** JD, 1979, Univ. of Cincinnati; **HOME ADD:** 6737 Murray Ave., Cincinnati, OH 45227, (513)561-5443; **BUS ADD:** 2012 Central Trust Twr., Cincinnati, OH 45202, (513)621-3993.

PORTER, Steven K.——**B:** Apr. 28, 1951, Oceanside, NY, *Assoc.*, Schulte Roth & Zabel; **PRIM RE ACT:** Attorney; **PREV EMPLOY:** Dreyer and Traub, 90 Park Ave., NY, NY; **PROFL AFFIL & HONORS:** ABA, Assn. of the Bar of the City of NY, NY State Bar Assn., NY Cty. Bar Assn.; **EDUC:** BA, 1973, Hist., Princeton Univ.; **GRAD EDUC:** JD, 1976, Law, Hofstra Univ. School of Law; **EDUC HONORS:** Outstanding Student in Corporate Law; **OTHER ACT & HONORS:** Lecturer at NYU RE Inst.; **HOME ADD:** 27 Palmer Ave.,

Mt. Vernon, NY 10552, (914)667-0428; **BUS ADD:** 460 Park Ave., New York, NY 10022, (212)758-0404.

PORTER, Thomas H., Jr.——B: Dec. 24, 1928, Atlanta, GA, *Project Mgr.*, The Coca-Cola Co., Atlanta Office Complex Devel. Dept.; **PRIM RE ACT:** Architect, Property Manager; **PREV EMPLOY:** Bothwell & Nash Architects, Atlanta; Millard and Spratline Devels., Atlanta; **PROFL AFFIL & HONORS:** Bldg. Owners & Mgmt. Inst., Atlanta; CSI, Atlanta, Bldg. Owners & Mgmt. Inst., Atlanta, Bd. of Dirs.; **EDUC:** 1951, Bldg. Const./Arch., GA Inst. of Tech.; **GRAD EDUC:** BA, 1966, Mgmt./RE, GA State Univ.; **MIL SERV:** US Army, 1946-1948; **OTHER ACT & HONORS:** Pres., N.W. Atlanta Bus. Assn., 1977-1979; Bd. Member, GA State Univ. Alumni Assn.; **HOME ADD:** 3648 Snapringer Rd., Lithonia, GA 30058, (404)981-2606; **BUS ADD:** PO Drawer 1734, Atlanta, GA 30301, (404)898-4061.

PORTER, Thomas J.——B: June 24, 1934, New Rochelle, NY, *Dir., RE*, Airco Inc.; **OTHER RE ACT:** Corp. RE Mgr.; **SERVICES:** Purchasing, selling, leasing of corp. RE; **PREV EMPLOY:** Asst. Mgr. RE, Amer. Standard; RE Coordinator, Gen. Foods Corp.; **PROFL AFFIL & HONORS:** Indus. Devel. Research Council; **EDUC:** 1957, Fin., Iona Coll.; **HOME ADD:** 54 Interlaken Ave., New Rochelle, NY 10801, (914)636-6371; **BUS ADD:** 85 Chestnut Ridge Rd., Montvale, NJ 07645.

PORTER, William J., Jr.——B: Sept. 9, 1909, Kalamazoo, MI, *Pres.*, Porter Realty Co.; **PRIM RE ACT:** Broker, Consultant, Appraiser, Property Manager; **PROFL AFFIL & HONORS:** Greater Lansing Bd. of Realtors, CPM; SREA; ASA; SIR; MAI; 1979 Greater Lansing Community Service Award; 1981 inducted into Capitol Area Bus. Hall of Fame; Realtor of the Year 1965; **EDUC:** BEE, 1932, Elec. Engrg., MI State Univ.; **OTHER ACT & HONORS:** Lansing Econ. Devel. Bd.; Lansing Hospital Fin. Authority; Trinity Lutheran Church; Tau Beta Pi; **HOME TEL:** (517)485-5993; **BUS ADD:** 109 W. Michigan Ave., Suite 800, Lansing, MI 48933, (517)485-7226.

PORTIS, John——*Exec. Secy.*, W. Virginia, WV Real Estate Commission; **PRIM RE ACT:** Property Manager; **BUS ADD:** 1033 Quarris St., Ste. 400, Charleston, WV 25301, (304)348-3555.*

PORTISS, Robert W.——B: May 13, 1943, Enderlin, ND, *Dir. Mktg. and Transportation*, Tulsa Port of Catoosa; **OTHER RE ACT:** Marketing; Advertising & Transportation; **SERVICES:** Site location analysis & foreign trade zones; **PREV EMPLOY:** Landmark land Inc.; Clarkdale Realty, Inc.; **PROFL AFFIL & HONORS:** S. Indus. devel. council; AR-OK Port Operation Assn., Grad. of Indus. Devel. Inst.; Univ. of OK, Certified Indus. Devel. (CID); **EDUC:** BS/ AA, 1970, Econ./Engrg., Bismarck Jr. Coll., ND; **GRAD EDUC:** MS, 1972, Econ., ND State Univ.; **MIL SERV:** USN, E-5, Good Conduct, Spec. Serv.; **OTHER ACT & HONORS:** Masonic & Shriner memberships, Church Comm.; **HOME ADD:** 10331 E. 26th St., Tulsa, OK 74129, (918)665-3371; **BUS ADD:** Catoosa, OK 74015, (918)266-2291.

PORTLE, Harold F., Jr.——B: Oct. 4, 1933, Worcester, MA, *Dir. of Leasing*, John Hancock Mutual Life Ins. Co., Bldg. Mgmt. & Constr.; **OTHER RE ACT:** Leasing office space in Home Office Complex, renting roof Antenna sites and overseeing operation of 1,800 car parking facility; **PROFL AFFIL & HONORS:** BOMA; **EDUC:** AS, 1954, Retail Merch., Becker Jr. Coll.; **GRAD EDUC:** Bus. Mgmt., Northeastern Univ.; **OTHER ACT & HONORS:** Back Bay Assn., Dir. 1975 to present; **HOME ADD:** 87 Thayer Cir., Randolph, MA 02368, (617)961-5534; **BUS ADD:** 200 Clarendon St., Boston, MA 02117, (617)421-2076.

POSILLICO, F. James——B: Mar. 30, 1921, Westbury, NY, *VP*, Posillico Const. Co., Inc.; **PRIM RE ACT:** Developer, Engineer, Builder, Property Manager; **PROFL AFFIL & HONORS:** NY State Soc. PE, NY State Lic. PE; **EDUC:** BCE, 1942, Civil Engrg., Polytech. Inst. Brooklyn; **EDUC HONORS:** Tau Beta Pi; **MIL SERV:** US Army, 1945, Pfc; **OTHER ACT & HONORS:** 1950-1959, 1975-1978, Tr., Westbury Bd. of Educ.; 1977-Present, Dir. Westbury Fed. S & L; 1974-Present, Member Village of Old Westbury Planning Bd.; 1980-Present, Member, Village of Old Westbury Bd. of Trustees; **HOME ADD:** 8 August Lane, Old Westbury, NY 11568, (516)626-2897; **BUS ADD:** 31 Tennyson Ave., Westbury, NY 11590, (516)333-0666.

POST, Gary M.——B: June 2, 1948, Boston, MA; **PRIM RE ACT:** Owner/Investor, Property Manager, Syndicator; **SERVICES:** Investment counseling; **REP CLIENTS:** Trusts, larger indiv. investors; **PREV EMPLOY:** McKinsey & Co., Union Bank; **EDUC:** AB, 1971, Hist., Stanford Univ.; **GRAD EDUC:** MBA, 1973, Fin., RE, UCLA; **EDUC HONORS:** Dept. Econ. honors; **BUS ADD:** 1403 Marinette Rd., Pacific Palisades, CA 90272, (213)454-7003.

POST, Robert A.——*VP Fin. & Treas.*, Champion Home Builders; **PRIM RE ACT:** Property Manager; **BUS ADD:** 5573 E. North St., Dryden, MI 48428, (313)796-2211.*

POSTAL, David R.——B: Jan. 12, 1945, Grand Rapids, MI, *Partner*, Holland & Postal; **PRIM RE ACT:** Consultant, Attorney, Instructor; **SERVICES:** Legal services to synds., and devels. covering all areas. Gen. course instruction; **REP CLIENTS:** Corp. Investment & Realty Inc., The Mgmt. Group Inc., Black Cloud Building Corp., Citadel Investment Group; **PREV EMPLOY:** Pres. Allstate School of RE; **PROFL AFFIL & HONORS:** State Bar ob AZ, ABA (Real Property and Probate Div.); **EDUC:** BA, 1968, Poli. Sci., Hist., MI State Univ.; **GRAD EDUC:** JD, 1975, Gen. Bus. and Real Prop., Univ. of MI Law School; **EDUC HONORS:** Regents Scholarship, Cum Laude; **MIL SERV:** US Army, Lt.; **OTHER ACT & HONORS:** Kiwanis, Pres. of the Bd. New Hope for the Blind; **HOME ADD:** 3709 West Morten, Phoenix, AZ 85021, (602)841-8961; **BUS ADD:** 3550 North Central Ave., Suite 1101, Phoenix, AZ 85012, (602)264-2712.

POSTEN, Blair J.——B: May 23, 1946, Hayward, CA, *Owner*, The Posten Co., Realtors; **PRIM RE ACT:** Broker, Syndicator, Consultant, Property Manager, Owner/Investor; **SERVICES:** RE Investment Counseling, Tax Planning, Sponsor of Single Family Home & Townhome Synd., Prop. Mgmt.; **REP CLIENTS:** Indiv. Investors; **PROFL AFFIL & HONORS:** CA Assn. of Realtors; NAR, RE Synd. Div., San Jose RE Bd. Million Dollar Sales Award 1975 & 1976; **EDUC:** BS, 1969, Bus. & Indus. Mgmt., San Jose State Univ.; **MIL SERV:** US Army, E-5, Purple Heart, Combat Infantryman's Badge, Army Accomodation Medal with 1st Oak Leaf Cluster; **HOME ADD:** 1410 Kew Gardens Ct., San Jose, CA 95120, (408)997-7842; **BUS ADD:** 2901 Moorpark Ave., Suite 270, San Jose, CA 95128, (408)241-3212.

POTAMKIN, Meyer P.——*Pres.*, Boulevard Mort. Co.; **PRIM RE ACT:** Broker, Lender, Owner/Investor; **PROFL AFFIL & HONORS:** MBAA; **EDUC:** BBA, 1932, Dickinson Coll.; **GRAD EDUC:** MA, 1941, Soc. Work, Temple Univ.; **EDUC HONORS:** Phi Epsilon Pi; **OTHER ACT & HONORS:** Pres. Blvd. Mort. Co, Bd. Trs. Phila. Coll. of Art, Tr. Phila. Museum Art, Pres. Crime Prevention Assn., BOD Settlement Music School, Jewish Youth Council, United Fund; **BUS ADD:** 2608 Cottman Ave., Phila., PA 19149, (215)335-7760.

POTENZIANI, Frank A.——B: Jan. 30, 1945, Aurora, IL, *Atty. at Law*; **PRIM RE ACT:** Attorney, Owner/Investor; **PREV EMPLOY:** United Bank of Denver, Albuquerque Nat. Bank, First Nat. Bank of Boston; **PROFL AFFIL & HONORS:** ABA, NM Bar Assn., Albuquerque Bar Assn., Amer. Jurisprudence Award, Estates 1978; **EDUC:** BA Arts and Letters, 1967, Econ., Pre-profl., Univ. of Notre Dame; **GRAD EDUC:** JD, 1978, Univ. of NM; **EDUC HONORS:** Amjur Award; **OTHER ACT & HONORS:** Dir., Mountain States Fin. Corp.; Dir., Grants State Bank, Dir., Evergreen Ins. Servs., Inc.; Bus. Advisory Council, Univ. of Notre Dame; Dir., Big Bros., Big Sisters of Amer.; **BUS ADD:** PO Box 4098, Albuquerque, NM 87196.

POTHIER, Rose——B: Mar. 8, 1943, *Atty.*, Pothier & Hinrichs; **PRIM RE ACT:** Attorney; **SERVICES:** Legal Services; **PREV EMPLOY:** Sr. VP with a mortgage banking company; **PROFL AFFIL & HONORS:** ABA, CA Bar Assn., CA Trial Lawyers Assn., Orange Cty. Bar Assn., CA Licensed RE broker, CA Escrow Assn., Assn. of Profl. Mort. Women, Charter 100; **GRAD EDUC:** BS, 1976, Law, Western State Univ.; JD, 1978, Law, Western State Univ., College of Law; **OTHER ACT & HONORS:** Speaker/lecturer on RE, fin., escrow & legal subject matters; **BUS ADD:** 2122 N. Broadway, Suite 100, Santa Ana, CA 92706, (714)953-8580.

POTT, Gordon A.——*Mgr. Corp RE*, American Cyanamid Co.; **PRIM RE ACT:** Property Manager; **BUS ADD:** Berdan Ave., Wayne, NJ 07470, (201)831-2000.*

POTTER, Charles J.——B: Sept. 6, 1946, Newton, MA, *VP*, Real Property Data Systems, Inc., Legal; **PRIM RE ACT:** Attorney, Appraiser, Property Manager; **SERVICES:** Statistical Analysis-Computer Assisted Mass Approval CAMA Valuations-RE Law; **REP CLIENTS:** Municipalities, Indivs., Comml. Devels.; **PREV EMPLOY:** RE Sales, Pvt. & Public Housing Mgmt., Consultants; **PROFL AFFIL & HONORS:** Boston Bar Assn. (Real Property), ABA, MA Bar Assn.; **EDUC:** BA, 1970, English/Hist., New England Coll., Henniker, NH; **GRAD EDUC:** JD, 1975, Law, New England Law School, Boston, MA; **MIL SERV:** USAR, E-5 1970-1976; **OTHER ACT & HONORS:** Lincoln Inst., Cambridge, MA; **HOME ADD:** 3 Timber Ln., Wayland, MA 01778, (617)653-0487; **BUS ADD:** Edgell Station

Box 2215, Framingham, MA 01701, (617)653-7703.

POTTER, George E.——**B:** May 11, 1921, Detroit, MI, *Dir. of Leasing*, C.W. Whittier & Bros.; **PRIM RE ACT:** Property Manager; **OTHER RE ACT:** Leasing & tenant relations; **PREV EMPLOY:** VP, Lang, Henan Inc., Detroit; Prop. Mgmt., all props.; **PROFL AFFIL & HONORS:** BOMA; Boston RD Bd., Boston & Cape Cod, Former Pres., Detroit BOMA; **EDUC:** 1947, Indus./Personnel, MI State Univ./Univ. of MI; **MIL SERV:** USAF, 1st Lt.; **HOME ADD:** 220 Haynes Rd., Sudbury, MA 01776, (617)443-2542; **BUS ADD:** One Federal St., Boston, MA 02110, (617)482-6000.

POTTER, James T.——**B:** Feb. 24, 1928, Madison, WI, *Pres.*, Potter, Lawson & Pawlowsky, Inc.; **PRIM RE ACT:** Architect; **SERVICES:** Complete Arch. & Design/Build Servs.; **REP CLIENTS:** CUNA Mutual Ins. Soc., Verex Ins. Co., WI Century Harbor; **PROFL AFFIL & HONORS:** AIA; **EDUC:** 1953, Arch., Univ. of MI; **OTHER ACT & HONORS:** Member Bd. of Dir. Natl. Mutual Benefit Ins., Madison W Rotary; **HOME ADD:** 3514 Lake Mendota Dr., Madison, WI 53705, (608)238-3948; **BUS ADD:** 15 Ellis Potter Ct., Madison, WI 53711, (608)274-2741.

POTTER, Richard B.——**B:** Jan. 17, 1947, Wash., DC, *Part.*, Compton, Compton & Potter, Litigation; **PRIM RE ACT:** Attorney; **SERVICES:** Legal counsel; zoning; subdiv.; comml. & resid. settlements; **REP CLIENTS:** Edward R. Carr & Assoc., Nat. Birchwood Corp., Sorrenson Constr. Corp., Battlefield Builders Co.; **PREV EMPLOY:** Assoc. Counsel, Compton, Latimer & Compton since law school grad. until 1979 partnership status; **PROFL AFFIL & HONORS:** ABA Member Probate & Prop. Sect.; VA State Bar Assn. Prince William Cty. Bar Assn.; ALTLA; **EDUC:** AB, 1969, Hist., Eng., Coll. of William & Mary, Williamsburg, VA; **GRAD EDUC:** JD, 1972, Marshall-Wythe Sch. of Law, Coll. of William & Mary; **EDUC HONORS:** Honor grad. ROTC; **MIL SERV:** USA R, Capt.; **OTHER ACT & HONORS:** Sons of Amer. Revolution, Nat. & State; Dir. Kiwanis Club of Manassas; Dir. Boys Club of Manassas; **HOME ADD:** 8811 Jackson Ave., Manassas, VA, (703)361-7823; **BUS ADD:** 9315 Grant Ave., Manassas, VA 22110, (703)361-2106.

POTTER, Robert C.——*Fac. Mgr.*, Nashua Corp.; **PRIM RE ACT:** Property Manager; **BUS ADD:** 44 Franklin St., Nashua, NH 03061, (603)880-2323.*

POTTNER, M. Richard——**B:** June 15, 1930, Gary, IN, *Operating VP*, Federated Dept. Stores, Inc.; **PRIM RE ACT:** Consultant, Appraiser; **SERVICES:** Appraisals and negotiations for RE taxes, purchases, sales and condemnations; **REP CLIENTS:** All Federated's divs. (Bloomingdale's, Bullock's, Abraham & Straus, etc.); **PREV EMPLOY:** Sears, Roebuck & Co., 1964-68; Nat. Coordinator of RE Taxes; **PROFL AFFIL & HONORS:** Intl. Assn. of Assessing Officers; Inst. of Prop. Taxation; Amer. Soc. of Appraisers; Nat. Retail Merchants Assn., AAE (Intl. Assn. of Assessing Officers); CMI (Inst. of Prop. Taxation), ASA (Amer. Soc. of Appraisers); **EDUC:** BS, 1956, Civil & Struct. Engrg., Chicago Tech. Coll.; **GRAD EDUC:** Appraisal, Amer. Inst. of RE Appraisers, Courses I and II and IV at IN Univ., Univ. of Chicago & Univ. of CT; **MIL SERV:** USMC, Cpl.; **HOME ADD:** 6311 Ridge Ave., Cincinnati, OH 45213, (513)631-6311; **BUS ADD:** 7 W 7th St., Cincinnati, OH 45202, (513)579-7315.

POTTS, Charles——**B:** Aug. 28, 1943, Idaho Falls, ID, *Potts*, Potts' Investment Properties; **PRIM RE ACT:** Owner/Investor, Property Manager; **PREV EMPLOY:** RE salesman/prop. mgmt. Maj. Realty, Sandpoint, ID; **PROFL AFFIL & HONORS:** Walla Walla Apt. Operators Assn., VP, 80-81, Bd. of Dir., 79-82; **EDUC:** BA, 1965, English/Soc. Sci., ID State Univ., Pocatello, ID; **HOME TEL:** (509)522-2889; **BUS ADD:** 525 Bryant, Walla Walla, WA 99362, (509)522-0766.

POTTS, John J.——**B:** July 22, 1947, Cambridge, MA, *Assoc. Prof. of Law*, Valparaiso Unlv., Sch. of Law; **PRIM RE ACT:** Attorney, Instructor; **SERVICES:** Tax advice; **PROFL AFFIL & HONORS:** Chmn., Bd. of Dir., Sect. of Taxation, NM State Bar Assn., June 1979-Oct, 1980; ABA; Comm. on Standards of Tax Practice, Sect. of Taxation, July, 1981-date; AICPA, Atty., CPA; **EDUC:** BA, 1969, Econ., Univ. of NM; **GRAD EDUC:** MS, 1975, Acctg., NE Univ. Grad. Sch. of Profl. Acctg.; JD, 1974, Boston Coll. Law Sch.; **EDUC HONORS:** Omicron Delta Epsilon (Nat. Econ. Hon.); **MIL SERV:** US Army; **OTHER ACT & HONORS:** Listed in *Marquis' Who's Who in Amer. Law* (2d ed., 1979); Author, 'Common Estate Planning Pitfall: New Mexico Needs a Rev. Proc. 64-19 Statute', State Bar of NM Bulletin & Advance Opinions No. 19, p. 1117 (December 11, 1980) (also in 80-81 New Mexico CPA Journal No.6, p.1 (October 1980)), Author, 'Tax Aspects of Simultaneous Death, A Limited Inquiry', 19 State Bar of New Mexico Bulletin & Advance Opinions No. 19, p. 420 (May 8, 1980) (also in 79-80 New Mexico CPA Journal No. 12, p.1 (April 1980)) & (80-81 New Mexico CPA Journal No.1, p. 3 (May 1980); Asst. Editor 3 Human Rights Nos. 1 & 2 (1973); **BUS ADD:** Valparaiso, IN 46383, (219)464-5447.

POTTS, Robert A.——**B:** Dec. 5, 1931, Washington, DC, *VP*, Management Associates, Inc.; **PRIM RE ACT:** Broker, Consultant, Developer, Owner/Investor, Property Manager; **SERVICES:** Prop. mgmt., devel. of comml. prop.; **REP CLIENTS:** Indiv. & institl. devel., investors, prop. owners, personal mgmt. counseling; **PREV EMPLOY:** Westgate Corp., McLean, VA, 1974-1978; City of NY, 1972-1974; **PROFL AFFIL & HONORS:** IREM of the Natl. Assn. of Realtors; No. VA Bd. of Realtors, CPM; **EDUC:** BGS, 1967, Econ./Language/Mil. Sci., Univ. of NE at Omaha; **MIL SERV:** US Army; Lt. Col.; LM, BS, AM, CR, 1952-1972; **OTHER ACT & HONORS:** Asst. Fire Commnr., City of NY, 1972-1974; Tysons Transp. Assn., Inc.; **HOME ADD:** 12392 Copenhagen Ct., Reston, VA 22091, (703)860-1862; **BUS ADD:** 1600 Anderson Rd., McLean, VA 22102, (703)356-2400.

POUCHER, Allen L., Jr.——**B:** July 28, 1954, Jacksonville, FL, Knight, Kincaid, Poucher & Harris, P.A.; **PRIM RE ACT:** Attorney, Developer; **SERVICES:** Legal opinions, closing servs.; **REP CLIENTS:** RE Devel., Inst. Investors, Pvt. Const. & Devel. Interests; **EDUC:** BA Bus. Admin., 1977, Fin./Intl. Fin./RE, Univ. of So. CA; **GRAD EDUC:** JD, 1980, Corp./Real Prop./Intl. Investment, Univ. of FL; **EDUC HONORS:** PAC-8 Conference Bus. Adm. Student, 1977, Pres. of Phi Delta Phi, Intl. Legal Frat.; **HOME ADD:** 1287 Avondale Ave., Jacksonville, FL 32205, (904)389-0297; **BUS ADD:** 1030 Amer. Heritage Life Bldg., 11 E Forsyth St., Jacksonville, FL 32202, (904)356-8321.

POWELL, Alex——**B:** Dec. 10, 1946, Frankfurt, Germany, *Atty.*, Alex Powell, A Professional Corp.; **PRIM RE ACT:** Attorney, Owner/Investor, Syndicator; **PROFL AFFIL & HONORS:** State Bar of AZ, State Bar of CA, *Who's Who in CA*; **EDUC:** BA, 1968, Poli. Sci., Temple Univ.; **GRAD EDUC:** JD, 1973, Univ. a phof Toledo Law School; **HOME ADD:** 2007 Mt. Shasta Dr., San Pedro, CA 90732, (213)548-1598; **BUS ADD:** Suite 210, 21515 Hawthornd Blvd., Torrance, CA 90503, (203)540-3375.

POWELL, Gene E.——**B:** May 7, 1939, Los Angeles, CA, *Pres.*, New West Devel. Corp.; **PRIM RE ACT:** Developer, Builder; **SERVICES:** Buy and devel. prop. using new tech.; **PREV EMPLOY:** Loan Officer, Home S&L; Amer. S&L; **PROFL AFFIL & HONORS:** Homebuilders Assn.; BIA, Man of Yr. Award by Sales & Mktg. Execs. Assn.; **MIL SERV:** USMC, E3, Good Conduct, 1958-1960; **HOME ADD:** 180 Newport Center Dr., Newport Beach, CA 92660; **BUS ADD:** 180 Newport Center Dr., Suite 180, Newport Beach, CA 92660, (714)760-8091.

POWELL, Jack——**B:** Dec. 21, 1921, Higginson, AR, *Owner*, Powell Realty, Inc.; **PRIM RE ACT:** Broker, Banker, Developer, Owner/Investor, Property Manager; **SERVICES:** RE Sales, Comml. devel.; **PREV EMPLOY:** Owned Powell Truck Lines for 33 yrs.; **PROFL AFFIL & HONORS:** NAR; **MIL SERV:** US Navy, 1st Class; **HOME ADD:** 916 Skyline Dr., Searcy, AR 72143, (501)268-8336; **BUS ADD:** 309 E. Race, Searcy, AR 72143, (501)268-2445.

POWELL, Jay——**B:** June 6, 1951, Atlanta, GA, *Sales Mgr.*, AL Cleaning Serv. & Supply Co.; **OTHER RE ACT:** Janitorial Serv.; **SERVICES:** Janitorial Work; Lawn Maintenence; Carpet Care; **PROFL AFFIL & HONORS:** Sales & Mktg. Exec. Club BOMA; **BUS ADD:** 228 2nd Ave. N, Birmnigham, AL 35204, (205)252-6497.

POWELL, Owen N.——**B:** July 28, 1930, Milwaukee, WI, *Pres.*, Diversified Prop, Inc.; **PRIM RE ACT:** Broker, Instructor, Property Manager; **REP CLIENTS:** DAON, Regis Homes, Inc.; **PREV EMPLOY:** Exec. VP, Southwest Prop., Inc.; Dir. of Mkt. Research & Dev. W. Region Gulf; **PROFL AFFIL & HONORS:** Stanford Bus. School Alum. Assn., BIA, Const. Indus. Alliance; **EDUC:** BA, 1952, Pol.Sci., Stanford Univ.; **GRAD EDUC:** MBA, 1954, Mktg., Stanford Univ.; **MIL SERV:** USA, Special Agent CIC; **OTHER ACT & HONORS:** Laguna Niguel Racquet Club, Univ. Athletic Club; Pres. Monarch Bay BIA Assn.; Tr., S. Coast Med. Ctr.; **HOME ADD:** 419 Monarch Bay, So. Laguna, CA 92677, (714)499-2095; **BUS ADD:** 18952 Mac Arthur Blvd., Suite 400, Irvine, CA 92715, (714)833-7767.

POWELL, Robert——**B:** Oct. 18, 1944, Elizabeth City, NC, *Divisional VP*, Sun Belt Properties Mgmt., Inc., Greenville Div.; **PRIM RE ACT:** Developer, Property Manager; **OTHER RE ACT:** Property Mgmt., Acquisition; **SERVICES:** Prop. mgmt., renovation, comml. sales; **PROFL AFFIL & HONORS:** Greenville Bd. of Realtors; Candidate, CPM; Candidate, CCIM; **EDUC:** BA, 1967, Sociology, Univ. of NC; **OTHER ACT & HONORS:** Rotary, Other Bus. Address: Box 16504, Greenville, SC, 29606; **HOME ADD:** 104 Lindmont Dr., Greenville,

SC 29607, (803)297-1677; **BUS ADD:** Ste. 218, Greenville, SC 296091 Chick Springs Rd., (803)233-3211.

POWELL, Wayne——B: Apr. 4, 1935, McMinnville, TN, *Owner*, Wayne Powell Realty; **PRIM RE ACT:** Broker; **SERVICES:** RE (resid.) brokerage; **REP CLIENTS:** DuPont, Relocation Realty, Merrill Lynch; **PROFL AFFIL & HONORS:** Bd. of Realtors, TAR, RNMI, NAR, GRI (TN), CRS, CRB, BD. Officer & Dir.; **EDUC:** BS, 1957, Acctg., W. KY Univ. Bowling Green, KY; **EDUC HONORS:** Beta Pi, Hon. Accounting Frat.; **MIL SERV:** USAR; **HOME ADD:** 1226 Mountain Brook Cir., Signal Mountain, TN 37377, (615)886-1870; **BUS ADD:** 250 Signal Mountain Road, Chattanooga, TN 37405, (615)756-2811.

POWELSON, Richard C.——B: July 25, 1929, Aurora, IL, *VP*, R. E. Investment Counselors, Ltd.; **PRIM RE ACT:** Broker, Consultant, Owner/Investor, Instructor; **SERVICES:** Book on RE fin.; **PREV EMPLOY:** Nat. known as a creative RE fin. expert, has taught courses in all phases of RE at coll. level - gives seminars nat. on fin., has taught Lowky/Nickerson RE course & presently teaching Robt. Allen "Nothing Down" course on RE Fi.; **PROFL AFFIL & HONORS:** Exchangers, GRI - CBC; **EDUC:** BA, 1951, Bus. & RE, IA Wesleyan-North Central-UT State; **GRAD EDUC:** PhD, 1981, Creative Fin., Rocknell Univ.; **EDUC HONORS:** BA - Bus., PhD - RE & RE Fin.; **MIL SERV:** US Army, Cpl.; **OTHER ACT & HONORS:** Past Pres. IL Assn. of Realtors, Past Dir. NAR, Past Realtor of the Year; **HOME ADD:** 2510 Grand Ave. #1405, Kansas City, MO 64108, (816)474-1534; **BUS ADD:** 2510 Grand, Suite 1405, Kansas City, MO 64108, (816)474-1534.

POWERS, Earl L.——B: Apr. 16, 1923, Bay City, MI, *Owner*, Earl L. Powers Realty Co.; **PRIM RE ACT:** Broker, Appraiser, Owner/Investor, Property Manager; **OTHER RE ACT:** Cert. RE appraiser; **SERVICES:** Complete RE and appraisals; **REP CLIENTS:** Dow, GM, Merrill Lynch Relocation, Relocation Realty, Argonaut Realty, Consumers Powers, Equitable Relocation Serv., Transamer., Home Equity; **PREV EMPLOY:** Self employed excess of 40 yrs.; **PROFL AFFIL & HONORS:** Past Pres. Bay Cty. Bd. of Realtors, 1966, Bay Cty. Bd. of Realtors, NAR, MLS, Multiple Listing System, Realtor, CREA, Cert. by Nat. Assn. of RE Appraisers; **EDUC:** 1942, Bus. Admin., Bay City Central; **GRAD EDUC:** RE Mgmt., RE Law, RE Appraisals, Delta Coll., Univ. of MI; **MIL SERV:** USAF, Sgt., Good Conduct, Amer. Defense; **OTHER ACT & HONORS:** Past Pres. Bay Cty. Bd. of Realtors, 1966; Sec. VP Bd. of Dir. Bay City Ctry. Club., Former member C of C; **HOME ADD:** 4659 Nicolet Pl., Bay City, MI 48706, (517)684-5052; **BUS ADD:** 406 7th St., Bay City, MI 48706, (517)895-8111.

POWERS, Esther S.——B: Apr. 16, 1929, Peninsula, OH; **PRIM RE ACT:** Broker, Appraiser, Owner/Investor; **SERVICES:** Appraisals-Resid. & Comml.; **REP CLIENTS:** Merrill Lynch Relocation Mgmt., Inc., State Exchange Bank-Culver, Tower Fed. S&L, S. Bend; First Nat. Bank, Mishawaka; **PREV EMPLOY:** 15 yrs. in active brokerage, Colver & S. Bend; **PROFL AFFIL & HONORS:** Dir.-St. Joseph Valley Chap. SREA, Dual Member S.-Mishawaka Bd. of Realtors and Marshall Cty. Bd. of Realtors, GRI, CRB, SRA; **EDUC:** Attended KS City Art Inst., 1948-50, Fine Arts; **OTHER ACT & HONORS:** Town Bd. Member - Culver - 1966-1969 order of E. Star, Tri-Kappa, Past Pres. - Marshall Cty. Bd. of Realtors, Past State Dir. - IN Assn. of Realtors; **HOME ADD:** 303 E Winfield, Culver, IN 46511, (219)842-2710; **BUS ADD:** Suite 413, Commerce Bldg., S. Bend, IN 46601, (219)233-2673.

POWERS, Norman R.——B: Oct. 30, 1924, Ft. Worth, TX, *Pres.*, Powers Investment, Inc.; **PRIM RE ACT:** Broker, Consultant, Developer, Owner/Investor, Property Manager, Syndicator; **EDUC:** BBA, 1949, Public Acctg., Univ. of TX; **HOME ADD:** 4007 Greystone, Austin, TX 78731; **BUS ADD:** 3636 Exec. Ctr. Dr., Austin, TX 78731, (512)346-2632.

POWERS, Theodore J.——B: Dec. 18, 1927, NJ, *Prin.*, Powers & Marshall Assoc., Inc.; **PRIM RE ACT:** Consultant, Appraiser; **SERVICES:** RE Appraising & consulting; **REP CLIENTS:** Attys., govt. agencies, corps., private indivs.; **PROFL AFFIL & HONORS:** MAI, ASA, AR/WA, NYSAS; **EDUC:** BA, 1952, RE, NY Univ.; **MIL SERV:** USN; **BUS ADD:** 170 Old Country Rd., Mineola, NY 11501, (516)248-5511.

POWTER, Colin J.——B: July 17, 1932, Parkes, Australia, *Pres.*, CP & Assoc., Inc.; **PRIM RE ACT:** Developer; **PREV EMPLOY:** Pres. Dusco, Inc., Park Ave., NY; **PROFL AFFIL & HONORS:** Intl. Council of Shopping Ctrs.; **EDUC:** 1954, Civil Engr., Sydney Univ., Sydney, Aust.; **HOME ADD:** 16325 Lauder Ln., Dallas, TX 75241, (214)386-9985; **BUS ADD:** 4488 Spring Valley Rd., Dallas, TX 75234, (214)661-1770.

PRANGE, James Robert——B: Apr. 27, 1936, Hammond, IN, *Pres.*, RE/MAX Lake Cty. Realty, Inc./Triangle Const., Inc./Prange Devel. Co.; **PRIM RE ACT:** Broker, Syndicator, Consultant, Appraiser, Developer, Builder, Property Manager, Owner/Investor; **SERVICES:** RE Brokerage, Investment counseling, valuation, devel. of land. Bldr. of Resid., Comml., Multi-family; Prop. Mgr.; **REP CLIENTS:** Lawyers, Lenders and indiv. or instnl. investors in RE, Mort. Cos. and banks; **PROFL AFFIL & HONORS:** NAIFA; NAR; Home Bldrs. Assn., Million Dollar Club; CRS; *Who's Who in RE in Midwest*; GRI; **MIL SERV:** US Army, Spec.; **OTHER ACT & HONORS:** C of C; **HOME ADD:** 349 Devon Rd., Valparaiso, IN 46383; **BUS ADD:** 8695 Broadway, Merrillville, IN 46410, (219)769-4111.

PRASLEY, James E.——*VP*, Herder Commercial Development Corp.; **PRIM RE ACT:** Developer; **BUS ADD:** 2033 East Speedway, Tucson, AZ 85719, (602)881-4377.*

PRATER, Richard Allan——B: June 1, 1947, Yakima, WA, *Pres.*, Coker, Kroeger, Prater, Inc.; **PRIM RE ACT:** Broker, Developer, Owner/Investor, Property Manager; **SERVICES:** Site selection counseling & sales, devel. of prop. & prop. mgmt.; **REP CLIENTS:** Natl. & indiv. retailers & investors in comml. props.; **PREV EMPLOY:** Jack Richey & Co., 1974-77, RE Inc., 1969-74; **PROFL AFFIL & HONORS:** NAR, CA Assn. of Realtors, Sacramento Assn. of Realtors; **EDUC:** BS, 1969, RE & Risk Mgmt., Sacramento State Coll.; **EDUC HONORS:** Dean's Hon. Roll; **OTHER ACT & HONORS:** Bd. of Dir. Sacramento Active 20-30 Club; **HOME ADD:** 5024 Kinross Rd., Carmichael, CA 95608, (916)481-8969; **BUS ADD:** 1900 Douglas Blvd., Roseville, CA 95678, (916)786-2411.

PRATESI, Edward E.——B: Dec. 5, 1948, NY, NY, *Pres.*, Real Estate Ventures; **PRIM RE ACT:** Syndicator, Consultant, Developer, Builder, Owner/Investor; **PROFL AFFIL & HONORS:** Planning Executives Inst., AICPA, CPA; **EDUC:** BS, 1970, Mktg., Univ. of New Haven; **GRAD EDUC:** MBA, 1976, Fin., Univ. of New Haven; **OTHER ACT & HONORS:** Past Pres., PEI Hartford Chap.; **HOME ADD:** 391 Farmhill Rd., Middletown, CT 06457, (203)346-1591; **BUS ADD:** 201 Regal Row, Dallas, TX 75247, (203)346-1591.

PRATHER, William C.——B: Feb. 20, 1921, Toledo, IL, *Gen. Counsel*, US League of Savings Associations; **PRIM RE ACT:** Consultant, Attorney, Lender, Regulator, Real Estate Publisher; **OTHER RE ACT:** Author and editor of various RE; **SERVICES:** Lending books and periodicals; **REP CLIENTS:** S & L trade org. for all thrift and home financing instns.; **PREV EMPLOY:** The First Nat. Bank of Chicago; **PROFL AFFIL & HONORS:** Nat. Lawyers Club, Phi Delta Phi, ABA, IL, Chicago Federal Intl. Bar Assns., Coll. of Mort. Attys., JD; **EDUC:** BA, 1938, Univ. of IL; **GRAD EDUC:** JD, 1947, Univ. of IL School of Law; **MIL SERV:** Military Govt., Lt., Bronze Star; **OTHER ACT & HONORS:** Cosmos Club, Univ. Club of Chicago, Exeter City Club, Phi Gamma Delta, Phi Eta Sigma, Phi Delta Chi; **HOME ADD:** Applewood Farm, Box 157, Toledo, IL 62468, (217)849-3537; **BUS ADD:** 111 E. Wacker Drive, Suite 2500, Chicago, IL 60601.

PRATT, Francis C., II——*VP, Mktg.*, The Evans Partnership; **OTHER RE ACT:** Sales & Leasing; **PROFL AFFIL & HONORS:** Nat. Assn. of Indus. & Office Parks; **EDUC:** BA, 1961, Yale Univ.; **GRAD EDUC:** MBA, 1967, Univ. of VA; **MIL SERV:** USMC, Lt.; **BUS ADD:** 4 Wood Hollow Rd., Parsippany, NJ 07054, (201)884-2800.

PRATT, Richard T.——*Chrmn*, Department of Housing and Urban Development, Federal Home Loan Bank Board; **PRIM RE ACT:** Lender; **BUS ADD:** 451 Seventh St., S.W., Washington, DC 20410, (202)377-6280.*

PRAYSON, Richard A.——B: Aug. 7, 1938, Cleveland, OH, *Staff Counsel*, Women's Fed. Savings and Loan Assn. of Cleveland; **PRIM RE ACT:** Attorney; **OTHER RE ACT:** RE Fin. and RE Titles; **SERVICES:** Legal counsel; **PREV EMPLOY:** Mellon Nat. Mort. Co. of OH; City of Cleveland, Dept. of Law (Land Acquisition) Chief Counsel for Dept. of Community Devel.; Lawyers Title Ins. Corp.; **PROFL AFFIL & HONORS:** Cuyahoga Bar Assn., Lectured at Cleveland Marshall Law School on Eminent Domain Trial Work; **EDUC:** AB, 1960, Major: Eng. Minors: Philosophy and Hist., John Carroll Univ.; **GRAD EDUC:** JD, 1964, Law, Cleveland Marshall Law School of Baldwin Wallace Coll.; **EDUC HONORS:** Cum Laude Grad., Dean's List, Land Title Co. Award for Excellence in Field of Real Prop. Law (1962); **OTHER ACT & HONORS:** Appointed Asst. Dir. of Law for City of Cleveland (1965-73); **HOME ADD:** 4353 West 60th St., Cleveland, OH 44144, (216)749-5376; **BUS ADD:** 320 Superior Ave., Cleveland, OH 44114, (216)687-8273.

PREBLE, Laurence G.——**B:** Apr. 24, 1939, Denver, CO, *Partner*, O'Melveny & Myers; **PRIM RE ACT:** Attorney; **SERVICES:** Legal rep. for RE and natural resources transactions; **REP CLIENTS:** Instnl. lenders, devels., owners, for. investors, comml. tenants; **PREV EMPLOY:** lecturer, author for Practicing Law Inst., CA Continuint Educ. of the Bar and other seminars; **PROFL AFFIL & HONORS:** ABA; LA Cty. Bar Assn., Chmn. Real Prop. Sect. 1979-80, Loyola Law School Alumni Assn., Pres. 1978-79; **EDUC:** Petroleum Refining Engr., 1961, CO School of Mines, Golden, CO; **GRAD EDUC:** JD, 1968, Loyola Univ. of LA School of Law; **EDUC HONORS:** Cum laude, Student Teaching Fellow 1967; J Rex Dibble Award 1968; **MIL SERV:** US Army 1962-64, Capt.; **OTHER ACT & HONORS:** La Canada-Flintridge C of C, Pres. 1974-75, Adjunct Prof. of Law, Southwestern Univ. School of Law 1970-75; **HOME ADD:** 863 Berkshire Ave., La Canada Flintridge, CA 91011; **BUS ADD:** 611 W 6th St., L.A., CA 90017, (213)620-1120.

PREISER, Richard C.——**B:** Aug. 30, 1941, NY, NY, *Sr. VP*, First Amer. Bank of Palm Beach Cty., RE Div.; **PRIM RE ACT:** Banker, Lender; **SERVICES:** Const. and interim loans, valuation, consulting; **REP CLIENTS:** Major owners, developers and builders in FL; **PREV EMPLOY:** Sterling Nat. Bank, 1972-1981, VP RE Div.; James Felt Realty Services, 1967-1970, RE Consult.; **PROFL AFFIL & HONORS:** Young Mort. Bankers Assn.; Young Mens RE Assn.; Various RE Bds.; FL Homebuilders Assn.; Steering Comm., Comml., Indus. Inst. Div. of Homebuilders Assn.; **EDUC:** BA, 1964, Poli. Sci., Univ. of VT; **GRAD EDUC:** MBA, 1968, Bus. Admin., American Univ.; **HOME ADD:** 4233 Magnolia Ct., Palm Beach Gardens, FL 33410, (305)626-2344; **BUS ADD:** 401 Northlake Blvd., N. Palm Beach, FL 33408, (305)848-0611.

PREISNER, A.J.——*Mgr. Adm. Services Div.*, Kennecott Copper Corp.; **PRIM RE ACT:** Property Manager; **BUS ADD:** 10 Stamford Forum, Stamford, CT 06904, (203)964-3000.*

PRENTISS, Donald K.——**B:** May 17, 1940, Evanston, IL, *VP, Profl. Books*, Development Systems Corp., RE Education Co.; **PRIM RE ACT:** Real Estate Publisher; **SERVICES:** Educational materials for the RE profl.; **REP CLIENTS:** RE, Acctg., Tax Profls.; **PREV EMPLOY:** Times Morror Corp. 1978-81; **PROFL AFFIL & HONORS:** RE Educators Assn.; **EDUC:** BA, 1964, Eng., Duke Univ.; **HOME ADD:** 948 Ridge Ave., Evanston, IL 60202, (312)328-3269; **BUS ADD:** 500 N. Dearborn, Chicago, IL 60610, (312)836-4400.

PRESLEY, Brian——**B:** Dec. 28, 1941, Evansville, IN, *Pres.*, CSG, Inc.; **PRIM RE ACT:** Broker, Owner/Investor, Property Manager, Syndicator; **SERVICES:** Investment counseling, RE sales, prop. mgmt., synd.; **PROFL AFFIL & HONORS:** NAR; RESSI; Apt. Council; Homebuilders, GRI designation in RE; **EDUC:** BS, 1963, Mktg/Fin., Univ. of Evansville; **GRAD EDUC:** MBA, 1964, Mktg./Fin., MI State Univ.; **EDUC HONORS:** Pi Sigma Epsilon Hon. Frat., Beta Gamma Sigma Hon. Frat.; **HOME ADD:** 1491 Vinton, Memphis, TN 38104; **BUS ADD:** 1032 S. Cooper St., Memphis, TN 38104, (901)272-2553.

PRESS, Fredric A.——**B:** Feb. 2, 1949, NY, NY, *Asst. Gen. Counsel*, The Rouse Co., Legal; **OTHER RE ACT:** RE Development; **SERVICES:** Legal advice & representation regarding RE financing, devel. & operations; **REP CLIENTS:** Devel. Div., The Rouse Co.; **PREV EMPLOY:** Assoc. of Dewey, Ballantine, Bushby, Palmer & Wood, NY, NY, 1973-77; Assoc. of Melrod, Redman & Gartlan, Wash. DC., 1977-79; **PROFL AFFIL & HONORS:** ABA, Assn of Bar of City of NY, NYS Bar Assn., NY Cty. Bar Assn., DC Bar Assn., Member MD Bar; **EDUC:** BA, 1970, Pol. Sci, Union Coll; **GRAD EDUC:** JD, 1973, Georgetown Univ. Law Ctr.; **EDUC HONORS:** Cum Laude with Honors in Pol. Sci., Editor, Law & Policy in Intl. Bus., Law Club Fellow; **HOME ADD:** 3604 Shepherd St., Chevy Chase, MD 20815, (301)986-1428; **BUS ADD:** 10275 Little Patuxent Pkwy, Columbia, MD 21044, (301)992-6405.

PRESTON, H. LeBaron——**B:** Nov. 8, 1943, NY, NY, *VP/Dir. of Fin./Devel. Dir.*, Gilbane Properties, Inc.; **PRIM RE ACT:** Developer, Owner/Investor, Property Manager; **OTHER RE ACT:** Fin.; Mkt. Research; **SERVICES:** Investment devel., multi-family resid., retail, office; **PREV EMPLOY:** The Rouse Co., 1972-1975; **PROFL AFFIL & HONORS:** ICSC; MD Bar; **EDUC:** BA, 1965, Arch., Yale Univ.; **GRAD EDUC:** JD, 1972, RE Law/Fin., Univ. of Chicago; **MIL SERV:** USMC Res., Capt., Bronze Star; **OTHER ACT & HONORS:** VP, Providence Preservation Soc. Revolving Fund; Dir. RI Grp. Health Assn.; **HOME ADD:** 251 Olney St., Providence, RI 02906, (401)861-7149; **BUS ADD:** 7 Jackson Walkway, Providence, RI 02940, (401)456-5894.

PRESTON, Joel R.——**B:** Dec. 29, 1940, Berkeley Twp., NJ, *Dir., Location Consulting*, Cushman & Wakefield, Inc.; **PRIM RE ACT:** Consultant; **SERVICES:** Facilities location consulting; RE feasibility analyses; **REP CLIENTS:** Fortune 1000; comml. and indus. devel.; **PREV EMPLOY:** The Fantus Co., 1978-1981; Citicorp, 1973-1978; **PROFL AFFIL & HONORS:** ULI, Nat. Assn. of Review Appraisers, C.R.A. Designation; **EDUC:** BA, 1968, Econ., Rutgers Univ.; **GRAD EDUC:** MBA, 1972, Fin. and Mktg., Rutgers Univ.; **EDUC HONORS:** Magna Cum Laude, Beta Gamma Sigma Bus. Honor Soc. Award for highest class G.P.A.; **HOME ADD:** 14 Douglass Dr., RD4, Princeton, NJ 08540, (201)329-3094; **BUS ADD:** 1166 Ave. of the Americas, New York, NY 10036, (212)841-7883.

PRESTON, John F.——**B:** May 25, 1943, San Francisco, CA, *Pres.*, White Oak Devel.; **PRIM RE ACT:** Broker, Consultant, Developer, Builder, Owner/Investor; **SERVICES:** Consultation and devel. for our own acct. of land and income props.; **REP CLIENTS:** Local investor groups and fin. instit. partners; **PREV EMPLOY:** Gerald D. Hines Interests; **PROFL AFFIL & HONORS:** ULI, Nat. Assn. of Homebuilders, Houston Bd. of Realtors, Asst. Prof. Rice Univ.; **GRAD EDUC:** MBA, 1970, Bus./RE, Harvard Univ.; **HOME ADD:** 10941 Beinhorn, Houston, TX 77024, (713)627-2400.

PRESTON, Marlow R.——**B:** Apr. 9, 1943, Abilene, TX, *Pres. (all three corporations)*, Mar-Nan Properties, Inc.; Marlow R. Preston, Inc.; Inco Properties, Inc.; **PRIM RE ACT:** Broker, Consultant, Attorney, Developer, Builder, Owner/Investor, Property Manager, Syndicator; **SERVICES:** Brokerage & consulting in small income props., devel. and building small income props.; **REP CLIENTS:** Conann Homes, indiv. and instit. investors in resid. and small income props.; **PREV EMPLOY:** City Atty., Bellaire, TX 1973-1975; RE Atty., Dallas, TX, 1969-1973; **PROFL AFFIL & HONORS:** NAR; RESSI; TX Bar Assn.; TX RE Broker, Phi Delta Phi (legal honor Frat.), GRI; **EDUC:** BA, 1968, Econ., Govt., Philosophy, Univ. of TX; **GRAD EDUC:** JD, 1969, RE Procedure, Unif. of TX; **EDUC HONORS:** Omicron Delta Kappa (leadership Honor Society), Atty. Gen., Univ. of TX Students Assn.; Order of the Barristers; Consul (Honor Society; **OTHER ACT & HONORS:** Sunday School Teacher to College Students, Hyde Park Baptist Church, Austin, TX; **HOME ADD:** 4114 Edwards Mt. Dr., Austin, TX 78731, (512)459-4411; **BUS ADD:** 11222 N. Lamar, Austin, TX 78758, (512)835-5555.

PRESTON, Richard L.——**B:** Sept. 29, 1949, Richmond, IN, *Chief Appraiser, Asst. VP*, State Fidelity Savings; **PRIM RE ACT:** Appraiser, Property Manager; **PROFL AFFIL & HONORS:** SREA, NARA, SRA, CRA; **EDUC:** BA, 1978, RE, Wright State Univ.; **OTHER ACT & HONORS:** VP Oakwood Optimist, Member of the Bd. of Dir. of SRA Chapter #81; **HOME ADD:** 149 Shenandoah Trail, W. Carrollton, OH 45449, (513)439-4706; **BUS ADD:** 100 W. Second St., Dayton, OH 45402, (513)461-5211.

PREVITE, Ernest L.——**B:** June 22, 1933, Leechburg, PA, *Pres.*, Citizens Federal; **OTHER RE ACT:** Managing Officer; **SERVICES:** Savings and Loan; **PREV EMPLOY:** Owner-Founder of The Atlantic Realty Cos.; **PROFL AFFIL & HONORS:** Cam. Co. Bd. of Realtors; Nat. Assn. Review Appraisers; NJ Savings League; Intl. Inst. of Valuers, CRA; SCV; **EDUC:** BA, 1955, Bus. Admin., Greenville Coll., Greenville, IL; **OTHER ACT & HONORS:** Nat. Task Force for Agr. Exports; Rotary Club; **HOME ADD:** 54 S White Horse Pike, Berlin, NJ 08009, (609)767-0442; **BUS ADD:** 150 S White Horse Pike, Berlin, NJ 08009, (609)767-5857.

PRICE, Billie B., Jr.——**B:** Sept. 3, 1943, Inglewood, CA, *Pres. - Broker*, New Horizons Realty & Investment, Inc.; **PRIM RE ACT:** Broker, Consultant, Developer, Owner/Investor, Instructor, Property Manager, Syndicator; **OTHER RE ACT:** Mort. Broker; **SERVICES:** Investment, exchange and joint venture consulting, purchases & sales of comml., indus., land and resid. income props., prop. mgmt.; **REP CLIENTS:** High income bracket investors - indiv. & corp.; **PREV EMPLOY:** 7 years, Efficiency Expert, Mgmt. Consultant; **PROFL AFFIL & HONORS:** Nat. Council of Exchangers, MLS, Nat., State and Local Bd. of Realtors, Valley of the Sun Exchangers, Broker, Mort. Broker; **EDUC:** 1963, Indus. Engrg., Flint Jr. Coll., General Motors Inst.; **OTHER ACT & HONORS:** C of C, Jaycees; **HOME ADD:** 1013 E Buena Vista Dr., Tempe, AZ 85284, (602)897-8745; **BUS ADD:** 2504 S. Rural, Tempe, AZ 85282, (602)894-0300.

PRICE, Gerald G.——**B:** Jan. 30, 1923, Ft. Smith, AR, *Broker, Owner*, Gerald Price Agency; **PRIM RE ACT:** Broker, Developer, Owner/Investor, Insuror; **SERVICES:** Sales, Devel., Prop. Mgmt.; **REP CLIENTS:** Home Buyers and Sellers, Indiv. and Corp. Comml. Investors; **PROFL AFFIL & HONORS:** NAR, ARA, NAHB, RNMI, GRI, CCIM, ROTY; **GRAD EDUC:** BS/BA, 1951, Mktg., Univ. of AR; **EDUC HONORS:** Grad. witb Honors; **MIL SERV:** US Army, Sgt.; **OTHER ACT & HONORS:** Optimist Intl., Ft. Smith C of C,

United Goddard Methodist Church; **HOME ADD:** 1300 N. 52nd St., Ft. Smith, AR 72901, (501)782-7053; **BUS ADD:** 3210 Grand Ave., Ft. Smith, AR 72901, (501)782-6057.

PRICE, John R.——**B:** July 25, 1928, Detroit, MI, *Realtor*, John Price, Realtors; **PRIM RE ACT:** Broker, Consultant, Appraiser, Developer, Builder, Owner/Investor, Property Manager, Insuror, Syndicator; **SERVICES:** Resid., comml. and indus. sales, devel & synd., appraisals and prop. mgmt.; **REP CLIENTS:** Indiv. and instnl. owners and purchasers of resid., comml., and indus. props.; **PROFL AFFIL & HONORS:** NAR, TN Assn. of Realtors, Knoxville Bd. of Realtors, Soc. of RE Appraisers (Assoc. Member), RNMI, CRB, CRS, GRI, Knoxville Realtor of the Year, 1975; **EDUC:** BEE, 1950, Univ. of TN; **MIL SERV:** US Army, 1945-1947, 1951-1953, 1st Lt.; **OTHER ACT & HONORS:** Tr. of the TN Realtor's Inst.; **HOME ADD:** P.O. Box 7007, Shaker Dr., Knoxville, TN 37921, (615)947-6918; **BUS ADD:** P.O. Box 7007, 7432 Oak Ridge Hwy, Knoxville, TN 37921, (615)690-7000.

PRICE, Leslie M., Jr.——**B:** Feb. 20, 1924, Chicago, IL, Leslie M. Price; **PRIM RE ACT:** Owner/Investor, Insuror; **EDUC:** BS, 1945, Univ. of MI, IL Tech., Northwestern Univ.; **HOME ADD:** 1640 E. 50th St., Chicago, IL 60615, (312)643-7177; **BUS ADD:** 1642 E. 56th St., Room 217, Chicago, IL 60637, (312)363-8800.

PRICE, Dr. Oliver Ray——**B:** Aug. 24, 1924, Springfield, MO, O.R. Price & Assoc.; **PRIM RE ACT:** Instructor, Syndicator, Consultant, Property Manager, Owner/Investor, Real Estate Publisher; **OTHER RE ACT:** Author: "High Leverage RE Investments"; **SERVICES:** Consulting/Writing; **REP CLIENTS:** Litton Ind., Inc.; Small Bus. Admin.; Pvt. Investors; **PREV EMPLOY:** Consultant to RE Dept. (Corp. Hdqtrs.) Litton Ind.; Give Seminars on "Creative RE Financing"; **PROFL AFFIL & HONORS:** Inst. Cert. Business Counselors; Rotary, SBA Award "Best Managed Small Co."; Pres. of Physics Hon Soc.; **EDUC:** BS, 1953, Physics, Math., CA Inst. of Tech., Pasadena; **GRAD EDUC:** PhD, 1958, Nuclear Physics, UCLA; **EDUC HONORS:** Upper 1/3; **MIL SERV:** USNR Air Corp., Lt. (j.g.), Navy Pilot; **OTHER ACT & HONORS:** Rotary Club; Pi Kappa DeLta; Author ("High Leverage RE Investments") Prentice-Hall, Inc. Englewood Cliffs, NJ 07632; **HOME ADD:** 703 S Norton Ave., Los Angeles, CA 90005, (213)388-5800; **BUS ADD:** 703 S Norton Ave., Los Angeles, CA 90005, (213)738-8129.

PRICE, Patrick Hilary——**B:** Feb. 1, 1928, Coos Bay, OR, *Exec. VP*, San Francisco Fed. S&L Assn.; **PRIM RE ACT:** Banker, Lender; **OTHER RE ACT:** Mort. Banker; **SERVICES:** S&L; **PROFL AFFIL & HONORS:** Bay Area Mort. Assn. (pres. 1964-65), San Francisco RE Bd. (past dir.); RE Research Council of N. CA (dir), (pres. 1979); **EDUC:** 1952, Univ. of OR, Sch. of Arch. & Allied Arts; **GRAD EDUC:** 1974, Grad. Sch. of Bus., IN Univ.; **MIL SERV:** USN, AC3; **OTHER ACT & HONORS:** St. Francis Yacht Club, San Francisco (Dir. 1979-80); **HOME ADD:** 491 Throckmorton, Mill Valley, CA 94941, (415)388-8837; **BUS ADD:** 85 Post St., San Francisco, CA 94104, (415)982-8100.

PRICE, Robert G.——**B:** Mar. 30, 1936, Elizabethtown, IL, *Atty.*, Kennedy & Price, Attys.; **PRIM RE ACT:** Consultant, Attorney; **REP CLIENTS:** First Carolina S&L, Hugh Ryall Realty, Haven-Wyman Realty, First Nat. Bank of SC; **PROFL AFFIL & HONORS:** SC Bar; Richland Cty. Bar; ABA; Sertoma; **EDUC:** BS, 1959, Chemistry, So. IL Univ.; **GRAD EDUC:** JD, 1969, Law, Univ. of SC; **MIL SERV:** USAF; Capt.; Air Medal w/clusters; **OTHER ACT & HONORS:** Boy Scouts; Columbia Music Festival Assn.; **HOME ADD:** 11 Lake Point, Columbia, SC, (803)782-0530; **BUS ADD:** POB 11628, Columbia, SC 29211, (803)799-2121.

PRICE, Sherman S.——**B:** Nov. 16, 1925, NY, NY, *Pres.*, Security Home Inspection Inc.; **PRIM RE ACT:** Engineer; **OTHER RE ACT:** Pre-purchase inspection of homes and bldgs.; **PROFL AFFIL & HONORS:** Dir. - Amer. Soc. of Home Inspectors; Member - NY State Soc. of Profl. Engrs.; Member - Brooklyn Engrs. Club; **EDUC:** BChem. Engrg., 1948, CCNY; Civil Engrg. Program, Polytech. Inst. of NY; **GRAD EDUC:** Advanced Grad. Work in Structural Engrg., CCNY, **OTHER ACT & HONORS:** I teach two seminar courses on home and bldg. inspection at the "New Sch. of Social Research" in NY; **HOME ADD:** 5905 Ave. T., Brooklyn, NY 11234, (212)763-5528; **BUS ADD:** 5906 Ave. T, Brooklyn, NY 11234, (212)763-5589.

PRICE, Thomas D., Jr.——**B:** June 2, 1954, Chicago, IL, *Atty.*, Sax & MacIver; **PRIM RE ACT:** Attorney; **REP CLIENTS:** Peoples Bank, Peoples Mort. Co., Walter E. Heller Western Inc., John Y Sato & Assoc. (lenders and devels.); **PREV EMPLOY:** Corp. Counsel, Northern CA S&L Assn., Palo Alto, CA (1978-80); **PROFL AFFIL & HONORS:** ABA, WA State Bar, State Bar of CA, Seattle-King Cty. Bar (Real Prop. Sects. of all Bars), Chairperson Housing Comm., 1980-82, Seattle Cty. Bar Assn. (Young Lawyers); **EDUC:** BA, 1975, Econ., Psych., Stanford Univ.; **GRAD EDUC:** JD, 1978, Stanford Law Sch.; **EDUC HONORS:** Grad. with distinction (Top 20 percent); **HOME ADD:** 13539 17th Ave. NE, Seattle, WA 98125, (206)367-6762; **BUS ADD:** 1700 Peoples Nat. Bank Bldg., Seattle, WA 98171, (206)624-1940.

PRICHARD, Gaylord E.——**B:** Mar. 4, 1922, Fresno, CA, *Owner*, Gaylord & Prichard Co.; **PRIM RE ACT:** Broker, Consultant, Developer, Owner/Investor; **SERVICES:** Fin. and econ. consulting including design/cost criteria, etc.; **REP CLIENTS:** Lenders, investors, devels. and joint venture partners covering comml., indus. and multifamily props.; **PREV EMPLOY:** Gaylord E. Prichard Co. and Assoc. Cos. since 1951; **PROFL AFFIL & HONORS:** Gen. Contractor Lic. #128081 CA, RE Broker - Lic. #0-216492-9 CA; **EDUC:** BA, 1944, Pre-Medical, Univ. of CA, Los Angeles; **GRAD EDUC:** 2 yrs. Post Grad. - no degree, 1944-45, UCLA; **HOME ADD:** 172 Juanita Way, San Francisco, CA 94127, (415)664-4796; **BUS ADD:** 500 Harbor Blvd., Belmont, CA 94002, (415)592-5500.

PRICHARD, Philip A.——**B:** May 31, 1945, Wheeling, WV, *Atty.*, Sole Practitioner; **PRIM RE ACT:** Attorney, Banker; **SERVICES:** Majority of work in areas of RE & estates. Legal Servs. - prepare deeds & other documents, title exams, etc.; **REP CLIENTS:** Lenders & Indivs. Note: Also on Bd. of First Exchange Bank, Mannington; **PROFL AFFIL & HONORS:** WV State Bar, ABA; **EDUC:** BA, 1967, Poli. Sci., Math., WV Univ.; **GRAD EDUC:** JD, 1971, WV Univ., Coll. of Law; **MIL SERV:** US Army; Sgt., Arcom. Bronze St., etc.; **OTHER ACT & HONORS:** City Atty. - 1972-1974, 1975-1979; City Council - 1979 to present; City Charter Bd. - 1974-1979; Nat. Space Inst., Planetary Soc.; **HOME ADD:** 107 High St., Mannington, WV 26582, (304)986-1528; **BUS ADD:** 107 High St., Mannington, WV 26582, (304)986-2255.

PRICHETT, Dean R.——*Pres.*, Federal Home Loan Bank of Des Moines; **PRIM RE ACT:** Banker; **BUS ADD:** 907 Walnut St., Des Moines, IA 50309, (515)243-4211.*

PRIDDY, Stephen P.——**B:** May 9, 1948, Anderson, IN, *Treas.*, Deci-Ma Corp.; **PRIM RE ACT:** Consultant, Developer, Owner/Investor, Property Manager, Syndicator; **SERVICES:** Indiv. RE planning, tax analysis and projection; **REP CLIENTS:** Indivs. and instit. investors in multi-family and comml. RE; **PREV EMPLOY:** Peat, Marwick, Mitchell & Co., CPA's; **PROFL AFFIL & HONORS:** Amer. Instit. of CPA's; IN Assn. of CPA; **EDUC:** BS, 1970, Acctg., Ball State Unic., Muncie, IN; **EDUC HONORS:** Price Waterhouse Award; **MIL SERV:** US Army, Sgt.; **HOME ADD:** 544 Village Dr., Carmel, IN 46032, (317)844-1505; **BUS ADD:** 8604 Allisonville Rd., Indianapolis, IN 46250, (317)842-7500.

PRIEHS, George W.——**B:** May 24, 1907, Mt. Clemens, MI, *Pres./Gen. Mgr.*, Priehs Realty Co., Inc.; **PRIM RE ACT:** Developer, Lender, Builder, Owner/Investor, Property Manager; **SERVICES:** Advisor, arch. advisor, fin. consultant; **PREV EMPLOY:** Dept. Mgr., R.C. Macys, NY; **PROFL AFFIL & HONORS:** Nat. Reailer Assn.; MI Retailers Assn., Past Pres., Small Stores Div., Nat. Retailers Assn.; Former Bd. Member, MI Retailers Assn.; Author of many trade articles for Fairchild Bus. Publications; Author of many articles - NY Times, Univ. of MI & Univ. of WI student papers; **EDUC:** BA, 1930, Univ. of MI; **MIL SERV:** USAF, Hon. Gen., 18 different medals; **OTHER ACT & HONORS:** Past Pres., Macomb Cty. C of C; Many local and state civic awards; **HOME ADD:** 24805 Crocker Blvd., Mt. Clemens, MI 48043; **BUS ADD:** 60-66 Macomb St., Mt. Clemens, MI 48043, (313)463-4567.

PRIEST, William G., Jr.——**B:** Feb. 2, 1940, Portland, OR, *Atty.*, The Priest Law Offices; **PRIM RE ACT:** Attorney, Instructor; **OTHER RE ACT:** Specialty: RE; **SERVICES:** Represent parties in RE Transactions/Litigation; **REP CLIENTS:** Transamerica Fin.; N. Amer. Equity Trust; CA Foreclosure Services; Tri Cty. Apt. Assn.; **EDUC:** BA, 1961, Pol. Sci., WA State Univ.; **GRAD EDUC:** JD, 1968, Law, Univ. of ID; **MIL SERV:** US Naval Reserve, CDR; **BUS ADD:** 20 N. 1st, Suite 100, San Jose, CA 95113, (408)279-3150.

PRIESTLEY, Allen E.——**B:** Jan. 22, 1917, Redford, MI, *Sr. VP*, St. Paul Title Ins. Corp., N Div.; **PRIM RE ACT:** Attorney; **SERVICES:** Title Ins. & escrow serv.; **PREV EMPLOY:** Gen. Counsel (retired), St. Paul Title Ins. Corp.; **PROFL AFFIL & HONORS:** State Bar of MI and ABA, Title Ins. Comm.; RP; P&Tr L Sec.; Title Standards Comm.; Editor, RP; R&Tr Journal; **EDUC:** Pre-Law, Detroit Inst. of Technology; **GRAD EDUC:** LLD, 1944, Law, Detroit Coll. of Law; **EDUC HONORS:** Cum Laude; **MIL SERV:** US Army; Counter-Intelligence Corps - Special Agent, Commendation Ribbon; **HOME ADD:** 2973 Edgefield Dr., Pontiac, MI 48054, (313)682-6553; **BUS ADD:** 1650 W Big Beaver Rd., PO Box 1289, Troy, MI 48099,

(313)643-4000.

PRIEUR, Kenneth M.——**B:** July 12, 1949, New Orleans, LA, *Dir. of Prop. Mgmt.*, AREFI Corp. of Louisiana; **PRIM RE ACT:** Broker, Consultant, Developer, Builder, Owner/Investor, Instructor, Property Manager, Syndicator; **SERVICES:** Analysis and acquisition of investments for clients, mgmt.; **REP CLIENTS:** Sale of props. of all types, also devel. and synd. of comml. props.; **PREV EMPLOY:** Westminster Mgmt. Co.; **PROFL AFFIL & HONORS:** NAR, GRI; **EDUC:** Univ. of New Orleans, 1972, Bus.; **MIL SERV:** US Navy Res.; **HOME ADD:** 6921 Lake Barrington Dr., New Orleans, LA 70128, (504)241-7383; **BUS ADD:** 111 Rue Iberville St., New Orleans, LA 70130, (504)524-4676.

PRIGAL, Kenneth B. K.——**B:** Mar. 2, 1957, Manhasset, NY, *Pres.*, Northcoast Corp.; Creative Grp., Ltd.; **PRIM RE ACT:** Broker, Consultant, Developer, Owner/Investor, Property Manager, Syndicator, Real Estate Publisher; **OTHER RE ACT:** Exchangor, columnist writer; **SERVICES:** Investment counseling, prop. acquisition, mgmt., sales; **PREV EMPLOY:** Philipson Corp., Ft. Lauderdale; **PROFL AFFIL & HONORS:** Interex; Lowry Nickerson Investment Group; Philadelphia Bd. of Realtors; Metro. Philadelphia RE Exchangers, PA/DE CCIM Chapt.; **EDUC:** BS, 1978, Mktg., Org. Beh., Boston Univ. Sch. of Mgmt.; **HOME ADD:** 221 Carpenter St., Philadelphia, PA 19147, (215)468-2867; **BUS ADD:** 221 Carpenter St., Philadelphia, PA 19147, (215)468-2867.

PRIGMORE, G. Daniel——**B:** Mar. 8, 1943, W. Springfield, MA, *Pres.*, FMR Properties; **PRIM RE ACT:** Consultant, Developer, Owner/Investor, Property Manager; **SERVICES:** Devel. and mgmt. of RE for parent co.; RE consulting services for selected corp. clients; **PROFL AFFIL & HONORS:** Amer. Soc. RE Counselors; Gr. Boston RE Bd.; Certified Appraiser, CRE; SRA; **EDUC:** BA, 1965, Econ., Union Coll.; **GRAD EDUC:** MBA, 1968, Fin., Harvard Bus. School; **EDUC HONORS:** with Distinction; **OTHER ACT & HONORS:** Tr., The Childrens' Museum, Boston; The Kingsley School, Boston; **HOME ADD:** 85 State St., Boston, MA 02109, (617)726-0370; **BUS ADD:** 7 Water St., Boston, MA 02109, (617)726-0370.

PRIKRYL, Latius R.——**B:** Dec. 3, 1949, Taylor, TX, *Atty.-at-Law*, Stubbeman, McRae, Sealy, Laughlin & Browder, Inc.; **PRIM RE ACT:** Attorney; **SERVICES:** Tax and RE, planning and documentation; **REP CLIENTS:** Lenders; indiv. and instnl. investors and devels. in and of resid. and comml. props.; **PREV EMPLOY:** Carneiro, Chumney & Co, CPA; San Antonio, TX; **PROFL AFFIL & HONORS:** State Bar of TX and ABA; **EDUC:** BA, 1972, Math., Univ. of TX at Austin; **GRAD EDUC:** JD, 1974, Law, St. Mary's Univ. of San Antonio, TX - School of Law; LLM - Taxation, 1975, SMU, Dallas, TX - School of Law; **HOME ADD:** 9903 Richelieu, Austin, TX 78750, (512)258-9912; **BUS ADD:** 1800 American Bank Tower; PO Box 2286, Austin, TX 78768, (512)476-3502.

PRIMLEY, Nanci C.——**B:** May 17, 1939, Bayard, NE, *Owner-Broker*, Worden Realty, Inc.; **PRIM RE ACT:** Broker, Appraiser, Property Manager, Owner/Investor; **SERVICES:** Investment Counseling, Appraisals, Prop. Mgmt.; **PREV EMPLOY:** Self-employed: Owned Grocery Store; **PROFL AFFIL & HONORS:** CRB, CRS, GRI Designations; **EDUC:** Fort Vancouver, 1957; **OTHER ACT & HONORS:** C of C, Cattlemans Assn., Womens Council of RE, Awards & Program Dir., Bd. of Realtors; **HOME ADD:** 16208 WE 33rd Ave., Ridgefield, WA 98642, (206)573-4062; **BUS ADD:** 7205 NE 219th St., Battle Ground, WA 98604, (206)687-3106.

PRIMM, Earl R.——**B:** June 11, 1931, Parsons, KS, *Pres.*, Cotter RE Agency, Inc., Cotter & Co.; **PRIM RE ACT:** Broker, Consultant; **SERVICES:** Buy, selling of stores, lease negotiations, new store; **REP CLIENTS:** True Value Hardware Stores & V&S Variety Stores; **MIL SERV:** US Army, Sgt., Various; **HOME ADD:** 632 S. Cleveland, Arlington Heights, IL 60005, (312)394-5412; **BUS ADD:** 2740 N Clybourn Ave., Chicago, IL 60614, (312)975-2725.

PRINCIPE, R. B.——**B:** Mar. 3, 1943, Evansten, IL, *Pres.*, Westoaks Realtors; **PRIM RE ACT:** Broker, Instructor, Syndicator, Consultant, Developer, Builder, Property Manager; **SERVICES:** Brokerage, Synd., Leasing, Prop. Man., Escrow, Mort. Comml. and Residential; **PROFL AFFIL & HONORS:** CAR, NAR, NASD, SEC, GRI, Past Pres. CUB of Realtors, Salesman of the Yr. 1966 Coneso Vaube Bd. of Realtors; Realtor of the Yr. - 1975 Coneso Vaube Bd. of Realtors; **OTHER ACT & HONORS:** Optimist Club; **HOME ADD:** 1873 Potrero Rd., Hiddeavauby, CA 91360, (850)496-1196; **BUS ADD:** 660 Hampshire Rd., Suite 200, Westlake Village, CA 91361, (213)889-2802.

PRINCIPE, Nicholas J.——**B:** June 3, 1943, Proctor, VT, *Pres.*, Michael Laurie & Partners, Inc.; **PRIM RE ACT:** Consultant, Appraiser, Developer, Owner/Investor, Property Manager; **OTHER RE ACT:** Investment advisor, valuations; **REP CLIENTS:** UK Insts., private investors, devels.; **EDUC:** BS, 1965, Sci.; **HOME ADD:** 1075 Park Ave., New York, NY 20028, (212)722-7165; **BUS ADD:** 500 Park Ave., New York, NY 10022, (212)688-0933.

PRINE, Charles W., Jr.——**B:** Apr. 23, 1926, Pittsburgh, PA, *Sr. VP - Staff Servs.*, Ryan Homes Inc.; **PRIM RE ACT:** Builder; **EDUC:** AB, 1948, Eng. Lit., Princeton Univ.; **EDUC HONORS:** Pres. - Univ. Press Club; **MIL SERV:** US Navy, Lt. J.G.; **OTHER ACT & HONORS:** Bd. of Dirs. - Pittsburgh Opera, Civic Light Opera, Transitional Serv., Housing Facilities, Inc., Parent and Child Guidance Ctr., Elder, Presbyterian Church; **HOME ADD:** 1108 Lindendale Dr., Pittsburgh, PA 15243; **BUS ADD:** 100 Ryan Ct., Pittsburgh, PA 15205, (412)276-8000.

PRINGLE, Mark L.——**B:** Oct. 22, 1957, Burlingame, CA, *Dir. of Prop. Mgmt./Mktg.*, The Raiser Organization; **PRIM RE ACT:** Property Manager; **OTHER RE ACT:** Mktg.; **SERVICES:** Lease-up and mgmt. of comml. prop., mkt. and feasability analysis; **REP CLIENTS:** Devels., pvt. investors; **PREV EMPLOY:** Mort. Banking; **PROFL AFFIL & HONORS:** San Mateo Cty. Devel. Assn.; **EDUC:** BS, 1979, RE, Fin., Univ. of S. CA; **HOME ADD:** 422 Highland Ave., San Mateo, CA 94401, (415)348-1660; **BUS ADD:** 800 S. Claremont St., San Mako, CA 94402, (415)342-9026.

PRINS, August W.——**B:** June 23, 1942, Amsterdam, Holland, *RE Broker*, Wm. Chuba Associates; **PRIM RE ACT:** Broker, Consultant, Owner/Investor, Property Manager, Insuror; **SERVICES:** All services of gen. brokerage; **PREV EMPLOY:** Insurance Broker Mktg. 7UP in Holland; **PROFL AFFIL & HONORS:** NAR, CAR, Sacramento Exchange Group, Local Realtors Bd., MLS, Nat. Mktg. Inst., GRI, CRS, Dir./VP MLS; **EDUC:** Coll. - 5 years, 1959, Hist. - Language - Mathematics, VHS - Amsterdam; **GRAD EDUC:** University - 4 years, 1964, Lang. - History - Mathematics, Univ. of Amsterdam; **MIL SERV:** Dutch Army, Corp.; **OTHER ACT & HONORS:** 1963 - Marketing Degree NTI - Rotterdam (one year); **HOME ADD:** 960 Squaw Valley Rd., Olympic Valley, CA 95730; **BUS ADD:** PO Box 2121, Olympic Valley, CA 95730, (916)583-3283.

PRISCOE, Robert V.——**B:** Apr. 18, 1949, New Brunswick, NJ, *Prin.*, Robert V. Priscoe R.E. Appraiser-Consultant; **PRIM RE ACT:** Consultant, Appraiser; **PREV EMPLOY:** Gino's Inc., R.E Representative comml. R.E. site selection 1977-80; **EDUC:** BA, 1972, Hist., Glassboro State Coll.; **HOME ADD:** 47 High St., Metuchen, NJ 08840; **BUS ADD:** 47 High St., Metuchen, NJ 08840, (201)548-3377.

PRITCHARD, Edwin D., Jr.——**B:** Nov. 29, 1946, Abington, PA, *Asst. VP*, Southeast National Bank of Pennsylvania, Comml. Lending; **PRIM RE ACT:** Banker, Lender; **SERVICES:** Const. lending and resid. mort. loans, project feasibility analysis, mktg.; **REP CLIENTS:** Corps., partnerships, and indivs., Support engaged in comml., indus. and resid. const.; **EDUC:** BBA, 1973, Econ. & Fin., New England Coll.; **EDUC HONORS:** Summa Cum Laude, Jameson Award, Wall Street Journal Student Achievement Award; **MIL SERV:** US Army; Spec. 5, Vietnam Serv. Ribbons; **HOME ADD:** 64 Candle Rd., Levittown, PA 19057, (215)945-2769; **BUS ADD:** 2 Country View Rd., Malvern, PA 19355, (215)648-1906.

PRITCHETT, Charles H., Jr.——**B:** July 12, 1951, Dothan, AL, *Partner*, Pritchett & Joseph RE Appraisers-Consultants; **PRIM RE ACT:** Appraiser; **SERVICES:** Appraising real prop., specifically comml., indus., condos. and apt. complexes; **REP CLIENTS:** Union Oil Co.; Texaco Inc.; First Nat. Bank of Birmingham; Metropolitan Prop.; Verex Assurance; Banks, S&L Assns., ins. cos., devel., bldrs., and indivs.; **PREV EMPLOY:** Staff Appraiser, Hearn Co., 1973-1980; **PROFL AFFIL & HONORS:** Past Pres., Birmingham Chap. 106 of SREA; Candidate Guidance Chmn. of AL Chap. 32 of AIREA, SRPA; MAI; Young Advisory Council for SREA; **EDUC:** BS, 1973, RE, Univ. of AL; **OTHER ACT & HONORS:** Bd. of Dir., AL Jubilee Barbershop Chorus; Bd. of Dir., Univ. of AL Baptist Student Union; Member, Sertoma (Sponsors Sertoma Nat. Power Hitting Championship w/Univ. of AL in Birmingham Comprehensive Cancer Center); **HOME ADD:** 5254 Paramont Dr., Birmingham, AL 35210, (205)956-5568; **BUS ADD:** 2117 Magnolia Avenue, Suite 103, Birmingham, AL 35205, (205)251-5180.

PRITCHETT, Clayton P.——**B:** June 7, 1927, Orange, NJ, *Sr. VP*, Landauer Associates, Inc., Valuation & Tech. Servs.; **PRIM RE ACT:** Consultant; **SERVICES:** Market, land use, feasibility analyses, investment counseling; **REP CLIENTS:** Devel./Investors, Fin. Instns., Corps., Non-profit Instns.; **PREV EMPLOY:** RE Research Corp., Chicago, IL, 1965-1968; **PROFL AFFIL & HONORS:** RE Bd. of NYC; ULI; Treas., NY Chap. of Lambda Alpha; Nat. Assn. of Indus. Office Parks, GRI Certificate; **EDUC:** BA, 1950, Math./Econ., Williams Coll.; **EDUC HONORS:** Dean's List; **MIL SERV:** USNR,

ET3, 1945-1946/1951-1952; **OTHER ACT & HONORS:** Elder and Consultant to various judicatories of the United Presbyterian Church; Lecturer, 1974-1975, NYU, SCE, RE Inst.; **HOME ADD:** 13 Barchester Way, Westfield, NJ 07090, (201)232-8171; **BUS ADD:** 200 Park Ave., New York, NY 10166, (212)687-2323.

PRITZ, Eldon G.——B: Mar. 10, 1926, Minot, ND, *Owner*, Eldon G. Pritz Appraisals; **PRIM RE ACT:** Consultant, Appraiser, Owner/Investor; **SERVICES:** RE appraisals - comml. - resid.; **REP CLIENTS:** IBM; Minneapolis Honeywell; Philco; Mountain Bell; CBS; CF & I; Transamerica; McGraw Hill; Exxon; **PREV EMPLOY:** Intl. Props., Sr. VP; Exchange Natl. Bank; Intermountain Mort.; **PROFL AFFIL & HONORS:** MAI, SRPA, CRA, Planning Comm. Bs. of Adjustment, Pres. SRA Chap. Colorado Springs, CO; Pres. Mort. Lenders Colorado Springs; **EDUC:** 1948, Bus., Luther Coll.; **GRAD EDUC:** Morg. Banking, appraising, CO Coll. of Ed., NW San Diego State; **OTHER ACT & HONORS:** Cty. Planning Commn., Cty. Ind. Bond Comm.; Trustee Colorado Springs School; **HOME ADD:** 1900 Constellation Dr., Colorado Springs, CO 80906, (303)473-4049; **BUS ADD:** 1422 No. Hancock Suite One So., Colorado Springs, CO 80903, (303)475-9200.

PRIZANT, Roger M.——B: Oct. 29, 1942, Louisville, KY, *Atty. at Law*, Roger M. Prizant Law Office; **PRIM RE ACT:** Attorney; **SERVICES:** Complete title ins. coverage and secv. & RE closings; **REP CLIENTS:** Baldwin United Mort. Co.; Citizens Fidelity Mort. Co.; Charter Mort. Co.; Churchill Mort. Co.; Collateral Investment Co., First Investment Co.; Kissell Mort. Co.; Lincoln Fed. S&L Assn. of Owensboro; Lincoln Serv. Corp., The Lomas & Nettleton Co., Realty Mort. Co. & Security Pac. Mort. Co.; Citizens Fidelity Bank, Liberty Nat. Bank & United Kentucky Bank; Legal counsel for KY Wing of the Civil Patrol; **PROFL AFFIL & HONORS:** Louisville Bar Assn., KY Bar Assn., ABA, KY Trial Lawyer and Amer. Trial Lawyer; **EDUC:** BSC, 1965, Mktg. Mgmt., Univ. of Louisville; **GRAD EDUC:** JD, 1968, Law, Univ. of Louisville; **OTHER ACT & HONORS:** 1973 to 1978 - City of Louisville Prosecuter; Dir.-Home Builders; Mort. Bankers Bd. of Realtors; Civil Air Patrol; **HOME ADD:** 4019 Woodstone Way, Louisville, KY 40222, (502)228-1128; **BUS ADD:** Suite 212 Semonin Building, 4812 US Hwy. 42, Louisville, KY 40222, (502)585-1111.

PRIZER, E.L.——*Publ.*, Orlando - Land Publishing, Co., Orlando - Land Magazine; **PRIM RE ACT:** Real Estate Publisher; **BUS ADD:** PO Box 2207, Orlando, FL 32802, (305)644-3355.*

PROCK, James E.——B: Nov. 3, 1935, St. Joseph, MO, *Pres.*, Keystate Props., Inc.; **PRIM RE ACT:** Broker, Consultant, Developer, Builder, Owner/Investor, Syndicator; **SERVICES:** Feasability analysis for devel. of indus., comml. and resid. land; investment counseling; **REP CLIENTS:** Land owners and indiv. or institl. investors in devel. projects; **PREV EMPLOY:** Southwest Properties, Inc., 1968-1975; The Bergheer Co., 1976-1981; **PROFL AFFIL & HONORS:** Nat. Assn. of Indus. and Office Parks, CA RE Broker; **EDUC:** BCE, 1957, Civil Engrg., Univ. of So. CA; **GRAD EDUC:** MBA, 1964, Fin./RE, Univ. of So. CA; **MIL SERV:** USN; Lt.; 1957-1960; **OTHER ACT & HONORS:** Palos Verdes Peninsula Community Ctr. Assn.; Peninsula Comm. of Childrens Hospital; **HOME ADD:** 26673 Honey Creek Rd., Rancho Palos Verdes, CA 90274, (213)377-8576; **BUS ADD:** 26673 Honey Creek Rd., Rancho Palos Verdes, CA 90274, (213)541-5156.

PROFETA, Paul V.——B: June 29, 1944, Maplewood, NJ, *Pres.*, Paul V. Profeta and Associates, Inc.; **PRIM RE ACT:** Broker, Consultant, Developer, Lender, Instructor, Property Manager, Syndicator, Owner/Investor; **SERVICES:** Investment analysis and acquisition, synd., prop. mgmt. consulting, mort. brokerage and mort. banking; **PREV EMPLOY:** Feist & Feist; **PROFL AFFIL & HONORS:** Assoc. Prof. of RE Fin. at Columbia Grad. School of Bus.; **EDUC:** AB, 1966, Hist., Harvard Coll.; **GRAD EDUC:** MBA, 1971, RE Fin., Harvard Bus. Sch.; **BUS ADD:** 769 Northfield Ave., W. Orange, NJ 07052, (201)325-1300.

PROGIN, James A.——B: Jan. 11, 1939, Fitchburg, MA, *Sr. VP, Treas.*, Spaulding and Slye Corp.; **OTHER RE ACT:** Brokerage, construction, consulting, devel., prop. mgmt.; **PREV EMPLOY:** Arthur Andersen & Co., Boston, MA; **PROFL AFFIL & HONORS:** CPA; Member, AICPA's; **EDUC:** AB, 1960, Dartmouth Coll.; **GRAD EDUC:** MBA, 1962, Amos Tuck School of Bus. Admin.; **HOME ADD:** 8 John Swift Rd., Acton, MA 01720, (617)263-3028; **BUS ADD:** 15 New England Exec. Park, Burlington, MA 01803, (617)523-8000.

PROHASKA, Mary Ann——B: Nov. 15, 1932, O'Fallon, IL, *Broker/Sales*, Wishing Well Realty; **PRIM RE ACT:** Broker; **SERVICES:** Listing, selling, consulting; **REP CLIENTS:** Indus., resid. & comml.; **PROFL AFFIL & HONORS:** Soc. of Las Vegas RE Exchangers, GRI; NIEC Gold Card #2678; **EDUC:** RE, Clark Cty. Comm. Coll. & pvt.; **OTHER ACT & HONORS:** Past Pres. Rainbow & Demolay Mother's Clubs, Chairperson RAND, NV Mining Council, Beta Sigma Pi; **HOME ADD:** 4045 Syracuse Dr., Las Vegas, NV 89121, (702)451-4226; **BUS ADD:** 4045 Syracuse Dr., Las Vegas, NV 89121, (702)361-2288.

PROPP, Robert R. S.——B: Jan. 16, 1947, Brooklyn, NY, *Pres.*, Robert R.S. Propp & Associates, Inc.; **PRIM RE ACT:** Broker, Consultant, Owner/Investor; **EDUC:** BBA, 1968, Pace Coll.; **BUS ADD:** 1320 Princeton St., Santa Monica, CA 90404, (213)828-3357.

PROUDLEY, Edward L.——B: Nov. 26, 1939, Pittsburgh, PA, *Gen. Mgr.*, Koppers Company, Inc., Building Operations; **PRIM RE ACT:** Broker; **OTHER RE ACT:** Gen. Mgr.; **SERVICES:** Manage office bldgs.; **PROFL AFFIL & HONORS:** BOMA of Pittsburgh; Amer. Soc. for Indus. Security; **HOME ADD:** 2665 Sunnyfield Dr., Pittsburgh, PA 15241, (412)833-8795; **BUS ADD:** 2312 Koppers Bldg., Pittsburgh, PA 15219, (421)227-2919.

PROUT, P.W.——*Mgr. Corp. RE*, American Motors Corp.; **PRIM RE ACT:** Property Manager; **BUS ADD:** 27777 Franklin Rd., American Center Bldg., Southfield, MI 48034, (313)827-1000.*

PRUDHOMME, Robert G.——B: Nov. 2, 1945, Providence, RI, *VP*, Equity Advertising Agency, Inc.; **OTHER RE ACT:** Advertising agency - full service; **SERVICES:** Graphic/advertising services for every stage of project devel. from conception to ongoing mktg. of prop., both comml. and resid. Related classified and display announcements, e.g., fin. record notices for brokers and banks. Established 1924.; **EDUC:** BA, 1968, Urban Sociology, Providence Coll.; **HOME ADD:** 444 Central Park West, New York, NY 10025, (212)749-1338; **BUS ADD:** 810 Seventh Ave., New York, NY 10019, (212)541-9000.

PRUETT, H. Shelby, Jr.——B: Apr. 5, 1932, St. Louis, MO, *Exec. VP*, SPIRE Corp.; **PRIM RE ACT:** Broker, Consultant, Architect, Developer, Builder, Owner/Investor, Property Manager, Syndicator; **OTHER RE ACT:** Profl. RE Devel. services; **SERVICES:** Devel. and synd. of comml./indus. prop.; devel. mgmt services; mkt. and fin. feasibility; build to suit and lease back; prop. mgmt.; **REP CLIENTS:** Corps., instns., railroads, banking and fin.; **PROFL AFFIL & HONORS:** AIA; NCARB; Nat. Assn. of Corp. Execs.; Nat. Trust for Hist. Preservation; RE Bd. of Metropolitan St. Louis, Registered Arch.; **EDUC:** BA, 1954, Arch., Yale Univ.; **GRAD EDUC:** BArch, 1960, Arch., WA Univ. School of Arch.; **MIL SERV:** US Army; Artillery; 1st. Lt.; **OTHER ACT & HONORS:** MO Athletic Club; Media Club; Bd. of Trustees, John Burroughs School; **HOME ADD:** St. Louis Cty., MO 63132; **BUS ADD:** 801 North Eleventh, St. Louis, MO 63101, (314)621-5850.

PRYOR, Barbara L.——B: Oct. 8, 1931, Boston, MA, *VP*, Julien J. Studley, Inc., Washington Office; **PRIM RE ACT:** Broker, Consultant; **SERVICES:** Tenant brokerage, RE consulting, bldg. agencies; **REP CLIENTS:** Major Aerospace, Fin. and Computer Firms; Agencies of the US and Local Govts.; **PREV EMPLOY:** Operations and Maintenance, NL Indus.; Facilities Management, Automation Indus.; Publishing and Sales; **PROFL AFFIL & HONORS:** Nat. Fed. of Bus. and Profl. Women; DC Federation; NAR, Life Member, Million Dollar Leasing Club; WBR Member; Editorial Bd., Southeast RE News; Active contributor to local and national RE publications; **EDUC:** School of Commerce and Fin.; RE, St. Louis Univ., St. Louis, MO 1954-1958; Amer. Univ. Washington, DC; **MIL SERV:** USMC, Sgt.; **OTHER ACT & HONORS:** Member of many wildlife conservation grps. and various local and civic and charitable orgs.; **HOME ADD:** 3707 Huntington St. NW, Washington, DC 20015, (202)363-6949; **BUS ADD:** 1333 New Hampshire Ave., NW, Washington, DC 20036, (202)296-6360.

PSOTA, Peter A.——B: April 19, 1937, NY, *Asst. Regional Mgr.*, The Equitable Life Assurance Soc. of the US, Realty Operations; **PRIM RE ACT:** Broker, Developer, Lender, Owner/Investor; **SERVICES:** Financing & RE Investments; **PREV EMPLOY:** Metropolitan Life Ins. Co., Travelers Ins. Co.; **PROFL AFFIL & HONORS:** Lic. RE Broker (NY); RE Board of NY; Young Mort. Bankers Assn.; **EDUC:** 1950, RE, Wagner Coll.; **EDUC HONORS:** Dean's Honor List; **MIL SERV:** USCG, Lcdr; **OTHER ACT & HONORS:** Dir., Settlement Housing Fund; Dir. & VP, Greenwich & Perry St. Housing Corp.; **HOME ADD:** 729 Greenwich St., New York, NY 10014, (212)243-7788; **BUS ADD:** 1350 Ave. of the Americas, New York, NY 10019, (212)541-5830.

PUDLO, William J.——B: Sept. 7, 1946, Holyoke, MA, *Pres.*, Ellis Title Company, Inc.; **PRIM RE ACT:** Attorney; **OTHER RE ACT:** Chief Exec. and Counsel for title and abstracting operation; **SERVICES:** Title Abstracting, Examining, Title Ins., Consultation on RE matters, Foreclosers, Zoning, Environmental Matters; **REP CLIENTS:** Exxon, Burger King, U-Haul, Equitable Life Assurance Soc., Digital,

MA Mutual Life Ins. Co., Lenders, developers, investors in RE; **PROFL AFFIL & HONORS:** ABA, MA Bar Assn.; MA Conveyances Assn.; Amer. Land Title Assn.; New England Land Title Assn.; **EDUC:** BA, 1968, Govt., Univ. of MA, Amherst; **GRAD EDUC:** JD, 1971, Law, Univ. of Toledo, Coll. of Law; **EDUC HONORS:** Amer. Jurisprudence Awain Taxation, Constitutional Law, Admin. Law, Pub. Article in World Law Review, Volume 5; **OTHER ACT & HONORS:** Greater Springfield C of C; Guest Lecturer, W. New England Coll. of Law; Adjunct Faculty, Springfield Tech. Community Coll.; **HOME ADD:** 653 Main Street, Hampden, MA 01036, (413)566-8444; **BUS ADD:** 55 State St., Springfield, MA 01103, (413)732-7451.

PUETT, Nelson——B: Feb. 23, 1920, Breckenridge, TX, *Owner*, Nelson Puett & Assocs.; **PRIM RE ACT:** Broker, Developer, Lender, Builder, Owner/Investor, Property Manager; **PROFL AFFIL & HONORS:** Pres., Austin RE Bd.; Nat. Dir., Nat. Assn. of Home Builders; **EDUC:** BBA, 1949, Univ. of TX, Austin; **MIL SERV:** USN Air Corp.; Lt. Comdr.; **OTHER ACT & HONORS:** Dir., Holy Cross Hospital; Chancellor's Council, Univ. of TX; **BUS ADD:** 5425 Burnet Rd., Austin, TX 78756, (512)453-6611.

PUFFER, John W., III——B: June 20, 1942, Miami Beach, FL, *Atty.*, Shackleford, Farrior, Stallings & Evans, P.A.; **PRIM RE ACT:** Attorney; **SERVICES:** Counseling, rep. before admin. agencies & litigation; **REP CLIENTS:** Lenders & indiv. or instnl. investors in comml. props.; **PROFL AFFIL & HONORS:** FL Bar ABA; **EDUC:** BSE, 1964, Indus. Engrg., Univ. of MI; **GRAD EDUC:** JD, 1967, Univ. of MI; **HOME ADD:** 3013 Villa Rosa Pk, Tampa, FL 33611, (813)839-8961; **BUS ADD:** PO Box 3324, Tampa, FL 33601, (813)273-5000.

PUGH, J.W.——B: Nov. 27, 1912, Reedley, CA, *Asst. VP*, Crocker National Bank; **PRIM RE ACT:** Banker; **OTHER RE ACT:** Instr. Amer. River Coll. 1955-1979; RE Fin., RE Appraisal, Writer; **REP CLIENTS:** Author with Wm. Hippaka "CA RE Fin." Prentice-Hall, Inc. publisher, 1966, first revision 1973, second revision 1978, fourth revision due 1983; **PREV EMPLOY:** Appraiser and Asst. Cashier Place Cty. Bank, Auburn, CA; Cashier and Exec. Officer and Appraiser The Suburban Bank of Fair Oaks, CA; **PROFL AFFIL & HONORS:** Soc. of RE Appraisers (affiliate member); **EDUC:** BA, 1934, Econ., Univ. of CA, Berkeley; **GRAD EDUC:** Cert. Engrg. Mgmt. & Sci., 1943-44, Engrg. and Mgmt., Grad. School of Bus., Stanford, and Grad. School of Engrg. Santa Clara Univ.; **OTHER ACT & HONORS:** Pres. CA Bankers Assn. and Pres. Nat. Assn. of Bank Auditors and Comptrollers; **HOME ADD:** 3820 San Juan Ave., Fair Oaks, CA 95628, (916)967-7329; **BUS ADD:** 3820 San Juan Ave., Fair Oaks, CA 95628, (916)967-7329.

PUGLIESE, William D.——B: Dec. 10, 1926, Ambler, PA, *Pres.*, William D. Pugliese, Inc.; **PRIM RE ACT:** Consultant, Appraiser; **SERVICES:** Brokerage, appraisals, feasibility studies; **REP CLIENTS:** Trevose Fed. S&L Assn.; Philadelphia Nat. Bank; US Life RE Serv. Corp.; PA Dept. of Transportation; Army Corps of Engrs.; **PROFL AFFIL & HONORS:** AIREA; Soc. of RE Appraisers; Intl. Right of Way Assn.; NAR, MAI, SREA, SR/WA; **EDUC:** BS, 1951, RE, Temple Univ.; **MIL SERV:** USAAF, Sgt. 1944-1946, Good Conduct Medal, European Medal; **OTHER ACT & HONORS:** Past Pres. CA Chap. #9, 1979 Intl. R/W Assn.; Philadelphia Chap. #2, SREA 1968; SREA Gov. 1969-1971; Realtor of the Year Award 1964 by N PA Bd. of Realtors; Ambrose J. Winder Memorial Award 1974 by Philadelphia Chap. #2, SREA; Profl. Recognition Award 1979-1980-1981 by AIREA; **HOME ADD:** 309 S Main St., North Wales, PA 19454, (215)699-5155; **BUS ADD:** 112 S Main St., North Wales, PA 19454, (215)699-3511.

PULKOWNIK, Patricia S.——B: Apr. 16, 1935, Windsor,Ontario, Can., *Salesperson-associate broker*, Schostak Bros. & Co., Inc., Office Bldg. Leasing & Sales; **OTHER RE ACT:** Salesperson; **SERVICES:** Sales & leasing, investment analysis & counseling; **REP CLIENTS:** Indiv. investors, doctors, attys., anxions for cashflow and shelter to buy own bldgs. Nat. as well as local users of office rental space, looking to lease or buy office bldg. & other investment props., Mony, ; Control Data, Medicus, Telephone Employees Credit Union, TRW; **PROFL AFFIL & HONORS:** CCIM Candidate; NAR; SOCBOR; DBR; PPBW; NAFE; **EDUC:** BBA, 1977, Mktg./RE, Eastern MI Univ., Ypsilanti; **EDUC HONORS:** With honors; **HOME ADD:** 1441 Woodland Place, Plymouth, MI 48170, (313)453-8106; **BUS ADD:** 17515 W. Nine Mile Rd., Southfield, MI 48075, (313)559-2000.

PURCELL, Henry, III——B: Dec. 21, 1929, Watertown, NY, *Pres.*, Henry Purcell Inc.; **PRIM RE ACT:** Broker, Consultant, Appraiser, Developer, Builder, Owner/Investor; **OTHER RE ACT:** Building & roof contractor; **SERVICES:** Profl. broker for Hyde Park in Tampa pioneering devel. of restorations of Hyde Park bldgs. and homes since 1976; **PROFL AFFIL & HONORS:** NAR, Realtor; State Cert. Bldg. Contractor; State Cert. Roofing Contractor; **EDUC:** BS, 1953, Mil. Engrg., US Mil. Acad.; **GRAD EDUC:** MBA, 1975, Econ./Fin., Univ. of UT; **MIL SERV:** Infantry, Lt. Col., Ret. (1974), DFC, Bronze Star w/Valor, VN Cross of Gallantry, Gold Star & Silver Star; **OTHER ACT & HONORS:** Dept. of the Army designated Foreign Area Specialist (Middle East), 1963; Princeton Univ., 1961, Middle East Studies; fluent in Turkish; **BUS ADD:** 800 W. Platt St., Tampa, FL 33606, (813)251-1698.

PURDON, H.P. Sandy——B: Nov. 3, 1942, NY, NY, *Pres.*, H.P. Purdon & Co., Inc.; **PRIM RE ACT:** Broker, Instructor, Syndicator, Consultant, Developer, Owner/Investor; **SERVICES:** All Residential & Investment RE Serv.; **REP CLIENTS:** Ocean & Coast Prop., Indiv. Investors; **PREV EMPLOY:** Sales Mgr. of "The Jelley Co.," Del Mar, CA; **PROFL AFFIL & HONORS:** NAR, CAR, RNMI, RESSI, Top Salesman "Townwoode Realtors" 1972, 73; Top Listing Salesman V.E. Howard & Co. Inc., 1974; Top Listing Agent "The Jelley Co." - 1975-76; Top Agent H.P. Purdon & Co. - 1977, 78, 79, 80; **EDUC:** BSAE, 1967, Auburn Univ.; **MIL SERV:** USMC, Capt., Many commendations with Combat "V"; **OTHER ACT & HONORS:** San Diego Yacht Club, Bd. of Dir. S CA Ocean Racing Assn.; MENSA; **HOME ADD:** 12839 Via Gremaldi, Del Mar, CA 92014, (714)755-7771; **BUS ADD:** 1247 Camina de. Mar, Del Mar, CA 92014, (714)481-3300.

PURSER, Lat Wesley, III——B: June 15, 1951, Charlotte, NC, *VP*, Lat Purser & Associates, Inc., Devel. and Mort.; **PRIM RE ACT:** Broker, Developer; **SERVICES:** Comml. Devel. and Brokerage; Mort. Brokerage; **REP CLIENTS:** Food Town, Eckerd's, Woolco, T.G. & Y.; CT Mutual, Capital Holding Corp., etc.; **PROFL AFFIL & HONORS:** MBA; ICSC; **EDUC:** BA, Commerce, Washington and Lee Univ.; **GRAD EDUC:** MBA, 1976, Fin., Univ. of NC; **HOME ADD:** 1427 Biltmore Dr., Charlotte, NC 28207, (704)375-7803; **BUS ADD:** P.O. Box 18067, Charlotte, NC 28218, (704)537-9583.

PURVIS, Robert L.——B: Nov. 13, 1934, Long Beach, CA, *VP Finance & Admin.*, Alcoa Prop., Inc.; **PRIM RE ACT:** Developer, Builder, Property Manager, Owner/Investor; **PROFL AFFIL & HONORS:** IREM, NAR, Greater Pgh. Bd. of Realtors; Nat. Assn. of Accountants; **EDUC:** BS - Bus. Admin., 1956, Accounting, Pepperdine Univ., Los Angeles, CA; **GRAD EDUC:** MBA, 1968, Personnel & Indus. Admin., Univ. of OR; **MIL SERV:** USCG, LCDR; **HOME ADD:** R.D. 3 - Grouse Ln., Sewickley, PA 15142, (412)741-2576; **BUS ADD:** 11501 Alcoa Bldg., Pittsburgh, PA 15219, (412)553-4600.

PUSATERI, Anthony V.——B: Nov. 8, 1945, Chicago, IL, *SW Region VP*, Fox & Carskadon Management Corp.; **PRIM RE ACT:** Property Manager; **OTHER RE ACT:** CSM, CPM; **PREV EMPLOY:** Lehndorff Mgmt. Group, USA; **PROFL AFFIL & HONORS:** CPM, CSM, BOMA, ICSC; **EDUC:** BA, 1967, Biology/Chemistry, St. Ambrose Coll.; **EDUC HONORS:** Biological Soc.; **OTHER ACT & HONORS:** Parish Council, ALl Saints Catholic Church, Dallas; **HOME ADD:** 6906 Brentfield, Dallas, TX 75248, (214)931-6094; **BUS ADD:** 5310 Harvest Hill, Suite 118, Dallas, TX 75230, (214)934-0050.

PUTMAN, Herbert D.——B: Sept. 30, 1915, Brooklyn, NY, *Sr. VP*, Pomeroy Appraisal Assoc., Inc., RE Appraising; **PRIM RE ACT:** Appraiser, Owner/Investor, Property Manager; **REP CLIENTS:** All governmental agencies, numerous banks, investment cos., attys., private indivs.; **PROFL AFFIL & HONORS:** AIREA, MAI, IRWA, SR/WA, Amer. Soc. of Farm Mgrs. & Rural Appraisers, ARA, NARA, CRA, Intl. Inst. of Valuers, SCV; **HOME ADD:** 2294 Mercer St., Baldwinsville, NY 13027, (315)638-4051; **BUS ADD:** Suite 780, One Lincoln Ctr., Syracuse, NY 13202.

PYBRUM, Steven M.——B: Santa Cruz, CA, *Tax Specialist*, Steven M. Pybrum and Assocs., Los Osos, San Luis Obispo, Atascudero; **PRIM RE ACT:** Consultant, Developer, Owner/Investor, Instructor, Syndicator; **OTHER RE ACT:** Professor of Taxation; **SERVICES:** Income tax planning of RE transactions, Rep. before IRS, Tax Return Prep., Income Tax Compliance of RE Trans.; **PREV EMPLOY:** Cost Accountant; Wm. Wrigley Jr. Co., Public Acctg. - Various firms; **PROFL AFFIL & HONORS:** CA Bar Assn.; CA Cattlemens Assn.; Western Growers Assn.; CA CPA Assn; Founder, "Controllers Round Table"; Founder Exec., Mangemt. Services, Tax & Fin. Planning Services to Corp. Execs, CPA; **EDUC:** BS, Acctg./RE, CA Polytech. State Univ.; **GRAD EDUC:** MBA, Taxation, Golden Gate Univ.; **OTHER ACT & HONORS:** Elks; Loyns; Exchange; J.C.'s, J.C.'s, Author, "Business Cents", "Agri - Business Tax Tips"; **HOME ADD:** 249 Vista Court, Los Osos, CA, (805)528-3652; **BUS ADD:** 249 Vista Ct., Los Osos, CA 93402, (805)541-2444.

PYHRR, Dr. Stephen A.——B: Mar. 11, 1944, Alexandria, LA, *Assoc. Prof.*, Dept. of Fin., The Univ. of TX; **PRIM RE ACT:** Consultant, Appraiser, Owner/Investor, Instructor; **SERVICES:** Seminar leader, investment counseling, feasibility studies, synd. of income properties; **REP CLIENTS:** Nat., state, and local RE trade assns.; indiv. and inst. investors; **PREV EMPLOY:** Affiliate positions with various RE investment, devel., and property mgmt. firms, 1968-present; **PROFL AFFIL & HONORS:** American RE and Urban Econ. Assn.; Fin. Mgmt. Assn.; Soc. of RE Appraisers; Amer. Instit. of RE Appraisers; Nat. Assn. of Review Appraisers, PhD; Honorary Degree, School of Mgmt. Banking, Northwestern Univ., CRA; **EDUC:** BS, 1966, Fin., The Univ. of IL; **GRAD EDUC:** MS, 1968, RE and Fin., Univ. of IL; PhD, 1971, RE and Fin., Univ. of IL; **OTHER ACT & HONORS:** Co-author of textbook, "RE Investment: Strategy, Analysis, Decisions", Warren, Gorham & Lamont, expected release Jan/Feb 1982; **HOME ADD:** 10806 River Terrace, Austin, TX 78746, (512)263-2654; **BUS ADD:** Austin, TX 78712, (512)471-4368.

PYSELL, Paul Edward——B: Jan. 20, 1944, Covington, VA, *Atty.*, Lotz, Black and Menk; **PRIM RE ACT:** Attorney; **SERVICES:** Title searches, certificates of title, closings, title ins. atty.; **PREV EMPLOY:** Div. Mgr. and Officer for Mid-sized corp. experienced in sales and sales mgmt. and in broadcast fields; **PROFL AFFIL & HONORS:** ABA; VA State Bar; Assn. of Amer. Trial Lawyers; VA Trial Lawyers Assn.; **EDUC:** BA, 1971, Govt./For. Affairs, Univ. of VA; **GRAD EDUC:** JD, 1974, Wash. and Lee Univ.; **EDUC HONORS:** Phi Beta Kappa w/distinction, Cum Laude; **MIL SERV:** U.S. Army, Capt., MSM, VSM, NDSL, GCM, Cross of Gallantry; **HOME ADD:** 16 N. Lynnhaven Dr., Staunton, VA 24401, (703)885-6292; **BUS ADD:** POB 1206, Staunton, VA 24401, (703)885-0888.

QUACKENBUSH, Stanley G.——B: Dec. 26, 1923, Boston, MA, *Exec. VP*, Worcester Cty. Inst. for Savings; **PRIM RE ACT:** Banker; **SERVICES:** Mort. loans, joint ventures; **EDUC:** BBA, 1948, Acctg. & Econ., Clark Univ.; **MIL SERV:** USAF, Cpl.; **HOME ADD:** 7 Bryant Ave., Shrewsbury, MA 02131, (617)842-6645; **BUS ADD:** 365 Main St., Worcester, MA 01608, (617)791-2272.

QUAIL, Beverly J.——B: June 19, 1949, Glendale, CA, *Partner*, Welborn, Dufford, Cook & Brown; **PRIM RE ACT:** Attorney; **REP CLIENTS:** Ingersoll-Rand Fin. Corp., First Nat. Bank in Grand Junction, Empire Savings, Building and Loan Assn.; **PROFL AFFIL & HONORS:** ABA, Section of Real Prop. Probate and Trust-Comm. on RE Litigation; CO Bar Assn., Legislative Comm. on RE; **EDUC:** BA, 1971, Univ. of S CA; **GRAD EDUC:** JD, 1974, Law, Univ. of Denver; **EDUC HONORS:** Magna Cum Laude, Phi Beta Kappa, Univ. of Denver-Denver Law Journal; **HOME ADD:** 19 Random Rd., Englewood, CO 80110, (303)781-6567; **BUS ADD:** 1100 United Bank Ctr., Denver, CO 80290, (303)861-8013.

QUARTARARO, Frank A.——B: July 28, 1931, Brooklyn, NY, *Pres.*, Century 21 Frank A. Quartararao Realty Corp.; **PRIM RE ACT:** Broker, Consultant, Appraiser, Owner/Investor, Property Manager, Insuror; **PROFL AFFIL & HONORS:** Brooklyn Bd. of Realtors; NY State Bd. of Realtors; Nat. Bd. of Realtors; Bay Ridge RE Bd.; MLS Serv.; **EDUC:** BBA, 1951; **MIL SERV:** USN, Storekeeper 2c; **OTHER ACT & HONORS:** Branch Office: 6407 Bay Parkway Brooklyn, NY; Tel: (212)CEN-TURY; **HOME ADD:** 7321 5 Ave., Brooklyn, NY 11209, (212)833-1776; **BUS ADD:** 7321 5 Ave., Brooklyn, NY 11209, (212)680-4800.

QUAST, Gerald D.——B: July 11, 1953, Aurora, IL, *Atty.*, Quast & Glenn; **PRIM RE ACT:** Attorney; **SERVICES:** Legal representation pertaining to the following: acquisitions, condos., loans, landlord-tenant, foreclosures, leases, construction contracts, etc.; **REP CLIENTS:** Banks, devels., builders, owner/investors, lenders, etc.; **PREV EMPLOY:** Geary, Stahl & Spencer, Attorneys at Law; **PROFL AFFIL & HONORS:** ABA; TX Bar Assn.; Dallas Bar Assn.; TX Young Lawyers Assn.; **EDUC:** BA, 1975, Fin., Western IL Univ.; **GRAD EDUC:** JD, 1978, Law, TX Tech, School of Law; **EDUC HONORS:** Dean's List, Student Ins. Award, TX Tech Law Review, Faculty Scholarship; **HOME ADD:** 9321 Leon Dr., Dallas, TX 75217, (214)286-6364; **BUS ADD:** 3000 Turtle Creek Plaza, Suite 203, Dallas, TX 75219, (214)528-4810.

QUAST, Richard D.——B: Apr. 20, 1930, Chicago, IL, *VP Corp. RE*, W. W. Grainger, Inc.; **PRIM RE ACT:** Developer, Builder, Owner/Investor, Property Manager; **OTHER RE ACT:** Devel. of corp. props. for W. W. Grainger, Inc.; **PROFL AFFIL & HONORS:** I.D.R.C., Nat. Assn. of Corporate RE Exec.; **EDUC:** BA, 1952, Geography/Geology, Beloit Coll.; **OTHER ACT & HONORS:** Chmn. Kildeer Plan. Commn., Chmn. Leaning Tower YMCA; **HOME ADD:** 21175 N. Middleton Dr., Kildeer, IL 60047, (312)438-2593; **BUS ADD:** 5500 W. Howard St., Skokie, IL 60077, (312)982-9000.

QUATE, Laurence W.——B: Aug. 25, 1925, Milford, UT, *Owner*, L.W. Quate, Realtor; **PRIM RE ACT:** Instructor, Syndicator, Developer; **PREV EMPLOY:** Entomologist, B.P. Bishop Museum, Honolulu, HI; **PROFL AFFIL & HONORS:** CCIM; **EDUC:** BS, 1949, Entomology, Univ. of CA, Berkeley; **GRAD EDUC:** PhD, 1952, Entomology, Univ. of CA, Berkeley; **MIL SERV:** USNR, PhM2C; **OTHER ACT & HONORS:** Rotary Club of Poway, CA Pres. 1979-80; Dir., San Diego Bd. of Dir.; Dir., Poway C of C; **HOME ADD:** 14755 High Valley Rd., Poway, CA 90264, (714)748-8856; **BUS ADD:** PO Box 51, Poway, CA 92064.

QUATTRIN, Gary L.——B: Jan. 22, 1943, Watsonville, CA, *Atty.*, Quattrin & Clemons; **PRIM RE ACT:** Consultant; **SERVICES:** Legal serv.; **REP CLIENTS:** Fed. Projects, Inc. - King Realty & Investment Co., PHA Realty Corp. - Fed. Prop. Mgmt., Inc.; **PREV EMPLOY:** Prop. mgmt. - FPR Community Devel.; **PROFL AFFIL & HONORS:** Sacramento Cty. Bar Assn.; ABA, Outstanding Alumni 1981 Lincoln Law Sch.; **EDUC:** 1965, Education, CA State Univ. Sacramento; **GRAD EDUC:** JD, 1975, Law, Lincoln Law Sch.; **OTHER ACT & HONORS:** Hornet Stinger Found. - Past Pres. CSUS, Outstanding Alumni, Lincoln Law School - 1981 - Outstanding Alumni CSUS Phys. Ed. 1980 & 81 - Hall of Fame CSUS 1979; **HOME ADD:** 8539 Emperor Dr., Fair Oaks, CA 95628; **BUS ADD:** 25 Cadellac Dr., Sacramento, CA 95825, (916)925-1081.

QUAY, Kenneth——B: Sept. 8, 1950, New York, NY, L. F. Rothschild, Untesberg, Towbin, Prop. Div.; **PRIM RE ACT:** Broker, Syndicator; **OTHER RE ACT:** Investment banker; **PREV EMPLOY:** Citibank, N.A. (RE Indus. Div.); **EDUC:** BBA, 1972, Acctg., Pace Univ.; **GRAD EDUC:** MBA, 1974, RE Fin., Wharton Grad. School; **HOME ADD:** 245 East 87th St., New York, NY 10028, (212)860-4822; **BUS ADD:** 55 Water St., New York, NY 10041, (212)425-3300.

QUEEN, Barry L.——B: Feb. 7, 1942, Springfield, MA, *Pres.*, Mutual Investment Group; **PRIM RE ACT:** Attorney, Banker, Developer, Lender, Owner/Investor, Property Manager; **OTHER RE ACT:** VP, Comml. RE, Mutual Bank for Savings; **SERVICES:** Financing, equity funds, joint ventures; **PROFL AFFIL & HONORS:** ABA; Nat. Assn. Mutual Savings Banks; Nat. Mort. Policy Comm.; Nat. Urban Investment Councilas . ; Amer. Bar Assn., MA Bar; **EDUC:** BA, 1963, Sociology, St. Lawrence Univ.; **GRAD EDUC:** LLB, 1969, Law, RE, Western New England; **EDUC HONORS:** Soc. and Psych. honorary, In RE, Criminal & Contract Law, Cum Laude; **OTHER ACT & HONORS:** Tr. & Dir., Local Devel. Corp. of Newton 1980-81; Temple Brotherhood Board, Mayor's Devel. Comm.; Instructor, Boston Arch. Center Continuing Educ.; Tr. Wedgestone Trust; President Chestnut Hill Development Corp.; **HOME ADD:** 958 Salem End Rd., Framingham, MA 01701, (617)872-2030; **BUS ADD:** 21 Merchants Row, Boston, MA 02109, (617)523-7170.

QUELER, Arthur N.——B: Aug. 7, 1946, NY, NY, *Managing Gen. Part.*, Berg Harquel Assoc.; **PRIM RE ACT:** Consultant, Owner/Investor, Syndicator; **SERVICES:** Tax planning; **REP CLIENTS:** Execs., prin. of closely-held corps., other profls.; **PREV EMPLOY:** 1975-80 Part. of Finkle & Co., CPA,s 1972-75, Peat, Marwick, Mitchell & Co., tax spec. & supervisor; **PROFL AFFIL & HONORS:** NY & NJ Soc. of CPA, MICPA; **EDUC:** BBA, 1969, Bus. Admin, Bernard M. Baruch Coll. of CUNY; **GRAD EDUC:** MBA, 1971, Bernard M. Baruch Coll. of CUNY; **HOME ADD:** 18 Massa Lane, Apt. D3 & 4, Edgewater, NJ 07020, (201)224-8353; **BUS ADD:** One Exec. Dr., Fort Lee, NJ 07024, (201)592-6700.

QUICK, Jacob D.——B: Nov. 9, 1938, Somerville, NJ, *Pres.*, Feist & Feist Realty Corp.; **PRIM RE ACT:** Broker; **SERVICES:** Indus. RE sales and leasing; **PROFL AFFIL & HONORS:** Active member SIR; **EDUC:** Rutgers Univ., 1960; **GRAD EDUC:** MBA, 1963, Fairleigh Dickinson Univ.; **MIL SERV:** US Army, 1st Lt.; **OTHER ACT & HONORS:** Former Mayor of Branchburg Twp., NJ, 1972 & 1975; **HOME ADD:** 42 SO. Branch Rd., Neshanic Sta., NY 08853, (201)369-4034; **BUS ADD:** 101 Eisenhower Parkway, Roseland, NJ 07068, (201)226-5000.

QUINLAN, Paul——*Dir.*, Nebraska Real Estate Commission; **PRIM RE ACT:** Property Manager; **BUS ADD:** 301 Centennial Mall, South, Box 94667, Lincoln, NE 68509, (402)471-2004.*

QUINN, Dennis J.——*Ed.-Publ.*, Apt. & Motel Assn. of Calif., The Apartment Reporter; **PRIM RE ACT:** Real Estate Publisher; **BUS ADD:** 3921 Wilshire Blvd., Los Angeles, CA 90010, (213)388-6136.*

QUINN, James. T.——**B:** Sept. 14, 1948, Tucson, AZ, *Rgnl. Dir./VP*, BJF Development, Inc., NE; **OTHER RE ACT:** Condo. Conversions; **SERVICES:** Prop. mgmt., condo. devel. & condo. conversions; **REP CLIENTS:** Prudential Ins. Co., CT Mutual; Aetna Life & Casuality; **PREV EMPLOY:** First Mort. Investors, First Mort. Advisors, VP; **PROFL AFFIL & HONORS:** Miami Bd. of Realtors, RE Broker, Mort. Broker; **EDUC:** BA, 1970, Econ., Rutgers Univ.; **GRAD EDUC:** MBA, 1973, Acctg., RE, Fin., Univ. of AZ; **EDUC HONORS:** Dean's List, Grad. Scholar; **MIL SERV:** USAF; 1st Lt.; **OTHER ACT & HONORS:** Miami Shores Ctry. Club; **HOME ADD:** 1218 NE 98th St., Miami Shores, FL 33138, (305)757-2799; **BUS ADD:** Village of Kings Creek, 7900 Camino Real, Miami, FL 33143.

QUINN, Michael D.——**B:** Sept. 4, 1936, Baltimore, MD, *Chmn. of the Bd.*, The Wye Group, Inc.; **PRIM RE ACT:** Broker, Consultant, Appraiser, Developer, Lender, Owner/Investor, Property Manager, Syndicator, Insuror; **SERVICES:** RE fin., joint ventures, ins., synd. of comml. prop., consulting; **REP CLIENTS:** Lenders and indiv. or instnl. investors in comml. prop.; **PROFL AFFIL & HONORS:** Baltimore Economic Soc., MD Mort. Bankers Assn., Nat. Assn. of Bus. Econ., Faculty, The Johns Hopkins Univ.; **EDUC:** 1960, Econ. and Fin., Univ. of MD; **MIL SERV:** USN, 1954-1956; **OTHER ACT & HONORS:** Ducks Unltd., Saints and Sinners of Amer.; **HOME ADD:** 8207 Robin Hood Court, Baltimore, MD 21204, (301)825-5678; **BUS ADD:** 28 Allegheny Ave., Baltimore, MD 21204, (301)296-7733.

RAAB, David A.——**B:** Feb. 12, 1955, York, PA, *Appraiser/Realtor*, Raab Agencies, Resid. Spec.; **PRIM RE ACT:** Broker, Consultant, Appraiser, Owner/Investor, Property Manager; **SERVICES:** Appraisal, brokerage, Mgmt.; **REP CLIENTS:** FHA; Banks; Attys.; lending instns.; realtors; indivs.; relocaton cos.; **PREV EMPLOY:** Thomasville Airport, Cert. FAA private pilot; **PROFL AFFIL & HONORS:** NAR, PA Realtors Assn., AACA, NARA, CRA, CAR, SCV; **EDUC:** BS, 1970, RE, York Coll. of PA; **OTHER ACT & HONORS:** Numerous; **HOME ADD:** 2800 Stillmeadow Ln., York, PA 17404, (717)764-8016; **BUS ADD:** 119E King St., York, PA 17403, (717)846-9550.

RABBIDEAU, Richard E.——**B:** Jan. 30, 1938, Ironwood, MI, *Partner*, Dykema, Gossett, Spencer, Goodnow & Trigg; **PRIM RE ACT:** Attorney; **PREV EMPLOY:** VP, H.F. Campbell Co. (Const./Devel.); **PROFL AFFIL & HONORS:** ABA; MI State Bar Assn.; Oakland Cty. Bar Assn.; Detroit Bar Assn., Council Member, Real Prop. Law Section, State Bar of MI; Member, Amer. Coll. of RE Lawyers; **EDUC:** BA, 1959, Eng., Univ. of MI; **GRAD EDUC:** JD, 1962, Univ. of MI; **HOME ADD:** 280 Touraine, Grosse Pointe Farms, MI 48236, (313)885-8836; **BUS ADD:** 35th Floor, 400 Renaissance Center, Detroit, MI 48243, (313)643-9640.

RABIN, Sol L.——**B:** Nov. 24, 1935, Philadelphia, PA, *Sr. VP*, Coldwell Banker, Consultation Servs.; **PRIM RE ACT:** Consultant; **OTHER RE ACT:** Mkt. research, investment counseling; **REP CLIENTS:** All maj. US developers; **PREV EMPLOY:** Professor, UCLA; **PROFL AFFIL & HONORS:** RE Counselor; **EDUC:** REED, 1957, Harvard Univ.; **GRAD EDUC:** MCP & PhD, 1960, City Planning, Univ. of PA; **HOME ADD:** 9315 Burton Way, Beverly Hills, CA 90210, (213)271-5275; **BUS ADD:** 533 Fremont Ave., Los Angeles, CA 90071, (213)613-3616.

RABINOWITZ, Alan James——**B:** Dec. 13, 1949, Revere, MA, *Prop. Atty.*, New England Electric System, New England Power Serv. Co.; **PRIM RE ACT:** Attorney; **SERVICES:** Legal advice & representation in all aspects of real prop. law including acquisition, sale, mgmt. and litigation; public utility clients; **PREV EMPLOY:** Private practice, 1974-1975; **PROFL AFFIL & HONORS:** ABA, Sects. on Real Prop., Probate & Trust Law, Corp., Banking & Bus. Law, Litigation; MA Conveyancers' Assn.; **EDUC:** BA, 1971, Govt., Norwich Univ.; **GRAD EDUC:** JD, 1974, New England School of Law; **MIL SERV:** US Army Res.; Capt.; 1971-1979; **HOME ADD:** 14 B Mayberry Dr., Westborough, MA 01581, (617)366-0113; **BUS ADD:** 25 Research Dr., Westborough, MA 01581, (617)366-9011.

RACE, Bradford J., Jr.——**B:** May 2, 1945, Hudson, NY, *Partner*, Seward & Kissell; **PRIM RE ACT:** Attorney; **PREV EMPLOY:** Dewey Ballantine Bushby Palmer & Wood; **EDUC:** AB, 1967, Hope Coll.; **GRAD EDUC:** JD, 1970, NW Univ.; **EDUC HONORS:** Cum Laude; **OTHER ACT & HONORS:** Bd. of Dir., Municipal Assistance Corp. for the City of NY; **HOME ADD:** 330 E 46th St., New York, NY; **BUS ADD:** Wall St. Plaza, Seward & Kissel, New York, NY 10005, (212)248-2800.

RACKOW, Julian P.——**B:** Dec. 16, 1941, Philadelphia, PA, *Partner*, Blank, Rome, Comisky & McCauley; **PRIM RE ACT:** Attorney; **PROFL AFFIL & HONORS:** ABA, Philadelphia & PA Bar Assns.; **EDUC:** AB, 1963, Govt., Cornell Univ.; **GRAD EDUC:** LLB, 1966, Harvard Law School; **EDUC HONORS:** Deans List; **BUS ADD:** Suite 1200, 4 Penn Ctr. Plaza, Philadelphia, PA 19103, (215)569-3700.

RACUSIN, Barry L.——**B:** May 26, 1949, Corpus Christi, TX, *Atty.*, Barry L. Racusin and Associates; **PRIM RE ACT:** Attorney; **SERVICES:** Gen. legal rep. on all phases of RE; **REP CLIENTS:** United Bank - Houston, United Bank - Metro of Houston; **PROFL AFFIL & HONORS:** Houston Bar Assn.; ABA; State Bar of TX; **EDUC:** AB, 1971, Govt./Econ., Univ. of TX, Austin; **GRAD EDUC:** JD, 1974, Corp./RE/Oil & Gas/Banking Law, Bates Coll. of Law, Univ. of Houston; **HOME ADD:** 7743 Portal, Houston, TX 77071, (713)981-0967; **BUS ADD:** 1990 Post Oak Blvd., Suite 1660, 1900 W Loop S, Houston, TX 77056, (713)222-6541.

RADCLIFFE, Clyde, III——*Asst. VP*, Universal Leaf Tobacco Co.; **PRIM RE ACT:** Property Manager; **BUS ADD:** 1501 North Hamilton St., at Broad, Richmond, VA 23260, (804)359-9311.*

RADER, F. Ronald——**B:** Sept. 18, 1943, NY, *Pres.*, The Rader Co., Inc.; **PRIM RE ACT:** Broker, Appraiser, Property Manager; **SERVICES:** Mkt. surveys, mkt. indus. & comml. props.; **REP CLIENTS:** Voi-Shan Int., The Antique Guild, Topa Mgmt., Zelman Devel., Burlington Northern Indus., Aeroquip Corp., Home Silk Shop, See's Candy, Funstriders; **PROFL AFFIL & HONORS:** RE Assn., Los Angeles Bd. of Realtors, CA Assn. of Realtors, Master of Indus. Brokerage, Soc. of Indus. Realtors; **EDUC:** El Camino Jr. Coll., Univ. of CA at Los Angeles; **OTHER ACT & HONORS:** History Preservation Soc., Past Pres. of Cheviot Hills Homeowners Assn., V.P. Amer. Indus. RE Assns.; **HOME ADD:** 2803 Forrester Dr., Cheviot Hills, CA 90064, (213)836-1710; **BUS ADD:** 2999 Overland Ave., Suite 103, Los Angeles, CA 90064, (213)204-3333.

RADER, Richard E.——**B:** Dec. 5, 1939, Wichita, KS, *Atty.-Owner*, Rader, Rader & Goulart; **PRIM RE ACT:** Attorney, Developer, Builder, Owner/Investor, Syndicator; **SERVICES:** Law in all phases of RE, including synd. and litigation; **REP CLIENTS:** Devels. and lenders; **PREV EMPLOY:** Trial Atty. with CA State Div. of Highways; **PROFL AFFIL & HONORS:** Licensed Atty. and Contractor; **EDUC:** BA, 1960, Pol. Sci., Radio and T.V., Univ. of Denver; **GRAD EDUC:** LLB, 1963, Law, Stanford Univ.; **OTHER ACT & HONORS:** VP, Bd. of Trustees, Sacramento Ctry. Day School; **HOME ADD:** 2340 Morley Way, Sacramento, CA 95825, (916)488-5839; **BUS ADD:** 2617 K St., Sacramento, CA 95816, (916)446-7577.

RADLOFF, Robert A.——**B:** Mar. 30, 1947, Chicago, IL, *Pres.*, The Boston Co. RE Counsel, Inc.; **OTHER RE ACT:** Investment Advisor to Pension Plans and Individuals; **SERVICES:** Advisory, Portfolio Mgmt., Portfolio Design, Synd.; **REP CLIENTS:** Instnl. Pension Plan Investors & Indiv. Investors; **PREV EMPLOY:** Kuras & Co., Inc., VP; **PROFL AFFIL & HONORS:** The Greater Boston RE Bd.; **EDUC:** BSBA, 1969, Fin., Boston Univ., School of Mgmt.; **OTHER ACT & HONORS:** Bd. of Mgrs. New England Home for Little Wanderers; **HOME ADD:** 75 Revere St., Boston, MA 02114, (617)227-6999; **BUS ADD:** One Boston Pl., Boston, MA 02106, (617)722-7102.

RADUNS, Edward B.——**B:** Oct. 1, 1930, Brooklyn, NY, *Pres.*, Southern Mort. Assoc., Inc.; **PRIM RE ACT:** Banker; **SERVICES:** FHA/VA Approved mort. banker; **REP CLIENTS:** FNMA; GNMA & 50 other S&L, comml. banks, pension funds; **PROFL AFFIL & HONORS:** MBA of Amer.; MBA of FL; MBA of Miami; Miami Bd. of Realtors, CMB; NFA; **EDUC:** BBA, 1952, Econ., Univ. of Miami; **GRAD EDUC:** MBA, 1972, Bus., Univ. of Miami; **MIL SERV:** US Army; Sgt.; **OTHER ACT & HONORS:** Member, Bd. of Dir., Nat. Assn. of CMB's; Member, Bd. of Dir., 1st City Bank of Coral Gables; **HOME ADD:** 10776 N Kendall Dr., Miami, FL 33176; **BUS ADD:** 1999 S.W. 27th Ave., Miami, FL 33145, (305)856-8000.

RAFFERTY, Michael Maurice——**B:** Mar. 3, 1953, Frankfurt, Germany, Mount Vernon Realty, Inc., Land, Comml. and Investment Div.; **PRIM RE ACT:** Broker, Consultant, Builder, Owner/Investor, Syndicator; **OTHER RE ACT:** Arch./Engrg. Consultant; **SERVICES:** Land packaging, devel. of resid. and comml. projects, investor counseling, synd. and technical design work; **REP CLIENTS:** Instl., corp. and indiv. devels./builders, investors; **PREV EMPLOY:** Dewberry, Nealon and Davis: largest arch./eng. consulting firm in Northern VA; **PROFL AFFIL & HONORS:** Assoc. Member AIA, AIP, Natl. Assn. of Realtors, Northern VA Builders Assn.; **EDUC:** BA, 1977,

Urban and Environmental Systems, VA Polytechnic Inst. and State Univ.; **EDUC HONORS:** Snibling Meritorious Scholarship; City of Blacksburg Planning Internship (Post-Grad.); **OTHER ACT & HONORS:** Citizen Comm.-Northern Sector, Southeastern Fairfax Cty. Redevel. Authority, Troop leader - Boy Scouts Troop 499, Artistry Found., Wash., DC; **HOME ADD:** 8602 Woodbine Lane, Annandale, VA 22003, (703)971-5613; **BUS ADD:** 6000 Stevenson Ave., Suite 303, Alexandria, VA 22304, (703)370-4100.

RAGOSA, C. Jerry——B: May 24, 1947, Norwalk, CT, *Tr./Exec. VP*, RE Investment Trust of Amer.; **OTHER RE ACT:** Tr. of Equity RE Investment Trust; **SERVICES:** Admin. Trust Activities; **PREV EMPLOY:** Dir./VP of Minot, DeBlois and Maddison, Inc.; **PROFL AFFIL & HONORS:** CPM, Realtor, ICSC Member; **EDUC:** BS, 1969, Econ., School of Mgmt.; **GRAD EDUC:** MBA, 1972, Boston Coll. School of Mgmt.; **OTHER ACT & HONORS:** American Arbitration Assc's Panel of Arbitrators.; **HOME ADD:** 51 Randolph Ave, Milton, MA 02187; **BUS ADD:** 294 Washington St., Boston, MA 02108, (617)426-2921.

RAHBAN, Frank——B: March 8, 1942, Iran, *Broker*, Beverly Hills Prop. & Mgmt. Co. & BHP Realty, Inc.; **PRIM RE ACT:** Broker; **GRAD EDUC:** BSCB, 1963, London Univ.; **HOME ADD:** 251 N. Bristol Ave., Los Angeles, CA 90049, (213)476-0407; **BUS ADD:** 433 N. Camden Dr., Beverly Hills, CA 90210, (213)550-0339.

RAHIYA, John C.——B: Jan. 4, 1944, Louisville, KY, *Asst. VP, Mktg.*, Equifax Services, Gen. Mgmt. Sys.; **OTHER RE ACT:** Supplying credit repts., mort. and prop. info. to lenders; **SERVICES:** Credit repts., loan services repts., dealing mort. contracts, prop. cond. and inspect. repts.; **REP CLIENTS:** Major resid. and comm. lenders; **PROFL AFFIL & HONORS:** Cobb Cty. Bd. of Realtors, GA Assn. of Realtors, NAR, Mort. Bankers Assn.; **EDUC:** BBA, 1966, Mgmt., Univ. of Notre Dame; **GRAD EDUC:** MBA, 1970, Mktg., Northwestern Univ.; **EDUC HONORS:** Deans List; **MIL SERV:** US Army, 1st Lt., Bronze Star, Army Commendation, Amer. Spirit Honor Medal; **OTHER ACT & HONORS:** Amer. Mktg. Assn., Amer. Soc. of Personnel Admin., named Man of the Year by the Atlanta Notre Dame Club; **HOME ADD:** 239 Woods Edge Ct., Marietta, GA 30067, (404)971-5813; **BUS ADD:** 1600 Peachtree St. N.W., Atlanta, GA 30309, (404)885-8095.

RAHL, Craig Thomas——B: Nov. 1, 1951, Morristown, NJ, *Dir. of Operations & Training*, Weichert Co. Realtors; **PRIM RE ACT:** Broker, Instructor, Property Manager; **OTHER RE ACT:** In charge of operations for largest RE Co. in NJ & Dir. of RE school; **PREV EMPLOY:** Dir. of Training, Weichert Realtors; Sales Assoc., Weichert Realtors; Sales, Suburban RE; **PROFL AFFIL & HONORS:** Morris Cty. Bd. of Realtors, NJAR, NAR, RE Trainers Assn., NJAR-State Million Dollar Club, Exec. Comm. Assoc. Dir. Morris Cty. Bd. of Realtors, Educ. Comm., Morris Cty. Bd. of Realtors; Fortune Co. Master Trainer Weichert Million Dollar Sales; **EDUC:** BA, 1974, Hist. & Poli. Sci., Bethany Coll., Bethany, WV; **GRAD EDUC:** Currently working toward MBA, Fairleigh Dickinson Univ., Madison, NJ; **EDUC HONORS:** Dean's List, Phi Alpha Theta (Nat. Hist. Frat.); **OTHER ACT & HONORS:** Kiwanis Club, Dir., 1978-79; Sigma Alpha Epsilon Frat., pledge trainer; **HOME ADD:** 85 Hillside Rd., Chester, NJ 07930, (201)879-7692; **BUS ADD:** 6 Dumont Pl., Morristown, NJ 07960, (201)267-7777.

RAI, Shambhu K.——B: June 22, 1937, Hoshangabad, M.P. INDIA, *Atty. at Law*; **PRIM RE ACT:** Broker, Consultant, Attorney, Developer, Owner/Investor, Property Manager, Syndicator; **OTHER RE ACT:** RE Law, Bus. Law, Corp. and Trusts; **SERVICES:** Civil and RE atty's services, synd. and devel. of comml. and RE projects, valuation, investment counseling, brokerage, prop. mgmt.; **PROFL AFFIL & HONORS:** ABA, MA Bar Assn., Boston and Middlesex Bar, Panel of Arbitrators, Amer. Arbitration Assn.; **EDUC:** LLB, 1959, Law, Sagar Univ., Sagar, INDIA; **GRAD EDUC:** LLM, 1974, Gen. Law, NY Univ. School of Law; **EDUC HONORS:** Univ. Gold Medal; **OTHER ACT & HONORS:** Indian Postal Serv., Govt. of India, Past Pres. of India Assn. of Greater Boston; **HOME ADD:** 25 Swan Rd., Winchester, MA 01890, (617)367-2108; **BUS ADD:** 18 Tremont St., Boston, MA 02108, (617)367-2108.

RAILSBACK, David P.——B: Aug. 21, 1950, Newton, MA, *Atty.*, Railsback Associates; **PRIM RE ACT:** Developer; **PROFL AFFIL & HONORS:** Amer. RI & MA Bar Assoc., RESSI; **EDUC:** BS, 1972, Acctg., Lehigh Univ.; **GRAD EDUC:** JD, 1978, Suffolk Univ. Law School; **EDUC HONORS:** Summa Cum Laude, Cum Laude; Law Review; **HOME ADD:** 631 Angell St., Providence, RI 02903, (401)751-8974; **BUS ADD:** 161 Walnut St., Boston, MA 02122, (617)288-5715.

RAINEN, Edward——B: Jul. 20, 1951, Malden, MA, Edward Rainen, Esq.; **PRIM RE ACT:** Attorney; **OTHER RE ACT:** Title Examiner; **SERVICES:** Title examination, title ins., closing servs.; **PROFL AFFIL & HONORS:** MA Conveyancers Assn.; MA Bar Assn.; ABA, Land Ct. Examiner; **EDUC:** BA, 1973, Econ., Hofstra Univ.; **GRAD EDUC:** JD, 1976, Boston Coll. Law School; **EDUC HONORS:** Cum Laude; **OTHER ACT & HONORS:** Bd. of Dirs., Temple Israel, Stoneham, MA; Fin. and Adv. Bd., town of Stoneham; **HOME ADD:** 18 Sparhawk Circ., Stoneham, MA 02180, (617)665-3193; **BUS ADD:** 18 Sparhawk Circ., Stoneham, MA 02180, (617)665-3193.

RAINER, James C., III——B: Feb. 14, 1933, Memphis, TN, *Pres.*, Rainer & Co.; **PRIM RE ACT:** Broker, Consultant, Appraiser, Owner/Investor, Property Manager; **SERVICES:** Specializes in agric. RE in Sunbelt states, evaluate, purchase, and devel. farm props., manage farms for others; **REP CLIENTS:** Investors, trust depts., & inst. which own or invest in farm RE with props. of 1,000 acres minimum; **PREV EMPLOY:** Dunavant Enterprises, 1971-78, Northwestern Mutual Life Ins. Co., 1961-64, farm mort. loan rep.; **PROFL AFFIL & HONORS:** Young Farmer of Yr., 60, Crittenden Cty., AK; **EDUC:** BA, 1954, Econ., Univ. of VA; **EDUC HONORS:** Phi Beta Kappa, Degree with distinction, Raven Soc.; **MIL SERV:** US Army, SP3; **OTHER ACT & HONORS:** Chm-. of Bd. St George's Day Sch., Bd. of Dir. Memphis Boy's Club, Tr. Episcopal Endowment Corp., Diocese of TN; **HOME ADD:** 626 S Shady Grove Rd., Memphis, TN 38119, (901)683-1822; **BUS ADD:** 871 Ridgeway Loop Rd., Suite 204, Memphis, TN 38119, (901)761-3652.

RAINES, Jack M.——B: Nov. 23, 1937, Port Arthur, TX, *Pres*, 3/D Intnl.; **PRIM RE ACT:** Architect; **OTHER RE ACT:** Planner; **SERVICES:** Arch., Engrg, planning, project mgmt, interior design, graphic design, Landscaping; **REP CLIENTS:** ARAMCO, Continental Airlines, Inc., Dow Chemical Co., Exxon Corp., Gen Electric Co., Gulf & Western Indus. Inc., IBM; **PROFL AFFIL & HONORS:** ABA, Houston Bar Assoc.; **EDUC:** BBA, 1960, TX A&M Univ.; **GRAD EDUC:** JD, 1967, Univ. of Houston; **MIL SERV:** USCG, Seaman; **OTHER ACT & HONORS:** Admitted to practice, Supreme Ct. of the US & Supreme Ct. of TX; **HOME ADD:** 635 Knipp, Houston, TX 77024, (713)871-7481; **BUS ADD:** 1900 W. Loop St., Houston, TX 77027, (713)871-7479.

RAINEY, Joseph S.——B: June 5, 1922, Ft. Collins, CO, *Owner*, Joseph S. Rainey & Assoc., Archs., Planners, Engs.; **PRIM RE ACT:** Architect, Consultant, Engineer; **SERVICES:** Arch., Planning, Eng., Insp., Testing; **EDUC:** BS Arch, 1950, Arch./Planning, GA Inst. of Tech., Atlanta, GA; **EDUC HONORS:** Student Design Prize Winner; **MIL SERV:** USAF, Capt./ Aircraft cmdr., multi-engine; DFC, Air Medal w/ Clusters, Unit Cit. CPI, European Theater, Alutian Theater; **OTHER ACT & HONORS:** Pres. Norristown Lions Club; Pres. PTL; Pres. Norristown Art League; Dir Comm. Homes Inc.; Dir. Comm. Missions Lutheran Church MO Synod, Phila., PA; **HOME ADD:** 625 Wayland Rd., Plymouth Meeting, PA 19462, (215)828-8389; **BUS ADD:** 625 Wayland Rd., Plymouth Meeting, PA 19462, (215)828-5315.

RAKOW, Michael G., Ph.D.——B: July 26, 1944, Fayetteville, NC, *Pres.*, Midas Realty, Rakow Enterprises Inc.; **PRIM RE ACT:** Broker, Consultant; **SERVICES:** Co. specializes in comml. re investments; **REP CLIENTS:** Indiv. and inst. investors of comml. re; **PREV EMPLOY:** Univ. prof., site locator for nat. chain store; **EDUC:** BA, 1966, Pol. Sci., AZ State Univ.; **GRAD EDUC:** MA, 1973, Politics/Govt., AZ State Univ.; Ph.D., 1973, Politics/Govt., AZ State Univ.; **EDUC HONORS:** Nat. Sci. Found. Fellowship, Nat. Sci. Found. Fellowship; **OTHER ACT & HONORS:** Phoenix C of C; **HOME ADD:** 7722 N. 3rd Ave., Phoenix, AZ 85021, (602)943-8100; **BUS ADD:** 205 E. Osborn Rd., Phoenix, AZ 85012, (602)265-1500.

RAKOW, Robert F.——B: June 12, 1938, Wausau, WI, *Facilities Mgr.*, Wausau Ins. Co.; **PRIM RE ACT:** Property Manager; **OTHER RE ACT:** Responsible for all Co. leased facilities; **PROFL AFFIL & HONORS:** CPM, IREM; **EDUC:** BS, 1960, Acctg. & Genl. Bus., Carroll Coll.; **MIL SERV:** USAR, Sgt., 1960-66; **OTHER ACT & HONORS:** D.C. Everest School Bd. 1975-78; Town of Weston Planning Commn. 1980-present; Direct SchooL Dist. Flag Football League; **HOME ADD:** 3811 Sternberg Ave., Schofield, WI 24476, (712)359-4524; **BUS ADD:** 2000 Westwood Dr., Wausau, WI 54401, (715)845-5211.

RAKUSIN, Beatryce——B: Apr. 18, 1926, Providence, RI, *Pres.*, Tira Realty Inc.; **PRIM RE ACT:** Broker; **SERVICES:** All areas of RE; **PROFL AFFIL & HONORS:** Miami Bd. of Realtors, FL State Bd. of Realtors, Nat. Bd. of Realtors, Realtor/Broker; **HOME ADD:** 1045 NE 170th Terr., N Miami, FL 33162, (305)651-7353; **BUS ADD:** 1745 NE 124th St., N. Miami, FL 33181, (305)895-0895.

RALLS, E. Scott——**B:** Dec. 9, 1950, Ralls, TX., *President*, Century 21 Ralls Realty, The E.S. Ralls Corp.; **PRIM RE ACT:** Broker, Consultant, Developer, Owner/Investor, Property Manager; **OTHER RE ACT:** Lease Broker; **SERVICES:** All RE related servs.; **PREV EMPLOY:** 4th Generation RE; **PROFL AFFIL & HONORS:** NAR, TX Assn. of Realtors; Dir. and 1982 Sec., Tyler Bd. of Realtors; **EDUC:** Associate + 3 semesters, 1973, Bus. and Psychology, Tyler Junior Coll., N. TX State Univ., Univ. of TX at Tyler; **OTHER ACT & HONORS:** Tyler C of C, Rotary, several social clubs; Chmn. of several Professional State Assn. Committees, Dir., All Saints Episcopal School; **HOME ADD:** 812 Foxcove, Tyler, TX 75703, (214)561-9253; **BUS ADD:** 3901 S. Broadway, Tyler, TX 75701, (214)561-4731.

RALSTON, Richard——*Dir. Fac.*, Storage Technology Corp.; **PRIM RE ACT:** Property Manager; **BUS ADD:** 2270 South 88th St., Louisville, CO 80027, (303)449-9950.*

RAMEY, Rose Marie——**B:** Sept. 12, 1929, Madison, WI, *Broker-Owner*, Rose Garden RE; **PRIM RE ACT:** Broker, Regulator, Property Manager, Owner/Investor; **PREV EMPLOY:** High School Teacher; **PROFL AFFIL & HONORS:** NAR; **EDUC:** BS, 1965, PE-Eng., Library, SD State Univ. - Brookings, SD; **GRAD EDUC:** Work Guidance & Counseling, 1968, SDSU; **EDUC HONORS:** Athletic Intercoll. Teams; **HOME ADD:** 829 7th Ave., Brookings, SD, (605)692-7575; **BUS ADD:** 515 Main Avenue South, Brookings, SD 57006, (605)692-7575.

RAMOS, Tony——**B:** Jan. 24, 1951, Laredo, TX, Tony Ramos, RE Broker & Counselor; **PRIM RE ACT:** Broker, Owner/Investor; **OTHER RE ACT:** Counselor; **SERVICES:** Brokerage of comml. investment RE; **PROFL AFFIL & HONORS:** NAR, State Bar of TX, JD, Univ. of Houston, 1975; **EDUC:** BS, 1972, Pol. Sci., Govt., Univ. of TX at Austin; **GRAD EDUC:** JD, 1975, Univ. of Houston, Houston, TX; **HOME ADD:** 1914 Longfield, San Antonio, TX 78248, (512)492-9239; **BUS ADD:** 8620 N. New Braunfelo, Suite 535, San Antonio, TX 78217, (512)826-2063.

RAMSAUR, James W.——**B:** Sept. 5, 1946, Oakland, CA, *Atty.*; **PRIM RE ACT:** Attorney; **SERVICES:** Legal; **PROFL AFFIL & HONORS:** Alameda Cty. Bar Assn., ABA, CA Trial Lawyers Assn.; **EDUC:** AB, 1971, Poli. Sci., Stanford Univ.; **GRAD EDUC:** MBA/JD, 1978, Univ. CA Berkeley/Univ. San Fran.; **MIL SERV:** US Army, SSG; **HOME TEL:** (415)658-0296; **BUS ADD:** Fidelity Plaza, 180 Grand Ave., Suite 900, Oakland, CA 94612, (415)834-8349.

RAMSAY, A.D., Jr.——*RE Dir.*, Olin Corp.; **PRIM RE ACT:** Property Manager; **BUS ADD:** 120 Long Ridge Rd., Stamford, CT 06904, (203)356-2000.*

RAMSEY, Hal——*Exec. VP*, Vantex Properties, Inc.; **PRIM RE ACT:** Developer; **BUS ADD:** 14001 E. Iliff Ave., Aurora, CO 80014, (303)755-7000.*

RAMSEY, Hal C.——**B:** Feb. 24, 1946, Bronxville, NY, *VP*, Dranguet-Helmer, Inc. (3 yrs.); **PRIM RE ACT:** Broker, Consultant, Builder; **OTHER RE ACT:** Mgmt. Multi Housing & Office; **PREV EMPLOY:** George O. Yamini Co. (5 yrs.) - Dev. & Mgmt. of Multi-Unit Housing; **PROFL AFFIL & HONORS:** IREM, Dallas Bd. of Realtors, CPM; **EDUC:** BBA, 1968, Finance, Mktg., Mgmt., Econ., Univ. of OK; **GRAD EDUC:** MBA, 1972, Mkt. Research, Finance, Mgmt., Univ. of Dallas - Braniff Grad. School; **EDUC HONORS:** 3.8; **HOME ADD:** 4113 Leadville Pl., Dallas, TX 75234, (214)934-3456; **BUS ADD:** 11300 N Central Ex.-Suite 521, Dallas, TX 75243, (214)369-8224.

RAMSEYER, William L.——**B:** July 18, 1941, Seattle, WA, *Exec. VP*, Questor Associates; **PRIM RE ACT:** Consultant; **SERVICES:** Valuation and appraisal, devel. feasibility, investment analysis and strategic planning; **REP CLIENTS:** Devels., investment mgrs., municipalities, investment bankers, attys.; **EDUC:** BA, 1965, Econ., Univ. of Puget Sound; **GRAD EDUC:** Advanced Mgmt. Program, 1979, Harvard Grad. School of Bus. Admin.; **MIL SERV:** USN, Lt., 1966-1970; **HOME ADD:** 17 Pacific Ave., Piedmont, CA 94611, (415)655-0503; **BUS ADD:** 115 Sansome St., Suite 600, San Francisco, CA 94104, (415)433-0300.

RAMSLAND, Maxwell O., Jr.——**B:** Aug. 13, 1939, Duluth, MN, *Pres.*, Ramsland & Vigen, Inc.; **PRIM RE ACT:** Consultant, Appraiser; **SERVICES:** Valuation Counsel, Condemnation Appraisals, etc.; **REP CLIENTS:** Corps., Attys., etc.; **PREV EMPLOY:** C. Robert Boucher & Assoc., Wash, D.C. Equitable Life Assurance Soc. of US (City Mort. Dept., Wash., DC); **PROFL AFFIL & HONORS:** AIREA; SREA; ASA (Sr. Member), MAI; SRPA; **EDUC:** BA, 1963, Econ. & Pol. Sci., Univ. of MN; **OTHER ACT & HONORS:** V Chmn., MN Higher Educ. Facilities Authority (1979-); Bd. of St. Luke's Hospital, Duluth (1978-); Duluth Grad. Med. Educ. Council; Pres. Bayfront Park Devel. Assn., Duluth; **HOME ADD:** 2401 E First St., Duluth, MN 55802, (218)728-3314; **BUS ADD:** The Torrey Bldg., Duluth, MN 55802, (218)727-8583.

RANDALL, Benjamin J.——**B:** Mar 21, 1948, Cleveland, OH, *Part.*, Marks Katz, Randall Weinberg & Blatt; **PRIM RE ACT:** Attorney; **REP CLIENTS:** Bennett & Kahnweiler Assocs., BA Mort. & Intl. Realty Corp., Saxon Paint & Home Care Ctrs. Inc.; **PROFL AFFIL & HONORS:** Chicago Mort. Attys., Chicago Bar Assn.; **EDUC:** BA, 1969, OH State Univ.; **GRAD EDUC:** JD, 1972, Case Western Res. Univ.; **HOME ADD:** 96 Glenwood, Winnetka, IL 60093, (312)835-3034; **BUS ADD:** Suite 1710, 208 S. LaSalle St., Chicago, IL 60604, (312)782-4912.

RANDALL, David——**B:** Sept. 6, 1931, Bronx, NY, *VP*, Royal Park Development Corp.; **PRIM RE ACT:** Broker, Consultant, Engineer, Appraiser, Developer, Builder, Owner/Investor, Property Manager, Insuror, Syndicator; **SERVICES:** Complete devel. services; **PROFL AFFIL & HONORS:** FABA; **EDUC:** BA, 1951, St. John's Univ.; **HOME ADD:** 10937 NW 17th Manor, Coral Springs, FL 33065, (305)752-5417; **BUS ADD:** 10937 NW 17th Manor, Coral Springs, FL 33065, (305)752-5417.

RANDALL, Roland Rodrock——**B:** Oct. 12, 1898, Doylestown, PA, *RE Counselor*, Jackson-Cross Co.; **OTHER RE ACT:** RE Counselor; **SERVICES:** Counseling; **PREV EMPLOY:** RE since 1925; **PROFL AFFIL & HONORS:** CRE, Founding Pres.; MAI, Nat. Chmn., 1947; SIR, Nat. Pres., 1949; RNMI; NAR; PA Realtor Assn., Pres., 1941; Philadelphia Bd. of Realtors; ULI, CRE, MAI, Nat. Assn. of Realtors' Distinguished Serv. Award, 1981; **EDUC:** BS, 1921, Econ., Wharton School, Univ. of PA; **MIL SERV:** US Army (315th Infantry); 2nd Lt.; WWI; **OTHER ACT & HONORS:** Lambda Alpha, (pres. 1980-82); **HOME ADD:** The Dorchester, 226 W. Rittenhouse Sq., Philadelphia, PA 19103, (215)546-7070; **BUS ADD:** 2000 Market St., Philadelphia, PA 19103, (215)561-8975.

RANDECKER, Allen W.——**B:** Sept. 10, 1938, Elizabeth, IL, *Pres.*, Hillcrest Constr.; **PRIM RE ACT:** Builder; **SERVICES:** Complete Home Building Service; **PROFL AFFIL & HONORS:** NAHB, Home Builders Assn. of IL; **MIL SERV:** US Army, Spec. 3, 1956-1964; **HOME ADD:** 8945 S. Massbach Rd., Elizabeth, IL 61028, (815)598-3369; **BUS ADD:** 8945 S. Massbach Rd., Elizabeth, IN 61028, (815)858-2358.

RANDLES, Lyle C.——**B:** Mar. 25, 1949, L.A. CA, *Pres.*, Wilkins Randles Assoc.; **PRIM RE ACT:** Broker, Property Manager; **PROFL AFFIL & HONORS:** BOMA, ICSC; **EDUC:** BA, 1971, Econ., UCLA; **BUS ADD:** 16255 Ventura Blvd., Encino, CA 91436, (213)986-4727.

RANDOLPH, Daniel P.——**B:** Sept. 13, 1946, Cincinnati, OH, *Atty.*, Ritter, Armstrong & Randolph; **PRIM RE ACT:** Attorney; **SERVICES:** Legal; **REP CLIENTS:** Westwood Homestead Bldg. & Loan; Allright Auto Park, Inc.; Geisken & Son Bldg. Co.; Geisken Devel. Co.; **PREV EMPLOY:** First Nat. Bank of Cincinnati; **PROFL AFFIL & HONORS:** ABA; OH State Bar Assn.; Cincinnati Bar Assn.; 6th Cir. Fed. Ct.; Internat'l. Assn. of Fin. Planners; **EDUC:** BA, 1969, Communication Arts, Xavier Univ.; **GRAD EDUC:** MS, 1972, Counseling, Troy State; 1977, Law, Chase Coll. of Law; **MIL SERV:** US Army; 1st Lt.; **OTHER ACT & HONORS:** Madeira City Solicitor; Prof. of Law, Chase Coll. of Law; Trustee, Intrnl. Assn. of Fin. Planners; Guest Lecture; Cincinatti Estate Planning Council; Past Member Madeira Planning Comm.; **HOME ADD:** 8133 Maxfield Ln., Madeira, OH, (513)271-4175; **BUS ADD:** 803 Dixie Terminal Bldg., Cincinnati, OH 45202, (513)381-5700.

RANKIN, J. Kenneth——**B:** Dec. 26, 1927, Sycamore, OH, *Manager, Corporate Real Estate*, United Technologies Corp.; **OTHER RE ACT:** Corp. RE Mgr.; **PROFL AFFIL & HONORS:** IREM; Nat. Assn. of Indus. and Office Parks; **EDUC:** BA, 1956, Bus. Admin., Heidelberg Coll., Tiffin, OH; **MIL SERV:** USCG, USAF, 1st. Lt.; **OTHER ACT & HONORS:** 3 yrs. City Council, Brown Deer, WI; **HOME ADD:** 2661 Beech Ln., Lancaster, PA 17601, (717)394-7830; **BUS ADD:** 1 Financial Plaza, Hartford, CT 06101, (203)728-7700.

RANKIN, Michael——**B:** Sept. 22, 1923, Toledo, OH, *In-House Legal Counsel*, Seaway Food Town, Inc., Gen.; **PRIM RE ACT:** Attorney, Property Manager; **OTHER RE ACT:** RE Investments; **SERVICES:** Providing legal serv. to Seaway Food Town on RE law matters; **REP CLIENTS:** Seaway Food Town, Inc.; **PREV EMPLOY:** Lucas Cty. Sheriff Dept.; **PROFL AFFIL & HONORS:** OH State Bar Assn., Lucas Cty. Bar Assn., Toledo Bar Assn., Nat. Sheriff's Assn., Atty. & Univ. Instr.; **EDUC:** BA, 1975, Criminology, Soc., OH State Univ.; **GRAD EDUC:** JD, 1979, Univ. of Toledo Sch. of Law; **EDUC**

HONORS: Pres. OH State Univ. Student Union, 1974, Outstanding Student Serv. Award, Pres. Phi Alpha Delta Profl. Law Frat.; **OTHER ACT & HONORS:** Former member Lucas Cty. Democratic Central Comm., Member Old Newsboys Assn.; **HOME ADD:** 3724 Talmadge Rd., Toledo, OH 43606, (419)472-7340; **BUS ADD:** 1020 Ford St., Maumee, OH 43537, (419)893-9401.

RANNEY, Eric D.——B: Aug. 28, 1949, Rochester, NY, *Partner*, Trotter, Bondurant, Miller & Hishon; **PRIM RE ACT:** Attorney, Owner/Investor; **SERVICES:** Legal advice concerning acquisition, devel., synd., secured lending; **REP CLIENTS:** Southmark Props., Inc., General Electric Credit Corp.; **PROFL AFFIL & HONORS:** ABA, GA Bar Assn.; **EDUC:** BA, 1971, Govt., Dartmouth Coll.; **GRAD EDUC:** JD, 1974, Columbia Univ. School of Law; **EDUC HONORS:** Phi Beta Kappa, Summa Cum Laude, Law Review; **HOME ADD:** 336 Lake Forrest Lane, NE, Atlanta, GA 30342, (404)252-9858; **BUS ADD:** 2200 First Atlanta Tower, Two Peachtree St. N.W., Atlanta, GA 30383, (404)688-0350.

RANNEY, Eugene A.——B: Apr. 11, 1933, Milwaukee, WI, *Mgr., RE Services*, Northwestern Mutual Life, Real Estate Investment Dept.; **PRIM RE ACT:** Attorney, Lender, Owner/Investor; **OTHER RE ACT:** Investment Admin.; **PREV EMPLOY:** Pvt. Law practice, 1959-1964; NML, Law Dept. 1964-1973; Mort. Loan Dept. 1973-1980; **PROFL AFFIL & HONORS:** WI Bar Assn.; **EDUC:** 1954, Econ., Marquette Univ.; **GRAD EDUC:** 1959, Law, Marquette Univ.; **EDUC HONORS:** Law Review; **MIL SERV:** US Army; Cpl.; **HOME ADD:** 2165 Pilgrim Pkwy., Brookfield, WI 53005, (414)786-3769; **BUS ADD:** 720 E. Wisconsin Ave., Milwaukee, WI 53202, (414)226-7044.

RANSDELL, Richard——*VP Fin. & Admin.*, Medford Corp.; **PRIM RE ACT:** Property Manager; **BUS ADD:** PO Box 550, Medford, OR 97501, (503)773-7491.*

RAPACKI, Lyle J.——B: June 14, 1951, New Brunswick, NJ, *Publisher and Chief Forecaster*, "Arizona Today" (a bimonthly letter on AZ's economy and business); **OTHER RE ACT:** Econ. Forecaster and Syndicated Radio Commentator; **SERVICES:** Market review or analysis; Demographic reports; **REP CLIENTS:** Held in confidence; **PREV EMPLOY:** SW Development Co. in Phoenix, AZ, 1974-1979 (Dir. of Prop. Mgmt. and Devel.) - opened own firm in 1980; **EDUC:** Bachelor's, Poli. Sci./Bus.; **GRAD EDUC:** MA, Bus. Mktg.; **OTHER ACT & HONORS:** Exec. Bd. of Boy Scouts; Salvation Army; C of C; Outstanding Young Man in Amer., 1980 Award; **HOME ADD:** 4509 Mtn. Meadow Dr., Flagstaff, AZ 86001, (602)526-9088; **BUS ADD:** 4509 Mtn. Meadow Dr., Flagstaff, AZ 86001.

RAPHAEL, Stephen M.——B: Nov. 9, 1941, New York, NY, *Partner*, Raphael and Marcus, P.C.; **PRIM RE ACT:** Attorney, Developer; **SERVICES:** Investment counseling and devel. of coop. and condo. plans; **REP CLIENTS:** Indiv. and instnl. investors in resid. and comml. props.; **PROFL AFFIL & HONORS:** Assn. of the Bar of City of NY; Chmn., Comm. of Coop. E Condos., Brooklyn Bar Assn. NY RE Bd.; **EDUC:** BA, 1963, Econ. and Hist., Columbia Univ.; **GRAD EDUC:** LLB/LLM, 1966/1971, Harvard/NY Univ.; **HOME ADD:** 601 Third St., Brooklyn, NY 10017, (212)965-3339; **BUS ADD:** 551 Fifth Ave., New York, NY 10017, (212)682-1480.

RAPIER, Reginald (Rex), Jr.——B: Feb. 18, 1911, Mobile, AL, *Broker, Owner*, Rapier Realty Co.; **PRIM RE ACT:** Consultant, Appraiser; **SERVICES:** Appraise all types of RE; **REP CLIENTS:** AL State Hwy. Dept., FHA, VA, Banks, S&Ls, Relocation Cos., Ins. Cos., Bus. Indivs., etc.; **PREV EMPLOY:** VP Home S&L Assn. of Mobile, Asst. VP Amer. Nat. Bank of Mobile, RE Specialist in Merchants Nat. Bank of Mobile; **PROFL AFFIL & HONORS:** AIREA, SRPA, NARA, Sr. RE Appraiser in SREA; Member of Mobile Cty. Bd. of Realtors and of NARA; Former Pres. of S AL, W FL Chapt. No. 49 of AIREA; Former Pres. of Mobile Chap. of SRA; **EDUC:** Amer. Inst. of Banking, several yrs., Univ. of Notre Dame - Appraisal #1, AIREA, Univ. of KY - Appraisal #II, AIREA, Univ. of GA - Appraisal #IV, AIREA; **GRAD EDUC:** Rutgers Univ., 1954, Grad. School of Banking in Comml. Banking; **MIL SERV:** US Army, S/Sgt., 2 Battle Stars; Served in N. Africa, Italy, Iran - during WWII; **OTHER ACT & HONORS:** Mobile Kiwanis Club, Alba Club; **HOME ADD:** 68 Byrnes Blvd., Mobile, AL 36608, (205)342-4285; **BUS ADD:** Suite 516A - 2 Office Park, Mobile, AL 36609, (205)344-7020.

RAPPAPORT, Herman H.——B: Sept. 24, 1916, New Haven, CT, *Pres.*, The Rappaport Co.; **PRIM RE ACT:** Developer, Builder, Owner/Investor; **REP CLIENTS:** Standard Oil Co. of NJ; Gen. Electric; Bechtel Corp.; Bank of Amer.; Rand Corp.; **EDUC:** BS, 1939, Chem. Engrg., CCNY; **BUS ADD:** 124 S. Lasky Dr., Beverly Hills, CA 90212, (213)550-8405.

RAPPOPORT, Stanley——B: Dec. 21, 1930, NY, NY, *Pres.*, NPI Management Corp., Nat. Prop. Investors Partnerships; **PRIM RE ACT:** Owner/Investor, Syndicator; **PREV EMPLOY:** Exec. VP, Investors Funding Corp.; **PROFL AFFIL & HONORS:** Nat. Realty Club; Lic. RE Broker; Lic. Ins. Broker (NY State), Lecturer, Practising Law Inst.; CRA; Articles Published in RE Forum; **EDUC:** BS, 1952, Banking/Fin., NYU; **OTHER ACT & HONORS:** Alumni Comm., NYU; Member, Bd. of Trs., Temple Israel of New Rochelle, NY; **HOME ADD:** 52 Harlan Dr., New Rochelle, NY 10804; **BUS ADD:** 666 Third Ave., NY, NY 10017, (212)878-9335.

RAPPORT, Roger J.——B: Sept. 30, 1937, Cleveland, OH, Old Mill Appraisal Co.; **OTHER RE ACT:** Appraiser; **SERVICES:** Appraisal of land prop. fixtures equipment, antiques, autos.; **REP CLIENTS:** VP of Bank of Amer., VP of Barclays Bank; Pres. Dowd's Moving & Storage, Mill Valley, CA; US Dept. of Army Insp. Gen. Office Damage Appraisal, Ceredio, CA; **PREV EMPLOY:** Bus. Adv. City of Oakland, CA; **PROFL AFFIL & HONORS:** IRWA, ASA, OH State, RE Degree, State of CA, Exec. Bd. IRWA; **EDUC:** BA/BS, 1960, RE, OH State Univ., Merritt Coll., Oakland, CA; **MIL SERV:** US Army, Medical Corps., PFC; **OTHER ACT & HONORS:** SCORE, SCCA, OSU Alumni Assn., Nat. Assn. of the Profl.; **HOME ADD:** PO Box 696, Mill Valley, CA 94941, (415)924-8968; **BUS ADD:** PO Box 646, Mill Valley, CA 94941, (415)388-8420.

RASIN, Alexander P., III——B: May 21, 1943, Chestertown, MD, *Judge*; **PRIM RE ACT:** Attorney; **OTHER RE ACT:** Agent, Safeco Title Ins. Co.; **SERVICES:** title searches, settlements; **REP CLIENTS:** Peoples Bank of Kent Cty., MD; FHA; Fed. Land Bank; Loyola Fed. S & L Assn.; **PROFL AFFIL & HONORS:** Kent Cty. Bar Assn.; MD State Bar Assn.; Amer. Bar Assn. (real prop., probate and trusts sect.); **EDUC:** BA, 1965, Amer. Hist., Washington & Lee Univ.; **GRAD EDUC:** LLB, 1968, Univ. of MD School of Law; **MIL SERV:** US Army, Lt.; **OTHER ACT & HONORS:** Pres., Kent School, Inc.; Pres., Kent Cty. Public Library; Pres., Chestertown Rotary Club; **HOME ADD:** Chestertown, MD 21620, (301)778-0027; **BUS ADD:** Court St., PO Box 228, Chestertown, MD 21620, (301)778-3515.

RASKIN, Edwin B.——B: Mar. 19, 1919, Savannah, GA, *Chmn.*, Edwin B. Raskin Co.; **PRIM RE ACT:** Broker, Consultant, Developer, Lender, Owner/Investor, Property Manager, Syndicator; **SERVICES:** Prop. mgmt., brokering, synd. of investment props.; **REP CLIENTS:** Indiv., instns., univ., banks, ins. cos.; **PROFL AFFIL & HONORS:** Nashville Bd. of Realtors, TN Assn. of Realtors, Nat. Assn. of RE Bds., IREM, Past. Pres. Middle TN Chapt., CPM; **EDUC:** BBA, 1940, Bus., Admin., Tulane Univ.; **MIL SERV:** USAF, Capt.; **OTHER ACT & HONORS:** Past. Pres. Traveller's Aid Soc., Past Pres., Nashville City Club; **HOME ADD:** 419 Ellendale, Nashville, TN 37205, (615)383-8131; **BUS ADD:** 12th Fl., Third Nat. Bank Bldg., Nashville, TN 37219, (615)244-4250.

RASMUSSEN, Gordon R.——B: Aug. 31, 1947, Fresno, CA, *Pres.*, Gordon Rasmussen, Inc.; **PRIM RE ACT:** Broker, Appraiser, Property Manager; **PREV EMPLOY:** 10 yrs. in RE; **PROFL AFFIL & HONORS:** CCIM, Cert. AZ Exchanger; **EDUC:** BS, 1969, Fin., Univ. of S. CA; **GRAD EDUC:** MBA, 1971, Fin., Univ. of S. CA; **BUS ADD:** 2020 E. Speedway, Tucson, AZ 85719, (602)327-9471.

RASMUSSEN, John A.——B: Feb. 15, 1937, Red Wing, MN, *Research Coordinator*, Feasibility Research Group, Ltd.; **PRIM RE ACT:** Consultant; **SERVICES:** RE market analysis, consumer survey research, fin. feasibility, site studies, target design analysis; **REP CLIENTS:** Chelsea Comm. Hospital, Delta Dental Plan of MI, Great Lakes Fed. Savings, Kohler Co., MI Nat. Bank, Realty Growth Investors, Union Oil Co. of CA,First Martin Corp., City of Ann Arbor; **PREV EMPLOY:** RE Appraisal and Consultant, 1963-1970; Instr./Lecturer: Appraisal Inst. of Can. and AIREA, 1978; Instr.: Soc. of RE Appraisers, 1978 to present; **PROFL AFFIL & HONORS:** Soc. of RE Appraisers; Amer. Soc. of Appraisers; ULI, SREA,ASA; **EDUC:** BBA, 1966, Univ. of MI, Grad. School of Bus. Admin.; **OTHER ACT & HONORS:** Pres., Ann Arbor Tomorrow, 1980; **HOME ADD:** 2808 Canterbury Rd., Ann Arbor, MI 48104; **BUS ADD:** 527 E. Liberty St., Suite 208, Ann Arbor, MI 48104.

RASMUSSEN, Lyle D.——B: July 13, 1950, Idaho Falls, ID, *Asst. VP*, United S&L Assn.; **PRIM RE ACT:** Lender; **SERVICES:** RE Mort., Savings; **EDUC:** BS, 1973, Soc., Brigham Young Univ.; **GRAD EDUC:** MBA, 1975, Brigham Young Univ.; **EDUC HONORS:** Honors Soc; Grad. Magna Cum Laude; **OTHER ACT & HONORS:** Layton C of C; **HOME ADD:** 1865 Bonneview Dr., Bountiful, UT 84010, (801)295-0628; **BUS ADD:** 75 N. Fort Lane, Suite 104, Layton, UT 84041, (801)766-1246.

RATCLIFFE, G.J., Jr.——*Sr. VP Fin. & Law.*, Harvey Hubbell Inc.; **PRIM RE ACT:** Attorney, Property Manager; **BUS ADD:** Derby-Milford Rd., Orange, CT 06477, (203)789-1100.*

RATHER, Dale L.——**B:** June 17, 1926, Wichita, KS, *Pres.*, Ankirk Devel. Corp.; **PRIM RE ACT:** Consultant, Owner/Investor, Property Manager, Syndicator; **SERVICES:** Prop. mgmt. and synd. sales; **REP CLIENTS:** Major REIT, Banks, Indiv., Trusts; **PROFL AFFIL & HONORS:** IREM, CPM; **EDUC:** BS, 1950, Bus. Admin., Univ. of OK; **OTHER ACT & HONORS:** Past Pres. of IREM, Los Angeles Chap.; **HOME ADD:** 4008 Calle Marlena, San Clemente, CA 92672, (714)498-1051; **BUS ADD:** 15 Brookhollow Dr., Santa Ana, CA 92705, (714)549-9066.

RATLIFF, JKV——**B:** Oct. 21, 1929, Birmingham, AL, *Asst. to the Pres.*, Collateral Investment Co.; **PRIM RE ACT:** Attorney, Developer, Lender, Owner/Investor; **OTHER RE ACT:** Mort. Banker; **PREV EMPLOY:** US Army; **EDUC:** BA, 1951, Univ. of AL; **GRAD EDUC:** LLB and JD, 1956, Univ. of AL; **MIL SERV:** Infantry, 1st Lt., 1953-1955; **HOME ADD:** 44 Greenway Rd., Birmingham, AL 35213, (205)871-3863; **BUS ADD:** 2100 1st Ave., N., Birmingham, AL 35203, (205)252-1000.

RATNER, Gershon M.——*Assoc. of Gen. Cnsl*, Department of Housing and Urban Development, Ofc. of Litigation; **PRIM RE ACT:** Lender; **BUS ADD:** 451 Seventh St., S.W., Washington, DC 20410, (202)755-1300.*

RATNER, Michael S.——**B:** Nov. 14, 1941, Springfield, MA, *Partner*, Bacon, Wilson, Ratner, Cohen, Salvage, Fialky & Fitzgerald, P.C.; **PRIM RE ACT:** Attorney; **SERVICES:** Basic RE, leasing, banking law, general civil law, conveyancing; **REP CLIENTS:** Ludlow Savings Bank, BayBank Valley Trust Co., Third National Bank of Hampden Cty., Shawmut First Bank and Trust Co., Springfield Institution for Savings, Community Savings Bank, United Cooperative Bank; Western New England Coll.; **PROFL AFFIL & HONORS:** Hampden Cty. Bar Assn (Exec. Bd. 1979-1981) President-Elect 1982, MA Bar Assn. (Chmn. Prop. Law Sec. 1980-1981), Commonwealth of MA Land Court Examiner; **EDUC:** BBA, 1963, Bus. Admin./Mktg., Univ. of MA; **GRAD EDUC:** JD, Boston Univ. School of Law; **OTHER ACT & HONORS:** Town of Longmeadow Park Commnr. - 1970-1973, Chmn. 1973; Charles C. Spellman Lodge of Masons; **HOME ADD:** 139 Shady Side Dr., Longmeadow, MA 01106, (413)567-0489; **BUS ADD:** 95 State St., Springfield, MA 01103, (413)781-0560.

RATNER, Morris——**B:** Dec. 3, 1905, NY, *Pres.*, Ratner Mgmt. Corp.; **PRIM RE ACT:** Owner/Investor, Property Manager; **PREV EMPLOY:** CPA for 40 yrs.; **PROFL AFFIL & HONORS:** NY State Soc. of CPAs; **EDUC:** BBA, 1927, Acctg./Fin., City Coll. of NY; **OTHER ACT & HONORS:** Bd. of Overseers, Jewish Theology Seminary; Former Treas. & VP, Beth El Synagogue; Chmn. Bd. of Governors, Jewish Community Center on the Palisades; **HOME ADD:** 27 Ridge Rd., Tenafly, NJ 07670; **BUS ADD:** 177 N. Dean St., Englewood, NJ 07631, (201)569-3711.

RATTERMAN, George W.——**B:** Nov. 12, 1926, Cincinnati, OH, *VP*, Jones Real Estate Colleges, Inc.; **PRIM RE ACT:** Instructor; **SERVICES:** Write courses; teach; do gen. admin. work; **PREV EMPLOY:** Securities and life ins.; **PROFL AFFIL & HONORS:** ABA, CLU; Author & Instr.; RE Broker; Editor-Publisher of *The Fin. Planner* Magazine; **EDUC:** RE Engrg. and Econ., Univ. of Notre Dame; **GRAD EDUC:** Masters, Fin. Servs., Amer. Coll., Bryn Mawr, PA; JD, Chase Coll., Cincinatti, OH; **MIL SERV:** US Naval Res., AS; **HOME ADD:** 750 Crescent Lane, Lakewood, CO 80215; **BUS ADD:** 2150 South Cherry St., Denver, CO 80222, (303)758-1033.

RATTRAY, James B.——**B:** July 26, 1950, Watertown, NY, *Dep. City Atty. for Devel.*, City of Hampton; **PRIM RE ACT:** Consultant, Attorney, Lender, Regulator; **SERVICES:** Negotiation and review of each transaction in area, contracts, title problems, fin. rehab. loans and indus. devel. bonds., compliance with land use restrictions both comml. and resid. projects; **REP CLIENTS:** Indivs., investors, devels., synds., resid. and comml. props.; **PROFL AFFIL & HONORS:** VA State Bar Assn., DC Bar Assn., ABA, Hampton Bar Assn.; **EDUC:** AB, 1972, Poli. Behav., Syracuse Univ.; **GRAD EDUC:** JD, 1975, Law, Marshall-Wythe School of Law, Coll. of William and Mary; **EDUC HONORS:** Cum Laude; **OTHER ACT & HONORS:** Author: "The Housing and Community Developement Act of 1974 As It Is Administered in VA and Attendant Problems" 41A NIMLO Municipal Law Review 182 (1978); **HOME ADD:** P O Box 146, Hampton, VA 23669, (804)722-2697; **BUS ADD:** 22 Lincoln St., Hampton, VA 23669, (804)727-6127.

RAUH, B. Michael——**B:** July 11, 1936, Washington, DC, *Sr. Partner*, Landis, Cohen, Singman & Rauh; **PRIM RE ACT:** Attorney; **EDUC:** BA, 1958, Econ., Univ. of MI; **GRAD EDUC:** LLB (JD), 1961, Univ. of WA; LLM, 1967, Trial Advocacy, Georgetown Univ.; **OTHER ACT & HONORS:** Nat. Bd. Member, Boys Clubs of Amer.; **HOME ADD:** 501 Slaters Lane 1011, Alexandria, VA 22314, (703)549-2022; **BUS ADD:** 1019 Nineteenth St. NW, Suite 500, Washington, DC 20036, (202)785-2020.

RAUSHENBUSH, Walter B.——**B:** June 13, 1928, Madison, WI, *Prof. of Law*, Univ. of WI Law School; **PRIM RE ACT:** Instructor, Consultant; **SERVICES:** Teaching Courses in Prop. & RE Law, occasional consulting with lawyers & trade assocs.; **PROFL AFFIL & HONORS:** Dane Cty. Bar Assoc., State Bar of WI, ABA; **EDUC:** AB, 1950, Govt., Harvard Coll.; **GRAD EDUC:** JD, 1953, Univ. of WI Law School; **EDUC HONORS:** Magna cum laude, High Honors; **MIL SERV:** USAF, Col. Active 1953-56, Reserve 1956-78; **OTHER ACT & HONORS:** Chmn. Advisory Comm. on WI Fair Housing Law, 1965-66, Dir., Amer. Bar Foundation Study of Resid. RE Transfer, 1968-70; **HOME ADD:** 3942 Plymouth Cir., Madison, WI 53705, (608)238-1370; **BUS ADD:** Univ. of WI Law School, Madison, WI 53706, (608)263-7413.

RAVEN, Larry Joseph——**B:** Jan. 25, 1939, Selma, CA, *Owner/Broker*, The Raven Co.; **PRIM RE ACT:** Broker, Consultant, Appraiser, Developer, Builder, Owner/Investor; **PREV EMPLOY:** Devel., created franchise and owned chain of convenience markets (R Pantry Mkts.) and meat markets (Holy Cow); **PROFL AFFIL & HONORS:** Fresno Bd. of Realtors, MLS-CA Assn. of Realtors; **EDUC:** Fresno City Coll.; **EDUC HONORS:** Amer. Farmer (highest national award, Future Farmers of Amer.); **MIL SERV:** US Army; **OTHER ACT & HONORS:** "Who's Who in Amer." W. Edition 1981; **HOME ADD:** Fresno, CA, 93702, (209)486-1710; **BUS ADD:** 3504 E. Huntington Blvd., Fresno, CA 93702, (209)486-1710.

RAVENEL, Arthur, III——**B:** Nov. 21, 1950, Charleston, SC, *Pres.*, Arthur Ravenel Jr. Co.; **PRIM RE ACT:** Broker, Owner/Investor, Property Manager, Insuror; **PROFL AFFIL & HONORS:** Gr. Charleston Bd. of Realtors, SC Bd. of Realtors, Nat. Bd. of Realtors, GRI; **EDUC:** 1972, Bus., The Citadel, Charleston, SC; **MIL SERV:** US Army, Lt.; **OTHER ACT & HONORS:** Charleston C of C, Exchange Club of Metro. Charleston; **HOME ADD:** 1286 W Vagabond Ln., Mt. Pleasant, SC 29464, (803)884-6593; **BUS ADD:** 635 E Bay St., Charleston, SC 29403, (803)723-7847.

RAVETTI, Silvio E.——**B:** Sept. 17, 1926, L.A., CA, *Pres.*, Select Income Mgmt. Co., Inc.; **PRIM RE ACT:** Broker, Syndicator, Property Manager; **SERVICES:** Shopping Ctr. mgmt./admin.; **PREV EMPLOY:** self employed since 1950; **PROFL AFFIL & HONORS:** IREM, NAREIT, S.F. Bd. of Realtors, CPM; **EDUC:** 1951, Bus.-Econ., Univ. of S.F.; **MIL SERV:** USMC, PFC, Sharpshooter; **OTHER ACT & HONORS:** Olympic Club, World Trade Club; **HOME ADD:** 242 Lake Merced Hill No., S.F., CA 94136, (415)239-7007; **BUS ADD:** 130 Bush St., S.F., CA 94104, (415)956-2233.

RAWLINGS, Jack——**B:** Jan. 9, 1947, Altoona, PA, *Assoc. Broker*, John Rawlings RE Inc.; **PRIM RE ACT:** Broker, Consultant, Appraiser, Instructor; **OTHER RE ACT:** Brokerage, appraising, investment consulting; **REP CLIENTS:** Indivs., Lenders, Merrill Lynch, Executrans, Employee Tranfer Corp.; **PROFL AFFIL & HONORS:** Pres. Altoona-Blair Cty. Bd. of Realtors, RPAC Tr., PA Assn. of Realtors, FLI, Nat. Assn. of Review Appraisers, Amer. RE and Urban Econ. Assn., 1977 PA Realtor Assoc. of The Year; **EDUC:** BS, 1968, RE, PA State Univ.; **MIL SERV:** US Army, 1968-70, S/Sgt.; **OTHER ACT & HONORS:** Exec. Bd. Boy Scouts, VP PA Economy League; **HOME ADD:** 704 Baynton Ave., Altoona, PA 16602, (814)942-9823; **BUS ADD:** 1111 12th Ave., Altoona, PA 16601, (814)944-2543.

RAWLINGS, William H.——**B:** Jan. 9, 1939, Long Beach, CA, *Pres.*, Hobie-Rawlings Devel. Co., Inc.; **PRIM RE ACT:** Broker, Consultant, Engineer, Developer, Builder, Owner/Investor; **SERVICES:** Land Devel. and Project Mgmt.; **REP CLIENTS:** Our own accts. and closed client list only; **PREV EMPLOY:** VP Engrg. Tech., Inc. VP Vector Dynamics, Inc.; VP Tanco Inc.; Pres. Tanco of OK; Dir. of Construction Kaiser-Aetna; **PROFL AFFIL & HONORS:** ASCE, NAR; **EDUC:** BA, 1968, Civil Engrg./Public Admin., CA State Univ., Long Beach, CA; **EDUC HONORS:** Cum Laude, Dean's List, Municipal Engrg. Scholarship, Student Body Scholarship; **MIL SERV:** USAF Security Service; **OTHER ACT & HONORS:** Temecula School Board Pres.; CA Republican Assembly; **HOME ADD:** PO Box 551, Temecula, CA 92390, (714)676-5309; **BUS ADD:** 37501 Glenoaks Rd., Rancho California, CA 92390, (714)676-5789.

RAWSON, David R.——**B:** Nov. 6, 1935, Lancster, WI, *Pres.*, Rawson, Blum & Co.; **PRIM RE ACT:** Broker, Consultant, Developer, Property Manager, Syndicator; **REP CLIENTS:** Indiv. & inst. investors in comml. props.; **PROFL AFFIL & HONORS:** ICSC; **EDUC:** BBA, 1957, Mktg., Univ. of WI; **MIL SERV:** USN, Lt. j.g.; **HOME ADD:** 2744 Green St., San Francisco, CA 94123, (415)931-3555; **BUS ADD:** 50 CA St., Suite 1235, San Francisco, CA 94123, (415)433-3380.

RAWSON, William——*VP Adm. & Law*, McGraw-Edison; **PRIM RE ACT:** Attorney, Property Manager; **BUS ADD:** 330 W. River Rd., Elgin, IL 60120, (312)981-3800.*

RAY, J. Charley——**B:** July 23, 1947, Harry Cty., *Pres.*, Ray Realty, Inc.; **PRIM RE ACT:** Broker, Consultant, Owner/Investor, Instructor, Property Manager; **SERVICES:** Sales, Devel. & Mgmt. of Comml. Investment Props.; **PROFL AFFIL & HONORS:** RNMI; SC RE Mktg. & Exchange Council, CCIM, GRI; **EDUC:** Assoc., Bus., Acctg., Univ. of SC; **MIL SERV:** USAF, S/Sgt.; **OTHER ACT & HONORS:** Member, Horry Cty. Council 1979; VP Conway C of C; **HOME ADD:** 181 Lakeland Dr., Conway, SC 29526, (803)248-9663; **BUS ADD:** 311 Beaty St., Conway, SC 29526, (803)248-6363.

RAY, Michael L.——*Exec. VP*, Vantage Companies; **PRIM RE ACT:** Developer; **BUS ADD:** 6220 S. Orange Blossom Trail, Orlando, FL 32809, (305)851-4500.*

RAYL, John E.——**B:** Nov. 27, 1947, Columbus, OH, *Pres.*, Leeward Capital Corp.; **PRIM RE ACT:** Consultant, Syndicator; **SERVICES:** Equity for Midwest Real Prop.; **REP CLIENTS:** Pvt. investors; **PREV EMPLOY:** Coopers & Lybrand 1969 to 1980; **EDUC:** BA, 1969, Bus., Capital Univ., Columbus; **GRAD EDUC:** MBA, 1977, Capital Univ.; **MIL SERV:** US Army; **BUS ADD:** Suite 101, 926 E. Broad St., Columbus, OH 43205, (614)252-0701.

RAYMOND, James W.——**B:** May 15, 1947, Chicago, IL, *Pres.*, The Raymond Co.; **PRIM RE ACT:** Broker, Developer, Builder, Syndicator; **SERVICES:** Gen. brokerage, devel. synd. of comml./indus. prop., investment counseling and gen. contracting; **PROFL AFFIL & HONORS:** RE Securities & Synd. Inst.; Farm & Land Inst.; **EDUC:** BS, 1969, Indus. Mgmt./Civil Engrg., Purdue Univ.; **HOME ADD:** 72 Denell Court, Crete, IL 60417, (312)672-6640; **BUS ADD:** 1965 Bernice Rd., Lansing, IL 60438, (312)895-4700.

RAYMOND, Patrick J.——**B:** Oct. 3, 1939, Buffalo, NY, *Atty*, Patrick J. Raymond; **PRIM RE ACT:** Attorney; **SERVICES:** Municipal defense & prop. owner prosecution, certioriri proceedings; **REP CLIENTS:** City of Binghamton, Spec. Counsel, Town of Salisbury, Village of Windsor, etc.; **PREV EMPLOY:** Former Corp. counsel, City of Binghamton; **PROFL AFFIL & HONORS:** State & Broome Cty. Bar Assn., NYS Assessors Assn., Who's Who in Amer. Law, Who's Who in Colls. & Univs. (1961); **EDUC:** BA, 1961, Sienna Coll., Loudonville, NY; **GRAD EDUC:** LLB, 1964, Albany Law Sch., Albany, NY; **OTHER ACT & HONORS:** 1974-77 Corp. counsel, Bing., NY; **HOME ADD:** 31 Brookfield Rd., Binghamton, NY 13903, (607)723-1355; **BUS ADD:** 27 Main St., Binghamton, NY 13905, (607)723-6664.

REA, George R., Jr.——**B:** Jan. 12, 1939, Meridian, MS, *Part.*, Rea, Shaw, Giffin & Stuart; **PRIM RE ACT:** Consultant, Instructor; **OTHER RE ACT:** CPA; **SERVICES:** Tax Analysis & Instr.;purchase & sale analysis; **PROFL AFFIL & HONORS:** Tax Div.- AICPA; 11 yr. participant in NYU tax inst.; member ICSC, Gold Medal for 1966 MS CPA exam; Former Sec. & Treas. of MS Soc. of CPAs; **EDUC:** BCE, 1961, Vanderbilt Univ.; **GRAD EDUC:** MA, 1966, Acctg., Univ. of AL; **EDUC HONORS:** Magna Cum Laude, Paul Garner Acctg. Award, Beta Gamma Sigma; **MIL SERV:** USMC, 1st. Lt.; **OTHER ACT & HONORS:** Bd. of Dirs, Museum of Art; Meridian Jr. Coll. Found; Meridian Speech & Hearing Ctr.; **HOME ADD:** PO Box 2090, Meridian, MS 39301, (601)485-4245; **BUS ADD:** PO Box 2090, Meridian, MS 39301, (601)693-2841.

REA, George W.——**B:** May 6, 1941, Harrison, AR, *Owner*, RE Appraisal Assocs.; **PRIM RE ACT:** Broker, Appraiser, Instructor; **SERVICES:** Appraisal, brokerage; **PREV EMPLOY:** Teacher on coll. and high school level; **PROFL AFFIL & HONORS:** RE Bd., SRA, SREA, AIREA, KORE Broker, MORE Broker; **EDUC:** BA, 1964, Hist. & Govt., Univ. of MO at Kansas City; **GRAD EDUC:** MA, 1968, Hist. & Educ., Univ. of MO at Kansas City; **OTHER ACT & HONORS:** Friends of Art; **HOME ADD:** 22 W. 68th Terr., Kansas City, MO 64110, (816)523-4841; **BUS ADD:** 4723 Troost Ave., Kansas City, MO 64110, (816)561-0050.

REA, John R.——**B:** Apr. 7, 1944, Los Angeles, CA, *Owner*, John Rea Realty; **PRIM RE ACT:** Broker, Owner/Investor; **SERVICES:** Residential Evaluation, Light Comm'l.; **REP CLIENTS:** 3rd Party Equity Companies; Banks; Relocation Services; **PREV EMPLOY:** Carter Realty, Monroe, LA, VP; **PROFL AFFIL & HONORS:** CRB; GRI; LA Realtors Assn.; NAHB, NFLI; SREA, CCIM candidate; **EDUC:** BA, 1968, Hist., NE LA Univ.; **OTHER ACT & HONORS:** Rotary; Jaycees (inactive); United Way; March of Dimes.

READ, Emerson B.——**B:** Aug. 9, 1925, Dobbs Ferry, NY, *COB*, Read and Read, Inc. Realtors; **PRIM RE ACT:** Broker, Instructor, Syndicator, Consultant, Appraiser, Property Manager, Owner/Investor, Real Estate Publisher; **PREV EMPLOY:** 1947, Proprietor Read & Read Realtors; 1950, Exec. VP and Gen. Sales Mgr., Carleton Dooley, Inc., Miami, FL; 1956 VP Comm. Sales Dept., The Keyes Co., Miami, FL, 1960; Exec. VP and Gen. Sales Mgr., The Keyes Co., Miami, FL, 1965; Part. Read & Read Realtors, Charleston, SC, and 1980 COB of Read & Read Inc., Realtors; 1972 Pres. Read Investment, Inc., RE Seceurities; **PROFL AFFIL & HONORS:** NAR, RNMI, IREM, IFA, Past Pres. of Greater Charleston Bd. of Realtors, 1972, Greater Charleston Bd. of Realtors of the Yr. 1979, CCIM, CPM; **GRAD EDUC:** BACE, 1950, The Citadel; **MIL SERV:** US Army, Air Corp., 1st Lt.; **OTHER ACT & HONORS:** Sons of Amer. Revolution, Huguenot Soc.; **HOME ADD:** 19 King St., Charleston, SC 29402, (803)723-3212; **BUS ADD:** P.O. Box 1089, 37 Broad St., Charleston, SC 29402, (803)577-5400.

READ, Walter N.——**B:** Feb. 8, 1918, Camden, NJ, *Atty. and Counselor at Law*, Archer, Greiner & Read, PC; **PRIM RE ACT:** Attorney; **SERVICES:** Legal rep. and counseling; **REP CLIENTS:** Banks, ins. and mort. cos., builders, devels. and RE brokers; **PROFL AFFIL & HONORS:** Real Property Probate & Trust Law Section - NJ State Bar Assn. and ABA, Pres. - Camden Cty. Bar Assn. 1966-1967; Pres. - NJ State Bar Assn. 1980-1981; **EDUC:** BA, 1939, Univ. of PA; **GRAD EDUC:** LLB, 1942, Univ. of PA; **MIL SERV:** US Naval Res.; LCDR, 1942-1946; **OTHER ACT & HONORS:** Member & Chmn. - Cinnaminson Twp. Zoning Bd.; Dir. - Continental Title Ins. Co.; **HOME ADD:** Moorestown Rd., Riverton, NJ 08077, (609)829-3049; **BUS ADD:** One Centennial Sq., E. Euclid Ave., Haddonfield, NJ 08033, (609)795-2121.

READE, Brian L.——**B:** Nov. 15, 1944, Anamosa, IA, *Sr. Assoc. Counsel*, Mitchell Energy and Development Corp., Legal Dept.; **PRIM RE ACT:** Attorney; **SERVICES:** Complete legal serv.; **PROFL AFFIL & HONORS:** ABA, TX Bar Assn., Houston Bar Assn.; **EDUC:** BA, 1969, Pol. Sci., Univ. of IA; **GRAD EDUC:** JD, 1969, Law, Univ. Of Houston; **EDUC HONORS:** Law Review; Order of the Barons; **HOME ADD:** 1014 Caspian, Houston, TX 77090, (713)537-2828; **BUS ADD:** 2001 Timberloch Pl., P.O. Box 4000, The Woodlands, TX 77380, (713)363-5679.

REAGAN, Gary Don——**B:** Aug. 23, 1941, Amarillo, TX, *Atty.*, Williams, Johnson, Reagan, Porter & Love, P.A.; **PRIM RE ACT:** Attorney, Developer, Instructor; **SERVICES:** Legal, devel., investment; **REP CLIENTS:** Plains Devel Co.; Hobbs Bd. of Realtors, Inc.; numerous local realtors; **PREV EMPLOY:** City Atty., Cities of Hobbs and Eunice; Asst. Dist. Atty. (Civil matters only); **PROFL AFFIL & HONORS:** State Bar of NM; Lea Cty. Bar Assn., ABA, Pres., Lea Cty. Bar Assn. 1978; **EDUC:** AB, 1963, Pre-Legal Curriculum, Stanford Univ. and Stanford in Italy (Florence); **GRAD EDUC:** JD, 1965, Law, Stanford Univ. School of Law; **OTHER ACT & HONORS:** Mayor, City of Hobbs 1972-1973, 1977; City Commnr., Pres., Jr. Achievement of Hobbs; Pres., Bd. of Trustees, Landsun Homes, Inc. (Retirement Community); **HOME ADD:** 200 Eagle Dr., Hobbs, NM 88240, (505)393-9072; **BUS ADD:** P.O. Box 1948, 113 N. Shipp, Hobbs, NM 88240, (505)397-3661.

REAGAN, Paul V.——**B:** Jan. 4, 1947, NY, *Asst. Gen. Counsel*, Bankers Trust Co., Legal Dept.; **PRIM RE ACT:** Attorney; **PREV EMPLOY:** Dewey Ballantine Rushby Palmer & Wood; **PROFL AFFIL & HONORS:** ABA, Assn. of The Bar-NYC; **EDUC:** BA, 1969, Hist., Rutgers Univ.; **GRAD EDUC:** JD, 1973, Notre Dame; **HOME ADD:** 607 Woodfield Rd., Wycoff, NJ 07481, (201)891-1868; **BUS ADD:** 280 Park Ave., New York, NY 10017, (212)850-1231.

REAGAN, Ray——**B:** Oct. 16, 1938, St. Petersberg, FL, *Dir. of Prop. Mgmt.*, Arvida Southern, Arvida Corp.; **PRIM RE ACT:** Consultant, Developer, Builder, Property Manager; **SERVICES:** Devel. bldg., & managing community assns. & consulting to others in indus.; **PREV EMPLOY:** Carlsberg Fin. Corp., LA, CA: Synd. and mgmt. of comml. props.; **PROFL AFFIL & HONORS:** CPA, NAR, CAI (Community Assn. Inst.), Cert. of Appreciation from IREM, 1977; **EDUC:** BS, 1958, Bus. Admin., Bryant Coll.; **HOME ADD:** 8717 SW 147 Pl., Miami, FL 33193, (305)382-1024; **BUS ADD:** 9400 S Dadeland Blvd., Suite PH, Miami, FL 33156, (305)667-1124.

REAL, Harold M., Esq.——**B:** Nov. 25, 1952, Philadelphia, PA, *Atty.*, Solo/Private Practice; **PRIM RE ACT:** Attorney; **SERVICES:** RE and Related Comml. Legal Servs.; **REP CLIENTS:** RE Investment

Trusts; Comml, Indus. & Resid. Devel. RE Mgmt. Cos. & Brokerage Agencies; Investors; **PREV EMPLOY:** Atty. w/Wolf, Block, Schorr & Solis-Cohen; **PROFL AFFIL & HONORS:** Nat. Homebuilders Assn. (& Local Affiliates); ABA, PA State & Philadelphia Bar Assns.; **EDUC:** AB, 1974, Eng. & Classics, Kenyon Coll.; **GRAD EDUC:** JD, 1977, Law, Temple Univ. School of Law; **EDUC HONORS:** Humanitarian Award; Cum Laude, Exec. Editor of Law Review; Received H. Reber Memorial Award; **BUS ADD:** 114 Forrest Ave., Narberth, PA 19072, (215)668-9510.

REAN, Richard——*Fac. & Adm. Mgr.*, Cadence Industries Corp.; **PRIM RE ACT:** Property Manager; **BUS ADD:** 21 Henderson Drive,, W. Coldwell, NJ 07006, (201)227-5100.*

REAP, William J.——**B:** Feb. 27, 1950, Richmond, VA, *Pres.*, William J. Reap Co., Inc.; **PRIM RE ACT:** Broker, Property Manager; **SERVICES:** Prop. mgmt., leasing & brokerage; **PROFL AFFIL & HONORS:** IREM, Natl. Bd. Realtors, No. VA Bd. Realtors, CPM; **EDUC:** 1972, Fin., Bus. Admin., Loyola Univ., Chicago, IL; **HOME ADD:** 8931 Victoria Rd., Springfield, VA 22151, (703)425-9782; **BUS ADD:** 927 S. Walter Reed Dr., Arlington, VA 22204, (703)892-4966.

REARDON, John J.——**B:** Feb. 12, 1946, Watertown, NY, *CEO*, IRCS Consultants, High Plains Research and Consulting Serv.; **PRIM RE ACT:** Consultant, Lender; **OTHER RE ACT:** Creative Fin. Packaging, Synd. of Props., Mktg.; **SERVICES:** Total project review, packaging and negotiations, including fin.; **REP CLIENTS:** In 1974-77 handled 8 million dollars in resid. comml. and indus.; 1977-78, 18 million in indus. and comml. and 78-81 64 million in indus. and comml.; **PREV EMPLOY:** Dir. City of Buffalo, NY and Erie Cty. Bus. Asst. Ctr., CEO Niagara Falls C of C, CEO, IRCS New York; **PROFL AFFIL & HONORS:** NACORE, QUED, AMA, ACCE, NYCE, positions held on 21 Econ., Indus. and commerce devel. bds.; **EDUC:** Poli. Sci., 1973, Urban Studies, S.U.C. Brockport NY; **GRAD EDUC:** 1974-80, Leadership and Mgmt., Notre Dame, Univ. of DE; **EDUC HONORS:** Served on campus planning and bldg. council; **MIL SERV:** USNR, E4, 6 NAM; **HOME ADD:** 1313 12th St., Sidney, NE; **BUS ADD:** 740 IL, Sindney, NE 69162, (308)254-4464.

REARDON, Timothy E.——**B** May 21, 1944, Sandusky, OH, *Dir. Bus. Devel Div.*, Michigan Dept. of Commerce., Travel Bur.; **OTHER RE ACT:** Mkt. Research/Mgmt. Consultant; **SERVICES:** Info., data. tech. asst., relevant to travel indus.; **REP CLIENTS:** Potential Investors/Devels., Limited Part., Units of Govt., Lenders Small Bus., Major. In-State Corps.; **PREV EMPLOY:** RE Research Corp., Chicago, IL, 1971-76; **PROFL AFFIL & HONORS:** Nat. Recreation & Park Assn., Nat. Assn. of Review Appraisers, SREA, Gr. Lansing Bd. of Realtors; Nat. Council on Urban Econ. Devel.; **EDUC:** BA, 1968, Econ., Public Fin., Univ. of Toledo; **GRAD EDUC:** MA, 1971, Geog., Urban Planning, Univ. of Toledo; **HOME ADD:** 758 N Kalamazoo Ave., Marhsall, MI 49068, (616)781-3589; **BUS ADD:** 5th Fl., Law Blgd., Lansing, MI 48909, (517)373-3323.

REATH, George——*Mgr. Legal Dept.*, Pennwalt Corp.; **PRIM RE ACT:** Property Manager; **BUS ADD:** Pennwalt Bldg., 3 Parkway, Philadelphia, PA 19102, (215)587-7000.*

REBACK, Forbes R.——**B:** Aug. 6, 1935, NY, NY, *Atty.*, Sole Practitioner; **PRIM RE ACT:** Attorney; **SERVICES:** All legal services in connection with acquisition, devel. & sales; **REP CLIENTS:** Lawyer's Title Ins. Corp.; **PREV EMPLOY:** Partner, Richmond and Fishburne, Attys., Charlottesville, 1967-1973; **PROFL AFFIL & HONORS:** VA State Bar; **EDUC:** BS, 1958, Agric./Econ., Cornell; **GRAD EDUC:** LLB, 1964, Law, Univ. of VA; **MIL SERV:** US Army; 1st Lt.; 1958-1961; **OTHER ACT & HONORS:** Dir., Nat. Beagle Club of Amer., Inc.; **HOME ADD:** Hunting Ridge Farm, Rte. 2, Charlottesville, VA 22901; **BUS ADD:** 230 Court Sq., Charlottesville, VA 22901, (804)295-1196.

REBER, John C.——**B:** Feb. 22, 1943, Portland, IN, *Atty.*, Rush, Marshall, Bergstrom and Robison, P.A.; **PRIM RE ACT:** Attorney; **REP CLIENTS:** Dade S&L Assn.; various RE devels. and matters pertaining to local RE acquisitions by various natl. and mult-state corps.; **PROFL AFFIL & HONORS:** ABA; FL Bar Assn.; Orange Cty. Bar Assn.; member various comms. and sects. of profl. assns., Author Chap. 3 'Searching for and Examination of Title' 'Real Prop. Title Examination and Ins. in FL', published The FL Bar Continuing Legal Educ.; **EDUC:** BS/BA, 1965, Econs./Eng.-Humanities, Univ. of S. FL; **GRAD EDUC:** JD, 1969, Law: Real Prop.; Corp./Bus.; Probate, Univ. of FL; **HOME ADD:** 966-B E. Michigan St., Orlando, FL 32806, (305)423-0874; **BUS ADD:** PO Box 3146, Orlando, FL 32806, (305)425-6624.

REBHOLZ, Howard——*RE Coord.*, Rath Packing; **PRIM RE ACT:** Property Manager; **BUS ADD:** Po Box 330, Waterloo, IA 50704, (319)235-8646.*

RECK, David E.——**B:** Feb. 4, 1953, Milwaukee, WI, *RE Consultant*, Merrill Lynch Realty; **PRIM RE ACT:** Broker, Consultant, Property Manager; **PROFL AFFIL & HONORS:** Nat. Bd. of Realtors; **EDUC:** Bs, 1975, Univ. of WI; **HOME ADD:** 2327E Bennett Ave., Milwaukee, WI 53207, (414)744-6077.

RECKTENWALD, R.J.——*VP Fin.*, Dinner Bell Foods, Inc.; **PRIM RE ACT:** Property Manager; **BUS ADD:** Drawer 388-West High St., Defiance, OH 43512, (419)782-9015.*

RECORDS, John W.——**B:** Jan. 16, 1945, Portland, OR, *VP*, Marquam Commercial Brokerage Co.; **PRIM RE ACT:** Broker, Consultant, Owner/Investor; **SERVICES:** Investment counseling, Dev. Consultation, Land Use Analysis; **REP CLIENTS:** Indiv. and Instit. Investors in, and Devel. of Comml. and Indust. Prop.; **PROFL AFFIL & HONORS:** Portland Brd. of Realtors, RESSI, RNMI; **EDUC:** BA, 1968, Intl. Bus., Univ. of WA; **MIL SERV:** USN, 1968-1970; **HOME ADD:** 6945 S.W. Gable Pkwy., Portland, OR 97225, (503)297-6263; **BUS ADD:** 813 S.W. Adler, Suite 400, Portland, OR 97205, (503)241-1155.

RECTOR, R. Dale——**B:** May 21, 1920, CO, *COB*, Realty Executives; **PRIM RE ACT:** Broker, Developer, Owner/Investor, Syndicator; **OTHER RE ACT:** Created and devel. the original 100% commission system; **PROFL AFFIL & HONORS:** Phoenix Bd. of Realtors, AZ Assn. of Realtors, NAR; **EDUC:** BA, 1942, CO Univ.; **OTHER ACT & HONORS:** Past Dist. Gov., Rotary Intl.; **HOME ADD:** 6121 N. 51 Pl., Scottsdale, AZ 85253, (602)959-8734; **BUS ADD:** 727 E. Maryland, Phoenix, AZ 85014, (602)264-4605.

RECTOR, Richard A.——**B:** Nov. 17, 1952, Pueblo, CO, *Pres./Chmn. of the Bd./Co-Owner*, Realty Executives/Exec-Systems, Inc./Real Estate - USA; **PRIM RE ACT:** Broker, Consultant; **OTHER RE ACT:** Franchisor & referral network owner; **SERVICES:** Originators of the 100 percent commission concept in RE; **REP CLIENTS:** RE cos. that need assistance with operations problems & RE cos. that need referrals from a nat. network; **PROFL AFFIL & HONORS:** RNMI; NAR; AAR; **EDUC:** BA, 1975, Psychology/Econ./Communication, Stanford Univ.; **OTHER ACT & HONORS:** Sigma Chi Frat.; **HOME ADD:** Scottsdale, AZ; **BUS ADD:** 727 E. Maryland Ave., Phoenix, AZ 85014, (602)264-4605.

RECZEK, John J.——**B:** Jan. 12, 1948, Miles City, MT, *Dist. Mktg. Rep.*, C.I.T. Corp., Billings, MT; **PRIM RE ACT:** Lender, Builder, Owner/Investor; **SERVICES:** Commercial & Indus. Lending; **REP CLIENTS:** Comml. & Indus. Bus.; **PREV EMPLOY:** Metropolitan Mort. Corp. 1974-1975; Bartlegon Mort. Corp. 1975-1980; **PROFL AFFIL & HONORS:** MT Econ. Advisory Bd., Comml. Lenders Assn., SBA; **EDUC:** BA Bus. Admin., 1970, Bus. Admin., Univ. of HI; **OTHER ACT & HONORS:** Revenue Sharing Bd. 1974-1976; Kiwanis, Advisory Bd. Key Club; **HOME ADD:** 752 Moccasin Tr., Billings, MT 59105, (406)245-7375; **BUS ADD:** P.O. Box 30816, Billings, MT 59107, (406)259-6909.

REDD, A. M., Jr.——**B:** Mar.11, 1937, Union Springs, AL, *Pres.*, A.M. Redd Jr., Inc.; **PRIM RE ACT:** Broker, Developer, Property Manager, Owner/Investor; **SERVICES:** Site selection and devel. for retail comml. clients; **REP CLIENTS:** Handy City, Kroger; **PREV EMPLOY:** Connolly & Redd Realty Servs.; **PROFL AFFIL & HONORS:** Member ICSC, Realtor; **EDUC:** BSIE, 1959, Auburn Univ.; **GRAD EDUC:** MSIM, 1963, GA Inst. of Tech.; **EDUC HONORS:** Phi Kappa Phi; **MIL SERV:** USN, Lt.; **OTHER ACT & HONORS:** Bulkhead Lions Club Pres. 1981; **HOME ADD:** 230O Bohler Rd. NW, Atlanta, GA 30327, (404)355-3654; **BUS ADD:** 2740 Bert Adams Rd., PO Box 19998, Atlanta, GA 30325, (404)434-8880.

REDDING, John R.——**B:** Feb. 15, 1941, Spokane, WA, *Sr. VP*, Sherwood & Roberts, Inc., Corp. Office; **PRIM RE ACT:** Broker, Lender, Insuror; **PREV EMPLOY:** US Army; **PROFL AFFIL & HONORS:** MBAA, OREE, MBA; **EDUC:** BA, 1964, Acctg., Wash. State Univ.; **MIL SERV:** US Army, Capt.; **HOME ADD:** 10604 NE 60th Place, Kirkland, WA 98033, (206)827-7625; **BUS ADD:** PO Box 1770, Seattle, WA 98111, (206)682-5400.

REDDING, Kim G.——**B:** June 8, 1955, Ft. Atkinson, WI, *Sr. RE Investment Analyst*, The Mutual Life Insurance Co. of New York, RE Investments; **OTHER RE ACT:** RE Financing; **SERVICES:** Joint Venture & Acquisition funds; **PROFL AFFIL & HONORS:** Bay Area Mort. Assn.; **EDUC:** BA, 1979, Bus. Admin., Fin., RE, CA State Univ., Fullerton; **EDUC HONORS:** Special Merit Award, Dept. of Fin.; **HOME ADD:** 750 Stierlin Rd. 3, Mountain View, CA 94043,

(415)969-6860; **BUS ADD:** 2988 Campus Dr., Suite 340, San Mateo, CA 94403, (415)573-0442.

REDDY, A. Thomas——B: Sept. 25, 1938, Columbus, OH, *Sales and Leasing*, Ramsey Shilling Commercial Brokerage; **PRIM RE ACT:** Broker, Appraiser; **SERVICES:** Sale, leasing, feasibility studies for office and comml. projects; **REP CLIENTS:** Great Western Cities, Attys. Office Mgmt., A & W Restaurants, Shakeys, Fortune 500 Cos.; **PREV EMPLOY:** VP Comml. & Indus. Devel., Great Western Cities; VP Sales & Mktg., Interim Prop. Devel.; **PROFL AFFIL & HONORS:** Senior Member, Nat. Assn. of Review Appraisers; **MIL SERV:** U.S. Army, 1st Lt.; **HOME ADD:** 5633 Colfax #106, N Hollywood, CA 91601, (213)763-1954; **BUS ADD:** 3360 Barham Blvd., Los Angeles, CA 90068, (213)851-6666.

REDEKER, M. Wayne——B: May 28, 1933, St. Louis, MO, *Pres.*, Amoco Realty Co., Wholly Owned subs. of Standard Oil Co. (Ind.); **PRIM RE ACT:** Developer, Builder, Owner/Investor; **SERVICES:** Full RE devel. and investment servs.; **REP CLIENTS:** All operating subs. of Standard Oil Co. (Ind.) and third party sales to Gen. Motors, Dow Jones, Union Carbide, Belden Corp., Oxford Devel., and many others; **PROFL AFFIL & HONORS:** MO Bar Assn.; ULI; Nat. Assn. of Corp. RE Execs.; Nat. Assn. of Indus. and Office Parks; **EDUC:** BSBA, 1956, Bus. Admin./Pre-Law, Washington Univ.; **GRAD EDUC:** JD, 1961, Corp. Law, Washington Univ. Law School; **EDUC HONORS:** Excellence in Negotiable Instruments Law; **MIL SERV:** US Army, Capt.; **OTHER ACT & HONORS:** Precinct Committeeman Republican Party, 1975-1979; Adm. Bd., Community United Methodist Church, Naperville, IL; **HOME ADD:** 64 Finch Ct., Naperville, IL 60565, (312)355-2479; **BUS ADD:** 200 E. Randolph Dr., MC2901A, Chicago, IL 60601, (312)856-6476.

REDER, Martin C.——B: Dec. 12, 1928, New York, NY, *Realtor*, Reder Investments; **PRIM RE ACT:** Broker, Consultant, Owner/Investor, Insuror; **OTHER RE ACT:** Exchanger; **SERVICES:** Investment counseling, fin. planning, exchanging; **PROFL AFFIL & HONORS:** Pres., Central Coast Exchangers, Dir., Nat. Council of Exchangers, FLI, Soc. of Exchange Counselors, Interex, GRI, Best Exchange Transaction, 1980, Central Coast Exchangers; **EDUC:** AB, 1950, Biochemistry, Univ. of CA, Berkeley; **MIL SERV:** US Navy, HM2; **OTHER ACT & HONORS:** Santa Barbara Cty. Democratic Central Comm. 1974-pres., Univ. Club; **HOME ADD:** 1959 Las Tunas Rd., Santa Barbara, CA 93103, (805)966-0034; **BUS ADD:** Box 30605, Santa Barbara, CA 93105, (805)965-1964.

REDLE, William D.——B: May 12, 1914, Sheridan, WY, *Sr. Partner*, Redle, Yonkee & Arney; **PRIM RE ACT:** Attorney; **SERVICES:** Advice re: sale or purchase of real prop. and preparation of contracts and related documents; **PROFL AFFIL & HONORS:** WY State Bar Assn., ABA, Amer. Judicature Soc., Amer. Coll. of Probate Counsel.; **GRAD EDUC:** LLB, 1938, Creighton Univ.; **EDUC HONORS:** Alpha Sigma Nu; **OTHER ACT & HONORS:** Currently serve on Bd. of Trustees of the B. F. & Rose H. Perkins Found., Thorne-Rider Found., Dodd & Dorothy L. Bryan Found., Vernon S. & Rowena W. Griffith Found., Sheridan Athletic Assn., Youth, Inc.; **HOME ADD:** 204 West Mountain View Dr., Sheridan, WY 82801, (307)674-8625; **BUS ADD:** 319 West Dow St., Sheridan, WY 82801, (307)674-7454.

REDLIN, E.J.——*Mgr. Retail Sales*, Murphy Oil Corp.; **PRIM RE ACT:** Property Manager; **BUS ADD:** 200 N. Jefferson, El Dorado, AR 71730, (501)862-6411.*

REDMAN, Arnold L.——B: Feb. 16, 1949, Evergreen Park, IL, *Asst. Prof. of RE*, Univ. of Cincinnati, Dept. of Finance; **PRIM RE ACT:** Instructor; **SERVICES:** Undergrad. real estate education; **PROFL AFFIL & HONORS:** Amer. Fin. Assn.; Amer. RE and Urban Econ. Assn.; Western Fin. Assn.; **EDUC:** BS, 1971, Fin./Banking/Investments, Univ. of IL at, Urbana; **GRAD EDUC:** MBA, 1973, Fin./Intl. Bus., NYU; Ph.D., 1979, RE/Urban Econ., Univ. of IL at Urbana; **EDUC HONORS:** NYU Scholarship; **HOME ADD:** 501 Vienna Woods Dr., Cincinnati, OH 45211, (513)481-4390; **BUS ADD:** Coll. of Bus. Admin., Dept. of Fin., Univ. of Cincinnati, Cincinnati, OH 45221, (513)475-5781.

REDMAN, James——*President*, Redman Industries, Inc.; **PRIM RE ACT:** Property Manager; **BUS ADD:** Redman Plaza East, 2550 Walnut Hill Lane, Dallas, TX 75229, (214)353-3600.*

REDMOND, John G., Sr.——B: Feb. 22, 1932, Paterson, NJ, *Broker*; **PRIM RE ACT:** Consultant, Owner/Investor, Property Manager; **SERVICES:** Investment evaluation; **PROFL AFFIL & HONORS:** Registered Profl. Engr.; **EDUC:** BA, 1954, Physics/Econ., Lafayette Coll.; **GRAD EDUC:** MS, 1962, EE, Northeastern Univ.; MBA, 1984, Bus. Admin., Northeastern Univ.; **MIL SERV:** Army Sig. Corps. 1st Lt.; **OTHER ACT & HONORS:** Winchester Capital Planning Comm. 1978/79; **HOME ADD:** One Nassau Dr., Winchester, MA 01890, (617)729-4966; **BUS ADD:** 1 Nassau Dr., Winchester, MA 01890, (617)729-4966.

REDMOND, Lee R., Jr.——B: Aug. 24, 1923, Cincinnati, OH, *Part.*, Thompson and Redmond; **PRIM RE ACT:** Attorney; **SERVICES:** Legal services, titles, foreclosures, and closings; **REP CLIENTS:** Mort. cos., The GA Co. Mort. Dept., Ins. Cos., John Hancock, Pilot Life, Gen. counsel, Trust Co. of Columbus; **PROFL AFFIL & HONORS:** GA Bar Assn., MBA, HBA, Columbus, RE Bd., Past Pres. Columbus Lawyers Club; **EDUC:** AB, 1947, Econ., Wash. and Lee Univ.; **GRAD EDUC:** LLB, 1949, Law, Wash. and Lee Univ.; **MIL SERV:** USAC, Lt.; **HOME ADD:** 2727 Foley Dr., Columbus, GA 31906, (404)327-7388; **BUS ADD:** PO Box 1538, Columbus, GA 31902, (404)327-4551.

REECE, Jerry D.——B: Mar. 7, 1940, Concordia, KS, *Sr. VP, Resid.*, Kroh Brothers Realty Co., Resid.; **PRIM RE ACT:** Broker; **SERVICES:** Resid. brokerage, closing, sales and mgmt. training, specialists in third party corp. marketing; **PREV EMPLOY:** Phillips Petroleum Co. (1966-70); **PROFL AFFIL & HONORS:** NAR, RNMI, KAR, MAR, CRB, GRI; **EDUC:** BS, 1963, Fin., Univ. of OR; **MIL SERV:** USMC, Lt. Col., Navy Commendation with Combat "V"; **OTHER ACT & HONORS:** KS City Bd. of Realtors Bd. of Dir.; **HOME ADD:** 6404 High Dr., Mission Hills, KS 66208, (913)432-3776; **BUS ADD:** 8900 Ward Parkway, Kansas City, MO 64114, (816)361-7300.

REED, C. Paul——B: Feb. 8, 1948, Minneapolis, MN, *Pres.*, Sundown Corp.; **PRIM RE ACT:** Developer, Builder, Property Manager; **EDUC:** BA, 1970, Geog./Hist., Middlebury Coll.; **EDUC HONORS:** Honor Soc; Blue Key, Jr. Yr.; **HOME ADD:** Box 215, Stowe, VT 05672; **BUS ADD:** POB 215, Stowe, VT 05672, (802)253-8261.

REED, Donald L.——B: June 16, 1928, Santa Cruz, CA, *Pres. & Broker*, Century 21 Central Realty Inc.; **PRIM RE ACT:** Broker, Consultant, Appraiser, Developer, Owner/Investor, Instructor, Property Manager, Syndicator; **OTHER RE ACT:** Bus. opportunity sales & analysis; **SERVICES:** Investment analysis & cash flow analysis; **REP CLIENTS:** Lenders and instnl. or indiv. investors in comml. & income props.; **PREV EMPLOY:** Site eval., bldg. insp., mech. insp. for City of Yakima, WA; **PROFL AFFIL & HONORS:** ICBO, AIM, Century 21, Realtor, AIM; **EDUC:** BA, 1949, Pol. Sci., Univ. of MD; **MIL SERV:** US Army, E-8 (1st Sgt.), 3 commendation medals with 2 oak leaf clusters, plus various other decorations; **OTHER ACT & HONORS:** Masonic Lodge, Elks, VFW, Rgnl. and area coordinator, Boy Scouts of Amer.; **HOME ADD:** 509 N 62nd St., Yakima, WA 98902, (509)966-3171; **BUS ADD:** 914 Summitview, Yakima, WA 98902, (509)575-0200.

REED, Douglas J.——B: Apr. 17, 1949, Hartford, WI, *RE Mgr.*, Allis-Chalmers Corp.; **OTHER RE ACT:** Corp. RE mgmt.; **SERVICES:** Site acquisition, surplus props. disposal, lease negotiation, etc.; **PREV EMPLOY:** Ravenhorst Corp., Minneapolis, MN; contr. devel.; **EDUC:** BBA, 1972, Fin., Mktg., Univ. of WI, Madison; **GRAD EDUC:** MS, 1974, RE & Urban Land Econ., Univ. of WI, Madison; **HOME ADD:** W223 N2481 Glenwood Ln., Waukesha, WI 53186, (414)544-6249; **BUS ADD:** 1126 S 70th St. W, Allis, WI 53214, (414)475-3387.

REED, Gregory L.——B: Oct. 20, 1945, Washington, DC, *Partner*, Frank, Bernstein, Conaway & Goldman; **PRIM RE ACT:** Attorney; **PREV EMPLOY:** Admitted to practice before Court of Appeals of MD, U.S.A., various federal courts; **PROFL AFFIL & HONORS:** ABA; MD State Bar Assn.; Bar Assn. of Baltimore City; **EDUC:** AB, 1967, Hist./Pol. Sci., Duke Univ.; **GRAD EDUC:** JD, 1971, Univ. of MD School of Law; **EDUC HONORS:** Editor-in-Chief, MD Law Review; **HOME ADD:** 5105 St. Albans Way, Baltimore, MD 21212, (301)435-2005; **BUS ADD:** 1300 Mercantile Bank and Trust Bldg., 2 Hopkins Plaza, Baltimore, MD 21201, (301)547-0500.

REED, H. Cullen, III——B: Aug. 20, 1953, Spartanburg, SC, *Partner*, Reed Construction Co.; **PRIM RE ACT:** Broker, Developer, Builder, Owner/Investor; **SERVICES:** Custom home const., subdiv. devel., RE sales and investments for resid., multi family & comml.; trade or equity exchanges; **REP CLIENTS:** Small investors, relocation cos., area bus. in both const. and sales, trade in or equity exchanges for clients; **PROFL AFFIL & HONORS:** NAR; Nat. Home Builders Assn.; RNMI; **EDUC:** BA, 1975, RE Fin./Econ., Univ. of SC, School of Bus. Admin.; **OTHER ACT & HONORS:** VP of Programs, Sertoma Club; Treas., Spartanburg Bd. of Realtors; Chap. Advisor at Wofford Coll. for Pi Kappa Phi Frat.; Member of the Bd. of Univ. of SC Alumni Assn. in Spartanburg, SC; Treas., Sigma Chap. of Pi Kappa Frat.; **HOME TEL:** (803)579-4471; **BUS ADD:** 114 S. Port Rd., Spartanburg, SC 29301, (803)574-3137.

REED, James M.——**B:** Mar. 24, 1947, Milwaukee, WI, *Atty., Partner*, Holland & Knight; **PRIM RE ACT:** Attorney; **SERVICES:** Legal, RE; **REP CLIENTS:** Resid. and comml. devels., const. lenders; **PROFL AFFIL & HONORS:** FL Bar; Hillsborough Cty. Bar Assn.; ABA; **EDUC:** BA, 1969, Econ., FL Presbyterian Coll. (now Eckerd Coll.); **GRAD EDUC:** JD, 1972, Law, FL State Univ., Coll. of Law; **EDUC HONORS:** Grad. with Honors; **OTHER ACT & HONORS:** Bd. of Visitors, Eckerd Coll.; Greater Tampa C of C; Urban Land Task Force; Leadership Tampa; Law Review, Articles Editor; **HOME ADD:** 5127 San Jose St., Tampa, FL 33609, (813)872-7351; **BUS ADD:** Ste. 1300, Exchange Bank Bldg., 610 N. Florida Ave., POB 1288, Tampa, FL 33601, (813)223-1621.

REED, John T.——**B:** July 5, 1946, Camden, NJ, *Sr. Editor*, The Real Estate Investing Letter; **PRIM RE ACT:** Owner/Investor, Instructor; **SERVICES:** Sell info. about RE, mgmt. for own acct. only; **REP CLIENTS:** Harcourt Brace Jovanovich, Changing Times, Personal Fin.; **PREV EMPLOY:** Agent with Pritchett & Co., 1972-74, Haddon Hts., NJ; Prop. Mgr. with Fox & Lazo Realtors, Cherry Hill, NJ, 1974-75; **PROFL AFFIL & HONORS:** NAR, NAREE, NAA, Authors Guild, TX Apt. Assn., Council for Competitive Econ., Intl. Platform Assn., Who's Who in CA, Who's Who in Hard Money Econ.; **EDUC:** BS, 1968, Mil. Sci., US Mil. Acad. at West Point; **GRAD EDUC:** MBA, 1977, Harvard Bus. Sch., Pres. of RE Club; **MIL SERV:** US Army, 1st Lt.; **OTHER ACT & HONORS:** Author of *Aggressive Tax Avoidance for RE Investors and Apt. Investing Checklists*; **HOME ADD:** 45 LaSalle Dr., Moraga, CA 94556, (415)376-8540; **BUS ADD:** 45 LaSalle Dr., Moraga, CA 94556, (415)376-1362.

REED, Julian S.——**B:** Sept. 25, 1932, Knoxville, TN, *Pres.*, Stan Reed, Inc. Realty; **PRIM RE ACT:** Broker, Consultant, Appraiser, Owner/Investor, Instructor, Property Manager, Insuror; **SERVICES:** Brokerage, consulting, valuation, prop. mgmt., ins., RE sch.; **REP CLIENTS:** Indiv., investors, attys., banks, lenders, relocation cos.; **PROFL AFFIL & HONORS:** NAR, GRI, Cert. RE Brokerage Mgr., Realtor of the Year; **MIL SERV:** US Army, 1950-54, A/2C, Good Conduct Medal, European Defense Medal, NATO Medal; **OTHER ACT & HONORS:** Optimist Club, Life Member; Optimist of the Year, Past Pres., 14 yrs. perfect attendance; also associated with AL Inst. of RE (Pres.); **HOME ADD:** 3801 Cabana Club, 204, Mobile, AL 36609, (205)343-4321; **BUS ADD:** 2102 Govt. St., Mobile, AL 36606, (205)479-7444.

REED, Lloyd H.——**B:** July 31, 1922, Wash. DC, *VP, RE Investment Counsel*, Mutual of NY, Law; **PRIM RE ACT:** Attorney; **PROFL AFFIL & HONORS:** ABA, Assn. of Life Ins. Counsel, Nat. Bar Assn.; **EDUC:** BA, 1943, Pol. Sci., Econ., Howard Univ.; **GRAD EDUC:** LLB, 1949, Harvard Law Sch.; **EDUC HONORS:** Magna Cum Laude; **HOME ADD:** 93 South Rd., White Plains, NY 10603, (914)761-0662; **BUS ADD:** 1740 Broadway, New York, NY 10019, (212)708-2260.

REED, Ronald A.——**B:** June 20, 1934, Dodge City, KS, *Pres.*, The Brokerage House Inc.; **PRIM RE ACT:** Broker, Developer, Builder, Owner/Investor, Instructor; **SERVICES:** Investment counseling, land devel. and subdiv. planning; **PREV EMPLOY:** Galley Realty 1969-74; **PROFL AFFIL & HONORS:** NAR; Nat. Assn. of Homebuilders, GRI; **OTHER ACT & HONORS:** Member WY Dept. of Econ. Planning and Devel.; Toastmasters; **HOME ADD:** 2900 Nord Ave., Chico, CA 95926, (916)345-0209; **BUS ADD:** PO Box 3193, Chico, CA 95927, (916)345-0209.

REED, Rosalind——**B:** Jan. 15, 1943, Lorain, OH, *VP*, Eastdil Realty, Inc.; **PRIM RE ACT:** Broker; **SERVICES:** RE fin. for corp. assets; **PREV EMPLOY:** Citibank, N.A., 1968-1973; **EDUC:** BA, 1965, Econs., Muskingum Coll.; **GRAD EDUC:** 1966-1968, Econs., NY Univ. Grad. School of Arts & Sci.; **OTHER ACT & HONORS:** Dir., First Women's Bank; **HOME ADD:** 1314 N. Dearborn, Chicago, IL 60610, (312)649-5530; **BUS ADD:** 30 N. LaSalle, Chicago, IL 60602, (312)984-6652.

REED, W. Lansing——**B:** Aug. 11, 1926, Boston, MA, *Pres.*, Occom, Reed and Company, Inc.; Rep., United Farm Agency, Inc.; **PRIM RE ACT:** Broker, Consultant; **SERVICES:** Investment analysis; **PREV EMPLOY:** Aluminum Company of America, 1948-1966; **PROFL AFFIL & HONORS:** Dartmouth Soc. of Engrs.; **EDUC:** BA, 1947, Engrg. & Sci., Dartmouth Coll.; **MIL SERV:** USN, Lt., 1951-53; **OTHER ACT & HONORS:** Harvard Club of Boston; United Way of the Upper Valley, and Dir. First VP; **HOME ADD:** P.O. Box 567, Hanover, NH 03755, (603)643-4100; **BUS ADD:** One Buck Rd., Hanover, NH 03755, (603)643-4100.

REEDER, George W.——**B:** Feb. 27, 1928, Cleveland, OH, *VP & Dir. of RE*, The Continental Corp., Systems & Procedures; **OTHER RE ACT:** In charge of large corp. RE dept., provide all RE servs., leasing, operations, mgmt., design, devel.,acquisition, disposal, appraising, etc. for our operating div.; **PREV EMPLOY:** Div. mgr. of office bldgs. for First Union Mgmt., Inc., Large REIT; **PROFL AFFIL & HONORS:** IREM; NACORE; BOMA; RE Bd. of NY; IDRC; **EDUC:** BBA, 1952, Mktg., Econ., Kent State Univ., OH; **EDUC HONORS:** Grad. Cum Laude, Amer. Mktg. Assn. award for Outstanding Mktg. Grad.; **MIL SERV:** USN, 1946-48, SM 3/c, Div. citations; **OTHER ACT & HONORS:** Ridgewood Ctry. Club; **HOME ADD:** 6 Ethelbert Pl., Ridgewood, NJ 07450, (201)447-4892; **BUS ADD:** 80 Maiden Ln., New York, NY 10038, (212)440-2260.

REEDER, Sally——**B:** Mar. 21, 1949, Pasadena, CA, *Owner-Pres.*, Reeder Appraisal Serv.; **PRIM RE ACT:** Appraiser; **SERVICES:** Appraising resid. comml. indus.; **PREV EMPLOY:** Chief Appraiser, Home S&L Assn.; Appraiser, Los Angeles Fed. S&L Assns.; **PROFL AFFIL & HONORS:** Soc. of RE Appraisers (Bd. of Dir., Orange Cty. Chapt.), SRA (First designated female in Orange Cty.); **EDUC:** BS, 1971, Urban Planning & Soc. Research, Univ. of CA, Davis; **EDUC HONORS:** Magna Cum Laude; **OTHER ACT & HONORS:** Dir. YMCA of Orange Cty.; **HOME ADD:** PO Box 107-A, Balboa Is., CA 92662, (714)673-7407; **BUS ADD:** PO Box 107-A, Balboa Is., CA 92662, (714)673-7407.

REES, Daniel L.——**B:** Feb. 21, 1928, Chicago, IL, *Owner*, Dan Rees & Assoc.; **PRIM RE ACT:** Broker, Appraiser; **SERVICES:** Gen. Brokerage; **REP CLIENTS:** Homequity, Executrans; **PREV EMPLOY:** 1950-1956 - Gen. Prop. Ins. (Underwriter, adjuster, agent); **PROFL AFFIL & HONORS:** RNMI, Cert. Residental Broker, 1967 and 1979 Realtor of the yr., 1978 MI Assoc. of Realtors, Pres., 1979 NAR, Regional VP; **EDUC:** AB, 1949, Bus. Admin. - Accounting & Econ., MI State Univ.; **HOME ADD:** 5044 Lakeshore Dr., Jackson, MI, (517)783-3222; **BUS ADD:** 222 W Prospect, Jackson, MI 49203, (517)782-9342.

REES, Terry L.——**B:** May 22, 1943, Logan, UT, *Corp. RE Mgr.*, Abbott Laboratories; **PRIM RE ACT:** Consultant, Property Manager, Owner/Investor; **SERVICES:** Buying, selling, leasing, managing and valuation of corp. prop.; **PREV EMPLOY:** RE Mgmt., Union Oil Co. of CA 1977-1979; **PROFL AFFIL & HONORS:** NACORE, IDRC.; **EDUC:** BA, 1969, Ger./PreLaw, UT State Univ.; **GRAD EDUC:** Post Grad. Study, 1975-1977, RE Mgmt./ Mktg., GA State Univ., Atlanta, GA; **EDUC HONORS:** Title IV Fellowship Rice Univ., Houston TX; **MIL SERV:** US Army Security Agency; Sp 5, Bronze Star; **OTHER ACT & HONORS:** Lindenhurt Planning Commn. 1981-1982, Scouting Co-ordinator Troop 74 Ingleside, IL; **HOME ADD:** 328 Lakeshore Dr., Lindenhurt, IL 60046, (312)356-6168; **BUS ADD:** Abbott Park, Dept. 540, N. Chicago, IL 60064, (312)937-5060.

REESE, Rostelle J., Jr.——**B:** Dec. 10, 1935, Chicago, IL, *Pres.*, C&R Enterprises Intl. Corp, Neo-Urban Devel. 21; **PRIM RE ACT:** Consultant, Engineer, Lender, Owner/Investor; **SERVICES:** Fin. arrangements - urban development; **REP CLIENTS:** Designers Ltd., White Top Cab Co., Indiv. Neighborhood Projects; **PREV EMPLOY:** US Govt., D/Div Eastern Comm. Region Autodin; **PROFL AFFIL & HONORS:** Nat. Assn. of Realty Investors, Inst. of Valuers, Doctor of Naporathy (DN); **EDUC:** BSCE, 1965-1957, Cryptographic Operations, USAF Inst. Denver, CO; **GRAD EDUC:** MBA, 1960, Auto Digital Network (Computers), Howard Univ.; **EDUC HONORS:** MSEE Nat. Honor Society; **MIL SERV:** USAF, Lt.Col., Pres. Unit Citation; **OTHER ACT & HONORS:** Notary DC 1979-present; Intercity Devel. Council; Advisory Council of Concerned Citizens; **HOME ADD:** 3542 Park Place NW, Washington, DC 20010, (202)726-5666; **BUS ADD:** 3628 Georgia Ave. NW, Washington, DC 20010, (202)723-9794.

REEVES, David M.——**B:** Sept. 1, 1939, St. Louis, MO, *Mgr., Indus. RE*, Ralston Purina Co., RE Div., Legal & Corp. Affairs Dept.; **PRIM RE ACT:** Instructor, Consultant, Developer, Property Manager; **SERVICES:** Overall Prop. Mgmt.; **PREV EMPLOY:** Asst. Dir., Agency & Branch Operations, St. Paul Title Ins. Corp.; **PROFL AFFIL & HONORS:** Indus. Dev. Research Council; Chmn. Indus. Dev. & Facility Planning, Mayor's Adv. Council, Cty. of St Louis; **EDUC:** BS Commerce & Fin., 1961, Indus. Relations, St. Louis Univ., School of Commerce and Fin.; **GRAD EDUC:** Law School, 1961-1964, Gen. Law, St. Louis Univ., School of Law; **OTHER ACT & HONORS:** Bd. of Educ., District 115, Whiteside School, Belleville, IL; **HOME ADD:** 117 San Mateo Dr., Belleville, IL 62221; **BUS ADD:** Checkerboard Sq., St. Louis, MO 63188, (314)982-2369.

REEVES, Melvin H.——**B:** Oct. 1, 1919, Flagler, CO, *Pres.*, Tillstrom Devel. Corp.; **PRIM RE ACT:** Developer, Builder; **SERVICES:** Land devel. and resid. and const.; **PROFL AFFIL & HONORS:** Natl. Assn. of Home Builders, OR Assn. of Home Builders, Home Builders Assn. of Metropolitan Portland; Portland Bd. of Realtors, OR Assn. of Realtors, National Assn. of Realtors; **EDUC:** ME, 1948, Univ. of CO; **MIL**

SERV: USAF, Aviation Cadet; **HOME ADD:** 2241 NE 205th, Troutdale, OR 97206, (503)667-7871; **BUS ADD:** 11160 N. E. Halsey St., Portland, OR 97220, (503)255-5420.

REEVES, Michael C.——**B:** Feb. 11, 1947, West Point, GA, *VP & SC State Mgr.*, AMIC Title Ins. Co.; **PRIM RE ACT:** Attorney; **OTHER RE ACT:** Title ins.; **SERVICES:** Title ins. for owners & lenders of resid. and comml. RE; **REP CLIENTS:** Attys., & lenders involved in resid. & comml. RE transactions; **PREV EMPLOY:** Kellogg, White & Reeves, Attys. at Law; **PROFL AFFIL & HONORS:** ABA, ALTA, NC Bar Assn., NC Land Title Assn.; **EDUC:** BA, 1969, Hist. & Poli. Sci., Presbyterian Coll., Clinton, SC; **GRAD EDUC:** JD, 1973, Wake Forest Univ School of Law, Winston-Salem, NC; **EDUC HONORS:** Dean's List; **HOME ADD:** 234 Fenton Pl., Charlotte, NC 28207; **BUS ADD:** 3455 NLNB Plaza, Charlotte, NC 28280, (704)376-3503.

REEVES, William R.——**B:** Feb. 8, 1937, Corbin, KY, *Pres.*; **PRIM RE ACT:** Consultant, Developer, Builder, Owner/Investor, Property Manager, Syndicator; **SERVICES:** Fin., const., manage indus. and comml. prop.; **REP CLIENTS:** St. Charles Assocs., Interstate Gen. Corp., Davis & McLeod (Law Firm); **PREV EMPLOY:** Fantus Div., Dun & Bradstreet, NYC, 1970-1972; Pres., Barnett Chem. Products, Inc., Philadelphia, 1972-1973; Cons., Nat. Ctr. for Resource Recovery, Washington, 1973-1980; VP, Interstate Gen. Corp., St. Charles, MD, San Juan, PR, 1973-; Dir., St. Charles Health Services, Inc., 1977-; Pres., Energetics Devel., Inc., 1980 to present; VP, IGC, 1973-1980; **PROFL AFFIL & HONORS:** Pres. Port Tobacco Restoration Soc., Pres., Dir., 1976-; Charles Cty., MD Heart Assn., Chmn., 1976-1977; Nat. Energy Resources Org., Met. Washington Bd. Trade, PE OH, MD; **EDUC:** BCE, 1959, Univ. of Cincinnati; **GRAD EDUC:** MBA, 1964, Univ. of VA; **MIL SERV:** US Army, Capt., 1960-1961; **OTHER ACT & HONORS:** Harvard Bus. School Club, WA; **HOME ADD:** Sunytop Farm, Pt. Tobacco, MD 20677; **BUS ADD:** 109 Post Office Rd., St. Charles, MD 20601, (301)645-2161.

REGAN, D. Thomas, Jr.——**B:** May 24, 1946, Washington, DC, *Pres.*, The Island Sound Corp.; **PRIM RE ACT:** Consultant, Developer, Owner/Investor, Property Manager, Syndicator; **SERVICES:** Investment counseling, equity placement, synd. of resid. and comml. devel.; **REP CLIENTS:** Indiv. investors, instns.; **PREV EMPLOY:** FL Fed. S&L Assn.; **EDUC:** BS, 1968, Econ., Wharton Sch. of Commerce & Fin., Univ. of PA; **GRAD EDUC:** MA, 1975, RE, Univ. of FL; **EDUC HONORS:** Phi Kappa Phi; **BUS ADD:** Suite One, 256 S. Nokomis Ave., Venice, FL 33595, (813)484-8421.

REGARDIE, William——*Ed.*, Real Estate Washington; **PRIM RE ACT:** Real Estate Publisher; **BUS ADD:** 1010 Wisconsin Ave., NW, Ste. 420, Washington, DC 20007, (202)342-0410.*

REGEVIK, Robert——**B:** Sept. 25, 1953, Brooklyn, NY, *Manager*, Morgan Stanley & Co., Inc.; **PRIM RE ACT:** Consultant, Owner/Investor; **OTHER RE ACT:** Tax law; **SERVICES:** Tax planning; **EDUC:** BS, 1976, Acctg., Northeastern Univ.; **GRAD EDUC:** MBA, 1979, Tax, Pace Univ.; **EDUC HONORS:** Dean's List - Beta Alpha Psi - Grad. with Honors; **HOME ADD:** 63-76 St., Brooklyn, NY 11209, (212)748-4189; **BUS ADD:** 1251 Ave. of the Americas, New York, NY 10020, (212)974-2392.

REGIER, Jarold W.——**B:** May 25, 1943, Newton, KS, *VP*, The Haskell Co., Law and Admin.; **PRIM RE ACT:** Attorney; **SERVICES:** Architects, engrgs., contractors, RE devels.; **REP CLIENTS:** Owners and devel. of shopping ctrs., warehouses, office bldgs., factories, hotels, apt. complexes, condos, indus. parks and PUDs; **PREV EMPLOY:** Rogers, Towers, Bailey, Jones & Gay, Attorneys, Jacksonville, FL; **PROFL AFFIL & HONORS:** ABA; The FL Bar; Jacksonville Bar Assn.; Amer. Mgmt. Assns.; **EDUC:** BA, 1966, Psych., econs., and acctg., Wichita State Univ., Wichita, KS; **GRAD EDUC:** JD and MBA, 1974, Law, Fin., RE and Gen. Bus. Admin., Univ. of KS; **EDUC HONORS:** Beta Gamma Sigma (Honorary Bus. Frat.); **MIL SERV:** USN Res.; Lt.; **OTHER ACT & HONORS:** Bd. of Dirs., Jr. Achievement; C of C Bus./Educ. Partnership Task Force; and Improved Air Service Task Force; **HOME ADD:** 7900 Concord Blvd. West., Jacksonville, FL 32208, (904)768-2733; **BUS ADD:** Haskell Bldg., Jacksonville, FL 32204, (904)358-1600.

REGIS, John A., Jr.——**B:** Jan. 21, 1944, San German, PR, *Dir. of Real Estate*, Pueblo Supermarkets; **OTHER RE ACT:** Prop. Mgmt., Leasing, Site Selection; **PREV EMPLOY:** RE Mgr. - Grand Union Supermarkets; **PROFL AFFIL & HONORS:** ICSC; PR Home Builders; **EDUC:** BS, 1967, Bus. Admin.; **GRAD EDUC:** MBA, 1974, Mktg. (additional concentration in Fin.), Inter Amer. Univ.; **MIL SERV:** US Army Nat. Guard, Spec. 4; **OTHER ACT & HONORS:** Dir., Ocean Park Resid. Assn.; Pres., Comm. for Beach Preservation; **HOME ADD:** 2012 Italia St., Ocean Park, Santurce, PR 00911, (809)726-2411; **BUS ADD:** GPO Box 3288, San Juan, PR 00936, (809)762-0590.

REGISTER, Sidney W, Jr.——**B:** Jan. 6, 1940, Savannah, GA, *Pres.*, Property Services, Inc.; **PRIM RE ACT:** Broker, Property Manager, Engineer, Owner/Investor; **SERVICES:** Brokerage, mgmt., consulting, invtmt.; **REP CLIENTS:** Maj. Ins. Co., Banks, Investors, etc.; **PROFL AFFIL & HONORS:** IREM, BOMA, NBR, CPM, Past Reg. Pres. of BOMA and IREM; **EDUC:** BS, 1962, Elec. Eng, The Citadel; **GRAD EDUC:** MBA, 1969, Mgmt/Fin, GA St. Univ.; **MIL SERV:** US Army, Capt.; **HOME ADD:** 3600 Julington Creek Rd., Jacksonville, FL 32223, (904)262-0717; **BUS ADD:** 815 S. Main St., Ste. 333, JacksonviLle, FL 32207, (904)396-1782.

REGULSKI, Lee——**B:** Nov. 19, 1926, Brooklyn, NY, *VP, Construction and Engrg.*, Wittner & Co.; **PRIM RE ACT:** Engineer; **SERVICES:** Construct and lease gen. office space; **REP CLIENTS:** Profl. servs. - attys., accts., banks, stock brokers, med.; **PREV EMPLOY:** Self employed - gen. contractor and consultant engr. 1968-1980; VP, Rutenberg Homes, Clearwater, FL 1962-1968, Caldwell & Cook, Construction Mgr., Rochester, NY 1954-1962; E.I. DuPont deNemours & Co., Cost and Construction Engr., 1950-1954; **PROFL AFFIL & HONORS:** ASCE, Past Branch Pres.; Nat. Soc. of Profl. Engrs., FL Engrg. Soc., Registered PE, FL, Arg. Gen. Contractor, FL; **EDUC:** BSCE, 1949, Cornell Univ.; **MIL SERV:** US Army, 1944-1945; **OTHER ACT & HONORS:** Municipal Code Enforcement Bd., Clearwater, FL Chmn. Bd. of Admustment Zoning and Appeals, Clearwater, Past member Kiwanis Club of Clearwater East, Past Pres.; Morningside Meadows Homeowners Assn., Clearwater, Past Pres.; Hope Presbyterian Church, Elder; **HOME ADD:** 1045 Chinaberry Road, Clearwater, FL 33516, (813)531-4259; **BUS ADD:** 5999 Central Ave., St. Petersburg, FL 33710, (813)384-3000.

REHLE, Daniel F.——**B:** July 1, 1933, New York, NY, *Pres.*, ERA Daniel F. Rehle Inc., Realtors; **PRIM RE ACT:** Broker, Consultant, Appraiser, Owner/Investor, Property Manager, Syndicator; **SERVICES:** Consulting; **REP CLIENTS:** Indiv. investors in comml. prop.; **PROFL AFFIL & HONORS:** Manchester Bd. of Realtors, Hartford Bd. of Realtors, Vernon Bd. of Realtors, Manchester, Vernon, Hartford, MLS, GRI, CRS; **EDUC:** AS, 1958, Bus. Mgmt., Hyllyr Coll.; **MIL SERV:** US Navy, Seaman First Class, 1951-1954; **OTHER ACT & HONORS:** Dir. - C of C; **BUS ADD:** 175 Main St., Manchester, CT 06040, (203)646-4525.

REI, Dr. Joseph D.——**B:** Sept. 29, 1948, Ft. Scott, KS, *Dir. of Student Family Housing*, Univ. of UT; **PRIM RE ACT:** Property Manager; **OTHER RE ACT:** Univ. Housing; **PREV EMPLOY:** Coordinator of Residence Life, IA State Univ., Residence Hall Dir., KS State Univ., Pres. Reico Mgmt., Inc.; **PROFL AFFIL & HONORS:** Assn. of Coll. and Univ. Housing Officers-Intl., Apt. Assn. of UT, Amer. Coll. Personnel Assn.; **EDUC:** 1970, Psych., Ottawa Univ.; **GRAD EDUC:** MS-1973;PhD-1978, Coll. Student Personnel, KS State Univ.; **MIL SERV:** US Army, Capt., Army Commendation with One Oak Leaf Cluster; **OTHER ACT & HONORS:** Kiwanis Intl.; **HOME ADD:** 4170 S. 530 East, Salt Lake City, UT 84103, (801)263-1610; **BUS ADD:** 1945 Sunnyside Ave., Salt Lake City, UT 84108, (801)581-6988.

REIBEL, Martin A.——**B:** Apr. 26, 1942, Brooklyn, NY, *Rgnl. VP - Acquisitions*, The Robert A. McNeil Corp.; **PRIM RE ACT:** Owner/Investor, Syndicator; **PREV EMPLOY:** Exec. VP, DLJ Realty Resources; **PROFL AFFIL & HONORS:** RE Bd. of NY; BOMA; Rho Epsilon; RE Securities & Synd. Inst.; **EDUC:** BS, 1963, RE/Fin., NYU; **EDUC HONORS:** Magna Cum Laude; **MIL SERV:** US Army; **OTHER ACT & HONORS:** Local Planning Bd.; **HOME ADD:** 130 Spruce St., Freehold, NJ 07728; **BUS ADD:** 1345 Ave. of Americas, New York, NY 10105, (212)245-8790.

REIBSTEIN, Saul V.——**B:** May 13, 1948, Philadelphia, PA, *Partner*, Laventhol & Horwath; **PRIM RE ACT:** Consultant; **GRAD EDUC:** BBA; **MIL SERV:** US Army, E-5; **HOME ADD:** 1118 Coventry Ln., Cheltenham, PA 19012, (215)782-1618; **BUS ADD:** 1845 Walnut St., Philadelphia, PA 19012, (215)299-1740.

REICH, James O.——**B:** Jan. 6, 1946, WI, *VP, Acquisitions*, The Gulledge Corp.; **PRIM RE ACT:** Attorney, Developer, Syndicator; **PROFL AFFIL & HONORS:** WI State Bar; MI State Bar; RESSI; ABA, Atty.; **EDUC:** BBA, 1969, RE, Univ. of WI; **GRAD EDUC:** MS, 1971, Investment analysis & APpraisal, Univ. of WI; JD, 1971, Univ. of WI; **MIL SERV:** MP, 2nd Lt.; **HOME ADD:** 10852 Weisbiger Lane, Oakton, VA, (703)533-0124; **BUS ADD:** 2 Skyline Pl., Ste. 101, 5203 Leesburg Pike, Falls Church, VA 22041, (703)931-6000.

REICH, Joseph A., Jr.——**B:** July 22, 1935, CO Springs, CO, *Pres.*, Reich-LeRoy & Assoc., Inc., Reich-LeRoy Comml. Brokerage Co.; **PRIM RE ACT:** Broker, Developer; **PROFL AFFIL & HONORS:**

CO Springs Bd. of Realtors; CCIM Chap. No. 5 (CAN); HBA Metropolitan CO Springs, GRI; **EDUC:** BS, 1957, Bus. Admin./Fin., Univ. of Notre Dame; **MIL SERV:** USNR, Capt.; **OTHER ACT & HONORS:** CO C of C, Airport Advisory Bd., Dir. First Amer. Bank; **HOME ADD:** 3330 Clubheights Dr., CO Springs, CO 80906, (303)576-3675; **BUS ADD:** 843 S. Circle Dr., CO Springs, CO 80910, (303)632-2120.

REICHEL, Harold I.——**B:** July 28, 1931, Brooklyn, NY, *Gen. Counsel*, The National Birchwood Cor.; **PRIM RE ACT:** Attorney, Developer, Builder, Property Manager; **OTHER RE ACT:** Negotiator; **PREV EMPLOY:** A.A. Hills & Co., Inc., VP-Counsel; **PROFL AFFIL & HONORS:** Queens & Nassau Bar Assn.; Brandeis Assn.; **EDUC:** BA, 1952, Poli. Sci., Yeshiva Univ.; **GRAD EDUC:** JD, 1956, Brooklyn Law School; **EDUC HONORS:** Grad. top quarter of class; **OTHER ACT & HONORS:** NY City School Bd., 1969-1972; **HOME ADD:** 110-34 67th Dr., Forest Hills, NY 11374, (212)261-3731; **BUS ADD:** 410 E Jericho Tpk., Mineola, NY 11501, (516)747-7880.

REICHELT, Ferdinand H.——**B:** Jan. 26, 1941, Chicago, IL, *Exec. VP*, Verex Corp.; **PRIM RE ACT:** Lender, Insuror; **SERVICES:** Mort. ins.; **PREV EMPLOY:** CPA with Peat, Marwick & Mitchell - 9 years (303 East Wacker Drive, Chicago, IL 60601); **PROFL AFFIL & HONORS:** Mortgage Ins. Cos. of Amer. (MICA) Nat. Investor Relations Inst., Ins. Acctg. & Statistical Assn., Amer. Inst. of CPAs, WI Inst. of CPAs, Financial Execs. Inst.; **EDUC:** BS, 1958-63, Acctg. and Fin., Univ. of IL; **MIL SERV:** USAF, Sgt.; **OTHER ACT & HONORS:** Madison Civic Ctr. Found., Madison Civic Repertory; Friends of Channel 21 (public TV); United Way; Madison Public Affairs Council; **HOME ADD:** 210 Shiloh Dr., Madison, WI 53705, (608)833-3444; **BUS ADD:** P O Box 7066, Madison, WI 53707, (608)257-2527.

REICHER, Leland J.——**B:** May 30, 1949, Los Angeles, CA, *Atty./CPA*, Leland J. Reicher, Atty. at Law; **PRIM RE ACT:** Attorney, Owner/Investor, Instructor; **SERVICES:** Atty., RE and tax law; **REP CLIENTS:** Investors and devel. and dealers in land, and improved comml., resid. & indus. props.; **PREV EMPLOY:** S.D. Leidesdorf & Co., CPA 1975-77; Mazirow, Schneider, Forer & Lawrence, Inc. Attys at Law 1977-79; **PROFL AFFIL & HONORS:** CA Bar Assn., L.A. Bar Assn., CA Soc. of CPA's; **EDUC:** BS, Acctg., 1972, Acctg. and Fin., Univ. of S. CA; **GRAD EDUC:** JD, 1975, RE Taxation Bus., Univ. of CA At L.A.; **EDUC HONORS:** Cum Laude, Haskins & Sells Found. Award, Touche Ross Srs. Award, Beta Gamma Sigma; **OTHER ACT & HONORS:** Instr. at UCLA Extension: RE Fin., RE Syndication, 1979 to Present; **HOME ADD:** 8401 Wyndham Rd., Los Angeles, CA 90046, (213)654-0926; **BUS ADD:** 2049 Century Park E. #710, Los Angeles, CA 90067, (213)277-9323.

REID, David J.——**B:** Mar. 28, 1941, The Dalles, OR, *VP & Mgr., Corp. Prop.*, Seattle Trust & Savings Bank, Prop.; **PRIM RE ACT:** Architect, Property Manager; **SERVICES:** Manage RE acquisition, design, const. and maintenance of bank facilities; **PREV EMPLOY:** Seattle - First Nat. Bank, 1975-1978; **PROFL AFFIL & HONORS:** AIA, BOMA; **EDUC:** BArch, 1966, Univ. of OR; **GRAD EDUC:** MArch, 1970, Urban Design & Planning, Univ. of WA; **MIL SERV:** USCG, LCDR, Vietnam Serv.; **HOME ADD:** 2271 NE 60th, Seattle, WA 98115, (206)522-2685; **BUS ADD:** 804 2nd Ave., Seattle, WA 98104, (206)223-2127.

REID, Katherine A.——**B:** Mar. 14, 1950, Long Beach, CA, *RE Spec.*, Jefferson Cty. School Dist. No. R-1, Facilities Planning & Const.; **OTHER RE ACT:** Acquisition & disposal and mgmt. of school dist. RE; **SERVICES:** Granting of easements, rights of way, consultation; **PREV EMPLOY:** Appraiser, City & Cty. of Denver Assessment Div., Deputy Assessor, Grand Cty. (Hot Sulphur Springs), CO; **PROFL AFFIL & HONORS:** CO Assn. of Tax Appraisers, Jefferson Cty. Assn. of School Bus. Officials, Cert. Tax Appraiser; **EDUC:** 1968/72, Anthro., Eng., Univ. of NM, Albuquerque, NM; **OTHER ACT & HONORS:** Deputy Assessor, Grand Cty. CO, 1973-77; **HOME ADD:** 642 Milky Way, Denver, CO 80221, (303)427-6383; **BUS ADD:** 809 Quail St., Lakewood, CO 80215, (303)231-2544.

REIDDA, Joseph J.——**B:** Sept. 15, 1942, Paterson, NJ, *Sr. RE Appraiser*, City Appraisal Serv., RE Investment; **PRIM RE ACT:** Consultant, Appraiser, Banker; **SERVICES:** Fee appraisal assignments; **REP CLIENTS:** Attys., Relocation cos., banks, brokers, ins. cos., mort. cos., pvt. indivs.; **PREV EMPLOY:** Franklin Soc. Fed. Savings & Loan, 217 Broadway, NYC, NY; **PROFL AFFIL & HONORS:** SREA, NARA, SRA, CRA; **EDUC:** BS, 1965, Bus. Admin., Fairleigh Dickinson Univ.; **MIL SERV:** US Army, E-5; **HOME ADD:** 84 N. Belair Ave., Cedar Knolls, NJ 07927, (201)539-7232; **BUS ADD:** Two Railroad Plaza, Whippany, NJ 07927, (201)428-8047.

REIDER, Jeffrey R.——**B:** Aug. 17, 1944, Cleveland, OH, *Counsel*, Tucker, Flyer, Sanger, Reider & Lewis; **PRIM RE ACT:** Consultant, Regulator; **OTHER RE ACT:** Dir./Tr., RE Investment Trust; **PROFL AFFIL & HONORS:** ABA; DC Bar Assn.; NAREIT; **EDUC:** 1966, Hist./Pol. Sci., OH State Univ.; **GRAD EDUC:** 1970, Law, Washington & Lee Univ. Sch. of Law; **EDUC HONORS:** Order of Coif, Magna Cum Laude; **MIL SERV:** US Army, Sp 4; **OTHER ACT & HONORS:** Tr., Fed. Realty Investment Trust; Dir., Washington Area Rgn., The Equitable Trust Co.; **HOME ADD:** 4805 Dorset Ave., Chevy Chase, MD 20815, (301)652-7552; **BUS ADD:** 1730 MA Ave., NW, Washington, DC 20036, (202)452-8600.

REIDY, Martin J.——**B:** May 2, 1938, Tulsa, OK; **PRIM RE ACT:** Appraiser, Owner/Investor; **SERVICES:** Resid., Comml. RE appraisal; **REP CLIENTS:** FHA, Mort. S & L's, Appraisal Assocs. of OK, US Dept. of Justice; **EDUC:** BA, 1968, Hist.-Liberal Arts, Univ. of Tulsa; **MIL SERV:** US Army, Sgt.; **BUS ADD:** PO Box 2164, Tulsa, OK 74101, (918)587-0559.

REILLY, George——**B:** Nov. 29, 1934, Waukegan, IL, *Partner*, Leonard, Street and Deinard; **PRIM RE ACT:** Attorney; **PROFL AFFIL & HONORS:** ABA, MN State Bar Assn.; **EDUC:** BA, 1956, Communications, IL Coll.; **GRAD EDUC:** MS, 1958, Comm., SD State Univ.; JD, 1964, Univ. of MN; **EDUC HONORS:** Magna Cum Laude, Law Review, Order of the Coif; **OTHER ACT & HONORS:** Formerly Chief Deputy Atty. Gen. of MN, Formerly Gen. Counsel to MN Housing Fin. Agency 1972-79; **HOME ADD:** 2304 Carter Ave., St. Paul, MN 55108, (612)645-6970; **BUS ADD:** 1200 National City Bank Bldg., Minneapolis, MN 55402, (612)339-1200.

REILLY, John——**B:** Mar. 25, 1942, NY, *VP*, Robbins & Reilly; **PRIM RE ACT:** Broker, Attorney, Instructor, Real Estate Publisher; **OTHER RE ACT:** Author; **SERVICES:** RE educ.; **REP CLIENTS:** Pre-licence students; **PREV EMPLOY:** Educ. consultant to RE Comm.; **PROFL AFFIL & HONORS:** REEA; **EDUC:** BA, 1963, Hist., Hamilton Coll.; **GRAD EDUC:** JD, 1966, Fordham Law School; **MIL SERV:** U.S. Army, Capt.; **OTHER ACT & HONORS:** Author: 'Language of Real Estate', 'Questions & Answers to Pass Real Estate Exam', 'Principles & Practices of Hawaiian Real Estate'; **HOME ADD:** 44-497 Kaneohe Bay Dr., Kaneohe, HI 96744, (808)235-6584; **BUS ADD:** 841 Bishop St. #2220, Honolulu, HI 96813, (808)524-2355.

REILLY, Paul J.——**B:** Sept. 30, 1954, Evergreen Pk, IL, *Dir. of Research*, Cook County Assessor's Office; **PRIM RE ACT:** Consultant, Attorney, Appraiser, Assessor; **PROFL AFFIL & HONORS:** Chicago Bar Assn.; IL Bar Assn., CIAO; **EDUC:** BS, 1976, Pol. Sci., Quincy Coll.; **GRAD EDUC:** JD, 1979, Loyola Univ. of Chicago; **HOME ADD:** 1636 N. Wells, Chicago, IL 60614, (312)649-9776; **BUS ADD:** 118 N. Clark, Chicago, IL 60602.

REILLY, Thomas J.——**B:** Oct. 21, 1937, Dubuque, IA, *VP*, American Trust and Savings Bank; **PRIM RE ACT:** Appraiser, Banker, Lender; **PREV EMPLOY:** Conservative Mort. Co. IA & MN; **PROFL AFFIL & HONORS:** Young IA Mort. Bankers; **EDUC:** BS, 1959, Math. & Physics, Loras Coll., Dubuque, IA; **MIL SERV:** US Army, E-5; **OTHER ACT & HONORS:** Lifetime Member Jaycees; **HOME ADD:** 951 Oxford St., Dubuque, IA 52001, (319)582-3963; **BUS ADD:** Town Clock Plaza, Dubuque, IA 52001, (319)582-1841.

REIMAN, Robert E.——**B:** Dec. 3, 1924, Rosalin, WA, *Certified Fin. Planner (Sr. Partner)*, Robert Reiman Associates; **PRIM RE ACT:** Developer, Owner/Investor; **OTHER RE ACT:** Reg. Prin.; Reg. Investment Advisor; **SERVICES:** Investment, estate, retirement planning; **REP CLIENTS:** Profls. & indus. with net worths in excess of $250,000, small businessmen; **PREV EMPLOY:** Gen. Part. & Synd. RE Devel., Fin. Planning Practice, RE Devel.; **PROFL AFFIL & HONORS:** Home Builders Assn., C of C, Inst. of Certified Fin. Planners, Intl. Assn. of Fin. Planners, Certified Fin. Planner, Reg. Investment Advisor, MBA, Reg. Prin. (Securities); **EDUC:** BS, Mech. Engrg., 1947, OR State Univ., Corvallis, OR; **GRAD EDUC:** MBA, 1967, Fin., OR State Univ., Corvallis, OR; **MIL SERV:** USN, AvCad; **OTHER ACT & HONORS:** Corvallis City Councilman 1978-1980; **HOME ADD:** 3510 NW Grant St., Corvallis, OR 97330, (503)753-7288; **BUS ADD:** PO Box 1617, 318 S.W. Washington, Corvallis, OR 97339, (503)757-1112.

REIMERS, Karl——*Sr. VP & Chief Fin. Off.*, OKC Corp.; **PRIM RE ACT:** Property Manager; **BUS ADD:** 4835 LBJ Freeway, PO Box 34190, Dallas, TX 75234, (214)233-7100.*

REIN, Samuel——Samuel Rein, Esq.; **PRIM RE ACT:** Attorney; **PROFL AFFIL & HONORS:** ABA, NYSBA; **EDUC:** BA, 1977, Poli. Sci., NYU; **GRAD EDUC:** JD, 1980, Brooklyn Law School; **BUS ADD:** 1855 E. 12th St., Brooklyn, NY 11229, (212)627-4338.

REINAUER, David——B: Sept. 5, 1940, Lake Charles, LA, *Pres.*, Reinauer RE Corp.; **PRIM RE ACT:** Broker, Consultant, Appraiser, Developer, Owner/Investor, Instructor, Property Manager, Syndicator; **PROFL AFFIL & HONORS:** NAR; RNMI; IREM; SIR; RESSI; FIABCI; Nat. Assn. of Home Builders, CRB; CPM; SIR; **EDUC:** BS, Econ./RE, Wharton School of Fin. and Commerce, Univ. of PA; **OTHER ACT & HONORS:** Pres., 1968, Young Men's Bus. Club of Lake Charles; Actor, Artists Civic Theatre & Studio and Lake Charles Little Theatre; 32nd degree Mason; Outstanding Citizen Award from YMBC, 1976; President of Lake Charles Chamber of Commerce, 1976; Past president of Greater Calcarier Board of Realtors and Louisiana Realtors Associations; Director of National Association of Realtors; Chairman, Professional Standards Committee, 1982; Regional Vice President-Elect, 1983.; **HOME ADD:** 813 Shell Beach Dr., Lake Charles, LA 70601, (318)436-4422; **BUS ADD:** POB CCC, Lake Charles, LA 70602, (318)433-4663.

REINGOLD, Herbert L.——B: Apr. 18, 1922, Pittsburgh, PA, *Owner*, Reingold RE Co.; **PRIM RE ACT:** Broker, Consultant, Appraiser, Property Manager; **SERVICES:** Sales mgmt., appraisals, bus. & indus. props.; **PROFL AFFIL & HONORS:** Nat. Assn. of RE Bds.; PA Assn. of Realtors; Gr. Pittsburgh Bd. of Realtors; **EDUC:** BS, 1943, Bus. Admin. & Indus. Engrg., Univ. of Pittsburgh; **MIL SERV:** US Army, 1943-46, Cpl.; **HOME ADD:** 5780 Fifth Ave., Pittsburgh, PA 15232, (412)441-0013; **BUS ADD:** 5100 Centre Ave., Pittsburgh, PA 15232, (412)261-3350.

REINGOLD, Jeffrey A.——B: Nov. 15, 1948, Portland, OR, *Owner/Broker*, Income Property Mgmt. Co.; **PRIM RE ACT:** Owner/Investor, Property Manager; **SERVICES:** Prop. Mgmt.; **PROFL AFFIL & HONORS:** Inst. of RE Mgmt.; State and Local Bds. of Realtors, CPM, Accredited Mgmt. Org.; **EDUC:** BFA, 1973, Fine Arts, Univ. of OR; **HOME ADD:** PO Box 3752, Eugene, OR 97403, (503)485-0539; **BUS ADD:** 1065 High St., Eugene, OR 97401, (503)485-8252.

REINHART, Peter S.——B: May 17, 1950, Mineola, NY, *VP and Gen. Counsel*, Hovnanian Enterprises, Inc.; **PRIM RE ACT:** Attorney; **PROFL AFFIL & HONORS:** ABA, NJ Bar Assn.; **EDUC:** AB, 1971, Govt., Franklin and Marshall Coll., Lancaster, PA; **GRAD EDUC:** JD, 1975, Rutgers - Camden School of Law; **EDUC HONORS:** PI Gamma Mu Natl. Soc. Sci. Honors Soc., Cum Laude; **MIL SERV:** Natl. Guard, S/Sgt.; **OTHER ACT & HONORS:** Past Pres. - Greater Red Bank Jaycees; **HOME ADD:** 67 Winchester Dr., Tinton Falls, NJ 07724, (201)542-3011; **BUS ADD:** 10 Highway 35, P.O. Box 500, Red Bank, NJ 07701, (201)747-7800.

REINHOLD, Robert C.——*Pres.*, R.C. Reinhold Co., Realtors; **PRIM RE ACT:** Broker, Consultant, Owner/Investor, Instructor, Property Manager, Syndicator; **SERVICES:** Leasing, consulting, sales; **REP CLIENTS:** Allstate Ins. Co., Cooper-Horowitz Inc., Divine Word Seminary, E.I. DuPont de Nemours & Co., Equitable Life Assurance Soc. of US; W.R. Grace Properties Inc., Gulf Oil Corp. John Hancock Mutual Life Ins. Co., Hospital Serv. Plan of NJ (BC-BS), Kendall Devel. Co., Marriott-Hot Shoppes Inc., Merrill Lynch, Pierce Fenner & Smith Inc., Prudential Ins. Co. of Amer., Shell Oil Co.; **PROFL AFFIL & HONORS:** Mercer Cty. Bd. of Realtors; NJ Assn. of Realtor Bds.; NAR Bds.; NJ Chap. No. 1, IREM, CPM; RE Broker; NJ State and Commonwealth of PA; Asst. Prof. of RE, Rider Coll., NJ; Past Pres., Mercer Cty. Bd. of Realtors; Former Dir., Mercer Cty. Bd. of Realtors; Exec. Comm., Mercer Cty. Econ. Devel. Commn.; **EDUC:** AB, 1950, Univ. of Miami; **OTHER ACT & HONORS:** Advisory Study Commn., City of Trenton; Recognized Mgmt. Broker, FHA; Former Member, Ewing Township Rent Control Bd.; **BUS ADD:** 134 Franklin Corner Rd., Lawrenceville, NJ 08648, (609)890-0999.

REININGS, John H., Jr.——B: Sept. 24, 1936, Toledo, OH, *Pres.*, Reininga Corporation; **PRIM RE ACT:** Developer, Property Manager; **SERVICES:** Devel. spec. in neighborhood & community shopping ctrs. in the W states; **PREV EMPLOY:** 1963-65 The Draper Companies, 1965-67 Desmond MacTavish & Assocs.; **PROFL AFFIL & HONORS:** VP Intl. Council of Shopping Ctrs., Member of the Advisory Bd/ of CA Bus. Props.; Member of Urban Land Institute, Cert. Shopping Ctr. Mgr. (CSM); Licensed CA RE Broker; **EDUC:** BS, 1958, Chem. Engrg., Univ. of CO; **GRAD EDUC:** MBA, 1960, Bus., Stanford Bus. Sch.; **EDUC HONORS:** VP of Class; **MIL SERV:** US Army, Pvt.; **OTHER ACT & HONORS:** Commonwealth Club, Bankers Club, Meadows Club (golf); **HOME ADD:** 120 Fairway Dr., San Rafael, CA 94901, (415)456-1964; **BUS ADD:** 425 California St., 2100, San Francisco, CA 94111, (415)391-2250.

REINSDORF, Jerry M.——B: 1936, *CEO, Gen. Partner, Chmn. & Pre.*, The Balcor Co.; **PRIM RE ACT:** Attorney; **OTHER RE ACT:** CPA; **PREV EMPLOY:** Carlyle RE Ltd. Partnerships; Altman, Kurlander & Weiss (law firm); Katten, Muchin, Zavis, Pearl & Galler; Atty. Chicago IRS; **PROFL AFFIL & HONORS:** RESSI, NAR, A Founder of the RESSI of NAR; CPA; Specialist in RE Securities; **BUS ADD:** Balcor Bldg., 10024 Skokie Blvd., Skokie, IL 60077, (312)677-2900.

REISDORF, Edward Gary——B: Mar. 8, 1941, Milwaukee, WI, *Pres.*, LR Equities, Inc.; **PRIM RE ACT:** Attorney, Developer; **SERVICES:** Legal serv.; devel. & synd. of real prop.; **PREV EMPLOY:** Pres., E.G. Reisdorf P.A.; **PROFL AFFIL & HONORS:** ABA; NJ Bar Assn., Who's Who in Fin. & Indus.; Who's Who in World; **EDUC:** BS, 1963, Pol. Sci., USAF Academy; **GRAD EDUC:** JD, 1968, Tax, Georgetown Law Ctr.; **MIL SERV:** USAF, Capt.; **HOME ADD:** 152 Fairmount Ave., Chatham, NJ 07928, (201)635-1918; **BUS ADD:** 8 Mountain Ave., Springfield, NJ 07081, (201)379-9000.

REISDORF, R.A.——B: Aug. 26, 1924, Pittsburgh, PA, *Exec. V.P.-Investments & Treas.*, Wisc. Life Ins. Co.; **PRIM RE ACT:** Attorney, Lender, Owner/Investor; **OTHER RE ACT:** Bd. Member; **SERVICES:** Comml. loans; **PREV EMPLOY:** Pure Oil Co., RE Mgr., 1955-1957; **PROFL AFFIL & HONORS:** Dane Co. & WI Bar Assn.; **EDUC:** BA, 1945, Pol. Sci. & Econ., PA State; **GRAD EDUC:** JD, 1949, WI Law School; **OTHER ACT & HONORS:** Lions; **HOME ADD:** 5702 Lake Mendota Dr., Madison, WI 53705, (608)233-5704; **BUS ADD:** 709 N. Segoe Rd. (Box-5099), Madison, WI 53705, (608)238-5841.

REISEMAN, Harvey I.——B: Sept. 8, 1930, NY, *Partner*, Reiseman & Lamont, P.A.; **PRIM RE ACT:** Attorney, Syndicator; **SERVICES:** All legal servs. including: zoning, land use law, pre-closing, closing & synd.; **PROFL AFFIL & HONORS:** Amer., FL and Dade Cty. Bar Assns., Amer. Arbitration Assn. Bd. of Arbitrators, Former Judge, V-Mayor of Dade Cty., FL, Sec.-Treas. of S. FL Rgnl. Planning Council; **EDUC:** BA, 1955, Sociology & Speech, The PA State Univ.; **GRAD EDUC:** JD, 1958, Law, Univ. of Miami Sch. of Law; **EDUC HONORS:** Dean's List; Pres., Phi Sigma Delta; Debate Team, Cum Laude, Editor-in-Chief, The Barrister, Assoc. Editor, Univ. of Miami Law Review; Pres., Tau Epsilon Rho; Pres., Wig 6 Robe; Omicrom Delta Kappa, Alpha Sigma Epsilon; Iron Arrow; **HOME ADD:** 600 NE 36th St., Penthouse 11, Miami, FL 33137, (305)325-1698; **BUS ADD:** 610 Executive Plaza, 3050 Biscayne Bldv., Miami, FL 33137, (305)576-9400.

REISERT, Charles E.——B: Apr. 5, 1941, New Albany, IN, *VP & Sec.*, Century 21 The Reisert Co., Inc.; **PRIM RE ACT:** Broker, Appraiser, Property Manager, Insuror, Syndicator; **REP CLIENTS:** Public Service IN, Denny Transport Serv., Equitable Life, Resid. Relocation, Robintech, Inc., Jeffboat, Inc., Amer. Comml. Barge Lines, Inc.; **PROFL AFFIL & HONORS:** So. IN Bd. of Realtors, IN Assn. of Realtors; NAR; RNMI, GRI; CRS; CRB; So. IN Bd. of Realtors - Current Pres., Past VP, Past Dir., Past Sec.-Treas., various comms.; IN Assn. of Realtors, Dir. Public Relations Comm.; Kentuckiana Brokers Council of Century 21, past Pres.; Listed, *The Best Realtors in America*; Realtor Pol. Action Comm., Life Member; **EDUC:** BS in Ed., 1963, Social Studies & Eng., IN Univ.; **GRAD EDUC:** MA, 1968, Amer. Hist., IN Univ.; **OTHER ACT & HONORS:** Rotary Club of Jeffersonville-Clarksville - Past Dir.; United Way of Clark Cty. - Past Pres., Past Campaign Pres., Present Dir.; Clark Cty. C of C - Dir.; RE Advisory Bd., Ivy Tech.; Bd. of Escot - IN Univ., Southeast; **HOME ADD:** 2005 Utica Pike, Jeffersonville, IN 47130, (812)288-9926; **BUS ADD:** 1302 E. 10th St., Jeffersonville, IN 47130, (800)457-6465.

REISING, Rich——*Legal Department*, Archer-Daniels-Midland Co.; **PRIM RE ACT:** Property Manager; **BUS ADD:** 4666 Farries Parkway, PO Box 1470, Decatur, IL 62525, (217)424-5200.*

REISMAN, Paul B.——B: Sept. 27, 1943, Paterson, NJ, *Pres.*, Reisman Property Interests, Inc.; **PRIM RE ACT:** Attorney, Developer, Property Manager, Syndicator; **OTHER RE ACT:** Since 1978, acquired 30 props. thru synd.; Asset value $125,000,000+; Equity investment $36,000,000+; **SERVICES:** Synd.; valuation; devel. & synd. of resid. and comml. props.; prop. mgmt.; **REP CLIENTS:** Indiv. investors; **PREV EMPLOY:** Banking Associate - Lehman Bros. Kuhn Loeb, Inc. 1973-1977; **EDUC:** BA, 1964, Liberal Arts - Combined degree program with School of Law; 3-yr. undergraduate program, Amer. Univ., Washington, DC; **GRAD EDUC:** Washington Coll. of Law, Wash., DC, 1967; **HOME ADD:** 11 White Pine Rd., Upper Saddle River, NJ 07458, (201)825-7745; **BUS ADD:** 114 Essex Suite, Rochelle Park, NJ 07662, (201)843-0233.

REISS, Abraham——B: Jan. 3, 1949, Antwerp, Belgium, *Managing Partner*; **PRIM RE ACT:** Broker, Consultant, Owner/Investor, Insuror, Property Manager; **EDUC:** BA, 1971, Econ., Brooklyn Coll.; **GRAD EDUC:** MBA, 1973, Fin. and Intl. Bus., Columbia Univ. Grad. School of Bus.; **EDUC HONORS:** Magma Cum Laude, Dept. Award for Excellence; **HOME ADD:** 320 Riverside Dr., New York, NY 10025, (212)222-7739; **BUS ADD:** 276 Riverside Dr., New York City, NY

10025, (215)865-5858.

REISS, Dale Anne——**B:** Sept. 3, 1947, Chicago, IL, *VP & Controller*, Urban Investment & Development Co., Corporate; **OTHER RE ACT:** Financial Control, Taxes, EDP; **PREV EMPLOY:** Arthur Young & Co. (Prin.), Dept. of Public Works/City of Chicago (Dir. of Fin.), City Coll. of Chicago (Asst. Controller); **PROFL AFFIL & HONORS:** AICPA, IL Soc. of CPA's, nareC, Officers Assn., Amer. Public Transit Assn., Inst. of Mgmt. Consulting, CPA, CMC; **EDUC:** BS, 1967, Econ./Acctg., IL Inst. of Tech.; **GRAD EDUC:** MBA, 1970, Fin. & Stat., Univ. of Chicago, Chicago, IL; **EDUC HONORS:** Dean's List; **HOME ADD:** 3100 N. Sheridan Rd., 14B, Chicago, IL 60657, (312)327-8698; **BUS ADD:** Suite 800, 845 N. Michigan Ave., Chicago, IL 60611, (312)440-3675.

REISS, Ronn——**B:** Mar. 17, 1932, St. Louis, MO, *Pres./Broker*, Reiss Corp., Realtors; **PRIM RE ACT:** Broker, Owner/Investor, Instructor, Syndicator; **SERVICES:** Investment counseling, synd.; **PROFL AFFIL & HONORS:** RESSI, FLI, Soc. of Las Vegas Exchangers, NAR, NV Assn. of Realtors, Las Vegas Bd. of Realtors, Realtor of the Year (Las Vegas)-1980; **EDUC:** BS, 1953, Secondary Educ., Wash. Univ. of St. Louis, MO; **OTHER ACT & HONORS:** Special Subcomm. Member - Subdiv. Law-City of Las Vegas, Special Subcomm. Member - Subdiv. Law-Clark Cty., NV; **HOME ADD:** 3128 Panocha St., Las Vegas, NV 89121, (702)735-2365; **BUS ADD:** 1516 S. Eastern Ave., Las Vegas, NV 89104, (702)384-3904.

REITTER, Karl L.——**B:** May 7, 1935, Vienna, Austria, *Broker*, Karl L. Reitter; **PRIM RE ACT:** Broker, Consultant, Developer, Owner/Investor, Syndicator; **SERVICES:** Investment & tax consulting, synd. & mgmt.; **REP CLIENTS:** Mostly european investors; **PREV EMPLOY:** Engrg. Economist, Can. Natl. Railways, Mktg. Analyst, Western Pac.; **EDUC:** B, Commerce, Fin. & Prod. Mgmt., Univ. of Manitoba, Can.; **EDUC HONORS:** Honors; **HOME ADD:** 25780 Tierra Grande, Carmel, CA 93923, (408)624-0454; **BUS ADD:** Midvalley Box 6555, Carmel, CA 93923, (408)625-0814.

REITZ, Elmer A.——*Exec. VP*, Greif Bros. Corp.; **PRIM RE ACT:** Property Manager; **BUS ADD:** 621 Pennsylvania Ave., Delaware, OH 43015, (614)363-1271.*

REMBERT, Paul——*Sr. VP of Oper.*, National Grape Co-Operative Assn.; **PRIM RE ACT:** Property Manager; **BUS ADD:** 2 South Portage St., Westfield, NY 14787, (716)326-3131.*

REMIJAN, David T.——**B:** Nov. 7, 1938, Gary, IN, *Pres.*, Remijan RE Inc.; **PRIM RE ACT:** Broker, Appraiser, Property Manager; **PREV EMPLOY:** VP, "CLM" Realtors, Inc.; **PROFL AFFIL & HONORS:** 1980 "Pres." - Hobart-Lake Station, N. Porter Cty. Bd. of Realtors; State Delegate, IN Bd. of Realtors, Grad. RNMI; CRB; Life Member-Realtors Political Action Comm.; 7 yr. Member Million Dollar Producer; **EDUC:** IN Univ. (2 yrs.); **MIL SERV:** US Army, 1956-1959, Sgt., Good Conduct Medal Europe; **OTHER ACT & HONORS:** Counselor - Youth Boxlng, Football and Little League; **HOME ADD:** 108 Calhoun Court, Balparaiso, IN 46383, (219)464-9094; **BUS ADD:** 11 West Ridge Rd., Hobart, IN 46342, (219)942-8534.

REMONDINO, Ben——*Plt. Mgr.*, Lea Ronal, Inc.; **PRIM RE ACT:** Property Manager; **BUS ADD:** 272 Buffalo Ave., Freeport, NY 11520, (516)868-8800.*

REMSEN, Alfred S., Jr.——**B:** Sept. 12, 1942, Buffalo, NY, *Sr. VP & Gen. Counsel*, Cushman & Wakefield, Inc.; **PRIM RE ACT:** Attorney; **PREV EMPLOY:** Schwartz, Remsen, Shapiro & Kelm, Columbus, OH; **PROFL AFFIL & HONORS:** ABA; NYSBA; ICSC; **EDUC:** BA, 1964, Lit., Univ. of MI; **GRAD EDUC:** JD, 1967, Law, Univ. of PA; **MIL SERV:** NYARNE; Sgt.; **OTHER ACT & HONORS:** Lecturer; ICSC, NACORE, BAR Assns.; **HOME ADD:** 25 Chasmars Pond Rd., Darien, CT 06820, (203)655-8481; **BUS ADD:** 1166 Ave. of the Americas, New York, NY 10036, (212)841-7797.

REMSTEDT, Walter E.——**B:** July 5, 1943, CA, *Gen Part.*, Remstedt Assoc.; **PRIM RE ACT:** Developer, Property Manager, Syndicator, Owner/Investor; **SERVICES:** Mgmt. of comml. props. & apt. complexes; **PREV EMPLOY:** Madison Props., San Francisco, 1969-current; **EDUC:** Bus., 1975, RE, CA State Univ., San Francisco; **MIL SERV:** US Army, E-5, Purple Heart; **OTHER ACT & HONORS:** Olympic Club, San Francisco, Anastasia's Club, Los Gatos; **HOME ADD:** 21919 Stagecoach Rd., Los Gatos, CA 95030, (408)353-4517; **BUS ADD:** 21919 Stagecoach Rd., Los Gatos, CA 95030, (408)353-2575.

RENARD, John S.——**B:** Mar. 13, 1938, New York, NY, *Exec. VP, Nat. Dir. Indus. Div.*, Cushman & Wakefield, Inc.; **PRIM RE ACT:** Broker, Consultant; **SERVICES:** Represent corp. and owner in buying, selling improved and unimproved RE; **PREV EMPLOY:** NY Central Railroad, Indus. Devel. Dept. 1960-1962; **PROFL AFFIL & HONORS:** SIR; Amer. Indus. Devel. Council; **EDUC:** BA, 1960, Engrg./Econ., Tufts Univ.; **GRAD EDUC:** MBA, 1969, Mktg./RE, CCNY; **MIL SERV:** USAR; **HOME ADD:** 48 Highland Cir., Bronxville, NY 10708; **BUS ADD:** 1166 Ave. of the Americas, New York, NY 10036, (212)841-7555.

RENAUD-WRIGHT, Michael S.——**B:** Mar. 24, 1917, Ireland, *VP*, Wolfson Brothers Realty Inc., Ventura-Santa Barbara Cty. Office; **PRIM RE ACT:** Broker, Consultant, Engineer, Owner/Investor, Instructor; **SERVICES:** Co. relocations to and from So. CA; all services are fee paid; **PREV EMPLOY:** Pres., CA Indus. Props. Inc.; Owner, Renaud-Wright Assocs., Consultants; **PROFL AFFIL & HONORS:** RE Consultant/Broker; **EDUC:** BA/BSc, 1935, Electronics Engrg./Mil. Electronics, Belfast Tech. Coll./Cambridge Extension Univ.; **MIL SERV:** RAF; Sqdn. Ldr.; **OTHER ACT & HONORS:** Santa Monica CA Indus. Planning Commn., 4 yrs.; Pres., Westchester Symphony Orchestra; **HOME ADD:** 720 Fillmore St., Santa Paula, CA 93060, (805)525-8780; **BUS ADD:** 8456 Allenwood Rd., Los Angeles, CA 90046, (213)275-4488.

RENFRO, Robert——**B:** July 29, 1948, Santa Ana, CA, *Pres.*, Renfro Investment Prop.; **PRIM RE ACT:** Broker, Syndicator, Consultant, Developer, Owner/Investor; **SERVICES:** Investment & dev. consultant; **PREV EMPLOY:** CPA; **PROFL AFFIL & HONORS:** RNMI, Pres., ID Chapt. CCIM; CPA; Bd. of Dir., ID Assn. of Realtors; **EDUC:** BS, 1970, Acctg., Woodbury Univ.; **HOME ADD:** PO Box 1085, Sun Valley, ID 83353; **BUS ADD:** PO Box 2100, Sun Valley, ID 83353, (208)726-4436.

RENKEN, Duane A.——**B:** Oct. 31, 1932, LeMars, IA, *Pres.*, Dajac, Inc.; **PRIM RE ACT:** Broker, Syndicator, Consultant, Developer, Property Manager, Owner/Investor; **SERVICES:** Investment mgmt. and counseling; **REP CLIENTS:** Indiv. investors in resid. and comml. prop.; **PREV EMPLOY:** Bendix Corp. - Space Systems Mktg. Mgr. - 10yrs.; **PROFL AFFIL & HONORS:** RESSI; **EDUC:** Aero Engineering, 1956, Aeronautical Engineering, IA State Univ.; **GRAD EDUC:** Bus., 1950-1960, Public Admin., Univ. of MI; **EDUC HONORS:** Sigma Gamma Tau, Knights of St. Patrick; **MIL SERV:** USAF, Capt., 1956-58; **OTHER ACT & HONORS:** Chmn. MI Bldg. Authority; Pres. Public School Bd.; State Hosp. Authority; **HOME ADD:** 2154 S. Seventh St, Ann Arbor, MI 48103, (313)633-9632; **BUS ADD:** 109 Miller, Ann Arbor, MI 48104, (313)688-1555.

RENNER, Robin L.——**B:** Oct. 8, 1932, Madison, SD, *Pres.*, Rennco Realty Investments, Inc.; **PRIM RE ACT:** Broker, Consultant, Attorney, Appraiser, Owner/Investor, Property Manager, Syndicator; **SERVICES:** Buyer's broker & 1031 exchanges; **REP CLIENTS:** Small investor grps.; **PREV EMPLOY:** RE Staff Atty & Asst. Gen. Counsel, 22 yrs., Paficic Lighting Dept., and ARCO; **PROFL AFFIL & HONORS:** Fed. CA & Phila Bar Assns.; **EDUC:** BA, 1954, Univ. of CA, Berkeley, Univ. of EA; **GRAD EDUC:** LLB, 1967, UC Berkeley, Boalt Hall Sch. of Law; **EDUC HONORS:** Poli. Sci. Hon. Soc., Grad. Cum Laude; **MIL SERV:** US Army, Capt., Army Commendation Medal; **HOME ADD:** 28208 Ridgepoint Ct., Rancho Palos Verdes, CA 90274, (213)541-2288; **BUS ADD:** 301 W. 64th Ave., 102, Anchorage, AK 99504, (907)277-0713.

RENNER, William B.——**B:** Oct. 29, 1949, Hackensack, NJ, *Venture Mgr.*, Legarde Eklund Interests; **OTHER RE ACT:** Acquistion specialist/venture mgr.; **SERVICES:** Analysis of acquisitions & subsequent mgmt. venture; **PREV EMPLOY:** Westinghouse Community Devel. Crp., 330 Univ. Dr., Coral Springs, FL, 1980-81; **EDUC:** BA, 1971, Phil., Pol. Sci, Bowdoin Coll.; **GRAD EDUC:** MS, 1980, Land & Devel. Planning, Harvard Univ.; **BUS ADD:** 777 29th St., Suite 100, Boulder, CO 80303, (303)443-2904.

RENNICK, Richard L.——*Public Relations Dir.*, Nat. Assn. of RE Investment Trusrs, Inc.; **OTHER RE ACT:** Public Relations for REIT indus.; **SERVICES:** Membership servs., publicity, fin. anaylst meetings, conferences, legislative relations, pubs., promotions, counseling, etc.; **PREV EMPLOY:** 13 yrs. as public relations dir. for advertising agencies; **PROFL AFFIL & HONORS:** Public Relations Soc. of Amer., Accredited Member of Public Relations Soc. of Amer.; **EDUC:** Journalism & Public Relations, Ampleforth Coll., York, Eng.; **MIL SERV:** Royal Air Force; **OTHER ACT & HONORS:** Amer. Heart Assn., VA Affiliate Bd. of Dirs.; **HOME ADD:** 1543 N. 19th St., Arlington, VA 22209, (703)525-7665; **BUS ADD:** 1101 17th St., Suite 700, Wash. DC 20036.

RENTON, David M.——B: May 15, 1946, Long Beach, CA, *Pres.*, Bildner-Renton Assoc., Inc.; **PRIM RE ACT:** Broker, Consultant, Owner/Investor; **SERVICES:** Hotel/motel, brokerage, fin., joint ventures; Properties having more than 200 rms., and chains; **REP CLIENTS:** Hotel/motel chains, investors (indiv. and instl.); **PROFL AFFIL & HONORS:** ULI; **BUS ADD:** 111 Prospect St., Stamford, CT 06901, (203)327-4365.

REPSOLD, Peter B.——B: Apr. 8, 1938, Evanston, IL, *Pres.*, Metropolitan Appraisal; **PRIM RE ACT:** Consultant, Appraiser, Developer, Owner/Investor, Instructor, Property Manager; **SERVICES:** RE appraisals, prop. mgmt., counseling; **PREV EMPLOY:** First Appraisal Co., RE Research Corp.; **PROFL AFFIL & HONORS:** Delta Sigma Pi; **EDUC:** Bus., RE, Northwestern Univ.; **OTHER ACT & HONORS:** Dir., Betty Thealen Memorial Educ. Loan Fund; **HOME ADD:** 396 Anita Pl., Wheeling, IL 60090, (312)459-1732; **BUS ADD:** 67 West Chestnut St., Chicago, IL 60610, (312)943-4036.

REPUCCI, Ron——*Corp. Fac. Mgr.*, Compugraphic Corp.; **PRIM RE ACT:** Property Manager; **BUS ADD:** 90 Industrial Way, Wilmington, MA 01887, (617)944-6555.*

RESCHKE, Valerie Juliette——B: Feb. 5, 1934, NY, *Broker/Owner*, RE/MAX Realtors, Walnut Creek; **PRIM RE ACT:** Broker, Consultant, Appraiser, Developer, Owner/Investor, Instructor, Insuror, Real Estate Publisher; **OTHER RE ACT:** Pres. appointment to CA Assn. of Realtors, Credentials Comm. 3 yrs.; Co-Chmn. Credentials Comm., 1982; **SERVICES:** Resid comml. devel.; **REP CLIENTS:** Candidate for the Sec. of State, VP of Transamerica, Bechtel; **PREV EMPLOY:** Teacher, Advertising Agency, Taught English to Japanese Execs. (Tobishiba, Mitsui, and Japanese Sch. Children for 3 yrs. in Japan); **PROFL AFFIL & HONORS:** GRI, CRS, CRB (First woman to hold this designation in Contra Costa); **EDUC:** BA, 1955, Biology, Chem., Math, Hofstra Univ.; **GRAD EDUC:** 1956-57, Columbia Univ., Juilliard Sch. of Music, Grace Downs Modeling Sch.; **EDUC HONORS:** Cum Laude, activities scholarship for 4 yrs., won Tri-Beta Nat. Research Paper 1955, Phi Beta Kappa; **OTHER ACT & HONORS:** Chmn. of Membership Comm. & Advanced Prof. Designations Comm. of Contra Costa Bd. of Realtors, Own RE co. RE/MAX, write RE column for weekly newspaper, Valley Pioneer in Who's Who in CA; **HOME ADD:** 1049 Alicante Dr., Danville, CA 94526, (415)837-5674; **BUS ADD:** 675 Ygnacio Valley Rd., Walnut Ck., CA 94596, (415)930-9800.

RESNICK, Franklin D.——B: June 6, 1936, NY, NY, *Atty.*, Resnick & Lawson; **PRIM RE ACT:** Consultant, Attorney, Developer, Owner/Investor; **SERVICES:** Devel. & synd. counseling, legal services; **REP CLIENTS:** Devel., contractors & lenders in multi-family & comml. prop.; **PREV EMPLOY:** Deputy Rgnl. Counsel FHA; Assoc. Rgnl. Counsel Dept. of Housing & Urban Devel., 1964-1970; **PROFL AFFIL & HONORS:** FL, GA & DC Bars; Mort. Bankers Assn.; **EDUC:** AA/BSBA, 1958, Indus./Mgmt./Acctg., Univ. of FL; **GRAD EDUC:** JD, 1964, Univ. of Miami; **HOME ADD:** 3437 Embry Cir., N.E., Atlanta, GA 30341, (404)455-8458; **BUS ADD:** 101 Marietta Tower, Suite 3306, POB 1765, Atlanta, GA 30301, (404)522-6430.

RESTAINO, Paul——B: July 26, 1944, Newark, NJ, *Pres.*, Paul Restaino Assoc.; **PRIM RE ACT:** Consultant, Owner/Investor, Syndicator; **OTHER RE ACT:** Co-op converter; **PREV EMPLOY:** VP, Bowery Savings Bank; **PROFL AFFIL & HONORS:** Young Mort. Bankers Assn.; **EDUC:** BS Eng., 1965, Case Western Reserve Univ.; **GRAD EDUC:** MBA, 1971, Fin., Harvard Univ.; MS Eng., 1967, Univ. of PA; **EDUC HONORS:** Dean's List, Distinction Grad.; **HOME ADD:** 104 E. 81st St., New York, NY 10028, (212)988-8738; **BUS ADD:** 717 Fifth Ave., Suite 2100, New York, NY 10022, (212)758-0202.

RESTON, Herbert D.——B: Jan. 4, 1931, New York City, *Owner-Pres.*, Reston-Sinco; **PRIM RE ACT:** Developer, Builder, Owner/Investor, Syndicator; **OTHER RE ACT:** Planner; **SERVICES:** Planning, devel., bldg. of comml. & indus., projects, prop. mgmt.; **REP CLIENTS:** Pvt. and instl. investors; **PROFL AFFIL & HONORS:** CA Licensed Contractors Assn., CA Licensed RE Broker/CA Licensed Bldg. Contractor; **EDUC:** BS, 1952, Bus. Admin. - Mktg., Univ. of CA, School of Bus. Admin.; **GRAD EDUC:** MBA, 1955, RE & Urban Land Econs., Grad. School of Mgmt., Univ. of CA, LA; Phd Candidate, 1955-1957, City & Rgnl. Planning, School of Public Admin., Univ. of So. CA; **EDUC HONORS:** I.Hellman Scholarship, Amer. Inst. of RE Appraisers-Grad. Scholarship & RE Award; **MIL SERV:** US Army, 1952-1954, Cpl.; Artillery School; **OTHER ACT & HONORS:** United Jewish Welfare Fund, Hebrew Univ. in Jerusaleum - Established Scholarship Endowment Fund; **HOME ADD:** 3435 Caribeth Dr., Encino, CA 91436; **BUS ADD:** 16255 Ventura Blvd., Ste. 509, Encino, CA 91436, (213)783-5292.

RETT, Donald A.——B: June 10, 1937, Newark, NJ, *Atty at Law*, Donald A. Rett, P.A.; **PRIM RE ACT:** Attorney; **SERVICES:** Securities Counsel to RE Synds.; **PREV EMPLOY:** Dir., Div. of Securities, State of FL 1975-77; Trial Atty., US Securities and exchange commn.; **PROFL AFFIL & HONORS:** RESSI; FL Bar; **EDUC:** BBA, 1970, Fin., Univ. of Miami; **GRAD EDUC:** JD, 1973, Securities Law, Univ. Of Miami; **MIL SERV:** US Army, E-4; **HOME ADD:** 2028 Ermine Dr., Tallahassee, FL 32308, (904)877-4372; **BUS ADD:** 421 E. Call St., Tallahassee, FL 32301, (904)222-6573.

REVITZ, Steven J.——*Atty. at Law*, Boren, Elperin, Howard & Sloan; **PRIM RE ACT:** Attorney; **SERVICES:** ME litigation; **REP CLIENTS:** Gulf & Western; General Mills; Walter E. Heller & Co.; **BUS ADD:** 9911 W. Pico Blvd., Ste. 1150, Los Angeles, CA 90035, (213)556-1032.

REXROTH, David K.——B: Nov. 5, 1951, Waterloo, IA, *Sr. Staff Appraiser*, US Appraisal & Research Corp.; **PRIM RE ACT:** Appraiser; **SERVICES:** Comml. & indus. RE appraisals, feasibility studies, investment counseling; **REP CLIENTS:** Comml. lending instns., accts., attys., govt. agencies, corps. & indivs.; **PREV EMPLOY:** IA Appraisal & Research Corp., 719 S&L Bldg., Des Moines, IA 50309; **PROFL AFFIL & HONORS:** AIREA, SREA, Lic. RE Broker in IA, Lic. RE salesman in MI, SRA (Sr. Res. Appraiser); MAI; **EDUC:** BA, 1973, Bus. Admin. & Econ., Olivet Nazarene Coll.; **HOME ADD:** 5490 Old Franklin Rd., Grand Blanc, MI 48439, (313)694-5998; **BUS ADD:** 120 W. First St., Flint, MI 48502, (313)232-1170.

REYER, Burton——B: Sept. 25, 1934, Albany, NY, *Pres.*, AFGO Engineering Corp.; **PRIM RE ACT:** Engineer; **OTHER RE ACT:** Mechanical contractor; **REP CLIENTS:** Tishman, Morse/Diesel; **PROFL AFFIL & HONORS:** NY Soc. of Profl. Engrs.; **EDUC:** BME, 1956, CCNY; **GRAD EDUC:** MME, 1963, Columbia Univ.; **HOME ADD:** 17 Foxwood Rd., Great Neck, NY 11024, (516)487-3086; **BUS ADD:** 287 Northern Blvd., Great Neck, NY 11021, (212)392-3301.

REYES, Michael V.——B: Sept. 30, 1956, Manila, Philippines, *Pres. and Chief Exec. Officer*, Urban Pacific Devel. Corp.; **PRIM RE ACT:** Developer; **SERVICES:** Devel. of major resid. and comml. structures; **PREV EMPLOY:** VP, The Reyes Group, Manila, Philippines; **EDUC:** BA, 1977, Econ., Univ. of CA at Los Angeles; **EDUC HONORS:** Cum Laude; **OTHER ACT & HONORS:** Rotary Club, Westwood Village (LA); **HOME ADD:** 1405 Bluebird Ave., Los Angeles, CA 90069, (213)858-1807; **BUS ADD:** 1875 Century Park East, Suite 1000, Los Angeles, CA 90067, (213)552-6934.

REYNOLDS, Anthony——B: Apr. 16, 1930, Rockville Centre, NY, *Prin.*, Reynolds & Reynolds, Inc.; **PRIM RE ACT:** Consultant; **SERVICES:** Advice; **PREV EMPLOY:** US Gen. Serv. Admin.; **PROFL AFFIL & HONORS:** Amer. Instit. of RE Appraisers; Amer. Soc. of RE Counselors; Lambda Alpha, MAI, CRE; **EDUC:** BS, 1952, Marketing, Univ. of MD; **GRAD EDUC:** MBA, 1961, The Amer. Univ.; **BUS ADD:** 725 Independence Ave., S.E., Washington, DC 20003, (202)544-2344.

REYNOLDS, Bryan P.——B: Mar. 17, 1936, Chicago, IL, *Pres.*, Reynolds Realty & Development Co.; **PRIM RE ACT:** Broker, Consultant, Developer, Builder, Syndicator; **OTHER RE ACT:** Designer and builder of racquetball courts; **SERVICES:** Devel. & sales of comml. prop.; **REP CLIENTS:** USAF; **PROFL AFFIL & HONORS:** FLI; RESSI, AFLM; **EDUC:** BA, 1960, Loyola Univ.; **MIL SERV:** US Army, SP-3; **HOME ADD:** 10428 Kilpatrick, Oak Lawn, IL 60453; **BUS ADD:** Rt. 83 & Rt. 171 S., Lemont, IL 60439, (312)257-7757.

REYNOLDS, J. Timothy——B: July 25, 1950, Gadsden, AL, *Prop. Mgr.*, Spaulding and Slye Corp., Prop. mgmt.; **PRIM RE ACT:** Property Manager; **SERVICES:** All areas of prop. mgmt. consulting; **PREV EMPLOY:** Prop. mgmt. for two large fin. instns. headquartered in Birmingham with respons. for prop. state-wide; **PROFL AFFIL & HONORS:** BOMA/Metropolitan Birmingham, VP BOMA; **EDUC:** BS, 1972, Mktg./econ., Jacksonville State Univ.; **GRAD EDUC:** Working on MBA, Fin., Univ. of AL in Birmingham; **MIL SERV:** USAF,E-4; **HOME ADD:** 1109 Fern St., Birmingham, AL 35209, (205)942-7626; **BUS ADD:** 1409 Bank for Savings Bldg., Birmingham, AL 35203, (205)251-6978.

REYNOLDS, Joseph C.——B: July 21, 1945, Columbia, SC, *Sr. VP*, August Kohn & Co., Inc., Income Prop. Dept.; **PRIM RE ACT:** Banker, Lender, Consultant; **PROFL AFFIL & HONORS:** MBAA; Pres. 1981-82 Mort. Bankers Assn. of the Carolinas, Inc.; **EDUC:** 1967, Banking & Fin., Bus. Admin., Univ. of SC; **HOME ADD:** 2108 O'Hara Ct., Columbia, SC 29204, (803)782-1787; **BUS ADD:** PO Box 225, Columbia, SC 29202, (803)771-3896.

REYNOLDS, Judith——B: July 16, 1936, LaCrosse, KS, *Prin.*, Reynolds & Reynolds, Inc.; **PRIM RE ACT:** Appraiser; **OTHER RE ACT:** Writer and lecturer on Topic of Appraising Historic Props.; **PREV EMPLOY:** Manufacturing Chemists Assn. (statistical compilations); **PROFL AFFIL & HONORS:** AIREA, Lambda Alpha, MAI, Editor in Chief, The Appraisal Journal 1980, 1981, Chmn. Nat. External Affairs Comm. for 1982; **EDUC:** 3 yrs., 1955-58, French, Phillips Univ., Enid OK, 1 yr., Univ. of MD 2 yrs.; **EDUC HONORS:** Honors curriculum in French and Lit.; **OTHER ACT & HONORS:** Bd. of Equalization and Review, 1975-1980, Appointed by Mayor of DC; **HOME ADD:** 723 Independence Ave. SE, Washington, DC 20003, (202)543-8490; **BUS ADD:** 725 Independence Ave. SE, Washington, DC 20003, (202)544-2344.

REYNOLDS, Judy Maxine——B: Dec. 3, 1938, Jackson, MI, *CPM*, McDevitt Mgmt. Co.; **PRIM RE ACT:** Property Manager; **SERVICES:** Resid. & comml. prop. mgmt.; **PROFL AFFIL & HONORS:** Bus. & Profl. Women, 1981 Realtor of the Year; Jackson Bd. of Realtors; 1980 Women of the Yr.; Women's Council of Realtors; NAR;; Michigan Chap.; **EDUC:** GRI, MI State Univ.; **OTHER ACT & HONORS:** Women's Council of Realtors, City Co-Chmn. for March of Dimes, School Volunteer; **HOME ADD:** 126 Robindale Ct., Brooklyn, MI 49230, (517)592-2598; **BUS ADD:** 1234 S. West, Box 862, Jackson, MI 49203, (517)787-1888.

REYNOLDS, Paul G., Jr.——B: Aug. 25, 1946, Chicago, IL, *VP, Interim Const., Chmn., RE Loan Comm.*, First National Bank & Trust of OK City, RE; **PRIM RE ACT:** Banker, Lender; **SERVICES:** Const. loans; RE Finance; **REP CLIENTS:** Devels.; RE Companies; **PREV EMPLOY:** RE Officer, Continental IL Nat. Bank, 1976-1980; VP, Mercantile Nat. Bank at Dallas, 1980-1982; **PROFL AFFIL & HONORS:** Assn. of RE Fin. Execs.; AMBA; **EDUC:** BS, 1972, Econ./Bus., IL Inst. of TechnoL.; **GRAD EDUC:** MBA, 1975, Fin., Univ. of Chicago; **MIL SERV:** US Army; Capt.; **HOME ADD:** 210 NW 16th St., Oklahoma City, OK 73103; **BUS ADD:** PO Box 25189, Oklahoma City, OK 73125, (405)272-4777.

REYNOLDS, Robert E.——B: Jan. 5, 1940, Tacoma, WA, *VP & Mgr.*, Rainier National Bank, Trust RE; **PRIM RE ACT:** Consultant, Banker, Property Manager; **OTHER RE ACT:** Investment Mgr.; **SERVICES:** RE Investment consultation, prop. mgmt. & equity & mort. acquisitions; **REP CLIENTS:** Personal Trust Clients and Pension Accounts; **PREV EMPLOY:** RE Brokerage 1963-70; **PROFL AFFIL & HONORS:** IREM, Amer. Inst. of Banking, Nat. Trust RE Assn., CPM; Past Pres. 1980-81 Nat. Trust RE Assn.; **EDUC:** BFA, 1963, Bus., Univ. of Puget Sound; **MIL SERV:** US Air Nat. Guard, 1960-66; **HOME ADD:** 3444 Magnolia Blvd. W, Seattle, WA 98199, (206)284-1232; **BUS ADD:** PO Box 3966, Seattle, WA 98124, (206)621-4376.

REYNOLDS, Thomas C., Jr.——B: Dec. 31, 1930, Delaware, PA, Gen. Appraisal Co.; **PRIM RE ACT:** Consultant, Appraiser; **SERVICES:** Appraise & advise on comml., indus. & resid. props.; **REP CLIENTS:** Fed., state agencies, corps. & banking instns.; **PREV EMPLOY:** HUD; **PROFL AFFIL & HONORS:** AIREA & SREA, MAI, SRPA; **EDUC:** BS, 1958, RE, Temple Univ. Philadelphia PA; **MIL SERV:** USMC, Sgt.; **HOME ADD:** 306 Whitby Dr., Wilmington, DE 19803, (302)478-1717; **BUS ADD:** 105 Webster Bldg. Concord Plaza, Silverside Rd., Wilmington, DE 19803, (302)478-1776.

REYNOLDS, Tom H.——B: May 30, 1920, Lewistown, MT, *Asst. VP Dir., RE Construction*, Lincoln National Life Insurance Co., Mort. Loan; **PRIM RE ACT:** Engineer, Appraiser, Lender; **SERVICES:** Construction supervision, appraising, farm loan underwriting, oil & gas leasing; **PREV EMPLOY:** US Army Corps of Engrs.; **PROFL AFFIL & HONORS:** MAI Candidate (expect to be awarded MAI designation in 1982); **EDUC:** BS, 1944, Engrg., US Naval Academy; **GRAD EDUC:** MS, 1955, Civil Engrg., Harvard Univ.; **MIL SERV:** US Navy, LT, Bronze Star, US Army, COL, Legion of Merit; **HOME ADD:** 11404 Westwind Dr., Ft. Wayne, IN 46825, (219)637-6782; **BUS ADD:** 1300 S. Clinton St., Ft. Wayne, IN 46801.

REYNOLDS, William H., Jr.——B: Feb. 28, 1949, NYC, NY, *Pres.*, City Assoc., Inc.; **PRIM RE ACT:** Broker, Developer, Owner/Investor; **SERVICES:** Primarily devel. of comml. RE; Also offer brokerage and prop. analysis services to pvt. and inst. investors; **REP CLIENTS:** Lenders and indiv. or inst. investors in comml. props.; **PREV EMPLOY:** VP, Devel. & Mktg., Portfolio Mgmt. of TX, Inc., 1976-1979; **PROFL AFFIL & HONORS:** Houston C of C; Old Woodbury CT Hist. Soc.; **EDUC:** BA, 1972, Eng., Trinity Coll.; **GRAD EDUC:** MPA, 1976, Urban/Rgnl. Planning, Univ. of New Haven; **EDUC HONORS:** Magna Cum Laude; **OTHER ACT & HONORS:** Planning Commn., Woodbury, CT, 1976-1977; **HOME ADD:** 2800 WI Ave. N.W., Washington, DC 20007, (202)362-3096; **BUS ADD:** 601 Sawyer 5th Flr., Houston, TX 77007, (713)622-2692.

RHAME, David P.——*Pres.*, Rhame Assoc. Inc.; **PRIM RE ACT:** Consultant, Developer, Builder, Owner/Investor; **PROFL AFFIL & HONORS:** Community Assoc. Inst. Nat. Assn. of Home-Builders, ULI; **EDUC:** BS, 1947, Bus. Admin., Univ. of CA at Los Angeles; **EDUC HONORS:** With Honors; **MIL SERV:** USAF, Lt. Col.; **OTHER ACT & HONORS:** Founder/COB Community Assoc. Inst., Life Dir. of NAHB, Council Exec. Grp. of ULI; **HOME ADD:** 3207 S. Fielder Rd., Arlington, TX 76015, (817)467-1807; **BUS ADD:** 1000 N. Bowen Rd., Arlington, TX 76012, (817)460-4071.

RHEA, D. Keith——B: June 12, 1948, Houma, LA, *Pres.*, Economic Advisory Services, Inc.; **PRIM RE ACT:** Developer, Builder, Owner/Investor, Property Manager; **OTHER RE ACT:** Venture & investment capital, oil & gas investments; **SERVICES:** Investment prop. mgmt. & mgmt. consulting, admin. mgmt.; **REP CLIENTS:** Const. Support Serv. Inc., Ashland and Partnership, Oak Leaf Investments, Pelican Pipeline, Co.; **PREV EMPLOY:** Mfrs. Hanover Trust Co. 1973-1976, Chromalog Natural Resources Co., 1976-1978; **PROFL AFFIL & HONORS:** Bayou Bd. of Realtors, Soc. of Petroleum Engrs., Profl. Fin. Planners of Greater New Orleans Tri-Parish Estate Planning Counsel, Nat. Assn. of Small Bus. Investment Cos.; **EDUC:** BS, Bus. Admin., 1971, Mktg., LA State Univ., Baton Rouge; **GRAD EDUC:** MBA, 1972, Fin., LA State Univ., Baton Rouge; **MIL SERV:** US Army, Capt., 1971-1981; **HOME ADD:** 1 Freeport Ct., Houma, LA 70360, (504)868-8094; **BUS ADD:** 301 Goode St., Houma, LA 70360, (504)851-3928.

RHODA, Richard L.——B: Apr. 17, 1943, Presque Isle, ME, *Atty.*, Pres. of Aroostook Land Titles & Insurance Agency; **PRIM RE ACT:** Attorney, Insuror; **SERVICES:** Legal and title insurance; **REP CLIENTS:** Chicago Title Co., Commonwealth Land Title Co., City Title Co.; **PROFL AFFIL & HONORS:** Aroostook Cty. Bar Assn.; **EDUC:** 1961, Hist. and Govt., Univ. of ME; **GRAD EDUC:** 1972, Law, Univ. of ME School of Law; **MIL SERV:** US Army, Sgt. 1966-1969; **OTHER ACT & HONORS:** Asst. Dist. Atty. - ME 1975-1978; Bd. of Dirs., Houlton Rgnl. Devel. Corp., Bd. of Dirs., Southern Aroostook Assn. of Retarded Citizens, Inc., Chmn. Bd. of Deacons, First Baptist Church, Houlton ME; **HOME ADD:** 45 Pleasant St., Houlton, ME 04730, (207)532-6849; **BUS ADD:** 5 Broadway, Houlton, ME 04730, (207)532-9000.

RHODES, Charles G., Jr.——B: Oct. 20, 1921, Alma, MI, *Pres.*, RE Mgmt. of Ft. Collins, Inc.; **PRIM RE ACT:** Property Manager; **OTHER RE ACT:** Comml. and off. leasing; **SERVICES:** Profl. prop. mgmt. & leasing of off. and warehouse space; **PROFL AFFIL & HONORS:** Ft. Collins Bd. of Realtors, IREM, AMO; **EDUC:** Univ. of CA at Davis, 1956, Agri. Econ.; **OTHER ACT & HONORS:** First Baptist Church; **HOME ADD:** 1401 Patton St., Ft. Collins, CO, (303)484-2303; **BUS ADD:** PO Box 1726, Ste. 660, Savings Bldg., Ft. Collins, CO 80522, (303)493-8303.

RHODES, Jeffrey J.——B: Feb. 25, 1947, *Exec. VP*, Urban Investment & Dev. Co.; **PRIM RE ACT:** Developer; **PREV EMPLOY:** Sea Pines Co., Aetna/Urban Indus. Parks; **PROFL AFFIL & HONORS:** ULI, SIR; **EDUC:** BA, 1969, Econ., Univ. PA; **GRAD EDUC:** MBA, 1971, Fin. and Ins., Univ. PA; **OTHER ACT & HONORS:** Exec. Club, Fin. Exec. Inst., Chicago Yacht Club, Carlton Club; **HOME ADD:** 1555 Astor St., Apt. 23SE, Chicago, IL 60610; **BUS ADD:** 845 N. Mich. Ave., Chicago, IL 60611.

RHODES, Joan LeBosquet——B: June 16, 1947, Chicago, IL, *Broker*, Rhodes & Rhodes Ltd.; **PRIM RE ACT:** Broker, Consultant, Owner/Investor, Property Manager, Syndicator; **OTHER RE ACT:** Exchangor; **SERVICES:** Prop. mgmt., RE investment counseling, investment RE brokerage & 1031 exchange broker; **PREV EMPLOY:** Public Relations; **PROFL AFFIL & HONORS:** No. VA Apt. Assn.; No. VA Bd. of Realtors, NAR, Nat. Inst. of RE Brokers; IREM; REMNI; RESSI; VA Assn. of Realtors; Alexandria C of C; AERE; **EDUC:** Sorbonne Cert., Journalism, Sorbonne, Paris, France; **GRAD EDUC:** Many Profl. Courses; **OTHER ACT & HONORS:** Alexandria Performing Arts, Little Theatre Alexandria, Jr. Friends of Alexandria Y; **BUS ADD:** 106 North Alfred St. 2, Alexandria, VA 22314, (703)836-8500.

RHODES, Richard M.——B: Sept. 14, 1929, Sacramento, CA, *Chmn. of the Bd.*, R.M. Rhodes Corp.; **PRIM RE ACT:** Broker, Consultant, Appraiser, Owner/Investor, Real Estate Publisher; **SERVICES:** Counseling, appraisal and acquisition of real prop., litigation spec.; **REP CLIENTS:** Instns., corps., indivs., attys.m devels., lenders, govts. interested in comml., agric., & recreational props.; **PREV EMPLOY:** CA Dept. of Transportation, 1952-58; **PROFL AFFIL & HONORS:** NAR, MAI, AIREA; **EDUC:** BA, 1952, Econ., Public Admin., Sacramento State Univ.; **EDUC HONORS:** With Honors; **OTHER ACT & HONORS:** City Councilman, Yuba City, CA 1960-64; **HOME ADD:** 2324 Swarthmore Dr., Sacramento, CA 95825,

(916)929-2500; **BUS ADD:** 601 University Ave., 119, Sacramento, CA 95825, (916)929-2327.

RHODES, Terry L.——B: Apr. 23, 1940, Los Angeles, CA, Rhodes, Kendall & Harrington; **PRIM RE ACT:** Attorney; **EDUC:** 1963, Long Beach State; **GRAD EDUC:** 1968, UCLA School of Law; **HOME ADD:** 2501 Lighthouse Ln., Newport Beach, CA 92660, (714)644-5296; **BUS ADD:** 4299 MacArthur Blvd., Ste 105, Newport Beach, CA 92660, (714)752-2282.

RHYNE, E. Earl——B: Nov. 20, 1935, Uniontown, AL, *Pres.*, Rhyne Companies; **PRIM RE ACT:** Broker, Engineer, Developer, Owner/Investor, Property Manager; **SERVICES:** Devel. and synd. of comml. props., prop. mgmt.; **REP CLIENTS:** Lenders and indiv. of inst. investors in comml. props.; **PREV EMPLOY:** Const. and Engrg. Mgmt.; Cox Craft Swimming Pool Co. 1970-73; Gen. Contractor 1965-73; Civil Engr. AFC Indus. 1960-63; **EDUC:** AB, 1958, Civil engrg., Univ. of AL; **MIL SERV:** USAR, S/Sgt.; **HOME ADD:** 2671 Swiss Ln., Birmingham, AL 35226, (205)822-6912; **BUS ADD:** PO Box 26370, Birmingham, AL 35226, (205)979-5050.

RIANDA, Brian I.——B: Feb. 17, 1940, San Jose, CA, *Pres.*, Brian Kianda, Inc.; **PRIM RE ACT:** Broker, Consultant, Owner/Investor; **PROFL AFFIL & HONORS:** NAREB, CCIM; **EDUC:** BS, 1965, Bus. Adm., CA St. Univ., Fresno; **MIL SERV:** USN, EM3; **HOME ADD:** 1218 San Angelo Dr., Salinas, CA 93901, (408)422-9787; **BUS ADD:** 680 E. Romie Ln., Salinas, CA 93901, (408)758-2728.

RIBLE, Charles H.——B: June 8, 1945, Oakland, CA, *Atty.*, Self-employed; **PRIM RE ACT:** Broker, Attorney; **SERVICES:** Legal service for RE brokers, synd. and investors; **PREV EMPLOY:** Gen. counsel, Pen-Pac Realty Co., Inc.; **PROFL AFFIL & HONORS:** R. Prop. Section, Tax Section, State Bar Assn. of CA, R. Prop. Sect. ABA; **EDUC:** BS, 1968, Civil Eng., Univ. of CA; **GRAD EDUC:** JD, 1974, RE Law, Golden Gate Univ. Law Sch.; **MIL SERV:** US Army, Lt.; **BUS ADD:** 702 Marshall St., Ste. 400, Redwood City, CA 94063, (415)367-0385.

RICCI, William J.——B: Aug. 17, 1927, Hartford, CT, Ricci Investment Realty; **PRIM RE ACT:** Broker, Consultant, Developer; **OTHER RE ACT:** Investment Mgr.; **SERVICES:** Investment counseling, valuation; **REP CLIENTS:** Indiv. corps., instns.; **PROFL AFFIL & HONORS:** NAR, CAR, CT-CID, Designated CCIM; **EDUC:** BS, 1950, Electrical Engrg., US Naval Acad.; BS, 1957, Aeronautical Engrg., USN Postgrad. School; **GRAD EDUC:** MS, 1958, Nuclear Engrg., IA State Univ.; **EDUC HONORS:** Hon.; **MIL SERV:** USN, LCDR; **OTHER ACT & HONORS:** Exchange Club of Deep River & Essex/Charter Pres. Valley Shore Toastmasters; **HOME ADD:** Woodland Dr., RFD 1, Centerbrook, CT 06409, (203)767-1339; **BUS ADD:** Woodland Dr., RFD 1, Centerbook, CT 06409, (203)767-1056.

RICE, Canice Timothy, Jr.——B: Apr. 4, 1950, St. Louis, *Atty. at Law*; **PRIM RE ACT:** Attorney; **PROFL AFFIL & HONORS:** MO Bar, IL Bar, ABA, Bar Assn. of Metropolitan St. Louis; **EDUC:** 1972, Eng., Holy Cross Coll.; **GRAD EDUC:** 1976, Law, Univ. of MO Law School; **EDUC HONORS:** Dean's List; **HOME ADD:** 6624 Kingsbury, St. Louis, MO 63130, (314)727-0477; **BUS ADD:** 408 Olive St., Suite 400, St. Louis, MO 63102, (314)241-8000.

RICE, F. Towers——B: July 2, 1931, Greenville, SC, *Pres.*, United Development Services, Inc.; **PRIM RE ACT:** Broker, Developer, Builder; **SERVICES:** Developing - innovative re-use of old structures; **PREV EMPLOY:** Quality Concrete Products, Inc.; Daniel Construction Co., Inc.; **PROFL AFFIL & HONORS:** NAIOP; **EDUC:** BS, 1953, Industrial Management, GA Tech., Atlanta, GA; **MIL SERV:** USMCR; Lt.Col.; **OTHER ACT & HONORS:** Kiwanis; **HOME ADD:** 107 Ridgeland Dr., Greenville, SC 29601, (803)271-1825; **BUS ADD:** 400 Mills Ave., 2d Level, Mills Centre, Greenville, SC 29601, (803)271-0215.

RICE, George——*Chmn.*, Vermont Real Estate Commission; **PRIM RE ACT:** Property Manager; **BUS ADD:** 7 E. State St., State Ofc. Building, Montpelior, VT 05602, (802)828-3228.*

RICE, Henry Hart——B: Mar. 2, 1911, NY, NY, *Chmn. of the Bd.*, James Felt Realty Serv. Inc.; **PRIM RE ACT:** Broker, Consultant, Owner/Investor, Instructor; **SERVICES:** Acquisition, mktg. investment props., tax-oriented trans., land use/feasibility surveys; devel. innovative fin. techniques, negotiation major lease trans.; **REP CLIENTS:** Lenders and indivs. or instnl. investors in comml. props.; **PREV EMPLOY:** Asst. Admin. Rent Dept., OPA; Tech. Advisor Nat. Housing Agency; Chief Conversion Mgmt. Div; Chief Sales Div. Fed. Public Housing Admin, Washington DC, 1942-46; Chief Appraiser NYC Reg. Office Fed. Public Housing Admin, 1947; VP J. Clarence Davies Realty, 1947-53; VP James Felt & Vo., 1953-69; Sr. VP 1969-73; Exec. VP James Felt Huberth & Huberth, 1973-75; **PROFL AFFIL & HONORS:** Assoc. Prof. Sch. Continuing Educ. & Ext. Servs., NY Univ.; Former Chmn. Sales Brokers Comm. REENY; Bd. Dirs. Realty Found. NY; Advisory Bd. NY Univ. RE Inst.; Member NYC RE Bd. (Former Gov. Dir. Brokerage Div.); Member Amer. Soc. RE Counselors; VP/Dir. 480 Park Ave. Corp.; Bd. of Dirs. East Side Assn., Recipient Most Inegnious Realtor Award 1957, 1969, 1979; **OTHER ACT & HONORS:** Past. TR. N. Castle Free Library, Former Dir. NYC Public Devel. Corp.; **HOME ADD:** 210 Hook Rd., Katonah, NY 10536, (914)232-3158; **BUS ADD:** 488 Madison Ave., New York, NY 10022, (212)421-2100.

RICE, Hulbert F.——B: Nov. 6, 1922, Cedar Rapids, IA, *Pres.*, Consultants West Corp.; **PRIM RE ACT:** Consultant, Appraiser, Instructor; **SERVICES:** Appraisal, marketability & feasibility reports; consultation; **REP CLIENTS:** S & L Assns.; banks; mort. bankers; city, state & fed. agencies; builders; devels. & lawyers; **PROFL AFFIL & HONORS:** AIREA; Soc. of RE Appraisers, MAI; **EDUC:** BA, 1947, Eng. & Sci., Grad. of Coe Coll.; attended Univ. of WI; **MIL SERV:** USN, Midshipman; **OTHER ACT & HONORS:** Kiwanis, Masonic Lodge, Consistory & Shrine; Bd. Member: Univ. Preparatory Academy, Seattle, WA; Eastside Referral & Treatment Center, Bellevue, WA; **HOME ADD:** 18311 NE 21st St., Redmond, WA 98052, (206)746-1318; **BUS ADD:** 20101 44th Ave. W., Lynnwood, WA 98036, (206)771-4880.

RICE, K. Wayne——B: Feb. 28, 1944, Richmond, VA, *Pres.*, Investment Research Group, Inc.; **PRIM RE ACT:** Broker, Developer, Owner/Investor, Property Manager, Syndicator; **OTHER RE ACT:** Investment advisor; **SERVICES:** Investment advice, consulting, synd., prop. mgmt.; **REP CLIENTS:** Individuals and bus.; **PROFL AFFIL & HONORS:** Dir., Construction Specifications Inst.; Pres. and Dir., Apt. Owners Assn.; Dir. East Bay Mktg. Group, Who's Who in Indus. and Fin. (1981); Who's Who in CA (1981); **EDUC:** Arch. Engrg, 1967, Structural Design, VA Polytechnic Inst.; **EDUC HONORS:** Top in Class in Curriculum; **MIL SERV:** US Army, 1st Lt., Bronze Star, Vietnam; **HOME ADD:** 165 Haven Hill Ct., Danville, CA 94526; **BUS ADD:** 22634 Second St., Suite 200, Hayward, CA 94541, (415)886-6001.

RICE, Matthew R.——B: Nov. 29, 1953, Westchester, PA, *Asst. Legal Counsel*, IL Dept. of Conservation; **PRIM RE ACT:** Attorney; **PREV EMPLOY:** Asst. Legal Counsel, IL Dept. of Admin. Servs., ABA Real Prop. Sect., Probate and Trust Law, IL Bar Assn. sect. on RE Law; **EDUC:** BA, 1975, Poli. Sci., So. IL Univ. at Carbondale; **GRAD EDUC:** JD, 1978, So. IL Univ. School of Law; **HOME ADD:** Apt. 234, 750 S. Durkin, Springfield, IL 62704, (217)787-2797; **BUS ADD:** Springfield, IL 62706 210, 524 S. 2nd. St., (217)782-1809.

RICE, Randolf J.——B: July 1, 1947, San Jose, CA, *Atty.*, Pillsbury, Madison & Sutco; **PRIM RE ACT:** Attorney; **OTHER RE ACT:** Litigation; **EDUC:** BA, 1969, Univ. of CA at Santa Cruz; **GRAD EDUC:** JD, 1978, Hastings Coll. of the Law, San Francisco; **EDUC HONORS:** Order of the Coif; **BUS ADD:** 101 Park Ctr. Plaza, San Jose, CA 95113, (408)287-2233.

RICE, Stephen C.——B: Nov. 4, 1949, Ann Arbor, MI, *VP Mktg. Dir.-Investment Props.*, Coldwell Banker Inc., Comml. RE Servs.; **PRIM RE ACT:** Broker; **SERVICES:** Brokerage & structuring of investment deals in the N.E.; **REP CLIENTS:** Maj. devel., ins. cos. pension funds, indiv. investors; **PREV EMPLOY:** Mort. Banker; Coldwell Banker, Jersey Mort., Peter F. Pasbjerg Co.; **EDUC:** BA, 1972, Econ., Lehigh Univ.; **HOME ADD:** 5 Puritan Rd., Acton, MA 01720, (617)897-9009; **BUS ADD:** 50 Staniford St., Boston, MA 02114, (617)367-7600.

RICH, David——B: Jan. 12, 1927, Houston, TX, *Pres.*, David Rich Co.; **PRIM RE ACT:** Broker, Consultant, Appraiser, Developer, Builder, Owner/Investor, Property Manager; **PROFL AFFIL & HONORS:** Metro Tulsa Bd. of Realtors; OK Assn. of Realtors; NAR; SIR, SIR Chap. Pres., OK Chap.; **EDUC:** BA, 1949, Chemistry, Univ. of TX; **MIL SERV:** US Army, M/Sgt., Good Conduct Medal, Victory Medal, Expert Rifleman, Amer. Theatre Medal; **OTHER ACT & HONORS:** Delta Masonic Lodge; Tulsa Consistory; **HOME ADD:** 3515 E. 66th St., Tulsa, OK 74136, (918)494-0143; **BUS ADD:** 2140 S. Harvard, Tulsa, OK 74114, (918)744-5474.

RICH, Howard L.——B: Aug. 22, 1918, Coleman, TX, Howard L. Rich, Realtor; **PRIM RE ACT:** Broker, Consultant; **PROFL AFFIL & HONORS:** San Antonio Bd. of Realtor, TX Assn. of Realtors, NAR, RNMI, C.C.I.M; **MIL SERV:** USN, CPO, Area,Ribbons,Battle Ribbons, SW Pacific WWII; **OTHER ACT & HONORS:** C of C; BS of A Regional Dir., Toastmaster Lions, Masons; **HOME ADD:** 5340 Hollyhock Rd., San Antonio, TX 78240, (512)696-2722; **BUS ADD:** 4203 Gardendale, San Antonio, TX 78229, (512)696-2722.

RICH, Thomas L.——**B:** Oct. 22, 1958, Stamford, CT, *Project Devel. Mgr.*, F.D. Rich Co., Inc., Devel. Grp.; **PRIM RE ACT:** Broker, Developer, Builder, Owner/Investor, Property Manager, Syndicator; **OTHER RE ACT:** Condo. devel.; **PREV EMPLOY:** TLRP Realty Tr., Condo. Devel.; **PROFL AFFIL & HONORS:** Amer. Mktg. Assn. Soc. for the Advancement of Mgmt.; **EDUC:** BS/BA, 1980, Fin. and Mktg., Boston Univ. Sch. of Mgmt.; **HOME ADD:** 310 Ocean Dr. E., Stamford, CT 06902; **BUS ADD:** 1 Landmark Sq., Stamford, CT 06901, (203)359-4440.

RICHARD, Howard M.——**B:** Sept. 20, 1944, Chicago, IL, *Partner*, Katten, Muchin, Zavis, Pearl & Galler; **PRIM RE ACT:** Attorney; **REP CLIENTS:** Synds., RE devels., lenders, mort. bankers, RE brokers; **PROFL AFFIL & HONORS:** Chicago Bar Assn., ABA (Probate and Real Prop. Sect.), ACLU (Participating Atty.); **EDUC:** BS, 1965, Econ., Cornell Univ.; **GRAD EDUC:** JD, 1968, Harvard Law Sch.; **EDUC HONORS:** Cum Laude, Deans List, Magna Cum Laude, Member of Bd. of Editors, Harvard Law Review; **HOME ADD:** 625 Sheridan Rd., Highland Pk., IL 60035, (312)432-7924; **BUS ADD:** 4100 55th St. E. Monroe, Chicago, IL 60603, (312)346-7400.

RICHARD, Joel——*VP Engineering*, Duplex Products, Inc.; **PRIM RE ACT:** Property Manager; **BUS ADD:** 228 Page St., Sycamore, IL 60178, (815)895-2101.*

RICHARDS, David Alan——**B:** Sept. 21, 1945, Dayton, OH, *Partner*, Coudert Brothers; **PRIM RE ACT:** Attorney; **SERVICES:** Legal representation for investors, owners; **REP CLIENTS:** Crouch Grp. Ltd.; London & Paris Holdings Ltd.; Mackenzie Hill Intl. Prop. Devel. Ltd.; Irish Life Assurance Co. Ltd.; Tiffany & Co.; **PREV EMPLOY:** Paul, Weiss, Rifkind, Wharton & Garrison, NY, 1972-1978; **PROFL AFFIL & HONORS:** ABA: Chmn. Comm. on For. Investment in US RE; Assn. of the Bar of the City of NY: Member, Real Prop. Comm., 1978-1980; **EDUC:** BA, 1967, Amer. Studies, Yale; **GRAD EDUC:** JD, 1972, Yale Law School; BA, 1969, Cambridge Univ.; MA, 1973, Cambridge Univ.; **EDUC HONORS:** Summa Cum Laude, First Class Honors; **OTHER ACT & HONORS:** Author: "Development Rights Transfer in NY City" 82 *Yale L.J.ln 338 (1972); "RE Counsel, Contract and Closing for the For. Investor" 14 Real Property, Probate & Trust J.* 257 (1979); **HOME ADD:** 18 Forest Ln, Scarsdale, NY 10583, (914)725-3254; **BUS ADD:** 200 Park Ave., New York, NY 10166, (212)880-4514.

RICHARDS, Edward J.——**B:** Mar. 22, 1936, Ontario, Can., *Pres.*, Los Angeles Urban Assoc.; **PRIM RE ACT:** Consultant, Developer; **PREV EMPLOY:** Cabot, Cabot & Forbes; Trizec Corp.; **EDUC:** BS, 1960, Civil Engrg., Queen's Univ.; **GRAD EDUC:** MBA, 1969, Fin., Suffolk Univ.; **HOME ADD:** 1310 Winston Ave., San Marino, CA 91108, (213)792-3967; **BUS ADD:** PO Box 8851, San Marino, CA 91108, (213)449-6909.

RICHARDS, Lawrence H.——**B:** Dec. 11, 1948, Youngstown, OH, *Corporate Tax Counsel*, The Cofaro Co.; **PRIM RE ACT:** Broker, Attorney; **OTHER RE ACT:** CPA; **SERVICES:** Entity formation, tax advice; **REP CLIENTS:** Indus. corps., partnerships; **PREV EMPLOY:** Peat, Marwick, Mitchell & Co., CPA's; **PROFL AFFIL & HONORS:** ABA, OH State Bar Assn., Amer. Inst. of CPA's, OH Soc. of CPA's; **EDUC:** BSA, 1970, Acctg., Youngstown State Univ.; **GRAD EDUC:** JD, 1976, Univ. of Akron; **EDUC HONORS:** Cum Laude, Youngstown Educational Found. scholarship, Amer. Jurisprudence Award for Estate Planning; **MIL SERV:** USMC, Sgt.; **HOME ADD:** 119 Sugar Cane Dr., Youngstown, OH 44512, (216)726-1495; **BUS ADD:** 2445 Belmont Ave., Youngstown, OH 44505, (216)747-2661.

RICHARDS, Maurice F.——**B:** Jan. 19, 1913, Rockland, MI, *Sole Prop. Richards Investment Co.*, Richards Investment Co.; **PRIM RE ACT:** Broker, Consultant, Property Manager, Syndicator; **SERVICES:** Investment counseling; income prop. synd. & prop. mgmt., oil & gas drilling programs; **REP CLIENTS:** Indiv. & grp. investors in income prop. synd.; **PREV EMPLOY:** Assoc. Prof. Univ. of CA, Santa Barbara 1950-64; **PROFL AFFIL & HONORS:** Member Natl. Assn. of Securities Dealers; Natl. Fed. of Independent Businessmen, Natl. Small Bus. Assn.; Channel City Club, Author: 7 Articles in Trade Magazines; Inventor; Electronic Training Aid for Cure of Enuresis (pat. pending); **EDUC:** BS, 1935, Indus. Arts & Math., No. MI Univ.; **GRAD EDUC:** MS, 1940, Indus. Education, Univ. of MI; PhD, 1950, Indus. Mgmt.; **EDUC HONORS:** Phi Delta Kappa; **MIL SERV:** US Naval Res., Lt., 11 Battle Stars on Pacific Campaign Ribbon; **OTHER ACT & HONORS:** Phi Delta Kappa 1940; Epsilon Pi Tau 1946; Suburban Kiwanis Club Pres.; Montecito Ctry. Club; Coral Casino 1970-71; **HOME ADD:** 1134 Dulzura Rd., Santa Barbara, CA 93108, (805)969-3965; **BUS ADD:** 1114 State St., Suite 233, Santa Barbara, CA 93101, (805)963-6688.

RICHARDS, Mildred V.——**B:** Dec. 5, 1918, Meriden, CT, *Owner*, Richards Agency, Realtors; **PRIM RE ACT:** Broker; **SERVICES:** RE Brokerage; **PROFL AFFIL & HONORS:** Central CT Bd. of Realtors, Pres. 1969-70. Realtor of the Yr. 1973-76; CT Assn. of Realtors, Pres. 1979; NAR, Dir. from 1978 to pres., V. Chmn. Realtors' Foundation; Charter Oak Chap. Women's Council, Pres. 1976; Nat. Nylaw Chmn. 1978-1980, GRI; CRB; CRS; **OTHER ACT & HONORS:** Meriden Bd. of Apportionment and Taxation; Neighborhood Revitalization Task Force; Commn. to Select a First City Mgr.; Dir. of C of C; Dir. of Public Health and Visiting Nurse Assn.; State of CT Task Force on Housing for the Aged; Dir., Meriden Chap. Red Cross; **HOME ADD:** 14 William Ave., Meriden, CT 06450, (203)634-3535; **BUS ADD:** 247 South St., Meriden, CT 06450, (203)634-1422.

RICHARDS, Robert L.——*Exec. VP*, Amer. Hotel and Motel Assn.; **OTHER RE ACT:** Public Service; **BUS ADD:** 888 Seventh Ave., New York, NY 10019, (212)265-4506.*

RICHARDS, Stanley——**B:** Oct. 11, 1933, Council Bluffs, IA, *Pres.*, Gen. Growth Props.; **PRIM RE ACT:** Attorney; **SERVICES:** Consultation shopping ctr. devel.; **PROFL AFFIL & HONORS:** IA Bar Assn.; **EDUC:** BSC, 1955, Acctg., Univ. of IA; **GRAD EDUC:** JD, 1958, Univ. of IA; **MIL SERV:** USAF, 1st Lt.; **HOME ADD:** 2923 Fox Run., Des Moines, IA 50321, (515)282-4218; **BUS ADD:** 215 Keo, PO Box 1536, Des Moines, IA 50306, (515)281-0117.

RICHARDSON, Edmund F.——**B:** Jan. 17, 1946, Fort Benning, GA, *Atty./Shareholder*, Robbins & Green, PA; **PRIM RE ACT:** Attorney; **SERVICES:** RE devel. documentation; **REP CLIENTS:** Winton & Scott Ltd., Universal Homes, Inc., Citicorp Homeowners, Inc., Kelp Corp., Seaward Props. Ltd.; **PREV EMPLOY:** Streich, Lang., Weeks & Cardon, PA; **PROFL AFFIL & HONORS:** ABA Sect. on Real Prop. Probate & Trusts; Corp., Banking & Bus. Law; **EDUC:** BS, 1970, Fin./Mgmt., AZ State Univ.; **GRAD EDUC:** JD, 1973, Comml. Law, AZ State Univ.; **EDUC HONORS:** Cum Laude, Managing Editor AZ State Law Journal; **MIL SERV:** US Air NG, Sgt.; **OTHER ACT & HONORS:** Maricopa Cty. Bar Assn.; Young Lawyers Bd. of Dir.; **BUS ADD:** 1800 United Bank Plaza, 3300 N. Central Ave., Phoenix, AZ 85012, (602)248-7999.

RICHARDSON, Howard——**B:** Sept. 6, 1921, Louisville, MS, *Pres.*, Richardson Realty; **PRIM RE ACT:** Broker, Developer, Owner/Investor; **PREV EMPLOY:** 31 yrs. USAF 1942-73, Ret. Col.; **PROFL AFFIL & HONORS:** FLI, NAR; **EDUC:** BS, 1947, Bus. Admin., MS State Univ.; **GRAD EDUC:** MBA, 1950, Fiscal Admin., Columbus Univ., now Catholic Univ., Wash., DC; **MIL SERV:** USAF, Col., Legion of Merit, 2 Distinguished Flying Cross's, 5 Air Medals, 2 AF Commendation Medals, WW II European campaign 5 Stars; **OTHER ACT & HONORS:** Past Pres. The Ret. Officers Assn.; Member Exchange Club, Military Order of World Wars; Order of Daedalians; Sigma Chi Soc. Frat.; **HOME ADD:** 4624 Kelton Dr., Jackson, MS 39211, (601)362-7151; **BUS ADD:** P.O. Box 16181, Jackson, MS 39236, (601)981-4144.

RICHARDSON, Robert E.——**B:** Jan. 28, 1943, Sheffield, AL, *Atty.*, Robert E. Richardson; **PRIM RE ACT:** Attorney, Syndicator; **PROFL AFFIL & HONORS:** NAR, CLU, Chartered Prop. and Casualty Underwriter; **EDUC:** BBA, 1971, Ins., Memphis State; **GRAD EDUC:** JD, 1978, John Marshall; **EDUC HONORS:** Outstanding Ins. Student; **MIL SERV:** USMC, Cpl.; **HOME ADD:** 3826 S. Atlanta Rd., Smyrna, GA 30080; **BUS ADD:** 3826 S. Atlanta Rd., Smyrna, GA 30080, (404)436-6336.

RICHARDSON, Thomas W.——**B:** May 30, 1940, Buffalo, NY, *Mgr.*, Russ Lyon Realty Co., Comml. Indus. Brokerage Div.; **PRIM RE ACT:** Broker; **SERVICES:** Comml./indus., retail. office, investment, land, and bus. brokerage servs.; **PROFL AFFIL & HONORS:** Natl. Assn. of Corp. RE Exec., BOMA; **EDUC:** BA, 1963, Econ., Coll. of William and Mary, Williamsburg, VA; **MIL SERV:** US Army, Infantry/Aviation, Capt., Numerous Decorations; **BUS ADD:** 2036 E. Camelback Rd., Phoenix, AZ 85016, (602)957-9830.

RICHARDSON, Wallace A.——**B:** Oct. 12, 1936, Bartlesville, OK, *Partner*, Knudsen, Berkheimer, Richardson & Endacott; **PRIM RE ACT:** Attorney, Owner/Investor; **REP CLIENTS:** Lenders, synds., devels.; **PROFL AFFIL & HONORS:** Amer. Coll. of RE Attys., Real Prop. Sect. ABA (Fin. Comm.), Title Standards Comm., NE Bar Assn.; **EDUC:** BBS, 1958, Acctg., Mgmt., Univ. of KS; **GRAD EDUC:** JD, 1963, Tax, Univ. of MI; **EDUC HONORS:** Beta Gamma Sigma, Alpha Kappa Psi, Mgmt. Award; **MIL SERV:** USN, Lt., 1958-60; **OTHER ACT & HONORS:** Consultant, Nat. Endowment for the Arts, Chmn. NE Arts. Council, Pres. Rotary Club; **HOME ADD:** 6911 Eastshore Dr., Lincoln, NE 68508; **BUS ADD:** 1000 NBC Ctr., Lincoln, NE 68508, (402)475-7011.

RICHERT, Clarendon G.——**B:** Apr. 6, 1924, Clarendon Hills, IL, *VP*, John Hancock Mutual Life Ins. Co. and John Hancock Realty Development Corp., Agricultural Investment; **PRIM RE ACT:** Appraiser, Lender; **PROFL AFFIL & HONORS:** Nat. Agricultural Credit Comm.; Mort. Bankers Assn. of America; Bd. of Dir. Informatics, Inc.; **EDUC:** BS, 1947, Gen. Agriculture, Univ. of IL; **GRAD EDUC:** MIT, AMP, 1964, Harvard Graduate School of Bus., Agribusiness Seminars (London & Boston); **MIL SERV:** USAF, 1st Lt., Air Medal, Distinguished Flying Cross; **OTHER ACT & HONORS:** Pres. & Exec. Comm., Norumbega Council, Boy Scouts of America; **HOME ADD:** 45 Summit Rd., Wellesley, MA 02181, (617)237-9191; **BUS ADD:** John Hancock Place, PO Box 111, Boston, MA 02117, (617)421-6012.

RICHERT, William F.——**B:** Dec. 8, 1950, Weatherford, OK, *Broker - Owner*, William F. Richert Co.; **PRIM RE ACT:** Broker, Consultant, Appraiser, Owner/Investor, Property Manager, Syndicator; **SERVICES:** Complete investment analysis for clients; **PREV EMPLOY:** Whiteside & Grant, Realtors 1974-78, Hardesty Co. 1978-80; **PROFL AFFIL & HONORS:** ICSC, RNMI, CCIM, NAR; **EDUC:** BBA, 1937, Fin. & RE, Univ. of OK; **OTHER ACT & HONORS:** Church Bd., Propellar Club; Toastmasters Intl., OK Divisional Lt. Gov.; **HOME ADD:** 6033 S. Quebec, Tulsa, OK 74135, (918)496-0332; **BUS ADD:** 7129 S. Yal, Tulsa, OK 74136, (918)496-1367.

RICHEY, Alvan E., Jr.——**B:** Jan. 11, 1936, TX, *VP*, American Buildings Co.; **PRIM RE ACT:** Builder; **PROFL AFFIL & HONORS:** Metal Bldg. Man. Assn.; Metal Bldg. Dealer Assn.; Indus. Devel. Assn.; **EDUC:** BS, 1958, Chem., TX A&M Univ.; **GRAD EDUC:** 1959, Meteorology; **MIL SERV:** USAF, Capt.; **HOME TEL:** (205)687-3076; **BUS ADD:** POB 800, Eufaula, AL 36027, (205)687-2032.

RICHMAN, Marvin Jordan——**B:** July 13, 1939, NYC, NY, *Pres.*, Olympia & York CA Equities Corp.; **PRIM RE ACT:** Developer, Builder; **SERVICES:** Devel. of comml., indus. & resid. props., prop. mgmt.; **PREV EMPLOY:** Sr. VP Urban Investment & Devel. Co., Chicago, 1969-79; Pres. First City Devel. Corp., Beverly Hills, 1979-80; **PROFL AFFIL & HONORS:** AIA, Amer. Planning Assn., Amer. Arbitration Assn., Panel of Constr. Arbitrators, Intl. Council of Shopping Ctrs.; **EDUC:** BArch, 1962, Arch., MIT; **GRAD EDUC:** MUP, 1966, Urban Planning, Public Admin., NY Univ.; MBA, 1977, Univ. of Chicago; **HOME ADD:** 3238 Fond Dr., Encino, CA 91436, (213)784-9687; **BUS ADD:** 261 S. Figueroa St., Los Angeles, CA 90012, (213)620-9195.

RICHMOND, Charles D.——**B:** Feb. 8, 1951, San Diego, *Charles D. Richmond, Esq.*, Ludecke, McGrath & Denton; **PRIM RE ACT:** Attorney, Owner/Investor, Syndicator; **SERVICES:** RE and tax planning, RE & tax litigation; **REP CLIENTS:** RE agents & gen. contractors; **PREV EMPLOY:** Formerly Employed by Fred Crane, Real Prop. Sales Associate; **PROFL AFFIL & HONORS:** Member of ABA Taxation and Real Prop. Comm. as well as San Diego Bar and CA Bar Assn. Comm. on Real Prop. and Taxation; **EDUC:** BA, 1974, Hist., Philosophy, USIU CA Western; **GRAD EDUC:** Grad. Work, RE, San Diego State Univ.; **HOME ADD:** 2721 Mission Blvd., San Diego, CA 92109, (714)488-2057; **BUS ADD:** 2333 First Ave., Suite 204, San Diego, CA 92109, (714)235-8020.

RICHMOND, F. Lynn——**B:** May 10, 1936, Long Beach, CA, *Owner/Developer*, LakeHills; **PRIM RE ACT:** Developer, Owner/Investor, Property Manager; **SERVICES:** Design, construct, sell & maintain home sites in a planned unit devel.; **PREV EMPLOY:** 20 yrs., Faculty, Univ. of OR; **EDUC:** BA, 1958, Soc. Sci., CA State Univ. at Long Beach; **GRAD EDUC:** MA, 1963, Sociology, Univ. of OR; PhD, 1970, Sociology, Univ. of OR; **EDUC HONORS:** 49'er & Alumni Awards 'Outstanding Grad. Student', Student Body Pres., Mis. Research Fellowships, Mis. Research Fellowships; **OTHER ACT & HONORS:** Pres., OR Bach Festival; Pres., W. Lane Forest Protective Assn.; VP, Eugene Opera; Advisory Council, BLM, Eugene District; **HOME ADD:** 24515 LakeHills Dr., Junction City, OR 97448, (503)998-6891; **BUS ADD:** 24515 LakeHills Dr., Junction City, OR 97448, (503)998-6891.

RICHMOND, Richard J.——**B:** Sept. 1, 1905, Westerly, RI, *Owner*, Richmond Realty; **PRIM RE ACT:** Broker, Consultant; **OTHER RE ACT:** Radio Station Mgmt. Consultant; **SERVICES:** Gen. RE sales; **PREV EMPLOY:** Richmond Realty, Westerly, RI (owner), Richmond Bros. Radio Stations - WMEX, Boston; WPGC, Washington, DC; KBML, Las Vegas; **PROFL AFFIL & HONORS:** Intl. Fed. of RE Brokers, Cty. Bd. of Realtors, NAB, Nat. Assn. of RE Brokers; **EDUC:** Univ. of CT; NY School of Interior Decoration; **OTHER ACT & HONORS:** Past Pres., Westerly Pawcatwell Bd. of Trade, Masonic - Elks, MA Broadcasters Assn., Nat. Broadcasters, Distinguished Serv. Award - St. Jude Children's Hospital - Memphis, TN; **HOME ADD:** 1000 Lowry St., Delray Beach, FL 33444; **BUS ADD:** 32 Canal St., Westerly, RI 02891, (401)596-4975.

RICHMOND, Roger W.——**B:** Sep. 22, 1939, Waterbury, CT, *VP*, Devoe, RE; **PRIM RE ACT:** Broker, Instructor, Consultant, Appraiser; **SERVICES:** Resid. devel., valuation, investment counseling; **REP CLIENTS:** Attys., banks, comms., indivs., bus.; **PREV EMPLOY:** Cost Supervisor, Data Processing Mgr.; **PROFL AFFIL & HONORS:** N.M. Econ. Devel. Comm., Chmn N.M. Conservation Comm. Sec., Charter Pres. N.M. Exchange, Past Pres. N.M. Bd. of Realtors, Realtor of the Yr. 1974-75; **OTHER ACT & HONORS:** Officer N.M. Little League, Advisor HS Bus. Advisory Comm.; **HOME ADD:** 24 Flower Hill Rd., New Milford, CT 06776, (203)354-4803; **BUS ADD:** 7 Kent Rd., New Milford, CT 06776, (203)354-5571.

RICKARD, Larry D.——**B:** June 11, 1943, Seneca, MO, *Pres./Broker*, Continental RE; **PRIM RE ACT:** Broker, Builder, Owner/Investor, Instructor; **SERVICES:** Brokerage, investing & contracting (Lic. Contractor), sales, rentals, mgmt.; **REP CLIENTS:** indiv., investors, self, builders; **PREV EMPLOY:** CA Sales License (1971-72) CA City, CA; Transamerican Investment Props., Dir. Coord. (1972) Wichita, KS; **PROFL AFFIL & HONORS:** Nat. Assoc. of Realtors, Realtors Nat. Marketing Instit., CRB, Cert. RE Brokerage Mgr.; **EDUC:** BBA, 1966, Mgmt., Wichita State Univ.; **GRAD EDUC:** MBA, 1969, Mgmt., Wichita State Univ.; **MIL SERV:** USAF, Capt.; **OTHER ACT & HONORS:** Dir., Wichita Bd. of Realtors; Crestview Cty. Club; Instr. Realty School of KS and Butler Cty. Community Coll.; Also assoc. with Continental Construction, Inc.; **HOME ADD:** Hillcreast Apts., 115 S. Rutan, Wichita, KS 67218, (316)682-4152; **BUS ADD:** PO Box 18552, Wichita, KS 67218.

RICKER, Judith C.——**B:** Apr. 27, 1947, Seattle, WA, *Pres.*, Invest West Mgmt. Co., Wholly owned sub. Invest West Fin. Corp.; **PRIM RE ACT:** Consultant, Property Manager, Owner/Investor; **SERVICES:** Prop. mgmt., analysis, mgmt, plans, market studies; **REP CLIENTS:** Indiv. & instl. income prop. owners, brokers and synds.; **PROFL AFFIL & HONORS:** IREM, CA Assoc of Realtors, CPM; **EDUC:** BA, 1969, Pol. Sci., Reed Coll., Portland, OR; **OTHER ACT & HONORS:** Published 'Journal of Prop. Mgmt.' 5/80; **HOME ADD:** 115 W. Junipero St., Santa Barbara, CA 93105, (805)682-2828; **BUS ADD:** 3916 St., PO Box 30460, Santa Barbara, CA 93105, (805)687-1588.

RICKER, Ruth B.——**B:** New York, NY, *Pres. and Owner*, Alta Mgmt. Consultants, Inc.; **PRIM RE ACT:** Consultant, Developer, Instructor, Property Manager; **SERVICES:** Prop. mgmt.; consulting; training; devel.; **REP CLIENTS:** Devel.; non-profit and conventional owners; public agencies; **PREV EMPLOY:** 14 year Prop. Mgmt.; **PROFL AFFIL & HONORS:** 1981 Pres. - Boston Chapter of Inst. of RE Mgmt. (IREM); Bd. of Dir. - Rental Housing Assn., CPM, Licensed RE Broker; 1981 Mgr. of the Yr. Boston Chap. of IREM; Elected-Bd. of Dirs. 2 Yr. Term (Effective 1982) Greater Boston RE Bd.; **EDUC:** RE courses, Burdett Coll. Northeastern Univ., IREM courses; **EDUC HONORS:** Certificates; **OTHER ACT & HONORS:** Ward 4 Boston, Ward Comm. - 4 years; YWCA and Facilities Comm.; **HOME ADD:** 14 Wessex Road, Newton, MA 02159, (617)965-2437; **BUS ADD:** 441 Stuart St., Boston, MA 02116, (617)965-4430.

RIDDLE, Joseph P., III——**B:** May 23, 1956, Fayetteville, NC, *Pres./VP*, Biltwell, Inc./March Development Corp., Homebuilding, Apt. Const., Comml. Duplexes, Townhomes; **PRIM RE ACT:** Broker, Consultant, Appraiser, Developer, Builder, Owner/Investor, Property Manager, Insuror; **SERVICES:** Rental locator, valuation, comml. deveL., investment counseling, new home consulting; **PROFL AFFIL & HONORS:** Nat. Assn. of Homebuilders; Fayetteville and NC Assn.; Fay Area Bd. of Realtors; NC Realtors; Nat. Bd. ERA (Electronic Realty Associates); **EDUC:** BS, 1977, Bus./Fin., Univ. of NC at Chapel Hill; **EDUC HONORS:** Dean's List; **OTHER ACT & HONORS:** YMCA; Haymount Meth. Church; TR., Fayetteville State Univ.; Bd. of Dir., Fayetteville Acad.; **HOME ADD:** 6843 Uppingham Dr., Fayetteville, NC 28306, (919)425-6231; **BUS ADD:** 238 N. McPherson Church Rd., Fayetteville, NC 28303, (919)864-3232.

RIDENOUR, James——*Dir. Admn.*, Great Lakes Chemical Corp.; **PRIM RE ACT:** Property Manager; **BUS ADD:** PO Box 2200, W. Lafayette, IN 47906, (317)463-2511.*

RIDGE, John E.——**B:** Feb. 13, 1914, Louisville, KY, *Sr. Partner, Chmn.*, Ridge-Porter Assoc., Ridge Porter Mort. Co.; **PRIM RE ACT:** Broker, Consultant, Appraiser, Developer, Lender; **SERVICES:** Appraising, consulting mort. banking; **REP CLIENTS:** Bank One N.A., Columbus, OH; Citizens Fidelity Bank & Trust Co., Louisville, KY; City Bank N.Y., Employee Transfer Co.; **PREV EMPLOY:** Chief Appraiser, Chief Underwriter and Dep. Dir., KY FHA Office; Dir. of Mgmt. HUD; **PROFL AFFIL & HONORS:** AIREA, Louisville Bd. of

Realtors, NAREB, MBA, MAI; **EDUC:** AB, 1936, Econ., Univ. of Louisville; **MIL SERV:** US Army, Col., 5 Bronze Battle Stars; **OTHER ACT & HONORS:** Kiwanis Club, Louisville Area C of C, Bd. of Dirs., three non-profit housing corps.; **HOME ADD:** 519 Dover Rd., Louisville, KY 40206, (502)895-1327; **BUS ADD:** Suite 1001 Kentucky Towers, Louisville, KY 40202, (502)587-6592.

RIDLOFF, Richard——**B:** July 18, 1948, NY, NY, *VP - Law/Sec.*, Mony Mort. Investors; **PRIM RE ACT:** Attorney, Consultant, Lender; **SERVICES:** Legal, investment counseling, systems devel.; **REP CLIENTS:** Lenders and indiv. or instnl. investors in Comml. props.; **PREV EMPLOY:** The Mutual Life Ins. Co. of NY, 1972 - 1979; **PROFL AFFIL & HONORS:** ABA; NYBA; ALTA; Member ABA Comm. on Real Prop. Fin., Sect. of Real Prop., Probate & Trust Law; Member of Editorial Bd. of the Real Prop. Fin. Newsletter Published by Said Comm.; Chmn. of the 1981/1982 Legislative Committee of NAREIT; **EDUC:** BA, 1969, Poli. Sci./Econ., Queens Coll.; **GRAD EDUC:** JD, 1972, Cornell Law School; **EDUC HONORS:** Cum Laude; Pi Sigma Alpha; Omicron Delta Epsilon; Alpha Epsilon Pi, Member Envir. Law Soc. & Legal Aid Clinic; **OTHER ACT & HONORS:** Secondary School Interviewing Comm. of Cornell Univ.; **HOME ADD:** 302 Nimitz St., Jericho, NY 11753, (516)822-9537; **BUS ADD:** 1740 Broadway, New York, NY 10019, (212)586-6716.

RIDPATH, James S.——**B:** Nov. 12, 1921, Haxton, CO, *Owner-Pres.*, Ridpath Insurance & Real Estate Investing; **PRIM RE ACT:** Consultant, Appraiser, Lender, Owner/Investor, Instructor, Property Manager, Insuror; **SERVICES:** Mgmt.; **PREV EMPLOY:** Self employed; **EDUC:** BA, Univ. of NB; **MIL SERV:** USN, First Class P.O.; **OTHER ACT & HONORS:** Big Brothers Assn. Pres. of Home Owners, Assn. Nat. Assn. of Life Underwriters-Shrine-Masonic Lodge, Pearl Harbor Survivors Association - Board of Directors of Phila. Housing Assn.; **BUS ADD:** 440 Eaton Rd., Drexel Hill, PA 19026, (215)622-4444.

RIEBESELL, H.F., Jr.——**B:** May 31, 1946, Denver, CO, *Atty.*, Law Office of H.F. Riebesell, Jr.; **PRIM RE ACT:** Attorney; **REP CLIENTS:** Bank of Denver, Hellmuth, Obata & Kassabaum, P.C., and other inst. and indiv. in comml. props.; **PROFL AFFIL & HONORS:** Arapahoe, CO and Amer. Bar Assn.; **EDUC:** BA, Econ., 1968, CO Coll.; **GRAD EDUC:** JD, 1971, Univ. of CO School of Law; **EDUC HONORS:** Cum Laude; **HOME ADD:** 8279 E. Otero Cir., Englewood, CO 80112, (303)779-0582; **BUS ADD:** 650 S. Cherry St., Suite 640, Denver, CO 80222, (303)320-1160.

RIECK, Thomas W.——**B:** July 10, 1045, Chicago, IL, *Pres.*, Rieck and Crotty, P.C., Attys. at Law; **PRIM RE ACT:** Attorney; **SERVICES:** Legal and tax consultation; **REP CLIENTS:** Lenders, devels., homeowners' assns., investors; **EDUC:** BBA, 1967, Acctg., Univ. of Notre Dame; **GRAD EDUC:** JD, 1971, Northwestern Univ.; **OTHER ACT & HONORS:** Chicago Athletic Assn., CPA Univ. of IL (1968); **HOME ADD:** 592 Provident Ave., Winnetka, IL 60093; **BUS ADD:** 55 West Monroe St., Chicago, IL 60603, (312)726-4646.

RIEDY, Dr. Mark J.——*Exec. VP*, Mortgage Bankers Assn. of Amer.; **PRIM RE ACT:** Banker; **BUS ADD:** 1125 15th St. NW, Washington, DC 20005, (202)785-8333.*

RIEKE, Forrest N.——**B:** May 26, 1942, Portland, OR, *Atty.*, Rieke, Geil & Savage, P.C.; **PRIM RE ACT:** Attorney, Owner/Investor, Property Manager; **SERVICES:** Legal counseling on RE problems, hist. renovation; **PREV EMPLOY:** Dept. of Fin., State of OR; **PROFL AFFIL & HONORS:** ABA, Real Prop. Probate and Trust Section, UDAG, Award of Excellence; **EDUC:** AB, 1968, Major Pol. Sci., Minor Econ., Stanford Univ.; **GRAD EDUC:** JD, 1971, Law, Willamette Univ., Coll. of Law; **EDUC HONORS:** Law Review, Contributing Member; **OTHER ACT & HONORS:** Chmn., Bd. of Dirs., Portland Public Schools, 1978-present; **HOME ADD:** 2758 NW Calumet Terr., Portland, OR 97210, (503)227-7294; **BUS ADD:** Suite 200, Historic Thomas Mann Bldg., 820 SW Second Ave., Portland, OR 97204, (503)222-0200.

RIEMER, Richard K.——**B:** Apr. 2, 1946, Cambridge, MA, *Pres*, RKR Properties, Inc.; **PRIM RE ACT:** Owner/Investor; **SERVICES:** Own and mgr. resid. hotels and rooming houses; **EDUC:** BA, 1968, Econ., Colby Coll.; **GRAD EDUC:** MBA, 1971, Fin., Wharton; **HOME ADD:** 882 Harvard Pl., Ridgefield, NJ 07657, (201)941-0667; **BUS ADD:** 882 Howard Pl., Ridgefield, NJ 07657, (201)941-0667.

RIEMONDY, Augustus——*Asst. to Chief Exec. Officer*, Hershey Foods Corp.; **PRIM RE ACT:** Property Manager; **BUS ADD:** 100 Mansion Rd. East, Hershey, PA 17033, (717)534-4200.*

RIFE, Thomas G.——**B:** Aug. 10, Bentonville, AR, *Fee Appraiser*, Appraisal Servs., Real Estate, Inc.; **PRIM RE ACT:** Appraiser, Owner/Investor; **SERVICES:** RE appraisal and investment analysis; **PREV EMPLOY:** Owner Rife & Co., Rogers, AR; **PROFL AFFIL & HONORS:** AIREA, RM; **EDUC:** BSE, 1973, Speech, Univ. of AR; **EDUC HONORS:** Who's Who in American Univs.; **HOME ADD:** 760 W Moorhead Cir., Boulder, CO 80303, (303)494-7514; **BUS ADD:** 1729 28th St., Boulder, CO 80301, (303)443-7990.

RIFKIN, Bernard M.——**B:** Sept. 18, 1924, *First VP & Chief Counsel*, The Title Guarantee Co., Pioneer Nat. Title Ins. Co.; **PRIM RE ACT:** Attorney, Insuror; **SERVICES:** Title ins.; **PROFL AFFIL & HONORS:** NY State Bar Assn., Cty Lawyers Bar Assn., Assn. of Bar of City of NY, Chm. Law Comm. of NY State Land Title Assn. & Member Law & Forms Comm. of Amer. Land Title Assn.; **EDUC:** AB, 1945, Hist., Brooklyn Coll.; **GRAD EDUC:** LLB, 1948, Columbia Univ. Law Sch.; LLM, 1972, NY Univ. Law Sch.; **EDUC HONORS:** Dean's List 2 yrs.; **OTHER ACT & HONORS:** Pres. (Past) CT Bd. of Title Underwriters, Vice Chmn. ABA Comm. on State & Local Taxation; **HOME ADD:** 1655 Flatbush Ave., Brooklyn, NY 11210, (212)253-7131; **BUS ADD:** 120 Broadway, New York, NY 10271, (212)964-1000.

RIFKIN, Henry A.——**B:** June 22, 1950, Griffin, GA, *Managing Partner*, Rifkin, Perling & Verner; **PRIM RE ACT:** Consultant, Owner/Investor; **OTHER RE ACT:** CPA; **SERVICES:** Acctg., tax and investment counseling; **REP CLIENTS:** Brokers and synds. of resid. and comml. props.; **PREV EMPLOY:** Coopers & Lybrand (Audit and tax senior); **PROFL AFFIL & HONORS:** GA Soc. of CPA's; AICPA, CPA; **EDUC:** BBA, 1973, Acctg., Univ. of GA; **GRAD EDUC:** MS, 1974, Acctg., Univ. of GA; **EDUC HONORS:** Beta Alpha Psi, Hon. Acctg. Frat.; **OTHER ACT & HONORS:** Recruiter, Univ. of GA Athletic Dept.; **HOME ADD:** 76 Putnam Circ., Atlanta, GA 30342, (404)231-1335; **BUS ADD:** 201 Allen Rd., NE, Suite 310, Atlanta, GA 30328, (404)256-6444.

RIGAS, John N.——**B:** Feb. 24, 1949, Muncie, IN, *Corp. Atty.*, Foremost Corp. of Amer., Legal Div.; **PRIM RE ACT:** Attorney, Developer, Builder, Owner/Investor, Lender; **REP CLIENTS:** Counsel for Foremost Ins. Co. (In-House); **PROFL AFFIL & HONORS:** ABA, Comml. Law League of Amer.; **EDUC:** BA, 1971, Eng., MI State Univ.; **GRAD EDUC:** MA & JD, 1972 & 1979, Hist.-Pol. Sci. & Law, Univ. of MI & Univ. of CT; **EDUC HONORS:** Honors Coll.; **HOME ADD:** 17 College N.E., Grand Rapids, MI 49503; **BUS ADD:** 5300 Foremost Dr. S.E., PO Box 2450, Grand Rapids, MI 49501, (616)942-3568.

RIGGS, Zennie Lawrence——**B:** Oct. 19, 1922, New Bern, N.C., *Atty.*, Practice; **PRIM RE ACT:** Attorney; **PROFL AFFIL & HONORS:** ABA; NC Bar Assn.; **EDUC:** BS in Commerce, 1942, Acctg., Univ. of NC, Chapel Hill, NC; **GRAD EDUC:** JD, 1950, Law, Univ. of NC, Chapel Hill, NC; **MIL SERV:** USN, QM 3/c; **OTHER ACT & HONORS:** Member NC General Assembly 1961, 1962; Masonic; Amer. Legion; **HOME ADD:** Rt. 1, Box 719, Maysville, NC 28555, (919)353-5207; **BUS ADD:** 234 New Bridge St., Jacksonville, NC 28540, (919)347-4129.

RILEY, Edward J.——**B:** Oct. 25, 1941, NYC, NY, *VP*, Amer. S&L Assoc. of FL, RE Ventures; **PRIM RE ACT:** Developer, Builder, Banker, Lender; **SERVICES:** In charge of RE ventures, devel. & joint ventures; **PREV EMPLOY:** 1975 - Date, Amer. S&L Assoc. of FL; 1966-1975, RE Appraiser, NYC; Wm. A White & Sons & Brown, Harris, Stevens AIRE; **PROFL AFFIL & HONORS:** RE & SFL Builders Assoc., MAI; SRPA; Bd. of Dir. & Sec. of S. FL Chap. - AIREA; **EDUC:** BBA, 1962, Bus., Econ., Pre-Law, Acctg., St. Johns Univ.; **HOME ADD:** 1901 NW 114th Ave., Pembroke Lakes, FL 33026, (305)431-7491; **BUS ADD:** 17801 NW 2nd Ave., Miami, FL 33169, (305)653-5353.

RILEY, James D.——**B:** Dec. 9, 1942, Chicago, IL, *Pres.*, Transcontinental Development Consultants; **PRIM RE ACT:** Consultant, Property Manager, Owner/Investor; **OTHER RE ACT:** Provide mktg., merchandising, sales and fin. consultation to lenders, builders/devel. for comml., indus. and resid. programs in new constr., rehabilitation and acquisition and disposition; **REP CLIENTS:** Builder assns., lender assns., major lender and builder/devel. converters and rehabilitation orgs.; **PREV EMPLOY:** VP of Mktg. and VP of Midwest Rgn. for mort. banking org.; **PROFL AFFIL & HONORS:** On Community Devel. Programs; Amer. Prop. Mgrs. Assn.; MBA; Nat. Assn. of Home Builders, 43 Mktg. and/or Merchandising and/or Sales Awards; **EDUC:** BS/BA, 1964, Mktg., LaSalle Extension Univ., Coll. of DuPage and other Correspondence Schools; **MIL SERV:** USN; **OTHER ACT & HONORS:** Bd. of Dirs. of a venture capital co., bank, trucking co.; Shaves Safer Found., Omni House, Big Brothers; **HOME ADD:** 2219 W. Nichols Rd., Arlington Heights, IL 60004, (312)843-

8205; **BUS ADD:** PO Box 973, Arlington Hights, IL 60006, (312)577-2864.

RILEY, Mark Barry——**B:** Sept. 3, 1955, Nashville, TN, King & Spalding, RE Dept.; **PRIM RE ACT:** Attorney; **PROFL AFFIL & HONORS:** Atlanta, GA and American Bar Assns.; **EDUC:** BA, 1977, Hist., Urban Studies, Vanderbilt Univ.; **GRAD EDUC:** JD, 1980, Vanderbilt Univ.; **EDUC HONORS:** Magna Cum Laude, Member, *Vanderbilt Law Review*, Order of the Coif; **HOME ADD:** 273 Peachtree Way NE, Atlanta, GA 30305, (404)237-2689; **BUS ADD:** 2500 Trust Co. Tower, Atlanta, GA 30303, (404)572-4600.

RILEY, Patrick C.——**B:** Oct. 2, 1951, Lancaster, PA, *Exec. VP*, Riley/Sherman & Walton Realtors; **PRIM RE ACT:** Broker, Appraiser, Developer, Owner/Investor; **SERVICES:** Administrative mgr., auction, relocation, resid. sales, new home const., investment, prop. mgmt.; **REP CLIENTS:** Homequity, Equitable, Executrans, Armstrong, Transamerica; **PROFL AFFIL & HONORS:** NAR; PAR; GLBR; RNMI, CRS; GRI; CRB; CCIM Candidate; **EDUC:** BS, 1972, Labor Arbitration & Mgmt., IN Univ.; **EDUC HONORS:** Member, President's Cabinet; **OTHER ACT & HONORS:** Member, Lancaster Cty. Planning Commn.; W. Lancaster Fire Co.; Chmn., PAR Convention 1981; **HOME ADD:** 3160 Briarwood Blvd., Lancaster, PA 17601, (717)285-3394; **BUS ADD:** 500 Delp Rd., Lancaster, PA 17601, (717)569-8781.

RINEY, Michael E.——**B:** Aug. 17, 1951, Lowell, MA, *Mgr. & RE*, The Talbots, Specialty Retailing Div./General Mills, Inc.; **OTHER RE ACT:** Act as rep. for corp.; **PROFL AFFIL & HONORS:** NACORE MA RE Broker; **EDUC:** BS, 1973, Mktg., Villanova; **HOME ADD:** 358 Commonwealth Ave., Boston, MA 02115; **BUS ADD:** 175 Beal St., Hingham, MA 02043, (617)749-7600.

RING, Dr. Alfred A.——**B:** Jan. 25, 1905, Beuthen, Germany, *Econ. Consultant*; **PRIM RE ACT:** Consultant, Appraiser, Instructor, Real Estate Publisher; **OTHER RE ACT:** Author, *RE Principles & Practices*; *Val. of RE*; **SERVICES:** Appraisal of railroad and public utility properties for ad valorem tax purposes; **REP CLIENTS:** Pacific Power & Light Co., Savannah Elec. & Power Co., No. Natural Gas Co., Seaboard RRG, Louisville & Nashville RR Co., Kansas RR Co., El Paso Nat. Gas Co., FL Power Co., WI Elec. Power Co., Burlington RR Co., Fed. Housing Admin., Veterans Admin.; **PREV EMPLOY:** Prof. & Head, Dept. of RE, Univ. of FL; Lecturer, NYU & Wichita State Univ.; **PROFL AFFIL & HONORS:** Life Member, FL Assn. of Realtors; Hon. Life Member, Gainesville Bd. of Realtors; Nat. Tax Assn.; Nat. Econ. Assn.; Hon. Life Member, Tax Chapter SREA, MAI; SRPA; **EDUC:** BS/BA, 1942, RE/Land Econ., NYU; **GRAD EDUC:** MBA, 1944, Public Utility Econ., NYU; PhD, 1947, Econ. Philosophy, NYU; **EDUC HONORS:** Magna Cum Laude, Beta Gamma Sigma, Lambda Alpha, Grad. Research Assist. and Lecturer, Grad. Research Assist. and Lecturer; **OTHER ACT & HONORS:** Nat. Tax Assn.; Nat. Econ. Assn.; Land Econ. Soc.; Soc. Ethics Professorship, U. of FL; Who's Who, Men of Science; Education and Int. Biography - London, England; **HOME ADD:** 1908 NW 7th Ln., Gainesville, FL 32603, (904)376-3434; **BUS ADD:** Box 13535, GainesvilLe, FL 32604, (904)376-3434.

RING, Charles B.——**B:** Nov. 3, 1947, W. Palm Beach, FL, *Partner*, Hollenbeck, Silc & Ring, Inc.; **PRIM RE ACT:** Broker, Consultant, Developer, Owner/Investor, Instructor, Syndicator; **SERVICES:** Sales, devel. and mgmt. of comml. props.; **REP CLIENTS:** Investors, law firms, devel.; **PROFL AFFIL & HONORS:** CCIM, local, state and nat. assn. member, CCIM; **EDUC:** BS, 1970, Bus., Mktg., Univ. of FL; **MIL SERV:** US Army, Capt., Distinguished Mil. Grad.; **OTHER ACT & HONORS:** Bd. of Dir. Univ. of FL Alumni, Flagler Natl. Bank Advisory Bd., RE Instr. Palm Beach Jr. Coll.; **HOME ADD:** 9707 Heather Cir., Palm Beach Gardens, FL 33410, (305)622-7944; **BUS ADD:** 2273 Palm Beach Lakes Blvd., W. Palm Beach, FL 33409, (305)686-1313.

RING, Michael W.——**B:** Feb. 14, 1943, Phoenix, AZ, *Partner*, Sheppard, Mullin, Richter & Hampton; **PRIM RE ACT:** Attorney; **SERVICES:** All legal services in connection with real prop. transactions; **PROFL AFFIL & HONORS:** ABA (Sect. on Real Prop., Probate & Trust Law); State Bar of CA; Los Angeles Cty. Bar Assn. (Real Prop. Sect., Gen. Real Prop. Practice Subsect.); **EDUC:** AB, 1964, Pol. Sci./Econ., Univ. of WA; **GRAD EDUC:** JD, 1968, Law, Univ. of CA, Berkeley School of Law; **EDUC HONORS:** High Distinction; **HOME TEL:** (213)397-6424; **BUS ADD:** 333 S. Hope St., 48th Floor, Los Angeles, CA 90071, (213)620-1780.

RINGEL, Thomas——**B:** Nov. 11, 1951, Hamilton, OH, *Partner*, Markowitz, Davis & Ringel; **PRIM RE ACT:** Attorney; **SERVICES:** Legal; **REP CLIENTS:** Keyes Co, Chemical Bank; **PROFL AFFIL & HONORS:** Kendall Perrine Bd. of Realtors, Dade Cty. Bar Assn. FL Bar Assn., ABA, S. Miami Kendall Bar Assn.; **EDUC:** BA, 1973, Poli. Sci., Univ. of MI; **GRAD EDUC:** JD, 1976, Univ. of Miami; **EDUC HONORS:** Cum Laude; **HOME ADD:** 12855 SW 110 Ter., Miami, FL 33186, (305)387-3078; **BUS ADD:** 9400 S Dadeland Blvd. 225, Miami, FL 33156, (305)666-1001.

RIORDAN, James M.——*Pres.*, The Aries Group Inc.; **PRIM RE ACT:** Developer; **BUS ADD:** 1647 Old Butler Plank Rd., Glenshaw, PA 15116, (412)489-3000.*

RIPLEY, Robert F.——**B:** Jan. 22, 1917, Mathews, VA, *Pres.*, Ripley Assocs., Inc. Realtors; **PRIM RE ACT:** Broker, Consultant, Appraiser, Developer, Owner/Investor; **SERVICES:** Comml., & investment RE; **PROFL AFFIL & HONORS:** Cert. Comml. Investment Member of RNMI; Norfolk/Chesapeake Bd. of Realtors; Tidewater Assn. of Homebuilders; VA Assn. of Realtors; Nat. Assn. of Realtors; Nat. Inst. of RE Brokers; Farm and Land Brokers; Tidewater VA Devel. Council; **EDUC:** Bus., Univ. of Richmond/Coll. of William & Mary; **MIL SERV:** USN, Lt., Bronze Star; **OTHER ACT & HONORS:** Viewers Comm. for RE, Norfolk City Council, 14 yrs.; Norfolk C of C; Chesapeake C of C; Chesapeake B&T, Bd. Member; Pres., Mid-Atlantic Chap. of Cert. Comml. Investment Members of Realtors Nat. Mktg. Inst. (VA, MD, DE, DC, 1979); Legal Action Comm., VA Assn. of Realtors, Chmn., 1977-1979; Chmn., 1979, Designations Comm., Norfolk/Chesapeake Bd. of Realtors; Realtors WA Comm., 2 yrs.; Appraisers' Comm., Norfolk RE Bd., 2 yrs.; Uniform Lic. Law Comm., VA Assn. of Realtors; Chmn., 3 yrs., Leg. Comm., Norfolk/Chesapeake Bd. of Realtors; Norfolk C of C State Legislative Comm., 2 yrs.; Norfolk City Council, 1952-1956; Commnr., Hampton Rds. Sanitation Dist. Comm., 1956-1970; Chmn., 2 yrs., Sports and Recreation Comm., Norfolk C of C; Bd. of Dir., United Communities Fund, 1961-1972; Chmn., 2 yrs., Mayor's Citizens Advisory Comm. for Community Planning, City of Norfolk; Chmn., 2 yrs., Norfolk Bd. of Realtors, Civic Affairs Comm. Designated, 1958, Realtor of Yr., Norfolk RE Bd.; Designated, 1966, Small Bus. Man of VA by the SBA; Member, 1968, Small Bus. Advisory Council of VA; Pres., 1969-1970, VA Council on Alcoholism and Drug Dependence; Member, Chesapeake Hospital Authority, 2 yrs.; Pres., 1969, Norfolk Bd. of Realtors; VP, Region 6, 1970, VA Assn. of Realtors; Member, Tidewater Community Project Group on Alcoholism; Chmn., Gov's. Advisory Council on Alcoholism for State of VA, 1973 thru 1976; VChmn., 1977-1978, VA Advisory Council on Susbtance Abuse Problems; Chmn., 1977, Personnel Task Force Study of the City Council, City of Chesapeake; Designated, 1978, First Citizen, City of Chesapeake; Member, 1979, Charter Study Comm., City of Chesapeake; Past Pres., Chesapeake C of C; **HOME ADD:** 277 Kempsville Rd., Chesapeake, VA, (804)547-5224; **BUS ADD:** 1515 N. Military Hwy., Norfolk, VA 23502, (804)853-6797.

RIPSIN, John J., Jr.——**B:** Mar. 1, 1925, Minneapolis, MN, *Pres.*, Evergreen Real Estate & Investment Co., Evergreen Land Servs. Co.; **PRIM RE ACT:** Broker, Consultant, Engineer, Appraiser, Owner/Investor, Instructor, Property Manager, Syndicator; **OTHER RE ACT:** Land and right of way acquisition; **SERVICES:** Prop. acquisition, land right acquisition, surveying & drafting; **REP CLIENTS:** Northern Natural Gas Co., Northern States Power Co., MN Gas Co.; **PREV EMPLOY:** Northern States Power Co.; **PROFL AFFIL & HONORS:** Intl. Right of Way Assn., SR/WA-R/W Assn.; **EDUC:** RE, Univ. of FL, Univ. of MN; Courses Presented by Intl. Right of Way Assn.; **MIL SERV:** US Army; **HOME ADD:** 10607 107th Place N, Maple Grove, MN 55369, (612)425-8303; **BUS ADD:** 3300 Bass Lake Rd., Suite #100, Brooklyn Center, MN 55429, (612)566-1036.

RISING, Austin——**B:** Sept. 11, 1918, NY, NY, *VP*, Beech Aircraft Corp.; **PRIM RE ACT:** Owner/Investor; **SERVICES:** Mfg. plants; comml. offices; fixed base operations at airports; **PROFL AFFIL & HONORS:** Rho Epsilon; Bd. of Dir., Sales & Mktg. Exec. Intl.-NY, Beta Gamma Sigma; **EDUC:** BS, 1941, Bus., NY Univ.; **EDUC HONORS:** Beta Gamma Sigma; Alpha Kappi Psi; **MIL SERV:** USN, Lt./s.g.; **OTHER ACT & HONORS:** Wichita Area Planning Commn. (5 yrs.); Past member Bd. of Dir. Wichita C of C; **HOME ADD:** 1440 N. Gatewood 7, Wichita, KS 67206, (316)685-4447; **BUS ADD:** 9709 E. Central, Wichita, KS 67201, (316)681-7149.

RISING, John S., Jr.——**B:** Sept. 12, 1932, San Francisco, *Pres.*, Prof. Sponsoring Fund, Inc.; **PRIM RE ACT:** Lender; **SERVICES:** Loans for bus. and investment to Drs.; **REP CLIENTS:** Physicians, Dentists, & Vets.; **EDUC:** BA, 1954, Econ. & Hist., Stanford Univ.; **GRAD EDUC:** MBA, 1957, Mktg. & Fin., Stanford Univ.; **MIL SERV:** USN, Lt., Korean Service United Nations; **HOME ADD:** 665 Hilary Dr., Tiburon, CA 94920, (415)435-4651; **BUS ADD:** 500 Sutter St., San Francisco, CA 94102, (415)421-4010.

RISKAS, Harry J.——**B:** Mar. 27, 1920, Shelton, WI, *President, Chmn. of the Bd.*, Sanfo-Bay Corp.; **PRIM RE ACT:** Consultant, Developer, Builder, Owner/Investor; **SERVICES:** Bldg., planning, consulting;

REP CLIENTS: Walgreen's, Safeway, Crocker Bank, Montgomery Ward, Tandem Computers, Remington Rand Comml. Life Ins. Co., Fred Harvey's, Ramada Inns, Howard Johnson's; **PREV EMPLOY:** Self; **PROFL AFFIL & HONORS:** Bayside Racquet Club, Admiral's Ambassadors Young Presidents, Bd. of Dirs., Comml. Life Ins. Co., Bd. of Dir., Inland Western Finance; **EDUC:** BS, 1949, Engrg., DePaw Univ.; **MIL SERV:** USN Air Corp., Lt. Cmdr., South Pacific, 8 Theater Ribbons; **OTHER ACT & HONORS:** Young Presidents Club 1963; Boys and Girl Scouts of America - Advisor; **HOME ADD:** 2020 Fairmont, San Mateo, CA 94402, (415)574-5230; **BUS ADD:** 1103 Juanita Ave., Burlingame, CA 94010, (415)342-7761.

RISNER, Willie R.——B: Sept. 20, 1931, Iron City, TN, *Broker-Owner*, Orange Coast RE; **PRIM RE ACT:** Broker, Property Manager; **PREV EMPLOY:** Broker-Salesman, Sydney Schwartz, Realtor 20 yrs.; **EDUC:** Certificate, 1966, RE, Univ. of TN; **MIL SERV:** USAF, S/Sgt, Several; **HOME ADD:** 2995 Briarwood Lane, Titusville, FL 3278O, (305)267-5646; **BUS ADD:** 500 N. Washington Ave. Suite 1, Titusville, FL 32780, (305)268-0520.

RISSER, Robin F.——B: Oct. 7, 1950, Greensville, OH, *Pres.*, Real-Invest. Corp.; **PRIM RE ACT:** Syndicator; **SERVICES:** Acquisition, synd., mgmt., devel.; **REP CLIENTS:** Equity investors; **PREV EMPLOY:** Pres. Real-Invest Corp., Real-Invest. Equities, 1979-Pres.; **PROFL AFFIL & HONORS:** CPA; **EDUC:** BA, 1973, Bus., Mt. Union Coll.; **GRAD EDUC:** MBA, 1978, Univ. of MI; **HOME ADD:** 2641 Geddes, Ann Arbor, MI 48104, (313)995-8358; **BUS ADD:** 412 E. Huron, Ann Arbor, MI 48104, (313)996-5930.

RITCH, Sanford E.——B: Dec. 17, 1935, Gainesville, FL, *V.P., Gen. Mgr.*, Metroplex Inc.; **PRIM RE ACT:** Broker, Instructor, Consultant; **SERVICES:** Resid. consultation, mgmt., training; **REP CLIENTS:** R.E. brokers, consumers, indiv.; **PREV EMPLOY:** Sperry-Rand Corp. and General Electric Corp.; **PROFL AFFIL & HONORS:** CRB, NAR, FAR, Realtor of the Yr., Bd. Pres.; **EDUC:** 1958, Mgmt., Bus,Admin., Univ. of FL; **OTHER ACT & HONORS:** Dir. and Past Pres. of Alachua Cty. Boys Clubs and Gainesville Lions Club, Past Dir. of C of C; **HOME ADD:** 3325-3 Palmetto, Alachua, FL 32615, (904)462-2320; **BUS ADD:** 3911 Newberry Rd., Gainesville, FL 32607, (904)372-2526.

RITLEY, Roger D.——B: May 16, 1941, OH, *Pres.*, Charles M. Ritley Associates, Inc.; **PRIM RE ACT:** Consultant, Appraiser; **SERVICES:** Appraisals of indus., comml., and large scale resid. devels.; RE consulting in matters of acquisition, disposition, market analysis and feasibility; **REP CLIENTS:** Maj. corps., fin. insts., govt. agencies, etc.; **PROFL AFFIL & HONORS:** Amer. Soc. of Appraisers; Amer. RE and Urban Econ. Assn.; Urban Land Inst.; Intl. Council of Shopping Ctrs.; NAR, 1st Honorable Mention in Soc. of RE Appraisers Manuscript Competition, 1977; **EDUC:** BBA, 1963, Urban Land Econ., Univ. of Pittsburgh; **GRAD EDUC:** MS, 1966, RE Investment Analysis & Appraisal, Univ. of WI; **HOME ADD:** 3702 Rawnsdale Rd., Shaker Hts., OH 44122, (216)921-0653; **BUS ADD:** 24755 Highpoint Rd., Beachwood, OH 44122, (216)464-8686.

RITTELMANN, P. Richard——B: Dec. 27, 1938, Pittsburgh, PA, *VP*, Burt Hill Kosar Rittelmann Assoc.; **PRIM RE ACT:** Architect, Developer, Engineer; **OTHER RE ACT:** Energy Mgmt. Consultant; **SERVICES:** Arch., engr., energy mgmt. design, const. documents, feasibility studies, consulting; **REP CLIENTS:** Prudential Ins. Co.; Westinghouse Corp.; US Dept. of Energy, Mellon Bank; Pullman-Standard Co.; Armco Steel Corp.; Amer. Hardware Co.; Calgon, Inc.; **PROFL AFFIL & HONORS:** AIA, ASHRAE, ACEC, Intl. Solar Energy Soc.; **EDUC:** BArch, 1960, RPI; **EDUC HONORS:** USN Holloway Scholarship; Kahn Memorial Scholarship TAI Beta Pi - Engrg. Hon.; Scarab - Arch. Design Hon.; **MIL SERV:** USN, Lt.; **OTHER ACT & HONORS:** Commissioner, PA State Art Commn.; **BUS ADD:** 400 Morgan Ctr., Butler, PA 16001, (412)285-4761.

RITTER, James J.——B: Nov. 27, 1923, Santa Barbara, CA, *VP*, Imperial Group, Inc.; **PRIM RE ACT:** Broker, Banker, Developer, Syndicator; **EDUC:** BA, 1946, Econ., Occidental Coll.; **GRAD EDUC:** MBA, 1963, Fin., Univ. of CA; **MIL SERV:** N.S.A.; **OTHER ACT & HONORS:** Pres. Holbrook Palmer Park Found.; **HOME ADD:** 49 Patricia Dr., Atherton, CA 94025, (415)365-3142; **BUS ADD:** 201 California St., San Francisco, CA 94111, (415)788-8889.

RITZAU, George S.——B: Nov. 6, 1924, San Francisco, CA, *VP*, T & S Development, Inc., Operations, Leasing, Const., Prop. Mgmt.; **PRIM RE ACT:** Developer, Property Manager; **PREV EMPLOY:** VP, Interstate Shopping Center, Inc.; VP, Downey S & L, RE Div.; **PROFL AFFIL & HONORS:** Intl. Council of Shopping Centers; **EDUC:** BS, 1948, Standord Univ.; **MIL SERV:** US Army; S/Sgt.; 6 Battle Stars; **HOME ADD:** 3551 Larchwood Pl., Riverside, CA 92506, (714)686-1131; **BUS ADD:** 5225 Canyon Crest Dr., Bldg. 100, Suite 150, Riverside, CA 92507, (714)686-1424.

RIZZI, Joseph V.——B: Dec. 5, 1949, Berwyn, IL, *Exec. VP*, TBR Enterprises, Inc.; **PRIM RE ACT:** Attorney; **SERVICES:** Legal and fin. analysis; **PREV EMPLOY:** Mayer, Brown & Platt, Chicago, 1975; Clerk, US Dist. Ct. for the No. Dist. of IL, 1976-1977; **PROFL AFFIL & HONORS:** IL & Amer. Bar Assns.; Nat. Retail Merchant's Assn.; Lic. for practice: IL Supreme Ct., US Dist. Ct. of N. Dist.; IL, and US Supreme Ct.; US Court of Appeal, 7th Dist., Who's Who in Fin. and Indus.; **EDUC:** BS, 1971, Fin., DePaul Univ.; **GRAD EDUC:** MBA, 1973, Fin., Univ. of Chicago; JD, 1976, Law, Univ. of Notre Dame; **EDUC HONORS:** Summa Cum Laude; elected to Delta Epsilum Sigma Nat. Hon. Soc., Dean's List, Magna Cum Laude, Assoc. Editor of the Notre Dame Lawyer; **OTHER ACT & HONORS:** Downers Grove C of C; Numerous publications; Union Club of Chicago; Alpha Phi Delta - Frat.; **HOME ADD:** 6824 Meadowcrest Dr., Downers Grove, IL 60516, (312)964-5544; **BUS ADD:** 7323 Lemont Rd., Downers Grove, IL 60516, (312)960-3900.

ROACH, Thomas A.——B: May 1, 1929, Akron, OH, *Partner*, Donovan Hammond Ziegelman Roach & Sotiroff; **PRIM RE ACT:** Attorney; **SERVICES:** Legal counsel; **REP CLIENTS:** Contractors, owners, comml. landlords; **PROFL AFFIL & HONORS:** MI Bar Assn., Real Prop. Law Section; ABA, Engrg. Soc. of Detroit; **EDUC:** BA, 1951, Letters and Law, Univ. of MI; **GRAD EDUC:** JD, 1953, Univ. of MI Law School; **EDUC HONORS:** Order of the Coif, With Distinction; **MIL SERV:** USCGR (Ret.), Capt., Comdt. Commendation; **OTHER ACT & HONORS:** Regent - The Univ. of MI, 1975; Torch Club of Detroit; Econ. Club of Detroit; **HOME ADD:** 151 Textile Rd., Ann Arbor, MI 48104, (313)429-4504; **BUS ADD:** 400 Renaissance Ctr., Suite 1100, Detroit, MI 48243, (313)259-7900.

ROBB, Michael Stephen——B: Nov. 14, 1947, Zanesville, OH, *Dir., Field Realty Investing*, Pacific Mutual Life Ins. Co., Realty Investing; **PRIM RE ACT:** Lender, Owner/Investor; **SERVICES:** RE acquisition & mort. lending; **REP CLIENTS:** Owners, investors, devels. of comml. RE; **PREV EMPLOY:** Lincoln Nat. Life Ins. Co.; **PROFL AFFIL & HONORS:** Intl. Council of Shopping Ctrs.; NAIOP, CRA; **EDUC:** BS, 1969, Mktg./Fin., OH State Univ.; **MIL SERV:** Army, 1st Lt., Bronze Star; **HOME ADD:** 67 Austin, Irvine, CA 9274, (714)857-4054; **BUS ADD:** 700 Newport Center Dr., Newport Beach, CA 92660, (714)640-3904.

ROBBINS, C. LaVern——B: May 21, 1913, Battle Creek, MI, *Pres./Treas.*, Robbins Cos. (now in 63rd yr.); **PRIM RE ACT:** Broker, Consultant, Appraiser, Banker, Developer, Builder, Instructor; **SERVICES:** Gen. brokerage, all type appraising; **REP CLIENTS:** Maj. corps., acquisition agents; **PREV EMPLOY:** Pres., Battle Creek Bd. of Reatlors 1959; Rep., Mutual Life of NY; Sports Editor, Battle Creek Moon-Journal; taught at Univ. of MI for 23 yrs.; **PROFL AFFIL & HONORS:** MI/NAR; AIREA (Pres., Ch. 10 in 1971), MI Assn. of Realtors Pres. 1977, MAI (Amer. Instit. of RE Appraisers); GRI (MI Assn. of Realtors); RAM (Univ. of MI); **OTHER ACT & HONORS:** Lions Intl. (Dir. 1962-1964); Pres., Battle Creek Unlimited 1979-1980; Pres., Calhoun Cty. Econ. Devel. Corp. 1981; **HOME ADD:** 650 E. Minges Rd., Battle Creek, MI 49015, (616)962-0437; **BUS ADD:** 2515 Capital Ave. SW, Battle Creek, MI 49015, (616)962-5504.

ROBBINS, Donald——*VP & Secy.*, Hasbro Industries, Inc.; **PRIM RE ACT:** Property Manager; **BUS ADD:** 1027 Newport Ave., Pawtucket, RI 02861, (401)726-4100.*

ROBBINS, Donald K.——B: Sept. 21, 1928, Portland, OR, *D. O. Broker; Principal*, Realty Exchange; DPP Securities Corp.; **PRIM RE ACT:** Broker, Owner/Investor, Instructor, Syndicator, Real Estate Publisher; **OTHER RE ACT:** RE Securities; **SERVICES:** Investment counsel & marketing; **PREV EMPLOY:** Mgr., Fireside Realty: RE Sales, F. M. Tarbell Co.; **PROFL AFFIL & HONORS:** RESSI, Nat. Assn. of Securities Dealers, Intl. Assn. of Fin. Planners; **GRAD EDUC:** BSEE, 1950, US Naval Academy, Annapolis, MD; **MIL SERV:** USN, Lt. (JG) 1945-55; **OTHER ACT & HONORS:** City of Portland, OR Rosarian; Bd. of Govs., RESSI, Rgnl. VP; Pres., OR Chap. RESSI; **HOME ADD:** 12 Greenridge Court, Lake Oswego, OR 97034, (503)244-0471; **BUS ADD:** 9 Mt. Jefferson Terrace, Lake Oswego, OR 97034, (503)635-3501.

ROBBINS, John R.——B: Sept. 2, 1942, Hawthone, CA, *Partner*, Lincoln Property Co.; **PRIM RE ACT:** Developer, Owner/Investor, Instructor; **SERVICES:** Devel. office & commercial bldgs., lecturer; **REP CLIENTS:** RE Investment Class for Univ. of Denver; Guest speaker NAHB seminars & Devel. Shopping Ctrs., Office Bldgs. & Indus. Bldgs. for own account; **PREV EMPLOY:** Sales Mgr., Sales Consultant - Coldwell Banker Comml. Brokerage Co.; **PROFL AFFIL & HONORS:** Intl. Council of Shopping Ctrs., Lic. Broker, CA & CO; **EDUC:** BS, 1965, Indus. Mgmt., San Jose State Univ.; **GRAD EDUC:**

MBA, 1967, Mktg., San Jose State Univ.; **MIL SERV:** US Army, Sgt.; **OTHER ACT & HONORS:** Bd. of Dirs. Wilderness Exper. Program 1976-78; Listed Who's Who, CA 1981, CA Teaching Credential; **HOME ADD:** 2330 Ostrosky Dr., Alamo, CA 94507, (415)820-6038; **BUS ADD:** 558 Pilgrim Dr., Foster City, CA 94404, (415)574-7676.

ROBBINS, Richard M.——B: Nov. 22, 1922, Stockton, CA, *Owner*, Richard M. Robbins, MAI; **PRIM RE ACT:** Consultant, Appraiser; **SERVICES:** Counseling re-valuation, arbitration, acquisition and mktg. of urban investment, special purpose, and problem props.; **REP CLIENTS:** Banks, private investors, corporate RE depts., law firms, instnl. lenders, govt. agencies, etc.; **PREV EMPLOY:** Rgnl. Appraiser, Equitable Life Assurance Soc. of the US, 1955-1965; **PROFL AFFIL & HONORS:** Amer. Soc. of RE Counselors, AIREA, CRE, MAI; **EDUC:** BS, 1944, Civil Engrg., Univ. of CA at Berkeley; **MIL SERV:** USN, 1942-1947, Lt.; **OTHER ACT & HONORS:** Lambda Alpha, Intl. Land Econs. Frat.; TR. of Transamer. Realty Investors; **HOME ADD:** 162 Prospect Ave., Sausalito, CA 94965, (415)332-2853; **BUS ADD:** 235 Montgomery St., Suite 1260, San Francisco, CA 94104, (415)434-3430.

ROBBINS, Richard W.——B: Apr. 6, 1939, Quincy, MA, *VP of Operations*, Marquis Hotels and Resorts, The Mariner Group of Affiliated Cos.; **PRIM RE ACT:** Broker, Consultant, Appraiser, Developer, Builder, Owner/Investor, Property Manager; **OTHER RE ACT:** Hotel and Resort Devels. and Mgr.; **SERVICES:** Consulting, mgmt., brokerage; **REP CLIENTS:** Hotel and Resort Owners, Devels., Lenders, Investors, etc.; **PREV EMPLOY:** VP, The Sheraton Corp.; VP, Great Amer. Mgmt. Corp.; **PROFL AFFIL & HONORS:** Amer. Hotel & Motel Assn.; Natl. Restaurant Assn.; Natl. Bd. of Realtors, IREM; Soc. of Mort. Consultants; Natl. Assn. Mort. Brokers, CPM; CHA; SMC; **HOME ADD:** 15797 Symphony Ct., SW, Ft. Myers, FL 33908, (813)489-0410; **BUS ADD:** 2075 Periwinkle Way, Suite 10, Sanibel Isl., FL 33957, (813)472-4176.

ROBBINS, William J., Jr.——B: Apr. 23, 1930, Sacramento, CA, *Pres.*, Robbins Land Co.; **PRIM RE ACT:** Broker, Consultant, Developer, Property Manager; **OTHER RE ACT:** Mgmt. and Comml. Devel.; **SERVICES:** Investment Counseling, Asset Mgmt. & Comml. Devel.; **REP CLIENTS:** Inst. & Corp. Investors in Comml. Real Props.; **PREV EMPLOY:** Pres., Comml. Div., McKeon Const., San Francisco 1971-74; VP W. Mort. Corp., San Francisco 1964-71; **PROFL AFFIL & HONORS:** AIREA; Natl. Assn. of Indus. & Office Parks; RNMI; BOMA, MAI; **EDUC:** BS, 1953, Pol. Sci., Hist. & Philosophy, Univ. of San Francisco; **MIL SERV:** USMC, 1st. Lt.; **HOME ADD:** 2727 Lacy Ln., Sacramento, CA 95821, (916)482-2603; **BUS ADD:** 601 University Ave., Ste. 135, Sacramento, CA 95825, (916)929-5745.

ROBERDS, C. Alvin, Jr.——B: Apr. 29, 1943, Mobile, AL, *Pres.*, Southern Realty Management, Inc. & Southern Realty Development, Inc.; **PRIM RE ACT:** Broker, Developer, Owner/Investor, Property Manager; **SERVICES:** Income prop. brokerage, apt. mgmt. & devel.; **PREV EMPLOY:** Arthur Andersen & Co. CPA; **PROFL AFFIL & HONORS:** AICPA, GA Soc. of CPA's, Atlanta Apt. Owners & Mgrs. Assn., CPA; **EDUC:** BS, 1965, Bus. & Acctg., Auburn Univ.; **MIL SERV:** USAF, Capt., Air Force Commendation & Viet Nam Serv. Medals; **OTHER ACT & HONORS:** Ansley Golf Club; Intl. Trade Club, Mobile AL; Outstanding Young Men of Amer. 1975; Who's Who in the S. & SW; **HOME ADD:** 1673 Executive Park Ln. NE, Atlanta, GA 30329, (404)634-9364; **BUS ADD:** 1600 Tullie Cir. NE, Suite 146, Atlanta, GA 30329, (404)325-0233.

ROBERSON, J. Clyde——Roberson Devel. Co./Roberson Realty Co.; **PRIM RE ACT:** Broker, Developer, Builder, Insuror; **SERVICES:** Const. of sub-div., multi- family, single family dwellings, churches, nursing homes, apartment complexes; **PREV EMPLOY:** RE Broker/Const.; **EDUC:** 1964, La Salle Univ., Law School; **GRAD EDUC:** 1967, TN Tech. Univ.; **HOME ADD:** Rte. 9, Cookeville, TN 38501; **BUS ADD:** 280 S. Jefferson St., Cookeville, TN 38501, (615)528-6551.

ROBERT, John——*Pres.*, John Robert Associates; **PRIM RE ACT:** Broker, Developer, Owner/Investor, Property Manager, Syndicator; **OTHER RE ACT:** Estate Bldg.; **SERVICES:** Investment RE & Asset mgmt.; **REP CLIENTS:** Location, purchase & sale of props. or bus. props. with upside potential for indiv. or grp. investors for equity growth & cash flow. Managed upgrading of these investments; **PROFL AFFIL & HONORS:** NAR, RESSI, Chmn. 1979-1980 Investment Comm., San Francisco Bd. of Realtors; **OTHER ACT & HONORS:** Commonwealth Club, Citizens Housing Forum; **BUS ADD:** 1686 Union St., San Francisco, CA 94123, (415)885-6880.

ROBERTS, Clifford F.——B: June 2, 1939, Brooklyn, NY, *VP Fin.*, Synco, Inc.; **PRIM RE ACT:** Developer, Builder, Property Manager, Syndicator; **PREV EMPLOY:** Hound Ears Lodge & Club Inc., WHB Devel. Corp., Coopers & Lybrand; **PROFL AFFIL & HONORS:** AICPA, Nat. Assn. of Accountants, NC Assn. of CPA's; **EDUC:** 1967, Acctg., Drexel Univ.; **MIL SERV:** USN, PO 2nd Class; **HOME ADD:** 2501 Tanglewood Ln., Charlotte, NC 28211, (704)364-2907; **BUS ADD:** PO Box 34487, Charlotte, NC 28234, (704)376-9500.

ROBERTS, David A.——B: May 4,1953, Melrose Park, IL, *Asst. VP*, Col. Fin. Serv., Inc., Comml. Loan Div.; **PRIM RE ACT:** Lender; **SERVICES:** First and Second Mort. Loans, Standby Commitments, Gap Commitments; **PREV EMPLOY:** First Nat. Bank of Chicago, Chicago, IL; **PROFL AFFIL & HONORS:** MBA, Certified Review Appraiser; **EDUC:** BS, 1975, Fin., Univ. of IL, Champaign, IL; **GRAD EDUC:** MBA, 1979, Fin. & RE, DePaul Univ., Chicago, IL; **OTHER ACT & HONORS:** Big Brothers/Big Sisters of Birmingham, AL; **HOME ADD:** 1533 Cape Cod Cir., Alabaster, AL 35007, (205)663-6892; **BUS ADD:** 3125 Independence DR. P.O. Box 6100, Birmingham, AL 35259, (205)870-4400.

ROBERTS, David D., Jr.——B: Apr. 2, 1947, Mobile, AL, *VP*, Roberts Brothers, Inc., Mgmt. Div.; **PRIM RE ACT:** Broker, Consultant, Developer, Property Manager, Owner/Investor; **OTHER RE ACT:** Shopping Ctr. Devel.; **SERVICES:** Investment counseling, devel. of comm; prop. mgmt. residential and comml. sales brokerage; **REP CLIENTS:** Indiv. or instit. investors in comml. or residential prop.; **PREV EMPLOY:** US Army; **PROFL AFFIL & HONORS:** Alabama Realtors Bd. of Dir. 1975-1976, 1981-1982; NAR; AL Realtors Inst. 1972; Pres. of the Gulf Coast Chap. of the CPM, 1980, Holder of the CPM designation from IREM, 1076. GRI Designated from AL, 1973, ICSC; **EDUC:** BS, 1970, Mgmt., Auburn Univ.; **GRAD EDUC:** 1971, Prop. Mgmt.; **MIL SERV:** US Army; **OTHER ACT & HONORS:** J.A. Council, 1972-1976; Mobile United Fund, 1975; State Bd. for C.F. Foundation, 1974-1978; Mobile Lions Club; Mobile County Bd. of Realtors - various directorships; Sigma Chi Frat. Alumni Council; Knights of Revelry - Mardi Gras Soc.; Comm. Chmn. for the Amer. Jr. Miss Pagent, 1979; **HOME ADD:** 4412 Winding Way, Mobile, AL 36609, (205)661-2102; **BUS ADD:** P.O. Box 6217, Mobile, AL 36660, (205)344-9220.

ROBERTS, Donald H.——B: Feb. 21, 1921, Ridgway, PA, *Pres.*, Don Roberts Real Estate Inc.; Sun Belt Investment Corp.; **PRIM RE ACT:** Broker, Consultant, Developer, Lender, Owner/Investor, Property Manager, Syndicator; **OTHER RE ACT:** CPA, SMC, CCIM; **REP CLIENTS:** Foreign investors, including underwriters; **PREV EMPLOY:** Instructor at Wharton, CPA Arthur Andersen & Co., Exec. VP The Kanter Corp., Pres. Keystone S&L, Pres. Alemonia S&L; **PROFL AFFIL & HONORS:** FAR, NAR, FAMB, NAMB, AICPA, PICPA, IACPA, RESSI, RNMI, FLI, CPA; SMC (Sr. Mort. Consultant); FL Mort. Broker of the Year 1977; Pres. FL Assn. of Mort. Brokers, 1981; CCIM; **EDUC:** BS, 1942, Bus. Admin., Univ. of Pittsburgh; **GRAD EDUC:** MBA (ex thesis), 1947, Acctg., Wharton School; **MIL SERV:** USNR, Lt. (jg); **OTHER ACT & HONORS:** Royal Palm Yacht Club, Founding CDR. Lee Co. MOWW, Lee Co. Comm. of 100; **HOME ADD:** 2324 Kent Ave., Ft. Myers, FL 33907, (813)939-1255; **BUS ADD:** 1620 Medical Ln., Ft. Myers, FL 33907, (813)936-3000.

ROBERTS, Douglas M.——B: June 25, 1947, Atlanta, GA, *Sales Mgr.*, McLester & Grisham; **PRIM RE ACT:** Broker; **PROFL AFFIL & HONORS:** NAR, TAR, ABOR, WCBOR, RESSI, 1 million sales from NHBA; **EDUC:** BBA, 1974, Fin., RE/Ins., Southwest TX State Univ.; **MIL SERV:** USN 1966-1970, E-5, Vietnam service; **OTHER ACT & HONORS:** Rotary, C of C; **HOME ADD:** 1005 Huntridge, Austin, TX 78758, (512)837-3295; **BUS ADD:** 905 NIH 35, Suite 101, Round Rock, TX 78664, (512)255-2561.

ROBERTS, Everett A.——B: Feb. 19, 1934, Ranger, TX, *Pres.*, IDI, Inc.; **PRIM RE ACT:** Broker, Consultant, Engineer, Developer, Builder, Owner/Investor, Property Manager, Insuror, Syndicator; **SERVICES:** Devel. & synd. of comml. props., investment counseling, prop. mgmt., construction mgmt.; **REP CLIENTS:** Comml. & indus. cos., instnl. lenders; **PROFL AFFIL & HONORS:** TSPE, NSPE, HIREB, Registered Profl. Engineer; **EDUC:** BSME, BBA, 1956-1968, Mechanical Engr., Acctg., Univ. of TX at Austin, Baylor Univ.; **GRAD EDUC:** MBA, 1963, TCU; **EDUC HONORS:** Beta Gamma Sigma, Beta Alpha Psi, Omega Delta Epsilon; **HOME ADD:** 4804 Boulder Run, Fort Worth, TX 76109, (817)731-2687; **BUS ADD:** 500 W. Thirteenth St., Fort Worth, TX 76102, (817)335-4500.

ROBERTS, Furman B.——B: Feb. 11, 1929, Safford, AZ, *City Atty.*, City of Orange; **PRIM RE ACT:** Attorney; **SERVICES:** Atty. for City of Orange, CA; **REP CLIENTS:** City of Orange, CA; **PREV EMPLOY:** Deputy Dist. Atty., Bakersfield (Kern Cty.); Deputy City Atty. City of Anaheim, CA; **PROFL AFFIL & HONORS:** ABA, CA

Bar, Orange Cty. Bar Assn.; **EDUC:** AB, 1951, Econ., Pre-Legal, Univ. of CA at Berkeley; **GRAD EDUC:** JD, 1954, Law, Univ. of CA at Berkeley; **EDUC HONORS:** Phi Beta Kappa; **MIL SERV:** USA, Sgt.; **OTHER ACT & HONORS:** Kiwanis Club, Boy Scouts; **HOME ADD:** 2504 E Paladin Ave., Anaheim, CA 92806, (714)772-6006; **BUS ADD:** 300 E Chapman Ave., Orange, CA 92666, (714)532-0351.

ROBERTS, Gary L.——B: Oct. 9, 1943, Riverside, CA, *Pres.*, Property Counselors, Inc.; **PRIM RE ACT:** Consultant, Appraiser; **SERVICES:** Valuation, evaluation, investment counseling, purchase/sale negotiations; **REP CLIENTS:** Instnl. investors, govt. agencies, public corps., devels., lenders and owners; **PREV EMPLOY:** First State Bank of OR 1975-78; Multnomah Cty. Assessor's Office 1973-75; **PROFL AFFIL & HONORS:** AIREA, Soc. of RE Appraisers, MAI, SRPA (Young Advisory Council 1979-80); **EDUC:** BS, 1965, Social Studies, OR State Univ.; **MIL SERV:** USN, Comdr., Air Medal; **HOME ADD:** 1108 S.W. Westwood Dr., Portland, OR 97204, (503)244-6913; **BUS ADD:** Suite 100, 220 S.W. Morrison, Portland, OR 97204, (503)227-0553.

ROBERTS, James Vincent——B: Sept. 17, 1950, Navasota, TX, *Atty.*, Solo; **PRIM RE ACT:** Broker, Attorney, Owner/Investor; **SERVICES:** Rep. before FMNA, FHA, VA, Comml. & Resid. Devel., Exchanges & Sales.; **REP CLIENTS:** Indiv. and inst. investors and devel. in resid. and comml. props.; **PROFL AFFIL & HONORS:** State Bar Sections on RE, Probate and Trust Law and Corp. Banking and Bus. Law, and Dallas Bar Assn. Sections on RE, taxation and probate; **EDUC:** BA, 1972, Math., Univ. of Tx of Austin; **GRAD EDUC:** JD, 1975, Univ. of TX School of Law, Austin, Tx; **EDUC HONORS:** Top 3% of coll. grad. degrees.; **OTHER ACT & HONORS:** Author "Changes in the Tax Treatment of Installment Sales", TX Bar Journal, 1981; **HOME ADD:** 419 Valencia, Dallas, TX 75223, (214)827-6374; **BUS ADD:** 2122 Southland Tower, 400 No. Olive, Dallas, TX 75201, (214)651-0421.

ROBERTS, James W.——B: Mar. 14, 1940, Cleveland, OH, *VP*, Dain Bosworth, Inc., Fixed Income; **PRIM RE ACT:** Lender, Owner/Investor; **SERVICES:** Improvement District Fin., Indus. Revenue Bonds, Mort. & Equity investments; **PREV EMPLOY:** Ex VP & Tr. Central Mort. & Realty Trust; **EDUC:** BUS, 1962, Miami Univ.; **GRAD EDUC:** MBA, 1964, IN Univ.; **HOME ADD:** 516 Timberland Dr., Burnsville, MN 55337, (612)890-6374; **BUS ADD:** 100 Dain Tower, Minneapolis, MN 55402, (612)371-2785.

ROBERTS, Jay——*Asst. Secy. & Treas.*, Ti-Caro Inc.; **PRIM RE ACT:** Property Manager; **BUS ADD:** PO Box 699, Gastonia, NC 28052, (704)867-7271.*

ROBERTS, John B.——B: May 2, 1929, Winchester, MA, *Pres.*, Bayfield Management Associates/Meredith Marina Inc.; **PRIM RE ACT:** Appraiser, Owner/Investor, Property Manager, Syndicator; **SERVICES:** Mgmt. Appraiser; **PREV EMPLOY:** Exec. Mgr., Niles Co., Inc.; **PROFL AFFIL & HONORS:** CPMC, CPMC, Realtor; **EDUC:** AB, 1952, Classics, Brown Univ.; **HOME ADD:** Bay Shore Dr., Meredith, NH 03253, (603)279-8852; **BUS ADD:** 114 Bay Rd., Manchester, NH 03253, (603)669-5554.

ROBERTS, John Perry——B: Apr. 22, 1944, Bartlesville, OK, *Attorney*, Kornfeld McMillin Phillips & Upp; **PRIM RE ACT:** Attorney; **SERVICES:** RE transactions; **REP CLIENTS:** Liberty Mort. Co., Penn Square Bank, N.A.; Sterling Property Investors; **PREV EMPLOY:** Liberty Nat'l Bank and Trust Co.; **PROFL AFFIL & HONORS:** Chmn. of OK Bar Assn. Banking Law Sect., ABA (Info. Member of RE Fin. Comm.), Adjunct Prof., Oklahoma City Univ. School of Law; Author "The Bankers Right of Set-Off;" Selected Problems 52 OK Bar Assn. Journal 723 (1981); **EDUC:** BA, 1966, Econ., Acctg., Univ. of OK; **GRAD EDUC:** JD, 1969, Law, Univ. of OK School of Law; **MIL SERV:** USA Reserves, Honorable Discharge, 1970-1976; **OTHER ACT & HONORS:** Oklahoma City C of C; **HOME ADD:** 3401 Cameron Dr., Oklahoma City, OK 73112, (405)947-4039; **BUS ADD:** 3037 N.W. 63rd, Suite 200 W., Oklahoma City, OK 73112, (405)840-9302.

ROBERTS, Nelson R.——B: Aug. 24, 1922, Cherokee, IA, *Pres.*, The Roberts Agency; **PRIM RE ACT:** Broker, Appraiser, Developer, Property Manager; **SERVICES:** Comml. & Resid. RE Broker, Appraiser, Devel., Counselor; **PROFL AFFIL & HONORS:** NAR; MN Assn. of Realtors; MN Multi-Housing Assn.; Past Pres., Brainerd Bd. of Realtors in 1960 and 1970; Dir., MN Assn. of Realtors; **EDUC:** 1942, Gates Coll.; **MIL SERV:** USN, Lt.j.g., Pilot; **OTHER ACT & HONORS:** Kiwanis Club, Past Pres.; Cmn. Bldg. Comm. Brainerd C of C; **HOME ADD:** 1819 S 7th St., Brainerd, MN 56401, (218)829-9075; **BUS ADD:** W Washington St., POB 404, Brainerd, MN 56401, (218)829-3513.

ROBERTS, Richard A.——B: Sept. 10, 1953, White Plains, NY, *Pres.*, Gee-Cee Realty, Inc.; **PRIM RE ACT:** Consultant, Property Manager, Owner/Investor, Syndicator; **SERVICES:** Synd. of Resid. Prop., Prop. Mgmt.; **REP CLIENTS:** Indiv. Investors; **PROFL AFFIL & HONORS:** Apt. Owners Advisory Council of Suburban NY, Urban Bankers Coalition; **EDUC:** BS, 1975, Acctg., Amer. Intl. Coll.; **GRAD EDUC:** MBA, 1979, Acctg., Iona Coll.; JD, 1984, RE Law, Brooklyn Law School; **HOME ADD:** 1 Hillside Terrace, White Plains, NY 10601; **BUS ADD:** P.O. Box 803, Main Station, White Plains, NY 10602, (914)946-2154.

ROBERTS, Robert B., Jr.——B: Sept. 13, 1950, St. Petersburg, *Pres.*, The R. B. Roberts Company; **PRIM RE ACT:** Syndicator, Consultant, Developer, Property Manager, Owner/Investor; **OTHER RE ACT:** Financial Planning; **PREV EMPLOY:** 2 yrs. Regional Leasing Dir., Amterre Mgmt., Inc., responsible over 17 shopping ctrs.; 1 yr. devel. and synd. small strip shopping ctrs., Berger-Samuels, Inc.; **PROFL AFFIL & HONORS:** Nat. Bd. of Realtors, RESSI, FL CCIM Chap. 9; **EDUC:** AA, 1973, Bus., St. Petersburg Jr. Coll.; **MIL SERV:** USN; **HOME ADD:** 6201 Bahama Shores Dr. S, St. Petersburg, FL 33705, (813)867-1567; **BUS ADD:** 405 Central Ave., 6th Floor, St. Petersburg, FL 33701, (813)823-0701.

ROBERTS, Thomas L.——B: Dec. 14, 1931, Asheville, NC, *Realtor/Appraiser*, Princeton Financial, Inc.; **PRIM RE ACT:** Appraiser; **SERVICES:** RE Appraisal; **REP CLIENTS:** Real Prop. Devels. and builders, public utilities and local, state and fed. agencies, attys., in prebuilder land and comml.-indus. props.; **PREV EMPLOY:** CA State Div. of Hwys, 1956-69; **PROFL AFFIL & HONORS:** AIREA; ASA; NARA; IR/WA; NAHB, MAI; ASA; Sr., IR/WA; Author of sev. articles, instrc. in RE Appraisal; **EDUC:** 1953, Public Admin., San Diego State Univ.; **EDUC HONORS:** With distinction in P.A.; **MIL SERV:** USMC-Res., Lt. Col.; **BUS ADD:** 3094 North Park Way, San Diego, CA 92104, (714)296-3103.

ROBERTS, William L.——B: Jan. 20, 1924, Boston, MA, *Pres.*, Burchett & Roberts Appraisers; **PRIM RE ACT:** Broker, Instructor, Consultant, Appraiser, Property Manager, Engineer, Owner/Investor; **OTHER RE ACT:** Data Processing; **SERVICES:** Appraisals, REDP Consulting, Lectures and Instructions; **PREV EMPLOY:** Pres. RCA, TRW, Sperry Rand - Mktg. Dir., Engrg. Mgr., Sales Rep., Merrill Lynch Realty; **PROFL AFFIL & HONORS:** Amer. Mgmt. Assoc.; AFCEA; SREA; NAR; TX Assoc. of Realtors; NARA, GRI, CRS, CRB, SRA, CRA, SVC; **EDUC:** Elec. Engrg., Northeastern Univ.; Bus. Admin., Rutgers Univ.; **GRAD EDUC:** LLB, Blackstone School of Law; **OTHER ACT & HONORS:** Who's Who in Fin. and Indus.; Intl. Men of Achievement; **HOME ADD:** 3021 Princeton Dr., Plano, TX 75075, (214)596-1386; **BUS ADD:** 1007 20th St., Plano, TX 75074, (214)423-7633.

ROBERTS, William Lee——B: May 5, 1947, Boston, MA, *Assoc.*, John McMahan Assoc. Inc.; **PRIM RE ACT:** Consultant, Developer, Owner/Investor, Property Manager; **SERVICES:** Fin. adv. devel. servs., acquisition and portfolio mgmt. for inst. and indiv. investors; **REP CLIENTS:** Maj. domestic & foreign inst., pension funds, and indivs.; **PREV EMPLOY:** Boston Redev. Auth., Gr. Portland (ME) Landmarks, Inc.; **PROFL AFFIL & HONORS:** APA, AICP, CSI, AICP; **EDUC:** BSAD, 1969, Arch. & Urban Planning, MIT; **GRAD EDUC:** MCP, 1972, City Planning, MIT; MBA, 1978, Harvard Bus. Sch.; **OTHER ACT & HONORS:** VP MIT Club of N CA Former a contributing ed. of RE Investing Letter (1977); **HOME ADD:** 1217 Waller St., San Francisco, CA 94117, (415)621-1526; **BUS ADD:** 201 California St., San Francisco, CA 94111, (415)433-7770.

ROBERTS, William S.——B: Feb. 1, 1930, Portland, OR, *Asst. VP*, Rainier National Bank, Income Prop. Lending; **PRIM RE ACT:** Banker, Lender; **SERVICES:** Openend constr. loans, participations, etc.; **REP CLIENTS:** Various indivs., partnerships, corps.; **PREV EMPLOY:** 27 years with Rainier Nat. Bank; **PROFL AFFIL & HONORS:** AIREA, MAI; **EDUC:** BA in Bus./Econ., 1954, Gen. Bus., WA State Univ.; **OTHER ACT & HONORS:** Dir., Chap. 8 AIREA - 1980, 1981, 1982; **HOME ADD:** 6805 83rd Ave. SE, Mercer Island, WA 98040, (206)232-3093; **BUS ADD:** PO Box 3966, Seattle, WA 98124, (206)621-5173.

ROBERTSON, Billy Perkins——B: July 23, 1915, Bangs, TX, *Owner*, Robertson Properties; **PRIM RE ACT:** Broker, Engineer, Appraiser; **OTHER RE ACT:** Analyst; **SERVICES:** Brokerage/Consulting; **REP CLIENTS:** Dennis-San Jacinto Corp.; Serv. Parts Investment Co.; Serv. Parts Warehouse, Inc.; **PROFL AFFIL & HONORS:** ASME, PE, NAR, TAR, FLI of NAR, (Houston Engrg. and Sci. Soc.), C of C, TFRA, TLMLS, IBA, ASME Council Certificate, ASME Commendation, HESS Meritorious; **EDUC:** BS, 1942, Mech. Engr., Univ. of TX; **GRAD EDUC:** Inst. for Mgmt. Certificate, 1964, Northwestern Univ.;Univ. of Pittsburgh; TX Realtors Inst. GRI;

EDUC HONORS: Pi Tau Sigma Honorary ME Frat.; **OTHER ACT & HONORS:** Bd. Member, Brazos Presbyterian Homes; Pres. and Dir. of HESS; Elder, Presbyterian Church; ASME Rgn. VIII Sections Comm.; **HOME ADD:** 606 West Thirteenth, Weslaco, TX 78596, (512)968-3747; **BUS ADD:** 606 West Thirteenth,, PO Box 537, Weslaco, TX 78596, (512)968-3433.

ROBERTSON, Gerald Decatur——B: Mar. 6, 1943, Newport News, VA, *Atty. at Law*, Gerald D. Robertson, Atty.; **PRIM RE ACT:** Attorney; **SERVICES:** Gen. practice of law with emphasis on RE; **EDUC:** BA, 1966, Poli. Sci., Hampden-Sydney Coll.; **GRAD EDUC:** JD, 1969, School of Law of Coll. of William & Mary; **HOME ADD:** 201 Mill Point Dr., Hampton, VA 23669, (804)722-3880; **BUS ADD:** 8 San Jose Dr., Newport News, VA 23606, (804)599-3993.

ROBERTSON, Joseph C.——B: Nov. 6, 1947, Marietta, OH, *Dir. of Acquisitions*, American Property and Mortgage; **PRIM RE ACT:** Owner/Investor; **OTHER RE ACT:** Acquisitions and Financing; **SERVICES:** RE Purchases - Sale/Leaseback and Mort. Brokerage; **PREV EMPLOY:** Past Asst. VP and Comml. Loan Officer for Mellon Nat. Mort. Co. of OH; Assoc. of Donald G. Culp Co. (Comml-Indus. Realtors-Columbus, OH); **PROFL AFFIL & HONORS:** NAR, Columbus, OH Chap.; Assoc. of Realtors; Columbus Comml. Indus. and Investment Realtors; **EDUC:** BS Bus. Admin., 1971, Fin. Mgmt. and Econ., Ashland Coll., OH; **EDUC HONORS:** Grad. with Dean's List Distinction; **OTHER ACT & HONORS:** Johnstown Village Council, 1977-1981, Pres. of Council; **HOME ADD:** 15A Westview Dr., Johnstown, OH 43031, (614)967-4461; **BUS ADD:** 500 W. Wilson Bridge Rd., Suite 200, Worthington, OH 43085, (614)436-4957.

ROBERTSON, Scott Jeffrey——B: Oct. 22, 1946, Waukesha, WI, *Pres.*, Kensington Group, Inc.; **PRIM RE ACT:** Consultant, Developer, Owner/Investor, Property Manager, Syndicator; **SERVICES:** Structure joint venture RE projects; **REP CLIENTS:** Self; **PREV EMPLOY:** Coughlin & Co. Inc., investment bankers, VP, Mgr. Mcpl. Underwriting Dept.; **PROFL AFFIL & HONORS:** CO Home Builders Assn.; Nat. Home Builders Assn.; Denver C of C; **EDUC:** BBS, 1968, Mktg., Univ. of CO; **OTHER ACT & HONORS:** Arvada Urban Renewal Authority (1st year of 5 year term); Seventies Pres., Church of Jesus Christ of Latter-Day Saints (Mormons); **HOME ADD:** 8295 Everett Way, Arvada, CO 80005, (303)424-7532; **BUS ADD:** 628 Sherman St., Denver, CO 80203, (303)830-1221.

ROBERTSON, Thomas V.——B: Sept. 15, 1932, Boston, MA, *Sales Mgr.*, Action RE; **PRIM RE ACT:** Broker, Property Manager; **OTHER RE ACT:** Selling Sales Mgr.; **SERVICES:** Homes for Living Referral Network, Guaranteed Sales Plan; **PREV EMPLOY:** Retired, USAF; **PROFL AFFIL & HONORS:** GRI, CRS, CRB; **EDUC:** BA, Bus. Admin., Univ. of MD; **EDUC HONORS:** W/high hon.; **MIL SERV:** USAF, Meritorious Service; **OTHER ACT & HONORS:** Kiwanis, Toastmasters, D.A.V.; **HOME ADD:** 114 Bellevue Blvd. North, Bellevue, NE 68005, (402)733-7444; **BUS ADD:** 1313 Harlan Dr., Bellevue, NE 68005, (402)291-3444.

ROBERTSON, William A.——B: Nov. 2, 1938, Long Beach, CA, *VP & Treas.*, Capitol Industries-EMI, Inc.; **PRIM RE ACT:** Property Manager, Owner/Investor, Insuror; **SERVICES:** Corporate RE, Internally and Landlord; **EDUC:** Bus./Fin., Long Beach State Coll.; **MIL SERV:** US Naval Reserves, YN2, 1958-1960; **HOME ADD:** 3097 Seahorse Ave., Ventura, CA 93001; **BUS ADD:** 1750 N. Vine St., Hollywood, CA 90028, (213)462-6252.

ROBIDEAUX, Robert W.——B: Apr. 8, 1943, *Treas.*, Kiemle & Hagood Co.; **PRIM RE ACT:** Broker; **SERVICES:** Sale, Devel., Mgmt., Consultation, Appraisal; **REP CLIENTS:** Fin. Instns., pvt. investors; **PROFL AFFIL & HONORS:** Bd. of Realtors, Bldg. Owners and Mgrs., Inst. of RE Mgrs., Spokane Community Coll. Advisory Bd. on RE Educ., CPM, RPA, Past Pres. of Inland Empire IREM, CCIM Candidate; **OTHER ACT & HONORS:** Past Pres. of the Inland Empire YMCA, Tr. Holy Family Hospital, Numerous other directorships and Pres. of community orgs.; **HOME ADD:** S. 5416 Morrill, Spokane, WA 99203, (509)448-8485; **BUS ADD:** 315 Washington Mutual Bldg., W. 601 Main Ave., Spokane, WA 99201, (509)838-6541.

ROBIN, Dean——B: Dec. 21, 1941, Brooklyn, NY, *Pres.*, OTC-Hawaii, Ltd., Revenue Advisors Real Estate, Ltd.; **PRIM RE ACT:** Broker, Consultant, Lender, Owner/Investor, Instructor, Syndicator; **SERVICES:** Investment advice and financing; **REP CLIENTS:** Grubb & Ellis; Oahu Corp.; Sunshine Jewelry of HI; Multi-Dimensional Industries; Laser Co. of HI; Terra Trade Grp.; Jerodin Electronics; **PREV EMPLOY:** Grubb & Ellis Comml. Brokerage; Oahu Corp.; Hugh Menefee Inc. (R); Hasegawa Kumenten, Ltd.; **PROFL AFFIL & HONORS:** NAR; Honolulu Bd. of Realtors; Hawaiian Bd. of Realtors; Account Exec., NASD, Diplomat of Intl. Assn. of Foreign Investors; **EDUC:** BA, 1964, Comml./Indus. Environments, Brooklyn Coll., CUNY; **GRAD EDUC:** MBA, 1966, Econ., Univ. of Edinburgh; **EDUC HONORS:** Debate Team; Pres., Law Club; Publisher, "Justice" Magazine, Cum Laude; **OTHER ACT & HONORS:** Republican Party; Advisor, Aloha Investment Club; Consultant, Nippon Kanaka Plutocratic Synd.; Account Exec., NASD; **HOME ADD:** 1535 Kupau St., Kailua, Oahu 96734, (808)262-0622; **BUS ADD:** 745 Fort St. Mall, Rm. 204, Honolulu, HI 96813, (808)526-2211.

ROBINETTE, William A.——B: Aug. 21, 1926, Pittsburgh, PA, *Pres.*, Foster International Development, Inc.; **PRIM RE ACT:** Developer, Owner/Investor, Property Manager; **SERVICES:** Suburban office complexes, Pittsburgh & Atlanta, Acquire commerical properties for European investors; **REP CLIENTS:** Xerox, L.B. Foster Co., Conrail, Mellon Bank, Transamerica Ins., Dun & Bradstreet, Incom Intl. Inc.; **PREV EMPLOY:** VP, L.B. Foster Co.; **PROFL AFFIL & HONORS:** Pittsburgh Bd. of Realtors; NARA; AMA; Nat. Assn. of Corp. RE Execs.; Nat. Assn. of Review Appraisers; **EDUC:** BS, 1951, Bus. Admin., Univ. of Pittsburgh; **GRAD EDUC:** MS, 1952, Econ., Univ. of Pittsburgh; **MIL SERV:** USN, RDM 1/C, Various; **OTHER ACT & HONORS:** Judge of Elections, Frankling Park, PA, 1958-1960; Atlanta Athletic Club; **HOME ADD:** 2909 Spalding Dr., Atlanta, GA 30338, (404)394-5575; **BUS ADD:** 415 Holiday Dr., Pittsburgh, PA 15220, (412)928-8904.

ROBINS, Roy S.——B: Apr. 23, 1938, Los Angeles, CA, *Pres.*, Rovi Pacific Corp.; **PRIM RE ACT:** Developer, Owner/Investor; **PREV EMPLOY:** VP, Bixby Ranch Co., Los Angeles/Long Beach, CA; **PROFL AFFIL & HONORS:** Member: Bd. of Dir. Several Companies; **EDUC:** BA, 1960, Econ./Mathematics, Stanford Univ.; **GRAD EDUC:** MBA, 1962, Fin./Mktg., Univ. of So. CA; **HOME ADD:** 10790 Wilshire Blvd, Los Angeles, CA 90024; **BUS ADD:** 1801 Century Park East, Suite 1111, Los Angeles, CA 90067, (213)553-8208.

ROBINSON, Charles G.——B: Dec. 29, 1929, St. Louis, MO, *Pres.*, CC Enterprises, Devel.; **PRIM RE ACT:** Lender, Builder, Owner/Investor, Instructor; **SERVICES:** Gen. purchaser & seller - lender; **PREV EMPLOY:** Family bus. 5 generations; **MIL SERV:** USAF, S/Sgt., HD; **BUS ADD:** 2049 Key West Dr., Arnold, MO 63010, (314)296-5311.

ROBINSON, Daniel T.——B: June 17, 1925, Los Angeles, CA, *Dir. of Bus. Devel.*, Merrill Lynch; **PRIM RE ACT:** Broker, Consultant, Developer, Builder, Owner/Investor, Syndicator; **SERVICES:** Investment counseling, synd.; **REP CLIENTS:** Large instnl. clients; **PREV EMPLOY:** Biom BRK Inc., self emp. broker; **EDUC:** BS-MBA, 1948, Chem., Univ. of S. CA; **GRAD EDUC:** MBA, 1950, Bus., Univ. of S. CA; **EDUC HONORS:** Deans List, Alumnus of Yr., Pharm. Bd.; **MIL SERV:** US Army; S/Sgt.; Purple Heart; **OTHER ACT & HONORS:** Bd. of Councillors-Univ. of S. CA; Bd. of Dir. School of Gerontology; Bd. Dir. Cardinal & Gold; Bd. of Trojan Club; **HOME ADD:** 6336 Vista Del Mar, Playa Del Rey, CA 90291, (213)821-1076; **BUS ADD:** 640 S Olive St., Los Angeles, CA 90014, (213)623-8400.

ROBINSON, Edward A.——B: Feb. 10, 1949, New York, *Pres.*, Edward A. Robinson Accountancy Corporation; **OTHER RE ACT:** CPA; **SERVICES:** Investment counseling; **REP CLIENTS:** Indivs., corps., partnerships; estates and trusts; **PREV EMPLOY:** Main Hurdman 1973-1977; **PROFL AFFIL & HONORS:** AICPA; CA Soc. of CPA's, Estate Planning Council, BS; MBA; CPA; **EDUC:** 1973, Acctg., St. Peter's Coll.; **GRAD EDUC:** Golden, 1979, Taxation, Golden Gate Univ.; **HOME ADD:** 4831 Rose Way, Union City, CA 94587, (415)489-0705; **BUS ADD:** 36604 Newark Blvd., Newark, CA 94560, (415)797-1787.

ROBINSON, Edward N.——B: Nov. 22, 1945, Savannah, GA, *Co-owner*, Robinson, Ross & Gallagher; **OTHER RE ACT:** RE Fin.; **SERVICES:** We arrange debt and equity fin. for maj. RE projects throughout the US; **PREV EMPLOY:** Atty., Tuttle & Taylor, L.A.; Law Clerk, The Hon. Warren Ferguson, US District Ct., Central District of CA; **PROFL AFFIL & HONORS:** Member, ULI; Occasional Lecturer on RE, Univ. of So. CA and Univ. of CA, **EDUC:** BA, 1967, Hist., Univ. of MI; **GRAD EDUC:** JD, 1974, Law, New York Univ.; **EDUC HONORS:** Honors Coll., Student Body Pres., Law Review, Order of the Coif; **HOME ADD:** 234 S. Kingsley Dr., Los Angeles, CA 90004, (213)382-4137; **BUS ADD:** 2049 Century Park East, Suite 1200, Los Angeles, CA 90067, (213)557-2311.

ROBINSON, Frank A.——B: July 14, 1945, Plainfield, NJ, *Dir., Corporate RE*, Computervision Corp.; **OTHER RE ACT:** Corporate RE; **SERVICES:** Various corporate RE activities; **REP CLIENTS:** Computervision Corp.; **PREV EMPLOY:** RE Mgr., Data Gen. Corp.; **PROFL AFFIL & HONORS:** Active member, Nat. Assn. of Corp. RE Execs., Indus. Devel. Research Council, SIR; **EDUC:** BA, 1967, Bus.

admin., Roanoke Coll., Salem, VA; **HOME ADD:** Bayberry Dr., Amherst, NH 03031, (603)673-3862; **BUS ADD:** Crosby Dr. Bldg. 14, Bedford, MA 01730, (617)275-1800.

ROBINSON, Gerald J.——**B:** Dec. 1, 1931, Baltimore, MD, *Atty.*, Carb, Luria, Glassner, Cook & Kufeld; **PRIM RE ACT:** Attorney; **SERVICES:** Legal and tax; **PROFL AFFIL & HONORS:** NY Bar Assn.; **EDUC:** BA, 1954, Amer. Studies, Cornell Univ.; **GRAD EDUC:** LLB, LLM, 1956, Tax Law, MD, NY Univ.; **EDUC HONORS:** Law Review; **MIL SERV:** US Army, SP-5; **OTHER ACT & HONORS:** Author: "Federal Income Taxation of Real Estate" (Book - WG&L), "Real Estate Tax Ideas" (Newsletter - WG&L); **HOME ADD:** Dogwood Ct., Stamford, CT 06903, (203)322-2138; **BUS ADD:** 529 5th Ave., NY, NY 10017, (212)986-3131.

ROBINSON, James——*Asst. Secy.*, Eastman Kodak Co.; **PRIM RE ACT:** Property Manager; **BUS ADD:** 343 State St., Rochester, NY 14650, (716)458-1000.*

ROBINSON, John T.——*Exec. Secy.*, Massachusetts, MA Real Estate Commission; **PRIM RE ACT:** Property Manager; **BUS ADD:** State House, Beacon St., Boston, MA 02133, (617)727-2121.*

ROBINSON, Lydia W.——**B:** Oct. 9, 1951, Detroit, MI, *RE Officer*, Continental Bank, Comml. Const.; **PRIM RE ACT:** Banker; **OTHER RE ACT:** RE Fin.; **SERVICES:** Devel. fin. for office and hotel props.; **REP CLIENTS:** Major devel. of comml. props.; **EDUC:** BA, 1973, Arch. Hist., Radcliffe Coll., Harvard Univ.; **GRAD EDUC:** Master in City & Rgnl. Plng., 1979, RE, Harvard Grad. School of Design; **EDUC HONORS:** Magna Cum Laude; **HOME ADD:** 1935 N. Bissell St., Chicago, IL 60614, (312)929-1029; **BUS ADD:** 231 S LaSalle St., Chicago, IL 60693, (312)828-5175.

ROBINSON, Michael G.——**B:** June 25, 1953, St. Louis, MO, *VP*, Colonial Savings Association, Comml.; **PRIM RE ACT:** Lender; **SERVICES:** Loans, income props.; **PREV EMPLOY:** Gulf Coast Investment Corp.; **PROFL AFFIL & HONORS:** Young Mort. Bankers; MBAA; **EDUC:** BBA, 1976, Fin., Univ. of TX; **EDUC HONORS:** Sigma Nu; **HOME ADD:** 6014 Valley Forge; **BUS ADD:** 6200 Savoy Suite 220, Houston, TX 77036, (713)784-2260.

ROBINSON, Michael J.——**B:** Jan. 4, 1940, NY, *Pres.*, M. J. Robinson & Co., Inc.; **PRIM RE ACT:** Syndicator, Consultant, Property Manager, Owner/Investor; **OTHER RE ACT:** Energy conservation consultant for large scale projects and high rise bldgs.; **SERVICES:** Energy saving systems; Prop. Mgmt., synd. of prop. in the N.E.; **PREV EMPLOY:** Former Sr. editor, House & Home Magazine; Former Pres. Anchor Realty Corp.; **PROFL AFFIL & HONORS:** RE Bd. of NY; Inst. of RE Mgt. (IREM) Associated Builders Org.; Community Housing Improvement Program, IREM, CPM, Chicago IREM 1976; **EDUC:** BA, 1963, Econ. & Journalism, Univ. of NC at Chapel Hill; **BUS ADD:** 501 Madison Ave., New York, NY 10022, (212)751-1152.

ROBINSON, Ned——**B:** Jan. 21, 1927, Oakland, CA, *Partner*, Stark, Stewart, Wells & Robinson; **PRIM RE ACT:** Attorney; **REP CLIENTS:** Sears; R.H. Macy; Rheam Mfg.; Port of Oakland Tele Prompter; Shell Oil; Moraga Country Club; City of Newark; Security Pac. Bank; Santa Barbara S & L; **PROFL AFFIL & HONORS:** ABA; CA Bar Assn.; Alameda & Contra Costa Bar Assn.; **EDUC:** 1947, Econ. & Engrg., Univ. of CA, Berkeley; **GRAD EDUC:** LLB, JD, 1951, Boalt Hall of Law, Univ. of CA, Berkeley; **EDUC HONORS:** Honors; **MIL SERV:** USN; Lt.; **OTHER ACT & HONORS:** Mayor/Council-Lafayette 1970-; ABAG Exec. Comm. Pres./Bd. YMCA; Bd. Boys Club; Pres. Legal Aid, etc.; **HOME ADD:** 1195 Glen Rd., Lafayette, CA 94549, (415)284-4950; **BUS ADD:** 180 Grand Ave., Suite 1400, Oakland, CA 94612, (415)834-2200.

ROBINSON, Peter C.——**B:** Nov. 16, 1938, Brighton, MA, *VP Planning/Mktg.*, Blount, Inc.; **PRIM RE ACT:** Builder; **PROFL AFFIL & HONORS:** Natl. Crushed Stone Assn., Amer. Mktg. Assn., Amer. Soc. Agricultural Engrs., Newcomer Soc., Engrg. Soc. of Detroit, Machinery & Allied Products Inst., Amer. Mgmt. Assn., Assn. Nat. Advertisers; **EDUC:** BS in For. Serv., 1961, Georgetown Univ.; **GRAD EDUC:** MBA, 1963, Babson Inst.; **OTHER ACT & HONORS:** Saginaw Club, Saginaw, MI; Capital City Club, Montgomery, AL; **HOME ADD:** Montgomery, AL; **BUS ADD:** 4520 Executive Park Dr., P.O. Box 949, Montgomery, AL 36192, (205)272-8020.

ROBINSON, Richard——*Corp. Dir. PH Engr.*, Genrad; **PRIM RE ACT:** Property Manager; **BUS ADD:** 300 Baker Ave., Concord, MA 01742, (617)369-4400.*

ROBINSON, Richard H.——**B:** Oct. 30, 1944, *VP*, Creative Investment Brokers, Inc.; **PRIM RE ACT:** Broker, Consultant, Property Manager, Owner/Investor; **OTHER RE ACT:** Exchg.; **SERVICES:** Brokerage and Investment Counseling; **REP CLIENTS:** Private Investors; **PROFL AFFIL & HONORS:** RNMI, CCIM; **EDUC:** BS, 1968, Agric. Engrg., MI State Univ.; **MIL SERV:** Reserves; **OTHER ACT & HONORS:** Optimist Intl.; **HOME ADD:** 100 Sterling, Lapeer, MI 48446, (313)664-9863; **BUS ADD:** 410 W Nepessing St., Lapeer, MI 48446, (313)664-1855.

ROBINSON, Ronald Redlich——**B:** July 15, 1946, So. Bend, IN, *VP*, Corley Real Estate Corp., Mgmt.; **PRIM RE ACT:** Broker, Consultant, Instructor, Property Manager, Insuror; **SERVICES:** Prop. mgmt., community assn. mgmt., ctry. club mgmt., ins., brokerage, mgmt. consulting, community assn. educ.; **REP CLIENTS:** Bd. and Members of Community Assns.; joint venturer of ctry. club, indiv. investors of resid. prop.; **PREV EMPLOY:** Baird and Warner, Inc., 1972-1978; **PROFL AFFIL & HONORS:** IREM; Community Assn. Inst.; Multi-family Housing Assn. of IL; NAR; Amer. Mgmt. Assn.; Amer. Soc. of Assoc. Exec., CPM; GRI; Rgn. Apt. Mgr.; **EDUC:** ABA, 1976, RE, Young Men's Christian Coll.; **MIL SERV:** US Army; Sgt.; Mil. Intelligence, Bronze Star; **OTHER ACT & HONORS:** IL RE Broker; IL Prop. & Casualty Broker; 1st V.P. Multi-Family Housing Assn. of IL, 1980-1981; Instr. for Community Assn. Inst., IL Chap.; Chmn., Program Comm., Multi-Family Housing Assn. of IL, 1981, 1982; Dir., Community Assn. Inst. of IL 1982-1984; Instrc. for Muti-Family Housing Assn. of IL; Chmn. Program and Education Comm., Community Assn. Inst. of IL 1982; Gen Mgr., Mission Hill Ctry. Club; **HOME ADD:** 1632 N. Chestnut Ave., Arlington Hts., IL 60004, (312)259-6622; **BUS ADD:** 1655 W. Mission Hills Rd., Northbrook, IL 60062, (312)498-3200.

ROBINSON, Steven C.——**B:** Oct. 14, 1956, St. Louis, MO, *Pres.*, Real Estate Professionals Ltd.; **PRIM RE ACT:** Broker, Consultant, Appraiser, Developer, Lender, Property Manager, Syndicator; **SERVICES:** Gen. purchaser & seller - lender; **PREV EMPLOY:** Family bus. - 5 generations; **EDUC:** 1980, Eng./Fin., MO State Univ.; **GRAD EDUC:** MBA, Fin., WA Univ., St. Louis, MO; **BUS ADD:** 2049 Key West Dr., Arnold, MO 63010, (314)296-5311.

ROBINSON, Walter——*VP Porch*, McLouth Steel; **PRIM RE ACT:** Property Manager; **BUS ADD:** 300 S. Livernois Ave., Detroit, MI 48209, (313).*

ROBINSON, Wayne——**B:** Nov. 12, 1943, Atlanta, GA, *VP, Devel.*, The Landmarks Group; **PRIM RE ACT:** Broker, Consultant, Developer, Owner/Investor, Property Manager; **SERVICES:** Aquisition, planning, devel., mktg., mgmt.; **REP CLIENTS:** IBM; **PREV EMPLOY:** Public Relations Profl.; Graphic Design Firm Owner; Resid. Devel.; Commercial Real Estate Broker; **PROFL AFFIL & HONORS:** NAR; Atlanta Bd. of Realtors; Nat. Assn. of Corporate RE Execs., CCIM; **EDUC:** BBA, 1978, Econ., GA State Univ.; **EDUC HONORS:** Dean's List with Distinction; **MIL SERV:** USMCR, E-3; **OTHER ACT & HONORS:** Pres., 1980-1982, Atlanta Track Club/Peachtree Rd. Race; **HOME ADD:** 1 Jefferson Hill Pl., NW, Atlanta, GA 30342, (404)256-0117; **BUS ADD:** 880 Johnson Ferry Rd., Atlanta, GA 30342, (404)252-6490.

ROCA, Ruben A.——**B:** Dec. 12, 1940, Santiago, Cuba, *VP and Dir., Research & Site Strategy*, The Rouse Co.; **PRIM RE ACT:** Developer; **SERVICES:** Direct the research and site selection activities for the Rouse Co. divs. and subs.; **PREV EMPLOY:** Dir. of Rgnl. Econ. for Hammer, Siler, George Assocs., DC; **PROFL AFFIL & HONORS:** Amer. Econ. Assn., ULI, Retail Research Soc., Intl. Council of Shopping Ctrs., and Soc. for Intl. Devel.; **EDUC:** BA, 1962, Econ. and Pol. Sci., N. Central Coll., Naperville, IL; **GRAD EDUC:** Masters, 1966, Econ., Amer. Univ., DC; **HOME ADD:** 11114 Ivy Bush Ln., Columbia, MD 21044, (301)997-0889; **BUS ADD:** 10275 Little Patuxent Pkwy., Columbia, MD 21044, (301)992-6290.

ROCCA, Felice A., Jr.——**B:** July 19, 1933, Philadelphia, PA, *Owner*, Rocca Assoc.; **PRIM RE ACT:** Broker, Consultant, Appraiser, Instructor; **SERVICES:** RE counseling and appraisal; **REP CLIENTS:** Maj. corps., banks, ins. cos.; **PREV EMPLOY:** Pennamco Inc. (Mort. Bankers); **PROFL AFFIL & HONORS:** Amer. Soc. of RE Counselors, AIREA, SREA (SREA), MTC Bankers Assn. (CMB), CRE, MAI; SREA; **EDUC:** 1959, Bus. Admin., RE, Temple Univ.; **HOME ADD:** 75 Carriage Hs. Dr., Holland, PA 18966, (215)355-1542; **BUS ADD:** 1004 Western Savings Bank, Philadelphia, PA 19107, (215)735-7600.

ROCHE, W. David, Jr.——**B:** Jan. 29, 1945, Pittsfield, MA, *Sr. VP & Sr. Mort. Officer*, City Savings Bank; **PRIM RE ACT:** Appraiser, Banker, Lender, Owner/Investor, Instructor; **PREV EMPLOY:** Currently Univ. of MA instr. in creative RE fin.; **PROFL AFFIL & HONORS:** Nat. Assn. of Review Appraisers, CRA; **EDUC:** BS, 1967, Bus., Stonehill Coll.; **GRAD EDUC:** 1981, Savings Banking, Fairfield Univ.; **MIL SERV:** USA 1967-1970, Capt.; **HOME ADD:** 325

Housatonic St., Lenox, MA 01240, (413)637-3585; **BUS ADD:** 116 North St., Pittsfield, MA 01201, (413)443-4421.

ROCHON, Ronald R.——B: June 6, 1935, *VP Constrc.*, Rauenhorst Corp., Constrc. Div.; **PRIM RE ACT:** Engineer, Builder; **SERVICES:** Design and constrc. of comml. & indus. props.; **REP CLIENTS:** Maj. US mfg., serv., and investment corps.; **PROFL AFFIL & HONORS:** Prof. Engrs. in Constr.; ASCE; **EDUC:** BS, 1958, Engrg., Univ. of MN; **GRAD EDUC:** MS, 1963, Engrg., Univ. of MN; **EDUC HONORS:** Cum Laude; **MIL SERV:** USAF; **HOME ADD:** 6528 Aster Tr., Excelsior, MN 55331, (612)474-6914; **BUS ADD:** 7900 Xerxes Ave. S., Suite 2200, Minneapolis, MN 55431, (612)830-4456.

ROCKWELL, Richard——B: June 26, 1922, Claremont, NH, *Partner*, Day, Berry & Howard, RE Dept.; **PRIM RE ACT:** Attorney; **PROFL AFFIL & HONORS:** Exec. Comm., Real Prop. Sect., CT Bar Assn.; **EDUC:** 1943, Hist., Yale Univ.; **GRAD EDUC:** 1949, Law, Yale; **HOME ADD:** 9 Thicket Ln., W. Hartford, CT 06107, (203)561-2247; **BUS ADD:** One Constitution Plaza, Hartford, CT 06103.

ROCKWOOD, Harry L.——B: Mar. 22, 1920, Cleveland, OH, *Gen. Mgr.*, Landau and Heyman, Inc., Mkt. Place Shopping Ctr.; **PRIM RE ACT:** Broker, Property Manager; **OTHER RE ACT:** GSM; CPM; Broker in OH, MI & IL; **SERVICES:** Comml. and leasing; **REP CLIENTS:** Landau and Heyman, Inc.; **PREV EMPLOY:** Arthur Rubloff & Co., Chicago; **PROFL AFFIL & HONORS:** ICSC, IREM; and Chicago RE Board, CSM & CPM; Contributor to "Prop. Mgmt." by Robt. Kykle (PhD), published 1979 by RE Educ. Corp.; **EDUC:** BBA, 1952, Mktg., Case W. Reserve Univ.; **MIL SERV:** USCG; SK2/C, Asiatic Theater; **OTHER ACT & HONORS:** E. Central Health Systems Agency - Dir. (elected at public elec.); Dir. of Green Meadows Girl Scout Council; 3 yrs. as Dir. of Champaign C of C; Pres. of Champaign Urbana Kiwanis Club (16th largest 'S' Club), 245 members; **HOME ADD:** 2301 Galen Dr., Champaign, IL 61820, (217)359-6081; **BUS ADD:** 2000 N. Neil St., Champaign, IL 61820, (217)356-2700.

ROCKWOOD, Michael L.——B: Sept. 20, 1954, KS, *Operating Mgr.*, FL Suncoast Mort.; **OTHER RE ACT:** Mort. broker; **SERVICES:** Permanent, constr., secondary fin. on resid., owner/investor prop.; **REP CLIENTS:** RE brokers, assoc. mort. brokers, builders & var. devel. & investors; **PREV EMPLOY:** Pitney Co. Mort. Bankers, Branch Mgr., 2 yrs.; **PROFL AFFIL & HONORS:** FL Assn. of Mort. Brokers, Nat. Assn. of Mortgage Brokers; **EDUC:** AA, 1976, Econ., Johnson Cty. Coll., Overland Park, KS; **OTHER ACT & HONORS:** Charter Member Clearwater Seritoma; **HOME ADD:** 9723 54th St. N, St. Petersburg, FL 33708, (813)393-7350; **BUS ADD:** 8225 46th Ave., N, St. Pete, FL 33709, (813)541-4161.

RODGERS, Douglas E.——B: Aug. 30, 1950, Manhattan, KS, *Dir. of Devel.*, Henderson Properties, Inc.; **PRIM RE ACT:** Consultant, Developer, Builder, Owner/Investor, Syndicator; **OTHER RE ACT:** RE Devel. comml., indus., retail, fin., packaging; Joint ventures, turnkey devel. services, RE consulting and advisory servs.; **SERVICES:** Turnkey Devel. Servs., Comml. and resid.; **PROFL AFFIL & HONORS:** NAR, Intl. Council of Shopping Centers, Nat. Assn. of Home Builders, ULI; **EDUC:** BS, 1972, Engrg., Univ. of KS; **MIL SERV:** USAF Academy; **HOME ADD:** 4708 Seabrook Ct., Oklahoma City, OK 73132, (405)721-4663; **BUS ADD:** 2629 N.W. 39th Expressway, Oklahoma City, OK 73112, (405)947-6801.

RODGERS, Peter J.——B: Sept. 16, 1939, Brooklyn, NY, *Pres.*, JALC RE Corp; Integrated Industries Inc. (VP); RCR Associates, INC. (Pres.); **PRIM RE ACT:** Consultant, Engineer, Developer, Builder, Property Manager, Syndicator; **SERVICES:** Feasibility analysis/fin. design, const., prop. mgmt. and synd.; **REP CLIENTS:** Public and private sector; **PREV EMPLOY:** VP, Capital Investment Devel. Corp.; **PROFL AFFIL & HONORS:** Amer.Planning Assn., Who's Who in Chester Cty.; Who's Who in Fin. & Indust.; **EDUC:** BEE, 1962, Cornell Univ.; **GRAD EDUC:** 1963-66, Math, San Jose State Coll.; 1972-73, RE Fin., Wharton School; **OTHER ACT & HONORS:** Chmn. East Pikeland Twp., Bd. of Supervisors 1972-78; Pres., Chester Cty. Assn. of Township Officials, Pres. Northern Chester Cty. Community Concert Assn.; Reg. PE; Lic. RE Salesperson; **HOME ADD:** RD #2 Yellow Springs Rd., Chester Springs, PA 19425, (215)827-7224; **BUS ADD:** 110 Pickering Way, Exton, PA 19341, (215)363-6100.

RODGERS, Timothy K.——B: Nov. 27, 1938, NYC, *RE Investment Officer*, John Hancock Mutual Life Ins. Co.; **PRIM RE ACT:** Owner/Investor; **SERVICES:** Oversee RE held in John Hancock's investment portfolio; **PROFL AFFIL & HONORS:** NAR, BOMA, IREM, Assoc. Member of Greater Boston RE Bd., SRPA, CPM, RPA, Lic. RE Broker; **EDUC:** BS, 1961, Lib. Arts., Springfield Coll., MA; **EDUC HONORS:** Cum Laude; **OTHER ACT & HONORS:** Bd. of Tr., United Church; **HOME ADD:** 105 Green St., Medfield, MA 02052, (617)359-6091; **BUS ADD:** One John Hancock Pl., Boston, MA 02117, (617)421-4323.

RODMAN, Kenneth L., Jr.——B: May 3, 1951, East Hartford, CT, *Pres. and Sole shareholder*, Kenneth L. Rodman, Jr., P.A., Atty. at Law; **PRIM RE ACT:** Attorney; **SERVICES:** Representing investors, lenders, drafting RE documents, RE litigation, mort. foreclosure; **REP CLIENTS:** Capital Nat. Bank; N.G.C. Enterprises, Inc.; Sun Coast Investment Soc.; Charlie's Plant Farm, Inc. Intl. Homes of Amer.; **PREV EMPLOY:** RE acquisitions for Charlie's Plant Farm, Inc.; **PROFL AFFIL & HONORS:** FL State Bar Assn. and ABA sect. on real prop. law; **EDUC:** 1971, Bus./Fin., Univ. of S. FL School of Poli. Sci.; **GRAD EDUC:** 1976, Gen. Law, Stetson Univ. College of Law; **OTHER ACT & HONORS:** Citizenship comm., Chmn. for Lt. Gov. Div. 7, Masonic Lodge, Demolay, Pres. Kiwanis Club of Tampa Bay, Past Pres. of Suncoast Investors Inc.; **HOME ADD:** 8221 La Serena Drive, Tampa, FL, (813)933-5544; **BUS ADD:** 501 E. Jackson St., Suite 208, PO Box 1316, Tampa, FL 33601, (813)228-6225.

RODRIGUEZ, James J.——B: Feb. 3, 1946, San Francisco, CA, *Broker/Atty., President*, Mission Properties; **PRIM RE ACT:** Broker, Attorney; **PREV EMPLOY:** Corp. RE Banking Officer, First Interstate Bank (UCB), interim const. lender; **PROFL AFFIL & HONORS:** ABA, CA Bar Assn., San Jose RE Bd., Educ. Comm./ SJREB, Los Altos RE Bd., CARET, RECI, Cty. Bar Assn., RE Broker, RECI, CARET, PSI CHI Hon. Soc.; **EDUC:** BA, 1969, Psych., Univ. of CA, Los Angeles, CA; **GRAD EDUC:** MBA, 1971, Fin., UCLA; JD, 1978, Law, RE, Santa Clara Univ. Law Sch.; **EDUC HONORS:** Cum laude, Cum laude; **OTHER ACT & HONORS:** Instr. San Jose State Univ., & De Anza Coll., Bus., Law & RE; **HOME ADD:** 1249 Sierra Ave., San Jose, CA 95126, (208)292-1448; **BUS ADD:** 900 Lafayette St., Suite 700, Santa Clara, CA 95050, (408)297-1684.

RODSTROM, Arthur R.——B: July 7, 1933, Chicago, IL, *Pres.*, Twenty North Wacker Corp.; **PRIM RE ACT:** Broker, Consultant, Property Manager; **SERVICES:** Prop. Mgmt., Leasing; **PROFL AFFIL & HONORS:** Bldg. Owners & Mgrs. Assn.; **EDUC:** BS/BA, 1962, Bus. Mgmt/RE, Roosevelt Univ.; **MIL SERV:** USA, PFC; **OTHER ACT & HONORS:** Rotary Club of Chic.; **BUS ADD:** 20 N. Wacker Dr., Chicago, IL 60606, (312)372-7800.

ROEBER, James E.——B: Feb. 24, 1929, Newark, NJ, *Owner/Broker*, , Northwest Properties Realty; **PRIM RE ACT:** Broker, Consultant, Developer, Owner/Investor, Instructor; **SERVICES:** Comml. & indus. sales, leasing & exchange, bus. opportunity brokerage, investment counseling, mgmt. consulting; **REP CLIENTS:** Rgnl. & natl. users and/or investors in retail, office, dist., and light mfrg. facilities and bus.; **PREV EMPLOY:** 23 yrs. bus. & indus. mgmt., 3 yrs. sec. Municipal Planning Commn., OH; **PROFL AFFIL & HONORS:** ICSC, RESSI, NAR, WAR, Spokane Bd. of Realtors, Devel. & conducted Small Bus. Clinic Seminar series for CA State Coll/San Bernardino and SBA; **EDUC:** BA, math/physics, Cornell Univ., Ithaca, NY; **GRAD EDUC:** MBA, Bus. admin. & mgmt., Xavier Univ., Cincinnati; **EDUC HONORS:** Cum Laude; **OTHER ACT & HONORS:** Rotary Intl., US Power Squadrons, Author of "Fin. Freedom & You" (personal/bus. fin. planning workbook) 1975; **HOME ADD:** W 1316 Cliffwood Ct., Spokane, WA 99218; **BUS ADD:** N 1010 Lake Rd., Spokane, WA 99206, (509)535-5556.

ROEBUCK, Thurman M.——B: June 3, 1942, Washington, DC, *Atty.*; **PRIM RE ACT:** Consultant, Attorney, Owner/Investor; **SERVICES:** Counseling, investing, appraising/assessing value; **PROFL AFFIL & HONORS:** ABA, PA Bar Assn., Cnty. Bar; **EDUC:** BS, 1966, Educ. (Psych./Hist.), D.C. Teachers Coll.; **GRAD EDUC:** M.Ed. and JD, 1970/1977, Educ. Admin./Tax Law, Amer. Univ./Georgetown Univ. Law Ctr.; **MIL SERV:** US Navy, PO; **OTHER ACT & HONORS:** Grad. Study in Econ., 1970-1973, Amer. Univ.; **HOME ADD:** 1800 Minnesota Ave. S.E., Washington, DC 20020, (202)678-4988; **BUS ADD:** 2401 E. St. NW, Washington, DC 20037, (703)756-6092.

ROESCH, Douglass R.——B: Aug. 26, 1916, Oyster Bay, LI, *VP and Chief Appraiser*, Suburbia Fed. S&L Assn, Appraisal; **PRIM RE ACT:** Broker, Appraiser, Property Manager, Banker, Lender; **SERVICES:** Mort. lending; **PREV EMPLOY:** Chief Appraiser, Mfrs., Hanover; Mort. Supr., Dry Dock Savings Bank; **PROFL AFFIL & HONORS:** SREA, Long Island Chap., SREA, Pres. of Chap. 1979-80; **EDUC:** BS, 1938, Econ., Stock brokerage, Mktg., Wharton Bus. School, Univ. of PA; **MIL SERV:** USNR, Lt.; **OTHER ACT & HONORS:** Member of Bd of Educ. 1953-54, Nat. Trustee of Leukemia Soc. of Amer., Kiwanis Club of Garden City, Pres. of Bd. of Trustees of United Meth. Church of Sea Cliff, Dir. of NY-CT Foundation of NY Annual Conf.; **HOME ADD:** 3 Sycamor Ave, Glen Head, NY 11545, (516)676-3794; **BUS ADD:** 1000 Franklin Ave., Garden City, NY 11530, (516)746-8500.

ROESKE, Ronald E.——B: Sept. 9, 1948, KS, *Leasing & Prop. Mgr.*, Del E. Webb Realty & Mgmt. Co.; **PRIM RE ACT:** Broker, Developer, Property Manager; **PROFL AFFIL & HONORS:** BOMA, Phx. Bd.; **HOME ADD:** 12820 N. 38th Ave., Phoenix, AZ 85003, (602)938-8310; **BUS ADD:** 3800 N. Central, Phoenix, AZ 85029, (602)264-8545.

ROETTGER, David Allen——B: July 5, 1934, Evansville, IN, *Arch.*, David Allen Roettger Arch.; **PRIM RE ACT:** Architect; **SERVICES:** Design through const. phases; **PROFL AFFIL & HONORS:** Const. Specifications Inst., Reg. Arch. (IN 1447); (NCARB 014189); **EDUC:** BS Arch., 1958, Univ. of Cincinnatti; **MIL SERV:** USA; **OTHER ACT & HONORS:** Optimist Club; **HOME ADD:** 8630 Carrollton Ave., Indianapolis, IN 46240, (317)846-6284; **BUS ADD:** 1009 Broadripple Ave., Indianapolis, IN 46220, (317)253-3092.

ROGENESS, Dean A.——B: July 19, 1940, Chicago, IL, *Second VP & Asst. Gen. Counsel*, Massachusetts Mutual Life Insurance Co., Law Div.(RE Sect.); **PRIM RE ACT:** Attorney; **SERVICES:** Counsel Co. reps. RE mort. loan and RE investments; **PROFL AFFIL & HONORS:** ABA; Amer. Land Title Assn.; **EDUC:** BA, 1962, Liberal Arts, Univ. of IL; **GRAD EDUC:** JD, 1968, Georgetown Univ. Law Ctr., Wash., DC; **HOME ADD:** 22 Warren Terr., Longmeadow, MA 01106, (413)567-5480; **BUS ADD:** 1295 State St., Springfield, MA 01111, (413)788-8411.

ROGERS, Carroll M.——B: Oct. 6, 1941, Glasco, KS, *Owner*, CMR & Assoc.; **PRIM RE ACT:** Consultant; **SERVICES:** Exec. Search; **PREV EMPLOY:** 1971-1975 Consultant to various comml. devels. on proposed devels. Assisted in determining econ. feasibility and arranging fin.; **PROFL AFFIL & HONORS:** AICPA, TX Soc. of CPA's, CPA; **EDUC:** BS, 1963, Acctg., Univ. of KS; **GRAD EDUC:** MBA, 1966, Acctg., N. TX State Univ.; **HOME ADD:** 3323 Darbyshire, Dallas, TX 75229, (214)358-5834; **BUS ADD:** 10300 N. Central Exp., Bldg. II, Suite 280, Dallas, TX 75231, (214)739-1382.

ROGERS, Chris——B: Aug. 15, 1955, Tupelo, MS, *RE Sales & Appraisals*, TRI Inc.; **PRIM RE ACT:** Appraiser; **OTHER RE ACT:** RE Sales; **SERVICES:** Appraisals, comml., indus., resid. farms.; **REP CLIENTS:** FMC Corp., Republic Nat. Bank of Dallas, Employee Transfer Corp., Van Rello, Inc. etc.; **PROFL AFFIL & HONORS:** NE, MS Bd. of Realtors, NAR; **EDUC:** MS State Univ.; **HOME ADD:** 106 Lewis Dr., Tupelo, MS 38801, (601)844-7336; **BUS ADD:** 600 W. Main St., Tupelo, MS 38801, (601)842-8283.

ROGERS, David H.——B: Oct. 28, 1945, Concord, MA, *VP, Devel. and Gen. Mgr.*, Spaulding and Slye Corp., Charlotte, NC; **PRIM RE ACT:** Developer, Builder, Property Manager; **SERVICES:** Full service RE investment, devel., mgmt.; **REP CLIENTS:** North Carolina National Bank, Wang, Exxon, ITT, International Paper; **PREV EMPLOY:** Arthur Andersen & Co., Boston, MA; **EDUC:** BS, 1972, Acctg., Lowell Tech. Inst., Lowell, MA; **GRAD EDUC:** MBA, 1973, Mgmt., Babson Coll., Wellesley, MA; **EDUC HONORS:** High Honors, Gillette Grad. Scholar, High Honors; **MIL SERV:** US Army, Sp.5, Army Commendation Medal; **HOME ADD:** 2318 Blakeford Lane, Charlotte, NC 28211, (704)365-2262; **BUS ADD:** Suite 1907, 400 South Tryon St., Charlotte, NC 28285, (704)333-6661.

ROGERS, H. Hugh——B: Oct. 30, 1930, Lexington, SC, *Partner*, Rogers, Duncan, Fullwood & Perrin, Attorneys at Law; **PRIM RE ACT:** Attorney, Developer, Builder, Owner/Investor, Property Manager; **SERVICES:** Legal services; **REP CLIENTS:** First Nat. Bank of SC; Lexington Cty. S&L Assn.; The Lexington State Bank; TranSouth Fin. Services; **PREV EMPLOY:** Rgnl. Counsel, SBA; **PROFL AFFIL & HONORS:** Lexington Cty., SC, Fed. Bar Assns.; ABA; SC Trial Lawyers Assn., AB, LLB, Wig and Robe Honorary Legal Society; **EDUC:** AB, 1951, Eng./Hist., Univ. of SC; **GRAD EDUC:** LLB, 1954, Univ. of SC, SchooL of Law; **MIL SERV:** US Army, JAGC, Col., US Army Res.; **OTHER ACT & HONORS:** Two terms Mayor of Lexington, various Bar comm. chmnships; Mt. Horeb United Methodist Church; **HOME ADD:** 1 Saxe Gotha Ln., Lexington, SC 29072, (803)359-6835; **BUS ADD:** 119 E. Main St., POB 396, Lexington, SC 29072.

ROGERS, Helene Sheppard——B: Mar. 18, 1925, Baltimore, MD, *Owner/Broker*, Helene Rogers RE; **PRIM RE ACT:** Broker, Property Manager, Owner/Investor; **SERVICES:** Residential brokerage combined with prop. mgmt.; **PROFL AFFIL & HONORS:** NAR; AZ Assn. of Realtors; Green Valley Bd. of Realtors; Nat. Mktg. Inst., Cert. RE Brokerage Mgr.; Cert. Residential Specialist; Grad., Realtors Inst. of AZ; **OTHER ACT & HONORS:** Ctry. Club of Green Valley; Past Pres., Green Valley Bd. of Realtors; **HOME ADD:** 282 Los Rincones, Green Valley, AZ 85614, (602)625-5493; **BUS ADD:** Green Valley Shopping Mall, Green Valley, AZ 85614, (602)625-4474.

ROGERS, Henry——B: Oct. 6, 1932, Jacksonville, FL, *VP*, Rogers, Taylor & Co.; **PRIM RE ACT:** Broker, Appraiser, Developer, Syndicator; **SERVICES:** Gen. brokerage of comml., indus., and acreage; **PROFL AFFIL & HONORS:** Realtors (Pres. Jacksonville 1979), SRA; FLI; CCIM; **GRAD EDUC:** AB, 1954, Phys. Sci., Harvard Univ.; **MIL SERV:** USN, Lt. (jg); **OTHER ACT & HONORS:** Civil Service Bd., Jacksonville, 1967-71, Chmn. 1969); Hist. Soc. (Pres. 1979-1981); Gateway Residence Inc. (Pres. 1966); Harvard Club of Jax (Pres. 1972-73); FL Yacht Club; **BUS ADD:** 1130 Atlantic Bank Bldg., Jacksonville, FL 32202, (904)355-3600.

ROGERS, James A.——B: Feb. 28, 1931, Upper Darby, PA, *Pres.*, Heritage Mort. Fin. Co.; **PRIM RE ACT:** Lender; **OTHER RE ACT:** Mort. Banking; **SERVICES:** Origination and Servicing; **PREV EMPLOY:** Kardon Investment Co. (1964-72), Lomas & Nettleton (1972-73); **PROFL AFFIL & HONORS:** MBA of NY, AICPA, PICPA, MBA of NJ, Philadelphia MBA, MBA of Amer.; **EDUC:** BS, 1952, Acctg., La Salle Coll.; **GRAD EDUC:** MS, 1955, Acct., Univ of PA; **MIL SERV:** USA; **HOME ADD:** 101 Hilldale Rd., Cheltenham, PA 19012, (215)635-5159; **BUS ADD:** 76 Euclid Ave., Haddonfield, NJ 08033, (609)795-2404.

ROGERS, James E.——B: Dec. 16, 1941, Bristol, VA, *Sr. VP and Div. Mgr.*, Stockton, White and Co., Real Estate Investment Div.; **PRIM RE ACT:** Broker, Consultant, Developer, Property Manager; **SERVICES:** Sales and mktg. of income producing props.; **PREV EMPLOY:** N.W. Fin. Investors 1975-1978; **PROFL AFFIL & HONORS:** Past Pres. NC Income Prop. Assn.; Bd. of Govs. of SPAAC, Charlotte, NC; Nat. Bd. of Realtors, Candidate , CCIM Designation; **EDUC:** BS, 1964, Mgmt., Econ., East TN State Univ.; **GRAD EDUC:** MBA, 1966, Mgmt., RE, East TN State Univ.; **MIL SERV:** USAF; **OTHER ACT & HONORS:** Chmn., Bd. of Dir., Leadership Charlotte; Chmn., Heart Fund Campaign, Bd. of Dir., Treas.; Pres., Charlotte Pops Orchestra; Bd. of Managers, YMCA; Bd. of Dir., Goodwill Indus.; Pres., East TN State Univ. Alumni Assn.; Advisory Bd., Big Brothers, Big Sisters; Grp. Chmn. for United Way Campaign; Nominated for Distinguished Serv. Award; Bd. of Dir., Charlotte Civitan Club; **HOME ADD:** 2909 Hampton Ave., Charlotte, NC 28207, (704)364-8083; **BUS ADD:** P O Box 11816, Charlotte, NC 28220, (704)525-6042.

ROGERS, R. Julian——B: Jan. 24, 1950, Tampa, FL, *Pres.*, AmeriFirst Devel. Co. of Central FL; **PRIM RE ACT:** Developer; **SERVICES:** Land devel. for resid. builders; **REP CLIENTS:** Tompkins Devel. Co., The Ryland Grp., Catalina Homes; **PREV EMPLOY:** SVP Fin. & Serv. Corp., Orlando Div., AmeriFirst FSLA; **EDUC:** BA, 1972, Mgmt., Operations Research, Univ. of S FL, Tampa; **EDUC HONORS:** Dean's Award for Academic Excellence; **HOME ADD:** 1630 Lasbury Ave., Winter Pk, FL 32789, (305)628-2497; **BUS ADD:** 455 S Orange Ave., Orlando, FL 32801, (305)237-2707.

ROGERS, Richard——*Pres.*, Mary Kay Cosmetics; **PRIM RE ACT:** Property Manager; **BUS ADD:** 8787 Stemmons Frwy., Dallas, TX 75247, (214)630-8787.*

ROGERS, Richard C.——*RE Dir.*, New York Times Co.; **PRIM RE ACT:** Property Manager; **BUS ADD:** 229 West 43rd St., New York, NY 10036, (212)556-1234.*

ROGERS, Richard E.——B: Dec. 8, 1929, Akron, OH, *Mgr. RE Field Personnel*, The Goodyear Tire & Rubber Co.; **OTHER RE ACT:** supervise 15 RE personnel in 11 cities in negotiating leases for Goodyear; **REP CLIENTS:** Manage corp. owned RE; **PROFL AFFIL & HONORS:** NACORE; **EDUC:** Soc. Sci., 1954, Hist., Houghton Coll., Houghton, NY; **HOME ADD:** 522 Hummel St., Akron, OH 44306, (216)253-8753; **BUS ADD:** 1144 E. Mkt. St, Akron, OH 44316, (216)796-7596.

ROGERS, Theodore C.——*Pres.*, NL Industries, Inc.; **PRIM RE ACT:** Property Manager; **BUS ADD:** 230 Avenue of the Americas, New York, NY 10020, (212)399-9400.*

ROGERS, William J.——B: July 16, 1921, NYC, *VP*, Continental Mort.; **PRIM RE ACT:** Broker, Property Manager; **PREV EMPLOY:** Prudential Ins. Co.; **EDUC:** BS, 1948, Fordham Univ.; **MIL SERV:** USN; **HOME ADD:** Oradell, NJ; **BUS ADD:** 545 Cedar Lane, Teaneck, NJ, (201)692-1776.

ROGOW, Nathan Mark——B: Dec. 16, 1939, Pittsburgh, PA, *Owner*, Nathan M. Rogow Co., Realtors; **PRIM RE ACT:** Broker, Consultant, Owner/Investor, Property Manager, Syndicator; **SERVICES:** Prop. Mgmt. & Estate Conservation & Accumulation Consulting, Synd.; **REP CLIENTS:** Nat. Corps., Rgnl. Synds., Corporate Execs., Profls.; **PROFL AFFIL & HONORS:** NAR, PA Assn. Realtors, Greater Pittsburgh Assn. of Realtors, RNMI, IREM, CPM; **EDUC:** BS in Bus.

Admin., 1963, Econ. & Retailing, Univ. of Pittsburgh; Youngstown State Univ.; **MIL SERV:** USAF Res., A1C; **OTHER ACT & HONORS:** United Jewish Federation Member of Affiliate Bds.; Allegheny Cty. Dept. of Planning-Four Rivrs Edge Park System; **HOME ADD:** 1420 Centre Ave., Pittsburgh, PA 15219; **BUS ADD:** Investment Bldg., Pittsburgh, PA 15222, (412)391-9211.

ROGOWSKI, Walter S.——*VP & Secy.*, Marmon Group, Inc.; **PRIM RE ACT:** Property Manager; **BUS ADD:** 39 South LaSalle St., Chicago, IL 60603, (312)372-9500.*

ROHDE, Alfred William, III (Tom)——**B:** Dec. 2, 1946, Atlantic City, NJ, *Owner/Principal Broker*, Tom Rohde Company, RE Brokerage & Devel.; **PRIM RE ACT:** Broker, Developer, Builder, Owner/Investor, Property Manager; **SERVICES:** Site selection, brokerage, inv. sales fin., managing; **REP CLIENTS:** Southland Corp., KWLK, Wash., Mr. Gattis; Albertsons; Godfathers Pizza; Volume Shoe; Chief Auto Parts; Sambos; Stop & Go; Baskin Robins; etc.; **PROFL AFFIL & HONORS:** SABUR, NAR, TAR, CCIM, CCIM; GRI; **EDUC:** BBA, 1970, Bus. Fin., Univ. of TX at Austin; **OTHER ACT & HONORS:** San Antonio C of C, Gr. Randolph Area C of C; Member, New America Network; **HOME ADD:** 206 Primera, Olmos Park, TX 78212, (512)828-5839; **BUS ADD:** 4139 Gardendale, St. 103, San Antonio, TX 78229, (512)699-0475.

ROKES, Richard L.——**B:** May 2, 1937, Natick, MA, *Treas.*, The Shelter Grp., Ltd.; **PRIM RE ACT:** Developer; **EDUC:** BS, 1960, Northeastern Univ.; **GRAD EDUC:** MBA, 1962, Northeastern Univ.; **MIL SERV:** USA, Sig. Corps., 1st Lt.; **HOME ADD:** 10655 NE Fourth, Bellevue, WA 98004; **BUS ADD:** 10655 NE 4th, No.510, Bellevue, WA 98004, (206)455-5555.

ROKOS, Ted G.——**B:** July 25, 1933, Los Angeles, CA, *VP*, Grubb & Ellis; **PRIM RE ACT:** Broker; **OTHER RE ACT:** Sales mgr. - 60 people; **SERVICES:** Comml./Indus. RE brokerage; **PREV EMPLOY:** Exec. VP, Mariners Savings & Loan; Pres., Ted Rokos & Co.; Pres., Univ. Mktg. Corp.; **PROFL AFFIL & HONORS:** NAIOP; ICSC; NACORE; **EDUC:** BS, 1956, Fin./RE, UCLA; **MIL SERV:** US Army; Cpl.; **OTHER ACT & HONORS:** Irvine Coast Country Club; Balboa Bay Club; **HOME ADD:** 2727 Windover Dr., Corona de Mar, CA 92625, (714)759-8982; **BUS ADD:** 4000 MacArthur Blvd., Newport Beach, CA 92660, (714)833-2900.

ROLFE, N. Anthony——**B:** Oct. 21, 1922, New York, NY, *Exec. VP*, Sulzberger - Rolfe Inc.; **PRIM RE ACT:** Broker, Consultant, Owner/Investor, Property Manager; **SERVICES:** Sales, cooperative/condo conversions, mgmt., consulting; **EDUC:** BS Economics, 1943, Bus. School, Univ. of MO; **MIL SERV:** USN, Lt.; **HOME ADD:** 1111 Park Ave., New York, NY; **BUS ADD:** 654 Madison Ave., New York, NY 10021, (212)593-7606.

ROLLER, Calvin L.——**B:** Aug. 25, 1948, Williamsport, PA, *Broker-assoc.*, ERA, Merrell & Co.; **PRIM RE ACT:** Broker, Consultant, Owner/Investor; **SERVICES:** Resid. income props.; **PROFL AFFIL & HONORS:** TX Assn. of Realtors; NE Tarrant Cty. Bd. of Realtors; **EDUC:** BS, 1970, Bus., Penn State Univ.; **GRAD EDUC:** MBA, 1975, Admin., Penn State Univ.; **HOME ADD:** 7116 Briar Dale Dr., Ft. Worth, TX 76180, (817)498-0070; **BUS ADD:** 505-B Bedford Rd., E Bedford, TX 76021, (817)268-2222.

ROMAIN, Joseph E.——**B:** June 25, 1933, St. Cloud, MN, *Pres.*, Romain Corp.; **PRIM RE ACT:** Developer, Owner/Investor; **PROFL AFFIL & HONORS:** MN Prop. Exchangers; Nat. Assn. Indus. & Office Parks; **EDUC:** BA, 1958, Acctg., St. Thomas Coll.; **MIL SERV:** US Navy, RM2; **OTHER ACT & HONORS:** V. Chmn. Lake Dist. IR Party; **HOME ADD:** 870 Windjammer Ln., Mound, MN 55364, (612)472-5964; **BUS ADD:** 710 Southgate Plaza, 5001 W. 80th St., Bloomington, MN 55437, (612)831-1286.

ROMAN, Douglas E.——**B:** Apr. 20, 1946, Winnipeg, Can., *Pres.*, The Cross Companies; **PRIM RE ACT:** Owner/Investor; **PREV EMPLOY:** Asst. to VP Engrg., Ceme Corp., 1969; Sr. Design/Estimator, Hood Corp., 1970; Estimator, Amer. Pipe Co., 1971; Mech. Engr., Exec., Kiemech Div., Peter Kewit, 1972; Owner, Environ. Contractors, 1973-74; Owner/Mgr., Cross Prodns. Co., Cross Trust Co., Timothy Enterprises, Amer. Mktg. Co., Crossroads Mfg. Ltd. (Can.), Crossroads Mfg. USA, Crossroads Prodns. Co., Creative Composition; **EDUC:** 1970, Biola Coll.; 1970, Cypress Jr. Coll.; **MIL SERV:** USMC, 1967-1968, Purple Heart; **OTHER ACT & HONORS:** Who's Who in the West; Who's Who in Finance and Industry; The Directory of Distinguished Americans; The International Who's Who of Intellectuals; **HOME ADD:** 415 N. Redrock, Anaheim, CA 92807; **BUS ADD:** POB 4179, Anaheim, CA 92803, (714)632-8224.

ROMANO, Donald F.——**B:** Sept. 2, 1942, Chicago, IL, *Broker Assoc.*, Tucson Realty & Trust Company; **PRIM RE ACT:** Broker, Consultant, Attorney, Real Estate Publisher; **SERVICES:** Non-resid. brokerage; **REP CLIENTS:** Devel.; **PREV EMPLOY:** Practicing RE Lawyer; **PROFL AFFIL & HONORS:** Tucson Tomorrow Land Use Comm.; **EDUC:** BS, 1964, Hist. Poli. Sci., Holy Cross; **GRAD EDUC:** JD, 1967, Loyola of Chicago; **HOME TEL:** (602)745-1387; **BUS ADD:** 2961 E Grant, Tucson, AZ 85716, (602)795-0500.

ROMANO, Joseph R.——**B:** Dec. 23, 1944, Passaic, NJ, *Dir. Sales & Mktg.*, Summit Assoc. Inc.; **PRIM RE ACT:** Broker, Consultant, Developer, Builder, Owner/Investor; **SERVICES:** Spec. & design build, indus. & office bldg. for sale or lease; **PROFL AFFIL & HONORS:** Nat. Assn. of Corp. RE Exec. (NACORE), Indus. RE Brokers Assn. of NY Metro. Area (IREBA), Intl. Coll. of RE Consulting Profls.; **EDUC:** BS, 1966, Eng. Lit., Seton Hall Univ., S Orange, NJ; **EDUC HONORS:** Dean's List; **HOME ADD:** 60 Prospect St., Metuchen, NJ 08840, (201)494-1993; **BUS ADD:** Raritan Plaza II, Raritan Ctr., Edison, NJ 08837, (201)225-2900.

ROMERO, Frank L.——**B:** Oct. 17, 1949, Falcon, Venezuela, *VP Arch. Mktg. Mgr. (Bd. of Dir.)*, Gemcraft Homes; **PRIM RE ACT:** Architect, Builder, Owner/Investor; **SERVICES:** Manage the resid. design, planning & mktg. for Gemcraft Homes, a Houston based homebuilder; **PREV EMPLOY:** VP, General Homes, Houston; Partner in Houston based Arch. Firm, Wauson & Williams Arch.; **PROFL AFFIL & HONORS:** Member, Greater Houston Builders Assn.; Consultant to Houston F.H.A. Arch. Section, Reg. Arch. TX 5931; **EDUC:** BArch., 1973, Univ. of Houston; **EDUC HONORS:** Grad. at top of Arch. Class of '73 (Cum Laude); Received AIA Scholastic Award and Scholarship; **OTHER ACT & HONORS:** Alief C of C; **HOME ADD:** 9406 Belasco, Houston, TX 77099, (713)495-2684; **BUS ADD:** 1304 Langham Creek Dr., Suite 170, Houston, TX 77084, (713)492-8043.

ROMERO, Steve G.——**B:** Oct. 2, 1947, Tucson, AZ, *Owner*, Steve Romero Investment Co.; **PRIM RE ACT:** Owner/Investor; **SERVICES:** Pvt. lending, selling etc.; **PROFL AFFIL & HONORS:** DBA; **MIL SERV:** USAF Reserve; **OTHER ACT & HONORS:** Precint Comm. #16, 9 yrs., NEA, AEA; **HOME ADD:** 2566 N. Shannon Rd., Tucson, AZ 85745, (602)882-8125; **BUS ADD:** 2566 N. Shannon Rd., Tucson, AZ 85745, (602)623-8750.

ROMINE, Christopher——**B:** July 1, 1952, Marysville, CA, *Chief Exec.*, Cara Corp.; **PRIM RE ACT:** Broker, Consultant, Builder, Property Manager, Syndicator; **OTHER RE ACT:** Practice consultant to doctors; **SERVICES:** Practice mgmt. for doctors, all phases RE; **REP CLIENTS:** Instns., indivs., and doctors; **PROFL AFFIL & HONORS:** NAR; **EDUC:** Bus. Admin., OK State Univ., Stillwater; **OTHER ACT & HONORS:** Member, Bd. Youth Service Tulsa Cty.; **HOME ADD:** 224 N. Rosedale, Tulsa, OK 74127, (918)582-8738; **BUS ADD:** 2734 N. Sheridan Rd., Tulsa, OK 74115, (212)494-4447.

ROMNEY, Keith, Jr.——**B:** June 15, 1940, NM, *Pres.*, Capitol Industries Inc.; Walden Hills Inc.; **PRIM RE ACT:** Developer, Builder, Owner/Investor, Property Manager; **REP CLIENTS:** Uniroyal; Hewlett Packard; Gen. Electric; Ford Motor; Gen. Motors, etc.; **PREV EMPLOY:** Acctg. Supr., State S & L, Salt Lake City; **PROFL AFFIL & HONORS:** Nat. Assn. of Home Builders, Life Spike, Nat. Assn. of Home Builders; Salt Lake Builder of the Year 1979; **EDUC:** BA, 1964, Bus. Admin., Brigham Young Univ.; **GRAD EDUC:** Law, George Washington Univ., Univ. of Heidelberg; Univ. of UT; **MIL SERV:** US Army, E-5; **OTHER ACT & HONORS:** Salt Lake City Housing Devel. Dir.; NAHB, Nat. Dir.; Dir., So. Salt Lake City C of C; **HOME ADD:** 2970 Devonshire Circ., Salt Lake City, UT 84108; **BUS ADD:** 2880 S. Main, Salt Lake City, UT 84115, (801)486-8409.

ROMNEY, Keith——*Chairman*, Resort Timesharing Council, c/o American Land Development Assn.; **OTHER RE ACT:** Profl. Assn. Admin.; **BUS ADD:** 1000 16th St. NW, Suite 604, Washington, DC 20036, (202)659-4582.*

RONDINONE, Serge W.——**B:** June 28, 1946, Munich, Germany, *Dir. of RE Devel.*, Bredero Consulting New York, Inc., Management Subsidiary of Bredero Grp. Netherlands; **PRIM RE ACT:** Developer, Owner/Investor, Property Manager; **OTHER RE ACT:** Investment of foreign funds into US RE; **SERVICES:** Establishment of joint venture devel. activities among and between intl. investors; **REP CLIENTS:** For. indiv. and instl. investors; **PREV EMPLOY:** Barkan Assoc., Inc., VP, 1976-1979; Anbar Corp., VP, 1973-1976; CUNY, Asst. Prof., 1968-1973; **PROFL AFFIL & HONORS:** Amer. Inst. RE Appraisers; Soc. of RE Appraisers; Nat. Assn. of Securities Dealers, NASD, 1974; **EDUC:** BA, 1968, Eng./Logical Analysis, SUNY; **GRAD EDUC:** MA, 1971, Adv. Critical Analysis, NYU; **EDUC HONORS:** Honor Roll, Summa Cum Laude, Who's Who Among Students in Amer. Coll. &

Univ., 1968, Rep. US at 7th Intl. Congress Aesthetics, Bucharest, Romania, 1972; **OTHER ACT & HONORS:** Member, Westchester Cty. Businessmans Assn.; Languages: Eng., German, French, Russian, Classical Greek and Latin; Fine Arts, Fencing, Sailing; **HOME ADD:** 2100 Linwood Ave., Ft. Lee, NJ 07024, (201)592-7219; **BUS ADD:** 342 Madison Ave., Suite 505, NY, NY 10173, (212)697-1575.

ROOF, William H.——**B:** Feb. 11, 1953, OH, *VP*, Dodge Investment Co., Aquisitions & Sales; **PRIM RE ACT:** Broker, Consultant, Owner/Investor, Property Manager, Syndicator; **SERVICES:** Prop. mgmt.; **PREV EMPLOY:** Comml. RE Broker; **EDUC:** BBA, 1975, Mgmt. and Psych., OH Univ.; **HOME ADD:** 307 Southwyke Condos., Maumee, OH 43537, (419)874-3550; **BUS ADD:** 1O8 1/2 W. Third St., Perrysburg, OH 43551, (419)874-3559.

ROOK, James F.——**B:** Nov. 28, 1927, Barberton, OH, *Mgr.*, Her, Inc.; **PRIM RE ACT:** Broker, Property Manager; **PROFL AFFIL & HONORS:** CRB; **EDUC:** BS, 1950, Spec. Ed.-Eng.-Hist., Ohio State Univ.; **OTHER ACT & HONORS:** Past Pres., Tri Village Lions; Past Pres., Central Community House Bd.; Past Member, Governing Bd.; First Community Church; Past Member, Gov. Bd. Pilot Dogs of Columbus; **HOME ADD:** 2693 Mt. Holyoke Rd., Columbus, OH 43221, (614)486-4984; **BUS ADD:** 1071 Fishinger Rd., Columbus, OH 43221, (614)451-7400.

ROONEY, John P.——**B:** May 1, 1932, Evanston, IL, *Prof.*, Cooley Law School; **PRIM RE ACT:** Instructor; **SERVICES:** Legal Consultation, Teach law of basic prop., modern R.E. transactions, banking; **PREV EMPLOY:** 16 yrs. pvt. law practice specializing in RE; **PROFL AFFIL & HONORS:** ABA; MI, CA, IL Bar Assns.; Real Prop. sections ABA, MI, CA; **EDUC:** BA, 1953, Math., Univ. of IL; **GRAD EDUC:** JD, 1958, Harvard Univ.; **EDUC HONORS:** Phi Beta Kappa; **MIL SERV:** USA, 1953-55, 1st Lt.; **HOME ADD:** 710 Chittenden Dr., E. Lansing, MI 48823, (517)332-0483; **BUS ADD:** 217 S. Capitol, Lansing, MI 48933, (517)371-5140.

ROONEY, Michael A.——**B:** July 15, 1938, Milwaukee, WI, *Pres.*, The Rooney Grp.; **PRIM RE ACT:** Broker, Consultant, Appraiser, Developer, Syndicator; **SERVICES:** RE consulting, appraisals, market studies, feasibility studies, cost allocation studies, site finding, devel. & mgmt.; **REP CLIENTS:** Lenders, owners and investors in comml., indus., and instnl. RE; **PREV EMPLOY:** Pres., Gen. Appraisal of Can. Ltd., Pres., Boeckh Co., subs. of Amer. Appraisal Co.; **PROFL AFFIL & HONORS:** Amer. Soc. of Appraisers, Designated Appraiser Amer. Soc. of Appraisers; **EDUC:** BS, 1960, Bus. Admin. RE, Marquette Univ.; **GRAD EDUC:** MS, 1964, RE Investment Analysis, Univ. of WI; **EDUC HONORS:** One of 20 outstanding grads.; **OTHER ACT & HONORS:** Rotary Club of Wauwatosa; **HOME ADD:** 8222 Jackson Park Blvd., Wauwatosa, WI 53213, (414)257-2296; **BUS ADD:** 933 North Mayfair Rd., Milwaukee, WI 53226, (414)476-6500.

ROOT, David R.——**B:** Dec. 31, 1946, PA, *Sr. Financial Analyst*, ITT Comm. Devel. Corp.; **PRIM RE ACT:** Appraiser, Developer; **OTHER RE ACT:** Comm. devel.; **SERVICES:** All facets of fin. analysis & project appraisal; **EDUC:** BS, 1970, Mgmt. Studies, Univ. of VA; **HOME ADD:** Box 1763, Palm Coast, FL 32037, (904)445-2184; **BUS ADD:** Palm Coast, FL 32037, (904)445-4900.

ROOT, Edgar Wilson——**B:** June 16, 1921, Seattle, WA, *Sr. VP*, US Life RE Servs. Corp.; **PRIM RE ACT:** Broker, Appraiser, Lender; **SERVICES:** Investment counseling, valuation, fin. comml. prop.; **PROFL AFFIL & HONORS:** SIR; **EDUC:** BA, 1948, RE Fin/, Univ. of WA; **MIL SERV:** USAF, Capt., 1942-46, 1951-52; **HOME ADD:** 21 Castle Ln., Oakland, CA 94611, (415)530-3287; **BUS ADD:** 614, 100 CA St., San Francisco, CA 94111, (415)956-7080.

ROOT, Stuart D.——**B:** Oct. 14, 1932, Chagrin Falls, OH, *Pres.*, The Bowery Savings Bank; **PRIM RE ACT:** Banker; **PREV EMPLOY:** Cadwalader, Wickersham & Taft 1960-81; Member 1969-81; **PROFL AFFIL & HONORS:** COB, The Harlem School of the Arts; Fin. Advisory Bd., Columbia Grad. School of Bus.; Econ. Club; Lecturer, Practicing Law Inst.; Lecturer, Amer. Law Inst./ABA; **EDUC:** BA, 1955, Philosophy, OH Wesleyan Univ.; **GRAD EDUC:** LLB, 1960, Law, Columbia Univ. School of Law; **MIL SERV:** US Army, E/M; **OTHER ACT & HONORS:** Capitol Hill Club, Pelham Ctry. Club, NY Genealogical & Biological Soc.; **BUS ADD:** 110 E. 42nd St., New York, NY 10017, (212)953-8000.

ROSADO, Jose F.——**B:** Nov. 27, 1948, Havana, Cuba, *Pres.*, Interholden Equities, Inc.; **PRIM RE ACT:** Broker, Consultant, Owner/Investor; **OTHER RE ACT:** RE Investment Banker for Large European Investors; **SERVICES:** Investment counseling, acquisition and disposition of lge. comml. props. for European investors in U.S. RE, European synds.; **REP CLIENTS:** Consortium of private Swiss banks; **PREV EMPLOY:** Shearson Props. Intl., Inc., Pres., Intl. RE Div. of Shearson, Loeb, Rhoades, Inc.; **PROFL AFFIL & HONORS:** Miami Bd. of Realtors; **EDUC:** BA, 1970, Psych., Univ. of Miami; **GRAD EDUC:** FL Intl. Univ., 1976, Fin., MBA, Bus. and Organizational Sciences; **EDUC HONORS:** Summa Cum Laude; 4.0 GPA; **HOME ADD:** 7600 SW 72 Ct., Miami, FL 33143, (305)667-4057; **BUS ADD:** 255 Alhabra Cir., Suite 845, Coral Gables, FL 33134, (305)447-8697.

ROSADO, Ronald D.——**B:** May 30, 1943, San Diego, CA, *Dir. of Mgmt. & Maintenance - CA*, Home Fed. Savings & Loan; **PRIM RE ACT:** Developer, Property Manager; **PREV EMPLOY:** Grubb & Ellis Property Services; **PROFL AFFIL & HONORS:** Candidate for CPM; **EDUC:** BA, 1969, Bus. & Pol. Sci.; **HOME ADD:** P.O. Box 368, San Diego, CA 92112, (714)942-1663; **BUS ADD:** P.O. Box 2070, San Diego, CA 92112.

ROSE, Jerome G.——**B:** July 4, 1926, NYC, NY, *Editor-in-Chief, RE Law Journal/Prof., Urban Planning*, Rutgers Univ., Dept. of Urban Planning; **PRIM RE ACT:** Consultant, Instructor, Real Estate Publisher; **SERVICES:** Consultant in land use regulation, environmental regulation; **REP CLIENTS:** Mcpl., cty., state govts.; **PROFL AFFIL & HONORS:** NY Bar; Profl. Planner in NJ; AICP, Prof. of Urban Planning; **EDUC:** AB, 1948, Pol. Sci./Econ., Cornell Univ.; **GRAD EDUC:** JD, 1951, Law, Harvard Law School; **EDUC HONORS:** Phi Beta Kappa; With Distinction in Govt., Cum Laude; **MIL SERV:** USN, PhM2/c; **OTHER ACT & HONORS:** Princeton Rgnl. Planning Bd., 1973-1981; **HOME ADD:** 21 Tyson Ln., Princeton, NJ 08540, (609)921-3263; **BUS ADD:** New Brunswick, NJ 08903, (201)932-4100.

ROSE, J.G.——**B:** May 10, 1933, TN, *Sr. VP & Sec.*, Johns Island Co. & Lost Tree Village Corp.; **PRIM RE ACT:** Architect, Developer, Builder, Owner/Investor, Property Manager; **PREV EMPLOY:** Sr. VP Alodex Corp.; **PROFL AFFIL & HONORS:** ULI, Reg. Arch. Various St.; **EDUC:** BArch, 1956, Yale Univ.; **MIL SERV:** USN, Lt.; **BUS ADD:** No. 1 Johns Island Dr., Vero Beach, FL 32960, (305)231-0900.

ROSE, Lawrence R.——*Gen. Mgr.*, Lockport Mall, General Growth Management Corp.; **PRIM RE ACT:** Owner/Investor, Property Manager; **SERVICES:** Shopping centers; **PREV EMPLOY:** Plaza Carolina, PR; Orlando Fashion Square, FL; Main Place Mall, Buffalo, NY; **PROFL AFFIL & HONORS:** Intl. Council of Shopping Centers, Cert. Shopping Center Mgr., Cert. Marketing Dir.; **EDUC:** BS, OH State Univ. Additional courses at Univ. of AZ and MI State Univ.; **MIL SERV:** USN; **OTHER ACT & HONORS:** Zoning Bd. of Appeals, Town of Amherst, NY, 2 terms; Pres. of Kiwanis Club of Lockport; Bd. of Govs., Kenan Center; **HOME ADD:** 102 Carriage Cir., Williamsville, NY 14221, (716)688-1698; **BUS ADD:** 5737 S. Transit Rd., Lockport, NY 14094, (716)434-6371.

ROSE, M. Zev——**B:** Oct. 10, 1937, Philadelphia, PA, *Pres.*, Rose, Miner & Podolsky, P.A.; **PRIM RE ACT:** Attorney; **SERVICES:** Legal; **REP CLIENTS:** Synd., dev., invest., owners of comml., indust. and resid. prop.; lenders, & title co.; **PROFL AFFIL & HONORS:** NJ State Bar Assn., ABA and Camden Cty. Bar Assn.; **EDUC:** BS - Econ., 1959, Univ. of PA, Wharton School; **GRAD EDUC:** JD, 1963, Rutgers Univ., School of Law; **OTHER ACT & HONORS:** Assist. Camden City, NJ, Solicitor 1964-1967, Assist. Camden Cty., NJ, Counsel 1967-1970; **BUS ADD:** 411 Rt. 70 E., Cherry Hill, NJ 08034, (609)428-6886.

ROSE, Marvin B., Jr.——**B:** May 30, 1945, Richmond, VA, *Pres.*, Rose & Assoc.; **PRIM RE ACT:** Broker, Syndicator, Consultant, Appraiser, Developer, Real Estate Publisher; **SERVICES:** Mkt. and fin. feasibility studies, land acquisition, publisher of resid. data reports, synd., dev.; **REP CLIENTS:** US Home; F & R; Levitt; Putte; Gen. Homes; **PREV EMPLOY:** VP & Reg. Mgr., Levitt Corp., Sr. Assoc., Econ. Research Assoc.; **PROFL AFFIL & HONORS:** NAHB; Natl. Bd. of Realtors; **EDUC:** BS, 1967, Civil Engrg., Duke Univ.; **GRAD EDUC:** M. Reg. Planning, 1970, Housing Mkt. & feasibility analysis, Univ. of NC; **EDUC HONORS:** Chi Epsilon, Dean's List, Outstanding Sr. Awards, Environmental Health Fellowship; **MIL SERV:** USNG; E-4; **OTHER ACT & HONORS:** Bd. of Dir., Big Brothers/Big Sisters; **HOME ADD:** 3236 San Bernadino St., Clearwater, FL 33519, (813)725-2007; **BUS ADD:** 3118 Gulf-to-Bay Blvd., Suite 200, Clearwater, FL 33519, (813)726-4948.

ROSE, Michael L.——**B:** Jan. 22, 1950, Muskegone, MI, *Gen. Mgr.*, Johns Island (Resid. Community); **PRIM RE ACT:** Developer, Property Manager; **SERVICES:** Complete prop. mgmt. & maintenance; **PREV EMPLOY:** Alstate Mgmt., Lansing, MI; **PROFL AFFIL & HONORS:** Dir., Community Assn. Instit. (Gold Coast Chapter) Treas., - Treas. Coast Condo. Assn., CPM, FL; **EDUC:** Bus. Admin., 1973, Bus. Mgmt., Acctg., Econ., MI State Univ.; **OTHER**

ACT & HONORS: Town Planning & Zoning Bd. 1979 & 1980; Dir. Vero Beach Yacht Club & Vero Beach Civic Assn.; **HOME ADD:** 854 Indian Ln., Vero Beach, FL 32960, (305)231-0485; **BUS ADD:** 7100 North AIA, Vero Beach, FL 32960, (305)231-1666.

ROSE, Richard Lindsay——B: Sept. 5, 1949, Knoxville, TN, *Atty.*, Leonard, Koehn, Rose & Hurt; **PRIM RE ACT:** Attorney; **REP CLIENTS:** Lexington Devel. Co., Transwestern Prop. Co., Markborough Props. Ltd., Sugerland Props., Inc.; **PROFL AFFIL & HONORS:** ABA, Sect. of Real Prop., Probate and Trust Law; Houston Bar Assn.; Dallas Bar Assn.; Natl. Assn. of Bond Lawyers; **EDUC:** BS, 1971, Mktg., Univ. of TN; **GRAD EDUC:** JD, 1974, Law, Univ. of TN; **EDUC HONORS:** High Honors, Order of the Coif; Editor-in-Chief, *TN Law Review*; **HOME ADD:** 268 Sugarberry Cir., Houston, TX 77024, (713)782-1255; **BUS ADD:** Suite 150, 6750 West Loop South, Bellaire, TX 77401, (713)661-3488.

ROSE, Robert E.——B: Dec. 10, 1946, *Pres.*, Foster & Marshall Realty Inc.; **PRIM RE ACT:** Developer, Syndicator; **SERVICES:** Devel. and investment banker in RE; **PROFL AFFIL & HONORS:** The Nat. Assn. of Indus. and Office Parks; Snohomis Cty. Econ. Devel. Council; **EDUC:** BS, 1968, Univ. Pittsburgh; **HOME ADD:** 4502 NE 33rd, Seattle, WA 98105, (206)524-0588; **BUS ADD:** 205 Columbia St., Seattle, WA 98104, (206)344-3515.

ROSE, Robert W.——B: Jan. 6, 1944, Terre Haute, IN, *Pres.*, Colter Assoc.; **PRIM RE ACT:** Consultant, Developer, Syndicator; **SERVICES:** Investment advisory servs., RE consulting, comml. prop. devel.; **REP CLIENTS:** Developers, indiv. investors; **EDUC:** BSCE, 1966, Rose Hulman; **GRAD EDUC:** MBA, 1971, Univ. of AZ; **HOME ADD:** 8402 N 18th St., Phoenix, AZ 85020, (602)943-5891; **BUS ADD:** 3443 N Central Ave., Suite 607, Phoenix, AZ 85012, (602)269-5357.

ROSE, William H.——B: Dec. 23, 1930, Flint, MI, *Part.*, Univ. Fin. Investors (UFI); **PRIM RE ACT:** Broker, Developer, Owner/Investor; **SERVICES:** Co-investor and devel. for investment market; **PREV EMPLOY:** RE brokerage & ins.; **PROFL AFFIL & HONORS:** Pheonix Bd. of Realtors, Valley of the Sun Exchangers, Phoenix Park Found., Member of Sun Angel Found, Member of Exec. Comm. for Fiesta Bowl; **HOME ADD:** 5339 N 29th St., Phoenix, AZ 85016, (602)956-2932; **BUS ADD:** 2930 E. Camelback, Suite 140, Phoenix, AZ 85016, (602)956-1041.

ROSEBERRY, Fred T., III——B: Mar. 31, 1938, Woodland, CA, *Atty. and counselor at Law*, Law Offices of Fred T. Roseberry III; **PRIM RE ACT:** Attorney, Owner/Investor, Instructor, Real Estate Publisher; **SERVICES:** Legal advice and counseling regarding real prop. matters and contracts, teach real prop. at San Joaquin Delta Coll.; **REP CLIENTS:** RE Brokers, Investors and devel.; **PREV EMPLOY:** Central Bank, Crocker Bank and Security Pacific Bank, Lending Officer & Operations; **PROFL AFFIL & HONORS:** State Bar of CA, San Joaquin Cty. Bar, RE Educ. Assn.; **EDUC:** BS, Agricultural Bus. mgmt., Cal Poly State Univ. Pomona; **GRAD EDUC:** JD, 1970, Humphreys School of Law; **OTHER ACT & HONORS:** North Stockton Rotary Club, Nu Beta Epsilon Nat. Law Frat.; **BUS ADD:** 1150 W Robinhood Dr. 11-A, Box 7362, Stockton, CA 95207, (209)478-8449.

ROSEMURGY, James M.——*Pres.*, Campbell Property Management & Real Estate Inc.; **PRIM RE ACT:** Broker, Property Manager; **PROFL AFFIL & HONORS:** Rgnl. RE Broker; CPA; **EDUC:** BBA, 1967, Acctg., Univ. of WI; **GRAD EDUC:** MBA, 1969, Fin., Univ. of CA; **OTHER ACT & HONORS:** Deerfield Housing Auth. Commnr.; **BUS ADD:** 1233 E. Hillsboro Blvd., Deerfield Beach, FL 33441, (305)427-8686.

ROSEN, Horace J.——B: Sept. 19, 1915, Milwaukee, WI, *Pres.*, R.G. Construction Cor., Harbor Investment Corp, Rosen Realty Co.; **PRIM RE ACT:** Broker, Consultant, Appraiser, Developer, Builder, Property Manager, Owner/Investor, Insuror; **OTHER ACT & HONORS:** Brynwood C of C, Boca Logo C of C, Metropolitan Bldrs. Assn., Award, Interior design, Parade of Homes; **HOME ADD:** 9596 N Regent Rd., Milwaukee, WI 53217, (414)352-0886; **BUS ADD:** 3950 S. Clement Ave., Milwaukee, WI 53007, (414)481-7050.

ROSEN, Kenneth D.——B: Mar. 21, 1929, Boston, MA, *Pres.*, The Kendar Companies; **PRIM RE ACT:** Broker, Developer, Owner/Investor; **SERVICES:** Condo. conversions, comml. & investment brokerage; **PROFL AFFIL & HONORS:** CCIM; Pres., Miami Bd. of Realtors 1971-72; Miami Realtor of the Year 1971; **EDUC:** BBA, 1952, Mktg., Boston Univ.; **MIL SERV:** US Army; **OTHER ACT & HONORS:** 32nd Degree Mason, Shriner, Past Master Miracle Lodge no. 321, Miami, FL; **HOME ADD:** 4730 Santa Maria, Coral Gables, FL 33146, (305)665-5347; **BUS ADD:** 1550 Madruga Ave., Coral Gables, FL 33146, (305)661-1550.

ROSEN, Lawrence——B: Jan. 11, 1938, Louisville, KY, *Chmn.*, Larry Rosen Co.; **PRIM RE ACT:** Broker, Consultant, Appraiser, Developer, Property Manager, Syndicator, Real Estate Publisher; **SERVICES:** Indus. & comml. prop. mgmt., brokerage, consulting, appraising; **REP CLIENTS:** US Dept. of HUD; GSA; Guerdon Industries; **PREV EMPLOY:** Executive Properties, VP - Investments; Rosen Enterprises, Inc. - Director; **PROFL AFFIL & HONORS:** KY RE Broker; Louisville Area C of C; **EDUC:** BS Bus., 1959, Fin., Econ., Miami Univ, OH; **EDUC HONORS:** Phi Beta Kappa, Omicron Delta Kappa, Cum Laude; **MIL SERV:** USN, 1959-1962, Lt. jg; **OTHER ACT & HONORS:** Standard Country Club; Author, "Calculator Mathematics for the Real Estate Professional" (1978); Dow Jones - "Irwin Guide to Interest" (1974, 1981); "How to Trade Put and Call Options" (1974); "When and How to Profit by Buying and Selling Gold" (1974); "Go Where the Money Is" (1967); Dow Jones - Irwin, Inc. Publisher; **HOME TEL:** (502)228-1933; **BUS ADD:** 7008 Springdale Rd., Louisville, KY 40222, (502)228-4343.

ROSEN, Lawrence N.——B: June 20, 1940, NYC, NY, *Pres.*, Lynx Corp.; **PRIM RE ACT:** Broker, Consultant, Attorney, Developer, Owner/Investor, Property Manager, Syndicator; **PREV EMPLOY:** 1979-80 (18 Mo.) J. I. Kislak, Inc. (Mort. Banking, RE); 1969-79 Thor Corp. (Pres.) Diversivied RE; **PROFL AFFIL & HONORS:** Fin. Execs. Inst.; NYS and FL Bar Assns.; NYS Soc. of CPA's, CPA; LLD; **EDUC:** BBA, 1962, Acctg., City Univ. of NY; **GRAD EDUC:** JD, 1965, Law, Fordham Univ., School of Law; **EDUC HONORS:** Law Review; **HOME ADD:** 21170 NE 22 Court, North Miami Beach, FL 33180, (305)932-7008; **BUS ADD:** 2241 Hollywood Blvd., Hollywood, FL 33020, (305)921-1978.

ROSEN, Michael Howard——B: May 22, 1943, New York City, NY, *Exec. VP*, The Town and Country Management Corp.; **PRIM RE ACT:** Developer, Owner/Investor, Property Manager; **PREV EMPLOY:** Morris Brickmasons Corp.; Rosen Prop. Inc.; Monumental Properties, Inc.; Monumental Properties Trust; **PROFL AFFIL & HONORS:** Metfair Rent Comm., Nat. Realty Comm., Amer. Home Builders Assn., Apt. Owners & Mgr. Assn., Who's Who in Bus. & Fin.; **EDUC:** AB, 1965, Econ., Tufts Univ.; **HOME ADD:** 110 Nob Hill Park Dr., Reisterstown, MD 21136, (301)833-8660; **BUS ADD:** 25 S. Charles St., Ste. 2121, Baltimore, MD 21201, (301)539-7600.

ROSEN, Michael P.——B: Sept. 18, 1946, Petaluma, CA, *Pres.*, M.P. Rosen, Inc.; **PRIM RE ACT:** Broker, Developer, Builder; **OTHER RE ACT:** Family-owned & operated dry cleaning bus.; RE agent; escrow bus.; bldg. construction; Re brokerage; **PROFL AFFIL & HONORS:** 20/30 Club; Pres. of Rohnert Park C of C, C of C Bd. Member; Sonoma Cty. Grand Jury; Dir. CA Jr. Miss Pageant; Member Petaluma Hosp. Advisory Bd.; Area Chmn. for Congressman Don Clausen; **EDUC:** AA, 1967, Santa Rosa Jr. Coll.; **HOME ADD:** 6061 Dolores Dr., Rohnert, CA 94928, (707)795-7883; **BUS ADD:** 6601 Commerce Blvd., Rohnert Park, CA 94928, (707)584-7484.

ROSEN, Nelson——B: Nov. 19, 1910, Boston, MA, *Partner*, Sandler and Rosen, Attorneys; **PRIM RE ACT:** Attorney; **REP CLIENTS:** Devels. and builders, investors, mort. bankers; **PROFL AFFIL & HONORS:** CA State Bar, ABA, Los Angeles Cty. Bar Assn., Beverly Hills Bar Assn.; **GRAD EDUC:** LLB, 1932, Univ. of OK School of Law; **EDUC HONORS:** Order of the Coif; **MIL SERV:** US Army, 1942-1945, Maj.; **HOME ADD:** 11630 Acama St., Studio City, North Hollywood, CA 91604, (213)763-6027; **BUS ADD:** 1801 Ave. of Stars, Gateway West Bldg. Suite 510, Los Angeles, CA 90067, (213)277-4411.

ROSEN, Randy——B: Feb. 18, 1950, Chicago, IL, *Pres.*, Klippel-Rosen & Assoc.; **PRIM RE ACT:** Broker, Consultant, Owner/Investor, Instructor, Property Manager, Syndicator; **SERVICES:** Brokerage, investment, counseling, synd., prop. mgmt.; **REP CLIENTS:** Indivs. & instns. in investment props. & mgmt.; **PROFL AFFIL & HONORS:** IREM, Northside RE Bd., Chicago RE Bd. (Member of Faculty), IL Assn. of Realtors, NAR, CPM; **EDUC:** BA, 1972, Econ., Univ. of IL; **HOME ADD:** 1638 Greenleaf, Chicago, IL 60622; **BUS ADD:** 5668 N Lincoln Ave., Chicago, IL 60659, (312)561-5531.

ROSEN, Col. Richard——B: Nov. 10, 1917, NYC, *Pres.*, Richard Rosen Group; **PRIM RE ACT:** Owner/Investor; **EDUC:** 1939, Banking, NY Univ.; **MIL SERV:** US Army, Col., 8 decorations; **HOME ADD:** 29 E. 21st St., NY, NY 10010, (212)777-3017; **BUS ADD:** 29 E. 21st St., NY, NY 10010, (212)777-3017.

ROSEN, Robert A.——B: June 19, 1936, Jackson Heights, Queens, NY, *Chmn. and Pres.*, Rosen Associates; **PRIM RE ACT:** Consultant, Developer, Builder, Owner/Investor; **OTHER RE ACT:** RE Investor and Devel. of Comml. Props.; **PROFL AFFIL & HONORS:** NACORE, ICSC, Hon. Member of Editorial Bd. of Natl. Mall Monitor; Prop. Consultants Soc., Great Britain, RESSI, Soc, for Intl. Devel., Intl. Inst. of Valuers with SCV designation; Assn. for a Better

NY, Young Pres. Org., NAR, Natl. Assn. of Review Appraisers; **EDUC:** BBA, 1957, Acctg. and Law, CUNY, Baruch Coll.; **GRAD EDUC:** MBA, 1960, Mktg. and Statistics, CUNY, Baruch Coll.; **MIL SERV:** Over 23 yrs. in the USAF & USNR, Presently Cmdr. in the US Naval Res.; **OTHER ACT & HONORS:** Assoc. Member of Naval War Coll.; Found., US Senatorial Bus. Advisory Bd.; Long Is. Council of the Albert Einstein Coll. of Med.; Public Relations Soc. of Amer. Faculty Member of New Sch. for Soc. Research; Pres. and Dean of the Intl. Inst. for RE Studies, Ltd.; Dir. of RE Inst., Adelphi Univ.; **HOME ADD:** 85-29 Wicklow Pl., Jamaica Estates, NY 11432, (212)454-6170; **BUS ADD:** 333 Jericho Tnpk., Jericho, NY 11753, (516)822-5350.

ROSEN, Robert J.——B: Nov. 23, 1947, New York, NY, *Partner*, Rosen, Hacker & Nierenberg; **PRIM RE ACT:** Attorney, Syndicator; **REP CLIENTS:** Cox Hotel Corp., Wilder-Richmon Corp., Lake Placid Club Resort, Conference Environments Corp., Horizon Hotels Ltd., N. Amer. Condo. Grp., J & C Lamb Corp.; **EDUC:** BA, 1969, Pol. Sci., Univ. of MA; **GRAD EDUC:** JD, 1972, Columbia Law School; **EDUC HONORS:** Phi Beta Kappa, Cum Laude, Harlan Fiske Stone Scholar; **HOME ADD:** 6 Creemer Rd., Armonk, NY 10504, (914)273-9336; **BUS ADD:** 342 Madison Ave., New York, NY 10173, (212)687-4444.

ROSEN, Stephen Daniel——B: Dec. 17, 1943, New York City, NY, *VP*, Steven Organization Corp.; **PRIM RE ACT:** Attorney, Developer, Owner/Investor; **PREV EMPLOY:** Fried, Frank, Harris, Shriver & Jacobson, Attys., 1975-1980; **EDUC:** AB, 1965, Philosophy, Univ. of Rochester; **GRAD EDUC:** LLB, 1968, Law, Harvard Law School; **EDUC HONORS:** Highest Distinction, Law Review; **HOME ADD:** 46 Remsen St., Brooklyn Heights, NY 11201, (212)852-3357; **BUS ADD:** 1995 Broadway, New York, NY 10023, (212)580-7200.

ROSENBAUM, Michael Gordon——B: Apr. 10, 1943, Boston, MA, *Prop. Mgr.*, Spaulding & Slye, Prop. Mgmt.; **PRIM RE ACT:** Property Manager; **SERVICES:** Full mgmt. services; **REP CLIENTS:** Hexalon RE, Inc.; **PREV EMPLOY:** Broker,Wheeler Realty Co., Inc., Boston, MA, 1968-1975; Involved with mgmt. of Prudential Center, Boston, MA for Prudential Mgr. of Comml./Resid. Div., 1975-1980; **PROFL AFFIL & HONORS:** BOMA, Greater Boston RE Bd.; **EDUC:** BA, 1967, Intl. Studies, OH State Univ.; **OTHER ACT & HONORS:** Bldg. and Land Acquisition Comm., Acton, MA, 1979-1981; **HOME ADD:** 84 Circuit Dr., Stow, MA 01775, (617)897-3111; **BUS ADD:** 225 Franklin St., Boston, MA 02110, (617)426-5326.

ROSENBAUM, Steven M.——B: Nov. 16, 1947, Cleveland, OH, *Pres.*, SMR Associates, SYNDEL Real Estate Development; **PRIM RE ACT:** Broker, Developer, Owner/Investor, Syndicator; **SERVICES:** Sales and consulting for RE investors; **REP CLIENTS:** Private and instl. investors in income producing props.; **PREV EMPLOY:** Arch. and Engrg. firms; **EDUC:** BS, 1973, Mktg. Communications, Design, OH State Univ.; **HOME ADD:** 15236 Count Fleet Court, Carmel, IN 46032, (317)846-5244; **BUS ADD:** 15236 Count Fleet Court, Carmel, IN 46032, (317)846-5244.

ROSENBERG, Burton X.——B: Jan. 21, 1941, Chicago, IL, *Part.*, Rosenberg, Savner & Unikel; **PRIM RE ACT:** Attorney; **SERVICES:** Legal; **REP CLIENTS:** Devel., synd., lenders; **PREV EMPLOY:** Partner, Levy & Erens; **EDUC:** BA, 1963, Econ., Univ. of PA; **GRAD EDUC:** JD, 1966, Northwestern Univ. Sch. of Law; **HOME ADD:** 406 Northwood, Glencoe, IL 60022, (312)835-5004; **BUS ADD:** 10 S. LaSalle St., Suite 1542, Chicago, IL 60603, (312)372-3100.

ROSENBERG, Jay A.——B: Oct. 23, 1939, Philadelphia, PA, *Partner*, Strauss, Troy & Ruehlmann Co., LPA; **PRIM RE ACT:** Attorney; **SERVICES:** Legal services, RE & bankruptcy law; **REP CLIENTS:** Central Trust Co., NA; First Nat. Bank of Cincinnati; Amer. Trust Co.; Title Ins. Co. of MN; **PROFL AFFIL & HONORS:** ABA; OH and Cincinnati Bar Assns., Tr., OH Land Title Assn.; **EDUC:** BS, 1961, Corp. Fin., Univ. of PA; **GRAD EDUC:** JD, 1965, Law, Univ. of MI; **EDUC HONORS:** With Distinction; **MIL SERV:** US Army; **HOME ADD:** 6539 Blue Ridge Ave., Cincinnati, OH 45213, (513)731-2265; **BUS ADD:** 2100 Central Trust Ctr., Cincinnati, OH 45202, (513)621-2120.

ROSENBERG, Jerome S.——B: Nov. 7, 1932, Los Angeles, CA, *Pres.*, Jero, Inc.; **PRIM RE ACT:** Developer, Builder, Owner/Investor; **PROFL AFFIL & HONORS:** Chmn. of a subcommittee for the NAHB, Wash.,D.C.; **OTHER ACT & HONORS:** Dev. of Aspen Hill, 500 million dev. Denver, CO; **HOME TEL:** (213)392-3046; **BUS ADD:** 723 Ocean Front Walk, Venice, CA 90291.

ROSENBERG, Sheli Z.——B: Feb. 2, 1942, NYC, NY, *VP & Gen. Counsel*, Equity Financial & Management Co.; **PRIM RE ACT:** Attorney; **SERVICES:** All services applicable to large RE practice; **PREV EMPLOY:** Partner, Schiff Hardin & Waite, Chicago, IL, 1970-1980; **EDUC:** BA, 1963, Hist./Pol. Sci., Jackson Coll. of Tufts Univ.; **GRAD EDUC:** JD, 1966, Northwestern Univ. School of Law; **EDUC HONORS:** Cum Laude; **HOME ADD:** 406 Northwood Dr., Glencoe, IL 60022, (312)835-5004; **BUS ADD:** 10 S. LaSalle St., Suite 900, Chicago, IL 60603, (312)782-8994.

ROSENBERG, Sidney B.——B: June 25, 1946, Jacksonville, FL, *VP*, Ackerman and Co., Devel.; **PRIM RE ACT:** Developer; **SERVICES:** Urban redevel. condos., office rennovation; **REP CLIENTS:** City of Atlanta; **PREV EMPLOY:** First Fidelity Mort. Corp, Marine Midland Realty Credit Corp.; **EDUC:** BA, 1968, Hist., Econ., Washington and Lee Univ.; **GRAD EDUC:** MBA, 1971, Fin., GA State Univ.; **HOME ADD:** 3464 Seven Pines Ct., Atlanta, GA 30339, (404)435-5730; **BUS ADD:** Tower Pl. Suite 100, Atlanta, GA 30026, (404)262-7171.

ROSENBERG, Steve——B: July 20, 1953, Chicago, IL, *Development Mgr.*, Smith-Ritchie/Landsing; **PRIM RE ACT:** Broker, Developer, Owner/Investor; **SERVICES:** Development mgmt., investment counseling; **PROFL AFFIL & HONORS:** Realtor, OR Lic. broker; **EDUC:** BA, 1975, Poli. Sci., CO Coll.; **GRAD EDUC:** MS, 1978, RE & Urban Econ., Univ. of WI; **EDUC HONORS:** Member Beta Gamma Delta, Natl. Honary Bus. Frat.; **OTHER ACT & HONORS:** Bd. of Dir., Jewish Community Ctr.; **HOME TEL:** (503)239-0318; **BUS ADD:** 133 SW Second, Portland, OR 97204, (503)227-2654.

ROSENBERG, Theodore M.——B: Dec. 27, 1941, Baltimore MD, *Pres.*, Twin Oaks Assts. Inc.; **PRIM RE ACT:** Consultant, Appraiser, Developer, Instructor, Syndicator; **OTHER RE ACT:** Preservation Consultant; **SERVICES:** Structuring, Planning, Econ. Feasibility, preservation, finanace; **REP CLIENTS:** Investors & Devels., Community & Nonprofit Organizations; **PREV EMPLOY:** The Chesapeake Life Ins. Co., The Chesapeake Fund; **PROFL AFFIL & HONORS:** Baltimore Neighorhood Preservation Council, Baltimore Sec., Traders Assn. Mid Atlantic Options Soc., Soc. of Fin. Examiners, League of Amer. Hist. Theaters, Preservation Action, Who's Who in Ind. & Fin., Who's Who in the World; Guest Lecturer on Preservation, Goucher Coll., Chmn Review Comm., Mt. Vernon Hist. Soc. (BAITO); **EDUC:** BS, Life Investment Officers Program, Univ. of Chicago; Investment Officers Program (ICI), S. Methodist Univ.; **OTHER ACT & HONORS:** Bd. Dir., Balto Opera Co; 5th Dist., New Theatre Project, Mt. Vernon Belvedere Assn., Baltimore Petach, Baltimore Learning Ctr.; **HOME ADD:** 5007 Forest Park Ave., Baltimore, MD 21207, (301)448-3134; **BUS ADD:** 521 St. Paul Pl., Baltimore, MD 21202, (301)685-4020.

ROSENBERG, Thomas B.——B: May 3, 1947, Chicago, IL, *Pres.*, Capital Associates Devel. Corp.; **PRIM RE ACT:** Developer; **PROFL AFFIL & HONORS:** Nat. Leased Housing Assn.; Housing Task Force of the Democratic Caucus; U.S. House of Representatives; ABA; **EDUC:** BA, 1968, Pol. Sci., Univ. of WI; **GRAD EDUC:** JD, 1972, Law, Univ. of CA; **EDUC HONORS:** Cum Laude; **HOME ADD:** 1310 Ritchie Ct., Chicago, IL 60610; **BUS ADD:** 1122 N. LaSalle Dr., Chicago, IL 60610, (312)856-0300.

ROSENBERG, William B.——B: Aug. 19, 1914, Harrisburg, PA, *Atty.*, Blumberg, Rosenberg, Mullen & Blumberg, Esqs.; **PRIM RE ACT:** Attorney; **SERVICES:** All legal services from negotiations through closing of title. Clearing of disputed titles; **REP CLIENTS:** Lofts Seed Inc., Pillar of Fire Church, Manville Nat. Bank; **PROFL AFFIL & HONORS:** ABA, NJ Bar Assn. and Somerset County Bar Assn, Past Pres. Somerset County Bar Assn.; **EDUC:** BA, 1935, Liberal Arts, Dickinson Coll., Carlisle, PA; **GRAD EDUC:** LLB, 1938, Law, Columbia Univ., New York, NY; **EDUC HONORS:** Phi Beta Kappa; **MIL SERV:** Intelligence, S/Sgr; **OTHER ACT & HONORS:** Judge, Mcpl. Court in Manville, NJ 1949-1955, Past Pres. Somerset County Vocational - Tech. Bd. of Educ.; Past Pres. NJ School Bds. Assn.; **HOME ADD:** 121 Agnes Pl., Bound Brook, NJ 08805, (201)356-8876; **BUS ADD:** 35 N Bridge St., P.O. Box 400, Somerville, NJ 08876, (201)526-5400.

ROSENBERGER, Herbert D.——B: Mar. 29, 1935, Bryn Mawr, PA, *VP*, First Nat. Bank of MD, Admin. Div.; **PRIM RE ACT:** Developer, Owner/Investor, Property Manager; **OTHER RE ACT:** VP RE/Const.; **SERVICES:** Manages and controls bank owned and leased property; **PREV EMPLOY:** MD Casulty Co., 1970-1981, Corp. Sec. & RE Dir.; **PROFL AFFIL & HONORS:** NACORE, Exec. VP & Sec./Treas., Greater Baltimore Comm.; Amer. Mgmt. Assn.; BOMA; **EDUC:** BS, 1957, EE, Temple Univ.; **GRAD EDUC:** MBA, 1961, Bus. Admin./Mktg./Fin., George Washington Univ.; **MIL SERV:** US Army, Medical Corp., 1957-1958; **OTHER ACT & HONORS:** Boy Scouts of Amer.; Baltimore Symphony Orch.; Baltimore Zoological Soc.; National Aquarium in Baltimore; **HOME ADD:** 5700 Rockspring Rd., Baltimore, MD 21209, (301)367-5700; **BUS ADD:** POB 1596, 25 S. Charles St., Baltimore, MD 21203, (301)244-4484.

ROSENBERRY, Paul E.——B: Aug. 18, 1935, Osceola, NE, *Agricultural Economist,* Self-employed; **PRIM RE ACT:** Consultant, Builder, Owner/Investor, Property Manager; **SERVICES:** Complete mgmt., taxes, acctg., renting, selling; **REP CLIENTS:** Homeowners, apt owners, landlords, farm owners; **PREV EMPLOY:** Aq. Econ. with US Dept. of Agriculture; **PROFL AFFIL & HONORS:** Cert. of Merit, Quality w/in Grades; **EDUC:** Voc. Educ., Univ. of NE; **GRAD EDUC:** M. Sci. & Phd, 1958 &1971, Ag. Econ., Math, IA State Univ.; **EDUC HONORS:** Alpha Tau Alpha, Gama Sigma Delta; **OTHER ACT & HONORS:** Bd. of Dir. Open Door Missions, Bd. of Dir. Wesley Found.; **HOME ADD:** RR1, Ames, IA 50010, (515)733-2139; **BUS ADD:** RRI, Ames, IA 50010, (515)733-2139.

ROSENBLATT, Fredric T.——B: Aug. 13, 1944, Minneapolis, MN, *Partner,* Leonard, Street and Deinard, Comml. RE; **PRIM RE ACT:** Attorney; **SERVICES:** Planning and negotiation of transactions and drafting of instruments in all aspects of RE acquisition, sale, fin., const., leasing and exchange; **REP CLIENTS:** Hyatt Minneapolis Corp. (owner, Minneapolis Hyatt Regency Hotel); Gelco Corp.; Peck & Peck Stores; La Maur, Inc.; Napco Indus., Inc.; Piper Jaffrey & Hopwood, Inc.; Budget Rent-A-Car; **PROFL AFFIL & HONORS:** Chmn. Real Prop. Sect., Hennepin Cty. Bar Assn.; Chmn., Condo. and Time-Sharing Sub-Comm., MN State Bar Assn., Real Prop. Sect.; Member, Hennepin Cty., MN and ABA Real Prop. Sections; **EDUC:** AB, 1966, Govt. and Hist., Dartmouth Coll.; **GRAD EDUC:** JD, 1969, Univ. of MI Law School; **EDUC HONORS:** Honors Major; **OTHER ACT & HONORS:** Bd. Member of: Guthrie Theatre Found., Minneapolis, MN and Associates of The Minneapolis Art Inst.; Member, Bd. of Mgmt., Minneapolis YMCA Camp Warren; **HOME ADD:** 3712 Zenith Ave. S., Minneapolis, MN 55410, (612)925-3712; **BUS ADD:** 1200 National City Bank Bldg., 510 Marquette Ave., Minneapolis, MN 55402, (612)339-1200.

ROSENBLATT, Harvey——B: Jan. 3, 1939, Brooklyn, NY, *Pres.,* Triton Group LTD; **PRIM RE ACT:** Broker, Owner/Investor; **OTHER RE ACT:** CPA; **PREV EMPLOY:** C.I. Realty Investors Nov.,1973- Nov.,1977 Tishman Realty & Const. Co., Inc. Jan.,1966- Nov.,1973; **PROFL AFFIL & HONORS:** Amer. Inst. CPA's & N.Y.C. Soc. of CPA's Dir.: Triton Group LTD & Palmas del Map Co.; **EDUC:** BS, 1961, Acctg., NYU; **HOME ADD:** 1431 Sylvia Lane, East Meadow, NY 11554, (516)538-7281; **BUS ADD:** New York, NY 100191 Pennsylvania Plaza, (212)736-3220.

ROSENFELD, Mark K.——B: Mar. 17, 1946, Jackson, MI, *Exec. VP,* Jacobson Stores, Inc.; **OTHER RE ACT:** Retail Exec.; **EDUC:** BA, 1968, Econ., Amherst Coll.; **GRAD EDUC:** SM, 1970, Sloan School (MIT); **EDUC HONORS:** Cum Laude; **MIL SERV:** US Army, 1st Lt., Commendation Medal; **HOME ADD:** 1812 Glen, Jackson, MI 49203, (517)789-7803; **BUS ADD:** 1200 N. West, Jackson, MI 49202, (517)787-3600.

ROSENFELD, Michael D.——B: June 27, 1947, Greensboro, NC, *Asst. VP,* First Interstate Mort. Co., National Div.; **PRIM RE ACT:** Consultant, Appraiser, Lender; **OTHER RE ACT:** Mort. Banker; **SERVICES:** Mort. loans for corporately sponsored RE projects; arrange joint ventures and consult on equity offerings; **REP CLIENTS:** Major corps./devels. across the US that are involved in RE; **PREV EMPLOY:** Bank of Amer., investment banking and Nat. Div.; **PROFL AFFIL & HONORS:** Treas., No. CA Mort. Bankers Assn.; Bay Area Mort. Bankers Assn.; **EDUC:** BS, 1970, Bus. Admin., Univ. of NV; **GRAD EDUC:** MS, 1973, Intl. Bus., Univ. of So. CA; MBA, 1981, RE, Golden Gate Univ.; **MIL SERV:** USN, Ens.; **HOME ADD:** 66 Beechwood Dr., Oakland, CA 94618, (415)652-3596; **BUS ADD:** One Embarcadero Ctr., Suite 2401, San Francisco, CA 94111, (415)544-5947.

ROSENSHINE, Marvin S.——*Treas.,* Sterndent Corp.; **PRIM RE ACT:** Broker, Property Manager; **BUS ADD:** 1455 East Putnam Ave., Old Greenwich, CT 06870, (203)637-5461.*

ROSENSTEIN, Joe——B: Feb. 17, 1922, NY, NY, *Realtor/Owner,* Sunstate Realty Assoc.; **PRIM RE ACT:** Broker, Instructor, Property Manager; **OTHER RE ACT:** Mort. Broker; **SERVICES:** Comml. & Resid. Investment Props., Land, Condos., Prop. mgmt.; **REP CLIENTS:** Indivs. & Group investors of FL Props.; **PREV EMPLOY:** Pres., Milrose Construction Co., NY; Pres., Townhouse Mgmt. & Maint. Servs., Inc.; **PROFL AFFIL & HONORS:** FL Bd. of Realtors; Manatee Cty. Bd. of Realtors; FL Assn. of Mort. Brokers; **EDUC:** Bus. Admin., RE, NY Univ., Manatee Jr. Coll.; **MIL SERV:** USN SeaBees, CM 3/C, Pac. Area, WW II; **OTHER ACT & HONORS:** Amer. Inst. of Parliamentarians; Navy Seabee Veterans of Amer.; Owner, Dir., Instr., Sunstate Inst. of RE (Lic. by FL Bd. of RE to offer all required FL RE licensing courses); **HOME ADD:** 2757 Mall Dr., Apt. 201, Sarasota, FL 33581, (813)921-4931; **BUS ADD:** 4220 60th St. Court W., Bradenton, FL 33529, (813)794-0471.

ROSENTHAL, Howard——B: Oct. 18, 1928, NYC, *Pres.,* Tribune Realty Inc., F and R Assoc., Inc.; **PRIM RE ACT:** Consultant, Appraiser, Property Manager; **PREV EMPLOY:** Self employed since 1959; **PROFL AFFIL & HONORS:** Realtor, CPM, IFA, CRA, Assoc. mbr. SRA, ASA; **EDUC:** BBA, 1950, RE and Genl., City Coll. of Bus. Adm.; **GRAD EDUC:** BBA, 1950; **BUS ADD:** 24 County Rd., Tennafly, NJ 07670, (212)594-4514.

ROSENTHAL, Leighton A.——*Pres.,* Work Wear Corp.; **PRIM RE ACT:** Property Manager; **BUS ADD:** 1768 East 25th St., Cleveland, OH 44114.*

ROSENTHAL, Richard J.——B: Mar. 10, 1940, New York, NY, *Owner,* R. J. Rosenthal & Assocs., Realtors; **PRIM RE ACT:** Broker, Consultant, Property Manager; **SERVICES:** Investment counseling and brokerage, fin. strategy and implementation, expert witness on RE custom and practice; **REP CLIENTS:** Pri. investors and devels., priv. lenders and profl. corp. qualified plans; **PREV EMPLOY:** Scientific Data Systems; Xerox Data Systems; Scientific Data Systems, Israel; MDR Investment Co.; **PROFL AFFIL & HONORS:** NAR, CCIM Candidate; Gold Card Exchangors Designation, NCE; CA RE Certificate, RECI, Realtor of the Year (1980); Regional VP and Member of Exec. Comm., CA Assn. of Realtors; **EDUC:** BBA, 1961, Mktg. and Advertising, Hofstra Univ., NY; **EDUC HONORS:** Dean's List 3 years; **MIL SERV:** US Army, Sgt.; **OTHER ACT & HONORS:** Marina del Rey Lodge B'nai B'rith; Charter Member, 1977, Bd. of Tr.; Venice C of C; Lecturer on RE Fin., CA Assn. of Realtors Speakers Bureau; **HOME ADD:** 140 Waterview, Playa del Rey, CA 90291, (213)392-3926; **BUS ADD:** 1340 W Wash. Blvd., Venice, CA 90291, (213)399-6562.

ROSENTHAL, Robert N.——B: Sept. 2, 1952, Chicago, IL, *Pres.,* Dunbar Corp.; **PRIM RE ACT:** Developer; **SERVICES:** Constr. and mktg. of resid. and comml. props.; **PROFL AFFIL & HONORS:** Home Builders Assn. of Gr. Chicago; **EDUC:** 1977, Hist., Reed Coll.; **HOME ADD:** 7631 N Eastlake Terr., Chicago, IL 60626, (312)973-2974; **BUS ADD:** 6033 N Sheridan Rd., Chicago, IL 60660, (312)275-4000.

ROSENTHAL, Stanley R.——B: Apr. 8, 1929, Brooklyn, NY, *Pres.,* All-State Properties Inc.; **PRIM RE ACT:** Broker, Developer, Builder; **SERVICES:** Land devel. for sale to builders; resid. builder; **PROFL AFFIL & HONORS:** Builders Assn. of S. FL; C of C, FL RE Broker; **EDUC:** BS, 1950, Acctg., NY Univ. School of Commerce; **EDUC HONORS:** Cum Laude; **MIL SERV:** US Army, 1st Lt., 1951-1953; **HOME ADD:** 19707 N.E. 36 Court, N. Miami Beach, FL 33180; **BUS ADD:** 4200 NW 16 St., Penthouse B, Ft. Lauderdale, FL 33313, (305)735-6300.

ROSENWALD, Robert L., Jr.——B: June 7, 1945, Jacksonville, FL, *CCIM,* Investment Realty; **PRIM RE ACT:** Broker, Consultant, Developer, Builder, Owner/Investor, Property Manager, Syndicator; **PREV EMPLOY:** Licensed Contractor; **PROFL AFFIL & HONORS:** NAR, American Land Development Association, Certified Commercial Investment Member of NAR; **EDUC:** BA, 1969, Philosophy & Mathematics, St. John's College, Santa Fe, NM; **OTHER ACT & HONORS:** Chairman, Education Committee, Santa Fe Bd. of Realtors; **HOME ADD:** Box 4, Galisted, NM 87540, (505)982-1506; **BUS ADD:** PO Drawer 1770, Santa Fe, NM 87501, (505)988-4474.

ROSENZWEIG, David L.——B: June 17, 1939, Pottsville, PA, *Atty.,* Rosenzweig & Schulz; **PRIM RE ACT:** Attorney; **PREV EMPLOY:** Union Commerce Corp., Cleveland, Ohio ($1.5 billion bank holding company - held positions of Exec. VP and General Counsel); **PROFL AFFIL & HONORS:** OH Bar Assn., Bar Assn. of Gr. Cleveland; **EDUC:** BS, 1962, Youngstown State Univ.; **GRAD EDUC:** JD, 1968, Case Western Reserve Univ. Law School; **EDUC HONORS:** Order of the Coif; Editor-in-Chief, Law Review; **OTHER ACT & HONORS:** Author: "Mortgages-Construction and Operation-Lien and Priority", 18 W. Res. Law Review 675, 1967; **HOME ADD:** 21349 Fairmount Blvd., Shaker Heights, OH 44118, (216)932-3334; **BUS ADD:** 720 Citizens Federal Tower, 2000 E. 9th St., Cleveland, OH 44115, (216)589-9300.

ROSENZWEIG, Martin L., Ph.D.——B: Nov. 3, 1932, New York, NY, *Chmn. and CEO,* University Group, Inc.; **PRIM RE ACT:** Owner/Investor, Syndicator; **SERVICES:** Synd. of large-scale public RE programs; **REP CLIENTS:** Indiv. & corp. investors; **PREV EMPLOY:** Pres., Univ. Group, Inc. 1967-1980; Partner, Univ. Advisory Co., 1969-present; Chmn., Univ. RE Trust, 1974-present; **PROFL AFFIL & HONORS:** RESSI; IAFP; Member of Exec. Comm., CA Synd. Forum; **EDUC:** BCE, 1955, Civil Engrg., Cornell Univ.; **GRAD EDUC:** PhD, 1959, Aeronautical Engrg., Mathematics, Physics, Cornell Univ.; **OTHER ACT & HONORS:** Dir., Peninsula

Symphony Assn.; Member, Cornell Univ. Council; **HOME ADD:** 27789 Palos Verdes Dr. E, Rancho Palos Verdes, CA 90274; **BUS ADD:** 666 E Ocean Blvd., Long Beach, CA 90802, (213)435-6344.

ROSEWATER, Robert David——**B:** June 24, 1939, Cleveland, OH, *Atty. - Partner*, Weston, Hurd, Fallon, Paisley & Howley; **PRIM RE ACT:** Attorney; **PROFL AFFIL & HONORS:** Bar Assn. of Greater Cleveland (Chmn., RE Sect.); OH State Bar Assn.; ABA; **EDUC:** AB, 1960, Govt., Harvard Univ.; **GRAD EDUC:** JD, 1965, Law, Harvard Law School; **EDUC HONORS:** Magna Cum Laude; **MIL SERV:** US Army, 1st Lt.; **HOME ADD:** 22231 Rye Rd., Shaker Heights, OH 44122, (216)295-2019; **BUS ADD:** 2500 Terminal Tower, Cleveland, OH 44113, (216)241-6602.

ROSOW, Lawrence M.——**B:** Oct. 20, 1923, San Antonio, TX, *Pres. & Chmn.*, Rosow & Kline, Realtors, Inc.; **PRIM RE ACT:** Broker, Insuror; **SERVICES:** Comml. Investment, Indus., Investment Counselling, Evaluation, Prop. Mgmt. and Resid.; **PROFL AFFIL & HONORS:** RNMI San Antonio Bd. of Realtors, TAR, NAR, IREF, Inter-City Relocation Servs., Greater San Antonio Builders Assn., San Antonio Apt. Assn.; **EDUC:** BS, Commerce, 1943, St. Mary's Univ.; **GRAD EDUC:** MS, 1948, Columbia Univ., Grad. Sch. of Bus., NY; **EDUC HONORS:** Honors, 1943; **MIL SERV:** TX Nat. Guard, Maj.; **HOME ADD:** 11431 Whisper Green, San Antonio, TX 78230, (512)492-2156; **BUS ADD:** 6836 San Pedro Ave., San Antonio, TX 78216, (512)828-9901.

ROSS, Barry J.——**B:** June 5, 1948, Los Angeles, CA, *Pres.*, Robinhood Homes, Inc.; **PRIM RE ACT:** Broker, Developer, Builder, Owner/Investor; **SERVICES:** Builder of SFD - San Diego Cty.; **PREV EMPLOY:** Touche Ross & Co., 1972-76; **PROFL AFFIL & HONORS:** AICPA, CA Soc. of CPA's; **EDUC:** BS, 1971, Bus. Mgmt., San Diego State Univ.; **GRAD EDUC:** MBA, 1972, Bus. Mgmt./Psych., San Diego State Univ.; **HOME ADD:** 630 Nardito Lane, Solana Beach, CA 92075, (714)755-3708; **BUS ADD:** 3648 Main St., Chula Vista, CA 92011, (714)422-0123.

ROSS, Eugene I.——**B:** Dec. 30, 1934, Chicago, IL, *Sr. VP*, Berger Realty Group; **PRIM RE ACT:** Broker, Consultant, Developer, Builder, Owner/Investor, Property Manager, Syndicator; **SERVICES:** Devel., counseling, investment, brokerage; **REP CLIENTS:** Public corps., banks, finl. instits., pension fund advisor, indivs.; **PREV EMPLOY:** Pres., Ross, Kotin & Co.; Pres., Seay & Thomas (Div. of IC Industries); VP, Arthur Rubloff & Co.; **PROFL AFFIL & HONORS:** Nat. Assn. of RE Counselors (CRE); Inst. of RE Mgmt. (CPM); Lambda Alpha; ULI, NAREB, HBA, CRE, CPM; **EDUC:** BS, 1956, Fin./Investment, Univ. of CO; **EDUC HONORS:** Alpha Kappa Psi; **MIL SERV:** USAF, Maj.; **OTHER ACT & HONORS:** Bd. of Dir., of Med. Research Inst.; Michael Reese Hosp.; Bd. of Dir., Treasure Lakes Co.; Young Presidents Org., Bd. of Dir., American Jewish Comm. (Chicago); **HOME ADD:** 875 Fairview Rd., Highland Pk., IL 60035; **BUS ADD:** 180 N. LaSalle St., Chicago, IL 60601, (312)558-3000.

ROSS, Fred D. (Bubba), Jr.——**B:** Oct. 6, 1949, Walterboro, SC, *VP*, Bankers Mortgage Corp., Comml.; **PRIM RE ACT:** Broker, Consultant, Appraiser, Lender, Property Manager; **OTHER RE ACT:** Mort. Banker; **SERVICES:** Investment placements; counseling; appraising; const. handling; prop. mgmt.; 221(d)(4) program; also work in FHA insured programs; **REP CLIENTS:** Instl. investors in comml. props.; nat. consulting firms; indivs.; & non-profit organs.; **PROFL AFFIL & HONORS:** AIREA, Soc. of RE Appraisers, SC RE Commn., Broker, MAI, SRPA; **EDUC:** BA, 1971, Psych., Erskine Coll.; **HOME ADD:** 2502 Wilmot Ave., Columbia, SC 29205, (803)771-4618; **BUS ADD:** P O Box 448, Columbia, SC 29202, (803)771-2670.

ROSS, Herbert A.——**B:** Jan. 31, 1935, Cleveland, OH, *Atty.*, Herbert A. Ross; **PRIM RE ACT:** Broker, Attorney, Owner/Investor; **SERVICES:** Represent brokers, owners, devel. and lenders as attys.; **REP CLIENTS:** Re/Max of Alaska, Inc.; Several other Re/Max; ERA/Glacer Realty; Allen P. Kirschbaum (developer); **PREV EMPLOY:** Self employment since 1969; **PROFL AFFIL & HONORS:** Alaska, American and Cleveland Bar Assn.; Assn. Trial Lawyers of Amer.; ABA; **EDUC:** AB, 1959, Psych., Western Reserve Univ. (Now Case Western Univ.); **GRAD EDUC:** LLB, 1964, Law, Univ. of San Francisco; **MIL SERV:** US Army, Res.; Pvt.; **OTHER ACT & HONORS:** RE Club, Univ. of Alaska at Anchorage; **HOME ADD:** P.O. Box 1331, Anchorage, AK 99510-1331, (907)272-8269; **BUS ADD:** 715 "L" St., Anchorage, AK 99501, (907)279-1574.

ROSS, Dr. Jay S.——**B:** Mar. 2, 1913, Philadelphia, PA, *Pres.*, J.S. Ross Co.; **PRIM RE ACT:** Broker, Instructor, Consultant, Developer, Builder, Owner/Investor; **SERVICES:** Acquisitions-Mergers; Consultant; **REP CLIENTS:** S CA Water Co.; Lucky Auto Supply; ETO; Urban Pacific Equities; **PREV EMPLOY:** Sec.-Treas. Superior Laminates-Superior Shower Door Co.; VP Nat. Housing Dev. Corp.; **PROFL AFFIL & HONORS:** Nat. Assn. of Bus. Econ.; NACPD; So. CA Corporate Planners, Chmn. RE & Regional Comm.-Los Angeles Chap., Natl. Assn.-Bus. Econ.; **EDUC:** AB, MBA, LLB, Econ., Accounting; **GRAD EDUC:** PhD, UCLA; USC; Braddock Univ.; **MIL SERV:** USCG; **OTHER ACT & HONORS:** St's. Orgs., Democratic Cty. Central Comm.; **BUS ADD:** 5067 San Feliciano Dr., Woodland Hills, CA 91364, (213)348-6249.

ROSS, Martha P.——**B:** Mar. 19, 1945, St. Louis, MO, *Housing Admin.*, City of Inglewood, CA, Housing; **OTHER RE ACT:** Municipal govt.; **SERVICES:** Varied; **PREV EMPLOY:** All city govt.; **PROFL AFFIL & HONORS:** Nat. Assn. of Housing and Redevel. Officials, Intl. City Mgmt. Assn., Amer. Soc. for Public Admin.; **EDUC:** BA, 1967, Poli. Sci., S. Methodist Univ.; **GRAD EDUC:** MA, 1972, Poli. Sci./Law, S. Methodist Univ.; **EDUC HONORS:** Mortar Bd., Who's Who in Amer. Univs., Kirkos Service Organization; **HOME ADD:** 660 Kingman Ave., Santa Monica, CA 90402; **BUS ADD:** One Manchester Blvd., Inglewood, CA 90301, (213)649-7221.

ROSS, Maxwell——*Dir. Purch.*, Gulton Industries, Inc.; **PRIM RE ACT:** Property Manager; **BUS ADD:** 101 College Rd. East, Princeton, NJ 08540, (609)452-1811.*

ROSS, Stephen M.——**B:** May 10, 1940, Detroit, MI, *Founder/Pres.*, Related Housing Cos., Inc.; **PRIM RE ACT:** Syndicator, Developer, Owner/Investor; **SERVICES:** Develop, own synd. and manage subsidized and conventional multi-family apt. devels.; **PREV EMPLOY:** CPA, Coopers & Lybrand, Detroit, MI; Asst. VP, Laird, Inc.; Bear, Stears & Co.; **PROFL AFFIL & HONORS:** MI & Fl Bar Assn.; Assn. of Builders and Owners of Greater NY, Master Builders Award, 1980, Assn. of Builders and Owners of Greater NY; **EDUC:** BA, 1962, Univ. of MI; **GRAD EDUC:** JD, 1965, Wayne State Univ., School of Law; LLM, 1966, Taxation, NY Univ.; **BUS ADD:** 645 Fifth Ave., New York, NY 10022, (212)421-5333.

ROSSER, Michael——**B:** Oct. 11, 1940, Denver, CO, *Nat. Sales Mgr.*, PMI Insurance Co.; **PRIM RE ACT:** Insuror; **SERVICES:** Secondary Mktg., Single Family Mort. Ins.; **REP CLIENTS:** Sales of various mort. ins. related products and servs.; **PREV EMPLOY:** Marketing officer United Mort. Co., Denver 1968-75; **PROFL AFFIL & HONORS:** Mort. Bankers Assn. of Amer., Chmn. Young Mort. Bankers Comm. 1978, Member Single Family Comm. 1978-81, Educ. Task Force 1980, Everett C. Spelman Award, CMBA 1981; **EDUC:** BS, 1964, Govt., CO State Univ.; **GRAD EDUC:** MA, 1972, Urban & Regnl. Planning, Univ. of No. CO; **EDUC HONORS:** Two Ford Found. grants, Local Govt. Studies, Grad. School of Mort. Banking, Northern Univ. 1978; **OTHER ACT & HONORS:** Advisory Bd., Univ. of Denver, RE & Const. Mgmt. Dept., Teaching Faculty various MBA programs, CO State Univ. Alumni Assn. Bd. of Dirs.; **HOME ADD:** 12478 E. Amherst Cr., Aurora, CO 80014, (303)751-2136; **BUS ADD:** 3201 S. Tamarac Dr. 205, Denver, CO 80231, (303)696-7505.

ROSSETTI, John——**B:** Dec. 18, 1950, Los Angeles, CA, *Pres.*, Terra Properties, Inc.; **PRIM RE ACT:** Broker, Developer, Owner/Investor, Syndicator; **EDUC:** BA, 1975, RE/Corporate Fin., Univ. of So. CA; **EDUC HONORS:** Dean's List, Cum Laude; **HOME ADD:** 3960 So. Higuera St. 62, San Luis Obispo, CA 93401, (805)543-9280; **BUS ADD:** 1303 Garden, Suite 2A, San Luis Obispo, CA 93401, (805)544-3900.

ROSSON, William M.——*Pres.*, Conwood Corp.; **PRIM RE ACT:** Consultant; **BUS ADD:** 813 Ridgelake Blvd., Memphis, TN 38117, (901)761-2050.*

ROSTEN, James A.——**B:** Dec. 30, 1956, Detroit, MI, *Realtor Assoc.*, Walter Neller Co.; **PRIM RE ACT:** Broker, Consultant, Owner/Investor, Property Manager; **SERVICES:** Specialize in exchanging, comml., office and retail income producing props., and mobile home parks; **PREV EMPLOY:** Self-employed managing own props. for over 4 years; **PROFL AFFIL & HONORS:** NAR, RNMI, IREM, MI Assn. Realtors, MAREX, MI Manufactured Housing Inst., Candidate for CPA, CCIM, CPM; **EDUC:** Bus. Admin., 1979, Fin./Econ., Central MI Univ.; AA,BS, Acctg., Central MI Univ.; **HOME ADD:** 6250 Rothburg Way, Apt. X-2, E. Lansing, MI 48823, (517)351-4010; **BUS ADD:** 122 S. Grand, Lansing, MI 48933, (517)489-6561.

ROSTER, Michael——**B:** Apr. 7, 1945, Chicago, IL, *Partner*, McKenna, Conner & Cuneo; **PRIM RE ACT:** Attorney; **REP CLIENTS:** S&L, Bank and Mort. Banking Firms; **PROFL AFFIL & HONORS:** Amer. Coll. of Mort. Attys.; ABA RE and Probate Sect.; Los Angeles Bar Assn. Comm. on RE Fin.; **EDUC:** AB, 1967, Pol. Sci. and Communication, Stanford, Univ.; **GRAD EDUC:** JD, 1973, Law, Stanford Law School; **EDUC HONORS:** Honors; **MIL SERV:** USN, Lt. j.g., Navy Commendation Medal; **OTHER ACT & HONORS:** Other bus. address: 1575 Eye St., NW Wash., DC 20005; Tel:

(202)789-7500; **HOME ADD:** 950 Glen Oaks Blvd., Pasadena, CA 91105, (213)795-9421; **BUS ADD:** 3435 Wilshire Blvd., Los Angeles, CA 90010, (213)384-3600.

ROTENBERG, Milton P.——B: July 29, 1940, Detroit, MI, *Pres.*, Rescom Development Corp.; **PRIM RE ACT:** Attorney, Developer, Builder; **OTHER RE ACT:** Planning, zoning, financing; **SERVICES:** Devel. & bldg. of resid. and comml. props.; **PROFL AFFIL & HONORS:** State Bar of MI, SE MI Home Builders Assn.; **GRAD EDUC:** LLB/JD, 1964, Detroit Coll. of Law; **HOME ADD:** 6868 Woodbank Dr., Birmingham, MI 48010, (313)626-5214; **BUS ADD:** 30100 Telegraph Rd., Suite 250, Birmingham, MI 48010, (313)644-1952.

ROTH, David A.——B: Dec. 13, 1937, St. Louis, MO, *Pres.*, David A. Roth & Assoc.; **PRIM RE ACT:** Broker, Attorney, Instructor, Consultant, Appraiser, Real Estate Publisher; **SERVICES:** RE Consultation & appraisals; **REP CLIENTS:** Execs, Crown Zellerbach, GM Argonaut; **PROFL AFFIL & HONORS:** SRA, AICP, MO Bar Assn., Lic. RE Broker, Recp. of Wm. Kinne Fellows Traveling Fellowship, NY; **EDUC:** BS, 1959, Lib. Arts, St. Louis Univ.; **GRAD EDUC:** MS/JD, 1963, Urban Planning, St. Louis Univ., MO; **MIL SERV:** USMC, Pfc.; **HOME ADD:** 169 Southdown, Chesterfield, MO 63017, (314)434-0858; **BUS ADD:** 7811 Carondelet, Suite 301, Clayton, MO 63105.

ROTH, Delbert N.——*Pres.*, Roth Realty, Inc.; **PRIM RE ACT:** Broker, Owner/Investor; **OTHER RE ACT:** Spec., Tax deferred exchanging; **PREV EMPLOY:** Teacher; **PROFL AFFIL & HONORS:** RNMI, CCIM; **EDUC:** BS, 1960, Math, Univ. of NE; **HOME ADD:** 3260 Williams Ln, Mound, MN 55364, (612)472-2334; **BUS ADD:** 6250 Wayzata Blvd., Minneapolis, MN 55416, (612)546-0919.

ROTH, Herbert L.——B: Aug. 26, 1937, NY, NY, *VP and Legal Counsel*, Thomas L. Karsten Associates; **PRIM RE ACT:** Attorney; **SERVICES:** Legal servs. to Thomas L. Karsten Assocs.; **REP CLIENTS:** Clients of Thomas L. Karsten Assocs. include Pension Funds, Banks and Instnl. Investors; **PREV EMPLOY:** VP, Legal, The May Stores Shopping Ctrs., Inc.; VP and Counsel, Ogden Devel. Corp.; **PROFL AFFIL & HONORS:** ABA; Los Angeles and Beverly Hills Bar Assns.; **EDUC:** BA, 1958, Amer. Studies, Syracuse Univ.; **GRAD EDUC:** JD, 1961, Yale Law School; **EDUC HONORS:** Phi Beta Kappa; **HOME ADD:** 333 S. Maple Dr., Beverly Hills, CA 90212, (213)273-2872; **BUS ADD:** 10960 Wilshire Blvd., Los Angeles, CA 90024, (213)473-1128.

ROTH, Lee B.——*Atty.*, Roth, Beeman & Savage; **PRIM RE ACT:** Attorney; **SERVICES:** Counseling, fin., govt. approvals; **PREV EMPLOY:** Amer. Nat. B&T of NJ, Instr. Cont. Legal Ed.; **PROFL AFFIL & HONORS:** ABA; NJSBA; Hunt. Co. BA, Chairman of SBA, Real Estate Section; **EDUC:** BA, 1959, Oberlin Coll.; **GRAD EDUC:** JD, Cornell Univ.; LLB, Cornell Univ.; **OTHER ACT & HONORS:** Hunter Cty. Camera Club, Hunterdon Cty. Hist. Soc., Amer. Cancer Soc., Hunterdon Cty. C of C; **HOME ADD:** Birch St., Flemington, NJ 08822, (201)782-5160; **BUS ADD:** 8 Main St., Flemington, NJ 08822, (201)782-5317.

ROTH, Peggy——*Ed.*, Community Development Svcs. Inc., Managing Housing Letter; **PRIM RE ACT:** Real Estate Publisher; **BUS ADD:** 399 Nat'l. Press. Bldg., Washington, DC 20045, (202)638-6113.*

ROTH, Richard, Jr.——B: Feb. 20, 1933, NYC, NY, *Pres.*, Emery Roth & Sons, P.C.; **PRIM RE ACT:** Architect; **SERVICES:** All phases of arch. & planning; **PROFL AFFIL & HONORS:** AIA, Royal Inst. of Brit. Archs.; **EDUC:** BArch., 1957, Arch., Miami Univ., Oxford, OH; **BUS ADD:** 845 Third Ave., New York, NY 19922, (212)753-1733.

ROTHACHER, Larry L.——B: Jan. 19, 1937, Dover, OH, *CCIM/Realtor*, Larry L. Rothacher, CCIM/Realtor; **PRIM RE ACT:** Broker, Consultant, Owner/Investor, Instructor, Syndicator; **OTHER RE ACT:** Exchanger; **SERVICES:** RE investment counseling, general brokerage, assistance, general partner in creation of synd., creation of exchange structuring; **PREV EMPLOY:** Pres. Bethom Corp. dba Better Homes Realty; **PROFL AFFIL & HONORS:** CCIM designee and instr. as part of RNMI; SEC member; 1982 Pres. of CCIM Chapter 1, N. CA; Vice Chmn. Investment Div., CA Assn. Realtors, CCIM, RNMI; **EDUC:** BA, 1965, Econ., Univ. of MD; **MIL SERV:** USA, PFC, Military Intelligence; **OTHER ACT & HONORS:** Commonwealth Club; **HOME ADD:** 2272 Gladwin Dr., Walnut Creek, CA 94596, (415)937-8110; **BUS ADD:** 1910 Olympic Blvd., Suite 205, Walnut Creek, CA 94596, (415)937-8110.

ROTHENBERG, Joel——B: June 3, 1937, NY, NY, *Pres.*, Ekstein-Rothenberg Corp.; **PRIM RE ACT:** Broker, Attorney, Owner/Investor, Syndicator; **SERVICES:** Mort. and equity fin., sale or synd. of comml. props.; **REP CLIENTS:** Instnl. lenders and investors in comml. props., indiv. devel. of comml. props.; **PROFL AFFIL & HONORS:** Intl. Council of Shopping Ctrs., Mort. Bankers Assn. of NY; **EDUC:** BA, 1959, Econ., Cornell Univ.; **GRAD EDUC:** LLB, MBA, 1962, Fin., Columbia Law Sch.; **EDUC HONORS:** Columbia Bus. Sch.; **BUS ADD:** 122 East. 42 St., New York, NY 10017, (212)682-0314.

ROTHERMEL, Daniel K.——*VP Gen. Coun. & Secy.*, Carpenter Tech. Corp.; **PRIM RE ACT:** Property Manager; **BUS ADD:** PO Box 662, Reading, PA 19603, (215)371-2000.*

ROTHKOPF, Gary S.——B: Dec. 24, 1957, NY, NY, *Pres.*, Garo Development Co.; **PRIM RE ACT:** Developer, Builder; **SERVICES:** RE builder, devel., const., sales, mktg., investment, mgmt.; **PROFL AFFIL & HONORS:** NAHB; Boston Builders Assn.; MA Re Broker; **EDUC:** BBA, 1979, Mktg./Fin., Boston Univ. School of Mgmt.; **HOME ADD:** 107 Brandeis Rd., Newton, MA 02159, (617)969-7747; **BUS ADD:** 56 Kearney Rd., Needham, MA 02194, (617)449-3202.

ROTHMAN, Noel N.——B: Jan. 16, 1930, *Chmn. of the Bd.*, Monticello Realty Corporation, Henry Crown & Company; **PRIM RE ACT:** Broker, Consultant, Appraiser, Developer, Property Manager; **PROFL AFFIL & HONORS:** NACRPA, Intl. Inst. of Valuers, NAIOP; **HOME ADD:** 2738 Euclid Park Pl., Evanston, IL 60201, (312)869-2874; **BUS ADD:** 300 W. Washington, Chicago, IL 60606, (312)236-6300.

ROTHSCHILD, Robert J.——B: Apr. 14, 1951, Brooklyn, NY, *VP*, Manufacturers Hanover Trust Co., RE and Mort. Dept.; **PRIM RE ACT:** Banker, Lender; **SERVICES:** Const. loans; **PREV EMPLOY:** Chase Manhattan Bank, N.A., 1972-1975; **EDUC:** 1972, Mgmt., St. John's Univ.; **GRAD EDUC:** 1977, Fin., St. John's Univ.; **OTHER ACT & HONORS:** Lecturer - NY Univ.; **HOME ADD:** 198-10 Pompeii Ave., Holliswood, NY 11423, (212)468-4666; **BUS ADD:** 270 Park Ave., NY, NY 10017, (212)286-6476.

ROTHSTEIN, Robert A.——B: Nov. 25, 1946, Lakewood, NJ, *Atty. At Law of NJ*, Rothstein Mandell and Strohm; **PRIM RE ACT:** Attorney; **REP CLIENTS:** Peoples Nat. Bank in Lakewood; **PROFL AFFIL & HONORS:** NJ Bar Assn., ABA, Ocean Cty. Bar Assn., Admitted NY, NJ Bar, US Supreme Ct., US Ct. of Appeals 2nd Circuit, Dist. Ct. for Dist. of NJ - for E. & So. Dist. of NY, Panel Tr. - US Tr. Bankruptcy Panel; **EDUC:** BA - History, 1968, Syracuse Univ.; JD, 1973, Brooklyn Law Sch.; **GRAD EDUC:** LLM, 1981, Corp. Law, NY Univ. Law Sch.; **OTHER ACT & HONORS:** Family YMCA of Ocean Cty.; Pres. Bd. of Dirs. Lakewood Jaycees, Lakewood Jaycees Found.; **HOME ADD:** 1432 Cedarview Ave., Lakewood, NJ 08701, (201)363-8311; **BUS ADD:** 219 Second St., Lakewood, NJ 08701, (201)363-0777.

ROTHWELL, Hank——B: Aug. 26, 1947, Chicago, IL, *Pres.*, Rothwell Dev. Co.; **PRIM RE ACT:** Broker, Syndicator, Consultant, Developer; **SERVICES:** Land acquisition and devel.; **PROFL AFFIL & HONORS:** NAIOP, Nat. RE Exchange, Nat. & Local Realtors, CCIM, GRI; **EDUC:** Bus. Mgmt., 1970, Fin., Univ. of UT; **MIL SERV:** USAR; **OTHER ACT & HONORS:** Holy Cross Hosp. Foundation, C of C; **HOME ADD:** 3650 Forest Hills Dr., Salt Lake City, UT 84106, (801)272-2475; **BUS ADD:** 79 S. State St., 110, Salt Lake City, UT 84111, (801)521-4238.

ROTKIN, Charles J.——B: Aug. 6, 1937, Los Angeles, CA, *Pres.; Chmn. of the Bd.*, San Val Dev. Corp.; **PRIM RE ACT:** Developer, Builder, Property Manager; **PREV EMPLOY:** Pres. Romax Const., Inc. MAXRO, Inc., San Val Restaurant Equip. Co., Inc.; **PROFL AFFIL & HONORS:** ICSC C of C, Sherman Oaks, Covina, CA, 26th Annual Food Facilities Design Award C of C 1972; **EDUC:** BA, 1959, Pol. Sci., UCLA; **MIL SERV:** USAFR, A/1C; **HOME ADD:** 5146 Topeka Dr., Tarzania, CA 91356; **BUS ADD:** 14651 Ventura Blvd., Sherman Oaks, CA 91403, (213)981-8900.

ROUDEBUSH, George M.——B: Jan. 25, 1894, Newtonsville, OH, *Atty.*, Roudebush, Adrion, Brown, Corlett & Ulrich & Roudebush, Brown & Ulrich Co.; **PRIM RE ACT:** Attorney, Developer, Owner/Investor, Property Manager; **OTHER RE ACT:** RE law, managing, dealing in, as owner & for clients; **REP CLIENTS:** Estates & Indiv. appraisers & valuations; **PREV EMPLOY:** Lifetime in same office; **EDUC:** 1915, Denison Univ.; **GRAD EDUC:** LLB, 1917, Univ. of Cincinnati Law Sch.; **MIL SERV:** USA Infantry, Capt., 2 yrs., Europe, 1st WW 1917-19; **OTHER ACT & HONORS:** ABA, Cleveland Bar, OH Bar, Bd. of Tr. Denison Univ., Chmn. Fin. Comm. 33 yrs., Dir. of many corps.; **HOME ADD:** 20101 Shelburne Rd., Shaker Heights, OH 44118, (216)321-5828; **BUS ADD:** 635 Nat. City Bank Bldg., Cleveland, OH 44114, (216)696-5200.

ROUGHLEY, Donald——**B:** Mar. 25, 1940, Toronto, Can., *Pres.*, Built Environment Co-ordinators Ltd.; **PRIM RE ACT:** Consultant, Engineer, Architect; **SERVICES:** Facility programming, interior planning, equipment design, project mgmt.; **REP CLIENTS:** Govt. agencies, instit., tech. indus.; **PROFL AFFIL & HONORS:** Bldg. Research Inst.; Environmental Design Research Assn.; Solar Energy Soc.; Arctic Inst.; **EDUC:** BArch., 1966, Univ. of Toronto; **EDUC HONORS:** Scholarships; **HOME ADD:** 17 Armour Blvd., Toronto, M5M4A2, Ont., Can., (416)488-2766; **BUS ADD:** 1947 Ave. Rd., Toronto, M5M4A2, Ont., Can., (416)783-4277.

ROUSE, Richard C.——**B:** Feb. 6, 1949, Richmond, VA, *Rgnl. Mgr., Evaluation*, Equitable Life Assurance Soc., Miami Rgnl. Office; **PRIM RE ACT:** Consultant, Appraiser, Lender; **SERVICES:** Investment counseling and review, valuation, equity and joint vanture devel.; **REP CLIENTS:** Major devels., pension funds, and owner/investors; **PREV EMPLOY:** Morton G. Thalhimer, Inc., 1974-1981, Sr. Appraiser; **PROFL AFFIL & HONORS:** Appraisal Inst.; Soc. of RE Appraisers; Soc. of Foresters, MAI; SRPA; **EDUC:** BS, 1972, Forest Resource Mgmt., VA Polytech. Inst. and State Univ.; **EDUC HONORS:** Co-operative Educ. Program, 1972; **OTHER ACT & HONORS:** Boca Raton Jaycees; **HOME ADD:** 22232 Alyssum Way, Boca Raton, FL 33233, (305)395-2158; **BUS ADD:** 1201 Brickell Ave., Miami, FL 33131, (305)371-4224.

ROUSE, Willard G., III——**B:** June 19, 1942, Baltimore, MD, *Managing Partner*, Rouse & Associates; **PRIM RE ACT:** Developer, Builder, Owner/Investor, Property Manager; **PROFL AFFIL & HONORS:** ULI; NAIOP; SIR; **EDUC:** 1966, Univ. of VA, Coll. of Arts & Sci.; **MIL SERV:** US Army; **HOME ADD:** RD#1, Copeland School Rd., Westchester, PA 19380; **BUS ADD:** Morehall Rd., Malvern, PA 19355, (215)647-7995.

ROUSSEAU, Edwin J.——**B:** Feb. 4, 1933, Ft. Wayne, IN, *Corp. Accounts*, Rousseau Realty House; **PRIM RE ACT:** Broker, Appraiser, Property Manager; **SERVICES:** List & sell resid. & comml.; **REP CLIENTS:** Homequity, Equitable Reloc., etc.; **PREV EMPLOY:** Mgr. Glenbrook Shopping Ctr., Fort Wayne, IN, 8 yrs.; **PROFL AFFIL & HONORS:** SREA, Realtor, SRA; **EDUC:** RE/Bus. Mgmt., IN Univ.; **MIL SERV:** USA, Spec. 3, Europe; **OTHER ACT & HONORS:** 8 yrs. city council, 8 years Cty CounciL, pres 5 yrs. Rotary, Sigma Alpha Epsilon; **HOME TEL:** (219)483-6777; **BUS ADD:** 5714 St. Joe Rd., Fort Wayne, IN 46815, (219)486-1515.

ROUSSEAU, John D.——**B:** Nov. 19, 1943, Milwaukee, WI, *Dir. Const. RE*, Honeywell, Corp.; **PRIM RE ACT:** Owner/Investor; **SERVICES:** In-house RE Activity; **EDUC:** BSEE, 1968, Automatic Control Theory, Univ. of WI; **OTHER ACT & HONORS:** Bd. Dir. Savathini Community Ctr.; **HOME ADD:** 8810 Elgin Pl., Golden Valley, MN 55427, (612)546-4935; **BUS ADD:** Honeywell Plaza, Mail Station, MN 55408, (612)870-2506.

ROUSSEAU, John J.——**B:** Apr. 23, 1920, Antran, Fr., *Pres.*, Century 21 Pacific, Ltd., Realtors; **PRIM RE ACT:** Broker, Instructor, Syndicator, Consultant, Appraiser, Developer, Owner/Investor, Real Estate Publisher; **SERVICES:** Gen. Brokerage, valuation, investment counseling, dev. & synd. economic RE letter.; **REP CLIENTS:** Safari Club, Hotels Kia Ora, Bishop Estate; **PREV EMPLOY:** Fin. Inspector Gen, French Gov. & European Econ. Community, 1955-67; **PROFL AFFIL & HONORS:** RNMI, RESSI; **EDUC:** BS, 1947, Math, Oceanography, Sea Academy of Nantes; **GRAD EDUC:** MS, 1954, Econ, Paris; Ph.D., Amer. Studies, Cambridge & Paris; **EDUC HONORS:** Cum Laude, Summa Cume Laude; **MIL SERV:** RAF & Fr. AF, Gen., 1940-67, Legion of Honor; **OTHER ACT & HONORS:** Consul of France, Las Vegas, 1969-71, Royal AF Assn., Shriner, Elder United Methodist Church, Kaneohe Yacht Club; **HOME ADD:** 1021 Noio St., Honolulu, HI 96816, (808)734-7876; **BUS ADD:** 1188 Bishop, 34th Floor, Honolulu, HI 96813, (808)538-3831.

ROUTH, Richard——*Mgr. RE*, Cone Mills Corp.; **PRIM RE ACT:** Property Manager; **BUS ADD:** 1201 Maple St., Greensboro, NC 27405, (919)379-6220.*

ROWAN, E.A.——**B:** Apr. 11, 1917, Dallas, TX, *Owner - Assoc.*, E.A. Rowan & Associates; **PRIM RE ACT:** Broker, Consultant, Appraiser; **SERVICES:** RE appraisal, analysis; **REP CLIENTS:** Mort. lenders, federal, state & cty. govts., indiv.; **PREV EMPLOY:** Asst. Chief Appriaser, Veterans, Appraiser Farmers Home Adm.; **PROFL AFFIL & HONORS:** Soc. of RE Appraisers; Assn. of Gov. Appraisers; Dallas Bd. of Realtors; Amer. Right of Way Assn., Sr. RE Analyst; Master Gov.; Appraiser; Realtor; **EDUC:** Engrg., TX A&M Univ.; **MIL SERV:** USN, CM/1C, Purple Heart; **OTHER ACT & HONORS:** Dallas C of C; **HOME ADD:** Rt. 1, Box 1020, Cedar Hill, TX 75104, (214)291-1816; **BUS ADD:** Suite 104, 1075 Griffin St. W., Dallas, TX 75215, (214)565-0324.

ROWE, B.A., III——**B:** Sept. 6, 1941, Bronxville, NY, *VP*, Rowe & Assoc., Inc.; **PRIM RE ACT:** Broker; **SERVICES:** Realtor; **EDUC:** BA, 1963, Bus., Yale Univ.; **MIL SERV:** USAR, 1st Lt.; **OTHER ACT & HONORS:** Notary; **HOME ADD:** 305 Mt. Laurel Rd., Fairfield, CT 06490, (203)255-4359; **BUS ADD:** 2600 Post Rd., Southport, CT 06490, (203)255-2210.

ROWE, Benjamin A.——*Chmn. of the Bd.*, Preferred Properties, Inc.; **PRIM RE ACT:** Broker, Consultant, Appraiser, Syndicator; **PREV EMPLOY:** Profl. Engr.; **PROFL AFFIL & HONORS:** VP FIABCI, GRI; **EDUC:** 1937, Rollins Coll.; **MIL SERV:** USA, Capt., 3 Silver Stars; **HOME ADD:** 23 Rockridge Ave., Greenwich, CT 06830, (203)869-7257; **BUS ADD:** 175 W. Putnam Ave, Greenwich, CT 06830, (203)869-5975.

ROWEN, David H.——*Pres.*, The Rowen Organization; **PRIM RE ACT:** Developer; **BUS ADD:** 9629 Brighton Way, Beverly Hills, CA 90210, (213)275-9700.*

ROWLAND, Joseph M.——*Pres.*, Rowland Financial Group, Inc.; **PRIM RE ACT:** Broker, Developer, Owner/Investor, Syndicator; **SERVICES:** RE investment opportunities, devel., synd.; **PROFL AFFIL & HONORS:** Bd. of Realtors, CCIM, SRS; **EDUC:** BA, 1969, RE, Univ. of WI, Madison; **HOME ADD:** 2913 Pelham Rd., Madison, WI 53713, (608)271-5339; **BUS ADD:** 1 Odana Ct., Madison, WI 53719, (608)273-2903.

ROWLAND, Thomas F., Jr.——**B:** Nov. 18, 1946, Greenwich, CT, *VP*, E.F. Hutton Real Estate Services, Inc.; **PRIM RE ACT:** Lender, Owner/Investor, Syndicator; **SERVICES:** Comml. prop. acquisitions & joint ventures; **REP CLIENTS:** Devels. & intermediaries representing proposed or existing comml. or multi-family props.; **PREV EMPLOY:** Sr. Fin. Officer, W. Mort. Loan Corp. (Aetna Correspondent); Coldwell Banker, RE Fin. Div.; GE Credit Corp., W. Rgnl. RE Rep.; **PROFL AFFIL & HONORS:** Nat. Mort. Bankers Assn.; CO Mort. Bankers Assn.; Comml. Comm.; **EDUC:** BA, 1969, Hist./Geography, Univ. of Denver; **GRAD EDUC:** attended, 1975-76, Mort. Banking, Costa Inst. of Mort. Banking at So. Methodist Univ.; **MIL SERV:** US Army, Res.; Sgt.; 1969-75; **OTHER ACT & HONORS:** Sons of the Revolution/State of NY; MAP Award, GE Credit Corp., most substantial new bus. contracts during 1977; **HOME ADD:** 7648 S. Detroit St., Littleton, CO 80122, (303)779-0438; **BUS ADD:** 5680 S. Syracuse Circ., 300, Englewood, CO 80111, (303)770-4646.

ROWLANDS, Hubert L.——**B:** Oct. 17, 1920, Emporia, KS, *Partner*, Dietrich, Davis, Dicus, Rowlands & Schmitt; **PRIM RE ACT:** Attorney; **SERVICES:** Preparation of documents, consultation and advice on legal matters, litigation, tax advice; **REP CLIENTS:** The Mutual Life Ins. Co. of NY; CT Mutual Life Ins. Co.; Northland Mort. Co.; Beneficial Standard Properties, Inc.; Boatmen's Bank and Trust Co. of KS City; **PREV EMPLOY:** With present firm 33 yrs.; **PROFL AFFIL & HONORS:** ABA (RE Sect.); Lawyers Assn. of KS City; The MO Bar; KS City Bar Assn.; Amer. Judicature Soc., Past Pres., Lawyers Assn. of KS City; **EDUC:** AB, 1941, Soc. Sci./Educ., Emporia State Univ.; **GRAD EDUC:** JD, 1948, Univ. of MI; **EDUC HONORS:** Kappa Delta Pi, Pi Kappa Delta, Order of the Coif, Bd. of Editors, MI Law Review; **OTHER ACT & HONORS:** Rgnl. Co-Chmn., Nat. Conference of Christians and Jews, 1965-1967; **HOME ADD:** 59 E. 107th Terr., Kansas City, MO 64114, (816)942-5543; **BUS ADD:** 1700 City Center Sq., 1100 Main, Kansas City, MO 64105, (816)221-3420.

ROWLEY, James C.——**B:** Nov. 6, 1946, Everett, WA, *Pres.*, Jeffrey Scott, Inc.; **PRIM RE ACT:** Broker, Consultant, Owner/Investor, Property Manager; **SERVICES:** Investment counseling, prop. evaluation, prop. mgmt.; **REP CLIENTS:** Attys. and other profls. with investment potential; **PROFL AFFIL & HONORS:** Bd. of Realtors, Treasurer Pac. NW RE Exchangers; First V.P. Realty World Brokers Council; F.L.I.; **EDUC:** BA, 1969, Econ., Social Research, Western WA State Univ., Univ. of WA; **EDUC HONORS:** Cum Laude, on Pres. List 6 times; **OTHER ACT & HONORS:** Bd. of Dirs. Marysville YMCA; **HOME ADD:** 11022 46th Ave. NE, Marysville, WA 98270, (206)659-7402; **BUS ADD:** 4922 72nd St. NE, Marysville, WA 98270, (206)653-2509.

ROWLSON, John F.——**B:** May 22, 1915, Burlington, VT, *Owner*, John F. Rowlson Co.; **PRIM RE ACT:** Appraiser; **OTHER RE ACT:** Appraisals & consultations, Analyst; **SERVICES:** Appraisals, feasibility mkt. studies; **REP CLIENTS:** Banks & Ins. Cos., Devs., Attys., Corps., City, State & Fed., including USN, GSA, USA Corp. of Engineers, IRS; **PROFL AFFIL & HONORS:** AIREA (MAI), AREVER (SREA); **EDUC:** BS, 1937, Dairy Prods., Chem., Univ. of CT; **GRAD EDUC:** MS, 1940, Dairy Production, Stats., Univ. of CT; **OTHER ACT & HONORS:** Hartford Cty HBA, ULI, Hartford

Kiwanis, CT 4-H Dev. Fund; **HOME ADD:** 109 Ledgewood Rd., W. Hartford, CT 06107, (203)521-3287; **BUS ADD:** 135 Day St., Newington, CT 06111, (203)547-1350.

ROWSON, Jack E.——B: Feb. 16, 1935, KS, *Chmn., Pres.*, First Natl. Bank; **PRIM RE ACT:** Appraiser, Banker, Developer, Lender, Owner/Investor, Insuror; **EDUC:** Brown Madcie Coll.; **GRAD EDUC:** 1955, Bus. Banking, CO Univ.; **MIL SERV:** US Army, Lt.; **OTHER ACT & HONORS:** Commnr. N.C.P.A. & P.P.L.; **HOME ADD:** 306 Grand, Alma, KS 66401, (913)765-2301; **BUS TEL:** (913)765-3311.

ROYALE, Don——B: Apr. 28, 1933, Toledo, OH, *Pres.*, Don Royale Co.; **PRIM RE ACT:** Broker, Syndicator; **SERVICES:** Brokerage, synd. & consulting; **PREV EMPLOY:** William Walters Co. (1962-71), Larwin Multihousing (1971-72); **PROFL AFFIL & HONORS:** Realtor CPM, Mgr. of yr. (1979), IREM, L.A. Chapt.; **GRAD EDUC:** BS, 1957, Bus. Admin., USC; **MIL SERV:** USA, Pfc.; **HOME ADD:** 1512 Gardena Ave., Glendale, CA 91204, (213)242-0111; **BUS ADD:** 1514 Gardena Ave., Glendale, CA 91204, (213)244-7271.

ROYCE, John F.——B: Arp. 7, 1943, Detroit, MI, *Pres.*, Prop. Consultants & Royce Construction, Inc.; **PRIM RE ACT:** Broker, Syndicator, Consultant, Developer, Builder, Property Manager, Owner/Investor; **PREV EMPLOY:** Boise Cascade Corp. 1968-71; **PROFL AFFIL & HONORS:** RESSI, NAR; **EDUC:** BS, 1965, Civil Engineering, Lehigh Univ.; **GRAD EDUC:** MBA, 1968, Fin., Columbia Univ.; **HOME ADD:** 4318 Clyde Court, Reno, NV 89504, (702)826-9213; **BUS ADD:** 275 Hill St., Reno, NV 89504, (702)322-5791.

ROYCO, Ray——*Corp. Counsel & Secy.*, Union Corp.; **PRIM RE ACT:** Property Manager; **BUS ADD:** Jones St., Verona, PA 15147, (412)362-1700.*

ROYER, M.N.——B: July 11, 1932, Lancaster, PA, *Owner*, Gateway Realty; **PRIM RE ACT:** Broker, Consultant, Developer, Syndicator; **OTHER RE ACT:** CPA, Instr., Author; **SERVICES:** Investment counseling, forming small-medium size partnerships for investment purposes, devel. of resid. subdivisions; **REP CLIENTS:** Individuals; **PROFL AFFIL & HONORS:** NAR, AICPA, State of OR for Authoring and Publishing Taxes of OR; **EDUC:** BS, 1959, Acctg./Econ., Penn. State Univ., Frankling & Marshall; **MIL SERV:** U.S. Army, Sgt.; **OTHER ACT & HONORS:** Lion of Year, 1972; **HOME ADD:** 33842 Brewster Rd., Lebanon, OR 97355, (503)258-5850; **BUS ADD:** 940 Main, Suite E, Lebanon, OR 97355, (503)258-2148.

ROZAN, Gerry M.——B: Dec. 24, 1934, Detroit, MI, *Sales*, Realty World, Wing & Assoc.; **PRIM RE ACT:** Broker, Appraiser, Developer, Builder, Instructor, Property Manager; **SERVICES:** Complete RE Serv.; **PREV EMPLOY:** Western College of RE; **PROFL AFFIL & HONORS:** GRI, CRS, MI, NAR; **EDUC:** BS, 1960, Commerce, Ferris State Coll., Big Rapids, MI; **MIL SERV:** USMC, Cpl.; **OTHER ACT & HONORS:** Optimist, Past Pres.; TEAM Past Pres.; Boy Scouts; B'nai B'rith Men, Past Pres.; **HOME ADD:** 523 N. LeSueur, Mesa, AZ 85202, (602)969-3140; **BUS ADD:** 20 W. 925 N. Stapley St., Mesa, AZ 85203, (602)964-1946.

RUANE, Michael J.——B: Aug. 29, 1946, Scranton, PA, Glassie, Pewett, Dudley, Beebe & Shanks; **PRIM RE ACT:** Attorney; **SERVICES:** All phases of comml. RE devel. & fin.; **REP CLIENTS:** Lenders & indivs. and instnl., investors in comml. prop.; **PREV EMPLOY:** US Dist. Ct. for DC, Law Clerk, 1973-74; **PROFL AFFIL & HONORS:** Real Prop., Trust & Probate Div. ABA; **EDUC:** BA, 1968, Hist., Eng., Univ. of Scranton; **GRAD EDUC:** JD, 1973, George Washington Univ. Law Sch.; **EDUC HONORS:** Cum Laude, Order of the Coif, Notes Editor, George Wash. Law Review; **BUS ADD:** 1737 H St., NW, Washington DC 20006, (202)466-4310.

RUBACHA, Paul D.——B: Aug. 17, 1950, Rochester, NY, *VP*, Citibank, N.A., RE Investment & Mgmt. Dept.; **PRIM RE ACT:** Developer, Property Manager, Owner/Investor; **SERVICES:** Acquire & Manage RE for Instl. Buyers; **REP CLIENTS:** Major US Pension Funds & Major Foreign Insts. and Indivs.; **PREV EMPLOY:** RE Dept., Prudential Ins. Co., 1973-81; **PROFL AFFIL & HONORS:** Guest lecturer, Cornell Univ., Harvard, NYU; **EDUC:** Econ. BS, 1972, Econ., Acctg., Cornell Univ.; **GRAD EDUC:** MBA, 1973, Fin., RE, Cornell Univ.; **EDUC HONORS:** Sr. Men's Honorary, Dean's List; **OTHER ACT & HONORS:** NYC Municipal Art Soc.; **HOME ADD:** 10 West 74th St. Apt. 9-A, New York, NY 10023, (212)362-0168; **BUS ADD:** 15th Floor, 153 E. 53 St., New York, NY 10043, (212)559-9024.

RUBEN, Lawrence——B: Sept. 28, 1926, Brooklyn, NY, *Pres.*, Lawrence Ruben Co.; **PRIM RE ACT:** Developer, Owner/Investor, Builder; **PROFL AFFIL & HONORS:** Assoc. Bldrs. & Owners of Greater NY; ABA; **EDUC:** BA, 1949, NY Univ.; **GRAD EDUC:** LLB, 1951, Brooklyn Law School; **MIL SERV:** US Army; **BUS ADD:** 600 Madison Ave., New York, NY 10022, (212)980-0910.

RUBENDALL, Floyd——B: Nov. 13, 1930, Cedar Falls, IA, *Pres.*, Tiffany Pacific Corp.; **PRIM RE ACT:** Consultant, Developer, Owner/Investor, Property Manager, Syndicator; **SERVICES:** Devel., synd. and mgr., income producing prop.; **REP CLIENTS:** VLF Fin. Corp., Reno, NV; Summit Capital Corp., Honolulu, HI and other instit. investors; **EDUC:** BA, 1953, Econs., Univ. N. IA; **MIL SERV:** US Navy, Lt., Korean Service Medal; **HOME ADD:** 250 Kawaihae, Honolulu, HI 96825, (808)395-3800; **BUS ADD:** 219 Portlock Rd., Honolulu, HI 96825, (808)395-2273.

RUBENSTEIN, Jeffrey C.——*Prin.*, Sachnoff Schrager Jones Weaver & Rubenstein, Ltd.; **PRIM RE ACT:** Attorney; **PROFL AFFIL & HONORS:** NAR; RESSI; ABA; Chicago BAr Assn., Coif Law Outline Series - Pres. 1966-1968; Chicago Council of Lawyers - Chmn. Ethics Comm. 1972-1974; ABA, Member - Comm. on Taxation 1976 - ; Active Participant - Sub-Comm. on RE 1976 and Sub-Comm. on Legislation - 1978- ; Contributor - of ABA 1978 and 1980 Revenue Acts - US Senate Fin. Comm.; IL Inst. of Technol., Kent School of Law Adjunct Prof. of Law; Taxation; Negotiations 1977-present; RESSI, VChmn. - Taxation 1980 and Comm. on Legislation 1978- , Rep. of RESSI 1977; Coif Outline Series - Author or Editor - "Sales and Secured Transactions"; "Bills and Notes", "Anti-Trust Law" and "Civil Procedure" 1966-1968; Practicing Law Institute - Lecturer & Co-Author of book, "Housing Programs", Chapter on Taxation - 1977; Chicago Bar Assn. - Lecturer - Author of Outline - "Real Estate Investments, Structuring the Transaction" 1979; IL Continuing Legal Eudcation Book, *"Financial Real Estate Transactions"* Author - Chapter on "Tax Implications of Financing a Real Estate Transaction" - published October, 1979; Journal of Real Estate Securities - Co-author of Regular articles - "Tax Update" 1980 - Author of published articles in the fields of taxation, real estate and securities laws; **EDUC:** AB, 1963, Univ. of MI; **GRAD EDUC:** JD, 1966, Univ. of MI; **OTHER ACT & HONORS:** Pro-Musica Soc. - Dir. - 1967-1969; Sen. Eugene McCarthy for Pres. - Delegate Liaison, Democratic Nat. Convention - 1968; Jewish United Fund, Young Peoples Div. - Dir. - 1972-1975; Univ. of MI Law School Development Comm. - 1968-1974 - VP and Dir. - 1972; United Jewish Appeal - Nat. Young Leadership Cabinet-Member of Cabinet 1974-1979; Jewish United Fund - Member, Community & Youth Servs. - 1974-1977, Leadership Devel. Comm. - 1974, Co-Chmn. Lawyers Div. - 1978; US Jaycees selected as one of Outstanding Young Men of America, 1978; Jewish Family and Community Servs. - Tr. and Treas. and Dir., 1979 -; **HOME ADD:** 1014 Elmwood Ave., Wilmette, IL 60091, (312)251-6395; **BUS ADD:** One IBM Plaza, Suite 4700, Chicago, IL 60611, (312)644-2400.

RUBENSTEIN, Mark E.——B: Jan. 9, 1941, Wilmington, DE, *Owner*, The Rubenstein Co.; **PRIM RE ACT:** Developer, Builder, Property Manager; **SERVICES:** Devel., contracting, managing, consulting; **REP CLIENTS:** Girard Bank, Wilmington Trust Co., PA Mutual Life Ins.; **PROFL AFFIL & HONORS:** Intl. Council of Shopping Centers, Rgnl. Dir., Intl. Council of Shopping Centers; 1980 Design Award, DE; **EDUC:** BES, 1962, Mech. Engrg., Johns Hopkins Univ.; **EDUC HONORS:** Honors; **OTHER ACT & HONORS:** Locust Club; Philmont C.C.; Bd., Children's Hospital; Orlowitz Cancer Inst.; Philadelphia Maritime Museum; Founder & Chmn. of Bd., Likoff Cardiovascular Inst.; **HOME ADD:** 1500 Washington Ln., Rydal, PA 19046, (215)886-1188; **BUS ADD:** 520 Three Penn Center, Philadelphia, PA 19102, (215)563-3558.

RUBENSTEIN, Mitchell——B: Feb. 4, 1954, Newark, NJ, *Partner*, Kane, Kessler, Rubenstein & Silvers; **PRIM RE ACT:** Attorney, Owner/Investor; **SERVICES:** Legal advice; tax planning; RE structuring; **PREV EMPLOY:** Clerk to prof. Boris Bittker of Yale Law School; Assoc., Markbys' Solicitors, London, England; **PROFL AFFIL & HONORS:** Palm Beach Cty., Amer., FL and NY Bar Assns.; Assoc. Member, Palm Beach Cty. Home Builders and Contractors Assn.; **EDUC:** BS, 1974, Bus. Admin., Boston Univ.; **GRAD EDUC:** JD, 1977, Univ. of VA School of Law; LLM, 1979, Taxation, NYU School of Law; **EDUC HONORS:** Cum Laude, Sr. Editor, VA Journal of Intl. Law; **OTHER ACT & HONORS:** Founder, Fellow, and Young Pres., Mt. Sinai Medical Ctr. of Gr. Miami; **HOME ADD:** 3543 S. Ocean Blvd., Palm Beach, FL 33480, (305)585-3690; **BUS ADD:** Gulfstream Bank Bldg., 2000 W. Glades Rd., Boca Raton, FL 33431, (305)395-7000.

RUBIN, Carolyn——B: Apr. 9, 1948, St. Louis, MO, *Asst. Dean*, Nova Law Ctr.; **PRIM RE ACT:** Attorney; **PREV EMPLOY:** Private Law Practice, Fort Lauderdale, FL; **PROFL AFFIL & HONORS:** FL Bar, ABA (Member, Real Prop. Sect.) Broward Cty. Bar Assn.; **EDUC:** BA, 1969, Hist., Maryville Coll., St. Louis, MO; **GRAD EDUC:** JD, 1979, Law, Nova Univ. Law Ctr.; **EDUC HONORS:** Magna cum laude,

Cum Laude; **HOME ADD:** 6110 White Oak Ln., Tamarac, FL 33319, (305)486-0965; **BUS ADD:** 3100 SW 9 Ave., Fort Lauderdale, FL 33312, (305)522-2300.

RUBIN, Larry Aryeh——**B:** July 7, 1950, NY, NY, *Pres.*, LA Rubin & Company; **PRIM RE ACT:** Consultant, Developer, Owner/Investor, Syndicator, Real Estate Publisher; **SERVICES:** Assist For. in acquiring prop. interests in U.S. for such clients; Publish "Overseas Financial News"; Duties include locating; acquiring; develop.; and synd.; **EDUC:** BA, 1972, Yeshiva Univ.; **BUS ADD:** 319 E. 53rd. St., New York, NY 10022, (212)826-6131.

RUBIN, Mahlon——**B:** Oct. 1, 1924, St. Louis, MO, *Managing Partner*, Rubin, Brown, Gornstein & Co., CPA's; **OTHER RE ACT:** CPA; **SERVICES:** Consultant, tax planning, investment analyst, synd.; **PROFL AFFIL & HONORS:** AICPA; MO and NY Socs. of CPA's, Served on many AICPA Comms.; Past Pres., MO Soc. of CPA's; Past Chmn., CPA Assocs.; **EDUC:** BSBA, 1948, Acctg., WA Univ.; **EDUC HONORS:** Magna Cum Laude, Beta Gamma Sigma; **MIL SERV:** USAF, Lt.; **HOME ADD:** 10866 Rondelay, St. Louis, MO 63141, (314)432-5141; **BUS ADD:** 230 S. Bemiston, St. Louis, MO 63105, (314)727-8150.

RUBIN, Norman A.——**B:** Sept. 6, 1929, Chicago, *Pres.*, Self Storage Co.; **PRIM RE ACT:** Developer; **SERVICES:** Consultant to Nat. Pension Fund for RE Investment; **PREV EMPLOY:** VP RE for MCA Devel., Univ. City, CA: 1958-1970; Exec. Dir., Admin., Ogden Devel. Co., 1970-present; **PROFL AFFIL & HONORS:** Member, Intl. Council of Shopping Ctrs., 1962-present; Member Self Serv. Storage Assn., Charter Dir. Rgn. II, Self Serv. Storage Assn., Member, State Bar of CA; **EDUC:** BS, 1951, Mktg. & Fin., Bus. Admin.; **GRAD EDUC:** LLD, 1954, UCLA; **EDUC HONORS:** Beta Gamma Sigma Honor Soc.; **MIL SERV:** US Army; Specialist III; **HOME ADD:** 532 N. Cherokee, Los Angeles, CA 90004, (213)462-5022; **BUS ADD:** 2525 Sawtelle Blvd., Los Angeles, CA 90064, (213)477-8255.

RUBIN, Sheldon——**B:** Mar. 30, 1936, Chicago, IL, Rubin, Eagan & Feder, A Profl. Corp.; **PRIM RE ACT:** Consultant, Attorney; **SERVICES:** Legal Services; workout counseling; **REP CLIENTS:** Indiv. and instit. lenders; guarantors and insurers; indiv. and corp. investors; **PREV EMPLOY:** Chicago Title and Trust Co. 1961-1973; **PROFL AFFIL & HONORS:** CA State Bar; IL Bar Assn., Beverly Hills Bar Assn., Los Angeles Bar Assn., Chicago Bar Assn., Amer. Bar Assn., Assn. of RE Attys., Pres., Assn. of RE Attys. (1980-1981); Faculty, PLI; **EDUC:** BS, 1957, Urban Land Econs., Univ. of IL; **GRAD EDUC:** JD, 1960, Law, Univ. of IL; **HOME ADD:** 522-25th St., Santa Monica, CA 90402, (213)395-7027; **BUS ADD:** 8383 Wilshire Blvd., Suite 950, Beverly Hills, CA 90211, (213)651-1200.

RUBIN, Steve——*Secy.*, General Binding Corp.; **PRIM RE ACT:** Property Manager; **BUS ADD:** One GBC Plaza, Northbrook, IL 60062, (312)272-3700.*

RUBINSTEIN, Manny A.——**B:** May 27, 1949, NY, *Pres.*, M.H.R. RE; **PRIM RE ACT:** Broker, Consultant, Appraiser, Developer, Builder, Owner/Investor, Property Manager, Syndicator; **EDUC:** BS, 1971, Computer Sci., Univ. of Miami; **HOME ADD:** Los Angeles, CA; **BUS ADD:** Rossway Rd., Pleasant Valley, NY 12569.

RUCCI, Peter Paul——**B:** Nov. 17, 1948, Norwalk, CT, *VP/Reg. Mgr.*, Shannon & Luchs, Res. Sales Div.; **PRIM RE ACT:** Broker; **OTHER RE ACT:** Mgr. of Mgrs.; **SERVICES:** Sale & leasing of resid. RE; **REP CLIENTS:** Sellers & purchasers of resid. prop. lessors and Lessees of resid. prop.; **PREV EMPLOY:** Sales Mgr. of resid. sales office (5 yrs), Asst. Dir. New Home Sales (2 yrs.); **PROFL AFFIL & HONORS:** Realtors Nat. Mktg. Inst. Montgomery Cty. Bd. of Realtors, Wash. DC Bd of Realtors, N. VA Bd. of Realtors, Inst. at Montgomery Coll., CRB Candidate 1979 'Outstanding Service' award from Wash. Bd. of Realtors; **EDUC:** BS, 1970, Pysch., Georgetown Univ.; **MIL SERV:** USA Res., E4; **HOME ADD:** 2831 Hurst Terr. NW, Washington, DC 20016, (202)244-7307; **BUS ADD:** 6410 Rockledge Dr., Suite 300, Bethesda, MD 20817, (301)897-8000.

RUDDER, Richard D.——**B:** Norwalk, CT, *Partner*, Brown, Wood, Ivey, Mitchell & Petty; **PRIM RE ACT:** Attorney; **SERVICES:** Special Fin. Counsel; **REP CLIENTS:** Ins. cos., banks, public and pvt. pension funds; **EDUC:** AB, 1963, English, Lafayette Coll.; **GRAD EDUC:** LLB, 1966, NY Univ.; MBA, 1971, Fin., Bernard Baruch Sch. of CCNY; **EDUC HONORS:** Dean's List, Honors Program; **BUS ADD:** One Liberty Plaza, New York, NY 10006, (212)349-7500.

RUDDY, Richard John, Jr.——**B:** Mar. 24, 1952, South Bend, IN, *Atty.*, Putbrese & Hunsaker; **PRIM RE ACT:** Attorney, Instructor; **SERVICES:** Tax advice, Re tax courses; **PROFL AFFIL & HONORS:** Amer. Bar Assn., Sec. of Taxation, RE Tax Problems Comm., DC Bar, Tax Comm., VA State Bar, Comm. on Taxation, Real Prop. & Bus., VA Bar Assn.; **EDUC:** BA, 1970-1974, Econ. major, Acctg. minor, Saint Vincent Coll., Latrobe, PA; **GRAD EDUC:** JD, 1974-1977, Law, Univ. of Richmond School of Law; LLM, 1980, Taxation, Georgetown Univ. Law center; **EDUC HONORS:** Magna Cum Laude, Who's Who Among Students in Amer. Univ. & Coll., 1974; **OTHER ACT & HONORS:** Springfield C of C, The Exchange Club of Capitol Hill, and The Lincoln Club of VA; **HOME ADD:** 8121 Willowdale Court, Springfield, VA 22153; **BUS ADD:** McLean House, Suite 100, McLean, VA 22101, (703)790-8400.

RUDES, George H.——**B:** Dec. 16, 1923, Genoa, OH, *Realtor*, George H. Rudes, Realtor; **PRIM RE ACT:** Broker, Insuror; **SERVICES:** Resid. & comml. & farms, sales & appraisals; **REP CLIENTS:** Bus., farmers, indivs., probate court, Villages, cities, etc.; **PREV EMPLOY:** Gen Ins. agent, Rudes & Reeder Ins. Agency Curtice, OH, 35 yrs.; **PROFL AFFIL & HONORS:** NBR, OH Bd. of Realtors, Cty. Bd. of Realtors, Ottawa Cty. Bd. of Realtors, NARA, Appraiser for IREA, Profl. Ins. Agents Assn. of OH; **EDUC:** BS, 1944, Engrg., Washington Jefferson Coll., Washington, PA; **MIL SERV:** USAF, S/Sgt., Good Conduct Medal, ETO Ribbon, ATO Ribbon; **OTHER ACT & HONORS:** Dir. Nat. Bank of Oak Harbor, Oak Harbor, OH; 31 yrs. Amer. Legion, Life Member VFW, Ottawa Cty. Conservation Club, Chippewa Ctry. Club; **HOME ADD:** 2631 N. First St., Martin, OH 43445, (419)855-8254; **BUS ADD:** 7165 N. Lucas St., Curtice, OH 43412, (419)836-2715.

RUDMAN, Pavi L.——**B:** Mar. 26, 1935, Bangor, ME, *Part.*, Rudman & Winchell; **PRIM RE ACT:** Attorney; **EDUC:** AB, 1957, Amer. Studies, Yale; **GRAD EDUC:** JD, 1960, George Wash. Univ. Law Sch.; **HOME ADD:** 454 Garland St., Bangor, ME 04401, (207)947-8288; **BUS ADD:** 84 Harlow St., Bangor, ME 04401, (207)947-4501.

RUDNIANYN, John S.——**B:** Apr. 24, 1950, Bronx, NY, *Pres.*, Intl. Property Services Corp.; **PRIM RE ACT:** Broker, Consultant, Developer, Owner/Investor, Syndicator; **SERVICES:** Consulting investors & other RE brokers; devel. & synd. of RE; **REP CLIENTS:** Investors, attys., RE brokers; **PROFL AFFIL & HONORS:** NAR; FL RE Securities and Synd. Inst.; Assn. of Realtors; FL RE Exchangers; Farm & Land Inst., CCIM; CRB; CRS; AFLM; GRI; **EDUC:** BA, 1973, RE, Univ. of FL; **EDUC HONORS:** High Honors, Phi Kappa Phi, Beta Gamma Sigma; **MIL SERV:** Army Nat. Guard; Spec. 4; **HOME ADD:** 3130 N.E. 7th Ln., Ocala, FL 32670, (904)629-5263; **BUS ADD:** 605 E. Silver Springs Blvd., Ocala, FL 32670, (904)732-7101.

RUDNICK, James S.——**B:** Nov. 21, 1940, Chicago, IL, *Sr. VP*, The Lomas & Nettleton Co.; **OTHER RE ACT:** RE investment banking; **SERVICES:** Joint venture synergism, equity sales, debt placement; **PREV EMPLOY:** Percy Wilson Mort. of Finance Corp.; Mellow Nat. Mort. Co.; **PROFL AFFIL & HONORS:** ILL; MBA; NAR; NAIOP; **EDUC:** BS, 1961, Hist., Univ. of WI; **GRAD EDUC:** JD, 1962, Univ. of Chicago, Law School; LLM, 1965, Tax, NYU School of Law; **HOME ADD:** 1324 Knollwood Way, Riverwoods, IL 60015, (312) 945-6877; **BUS ADD:** 230 W. Monroe St., Chicago, IL 60606, (312)346-6153.

RUDNIK, Shirley L.——**B:** Aug. 2, 1932, Chicago, IL, *Broker*, J.W. Reedy; **PRIM RE ACT:** Broker; **PROFL AFFIL & HONORS:** CRS, Life member million dollar club, Member 2 Million Dollar Club, Pres. Club, Silver Award; **HOME ADD:** 311 S. Riverside Dr., Villa Park, IL 60181, (312)279-7792; **BUS ADD:** 8E. St. Charles Rd., Villa Park, IL 60181, (312)832-7100.

RUDOFF, Arnold G.——**B:** Oct. 31, 1938, Chicago, IL, *Pres.*, Spectrum Fin. Co's., Ltd. Partners Letter; **PRIM RE ACT:** Attorney, Instructor, Consultant, Owner/Investor, Real Estate Publisher; **OTHER RE ACT:** CPA, Editor; **SERVICES:** Counseling in partnership structuring, mktg. analysis of offerings, expert witness on valuation and litigation; **REP CLIENTS:** Synd., attys., CPA's, investors; **PREV EMPLOY:** Author and lecturer; **PROFL AFFIL & HONORS:** Atty. - CA; CPA - IL; **EDUC:** BS, 1959, Acctg., Roosevelt Univ.; **GRAD EDUC:** JD, 1963, Univ. of CA; **BUS ADD:** 1225 Crane St., Suite 104, Menlo Park, CA 94025, (415)321-9110.

RUDSINSKI, Gary L.——**B:** Dec. 28, 1944, Elgin, IL, *Broker-Mgr.*, Byrnes Bros. Inc., Better Homes and Gardens; **PRIM RE ACT:** Broker; **PREV EMPLOY:** Alden-Hebron High School, Hebron, IL, Teacher; **PROFL AFFIL & HONORS:** GRI, CRS, RNMI, McHenry C of C; **EDUC:** BSEd, 1968, Secondary Educ., Northern IL Univ.; **OTHER ACT & HONORS:** Kiwanis of McHenry, Notary Assoc.; **HOME ADD:** 1205 3rd St., McHenry, IL 60050, (815)385-7271; **BUS ADD:** 4507 W. Elm, PO 385, McHenry, IL 60050, (815)385-6900.

RUDY, Michael D.——**B:** Feb. 20, 1948, Berkeley, CA, *Part.*, Deloitte Haskins & Sells; **OTHER RE ACT:** CPA; **SERVICES:** Acctg. auditing, tax & mgmt. advisory services; **REP CLIENTS:** Fox & Carskadon Fin. Corp.; Foremost McKesson Prop. Co.; McKeon Const.; Kacor Realty; Sn. Pacific Devel. Co.; Montgomery Realty Investors; Codding Enterprises; **PROFL AFFIL & HONORS:** CA Soc. of CPA's, East Bay Chap. R.E. Comm.; AICPA; RESSI; **EDUC:** BS, 1970, Acctg., Univ. of CO; **HOME ADD:** 19 Gary Way, Alamo, CA 94507, (415)837-6815; **BUS ADD:** 44 Montgomery St., San Francisco, CA 94104, (415)393-4321.

RUETHER, Eugene F., Jr.——**B:** July 30, 1926, Columbia, MO, *Pres.*, Rutter & Ruether, Inc., Realtors; **PRIM RE ACT:** Broker, Appraiser, Developer; **SERVICES:** Resid. and comml. sales, leasing, appraisals; **PROFL AFFIL & HONORS:** Columbia Bd. of Realtors; MO and NAR; Realtors Nat. Mktg. Inst., GRI; CRB; **EDUC:** BS, 1949, Bus. Admin., Univ. of MO; **OTHER ACT & HONORS:** Columbia City Councilman, 1967-1971; Columbia C of C, Pres., 1965-1966; Lions Club Pres., 1974-75; Bd. of Zoning Adjustment Chmn. 1981-82; **HOME ADD:** 912 S. Glenwood, Columbia, MO, (314)449-4475; **BUS ADD:** 101 Executive Bldg., Columbia, MO 65205, (314)443-4545.

RUFF, Arthur L.——*Pres.*, Vantage Cos.; **PRIM RE ACT:** Developer; **BUS ADD:** 2525 Stemmons Freeway, Dallas, TX 75207, (214)631-0600.*

RUFF, Jere——**B:** Dec. 26, 1935, Longview, TX, *Pres.*, Ruff Realtors, Inc.; **PRIM RE ACT:** Broker, Consultant, Developer, Owner/Investor, Syndicator; **REP CLIENTS:** First Nat. Bank - Trust Dept., Southwestern Bell Telephone; **PROFL AFFIL & HONORS:** Cert. Comml. Investment Member, NAR, CCIM; **EDUC:** BBA, 1957, RE, SMU; **OTHER ACT & HONORS:** Past Pres. Longview C of C; **HOME ADD:** 1917 Willis, Longview, TX 75601, (214)753-6079; **BUS ADD:** PO Box 2422, 400 So. Fredonia, Longview, TX 75601, (214)753-4444.

RUFF, John T.——**B:** Feb. 5, 1954, Rome, GA, *Atty.*, Neely & Player; **PRIM RE ACT:** Attorney; **OTHER RE ACT:** Comml. Litigation; **SERVICES:** Acquisition & tax consultation & RE closing; **REP CLIENTS:** S RY System, Deutz Corp.; Corp. Travel Intl, Inc.; AIIE; Moore Grp. Inc.; **PROFL AFFIL & HONORS:** State Bar of GA; ABA; Atlanta Bar Assn.; **EDUC:** BS, 1976, Pol. Sci., GIT & GA So. Coll.; **GRAD EDUC:** JD, 1979, Univ. of VA; **EDUC HONORS:** Nat. Merit Scholar, Phi Kappa Phi; **HOME ADD:** 1709 Belle Isle Cir., Atlanta, GA 30329, (404)636-3257; **BUS ADD:** 401 W. Peachtree St., Atlanta, GA 30365, (404)681-2600.

RUFFER, Donald O.——**B:** Apr. 10, 1929, Wauseon, OH, *Pres.*, Donald O. Ruffer, Inc.; **PRIM RE ACT:** Broker, Appraiser, Developer, Owner/Investor, Property Manager, Instructor, Syndicator; **SERVICES:** Prop. sale, leasing, appraising, managing, investment counseling; **PREV EMPLOY:** 15 yrs. in Mgmt. of Various C of C in NE and the Mid-West, specializing in Comml. and Indus. Devel.; **PROFL AFFIL & HONORS:** MAR, NAR, RNMI, Berkshire Cty. Bd. of Realtors, NRE, Berkshire Cty. Bd. Realtor of the Year 1974, CCIM, GRI, CRB; **MIL SERV:** US Army Sgt. Major; **OTHER ACT & HONORS:** Rotary Club of Pittsfield; **HOME ADD:** 1000 William St., Pittsfield, MA 01201, (413)499-1761; **BUS ADD:** 163 N. St., Pittsfield, MA 01201, (413)445-5661.

RUFRANO, Glenn J.——**B:** Jan. 20, 1950, Brooklyn, NY, *Sr. VP*, Landauer Assoc., Inc.; **PRIM RE ACT:** Consultant, Appraiser; **SERVICES:** Investment counseling, prop. mktg.; **REP CLIENTS:** Major corp., lending instit.; **PREV EMPLOY:** Asst. Treas., Morgan Guaranty Trust Co.; **PROFL AFFIL & HONORS:** Asst. Adjunct Prof., NY Univ., Broker, FL, Member AIREA; **EDUC:** BA, 1971, Computer Sci./Bus., Rutgers Univ.; **GRAD EDUC:** MSM, 1975, RE, FL Intl. Univ.; **OTHER ACT & HONORS:** Research Comm., NYU & RE Bd. of NY; **HOME ADD:** 2453 Soma Ave., Bellmore, NY 11710; **BUS ADD:** 200 Park Ave., NY, NY 10010, (212)687-2323.

RUGG, Frank J.——*RE Mgr.*, International Harvester Co.; **PRIM RE ACT:** Property Manager; **BUS ADD:** 402 N. Michigan Ave., Chicago, IL 60611, (312)836-2000.*

RUGGLES, Richard M.——**B:** May 22, 1929, Chicago, IL, *Prop. Mgr.*, Mayfair Mgmt. Co.; **PRIM RE ACT:** Broker, Property Manager, Insuror; **SERVICES:** Mgmt. of RE holdings including office and specialty Bldgs., vacant lands, etc.; **PROFL AFFIL & HONORS:** BOMA, SORPA, Real Prop. Admin. designation from BOMA; **EDUC:** BS, 1954, Bus. Admin. and Soc. studies, Morningside Coll., Sioux City, IA; **GRAD EDUC:** Did grad. work at Northwestern Univ., Chicago RE Bd., Amer. Inst. of Banking and Chicago Ins. School; **MIL SERV:** USA, Cpl.; **HOME ADD:** 2710 Central St., Evanston, IL 60201, (312)869-3155; **BUS ADD:** 5 N. Wabash Ave, Chicago, IL 60602, (312)236-4669.

RUGGLES, Robert K., III——**B:** Dec. 3, 1950, Ware, MA, *VP/Prin.*, L.W. Ellwood & Co.; **PRIM RE ACT:** Consultant, Appraiser; **SERVICES:** RE Counseling & Valuation; **PROFL AFFIL & HONORS:** AIREA, Soc. of RE Appraisers, Nat. Assn. of Corporate RE Execs., MAI; SRPA; **EDUC:** BS, 1972, Fin. & RE & Urban Econ. Studies, Univ. of CT; **GRAD EDUC:** MBA, 1975, Fordham Univ.; **EDUC HONORS:** Distinction Award in Fin., Beta Gamma Sigma Honorary Bus. Frat., Cited for Distinguished Academic Achievement in RE Fin.; **HOME ADD:** 143 Fairmount Rd., Ridgewood, NJ 07450, (201)652-4667; **BUS ADD:** 1270 Ave. of the Americas, Suite 1902, Rockefeller Center, New York, NY 10020, (212)246-0049.

RUHL, Charles A.——**B:** Apr. 17, 1927, Davenport, IA, *Pres.*, Ruhl & Ruhl Realtors, Inc.; **PRIM RE ACT:** Broker, Developer, Owner/Investor, Property Manager; **SERVICES:** Valuation, negotiation, devel., lease & sales; **REP CLIENTS:** Resid., comml. - 5 offices in IA and IL Quad Cities; **PROFL AFFIL & HONORS:** CPM (prop. mgmt.); past pres. IA Assn. Realtors & Gr. Davenport Bd. and IA Inst. RE Mgmt.; **EDUC:** BS Commerce, 1950, RE, Insurance, Univ. of IA; **MIL SERV:** USN, Petty Officer, WWII; **OTHER ACT & HONORS:** Chmn. Bd. of Adjustment 15 years; Rotary; **HOME ADD:** 112 Forest Rd., Davenport, IA 52803; **BUS ADD:** 112 Brady St, Davenport, IA 52801, (319)324-1981.

RUKAB, Tony——**B:** Dec. 7, 1935, Palestine, *Pres.*, Tony Rukab & Assoc. Inc.; **PRIM RE ACT:** Broker; **OTHER RE ACT:** Business opportunities; **PROFL AFFIL & HONORS:** Realtor; **MIL SERV:** USA, Corp. 1955-57; **OTHER ACT & HONORS:** Mason, Shriner, Pvt. Club; **HOME ADD:** 1831 Woodmere Dr., Jackson, FL 32205, (904)389-2976; **BUS ADD:** 2219 Park St., Jackson, FL 32205, (904)384-4577.

RULE, Peter W.——**B:** Aug. 26, 1939, Oakland, CA, *General Counsel*, First Interstate Bank of Washington, Law Dept.; **PRIM RE ACT:** Attorney; **SERVICES:** Documentation, negotiation, litigation; **REP CLIENTS:** First Interstate Banks of Wash. & CA; **PROFL AFFIL & HONORS:** Wash. State Bar Assn.; CA State Bar Assn.; ABA; **EDUC:** BA, 1962, Hist., Geography, CA State Univ., S.F.; **GRAD EDUC:** JD, 1965, UC Hastings Coll. of the Law; **OTHER ACT & HONORS:** Chmn., Morage, CA Planning Commn.; **HOME TEL:** (206)883-3160; **BUS ADD:** PO Box 160, Seattle, WA 98111, (206)292-3627.

RULIS, Robert A.——**B:** Feb. 8, 1928, PA, *Pres.*, Rulis Realty Co.; **PRIM RE ACT:** Broker, Instructor, Syndicator, Consultant, Developer, Property Manager, Owner/Investor; **OTHER RE ACT:** Lecturer Tax Shelters; **PREV EMPLOY:** 30 yrs. Exp.; **EDUC:** BS, 1956, Gov., Univ. of MD.; **GRAD EDUC:** Public Admin., Univ. of OK; **MIL SERV:** USN, Cmdr., Various decorations; **HOME ADD:** 12815 Dewey St., Omaha, NE 68154, (402)334-2810; **BUS ADD:** 2201 Jones St., Omaha, NE 68102, (402)346-6411.

RUMFORD, Frances R. Senfeld——*Exec. VP*, Rosenfeld Realty Co., Inc.; **PRIM RE ACT:** Developer, Owner/Investor, Property Manager; **SERVICES:** Leasing, mgmt. devel., synd. of comml. props., shopping ctrs.; **REP CLIENTS:** Inst. investors, pvt. owners; **PROFL AFFIL & HONORS:** Intl. council of shopping ctrs., Former State Dir. of MD, DE, DC & VA; **BUS ADD:** 7101 Wisconsin Ave. #1000, Bethesda, MD 20014, (301)986-0700.

RUNBAUGH, Thomas N.——**B:** May 5, 1944, Ashland, OH, *Pres.*, Rumbaugh & Assocs., Inc.; **PRIM RE ACT:** Broker, Appraiser, Property Manager; **SERVICES:** Renter assistance, Rental mgmt., MLS, APRS Referral Serv.; **REP CLIENTS:** Indiv. home buyers & sellers & local lender foreclosures; **PROFL AFFIL & HONORS:** Local, State & Natl NAR, RNMI, GRI, CRS, CRB, Served 2 consec. terms as Pres. Ashland Bd. of Realtors; **MIL SERV:** USA, Specialist 5th class, 1965-69; **OTHER ACT & HONORS:** Ashland Rotary Club, Bd. of Tr. of Ashland United Appeal, YMCA Bd. of Dir., Charter Member of Ashland City Cty Council; **HOME ADD:** 128 College Ave., Ashland, OH 44805, (419)289-0433; **BUS ADD:** 1250 Claremont Ave., Ashland, OH 44805, (419)289-2828.

RUNDEL, James A.——*Atty.*, Law Offices of James A. Rundel; **PRIM RE ACT:** Attorney, Syndicator; **SERVICES:** RE law and synd.; **PREV EMPLOY:** 10 yrs. practice of law; **PROFL AFFIL & HONORS:** ABA, JD; **EDUC:** BA, 1967, Bus. Admin., Univ. of Redlands; **GRAD EDUC:** LLM, 1970, Univ. of CA, Hastings Coll. of the Law; **EDUC HONORS:** Thurston Soc.; Publications Editor Hastings Law Journal; Published in 21 Hastings law journals, 216 on Mech. Liens; **OTHER ACT & HONORS:** CSSA, AFA; **BUS ADD:** 114 Pierce St., Santa Rosa, CA 95404, (707)542-1921.

RUNDELL, Richard F.——**B:** Feb. 12, 1927, Albany, NY, *VP*, Ostendorf-Morris Co., MGMI; **PRIM RE ACT:** Property Manager, Engineer; **SERVICES:** Prop. Mgmt.; **REP CLIENTS:** All types of prop. owners-office bldgs., warehouse props., shopping ctrs., apts.; **PREV EMPLOY:** Standard Oil Co.(OH) 1956-69; **PROFL AFFIL & HONORS:** CPM(IREM) Tr. BOMA Reg. Prof. Engrg. (OH), Past Pres.-Cleveland Chap. IREM; **EDUC:** BCE, 1948, Cornell Univ.; **EDUC HONORS:** Tau Beta Phi; **MIL SERV:** USN, Lt.(j.g.); **HOME ADD:** 6316 Elmcrest Dr., Hudson, OH 44236, (216)653-5902; **BUS ADD:** 1100 Superior Ave., Cleveland, OH 44114, (216)861-7200.

RUNGE, John R.——**B:** Aug. 16, 1953, Keokuk, IA, *Pres.*, Runge; **PRIM RE ACT:** Broker, Developer, Builder, Property Manager; **SERVICES:** custom home building (solar design); **BUS ADD:** RR 1, Box 275B, Keokuk, IA, (319)524-6118.

RUPEL, James B.——**B:** June 17, 1954, Piqua, OH, *Exec. VP*, Hidden Valley Lake, Inc.; **PRIM RE ACT:** Developer, Builder; **SERVICES:** Lake Resort Communities, Water & Sewer Utilities; **PREV EMPLOY:** Touche Ross & Co., Dayton, OH 1976-1977; **PROFL AFFIL & HONORS:** AICPA, OH Soc. CPA; **EDUC:** BA, 1976, Bus./Acctg., Wittenberg Univ.; **GRAD EDUC:** MBA, 1979, Fin./Acctg., IN Univ.-Bloomington; **EDUC HONORS:** Cum Laude; **HOME ADD:** R 3, Lawrenceburg, IN 47025, (812)537-3468; **BUS ADD:** R 3, Lawrenceburg, IN 47025, (812)537-3333.

RUPEL, James J.——**B:** Feb. 5, 1926, Jay Co., IN, *Pres.*, Hidden Valley Lake, Inc.; **PRIM RE ACT:** Developer; **SERVICES:** RE Devel. & Sales; **PREV EMPLOY:** Pres. COB, Lloyds Acceptance Corp.; **EDUC:** BCE, 1948, Purdue Univ.; **GRAD EDUC:** MBA, 1950, Mgmt., IN Univ.; **MIL SERV:** USA 1944-1946, Pfc. Bronze Star (combat); **HOME ADD:** RR3 Hidden Valley Lake, Lawrenceburg, IN 47025; **BUS ADD:** RR3 Hidden Valley Lake, Lawrenceburg, IN 47025, (812)537-3333.

RUPORT, Scott H.——**B:** Nov. 22, 1949, *Atty.*, Skidmore, Ruport & Haskins; **PRIM RE ACT:** Attorney, Instructor; **PROFL AFFIL & HONORS:** ABA; OH State Bar Assn.; Akron Bar Assn.; OH Academy of Trial Lawyers; The Association of Trial Lawyers of America, Admitted to practice before the US Supreme Court 1978; Admitted to practice before the District Court for NE OH; Sixth Circuit Court of Appeals; Ohio Supreme Court 1974; **EDUC:** BS, 1971, Pre-law, Bowling Green State Univ.; **GRAD EDUC:** JD, 1974, Univ. of Akron School of Law; **EDUC HONORS:** Beta Gamma Sigma, Phi Alpha Delta; **MIL SERV:** Fin., Capt., Distinguished Military Grad.; **HOME ADD:** 138 Overwood Rd., Akron, OH 44313, (216)864-2439; **BUS ADD:** 815 Centran Bldg., Akron, OH 44308, (216)253-1550.

RUPP, Paul W.——*VP Fin. & Treas.*, National Standard Co.; **PRIM RE ACT:** Property Manager; **BUS ADD:** 1618 Terminal Rd., Niles, MI 49120, (616)683-8100.*

RUPWANI, Kanayo N. "Rupi"——**B:** Nov. 13, 1940, Tando Jam, Pakistan, *Broker - Owner*, Century 21 Rupwani Associates; **PRIM RE ACT:** Broker, Consultant, Appraiser, Developer, Builder, Owner/Investor, Property Manager, Insuror, Syndicator; **SERVICES:** Buying, selling, bldg., mgmt., secondary fin.; **REP CLIENTS:** HUD and VA; **PREV EMPLOY:** Retail & wholesale sales (1960-1972); **PROFL AFFIL & HONORS:** The Greater Waterbury Bd. of Realtors, Broker's Council of Century 21 Brokers of New Haven Cty, CT and NAR; CAR and Educ. Comm. of the Greater Waterbury Bd. of Realtors, GRI; **OTHER ACT & HONORS:** Elks, Lions; **HOME ADD:** 817 May St., Naugatuck, CT 06770, (203)723-1262; **BUS ADD:** 1360 New Haven Rd., Naugatuck, CT 06670, (203)723-7423.

RUSCHMAN, Richard C.——**B:** May 6, 1953, Lewistown, PA, *Atty.*, Law Offices of Ronald L. Evans, P.C.; **PRIM RE ACT:** Attorney, Developer, Syndicator; **SERVICES:** Legal counseling and representation, devel. and synd. of comml. props.; **REP CLIENTS:** Paul Broadhead & Assoc., Inc.; Jacobs/Kahan and Co.; CP & Assoc., Inc., Commerce Title Company of Dallas, Inc.; **PREV EMPLOY:** Tenney & Bentley, Chicago 1978-80; **PROFL AFFIL & HONORS:** ABA, IL State Bar Assn.; TX State Bar Assn.; **EDUC:** AB, 1975, Pol. Sci., Univ. of MI, Ann Arbor MI; **GRAD EDUC:** JD, 1978, Univ. of MI, Ann Arbor, MI; **EDUC HONORS:** High honors; **HOME ADD:** 333 Melrose #30B, Richardson, TX 75230, (214)238-8543; **BUS ADD:** 16475 Dallas Pkwy., Ste. 520, Dallas, TX 75248, (214)931-0123.

RUSH, Fred L.——**B:** July 13, 1925, Honaker, VA, *Part.*, Bernstein, Bernstein, Feinman & Rush, P.A.; **PRIM RE ACT:** Attorney; **SERVICES:** All legal services plus tax advice & asst. in structuring deals; **PREV EMPLOY:** Citibank (NYC); NCNB (Charlotte, NC); SE Banks Tr. Co.; NA (Miami, FL); **PROFL AFFIL & HONORS:** The FL Bar; VA Bar; Dist of Columbia Bar; ABA; Intl. Assn. of Fin. Planning, LLB; **EDUC:** BA, 1948, Pol. Sci. & Econ., Wash. & Lee Univ., Lexington, VA; **GRAD EDUC:** LLB, 1950, Wash. & Lee Univ., Lexington, VA; **MIL SERV:** USN; Lt. (jg); **OTHER ACT & HONORS:** Comm. Atty. Buchanan Cty., VA (1951-55); Town Atty., Grundy VA, (1951-55), Rotary Club, Estate Planning Council of NYC, Pres. (65-66); Thesis Examiner, Nat. Grad. Trust School, NW Univ.; Frequent lecturer on tax, tax shelters, fin planning before prof. seminars throughout US; **HOME ADD:** 2745 SW 6th St., Delray Beach, FL 33445, (305)276-0534; **BUS ADD:** 2740 E Oakland Park Blvd., Suite 302, Ft. Lauderdale, FL 33306, (305)563-3205.

RUSH, James W.——**B:** Jan. 18, 1929, Chicago, IL, *Pres.*, Fountain Hills Development Corp., MCO Holdings, Inc.; **PRIM RE ACT:** Developer, Builder, Property Manager; **PREV EMPLOY:** Pres.-Houston Prop. Interests, Inc.; VP-Woodlands Devel. Corp.-Mitchell Energy & Devel. Corp.; VP-Sugarland Props.-Gerald D. Hines Interests; Dir. of Mktg.-AVCO Comml. Devels., Inc.; **PROFL AFFIL & HONORS:** Natl. Assn. of Office and Indus. Parks, Natl. Assn. of Corp. RE Execs., Inst. of Resid. Mktg., Bonded and Registered Home Builder-Greater Houston Home Builders Assn., Natl. Assn. of Home Builders; **EDUC:** Bus. Admin., Lake Forest Coll. - Northwestern Univ.; **GRAD EDUC:** 1963, Bus. - Mktg., Syracuse Univ.; **MIL SERV:** USAF-50-55, 1st Lt., DFC, Air Med., Korean Theater; **OTHER ACT & HONORS:** Acted recently as Liaison Officer between KUHT-Channel 8 (public TV) and the Greater Houston Home Builders who constructed and auctioned a new home which raised $55,000; **HOME ADD:** 16838 E. Palisades Blvd., Fountain Hills, AZ 85268, (800)528-0292; **BUS ADD:** 16838 E. Palisades Blvd., Fountain Hills, AZ 85268, (800)528-0292.

RUSH, James W.——*Office Service Mgr.*, Lever Brothers; **PRIM RE ACT:** Property Manager; **BUS ADD:** 390 Park Ave., New York, NY 10022, (212)688-6000.*

RUSHFORTH, Randy——**B:** Aug. 27, 1946, Tacoma, WA, *Pres.*, Rushforth Constr. Co. Inc.; **PRIM RE ACT:** Consultant, Developer, Builder, Owner/Investor; **SERVICES:** Gen. contr., design; **REP CLIENTS:** Comml. owners & devels.; **PREV EMPLOY:** Careage Corp., Bellevue, WA, 1971-76; **EDUC:** Const. Mgmt., 1971, Bus. Engrg., Univ. of WA; **OTHER ACT & HONORS:** Rotary, Tacoma, WA; **BUS ADD:** 702 Alexander Ave., Tacoma, WA 98421, (206)572-4774.

RUSHKIN, Kate——**B:** Oct. 13, 1952, Boston, *Jr. VP*, The Copeland Corp., Investments; **PRIM RE ACT:** Owner/Investor; **SERVICES:** Investing, developing; **EDUC:** BS, 1974, Econ., Univ. of Chicago; **GRAD EDUC:** PhD, 1976, Econ., Univ. of Chicago; **EDUC HONORS:** Magna Cum Laude, Summa Cum Laude; **HOME ADD:** 355 School St., Marshfield, MA 02050; **BUS ADD:** 35 Copeland St., Quincy, MA 02169.

RUSHMORE, Stephen——**B:** Mar. 18, 1945, Glen Cove, NY, *Pres.*, Hospitality Valuation Services, Inc.; **PRIM RE ACT:** Broker, Consultant, Appraiser, Instructor; **SERVICES:** Specializes in hotel-motel valuations, mkt. studies and counseling; **REP CLIENTS:** Maj. lenders and hotel chains and investors; **PROFL AFFIL & HONORS:** AIREA; Soc. of RE Appraisers; Cornell Soc. of Hotelmen; RE Bd. of NYC; Amer. Hotel & Motel Assn.; ASREC, MAI; SRPA; CSA; CRE; **EDUC:** BS, 1967, Hotel Admin., Cornell Univ.; **GRAD EDUC:** MBA, 1971, Fin., Univ. of Buffalo; **OTHER ACT & HONORS:** Author; *The Valuation of Hotels and Motels*, text of AIREA; **HOME ADD:** 22 Shepherd Ln., Roslyn Hts., NY 11577, (516)621-1918; **BUS ADD:** 128 Front St., Mineola, NY 11501, (516)248-8828.

RUSSELL, Georgann——**B:** Nov. 12, 1946, NYC, *Owner/Mgr.*, RE Mgmt. & Investment Company; **PRIM RE ACT:** Broker, Consultant, Property Manager, Owner/Investor; **PREV EMPLOY:** VP D. Russel & Assoc. 1968-72, R.W. Zukin Corp. 1972-75; **PROFL AFFIL & HONORS:** CA Assn. Realtors, Natl. Inst. RE Brokers, REaltors Mktg. Inst.; **OTHER ACT & HONORS:** Santa Cruz Coalition against rent control, women entrepreneurs, bus. & prof. women's; **HOME ADD:** 1708 Escalona Dr., Santa Cruz, CA 95060; **BUS ADD:** 104 Walnut Ave. #200, Santa Cruz, CA 95060, (408)423-1340.

RUSSELL, James E., Jr.——**B:** June 30, 1931, High Point, NC, *Pres.*, United Assoc., Inc.; **PRIM RE ACT:** Broker, Developer, Builder, Property Manager, Owner/Investor; **SERVICES:** Developing & operating RE for Profit; **PREV EMPLOY:** in this Bus. since 1955; **PROFL AFFIL & HONORS:** NHBA, NARER, RAM, NNBA - Dir. Atlantic Bank of Orlando; **HOME ADD:** 2403 Norfolk Rd., Orlando, FL 32803, (305)896-4763; **BUS ADD:** 1215 E. Amelia St., Orlando, FL 32802, (305)896-7121.

RUSSELL, John A.——**B:** June 15, 1948, Jersey City, NJ, *Owner/Broker*, Century 21 Jack Associates; **PRIM RE ACT:** Broker, Developer, Builder, Owner/Investor; **SERVICES:** RE Mktg. & Sales, Resid. Devel.; **PROFL AFFIL & HONORS:** NAR, VAR, NW VT Bd. of Realtors; Franklin Cty. Bd. of Realtors, CRS, GRI; **EDUC:** BA, 1970, Eng., St. Michael's Coll., Winooski, VT; **OTHER ACT &**

HONORS: Home builders Assn.; **HOME ADD:** 5 Gilbert St., S. Burlington, VT 05468, (802)863-3430; **BUS ADD:** Rte. 7, PO Box 8, Milton, VT 05468, (802)893-2415.

RUSSELL, John K.——B: Aug. 14, 1946, Nassawadox, VA, *Escrow & Const. Disbursement Area Mgr.*, Lawyers Title Insurance Corp.; **PRIM RE ACT:** Consultant, Insuror; **SERVICES:** Title Ins. Escrow & disbursement of funds on const. loans on behalf of lenders, borrowers; **REP CLIENTS:** Any size builder, devel., investor, lender, gen. contractor, realtor, subcontractor or supplier; Architect; **PREV EMPLOY:** State Comml. Loan Officer, First Mort. Corp. 1971-77, Mort. Banking Firm; **PROFL AFFIL & HONORS:** VA Mort. Bankers Assn.; Amer. Arbitration Assn.; Nat. Assn. of Review Appraisers; Bd. of Dirs., Richmond How Corp.; **EDUC:** AA, 1970, Bus. Mgmt., Univ. of VA; **MIL SERV:** US Army, SSG, Army Commendation Medal; **OTHER ACT & HONORS:** Advisor, Boy Scouts, Troop 874, Richmond, VA; **HOME ADD:** 10013 Copperwood Ct., Richmond, VA 23236, (804)320-3546; **BUS ADD:** 9th & Main Sts., PO Box 1456, Richmond, VA 23212, (804)643-3594.

RUSSELL, Michael P.——B: June 1, 1945, Los Angeles, CA, *Pres.*, The Russell Development Company; **PRIM RE ACT:** Consultant, Developer; **OTHER RE ACT:** Investment; **SERVICES:** Market & Fin.; **REP CLIENTS:** Mobil, Prudential, Transamerica, The Irvine Co., Maguire Partners; **PREV EMPLOY:** Booz, Allen Hamilton; **PROFL AFFIL & HONORS:** ULI, Lamda Alpha; **EDUC:** BA, 1967, Pol. Sci./Econ., USC; **GRAD EDUC:** MPL, 1967, Urban Regional Planning, Univ. S. CA; **OTHER ACT & HONORS:** ULI, HUD and NIH Fellowships; **BUS ADD:** 723 Greentree Rd., Pacific Palisades, CA 90272, (213)972-4000.

RUSSELL, Patrick J.——B: Aug. 30, 1948, Houston, TX, Cogsell and Wehrle; **PRIM RE ACT:** Attorney; **REP CLIENTS:** RE Devels. and Synds.; **PROFL AFFIL & HONORS:** ABA, CO and Denver Bar Assns.; **EDUC:** BA, 1971, Econ., Claremont Men's Coll.; BS, 1971, Indus. Engrg., Stanford Univ.; **GRAD EDUC:** MS, 1971, Indus. Engrg., Stanford Univ.; MBA, 1974, Fin., Univ. of Denver; JD, 1974, Law, Univ. of Denver; **EDUC HONORS:** Cum Laude; **HOME ADD:** 1125 S. Vine, Denver, CO 80210, (303)244-9373; **BUS ADD:** 1910 Lincoln Ctr. Bldg., Denver, CO 80264, (303)861-2150.

RUSSELL, Ralph S.——B: July 23, 1928, Sutherland, NE, *Broker-Appraiser-Inst.*, Moraine Park Tech. Inst. & Casey & Co.; **PRIM RE ACT:** Broker, Instructor, Consultant, Appraiser, Owner/Investor; **SERVICES:** Valuation-residential brokerage-investment consultant-prelicensing and advanced R.E. sales instruction; **PROFL AFFIL & HONORS:** SREA; NAR; Wisconsin Realtors Assn.-Amer. Vocational Assn., Member-Wisconcin Realtors Honor Soc.; **EDUC:** BS, 1953, Communications, Boston Univ.; **GRAD EDUC:** M. ED., 1962, Boston Univ.; **EDUC HONORS:** Cum Laude; **OTHER ACT & HONORS:** Pres.-Kiwanis Early Risers of West Bend; **HOME ADD:** 5628 Scenic Dr., West Bend, WI 53095, (414)338-8768; **BUS ADD:** 2151 N. Main St., West Bend, WI 53905, (414)334-3413.

RUSSELL, Richard C. (Dick)——B: Oct. 23, 1946, Johnson City, TN, *RE Mgr.*, Jack Eckerd Corp. (1980 to present), So. FL Drug Div. and J. Byrons Div.; **OTHER RE ACT:** Retail site selection and lease negotiations; **PREV EMPLOY:** RE Field Leasing Rep for J.C. Penney's, Eastern Region in Pittsburgh, PA (1974-1980); **PROFL AFFIL & HONORS:** NACORE; ICSC; **EDUC:** BS, 2973, Indus. Technol., East TN State Univ.; **MIL SERV:** USN - Submarines, E-5 (1966-1970), several non-combat; **OTHER ACT & HONORS:** Sigma Chi Alumni Chapter (Ft. Lauderdale); 1980 Delegate to Republican National Convention; **HOME ADD:** 9380 B. SW 61st Way, Boca Raton, FL 33433; **BUS ADD:** 1471 W. Hillsboro Blvd., Deerfield Beach, FL 33441, (305)428-2830.

RUSSELL, Richard F.——B: Apr. 5, 1940, Springfield, MA, *Asst. VP*, Connecticut Mutual Life Insurance Company, Urban Investment; **PRIM RE ACT:** Owner/Investor, Instructor, Property Manager, Insuror; **PROFL AFFIL & HONORS:** IREM, CPM; **EDUC:** BBA, 1968, Gen. Bus. & Acctg., Amer. Intl. Coll.; **GRAD EDUC:** MBA, 1972, Bus., Western New England Coll; **MIL SERV:** USN, E-5; **OTHER ACT & HONORS:** Chmn., East Longmeadow School Comm. 3 yrs.; Chmn., East Longmeadow Building Comm. 3 yrs.; **HOME ADD:** 291 Prospect St., East Longmeadow, MA 01028, (413)525-4337; **BUS ADD:** 140 Garden St., Hartford, CT 06115, (203)727-6532.

RUSSELL, Robert L.——B: Mar. 4, 1954, Monroe, LA, *R.E. Appraiser/Consultant*, Robert Jenkins and Assoc.; **PRIM RE ACT:** Broker, Instructor, Consultant, Appraiser; **SERVICES:** R.E. Appraisal, Counseling and Research (throughout LA including Baton Rouge, New Orleans, Shreveport and Lafayette); **EDUC:** BS, 1975, Soc. Sci., Econ., Fin., R.E., LA State Univ., Baton Rouge; **GRAD EDUC:** 6 sem. Grad. hrs., Investment Analysis, Shreveport Centenary Coll.; **OTHER ACT & HONORS:** Lambda Chi Alpha, Cert. RE Instructor; AIREA; Soc. of RE Appraisers; **HOME ADD:** 1217 Beckenham, Baton Rouge, LA 70808, (504)293-3667; **BUS ADD:** 4314 S. Sherwood Forest, Suite 125, Baton Rouge, LA 70816, (504)293-6083.

RUSSELL, Roger S.——B: May 4, 1944, Washington, DC, *Pres. and Chmn.*, Grove Realty, Inc. and Westwood Mort. Exchange, Inc.; **PRIM RE ACT:** Broker, Consultant, Lender, Owner/Investor, Instructor, Property Manager, Syndicator; **OTHER RE ACT:** Mort. broker; **SERVICES:** Brokerage, consulting, mort. banking/brokerage; **REP CLIENTS:** All private clients; **PREV EMPLOY:** 12 yrs. of sales, prop. mgmt., synd., construction; **PROFL AFFIL & HONORS:** NAR; IREM; Mort. Banker's Assn. of OH, CPM; State VP, Oregon Assn. of Realtors; **EDUC:** BS, 1972, RE/Fin., Univ. of S. CA; **GRAD EDUC:** MBA, 1974, RE/Fin., Univ. of S. CA Grad. School of Bus.; **EDUC HONORS:** Magna Cum Laude, Beta Gamma Sigma, Beta Gamma Sigma, 4.0 average; **MIL SERV:** USN, Vietnam; **OTHER ACT & HONORS:** Founder of bank, escrow co., and mort. banking firm; **HOME ADD:** 2040 Dogwood Dr., Eugene, OR 97405; **BUS ADD:** 1137 E. Main, Cottage Grove, OR 97424, (503)942-5535.

RUSSO, Adrian——*VP Ind. Rel.*, Chamberlain Manufacturing Co.; **PRIM RE ACT:** Property Manager; **BUS ADD:** 845 Larch Ave., Elmhurst, IL 60126, (312)279-3600.*

RUSSO, Edmund Peter——B: Apr. 23, 1923, Middletown, CT, *Sr. Partner (Pres.)*, Russo, Allen & Baker, P.A.; **PRIM RE ACT:** Attorney, Owner/Investor; **REP CLIENTS:** Coral Gables Bd. of Realtors; Sheraton Corp. of Amer.; ITT-South FL Devel. Corp.; **PROFL AFFIL & HONORS:** Coral Gables Bar Assn.; Dade Cty. Bar Assn.; FL Bar Assn.; ABA; **EDUC:** BA, 1947, Romance Languages, Hist., Wesleyan Univ.; **GRAD EDUC:** JD, Law, Univ. of Miami, Miami, FL; **EDUC HONORS:** Phi Beta Kappa; **MIL SERV:** USAAF, USAF; Capt.; **OTHER ACT & HONORS:** Dir., Flagship Nat. Bank of Miami; **HOME ADD:** 625 Biltmore Way, Coral Gables, FL 33134, (305)448-2392; **BUS ADD:** Riviera Prof. Bldg. 4675, Ponce De Leon Blvd., Coral Gables, FL 33146, (305)665-0414.

RUTEMEYER, E.F.——B: Dec. 21, 1923, Cincinnatti, OH, *Pres.*, A&E Design Grp., Inc.; **PRIM RE ACT:** Architect; **SERVICES:** Planning, Arch., Landscape Archit. and Engrg.; **PREV EMPLOY:** E.F. Rutemeyer, Architect Self-Employed; **PROFL AFFIL & HONORS:** AIA; **MIL SERV:** USN, Lt.; **HOME ADD:** 6375 Evans Mill Way, Lithonia, GA 30058, (404)482-1569; **BUS ADD:** 2840 Profl. Pkwy, Atlanta, GA 30339, (404)952-1009.

RUTH, Craig——B: July 18, 1930, Akron, PA, *Executive Vice-President*, Tooley & Company, (Bill Tooley & Craig Ruth, Owners); **PRIM RE ACT:** Consultant, Developer, Owner/Investor, Property Manager; **OTHER RE ACT:** Mktg. (Leasing); **SERVICES:** Deve., Consulting, Leasing, Mgmt.; **REP CLIENTS:** Union Pacific Corp., Lloyd's Bank, Santa Fe Intl. Corp., Frank B. Hall & Co. of CA, Devel. Hi-Rise Office Bldgs. & Hotels Most Prestigious-55 story security Pacific Nat. Bank Bldg. & 1500 Room Bonaverture Hotel; **PREV EMPLOY:** Ketchum, Peck & Tooley, Investment Builders-Owner-Craig/Frank Co.-Murdock Dev. Co.; **PROFL AFFIL & HONORS:** Past Dir.-BOMA, 1965-Nominated-Outstanding Young Men of America 1965-Construction Award For: Yorba Linda Village; **EDUC:** AB of Arts, 1952, Speech, Psy., Muskingum Coll.-New Concord, OH, Northwestern Univ.-Evanston, IL; **MIL SERV:** USMC, Capt., 1953-1955; **OTHER ACT & HONORS:** Staff Position 1956-1957, Lectorer-Teaching-Grad. School of RE at Stanford & USC; **HOME ADD:** 4045 Miraleste Dr., Rancho Palos Verdes, CA 90274, (213)831-4663; **BUS ADD:** 3303 Wilshire Blvd., Los Angeles, CA 90010, (213)382-8211.

RUTHERFORD, Kenneth——*Mgr. RE & Prop. Services*, Deere & Co.; **PRIM RE ACT:** Property Manager; **BUS ADD:** John Deere Rd., Moline, IL 61265, (309)752-8000.*

RUTLEDGE, James C.——B: Mar. 20, 1947, Laurel, MS, *Sec.-Treas.*, Exec. RE Services, Inc.; **PRIM RE ACT:** Broker, Developer, Owner/Investor, Syndicator; **SERVICES:** RE portfolio mgmt.; **PROFL AFFIL & HONORS:** Sarasota Bd. of Realtors; Nat. Assn. of Realtors; Realtors Nat. Mktg. Inst., CCIM Candidate; **EDUC:** BBA, 1969, Mktg., Univ. of MS; **MIL SERV:** US Army (ASA), E-5; **HOME ADD:** 1430 Kimlira La., Sarasota, FL 33581; **BUS ADD:** 1770 Wood St., Sarasota, FL 33577, (813)365-0900.

RUTLEDGE, John K.——B: Feb. 13, 1945, Springfield, IL, *VP-Mgr. Trust Real Props.*, Continental Illinois National Bank and Trust Co. of Chicago, Trust; **PRIM RE ACT:** Banker; **OTHER RE ACT:** RE investment servs.; **SERVICES:** Urban and agricultural prop. investment and mgmt.; **REP CLIENTS:** Personal trusts, pension plans, intl. investors; **PREV EMPLOY:** Const. lending; **PROFL AFFIL &**

HONORS: IL Chap. Amer. Soc. of Farm Mgrs. and Rural Appraisers; **EDUC:** BS Agricultural Sci., 1967, Farm Mgmt., Univ. of IL; **GRAD EDUC:** MS, 1969, Agricultural Fin., Univ. of IL; **EDUC HONORS:** High Honors, Alpha Zeta, Phi Eta Sigma, Gamma Sigma Delta; **MIL SERV:** IL Army Nat. Guard, Sgt., 1967-73; **OTHER ACT & HONORS:** Chmn.-Capital Needs Task Force-Presbytery of Chicago; **BUS ADD:** 30 N. LaSalle St., Chicago, IL 60693, (312)828-3971.

RUTLEDGE, Paul R.——**B:** Mar. 13, 1953, Johnstown, PA, *Gen. Mgr. and Leasing Consultant*, A.E. Le Page, Shopping Ctr. Div.; **PRIM RE ACT:** Consultant, Property Manager; **SERVICES:** Leasing-Prop. Mgr.; **REP CLIENTS:** Amlea of FL; **PREV EMPLOY:** Gen. Mgr. Palm Beach Mall of Edward J. DeBartolo Corp. Largest Ctr. Dev. in US; **PROFL AFFIL & HONORS:** North Palm Bd. of RE Member I.C.S.C., Member of BOMA Intl., Sgrafic Award - AD Design, Natl. Research Bureau Retail Mktg. Award, Who's Who in the Southeast, 1980-81; **EDUC:** BS, Advertising-Bus., Univ. of S. FL; **EDUC HONORS:** Who's Who in Coll. and Univ., Dean's List; **HOME ADD:** 3845 Coelebs Ave., Boynton Bch., FL 33436, (305)499-8510; **BUS ADD:** 11594 U.S. One, Palm Beach Gardens, FL 33408, (305)626-3880.

RUTLEDGE, Richard G.——**B:** Apr. 5, 1933, Sayre, PA, *Part Owner, Exec. VP*, Gilbert Rayner, Inc.; **PRIM RE ACT:** Broker, Owner/Investor; **SERVICES:** All aspects of managing an active multiple office resid. brokerage firm, prop. mgmt.; **REP CLIENTS:** Major third party cos.; **PREV EMPLOY:** Part owner of major multiple office RE firm in Chicago (1965-1980); **PROFL AFFIL & HONORS:** GRI, CRB; **EDUC:** BME, 1956, Bus. mgmt., Cornell Univ., Ithaca, NY; **GRAD EDUC:** MBA, 1960, Gen. Bus., Univ. of HI, Honolulu; **MIL SERV:** US Naval Res., Lt. JG; **OTHER ACT & HONORS:** Rotary Club of Lake Forest, MI Shores Club, Wilmette; Geneva Lake Yacht Club.; **HOME ADD:** 826 Forest Ave., Wilmette, IL 60091, (312)251-5873; **BUS ADD:** 300 E. IL Rd., Lake Forest, IL 60045, (312)234-9300.

RUTSCHOW, Robert F.——**B:** June 1, 1931, Herkimer, NY, *Atty.*, Gordon, Marshall and Rutschow; **PRIM RE ACT:** Attorney; **SERVICES:** RE closings; second mort. closings; **PREV EMPLOY:** Boeing Airplane Co. 1955-1959; Instr. VA Military Inst. 1960-1967; **PROFL AFFIL & HONORS:** VA State Bar; ABA; **EDUC:** BS, 1953, Civil Engrg., VA Military Inst.; **GRAD EDUC:** JD, 1968, Law, Washington and Lee Univ.; **MIL SERV:** USAF; Lt.; 1953-1955; **HOME ADD:** 335 Key West Dr., Charlottesville, VA 22901, (801)296-2597; **BUS ADD:** 801 E. Jefferson St., Charlottesville, VA 22901, (804)295-7113.

RUTTAN, Charles D.——**B:** July 21, 1943, Oakland, CA, *Lawyer*, Morrison, Dunn, Cohen, Miller & Carney; **PRIM RE ACT:** Attorney; **REP CLIENTS:** Emkay Devel. Co., Inc., a subsidiary of Morrison-Knudsen; Winmar Pacific, Inc., a subsidiary of Safeco Ins. Co. of Amer.; Miller Brewing Co.; Carnation Co.; **PROFL AFFIL & HONORS:** ABA - Sections: Real Prop., Corp., Banking and Bus. Law; OSB - Sections Corps., RE, Securities; USDC, 9th Circuit; **EDUC:** BS, 1966, Acctg., CA State Univ., Chico; **GRAD EDUC:** JD, 1972, Willamette Univ.; **MIL SERV:** Army, Lt.; **HOME ADD:** 17100 Bryant Rd., Lake Oswego, OR 97034, (503)636-1312; **BUS ADD:** 851 SW Sixth Ave., Portland, OR 97204, (504)224-6440.

RUTTENBERG, Roger F.——**B:** Jan. 8, 1944, Chicago, IL, *Pres.*, Lakewest Equity, Inc.; **PRIM RE ACT:** Developer, Owner/Investor, Syndicator; **SERVICES:** Redevel. and synd. of comml. prop.; **REP CLIENTS:** Indiv. investors and Nat. retail chains; **PREV EMPLOY:** Abacus Group, Tishman Realty and Construction Co., Inc.; **PROFL AFFIL & HONORS:** Intl. Council of Shopping Ctrs., RESSI, Beta Gamma Sigma; **EDUC:** AB, 1966, Econ., Univ. of PA; **GRAD EDUC:** MBA, 1971, Mktg., Northwestern Univ.; **EDUC HONORS:** with distinction; **MIL SERV:** US Navy, Lt.; **HOME ADD:** 10 Crescent Dr., Glencoe, IL 60022, (312)835-3384; **BUS ADD:** 55 East Monroe St., Suite 3950, Chicago, IL 60603, (312)332-1150.

RUZIC, John F.——**B:** Aug. 6, 1950, Chicago, IL, *Assoc.*, Laventhol & Horwath, Mgmt. Advisory Servs.; **PRIM RE ACT:** Consultant; **OTHER RE ACT:** Feasibility analysis, Mkt. studies, Fin./cash flow projections, prop. valuation, project planning, deal structuring, community/econ. devel., strategic planning; **REP CLIENTS:** Hyatt Hotels, Hilton Hotels, Sheraton, Holiday Inns, Ramada Inns, Quality Inns, Days Inns of Amer., Four Seasons Hotels, Meridian Hotels, Playboy Clubs Intl., General Mills-Restaurant Grp. - lenders and indiv. or instnl. investors/devels. of comml. and resid. props.; **PREV EMPLOY:** Pillsbury, Inc./Intl. Multi-Food Corp.; **PROFL AFFIL & HONORS:** Amer. Hotel & Motel Assn.; Nat. Restaurant Assn.; Intl. Food Serv. Exec. Assn.; Intl. Assn. of Hospitality Accountants; **EDUC:** BS, Hotel & Restaurant Mgmt., Minor: Acctg. & Mktg., FL Intl. Univ.; **GRAD EDUC:** MS, Maj.: Hotel & Food Mgmt. Minor: Fin., FL Intl. Univ.; **EDUC HONORS:** Dean's List, GPA 3.6/4.0 (no distinctions are made at F.I.U. on the graduate level); **OTHER ACT & HONORS:** Income Tax Assistance - IRS (VITA), Writings: 1) Co-author - *Laventhol & Horwath-FL Ctry. Club/Yacht Club Study, a Statistical Analysis of Club Operations*; 2) *Evaluating Franchise Investments-A Self-Evaluation Method for Franchisees and Investors*, a Thesis Prepared at FL Intl. Univ., Grad. School of Hospitality Mgmt.; **HOME ADD:** 11713 Lovejoy St., Silver Spring, MD 20902, (301)593-4961; **BUS ADD:** 2115 E. Jefferson St., Suite 500, Rockville, MD 20852, (301)468-0888.

RUZICKA, Len——**B:** May 6, 1945, St. Louis, MO, *RE Counsel*, The Seven-Up Co.; **PRIM RE ACT:** Attorney; **SERVICES:** All phases of RE law affecting the Seven-Up Co. and its subs.; **PREV EMPLOY:** Title Counsel, Pioneer Mat. Title Ins. Co., Private Practice; **PROFL AFFIL & HONORS:** ABA; MO Bar Assn.; St. Louis Metro Bar Assn.; Amer. Arbitration Assn.; **EDUC:** BA, 1967, Econ., Georgetown Univ.; **GRAD EDUC:** JD, 1974, Law, St. Louis Univ.; **MIL SERV:** USN, Lt.; **HOME ADD:** 776 Hawthicket, St. Louis, MO 63105, (314)862-3978; **BUS ADD:** 121 S. Meramel, St. Louis, MO 63105, (314)889-7763.

RYAN, Arthur N.——*Pres.*, Technicolor, Inc.; **PRIM RE ACT:** Property Manager; **BUS ADD:** Century City, 2049 Century Park East, Ste. 2400, Los Angeles, CA 90067, (213)553-5200.*

RYAN, David E.——**B:** Sept. 2, 1936, Santa Monica, CA, *VP/Partner*, Penta Pac. Props.; **PRIM RE ACT:** Broker, Developer, Owner/Investor; **SERVICES:** Specialize in leasing, selling & devel. warehouse, mfg. facilities & office bldgs.; **PROFL AFFIL & HONORS:** SIR; Past Pres., S. CA Chap., currently Dist. Dir., Los Angeles Realty Bd., Los Angeles Realty Bd., Award, Realtor of the Year; **EDUC:** BS, 1960, RE, Fin., USC; **GRAD EDUC:** Cert. in RE, 1961, UCLA; **MIL SERV:** US Navy; QM 1st Cl.; **OTHER ACT & HONORS:** Guest Speaker, lecturer to various RE groups; **HOME ADD:** 9214 La Alba Dr., Whittier, CA 90603, (213)947-3163; **BUS ADD:** 918 Town & Country Rd., Orange, CA 92668, (714)558-1188.

RYAN, Frank——*Newmont Mining*; **PRIM RE ACT:** Property Manager; **BUS ADD:** 300 Park Ave. 12th Flr., New York, NY 10022, (212)980-1111.*

RYAN, J. Kevin——**B:** Jan. 1, 1953, NYC, NY, *Appraisal Officer*, Dime Savings Bank of NY, Real Estate Dept.; **PRIM RE ACT:** Banker; **PROFL AFFIL & HONORS:** Assoc., Soc. of RE Appraisers; Member, Young Mort. Bankers Assn. of NY; Candidate, Amer. Instit. of RE Appraisers; **EDUC:** BBA, 1977, Mgmt., Hofstra Univ.; **GRAD EDUC:** MBA, 1981, Fin., Fordham Univ.; **OTHER ACT & HONORS:** Adjunct Asst. Prof. of Mgmt., St. John's Univ., Jamaica, NY; **HOME ADD:** 1 Bryant Ave., New Hyde Park, NY 11040, (516)488-4680; **BUS ADD:** 9 DeKalb Ave., Brooklyn, NY 11201, (212)643-5180.

RYAN, James N.——*Director Purchasing & Manufacturing*, Barber-Green Co.; **PRIM RE ACT:** Property Manager; **BUS ADD:** 400 N. Highland Ave., Aurora, IL 60507, (312)859-2200.*

RYAN, James P.——**B:** June 14, 1941, Arlington, SD, *Pres.*, James P. Ryan & Co., Inc.; **PRIM RE ACT:** Broker, Consultant; **PREV EMPLOY:** CT Gen. Life Ins. Co. 1969-72; CONT RE Equities 1972-74; **EDUC:** BS, 1964, Mil. Engrg., US Military Acad. at West Point; **EDUC HONORS:** Mil. Serv.; **MIL SERV:** US Army Corps of Engrs., Capt., Bronze Star; **HOME ADD:** 9 Clubhouse Cir., Darien, CT 06820, (203)655-4026; **BUS ADD:** 777 Boston Post Rd., Darien, CT 06820, (203)655-6048.

RYAN, Robert A.——**B:** Jan. 8, 1941, NYC, *Managing Part.*, R.E. Advisors; **PRIM RE ACT:** Consultant; **SERVICES:** Appraisal, Feasibility Analysis, Mktg., Fin.; **PREV EMPLOY:** V.P., Gilbane Properties, VA, Cross & Brown Co. Asst. V.P. Galbreath-Ruffin Corp.; **PROFL AFFIL & HONORS:** Providence RI Bd. of Realtors and ROMA; **EDUC:** BS, Econ., Coll. of the Holy Cross, Worcester, MA; **MIL SERV:** U.S.N.R., Ltjg., Unit Citations-Cuba 62; **HOME ADD:** 10 Henry Dr., Barrington, RI 02806, (401)245-5513; **BUS ADD:** P. O. Box 28, Barrington, RI 98665, (401)247-0485.

RYAN, Robert L.——**B:** Sept. 3, 1933, Owosso, MI, *Pres.*, Briarcrest Realty Inc.; **PRIM RE ACT:** Broker; **SERVICES:** Full Range of RE Activity; **PREV EMPLOY:** Former Sales Mgt. (8 yrs.) Largest Realtor in NW OH; Nat. Sales Mgr.- American Lincoln Corp. (14 yrs.); **PROFL AFFIL & HONORS:** Bd. of Trustees-State of OH Realtors/Toledo Bd. of Realtors, Broker, Life Member OH Million Dollar Club; **EDUC:** BA, 1958, Econ./Bus., MI State Univ.; **MIL SERV:** USN, E-4, STD; **OTHER ACT & HONORS:** Tol. Sales/Mktg. Execs. Club; **HOME ADD:** 3752 Dewlawn Dr., Toledo, OH 43614, (419)382-8222; **BUS ADD:** 5345 Heatherdowns Bl., Toledo, OH 43614, (419)866-8888.

RYAN, Thomas N., III——B: Sept. 20, 1943, Louisville, KY, *Sr. VP*, Union Planters Nat. Bank, RE; **PRIM RE ACT:** Broker, Consultant, Banker, Developer, Lender, Builder, Property Manager, Syndicator; **SERVICES:** Full range of RE Services; **REP CLIENTS:** Numerous Maj. Fin. Inst., Pension Funds, Savings & Loans, etc.; **PREV EMPLOY:** Citizens Fidelity Mort. Co., Louisville, KY, Exec. VP; **PROFL AFFIL & HONORS:** MBA, TN MBA, HBA, of Memphis; **EDUC:** BS, 1966, Mktg./RE, Western KY Univ.; **GRAD EDUC:** IN Univ. Grad. Mgmt. School; Nat. School RE Fin.; **OTHER ACT & HONORS:** Bd. of Dirs., KY MBA, Past Sec. VP Louisville Chapter MBA Pres. Elect.; **HOME ADD:** 431 Kirbi Oaks, Memphis, TN 38111, (901)767-3588; **BUS ADD:** PO Box 387, Memphis, TN 38101, (901)523-6047.

RYAN, Thomas S.——B: Sept. 4, 1947, Olean, NY, *Asst. VP*, Continental Amer. Life Ins. Co., RE Financing; **PRIM RE ACT:** Lender; **SERVICES:** Mort. Financing & RE Equities; **PREV EMPLOY:** Metropolitan Life Ins. Co., 1973-1978; US Treasury Dept., 1969-1973; **PROFL AFFIL & HONORS:** MBAA, SREA; **EDUC:** BA, 1969, Bus. Admin., St. Bonaventure Univ.; **GRAD EDUC:** MBA, 1977, No. Ill. Univ.; **HOME ADD:** 1920 Dorset Rd., N. Graylyn Crest, Wilmington, DE 19810, (302)475-1467; **BUS ADD:** 1100 King St., Wilmington, DE 19899, (302)421-5823.

RYAN, Thomas W.——B: Dec. 4, 1948, Scranton, PA, *Sr. VP*, Fidelity Union Bank, RE; **PRIM RE ACT:** Banker, Lender; **PROFL AFFIL & HONORS:** MBA of NJ, NJ Bankers Assn., Indus. RE Brokers Assn., NAIOP, James St. Commons Urban Renewal Corp.; **EDUC:** BA, 1971, Econ., Mktg., Villanova Univ., PA; **GRAD EDUC:** MBA, 1974, Rutgers, The State Univ., NJ; The Stonier Grad. School of Banking, Rutgers, Grad. 1980; **HOME ADD:** 4 Joanna Way, Chatham Township, NJ 07928, (201)635-4785; **BUS ADD:** 765 Broad St, Newark, NJ 07101, (201)430-4219.

RYBCZYK, Edward J.——B: Nov. 20, 1936, Bridgeport, CT, *Sr. VP*, Raymond, Parish, Pine & Weiner, Inc.; **PRIM RE ACT:** Consultant; **SERVICES:** Land devel. & environmental servs.; **REP CLIENTS:** Devels., builders, maj. corps., local, state and fed govts.; **PREV EMPLOY:** Dir. Redevel. Agency, Manchester, CT; **EDUC:** BSCE, 1958, Civil Engrg., Rensselaer Polytechnic Inst.; **HOME ADD:** 83 Rockledge Rd., Apt. 2A, Hartsdale, NY 10530, (914)723-7514; **BUS ADD:** 555 White Plains Rd., Tarrytown, NY 10591, (914)631-9003.

RYDSON, Marlyn D.——B: Oct. 30, 1930, Britt, IA, *Pres.*, Northern IN Mort. Co., Inc., Also The Chamberlain Agency; **PRIM RE ACT:** Broker, Appraiser, Developer, Property Manager, Owner/Investor, Insuror; **PROFL AFFIL & HONORS:** MBA, Bd. of Realtors, MLS; **EDUC:** BA, 1955, Actuarial Sci., Univ. of IA; **GRAD EDUC:** MA, 1956, Secondary School Admin., Univ. of IA; **MIL SERV:** USAF, Sgt.; **OTHER ACT & HONORS:** Member & Sec. of Redevel. Commn., Rotary, Shrine, Elcona Ctry. Club, Four Lakes Ctry. Club; **HOME ADD:** 1824 Brookwood Dr., Elkhart, IN 46514, (219)264-5338; **BUS ADD:** 314 S. Fourth St., Elkhart, IN 46516, (219)295-8205.

RYMER, S.E., Jr.——*Pres.*, Magic Chef, Inc.; **PRIM RE ACT:** Property Manager; **BUS ADD:** 740 King Edward Ave., Cleveland, TN 37311, (615)472-3371.*

RYPKEMA, Donovan D.——B: Apr. 30, 1948, Agana, Guam, *Owner*, The Real Estate Services Group; **PRIM RE ACT:** Broker, Consultant, Appraiser, Developer, Owner/Investor, Instructor; **SERVICES:** Valuation, devel., particularly historic props.; **REP CLIENTS:** Lenders, fed. govt. agencies, indiv. investors; **PREV EMPLOY:** Asst. to the Pres., Northwestern Engrg. Co.; **PROFL AFFIL & HONORS:** Candidate, AIREA, NAR, SD Assn. of Realtors; **EDUC:** BA, 1970, Poli. Sci., Hist., Univ. of SD; **OTHER ACT & HONORS:** Branch Advisory Bd., United National Bank, Rapid City, SD; **HOME ADD:** 612 St. James St., Rapid City, SD 57701, (605)348-3953; **BUS ADD:** 630 St. Joe St., Suite 202, Rapid City, SD 57701, (605)348-3780.

RYTHER, A. Harold, Jr.——B: Feb. 20, 1937, Youngstown, OH, *Dir. of Mktg.*, Wedgewood Apts. Inc.; **PRIM RE ACT:** Instructor, Consultant, Property Manager; **SERVICES:** Condo conversion consultant; **PROFL AFFIL & HONORS:** HBA, IREM, CPM; **EDUC:** 1959, RE, Youngstown St. Univ.; **OTHER ACT & HONORS:** Past Pres. Optimist Club; **HOME ADD:** 5315 Cottage Dr., Cortland, OH 44410, (216)637-9500; **BUS ADD:** 1839 S. Raccoon Rd., Youngstown, OH 44515, (216)792-3801.

RYTTER, Edward R.——B: July 10, 1939, Jersey City, NJ, *VP-Design & Construction*, Amer. Express; **OTHER RE ACT:** Corp. officer, constrc.; **SERVICES:** Project mgmt.; **PROFL AFFIL & HONORS:** Assn. of Energy Engrs., Constr. Spec. Inst., Wings Club, Amer. Arbitration Assn.; **EDUC:** BS, 1967, ME, Fairleigh Dickinson Univ.; **GRAD EDUC:** MBA, 1976, Mgmt., Fairleigh Dickinson Univ.; **EDUC HONORS:** Magna Cum Laude; **MIL SERV:** USA, Spec. 5; **HOME ADD:** 19 Cider Hill, Upper Saddle River, NJ 07458, (201)327-7312; **BUS ADD:** Amer. Express Plaza, NY, NY 10004, (212)323-2332.

SAACKE, Robert W. "Bob"——B: Oct. 8, 1936, New York, NY, *Owner*, Bob Saacke Realtor; **PRIM RE ACT:** Broker, Consultant; **SERVICES:** Comml. and investment brokerage, site evaluation and acquisition, synd. Rep. clients: indiv. and instnl. investors in comml. props.; **PROFL AFFIL & HONORS:** 1982-84 Dir., NAR, 1970 Pres. TN Assn. of Realtors, 1968, 1970, 1978, Bristol, TN/VA Realtor of the Year., CCIM, CRS, Omega Tau Rho, Sr. Cert. Valuer, Intl. Inst. of Valuers.; **EDUC:** Bach Indus. Engrg., 1960, GA Tech.; **OTHER ACT & HONORS:** Former Sullivan Cty. Commnr., 1970 Pres. Bristol Host Lions Club, Member Nat. RE Exchange; **HOME ADD:** Ten Brentwood, Bristol, TN 37620, (615)878-3252; **BUS ADD:** 900 Volunteer Pkwy., Bristol, TN 37620, (615)968-5558.

SABADIE, Louis——B: Apr. 25, 1920, New Orleans, LA, *V.P. & Dir. of Corp. R.E.*, Brown Grp., Inc.; **OTHER RE ACT:** Primary function leasing corp., retail store locations; **REP CLIENTS:** Within co. exclusively; **PROFL AFFIL & HONORS:** ICSC; **EDUC:** BS, 1940, Bus. Admin., Tulane Univ. New Orleans, LA; **MIL SERV:** USAF; Capt.; **HOME ADD:** 800 N. Spoede Rd., Creve Coeur, MO 63141, (314)432-4830; **BUS ADD:** 8400 Maryland Ave., St.Louis, MO 63105, (314)997-7500.

SABBEY, John G.——B: Apr. 9, 1941, Boston, *CPA*, John G. Sabbey & Co.; **PRIM RE ACT:** Consultant, Developer, Property Manager, Owner/Investor; **PROFL AFFIL & HONORS:** MA Soc. CPA; Amer. Inst. CPA; **EDUC:** Northeastern Univ., 1963, Acctg. & Econ., Bus.; **MIL SERV:** USA (63-65), 1st Lt.; **OTHER ACT & HONORS:** TRIM, John Birch Soc.; **HOME ADD:** 13 Mohawk Dr., Acton, MA 01720, (617)263-3702; **BUS ADD:** 13 Mohawk Dr., Acton, MA 01720, (617)263-1768.

SABELLA, Thomas A.——B: Aug. 11, 1943, Jersey City, NJ, *Mgr. Corp. RE*, Amerada Hess Corp.; **PRIM RE ACT:** Property Manager, Owner/Investor, Attorney; **SERVICES:** Purchase, sale & leasing, mgmt. of RE; **PREV EMPLOY:** Prudential Ins. Co.(RE Ins. Dept.) Gen. Resources Assoc.(Mort. Banking); **PROFL AFFIL & HONORS:** CPA; **EDUC:** BS, 1965, Acctg., Univ. of Bridgeport; **GRAD EDUC:** JD, 1969, Fordham Law School; **HOME ADD:** 9 Wren Ct., Middletown, NJ 07748; **BUS ADD:** 1185 Ave. of the Amer., NY, NY 10036, (212)997-8657; **BUS TEL:** (201)671-5706.

SACCO, George L.——B: July 19, 1938, Medford, MA, *Atty. - Consultant*, Law Offices of George L. Sacco; **PRIM RE ACT:** Broker, Consultant, Attorney; **OTHER RE ACT:** Atty. for elderly housing; moderate & family; **SERVICES:** Housing; Nursing Home devel.; private and public; **REP CLIENTS:** Housing apts. and condos.; **PREV EMPLOY:** 1962-1974, State Rep., MA House of Reps.; 1963-1974, Comm. on Educ., Clerk; 1965-1966, Comm. on Rules, Asst. Majority Leader; **PROFL AFFIL & HONORS:** Member, MA Bar Assn., MA Academy of Trial Attys., MA Assn. of Criminal Defense Lawyers, MA Continuing Legal Educ. - NE Law Inst., Inc., Middlesex Cty. Bar Assn., Nat. Assn. of Criminal Defense Lawyers, and Amer. Judicature Soc., "Man of the Year" Award, MA Italian-Amer. Civic League 1973; "Ten Outstanding Young Leaders" Award, one of ten selected by the Greater Boston Junior C of C, 1972; "Dr. Enrico Fermi Award" (Man of the Year), MA Italian-American Veterans Assn., 1969; Medford Mental Health Public Service Award, 1964; Sr. Citizens and Assocs. Public Serv. Award, 1963; Special Citation, United Fund—Outstanding Leadership and Achievement in behalf of community health and social agencies, 1962; **EDUC:** AB, 1956-1960, Govt.-Public Serv. Hist. Govt., Northeastern Univ. & Suffolk Univ.; **GRAD EDUC:** JD, LLB, 1961-1963, Debating Soc., Suffolk Law School; **OTHER ACT & HONORS:** Former VChmn. of House Ways and Means Comm. State Legis. 1962-1974; City Govt., City of Medford (1959-1963); MA Bar Assn.; MA Leg. Assn.; Zoning Comm.; Dir., Greater Boston Assn. for Retarded Children; Dir., Adolescent Counseling in Devel.; Gen. Co-Chmn., Cancer Crusade; Member, Amer. Cancer Soc.; Member, Suffolk Law School Annual Fund; Member, Irish-American Club; Member, Sons of Italy; Member, West Medford Community Center; Member, Bd. of Tr., Medford Draft Info. Ctr.; Member, Medford Mustang Athletic Assn.; Founder, Pop Warner Football Conf. in Medford; five years, Little League and Pop Warner coach; recreational leader in city playgrounds; **HOME ADD:** 60 Wedgmere Ave.,

Winchester, MA 01890, (617)729-8282; **BUS ADD:** 10 High St., Medford, MA 02155, (617)391-4488.

SACHEN, Joseph L.——B: June 5, 1950, Aurora, IL, *Mgr.*, Sachen Real Estate, Batavia Branch; **PRIM RE ACT:** Broker, Consultant, Appraiser, Owner/Investor; **SERVICES:** Mktg., appraising, investment analysis; **REP CLIENTS:** Indiv.; **PROFL AFFIL & HONORS:** NAR, Aurora C of C; **EDUC:** BA, 1973, Econ., Northwestern Univ.; **OTHER ACT & HONORS:** Jaycees, Fox Valley Rugby Club; **HOME ADD:** 932 Liberty St., Aurora, IL 60505, (312)898-2478; **BUS ADD:** PO Box 643, Autora, IL 60507, (312)879-0660.

SACHS, Gary Allen——B: June 1936, MN, *Sr. VP*, Treco Property Services Inc., Comml.; **PRIM RE ACT:** Property Manager; **OTHER RE ACT:** Leasing, mgmt., sales & devel. of comml. income props.; **PREV EMPLOY:** VP Comml. Dept., The Ervin Co.; **PROFL AFFIL & HONORS:** Designated CPM by IREM; **EDUC:** BBA, 1958, Bus. mktg. & sales, Univ. of MN; **HOME ADD:** 74 Belmont Blvd., Orange Park, FL 32073, (904)272-0243; **BUS ADD:** 1325 San Marco Blvd., Jacksonville, FL 32207, (904)396-1600.

SACHS, Henry A.——B: Apr. 5, 1949, Detroit, MI, *Partner*, Hetchler & Sachs; **PRIM RE ACT:** Broker, Attorney, Developer, Owner/Investor, Instructor, Property Manager; **PROFL AFFIL & HONORS:** ABA; State Bar of MI; Macomb Cty. Bd. of Realtors; **EDUC:** BA, 1970, Mgmt., MI State Univ.; **GRAD EDUC:** JD, 1975, RE, Detroit Coll. of Law; **EDUC HONORS:** Evans Scholars; **OTHER ACT & HONORS:** Elks; **HOME ADD:** 15323 Amore, Mt. Clemens, MI 48044; **BUS ADD:** 20095 Mack, Grosse Pointe Woods, MI 48236, (313)882-8200.

SACHS, Jerry M.——B: Sept. 18, 1948, Jacksonville, FL, *Pres.*, Jerry M. Sachs & Assoc., Inc.; **PRIM RE ACT:** Broker, Consultant, Property Manager; **SERVICES:** Sales, Consulting, Prop. mgmt., Leasing; **REP CLIENTS:** Major Nat. Ins. Cos., Local investors, St. of FL, etc.; **PROFL AFFIL & HONORS:** Local, State, & Natl. Bd. of Realtors, IREM, CPM; **EDUC:** AA, 1969, Bus., N. FL Jr. Coll.; **MIL SERV:** USAR, SP/5; **OTHER ACT & HONORS:** Congregation Shomrei Torah Synagogue, Pres., 1980-82; **HOME ADD:** 2520 Limerick Dr., Tallahassee, FL 32308, (904)893-5027; **BUS ADD:** 1449 Thomasville Rd., PO Box 12939, Tallahassee, FL 32308, (904)224-8822.

SACK, Burton M.——B: Dec. 13, 1937, Melrose, MA, *Sr. VP*, Howard Johnson Co.; **OTHER RE ACT:** Dev. of restaurants, motor lodge facilities, etc., for the Howard Johnson Co., Intl. Devel. Acquisitions; **PROFL AFFIL & HONORS:** Natl. Assn. of corporate exec. (former Pres., NE Chapt); **EDUC:** 1961, Hospitality Indus., Cornell Univ., School of Hotel & Restaurant Admin.; **GRAD EDUC:** PMD Prog, 1967, Harvard Bus. School; **EDUC HONORS:** Grad. with distinction; **MIL SERV:** USMC, Sgt.; **OTHER ACT & HONORS:** Former Member of the Bd. of Dirs., Broadcasting Exec. Club of New England, Former Member of the Bd. of Dirs. Greater Boston Assn. for Retarded Children, Marshfield MA, Ind. & Dev. Comm., Jaycees OYM Award, 1963; **HOME ADD:** 10 Christmas Tree Lane, Marshfield, MA 02050, (617)834-7894; **BUS ADD:** 220 Forbes Rd., Braintree, MA 02184, (617)848-2350.

SACK, Nathaniel——B: Feb. 14, 1941, Chicago, IL, *Atty.*, D'Ancona & Pflaum; **PRIM RE ACT:** Attorney; **SERVICES:** Legal & Tax Advice; **REP CLIENTS:** Devel. Synd., pension fund investors, prop. mgrs. home builders; **PROFL AFFIL & HONORS:** ABA, Tax Sect.; Chicago BAr Assn., Real Prop and Tax Sections; Chicago Mort. Attys. Assn.; **EDUC:** BA, 1962, Eng., Univ. of MI; **GRAD EDUC:** JD, 1965, Harvard Law School; **MIL SERV:** USAR, Capt.; **HOME ADD:** 3000 Sheridan Rd., Chicago, IL, (312)549-4542; **BUS ADD:** 30 N. LaSalle St., Suite 3100, Chicago, IL 60602, (312)580-2012.

SACRE, Robert Knowles——B: Sept. 11, 1941, Atlanta, GA, *Broker*, RE/MAX 100 of Sandy Springs, Inc.; **PRIM RE ACT:** Broker, Consultant, Developer, Regulator; **OTHER RE ACT:** Salesman in resid., comml., indus. and income props.; **SERVICES:** New Home Constr., Relocation, Resale; **PROFL AFFIL & HONORS:** NAR, GA Assn., Atlanta Bd., GRI, CRS, CRB, Life Member of the Dekalb Bd. of Realtors; Million Dollar Club; Realtors Assoc. of the Year for 1979 Dekalb Bd.; **HOME ADD:** 2320 Wineleas Rd., Decatur, GA 30033, (404)636-0647; **BUS ADD:** 1150 Hammond Dr., Bldg. D, Suite 4295, Atlanta, GA 30328, (404)396-7770.

SADDINGTON, Hugh M.——B: Nov. 12, 1943, Syracuse, NY, *VP*, The Pacific Co.; **PRIM RE ACT:** Developer, Builder, Owner/Investor, Property Manager; **SERVICES:** Corp. devel. including project information, fin. structuring, tax planning, acquisitional evaluations and operational responsibility for certain required entities; **PREV EMPLOY:** Tax Partner, Kenneth Leventhal & Co.; **PROFL AFFIL & HONORS:** Home Builders Council; Intl. Council of Shopping Ctrs.; Pacific Coast Builders Conference; Amer. Instit. of CPA's; CA Soc. of CPA's; **EDUC:** BS, 1966, Acctg., San Diego State Univ.; **OTHER ACT & HONORS:** Dir., Orange Cty. Music Ctr.; Dir., Aztec Athletic Found.; Dir., Dorado Growth Industries; Dir., Western Facilities Mgmt. Inc.; **HOME ADD:** 2514 Lake Park Ln., Newport Beach, CA 92660, (714)646-6133; **BUS ADD:** 17911 Mitchell Ave., Irvine, CA 92714, (714)957-2519.

SADLER, Wade B.——B: Mar. 29, 1946, Greenville, SC, *Pres.*, Equity Mgmt. Corp.; **PRIM RE ACT:** Broker, Consultant, Owner/Investor, Property Manager, Syndicator; **OTHER RE ACT:** Time-Sharing Consulting; **SERVICES:** Synd. of multi-family resid. props., prop. mgmt.; Time-Sharing Consulting, Loan Placement; **REP CLIENTS:** Investors, owners & devels. of multi-family resid. props.; **PREV EMPLOY:** United Capital Securities, Exec. VP; **PROFL AFFIL & HONORS:** RESSI; **EDUC:** BS, 1968, Bus. Admin., Auburn Univ.; **GRAD EDUC:** MBA, 1972, Fin., Auburn Univ.; **HOME ADD:** 4004 Toney Ct., Huntsville, AL 35802, (205)881-5976; **BUS ADD:** 106 Central Ave., Huntsville, AL 35801, (205)533-7762.

SADOCK, James, Jr.——B: Jan 3, 1946, NY, NY, *Atty.*, Coral Ridge Props., Inc., a subs. of Westinghouse Electric Corp.; **PRIM RE ACT:** Attorney; **OTHER RE ACT:** RE and Corporate Law; **PREV EMPLOY:** Gen. Counsel, Magna Props., Inc.; Gen. Atty., Investment Corp. of FL; **PROFL AFFIL & HONORS:** FL State Bar; US Supreme Court; **EDUC:** BA, 1967, Hist., Univ. of Miami, FL; **GRAD EDUC:** JD, 1971, Univ. of Tulsa, OK; **EDUC HONORS:** Dean's list, delegate to student bar; **HOME ADD:** 1400 NE 56th St., Ft. Lauderdale, FL 33334; **BUS ADD:** 3300 University Dr., Coral Springs, FL 33065, (305)752-1100.

SADOWSKY, Howard D.——B: Oct. 19, 1941, NY, *Sr. VP*, Julien J. Studley, Inc.; **PRIM RE ACT:** Broker, Consultant; **SERVICES:** Consulting & brokerage servs. for users & devels. of office space; **BUS ADD:** 10850 Wilshire Blvd., Los Angeles, CA 90024, (213)475-5761.

SAENGER, George W.——B: Nov. 8, 1946, New York, NY, *Atty. at Law*, Adams, Hendon, Carson & Crow, P.A.; **PRIM RE ACT:** Attorney; **SERVICES:** Title examinations, certification and document preparation and synd.; **PROFL AFFIL & HONORS:** ABA, NC Bar Assn., NC State Bar; **EDUC:** BS, 1968, Econ., Univ. of NC, Chapel Hill; **GRAD EDUC:** JD, 1976, Law, Univ. of NC, Chapel Hill; **MIL SERV:** USAF, Capt., Air Medal, Second Oak Leaf Cluster; **HOME ADD:** 15 Summer St., Asheville, NC 28804, (704)253-9049; **BUS ADD:** 601 First Union National Bank Bldg., 82 Patton Avenue, Asheville, NC 28801, (704)252-7381.

SAFER, Fredrick J.——B: Dec. 28, 1934, Milwaukee, WI, *Atty.*, Safer Legal Services, S.C.; **PRIM RE ACT:** Attorney; **SERVICES:** Legal; **PROFL AFFIL & HONORS:** ABA; WI and Milwaukee Bar Assns.; **EDUC:** BA, 1957, Econ., Boston Univ.; **GRAD EDUC:** JD, 1970, Marquette Univ. Law School; **MIL SERV:** U.S. Army, E-5; **OTHER ACT & HONORS:** Pres., Bd. of Trustees, Congregation Beth Israel, Glendale WI; Pres., Bd. of Dir., Hillel Academy, Milwaukee WI; **HOME ADD:** 2510 W. Brantwood Ave., Glendale, WI 53209, (414)351-0161; **BUS ADD:** 633 W. Wisconsin Ave., Suite 1703, Milwaukee, WI 53203, (414)276-2260.

SAFT, Stephen J.——B: July 21, 1944, New York, NY, *Tax Part.*, Kleban & Samor, PC; **PRIM RE ACT:** Attorney; **SERVICES:** Legal Servs., RE Synd., Tax, Bus.; **PREV EMPLOY:** Touche, Ross & Co., CPA's, NY; **PROFL AFFIL & HONORS:** ABA, CT Bar Assn., AICPA, CSCPA; **EDUC:** BS, 1966, Acctg., Univ. of RI; **GRAD EDUC:** JD/LLM, 1970, Taxation, Brooklyn Law Sch., NYU. Grad. Sch. of Law; **EDUC HONORS:** Dean's List; **OTHER ACT & HONORS:** Public Speaker & Author on Tax Subjects; **HOME ADD:** 59 Vixen Rd., Trumbull, CT 06611, (203)261-0001; **BUS ADD:** 2425 Post Rd., Southport, CT 06490, (203)255-4646.

SAFT, Stuart M.——B: Feb. 17, 1947, New York, NY, *Partner*, Powsner Saft & Powsner, P.C.; **PRIM RE ACT:** Attorney; **SERVICES:** Legal; **REP CLIENTS:** Investors, Inst. and Second Mort. Lenders, Synds., Devels., Mort. Brokers, Cooperative Converters, Cooperative Bldgs., Publicly Owned Cos., and For. Investors.; **PREV EMPLOY:** Partner, Brauner Baron Rosenweig Kligler & Sparber; **PROFL AFFIL & HONORS:** ABA, NY Bar Assn., FL Bar; **EDUC:** BA, 1968, Pol. Sci., Hofstra Univ.; **GRAD EDUC:** JD, 1971, Law, Columbia Univ., School of Law; **EDUC HONORS:** Dean's List, Bovenaan Honor Soc., Articles Ed., Journal of Transnational Law; **MIL SERV:** Army, Capt.; **OTHER ACT & HONORS:** Bd. of Dirs., Council of NY Cooperatives; **HOME ADD:** 935 Park Ave., New York, NY 10028, (212)628-4486; **BUS ADD:** 3 East 54th St., New York, NY 10022, (212)759-9212.

SAGE, Bill——*Dir. Legal Serv.*, Texfi Industries, Inc.; **PRIM RE ACT:** Property Manager; **BUS ADD:** PO Box 20348, Greensboro, NC 27420, (919)378-6400.*

SAHAGIAN, Ted——**B:** Feb. 10, 1939, Watertown, MA, *Pres.*, Wellington Props., Inc.; **PRIM RE ACT:** Broker, Appraiser, Developer, Owner/Investor, Property Manager, Syndicator; **OTHER RE ACT:** Mort. broker; **SERVICES:** devel. & synd. of comml. props., prop. mgmt., resid. & comml. sales, maj. corp. site locators; **REP CLIENTS:** US & For. indiv. & inst. comml. props.; **EDUC:** 1961, Babson Inst.; **MIL SERV:** USA, Capt.; **OTHER ACT & HONORS:** FL Air Acad. Tr.; **HOME ADD:** 2715 N. Ocean Blvd., Ft. Lauderdale, FL 33308, (305)527-1343; **BUS ADD:** 2455 E. Sunrise Blvd., Ft. Lauderdale, FL 33304, (305)565-0962.

SAHLEIN, Stephen——*Ed.*, HBJ Newsletter, Inc., Real Estate Investing Letter; **PRIM RE ACT:** Real Estate Publisher; **BUS ADD:** 757 Third Ave., New York, NY 10017, (212)888-3335.*

SAINT, John B.——**B:** Sept. 7, 1946, Huntsville, AL, *Gen. Mgr. of Comml. Fin.*, The Mitchell Co.; **PRIM RE ACT:** Consultant, Developer, Property Manager; **OTHER RE ACT:** Shopping Ctr. Devel.; **SERVICES:** Devel., leasing, sales & mgmt.; **REP CLIENTS:** Lenders, indiv. & instnl. investors as well as US and For. Pension Funds; **PROFL AFFIL & HONORS:** Intl. Council of Shopping Centers; **EDUC:** BA, 1968, Fin. and Acctg., Univ. of AL; **GRAD EDUC:** MBA, 1974, Fin., Univ. of S. AL; **MIL SERV:** US Army, Capt.; **OTHER ACT & HONORS:** Co. is ranked ninth in nat. for open shopping center devels.; **HOME ADD:** 6601 Chimney Top Dr. S., Mobile, AL 36609, (205)344-8165; **BUS ADD:** PO Box 160306, Mobile, AL 36616, (205)476-1200.

ST. GEORGE, E.W.——**B:** Nov. 21, 1948, Rochester, PA, *RE Broker*, Props. Unlimited; **PRIM RE ACT:** Broker, Syndicator, Property Manager, Owner/Investor; **PREV EMPLOY:** Admin. Co-ordinator for W. Devel. and investment Corp.; **EDUC:** BA, 1970, Pre-Law, PA State Univ.; **MIL SERV:** PA ANG, S/Sgt.; **HOME ADD:** 105 Fairland Dr., Industry, PA 15052, (412)643-4130; **BUS ADD:** 1301 Midland-Beaver Rd., Industry, PA 15052, (412)643-5230.

ST. GEORGE, Michael F.——**B:** July 18, 1940, NY, *CRB*, St. George Realty; **PRIM RE ACT:** Broker, Appraiser; **SERVICES:** Sales and leases; **PROFL AFFIL & HONORS:** Realtors Nat. Mktg. Inst.; Nat. Assn. of Realtors; Builders Inst. of No. Westchester & Putnam Ctys.; NY State Assn. of Realtors, GRI; CRS; CRB; **BUS ADD:** 1928 Commerce St., Yorktown Hts., NY 10598, (914)962-5531.

ST. GEORGE, Nicholas J.——**B:** Feb. 11, 1939, Waltham, MA, *Pres. and CEO*, Oakwood Homes Corp.; **OTHER RE ACT:** Mfr. and retailer of manufactured housing; **PREV EMPLOY:** 1977-1979, VP, Corp. Devel., Ferguson Enterprises, Inc.; 1966-1976, Grp. VP in charge of Investment Banking, Legg Mason Wood Walker, Inc.; **PROFL AFFIL & HONORS:** Bd. of Dirs., Manufactured Housing Instit.; Legislative Comm., NC Manufactured Housing Instit., ABA; VA State Bar Assn.; Who's Who in Bus. & Fin., 1981; **EDUC:** BA, 1960, Econ., Coll. of William & Mary; **GRAD EDUC:** LLD, 1965, Marshall Wythe School of Law, Coll. of William & Mary; **MIL SERV:** U.S. Army, Lt., Airborne Distinguished Service Award; **HOME ADD:** 201 W Bessemer Ave., Greensboro, NC 27401, (919)272-6248; **BUS ADD:** PO Box 7386, 2225 S. Holden Rd., Greensboro, NC 27407, (919)292-7061.

ST. GERMAIN, Philip M.——**B:** Oct. 25, 1936, Boston, MA, *Pres.*, Faneuil Associates, Inc.; **PRIM RE ACT:** Attorney, Developer, Owner/Investor, Syndicator; **SERVICES:** Hotel devel., synd. and mgmt.; **REP CLIENTS:** Hotel owners and investors; **PREV EMPLOY:** Asst. to Pres. of Sheraton Corp.; Sr. VP & Treas., Archris Hotel Corp.; VP & Treas. of Acton Corp.; **PROFL AFFIL & HONORS:** ABA; **EDUC:** BS, 1961, Acctg., Boston Coll.; **GRAD EDUC:** JD, 1965, Boston Coll., Law School; **EDUC HONORS:** Cum Laude; **MIL SERV:** U.S. Army, Sgt.; **OTHER ACT & HONORS:** Dir. of Acton Corp.; Trustee, Chamberlayne Coll.; Dir., Middlesex Club; **HOME ADD:** 35 Dutton Rd., Sudbury, MA 01776, (617)443-8494; **BUS ADD:** 35 Dutton Rd., Sudbury, MA 01776, (617)443-8494

ST. JOHN, Richard J.——*VP Adm.*, Royal Crown Cola Co.; **PRIM RE ACT:** Property Manager; **BUS ADD:** 41 Perimeter Center East NE, Atlanta, GA 30346, (404)394-6120.*

ST. LAURENT, Louis S., II——**B:** Nov. 11, 1938, Que. City, Canada, *Pres. & Dir.*, Can-Am Investments, Inc.; **PRIM RE ACT:** Broker, Consultant, Developer; **OTHER RE ACT:** Devel. & Marketer & Consultant; **SERVICES:** Timeshare Resorts; **REP CLIENTS:** Topsider Resort, Key Largo Yacht & Tennis Club, FL Keys; **PROFL AFFIL & HONORS:** FL Bar (Atty.) Salesmen, Broker, FL RE Commn.; **EDUC:** Loyola (Montreal) Univ. of Tampa (FL); **GRAD EDUC:** Law-Stetson Coll. of Law, 1964; **OTHER ACT & HONORS:** 20th Circuit-Fort Myers, FL Chief Asst. State Atty. 11 yrs.; **HOME ADD:** 117 Dove Lake Dr., Tavernier, FL 33070, (305)852-5075; **BUS ADD:** Ste 7 Damhren Bldg. 99198 Overseas Hwy., Key Largo, FL 33037, (305)451-1520.

ST. LAWRENCE, Charles V.——*Dir. (Actg.)*, Department of Housing and Urban Development, Organization & Management Info.; **PRIM RE ACT:** Lender; **BUS ADD:** 451 Seventh St., S.W., Washington, DC 20410, (202)755-5208.*

ST. PETER, Steven——*RE Mgr.*, Clark Oil & Refining Corp.; **PRIM RE ACT:** Property Manager; **BUS ADD:** 8530 W. National Ave., PO Box 1994, Milwaukee, WI 53201, (414)321-5100.*

SAKAI, Hiroshi——**B:** July 2, 1925, Lihue, Kauai, HI, *Atty. at Law*, Self, PC; **PRIM RE ACT:** Consultant, Attorney; **SERVICES:** Atty., structuring of projects; **REP CLIENTS:** Devel. of subdiv., condos. co-ops, time sharing, represent bank, also member of the bd.; **PROFL AFFIL & HONORS:** Commr. from State of HI NCCUSL, Co-Author, "Modern Condo. Forms", "Condo. Owner's Handbook"; **EDUC:** AA, 1948, George Washington Univ.; **GRAD EDUC:** LLB, LLM, 1950, George Washington Univ. Law Sch.; **MIL SERV:** US Army; S/Sgt., 1944-47; **HOME ADD:** 3773 Diamond Head Cir., Honolulu, HI 96815; **BUS ADD:** 602 City Bank Bldg., Honolulu, HI 96813, (808)531-4171.

SAKAL, Jeffrey——**B:** Mar. 27, 1946, NY, NY, *RE Counsel, Corp. Staff*, The Singer Co., World Headquarters; **PRIM RE ACT:** Attorney; **SERVICES:** Counseling on all RE matters; **REP CLIENTS:** The Singer Co., its divs. and subs.; **PREV EMPLOY:** Lasser, Lasser, Sarokin & Hochman; **PROFL AFFIL & HONORS:** NJ, NY City Bar Assns.; ABA; Beta Gamma Sigma; NJ Bar; **EDUC:** BA, 1967, Hist./Poli. Sci., Rutgers Univ.; **GRAD EDUC:** JD, 1972, Rutgers Law School; MBA, 1972, Rutgers Grad. School of Bus. Admin.; **EDUC HONORS:** Beta Gamma Sigma; **HOME ADD:** 33 Northern Dr., Upper Saddle River, NJ 07458, (201)825-9619; **BUS ADD:** 8 Stamford Forum, Stamford, CT 06904, (203)356-4200.

SAKATA, Gary——*Mgr. Treas. Oper.*, Staley, A.E. Mfg. Co.; **PRIM RE ACT:** Property Manager; **BUS ADD:** 2200 East Eldorado St., Decatur, IL 62525, (217)423-4411.*

SALAS, Nestor A.——**B:** Aug. 22, 1947, Havana, Cuba, *Assoc.*, The Klock Comp. Realtors, Kendall W; **PRIM RE ACT:** Broker, Consultant, Owner/Investor, Property Manager; **OTHER RE ACT:** Invest. counselor; exporter, pre-fabricated houses and bldgs.; **SERVICES:** Sales,consultant, mgr.; **REP CLIENTS:** NASA Trading Corp.; **PREV EMPLOY:** Pres. NASA Trading Exporters, Pre-Fab Housing & Bldg. Materials; **PROFL AFFIL & HONORS:** Miami Bd. of Realtors, FL License, Realtor; **EDUC:** 1970, Interior Design, Bus. Admin. & Interior Design, Miami Dade Jr. Coll., NY School of Interior Design, Rutgers Univ.; **OTHER ACT & HONORS:** Past. Pres., Spanish C of C of NJ; AMA; World Trade Assn.; Fairchild Tropical Garden; **HOME ADD:** 6845 SW 85th Ave., Miami, FL 33143, (305)595-3600; **BUS ADD:** 10677 N. Kendall Dr., Suite 5A, Miami, FL 33176, (305)596-3333.

SALERNO, Bernard——*Fac. Mgr.*, Management Assistance, Inc.; **PRIM RE ACT:** Property Manager; **BUS ADD:** 560 Lexington Ave., New York, NY 10022, (212)909-1400.*

SALERNO, Bob——*Admin.*, Washington Dept. of Licensing, Real Estate Division; **PRIM RE ACT:** Insuror; **BUS ADD:** PO Box 247, Olympia, WA 98504, (206)753-6681.*

SALERNO, Michael J.——**B:** May 30, 1936, Jamesburg, NJ, *VP*, Midlantic Nat. Bank/Merchants, Mort.; **PRIM RE ACT:** Banker, Lender; **SERVICES:** All phases of RE lending; **PROFL AFFIL & HONORS:** MBAA, Central Jersey Builders Assn., NJ Bankers Assn.; **HOME ADD:** 21 Sedgwick St., Jamesburg, NJ 08831, (212)521-1475; **BUS ADD:** 60 Neptune Blvd., Neptune, NJ 07753, (212)775-3434.

SALIBA, Jacob——*Pres.*, Katy Industries, Inc.; **PRIM RE ACT:** Property Manager; **BUS ADD:** 853 Dundee Ave., Elgin, IL 60120, (312)697-8900.*

SALISBURY, Daniel J.——**B:** Nov. 21, 1924, Syracuse, NY, *VP*, Lindrick Corp.; **PRIM RE ACT:** Broker, Developer, Builder; **PREV EMPLOY:** Realtec, Inc.; **PROFL AFFIL & HONORS:** FL Assn. Realtors, Pasco Bldrs. Assn.; **EDUC:** Syracuse Univ.; **MIL SERV:** USAF, 1st Lt.; **HOME ADD:** 180 Water Oak Way, Oldsmar, FL 33557, (813)784-6946; **BUS ADD:** PO Box 1176, New Port Richey, FL 33552, (813)849-2266.

SALISBURY, Ron O.——B: Oct. 16, 1943, Bangor, ME, *Dist. Chief Appraiser*, Security Pacific National Bank, N. Coastal Div.; **PRIM RE ACT:** Instructor; **SERVICES:** Valuation, feasibilty analysis; **PROFL AFFIL & HONORS:** Assoc. Member, Soc. of RE Appraisers; Candidate, Amer. Soc. of Appraisers; **OTHER ACT & HONORS:** Bd. of Dir., San Diego Poet's Press; **HOME ADD:** 2930 Fulton St., Berkeley, CA 94705; **BUS ADD:** One Embarcadero Ctr., San Francisco, CA 94111, (415)445-4401.

SALLEE, Lynn F., II——B: Apr. 21, 1943, Alexandria, VA, *Pres.*, Sallee Construction; **PRIM RE ACT:** Builder, Owner/Investor; **SERVICES:** Gen. contracting, light comml.; **REP CLIENTS:** Wendy's Old Fashion Hamburgers, Pizza Inn, Nat. Pride Car Wash, Laesch Dairy, Theta Chi Frat., Foxy's Ice Cream; **PREV EMPLOY:** Comml. Banker (Union Nat. Bank), Waller Bros. Inc. (tract builders) Appraiser; **PROFL AFFIL & HONORS:** Bloomington, Normal Homebuilders, VP Bd. Member-Home Builders Assn. of IL; **EDUC:** BS, 1966, Sci., Physical Educ., Western IL Univ.; **HOME ADD:** RR 4, Bloomington, IL 61701, (309)963-4578; **BUS ADD:** RR #4 Lara Trace, Bloomington, IL 61701, (309)963-4578.

SALLEN, Marvin——B: Oct. 15, 1930, Detroit, *VP*, Sonnenblick-Goldman Corp. of Mich.; **OTHER RE ACT:** Mort. Banker; **SERVICES:** Comml. RE fin.; **EDUC:** AB, 1952, Econs., Univ. of MI; **HOME ADD:** 800 Covington, Birmingham, MI 48010, (313)642-4980; **BUS ADD:** 555 S. Woodward Ave., Suite 508, Birmingham, MI 48011, (313)647-3440.

SALLY, Donald W.——B: June 22, 1930, Rolla, MO, *Pres.*, Drexel Mgmt., Inc.; **PRIM RE ACT:** Broker, Consultant, Property Manager; **OTHER RE ACT:** Condo. conversions; **SERVICES:** Condo. conversions mktg. service, multi-family prop. mgmt. consulting; **REP CLIENTS:** The Vantage Cos.,(3rd Largest RE devel. in the U.S.-1980); **PREV EMPLOY:** Div. VP & Charter Tr. of Baird & Warner RE Investment Trust(REIT), Chicago, IL; **PROFL AFFIL & HONORS:** Past Bd. of Govs. of IREM OF NAR, Editor of the Journal of Prop. Mgmt., Charter Member of the Academy of Authors of both IREM AND CAI, Past Pres. of Prop. Mgmt. Council of Chicago RE Bd., Chicago Apt. BOMA, CPM, Twice awarded Article of the year by IREM; **EDUC:** BS, Bus. & Public Admin., Univ. of MO; **MIL SERV:** USA, Cpl., Korean Theatre, two battle stars; **OTHER ACT & HONORS:** Brookhaven Ctry. Club; **HOME ADD:** 3525 Turtle Creek 18-D, Dallas, TX 75219, (214)522-5358; **BUS ADD:** 2880 LBJ Freeway, Suite 503, Dallas, TX 75234, (214)247-9737.

SALMON, William C.——B: Feb. 11, 1950, Norwalk, CT, *Atty.*, Rucci & Rearden; **PRIM RE ACT:** Attorney; **SERVICES:** Legal servs. & counseling in RE matters; **REP CLIENTS:** Lenders, devels., investors, title cos. in comml. & resid. RE; **PROFL AFFIL & HONORS:** CT Bar Assn., Member of RE Sect., Darien Bar Assn., New Canaan Bar Assn.; **EDUC:** BA, 1972, Eng., Phil., Univ. of CT; **GRAD EDUC:** JD, 1975, Pettit Coll. of Law, OH No. Univ.; **EDUC HONORS:** Assoc. Ed. of Law Review, published three times; **HOME ADD:** Unit D-13 Beachcomber Condo., 637 Cove Rd., Stamford, CT 06902, (203)324-0649; **BUS ADD:** PO Box 1107, 1003 Post Rd., Darien, CT 06820, (203)655-7695.

SALOMON, Muriel——B: Oct. 10, 1933, New Haven, CT, *Realtor-Owner*, Fort Hale Realty; **PRIM RE ACT:** Broker, Consultant, Appraiser, Builder, Owner/Investor, Instructor, Real Estate Publisher; **OTHER RE ACT:** Resid. & comml. counseling - modular home builder; **SERVICES:** Sales & RE counseling, complete installation of modular housing, editing RE newsletters & column, teaching sales & RE; **PREV EMPLOY:** Columnist, New Haven Journal Courier; Long Wharf Theatre Newsletter; Branch Mgr., Royal of Amer. RE; Arthur Murrays, Sales Rep.; W.A.V.Z. Radio, Time Sales; **PROFL AFFIL & HONORS:** Realtor; GRI; CRS, 1982 VP; Women's Council; Realtor of Greater New Haven; Bd. of New England Appraisers Assn.; CT Assn. of Realtors; NAR; CT Homebuilders Assn., Nat. Homebuilders Assn.; Member of Independent Realtors; CARE 1982; Treas. of CRS Chmn. Communications Comm. - Greater New Haven Bd. of Realtors for state of CT; Realtor Dir. CN Assoc. Realtors, 1982; **EDUC:** Adv. Sales Techniques and Communication Interpretation, Yale Univ.; **OTHER ACT & HONORS:** Ombudsman Program, Nursing Homes; State of CT 1978-1979, East Haven and New Haven C of C; Secretary Fort Hele Fuel; -99 RPAC Club; 1st Prize CAR Sales Ads Competition, 1980; REEA; New Haven and CT Comml. Investment Div.; CT Based Journalist; **HOME ADD:** 40 Morris Ave., New Haven, CT 06512, (203)467-4150; **BUS ADD:** 575 Main St., East Haven, CT 06512, (203)467-1135.

SALOMON, Robert J.——B: Apr. 19, 1925, Brooklyn, NY, *VP*, Warner Communications Inc.; **PRIM RE ACT:** Consultant, Property Manager; **PREV EMPLOY:** Asst. VP Rockefeller Ctr., Inc.; **PROFL AFFIL & HONORS:** NACORE, Former Pres. NY chapt.; **EDUC:** BS, 1949, US Naval Acad.; **MIL SERV:** USN, Lt.; **HOME ADD:** 756 Bowne Rd., Ocean, NJ, 07712, (201)493-2157; **BUS ADD:** 75 Rockefeller Plaza, New York, NY 10019, (212)484-6540.

SALOMON, Suzanne E.——B: Mar. 15, 1947, Chicago, IL, *VP*, Sybedon Equities Corp.; **PRIM RE ACT:** Broker, Consultant, Developer, Owner/Investor, Syndicator; **SERVICES:** Re investment banking firm involved in ltd. partnerships; various types of comml. RE; Brokerage & Investments; Developments, Joint Ventures; **REP CLIENTS:** Indiv. or instnl. investors or advisors in comml. RE; lenders; **PREV EMPLOY:** Intl. Corporate Strategies, Pres.; Chase Manhattan Bank, VP; Intl. Paper Co., Gladstone Assocs.; **PROFL AFFIL & HONORS:** Assn. of RE Women, Fin. Women's Assn. of NY, RESSI; **EDUC:** BA, 1969, Hist., Wellesley Coll.; **GRAD EDUC:** MPA, 1971, Public Affairs & Urban Planning, Princeton Univ. (Woodrow Wilson School of Public & Intl. Affairs); **EDUC HONORS:** Summa Cum Laude, Woodrow Wilson School Fellow; **OTHER ACT & HONORS:** Bd. of Dirs., NY Comm. for Young Audiences, Bd. of Tr., McBurney School; **HOME ADD:** 320 E. 57th St., New York, NY 10022, (212)688-8196; **BUS ADD:** 1211 Ave. of the Americas, New York, NY 10036, (212)354-5756.

SALONY, Jon R.——B: Jan. 9, 1946, NYC, *VP*, Chemical Bank, RE Div.; **PRIM RE ACT:** Banker, Lender; **SERVICES:** Project Fin., Mort. Banking & RE; **REP CLIENTS:** Servicing Nationwide Client Base; **EDUC:** BA, 1968, Econ., Franklin & Marshall Coll.; **GRAD EDUC:** MBA, 1974, RE, Fordham Univ.; **MIL SERV:** USAR; **HOME ADD:** 200 E. 78th St., New York, NY 10021, (212)472-2493; **BUS ADD:** 633 Third Ave., New York, NY 10017, (212)878-7566.

SALOWE, Allen E.——B: Apr. 2, 1933, Plainfield, NJ, *VP*, ITT Community Development Corp.; **PRIM RE ACT:** Developer; **SERVICES:** Planning land devel., community devel., housing const. comml. and indiv.; **PREV EMPLOY:** Profl. consulting 1972-74, Champion Bldg. Products 1966-72; **PROFL AFFIL & HONORS:** Urban Land Inst.; **EDUC:** AB, 1955, Econ./Mktg., Univ. of Miami; **GRAD EDUC:** MBA, 1957, Bus., Rutgers Univ.; **MIL SERV:** US Air Force; **OTHER ACT & HONORS:** Pres., Plainfield (NJ) Bd. of Educ. 1974-75; Chmn., Plainfield (NJ) Planning Bd. 1972-73; Bd. of Dir. Daytona Beach Symphony Soc.; **HOME ADD:** 6 Cynthia Ct., Palm Coast, FL 32037, (904)445-3824; **BUS ADD:** Exec. Offices, Palm Coast, FL 32051, (904)445-4900.

SALVADORE, Guido R.——B: Oct. 24, 1927, Norton, MA, *Partner*, Higgins, Cavanagh & Cooney; **PRIM RE ACT:** Attorney, Developer; **SERVICES:** Legal; **PROFL AFFIL & HONORS:** ABA, Rhode Island Bar Assn.; **EDUC:** AB, 1951, Econs., Poli. Sci., Brown Univ.; **GRAD EDUC:** LLB, 1954, Law, Harvard Law School; **MIL SERV:** USN, ETM 2C; **HOME ADD:** 38 Sunset Dr., E. Greenwich, RI 02818, (401)884-5413; **BUS ADD:** 123 Dyer St., Providence, RI 02903, (401)272-3500.

SALVAY, Craig L.——B: Jan. 29, 1951, Kansas City, MO, *Pres.*, Craig L. Salvay and Co., Inc.; **PRIM RE ACT:** Broker, Consultant, Owner/Investor, Syndicator; **SERVICES:** Site selection, negotiation, fin.; **REP CLIENTS:** Gen. KS Bankshares, Wendy's Old-Fashioned Hamburgers of KS City; **PREV EMPLOY:** Formerly assoc. with Roger L. Cohen and Co., KS City, MO; **PROFL AFFIL & HONORS:** Nat. Assns. of Realtors; MO Assn. of Realtors; Realtors Nat. Marketing Inst. (CCIM Div.); ABA; MO Bar Assn., JD; **EDUC:** BA, 1974, Econ., Univ. of PA; **GRAD EDUC:** JD, 1978, Law, St. Louis Univ.; **OTHER ACT & HONORS:** Big Bros. and Sisters of KS City, MO; **BUS ADD:** 8600 W. 63rd St., Suite 305, Shawnee Mission, KS 66202, (913)362-8180.

SALVETTI, Don A., Jr.——B: May 13, 1931, Midway, PA, *Sr. VP, Indus. Grp.*, Joseph C. Canizaro Interests; **PRIM RE ACT:** Developer, Owner/Investor; **SERVICES:** Land devel., build to suit and joint venture devel.; **REP CLIENTS:** Amer. Hospital Supply, Whirlpool Corp., Nabisco; **PREV EMPLOY:** VP, The Korman Corp., Philadelphia, PA; **PROFL AFFIL & HONORS:** Dir., Nat. Assn. of Office and Indus. Parks, PE-PA, TX, LA; **EDUC:** BCE, 1953, Civil & Structures, Univ. of VA; **GRAD EDUC:** MS, 1954, 1962, Structural Engrg., Indus. Mgmt., RPI, Carnegie-Mellon Univ.; **EDUC HONORS:** Tau Beta Pi - Chap. Pres., Soc. of Sigma Xi; **MIL SERV:** USN, Lt. JG; **OTHER ACT & HONORS:** Beau Chene Country Club, Dir., New Orleans Traffic & Transportation Bureau; **HOME ADD:** 711 Bocage Ln., Mandeville, LA 70448, (504)845-3749; **BUS ADD:** 300 Poydras St., New Orleans, LA 70130, (504)469-0900.

SALZMAN, Lester W.——B: Oct. 7, 1952, New York City, NY, *Pres.*, Towers Associates, Inc.; **PRIM RE ACT:** Broker, Consultant, Appraiser, Developer, Lender, Builder, Owner/Investor, Property Manager, Syndicator; **OTHER RE ACT:** Columnist, weekly RE and investment; **SERVICES:** Comprehensive RE devel. and sales serv.; **REP CLIENTS:** Cavagnan Communities, Inc., Berel Co., Community

Realty Mgmt., Previte, Todd, and Genmel, Family of Homes, Inc., others; **PREV EMPLOY:** Dir. of Medical Social Work at two General Hospitals, Journalist - The Atlantic City Press; **PROFL AFFIL & HONORS:** Soc. of RE Appraisers, Nat. Bd. of Realtors, NJ Pressman's Assn., Soc. of Prop. Mgmt. Profls.; Licensed to practice in NJ and FL, Million Dollar Sales; **EDUC:** Stockton State Coll., 1974, Sociology; **GRAD EDUC:** M.Ed., 1978, Admin.; **EDUC HONORS:** Managing Editor, School Newspaper; Student Gov., VP; Varsity Baseball, Magna Cum Laude; **OTHER ACT & HONORS:** VP - Atlantic City Jaycees; Pres. - NJ Assn. Hosp. Soc. Work; **HOME ADD:** 212 N. Newark Ave., Ventnor, NJ 08406, (609)823-0959; **BUS ADD:** The Margate Towers, 9400 Atlantic Ave., Margate, NJ 08402, (609)822-9477.

SAMBER, David M.——B: Sept. 15, 1949, New York, NY, *VP*, Kimco Development Corp.; **PRIM RE ACT:** Attorney, Developer, Owner/Investor, Property Manager, Syndicator; **PROFL AFFIL & HONORS:** Intl. Council of Shopping Ctrs.; **EDUC:** 1971, Univ. of Toledo; **GRAD EDUC:** JD, 1974, St. Johns Univ., School of Law; **HOME ADD:** 2064 Stratford Dr., Westbury, NY 11590, (516)334-4023.

SAMEC, Donald G.——B: May 28, 1943, Berwyn, IL, *Appraiser/Broker*, Donald G. Samec, Appraising; **PRIM RE ACT:** Appraiser, Instructor; **SERVICES:** Appraising, consultant of resid., income and comml. prop.; **REP CLIENTS:** Fin. inst., attys., corps. and indiv.; **PREV EMPLOY:** RE sales, instr. & lecturer in RE, appraising, & investment props.; **PROFL AFFIL & HONORS:** Portland, OR, & NAR, NAREA, RNMI, NAIFa SREA, MLS, CREA, GRI, CRS, MLS (Bd. of Tr./Officer); **EDUC:** Assoc. in RE Appraisal, 1975, Portland Comm. Coll.; Associate in Electronic Engrg., 1972, Portland Comm. Coll.; BAEE, 1969, Oregon Technical Inst.; **GRAD EDUC:** MED, 1974, Psych., Counseling & Curriculum Devel., Univ. of Portland; **MIL SERV:** USN, NCO, USAR; **HOME ADD:** 4217 NE Flanders, Portland, OR, (503)232-1933; **BUS ADD:** 4217 NE Flanders, Portland, OR 97213, (503)232-1933.

SAMLOFF, Harold——B: Apr. 29, 1937, Rochester, NY, *Partner*, Buckingham Properties; **PRIM RE ACT:** Attorney, Developer, Builder, Owner/Investor, Property Manager; **SERVICES:** Mixed use devel., rehab. and indus. park devel.; **PREV EMPLOY:** Atty.; **EDUC:** BA, 1959, Govt., Cornell; **GRAD EDUC:** LLD, 1962, Columbia Law School; **EDUC HONORS:** Bd. of Editors, Law Review; **MIL SERV:** US Army, Infantry, Sp. 5, 1962-1968 (Reserves); **HOME ADD:** 42 Framingham Lane, Pittsford, NY 14534, (716)461-3539; **BUS ADD:** 687 Monroe Ave., Rochester, NY 14607, (716)271-5343.

SAMMIS, Jesse F., III——B: May 12, 1938, Pittsburgh, PA, *Pres.*, New England Land Co., Ltd.; **PRIM RE ACT:** Broker, Developer, Owner/Investor, Syndicator; **PREV EMPLOY:** VP, Laird Properties, Inc.; Cross & Brown Co.; **PROFL AFFIL & HONORS:** IREF; Greenwich Bd. of Realtors; NY Bd. of Realtors; Nat. Assn. of RE Brokers; **EDUC:** 1960, Eng./Bus., St. Lawrence Univ.; **MIL SERV:** US Army; **BUS ADD:** 151 Railroad Ave., Greenwich, CT 06830, (203)661-6004.

SAMNICK, Robert L.——B: Feb. 10, 1946, Brooklyn, NY, *Partner*, Lieb, Samnick & Lukashok; **PRIM RE ACT:** Attorney; **SERVICES:** Atty. for devel. & synd., Coop & condo. filings; **REP CLIENTS:** Devel., synd. owner of resid. prop. being converted for coop. or condo. ownership and new const. coop. and condo.; **PREV EMPLOY:** Atty. with Stroock & Stroock & Lavan, NYC Law Clerk, US Dist. Ct. So. Dist. NY; **PROFL AFFIL & HONORS:** Member of Bar of NY, NJ, US Dist. Cts., SD NY, ED NY, Dist. NJ, US Supreme Ct. ABA, NYS Bar Assn.; **EDUC:** BA, 1968, Poli. Sci. & Hist., Long Is. Univ.; **GRAD EDUC:** JD, 1972, Brooklyn Law Sch.; **EDUC HONORS:** Research Editor Brooklyn Law Review; **HOME ADD:** 20 Dorothea St., Plainview, NY 11803, (516)938-4608; **BUS ADD:** 1133 Ave. of the Americas, New York, NY 10036, (212)391-1260.

SAMOWSKI, Don——B: 1937, Lowell, MA, *Sr. City Planner*, City of Lowell, Planning and Devel.; **PRIM RE ACT:** Broker, Regulator, Builder, Owner/Investor, Property Manager, Syndicator; **SERVICES:** City Planning Spec. in Zoning and Subdivision Control; **REP CLIENTS:** Admin. of subdivision and zoning regulations and coordination of major dev. project; **PREV EMPLOY:** RE Broker MA; Home Builder - MA; **PROFL AFFIL & HONORS:** APA, BOMA, Cert. Appreciation U.S. Bureau of Census; **EDUC:** Assoc., 1970, CE, Univ. of Lowell; **MIL SERV:** US Army, Sgt.; **OTHER ACT & HONORS:** Sec. Lowell Planning Bd.; Co-Chmn., Greater Lowell Regatta Festival Commn.; Sailing Program; **BUS ADD:** 50 Arcand Dr., Lowell, MA 01852, (617)454-8821.

SAMPLE, Bob E.——B: Mar. 27, 1935, Monte Vista, CO, *Exec. VP-CEO*, Innovative Inv. Ltd.; **PRIM RE ACT:** Broker, Instructor, Syndicator, Consultant, Developer, Builder, Insuror, Owner/Investor; **OTHER RE ACT:** Fin. Planning, Pension Fund Mgmt.; **SERVICES:** Inv. counseling, dev. of inv. props., comml. & bus. brokerage pension fund mgmt.; **REP CLIENTS:** Indiv. and inst. investors; **PROFL AFFIL & HONORS:** Intl. Assn. of Fin. Planners, RE Securities & Exch. Inst., Intl. Motel Brokers of USA, Farm & Land Inst.; **EDUC:** BA, 1955, Ed., Univ. of CO; **HOME ADD:** 610 W. Main St., W. Dundee, IL 60118, (312)426-9643; **BUS ADD:** 400 Federation Pl., Elgin, IL 60120, (312)888-1580.

SAMPSON, Curtis H.——B: June 11, 1912, Germany, *Realtor*, Curtis H. Sampson, Realtor; **PRIM RE ACT:** Broker; **SERVICES:** Comm. RE Brokerage and Exchanging; **PREV EMPLOY:** Self employed 1946-1955 Electrical Design and Const. - Contractor RNMI, CA; **PROFL AFFIL & HONORS:** Assoc. of Realtors, Nat. Council of Exchangors Interex, CCIM, GRI; **GRAD EDUC:** BBA, 1933, Univ. of Hamburg, Germany; **MIL SERV:** Investom, Devs., Trusts; **OTHER ACT & HONORS:** Masonic 32, Member of Shrine; **HOME ADD:** 4546 Hazeltine Ave., #6, Sherman Oaks, CA 91423, (213)986-2122; **BUS ADD:** 99 East Magnolia Blvd., Suite 240, Burbank, CA 91502, (213)846-3260.

SAMPSON, John——*VP Corp. Plng. & Dev.*, Central Soya; **PRIM RE ACT:** Property Manager; **BUS ADD:** 1300 Ft. Wayne National Building, Fort Wayne, IN 46802, (219)425-5100.*

SAMPSON, Russell S.——B: Oct. 18, 1955, Summit, NJ, *Indus. Salesman*, Coldwell Banker; **PRIM RE ACT:** Broker; **EDUC:** BA, 1978, Econ., OH Wesleyan Univ.; **HOME ADD:** 68 Southgate, Murray Hill, NJ 07971, (201)464-6692; **BUS ADD:** 433 Hackensack Ave., Hackensack, NJ 07601, (201)488-6000.

SAMS, Gerald N.——B: Sept. 11, 1937, Milligan Coll., TN, *Admin. RE and Procurement*, The Coca Cola Co.; **OTHER RE ACT:** Admin. of Co. owned Indus. RE; **SERVICES:** Coord. the acqn. and sale of co. prop. in US; **PROFL AFFIL & HONORS:** Assoc. mbr. SIR; **EDUC:** BS Indus. Arts, 1962, E. TN State Univ.; **MIL SERV:** USA, SP4; **BUS ADD:** PO Drawer 1734, Atlanta, GA 30301, (404)898-4493.

SAMUELS, Leslie Eugene——B: Nov. 12, 1929, VI, *Pres.*, Samuels & Co., Stull Mort. Bankers; **PRIM RE ACT:** Consultant, Attorney, Property Manager; **OTHER RE ACT:** Fin. broker; **SERVICES:** Fin. & mgmt. consultant; **PREV EMPLOY:** NYC Dept. of Bldgs., 1966-70; **PROFL AFFIL & HONORS:** Intl. Bus. Assn.; **EDUC:** BS, 1955, Music Educ., NY Univ., Carnegie Hall Sch. of Music; **GRAD EDUC:** LLB, 1974, Blackstone Sch. of Law; JD, 1975, Contract Law, Blackstone Sch. of Law; **MIL SERV:** USA; Pvt.; 1951-53; **OTHER ACT & HONORS:** Dist. Leader (Bronx 86th AD), 1969-73; Bd. of Advisors of Aster Home for Children, Advisor Brownsville C of C; **HOME ADD:** 2814 Bruner Ave., Bronx, NY 10469, (212)379-0595; **BUS ADD:** PO Box 195, Bronx, NY 10469, (212)379-0595.

SAMUELSON, Harold M.——B: Oct. 17, 1919, Los Angeles, CA, *Co-owner*, Hunter-Samuelson Appraisal Co.(est.1958); **PRIM RE ACT:** Instructor, Appraiser; **REP CLIENTS:** Banks, S&L, Attys., Cities; **PREV EMPLOY:** Right of way agent, CA Div. of Hwys.; **PROFL AFFIL & HONORS:** NARA: ASA: SREA; Monterey Peninsula Bd. of Realtors; CAR; NAR, SRA, ASA, CRA; **EDUC:** BA, 1949, Bus. Admin., San Jose State Univ.; **MIL SERV:** USMC, Maj., 3 Air medals; **HOME ADD:** 1330 Skyline Dr., Monterey, CA 93940, (408)372-5135; **BUS ADD:** 886 Abrego, Monterey, CA 93940, (408)373-3443.

SAMUELSON, Larry——B: Mar. 7, 1938, Cleveland, OH, *VP*, Turner Development Corp., SW Rgn.; **PRIM RE ACT:** Developer, Owner/Investor; **SERVICES:** Devel. of income props.; **REP CLIENTS:** Instnl. investors; **PREV EMPLOY:** Century Devel. Corp., Heritage Devel. Group; **PROFL AFFIL & HONORS:** Urban Land Inst., AIA, Houston C of C, Rice Design Ctr., Lic. Arch., RE Broker, State of TX; **EDUC:** BArch., 1959, Arch., Rice Univ.; **GRAD EDUC:** BS, 1960, Arch., Rice Univ.; **OTHER ACT & HONORS:** Inst. for Urban Design; **HOME ADD:** 10047 Ella Lee Lane, Houston, TX 77042, (713)782-3788; **BUS ADD:** 10000 Richmond, Suite 650, Houston, TX 77042, (713)266-4430.

SANDBOTHE, Norbert Paul——B: Apr. 25, 1936, Vienna, MO, *Pres.*, Sandfam Corp.; **PRIM RE ACT:** Broker, Consultant, Developer, Owner/Investor, Property Manager, Syndicator; **OTHER RE ACT:** Develop & own shopping ctrs.; **SERVICES:** Manage own ctrs.; **PREV EMPLOY:** RE & Sales Mgmt., Shell Oil Co.; **PROFL AFFIL & HONORS:** W. St. Louis Cty. C of C; **EDUC:** BS, 1960, Bus. Mgmt./Econ. Phy., Central MO State Univ.; **EDUC HONORS:** Dean's Hon. Roll; **MIL SERV:** US Army, SP-3; **OTHER ACT & HONORS:** Bd. of Dir., Ellisville Metro Bank; **HOME ADD:** 12348 Country Glen Ln., Creve Coeur, MO 63141, (314)434-1202; **BUS ADD:** 300 Ozark Trail Dr., Suite 201, St. Louis, MO 63011, (314)394-5100.

SANDERS, D. Faye——B: Jan. 29, 1944, Columbus, MS, *Community Relations Officer*, Citizens Bank, Community Reinvestment; **PRIM RE ACT:** Banker, Lender; **SERVICES:** Counseling re: urban reinvestment; **PREV EMPLOY:** Model Cities Program, Program Evaluator, New Orleans, LA; Council for Community Serv., Planning Dir., Providence; **PROFL AFFIL & HONORS:** Nat. Assn. of Bank Women; **EDUC:** BS, 1968, Sociology, Spring Hill Coll.; **GRAD EDUC:** MSW, 1971, Urban Planning/Community Org., Tulane Univ.; **OTHER ACT & HONORS:** Bd. of Dir., Stop Wasting Abandoned Property, Inc.; Bd. of Dir., Planned Parenthood of RI; Fin. Inst. Rep. to Citizens Review Bd.; Providence Mayor's Office of Community Devel.; **HOME ADD:** 265 Atwells Ave., Providence, RI, (401)272-3786; **BUS ADD:** 870 Westminster St., Providence, RI 02903, (401)456-7285.

SANDERS, G. Clarke——B: Jan. 31, 1951, Memphis, TN, *VP & Dir. of Loan Admin.*, Sec. Fed. S&L Assn., Mort. Lending; **PRIM RE ACT:** Banker, Lender, Owner/Investor; **SERVICES:** Mort. lending, banking, investments; **REP CLIENTS:** All major instln. investors; **PREV EMPLOY:** Atlantic Nat. Bank of Jacksonville, FL; Third Nat. Bank of Nashville; **PROFL AFFIL & HONORS:** C of C; Mort. Bankers Assn.; **EDUC:** BA, 1973, Bus. Admin., & Amer. Hist., Vanderbilt Univ.; **EDUC HONORS:** VP of Student Assn., Pres. of newspaper, US Jaycees, 1981 Outstanding Young Amer.; **MIL SERV:** Naval ROTC, Cadet, Hon. Discharge; **OTHER ACT & HONORS:** YMCA, Vanderbilt Alumni Assn.; **HOME ADD:** 4505 Harding Rd., 175, Nashville, TN 37205, (615)297-6088; **BUS ADD:** 4235 Hillsboro Rd., Nashville, TN 37215, (615)383-6130.

SANDERS, Jerry L.——B: Aug. 5, 1937, Brady, TX, *Supt.*, Aberdeen Builders; **PRIM RE ACT:** Developer, Builder; **SERVICES:** Const. Mgmt.; **PROFL AFFIL & HONORS:** NAHB; **HOME ADD:** 109 Wynnmeade Pkwy., Peachtree City, GA 30269, (404)487-6017; **BUS ADD:** 23 Eastbrook Bend, Peachtree City, GA 30269, (404)487-4070.

SANDERS, John K., Jr.——B: Oct. 15, 1947, NJ, *Chmn. of Bd.*, JKS Capital Corp.; **PRIM RE ACT:** Broker, Syndicator, Consultant, Owner/Investor; **PREV EMPLOY:** Sanders & Co., W. End, NJ & NY & CA & FL; **PROFL AFFIL & HONORS:** Nat. Assn. of Acct./ ABA/ Fed. Bar Assn./ Assn. of Gov. Acct./ Amer. Arbitration Assn./ Amer. Mgmt. Assn.; **EDUC:** BA, 1968, Bus. Mgmt./Fin.Acctg., Univ. of Maryland, Coll. Park, MD.; **GRAD EDUC:** MBA, 1971, Law, Seton Hall Univ., Newark NJ; JD, 1975, Bus. Mgmt./Finance/Acct., Seton Hall Univ., Newark, NJ; **EDUC HONORS:** Magna Cum Laude; **MIL SERV:** USAF, Maj., Bronze Star/Flying Cross/Purple Heart Air Medal/Air Force Commendation Medal; **OTHER ACT & HONORS:** VFW Past Comdr., Disabled Amer. Vets.; **HOME ADD:** P.O. Box 3117, West End, NJ 07740; **BUS ADD:** 135 Brighton Ave., W.End, NJ 07740, (201)870-3600.

SANDERS, John M.——B: Aug. 13, 1925, Harperville, MS, *Mgr. RE*, Baddour, Inc. (Fred's Discount Stores); **PRIM RE ACT:** Developer, Property Manager; **GRAD EDUC:** Sci., 1950, B.S. State Coll.; **MIL SERV:** USN; HM 2/C; **HOME ADD:** 2602 Greenbriar Dr., Columbus, MS 39701, (601)328-4769; **BUS ADD:** 4300 New Getwell Rd., Memphis, TN 38118, (901)365-8880.

SANDERS, Michael Leo——B: Aug. 28, 1954, Salzburg, Austria, *Corp. Counsel*, Wood Bros. Homes, Inc., Corporate Div.; **PRIM RE ACT:** Consultant, Attorney, Developer, Builder, Insuror; **OTHER RE ACT:** CPA/RE Acct.; **SERVICES:** Consultant on legal/fin./tax issues; **PREV EMPLOY:** Deloitte Haskins & Sells; Panell Kerr & Forester; Stelle Industries, Inc.; US Dept. of HUD; **PROFL AFFIL & HONORS:** ABA, AICPA, Amer. Assn. of Atty. - CPA's, JD, CPA; **EDUC:** BBA, 1976, Acctg./Tax/Systems Analysis, Bus. Coll., Western IL Univ.; **GRAD EDUC:** JD, 1980, Law/Corp., Univ. of IL; **EDUC HONORS:** Grad. with honors, Dean's List; **HOME ADD:** 17655 Snowberry Way, Parker, CO 80134, (303)690-9036; **BUS ADD:** 1658 Cole Blvd., Golden, CO 80401, (303)232-2100.

SANDERS, Nield J.——B: Aug. 21, 1914, Aubrey, TX, *Pres.*, McDonald Meadows, Inc., Main Office; **PRIM RE ACT:** Broker, Appraiser, Developer, Builder, Owner/Investor, Instructor, Property Manager; **SERVICES:** RE devel. & appraising, RE broker and counseling; **PREV EMPLOY:** Prod. & Material Control Mgr., The Bendix Corp. & Litton Indus. Systems, Mgr. var. cos.; **PROFL AFFIL & HONORS:** NAR, NAHB, Amer. Prod. & Material Cont. Soc., Amer. Mgmt. Soc., Realtor, Past Pres AR Realtors Assn., RE Frat Omega Tau Rho Member, Rotary Fellow, GRI; **EDUC:** AA, 1933, Univ. of MO, Kansas City, NE Jr., Coll. & Univ. of NM; **MIL SERV:** US Army Air Force, S/Sgt.; **OTHER ACT & HONORS:** County Water Comm., Planning Comm., BPOE, POE, Rotary Intl.; **HOME ADD:** PO Box 93, Lakeview, AR 72642, (501)431-5628; **BUS ADD:** PO Box 135, Bull Shoals, AR 72642, (501)445-4354.

SANDERS, Raymond Carter, Jr.——B: Sept. 12, 1942, Atlanta, GA, *Assoc. Gen. Dep. Asst. Sec.*, Dept. of Housing and Urban Devel., Housing; **PRIM RE ACT:** Broker, Attorney, Developer; **PREV EMPLOY:** Shifflet, Sharp & Sanders, Attys. at Law, San Diego; **PROFL AFFIL & HONORS:** State Bar of CA, CA RE Broker, Amer. Arbitration Assn., San Diego Cty. Bar Assn., CA Bd. of Realtors; **EDUC:** BBA, 1965, Bus./RE, Univ. of GA; **GRAD EDUC:** JD, 1971, Law, Univ. of San Diego, School of Law; **MIL SERV:** USNR, Lt., Vietnam; **OTHER ACT & HONORS:** Bd. of Dirs. Amer. Cancer Soc. (San Diego Cty.), Bd. of Trustees, San Diego Found. for Blind; **HOME ADD:** 302 W. Glendale, Alexandria, VA 22301, (703)548-4496; **BUS ADD:** 451 7th St. S.W., Washington, DC 20410, (202)755-7366.

SANDERS, Scott——Safeguard Industries, Inc.; **PRIM RE ACT:** Property Manager; **BUS ADD:** 630 Park Ave., King of Prussia, PA 19406, (215)265-4000.*

SANDERSON, David V.——B: July 27, 1949, Alhambra, CA, *Assoc.*, Streich Lang Weeks & Cardon; **PRIM RE ACT:** Attorney; **SERVICES:** Foreclosure litigation and proceedings, RE devel.; **PREV EMPLOY:** 1976-1980, Atty., Marriott Corp., Washington, DC (Comml./restaurant RE devel.); **PROFL AFFIL & HONORS:** ABA and AZ State Bar Assn., Member AZ, MD, and U.S. Ninth Circuit Ct. of Appeals Bars; **EDUC:** BA, 1973, Amer. Studies, CA State Univ., Fullerton; **GRAD EDUC:** JD, 1976, Law, J. Reuben Clark Law School, Brigham Young Univ.; **EDUC HONORS:** Dean's List, Grad. with Honors, Cum Laude; Assoc. Editor Brigham Young Univ. Law Review; **HOME ADD:** 4507 W. Lewis Ave., Phoenix, AZ 85035; **BUS ADD:** 2100 First Interstate Bank Plaza, 100 W. Washington, Phoenix, AZ 85003, (602)257-0999.

SANDERSON, William H.——B: Oct. 6, 1917, Phillipsburg, NJ, *Realtor, Sec./Treas., Owner*, Century 21 Acacia Realty, Inc.; **PRIM RE ACT:** Broker, Syndicator, Consultant, Appraiser; **SERVICES:** Counseling, Investment Analysis, Sales; **PROFL AFFIL & HONORS:** FLI, RNMI, CRB, CRS, GRI; **EDUC:** BS, 1959, Physics - Math - Eng., Fairleigh Dickinson Univ.; **EDUC HONORS:** Cum Laude; **HOME ADD:** 125 Seville Pl. SW, Port Charlotte, FL 33952, (813)625-3494; **BUS ADD:** 2195 Tamiami Trail - PO Box 2648, Port Charlotte, FL 33952, (813)629-8770.

SANDLEMAN, Joel——*VP Adm. & Asst. Secy.*, Puritan Fashions Corp.; **PRIM RE ACT:** Property Manager; **BUS ADD:** Broadway, New York, NY 10018, (212)575-0800.*

SANDLIAN, Colby B.——B: Dec. 18, 1930, Dodge City, KS, *owner*, Sandlian Realty; **PRIM RE ACT:** Broker, Instructor, Consultant, Developer, Property Manager; **SERVICES:** Sale and investments of comml. and investment props., counseling; **PROFL AFFIL & HONORS:** CCIM, Pres. of Soc. of Exchange Counselors; Past Pres. of Wichita Metro. Area Bd. of Realtors, Realtor of the Year Wichita Metro. Area Bd. of Realtors 1970, Counselor of the Year 1979, 1977 Clifford P. Weaver Award from Educ. Foundation; **EDUC:** Attended Wichita State Univ.; **MIL SERV:** USN, 1949-50; **OTHER ACT & HONORS:** Scottish Rite Free Masonry and Midian Shrine; **HOME ADD:** 1500 Fairfield, Wichita, KS 67208, (316)683-3912; **BUS ADD:** 435 North Broadway, Wichita, KS 67202, (316)263-0118.

SANDLIN, Geo. W.——B: May 13, 1912, Glen Rose, TX, *Owner*, Sandlin & Co.; **PRIM RE ACT:** Broker, Consultant, Appraiser, Lender, Owner/Investor, Property Manager, Insuror; **PREV EMPLOY:** Sandlin & Co. - since 1936; Holc Inc.; **PROFL AFFIL & HONORS:** Austin Bd. of Realtors (Past Pres.), TX Assn. of Realtors (Past Pres.), Natl. Assn. of Realtors (Dir.), Mort. Bankers of Amer. (Sandlin Mort. Corp.), RE Broker; Mort. Banker; IFA; CPM; **MIL SERV:** USNR, Comdr., Amer. Legion, Veterans of For. Wars; **HOME ADD:** 1801 Lavaca St. #7L, Austin, TX 78701; **BUS ADD:** 308 W. 15th St., Austin, TX 78701, (512)478-5621.

SANDLIN, Geo. W.R. (Buck)——B: Nov. 27, 1943, Austin, TX, Sandlin & Co., Realtors; **PRIM RE ACT:** Broker, Consultant, Lender, Owner/Investor, Insuror, Property Manager, Syndicator; **SERVICES:** Prop. Mgmt., Investment Counseling, Improved Prop. Synd. & Mort. Banking; **REP CLIENTS:** Indiv. investors, instit. investors, and lenders for improved income producing props.; **PROFL AFFIL & HONORS:** Austin Bd. of Realtors, TX Assn. of Realtors, Inst. of RE Mgmt., Nat. Assns. of Realtors, Dir., Austin Bd. of Realtors, 1979-1981; Chmn., Bd. of Gov. of Comml. Investment Div. of the Austin Bd. of Realtors, 1978 & 1979; Board of Governors 1978-1982; **MIL SERV:** USN 1966-1970, Special Citation from M.F. Weisner, Vice Admiral Seventh Fleet for Combat Duty Vietnam; **HOME ADD:** 1402 Northwood Rd., Austin, TX 78703, (512)474-1722; **BUS ADD:** 308 W. 15th St., Austin, TX 78701, (512)478-5621.

SANDRON, Ira——B: Sept. 13, 1949, Brooklyn, NY, *Broker*, Pacific Sands Equities; **PRIM RE ACT:** Broker, Attorney; **PREV EMPLOY:** ABA, L.A. Cty. Bar Assn., Beverly Hills Bar Assn., Indus. Relations Research Assn.; **EDUC:** BA, 1971, Pol. Sci., Occidental Coll.; **GRAD EDUC:** JD, 1974, Law, Duke Law School; **EDUC HONORS:** Cum Laude, Argonaut Award, President's Honor Roll; **HOME ADD:** 3528 Maplewood Ave., Los Angeles, CA 90066, (213)397-1834; **BUS ADD:** 2800 Neilson Way, Ste. 505, Santa Monica, CA 90405, (213)399-1506.

SANDS, Dr. Ralph S.——B: Aug. 23, 1930, Detroit, MI, *Pres.*, Rallen Prop.; **PRIM RE ACT:** Broker, Consultant, Developer, Builder, Owner/Investor, Property Manager, Syndicator; **SERVICES:** Plan, design, devel., comml. medical, etc.; **PROFL AFFIL & HONORS:** RESSI; Amer. Dental Assn., 1980 Civic Award from San Fernando Valley Bd. of Realtors, Beautification Comm.; **EDUC:** BBA, Fresno State Coll.; **GRAD EDUC:** DDS, Dentistry, Univ. of Detroit; **MIL SERV:** USN; PO, Pres. Unit Citation, Good Conduct Medal; **OTHER ACT & HONORS:** Past Pres., Amer. Cancer Soc., San Fernando Valley Unit; Past Pres., Toastmasters Intl., Encino, CA; Past Dir., Encino C of C; Past Chief, Dept. of Dentistry, Encino Hospital; Past Member, Planning Advisory Bd., W. Valley Community Hospital; Past Member, Mayor's Advisory Council, Non-Profit Charitable Org., Los Angeles, CA; Past Chmn., Annual Community Health Fair, Encino, CA; **BUS ADD:** 18065 Ventura Blvd., Encino, CA 91316, (213)783-1882.

SANDSTAD, Kenneth D.——B: May 22, 1946, Faribault, MN, *VP & Resid. Mgr. (1979-Present)*, Coldwell Banker Commercial Real Estate Services; **OTHER RE ACT:** Mgr.; **REP CLIENTS:** Comml. RE users, indiv. and instnl. investors; **PREV EMPLOY:** VP, Kelly Sandstad & Co., Inc. (1973-74); Sales Mgr., Coldwell Banker Comml. RE Servs. (1974-79); **PROFL AFFIL & HONORS:** Member, MN Bar; **EDUC:** BA, 1968, Eng., St. Olaf Coll.; **GRAD EDUC:** JD, 1971, Univ. of MN Law School; **OTHER ACT & HONORS:** Bd. Member, St. Olaf Coll. Alumni Assn. (1980-Present); Trustee, Breck School (1981-Present); Bd. Member, Hennepin Ctr. for the Arts; **HOME ADD:** 330 West Elmwood Pl., Minneapolis, MN 55409; **BUS ADD:** 6600 France Ave. S., Minneapolis, MN 55435, (612)920-8611.

SANDYS, Syd——B: June 4, 1931, Montreal, Can., *Partner, Managing Dir.*, Carleton Development Ltd.; **PRIM RE ACT:** Developer, Property Manager; **OTHER RE ACT:** Developers of office/warehouse parks in southwest; **HOME ADD:** 229 E. Desert Park Ln., Phoenix, AZ 85004, (602)997-8144; **BUS ADD:** 2035 N. Central Ave. #108, Phoenix, AZ 85004, (602)252-3964.

SAN FILIPPO, Steven——B: Nov. 25, 1950, San Francisco, CA, *Partner*, San Filippo, Krause & Baldanzi; **PRIM RE ACT:** Consultant, Owner/Investor, Syndicator; **OTHER RE ACT:** CPA; **SERVICES:** Tax consultant involved in RE synds.; **PREV EMPLOY:** Laventhol & Horwath, CPA's; **PROFL AFFIL & HONORS:** CA Soc. of CPA's; AI of CPA's; **EDUC:** BS, 1973, Acctg., Specialist, Univ. of San Francisco; **EDUC HONORS:** Beta Alpha Si, Honorary Member; **OTHER ACT & HONORS:** Redwood City Rotary; Beta Alpha Si; **HOME ADD:** 35 King St., Redwood City, CA 94062, (415)364-2650; **BUS ADD:** 1250 San Carlos Ave. #208, San Carlos, CA 94070, (415)595-4560.

SANFORD, Kendall T.——B: May 18, 1943, Joplin, MO, *Gen. Atty.*, The Denver and Rio Grande Western Railroad Co.; **PRIM RE ACT:** Attorney; **SERVICES:** Rep. Railroad in all land and right of way matters; **PREV EMPLOY:** Holland & Hart, Attys., Denver; **PROFL AFFIL & HONORS:** ABA, CO Bar Assn., Admitted to CO, 10th Circuit, D.C. Circuit, and U.S. Supreme Ct.; **EDUC:** 1970, Poli. Sci. & Hist., Univ. of Denver; **GRAD EDUC:** JD, 1974, Univ. of Denver Coll. of Law; **EDUC HONORS:** Law Journal Editor, Order of St. Ives; **HOME ADD:** 3175 S. Xanthi, Denver, CO 80231, (303)750-6432; **BUS ADD:** PO Box 5482, Denver, CO 80217, (303)629-5533.

SANFORD, Vernon T., Jr.——B: July 17, 1933, Verden, OK, *Sr. VP*, Citizens Frost Bank, N.A., Lending Group; **PRIM RE ACT:** Broker, Attorney, Banker, Lender, Owner/Investor, Instructor; **EDUC:** BBA, 1957, Univ. of TX, Austin; **GRAD EDUC:** JD, 1965, Univ. of TX, Austin; **MIL SERV:** USAF, Capt.; **HOME ADD:** 11303 Mystery Dr., San Antonio, TX 78216, (512)342-6746; **BUS ADD:** PO Box 29009, San Antonio, TX 78284, (512)344-0141.

SANFORD, Walter Scott——B: Mar. 5, 1956, Pasadena, CA, *Broker*, J.T.M. Brokerage Corp.; **PRIM RE ACT:** Broker, Consultant, Owner/Investor, Syndicator; **SERVICES:** Exchanges, synd., high priced brokerage, expert in Long Beach, consultation; **REP CLIENTS:** Profls.; **PREV EMPLOY:** Pres. of N and S Enterprises, Inc. (a firm involved in the rehabilitation of older residential and comml. bldgs. in Phoenix, Los Angeles, and Seattle); **PROFL AFFIL & HONORS:** Long Beach Traders; CAR; NAR; **EDUC:** BS, 1979, Econ., Bus., RE Fin., Univ. of S. CA; **EDUC HONORS:** Top 5% of Class; **OTHER ACT & HONORS:** Various community orgs.; **HOME ADD:** 275 Park Ave., Long Beach, CA 90803, (213)438-4600; **BUS ADD:** 312 Redondo Ave., Long Beach, CA 90814.

SANGER, Scott H.——B: Nov. 8, 1948, Chicago, IL, *Pres.*, The Taos Group, Ltd.; **PRIM RE ACT:** Consultant, Attorney, Developer, Builder, Owner/Investor, Property Manager, Syndicator; **SERVICES:** RE Investment Counseling, devel., synd., prop. mgmt., construction; **REP CLIENTS:** Taos Inn Assoc.; **PREV EMPLOY:** Atty: Offices of Scott H. Sanger, Atty. at Law, specializing in RE Law, NM; Newman, Stahl & Shadur, Chicago, specializing in RE Law; **PROFL AFFIL & HONORS:** ABA; MN State Bar Assn.; Chicago Bar Assn.; IL State Bar Assn.; **EDUC:** BA, 1970, Hist., Tulane Univ.; **GRAD EDUC:** JD, 1973, RE Law, Bus. Law, Tax Law, Northwestern Univ. School of Law; **EDUC HONORS:** Who's Who In American Colls. and Univs., Nat. Student Register; **HOME ADD:** PO Box 3097, 5O8 Hinde Pl., Taos, NM, (505)758-9056; **BUS ADD:** PO Drawer N, Taos, NM 87571, (505)758-9104.

SANGIULIANO, George A.——B: Oct. 2, 1947, Elizabeth, NJ, *Pres.-Owner of Carasan Inc.*, Sangiuliano Bros. Const. & Fire Rebuilders; **PRIM RE ACT:** Syndicator, Consultant, Builder, Owner/Investor; **PREV EMPLOY:** Electrical Contractor; **PROFL AFFIL & HONORS:** Natl. Remodelers Assoc.(NRA), BCB, Contractor of the year 1981 NRA; **EDUC:** Profl. School of Bus., 1978; **MIL SERV:** USAF; **OTHER ACT & HONORS:** Presently- Councilman-at-large Clark (Elected 1980-1984); Pres. Clark Unico; Kiwanis, K of C, Republican Club, Gran Centurions; **HOME ADD:** 500 Parkway Dr., Clark, NJ 07066, (201)382-0334; **BUS ADD:** 138 Westfield Ave., Clark, NJ 07066, (201)574-9057.

SANGUNETT, Jack B.——B: May 24, 1945, Wichita, KS, Jack B. Sangunett & Assoc.; **PRIM RE ACT:** Consultant, Owner/Investor; **OTHER RE ACT:** Resort & condo. conversion mktg.; **SERVICES:** Advertising, mktg., public relations; **REP CLIENTS:** Resid. Resource Grp., Adelphi, MD; Key Colony Key Biscayne, FL; Blaeser Devel. Dallas, TX; Joshua Muss & Assoc. Dallas, TX; Sparta Brook Homes, Charlotte, NC; Prop. Mgmt. Servs. Adelphia, MD; Sparta Brook Homes of MD Germantown, MD; Arlen Realty & Devel. NY, NY; **PREV EMPLOY:** VP, Hoffman Advertising Grp., Inc., NYC; **PROFL AFFIL & HONORS:** Dir. API Trust, Boston, MA, Outstanding Young Men of Amer., 1979; Dir. The Ad Agency, Alexandria, VA; **EDUC:** 1963-66, Journalism, Broadcast, Univ. of Tulsa; **EDUC HONORS:** Alpha Epsilon Rho Hon. Broadcast Comm. Frat.; **MIL SERV:** USN, 1966-69, Journalist SN, Vietnam Serv. Medal, Vietnam Campaign Medal, Presidential Unit Citation; **OTHER ACT & HONORS:** Alexandria C of C; **HOME ADD:** 4717 S. 31st St., Arlington, VA 22206, (703)671-3679; **BUS ADD:** 3543 W. Braddock Rd., Alexandria, VA 22302, (703)998-8096.

SANI, Hamid H.——B: Dec. 25, 1942, Bombay, India, United Investments; **PRIM RE ACT:** Broker, Consultant, Instructor, Property Manager; **OTHER RE ACT:** Exchangor; Estate Planning; **SERVICES:** Bus. Op. Fin. advisor; RE counselor; **REP CLIENTS:** Profl. Clients; RE Brokers, Non-Profit organizations and single proprietor bus.; **PREV EMPLOY:** Mgmt./Engrg. in construction industry and computer companies; **PROFL AFFIL & HONORS:** NAR; Charter Member/Inst. of Cert. Bus. Counselors, Member NCE, Million Dollar Exchangor; Pres. of Verdugo Exchangors; CBC; **EDUC:** BEE, 1964, Elec. Engrg., Coll. of Eng., Poona, India; **GRAD EDUC:** MS, 1968, E.E., Worcester Polytechnic Inst. Mass.; **EDUC HONORS:** 4th rank in Univ. of Poona; J.N. Tata Scholar; **OTHER ACT & HONORS:** Member Affiliation, Nat. Exchange Grps.; Grad. Level Courses in Fin. & Law; have published articles in exchange periodicals; **HOME ADD:** 29373 Hillrise Dr., Agoura, CA 91301, (213)889-5882; **BUS ADD:** 29373 Hillrise Dr., Agoura, CA 91301, (213)991-8351.

SANSONE, Steven A.——B: July 30, 1953, St. Louis, MO, *Natl. Account Mgr.*, Property Tax Research; **PRIM RE ACT:** Consultant, Appraiser; **OTHER RE ACT:** Prop. tax consultant; **SERVICES:** Reduction of comml., indus. prop. taxes; **REP CLIENTS:** Comml., indus. prop. owners; **PROFL AFFIL & HONORS:** Natl. Assn. of Review Appraisers, CRA; **EDUC:** BA, 1976, Econ., Westminster Coll., Fulton MO; **OTHER ACT & HONORS:** Atlanta C of C; **HOME ADD:** 2047 E. Powers Ferry Rd., Marietta, GA 30067, (404)952-4488; **BUS ADD:** 930 S. Omni Intl., Atlanta, GA 30303, (404)522-0600.

SANTOMAURO, Michael——*Executive Officer*, National Roomate Association; **OTHER RE ACT:** Profl. Assn. Admin.; **BUS ADD:** 315 Fifth Ave., New York, NY 10016, (212)686-9870.*

SANTYE, Anthony J., Jr.——B: Jan. 26, 1951, Plainfield, NJ, *Managing Partner*, A.J. Santye & Co. P.A.; **OTHER RE ACT:** Public accountant; **SERVICES:** Formation of synds. for client as genl. partners, equity & debt fin., gen. partner for synds., Advisor to clients investry as unit partners; **PROFL AFFIL & HONORS:** NJ Soc. of Public Accountants, Nat. Assn. of Public Accountants, NJ Reg. Public Acct., IRS Enrolled Agent; **EDUC:** BS Rider Coll., 1977, Acctg., NYU RE Inst.-courses; **GRAD EDUC:** Fairleigh Dickinson Univ., MBA - courses; **HOME ADD:** 717 Marlborough Common, Somerville, NJ 08876, (201)874-6869; **BUS ADD:** 176 Cedar St., N. Plainfield, NJ 07060, (201)755-5000.

SAPERSTON, Howard T., Jr.——B: Oct. 4, 1949, Buffalo, NY, *VP*, D'Ambrosia, Hogan, Oppenheimer, Saperston & Voit RE Associates, Inc.; **PRIM RE ACT:** Broker, Consultant, Appraiser, Property Manager; **SERVICES:** Comml. & indus. RE; **REP CLIENTS:** Many of the Fortune 500; **PROFL AFFIL & HONORS:** SIR, Greater Buffalo Bd. of Realtors, Buffalo C of C Industrial RE Council; **EDUC:** BA, 1963, Bus. & Admin., Franklin & Marshall Coll.; **OTHER ACT & HONORS:** Dir. Buffalo Sabres Hockey Team; Dir., Boys Clubs of Buffalo; Chmn., WNY Olympic Comm.; Dir., Arthritis Foundation, Tr., The Nichols School; Member, The Buffalo Club; **HOME ADD:** 100 Morris Ave., Buffalo, NY 14214, (716)835-0046; **BUS ADD:** 560 Delaware Ave., Buffalo, NY 14202, (716)884-7000.

SAPP, Jonathan W.——B: Oct. 22, 1948, Los Angeles, CA, *Pres.*, California Merchant Builders (Incorporated); **PRIM RE ACT:** Developer; **SERVICES:** Dev. of single family subdivs., condos, comml. & indus. ctrs & bldgs.; **PROFL AFFIL & HONORS:** Bldg. Indus. Assn. of Superior CA, Placer County Contr. Assn.; **EDUC:** Univ. of Nev., CA State Univ. at San Diego; **HOME ADD:** 11756 Red Dog Rd., Nevada City, CA 95959, (916)265-6655; **BUS ADD:** 11756 Red Dog Rd., Nevada City, CA 95959, (916)265-4542.

SAPUTO, Peter T.——B: July 21, 1954, Walnut Creek, CA, *Atty. at Law*, Van Voorhis & Skaggs; **PRIM RE ACT:** Attorney; **SERVICES:** Real prop. devel., tax planning, tax deferred exchanges; **REP CLIENTS:** Devel., converters, investors; **PROFL AFFIL & HONORS:** Bldg. Indus. Assn.; Dept. of RE Task Force; ABA; Contra Costa Cty. Bar Assn.; Admitted to practice law in the state of CA in US Dist. Ct. and in US Tax Ct.; **EDUC:** BS, 1976, Fin., Univ. of CA at Berkeley; **GRAD EDUC:** JD, 1979, tax, Golden Gate Univ.; MBA, (tax)1979, Golden Gate Univ.; LLM, (tax)1980, Golden Gate Univ.; **EDUC HONORS:** with honors; **BUS ADD:** 1855 Olympic Blvd., Suite 111 PO Box 'V', Walnut Creek, CA 94596, (415)937-8000.

SARGENT, Paul E.——B: July 18, 1954, UT, *Mort. Loan Spec.*, Amley & Assoc.; **PRIM RE ACT:** Broker, Owner/Investor; **SERVICES:** Handle fin. arrangements for parts.; **PREV EMPLOY:** Cardon Corp. Fin. Analyst; Valley Nat. Bank, Comml. Credit Program; **EDUC:** BA, 1978, Bus. Admin, UT State Univ.; **GRAD EDUC:** MBA, 1979, Fin., AZ State Univ.; **EDUC HONORS:** Grad. Asst.ship; **HOME ADD:** 1740 E. Hilton St., Mesa, AZ 85204, (602)892-2995; **BUS ADD:** 4350 E. Camelbeck, Suite 190B, Phoenix, AZ 85018, (602)959-1792.

SARHANGIAN, Ted——B: July 7, 1945, *Gen. Partner*, Summerhill; **PRIM RE ACT:** Developer, Owner/Investor, Syndicator; **EDUC:** Bus. Admin., 1969, Fin., Pepperdine Univ.; **GRAD EDUC:** MBA, 1973, Fin., Pepperdine Univ.; **OTHER ACT & HONORS:** Pres., Beverly Hills Equities, Inc., RE Synd.; **BUS ADD:** 10850 Wilshire Blvd., Ste. 770, Los Angeles, CA 90024, (213)474-4553.

SARKIN, Harold——B: Jan. 17, 1929, Syracuse, NY, Sarkin RE, Inc.; Florida and NY Brokerage; **PRIM RE ACT:** Broker, Consultant, Appraiser, Developer, Builder, Owner/Investor, Property Manager, Syndicator; **SERVICES:** Prop. mgmt. & devel. of multi-family housing; hotel and motel consultant; **REP CLIENTS:** Indiv. investors in comml. props.; **PROFL AFFIL & HONORS:** AOMA, NHBA; **EDUC:** BS, 1950, Syracuse Univ.; **OTHER ACT & HONORS:** AOMA, NHBA; **HOME ADD:** 217 Edgemont Dr., Syracuse, NY 13014, (305)446-2714; **BUS ADD:** 711 E. Genesee St., Syracuse, NY 13210, (305)971-5728.

SARLES, B. Dave, Jr.——B: Oct. 29, 1926, Bakersfield, CA, *Gen. Counsel*, Morgage and Trust, Inc.; **PRIM RE ACT:** Attorney, Lender; **SERVICES:** Loan documentation, creditor's rights; **PROFL AFFIL & HONORS:** State Bar of TX, Title Ins. Comm.; Houston Bar Assn., Bankruptcy Forum, Corp. Counsel Section; **EDUC:** BBA, 1949, Bus./Econ., Univ. of TX; **GRAD EDUC:** JD, 1963, S. TX Coll. of Law; **MIL SERV:** U.S. Army, 1944-1946; **OTHER ACT & HONORS:** Gethsemane United Methodist Church; **HOME ADD:** 5651 Sylmar, Houston, TX 77081; **BUS ADD:** POB 2885 (3100 Travis), Houston, TX 77001, (713)525-8000.

SAROSKY, William J.——B: Nov. 23, 1942, Hazelton, PA, *Pres.*, Remax Mountain West Inc.; **PRIM RE ACT:** Broker, Consultant, Lender, Builder, Owner/Investor, Property Manager; **SERVICES:** Investment counseling, motel brokerage & fin.; **REP CLIENTS:** Comml. investors; **PROFL AFFIL & HONORS:** NAR, RESSI, RN, Grand Junction Bd. of Realtors, GRI, CRB; **EDUC:** BS, 1971, Bus., Univ. of MD; **EDUC HONORS:** Cum Laude; **HOME ADD:** 581 36 Rd., Palisade, CO 81526, (303)464-7298; **BUS ADD:** 915 N. 7th St., Grand Junction, CO 81501, (303)245-9510.

SATHRE, Martin R.——B: July 30, 1925, Bemidji, MN, *Pres.*, Sathre Abstracters Inc.; **OTHER RE ACT:** Title evidence & title insurance also dir. of local savings and loan assn.; **PROFL AFFIL & HONORS:** Amer. Land Title Assn. & MN Land Title Assn., MN Cty. Recorders Assn.; **MIL SERV:** US Army, T Sgt.; **OTHER ACT & HONORS:** Cty. Recorder for Beltrami Cty., MN 1961-1982; **HOME ADD:** PO Box 146, Bemidji, MN 56601, (218)751-3546; **BUS ADD:** PO Box 146, Bemidji, MN 56601, (218)751-4565.

SATIAN, Sarkis A.——B: Oct. 5, 1938, Alexandria, Egypt, *Pres.*, Matian Enterprises Inc.; **PRIM RE ACT:** Developer, Builder; **PREV EMPLOY:** Project Superintendent, Norair Engineering, Wash., DC; **PROFL AFFIL & HONORS:** Change of land use, devel. of residential lots & building s/f homes; **EDUC:** BCE, Const. Mgmt., Intl. Correspondence School; **MIL SERV:** Medical Corp, Pfc., Sharpshooter; **OTHER ACT & HONORS:** Parish Council Member, St. Mary's Armenian Apostle Church of Wash., DC; **HOME ADD:** 721 Lawton St., McLean, VA 22101, (703)356-1177; **BUS ADD:** 721 Lawton St., McLean, VA 22101, (703)893-1477.

SATTER, Robert A.——B: Dec. 15, 1943, St. Louis, MO, *Pres.*; **PRIM RE ACT:** Broker, Developer, Builder; **PROFL AFFIL & HONORS:** FL lic. State Gen. Contractor, RE Broker and Mort. Broker, Dir., Better Bus. Bureau of Palm Beach Cty., Dir., Nat., State, and Local Home Builders Assn., Dir., First Amer. Bank of Palm Beach, Dir., Economic Council of Palm Beach Cty., Designated as Palm Beach Cty's. Builder of the Yr. both 1977 and 1979 by Homebuilder's and Contractor's Assn. of Palm Beach County; **EDUC:** BS in Engin., 1966, West Point; **GRAD EDUC:** MS in Engin., 1971, Univ. of MA; **MIL SERV:** USA, Capt., Bronze Star Meritorious Service Medal, Army Commendation Medal; **OTHER ACT & HONORS:** W. Palm Beach S Rotary/Vets. of Foreign Wars; **HOME ADD:** 537 Murifield Dr., Atlantic, FL 33462, (305)968-0515; **BUS ADD:** 2328 S. Congress Ave., W Palm Beach, FL 33406, (305)968-0750.

SATTERLEE, Alan——B: May 1, 1939, Akron, OH, *Pres.*, Alan Satterlee Enterprises; **PRIM RE ACT:** Broker, Developer, Builder, Owner/Investor, Property Manager; **PROFL AFFIL & HONORS:** Bd. Member, Concerned Citizens for Prop. Rights; Member, CA Coastal Council; Member, Advocates for Balanced CA Devel.; Member, Malibu/Santa Monica Mountains Citizens Planning Comm.; **EDUC:** BS, 1961, Mktg./Gen. Bus., Univ. of AZ; **OTHER ACT & HONORS:** Founder and Chmn. of Bd., Liberty Canyon Christian Sch.; **BUS ADD:** 26560 Rondell St., Suite 201, Calabasas, CA 91302, (213)880-5366.

SATTERWHITE, P. Roy——B: June 3, 1920, Jemison, AL, *Sr. VP & Mgr., S RE*, Mead Land Services and The Mead Corp.; **PRIM RE ACT:** Broker, Developer, Property Manager; **PREV EMPLOY:** U.S. Steel Corp.; **PROFL AFFIL & HONORS:** Indus. Dev. Research Inst.; **EDUC:** BS, 1951, Agric. Sci., Auburn Univ.; **EDUC HONORS:** Comer Medal for excellence in Nat. Sci.; Alpha Zeta; Gama Sigma Delta; Phi Kappa Phi; **MIL SERV:** USN, Yeoman; **HOME ADD:** 142 Lindberg Rd., Hueytown, AL 35023, (205)491-4088; **BUS ADD:** POB 668, Bessemer, AL 35021, (205)424-1595.

SATULOFF, Barth——B: Dec. 13, 1945, Buffalo, NY, *CPA*, Barth Satuloff, CPA; **OTHER RE ACT:** CPA; **SERVICES:** Acctg. serv., auditing, fin. forecasting, tax planning, compliance & representation for RE clients; **REP CLIENTS:** Indiv. & bus. investors - both domestic & foreign; **PREV EMPLOY:** Price Waterhouse & Co., Miami, FL; Laventhol & Horwath, Miami, FL; **PROFL AFFIL & HONORS:** AICPA, FICPA, NYSSCPA, ISCPA, SLCPA, ARA, BAX, CPA: FL, NY, IL & LA; **EDUC:** BBA, 1967, Acctg., Univ. of Miami, Coral Gables, FL; **GRAD EDUC:** MBA, 1969, Acctg. & taxation, Univ. of Miami, Coral Gables, FL; **EDUC HONORS:** Beta Alpha Psi Natl. Acctg. Honorary Frat.; **MIL SERV:** FL Army Nat. Guard, Spec. 5, Armed Forces Reserve Commendation Medal; **OTHER ACT & HONORS:** Pres. & Chmn. of the Bd., Chartered Investment Research Corp.; Pres. Satuloff Bros., Inc., Buffalo, NY; **HOME ADD:** 9614 SW 134th Ct., Miami, FL 33143; **BUS ADD:** Kings Creek Village Pl., 8024 SN 81 Dr., Miami, FL 33143, (305)595-4695.

SAUDER, Kenneth R.——B: Nov. 19, 1940, Peoria, IL, *Dir. of Training*, Noah Herman Sons Realtors; **PRIM RE ACT:** Broker, Consultant, Owner/Investor, Instructor, Property Manager; **OTHER RE ACT:** Relocation dir. RELO; **PREV EMPLOY:** Owner of furniture bus.; **PROFL AFFIL & HONORS:** GRI, Fortune Master Trainer RE Educ. Assn., Assn. of IL RE Educ. RE Trainers Assn., GRI; ARC; **EDUC:** BBA, 1963, Acctg., Bradley Univ.; **MIL SERV:**

US Army, SP5; **OTHER ACT & HONORS:** Chmn. of Educ. Comm. Peoria Bd. Realtors, Instr. Dale Carnegie Course; **HOME ADD:** RR #1 300 Spring Creek Rd., Washington, IL 61571, (309)745-9455; **BUS ADD:** 31000 N. Dries Ln., Peoria, IL 61604, (309)686-2215.

SAUERBRUNN, Kathleen H.——B: Oct. 18, 1917, Little Silver, NJ, *Assoc. Gen. Counsel*, Dept. of Housing & Urban Devel., Gen. Counsel's Office, Regulatory Programs; **PRIM RE ACT:** Attorney, Regulator; **SERVICES:** Legal counsel, regulatory & statutory drafting; **PROFL AFFIL & HONORS:** Fed. Bar Assn.; ABA; TX Bar Assn.; US Supreme Court; DC Court of Appeals; Court of Claims; **EDUC:** BA, 1939, Eng., Rutgers Univ.; **GRAD EDUC:** JD, 1962, Law, So. Methodist School of Law; **EDUC HONORS:** Cum Laude; **OTHER ACT & HONORS:** Tantallon Golf-Ctry. Club; **HOME ADD:** 1315 Swan Harbour Rd., Ft. Washington, MD 20744, (301)292-3025; **BUS ADD:** 451 Seventh St., SW, Washington, DC 20410, (202)755-6999.

SAUERTEIG, Paul J.——B: May 9, 1917, Ft. Wayne, IN, *Atty.*; **PRIM RE ACT:** Attorney; **PREV EMPLOY:** Lincoln Nat. Corp., VP and Sec.; The Lincoln Nat. Life Ins. Co., Assoc. Gen. Counsel; Amer. Soc. of Hospital Attys.; **EDUC:** AB, 1939, Columbia Coll. NYC; **GRAD EDUC:** LLB, 1942, Columbia Univ. Law School; **MIL SERV:** USA, S/Sgt.; **HOME ADD:** 1830 Hawthorne Rd., Ft. Wayne, IN 46804, (219)432-5075; **BUS ADD:** 222 Utility Bldg., Ft. Wayne, IN 46802, (219)426-2244.

SAUNDERS, Donald L.——B: Jan. 28, 1935, Boston, MA, *Pres. and CEO*, Saunders & Assoc.; **PRIM RE ACT:** Broker, Consultant, Appraiser, Property Manager, Owner/Investor; **SERVICES:** Prop. mgmt.; **REP CLIENTS:** Managing, Statler Office Bldg., Boston, MA; Greater Providence Bank Bldg., Providence, RI; Fresh Pond Shopping Ctr., Cambridge, MA; **PROFL AFFIL & HONORS:** IREM; NACORE; Greater Boston RE Bd.; Mass. Bd. of RE Appraisers; Back Bay Architectural Commn.; Int'l. Inst. of Valuers, CPM; SCV; MRA; **EDUC:** 1957, AIREA - Course I. II & V, Brown Univ.; **EDUC HONORS:** IREM - Course I & II; **OTHER ACT & HONORS:** Bd. of Fire Prevention, MA; Lotos Club; Hope Club; Back Bay Assn.; Hundred Club of MA; Tru. Emeriti: Brown Univ., Pres. Farview, Inc. (Brown U. RE holding Co.); Vice Chmn. of Planning and Bldg. Comm. of Brown U.; **HOME ADD:** 1501 Beacon St., Brookline, MA 02135, (617)232-1868; **BUS ADD:** 229 Newbury St., Boston, MA 02116, (617)536-1620.

SAUNDERS, Monte L.——B: Mar. 22, 1954, Alameda, CA, *Investment Consultant*, McDaniel & Assoc., RE; **PRIM RE ACT:** Broker, Consultant, Developer, Owner/Investor; **SERVICES:** Consulting, devel., brokerage; **PREV EMPLOY:** Personal experience; **PROFL AFFIL & HONORS:** So Lake Tahoe Bd. of Realtors, Sacramento Exchange Group, Sierra-Reno Exchange Groups, etc.; **HOME ADD:** PO Box 5258, S. Lake Tahoe, CA 95729, (916)544-8565; **BUS ADD:** PO Box 10138, So. Lake Tahoe, CA 95731, (916)544-0900.

SAUNDERS, Ron——B: Oct. 30, 1954, Key West, FL, Saunders & Saunders P.A.; **PRIM RE ACT:** Attorney; **SERVICES:** Legal, RE & Corp.; **REP CLIENTS:** Key West Bd. of Realtors; 1st Fed. S&L of The FL Keys; First Title Serv. Corp.; **PROFL AFFIL & HONORS:** FL Bar, ABA, Real Prop. Probate & Tr. Sect., RE & Corp. Law; **EDUC:** BS, 1976, Econ. & Fin., Univ. of FL; **GRAD EDUC:** JD, 1979, Law, Univ. of FL; **EDUC HONORS:** High Honors, ODK, Blue Key, Savant; **OTHER ACT & HONORS:** Vice Chmn. Career Serv. Council; Pres. Key West Jaycees; Elks; Rotary, Moose; **HOME ADD:** 3312 Northside Dr., Key West, FL 33040, (305)296-2241; **BUS ADD:** 516 Southard St., Key West, FL 33040, (305)296-3289.

SAUNDERS, William P., Jr.——B: Sept. 15, 1928, Flemingsburg, KY, *Pres.*, Gouger, O'Neal & Saunders Realty; **PRIM RE ACT:** Broker, Appraiser, Developer, Owner/Investor, Insuror, Syndicator; **SERVICES:** Condo devel. & mgmt.; **REP CLIENTS:** Exclusive rep. Ctry. Club of NC, Brooks & Perkins Inc., New Indus.; **PREV EMPLOY:** VP E-Z Flo Chem. Co., Sub Union Carbide Copr.; **PROFL AFFIL & HONORS:** NAR, RMNI, NC Assn. of Realtors, RESSI, Farm & Land Inst., GRI, CRS, CRB; **EDUC:** BS, 1950, Agric. Econ., Univ. of KY; **MIL SERV:** USA, 1951-54, Capt.; **OTHER ACT & HONORS:** Pres. Sandhills C of C, 1973, Dist. Chmn. Moore Dist. Boy Scouts of Amer.; **HOME ADD:** Brookline Dr., PO Box 370, Ctry. Club of NC, S Pines, NC 28387, (913)692-7391; **BUS ADD:** PO Box 985, Pinehurst, NC 28374, (919)295-5504.

SAUVE, Richard M.——B: July 9, 1919, Minneapolis, MN, *Owner*, Sauve Appraisals; **PRIM RE ACT:** Appraiser, Owner/Investor; **SERVICES:** Spec. in assignments involving litigation i.e., condemnation, tax abatement, etc.; **PREV EMPLOY:** Pres. The Beecher Co., Inc. 1957-75 (Realtors); **PROFL AFFIL & HONORS:** AIREA, NAR, MN Assn. of Realtors, Gr. Minneapolis Bd. of Realtors, MAI Past Pres. (1961), Minneapolis Bd. of Realtors; **EDUC:** Univ. of MN, 1937-40; **MIL SERV:** USA Air Corps., Maj., DFC, with OLC, Air Medal with 6 OLC; **HOME ADD:** 6566 France Ave. S, Edina, MN 55435, (612)926-8263; **BUS ADD:** 4005 W. 65th St., Minneapolis, MN 55435, (612)925-4650.

SAVAS, E.S.——*Asst. Sec. for Policy Devel. & Research*, US Dept. of HUD; **PRIM RE ACT:** Regulator; **SERVICES:** Works closely with HUD program officials in improving program operations and setting departmental policies, goals, and priorities and is prin. advisor to the Sec. on overall departmental policy, program evaluation and research; **PREV EMPLOY:** Dir. of Center for Gov. Studies and Prof. at Grad. School of Bus., Columbia Univ., First Deputy City Admin. of NY (1970-1972); Deputy City Admin. (1967-1969); **PROFL AFFIL & HONORS:** Author of numerous articles & 6 books. Recipient of Louis Brownlow Memorial Award - Amer. Soc. of Public Admin.; **EDUC:** BA, 1951, Univ. of Chicago, With Honors; BS, 1953, Univ. of Chicago; **GRAD EDUC:** MS, 1956, Columbia Univ.; PhD, 1960, Columbia Univ.; **MIL SERV:** US Army 1953-1955 (Korea); **BUS ADD:** HUD Bldg. 451 7th St., Washington, DC 20410.

SAVITS, Irving A.——B: Aug. 28, 1920, Philadelphia, PA, *Owner*, Irving Savits Agency; **PRIM RE ACT:** Broker, Consultant, Attorney, Appraiser, Owner/Investor, Property Manager, Insuror, Syndicator; **OTHER RE ACT:** DE Cty. C of C; **SERVICES:** Assessment appeals, RE appraising, consultant; **REP CLIENTS:** Indivs. and cos. on comml. and indus. investments; **PREV EMPLOY:** RE self employment; went into RE ins. bus. after grad. law sch.; **PROFL AFFIL & HONORS:** ASA, SREA, Right of Way, Man of the Year, Chester RE Bd., 1956, 1964; **EDUC:** BS, 1942, Univ. of AL; **GRAD EDUC:** JD, 1949, Temple Univ. Law Sch.; **EDUC HONORS:** Tau Epsilon Rho; **MIL SERV:** USAF, Pvt. 1st class, Good Conduct; **OTHER ACT & HONORS:** Pres (Past) DE Cty. Appraisal Soc., Dir. 1956-73 Chapt. of DE Cty. Bd. of Realtors, Masons, B'nai B'rith, Aston Bus. & Profl. Assn., DE Cty. C of C; **HOME ADD:** 208 Fairfield Dr., Wallingford, PA 19086, (215)506-3133; **BUS ADD:** 2745 Weir Rd., Aston, PA 19014, (215)497-4550.

SAVLICK, Albert——B: Feb. 28, 1914, NY, NY, *Managing Dir.*, Heartland Indus. Park; **PRIM RE ACT:** Broker, Developer, Builder; **SERVICES:** All phases of const.; **PROFL AFFIL & HONORS:** Brokers; **EDUC:** BS, 1934, Coll. of City of NY; **EDUC HONORS:** Dean's List; **MIL SERV:** US Army Corps of Engrs., Capt.; **HOME ADD:** 3058 Morgan Dr., Wantagh, NY 11793; **BUS ADD:** 150 Oser Ave., Hauppauge, NY 11788, (516)273-5900.

SAVO, Peg——B: June 2, 1924, Throop, PA, *Mgr.*, Hinerfeld Realty Co., Suburban; **PRIM RE ACT:** Broker, Appraiser, Owner/Investor; **PROFL AFFIL & HONORS:** Greater Scranton Bd. of Realtors, PA Bd. of Realtors, Nat. Institute of Realtors; **EDUC:** Exec. Sec., Powell School of Bus.; Univ. of Bridgeport, PA State Univ. & Marywood Coll.; **OTHER ACT & HONORS:** Chmn.; Newton Township Planning Commn., Elks Club, Waverly Community Club, Newton Twp. Zoning Bd.; **HOME ADD:** RD 2 Box 395, Clarks Summit, PA 18411, (717)587-2984; **BUS ADD:** 120 S State St., Clarks Summit, PA 18411, (717)586-0756.

SAWYER, Heywood A.——B: Apr. 18, 1925, Portland, ME, *Pres.*, Sawyer Appraisal Co.; **PRIM RE ACT:** Appraiser; **REP CLIENTS:** Lenders & indiv. and/or instnl. investors in RE; **PROFL AFFIL & HONORS:** SRA, Soc. of RE Appraisers; **EDUC:** BS, 1949, Bus. Admin., Boston Univ.; **MIL SERV:** USAF, 2nd Lt.; **OTHER ACT & HONORS:** Member Nat. Alumni Council of Boston Univ.; VP, Pine Tree Council, Boy Scouts of Amer.; **HOME ADD:** 5A Indian Ridge, Yarmouth, ME 04096, (207)846-5856; **BUS ADD:** PO Box 8055, Portland, ME 04104, (207)772-8381.

SAWYER, James L.——B: Aug. 10, 1951, Detroit, *Partner*, Prendergast & Sawyer, Architects; **PRIM RE ACT:** Consultant, Architect; **SERVICES:** Site selection, feasibility, budgeting, arch.; **REP CLIENTS:** NYU Medical Ctr., The City of NY, The Staten Is. Children's Museum; **PREV EMPLOY:** I.M. Pei & Partners, Architects, 1974-1979; **PROFL AFFIL & HONORS:** Registered NY State, Cert. NCARB; **EDUC:** BArch., 1974, Profl. Program (5 year), Cornell; **GRAD EDUC:** MBA, 1979, Intl., NYU, GBA; **EDUC HONORS:** Owing's Prize 1974, Eggers Prize 1971, Certificate in Intl. Mgmt. (IMP.); **HOME ADD:** 166 Midwood St., Brooklyn, NY 11225, (212)856-6011; **BUS ADD:** 136 Church St., New York, NY 10007, (212)732-1081.

SAWYER, Paul——*Dir.*, Maine Real Estate Commissioner; **PRIM RE ACT:** Property Manager; **BUS ADD:** State House, Ste. #35, Augusta, ME 04333, (207)289-3735.*

SAWYER, Richard Lewis——**B:** Oct. 1, 1929, Auburn, ME, *Owner*, Richard Lewis Sawyer S.R.A.; **PRIM RE ACT:** Consultant, Appraiser; **SERVICES:** RE Appraisals (Resid., Comml., Indivs.); **REP CLIENTS:** State and Local agencies, banks, attys., corps., reloc. cos. & other private clients; **PROFL AFFIL & HONORS:** SREA; Nat. Assn. of Review Apparaisers, SRA; CRA; **EDUC:** BS, 1951, Forestry, Univ. of ME; **MIL SERV:** US Army; Capt.; **HOME ADD:** 151 Main St., Gorham, ME 04038, (207)839-4454; **BUS ADD:** PO Box 44, 39 Main St., Gorham, ME 04038, (207)839-3376.

SAYER, Colin——*Secy.*, Riegel Textile Corp.; **PRIM RE ACT:** Property Manager; **BUS ADD:** Green Gate Park, Ste. 800, 25 Woods Lake Rd., Greenville, SC 29607, (803)242-6050.*

SAYERS, Clinton P.——**B:** Mar. 7, 1950, San Antonio, TX, *Pres.*, Sayers & Assoc. Inc.; **PRIM RE ACT:** Broker, Consultant, Appraiser, Developer; **SERVICES:** Resid. & Comml. Appraisals, Condo & Office Devel.; **PROFL AFFIL & HONORS:** SREA, AIREA, Austin Bd. of Realtors, Amer. Assn. of Petroleum Landmen, SRA, 1975; SRPA, 1978; RM 1979; **EDUC:** BBA, 1973, Gen. Bus., Univ. of TX; **OTHER ACT & HONORS:** Young Men's Bus. League, 1981 Pres., 1980 VP, 1979 Treas., SREA, Chapt. 80; **HOME TEL:** (512)478-9212; **BUS ADD:** 1504 Robin Hood Trail, Austin, TX 78703, (512)478-9991.

SAYLER, Diana C.——**B:** May 2, 1946, Scotland, SD, *Mgr.*, Key Real Estate; **PRIM RE ACT:** Broker, Owner/Investor, Instructor; **SERVICES:** Resid. investment counseling, fin. instr.; **PROFL AFFIL & HONORS:** WCR, Local & State Pres., (1978-1982), GRI; CRB; **EDUC:** BA, 1968, Eng., Educ., Midland Coll., Fremont NE; **EDUC HONORS:** Magna Cum Laude; **HOME ADD:** 831 Hidden Hill Dr., Bellevue, NE 68005, (402)291-9606; **BUS ADD:** 11531 S. 36th, Omaha, NE 68123, (402)292-2200.

SAYLOR, Paul H.——**B:** May 23, 1942, NJ, *Pres.*, Ackerman Advisory Associates; **PRIM RE ACT:** Consultant, Lender, Owner/Investor, Property Manager; **OTHER RE ACT:** Advisor and asset mgr. to domestic and foreign instns. investing in U.S. RE; **SERVICES:** Selection of investments, structuring of transactions, contract negotiations, asset mgmt., operational and fin. reporting various domestic and foreign pension funds, insurance cos. and banks; **PREV EMPLOY:** Pres., Saylor Prop. 1972-1979, Sr. VP & Bd. Member, Calprop Corp. 1969-1972; **PROFL AFFIL & HONORS:** Licensed RE broker, inst. for Mort. Banker's Assn. Seminars, licensed gen. contractor; **EDUC:** BA, 1964, Econ., Soc., Univ. of VA; **GRAD EDUC:** None - Various RE, 1965-1970, courses completed at Univ. of CT and UCLA; **EDUC HONORS:** Dean's List; **OTHER ACT & HONORS:** Advisory Comm. Special Olympics, YMCA Bd., End World Hunger Assn.; **BUS ADD:** 3340 Peachtree Rd. NE, Atlanta, GA 30026, (404)266-0800.

SCALA, James Robert——**B:** Oct. 5, 1948, Detroit, MI, *Assoc.*, Simpson Thacher & Bartlett; **PRIM RE ACT:** Attorney; **SERVICES:** Legal; **REP CLIENTS:** Lenders - Comml. Props.; **PREV EMPLOY:** Dewey, Ballantine, Bushby, Palmer & Wood 1974-78; Fried, Frank, Harris, Shriver & Jacobson 1978-80; **PROFL AFFIL & HONORS:** ABA; NYBA; **EDUC:** AB, Magna Cum Laude, 1970, Hist. (Honors), Georgetown Univ.; **GRAD EDUC:** JD, 1974, Columbia Univ. - School of Law; **EDUC HONORS:** Phi Beta Kappa, Harlan Fiske Stone Scholar; Articles Editor-Columbia Journal of Law and Social Problems; **MIL SERV:** Army National Guard, SP-5; **HOME ADD:** 1641 Third Ave., Apt. 12G, New York, NY 10028, (212)860-4667; **BUS ADD:** 350 Park Ave., New York, NY 10022, (212)753-8700.

SCANLON, Thomas J., Jr.——**B:** Aug. 21, 1946, Buffalo, NY, *VP*, Marine Midland Bank, Construction Loan Div.; **PRIM RE ACT:** Banker; **SERVICES:** Provide construction and interim RE loans; **REP CLIENTS:** Major U.S. devels./investors; **PROFL AFFIL & HONORS:** Mort. Bankers Assn., Amer. Inst. of Banking; **EDUC:** BS, 1968, Soc., Canisius Coll.; **GRAD EDUC:** MBA, 1970, Fin., State Univ. of NY at Buffalo; **HOME ADD:** 68 Lowell Rd., Kenmore, NY 14217, (716)874-3708; **BUS ADD:** Buffalo, NY 142401 M M Ctr., (716)843-2768.

SCANNAPIECO, Thomas——**B:** Aug. 15, 1949, Philadelphia, PA, *Pres.*, Historical Developers, Inc.; **PRIM RE ACT:** Developer, Builder, Syndicator; **SERVICES:** Investment counseling, devel. of historic prop; **REP CLIENTS:** Indiv. investors seeking tax sheltered RE investments; **PREV EMPLOY:** Pres. of Philatech Corp. resid. and light comml. builders; **PROFL AFFIL & HONORS:** Associate member AIA; active member Nat. Trust for Historic Preservation; **EDUC:** BS, 1971, St. Joseph's Coll., Philadelphia, PA; **OTHER ACT & HONORS:** Big Brothers Assn.; **HOME ADD:** 2007 Wallace St., Philadelphia, PA 19130, (215)765-7660; **BUS ADD:** 2005 Wallace St., Philadelphia, PA 19130, (215)765-7665.

SCAPILLATO, Thomas A.——**B:** Jan. 9, 1942, Chicago, IL, *Pres.*, TUSC; **PRIM RE ACT:** Owner/Investor, Instructor, Property Manager, Syndicator, Real Estate Publisher; **SERVICES:** Synd. & prop. mgmt.; **REP CLIENTS:** Lenders and indiv. or instnl. investors in income producing props.; **PREV EMPLOY:** The Balcor Co., 1978-80; The First Nat. Bank of Chicago 1974-78; Continental Bank 1971-74; **PROFL AFFIL & HONORS:** IREM; RESSI; Lambda Alpha; ICSC; Nat. Assn. of Review Appraisers, CPM, CRA; **EDUC:** BS, Civil & Mech. Engrg., IL Inst. of Tech.; **BUS ADD:** Suite 105, 825 N. Cass Ave., Westmont, IL 60559, (312)654-8080.

SCARDILLI, Dennis A.——**B:** Jul. 7, 1949, Irvington, NJ, *Appraiser/ Consultant*, J.A. Scardilli RE Inc., Appraisal Div.; **PRIM RE ACT:** Consultant, Appraiser; **OTHER RE ACT:** Land Use Planning; **SERVICES:** RE Appraisals, Counseling, Econ. Anal., Planning Anal.; **REP CLIENTS:** Law Firms, Fin. Inst. and Dev. in the Atlantic City Area; **PREV EMPLOY:** HUD; NJHFA, Atlantic City Planning Dept.; **PROFL AFFIL & HONORS:** Atlantic City & Cty. Bd. of Realtors; APA; ULI; **EDUC:** BA, 1971, Speech, Wheaton Coll., Wheaton, IL; **GRAD EDUC:** Cand. for MUP, projected 1982, Housing and Econ., NYU; **MIL SERV:** USAR, Capt.; **HOME ADD:** 310 Coolidge Ave., Absecon, NJ 08201, (609)646-0591; **BUS ADD:** 337 E. White Horse Pike, Absecon, NJ 08201, (609)652-8000.

SCARDINA, Frank Joseph——**B:** Feb. 18, 1948, Chicago, IL, *Pres.*, Kaufman and Broad Communities, Inc., Subs. of Kaufman and Broad, Inc.; **PRIM RE ACT:** Developer, Builder; **SERVICES:** Devel., builder of single family housing communities; **PREV EMPLOY:** VP and Gen. Counsel, Kaufman and Broad, Inc. (NYSE Co.), 1979-1981; private practice as atty.; **PROFL AFFIL & HONORS:** CA State Bar; ABA; **EDUC:** BA, 1969, Econ./Philosophy, Univ. of Denver; **GRAD EDUC:** JD, 1972, Law, Univ. of CA at Berkeley, Boalt Hall School of Law; **HOME ADD:** 4524 Poe Ave., Woodland Hills, CA 91364, (213)346-8398; **BUS ADD:** 10801 National Blvd., Los Angeles, CA 90064, (213)475-6711.

SCARRITT, Richard W.——**B:** Dec. 13, 1938, Enid, OK, *Partner*, Spencer, Fane, Britt & Browne; **PRIM RE ACT:** Regulator; **OTHER RE ACT:** Financing, Zoning; **SERVICES:** Legal; **PROFL AFFIL & HONORS:** Kansas City, MO and Amer. Bar Assns.; Bar of U.S. Supreme Court; RE Bd. of Kansas City (Affiliate); **EDUC:** BA, 1960, Econ., Fin., Philosophy & Poli. Sci., Univ. of OK; **GRAD EDUC:** JD, 1963, Harvard Law School; **EDUC HONORS:** Dean's List; **OTHER ACT & HONORS:** Mensa; Panel of Arbitrators, Amer. Arbitration Assn.; MO C of C; **HOME ADD:** 5236 Mercier, Kansas City, MO 64112, (816)523-8181; **BUS ADD:** 1000 Power & Light Bldg., Kansas City, MO 64105, (816)474-8100.

SCATENA, Gerald W.——**B:** Oct. 8, 1947, Oakland, CA, *Div. Counsel*, Systech Financial Corporation; **PRIM RE ACT:** Broker, Attorney; **EDUC:** BS, 1969, Econs., Saint Mary's Coll.; **GRAD EDUC:** JD; MBA, 1972; 1980, Law; RE, Hastings; Golden Gate Univ.; **EDUC HONORS:** Cum Laude; **OTHER ACT & HONORS:** Alameda Bar Assn., Contra Costa Bar Assn.; **HOME ADD:** 751 Glen Eagle Court, San Ramon, CA 94583, (415)838-9514; **BUS ADD:** 115 Ryan Indus. Court, San Ramon, CA 94583, (415)838-8600.

SCERBO, Carmine——**B:** Mar. 3, 1928, Italy, *Pres.*, Scerbo Devel. Corp.; **PRIM RE ACT:** Developer; **PREV EMPLOY:** Self-employed for 30 yrs.; **PROFL AFFIL & HONORS:** Various builder orgs.; **GRAD EDUC:** Elementary, tech. & mil. schools in Italy; **MIL SERV:** Armed Corps. of Engrgs.; **HOME ADD:** P O Box 8209, Newport Beach, CA 92660; **BUS ADD:** PO Box 8209, Newport Beach, CA 92660, (714)730-1611.

SCHAAL, Gary G.——**B:** Apr. 1, 1950, *Gen. Sales Mgr.*, Scarborough Corp.; **PRIM RE ACT:** Broker, Developer, Builder; **PROFL AFFIL & HONORS:** NAHB, Million Dollar Lifetime Cir. Recipient; **EDUC:** BA, 1972, Econ./Pol. Sci., Ursinus, Collegeville, PA; **MIL SERV:** USAFNG, S/Sgt., 1972-1978; **OTHER ACT & HONORS:** Pres., Sturbridge Lakes Home Owners Assn.; **HOME ADD:** 8 Addington Ct., Voorhees, NJ 08043, (609)768-0274; **BUS ADD:** POB 387, Marlton, NJ 08053, (609)768-1010.

SCHAEFER, Gene R.——*Exec. VP*, National Housing Conference; **PRIM RE ACT:** Regulator; **BUS ADD:** 1126 16th St. NW, Ste. 211, Washington, DC 20036, (202)223-4844.*

SCHAEFER, Howard G.——**B:** July 17, 1945, Buffalo, NY, *Lawyer*, Howard G. Schaefer; **PRIM RE ACT:** Attorney, Owner/Investor, Syndicator; **SERVICES:** Tax & legal consultation, document drafting, prop. synd.; **REP CLIENTS:** Investors; **PREV EMPLOY:** Tax Dept. with Coopers & Lybrand 1971-1980; **PROFL AFFIL & HONORS:** CA State Bar Assn., L.A. County Bar Assn., ABA, CA Soc. of CPA's, AICPA, L.A. CPA Soc.; **EDUC:** BS Acctg., 1967, Acctg., CA State

Univ. at Los Angeles; **GRAD EDUC:** JD, 1971, Tax Law, Univ. of Southern CA; **MIL SERV:** CA Natl. Guard, SP-5; **OTHER ACT & HONORS:** 1978 Republican Party Nominee for Congress, 24th CD.; CA Republican State Central Comm.; **HOME ADD:** 7300 Franklin St. #653, Los Angeles, CA 90046; **BUS ADD:** 1801 Century Park East, Suite 1801, Los Angeles, CA 90067, (213)552-5310.

SCHAEFER, James T.——B: Aug. 29, 1937, Evanston, IL, *Pres.*, UOP Realty Development Co., a subsidiary of UOP Inc.; **PRIM RE ACT:** Developer; **OTHER RE ACT:** Corp. RE; **SERVICES:** Devel. & manage lands owned by parent co. only; **PREV EMPLOY:** Land Acquisition Mgr., Material Serv. Div. of Gen. Dynamics Corp.; **PROFL AFFIL & HONORS:** Indus. Devel. Research Council; ULI, 1981-82 Who's Who in Amer. Bus. & Fin.; **EDUC:** BSC, 1959, Bus. Mgmt., DePaul Univ.; **GRAD EDUC:** MBA, 1966, Mktg., Fin., Northwestern Univ.; **MIL SERV:** US Army; **OTHER ACT & HONORS:** Alderman, City of Park Ridge, 1979-present; Park Ridge Fine Arts Soc., Pres.; DePaul Univ. Alumni Assn., VP; DePaul Univ. Distinguished Alumni Award, 1973; **HOME ADD:** 618 Wisner St., Park Ridge, IL 60068, (312)825-0482; **BUS ADD:** 10 UOP Pl., Des Plaines, IL 60016, (312)391-2277.

SCHAEFER, Keith F.——B: July 20, 1943, Phil., PA, *Broker*, Moore & Co., Comm. Investment; **PRIM RE ACT:** Broker, Syndicator, Developer, Builder; **EDUC:** Mankato Univ., 1965; **MIL SERV:** USN, P.O.3; **HOME ADD:** 844 Marion St., Denver, CO 80218, (303)832-7771; **BUS ADD:** 390 Grant St., Denver, CO 80203, (303)778-1600.

SCHAEFFER, Louis B.——B: Dec. 15, 1937, Chicago, IL, *Sec. and House Counsel*, Security Mort. Co., Inc.; **PRIM RE ACT:** Attorney, Property Manager, Syndicator; **OTHER RE ACT:** Mort. Banker; **PREV EMPLOY:** Partner, Gerst, Campo & Schaeffer Attorneys at Law; **PROFL AFFIL & HONORS:** State Bar of AZ; Maricopa County Bar Assn.; State Bar Committee on Arbitration; **EDUC:** Hist., Univ. of AZ; **GRAD EDUC:** JD, 1961, Univ. of AZ; **EDUC HONORS:** American Jurisprudence Awards in Insurance & Equity; Pima County Bar Auxiliary Award; **HOME ADD:** 5830 N. 12th Place, Phoenix, AZ 85014, (602)277-0731; **BUS ADD:** 3507 N. Central, Suite 200, Phoenix, AZ 85012, (602)277-1416.

SCHAFER, H. James——B: June 18, 1944, Englewood, NJ, *VP*, Coldwell Banker, Coldwell Banker Comml. RE Servs.; **PRIM RE ACT:** Broker, Consultant; **SERVICES:** Brokerage, consultation, management; **REP CLIENTS:** Large ins. cos., pension funds, maj. indus. cos., nat. devels.; **PROFL AFFIL & HONORS:** Active member, SIR; Member, Boston RE Bd.; Member, Intl. Comm., Brokers Lics., MA, RI, NH, CA; **EDUC:** BA, 1966, Psych., St. Mary's Coll. of CA; **GRAD EDUC:** MBA, 1977, Mgmt., St. Mary's Coll. of CA; **MIL SERV:** US Army; Lt.; **OTHER ACT & HONORS:** Bd. of Dir., Boys' Clubs Boston; Biltmore Racquet Club; **HOME ADD:** 137 Forest St., Sherborn, MA 01770, (617)653-8090; **BUS ADD:** 50 Staniford St., Suite 1000, Boston, MA 02114, (617)367-7620.

SCHAFER, Hans——B: Sept. 22, 1934, Baltimore, MD, *Pres.*, Hans Schafer, Inc.; **OTHER RE ACT:** Designer/Constr. Mgr.; **SERVICES:** Facility planning & const.; **PREV EMPLOY:** Union Memorial Hospital, Baltimore, MD, 1967-1971; Richland Mem. Hospital; **PROFL AFFIL & HONORS:** Amer. Hosp. Assn.; **MIL SERV:** USMC, Sgt., 1957-1959; **HOME ADD:** 183 Mariners Row, Columbia, SC 29210, (803)781-5351; **BUS ADD:** 183 Mariners Row, Columbia, SC 29210, (803)781-5351.

SCHAFER, Robert——B: Sept. 13, 1942, Syracuse, NY, *Atty.*, Casplar & Bok, RE; **PRIM RE ACT:** Attorney; **SERVICES:** Legal serv. for the entire range of RE devel. and mgmt. issues; **REP CLIENTS:** Owners, mgrs. and devel. of RE, lenders, arch., consultants; **PREV EMPLOY:** Prof. of Urban Planning, Harvard Univ., 1971-1979; Faculty Assoc., Joint Ctr. for Urban Studies of MIT and Harvard Univ., 1971-1979; **PROFL AFFIL & HONORS:** ABA; MA Bar Assn.; Amer. Econ. Assn., Listed in Who's Who in Amer. Law; **EDUC:** BS, 1961, Physics, Union Coll., **GRAD EDUC:** MS, 1965, Physics, Yale Univ.; JD, 1968, Law, Harvard Law School; PhD, 1973, Urban Econ., Harvard Univ.; **EDUC HONORS:** Summa Cum Laude, Phi Beta Kappa, Soc. of Sigma Xi, Nott Scholar, Prize Scholar, Editor in Chief, Harvard Civil Rights-Civil Liberties Law Review, Cum Laude, Grad. Prize Fellow, Travelling Fellow; **OTHER ACT & HONORS:** Citizens Housing and Planning Assn. of MA; Author of "Discrimination in Mort. Lending" (MIT Press, 1981); "Housing Urban Amer." (Aldine, 2nd ed., 1980) "The Suburbanization of Multifamily Housing" (Lexington Books, 1974); "A Place to Live: Housing Policy in the States" (Council of State Govts., 1974) and numerous articles; **HOME ADD:** 161 Lewis Rd., Belmont, MA 02178, (617)484-2589; **BUS ADD:** One Winthrop Sq., Boston, MA 02110, (617)357-4400.

SCHAFFER, Arnold C.——B: Apr. 26, 1925, Dayton, OH, *Owner*, Arnold C. Schaffer, Realtors; **PRIM RE ACT:** Broker, Appraiser, Developer, Builder, Owner/Investor, Property Manager; **SERVICES:** Comml., Warehouse/Distribution, Indus. Sites; **REP CLIENTS:** GMC, US Steel, E.F. MacDonald, Major Oil Cos.; **PREV EMPLOY:** US Navy, 1943-46 and 1950-52; **PROFL AFFIL & HONORS:** Nat., OH, Dayton Area Bds. of Realtors, Realtor; **EDUC:** BS, 1950, Bus. Admin., Univ. of Dayton; **MIL SERV:** USN; **OTHER ACT & HONORS:** Personnel Advisor, Awards Chmn., Sugarcreek Ski Patrol; Member of the Nat. Ski Patrol System; Voted the National Outstanding Ski Patrol 1980-81 Season; **BUS ADD:** 505 East Stroop Rd., Dayton, OH 45429, (513)294-1000.

SCHAFFER, Fred W.——*Treasurer*, Rohm & Haas Co.; **PRIM RE ACT:** Property Manager; **BUS ADD:** Independence Mall West, Philadelphia, PA 19105, (215)592-3000.*

SCHAFFRAN, E. Morton——B: Apr. 21, 1917, Brooklyn, NY, *Pres.*, E. M. Schaffran and Co.; **PRIM RE ACT:** Consultant, Developer; **SERVICES:** Research and devel. in multifamily housing; **REP CLIENTS:** Sponsors of multifamily housing projects, local governing bodies; **PREV EMPLOY:** Deputy Dir., Marin Cty. Housing Auth. and Redev. Agency 1957-58; Public Housing Admin. 1938-56; **PROFL AFFIL & HONORS:** Lambda Alpha (an Econ. Fraternity); **EDUC:** AB, 1937, Econ., Swarthmore Coll.; **GRAD EDUC:** MA, 1939, Housing and Planning, Columbia Univ.; **OTHER ACT & HONORS:** Past Pres., Mt. Diablo Council, Boy Scouts of Amer.; **HOME ADD:** 700 Hancock Way, El Cerrito, CA 94530, (415)525-5773; **BUS ADD:** 518 El Cerrito Plaza, El Cerrito, CA 94530, (415)526-1200.

SCHAFLER, Norman I.——*Chairman of the Board*, Condec Corp.; **PRIM RE ACT:** Property Manager; **BUS ADD:** 1700 E. Putnam Rd., Old Greenwich, CT 06870, (203)637-4511.*

SCHAIMAN, David S.——B: Oct. 4, 1933, Brooklyn, NY, *Sr. VP, Advisory Dir.*, Sonnenblick-Goldman Corp. and Lehman Bros. Kuhn Loeb, Inc.; **PRIM RE ACT:** Broker, Attorney, Owner/Investor; **OTHER RE ACT:** CPA; **SERVICES:** Sale and fin. of RE prop. by way of mort. loan, joint venture and equity participation; **REP CLIENTS:** Lenders, owners, devels. and instnl. and indiv. investors in income-producing RE props.; **PROFL AFFIL & HONORS:** Bar Assn. of the City of NY; MBA; NY RE Bd.; **EDUC:** BS, 1955, Econ., Wharton School, Univ. of PA; **GRAD EDUC:** JD, 1961, Law, Harvard Law School; **EDUC HONORS:** Beta Alpha Psi; Beta Gamma Sigma; **MIL SERV:** US Army; 1st Lt.; **HOME ADD:** 12 Old Farm Lane, Hartsdale, NY 10530, (914)428-0332; **BUS ADD:** 1251 Ave. of the Americas, New York, NY 10020, (212)541-4321.

SCHALL, John H.——B: Dec. 20, 1933, OH, *Broker*, Polk Realty; **PRIM RE ACT:** Broker; **SERVICES:** Appraisals, consulting; **PROFL AFFIL & HONORS:** NAR: Salem Multiple Listing Bureau; **OTHER ACT & HONORS:** Dallas Rotary Club; **HOME ADD:** 649 S.W. Hayter St., Dallas, OR 97338, (503)623-8779; **BUS ADD:** 990 E. Ellendale, Dallas, OR 97338, (503)623-8369.

SCHANG, Donald C.——B: Jan. 13, 1931, Louisville, KY, *Owner*, Donald C. Schang, Realtor; **PRIM RE ACT:** Broker; **SERVICES:** Comml., investment brokerage; **REP CLIENTS:** Major income prop. purchasers; **PROFL AFFIL & HONORS:** NAR; St. Pete. Bd. of Realtors; FL Assn. of Realtors; RNMI, Realtor; **EDUC:** BS, 1955, Commerce/Law, Univ. of KY; **MIL SERV:** USAF, Capt.; **HOME ADD:** 2149 Bayou Grande Blvd. N.E., St. Petersburg, FL 33703, (813)522-9954; **BUS ADD:** 2149 Bayou Grande Blvd. N.E., St. Petersburg, FL 33703, (813)522-2816.

SCHANK, David L.——B: Dec. 13, 1952, Louisville, KY, *RE Broker*, The Kessler Co's; **PRIM RE ACT:** Broker, Consultant, Developer, Builder, Owner/Investor, Property Manager, Syndicator; **OTHER RE ACT:** Exchanger; **REP CLIENTS:** Been involved in RE over 10 yrs.; **PREV EMPLOY:** Bass & Weisberg Comml. Investment Div.; **PROFL AFFIL & HONORS:** CO, RI, LA Bd.of Realtors; So. IN Bd. of Realtors; NAR; KY RE Exchangers; **HOME ADD:** 1129 Everett Ave., Apt. 1, Louisville, KY 40204, (502)454-4019; **BUS ADD:** 225 N. Clifton Ave., Louisville, KY 40206, (502)897-5284.

SCHAPIRO, Mervin B.——B: May 26, 1920, NY, NY, *Mgr.*, Dial Assoc., Inc. and Maxim Homes Inc.; **PRIM RE ACT:** Broker, Appraiser, Builder; **SERVICES:** Brokerage, appraising, bldg.; **PROFL AFFIL & HONORS:** NAHB; **EDUC:** BBA, 1947, Acctg., CCNY; **GRAD EDUC:** 1951, Mktg./Mgmt., NYU Grad. School of Bus. Admin.; **MIL SERV:** USA, S/Sgt.; **HOME ADD:** 30 Brookline Dr., Massapequa, NY 11758, (516)731-3669; **BUS ADD:** 4180 Sunrise Hwy., Massapequa, NY 11758, (516)541-4550.

SCHARCK, Ronald A.——**B:** Oct. 29, 1942, Houston, TX, *Pres.*, Ronald A. Scharck, Inc.; **PRIM RE ACT:** Broker, Consultant, Owner/Investor, Property Manager; **SERVICES:** Comml. investment sales, acquisitions, exchanges & Counseling; **PROFL AFFIL & HONORS:** NAR, RNMI, CCIM; **EDUC:** BBA, 1969, Fin., TX A & M Univ.; **HOME ADD:** 5218 Theall, Houston, TX 77066, (713)893-6941; **BUS ADD:** 5271 Memorial Dr., Houston, TX 77007, (713)869-7236.

SCHARF, Roy H.——**B:** May 30, 1928, Newark, NJ, *Atty. at Law*; **PRIM RE ACT:** Attorney; **SERVICES:** Law; **REP CLIENTS:** Builders and devels.; **PROFL AFFIL & HONORS:** ABA, CT Bar Assn., New Haven Cty. Bar Assn., Nat. Assn. of Home Builders; **EDUC:** BA, 1949, Univ. of CT; **GRAD EDUC:** LLB, 1952, Harvard Law Sch.; **HOME ADD:** 22 Beverly Rd., Hamden, CT 06514, (203)288-2949; **BUS ADD:** 127 Cedar St., PO Box 608, Branford, CT 06405, (203)481-5532.

SCHARLACH, Adrian E.——**B:** Nov. 10, 1917, San Francisco, CA, *Pres.*, S&H Prop. Inc., Adrian Rentals, Inc.; Remington Oil Co.; **PRIM RE ACT:** Owner/Investor; **OTHER RE ACT:** Corporate Executive/Investments; **EDUC:** 1938, Econ., Univ. of CA, Berkeley; **MIL SERV:** US Army, Capt., Bronze Star, 1943-46; **OTHER ACT & HONORS:** VP/Sec. Concordia Argonaut Club, Pres. E. Bay Hotel Assn.; **BUS ADD:** PO Box 15428, San Francisco, CA 94115, (415)435-2687.

SCHATTON, Norman P.——**B:** May 19, 1917, NYC, NY, *Mgr. Comml. Dept. (Sr. VP)*, Alexander Summer Co.; **PRIM RE ACT:** Broker, Consultant, Owner/Investor; **OTHER RE ACT:** Shopping Ctr. Sales & Leasing Spec.; **REP CLIENTS:** Prud. Insurance Co.; Allied Stores Corp.; **PREV EMPLOY:** 26 years in present position; **PROFL AFFIL & HONORS:** NAREB; ICSC; **EDUC:** 1937, Econ., Brooklyn Coll.; **GRAD EDUC:** LLB, 1940, Law, Brooklyn Law School; **MIL SERV:** Completion Corps Military Police, 1943-46, 1st Lt., Pacific Theatre, Good Conduct, etc.; **OTHER ACT & HONORS:** Jewish War Veterans, I.O.O.F.; Bergen Symphony Soc.; **HOME ADD:** 4 Horizon Rd., Fort Lee, NJ 07024, (201)886-9132; **BUS ADD:** 222 Cedar Ln., Teaneck, NJ 07666, (201)836-4500.

SCHATZBERG, Sy——**B:** Mar. 18, 1925, NYC, *VP*, J.I. Kislak Realty Corp., Investment Dept.; **PRIM RE ACT:** Broker; **EDUC:** BS, 1953, RE, NY Univ.; **MIL SERV:** USAF, Cpl.; **HOME ADD:** 37-02 Lenox Dr., Fair Lawn, NJ 07410, (201)791-1417; **BUS ADD:** 581 Broad St., Newark, NJ 07102, (201)624-8000.

SCHAUB, James K.——**B:** June 11, 1953, Chicago, IL, *VP, Planning and Acquisitions*, International Development and Marketing, Inc.; **PRIM RE ACT:** Broker, Developer; **OTHER RE ACT:** Restaurant site location, resid. land devel., cost appraisal; **EDUC:** BA, RE Fin. Appraisal, Law, Devel., FL State Univ.; **HOME ADD:** 5550 NW 44th St. 412B, Ft. Lauderdale, FL 33319; **BUS ADD:** 3300 Inverrary Blvd., Lauderhill, FL 33319, (305)739-6650.

SCHAUDER, Frederick——*VP Fin. & Treas.*, Raybestos-Manhattan, Inc.; **PRIM RE ACT:** Property Manager; **BUS ADD:** 100 Oakview Drive, Trumbull, CT 06611, (203)371-0101.*

SCHEBOR, Ronald R.——**B:** Jan. 8, 1937, Dearborn, MI, *VP*, Hometrend of MI, Inc.; **PRIM RE ACT:** Broker; **SERVICES:** RE Franchise; **PREV EMPLOY:** Ladd's Inc., Hometrent (RE Mgmt).; **PROFL AFFIL & HONORS:** NAR, RNMI, MI Assn. of Realtors, CRB, CRS, GRI designations; **HOME ADD:** 18 N. Holcomb, Clarkston, MI 48016, (313)625-1591; **BUS ADD:** 4086 Rochester Rd., Troy, MI 48098, (313)689-1515.

SCHECHTER, Howard——**B:** Feb. 11, 1952, New York, NY, *Atty.*, Law Offices of Howard Schechter; **PRIM RE ACT:** Attorney, Consultant; **OTHER RE ACT:** Co-op/Condo Conversion Specialist; **PROFL AFFIL & HONORS:** Dir. NY State Assn. of Renewal & Housing Officials, Inc.; Real Prop. Law Section of NY State Bar Assn.; **EDUC:** BA, 1972, NY Univ.; **GRAD EDUC:** JD, 1975, NY Univ. Law School; **EDUC HONORS:** Phi Beta Kappa, Cum Laude; **OTHER ACT & HONORS:** Pres. Marchant Park Civic Assn.; **BUS ADD:** 10 Columbus Cir., Room 1200, New York, NY 10019, (212)957-7900.

SCHECHTER, Robert——**B:** June 20, 1922, New York City, NY, *Pres.*, Robert Schechter & Co., Pres., Monmouth Freehold Indus. Park Inc.; **PRIM RE ACT:** Broker, Consultant, Developer, Owner/Investor, Property Manager; **SERVICES:** Indus. prop. devel. and mgmt. of over 1,000,000 sq. feet of buildings, consultant; **REP CLIENTS:** Koppers Co., Titeflex Co., Lear-Siegler Inc. Lehigh Valley Indus. Inc., Newell Cols Inc., various other natl. listed cos.; **EDUC:** BS, 1948, Acctg. & Fin., Rutgers Univ.; **EDUC HONORS:** SBA Honors Award; **MIL SERV:** US Army; Lt.; Field Commission, Europe; **OTHER ACT & HONORS:** Trustee, Amer. Jewish Comm., Essex Cty., NJ; **HOME ADD:** 8 Windsor Dr., Livingston, NJ, (201)992-5989; **BUS ADD:** 600 S. Livingston Ave., Livingston, NJ 07039, (201)678-6600.

SCHECHTER, Stuart A.——**B:** Mar. 24, 1943, Brooklyn, NY, *Partner*, Jacobson, Schechter and Lewis; **PRIM RE ACT:** Consultant, Attorney, Owner/Investor; **SERVICES:** Investment counseling, deal structuring; **REP CLIENTS:** Indiv. investors in various types of RE investments; **PREV EMPLOY:** Dreyer & Traub, 1968; **PROFL AFFIL & HONORS:** So. Broward Bar Assn.; FL Bar; Lawyers Title Guaranty Fund; New York Bar, Designated Specialist in Real Prop. Law; **EDUC:** BA, 1964, Govt., Clark Univ.; **GRAD EDUC:** JD, 1967, NY Univ. School of Law; **HOME ADD:** 3140 N. 52nd Ave., Hollywood, FL 33021, (305)981-7117; **BUS ADD:** 3363 Sheridan St., Hollywood, FL 33021, (305)962-1600.

SCHECTER, Jack H.——**B:** Mar. 22, 1916, Montgomery, AL, *Architect*, Office of Jack H. Schecter-AIA-Architect; **PRIM RE ACT:** Architect; **SERVICES:** Planning, site design, gen. arch.; **REP CLIENTS:** Bridgeport Housing Authority, New Haven Housing Authority; **PROFL AFFIL & HONORS:** CT Chap. of the AIA; Bridgeport Assn. of Architects; **EDUC:** Brooklyn Tech.; **GRAD EDUC:** Pratt Inst. Arch.; **EDUC HONORS:** First Award, Registered Architect CT, NY, NJ, FL; **OTHER ACT & HONORS:** VP Arch. Reg. Bd. State of CT Emeritus; Head of Research CT Ch. of AIA; Bd. of Govs. AIA Emeritus; Arch. Advisor, YMCA Boys Club; Jewish Community Center; Bridgeport BD. of Govs.; **HOME ADD:** 20 Cedarwoods Lane, Fairfield, CT 06432, (203)372-6981; **BUS ADD:** 144 Goldenhill St., Bridgeport, CT 06604, (203)334-0189.

SCHEELER, John E.——**B:** Dec. 26, 1930, Baltimore, MD, *Corp. Mgr./Asst. VP*, Honolulu Ltd./3900 Corp.; **PRIM RE ACT:** Consultant, Property Manager; **OTHER RE ACT:** Acct.; **PREV EMPLOY:** The Hentschel Org., RE Lic., Comml. RE Appraiser & Broker; **PROFL AFFIL & HONORS:** The Greater Baltimore Bd. of Realtors; MD RE License, Assoc. Realtor; **EDUC:** AA, 1976, Fin. Acctg.; BS, 1980, Acctg., Thomas A. Edison Coll.; **MIL SERV:** USMC, E-7, 1947-1970; **OTHER ACT & HONORS:** Knights of Columbus, 3rd Degree, Council 7025; Fleet Reserve Assn.; Marine Corp. Assn.; **HOME ADD:** 7624 3rd Ave., Glen Burnie, MD 21061, (301)766-7996; **BUS ADD:** 5518 Baltimore Nat. Pike, Baltimore, MD 21228, (301)744-6142.

SCHEFMEYER, Donald H.——**B:** Aug. 29, 1947, Nyack, NY, *VP, Dept. Mgr.*, Tower Fed. S & L Assn., Comml. RE Fin., Mort. Banking; **PRIM RE ACT:** Broker, Instructor, Syndicator, Consultant, Appraiser, Developer, Lender, Owner/Investor; **REP CLIENTS:** Major instl. investors nationwide; **PREV EMPLOY:** 1977-80 Sr. VP Whitcomb & Keller Mort. Co., Inc., S. Bend, IN; 1972-77 V.P., H.J. Ludington, Inc., Rochester, NY; **PROFL AFFIL & HONORS:** SREA, Natl. Assn. of Review Appraisers, Mort. Bankers Assn., Awarded SRPA designation 1979, CRA designation 1980; **EDUC:** BA, 1969, Engrg., Syracuse Univ.; **EDUC HONORS:** Cum Laude (Eng.); **MIL SERV:** USAR; E-5, 1971-76; **OTHER ACT & HONORS:** Sigma Chi Frat. Alumni; Masons; Cert. Instr. for the SREA; Lecturer for Mort. Bankers Assn. on Income Prop.; **HOME ADD:** 19325 Sundale Dr., S. Bend, IN 46614, (219)291-2366; **BUS ADD:** 216 W. Wash. Ave., S. Bend, IN 46614, (219)234-7171.

SCHEIDLER, Donald——*VP*, KDI Corp.; **PRIM RE ACT:** Property Manager; **BUS ADD:** Dragon Way, Cincinnati, OH 45227, (513)272-1421.*

SCHEIDT, Virgil——*Chmn*, Indiana, Indiana Real Estate Commission; **PRIM RE ACT:** Property Manager; **BUS ADD:** 636 3rd St., Columbus, IN 47201, (812)372-8201.*

SCHEK, Leslie G.——*VP Adm. & Fin.*, Noxell Corp.; **PRIM RE ACT:** Property Manager; **BUS ADD:** PO Box 1799, Baltimore, MD 21203, (301)628-7300.*

SCHEMBRI, Stephen A.——**B:** Mar. 9, 1940, NY, NY, *Asst. VP/RE Spec.*, Citibank N.A., Brooklyn-Staten Is. Region; **PRIM RE ACT:** Instructor, Consultant, Appraiser, Banker; **SERVICES:** Officer in charge of RE, Bus. Devel., lending for Brooklyn/SI Reg. of Citibank; **PROFL AFFIL & HONORS:** AIREA, SREA, MAI, SREA; **MIL SERV:** USMCR, E-5; **HOME ADD:** 10 Robin Ln., Kings Park, NY 11754, (516)269-3835; **BUS ADD:** 181 Montague St., Brooklyn, NY 11201, (212)330-9568.

SCHENCK, Harold E., II——**B:** June 29, 1943, Dayton, OH, *Chief Appraiser*, Muskegon Fed. S&L Assn.; **PRIM RE ACT:** Appraiser; **SERVICES:** Appraisals for mort. lending; **PREV EMPLOY:** Staff Appraiser for Gem City Savings, Dayton, OH 1968-1977; **PROFL AFFIL & HONORS:** Sr. Resid. Appraiser - SREA, VP Chap. 91,

SREA; **EDUC:** Jr. Acct., 1962, Miami Jacobs Coll.; **OTHER ACT & HONORS:** Pres.-Muskegon Noon Y's Men's Club; **HOME ADD:** 2087 Seminole Rd., Muskegon, MI 49441, (616)780-2111; **BUS ADD:** 880 First St., Muskegon, MI 49440, (616)726-4461.

SCHENK, Walter H.——B: Nov. 3, 1937, Philadelphia, PA, *Sec. Partner, Owner*, Wm. Schenk Const. Co., Inc., Wm. Shenk & Sons; **PRIM RE ACT:** Consultant, Developer, Lender, Builder, Owner/Investor, Property Manager, Syndicator; **SERVICES:** All phases of const. programs & mgmt.; **EDUC:** PA State Univ., 1960, RE & Bus. Fin.; **MIL SERV:** USNR, 3rd. Class; **OTHER ACT & HONORS:** Past Pres., Philmont Kiwanis; **HOME ADD:** 2331 Stahl Rd., Huntington Valley, PA 19006; **BUS ADD:** Shady Ln. & Rockledge Ave., Rockledge, PA 19111, (215)379-5505.

SCHENKEL, James J.——B: Mar. 21, 1933, Ft. Wayne, IN, *Pres.*, Schenkel & Shultz, Inc.; **PRIM RE ACT:** Architect, Owner/Investor; **SERVICES:** Arch., int. design & space planning, mech. elec., struct. & civil engrg.; **REP CLIENTS:** Office bldgs., shopping ctrs., comml. bldgs.; **PROFL AFFIL & HONORS:** AIA; NCARB; Bd. Member, IN Arch. Found.; **EDUC:** BA, 1956, Arch., Univ. of Notre Dame; **MIL SERV:** US Army, Capt., 1957-1959; **OTHER ACT & HONORS:** Member Bd. of Dir., Anthony Wayne Bank; **HOME ADD:** 5022 Midlothian Dr., Ft. Wayne, IN 46815, (219)485-5012; **BUS ADD:** 3702 Rupp Dr., Ft. Wayne, IN 46815, (219)484-9080.

SCHENKER, Michael S.——B: Oct. 23, 1946, Hartford, CT, *Partner, Hempstead & Schenker*; **PRIM RE ACT:** Attorney; **SERVICES:** Legal rep. with regard to the purchase and sale of prop.; **REP CLIENTS:** Title ins. cos. and special counsel to devels.; **PROFL AFFIL & HONORS:** ABA, CT Bar Assn., New England Land Title Assn.; **EDUC:** BChE, 1969, Cornell Univ.; **GRAD EDUC:** JD, 1974, Cornell Law School; **HOME ADD:** 51 Munnisunk Dr., Simsbury, CT 06070, (203)658-6957; **BUS ADD:** 60 Washington St., Hartford, CT 06106, (203)522-2500.

SCHENKER, Sidney——B: Jan. 22, 1908, Paterson, NJ, *Partner*, Schenker & Schenker Architects & Planners; **PRIM RE ACT:** Consultant, Architect, Developer, Owner/Investor, Property Manager; **SERVICES:** Planning, Arch., Des. Building, Merchandising Layout Consultant Retail Stores, Energy Consultant, Motion Picture Theatre Consultant; **PROFL AFFIL & HONORS:** AIA, Amer. Instit. of Theatre Technol.; **EDUC:** BArch, 1931, Design & Construction, NY Univ. Coll. of Arch. & Allied Arts; **EDUC HONORS:** Grad. - Magna Cum Laude, Winner - Vegliante Award - Arch. League, NJ Chap. AIA; **OTHER ACT & HONORS:** Pres. - NJ State Bd. of Arch.; Bd. Member - Jewish Family Serv. '80-'81 of NJ; Bd. Member - Jewish Fed. of NJ; **HOME ADD:** 130 E. 39th St., Paterson, NJ 05714, (201)278-4818; **BUS ADD:** Thirty Five Church St., Paterson, NJ 07505, (201)278-7171.

SCHENKMAN, Eugene——B: Aug. 5, 1923, NJ, *Partner*, Campus Dr. Assocs., Hocroft Assocs., Somerville Industrial Park; **PRIM RE ACT:** Attorney, Developer, Builder, Owner/Investor; **SERVICES:** Devel. of comml. & indus. prop.; **PROFL AFFIL & HONORS:** Somerset Cty. Bar Assn.; NJ State Bar Assn.; **EDUC:** BA, 1950, Rutgers Univ.; **GRAD EDUC:** LLB, 1950, Rutgers Law School; **MIL SERV:** USN; **HOME ADD:** 16 Northern Dr., Bridgewater, NJ 08807, (201)725-1997; **BUS ADD:** 1011 Rt. 22, PO Box 6622, Bridgewater, NJ 08807, (201)725-8100.

SCHETTL, Gary S.——B: Feb. 10, 1949, Dearborn, MI, *Dir. of Consulting Services*, Laventhol & Horwath, Management Advisory Services; **PRIM RE ACT:** Consultant; **SERVICES:** Investment analysis, feasibility consulting; valuation, project analysis; **REP CLIENTS:** Lenders, devels., synds., hotel co's., land use planners, resort lenders/devels.; **PROFL AFFIL & HONORS:** MBA; CO/WY Hotel Assn.; Resort and Condo. Comm.; **EDUC:** BS, Bus. Admin., 1971, Hotel, Restaurant and Instnl. Mgmt., MI State Univ.; **GRAD EDUC:** MBA, 1973, Fin., MI State Univ.; **EDUC HONORS:** Cum Laude; **HOME ADD:** 1583 Ogden St., Denver, CO 80218, (303)837-9838; **BUS ADD:** 1800 Emerson St., Denver, CO 80218, (303)861-2500.

SCHIEBER, Frank W.——B: June 18, 1928, Phila., PA, *Pres, Sec. Treas.*, Gould Realty Corp.; **PRIM RE ACT:** Broker, Consultant, Appraiser, Owner/Investor, Instructor, Syndicator; **OTHER RE ACT:** Mort. Broker, fin. consultant; **SERVICES:** Consulting, exchanges, appraisals, comml. investments, land assemblage, joint ventures, const. & permanent loans, refinancing refunding, wraparound morts.; **REP CLIENTS:** Indivs., instnl. investors and corps. in RE and non-RE related investments and/or loans; **PREV EMPLOY:** Simplified Tax Records, 1954-58, Owner; H & M Const. Co., 1962-63; Gen. Sales Mgr.; Gulf Amer. Land Corp., 1963-65, Housing sales; **PROFL AFFIL & HONORS:** FL Assn. of Realtors, NAR, Cape Coral Bd. of Realtors, Nat. Assn. of Mort. Brokers, FL Assn. of Mort. Brokers, RNMI, FLI, RESSI, IREF, Int. Council of Shopping Ctrs., GRI, FL Cert. 4, CCIM 555, AFLM 438, CRS; **EDUC:** BS, 1951, Mktg., Econ. & Fin., Babson Coll.; **MIL SERV:** USAF, Aviation Cadet; **OTHER ACT & HONORS:** Ex-adjunct prof., Univ. of FL, teaching RE investments, fin. & appraisals, VP, FL Assn. of Realtors, 1979; Pres. Cape Coral Bd. of Realtors, 1951; Realtor of the Yr., 1951; Nat. Sec. Assn. Boss of the Year, 1951; VP Cape Coral C of C, 1970; Pres. Cape Coral Dad's Club, 1965; Co-chmn. Cape Coral Parks and Rec. Comm., 1970; Charter Dir. Cape Coral Republican Club, 1965; Charter Dir. Cape Coral Swim Assn., AAU, 1966; **HOME ADD:** 5929 SW 1st Ct., Cape Coral, FL 33904, (813)542-4653; **BUS ADD:** Ste. 325, First Fed. Bldg., 4732 Del Prado Blvd., Cape Coral, FL 33904, (813)542-2033.

SCHIEFELBEIN, Wayne L.——B: Sept. 27, 1953, Manhattan, NYC, *VP Regulatory Affairs; Interval International, Inc.*, VP Regulatory Affairs for Interval International, Inc.; **PRIM RE ACT:** Attorney, Regulator, Real Estate Publisher; **SERVICES:** Exec. Editor of the *Time Sharing Encyclopedia*, authoritative Indus. Reference work, and the *Time Sharing Indus. Review*, Monthly indus. periodical; **PREV EMPLOY:** Legal Asst., Davis and Langer, P.A., S. Miami FL, specialists in time share project documentation; **PROFL AFFIL & HONORS:** FL Bar, ABA, Dade Cty. Bar Assn.; **EDUC:** BA, 1975, Intl. Relations, Univ. of AZ; **GRAD EDUC:** JD, 1978, Law, Univ. of Miami School of Law; **EDUC HONORS:** Degree awarded "with distinction"; **HOME ADD:** 9896 N. Kendall Dr. C-108, Miami, FL 33176, (305)595-1197; **BUS ADD:** 7000 S.W. 62nd Ave., Ste. 306, Coral Gables, FL 33143, (305)667-0202.

SCHIEFFEN, Michael——*Dir. Corp. Dev.*, Sybron Corp.; **PRIM RE ACT:** Property Manager; **BUS ADD:** 1100 Midtown Tower, Rochester, NY 14604, (716)546-4040.*

SCHIFFER, Joseph Gill——B: July 27, 1934, New York, NY, *Pres.*, Joseph Gill Schiffer and Associates, Market Dynamics; **PRIM RE ACT:** Broker, Consultant, Developer, Instructor, Property Manager; **SERVICES:** Co-op and condo conversion of existing props., feasibility/mkt. analysis for investors & builders, prop. search, negotiation & devel.; **REP CLIENTS:** Investors domestic and intl., builders; **PREV EMPLOY:** VP, Mktg., The Gale Org.; Mktg. Dir., Levitt & Sons; **EDUC:** BS, 1956, NY Univ.; **GRAD EDUC:** 1977, RE Inst., C.W. Post, Sch. of Bus. Admin.; **MIL SERV:** US Army, Lt.; **OTHER ACT & HONORS:** Instr., RE, South Huntington (NY) Public School Adult Educ.; **HOME ADD:** 27 Craig Dr., South Huntington, NY 11746; **BUS ADD:** 10 Mitchell Rd., Westhampton Beach, NY 11746, (516)288-1818.

SCHIFFER, Tom R.——B: Oct. 17, 1933, Cincinnati, OH, *Sales Counselor, Assoc. Broker*, Albuquerque Gallery of Homes; **PRIM RE ACT:** Broker; **SERVICES:** Relocation expertise, equity advance, luxury rentals, land & comml.; **REP CLIENTS:** IBM, GTE-Lenkurt Div., Xerox, Sandia Labs; **PROFL AFFIL & HONORS:** National Asso. of Realtors, Realtors Asso. of NM, Albuquerque Bd. of Realtors, GRI, CRB, CRS, also Albuquerque Bd. of Realtors-Leading Producer 1977 & 1979, Albuquerque Bd. of Realtors-Salesman of The Year 1979, Gallery of Homes Lifetime Member Pres. Sales Counselor (Highest Award on Nat. Level)-honored 5 years consecutively; **EDUC:** BBA, 1955, Marketing & Merchandising, Miami Univ., Oxford, OH; **MIL SERV:** US Army, M/Sgt.; **HOME ADD:** 1436 Catron SE, Albuquerque, NM 87123, (505)292-3222; **BUS ADD:** 12800 Lomas Blvd. NE, Albuquerque, NM 87123, (505)298-7438.

SCHIFFMAN, Martin——B: Feb. 15, 1949, New York, NY, *Pres.*, Lehman Realty Corp.; **PRIM RE ACT:** Broker, Consultant, Syndicator; **SERVICES:** RE Investment Banking; **REP CLIENTS:** Clients and Partners of Lehman Brothers Kuhn Loeb Inc.; **PREV EMPLOY:** VP, Manchester Advisory Corp.; VP, Sonnenblick Goldman Advisory Corp.; **PROFL AFFIL & HONORS:** Young Mort. Bankers Assn.; RE Bd. of NY; **EDUC:** BBA, 1970, Econ., Bernard Baruch Coll.; **GRAD EDUC:** MUP, 1972, Econ., NYU; **HOME ADD:** 555 North Ave., Fort Lee, NJ 07024, (201)947-9871; **BUS ADD:** 1251 Ave. of Americas, New York, NY 10020, (212)245-5790.

SCHILKE, Neil W.——B: Jan. 30, 1934, Tobias, NE, *Partner*, Sidner, Svoboda, Schilke, Wiseman & Thomsen; **PRIM RE ACT:** Attorney; **SERVICES:** Legal rep.; **REP CLIENTS:** NE State S&L Assn., First Natl. Bank of Hooper, First Natl. Bank & Trust, Fremont, NE, First State Bank, Fremont, NE; **PREV EMPLOY:** Legal counsel Phillips Petroleum; **PROFL AFFIL & HONORS:** ABA; **EDUC:** BA, 1958, Eng. and Hist., Midland Coll.; **GRAD EDUC:** LLB, 1961, Law, Coll. of William and Mary; **EDUC HONORS:** Blue Key Honorary, Outstanding Student Award, Law Review, Winner Richmond Title Will Contest, Moot Court, Outstanding Student Award; **MIL SERV:** Army Air Borne, Corp.; **OTHER ACT & HONORS:** Bd. of Trustees, Midland Coll., YMCA, YMCA Found., Community Found., Salvation Army Advisory Bd., First National Bank, Hooper; **HOME ADD:** Rt. 5, Fremont, NE 68025, (402)628-8139; **BUS ADD:** 505 N. Main St.,

Fremont, NE 68025, (402)721-7111.

SCHILLING, Christopher J.——**B:** July 10, 1951, Medina, NY, *Atty.*, Jones & Foster PA; **PRIM RE ACT:** Attorney; **SERVICES:** Gen. RE practice; **PROFL AFFIL & HONORS:** Real prop., probate & trust law sects. of ABA & the FL Bar Assn.; **EDUC:** BA, 1974, Econ., Univ. of FL; **GRAD EDUC:** JD, 1976, Univ. of FL; **EDUC HONORS:** with honors, order of the coif; **HOME ADD:** 902 Orange Dr., Lake Park, FL 33403, (305)844-8414; **BUS ADD:** 601 Flagler Dr. Ct., Drawer E, W. Palm Beach, FL 33402, (305)659-3000.

SCHILPP, Frank O., Jr.——**B:** Sept. 3, 1937, Philadelphia, PA, *Owner*, F.O. Schilpp Realty; **PRIM RE ACT:** Broker, Consultant; **SERVICES:** Full serv. comml. indus. RE; **PROFL AFFIL & HONORS:** Soc. of Indus. Realtors, Mrkt. Inst. of the Nat. Assn. of Realtors, Soc. of Indus. Realtors; CCIM Candidate; **EDUC:** BS, 1973, Bus., Inter-Amer. Univ./St. German, PR; **MIL SERV:** USAF, Capt.; **HOME ADD:** 9513 Tee Ln., Wichita, KS 67212, (316)722-1142; **BUS ADD:** Fourth Fin. Ctr., Suite 645, Wichita, KS 67202, (316)265-7047.

SCHIMMEL, Alfred——**B:** Sept. 22, 1915, NY, NY, *RE Appraiser and Econ. Analyst*, Alfred Schimmel A.S.A.; **PRIM RE ACT:** Consultant, Appraiser, Instructor; **SERVICES:** RE appraisals; feasibility studies; **REP CLIENTS:** Banks, govt. agencies, comml. lenders, pvt. indiv.; **PREV EMPLOY:** VP and Chief Appraiser - Douglas L. Elliman Co., N.Y.S. Banking Dept., NYC Planning Dept.; **PROFL AFFIL & HONORS:** Amer. Soc. of Appraisers, RE Bd. of NY, Amer. Fin. Assn., NY State Inst. of Assessors, Fellow - NY State Inst. of Assessors, Sr. Member and Past Pres. NY Chap. of Amer. Soc. of Appraisers; **EDUC:** BSS, 1935, Soc. Sci., CUNY; **GRAD EDUC:** MS, 1932, Education, CUNY; **MIL SERV:** US Army, T/Sgt., Bronze Star; **HOME ADD:** 1005 Jerome Ave., Bronx, NY 10452, (212)538-4321; **BUS ADD:** 250 W. 57th St., NY, NY 10107, (212)489-9553.

SCHIMPFF, Thomas F., Jr.——**B:** Nov. 12, 1939, Cincinnati, OH, *Asst. RE Mgr.*, Cincinnati Milacron Inc., Corporate; **PRIM RE ACT:** Consultant, Property Manager; **SERVICES:** Negotiate leases, assist in purchase & sale of RE; **EDUC:** Engrg., Acctg., & RE, Univ. of Cincinnati; **OTHER ACT & HONORS:** Councilman/Woodlawn, OH/1967-69; **HOME ADD:** 5040 St. Rt. 222, Batavia, OH 45103, (513)732-0352; **BUS ADD:** 4701 Marburg Ave., Cincinnati, OH 45209, (513)841-8924.

SCHINDLER, Elmer V.——**B:** Nov. 21, 1923, Akron, OH, *N.E. Regional Prop. Mgr.*, The Equitable Life Assurance Soc. of the US, RE Operations; **PRIM RE ACT:** Instructor, Consultant, Property Manager, Owner/Investor; **OTHER RE ACT:** Prop. mgmt., supervise corp. mgmt.; monitor mgmt agents; **SERVICES:** Leasing, accounting, operations, training; **REP CLIENTS:** Soc. prop. only; **PREV EMPLOY:** Oliver Tyrone Corp. RE Dev., 1965-1977; Bates & Springer, Inc., managing agents, 1960-1965; **PROFL AFFIL & HONORS:** NY BOMA, Amer. Arbitration Assn., Soc. of Real Prop Admin., founding member; **EDUC:** AB, 1949, Eng., Soc, Yale Univ; **EDUC HONORS:** Sr. Thesis; **MIL SERV:** USAF, Capt., DFC, Air Medal; **HOME ADD:** 41 Polly Dr, Huntington, NY 11743, (516)549-5170; **BUS ADD:** 1350 Ave. of the Americas, NY, NY 10019, (212)307-0296.

SCHINDLER, Tobias——**B:** Mar. 29, 1921, Sioux City, IA, *Pres.*, Schindlers, Inc.; **PRIM RE ACT:** Developer, Owner/Investor, Property Manager; **SERVICES:** Resid. devel.-both rental and sales; **REP CLIENTS:** Presently operate 4 sect. 08 projects-291 units, 100 additional units scheduled for const. in immediate future. also working on 420 units townhouse build & sell; **EDUC:** 2 yrs.-Bus. Admin.; **MIL SERV:** USAF, Lt. Col., Retired, 23 yrs., Pilot & Fin. Mgmt.; Distinguished Flying Cross, 7 Air Medals, French Croix de Guerre, plus many others; **HOME ADD:** 2875 Sunset Dr., Camp Hill, PA 17011, (717)737-9908; **BUS ADD:** 451 N. 21st St., Camp Hill, PA 17011, (717)763-7193.

SCHINKEL, Douglas A.——**B:** Apr. 12, 1951, Webster, SD, *RE Broker*, Investment Broker Assoc.; **PRIM RE ACT:** Broker, Instructor, Consultant, Appraiser, Property Manager, Owner/Investor; **SERVICES:** RE Investment planning and lecturing; **PROFL AFFIL & HONORS:** State and Nat. Realtor Assn. and Local Bd., GRI; **EDUC:** BS, 1973, Bus./Fin., Northern State Coll., SD; **HOME ADD:** 9755 Cavell Ave., S. Bloomington, MN 55438, (612)941-2070; **BUS ADD:** 5100 Industrial Blvd., Suite +201, Edina, MN 55435, (612)835-0165.

SCHLAIFER, Jack I.——**B:** Sept. 12, 1929, Los Angeles, CA, *Dir.*, Brokers & Builders, Inc., Indus. Grp.; **PRIM RE ACT:** Broker, Developer, Owner/Investor, Property Manager, Syndicator; **SERVICES:** Brokerage, indus. & comml. RE, gen partner, devel., prop. mgmts., leasing & sales; **REP CLIENTS:** Investors and users, manufacturers, warehouse, distributors, R&D firms; **PREV EMPLOY:** Sales Assoc., Indus Park. Assocs., 1976-80; Exec. VP, Partner, Alfred J. Allen & Assoc., 1970-76; **PROFL AFFIL & HONORS:** AIREA; Indus. Assn. of San Fernando Valley; **EDUC:** 1948-51, Bus. Admin., CA State at Los Angeles; **MIL SERV:** USA; S/Sgt.; 1951-53, Army of Occupation; **OTHER ACT & HONORS:** VP Bd. of Dirs. Temple Beth Hillel, N. Hollywood; **HOME ADD:** 5222 Longridge Ave., Van Nuys, CA 91401, (213)986-0562; **BUS ADD:** 5850 Canoga Ave., Suite 210, Woodland Hills, CA 91367, (213)992-8322.

SCHLANBUSCH, Ernest G.——**B:** June 12, 1921, MN, *Broker/Salesman*, Wm. L. Kunkel & Co., Realtors, Comml. Investment; **PRIM RE ACT:** Broker, Consultant, Owner/Investor; **OTHER RE ACT:** RE Exchangor; **SERVICES:** RE Sales, Leasing, Exchanging, Devel., Investment Counseling; **REP CLIENTS:** Indiv. Investors, Prop. Owners, Lenders, Corp's., Non-Profit Instn's.; **PROFL AFFIL & HONORS:** RNMI; RESSI; IL Assn. of Realtors; Central Assn. of RE Exchangors; O'Hare Grp. Realtors for Bus. & Indus., GRI; CCIM; **EDUC:** BA, 1943, Phys. Sci/Psych., St. Olaf Coll., MN; **GRAD EDUC:** Grad. Study, 1947-1949, Bus./Indus. Psych., OH State Univ.; **MIL SERV:** USAF, Capt., 1943-1947; **OTHER ACT & HONORS:** Pres., O'Hare Grp. - Realtors for Bus. and Indus.; **HOME ADD:** 851 E. Grant Dr., Des Plaines, IL 60016, (312)827-4790; **BUS ADD:** 880 Lee St., Des Plaines, IL 60016, (312)298-9555.

SCHLANGEN, William M.——**B:** Apr. 20, 1929, Chicago, IL, *Pres.*, Columbia Pacific Construction; **PRIM RE ACT:** Broker, Developer, Builder, Owner/Investor, Property Manager, Syndicator; **SERVICES:** RE brokerage, prop. mgmt., RE investments and construction; **REP CLIENTS:** Indiv. investors in comml. props.; **PROFL AFFIL & HONORS:** Sonoma County Bd. of Realtors, CA Assn. of Realtors, ICSC, Intl. RE Fed., North Coast Builders Exchange, FIABCI; **EDUC:** BA, 1951, Hist. and Philosophy, Amherst Coll.; **GRAD EDUC:** MBA, 1957, Mktg., Harvard Bus. School; **MIL SERV:** USN, Lt., Korean Service Medal w/7 Battle Stars & President's Unit Citation Medal; **OTHER ACT & HONORS:** President Geyserville Unified School Bd.; Univ. Club of San Francisco; Wild Oak Saddle Club; Sonoma Cty. Trailblazers; Rotary Intl.; **HOME ADD:** 1000 Buckeye Rd., Kenwood, CA 95452, (707)539-7157; **BUS ADD:** 290 B Street, Suite 220, Santa Rosa, CA 95401, (707)546-5753.

SCHLECTE, William M.——**B:** Oct. 21, 1947, Pontiac, MI, *VP/Sec.*, Brimacombe & Schlecte, P.C.; **PRIM RE ACT:** Attorney, Instructor; **SERVICES:** Legal counseling; **REP CLIENTS:** Indiv., RE licensees, devels.; **PROFL AFFIL & HONORS:** ABA, Real Prop. & Litigation Sects., State Bar of MI, Amer. Trial Lawyers Assn., Lawyer-Pilot Bar Assn.; **EDUC:** BA, 1969, Econ., Univ. of MI; **GRAD EDUC:** JD, 1972, Univ. of MI Law Sch.; **EDUC HONORS:** Cum Laude; **HOME ADD:** 2100 Devonshire, Ann Arbor, MI 48104; **BUS ADD:** 3135 S. State, Suite 208, Ann Arbor, MI 48104, (313)769-3330.

SCHLEE, Merrill O.——**B:** June 23, 1944, Lyons, NY, *Atty.*, Merrill O. Schlee; **PRIM RE ACT:** Attorney; **SERVICES:** Legal Serv.; **REP CLIENTS:** Mort. closings for lending instns. and all legal serv. for indiv.; **PROFL AFFIL & HONORS:** NY State Bar Assn.; Wayne Cty. Bar Assn. (VP); **EDUC:** BA, 1966, Liberal Arts, St. Lawrence Univ.; **GRAD EDUC:** JD, 1969, Law, Albany Law School of Union Univ.; **OTHER ACT & HONORS:** Asst. Dist. Atty. Wayne Cty., 1973-1979; Acting Justice Village of Sodus, 1972-73; **HOME ADD:** 5767 Lasher Rd., Wolcott, NY 14590, (315)594-2940; **BUS ADD:** 46 W. Main St., P.O. Box 249, Sodus, NY 14551, (315)483-6733.

SCHLEGEL, William J.——**B:** Oct. 21,1925, Jacumba, CA, *Broker*, Totem Realty Inc.; **PRIM RE ACT:** Broker, Syndicator, Consultant, Developer, Builder; **SERVICES:** RE Counseling, Synd. of Props., Dev. of Lands & Comml. Prop. Builder; **REP CLIENTS:** Home & Comml. Builder Rep., Investors; **PREV EMPLOY:** 20 Yrs. as a utility Engr. Supr.; **PROFL AFFIL & HONORS:** Pres. & Reg. Chmn. of RESSI; **MIL SERV:** USAF; **OTHER ACT & HONORS:** Past Pres. of the local MLS, Past Bd. Member of Local Bd. of Realty, Past Div. Chmn. AK Div. Nat. Ski Patrol, Past Dep. Dis. Gov. Dist. 49 Intl. Lions Club, Past Rgnl. Chmn. Ressi; **HOME ADD:** 1921 S. Salem Dr., Anchorage, AK 99504, (907)276-6348; **BUS ADD:** 724 E. 15th, Anchorage, AK 99501, (907)272-0571.

SCHLENGER, Robert D.——**B:** Jan. 17, 1927, Newark, NJ, *Pres.*, Robert D. Schlenger Co.; **PRIM RE ACT:** Broker, Consultant, Property Manager; **SERVICES:** Sales, leases and mgmt. of comml. & investment props.; **REP CLIENTS:** Fin. instns. and private owners, users and investors; **PREV EMPLOY:** Feist & Feist, NY and NJ, 1950-55; **PROFL AFFIL & HONORS:** Nat. Inst. of Realtors; Charter Member of Comml. and Inv. Div., NJ Condemnation Commnr.; **EDUC:** BA, 1949, Hist., Brown Univ.; **MIL SERV:** Maritime Service, WO; **OTHER ACT & HONORS:** Orange Lawn Tennis Club; **HOME ADD:** South Orange, NJ; **BUS ADD:** 75 Main St., Millburn, NJ 07041, (201)379-1300.

SCHLESINGER, Frank A.——B: April 17, 1922, Newark, NJ, *Pres.*, Louis Schlesinger Co.; **PRIM RE ACT:** Broker, Consultant, Appraiser, Owner/Investor, Syndicator; **SERVICES:** Relocation, prop. appraisals, corp. consulting; **PROFL AFFIL & HONORS:** SIR, ASCRE, MAI; **EDUC:** AA, 1944, Univ. of WI; **MIL SERV:** Inf, Sgt., Bronze Star; **OTHER ACT & HONORS:** Red Cross, Boys Club (Tr.), Tr., Newark Medical Ctr., YM-YWHA, Metropolitan NJ (Bd. Member); **HOME ADD:** 166 Forest Hill Rd., W. Orange, NJ 07052, (201)931-6627; **BUS ADD:** 1373 Broad St., Clifton, NJ 07013, (201)473-3400.

SCHLESINGER, Tod Michael——B: Sept. 29, 1947, San Francisco, CA, *VP, Project Devel.*, Schlesinger Investments; **PRIM RE ACT:** Broker, Consultant, Appraiser, Developer, Owner/Investor, Property Manager; **SERVICES:** Comml. brokerage, prop. mgmt., consultation, land devel., appraisals; **PREV EMPLOY:** 2 yrs. with Saxe Realtors, A Div. of Amer. Invsco. Inc., Chicago, IL; **PROFL AFFIL & HONORS:** Member San Francisco Bd. of Realtors, CA Assn. of Realtors, NAR; **HOME ADD:** 647 26th Ave., #1, San Francisco, CA 94121, (415)751-6358; **BUS ADD:** 17 Lupine Ave., San Francisco, CA 94118, (415)668-1113.

SCHLESSLER R.W., *Gen. Mgr. RE Dept.*, Mobile Corp.; **PRIM RE ACT:** Property Manager; **BUS ADD:** 150 E. 42nd St., New York, NY 10017, (212)883-4242.*

SCHLICKE, Gordon W.——B: 1935, *Corp. Compliance Officer, AVP*, Rainier Mortgage Co., Rainier Bancorp.; **PRIM RE ACT:** Broker, Consultant, Builder, Owner/Investor, Instructor, Real Estate Publisher; **OTHER RE ACT:** Pres., Gordon & Standlee, Inc.; **SERVICES:** RE Fin. Consulting, Bldg. & Devel.; **REP CLIENTS:** RE Brokers, Devel., Lenders; **PROFL AFFIL & HONORS:** Chmn., WMBA Educ. Comm., Bd. of Dir. WMBA, Single Family Comm. MBA of Amer. Apr.; **EDUC:** BS, 1958, Fin., Univ. of WI; **GRAD EDUC:** MBA, 1974, Northwestern Univ.; **BUS ADD:** 2nd & Spring St., Seattle, WA 98111, (206)621-5230.

SCHLITZ, R.J.——*Secy.*, Ohio Ferro-Alloys Corp.; **PRIM RE ACT:** Property Manager; **BUS ADD:** PO Box 817, Canton, OH 44711, (216)492-5110.*

SCHLOEMER, James H.——B: Nov. 26, 1958, West Bend, WI, *Pres.*, Continental Properties Co., Inc.; **PRIM RE ACT:** Broker, Developer, Property Manager; **SERVICES:** Comml. and resid. devel., sales, comml. site location, prop. mgmt.; **REP CLIENTS:** Comml. tenants/owners, indiv. investors; **PREV EMPLOY:** Pres., Westbrook Devel. Co., West Bend, WI; Comml. Sales, Swenson Realty, West Bend, WI; **PROFL AFFIL & HONORS:** NAR, Chmn., Serv. Enterprise Devel., West Bend, WI, Outstanding Young Men of America 1981; **EDUC:** BS, 1981, Acctg., Valparaiso Univ.; **GRAD EDUC:** Currently attending Univ. of Chicago; **EDUC HONORS:** Cum Laude; **OTHER ACT & HONORS:** Chmn. Serion Gift Comm., Valparaiso Univ.; Chmn., Sr. Steering Comm., Valparaiso Univ.; **HOME ADD:** 535 Highland View Dr., West Bend, WI 53095, (414)334-3891; **BUS ADD:** 2419 W. Washington St., P.O. Box 435, West Bend, WI 53095, (414)334-0800.

SCHLOSS, Nathan——B: Jan. 14, 1927, Baltimore, MD, *VP-Treas.*, RE Research Corp.; **PRIM RE ACT:** Consultant; **OTHER RE ACT:** Econ. and Fin. Analyst; **SERVICES:** RE and Urban Market/Econ. Analysis, Fin. Analysis, Investment/Portfolio Evaluation & Counseling; **REP CLIENTS:** Fortune 1,000 Corps., Major Fin. Institu., Large Devel. and Public Agencies; **PREV EMPLOY:** Sears, Roebuck & Co. (1950-1963), Montgomery Ward and Co. (1963-1965), The Walgreen Co. (1970-1972); **PROFL AFFIL & HONORS:** Intl. Frat. of Lambda Alpha, Member-Comm. on Price Indexes, Productivity and Employment & Unemployment of the Bus. Research Advisory Council to the Bureau of Labor Statistics, US Dept. of Labor (1979-Present), Member-IL Employ. and Training Council Technical Advisory Comm. on Employment & Training Data, State of IL (1979-Present), Member Amer. Marketing Assn.; **EDUC:** BS, 1950, Bus., The Johns Hopkins Univ.; **EDUC HONORS:** Grad. with Honors; **OTHER ACT & HONORS:** Members-Plan Comm., Wilmette, IL (1975-1977); **HOME ADD:** 115 Hollywood Ct., Wilmette, IL 60091, (312)251-9582; **BUS ADD:** 72 W. Adams St., Chicago, IL 60603, (312)346-5885.

SCHLOSSER, Bryon R.——B: Mar 17, 1946, Kansas City, KS, *Atty.*, Hardesty, Hall, Schlosser & Puckett-Chartered; **PRIM RE ACT:** Attorney; **SERVICES:** Legal consultation, valuation, synd., tax projections & analysis; **PROFL AFFIL & HONORS:** Topeka, KS, Amer. Bars; Member Exec. Comm, KS Tax Sect.; Member ABA Comm. on RE Problems of Tax Sect.; Member Topeka & Nat. Home Builders Assn.; **EDUC:** BS, 1968, Acctg., KS State Univ.; **GRAD EDUC:** JD, 1971, Tax, Washburn Univ., Sch. of Law; **HOME ADD:** 2262 Llandovery Lane, Topeka, KA, (913)272-7569; **BUS ADD:** 2201 W. 29th St., Topeka, KS 66611, (913)266-4595.

SCHLOSSMAN, William A.——B: Nov. 1, 1919, Chicago, IL, *Pres.*, The George A. Black Co.; **PRIM RE ACT:** Broker, Property Manager; **PREV EMPLOY:** IL Bell Co.; **PROFL AFFIL & HONORS:** NAR; MN Assoc. of Realtors; ND Assn. of Realtors; Fargo - Moorehead Bd. of Realtors; IREM; ICSC; USC. of C.; Nat. Parking Assn.; BOMA; GNDA, CPM, "Outstanding Bus. Leader" in ND - ND State Univ.; Dist. Service Award from US Jr. C. of C. - 1950, "Golden Hammer Award", "Marketer of the Yr.", Greater ND Assn. of Bus. & Ind. Devel. Award, 1976; **MIL SERV:** USN, Lt.; **OTHER ACT & HONORS:** Past Pres., Fargo C. of C., Past Pres., Fargo YMCA, Past Pres. & Campaign Chmn., United Way, Past Co-Chmn. - Citizens for City Planning, Past Memeber of ND Exec. Comm. of the Upper Midwest R & D Co., Read Feather Award, Pres. Council & Patron Jamestown Coll., Pres. Award, Concordia Coll.; **HOME ADD:** 1414 S. River Rd., Fargo, ND 58103, (701)293-0071; **BUS ADD:** Suite 305, Black Bldg., Fargo, ND 58102, (701)232-7102.

SCHLOTT, Richard——B: June 28, 1937, Rochester, NY, *Pres.*, Richard L. Schlott Realtors Inc.; **PRIM RE ACT:** Broker, Consultant, Owner/Investor, Instructor; **SERVICES:** RE Sales (new- resale), condo sales, third party co.; **REP CLIENTS:** Homequity/Homerica, Merrill Lynch Real Mgmt., Employee Transfer, Equitable Rel.; **PROFL AFFIL & HONORS:** GRI, CRS, CRB; **OTHER ACT & HONORS:** NJ Assn. of Realtors, Treas. 1980, Sec. 1979, RPAC State Chmn. 1979-80-81, Pres. Schlott Realtors; **HOME ADD:** 435 Clinton Ave., Wyckoff, NJ 07481, (201)891-2646; **BUS ADD:** 2100 Route 208, Fairlawn, NJ 07410, (201)791-3000.

SCHLUSSEL, Mark E.——B: Dec. 14, 1940, Detroit, MI, *Sr. Part.*, Schlussel, Lifton, Simon, Rands, Kaufman, Lesinski & Jackier; **PRIM RE ACT:** Attorney; **SERVICES:** Zoning, FHA, State Housing work; Gen. RE; **REP CLIENTS:** Forest City Enterprises; Sheffield Assn.; McDonald Corp.; Burger Chef; **PREV EMPLOY:** MI Court of Appeals, 1965-66; **PROFL AFFIL & HONORS:** Bd. member, Southfield C of C; Bd. of Dir., Southfield Econ. Devel. Corp.; **EDUC:** BA, 1962, Amer. Hist., Wayne State Univ.; **GRAD EDUC:** JD, 1965, RE, Univ. of MI Law School; **OTHER ACT & HONORS:** Southfield City Councilman, 1972-73; Chmn. Culture & Educ. Div.; Bd. of Govs. and Exec. Comm. of Jewish Welfare Fed., Detroit; Bd. Member of Jewish Nat. Fund of Detroit; **HOME ADD:** 28755 Bell Rd., Southfield, MI 48034, (313)355-2270; **BUS ADD:** 29201 Telegraph Rd., Suite 500, Southfield, MI 48034, (313)353-9500.

SCHMAEDICK, Ronald Albert——B: Sept. 29, 1935, Chicago, IL, *Pres.*, Rams Realty Inc. & Assured Realty Services Co.; **PRIM RE ACT:** Broker, Instructor, Property Manager, Owner/Investor; **PREV EMPLOY:** Commonwealth Mort. Fin. & Nat. Homes Corp.; **PROFL AFFIL & HONORS:** Home Bldrs. Assn.; Nat., State & Local Bd. of Realtors, Local Pres. of Realtors, 1974; State Pres. of Realtors, 1977; Local HBA Pres., 1968; Eugene Realtor of the Yr., 1976; **EDUC:** BA, 1958, Indus. Mgmt., Univ. of WI, Madison; **MIL SERV:** USN, Lt., Antarctic Serv.; **OTHER ACT & HONORS:** Rotary; Elks; Town Club of Eugene; **HOME ADD:** 1742 W. 34th Pl., Eugene, OR 97405, (503)485-4983; **BUS ADD:** 315 W. Broadway, Eugene, OR 97401, (501)485-6200.

SCHMELTZER, Robert W.——B: Sep. 4, 1933, Oak Park, IL, *Mgr. Real Estate & Ins.*, A.B. Dick; **PRIM RE ACT:** Broker, Consultant, Appraiser, Developer, Builder, Property Manager, Owner/Investor, Insuror; **PREV EMPLOY:** Amer. Oil Co, R.E. & Const.; **PROFL AFFIL & HONORS:** Indus. Devel. Research Council; **EDUC:** BCE, 1956, Univ. of IL; **GRAD EDUC:** R.E., Northwestern Univ., Univ. of Chicago.; **MIL SERV:** Corp. of Engrs., Capt.; **OTHER ACT & HONORS:** Lombard Plan Commn.; **HOME ADD:** 504 So. School St., Lombard, IL 60148, (312)627-4563; **BUS ADD:** 5700 W. Touhy, Chicago, IL 60648, (312)647-8800.

SCHMELZER, Charles J., III——B: Nov. 4, 1945, Kansas City, MO, *Partner*, Linde Thomson Fairchild Langworthy Kohn & Van Dyke, PC; **PRIM RE ACT:** Attorney; **SERVICES:** Gen. RE matters; **REP CLIENTS:** Varnun, Armstrong, Deeter, Inc.: Coldwell Banker; **PROFL AFFIL & HONORS:** ABA, MO Bar Assn., Kansas City Bar Assn., Lawyers Assn. of Kansas City; **EDUC:** MA, 1967, Phil., Beloit Coll.; **GRAD EDUC:** JD, 1970, MO Univ.; **MIL SERV:** USA, 1st Lt.; **OTHER ACT & HONORS:** Chmn. Fair Housing Comm. of Kansas City, 1980-81; Pres. Bd. of Dirs., Kansas City Chapt. of Young Audiences, Inc.; **HOME ADD:** Kansas City, 1003 Huntington Rd., MO 64113, (816)363-5014; **BUS ADD:** 2700 City Ctr. Sq., PO Box 26010, Kansas City, MO 64196, (816)474-6420.

SCHMIDT, Andrea Larson——B: Feb. 21, 1944, Chicago, IL, *Broker/Owner*, Landmark Real Estate; **PRIM RE ACT:** Broker, Owner/Investor; **PROFL AFFIL & HONORS:** State Pres.-WCR - Vice Chairman-congressional Liason Subcommittee-NAR District 7 Vice President, IAR, GRI; CRS; CRB; **EDUC:** BA, 1965, Spanish,

Univ. of IL; **GRAD EDUC:** MA, 1966, Univ. of IL; 6 yrs. on PHd 1971; **OTHER ACT & HONORS:** Bd. of Dir.-Champaign C of C; Bd. of Dir. Champaign Cty. Bd. of Realtors; **HOME ADD:** 1915 McDonald, Champaign, IL 61820, (217)356-0977; **BUS ADD:** 1708 S. Neil, Champaign, IL 61820, (217)352-1933.

SCHMIDT, C.L. Mike——B: June 15, 1940, Lamesa, TX, *Pres.*, Schmidt Investments; **PRIM RE ACT:** Broker, Attorney; **PROFL AFFIL & HONORS:** ABA, TX Bar Assn., Amer. Bd. Trial Advocates; **EDUC:** BA, 1962, Hist., So. Methodist Univ., Dallas, TX; **GRAD EDUC:** LLB, 1965, Litigation, So. Methodist Univ., Dallas, TX; **EDUC HONORS:** Who's Who in Amer. Colls., Ex VP Amer. Law Student Assn.; **OTHER ACT & HONORS:** Guest lecturer, teacher; **HOME ADD:** 3111 Beverly Dr., Dallas, TX 75205, (214)528-1828; **BUS ADD:** P.O. Box 1170, Dallas, TX 75221, (214)748-4541.

SCHMIDT, Eno A.——B: Mar. 19, 1952, Orange, CA, *CPA*, Eno A. Schmidt; **PRIM RE ACT:** Consultant, Owner/Investor; **OTHER RE ACT:** CPA; **SERVICES:** Full range of investment consultation; **REP CLIENTS:** Lenders and indiv. investors in resid. income prop.; **PREV EMPLOY:** 5 yrs. with Peat, Marwick, Mitchell & Co., CPA's; **PROFL AFFIL & HONORS:** CA Soc. of CPA's; Apt. Assn. of Los Angeles Cty.; S. CA Assn. of RE Investors, CPA; **EDUC:** BA, 1973, Econ., Univ. of CA, Los Angeles; **GRAD EDUC:** MBA, 1975, Fin., Univ. of Chicago; **EDUC HONORS:** Phi Beta Kappa, Summa Cum Laude; **OTHER ACT & HONORS:** UCLA Alumni Assn.; **HOME ADD:** 4140-172 Workman Mill Rd., Whittier, CA 90601, (213)692-7307; **BUS ADD:** 4140-172 Workman Mill Rd., Whittier, CA 90601, (213)692-7307.

SCHMIDT, Michael R.——B: Jan. 17, 1943, NY, *Pres.*, Michael R. Schmidt Assoc.; **PRIM RE ACT:** Broker, Appraiser; **SERVICES:** Independent Fee Appraiser, appraisals, brokerage and consulting; **REP CLIENTS:** Homequity, Merrill Lynch, Executrans, Bell Telephone, Midlantic Mort. Co., S&L, Attys., pvt. indivs., banks; **PROFL AFFIL & HONORS:** Realtor, Member NJ Bd. of Realtors, Candidate IFA, Realtor; **EDUC:** RE and Appraisal Courses; **MIL SERV:** USN; **OTHER ACT & HONORS:** Kiwanis; **HOME ADD:** 21 Nunn Ave., Washington, NJ 07882, (201)689-5674; **BUS ADD:** 111 W. Washington Ave., Washington, NJ 07882, (201)689-5650.

SCHMIDT, Norman K.——B: Nov. 8, 1936, Waterbury, CT, *Pres.*, Rosa & Schmidt Assoc.; **PRIM RE ACT:** Broker, Insuror; **SERVICES:** Resid. & Comml. RE & Ins.; **PREV EMPLOY:** 10 yrs. RE & Ins. Broker, The Schmidt Agency, Southbury, CT; **PROFL AFFIL & HONORS:** Pres. Greater Waterbury Bd. Realtors, 1981, 3 yr. State CT Assn., Realtor 1980-82, Dir. Waterbury Greater C of C 1980-83; **EDUC:** AA, 1958, Bus. Mgmt., Post Jr. Coll.; **MIL SERV:** USAR, 1957-64, Sgt.; **HOME ADD:** 58 Robinson La., Southbury, CT, (203)264-5227; **BUS ADD:** 113 Homer St., PO Box 4307, Waterbury, CT 06704, (203)755-7764.

SCHMIDT, R. Denny——B: Sept. 19, 1940, NYC, *1st V.P.*, J. Henry Schroder B and T Co.; **PREV EMPLOY:** Chase Manhattan Bank, 1966-1979; **EDUC:** AB, 1962, Govt., Hamilton Coll; **EDUC HONORS:** Summa Cum Laude; **MIL SERV:** USA, 1st Lt.; **HOME ADD:** 2 Meadow Dr., Port Washington, NY, (516)767-1080; **BUS ADD:** 1 State St, NY, NY 10015, (212)269-6500.

SCHMIDT, Robert A.——*Chmn., Acting Pres.*, Olympia Brewing Co.; **PRIM RE ACT:** Property Manager; **BUS ADD:** PO Box 947, Olympia, WA 98507, (206)754-5000.*

SCHMIDT, Robert Earl——B: Aug. 25, 1948, Waseca, MN, *Atty. at Law*, Schmidt Law Office; **PRIM RE ACT:** Attorney; **SERVICES:** Complete RE rep. of buyers and sellers of RE; **PROFL AFFIL & HONORS:** ABA and MN Bar Assn.; **EDUC:** BS, 1970, Fin. and Acctg., Creighton Univ., Omaha, NE; **GRAD EDUC:** JD, 1974, Creighton Univ. School of Law; **EDUC HONORS:** Grad. Cum Laude; **HOME ADD:** 721 10th Ave. N.E., Waseca, MN 56093, (507)835-3742; **BUS ADD:** PO Box 502, Waseca, MN 56093, (507)835-4884.

SCHMITT, Michael J.——B: Jan. 10, 1950, St. Cloud, MN, *Bus. Broker*, Orion Commercial; **PRIM RE ACT:** Broker; **SERVICES:** Exclusive Broker of bus. opportunities; **REP CLIENTS:** Motel, resort, mfg. type buyers; **PROFL AFFIL & HONORS:** NAR, State Assn. of Realtors, Bus. Broker; **EDUC:** BS, 1972, Bus. Mgmt. & Econ., St. Cloud State Univ.; **OTHER ACT & HONORS:** Lions, Elks, Moose, Area Bd. of Realtors; **HOME ADD:** Rte. #2, Rice, MN 56367, (612)252-7899; **BUS ADD:** 1124 St. Germain St., St. Cloud, MN 56301, (612)251-1177.

SCHMITT, Vincent J.——B: Dec. 29, 1911, NY, NY, *Realtor*, V.J. Schmitt & Co.; **PRIM RE ACT:** Broker, Appraiser, Developer, Builder, Property Manager, Insuror; **PREV EMPLOY:** Realtor since 1947: Pan Amer. Refining in TX city, TX; Foreman Planning and Scheduling Mech. Dept.; **PROFL AFFIL & HONORS:** NAR, RNMI, TAR, Tr. NAR Ins. Trusts, past Pres. and Dir. of TX Assoc. Realtors in TX City, and Lamarque Bd. Realtors; **EDUC:** Arch Engrg., Univ. of MI, Ann Arbor; **OTHER ACT & HONORS:** Chmn. City Planning Commn. for 20 yrs., Chmn. Galveston Cty. Research Council for 1 yr., TX City Noon Lions Club, Main Land Chap. Heart Assoc., C of C in TX City-La Marque, Knights of Columbus; **HOME ADD:** 1121 Mainland Dr., Texas City, TX 77590, (713)945-6253; **BUS ADD:** 908 6th St., N. Texas City, TX 77590, (713)948-3554.

SCHMITZ, John W.——B: May 29, 1953, Chicago, IL, *Pres.*, John W. Schmitz, Inc.; **PRIM RE ACT:** Syndicator, Developer, Property Manager, Owner/Investor; **SERVICES:** Devel., synd. & mgmt. of comml. & indus. props.; **REP CLIENTS:** Miami Dade Indus. Park, Inc., Schmitz Devel. Co.; **PREV EMPLOY:** Farina, Wiener & Schmitz, Attys. at Law; **PROFL AFFIL & HONORS:** RNMI, RESSI; **EDUC:** BA, 1975, Comm., Stanford Univ.; **GRAD EDUC:** JD, 1978, Univ. of Miami; MBA, 1980, Univ. of Miami; **HOME ADD:** 16951 SW 80th Ct., Miami, FL 33157, (305)232-1274; **BUS ADD:** 4450 NW 135th St., Miami, FL 33054, (305)685-5191.

SCHMITZ, Thomas Wayne——B: Sept. 24, 1949, Madison, WI, *VP, Marketing*, Fisher & Fisher Investment Co., Marketing; **PRIM RE ACT:** Broker, Consultant, Developer, Owner/Investor, Instructor, Property Manager, Assessor; **SERVICES:** Mktg. specialist, devel. procurement; **REP CLIENTS:** Gross Investments, Inc., Sunbelt RE Props., New Homes Mktg. Corp., Tosh Devel./Investment Co.; **PREV EMPLOY:** Dyson Systems; Empire Soc. of Amer., BCM Devel. Co.; **PROFL AFFIL & HONORS:** Member, Nat. Assn. of Home Builders, NAA, Madison & Nat. REAA, Madison, Consultant to WI Landmarks Assn., PhD RE Mgmt; Marketing-Univ. of WI, Past Pres. of RE Mktg. Specialists Assn.; **EDUC:** BA, 1972, RE Mgmt.-Mktg., Univ. of WI; **GRAD EDUC:** PhD, 1978, RE, Univ. of WI, Madison; **EDUC HONORS:** Sigma Phi Delta-Man of Year-1971, Evans Scholar; **MIL SERV:** USMC, Sgt., Purple Heart; **OTHER ACT & HONORS:** Alderman, 1980-81; Dist. Party Res. Democrat 1979; Boys Club, YMCA; Home for Battered Children; German-American Club; **HOME ADD:** 6126 Hammersley Rd., Madison, WI 53711, (608)271-6739; **BUS ADD:** 3205 Stevens Street, Madison, WI 53705.

SCHMOOK, J. Lynn——B: Oct. 9, 1949, Cherokee, OK, J. Lynn Schmook; **PRIM RE ACT:** Consultant, Appraiser, Banker, Lender; **SERVICES:** Consultation, appraisal background of lending as banker; **PREV EMPLOY:** Sooner Fed. S&L, 1972-74; Mid-Amer. Fed S&L, 1974-78; First Nat. Bank Tulsa, 1978-81; **PROFL AFFIL & HONORS:** AIREA, SREA, NBR, MAI, SRPA; **EDUC:** BS, 1972, Agric. Econ., OK State Univ.; **EDUC HONORS:** Alpha Zeta; **MIL SERV:** USMC, E-1; **HOME ADD:** 7951 S. Toledo Ave., Tulsa, OK 74136, (918)492-9637; **BUS ADD:** 7951 S. Toledo Ave., Tulsa, OK 74136, (918)494-4930.

SCHMUCKAL, Ralph P., Jr.——B: Apr. 18, 1947, Detroit, MI, *Broker/Owner*, Cumberland Realty; **PRIM RE ACT:** Broker, Instructor, Syndicator, Builder, Property Manager, Owner/Investor; **PREV EMPLOY:** Chmn., Bldg. Authority, Charter Township of Pittsfield; Instr., Eastern MI Univ., Coll. of Bus.; Pres., Econ. Dev. Corp., Charter Township of Pittsfield; Sec., Pittsfield Bldg. Authority; **PROFL AFFIL & HONORS:** RESSI; Realtors, Alpha Kappa Psi, RE Alumnae of MI; **EDUC:** BBA, 1969, Gen, Bus. & Fin., Eastern MI Univ.; **GRAD EDUC:** MBA, 1972, Cert. in RE, Univ. of MI; MBA, Mktg., E. MI Univ.; **MIL SERV:** US Army; S/Sgt.; **OTHER ACT & HONORS:** TR, Charter Township, 1977-1980; Amer. Legion; Kiwanis (Past Pres.); Jaycees; Bd of Dir, C of C; **HOME ADD:** 3461 Maple Dr., Ypsilanti, MI 48197, (313)434-1361; **BUS ADD:** 11 N. Hamilton St. P.O. Box 163, Ypsilanti, MI 48197, (313)483-3890.

SCHMUS, Gilbert D.——*Treas.*, Harnischfegar Corp.; **PRIM RE ACT:** Property Manager; **BUS ADD:** PO Box 554, Milwaukee, WI 53201, (414)671-4400.*

SCHNABEL, Donald——B: July 28, 1933, *Sr. VP*, Julien J. Studley, Inc., Consulting Group; **PRIM RE ACT:** Consultant; **HOME ADD:** 300 East 57th St., New York, NY 10022, (212)832-3518; **BUS ADD:** 342 Madison Ave., New York, NY 10017, (212)949-0126.

SCHNALL, Flora——B: Brooklyn, NY, *Partner*, Rosenman Colin Freund Lewis & Cohen; **PRIM RE ACT:** Attorney; **SERVICES:** Legal Services; **REP CLIENTS:** John C. Portman, Jr., Sony Corp., Paramount Grp., Inc., York-Hanover, Inc.; **PROFL AFFIL & HONORS:** NYC Bar Assn., NY State Bar Assn., ABA, Editor of Real Prop. Newsletter, NY State Bar Assn.; Member of Exec. Comm. of Real

Prop. Sect., NY State Bar Assn.; **EDUC:** BA, 1956, Poli. Sci., Smith Coll.; **GRAD EDUC:** JD, 1959, Law, Harvard Law School; **EDUC HONORS:** Magna Cum Laude; **OTHER ACT & HONORS:** Asst. Counsel to Gov. Nelson A. Rockefeller Dir. - Northside Ctr. for ChiLd Dev. Inc. VP and Dir. of The Common; **BUS ADD:** 575 Madison Ave., New York, NY 10022, (212)940-8570.

SCHNEE, William M.——B: Jan. 10, 1924, Cleveland, OH, *Bd. Chmn.*, Bergman, Schnee & Company, Inc.; **PRIM RE ACT:** Broker, Consultant; **SERVICES:** Indus. and office brokerage and counseling; **REP CLIENTS:** Xerox; FMC; Plessey Corp. & many others; **PROFL AFFIL & HONORS:** SIR; AIREA, Master of Indus. Brokerage from AIR; **EDUC:** BS, 1950, Public & Admin., Univ. of So. CA; **MIL SERV:** USN; Seabees, Petty Officer; One battle star; **OTHER ACT & HONORS:** Dir., Los Angeles Realty Bd. 1979-80; VP, Amer. Indus. RE Assn.; **HOME ADD:** 9825 Wish Ave., Northridge, CA, (213)349-9825; **BUS ADD:** 2716 Ocean Park Blvd. 1025, Santa Monica, CA 90405, (213)870-4751.

SCHNEEWEISS, Samuel——B: June 27, 1919, New York, NY, *Part.*, Becker, Ross & Stone; **PRIM RE ACT:** Attorney; **SERVICES:** Legal; **REP CLIENTS:** Indiv. & corp. investors and users; **PROFL AFFIL & HONORS:** ABA, Sect. of Real Prop. Law; NYS Bar Assn., Real Prop. Law Sect., Comm. on Condos & Coops; Assn. of the Bar of NYC; NY Cty. Lawyers Assn.; **EDUC:** BS, 1941, Econ., Commerce, NY Univ.; **GRAD EDUC:** JD, 1948, NY Univ.; **MIL SERV:** USA Corps. of Engrs., Civilian Sec. Officer, 1942-44; **OTHER ACT & HONORS:** Henry St. Settlement Bd. of Dir., 1952-79; Real Prop. Comm. (Chmn.), 1960-79; **HOME ADD:** 303 Mercer St., New York, NY 10003, (212)533-9235; **BUS ADD:** 41 E. 42nd St., New York, NY 10017, (212)697-2310.

SCHNEIDER, Eric S.——B: May 10, 1948, New York, NY, *Exec. VP & Grp. Publisher*, CMP Publications, Inc., The Bldgs. Journal; **PRIM RE ACT:** Real Estate Publisher; **SERVICES:** Publish nat. bus. newspaper of the bldgs. indus.; **REP CLIENTS:** contractor, George Fuller; product supplier, Flour City; RE title ins., First Amer. Title; **PROFL AFFIL & HONORS:** Who's Who in the East; **EDUC:** BA, 1970, Eng. & Philosophy, NY Univ.; **MIL SERV:** US Army Res., SP-4; **HOME ADD:** 73 Holbrook Rd., Briarcliff, NY 10510, (914)762-1468; **BUS ADD:** 333 E. Shore Rd., Manhasset, NY 11030, (516)829-5880.

SCHNEIDER, Herbert M.——B: July 27, 1924, Boston, MA, *Pres.*, Schneider Group; **PRIM RE ACT:** Broker, Architect, Syndicator, Developer, Property Manager, Owner/Investor; **SERVICES:** Integrated RE Servs., specializing in adaptive reuse of older bldgs.; **PREV EMPLOY:** Licensed Realtor State of MI, Licensed Builder State of MI; **PROFL AFFIL & HONORS:** SEC, State of MI, Reg. broker/dealer/Real Estate Syndications, RESSI, Nat. Assoc. Sec. Dealers; **EDUC:** BS, 1948, Engrg., Northeastern Univ.; **HOME ADD:** 1021 Arlington Blvd., Ann Arbor, MI 48104, (313)971-4255; **BUS ADD:** P.O.Box 8420, 410 S. Main St., Ann Arbor, MI 48107, (313)995-2169.

SCHNEIDER, James E.——B: Jul. 15, 1938, Milwaukee, WI, *VP*, First Wisconsin National Bank of Milwaukee, RE Fin. Div.; **OTHER RE ACT:** Comml. mort. banking; **SERVICES:** Loan placements, const. loans; **REP CLIENTS:** RE devel., ins. cos.; **PREV EMPLOY:** Equitable Life Assurance Soc.; **PROFL AFFIL & HONORS:** WI Mort. Bankers Assn., Milwaukee Bd. Realtors; Amer. Inst. RE Appraisers, Building Owners & Mgrs. Assn., MAI; **EDUC:** BBA, 1960, Fin., Univ. of Miami (FL); **MIL SERV:** US Army Reserve, Sgt.; **OTHER ACT & HONORS:** Past Pres. and current Dir. of WI Mort. Bankers Assn.; Sec. and Dir. of WI Chap. of Amer. Inst. RE Appraisers; **HOME ADD:** 6027 N. Apple Blossom Ln., Glendale, WI 53217, (414)962-7212; **BUS ADD:** 777 E. Wisconsin Ave., Milwaukee, WI 53202, (414)765-4863.

SCHNEIDER, Julius——B: Mar. 31, 1926, Inwood, NY, *Pres. of RE Firm; Atty.*, J. Schneider Realty Corp. (RE Broker), Julius Schneider, Esq. (Atty.); **PRIM RE ACT:** Broker, Consultant, Attorney, Developer, Owner/Investor, Property Manager, Syndicator; **SERVICES:** Mgmt., brokerage, devel., consulting, legal; **PREV EMPLOY:** Self-employed many years; **PROFL AFFIL & HONORS:** Nassau Cty. Bar Assn.; **EDUC:** BA, 1949, Eng. & Mathematics, Hofstra Unlv., Hempstead, NY; **GRAD EDUC:** LLB, 1957, NY Univ.; **EDUC HONORS:** Cum Laude - Honors in Eng.; **MIL SERV:** USA, Tech. Sgt.; **OTHER ACT & HONORS:** Village Tr. 9 years; Village Atty. 1 year; Tr. L.I. Jewish Hillside Medical Ctr.; Former Pres. Hon. Bd. Member 5 Towns Comm. Chest; Former Pres. 5 Towns Comm. Council; **HOME ADD:** 278 Linwood Ave., Cedarhurst, NY 11516, (516)295-4941; **BUS ADD:** 124 Cedarhurst Ave., Cedarhurst, NY 11516, (516)569-2525.

SCHNEIDER, Kenneth B.——B: Dec. 4, 1943, Brooklyn, NY, *Asst. Prof. of Mgmt. & Mktg.*, Canisius Coll., Sch. of Bus. Admin.; **PRIM RE ACT:** Consultant, Appraiser, Instructor; **OTHER RE ACT:** RE and Prop. Mktg. Research & Planning; **SERVICES:** Valuation studies, mktg. studies and reseach in RE mkt. analysis; **REP CLIENTS:** Devel., fin. instit., attys.; **PROFL AFFIL & HONORS:** AREAUEA, AEA; **EDUC:** Bus., 1976, Econ., Univ. of NE; **GRAD EDUC:** MA, 1977, Econ., Univ. of NE; Cert. in RE and land use econ., 1978, RE, Univ. of NE; **EDUC HONORS:** Omicron Delta Epsilon; **MIL SERV:** US Army Res., sp. 4; **HOME ADD:** 160 Lakewood Pkwy., Snyder, NY 14226, (716)839-2830; **BUS ADD:** 2001 Main St., Buffalo, NY 14208, (716)883-7000.

SCHNEIDER, Melvin L.——B: Oct. 23, 1939, Frostburg, MD, *Atty. at Law*, Schneider and Higdon; **PRIM RE ACT:** Attorney; **SERVICES:** All RE law and title servs.; **PROFL AFFIL & HONORS:** MD State Bar Assn.; Amer. Assn. of Trial Lawyers; **EDUC:** BS, 1962, Physics, Univ. of MD; **GRAD EDUC:** JD, 1967, Law, Univ. of MD; **EDUC HONORS:** Law Review; **HOME ADD:** 7001 Good Luck Rd., New Carrollton, MD 20784; **BUS ADD:** 7338 Baltimore Ave., College Park, MD 20740, (301)864-3151.

SCHNEIDER, Michael E.——B: June 11, 1944, Long Beach, CA, *Atty.*, Diemer, Schneider & Luce; **PRIM RE ACT:** Attorney; **SERVICES:** Legal and tax advice; **PROFL AFFIL & HONORS:** Bar Assns.; **EDUC:** BA, 1966, Pol. Sci./Econ., UCLA; **GRAD EDUC:** JD, 1969, Law, Univ. of Santa Clara; **EDUC HONORS:** Scholarship; **OTHER ACT & HONORS:** Palo Alto Adolescent Servs. Corp.; **BUS ADD:** 750 Welch Rd., Suite 301, Palo Alto, CA 94304, (415)321-4240.

SCHNEIDER, Robert A.——*Partner*, Sherman & Yegelwel, CPA's; **PRIM RE ACT:** Consultant, Developer, Owner/Investor, Property Manager, Syndicator; **OTHER RE ACT:** Tax Shelter Acct.; **SERVICES:** Acctg., mgmt., consultant Hotels & Motels & Apts.; **BUS ADD:** SCN Ctr., Corner Main & Lady St., Columbia, SC 29211, (803)779-4292.

SCHNIEDERS, Edmund F., Jr.——B: Mar. 12, 1935, Los Angeles, CA, *Chmn. of the Bd. and Pres.*, Amer. Nat. Grp.; **PRIM RE ACT:** Broker, Developer, Property Manager, Syndicator; **OTHER RE ACT:** Const.; **SERVICES:** RE investment, devel., synd. & mgmt.; **PREV EMPLOY:** VP & Dir., John D. Lusk & Son. Inc., 1962-65; **PROFL AFFIL & HONORS:** Loyola Marymount Bd. of Regents, 1978-present, Young Pres. Org., 1973-present; **EDUC:** BA, 1956, Stanford Univ.; **EDUC HONORS:** Cum Laude; **MIL SERV:** USA, Capt.; **HOME ADD:** 1590 Stone Canyon Rd., Los Angeles, CA 90024, (213)270-4891; **BUS ADD:** 405 S. Beverly Dr., Beverly Hills, CA 90212, (213)879-0900.

SCHNITZER, Jordan D.——B: May 8, 1951, Portland, OR, *Exec. VP/Pres.*, Harsh Inv. Corp./No. Specialty Sales Co.; **PRIM RE ACT:** Attorney, Developer, Builder, Owner/Investor, Property Manager; **EDUC:** 1973, Lit., Univ. of OR; **GRAD EDUC:** JD, 1976, Lewis & Clark, Northwestern School of Law; **OTHER ACT & HONORS:** 1981, Outstanding Young Men of Amer.; **BUS ADD:** 811 N.W. 19th, POB 2708, Portland, OR 97208.

SCHOCHET, Jay R.——B: June 10, 1930, NYC, NY, *Gen. Part.*, Schochet Assoc.; **PRIM RE ACT:** Broker, Developer, Builder, Property Manager; **PROFL AFFIL & HONORS:** NAR; NAHB; **EDUC:** AB, 1952, Econ./Soc., Dartmouth; **MIL SERV:** USAF, 1st Lt.; **HOME ADD:** 14 Byron St., Boston, MA 02108, (617)523-6085; **BUS ADD:** 20 Providence St., Boston, MA 02116, (617)482-8925.

SCHOEFFEL, Rudd——B: May 1, 1939, Pasadena, CA, *Owner*, Rancho Buena Vista; **PRIM RE ACT:** Developer, Builder, Owner/Investor, Property Manager, Syndicator; **OTHER RE ACT:** Gen. Contr.; **PREV EMPLOY:** Hornblower, Weeks, Hemphill Noyes, S CA First Natl. Bank; **EDUC:** BA, 1965, Phil., Occidental Coll., Los Angeles; **GRAD EDUC:** MA, 1967, Phil., Pol., Econ., Oxford Univ., England; **EDUC HONORS:** Cum Laude, Woodrow Wilson Fellow, Oxford Blue; **OTHER ACT & HONORS:** Planning Commissioner, City of Vista, 1977-81, Phi, Gamma Delta; **HOME ADD:** 640 Alta Vista Dr., Vista, CA 92083; **BUS ADD:** 110 Escondido Ave., Suite 103, Vista, CA 92083, (714)758-9850.

SCHOEN, Robert M.——B: Sept. 6, 1920, New Holstein, WI, *Atty.*; **PRIM RE ACT:** Attorney; **PREV EMPLOY:** Atty. US Veterans Admin. (now retired); part-time private law practice only; **PROFL AFFIL & HONORS:** WI State Bar Assn.; ABA; Monroe Cty. Bar Assn.; **EDUC:** PhB, 1943, Philosophy, Econ., Marquette Univ., Milwaukee, WI; **GRAD EDUC:** JD, 1944, Law, Marquette Univ., Milwaukee, WI; **EDUC HONORS:** Secy. Marquette Union Bd.; **HOME ADD:** Sparta, WI 54656, (608)269-4692; **BUS ADD:** PO Box 386, 111 W. Oak, Sparta, WI 54656, (608)269-4692.

SCHOENFELD, Norman——**B:** May 22, 1929, New York, NY, *VP*, Sybedon Corporation, Loan Placement; **OTHER RE ACT:** Inst. Loan Placement; **PREV EMPLOY:** VP Bankers Trust, Advanced Mortgage, Citicorp subsidiary; **PROFL AFFIL & HONORS:** NY Mort. Bankers Assn., NYS Bar, NYS RE Broker; **EDUC:** AB, 1949, History, NYU; **GRAD EDUC:** JD, 1952, Harvard Univ.; **MIL SERV:** US Army Sgt.; **OTHER ACT & HONORS:** NYU Real Estate Institute, Instructor; Co-author "Modern Real Estate", articles published: "Appraisal Journal, American Banker", "Real Estate Outlook"; **HOME ADD:** 320 W. 76th St., New York, NY 10023; **BUS ADD:** 1211 Ave. of Amercias, New York, NY 10023, (212)752-7510.

SCHOFIELD, Donald S.——**B:** Dec. 5, 1928, Stoneham, MA, *Pres. & CEO*, First Union RE Investments; **OTHER RE ACT:** RE Investment Trust; **PREV EMPLOY:** Windsor Investment Co., Boston MA 1968-1978; **PROFL AFFIL & HONORS:** AICPA; **EDUC:** BS, 1956, Bus. Admin., Boston Univ.; **GRAD EDUC:** MBA, 1957, Boston Univ.; **EDUC HONORS:** Summa Cum Laude; **MIL SERV:** USA, 1951-1952; **OTHER ACT & HONORS:** Beta Gamma Sigma; **HOME ADD:** 8837 Camelot Dr., Chesterland, OH 44026; **BUS ADD:** 55 Public Sq., Suite 1900, Cleveland, OH 44113, (216)781-4030.

SCHOMAEKER, James B.——**B:** Sept. 9, 1936, Lima, OH, *Pres.*, The Gooding Co.; **PRIM RE ACT:** Broker, Instructor, Property Manager; **REP CLIENTS:** Westinghouse Electric Corp., Procter & Gamble, Merrill Lynch, Homequity, Employee Transfer Corp.; **PROFL AFFIL & HONORS:** Nat. Assn. of Home Builders, Nat. Mgmt. Assn., GRI, CRB, CRS; **EDUC:** BS, 1958, Bus. Admin., Bowling Green State Univ.; **EDUC HONORS:** Sr. Class, VP, Omicron Delta Kappa; **MIL SERV:** US Army, Sgt.; **OTHER ACT & HONORS:** Pres., Lima Better Bus. Bureau 1979-80; Bd. of Dirs. United Telephone Co. of OH, YMCA, Lima C of C; **HOME ADD:** 3923 Odema Dr., Lima, OH 45806, (419)999-1706; **BUS ADD:** 406 S. Cable Rd., Lima, OH 45806, (410)227-4666.

SCHOOLER, David——**B:** Sept. 22, 1949, Chicago, IL, *Dir., RE Div.*, Sterling Recreation Organization; **PRIM RE ACT:** Attorney, Developer, Regulator, Builder, Owner/Investor, Property Manager; **PREV EMPLOY:** City of Bellevue Planning Dept.; **PROFL AFFIL & HONORS:** WA State Bar Assn.; **EDUC:** BS, 1971, Geo., Univ. of WI; **GRAD EDUC:** MS, 1973, Urban & Rbnl. Planning, Univ. of WI; JD, 1976, Univ. of Denver; **EDUC HONORS:** Honors; **OTHER ACT & HONORS:** VP, Kirkland Bd. of Adjustment; **HOME ADD:** 1015 2d St., Kirkland, WA 98033, (206)822-4996; **BUS ADD:** PO Box 1723, Bellevue, WA 98009, (206)455-8167.

SCHOOLFIELD, William C., Jr.——**B:** Jan. 7, 1948, Bridgeport, CT, *VP*, Corrigan Properties, Inc.; **PRIM RE ACT:** Developer, Owner/Investor, Property Manager; **PROFL AFFIL & HONORS:** ULI; Intl. Council of Shopping Centers; IREM; Greater Dallas Bd. of Realtors, CPM, CSM; **EDUC:** BBA, 1970, Gen. Bus., Univ. of TX; **GRAD EDUC:** MBA, 1973, RE, So. Methodist Univ.; **OTHER ACT & HONORS:** Big Brothers & Sisters; **HOME ADD:** 4518 Roland, Apt. #1, Dallas, TX 75219, (214)528-0985; **BUS ADD:** 1200 Mercantile Dallas Bldg., Dallas, TX 75201, (214)747-0391.

SCHORR, Bernard W.——**B:** Jan. 26, 1920, Worcester, MA, *Pres. -Treas., Realtor*, Prestige, Inc. D/B/A Prestige Realty; **PRIM RE ACT:** Broker, Appraiser, Property Manager; **PROFL AFFIL & HONORS:** NIREB; MAREB; NAREB; **EDUC:** Northeastern Univ., Shrivenham Army Univ., Shrivenham, England; **GRAD EDUC:** Univ. of CT - Resid. Appraisal; **MIL SERV:** USA 1942-1946, Tec 5, ETO 2 clusters; **OTHER ACT & HONORS:** Past Pres. Springfield Bd. of Realtors 1974; Realtor of the Year 1975; Past Pres. USO; Past Pres. Two Lions Clubs; Past Pres. Heat Council; Past Pres. Beth El Brotherhood; Past Pres. Melpha Shrine Temple Guard; **HOME ADD:** 136 Webber St., Springfield, MA 01108, (413)739-0106; **BUS ADD:** 392 Dickinson St., Springfield, MA 01108, (413)788-0985.

SCHRECK, William R.——**B:** Apr. 25, 1948, Evanston, IL, Schreck Co., Realtors; **PRIM RE ACT:** Broker; **SERVICES:** Comml. sales, leasing, site; **REP CLIENTS:** Indiv. and instnl. users; **PROFL AFFIL & HONORS:** RNMI, RESSI, CCIM; **EDUC:** BA, 1970, No. IL Univ.; **HOME ADD:** SRA Box 4029Z, Anchorage, AK 99507, (907)345-3330; **BUS ADD:** 2601 Blueberry Rd., Anchorage, AK 99503, (907)276-7048.

SCHREIBER, Allan C.——**B:** Jan. 23, 1941, Mineola, NY, *Sr. VP, Exec. Div.*, Nat. Bank of North Amer., RE Loan Div.; **PRIM RE ACT:** Lender; **SERVICES:** All banking ser.; **PREV EMPLOY:** The Chase Manhattan Bank, VP 1966-1979; **PROFL AFFIL & HONORS:** RE Bd. of NY; ABA; Young Men's RE Assn. of NY; MBA; ULI; Amer. Management Assn.; **GRAD EDUC:** BS, 1962, Bus., The Citadel; **EDUC HONORS:** Dean's List Econ. Honor Soc.; **MIL SERV:** US Army, LT; **OTHER ACT & HONORS:** Member, Planning Bd., Harrington Park, NJ; Chmn., Cub Scout Comm., Harrington Park; **HOME ADD:** Harrington Park, NJ; **BUS ADD:** 44 Wall St., New York, NY 10005, (212)623-2958.

SCHREIBER, Glenn P., Jr.——**B:** May 31, 1948, McKeesport, PA, *VP, RE*, Specialty Consultants, Inc.; **PRIM RE ACT:** Consultant; **SERVICES:** Spec. Consults., Inc. is the largest nat. exec. search firm in the country that specializes exclusively in the RE industry; **REP CLIENTS:** Devels., investors., contractors, synd., prop. mgrs., brokers, and lenders; **PROFL AFFIL & HONORS:** ICSC; RESSI; NACORE; BOMA; MBA, Numerous articles published in various RE trade journals; Guest lecturer, Nat. Assoc. of RE Execs. (Nat. Annual Conference); **EDUC:** BS, 1970, Slippery Rock State Coll.; **HOME ADD:** 124 Thunderbird Dr., McKeesport, PA 15135, (412)751-3298; **BUS ADD:** 2710 Gateway Towers, Pittsburgh, PA 15222, (412)355-8200.

SCHREIBER, Irving——**B:** July 29, 1921, NY, NY, *Publisher*, Panel Publishers; **PRIM RE ACT:** Attorney, Real Estate Publisher, Instructor; **OTHER RE ACT:** Prof. of Tax.; Author of RE Publications; **PREV EMPLOY:** Exec. Editor, Inst. for Bus. Planning; **PROFL AFFIL & HONORS:** ABA, AICPA, NY State Soc. CPA; NY Bar Assn.; **EDUC:** BBA, 1946, Acctg., CCNY (Now Baruch Coll., CUNY); **GRAD EDUC:** JD, 1948, Law, Columbia Univ. Law School; **EDUC HONORS:** Cum Laude; **MIL SERV:** US Air Corps., 1st Lt., Air Medal (4 oak leaf clusters); **HOME ADD:** 164-45 75 Ave., Flushing, NY 11366, (212)591-4972; **BUS ADD:** 14 Plaza Rd., Greenvale, NY 11548, (516)484-0006.

SCHREIBER, William D.——**B:** Jan. 5, 1938, Milwaukee, *VP*, Grootemaat Corp., RE Mgmt.; **PRIM RE ACT:** Broker, Property Manager; **PREV EMPLOY:** Past Exec. Dir. BOMA-Milwaukee; **PROFL AFFIL & HONORS:** BOMA, IREM, Milwaukee Bd. of Realtors; **EDUC:** BA, 1959, Bus. Admin.-RE, Valparaiso Univ.; **HOME ADD:** 590 E. Ravenswood Hill Cir., Waukesha, WI 53186, (414)786-5318; **BUS ADD:** 735 N. Water St., Milwaukee, WI 53202, (414)271-5690.

SCHRIEBER, Brian C.——**B:** Nov. 28, 1948, Pittsburgh, PA; **PRIM RE ACT:** Attorney, Owner/Investor, Broker; **SERVICES:** Legal, Indus. & Resid. leasing; **EDUC:** BA, 1970, Hist., Univ. of WI; **GRAD EDUC:** JD, 1973, Georgetown Univ. Law Ctr.; **HOME ADD:** 1330 Squirrel Hill Ave., Pittsburgh, PA 15217, (412)621-4273; **BUS ADD:** 1360 Old Freeport Rd., Suite 300, Pittsburgh, PA 15238, (412)963-1000.

SCHROCK, Lyle E.——**B:** June 26, 1931, Topeka, IL, *Pres.*, Gilbert Rayner, Inc.; **PRIM RE ACT:** Broker; **SERVICES:** Complete RE serv.; **REP CLIENTS:** Home buyers and sellers, and RE investors; **PROFL AFFIL & HONORS:** Dir., IL Assn. of Realtors; NAR; Pres., North Shore Bd. of Realtors, GRI, CRB; **OTHER ACT & HONORS:** Dir. Lake Forest S & L Assn., Pres. Council, Barat Coll, Exec. Bd., BSA; **HOME ADD:** 160 E. Onwentsia Rd., Lake Forest, IL 60045, (312)234-1130; **BUS ADD:** 300 E. IL Rd., Lake Forest, IL 60045, (312)234-9300.

SCHROEDER, Cliff——**B:** MN, *Owner-Broker*, Cliff Schroeder, Realtors-Consultants-Devels.; **PRIM RE ACT:** Broker, Consultant, Developer, Insuror, Syndicator; **OTHER RE ACT:** Financial Planning; **SERVICES:** RE services, Consulting, Fin. Planning; **PROFL AFFIL & HONORS:** NAR, CA Assn. of Realtors, Realtors Natl. Mktg. Instit., Los Angeles, CA CCIM Chap., Assn. of RE Attys., Amer. Soc. of Chartered Life Underwriters & LA Chap., Sales & Mktg. Council of the NAHB; **EDUC:** BA, Differential Psych./Indus. Relations, Univ. of MN; **GRAD EDUC:** RE, Ins., Fin. Planning, Mktg., Univ. of CA, CA State Univ.; **HOME ADD:** 5265 Greenmeadow Rd., Long Beach, CA 90808, (213)429-1745; **BUS ADD:** 2750 Bellflower Blvd., Suite 206, Long Beach, CA 90815, (213)420-2880.

SCHROEDER, Daniel——*Admin.*, Mississippi, MS Real Estate Commission; **PRIM RE ACT:** Property Manager; **BUS ADD:** 1920 Dumbarton St., Jackson, MS 39216, (601)982-6300.*

SCHROEDER, K. Ronald——**B:** Aug. 20, 1947, Los Angeles, CA, Walter Uccellini Enterprises, Inc., Devel./Prop. Mgmt.; **PRIM RE ACT:** Developer, Property Manager; **SERVICES:** Devel./Prop. mgmt.; **PREV EMPLOY:** Ten years exper. in prop. mgmt./const./land devel. for private firms; **PROFL AFFIL & HONORS:** IREM, CPM Candidate/NY State RE Lic., Notary Public; **EDUC:** BS Econ., 1970, Econs./Acctg., State Univ. of NY at Albany; **GRAD EDUC:** Course work completed for MS, 1971, Econs., State Univ. of NY at Albany; **EDUC HONORS:** Dean's List; **HOME ADD:** 27 Ableman Ave., Albany, NY 12203, (518)456-2736; **BUS ADD:** 5 Broadway, Suite 206, PO Box 305, Troy, NY 12180, (518)271-7564.

SCHROEDER, William R., Jr.——**B:** June 20, 1944, Denver, CO, *Sec.-Treas.*, Schroeder & Co., Inc.; **PRIM RE ACT:** Broker, Consultant, Appraiser, Property Manager; **SERVICES:** RE Sales, Prop. Mgmt.; **PROFL AFFIL & HONORS:** Nat. Assn. of Realtors, Denver Bd. of Realtors, GRI; CRS; CRB; **EDUC:** Engrg. and RE, Univ. of CO.; **EDUC HONORS:** Grad. Realtors Inst. (GRI); **MIL SERV:** USN (1965-67), E-4 (RD-3) PO; **OTHER ACT & HONORS:** Rep. Party (Comm. Man, Dist. 28 House of Rep. Sec.); Pres. 1980-81 The Terrace Club (Swim and Tennis and Club), Soccer Coach 7-10 year old Boys; **HOME ADD:** 4420 S Braun Ct., Morrison, CO 80465, (303)697-8321; **BUS ADD:** 4393 W Florida Ave., Denver, CO 80219, (303)934-2391.

SCHROEDER, William R., Sr.——**B:** May 20, 1923, Faribault, MN, *Pres./Broker*, Schroeder & Co., Inc.; **PRIM RE ACT:** Broker, Consultant, Appraiser, Developer, Lender, Owner/Investor, Instructor, Property Manager, Insuror; **SERVICES:** A full service realty co.; **PREV EMPLOY:** Schroeder & Co. Celebrates its 35th Anniversary in 1982; **PROFL AFFIL & HONORS:** Denver Bd. of Realtors; CO Assn. of Realtors; The Nat. Assn. of RE Bds.; Denver-Metro Realty Bd., Past Dir. and Past Treas. of the Denver Bd. of Realtors; Past Pres., Metro Denver Realty Bd.; Past Pres., Optimist Club of W. Denver; **EDUC:** RE Fin., Univ. of CO Extension; **OTHER ACT & HONORS:** Denver Bd. of Educ. (1979-1985); **HOME ADD:** 1620 S. Perry St., Denver, CO 80219, (303)935-5775; **BUS ADD:** 4393 W. Florida Ave., Denver, CO 80219, (303)934-2391.

SCHROETER, Thomas G.——**B:** June 30, 1948, Detroit, MI, *Atty.*, Miller, Canfield, Paddock & Stone; **OTHER RE ACT:** RE lending, reorganizations, work outs; **PROFL AFFIL & HONORS:** ABA, State Bar of MI (Real Prop. Law Sect., Comm. on Seminars & Workshops), Detroit Bar Assn.; **EDUC:** AB, 1970, Govt., Georgetown Univ.; **GRAD EDUC:** JD, 1973, Georgetown Law Ctr.; **EDUC HONORS:** Editor, Law Review; **HOME ADD:** 1390 Whittier, Grosse Pointe Pk., MI; **BUS ADD:** 300 Wabeck Bldg., Birmingham, MI 48012, (313)645-5000.

SCHROUF, M. H.——**B:** May 28, 1936, Oklahoma City, OK, *Chmn.*, Realty Group; **PRIM RE ACT:** Broker, Developer, Builder, Owner/Investor, Property Manager; **PREV EMPLOY:** Exec. VP - Forward Oil & Gas, Inc.; VP & Gen. Mgr. Indus. Brokers, Inc. & Star Realty Mgmt., Inc.; **PROFL AFFIL & HONORS:** NAR; **EDUC:** BBA, 1960, Mktg., OK Univ.; **EDUC HONORS:** Dean's & Pres's. Honor Rolls; Outstanding Salesmanship Student; Outstanding Advertising/Mktg. Student; **OTHER ACT & HONORS:** COMCERT - Chmn.; Chmn. Major Bond Issue Comm.; **HOME ADD:** 2720 Cypress, Norman, OK 73069, (405)360-0716; **BUS ADD:** 1215 Crossroads Blvd., Ste. 121, PO Box 5087, Norman, OK 73070, (405)360-6545.

SCHUCKMAN, Stanley H.——**B:** Aug. 18, 1944, Brooklyn, NY, Schuckman Realty Co.; **PRIM RE ACT:** Broker; **SERVICES:** Lic. RE broker and consultant specializing in retail store planning, leasing & devel.; **REP CLIENTS:** Channel Home Centers, Rickel Home Centers, Pergament Home Centers, Toys R Us, Child World, Playworld, supermarkets, etc.; **PREV EMPLOY:** Breslin Realty; **PROFL AFFIL & HONORS:** Intl. Council of Shopping Centers; **EDUC:** 1968, Acctg., C.W. Post Coll.; **HOME ADD:** 15 Firelight Ct., Dix Hills, NY 11746, (516)499-8976; **BUS ADD:** 390 N. Broadway, Jericho, NY 11753, (516)931-3443.

SCHUHMANN, Barbara L.——**B:** Jan. 26, 1949, Louisville, KY, *VP*, Merdes, Schiable, Staley & DeLisio; **PRIM RE ACT:** Attorney, Instructor; **OTHER RE ACT:** RE Law, U. of AK, 1980; Business Law, 1982; **SERVICES:** Counseling; document preparation; litigation; **REP CLIENTS:** Lenders, condo. assns., devel., indiv.; **PREV EMPLOY:** Legislative assist., US Senator Marlow Cook; Govt. Affairs, Republic Steel Corp.; **PROFL AFFIL & HONORS:** Amer. AK, Tanana Valley & DC Bar Assns.; **EDUC:** BA, 1971, Hist., Amer. Univ.; **GRAD EDUC:** JD, 1974, Georgetown Univ.; **EDUC HONORS:** Cum Laude; **OTHER ACT & HONORS:** Chairperson, AK Commission on the Status of Women, 1981, 1982; **HOME ADD:** Fairbanks, AK 99701SR Box 40465; **BUS ADD:** PO Box 810, Fairbanks, AK 99707, (907)452-1855.

SCHULER, Dominic A.——**B:** Jan. 1, 1920, Louisville, KY, *Dir. of Housing*, Dept. of Housing & Urban Development, Housing; **PRIM RE ACT:** Lender, Regulator, Property Manager; **SERVICES:** Mort. Insurance, Mort. Underwriting, Property Mgmt.; **REP CLIENTS:** Builders, Devel., Owners, Managers; **PROFL AFFIL & HONORS:** IREM, CPM; **EDUC:** BA, 1955, Arch.-Chemistry, Univ. IL, Univ. of Louisville; **MIL SERV:** USAF, S/Sgt.; **HOME ADD:** 541 Sunnyside Dr., Louisville, KY 40206, (502)895-0108; **BUS ADD:** HUD PO Box 1044, Louisville, KY 40201, (502)582-5266.

SCHULMAN, Albert——**B:** Oct. 7, 1929, Chicago, IL, *VP*, Arthur Rubloff & Company, Indus. Properties Group; **PRIM RE ACT:** Broker; **PROFL AFFIL & HONORS:** RNMI, Chicago RE Bd., NAR, IL RE Assn. IREB, Cert. Comml. Investment Member; **EDUC:** Bus., Northwestern Univ.; **MIL SERV:** US Army, Cpl.; **OTHER ACT & HONORS:** Past Pres. 1978 CCIM Chap. State of IL. Past Pres. 1971-1972 Salesman Club of the Chicago Real Estate Board; **HOME ADD:** 399 Sunset Ln., Glencoe, IL 60022, (312)835-2602; **BUS ADD:** 8600 W. Bryn Mawr 100, Chicago, IL 60631, (312)399-7021.

SCHULMAN, Robert P.——**B:** Nov. 22, 1927, New York, NY, *Gen. Counsel*, Kimco Development Corp.; **OTHER RE ACT:** RE and Corp. Law; **SERVICES:** Atty.; **REP CLIENTS:** The Kimco Corp., Kimco Devel. Corp.; **PREV EMPLOY:** Partner: Kahr & Spitzer & Howard, NYC; **PROFL AFFIL & HONORS:** ABA, NY State Bar Assn.; **EDUC:** BA, 1949, Poli. Sci., NYU; **GRAD EDUC:** LLB, 1952, Law, NYU; **EDUC HONORS:** Law Review Editor; **MIL SERV:** USAF, Cpl.; **OTHER ACT & HONORS:** Asst. Prof., The RE Inst., NYU; **HOME ADD:** 129 Grace St., Plainview, NY 11803, (516)938-2913; **BUS ADD:** 1044 Northern Blvd., Roslyn, NY 11576, (516)484-5865.

SCHULTHEIS, Ralph William, Jr.——**B:** Jan. 9, 1938, Woodbury, NJ, *Principal*, First Southern Systems; **PRIM RE ACT:** Consultant, Owner/Investor, Syndicator; **OTHER RE ACT:** Electronic systems for the RE community; **EDUC:** 1960, Econ., Princeton Univ.; **GRAD EDUC:** 1962, Mktg., Wharton Bus. School, Univ. of PA; **MIL SERV:** US Army; **OTHER ACT & HONORS:** Orlando Area C of C; AUSA; Navy League; SCS; NSIA; **HOME ADD:** 1921 Hobson St., Longwood, FL 32750; **BUS ADD:** PO Box 2105, Winter Park, FL 32790, (305)331-0939.

SCHULTZ, Harvey——**B:** May 14, 1941, LongBranch, NJ, *Exec. VP*, M. Alrieri Co., Inc.; **PRIM RE ACT:** Developer, Builder, Property Manager, Owner/Investor; **PROFL AFFIL & HONORS:** MAIP, QRELA; **EDUC:** BA, 1963, Bus. Admin., Boston Univ.; **HOME ADD:** 2 Pal Dr., Wayside, NJ 07083, (201)493-3046; **BUS ADD:** 2401 Morris Ave., Union, NJ 07083, (201)687-2530.

SCHULTZ, H.L.——**B:** Dec. 14, 1918, Williamsport, PA, *Broker/Affiliate*, Jimmie Taylor & Co., Inc., Comml. - Indus.; **PRIM RE ACT:** Broker, Consultant, Appraiser, Instructor, Syndicator; **SERVICES:** RE brokerage, counseling, appraising, synd.; **REP CLIENTS:** Garland Coal Co., Don Rey Media Group, Southwest Explorers, US Forgecraft; **PREV EMPLOY:** Chief Acct., Mayflower Hotel, Washington, DC; Cost Acct., GE, Fort Smith; **PROFL AFFIL & HONORS:** NAR; RMI; AK Realtors Assn.; Cert. RE Counser; **EDUC:** BS, Georgetown Univ.; **GRAD EDUC:** LLB, 1941, Nat. Univ.; **OTHER ACT & HONORS:** Ft. Smith C of C; The Exchange Club of Ft. Smith; Razback Club; Wild Hogs; Ft. Smith Quarterback Club; Masonic Bodies; R.O.Y. State of AR 1967; **HOME ADD:** 8511 Royal Ridge Dr., Ft. Smith, AR 72913, (501)452-1645; **BUS ADD:** 4611 Rogers Ave., Ft. Smith, AR 72913, (501)782-8871.

SCHULTZ, Mortimer L.——**B:** Feb. 12, 1918, Newark, NJ, *Pres.*, M.L. Schultz Co.; **PRIM RE ACT:** Broker, Appraiser, Developer, Builder, Owner/Investor, Property Manager, Syndicator; **REP CLIENTS:** Attys., banks, indus. firms, Comml. firms; Security Firms; **PREV EMPLOY:** Shopping Ctr. Owner; Pres. Diversified RE Co.; RE Synd.; Gen. Contractor; **PROFL AFFIL & HONORS:** Somerset Cty. Bd. of Realtors; NJ Assn. of Realtors; NAR, Lic. RE Broker, NJ; **MIL SERV:** US Army Air Force, 2nd Lt.; **HOME ADD:** 1106 Park Ave., Plainfield, NJ 07060, (201)756-5887; **BUS ADD:** 700 Somerset St., Watchung, NJ 07060, (201)753-6770.

SCHULTZ, Richard A.——**B:** Sept. 22, 1939, Jacksonville, FL, *Pres.*, Atwater Company; **PRIM RE ACT:** Broker, Consultant, Property Manager; **SERVICES:** Office Bldg. Mgmt., Investment Counseling, Valuation, Office Bldg. Leasing; **REP CLIENTS:** Lenders, Inst., & Indiv. Investors in office bldgs.; **PREV EMPLOY:** FL Fed. S&L Assn., 1972-78; Justice Corp., 1978-81; **PROFL AFFIL & HONORS:** IREM, Realtor, CPM; **EDUC:** BSBA, 1964, Bus. Admin., Jacksonville Univ.; **OTHER ACT & HONORS:** Rotary; **HOME ADD:** 6055 Bayou Grande Bl., St. Petersburg, FL 33703, (813)525-5463; **BUS ADD:** 6055 Bayou Grande Blvd. NE, St. Petersburg, FL 33703, (813)525-5463.

SCHULZ, Dennis——*Secy./Treas.*, North Dakota Real Estate Commission; **PRIM RE ACT:** Property Manager; **BUS ADD:** PO Box 727, Bismarck, ND 58502, (701)224-2749.*

SCHULZ, Henry C.——**B:** Jan. 14, 1931, Huntington, NY, *Principal*, Commercial Brokerage Co.; **PRIM RE ACT:** Broker; **SERVICES:** Comml. & indus. RE brokerage; **REP CLIENTS:** Pacific Tel. Co., Gen. Mills, Amer. Airlines; **EDUC:** BA, 1952, Econ., Univ. of VA; **MIL SERV:** US Army, 1st. Lt.; **OTHER ACT & HONORS:** past Pres. Oyster Bay NY Bd. of Educ. 1965-68; **HOME ADD:** 4559 Ben Ave., N. Hollywood, CA 91607, (213)985-2773; **BUS ADD:** 3243 Wilshire Blvd., Los Angeles, CA 90010, (213)487-7600.

SCHUMACHER, George——Penta Pacific Properties; **PRIM RE ACT:** Developer; **BUS ADD:** 14714 Carmenita Rd., Norwalk, CA 90650, (213)921-7914.*

SCHUMACHER, Stephen J.——**B:** Feb. 5, 1942, Los Angeles CA, *Atty.*, Schumacher and Evans; **PRIM RE ACT:** Attorney; **SERVICES:** Real prop. and tax advise; **PROFL AFFIL & HONORS:** ABA, Real Prop. & Tax Sect.; CA State Bar Assn., RP & Tax; LA Bar Assn. Orange Cty. Bar Assn.; **EDUC:** AB, 1963, Econ., U.S.C.; **GRAD EDUC:** JD, 1967, Univ. of CA at Hastings; LLM, 1969, Taxation, NYU; **EDUC HONORS:** Schwed Memorial Scholar; **OTHER ACT & HONORS:** Balboa Bay Club; Back Bay Club; Instructor, RE Taxation, UCI Co-Author of publication on RE Taxation; Author of various articles for legal periodicals; Lecturer CA Continuing Educ. of Bar on RE Topics; Who's Who in Orange Cty.; **HOME ADD:** 2031 Yacht Defender, Newport Beach, CA 92660, (714)760-3661; **BUS ADD:** 3151 Airway Ave. A-1, Costa Mesa, CA 92626, (714)850-1190.

SCHUMAN, David M.——**B:** Apr. 20, 1944, Los Angeles, CA, *Partner*, First City Equities; **PRIM RE ACT:** Developer, Owner/Investor; **SERVICES:** RE investment and devel.; **PREV EMPLOY:** Barsa Inc., Seattle, WA, 1977-1978; Sonnenblick-Goldman Corp. of CA, 1973-1977, Seattle & 1970-1973, CA; **PROFL AFFIL & HONORS:** Intl. Council of Shopping Centers; Nat. Assn. of RE Brokers; Mort. Bankers Assn., Mayor's Task Force on In-City Living, Seattle, WA; **EDUC:** BA, 1969, Bus. Admin./Fin., Univ. of WA/CA State Coll./Los Angeles City Coll.; **MIL SERV:** U.S. Army, M/Sgt.; **HOME ADD:** 9438 Southeast 52nd St., Mercer Island, WA 98040, (206)232-7484; **BUS ADD:** Suite 4040, 800 Fifth Ave., Seattle, WA 98104, (206)624-9223.

SCHUPE, H.E.——*Mgr. RE*, Republic Steel Co.; **PRIM RE ACT:** Property Manager; **BUS ADD:** PO Box 6778, Cleveland, OH 44101, (216)622-5000.*

SCHURGER, David L., Jr.——**B:** Sept. 2, 1944, Lubbock, TX, *Prof.*, S OK City Jr. Coll.; **PRIM RE ACT:** Broker, Instructor, Syndicator, Consultant, Appraiser, Developer, Property Manager, Owner/Investor; **OTHER RE ACT:** Petroleum land titles; Coordinator of RE and petroleum land mgmt. program offering adult education degrees.; **SERVICES:** Investment counseling, Oil property valuation; Commercial real estate; **REP CLIENTS:** S&L, Life Ins. Co's., Specialized Oil and Gas Leases, Individual investors; **PREV EMPLOY:** Builder/Devel., Resid. and Comm'l. Brokerage Firm; **PROFL AFFIL & HONORS:** RESSI; AREUEA; Bd. of Dir., 3 yr. term (80-83), REEA; Sr. Member, NARA; **EDUC:** BSBA, 1971, RE/Mktg., Univ. of FL; **GRAD EDUC:** Grad. Study, Human Relations, Univ. of OK; **EDUC HONORS:** Beta Gamma Sigma, Phi Kappa Phi; **OTHER ACT & HONORS:** Also assoc. with Professional RE Consultants; **HOME ADD:** 7833 S. Youngs, Oklahoma City, OK 73159, (405)681-5278; **BUS ADD:** 7777 S. May, Oklahoma City, OK 73159, (405)682-7550.

SCHURGOT, Paul D., Jr.——*President*, Walco National Corp.; **PRIM RE ACT:** Property Manager; **BUS ADD:** 743 Fifth Ave., New York, NY 10022, (212)688-4685.*

SCHUSTER, Meryl A.——**B:** Nov. 19, 1953, Pico Rivera, CA, *RE Sales Assoc.*, IDM Corp., RE Investments; **PRIM RE ACT:** Owner/Investor; **PREV EMPLOY:** CA Mort. Serv., Charter Mort. Co., Allstate Enterprises & Mort. Corp.; **PROFL AFFIL & HONORS:** NAR, CAR, Political Affairs Comm., Long Beach Bd. of Realtors, RECI; **EDUC:** Pre-Law & RE Investment Analysis, CA State, LA, Long Beach City Coll.; **OTHER ACT & HONORS:** Assoc. Member, Republican Central Comm.; **HOME ADD:** 4014 Colorado St., Long Beach, CA 90805, (213)433-6688; **BUS ADD:** 4647 Long Beach Blvd., Long Beach, CA 90805, (213)595-4565.

SCHUSTERMAN, Allen——*Asst. Secy.*, M. Lowenstein & Sons, Inc.; **PRIM RE ACT:** Property Manager; **BUS ADD:** 1430 Broadway, New York, NY 10018, (212)930-5000.*

SCHUTTE, Betty——**B:** July 25, 1934, Louisville, KY, *Pres.*, Century 21 Betty Schutte Realtors; **PRIM RE ACT:** Broker, Property Manager; **REP CLIENTS:** Area Mgr. Broker for HUD; **PROFL AFFIL & HONORS:** NAR, KAR, Louisville Bd. of Realtors, BPWC, Women's Council, Pres. 1972; CPM; GRI; **EDUC:** CPM, 1976, GRI, 1970, 1952, Holy Rosary Academy; **HOME ADD:** 913 Albemarle Ct, Louisville, KY 40222, (502)425-8629; **BUS ADD:** 3309 College Dr, Louisville, KY 40299, (502)267-5403.

SCHWAB, C.H.——*Manager, RE*, Atlantic Richfield Co.; **PRIM RE ACT:** Property Manager; **BUS ADD:** 515 So. Flower Street, Los Angeles, CA 90071, (213)486-3511.*

SCHWADERER, Charles B., II——**B:** Jan 19, 1946, Detroit, MI, *Pres.*, Sunbelt Assoc., Inc., Realtors; **PRIM RE ACT:** Broker, Consultant; **SERVICES:** Gen. brokerage-sales, leasing, consulting-comml.props.-vacant or improved; **REP CLIENTS:** Investors and devel.; **PREV EMPLOY:** Keyes Co. Realtors-Dist. Sales Mgr. & Corp. officer 1979-72; **PROFL AFFIL & HONORS:** FLI, RESSI, Boca Raton Bd. of Realtors, Pres. Elect, 1981-Boca Raton Bd. of Realtors; Dir., 1980-81 FL Assn. of Realtors; **EDUC:** BS, BA, 1968, Fin., Univ. of FL-Bus. School; **GRAD EDUC:** 1971-72, R.E., FL Atlantic Univ., Univ. of FL; **MIL SERV:** US Army; Lt., Combat Infantry Badge; Bronze Star, Air Medal, Army Commendation Medal, Vietnam campaign medals; **HOME ADD:** 1080 N.W. 3rd St., Boca Raton, FL 33432, (305)368-8690; **BUS ADD:** 235 S. Fed. Hwy., Boca Raton, FL 33432, (305)368-8317.

SCHWALL, Leonard——**B:** Aug. 27, 1926, Boston, MA, *Part.*, Schwall & Becker; **PRIM RE ACT:** Attorney; **SERVICES:** Mort. Foreclosures, Title Closings & Mortgs. on Comml. & Resid. RE; **REP CLIENTS:** Citibank, NA; Newburgh Savings Bank; W. Side Fed. S&L Assn.; Equitable Life Assurance Soc.; **PREV EMPLOY:** Housing & Home Fin. Agency 1950-52, Assessor, Town of Clarkstown 1957-59; **PROFL AFFIL & HONORS:** ABA, Attys. Comm. US League of Savings Assns, Attys. Comm. Savings Assn. League of NY Amer. Clg of Mtg Attys.; **EDUC:** AB, 1947, Harvard; **GRAD EDUC:** LLB, 1950, Columbia Univ.; **MIL SERV:** USNR, Aviation Cadet; **HOME ADD:** Roselawn Rd., Highland Mills, NY 10930, (914)928-2122; **BUS ADD:** 49 Maple Ave., New City, Rockland Cty., NY 10956, (914)634-3696.

SCHWAMM, Jay Marc——**B:** Apr. 17, 1930, New York, NY, *Pres.*, Redafco, Inc.; **PRIM RE ACT:** Developer, Owner/Investor; **REP CLIENTS:** Instnl. joint venture participants; **PREV EMPLOY:** Chmn. of the Bd., Amer. Trust Co. (NY); **EDUC:** AB, 1951, Public & Intl. Affairs, Princeton Univ. (Woodrow Wilson School); **GRAD EDUC:** MBA, 1953, Fin., Harvard Bus. School; **EDUC HONORS:** Magna Cum Laude, Phi Beta Kappa, Grad. with Distinction, Century Club; **MIL SERV:** US Army, Res.; 1st Lt.; **OTHER ACT & HONORS:** Special Asst. to VP of the US (1968); Consultant to the Asst. Sec. of Commerce (Economic Devel.) 1966-1969; **HOME ADD:** 211 Central Park W., New York, NY 10024; **BUS ADD:** 251 West 57th St., New York, NY 10019, (212)582-9595.

SCHWANDER, Robert H.——**B:** Oct. 21, 1926, Berwyn, IL, *Pres.*, Schwander & Co.; **PRIM RE ACT:** Developer, Builder, Property Manager, Owner/Investor; **SERVICES:** Develop, build and manage mid-rise combination apt. & comml. bldgs.; **PREV EMPLOY:** 26 yrs. with Schwander & Co.; **EDUC:** BBA, 1950, Acctg. & fin., Northwestern Univ.; **MIL SERV:** US Army, 1943-44, Pvt.; USN 1944-46, S/1/c; **OTHER ACT & HONORS:** Air Force Assn., US Naval Inst., Nat. Rifle Assn.; **HOME ADD:** 22 W 470 Glen Park Rd., Glen Ellyn, IL 60137; **BUS ADD:** 5107A Washington St., Downers Grove, IL 60515, (312)969-5521.

SCHWARTZ, Gerald——**B:** Feb. 22, 1945, Chicago, IL, *Dir. of Real Estate*, Seraco Group; **PRIM RE ACT:** Developer; **PREV EMPLOY:** VP, Gladstone Assoc.; Directed firms practice for retailers & devel. of shopping centers; **PROFL AFFIL & HONORS:** ULI; Intl. Council of Shopping Centers; **EDUC:** BS, 1967, European Hist., Univ. of WI; **GRAD EDUC:** MBA, 1970, RE, Univ. of WI; **EDUC HONORS:** Research Grant - Student Housing; **OTHER ACT & HONORS:** Publications: contributing author to: *Mkt. Research for Shopping Centers* (ICSC); *Retail Developers Handbook* (ULI); *Shopping Centers 1988: Answers for Next Decade* (ICSC); **HOME ADD:** 143 Cary Ave., Highland Park, IL 60035, (312)432-6412; **BUS ADD:** 55 W. Monroe Ave., Xerox Centre, Chicago, IL 60603, (312)875-0323.

SCHWARTZ, Gilbert Sumner——**B:** June 1, 1924, NY, NY, *Pres.*, Sahara, Realtors; **PRIM RE ACT:** Broker; **SERVICES:** All phases of resid., comml. and investment RE; **REP CLIENTS:** NV S & L, NV Power, Radio Shack, Lafayette Electronics, Howard Hughes, NV State Rehab. & Rest. Ctr.; **PREV EMPLOY:** Lic. RE salesman in NY - 1945 worked with father, Emanuel Schwartz in comml. & investment brokerage bus.; Opened own RE firm in 1964 - currently Pres. of same; **PROFL AFFIL & HONORS:** Las Vegas Bd. of Realtors, NV Ass. of Realtors; NAR, Sr. Instr., RNMI Mktg. Mgmt.; Instr., NV Assn. of Realtors; Realtor of the Year 1974; Nat. Omega Tau Tho 1973; Personalities of the West & Midwest 1972; Who's Who in the West 1975 & 1976; GRI, CRB, CRS; Pres., Las Vegas Bd. of Realtors 1969; Pres., NV Assn. of Realtors 1972; VP, Nat. Assn. of Realtors 1974; **EDUC:** Clarkson Coll. of Tech., Potsdam NY 1942-43; **MIL SERV:** USN; **OTHER ACT & HONORS:** Advisory Council Clark Cty. Community Coll.; Elks Lodge; Sheriff's Possee 1961; Tr., NV Devel. Authority; **HOME ADD:** 2841 Queens Courtyard Dr., Las Vegas, NV 89109, (702)731-0852; **BUS ADD:** 1095 E. Sahara Ave., Las Vegas, NV 89121, (702)733-1000.

SCHWARTZ, Harvey——B: July 16, 1941, New York, NY, *Partner*, Shapiro, Mortman & Schwartz, P.C.; **PRIM RE ACT:** Attorney; **SERVICES:** Tax planning & structuring; **REP CLIENTS:** Purchasers, sellers, devels. and syndicators of Real props.; **PROFL AFFIL & HONORS:** ABA; NY State Bar Assn.; Assn. of the Bar of City of NY; **EDUC:** BBA, 1963, Acctg., CCNY; **GRAD EDUC:** JD, 1967, Columbia Law School; **EDUC HONORS:** Magna Cum Laude, Cum Laude; **HOME ADD:** 421 Westwood Rd., Woodmere, NY 11598; **BUS ADD:** 800 Third Ave., New York, NY 10022, (212)371-6100.

SCHWARTZ, Jacob——B: Dec. 10, 1917, NYC, *Realtor*, J. Schwartz, RE Co.; **PRIM RE ACT:** Broker, Appraiser; **PREV EMPLOY:** IRS Tax Auditor; **PROFL AFFIL & HONORS:** Masonic Lodge; **EDUC:** Johns Hopkins Appraisal Courses; **HOME ADD:** 6243 Robin Hill Rd., Baltimore, MD 21207, (301)944-1739; **BUS ADD:** 6243 Robin Hill Rd., Baltimore, MD 21207, (301)944-1739.

SCHWARTZ, J.F.——*Secy.*, Federal Signal Corp.; **PRIM RE ACT:** Property Manager; **BUS ADD:** 1415 W. 22nd St., Oak Brook, IL 60514, (312)920-2700.*

SCHWARTZ, Joseph Harold——B: Aug. 16, 1950, Los Angeles, CA, *VP*, Angeles Realty Corp.; **PRIM RE ACT:** Owner/Investor, Syndicator; **PREV EMPLOY:** Asst. const. supt. 1974-77, Shapell Indus., Inc.; **EDUC:** BA, 1974, Law And Soc., Univ.of CA, Santa Barbara; **GRAD EDUC:** MBA, 1979, Housing, RE, Urban Land Econ., UCLA; **EDUC HONORS:** Cum Laude; **OTHER ACT & HONORS:** Bd. of Dir. Gateways Hospital; President's Asvisory Council of the City of Hope; **HOME ADD:** 12579 Westminster Ave., Los Angeles, CA 90066, (213)390-9362; **BUS ADD:** 1888 Century Park E, Los Angeles, CA 90067, (213)277-4900.

SCHWARTZ, Lawrence B.——B: May 17, 1929, Bridgeport, CT, *Atty., CPA*, Gladstone, Schwartz, Baroff and Blum; **PRIM RE ACT:** Consultant, Attorney, Syndicator, Banker, Owner/Investor; **SERVICES:** Full legal, fin. and consultation services; **REP CLIENTS:** Baker-Firestone, Inc.; Hyman J. Goldfeld, Largo, Inc.; Lafayette Bank & Trust Co., Bridgeport, CT; Claridge Hotel/Casino, Atlantic City, NJ; **PROFL AFFIL & HONORS:** Member, Bridgeport Bar Assn.; CT Bar Assn.; ABA, JD in Law, Member Beta Alpha Psi, Nat. Honorary Acctg. Soc.; **EDUC:** BS Econ., 1951, Wharton School of Fin., Univ. of PA; **GRAD EDUC:** JD, 1954, Law, Univ. of CT; **EDUC HONORS:** Cum Laude, Magna Cum Laude; **OTHER ACT & HONORS:** Sec., CT Bd. of Pardons, 1969, 1976; Treas., Town of Trumbull, 1958, 1959; **HOME ADD:** 1037 Fairfield Beach Rd., Fairfield, CT, (203)255-5252; **BUS ADD:** 333 State St., Bridgeport, CT 06604, (203)368-6746.

SCHWARTZ, Michael L.——B: July 15, 1948, NY, *Executive Vice President, Real Estate*, Sherman Clay & Co., Real Estate Division; **OTHER RE ACT:** Acquisitions, Redevelopment; **PREV EMPLOY:** Morgan Guaranty Trust Co., New York, NY; **PROFL AFFIL & HONORS:** The Intl. Council of Shopping Ctrs., Urban Land Inst.; **EDUC:** BA, 1970, Hist., Stanford Univ.; **GRAD EDUC:** MBA, 1974, Fin., Harvard Bus. School; **EDUC HONORS:** Hist. with honors; **OTHER ACT & HONORS:** Bd. of Trustee Member, Pomfret School, Pomfret Conn.; **HOME ADD:** 132 Locust St., San Francisco, CA 94118, (415)929-0971; **BUS ADD:** 851 Traeger Ave Suite 200, San Bruno, CA 94066, (415)952-2300.

SCHWARTZ, N. Willard——B: June 3, 1924, N. Plainfield, NJ, *VP*, Premier Financial Group; **PRIM RE ACT:** Broker; **OTHER RE ACT:** Mort. broker; **SERVICES:** Broker mort. from one fin. instn. to another; **PREV EMPLOY:** Former VP, Peoples Nat. Bank of No. Jersey; Member, Bd. of Dir. of United Jersey Bank; Dir., City Federal S&L; **PROFL AFFIL & HONORS:** NJ Assn. of Realtors; RNMI; Nat. Assn. of Realtors; Indus. RE Brokers Assn. of the NY Metropolitan Area; Inter-City Relocation Serv.; Former VP, Nat. Assn. of RE Lic. Law Officials; Member, Past Pres., Newark-No. Jersey Chap. of the Nat. Assn. of Indep. Fee Appraisers; Fee Appraiser for the US Fed. Housing Admin.; Fee Appraiser for the US Vet. Admin.; Member, Continental Assn. of Appraisers; Member, Nat. Assn. of Review Appraisers; **MIL SERV:** US Army, 1st Lt.; **OTHER ACT & HONORS:** Community Devel. Block Grant Comm. (Parsippany); No NJ and US Power Squadrons; Amer. Legion and VFW; B'nai B'rith; Member, Temple Sholem of W. Essex; Former Chmn., Parsippany Indus. Comm.; Past Pres., Parsippany C of C; Former Chmn., W. Essex Boy Scouts of Amer.; Former Commnr. of RE, State of NJ; **HOME ADD:** 53 Brookside Terr., No. Caldwall, NJ 07006, (201)226-5776; **BUS ADD:** 20 Evergreen Pl., E. Orange, NJ 07018, (201)672-9000.

SCHWARTZ, Norman A.——B: Jan. 29, 1922, NY, *Pres.*, Norman A. Schwartz Inc.; **PRIM RE ACT:** Broker, Consultant, Appraiser, Owner/Investor, Property Manager; **PROFL AFFIL & HONORS:** RE Bd. of Rochester, NY State Assn. of Realtors, NAR, GRI; **MIL SERV:** USAF, Cpl., WW II; **OTHER ACT & HONORS:** Knights of Pythias, B'nai B'rith; **HOME ADD:** 65 Towpath Ln., Rochester, NY 14618, (716)271-5770; **BUS ADD:** 1664 Monroe Ave., Rochester, NY 14618, (716)244-0200.

SCHWARTZ, Richard J.——*Pres.*, Jonathan Logan Inc.; **PRIM RE ACT:** Property Manager; **BUS ADD:** 1411 Broadway, New York, NY 10018, (212)840-9400.*

SCHWARTZ, Ronald M.——B: Feb. 7, 1933, Stamford, CT, *Atty. at Law*, Self-employed; **PRIM RE ACT:** Attorney, Owner/Investor, Property Manager, Developer; **EDUC:** AB, 1953, Duke Univ.; **GRAD EDUC:** JSD, 1956, Duke Law School; **OTHER ACT & HONORS:** Asst. Corp. Counsel/Bd. of Representatives, Pres.; **HOME ADD:** 195 Guinea Rd., Stamford, CT 06807, (203)322-3996; **BUS ADD:** 1017 Washington Blvd.,, Stamford, CT 06901, (203)327-0444.

SCHWARTZ, Sheldon——*Attorney*, Sheldon Schwartz; **PRIM RE ACT:** Attorney; **OTHER RE ACT:** Tax Editor at Real Estate Review; **SERVICES:** Tax and RE Law; **PROFL AFFIL & HONORS:** NY Bar Assn. (Tax Committee), Who's Who in American Law - 1st Edition; Co-author of "Tax Savings Opportunities in RE Deals" Prentice Hall, 1970; Frequent lecturer on RE Tax; **EDUC:** 1959, Hunter College; **GRAD EDUC:** LLB/LLM, 1962, 1963, Law, New York School of Law; **OTHER ACT & HONORS:** Adjunct Professor of Taxation at NYU; **BUS ADD:** New York, NY 10017, (212)687-0400.

SCHWARTZ, Stephen C.——B: Apr. 24, 1942, Philadelphia, PA, *Pres.*, United Mort. & Equity Corp.; **PRIM RE ACT:** Developer, Lender, Owner/Investor; **REP CLIENTS:** Synd. and principles in income producing comml. prop.; **PREV EMPLOY:** Anglo-Amer. Equity Corp, Warwick Realty Group; **PROFL AFFIL & HONORS:** Intl. Assn. of Fin. Counselors; **EDUC:** BS, 1965, Fin., Philadelphia Coll. of Textile Sciences; **GRAD EDUC:** Diploma, 1966, Fin., NY Inst. of Fin.; **OTHER ACT & HONORS:** Community Leaders of Amer.; **HOME ADD:** 1366 Revelation Rd., Meadowbrook, PA 19046, (215)947-5650; **BUS ADD:** The Warwick, Suite 1917, 17th & Locust Sts., Philadelphia, PA 19103, (215)735-3313.

SCHWARTZ, Thomas D.——B: Apr. 1, 1932, Carbondale, IL, *VP, Admin. & Sec., Alton Packaging Corp. and President, Alton Pension Management Co.*; **PRIM RE ACT:** Attorney; **PROFL AFFIL & HONORS:** RE Sect. ABA; IL Bar Assn.; Bar Assn. of Metropolitan St. Louis; **EDUC:** BA, 1956, Eng., Physics, Math & German, Southern IL Univ., Carbondale; **GRAD EDUC:** JD, 1961, Law, Univ. of Chicago Law School; **MIL SERV:** US Army, Spec. 3; **OTHER ACT & HONORS:** Dir., First Nat. Bank & Trust, Carbondale, IL; Elder, First Presbyterian Church, Alton, IL; Chmn., Bd. of Dirs., St. Anthony's Hospital, Alton, Il; **HOME ADD:** 1402 D'Adrian Dr., Godfrey, IL 62035, (618)466-1215; **BUS ADD:** 401 Alton St., Alton, IL 62002, (618)463-6114.

SCHWARTZ, William Thomas——B: Apr. 2, 1940, Kansas City, MO, *VP & Gen. Mgr.*, Security Pac. Intl. Bank; **PRIM RE ACT:** Banker, Owner/Investor, Instructor; **PREV EMPLOY:** 1967-69 Coldwell Banker & Co., San Francisco, CA; 1971-75 Bankers Trust Co., NY, NY, 1975-76 Abbott Labs., N. Chicago, IL., 1976-81 Sunbeam Corp., Oak Brook, IL; **PROFL AFFIL & HONORS:** Pres. Wharton Alumni Assn. of Chicago, 1978-81, Member. Bd. of Dirs. Nat. Wharton Alumni Assn., 1978-81.; **EDUC:** AB, 1962, Harvard Univ.; **GRAD EDUC:** MBA, 1970, Wharton Scbool, Univ. of PA, Univ. of S. CA; **MIL SERV:** USN, Lt.; **HOME ADD:** 1306 Rosalie St., Evanston, IL 60201, (312)866-8280; **BUS ADD:** 55 W Monroe St., Chicago, IL 60603, (312)580-7023.

SCHWARTZBERG, Hugh J.——B: Feb. 17, 1933, Chicago, IL, *Partner*, Schwartzberg, Barnett & Cohen; **PRIM RE ACT:** Attorney, Owner/Investor, Property Manager; **PROFL AFFIL & HONORS:** Chicago Bar Assn.; IL State Bar Assn.; ABA; World Assn. of Lawyers; Tau Epsilon Rho Law Frat.; **EDUC:** BA, 1953, Hist., Govt. and Econ., Harvard Coll.; **GRAD EDUC:** LLB, JD, 1956, Yale Law School; **EDUC HONORS:** Cum Laude; **OTHER ACT & HONORS:** Treas. B'nai B'rith Dist. 6, 1980-present; Who's Who in Amer. Law; **HOME ADD:** 853 W. Fullerton Ave., Chicago, IL 60614, (312)525-5256; **BUS ADD:** 11 S. LaSalle St., Chicago, IL 60603, (312)726-3555.

SCHWARZ, A. David, III——B: Apr. 29, 1948, Houston, TX, *Pres.*, A. David Schwarz III, Inc.; **PRIM RE ACT:** Broker, Owner/Investor; **SERVICES:** Investment counseling, research, comml. indus. and income prop. brokerage; **REP CLIENTS:** Comml. & indus. devel., investors in income producing prop.; **PROFL AFFIL & HONORS:** Houston Bd. of Realtors, Houston Apt. Assn., TX Assn. of Realtors, Houston Realty Breakfast Club; **EDUC:** BBA, 1970, Acctg., Univ. of TX at Austin; **OTHER ACT & HONORS:** Houston C of C, Rotary Club of Houston , Houston Livestock Show & Rodeo Life Member,

Univ. of TX Alumni Assn., Life Member, Sunrisers Breakfast Club, Century Club, Univ. of TX; **HOME ADD:** 2436 Chimney Rock, Houston, TX 77056, (713)977-3027; **BUS ADD:** 817 S Ripple Creek, Houston, TX 77057, (713)467-5200.

SCHWARZ, Michael——B: Apr. 29, 1937, Breslau, Germany, *Partner*, Arthur Andersen & Co., Tax RE; **OTHER RE ACT:** CPA; **SERVICES:** RE indus. tax practice; **REP CLIENTS:** Indiv. & corp RE devels. & investors; **PROFL AFFIL & HONORS:** AICPA, GA Soc. of CPA's, CPA Gold Medal; **EDUC:** BBA, 1958, Acctg., Univ. of GA; **OTHER ACT & HONORS:** VP of Atlanta Jewish Fed., Leadership Atlanta; Young Leadership, UJA; Co-author of *Federal Taxes Affecting RE*; **HOME ADD:** 1134 Swathmore Dr., NW, Atlanta, GA 30327, (404)266-9735; **BUS ADD:** 25 Park Pl., NE, Atlanta, GA 30303, (404)658-1776.

SCHWARZ, Roy M., Jr.——B: Feb. 15, 1938, New Orleans, LA, *Pres.*, Schwarz & Assoc., Inc., Realtors; **PRIM RE ACT:** Broker, Consultant, Appraiser, Owner/Investor; **SERVICES:** Sales, leasing, appraising/counseling in comml., indus., investment props.; **REP CLIENTS:** Law firms, nat. and local cos.; **PREV EMPLOY:** Latter & Blum, Inc. 1964-75; **PROFL AFFIL & HONORS:** SIR, MAI; **EDUC:** BA, 1960, Amer. Studies, Yale Univ.; **MIL SERV:** US Army, Pvt.; **OTHER ACT & HONORS:** Pres., Cancer Assn. of Greater New Orleans, Bd. of Dir., United Way of Greater New Orleans; **HOME ADD:** 6025 Coliseum St., New Orelans, LA 70118, (504)891-7356; **BUS ADD:** 408 Magazine St., New Orleans, LA 70130, (504)529-5515.

SCHWARZ, Sidney M.——B: Dec. 15, 1912, Orange, NJ, *Pres.*, Harry I. Schwarz & Co.; **PRIM RE ACT:** Broker, Consultant, Appraiser, Instructor, Property Manager; **SERVICES:** Appraisal servs., broker & prop. mgmt.; **PREV EMPLOY:** Appraiser with Army Corps. of Engrs., 1946; **PROFL AFFIL & HONORS:** Amer. R/W Assn.; Morris Cty. Bd. of Realtors; MAI, NJ Chap. Pres., 1958, MAI; CPM; SRPA; **EDUC:** BS, 1935, Econ., Lehigh Univ.; **MIL SERV:** US Army Corps. of Engrs.; Tech. Sgt., Army Commendation Medal; **OTHER ACT & HONORS:** Morris Cty. Housing Authority; Dover Ind. Comm.; Dover C of C, Past Pres.; Dover Lions Club (Founder Member); Mt. Sinai Cemetery Assn., Pres.; Dover 250 Anniversary Comm., V.Chmn.; Dover Gen. Hospital, Member of Bd. of Tr.; Temple B'Nai Or Morristown, Member of Bd. of Tr.; Dover Jewish Ctr.; Colonial Lodge #254 F&AM; **HOME ADD:** 85 Linwood Ave., Dover, NJ 07801, (201)366-7878; **BUS ADD:** 28-30 N. Sussex St., Dover, NJ 07801, (201)366-5600.

SCHWARZBAUM, Leon——*Dir. of RE*, Cluett, Peabody & Co., Inc.; **PRIM RE ACT:** Property Manager; **BUS ADD:** 510 5th Ave., New York, NY 10036, (212)930-3000.*

SCHWEIGER, Anthony W.——B: Nov. 25, 1941, Phila., PA, *Pres.*, Schweiger & Assocs.; **PRIM RE ACT:** Broker, Consultant; **SERVICES:** Specialized mgmt. services for mort. bankers & fin. instns.; **PREV EMPLOY:** Sr. VP Arvida Mort. Co., Pres. Mtg. Investment Securities, Sr. Mgmt. positions with Bowest Corp. & Assoc. Mort. Cos., First Fed'l Savings-Phila.; **PROFL AFFIL & HONORS:** MBA; **EDUC:** BS, 1964, RE Fin., Wharton School., Univ. of PA; **GRAD EDUC:** MBA, 1967, Mktg., Temple Univ.; **HOME ADD:** 120 Society Hill, Cherry Hill, NJ 08003; **BUS ADD:** Box 2656, Cherry Hill, NJ 08003, (609)663-4494.

SCHWEIGER, H. Denny——B: Apr. 1, 1926, NYC, NY, *Pres.*, The Alison Co.; **PRIM RE ACT:** Owner/Investor; **SERVICES:** Purchase of our own acct. only; **EDUC:** BS, 1947, Mgmt., Univ. of PA, Philadelphia, PA; **MIL SERV:** USN, Lt.; **OTHER ACT & HONORS:** Jockey Club, Grove Isle Club, AEGU, London; **HOME ADD:** 325 NE 122nd St., N Miami, FL 33161, (305)681-6815; **BUS ADD:** 1983 Broad Causeway, N Miami, FL 33181, (305)893-6255.

SCHWEIGER, Robert E.——B: Feb. 14, 1933, Prairie du Chien, WI, *Comml. Mgr.*, Merrill Lynch Realty; Rodgers & Cummings, Inc.; **PRIM RE ACT:** Broker, Developer, Owner/Investor, Syndicator; **SERVICES:** Sales of comml. & indus. props.; **REP CLIENTS:** Exchange, leasing & synd. of investment prop.; **PROFL AFFIL & HONORS:** CCIM; **EDUC:** 1951, Univ. of WI, Madison; 1955, Marguette Univ., Milwaukee; **MIL SERV:** US Army; Sgt.; **HOME ADD:** 1846 Oak Park Dr., Clearwater, FL 33516, (813)531-8146; **BUS ADD:** 1988 Gulf to Bay Blvd., Clearwater, FL 33515, (813)442-4111.

SCHWENKE, Roger D.——B: Oct. 18, 1944, Wash., DC, *Partner/Administrator, RE Dept.*, Carlton, Fields, Ward, Emmanuel, Smith & Cutler, PA; **PRIM RE ACT:** Attorney; **SERVICES:** Legal advice, transaction negotiation and documentation; environmental permitting; **REP CLIENTS:** Lenders and comml. devels.; **PREV EMPLOY:** Instr. of Law, Univ. of FL, Coll. of Law, 1969-1970; **PROFL AFFIL & HONORS:** ABA (Real Prop. Sect.); (Standing Comm. on Environmental Law); The FL Bar (Chmn., Environmental and Land Use Sect., 1980-1981), Amer. Coll. of RE Lawyers; **EDUC:** BA, 1966, Intl. Studies, OH State Univ.; **GRAD EDUC:** JD, 1969, Law, Univ. of FL; **EDUC HONORS:** Arts and Sci., Honors Program; Sphinx Sr. Men's Hon.; Pi Sigma Alpha, With Honors; Law Review Editorial Bd.; Order of Coif; **OTHER ACT & HONORS:** Greater Tampa C of C (Chmn., Environment Council, 1981); Diocesan Council, Episcopal Diocese of S.W. FL; **HOME ADD:** 4939 San Rafael, Tampa, FL 33609, (813)876-4252; **BUS ADD:** PO Box 3239, 610 N. Florida Ave., Tampa, FL 33601, (813)223-5366.

SCHWERIN, Thomas R.——B: Mar. 23, 1940, NY, *Pres.*, Brown Van Allen, Inc.; **PRIM RE ACT:** Consultant, Developer, Owner/Investor, Property Manager; **SERVICES:** Acquisitions of major office buildings & leasing & renovation of same, 1976 to present; **PROFL AFFIL & HONORS:** Member, RE Bd. of NY; **EDUC:** BA, 1963, Poli. Sci., Univ. of VA; **MIL SERV:** USNR, Lt.; **BUS ADD:** 345 Park Ave., New York, NY 10154, (212)980-5189.

SCHWETHELM, A.C.——B: Aug. 6, 1931, Comfort, TX, *Owner*, A.C. Schwethelm and Assoc.; **PRIM RE ACT:** Broker, Consultant, Appraiser, Developer, Owner/Investor, Instructor; **SERVICES:** Appraisal, brokerage, consultation; **REP CLIENTS:** TX Dept. of Highways and Public Transportation; TX Parks and Wildlife Dept., Bankers, Attys.; **PROFL AFFIL & HONORS:** Intl. Right of Way Assn.; TX Soc. of Farm & Ranch Mgrs. and Appraisers, RM, Amer. Inst. of RE Appraisers; SRA, Soc. of RE Appraisers; **OTHER ACT & HONORS:** Dir., Guadalupe Blanco River Auth., 1976 to present; Dir., Comfort State Bank; RE Instr., Schreiner Coll.; **HOME ADD:** 547 Chaparral Dr., Comfort, TX 78013, (512)995-3313; **BUS ADD:** 801 Front St., Comfort, TX 78013, (512)995-3313.

SCIARA, Joseph F.——B: Mar. 7, 1920, Chicago, IL, *Pres., Broker*, House of Sciara Realty; **PRIM RE ACT:** Broker, Builder, Property Manager; **PREV EMPLOY:** RE Broker, Exc. Officer Post Tribune newspapers, Chicago; **PROFL AFFIL & HONORS:** AMA, Ind. Bus. Assn.; **EDUC:** 1948, Law, Bus., RE, Law Acctg., IL Coll Commerce; **MIL SERV:** USA, Sgt., Bronze Star, Purple Heart; **OTHER ACT & HONORS:** DAV, VFW, Amer. Italian Vets; **HOME ADD:** 9222 Courtland Dr., Niles, IL 60648, (312)965-4720; **BUS ADD:** 9222 Courtland Dr., Niles, IL 60648, (312)965-4720.

SCINTO, John J——B: May, 23, 1947, Bridgeport, CT, *Owner*, John J. Scinto, CPA; **PRIM RE ACT:** Broker, Consultant, Owner/Investor, Instructor, Syndicator; **OTHER RE ACT:** Tax Planner; Fin. Planner; Acct.; **PREV EMPLOY:** IRS, auditor of RE synd.; **PROFL AFFIL & HONORS:** CT Soc. of CPA's, Amer. Inst. of CPA's, CPA; **EDUC:** BA, 1969, Bus. Admin., Sacred Heart Univ.; **GRAD EDUC:** MBA, 1976, Bus. Admin., Univ. of Bridgeport; MS, 1975, Criminal Justice, Univ. of New Haven; **OTHER ACT & HONORS:** Univ. of Bridgeport's MBA Assn., 1st VP; **BUS ADD:** PO Box 5194, Hamden, CT 06518, (203)248-3947.

SCISCIO, Leonardo F.——B: June 26, 1934, NYC, NY, *Pres.*, Avanti Equity, RE; **PRIM RE ACT:** Broker, Consultant; **OTHER RE ACT:** Co-broker and Co-consultant in inst. sales; **SERVICES:** Inst. investor liaison, advisory & agency servs.; **REP CLIENTS:** Builders and lenders, and corp. or inst. investors in income prop. and land, pension funds; **PREV EMPLOY:** Leonardo Homes, Inc., 1970-78, Standard & Poor's Investment Counseling Corp. 1967-70; **PROFL AFFIL & HONORS:** Nat. Assn. of Review Appraisers, Sr. Member, CRA, Licensed RE Broker; **EDUC:** BS, 1957, Fin. & Macro Econ., School of Bus. Admin., Syracuse Univ.; **GRAD EDUC:** MBA, 1964, Fin., banking & investment, RE minor, Grad. School of Bus. Admin., NY Univ.; Law School, Fordham Univ.; **MIL SERV:** US Army, Sgt., 1962-64; **OTHER ACT & HONORS:** NYU, Grad. School of Bus. Admin. Alumni Member; **HOME ADD:** 248 Fairhaven Blvd., Woodbury Long Island, NY 11797, (516)921-6880; **BUS ADD:** Box 402, Woodbury, Long Island, NY 11797, (516)921-6880.

SCOFIELD, Lawrence F., Jr.——B: Oct. 6, 1944, Malden, MA, *Atty.*, Rockemann Sawyer & Brewster; **PRIM RE ACT:** Attorney, Instructor; **SERVICES:** all phases of RE Law; **PREV EMPLOY:** Div. Counsel, Pioneer Nat. Title Insurance Co. (Regional Claims Counsel); **PROFL AFFIL & HONORS:** ABA, MBA, MA Conveyancers Assn., The Abstract Club; **EDUC:** BA, 1966, English, Boston Coll.; **GRAD EDUC:** MA, 1967, English, Boston Coll.; JD, 1973, Suffolk Univ. Law School; **HOME ADD:** 7 Hawes Ave., Melrose, MA 02176, (617)665-2813; **BUS ADD:** 28 State St., Boston, MA 02109, (617)523-3550.

SCOLNIK, Glenn——B: June 16, 1951, Munster, IN, *Atty.*, Sommer & Barnard, P.C.; **PRIM RE ACT:** Attorney; **SERVICES:** Counseling on acquisition, disposition or synd. of RE; **REP CLIENTS:** RE synd. firms, pvt. investors; **PROFL AFFIL & HONORS:** Indianapolis, IN, Amer. Bar Assns.; **EDUC:** BS, 1974, Bus. Econ., IN Univ.; **GRAD**

EDUC: 1978, IN Univ. Law School; **EDUC HONORS:** Beta Gamma Sigma, Cum Laude; **HOME ADD:** 5304 N. Park Ave., Indianapolis, IN 46220, (317)283-7775; **BUS ADD:** 1100 Merchants Bank Bldg., Indianapolis, IN 46204, (317)639-3454.

SCOTT, Ben A., Jr.——B: Apr. 14, 1922, Danville, VA, *Mgr. Residential Dept.*, Harrison & Bates, Inc.; **PRIM RE ACT:** Consultant, Property Manager; **SERVICES:** Mgmt. Agent for Apts., Condominiums and Townhouse Assoc.; **REP CLIENTS:** Prop. Owners and Homemakers Assoc.; **PREV EMPLOY:** RE Dept. of United VA Bank 1970-1978; **PROFL AFFIL & HONORS:** IREM, NAR; **EDUC:** BS, 1948, Chem. and Lang., Randolph-Macon Coll., Ashland,VA; **MIL SERV:** USAF, (1943-1946, 1952-1969), Maj., Air Medal, Commendation Medal; **HOME ADD:** 9305 Donora Dr., Richmond, VA 23229, (804)270-7016; **BUS ADD:** Richmond Plaza Bldg., 111 S. Sixth St., Richmond, VA 23219, (804)788-1000.

SCOTT, James F.——B: June 30, 1921, Geneva, NY, *Pres.*, Scott Appraisal Serv. Inc.; **PRIM RE ACT:** Consultant, Appraiser; **SERVICES:** RE Appraisal & consultation serv. in E. US Special emphasis on condemnation, tax litigation, condo. conversion; **REP CLIENTS:** Xerox, Kodak, Sundstrand, General Tire, Amer. Invsco, I.D. Devel., Coca Cola, Western Elec.; **PREV EMPLOY:** In business as Scott Appraisal Serv., Atlanta, GA since 1973. Rochester, NY 1967-1972; **PROFL AFFIL & HONORS:** Designations: SRA; SRPA; Society of RE, CRA, Who's Who in Indus. & Fin.; Who's Who in World; **MIL SERV:** USAAF, Pac. Theater, Major, Silver Star (2), Air Medals (6); **HOME ADD:** 3844 Longview Dr., Altlanta, GA 30341, (404)457-5978; **BUS ADD:** 6695 Peachtree Indus. Blvd., Suite 212, Atlanta, GA 30360, (404)449-4669.

SCOTT, James N.——B: Aug. 9, 1947, Omaha, NE, *Owner/Broker*, David James Realty; **PRIM RE ACT:** Broker; **SERVICES:** Comml./ Investment Brokerage; Buyer's Broker; **REP CLIENTS:** Indiv. users and investors, pension funds, rgnl. chains; **PROFL AFFIL & HONORS:** NAR; CCIM; CRS; **EDUC:** BA, 1969, Psychol./Eng., Univ. of Omaha; Univ. of WA; **OTHER ACT & HONORS:** Rotary; WA Assn. of Bus.; **HOME ADD:** 2357 Crosby Dr., Mr. Vernon, WA 98273, (206)424-8440; **BUS ADD:** 1010 E. College Way, Mt. Vernon, WA 98273, (206)424-4901.

SCOTT, J.R.——B: Oct. 22, 1926, Amarillo, TX, *VP-RE*, Santa Fe Railway Co., A Santa Fe Industries Co.; **OTHER RE ACT:** RE; **PREV EMPLOY:** 32 years exper. in RE activities of Santa Fe Indus. Cos.; **PROFL AFFIL & HONORS:** Exec. Grp. of the Indus. & Office Park Devel. Council of the ULI; Nat. Assn. of Corporate RE Execs.; **EDUC:** BS Bus., 1949, Land Mgmt., Univ. of CO; **HOME ADD:** 20440 Kedzie Ave., Olympia Fields, IL 60461, (312)748-6361; **BUS ADD:** 224 S. MI Ave., Chicago, IL 60604, (312)427-4900.

SCOTT, Lorett J.——B: Aug. 13, 1923, Springfield, MA, *Sales Mgr.*, Century 21 Dean Associates; **PRIM RE ACT:** Broker; **OTHER RE ACT:** Relocation coordinator; **PROFL AFFIL & HONORS:** RNMI; NAR; MA Assn. of Realtors; N.E. Chapt. of CRB; Greater Salem Bd. of Realtors; Women's Council of Realtors; Intl. Relocation Consultants, Inc., GRI; CRS; CRB; **HOME ADD:** 41 Carriage Way, Danvers, MA 01923, (617)774-7723; **BUS ADD:** 494 Lowell St., Peabody, MA 01960, (617)535-6500.

SCOTT, Mae Rankin——B: Jan. 1, 1940, Birmingham, AL, *VP*, Pan Amer. Mort. Corp., Mort. Lending; **PRIM RE ACT:** Appraiser, Banker, Lender; **OTHER RE ACT:** Member of various So. FL RE Bds.; **SERVICES:** Land acquisition & devel., const. loan fin., mort. loan processing & etc.; **PREV EMPLOY:** Exec. VP, King's Way Mort. Co.; Corp. Sec., Veritas Ins. Co.; Corp. Sec., Alpha, Inc.; Heritage Corp. of NY; **PROFL AFFIL & HONORS:** Mort. Bankers of So. FL; Mort. Bankers Assn.; So. FL Bldrs. Assn; Nat. Assn. of Review Appraisers; CRA; **EDUC:** Mort. Banking field, Ext. Univ. of AL; **OTHER ACT & HONORS:** Prevention of Blindness; **BUS ADD:** 150 S.E. Third Ave., Miami, FL 33131, (305)577-5911.

SCOTT, Michael A.——B: Aug. 22, 1950, Kingman, AZ, *Pres.*, S&T Investment Realty & Management, Inc., In charge of Sales & Computer Operations; **PRIM RE ACT:** Broker, Consultant, Developer, Owner/Investor, Syndicator; **SERVICES:** Our firm provides comml. brokerage, synd., prop. mgmt., consulting to devels. & devel.; **REP CLIENTS:** R.E.I.T.'s, Instnl. buyers, devels., synd. & owners of comml. props.; **PREV EMPLOY:** Heywood Realty, Merrill Lynch Fannin Realty; **PROFL AFFIL & HONORS:** Member of Local and Natl. RE Bds., Salesman of the month, Grad. from Profile of a Champion; **OTHER ACT & HONORS:** Member of Save the Whales Found. & The Planetary Soc.; **HOME ADD:** 1907 S. Beverly, Mesa, AZ 85202, (602)838-7873; **BUS ADD:** 325 E. So. #5, Tempe, AZ 85282, (602)968-9241.

SCOTT, Michael R.——B: Dec. 15, 1956, Joliet, IL, *V.P. - Comm'l. Investment*, Century 21 Vic Scott & Assoc.; **PRIM RE ACT:** Broker, Consultant, Developer, Property Manager, Owner/Investor; **SERVICES:** Comm'l. - Investment brokerage, prop. mgmt., dev. of comm'l. prop.; **PROFL AFFIL & HONORS:** Will Cty. Bd. of Realtors, Will-Grundy Cty. Home Builders Assn.; **EDUC:** BA, 1979, Econ., Dartmouth Coll.; **OTHER ACT & HONORS:** Big Brothers of Will County; **HOME ADD:** 1020 John St., Joliet, IL, (815)723-7302; **BUS ADD:** 2317 W. Jefferson St., Joliet, IL, (815)729-9200.

SCOTT, O.V.——B: Oct. 19, 1929, Dallas, TX, *Atty.*, Crenshaw DuPree & Milam, Atty.; **OTHER RE ACT:** Acquisition; Devel.; Mgmt.; **SERVICES:** Legal; **REP CLIENTS:** RE Brokers & Sales Organizations, Bus. Investors in Real Property, RE Prop. Mgrs.; **PROFL AFFIL & HONORS:** ABA; TX Bar Assn.; Lubbock Cty. Bar Assn.; **EDUC:** BS, 1953, Petroleum Exploration, Univ. of OK; **GRAD EDUC:** LLB, 1961, Real Property/Bus., Univ. of TX; **MIL SERV:** USMC, Lt.; **HOME ADD:** 3301 45th St., Lubbock, TX 79413, (806)795-5886; **BUS ADD:** POB 1499, Lubbock, TX 79408, (806)762-5281.

SCOTT, Raymond L.——B: July 14, 1949, Philadelphia, PA, *Princ./Pres.*, Catalyst Inc. Architectures, Bus. Devel. & Fin. Consultant; **PRIM RE ACT:** Architect, Regulator, Instructor, Syndicator, Consultant, Developer, Property Manager, Owner/Investor; **OTHER RE ACT:** Fin. Consultant, Code Analysis; **SERVICES:** Arch., Feasibility Analysis, Investor; **REP CLIENTS:** Prudential, Attys., Investors; **PREV EMPLOY:** Arch., Bldg.; **PROFL AFFIL & HONORS:** AIA, OCBD, AIA Design & Honor Awards; **EDUC:** BArch, 1973, Arch. & Bus., LA State Univ.; **OTHER ACT & HONORS:** Core Area Task Forces; Orlando Growth Mgt. Plan; **HOME ADD:** 721 Woodbridges Pl., Longwood, FL 32750, (305)834-5514; **BUS ADD:** PO Box 2769, Orlando, FL 32802, (305)841-1925.

SCOTT, Richard E.——B: Sept. 5, 1947, Chicago, IL, *Pres.*, IRE, Inc.; **PRIM RE ACT:** Broker, Consultant, Developer, Owner/Investor, Property Manager, Syndicator; **OTHER RE ACT:** Registered prin., securities; **PROFL AFFIL & HONORS:** RESSI; IREM; **EDUC:** BA, 1969, Bus. and Econ., Wheaton Coll.; **GRAD EDUC:** MA; MBA, 1974, 1978, Communications (MA), Fin.(MBA), Wheaton Coll. Grad. School (MA), No. IL Univ. (MBA); **HOME ADD:** 712 N. Cherry, Wheaton, IL 60187, (312)665-0228; **BUS ADD:** 1123 Wheaton Oaks Ct., Wheaton, IL 60187, (312)653-3220.

SCOTT, Robert E., Jr.——B: Nov. 17, 1940, Rahway, NJ, *Pres.*, R.E. Scott Mort. Co.; **PRIM RE ACT:** Broker, Appraiser, Developer, Lender, Builder, Instructor; **SERVICES:** Mort. banking, RE brokerage, resid. bldg.; **REP CLIENTS:** Numerous banks, savings and loans, savings banks and Fed. Nat. Mort. Assn.; NJ Mort. Fin. Agency; **PROFL AFFIL & HONORS:** NJ Assn. of Realtors; Nat. Assn. of Realtors; Mort. Bankers Assn. of NJ; MBA of Amer., Past Pres., MBA of NJ; Past Pres., Eastern Union Cty. Bd. of Realtors; **EDUC:** BA, 1962, Intl. Relations, Dartmouth Coll.; **HOME ADD:** 42 Laurel Brook Rd., Lincroft, NJ 07208; **BUS ADD:** 400 Westfield Ave., Elizabeth, NJ 07208, (201)355-8100.

SCOTT, Robert H.——B: Nov. 5, 1927, Fall River, MA, *Owner*, Real Estate Appraiser and Consultant; **PRIM RE ACT:** Broker, Consultant, Appraiser, Owner/Investor, Property Manager; **SERVICES:** RE appraising & consultation; **REP CLIENTS:** MI Dept. of Transportation; **PROFL AFFIL & HONORS:** Soc. of RE appraisers, Amer. Soc. of Appraisers, Amer. ROW Assn., SRPA, Soc. of RE Appraisers, Past pres.; **EDUC:** BS, 1949, Nautical Sci., MA Maritime Acad.; **MIL SERV:** USN, Lt. Comdr., Korean Theatre; **OTHER ACT & HONORS:** Past Commodore-Albatross Yacht Club, Mt. Clemens, MI, Past Pres. RE Appraisers Assn. of Detroit; **HOME ADD:** 5065 Crooks Rd., Royal Oak, MI 48073, (313)280-0295; **BUS ADD:** 2820 W. Maple Rd., Troy, MI 48084, (313)643-0412.

SCOTT, Roger——*VP*, Kerr Glass Mfg. Corp.; **PRIM RE ACT:** Property Manager; **BUS ADD:** 501 S. Shatto Place, Los Angeles, CA 90020, (213)487-3250.*

SCOTT, Walter——*Exec. VP & Secy*, Savannah Foods & Industries, Inc.; **PRIM RE ACT:** Property Manager; **BUS ADD:** PO Box 339, Savannah, GA 31402, (912)234-1261.*

SCRIMA, Thomas Charles——B: Mar. 6, 1947, Tribes Hill, NY, *Pres.*, Centers America Ltd.; **PRIM RE ACT:** Consultant, Owner/Investor; **SERVICES:** Consulting, joint venture; **REP CLIENTS:** First Nat. Bank of Boston, Bassett Const., Arthur Rubloff Co, Price Indus.; **EDUC:** BA, 1968, Chem., Soc., Univ. of Notre Dame; **EDUC HONORS:** Cum Laude; **OTHER ACT & HONORS:** CO Springs Econ. Devel. Comm.; **HOME ADD:** 13802 Perry Park Rd., Palmer Lake, CO 80133, (303)481-3931; **BUS ADD:** 5775 N. Union Blvd.,

Colorado Springs, CO 80918, (303)598-2855.

SCROGGINS, Richard M.——**B:** Dec. 11, 1932, Highland Park, MI, *VP*, Amer. Express Co., RE; **PRIM RE ACT:** Architect, Consultant, Appraiser, Developer, Builder, Property Manager, Engineer, Owner/Investor; **OTHER RE ACT:** The Above are under an umbrella of corp. RE for all Subs. and operating units of the co., Leasing; **PREV EMPLOY:** Ford Motor Co. 1963-1975, Shell Oil Co.; **PROFL AFFIL & HONORS:** NACORE, ULI; **EDUC:** BBA, 1955, Mktg., Univ. of MI; **MIL SERV:** USMC, 1st Lt., 1955-1958; **OTHER ACT & HONORS:** Chmn., Myasthenia Gravis Foundation of Greater NY; Past Dir. Dearborn C of C; **HOME ADD:** 15 Rockview Dr., Greenwich, CT 06830, (203)622-9295; **BUS ADD:** Amer. Express Plaza, NY, NY 10004, (212)323-2326.

SCRUGGS, William C., Jr.——**B:** July 24, 1927, Asheville, NC, *Broker*, Scruggs & Maddox; **PRIM RE ACT:** Broker, Instructor, Syndicator, Consultant, Appraiser, Developer, Owner/Investor; **PROFL AFFIL & HONORS:** FLI; RNMI; NAR; SIR; SREA; RESSI; AIREA, CCIM; GRI; AFLM; CRS; CRB; Omega Tau Rho; **EDUC:** BA, 1948, Math., Bob Jones Univ., Greenville, SC; **GRAD EDUC:** 3 years, Church hist., New Orleans Baptist Theological Seminary; **HOME ADD:** 3929 Woodmont Dr., Mobile, AL, (205)666-2877; **BUS ADD:** One Office Park, Suite 103, Mobile, AL 36009, (205)344-7700.

SCURFIELD, Ralph Thomas——**B:** Jan. 7, 1928, Broadview, SK, *Chmn. & CEO*, Nu-West Group Ltd.; **PRIM RE ACT:** Developer, Property Manager; **OTHER RE ACT:** Oil and Gas Indus. (Voyager Petroleums Ltd., a subs. of Nu-West Grp. Ltd.); **SERVICES:** Const. and sale of resid. houses, land assembly, land devel., contract bldg., revenue producing props., petroleum and natural gas; **PREV EMPLOY:** Taught school and worked as const. supervisor for several years prior to becoming Pres. of Nu-West in 1957; **PROFL AFFIL & HONORS:** Member, Bd. of Dirs., Carma Ltd., MICC Investments Ltd. and The Mort. Ins. Co. of Canada; Allarco Devels. Ltd. and Alberta Gas Chemicals Ltd.; Transalta Utilities, Past Pres., HUDAC and HUDAC Assn. of Calgary; Past Chmn., Resid. Devel. Council of HUDAC; Member, ULI; **EDUC:** BS, 1948, Univ. of Manitoba; **GRAD EDUC:** Grad., Advanced Mgmt. Program, Harvard Bus. School; **OTHER ACT & HONORS:** Member of Bus. Advisory Bd. of Univ. of Calgary School of Bus.; Member of the Bd. of Govs. of the Banff Centre; Past Pres of the N. Calgary Bus. Assn.; Member of Ranchmen's Club; Silver Springs Golf & Ctry. Club; Calgary Winter Club; **HOME ADD:** 1640 Cayuga Dr., N.W., Calgary, T2L0N3, Alb., Canada, (403)289-7288; **BUS ADD:** POB 6958, Postal Station D, Calgary, T2P2R6, Alb., Canada, (403)235-7603.

SEABORN, James L., Jr.——**B:** June 19, 1931, Norfolk, VA, *Sr. VP*, VNB Mort. Corp., Resid. Loan Div.; **PRIM RE ACT:** Lender; **SERVICES:** Resid. Mort. lending; **REP CLIENTS:** Life ins. cos., mutual savings banks, S&L Assns., FNMA, FHLMC, Instnl. investors; **PREV EMPLOY:** First Mort. Corp.; **PROFL AFFIL & HONORS:** SREA, SRA; **EDUC:** BBA, 1961, Bus. Mgmt., Richmond Profl. Inst. (Now VA Commonwealth Univ.); **EDUC HONORS:** Wall St. Journal Award; **MIL SERV:** USAF, S/Sgt.; **OTHER ACT & HONORS:** Member Bd. of Dirs., VA Commonwealth Univ. Bus Sch. Alumni Assn.; **HOME ADD:** 8670 Trabue Rd., Richmond, VA 23235, (804)272-7682; **BUS ADD:** 201 E. Cary St., Richmond, VA 23275, (804)782-0360.

SEABURY, Glen N., Jr.——**B:** Nov. 27, 1945, Ft. Eustis, VA, *Pres.*, Apple Development Corp.; **PRIM RE ACT:** Broker, Consultant, Appraiser, Developer, Owner/Investor, Property Manager, Syndicator; **PROFL AFFIL & HONORS:** RESSI; **EDUC:** BS, 1971, Normal Psych., Brigham Young Univ.; **OTHER ACT & HONORS:** Mensa Intl., SAR, Optimist Club, Who's Who in So. & S.W., 1980-81; **HOME ADD:** 4263 Delmar Dr., Montgomery, AL 76109; **BUS ADD:** 1230 Perry Hill Rd., Ste 1-A, Montgomery, AL 36109, (205)272-2356.

SEAL, R.L.——*VP Admin.*, W.A. Krueger Co.; **PRIM RE ACT:** Assessor; **BUS ADD:** 7301 East Helm Dr., Scottsdale, AZ 85260, (602)948-5650.*

SEALEY, John Charles——**B:** Jan. 16, 1925, Ottawa, KS, *Gen. Mgr.*, Shell Oil Company, Corp. RE and Gen. Servs.; **OTHER RE ACT:** Manage corp. real assets including a land investments div.; **PROFL AFFIL & HONORS:** Nat. Assn. of Corporate RE Execs., IDRC, Exec. Comm. - So. Main Center Assn., Exec. Comm. - West Houston Assn.; **EDUC:** BS - ME; BA - Bus. Admin., 1947, Univ. of CA; **MIL SERV:** USN, Ens.; **HOME ADD:** 12422 Boheme, Houston, TX 77024, (713)464-7882; **BUS ADD:** PO Box 2099, Houston, TX 77001, (713)241-5911.

SEALY, J. Pollard, Jr.——**B:** Sept. 24, 1924, Shreveport, LA, *Pres. - since 1946*, Sealy Realty Co., Inc.; **PRIM RE ACT:** Broker, Consultant, Developer, Owner/Investor, Property Manager, Syndicator; **SERVICES:** Sale, lease, mgmt., synd. and ownership of comml. and investment props.; **REP CLIENTS:** Indivs. and Instit. investors in investment props.; **PROFL AFFIL & HONORS:** SIR, Comml. Investment Member; RMI; IREA; Inst. RE Mgrs.; RESSI, CCIM; CPM; MAI; SIR; **MIL SERV:** US Army; Sgt., 1943-1946; **OTHER ACT & HONORS:** Past Pres., Shreveport, Bossier Bd. of Realtors; Shreveport Jr. C of C.; Shreveport Gun Club; **HOME ADD:** 833 River Rd., Shreveport, LA 71105, (318)868-1229; **BUS ADD:** 1401 Petroleum Tower, Shreveport, LA 77101, (318)222-8700.

SEAMAN, R.N.——**B:** Nov. 6, 1934, Toledo, OH, *Exec. VP*, Sunco-Tampa, Inc.; **PRIM RE ACT:** Consultant, Developer, Owner/Investor, Syndicator; **EDUC:** Univ. of Toledo; **GRAD EDUC:** BS, 1954, Univ. of Toledo; **MIL SERV:** USMC; **HOME TEL:** (813)251-2215; **BUS ADD:** PO Box 22203, Tampa, FL 33622.

SEARLES, David S., Jr.——**B:** Aug. 5, 1946, Detroit, MI, *Pres.*, Chase Properties, Inc.; **PRIM RE ACT:** Developer, Builder, Owner/Investor, Syndicator; **PREV EMPLOY:** VP of Fin. - United Resources, Inc. and Country Club of Miami Corp.; **PROFL AFFIL & HONORS:** NAR, NAHB; **EDUC:** BA, 1968, Fin., Univ. of South FL; **GRAD EDUC:** MBA, 1970, Fin., Harvard Bus. School; **OTHER ACT & HONORS:** Intl. Order of St. Luke; **HOME ADD:** 5030 Nesbit Ferry Ln., Atlanta, GA 30360, (404)393-2593; **BUS ADD:** 7710 Spalding Dr., Norcross, GA 30092, (404)447-5554.

SEARLES, Sidney Z.——**B:** Aug. 25, 1914, New York, NY, *Sr. Atty.*, Searles and Sachman, P.C.; **PRIM RE ACT:** Consultant, Attorney; **REP CLIENTS:** Columbia Univ.; ASPCA; Ford Motor Co. (Special Condemnation Counsel); **PREV EMPLOY:** Sr. Partner, Raphael, Searles & Vischi; **PROFL AFFIL & HONORS:** ABA; Assn. of Bar of City of NY; NY State Bar Assn., Chmn. of Comm. of Condemnation Assn. of Bank of City of NY; Chmn. of Seminars on Condemnation, under auspices of ALI ABA, PLI; **EDUC:** BS, 1934, Pol. Sci., St. John's Univ.; **GRAD EDUC:** JD, 1937, Law, Columbia Univ. Law School; **MIL SERV:** US Army; **HOME TEL:** (516)374-0005; **BUS ADD:** Bar Bldg., 36 W. 44 St., New York, NY 10036, (212)869-8274.

SEARS, James W.——**B:** Nov. 26, 1949, Witchita Falls, TX, *Atty.*, Butler, McDonald, Moon & Sears, PA; **PRIM RE ACT:** Attorney; **OTHER RE ACT:** Investor, Law Practice; **SERVICES:** Legal representation in RE investment; **PROFL AFFIL & HONORS:** Central FL investment soc.; The FL Bar, Real Prop., Probate and Trust Law Sect., Land Trust Comm.; ABA, Real Prop., Probate and Trust Law Section; **EDUC:** BBA, 1971, Fin., Stetson Univ.; **GRAD EDUC:** JD, 1974, Univ. of FL; **EDUC HONORS:** Practice Court Award; **OTHER ACT & HONORS:** Assistant State Atty. 1976-78; **HOME ADD:** 1309 Radclyffe Rd., Orlando, FL 32804, (305)425-7427; **BUS ADD:** 1218 E. Robinson St., Orlando, FL 32801, (305)896-9068.

SEARS, Warren——*RE Mgr.*, Keller Industries, Inc.; **PRIM RE ACT:** Property Manager; **BUS ADD:** 18000 State Rd. 9, Miami, FL 33162, (305)651-7100.*

SEATON, John E.——**B:** Mar. 3, 1944, Washington, DC, *VP*, Citicorp Real Estate, Inc., Tampa; **PRIM RE ACT:** Banker, Lender; **SERVICES:** Fin. of major RE projects; **REP CLIENTS:** Devels. of comml. props.; **PROFL AFFIL & HONORS:** MBAA - Income Comm.; **EDUC:** BA, 1966, Econ., NC State Univ.; **GRAD EDUC:** MBA, 1971, Fin., GA State Univ.; **MIL SERV:** USAF, Capt., Distinguished Flying Cross, Airmedal; **HOME ADD:** 1650 Honeybear Ln., Dunedin, FL 33528, (813)785-3146; **BUS ADD:** One Countryside Office Park, Suite 310, Clearwater, FL 33515, (813)796-2451.

SEATON, Martin——**B:** Nov. 24, 1936, Toronto, Can., *Pres.*, Cadillac Fairview US Western Region, Inc.; **PRIM RE ACT:** Developer, Owner/Investor; **SERVICES:** RE Devel. and investors; **PROFL AFFIL & HONORS:** Inst. of Chartered Accountants of ON, Chartered Accountant; **HOME ADD:** 3087 Deep Canyon Dr., Beverly Hills, CA 90210, (213)858-8776; **BUS ADD:** 1800 Ave. of The Stars 730, Los Angeles, CA 90067, (213)557-2252.

SEAY, Thomas P.——**B:** Oct. 21, 1941, Little Rock, AR, *VP*, Wal-Mart Stores,Inc., RE; **PRIM RE ACT:** Developer, Builder, Owner/Investor, Property Manager; **OTHER RE ACT:** Maj. Tenant of shopping centers - Mall and Strip Centers; **PREV EMPLOY:** Cooper Communities, Inc. 1971-1973; **PROFL AFFIL & HONORS:** Intl. Council of Shopping Centers; Nat. Assn. of Corporate RE Execs.; **EDUC:** BSBA, 1963, Bus., Mktg., Fin., Univ. of AR; **GRAD EDUC:** MBA, 1974, Fin., Univ. of AR; **EDUC HONORS:** Psi Epsilon, SBA Award; **MIL SERV:** US Army, Capt. 1963-1970, Bronze Star, Army Commendation Award, Valorous Unit Citation, Armed Forces

Expenditory Service Republic of Vietnam Service, Vietnam Defense Medal; **OTHER ACT & HONORS:** Kiwanis; **HOME ADD:** 702 King Dr., Bentonville, AR 72712, (501)273-3917; **BUS ADD:** PO Box 116, Bentonville, AR 72712, (501)273-4000.

SEBASTIAN, James J.——B: Apr. 20, 1947, Warren, OH, *Pres.*, The James J. Sebastian Co.; Ohio Brokers, Inc.; **PRIM RE ACT:** Consultant, Developer; **SERVICES:** Brokerage, consulting, fin. devel.; **PREV EMPLOY:** Red Roof Inns., Dir. of Support Servs.; **EDUC:** BS, 1969, Indus. Tech., OH State Univ.; **GRAD EDUC:** MBA, 1978, Mktg.; **OTHER ACT & HONORS:** Little Turtle CC; Columbus Athletic Club; **HOME ADD:** 103 Nob Hill Dr. N., Gahanna, OH 43230, (614)476-4586; **BUS ADD:** The Borden Bldg., 180 E. Broad St., Columbus, OH 43215, (614)461-0503.

SEBASTIANELLI, Mario J., MD——B: Sept. 14, 1935, Jessup, PA, *Sole Prop.*; **PRIM RE ACT:** Consultant, Developer, Owner/Investor, Property Manager; **SERVICES:** Rental space for doctors of medicine and other health serv. profls. in professionally fully prepared suites or prepared to meet spec. needs. Provision for assistance in interior design, purchase of furniture and equipment, fin. aspects of practice mgmt, employee recruitment. Beach front condos & homes for rent in the FL sunbelt. Inventory of comml. & resid. devel. land in PA & FL for future medical offices, apts. & vacation homes. Consultant to health serv. profls. for starting practice and indep. devel. of med. offices; **REP CLIENTS:** Drs. of Medicine and related health field profls., affluent FL vacationers, health serv. consumers; **EDUC:** BS, 1958, Biology & Chem., Univ. of Scranton; **GRAD EDUC:** MD, 1962, Medicine, Jefferson Medical Coll.; **EDUC HONORS:** Magna Cum Laude, Valedictory address, Alpha Omega Alpha, Nat. Medicine Hon. Soc.; **MIL SERV:** USN, Lt., MC; **OTHER ACT & HONORS:** Knights of Columbus, Intl. Platform Assoc., Biographee of Who's Who in the East, Men of Achievement; Comm. Leaders and Noteworthy Americans; Dir. of Intl. Biography; Intl. Who's Who of Intellectuals; Who's Who Among Students in Amer. Univs. & Colls.; Biographical Dir. of Amer. Coll. of Physicians; Dir. of Medical Specialists; Intl. Who's Who in Comm. Serv.; Notable Personalities of Amer.; Fellowship in Amer. Coll. of Physicians; Amer. Coll. of Angiology; Amer. Biographical Research Assn. & Intl. Biographical Assn.; **HOME ADD:** 176 Constitution Ave., Jessup, PA 18434; **BUS ADD:** 1416 Monroe Ave., Dunmore, PA 18509, (717)347-5212.

SEBESTA, James A.——B: Aug. 24, 1935, Pontiac, IL, *Pres.*, Sebesta RE Co. & Sebesta Mort. Co.; **PRIM RE ACT:** Broker, Consultant, Banker, Developer, Builder, Owner/Investor, Property Manager; **REP CLIENTS:** Chase Devel. Corp., VP; **PREV EMPLOY:** St. Johns Management: Jacksonville, FL Pres.; **PROFL AFFIL & HONORS:** Bd. of Dir., Jacksonville Apt. Assn., CCIM Candidate, Ressi, FL RE Broker, FL Mortgage Broker: Sales & Marketing Exec. of Jacksonville; **EDUC:** BS, 1957, Mgmt., Loyola Univ.; **GRAD EDUC:** MBA, 1968, Indus. Mgmt., DePaul Univ.; **MIL SERV:** US Navy, CTSN; **OTHER ACT & HONORS:** 1965 Lake Wales, FL City Commn.: Supervisor of Elections - Hillsborough Cty. (1970-1974) Statewide Candidate; Sec. of State (1974); 1975-77 State of FL - Ethics Commn./ 1980 - State of FL Compensation Review Commn./1980 Reagan/Bush Chmn., Duval County FL; **HOME ADD:** 1403 Sommerville Rd., Jacksonville, FL 32207, (904)399-0635; **BUS ADD:** 51 West Forsyth St., Jacksonville, FL 32202, (904)359-7253.

SEBOLD, John D.——B: Feb. 28, 1933, NE, *VP of Devel.*, Carlson Properties, Inc.; **PRIM RE ACT:** Broker, Developer, Owner/Investor, Property Manager; **SERVICES:** Sale/leaseback - turn key devel.; **PROFL AFFIL & HONORS:** NAIOP, AEDC, SIR, AIDC, NAR, MIDA, CID; **EDUC:** BS, 1955, Econ.-Bus. Admin., Univ. of NE; **OTHER ACT & HONORS:** Gov. Indus. Awards 1967 & 1970; Past Pres. MN Indus. Devel. Assn.; **HOME ADD:** 17500 25 Ave. N., Minneapolis, MN 55447, (612)473-3239; **BUS ADD:** 12805 State Hwy. 55, Plymouth, MN 55441, (612)540-5541.

SECREST, L. Ramon——B: Dec. 29, 1926, IN, *Mgr., Indus. RE and Const.*, Eli Lilly and Co.; **PRIM RE ACT:** Architect, Consultant, Appraiser, Engineer; **PREV EMPLOY:** Engineer; **PROFL AFFIL & HONORS:** ASCE; NACORE; RE Broker (IN), Profl. Engrs. Soc. (IN); **EDUC:** BS-Civil Engrg., 1951, Structural Engrg., Purdue Univ.-W Lafayette, IN; **EDUC HONORS:** Chi Epsilon (Hon. Civil Engrg.); **HOME ADD:** 7025 Keston Cir., Indianapolis, IN 46256, (317)849-0677; **BUS ADD:** 307 E McCarty St., Indianapolis, IN 46285, (317)261-3739.

SEDWAY, Lynn M.——B: Nov. 26, 1941, Washington, DC, *Principal*, Lynn Sedway & Assoc.; **PRIM RE ACT:** Consultant, Appraiser; **SERVICES:** Consultant servs, in urban and RE econ. to public and private sector clients; **REP CLIENTS:** City of Palo Alto, Fireman's Fund, Marin Cty.; **PROFL AFFIL & HONORS:** ULI, Lambda Alpha, MBA; **EDUC:** BA, 1963, Econ., Univ. of MI; **GRAD EDUC:** MBA, 1976, Urban & RE Econ., Univ. of CA at Berkeley; **OTHER ACT & HONORS:** Overall Econ. Devel. Comm., Marin Symphony Bd., Dominican Coll. Citizens Adv. Comm.; **HOME ADD:** 79 Moncade Way, San Rafael, CA 94901, (415)454-7979; **BUS ADD:** 10O0 4th St., Ste. 500, San Rafael, CA 94901, (415)457-4202.

SEE, Robert F., Jr.——B: Apr. 23, 1942, Kansas City, MO, *Shareholder/Dir.*, Locke, Purnell, Boren, Laney & Neely, A Professional Corp.; **PRIM RE ACT:** Attorney; **SERVICES:** Legal; **REP CLIENTS:** Various lenders, devels., contractors, investors, and brokers; **PROFL AFFIL & HONORS:** ABA, TX Bar Assn. and Dallas Bar Assn.; **EDUC:** BA, 1964, Liberal Arts, Univ. of TX at Austin; JD, 1966, Univ. of TX at Austin; **EDUC HONORS:** with Honors, with Honors (Assoc. Editor, TX Law Review); **HOME ADD:** 7418K Fair Oaks Ave., Dallas, TX 75231, (214)369-4374; **BUS ADD:** 3600 RepublicBank Tower, Dallas, TX 75201, (214)746-7400.

SEE, Ronald L.——B: Nov.16, 1942, Marion Cty., IL, *Pres.*, Myers, Robinson, See R.E. & Devel., Inc.; **PRIM RE ACT:** Broker, Syndicator, Developer, Owner/Investor; **SERVICES:** Brokerage, synd, investment analysis; **REP CLIENTS:** Indiv. and Inst. Investors; **PROFL AFFIL & HONORS:** NAR, RNMI, State Chmn.- IL. Assoc. of Realtors Legislative Fin. Sub-Comm., Serve on local Bds. Long Range Planning Comm.; **EDUC:** BA, 1964, Fin. Mgmt., S. IL Univ.; **OTHER ACT & HONORS:** Kiwanis (past Pres.) Springfield Schools Fin. Advisory Comm. (Past Chmn.); **HOME ADD:** 3001 Battersea Pt., Springfield, IL, (217)787-2401; **BUS ADD:** 2001 W. Monroe, Springfield, IL 62704, (217)787-6761.

SEELEY, Fred C.——B: Mar. 23, 1942, Ann Arbor, MI, *VP*, Perry Drug Stores, Inc., RE; **PRIM RE ACT:** Consultant, Developer, Property Manager; **OTHER RE ACT:** Site Selector; **SERVICES:** Manage RE & Mktg. Functions; **PROFL AFFIL & HONORS:** NACORE, ICSC, Bd. of Dirs. Pontiac Econ. Dev. Corp, Oakland Cty.; Bd. of Dirs. & Chmn. Oakland Cty. C of C; Bd. of Dirs. Oakland City Econ. Dev. Corp.; Trustee Oakland City Local Dev. Co.; **EDUC:** BA, 1965, Mktg., Fin., Mich. State Univ.; **GRAD EDUC:** MBA, Fin., Mich. State Univ.; **MIL SERV:** USNG, Sgt.; **HOME ADD:** 950 Cragin, Bloomfield Hills, MI 48013, (313)851-5543; **BUS ADD:** PO Box 1957, Pontiac, MI 48056, (313)334-1300.

SEELEY, Frederick P.——B: Jan 19, 1940, Greenwich, CT, *Tucson Regl. Mgr.*, Del E. Webb Realty and Mgmt. Co.; **PRIM RE ACT:** Consultant, Property Manager; **OTHER RE ACT:** Leasing Specialist; **PROFL AFFIL & HONORS:** Mason-BOMA, Tuscon Bd. of RE, IREM, CPM; **EDUC:** BA, 1964, Bus. Mgmt., CO State Univ.; **MIL SERV:** USA, Sgt.; **HOME ADD:** 8130 E. Ridgebrook Dr., Tucson, AZ 85701, (602)885-8963; **BUS ADD:** 32 N. Stone, Suite 512, Tucson, AZ 85701, (602)792-2444.

SEELY, Arthur W.——B: Oct. 1, 1954, Las Vegas, NV, *Pres.*, Real Equity Diversification, Inc.; **PRIM RE ACT:** Developer, Owner/Investor, Syndicator; **SERVICES:** Develop-Construct & Sell Pvt. Security Ctrs. to Indiv. Sales are as Condos or Coops., Syndication of Income Property; **PROFL AFFIL & HONORS:** Charter Member-Natl. Assn. of Independent Security Ctrs., CO Safe Deposit Assn., NY Safe Deposit Assn., US Safe Deposit Assn., Denver Apt. Assn., CO Apt. Assn.; **EDUC:** Bus. Econ., 1975, Univ. of CA at Santa Barbara; **HOME ADD:** 2 Cypress Point Way, Littleton, CO 80123, (303)861-1614; **BUS ADD:** 655 Broadway Penthouse 1000, Denver, CO 80203, (303)861-1614.

SEELY, Don——*Treasurer*, Searle, G.D. & Co.; **PRIM RE ACT:** Property Manager; **BUS ADD:** Box 1045, Skokie, IL 60076, (312)982-7000.*

SEEVAK, Sheldon——B: May 28, 1929, Boston, MA, *Partner*, Goldman, Sachs & Co., RE; **PRIM RE ACT:** Broker, Consultant, Owner/Investor, Syndicator; **PROFL AFFIL & HONORS:** ULI; NY City RE Bd.; Intl. Council of Shopping Centers; Nat. Assn. of Indus. & Office Parks; **EDUC:** BA, 1950, Univ. of IL; **GRAD EDUC:** 1961, Taxation, NY Univ. Law School; 1953, Harvard Law School; **EDUC HONORS:** Honors; **MIL SERV:** USCG, Lt.; **OTHER ACT & HONORS:** Tr. - Newark Beth Israel Medical Center; Dir., Univ. of Chicago Found. for Emotionally Disturbed Children; **HOME ADD:** 56 Duffield Dr., So. Orange, NJ 07079, (201)762-3892; **BUS ADD:** 55 Broad St., New York, NY 10004, (212)676-5001.

SEGAL, David F.——B: May 27, 1950, NYC, NY, *Partner*, Jaffe & Segal; **PRIM RE ACT:** Attorney; **SERVICES:** Representing brokers in comml. & indus. transactions; **REP CLIENTS:** R.B. Schlesinger & Co., Inc.; Andover Realty Inc.; **EDUC:** BA, 1972, Pol. Sci., NYU; **GRAD EDUC:** JD, 1975, Law, Brooklyn Law School; Master of Law Program, NYU; **HOME ADD:** 2077 Center Ave., Ft. Lee, NJ 07024, (201)944-0188; **BUS ADD:** 509 Madison Ave., Suite 506, NY, NY

10022, (212)980-9190.

SEGAL, David P.——**B:** Sept. 23, 1931, Cambridge, MA, *VP, Corp. RE*, Dunkin' Donuts of America, Inc.; **PRIM RE ACT:** Property Manager; **OTHER RE ACT:** Mgr. of corp. RE assets; **PROFL AFFIL & HONORS:** NACORE; **EDUC:** BS, 1954, Food Tech., Univ. of MA; **GRAD EDUC:** MBA, 1959, Mktg., Columbia Grad. School of Bus.; PhD., 1968, Harvard Grad. School of Bus.; **MIL SERV:** US Army; SP 4, 1955-1956; **OTHER ACT & HONORS:** Bd. of Dir. & Tr., NACORE; **HOME ADD:** 139 Country Dr., Weston, MA 02193, (617)891-1188; **BUS ADD:** POB 317, Randolph, MA 02368, (617) 961-4000.

SEGAL, Donald——**B:** Mar. 20, 1928, Philadelphia, PA, *Pres.*, Segal Assoc. Inc.; **PRIM RE ACT:** Developer, Builder, Syndicator; **SERVICES:** Land devel., bldg., constr. mgmt.; **REP CLIENTS:** Synd.; **PROFL AFFIL & HONORS:** Nat. Assn. Home Builders; **EDUC:** BS, 1970, Acctg. & Fin., Wharton Sch. of Univ. of PA; **OTHER ACT & HONORS:** Pres. Bd. of Commrs. Lower Merion Twp., PA, 1974-79; Bd. Member Moore Inst. of Art, Philadelphia, PA; Bd. Member Philadelphia Child Guidance Clinic, Philadelphia, PA; Bd. Member of All Star Forum, Philadelphia, PA; **HOME ADD:** 928 Bryn Mawr Ave., Narberth, PA 19072, (215)664-3666; **BUS ADD:** 560 Benigno Blvd., Bellmawr, NJ 08031, (609)931-0056.

SEGAL, John E.——**B:** Mar. 29, 1955, Philadelphia, PA, *VP*, Donald Segal Assoc., Inc.; **PRIM RE ACT:** Consultant, Developer, Builder, Owner/Investor; **SERVICES:** Land Devel. & consulting, constr., mgmt., & bldg.; **PROFL AFFIL & HONORS:** Nat. Assn. of Home Builders; Home Builders League of S. Jersey; **EDUC:** BA, 1977, Bio Physics, Univ. of PA, Philadelphia, PA; **HOME ADD:** 425 Williams Rd., Wynnewood, PA 19096, (215)649-6528; **BUS ADD:** 560 Benigno Blvd., Bellmawr, NJ 08031, (609)931-0056.

SEGAL, Robert M.——**B:** Apr. 7, 1935, Atlantic City, NJ, *Partner, Chmn. of Exec. Comm.*, Wolf, Block, Schorr & Solis-Cohen, RE Dept.; **PRIM RE ACT:** Attorney; **SERVICES:** Legal counseling and rep.; **REP CLIENTS:** Shopping ctr. devels., office bldg. devels., resid. devels., gen. cntrs., brokers and managing agents, arch., synds., instnl. lenders, ins. cos., hotel and conference ctr. operators; **PROFL AFFIL & HONORS:** Philadelphia, PA Bar Assns., ABA, ICSC, Rated 'av' in Martindale-Hubbell Legal Dir., Listed in current ed. of Who's Who in Amer. Law; **EDUC:** BS, 1957, Fin. & Investment, Wharton Sch. of Fin. & Commerce of Univ. of PA; **GRAD EDUC:** LLB, 1960, Law, Harvard Univ. Law Sch.; **EDUC HONORS:** Beta Gamma Sigma Award for highest scholastic average in class, Herbert S. Steuer Award, Cum Laude; **MIL SERV:** USA, 1st Lt.; **OTHER ACT & HONORS:** Former Constable of Elections, Lower Merion Township, Bds. of Dirs. of Jewish Employment and Vocational Serv. of Philadelphia, (Pres), Nat. Assn. of Jewish Vocational Servs., Jewish Family Serv. of Philadelphia (Chmn. of Investment Comm), Amer. Jewish Comm., Fed. of Jewish Agencies of Gr. Philadelphia. Member of B'nai B'rith, Harvard Club, Green Valley Ctry. Club, Locust Club, Member of Bds. of Dirs. and Officer of var. pvt. bus. corps. and pvt. charitable found.; **HOME ADD:** 1130 Red Rose Ln., Villanova, PA 19085, (215)525-6815; **BUS ADD:** 12th Fl., Packard Bldg., Philadelphia, PA 19102, (215)977-2230.

SEGAL, Stephen M.——**B:** Feb. 19, 1928, Phila., PA, *Pres.*, Stephen M. Segal, Inc.; **PRIM RE ACT:** Broker, Consultant, Appraiser; **SERVICES:** Marketing, cons., appraising of indus. comml. & investment props., site selection & land assemblage, fin. & prep. of market & feasibility studies; **REP CLIENTS:** Indus., fin. instns., attys, govt. agencies, utilities & indivs.; **PROFL AFFIL & HONORS:** SURM Former Pres. of NJ Chap. & Member of Bd. of Dir. Amer. Inst. of RE Appraisers (MAI), Former pres. NJ Chapt. & Member of Natl. Governing Council Amer. Soc. of RE CRE, Recipient of Profl. Recognition Award from AIREA; **EDUC:** BA, 1949, Commerce & Fin., PA State Univ.; **MIL SERV:** USN, Lt. JG; **OTHER ACT & HONORS:** 1966-70 Chmn. Lower Makefield Twp., PA Planning Comm.; Former Tr. Princeton Day School., Princeton, NJ; Former Dir. Trenton Chapt. Amer. Red Cross; Former Dir. Trenton Central YMCA; **HOME ADD:** 2211 Yardley Rd., Yardley, PA 19067, (215)493-2397; **BUS ADD:** 28 W State St., Trenton, NJ 08608, (609)989-7470.

SEGEL, M. Nelson——**B:** Jan. 26, 1952, Toledo, OH, M. Nelson Segel, Chartered; **PRIM RE ACT:** Attorney, Regulator, Owner/Investor; **SERVICES:** Legal documentation & structure, fin. consultation; **PREV EMPLOY:** Counsel to Commr. OH Div. of Securities; **PROFL AFFIL & HONORS:** ABA, OH, NV & Clark Cty. Bar Assns., RESSI; **EDUC:** BA, 1974, Psych., Univ. of Toledo; **GRAD EDUC:** MBA, 1975, Fin., Univ. of Toledo; JD, 1978, Univ. of Toledo; **HOME ADD:** 939 E. Flamingo, 78, Las Vegas, NV 89109, (702)731-1392; **BUS ADD:** 101 Convention Ctr. Dr., Suite 900, Las Vegas, NV 89125, (702)369-5990.

SEGHEZZI, Alan R.——**B:** Jan. 12, 1954, Boston, MA, *Atty.*, Murphy, Lamere & Murphy; **PRIM RE ACT:** Attorney; **SERVICES:** Representation of lessors, lessees, buyers, sellers and Mortgages; **REP CLIENTS:** Buyers, sellers, lenders, both resid. and comml.; **PROFL AFFIL & HONORS:** ABA, MBA; **EDUC:** BA, 1976, Econ. and Pol. Sci., Arts and Sciences, Boston Coll.; **GRAD EDUC:** 1979, Law, Boston Coll. Law School; **EDUC HONORS:** Magna Cum Laude; **OTHER ACT & HONORS:** Boston Univ. Grad. Tax Program, Candidate for LLM in Taxation, June 1983; **HOME ADD:** 126 W. St., Brockton, MA 02401, (617)584-1760; **BUS ADD:** S. Shore Plaza, P.O. Box 356, Braintree, MA 02184, (617)848-1850.

SEIBEL, John P.——**B:** May 3, 1936, Detroit, MI, *Pres.*, Champion Home Communities, Inc.; **PRIM RE ACT:** Developer, Property Manager; **OTHER RE ACT:** Developer, Housing Mfg.; **PREV EMPLOY:** Gen. Mgr. of Chateau Estates/Chateau Enterprises, Inc.; Asst. VP, Detroit & Northern S & L Assn.; Admin. VP of Metropolitan Fed. Savings; **PROFL AFFIL & HONORS:** MI Manufactured Housing Inst.; MI Mobile Home & Rec. Vehicle Inst.; Nat. Housing Fed.; **EDUC:** BBA, 1959, Econ., MI State Univ.; **OTHER ACT & HONORS:** Detroit Yacht Club, Clinton River Boat Club, Burbon Barrel Hunt Club; **HOME ADD:** 38840 Lagae, New Baltimore, MI 48047, (313)725-4322; **BUS ADD:** 2886 Fair Lane, Liuonia, MI 48150, (313)522-6906.

SEIDEL, Joseph S.——**B:** June 30, 1928, Elizabeth, NJ, *Atty.*, Joseph S. Seidel, P.A.; **PRIM RE ACT:** Attorney; **SERVICES:** Legal; **REP CLIENTS:** Bellemead Devel. Corp., Eastman Constr. Co. Inc., Jersey City Redevel. Agency; **PREV EMPLOY:** Partner, Hannoch, Weisman, Stern & Besser, Newark, NJ; **PROFL AFFIL & HONORS:** Right-of-Way Assn., Chmn. 1974-75, Profl. Devel. Comm., Member, Sussex Cty. Bar Assn., NJ State (Chmn. Comm. on Revision of Law of Eminent Domain, 1968, 1969, 1970, Amer. Panel Member, 1978 convention Bar Assns.; **EDUC:** AB, 1950, Poli. Sci., Rutgers Univ.; **GRAD EDUC:** JD, 1956, Rutgers Univ.; **MIL SERV:** USAF Res.; Capt., JAGD; **OTHER ACT & HONORS:** Mcpl. Prosecutor, Township of Springfield, 1962-67, Borough of Hopatcong, 1981-; **HOME ADD:** 25 Air Castle Isles, PO Box 1003, Hopatcong, NJ 07843, (201)770-0567; **BUS ADD:** 25 Air Castle Isles, PO Box 1003, Hopatcong, NJ 07843, (201)770-0456.

SEIFERT, Donald P.——*Manager RE Dept.*, Anheuser-Busch, Inc.; **PRIM RE ACT:** Property Manager; **BUS ADD:** 721 Pestalozzi St., St. Louis, MO 63118, (314)577-3353.*

SEIFFERT, W.W.——**B:** Aug. 20, 1920, S. St. Paul, MN, *Mgr., RE*, Superamerica Stations, Inc., Div. of Ashland Oil, Inc.; **PRIM RE ACT:** Broker, Appraiser, Property Manager; **PREV EMPLOY:** 20 yrs., Cities Service Oil Co., Mgr. of Operations; **PROFL AFFIL & HONORS:** Minneapolis Bd. of Realtors; Soc. of RE Appraisers; Member of NACORE; Nat. Assn. of Corp. RE Execs.; **EDUC:** Univ. of MN; **MIL SERV:** US Army, 1st Lt.; **HOME ADD:** 745 Hilltop Rd., Mendota Heights, MN 55118; **BUS ADD:** 1240 W. 98th St., Bloomington, MN 55431, (612)887-6141.

SEIGER, Joseph R.——**B:** Apr. 12, 1942, Washington, D.C., *Part.*, Vintage Prop.; **PRIM RE ACT:** Broker, Attorney, Developer, Builder, Property Manager, Owner/Investor; **PREV EMPLOY:** HUD, 1966-67; SFO Redev. Agy., 1968-70; Asst. Genl. Counsel, L. B. Nelson Corp.; Menlo Pk., CA, Genl. Counsel; **PROFL AFFIL & HONORS:** Bar Assoc. Dist. of Columbia, State of CA; **EDUC:** AB, 1964, Econ., Fin., Univ. of Pittsburgh; **GRAD EDUC:** JD, 1967, Univ. of MI; LLM, 1968, George Washington Univ. Law School; **EDUC HONORS:** O.D.E. Natl. Econ. Honor Soc.; **BUS ADD:** 3000 Sand Hill Rd., Bldg. 3, Suite 255, Menlo Pk., CA 94025, (415)854-5681.

SEITL, Wayne F.——**B:** Mar 10, 1950, Warren, OH, *Atty.*, Wood, Whitesell, Karp, Wellbaum, Miller & Seitl, PA; **PRIM RE ACT:** Attorney; **SERVICES:** Legal Counseling Tax and Securities Fields; **REP CLIENTS:** Allen RE Servs., Inc., Sarasota, FL; **PROFL AFFIL & HONORS:** Adjunct member ABA, Comm. on Special Tax Problems of RE, Author Tax Bus. and Estate Planning Aspects of FL RE Transactions, May 1980 Tax Planning Press; **EDUC:** BS, 1971, Public Relations, Univ. of FL; **GRAD EDUC:** JD, 1974, General Law, Univ. of FL; LLM, 1977, Tax Law, Univ. of Miami; **EDUC HONORS:** Graduate with honors, Honors Grad.; **OTHER ACT & HONORS:** Dir. Sarasota Family YMCA, YMCA Found.; **BUS ADD:** 3100 S. Tamiami Trail, Sarasota, FL 33579, (813)366-9110.

SELBER, Leonard——**B:** July 19, 1934, Shreveport, LA, *VP*, Selber Bros., Inc.; **PRIM RE ACT:** Developer, Owner/Investor; **EDUC:** 1956, Tulane Univ.; **MIL SERV:** USAF, Capt.; **HOME ADD:** 6021 Gilbert Dr., Shreveport, LA 71106, (318)868-2205; **BUS ADD:** Box

21830, Shreveport, LA 71120, (318)221-2561.

SELBER, Marilyn Golomb——**B:** Apr. 9, 1945, Youngstown, OH, *Atty.-at-Law*, Selber & Selber; **PRIM RE ACT:** Attorney; **SERVICES:** Financing, conveyancing, title search and title ins., regarding resid. and comml. real prop.; **REP CLIENTS:** Duval Fed. S&L Assn. of Jacksonville; FL Nat. Bank of Jacksonville; Pic N' Save Drug Co., Inc.; Nat. Merchandise Co., Inc.; Brierwood Builders, Inc.; Brierwood Apts.; Anastasia Condo. Assn., Inc.; Schurgin Realty & Devel. Co.; **PREV EMPLOY:** Assoc., Davis, Polk & Wardwell, Attys. (NY) 1970-72; Assoc. Selber & Ansbacher, Attys. 1972-73; Partner, Selber & Selber, Attys. 1973-present; **PROFL AFFIL & HONORS:** Jacksonville & Amer. Bar Assns. (Member, Committees on: Title Ins., 1975 to present; Conveyancing, 1976 to present, Real Prop. Div., Section on Real Prop. Probate & Trust Law); The FL Bar (Member: Committees on: Title Aspects of FL Probate Code, 1977 to present; Liaison with Title Insurers, 1978 to present; Liaison with Corp. Fiduciaries, 1978-80, Real Prop., Probate and Trust Law Sect.); **EDUC:** BA, 1966, Hist., Stern Coll. of Yeshiva Univ.; **GRAD EDUC:** JD, 1969, NYU School of Law; **EDUC HONORS:** Dean's List, Hist. Award, Member Moot Ct. Bd. 1967-69; **OTHER ACT & HONORS:** Amer. Mizrachi Women, Hadassah, Young Israel, Zionist Org. of Amer.; Public speaking in areas of RE and in areas relating to Judaism; **HOME ADD:** 8880 Old Kings Rd. S., Apt. 59W, Jacksonville, FL 32217, (904)737-2068; **BUS ADD:** 427 Edward Ball Bldg., Jacksonville, FL 32202, (904)358-3830.

SELBO, Lyle W.——**B:** July 8, 1926, Jamestown, ND, *Atty.*, Nilles, Hansen, Selbo, Magill & Davies, Ltd.; **PRIM RE ACT:** Attorney; **SERVICES:** Representation of clients re: acquisition, sale, mortgaging, devel.; **PROFL AFFIL & HONORS:** ABA, ND Bar Assn. and Sects. thereof; Amer. Coll. of Probate Counsel; **EDUC:** Bachelor of Philosophy, 1948, Pre-Law and Mathematics, Univ. of ND; **GRAD EDUC:** JD, 1950, Law, Univ. of ND; **EDUC HONORS:** with Distinction; **MIL SERV:** US Naval Res., Lt. j.g.; **OTHER ACT & HONORS:** School Bd., Fargo, ND 1970-1976; Dir., First Bank of ND, Fargo; **HOME ADD:** 501 7th St. S., Fargo, ND, (701)293-5535; **BUS ADD:** 415 3rd Ave. N., PO Box 2626, Fargo, ND 58108, (701)237-5544.

SELDEN, Dr. Basil H.——**B:** May 23, 1927, Philadelphia PA, *Pres., Dir.*, Selden Enterprises Inc.; **PRIM RE ACT:** Consultant, Owner/Investor; **SERVICES:** Consultation, Investment Advice; **EDUC:** AB, 1956, Physics & Math, Lincoln Univ.; **GRAD EDUC:** Ms Ed. & EdD, 1967, Educ., Admin. & Bus., Univ. of PA; Univ. of NV; Temple Univ.; Villanova Univ.; Univ. of DE; Widener Coll.; **OTHER ACT & HONORS:** Notary Public PA 8 yrs; Author, *More For Your Money, Or More Money For Your*; Dir. & Founder - World Wide Benevolent Soc.; Other Office: 2644 Capitol Trail, Suite J, Newark, DE 197a oh11, (302)368-1652; **HOME ADD:** 2307 Graywood Rd. Northshire, Wilmington, DE 19810; **BUS ADD:** 30 Mary St., Suite 3, Reno, NV 89509, (702)329-4304.

SELDIN, Stephen——**B:** June 4, 1935, Brooklyn, NY, *Atty.*, Bell, Kalnick, Beckman, Klee & Green 1980 - pres.; **PRIM RE ACT:** Consultant, Attorney; **OTHER RE ACT:** RE; **SERVICES:** RE Atty. and consultant; **REP CLIENTS:** Misc. RE devel. and lenders; **PROFL AFFIL & HONORS:** RE Bd. of NY, Inc., Member, Legislation and Adaptive Reuse Comm.; NY State Bar Assn.; NY Cty. Lawyers Assn.; **EDUC:** BBA, 1956, Econs., CCNY; **GRAD EDUC:** LLB, 1959, The Yale Law School; **EDUC HONORS:** Cum Laude, Beta Gama Sigma; **HOME ADD:** 325 W 13th St., New York, NY 10014, (212)421-3311; **BUS ADD:** 501 Madison Ave., New York, NY 10022, (212)421-3311.

SELL, Jan A.——**B:** Aug. 27, 1952, Pittsburgh, PA, *Pres.*, Sell, Huish, & McFadden Inc.; **PRIM RE ACT:** Consultant, Appraiser, Property Manager, Syndicator; **SERVICES:** Appraisal, Consultation, Analysis, Synds.; **REP CLIENTS:** Fin. instns., Investors, Attys., Accountants, Govt. Agencies; **PREV EMPLOY:** Pres., JA Sell Corp 1980-1981; Pres., Appraisal Research Consultants 1978-1980; Staff Appraiser Valley Natl. Bank 1974-1978; **PROFL AFFIL & HONORS:** AIREA, Appraisers-Soc. of RE Appraisers, MAI, SRPA, SRA; **EDUC:** Gen. Bus., Bus., 1974, RE, AZ State Univ.; **EDUC HONORS:** Outstanding Appraisal Student, 1974; **HOME ADD:** 2020 S. El Marino, Mesa, AZ, (602)839-4177; **BUS ADD:** 2111 E. Baseline Rd., C-5, Tempe, AZ 85283, (602)838-0500.

SELLARS, W. M.——**B:** Sept. 25, 1923, Recovery, GA, *Brd. Chmn.*, Ward Wight Co.; **PRIM RE ACT:** Broker, Syndicator, Developer, Owner/Investor; **PROFL AFFIL & HONORS:** NAR, RESSI; **GRAD EDUC:** BS Agricu., 1949, Animal Husbandry, Bus., Univ. of GA; **EDUC HONORS:** Ag-Hon, Gridiron; **MIL SERV:** USN, RM 3/C; **HOME ADD:** 619 Fairfield Dr., Marietta, GA 30067, (404)973-2844; **BUS ADD:** 3340 Peachtree Rd., Suite 2310, Atlanta, GA 30326, (404)261-9300.

SELLERS, James R.——**B:** Jan. 28, 1934, Barberton, OH, *SR. VP*, Western Amer. Mort. Co. Comml.; **PRIM RE ACT:** Broker, Lender, Owner/Investor, Property Manager; **SERVICES:** Arrange joint ventures and loans; invest in RE for Corp. account; **PREV EMPLOY:** Apt. devel. and mgr. (W.R. Schulz & Assoc. Phoenix 1970-73); 1958-70, Title ins. (Pres.- Tucson Title Ins. Co. 1968, 69, 70); **PROFL AFFIL & HONORS:** Mort. Bankers Assn. of Amer., AZ Mort. Bankers Assn.; Member Bd. of Dir., AZ Multi-Housing Assn., Outstanding Young Men of Amer. 1967; **EDUC:** BS, 1955, AZ State Univ.; **EDUC HONORS:** Assoc. Men Students Officer; **MIL SERV:** US Infantry, 1st Lt.; **OTHER ACT & HONORS:** Pres., Skyline Ctry. Club, Tucson; Bd. of Dir., Pima Cty. RE Research Council; **HOME ADD:** 6601 N. Montezuma, Tucson, AZ 85718, (602)299-1919; **BUS ADD:** PO Box 12547, Tucson, AZ 85732, (602)747-9000.

SELLERS, Ralph W., Jr.——**B:** July 26, 1926, Del Rio, TX, *Owner*, Ralph Sellers & Assoc.; **PRIM RE ACT:** Broker, Consultant, Appraiser, Owner/Investor; **SERVICES:** Appraisals, consultation, comml. brokerage; **REP CLIENTS:** Manufacturers Hanover Trust, local lending instns. & banks, Fed. Home Loan Bank; **PROFL AFFIL & HONORS:** AIREA, Amer. Soc. of RE Counselors, El Paso Bd. of Realtors, MAI, CRE; **MIL SERV:** USN; **OTHER ACT & HONORS:** Gov. District 7 - 1978-1980, Soc. of RE Appraisers; **HOME ADD:** 400 Ridgemont, El Paso, TX 79912, (915)584-2422; **BUS ADD:** 6604 Westwind, El Paso, TX 79912.

SELLGREN, Arthur——*Adm. Prop. Mgmt.*, Rohr Industries, Inc.; **PRIM RE ACT:** Property Manager; **BUS ADD:** Box 878, Chula Vista, CA 92012, (714)575-4111.*

SELLING, John——**B:** May 21, 1916, Portland, OR, *Pres.*, ESP Prop. Factors; **PRIM RE ACT:** Broker, Consultant, Developer, Owner/Investor, Instructor, Property Manager; **PROFL AFFIL & HONORS:** IREM, Regional VP, CPM; **MIL SERV:** Infantry, PFC, 1942-1945, Good Conduct Medal; **OTHER ACT & HONORS:** Rotary Club, CPM Professional Achievement Award; **HOME ADD:** 3730 S.W. Shattuck, Portland, OR 97221, (503)292-3851; **BUS ADD:** 1101 S.E. Salmon, Portland, OR 97214.

SELSOR, L. Grant——**B:** June 7, 1947, Springfield, MO, *Shareholder - Employee*, Barstow, Selsor & Barstow, PC; **PRIM RE ACT:** Attorney; **SERVICES:** Title servs., RE documents, RE investment planning; **REP CLIENTS:** First Nat. Bank & Trust of Menominee; Superior State Devel. Co. (a RE ltd. partnership); D-C Equipment, Inc.; Santo Indus., Inc.; **PROFL AFFIL & HONORS:** MI Bar Assn., ABA, Menominee Cty. Bar Assn., Member-Real Prop. Law Sect. of ABA; **EDUC:** BA, 1969, Poli. Sci. & Hist., Drury Coll.; **GRAD EDUC:** JD, 1973, Law, Univ. of KY; **EDUC HONORS:** Honor Roll, Kiwanis Club Scholarship, Asst. in Poli. Sci. Dept.; **MIL SERV:** USAR, Sgt.; **OTHER ACT & HONORS:** Chmn. Menominee Cty. Mental Health Bd.; Menominee Econ. Devel. Corp.; Menominee Indus. Devel. Corp.; Bds: C of C, YMCA, Riverside Ctry. Club; **HOME ADD:** Star Route, Box 202, Menominee, MI 49858, (906)864-2532; **BUS ADD:** First National Bank & Trust Bldg., Menominee, MI 49858, (906)863-9959.

SELTZER, Dean B.——**B:** Sept. 20, 1937, Philadelphia, PA, *F VP Grouphead*, Barclays Bank International Limited, Real Estate Financial Services Group; **PRIM RE ACT:** Banker; **OTHER RE ACT:** RE Finance; **SERVICES:** RE Financing for builders, developers and investors; **REP CLIENTS:** Industry Leaders and Middle Management; **EDUC:** BA, 1959, Fin., PA State Univ.; **GRAD EDUC:** MBA, 1960, Fin., Grad. School of Bus. Columbia Univ.; **HOME ADD:** Woodbrook Rd., Pleasantville, NY 10570, (914)769-9198; **BUS ADD:** Head Office North America, Pan Am Building, 200 Park Ave., New York, NY 10166, (212)573-4577.

SEMAS, Leonard A.——**B:** Feb. 2, 1947, Taunton, MA, *Owner*, Len Semas RE; **PRIM RE ACT:** Broker, Appraiser, Developer, Builder, Owner/Investor, Property Manager, Syndicator; **OTHER RE ACT:** General Contractor; **PREV EMPLOY:** Amer. Hosp. Supply Corp.; **PROFL AFFIL & HONORS:** San Jose RE Bd., Sacramento Bd. of Realtors, CAR, NAR, CAR Synd. Div., CAR Investment Div., Assoc. Builders & Contractors; **EDUC:** BS, 1968, Bio., Phil., Univ. of Santa Clara; **GRAD EDUC:** MBA, 1975, Fin., Univ. of Santa Clara; **EDUC HONORS:** Dean's List; **MIL SERV:** USA, 1st Lt.; **OTHER ACT & HONORS:** Dist. Mil. Grad. Engr. Office Candidate School, US Army; **HOME ADD:** 1696 Husted Ave., San Jose, CA 95124, (408)723-2598; **BUS ADD:** 1276 Lincoln Ave., Suite 203, San Jose, CA 95125, (408)947-1888.

SENF, Charles K.——**B:** Feb. 25, 1946, New York, NY, *Pres.*, Real Estate Counseling & Exchange; **PRIM RE ACT:** Consultant; **OTHER RE ACT:** Real Prop. Exchange; **SERVICES:** Const., Fin., Arch., Synd., Consultation; **PREV EMPLOY:** All employment in the field of RE Sales, Exchange and Counseling; **PROFL AFFIL & HONORS:**

Broward RE Exchangors, FREE, PBNB Realtors, NML, ASPC, Exchangor, Counselor; **EDUC:** AA, BBA, 1970, 1972, RE/Computers, MD, FL Atl. Univ.; **GRAD EDUC:** MA, 1981, Community Coll./Computer Educ., FL Atl. Univ.; **EDUC HONORS:** MCCSA; **MIL SERV:** US Army, NDSM, OSEM, GCM; **OTHER ACT & HONORS:** Pres., Palm Beach RE Exchangors; **HOME ADD:** PO Box 952, Boca Raton, FL 33432; **BUS ADD:** 903 SE First Way, Deerfield Beach, FL 33441, (305)278-7418.

SENTER, Bill——**B:** May 11, 1930, Aspermont, TX, *Pres., Chmn. of Bd.*, Synergism, Inc.; **PRIM RE ACT:** Broker, Developer, Builder, Owner/Investor, Property Manager, Syndicator; **PREV EMPLOY:** Owner, Senter Ins. Co.; **PROFL AFFIL & HONORS:** CCIM; Cert. Residential Broker; RNMI; Accredited Farm and Land Member; CRI, Pres., Abilene Bd. of Realtors, Realtor of Year; **EDUC:** BBA, 1951, Fin., TX Tech. Univ.; **OTHER ACT & HONORS:** TX RE Commn. 1978-84 (chmn. 1981); Outstanding Young Man of Abilene; Boss of the Year; **HOME ADD:** 140 Hedges, Abilene, TX 79605, (915)692-3221; **BUS ADD:** 2901 S. 1st, Abilene, TX 79605, (915)677-1811.

SENTIVANY, Edward K., Jr.——**B:** July 25, 1944, New Britain, CT, *First VP*, State Nat. Bank of CT, RE & Mort. Admin.; **PRIM RE ACT:** Consultant, Banker, Lender; **OTHER RE ACT:** Mort. banker; **SERVICES:** RE investment counseling; **REP CLIENTS:** Devels., owners, major RE investors; **PREV EMPLOY:** Pres. MAC Investment Grp. Inc., Boston, MA; Chmn. Dir. CT Housing Fin. Auth; **PROFL AFFIL & HONORS:** CT Bankers Assn., MBA; **EDUC:** BS, 1967, RE & Fin., Univ. of CT; **OTHER ACT & HONORS:** Lions Club; **HOME ADD:** 151 Rockwood Dr., Southington, CT 06489, (203)621-4235; **BUS ADD:** 1 Atlantic St., PO Box 181, Stamford, CT 06904, (203)356-0234.

SENTURIA, Richard H.——**B:** Aug. 14, 1938, W. Frankfort, IL, *Pres.*, Investment Capital Associates, Inc.; **PRIM RE ACT:** Consultant, Developer, Owner/Investor, Syndicator; **SERVICES:** Fin. planning - product acquisition & mktg. consulting for investment firms; **REP CLIENTS:** Regional Investment Brokerage Firms, Synd., Investors; **PREV EMPLOY:** VP Tax Shelters, R. Rowland & Co., Inc. 1976-79; **PROFL AFFIL & HONORS:** IAFP, Am. Assn. of Reg. Reps.; **EDUC:** 1956-57, Southern IL Univ.; **GRAD EDUC:** 1957-59 and 1960-61, Washington Univ. (St. Louis) Bus. School; 1959-60, Washington Univ. Law School; **MIL SERV:** US Army, Sp 5, 1961-62; **OTHER ACT & HONORS:** Bd. of Dir., Forsyth School, Congregation B'Nai Amoona; V.P. Wharfside Redevel. Corp.; **HOME ADD:** 425 Shadybrook Dr., Creve Coeur, MO 63141, (314)567-1224; **BUS ADD:** 707 N 2nd St., Suite 200, St. Louis, MO 63102, (314)231-1242.

SENZ, John——*Mfg. Dept.*, Lubrizol Corp.; **PRIM RE ACT:** Property Manager; **BUS ADD:** 29400 Lakeland Blvd., Wickliffe, OH 44092, (216)943-4200.*

SERMERSHEIM, Michael D.——**B:** Dec. 24, 1948, Akron, OH, *Attorney; Office of University Legal Serv.; Lecturer (faculty member)*, University of Akron; **PRIM RE ACT:** Consultant, Attorney; **SERVICES:** Legal Advice, Lecturing, Consulting; **REP CLIENTS:** Univ. of Akron, certain private corps. and partnerships, and private indiv.; **PROFL AFFIL & HONORS:** Akron Bar Assn.; Tr. of Metro Regional Transit Auth. (Akron, OH) and Chmn. of its Planning, Service and Mktg. Comm.; **EDUC:** BA, 1970, Arts, Bus., Acctg., Univ. of Akron; **GRAD EDUC:** JD, 1973, Comml., Univ. of Akron; **EDUC HONORS:** National Order of Barristers; **MIL SERV:** Army (JAGC), Capt., ARCOM; **HOME ADD:** 2068 25th St., Cuyahoga Falls, OH 44223, (216)929-1965; **BUS ADD:** Buchtel Hall, Rm. 212, Office of Legal Services, Univ. of Akron, Akron, OH 44325, (216)375-7830.

SERSZEN, Jerome A.——**B:** Apr. 4, 1944, Chicago, IL, *Staff Appraiser*, Evalucor, Inc.; **PRIM RE ACT:** Appraiser, Owner/Investor; **OTHER RE ACT:** Review Appraiser; **SERVICES:** Evals., consultation, mgmt.; **REP CLIENTS:** Lenders, lawyers, indivs., transfer employee cos., Fed. and local govts.; **PROFL AFFIL & HONORS:** Chicago RE Bd.; North Shore Bd. of Realtors; Soc. RE Appraisers; Review Appraisers; Intl. Right-of-Way, SRA, CRA, IRLWA; **EDUC:** BA, 1969, Econ. & RE, Loyola Univ.; **GRAD EDUC:** MBA, 1972, Econ., Statistics, RE, DePaul Univ.; **HOME ADD:** 4104 Odell Ave., Norridge, IL 60634, (312)452-0485; **BUS ADD:** 1001 Lake St., Oak Park, IL 60301, (312)524-1095.

SESSIONS, Michael A.——*RE Mgr.*, U.N.C. Resources, Inc.; **PRIM RE ACT:** Property Manager; **BUS ADD:** UNC Crescent Plaza, 700, Leesburg Pike, Falls Church, VA 22043, (703)821-7900.*

SETH, Jack C.——**B:** Jan. 20, 1927, Fullerton, CA, *Sales Agent*, Kidder, Mathews & Segner, Inc., Indus. & Comml.; **PRIM RE ACT:** Broker; **EDUC:** BA, 1951, Econ. & Bus. Admin., Univ. of WA; **MIL SERV:** USMC, Sgt., M44-47, Pres. Unit Citation with 1 star; **HOME ADD:** 4635 138th Ave. SE, Bellevue, WA 98006, (206)746-0733; **BUS ADD:** 9930 Evergreen Way Suite C-105, Everett, WA 98204, (206)347-4000.

SETTLE, Joseph——*Pres.*, Federal Home Loan Bank of Little Rock; **PRIM RE ACT:** Banker; **BUS ADD:** 1400 Tower Bldg., Little Rock, AR 72201, (501)372-7141.*

SEWALL, Nancy C.——**B:** Nov. 23, 1946, Boston, MA, *Exec. Mktg. Dir.*, Action Committee of 50 Inc.; **PRIM RE ACT:** Developer; **OTHER RE ACT:** Economic Devel.; **SERVICES:** Site location information, labor mkt. information; **REP CLIENTS:** Site selection, RE officers; **PREV EMPLOY:** RE Brokerage; **PROFL AFFIL & HONORS:** Ind Dev. Council ME, Northeast Ind. Dev. Assn.; **EDUC:** BA, 1968, Psych/Sociology, Univ. of ME; **GRAD EDUC:** MBA (enrolled), Univ. of ME; **HOME ADD:** 94 Mill St., Orono, ME 04473, (207)866-3128; **BUS ADD:** 151 Broadway, Bangor, ME 04401, (207)947-3535.

SEWING, Charles E.——**B:** Feb. 3, 1942, White Plains, NY, *VP and Chief Appraiser*, Wells Fargo Bank 1968-present; **PRIM RE ACT:** Appraiser; **SERVICES:** Appraisal servs. to Wells Fargo Co. & subsid.; **PREV EMPLOY:** Assessor's Office, Sonoma Cty., CA 1965-68; **PROFL AFFIL & HONORS:** AIREA; Bd. of Realtors, Marin Cty., CA; Bd. of Realtors, San Francisco CA, MAI; **EDUC:** BS, 1965, Mktg., Pomona, CA State Polytechnic Univ., CA; **HOME ADD:** P.O. Box 1246, Novato, CA 94948, (415)892-6871; **BUS ADD:** 475 Sansome St., AU 8751, San Francisco, CA 94111, (415)396-7250.

SEYBOLD, Donald A.——**B:** Nov. 7, 1931, Chico, CA, *Owner, Branch Office, Strout Realty, Inc.*; **PRIM RE ACT:** Broker, Developer, Builder, Owner/Investor, Instructor; **PREV EMPLOY:** Owner Castberg RE; **PROFL AFFIL & HONORS:** NAR; Rotary; **EDUC:** 1953, Univ. of Santa Clara, CA; **MIL SERV:** US Army; Lt. Col.; Bronze Star, Joint Service Commendation, Army Commendation w/3 OLC; **HOME ADD:** 628 Meadow Ct., Powell, WI 82435, (307)754-5345; **BUS ADD:** 116 N. Rent, Powell, WI 82435, (307)754-9363.

SEYFERTH, Harold H.——**B:** Jan. 22, 1922, Stockton, CA, *Pres.*, H. Seyferth Associates; **PRIM RE ACT:** Consultant, Appraiser; **SERVICES:** Appraisals, consultation, right of way, fiscal & econ. analysis; **REP CLIENTS:** Law offices, public agencies, ins. cos., fin. cos., gen. cos.; **PROFL AFFIL & HONORS:** Intl. Right of Way Assn.; Nat. Assn. of Review Appraisers; Amer. Assn. of Cert. Appraisers; Intl. Coll. of RE Consulting; Intl. Inst. of Valuers, Sr. Member; Intl. Org. of RE Appraisers; Nat. Assn. of Cert. Real Prop. Appraisers; Nat. RE Educ. Assn., Indiv. Charter Member; ULI, Member, CAS; CRA; SCU; ICA; CRPA; APA; RECP; RECI; San Jose State Univ.; Golden Gate Univ.; Hartnell Coll.; Monterey Peninsula Coll.; Pacific Western Univ.; **EDUC:** BA, 1948, Psych./Econ., San Jose State Univ.; **GRAD EDUC:** Cert./MBA, 1950/1981, Mcpl. Govt./RE, Coro Found./Pac. Western Univ.; **EDUC HONORS:** Psych., Fellow; **MIL SERV:** USN, WWII; **OTHER ACT & HONORS:** All-Amer. City Citizen Award, City of San Jose; Outstanding Citizen Award, City of San Jose; Chmn., Bd. of Dirs., Carmel Riviera Mutual Water Co.; Chmn., Citizens Advisory Comm., Local Coastal Program, Carmel Area; Bd. of Dirs., Boy's City Boy's Club, San Jose; Bd. of Dirs., Amer. Cancer Soc., San Jose; Charter Revision Comm., City of San Jose, Bd. of Trs., Enterprise School Dist.; Charter Member, Council of Monterey Bay; Charter Member, San Antonio Valley Hist. Assn.; Chmn., Monterey Cty. Parks Commn.; **HOME ADD:** 50 Yankee Point Dr., Carmel, CA 93923, (408)624-0740; **BUS ADD:** 1015 Cass St., Monterey, CA 93940, (408)649-1838.

SEYMOUR, Bruce A.——**B:** June 13, 1933, New York, NY, *C.E.O. Pres.*, B.A. Seymour Development Group; **OTHER RE ACT:** RE Devel., Investment; **SERVICES:** Devel. and mgmt. of comml. props.; **REP CLIENTS:** State of CA, Del Monte Foods, Other Nat. Cos.; **PREV EMPLOY:** Pres. COE, Land Resource Devel. Corp.; **PROFL AFFIL & HONORS:** Assoc. Builders and Contractors, Inc.; BOMA, Amer. Mgmt. Assn.; **EDUC:** BA, 1960, Bus., RE, UCLA; **MIL SERV:** USAF, Sgt.; **HOME ADD:** 15 Edward Ct., San Rafael, CA 94901, (415)457-3394; **BUS ADD:** 1455 Francisco Blvd., San Rafael, CA 94901, (415)453-6575.

SEYMOUR, Charles F.——**B:** Nov. 15, 1921, Swarthmore, PA, *Pres. & CEO*, Jackson-Cross Co.; **PRIM RE ACT:** Broker, Consultant, Appraiser; **PREV EMPLOY:** Arthur W. Binns, Inc.; **PROFL AFFIL & HONORS:** AIREA; ASREC; **EDUC:** 1949, Univ. of Penn.; **HOME ADD:** 1131 Putnam Blvd., Wallingford, PA 19086, (215)874-9791; **BUS ADD:** 2000 Market St., Philadelphia, PA 19103, (215)561-8910.

SFOUGGATAKIS, Nicholas A.——**B:** Mar. 22, 1947, New York, NY, *CPA*, N.A. Sfouggatakis & Co.; **PRIM RE ACT:** Consultant, Developer, Owner/Investor, Property Manager; **OTHER RE ACT:** Acct. - Tax Specialist Fin. Cons.; **REP CLIENTS:** Danae Realty

Corp., Sfouggatakis Realty Co.; **PREV EMPLOY:** Arthur Andersen & Co., CPA's, Nicholas Estates Realty Co.; **PROFL AFFIL & HONORS:** AICPA, NYS, CPA's; **EDUC:** BS, 1968, Acctg., Brooklyn, Coll.; **GRAD EDUC:** M.B.A., 1970, Fin. and Investments, NYU Grad. School of Bus.; 1970-1974, Brooklyn Law School; **OTHER ACT & HONORS:** VP - Pancretan Assn. of Amer.; **HOME ADD:** 20 89th St., Brooklyn, NY 11209, (212)238-5153; **BUS ADD:** 19 Rector St., New York, NY 10016, (212)238-5153.

SHAAK, J. Franklin——B: Dec. 20, 1923, Kearny, NJ, *RE Consultant*, Eric Bram & Co.; **PRIM RE ACT:** Broker, Appraiser, Consultant; **SERVICES:** Investment counseling, appraisal, site location and leasing for maj. indus., distribution, office users in NJ; **REP CLIENTS:** State of NJ; Garden State Pkwy. Auth.; Campbell Soup Co.; GeneraL Services Admin.; Colonial Life Ins. Co.; Home Life Ins. Co. and various indus. corps.; **PREV EMPLOY:** Former VP, US LIFE, RE Services; VP, Sanders A. Kahn Assoc.; Chief Appraiser, Equitable Life Assur. Soc.; **PROFL AFFIL & HONORS:** MAI; GRI; **EDUC:** BS, RE Studies, NYU; 1946, US Merchant Marine Acad.; **MIL SERV:** USN, Res.; Lt.j.g.; **HOME ADD:** 447B New Haven Way, Jamesburg, NJ 08831, (609)655-1854; **BUS ADD:** 77 Milltown Rd., E. Brunswick, NJ 08816, (201)238-3500.

SHACHAT, Joseph M.——B: June 11, 1929, Newark, NJ, *V.P.*, Heller Constr. Co.; **PRIM RE ACT:** Broker, Consultant, Developer, Builder, Owner/Investor; **EDUC:** BBA, 1953, Advt., Mktg., Fairleigh Dickinson Univ.; **GRAD EDUC:** Rutgers Univ.; **MIL SERV:** USN; SFC; **OTHER ACT & HONORS:** Bd. of Ed., Indus. Comm.; **HOME ADD:** 66 Katydid Dr., N. Branch, Somerville, NJ 08876, (201)722-1667; **BUS ADD:** 205 Mill Rd., Edison, NJ 08817, (201)287-4880.

SHACK, Norman M.——Norman M. Shack; **PRIM RE ACT:** Attorney; **PROFL AFFIL & HONORS:** ABA, MBA, MA Conveyancers Assn.; **EDUC:** BS, 1948, Tufts Univ.; **GRAD EDUC:** LLB, 1951, Boston Univ.; **BUS ADD:** 420 Common St., Lawrence, MA 01840, (617)688-0292.

SHAEVITZ, Robert M.——B: Jan. 14, 1933, Cleveland, OH, *Pres.*, RMS Companies; **PRIM RE ACT:** Developer, Owner/Investor, Property Manager, Syndicator; **SERVICES:** Devel. office, apts., bldgs. & mgmt. of them; **REP CLIENTS:** Indiv. & ltd. partners; **PROFL AFFIL & HONORS:** CAA; CPM; **EDUC:** BA, 1955, RE, OH State Univ.; **MIL SERV:** U.S. Army; Pfc.; **HOME ADD:** 61 Fruit Hill Dr., Chillicothe, OH 45601, (614)775-6226; **BUS ADD:** Foulke Block Bldg., Chillicothe, OH 45601, (614)773-8686.

SHAFER, Pauline M.——B: Mar. 21, 1925, Liberty Township, PA, *Pres.*, P & S Developments, Inc.; **PRIM RE ACT:** Developer, Owner/Investor; **SERVICES:** Devel. of land for comml. and resid. const.; **REP CLIENTS:** Home builders and comml. construction cos.; **PREV EMPLOY:** VP/Sec., Oscar F. Shafer, Inc. (Home Builders); Treas./Comptroller, Cumberland Construction Co. and RSE Inc.; **PROFL AFFIL & HONORS:** Nat. Assn. of Home Builders Auxiliary, Nat. Pres., NAHB Aux. (1964); **EDUC:** BS, 1944, Acctg./Bus. Mgmt., IN Univ. of PA; **OTHER ACT & HONORS:** ACLD (Assn. for Children with Learning Disabilities); DDAN (Devel. Disabilities Advocacy Network); Citizens Curriculum Comm., Cumb. Valley School Dist.; Elder, United Presbyterian Church USA; **HOME ADD:** 43 Green Ridge Rd., Mechanicsburg, PA 17055, (717)766-7303; **BUS ADD:** 43 Green Ridge Rd., Mechanicsburg, PA 17055, (717)766-7303.

SHAFER, Thomas W.——B: Dec. 3, 1941, Wenatchee, WA, CEO T.W. Shafer & Associates, Inc.; **PRIM RE ACT:** Broker, Engineer, Developer, Instructor; **SERVICES:** Feasibility studies, fin. analysis & structuring; **REP CLIENTS:** Out of area investors, instnl. investors and lenders, indiv. in need of outside expertise; **PROFL AFFIL & HONORS:** ULI, CAR, WTA; **EDUC:** 1965, Econ., WA State Univ.; **GRAD EDUC:** MBA, 1972, Fin., San Diego State Univ.; **MIL SERV:** USN/USMC, HM2, several decorations; **OTHER ACT & HONORS:** La Jolla Profl. Mens Club, Author *RE & Econ.*, *Urban Growth & Econ.*, both published by Reston Publishing Co.; **HOME TEL:** (714)450-1264; **BUS ADD:** PO Box 1721, La Jolla, CA 92038.

SHAFER, W. Bruce——B: May 26, 1936, San Francisco, CA, *Cty. Assessor, Recorder*, County of Marin; **PRIM RE ACT:** Consultant, Appraiser, Instructor, Assessor; **OTHER RE ACT:** County Recorder; **SERVICES:** Valuation and assessment of 86,000 parcels with a restricted role value of 8.1 billion dollars; creation and maintenance of all official documents, notices, and papers filed in the cty.; **PREV EMPLOY:** Indep. fee appraiser & consultant, 1964-1978; **PROFL AFFIL & HONORS:** Intl. Assn. of Assessing Officers, IREF, AIREA, SRPA, NARA, Assn. of Fed. Appraisers (Sr. Member), Soc. of Govt. Appraisers (SGA), Amer. Arbitration Assn. (comml. panel), Profl. Recognition Award, 1978-89, Amer. Instit. RE Appr.; **EDUC:** BS, 1958, Bus. Admin., Univ. of San Francisco; **OTHER ACT & HONORS:** Marin Cty. Assessment Appeals Bd., 1970-1978; Guardsmen of S.F.; US Navy League; Commonwealth Club; Rotary; Pres., Marin Bd. of Realtors, 1970; Dir., CA Assn. of Realtors, 1968-1972; Instr., appraisal courses, Coll. of Marin, 1974-1978; **HOME ADD:** 52 Peninsula Rd., Belvedere, CA 94920, (415)435-4217; **BUS ADD:** Admin. Bldg., Civic Ctr., San Rafael, CA 94903, (415)499-7198.

SHAFFER, Don B.——B: July 4, 1946, Seattle, WA, *Pres.*, D.B. Shaffer Co.; **PRIM RE ACT:** Broker, Consultant, Developer, Owner/Investor; **SERVICES:** Feasibility analysis & project mgmt. services; **PREV EMPLOY:** Devel. mgr. (The Quadrant Corp.); VP & Gen. Mgr. (Environment NW Inc.); **PROFL AFFIL & HONORS:** NAHB, Seattle Master Bldrs., Seattle C of C; **EDUC:** BS, 1969, Arch., Constr. & Land Planning, Coll. of Architecture & Urban Planning, Univ. of WA; **OTHER ACT & HONORS:** Big Bros. of America (11 yrs.); **HOME ADD:** 2070 N 78th St., Seattle, WA 98103, (206)522-7852; **BUS ADD:** Northgate Exec. Ctr., 155 NE 100th Suite 403, Seattle, WA 98125, (206)524-5535.

SHAFFER, Jack A.——B: Jan. 15, 1930, Chicago, IL, *Sr. VP*, Sonnenblick-Goldman Corp., Lehman Bros. Kuhn Loeb Inc.; **PRIM RE ACT:** Broker, Consultant, Banker, Lender; **PROFL AFFIL & HONORS:** ULI, MBA; **EDUC:** 1951, Fin., Univ. of Miami; **GRAD EDUC:** JD, 1953, Northwestern Univ.; **EDUC HONORS:** Wigmore Key; **MIL SERV:** Judge Advocate, Gen.; **HOME ADD:** 300 E 56th St. #30F, New York, NY 10022, (212)838-2315; **BUS ADD:** 1251 Ave. of The Americas, New York, NY 10022, (212)541-4321.

SHAFFER, N. Manfred——B: Oct. 10, 1927, Somerville, MA, STS: Land Use and Real Estate Consultants; **PRIM RE ACT:** Consultant, Syndicator, Instructor, Developer, Broker; **OTHER RE ACT:** Exchangor; **SERVICES:** Consulting; Ltd. partnerships, Legislative advocate, investment; **PREV EMPLOY:** Prof., Environmental studies & geography, Univ. of CA; **PROFL AFFIL & HONORS:** RESSI, FIABCI, APA, Santa Cruz Bd. of Realtors, Santa Cruz City Planning Commn.; **EDUC:** BS, 1955, Geography, Columbia Univ.; **GRAD EDUC:** MS, 1957, Geog., Univ. of WI (Madison); PhD, 1963, Geog., Planning Housing, Columbia Univ.; **EDUC HONORS:** Nat. Acad. of Sc. For. Field Research Fellow; **MIL SERV:** US Marines, Sgt.; **OTHER ACT & HONORS:** Chmn., Monterey Bay Unified Air Pollution Control Dist. Hearing Bd., since 1974, Pres., Santa Cruz Area C of C; **HOME ADD:** 80 Alta Vista Dr., Santa Cruz, CA 95060, (408)423-1175; **BUS ADD:** 147 River St. S. #221, Santa Cruz, CA 95060, (408)426-6055.

SHAFFER, Ralph——*RE Dept.*, Outboard Marine Corp.; **PRIM RE ACT:** Property Manager; **BUS ADD:** 100 Sea Horse Dr., Wakegan, IL 60086, (312)689-6200.*

SHAFRON, Shelly Jay——B: Feb. 9, 1950, Los Angeles, CA, *Atty.*, Rich & Ezer; **PRIM RE ACT:** Consultant, Attorney, Owner/Investor; **SERVICES:** Legal services, both transaction and litigation with emphasis on trial and appellate work; counseling RE and Mort. Brokerage Firms and Investors; Teaching RE Brokerage Law; Speaking and lecturing; **REP CLIENTS:** Coldwell Banker & Co.; Forest E. Olson, Inc.; Gamson & Flans, RE Auctioneers; The Robert McNeil Corp.; The Northrop Corp. (RE only); The George Elkins Co.; Statewide Home Loan Co.; Franklin Home Loan Co.; **PREV EMPLOY:** 5 yrs. as Staff Atty. and Rgnl. Counsel for Coldwell Banker & Co., a diversified nat. brokerage and RE services co.; **PROFL AFFIL & HONORS:** CA Bar; ABA; Licensed Broker; Various Civic, RE and Legal Assns.; Instr., Golden Gate Univ., Ctr. for Profl. Devel., Approved Instr., CA Dept. of RE; Who's Who in CA; **EDUC:** BA, 1972, Poli. Sci./Hist., Univ. of S. CA; **GRAD EDUC:** LLM, 1975, Law, Loyola Law School of Los Angeles; **EDUC HONORS:** Grad. Cum Laude, six times on Dean's List, Grad. Cum Laude; Editor of Loyola Law Review; **OTHER ACT & HONORS:** Town Hall of Los Angeles; Univ. of S. CA Alumni; Guest Lecturer at Univ. of S. CA on RE; Guest Lecturer to various Realty Bds.; **HOME ADD:** 5435 Yarmouth Ave. #3, Encino, CA 91316, (213)344-7041; **BUS ADD:** 1888 Century Park E. #1204, Los Angeles, CA 90067, (213)277-7747.

SHAH, Indrawadan K.——B: Aug. 4, 1939, Mandal, India, *Associate Regional Counsel*, Chicago Title Insurance Co., Great Lakes; **PRIM RE ACT:** Consultant, Attorney, Instructor, Insuror, Real Estate Publisher; **SERVICES:** Counseling on RE Title matters; **REP CLIENTS:** Attys., Brokers, Lending Instn.; **PREV EMPLOY:** Asst. VP and Asst. Counsel Mellon Natl. Mtg. Co., Cleveland, OH 44114; **PROFL AFFIL & HONORS:** Amer. Bar Assn. 1974, OH Bar Assn. 1974, Cuyahoga Cty. Bar Assn. 1974, Cleveland Bar Assn. 1974, Chmn., Real Prop. Comm., Cuyahoga Cty. Bar 1980-1981; **EDUC:** BS, 1959, Bus. Admin., Gujarat Univ, India; **GRAD EDUC:** M.Com., 1962, Bus. Admin., Gujarat Univ., India; LLM, 1967, Comml. Law, Gujarat Univ., India; **EDUC HONORS:** Stood Second; **OTHER ACT & HONORS:** Chmn., India Community Ctr. 1981-1982, Contributory Editor "Law & Fact"

Published by Cuyahoga Cty. Bar, Editor of "The Lotus" for 4 years Published by I.C.C.; **HOME ADD:** 577 St. Lawrence Blvd., Eastlake, OH 44094, (216)946-3946; **BUS ADD:** 1275 Ontario St., Cleveland, OH 44113.

SHAHEEN, Shouky A.——**B:** July 17, 1929, Chicago, IL, *Owner*, Shaheen Co.; **PRIM RE ACT:** Developer; **SERVICES:** Build & Lease Offices & Warehouses - Own Account; **EDUC:** AB, 1950, Lib. Arts, Univ. of Chicago; **GRAD EDUC:** MBA, 1952, Bus. Admin., Univ. of Chicago; **HOME ADD:** 3792 Dumbarton Rd. NW, Atlanta, GA 30327, (404)262-3232; **BUS ADD:** Suite 710 - 300 Northcreek Office Park, 3715 Northside Pkwy NW, Atlanta, GA 30327.

SHAIR, Mark A.——**B:** Sept. 12, 1943, Boston, MA, *VP*, Kelly & Picerne Inc.; **PRIM RE ACT:** Developer, Builder, Owner/Investor, Property Manager; **OTHER RE ACT:** Acquisition and Devel. Mgr.; **PREV EMPLOY:** Federated Dept. Stores, Divisional RE Mgr.; **PROFL AFFIL & HONORS:** Intl. Council of Shopping Centers; RI Bd. of Realtors, CSM Candidate; **EDUC:** BSBA, 1967, Mktg./Adv., Northeastern Univ.; **GRAD EDUC:** MBA, 1968, Mktg., Babson Coll.; **EDUC HONORS:** Magna Cum Laude, Cum Laude; **OTHER ACT & HONORS:** B'Nai B'Rith; Realty Lodge, Boston; RE Broker - MA & RI; **HOME ADD:** 2 Fox Hollow Ln., Sharon, MA 02007, (617)784-2318; **BUS ADD:** 1265 Reservoir Ave., Cranston, RI 02920, (401)944-1500.

SHALIT, Michael——**B:** June 23, 1948, Newark, NJ, *Pres. & Owner*, Eric Bram & Co., RE; **PRIM RE ACT:** Broker, Syndicator, Consultant, Developer, Property Manager, Owner/Investor; **PREV EMPLOY:** Construction Supr.-1967; **PROFL AFFIL & HONORS:** SIR, areba, NAIDP, Realtors; **EDUC:** Psych., 1970, KS State Tchrs. Coll.; **OTHER ACT & HONORS:** C of C, Lions Club; **HOME ADD:** 30 Rebel Run Dr., E Brunswick, NJ 08816; **BUS ADD:** 77 Milltown Rd., E Brunswick, NJ 08816, (201)238-3500.

SHANAHAN, John E.——**B:** Sept. 4, 1926, Chicago, IL, *Pres.*, John E. Shanahan & Assocs. Ltd.; **PRIM RE ACT:** Consultant, Appraiser; **SERVICES:** RE Appraisers; **REP CLIENTS:** Touche Ross & Co., Intl. Harvester, Fort Motor Co., Bell & Howell, Coca-Cola, JC Penney, Sears, Roebuck & Co., IRS; **PREV EMPLOY:** 1956-62 VP HO Walther Co., A RE Appraisal firm; **PROFL AFFIL & HONORS:** AIREA, RESSI, Soc. of RE Appraisers, Soc. of RE Counselors, Lamda Alpha, Land Econ. Frat; **EDUC:** BS, 1960, Math, Loyola Univ.; **MIL SERV:** US Army, Sgt.; **HOME ADD:** 10137 S Karlov, Oak Lawn, IL 60453, (312)636-4793; **BUS ADD:** 4550 W 103rd St., Oak Lawn, IL 60433, (312)857-8020.

SHANAHAN, Thomas——*R.E. Mgr.*, Computervision Corp.; **PRIM RE ACT:** Property Manager; **BUS ADD:** 201 Burlington Rd., Bedford, MA 01730, (617)275-1800.*

SHANAMAN, William P.——**B:** Jan. 24, 1947, W. Chester, PA, *VP*, Binswanger Co., Binswanger Mgmt. Corp.; **PRIM RE ACT:** Broker, Consultant, Property Manager; **OTHER RE ACT:** Leasing consultant/agent; **PREV EMPLOY:** Stock Broker, Kidder Peabody, 1972-1974; Mgr., RE, Binswanger/Herman RE, 1974-1979; Left for Consulting Contract at Conrail, 1979-1981 then returned to Binswanger 1981; **PROFL AFFIL & HONORS:** Philadelphia Bd. of Realtors; BOMA; NACORE; **EDUC:** BS, 1972, Econ./Fin., Widener Univ.; **MIL SERV:** US Army; Inf., Capt., Purple Heart, Bronze Star, Silver Star; **HOME ADD:** 220 Quite Hollow Ln., Media, PA 19063, (215)565-4004; **BUS ADD:** 1845 Walnut St., Philadelphia, PA 19103, (215)448-6000.

SHANEDLING, Phil——**B:** June 17, 1913, Virginia, MN, *Owner*, Phil Shanedling Investments; **PRIM RE ACT:** Developer; **SERVICES:** Devel. of comml. prop.; **REP CLIENTS:** Pitney Bowes, AB Dick, IBM, Arden Mayfair, Lucky Stores (have developed buildings for above); **EDUC:** BA, 1936, Bus., Univ. of PA (Wharton Sch); **EDUC HONORS:** Beta Gamma Sigma; **OTHER ACT & HONORS:** Cedars, Sinai Bd. of Gov.; Pres. of Pomona Mall; Dir., Los Angeles Psychiatric Serv.; **BUS ADD:** 9350 Wilshire Blvd., Beverly Hills, CA 90212, (213)272-4138.

SHANHOLTZER, Stephen H.——**B:** Apr. 23, 1946, Springfield, MO, *Supr. of Right of Way*, City of Springfield, MO, Public Works Dept.; **PRIM RE ACT:** Appraiser; **SERVICES:** Right of Way appraisal, acquisition and disposition; **PROFL AFFIL & HONORS:** SR/WA (Sr. Member, Intl. Right of Way Assn.), Member, Intl. Profl. Devel. Comm. of the Intl. Right of Way Assn.; Past Pres. S. W. MO Chapter 165 of Soc. of RE Appraisers, SRA; **EDUC:** BS, 1969, Indus. Tech, S.W. MO State Univ.; BS, 1978, Bus. Admin., Drury; **GRAD EDUC:** MBA, 1981, Mgmt., SW MO State Univ.; **MIL SERV:** USA, E-4; **OTHER ACT & HONORS:** Instr. of RE Appraisal courses at SW MO State Univ.; **HOME ADD:** 2379 E. Berkeley, Springfield, MO 65804, (417)887-2859; **BUS ADD:** 830 Boonville Ave., Springfield, MO 65801, (417)864-1935.

SHANKS, Alexander Graham——**B:** Dec. 8, 1934, Birmingham, AL, *Pres.*, Graham Shanks Inc.; **PRIM RE ACT:** Broker, Owner/Investor; **SERVICES:** Resid. and comml. RE investment & brokerage; **PROFL AFFIL & HONORS:** Washington Bd. of Realtors, NAR, GRI; **EDUC:** AB, 1956, US Hist., Univ. of NC; **GRAD EDUC:** MA, 1959, PhD, 1965, US Hist., Univ. of WI, Univ. of NC; **EDUC HONORS:** Grad. with Honors, Phi Beta Kappa; **MIL SERV:** USN, Lt. (jg); **HOME ADD:** 910 17th St. NW, #901, Washington, DC 20006, (202)333-5259; **BUS ADD:** 901 Barr Bldg., 910 17th St. NW, Washington, DC 20006.

SHANKS, Hershel——**B:** Mar. 8, 1930, Sharon, PA, *Sr. Partner*, Glassie, Pewett, Dudley, Beebe & Shanks; **PRIM RE ACT:** Attorney; **EDUC:** BA, 1952, Eng. Lit., Haverford Coll.; **GRAD EDUC:** MA, 1953, Sociology, Columbua Univ.; LLB, 1956, Harvard Law Sch.; **EDUC HONORS:** Cum Laude; **OTHER ACT & HONORS:** *The Art and Craft of Judging*, Macmillan, 1968; 'Special Usury Problems Applicable to National Banks' Banking Law Journal (Apr. 1970), reprinted in Ian R. MacNeil, *Cases and Materials on Contracts*, Foundation Press, Inc. (1971); 'State Action and the Girard Estate Case', 105 Univ. of PA L. Rev. 213; 'The Tax Lien Tamed', 8 UCLA L. Rev. 339; 'Practical Problems in the Application of Archaic Usury Statutes', 53 Univ. of VA L. Rev. 327; 'The District of Columbia 8 Percent Usury Law', *The Realtor*; 'Out of State Mort. Money', *The Realtor*; **HOME ADD:** 5208 38th St. NW, Washington, DC 20015, (202)966-9434; **BUS ADD:** 1737 H St. NW, Washington DC 20006, (202)466-4310.

SHANNON, Gerald T.——*Mgr. Corp RE*, American Home Products; **PRIM RE ACT:** Property Manager; **BUS ADD:** 685 Third Ave., New York, NY 10017, (212)968-1000.*

SHANOSKI, Daniel P.——**B:** Jan. 25, 1946, Detroit, MI, *Atty.*, Schouman & Tindall; **PRIM RE ACT:** Broker, Attorney; **SERVICES:** All phases of real prop. acquisition & devel., including synd.; **REP CLIENTS:** Devels., mfg. concerns, investor grps; **PREV EMPLOY:** Atty, Kemp, Klein, Endelman & Beer, P.C., primarily responsibility for all real prop. transactions, including leasing; **PROFL AFFIL & HONORS:** ABA; MI State Bar, Real Prop. Sects., Dir., Fed. Securities Bar Assn.; **EDUC:** BA, 1968, Econ., Wayne State Univ.; **GRAD EDUC:** JD, 1977, Real Prop. & Securities Law, Univ. of Detroit Sch. of Law; **EDUC HONORS:** Editor In Brief (Student Newspaper); Editor, the Docket (Alumni Pub.); Managing Editor, 'The Journal of the State Bar of MI', Corp. Fin. & Bus. Law Sect.; **HOME ADD:** 5189 Forestdale Ct., W Bloomfield, MI 48033, (313)661-5740; **BUS ADD:** 21633 E Nine Mile Rd., St. Clair Shores, MI 48080, (313)776-6670.

SHANSBY, Vernon E.——**B:** Feb. 5, 1928, Spokane, WA, *Branch Mgr. & Assoc. Broker*, Kidder, Mathews & Segner, Inc.; **PRIM RE ACT:** Broker, Consultant, Owner/Investor; **SERVICES:** Indus. & comml. RE leasing, sales & Consulting; **REP CLIENTS:** Users, owners & tenants of indus. and comml. facilities and investors and devels. of indus. and comml. sites; **PROFL AFFIL & HONORS:** Nat. Assn. of Indus. & Office Parks; **EDUC:** BA, 1949, Soc. Sci., Univ. of WA; **MIL SERV:** USN; **HOME ADD:** 16548 35th Ave. NE, Seattle, WA 98155, (206)363-1887; **BUS ADD:** 9930 Evergreen Way, Suite C-105, Everett, WA 98204, (206)347-4000.

SHAPIRO, Brian G.——**B:** Aug. 4, 1953, Oshkosh, WI, *Tax Mgr.*, Arthur Young and Co.; **PRIM RE ACT:** Consultant; **SERVICES:** Tax and fin. consulting; **PROFL AFFIL & HONORS:** CA Soc. CPA, AICPA, Nat. Assn. of Accts., visiting lecturer UCLA Grad. Sch. of Mgmt., CPA; **EDUC:** BBA, 1975, Acctg. and Information Systems, Fin. & Investment Banking, Univ. of WI - Madison; **GRAD EDUC:** MBA, 1976, Fin. & Investment Banking, Univ. of WI - Madison; MBT, 1980, Taxation, Univ. of So. CA; **EDUC HONORS:** Beta Alpha Psi, Beta Gamma Sigma, Phi Kappa Phi; **OTHER ACT & HONORS:** Tr., Zeta Beta Tau Frat., Pres., Univ. of WI Alumni Club of Los Angeles; **HOME ADD:** 15457 Moorpark St., Sherman Oaks, CA 91403; **BUS ADD:** 433 N. Camden Dr., Suite 1000, Beverly Hills, CA 90210, (213)278-9600.

SHAPIRO, Burt——**B:** June 18, 1947, New York, NY, *VP*, Wallach Enterprises; **PRIM RE ACT:** Attorney; **SERVICES:** Investment Counseling; **REP CLIENTS:** Profl. Athletes; **PREV EMPLOY:** Partner & Jerry LeVias Mgmt. Enterprises, Atty. for Lo-vaca Gathering Co.; **PROFL AFFIL & HONORS:** Phi Delta Phi Legal Frat., State Bar of TX, Supreme Court of US, 5 Circuit Ct. of Appeals, Fed. Dist. Ct. for So. Dist. of TX; **EDUC:** BA, 1969, Poli. Sci., State Univ. of NY at Stony Brook; **GRAD EDUC:** JD, 1972, Law, Bates Coll. of Law, Univ. of Houston; **EDUC HONORS:** Dean's List; **HOME ADD:** 930 N. Palm, Los Angeles, CA 90069, (213)659-1755;

BUS ADD: 1400 Braeridge Dr., Beverly Hills, CA 90210, (213)278-4574.

SHAPIRO, Donald L.——**B:** Apr. 17, 1935, NY, *Pres.*, Vector RE Corp.; **PRIM RE ACT:** Developer, Builder, Owner/Investor; **PREV EMPLOY:** VP, RE, Levitt & Sons., 1961-71, Exec VP, Peerage; **PROFL AFFIL & HONORS:** ICSC, ULI, RE Bd. of NY, Reg. Plan. Assn., CSM, ICSC; **EDUC:** AB, 1957, Econ., Harvard; **GRAD EDUC:** MBA, 1961, Mktg., Fin., Harvard Grad. Sch. of Bus.; **EDUC HONORS:** Cum Laude; **MIL SERV:** USN, Lt. (JG); **HOME ADD:** 105 Eddy Dr., Huntington Sta., NY 11746, (516)271-3039; **BUS ADD:** 666 5th Ave., NY, NY 10103, (212)581-2400.

SHAPIRO, Donn——**B:** Sept. 28, 1933, Chicago, IL, *Pres.*, Donn Shapiro & Co; **PRIM RE ACT:** Broker, Consultant, Property Manager; **PREV EMPLOY:** 15 yrs Brokerage Loading Chicago Firm; **PROFL AFFIL & HONORS:** BOMA; **EDUC:** 1956, F.S.C.; **MIL SERV:** USA; **HOME ADD:** 228 Lincoln Dr, Glencoe, IL 60022, (312)835-5121; **BUS ADD:** Suite #440-620 N. Michigan Ave., Chicago, IL 60611, (312)787-0344.

SHAPIRO, Irving——**B:** Jan. 31, 1909, New York, NY, *Counsel*, Royal Abstract Corp.; **PRIM RE ACT:** Attorney, Consultant; **OTHER RE ACT:** Counsel to Lawyers in foreclosure; **SERVICES:** Actions & Closings; **REP CLIENTS:** Operators & Banks; **PROFL AFFIL & HONORS:** NYC Lawyers Assn.; **EDUC:** CCNY; **GRAD EDUC:** LLB, 1931, RE, BrookLyn Law School; **OTHER ACT & HONORS:** RE Square Club; Masonic Organizations; Lawyers Square Club; **HOME ADD:** 370 W Bway, Long Beach, NY, (516)432-0085; **BUS ADD:** 280 Broadway, NYC, NY 10007, (212)962-7900.

SHAPIRO, Jacob——*Ed.*, Greater NY Taxpayers Assoc., Real Estate News (Greater NY); **PRIM RE ACT:** Real Estate Publisher; **BUS ADD:** 770 Broadway, New York, NY 10003, (212)677-9600.*

SHAPIRO, Joel G.——**B:** May 10, 1948, Jersey City, NJ, *Mgr.*, Seidman & Seidman; **OTHER RE ACT:** Acct.; **SERVICES:** Acctg. & Tax advice on structuring of synd. of RE equity offerings; **REP CLIENTS:** RE synd. & builder/devel.; **PROFL AFFIL & HONORS:** AICPA, NYSSCPA; **EDUC:** BS, 1971, Acctg., NY Univ.; **GRAD EDUC:** MBA, 1976, Taxation, CUNY; **MIL SERV:** USA Nat. Guard 1970-78; **OTHER ACT & HONORS:** Bd. of Dir., Soc. for the Advancement of Judaism; **HOME ADD:** 15 Columbus Circle, New York, NY 10023, (212)765-7500; **BUS ADD:** 15 Columbus Cir., New York, NY 10023, (212)765-7500.

SHAPIRO, Michael J., Esq.——**B:** Feb. 1, 1951, Brooklyn, NY, *Assoc.*, Kurzman Karelsen & Frank; **PRIM RE ACT:** Attorney; **SERVICES:** Representation of maj. condo. and coops. in metropolitan NY area; preparation of offering plans to convert to coop. or condo. ownership apt. bldgs.; **REP CLIENTS:** Major sponsor-sellers and condo./coop. apt. corps. in metropolitan NY area; **PROFL AFFIL & HONORS:** Amer. and NY State Bar Assns.; Coop. Housing Lawyers Group; Assn. of the Bar of the City of NY; **EDUC:** BA, 1973, English, Columbia Coll.; **GRAD EDUC:** JD, NYU School of Law; **EDUC HONORS:** Henry Evans Traveling Fellowship; Dean's List; **OTHER ACT & HONORS:** Amer. Soc. of Composers, Authors & Publishers, Central Opera Serv., Volunteer Lawyers for the Arts; **HOME ADD:** 1725 York Ave., #23H, New York, NY 10028; **BUS ADD:** 230 Park Ave., Suite 2300, New York, NY 10169, (212)867-9500.

SHAPIRO, Richard J.——**B:** May 14, 1949, Providence, RI, *Atty.*, Demov, Morris, Levin & Shein; **PRIM RE ACT:** Attorney; **OTHER RE ACT:** Taxation; **PREV EMPLOY:** Stroock & Stroock & Lavan, 1978-1980; Shearman & Sterling, 1973-1978; **PROFL AFFIL & HONORS:** NY State Bar Assn.; Amer. Bar Assn.; New York City Bar Assn.; **EDUC:** AB, 1970, Pol. Sci., Brown Univ.; **GRAD EDUC:** JD, 1973, Columbia Univ. Law School; LLM, 1977, Taxation, NYU; **EDUC HONORS:** Cum Laude w/Honors in Pol. Sci.; **HOME ADD:** 120 Country Ridge Dr., Port Chester, NY 10573, (914)937-0576; **BUS ADD:** 40 West 57th St., New York, NY 10019, (212)757-5050.

SHAPIRO, Robert I.——**B:** July 11, 1936, New York, NY, *Sr. VP*, Merrill Lynch Realty, Comm. Service of NY; **PRIM RE ACT:** Broker, Consultant, Engineer, Owner/Investor; **OTHER RE ACT:** Chief Operations Officer; **SERVICES:** Gen. comml. RE brokerage; **PREV EMPLOY:** Williams & Co. RE; City Center RE; **PROFL AFFIL & HONORS:** RE Bd. of NY, Dir. Realty Found, Rgnl. Plan Assn., Adj. Asst. Prof. of RE, NY Univ., Young Man of Yr. Award, RE Bd. of NY, 1973; **EDUC:** BS, 1959, Engrg., West Point; **GRAD EDUC:** MBA, 1961, Fin., Grad. Sch. of Bus., Columbia, Univ.; **HOME ADD:** 1010 Fifth Ave., New York, NY 10028, (212)988-0256; **BUS ADD:** 919 Third Ave., New York, NY 10022, (212)421-7000.

SHAPIRO, Robert Lee——**B:** Nov. 15, 1945, Philadelphia, PA, *Atty.-Partner*, Levy, Shapiro, Kneen & Kingcade, P.A., RE; **PRIM RE ACT:** Attorney; **REP CLIENTS:** Cenvill Communities, Inc.; Hovnanian Enterprises, Inc., and rep. of brokers, architects, devl., builders, prop. mgrs., lenders and owner/investors; **PROFL AFFIL & HONORS:** Palm Beach Cty. and ABA, FL Bar, Corp. and Bus. and Real Prop. Law; **EDUC:** BBA, 1968, Stetson Univ.; **GRAD EDUC:** JD, 1970, Cumberland School of Law, Stanford Univ.; **EDUC HONORS:** Magna Cum Laude; **BUS ADD:** 218 Royal Palm Way, Palm Beach, FL 33480, (305)655-3751.

SHAPIRO, Ronald M.——**B:** May 13, 1951, Brooklyn, NY, *Investment Mgr., RE Operations*, Prudential Insurance Co. of America, Eastern Div.; **OTHER RE ACT:** RE Accountant; **SERVICES:** Tax, acctg. and other fin. serv. to RE industry, RE invest., prop. mgmt., devel. serv. to RE indus.; **PREV EMPLOY:** Arthur Young & Co., 1976-1979; **PROFL AFFIL & HONORS:** Membership in AICPA, NYSSCPA, NJSSCPA; **EDUC:** BA, 1973, Econ., SUNY, Stony Brook; **GRAD EDUC:** MBA, 1976, Fin./Acctg., Columbia Grad. School of Bus.; **HOME ADD:** 10 Yardley St., Edison, NJ 08820; **BUS ADD:** 10 Bank St., Newark, NJ 07102, (201)877-4375.

SHAPIRO, Steven M.——**B:** Jan 27, 1951, Miami Beach, FL, *Exec. VP*, Limited Editions of Palm Bch., Inc.; **PRIM RE ACT:** Broker, Syndicator, Developer, Builder, Owner/Investor; **SERVICES:** Dev. Bldg.; **PREV EMPLOY:** Presently Prin. of Southfields Ltd., Inc., R&S Equip. Corp.; Prin. of PDC Dev. Corp.; Prin. of Elysium Associates; **PROFL AFFIL & HONORS:** NAHB; Contractors Assn. of Palm Beach Cty.; W Palm Bch C of C; Sales and Marketing Council NAHB; HBIC; **EDUC:** BA, 1973, Motion Pictures, Univ. of Miami; **EDUC HONORS:** Honor Roll; **HOME ADD:** 12689 Headwater Cir., West Palm Beach, FL 33411, (305)793-2680; **BUS ADD:** 12661 Headwater Cir., West Palm Beach, FL 33411, (305)793-2003.

SHAPKIN, Barton E.——**B:** Jan. 25, 1945, *Atty.*; **PRIM RE ACT:** Consultant, Property Manager, Syndicator; **SERVICES:** Overseas investments in So. CA; **PREV EMPLOY:** Prof. of Contracts/Evidence; **PROFL AFFIL & HONORS:** State Bar, Fed. Bar (Central Dist.); **EDUC:** 1965, Physiological Psych., Univ. of WI; **OTHER ACT & HONORS:** Arch. Review Bd., Oxnard, CA; Santa Monica Planning, Main St., Various Homeowners Groups; **BUS ADD:** 169 Pier Ave., Top Floor, Santa Monica, CA 90405, (213)396-7400.

SHARP, Jack L.——**B:** Oct. 3, 1941, Springfield, OH, *Chmn.*, Epoch Devel. Corp.; **PRIM RE ACT:** Broker, Syndicator, Developer, Builder, Property Manager, Owner/Investor, Insuror; **SERVICES:** Tax shelter apt. projects; **REP CLIENTS:** Major brokerage houses & pvt. synds.; **PREV EMPLOY:** Coopers & Lybrand, CPAs; **PROFL AFFIL & HONORS:** Amer. Inst. of CPA's, Natl. Assn. of Realtors, CPA; **EDUC:** BS, 1968, Bus. Admin. Acctg., OH State Univ.; **MIL SERV:** USAF, E4; **OTHER ACT & HONORS:** Natl. Assoc. of Accountants; **HOME ADD:** 134 Willow Creek, Lewisville, TX 75067, (214)221-3245; **BUS ADD:** 1720 Westminster Dr., Denton, TX 76201, (817)383-2326.

SHARPE, Jeremy Carl——**B:** Apr. 6, 1950, Spokane, WA, Belin Harris Helmick & Heartney; **PRIM RE ACT:** Attorney; **SERVICES:** Abstract examination; drafting and review of all types of RE documentation on behalf of buyers, sellers, and lenders; **REP CLIENTS:** IA, Des Moines Natl. Bank; John Hancock Mutual Life Insurance Co.; **PROFL AFFIL & HONORS:** ABA (Probate and Real Property Section), IA State Bar Assn., Polk Cty. Bar Assn.; **EDUC:** BA, 1972, Poli. Sci., Columbia Coll., New York, NY; **GRAD EDUC:** JD, 1975, Law, Columbia Law School; **EDUC HONORS:** Magna Cum Laude, Phi Beta Kappa, Harlan Fiske Stone Scholar; Articles Editor - Columbia Journal of Law and Social Problems; **OTHER ACT & HONORS:** Asst. District Commnr. (Walnut Creek District), Boy Scouts of Amer.; **HOME ADD:** 1425 NW 105th, Des Moines, IA 50322, (515)223-5798; **BUS ADD:** 2000 Financial Center, Des Moines, IA 50309, (515)243-7100.

SHARPE, Patrick M.——**B:** Oct. 30, 1934, Greensboro, NC, *Atty.*, Faw Folger Sharp & White; **PRIM RE ACT:** Attorney; **SERVICES:** Legal; **PREV EMPLOY:** Asst. to NC Commnr. of Revenue; Trust Officer, First Citizens Bank & Trust Co.; **PROFL AFFIL & HONORS:** ABA; NC Bar Probate and RE Sect. of both assns., Lecturer, NC Bar Assn. on use of microcoputers; **EDUC:** BA, 1957, Acctg., Wake Forest Univ.; **GRAD EDUC:** LLB, 1959, Law, Wake Forest Univ.; **HOME ADD:** 342 W. Pine St., Mt. Airy, NC 27030, (919)786-7200; **BUS ADD:** PO Box 512, Mt. Airy, NC 27030, (919)786-2149.

SHARPE, Richard——**B:** Aug. 7, 1930, New Haven, CT, Richard Sharpe Assoc./Architects; **PRIM RE ACT:** Architect; **SERVICES:** Architecture/interiors/urban design; **REP CLIENTS:** Gen. Dynamics

Corp.; USN; CT Coll.; New England Telephone Co.; Bunker Rameo; Borg Fabrics Div.; **PROFL AFFIL & HONORS:** AIA; CT Soc. of Architects; Pan Am Fed.of Architects, Coll. of Fellows, AIA; Hon. Membership, Mexico, Guatamala, Panama, Columbia, Venezuela, Brazil, Argentine, Uruguay, Peru; **EDUC:** BArch, 1953, Univ. of PA; **GRAD EDUC:** 1953, Univ. of Liverpool, Grad. School of Civic Design; **OTHER ACT & HONORS:** Pres., Thames River Devel. Corp.; E. CT Develop Corp., Advisory Bd., CT Telecomm. Corp.; **HOME ADD:** 47 Canterbury Turnpike, Norwich, CT 06360, (203)887-7716; **BUS ADD:** 30 Connecticut Ave., Norwich, CT 06360, (203)889-7314.

SHARPE, Savoie——B: June 10, 1937, Sherbrooke, Que., Can., *Financial Analyst, Corp. Services*, Societe d'Investissement Desjardins; **PRIM RE ACT:** Consultant; **OTHER RE ACT:** Pres., Quebec Condo. Assn., condominium consultant; **SERVICES:** The assn. is responsible for dissemination of info. on condos. on a province-wide basis; it provides collective support and representation of co-owners views and interests with respect to legislation and other aspects of co-ownership; **PROFL AFFIL & HONORS:** Order of Engrs., Quebec; **EDUC:** BA, 1959, Mech. Engrg., Universite de Sherbrooke; BSc., 1964, Mech. Engrg., Universite de Sherbrooke; **HOME ADD:** 1030 Legault, Greenfield Park, J4V3C4, Que., Can., (514)656-3886; **BUS ADD:** 1, Complexe Desjardins, Rm. 1222, PO Box 760, Desjardins Branch, Montreal, Que., Can., (514)281-7676.

SHARPE, Wayne G., Jr.——B: Sept. 12, 1942, Newton MA, *Exec. VP*, Cambridge Savings Bank, Loan Div.; **PRIM RE ACT:** Broker, Appraiser, Banker, Lender, Instructor; **SERVICES:** Complete mort. lending services; **PROFL AFFIL & HONORS:** Cambridge Energy Comm.; Treas., Cambridge C of C; VP Cmml. Mort. Servicing, Comm., MBA; **EDUC:** BS, 1973, Fin., Northeastern Univ.; **GRAD EDUC:** MBA, 1981, Fin., Babson Coll.; **EDUC HONORS:** with Distinction; **MIL SERV:** US Army; Capt.; **HOME ADD:** 119 Drake Rd., Burlington, MA 01803; **BUS ADD:** 1374 MA Ave., Cambridge, MA 02138, (617)864-8700.

SHATKEN, Stuart B.——B: Apr. 11, 1944, Newark, NJ, *Sr. VP/Dir. of Dev.*, David H. Feinberg & Co., Inc.; **PRIM RE ACT:** Developer; **SERVICES:** Major mixed-use devel., all aspects of acquisition, planning, design, mktg., leasing and mgmt.; **PREV EMPLOY:** Rose Assoc. (VP RE Devel.); HRH Const. (VP Mgmt.); Loews Corp. (RE Dept.); **PROFL AFFIL & HONORS:** Member - RE Bd. of NY; Amer. Mgmt. Assn., Sec., Young Men's RE Assn.; Intl. Council of Shopping Ctrs.; NY State Bar Assn., Chmn. of the Bd., Young Men's RE Assn.; RE Consultant, Metropolitan Museum of Art; Spec. Consultant, Volunteer Urban Consultant Grp., Inc.; Program Chmn. of Stores Comm., RE Bd. of NY; **EDUC:** Bus. Admin., 1966, Mktg., The Amer. Univ.; **GRAD EDUC:** JD, 1969, RE, Brooklyn Law Sch.; **EDUC HONORS:** Mktg. & Bus.; Class Pres.; **OTHER ACT & HONORS:** Co-Chmn. RE Exec. Div. of United Jewish Appeal/Fed. Campaign United Jewish Appeal Young Leadership Cabinet; **HOME ADD:** 11 Riverside Dr., Apt. 5 BE, New York, NY 10023, (212)595-3554; **BUS ADD:** 250 Park Ave., New York, NY 10077, (212)697-5540.

SHAVER, Jesse M.——B: Nov. 16, 1919, Nashville, TN, *Consultant & Exec. VP*, Allis-Chalmers Corp.; **PRIM RE ACT:** Owner/Investor; **PREV EMPLOY:** Chmn. and Pres., Amer. Air Filter Co., Inc., Louisville, KY (1968-80); **PROFL AFFIL & HONORS:** IEEE, ASHRAE; **EDUC:** BS, 1942, Engrg., Purdue Univ.; **GRAD EDUC:** MBA, 1955, Bus. Admin., Univ. of Chicago; **MIL SERV:** Field Art., Maj., Bronze Star; **HOME ADD:** 3105 Boxhill Ln., Louisville, KY 40222; **BUS ADD:** 455 S. 4th St., Louisville, KY 40202, (502)589-2108.

SHAW, Arthur F.——B: Mar. 3, 1943, MI, *Pres.*, Catalano/Shaw & Associates, Inc.; **PRIM RE ACT:** Broker, Consultant; **SERVICES:** Specialized in office/indust. RE; **REP CLIENTS:** Currently exclusive agent for approximately 1,000,000 sq. ft. of office/indust. space; **PREV EMPLOY:** 4 years Ford Land Development; 2 years Burroughs Corp. (RE); 6 years A.F. Shaw & Associates, Pres.; **EDUC:** BS, 1969, Acctg., Lawrence Inst. of Technol.; **MIL SERV:** US Army, E-6, 1963-1968 Nat'l Guard; **OTHER ACT & HONORS:** Great Oaks Country Club; **HOME ADD:** 5755 Becker Dr., Rochester, MI 48063; **BUS ADD:** 29201 Telegraph Rd., #302, Southfield, MI 48034, (313)354-3820.

SHAW, David M.——B: Dec. 4, 1948, New York, NY, *Atty.*, Arky, Freed, Stearns, Watson & Greer, RE; **PRIM RE ACT:** Attorney; **SERVICES:** All aspects of Comml. RE and secured fin., public & pvt. syndication; **REP CLIENTS:** State and Nat. lenders; for. and domestic investors; Nat. and local devels.; **PREV EMPLOY:** Hunton & Williams, Richmond, VA; **PROFL AFFIL & HONORS:** FL & VA Bar Assns., ABA (Real Prop. Div.), FL Bar Assn. (Real Prop. Div.), Condo. Comm.; **EDUC:** BA, 1970, Govt. and for. affairs, Univ. of VA; **GRAD EDUC:** JD, 1973, RE Transactions, Columbia Univ.; **EDUC HONORS:** Phi Beta Kappa; Summa Cum Laude; **HOME ADD:** 9925 Southwest 57 Ct., Miami, FL 33156, (305)661-0022; **BUS ADD:** Suite 2800, One Biscayne Tower, Miami, FL 33131, (305)374-4800.

SHAW, E. Kenneth——B: Nov. 19, 1944, Portland, OR, *VP, Comml.-Investment Div.*, Century 21 - Heritage Homes & Investments, Inc.; **PRIM RE ACT:** Broker, Owner/Investor, Instructor, Syndicator; **SERVICES:** Investment analysis, project devel., brokerage, small pvt. synd., speaking and seminars; **REP CLIENTS:** Bds. of Realtors, SBA, Univ. of AK - Anchorage, Investors; **PROFL AFFIL & HONORS:** RESSI; AK Creative RE Exchangors, Interex, CCIM; **OTHER ACT & HONORS:** Jaycees, Toastmasters, Recipient of Outstanding Project Award for Elderly Assistance, U.S. Jaycees, 1974-1975; **HOME ADD:** POB 3-604 (ECB), Anchorage, AK 99503, (907)272-4201; **BUS ADD:** 207 E. Northern Lights Blvd., Anchorage, AK 99503, (907)276-1333.

SHAW, Michael W.——B: Sept. 12, 1930, Buffalo, NY, *Owner*, Shaw Development and Equipment Co.; **PRIM RE ACT:** Consultant, Developer, Regulator, Owner/Investor, Property Manager; **OTHER RE ACT:** Sales assoc. (ERA Realtor); **SERVICES:** Land sales and devel., Equipment Sales & Rentals; **REP CLIENTS:** Houston Oil & Mineral, Gulf Resources Corp.; **PREV EMPLOY:** Maintenance Supt. Cibola Cty. Schools; **PROFL AFFIL & HONORS:** Plumbing & Electrical Contractors Lic., State of NM; NM State Univ., Alumni-Class of 1978, Notary Public, State of NM; **EDUC:** AA, 1978, Bus. admin, NM State Univ.; BA, 1952, Indus. Arts, Educ., Univ. State of NY, Buffalo; **OTHER ACT & HONORS:** Village of Milan, Planning & zoning bd.; Lions Club; Milan Citizens Comm., Inc.; Chmn. Member, NM Conference of Building Officials, a chap. of ICBO; **HOME ADD:** Box 2985, Milan, NM 87021, (505)287-2772; **BUS ADD:** Box 1750, Grants, NM 87020, (505)287-2772.

SHAW, Richard A.——B: Oct. 14, 1937, Portland, OR, *VP*, Shenas, Robbins, Shenas & Shaw, A Prof. Corp.; **PRIM RE ACT:** Attorney, Instructor; **SERVICES:** Tax Law Specialist; **PROFL AFFIL & HONORS:** Chair, CA State Bar, Tax Section (1981-1982); Chmn. ABA, Tax Sect. Comm. on Subchapter S Corp., Delegate, CA State Bar Conf. of Delegates (1976-1981); **EDUC:** BS, 1959, Liberal Arts/Econ., Univ. of OR; **GRAD EDUC:** JD, 1962, Univ. of OR; **EDUC HONORS:** Master of Laws (Taxation) 1963, Tax Law NY Univ. Teaching Fellow/Ford Foundation; **MIL SERV:** USA, Capt., USA Commendation Medal, Judge Advocate General's Corps.; **OTHER ACT & HONORS:** VP, San Diego Cty. Council, Boy Scouts of America; VP, Area IV, W. Region, Boy Scouts of America; Member of Natl. Council, Boy Scouts; **HOME ADD:** 4409 Brindisi St., San Diego, CA 92101, (714)224-7259; **BUS ADD:** 110 West A St. Suite 1500, San Diego, CA 92101, (714)236-1777.

SHAW, Robert——*Mgr. Fac.*, Fischer & Porter Co.; **PRIM RE ACT:** Property Manager; **BUS ADD:** One Gibralter Plaza, Horsham, PA 19044, (215)674-6109.*

SHAW, V.E.——B: Nov. 19, 1916, AL, *Sr. V.P.*, First Federal Savings & Loan Association; **PRIM RE ACT:** Appraiser; **SERVICES:** Available on part-time basis for appraisals; **PREV EMPLOY:** 3 years in bookkeeping and estimator for construction contractor; **PROFL AFFIL & HONORS:** Assoc. Member, Soc. of RE Appraisal; CRA, NARA; Assoc. Member Birmingham, AL Bd. of Realtors; Assoc. Member Walker Cty. Home Builders Assn.; **MIL SERV:** US Army, TSgt.; **OTHER ACT & HONORS:** Member Jasper Bd. of Educ. for 15 years; Past Pres. Jasper Kiwanis Club; Past Lt. Gov., AL District Kiwanis Club; 15 years Boy Scout work; Methodist Church; **HOME ADD:** 1204 Quarry Hills Rd., Jasper, AL 35501, (205)384-6549; **BUS ADD:** PO Box 1388, Jasper, AL 35501, (205)221-4111.

SHAW, Victor Hsia——B: June 25, 1939, China, *Pres.*, Pacific Investment Co.; **PRIM RE ACT:** Broker, Owner/Investor, Property Manager, Syndicator; **SERVICES:** Gen. partner of 12 ltd. partnerships; real prop. research, selection, ownership & brokerage; **REP CLIENTS:** Ltd. partnerships, for. investors; **PREV EMPLOY:** Econ. Research Assocs.; **PROFL AFFIL & HONORS:** NAR, CA Realtors Assn. (investment div.), Beverly Hills Bd. of Realtors, Urban Environmental Design Nat. Award by Hud 1980; **EDUC:** BA, 1963, Design, UCLA; **GRAD EDUC:** MA, 1965, Indus. Design, UCLA; MS, 1968, Arch. Psych., Univ. of UT; **EDUC HONORS:** Nat. Student Design Award; **OTHER ACT & HONORS:** Bd. of Mgrs., Westside YMCA; So. CA Chinese Businessmen Assn.; Rotary Club of Westwood Village; Dir., Trans Amer. Nat. Bank, Los Angeles; Author *CA RE,* 1980 (in chinese, published in US); **HOME ADD:** 2656 Claray Dr., Los Angeles, CA 90077; **BUS ADD:** 9300 Wilshire Blvd., Beverly Hills, CA 90212, (213)272-7006.

SHEA, Charles T.——B: Nov. 28, 1921, Milwaukee WI, *VP & Counsel*, New England Mutual Life Ins. Co., Fin. Law Dept.; **OTHER RE ACT:** Legal counsel for instnl investor/lender; **SERVICES:** Legal advice on structuring of devel. RE, joint ventures and on comml. mort. lending; **PROFL AFFIL & HONORS:** ABA, Sect. Real Prop. Probate

& Trust Law, Corp. Banking & Bus. Law; **EDUC:** 1943, Hist., Williams Coll.; **GRAD EDUC:** LLB, 1950, Harvard Law Sch.; **MIL SERV:** USA, 1st Lt., 1942-46, Battlefield Commission; **OTHER ACT & HONORS:** Gore Place Soc. (SPNEA Affiliate), St. Elmo Hall, Delta Phi, Harvard Club of Boston, US Parachute Assn.; **HOME ADD:** Wilson's Mill, Wilsondale St., Dover, MA 02030; **BUS ADD:** 501 Boylston St., Boston, MA 02117, (617)266-3700.

SHEA, Daniel C.——B: Mar. 21, 1922, Cambridge, MA, *Sr. VP, Gen. Counsel and Sec.*, Eureka Fed. S & L Assn. of S F; **PRIM RE ACT:** Attorney, Developer, Lender, Owner/Investor; **SERVICES:** Legal, prepare documents and related activity; **PREV EMPLOY:** Chief Hearing Officer, Federal Home Loan Bank Bd.; **PROFL AFFIL & HONORS:** ABA, FBA, Am. Judicature Soc. CA Bar, D of C Bar; **EDUC:** BS, 1951, Mgmt., Boston Coll.; **GRAD EDUC:** JD, LLM, 1955, 1957, Law, Georgetown Univ.; **MIL SERV:** US Army; **OTHER ACT & HONORS:** Pres. FBA San Francisco Chap. 1979-80; **HOME ADD:** 70 Turnsworth Ave., Redwood City, CA 94062, (415)366-6619; **BUS ADD:** 1250 San Carlos Ave., San Carlos, CA 94070, (405)595-3200.

SHEA, David B.——B: Oct. 18, 1946, Vallejo, CA, Goodloe-Wagner Engerprises, Inc.; **PRIM RE ACT:** Consultant, Appraiser, Owner/Investor, Syndicator; **SERVICES:** Investment counseling, valuation, sales, leasing, prop. mgmt., devel.; **PREV EMPLOY:** Ernst & Whinney, CPA's; **PROFL AFFIL & HONORS:** Nat. and local Assn. of Realtors, RNMI, CPA, RE Broker; **EDUC:** BS, 1972, Acctg., Bus. Mgmt., Univ. of VA; **MIL SERV:** USA, Sgt., Bronze Star; **HOME ADD:** 2221 Hanover Ave., Richmond, VA, (804)353-4267; **BUS ADD:** 500 Libbie Ave., Richmond, VA 23226, (804)282-2010.

SHEA, Kevin R.——B: Sept. 7, 1946, Quincy, MA, *Pres.*, FMK Design-Build, Inc.; **PRIM RE ACT:** Architect, Developer, Builder; **SERVICES:** Devel./arch. design/const.; **PREV EMPLOY:** Project Mgr., Dusco Inc., Dallas, TX; **PROFL AFFIL & HONORS:** Registered Arch., Licensed RE Broker; **EDUC:** BA, 1968, Arch., Univ. of Notre Dame; **GRAD EDUC:** Master of Arch., 1975, Harvard Univ. Grad. School of Design; MBA with Honors, 1978, Boston Univ. Grad. School of Mgmt.; **MIL SERV:** US Army; 1 Lt.; Corps of Engrs.; **HOME ADD:** 357 Harvard St., Cambridge, MA 02138, (617)868-4034; **BUS ADD:** 357 Harvard St., Cambridge, MA 02138, (617)868-4034.

SHEA, Leo G.——B: Jan. 17, 1929, Chicago, IL, *Pres.*, Louis G. Redstone Associates, Inc.; **PRIM RE ACT:** Consultant, Engineer, Architect, Developer, Owner/Investor; **OTHER RE ACT:** Rehab. & hist. preservation consultation; **SERVICES:** Feasibility Studies, land planning, A/E & interior design servs.; **REP CLIENTS:** Detroit Mort. & Realty Co., The Taubman Co., E.N. Maisel & Assoc., First Fed. Savings of Detroit, Winkelman Stores, Inc., The Center Cos., Moceri Mgmt. Co.; **PROFL AFFIL & HONORS:** AIA; ULI; ACA; CSI; ESD, FAIA; **EDUC:** BArch, 1951, Rensselaer Polytechnic Inst.; **GRAD EDUC:** MBA, 1959, Fin., Univ. of Chicago; **MIL SERV:** USMC, Capt.; **BUS ADD:** 28425 W. Eight Mile Rd., Livonia, MI 48152, (313)476-6620.

SHEA, Vernon T.——B: July 4, 1928, Asbury Park, NJ, *Pres.*, Southeastern R.E. Appraisal Corp.; **PRIM RE ACT:** Consultant, Appraiser, Owner/Investor; **SERVICES:** Appraisal service throughout FL; **PREV EMPLOY:** Appraisal field since 1952; **PROFL AFFIL & HONORS:** AIREA, SREA, MAI, SRPA; **EDUC:** BSBA, 1952, R.E., Univ. of FL; **GRAD EDUC:** S&L School for Exec. Devel. IN; **OTHER ACT & HONORS:** St. Petersburg Yacht Club, C of C, Pinellas Cty. Comm. of 100; **HOME ADD:** 6527-31st Ave. N., St. Petersburg, FL 33710, (813)347-5331; **BUS ADD:** 41 Beach Dr. S.E., St. Petersburg, FL 33701, (813)893-1471.

SHEA, William——*Pres.*, Government Employee Real Estate of America; **PRIM RE ACT:** Syndicator; **BUS ADD:** 6000 Stevenson Ave., Alexandria, VA 22304.*

SHEALY, Phil——*City Mgr. for Community Devel.*, Mankato Economic Development; **PRIM RE ACT:** Developer; **BUS ADD:** PO Box 3368, Mankato, MN 56001, (507)625-3161.*

SHEARER, Angus T., Jr.——B: Apr. 1, 1936, Tulsa, OK, *Pres. & CEO*, Wallace Assoc. Inc.; **PRIM RE ACT:** Consultant, Owner/Investor, Instructor, Property Manager; **SERVICES:** Investment, research & consulting, prop. mgmt.; **PREV EMPLOY:** Litton Indus., Wallace Assoc., Inc., Univ. of UT, Pioneer Bank; **PROFL AFFIL & HONORS:** Who's Who in Fin. & Indus., Who's Who in the West, Adjunct Prof. Coll. of Bus., Dept. of Fin., Univ. of UT (RE related), Dir. Pioneer Bank & Pioneer State Bank, Dir. Comm. Fin. Servs. & Western Home Fin. Servs., Dir. Fed. Resources Corp., Dir. First Fed. S&L of Rochester; **EDUC:** BS, 1959, Engrg., Univ. of Tulsa; **GRAD EDUC:** MBA, 1972, Univ. of UT; Grad Studies, 1963-67, Math., Univ. of UT; **EDUC HONORS:** Xi Omicron, Acad. Scholarship Dow Chem. Co., Who's Who in Amer. Colls. & Univs.; **HOME ADD:** 3700 Gilroy Rd., Salt Lake City, UT 84109, (801)277-6644; **BUS ADD:** 1518 Walker Bldg., Salt Lake City, UT 84111, (801)355-1791.

SHEARER, Marilyn——B: Aug. 26, 1936, Gary, IN, *Pres., WA Mgmt., Treas., Wallace Assoc.*; **PRIM RE ACT:** Consultant, Property Manager, Syndicator; **SERVICES:** RE investment, econ. research & consulting, prop. mgmt., site analysis & selection; RE investment consultation; **REP CLIENTS:** Prudential Fed. Savings, First Security Bank, First Interstate Bank, Pioneer Bank & Trust, Salt Lake City Redev. Agency, Chase Manhatten Bank, UT Valley Land Co., Wasatch Towers, Moyle & Draper, Ray Quinney & Nebeker, Salt Lake City C of C, various other investors and prop. owners; **EDUC:** BA, 1958, Univ. of Tulsa; **GRAD EDUC:** Additional studies, Acctg., Computer Systems, Univ. of UT; **EDUC HONORS:** Mortar Bd., Phi Gamma Kappa; **HOME ADD:** 3700 Gilroy Rd., Salt Lake City, UT 84109, (801)277-6644; **BUS ADD:** 1518 Walker Bldg., Salt Lake City, UT 84111, (801)355-1791.

SHEARER, Robert A.——B: Feb. 15, 1947, Seattle, WA, *Gen. Mgr.*, Central Park; **PRIM RE ACT:** Broker, Developer, Property Manager; **PROFL AFFIL & HONORS:** IREM, CPM; **EDUC:** 1969, Eng./Educ., Hillsdale Coll.; **GRAD EDUC:** 1970, Eng. Lit., Western IL Univ.; **EDUC HONORS:** Pres., ODK (Leadership Hon.); Pres., LIT (Lit. Hon.); Who's Who in Amer. Univs. & Colls.; **HOME ADD:** 408 Park Dr., San Antonio, TX 78212; **BUS ADD:** 243 Central Park, San Antonio, TX 78216, (512)341-3351.

SHEARS, John J.——*Ins. Mgr.*, Handy & Harman; **PRIM RE ACT:** Insuror; **BUS ADD:** 850 Third Ave., New York, NY 10022, (212)752-3400.*

SHEDD, Peter J.——B: Feb. 15, 1953, Ponca City, OK, *Asst. Prof. of Legal Studies*, Univ. of GA, Coll. of Bus., Dept. of RE & Legal Studies; **PRIM RE ACT:** Attorney, Instructor; **OTHER RE ACT:** Researcher and Author; **SERVICES:** Teaching, consulting, legal transactions; **PROFL AFFIL & HONORS:** ABA, Amer. Bus. Law Assn., State Bar of GA, 1980 Amer. Bus. Law Assn's. Faculty Award of Excellence; **EDUC:** BBA, 1974, Mktg., Univ. of GA; **GRAD EDUC:** JD, 1974, Univ. of Georgia; **EDUC HONORS:** Magna Cum Laude, Order of the Barristers; **HOME ADD:** 187 Milledge Terrace, Athens, GA 30606, (404)543-0360; **BUS ADD:** Brooks Hall, Athens, GA 30602, (404)542-2126.

SHEEHAN, Daniel F., Sr.——B: Nov. 16, 1903, St. Louis, MO, *Chmn. Exec. Comm.*, Dolan Company Realtors; **PRIM RE ACT:** Broker, Consultant, Attorney; **SERVICES:** Brokerage and consultant; **PROFL AFFIL & HONORS:** Past Pres. NAR; PP, RNMI; IFA; P. Pres., RE Bd. of Met. St. Louis; PP Mort. Bankers Assn. of St. Louis, CRB; CCIM; CRS; JD; IFAS; **GRAD EDUC:** JD, 1925, St. Louis Univ. Law School; **OTHER ACT & HONORS:** Knight of Malta; Knight of Equestrian Order of Holy Sepulchre; Member Archdiocesan Devel. Council, Archdiocese of St. Louis; Member Bd. of Dirs. Mary Queen & Mother Assn. of St. Louis; Member Bd. Dirs. Our Lady of Life Apts.; Member Bd. of Dirs. Commerce-West County Bank; Glen Echo C C; Clayton Club, MO Athletic Club; **HOME ADD:** 14 Brentmoor Park, Clayton, MO 63105, (314)725-0005; **BUS ADD:** 6401 Manchester, St. Louis, MO 63139, (314)645-2610.

SHEEHAN, Thomas J.——B: NY, *Pres.*, Metropolitan Realty Management, Inc.; **PRIM RE ACT:** Consultant, Appraiser, Property Manager; **SERVICES:** Leasing & Mgmt. of office bldgs.; **REP CLIENTS:** Metropolitan Life Insurance Co.; **PROFL AFFIL & HONORS:** RE Bd. of NY; IREM; Citizens Tax Council; ULI; Fed. Policy Council; BOMA; NY Building Congress; **EDUC:** BS, 1965, Bus. Admin., C.W. Post Coll., Brookville, NY; **GRAD EDUC:** MBA, 1967, Mgmt., Arthur T. Roth Grad. School of Bus.; **OTHER ACT & HONORS:** Chmn., RE Comm.; Greater NY Council, Boy Scouts of Amer.; Instr. NYU; **HOME ADD:** 1608 Rockwin Rd., Rockville Ctr., NY 11570; **BUS ADD:** 200 Park Ave., NY, NY 10166, (212)986-2100.

SHEEHY, Robert F.——*Dir. RE*, International Telephone & Telegraph Corp.; **PRIM RE ACT:** Property Manager; **BUS ADD:** 320 Park Ave., New York, NY 10022, (212)752-6000.*

SHEETS, Carleton Hunter——B: Aug. 25, 1939, Olney, IL, *Pres.*, FL Equity Resources Corp.; **PRIM RE ACT:** Broker, Consultant, Owner/Investor, Instructor, Syndicator; **OTHER RE ACT:** Nat. recognized lecturer in the area of creative re finance - 150 lectures annually; **SERVICES:** Consultant to synd. and educ.; **REP CLIENTS:** Bert Rodgers Schools of RE - Orlando, FL; **PROFL AFFIL & HONORS:** RE Securities and Synd. Instit., SRS designation from RESSI; **EDUC:** BA, 1961, Psych./Bus./Speech, OH Wesleyan Univ.;

OTHER ACT & HONORS: Former Rgnl. VP, RESSI; Bd. of Govs., RESSI; Fl. Chap. Pres., RESSI; Presently Bd. of Gov's., FL Chap., RESSI; Who's Who in Creative RE Finance; **HOME ADD:** 4477 Maurice Dr., Delray Beach, FL 33445, (305)498-8565; **BUS ADD:** 312 Southeast First St., Delray Beach, FL 33444, (305)276-0054.

SHEGA, Frank A.——B: Aug. 14, 1944, Cleveland, OH, *Mgr. - RE*, Cook United, Inc.; **PRIM RE ACT:** Property Manager; **EDUC:** BBA, 1968, Personnel, Kent State Univ.; **MIL SERV:** US Army, E-5; **HOME ADD:** 10233 Pirates Trail, Aurora, OH 44202; **BUS ADD:** 16502 Rockside Rd., Maple Heights, OH 44137, (216)475-1000.

SHELBRICK, Jack——B: Sept. 22, 1941, Red Bank, NJ, *VP, Comml. Props.*, ERA-Unica Realty, Inc.; **PRIM RE ACT:** Broker, Consultant, Owner/Investor; **OTHER RE ACT:** Subdivider; **SERVICES:** Subdiv. devel. & mktg.; synds. of comml./inv props.; site locating; **REP CLIENTS:** Large land owners, investors, devels., comml. prop. users; **PROFL AFFIL & HONORS:** Member: local, state and nat. realtor assns. and various comms; chamber legislative affairs comm.; Albuquerque quality growth comm., GRI, 1976; **EDUC:** BA, 1972, Bus. and Acctg., Univ. of Albuquerque; **MIL SERV:** USAF; 1st Lt.; **OTHER ACT & HONORS:** Planning Bd., NM Health Care Coalition; **HOME ADD:** PO Box 11939, Albuquerque, NM 87192, (505)345-1226; **BUS ADD:** 9312 Montgom., NE, Albuquerque, NM 87111, (505)293-8400.

SHELDON, Terry E.——B: June 22, 1945, Sacramento, CA, *Gen. Counsel & Sr. VP*, Consolidated Capital Cos.; **PRIM RE ACT:** Attorney; **OTHER RE ACT:** Trustee & gen. counsel & sec. for 3 active RE investment trusts: Consolidated Capital Realty Investors, Consolidated Capital Income Trust, Consolidated Capital Special Trust In charge of all Corp. Admin.; **PREV EMPLOY:** Atty. Bronson, Bronson & McKinnon law firm, San Francisco (1970-74); **PROFL AFFIL & HONORS:** ABA, Member CBA, Amer. & San Francisco Ctys. Bar Assns.; **EDUC:** BS, 1967, Bus. Admin., Abilene Christian Univ., Abilene TX; **GRAD EDUC:** JD, 1970, So. Methodist Univ., Dallas, TX; **EDUC HONORS:** Magna Cum Laude, Dean's List, Law Review, Southwestern Law Journal; **HOME ADD:** 451 Montcrest Pl., Danville, CA 94526, (415)837-9445; **BUS ADD:** 1900 Powell, Emeryville, CA 94608, (415)652-7171.

SHELL, Robert D.——B: Sept. 4, 1948, Erie, PA, *Pres.*, Shell-Westerman Realtors, RE/MAX Professional Realtors; **PRIM RE ACT:** Broker, Consultant, Developer, Builder, Owner/Investor, Instructor, Property Manager; **OTHER RE ACT:** Condo. Conversions; **SERVICES:** RE mktg. & sales; **PROFL AFFIL & HONORS:** Local & Nat. Bd. of Realtors, Local and Nat. Home Bldrs. Assn.; **EDUC:** BS, 1971, Mktg., Univ. of Louisville; **MIL SERV:** KY Air Nat. Guard, Tsgt.; **OTHER ACT & HONORS:** Scout Master, Boy Scouts of Amer.; 1978 Pres. Louisville Condo. Council; **HOME ADD:** 10303 Statia Lynn Ct., Louisville, KY 40223, (502)245-2933; **BUS ADD:** 207 Willow Stone Way, Louisville, KY 40223, (502)245-1591.

SHELLEY, Daniel W.——B: Jan. 8, 1943, *Pres.*, FL Equities Corp.; **PRIM RE ACT:** Developer, Owner/Investor, Property Manager; **PREV EMPLOY:** Mgmt. Consultant Mobil Oil Corp.; **PROFL AFFIL & HONORS:** ICSC; **EDUC:** BS, 1963, Physics, MIT; **GRAD EDUC:** MS, 1966, Mgmt., Sloan Sch., MIT; **OTHER ACT & HONORS:** Chmn. Dist. Export Council, US Dept. Commerce, 1979-81; **HOME ADD:** Dorado Beach, Dorado, PR 00646, (809)796-3758; **BUS ADD:** 1013 Banco Popular Ctr., Hato Rey, PR 00918, (809)763-7980.

SHELLOOE, Daniel P.——B: Sept. 2, 1939, Salinas, CA, *Owner*, Daniel P. Shellooe, Real Estate; **PRIM RE ACT:** Broker, Consultant, Owner/Investor, Syndicator; **OTHER RE ACT:** Managing partner of Rehab projects; **SERVICES:** Real prop. brokerage, comml. lands & bldgs.; **REP CLIENTS:** Many San Francisco Bay area attys. and physicians; indiv. investors in comml. prop.; **PREV EMPLOY:** First S & L Assn., Great W. Fin. Corp.; **EDUC:** BA, 1961, Econ., Univ. of Santa Clara; **EDUC HONORS:** Who's Who Among Univ. Students; **MIL SERV:** US Army; **HOME ADD:** 1449 Casa Vallecita, Alamo, CA 94507, (415)934-3240; **BUS ADD:** 1449 Casa Vallecita, Alamo, CA 94507.

SHELTON, Charles W.——B: Dec. 29, 1950, Hobbs, NM, *Pres.*, KS Mortgage Co.; **PRIM RE ACT:** Consultant, Banker, Lender; **SERVICES:** Comml. Mort. Loan Placements, Construction Lending, Secondary Marketing; **REP CLIENTS:** Builders, Devels., Invest. Investors and Lenders; **PREV EMPLOY:** First National Bank in Dallas, Dallas, TX; **PROFL AFFIL & HONORS:** MBAA; **EDUC:** BS, 1974, RE, East TN State Univ.; **HOME ADD:** 5612 N Mayview, Kansas City, MO 64151, (816)741-4850; **BUS ADD:** PO Box 1564, Kansas City, KS 66117, (913)299-3400.

SHELTON, Harroll——B: June 28, 1916, Greenwood, MS, *Broker Assoc.*, LeClare Props.; **PRIM RE ACT:** Broker, Consultant, Owner/Investor; **SERVICES:** Investment counseling & other RE problems; **PROFL AFFIL & HONORS:** RNMI; RESSI; NV Bd. of Realtors; Research Inst. for Counselists, Inc.; Soc. of Las Vegas Exchangers, GRI; **EDUC:** Bowling Green Coll. of Commerce; **GRAD EDUC:** 1935, Bus. Admin.; **MIL SERV:** US Army; Capt.; **HOME ADD:** 3705 Tennis Ct., Las Vegas, NV 89121, (702)458-6394; **BUS ADD:** 1785 E Sahara Ave., Suite 190, Las Vegas, NV 89104, (702)733-3932.

SHELTON, Howard P.——*Pres.*, Howard P. Shelton, Inc.; **OTHER RE ACT:** Machinery & equipment appraiser; **SERVICES:** Fee appraiser; **REP CLIENTS:** Banks, municipalities, corps., attys.; **PROFL AFFIL & HONORS:** Sr. Member, Amer. Soc. of Appraisers, ASA, CRA; **BUS ADD:** 17291 Irvine Blvd., Tustin, CA 92680, (714)838-9427.

SHELTON, Kenneth L.——B: Jan. 8, 1941, Evansville, IN, Kenneth L. Shelton, SRA and Associates, Real Estate Appraisers; **PRIM RE ACT:** Consultant, Appraiser; **SERVICES:** Appraising, Investment Counseling, Devel. Valuation; **REP CLIENTS:** Banks, Devel., Relocation Agencies; **PREV EMPLOY:** Fifteen years appraisal experience with the U.S. Fish and Wildlife Serv., Corps of Engrs., KY Dept. of Hwys., and as an indep. fee appraiser; **PROFL AFFIL & HONORS:** NARA; Soc. of RE Appraisers, CRA, SRA; **EDUC:** Indus. Technology (BS), 1965, Murray State Univ.; **GRAD EDUC:** Higher Education, 1973, RE Appraising, Admin. and Supervision, Morehead State Univ.; **EDUC HONORS:** Recipient Land Acquisition Achievement Award - US Fish & Wildlife Serv. 1979; **OTHER ACT & HONORS:** Grad. of the Dept. Mgr. Devel. Program of the Dept. of the Interior, 1980; Bd. of Dir., Boeuf Sauvage Investment Club, 1981; **HOME ADD:** 15766 W. Bunker Way, Morrison, CO 80465, (303)697-8358; **BUS ADD:** 1976 S. Urban St., Lakewood, CO 80228, (303)988-0212.

SHENDLEMAN, Jack——B: Aug. 4, 1932, New York, NY, *Pres.*, RIC Corp. (Real Estate & Investment Consultants); **PRIM RE ACT:** Broker, Consultant, Owner/Investor, Instructor, Real Estate Publisher; **OTHER RE ACT:** Leasing; **SERVICES:** Investment counseling, planning, re-organizing and mktg. bus. opportunities; **REP CLIENTS:** Indiv. investors, several natl. restaurant chains; **PROFL AFFIL & HONORS:** NAR, CAR, Denver Bd. of Realtors, Chap. No. 6, CCIM, contributing author "Denver Bus. World"; **EDUC:** BA, 1954, Acctg., Queens Coll. of the City of NY; **MIL SERV:** USA, Sgt.; **OTHER ACT & HONORS:** Chap. Chmn., Metro Denver March of Dimes, Member RE Advisory Bd., Emily Griffith Opportunity School; **HOME ADD:** 11932 E. Maple Ave., Aurora, CO 80012, (303)343-9955; **BUS ADD:** 1777 S. Harrison St., Penthouse 312, Denver, CO 80210, (303)759-5559.

SHENEHON, Howard E.——B: Aug. 28, 1914, Minneapolis, MN, *Pres.*, Howard E. Sbenehon & Assoc., Inc.; **PRIM RE ACT:** Consultant, Appraiser; **SERVICES:** RE Valuation, consulting & appraising; **REP CLIENTS:** Attys., local govts., lenders, buyers, sellers; **PREV EMPLOY:** Partner Shenehon Goodlund Taylor Fruen, Inc., Appraisers, Minneapolis; **PROFL AFFIL & HONORS:** AIREA (MAI), SREA; ARWA; SRPA; Realtor, Omega Tau Rho Realtor Award in 1979 (Serv. recognition); Partner RE Counselors Grp. of Amer., Inc., a national valuation and consultation service, nationwide, with 20 partners; 25 yrs. teaching.; **EDUC:** AA, 1936, Univ of MN; **OTHER ACT & HONORS:** Unif. of MN Ext. Class Teaching for 25 yrs. in RE & fundamentals of appraising, Tr. Hennepin Ave. United Methodist Church, Minneapolis, Urban League Bd., MN Hearing Soc., Past Pres., PTA Pres.; **HOME ADD:** 1944 Penn Ave. S, Minneapolis, MN 55405, (612)374-5891; **BUS TEL:** (612)333-6533.

SHENFELD, Sandra Manno——B: Dec. 20, 1940, Atlantic Cty, NJ, *VP, RE*, Resorts Intl. Hotel Casino; **PRIM RE ACT:** Owner/Investor; **EDUC:** BA, 1962, Rosemont Coll.; **HOME ADD:** 29 N Kingston Ave., Atlantic City, NJ 08404, (609)347-4500; **BUS ADD:** Boardwalk at N. Car. Ave., Atlantic City, NJ 08404, (609)340-6693.

SHENK, John C., Jr.——B: May 7, 1926, Evanston, IL, *Chmn. and CEO*, First Fed. Savings and Loan Assn. of Davenport; **PRIM RE ACT:** Lender; **PREV EMPLOY:** Comml. banking, practicing atty.; **EDUC:** AB, 1950, Hist., Econ., Poli. Sci., Liberal Arts, Wash. Univ.; **GRAD EDUC:** JD, 1955, Univ. of IA; **EDUC HONORS:** Bd. of Editors, IA Law Review; **MIL SERV:** USA, Agent, CIA; **HOME ADD:** 1730 Harmony Ct., Bettendorf, IA 52722, (319)355-0197; **BUS ADD:** 131 W 3rd St., Davenport, IA 52801, (319)326-0121.

SHEPARD, Bruce L.——B: May 16, 1948, New York, NY, *VP of RE*, The Felsway Corp., Shoe-Town; **OTHER RE ACT:** Retail sites; **SERVICES:** RE and const. decisions; **PREV EMPLOY:** E. Coast Rep. to Hit or Miss; **PROFL AFFIL & HONORS:** NACORE, ICSC,

VP OF NACORE, NJ Chapt.; **EDUC:** BS, 1970, Fin. & Mktg., NY Univ.; **EDUC HONORS:** Deans List; **HOME ADD:** 201 East 77th St., New York, NY 10021, (212)734-9714; **BUS ADD:** 994 Riverview Dr., Totowa, NJ 07512, (201)785-1900.

SHEPARD, Edward F.——B: July 10, 1945, Darby, PA, *Dir. of Mktg.*, Lockwood & Lehr, Comml. Div.; **PRIM RE ACT:** Broker, Consultant, Owner/Investor, Syndicator; **SERVICES:** Mkt. analysis, mktg., RE investment counseling, land trusts, syd. of comml. props.; **REP CLIENTS:** Pvt. indivs. (domestic and interl.), instl. investors; **PREV EMPLOY:** VP Operations & Mkg. Merchants Intl. Inc., Wash., DC 1968-74 (Interl. Transportation household goods, electronic aircraft parts, major accounts I.R.B.D., I.M.F., U.S. State Dept.); **PROFL AFFIL & HONORS:** Ft. Laud. Bd. of Realtors, NAR, presently fulfilling reg. for S.I.R. CCIM, RESSI; **EDUC:** BS, 1968-1978, Mktg./Anatomy & Physiology, Univ. of KY/VA Polytechnic Inst.; **GRAD EDUC:** 20 hours of 72 required courses, Reproductive Physiology, VA Polytechnic Inst.; **EDUC HONORS:** Dean's List; **OTHER ACT & HONORS:** VP Young Democrats & Various Comms. (State Level) 2 yrs., Vol. teacher (sub.) & community youth group activities; **HOME ADD:** 1481 S. Ocean Blvd. #421, Pompano Beach, FL 33062, (305)782-1620; **BUS ADD:** 2000 East Oakland Park Blvd., Ft. Lauderdale, FL 33306, (305)566-7802.

SHEPARD, Richard A.——B: Nov. 4, 1948, New York, NY, *Counsel - Land Utilization*, International Paper Co., Wood Products & Resource Bus.; **PRIM RE ACT:** Attorney; **SERVICES:** Legal advice concerning contracts, litigation, leases, review govt. requests; drafting of legal instruments; **PREV EMPLOY:** Mgr., RE Admin., GAF Corp.; **EDUC:** BA, 1970, Poli. Sci., Drew Univ.; **GRAD EDUC:** JD, 1973, NY Law School; **BUS ADD:** 77 West 45th St., New York, NY 10036, (212)536-5590.

SHEPHERD, Everett, Jr.——B: Sept. 9, 1926, Birmingham, AL, *Proprietor, Brookwood Village; V.P. Shepherd Realty Co., Inc.*; **PRIM RE ACT:** Broker, Developer, Builder, Property Manager, Engineer, Owner/Investor, Insuror; **SERVICES:** Valuation dev. of comml prop.; **REP CLIENTS:** Lenders and indiv. or instl. investors in comml. prop.; **PREV EMPLOY:** Five Points West Shopping Center; Constr. Engr., Texaco Inc.; **PROFL AFFIL & HONORS:** B'ham Bd. of Realtors, GRI; **EDUC:** BS Civil Engr., 1950, VA Military Inst.; **EDUC HONORS:** Varsity Football Letter; **MIL SERV:** USAR, 2nd Lt.; **HOME ADD:** 2744 Cherokee Dr., Birmingham, AL 35216, (205)871-0871; **BUS ADD:** 504 C Brookwood Blvd., Birmingham, AL 35209, (205)870-1213.

SHEPHERD, James McMenanin——B: July 14, 1917, Hampton, VA, *Pres.*, Landell Corp.; **OTHER RE ACT:** Bldg. Consultant; **SERVICES:** Advisor to home owners in regard to all aspects of house const.; **EDUC:** BS, 1939, US Military Academy, West Point, NY; **MIL SERV:** USA, Brig. Gen., Fistful; **HOME ADD:** 100 Sheriffs Pl., Williamsburg, VA 23185, (804)229-0661; **BUS ADD:** PO Box 307, Williamsburg, VA 23185, (804)229-0661.

SHEPPARD, Mark——B: Aug. 13, 1948, NJ, *Managing Partner*, Law Offices of Mark Sheppard; **PRIM RE ACT:** Consultant, Attorney, Instructor; **REP CLIENTS:** Golden West Fin.; Kohn, Loeb & Hoffman; Westborough Assoc.; Internal Loss Prevention; **PROFL AFFIL & HONORS:** State & Federal Bar; Tax Bar; Amer. Bar Assn., Recipient of Cohen Award 1979; **EDUC:** BA, 1970, Econ., Engrg., Univ. of CA; **GRAD EDUC:** JD, 1973, Law, NYU School of Law & LLM, Tax; **EDUC HONORS:** Phi Beta Kappa; **BUS ADD:** 2648 Park Wilshire, S-400, San Jose, CA 95124, (408)267-1218.

SHER, David——B: Jan. 21, 1930, New York, NY, *Pres./Visiting Assoc. Prof.*, David Sher Assoc, Inc./Cornell Univ. School of Hotel Admin.; **PRIM RE ACT:** Broker, Consultant, Instructor; **SERVICES:** RE, Mktg., fin., corp. mgmt., investment & bus. analysis; **REP CLIENTS:** Sun Oil, Bankers Trust, Dunkin Donuts, Clorox, Collins Foods; **PREV EMPLOY:** Carrols Devel. Corp., Star Market, Food Fair; **PROFL AFFIL & HONORS:** NACORE, Nat. Restaurant Assoc., AREVEA, REEA; **EDUC:** BS, 1950, Econ., Coll. of the City of NY; **GRAD EDUC:** MS, 1954, Bus./econ., Columbia Univ.; **EDUC HONORS:** Cum Laude, Phi Beta Kappa, Ward Medal in Econ.; **OTHER ACT & HONORS:** Chmn. of the Task Force for Jamesville-DeWitt Bd. of Educ. 1977; **HOME ADD:** 7 Lynacres Blvd., 13066, Fayetteville, NY 13066, (315)446-7212; **BUS ADD:** 7 Lynacres Blvd., Fayetteville, NY 13066, (315)446-2077.

SHERBURNE, Mary L.——B: June 21, 1926, NC, *Assoc. Broker*, The Braedon Co's., Comml. Sales; **PRIM RE ACT:** Broker, Consultant, Appraiser, Syndicator; **OTHER RE ACT:** Fin. Analyst; **SERVICES:** Sales, land acquisition, project analysis; **REP CLIENTS:** Specialize in downtown office, apts., acquisition by foreign sources; **PREV EMPLOY:** CBS Realty; Nat. Center for Housing Mgmt.; **PROFL AFFIL & HONORS:** Washington Bd. of Realtors; Apt. Owners Mgrs. Assn.; AIREA, Broker, DC; Sales Agent, MD & VA; **EDUC:** BS, 1957, Sci./Eng., Univ. of NC; **GRAD EDUC:** MS, 1983, RE, Amer. Univ.; **EDUC HONORS:** Phi Beta Kappa; **HOME ADD:** 3110 Hawthorne St. NW, Washington, DC 20008, (202)338-6407; **BUS ADD:** 1150 17th St. NW, Washington, DC 20036, (202)466-2130.

SHERBUT, James John——B: Jan. 5, 1956, Winnipeg, Manitoba, *Pres.*, Britgary Props. Ltd.; **PRIM RE ACT:** Developer, Owner/Investor, Property Manager; **SERVICES:** Prop. mgmt. consulting; **PROFL AFFIL & HONORS:** IREM; **HOME ADD:** 60 Brookpark Rise SW, Calgary, T2H 0L3, Alberta, Can., (403)281-0126; **BUS ADD:** PO Box 5143, Sta. A, Calgary, T2H 0L3, Alta., Can., (403)253-2400.

SHERF, Stephen W.——B: Jan. 9, 1948, Lincoln, NE, *Mgr.*, Laventhol & Horwath, Mgmt. Advisory Services; **PRIM RE ACT:** Consultant; **SERVICES:** Feasibility studies, fin. projections, fin. analysis; **REP CLIENTS:** Devels., lendors, investors; **PROFL AFFIL & HONORS:** AICPA; Greater Minneapolis Bd. of Realtors; MN Multi-Housing Assn.; **EDUC:** BA, 1970, Econ., Cornell Univ.; **GRAD EDUC:** MBA, 1974, Fin., Cornell Univ.; **MIL SERV:** Nat. Guard, Sgt.; **HOME ADD:** 5150 Gladstone Ave., Minneapolis, MN 55419, (612)824-8187; **BUS ADD:** Ste. 1650, 100 Washington Sq., Minneapolis, MN 55401, (612)332-5500.

SHERIDAN, Donald T.——B: July 26, 1922, Evanston, IL, *Chmn. and Chief Exec. Officer*, L. J. Sheridan & Co.; **PRIM RE ACT:** Broker, Consultant, Developer, Owner/Investor, Property Manager; **PROFL AFFIL & HONORS:** BOMA, CRE, CCIM, RPA, CPM; **EDUC:** Dartmouth Coll.; **MIL SERV:** USAF, 1st Lt.; **BUS ADD:** 111 W Washington St., Chicago, IL 60602, (312)726-7743.

SHERIDAN, James C., Jr.——B: July 13, 1923, New York, NY, *VP*, Harlem Savings Bank, Mort. Origination; **PRIM RE ACT:** Appraiser, Banker, Lender; **PREV EMPLOY:** Realty Consultant NY State Banking Dept.; **PROFL AFFIL & HONORS:** Sr. member Long Island Soc. of RE Appraisers; Peter Minuit Post No. 1247; The RE Post of the Amer. Legion; MBA, Sr. Member NARA; **EDUC:** AB, 1947, Eng., Univ. of Notre Dame; **MIL SERV:** US Army, Sgt., Two Battle Stars; **HOME ADD:** 119 Harrow Ln., Manhasset, NY 11030, (516)627-1255; **BUS ADD:** 205 E. 42nd St., New York, NY 10017, (212)573-8027.

SHERIDAN, Marie M.——B: Apr. 4, 1926, Ladonia, TX, *Pres.*, Wm. Rigg, Inc.; **PRIM RE ACT:** Broker, Owner/Investor, Instructor; **PROFL AFFIL & HONORS:** Intl. Federation RE Brokers NAR, TAR, Ft. Worth Bd. of Realtors, Arlington B of D, NETC Box D, CRB, CRS; **EDUC:** BA, Spanish, Univ. of TX-Austin; **HOME ADD:** 8800 Royal Harbor Ct., Ft. Worth, TX 76179, (817)236-7059; **BUS ADD:** 6148 Camp Bowie Blvd., Ft. Worth, TX 76179, (817)731-0761.

SHERIDAN, Vincent G.——B: Apr. 15, 1921, New York, NY; **PRIM RE ACT:** Broker, Consultant, Appraiser, Property Manager, Owner/Investor, Insuror; **OTHER RE ACT:** Adjuster, PE; **SERVICES:** RE investment & feasibility reports, title engrg, site planner; **REP CLIENTS:** NY State Dept. of Public Works, appraiser for Chase-Manhattan Bank, Design Consultant for Alta Industries; **PROFL AFFIL & HONORS:** APA, SRA, Sr. Member CAS, IFAS, Pres. Hudson Valley IFAA, CREA, SR/WA, ASA, CCE, CPM, AFLM, ACEC, Tau Beta Pi, Sigma Tau, Chi Epsilon, Alpha Psi Omega; **EDUC:** BSCE, BS, 1951, Bus., Univ. of CO; **GRAD EDUC:** MBA, 1979, Farleigh Dickinson; **MIL SERV:** USNR, 1942-1951; **OTHER ACT & HONORS:** Chmn. Cty. Planning Comm.; V. Chmn. & Exec. Comm.; Greene Cty. Conserv. Party; Faculty Ulster City Community Coll.; Faculty, Business Planning Inst., Delhi Ag. & Tech. Com. Coll.; Commissioner in Condemnation, Urban Renewal; Member, The Explorer's Club; **HOME ADD:** RD 2, Box 500, Catskill, NY 12414, (518)943-3308; **BUS ADD:** 305 Main St., Catskill, NY 12414, (518)943-3061.

SHERIFF, Fred A.——B: Apr. 14, 1948, Santa Monica, CA, *VP/Resident Mgr.*, Coldwell Banker Comml. RE Servs.; **PRIM RE ACT:** Broker; **SERVICES:** Comml. brokerage of indus., office, retail & investment RE; **REP CLIENTS:** Devels., investors, bldg. & land owners & users; **EDUC:** BS, 1970, Mktg., Fresno State Univ.; **GRAD EDUC:** MBA, 1971, Mgmt., Univ. of S. CA; **HOME ADD:** 1700 Coventry Ln., Oklahoma City, OK 73120, (405)843-8555; **BUS ADD:** 110 N. Robinson, Suite 500, Oklahoma City, OK 73102, (405)272-5300.

SHERIFF, Garth I.——B: Feb. 7, 1946, Los Angeles, CA, *Sr. Part.*, Allen & Sheriff; **PRIM RE ACT:** Architect, Syndicator, Consultant, Developer, Engineer; **SERVICES:** Arch., space and feasibility planning, dev. and synd. of comml. and multi-unit resid. props.; **PROFL AFFIL & HONORS:** Corp. member AIA, NCARB; **EDUC:**

BArch, 1969, Arch., Univ. of S. CA; **EDUC HONORS:** Pres. Tau Sigma Delta, Natl. Arch. Honorary, Degree Cum laude; **OTHER ACT & HONORS:** Co-Chmn. Citizens Initiative to Preserve Santa Monica Piers; **HOME ADD:** 823 19th St. C, Santa Monica, CA 90403, (213)929-0949; **BUS ADD:** 3020 S. Robertson Blvd. 4, Los Angeles, CA 90034, (213)837-7227.

SHERMAN, Dennis H.——B: July 20, 1939, Cleveland, OH, *Profl. Engr. and Atty.*, Private Practice; **PRIM RE ACT:** Engineer, Attorney; **SERVICES:** Legal services and expert witness in RE matters especially related to matters involving architects, engineers, and construction contractors; **REP CLIENTS:** Arch., engrs., contractors, devel., investors, realtors, RE mgmt. co., landlords, tenants; **PREV EMPLOY:** Dalton Dalton Newport Inc., Architects, Engrs., and Planners, Principal, Corporate Counsel, and Asst. Secretary; **PROFL AFFIL & HONORS:** ABA, OH Bar Assn., Cuyahoga County Bar Assn., Amer. Soc. of Civil Engrs., Amer. Arbitration Assn., Registered Profl. Engr. in OH and Nationally, Atty. in Ohio; **EDUC:** BCE, 1962, OH State Univ.; **GRAD EDUC:** JD, 1966, Cleveland State Univ.; **EDUC HONORS:** Best Student in Real Prop. Law; **MIL SERV:** USAR, Pfc; **HOME ADD:** 26711 Fairmount Blvd., Cleveland, OH 44122, (216)831-1270; **BUS ADD:** 26711 Fairmount Blvd., Cleveland, OH 44122, (216)283-4000.

SHERMAN, Jefferson L.——B: June 9, 1951, Battle Creek, MI, *Assoc. Broker*, Sherman Assoc., Realtors; **PRIM RE ACT:** Broker, Appraiser; **PROFL AFFIL & HONORS:** NAR, MI Assn. Realtors, RNMI, Battle Creek Bd. of Realtors Pres. 1981 and 1982, CRS, Cert. RE Broker Mgr.; **EDUC:** BA, 1973, Soc. Sci., Bowling Green State Univ.; **HOME ADD:** 603 Manor Dr., Albion, MI 49224, (517)629-5500; **BUS ADD:** 309 W. Michigan Ave., Marshall, MI 49068, (616)781-4288.

SHERMAN, John S., Jr.——B: Aug. 13, 1928, Charleston, WV, *Pres.*, Realty World Jack Sherman, Inc., Realtor; **PRIM RE ACT:** Broker, Instructor, Appraiser; **OTHER RE ACT:** RE School Operator; **SERVICES:** Realty Sales, Mgmt. & Consultation; **PREV EMPLOY:** 1966-71 and 1974-79, Private Appraisal Practice in Vero Beach, 1972-73 Chief Appraiser Indian River Fed. S&L; **PROFL AFFIL & HONORS:** Vero Beach Bd. of Realtors (Pars. 1969) SRA Pres., Realty World Gold Coast Broker Council, 1980-81; **EDUC:** BA, 1952, Eng. Lit., Univ. FL - Gainesville; **EDUC HONORS:** Phi Eta Sigma; **MIL SERV:** USA, Cpl. 1946-48; **HOME ADD:** 4049 Ocean Drive, Apt. No. 303, Vero Beach, FL 32960, (305)567-1924; **BUS ADD:** 2080 Sixth Ave., Vero Beach, FL 32960, (305)567-1924.

SHERMAN, Michael B.——B: Quincy, MA, *Sr. VP, Dir. of Mktg.*, Spaulding and Slye Corp.; **PRIM RE ACT:** Broker, Developer, Builder, Property Manager; **PREV EMPLOY:** The Codman Co., Boston, MA; **PROFL AFFIL & HONORS:** NAR; Nat. Assn. of Indus. and Office Parks; Greater Boston RE Bd.; Former Dir. and Past Pres. of Boston Brokers Inst. Council CII, Serves on the Bd. of Advisors of the New England RE Directory; **EDUC:** BS, 1964, Psych., Bowdoin Coll.; **MIL SERV:** US Army, Private 1st Class; **OTHER ACT & HONORS:** Eastern Yacht Club, Marblehead, MA - Gut n' Feathers Club; **HOME ADD:** Seven Lookout Ct., Marblehead, MA 01945, (617)631-3567; **BUS ADD:** 15 New England Executive Park, Burlington, MA 01803, (617)523-8000.

SHERMAN, Robert A.——*VP Gen. Couns. & Secy.*, Wallace-Murray Corp.; **PRIM RE ACT:** Property Manager; **BUS ADD:** 299 Park Ave., New York, NY 10177, (212)486-6400.*

SHERMAN, William H.——B: Nov. 18, 1927, St. Paul, MN, *Owner*, William Sherman Co., Golf Course Brokers, Appraisers & Consultants; **PRIM RE ACT:** Broker, Consultant, Appraiser; **SERVICES:** Consulting, brokerage & appraisal services to golf course indus.; **REP CLIENTS:** Land developers, public agencies, golf course owners & investors; **PREV EMPLOY:** Rgnl. Dir., Nat. Golf Found., Chicago, IL & San Francisco, CA 1955-1963; **EDUC:** 1949, Journalism, Univ. of Notre Dame; **GRAD EDUC:** RE Cert., 1966, Univ. of CA; **MIL SERV:** US Army; **OTHER ACT & HONORS:** Honorary Life Member, So. CA PGA; VP, Univ. of Notre Dame Nat. Alumni Bd., 1976-1980; **HOME ADD:** 625 Belle, San Rafael, CA 94901, (415)454-8550; **BUS ADD:** 880 Las Gallinas, San Rafael, CA 94903, (415)472-6232.

SHERMER, Howard——B: June 16, 1925, Merlin, OR, *Pres.*, Shermer Cochran, Inc.; **PRIM RE ACT:** Broker, Syndicator, Consultant, Appraiser, Property Manager, Owner/Investor; **SERVICES:** Investment counseling, synd. of comml. prop.; **REP CLIENTS:** Resid. & comml. investors; **PREV EMPLOY:** Stevenson Dilbeek (Realtors) 1970-78, Howard Shermer Interiors, 1957-69; **PROFL AFFIL & HONORS:** RNMI, 6 yrs. Salesman of Yr.; MLS co-op sales & listing awards; CRB; **EDUC:** 1961, Interior design, Glendale Coll.; **MIL SERV:** USN, Bosn Fc., 1942-46; **OTHER ACT & HONORS:** Veedugo Club (Bus.); **HOME ADD:** 1729 Foothill Dr., Glendale, CA 91201, (213)244-1729; **BUS ADD:** 1125 N Pacific Ave., Glendale, CA 91202, (213)240-3333.

SHERN, Mary Steeves——B: Jan. 21, 1921, New York, NY, *Pres.*, Subdividerx, Inc. Barefoot Realty Inc.; **PRIM RE ACT:** Broker, Consultant, Developer, Instructor; **SERVICES:** Cond. project Bldg. and mktg.; **PROFL AFFIL & HONORS:** HI Assn. of Realtors, Honolulu Transit Coalition, GRI, CRS, CRB, Pres. HI Assn. of Realtors, NAR Dir.; **EDUC:** 1942, Econ., Swarthmore Coll.; **OTHER ACT & HONORS:** HI Commn. on the Handicapped; **HOME ADD:** 1487 Hiikala Pl. #11, Honolulu, HI 96816, (808)735-4911; **BUS ADD:** 4747 Kilauea Ave. #103, Honolulu, HI 96816, (808)734-2291.

SHERR, S. Sy——B: Aug. 31, 1937, New York, NY, *Atty.*, Sherr & Wallach; **PRIM RE ACT:** Broker, Attorney, Developer, Owner/Investor, Instructor, Syndicator; **SERVICES:** RE contracts, title ins. and closing, devel. and synd. of comml. props.; **PREV EMPLOY:** Instructor, FL RE Salesman Course; Sr. Partner, 1963-1980, Bernstein, Sherr, Hodges, Lancer & Vandroff, P.A.; **PROFL AFFIL & HONORS:** FL and Amer. Bar Assns.; FL RE Broker; Lawyers Title Guaranty Fund, Bar Specialization - Real Prop.; **EDUC:** BBA, 1959, Acctg., CCNY; **GRAD EDUC:** JD, 1962, Law/Comml. Courses, Univ. of FL; **EDUC HONORS:** Beta Alpha Psi, Nat. Hon., Acctg., Law Review; **HOME ADD:** 614 Owl Way, Sarasota, FL 33577, (813)366-5923; **BUS ADD:** 806 United First Federal Bldg., Sarasota, FL 33577, (813)955-4111.

SHERRER, James——*Pres.*, Huyck Corp.; **PRIM RE ACT:** Property Manager; **BUS ADD:** Wake Forest, NC 27587, (919)556-2071.*

SHERRILL, Rodolph G.——B: Feb. 19, 1938, Chattanooga, TN, *VP, RE*, The Krystal Co.; **OTHER RE ACT:** Corp. fast food; **PROFL AFFIL & HONORS:** NACORE, Pres., Chattanooga Chap. NACORE; **EDUC:** BA, 1961, Econ., MI State Univ.; **MIL SERV:** USNR, Lt.j.g.; **HOME ADD:** 1039 Ft. Stephenson, Lookout Mtn., TN 37350, (404)820-9431; **BUS ADD:** 100 W. 9th St., Chattanooga, TN 37402, (615)756-5100.

SHERWIN, Samuel R.——B: June 3, 1919, Viola, IL, *Pres.*, Sherwin RE Inc., and Sherwin Mgmt., Inc.; **PRIM RE ACT:** Broker, Owner/Investor, Property Manager, Insuror, Syndicator; **PROFL AFFIL & HONORS:** CPM (IREM); **EDUC:** BA, 1948, Econ.; MA, 1949, Econ.; **MIL SERV:** USN, SK3c; **OTHER ACT & HONORS:** Pres., N. Side RE Bd. 1980-1981; **HOME ADD:** 1123 Ridge Ave., Evanston, IL 60202, (312)864-2227; **BUS ADD:** 565 Howard St., Evanston, IL 60202.

SHERWOOD, Clifton A.——B: June 1, 1943, Los Angeles, CA, *Gen. Partner*, S.B. Development Co.; **PRIM RE ACT:** Broker, Developer, Owner/Investor; **SERVICES:** Devel. & sales or comml. & indus. props.; **PREV EMPLOY:** Norris, Beggs & Simpson 1974-79; **PROFL AFFIL & HONORS:** S.S.S.A.; **EDUC:** BS, 1968, Mgmt., Univ. of UT; **GRAD EDUC:** MBA, 1970, Fin., Univ. of UT; **OTHER ACT & HONORS:** Castro Valley Municipal Advisory Council 1981-; **HOME TEL:** (415)582-3666; **BUS ADD:** 22300 Foothill Blvd., Suite 311, Hayward, CA 94541.

SHERWOOD, Paul T.——B: Nov. 5, 1919, Nutley, NJ, *Dir. of Corporate Servs.*, The Singer Co.; **OTHER RE ACT:** Corporate RE Exec.; **PREV EMPLOY:** 1972-1975, Treasurer, Arden Mayfair Inc., City of Commerce, CA; 1965-72, VP Fin., Hunt Wesson Foods, Fullerton, CA; 1960-65, Controller, Indus. Products Div. Singer Co., New York City; **PROFL AFFIL & HONORS:** Dir. Nat. Assn. Corp. RE Execs.; **EDUC:** 1942, Acctg., Amer. Inst. of Banking; **HOME ADD:** 33 Pinnacle Rock Rd., Stamford, CT 06903, (203)322-4513; **BUS ADD:** 8 Stamford Forum, Stamford, CT 06904, (203)356-4200.

SHERWOOD, Robert E.——B: Dec. 28, 1928, Linton, IN, *Pres.*, Sebring Shores Devel., Inc.; **PRIM RE ACT:** Broker, Consultant, Appraiser, Developer, Builder; **PREV EMPLOY:** Dir. of Barnett Bank of Highlands Cty., Pres. of Lakeview Memorial Gardens, Inc.; **EDUC:** 1950, Bus. Admin., IN Univ.; **BUS ADD:** 2137 Memorial Dr., Sebring, FL 33870, (813)385-4335.

SHEVIN, Arnold D.——B: Jan. 19, 1946, Miami, FL, *VP - (Partner), Atty.*, Sparber, Shevin, Rosen, Shapo & Heilbronner, P.A., RE and Corp.; **PRIM RE ACT:** Attorney; **SERVICES:** Represent clients in all aspects of RE transactions including lending transactions, devel. of comml., condo. and single family type projects, synd.; **REP CLIENTS:** Sunset Commercial Bank, Lincoln S&L Assn., Lazarus Communities, Marc Firestone Construction, Inc., Villa Regina Condo's.; **PROFL AFFIL & HONORS:** FL Bar (RE and Trust Law Sect.); ABA (RE Sect.); Dade Cty. Bar Assn.; Member, Sports Lawyers Assn.; **EDUC:** BA, 1967, Hist., Emory Univ.; **GRAD EDUC:** JD, 1970, RE, Corp.,

Univ. of FL; **EDUC HONORS:** Dean's List, Biology Honor Soc., Law Review - John Marshall Bar Assn., several book awards; **OTHER ACT & HONORS:** Member Super Bowl Subcomm. of Gr. Miami Dade Sports Authority; **HOME ADD:** 7375 Southwest 154th Terr., Miami, FL 33157, (305)235-2119; **BUS ADD:** 30th Floor, AmeriFirst Bldg., One Southeast 3rd Ave., Miami, FL 33131, (305)358-7990.

SHIDLER, Jay H., II——B: Apr. 20, 1946, Pasadena, CA, *Sr. Partner*, Shidler & Company, Also Shidler & Shidler (San Francisco), McDade & Shidler (Los Angeles), Meringoff & Shidler (New York); **PRIM RE ACT:** Developer, Owner/Investor; **PREV EMPLOY:** Partner, Shidler & Petty; **EDUC:** BA, 1968, RE, Univ. of HI; **MIL SERV:** US Army, Lt. 1969-1971; **OTHER ACT & HONORS:** Pac. Club, Outrigger Canoe Club, Mokuleia Polo Club, HI Polo Found.; **HOME ADD:** 3233 Diamond Head Rd., Honolulu, HI 96815, (808)923-5975; **BUS ADD:** 733 Bishop St., Suite 2730, Honolulu, HI 96813, (808)536-6947.

SHIEFMAN, Saul——B: July 24, 1917, Detroit, MI, *Pres.*, Shiefman & Assoc.; **PRIM RE ACT:** Consultant, Real Estate Publisher; **SERVICES:** Public Relations; Editor, U.S. Housing Markets; **REP CLIENTS:** Advance Mortgage Corp., Citicorp RE, Inc., Hall RE Group; **PROFL AFFIL & HONORS:** Public Relations Soc. of Amer., Counselors Academy, Silver Anvil, PRSA; **EDUC:** BA, 1941, Sociology, Wayne State Univ.; **OTHER ACT & HONORS:** Past Pres., Jewish Parents Inst. of Detroit; Dir., Neighborhood Serv. Org. of Detroit; **HOME ADD:** 1539 Chateaufort, Detroit, MI 48207, (313)393-8429; **BUS ADD:** 406 City Nat. Bank Bldg., Detroit, MI 48226, (313)963-9441.

SHIELD, William C.——B: Dec. 17, 1939, Crockett, CA, *Pres.*, Pacific Investment RE; **PRIM RE ACT:** Broker, Lender, Syndicator; **SERVICES:** Investment consulting, selection, packaging & mktg. synd.; **PREV EMPLOY:** Project admin., Food Machinery Corp., Pres. Madison & Burke Fin. Inc.; **EDUC:** BA, 1963, Econ., St. Mary's Coll., CA; **OTHER ACT & HONORS:** ACM; **HOME ADD:** 1196 Danville Blvd., Alamo, CA 94507, (415)837-6761; **BUS ADD:** 375 Diablo Rd., 104, Danville, CA 94526, (415)820-3939.

SHIELDS, Charles O.——B: Jan. 2, 1917, Ballinger, TX, *Sr. Law Partner*, Ray Anderson Shields Trotti & Hemphill; **PRIM RE ACT:** Attorney; **SERVICES:** Gen. counsel, legal servs.; **REP CLIENTS:** Greater Dallas Bd. of Realtors, Inc., Henry S. Miller Resid. Corp., Judge B. Fite, Realtors; **PROFL AFFIL & HONORS:** Local, state and ABA; **EDUC:** 1938, N. TX Coll., Arlington, TX; **GRAD EDUC:** JD, 1942, Law, Univ. of TX at Austin, TX; **OTHER ACT & HONORS:** Asst. Dist. Atty. of Dallas Cty., TX 1946-1947; Kiwanis Club, Pres. N. Dallas Park Cities 1958; **HOME ADD:** 7000 Lavendale, Dallas, TX 75230, (214)361-1333; **BUS ADD:** 1300 Fidelity Union Tower, Dallas, TX 75201, (214)742-1161.

SHIELDS, Claude J.——B: Jan. 2, 1919, Sevier Cty., TN, *RE Developer*, Shields Mountain Estates; **PRIM RE ACT:** Consultant, Appraiser, Developer, Builder, Syndicator; **REP CLIENTS:** Appraisals for banks , estates, indiv. and cts.; **EDUC:** Smith Coll.; **MIL SERV:** US Air Corp., S/Sgt.; **HOME ADD:** PO Box 2, Pigeon Forge, TN 37862, (615)453-5181; **BUS ADD:** N. Parkway Box 2, Pigeon Forge, TN 37863, (615)453-5181.

SHIELDS, H. Richard——B: NY, *Pres.*, Regal Consultants Ltd.; **PRIM RE ACT:** Consultant, Owner/Investor; **PREV EMPLOY:** Amer. Diversified Indus. Corp. (O.T.C.) Pres., CEO; **PROFL AFFIL & HONORS:** Natl. Tax Assn., Amer. Inst. of Mgmt. Natl. Assn. of Accountants; Amer. Tax Inst.; **EDUC:** AB, Polit. Sci., Brooklyn Coll.; **GRAD EDUC:** LLB, JD, NY Univ. School of Law; Bus. Admin. MBA, Harvard Univ. School; **MIL SERV:** USAF, Maj., Commendation Medal Legion of Merit; **OTHER ACT & HONORS:** Referee & Arbitrator, Civil Ct. NYC, 10 yrs.; Harvard Club; Natl. Assn. of Corp. Directory; Who's Who in Amer.; Who's Who Commerce & Indus.; **HOME ADD:** Great Neck, NY 11021; **BUS ADD:** 98 Cutter Mill Rd., Great Neck, NY 11021, (516)482-4747.

SHIELDS, Robert L., III——B: Oct. 19, 1945, Birmingham, AL, *Atty. at Law*; **PRIM RE ACT:** Consultant, Attorney, Owner/Investor; **REP CLIENTS:** Local RE and resid. bldg. contractors and sub-contractors; lenders & investors closing agent; **PROFL AFFIL & HONORS:** ABA; Birmingham MBAA; **EDUC:** BS, 1967, Liberal Arts, Univ. of AL; **GRAD EDUC:** JD, 1975, Cumberland School of Law; **EDUC HONORS:** Cum Laude; **MIL SERV:** USN, Lt., Navy Commendation Medal; **HOME ADD:** 2145 Mountain View Dr., Birmingham, AL 35216, (205)979-9272; **BUS ADD:** 2220 Highland Ave., POB 3305-A, Birmingham, AL 35255, (205)933-2756.

SHIFFMAN, Michael A.——B: July 23, 1941, Newark, NJ, *Atty.*, Michael A. Shiffman, P.C.; **PRIM RE ACT:** Attorney, Consultant, Broker; **SERVICES:** Active legal practice with RE emphasis, RE consulting; **REP CLIENTS:** Torino Indus., Collins Devel., Gothard Bank (Switzerland), RE devel. & major foreign prop. acquirers; **PROFL AFFIL & HONORS:** ABA, CA State Bar, Intl. Bar; **GRAD EDUC:** LLB, 1974, Lincoln Law School; **EDUC HONORS:** Magna Cum Laude, class valedictorian; **HOME ADD:** 109 Oak Ave., Kentfield, CA 94904, (415)456-9654; **BUS ADD:** 900 Larkspur Landing Cir. #219, Larkspur, CA 94939, (415)461-9255.

SHIFMAN, Arnold R.——B: Jan. 19, 1940, Canton, OH, *Atty.*, Shifman & Friedman; **PRIM RE ACT:** Attorney; **SERVICES:** All areas of RE Law; **REP CLIENTS:** First Fed. S&L Assn. of Canton; **PROFL AFFIL & HONORS:** ABA, OSBA; **EDUC:** BA, 1961, Anthroplogy Sociology, OH State Univ.; **GRAD EDUC:** Law, 1964, OH State Univ.; **EDUC HONORS:** Alpha Kappa Delta Hon. Frat.; **BUS ADD:** 548 Citizens Savings Bldg., Canton, OH 44702, (216)456-2852.

SHIGEOKA, Dennis K.——B: Dec. 7, 1945, Hilo, HI, *VP/Treas.*, Okahara, Shigeoka & Associates, Inc.; **PRIM RE ACT:** Consultant, Engineer; **SERVICES:** Planning and Consulting Engr.; **PROFL AFFIL & HONORS:** HI Soc. of Profl. Engrs.; Nat. Soc. of Profl. Engrs.; Amer. Soc. of Civil Engrs.; **EDUC:** BCE, 1968, Civil Engrg., Univ. of HI; **MIL SERV:** US Army, E-5; **OTHER ACT & HONORS:** Rotary; **HOME ADD:** 250 Naniakea St., Hilo, HI 96720, (808)959-6135; **BUS ADD:** 200 Kohola St., Hilo, HI 96720, (808)961-5527.

SHIMA, Richard R.——B: Jan. 9, 1950, New York, NY, *VP*, Morgan Guaranty Trust Co. of NY, RE Investment Dept.; **PRIM RE ACT:** Consultant, Appraiser; **SERVICES:** Investment analysis, prop. disposition, appraisals, and mkt./econ. feasibility studies involving maj. comml. corps.; **REP CLIENTS:** Maj. corps. and high net worth domestic and foreign indivs.; **PREV EMPLOY:** Asst. Project Mgr. Citicorp; **PROFL AFFIL & HONORS:** Candidate, AIREA & Assoc., SREA; **EDUC:** BA, 1972, Econ., Rutgers Coll.; **GRAD EDUC:** MS, 1973, RE/Equity Analysis, U of WI Grad. School of Bus.; **MIL SERV:** Transportation, Capt. (retired); **HOME ADD:** 3 Indian Trial, Sparta, NJ 07871, (201)729-9544; **BUS ADD:** 9 W 57th St., New York, NY 10017, (212)826-7110.

SHINALL, John M.——B: Feb. 26, 1944, Atlanta, GA, *Part.*, Shinall, Kuckleburg & Kell, Attys.; **PRIM RE ACT:** Attorney; **PREV EMPLOY:** Boling, Nevill & Shinall, Attys. - 1971-1975; Swertfeger, Scott, Pike & Simmons, Attys. - 1968-1970; **PROFL AFFIL & HONORS:** ABA, State Bar of GA, Past Pres., Blue Ridge Circuit Bar Assn.; **EDUC:** BA, 1966, Poli. Sci., Emory Univ.; **GRAD EDUC:** JD, 1969, Lumpkin Law School - Univ. of GA; **HOME ADD:** 1036 Strawberry Dr., Cumming, GA 30130, (404)889-1982; **BUS ADD:** PO Box 240, Cumming, GA 30130, (404)887-0400.

SHINDLER, Donald Alan——B: Oct. 15, 1946, New Orleans, LA, *Chmn. & Partner*, CBA, YLS Housing & Urban Affairs Comm. 1980-81, Rudnick & Wolfe; **PRIM RE ACT:** Attorney; **SERVICES:** Legal Rep. & Advice Counseling on Acquisitions, Speaker at RE Seminars; **REP CLIENTS:** Lenders, RE Devel, and Synd., Indiv. Investors, Comm. Enterprises; **PROFL AFFIL & HONORS:** ABA Chicago Bar Assn., IL & LA State Bar Assocs., CPA; **EDUC:** BSBA, 1968, Acctg. and Fin., WA Univ., St. Louis, MO; **GRAD EDUC:** JD, 1971, Tulane Univ. School of Law, New Orleans, LA; **EDUC HONORS:** Final Honors, Beta Gamma Sigma, Order of the Coif., Tulane Law Review, Tulane Moot Court; **MIL SERV:** USNR, Lt., J.A.G.C. 1971-1975; **OTHER ACT & HONORS:** Dir. Library Bd., Glencoe, IL 1981 - 86; **BUS ADD:** 30 N. La Salle St., Chicago, IL 60602, (312)368-4000.

SHINDLER, Michael C.——B: Sept. 30, 1951, New Orleans, LA, *Associate*, Katten, Muchin, Zavis, Pearl & Galler, Real Estate Dept.; **PRIM RE ACT:** Attorney; **PROFL AFFIL & HONORS:** ABA; Chicago Bar Assn.; **EDUC:** AB, 1973, Pol. Sci., Univ. of NC; **GRAD EDUC:** JD, 1976, Wash. Univ. (St. Louis); **EDUC HONORS:** Editor, Washington Univ. Law Quarterly; **MIL SERV:** US Army Res.; 1971-77; **HOME ADD:** 4200 Marine Dr. #801, Chicago, IL 60613; **BUS ADD:** 55 E. Monroe St., Ste. 4100, Chicago, IL 60603, (312)346-7400.

SHINE, James P.——B: Detroit, MI, *VP - RE*, Bickford Corp.; **PRIM RE ACT:** Attorney, Consultant, Developer, Builder, Property Manager, Owner/Investor; **PREV EMPLOY:** Intl. Tel. and Tel., 320 Park Ave., NYC, NY, Mgr. of RE; **EDUC:** PhB, 1958, Journalism & Phil., Univ. of Detroit; **GRAD EDUC:** LLD, 1962, Detroit Coll. of Law.; **MIL SERV:** USA, 1952-1954; **BUS ADD:** 1330 Soldiers Field Rd., Brighton, MA 02135, (617)782-4010.

SHINEHOUSE, B.R.——B: Sept. 23, 1947, PA, *Atty./CPA*; **PRIM RE ACT:** Attorney, Instructor, Owner/Investor, Syndicator; **SERVICES:** Atty./CPA; **PREV EMPLOY:** Arthur Anderson & Co.; **PROFL**

AFFIL & HONORS: AAA-CPA; State Bar of NV & CA; Instr. in Real Prop. Law, Fin. Taxation at Univ. of NV; **EDUC:** BS/BA, 1969, Univ. of NV at Las Vegas; **GRAD EDUC:** JD, 1974, Univ. of CA at Davis Law School; MBA, 1970, Univ. of NV at Las Vegas; **EDUC HONORS:** Grad. with Honors, Phi Kappa Phi; Deans Grad. Fellowship in Bus. and Econ. Award; Chancellor's Distinguished Scholar; **BUS ADD:** 302 E. Carson Ave., First Interstate Bank Bldg., Suite 620, Las Vegas, NV 89101, (702)386-5054.

SHIPE, Douglas V.——B: May 27, 1951, Kansas City, MO, *Sr. Tax Analyst*, Cook Paint & Varnish Co., Tax & Insurance; **PRIM RE ACT:** Consultant; **SERVICES:** Investment and tax shelter analysis; **REP CLIENTS:** Limited partnerships and indiv.; **PREV EMPLOY:** IRS Agent, MO Dept. of Revenue; **PROFL AFFIL & HONORS:** Nat. Assn. of Accountants; Tax Executives Inst.; **EDUC:** BBA, 1973, Acctg., Univ. of MO, Columbia; **MIL SERV:** US Army, Lt.; **HOME ADD:** 12900 Smalley, Grandview, MO 64030; **BUS ADD:** POB 389, Kansas City, MO 64141, (816)391-6294.

SHIPMAN, Sally Stevens——B: Mar. 23, 1940, Beaumont, TX, *Principal*, Shipmen and Associates; **PRIM RE ACT:** Consultant; **OTHER RE ACT:** Urban planning; **SERVICES:** Zoning summaries City of Austin, land use planning, devel. feasibility, demographics; **REP CLIENTS:** Architects, attys., lenders, school district, neighborhoods, those seeking zoning change; **PROFL AFFIL & HONORS:** City of Austin Planning Commn., Amer. Inst. Certified Planners, Amer. Planning Ass. TX Chap., Educ. Found. Bd.; **EDUC:** BA, 1960, Hist., Univ. of TX; **GRAD EDUC:** MS Community Rgn. Planning, 1978, Land use, Univ. of TX; **OTHER ACT & HONORS:** League of Women Voters, WE Care Austin Women's Environmental Coalition Bd., PTA (Officer), Camp Fire (leader), Neighborhood correspondent Austin Amer.-Statesman, Heritage Soc., Symphony League, West Austin Neighborhood Grp. Bd.; **HOME ADD:** 2705 Moonlight Bend, Austin, TX 78703, (512)476-9954; **BUS ADD:** PO Box 5938, Austin, TX 78763, (512)472-3401.

SHIPP, James——*Exec. Dir. Central Facilities*, Cummins Engine Co., In.; **PRIM RE ACT:** Property Manager; **BUS ADD:** 1000 Fifth St., Columbus, IN 47201, (812)379-5981.*

SHIRER, Mary Lou——*Pres.*, Mary Lou Shirer Co. Realtors; **PRIM RE ACT:** Broker, Owner/Investor, Instructor, Property Manager; **OTHER RE ACT:** Guest lectures Univ. of TX; **SERVICES:** Coll. of Bus. Admin.; **PROFL AFFIL & HONORS:** U.T. RE Soc.; TX Assn. of Realtors; NAR; ABOR; Austin Apt. Assn., also TX & Nat. Comml. Investment Div., First woman on RE Comm. for City of Austin; First woman in Comml. Investment Div., CRB, CRS, GRI, CID; **EDUC:** BS, Physical Therapy, Boston Univ.; Physical Therapy, Harvard Univ.; **HOME ADD:** 8510A Mesa Dr., Austin, TX 78759, (512)345-2375; **BUS ADD:** Shirer Sq., 8105A Mesa Dr., Austin, TX 78759, (512)345-2375.

SHIRLEY, Kim R.——B: June 29, 1942, Altadena, CA, *Pres.*, Crookall, Shirley & Co.; **PRIM RE ACT:** Broker, Developer, Owner/Investor, Property Manager; **REP CLIENTS:** Roadway Express, Inc., Teledyne Indus., Pac. Telephone; **PREV EMPLOY:** Penta Pac. Props.; **PROFL AFFIL & HONORS:** Soc. of Indus. Realtors; **EDUC:** BA, 1965, Econ., UCLA; **MIL SERV:** USAF, Capt.; **HOME ADD:** 23742 Via Porton, Mission Viejo, CA 92691, (714)830-6003; **BUS ADD:** 601 North Park Center, Suite 205, Santa Ana, CA 92701, (714)558-1517.

SHIRLEY, Ralph——*Pres.*, Shirley Houston, Inc.; **PRIM RE ACT:** Broker, Consultant, Developer, Builder, Owner/Investor, Property Manager; **SERVICES:** Brokerage, design, devel. & mgmt.; **HOME ADD:** 217 Woener Rd., Houston, TX 77068, (713)444-4610; **BUS ADD:** 2301 FM 1960 W 202, Houston, TX 77068, (713)444-2582.

SHIVE, Richard B.——B: Jan. 16, 1933, Cleveland, OH, *Part.*, Scrimenti/Shive/Spinelli/Perantoni/Architects; **PRIM RE ACT:** Architect; **SERVICES:** Feasibility Studies, Architectural & Site Design; **REP CLIENTS:** AT&T - Long Lines, Baker & Taylor; **PROFL AFFIL & HONORS:** AIA; Const. Specifications Inst.; Illuminating Engineers Soc.; Amer. Concrete Inst.; Amer. Soc. of Heating, Refrigerating, and Air Conditioning Engineers; ASTM; **EDUC:** BS, 1954, Bldg. Sci., RPI, Troy, NY; **GRAD EDUC:** Post Grad. Study, Structural Design, Newark Coll. of Engin., 1957, Paint Tech., Struct. Design, Landscape Design, Rutgers 1960-63; **OTHER ACT & HONORS:** Pres. Bd. of Trs., Somerset Medical Ctr.; James F. Lincoln ARC Welding Found. Award 1973; **HOME ADD:** RD1s#1 N. Mountain Ave., Bound Brook, NJ 08805, (201)469-2682; **BUS ADD:** P.O. Box 758, 350 Grove St., Somerville, NJ 08876, (201)725-7000.

SHLAES, Jared——B: July 7, 1930, Chicago, IL, *Pres.*, Shlaes & Co.; **PRIM RE ACT:** Consultant, Appraiser; **SERVICES:** Real estate consulting and appraisal; **REP CLIENTS:** NAR, HUD, US Postal Serv., Chicago Bd. of Education, City of Chicago, IL, McDonalds Corp., Continental Bank, First National Bank of Chicago, Harris Bank, Amer. Nat. Bank, leading law firms and devels.; **PREV EMPLOY:** Sr. VP, Arthur Rubloff & Co. 1971-74; **PROFL AFFIL & HONORS:** Amer. Soc. of RE Counselors; AIREA; Amer. Planning Assn.; Chicago RE Bd., CRE; MAI; Lambda Alpha; Louise & Y.T. Lum award of AIREA; Past. VP ASREC; **EDUC:** BA, 1948, Liberal Arts, Univ.of Chicago; **GRAD EDUC:** MBA, 1950, Fin., Univ. of Chicago; **EDUC HONORS:** Gen. Honors; **MIL SERV:** Army, Cpl.; **OTHER ACT & HONORS:** Past Advisor, Nat. Trust for Historic Preservation; Editor-in-Chief, "Real Estate Issues"; **HOME ADD:** 235 Eugenie St., Chicago, IL 60614; **BUS ADD:** 405 N. Wabash, Chicago, IL 60611, (312)467-1000.

SHLONSKY, Roger B.——B: Apr. 28, 1938, Columbus, OH, *Partner*, R.B. Shlonsky & Co.; **PRIM RE ACT:** Developer, Consultant; **OTHER RE ACT:** CPA; **SERVICES:** Devel., Investment Analysis, Fin. acctg., Litigation relative to Nat. and Intl. Const.; **REP CLIENTS:** US Dept. of Justice, Intl. Communications Agency, Robert Sheridan & Partners, Law firms on E. Coast; **PREV EMPLOY:** VP-Fin. and Partner, Robert Sheridan's & Partner, Price Waterhouse & Co.; **PROFL AFFIL & HONORS:** AICPA's; IL Soc. of CPA's; MD Assn. of CPA's, CPA in states of IL and MD; **EDUC:** BBA, 1960, Acctg., Syracuse Univ.; **MIL SERV:** US Army/Infantry, Capt.; **HOME ADD:** 9028 Willow Valley Dr., Potomac, MD 20854, (301)340-7111; **BUS ADD:** 9028 Willow Valley Dr., Potomac, MD 20854, (301)340-7111.

SHOBBROOK, Thomas W.——B: Oct. 11, 1932, Lewiston, ID, *VP, Div. Mgr.*, Prop. Mgmt. Systems; **PRIM RE ACT:** Property Manager; **SERVICES:** Mgmt. of office bldgs. & office parks; **REP CLIENTS:** Major ins. cos., foreign investment grps., major oil cos.; **PREV EMPLOY:** Mgr. RE Trust Dept. of major reg. bank; **PROFL AFFIL & HONORS:** CPM; **EDUC:** BS, 1954, Psych., U. of ID; **MIL SERV:** USA, 1st Lt.; **HOME ADD:** 14728-B Perthshire, Houston, TX 77092, (713)497-5587; **BUS ADD:** Suite 600, 2900 N. Loop W, Houston, TX 77092, (713)683-1405.

SHOCKLEY, Hugh U.——B: Jan. 31, 1920, Patchoque, NY, *Pres.*, Affiliated Properties Corp.; **PRIM RE ACT:** Broker, Syndicator; **SERVICES:** Provide investments for high-bracket taxpayers thru. synd. mgmt.; **REP CLIENTS:** Execs. of major corps. & lending inst. in metro. Denver area; **PREV EMPLOY:** Real estate 22 yrs.; **PROFL AFFIL & HONORS:** NAR, Realtors Nat. Mktg. Inst., RE Sec. Synd. Inst., CO Assn. of Realtors, Denver Bd. of Realtors; **EDUC:** BS, 1952, Speech Pathology, Univ. of Denver; **MIL SERV:** USA, Capt.; **OTHER ACT & HONORS:** Denver Athletic Club, Cherry Hills Ctry. Club, Denver Petroleum Club, Advisor CO Women's Coll. Found.; **HOME ADD:** 6431 E Cornell Ave., Denver, CO 80222, (303)757-2436; **BUS ADD:** 110-16th St., Denver, CO 80202, (303)623-6651.

SHOCKLEY, Robert E.——B: May 31, 1933, Hot Springs, AR, *Owner*, Shockley Realty & Appraisal Co.; **PRIM RE ACT:** Broker, Instructor, Consultant, Appraiser, Owner/Investor; **OTHER RE ACT:** Specializing in condemnation appraising & court testimony; **SERVICES:** Gen. comml. brokerage, counseling & appraising.; **REP CLIENTS:** Numerous law firms, mort. & invest. co's. & accounting firms; **PREV EMPLOY:** AR Highway Dept.; **PROFL AFFIL & HONORS:** SREA; NAR, Past Pres. of Central AR, SREA; Past Pres. of Hot Springs Bd. of Realtors; **OTHER ACT & HONORS:** Sertoma Intl.; **HOME TEL:** (501)525-3293; **BUS ADD:** 316 Long Island Dr., Hot Springs, AR 71901, (501)525-3293.

SHOLLENBERGER, Brian D.——B: Dec. 4, 1949, Norristown, PA, *VP*, Univ. Natl. Bank, RE; **PRIM RE ACT:** Banker, Lender; **SERVICES:** Comml. construction lending; **PREV EMPLOY:** United Bank of Denver, Denver, CO; Colonial Bank & Trust, Waterbury, CT; **PROFL AFFIL & HONORS:** Home Builders Assn.; Assoc. Gen. Contractors; Assoc. Bldg. Contractors; Robert Morris Assoc.; **EDUC:** BS, 1971, Mgmt./Computer Sci., Bloomsburg State Coll., Bloomsburg, PA; **GRAD EDUC:** MBA, 1974, Fin., Univ. of CT, Storrs, CT; **HOME ADD:** 1334 Marion St., Denver, CO 80218; **BUS ADD:** 4201 E. Yale, Denver, CO 80222, (303)757-7272.

SHOROBURA, R. George——B: Mar. 23, 1950, Cleveland, MS, *Architect*, R. George Shorobura & Assoc.; **PRIM RE ACT:** Architect, Developer; **PREV EMPLOY:** Sr. Designer, Chicago Office, Skidmore, Owings & Merrill; **EDUC:** BS Arch., 1973, Design, Hi Rise Resid., Comml. Structures, U. of IL; **EDUC HONORS:** First Place, State of IL Indus. Arts Exhibition held at Western IL Univ., Category: Architecture; **OTHER ACT & HONORS:** Ukrainian Inst. of Modern Art., E. Humboldt Park Urban Renewal Comm Tech. Consultant &

Advisor; **HOME ADD:** 339 Armitage, Chicago, IL 60614; **BUS ADD:** 339 Armitage, Chigago, IL 60614, (312)871-4835.

SHORT, Alexander C.——B: July 26, 1940, Wash., DC, *Atty.*, Miles & Stockbridge; **PRIM RE ACT:** Attorney; **SERVICES:** Rep. of Lenders and Dev.; **REP CLIENTS:** Lenders and indiv. instnl. investors and dev. of comm'l. prop.; **PREV EMPLOY:** HUD 1963-1969; **PROFL AFFIL & HONORS:** ABA, Maryland State Bar Assn.; **EDUC:** BA, 1963, Amer. His., Amherst Coll.; **GRAD EDUC:** MA, 1968, Pol. Sci. and Public Admin., Univ. of PA; JD, 1972, Law, Univ. of VA; **HOME ADD:** 341 Turnbridge Rd., Baltimore, MD 21212, (301)323-6519; **BUS ADD:** 10 Light St., Baltimore, MD 21202, (301)727-6464.

SHORT, Audrey C.——B: Nov. 1, 1933, MA, *Pres.*, Realty World - Audrey Short, Inc.; **PRIM RE ACT:** Broker, Consultant, Appraiser; **OTHER RE ACT:** Gen. RE brokerage; **SERVICES:** Resid. sales, listing and fin. assistance; comml. rental and sales; resid. rental mgmt; appraisals; **PROFL AFFIL & HONORS:** Natl. State and Mercer Cty. Bd. of Realtors; NJ Chap. of Cert. Resid. Brokers, CRS, CRB, IFA Candidate; Officer and Dir. Mercer Cty. Bd. of Realtors; Former Pres. Princeton RE Grp; Realty World Broker of the Year 1977 and 1978, PA Region; **EDUC:** AA, Stephens Coll.; **OTHER ACT & HONORS:** Pres. Princeton Area C of C 1975; Pres. Princeton Communities United Way 1980; **HOME ADD:** 50 Fackler Rd., Princeton, NJ 08540, (609)921-8897; **BUS ADD:** 163 Nassau St., Princeton, NJ 08540, (609)921-9222.

SHORT, Keith——B: Apr. 15, 1947, Wichita Falls, TX, *Atty. at Law*, Foreman & Dyess; **PRIM RE ACT:** Attorney; **SERVICES:** Legal services dealing with various aspects of RE; **REP CLIENTS:** Land devel., prop. owners; **PROFL AFFIL & HONORS:** CA, TX, and Houston Bar Assns.; ABA; **EDUC:** BA, 1968, Univ. of TX; **GRAD EDUC:** JD, 1971, Univ. of TX; **EDUC HONORS:** Cum Laude; **MIL SERV:** US Army Res., Capt.; **OTHER ACT & HONORS:** Assoc. Editor, TX Law Review, 1971; **HOME ADD:** 6435 Brompton, Houston, TX 77005, (713)663-6834; **BUS ADD:** First International Plaza, Houston, TX 77002.

SHORY, Nolan L.——B: June 17, 1915, Birmingham, AL, *Owner*, ABC Realty; **PRIM RE ACT:** Broker, Attorney, Developer, Builder, Owner/Investor, Property Manager; **PREV EMPLOY:** Dept. of Defense, Procurement; **PROFL AFFIL & HONORS:** ALA Bar Assn., Birmingham Bar Assn.; **EDUC:** BBA, 1951, Acctg., admin., Univ. of GA; **GRAD EDUC:** JD, 1955, Gen. law, RE, Birmingham School of Law; **MIL SERV:** US Army, Sgt.; **HOME ADD:** 1540 Shades Crest Rd., Birmingham, AL 35226, (205)979-0960; **BUS ADD:** 426 Woodward Bldg., Birmingham, AL 35203, (205)323-2445.

SHOUHAYIB, Kamal——B: Jan 13, 1946, Aley, Lebanon, *Pres.*, Shoubahib Investment Co.; **PRIM RE ACT:** Syndicator, Owner/Investor; **PROFL AFFIL & HONORS:** RESSI, MI Apt. Assn.; **EDUC:** BCE, 1969, Civil Engrg.; **HOME ADD:** 3858 Old Creek Rd., Troy, MI, (313)362-0866; **BUS ADD:** 755 W. Big Beaver Rd., Toy, MI 48084, (313)362-4150.

SHOWMAKER, L.E.——B: Feb 27, 1941, Kokomo, IN, *Pres.*, The Synds. Corp.; **PRIM RE ACT:** Broker, Instructor, Syndicator, Consultant, Owner/Investor; **SERVICES:** R.E. securities & synds., RE broker, fin. advisor; **REP CLIENTS:** Health care profs., RE investors; **PREV EMPLOY:** Pres./CEO Elsan Co., Marsan Co.; **PROFL AFFIL & HONORS:** NAR, RNMI, RESSI, MI Assn. of Realtors Exchange Div., CCIM; **EDUC:** BS, 1964, Pre-med., Ball State Univ.; **GRAD EDUC:** Mgmt. operations, Univ. of S. CA; **EDUC HONORS:** In the honors program for a period of time; **MIL SERV:** USAF, Capt, Numerous Decorations; **OTHER ACT & HONORS:** Assoc. Dir., USDA Soil Conservation Dist., U.S. Jaycees; **HOME ADD:** 2271 S. Long Lake Rd., Fenton, MI 48430, (313)629-2591; **BUS ADD:** G-3200 Beecher Rd., Suite A, Flint, MI 48504, (313)733-6810.

SHRAGO, Jeffrey Kazis——B: Mar. 12, 1953, Boston, MA, *VP*, Julien J. Studley, Inc.; **PRIM RE ACT:** Broker, Consultant; **SERVICES:** Comml. sales, leasing and devel.; **REP CLIENTS:** Comml. devels. and all users of comml. office space; **PREV EMPLOY:** The New England Merchants Nat. Bank 1974-1975; **PROFL AFFIL & HONORS:** NAR; WA Bd. of Realtors, Recipient of the WA Bd. of Realtors Million Dollar Leasing Club Award 1976-1980; Recipient of the WA Bd. of Realtors New Leasing Agent of the Year Award 1976; Designated a Life Member of the WA Bd. of Realtors Million Dollar Leasing Club, 1980; **EDUC:** BA, 1975, Econ., Boston Univ.; **EDUC HONORS:** Cum Laude; **HOME ADD:** 2555 Pennsylvania Ave., NW, Washington, DC 20037, (202)296-0820; **BUS ADD:** 1333 New Hampshire Ave., NW, Washington, DC 20036, (202)296-6360.

SHREVE, Robert D.——B: Nov. 20, 1930, Omaha, NE, *VP*, Maenner Co., Investment Prop. Mgmt.; **PRIM RE ACT:** Property Manager; **REP CLIENTS:** Pension plans, banks, private investors; **PROFL AFFIL & HONORS:** IREM; BOMA; Intl. Council of Shopping Centers; AMO, CPM; **HOME ADD:** 2659 S. 96th Cir., Omaha, NE 68124, (402)391-1309; **BUS ADD:** 10050 Regency Cir., Suite #100, Omaha, NE 68114, (402)393-3200.

SHUBIN, Bill——B: Sept. 16, 1934, Bell, CA, *VP & Gen. Mgr.*, Arvida Corp., Comml./Indus. Div.; **PRIM RE ACT:** Broker, Developer, Builder, Owner/Investor, Property Manager; **SERVICES:** Resid. devels.; resort recreational devels.; comml./indus. devels.; **PREV EMPLOY:** VP & Gen. Mgr. The City, a 200-acre master planned urban center in Orange Cty. CA, devel. by partnership of Kaiser Aluminum & Metropolitan Life; **PROFL AFFIL & HONORS:** ULI, Nat. Assn. of Indus. & Office Parks, Nat. Assn. of Corporate RE Execs., Intl. Council of Shopping Ctrs.; **EDUC:** BS, 1958, Fin., Univ. of So. CA; **MIL SERV:** USA; **OTHER ACT & HONORS:** Member, 1981 Historic Boca Raton Preservation Bd. of Commnrs.; Local & state C of C; Past Chmn. of United Way; **HOME ADD:** 175 NE Spanish Trail, Boca Raton, FL 33432, (305)368-0864; **BUS ADD:** 5550 Glades Rd., PO Box 100, Boca Raton, FL 33432, (305)395-2000.

SHUCART, James——B: May 19, 1946, St. Louis, MO, *Pres.*, Property Consultants, Inc.; **PRIM RE ACT:** Broker, Consultant, Developer, Owner/Investor, Property Manager, Syndicator; **OTHER RE ACT:** Condo. conversions; **SERVICES:** Investment counselling; analysis of income props.; **REP CLIENTS:** Pvt. and instnl. investors; **PREV EMPLOY:** Ira E. Berry Realtors, Inc. 1976-79; **PROFL AFFIL & HONORS:** NAR; CCIM Candidate; MO Assn. of Realtors; **EDUC:** BBA, 1969, Fin., Kansas State Univ.; **MIL SERV:** US Army; 1st Lt.; **OTHER ACT & HONORS:** St. Louis RE Exchange; **HOME ADD:** 9 Brentmoor Park, Clayton, MO 63105, (314)726-4565; **BUS ADD:** P.O. Box 11718, St. Louis, MO 63105, (314)725-9540.

SHULER, (Samuel) Mark——B: Oct. 13, 1948, Edmonton, Alb., Can., Mark Shuler, Barrister & Solicitor; **PRIM RE ACT:** Attorney; **PREV EMPLOY:** Eden, Pirie & Shuler, Barristers and Solicitors, 615 3rd Ave. SW, Cmlgary, Alb., Can.; **PROFL AFFIL & HONORS:** Law Soc. of Alberta; Can. Bar Assn.; Can. Civil Liberties Assn.; **EDUC:** BA, 1970, Political Philosophy, Univ. of Alberta (Edmonton, Can.); **GRAD EDUC:** LLB, 1974, Univ. of Toronto (Toronto, Can.); **EDUC HONORS:** Honors Standing; **OTHER ACT & HONORS:** Chmn., Bus. Law Sect., Can. Bar Assn. (S. Alberta Branch), 1979-1981; Pres., Calgary Jewish Family Serv. (United Way Agency), 1979-1981; Author: "Leasing as Subdivision" 1979 Legal Educ. Soc. of Alberta; Author: "Attitudinal Analysis of Supreme Court of Canada Justices" 32 U. of T. Fac. LR1 1974; Lecturer 1981 Legal Educ. Soc. of Alberta/Alberta Inst. of Law Reform Special Lectures on "Business Corp. Act., 1981"; Lecturer/Author: "Lawyers Liens and Partnership Liens" 1981/1982 Can. Bar Assn. (Alberta Branch) Proceedings; **HOME ADD:** Ste. 510, Mission Profl. Ctr., 2303 4th. St. SW, Calgary, T2S2S7, Alb, Canada, (403)252-2187; **BUS ADD:** Ste. 510, Mission Profl. Ctr., 2303 4th St. SW, Calgary, T2S2S7, Alb, Canada.

SHULL, James——*SIR, Manager*, Armco Steel Corp.; **PRIM RE ACT:** Property Manager; **BUS ADD:** 703 Wais St., Middletown, OH 45042, (513)425-2346.*

SHULMAN, James H.——B: Apr. 5, 1946, Hartford, CT, *Principal*, Byrne, Shechtman, & Slater, P.C.; **PRIM RE ACT:** Attorney; **SERVICES:** All aspects of RE law; **REP CLIENTS:** RE depts. of major New England supermarkets; CT devels. of suburban office parks; area lenders and devels.; **PREV EMPLOY:** Partner, Ribicoff & Kotkin law firm, Hartford, CT; **PROFL AFFIL & HONORS:** ABA, CT Bar Assn., Hartford Cty. Bar Assn.; **EDUC:** 1968, George Washington Univ.; **GRAD EDUC:** 1971, George Washington Law School; **EDUC HONORS:** Law Review, grad. with honors; **OTHER ACT & HONORS:** Zoning Alternate, W. Hartford Town Council; **BUS ADD:** P O Box 3216, 111 Pearl St., Hartford, CT 06103, (203)525-4700.

SHULSKY, Marvin R.——B: Jan. 10, 1943, New York, NY, *VP*, Region Holding Corp.; **PRIM RE ACT:** Broker; **OTHER RE ACT:** Mgr., Investor; **PROFL AFFIL & HONORS:** RE Bd. of NY, ICSC Midtown Realty Owners Fifth Ave. Assn.; **EDUC:** 1963, Lib. Arts., Eng., Boston Univ.; **HOME ADD:** 1165 Park Ave., New York, NY; **BUS ADD:** 307 Fifth Ave., New York, NY 10016, (212)685-1514.

SHULTZ, E. Alison——B: Aug. 11, 1945, Zurich, Switz., *Asst. Dir.*, Gibson Assocs. Inc.; **PRIM RE ACT:** Regulator, Real Estate Publisher; **SERVICES:** All aspects of RE publishing and regulation; **REP CLIENTS:** James L. Burrows Esq., L. Marie Scenna, private clientele; **EDUC:** BA, 1967, Arch., Cornell Univ.; **GRAD EDUC:** MS, 1971, Arch., Hofstra Univ.; JD, 1985, Suffolk Univ.; **EDUC HONORS:** Magna Cum Laude, Summa Cum Laude; **BUS ADD:** 53

Chestnut Hill Ave., Brighton, MA 02135, (617)782-4090.

SHUTTLEWORTH, J.E.——*Dir. of Corp. RE*, General Foods Corp.; **PRIM RE ACT:** Property Manager; **BUS ADD:** 250 North St., White Plains, NY 10625, (914)683-2500.*

SHUTZ, Byron T.——**B:** June 26, 1899, New Philadelphia, OH, *Honorary Chmn.*, The Byron Shutz Co.; **PRIM RE ACT:** Broker, Consultant, Lender, Owner/Investor, Property Manager; **OTHER RE ACT:** Mort. banker; **REP CLIENTS:** Crown Center Redevel. Corp.; Hallmark Cards, Inc.; **PREV EMPLOY:** Sr. Partner, Herbert V. Jones & Co.; Chmn., Byron Shutz Co.; **PROFL AFFIL & HONORS:** RE Bd. of Kansas City, MO, former Pres.; MO RE Assn., former Pres.; Chmn., MO License Comm. RE, Former Pres., Mtg. Bankers Assn. of Amer.; Permanent Member, Bd. of Governonrs of Mktg. Bankers Assn. of Amer.; Realtor Emeritus; **EDUC:** 1919, Univ. of KS; **MIL SERV:** USN; Seaman, WW I; **OTHER ACT & HONORS:** Trustee, Jacob & Ella Loose Charitable Trusts; Trustee, Andrew Drum Inst. for Boys; Dir., Farm & Home Savings Assn., 22 yrs.; Dir., First Nat. Bk. of KC, MO; Former Dir. & V. Chmn., Midwest Research Instit.; Past Pres., KC & Jackson City Chapt. Am. Red Cross; Dir., KC Assn. of Trust & Foundations; Member of Bd. of Trustees, K.U. Endowment Assn.; Citation for Distinguished Service from Univ. of KS, June 1963; 15 yrs., Dir. of K.C. Power & Light Co.; **HOME ADD:** 1000 W. 66th St., Kansas City, MO 64113, (816)444-9184; **BUS ADD:** 800 W. 47th St., Suite 212, Kansas City, MO 64112, (816)531-2195.

SHWEIKI, Jacob——**B:** Jan. 3, 1933, Jerusalem, Israel, *Pres.*, Jacob Shweiki, Realty; **PRIM RE ACT:** Broker, Consultant, Developer, Owner/Investor; **OTHER RE ACT:** Investor; **PREV EMPLOY:** San Antonio Bd. of Realtors; TX Assn. of Realtors; **PROFL AFFIL & HONORS:** NAR; San Antonio Apt. Assn.; **EDUC:** BA, 1964, Educ., Hebrew Univ., Jerusalem, Israel; **GRAD EDUC:** MS, 1972, Counseling, Psych., Butler Univ., Indianapolis, IN; **HOME TEL:** (512)696-8392; **BUS ADD:** 9315 Ranchero, San Antonio, TX 78240, (512)349-5555.

SHYNE, C. Michael——**B:** May 18, 1949, St. Louis, MO, *Pres.*, West Source Realtors, Inc.; **PRIM RE ACT:** Broker, Syndicator, Developer, Builder, Property Manager, Owner/Investor; **SERVICES:** Investment Advising of Sunbent RE, Synd. of Comml. RE, Subdiv., Devel. and Mktg, Pro. Mgmt.; **REP CLIENTS:** Indiv. and Retirement Funds Investing in Raw Comml. Land for Capital Gains only; **PREV EMPLOY:** Subdiv. Devel. Prop. Mgmt., Shyne Realtors, 1964-1973; RE Broker, Shyne Realtors 1972-1974; **PROFL AFFIL & HONORS:** RNMI; **EDUC:** BA, 1972, Educ. & Arch., AZ State Univ.; **OTHER ACT & HONORS:** Pres. and Founder, Southwest Humanities, Pvt. Charitable Found.; **BUS ADD:** 1211 Cuba Ave., PO Box 1705, Alamogordo, NM 88310, (505)437-0220.

SIBBALD, James W.——**B:** Feb. 19, 1948, Longview, WA, *Asst.-Secretary Manager, Douglas Cty.*, Transamerica Title Ins. Co.; **PRIM RE ACT:** Insuror; **SERVICES:** Title insurance, escrow closing, builder's servs.; **REP CLIENTS:** Lenders, brokers, builders, investors, attys.; **PREV EMPLOY:** Assocs. Fin. Servs. of OR, Inc. 1975-76; **PROFL AFFIL & HONORS:** Amer. Land Title Assn.; OR Escrow Council, Inc.; OR Land Title Assn.; OR Assn. of Realtors; Nat. Assn. of Homebuilders, Pres. - Oregon Escrow Council, Inc. (1981-82); **OTHER ACT & HONORS:** BPOE; Optimists Intl., Sutherlin Knolls Golf Assn.; **BUS ADD:** 308 S.E. Jackson St. (P.O. Box 1609), Roseburg, OR 97470, (503)672-6651.

SIBELMAN, Howard——**B:** Jan. 18, 1948, Brooklyn, NY, *Partner*, Laventhol & Horwath; **OTHER RE ACT:** CPA; **SERVICES:** Acctg., Auditing, Private and Public Offerings; **REP CLIENTS:** RE Syndicators, Devels., Mgmt. Cos., Public RE Partnerships; **PROFL AFFIL & HONORS:** AICPA; CA Soc. of CPAs; **EDUC:** BS, 1968, Acctg., Brooklyn Coll.; **GRAD EDUC:** MBT, In Progress, Taxation, Univ. of So. CA; **EDUC HONORS:** Cum Laude; Honors in Economics; **MIL SERV:** USAR, Sgt.; **OTHER ACT & HONORS:** Bd. of Trustees, Temple Judea, Tarzana, CA; **BUS ADD:** 3700 Wilshire Blvd., Ste. 900, Los Angeles, CA 90010, (213)381-5393.

SIBLEY, Donald A.——**B:** Sept. 4, 1935, Buffalo, NY, *Asst. Mgr. RE & Prop. Devel.*, Agway, Inc., Fin. & Control; **PRIM RE ACT:** Engineer, Developer, Owner/Investor, Property Manager; **OTHER RE ACT:** Corp. RE - Asst. Mgr.; **SERVICES:** Manage corp. RE & prop. devel.; **PROFL AFFIL & HONORS:** NACORE, Profl. Engr. in 11 N.E. States; **GRAD EDUC:** Assoc. in Applied Sci. - Engrg., 1975, Engrg., Univ. of Buffalo; **MIL SERV:** US Army, Specialist II; **OTHER ACT & HONORS:** Syracuse Track Club - Member; **HOME ADD:** 5830 S. Coventry Rd., E. Syracuse, NY 13215, (315)656-8435; **BUS ADD:** Box 4933, Syracuse, NY 13221, (315)477-7386.

SIBLEY, Harper, Jr.——**B:** May 2, 1927, Rochester, NY, *Pres*, FMI Financial Corp.; **PRIM RE ACT:** Developer, Builder, Owner/Investor, Property Manager; **OTHER RE ACT:** Chmn. Ocean Reef Club, Key Largo, FL, Hotel & Resort Op; **EDUC:** 1949, Hist., Princeton Univ.; **MIL SERV:** US Army, Lt.; **OTHER ACT & HONORS:** Also associated with, Boca Grande Club, Boca Grande, FL, Pres.; **HOME ADD:** 10640 S.W. 53rd Ave., Miami, FL 33156, (305)665-6523; **BUS ADD:** 801 41st St., Miami, FL 33140, (305)532-7361.

SIBLEY, Robert Dale——**B:** Nov. 3, 1948, Bogalusa, LA, *Owner*, Dale Sibley and Assoc.; **PRIM RE ACT:** Broker, Appraiser, Property Manager, Owner/Investor; **EDUC:** BA, 1970, Poli. Sci. & Hist., S.E. LA Univ.; **HOME ADD:** 111 Herwig Bluff Rd., Slidell, LA 70458, (504)641-4634; **BUS ADD:** 1825 Old Spanish Trail, Slidell, LA 70458, (504)641-7691.

SICHERMAN, Marvin Allen——**B:** Dec. 27, 1934, Cleveland, OH, *Atty. and Pres.*, Dettelbach & Sicherman Co., L. P. A.; **PRIM RE ACT:** Attorney; **SERVICES:** Legal representation; **REP CLIENTS:** Comml. and instnl. lenders, corporate and indiv. investors and owners; **PROFL AFFIL & HONORS:** Amer., OH, Greater Cleveland and Cuyahoga Cty. Bar Assns., and Comml. Law League of Amer., Contributor to legal journals and lecturer at educ. seminars and programs; **EDUC:** BA, 1957, Liberal Arts, Case-Western Reserve Univ. (Adelbert Coll.); **GRAD EDUC:** LLB and JD, 1960 and 1968, Law, Case-Western Reserve Univ. (Law School); **EDUC HONORS:** Poli. Sci. Hon., Debate Team, Editorial Bd. of Law Review, Moot Ct. Bd. 1958-60; **OTHER ACT & HONORS:** Member Bd. of Educ., Beachwood, OH 1978-198- & Pres. 1981; Jewish Chautaqua Soc.; Zeta Beta Tau; Fairmount Temple (Bd. of Tr. of Brotherhood 1968-76); Beachwood Civil League; Beachwood Arts Council, Bd. of Tr. 1975-198-; **HOME ADD:** 24500 Albert Lane, Beachwood, OH 44122, (216)464-1244; **BUS ADD:** 1300 Ohio Savings Plaza, 1801 East Ninth St., Cleveland, OH 44114, (216)696-6000.

SIDERS, Ron——*VP Corp Dev.*, Robbins & Myers, Inc.; **PRIM RE ACT:** Property Manager; **BUS ADD:** 1400 Winters Bank Tower, Dayton, OH 45423.*

SIDES, Dorothy Hunt——**B:** Jan. 20, 1933, Norfolk, VA, *Pres.*, Quality RE, Inc. Gallery of Homes; **PRIM RE ACT:** Broker; **SERVICES:** Residential & Comml. RE; **REP CLIENTS:** Kraft, Travomatic, Homequity; **PROFL AFFIL & HONORS:** NAR, RNMI, WCR, AAWW, CCBR, CRB, Who's Who of Amer. Women; **EDUC:** BA, 1955, Hist. & Educ., Meredith Coll., Raleigh, NC; **GRAD EDUC:** Admin., Not complete, Calif. State; **OTHER ACT & HONORS:** Pres. of AAWW (CU Branch), C of C; **HOME ADD:** Lyndhurst Village Court, Champaign, IL 61820, (217)359-4437; **BUS ADD:** 501 S Mattis Ave., Champaign, IL 61820, (217)351-1988.

SIEBRECHT, James K.——**B:** Nov. 2, 1918, Rome, GA, *Owner*, James K. Siebrecht Agency; **PRIM RE ACT:** Broker, Consultant, Appraiser, Banker, Developer, Syndicator; **PREV EMPLOY:** Own business since 1950; **PROFL AFFIL & HONORS:** AIREA; Amer. Soc. of RE Counselors; **EDUC:** BS/BA, 1941, Univ. of FL; **MIL SERV:** US Army, Capt., WWII, 1941-1945; **HOME ADD:** 425 Brazilian Ave., Palm Beach, FL 33480, (305)655-1290; **BUS ADD:** 320 Royal Palm Way, Palm Beach, FL 33480, (305)655-7034.

SIEFEL, Robert H.——**B:** Feb. 23, 1948, New Britain, CT, *Pres.*, Century 21 Har-Bur Realty; **PRIM RE ACT:** Broker, Appraiser; **SERVICES:** RE brokerage and appraising; **PROFL AFFIL & HONORS:** Gr. Hartford Bd. of Realtors, Realtor; **EDUC:** BBA, 1970, Mktg., Central CT State Coll.; **MIL SERV:** Nat. Guard, Sgt.; **OTHER ACT & HONORS:** Burlington Jaycees; **HOME ADD:** Stafford Rd., Burlington, CT 06013, (203)673-0589; **BUS ADD:** Harwinton Profl. Bldg., Harwinton, CT 06791, (203)485-1805.

SIEGEL, Leonard——**B:** Apr. 12, 1950, Inglewood, CA, *Principal*, Kehr, Siegél & DeMeter, PC; **PRIM RE ACT:** Attorney; **SERVICES:** RE Law and Condo. Law; **REP CLIENTS:** Condo. Assns. and Devels.; **PROFL AFFIL & HONORS:** Community Assns. Inst., Pres. (1980-81, 1981-82) Los Angeles/San Fernando Valley Chap.; Member CA State Bar Comm. on Cooperatives and Condos.; **EDUC:** BS, 1971, Econ., UCLA; **GRAD EDUC:** JD, 1974, Loyola Law School Los Angeles; **EDUC HONORS:** Note Editor Loyola Law Review, St. Thomas More Honor Soc.; **OTHER ACT & HONORS:** Publication: "Aliens & Practice of Law", Loyola Law Review (1973); **HOME ADD:** 5405 Senford Ave., Los Angeles, CA 90056, (213)390-6749; **BUS ADD:** Suite 1760, 1875 Century Park East, Los Angeles, CA 90067, (213)552-9681.

SIEGEL, Leonard S.——B: June 21, 1918, Winooski, VT, *Gen. Counsel, Exec. VP, Legal*, MEGO Intl. Inc.; **PRIM RE ACT:** Attorney; **SERVICES:** Handle RE matters for Mego Intl., Inc. & subs. worldwide; **PREV EMPLOY:** 25 yrs. was in Gen. practice of law, specializing in RE; **PROFL AFFIL & HONORS:** ABA, Amer. Importers Assn., Harvard Legal Aid Soc.; **EDUC:** BA, 1939, Poli. Soc., Hist., NYU; **GRAD EDUC:** LLB/JD, 1942, Harvard Law School; **EDUC HONORS:** Won scholarships for each of 3 yrs., Member of Harvard Legal Aid.; **MIL SERV:** USAAF, Sgt.; **OTHER ACT & HONORS:** Past Master Masonic Lodge, Grand Rep. of ND (Masons), Past Comdr. of Masonic War Vets., Controller of 8th Masonic Dist. Assn. of Man.; **HOME ADD:** 1 Stuyvesant Oval, New York, NY 10009, (212)673-0432; **BUS ADD:** 41 Madison Ave., New York, NY 10010, (212)532-6333.

SIEGEL, Michael H.——B: Sep. 24, 1948, Bronx, NY, *VP & Branch Mgr.*, Cushman & Wakefield of CT. Inc.; **PRIM RE ACT:** Broker, Consultant, Property Manager; **SERVICES:** RE Brokerage, Consulting Inc.; **MIL SERV:** USA, 1967-69, Sgt., E-5, Purple Heart, Combat Infantry Badge, Good Conduct, Unit Citation; **OTHER ACT & HONORS:** RE Bd. NYC; **HOME ADD:** 403 Pinetree Dr., Orange, CT 06477, (203)795-3905; **BUS ADD:** 1111 Summer St., Stamford, CT 06905, (203)348-8550.

SIEGELBAUM, David A.——*Mgr. of Info. Services*, Fifield Palmer & Co.; **PRIM RE ACT:** Developer; **BUS ADD:** 101 N. Wacker Dr., Ste 1200, Chicago, IL 60606, (312)853-3700.*

SIEGLER, S.——*Gen. Mgr. Prop. Bldgs. & Services*, The Foxboro Co.; **PRIM RE ACT:** Property Manager; **BUS ADD:** 38 Neponset Ave., Foxboro, MA 02035, (617)543-8750.*

SIEGMAN, Jerome——B: May 1, 1941, New York, NY, *Atty.*, Ireland, Stapleton & Pryor, P.C.; **PRIM RE ACT:** Attorney; **SERVICES:** Legal advice; **REP CLIENTS:** The Snowmass Co., Ltd.; Harold A. Simpson & Assoc. Development Co.; **PROFL AFFIL & HONORS:** Denver, CO and ABA; RESSI; **EDUC:** AB, 1961, Hist., Cornell Univ.; **GRAD EDUC:** LLB, 1964, Law, Fordham Univ. School of Law; **EDUC HONORS:** Law Review; **OTHER ACT & HONORS:** Law Clerk to Hon. Ben J. Rabin, App. Div. 1st Dept. New York; Frequent Lecturer on Securities Aspects of RE Synds.; Structuring RE Synd.; Author, *Federal State Securities Law Aspects of RE Synd.; Structuring the RE Synd.*, Published by CO RESSI; Northwest Ctr. for Continuing Legal Education; **HOME ADD:** 5600 E. Oxford Ave., Englewood, CO 80111, (303)757-5348; **BUS ADD:** 1675 Broadway, Denver, CO 80202, (303)623-2700.

SIEVERT, Clarence C.——B: Jan. 16, 1921, Seattle, WA, *Owner-Broker*, Sievert's Realty; **PRIM RE ACT:** Broker, Consultant, Owner/Investor; **SERVICES:** Investment counseling, Comml., Indus. and Land Sales; **REP CLIENTS:** Lenders and indiv. or instnl. investors in Comml. prop.; **PROFL AFFIL & HONORS:** CCIM; NAR; Cert. Prop. Exchanger, Realtor of the yr. 1960; **MIL SERV:** USN, Seaman 1st Class; **OTHER ACT & HONORS:** Planning Commnr., Lynnwood, WA 1967, Elks Club, S. Snohomish Cty. C. Of C. Snohomish Cty. Econ. Council; **HOME ADD:** 18532 - 52nd Ave. W. #E-8, Lynnwood, WA 98036, (206)771-3323; **BUS ADD:** 3810 - 196th SW Suite 12, Lynnwood, WA 98036, (206)776-2124.

SIGAL, Gerald——B: May 8, 1935, Bethlehem, PA, *Atty.*, Bingaman, Hess, Coblentz & Bell; **PRIM RE ACT:** Attorney; **SERVICES:** Legal; **REP CLIENTS:** Banks, borrowers, devels., sellers, mcpl. planning commns., zoning hearing bds., mcpl. tax assessors; **PROFL AFFIL & HONORS:** PA Bar Assn., Berks Cty. Bar Assn.; **EDUC:** AB, 1955, Econ. - Govt., Lafayette Coll.; **GRAD EDUC:** LLB, 1958, Corps. - Investment Banking, Univ. of VA; **HOME ADD:** 520 Stephen Rd., Greenfields, Reading, PA 19601, (215)372-7335; **BUS ADD:** 601 Penn St., Reading, PA 19601, (215)374-2261.

SIGLER, John N.——B: Jan. 19, 1944, Columbus, OH, *Pres.*, Sigler & Co., Inc.; **PRIM RE ACT:** Broker, Attorney, Syndicator, Consultant, Appraiser, Developer, Property Manager, Owner/Investor; **EDUC:** AB, 1965, Math./Econ., Princeton Univ.; **GRAD EDUC:** MS, MBA, JD, 1965, 1970, 1976, Mgmt. Sci. - Bus. Fin. Law, Johns Hopkins, Columbia, MD; **OTHER ACT & HONORS:** CPA, MD; **BUS ADD:** 2433 Maryland Ave., Baltimore, MD 21218, (301)235-7777.

SIKORSKI, Robert S.——B: June 20, 1948, New York, NY, *Atty./Broker*, Robert S. Sikorski; **PRIM RE ACT:** Broker, Attorney; **PROFL AFFIL & HONORS:** ABA; **EDUC:** BA, 1969, Poli. Sci., SUNY- Buffalo; **GRAD EDUC:** JD, 1972, Law, St. John's Univ. Sch. of Law; **MIL SERV:** US Army/Jag, Capt.; **HOME ADD:** 62-31 82nd St., Middle Village, NY 11379, (212)458-5427; **BUS ADD:** 66-12 Fresh Pond Rd., Ridgewood, NJ 07485, (212)386-5008.

SILBER, Mark E.——B: June 11, 1944, Cleveland, OH, *Pres.*, Lexington Capital Corp.; **PRIM RE ACT:** Consultant, Owner/Investor, Syndicator; **SERVICES:** Invest. consultation, development & synd.; **REP CLIENTS:** Indiv., instit. and for. investors in comml. props.; **PREV EMPLOY:** VP of Acquisitions for Oppenheimer Props., Inc. and Integrated Resources, Inc.; **PROFL AFFIL & HONORS:** NASD, RE Broker; **EDUC:** BBA, 1966, Fin., Acctg., Univ. of WI; **GRAD EDUC:** MS, 1969, Urban Land Econ., Invest., Corp. Fin., Univ. of IL; **EDUC HONORS:** Teaching Instr. of Research Asst.; **HOME ADD:** Chappaqua, NY; **BUS ADD:** 441 Lexington Ave., Suite 1501, New York, NY 10017, (212)286-9770.

SILBER, Norman J.——B: Apr. 18, 1945, Tampa, FL, *Atty.-at-Law*, Norman J. Silber, P.A.; **PRIM RE ACT:** Attorney; **SERVICES:** Gen. legal serv., including securities and litigation; **REP CLIENTS:** Indiv. and instnl. investors, lenders and synd. (private and public); **PREV EMPLOY:** Exec. VP - I.R.E. Fin. Corp. (synd.) 1972-76; **PROFL AFFIL & HONORS:** FL Bar Assn. (Comm. on Securities), ABA, Dade Cty. Bar Assn., Assn. of Trial Lawyers of Amer. and Academy of FL Trial Lawyers; **EDUC:** BA, 1967, Eng., Chemistry, Tulane Univ.; **GRAD EDUC:** JD, 1969, Law, Tulane Univ. School of Law; **EDUC HONORS:** Omicron Delta Kappa; Kappa Delta Phi; **HOME ADD:** 1232 Palermo Ave., Coral Gables, FL 33134, (305)447-9712; **BUS ADD:** 100 N. Biscayne Blvd., Suite 2702, Miami, FL 33132, (305)371-2130.

SILER, Robert W., Jr.——B: Aug. 16, 1928, Siler City, NC, *Pres.*, Hammer, Siler, George Assoc.; **PRIM RE ACT:** Consultant, Developer, Owner/Investor; **SERVICES:** Mkt. Analysis, Pre-devel. planning, Econ. feasibility studies for R.E.; **REP CLIENTS:** Comml. banks, Lenders; devel., retail stores, local govts.; **PROFL AFFIL & HONORS:** ULI; APA; Lamba Alpha; **EDUC:** AB, 1953, Pol. Sci., Univ. of NC; **GRAD EDUC:** M in Urban planning, 1955, Univ. of NC; **EDUC HONORS:** Phi Beta Kappa; **MIL SERV:** USN, PO1; **HOME ADD:** 601 G St., S.W., Wash., DC 20024, (202)554-2018; **BUS ADD:** 1140 Connecticut Ave., Washington, DC 20036, (202)223-1100.

SILLCOCKS, H. Jackson——B: Mar. 30, 1907, New York, NY, *Counsel, Partner, 1962-77*, Trubin, Sillcocks, Edelman & Knapp; **PRIM RE ACT:** Consultant, Attorney, Real Estate Publisher; **SERVICES:** Preparation & supv. of RE legal forms; surv. of foreclosures; advice to partners and assoc. on RE matters; handling certain indiv. matters; **PREV EMPLOY:** Gould & Wilkie, 1931-34; Tanner Sillcocks & Friend, 1934-49, Partner 1949-54; VP and Assoc. Counsel, Webb & Mnapp, Inc. 1954-62; **PROFL AFFIL & HONORS:** Assn. of the Bar of the City of NY; NY State Bar; ABA; **EDUC:** BA, 1928, Eng., Yale Univ.; **GRAD EDUC:** LLB, 1931, Harvard Law School; **OTHER ACT & HONORS:** Dir., First Capital Props. Corp., Coral Beach, FL; **HOME ADD:** 45 W. 54th St., New York, NY 10019, (212)581-7164; **BUS ADD:** 375 Park Ave., New York, NY 10152, (212)759-5400.

SILNY, Fred——*RE Mgr.*, Carnation Co.; **PRIM RE ACT:** Property Manager; **BUS ADD:** 5045 Wilshire Blvd., Los Angeles, CA 90036, (213)932-6000.*

SILVER, Bernard F.——B: June 24, 1943; **PRIM RE ACT:** Consultant, Attorney, Developer, Lender; **REP CLIENTS:** Lenders & indiv. investors in comml. props.; **EDUC:** BS, 1964, Econ., Wharton Sch., Univ. of PA; **GRAD EDUC:** JD, 1969, Columbia Sch. of Law; LLM, 1981, Tax., Univ. of Miami Sch. of Law; **MIL SERV:** USAR, 1st Lt., 1965-67; **BUS ADD:** 3550 W Fairview St., Miami, FL 33133, (305)856-3065.

SILVER, Robert C.——B: Jan. 26, 1930, NY, *Atty.*, Hale, Sanderson, Byrnes & Morton; **PRIM RE ACT:** Attorney; **OTHER RE ACT:** Investor; Tax Advisor; **SERVICES:** Legal, Tax and Investment Planning; **PROFL AFFIL & HONORS:** ABA, Real Prop. Sect.; MA Bar Assn.; Boston Bar Assn.; Amer. Judicature Soc.; **EDUC:** AB, 1951, Columbia Univ.; **GRAD EDUC:** JD, 1960, Harvard Law School; **MIL SERV:** USN, Lt. Comdr.; **HOME ADD:** 16 Emerson Pl., Boston, MA 02114; **BUS ADD:** Ten Post Office Sq., Boston, MA 02109, (617)402-1107.

SILVERANG, Kevin J.——B: Apr. 22, 1955, Brooklyn, NY, *Atty.*, Pepper, Hamilton & Scheetz; **PRIM RE ACT:** Attorney; **SERVICES:** Legal representation, Negotiation; **REP CLIENTS:** Lenders, Inst. Investors in comml. props., Devel. of Condo./Time Sharing Props.; **PROFL AFFIL & HONORS:** ABA, RE & Probate Section; PA Bar Assn., RE Section; **EDUC:** BA, 1977, Gvt., Local Gvt., Pol. Sci., Franklin & Marshall Coll.; **GRAD EDUC:** JD, 1980, Real Prop. Law, Villanova; **EDUC HONORS:** Cum Laude, Law Review-Assoc. Editor, Order of the Coif; **HOME ADD:** 219 Sugartown Rd., Wayne, PA 19087, (215)964-9119; **BUS ADD:** 123 S Broad St., Philadelphia, PA 19109, (215)893-4507.

SILVERFIELD, Gary Daniel——**B:** May 10, 1947, Columbia, SC, *Pres.*, Stokes & Company Realty Group, Inc.; **PRIM RE ACT:** Broker, Developer; **SERVICES:** RE devel. and sales; **PREV EMPLOY:** Sr. Appraiser, Prudential Ins. Co., 1971-1973; VP, Barnett Winston Co., 1973-1975; VP, Mercury Luggage Mfg. Co., 1975-1978; **PROFL AFFIL & HONORS:** Nat. Assn. of Homebuilders, MBAA, NAR, Council for Rural Housing and Devel.; **EDUC:** BS, 1969, Bus. and Fin., Washington & Lee Univ.; **GRAD EDUC:** MBA, 1971, Fin. and Mktg., Univ. of SC; **EDUC HONORS:** Who's Who in Amer. Colls. & Univs., Outstanding Coll. Athletes of Amer., Beta Gamma Sigma; **MIL SERV:** US Air Nat. Guard, Staff Sgt.; **OTHER ACT & HONORS:** Jacksonville Zoning Bd. (apptd.), The Deerwood Club, The Univ. Club, Beauclerc Ctry. Club, The Tournament Players Club and The Meninak Club; **HOME ADD:** 8028 Acorn Ridge Rd., Jacksonville, FL 32216, (904)641-0954; **BUS ADD:** 4319 Salisbury Rd., Jacksonville, FL 32216, (904)731-8170.

SILVERMAN, Alexander——*Secretary*, American Association of Business Brokers; **OTHER RE ACT:** Profl. Assn. Admin.; **BUS ADD:** 41 State St., Suite 508, Albany, NY 12207, (518)462-0395.*

SILVERMAN, Leon——**B:** Apr. 14, 1940, New York, NY, *Sr. VP/Treas.*, The Lansco Corporation; **PRIM RE ACT:** Broker, Builder, Owner/Investor; **SERVICES:** We build, lease and manage office bldgs. & shopping ctrs.; **PROFL AFFIL & HONORS:** RE Bd. of NY - BOMA; Intl/Council of Shopping Centers; **EDUC:** BS, 1962, Fin., NY Univ.; **MIL SERV:** U.S. Army; **HOME ADD:** New York, NY; **BUS ADD:** 122 E. 42nd St., New York, NY 10168, (212)867-5555.

SILVERMAN, Ronald H.——**B:** Aug. 18, 1938, Toledo, OH, *VP, RE Devel. & Mktg.*, Security Mortgage Co./Turco Devel. Co.; **PRIM RE ACT:** Developer, Owner/Investor, Property Manager; **SERVICES:** full serv. RE develop., subs. of mort. banker; **PREV EMPLOY:** May Department Stores, Beneficial Standard Properties; **EDUC:** BA, Pre-law, Univ. of San Fernando Valley; **GRAD EDUC:** LLB, 1966, Law, Univ. of San Fernando Valley; **MIL SERV:** USAF Res.; **HOME ADD:** 7544 York, Apt. 3W, Clayton, MO 63105; **BUS ADD:** 929 Fee Fee Rd., Suite 200, Maryland Heights, MO 63043, (314)434-6300.

SILVERSHEIN, Bennett——**B:** July 17, 1933, Brooklyn, NY, Silvershein Assoc.; **PRIM RE ACT:** Developer, Builder, Owner/Investor; **PREV EMPLOY:** Treas., Furman Wolfson Investment Trust Assoc., Realty Investors Dev. Corp.; **PROFL AFFIL & HONORS:** ICSC; **EDUC:** 1955, Bus. Admin./Mktg.-Fin., Rider Coll.; **MIL SERV:** USA, Specialist 4; **OTHER ACT & HONORS:** Bd. Membership, St. Clares Hosp., Denville, NJ, White Meadow Temple Rockaway, NJ, Community Mental Health Ctr., Denville, NJ; **HOME ADD:** 23 Lake Shore Dr., Rockaway, NJ 07866, (201)627-1240; **BUS ADD:** 11 East 44th St., NY, NY 10017, (212)599-0550.

SILVERSTEIN, Cathy——*Ed.*, Mattco Equities, Apt. Management Newsletter; **PRIM RE ACT:** Real Estate Publisher; **BUS ADD:** 48 W. 21st St., New York, NY 10010, (212)741-2100.*

SILVERSTEIN, F. Jerome——**B:** Mar. 7, 1921, Hartford, CT, *Owner*, F. Jerome Silverstein, Realty; **PRIM RE ACT:** Broker, Appraiser; **SERVICES:** Appraisals; **REP CLIENTS:** Lending instns., investors, attys.; **PROFL AFFIL & HONORS:** AIREA; Soc. of RE Appraisers; NAR, MAI; SRPA; **EDUC:** BS, 1947, RE, Univ. of CT; **MIL SERV:** USAF, S/Sgt., 1941-1944; **OTHER ACT & HONORS:** Chmn., New London Redevel. Agency 1958-1978; CT RE Commn. 1964-present; Masons, Shrine, Elks; **HOME ADD:** 1065 Ocean Ave., New London, CT 06320, (203)442-8827; **BUS ADD:** 228 Captains Walk, P.O. Box 150, New London, CT 06320, (203)444-7000.

SILVERSTEIN, Stephen——**B:** July 5, 1948, Lowell, MA, *Sr. VP, Fin. Operations*, Playboy Enterprises, Inc.; **PRIM RE ACT:** Developer, Builder, Owner/Investor, Syndicator; **EDUC:** BBA, 1970, Econ., Univ. of MA; **GRAD EDUC:** MBA, 1972, Fin., Univ. of Chicago; **EDUC HONORS:** Magna Cum Laude, Dean's List; **MIL SERV:** USAF, 2nd Lt.; **OTHER ACT & HONORS:** Amer. Mgmt. Assn.; Amer. Fin. Assn.; Soc. of Intl. Treasurers; **HOME ADD:** 1780 Robinwood Ln., Riverwoods, IL 60015, (312)945-3733; **BUS ADD:** 919 N. Michigan Ave., Chicago, IL 60611, (312)751-8000.

SILVEY, Frederic R.——**B:** Apr. 24, 1912, San Francisco, CA, *Pres.*, Americus Inc.; **PRIM RE ACT:** Broker, Developer, Builder, Owner/Investor, Property Manager, Syndicator; **SERVICES:** Devel. subdivs. and income props.; **REP CLIENTS:** Americus Intl. and Silvan Co.; **PROFL AFFIL & HONORS:** IREM; County Costa Bd. of Realtors; Assoc. Bldg. Indus.; Sonoma Cty. Bd. of Realtors, CPM; **EDUC:** AA, 1932, Chem. Engrg., Diablo Valley Coll.; AA, 1980, Hotel & Rest. Mgmt., Diablo Valley Coll.; **OTHER ACT & HONORS:** Past Dist. Gov., Kiwanis Intl.; Walnut Creek Kiwanis Club; Redwood City F&AM, #168; **HOME ADD:** 103 Starlyn Dr., Pleasant Hill, CA 94523, (415)934-7589; **BUS ADD:** 1710 Linda Dr., Pleasant Hill, CA 94523, (415)825-3595.

SIMEONE, Victor R.——**B:** Jan. 20, 1929, Buffalo, NY, *Pres.*, Victor R. Simeone, SRA; **PRIM RE ACT:** Consultant, Appraiser; **SERVICES:** RE Appraisals; **REP CLIENTS:** Major lenders, devel., private parties; **PREV EMPLOY:** 25 yrs. of appraisals; **PROFL AFFIL & HONORS:** SREA, SRA, Class IV State of CA; **EDUC:** AA, 1964, RE, Long Beach City Coll.; **MIL SERV:** US Signal Corps, Cpl.; **OTHER ACT & HONORS:** Past Pres., Chapter 94, SREA, Long Beach, CA; **HOME ADD:** 1060 Alejo Rd., Palm Springs, CA 92262; **BUS ADD:** POB 285, Cypress, CA 90630, (714)323-2109.

SIMI, Dante R.——**B:** July 20, 1939, Lancaster, CA, *Pres.*, Simi RE Co.; **PRIM RE ACT:** Broker, Consultant, Developer, Syndicator; **SERVICES:** Resid. and Devel. Sales, Mktg. Research and Analysis; **REP CLIENTS:** Lenders and indiv. or instit. investors in resid. devel.; **PROFL AFFIL & HONORS:** Building Industry Assn. of San Joaquin Valley, CA Assn. of Realtors; **EDUC:** BA, 1962, Liberal Arts, Bus. & Mktg. Minors, Fresno State Univ.; **GRAD EDUC:** MBA, Tulane Univ.; **OTHER ACT & HONORS:** Dir. of Fig Garden Rotary; Dir., Fresno Metropolitan Mus.; **BUS ADD:** 225 W. Shaw, Fresno, CA 93711, (209)226-1190.

SIMKINS, James H.——**B:** Knoxville, TN, *Pres.*, James H. Simkins Co., Inc.; **PRIM RE ACT:** Broker, Property Manager; **SERVICES:** Mgmt. Sales; **PROFL AFFIL & HONORS:** IREM, CPM; **EDUC:** BA, 1942, Furman Univ.; **MIL SERV:** USAF, Pvt.; **OTHER ACT & HONORS:** 14 Yrs, Greenville, SC Cty. Council Interim Mayor, Past Pres. Greeneville Jaycees, Past Pres. SC Jaycees, Past Pres. Greenville Cty Mental Health Assoc., Past Pres. SC Mental Health Assoc.; **HOME ADD:** 105 Morningdale Dr., Greenville, SC 29609, (803)233-5692; **BUS ADD:** 1922 Augusta St., Greenville, SC 29605, (803)271-2323.

SIMMER, Barry——*VP*, IRF Financial Corp., Private Synd.; **PRIM RE ACT:** Syndicator; **OTHER RE ACT:** Packaging & mktg. of private placement; **SERVICES:** Mktg, synd., seminar lectures, broker/dealer visit, broker dealer comm.; **BUS ADD:** 200 So. Dixie Hwy, Miami, FL 33313, (305)858-6750.

SIMMONS, Lawrence F.——**B:** Nov. 24, 1945, Philadelphia, PA, *Prop. Mgr.*, Zalco Realty, Inc.; **PRIM RE ACT:** Property Manager; **SERVICES:** Complete prop. mgmt. servs.; **PREV EMPLOY:** Amer. Invesco, Landon & Co.; **PROFL AFFIL & HONORS:** PMA, AOBA, Landlord/Tenant Comm., Prin. George Cty., Lic. Stationary Engrg. Outstanding Young Men of Amer., 1977; **EDUC:** 1977, Bus. Admin., MD Univ.; **MIL SERV:** USA, E-4, Good Conduct; **HOME ADD:** 14954 Belle Ami Dr., Laurel, MD, (301)953-9269; **BUS ADD:** 8555 16th St., Silver Spring, MD 20910, (301)588-5055.

SIMMONS, Raymond J.——*Group VP*, Tokheim; **PRIM RE ACT:** Property Manager; **BUS ADD:** PO Box 360, Fort Wayne, IN 46801, (219)423-2552.*

SIMMONS, Richard D.——**B:** May 20, 1922, Fall River, MA, *Prin.*, Simmons Associates; **PRIM RE ACT:** Broker, Consultant, Appraiser, Owner/Investor, Instructor, Syndicator; **OTHER RE ACT:** Faculty & Curriculum Advisor, Bentley Coll., Dept. of Cont. Educ.; **SERVICES:** Counseling, appraisals, ltd. partnerships; **REP CLIENTS:** Atty, bus. firms, corp., indiv., mcpl. govt., inst., govt. entities, quasi-judicial & govt. entities; **PROFL AFFIL & HONORS:** Amer. Soc. RE Counselors; Nat. Assn. Review Appraisers; MA Bd. of RE Appraisers, CRE; CRA; MRA; **MIL SERV:** US Army, 1st Lt.; **OTHER ACT & HONORS:** Conservation Commn., Lynnfield, 1980-1981; Downtown Club; **HOME ADD:** 45 Walnut St., Lynnfield, MA 01940, (617)334-4558; **BUS ADD:** POB 671, Lynnfield, MA 01940, (617)246-3288.

SIMMONS, Roger——*Mgr. Asset Adm.*, Reynolds, R.J., Industries; **PRIM RE ACT:** Property Manager; **BUS ADD:** World Headquarters Bldg., PO Box 2959, Winston-Salem, NC 27102, (919)773-2000.*

SIMMONS, T. Freddie——**B:** Dec. 7, 1934, Toccoa, GA, *Pres.*, T. Freddie Simmons, MAI Appraisers & Consultants; **PRIM RE ACT:** Consultant, Appraiser; **SERVICES:** RE Appraising & Consulting; **REP CLIENTS:** Decatur Fed. S & L Assn.; Trust Co. Bank; C & S Natl. Bank; GA Dept. of Trans; Dept. Nat. Resources; Atlanta Gas Light Co.; Wms. Bros. Lumber Co.; US Postal Serv.; Aetna Bus. Credit Inv.; Scripto Inc.; Republic Airlines; **PREV EMPLOY:** Frank B. Roberts & Assoc.; **PROFL AFFIL & HONORS:** AIREA, MAI, SRPA; **EDUC:** 1962, RE Maj., GA State Univ.; **MIL SERV:** US Army, SP4; **HOME ADD:** 3993 Bontura Ct., Stone Mt., GA 30083; **BUS ADD:** 315 W. Ponce De Leon Ave., Suite 369, Decatur, GA 30030, (404)374-1423.

SIMMONS, Wilbur E., Jr.——**B:** Dec. 29, 1939, Baltimore, MD, Venable, Baetjer & Howard; **PRIM RE ACT:** Attorney, Consultant; **OTHER RE ACT:** Investment advisor; **SERVICES:** Legal rep. & advice, synd. advice, RE investment advice; **PROFL AFFIL & HONORS:** ABA, MD Bar Assn., RESSI; **EDUC:** BA, 1961, Poli. Sci., Univ. of MD; **GRAD EDUC:** LLB, 1963, Univ. of MD Sch. of Law; LLM, 1965, Yale Univ. Sch. of Law; **EDUC HONORS:** Grad. with Honors, Order of the Coif, Law Review Editor; **OTHER ACT & HONORS:** Asst. Atty. Gen., State of MD, 1969-71; **BUS ADD:** 1800 Mercantile Bank & Tr. Bldg., Two Hopkins Plaza, Baltimore, MD 21201.

SIMMS, William S.——*Pres.*, Cochise Development Corp.; **PRIM RE ACT:** Broker, Developer, Builder, Owner/Investor; **BUS ADD:** 4335 Cobb Pkwy NW, Atlanta, GA 30339.

SIMON, Arnold N.——**B:** Mar. 22, 1932, Philadelphia, PA, *Owner*, Arnold N. Simon; **PRIM RE ACT:** Broker, Property Manager, Syndicator; **PROFL AFFIL & HONORS:** NAHM, RAM; **MIL SERV:** US Army, S/Sgt.; **BUS ADD:** 371 Merrick Rd., Rockville Ctr., NY 11570, (516)764-3010.

SIMON, David E.——**B:** Apr. 1, 1943, Vallejo, CA, *Owner*, David E. Simpson, A Professional Corporation; **PRIM RE ACT:** Attorney, Developer, Syndicator; **SERVICES:** Legal counseling, synd. and devel. of props.; **REP CLIENTS:** Devel., investors; **PROFL AFFIL & HONORS:** ABA, CA Bar Assn., Los Angeles Cty. Bar Assn., Inglewood Bar Assn. (Dir.), Hawthorne/Lawndale Bd. of Realtors (Dir.); **EDUC:** BS, 1965, U.C.L.A.; **GRAD EDUC:** JD, 1968, Law, Univ. S.CA; **OTHER ACT & HONORS:** Kiwanis Club of Hawthorne (Dir.), Hawthorne Family YMCA (Pres.); **BUS ADD:** 12730 Hawthorne Plaza, Hawthorne, CA 90250, (213)973-0474.

SIMON, Franklin Wallace——**B:** June 2, 1924, Boston, MA, *Pres*, Franklin W. Simon Enterprises, Comm. Planning & Devel. Assoc.; **PRIM RE ACT:** Syndicator, Consultant, Developer, Builder, Property Manager; **SERVICES:** Devel., bldr., prop. mgr., synd., RE Advisor; **PREV EMPLOY:** 20 yrs. in RE Devel.; **PROFL AFFIL & HONORS:** Apt. Owners & Mgrs. Assn., Natl. Soc. Home & Bldrs.; **EDUC:** BSME, 1950, Univ. of RI; **GRAD EDUC:** MBA, 1952, Bus., Harvard Grad. School. of Bus.; **EDUC HONORS:** Summa Cum Laude, Tau Beta Pi, Phi Kappa Phi; **MIL SERV:** US Army, Inf. Rangers, Pfc, Silver Star, Bronze Star, Purple Heart with Cluster, 5 Battle Stars; **HOME ADD:** 42 Priscilla Ln., Quincy, MA 02169, (617)479-3410; **BUS ADD:** 10 Forbes Rd., Braintree, MA 02184, (617)848-2500.

SIMON, Howard I.——**B:** Feb. 1, 1931, *Pres.*, Weston Equities, Inc.; **PRIM RE ACT:** Developer, Builder, Owner/Investor; **PROFL AFFIL & HONORS:** RE Bd. of NY, Young Presidents Org., Tr. of Human Resources Ctr., Pres. Advisory Council of Wholsale and Retail Activity; **EDUC:** BS, 1953, Econ., Wharton School, Univ. of PA; **OTHER ACT & HONORS:** Glen Oaks Ctry. Club; **HOME ADD:** 40 Fern Dr., Roslyn, NY 11576, (516)484-2040; **BUS ADD:** One Penn Plaza, Suite 4527, New York, NY 10119, (212)239-1400.

SIMON, Kenneth D.——**B:** Mar. 25, 1918, St. Paul, MN, *Chmn. of Bd. & CEO*, Air Conditioning Co., Inc. (ACCO), Devel.; **PRIM RE ACT:** Developer, Engineer, Builder, Owner/Investor; **SERVICES:** Bldg. (sub-contracting) & servicing (maintenance); Mechanical Contracting (process piping); **REP CLIENTS:** Indus., Comml., Instnl.; **PREV EMPLOY:** With ACCO since 1950; **PROFL AFFIL & HONORS:** Amer. Soc. of Heating, Refrigeration & Air Conditioning; CA Soc. of PE, Profl. CA ME; Registered Engr.; **EDUC:** ME, 1947, Air Conditioning, Heating & Ventilation, Inst. of Technol., Univ. of MN; **GRAD EDUC:** Bus. Admin., 1947, Indus. Engrg. & Mgmt., School of Bus. Admin. - Univ. of MN; **EDUC HONORS:** Hon. Engrg. Soc.; **MIL SERV:** USNR, Lt., Comdr., Bronze Star, Combat Ribbons, Purple Heart, Pre-Pearl Harbors, Overseas Ribbon; European & Pacific Theatre; **OTHER ACT & HONORS:** VP - Glendale C of C; Bd. of Dirs. - Encino S&L; Rgnl. Bd. of Dirs. - Union Bank; Various other corps., religious, charitable, & profl. grps.; Pres., Mechanical Development Corp.; VP - Encino Bowl Corp.; **HOME ADD:** 4156 Longridge Ave., Sherman Oaks, CA 91423, (213)789-2500; **BUS ADD:** 6265 San Fernando Rd., Glendale, CA 91201, (213)244-6571.

SIMON, Mitchell J.——**B:** Jan. 8, 1948, Sturgeon Bay, WI, *Atty. At Law*, Simon & Geres Law Office; **PRIM RE ACT:** Attorney; **SERVICES:** Legal servs. - comml. & resid. RE purch/sale/devel.; **REP CLIENTS:** Comml. Bank, Whitewater, WI., First State S&L Assoc., DLK Enterprises, Inc., Steck Realty; **PROFL AFFIL & HONORS:** WI Bar Assn., Walworth Cty. Assn., ABA & RE Sects. of ABA & WBA; **EDUC:** BS, 1970, Bus. Admin. (Fin., Econ., Mgmt. Sci.), Marquette Univ. School of Bus. Admin.; **GRAD EDUC:** JD, 1973, Law, Marquette Univ. Law School; **EDUC HONORS:** Beta Gamma Sigma (Bus. Hon. Frat.); **HOME ADD:** 211 N. Park St., Whitewater, WI 53190, (414)473-7262; **BUS ADD:** 304 W. Main St., Whitewater, WI 53190, (414)473-6940.

SIMON, Ronald I.——**B:** Nov. 4, 1938, Cairo, Egypt, Ronald I. Simon Inc.; **PRIM RE ACT:** Owner/Investor, Syndicator; **SERVICES:** Fin. consultant, arrange fin.; **PREV EMPLOY:** Exec. VP, Treas., Dir. - Avco Community Devels., Inc. - 1970-1973; **EDUC:** BA, 1960, Econ., Harvard Univ.; **GRAD EDUC:** MA, 1962, Hist., Columbia Univ.; PhD, 1968, Fin. & Acctg., Columbia Univ. Grad. School of Bus.; Ford Foundation Fellowship; **EDUC HONORS:** Cum Laude; **OTHER ACT & HONORS:** Univ. Club - New York City; **HOME ADD:** PO Box 1986, LaJolla, CA 92037, (714)459-1893; **BUS ADD:** 7911 Herschel Ave., LaJolla, CA 92037, (714)459-9764.

SIMONI, Carl David——**B:** May 24, 1947, Philadelphia, PA, *Sr. Assoc.*, Goldschmidt, Fredericks & Oshatz; **PRIM RE ACT:** Attorney; **SERVICES:** Provide legal counseling regarding all facets of RE law; **REP CLIENTS:** Lenders, comml. landlords & tenants, devels., cooperative converters, synds., investors in comml. prop.; **PREV EMPLOY:** Cravath, Swaine & Moore, RE Assoc., 1973-1978; The Ford Found., RE Counsel, 1978-1980; **PROFL AFFIL & HONORS:** ABA, member of RE, Probate & Trust Sec.; FL Bar; NY Bar; **EDUC:** BS, 1969, Econ., St. John's Univ.; **GRAD EDUC:** JD, 1972, Law, St. John's Univ. School of Law; **EDUC HONORS:** Dean's List, Bus. Honors Program, Dean's List, Law Review Member & Editor; **MIL SERV:** US Army, 1st Lt.; **HOME ADD:** 32 Kingsbury Rd., Garden City, NY 11530, (516)742-0275; **BUS ADD:** 655 Madison Ave., New York, NY 11021, (212)838-2424.

SIMONSON, Dale A.——**B:** Mar. 12, 1936, Minneapolis, MN, *Pres.*, Simonson Realty, Inc.; **PRIM RE ACT:** Broker, Consultant, Attorney, Property Manager; **SERVICES:** Brokerage and consulting for comml. indus., and investment props., mgmt. servs.; **REP CLIENTS:** Sellers, users and indiv. and corp. investors; **PREV EMPLOY:** Pvt. law practice; **PROFL AFFIL & HONORS:** RNMI; Upper Midwest CCIM Chapt.; MN Prop. Exchangers; Gr. Minneapolis Bd. of Realtors; **EDUC:** BLL, 1959, Law, Univ. of MN; **GRAD EDUC:** JD, 1959, Univ. of MN Law Sch.; **MIL SERV:** USN Res.; Lt.; **OTHER ACT & HONORS:** Hennepin Cty, Ct. Commn., 1967-70; Kiwanis; Bloomington C of C Bd. of Dirs.; Bloomington Econ. Devel. Commn.; **HOME ADD:** 2815 Overlook Dr., Bloomington, MN 55431, (612)881-5975; **BUS ADD:** 686 W 92nd St., Bloomington, MN 55420, (612)884-7152.

SIMONTON, G. Scott——**B:** Nov. 29, 1946, Jacksonville, FL, *Pres.*, Simonton RE Appraisals; **PRIM RE ACT:** Consultant, Appraiser, Builder, Owner/Investor; **REP CLIENTS:** Lenders; Indiv. and Synd. Investors; **PREV EMPLOY:** Pres. - Antigua Const., Inc.; Part. - Donn & Simonton RE Appraisals; CPA - Haskins & Sells; **PROFL AFFIL & HONORS:** SRA, CRA, CPA; **EDUC:** BS, 1971, Acctg./Fin., Brigham Young Univ.; **HOME ADD:** 2055 E. Kenwood Cir., Mesa, AZ 85203, (602)964-1597; **BUS ADD:** 2055 E. Kenwood Cir., Mesa, AZ 85203, (602)833-5401.

SIMPKINS, R. Douglas, Jr.——**B:** Aug. 16, 1941, Nashville, *Partner*, Dienna/Simpkins Co.; **PRIM RE ACT:** Developer; **SERVICES:** RE Devel., Devel. Consultation; **PREV EMPLOY:** First Mort. Co. of TX, Inc.; Ben G. McGuire & Co.; **PROFL AFFIL & HONORS:** MBA; **EDUC:** BBA, 1964, Bus. Admin., TX Tech. Univ.; **OTHER ACT & HONORS:** Houston Racuet Club, River Oaks Breakfast Club (Pres.-1981); **HOME ADD:** 2921 Avalon Place, Houston, TX 77019, (713)522-2105; **BUS ADD:** 515 S. Post Oak Rd., Suite 810, Houston, TX 77027, (713)621-4343.

SIMPSON, A. Boyd——**B:** Nov. 24, 1948, Lakeland, FL, *Pres.*, Hooker/Barnes, Comml. Div.; **PRIM RE ACT:** Broker, Consultant, Developer; **SERVICES:** Devel. of comml. prop., investment Brokerage counseling; **REP CLIENTS:** Instnl. and significant pvt. investors, Natl. and Local tenants; **PREV EMPLOY:** VP, B.F. Saul Co. (1973-1979); **PROFL AFFIL & HONORS:** NAOIP; NARA; US C of C ; Various RE Bds.; AIIE, CRA; Profl. Engrs.; **EDUC:** BS, 1970, Information and Control Systems, GA Tech.; **GRAD EDUC:** MA, 1972, Fin., Wharton School of Fin. & Commerce; **EDUC HONORS:** Dean's List, Top 20%, Top 15%, Dean's List; **OTHER ACT & HONORS:** Cherokee Town & Ctry.; Atlanta City Club; *Who's Who in Fin. in US*; **HOME ADD:** 1140 Rosedale Rd., Atlanta, GA 30306, (404)876-1741; **BUS ADD:** 2175 Parklake Dr., Suite 250, Atlanta, GA 30345, (404)939-8780.

SIMPSON, Clarence C.——**B:** Aug. 2, 1943, San Antonio, TX, *Nat. Dir. of RE*, Church's Fried Chicken, Inc., Nat. Hdqtrs.; **OTHER RE ACT:** Responsible for the devel. of at least 100 new restaurants per year, Corporate RE Mgmt.; **SERVICES:** Research, identification, negotiation, devel., crop. mgmt. of restaurant locations; **PREV EMPLOY:** Self Employed RE Broker & Appraiser specializing in investment props., 1968-1975; **PROFL AFFIL & HONORS:**

NACORE; NRA; NARA, CRA; **OTHER ACT & HONORS:** Democratic Cty. Chmn., 1972; Outstanding Young Men of Amer., 1975; **HOME ADD:** 111 Lemonwood, San Antonio, TX 78213, (512)344-8892; **BUS ADD:** 302 Spencer Ln., San Antonio, TX 78284, (512)735-9392.

SIMPSON, Fred——*Dir. Fac. & Maint.*, Franklin Mint Corp.; **PRIM RE ACT:** Property Manager; **BUS ADD:** Franklin Center, PA 19091, (215)459-6000.*

SIMPSON, Jerry——*VP*, Harsco Corp.; **PRIM RE ACT:** Property Manager; **BUS ADD:** Camp Hill, PA 17011, (717)763-7064.*

SIMPSON, Joseph J.——**B:** Dec. 17, 1937, New York, NY, *A.V.P.*, Eastern Savings Bank, Construction & Joint Venture; **PRIM RE ACT:** Appraiser, Banker, Developer, Lender, Owner/Investor; **OTHER RE ACT:** Joint Venture Devel.; **SERVICES:** Lending, valuation, joint venture, comml. props., investment counseling; **REP CLIENTS:** Nationwide builders in comml. props.; **PREV EMPLOY:** Marine Midland Realty Credit Corp.; **PROFL AFFIL & HONORS:** Sr. Member Columbia SREA; Rho Epsilon (National RE Fraternity NYC Professional Chapter), CSA; **EDUC:** BS, 1960, Bus. Admin. & Fin., WV Wesleyan Coll.; **MIL SERV:** USA R., Lt.; **HOME ADD:** Wakeman Farms, Sherman, CT 06784, (203)355-0274; **BUS ADD:** 1075 Central Park Ave., Scarsdale, NY 10583, (914)725-5600.

SIMPSON, Lee——*VP Operations*, Louisiana-Pacific Corp.; **PRIM RE ACT:** Property Manager; **BUS ADD:** 1300 SW Fifth Ave., Portland, OR 97201, (503)221-0800.*

SIMPSON, Robert——*VP Fin. & Corp. Dev.*, Southland Royalty Co.; **PRIM RE ACT:** Property Manager; **BUS ADD:** 1000 Fort Worth Club Tower, Fort Worth, TX 76102, (817)390-9200.*

SIMPSON, Robert C.——*VP Industrial Relations*, Twin Disc Inc.; **PRIM RE ACT:** Consultant; **BUS ADD:** 1328 Racine St., Racine, WI 53403, (414)634-1981.*

SIMPSON, Robert L.——**B:** May 16, 1921, Tacoma, Washington, *Pres.*, Robert Simpson Investments, Inc.; **PRIM RE ACT:** Broker, Consultant, Owner/Investor, Instructor; **OTHER RE ACT:** RE Exchange Couselor; **SERVICES:** Author of: "How to Be a Successful RE Exchange Counselor" to be published by Reston Publishing Co. in 1982; **PREV EMPLOY:** Instructor Coastline Community Coll. Dist. Courses taught; Basic RE Exchanging, Advanced RE Exchanging and Creative RE; **PROFL AFFIL & HONORS:** CAR, NAR Orange Coast Exchangors; Magic; Pacific Coast Exchangors, Natl. Exchangors, Ph.D.; **EDUC:** BEd, 1948, Educ., Univ. of WA; **GRAD EDUC:** MA, 1962, Educ. Psych., CA Sate Univ. Los Angeles; PH.D, 1968, Educ. Psych, Univ. of So. CA; **MIL SERV:** USAF, Lt., Usual Cluster; **OTHER ACT & HONORS:** Prof. Emeritus CA State Univ. Fullerton; Lic. Clinical Psych. Neuropsychologist at Rancho Los Amigos Hosp. until 1976. Twenty yrs. in private practice clinical psych. Retired 1977; **HOME ADD:** 16851 Saybrook Lane, Huntington Beach, CA 92649, (213)592-1903; **BUS ADD:** 16851 Saybrook Lane, Huntington Beach, CA 92649, (714)846-7543.

SIMPSON, Wayne E.——*VP - Operations & Planning*, Olin-American, Inc., Subs. of Olin Corp.; **PRIM RE ACT:** Developer, Builder; **SERVICES:** For-sale resid. housing, nat.; **PREV EMPLOY:** Dir. Fin., Member Investment Comm., Olin Corp., Stamford, CT; **PROFL AFFIL & HONORS:** CPA; **EDUC:** BS in Commerce, 1949, Acctg., TX Christian Univ.; **GRAD EDUC:** MBA, 1951, Fin., Harvard Bus. School; **EDUC HONORS:** With Distinction; **HOME ADD:** 897 Dolphin Ct., Danville, CA 94526; **BUS ADD:** PO Box 23172, Pleasant Hill, CA 94523, (415)798-9150.

SIMS, Albert H.——**B:** NYC, *Pres.*, Albert H. Sims Co. Inc.; **PRIM RE ACT:** Broker, Instructor, Consultant, Property Manager; **PROFL AFFIL & HONORS:** IREM, CPA, CPM; **EDUC:** BBA, 1948, CUNY; **GRAD EDUC:** MBA, 1956, CUNY; **MIL SERV:** US Army, Sgt., Pacific & Phillipines Ribbons; **HOME ADD:** 3020 Cpl. Kenney St., Rayside, NY 11361, (212)225-5154; **BUS ADD:** 107 Northern Blvd., Great Neck, NY 11022, (516)482-5756.

SIMS, Charles F.——**B:** Oct. 12, 1936, Greenwood, SC, *VP - Owner*, Cothran, Sims, Barker, Inc.; **PRIM RE ACT:** Broker; **REP CLIENTS:** Merrill Lynch Relocation Mg., etc.; First National Bank of Bartlesville, Equitable Relocation Mgmt.; **PROFL AFFIL & HONORS:** NAR, CRB, GRI, Realtor of the Year in Greenville Bd. (1977); Past Pres. of Same Bd.; **EDUC:** BA, 1958, Furman Unvi.; **OTHER ACT & HONORS:** Lions Club; **HOME ADD:** 408 Sweetwater Rd., Greer, SC 29651, (803)292-2945; **BUS ADD:** 333 Wade Hampton Blvd., Greenville, SC 29609, (803)242-5095.

SIMS, Dennis C.——**B:** Feb. 11, 1942, *Dir.*, Alto Sol Enterprises; **PRIM RE ACT:** Consultant, Owner/Investor, Syndicator; **SERVICES:** Fin. advice, investment mgmt., synd., multiple state diversification; **REP CLIENTS:** indivs. and partnerships, intnl. investors; **PROFL AFFIL & HONORS:** Clinical Member ITAA; **EDUC:** BSFS, 1960, Pol. Sci., Sch. of For. Serv., Georgetown Univ.; **GRAD EDUC:** MA, 1965, Soc. & Instnl. Devel., Stanford Univ.; PhD, 1970, Soc. & Instnl. Devel., Stanford Univ.; **EDUC HONORS:** Cum Laude; **OTHER ACT & HONORS:** Co-author of *OK Saleswoman* with Angela Garcia & Marty Caro; Author of 'Context Sensitive Evaluation'; Designer of SIBOM eval. procedure; **BUS ADD:** 641 Towle Way, Palo Alto, CA 94306, (415)493-3628.

SIMS, Gordon L.——**B:** June 20, 1938, Indianapolis, IN, *VP*, Jefferson Nat. Life Ins. Co.; **PRIM RE ACT:** Insuror; **SERVICES:** Mort. lending; **PREV EMPLOY:** Equitable Life 1962-69; Galbraith Mort. 69-72; **PROFL AFFIL & HONORS:** MAI, MBAA, MBA of IN; **EDUC:** BS, 1960, RE, IN Univ.; **HOME ADD:** 10920 Lakeview Dr., Carmel, IN 46032; **BUS ADD:** 1 Virginia Ave., Indianapolis, IN 46204, (317)267-8130.

SIMS, Hugo S., III——**B:** Aug. 18, 1943, Orangeburg, SC, *VP*, Mgmt. & Inv. Corp.; **PRIM RE ACT:** Attorney, Developer, Property Manager; **SERVICES:** RE Mgmt and Dev., also Co. Cont.; **PREV EMPLOY:** Atty., US Dept. of Justice, Anti-trust Div.; **PROFL AFFIL & HONORS:** IREM, CPM; **EDUC:** BA, 1965, Hist. & Eng., Wofford Coll., SC; **GRAD EDUC:** JD, 1967, Law, Univ. of SC; **EDUC HONORS:** Dean's List; **OTHER ACT & HONORS:** Rotary Club; **HOME ADD:** 399 Plantation Dr., Orangeburg, SC 29115, (803)536-5089; **BUS ADD:** 900 Chestnut St., PO Box 2817, Orangeburg, SC 29115, (803)534-4131.

SIMS, Maurine D.——**B:** Sep. 10, 1917, Neshoba Cty, MS, *Realtor*, Sims Realty; **PRIM RE ACT:** Broker; **PREV EMPLOY:** Math. Teacher, Meridian Public Schools, 10 Yrs., Math. & Sci. Teacher, Lauderdale Co. Schools, 6 Yrs.; **PROFL AFFIL & HONORS:** Meridian Bd. of Realtors, MS Assn. of Realtors, NAR; **EDUC:** BS, 1940, Math. & Gen. Sci., Univ. of So. MS; **GRAD EDUC:** MEd., 1968, Math., MS State Univ.; **HOME ADD:** 1842 36th St., Meridian, MS 39301, (601)482-3988; **BUS ADD:** 417 Russell Dr., PO Box 1528, Meridian, MS 39301, (601)482-3628.

SIMS, Wallen——*VP Adm.*, Shaw Industries, Inc.; **PRIM RE ACT:** Property Manager; **BUS ADD:** PO Drawer 2128, E. Franklin St., Dalton, GA 30720, (404)278-3812.*

SIMVOULAKIS, George——**B:** Oct. 19, 1950, Modesto, CA, *Pres.*, E.G. Devel.; **PRIM RE ACT:** Consultant, Developer, Builder, Owner/Investor, Syndicator; **OTHER RE ACT:** RE Salesman; **SERVICES:** Complete service from synd. and acquisition through zoning, devel., const., leasing and/or sales; **REP CLIENTS:** local, natl. and intl. clientele; **PREV EMPLOY:** Frank Howard Allen Comml. Investments Stanislaus Co. Div., CA; **PROFL AFFIL & HONORS:** Local and Nat. Bd. of Realtors, Assn. of Independent Amer. Investors; **EDUC:** BS, 1973, Philosophy, Univ. of UT; **GRAD EDUC:** Two yrs., Western State Univ., Coll. of the Law, Los Angeles, CA; **HOME ADD:** 2645 El Goya Dr., Modesto, CA 95354, (209)521-0476; **BUS ADD:** PO Box 1031, 213 Primo Way, Modesto, CA 95353, (209)538-1966.

SINCLAIR, Joseph T.——**B:** Nov. 17, 1940, Detroit, MI, *Sr. Partner*, Commercial Investment RE Co.; **PRIM RE ACT:** Broker, Consultant, Developer, Owner/Investor, Instructor, Property Manager, Syndicator; **SERVICES:** Full investment RE serv.; **REP CLIENTS:** Indiv. investors in income and investment props.; **PREV EMPLOY:** Harshman & Sinclair Atty., Dyer, Meek, Ruegsegger & Bullard Atty.; **PROFL AFFIL & HONORS:** RNMI, RESSI, FLI, NAR, CO W. Exchange Counselors, Inst. of Cert. Bus. Counselors, Intl. Inst. Valuers, Mesa Cty. Bar Assn., CCIM, Sr. Cert. Valuer; **EDUC:** BA, 1964, Poli. Sci., Univ. of MI; **GRAD EDUC:** JD, 1971, Law, Univ. of MI Law School; **MIL SERV:** USN, Lt., 1965-68; **HOME ADD:** PO Box 2860, Grand Junction, CO 81502, (303)434-6182; **BUS ADD:** PO Box 2860, Grand Junction, CO 81502, (303)245-6543.

SINCLAIR, Michael D.——**B:** July 26, 1948, New York, NY, *Atty.*, Csaplar & Bok; **PRIM RE ACT:** Attorney; **SERVICES:** Legal Advice to Lenders, Devels., and Govt. Agencies with respect to RE Devel.; **REP CLIENTS:** Private Devels., Municipalities and Govt. Agencies, Instnl. Lenders; **PREV EMPLOY:** Substantial prior Exper. as an Architect with Private Arch. Firms and Educ. Instns. in NY and MA; **PROFL AFFIL & HONORS:** ABA, Boston Bar Assn., AIA, Boston Soc. of Architects, Amer. Planning Assn.; **EDUC:** BArch, 1970, Arch., Cornell Univ.; **GRAD EDUC:** MCRP, 1977, Housing Policy, Harvard Univ.; JD, 1977, Law, Boston Univ.; **HOME ADD:** 652 Washington St., Brookline, MA 02146, (617)738-4437; **BUS ADD:** One Winthrop Sq., Boston, MA 02110, (617)357-4400.

SINCLAIR, Richard C.——**B:** July 15, 1948, Modesto, CA, *Atty. at Law; Pres., Sinclair Enterprises, Inc.*, Law Offices of Richard C. Sinclair; **PRIM RE ACT:** Attorney, Owner/Investor, Property Manager; **OTHER RE ACT:** Tax consultant, lecturer, coll. instr. in RE and Law; **SERVICES:** RE Law, Tax planning and investment counseling, devel. & synd. of resid. & comml. prop.; **REP CLIENTS:** Devels., Realtors and indiv., corp. and synd. investors; **PREV EMPLOY:** Realtor, 1970 to present; Lecturer & CA Community Coll. Instr.; RE Law and Tax; **PROFL AFFIL & HONORS:** ABA, CA Bar Assn., Stanislaus Cty. Bar Assn., NAR, Modesto Bd. of Realtors, CA Assn. of Realtors, *Who's Who in Amer. Law 1979*; **EDUC:** BA, 1970, Soc. Psych., Univ. of CA; **GRAD EDUC:** JD & LLM, 1975 & 1976, RE, Bus. and Tax Law, Univ. of Pac., McGeorge School of Law, Univ. of Miami, School of Law; **HOME ADD:** 8212 Oak View Dr., Oakdale, CA 95361; **BUS ADD:** 8212 Oak View Dr., Oakdale, CA 95361, (209)847-7077.

SINCLAIR, William F.——**B:** Apr. 3, 1946, Washington, DC, *Pres.*, Perpetual Amer. Fed. S&L Assn.; **PRIM RE ACT:** Banker, Lender; **PROFL AFFIL & HONORS:** Dir. of Perpetual Amer. Bd. of Realtors, DC Soc. for Crippled Children, Wash. Downtown Kiwanis Club, Firemen's Ins. Co., Fifth Fed. Reserve Dist Operations Advisory Comm., Republic Mort. Ins. Corp., Man of The Yr., 1975; Outstanding Young Men of Amer., 1979; **EDUC:** 1968, Econ., Fin. & Banking, Randolph-Macon; **GRAD EDUC:** 1973, Computer Sci., Mgmt. Information Systems, Amer. Univ.; **MIL SERV:** USN, Lt.; **HOME ADD:** 300 Pennsylvania Ave., Washington, DC 20003; **BUS ADD:** 50 11th St., NW, Washington, DC 20004, (202)783-7700.

SINGER, Bernard——**B:** Apr. 18, 1917, Cambridge, MA, *Owner*, Singer Assoc.; **PRIM RE ACT:** Consultant, Appraiser; **SERVICES:** Appraising, consulting; **PROFL AFFIL & HONORS:** SREA, CRE, CPM, ASA, MRA; **EDUC:** BS Econ., 1938, RE, Wharton School, Univ. of PA; **MIL SERV:** USAF, Capt., WWII; **OTHER ACT & HONORS:** VChmn. MHFA 1980-81; **HOME ADD:** 71 Colchester St., Brookline, MA 02146, (617)734-4011; **BUS ADD:** 1425 Beason St., Brookline, MA 02146, (617)566-2200.

SINGER, Bruce——**B:** Feb. 22, 1939, Duluth, MN, *Atty.*, Van Voorhis & Skaggs; **PRIM RE ACT:** Consultant, Attorney; **SERVICES:** Evaluation, structure, negotiations & documentation of resid. and comml. RE trans.; **REP CLIENTS:** Lenders, investors and devels. with respect to comml. & resid. real prop.; **PREV EMPLOY:** Bankamerica Realty Servs., 1970-75, Robert A. McNeil Corp., 1975-80; **PROFL AFFIL & HONORS:** CA Bar Assn., ABA; **EDUC:** BA, 1961, Geog., UCLA; **GRAD EDUC:** MBA, 1965, RE, UCLA; JD, 1979, Law, Boalt Hall, UC, Berkeley; **EDUC HONORS:** Phi Beta Kappa, Pi Gamma Mu, Beta Gamma Sigma, Order of the Coif; **OTHER ACT & HONORS:** Lecturer RE Law & Econ., Merritt Coll., Oakland, CA; **HOME ADD:** 39 Clarewood Ln., Oakland, CA 94618, (415)547-2071; **BUS ADD:** 1855 Olympic Blvd., Walnut Creek, CA 94596, (415)937-8000.

SINGER, Daniel M.——**B:** Oct. 10, 1930, Brooklyn, NY, *Partner*, Fried, Frank, Harris, Shriver & Kampelman, RE Dept.; **PRIM RE ACT:** Attorney; **SERVICES:** All types; **PREV EMPLOY:** Law Clerk - U.S. Court of Appeals for the DC Circuit 1956-58; **PROFL AFFIL & HONORS:** ABA; ICSC; **EDUC:** BA, 1951, Swarthmore Coll.; **GRAD EDUC:** LLB, 1954, Yale Law School; **EDUC HONORS:** Cum Laude; Editor in Chief of Weekly Campus Newspaper, Editorial Bd. Yale Law Journal; **MIL SERV:** US Army, 1954-1956, Signal Corps, SP/5, 3 Letters of Commendation; **OTHER ACT & HONORS:** Several publications; **HOME ADD:** 5410 39th St., N.W., Washington, DC 20015; **BUS ADD:** 600 New Hampshire Ave., NW, Suite 1000, Washington, DC 20037, (202)342-3500.

SINGER, Harold——**B:** Nov. 17, 1915, Dayton, OH, *Pres.*, Dayton Co.; **PRIM RE ACT:** Broker, Attorney, Developer, Builder, Owner/Investor, Property Manager, Insuror; **PREV EMPLOY:** Lawyer, Realtor, Devel., Soldier, Farmer; **PROFL AFFIL & HONORS:** OH Bar Assn., Dayton RE Assn., Intl. Council Shopping Ctrs., NAIOP; **MIL SERV:** USAF, Capt., Bronze Star & various others; **OTHER ACT & HONORS:** Masons, Scottish Rites, Shrine, YMCA, B'nai B'rith; **HOME ADD:** 5720 Heather Hollow, Dayton, OH 45415, (513)276-3991; **BUS ADD:** 120 W. Second St., Dayton, OH 45402, (513)222-1313.

SINGLETON, James M.——**B:** Dec. 19, 1939, Warsaw, MO, *Dir., Housing Div.*, H.U.D., Housing; **PRIM RE ACT:** Regulator, Consultant, Appraiser, Property Manager, Assessor; **PREV EMPLOY:** HUD Field Offices, 1962-1971; 1962-1971; Atlanta Regnl. Office, 1971-1976; HUD Central Office; 1976-1978; **PROFL AFFIL & HONORS:** IREM, NARA, Assn. of Government Appraisers, Certificate of Merit from HUD Sec., 1972; CPM; CRA; **EDUC:** BS, 1962, Banking and Fin., Univ. of MO - Columbia; **HOME ADD:** 14124 Cross Trails Dr., Chesterfield, MO 63017, (314)275-2312; **BUS ADD:** 210 N Tucker Blvd., St. Louis, MO 63101, (314)425-5645.

SINGLETON, Richard R.——**B:** May 4, 1947, So. Bend, IN, *VP*, The Oxford Grp., Project Fin./Investor Servicing; **PRIM RE ACT:** Developer, Builder, Property Manager, Syndicator; **OTHER RE ACT:** Investor servicing; **SERVICES:** Fin. analysis, debt & equity placement for muLti-family props.; investor servicing for equity partners; **REP CLIENTS:** Devel., const. & mgmt. of apts.; **PREV EMPLOY:** Arthur Andersen & Co., 1972-1978; **PROFL AFFIL & HONORS:** AICPA; IN CPA Soc.; **EDUC:** BA, 1970, Econ., IN Univ.; **GRAD EDUC:** MBA, 1972, Acctg./Fin., Univ. of MI Grad. School of Bus.; **EDUC HONORS:** Dean's List; **HOME ADD:** 3778 E. 62nd St., Indianapolis, IN 46220, (317)257-8975; **BUS ADD:** 3919 Meadows Dr., Indianapolis, IN 46205, (317)547-1311.

SINNARD, Herbert R.——**B:** Nov. 13, 1903, Chicago, IL, *Environmental Site Planner*, Architect, Solar Estates; **PRIM RE ACT:** Architect, Consultant, Developer; **OTHER RE ACT:** Site Orientation Planning; **SERVICES:** Consulting-Preliminary Planning-Site; **PREV EMPLOY:** Educator-Professor of Architecture Chmn.-Dept.; **PROFL AFFIL & HONORS:** AIA, ASAE, Lake Forest Found. for Architects LA; **EDUC:** BS, 1927, Arch. and Enginrg., IA State Univ., Ames, IA; **GRAD EDUC:** MS, 1929, Arch. Design, IA State Univ.; **EDUC HONORS:** Phi Kappa Phi; **MIL SERV:** US Army, Lt. Colonel; **OTHER ACT & HONORS:** City Planning Commn., Corvallis, OR 17 yr., Sigma Chi Fraternity L.M. Masonic Lodge, Elks Lodge, Triad Serv. Club O.S.U., Ret. Officers Club LM; **HOME ADD:** 2930 NW Highland Dr., Corvallis, 97330, OR, (503)753-6235; **BUS ADD:** 2930 NW Highland Dr., Corvallis, OR 97330, (503)994-5628.

SIPP, James F.——**B:** Apr. 24, 1937, Chicago, IL, *Dir. of RE*, White Castle System, Inc.; **OTHER RE ACT:** Propose and devel. growth strategy for corp. with regard to RE, coord. and direct acq. of new prop., oversee prop. records, devel. plans for devel. or dispostion of excess prop.; **PREV EMPLOY:** John W. Galbreath and Co., Multicon; **PROFL AFFIL & HONORS:** NACORE, NARA, Columbus Bd. of Realtors, ICSC; **EDUC:** BS, 1959, Fin., OH State Univ.; **GRAD EDUC:** MBA, 1961, Fin., Harvard Business School; **MIL SERV:** US Army, Capt.; **OTHER ACT & HONORS:** Governing Bd. of Church; **HOME ADD:** 4010 New Hall Rd., Columbus, OH 43220, (614)457-5469; **BUS ADD:** PO Box 1498, 555 W. Goodale St., Columbus, OH 43216, (614)228-5781.

SIRES, Bruce David——**B:** Mar. 29, 1948, Milwaukee, WI, *Partner*, Halperin & Halperin; **PRIM RE ACT:** Attorney; **SERVICES:** Tax planning; **PROFL AFFIL & HONORS:** Real Property, probate and Trust law Sect./ABA; Taxation & Probate Trust and Estate Planning Sect./CA State Bar; and local bar assns.; **EDUC:** AB Econ., 1969, Acctg. and econ., UCLA; **GRAD EDUC:** JD, 1972, Hastings Coll. of the Law; LlM, 1976, Law and Taxation, NY Univ.; **EDUC HONORS:** Omicron Delta Epsilon; **HOME ADD:** 1263 S. Woodruff Ave., Los Angeles, CA 90024, (213)475-9275; **BUS ADD:** 2049 Century Park E, Suite 4000, Los Angeles, CA 90067, (213)552-1164.

SIRLIN, Alan Robert——**B:** Jan. 20, 1952, Brooklyn, NY; **OTHER RE ACT:** Real estate practice; **SERVICES:** Comml. RE Mort. leasing, conveyancing, coop. conversions; **PREV EMPLOY:** NY Life Ins. Co., 1978-80, Atty. Gen. Counsel's office, Comml. RE & Mort. loans; **PROFL AFFIL & HONORS:** NY City Lawyer's Assn., JD; **EDUC:** BA, 1973, Poli. Sci., Bucknell Univ., Lewisburg, PA; **GRAD EDUC:** JD, 1976, NYU Sch. of Law; **EDUC HONORS:** Hons. in Poli. Sci.; **HOME ADD:** 40 Clinton St., Brooklyn, NY 11201, (212)596-5537; **BUS ADD:** 40 Clinton St., Brooklyn, NY 11201, (212)596-5537.

SIRMANS, Clemon F.——**B:** July 2, 1949, Douglas, GA, *Associate Prof.*, Univ. of GA, Dept. of RE; **PRIM RE ACT:** Consultant, Appraiser, Owner/Investor, Instructor, Syndicator, Real Estate Publisher; **SERVICES:** Investment counseling, valuation, instruction; **REP CLIENTS:** Indivs., instns., lenders for income-producing props.; **EDUC:** BS, 1971, Econ., Valdosta State Coll.; **GRAD EDUC:** MA and PhD, 1975, RE and Urban Devel., Univ. of GA; **EDUC HONORS:** Grad. with Honors; **HOME ADD:** 255 Hill Crest Dr., Watkinsville, GA 30677, (404)769-6094; **BUS ADD:** Coll. of Bus. Admin., Univ. of GA, Athens, GA 30602, (404)542-2126.

SIRMON, Wm. W., Jr.——*Pres.*, Pmni Properties, Inc.; **PRIM RE ACT:** Developer; **BUS ADD:** PO Box 3343, Spartanburg, SC 29304, (803)585-8777.*

SIROTA, David——**B:** May 25, 1928, Detroit, MI, David Sirota, PhD, Real Estate Consultant; **PRIM RE ACT:** Broker, Consultant, Instructor; **OTHER RE ACT:** Author RE Books; **PREV EMPLOY:** Univ. NE, Omaha and CA St., Fullerton; **PROFL AFFIL & HONORS:** REEA; **EDUC:** BS/BA, 1965, RE, Univ. AZ, Tucson;

GRAD EDUC: MBA, PhD, 1966-1971, Area Devel., Univ. AZ, Tucson; **EDUC HONORS:** Mtg. Bankers Scholarship 1965; **OTHER ACT & HONORS:** Author: *Essentials of RE*; *Essentials of RE Fin.*; *Essentials of RE Investment*; *Creative RE Fin.*; **BUS ADD:** 564 S. Corpino De Pecho, Green Valley, AZ 85614, (602)625-6417.

SISK, John K.——B: Feb. 19, 1941, Greenville, SC, *Partner/Mgr.*, Sisk & Assoc.; **PRIM RE ACT:** Developer; **EDUC:** BS, 1964, Bus. Admin., The Citadel; **GRAD EDUC:** MBA, 19067, Fin., Emory Univ.; **MIL SERV:** US Army, 1st Lt.; **HOME TEL:** (904)387-1545; **BUS ADD:** 4380 Lakeside Dr., Jacksonville, FL 32210, (904)384-8080.

SISKIND, Donald H.——B: Dec. 25, 1937, Providence, RI, *Sr. Partner*, Marshall Bratter Greene Allison & Tucker; **PRIM RE ACT:** Attorney; **REP CLIENTS:** The Cadillac Fairview Corp., Ltd.; Jones Long Wooton, Bank of Montreal; **PROFL AFFIL & HONORS:** ABA; NY State Bar Assn.; ICSC; Bar Assn. of the City of NY; **EDUC:** BS, 1959, Acctg. and Fin., Wharton School of Fin. and Commerce, Univ. of PA; **GRAD EDUC:** LLB, 1962, Columbia Univ. School of Law; **EDUC HONORS:** Phi Alpha Psi, Honorary Acctg. Soc.; **HOME ADD:** 349 Fort Hill Rd., Scarsdale, NY 10583, (914)472-3538; **BUS ADD:** 430 Park Ave., New York, NY 10036, (212)421-7200.

SISLER, Gary——B: June 8, 1934, ID, *Pres.*, Sisler-Baal, Inc.; **PRIM RE ACT:** Broker, Syndicator, Consultant, Developer, Property Manager, Owner/Investor; **SERVICES:** investment counseling; Synd. and dev. of comml. prop., prop. mgmt., leasing/sales, foreign investors, institutional investors in comml. prop.; **PREV EMPLOY:** ESSO (Latin Amer.); **PROFL AFFIL & HONORS:** SIR, CCIM; **EDUC:** BA, 1956, Univ. of WA; **GRAD EDUC:** BA, 1959, Amer. Inst. of Foreign Trade; **MIL SERV:** US Army, SP3; **HOME ADD:** 7961 SW 148th St., Miami, FL 33158, (305)233-1455; **BUS ADD:** 7235 Corporate Ctr. Dr., Miami, FL 33126, (305)591-4400.

SJOGREN, Per H.——B: Apr. 22, 1922, Lulea, Sweden, *Pres.*, King's View Realty, Inc.; **PRIM RE ACT:** Broker, Consultant, Developer, Owner/Investor; **SERVICES:** R.E. investment analysis & planning; **REP CLIENTS:** Comml RE Investors; **PREV EMPLOY:** Assoc. Prof. & Chmn., School of Bus., OR State Univ. (1959-1968); Consulting Economist for Checchi & Co., Wash., D.C. and Union of C. of C. & Indus., Turkey (1966-1967); **PROFL AFFIL & HONORS:** OAR; NAREB; Corvallis Bd. of Realtors (Pres. - 1975), Realtor of Yr., Corvallis Bd., 1977; **EDUC:** BA, 1947, Eng., Univ. of Uppsala, Sweden; **GRAD EDUC:** MA, 1948, Eng., Univ. of Uppsala, Sweden; PhD, 1964, Fin./Banking/Econ. Theory, Grad. School of Bus., Columbia Univ., NYC; **EDUC HONORS:** Grad. Study Award (1958-1959); Two Ford Foundation Post-Grad. Grants; **MIL SERV:** Swedish Army; Vice Cpl., 1941-1943; **OTHER ACT & HONORS:** Chmn., Benton Cty., OR Planning Commn.; Amer. Contr. Bridge League; Elks; **HOME ADD:** 1225 N.W. Fernwood Cir., Corvallis, OR 97330, (503)764-3106; **BUS ADD:** 150 S.W. Monroe, Corvallis, OR 97330, (503)753-2233.

SKARYD, William C.——B: June 18, 1947, Cleveland, OH, *CPA*, William C. Skaryd & Co.; **OTHER RE ACT:** CPA; **SERVICES:** Tax and fin. consultant to devels., synds. and brokers; **PREV EMPLOY:** Part. with Lewandowski, Veres & CO, CPA's; **PROFL AFFIL & HONORS:** AICPA's; OH Soc. of CPA's; **EDUC:** BS, 1969, Acctg., John Carroll Univ.; **GRAD EDUC:** MBA, 1975, Fin., Cleveland State Univ.; **MIL SERV:** US Army, 1st Lt., Bronze Star; **OTHER ACT & HONORS:** C of C; **HOME ADD:** 28300 Lincoln Rd., Bay Village, OH 44140, (216)835-1129; **BUS ADD:** 24600 Center Ridge Rd., 490, Westlake, OH 44145, (216)871-3724.

SKELLY, Joseph G.——B: June 21, 1935, Oil City, PA, *Partner*, Ball & Skelly; **PRIM RE ACT:** Attorney; **SERVICES:** Legal; **REP CLIENTS:** Central Penn Multi-List, Inc.; Home Prot. Corp.; Texaco, Inc.; Pfizer, Inc.; Cemetery Assn. of PA; Cumberland Restaurant Corp.; Generally corp. and indiv. clients involved in RE and comml. matters, matters involving state admin. agencies, civil litigation, zoning; **PROFL AFFIL & HONORS:** Admitted to Practice; PA Supreme; Superior and Commonwealth Courts; Local Courts; US Supreme Court; US District Courts; Middle and Eastern Dist. PA & ABA (Member Sects. on Real Prop., Probate & Tr. Law); PA Trial Lawyers Assn., *Marquis, Who's Who in Amer. Law*; **EDUC:** BS, 1957, Sci., Univ. of Notre Dame, Notre Dame, IN; **GRAD EDUC:** JD, 1962, Law, Villanova Univ. School of Law, Villanova, PA; **OTHER ACT & HONORS:** Bd. of Dir. Keystone Council; Boy Scouts of Amer.; Bd. of Dir. Alcoholism Services; Inc., YMCA; **HOME ADD:** 232 Poplar Ave., New Cumberland, PA 17070, (717)774-2720; **BUS ADD:** 511 N. 2nd St., PO Box 1108, Harrisburg, PA 17108, (717)232-8731.

SKIDD, Thomas P., Jr.——B: Jul. 2, 1936, Norwalk, CT, *Partner*, Cummings & Lockwood, RE Dept.; **PRIM RE ACT:** Attorney; **SERVICES:** Comml. RE; **PROFL AFFIL & HONORS:** CT and Stamford Bar Assns., Admitted to CT, US Dist. Ct. and US Supreme Ct. Practice; **EDUC:** AB, 1958, Econ., Georgetown Univ.; **GRAD EDUC:** LLB, 1961, Yale Univ.; **EDUC HONORS:** Cum Laude; **MIL SERV:** USN, NCO; **OTHER ACT & HONORS:** Wilton Democratic Town Comm. 1971-1974; Dir., CT Attys. Title Guar. Fund, Inc. 1974- ; Bd. of Dir. Stamford Red Cross (1967-71) and Stamford United Fund (1974-75); Biographee in *Who's Who in American Law.*; **HOME ADD:** 23 Stonebridge Rd., Wilton, CT 06897, (203)762-0156; **BUS ADD:** Ten Stamford Forum Box 120, Stamford, CT 06904, (203)327-1700.

SKILLERN, Lynn T.——*VP*, Coldwell Banker Barton & Ludwig Realtors, Inc., Resid.; **PRIM RE ACT:** Broker; **PROFL AFFIL & HONORS:** GA Realtors Inst., DeKalb Bd. of Realtors, Pres. DeKalb Chap. Women's Council of Realtors (1975); CRB; CRS; GRI; **EDUC:** AB, Chem., Maryville Coll.; **HOME ADD:** 1132 Forest Heights Rd., Stone Mountain, GA 30083, (404)292-6027; **BUS ADD:** 3399 Chamblee-Tucker Rd., Atlanta, GA 30341, (404)451-8282.

SKILLMAN, Ernest Edward, Jr.——B: Oct. 3, 1937, New Orleans, LA, *Realtor and Broker*, Skill RE, Comml. and Land Div.; **PRIM RE ACT:** Broker, Consultant, Appraiser, Lender, Owner/Investor, Property Manager; **EDUC:** BA, 1960, Social Sciences (Hist.), LA State Univ., Southeastern Coll. (Hammond, LA); **GRAD EDUC:** MBA, Bus. Admin., LA State Univ. of Baton Rouge; **MIL SERV:** USN, Comdr., Vietnam War Medal; **OTHER ACT & HONORS:** Sec. & Treas., Audubon Kiwanis Club; ROA; (Life Member) Military; Order of World Wars (Life Member); 1981-1982, *Who's Who in Amer. Bus. and Indus.*; Sigma Chi Social Frat. (Life Member); **HOME ADD:** 753 Kenilworth Parkway, Baton Rouge, LA 70808, (504)766-5380; **BUS ADD:** 1970 Staring Lane, Baton Rouge, LA 70810, (504)769-4170.

SKINNER, Michael——B: Aug. 30, 1946, San Francisco, CA, *Pres.*, M.G. Skinner & Associates; **PRIM RE ACT:** Owner/Investor, Insuror; **SERVICES:** Admin. of insurance and risk mgmt. programs; **REP CLIENTS:** Various of the largest RE owners, devels. or mgmt. firms in the state of CA and the US; **PREV EMPLOY:** Comml. Insurance Brokerages; **PROFL AFFIL & HONORS:** Profl. Insurance Agents Assn.; RESSI Affiliate; **EDUC:** BSC, 1968, Mgmt., Mktg., Santa Clara Univ.; **HOME ADD:** 1834 Michael Ln., Pacific Palisades, CA 90272, (213)459-6123; **BUS ADD:** 11340 W. Olympic Blvd. #207, Los Angeles, CA 90064, (213)473-2984.

SKINNER, Robert S., Jr.——B: Dec. 18, 1927, Baltimore, MD, *Pres.*, Robert S. Skinner & Son, Inc.; **PRIM RE ACT:** Appraiser; **OTHER RE ACT:** Bd. member Metropolis S&L; Advisory Bd. of John Hanson S&L; **PREV EMPLOY:** Nat. City Bank of NY; **EDUC:** BA, 1952, Econ., Trinity Coll. - Hartford, CT; **GRAD EDUC:** Fin., Johns Hopkins, Univ. of GA; **MIL SERV:** US Army, USAF, S/Sgt., 2d Lt., Several; **OTHER ACT & HONORS:** Bd. member, Reston Travel, Metropolis B&L, Past Pres. Soc. of RE Appraisers, Baltimore Chap.; **HOME ADD:** 614 Hastings Rd., Towson, MD 21204, (301)823-0683; **BUS TEL:** (301)366-7711.

SKIPWORTH, Larry——B: Sept. 19, 1944, Columbia, SC, *Sr. Counsel*, The Abacus Group; **PRIM RE ACT:** Banker, Attorney, Developer, Property Manager, Owner/Investor; **SERVICES:** Loans, devel. advice, investment counseling, prop. mgmt., legal, consulting, synd., acquistion, exchanges; **REP CLIENTS:** Devels., indivis., lenders, builders in RE investments nationwide; **PREV EMPLOY:** Philadelphia RE Investment Co.; DE Devel.; Chicago Loop, law firm; **PROFL AFFIL & HONORS:** IL Mort. Bankers Assn.; ABA; IL, Chicago & DuPage Bar Assns.; Chicago RE Club; Chicago Mortgage Atty. Assn., Publications in RE fin., zoning, and pension plans; Speaker and Author for Bar Assn. Seminars & Fin. Grps.; **EDUC:** BS, 1967, Econ./Math, Western IL Univ.; **GRAD EDUC:** MCP, 1975, RE Fin. & Planning, Wharton; MA, 1968, Econ., Univ. of IL; **EDUC HONORS:** Woodrow Wilson (Hon.) Fellowship, Mellon Fellowship in Urban Renewal, Nat. Sci. Found. Fellowship; **OTHER ACT & HONORS:** Faculty member, Elmhurst Coll., Mgmt. Program; Council on For. Relations; Rydall YMCA; Amer. Soc. of Planning Officials; Ed. & Publisher, Econ. Sense, Fin. Newsletter; Faculty Member, IL Inst. of Tech/Kent Coll. of Law; **HOME ADD:** 487 Ridgewood, Glen Ellyn, IL 60137, (312)858-3570; **BUS ADD:** 10 S LaSalle St., Chicago, IL 60603, (312)346-9172.

SKLAR, Stanley P.——B: Apr. 25, 1938, Brooklyn, NY, *Partner*, Mann, Cogan, Sklar & Lerman; **PRIM RE ACT:** Attorney, Instructor; **SERVICES:** Legal Services; **PROFL AFFIL & HONORS:** Member, Village of Northbrook Zoning Bd. of Appeals, 1973-, Atty., Northbrook Park Dist., 1974-1979 , Chicago Bar Assn., Mechanics' Lien Comm., Chmn., 1973-1975; RE Const. Comm.; ABA, Const. Contracts Comm., Real Prop. Litigation Comm.; Forum Comm. on Const. Indus.; Chicago RE Bd., Amer. Arbitration Assn., Const. Panel, Lic. RE Broker, Atty., Arbitrator ; Instr., Oakton Community Coll.; Co-Author, IL Mechanics' Liens, IL Inst. for Continuing Legal Educ. (1979);

Author, *Liability of RE Brokers for Misrepresentation*, "Realty Today, 1980"; **EDUC:** BS, 1960, Indus. Admin., Univ. of IL; **GRAD EDUC:** JD, 1964, Law, Northwestern Univ. School of Law; **MIL SERV:** USAF; **HOME ADD:** 1890 Phillips, Northbrook, IL 60062; **BUS ADD:** 29 So. LaSalle St., Suite 440, Chicago, IL 60603, (312)372-4500.

SKLAR, William Paul, Esq.——B: Sept. 10, 1958, NY, NY, *Atty. at Law/Prof. of Law*, Wood, Cobb, Murphy and Craig; **PRIM RE ACT:** Attorney, Instructor; **SERVICES:** Legal representation of RE devels., investors and lenders; **REP CLIENTS:** Same as services provided; **PROFL AFFIL & HONORS:** The FL Bar; Palm Beach Cty. Bar Assn.; ABA; Member, Real Prop., Probate and Trust Sect., Condo. and Cooperative Housing Comm., ABA and FL Bar; Member Advisory Bd., Univ. of Miami Condo. and Cluster Housing Inst.; **EDUC:** BBA, 1977, Bus. Admin./Politics/Public Affairs, Univ. of Miami; **GRAD EDUC:** JD, 1980, Real Prop. Law, Univ. of Miami, School of Law; **EDUC HONORS:** Pi Sigma Alpha, Nat. Pol. Sci. Hon.; Magna Cum Laude, Phi Delta Phi; Faculty Research Asst., 1979-1980; **OTHER ACT & HONORS:** Adjunct Prof. of Law, Univ. of Miami School of Law; Author: "Cases and Materials on Condo. and Cluster Housing" - 1980; "The Wrap-Around Mortgage - Its Uses and Consequences - Lawyers Title Guaranty Fund Notes" - 1979; Contributing Editor - "Florida Real Estate Transactions" - 1980.; **HOME ADD:** 20797 Cipres Way, Boca Raton, FL 33433, (305)483-8409; **BUS ADD:** 319 Clematis St., W. Palm Beach, FL 33401, (305)655-8616.

SKLARZ, Michael A.——B: Nov. 22, 1947, Newark, NJ, *Dir. of Research*, Locations, Inc.; **OTHER RE ACT:** RE Research & Econ. Forecasting; **SERVICES:** Author of 'HI RE Indicators'; **REP CLIENTS:** Most maj. banks, S&L and devels. in HI; **EDUC:** BS, 1969, Applied Math., Columbia Univ.; **GRAD EDUC:** MS, 1971, Applied Math., Univ. of HI; PhD, 1975, Ocean Engrg., Univ. of HI; **HOME ADD:** 19 Makaweli St., Honolulu, HI 96825, (808)395-7010; **BUS ADD:** 1339 Hunakai St., Honolulu, HI 98816, (808)735-4200.

SKRIVAN, Albert N.——B: June 20, 1920, Valpraiso, NE, *Designer - Teacher*, Self; **PRIM RE ACT:** Instructor; **SERVICES:** Educ. (Vo.-Tech.) arch.; **REP CLIENTS:** Post Secondary; **PREV EMPLOY:** Const. estimator; **PROFL AFFIL & HONORS:** Amer. Inst. of Design & Drafting, Intl. Assn. of Housing Sci.; **EDUC:** 1938, Denver Univ.; **MIL SERV:** US Navy, Sp Y1C, 11 Naval Engagements, 11 Stars on Asiatic-Pac. Area Serv. Medals; **HOME ADD:** 1236 Sumner, Longmont, CA 80501, (505)776-2630; **BUS ADD:** 1236 Sumner, Longmont, CO 80501, (505)776-2630.

SLATER, Adair——*Mktg. Dir.*, Redwood Shores, Inc.; **PRIM RE ACT:** Developer; **BUS ADD:** 350 Marine World Pkwy., Redwood City, CA 94065, (415)592-4170.*

SLATER, John W., Jr.——B: May 10, 1948, Memphis, TN, *Part.*, Winchester, Huggins, Charlton, Leake, Brown & Slater; **PRIM RE ACT:** Attorney; **SERVICES:** Represent devel. & lenders in RE fin., act as bond counsel in indus. revenue bond fin.; **REP CLIENTS:** Devels., private firms & lenders in connection with comml. RE devels; The Indus. Devel. Bd. of City of Memphis & Cty. of Shelby; TN Memphis Ctr. City Revenue Fin. Corp.; **PROFL AFFIL & HONORS:** ABA, Sect. of Real Prop. Probate & Tr. Law; **EDUC:** BA, 1970, Econ., Princeton Univ.; **GRAD EDUC:** JD, 1973, Fin. & Tax Law, Univ. of VA; **MIL SERV:** USA R, Capt.; **OTHER ACT & HONORS:** Sec. Memphis Area C of C; **HOME ADD:** 4212 Woodmere Cove, Memphis, TN 38117, (901)682-6493; **BUS ADD:** 1900 First TN Bank Bldg., 165 Madison Ave., Memphis, TN 38103, (901)526-7374.

SLATER, Martin——*VP Oper.*, Chock Full of Nuts Corp.; **PRIM RE ACT:** Property Manager; **BUS ADD:** 425 Lexington Ave., New York, NY 10017, (212)532-0300.*

SLATER, Robert——B: July 6, 1940, Newark, NJ, *Pres.*, LRF Slater Cos. Inc. and Affil. Cos.; **PRIM RE ACT:** Consultant, Developer, Property Manager, Owner/Investor; **OTHER RE ACT:** Comml. indus., shopping ctrs.; **SERVICES:** Site acquisition, project planning and execution, prop. mgmt.; **REP CLIENTS:** F.W. Woolworth; W.R. Grace; Amer. Stores; Channel House Ctrsl; Honeywell; Gen. Services Admin.; Prince Range Stores; Toys R Us; Rite Aid; Thom Mean Charming Shoppes; Marriott Corp.; Radio Shack; **PREV EMPLOY:** CEO; Channel Home Centers; **PROFL AFFIL & HONORS:** ICSC, Indus. Serv. Award - ICSC; **EDUC:** BS, 1962, Fin., Lehigh Univ.; **GRAD EDUC:** Grad. Courses, Various, Harvard U., Seton Hall U.; **EDUC HONORS:** Cum Laude; **MIL SERV:** Fin. Corps.; 1st Lt.; Commendation Citation; **OTHER ACT & HONORS:** Commnr., Essex Cty. NJ Improvement Authority; Bd. of Govs., D of I Home for the Aging Devel. Council; St. Barnabas Hosp.; **HOME ADD:** 6 Sylvan Ct., Livingston, NJ 07039, (201)992-5741; **BUS ADD:** 2 W Northfield Rd., Livingston, NJ 07039, (201)994-2400.

SLATKIN, Jean——B: June 1, 1922, Philadelphia, PA, *VP*, Lou-Town Realty; **PRIM RE ACT:** Broker; **SERVICES:** Sales, Appraisals, Financing; **PROFL AFFIL & HONORS:** LI Bd. of Realtors, NYS Assn. of Realtors, NAR, RNMI, WCR, Realtor of the Yr., 1980 (LI Bd. of Realtors); Distinguished Serv. Award, (NYS Assn. of Realtors 1980); GRI; CRS; CRB; **OTHER ACT & HONORS:** VP, LI Bd. of Realtors, Dir. of NYS Assn. of Realtors; **HOME ADD:** 661 Miriam Pkwy,, Elmont, NY 11003, (516)825-1855; **BUS ADD:** 753 Hempstead Tpk., Franklin Square, NY 11010, (516)538-7055.

SLATTERY, Joseph P., Jr.——B: Sept. 18, 1941, Rockville Ctr., NY, *Dir. - Corporate Facilities*, PPD Property, Inc.; **PRIM RE ACT:** Owner/Investor; **OTHER RE ACT:** RE & Const.; **SERVICES:** Corp. RE; **REP CLIENTS:** The Corp.; **PREV EMPLOY:** Grumman Aerospace Corp., Bethpage, NY; Mgr. of Project Engrg.-Corporate Facilities 1965-79; **PROFL AFFIL & HONORS:** AIPE, Amer. Inst. of Indus. Engrs.; **EDUC:** BS, 1974, Const. Mgmt., Pratt Inst.- Brooklyn, NY; **EDUC HONORS:** Arthur Goeller Award and Cavanaugh Assn. Award; **MIL SERV:** US Army, S/Sgt. 1959-63; **OTHER ACT & HONORS:** Dist. Comm. Boy Scouts-Nassau Cty. Council BSA; **HOME ADD:** 8 Lynn Ct., Plainview, NY 11803, (516)433-4227; **BUS ADD:** 3333 New Hyde Park Rd., New Hyde Park, NY 11042, (516)684-3520.

SLAVIK, Stephan F., Sr.——B: May 30, 1920, Detroit, MI, *Pres.*, Slavik Co.; **PRIM RE ACT:** Developer, Builder, Property Manager, Owner/Investor; **PROFL AFFIL & HONORS:** Bldrs. Assn. of Detroit, MI; **MIL SERV:** USAF, Sgt., Purple heart, 4 Oak Clusters; **HOME ADD:** 1208 Oakwood Ct., Rochester, MI 48063; **BUS ADD:** 31555 W. 14 Milerd, Suite 203, Farmington, MI 48018.

SLAVIN, Sherman R.——B: Jan. 16, 1922, Watertown, NY, *Atty.*, Slavin & Stauffacher; **PRIM RE ACT:** Attorney; **SERVICES:** Title and RE purchases, closings, morts. and fin.; **REP CLIENTS:** Thomaston Savings Bank, Gray Electric Co.; **PROFL AFFIL & HONORS:** Amer. Bar Assn., CT Bar Assn., Waterbury Bar Assn.; **EDUC:** AB, 1942, Govt., Harvard Coll.; **GRAD EDUC:** LLB, 1949, Harvard Law School; **EDUC HONORS:** Cum Laude; **MIL SERV:** Army, Sgt.; **OTHER ACT & HONORS:** Town Atty., Watertown 6 Yrs.; Bd. of Education, Watertown 9 Yrs.; Presently Atty. for Watertown Fire Dist.; Litchfield Cty. Univ. Club; Harvard Club of Northern CT; Bd. of Tr., United Methodist Church of Watertown; **HOME ADD:** 55 Woolson St., Watertown, CT; **BUS ADD:** 48 Woodruff Ave. Box A, Watertown, CT 06795, (203)274-2511.

SLAVIN, Thomas P.——B: Aug. 18, 1941, Cleveland, OH, *Pres.*, CIDCO Mgmt. Co., Inc.; **PRIM RE ACT:** Attorney, Developer, Owner/Investor, Property Manager, Syndicator; **SERVICES:** Synd. & mgmt. of hotels and office bldgs.; **REP CLIENTS:** Indiv. and fin. advisory firms investing in comml. props.; **PREV EMPLOY:** Fraser Mort. Co.; **EDUC:** BS, 1963, Forest Sci.; **GRAD EDUC:** JD, 1970, Marshall Law Sch., Div. of Cleveland State Univ.; **EDUC HONORS:** *Who's Who Among Students in Amer. Colls. & Univs.*, Alpha Chi; **OTHER ACT & HONORS:** Rowfant Club, Cleveland Athletic Club; **HOME ADD:** 2906 Winthrop, Shaker Heights, OH 44120, (216)751-0784; **BUS ADD:** 1250 Superior Ave., The Park Mall, Cleveland, OH 44114, (216)574-4949.

SLAVITT, Earl B.——B: Sept. 12, 1939, Chicago, IL, *Partner*, Katten, Muchin, Zavis, Pearl & Galler, RE; **PRIM RE ACT:** Attorney; **SERVICES:** Legal Services; **REP CLIENTS:** Lenders, pension funds and indiv. or private investors in comml. and resid. props.; indus. props.; **PREV EMPLOY:** Principal in Tash, Slavitt and Silberman (1978-1981); Partner, Levy and Erens (1969-1978); **PROFL AFFIL & HONORS:** Chicago Bar Assn.; IL State Bar Assn.; American Bar Assn; Chicago Council of Lawyers, Sit on number of RE related bar assn. committees; **EDUC:** BS, 1961, Acctg./Pre-Law, Univ. of PA, Wharton School of Bus.; **GRAD EDUC:** JD, 1964, Univ. of PA; **OTHER ACT & HONORS:** Bd. of Gov's., Lawyers in Mensa; Published articles on matters of legal interest; Speaker at ISBA mid-year meeting; **HOME ADD:** 405 Darrow Ave., Evanston, IL 60202, (312)491-1208; **BUS ADD:** 55 E. Monroe St., Suite 4100, Chicago, IL 60603, (312)346-7400.

SLAZAS, James A.——B: Dec. 18, 1930, Cleveland, OH, *Sec./Treas.*, Paxall, Inc.; **PRIM RE ACT:** Owner/Investor; **OTHER RE ACT:** Handling RE for a Mfr.; **PREV EMPLOY:** Sangenio Electric Co., 1966-1969; **PROFL AFFIL & HONORS:** Nat. Assn. of Accountants, Tax Exec. Inst., Risk Ins. Mgrs. Soc., Intl. Bus. Council; **EDUC:** BS, 1953, Accounting, John Carroll Univ.; **MIL SERV:** USAF, Sgt.; **OTHER ACT & HONORS:** Union League Clubs of Chicago; **HOME ADD:** 908 No. Greenwood, Park Ridge, IL 60068, (312)696-0582; **BUS ADD:** 100 W Monroe St., Chicago, IL 60603, (312)332-5580.

SLEEPER, Neal D.——**B:** Jan. 21, 1946, Dallas, TX, *VP, Comml. Devel.*, Murray Props. Co.; **PRIM RE ACT:** Developer; **SERVICES:** All devel. related servs.; **PREV EMPLOY:** Murray Mgmt. Corp., Pres.; **PROFL AFFIL & HONORS:** BOMA, IREM, CPM, Pres. Dallas/Ft. Worth Chapt. IREM; **EDUC:** BBA, 1968, Fin., Univ. of TX at Austin; **HOME ADD:** 3448 Stanford, Dallas, TX 75225, (214)363-9791; **BUS ADD:** 5520 LBJ Frwy, Dallas, TX 75240, (214)385-2645.

SLEET, Phillip Milton, Sr.——**B:** Mar. 1, 1914, Alexandria, LA, *Realtor*, Phil Sleet Realty Inc.; **PRIM RE ACT:** Broker, Consultant, Appraiser; **OTHER RE ACT:** Relocation; **PROFL AFFIL & HONORS:** NAR, Cert. RE Brokerage Mgr. and CRS, Realtor of the Year, Alexandria, LA; **EDUC:** BS, 1938, Bus. Coll. of Commerce, LA State Univ.; **MIL SERV:** US Army, Lt. Col., Bronze Star; **OTHER ACT & HONORS:** Lay Advisory Comm., LSU Alexandria; Pres. Lay Advisory Comm. of St. Francis Cabrini Hosp., Kiwanis, Past Pres.; **HOME ADD:** 2000 White St., Alexandria, LA 71301, (318)442-5982; **BUS ADD:** 4121 Parliament Dr., Alexandria, LA 71301, (318)445-7800.

SLEET, Phillip "Phil" M., Jr.——**B:** July 10, 1942, Augusta, Richmond, GA, *Part./Owner*, Phil Sleet Realty Inc.; **PRIM RE ACT:** Broker, Consultant, Appraiser, Property Manager; **OTHER RE ACT:** Relocation; **REP CLIENTS:** Proctor & Gamble, Homeequity, Merrill-Lynch; **PROFL AFFIL & HONORS:** NAR, RNMI, Recipient, W. Max Moore Trophy, RNMI, NAR, 1980; **EDUC:** BS, 1964, Engrg., U.S. Mil. Academy, West Point, NY; **GRAD EDUC:** 1970-71 incomplete, Bus. Admin., LA State Univ., Baton Rouge, LA; **MIL SERV:** US Army, Capt., Bronze Star; **OTHER ACT & HONORS:** Kiwanis, Soc. of the War of 1812; **HOME ADD:** PO Box 1826, Alexandria, LA 71301, (318)448-0095; **BUS ADD:** 4121 Parliament Dr., Alexandria, LA 71301, (318)445-7800.

SLICER, Paul A.——**B:** Aug. 17, 1928, Kennett, MO, *Counsel*, Citicorp Person-to-Person, Inc. and Citicorp Homeowners, Inc., Legal Dept.; **PRIM RE ACT:** Attorney; **SERVICES:** Interface with bus. mgrs. to develop loan products secured by RE., to include instructions and documentation, taking into consideration state and fed. laws and regulations; **PREV EMPLOY:** VP, City Fin. Co., HQ in Memphis, TN, subs. of James Talcott, Inc.; Assoc. Gen. Counsel, ISC Fin. Corp., HQ Kansas City, MO; **PROFL AFFIL & HONORS:** Phi Delta Phi-Legal Frat., ABA, MO Bar Assn.; **EDUC:** BA, 1951, Hist. Pol. Sci.-Econ., Univ. of MO-Columbia; **GRAD EDUC:** LLB, 1954, Univ. of MO-Columbia; **MIL SERV:** US Army-JAGC, Maj.; **OTHER ACT & HONORS:** Asst. Gen. State of MO, 1961-62; Corp. Counsel and Supervisor, Office of Sec. of State, State of MO 1962-65; **HOME ADD:** 37 Champagne; Lake St. Louis, MO 63367, (314)625-2573; **BUS ADD:** 670 Mason Ridge Ctr. Dr., St. Louis, MO 63141, (314)851-1400.

SLIWINSKI, Teddy——**B:** Oct. 22, 1951, Cleveland OH, *Atty. at Law*; **PRIM RE ACT:** Broker, Consultant, Attorney, Appraiser, Developer, Owner/Investor, Instructor, Syndicator; **OTHER RE ACT:** Urban devel.; **SERVICES:** Investment counseling - synd. - neighborhood devel.; **REP CLIENTS:** Slavic Village Assn., Detroit Shoreway Devel. Corp., various neighborhood corps.; **PREV EMPLOY:** Instructor in RE law, principles & practices & investments at Cuyahoga Community Coll.; **PROFL AFFIL & HONORS:** Cleveland - Cuyahoga Cty. & State of OH Bar Assns. RE Section, Acad. of RE Inst., NAR, OH Assn. of Realtors; **EDUC:** BA, 1973, Poli. Sci., Cleveland State Univ.; **GRAD EDUC:** JD, 1975, Law, Cleveland State Law Sch.; **EDUC HONORS:** Dean's List, Dean's List; **MIL SERV:** USMC, Platoon Leaders Class, Officer Candidate Sch., Quantico, VA, Commn. 2nd Lt.; **OTHER ACT & HONORS:** *Who's Who Among Amer. Students 1974-1975*; **HOME ADD:** 6502 Chambers Ave., Cleveland, OH 44105, (216)641-1782; **BUS ADD:** 6514 Fleet Ave., Cleveland, OH 44105, (216)641-9191.

SLOAME, Stuart——*Dpty. Asst. Secy.*, Department of Housing and Urban Development, Field Operatons & Environment/Energy Programs; **PRIM RE ACT:** Lender; **BUS ADD:** 451 Seventh St., S.W., Washington, DC 20410, (202)755-6082.*

SLOAN, Jim——**B:** July 29, 1937, Stillwater, IL, *Owner/Partner Mgr. Broker*, ERA Scott & Sloan Realty; **PRIM RE ACT:** Broker, Appraiser, Builder, Owner/Investor, Property Manager, Syndicator; **SERVICES:** Full Serv. Realty & Custom Homebuilding; **REP CLIENTS:** RELO, Merrill Lynch Relocation, Bank of St. Louis; **PREV EMPLOY:** Former Prof. at OK State Univ. Agency for Intl. Devel.-Thailand Assignment; **PROFL AFFIL & HONORS:** OAR, NAR, RESSI, GRI; CRS; **EDUC:** BS, 1960, Indus. Education, OK State Univ.; **GRAD EDUC:** MS, 1974, Indus. Arts Education, OK State Univ.; **EDUC HONORS:** Outstanding Sr. Award; *Who's Who Among Students in Amer. Univ. & Coll.*; **MIL SERV:** USMCR,Cpl., 1955-1963; **OTHER ACT & HONORS:** OSU Alumni, Phi Delta Kappa, Iola Lambda Sigma, Past Pres. OIAA; Past VP OVA; **HOME ADD:** 302 E. Redbud, Stillwater, OK 74074, (405)377-9870; **BUS ADD:** 408 S. Main, Stillwater, OK 74074.

SLOANE, Ronald L.——**B:** July 10, 1946, Milwaukee, WI, *President*, Affiliated Financial Services, Inc.; **PRIM RE ACT:** Broker, Owner/Investor; **SERVICES:** Real estate consulting services; financial planning; development and synd. of residential and commercial properties; Broker/Dealer Securities Firm; **PROFL AFFIL & HONORS:** Amer. Institute of CPA's (AICPA); WI Instit. of CPA's (WICPA); RESSI, Nat. Synd. Forum, CPA; **EDUC:** BBA, 1969, Acctg., Univ. of WI, Milwaukee; **GRAD EDUC:** MBA, 1971, Bus. Mgmt., Univ. of WI, Milwaukee; **EDUC HONORS:** Magna Cum Laude; **OTHER ACT & HONORS:** Member, Univ. of WI Milwaukee Alumni Assn., Bd. of Trustees; **HOME ADD:** 2980 Monterey Blvd., Brookfield, WI 53005, (414)784-1283; **BUS ADD:** 2980 Monterey Blvd., Brookfield, WI 53005, (414)784-1283.

SLONE, Russell J.——**B:** Jan. 22, 1943, Lexington, KY, *Projects Mgr.*, Kentucky Commerce Cabinet, Industrial Development Division; Industrial Marketing Branch; **OTHER RE ACT:** Govt. Agency for Economic Devel.; **SERVICES:** Recommendations & evaluations for plant locations; **PREV EMPLOY:** Dir. of Mktg., Const. Firm; Indus. Devel. Rep., Elec. Utility; **PROFL AFFIL & HONORS:** KY Indus. Devel. Council; So. Indus. Devel. Council; **EDUC:** BBA, 1970, Production, Office & Personnel Mgmt., E. KY Univ., Richmond, KY; **HOME ADD:** 2135 Tamarack Dr., Lexington, KY 40504, (606)277-2726; **BUS ADD:** Capital Plaza Tower, Frankfort, KY 40601, (502)564-7140.

SLOSBURG, D. David——**B:** Sept. 7, 1952, Omaha, NE, *Partner*, Slosburg Co.; **PRIM RE ACT:** Developer, Builder, Owner/Investor, Property Manager; **SERVICES:** Building and leasing to Natl. tenants office Space/Shopping Ctrs.; **EDUC:** BS, 1974, Fin., Wharton School of Fin. and Commerce, Univ. PA; **OTHER ACT & HONORS:** Omaha Symphony Council, Bd. of Dirs., Douglas Cty. Hist. Soc.; **HOME ADD:** 3102 N. 97th St., Omaha, NE 68144, (402)571-1316; **BUS ADD:** 13023 Arbor St., Omaha, NE 68144, (402)334-7900.

SLYE, George E.——**B:** Mar. 16, 1931, Boston, MA, *VChmn. and Part.*, Spaulding and Slye Corp.; **PRIM RE ACT:** Broker, Consultant, Developer, Builder, Property Manager, Owner/Investor; **SERVICES:** Brokerage, const., devel., prop. mgmt., energy mgmt.; **REP CLIENTS:** 300 maj. US clients, lenders, inst.; **PREV EMPLOY:** Dwight Bldg. Co., New Haven, CT; Amer. Urgan Corp., New Haven, CT; **PROFL AFFIL & HONORS:** ULI, ICSC, NIDA, NAR, Pres. of Gtr. Boston RE Bd., 1977 Boston Realtor of Yr.; 1978 MA A.R. Realtor of Yr.; **EDUC:** BS in BA, 1953, Fin. & Mktg., Babson Coll.; **GRAD EDUC:** Econ., 1952, Wesleyan Univ., Middletown,CT; **EDUC HONORS:** Cum Laude; **MIL SERV:** USNR, LCDR, Service Ribbons; **OTHER ACT & HONORS:** Boston - Mayor's Fair Hsg. Comm.; MA.- Gov's. Energy Adv. Comm.; Dir. Univ. Hosp. - Boston; Tr., Boston Five Savings Bank; Dir. Big Brother Assn. of Boston; Dir. Hill Devel. Co., Wesleyan Univ.; **HOME ADD:** Box 107, Mirror Lake, NH 03853, (603)569-3957; **BUS ADD:** 15 New England Exec. Park, Burlington, MA 01803, (617)523-8000.

SMALL, Harold S.——**B:** Jan. 22, 1945, Chicago, IL, *Mgng Part.*, Roseman & Small; **PRIM RE ACT:** Attorney, Instructor; **OTHER RE ACT:** Univ. Instr.; **REP CLIENTS:** Shapell Indus. of San Diego, Inc.; ADMA Co. Inc.; **PROFL AFFIL & HONORS:** ABA, State Bar of CA, San Diego Cty. Bar Assn., AICPA, CA Soc. of CPA's, CPA; **EDUC:** BS, 1967, Acctg., San Diego State Univ.; **GRAD EDUC:** JD, 1970, Law, Univ. of CA, Hastings Coll. of Law; **OTHER ACT & HONORS:** Chmn. Taxation Sect. of San Diego Cty. Bar Assn., 1980; Chmn. Law Office Mgmt.Comm. of San Diego Cty. Bar Assn. 1978-1980; Chmn. Ins. Comm. of San Diego Cty. Bar Assn. 1977-1978; **HOME ADD:** 5558 Avenida Fiesta, La Jolla, CA 92037; **BUS ADD:** 225 Broadway, Central Fed. Tower, Suite 1313, San Diego, CA 92101, (714)231-8848.

SMALL, John L.——**B:** July 22, 1951, Huntingburg, IN, *Pres.*, Small Dreams Realty, Inc.; **PRIM RE ACT:** Broker; **PREV EMPLOY:** Asst. Cashier & Auditor HoLland Natl. Bank, Holland, IN 47541, 1974-76; **PROFL AFFIL & HONORS:** 1979 Sec. Dubois Co. Bd. of Realtors & VP in 1981; **EDUC:** BA, 1973, Bus. Fin., IN State Univ.; **HOME ADD:** RR 2, Box 203, A-11, Huntingburg, IN 47542; **BUS ADD:** RR1, BOX 59, Celestine, IN 47251, (812)389-2333.

SMALL, Peter M.——**B:** Dec. 20, 1942, Glen Ridge, NJ, *Pres. and Chief Exec. Officer*, Spaulding and Slye Corp.; **PRIM RE ACT:** Broker, Consultant, Property Manager, Developer, Builder; **SERVICES:** Brokerage/Const./Consulting/Devel./Prop. Mgmt.; **PREV EMPLOY:** The Codman Co., Boston, MA; **PROFL AFFIL & HONORS:** Greater Boston RE Bd.; BOMA; Greater Boston Bd. of Dirs.; Nat. Assn. of

Indus. and Office Parks; Young Pres. Org.; NAR; Assoc. Member, Nat. Assn. of Corp. RE Execs.; **EDUC:** BA, 1964, Amer. Hist., Bowdoin Coll.; **MIL SERV:** USCG, Lt.; **HOME ADD:** 132 Park Ln., Concord, MA 01742, (617)369-7209; **BUS ADD:** 15 New England Executive Pk., Burlington, MA 01803, (617)523-8000.

SMALL, Ricardo——B: Dec. 18, 1946, Barranquilla, Colombia, S.A., *Broker Assoc.*, Realty Exec. of Tucson; **PRIM RE ACT:** Broker, Owner/Investor, Property Manager; **SERVICES:** All, with spec. in SFR investment & mgmt.; **REP CLIENTS:** Dentists, doctors, vets., and other profls.; **PREV EMPLOY:** ERA Winston & Co. Realtors, Sales Assoc.; **PROFL AFFIL & HONORS:** Candidate for CCIM, First 3 of 5 classes completed, 1977: Outstanding New Assoc. of Most Listings Sold, 1978 & 1979 Million Dollar Club; **EDUC:** BS, 1969, Wildlife Biology, Univ. of AZ; **GRAD EDUC:** MS, 1971, Wildlife Biology, Univ. of AZ; **EDUC HONORS:** Tucson Rod & Gun Club Scholarship, Nat. Wildlife Fed. Fellowship; **OTHER ACT & HONORS:** Tucson Rod & Gun Club, Speak Spanish; **HOME ADD:** 9401 E Creek, Tucson, AZ 85730, (602)298-3342; **BUS ADD:** PO Box 17296, Tucson, AZ 85731, (602)298-3342.

SMALL, Sylvester J.——B: Dec. 31, 1912, Westbury, NY, *Pres.*, S.J. Small Realty Co.; **PRIM RE ACT:** Broker; **SERVICES:** Comml. Prop. & Indus. Props.; **EDUC:** BS, 1936, RE & Fin., Econ., Wharton Sch., Univ. of PA; **HOME ADD:** PO Box 182, Bright Waters, NY 11718, (516)277-6870; **BUS ADD:** 2453 Union Blvd., Bldg. G-26A, Islip, NY 11751, (516)277-6870.

SMALLEY, James A.——*Pres.*, Smalley Inc.; **PRIM RE ACT:** Broker, Consultant, Appraiser, Owner/Investor, Instructor, Property Manager, Syndicator; **SERVICES:** Brokerage, consultation, appraisal; **PROFL AFFIL & HONORS:** CCIM; GRI; IFA; CRS; SEC; RAM.; **BUS ADD:** 2660 S. Rochester Rd., Rochester, MI 48063, (313)852-1700.

SMALLOW, Stevan A.——B: Sept. 29, 1948, Philadelphia, PA, *VP*, Smallow Mgmt. Co.; **PRIM RE ACT:** Syndicator, Property Manager, Owner/Investor; **SERVICES:** Prop. Mgmt. for Apts. & Condos. Synd. of Investment RE; **REP CLIENTS:** Indiv., Cos., Instns., Condo Assns.; **PROFL AFFIL & HONORS:** CPM, Firm is an accredited mgmt. org.; **EDUC:** BS, 1970, RE, PA State Univ.; **EDUC HONORS:** Deans List; **MIL SERV:** US Army, SP/5; **HOME ADD:** 622 Bob White Lane, Huntingdon Valley, PA 19006; **BUS TEL:** (215)343-4500.

SMART, Eric——*Ed.*, Urban Land Inst., Urban Land; **PRIM RE ACT:** Real Estate Publisher; **BUS ADD:** 1200 18th St., NW, Washington, DC 20036, (202)331-8500.*

SMART, James Lee——B: July 14, 1940, Spanish Fork, UT, *Owner & Pres.*, Smart Projections West Construction and Development, Inc.; **PRIM RE ACT:** Consultant, Developer, Builder, Owner/Investor, Instructor, Property Manager, Syndicator; **SERVICES:** Devel. - subdiv. lots & townhouses, RE consultant, seminar instr. - RE investing; **PREV EMPLOY:** 12 years as Prof. with the L.D.S. Church School System, Dir. of Pre-Service Teacher Training - UT State Univ.; **PROFL AFFIL & HONORS:** Member, PDK Educational Frat.; Member, NHBA, Selected for *Who's Who in the West*; Pres. No. UT Home Bldrs. Assn.; **EDUC:** BS, 1964, Mathematics, Secondary Education, Sociology, Brigham Young Univ.; **GRAD EDUC:** MS, 1968, Educ., Eastern OR State Coll., LaGrande, OR; EdD, 1978, Educ. Admin., Brigham Young Univ., Provo, UT; **EDUC HONORS:** VP of Student Housing, Assoc. Men's Student Council, Scored 93rd percentile on Grad. Rec. Exam in Educ. 3.72 GPA; **OTHER ACT & HONORS:** High Council - LDS Church; **HOME ADD:** 1569 Brittany Place, Logan, UT 84321, (801)752-0097; **BUS ADD:** 1569 Brittany Place, Logan, UT 84321, (801)752-0097.

SMATHERS, Joseph F., Jr.——B: Sept. 20, 1946, Canton, NC, *VP Development Operations*, Hardees Food Systems Inc.; **OTHER RE ACT:** Corporate RE Officer; **PREV EMPLOY:** Site Devel., British Petroleum, Washington, DC; **PROFL AFFIL & HONORS:** Founding Member, NACORE, Nat. Assn. of Review Appraisers, Sr. Member; Sr. Member., Intl. Inst. of Valuers; **EDUC:** BS, 1969, Econ., Mars Hill Coll.; **GRAD EDUC:** Grad. Work, Johns Hopkins Univ., Univ. of NC, Chapel Hill; **HOME ADD:** 3516 Sheffield Dr., Rocky Mount, NC 27801; **BUS ADD:** 1233 North Church St., Rocky Mount, NC 27801, (919)977-2060.

SMEDBERG, Gerald D.——B: Apr. 11, 1930, Minneapolis, MN, *Pres.*, Smedberg & Assocs., Inc.; **PRIM RE ACT:** Broker, Consultant, Appraiser, Owner/Investor, Instructor, Insuror; **SERVICES:** Broker-instr., consultant, appraiser, ins., owner, investor; **PROFL AFFIL & HONORS:** NAR; RNMI; Nat. Assn. Ind. Fee Appraisers; Nat. Speakers Assn., CRB; CRS; IFA; Past Pres., Metro. Area Ind. Fee Appraisers; Sec. & Dir. Minneapolis Bd. of Realtors; Dir. Minneapolis MLS; State Membership Chmn. as well as chmn. of numerous other comms.; VP Membership & Member of Exec. Comm. RNMI; RNMI Convention Comm.; VChmn. (Honolulu Convention); NAR Membership Comm.; Nat. Speakers Assn.; Sales & Mktg. Execs.; Instr. and coordinator of RE lic. course at Voc-Tech Inst.; State approved instr. MN, LA, ME & SD Realtor courses; **MIL SERV:** USN; PO 3rd.; **OTHER ACT & HONORS:** Jaycee Intl. Senator; Dir. Minneapolis Jaycees, Lifetime member; PTA Pres.; Mt. Olivet Men's Club Dir.; Boy Scout and Cub Scout Comm. Chmn.; **HOME ADD:** 4026 York Ave. S, Minneapolis, MN 55410, (612)926-4506; **BUS ADD:** 4500 Excelsior Blvd., Minneapolis, MN 55416, (612)925-4020.

SMEDLEY, James K.——B: June 28, 1938, Poteau, OK, *Pres.*, Smedley Realty & Management Co., Inc.; **PRIM RE ACT:** Broker, Consultant, Instructor, Property Manager, Syndicator; **SERVICES:** Multi-Family & Comml. Brokerage, Leasing & Mgmt.; **REP CLIENTS:** Investors, Synd. and Major Fin. Instit.; **PREV EMPLOY:** Republic Nat. Bank of Dallas, 1969-1978; **PROFL AFFIL & HONORS:** Instit. of RE Mgmt., Nat. Assn. of RE Boards, CPM; **EDUC:** BS, 1960, Forest Mgmt., OK State Univ.; **MIL SERV:** US Army, Sgt.; **OTHER ACT & HONORS:** Approved Instr., RE, Texarkana Coll. System; **HOME ADD:** 928 E New Boston Rd., Nash, TX 75569, (214)832-3883; **BUS ADD:** 4112 McKnight Rd., Texarkana, TX 75503, (214)832-5486.

SMENT, Michael R.——B: Sept. 29, 1954, Inglewood, CA, *Atty.*, Borton, Petrini & Conron; **PRIM RE ACT:** Attorney, Owner/Investor, Property Manager, Real Estate Publisher; **SERVICES:** Legal and Bus. planning advice; drafting of documents; negotiating transactions; all types of plaintiff and defense litigation; foreclosures; etc.; **REP CLIENTS:** Lenders, indiv. and instnl. investors, devels, brokers; salespeople; contractors; indiv. and corporate pro. owners, bus. lessees and lessors, govt. entities, and non-profit corps.; **PREV EMPLOY:** State of CA, 4th Dist., Ct. of Appeal 1978-1980; **PROFL AFFIL & HONORS:** State Bar of CA (Real Prop. Law Sect., Asst. Editor, State Bar Real Prop. Newsletter, 1980-1981); Kern Cty. Bar Assn., ABA, (Real Prop. and Bus. Law Sect.); Assn. of Southern CA Defense Counsel; **EDUC:** BA, Cum Laude,1976, Public Relations/Journalism, Univ. of Southern CA (School of Journalism); **GRAD EDUC:** JD, 1979, Bus. and RE Law, Univ. of San Diego, Sch. of Law; **EDUC HONORS:** Dean's List, 1972-1976; Delta Chi Educ. Award, 1975 & 1976; Blackstonian Honor Soc., 1975-1976, Member, San Diego Law Review '78-79, Semi-Finalist, Atty.-Client Competition, 1977; **OTHER ACT & HONORS:** Public Relations Soc. of Amer. 1976-1981, Republican Natl. Comm. 1978-1981; **HOME ADD:** 2421 Planz Rd., 13, Bakersfield, CA 93304; **BUS ADD:** 1712-19th St., Bakersfield, CA 93302, (805)322-3051.

SMETHURST, Robert Guy——B: May 28, 1929, Calgary, Alberta, Can., *Managing Partner*, D'Arcy and Deacon; **PRIM RE ACT:** Attorney, Owner/Investor; **SERVICES:** Legal advice, drafting of documents, etc.; **REP CLIENTS:** RE, condo. and timeshare devels., mort. lenders; **PROFL AFFIL & HONORS:** Can. Bar Assn.; Uniform Law Conference, Queen's Counsel; **EDUC:** LLB, 1952, Univ. of MB; **MIL SERV:** Can. Army; Maj.; Can. Forces Decoration; **HOME ADD:** 308 Lamont Blvd., Winnipeg, R3P 0G1, MB, (204)885-1057; **BUS ADD:** 300-286 Smith St., Winnipeg, R3C 1K6, Manitoba, (204)942-2271.

SMILES, Scott T.——B: Jan. 9, 1953, Paterson, NJ, *Prop. Appraisal Supervisor*, Palm Bch. Prop. Appraisers Office; **PRIM RE ACT:** Appraiser; **SERVICES:** spec. assignment, reappraisal of central bus. dist.; Comml. and Residential Appraisals and Reviews; **PROFL AFFIL & HONORS:** Nat. Assn. of Ind. Fee Appraisers, Intl. Assn. of Assessing Officers, NARA; International Institute of Public Appraisers, Ltd., CRA, Cert. FL Evaluator; RPA; **EDUC:** BA, 1976, Pol. Sci., Montclair State Coll., Upper Montclair, NJ; **EDUC HONORS:** Magna Cum Laude, Nat. Pol. Sci. Hon. Soc. Award, Nat. Soc. Sci. Honor Soc. Award; **HOME ADD:** 2097 SW 13 Terr., Boynton Bch., FL 33435, (305)732-8528; **BUS ADD:** Cty. Ct. House, Rm. #214, W Palm Beach, FL 33401.

SMILEY, Thomas B., III——B: Feb. 3, 1949, *Pres.*, Smiley, Fay & Poe, Inc.; **PRIM RE ACT:** Broker, Owner/Investor, Syndicator; **SERVICES:** Comml. RE Brokerage, Synd., Devel.; **REP CLIENTS:** Comml. Prop. owners & investors; **EDUC:** Bus. Admin. & Econ., 1972, John Brown Univ.; **BUS ADD:** 1853 Lexington, Houston, TX 77098, (713)358-5204.

SMITH, Albert C.——B: Mar. 6, 1927, Macon, Bibb Cty., GA, *Sec.-Treas.*, Enota Realty, Inc.; **PRIM RE ACT:** Broker, Consultant, Developer, Insuror; **OTHER RE ACT:** Comml. Brokerage & Acquisitions in confidence; **SERVICES:** Comml. brokerage & acquisitions; land & timber mgmt., auctions; **REP CLIENTS:** Indiv. & corporate investors, landowners, estates; **PREV EMPLOY:** RE & Ins.; **PROFL AFFIL & HONORS:** DeKalb Cty. GA & NAR, FLI; **EDUC:**

BS, 1948, Emory Univ., Univ. of GA, Emory Univ. School of Law; **HOME ADD:** 3117 Randolph Rd., Atlanta, GA 30345; **BUS ADD:** 2256 Northlake Pkwy, Suite 313, Tucker, GA 30084, (404)491-0077.

SMITH, Ben H.——B: July 8, 1936, Albany, OR, *Broker-Owner*, Western Investors Realty; **PRIM RE ACT:** Broker, Instructor, Consultant, Owner/Investor; **SERVICES:** Spec. in comml. invest. props., exchanging, sale-leaseback; **REP CLIENTS:** Pension funds, investor grps., indivs. needing tax shelter; **PREV EMPLOY:** Lic. 1959, background in Ins. & Adv. Owned own Mktg./Adv. agency for 5 yrs.; **PROFL AFFIL & HONORS:** OAR, NAR, FLI, New America Network, Interex, FIABCI, RESSI, Currently Pres. of OR CCIM Chap. 36; CCIM Designee; **MIL SERV:** US Army; **HOME ADD:** 3475 Chambers St., Eugene, OR 97405, (503)485-8858; **BUS ADD:** Suite 990, 975 Oak St., Eugene, OR 97401, (503)485-8550.

SMITH, Bill——B: July 29, 1927, FL, *Pres.*, Century 21, Town and Country Realty; **PRIM RE ACT:** Broker, Consultant, Owner/Investor, Developer, Instructor; **SERVICES:** Sales, mgmt., devel., of comml. investment RE, resid. invest.; **PREV EMPLOY:** Seventeen yrs. in the RE profession; **PROFL AFFIL & HONORS:** NAR, TAR, Victoria Bd. of Realtors, Grad. of RE Inst.; GRI; CCIM; **EDUC:** Various RE schools and seminars including successful completion of all CCIM study courses (Requirements of designation NOT completed); **MIL SERV:** USN; HC 3/C, Pacific Theatre, Good Conduct; **OTHER ACT & HONORS:** Dir., Victoria Mexican Amer. C of C; **HOME ADD:** 2803 Bluebonnet Dr., Victoria, TX 77901, (512)575-6715; **BUS ADD:** 911 E. Airline Rd., PO Box 3432, Vicoria, TX 77903, (512)575-8221.

SMITH, Blair E.——B: June 3, 1932, Bangor, ME, *VP & Prop. Mgr.*, ERA Libby Bloxam, Inc.; **PRIM RE ACT:** Broker, Property Manager; **SERVICES:** Resid. sales, prop. mgmt., comml.; **PROFL AFFIL & HONORS:** NAR, RNMI, GRI, CRB; **EDUC:** BS, 1974, Mgmt., Econ., Hampton Inst.; **MIL SERV:** Army, 1952-73, Lt. Col., DSM, Air Medal with 16 OLC, Army Commendation Medal; **OTHER ACT & HONORS:** Newport News/Hampton Tax Payers Assn.; Mason; Truth & Friendship 828 AF&AM; Pres. Newport News/Hampton Bd. of Realtors, 1981; **HOME ADD:** 924 Etna Dr., PO Box 2265, Newport News, VA 23602, (804)877-7801; **BUS ADD:** 14801 Warwick Blvd., Newport News, VA 23602, (804)874-2545.

SMITH, Brian J.——B: Jan. 3, 1952, Albany, NY, *Sr. Atty.*, NY State Dept. of Law, Real Prop. Bureau; **PRIM RE ACT:** Attorney; **SERVICES:** RE Apprpriations; **PROFL AFFIL & HONORS:** ABA; NY State Bar Assn.; **EDUC:** BS, 1974, Pol. Sci., SUNY Brockport; **GRAD EDUC:** JD, 1977, Law, Catholic Univ. of America; **EDUC HONORS:** Cum Laude; **OTHER ACT & HONORS:** Albany County Democratic Committee (1978-82); **HOME ADD:** 185 Lancaster St., Albany, NY 12210; **BUS ADD:** The Capitol, Albany, NY 12224, (518)474-2117.

SMITH, Charles G., Jr.——B: July 28, 1942, Baltimore, MD, *Dir. of Fin.*, Homestead Props.; **PRIM RE ACT:** Developer, Builder; **OTHER RE ACT:** CPA; **SERVICES:** Resid. const. and sale of devel. lots to builders for resid. const.; **REP CLIENTS:** Indivs. & builders; **PREV EMPLOY:** VP Fin., Treas. & Controller - Context Indus. Inc., 5 yrs.; **PROFL AFFIL & HONORS:** AICPA; FL Insts. of CPA's; Nat. Assn. of Accountants, CPA; **EDUC:** BS/BA, 1969, Acctg., FL Atlantic Univ.; **EDUC HONORS:** Dean's List; **MIL SERV:** USCG, PO; **OTHER ACT & HONORS:** Past Member, So. Miami Kendale J.C.S.; **HOME ADD:** 10721 S.W. 124 St., Miami, FL 33176, (305)233-7447; **BUS ADD:** 311 N.E. 8th St., Homestead, FL 33030, (305)245-3030.

SMITH, Charles H., Jr.——B: Dec. 23, 1926, Charlottesville, VA, *Pres.*, Montague, Miller & Co., Realtors; **PRIM RE ACT:** Broker, Consultant; **SERVICES:** Operation of RE sales org.; **PREV EMPLOY:** 20 yrs. in radio broadcasting; **PROFL AFFIL & HONORS:** Past Pres. Charlottesville Albemarle of Realtors; Past Chmn. VAR Awards Comm.; Past Chmn. Local MLS; Member of Profl. Standards Comm., Realtor Best Exemplifying Code of Ethics (local award) 1974; Outstanding board President-Region III (States Award9 1970; **EDUC:** BA, 1950, Hist., Univ. of VA; **EDUC HONORS:** Dean's List last 2 yrs.; **MIL SERV:** US Army, 2nd lt.; **OTHER ACT & HONORS:** Past Pres. Charlottesville, Albemarle C of C; Past Pres. Charlottesville, Albemarle Beekeepers Assn.; Dir. of Greater Charlottesville area Devel. Corp.; **HOME TEL:** (804)293-8828; **BUS ADD:** 500 Westfield Rd., Charlottesville, VA 22906, (804)973-5393.

SMITH, Charles M.——B: May 5, 1954, Marietta, GA, *RE Appraisers*, Claiborne, Lothrop and Sample; **PRIM RE ACT:** Appraiser, Instructor; **SERVICES:** RE appraisals, appraisal course instruction; **REP CLIENTS:** Lenders, relocation companies, dept. of transportation; **PREV EMPLOY:** The Fidelity Corp.; **PROFL AFFIL & HONORS:** AIREA; Soc. of RE Appraisers (SRA); Amer. Soc. of Appraisers, RM; SRA; **EDUC:** BS, 1976, RE Appraisal & Fin., Univ. of TN; **HOME ADD:** 8229 Hunterhill Dr., Knoxville, TN, (615)693-5940; **BUS ADD:** 707 Market St., Knoxville, TN 37902, (615)637-4011.

SMITH, Charles W., Jr.——B: Oct. 14, 1926, Richmond, VA, *Partner*, Charles W. Smith Co. Realtors; **PRIM RE ACT:** Broker, Appraiser, Lender, Builder, Owner/Investor, Property Manager; **EDUC:** 2 years at Hampden Sydney Coll.; **MIL SERV:** USN; **HOME ADD:** 206 Tarrytown Dr., Richmond, VA 23229, (804)740-8210; **BUS ADD:** 114 N. 7th St., Richmond, VA 23219, (804)643-5381.

SMITH, Claude R.——B: Nov. 30, 1942, Birmingham, AL, *Atty. & Notary Public*; **PRIM RE ACT:** Attorney; **PREV EMPLOY:** Sr. Atty. Fed. Land Bank of New Orleans; Gen. Counsel Fed. Intermediate Credit Bank of New Orleans; **PROFL AFFIL & HONORS:** Amer., AL & LA Bar Assns.; Phi Alpha Delta Law Frat. and Jefferson Parish Bar Assns.; **EDUC:** AB, 1964, Poli. Sci. - Minor in Math., Univ. of AL - Tuscaloosa, AL; **GRAD EDUC:** JD, 1967, Cumberland School of Law, Samford Univ. - Birmingham, AL; **EDUC HONORS:** Alpha Phi Omega; **MIL SERV:** Further study - Loyola Univ. School of Law - New Orleans; **OTHER ACT & HONORS:** LA Coalition of Handicapped Children & Cystic Fibrosis Foundation; **HOME ADD:** 4317 Troy St., Metairie, LA 70001, (504)455-8012; **BUS ADD:** 4408 Yale St., Metairie, LA 70002, (504)889-0408.

SMITH, Curtis B.——B: Mar. 26, 1945, Bakersfield, CA, *Pres., Chief Fin. Officer, Member Bd. Dir*, Calafia Devel. Corp.; **PRIM RE ACT:** Developer, Owner/Investor, Syndicator; **SERVICES:** Formation & operation of CA ltd. partnerships for investment in real property; **REP CLIENTS:** Indiv., corp. & pension plan investors; **PROFL AFFIL & HONORS:** Member Bd. of Dir., Apt. Assn. of Greater Los Angeles; **EDUC:** BS, 1973, Geog., Ecosystems, Univ. of CA at Los Angeles; **EDUC HONORS:** Dean's List; **MIL SERV:** USAF, E-4, Air Force Commendation Medal; **BUS ADD:** 3685 Motor Ave., Ste. 200, Los Angeles, CA 90034, (213)558-0543.

SMITH, Dane F.——B: Nov. 7, 1951, *Nat. Leasing Mgr.*, The MaceRich Co.; **PRIM RE ACT:** Developer; **PREV EMPLOY:** Alexander Summer Mort. Co., Teaneck, NJ 1973-1974; **EDUC:** BS, 1973, Computer Sci., Boston Coll., Chestnut Hill MA; **GRAD EDUC:** MBA, 1978, Gen. Bus., MS Coll. Clinton MS; **EDUC HONORS:** Cum Laude; **HOME ADD:** 7317 Campbell Rd., Dallas, TX 75240, (214)233-6747; **BUS ADD:** 5501 LBJ Freeway, Suite 500, Dallas, TX 75240, (214)385-9858.

SMITH, Donald W.A.——B: Feb. 11, 1940, Monterey, CA, *Prin.*, D.J. Wilson & Co., Inc.; **PRIM RE ACT:** Property Manager, Broker, Consultant, Instructor; **SERVICES:** Broker, prop. mgr., leasing agent, consultant of comml. props.; **REP CLIENTS:** Instnl. and foreign investors in comml. props.; **PREV EMPLOY:** Exec. VP, Fox & Carskadon Mgmt. Corp., 1976-1980; VP, Grubb & Ellis Prop. Servs., Inc., 1972-1976; Dir. of Prop. Mgmt., Grubin Morth & Lawless, Inc., 1968-1972; **PROFL AFFIL & HONORS:** IREM; RESSI; Intl. Council of Shopping Ctrs.; Intl. Inst. of Valuers; BOMA, CPM; CSM; SCV; 1981 Mgr. of the Yr., Orange Cty. Chap., IREM; **EDUC:** BA, 1961, Indus. Mgmt./Bus., Univ. of CA, Santa Barbara; **MIL SERV:** US Army Res., Lt. Col., 1961 to present; **HOME ADD:** 535 Poplar St., Laguna Beach, CA 92651; **BUS ADD:** 1151 Dove St., Ste. 140, Newport Beach, CA 92660, (714)851-1244.

SMITH, Drayton Beecher, II——B: Apr. 15, 1949, Memphis, TN, *Atty. at Law*, Glanker, Brown, Gilliland, Chase, Robinson & Raines, Tax Dept.; **PRIM RE ACT:** Attorney, Owner/Investor; **SERVICES:** Investment counseling, tax planning, prop. mgmt., liquidation of decedent's estates; **REP CLIENTS:** Individual investors in comml. props.; decedent's estates; **PROFL AFFIL & HONORS:** Member of ABA-Taxation Section and Real Prop. Probate and Trust Sect., Member of Comm. on Income of Estates and Trusts-Special Partnership Project; **EDUC:** BA, 1971, Eng. and Hist., Milsaps Coll.; **GRAD EDUC:** JD, 1974, Real Prop., probate, trust and tax law, Univ. of TN, George C. Taylor Coll. of Law; **EDUC HONORS:** Dean's List; **OTHER ACT & HONORS:** Notary Public (1975 to present); Sec./Treas. Northeast Memphis Optimist Club (1977-78); **HOME ADD:** 237 Windover Rd., Memphis, TN 38111, (901)327-4822; **BUS ADD:** 1700 One Commerce Square, Memphis, TN 38103, (901)525-1322.

SMITH, Edward T.——B: Oct. 24, 1934, Hartford, CT, Healy-Smith Development Inc.; **OTHER RE ACT:** Shopping Center Development; **PREV EMPLOY:** Friendly Ice Cream Corp. 1962-1968, W.T. Grant Co. 1968-1975, Great Atl. & Pac. Tea Co. 1975-1977; **PROFL AFFIL & HONORS:** ICSC 1963-Present; **EDUC:** 1960, Arts & Sci., Univ. of CT; **HOME ADD:** 96 Ardmore Rd., West Hartford, CT, (617)329-

7616; **BUS ADD:** 850R Providence Hwy., Dedham, MA 02026.

SMITH, Edwin A.——**B:** Aug. 15, 1931, Boston, MA, *Owner*, Edwin Smith, Realtor; **PRIM RE ACT:** Broker, Syndicator; **SERVICES:** Investments for Estate Building Representing the Buyer; **REP CLIENTS:** Profls., Corp. Exec. & Small Bus. Owners; **PROFL AFFIL & HONORS:** NAR, Intl. Real Estate Exchangers, New England RE Exchangers, Realtors, Comml.-Investment Div., *Who's Who in Creative R*; **EDUC:** BBA, 1957, Acctg. and Fin., Babson Coll.; **GRAD EDUC:** MBA, 1974, Mgmt. and Behavorial Sci., Babson Coll.; **EDUC HONORS:** Grad. with Distinction; **MIL SERV:** USN, Yeoman; **OTHER ACT & HONORS:** Beverly Rotary Club, Dir., N. Shore C of C, Pres., MA Assn. of Realtors, Commercial Investment Div.; **HOME ADD:** 12 Pickman Rd., Beverly, MA 01915, (617)927-3424; **BUS ADD:** 12 Pickman Rd., Beverly, MA 01915, (617)927-5444.

SMITH, Eugene P.——**B:** Oct. 8, 1921, York, PA, *Partner*, Weinberg and Green, RE; **PRIM RE ACT:** Attorney; **SERVICES:** All serv. relating to acquisition, devel., improvement, operation, and sale of RE projects; **PROFL AFFIL & HONORS:** ABA, MD State Bar Assn., Baltimore City Bar Assn., Homebuilders Assn. of MD.; **EDUC:** BA, 1943, Philosophy, St. Mary's Seminary and Univ.; **GRAD EDUC:** LLB, 1949 subsequently changed to JD, Law, Univ. of Baltimore, Heisler Soc.; **EDUC HONORS:** Magna Cum Laude; **OTHER ACT & HONORS:** Dir., VP and Pres. of Baltimore Assn. for Retarded Citizens; **HOME ADD:** 409 Gittings Ave., Baltimore, MD 20212, (301)435-7534; **BUS ADD:** 100 S. Charles St., Baltimore, MD 21201, (301)332-8713.

SMITH, Forrest C.——**B:** Aug. 4, 1940, Wallace, NC, *RE Prop. Mgr. - Asst. VP*, Integon Corp., RE; **PRIM RE ACT:** Property Manager; **OTHER RE ACT:** Acquisition of new props. for firm; **SERVICES:** Mgmt. of investor owned props.; **REP CLIENTS:** Integon RE Props.; **PREV EMPLOY:** Controller, Integon Realty, Integon Computer Corp.; **PROFL AFFIL & HONORS:** IREM/W-S7; Nat Bd. of Realtors, CPM; **EDUC:** BS, 1962, Bus. Admin., E Carolina Univ.; **EDUC HONORS:** Dean List; **HOME ADD:** 131-2 Dalewood Dr., Winston-Salem, NC 27104, (919)768-9289; **BUS ADD:** 500 W Fifth St., Winston-Salem, NC 27102, (919)725-7261.

SMITH, Frank James——**B:** June 10, 1938, Saskatchenan, CAN, *Gen. Mgr. (EO)*, Canapen Investments Ltd. (The Canapen Grp.); **PRIM RE ACT:** Consultant, Owner/Investor; **SERVICES:** RE Investment Advisors; **REP CLIENTS:** CAN Natl. Railways Employees Pension Trust Fund; **PREV EMPLOY:** Paragon Props. Limited 1968-1970; Frank J. Smith & Assocs. Ltd. 1970-1982; Canaden Investments 1976 to date; **PROFL AFFIL & HONORS:** CAN Inst. of Chartered Accountants, BOMA, Intl. Council of Shopping Centres, Chartered Accountant; **OTHER ACT & HONORS:** Bd. of Advisors-Grant McEwan Community Coll.; **HOME ADD:** 9515 Ottewell Rd., Edmonton, Alberta, CAN, (403)466-2046; **BUS ADD:** 680 Phipps-McKinnon Bldg., 10020 101A Ave., Edmonton, T53-3G2, Alberta, CAN, (403)428-0511.

SMITH, Gary W.——**B:** Aug. 31, 1952, *Exec. Dir.*, Chester County Development Council; **SERVICES:** Cty. Economic Devel. Agency, specifically in indus. & comml. devel.; **PROFL AFFIL & HONORS:** NAIOP; AEDA; Bd. of Dirs., NIDA & PEDA; **EDUC:** BA, 1974, Geography/Planning, West Chester State Coll.; **EDUC HONORS:** Cum Laude with a GPA of 3.35; **OTHER ACT & HONORS:** Explorer Div. of Boy Scout Chester Cty. Council; **HOME ADD:** 1907 Chestnut Ln., Downingtown, PA 19335, (215)384-6025; **BUS ADD:** 750 Pottstown Pike, Exton, PA 19341, (215)363-6110.

SMITH, George R.——**B:** Jan. 29, 1913, Arcadia, FL, *Sec.-Treas.*, Arcadia Shopping Plaza, Inc.; **PRIM RE ACT:** Broker, Appraiser, Owner/Investor, Insuror; **PROFL AFFIL & HONORS:** FL Assn. of Realtors, NAR, FL AIA, NAIA; **MIL SERV:** US Army, Col. (Retired); **OTHER ACT & HONORS:** C of C, Kiwanis, Amer. Legion; **HOME ADD:** 300 Smith Ave., Arcadia, FL 33821; **BUS ADD:** PO Drawer 150, Arcadia, FL 33821, (813)494-3511.

SMITH, George T.——**B:** Sept. 21, 1924, Wadley, GA, *Real Prop. Admin.*, Joint City - County Bd. of Tax Assessors, Atlanta-Fulton County; **PRIM RE ACT:** Appraiser, Assessor; **PROFL AFFIL & HONORS:** IAAO; GA Assn. of Assessing Officials, CAE; GCA; **EDUC:** Attended the Univ. of GA; **HOME ADD:** 1921 Arnold Dr., Austell, GA 30001, (404)941-9447; **BUS ADD:** 165 Central Ave. SW, Room 100, Atlanta, GA 30335, (404)572-2940.

SMITH, Gibson L.——**B:** Feb. 26, 1914, Charlotte, NC, *Pres.*, Gibson Smith Realty Co.; **PRIM RE ACT:** Broker, Consultant, Appraiser, Syndicator; **SERVICES:** Comml. RE, sales, leases, mgmt.; **REP CLIENTS:** Chain stores, banks, trusts; **PREV EMPLOY:** Mgr., Belkstores RE, 1940-1964, Charlotte, NC; **PROFL AFFIL & HONORS:** Realtor; **EDUC:** 1932, Math., Darlington School, Rome, GA; AB, 1937, Pol. Sci./Hist., Davidson Coll.; **EDUC HONORS:** Cum Laude, Dean's List; **MIL SERV:** USN Res.; Lt.; Minesweeping, WWI; **OTHER ACT & HONORS:** City Councilman, Charlotte, 1959-1969; Amer. Legion; Amer. Defense Assn.; Charlotte City Club; Myers Park Presbyterian Church; **HOME ADD:** 2633 Richardson Dr.#4, Charlotte, NC 28211, (704)366-4652; **BUS ADD:** Suite 1710, NCNB Plaza, Charlotte, NC 28280, (704)333-7151.

SMITH, Gordon L., Jr.——*Secy. & Treas.*, North American Royalties Inc.; **PRIM RE ACT:** Property Manager; **BUS ADD:** 200 E. Eighth St., Chatanooga, TN 37402, (615)265-3181.*

SMITH, Gordon V.——**B:** July 3, 1932, Gary, IN, *Pres.*, Miller and Smith, Inc.; **PRIM RE ACT:** Broker, Developer, Builder, Owner/Investor, Instructor, Property Manager; **OTHER RE ACT:** Mort. Banking; **PROFL AFFIL & HONORS:** Nat. Assn. of Home Builders; **EDUC:** BA, 1954, Econ., OH Wesleyan Univ.; **GRAD EDUC:** MBA, 1959, Fin., Harvard Bus. School; **EDUC HONORS:** Phi Beta Kappa; **MIL SERV:** USAF, 1st Lt., Pilot; **OTHER ACT & HONORS:** Bd. of Trs., OH Wesleyan Univ.; **HOME ADD:** 8716 Crider Brook Way, Potomac, MD 20854, (301)469-8597; **BUS ADD:** 1301 Beverly Rd., McLean, VA 22101, (703)821-2500.

SMITH, H. Derrell——**B:** Aug. 4, 1945, Salt Lake City, UT, *VP & Mgr., RE*, Alaska Statebank, RE; **PRIM RE ACT:** Banker; **SERVICES:** Comml., constr. & resid. RE loans; **PROFL AFFIL & HONORS:** ABA; AREA; **EDUC:** 1970, Econ., Brigham Young Univ.; **MIL SERV:** US Army, Sgt. E-4; **OTHER ACT & HONORS:** Taught Econ. & Math at AK Pacific Univ., 1971-1973; **HOME ADD:** SRA Box 199-Y, Anchorage, AK 99502, (907)344-8035; **BUS ADD:** 310 E. Northern Lights Blvd., Anchorage, AK 99502, (907)277-5661.

SMITH, Halbert C.——**B:** July 25, 1934, Libertyville, IL, *Prof. & Dir. RE Research Ctr.*, Univ. of FL, Coll. of Bus. Admin.; **PRIM RE ACT:** Consultant, Instructor; **SERVICES:** Teaching, research, investment analysis; **REP CLIENTS:** Profl. orgs., public agencies, private investors; **PREV EMPLOY:** Dir. of Econ. Research, Fed. Home Loan Bank Bd.; **PROFL AFFIL & HONORS:** Amer. RE & Urban Econ. Assn., Soc. of RE Appraisers; Amer. Soc. of RE Counselors, Sr. RE Analyst (SREA); CRE; **EDUC:** BS, 1956, Agric. Econ., Purdue Univ.; **GRAD EDUC:** MBA, 1959, Bus., Indiana Univ.; DBA, 1962, Univ. of IL; **EDUC HONORS:** Beta Gamma Sigma; **MIL SERV:** Army, Lt.; **OTHER ACT & HONORS:** 1970 Pres., Amer. RE & Urban Econ. Assn.; **HOME ADD:** 701 NW 28th St., Gainesville, FL 32607, (904)373-7411; **BUS ADD:** Gainesville, FL 32611, (904)392-0157.

SMITH, Harlan W.——*Pres.*, Dyneer Corp.; **PRIM RE ACT:** Property Manager; **BUS ADD:** Riverside Bldg., Westport, CT 06880, (203)226-1071.*

SMITH, Harold D.——**B:** Nov. 12, 1939, Shakopea, MN, *Pres.*, H.D. Smith & Associates; **PRIM RE ACT:** Consultant; **SERVICES:** RE tax consultant; **REP CLIENTS:** Taxpayers of comml. prop.; **PREV EMPLOY:** Tax Representative, Dayton Hudson Corp.; **PROFL AFFIL & HONORS:** Accredited Assessment Evaluator, Intl. Assn. of Assessing Officers; SRA; **HOME ADD:** 3525 Chippewa Rd., Loretto, MN 55357, (612)478-6625; **BUS ADD:** 3525 Chippewa Rd., Loretto, MN 55357, (612)478-6625.

SMITH, Harry A., III——**B:** July 3, 1945, Natrona Hgts., PA, *Atty.*; **PRIM RE ACT:** Attorney; **SERVICES:** Legal Services, Inc. Title Research, Litigation; **REP CLIENTS:** Bank of Mill Creek, WV; Mountain State Fed. S & L Assn., Clarksburg WV; Belington Bank, Belington, WV; First Fed. S & L Assn. of Cumberland, MD; **PREV EMPLOY:** Law Clerk, Chief Judge Robert E. Maxwell, US Dist. Court, N. Dist. of WV (1972-1973); **PROFL AFFIL & HONORS:** ABA; WV State Bar; Randolph Cty. WV Bar Assn.; Admitted to Bar in OH (1972) and WV (1973); **EDUC:** BA, 1967, English, Univ. of Pittsburgh, PA; **GRAD EDUC:** JD, 1972, Case Western Reserve Univ. School of Law, Cleveland, OH; **HOME ADD:** 102 Henry Ave., Elkins, WV 26241, (304)636-7623; **BUS ADD:** PO Box 1905, Elkins, WV 26241, (304)636-4042.

SMITH, Harry G.——**B:** Sept. 12, 1942, Rockford, IL, *Pres.*, Smith/Cantrell & Associates, Inc.; **PRIM RE ACT:** Broker, Consultant, Developer, Builder, Owner/Investor; **PREV EMPLOY:** Mgr./broker, Rombek Goulb & Co.; **PROFL AFFIL & HONORS:** Chicago RE Bd.; **EDUC:** BS, 1965, Econ., So. IL Univ.; **MIL SERV:** US Army, Capt., Bronze Star, Purple Heart, army commendation, 4 campaign ribbons; **OTHER ACT & HONORS:** VP-Sky Soaring, Inc.; **HOME ADD:** 111 S. Haman Rd., Inverness, IL 60067, (312)358-9206; **BUS ADD:** 2720 Des Plaines Ave., Des Plaines, IL 60018, (312)297-8710.

SMITH, Harry R., Jr.——**B:** June 26, 1926, Baltimore, MD, *VP*, Yost & Smith, P.A., Attorneys at Law; **PRIM RE ACT:** Consultant, Attorney, Developer, Owner/Investor; **OTHER RE ACT:** Civil Engr.; **SERVICES:** Consulting and legal services for devel., synd. and leasing of prop.; **REP CLIENTS:** Indiv., corps., partnerships and ltd. partnerships; **PREV EMPLOY:** Self-Employed Atty. and Civil Engr.; **PROFL AFFIL & HONORS:** ABA, MD Bar Assn.; Amer. Soc. of Civil Engrs., Engrg. Soc. of Baltimore; **EDUC:** BS, 1950, Civil Engrg., Univ. of MD; **GRAD EDUC:** JD, 1968, Univ. of Baltimore; **EDUC HONORS:** Honor Court 1968; **MIL SERV:** US Navy, Quartermaster, 2nd class 1944-1946; **OTHER ACT & HONORS:** St. Christopher's Episcopal Church; Member of Consultant Network of the Episcopal Diocese of Washington; Bd. Member of Life Care Community Presently Under Devel.; **HOME ADD:** 6500 Bell Station Road, Glenn Dale, MD 20769; **BUS ADD:** Arundel Law Center, 105 S. Crain Highway, Glen Burnie, MD 21061, (301)768-5656.

SMITH, Ira R.——**B:** Oct. 18, 1927, Chicksha, OK, *Pres.*, CBS RE Co.; **PRIM RE ACT:** Broker, Appraiser, Developer, Owner/Investor, Syndicator; **EDUC:** BS, 1954, Mktg., Drake Univ.; **MIL SERV:** USN, Lt.; **OTHER ACT & HONORS:** 1981 Small Bus. Award presented by the Midlands Bus. Journal; **HOME ADD:** 3614 S. 94th St., Omaha, NE 68124, (402)397-6222; **BUS ADD:** 9202 W. Dodge Rd., Ste. 302, Omaha, NE 68114, (402)397-6222.

SMITH, Irv——**B:** Dec. 5, 1927, Denver, CO, *Pres.*, AAA Co., Inc., Comml. Investment Prop.; **PRIM RE ACT:** Broker, Banker, Builder, Instructor; **OTHER RE ACT:** Author, lecturer, seminar conductor, instr., Univ. of CO; **PROFL AFFIL & HONORS:** RNMI; CO Assn. of Realtors; Aurora Bd. of Realtors, CCIM; GRI; Univ. Instr.; Nationally known newspaper columnist; **EDUC:** 1945, Univ. of CO; **OTHER ACT & HONORS:** Housing, Rehab. Dir., Civil Defense; Advisor, Federally Funded FACE; Div. Gov., Toastmasters; Chmn., Comm./Investment, Aurora Bd. of Realtors; Dir., Exchange Grp. Co.; **HOME ADD:** 15697 E. Monmouth Pl., Aurora, CO 80015, (303)693-8550; **BUS ADD:** 15697 E. Monmouth Pl., Aurora, CO 80015, (303)750-3000.

SMITH, Ivan J.——**B:** Apr. 9, 1930, Corbin, KY, *Pres.*, Ivan J. Smith & Co., Inc. Realtors; **PRIM RE ACT:** Broker, Developer, Lender, Syndicator; **SERVICES:** All gen. RE brokerage servs.; **PROFL AFFIL & HONORS:** NAR, FL Assn. of Realtors, Nat. Inst. of RE Brokers, CID, Past Pres., Pompano Beach, Deerfield Bd. of Realtors; **EDUC:** 1948-51, Bus. Admin., Univ. of FL; **MIL SERV:** USCG, 2nd Class PO; **OTHER ACT & HONORS:** Chmn. of the Bd., First Bankers NA, Pompano Beach, Dir. First Bankers Corp. of Fl; **BUS ADD:** 3350 E Atlantic Blvd., Pompano Beach, FL 33062, (305)946-0800.

SMITH, J. Michael——**B:** Jan. 21, 1944, Pittsburgh, PA, *Pres.*, The Cabot Group; **PRIM RE ACT:** Developer, Owner/Investor, Syndicator; **SERVICES:** Investment counseling/devel., brokerage, and synd. of comml. props./prop. mgmt.; **REP CLIENTS:** Indiv. or inst. investors or conventures in comml. props.; **PROFL AFFIL & HONORS:** Inst. of RE Mgmt./Mort. Bankers Assn.; **EDUC:** BS, 1967, Mktg., Miami Univ. (OH); **EDUC HONORS:** Dean's List; **OTHER ACT & HONORS:** Bd. of Tr. of Keuka Coll./Bd. Chmn. Rochester Midtown YMCA; **BUS ADD:** 1230 First Federal Plaza, Rochester, NY 14614, (716)546-7440.

SMITH, James G.——**B:** Jun. 28, 1918, Queens, NY, *Sr. VP*, East New York Savings Bank; **PRIM RE ACT:** Banker; **PREV EMPLOY:** European Amer. Bank; Franklin Natl. Bank; **PROFL AFFIL & HONORS:** SREA; **HOME ADD:** 7 Jefferson St., West Hampstead, L.I., NY 11552, (516)481-4151; **BUS ADD:** 1244 Atlantic Ave., Brooklyn, NY 11207, (212)270-6351.

SMITH, James T.——**B:** Jan. 27, 1938, Oak Park, IL, *Owner/Broker, Pres.*, James T. Smith, Inc., Realtor; **PRIM RE ACT:** Broker, Instructor, Consultant, Appraiser, Builder, Insuror; **SERVICES:** Gen. RE Brokerage, Appraisals, Contractor Consultant; **REP CLIENTS:** Resid., Comml., and Investment Clients; **PREV EMPLOY:** Symons Mfg. Co. 1962-1971, Marcor Housing Systems 1971-1972; **PROFL AFFIL & HONORS:** Denver Bd. of Realtors, CO Assn. of Realtors, NAR, CRB, CRS, GRI, CRPA, 1982 Pres., Denver Bd. of Realtors; **EDUC:** BS/BA, 1959, Bldg. Indus. & RE, Univ. of Denver; **MIL SERV:** USMC, Sgt. E-5, Good Conduct Medal, Reserve Medal; **OTHER ACT & HONORS:** Commnr., CO Div. of Wildlife 1979-1983, Life Member Natl. Rifle Assn., Amateur Trap Assn.; **HOME ADD:** 7405 E Kenyon Ave., Denver, CO 80237, (303)771-6117; **BUS ADD:** 6740 E Hampden Ave., Suite 308, Denver, CO 80224, (303)759-9905.

SMITH, Jeanette——*Ed.-Adv. Dir.*, American Land Development Assn., ALDA; **PRIM RE ACT:** Real Estate Publisher; **BUS ADD:** 604 Solar Bldg., 1000 16th St., NW, Washington, DC 20036, (202)659-4582.*

SMITH, Jim——**B:** May 22, 1942, Chicago, IL, *Partner*, Woodland Farms Real Estate; **PRIM RE ACT:** Broker, Developer, Lender, Builder, Owner/Investor; **EDUC:** BS, 1970, Acctg., St. Joseph's Coll.; **GRAD EDUC:** MBA, 1972, Acctg., DePaul Univ.; **HOME ADD:** PO Box 183, Eastman, WI 54626, (608)734-3933; **BUS ADD:** PO Box 96, DeSoto, WI 54624, (608)648-3326.

SMITH, Joanne S.——**B:** July 3, 1927, Pine Bluff, AR, *VP*, Theis-Smith Prop. Mgmt. Inc.; **PRIM RE ACT:** Syndicator, Property Manager; **PROFL AFFIL & HONORS:** IREM, AR Chap. Past Pres., GRI, CPM, CCIM Candidate, RAM of NAHB; **EDUC:** BS, 1950, Bus. Admin., Univ. of AR; **EDUC HONORS:** Cum Laude; **OTHER ACT & HONORS:** Dir. Pine Bluff C of C; Also associated with Midland Corp. - Dir. & VP; **HOME ADD:** 17 Elm Woods Cir., Pine Bluff, AR 71603, (501)535-0045; **BUS ADD:** 5th at Walnut St., Pine Bluff, AR 71601, (501)534-7010.

SMITH, John Charles——**B:** Dec. 31, 1942, Los Angeles, CA, *Pres.*, Pioneer Investments Co.; **PRIM RE ACT:** Broker, Consultant, Attorney, Instructor; **SERVICES:** Broker servs (comml. & investment), attys. servs.; **PREV EMPLOY:** Ed Moore Realty, Inc. (salesman); Instr. in law & RE Fullerton & Cypress Comm. Colls.; **PROFL AFFIL & HONORS:** Member of CA Bar, and admitted to practice before the US Supreme Court; **EDUC:** BS, 1968, Fin. & Banking (Bus. Mgmt.), Brigham Young Univ., Provo, UT; **GRAD EDUC:** JD, 1974, Pepperdine Univ. Sch. of Law, Malibu, CA; **EDUC HONORS:** Amer. Jurisprudence Award in Labor Law; **OTHER ACT & HONORS:** Bd. of Dirs.: Norwalk Food Assn.; Cypress Coll., Patrons for the Performing Arts; **HOME ADD:** PO Box 955, La Mirada, CA 90637; **BUS ADD:** PO Box 955, La Mirada, CA 90637, (714)522-4742.

SMITH, Ken——*Asst. VP Mgmt. Serv.*, Paller Inc.; **PRIM RE ACT:** Property Manager; **BUS ADD:** Business Center Bldg., PO Box 1518, Bellevue, WA 98009, (206)455-7444.*

SMITH, Kenneth J.——**B:** July 30, 1934, Cleveland, OH, *Econ. Devel. Dir.*, City of Coral Gables; **OTHER RE ACT:** Econ. Devel. Dir.; **SERVICES:** Mktg. Coral Gables as a business location and Providing info. to industry; **PROFL AFFIL & HONORS:** Amer. Econ. Devel. Council; So. Indus. Devel. Council; FL Indus. Devel. Council, Soc. of Profl. Journalists; **EDUC:** BA, 1959, Journalism, Univ. of Miami; **MIL SERV:** USCG, PO; **OTHER ACT & HONORS:** Jr. Orange Bowl Comm.; **HOME ADD:** 480 NE 143rd St., N. Miami, FL 33161, (305)891-5023; **BUS ADD:** 405 Biltmore Way, Coral Gables, FL 33134, (305)442-6441.

SMITH, Lamar E.——**B:** Aug. 21, 1945, Xenia, OH, *Exec. VP, Treas., Pres.*, Dayton Fin. Serv.; Columbus Serv. & Mort. Co.; **PRIM RE ACT:** Developer, Builder, Property Manager; **SERVICES:** Land devel., const. and bldg. mgmt.; **REP CLIENTS:** Builders and parent Co.; **PROFL AFFIL & HONORS:** ULI; Partners, Coll. of Admin.; OH State Univ., Grad. Sch., S & L, IN Univ.; **EDUC:** 1967, Fin., OH State Univ.; **MIL SERV:** US Army; 1st Lt.; ACM; ACM 1st OAK; **OTHER ACT & HONORS:** Dayton Kiwanis Club; Dayton Area C of C; **HOME ADD:** 3951 Ephrata Ct., Dayton, OH 45430, (513)429-2365; **BUS ADD:** 110 N. Main St., Dayton, OH 45402, (513)228-7273.

SMITH, Larry J.——**B:** Apr. 2, 1936, Chicago, IL, *Exec. VP*, Romanek Golub & Co.; **PRIM RE ACT:** Broker, Consultant, Developer, Owner/Investor, Property Manager; **PROFL AFFIL & HONORS:** Chicago RE Bd., Natl. Assn. of RE Bds., RNMI, IREM, CCIM, CPM; **EDUC:** BS, 1957, Econ., Univ. of PA; **MIL SERV:** US Army, Capt.; **BUS ADD:** 625 N. Michigan Ave., Chicago, IL 60611, (312)440-8800.

SMITH, Manning J., III——*VP*, Woodside Corp.; **PRIM RE ACT:** Owner/Investor, Property Manager, Syndicator; **SERVICES:** Pvt. ltd. partnerships; **PROFL AFFIL & HONORS:** CPA, CA, 1970; **EDUC:** BA, 1962, Dartmouth Coll.; **GRAD EDUC:** MBA, 1967, Wharton Sch. Univ. of PA; **MIL SERV:** USMC, Capt.; **BUS ADD:** 3000 Sand Hill Rd., Menlo Park, CA 94025, (415)854-1550.

SMITH, Mark R.——**B:** Mar. 16, 1949, Dallas, TX, *Pres.*, Mark R. Smith Props.; **PRIM RE ACT:** Broker, Developer, Property Manager; **REP CLIENTS:** Inst. and indivs.; **PROFL AFFIL & HONORS:** Dallas Bd. of Realtors; N. TX RE Investors; **EDUC:** RE, Bus., Tyler Jr. Coll., Dallas Baptist, SMU; **MIL SERV:** USMC; **OTHER ACT & HONORS:** Rotary Intl., Bd. of Dir.; **HOME ADD:** 2800 Purdue, Dallas, TX 75225; **BUS ADD:** 2900 Turtle Creek Plaza, 230, Dallas, TX 75219.

SMITH, Mary Elizabeth——**B:** Mar. 12, 1939, S. Pines, NC, *RE Salesperson*, Webb & Brooker, Inc., Resid. sales; **OTHER RE ACT:** RE Salesperson; **SERVICES:** Devel. and synd. of resid. props.; **REP**

CLIENTS: Indiv. or instnl. investors in resid. prop.; **PROFL AFFIL & HONORS:** The RE Bd. of NY, in Greater NY RE Bd.; **EDUC:** BA, 1975, Eng. lit., Columbia Univ.; **GRAD EDUC:** MA, 1977, Educ. admin., NY Univ.; **OTHER ACT & HONORS:** NAACP; **HOME ADD:** 2110 1st Ave., #1902, New York, NY 10029, (212)876-2070; **BUS ADD:** 2534 Adam Clayton Powel Jr.l Blvd., New York, NY 10039, (212)926-7100.

SMITH, Michael G.——**B:** Nov. 12, 1942, Hanover, NH, *Partner*, Madway, Blumberg, Bishop & Smith; **PRIM RE ACT:** Consultant, Attorney; **SERVICES:** Legal representation, fin. & investment analysis; **REP CLIENTS:** Fed, state & local govts.; devels.; housing devels.; corps.; condo, co-op & homeowners' assns.; **PREV EMPLOY:** Nat. Housing Law Project, 1977-present; **PROFL AFFIL & HONORS:** ABA, Sect. Advisor to the Spec. Comm. on the Model RE Coop. Act of the Nat. Conf. of Commnrs. on Uniform State Laws, 1980-81; Vice Chmn. of Condos., Co-ops, & Homeowner Assns., Comm. ABA; **EDUC:** BS, 1965, Math. & Econ., Yale Univ.; **GRAD EDUC:** JD, 1969, Columbua Law Sch.; MBA, 1969, Fin., Columbia Bus. Sch.; **HOME ADD:** 1501 Beverly Pl., Albany, NY 94706, (415)527-9240; **BUS ADD:** 2150 Shattuck Ave., Suite 300, Berkeley, CA 94704, (415)548-9400.

SMITH, Neil——**B:** July 10, 1937, Gardner, MA, *V.P.*, CC&F Prop. Mgmt. Co., Inc.; **PRIM RE ACT:** Property Manager; **SERVICES:** Full service prop. mgmt. for comml. owners; **REP CLIENTS:** Pension funds, ins. cos., condo. assns., private investors; **PREV EMPLOY:** Sperry Rand Corp. 1961-1971; **PROFL AFFIL & HONORS:** BOMA - Past President, Greater Boston RE Bd. - V.P. & Dir.; **EDUC:** BS, 1960, Elec. Engr., Northeastern Univ., Boston, MA; **GRAD EDUC:** MBA, 1968, Northeastern Univ.; **MIL SERV:** US Army, 2nd Lt.; **OTHER ACT & HONORS:** Registered Prof. Engineer (MA); **HOME ADD:** 6 Morse Rd., Wayland, MA 01778; **BUS ADD:** Sixty State St., Boston, MA 02109, (617)742-7600.

SMITH, Ormond N.——**B:** Dec. 17, 1943, Harrisburg, PA, *Sole Prop.*, Ormond N. Smith, Esq.; **PRIM RE ACT:** Attorney; **SERVICES:** Foreclosure of mort.; **PROFL AFFIL & HONORS:** Richmond Cty. Bar Assn.; NY City Lawyers Assn.; NY State Bar Assn.; ABA; **EDUC:** 1967, Econ., Univ. of Pittsburgh; **GRAD EDUC:** JD, 1974, NY Law Sch.; **OTHER ACT & HONORS:** Pres. New Brighton Jewish Congregation; **HOME ADD:** 85 Birchard Ave., Staten Island, NY 10314, (212)698-0299; **BUS ADD:** 25 Sheraden Ave., Staten Island, NY 10314, (212)761-2700.

SMITH, Owen T.——**B:** June 29, 1937, Brooklyn, NY, *Dep. Cty. Exec.*, County of Nassau (NY); **PRIM RE ACT:** Developer, Regulator; **OTHER RE ACT:** Govt. ofcl.; **SERVICES:** Responsible for RE devel. in Nassau Cty., Long Island, NY; **PREV EMPLOY:** Editor, Inst. for Bus. Planning, RE & Investment Ideas; **PROFL AFFIL & HONORS:** ABA, NY State Bar Assn., Chmn. Nassau Cty. Planning Commn.; **EDUC:** BA, 1959, Econ. & Govt., Trinity Coll., Hartford, CT; **GRAD EDUC:** LLD-JD, 1964, St. John's School of Law; **OTHER ACT & HONORS:** Dep. Cty. Exec., Cty. of Nassau 1980-; VP - Props.- Boy Scouts of Amer.; **HOME ADD:** Mill River Rd., Oyster Bay, NY 11771, (516)922-0028; **BUS ADD:** 1 West St., Mineola, NY 11501, (516)535-3333.

SMITH, Paul J.——*Dir. RE*, Goodyear Tire & Rubber Co.; **PRIM RE ACT:** Property Manager; **BUS ADD:** 1144 E. Market St., Akron, OH 44316, (216)794-4286.*

SMITH, Peter A.——**B:** Sept. 21, 1945, Birmingham, MI, *Asst. VP*, Chemical Mortgage Co., Const. Loans/Asset Mgmt.; **PRIM RE ACT:** Lender; **PREV EMPLOY:** Inland Steel Development Corporation 1972-1977; **PROFL AFFIL & HONORS:** Profl. Engr. Registered in the State of OH; **EDUC:** BS, 1967, CE, MI State Univ.; **GRAD EDUC:** MBA, 1971, MI State Univ.; **EDUC HONORS:** Beta Gamma Sigma Honorary Scholarship Soc.; **HOME ADD:** 872 College Ave., Columbus, OH 43209, (614)235-4760; **BUS ADD:** 101E Town St., Columbus, OH 43215, (614)460-3096.

SMITH, Peter C.——**B:** Mar. 20, 1940, Cleveland, OH, *Pres.*, Peter C. Smith & Associates, Inc.; **PRIM RE ACT:** Developer, Owner/Investor, Property Manager; **SERVICES:** Owners and devel. of comml. props.; **REP CLIENTS:** Winn-Dixie, Eckerd Drugs, U.S. Postal Service, Long John Silver's, Cobb Theaters, Publix Super Mkts., Super-X Drugs, 7-Eleven Food Stores, etc.; **PREV EMPLOY:** Admin. of Contracts and Leases for Nat. Airlines 1967-72; **PROFL AFFIL & HONORS:** Various, Various; **EDUC:** BA, 1965, Econ., Union Coll., Schenectady, NY; **MIL SERV:** US Army, Lt.; **OTHER ACT & HONORS:** Past Commodore, Fort Pierce Yacht Club; Member, Racquet Club of Philadelphia; **HOME TEL:** (305)465-6691; **BUS ADD:** P.O. Box 4373, Fort Pierce, FL 33454, (305)465-1440.

SMITH, R. Jeffrey——**B:** Mar. 30, 1953, New Haven, CT, *Atty.*, Barclays American/Business Credit, Inc., Law Dept.; **PRIM RE ACT:** Attorney; **SERVICES:** Legal Counsel; **PREV EMPLOY:** MA Mutual Life Insurance Co. (1978-1979) Atty. in Law Dept.; **PROFL AFFIL & HONORS:** Member of MBA, ABA (Member of Corp., Banking and Business Law and Real Prop., Probate and Trust Law Divisions); **EDUC:** BA (Hist.), 1975, Hist., Poli. Sci., Duke Univ., Durham, NC; **GRAD EDUC:** JD, 1978, Law, Georgetown Univ. Law Ctr., Washington, DC; **EDUC HONORS:** Graduated Cum Laude, Dean's List and Class Honors; **HOME ADD:** 100 Susan Dr., Suffield, CT 06078, (203)668-1433; **BUS ADD:** PO Box 118, Hartford, CT 06101, (203)528-4831.

SMITH, Ralph C.——**B:** July 6, 1924, Flint, MI, *Sr. VP*, Commonwealth Land Title Ins. Co., Nat. Title Serv. Div.; **OTHER RE ACT:** Title Insurance; **SERVICES:** Title insurance & closing serv. - nationwide; **REP CLIENTS:** Marriott, Prudential, B.F. Saul Reit, Ernest F. Hahn Co., Exxon, McCormick Props., McDonalds, PPG, Law Firms; **PREV EMPLOY:** Lawyers Title Ins. Corp., 1961-1969; **PROFL AFFIL & HONORS:** NAREB; NAREIT; NAHB; MBA; ALTA; ICSC; NACORE; NAIOP; ABA; **EDUC:** AB, 1948, Law, Univ. of MI; **GRAD EDUC:** JD, 1950, Univ. of MI, Law School; **MIL SERV:** US Army, T/5, Several decorations, 1943-1946; **OTHER ACT & HONORS:** Nat. Press Club; **HOME ADD:** 620 Rivercrest Dr., McLean, VA 22101, (703)356-5298; **BUS ADD:** 8150 Lessburg Pike, Suite 513, Vienna, VA 22180, (703)790-1240.

SMITH, Richard, Sr.——**B:** Apr. 13, 1943, Cleveland, OH, *Pres.*, Smith Brothers, Inc.; **PRIM RE ACT:** Developer, Owner/Investor, Property Manager, Syndicator; **OTHER RE ACT:** Prop. Mgr.; **SERVICES:** Synd. of comml. props., prop. mgmt. & condo. conversion; **PREV EMPLOY:** Centennial Realty Co.; **PROFL AFFIL & HONORS:** Natl. State and Atlanta Bd. of Realtors; C of C; AOMA; **EDUC:** BBS, 1971, GA State Univ.; BBA, 1969, FL State Univ.; **EDUC HONORS:** Dean's List with Distingtion, Deans List with Distinction; **OTHER ACT & HONORS:** GA Assn. of Condo. Owners; **HOME ADD:** 1547 Hidden Hills Pkwy., Atlanta, GA 30088; **BUS ADD:** 3177 Peachtree Rd., Suite 217, Atlanta, GA 30305.

SMITH, Richard——*VP*, Toro Manufacturing Corp.; **PRIM RE ACT:** Property Manager; **BUS ADD:** One Appletree Square, 8009 34th Ave., South, Minneapolis, MN 55420, (612)887-8580.*

SMITH, Richard G.——**B:** Nov. 7, 1928, Chicago, IL, *Counsel and Asst. Sec.*, Avco Community Developers, Inc., Laguna Niguel; **PRIM RE ACT:** Broker, Attorney, Developer, Builder, Owner/Investor; **OTHER RE ACT:** Bldg. Contractor; Mgmt; **PREV EMPLOY:** Gen. Counsel & Sec., Occidental Land, Inc., (The RE Subsidiary of Occidental Petroleum Corp.); **PROFL AFFIL & HONORS:** ABA; CA Bar Assn.; Orange Cty. Bar Assn.; Amer. Bd. of Realtors, San Fernando Valley Realty Bd.; **EDUC:** BA, 1950, Econ., UCLA; **GRAD EDUC:** LLB, 1956, Law, DePauL Univ. Coll. of Law; **MIL SERV:** USAF, 1950-1952; **HOME ADD:** 29622 Quigly Dr., Laguna Niguel, CA 92677; **BUS ADD:** 3 Monarch Bay Plaza, Laguna Niguel, CA 92677, (714)830-5050.

SMITH, Richard L.V.——**B:** Dec. 27, 1933, Bismarck, ND, *Pres.*, Smith & Gabbert, Inc.; **PRIM RE ACT:** Broker, Consultant, Developer, Owner/Investor, Property Manager, Syndicator; **REP CLIENTS:** Contractors, investors (major); **PREV EMPLOY:** Devel., broker 16 yrs.; **PROFL AFFIL & HONORS:** NACOR; NAR; CAR; P.R.I.D.E.; **EDUC:** BS, 1954, Univ. of OR; **OTHER ACT & HONORS:** Grand Jury 1975/76; **HOME ADD:** 3351 Cambridge Rd., Cameron Park, CA 95682, (916)933-2108; **BUS ADD:** 3377 Coach Ln., Cameron Park, CA 95682, (916)933-0674.

SMITH, Robert J.——**B:** May 13, 1936, Punxsutawney, PA, *Supervisor, RE Services*, Baltimore Gas & Electric Co., Gen. Servs. Div.; **OTHER RE ACT:** Acquisition of prop. for utility; **SERVICES:** Acquisition, sales, leasing; **PROFL AFFIL & HONORS:** Greater Baltimore Bd. of Realtors; Intl. Right of Way Assn., RE Broker, MD; **EDUC:** BA, BS, 1958, 1971, Mineral Econ., Fuels; Mech. Eng., PA State Univ. & Johns Hopkins Univ.; **GRAD EDUC:** MBA, 1970, Mgmt., Univ. of Baltimore; **MIL SERV:** US Army; SP5; **OTHER ACT & HONORS:** Bd. of Trs. Central Presbyterian Church, Towson, MD, Pres. of Bd. 1979 & 80; **HOME ADD:** 535 Dunkirk Rd., Baltimore, MD 21212, (301)377-6795; **BUS ADD:** Cromwell Ctr., PO Box 1475, Baltimore, MD 21203, (301)583-4840.

SMITH, Robley W.——**B:** Apr. 14, 1927, NYC, *Pres. thru 1980*, Cert. Mgmt., AR Corp.; **PRIM RE ACT:** Consultant, Property Manager, Engineer, Insuror; **SERVICES:** All types of R.E. brokerage; **REP CLIENTS:** Makaha Valley Towers; Mariners Village III; Kapiolani Manor; Kukui Plaza; **PREV EMPLOY:** US Army Corps of Engrs. 32 yrs; **PROFL AFFIL & HONORS:** ASCE, ASME, Member Pi Tau

Sigma Natl. Hon.; Mech. Engrg. Frat.; **EDUC:** BSCE, BSME, 1950/1967, IN Inst. of Engrg., AZ State; **GRAD EDUC:** MSE, 1968, Heat Transfer, AZ State Univ.; **EDUC HONORS:** Pi Tau Sigma; **MIL SERV:** US Army Corps. of Engrg., Ltc., Legion of merit w/ oak leaf cluster; **OTHER ACT & HONORS:** Member Oahu Hearing Bds., Rotarian, Bd. of Realtors; **HOME ADD:** 98-1716 A Kaahumanu St., Pearl City, HI 96782, (808)456-3388; **BUS ADD:** Box 547, Pearl City, HI 96782, (808)487-7941.

SMITH, Roger L.——B: Mar. 21, 1950, Forte Meade, MD, *Asst. Dir. of Bldg., Mgmt.*, John W. Galbreath & Co., Home Office; **PRIM RE ACT:** Broker, Consultant, Developer, Property Manager, Owner/Investor; **SERVICES:** Devel. and Const. Mgmt., Devel. of Downtown Highrise Office and Mixed-Use Projects, Prop. Mgmt.; **REP CLIENTS:** Large Corps. and Instnl. Investors, and Prominent Local Fin. Instns.; **PROFL AFFIL & HONORS:** IREM; BOMA; NAR; Agency Mgmt. Council (BOMA, Intl.), CPM; **EDUC:** BS, 1972, Bus. Admin. - Corp. Fin., OH State Univ.; **EDUC HONORS:** Grad. Cum Laude; **OTHER ACT & HONORS:** Treas. of Westerville Amateur Soccer Program; **HOME ADD:** 5956 Dakar Rd. E, Westerville, OH 43081, (614)891-0369; **BUS ADD:** 180 E. Broad St., Columbus, OH 43215, (614)460-4420.

SMITH, Roland M.——B: Feb. 24, 1893, CLear Lake, IA, *Pres.*, Roland M. Smith, Inc., Realtors, Resid. and Comml.; **PRIM RE ACT:** Broker, Appraiser, Developer, Owner/Investor; **OTHER RE ACT:** Appraiser; **PROFL AFFIL & HONORS:** SRA; Appraiser; State, Nat. and Local RE Assns.; **MIL SERV:** USAF, Maj.; **OTHER ACT & HONORS:** Masons; Odd Fellows; Knights of Pythias; Elks; Jesters; Lettermans Club; **HOME ADD:** 330 Golfview Ave., Iowa City, IA 25240, (319)337-3522; **BUS ADD:** 10 Paul-Helen Bldg., Iowa City, IA 52240, (319)351-0123.

SMITH, Ronald R.——B: Oct. 11, 1950, Minneapolis, MN, *Asst. VP*, Coldwell Banker RE Mgmt. Serv.; **PRIM RE ACT:** Property Manager, Broker; **SERVICES:** Continuous RE mgmt. and advisory serv.; **REP CLIENTS:** Inst. and pvt. prop. owners; **PROFL AFFIL & HONORS:** IREM; BOMA; Nat. Assn. of Office and Indus. Parks; Nat. Apt. Assn. CPM; **EDUC:** BA, 1972, Mktg., Mankato State Univ.; **HOME ADD:** 15311 La Paloma, Houston, TX 77027, (713)840-6676; **BUS ADD:** 2500 W. Loop S., Houston, TX 77027, (713)840-6676.

SMITH, Ronald R.——B: July 29, 1948, Ripon, WI, *Partner*, Koberstein, Smith & Chvala; **PRIM RE ACT:** Attorney; **PREV EMPLOY:** Credit analyst and RE underwriter with Ford Motor Credit Co. 1973-75; **PROFL AFFIL & HONORS:** ABA, WI Bar Assn., Dane Cty. Bar Assn.; **EDUC:** BA, 1971, Soc., Univ. of WI; **GRAD EDUC:** MBA, 1973, RE and Fin., Univ. of WI; JD, 1978, Univ. of WI; **EDUC HONORS:** Grad.Cum Laude,Phi Eta Sigma, Freshman honorary frat., Grad. Cum Laude, Beta Gamma Sigma frat. (open to top 10%), Grad. Cum Laude, recipient of Jacob H. Beuscher Memorial Scholarship for academic achievement and interest in RE law; **OTHER ACT & HONORS:** Alumni Chap. of Alpha Delta Phi frat., Licensed RE broker for WI, former candidate for MAI designation; **HOME ADD:** 4242 Mandan Crescent, Madison, WI 53711, (608)274-9736; **BUS ADD:** 106 King St. Box 2599, Madison, WI 53701, (608)251-8787.

SMITH, Russell B., III——B: June 29, 1948, Ajo, AZ, *Pres. Atty./Counselor*, The Law Offices of Russell B. Smith III, PC; **PRIM RE ACT:** Consultant, Attorney, Regulator, Instructor; **OTHER RE ACT:** Lic. in both AZ & TX, inc. RE licenses; **SERVICES:** Full serv. atty. for comml. & resid. RE including income tax; **REP CLIENTS:** Mel York, Ltd. (Can.), Diversified Holdings, Inc., & Investors Devel. Energy Corp. (UT), Camway Investments, Inc. (UT), & Tiger Realtors; **PREV EMPLOY:** A successful comml. & resid. sales agent, & house counsel for comml. brokerage in Houston, TX, underwriter for the Tucson Realtor Review, tax & RE instr. for Western Coll.; **PROFL AFFIL & HONORS:** ABA (Tax Sect.), AZ Bar, Fed. Bar, Maricopa Cty. Bar, Pima Cty. Bar, TX Bar, US Tax Ct.; **EDUC:** 1976, Acct. & Hist., Univ. of UT, Univ. of MD (Europe); **GRAD EDUC:** JD, 1979, RE Law, Water Law & Natural Resources, Univ. of UT Law Sch.; **EDUC HONORS:** Phi Kappa Phi, Merit Scholarships, Tech. editor, Journal of Contemporary Law, Soc. of Bar & Gavel (Service); **MIL SERV:** US Army, S/Sgt.; **OTHER ACT & HONORS:** Pop Warner Football, BSA; **HOME ADD:** 6338 N. 85th St., Scottsdale, AZ 85253, (602)998-2100; **BUS ADD:** 7975 N. Hayden Rd., Ste. B-128, Scottsdale, AZ 85258.

SMITH, Squier——B: Sep. 18, 1942, Palo Alto, CA, *VP, Office Leasing*, Bullier & Bullier, Inc.; **PRIM RE ACT:** Broker, Property Manager; **PREV EMPLOY:** US Nat. Bank, Trust Dept. (1964-66); **PROFL AFFIL & HONORS:** BOMA, Portland Bd. of Realtors, RPA (1977); **EDUC:** BS, 1964, Hist., Univ. of OR; **OTHER ACT & HONORS:** Dir. Portland Rose Festival Assn., Member Citizen Adv. Comm. to the Downtown Plan; **HOME ADD:** 7485 SW 93rd, 97223, Portland, OR, (503)246-1172; **BUS ADD:** 707 SW Wash. St., Portland, OR 97205, (503)223-3123.

SMITH, Stephen T.——B: Oct. 19, 1945, Glendale, CA, *VP*, Property Counselors, Inc.; **PRIM RE ACT:** Consultant, Appraiser; **SERVICES:** RE appraisal, counseling, feasibility analysis; **REP CLIENTS:** OR State Hwy. Div.; Portland Metro. Serv. District; major banks, S&L assns., private devel. and nat. corp.; **PREV EMPLOY:** Equitable S&L Assn., Portland, OR, 1976-1977; Multnomah Cty. Div. of Assessment and Taxation, 1971-1976; **PROFL AFFIL & HONORS:** AIREA; SREA; IRWA, MAI; SRPA; **EDUC:** BA, 1971, Poli. Sci., Univ. of CA, Los Angeles; **MIL SERV:** US Army; SP 5 (E-5), Nat. Defense Service Medal, 1963-1966; **OTHER ACT & HONORS:** Academy of Pol. Sci.; Grange; UCLA Alumni Assn.; **HOME ADD:** 4119 S.E. Malden St., Portland, OR 97202, (503)771-3842; **BUS ADD:** 220 S.W. Morrison St., Suite 100, Portland, OR 97204, (503)227-0553.

SMITH, Steven C.——B: Dec. 1949, CA, *Atty./Prof. of Bus. Law: and RE Law*, Rich & Ezer, Attys, and Loyola Marymount Univ. Coll. of Bus.; **PRIM RE ACT:** Broker, Consultant, Attorney, Instructor; **SERVICES:** Legal and analytical serv. for devels., bankers and builders; **PROFL AFFIL & HONORS:** Admitted to practice law before CA State and Fed. cts. and US Supreme Ct., LA cty. Bar Member, Amer. Trial Lawyers Assn., Member; Arbirtator, Amer. Arbitration Assn., Commercial Law Panel; Member of Amer. Assn. of Univ. Profs.; **EDUC:** BA, 1975, Urban studies and Bus. Admin., CA State Univ.; **GRAD EDUC:** JD, 1977, Southwestern Univ.; **EDUC HONORS:** Alpha Gamma Sigma Hon. Soc. Award, ABA Moot Court Award 1977; **MIL SERV:** Army & Army Reserve, Aviator, 1968-present; **BUS ADD:** 1888 Century Park East, Suite 1204, Century City, Los Angeles, CA 90067, (213)277-7747.

SMITH, Terrence F.——B: Nov. 13, 1948, Enid, OK, *Pres.*, Terry Smith and Co. Ltd.; **PRIM RE ACT:** Broker, Syndicator, Consultant, Owner/Investor; **SERVICES:** Brokerage, Acquisition & Consulting & Synd. of Invest. Prop.; **REP CLIENTS:** Private and Instnl. Investors in Comml. Props.; **PREV EMPLOY:** Moore and Co.; **PROFL AFFIL & HONORS:** RNMI, CO Assn. of Realtors, Recipient of Century Club Award 1977, 78, 79, 80,81 Denver Bd. of Realtors Roundtable 1977, 78, 79, 80,81; CCIM; **MIL SERV:** USN, E-5; **HOME ADD:** 9950 Yates St., Denver, CO 80030, (303)469-7449; **BUS ADD:** 390 Grant St., Denver, CO 80030, (303)778-1600.

SMITH, Thomas M.——B: Jan. 29, 1952, Kansas City, MO, *Partner*, Robinson and Smith Attys. at Law; **PRIM RE ACT:** Attorney, Owner/Investor; **OTHER RE ACT:** Comml. closings (Dallas Title Co.); **SERVICES:** Gen. RE practice with RE litigation emphasis; **REP CLIENTS:** Indiv. & instnl. investors; **PREV EMPLOY:** Stewart Title Nat. Closing Office, Dallas, TX; **PROFL AFFIL & HONORS:** ABA, Real Prop./Trust Div.; **EDUC:** Econ./Poli. Sci., 1974, TX Tech; **GRAD EDUC:** JD, 1978, Tax, TX Tech School of Law; **EDUC HONORS:** Honors Program, Dean's List; **HOME ADD:** 4005 Rosa Rd., Dallas, TX 75220, (214)351-2097; **BUS ADD:** 4054 McKinney Ave. Ste A, Dallas, TX 75204, (214)559-3680.

SMITH, Traver Clinton, Jr.——B: Feb. 25, 1946, Detroit, MI, *Atty.*, Esdaile, Barrett & Esdaile; **PRIM RE ACT:** Consultant, Attorney; **SERVICES:** Legal counsel; **REP CLIENTS:** Lenders and investors in comml. & resid. props., devels.; **PROFL AFFIL & HONORS:** ABA, MBA, Boston Bar Assn.; **EDUC:** 1968, Govt., Harvard Coll.; **GRAD EDUC:** JD, 1974, Boston Coll. Law Sch.; **EDUC HONORS:** Cum Laude; **HOME ADD:** 10 Kirkland Pl., Cambridge, MA 02138, (617)547-4283; **BUS ADD:** 75 Fed. St., Boston, MA 02110, (617)482-0333.

SMITH, Wallace G.——B: Mar. 5, 1937, *Pres. & Founder*, Colony Resorts, Inc.; **PRIM RE ACT:** Consultant, Property Manager; **OTHER RE ACT:** Condo & Resort Mgmt.; **SERVICES:** Feasibility & planning in opening of new resorts, prop. & rental mgmt. & consulting; **REP CLIENTS:** Devel., indiv. condo. homeowners, the Bds. of Dirs. of those resort assns.; the assns. of homeowners of those resorts; **PREV EMPLOY:** Pres., Ambassador Hotel Co., 1972-1975; Chmn., Office of the Pres., First Travel Corp., 1979-1980; **PROFL AFFIL & HONORS:** Newcomen Soc.; Jonathan Club; Jonathan Club Personnel & Pension Comm.; Bd. of Gov. Arthritus Found.; Bd. of Dir. St. John of God Hospital; **EDUC:** BA, 1959, Bus. Admin., Univ. of Santa Clara; **OTHER ACT & HONORS:** Calabasas Park Ctry. Club; Regency Club; **HOME ADD:** 4370 Park Milano, Calabasas, CA 91302, (213)888-8415; **BUS ADD:** 7833 Haskell Ave., Van Nuys, CA 91406, (213)988-0530.

SMITH, Walstein, Jr.——B: Jan. 31, 1920, Frost, TX, *Pres.*, Smith Real Estate Associates, Inc.; **PRIM RE ACT:** Broker, Attorney, Appraiser, Owner/Investor, Instructor; **SERVICES:** Legal advice, valuation, investment counseling; **REP CLIENTS:** Baylor Univ.; The city of Waco; Corp. Employers; Instnl. Investors and Lenders, CPAs; **PREV EMPLOY:** Prof. of RE, Baylor Univ.; **PROFL AFFIL & HONORS:** TX Bar Assn., McLennan Cty. Bar Assn., Waco Bd. of Realtors, MAI; Soc. of RE Appraisers; **EDUC:** BBA, 1941, Mgmt., Baylor Univ.; **GRAD EDUC:** JD, 1942, Law, Baylor Law School, Univ. of TX at Austin; MBA, 1951, RE, Baylor Law School; PhD, 1969, Fin., Baylor Law School, Univ. of TX at Austin; **EDUC HONORS:** Beta Gamma Sigma; **MIL SERV:** USAF; Capt., Bronze Star; **OTHER ACT & HONORS:** Mayor Protem City of Waco, 1950; Dist. Gov., Soc. of RE Appraisers 1972-74; Pres. Ft. Worth Chap. Amer. Inst. of RE Appraisers - 1982; **HOME ADD:** 5831 Mt. Rockwood, Waco, TX 76710; **BUS ADD:** 6613 Sanger Ave., Waco, TX 76710, (817)772-2222.

SMITH, Walter James——B: Jan. 31, 1945, Naples, FL, *Pres.*, Investors Research & Devel. Corp.; **PRIM RE ACT:** Broker, Syndicator, Consultant, Appraiser, Developer, Property Manager, Owner/Investor; **OTHER RE ACT:** Bank Dir.; **SERVICES:** Research Feasibility and Consulting - Devel. (Land Acquisition - Project Coordination); **REP CLIENTS:** Pvt. (Synd.); **PROFL AFFIL & HONORS:** Realtor, Land Studies Soc., ULI, Receipient of Gorton Award, 1967; **EDUC:** BS/BA, 1966, Fin., Univ. of FL; **GRAD EDUC:** MA, 1971, RE and Urban Studies, Univ. of FL; **EDUC HONORS:** Cum Laude, Beta Gamma Sigma, Phi Kappa Phi; **OTHER ACT & HONORS:** Member-FL Judicial Nominating Comm.; Alpha Kappa Psi; Pres., Naples Bd. of Realtors; Dir., FL Assn. of Realtors; **HOME ADD:** 3355 Gordon Dr., Naples, FL 33940; **BUS ADD:** 797 Fifth Ave, PO Box 247, Naples, FL 33938, (813)262-7215.

SMITH, William——*Pres.*, Pabst Brewing Co.; **PRIM RE ACT:** Property Manager; **BUS ADD:** Juneau Ave., Milwaukee, WI 53201, (414)347-7300.*

SMITH, William B.——B: Aug. 5, 1929, Birmingham, AL, *First VP*, Financial Federal Savings & Loan, Investments; **PRIM RE ACT:** Consultant, Appraiser, Lender; **SERVICES:** Fin., consultant, appraiser; **EDUC:** BA, 1950, Bus. Admin., Duke Univ.; **GRAD EDUC:** MBA, 1951, RE, Univ. of FL; **MIL SERV:** USAF, 2nd Lt.; **HOME ADD:** 8410 Menteith Terr., Hialeah, FL 33016, (305)557-6817; **BUS ADD:** 6625 Miami Lakes Dr., Miami Lakes, FL 33014, (305)883-7176.

SMITH, William J.——B: Oct. 7, 1928, Pleasanton, TX, *Pres.*, Four Winds RE Co.; **PRIM RE ACT:** Broker, Consultant, Appraiser, Owner/Investor; **SERVICES:** RE Analyst & Investment Consultant; **PREV EMPLOY:** S. Western Consolidated Mort. Investments, VP; Sabco Land Co., Pres.; **PROFL AFFIL & HONORS:** NARA, ASREC, CRA; **EDUC:** BS, 1950, Psych., Trinity Univ.; **GRAD EDUC:** MS, 1977, Human Resources, St. Mary's Univ.; **OTHER ACT & HONORS:** Bd. of Dir. ACLU: Assn. for Supervision & Curriculum Dev., Nat. Council on Alcoholism; San Antonio Literary Council; **HOME ADD:** 157 Medicine Rock, San Antonio, TX 78216, (512)349-1878; **BUS ADD:** 7115 Blanco Rd., Suite 114, San Antonio, TX 78216, (512)271-1565.

SMITH, William R.——B: May 5, 1929, Columbus, OH, *Pres.*, TDRC Realty Corp.; **PRIM RE ACT:** Broker, Owner/Investor, Syndicator; **PREV EMPLOY:** Exec. VP, Canton Co. of Baltimore & Canton RR Co., Dir. of Both cos.; **PROFL AFFIL & HONORS:** Home Builders Assn. of MD; **EDUC:** BS, 1953, Bus. Admin., Trans., OH State Univ.; **EDUC HONORS:** Beta Gamma Sigma; **MIL SERV:** Army; Sgt., 1947-48; **OTHER ACT & HONORS:** Chmn., Econ. Devel. Comm., Baltimore Cty., MD, 1965-66; Dir., The Merchants Club of Baltimore City; Member, The Port Comm., Gr. Baltimore Comm.; **HOME ADD:** 1804 Roland Ave., Baltimore, MD 21204, (301)321-1619; **BUS ADD:** 2526 N. Charles St., Baltimore, MD 21218, (301)235-5400.

SMITH, William S.——B: Feb. 11, 1931, Tillamoor, OR, *Pres./Broker*, Mother Lode Realty; **PRIM RE ACT:** Broker, Property Manager; **OTHER RE ACT:** Exchanges & investment RE; **EDUC:** BS, 1953, Educ., OR State Univ.; **MIL SERV:** US Army, Lt.; **HOME ADD:** PO Box 1185, Auburn, CA 95603, (916)885-3302; **BUS ADD:** PO Box 629, Auburn, CA 95603, (916)823-9111.

SMITH, Wm. A.——B: Oct. 26, 1922, Grant, NE, *Pres.*, Wm. Smith Co.; **PRIM RE ACT:** Consultant, Appraiser, Owner/Investor; **SERVICES:** Primarily appraisals of income producing RE; **REP CLIENTS:** Govt. agencies, instnl. investors, pvt. investors and mort. loan firms; **PREV EMPLOY:** Sr. VP Coast Mort. Co., now known as Rainier Mort. Co.; **PROFL AFFIL & HONORS:** Member of AIREA, MAI; **EDUC:** 1953, Bus. Fin. & RE, Univ. of WA, Seattle, WA; **MIL SERV:** USN, Lt., Air Medal, Pres. Unit Citation; **HOME ADD:** 16530 Shore Dr., NE, Seattle, WA 98155, (206)362-4363; **BUS ADD:** 16530 Shore Dr., NE, Seattle, WA 98155, (206)363-7454.

SMITHER, John Rowland——B: May 29, 1931, Lexington, KY, *Supervisory Appraiser*, USA Corps of Engr., Savannah Dist., RE Div.; **PRIM RE ACT:** Appraiser; **PREV EMPLOY:** Appraiser, M.L. Garrison Co., Lexington, KY 1965-1973, Appraiser, City of Lexington, KY 1961-1965; **PROFL AFFIL & HONORS:** SREA, SRA; **MIL SERV:** USAF, Sgt.; **HOME ADD:** 5216 Sweetbriar Dr., Raleigh, NC 27609, (919)787-7783; **BUS ADD:** 109 Ward St., Cary, NC 27511, (919)467-8112.

SMOLEN, Michael H.——B: Mar. 30, 1939, New York City, NY, *VP RE*, US Indus., Inc., U.S.I. Prop. Corp.; **PRIM RE ACT:** Broker, Consultant, Owner/Investor, Property Manager; **OTHER RE ACT:** Corp. Fortune 200 Dir., Consultant; **SERVICES:** Acquisition, divestitures, sales, leasing; consulting; **REP CLIENTS:** 70 divs. in indus., apparel, consumer, financial, business; **PREV EMPLOY:** Goodyear, New England Indus., Thomas Mellon Evans (leading US indus., controlling several fortune 500 co's.); **PROFL AFFIL & HONORS:** Indus. Devel. Research Council; IREM, RE Broker NY State; **EDUC:** AAS-BBA, 1963, RE, Ins., Fin.,Acctg., Syracuse, CUNY; **MIL SERV:** US Army; Pvt.; **HOME ADD:** 82 Hanson Ln., New Rochelle, NY 10804, (914)576-1952; **BUS ADD:** 733 Third Ave., New York City, NY 10017, (212)986-4710.

SMOLINSKY, Ronald J.——B: July 9, 1947, Manhattan, NY, *VP - Controller*, Julien J. Studley, Inc., Headquarters; **PRIM RE ACT:** Broker, Consultant, Owner/Investor; **SERVICES:** Comml. office space leasing; **PREV EMPLOY:** Alexander Grant; **PROFL AFFIL & HONORS:** AICPA, NYSSCPA, CPA; **EDUC:** BBA, 1969, Acctg., CCNY - Baruch; **MIL SERV:** US Army, Sgt.; **HOME ADD:** 3341 Yost Blvd., Oceanside, NY 11572, (516)766-6190; **BUS ADD:** 342 Madison Ave., New York, NY 10002, (212)949-0139.

SMOLKER, Gary——B: Nov. 5, 1945, Los Angeles, CA, *Prin.*, Law Offices of Gary Smolker; **PRIM RE ACT:** Consultant, Attorney; **SERVICES:** Legal and bus. counsel; litigation; **REP CLIENTS:** American Devel. Corp.; Montgomery Ross Fisher Inc.; Transamerica Title Insurance Co.; Chicago Title Ins. Co.; American Intl. Mort.; Beverly Hills Escrow Co.; Innovac Investments Intl., Inc.; Pan Financial Alliance; Attorneys Office Management Inc. (Paul Fegen): RE devels., title copmanies, escrows, lenders, brokers, owners, investors; **PROFL AFFIL & HONORS:** Contributing Editor Beverly Hills Bar Assn. Journal; Assn. of RE Attys.; National Assn. of Homebuilders; Building Industry Assn. of So. CA; CA State Bar Assn.; ABA, Frequent guest at RE indus. conventions and meetings in Southern CA; listed in *Who's Who in CA*; *Lawyer's Register by Specialties and Fields of Law*, and *The Lawyer to Lawyer Consultation Panel Directory*; **EDUC:** BS, 1967, Chem. Engrg., U.C. Berkeley; **GRAD EDUC:** MS, 1968, Chem. Engrg., Cornell Univ.; JD, 1973, Law, Loyola Law School; **EDUC HONORS:** Honor Student, Cum Laude; **OTHER ACT & HONORS:** Audubon Soc.; Metropolitan Art Museum, Sponsor of local youth soccer team; **HOME ADD:** 15-63rd Ave., Playa del Rey, CA 90219, (213)822-9383; **BUS ADD:** Penthouse-Glendale Federal Bldg., 9454 Wilshire Blvd., Beverly Hills, CA 90212, (213)273-2200.

SMOOKE, Michael G.——B: Oct. 2, 1945, Los Angeles, CA, *Part.*, Buchalter, Nemer, Fields, Chrystie & Younger, Chmn., RE Dept.; **PRIM RE ACT:** Attorney; **SERVICES:** Representation of devels., synds., brokers, investors, contractors and lenders in comml., indust. and resid. RE transactions; **REP CLIENTS:** Devels., syndicators, brokers, banks, insurance cos., contractors, indivs.; **PROFL AFFIL & HONORS:** Real Prop. Sections, Los Angeles Cty. and CA State Bar Assns.; ABA; Mortage Realtors Assn., Lecturer; **EDUC:** BA, 1967, Econ., UCLA; **GRAD EDUC:** JD, 1970, Law, Harvard Law School; **EDUC HONORS:** Magna cum laude, Phi Beta Kappa, Pi Gamma Mu, Omicron Delta Epsilon, Note Editor, Harvard Journal on Legislation; **OTHER ACT & HONORS:** Exec. Bd., Modern and Comtemporary Art Council, Los Angeles Cty. Museum of Art; **HOME ADD:** 3011 McConnell Dr., Los Angeles, CA 90064, (213)626-6700; **BUS ADD:** 700 S. Flower, Ste. 700, Los Angeles, CA 90017, (213)626-6700.

SMOOKE, Nathan——*Pres.*, Wellman Properties; **PRIM RE ACT:** Developer; **BUS ADD:** 405 Mateo St., Los Angeles, CA 90013, (213)624-8361.*

SMUCKLER, Gary S.——B: Jan. 29, 1949, Milwaukee, WI, *Assoc. Gen. Counsel, RE*, Federal Home Loan Mortgage Corp., Legal Dept.; **PRIM RE ACT:** Attorney; **PREV EMPLOY:** Asst. VP, Mort. Servicing, Amer. Fed. S&L Assn., Southfield, MI; **PROFL AFFIL & HONORS:** Member of MI and DC Bars; ABA; IntL. Bar Assn.; **EDUC:** BA, 1971, Hist., Univ. of MI; **GRAD EDUC:** JD, 1974, Wayne State Univ. Law Sch.; **BUS ADD:** 1776 G St., N.W., PO Box 37248, Washington, DC 20013, (202)789-4736.

SMURDON, Thomas J.——**B:** March 27, 1933, Gary, IN, *Pres.*, Thomas J. Smurdon And Assoc., Comml.; **PRIM RE ACT:** Broker, Developer, Builder, Syndicator; **EDUC:** 1956, Mech. Engrg., AZ State Univ.; **MIL SERV:** Army, Cpl.; **HOME ADD:** 407 E. 69th Pl., Merrillville, IN 46410, (219)769-6844; **BUS ADD:** 8300 Mississippi St., Suite C, Merrillville, IN 46410, (219)769-1818.

SMYER, Sidney W.——**B:** June 4, 1928, Birmingham, AL, *Chmn. & CEO*, Birmingham Realty Co.; **PRIM RE ACT:** Broker, Developer, Owner/Investor, Property Manager; **SERVICES:** Devl. own. RE for own account; **PROFL AFFIL & HONORS:** Bd. of Realtors; **EDUC:** BS, 1949, Univ. of AL; **GRAD EDUC:** LLB, 1951, Univ. of AL; **MIL SERV:** US Army; Capt.; **HOME ADD:** 2780 Comer Cir., Birmingham, AL 35216; **BUS ADD:** 2118 1st Ave. N., Birmingham, AL 35204, (205)322-7789.

SMYLIE, Robert Owen——**B:** June 12, 1948, LA, *Atty.*, Smylie & Selman; **PRIM RE ACT:** Attorney; **REP CLIENTS:** Watt Ind. Subsidiarys: Wilshire Diversified; MJ Brock & Sons; The Wilshire House; Hotel Del Cronado; The Mather Corp.; **PREV EMPLOY:** CA Dept. of RE, Dep. RE Comm.; Freshman Marantz, Comsky & Deutsch (Beverly Hills); **PROFL AFFIL & HONORS:** Builders Indus. Assn., Beverly Hills Bar Assn., CA State Bar, LA Cty Bar Assn., ABA (RE Sect. of each of bars); **EDUC:** 1966-70, Univ. of CA, Berkeley; **HOME ADD:** 156 Hart Ave., 4, Santa Monica, CA 90805, (213)399-1420; **BUS ADD:** 1875 Century Park E, S. 1610, Los Angeles, CA 90067, (213)553-3758.

SMYTH, David N.——**B:** Oct. 12, 1942, Toronto, Canada, *Principal*, Urbacor Props. Ltd.; **PRIM RE ACT:** Consultant, Developer, Owner/Investor, Syndicator; **OTHER RE ACT:** Pension fund advisor; devel. mgr.; **SERVICES:** Prop. acquisition; devel.; asset mgmt.; **PREV EMPLOY:** VP: The Cadillac Fairview Corp. Ltd.; **PROFL AFFIL & HONORS:** Canadian Instit. of Chartered Accountants; Soc. of Mgmt. Accountants, CA, RIA; **BUS ADD:** 102 Larkfield Dr., Don Mills, Ontario, Canada, (416)444-1523.

SNAIDER, Benson A.——**B:** Oct. 2, 1937, New Haven, CT, *Atty.*, Benson A. Snaider, P.C.; **PRIM RE ACT:** Attorney; **SERVICES:** RE devel. and zoning law; **REP CLIENTS:** Rgnl. Devel. of CT, Inc.; Broncos; Bank of New Haven; Union Trust Co.; **PROFL AFFIL & HONORS:** Amer. Right of Way Assn.; ABA; CT Bar Assn.; **EDUC:** BA, 1959, Pol. Sci., Univ. of VT; **GRAD EDUC:** LLB, 1962, Real Prop., Univ. of VA Law Sch.; **MIL SERV:** US Army; Capt.; **OTHER ACT & HONORS:** Author: 'Condemnation Law,' CT Bar Journal; **HOME ADD:** 59 Alston Ave., New Haven, CT 06515, (203)397-1276; **BUS ADD:** 152 Temple St., New Haven, CT 06510, (203)777-6426.

SNEDDON, John L.——*SIR Mgr. RE*, Wheeling-Pittsburgh Steel Corp.; **PRIM RE ACT:** Property Manager; **BUS ADD:** 1134 Market St., Wheeling, WV 26003, (304)234-2313.*

SNEDEGAR, Kenneth T.——**B:** May 24, 1918, Indianapolis, IN, *Pres.*, Foremost Real Estate Company, Div. of Foremost Corp. of America; **PRIM RE ACT:** Broker, Consultant, Attorney, Developer, Owner/Investor, Property Manager, Insuror; **PREV EMPLOY:** 1952-56 Claims Mgmt., Mfrs. & Merchants Indemnity Co.; **PROFL AFFIL & HONORS:** ABA, OH State Bar, GA Bar Assn., Pres., OH Central Mobile Home Assn. 1963-64, Treas., FL M/H Assn. 1960-62; **EDUC:** RE Practice, Bus. Admin., Chase Coll. of Commerce, Univ. of Cincinnati; **GRAD EDUC:** LLB, 1953, Salmon P. Chase Coll. of Law; **EDUC HONORS:** Iota Lamba Pi Soc.; **MIL SERV:** USAAF, 1942-46, A/C, ETO; **OTHER ACT & HONORS:** Jr. Achievement of Grand Rapids, Advisor, *Who's Who in Insurance 1974*; **HOME ADD:** 2559 Shagbark SE, Grand Rapids, MI 49506; **BUS ADD:** 5800 Foremost Dr., SE, Grand Rapids, MI 49506, (616)942-3516.

SNEDIKER, David E.——**B:** Oct. 2, 1947, Chicago, IL, *Atty./Partner*, Doran, Buckley, Kremer, O'Reilly & Pieper, Corp./RE Dept.; **PRIM RE ACT:** Attorney; **REP CLIENTS:** Lenders, brokers, devel. and investors, including Merrill Lynch Realty Comml. Services, Inc. and its subsid., Merrill Lynch, Hubbard Inc. and its subsid., and other affiliated Merrill Lynch Companies; Citibank, Dime, Chase and several Long Island S&L's; Kalicow, Peabody, and various private investors; **PROFL AFFIL & HONORS:** Amer., NY and Nassau Cty. Bar Assns. and various committees of each; **EDUC:** BS, 1969, Biology, Univ. of Notre Dame; **GRAD EDUC:** JD, 1975, St. John's Univ. School of Law; **EDUC HONORS:** Dean's List, US Law Week Award, Various Amer. Jurisprudence Awards; **OTHER ACT & HONORS:** NYU, RE Inst. Cert., 1978; **HOME ADD:** 6 Libby Dr., Glen Cove, NY 11542, (516)759-0846; **BUS ADD:** 1505 Kellum Pl., Mineola, NY 11501, (516)741-3100.

SNELL, Nancy——*Ed.*, Communication Channels, Inc., Southeast Real Estate News; **PRIM RE ACT:** Real Estate Publisher; **BUS ADD:** 6285 Barfield Rd., Atlanta, GA 30328, (404)256-9800.*

SNELL, William N.——*Corp. Secy.*, Vendo Co.; **PRIM RE ACT:** Property Manager; **BUS ADD:** 1967 North Gateway Blvd., Fresno, CA 93727, (209)252-9531.*

SNIDER, Donald J.——**B:** Jan. 29, 1947, DC, *VP*, Snider Bros., Inc.; **PRIM RE ACT:** Broker; **SERVICES:** RE Brokerage; **PREV EMPLOY:** Mont. Cty. Bd. of Realtors Prince George Cty. Bd. of Realtors; Wash. DC Bd. of Realtors NAR; MD Assn Realtors; **PROFL AFFIL & HONORS:** CRB; **EDUC:** BA, 1968, Electrical Eng., Case Inst. of Tech.; **HOME ADD:** 9129 Cranford Dr., Potomac, MD 20854, (301)299-6555; **BUS ADD:** 7000 Wisc. Ave., Bethesda, MD 20015, (301)652-4570.

SNODDY, Charles E., Jr.——**B:** Aug. 11, 1923, Buies Creek, NC, *VP*, Metropolitan Life Insurance Co., RE Investments; **PRIM RE ACT:** Appraiser, Developer, Owner/Investor, Property Manager; **SERVICES:** Fin., construction loans, Equity Investment Co.; **REP CLIENTS:** RE Devel., Brokers, Owners; **PREV EMPLOY:** In RE Since 1954 as appraiser, builder, devel., Built Devel. 2,000,000 office; **EDUC:** BS, 1952, Mgmt., NYU; **MIL SERV:** USN, Lt.; **HOME ADD:** 530 East 23rd St., New York City, NY 10010, (212)982-5827; **BUS ADD:** 1 Madison Ave., New York, NY 10010, (212)578-2751.

SNODDY, Ken James, Sr.——**B:** Aug. 10, 1918, Coalgate, OK, *Pres.*, Oceanview Acres 1977 2nd 'C' Acres Corp. 1977; **PRIM RE ACT:** Consultant, Developer, Builder, Owner/Investor, Instructor, Property Manager; **SERVICES:** Teach drafting - land and comml. devel., bldr. of homes, bus., owner of profl. bldgs.; **PREV EMPLOY:** Teacher 15 years, logger, cattle rancher, contractor; **PROFL AFFIL & HONORS:** Multi-family Housing Council; Councilman, Precinct Comm. man - 4th dist. delegate; State Fin. Comm.; **EDUC:** BS, 1948, Ind. Arts, Tahlequah, OK; **GRAD EDUC:** MS, 1963, Ind. Arts, OR State; **MIL SERV:** Seabee's, CM3/c, 1942-1945; **OTHER ACT & HONORS:** Dir., Keep OR Free of Gambling; Church of the Nazarene; Served as Trustee Bd. Member - Fin. Comm. Bld. Comm.; **HOME ADD:** 2494 Broadway, North Bend, OR 97459, (503)756-7117; **BUS ADD:** PO Box 50, North Bend, OR 97459, (503)756-7117.

SNODGRASS, Larry L.——**B:** Mar 16, 1947, Fayetteville, AR, *Asst. General Counsel*, Cooper Communities, Inc.; **PRIM RE ACT:** Attorney, Property Manager; **SERVICES:** Corporate Counsel in all phases of RE for major RE developer with over 130,000 acres under devel. in three states. Legal advisor for wholly owned subsidiary that is the largest homebuilder in AR. Prop. Mgr. for all comml. prop. in three completely self contained villages; **PROFL AFFIL & HONORS:** AR Bar Assn.; ABA; **EDUC:** BABA, 1969, Mktg./Fin., Univ. of AR, Fayetteville, AR; **GRAD EDUC:** JD, 1974, Law, Univ. of AR School of Law; **MIL SERV:** USAF; **OTHER ACT & HONORS:** Municipal Judge, City of Lincoln, AR; **HOME ADD:** 215 W. Pine St., Rogers, AR 72756, (501)636-6879; **BUS ADD:** PO Box 569/103 S. Main St., Bentonville, AR 72712, (501)273-3365.

SNOW, E. Ned——*Dir. Mfg. Staff. Opers.*, Hyster Co.; **PRIM RE ACT:** Property Manager; **BUS ADD:** Lloyd Bldg. PO Box 2902, Portland, OR 97208, (503)280-7000.*

SNOWDEN, Robert G.——**B:** Aug. 30, 1917, Memphis, TN, *Pres.*, Wilkinson & Snowden, Inc.; **PRIM RE ACT:** Broker, Consultant, Developer, Builder, Owner/Investor, Property Manager, Syndicator; **REP CLIENTS:** Cleo Wrap, Dover Elecator, Nat. Bank of Commerce, New Holland, Ryder Truck Lines, Memphis Univ. Sch.; **PROFL AFFIL & HONORS:** Realtor, Past Pres Home Bldrs. Memphis Chap.; **EDUC:** BS, 1940, Phys. & Math., Univ. of the South, Sewanee, TN; **EDUC HONORS:** Hon. Degree, Doctor Civil Law 1972; **MIL SERV:** USMC, Lt. Col.; **HOME ADD:** 3170 Southern, Memphis, TN 38111, (901)323-1044; **BUS ADD:** 65-50 2nd St., Memphis, TN 38103, (901)522-1190.

SNYDER, David F., AIA——**B:** Jan. 20, 1927, Swiftown, MS, *Architect*, David F. Snyder, Architect; **PRIM RE ACT:** Architect, Syndicator, Consultant, Developer; **SERVICES:** Architectural/Construction Mgmt. Serv., etc.; **REP CLIENTS:** Local Housing Authorities, Dev. Madison Housing Authority, Madison, AR, Maj. Assoc., Jackson MS, Lisman Housing, Authority, Lisman, AL; **PREV EMPLOY:** Private Arch. Practice 1964-1976, IN, Other Midwest States, since 1976 in SE US; **PROFL AFFIL & HONORS:** AIA, HUD Honor Award, Operation Breakthrough Assoc. Architect; **EDUC:** BS, 1951, Architectural Engineering, Univ. of IL; **MIL SERV:** US Army, E-4; **HOME ADD:** 4651 Greenleaf Cir., SW, Atlanta, GA 30331, (404)346-1485; **BUS ADD:** PO Box 41108, 4651 Greenleaf Cir., SW, Atlanta, GA 30331, (404)346-1485.

SNYDER, Edward S.——B: Mar. 11, 1935, Philadelphia, PA, *Owner*, Edward S. Snyder Real Estate; **PRIM RE ACT:** Broker, Appraiser, Instructor, Property Manager; **PROFL AFFIL & HONORS:** AIREA, Amer. Soc. of Appraisers, Sr. Member - ASA, IREM, CPM Member, Assn. of Fed. Appraisers, CPM, RM; **EDUC:** BS, 1957, RE & Ins., Temple Univ.; **GRAD EDUC:** PhD, 1976, Bus., Pac. Coll.; **MIL SERV:** US Army, Spec 4, Good Conduct; **OTHER ACT & HONORS:** Co-Editor - IREM Text Book; **HOME ADD:** 1113 Morefield Rd., Philadelphia, PA 19152; **BUS ADD:** 8400 Bustleton Ave., Philadelphia, PA 19152, (215)725-2320.

SNYDER, Gary L.——B: July 22, 1947, Ottawa, KS, *Broker/Dir. of RE*, Ruffin Prop.; **PRIM RE ACT:** Broker, Developer, Property Manager; **SERVICES:** Design & build for client, prop. mgmt., investment counseling, mkt. studies; **REP CLIENTS:** Town & Cty. Convenience stores; **PREV EMPLOY:** 4 yrs. prop. mgmt. experience prior to brokerage; **PROFL AFFIL & HONORS:** CCIM Candidate; Realtor; **EDUC:** Psych./Study of RE, Wichita State Univ.; **HOME ADD:** 6934 El Robelai, Wichita, KS 67209, (316)943-8889; **BUS ADD:** 1725 E. Douglas, Wichita, KS 67209, (316)265-7201.

SNYDER, Harry Y.——B: May 21, 1922, Palestine, *Realtor*, White House Props.; **PRIM RE ACT:** Broker, Consultant, Instructor; **OTHER RE ACT:** Exchangor; **SERVICES:** Exchanging; investment counseling; RE problem solving; **REP CLIENTS:** Problemed prop. owners; **PROFL AFFIL & HONORS:** San Fernando Valley Bd. of Realtors; CA Assn. of Realtors; NAR; Central Coast Exchangors; San Fernando Valley Exchangors; **EDUC:** BBA, 1955, UCLA; **MIL SERV:** US Army, Sgt.; **HOME ADD:** PO Box 8466, Van Nuys, CA 91409, (213)789-2277; **BUS ADD:** 14649 Ventura Blvd., Sherman Oaks, CA 91423, (213)789-2277.

SNYDER, James E.——B: Jan. 31, 1951, Seattle, WA, *Appraiser/Investment Analyst*, NY Life Ins., RE & Mort. Loan Dept.; **PRIM RE ACT:** Appraiser, Lender; **SERVICES:** Appraisal, investment analysis, loan underwriting; **EDUC:** BS, 1974, Econ., OR State Univ.; **GRAD EDUC:** MS, 1980, RE, Univ. of WI; **HOME ADD:** 4433 Evans Ave., Oakland, CA 94602, (415)530-7154; **BUS ADD:** 201 CA St., Suite 575, San Francisco, CA 94111, (415)433-1240.

SNYDER, Richard J.——B: June 18, 1939, Boston, MA, *Partner*, Goldstein & Manello; **PRIM RE ACT:** Attorney; **OTHER RE ACT:** Lecturer, Babson Grad. School of Bus. Admin.; **SERVICES:** Real Prop. Law; **PREV EMPLOY:** US Dept. of Justice, 1963-1966; Private Practice 1966-present; **PROFL AFFIL & HONORS:** MA Conveyancers Assn.; Boston, MA Bar Assns. and ABA (Member Sect. of Real Prop. Probate & Trust Law); Member, North Atlantic Bus. Law Assn.; Amer. Bus. Law Assn.; Amer Assn. of College and Univ. Attys.; US Supreme Ct.; MA Supreme Judicial Ct.; US Ct. of Appeals, First Circuit; US Dist. Ct., District of MA; US Ct. of Claims; US Tax Ct., Listed: Who's Who in Amer. Law; Former Pres., North Atlantic Bus. Law Assn.; Former Chmn., Real Prop. Comm., Amer. Bus. Law Assn.; **EDUC:** BBA, 1960, Acctg., Babson Coll.; **GRAD EDUC:** JD, 1963, Boston Univ. School of Law; LLM, 1966, Georgetown Univ. School of Law; **EDUC HONORS:** Cum Laude; **OTHER ACT & HONORS:** Pres., The Sunday School, Inc.; Trustee, Babson Coll.; Outstanding Young Men in Amer., 1970; Former Pres., Babson Coll. Alumni Assn.; **HOME ADD:** 142 Comml. St., Boston, MA 02109, (617)227-5858; **BUS ADD:** 1 Federal St., Boston, MA 02110, (617)426-3700.

SNYDER, Robert J., Jr.——B: Jsn. 6, 1930, Pittsburgh, PA, *Atty.*, Robert J. Snyder Jr., Attorney at Law; **PRIM RE ACT:** Attorney; **EDUC:** AB, 1952, Econ., Oberlin Coll.; **GRAD EDUC:** LLD, 1957, Law, Univ. of MI; **HOME ADD:** 4533 Aspen Dr., Sierra Vista, AZ 85635, (602)458-4068; **BUS ADD:** 202 N. Canyon Dr., Sierra Vista, AZ 85635, (602)458-4292.

SNYDER, Russell E.——B: Feb. 17, 1923, Phila, PA, *Sr. VP*, Jackson-Cros Co.; **PRIM RE ACT:** Broker, Consultant, Appraiser, Instructor, Insuror; **SERVICES:** RE appraisal and counseling service, also machinery and equipment valuation serv.; **REP CLIENTS:** Penn Central Corp. since before 1970; **PROFL AFFIL & HONORS:** AIREA, Appraisers, Intl. Right of Way Assn., MAI, IR/WA; **EDUC:** AB, 1953, RE Const. and Bus. Courses, Temple Univ.; **MIL SERV:** USN; **OTHER ACT & HONORS:** VP, Sr. Div. of Little League Baseball Trustee/Deacon - First Presbyterian Church of Haddonfield; **HOME ADD:** 410 Beechwood Ave., Haddonfield, NJ 08033, (609) 429-1115; **BUS ADD:** 2000 Market St., Philadelphia, PA 19103, (215)561-8971.

SOARES, Carol A.——B: Elizabeth, NJ, *Asst. VP*, Jersey Mort. Co.; **PRIM RE ACT:** Appraiser, Lender, Property Manager, Insuror; **SERVICES:** Prop. mgmt., ins., const. and resid. and income prop. originators, serv. of resid. and income prop.; **REP CLIENTS:** Instnl. investors in resid. and income loans; **PROFL AFFIL & HONORS:** Soroptimist Intl. of Elizabeth, NJ MBAA; **EDUC:** Law, Prof. Bus. School, Union Coll.; **HOME ADD:** 910 Adams Ave., Elizabeth, NJ 07201, (201)289-7892; **BUS ADD:** 430 Westfield Ave., Elizabeth, NJ 07207, (201)354-8000.

SOBEL, Joseph J.——B: Aug. 10, 1944, Chicago, IL, *Partner*, Laventhol & Horwath; **PRIM RE ACT:** Consultant; **OTHER RE ACT:** Acctg., auditing and tax services; **SERVICES:** Accounting, auditing, tax planning, market and econ. feasibility studies, fin. projections and other consulting services; **REP CLIENTS:** Major resid. and comml. devels., synds., and investors; **PROFL AFFIL & HONORS:** AICPA; IL CPA Soc.; Jr. RE Bd. of Chicago, Chmn., IL CPA Soc., Comm. on RE., 1981-1982; **EDUC:** AA, 1964, Acctg., Wright Jr. Coll.; BS/BA, 1967, Acctg., Roosevelt Univ.; **EDUC HONORS:** Summa Cum Laude, Phi Theta Kappa; **OTHER ACT & HONORS:** TR., Arlington Hts. Police Pension Bd., 8 yrs.; Treas., No. IL Apple Users Grp.; **HOME ADD:** 1826 E. Canterbury Dr., Arlington Heights, IL 60004, (312)398-1826; **BUS ADD:** 111 E. Wacker Dr., Chicago, IL 60601, (312)644-4570.

SOBEL, Lester——*Ed. - Mng. Ed.*, Leader Observer, Inc., Realty; **PRIM RE ACT:** Real Estate Publisher; **BUS ADD:** 80-34 Jamaica Ave., Woodhaven, NY 11421, (212)296-2233.*

SOBRATO, John A.——B: May 23, 1939, San Francisco, CA, *Owner*, Sobrato Devel. Co.; **PRIM RE ACT:** Developer, Builder, Property Manager; **SERVICES:** Devel., builder, & mgr. of 3 million sq. ft. of high tech. space in Santa Clara Cty.; **REP CLIENTS:** Amdahl, GE, Fairchild, Tymshare, Sylvania, ESL, Northern Telecom, Storage Tech., Four Phase Systems; **PROFL AFFIL & HONORS:** NAIOP, Pres. Palo Alto RE Bd., 1872, VP Bd. Pres. Comm. CREA, 1973; **EDUC:** 1960, Bus. Admin., Univ. of Santa Clara; **EDUC HONORS:** Magna Cum Laude; **OTHER ACT & HONORS:** Regent Univ. of Santa Clara, V Chmn. Found. Bd. St. Francis High Sch.; **BUS ADD:** 20700 Valley Green Dr., Cupertino, CA 95014, (408)446-0700.

SOCOLOFSKY, David B.——B: June 24, 1944, Woodbury, NJ, *Pres.*, Socolofsky & Co., Realtors; **PRIM RE ACT:** Broker; **SERVICES:** RE Mgtg., Appraisal; **PROFL AFFIL & HONORS:** RNMI, NAR, OR Assn. of Realtors, Portland Bd. of Realtors, CRB; **EDUC:** Econ. - AB, 1966, Oberlin Coll.; **GRAD EDUC:** Econ. - MA, 1969, WA State Univ.; **HOME ADD:** 6040 SW Cross Creek Dr., Aloha, OR 97007, (503)642-1871; **BUS ADD:** 7405 SE Powell Blvd., Portland, OR 97206, (503)777-5628.

SODEN, James A.——B: Oct. 20, 1922, Montreal, Quebec, Can., *Chmn./CEO*, Sonco Prop. Devel. and Services Co. Inc.; **PRIM RE ACT:** Developer, Property Manager; **PREV EMPLOY:** Formerly Chmn. and CEO, Trizec Corp. Ltd.; **PROFL AFFIL & HONORS:** Founding Chmn. of Can. Inst. of Public RE Co's.; **EDUC:** Bach. of Civil Laws, 1950, RE, McGill Univ.; **EDUC HONORS:** 1st Class Honors; **MIL SERV:** Royal Canadian Air Force; Squadron Leader; Mention in Despatches; **HOME ADD:** 55A Ave. Rd., Suite 2200, Toronto, Ont., Can., (416)960-0602; **BUS ADD:** 55A Ave. Rd., Suite W602, Toronto, M5R2G3, Ont., Can., (416)960-8388.

SOFFERMAN, David——B: Jul. 6, 1935, New York City, *Sr. Vice Pres.*, Arbor House Properties. LTD; **PRIM RE ACT:** Consultant, Developer, Broker, Owner/Investor, Syndicator; **SERVICES:** Synd., consultant and devel. activities; **PREV EMPLOY:** Sr. VP, Arthur Rubloff & Co.; CFO, Gen. Growth Companies; **PROFL AFFIL & HONORS:** CPA in NY, IL, IA, Nacore and Fin. Execs. Inst., CPA; **EDUC:** BS in Econ., 1955, Fin. and Acctg., Wharton School, Univ. of PA; **MIL SERV:** US Army; E-5; **HOME ADD:** 25 W. Brookwood Dr., Arlington Heights, IL 60004, (312)259-2526; **BUS ADD:** 666 Old Country Rd., Garden City, NY 11530, (516)222-2545.

SOGG, Wilton S.——*Partner*, Guren, Merritt, Feibel, Sogg & Cohen; **PRIM RE ACT:** Attorney, Instructor, Syndicator; **SERVICES:** Legal serv.; **PROFL AFFIL & HONORS:** Amer. Law Inst.; ABA; OH Bar Assn.; DC Bar Assn.; FL Bar Assn.; US Tax Ct.; US Supreme Ct., Who's Who in Amer.; Finalist: White House Fellowship; **EDUC:** BA, Dartmouth; **GRAD EDUC:** LLB, JD, Harvard Law School; **EDUC HONORS:** Magna Cum Laude, Phi Beta Kappa, Tau Epsilon Phi Pres., Editor: Harvard Law Review; **OTHER ACT & HONORS:** Pres. Commn. on Holocaust; Kane Memorial Award, Jewish Comm. Fed. of Cleveland (Bd., Chmn., Exec. Comm.); *Co-authoriSmith's Review Real and Personal Prop., Conveyancing and Future Interests* published by West (1978); Fulbright Fellowship; London School of Economics, University of London; London 1959-1960; Graduate School of Credit and Financial Management, The London Graduate School of Business Studies, Graduate Award, 1976; also assoc. with Cleveland Marshall Coll. of Law, adjunct Prof.; **BUS ADD:** 650 Terminal Tower, Cleveland, OH 44113, (216)696-8550.

SOHMER, David H.——**B:** May 2, 1941, Montreal, Can., *Partner*, Spiegel & Kravetz; **PRIM RE ACT:** Attorney; **SERVICES:** Tax, corporate and RE; **REP CLIENTS:** Devels. and investors (Can. and for.); **PROFL AFFIL & HONORS:** Can., Que., NS Bars; Can. Tax Found., Intl. Fiscal Assn.; **EDUC:** B.Com., BA, 1962, 1963, Econ.; **GRAD EDUC:** BCL, LLB, 1966, 1967; **OTHER ACT & HONORS:** Sessional Lecturer, Bus. Assns., Faculty of Law, McGill Univ.; **HOME ADD:** 5567 Rosedale Ave., Cote St. Luc, Que., Canada, (514)482-0115; **BUS ADD:** 1155 Dorchester Blvd. W., Suite 3406, Montreal, Que., Can., (514)875-2100.

SOIFER, Lawrence M.——**B:** July 15, 1927, New York, NY, *VP*, R.H. Macy & Co., Inc.; **PRIM RE ACT:** Attorney; **SERVICES:** Legal activities of R.H. Macy & Co., Inc. with emphasis on shopping ctrs. and other RE transactions; **PREV EMPLOY:** Chase Manhattan Mort. and Realty Trust, VP; Levitt and Sons, Inc., VP and Gen. Counsel; **PROFL AFFIL & HONORS:** ABA; NY State Bar Assn.; **EDUC:** BA, 1949, Pol. Sci., Queens Coll.; **GRAD EDUC:** JD, 1951, Law, Columbia Law School; **HOME ADD:** 48 Deepdale Dr., Great Neck, NY 11021, (516)466-3531; **BUS ADD:** 151 W 34th St., New York, NY 10001, (212)560-4072.

SOKOL, Bruce S.——**B:** Aug. 25, 1950, Lakewood, CA, *Dir. of Appraisals*, Citibank, Bronx, Westchester, Mid Hudson Reg.; **PRIM RE ACT:** Appraiser; **SERVICES:** RE Appraiser; **PROFL AFFIL & HONORS:** NAIFA, SREA, NY State Soc. of RE Appraisers, IFA; **EDUC:** BS, 1973, U. of CA, at Riverside; **GRAD EDUC:** MBA, 1976, Coll. for Human Serv.; **OTHER ACT & HONORS:** Lecturer at Rockland Comm. Coll., Mort. Fin. & RE; **HOME ADD:** 26 Cedar Ln., Monsey, NY 10952, (914)425-8424; **BUS ADD:** 4377 Bronx Blvd., Bronx, NY 10466, (212)579-3138.

SOKOL, Jerry L.——**B:** July 22, 1931, Chicago, IL, *Pres.*, Sokol Investment, Inc.; **PRIM RE ACT:** Broker, Consultant, Owner/Investor, Instructor, Syndicator; **SERVICES:** Brokerage & Synd. of Investment Props. Consultant in Synd. Instr. in Synd. & Investment; **REP CLIENTS:** Indivs. & Firms involved in Comml. & Investment Props.; **PROFL AFFIL & HONORS:** RESSI, Nat. Assn. of Realtors, GRI; **EDUC:** BSEE, 1954, EE, Purdue Univ.; **GRAD EDUC:** MBA, Not Completed, Fin., CA State Coll., Fullerton; **MIL SERV:** US Army Sig. Corps, 1st LT; **BUS ADD:** 32122 Paseo Adelanto, Suite 3B, San Juan Capistrano, CA 92675, (714)661-7050.

SOKOL, Loretta D.——**B:** Ephrata, WA, *Broker/Owner*, Century 21 Royal Realty; **PRIM RE ACT:** Broker, Consultant; **SERVICES:** RE sales, mktg. and mgmt. consultant; **PROFL AFFIL & HONORS:** Realtor & RNMI member, Realtor of the Yr., AK 1978; Pres. AK Assn. of Realtors 1980; **EDUC:** B. Educ., 1960, Lit., Drama, Univ. of HI; **GRAD EDUC:** Psych.- Grad. School, Central WA Univ.; **OTHER ACT & HONORS:** Salvation Army Advisory Bd.; **HOME ADD:** 2716 McKenzie Dr., Anchorage, AK 99503, (907)243-3695; **BUS ADD:** 1317 W. Northern Lights Blvd., Anchorage, AK 99503, (907)276-6368.

SOKOLOFF, Charles S.——**B:** June 9, 1942, Brooklyn, NY, *Partner*, Tobin & Silverstein Inc.; **PRIM RE ACT:** Attorney; **SERVICES:** Legal representation in fin. & tax planning, leasing, devel., conversions, etc.; **REP CLIENTS:** Instit. construction and permanent lenders, RE devels,, contractors and investors; **PROFL AFFIL & HONORS:** Amer. Coll. of RE Lawyers, ABA and RI Bar Assn.; **EDUC:** AB, 1963, Econ., Brown Univ.; **GRAD EDUC:** JD & LLM, 1966 & 1970, Law & Taxation, Univ. of PA & Boston Univ.; **OTHER ACT & HONORS:** Member, Planning Bd. City of Woonsocket, RI; **BUS ADD:** 1122 Indus. Bank Bldg., Providence, RI 02903, (401)274-6300.

SOKOLOV, Richard Saul——**B:** Dec. 7, 1949, Philadelphia, PA, *Partner, Atty.*, Weinberg and Green; **PRIM RE ACT:** Attorney; **REP CLIENTS:** Devels., investors, broker-dealers, synds., const. and permanent lenders, gen. contractors; **PROFL AFFIL & HONORS:** ABA, MD State Bar Assn., Baltimore City Bar Assn., ABA Sect. on Real Prop., Probate & Trust, MD State Bar Sect. on Real Prop. and Zoning; **EDUC:** BA, 1971, Psych., PA State Univ.; **GRAD EDUC:** JD, 1974, Law, Georgetown Univ.; **EDUC HONORS:** Phi Beta Kappa, Phi Kappa Phi, Grad. with high distinction, honors in Psych., Editor, Law and Policy in Intl. Bus.; **HOME ADD:** 6375 Tinted Hill, Columbia, MD 21045; **BUS ADD:** 14th Floor, 100 S. Charles St., Baltimore, MD 21201, (301)332-8712.

SOKOLOW, Gerry——*RE Dept.*, Keystone International; **PRIM RE ACT:** Property Manager; **BUS ADD:** PO Box 40010, Houston, TX 77040, (713)466-1176.*

SOLEM, Richard Ray——**B:** Williston, ND, *Pres.*, Equity Fund Grp [4 Co's: Equity Fund Realty (a brokerage), Equity Fund Investors (Partnership Mgmt.), Equity Fund Mgmt. (Prop. Mgmt.) and Equity Fund Securities; **PRIM RE ACT:** Broker, Syndicator, Property Manager; **PREV EMPLOY:** Project Dev. Officer, Agency for Intl. Dev. (package projects in Spanish & Portuguese language countries in Africa, Latin America & Europe); **PROFL AFFIL & HONORS:** RESSI, RNMI, Hold SRS designation from RESSI, Candidate for CCIM; **EDUC:** BA, 1966, Latin Amer. Hist., Univ. of TX; **GRAD EDUC:** MA, 1968, Latin Amer. Studies, Univ. of TX; **OTHER ACT & HONORS:** Pres. of DC, DE, MD RESSI, Member of Bd. of Dir. & Treas. of Lafayette Fed. Credit Union; **HOME ADD:** 5712 Whittier Blvd., Bethesda, MD 20034, (301)229-1671; **BUS ADD:** 7512 Whittier Blvd., Bethesda, MD 20034, (301)229-1621.

SOLES, Christopher X.——**B:** Feb. 11, 1949, Winchester, MA, *VP*, Dead River Properties, Inc.; **PRIM RE ACT:** Attorney, Property Manager, Owner/Investor; **SERVICES:** Involved in managing and investing in RE; **REP CLIENTS:** Nat. Basis for Privately held corps. headquartered in Portland, ME; **PREV EMPLOY:** Mgr. 1976-81, RE Devel., Hannaford Bros. Co., S. Portland, ME, Operator of Shop N Save Supermarkets & Wellby Drug Stores; **PROFL AFFIL & HONORS:** ICSC, ME Bar Assn.; **EDUC:** AB, 1971, Pol. & Near East Studies, Princeton Univ.; **GRAD EDUC:** JD, 1976, Bus. Law & Taxation, Univ. of ME School of Law; **EDUC HONORS:** Cum Laude; **OTHER ACT & HONORS:** Middle East Ctr. for Arab Studies, Shemlan, Lebanon 1970-71, Concentration, Arabic Language Training, Grad. With Distinction; **HOME ADD:** Beech Hill Rd. Box 359, Freeport, ME 04032; **BUS ADD:** 415 Congress St., Portland, ME 04104, (207)773-5841.

SOLIE, Robert "Bob" L.——**B:** Jan. 8, 1948, Olympia, WA, *Sales Assoc.*, Evergreen Olympic Realty, Inc.; **PRIM RE ACT:** Owner/Investor; **OTHER RE ACT:** Comml. & investment RE sales; **SERVICES:** Investment counseling, prop. mgmt., devel.; **EDUC:** BS, 1970, Geology & Chemistry, Univ. of Puget Sound; **GRAD EDUC:** MBA, 1975, Mktg., Mgmt., Intl. Bus., Univ. of Puget Sound; **HOME ADD:** 3001 Country Club Loop N.W., Olympia, WA 98502, (206)866-2669; **BUS ADD:** 3309 Capital Blvd., Olympia, WA 98501, (206)352-7651.

SOLOMON, Douglas P.——**B:** Nov. 13, 1944, Far Rockaway, NY, *Atty. (Pres.)*, Douglas Paul Solomon, P.A.; **PRIM RE ACT:** Broker, Attorney, Syndicator; **SERVICES:** All legal aspects of acquisition and fin. transactions; site selection; litigation; **REP CLIENTS:** Indiv. or corp. devel. or investors; **PROFL AFFIL & HONORS:** ABA, FL Bar Assn., RE Assn. of Prof.; **EDUC:** BA, 1966, Pol. Sci., Univ. of Rochester; **GRAD EDUC:** JD, 1969, NYU Law School; **EDUC HONORS:** Mendicants; **BUS ADD:** Suite 4A, Mayfair II in the Grove, 2911 Grand Ave., Coconut Grove, FL 33133, (305)444-6988.

SOLOMON, Gerald——*Dpty. Asst. Secy.*, Department of Housing and Urban Development, Enforcement & Compliance; **PRIM RE ACT:** Lender; **BUS ADD:** 451 Seventh St., S.W., Washington, DC 20410, (202)755-5735.*

SOLOMON, Gerald H.——**B:** Sept. 18, 1923, New Castle, PA, *Chief Appraiser, Baltimore Dist.*, US Army Corps of Engrs., RE Div., Baltimore; **PRIM RE ACT:** Appraiser; **SERVICES:** Supervisory (appraisals and review); **REP CLIENTS:** US govt., civil and military assignments; **PREV EMPLOY:** Appraiser Gen. Servs. Admin., Washington DC; PA Dept. of Highways; Right of Way Div.; **PROFL AFFIL & HONORS:** MAI; SREA; MGA (Assn. of Govt. Appraisers); CRA (NARA); Member Int. Right of Way Assn., SRPA; Who's Who in the East, 1979-80, 1977-78; **EDUC:** BA, 1950, Bus. Admin., Transylvania Coll., Lexington, KY; **MIL SERV:** USAAF; Sgt.; 1943-46; **HOME ADD:** 8 Charles Plaza, Apt. 801NT, Baltimore, MD 21201, (301)385-1141; **BUS ADD:** PO Box 1715, Baltimore, MD 21203, (301)962-3002.

SOLOMON, Maurice H.——**B:** June 5, 1928, New York, NY, *Sr. VP, Dir.*, Julien J. Studley, Inc.; **PRIM RE ACT:** Broker; **OTHER RE ACT:** Leasing agent; **SERVICES:** Instituting renting programs for office bldgs.; establishing standards and procedures for tenant alterations and space selection; coordinating lease analysis with attys. and preparing material for negotiation; **PROFL AFFIL & HONORS:** RE Bd. of NY; **EDUC:** BA, 1950, Eng. & Drama, Syracuse Univ.; **MIL SERV:** US Army, Pfc; **HOME ADD:** 530 Park Ave., New York, NY 10021, (212)486-1202; **BUS ADD:** 342 Madison Ave., New York, NY 10173, (212)949-0128.

SOLOMON, Ralph——**B:** Dec. 28, 1934, New York, NY, *Pres.*, Ralph Solomon, MAI, SRPA, RE Appraiser & Consultant; **PRIM RE ACT:** Consultant, Appraiser; **SERVICES:** RE appraisals, reports & consultations; **REP CLIENTS:** Banks, corps., attys., indiv. & govt.; **PREV EMPLOY:** Former Chief Appraiser, Mfrs. Hanover Trust Co.; Formerly VP & Chief Appraisal Officer, Lincoln Savings Bank; **PROFL AFFIL & HONORS:** AIREA; SREA; NARA, MAI; SRPA; SRA; CRA; NYSAS; MLIS; Rho Epsilon; **EDUC:** BBA, 1960, Mgmt., City Coll. of NY; **GRAD EDUC:** Post Grad. Courses, 1962-1981, RE

Appraising, Tulane Univ., Univ. of CT, NYU; **OTHER ACT & HONORS:** Bd. of Dir. & Officer, City Coll. Bus. School Alumni; Listed in Who's Who in Fin. & Indus., 1979; **HOME ADD:** 3 Cardiff Run, Mt. Sinai, NY 11766, (516)928-2127; **BUS ADD:** 3 Cardiff Run, Mt. Sinai, NY 11766, (516)928-2127.

SOLOMON, Robert Donald——B: July 25, 1949, New York, NY, *VP*, Refco Partners; **PRIM RE ACT:** Consultant, Banker, Lender, Syndicator; **SERVICES:** Investment bankers for RE projects, focusing on tax-exempt fin. of housing, health care, & comml. facilities; **REP CLIENTS:** Devels., non-profit instns., mort. bankers; **PREV EMPLOY:** VP, Bear Stearns & Co.; VP, First Pennco Securities; **EDUC:** AB, 1971, Amer. Hist., Brown Univ.; **GRAD EDUC:** MBA, 1973, Harvard Bus. School; **HOME ADD:** 4 Atkinson Road, Rockville Center, NY 11570, (516)764-8357; **BUS ADD:** Suite 9625, 1 World Trade Center, New York, NY 10048, (212)466-3884.

SOLOMON, Steven A.——B: Dec. 31, 1946, Newark, NJ, *Nix and Wendell*; **PRIM RE ACT:** Attorney; **REP CLIENTS:** Banks & instnl. lenders, devels., investors, prop. mgrs., synds.; **EDUC:** 1968, Econ., Univ. of Chicago; **GRAD EDUC:** JD, 1971, Univ. of MI; **EDUC HONORS:** Special Honors in Econ.; **HOME ADD:** 36 Heather St., Manchester, NH 03104, (603)627-4282; **BUS ADD:** 50 Bridge St., Manchester, NH 03101, (603)625-4100.

SOLOT, Sanders K.——B: Nov. 10, 1926, Tucson, AZ, *Pres.*, Sanders K. Solot & Assoc., RE Appraisers & Consultants; **PRIM RE ACT:** Consultant, Appraiser; **PROFL AFFIL & HONORS:** AIREA; MAI; Sr. RE Analyst of the SREA, Prof. Recognition Award of the AIREA; **EDUC:** BS, 1950, Bus. Admin, Univ. of AZ; **MIL SERV:** USN; Yeoman 2C; **HOME ADD:** 4142 E Poe St, Tucson, AZ 85711; **BUS ADD:** 5301 E Broadway, PO Box 12339, Tucson, AZ 85732, (602)745-1111.

SOMMER, Frank R——B: July 30, 1923, New York City, NY, *Dir.-RE*, AMF Inc.; **OTHER RE ACT:** Involved in all phases of RE & Constr. including Indus., Comml., Resid and Leasing; **PROFL AFFIL & HONORS:** Past Pres. - Indus. Devel. Research Council; Past Dir. Employee Relocation Council,Past Assoc. Member SIR; **EDUC:** BA, 1943, Econs., Cornell Univ.; **MIL SERV:** Artillery, Maj., presently in Retd. Res., European Theatre, 3 Battle Stars, Gtc; **HOME ADD:** 30 Greenridge Ave., White Plains, NY 10605, (914)946-5626; **BUS ADD:** 777 Westchester Ave., White Plains, NY 10604, (914)694-9000.

SOMMER, Roselle L.——B: Sept. 6, 1921, Chicago, IL, *RE Broker*, The Sommer Off.; **PRIM RE ACT:** Broker, Syndicator, Consultant, Developer, Property Manager, Lender; **OTHER RE ACT:** 2nd Trust Deeds Exchanges; **SERVICES:** Investment Counseling; **PROFL AFFIL & HONORS:** CCIM, GRI, Int'l. Coll. RE Consulting Prof., Exchange Awards; **EDUC:** 3 yrs., 1938-1940, Bus. Adm., Northwestern Univ.; **OTHER ACT & HONORS:** NCCJ Award, Pres. Long Beach Jewish Commonwealth Fed. Ctr., Secretary, NCCJ; **HOME ADD:** 4471 Green Ave., Los Alamitos, CA, (213)431-1538; **BUS ADD:** 11232 Los Alamitos Blvd., Los Alamitos, CA 90720, (213)430-3588.

SOMMER, Scott A.——B: May 26, 1950, Rockville Center, NY, *Atty.*, Tobin & Tobin; **PRIM RE ACT:** Attorney; **SERVICES:** Rep. in purchase and sales, subdivs., and comml. leasing and secured transactions; **REP CLIENTS:** The Hibernia Bank, Bank of Trade; Chicago Title Ins. Co., Founders Title Co., Title Ins. Co. of MN, St. Paul Title Co.; **PROFL AFFIL & HONORS:** Real Prop. Sect., San Francisco Bar Assn.; Real Prop. Sect., State Bar of CA; **EDUC:** BA, 1972, Modern European Hist., Univ. of CA; **GRAD EDUC:** JD, 1976, Univ. of CA, Hastings Coll. of Law; **BUS ADD:** 2600 Crocker Plaza, One Post St., San Francisco, CA 94104, (415)433-1400.

SOMMERS, Norman S.——B: Dec. 12, 1919, Detroit, MI, *1st VP*, Sommers, Schwartz, Silver & Schwartz, P.C.; **PRIM RE ACT:** Attorney; **REP CLIENTS:** Chatham Super Markets, Inc., Woodland Med. Crp., P.C., Memorial Med. Ctr., Vlasic Foods., Inc., (local counsel for Campbell Soup Co); Herman Frankel Companies; Bravo Homes, Inc.; **PROFL AFFIL & HONORS:** Amer. Coll. of RE Lawyers, State Bar of MI, ABA, Research Clerk for Justice of MI Supreme Ct.; **EDUC:** 1939, Detroit Inst. of Tech.; **GRAD EDUC:** JD, 1942, Detroit Coll. of Law; **EDUC HONORS:** Cum Laude; **HOME ADD:** 1196 Stuyvessant, Birmingham, MI 48010, (313)646-8987; **BUS ADD:** 1800 Travelers Tower, Southfield, MI 48076, (313)355-0300.

SONNE, Ross N., Jr.——B: May 29, 1929, Rockford, IL, *Pres.*, R.N. Sonne & Co.; **PRIM RE ACT:** Broker, Appraiser, Developer, Owner/Investor, Property Manager, Syndicator; **PROFL AFFIL & HONORS:** IREM, CPM Designation; Assoc. Member SREA, Nat. Assn. of Review Appraisers, CRA, NRAB; **EDUC:** BA, 1952, Bus. & Liberal Arts, Univ. of S. CA; **GRAD EDUC:** Univ. S. CA Grad School, 1953-54; **HOME ADD:** 1425 Laurel, South Pasadena, CA 91030, (213)682-2281; **BUS ADD:** 1104 Fremont, South Pasadena, CA 91030, (213)682-1144.

SONNENBLICK, Arthur I.——B: Dec. 16, 1931, New York, NY, *Pres.*, Sonnenblick - Goldman Corp.; **PRIM RE ACT:** Broker, Consultant; **SERVICES:** Fin. and sales of income producing prop.; **REP CLIENTS:** Indiv. and instnl. devels. and investors in income producing props.; **EDUC:** BS in Econ., 1953, RE, Wharton Sch. of Fin. & Commerce, Univ. of PA; **MIL SERV:** USN, Lt. jg 1953-57; **HOME ADD:** 4 Hampton Rd., Scarsdale, NY 10583; **BUS ADD:** 1251 Ave. of the Americas, New York, NY 10020, (212)541-4121.

SONNENBLICK, Jack E.——B: Oct. 1, 1923, New York, *Chmn. of the Bd.*, Sonnenblick-Goldman Corp., S-G Corp., a subsidiary of Lehman Bros. Kuhn Loeb Inc.; **PRIM RE ACT:** Broker, Consultant; **SERVICES:** Arranges fin. for maj. income producing props. as well as joint ventures and equity investments; **REP CLIENTS:** All maj. builders and owners of RE as well as instnl. investors and lenders; **MIL SERV:** US Army Corps. of Engrs., 1st Lt.; **BUS ADD:** 1251 Avenue of the Americas, New York, NY 10020, (212)541-4321.

SONNENSCHEIN, Irving——B: June 3, 1920, New York, *Partner*, Sonnenschein, Sherman & Deutsch; **PRIM RE ACT:** Attorney; **SERVICES:** Legal services relating to all phases of RE including acquisitions, sales, cooperative conversions, RE tax assessment reduction proceedings; **REP CLIENTS:** RE investors and operators including instit. investors; **PROFL AFFIL & HONORS:** Bar Assn. of the City of NY, ABA, RE Tax Review Bar Assn., Member of NY State Temporary State Leg. Commn. on the Real Prop. Tax; **EDUC:** BS, 1938, CCNY; **GRAD EDUC:** LLB, 1941, Columbia Law School; **EDUC HONORS:** With Honors, Cum Laude, Phi Betta Kappa, Kent Scholar; **HOME ADD:** 10 West 86 St., New York, NY 10024, (212)724-0286; **BUS ADD:** 10 Columbus Circle, New York, NY 10019, (212)245-6754.

SOO, Charles Edward——B: Dec. 12, 1931, Washington, DC, *Asst. Sec.*, The Life Ins. Co. of Virginia, Agency Dept., Div. of Field Prop. and Leasing; **PRIM RE ACT:** Property Manager, Insuror; **OTHER RE ACT:** Leasing and negotiation; **SERVICES:** Leasing and Prop. Management, Estate Planning - preserving life estates.; **REP CLIENTS:** Personal clients on estate conservation, trustees for prop. evaluation and mgmt.; **PROFL AFFIL & HONORS:** IREM, Bd. of Realtors, Chartered Life Underwriters Designations, CLU, CPM; **EDUC:** 2 Yrs. Coll. - math/engineering, Montgomery Jr. Coll., Benjamin Franklin Univ.; **MIL SERV:** USN, Airman 1st Class, Natl. Defense; **OTHER ACT & HONORS:** Past Commander Amer. Legion, Masonic Member Scottish Rite Chmn. of the Bd. semi-pro football team, Richmond Bruins; **HOME ADD:** 11804 Pleasant Hill Court, Richmond, VA 23236, (804)794-1206; **BUS ADD:** P.O. Box 27601, Richmond, VA 23261, (804)281-6568.

SOPP, Brian W.——B: Feb. 21, 1942, Can., *Sr. VP*, US Trust Co., RE; **PRIM RE ACT:** Banker, Lender; **OTHER RE ACT:** Constr., conversion, interim loans, equity participations, joint ventures; **PREV EMPLOY:** Exec/ VP & Sr. RE Officer, Union Nat. Bank, Lowell, MA; **PROFL AFFIL & HONORS:** MA Bankers Assn., Mort. Fin., Comm., Gr. Boston RE Bd., MA Bldg. Congress; **EDUC:** B Comm., 1965, Econ., McGill Univ.; **GRAD EDUC:** MBA, 1968, Fin., Harvard Univ.; **HOME ADD:** 10 Sheffield Ctr., Andover, MA 01810, (617)470-0880; **BUS ADD:** 40 Court St., Boston, MA 02108, (617)726-7158.

SORGEN, Richard Jesse——B: Aug. 4, 1945, Toledo, OH, *Arch./Part.*, The Richard Troy Partnership; **PRIM RE ACT:** Architect; **SERVICES:** Site feasibility, project design, cost estimating; **REP CLIENTS:** Developers, investors, owners of all type structures; **PREV EMPLOY:** VP of Devel./Const. Firm (1976-1977); Project Mgr., SSOE Arch. (1972-1976); **PROFL AFFIL & HONORS:** AIA - 1975 current, AIA, Scholastic Award, 1972; **EDUC:** BS, 1972, Arch., Univ. of MI; Univ. of Toledo; **GRAD EDUC:** MArch., 1973, Arch. Design, Univ. of MI; **EDUC HONORS:** Dean's List, 1970, Degree with high distinction; **MIL SERV:** USN, TDPO3; **OTHER ACT & HONORS:** Rotary, 1979 - current; BPOE Elks, 1967 - 1969; Outstanding Young Men of Amer., 1980; **HOME ADD:** 2326 Pemberton Dr., Toledo, OH 43606; **BUS ADD:** 4841 Monroe St., Toledo, OH 43623, (419)474-5775.

SORGIE, Frank A.——*Sr. Audit Mgr.*, Price Waterhouse; **OTHER RE ACT:** CPA; **SERVICES:** Acctg., auditing and tax serv.; **BUS ADD:** 100 Jericho Quadrangle, Jericho, NY 11753, (516)681-7114.

SORLEY, Michael Garland——B: Oct. 21, 1943, Plainview, TX, *Broker Assoc.*, Laguarta, Gavrel & Kirk, Inc., Realtors, Comm'l.; **PRIM RE ACT:** Broker; **SERVICES:** Sales of income producing (investment) RE; **PREV EMPLOY:** Henry S. Miller Co., Realtors (1972-1975); **PROFL AFFIL & HONORS:** RNMI; CCIM; **EDUC:** BA, 1966, Bus. Admin., Principia College, Elsah, IL; **GRAD EDUC:**

1968, Soc. Sci., Boston Univ.; **EDUC HONORS:** VP, Freshman Class; Pres., Sophmore Class, On scholarship; **MIL SERV:** USAFR; 2nd Lt.; **HOME ADD:** 7447 Cambridge 120, Houston, TX 77054, (713)795-5230; **BUS ADD:** 2737 Buffalo Speedway, Houston, TX 77098, (713)622-2200.

SORVAAG, C.M.——B: Sep. 20, 1916, Portland, OR, *Pres.*, Brookings Harbor Realty, Inc.; **PRIM RE ACT:** Broker, Consultant, Appraiser; **SERVICES:** Sales, appraising; **REP CLIENTS:** Banks, Attys., VA, OR Dept. of Vet. Affairs, Devels.; **PROFL AFFIL & HONORS:** NAR; **EDUC:** BEE, 1939, OR State Univ.; **GRAD EDUC:** MBA, 1970, Mgmt., Univ. of Santa Clara; **EDUC HONORS:** Eta Kappa Nu, Tau Beta Pi, Sigma Xi; **OTHER ACT & HONORS:** Reg. Prof. Engineer, Electrical, State of CA; **HOME ADD:** P.O. Box 1074, Brookings, OR 97415, (503)469-4949; **BUS ADD:** P.O. Box 1074, 605 Chetco Ave., Brookings, OR 97415, (503)469-2194.

SOSZKA, Kenneth R.——B: Feb. 25, 1946, Huntington, NY, *Dir. of Fin. - Controller*, Cadillac Fairview, Urban Devel.; **PRIM RE ACT:** Developer, Owner/Investor; **OTHER RE ACT:** Fin.; **PREV EMPLOY:** Kaufman and Broad, Inc.; **PROFL AFFIL & HONORS:** AICPA; **EDUC:** BS, 1967, Bus. Admin./Fin., Providence Coll.; **EDUC HONORS:** Dean's List; Cum Laude; **HOME ADD:** 19 Whitehall Ct., Holbrook, NY 11741, (516)472-0353; **BUS ADD:** Suite 2606, 375 Park Ave., New York, NY 10022, (212)755-3070.

SOUCY, Thomas E.——B: Feb. 19, 1945, E St. Louis, IL, *Owner, Pres.*, Soucy RE, Prosper-Marcel, Ltd.; **PRIM RE ACT:** Broker, Consultant, Developer, Owner/Investor, Syndicator; **OTHER RE ACT:** Appraisals, mgmt., exchanging, RE loans; **SERVICES:** Consulting, tax deferred exchanges, RE problem solving; **REP CLIENTS:** Commonwealth Life & Accident Ins. Co., Frito-Lay, Inc., Fruin Colron Corp., Gen. Amer. Life Ins. Co., John Harland Co., IL Power Co., Prudential Life Ins. Co., Transamerica Ins. Grp., GW Bell Telephone Co.; **PREV EMPLOY:** Thomas J. White Devel. Co., Bakewell Corp.; **PROFL AFFIL & HONORS:** NAR, IL Assn. of Realtors, Belleville Bd. of Realtors, S IL RE Exchangors, Intl. RE Exchangors, CCIM, RNMI, 1977 Exchangor of the Yr., St. Louis RE Exchange, "1981 Sale of Year", So. IL RE Exchange; **EDUC:** BS, 1967, Sci., Univ. of Notre Dame; **GRAD EDUC:** Law, St. Louis Univ. Law Sch.; **MIL SERV:** USAR, 1968-75, S/Sgt.; **OTHER ACT & HONORS:** Past Pres. Kiwanis; **BUS ADD:** 8525 W. Main, Belleville, IL 62223, (618)397-8666.

SOUDRIETTE, James W.——B: Mar. 26, 1928, Kalamazoo, MI, *Pres.*, The Galaxy Organization; **PRIM RE ACT:** Broker, Consultant, Engineer, Developer, Owner/Investor, Syndicator; **OTHER RE ACT:** Equity/Asset Mgr.; **SERVICES:** Feasibility through devel. of indus. parks.; Second home projects; **REP CLIENTS:** Equity/Asset Mgr. for Hi Rise, comml., indus. parks & second home (resid.) props.; **EDUC:** BBA, 1950, W MI Univ.; **MIL SERV:** USAF; **BUS ADD:** 11 W Jefferson, 224, Phoenix, AZ 85003, (602)254-5246.

SOUED, Frederick A.——B: Aug. 17, 1948, New York, *Gen. Partner*, Entreprises Entre Nous; **PRIM RE ACT:** Broker, Consultant, Developer, Owner/Investor, Property Manager, Syndicator; **EDUC:** AB, 1970, Econ., Hamilton Coll.; **GRAD EDUC:** MA, 1976, Eng., Hayward St.; MPH, 1978, Admin., Berkeley; **EDUC HONORS:** Phi Beta Kappa; **MIL SERV:** QMC, 1st Lt.; **BUS ADD:** 2400 Sycamore Dr., Suite 8, Antioch, CA 94509, (415)778-3366.

SOUKUP, John F.——B: Mar. 4, 1948, Burbank, CA, *Lawyer*, Law Office of John F. Soukup; **OTHER RE ACT:** Legal representation; **SERVICES:** Legal Representation of Buyers, Sellers of Comml. RE, Landlord-Tenant; **PREV EMPLOY:** Tyre & Kamins, Lawyers; **PROFL AFFIL & HONORS:** Los Angeles Cty. Bar; **EDUC:** 1970, Intl. Relations, Univ. of S. CA; **GRAD EDUC:** JD, 1973, Univ. of S. CA; **EDUC HONORS:** Law Review; **OTHER ACT & HONORS:** Author, 'Purchase & Sale Agreements,' CA Real Property Sales Transactions; CA Continuing Education of the Bar, 1981; **BUS ADD:** 433 N. Camden Dr., Suite 400, Beverly Hills, CA 90210, (213)276-2026.

SOULE, Wesley——*Treasurer*, Rexham Corp.; **PRIM RE ACT:** Attorney; **BUS ADD:** 90 Park Ave., New York, NY 10016, (212)883-0915.*

SOUTH, Jerry G.——B: Dec. 1, 1932, Frankfort, KY, *Pres.*, BA Mort. & Intnl. Realty Corp., Wholly Owned sub. of BankAmerica Corp.; **OTHER RE ACT:** Mort. banking; **SERVICES:** Constr. & standby lending, permanent debt & equity fin. for comml. prop.; **REP CLIENTS:** Comml. props. devel., instns. lenders & investors in comml. props.; **PREV EMPLOY:** VP Bank of Amer.; **PROFL AFFIL & HONORS:** Mort. Bankers Assn. (Dir. N. CA) (Nat. N. CA), NARA, CA & KY State Bars, Atty; **EDUC:** AB, 1954, Econ., Wash & Lee Univ.; **GRAD EDUC:** LLB, 1958, Law, Stanford Univ. Law Sch.; **EDUC HONORS:** Cum Laude, Adv. mgmt. program, Harvard Bus. Sch., 1976; **MIL SERV:** USN, 1954-56, Lt. j.g.; **OTHER ACT & HONORS:** Tr. Wash. & Lee Univ., Bankers Club of San Francisco; **BUS ADD:** 555 CA St., San Francisco, CA 94104, (415)622-6524.

SOUTHMAYD, Daniel B.——B: Apr. 13, 1951, Cleveland, OH, *Mktg./Sales Dir.*, Sign Systems, Inc.; **SERVICES:** Custom Arch. Signage Fabricator; **REP CLIENTS:** Office complexes,, bldgs., univs., hotels, hospitals; **EDUC:** BA, 1973, Journalism/Psych., OH Univ.; **HOME ADD:** 5187 Olivia Trail, Stone Mtn., GA 30088, (404)987-3394; **BUS ADD:** 1016 Monroe Dr. NE, Atlanta, GA 30306, (404)875-6412.

SOUTHWELL, Lawrence G.——B: July 30, 1937, Flint, MI, *VP*, Citizens Comml. & Savings Bank, Mort. Dept.; **PRIM RE ACT:** Appraiser, Banker, Lender, Instructor; **PROFL AFFIL & HONORS:** Mort. Bankers Assn. of MI; E. MI Mort. Bankers; MN Bankers Assn.; Soc. of RE Appraisers; Flint Bd. of Realtors; Genesee Valley Bd. of RE; **OTHER ACT & HONORS:** Tr. Cystic Fibrosis Found.; Instr. in RE Fin. at N. MI Univ., & Ctr. MI Univ.; **HOME ADD:** 3307 Mackin Rd., Flint, MI 48504, (313)235-4487; **BUS ADD:** One Citizens Banking Ctr., Flint, MI 48502, (313)766-7633.

SOUTO, Ric A.——B: Jan. 11, 1948, Havana, Cuba, *Partner/Broker*, Equity Investments International; **PRIM RE ACT:** Broker, Consultant, Owner/Investor; **SERVICES:** RE Counseling; **REP CLIENTS:** For. and local investors; **PREV EMPLOY:** Mgmt. Analyst, U.S. Dept. of Defense (assigned in Germany working with local labor forces and US personnel); **PROFL AFFIL & HONORS:** Vail Bd. of Realtors; **EDUC:** B of Bus. Admin., 1970, Mktg., OH Univ.; **GRAD EDUC:** MA Mgmt., 1972, Intl. Mktg., Amer. Grad. Schl. of Intl. Mgmt.; **MIL SERV:** US Army, 1st Lt.; **HOME ADD:** PO Box 257, Avon, CO 81620; **BUS ADD:** 108 S. Frontage Rd. W, Suite 208, Vail, CO 81657, (303)476-7450.

SOVA, Richard S.——B: Aug. 4, 1946, Marshalltown, IA, *VP-Finance*, Amer. Invsco Devel. Corp.; **PRIM RE ACT:** Broker, Consultant, Developer, Owner/Investor; **SERVICES:** Devel. of comml. & resid. RE; **PREV EMPLOY:** Pres. United Mort. Corp., 1975-80; Nat. Homes Acceptance Corp., 1972-74; **PROFL AFFIL & HONORS:** MBA, IL Mort. Bankers Assn., Cert. Mort. Banker Designation; MBA; **EDUC:** BS, 1968, Bus., Econ., Indus. Admin., IA State Univ.; **GRAD EDUC:** MBA, 1972, Fin., Univ. of IA; **MIL SERV:** USA, E-5; **OTHER ACT & HONORS:** Licensed RE Broker, IL; **HOME ADD:** 2131 N Clark, Chicago, IL 60614; **BUS ADD:** 120 S LaSalle St., Suite 2200, Chicago, IL 60603, (312)621-8660.

SOWARDS, Nelson Gary——B: Dec. 16, 1943, Provo, UT, *VP*, Coates & Sowards, Inc.; **PRIM RE ACT:** Broker, Instructor, Property Manager; **PREV EMPLOY:** Regional Prop. Mgr., Norris, Beggs & Simpson 1972-1977; **PROFL AFFIL & HONORS:** CPM; IREM; Realtor; San Jose Bd. Assn. of S Bay Brokers (A.S.B.B.) RE; ICSC; **EDUC:** BS, 1971, Bus. Mgmt., CA State Univ. at Hayward; **MIL SERV:** US Army; SP-5, Vietnam Campaign ribbons; **HOME ADD:** 5866 Zileman Ct., San Jose, CA 95123, (408)578-8158; **BUS ADD:** 1530 Meridian Ave., San Jose, CA 95125, (408)267-4600.

SOWELL, James E.——B: July 5, 1948, Bryan, TX, *Pres.*, Jim Sowell Construction Co. Inc.; **PRIM RE ACT:** Developer, Builder, Owner/Investor; **SERVICES:** Devel. and const. of comml. properties; **REP CLIENTS:** Southland Corp., Wood Bros. Homes, US Homes, Gulf Oil Co., Cities Serv. Oil Co., Kroger Food Stores, Tandy Corp., Allstate Ins., Trammel Crow; **PROFL AFFIL & HONORS:** Nat. Assn. of Home Builders; Intl. Council of Shopping Ctrs., Dir., Arlington Savings Assn.; **EDUC:** BBA, 1970, Fin., Texas Tech.; **EDUC HONORS:** Pres., Sigma Alpha Epsilon; **MIL SERV:** US Army, Sp. 5; **HOME ADD:** 3600 Drexel, Dallas, TX 75205, (214)526-1007; **BUS ADD:** 711 E. Lamar Blvd., Suite 100, Arlington, TX 76012, (817)261-4936.

SOWELS, David——B: Feb. 20, 1951, Ft. Worth, TX, *Pres.*, Force Inc., Financial Organizers Realty, Devel.; **PRIM RE ACT:** Developer, Syndicator; **OTHER RE ACT:** Condo. Devel.; **PROFL AFFIL & HONORS:** NAR, GRI; **MIL SERV:** US Army, E-4; **OTHER ACT & HONORS:** Men of Tomorrow, VChmn.; **HOME ADD:** 5822 Buena Vista Ave., Oakland, CA 94618, (415)655-6855; **BUS ADD:** 1128 Broadway, Oakland, CA 94607, (415)465-9400.

SOYBEL, Arthur——B: June 16, 1925, Brooklyn, NY, *Owner*, Arthur Soybel Realty; **PRIM RE ACT:** Attorney, Owner/Investor, Property Manager; **SERVICES:** Total legal servs. in RE; **REP CLIENTS:** Sellers, purchasers, owner mgrs.; **PROFL AFFIL & HONORS:** Bar Assn., City of NY, NY State Bar Assn., CHIP; **EDUC:** BA, 1947 1950, Music, Manhattan Sch. of Music, Univ. of NC; **GRAD EDUC:** JD, 1954, NY Law Sch.; **MIL SERV:** USN, Lt. JG, 1943-46; **OTHER ACT & HONORS:** Member Community Bd. 7, 1967-68; **HOME**

ADD: 393 W End Ave., New York, NY 10024, (212)787-6063; **BUS ADD:** 36 W 44th St., New York, NY 10036, (212)840-6543.

SPAGAT, Martin——**B:** June 22, 1940, Chicago, IL, *Atty. at Law*, Spagat and O'Brien LTD.; **PRIM RE ACT:** Attorney; **SERVICES:** All Phases of Legal RE Rep.; **REP CLIENTS:** N.R.E. Bd.; Northwestern S&L, Assn.; **PROFL AFFIL & HONORS:** Chicago R.E. Bd., ABA Northwest R.E. Bd., Chicago Bar Assn., IL Bar Assn.; **GRAD EDUC:** JD, 1964, Univ. of IL; **HOME ADD:** 216 Charles Pl., Wilnelte, IL 60091; **BUS ADD:** 39 S. LaSalle, Suite 808, Chicago, IL 60603, (312)641-1230.

SPAGNA, Arthur O.——**B:** June 25, 1911, New York, NY, Spagna & Spagna; **PRIM RE ACT:** Broker, Attorney, Property Manager, Insuror; **SERVICES:** RE Law; **PROFL AFFIL & HONORS:** Bay Ridge RE Bd., Columbian Attys., Bay Ridge Attys., Brooklyn Bar Assn., ABA; **EDUC:** Law Certificate, 1929, Pre-Legal, St. Johns; **GRAD EDUC:** LLB, 1932, Law, St. Johns; **MIL SERV:** USAF-Judge Advocate Capt.; **OTHER ACT & HONORS:** Civil Court Administrator Judge; **HOME ADD:** 1246 5th St., Brooklyn, NY, (212)436-4400; **BUS ADD:** 4504 New Utrecht Ave., Brooklyn, NY 11219, (212)436-4400.

SPAHR, Gary M.——**B:** July 12, 1954, Loveland, CO, *RE Loan Officer*, First Wyoming Bank, NA, Cheyenne; **PRIM RE ACT:** Banker, Lender, Regulator, Instructor; **OTHER RE ACT:** Loan Servicer; **SERVICES:** Resid. & comml. const.; perm. and land devel. loans; escrow and loan servicing; mort. ins. and loan counseling; **PREV EMPLOY:** Mgr. for Western States Mort. Co. 1976-78; Asst. Mgr. for Northern Colorado Mort. Co. 1975-76; **PROFL AFFIL & HONORS:** Bd. of Realtors, Amer. Inst. of Banking; S.E. WY Homebuilders; Assoc. Gen. Contractors of WY, FNMA Level 2 Underwriter; Delegated Underwriter for AMIC; State Chmn. for Amer. Inst. of Banking; Grad. of Nat. School of RE Fin.; Earned the Basic, Standard, Advance & General Cert. from AIB; Retail and General Banking Diplomas; **EDUC:** BBA, 1976, Fin. and RE, CO State Univ., Ft. Collins, CO; **OTHER ACT & HONORS:** Instructor for AIB RE Lending and Consumer Compliance Courses; Treasurer, Exchange Club of Cheyenne; V.P., CSU Alumni Assn.; Ins. Agent & Notary Public for State of WY; **HOME ADD:** 3512 Randy Rd., Cheyenne, WY 82001, (307)635-0494; **BUS ADD:** P.O. Box 1227, Cheyenne, WY 82001, (307)634-5961.

SPAHR, J. Alan——**B:** Mar. 18, 1934, Carlisle, PA, *Pres.*, Alan Spahr Associates, Inc.; **PRIM RE ACT:** Broker, Consultant, Engineer, Appraiser, Developer, Builder, Owner/Investor, Instructor, Syndicator; **SERVICES:** Devel. & mktg. of indus. props.; **REP CLIENTS:** Indus., Lenders and Investors; **PREV EMPLOY:** Davis Forest Indus., VP & Gen. Mgt.-Ledgewood Props. Div.; **EDUC:** BS, ME, 1956, Mechanical Engrg. & Indus. Mgmt., MIT; **EDUC HONORS:** Pi Tau Sigma; **HOME ADD:** Bible Hill Rd., Claremont, NH 03743, (603)542-8440; **BUS ADD:** Box 958, Bible Hill Rd., Claremont, NH 03743, (603)543-0595.

SPAINHOUR, Kenneth F.——**B:** Oct. 4, 1938, Winston Salem, NC, *VP and Dir. of Physical Resources*, Fast Fare, Inc., Corporate Office; **PRIM RE ACT:** Broker, Developer, Owner/Investor, Instructor, Property Manager; **PREV EMPLOY:** North Hills, Inc. Shoppig Ctr. Devel.; **PROFL AFFIL & HONORS:** NC Assn. of Realtors, Inc.; NAR; RNMI; Nat. Assn. of Corporate RE Execs.; Raleigh Bd. of Realtors and NACS Educ. Adv. Comm., GRI; **EDUC:** BS, 1963, Math.; **GRAD EDUC:** Wake Forest Univ.; **MIL SERV:** USAF; Air Nat. Guard; **HOME ADD:** 8301 Meadow Ridge Ct., Raleigh, NC 27609, (919)847-1509; **BUS ADD:** P.O. Box 907, Ruin Creek Rd., Henderson, NC 27536.

SPAK, Jude——*Asst. Treas.*, Joy Manufacturing Co.; **PRIM RE ACT:** Property Manager; **BUS ADD:** Henry W. Oliver Bldg., Pittsburgh, PA 15222, (412)562-4500.*

SPALDING, Edward C., Jr.——**B:** Feb. 5, 1949, Lake Forest, IL, *Branch Mgr.*, Lawyers Title Insurance, Continental Financial Servs. (Continental Grp.); **PRIM RE ACT:** Insuror; **OTHER RE ACT:** Title Ins.; **SERVICES:** Searches, examinations, commitments, policies, closing; **EDUC:** BS, 1971, Pol. Sci./Bus., Univ. of Denver; **HOME ADD:** Apt. 2204, Palm Beach House, W. Palm Beach, FL 33401, (305)522-1861; **BUS ADD:** 1665 Palm Beach Lakes Blvd., W. Palm Beach, FL 33401.

SPALDING, Mona T.——**B:** Oct. 2, 1928, Newburyport, MA, *Owner, Mgr.*, Mona's Realty; **PRIM RE ACT:** Broker, Owner/Investor; **PREV EMPLOY:** Hart & Co., Realty World; **PROFL AFFIL & HONORS:** Greater Newburyport Bd. of Realtors, GRI Realtor of Yr., Professional Women's Club (1979); **EDUC:** BA, 1976, Art Hist., NSCC & Lowell Univ.; **EDUC HONORS:** Summa Cum Laude; **OTHER ACT & HONORS:** VP G.N. Bd. of Realtors, IC Church; **HOME ADD:** 19 Broad St., Newburyport, MA, (617)465-0027; **BUS ADD:** 8 Harris St., Newburyport, MA 01950, (617)462-8088.

SPALLA, Dennis J.——**B:** Jan. 18, 1941, Detroit, MI, *VP*, Kraus Anderson Devel. Corp., Part of Kraus Anderson Group of Construction & RE Firms; **PRIM RE ACT:** Broker, Consultant, Developer, Builder, Owner/Investor; **SERVICES:** Devel. comml. props. for others and for our own portfolio; **PREV EMPLOY:** Dayton Hudson Corp.; **PROFL AFFIL & HONORS:** ABA, MN & ND Bar Assns.; Intl. Council of Shopping Centers; **EDUC:** BA, 1963, English, Univ. of MI; **GRAD EDUC:** JD, 1967, Wayne State Univ. Law School; **EDUC HONORS:** Tribe of Michigamua Honorary Soc.; **HOME ADD:** 440 Vinewood Ln., Plymouth, MN 55441, (612)545-4100; **BUS ADD:** 2510 Minnehaha Ave., Minneapolis, MN 55404, (612)721-4877.

SPANGLER, Charles Bishop——**B:** Jan. 7, 1932, VA, *Pres.*, C. B. Spangler, Inc.; **PRIM RE ACT:** Developer, Owner/Investor, Syndicator; **SERVICES:** Investment counselling, synd., devel. of sunbelt investment props.; **REP CLIENTS:** Medical/profl.; **PREV EMPLOY:** Dir., Advanced Systems Teledyne Ryan; **PROFL AFFIL & HONORS:** Who's Who in the West; **EDUC:** BS, 1953, Mathematics & Physics, Berea Coll., KY; **GRAD EDUC:** MS, PhD, 1955, 1963, Mathematics & Physics, The Univ. of Pittsburgh; **EDUC HONORS:** Clark Prize in Physics; **OTHER ACT & HONORS:** Deacon, Tomey Pines Church; **HOME ADD:** 335 Fern Glen, La Jolla, CA 92037; **BUS ADD:** 335 Fern Glen, La Jolla, CA 92037, (714)454-0062.

SPANGLER, Leonard L., Jr.——**B:** July 17, 1939, Hagerstown, MD, *Pres.*, Atlantic Coastal Title Corp.; **OTHER RE ACT:** Title Ins.; **SERVICES:** Title insurance and closing serv.; **REP CLIENTS:** PGA Nat., U.S. Homes, Transar Realty of FL, various S&L and lending inst.; **PREV EMPLOY:** Cty. Mgr., Lawyers Title Insurance Corp., 1968-1980; **PROFL AFFIL & HONORS:** Palm Beach Cty. Title Assn.; FL Land Title Assn.; Mort. Bankers Assn.; Various RE Bds.; **MIL SERV:** USAF, S/Sgt.; **OTHER ACT & HONORS:** Chmn., Charter Review Commn., N. Lauderdale, FL, 1970-1971; Rotary and other civic assns.; **HOME ADD:** 936 47th Ave., Vero Beach, FL 32960, (305)569-4364; **BUS ADD:** 936 47th Ave., Vero Beach, FL 32960, (305)569-4364.

SPANO, Mary Marleen——*Pres.*, Sterling Realty Co.; **PRIM RE ACT:** Broker, Appraiser; **SERVICES:** RE sales, rentals, ins. sales, appraisals; **REP CLIENTS:** Fellowship Savings, Bergen State Bank, GM, Employees Relocation Serv., Equitable Relocation, Relocation Realty, Mercury Mort. Co., Cateract Savings, Boiling Springs Mort., United Jersey Mort., Globe Mort. Co., Forman Mort. Co., Lawyers Mort. Co., many attys. in area; **PREV EMPLOY:** RE broker since 1960 and salesman from 1955-60; **PROFL AFFIL & HONORS:** Eastern Bergen Cty. Bd. of Realtors, Bergen Cty. Multiple Listing Service, NAIFA, Outstanding Appraiser of yr, 1971 by E. Bergen Bd. of Realtors Community Serv. Award nominee for 1970 by E. Bergen Bd. of Realtors; **GRAD EDUC:** 1948, all appraisal courses, Rutgers Univ., Fairleigh Dickinson Univ. & Bergen Community Coll.; **OTHER ACT & HONORS:** State Dir. 1982 NJ Assoc. of Ind. Fee Appraisers, European Health Spa; National Man of the Year Award - 1981 (to be changed to National Appraiser of the Year); **HOME ADD:** 332 Teaneck Rd., Teaneck, NJ 07666, (201)833-1692; **BUS ADD:** 332 Teaneck Rd., Teaneck, NJ 07666, (201)833-1692.

SPANOS, George——**B:** July 2, 1936, Lansing, MI, Burns and Spanos; **PRIM RE ACT:** Attorney, Developer, Owner/Investor, Syndicator; **REP CLIENTS:** Owner/investors, devel., synd.; **PROFL AFFIL & HONORS:** ABA Real Prop., Probate and Trust Section; State Bar of MI, Real Property Section; **EDUC:** BA, 1958, Pre-Law, Acctg., Albion Coll.; **GRAD EDUC:** JD, 1961, Law, Northwestern Univ. School of Law; **HOME ADD:** 730 Winter Park Lane, Petoskey, MI 49770, (616)347-2482; **BUS ADD:** 410 Petoskey, Petoskey, MI 49770, (616)347-2566.

SPARKS, John O.——**B:** Apr. 7, 1939, Woodward, OK, *Atty.*, Sparks, Liles & Starke, Inc.; **PRIM RE ACT:** Attorney; **SERVICES:** Title exam., sale of RE contrs., consultation, estate planning; **REP CLIENTS:** Group Title Examiner for Bank of Woodward, OK; NW Fed. S&L Assn.; Amer. First Title & Trust Co.; Chicago Title Ins. Co.; SW Title & Trust Co.; Lawyers Title Ins. Corp.; **EDUC:** AB, 1961, Journalism, Univ. of OK; **MIL SERV:** US Army, 1st Lt.; **OTHER ACT & HONORS:** Asst. DA, Woodward Cty., OK, Jan. 1967 to April 1968; Asst. DA OK Cty., OK, Apr. 1968 to June 1969; Asst. US DA, Western Dist. of OK, June 1969 to July 1970; City Atty., City of Woodward, OK, May 1974 to July 1978; **HOME ADD:** 3611 Cedar Ridge Ln., PO Box 968, Woodward, OK 73801, (405)256-6524; **BUS ADD:** PO Box 968, 1715 Main, Woodward, OK 73801, (405)256-8647.

SPARR, Olive M.——**B:** Oct. 10, 1920, DeKalb, IL, *Broker/Owner*, Golden Rule Realty Enterprises, Inc.; **PRIM RE ACT:** Broker, Owner/Investor; **SERVICES:** Listing and selling; **PROFL AFFIL & HONORS:** RNMI, CRB, NAR, CAR, GRI, CRS; **EDUC:** Diablo Valley Jr. Coll., CA; Oakland Community Coll., CA; **OTHER ACT & HONORS:** Bus. Prof. Womens Assn., Delta Cty. Golf Assn., Volunteer Pink Lady, Delta Cty. Memorial Hospital; **HOME ADD:** 1676 H 75 Rd., Delta, CO 81416, (303)874-3035; **BUS ADD:** 424 Main St., Delta, CO 81416, (303)874-7572.

SPARROW, David J.——**B:** July 5, 1927, Detroit, MI, *Partners*, Rowin & Sparrow; **PRIM RE ACT:** Attorney, Owner/Investor, Property Manager, Syndicator; **PROFL AFFIL & HONORS:** State Bar of MI; ABA; Detroit Bar Assn.; MI Apt. Owners Assn.; **EDUC:** Highland Park Jr. Coll.; **GRAD EDUC:** JD, 1951, Detroit Coll. of Law; **OTHER ACT & HONORS:** Oakland Schools B.O.E. - 10 years; **HOME ADD:** 5880 Tootmoor, Bloomfield Hills, MI 48013, (313)526-5073; **BUS ADD:** 100 W. Long Lake Rd., Bloomfield Hills, MI 48013, (313)642-7600.

SPEARS, W.E.——*RE Mgr.*, Marathon Oil; **PRIM RE ACT:** Property Manager; **BUS ADD:** 539 S. Main St., Findlay, OH 45840, (419)422-2121.*

SPEARS, William J.——**B:** Jan. 9, 1943, Panama City, FL, *Partner*, Laventhol & Horwath, Audit; **OTHER RE ACT:** CPA; **SERVICES:** Acctg., audit, tax, consulting; **PROFL AFFIL & HONORS:** AICPA; FICPA; NCACPA; NAA; **EDUC:** BS, 1965, Acctg., FL State Univ.; **MIL SERV:** US Army, Sp5, 1966-1968; **HOME ADD:** 3016 Hanson Dr., Charlotte, NC 28207, (704)366-4257; **BUS ADD:** One NCNB Plaza, Ste. 3420, Charlotte, NC 28280, (704)377-0220.

SPEER, Erling Dick——**B:** May 12, 1940, Augusta, GA, *Pres.*, Environmental Ventures, Inc.; **PRIM RE ACT:** Developer, Builder, Owner/Investor, Property Manager; **SERVICES:** Devel. mgmt. of RE projects for clients and joint venture partners; **REP CLIENTS:** Great Amer. Mgmt. & Investment Inc., Atlanta, GA; Van Rinkle Construc. Co., Atlanta, GA; **PROFL AFFIL & HONORS:** NAHB; ALDA; ULI, Chmn., Recreational Devel. Council; **EDUC:** BS, 1963, Bus. Mgmt., Univ. of SC; **HOME ADD:** 5190 Burning Tree Cir., Stuart, FL 33494, (305)287-4577; **BUS ADD:** 6500 Mariner Sands Dr., Stuart, FL 33494, (305)283-7500.

SPEIER, Peter——**B:** Dec. 29, 1937, New York City, NY, *Sr. VP*, Julien J. Studley, Inc.; **PRIM RE ACT:** Broker, Consultant; **SERVICES:** Represent tenants looking to develop or lease office bldgs., Represents national Companies throughout the US.; **REP CLIENTS:** Specialize with law firms assns., Acctg. firms; **PROFL AFFIL & HONORS:** WA, NY RE Bds.; Bd. of Trade; **EDUC:** BS, 1959, Acctg., Univ. of Buffalo; **MIL SERV:** US Army, Sgt.; **HOME ADD:** 9034 Congressional Pkwy., Potomac, MD 20856, (301)299-7198; **BUS ADD:** 1333 New Hampshire Ave. NW, Washington, DC 20036, (202)296-6360.

SPEIK, Robert L.——**B:** June 2, 1928, Pasadena, CA, *VP, Income Prop. Dept.*, Rainier Mortgage Co., A Subsidiary of Rainier Ban Corporation; **PRIM RE ACT:** Broker, Instructor, Consultant, Appraiser, Lender, Owner/Investor; **SERVICES:** Fin. for non-residential projects; **REP CLIENTS:** Metropolitan Life, MA Mutual Life, Soc. for Savings, CA Fed. Savings; **PROFL AFFIL & HONORS:** Nat. Ass. of Review Appraise; Intl. Inst. of Valuers, MBAA,CA, S. CA and Orange Cty. MBA, at Irvine; Charter Member of Orange Cty. fin. Exe., Charter Chmn. of Orange Mort. Bankers; **EDUC:** BA, 1950, Liberal Arts, Pomona Coll., Claremont, CA; **GRAD EDUC:** Certificate in RE with specialization in Fin, 1975, UCLA; **EDUC HONORS:** Cert.CA; **MIL SERV:** US Army, Lt.; **OTHER ACT & HONORS:** Treas. Mountaineering Training Comm. Sierra Club; **HOME ADD:** 3030 Anacapa Pl., Fullerton, CA 92635, (714)680-0330; **BUS ADD:** 1900 East Fourth St., Suite 120, Santa Ana, CA 92705, (714)973-1541.

SPEIZER, Harry——**B:** Apr. 15, 1947, Steyer, Austria, *Pres.*, The Speizer Company; **PRIM RE ACT:** Broker, Consultant, Developer, Builder, Owner/Investor, Syndicator; **SERVICES:** Comml./Investment Brokerage, Investment Counseling, Feasibility and Mkt. Research Studies; Synd. and Devel. of Comml. Props.; **REP CLIENTS:** RE Devel. and Bldg. Firms, Indiv. and Instnl. Investors in Comml. Props.; **PREV EMPLOY:** The Keyes Co. 1972-76; The Arvida Corp., 1976-78; Goodkin Research Corp. 1978-79; The Speizer Co. 1979 to present; **PROFL AFFIL & HONORS:** Lic. RE Broker, Lic. Gen. Contractor, Realtors Nat. Mktg. Inst.; RESSI; Builders Assn. of S. FL; RE Assn. of Profls., Econ. Soc.; Nat. Assn. of Realtors; **EDUC:** BS, 1968, Communications, Univ. of Houston; **GRAD EDUC:** MA & MBA, 1970 & 1976, Communications & Bus. Admin., Univ. of Houston & Univ of Miami; **OTHER ACT & HONORS:** Awarded GRI and CCIM designations; lectured in real estate commercial - investment seminars; authored articles in real estate, served on Advisory board to Sunset Commerical Bank; **HOME ADD:** 11301 SW 109th Rd., Miami, FL 33176, (305)596-0305; **BUS ADD:** 10651 N. Kendall Dr., Suite 110, Miami, FL 33176, (305)274-2050.

SPELMAN, Harold J.——**B:** Aug. 12, 1923, Chicago, IL, *Atty. at Law*, Harold J. Spelman & Assoc.; **PRIM RE ACT:** Attorney; **PROFL AFFIL & HONORS:** DuPage Bar Assn.; IL Bar Assn. Chmn. RE Sect.; Amer. Bar Assn.; **EDUC:** AB, 1946, Hist., Univ. of Chicago; **GRAD EDUC:** JD, 1948, Law, Univ. of Chicago; **EDUC HONORS:** Pres., Student Body; Law Review; **MIL SERV:** USN, Air Cadet; **OTHER ACT & HONORS:** City Atty., 1952 to present; Police Mag., 1948-1952; AF&AM; Rotary; Editor Real Property News Letter; Chmn. IL Broker/Lawyer Accord Comm.; Author Numerous Articles; **HOME ADD:** 2O0 High St., W. Chicago, IL 60185, (312)231-1580; **BUS ADD:** 200 High St., W. Chicago, IL 60185, (312)231-1580.

SPENCER, Donald G.——**B:** June 9, 1935, Los Angeles, CA, *Mgr., RE Investment Services*, Seattle First National Bank, Trust; **PRIM RE ACT:** Consultant, Appraiser, Lender, Instructor; **OTHER RE ACT:** RE Asset Mgt., Acquisitions; **SERVICES:** Acquisition, consulting, asset mgmt.; **PROFL AFFIL & HONORS:** IREM, Nat. Assn. of Corporate RE Execs.; Soc. of RE Appraisers; Nat. Trust RE Assn.; Amer. Arbitration Assn.; **EDUC:** Bus. Admin., 1958, Bus., Seattle Pacific Univ.; **HOME ADD:** 1015 144th Pl. SE, Belleville, WA 98007, (206)747-4198; **BUS ADD:** PO Box 3586, Seattle, WA 98124, (206)583-7317.

SPENCER, Joan H.——**B:** May 2, 1934, St. Louis, MO, *Owner*, Joan Harris Spencer; **PRIM RE ACT:** Broker, Appraiser, Instructor, Property Manager; **REP CLIENTS:** Resid. Sellers, also Comml.; **PREV EMPLOY:** 15 yrs RE sales & mgmt.; **PROFL AFFIL & HONORS:** Westchester Cty. Bd. of Realtors; NY State Assn. of Realtors; NAR; RNMI, CRS; GRI; **EDUC:** Vassar Coll., 1956, Sociology, Psych.; **OTHER ACT & HONORS:** Dir. of Eastchester Family Consultants Serv.; Jr. League of Bronxville; **HOME ADD:** 8 Midland Gardens, Bronxville, NY 10708, (914)793-5834; **BUS ADD:** 9 Park Pl., Bronxville, NY 10708, (914)779-1717.

SPENCER, Ralph D.——**B:** June 11, 1947, Richmond, VA, *VP*, Harrison & Bates, Inc.; **PRIM RE ACT:** Broker, Instructor; **SERVICES:** Gen. comml., indus. & investment brokerage; **REP CLIENTS:** Amer. Brands, Western Electric, Wards Co., Hechinger Co., Marriott; **PREV EMPLOY:** Larasan Realty, Virginia Beach, VA; **PROFL AFFIL & HONORS:** Member, RNMI; ULI; Nat. Assn. of Office & Indus. Parks; SIR, CCIM; **EDUC:** BS, 1969, Bus./Mktg., Old Dominion Univ.; **GRAD EDUC:** MS, 1979, Bus. (RE & Urban Land Dev.), VA Commonwealth Univ.; **MIL SERV:** US Army, E-5; **HOME ADD:** 4429 Old Fox Trail, Miplothian, VA 23113, (804)744-3138; **BUS ADD:** Richmond Plaza, 111 S. 6th St., Richmond, VA 23219, (804)788-1000.

SPENCER, Richard I.——**B:** Feb. 6, 1930, Medford, MA, *Prop.*, Spencer & Co.; **PRIM RE ACT:** Broker, Consultant, Appraiser; **PREV EMPLOY:** Sr. VP & Part. Hunneman & Co., Inc. to Jan. 1981; **PROFL AFFIL & HONORS:** SIR; NAR; NH Assn. of Realtors, SIR; **HOME ADD:** RD 2, Box 6, Chester, NH 03036, (603)887-3615; **BUS ADD:** RD 2, Box 6, Chester, NH 03036, (603)887-3615.

SPENCER, Thomas A.——**B:** Oct. 24, 1953, Indianapolis, *Comml. Prop. Mgr.*, Oxford Devel. Corp.; **PRIM RE ACT:** Broker, Property Manager; **EDUC:** BBA, 1976, Mktg., Univ. of Notre Dame; **HOME ADD:** 210 E. 82nd St., Indianapolis, IN 46240; **BUS ADD:** 3919 Meadows Dr., Indianapolis, IN 46205, (317)542-0128.

SPERA, Charles C.——**B:** Sept. 11, 1942, St. Louis, MO, *VP*, Schostak Bros. & Co., Inc., Investor Services Div.; **PRIM RE ACT:** Broker, Consultant, Owner/Investor; **SERVICES:** Acquisition and sales of income producing props., consultation, valuation, merger transactions; **REP CLIENTS:** Indivs. and instl. clients; **PREV EMPLOY:** Prudential Ins. Co. of America; Honeywell, Inc.; **PROFL AFFIL & HONORS:** RESSI, RNMI, CCIM; **EDUC:** BA, 1964, Univ. of Buffalo, Buffalo, NY; **HOME ADD:** 21170 Chubb Rd., Northville, MI 48167, (313)348-0785; **BUS ADD:** 17515 W. 9 Mile Rd., Southfield, MI 48075, (313)559-2000.

SPERLING, Gary H.——**B:** July 14, 1945, Newark, NJ, *First Deputy Commissioner/Gen. Counsel*, City of New York, Dept. of Ports and Terminals; **PRIM RE ACT:** Attorney, Regulator; **SERVICES:** Ownership and regulation of City waterfront props.; **EDUC:** BA, 1966, Govt., Columbia Univ.; **GRAD EDUC:** JD, 1969, Law, Columbia Univ.; **EDUC HONORS:** Cum laude, Bennett Prize, Curtis Medal, Cum laude, Stone Scholar; **OTHER ACT & HONORS:** Pres. US Chess Federation; US Delegate; Intl. Chess Federation; **HOME ADD:** 117 Beverly Ave., Staten Island, NY 10301; **BUS ADD:** Battery

Maritime Bldg., New York, NY 10004, (212)248-8239.

SPETH, Paul H.——B: Feb. 19, 1935, New Albany, IN, Speth Appraisal Co.; **PRIM RE ACT:** Broker, Appraiser, Builder; **OTHER RE ACT:** Ins. & RE appraisal; **PROFL AFFIL & HONORS:** RE Bd., NAR; **EDUC:** BS, 1958, Educ., IN Univ.; **EDUC HONORS:** Little 500 Scholarship; **OTHER ACT & HONORS:** Jaycee VP & Dir., New Orleans Credit Bureau Arbitrator Member, Broker License IN & KY; **HOME ADD:** 2632 Joy Ann Dr., Marrero, LA 70072, (504)340-6059; **BUS ADD:** 2632 Joy Ann Dr., Marrero, CA 70072, (504)340-3623.

SPEVAK, Irving——B: Dec. 10, 1917, Albany, NY, *Pres.*, Irving B. Spevak Inc.; **PRIM RE ACT:** Broker, Instructor, Property Manager; **OTHER RE ACT:** Specialist in site acquisition and evaluation for Comml., Office and Indus., Clients - since 1951; **SERVICES:** Prop., search, traffic analysis and demographics; **REP CLIENTS:** Metropolitan Life Ins. Co., Macys, Holiday Inns., Wendys, KY Fried Chicken; **PREV EMPLOY:** VP - Corbetta Enterprises, Inc. 1969-1973, Full Charge of Mgmt. of Operations-New Apt. Constr.; **PROFL AFFIL & HONORS:** Dutchess Cty. Bd. of Realtors (Pres. 1969 and 1970); NY State Assn. of Realtors (State Dir. 1979 to Present) Comml. & Investment Div. NYSAR Bd. of Gov. 1980 and 1981; **EDUC:** Bus. Admin., Univ. of NE and Vassar Coll.; **MIL SERV:** USN, Ph.M 2nd Class, Served in Pacific Theatre; **OTHER ACT & HONORS:** Past Pres.-Masons, Past Commander-Jewish War Veterans, Lic. Instr.-RE Licensing and Continuing Educ. Courses; **HOME ADD:** 287 New Hackensack Rd., Poughkeepsie, NY 12603, (914)454-4280; **BUS ADD:** 287 New Hackensack Rd., Poughkeepsie, NY 12603, (914)454-4280.

SPEZIO, Arthur J.——B: Apr. 14, 1948, Rochester, NY, *CPA*, Arthur J. Spezio, CPA; **OTHER RE ACT:** Tax consultant; **SERVICES:** Investment counseling RE: tax aspects; **PROFL AFFIL & HONORS:** Member, AICPA; NY State Soc. of CPA's, Chairperson, MAS Comm., 1979-1980; **EDUC:** BS, 1974, Acctg., Rochester Inst. of Tech.; **EDUC HONORS:** Cum Laude; **MIL SERV:** USAF, S/Sgt.; **OTHER ACT & HONORS:** Adjunct Instr., School of Bus., SUNY Geneseo; **HOME ADD:** 545 Clay Ave., Rochester, NY 14613, (716)254-9038; **BUS ADD:** 1577 Ridge Rd., Suite 204, Rochester, NY 14615, (716)621-7277.

SPIALTER, Howard D.——B: Apr. 29, 1954, Newark, NJ, *Atty.*; **PRIM RE ACT:** Consultant, Attorney, Owner/Investor; **SERVICES:** Legal and Counselling; **REP CLIENTS:** Investors in miscellaneous types of RE prop.; **PROFL AFFIL & HONORS:** ABA, NJ State Bar Assn.; **EDUC:** BA, 1974, Econ., Acctg., Rutgers Univ.; **GRAD EDUC:** JD, 1977, Law, Rutgers Univ.; **EDUC HONORS:** Econ. Honor Soc., Cum Laude; **OTHER ACT & HONORS:** Temple Beth, Clark, NJ, (Officer,) B'nai Brith Clark, NJ (VP); **HOME ADD:** 37 Dorset Dr., Clark, NJ 07066, (201)574-9540; **BUS ADD:** 203 Amboy Ave., PO Box 472, Metuchen, NJ 08840, (201)548-0575.

SPIDELL, Bob——B: Nov. 12, 1933, Andover, ME, *Editor and Publisher*, Spidell Publishing; **PRIM RE ACT:** Real Estate Publisher; **SERVICES:** Editor and publisher of the RE Taxletter; The CA Taxletter, numerous books and special reports on taxes. Also lectures extensively on CA and Fed. taxes; **PROFL AFFIL & HONORS:** Nat. Soc. of Public Accts., Nat. Assn. of Enrolled Agents; **EDUC:** BA, 1965, Econ., Long Beach State Coll.; **MIL SERV:** USMC, 1953-56, Sgt.; **HOME ADD:** 407 S. Archer St., Anaheim, CA 92804; **BUS ADD:** 239 S. Magnolia Ave., Anaheim, CA 92804, (714)821-6950.

SPIECKERMAN, E.W.——B: May 27, 1933, West Germany, *VP*, Tandy Corp., Radio Schck; **OTHER RE ACT:** Retail RE Exec.; **SERVICES:** leasing of retail stores, distribution ctrs.; **REP CLIENTS:** factories for Radio Schck, constr., interior design, etc.; **PROFL AFFIL & HONORS:** Intl. Council of Shopping Ctrs.; Nat. Assn. of Corp. RE Execs.; **EDUC:** BA, 1959, Arts and Sci., Bus. Mgmt., So. Methodist Univ.; **EDUC HONORS:** Dean's List; **MIL SERV:** USN, Pacific Fleet; **OTHER ACT & HONORS:** Shady Oaks Ctry. Club, Ft. Worth; YMCA, Univ. Christian Church; **HOME ADD:** Rt. 3, Box 88, Azle, TX 76020, (817)444-3724; **BUS ADD:** 1600 One Tandy Ctr., Ft. Worth, TX 76102, (817)390-3224.

SPIEGEL, Siegmund——B: Nov. 13, 1919, Gera, Germany, *Arch./ Owner*; **PRIM RE ACT:** Architect; **PROFL AFFIL & HONORS:** AIA; NY State Assn. of Architects; Long Is. Chap., AIA; **EDUC:** Columbia Univ., NY; **MIL SERV:** US Army/Infantry, M/Sgt., The Bronze Star, Purple Heart, Belgium Law Croix de Guerre avec Palme; **OTHER ACT & HONORS:** Nassau Cty. Rent Guidelines Bd., 1974 - ; Nat. Assn. of Home Builders, Long Island Builders Inst., Life Dir.; **HOME ADD:** 1508 Hayes Ct., East Meadow, NY 11554; **BUS ADD:** 2035 Hempstead Tpk., East Meadow, NY 11554, (516)794-8050.

SPIEKER, Warren E. "Ned", Jr.——B: May 9, 1944, Orange, CA, *Managing Gen. Partner*, Trammell Crow Co., Pacific Northwest States; **PRIM RE ACT:** Developer; **PREV EMPLOY:** Dillingham Corp.; **PROFL AFFIL & HONORS:** ULI; SIR; **EDUC:** BS, 1966, BA, Univ. of CA, Berkeley; **HOME ADD:** 475 Selby Ln., Atherton, CA 94025, (415)327-3626; **BUS ADD:** 2180 Sand Hill Rd., Menlo Park, CA 94025, (415)854-5333.

SPIERER, Steven F.——B: May 13, 1953, Los Angeles, CA, *Atty.*, Spierer & Woodward; **PRIM RE ACT:** Attorney, Owner/Investor; **SERVICES:** Legal concerning only RE & Bus.; **REP CLIENTS:** Transamerica Title Ins.; Title Ins. & Trust; Spring Realty; **EDUC:** BA, 1975, Pre Law Studies, Poli. Sci, CA State Univ., Dominguez Hills, CA; **GRAD EDUC:** JD, 1977, Southwestern Univ. Sch. of Law; **EDUC HONORS:** Grad. with distinction in gen. scholarship, Grad. of SCALE Project, Pilot Yr.; **BUS ADD:** 21535 Hawthorne Blvd., 532, Torrance, CA 90503, (213)540-3199.

SPIESS, Paul D.——B: June 22, 1949, Cleveland, OH, *Pres.*, First Bank Mort. Corp.; **PRIM RE ACT:** Banker, Lender; **OTHER RE ACT:** Mort. Banking, Loan Serv., Construction Lending; **REP CLIENTS:** Resid. and Comml. Devel., S&L Assn., Life Ins. Corps., State Housing Agency; **PREV EMPLOY:** VP - Baybank Harvard Trust Co., Cambridge, MA; **PROFL AFFIL & HONORS:** Mort. Bankers of Amer., Greater Boston RE Bd.; **EDUC:** BA, 1971, Govt., Colby Coll., Waterville, ME; **GRAD EDUC:** MBA, 1977, Fin., Boston Univ.; **EDUC HONORS:** Cum Laude; **HOME ADD:** Madison Ln., Amherst, NH 03031; **BUS ADD:** 111 Charles St., Manchester, NH 03105, (603)623-3530.

SPIESSBACH, Michael F.——B: Sept. 25, 1943, Newark, NJ, *Assoc. Dir., Intl. RE Mktg. & Fin.*, Merrill Lynch Hubbard Intl.; **PRIM RE ACT:** Attorney; **OTHER RE ACT:** Intl. Product Devel. & Mktg.; **SERVICES:** All servs.; **REP CLIENTS:** Numerous maj. foreign corps. and indivs. of personal wealth; **PREV EMPLOY:** Pres., Mexus, Inc.; **PROFL AFFIL & HONORS:** ABA; **EDUC:** BA, 1967, Hist./Art, Rutgers Univ., Newark, NJ; **GRAD EDUC:** JD, 1972, Law, Seton Hall Law School, Newark, NJ; **EDUC HONORS:** Scholarship recipient & Editor, Seton Hall Law Review; **OTHER ACT & HONORS:** Member Bd. of Dirs. & Exec. Comm., NJ Chap. of the Arthritis Found.; **HOME ADD:** 52 Mountain View Rd., Millburn, NJ 07041; **BUS ADD:** 2 Broadway, New York, NY 10004, (212)908-8640.

SPILLER, Sol. L.——B: Oct. 15, 1924, Wilmington, DE, *Mgr., Capital Assets*, Whittaker Corp.; **OTHER RE ACT:** Dir., Corp. RE; Mgmt. of Capital Assets; **SERVICES:** Buying, selling, leasing, sub-leasing, construction, project mgmt. fin. review, facility mgmt.; **PREV EMPLOY:** Engrg.; Gen. Mgmt.; **PROFL AFFIL & HONORS:** Indus. Devel. Research Council; **EDUC:** BS, 1944, Chem. Engrg., Univ. of Delaware; **GRAD EDUC:** MBA, 1947, Indus. Mgmt., Univ. of PA, Wharton Graduate School; **EDUC HONORS:** Phi Kappa Phi; **MIL SERV:** USN; Lt.j.g.; **HOME ADD:** 2915 Woodwardia Dr., Los Angeles, CA 90024, (213)986-2742; **BUS ADD:** 10880 Wilshire Blvd., Los Angeles, CA 90024, (213)475-9411.

SPINGLER, Frank J.——B: Dec. 29, 1944, Poughkeepsie, NY, *Dir., RE*, Southern Railway System, Law and Finance; **PRIM RE ACT:** Attorney; **PROFL AFFIL & HONORS:** ABA; DC Bar Assn.; **EDUC:** BA, 1967, English, St. Bonaventure Uiv.; **GRAD EDUC:** JD, 1970, Law, Georgetown Univ.; **MIL SERV:** US Army, Capt.; **HOME ADD:** 611 Fifth St., N.E., Washington, DC 20002; **BUS ADD:** 920 Fifteenth St., NW, Washington, DC 20005, (202)383-4414.

SPINKELINK, Lyle——B: June 7, 1941, Sioux Center, IA, *Pres.*, Woodview Props., Inc.; **PRIM RE ACT:** Developer, Builder; **EDUC:** BS, 1964, Econ., Morningside Coll; **HOME ADD:** 31071 Monterey, S. Laguna, CA 92677, (714)499-3694; **BUS ADD:** 1701 E. Edinger Ave., Bldg. A-3, Santa Ana, CA 92705, (714)955-1550.

SPINNER, Leslie P.——B: Feb. 8, 1943, Oak Park, IL, *VP, Fin.*, Pain Wetzel Assoc., Inc.; **PRIM RE ACT:** Broker, Consultant; **SERVICES:** Comml./Indus. RE Brokerage and Consulting; **PREV EMPLOY:** Accounting, consulting and tax work, Touche Ross & Co. (Nat. CPA firm); **EDUC:** BBA, 1965, Fin., Loyola Univ., Chicago; **GRAD EDUC:** MBA, 1966, Fin., IL Inst. of Tech.; **EDUC HONORS:** Blue Key Nat. Honor Frat.; **HOME ADD:** Bow Lane, Rt. 2, Barrington Hills, IL, (312)382-2910; **BUS ADD:** 100 S. Wacker, Chicago, IL 60606, (312)332-5834.

SPIRA, Seymour L.——B: Dec. 10, 1924, Paterson, NJ, *Pres.*, Kew Management Corp.; **PRIM RE ACT:** Owner/Investor; **PROFL AFFIL & HONORS:** RE Bd. of NY; Midtown Prop. Owners Assn.; **EDUC:** BS, 1944, Cornell Univ.; **MIL SERV:** USN, Lt.; **HOME ADD:** 164 Beechwood Rd., Ridgewood, NJ 07450, (201)445-2273; **BUS ADD:** 1123 Broadway, New York, NY 10010, (212)255-3346.

SPITLER, LaRue G.——B: July 5, 1925, Owosso, MI, *Const. Loan Officer*, Capitol Fed. S&L Assn.; **PRIM RE ACT:** Appraiser, Lender; **SERVICES:** Appraisals, consultations, mort.; **REP CLIENTS:** Capitol Fed. S&L; **PROFL AFFIL & HONORS:** SREA; Greater Lansing Home Bldrs. Assn. (Dir.), SRA; **EDUC:** MSU (Seminar-201 - Income Approval), Univ. of KY; **HOME ADD:** 1002 E. Walker St., St. Johns, MI 48879, (517)224-2574; **BUS ADD:** 112 E. Allegan St., Lansing, MI 48910, (517)374-3549.

SPITZ, Fred M.——B: Sept. 29, 1942, NY City, *Pres.*, Somerset Properties, Inc.; **PRIM RE ACT:** Owner/Investor, Property Manager, Syndicator; **OTHER RE ACT:** Investment Banker; **PREV EMPLOY:** VP, Merrill Lynch, Hubbard Inc. (1975-81); VP, Arlen Relty & Devel. Corp. (1969-75); **PROFL AFFIL & HONORS:** Member of NY and FL Bars; **EDUC:** BA, 1964, Govt., Dartmouth Coll.; **GRAD EDUC:** JD, 1967, Law, St. John's Univ. Law School; **HOME ADD:** 7850 NW 5th Place, Plantation, FL 33324, (305)472-8658; **BUS ADD:** Suite 215, 4740 North State Rd. 7, Fort Lauderdale, FL 33319, (305)472-3799.

SPITZER, Max D.——B: Feb. 8, 1906, *Partner*, Burns Jackson Summit Robins Spitzer & Feldesman; **PRIM RE ACT:** Attorney; **OTHER RE ACT:** RE in 1924 and upon graduation continued to date; **REP CLIENTS:** Office bldgs., shopping centers, apt. houses, etc.; **PROFL AFFIL & HONORS:** RE Bd. of NY; Member of RE Comm.; Bar Assn. of the City of NY, NY Cty. Lawyers Assn.; **EDUC:** BS, 1927, Comml. Sci.; **GRAD EDUC:** JD, 1928, NY Univ.; **MIL SERV:** US Army, S/Sgt., 1943-45; **OTHER ACT & HONORS:** Philanthropic and religious orgs.; **HOME ADD:** 1025 Fifth Ave., New York, NY 1O028, (212)879-9585; **BUS ADD:** 445 Park Ave., New York, NY 10022, (212)980-3200.

SPITZER, Robert C.——B: Sept. 25, 1941, *Atty.*, Campbell, Spitzer, Davis & Turgeon; **PRIM RE ACT:** Attorney; **PREV EMPLOY:** Nauman, Smith, Shissler & Hall, Attys. at Law; Asst. Dist. Atty., Legislative Ref. Bureau, PA Constitutional Convention; McNees, Wallace and Nurick, Attys. at Law; **PROFL AFFIL & HONORS:** Dauphin Cty., PA and ABA; 1969 Easter Seal Campaign, Chmn.; Bd. of Dirs., Tri-County Easter Seal Soc.; Former Member, Draft Bd. #55; **EDUC:** BA, 1963, Hist., Trinity Coll.; **GRAD EDUC:** JD, 1966, Univ. of Chicago Law School; **EDUC HONORS:** Pi Gamma Mu; **HOME ADD:** 399 N. 26th St., Camp Hill, PA 17011, (717)761-1555; **BUS ADD:** 130 State St., Box 1000, Harrisburg, PA 17108, (717)232-1876.

SPITZER, Robert Damon——B: July 28, 1946, Hot Springs, AR, *Atty.*, Hale, Lane, Peek, Dennison & Howard; **PRIM RE ACT:** Attorney; **REP CLIENTS:** First Amer. Title Co.; **PROFL AFFIL & HONORS:** Bar of NV, Bar of CA, AIME; **EDUC:** BS, 1968, Mining Engrg., Stanford Univ.; **GRAD EDUC:** JD, 1975, Hastings Coll. of Law, Univ. of CA; **MIL SERV:** USN, Lt.; **HOME ADD:** PO Box 3412, Incline Village, NV 89450, (702)831-6539; **BUS ADD:** 50 W. Liberty St., Suite 650, Reno, NV 89501, (702)786-7900.

SPIVA, Judy "Breezy" P.——B: Mar. 27, 1944, Savannah, GA, *Exec. VP & Gen. Mgr.*, Century 21 Ambassador Realty, Inc.; **PRIM RE ACT:** Broker, Consultant, Property Manager; **OTHER RE ACT:** Life Ins.; **SERVICES:** Prop. mgmt., referral serv., valuation of props., mktg. & selling of resid. new and re-sales, notary serv., fin. qualifying serv.; **REP CLIENTS:** Indivs.; **PROFL AFFIL & HONORS:** NAR, AL Assn. of Realtors; Huntsville Bd. of Realtors; RNMI, AL Chap., Cert. Resid. Specialists; Century 21 North AL Brokers Council; Century 21 Nat. Brokers Congress; MLS, CRS, GRI; **OTHER ACT & HONORS:** Daughters of the Amer. Revolution; Amer. Bus. Women's Assn.; Beta Sigma Phi; ABWA Heart of Dixie Chap., Woman of the Year 1980-81, Girl of the Year, Nu Chapter, Beta Sigma Phi, 1972-73; **HOME ADD:** 8015 Randall Road SW, Huntsville, AL 35802, (205)883-7145; **BUS ADD:** 7910 So. Memorial Pkwy. SW, Huntsville, AL 35802, (205)883-9400.

SPIVACK, Harvey——B: Feb. 25, 1931, NYC, *Partner*, S&H Realty Co.; **PRIM RE ACT:** Developer, Owner/Investor, Builder, Property Manager; **PROFL AFFIL & HONORS:** Long Is. Bd. Realtors IREM, CPM; **EDUC:** AB, 1953, Cornell Univ.; **MIL SERV:** US Army, Lt., 1953-55; **HOME ADD:** 90 Spruce Dr., Rsolyn, NY 11576, (516)621-5789; **BUS ADD:** 7 Wildwood Gardens, Port Washington, NY 11050, (516)767-4940.

SPLICHAL, John F.——B: Oct. 20, 1930, Rosenberg, TX, *VP*, Mortgage Investment Corp., Comml.; **PRIM RE ACT:** Broker, Appraiser; **OTHER RE ACT:** Mort. Banking; **SERVICES:** Comml. Mort. Loan Placement; **REP CLIENTS:** Devels. and instnl. Lenders; **PREV EMPLOY:** Mort. banking snd RE appraising since 1956; **PROFL AFFIL & HONORS:** Soc. of RE Appraisers; San Antonio Mort. Bankers Assn.; Nat. Assn. of Review Appraisers, SRA; CRA; Lic. TX RE Broker; **EDUC:** Univ. of TX; **MIL SERV:** USAF, 1st. Lt.; **HOME ADD:** PO Box 32501, San Antonio, TX 78216, (512)653-1414; **BUS ADD:** PO Box 32668, San Antonio, TX 78286, (512)822-5000.

SPOERL, Robert E.——B: July 2, 1952, Dayton, OH, *Research Assoc.*, Ctr. for RE & Land Use Analysis; **OTHER RE ACT:** Research RE & land use, published reports & studies; **PROFL AFFIL & HONORS:** Amer. RE & Urban Econ. Assn., Natl. Assn. of Review Appraisers, RE Educ. Assn., Natl. Assn. of Realtors, Cert. Review Appraiser (CRA); **EDUC:** BA, 1974, Econ., Univ. of KY; **GRAD EDUC:** MS, 1976, Econ., Univ. of KY; **EDUC HONORS:** Omicron Delta Epsilon (Econ. Hon.); **HOME ADD:** 984 Pinebloome Dr., Lexington, KY 40504, (606)276-4009; **BUS ADD:** 103 Commerce Bldg., Coll. of Bus. & Econ., Univ. of KY, Lexington, KY 40506, (606)258-4827.

SPOONER, Linda Greer——*Assoc. Atty.*, Stroock, Stroock & Lavan, RE; **PRIM RE ACT:** Attorney; **SERVICES:** Federally insured & uninsured housing programs; admin. & regulatory practice; Small bus. advising; Mort. workouts & increases; RE Fin.; Foreclosure suits; **PREV EMPLOY:** Staff Atty., US Dept. of HUD, Washington, DC 1975-79; **PROFL AFFIL & HONORS:** Dist. of Columbia Bar Assn.; Nat. Assn. of Black Women Attys., Member, Bd. of Dir.; Outstanding Young Woman of America, 1976 & 1977; Who's Who in American Law, 1979; **BUS ADD:** 1150 17th St., NW, Suite 600, Washington, DC 20036, (202)452-9250.

SPORT, Haywood M.——B: Feb. 17, 1937, Montgomery, AL, *VP & Mort. Loan Officer*, The Alabama National Bank of Montgomery; **PRIM RE ACT:** Banker; **EDUC:** BBA, 1960, Auburn Univ.; **GRAD EDUC:** 1970, School of Banking of the South; **OTHER ACT & HONORS:** Montgomery Homebuilders Assn.; **HOME ADD:** 3413 Drexel Rd., Montgomery, AL 36106, (205)272-8279; **BUS ADD:** PO Drawer 431, Montgomery, AL 36195, (205)834-9500.

SPOTTS, James L.——B: Jan. 10, 1934, Santa Cruz, CA, *Prop. Dir.*, City of San Diego; **PRIM RE ACT:** Broker, Property Manager; **EDUC:** BS, 1955, Nautical Sci., CA Maritime Academy; **GRAD EDUC:** MS, 1972, Bus., San Diego State Coll.; **MIL SERV:** USNR, Capt. Retired; **OTHER ACT & HONORS:** Various econ. devel. organizations; **HOME ADD:** 3944 Milan St., San Diego, CA 92107, (714)222-2210; **BUS ADD:** Mail Station 9B, Community Concourse, San Diego, CA 92107, (714)236-6144.

SPRAGGINS, Ronald F.——B: Nov. 9, 1942, Yale, IL, *Pres.*, Commonwealth Investment Corp.; **PRIM RE ACT:** Broker, Owner/Investor, Syndicator; **SERVICES:** Ownership & mgmt. of props.; **PREV EMPLOY:** Weidman & Co., 1969; Scurr-Messenger & Assocs., 1970; **PROFL AFFIL & HONORS:** CCIM; Pres. of CO-WY Chap., 1981; Past Pres. for the Pikes Peak Apt. Assn., 1979-1980; Pres. and member of Bd. of Dirs., CO Apt. Assn. 1980-1981; Nat. Inst. for RNMI; Who's Who in RE; Outstanding Sales Award for Colorado Springs; Instr. for the Univ. of CO Advanced RE Investment Courses; Author of articles in RE Today and RE Observer magazines; Instr. for OK State Univ.; GRI; **EDUC:** BS, 1965, Bus. Admin., Eastern IL Univ.; **GRAD EDUC:** Masters, Bus. Admin., IN State Univ./Univ. of CO/ Eastern IL Univ.; **HOME ADD:** 3120 Bonne Vista Dr., Colorado Springs, CO 80906, (303)598-8092; **BUS ADD:** 830 N. Tejon, Suite 100, Colorado Springs, CO 80903, (303)473-6400.

SPRINGER, Byron E.——B: June 25, 1932, Lawrence, KS, *Partner*, Barber Emerson Six Springer & Zinn; **PRIM RE ACT:** Attorney; **SERVICES:** Legal serv. approval of title, synd. of resid. & comml. proj.; **REP CLIENTS:** Lawyers Title Ins. Co., Chicago Title Ins. Co., First Nat. Bank of Lawrence, Lawrence, KS; Kaw Valley State Bank, Fed. Land Bank of Wichita; **PROFL AFFIL & HONORS:** KS Bar Assn., ABA; **EDUC:** BA, 1955, Univ. of KS; **GRAD EDUC:** JD, 1960, Univ. of KS; **OTHER ACT & HONORS:** KS House of Reps. 1961-62; **HOME ADD:** 127 Providence Rd., Lawrence, KS 66044, (913)843-1222; **BUS ADD:** MA at S. Park, PO Box 666, Lawrence, KS 66044, (913)843-6600.

SPRINGER, Clement D.——B: July 31, 1931, Mankato, MN, *Dir. of Dev.*, The Kahler Corp., Devel.; **PRIM RE ACT:** Property Manager, Owner/Investor; **REP CLIENTS:** To Corp. only; **PREV EMPLOY:** Dayton Hudson Corp., MPLS, MN 1966-75 Metropolitan Council; **PROFL AFFIL & HONORS:** Am. Inst. of Cert. Planners; member NACORE; Amer. Assoc. of Geographers; **EDUC:** BA, 1955, Geography, Univ. of MN; **GRAD EDUC:** MA, 1957, Geog., St. Univ. of IA; **MIL SERV:** US Army, Cpl. 1951-53; **OTHER ACT & HONORS:** Councilman, St. Anthony MN 1966-69; **HOME ADD:** 1811 Walden Lane SW, Rochester, MN 55901, (507)289-5570; **BUS ADD:** 20 Second Ave. SW, PO Box 1028, Rochester, MN 55903, (507)285-2786.

SPRINGER, Jean R.——*Owner/Broker*, Springer Realty; **PRIM RE ACT:** Broker, Owner/Investor, Insuror; **PROFL AFFIL & HONORS:** Amer. Soc. of Relocation Broker; Mktg. Inst. of NAR, GRI, CRS, CRB; **EDUC:** Bus. Admin., Univ. of Miami; **OTHER ACT &**

HONORS: C of C; **HOME ADD:** 8201-SW 27th Pl., Fort Lauderdale, FL 33328, (305)475-9044; **BUS ADD:** 2331 N. State Rd. 7, Suite 115, Fort Lauderdale, FL 33313, (305)739-3000.

SPRINGER, Lowell W.——B: Nov. 24, 1947, Havre, MT, *Prin.*, Springer Grp. Architects; **PRIM RE ACT:** Architect, Developer, Owner/Investor; **SERVICES:** Planning, Arch. design; **PREV EMPLOY:** Richard Prows; Total Concept; Environmental Design Corp.; Korell and Iverson; **PROFL AFFIL & HONORS:** NCARB; Fred Willson Soc. of Architects, Past Pres. - Fred Willson Soc. of Architects; **EDUC:** B.Arch., 1970, Mont. State Univ., Bozeman; **EDUC HONORS:** Post-graduate work through the Nat. Sci. Found. to study the Gallatin Canyon impact of the Big Sky resort area; **OTHER ACT & HONORS:** Gallatin Empire Lions Club; Bd. of Dir. - Salvation Army; Bd. of Dir. - Jr. Achievement; Bd. of Dir. - Bozeman Wrestling Club; **HOME ADD:** 117 Hoffman, Bozeman, MT 59715, (406)587-8547; **BUS ADD:** 109 E. Main, Suite 11, Bozeman, MT 59715, (406)587-5409.

SPRINKLES, Catherine C.——B: Nov. 13, 1941, San Antonio, TX, *Atty.*, Ferrari, Alvarez, Olsen & Otioboni; **PRIM RE ACT:** Attorney; **SERVICES:** Legal serv. in structuring & closing transactions; partnership formation; exchanges; **REP CLIENTS:** Private; **PROFL AFFIL & HONORS:** Santa Clara Cty. Bar Assn.; **EDUC:** 1965, Poli. Sci., San Jose State Univ.; **GRAD EDUC:** JD, 1973, Univ. of Santa Clara; **EDUC HONORS:** With Distinction, Summa Cum Laude; **HOME ADD:** 24100 Deerpath Rd., Saratoga, CA 95070; **BUS ADD:** 101 Park Ctr. Plaza, 1007, San Jose, CA 95113, (408)294-0174.

SPROTT, Rodney M.——B: Jul. 7, 1953, Charlotte, NC, *Atty.*, Weinberg, Brown & McDougall; **PRIM RE ACT:** Attorney; **SERVICES:** Title exams., document prep., loan closings; **REP CLIENTS:** All banks and S&L Assoc. in Sumter, SC and many mort. bankers in SC; **PROFL AFFIL & HONORS:** ABA, SC Bar, Sumter Cty. Bar Assoc., Sumter Bd. of Realtors; **EDUC:** BA, 1975, Poli. Sci., Clemson Univ.; **GRAD EDUC:** JD, 1978, Univ. of SC; **EDUC HONORS:** Cum Laude; **OTHER ACT & HONORS:** Sumter Rotary Club; **HOME ADD:** 14 Wactor St., Sumter, SC 29150, (803)775-4936; **BUS ADD:** 109 N. Main St., PO Box1289, Sumter, SC 29150, (803)775-1274.

SPROUSE, James M.——*Exec. VP*, Associated General Contractors of America; **PRIM RE ACT:** Builder; **BUS ADD:** 1957 E St., NW, Washington, DC 20006, (202)393-2040.*

SPRUTE, Herbert A.——B: Sept. 2, 1947, Cottonwood, ID, *Partner*, Sprute & Sprute; **OTHER RE ACT:** CPA; **SERVICES:** Income tax and investment counseling; **REP CLIENTS:** Corps., indivs. and partnerships; **PREV EMPLOY:** Touche Ross & Co.; **PROFL AFFIL & HONORS:** AICPA; Washington Soc. of CPA's, CPA; **EDUC:** BS, 1972, Acctg., Univ. of ID; **GRAD EDUC:** Masters, In Progress, Taxation, Golden Gate Univ., Seattle, WA; **EDUC HONORS:** Summa Cum Laude, Phi Kappa Phi, Top Grad. in Bus. School; **MIL SERV:** USN, E-5, Vietnam; **HOME ADD:** 8817 28th Ave. NW, Seattle, WA 98117, (206)782-3171; **BUS ADD:** 5711 20th Ave. NW, Seattle, WA 98107, (206)782-6420.

SPUNGIN, Lawrence D.——B: July 21, 1939, Chicago, IL, *VP*, MCA Dev. Co.; **PRIM RE ACT:** Broker, Attorney, Developer, Owner/Investor; **PROFL AFFIL & HONORS:** CA and IL State Bar Assn.; **EDUC:** BS, 1960, Hist./Lit., Univ. of WI; **GRAD EDUC:** JD, 1963, Univ. of Chicago; **HOME ADD:** 1533 S. Doheny Dr., Los Angeles, CA 90035, (213)556-0568; **BUS ADD:** 100 Universal City Plaza, Universal City, CA 91608, (213)508-3434.

SPUNT, Linda L.——B: Chicago, IL, *RE Broker & CPA*, Sheldon F. Good & Co., Comml. Investment; **PRIM RE ACT:** Broker, Consultant, Instructor; **OTHER RE ACT:** CPA; **SERVICES:** Investment counseling & brokering of comml. props.; **REP CLIENTS:** Indivs., lenders & investors of comml. props.; **PREV EMPLOY:** Internal Revenue Field Agent, Chicago Dist.; **PROFL AFFIL & HONORS:** IL CPA Soc.; AICPA; Chicago RE Bd., CPA; RE Broker; **EDUC:** BS, 1965, Acctg./Bus. Law, Roosevelt Univ.; **GRAD EDUC:** MS, 1970, Acctg./Bus. Law, Roosevelt Univ.; **OTHER ACT & HONORS:** Art Inst. of Chicago; Chicago Council on For. Relations; **HOME ADD:** 655 Irving Park Rd., Chicago, IL 60613, (312)348-6719; **BUS ADD:** 11 N. Wacker Dr., Chicago, IL 60606, (312)346-1500.

SQUIRES, Bruce Victor——B: Apr. 13, 1958, Santa Fe, NM, *Broker/Contr.*, Squires & Assoc.; **PRIM RE ACT:** Broker, Builder, Property Manager; **PROFL AFFIL & HONORS:** Realtor, Nat. Assn. of Home Builders; **EDUC:** BSBA, 1980, RE & Constr. Mgmt., Univ. of Denver; **HOME ADD:** 804 Calle Romolo, Santa Fe, NM 87501, (505)983-1473; **BUS ADD:** PO Box 876, Santa Fe, NM 87501, (505)983-1473.

STACHEL, Gary R.——B: Jan. 29, 1952, Detroit, MI, *Dir. of Corp. RE*, Cunningham Drug Stores; **PRIM RE ACT:** Broker; **PREV EMPLOY:** Ford Motor Land Devel. Corp.; **PROFL AFFIL & HONORS:** NACORE, ICSC; **EDUC:** 1975, Mktg., Western MI Univ.; **HOME TEL:** (313)774-0899; **BUS ADD:** 1927 Rosa Parks Blvd., Detroit, MI 48216, (313)963-7764.

STACHEL, Robert D., Sr.——B: Feb. 2, 1934, Knoxville, TN, *Pres.*, Century 21 Great Amer. Realty; **PRIM RE ACT:** Broker, Consultant, Developer, Owner/Investor, Instructor, Property Manager, Syndicator; **OTHER RE ACT:** Securities; **SERVICES:** Comml. and Indus. devel.; Structure and Mgmt. of Syndications; RE Investment Consultant, Mgmt. for and operation of a full-time resid. brokerage; **PROFL AFFIL & HONORS:** RNMI/NAR; Ressi-Pres. AZ Chap.; Cochise Bd. of Realtors-Pres. 1980, 1981; AZ Assn. of Realtors-Dir. 1980, !981 AZ Realtors Inst. Faculty; 1980 AZ Realtor of the Yr., CCIM; GRI; **EDUC:** BS, 1956, Soc. Studies, Econ., E. TN State Univ.; **MIL SERV:** US Army, Lt. Col., Legion of Merit Bronze Star, Air Medal 'V', 1953-1977; **OTHER ACT & HONORS:** Sierra Vista Indus. Devel. Auth. 1976-78; City of Sierra Vista Airport Devel. Coord. 1977-1980; **HOME ADD:** 2613 San Juan Capistrano Dr., Sierra Vista, AZ 85635, (602)458-5456; **BUS ADD:** 741 Fry Blvd., Sierra Vista, AZ 85635, (602)458-2100.

STACK, Daniel——B: July 29, 1928, Brooklyn, NY, *Sr. VP, Counsel and Sec.*, The Greenwich Savings Bank; **PRIM RE ACT:** Attorney, Regulator, Consultant, Banker, Lender, Owner/Investor; **SERVICES:** Legal, Structuring, Fin.; **PREV EMPLOY:** 25 yrs. as counsel, pension fund mgr., acquisitions exec., lecturer, and fin. consultant; **PROFL AFFIL & HONORS:** ABA, NY State Bar Assn., NYC Lawyers Assn.; **EDUC:** BA, 1949, Econ. & Poli. Sci., Brooklyn Coll.; **GRAD EDUC:** LLB; LLM, 1952; 1955, Columbia Univ.; Georgetown Univ.; **EDUC HONORS:** Cum Laude; Dept. Honors in Econ. & Poli. Sci.; **MIL SERV:** USN, USNR, Capt., Joint Serv. Commendation Medal; **OTHER ACT & HONORS:** Gen. Counsel, Greater NY Safety Council; Congressman's Serv. Academy Nominations Comm.; **HOME ADD:** 8 Linda Dr., Suffern, NY 10901, (914)357-3149; **BUS ADD:** 1356 Broadway, New York, NY 10018, (212)868-6907.

STACK, Geoffrey L.——B: Sept. 16, 1943, Trinidad, B.W.I., *Pres.*, Regis Homes, Inc., Newport Beach Headquarters; **PRIM RE ACT:** Developer, Owner/Investor, Syndicator; **SERVICES:** Condo. conversions is main bus.; also synd. comml. and resid. props.; **PREV EMPLOY:** Dir. of Acquisitions, J.H. Snyder Co., 1100 Glendon Ave., Los Angeles, CA, 1972 to 1975; **PROFL AFFIL & HONORS:** Bldg. Indus. Assn.; Const. Indus. Alliance; Bd. of Dir., Nat. Multi-Housing Council, Washington, DC, Registered Nat. Assn. of Securities Dealers, Inc.; **EDUC:** BA, 1965, Govt., Georgetown Univ.; **GRAD EDUC:** MBA, 1972, RE Fin., Wharton Sch., Univ. of PA; **EDUC HONORS:** Dean's Honor List, Pres. of MBA Assn.; **MIL SERV:** USMC; Capt.; **OTHER ACT & HONORS:** Bd. of Tr., S. Coast Repertory Theate; Bd. of Dir., Enterprise Nat. Bank; Bd. of Tr., Harbor Day Sch.; Nat. Bd. of Dir., Wharton Grad. Sch. Alumni Assn.; **BUS ADD:** 5120 Campus Dr., PO Box 7090, Newport Beach, CA 92660, (714)975-0727.

STACKHOUSE, Philip E.——B: Aug. 1, 1947, Baltimore, MD, *VP, Div. Officer*, First National Bank of MD, Mort. Div.; **PRIM RE ACT:** Consultant, Banker, Lender; **OTHER RE ACT:** Mort. banker; **SERVICES:** Resid. & comml. mort. credit; **REP CLIENTS:** Mort. investors, devel., banks and savings & loans; **PROFL AFFIL & HONORS:** Amer. Bankers Assn.(Housing & RE Fin. Div.); Mort. Bankers Assn. of Amer., MD Mort. Bankers Assn., Bd. of Regents; Natl. School of RE Fin. & Faculty (OH State); **EDUC:** BA, 1972, Econ., Washington and Lee Univ.; **EDUC HONORS:** Honors; **MIL SERV:** US Army, S/Sgt., E-6, Arcom, Bronze star; **HOME ADD:** 347 Greenlow Rd., Baltimore, MD 21228, (301)744-7650; **BUS ADD:** PO Box 1596, Baltimore, MD 21203, (301)244-4570.

STACKLER, Robert W.——B: Sept. 29, 1931, Jamaica, NY, SF&G Associates; **PRIM RE ACT:** Broker, Developer, Builder, Owner/Investor; **PROFL AFFIL & HONORS:** Dir. of Long Island Trust Co., Past Pres. and Life Dir. Long Island Builders Inst., Life Dir. NAHB; **EDUC:** 1953, NY State Univ.; **OTHER ACT & HONORS:** Past Pres. Hicksville Kiwanis Club; **HOME ADD:** 469 Woodbury Rd., Huntington, NY 11743, (516)692-6210; **BUS ADD:** PO Box 319, Rockville Ctr., NY 11571, (516)678-3888.

STAFFA, Charles V.——B: Jan. 27, 1934, Newgulf, TX, *Pres.*, Houston Ctr. Corp.; **PRIM RE ACT:** Developer; **PROFL AFFIL & HONORS:** ABA; Houston Bar Assn.; NACORE; Houston C of C; **EDUC:** BS, 1956, Mechanical Engrg., LA State Univ.; **GRAD EDUC:** JD, 1966, S. TX SchooL of Law; **MIL SERV:** US Corp. of Eng.; Cmdr.; **HOME ADD:** 3127 Tangley Rd., Houston, TX 77005, (713)666-5750; **BUS ADD:** PO Box 2521, Houston, TX 77001, (713)654-4444.

STAFFORD, C.B.——*Exec. Dir.*, Florida Real Estate Commission; **PRIM RE ACT:** Property Manager; **BUS ADD:** PO Box 1900, Orlando, FL 32802, (305)423-6071.*

STAFFORD, Jean F.——**B:** Apr. 23, 1934, Greenville, SC, *Broker/Mgr.*, Century Associates, Inc.; **PRIM RE ACT:** Broker; **SERVICES:** Residential mgmt., sales and valuation; **PROFL AFFIL & HONORS:** NAR, NAHB, CRS, RNMI, GRI, CRB; **HOME ADD:** 514 Trinity Way, Greenville, SC 29609, (803)246-5643; **BUS ADD:** 2502 Wade Hampton Blvd., Greenville, SC 29609, (803)292-1700.

STAFFORD, P. Gordon——*VP, Sec. & Gen. Counc.*, Elcor Corp.; **PRIM RE ACT:** Attorney, Property Manager; **BUS ADD:** 2100 Wilco Bldg., Midland, TX 79701, (915)685-0200.*

STAGG, Howard J.——**B:** Sept. 4, 1941, Glen Ridge, NJ, *Atty. at Law*, Howard J. Stagg IV, Esq., A Professional Corp.; **PRIM RE ACT:** Attorney; **OTHER RE ACT:** RE brokers, contractors and other persons dealing in RE; **PROFL AFFIL & HONORS:** CA State Bar Assn.; ABA; Sacramento Cty. Bar Assn.; Amer. Trial Lawyers Assn.; CA Trial Lawyers Assn.; Capitol City Lawyers; **EDUC:** BA, 1963, Econ. & Hist., Univ. of AZ; **GRAD EDUC:** JD, 1970, Law, Univ. of Pac., McGeorge School of Law; **MIL SERV:** US Air Force, Capt., Vietnam Service Medal; **OTHER ACT & HONORS:** Managing Editor of Pac. Law Journal; **HOME ADD:** 3611 Arden Creek Rd., Sacramento, CA 95825, (916)481-0274; **BUS ADD:** 1526 River Park Dr., Sacramento, CA 95815, (916)924-8400.

STAHL, David E.——*Exec. VP*, National Assn. of Homebuilders of the US; **PRIM RE ACT:** Builder; **BUS ADD:** 15th & M St., NW, Washington, DC 20005, (202)452-0200.*

STAHL, Michael——**B:** Feb. 26, 1950, NYC, *Pres.*, Stahl Mgmt. Corp.; **PRIM RE ACT:** Syndicator, Consultant, Developer, Property Manager, Owner/Investor; **SERVICES:** Rehabilitation planing, devel. and supervision, Prop. Mgmt. with special emphasis on energy control and mgmt.; **PROFL AFFIL & HONORS:** RE Bd. of NY, CHIP & BOMA; **EDUC:** BArch., 1977, Pratt Inst.; **BUS ADD:** 4951 Broadway, New York, NY 10034, (212)942-6800.

STAKES, Gary E.——**B:** Sept. 22, 1943, Wash., DC., *VP Prop. Devel. & Mort. Fin.*, HBE Corp., Adam's Mark Hotels & HBE Props.; **PRIM RE ACT:** Developer; **SERVICES:** Design, build, own, operate & manage hotels & office bldgs.; **REP CLIENTS:** For our own account and in joint venture with maj. instnl. investors; **PREV EMPLOY:** Holiday Inns, Inc., Cameron-Brown Mort. Co.; **EDUC:** BSBA, 1969, Gen. Bus., E. Carolina Univ.; **EDUC HONORS:** Econ. Honors, Omicron Delta Epsilon, Phi Theta Kappa; **MIL SERV:** US Army, Sgt., Vietnam Occupational Medals; **HOME ADD:** 2106 Willow Way Ct., Chesterfield, MO 63017, (314)532-4961; **BUS ADD:** 717 Office Parkway, Saint Louis, MO 63141, (314)567-9000.

STALEY, Charles Wesley——**B:** Feb. 28, 1921, Greensboro, NC, *VP, RE*, McLean Trucking Co.; **PRIM RE ACT:** Consultant, Builder, Property Manager, Engineer; **PROFL AFFIL & HONORS:** VP RE of McLean; VP of Malja Corp.; Bd. of Tr. of TPE; Member of NC Motor Carriers Assn.; & Ops. Council of Amer. Trkg. Assn.; Charter Member of Natl. Assn. of RE Appraisers; **EDUC:** BS, 1948, Civil Engrg., NC State Univ.; **MIL SERV:** US Army; **OTHER ACT & HONORS:** Forsyth Ctry. Club, BPOE; **HOME ADD:** 3242 Merion Ct., Winston-Salem, NC 27154, (919)765-7056; **BUS ADD:** PO Box 213, Winston Salem, NC 27154, (919)721-2440.

STALKER, Hobart C.——**B:** Dec. 3, 1939, San Diego, CA, *Second VP, Mort. & RE*, The Midland Mutual Life Ins. Co.; **PRIM RE ACT:** Consultant, Lender, Owner/Investor, Property Manager; **SERVICES:** RE Investing; **PREV EMPLOY:** Lincoln Liberty Life, 1977-79, John Burnham Co., 1976-77, Home Fed. Savings, 1972-76, Oceanside Fed. Savings, 1965-72; **PROFL AFFIL & HONORS:** Mort. Bankers Assn., RE Instr. Inst., CA RE Broker; **EDUC:** Grad. Diploma, 1971, Bus. & RE, Inst. of Fin. Educ.; **GRAD EDUC:** RE & Escro Cert., 1972, RE & Escrow, Palomar Coll.; **HOME ADD:** 1150 Rockport Ln., Columbus, OH 43215, (614)451-4815; **BUS ADD:** 250 E. Broad St., Columbus, OH 43215, (614)228-2001.

STALLINGS, William Ralph——**B:** Dec. 27, 1909, Mattoon, IL, *Pres.*, Ralph Stallings Co.; **PRIM RE ACT:** Broker, Appraiser, Owner/Investor; **PROFL AFFIL & HONORS:** Local, State and Nat. Bd. of Realtors; OK City C of C, 10 years (5 terms) Bd. of Dir. of Local Realtors Bd.; Pres. 1952; Nat. Ethics Comm. 1953; **EDUC:** BS, 1946, Math., OK City Univ.; **OTHER ACT & HONORS:** Mason; Shriner; Sons of the American Revolution; Presbyterian Church; Nat. Cowboy Hall of Fame; OK County Historical Soc.; Past Member: Soc. of RE Appraisers; Amer. Instit. of RE Appraisers; Civitans; Toastmasters; Coon and Possum Hunters Club; **HOME ADD:** 2513 NW 25th St., Oklahoma City, OK 73107; **BUS ADD:** 2410 NW 23rd St., Oklahoma City, OK 73107, (405)528-5561.

STAMBERG, Frank——*Group VP*, Chesebrough - Ponds; **PRIM RE ACT:** Property Manager; **BUS ADD:** 33 Benedict Place, Greenwich, CT 06830, (203)661-2000.*

STAMPAHAR, Richard J.——**B:** Aug. 5, 1931, Pittsburgh, PA, *Brokerage Mgr.*, Oliver Realty Inc.; **PRIM RE ACT:** Broker; **SERVICES:** Sales and leasing of comml. & indus. prop.; **PREV EMPLOY:** Realty Growth Corp. 1966, Westinghouse Electric 1963-1966, Heppenstall Steel Co. 1951-1963; **PROFL AFFIL & HONORS:** IREM; **EDUC:** BS, 1953, Indus. Mgmt., Duquesne Univ.; **GRAD EDUC:** MBA, 1961, Mktg. and Adv., Univ. of Pittsburgh; **MIL SERV:** US Army Artillery, 1st Lt.; **OTHER ACT & HONORS:** Commnr. First Class Township 1966-1975, Amen Corner, Pres. IREM Chap. 7; **HOME ADD:** 215 Falconhurst Dr., Pittsburgh, PA 15238, (412)828-6567; **BUS ADD:** 2800 Two Oliver Plaza, Pittsburgh, PA 15222, (412)434-1056.

STANARD, Chandler Kite——**B:** Feb. 26, 1946, Mobile, AL, *Senior Partner*, Stanard & Mills; **PRIM RE ACT:** Attorney, Developer, Owner/Investor, Syndicator; **REP CLIENTS:** Lenders and Investors/Developers; **EDUC:** 1968, Acctg./Fin., Univ. of AL; **GRAD EDUC:** JD, 1971, Tax-Corp., Univ. of AL; **HOME ADD:** 500 E. Barksdale Dr., Mobile, AL 36606; **BUS ADD:** Suite 1802 First Nat. Bank Bldg., Mobile, AL 36601, (205)432-0701.

STANDRING, James D.——**B:** Dec. 2, 1951, Fresno, CA, *Pres.*, Westland Industries, Inc.; **PRIM RE ACT:** Consultant, Developer, Builder, Owner/Investor; **SERVICES:** Investment counseling, devel. counseling; **PROFL AFFIL & HONORS:** Portland Metropolitan Homebuilders Assn., OR Homebuilders Assn., Nat. Homebuilders Assn.; **EDUC:** BS, 1975, Poli. Sci., Bus. Admin., CA State Univ.; **HOME ADD:** 20 Walking Woods Dr., Lake Oswego, OR 97034, (503)635-3015; **BUS ADD:** 11830 SW Kerr Pkwy., Lake Oswego, OR 97034, (503)245-9715.

STANFIELD-PINEL, Bertrand——**B:** Oct. 27, 1950, Paris, France, *VP/Gen. Mgr./Designated Broker*, Feau Realty Devel. & Mgmt., Inc.; **PRIM RE ACT:** Broker, Consultant, Developer, Builder, Property Manager; **SERVICES:** Investment counseling, devel. - construction mgmt. of multi-family and garden office complex; **REP CLIENTS:** Indivs., lenders, instnl. investment groups; **PROFL AFFIL & HONORS:** Realtor, FIABCI, AZ Multi-Family Assn., State of AZ Licenses: RE Broker, Mort. Broker; **EDUC:** BS-EE, 1972, Worcester Polytechnic Inst., Worcester, MA; **HOME ADD:** 5320 N. 25 St., Phoenix, AZ 85016, (602)957-0623; **BUS ADD:** 6900 E. Camelback Rd. #240, Scottsdale, AZ 85251, (602)949-7960.

STANGER, Robert A.——*Pres.*, Robert A. Stanger & Co.; **PRIM RE ACT:** Consultant, Real Estate Publisher; **SERVICES:** Investment analysis, RE due diligence studies; **REP CLIENTS:** Brokerage firms, indiv. investors; **BUS ADD:** 623 River Rd., Fair Haven, NJ 07701, (201)747-7566.

STANINGER, Ken A.——**B:** May 15, 1949, Missoula, MT, *Pres./Owner*, ERA Staninger & Assoc., Missoula Div.; **PRIM RE ACT:** Broker, Consultant, Appraiser, Developer, Owner/Investor, Instructor; **PREV EMPLOY:** Sec. Agency, 1971-76 Staninger & Assoc., 1976-80, ERA Staninger & Assoc., 1980-present; **PROFL AFFIL & HONORS:** Local, State & Nat. Assn. of Realtors, RNMI, FLI, Broker, CRS, GRI; **EDUC:** BS, 1971, Bus. Fin., CO State Univ.; **OTHER ACT & HONORS:** Kiwanis Club, Elks Club, Missoula Mavericks, JC's, Missoula Golf Course Bd.; **HOME ADD:** 8455 St. Vrain Way, Missoula, MT 59802, (406)549-5804; **BUS ADD:** 2806 Garfield, PO Box 4865, Missoula, MT 59806, (406)728-8850.

STANKEVICH, George Cochran, Esq.——**B:** Oct. 14, 1940, New York, NY, *Partner*, George Cochran Stankevich Assocs.; **PRIM RE ACT:** Attorney, Developer; **SERVICES:** Time share devel.; **GRAD EDUC:** JD, 1965, Law, Univ. of MD; **BUS ADD:** West Neck Mews, Shelter Is., NY 11964, (516)756-3838.

STANLEY, Ginna——**B:** Jan. 11, 1924, Warwick, RI, *Owner*, Ginna Stanley Income Tax Serv.; **PRIM RE ACT:** Broker; **OTHER RE ACT:** Real estate, income tax consultant; **SERVICES:** Investment, tax counseling, resid. & comml.; **REP CLIENTS:** Owners of farms, small businesses sales; **PROFL AFFIL & HONORS:** IN Soc. Public Acctg., Knox Cty. C of C, Knox Cty. Bd. Realtors, IN Assn. of Realtors, Vincennes Univ. Fellows and Sponsors; **EDUC:** BA, 1944, Pembroke Coll. in Brown Univ.; **OTHER ACT & HONORS:** Amer. Assn. of Univ. Women, Amer. Red Cross, Fortnightly Club, YMCA Auxiliary; **HOME ADD:** 104 Shawnee Dr., Vincennes, IN 47591, (812)886-4885; **BUS ADD:** 506 Broadway, Vincennes, IN 47591, (812)882-1409.

STANSON, Richard S.——B: Oct. 15, 1933, Akron, OH, *Pres.*, S.D. Stanson and Co.; **PRIM RE ACT:** Broker, Consultant, Property Manager; **SERVICES:** Consulting in historic restoration and adaptive reuse, corp. RE functions; **PROFL AFFIL & HONORS:** SIR, Amer. Assn. of RE Counselors, NACORE, Omega Tau Rho; **EDUC:** BA, 1956, Hist., Trinity Coll, Hartford, CT.; **MIL SERV:** USAF, Pilot, Capt.; **HOME ADD:** 874 Merriman Rd., Akron, OH 44305, (216)836-7336; **BUS ADD:** 137 S. Main St., Akron, OH 44308, (216)376-2181.

STANUSH, Frank A.——B: June 24, 1914, San Antonio, TX, *Pres.*, Huntleigh Park, Inc./Modern Builders, Inc.; **PRIM RE ACT:** Developer, Builder; **SERVICES:** Developing & Building; **PROFL AFFIL & HONORS:** Home Builders, Home Builders Assn.; **HOME ADD:** 210 Northeast, San Antonio, TX 78213, (512)342-7307; **BUS ADD:** 240 W. Josephine, San Antonio, TX 78212, (512)732-8265.

STANWYCK, Steven J.——B: Sept. 21, 1944, NY, NY, *Lawyer*, Steven J. Stanwyck, PC; **PRIM RE ACT:** Attorney, Broker; **OTHER RE ACT:** Investments; **SERVICES:** Legal counsel, investment structure & review; **PREV EMPLOY:** Dewey, Ballantine, Bushby, Palmer & Wood, NY, NY; Kadison, Pfaelzer, Woodard, Quinn & Rossi, Los Angeles; **PROFL AFFIL & HONORS:** Assn. of Bar City of NY; NY State Bar; State Bar of CA; Los Angeles Cty. Bar; **EDUC:** BA, 1967, Econ./Poli. Sci./Sci., Univ. of Denver; **GRAD EDUC:** JD, 1970, Univ. of CA; MBA, 1971, RE/Fin., Univ. of CA; **MIL SERV:** US Army Security Agency, SP4; **BUS ADD:** 9734 Wendover Dr., Beverly Hills, CA 90210, (213)550-7582.

STAPLETON, Robert J.——B: Jan. 1, 1922, Ft. Wayne, IN, *Pres.*, Scioto Econ. Devel. Corp.; **PRIM RE ACT:** Developer; **SERVICES:** Site & bldg. selection, fin., data Prep. etc.; **PREV EMPLOY:** Jobs Div., La Salle, IL, Northern Nat. Gas Co. (Mgr. Petrochem. Ind Park); Com Ed Co., Chicago; Pres. Clinton (IA) Devel. Co.; **PROFL AFFIL & HONORS:** Nat. Assn. of Corp. RE Execs., ULI, Council Urban Econ. Devel., OH, Devel. Assn. Great Lakes Area Devel. Council., Amer. Econ. Devel. Council, Lifetime Member IL Devel. Council; Nat. Devel. Council; Nat. Waterways Conference, Cert. Indus. Devel.; **EDUC:** BA, 1946, Econ., Geog., Bus. Admin., Valpararso Univ.; **GRAD EDUC:** MS, 1947, Geog., Econ., Bus. Admin., Univ. of WI, Univ. of MI, Columbia Univ.; **EDUC HONORS:** Pi Gamma Mu (Nat. Hon. Soc.); **MIL SERV:** Capt. (USNR-Retd.); **OTHER ACT & HONORS:** Rotary Club, Portsmouth Growth Fnd., Gr. Portsmouth Growth Corp., Portsmouth Area C of C; **HOME ADD:** 3219 Old Post Rd., Portsmouth, OH 45662, (614)353-4953; **BUS ADD:** Court House, Suite 1 & 2, Portsmouth, OH 45662, (614)354-7779.

STAPP, William B.——B: Aug. 10, 1940, Philadelphia, PA, *Broker-Owner*, Bill Stapp and Associates, Inc., Comml. Investment; Property Management; **PRIM RE ACT:** Broker, Consultant, Developer, Property Manager, Lender, Owner/Investor; **SERVICES:** Apt. specialists, gen. comml. specialists, brokerage and prop. mgmt.; **REP CLIENTS:** Indiv. investors in comml. prop.; **PREV EMPLOY:** General Ins. Brokerage; **PROFL AFFIL & HONORS:** NAR; RESSI; RNMI; OR Assn. of of Realtors, Portland; Bd. of Realtors; OR Apt. Assn; Multi-Family Housing Council; RE Member of OR Chap. of CCIM; **EDUC:** BA, Econ., Poli. Sci., Univ. of CO; **OTHER ACT & HONORS:** Lake Oswego Soccer Club Coach; **HOME ADD:** 12606 SW Edgecliff Rd., Portland, OR 97219; **BUS ADD:** 12606 SW Edgecliff Rd., Portland, OR 97219, (503)635-6621.

STARK, Mark J.——B: Aug. 22, 1933, Chicago, IL, *VP*, Sudler & Co., Mgr. John Hancock Ctr.; **PRIM RE ACT:** Broker, Property Manager; **PREV EMPLOY:** US Gypsum Co. 1958-1973, Seay & Thomas RE(Sub of IC Indus.) 1973; **PROFL AFFIL & HONORS:** CPM - IREM; Chicago RE Bd., Chicago - Boma; **EDUC:** BSBA, 1958, Acctg., Northern IL Univ.; **MIL SERV:** US Army; **BUS ADD:** 875 N. Michigan Ave., Chicago, IL 60611, (312)751-3678.

STARK, William L.——B: Jan. 8, 1927, Oxford, NC, *Investment & Prop. Mgr.*, Rosemyr Corp.; **PRIM RE ACT:** Broker, Consultant, Developer, Property Manager, Engineer, Owner/Investor; **SERVICES:** Investment Counseling, Devel., Prop. Mgmt.; **PROFL AFFIL & HONORS:** CPA; **EDUC:** BS in Bus. Admin., 1951, Acctg., Univ. of NC; **GRAD EDUC:** Certificate - The Exec. Program, 1964, Bus. Mgmt., Univ. of NC; **MIL SERV:** USN; **OTHER ACT & HONORS:** Chmn. Local Planning Bd., Kiwanis Club, Realtor; **HOME ADD:** 201 Beechwood Trail, Henderson, NC 27536, (919)438-7510; **BUS ADD:** 704 S. Garnett St., PO Box 911, Henderson, NC 27536, (919)492-0009.

STARK, William W., Jr.——B: Oct. 28, 1941, Chicago, IL, *Sr. VP*, Fox & Carskadon Financial Corp., Investor & Legal Servs. Div.; **PRIM RE ACT:** Attorney, Syndicator; **PROFL AFFIL & HONORS:** SRS; **EDUC:** BS, 1963, EE, Standord Univ.; **GRAD EDUC:** JD, 1966, Stanford Univ.; MBA, 1972, Stanford Univ.; **MIL SERV:** US Naval Res., Lt.; **BUS ADD:** 2755 Campus Dr. #300, San Mateo, CA 94403, (415)574-3333.

STARKE, John E.——B: Dec. 19, 1943, London, England, *Pres.*, Texas Investment Properties; **PRIM RE ACT:** Broker, Consultant, Developer, Builder, Owner/Investor, Instructor, Property Manager, Syndicator, Real Estate Publisher; **SERVICES:** Synd. of comml. & income producing props.; comml. const.; investment counseling; RE author; conduct RE seminars; teach at 3 colleges (RE courses); own over 320 units in TX; 7 in MO; prop. mgmt.; **REP CLIENTS:** For. and domestic comml. investors - -100,000 to -25,000,000+, office bldgs., shopping malls, hotels, large seasoned apt. complex, spec. land devel.; **PREV EMPLOY:** Housing Systems Intl. Exec. VP, 1963-1968; **PROFL AFFIL & HONORS:** GDBR; TAR; NAR; SMEI; Interex; N. TX Exchangors Assn.; RE Career Coll.; Comml. Coll. RE Inst., GREA; **MIL SERV:** USAF; Sgt.; **OTHER ACT & HONORS:** MENSA; **HOME ADD:** 3420 Country Sq. Dr., Carrollton, TX 75006; **BUS ADD:** PO Box 233, Carrollton, TX 75006, (214)242-6884.

STARKE, John W.——B: July 1, 1944, Louisville, KY, *Managing Dir.*, Mort. Systems Corp.; **PRIM RE ACT:** Consultant; **SERVICES:** Set up mort. lending operation for new entrants to secondary market; **REP CLIENTS:** Major banks and trade assns.; **PREV EMPLOY:** Dir., Corp. Planning, GNMA; **PROFL AFFIL & HONORS:** Nat. Press Club, Nat. Economists Club; **EDUC:** BS, 1966, Electrical Engrg., George Washington Univ.; **GRAD EDUC:** MS (Mgmt.) Sloan School - MIT, 1968; MS (Operations Research), 1973, George Washington Univ.; **EDUC HONORS:** Tau Beta Pi; **BUS ADD:** 4813 Bethesda Ave., Bethesda, MD 20814, (301)654-4310.

STARKEY, Dan B.——B: May 7, 1942, Canton, OH, *Pres. and CEO*, Starkey, Bright & Willis; **PRIM RE ACT:** Consultant, Developer, Owner/Investor, Property Manager, Syndicator; **SERVICES:** Investment counseling, devel., synd. & indiv., prop. mgmt.; **REP CLIENTS:** Pension Funds, Corp. Clients; **PREV EMPLOY:** Innisfree Corp. 1972-74, William Messenger Corp. 1975-78; **PROFL AFFIL & HONORS:** RESSI; CARE Assocs. (investment div.); NAR; INH. Exchangors Assn.; Nat. Council RE Exchangors, Nat. Notary Assn.; Apt. Assn. of Orange Cty., Apt. Assn. of Phoenix, CCIM, RNMI; **EDUC:** BBA, 1967, Mgmt., OH State Univ.; Kent State Univ.; **MIL SERV:** US Army, Spc. 5, Honorable Discharge; **OTHER ACT & HONORS:** US Power Squadron; Balboa Power Squadron; Univ. Athletic Club; **HOME ADD:** 14 Urbino, Irvine, CA 92714, (714)731-0611; **BUS ADD:** 18023 Sky Park Cir., Suite F-2, Irvine, CA 92714, (714)549-1930.

STARKEY, John P.——B: Feb. 13, 1928, San Diego, CA, *Pres.*, John P. Starkey Co.; **PRIM RE ACT:** Broker, Consultant, Appraiser, Developer, Owner/Investor, Property Manager; **PROFL AFFIL & HONORS:** San Diego Bd. of Realtors; San Diego C of C; San Diego Rotary Club; **EDUC:** BA, 1950, Bus. Admin., Univ. of UT, San Diego State Univ.; **MIL SERV:** US Army; **OTHER ACT & HONORS:** Dir., Metro. Water Dist. of So. CA and San Diego Cty. Water Authority; Past Chmn., CA State Parks and Recreation Commn.; Past Chmn., CA State Parks Found.; Sigma Alpha Epsilon, Also affiliated with: So. Mort. Co. (Pres.); Homestar Investment Corp. (Pres.); Star Venture Corp. (Pres.); **BUS ADD:** 770 B St., Suite 404, San Diego, CA 92101, (714)231-6709.

STARKWEATHER, Thomas L.——B: May 19, 1942, Saginaw, MI, *2nd VP; Mortgage loan Production*, New York Life Insurance Co., RE Mort. Loan Dept.; **PRIM RE ACT:** Lender, Owner/Investor; **SERVICES:** Mort. loans, equity purchases and joint ventures; **PREV EMPLOY:** 1966-68 Center for Real Estate and Urban Economic Studies, Univ. of Conn. - Research Assistant; 1968-72 New York Life Insurance, Real Estate and Mortgage Loan Dept., Detroit Michigan, - Appraiser/analysist; 1972-74 New York Life, Chicago, Ill - Regional Appraiser; 1974-77 New York Life, New York, NY - Assistant Chief Appraiser; 1977-78 New York Life, New York, NY - Assistant VP.; 1978-Current New York Life, New York, NY - 2nd VP., **EDUC:** BS, 1968, RE, Fin. and Urban Econ., Univ. of CT; **HOME ADD:** 367 Cedar Ln., New Cannan, CT 06840, (203)966-8606; **BUS ADD:** 51 Madison Ave., New York, NY 10010, (212)576-6315.

STARLING, Kenneth H.——B: Dec. 10, 1948, Pasadena, CA, *Pres.*, Starling & Associates; **PRIM RE ACT:** Consultant, Developer; **SERVICES:** Subdivs., specializing in condos.; **REP CLIENTS:** The Knowleton Corp.; G.A. Devel., Inc.; Wallace Investment Co.; I.F. Devel., Inc.; Arken Devel., Inc.; **PROFL AFFIL & HONORS:** SCBIA; **EDUC:** 1971, Eng./Bus. Admin., CA State Univ., Los Angeles; **BUS ADD:** PO Box 8557, San Marino, CA 91108, (213)797-8123.

STARNES, James L.——**B:** Feb. 12, 1921, Little Rock, AR, *Chmn. and Pres.*, Starnes Properties, Inc.; **PRIM RE ACT:** Attorney, Instructor, Consultant, Appraiser, Banker, Lender, Owner/Investor; **OTHER RE ACT:** Mortgage banker; **SERVICES:** RE fin. and evaluation; **REP CLIENTS:** Nat. and Intl. corps., indiv. attys., and banks; **PREV EMPLOY:** 1976-1981 Pres. NCNB Mort. Corp., 1974 to 1976 Phipps Land Co., Atlanta GA, Sr. V.P., 1962 to 1974 Phipps Harrtington Corp., Atlanta, GA., Pres. and CEO, 1951 to 1961 Starnes Robert Co., Atlanta, GA, Pres.; **PROFL AFFIL & HONORS:** MBAA, MBA, GA Member Atlanta RE Bd., CMB, AIREA, MAI; **EDUC:** 1938-41, Emory Univ., Atlanta; **GRAD EDUC:** LLB, 1949, Law, Emory Univ., Atlanta; **MIL SERV:** USN, Lt. Cmdr.; **HOME ADD:** 1530 Queens Rd., Charlotte, NC 28207, (704)372-9535; **BUS ADD:** 1530 Queens Rd., Charlotte, NC 28207, (704)372-9535.

STARR, Harold H.——**B:** Mar. 22, 1925, Detroit, MI, *Realtor/Gen. Partner*, Starr Property Management Co.; **PRIM RE ACT:** Broker, Developer, Owner/Investor, Instructor, Property Manager, Syndicator; **SERVICES:** Synd. of various size properties; **REP CLIENTS:** Instr. at UCLA Extension; Teacher at W. Los Angeles Comm. Coll.; indiv. investors; Amer. Medical Intl.; pension funds; **PROFL AFFIL & HONORS:** NAR; CA Assn. of Realtors; Los Angeles Realty Bd.; Nat. Soc. of Public Accountants; CA Soc. of Public Accountants, PA; CPCU; Realtor; **EDUC:** AA, 1946, Mktg./Acctg., UCLA; BS, 1947, Mktg./Acctg., UCLA; **MIL SERV:** USN; **OTHER ACT & HONORS:** Pres. of Bus. Contemporaries, Common Cause, ACLU, Federal Advisory Committee under Sec. Commerce Hodges (1961-1965); **BUS ADD:** 1810 Smyrna-Roswell Rd., Smyrna, GA 30080.

STARR, Joe Fred——*VP New Corp. Ventures*, Tyson Foods, Inc.; **PRIM RE ACT:** Property Manager; **BUS ADD:** 2210 West Oaklawn Dr., Drawer E., Springdale, AR 72764, (501)756-4000.*

STARRETT, Andre V.——**B:** Dec. 27, 1935, Tokyo, Japan, *Pres.*, Woodway Realty Corp.; **PRIM RE ACT:** Consultant, Developer, Owner/Investor; **REP CLIENTS:** Primarily European fin. instns.; **PREV EMPLOY:** Intl. Banking Dept. of Marine Midland Bank, Corporate Fin. Dept. of Eastman Dillon Union Securities & Co.; **PROFL AFFIL & HONORS:** ULI; **EDUC:** AB, 1958, Liberal Arts and Econ., Columbia Coll.; **GRAD EDUC:** MBA, 1960, Fin. and Intl. Bus., Columbia Grad. School of Bus.; **MIL SERV:** US Army, Sgt.; **HOME ADD:** 11 East 86th St., New York, NY 10028, (212)534-5012; **BUS ADD:** 450 Park Ave., New York, NY 10022, (212)355-5050.

STATKIEWICZ, Robert E.——*Exec. VP*, Devel. Gen. Corp.; **PRIM RE ACT:** Broker, Developer, Owner/Investor, Property Manager; **PREV EMPLOY:** First PA Bank; Blvd. Mort. Co.; **PROFL AFFIL & HONORS:** Nat. Assn. of Review Appraisers; Intl. Council of Shopping Ctrs.; Sigma Kappa Phi Honor Fraternity; Univ. of PA RE Soc., Cert. Review Appraiser; Shopping Ctr. Mgr.; **EDUC:** School of Mort. Banking, Wharton School, Univ. of PA; **EDUC HONORS:** Cum Laude; **BUS ADD:** 8725 Loch Raven Blvd., Towson, MD 21204, (301)821-8500.

STAUB, John T.——**B:** Nov. 8, 1943, Chicago, IL, *Partner*, Jensen, Fore and Staub Architects; **PRIM RE ACT:** Architect; **SERVICES:** Complete arch. and constr. mgmt. serv.; **REP CLIENTS:** Major Food and dept. store chains, churches, and pvt. devels.; **PROFL AFFIL & HONORS:** AIA, NCARB; **EDUC:** B Arch, 1966, Design and Engrg., Univ. of Notre Dame; **MIL SERV:** USN; Lt.; 1966-1968; **HOME ADD:** 1113 Del Mar Dr., Palatine, IL 60067, (312)359-0462; **BUS ADD:** 2000 Spring Rd., Ste 620, Oakbrook, IL 60521, (312)887-1770.

STAUDT, J.N.——*Fin. Dir.*, Lee Enterprises; **PRIM RE ACT:** Property Manager; **BUS ADD:** 130 E. Second St., Davenport, IA 52801, (319)383-2202.*

STAVAST, Joseph John——**B:** July 21, 1941, Denver, CO, *VP*, Moore and Co., Resid.; **PRIM RE ACT:** Broker, Instructor, Owner/Investor; **SERVICES:** Resid. sales; **PREV EMPLOY:** Mktg. Dir., Wood Bros. Homes; **PROFL AFFIL & HONORS:** NAR, RNMI, CRS, CRB, GRI; **EDUC:** BA, 1967, Geography, Econ., Poli. Sci., CO Univ.; **EDUC HONORS:** Deans List, Pres. Honor Roll; **MIL SERV:** USNR, Lt.; **OTHER ACT & HONORS:** Mensa, Intertel; **HOME ADD:** 2468 Ward Dr., Lakewood, CO 80215, (303)232-0303; **BUS ADD:** 2081 Youngfield, Golden, CO 80401, (303)232-5511.

STAYTON, Jack——*Purchasing Agent*, Monarch Machine Tool; **PRIM RE ACT:** Property Manager; **BUS ADD:** N. Oak Ave., Sidney, OH 45365, (513)492-4111.*

STEARNS, George——*Ed.*, Realty & Building; **PRIM RE ACT:** Real Estate Publisher; **BUS ADD:** 12 E. Grand Ave., Chicago, IL 60611, (312)944-1204.*

STEARNS, Howard M., Jr.——**B:** April 15, 1928, Hartford, CT, *First VP & Rgnl. Mgr.*, Coldwell Banker, RE Fin. Serv.; **OTHER RE ACT:** RE Fin.; **SERVICES:** Permanent and short term debt and/or equity for income producing RE; **REP CLIENTS:** Major nat. and rgnl. RE devel., life ins. cos., thrift inst. and pension funds; **PREV EMPLOY:** CT Gen. Life Ins. Co. 1951-59, First Mktg. Co. of TX, Inc. 1959-74, Rotan Mosle 1974-76, Dorman & Wilson, Inc. 1976-78; **PROFL AFFIL & HONORS:** Mort. Bankers Assn. of Amer., The Amer. Assn. of Cert. Appraisers, Nat. Assn. of Review Appraisers, Intl. Inst. of Valuers, CMB; **EDUC:** BA, 1951, Soc. Sci., Earlham Coll.; **MIL SERV:** US Army, Cpl.; **HOME ADD:** 243 Cupsaw Dr., Ringwood, NJ 07456, (201)962-7251; **BUS ADD:** 433 Hackensack Ave., Hackensack, NJ 07601, (201)488-6000.

STEARNS, Richard D.——**B:** Nov. 3, 1945, Willard, OH, *Dir., Mort. Fin.*, Cardinal Indus.; **PRIM RE ACT:** Attorney, Developer; **SERVICES:** Full serv. devel. operating in 6 states, manage 13,000 apts., 3000 motel rooms, single family, condos., corp. offices in Columbus, OH. Other offices in Orlando, FL & Atlanta, GA; **PREV EMPLOY:** Midland Mutual Life Ins. Co., Columbus, OH, Investment Dept., Galbreath Mort. Co., (Now Chemical Mort. Co.), Columbus, OH, Comml. Loan Officer; **PROFL AFFIL & HONORS:** Columbus Bar, OH Bar, Atty, OH Re Broker; **EDUC:** BA, 1968, Econ., OH State Univ.; **GRAD EDUC:** JD, 1971, Univ. of Toledo; **MIL SERV:** Army, Capt.; **HOME ADD:** 2391 Brentwood Rd., Columbus, OH 43209, (614)231-5969; **BUS ADD:** 2040 S. Hamilton Rd., Columbus, OH 43227, (614)861-3211.

STEELE, Herbert D.——**B:** Aug. 18, 1943, McKeesport, PA, *Vice President-Branch Mgr.*, Ralph C. Sutro Co., Income Prop. Loan Div.; **OTHER RE ACT:** Mort. Broker; **SERVICES:** Debt; Equity Fin. of Major Comml. Prop.; **REP CLIENTS:** Major Regional RE Devel.; **PREV EMPLOY:** The Alison Co., Newport Beach, CA (Mort. Banking); Monarch Life Ins. Co., Springfield, MA (RE Investment); **PROFL AFFIL & HONORS:** ULI; **EDUC:** BA, 1965, Eng. Lit., Duke Univ.; **GRAD EDUC:** MBA, 1971, RE Fin., Univ. of CT.; **MIL SERV:** USNR, Lt., Vietnam Serv.; **OTHER ACT & HONORS:** The Back Bay Club; **BUS ADD:** 1300 Quail St. #105, Newport Beach, CA 92660, (714)752-2281.

STEELE, John W., III——**B:** Oct. 21, 1937, Marlow, OK, *VP, Assoc. Gen. Counsel*, The Rouse Co., Legal Div.; **PRIM RE ACT:** Attorney; **SERVICES:** Legal Counsel; **REP CLIENTS:** All services are performed for The Rouse Co. and affiliated entities; **PROFL AFFIL & HONORS:** ABA, MD State Bar Assn., Bar Assn. of Baltimore City; **EDUC:** BA, 1958, Poli. Sci., Amer. Hist., Univ. of Baltimore; **GRAD EDUC:** LLB, 1961, Univ. of Baltimore, School of Law; **EDUC HONORS:** Magna Cum Laude, Ranked 2nd in Class, Magna Cum Laude, Heuisler Honor Soc.; **OTHER ACT & HONORS:** Instr., Univ. of MD, School of Law 1974-Present, Lecturer, CLE Programs; **HOME ADD:** 1019 Timber Trail Rd., Towson, MD 21204, (301)337-0138; **BUS ADD:** 10275 Little Patuxent Parkway, Columbia, MD 21044, (301)992-6407.

STEELE, S.S.——**B:** Oct. 9, 1916, NY, *CEO*, S.S. Steele & Co., Inc., Main Office; **PRIM RE ACT:** Broker, Developer, Banker, Builder, Insuror; **SERVICES:** Mort. loan assistance; **REP CLIENTS:** Central Bank of Mobile, First Southern Fed. S&L; **PROFL AFFIL & HONORS:** Home Builders Assn., RE Bd. (Inactive), US C of C, Leadership Award by Home Builders Assn. of Metro Mobile, Cert. of Commendation by City of Mobile, Cert. of Appreciation by Univ. of S, AL Medical Ctr.; **EDUC:** Univ. of CA, Berkeley; **MIL SERV:** USAF, 1st Lt.; **OTHER ACT & HONORS:** Chmn. Housing Bd. of Mobile, 1959-64; Bd. Member of Mobile Gen Hospital; Skyline Ctry. Club; Bd. of Dirs., Central Bank of Mobile, Member of MENSA.; **HOME ADD:** 1116 Pace Pkwy, Mobile, AL 36609, (205)666-7429; **BUS ADD:** 5555 Govt. Blvd., Mobile, AL 36609, (205)661-9600.

STEELE, Thomas A.——**B:** May 17, 1940, Cumberland, MD, *Pres.*, Perini Land & Devel. Co.; **PRIM RE ACT:** Consultant, Developer, Builder, Owner/Investor; **SERVICES:** Primarily devel. major projects cos. accounts; **PROFL AFFIL & HONORS:** Reg. Broker, MA; **EDUC:** BA, 1962, Liberal Arts, Harvard Univ.; **GRAD EDUC:** MBA, 1969, Fin., Harvard Bus. School; **EDUC HONORS:** Magna Cum Laude, Distinction; **MIL SERV:** USN, Lt.; **OTHER ACT & HONORS:** V Chmn., Fin. Comm., Boxboro; **HOME ADD:** 797 Depot Rd., Foxboro, MA 02035, (617)263-5041; **BUS ADD:** 73 Mt. Wayte Ave., Bellingham, MA 01701, (617)875-6171.

STEELE, William L.——**B:** Oct. 7, 1918, Hartford, AR, *Broker*, Steele Realty Co.; **PRIM RE ACT:** Broker, Appraiser, Owner/Investor, Property Manager; **OTHER RE ACT:** Leasing Agent for 2 shopping centers; **PREV EMPLOY:** Drycleaning for 5 years, Police Officer for 23 years previous. RE bus. past 8 years.; **PROFL AFFIL & HONORS:** Soc. of RE Appraisers, Nat. Assn. of RE Appraisers, Broker in State of

OK, and Broker in State of AR; **EDUC:** 1979, Fin., Univ. of Tulsa; **MIL SERV:** USN WWII, Rdm. 2/C; **OTHER ACT & HONORS:** Masonic Lodge, Shriner, York Rite Bodies, Grotto, Assemby of God Church; **HOME ADD:** 10110 East 27th St., Tulsa, OK 74129, (918)627-2139; **BUS ADD:** 2615-C S. Memorial Dr., Tulsa, OK 74129, (918)664-6212.

STEEN, Harold W.——B: July 30, 1911, Osseo, WI; **PRIM RE ACT:** Consultant, Appraiser, Instructor; **OTHER RE ACT:** Accept assignments in indus. and comml. prop. only; **SERVICES:** Feasibility analysis; **REP CLIENTS:** Lenders, indus. and comml. interests; **PREV EMPLOY:** VP of S&L in charge of Appraisal Dept.; Assoc., F.J. Frank and Assocs.; **PROFL AFFIL & HONORS:** Sr. RE Analyst, Soc. of RE Appraisers, SREA; **EDUC:** BS, 1933, Arch./Gen. Metal/Indus. Educ., Stout State Univ.; **GRAD EDUC:** 1935, Admin., Univ. of WV; **MIL SERV:** USN; Lt. Sr. Gr.; **OTHER ACT & HONORS:** Active Member of SCORE; **HOME ADD:** 1914 Ray Ave., Caldwell, ID, (208)454-1783; **BUS ADD:** 1914 Ray Ave., Caldwell, ID 83605, (208)454-1783.

STEENBAKKERS, H. John——B: Oct. 21, 1942, Rotterdam, the Neth., *Pres.*, H.J. Steenbakkers Co.; **PRIM RE ACT:** Broker, Consultant, Developer, Owner/Investor, Instructor; **OTHER RE ACT:** Investment planner; **SERVICES:** RE brokerage, consulting to developers, loan broker, investment planning; **REP CLIENTS:** Consultant in retirement indus., investment planner to well-to-do indivs., brokerage to the general public, develop for my own acct. and acct. of investors; **PREV EMPLOY:** VP, The Danmor Co., Devels. of Retirement Housing; VP, Medifac West, Devel. of Nursing Homes & Retirement Housing; Deloitte, Haskins & Sells, Accountant; **EDUC:** BS, 1969, Acctg./Econ., Brigham Young Univ.; **HOME ADD:** 3004 177th Ave., N.E., Redmond, WA 98052, (206)885-9133; **BUS ADD:** 1801 130th Ave. N.E., POB 1902, Bellevue, WA 98009, (206)883-3333.

STEENSON, Scott R.——B: Dec. 5, 1946, Beaumont, TX, *Pres.*, Steenson Props., Inc.; **PRIM RE ACT:** Broker, Developer, Owner/Investor; **SERVICES:** Comml. brokerage/comml. devel./prop. mgmt.; **REP CLIENTS:** Indiv. and instnl. investors; **PROFL AFFIL & HONORS:** Greater Dallas Bd. of Realtors, Instit. Affiliate; **EDUC:** BS, 1970, Sec. Ed. (Biology/Chemistry Concentration), N. TX State Univ.; **OTHER ACT & HONORS:** SW Officials Assn.; **HOME ADD:** 5101 N. Ave. "A" #266, Midland, TX 79701, (214)826-6538; **BUS ADD:** 210 N. Big Spring, Midland, TX 79701, (915)682-1287.

STEFAN, Chester J.——B: Nov. 1, 1945, Chicago, IL, *Gen. Mgr.*, The Mitchell Co., Apt. Devel.; **PRIM RE ACT:** Broker, Consultant, Developer, Lender, Builder, Owner/Investor, Property Manager, Syndicator; **SERVICES:** Income prop. devel., mort. banking to include origination of FHA insured loans & tax exempt fin., synd. of income producing prop. and gen. RE brokerage & devel.; **PREV EMPLOY:** HUD, Birmingham Area Office, Fin. Analyst; **PROFL AFFIL & HONORS:** Nat. Leased Housing Assn.; Homebuilders Assn. of AL; **EDUC:** BA, 1967, Psych./Philosophy, DePaul Univ.; **GRAD EDUC:** MBA, 1971, Mgmt./Fin., FL State Univ.; **EDUC HONORS:** Dean's List 3 yrs., Psy Chi Psych. Honor Soc., Grad. 1st in class, Summa Cum Laude; **MIL SERV:** US Army, Capt., Nat. Defense Service Ribbon, Vietnamese Service Ribbon, Vietnamese Campaign Ribbon with Three Stars, Army Commendation Medal and Bronze Star; **HOME ADD:** 613 Highland Woods Dr. E., Mobile, AL 36608, (205)342-9084; **BUS ADD:** POB 160306, Mobile, AL 36616, (205)476-1200.

STEFEK, W.F. Bill——B: Apr. 16, 1930, Granger, TX, *Owner*, Stefek; **PRIM RE ACT:** Developer, Owner/Investor, Property Manager; **OTHER RE ACT:** Planner, recreation facilities; Div. of US Army Recreation Sports; **SERVICES:** Manage prop. by planning devel.; **REP CLIENTS:** Investors, mgrs. of comml. recreation and comml. light indus.; **PREV EMPLOY:** Dir. Planner US Army Recreation, 1964-72; **PROFL AFFIL & HONORS:** Nat. Parks and Recreation Assn. (NRPA), 1964 to present, Dept. of Army Outstanding Performance 1964, 1966, 1967, 1968, 1970, 1972, 1973, 1976, 1980; **EDUC:** Recreation Facilities & Human Relations, Spec. Educ., 1970-present; **GRAD EDUC:** Human Behavior in Recreation, Spec. Educ., 1975 to present; **MIL SERV:** US Army, Sgt., 1948-52; **OTHER ACT & HONORS:** Bd. of Dir., Water Supply Corp., 1969-present; Dist. Pres. Catholic Union of TX, 1978 to present; SIR 4th Degree; Knights of Columbus, 1971 to present; **HOME ADD:** 606 Elms Rd., Killeen, TX 76541, (817)634-3330; **BUS ADD:** 606 Elms Rd., Killeen, TX 76541, (817)634-3330.

STEFFEL, Charles S. (Steve)——B: Aug. 16, 1943, OH, *Owner*, Steffel Realty; **PRIM RE ACT:** Broker, Instructor, Syndicator, Consultant, Owner/Investor; **SERVICES:** Apt., office and shopping ctr. brokerage; **REP CLIENTS:** Condo. converters, ins. cos., pension funds; **PROFL AFFIL & HONORS:** RESSI; **EDUC:** BS, 1965, Bus. Admin., The Defiance Coll., Defiance, OH; **GRAD EDUC:** MBA, 1975, Fin., Mktg., Bowling Green State Univ., OH; **MIL SERV:** USAR; **HOME ADD:** 6969 Oak Ln., Indianapolis, IN 46220, (317)257-5133; **BUS ADD:** 9101 Wesleyan Rd., Suite 108, Indianapolis, IN 46268, (317)875-8055.

STEFFEY, John W., Jr.——B: Feb. 24, 1951, Baltimore, MD, *VP*, Chas H. Steffey Inc.; **PRIM RE ACT:** Broker, Consultant, Appraiser, Developer, Builder, Instructor; **SERVICES:** Full service RE; **PROFL AFFIL & HONORS:** NAREA, Sec. Bd. of Realtors, Dir. of Rgnl. Planning Comm.; Chmn. Profl. Standards; CRB; BRS; GRI; **EDUC:** 1972, Bus. Admin., Anne Arundel Simmond Coll.; **OTHER ACT & HONORS:** Elks Club, Kiwanis Club, Indus. Advisory Council, Anne Arundel Cty.; **HOME ADD:** 1218 Driftwood Ct., Arnold, MD 21202, (301)544-3896; **BUS ADD:** 2 E. Fayette St., Baltimore, MD 21202, (301)685-2412.

STEFFKE, Glenn T.——B: Nov. 24, 1938, Wyandotte, MI, *VP*, Southeast Properties, Inc. (affil. of Southeast Banking Corp.); **OTHER RE ACT:** Corporate RE; **SERVICES:** Acquisitions, leasing, admin. of corp. RE assets of Southeast Banking Corp. and affiliates; **PREV EMPLOY:** Investors Funding Corp. of NY 1969-73; **PROFL AFFIL & HONORS:** BOMA, NACORE (Nat. Assn. of Corporate RE Execs.), S. FL Building & Zoning Assn., Pres., Miami Chapter NACORE; **EDUC:** 1960, Bus. Admin., Ferris State Coll.; **GRAD EDUC:** 1979, Corp. RE, Notre Dame; **MIL SERV:** US Army, Sgt. E-5, Army Commendation Medal; **OTHER ACT & HONORS:** Cirtus Club, Bachelors Club, Harbor Beach Surf Club; **HOME ADD:** 3737 Kent Rd., Miami, FL 33133, (305)442-8504; **BUS ADD:** 1699 Coral Way, Miami, FL 33133, (305)577-4094.

STEFL, Allan H.——B: Aug. 24, 1943, Manitowoc, WI, *Pres.*, *Allan H. Stefl, Inc.*, Partner, Stefl & Co.; **PRIM RE ACT:** Broker, Consultant, Owner/Investor, Property Manager, Syndicator; **PROFL AFFIL & HONORS:** CA and TX RE Broker Licenses; NAR; CA Assn. of Realtors, Investment Div., Synd. Div., Prop. Mgmt. Div., Certificate Inst.; Malibu Bd. of Realtors; Nat., TX, and Houston Apt. Assns.; **EDUC:** BBA, 1965, For. Trade, Univ. of WI, Madison; **GRAD EDUC:** MBA, 1970, Gen., Univ. of S. CA; **MIL SERV:** USMC, Capt., Bronze Star w/Combat V and six others, 1965-1968; **OTHER ACT & HONORS:** Kappa Sigma Frat., MENSA, CA Jr. Coll. Teaching Certificate; **HOME ADD:** 20239 Inland Ln., Malibu, CA 90265; **BUS ADD:** POB 79789, Houston, TX 77079, (713)461-5951.

STEFOIN, David E.——*Pres.*, Clark, Harris & Stefan Enterprises, Inc.; **PRIM RE ACT:** Developer; **BUS ADD:** 950 County Line Rd, Rosemont, PA 19018, (215)525-6630.*

STEGMEYER, Joseph——*VP Corp. Dev.*, Worthington Industries, Inc.; **PRIM RE ACT:** Property Manager; **BUS ADD:** 1205 Dearborn Dr., Columbus, OH 43085, (614)328-3210.*

STEHLIK, Galen E.——B: Apr. 6, 1952, Crete, NE, *VP/Sr. Tr. Officer*, The Overland National Bank, Tr. & Estates; **PRIM RE ACT:** Attorney, Banker, Property Manager; **OTHER RE ACT:** Tr. investments; **SERVICES:** Mgmt., investments & sales; **PREV EMPLOY:** Assoc. in law firm of Stinacher & Vosoba, Wilber, NE; **PROFL AFFIL & HONORS:** ABA; NE and Hall Cty. Bar Assns.; ABA Sect. on Real Property, Probate and Trust Law; Young Lawyers Sect.; NE Bar Assn.; **EDUC:** BS, 1974, Econ., Pol. Sci. and Hist., Univ. of NE, Lincoln; **GRAD EDUC:** JD, 1977, Law, Univ. of NE Coll. of Law, Lincoln; **EDUC HONORS:** Grad. with Distinction; C.S. Boucher Memorial Award; Magna Cum Laude; **MIL SERV:** USAF, 1st Lt.; **OTHER ACT & HONORS:** Bd. Member, Hall Cty. Rgnl. Airport Auth.; **HOME ADD:** 37 Chantilly Ave., Grand Island, NE 68801, (308)381-2695; **BUS ADD:** 304 West 3rd St., Grand Island, NE 68801, (308)382-4800.

STEHLIK, L. Joe——B: Dec. 20, 1946, Humboldt, NE, *Owner*, Stehlik Law Office; **PRIM RE ACT:** Attorney; **OTHER RE ACT:** Abstracter; **SERVICES:** Gen. legal and abstracting; **REP CLIENTS:** Indiv. homeowners and farm landowners; realtors and lenders; **PROFL AFFIL & HONORS:** NE Land Title Assn.; Member, RE, Probate and Trust Section of ABA; Member NE State Bar Assn.; **EDUC:** BBA, 1968, Gen. Bus., Univ. of NE, Lincoln; **GRAD EDUC:** JD, 1971, Univ. of NE; **EDUC HONORS:** Cum Laude; Beta Gamma Sigma; **MIL SERV:** US Army Res., Capt.; **OTHER ACT & HONORS:** Cty. Atty./Pawnee Cty., NE/1974 to present; I.O.O.F., Sertoma, Jaycees, Rotary; **HOME ADD:** 734 2nd St., Pawnee City, NE 68420, (402)852-2240; **BUS ADD:** 653 G. St., PO Box 187, Pawnee City, NE 68420, (402)852-2973.

STEICHEN, C. Everett——B: Aug. 11, 1925, Oregon City, OR, *Prin.*, Wallace & Steichen, Inc.; **PRIM RE ACT:** Broker, Consultant, Syndicator; **REP CLIENTS:** Comml. & large scale devel., corporations, retailers; **PREV EMPLOY:** Larry Smith & Company - 22 years; **PROFL AFFIL & HONORS:** ICSC, ULI, Nat. Retail Merchants Assn.; **EDUC:** BA, 1952, Hist., Reed Coll.; **GRAD EDUC:** MA, 1955, Econ., Univ. of WA; **MIL SERV:** USAF, 1st Lt.; **HOME ADD:** 46 Douglass Way, Atherton, CA 94025; **BUS ADD:** 261 Hamilton Ave., Palo Alto, CA 94301, (415)328-0447.

STEIGELMAN, Keanneard L.——B: Phila., PA, *Pres.*, Steigelman & Assoc., Inc., Realtors; **PRIM RE ACT:** Broker, Syndicator, Consultant; **SERVICES:** Ind./comml. brokerage, investment analysis; **PROFL AFFIL & HONORS:** NAR, PA Assoc. Realtors, Bucks Cty. Bd. of Realtors, GRI, CCIM, SRS; **EDUC:** BS/BA, 1963, Econ. & Fin., Boston Univ.; **MIL SERV:** US Army; **OTHER ACT & HONORS:** Pres. Langdale Rotaty Club; VP N. PA C of C; **HOME ADD:** 62 Old Church Rd., N. Wales, PA 19454; **BUS ADD:** Box 27, Line Lexington, PA 18932, (215)822-3345.

STEIKER, Jerome J.——B: May 3, 1922, New York, NY, *Sr. VP, Treas., & Dir.*, Sonnenblick-Goldman Corp., and Dir. of its affiliate - Lehman Brothers Kuhn Loeb Inc.; **PRIM RE ACT:** Broker, Consultant; **OTHER RE ACT:** Mort. banker; **SERVICES:** Arrange fin., equity & sales of major RE projects; **PREV EMPLOY:** Formerly Pres. & CEO of First Nat. Bank of Rochester, NY; VP of Royal Nat. Bank of NY; Dir. of Mktg. of Lincoln Rochester Trust Co., Rochester, NY; **PROFL AFFIL & HONORS:** Amer. Inst. of CPA's; NY's Soc. of CPA's; NY RE Bd.; ICSC; Intl. Downtown Executives Assn.; MBA; Nat. Assn. of Corp. RE Execs., CPA - NYS; Townsend Harris Medal - City Coll. of NY; Beta Gamma Sigma (Nat. Honoroary Bus. Frat.); **EDUC:** BBA, 1941, Acctg., City Coll. of NY, Cum Laude; ME, 1942, Mech. Engrg., Pratt Inst.; CTF in Advanced Math, 1943, Advanced Mathematics, State Univ. of IA; **GRAD EDUC:** MBA, 1947, Fin., Harvard Univ. (Graduate School of Business Administration; **EDUC HONORS:** Grad. with distinction; **MIL SERV:** USAF, Dir. of Communications Intelligence - CBI Theater of Operations; **OTHER ACT & HONORS:** Dir., Washington Nat. Life Ins Co. of NY; Design Craft Jewel Industries, Inc.; Riverdale YMHA; Federation of Jewish Philanthropies - NY; City Coll. Fund; NY State Soc. of CPA's; Harvard Business School Exec. Council; Pres. of City Coll. Alumni Assn.; **HOME ADD:** 45 E 66th St., New York, NY 10021, (212)249-0406; **BUS ADD:** 1251 Avenue of the Americas, New York, NY 10020, (212)541-4321.

STEIN, Arthur——B: Aug. 14, 1945, Bayonne, NJ, *Atty.*, Curry & Stein, A Profl. Corp.; **PRIM RE ACT:** Attorney, Owner/Investor; **SERVICES:** Legal counsel in all phases of RE; **REP CLIENTS:** Planning Bds., indiv. investors, RE brokers, Planning Bd. of Township of Dover (Toms River), NJ; Planning Bd. of Township of Lacey (Forked River), NJ; Planning Bd. of Township of Berkeley, NJ; **PREV EMPLOY:** Atty. for Planning Bd. of Borough of Seaside Heights, NJ; Atty. for Planning Bd. Borough of Pine Beach, NJ; **PROFL AFFIL & HONORS:** ABA; NJ State Bar Assn.; Ocean Cty. Bar Assn.; **EDUC:** BS, 1966, Bus./Acctg./Econ., Seton Hall Univ.; **GRAD EDUC:** JD, 1969, Seton Hall School of Law; **EDUC HONORS:** Who's Who in Amer. Coll. & Univ.; **MIL SERV:** US Army, Capt., 1970-1972; **OTHER ACT & HONORS:** Asst. Ocean Cty. Counsel, 1978-1980; Asst. Bergen Cty. Pros., 1972-1974; **HOME ADD:** 885 Ocean View Dr., Toms River, NJ 08753, (201)929-1850; **BUS ADD:** 535 W. Lacey Rd., POB 131, Forked River, NJ 08731, (609)693-9194.

STEIN, David E.——B: June 22, 1951, Newark, NJ, *Publisher*, New England RE Directory; **PRIM RE ACT:** Real Estate Publisher; **SERVICES:** Comml. RE mkt. data and articles; **EDUC:** BA, 1973, Amer. Politics and Culture, Bucknell Univ.; **GRAD EDUC:** MBA, 1979, Mktg., Boston Univ.; **EDUC HONORS:** with Honors; **HOME ADD:** 23 Magazine St., Cambridge, MA 02138, (617)661-7249; **BUS ADD:** 227 Statler Office Bldg., Boston, MA 02116, (617)482-7920.

STEIN, David Jerome——B: Aug. 10, 1934, Fairbury, IL, *Fin. Consultant*; **PRIM RE ACT:** Broker, Consultant, Developer, Owner/Investor; **SERVICES:** Fin. consulting and comml. mort. brokerage; **REP CLIENTS:** Lenders, indiv., devel. and instnl. investors in comml. prop.; **PREV EMPLOY:** Owner, Stein Enterprises, Inc. and D & R Marketing; Pres., Medical Condos, Inc.; Exec. VP & Gen. Mgr., Roy Demanes Industries; Corp. Sec., IL Valley S & L Assn.; Asst. to VP for Farm Mortgages-Mutual of New York Life; Regional Sales Mgr., Agri. Div., Monsanto Co.; Credit Supr Int. Harvester Credit Corp.; Retail Credit Dir., FS Services, Inc.; Asst. Sec.-Treas. Champaign Production Credit Assn.; **PROFL AFFIL & HONORS:** Exec. Award - Grad. School of Credit and Fin. Mgmt., Dartmouth Coll.; **EDUC:** 1959, Agricultural Econ. and Fin., Univ. of IL; **GRAD EDUC:** 1968, Dartmouth Coll., Grad. School of Credit and Fin. Mgmt.; **EDUC HONORS:** Exec. Award; **MIL SERV:** US Army, Sgt. 1953-55; **HOME ADD:** 906 W. Kensington Dr., Peoria, IL 61614, (309)692-4700; **BUS ADD:** P.O. Box 3881, 906 W. Kensington Dr., Peoria, IL 61614, (309)692-5100.

STEIN, Franklin D.——B: May 9, 1937, New York City, NY, *Sole Assessor*, Town of Haverstraw, Assessors Office; **PRIM RE ACT:** Consultant, Appraiser, Property Manager, Assessor; **SERVICES:** Valuation, investment counseling, prop. mgmt.; **REP CLIENTS:** Gov. Agencies, indiv. investors; **PREV EMPLOY:** Housing & Devel. Admin. - City of NY; Lefrak Organization-Queens, NY; **PROFL AFFIL & HONORS:** Society of RE Appraisers, Amer. Soc. of Appraisers, NY State Assessors Assn., NARA, SRPA, ASA, IAO, CRA; **EDUC:** BBA, 1959, RE, Bernard Baruch School of Bus. and Public Admin.; **GRAD EDUC:** Advanced RE Appraisal Course, Amer. Instit. of RE Appraisers, Soc. of RE Appraisers; **MIL SERV:** US Army Reserve, Spec. 4/c; **OTHER ACT & HONORS:** Cty. Govt. Operations Comm.; **HOME ADD:** 34 Morton St., Garnerville, NY 10923, (914)947-3066; **BUS ADD:** One Rosman Rd., Garnerville, NY 10923, (914)429-2000.

STEIN, Fredric C.——B: Oct. 16, 1950, New York City, NY, Greiner-Maltz Co., Inc.; **PRIM RE ACT:** Broker, Consultant, Appraiser, Owner/Investor; **SERVICES:** Indus. RE specialist; **PREV EMPLOY:** Self employed developer; **EDUC:** BS, 1979, Bus. Fin., NYU; **HOME ADD:** 7 East 14th St., New York, NY 10003, (212)242-0366; **BUS ADD:** 2525 Queens Plaza North, Long Island City, NY 10003, (212)786-5050.

STEIN, Leonard R.——B: Oct. 8, 1948, Bayonne, NJ, *Divisional VP/Controller*, Integrated Resources Inc., Private Placement Acctg. & Tax; **PRIM RE ACT:** Owner/Investor, Syndicator; **SERVICES:** Tax shelters; **REP CLIENTS:** J.C. Penny; M. Ward; Sears; Abertsons; Skaggs; etc.; **PREV EMPLOY:** Touche Ross & Co.; Ernst & Whitney; **PROFL AFFIL & HONORS:** NAA; **EDUC:** BS, 1970, Acctg., Fairleigh Dickinson Univ.; **MIL SERV:** US Army 1970-73; Spec. 4; **HOME ADD:** 32 Sharon Ct., Metuchen, NJ 08840, (201)549-8918; **BUS ADD:** 666 3rd Ave., New York, NY 10017, (212)878-9383.

STEIN, Peter R.——B: Sep. 3, 1953, NYC, *VP & Dir. of Urban Land Program*, Trust for Public Land, Urban Land Program; **OTHER RE ACT:** Nonprofit land conservation & acquisition specs.; **SERVICES:** Assist in transfer of lands from private sector to public sector, provide tech. asst. to community grps. regarding nonprofit land acquisition techniques.; **REP CLIENTS:** Fed., state, city, agencies, community & neighborhood grps., corps., indivs.; **PREV EMPLOY:** Paul Props. 1971-73; Suburban Action Inst., 1974; **PROFL AFFIL & HONORS:** Parts. for Livable Places, Founding Bd. Member, 1977-Present; **EDUC:** BA, 1975, Reg. Planning, Univ. of CA at Santa Cruz; **GRAD EDUC:** Cert in Advanced Envir. Studies, 1981, Grad. School of Design, Harvard Univ.; **EDUC HONORS:** Highest Hons., Loeb Fellowship; **HOME ADD:** 423 Atlantic Ave., Brooklyn, NY 11217, (212)625-0361; **BUS ADD:** 254 W. 31st St., New York, NY 10001, (212)563-5959.

STEIN, Terrance W.——B: July 24, 1947, Duluth, MN, *Nat. Field Mgr.*, Honeywell, Building Mgmt. Services; **PRIM RE ACT:** Property Manager; **SERVICES:** Prop. mgmt., leasing, consulting; **REP CLIENTS:** Prudential Ins. Co., Mutual of NY, Crocker Bank, Hexalon B.V., Liberty Mutual, NY Life; **PREV EMPLOY:** Coldwell Banker, Mgr. of Minneapolis/St. Paul Property Mgmt. Office; **PROFL AFFIL & HONORS:** IREM; BOMA; NAIOP, CPM; RPA; **EDUC:** BA, 1969, Bus. Admin., Univ. of MN; **MIL SERV:** USNR, Ens.; **HOME ADD:** 8270 Havelock Ct., Apple Valley, MN 55124, (612)432-2661; **BUS ADD:** Honeywell Plaza, Minneapolis, MN 55408, (612)870-5488.

STEIN, Theodore E.——B: Dec. 25, 1917, Newark, NJ, *Exec. VP*, The Blau and Berg Company, Div. of Berg Enterprises, Inc. (Amex); **PRIM RE ACT:** Broker, Appraiser, Developer, Owner/Investor, Syndicator; **SERVICES:** Indus. and comml. brokerage consulting; **REP CLIENTS:** Prop. owners, devels., corp. execs.; **PREV EMPLOY:** All phases RE from 3/1/35 to date; **PROFL AFFIL & HONORS:** Active Member SIR, Indus. RE Brokers Assn. of Metro NY Area; **MIL SERV:** US Coast Guard, CPO, 4 Stars, 3 Theaters of War, WW II; **HOME ADD:** 177 Mitchell St., West Orange, NJ 07052, (201)731-5463; **BUS ADD:** 75 Lincoln Hyw. Rt. 27, Iselin, NJ 08830, (201)494-3100.

STEINBERG, Bernard L.——B: Sept. 27, 1927, Phila, PA, *Pres.*, Parkshore Devel. Corp.; **PRIM RE ACT:** Developer, Builder, Owner/Investor; **PROFL AFFIL & HONORS:** NAHB; **EDUC:** BS, 1948, Acctg., Temple Univ.; **HOME ADD:** 8209 Bayshore Dr. West, Margate, NJ 08402, (609)822-4768; **BUS ADD:** New Road & Central Ave, Linwood, NJ 08221, (609)641-7881.

STEINBERG, Michael L.——B: May 18, 1953, Brooklyn, NY, *Pres.*, Prestige Props. Inc.; **PRIM RE ACT:** Broker, Consultant, Developer, Owner/Investor, Property Manager; **SERVICES:** Buyer's, broker, devel. of comml. prop., joint ventures, mgmt. of comml., indus., and resid. props.; **PROFL AFFIL & HONORS:** NAR, FL Assn. of Realtors, Gainesville Bd. of Realtors; **EDUC:** 1975, Univ. of FL;

HOME ADD: 2727 NW 43rdl St., Gainesville, FL 32601, (904)377-5140; **BUS ADD:** 2727 NW 43rd St., Gainesville, FL 32601, (904)373-1700.

STEINBERG, Morton M.——B: Feb. 13, 1945, Chicago, IL, *Part.*, Arnstein, Gluck & Lehr; **PRIM RE ACT:** Attorney; **SERVICES:** Legal rep.; **REP CLIENTS:** Continental IL ;Nat. B&T Co. of Chicago; Sears B&T Co.; Leucadia Nat. Corp., and other Amer. and Can. indivs. and instnl lenders, investors and devels.; **PROFL AFFIL & HONORS:** US Supreme Court; US Court of Appeals, Seventh Circuit; Chicago Bar Assn.; **EDUC:** AB, 1967, Hist. & Pol. Sci., Univ. of IL; **GRAD EDUC:** JD, 1971, Northwestern Univ. Sch. of Law; **EDUC HONORS:** w/Honors, Sr. Editor *Journal of Criminal Law and Criminology*; **MIL SERV:** US Army, Res.; 1969-75; **OTHER ACT & HONORS:** VP & Dir. Camp Ramah, Inc.; **HOME ADD:** 1320 Lincoln Ave. S, Highland Pk., IL 60035, (312)433-6775; **BUS ADD:** Sears Tower, 75th Fl., Chicago, IL 60606, (312)876-7100.

STEINEGGER, Frank J., III——B: July 27, 1952, Stamford, CT, *Proj. Mgr., Great Western Bank Plaza*, Iliff, Thorn & Co.; **PRIM RE ACT:** Broker; **SERVICES:** Comml. RE brokerage, sale and leasing of office bldg. projects; **PREV EMPLOY:** Dir. of Leasing, Denver Nat. Bank Plaza for L.C. Fulenwider, Inc., Denver, CO; **EDUC:** BS/BA, 1974, RE and Const. Mgmt., Univ. of Denver; **OTHER ACT & HONORS:** Beta Theta Pi Frat.; **HOME ADD:** 12 E. Echo Ln., Phoenix, AZ 85020; **BUS ADD:** 2400 N. Central Ave., Ste. 400, Phoenix, AZ 85004, (602)253-3110.

STEINEL, Russell L.——*VP*, Helmsley-Spear, Inc. of Connecticut; **PRIM RE ACT:** Developer; **BUS ADD:** One Landmark Sq., Ste 420, Stamford, CT 06901, (203)356-9650.*

STEINER, David S.——B: Sept. 29, 1929, Newark, NJ, *Exec. VP*, The Sudler Cos.; **PRIM RE ACT:** Developer; **SERVICES:** Devel. & owner of office & indus. parks & mixed use projects; **EDUC:** BS, 1951, Civil Engrg., Carnegie Inst. of Tech.; **EDUC HONORS:** Cum Laude; **MIL SERV:** Army Corp. Engrg., 1st Lt., 1951-53, Pres. Unit Commendation; **OTHER ACT & HONORS:** Chmn. Econ. Devel. Council, State of NJ; National Assn. of Indus. & Office Parks; Nat. Pres. 1973-74; Bd. of Dir. ULI; Amer. Econ Devel. Counsel; N.E. Ind. Devel. Assn.; NJ Ind. Devel. Assn.; Amer. Soc. of Civil Engrs.; Treas. Soc. for Environ. & Econ. Devel.; Tri-State Council of Economic Advisors, Tristate Regional Planning Commission (CT, NJ and NY); Member Commission on Commerce, State of NJ; **HOME ADD:** Rocky Way, Llewellyn Pk, W. Orange, NJ 07052; **BUS ADD:** 32 Commerce St., Newark, NJ 07102, (201)622-3330; **BUS TEL:** (201)731-9891.

STEINER, John S.——*Partner*, Fordyce and Mayne; **PRIM RE ACT:** Consultant; **EDUC:** BA, 1967, Hist., Univ. of MO; **GRAD EDUC:** MA, 1968, Hist., Univ. of MO; JD, 1971, Law, Tulane Univ.; **OTHER ACT & HONORS:** Municipal Judge, City of Ladue, 1979 to present; Gen. Counsel, Jr. Achievement of MS Valley, Inc.; **HOME ADD:** 64 Fair Oaks, Ladue, MO 63124, (314)993-3484; **BUS ADD:** 120 S. Central, Suite 1100, Clayton, MO 63105.

STEINER, Mark S.——B: Nov. 1, 1947, Hartford, CT, *Pres.*, General Health Management, Inc.; **PRIM RE ACT:** Consultant, Developer, Owner/Investor, Property Manager; **EDUC:** BS, 1969, Econ., Univ. of CT; **GRAD EDUC:** MBA, 1972, RE, Syracuse Univ.; **HOME ADD:** 237 New Rd., Avon, CT 06001, (203)693-6085; **BUS ADD:** 111 Founders Plaza, E. Hartford, CT 06108, (203)528-9344.

STEINFELS, Victor E., III——B: July 26, 1937, East Orange, NJ, *VP, Operations*, Cardinal Indus. Inc.; **PRIM RE ACT:** Consultant, Developer, Builder, Owner/Investor, Instructor, Property Manager; **PREV EMPLOY:** VP, Prop. Mgmt. Div.; VP, Const. Div.; VP, Land Acquisition and Devel. Divs.; Owner of 45 Unit apt. complex; Lecturer, Nat. Apt. Builders and Devel. Assn.; **PROFL AFFIL & HONORS:** Assoc. Builders and Contractors/NAHB, NAA; **EDUC:** BS, 1961, Bus. Admin., Seton Hall Univ., South Orange, NJ; **GRAD EDUC:** MBA, 1965, Bus. Admin., Seton Hall Univ., South Orange, NJ; **EDUC HONORS:** Dean's List; **MIL SERV:** USMC, PFC, Expert Rifleman; **OTHER ACT & HONORS:** Dir., Manuscript Comm., Amer. Systems Mgmt.; **HOME ADD:** 1250 Briarmeadow, Worthington, OH 43085, (614)846-4185; **BUS ADD:** 2040 S. Hamilton Rd., Columbus, OH 43227, (614)861-3211.

STEINKRAUSS, Daniel——*Corp. Fac. Mgr.*, M/A Com. Inc.; **PRIM RE ACT:** Property Manager; **BUS ADD:** 7 New England Executive Park, Burlington, MA 01803, (617)272-9600.*

STEINMAN, David W.——B: July 16, 1940, Kew Gardens, NY, *VP & Chief Real Estate Lending Officer*, Bank One of Columbus N.A., Mort. Lend.; **PRIM RE ACT:** Banker; **SERVICES:** Mort. loans for comm'l. and resid. prop.; **PREV EMPLOY:** BA Mort. of Ohio (Bankamer. Corp.) 1974-1981; East Dil Realty, Inc. 1970-1974; Lincoln Nat. Life Ins. Co. 1962-1970; **PROFL AFFIL & HONORS:** MBA, Certified Mortgage Banker; **EDUC:** BS, 1962, Fin., Bowling Green State Univ.; **OTHER ACT & HONORS:** City Councilman, City of Worthington, 1979-81; Exec. Comm. of Mid Ohio Regional Planning Comm., 1980-81; **HOME ADD:** 177 Greenglade Ave., Worthington, OH 43085, (614)436-1301; **BUS ADD:** 100 E. Broad St., Columbus, OH 43271, (614)463-6856.

STEINMETZ, Charles P.——B: Aug. 27, 1931, Wheeling, WV, *Pres.*, Steinmetz & Associates, Inc.; **PRIM RE ACT:** Broker, Consultant, Developer, Owner/Investor, Insuror; **PROFL AFFIL & HONORS:** San Antonio Bd. of Realtors; **EDUC:** BS-Bus., 1955, Ins., West VA Univ.; **GRAD EDUC:** MBA, 1973, Fin. Mgmt., St. Mary's Univ. of San Antonio; **MIL SERV:** US Army; LTC; BS, AM, Army Comm. Meritorious Service; **OTHER ACT & HONORS:** Charter Member & Member of Bd. of Dirs. of the Oak Hills Rotary Club; **HOME ADD:** 6319 Cornplanter Dr., San Antonio, TX 78238, (512)684-6412; **BUS ADD:** 1603 Babcock Rd., Suite 141, San Antonio, TX 78229, (512)340-2121.

STEINMETZ, George C., Jr.——B: Mar. 28, 1924, Wheeling, WV, *Exec. VP*, Steinmetz & Assoc., Inc.; **PRIM RE ACT:** Consultant, Developer, Owner/Investor, Syndicator; **SERVICES:** Prop. mgmt., fin. consulting; **PREV EMPLOY:** Mktg. Specialist; **EDUC:** 3 yrs. Bus. Admin., Mktg., WV Univ.; **MIL SERV:** USN Air Corps. 1942-45; **OTHER ACT & HONORS:** Phi Kappa Psi, Rotary Intl., C of C, Chmn.of Task Force for Chamber's Annual Office Bldg. Dir.; **HOME ADD:** 3410 River Way, San Antonio, TX 78230, (512)692-1318; **BUS ADD:** 1603 Babcock Rd. 141, San Antonio, TX 78229, (512)340-2121.

STEINMETZ, William A.——B: Jan. 30, 1928, Wheeling, WV, *VP/Sec./Treas.*, Steinmetz & Assoc., Inc.; **PRIM RE ACT:** Developer, Builder, Owner/Investor, Property Manager; **SERVICES:** Manage comml. prop., invest, develop & supervise const.; **PREV EMPLOY:** 30 years in Mil.; **PROFL AFFIL & HONORS:** IREM; San Antonio Apt. Assn., CPM; **GRAD EDUC:** BGE, 1966, Mil. Sci., Univ. of NE at Omaha; **MIL SERV:** USAF; Lt. Col.; Bronze Star, Meritorious Service w/OLC, AFCM, Joint Serv. Commendation w/OLC; **OTHER ACT & HONORS:** AFA; **HOME ADD:** 15206 Summerton Oak, San Antonio, TX 78232, (512)496-2851; **BUS ADD:** 1603 Babcock Rd., Suite 141, San Antonio, TX 78229.

STELLE, Roger T.——B: Sept. 19, 1944, Springfield, IL, *Partner*, Holmstrom & Green Profl. Corp.; **PRIM RE ACT:** Attorney; **SERVICES:** Legal services in all phases of RE devel. and synd.; **REP CLIENTS:** Lenders and devels. engaged in comml. and resid. RE fin. and devel.; **PREV EMPLOY:** Thomas F. Seay & Assoc., Chicago Title & Tr. Co.; **PROFL AFFIL & HONORS:** ABA, IL State Bar Assn., Chicago Bar Assn.; **EDUC:** BS, 1966, Bus. Admin., Northwestern Univ.; **GRAD EDUC:** MBA, 1967, Northwestern Univ.; JD, 1970, IN Univ.; LLM, 1975, John Marshall Law Sch.; **MIL SERV:** USAR, JAGC, Maj.; **HOME ADD:** 81 Minnie St., Crystal Lake, IL 60014, (815)455-3469; **BUS ADD:** 145 Virginia St., Crystal Lake, IL 60014, (815)459-8440.

STELLMACHER, Herbert Bob——B: June 11, 1914, Dallas, TX, *RE Mktg. Coordinator*, Bishop Trust Co., Ltd., Land Use & Devel. Div.; **PRIM RE ACT:** Broker, Consultant, Appraiser, Owner/Investor, Instructor; **OTHER RE ACT:** Analyst, Economist; **SERVICES:** Appraisal, feasibility analysis & mktg. of RE; **PREV EMPLOY:** 27 yrs. a prof. at Univ. of HI, N TX State Univ., Univ. of Houston & IL Tech.; **PROFL AFFIL & HONORS:** SREA, NARA, NAR, HI Assn. of Realtors, Honolulu Bd. of Realtors, SRPA, CRA, GRI, Realtor; **EDUC:** BA, 1935, Pure Math., Univ. of TX; **GRAD EDUC:** MBA, 1952, Admin. Mgmt., So. Methodist Univ.; **EDUC HONORS:** With Honors, Beta Gamma Sigma, Sigma Iota Epsilon; **MIL SERV:** USN, Lt.; **OTHER ACT & HONORS:** Member Environmental Quality Comm., 1980-81; **HOME ADD:** 2416 Ferdinand Ave., Honolulu, HI 96822, (808)949-4239; **BUS ADD:** Bishop & King St., PO Box 2390, Honolulu, HI 96804, (808)523-2269.

STEMAN, Robert E.——B: Apr. 12, 1908, Cincinnati, OH, Peck, Shaffer & Williams; **PRIM RE ACT:** Attorney; **SERVICES:** Bond counsel, FHA counsel; **PREV EMPLOY:** Chief Trial Counsel City of Cincinnati (1946-1948); City of No. College1955-1961; Judge Advocate Gen. 1965-1967; **PROFL AFFIL & HONORS:** Cincinnati, OH State Bar Assns.; ABA; Lawyers Club of Cincinnati, Commander-in-Chief (1970-1971) Military Order of World Wars; **EDUC:** AB, 1931, Miami Univ.; **GRAD EDUC:** JD, 1933, Univ. of Cincinnati; **EDUC HONORS:** Phi Delta Phi Frat.; **OTHER ACT & HONORS:** Special legal counsel; Bd. Educ. City of Cincinnati; **BUS ADD:** 2200 First National Bank Center, 425 Walnut St., Cincinnati, OH 45202, (513)621-3394.

STEMMER, Wayne J.——**B:** Oct. 29, 1942, Eliz., NJ, *VP*, Citicorp RE (Citibank NA), SW; **PRIM RE ACT:** Banker; **SERVICES:** Const. lending; **REP CLIENTS:** Major devels.; **PROFL AFFIL & HONORS:** SRA; **EDUC:** BA, 1964, Bus., Rutgers Univ.; **MIL SERV:** US Army, Capt.; **HOME ADD:** 13719 Tosca Ln., Houston, TX 77079, (713)468-1736; **BUS ADD:** Ste. 1800, One Riverway, Houston, TX 77056, (713)621-7661.

STENDERUP, James K.——**B:** June 28, 1945, Los Angeles, CA, *VP & Dist Mgr.*, Grubb & Ellis Co., Comml. Brokerage Co.; **PRIM RE ACT:** Broker; **SERVICES:** Office, indus., comml. sales & leasing; **PREV EMPLOY:** Ryder, Stilwell Inc. 1970-74; **PROFL AFFIL & HONORS:** ULI, ICSC, NAIOP, San Diego Econ. Devel. Corp., Pres. Award, Grubb & Ellis 1980; **EDUC:** AB, 1966, Econ., UCLA; **GRAD EDUC:** MBA & MS, 1969 & 1970, Mgmt., Fin., Econ., CA State Univ., Long Beach & Univ. S. CA; **EDUC HONORS:** Beta Gamma Sigma; **HOME ADD:** 3320 Camino E. Bluff, La Jolla, CA 92037, (714)455-7672; **BUS ADD:** 2299 Camino Del Rio, San Diego, CA 92108, (714)297-5500.

STENSETH, David L.——**B:** Dec. 22, 1936, Crookston, MN, *Pres.*, Sioux Falls Devel. Found.; **PRIM RE ACT:** Appraiser, Developer, Property Manager; **OTHER RE ACT:** Overall admin. of indus. park devel. (520 acre tract) Admin. of ind. devel. of city and surrounding area. Work with firms in fin., training, site location, const., const. mgmt., and bldg.; **PREV EMPLOY:** 1964-1970 Dir. of Devel., VP of Devel. at Augustana Coll., Sioux Falls, SD; 1961-1964 Field Rep. and Dir. of Fin., Minnesota Republican Party, Minneapolis MN; 1958-61 Admin. Asst. Congressman Odin Langen, MN, Washington, DC; **PROFL AFFIL & HONORS:** Dir., North Amer. Nat. Corp., Columbus, OH; Dir., Brookings Intl. Life Ins. Co., Brookings, SD; Dir., Parkview Nursing Home, Volga, SD; Pres./Dir., Sioux Land Dev. Corp., Sioux Falls, SD; Member, SECOG Econ. Dev. Comm., Vice Chmn, Comm. for Econ. Growth; Fin. Chmn., Sioux Council, Boy Scouts of America; Dir., Bd. of Regents, Indus. Devel. Inst., Univ. of OK; Dir., SD Manu. & Proc. Assoc.; Member, NARA; Licensed Realtor in SD; Dir., PIC; Dir./Treas. of SD Alcohol Fuels Assn.; Pres., SD Indus. Dev. Assn.; **EDUC:** BA, 1958, Econ., Pol. Sci. and Hist., Grad. Indus. Devel. Instn., Univ. of OK 1974; **OTHER ACT & HONORS:** Rotary; Elks; Bd. of Realtors; Transportation Club; Member, Amer. Indus. Dev. Council; Nat. Assn. of Ind Parks; Gov's. Comm. on Juvenile Delinquency; Dir., Westward Ho Country Club; Dir., South East Area Vocational School; Dir., VP Sioux Falls Boys Club; Dir., Nordland Heritage Assn.; **HOME ADD:** 2308 Wayland Court, Sioux Falls, SD 57105, (605)338-9923; **BUS ADD:** 131 East 10th St., Sioux Falls, SD 57102, (605)339-0103.

STENTON, Richard R.——*Pres.*, Mission Equity; **PRIM RE ACT:** Property Manager, Owner/Investor, Syndicator, Broker; **OTHER RE ACT:** Comml./Indus. Devel./Contractor; **SERVICES:** Purchase land, planning, building & prop. mgmt., tax planning for private investors; **REP CLIENTS:** Private indiv. and public synd. plus personal ownership; **BUS ADD:** 27285 Las Ramblas, Suite 200, Mission Viejo, CA 92691, (714)643-0120.

STENZHORN, Robert F.——*Pres.*, Robert F. Stenzhorn Inc.; **PRIM RE ACT:** Developer; **BUS ADD:** 3943 Fountainbleau Dr., Tampa, FL 33615, (813)884-6426.*

STEPHANO, Stephen C.S.——**B:** Oct. 18, 1933, Philadelphia, PA, *Gen. Partner*, Stephano Brothers Real Estate Inv. Assoc.; **PRIM RE ACT:** Developer, Property Manager, Syndicator, Owner/Investor, Consultant; **SERVICES:** Own, operate, synd., and devel. apts.; **EDUC:** 1952, Wm. Penn Charter School; BA, 1956, Economics, Int. Law, Univ. of Pennsylvania; **MIL SERV:** US Army, Cpl.; **HOME ADD:** 200 Woodspring Rd., Gwynedd Valley, PA 19437, (215)699-9219; **BUS ADD:** 7 Sheble La., Spring House, PA 19477.

STEPHENS, James A., Jr.——**B:** Dec. 27, 1945, West Point, GA, *Pres. & Prin. Broker*, Century 21 The Property Shop; **PRIM RE ACT:** Broker, Consultant, Owner/Investor, Instructor, Property Manager; **SERVICES:** Valuation, resid. mktg., prop. managing, prelicense instruction; **REP CLIENTS:** Third party home buying corp.; local builders; members of ERC; **PREV EMPLOY:** Relocation Mgr., TICOR Relocation Mgmt. Co., FL, GA & AL, 1973-1974; **PROFL AFFIL & HONORS:** NAR; Realtors Nat. Mktg. Inst.; GA Assn. of Realtors; GA Chap. Cert. Resid. Specialists, CRB; CRS; GRI; 1980 President's Award GA CRS Chap.; **EDUC:** BS, 1967, Engrg., GA Inst. of Tech.; **MIL SERV:** US Army, Air Defense Artillery, 1st Lt.; **OTHER ACT & HONORS:** RE Inst., Dekalb Community Coll.; **HOME ADD:** 970 Deer Chase Court, Stone Mountain, GA 30088, (404)469-3766; **BUS ADD:** 5062 Memorial Dr., Stone Mountain, GA 30083, (404)296-9191.

STEPHENS, Leland Griffin——**B:** Mar. 20, 1935, Lawrenceburg, TN, *Owner*, Lee Stephens; **PRIM RE ACT:** Consultant, Real Estate Publisher; **OTHER RE ACT:** Exec. search consultant; **SERVICES:** Compensation, exec. search; **REP CLIENTS:** The Taubman Co.; Bankers Trust Co.; Mobil Land Devel. Co.; Romanek Golub & Co.; **PREV EMPLOY:** VP, Nat. RE Search Div. of Korn/Ferry Intl.; **EDUC:** BS, 1962, Personnel/Indus. Relations, Univ. of CA, Los Angeles; **GRAD EDUC:** MBA, 1965, Mktg./Fin., Univ. of MI; **EDUC HONORS:** Grad. with Honors, Beta Gamma Sigma, Grad. with Distinction, Beta Gamma Sigma; **MIL SERV:** USN; 2nd Class, Korean Serv., 1953-1957; **HOME ADD:** 6655 La Jolla Blvd., La Jolla, CA 92037, (714)459-9754; **BUS ADD:** 7825 Ivanhoe, Suite 203, La Jolla, CA 92037, (714)459-9754.

STEPHENS, Rolland R.——**B:** Sept. 17, 1938, Muncie, IN, *RE Investment Analyst*, Indep. Appraiser; **PRIM RE ACT:** Broker, Instructor, Appraiser; **SERVICES:** Consulting & Appraisal of Comml. & Indus. Prop.; **REP CLIENTS:** Tchrs. Ins. & Annuity Assoc. of Amer., Title Ins. & Trust Co., Lawyers, Investors, Bankers, Large Corps.; **PROFL AFFIL & HONORS:** AIREA (1979 Pres. So. CA Chap. No. 5); SREA: Pasadena Bd. of Realtors; **EDUC:** BS, 1960, IN Univ.; **OTHER ACT & HONORS:** Rotary Club; **HOME ADD:** 823 Green Lane, La Cañada, CA 91011, (213)790-1123; **BUS ADD:** 61 W. California Blvd., Pasadena, CA 91105, (213)793-3101.

STEPHENS, Ronald L.——**B:** Apr. 2, 1934, Ocean View, DE, *Pres.*, Stephens Management Corp.; **PRIM RE ACT:** Broker, Consultant, Appraiser, Developer, Owner/Investor, Property Manager, Syndicator; **PREV EMPLOY:** DE State Housing Authority (1968-1973); **PROFL AFFIL & HONORS:** Assoc. Member SREA, AIREA, RMMI, Member NAR, State Dir. DE Bd. of Realtors, CPM; RM Candidate; CCIM Candidate; **EDUC:** AA, 1954, Fin.; **OTHER ACT & HONORS:** Cambridge Yacht Club, Eastern Shore Sailing Assn.;Also affil. with Stephens-Durham Real Estate (pres.); **HOME ADD:** 110 Anchor Way, P O Box 527, Rehoboth Beach, DE 19971, (302)227-4789; **BUS ADD:** P O Box 351, Laurel, DE 19956, (302)856-7327.

STEPHENSON, Cosette——**B:** Jan. 1, 1925, Birmingham, AL, *Director, Training & Development*, First RE Corp. of AL, The Gallery of Homes; **PRIM RE ACT:** Broker, Instructor; **SERVICES:** Train & devel. RE agents for all our offices and devel. through statistical research market areas for new offices; **PREV EMPLOY:** Broker-manager resid. RE office, First Real Estate; **PROFL AFFIL & HONORS:** NAR; Realtors Nat. Mktg. Instit.; Birmingham Areas Bd. of Realtors; Women's Council of Realtors, CRB, CRS, GRI; **EDUC:** AB, 1946, Hist., Research, Bus., Birmingham-Southern Coll., Univ. of AL in Birmingham (Post-Grad.); **OTHER ACT & HONORS:** 1982 Local Chap. Pres., Women's Council of Realtors, Birmingham; **HOME ADD:** 901 Greenbriar Circle, Birmingham, AL 35213, (205)871-5717; **BUS ADD:** 2964 Columbiana Rd., Birmingham, AL 35216, (205)822-2364.

STEPHENSON, John S.——**B:** May 2, 1944, Holland, MI, *VP of RE*, Meijer, Inc., Props.; **PRIM RE ACT:** Developer, Owner/Investor, Property Manager; **SERVICES:** In-house devel. of retail stores, prop. mgmt., peripheral sales; **PROFL AFFIL & HONORS:** Nat. Assn. of Corp. RE Execs.; Intl. Council of Shopping Ctrs.; Detroit Bd. of Realtors; **EDUC:** BS, 1966, Chem. Engrg., MI State Univ.; **GRAD EDUC:** MBA, 1969, Mktg., MI State Univ.; **HOME ADD:** 2430 Maplewood SE, Grand Rapids, MI 49506, (616)949-7817; **BUS ADD:** 2727 Walker N.W., Grand Rapids, MI 49504.

STEPHENSON, Robert C.——**B:** Sept. 21, 1938, Meadville, PA, *Part.*, Liberati, Davenport, Stephenson Assoc.; **PRIM RE ACT:** Broker, Consultant, Developer, Owner/Investor; **OTHER RE ACT:** Indus. & comml. R.E.; **SERVICES:** Project devel. mgmt., investment prop. Sales/Acquisition, Investment Counseling of Indus. and Comm. Props.; **REP CLIENTS:** Corporate, inst. and indiv. investors; **PREV EMPLOY:** Oliver Realty Inc., Exec. VP; Donovan Co.; CT Gen. Life Ins. Co.; **PROFL AFFIL & HONORS:** IREM, SIR, NAR, NAIOP, CPA; **EDUC:** BA, 1962, Pol. Sci., Secondary Educ., Allegheny Coll.; **OTHER ACT & HONORS:** Bower Hill Presbyterian Church Elder, Republican Party Committeeman, Jr. Achievement of S.W. PA, United Way; **HOME ADD:** 1895 Tilton Dr., Upper St. Clair, PA 15241, (412)221-2058; **BUS ADD:** Suite 333, 125 Seventh St., Pittsburgh, PA 15222, (412)288-8666.

STEPHENSON, Ronald L.——**B:** Apr. 5, 1942, Tulare, CA, *Partner*, Hahn Cazier & Leff; **PRIM RE ACT:** Attorney; **SERVICES:** Representation in acquisition, fin. devel., synd. and other dispositions of real prop. and interests therein (e.g. mort., leaseholds, time-shares); **REP CLIENTS:** Gen. partner synd., RE investment trusts, S&L assns., banks, pass-through and pay-through servicers and originators, and indivs.; **PROFL AFFIL & HONORS:** Member, Los Angeles Cty. and (member, sect. on: Corp., bus. and banking law, real prop., probate and trust law), ABA, and the State Bar of CA; **EDUC:** BA, 1964, Bus. Admin./Econ., Occidental Coll.; **GRAD EDUC:** JD, 1967, Boalt Hall School of Law, Univ. of CA, Berkeley; **EDUC HONORS:** Econ. Dept. Honors at Grad. and Omicron Delta Epsilon Honor Soc. in Econ.; **HOME ADD:** 3706 Stone Canyon Ave., Sherman Oaks, CA 91403, (213)995-3348; **BUS ADD:** 555 S. Flower St. 42nd Fl., Los Angeles, CA 90071, (213)485-9001.

STEPHENSON, William V.——*Exec. Dir.*, Tucson Economic Development Corp.; **PRIM RE ACT:** Developer; **BUS ADD:** 465 W St. Mary's Rd., Ste. 200, Tucson, AZ 85705, (602)623-3673.*

STEPHENSON, Willis W.——**B:** Sept. 9, 1928, Severn, NC, *Pres.*, Atlantic Permanent Fed. S&L Assn.; **PRIM RE ACT:** Lender; **SERVICES:** First and second mort. loans; prop. improvement loans; appraisales, insurance; savings accts; investment checking; **PREV EMPLOY:** VA Natl. Bank 1957-1974; **PROFL AFFIL & HONORS:** Instit. of Fin. Educ., Legislative Comm., VA S&L League; Public Relations & Consumer Affairs Comm., US League of Savings Assn.; **EDUC:** BS, 1951, Univ. of NC, Chapel Hill; **GRAD EDUC:** 1964, Rutgers Univ., Stonier Grad. School of Banking; 1975, IN Univ., Grad. School of S&L; **MIL SERV:** US Army, Sgt., 1946-1948; **OTHER ACT & HONORS:** Bd. Member-Natl. Soc. to Prevent Blindness, Endowment Comm.-Chowan Coll., VP & Dir.-VA Coll. Fund; **HOME ADD:** 1414 Five Hill Trail, VA Beach, VA 23452, (804)463-2765; **BUS ADD:** 740 Boush St., Norfolk, VA 23510, (804)622-1897.

STEPKE, Russell R.——**B:** May 7, 1942, Milwaukee, WI, *Pres.*, Resource Financial Corp.; **PRIM RE ACT:** Broker, Appraiser, Banker, Owner/Investor, Property Manager; **SERVICES:** RE acquisition negotiation, lease negotiation, fin. & investment banking & bldg. devel.; **REP CLIENTS:** Amer. Devel. Co., Nat. Maintenance Corp.; Adelman Laundry & Cleaners, Inc.; Skokie Valley Laundry & Clearners, Inc.; Nevens Co., Resource Realty Corp.; Computer Enterprises, Inc. & Math Box, Inc.; **PREV EMPLOY:** Managing Part., Stepke, Trebon & Schoenfeld; **PROFL AFFIL & HONORS:** ABA; Milwaukee Bar Assn.; WI Bar Assn.; Corp. Banking & RE Sect. ABA; **EDUC:** BA, 1965, Phil., Psych., Marquette Univ.; **GRAD EDUC:** JD, 1968, Tax & Real Prop., Marquette Univ. Law Sch.; **OTHER ACT & HONORS:** TR. Village of Fox Point, 1978-80; Pres. Fox Point-Bayside Joint Library, 1979-80; Dir. Inner City Redevel. Corp.; Lecturer Inst. for Community Bankers, 1977-80; **HOME ADD:** 1221 E. Bywater Ln., Fox Point, WI 53217, (414)352-1049; **BUS ADD:** 627 E. Henry Clay St., Whitefish Bay, WI 53217, (414)963-2015.

STERLING, Richard H.——**B:** June 24, 1918, Detroit, MI, *Pres.*, Radnor Corp.; **PRIM RE ACT:** Developer; **PREV EMPLOY:** Sun Co., Inc. Dir. Materials Mgmt. and Gen. Mgr., Mktg. Div.; **EDUC:** Bus. Admin., Univ. of W MI; **HOME ADD:** 710 Harriton Rd., Bryn Mawr, PA; **BUS ADD:** Two Radner Corp. Ctr., Ste. 420, 100 Matsonford Rd., Radnor, PA 19087, (215)293-6900.

STERN, Benjamin S.——**B:** Sept. 29, 1941, Green Bay, WI, *Atty.*, Benjamin S. Stern; **PRIM RE ACT:** Attorney; **SERVICES:** All facets of RE and gen. bus. law; **REP CLIENTS:** MGIC Investment Corp., Comml. Loan Ins. Corp., MGIC Devel. Corp., Preferred RE Investments of Milwaukee, Mil-Mar Shoe Co., Inc. Gentron Corp., Amer. Municipal Bond Ass. Corp.; **PREV EMPLOY:** Gen. Counsel Comml. Loan Ins. Corp., Sr. Counsel MGIC Investment Corp., RE Fin. Atty. McDonald's Corp., Assoc. Counsel BB Cohen & Co.; Counsel Chicago Title Ins. Co.; **PROFL AFFIL & HONORS:** WI Bar Assn., Milwaukee Bar Assn., Member IL Bar; **EDUC:** BA, 1963, Univ. WI; **GRAD EDUC:** JD, 1966, Univ. of WI; **HOME ADD:** 7300 N. Wayside Dr., Glendale, WI 53209, (414)352-7287; **BUS ADD:** 700 N. Water St., Milwaukee, WI 53202, (414)276-4080.

STERN, Stuart I.——**B:** Feb. 15, 1916, Lublin, Poland, *Pres.*, MJL Realty Sales Inc.; **PRIM RE ACT:** Broker, Attorney, Developer, Owner/Investor, Syndicator; **PREV EMPLOY:** VP, Oxford Devel. Corp., Indianapolis, IN; **PROFL AFFIL & HONORS:** Intl. Council of Shopping Ctrs.; NY Bar; IN Bar; RE & Mort. Broker, FL, Atty., Broker, Synd.; **EDUC:** Pre-Law, Bkly. Coll., **GRAD EDUC:** LLB, 1939, St. John's School of Law; **MIL SERV:** US Army; Capt., Bronze Star; **HOME ADD:** 18071 Biscayne Blvd., Miami, FL 33160, (305)931-4238; **BUS ADD:** 1250 E. Hallandale, Hallandale, FL 33009, (305)454-0301.

STERN, Theodore——**B:** Oct. 9, 1932, Los Angeles, CA, *Sr. VP*, JMB/California, JMB Realty Corp.; **PRIM RE ACT:** Owner/Investor, Syndicator; **OTHER RE ACT:** Income prop.; **SERVICES:** Investment, mgmt. & devel. of income props.; **REP CLIENTS:** Devel. & owners of major income props.; **PREV EMPLOY:** VP Pacific Coast Properties; **PROFL AFFIL & HONORS:** NASD, ICSC, ULI, RE Broker; **EDUC:** BS, 1955, Mktg., UCLA; **EDUC HONORS:** Mark Rashmir Travelling Award in Mktg.; **HOME ADD:** 2556 Almaden Ct., Los Angeles, CA 90077, (213)550-0660; **BUS ADD:** 8383 Wilshire Blvd., Beverly Hills, CA 90211, (213)655-2634.

STERN, William H.——**B:** Apr. 13, 1930, NYC, *Exec. VP*, Sonnenblick-Goldman Corp.; **PRIM RE ACT:** Broker; **PROFL AFFIL & HONORS:** Chmn., Mort. Comm. N.Y.R.E. Bd. 1982, recipient of 'Most Ingenious Award' NYSREB 1978; **GRAD EDUC:** JD & LLM, 1952, Syracuse U. Coll. of Law & NYU School of Law; **EDUC HONORS:** Law Review; **MIL SERV:** USAF, Capt.; **HOME ADD:** 400 E. 56th St., New York, NY 10022, (212)486-0630; **BUS ADD:** 1251 Ave. of the Americas, New York, NY 10020, (212)541-4321.

STERNBERG, Cary B.——**B:** Jan 1, 1951, Williamsburg, VA, *Dir. of Resid. Sales*, Drucker and Falk, Realtors; **PRIM RE ACT:** Broker, Instructor; **OTHER RE ACT:** Brokerage Mgr.; **SERVICES:** Resid. Sales, Mktg., Dev., Conversions, Relocation; **REP CLIENTS:** Indiv., Bldr. and Corp. Clients; **PROFL AFFIL & HONORS:** NAR; RNMI; VA Assoc. of Realtors (Dir.) Newport News; Hampton Bd. of Realtors, VP-Dir., MLS Leadership Award, 1980; CRB; CRS; GRI; **EDUC:** BA, 1973, History, Univ. of VA; **OTHER ACT & HONORS:** Notary Public/State of VA/6yrs.; Exchange Club of Hampton Rds. (Immediate Past Pres.); **HOME ADD:** 75 Colombia Dr., Newport News, VA 23602, (804)874-2264; **BUS ADD:** 9286 Warwick Blvd., Newport News, VA 23607, (804)245-1541.

STERNBERG, Steven A.——**B:** Feb. 27, 1946, Brooklyn, NY, *Broker*, Merrill Lynch Realty/Barrows Co., Comm'l. Investment; **PRIM RE ACT:** Broker, Syndicator, Consultant, Appraiser, Owner/Investor; **OTHER RE ACT:** Condo. Conversions; **SERVICES:** Investment brokerage & consulting, representation of buyers and/or sellers, fee appraiser, condo. conversion studies/analysis; **REP CLIENTS:** Private investors, synd., instnl. and corp. investors; **PROFL AFFIL & HONORS:** Community Assoc. Inst., RNMI, GRI; **EDUC:** BPA, 1972, Photography, Brooks Inst. of Photography; **MIL SERV:** USN, PO 2; **OTHER ACT & HONORS:** Fair Rent Commnr.-Town of Rocky Hill/80-81, Lecturer and Author on RE Investments; **HOME ADD:** 302 Cedar Hollow Dr., Rocky Hill, CT 06067, (203)563-0898; **BUS ADD:** Hartford, CT 0610654 Elm St., (203)728-3000.

STERZER, Herbert——**B:** Aug. 25, 1918, NY, NY, *RE Appraiser and Consultant*; **PRIM RE ACT:** Consultant, Appraiser; **SERVICES:** RE consulting; **REP CLIENTS:** Attys., investors, corps., partnerships; **PREV EMPLOY:** Superv. Appraiser, Dept. of Savings and Loan, State of CA; **PROFL AFFIL & HONORS:** SREA (Sr. RE Analyst); ASA (Sr. Member, ASA; **EDUC:** BA, Bus. Psych.; **GRAD EDUC:** MA, 1980, Phil. & Lit., Intl. Coll.; **HOME ADD:** 818 N. Doheny Dr., Los Angeles, CA 90069, (213)271-1342; **BUS ADD:** 818 N. Doheny Dr., Los Angeles, CA 90069, (213)273-8300.

STEUBEN, Norton L.——**B:** Feb. 14, 1936, Milwaukee, WI, *Prof.*, Univ. of CO Law School of Counsel, Ireland, Stapleton & Pryor, PC; **PRIM RE ACT:** Attorney, Instructor; **PREV EMPLOY:** Hodgson, Russ, Andrews, Wood & Goodyear; **PROFL AFFIL & HONORS:** ABA; CO Bar Assn.; NY Bar Assn.; Boulder Cty. Bar Assn.; Amer. Assn. of Univ. Prof.; Sau Epsilon Rho, S.I. Goldberg Award; Order of the Coif, Barristers Soc.; **EDUC:** BA, 1958, Univ. of MI; **GRAD EDUC:** JD, 1961, Univ. of MI Law School; **EDUC HONORS:** Grad. with Distinction; **HOME ADD:** 845 8th St., Boulder, CO 80302, (303)447-1581; **BUS ADD:** Campus Box 401, Univ. of CO, Boulder, CO 80309, (303)492-7963.

STEVENS, Chester W.——**B:** May 14, 1925, Milwaukee, WI, *Pres.*, C. W. Stevens Co., Inc.; **PRIM RE ACT:** Broker, Property Manager; **SERVICES:** Prop. mgmt. and leasing project devel., mgmt. counseling for high risk office bldgs.; **REP CLIENTS:** Large devel. and indiv. investors in comml. prop.; **PREV EMPLOY:** V.P. First WI Natl. Bank, Prop. Mgmt. and Leasing, Stevens Carley Co., Inc., Pres. & C.E.O.; **PROFL AFFIL & HONORS:** BOMA, IREM, Bd. of Realtors, 1980 Mgr. of the Yr. Award, IREM Milwaukee Chap., CPM, RPA; **MIL SERV:** US Army, USAF, 1943 to 1946, SSgt.; **OTHER ACT & HONORS:** Bd. Mbr. Milwaukee Convention Ctr. and Vistors Bureau, Bd. Mbr. BOMI Institute; **HOME ADD:** 2505 Stonfield Ct., Waukesha, WI 53186, (414)544-4971; **BUS ADD:** 170 S. 2nd St., Milwaukee, WI 53202, (414)765-0604.

STEVENS, H.C.——**B:** Oct. 30, 1933, Sharkey Cty, MS, *Realtor*, H.C. Stevens, Realtor; **PRIM RE ACT:** Appraiser; **PREV EMPLOY:** Deer Creek Ins. Agency; **PROFL AFFIL & HONORS:** FLI, Nat. Soc. of Farm Mgrs. & Rural Appraisers, NARGA, NAREB; **EDUC:** BBA, 1955, Univ. MS; **HOME ADD:** Church St., Box 54, Anguilla, MS 38721, (601)873-4996; **BUS ADD:** P.O. Box 126, 105 East Ave. S., Hollandale, MS 38748, (601)827-2269.

STEVENS, Marshall H.——B: Dec. 15, 1933, VA, *Pres. & Chief Exec. Officer*, Hamilton Devel. Corp.; **PRIM RE ACT:** Engineer, Developer, Builder, Owner/Investor; **SERVICES:** RE devel. and construction; **REP CLIENTS:** Fin. insts.; **PREV EMPLOY:** Webb & Knapp; Hammerson Prop. Corp.; James Landauer Associates; **PROFL AFFIL & HONORS:** ULI; **EDUC:** 1956, Indus. Admin., Yale Univ.; **MIL SERV:** U.S. Army, Lt.; **OTHER ACT & HONORS:** Yale Club; **HOME ADD:** 16 Comstock Trail, Brookfield Ctr., CT 06805, (203)775-1918; **BUS ADD:** 57 North St., Danbury, CT 06810, (203)797-8811.

STEVENS, Norton——*Pres.*, Norlin Industries; **PRIM RE ACT:** Property Manager; **BUS ADD:** 44 So. Broadway, White Plains, NY 10601, (914)683-0001.*

STEVENS, Norton——B: June 1, 1933, Philadelphia, PA, *Branch Mgr.*, Lomas & Nettleton; **PRIM RE ACT:** Owner/Investor; **SERVICES:** FHA, VA CONV. MORT.; **MIL SERV:** US Army, Sgt.; **OTHER ACT & HONORS:** Committee Man 1979-1981; **HOME ADD:** 301 Avon St., Philadelphia, PA 19116, (215)698-2961; **BUS ADD:** 21 N.Y. Rd., Willow Grove, PA 19090, (215)657-1660.

STEVENS, Stanley M.——B: Dec. 21, 1948, Keokuk, IA, *Part.*, Rudnick & Wolfe; **PRIM RE ACT:** Attorney; **REP CLIENTS:** Continental IL Nat. B&T Co. of Chicago; **PROFL AFFIL & HONORS:** ABA, Chicago Bar Assn., IL Bar Assn., Chicago Council of Lawyers; **EDUC:** BA, 1970, Pol. Sci., Univ. of MO; **GRAD EDUC:** JD, 1973, Univ. of Chicago; **EDUC HONORS:** Phi Beta Kappa, With Honors; **HOME ADD:** 50 E. Bellevue Pl., Chicago, IL 60611, (312)664-3425; **BUS ADD:** 30 N. LaSalle St., Chicago, IL 60602, (312)368-4039.

STEVENS, Thomas E.——B: Feb. 10, 1938, Columbus, NE, *RE Appraiser*, Thomas E. Stevens and Associates; **PRIM RE ACT:** Broker, Consultant, Appraiser; **SERVICES:** appraisal of RE - resid., comml., indus. & special purpose props.; **REP CLIENTS:** lending instns., ins. cos., mfgs., federal, state and cty. agencies, tax and estate purposes. Qualified Dir. Fee & Cert. Agency Program Appraiser for Housing & Urban Devel.; **PROFL AFFIL & HONORS:** AIREA; Soc. NE RE Assn.; Omaha RE Bd. and Rho Epsilon Nat. RE Frat., MAI, SRPA; **EDUC:** BBA, 1964, RE, Univ. of NE at Omaha; **HOME ADD:** 6803 N. 60th St., Omaha, NE 68152, (402)571-6362; **BUS ADD:** 7701 Pacific St., Suite 111, Omaha, NE 68114, (402)393-9774.

STEVENS, Timothy N.——B: July 8, 1941, Fitchburg, MA, *VP & Mgr.*, Union Bank, Mort. Investment Div.; **PRIM RE ACT:** Broker, Appraiser, Lender, Banker; **SERVICES:** RE investment banking servs., resid. lending., mort. banking & brokerage; **REP CLIENTS:** Instnt. lenders & investors, devel. pvt. investors; **PREV EMPLOY:** MA Mutual LIfe Ins. Co., Metropolitan Life Ins. Co.; **PROFL AFFIL & HONORS:** Mort. Bankers Assn. of Amer., CA Mort. Bankers Assn., LA World Affairs Council, Licensed CA RE Broker, Intnl. Council of Shopping Ctr.; **EDUC:** BS, 1966, Mktg. & Fin., Wharton Sch., Univ. of PA; **GRAD EDUC:** MBA, 1971, Fin., Grad. Sch., Univ. of MA; **MIL SERV:** US Army, 1959-62, Spec. 5th, Distinguished Service; **OTHER ACT & HONORS:** LA Athletic Club, Credentialed RE Instr. for CA Coll. System; **HOME ADD:** 15461 Albright St., Pacific Palisades, CA 90272, (213)459-2669; **BUS ADD:** 760 S. Hill St., Los Angeles, CA 90014, (213)687-6322.

STEVENS, Walter A.——B: March 27, 1926, Brunswick, GA, *Pres.*, C.B. Snyder Realty, Inc.; **PRIM RE ACT:** Broker; **SERVICES:** Indus., and comml. R.E. sales and leasing; **REP CLIENTS:** Small and large bus.; **EDUC:** AS, 1968, Indus. mgmt., Fairleigh Dickinson Univ.; **MIL SERV:** USAF, Sgt.; **HOME ADD:** 521 Piermont Ave., Apt. 401, River Vale, NJ 07675, (201)666-5441; **BUS ADD:** Paramus, NJ 0765215 Prospect St., (201)368-1200.

STEVENS, William F.——B: Nov. 3, 1937, Detroit, MI, *Sales Assoc.*, Fuller and Co.; **PRIM RE ACT:** Broker; **SERVICES:** Comml., indus., and investment RE sales and leasing; **PREV EMPLOY:** Doug Morrison and Co., Denver, 1971-1976; Comml. RE sales and leasing; **PROFL AFFIL & HONORS:** Denver Bd. of Realtors, Indus. for Jefferson Cty., CO Nat. Assn. of Realtor, RNMI, Denver Bd. of Realtor Million Dollar Roundtable; **MIL SERV:** USAR, Pvt.; **OTHER ACT & HONORS:** Lankwood, CO C of C; **HOME ADD:** 290 S. Oneida, Denver, CO 80024, (303)756-5613; **BUS ADD:** One Park Central, 1515 Arapahoe, Denver, CO 80202, (303)292-3700.

STEVENS, Winfred A.——B: Aug. 23, 1943, Bangor, ME, *RE Partner*, Rudman & Winchell; **PRIM RE ACT:** Attorney, Insuror; **SERVICES:** All servs. regarding RE law, including title; **REP CLIENTS:** Lending inst., RE brokers, investors and devel.; **PROFL AFFIL & HONORS:** ABA, FL Bar Assn., ME Bar Assn., Bangor Bd. of Realtors; **EDUC:** BA, 1965, Liberal Arts, Univ. of ME; **GRAD EDUC:** JD, 1968, Univ. of FL, Coll. of Law; **MIL SERV:** US Army, Capt.; **OTHER ACT & HONORS:** Bd. of Dir., YMCA (Bangor), RE Instr., Pres., Penobscot Title Co.; **HOME ADD:** 251 Nowell Rd., Bangor, ME 04401, (207)942-5894; **BUS ADD:** 84 Harlow St., Bangor, ME 04401, (207)947-4501.

STEVENSON, Allen W.——B: Oct. 28, 1952, Syracuse, NY, *Dir. of Taxation & Controller*, Drever McIntosh & Co.; **PRIM RE ACT:** Consultant, Developer, Owner/Investor, Syndicator; **SERVICES:** Synd. & mgmt. of comml. & Resid. property; **REP CLIENTS:** Indiv. investors in resid. & comml. RE projects; **PREV EMPLOY:** Arthur Andersen & Co. '76-80; **PROFL AFFIL & HONORS:** CPA, CA CPA Society, AICPA; **EDUC:** BA, 1973, Econ., SUNY, Stony Brook; **GRAD EDUC:** MBA, 1976, Fin./Acctg., UC Berkeley School of Bus.; **EDUC HONORS:** UC Honor Soc.; **HOME ADD:** 829 Wawona Ave., Piedmont, CA 94610; **BUS ADD:** 110 Sutter St. Suite 905, San Francisco, CA 94104, (415)433-1773.

STEVENSON, Eric——B: June 27, 1926, New York, NY, *Sr. VP*, Mortgage Bankers Association of America, Income Property Dept.; **OTHER RE ACT:** Profl. assn. admin.; Income prop./comml. & industrial; **REP CLIENTS:** Mortgage bankers; **PREV EMPLOY:** Pres., Stevenson & Kittredge, consultant for HUD, Natl. S&L League, Ford Foundation, ABA; **PROFL AFFIL & HONORS:** Member DC & CT Bar, Administrator of 2 million dollar investment program, Life Insurance (1969-1973), Licensed RE Broker & Atty.; **EDUC:** BA, 1947, Intl. Relations, Yale Univ.; **GRAD EDUC:** LLB, 1950, Yale Univ. Law School; **MIL SERV:** USN, Lt.; **OTHER ACT & HONORS:** Gen. Council, Peace Corps; **HOME ADD:** 2713 34th Pl., Washington, DC 20007, (202)337-4813; **BUS ADD:** 1125 15th St. NW, Washington, DC 20005, (202)861-6586.

STEVENSON, Horace E.——B: Apr. 14, 1935, Huntsville, TX, *Design & Planning Consultant*, Horrace E. Stevenson & Assoc.; **OTHER RE ACT:** Architectural Consultant; **SERVICES:** Design & planning counseling, plans, specifications & supervision; **REP CLIENTS:** Churches, instl., resid.; **PREV EMPLOY:** John S. Chase FAIA, Architect, 1957-68; **EDUC:** BS, 1957, Arch., Tuskegee Inst., Tuskegee, AL; **MIL SERV:** US Army, 1st Lt., Artillery & Missile School Diploma; **OTHER ACT & HONORS:** Notary Public, State of TX; **BUS ADD:** 8705 Autumn Lane, Houston, TX 77016, (713)631-1660.

STEVENSON, Howard H.——B: June 27, 1941, Salt Lake City, UT, *Professor*, Harvard Grad. School of Bus.; **PRIM RE ACT:** Consultant, Owner/Investor; **REP CLIENTS:** Realty Income Trust, CT Gen., RE Mortgage Investors; **PREV EMPLOY:** VP, Preco Corp.; VP, Simmons Assocs. Investment Bankers; **PROFL AFFIL & HONORS:** ULI; Tr. CT Gen. RE & Mort. Investors, Tr. Realty Income Trust; Dir. Eastern Realty Investment Co.; Dir. HCR Inc.; Dir. Wolfe Indus. Inc.; The Land Conservancy Amer. Forestry Soc.; **EDUC:** BS, 1963, Mathematics, Stanford Univ.; **GRAD EDUC:** MBA, DBA, 1965, 1969, Bus. Admin., Harvard Univ.; **EDUC HONORS:** Distinction, High Distinction, George F. Baker Scholar; **OTHER ACT & HONORS:** Dir. Suffield Land Conservancy; Dir., Timber Owners of New England; **HOME TEL:** (203)668-0877; **BUS ADD:** Soldiers Field Station, Boston, MA 02163, (617)495-6000.

STEVENSON, John D.——B: Mar. 26, 1929, Cobalt, Ont., Can, *Partner*, Smith, Lyons, Torrance, Stevenson & Mayer; **PRIM RE ACT:** Attorney; **SERVICES:** Legal documents for devel. and synd. of comml. props.; **REP CLIENTS:** Lenders and instn. clients in comml props.; **PROFL AFFIL & HONORS:** Member, Can. Bar Assn., Can. Tax Found.; **EDUC:** BA, 1950, Econ., Univ. of Toronto; **GRAD EDUC:** LLB, 1953, Univ. of Toronto; **OTHER ACT & HONORS:** Gov., Upper Can. Coll.; **HOME ADD:** 166 Forest Hill Rd., Toronto, Ont., Can., (416)485-3040; **BUS ADD:** PO Box 420, 2 First Canadian Place, Toronto, M5X 1J3, Ont., Canada, (416)369-7200.

STEVENSON, William G.——B: Mar. 11, 1933, Toronto, Can., *Pres.*, William G. Stevenson Projects Ltd.; **PRIM RE ACT:** Developer, Builder, Property Manager; **PREV EMPLOY:** Law Dept. Esso Canada; **PROFL AFFIL & HONORS:** ULI; **EDUC:** BA, 1955, Econ., Univ. of Toronto; **GRAD EDUC:** 1959, Osgoode Hall Law School; **HOME ADD:** 35 Rykert Cr., Toronto, Can., (416)425-3781; **BUS ADD:** 44 St. Clair Ave. E, Toronto, M4T 1M9, Can., (416)962-7921.

STEVENSON, William W.——B: Sept. 21, 1927, Pittsburgh, PA, *Pres.*, Eglington Investment Co.; **PRIM RE ACT:** Attorney, Banker, Developer, Owner/Investor, Property Manager; **SERVICES:** For own account or trusts and land trusts managed; **PREV EMPLOY:** Acting Chmn., Econ. Warfare Comm., US Mission to S. Vietnam; **EDUC:** AB, 1950, Hist., Princeton Univ.; **GRAD EDUC:** LLB, 1959, VA Law School; **EDUC HONORS:** Cum Laude; **MIL SERV:** Psywar, Pvt.; **OTHER ACT & HONORS:** Dir. of two homeowners assns., Trustee of three land trusts, Dir. of two civic orgs., formerly on SBA Advisory Bd. and Indus. Devel. Commn.; Chmn., First VA Bank Central; **HOME ADD:** 406 Wellington Dr., Charlottesville, VA 22901, (804)293-6731; **BUS ADD:** 406 Wellington Dr., Charlottesville, VA 22901, (804)293-6731.

STEWARD, James A.——B: Sep. 8, 1917, San Franscisco, CA, *Sr. VP*, The Travelers Ins. Co., R.E. Invest.; **PRIM RE ACT:** Lender, Insuror; **EDUC:** AB, 1939, Econ., Amherst Coll.; **MIL SERV:** USN, Lt.jg.; **HOME ADD:** 9 Parish Rd., Farmington, CT 06032, (203)677-9236; **BUS ADD:** 1 Tower Sq., Hartford,, CT 06115, (203)277-4888.

STEWARD, Wendell——*Pres.*, Texas International Co.; **PRIM RE ACT:** Property Manager; **BUS ADD:** Greenbriar Mgmt. Corp., 11101 Greenbriar Chase, Oklahoma City, OK 73170, (405)947-8661.*

STEWART, Barbara C.——B: Nov. 7, 1932, Livingston Cty., IL, *Realtor*, William Frakes Agency; **PRIM RE ACT:** Consultant, Appraiser, Property Manager; **SERVICES:** RE sales serv., appraising & prop. mgmt.; **REP CLIENTS:** Gen. public in purchase or sale of resid. or invest. props.; **PREV EMPLOY:** Travel Agent, Prop. Mgmt.; **PROFL AFFIL & HONORS:** Amer. Bus. Women's Assoc., Pilot Internatl., KS Assoc. of Realtors, Manhattan Bd. of Realtors; **EDUC:** Private Sec. Sch. Degree, 1952, Private Sec. Work, Katharine Gibbs Secretarial School, Chicago, IL; **EDUC HONORS:** Excellent Rating; **OTHER ACT & HONORS:** Girl Scouts, Boy Scouts, Kidney Found., Heart Fund; **HOME ADD:** 2062 College Hts. Rd., Manhattan, KS 66502, (913)539-2663; **BUS ADD:** 1619 Poyntz Ave., Manhattan, KS 66502, (913)539-0507.

STEWART, D. Wayne——B: Sept. 13, 1946, Franklin, KY, *Atty.*, Solo Practice; **PRIM RE ACT:** Attorney, Owner/Investor; **SERVICES:** RE counsel and litigation, lien law; **REP CLIENTS:** Net Realty Holding Co.; ReMax-Aurora Mall; Northstar Fire Protection Co.; **PROFL AFFIL & HONORS:** ABA; CO and Denver Bar Assns., Real Estate Sect.; CO Trial Lawyers Assn.; **EDUC:** BA, 1971, French Lit., Languages, Brigham Young Univ.; **GRAD EDUC:** JD, 1976, RE Planning, Brigham Young Univ., J. Reaben Clark School of Law; **EDUC HONORS:** Cum Laude, Pi Delta Phi and Phi Kappa Phi; **OTHER ACT & HONORS:** Chmn., J. Reuben Clark Law Soc. - CO; **HOME ADD:** 5440 S. Havana Ct., Englewood, CO 80111, (303)771-4849; **BUS ADD:** 5440 S. Havana Ct., Englewood, CO 80111, (303)779-0086.

STEWART, David——*VP & Gen. Mgr.*, Steward & Stevenson Services, Inc.; **PRIM RE ACT:** Property Manager; **BUS ADD:** PO Box 1637, Houston, TX 77001, (713)225-5341.*

STEWART, James W.——B: Mar. 10, 1934, Dallas, TX, *Dir. of Servicing*, Gulfco Capital Mgmt., Inc., Dallas Office; **PRIM RE ACT:** Broker, Consultant, Appraiser, Lender; **SERVICES:** Sale & manage & admin. real estate for three ins. co's.; **REP CLIENTS:** Gulf United Corp., Republic Nat. Life Ins. Co., or any instit. investor in comml. prop.; **PREV EMPLOY:** Mortg. Loan Officer for Republic Nat. Life Ins. Co., 1973-1981; **PROFL AFFIL & HONORS:** Assoc. Member., Soc. of RE Appraisers; **EDUC:** BS, 1959, Bus./Econ., E TX State Univ.; **MIL SERV:** U.S. Army, Sgt., Nat. Defense, Good Conduct, Parachute Wings, 1953-1956; **OTHER ACT & HONORS:** NRA; BASS; **HOME ADD:** 1608 University Dr., Richardson, TX 75081, (214)238-0262; **BUS ADD:** Suite 412, Valley View Bank Bldg., POB 401249, Dallas, TX 75240, (214)233-2334.

STEWART, Michael Jay——B: July 3, 1947, Muncie, IN, *Dir. of Leasing*, Johnstown Props.; **PRIM RE ACT:** Broker, Attorney; **SERVICES:** Feasibility analysis, asset mgmt., comml. leasing; **REP CLIENTS:** indiv., synds, public trusts; **PREV EMPLOY:** VP Knowlton Realty Ltd., Newport Bch., CA; **PROFL AFFIL & HONORS:** CA, Orange Cty. & Amer. Bar Assns.; RE Soc., Orange Cty. & ABA, Licensed RE Broker in CA; **EDUC:** BA, 1971, Mktg., CA State Univ., Fullerton, CA; **GRAD EDUC:** JD, 1976, Real Prop., CA State Univ., Fullerton, CA; **HOME ADD:** 2335 Littleton Cir., Costa Mesa, CA 92626, (714)546-1716; **BUS ADD:** 1101 Dove St., Suite 120, Newport Beach, CA 92660, (714)752-0150.

STEWART, Susan Hastings——B: Aug. 24, 1945, Niagara Falls, NY, *VP*; **PRIM RE ACT:** Broker; **SERVICES:** Counseling, brokerage, financing; **PREV EMPLOY:** Comml. Underwriting - Ins.; **PROFL AFFIL & HONORS:** RNMI, ICSC, CCIM; **EDUC:** BS, 1978, Finance, Econ., Bus. Admin., FL State Coll.; **OTHER ACT & HONORS:** State V. Chmn., FL Gop '74-79; **HOME ADD:** 1462 Granville, Winter Park, FL 32789, (305)628-3914; **BUS ADD:** Suite 1401 SNA Tower, Orlando, FL 32801, (305)422-4466.

STEWART, W. Douglas——B: April 8, 1938, Paterson, NJ, *Dir., Div. of Housing*, City of Paterson, NJ, Div. of Housing; **PRIM RE ACT:** Regulator; **SERVICES:** Full municipal housing servs.; **PREV EMPLOY:** Banker; **PROFL AFFIL & HONORS:** Nat. Assn. of Housing & Redevel. Officials; Amer. Planning Assn.; **EDUC:** BS, 1970, Bus. Admin., Fairleigh Dickinson Univ.; **MIL SERV:** US Army; Spec. 4; **OTHER ACT & HONORS:** Rotary; NAACP; **HOME ADD:** 84 East 39th St., Paterson, NJ 07514, (201)345-3593; **BUS ADD:** 133 Ellison St., Paterson, NJ 07505, (201)881-3671.

STIEBEL, Michael S.——B: Mar. 22, 1949, NY, *Asst. Counsel*, CBT Corporation, The Connecticut Bank and Trust Co.; **PRIM RE ACT:** Attorney; **SERVICES:** Legal presentation; **REP CLIENTS:** The CT Bank and Trust Co., CBT Realty Corp., CBT Corp.; **PREV EMPLOY:** Schatz & Schatz Ribicoff & Kotkin, Hartford, CT; **PROFL AFFIL & HONORS:** Exec. Comm. Real Prop. Sect. of CT Bar Assn., Wesfalla Real Prop. Sect., ABA, Hartford, Cty. Bar; **EDUC:** BA, 1971, Hist., Econ., VA Commonwealth Univ., St. Mary's Univ. School of Law; **GRAD EDUC:** JD, 1975, Law, Coll. of William and Mary; **EDUC HONORS:** Law Journal; **OTHER ACT & HONORS:** VChrmn. Rocky Hill Housing Authority; **HOME ADD:** 75 Ridgewood Dr., Rocky Hill, CT 06067, (203)563-4135; **BUS ADD:** 1 Constitution Plaza, Hartford, CT 06115, (203)244-4608.

STIEMSMA, Steven J.——B: Mar. 9, 1955, Fond du lac, WI, *Pres.*, Steven J. Stiemsma, Arch. Design; **PRIM RE ACT:** Architect, Builder; **SERVICES:** Arch. Design/consultation; **REP CLIENTS:** Select indiv. clients & housing tract devels.; **PREV EMPLOY:** Red Moltz & Assoc., Irvine, CA; **HOME ADD:** 1030 Silent Cir., Corona, CA 91720, (714)737-1577; **BUS ADD:** 1030 Silent Cir., Corona, CA 91720, (714)737-4020.

STIFF, Thomas——*Executive Director*, National Association of Housing Cooperatives; **OTHER RE ACT:** Profl. Assn. Admin.; **BUS ADD:** 1012 14th St. NW, Suite 804, Washington, DC 20005, (202)628-6242.*

STILB, Michael A.——B: July 18, 1948, Princeton, NJ, *VP*, Haven Corp., Devel.; **PRIM RE ACT:** Developer, Builder; **SERVICES:** Acquisition, mktg., bldg., packaging; **REP CLIENTS:** Limited and gen. partnerships; **PREV EMPLOY:** Tekton Corp.; **PROFL AFFIL & HONORS:** ICSC; **EDUC:** BS, 1966-1972, Land Planning/Landscape Arch., Univ. of AZ; **OTHER ACT & HONORS:** The M.O. Oyster Club; Los Charros del Desierto, Trunk 'n Tusk; Ducks Unlimited; Boy Scouts of Amer.; **HOME ADD:** 3750 N. Ctry. Club, 8, Tucson, AZ 85716, (602)325-3831; **BUS ADD:** 231 W. Esperanza Blvd., (PO Box 649), Green Valley, AZ 85614, (602)791-2866.

STILES, William R.——B: Jan. 18, 1946, Stewartville, MN, *Atty.*, Smith, Schneider & Stiles, P.C.; **PRIM RE ACT:** Attorney; **SERVICES:** RE fin., synd., condo. & co-op conversions; **REP CLIENTS:** Lenders and RE devels. and owners; **PROFL AFFIL & HONORS:** Member of Real Prop., Probate & Trust Div. of ABA, Published Article on RE Synd., 23 Drake Law Review 483 (1974); **EDUC:** BA, 1969, Poli. Sci., Drake Univ., Des Moines, IA; **GRAD EDUC:** JD, 1973, Law, Drake Univ., Des Moines, IA; **EDUC HONORS:** Order of Coif, Order of Barristers, Editor-in-Chief, Drake Law Review, Who's Who in Amer. Coll. & Univs.; **OTHER ACT & HONORS:** Member, Parks & Recreation Dept., Clive, IA 1975-1980; **HOME ADD:** 3812 Greenbranch Dr., W. Des Moines, IA 50265, (515)225-3499; **BUS ADD:** 4717 Grand Ave., Des Moines, IA 50312, (515)274-2345.

STILLERMAN, L. M. (Larry)——B: Dec. 24, 1924, Indianapolis, IN, *Pres.*, Stillerman Jones & Lobaugh, Inc.; **PRIM RE ACT:** Consultant, Instructor, Property Manager, Real Estate Publisher; **OTHER RE ACT:** Leasing Representative; **SERVICES:** Mktg./leasing consultation; leasing/mgmt. services; **REP CLIENTS:** Shopping center devels./mgrs.; retailers; **PREV EMPLOY:** Melvin Simon & Assoc., 1966-78; Stillerman Group, marketing/sales, 1956-65; RE Editor, The Indianapolis Times, 1948-55; **PROFL AFFIL & HONORS:** ICSC, Sigma Delta Chi, Pi Sigma Alpha; **EDUC:** BA, 1948, Govt./Pre-Law, Indiana Univ.; **MIL SERV:** US Army Air Corps, 8th Air Force, T/Sgt., American, European Theatre Battle Ribbons; Air Medal w/Clusters; Unit Congressional Citation; **OTHER ACT & HONORS:** Lecturer, Seminar Leader, ICSC; Nat. Assn. of Merchants Assn, NACO, Officer and Director of Jones Report, Inc.; Carlson Report, Inc.; Budge Type; Centermation Systems, Inc. RE; **HOME ADD:** 3039 Bush Pkwy., Carmel, IN 46032, (317)844-4125; **BUS ADD:** 50 E. 91st St., (Suite 102), P O Box 40004, Indianapolis, IN 46240, (317)844-4960.

STILLMAN, Abbott——B: Mar 14, 1947, New York, NY, *Partner/Principal*, The Stillman Group; **PRIM RE ACT:** Developer, Builder, Owner/Investor, Property Manager; **SERVICES:** RE devel., const. mgmt. & investment; **PREV EMPLOY:** Sea Pines Co., Hilton

Head, SC, Asst. to Pres.; Hare, Brewer and Kelley, Palo Alto, CA, Vice Pres.; **EDUC:** BA, 1969, Poli./Literature, Union Coll.; **GRAD EDUC:** MCP, 1973, Design & City Planning, MIT; **EDUC HONORS:** Phi Beta Kappa, Mellon Fellow; **BUS ADD:** 440 East 62nd St., New York, NY 10021, (212)832-8815.

STIMAC, Steven P.——**B:** Dec. 12, 1954, Reno, NV, *Right-of-Way Agent II (Staff Appraiser)*, NV Dept. of Trans., Right-of-Way; **PRIM RE ACT:** Broker, Consultant, Appraiser, Owner/Investor; **SERVICES:** RE appraiser, brokerage, RE consultation; **REP CLIENTS:** Jim Skaggs RE, NV Dept. of Trans., Norma Fink Realty, var. appraisal firms, John Dermondy Inc.; **PROFL AFFIL & HONORS:** Soc. of RE Appraisers, current 2nd VP; **EDUC:** Managerial Sci., Univ. of NV, Reno; **OTHER ACT & HONORS:** Soc. of RE Appraisers; **HOME ADD:** 1816 N. Division St., Carson City, NV 89701, (702)883-1949; **BUS ADD:** Box 1380, Carson, NV 89701, (702)885-5530.

STINCHFIELD, John Edward——**B:** July 31, 1947, Alameda, CA, *Corporate Counsel*, Donohoe Construction Co., Inc.; **PRIM RE ACT:** Attorney; **REP CLIENTS:** Donohoe Construction Co., Inc., John F. Donohoe & Sons, Realtors, Complete Bldg. Services, Inc., Taylor Tool Rental Co., Inc., Beaver Mill & Supply Co., Inc., Gen. Contractor/Investment Builder/Realtor/Prop. Mgmt.; Mechanical and Janitorial Services; **PREV EMPLOY:** Bueau of Competition, US Fed. Trade Comm. 3/77-3/79; Div. of Corp. Fin., US Securities & Exchange Comm. 3/74-3/77; **PROFL AFFIL & HONORS:** State Bar of CA, Dist. of Columbia Bar, ABA; **EDUC:** BA, 1969, Econ./Govt., Wesleyan Univ., Middletown, CT; **GRAD EDUC:** JD, 1973, Law, Univ. of CA, Hastings Coll. of the Law; **HOME ADD:** 3608 Ordway St. NW, Washington, DC 20016; **BUS ADD:** 2101 WI Ave., NW, Washington, DC 20007, (202)333-0880.

STOCKHAM, Ronald L., Esquire——**B:** Apr. 14, 1942, Trenton, NJ, *Pres. and Sr. Lawyer*, Ronald L. Stockham, P.C.; **PRIM RE ACT:** Attorney; **OTHER RE ACT:** Title Ins., All legal servs. re the sale and/or purchase of RE; Approved Atty. of Commonwealth Land Title Ins. Co.; **REP CLIENTS:** NJ Nat. Bank; The Trenton Saving Fund Soc.; Delaware Valley Abstract Co.; 1st Nat State Bank of Central Jersey; Princeton B&T Co.; **PREV EMPLOY:** Asst. District Atty., Bucks Cty., PA; **PROFL AFFIL & HONORS:** Amer. PA, and Bucks Cty. Bar Assns., PA Bar Assn., Corp. Law Comm. & Membership Comm., Life Member, Phi Alpha Delta Legal Frat., Member, Bucks Cty. Estate Planning Council, Panel of Arbitrators, Amer. Arbitration Assn., Former Tr. & Former Solicitor, Morrisville Free Library Assn.; **EDUC:** BA, 1964, Bio. & Liberal Arts, Univ. of PA, Philadelphia, PA; **GRAD EDUC:** JD, 1968, Law, Temple Univ. School of Law, Philadelphia, PA; **EDUC HONORS:** Varsity Boat Club (Crew); **OTHER ACT & HONORS:** Member & Past Pres., Morrisville Rotary Club; former Comm. Chmn., Bucks Cty. Friends of Scouting; Past Bd. Member & Past VP, The Pennsbury Soc.; **HOME ADD:** 651 N. Pennsylvania Ave., Morrisville, PA 19067; **BUS ADD:** 651 N. Pennsylvania Ave., Morrisville, PA 19067, (215)736-0031.

STOCKING, Von K.——**B:** Apr. 1, 1946, Boise, ID, *VP*, Columbia Investment Group/Osmond R.E. & Development of S.L.; **PRIM RE ACT:** Broker, Consultant, Developer, Owner/Investor, Property Manager, Syndicator; **OTHER RE ACT:** Writes RE analysis, fin. and leasing programs, Tax Planning; **SERVICES:** For investors, consultants, banks on Hewlett Packard 97; **REP CLIENTS:** UT Bank corporation, Ut Industrial Development Co.; **PREV EMPLOY:** Key 980 Assoc.; Emporium Management (Co-Developer); The Southwestern Co.; **PROFL AFFIL & HONORS:** RNMI; ICSC; **EDUC:** BSEE, 1973, EE, Utah State Univ.; **GRAD EDUC:** 1 year, Fin., RE, Bus. Mgmt., UT State Univ.; **EDUC HONORS:** Sigma Phi Eta, I.K. (Service Frat.) Nat. VP; **OTHER ACT & HONORS:** Exchange Club; Comstock Trading Co.; LDS Church; Ruff Community Forum Chmn.; **HOME ADD:** 415 N. 225 E., North Salt Lake, UT 84054; **BUS ADD:** 415 Cloverdale Rd., N. Salt Lake, UT 84054, (801)295-5445.

STOCKWELL, Paul W.——**B:** June 19, 1954, Alexandria, VA, *Devel. Officer*, CF Southern Region, Inc. (a Subs. of Cadillac Fairview), Houston Office; **PRIM RE ACT:** Developer, Owner/Investor; **SERVICES:** Devel./ownership of all types of RE; **PREV EMPLOY:** Coldwell Banker Comml. Brokerage Co.; **PROFL AFFIL & HONORS:** Intl. Council of Shopping Ctrs.; **EDUC:** BArch., 1976, Arch., Univ. of CA - Berkeley; **GRAD EDUC:** MBA, 1979, RE/Fin., Univ. of CA - Berkeley; **EDUC HONORS:** Received Scholarship from Acad. of Model Aeronautics 1973, Received Scholarship from CA Assn. of Realtors 1978; **OTHER ACT & HONORS:** Kappa Sigma Frat.; **HOME ADD:** 7950 N. Stadium Ave., #234, Houston, TX 77030, (713)790-9455; **BUS ADD:** 1 Houston Ctr., Suite 1400, Houston, TX 77010, (713)654-4444.

STOEVER, M.D.——*Sales Mgr.*, John Crosland Co.; **PRIM RE ACT:** Developer; **BUS ADD:** PO Box 11231, Dept MD, Charlotte, NC 28220, (704)523-8111.*

STOKER, James William——**B:** Dec. 27, 1934, Council Bluffs, IA, *Mgr. of RE*, MN Mining and Mfg. Co.; **PRIM RE ACT:** Developer, Property Manager, Engineer, Owner/Investor; **OTHER RE ACT:** Mgr. of corp. indus. RE; **PREV EMPLOY:** Ellerbe Arch. & Engrs., St. Paul, MN; **PROFL AFFIL & HONORS:** Indus. Devel. Research Council, MN Indus. Devel. Assn.; **EDUC:** BCE, 1958, IA State Univ., Ames, IA; **MIL SERV:** USCG; 1953-1955; **HOME ADD:** 11640 Lockridge Ave. S., Hastings, MN 55033, (612)437-1055; **BUS ADD:** PO Box 33331, Bldg. 42-8W, St. Paul, MN 55133, (612)778-4752.

STOKES, James F.——**B:** Dec. 23, 1932, Chicago, IL, *Exec. VP*, Nicolson, Porter & List, Inc.; **PRIM RE ACT:** Broker, Consultant, Appraiser, Developer, Owner/Investor, Property Manager; **SERVICES:** Indus. RE only; **REP CLIENTS:** Mfrg. and warehousing cos., insurance cos. and pension fund investments; **PROFL AFFIL & HONORS:** Past Pres. Chgo. Chap. & Nat. Bd. Member of SIR, Chicago RE Bd., Lambda Alpha Land Econs. Frat., NAR, OMEGA, TAU, RAO AWARD; **EDUC:** BS, 1955, Eng./Phil., Loyola Univ.; **GRAD EDUC:** MS, 1957, Bus. - Law, Northwestern Univ.; **OTHER ACT & HONORS:** Zoning Bd. of Appeals 1981-84; **HOME ADD:** 1116 Valley Rd., Lake Forest, IL 60045, (312)234-5665; **BUS ADD:** 125 S. Wacker Dr., Rm. 1850, Chicago, IL 60606, (312)782-7755.

STOKES, Randall L.——**B:** July 29, 1950, Rome, GA, *Pres.*, Randall Stokes & Assoc., Inc.; **PRIM RE ACT:** Consultant, Appraiser; **SERVICES:** RE appraisal & consultation; **REP CLIENTS:** Gov. agencies, mort. lenders, attys. trust depts., devels.; **PROFL AFFIL & HONORS:** MAI designation (AIREA) SRPA designation (SREA), Atlanta Bd. of Realtors, Atlanta MBA; **EDUC:** BBA, 1972, RE & Urban Dev., Univ. of GA; **HOME ADD:** 5896 Western Hills Dr., Norcross, GA, (404)447-9751; **BUS ADD:** 3783 Presidential Dr., Suite 11, Atlanta, GA 30340, (404)458-0361.

STOKKE, Diane R.——**B:** Jan. 29, 1951, Kansas City MO, *Atty.*, Preston, Thorgrimson, Ellis & Holman, Seattle Office; **PRIM RE ACT:** Attorney; **SERVICES:** Legal; **REP CLIENTS:** Instnl. and other lenders in comml. prop.; **PROFL AFFIL & HONORS:** WA State, Seattle King Cty. Bar Assns., ABA, Member Real Prop. Sects.; **EDUC:** BA, 1972, Poli. Sci., Gonzaga Univ.; **GRAD EDUC:** JD, 1976, Univ. of WA; **EDUC HONORS:** Magna Cum Laude, Notes editor, WA Law Review 1975-76; High Honors, Order of the Coif; **HOME ADD:** 2342 N. 50th, Seattle, WA 98116, (206)633-5622; **BUS ADD:** 2000 IBM Bldg., Seattle, WA 98101, (206)623-7580.

STOKLOSA, Raymond J.——**B:** Aug. 27, 1942, Chicago, IL, *Owner*, Stoklosa & Assoc.; **PRIM RE ACT:** Owner/Investor; **OTHER RE ACT:** Buyer's Broker; **EDUC:** 1966, WI State Univ. (Whitewater); **HOME ADD:** 1754 Terrace Dr., Belmont, CA 94002, (415)591-6807; **BUS ADD:** 1700 S. El Camino Real, San Mateo, CA 94403, (415)572-1515.

STOLL, Edwin L.——**B:** May 16, 1915, Mt. Pulaski, IL, *Dir. of Corp. Affairs*, Nat. Corp. for Housing Partnerships; **PRIM RE ACT:** Developer, Builder, Property Manager, Syndicator; **SERVICES:** As largest priv. producer of low & moderate income housing in nation, co. provides equity capital, joint venture funds, and expertise to its partners; **REP CLIENTS:** Builders, devel., non-profit, and community groups with whom NCHP goes into partnership for the construction of housing, both multifamily rental and single-family sales; **PREV EMPLOY:** VP for Public Affairs, Dir. of Washington Office, and Dir. of Public Relations while with Nat. Assn. of RE Bds. for 26 yrs., 1946-1972; Reporter, Chicago Tribune, 1937-41; **PROFL AFFIL & HONORS:** Past Pres., Nat. Capital Chap., Public Relations Soc. of Amer.; **EDUC:** BS, 1937, Journalism, IL; **EDUC HONORS:** Kappa Tau Alpha (journalism scholarship honorary), MaWanDa and Sachem (senior and junior extracurricular honoraries), Phi Eta Sigma (freshman scholarship honorary); **MIL SERV:** US Army 1941-46, Lt. Col., Army Commendation Ribbon; **OTHER ACT & HONORS:** Nat. Press Club; Kenwood Ctry. Club; **HOME ADD:** 7705 Hackamore Dr., Potomac, MD 20854, (301)299-3699; **BUS ADD:** 1133 Fifteenth St., N.W., Wash., DC 20005, (202)857-5848.

STOLLMAN, Israel——**B:** Mar. 15, 1923, NYC, NY, *Exec. Dir.*, American Planning Association; **OTHER RE ACT:** City & Regional Planner; **SERVICES:** Admin. nat. organization; **PREV EMPLOY:** Exec. Dir. Amer. Soc. of Planning Off. 1968-1978, Chmn. of City & Reg. Planning, OH State Univ., 1957-1968; **PROFL AFFIL & HONORS:** AICP, AICP; **EDUC:** BSS, 1947, Housing and Planning, CCNY; **GRAD EDUC:** MCP, 1948, City and Regional Planning, MIT; **MIL SERV:** US Army, Air Cadet, 1943-45; **HOME ADD:** 215 W. Menomonee St., Chicago, IL 60614, (312)943-0427; **BUS ADD:**

1776 Mass. Ave., N.W., Wash., DC 20036, (202)872-0661.

STOLPMAN, Ronald B.——**B:** Dec. 31, 1939, Kellogg, MN, *Pres.*, The Jefferson Co.; **PRIM RE ACT:** Developer; **EDUC:** BA, 1961, Bus. Admin., St. Thomas Coll.; **GRAD EDUC:** MA, 1966, Bus. Admin., Mankate State Coll.; **MIL SERV:** USMC, 1st Lt.; **BUS ADD:** 219 Main St. SE, Minneapolis, MN 55414, (612)379-1316.

STOLTZ, Bob——**B:** Dec. 31, 1944, Rolla, MO, *Broker*, Stoltz Realtor; **PRIM RE ACT:** Broker; **REP CLIENTS:** Gen. public; **PREV EMPLOY:** Education; **PROFL AFFIL & HONORS:** MO Assn. of Realtors; US Chamber; NAR; **EDUC:** BS, 1966, Math, Hist., MO Valley Coll.; **GRAD EDUC:** MEd, 1973, Admin., Lincoln Univ.; **MIL SERV:** Quartermaster Corps. Engr.; Capt.; **OTHER ACT & HONORS:** Educ. organizations; **HOME ADD:** RFD 4m Box 129, (314)364-6462; **BUS ADD:** 8255 Bishop, Rolla, MO 65401, (314)364-7100.

STOLTZ, Jack P.——**B:** Jan. 6, 1941, Philadelphia, PA, *Pres.*, Stoltz Realty Co., Comml. and Indus.; **PRIM RE ACT:** Broker, Consultant; **SERVICES:** Investment counseling, brokerage, and synd. of income producing prop., joint ventures and indus. and comml. leasing; **REP CLIENTS:** European investment groups, pension funds, pvt. investors, lending instns. and maj. indus. office users; **PROFL AFFIL & HONORS:** Comml. and Indus. Council New Castle Cty., Natl Assn. Realty Bds., ULI, Natl. Assn. of Office and Indus. Parks, REESI, NE Indus. Devel. Assn., Past Pres. Comml. & Indus. Council, New Castle Cty.; **EDUC:** 1962, Arts and Sci., Univ. of DE; **HOME ADD:** 3815 Valley Brook Rd., Oakwood Rd., Oakwood Hills, Wilmington, DE 19803, (302)239-7354; **BUS ADD:** 1600 Pennsylvania Ave., Wilmington, DE 19806, (302)658-6681.

STONE, Carol A.——*Office Admin.*, Miller, Starr & Regalita; **PRIM RE ACT:** Attorney; **SERVICES:** Litigation and bus. representation in the area of RE and bus.; **REP CLIENTS:** Amer. S&L Assn., World S&L Assn., Great Western S&L Assn., Central Bank, First Amer. Title Ins. Co., Safeco Title Ins. Co., Berkeley, Contra Costa, E. Contra Costa, W. Contra Costa & Menlo Park Bd. of Realtors, DiGiorgio Devel. Corp., Broadmoor Homes, Div. of Genstar, Kaiser Sand & Gravel Co., Holland Oil, Shapell Indus. of No. CA, Boise Cascade Corp.; **BUS ADD:** One Kaiser Plaza, Suite 1650, Oakland, CA 94612, (415)465-3800.

STONE, David E.——**B:** July 24, 1935, Chicago, IL, *Pres.*, Acad. of RE Training, Creative RE Consultants; **PRIM RE ACT:** Broker, Consultant, Instructor; **OTHER RE ACT:** Education; **SERVICES:** Counseling, lecturing, cont. educ. sch.; **REP CLIENTS:** ERA of Cleveland, ERA of Columbus, ERA of Toledo, Realty World of N. OH, Realty World of S. OH, Cleveland Area Bd. of Realtors, Zanesville Bd. of Realtors, Portage Cty. Bd. of Realtors, Kent State Univ., Ashtabula Branch, John Carrol Univ.; **PREV EMPLOY:** Broker, lic. instr. of various RE topics including RE law, gen. mgr., of multi-ofc. co., land devel., and founder of two RE cos.; **PROFL AFFIL & HONORS:** NAR, State/Cleveland Area Bds. of Realtors, RNMI, GRI, CRS, CRA; **EDUC:** BS, 1962, Bus., Western Res. Univ.; **MIL SERV:** Army, Sgt.; **OTHER ACT & HONORS:** Precinct Committeeman, Optimist Club, Boy Scouts; **HOME ADD:** 17700 Windslow Rd., Shaker Hts., OH 44122, (216)751-1821; **BUS ADD:** PO Box 39611, Solon, OH 44139, (216)248-7591.

STONE, Frederick L.——**B:** Dec. 18, 1944, Oshkosh, WI, *Owner/Pres.*, Stone RE Serv./Stone Mort. Co. (Stone Securities Ltd.: Sole Proprietorship); Stone Dev. Co. Inc.; **PRIM RE ACT:** Broker, Syndicator, Consultant, Appraiser, Developer, Property Manager, Lender, Owner/Investor; **SERVICES:** Complete capabilities in all RE activities; **PREV EMPLOY:** 5 yrs. - Pres., Citizens Mort. Co., Sheboygan, WI, 5 yrs - Mort. Banking Officer, First WI Nat. Bank of Milwaukee, WI; **PROFL AFFIL & HONORS:** NAR, RESSI, Int. Assn. of Fin. Planners; **EDUC:** BBA, 1968, Fin. and Investments, Univ. of WI-Madison; **GRAD EDUC:** MBA, 1969, Fin. and Investments, Univ. of WI-Madison; **OTHER ACT & HONORS:** 5 yrs. - Town of Wilson Planning Commn. - V Chmn. Rotarian, Mason, Membership Chmn. - Pine Hills Ctry. Club, Boy Scouts of Amer. - Capital Contribution Campaign, YMCA - Y's Men Club, Sheboygan County Landmarks (Historic Preservation); **HOME ADD:** 1730 Sunnyside Ct., Sheboygan, WI 53081, (414)452-3100; **BUS ADD:** 927A Plaza 8, Sheboygan, WI 53081, (414)459-9444.

STONE, John Wayne——**B:** Aug. 19, 1952, Herrin, IL, *VP*, Goss Realty Inc.; **PRIM RE ACT:** Broker, Developer, Property Manager; **SERVICES:** Appraisal; investment analysis; **PREV EMPLOY:** Sold vacuum cleaners for 3 years; **PROFL AFFIL & HONORS:** Realtor, Egyptian Bd. of Realtors, RESSI, GRI; **EDUC:** Univ. of Southern IL, SIU; **HOME ADD:** RR 2 Box 291-B, Murphysboro, IL 62966, (618)684-3639; **BUS ADD:** Westown Mall, P O Box 1240, Carbondale, IL 62901, (618)457-8177.

STONE, Keith J.——**B:** 1943, England, *Sr. VP*, Folsom Investments Inc.; **PRIM RE ACT:** Developer; **SERVICES:** Devel., construction mgmt., leasing; **PREV EMPLOY:** Pres., Crow Hotel Devel. Co.; Partner, Trammell Crow Co.; **PROFL AFFIL & HONORS:** English Bar, Thoron Fellowship Recipient; **EDUC:** BA, 1965, Math./Physics, Cambridge Univ.; **GRAD EDUC:** MA, 1966, Law, Cambridge Univ.; MBA, 1969, Wharton School; **HOME ADD:** 4716 St. Johns Dr., Dallas, TX 75205, (214)522-4563; **BUS ADD:** 16475 Dallas Pkwy., Dallas, TX 75248, (214)931-7400.

STONE, Lewis M.——*Dri. of Mktg.*, Richard I. Rubin & Co.; **PRIM RE ACT:** Developer; **BUS ADD:** Ste 3806, 1700 Market St., Philadelphia, PA 19103, (215)963-1200.*

STONE, Michael B.——**B:** Dec. 18, 1935, NY, NY, *Pres.*, Micahel B. Stone, Inc.; **PRIM RE ACT:** Consultant; **OTHER RE ACT:** RE advisor; **SERVICES:** RE Counseling & investment advisory servs.; **REP CLIENTS:** Fin. insts., maj. corp., pension funds, attys., RE devels., owners & investors; **PROFL AFFIL & HONORS:** Amer. Soc. of RE Counselors, ULI, NAR, GA Assn. of Realtors, Atlanta Bd. of Realtors, CRE; **EDUC:** BA, 1957, Econ., Govt., Cornell Univ., Naval Justice Inst.; **MIL SERV:** USN, Lt. JG., 1957-59; **HOME ADD:** 1671 Manhasset Dr., Dunwoody, GA 30338, (404)394-3847; **BUS ADD:** 180 Interstate N. Prkwy, Suite 400, Atlanta, GA 30339, (404)955-0662.

STONE, Raymond W., Jr.——**B:** Dec. 2, 1919, Brooklyn, NY, *Exec. Asst.*, Orange & Rockland Utilities, Inc., Area Devel. Dept.; **OTHER RE ACT:** Mgr. Area Devel.; **SERVICES:** Maintain prop. listings, tax and labor information; **PREV EMPLOY:** Joseph Garabaldi - Indus. Realtor; **PROFL AFFIL & HONORS:** SIR, AREBA, NYAIDA, NJAIDA, VP NYC Chapter SIR; **EDUC:** BA, 1950, Econ., Yale University; **MIL SERV:** USAF, 1st LT, DFC; **HOME ADD:** 12 Yorkshire Dr., Suffern, NY 10901, (914)357-6252; **BUS ADD:** One Blue Hill Plaza, Pearl River, NY 10965, (914)627-2746.

STONE, Richard P.——**B:** Jan. 11, 1934, NYC, *Pres.*, Stone-Erlanger, Inc.; **PRIM RE ACT:** Broker, Syndicator, Consultant, Property Manager, Owner/Investor; **OTHER RE ACT:** Estate and Trust Admin.; **SERVICES:** Mgmt., site acquisition, negotiator, mktg., leasing; **REP CLIENTS:** Adminr. c.t.a. Estate of S. Klein, Consultant to chains re site acquisition, shopping ctr. locations and lease negotiation; **PREV EMPLOY:** All-States Realty Corp., A&P Tea Co., Vornado, Inc., Mort. Investment Co.; **PROFL AFFIL & HONORS:** NY & Westchester Realty Bds.; **EDUC:** AB, 1956, Govt. and Comparative Lit., Harvard; **GRAD EDUC:** 2 yrs., Denver Law School; **OTHER ACT & HONORS:** Sweet 14 LDC Bd. of Dir., 1981, 14th St.-Union Sq. Area Project: Bd. of Dir., Executive Steering Comm., Task Force Chmn.; 1977-1981, 14th St. Assoc. Bd. of Dir. Chmn. 1977-1981, United Way of Purchase: Chmn. 1977-1980; Pres. 1981 United Way of Weschester: Bd. of Dir. 1981, Purchase Association: Bd. of Dir. 1977-1981; **HOME ADD:** Purchase St., Purchase, NY 10577, (914)428-4628; **BUS ADD:** 88 Purchase St., Rye, NY 10580, (914)967-1000.

STONE, Robert L.——*Exec. VP*, Columbia Pictures Industries, Inc.; **PRIM RE ACT:** Property Manager; **BUS ADD:** 711 Fifth Ave., New York, NY 10022, (212)751-4400.*

STONE, Roger W.——*Pres.*, Stone Container Corp.; **PRIM RE ACT:** Property Manager; **BUS ADD:** 360 N. Michigan Ave., Chicago, IL 60601, (312)346-6600.*

STONE, Ronald M.——**B:** Feb. 28, 1943, Boston, MA, *Pres./CEO*, DBG Property Development Corp.; **PRIM RE ACT:** Attorney, Developer, Owner/Investor, Syndicator; **SERVICES:** Devel. and synd. prog.; luxury, condos., office bldgs.; **REP CLIENTS:** Many Wall St. Houses - Herzfeld & Stern, Lehman Brothers, etc.; **PREV EMPLOY:** Chairman & COO of the Kirkwood Grp.; Dir. of RE Div. of Prescott, Ball, Turben; **PROFL AFFIL & HONORS:** Member, NY Stock Exchange with offices in 12 states; **EDUC:** BBA, 1964, Bus. Admin., Univ. of MA, Amherst; **GRAD EDUC:** JD, 1967, RE/Tax/Securities Law, George Washington Law School; **OTHER ACT & HONORS:** Soc. for Advancement of Mgmt.; NY Realty Bd.; Greater Boston RE Bd.; **HOME ADD:** 245 E. 63 St., New York, NY 10021, (212)888-6129; **BUS ADD:** 850 Third Ave., New York, NY 10022, (212)486-0040.

STONE, Warner E.——**B:** Sept. 28, 1943, Galveston, TX, *Sr. VP*, Ben G. McGuire & Co. (Subsidiary Wells Fargo); **OTHER RE ACT:** Mort. Banker; **SERVICES:** Equity and Mort. Financing; **PREV EMPLOY:** Former VP BA Mort. of TX (subsidiary Bank of Amer.); **PROFL AFFIL & HONORS:** CPA; **EDUC:** BBA, 1965, Fin. - RE, Univ. of TX at Austin; **GRAD EDUC:** MS, 1969, Urban Land Econ. (RE), Univ. of WI; **EDUC HONORS:** Deans List, etc., Scholarship,

NASA Fellowship; **MIL SERV:** USN, Lt.; **HOME ADD:** 1222 Mohawk Trail, Richardson, TX 75080, (214)783-4782; **BUS ADD:** 12700 Park Central Dr., Suite 304, Dallas, TX 75251, (214)386-5677.

STONEBURNER, Craig B.——B: Apr. 21, 1946, Canton, OH, *Owner*, Stoneburner Properties; **PRIM RE ACT:** Owner/Investor; **OTHER RE ACT:** Investment Devel.; **SERVICES:** Pvt. RE broker RE investment & joint ventures; **PREV EMPLOY:** Pat Tobias & Co., Diran Corp. (Diversified RE Analysts); **EDUC:** BS Bus. Admin., 1968, Presbyterian Coll.; **GRAD EDUC:** 1968-1971, Law, Univ. of SC Law School; **MIL SERV:** US Army Reserves, SP-4; **OTHER ACT & HONORS:** Past-Columbia Bd. of Realtors; Past-Columbia & SC , Mktg. & Exchange Councils; **HOME ADD:** 2515 Canterbury Rd., Columbia, SC 29204, (803)254-9963; **BUS ADD:** 700 Keenan Bldg., 1310 Lady St., Columbia, SC 29201, (803)799-9483.

STOREY, Albert E., Jr.——B: June 8, 1928, Lynndyl, UT, *Broker, Treas.*, Award Realty, Inc.; **PRIM RE ACT:** Broker, Syndicator, Property Manager, Owner/Investor; **OTHER RE ACT:** Residential Ubcine; **SERVICES:** Complete RE services; **PREV EMPLOY:** Retired from Western Union, Last active position Dir. of Mktg.; **PROFL AFFIL & HONORS:** NAR, Armed Forces Communications & Electronics Assn., Chmn. NV State Energy Comm., NV Assn. of Realtors; **EDUC:** 1951, Pol. Sci., Univ. of NV-Reno, NV; **MIL SERV:** US Army, PFC 1946-47; **OTHER ACT & HONORS:** Chmn., NV State Energy Comm.; **HOME ADD:** 6150 Peppermill Dr., Las Vegas, NV 89102; **BUS ADD:** 801 S. Rancho Dr., Las Vegas, NV 89106, (702)385-7400.

STOREY, M. Bert——B: June 10, 1929, Columbia, SC, *Owner*, Bert Storey Assoc.; **PRIM RE ACT:** Broker, Syndicator, Consultant, Developer, Property Manager, Engineer, Owner/Investor; **PREV EMPLOY:** E.I. DuPont deNemours & Co.; **PROFL AFFIL & HONORS:** Prof. Engr., GA & SC; CCIM of RNMI, Amer. Soc. of Civil Engrs.; **EDUC:** BS, 1951, Civil Engrg., Univ. of SC; **MIL SERV:** US Army; **OTHER ACT & HONORS:** Bd. of Dir, GA Assn. of Realtors; **HOME ADD:** 502 Scotts Way, Augusta, GA 30909, (404)733-3014; **BUS ADD:** 825 Russell St., Augusta, GA 30904, (404)736-8401.

STOREY, R. Keith——*SIR Mgr. RE West*, Weyerhauser Co.; **PRIM RE ACT:** Property Manager; **BUS ADD:** Tacoma, WA 98477, (206)924-2345.*

STORKE, Tara D.——B: Nov. 23, 2944, Oakland, CA, *Sales Assoc.*, Roy H. Long Realty, Comml.; **PRIM RE ACT:** Broker, Property Manager, Syndicator; **OTHER RE ACT:** Exchanger; **SERVICES:** Investment counseling, synd., exchange counseling, valuation, prop. mgmt.; **PROFL AFFIL & HONORS:** Tucson RE Exchangors; AZ Assn. of RE Exchangors, CCIM Candidate, Million Dollar Club; **EDUC:** BA, 1966, Poli. Sci., Univ. of CA at Santa Barbara; **EDUC HONORS:** Dean's List, Poli. Sci. Honorary; **OTHER ACT & HONORS:** Pres., Bd. of Dir., Townhouse Assn.; **BUS ADD:** 5671 N. Oracle Rd., Tucson, AZ 85704, (602)297-1186.

STORMS, John W.——*Dir. Adm. Serv.*, Times Mirror Co.; **PRIM RE ACT:** Property Manager; **BUS ADD:** Times Mirror Square, Los Angeles, CA 90053, (213)972-3700.*

STORY, John, Jr.——B: July 26, 1924, Cleveland, OK, *Sr. Partner*, Story & Associates; **PRIM RE ACT:** Broker, Appraiser, Instructor; **OTHER RE ACT:** Expert Witness; **SERVICES:** RE Valuation for lititation and condemnation; appraisals; Comml. and indus. brokers; appraisal instr.; **REP CLIENTS:** Gov't agencies; maj. utility & energy cos.; attys.; **PROFL AFFIL & HONORS:** Nat. Assn. of Independent Fee Appraisers; Nat. Assn. of Review Appraisers; NAR; Nat. Forensic Ctr., IFAS; CRA; Realtor; Expert Witness; NAIFA Instr.; **EDUC:** 1950, Bus. Admin., Univ. of Tulsa; **MIL SERV:** USAF; Tech./Sgt.; **OTHER ACT & HONORS:** Elder, Presbyterian Church; Pres., Tulsa Fin & Feather Club, Inc.; Past Pres., Port of Tulsa Propeller Club; **HOME ADD:** 2619 E. 15th St., Tulsa, OK 74104, (918)742-6936; **BUS ADD:** 2619 E. 15th St., Tulsa, OK 74104, (918)749-3321.

STOTHERS, Hilton H., Jr.——B: Nov. 7, 1946, NY, NY, *Atty.*, Chadbourne Parke Whiteside & Wolff; **PRIM RE ACT:** Attorney; **SERVICES:** Legal counseling; **REP CLIENTS:** domestic and for. investors and dealers in RE; **PROFL AFFIL & HONORS:** Assn. of the Bar of the City of NY, ABA; **EDUC:** AB, 1968, 1968, Princeton Univ.; **GRAD EDUC:** JD, 1972, Columbia Law School; Cert. in Law, 1973, Univ. of Paris, France; **HOME ADD:** 192 E. 75th St., New York, NY 10021, (212)472-3283; **BUS ADD:** 30 Rockefeller Plaza, New York, NY 10112, (212)541-5800.

STOTTER, Morton M.——B: May 8, 1909, Cleveland, OH, *Counsel*, Benesch, Friedlander, Coplan & Aronoff; **PRIM RE ACT:** Attorney; **PREV EMPLOY:** 50 yrs. in practice of law; **PROFL AFFIL & HONORS:** ABA; OH State Bar Assn.; Cleveland Bar Assn.; Cuyahoga Bar Assn.; **GRAD EDUC:** LLB, 1930, Cleveland Marshall Law School of CSU; LLM, 1958, Case Western Res. Univ.; **HOME ADD:** 2 Bratenahl Pl., Bratenahl, OH 44108, (216)681-8866; **BUS ADD:** 1100 Citizens Bldg., Cleveland, OH 44114.

STOUFFER, James P.——B: Sept. 27, 1944, Fort Smith, AR, *Atty.*, Hutchins and Wells, P.C.; **PRIM RE ACT:** Attorney; **SERVICES:** All gen. legal servs. relating to RE; **PROFL AFFIL & HONORS:** ABA; CO Bar Assn.; Denver Bar Assn.; Boulder Cty. Estate Planning Council; **EDUC:** BS, 1966, Econ., Univ. of WI; **GRAD EDUC:** JD, 1969, Univ. of WI; **HOME ADD:** 285 Iroquois Dr., Boulder, CO 80303, (303)494-4756; **BUS ADD:** 1750 Gilpin St., Denver, CO 80218, (303)399-1122.

STOUGH, R. Maxine——*Ed.*, American Load Title Assn., Title News; **PRIM RE ACT:** Real Estate Publisher; **BUS ADD:** 1828 L. St., NW, Washington, DC 20016, (202)296-3671.*

STOUGHTON, Robert E.——B: Jan. 25, 1937, Hartford, CT, *VP*, First Essex Savings Bank; **PRIM RE ACT:** Banker, Lender; **SERVICES:** Consumer, investor RE counseling, valuation, comml. RE lending; **REP CLIENTS:** Indiv. or instnl. investors in comml., investment props., consumer owner - occupants, other lenders; **PREV EMPLOY:** Lending and valuation experience, Northeast/Freedom Federal Savings, Home Federal Savings; **PROFL AFFIL & HONORS:** MBA; MA, Mort. Bankers; Lawrence Devel. Fin. Corp.; Lawrence Neighborhood Housing Services; AIREA; **EDUC:** BA, 1959, Bus. Admin. and Communications, Emerson Coll.; **GRAD EDUC:** Grad. School of Savings Banking, 1981, Fin. Mgmt.; **EDUC HONORS:** Grad. GSSB with Honors; **OTHER ACT & HONORS:** Commnr. - Belmont Recreation Dept.; Auditor - Plymouth Congregl. Church; **HOME ADD:** 688 Concord Ave., Belmont, MA 02178, (617)489-1411; **BUS ADD:** 296 Essex St., Lawrence, MA 01840, (617)681-7500.

STOUT, Donald E.——B: Mar. 16, 1926, Dayton, OH, *Pres.*, Donald E. Stout, Inc.; **PRIM RE ACT:** Broker, Consultant, Appraiser, Developer, Owner/Investor, Property Manager; **SERVICES:** Appraisals, comm. prop. mgmt., devel.; **REP CLIENTS:** US Steel, US PO Dept., Penn Central RR, Exxon Co., Firestone, IBM, Atlantic Richfield Oil Co.; **PREV EMPLOY:** Currently devel. Wright-Gate Research/Indus./Mall, 280 acres, 'The Falls', 50 acres, & other related exp.; **PROFL AFFIL & HONORS:** Local State & Nat. Bds. of Realtors, Listed Marquis Who's Who in Fin. & Indus., & Who's Who in the World, Dun & Bradstreet Million Dollar Dir., MAI, SREA, SIR, CRA; **GRAD EDUC:** 1950, Bus. & RE, Miami Univ., Notre Dame, Cornell; **MIL SERV:** US Army, Enlisted status, 1944-45, Navy, Enlisted status, 1945-46, Currently ret. Navy Supply Officer; **OTHER ACT & HONORS:** Various Flying Club Memberships, 32 Deg. Shrine, Phi Delta Theta Alumni, Res. Officer's Assn.; **HOME ADD:** 759 Plantation Ln., Dayton, OH 45419, (513)293-9955; **BUS ADD:** 1340 Woodman Dr., Dayton, OH 45432, (513)223-3000.

STOUT, Gary E.——B: Apr. 23, 1941, Burlington, IA, *Econ. Devel. Consultant*, Gary E. Stout Assoc.; **PRIM RE ACT:** Consultant, Developer, Instructor; **SERVICES:** Public/private fin. packaging, devel. counseling; **REP CLIENTS:** Private devels., private corps., cities; **PREV EMPLOY:** Devel. Dir., St. Paul, MN and Portland, OR; **PROFL AFFIL & HONORS:** ULI' CUED; NAHRO; **EDUC:** BS, 1964, Urban Planning, Univ. of IA; **GRAD EDUC:** MPA, 1973, Fin., PA State Univ.; **HOME ADD:** Suite 332, 4 Pine Tree Dr., Arden Hills, MN 55112, (612)483-2989; **BUS ADD:** Suite 332, 4 Pine Tree Dr., Arden Hills, MN 55112, (612)291-7728.

STOUT, Mark——B: Oct. 10, 1950, Denver, CO, *Pres.*, Mark Stout Inc.; **PRIM RE ACT:** Broker, Owner/Investor, Property Manager, Syndicator; **PROFL AFFIL & HONORS:** Soc. of Las Vegas Exchangers (SOLVE); RESSI; **EDUC:** BS, 1972, RE Fin., AZ State Univ.; **OTHER ACT & HONORS:** NV Apt. Assn.; 76ers Exchange Club; **HOME ADD:** 5151 Tennis Ct., Las Vegas, NV 89120, (702)451-3336; **BUS ADD:** 1700 E. Desert Inn., Suite 108, Las Vegas, NV 89109, (702)369-7115.

STOVER, Phillip J.——B: Dec. 29, 1938, Kansas City, MO, *Pres.*, Stover and Co.; **PRIM RE ACT:** Broker, Syndicator, Developer, Property Manager; **OTHER RE ACT:** Office space leasing; **SERVICES:** Office space leasing, dev. and synd. of comml. prop., prop. mgmt.; **REP CLIENTS:** Mjr. corp. tenants; indiv. or instnl. investors in comml. prop.; **PREV EMPLOY:** Arthur Rubloff and Co., 1967-77; Capital Resources 1974-1975; Collaborative Dev. Ltd. 1971-1973; Draper and Kramer, Inc. 1962-1969; **PROFL AFFIL & HONORS:**

IREM; Who's Who in R.E., CPM; **EDUC:** BA, 1961, Hist. of Arts and Arch., Yale; **GRAD EDUC:** MBA, 1971, Urban Studies, Univ. of Chicago; **MIL SERV:** U S Army; SP, 1962; **OTHER ACT & HONORS:** Assoc. mbr. of the Bd. of DR. of the Univ. of Chicago Cancer Research Found.; Publications,; Univ. of Chicago Urban Econ. Rpt. No. 52, Speeches Chicago Chptr. of the IREM, Office Bldg. Leasing and Mgmt, Seminar Office Leasing Space, October 24, 1973; **HOME ADD:** 20 E. Cedar, Chicago, IL 60611, (312)943-3666; **BUS ADD:** 20 N. Clark St. Ste. 502, Chicago, IL 60602, (312)372-9000.

STOWELL, John D.——B: Dec. 30, 1938, Rumford, ME, *Pres.*, Webb River Land Co.; **PRIM RE ACT:** Broker, Appraiser; **OTHER RE ACT:** Land Surveyor, Forester; **SERVICES:** Complete forest mgmt. ser. to include roadbuilding & timber harvesting, also wood lot surveying; **REP CLIENTS:** Indiv. woodlot owners and corps., not large enough to support a forest management div.; **PROFL AFFIL & HONORS:** ME Soc. of Land Surveyors, Amer. Congress Surveying & Mapping, Amer. Soc. of Photogrammetry; **EDUC:** AB, 1961, Dartmouth Coll.; **MIL SERV:** USMC, Res. Cpl., 1961-67; **HOME ADD:** Stewart Ave., Farmington, ME 04938, (207)778-3905; **BUS ADD:** Pine St., Dixfield, ME 04224, (207)567-7221.

STRACHOTA, Robert J.——B: July 7, 1953, Milwaukee, WI, *Treas.*, Shenehon and Assoc.; **PRIM RE ACT:** Consultant, Appraiser; **SERVICES:** RE consultation and appraisal servs.; **REP CLIENTS:** Dain Bosworth, Fed. Home Loan Bank Bd., Prudential Ins., Gen. Mills, Munsingwear, IRS, K-Mart, etc.; **PREV EMPLOY:** Mgr. of RE at Patchin Appraisals, Minneapolis; **PROFL AFFIL & HONORS:** AIREA, Soc. of RE Appraisers; MN Indus. Dev. Assn., Nat. Assn. of Indus. and Office Parks, MAI, SRPA; **EDUC:** BA, 1975, Fin., Coll. of St. Thomas; **GRAD EDUC:** MBA, 1980, Fin., Univ. of MN; **EDUC HONORS:** Cum Laude; **HOME ADD:** 4506 Dak Dr., Edina, MN 55424, (612)922-4588; **BUS ADD:** 505 E. Grant St., Minneapolis, MN 55404, (612)333-6533.

STRADAL, Walter J., Jr.——B: Oct. 3, 1927, St. Louis, MO, *Exec. VP*, RE Bd. of Metro. St. Louis; **OTHER RE ACT:** Admin. officer; **SERVICES:** Trade Assn.; **REP CLIENTS:** 7,000 Licensed St. Louis & St. Louis Cty. RE Agents; **PREV EMPLOY:** Wash. Univ., St. Louis, MO; **EDUC:** BFA, 1952, Wash. Univ.; **EDUC HONORS:** Jr. Men's Hon. (Thurtene); **MIL SERV:** USN, WW II, S 1/C, Victory Medal, S. Pac. Ops.; **OTHER ACT & HONORS:** Alderman, City of Creve Coeur, 6 yrs.; Member Advisory Bd. Deaconess Hosp.; **HOME ADD:** 510 N. Spoede Rd., Creve Coeur, MO 63141, (314)432-3874; **BUS ADD:** 8027 Forsyth Blvd., St. Louis, MO 63105, (314)727-2400.

STRANG, Ronald A.——B: July 16, 1935, St. Paul, MN, *R.E. Appraiser*, Strang and Sampair Co.; **PRIM RE ACT:** Consultant, Appraiser, Developer, Builder, Property Manager, Owner/Investor; **PREV EMPLOY:** Dep. Assessor and S and L Appraiser; **PROFL AFFIL & HONORS:** SREA, SRA; **EDUC:** Eng., Math, Psych., Univ. of MN; **MIL SERV:** USN, 2nd Class Petty Officer; **HOME ADD:** 14080 Old Holt Ct., Lindstrom, MN 55113, (612)257-6084; **BUS ADD:** 2489 N. Rice St., Roseville, MN 55113, (612)484-3080.

STRANGE, Robert T.——B: Apr. 10, 1929, Annapolis, MD, *Pres.*, Charter Mgmt., Inc.; **PRIM RE ACT:** Broker, Consultant, Property Manager; **SERVICES:** Prop. mgmt. serv. to condo., comml., indus. and resid. Prop.; **REP CLIENTS:** Condo. assns., bldg. owners, etc.; **PREV EMPLOY:** Formerly VP of RE firm responsible for prop. mgmt. functions; **PROFL AFFIL & HONORS:** IREM; Comm. Assoc. Inst.; NAR; State and Local RE Bds., CPM; **MIL SERV:** US Air Force, Lt. Col.; **HOME ADD:** 412 Ferry Point Rd., Annapolis, MD 21403, (301)268-8289; **BUS ADD:** 134 Holiday Ct. 308, Annapolis, MD 21401, (301)841-6555.

STRATEMEIER, Ed.——*Legal Counsel & RE*, Russell Stover Candies, Inc.; **PRIM RE ACT:** Attorney; **BUS ADD:** 1004 Baltimore Ave., Kansas City, MO 64105, (816)842-9240.*

STRATHBUCKER, Jerry——*Corp. Const. Mgr.*, Intel Corp.; **PRIM RE ACT:** Property Manager; **BUS ADD:** 3065 Bowers Ave., Santa Clara, CA 95051, (408)987-8080.*

STRATTON, James Malcolm, Jr.——B: Aug. 24, 1928, San Francisco, CA, *Area Mgr.-Western Area*, Vorelco Inc., Western Area & Vorelco of CA Inc.; **PRIM RE ACT:** Developer, Property Manager; **SERVICES:** Corporate RE & acquisition, mgmt., devel.; **PREV EMPLOY:** Roth Props., Western Reneline, Ghirardelli Sq.; **PROFL AFFIL & HONORS:** Natl. Assn. of Corporate RE Execs.; **EDUC:** Pre-Med, Bus. Admin., Univ. of CA, Berkeley; **MIL SERV:** US Naval Reserves, Lt. Comdr., Air Medal; **OTHER ACT & HONORS:** Univ. Club San Francisco, S.F. Air Sheriffs Sq. Den., Sierra Club Bd. of Dir. Planned Parenthood, Far West Ski Assn.; **HOME TEL:** (415)839-6162; **BUS ADD:** 7106 Johnson Suite A, Pleasanton, CA 94566, (415)462-3342.

STRATTON, John C.——B: July 11, 1920, Chicago, IL, *Pres.*, Stratton Realty; **PRIM RE ACT:** Broker, Consultant, Appraiser; **OTHER RE ACT:** Lecturer at Univ. of CT, 1968-74; W. CT State Coll. 1975-80; **PROFL AFFIL & HONORS:** New Milford Bd. Realtors, Dir.; NAR; Nat. RE Exchange; Realtors Nat. Mktg. Inst.; Nat. Inst. of Farm & Land Brokers; Comml. Investment Div. of CT Assn. of Realtors; CT CCIM; Intl. RE Fed.; Intl. Inst. Valuers; NARA; SRPA; World-Wide Prop. Unlimited, CRB; CRS; GRI; CRA; SCV; **EDUC:** BS, 1949, ME, Princeton Univ.; **GRAD EDUC:** MBA, 1980, Univ. of New Haven, CT; **EDUC HONORS:** Cum Laude; Soc. of Sigma XI; **MIL SERV:** USAAF, 1st Lt., Air Medal, Oak Leaf Cluster, Distinguished Flying Cross; **OTHER ACT & HONORS:** Chmn., Zoning Commn., Newtown, CT, 1968 - 1973; Princeton Club of NY; "Who's Who in Amer."; "Who's Who in the East"; "Who's Who in Fin. & Indus."; "Who's Who in the World"; **HOME ADD:** Squire Rd., Roxbury, CT 06783, (203)355-1098; **BUS ADD:** Squire Rd., Roxbury, CT 06783, (203)355-2185.

STRATTON, John X.——B: Nov. 18, 1927, Birmingham, AL, *Pres.*, Stratton Realty, Inc. - Stratton Development Corp.; **PRIM RE ACT:** Broker, Consultant, Appraiser, Developer, Builder, Owner/Investor, Instructor, Property Manager, Syndicator; **OTHER RE ACT:** Bus. acquisitions and mergers; **REP CLIENTS:** Nat. clients; **PROFL AFFIL & HONORS:** CBC, Revest., IMBUSA, NAR, INTEREX, CBC; **EDUC:** BA, 1949, Bus. Admin., Univ. of AL; **OTHER ACT & HONORS:** Rotary, Blue Lodge, Shrine, Grato, C of C; **HOME ADD:** 3021 Fernwood, Davenport, IA 52807, (319)359-0263; **BUS ADD:** 3901 Marquette St., Davenport, IA 52806, (319)386-6050.

STRAUS, Joseph, Jr.——B: Sept. 26, 1921, New York, NY, *Partner*, Strouse Greenberg and Co., Investment Div.; **PRIM RE ACT:** Broker, Consultant, Developer, Owner/Investor, Syndicator; **OTHER RE ACT:** Specializes in the sale of investment-grade RE to instns., corps. and indiv., and the organization and sponsorship of limited parnerships which acquire income producing props., provides consultation services to comml. banks, major corps., insurance cos., and other fin. instn., and pension funds; **PROFL AFFIL & HONORS:** Trustee, The ULI; Trea., The Urban Land Research Found.; Dir., Natl. Realty Comm.; Member, Mort. Comm. of the RE Bd. of NY, Inc.; Member, ASREC; Member Lamda Alpha The Honorary Profl. Land Econs. Frat.; **EDUC:** BS, 1942, RE and Corporate Fin., The Wharton School of Fin. and Commerce, Univ. of PA; **MIL SERV:** USN, Lt.; **OTHER ACT & HONORS:** Tr., Delaware Valley Coll.; Chmn., Rolling Hill Hospital, Philadelphia; Tr., Philadelphia Psych. Ctr.; Tr., United Hosp. Corp.; Dir., Natl. Council of Christians and Jews; **HOME ADD:** 8323 High School Rd., Elkins Park, PA 19117, (215)635-4046; **BUS ADD:** 1626 Locust St., Philadelphia, PA 19103, (215)985-1100.

STRAUS, Stanley S.——B: Feb. 24, 1914, Cincinnati, OH, *Pres.*, Espy & Straus, Inc.; **PRIM RE ACT:** Broker; **SERVICES:** Sales, leasing, fin., consulting; **REP CLIENTS:** Nat. & local corp. & indiv. investors; **PROFL AFFIL & HONORS:** SIR; **EDUC:** AB, 1936, Econ., Yale Univ.; **MIL SERV:** USAF, Maj., Battle Stars, etc.; **OTHER ACT & HONORS:** Former Tr., Amer. Heart Assn.; Past Member Yale Devel. Bd.; Member, S. OH Bank Bd.; **HOME ADD:** 1111 Rookwood Dr., Cincinnati, OH 45208, (513)321-7127; **BUS ADD:** 1077 Celestial St., Cincinnati, OH 45202, (513)721-6315.

STRAUSS, Jay J.——B: Jan. 30, 1936, *Pres.*, The Abacus Grp.; **PRIM RE ACT:** Banker, Lender; **PROFL AFFIL & HONORS:** Past Pres. IL MBA; Member MBA; IREM, Chicago R.E. Bd.; Jr. R.E. Bd. Chicago-Past Pres., CPM, ICSC, D.F. of Nat. Assn. of CMB; **EDUC:** BS, 1957, Indus. Engrg., Univ. of IL; **MIL SERV:** US Army Corps. Engrs., Lt. 1957-59; **HOME ADD:** 2347 Meadow Dr. S., Wilmette, IL 60091; **BUS ADD:** 10 S. LaSalle St., Chicago, IL 60603, (312)346-9172.

STRAUSS, Joseph——*Special Asst.*, Department of Housing and Urban Development, Ofc. of Secy/Under Secy.; **PRIM RE ACT:** Lender; **BUS ADD:** 451 Seventh St., S.E., Washington, DC 20410, (202)755-3636.*

STRAUSS, Marc J.——B: Mar. 29, 1953, Chicago, IL, *Partner*, Strauss, Sulzer, Shapiro & Wilkins; **PRIM RE ACT:** Attorney; **SERVICES:** Legal rep.; **REP CLIENTS:** Amer. Invsco, Chicago S&L Assn., Mutual Fed. S&L, Avondale S&L Assn.; **PROFL AFFIL & HONORS:** Chicago, IL & Amer. Bar Assns.; **EDUC:** BA, 1975, Econ., Pol. Sci., Northwestern Univ.; **GRAD EDUC:** MM, 1976, Strategic Planning, Fin., Northwestern Univ.; JD, 1979, Northwestern Univ.; **EDUC HONORS:** Clarion DeWitt Hardy Scholar, Cumnock Prize, Honors Degree, Cum Laude; **HOME ADD:** 711 W. Diversey, Chicago, IL 60602, (312)248-8456; **BUS ADD:** 20 N. Clark, Suite 808, Chicago, IL 60602, (312)726-9060.

STRAUSS, Michael S.——**B:** Apr. 10, 1951, Lynn, MA, *Atty.*, W. R. Grace & Co., Legal Div.; **OTHER RE ACT:** Commercial RE Development; **PREV EMPLOY:** RE and Mort. Atty. - The Manhattan Life Ins. Co.; **PROFL AFFIL & HONORS:** Boston Bar Assn., Phi Alpha Delta Law Frat., Intl. Council of Shopping Centers, Bar Membership: MA, NY, US Dist. Ct., Dist. of MA, US Supreme Ct.; **EDUC:** BA, 1973, Eng., Univ. of MA, Amherst, MA; **GRAD EDUC:** JD, 1976, Western New England Coll., Springfield, MA; **EDUC HONORS:** Phi Kappa Phi, Commonwealth Scholar; **HOME ADD:** 3671 Hudson Manor Terr., Riverdale, NY 10463, (212)548-9150; **BUS ADD:** 1114 Ave. of the Americas, New York, NY 10036, (212)764-6491.

STRAUSS, William V.——**B:** July 5, 1942, Cincinnati, OH, *Partner*, Strauss, Troy and Ruehlmann Co., L.P.A.; **PRIM RE ACT:** Attorney; **OTHER RE ACT:** VP, Security Title and Guaranty Agency, Inc.; **REP CLIENTS:** Devels. mortgagees and synds. relative to FHA multi-family and comml. projects; **PROFL AFFIL & HONORS:** ABA, Comm. on Housing and Community Devel.; OH State Bar Assn.; Cincinnati Bar Assn., Housing Comm.; Greater Cincinnati C of C Housing Comm.; Queen City Housing Bd.; **EDUC:** AB, 1964, Govt., Harvard Coll.; **GRAD EDUC:** 1967, Univ. of PA Law School; **EDUC HONORS:** Cum Laude; **HOME ADD:** 40 Walnut Ave., Wyoming, OH 45215, (513)821-4927; **BUS ADD:** 2100 Central Trust Center, Cincinnati, OH 45202, (513)621-2120.

STRECKER, Raymond F.——**B:** June 18, 1929, Philadelphia, PA, *Pres.*, East Girard Savings Assn.; **PRIM RE ACT:** Banker, Lender; **PREV EMPLOY:** 1953-55, Benjamin Franklin Federal S & L, Philadelphia; 1955-67, Trevose S & L Assn., Trevose, PA; **PROFL AFFIL & HONORS:** Dir., Fed. Home Loan Bank of Pittsburgh; Advisory Comm. Member, Fed. Home Loan Mort. Corp., 1969, Special Leadership Award from Philadelphia, Chapter 91 Amer. S & L Inst.; 1979, Man of the Year, Soc. of S & L Mort. Officers; **EDUC:** BA, 1950, Amer. Lit., Univ. of PA; **GRAD EDUC:** S & L, 1962, IN Univ.; **EDUC HONORS:** Maj. Honors; **MIL SERV:** USN; Lt.j.g., 1950-53; **OTHER ACT & HONORS:** Chmn., Amer. Nat. Red Cross, Bucks County Chap. 1974-76; Past Pres., Rotary Club of NE Philadelphia; Member, various RE and C of C; Member, Comly Rich House Restoration Comm.; Past Pres., PA S&L League, Inc.; Past Pres., Insured S&L of Deleware Valley; Past Pres., Philadelphia Chap. of the Inst. of Fin. Edu.; Chmn., US League of Savings Assn. (Constit. Comm.); **HOME ADD:** Newtown, PA; **BUS ADD:** 7048 Castor Ave., Philadelphia, PA 19149, (215)722-3300.

STREHLKE, Richard B.——The Strehlke Company; **PRIM RE ACT:** Developer, Builder, Owner/Investor, Property Manager; **PROFL AFFIL & HONORS:** Gr. Boston RE Bd., Bldg. Owners and Mgrs. Assn.; **EDUC:** BS, Civil Engrg., Tufts Univ.; **BUS ADD:** Framingham Exec. Park - 20 Speen St., Framingham, MA 01701, (617)653-8690.

STREICH, Richard G.——**B:** Mar. 12, 1930, Buffalo, NY, *Pres.*, Eastland Properties, Inc.; **PRIM RE ACT:** Broker; **OTHER RE ACT:** Comml. Props. and Land; **EDUC:** BA, 1952, Bus. Admin., Colby Coll.; **OTHER ACT & HONORS:** Broward Cty. School Bd., Member 70-71; **HOME ADD:** 4821 NE 29th Ave., Ft. Lauderdale, FL 33308, (305)772-0328; **BUS ADD:** 1915 NE 45th Street, Ft. Lauderdale, FL 33308, (305)491-4315.

STREICHER, Sharon A.——**B:** Nov. 10, 1947, NYC, NY, *Atty.*, Panasonic Co, Div. of Matsushita Electric, Corp. of Amer.; **PRIM RE ACT:** Attorney; **SERVICES:** Negotiation, drafting & review of leases and other RE documents; **PREV EMPLOY:** Asst. VP & Corp. Counsel to Sonesta Intl. Hotels Corp.; **PROFL AFFIL & HONORS:** CA Bar & MA Bar; **EDUC:** BA, 1968, Poli. Sci., Brooklyn Coll. of CUNY; **GRAD EDUC:** JD, 1971, Hastings Coll. of the Law, Univ. of CA; **EDUC HONORS:** Cum Laude; **BUS ADD:** One Panasonic Way, Secaucus, NJ 07094, (201)348-7000.

STRENG, G. William——**B:** June 19, 1926, Scranton, PA, *Pres.*, Ich, Inc.; **PRIM RE ACT:** Broker, Developer, Builder; **SERVICES:** Gen. brokerage; devel. lots; **PREV EMPLOY:** Heraty & Gannon Org. 1954-1957; **PROFL AFFIL & HONORS:** Sacramento Bldg. Indus. Assn.; CA Soc. of CPA; **EDUC:** AB, 1950, Liberal Arts, Dartmouth Coll.; **GRAD EDUC:** MBA, 1951, Bus. Acctg., Amos Tuck School at Dartmouth Coll.; **EDUC HONORS:** Phi Beta Kappa, Magna Cum Laude; **MIL SERV:** US Army, 1944-1946, M/Sgt.; **OTHER ACT & HONORS:** Woodland C of C; Davis C of C; **HOME ADD:** 528 Hermosa Pl., Davis, CA 95616, (916)756-3795; **BUS ADD:** 835 W. Eldorado Ave., Woodland, CA 95695, (916)666-0901.

STRENKOWSKI, Edward A.——**B:** Sept. 14, 1953, Elizabeth, NJ, *Atty.*, Cities Serv. Co., Energy Resources Grp.; **PRIM RE ACT:** Attorney; **SERVICES:** In charge of title work, legal work relating to prop. closings and contracting, contract negotiation; **REP CLIENTS:** Cities Service Co., Real Prop. & Oil & Gas Law; **PROFL AFFIL & HONORS:** ABA; OK Bar Assn.; Delta Theta Phi Legal Frat.; Tulsa Cty. Bar Assn.; Mineral Law Sect.; **EDUC:** BA, 1975, Hist., Pol. Sci., Niagara Univ., NY; **GRAD EDUC:** JD, 1978, Law, Univ. of AR, Sch. of Law; **EDUC HONORS:** Magna Cum Laude, Law Review, Grad. with Hons.; **HOME ADD:** 1921 N. Desert Palm, Tulsa, OK 74133, (918)252-0139; **BUS ADD:** PO Box 300, Tulsa, OK 74102, (918)561-2559.

STRIBLING, J. H.——**B:** July 16, 1936, Jackson, MS, *Pres.*, Stribling Realty Corp.; **PRIM RE ACT:** Broker, Developer, Builder, Owner/Investor, Property Manager, Syndicator; **SERVICES:** Site selections and devel. for major clients; sales, devel. and synd. of comml. and indus. prop.; **PROFL AFFIL & HONORS:** MS and Nat. Bd. of Realtors; Realtor Nat. Mktg. Inst., Comm. Dev.; Int. Council of Shopping Ctrs., FLI, GRI; **EDUC:** BS, 1961, Acctg., MS Coll.; Univ. of MS; **HOME ADD:** 1034 Hallmark Dr., Jackson, MS 39206, (601)981-9166; **BUS ADD:** 5440 Executive Place, P O Box 16607, Jackson, MS 39206, (601)981-2200.

STRICKLAND, Charles Edward——**B:** Aug. 8, 1949, Nash Cty, NC, *VP*, Wimberley, Gregory & Co. Inc.; **PRIM RE ACT:** Broker, Instructor, Consultant, Appraiser, Property Manager, Owner/Investor; **SERVICES:** Sales, counseling for appraisals, long term planning for invest. props., mgmt.; **PREV EMPLOY:** Pres., Preventative Maint. Indus. of Rocky Mt. Inc.; **PROFL AFFIL & HONORS:** Grad. of Realtors Inst., CPM, Gov. PMD-NCAR parade of Appreciation Awarded (2), IREM Piedmont Chap. 56 Appreciation Award (2); **EDUC:** AB, 1971, Bus. Admin, Acctg., Nash Tech. Inst.; **OTHER ACT & HONORS:** Chm/Rocky Mt. Housing Bd., 3 yrs., RE Instr. Inst. of REM, Chicago, Meredith Coll. Raleigh, Nash Tech. Inst., NCRE, Licensing Bd.; **HOME ADD:** 2801-A-3 Sunset Ave., Rocky Mount, NC 27801, (919)443-6792; **BUS ADD:** 118 S. Franklin St., Rocky Mount, NC 27801, (919)446-6195.

STRICKLAND, Wilbur H.——**B:** Alachoq Cty., FL, *Realtor (Owner)*; **PRIM RE ACT:** Broker, Consultant; **OTHER RE ACT:** Indus. Sales/Leases; **SERVICES:** Sales, leasing, exchanges, counselling; **PREV EMPLOY:** Accountant, Employed by Roy L. Purvis, CPA, Gainesville, FL; **PROFL AFFIL & HONORS:** RNMI, Chicago, Pres. Orlando - Winter Park Bd. of Realtors, 1973; **EDUC:** Univ. of FL; Inst. of Bus. & Acctg., Atlanta; **MIL SERV:** USCG, Q.M. 3rd, 1929-1933; **OTHER ACT & HONORS:** Commnr., Orlando, FL - 7 yrs - 1953-1960; Orlando-Orange Cty. Airport Zoning Bd. of Adjustment; **HOME ADD:** 3504 Finch St., Orlando, FL 32803, (305)894-6175; **BUS ADD:** 401 S. Eola Dr., Orlando, FL 32801, (305)894-3931.

STRINGER, Robert G.——**B:** Nov. 13, 1930, Monroe, LA, *Owner*, CA National Appraisal Co.; **PRIM RE ACT:** Consultant, Appraiser; **PROFL AFFIL & HONORS:** Sr. Member Amer. Soc. Appraisers; **EDUC:** AA, 1954, Bus., Yuba Jr. Coll.; BA, 1956, Bus. Econ. Psych., Sacramento State Univ.; **MIL SERV:** USAF, AZC; **HOME ADD:** 4531 Amer. River Dr., Sacramento, CA 95825, (916)488-3197; **BUS ADD:** 4531 American River Dr., Sacramento, CA 95825, (916)486-1142.

STROBECK, Charles L.——**B:** June 17, 1928, Chicago, IL, *Pres.*, Strobeck Reiss & Co.; **PRIM RE ACT:** Broker, Consultant, Developer, Owner/Investor, Property Manager, Syndicator; **SERVICES:** Gen. RE serv. comml. & indus.; **REP CLIENTS:** Blue Cross, Continental Bank, Duff & Phelps, Federal Hamilton Bank, Alexander & Alexander; **PREV EMPLOY:** Sudlerd Co., Partner; **PROFL AFFIL & HONORS:** Chicago RE Bd., IREM; Amer. Soc. of RE Counselors, CPM, CRE; **EDUC:** AB, 1949, Bus. Admin. & Econ., Wheaton Coll.; **MIL SERV:** US Army, Corp.; **OTHER ACT & HONORS:** TR. & Pres. Wheaton Sanitary Dis..; Pres. Union League Club of Chicago 1973-74; Pres. Wheaton Christian High School; Pres. Chicago Youth Centers 1980; **HOME ADD:** Hawthorne Rd., Wheaton, IL 60187, (312)668-7675; **BUS ADD:** Ste. 1600, 134 S. LaSalle St., Chicago, IL 60603, (312)644-4800.

STROEBE, Conrad F.——*Partner*, Conrad & Brown; **PRIM RE ACT:** Consultant, Developer, Builder, Owner/Investor; **OTHER RE ACT:** CPA; **SERVICES:** Fin. review & evaluation of comml. prop., planning, const. mgmt.; **REP CLIENTS:** Smaller corp./profl. bus. and indiv. investors; **PREV EMPLOY:** Arthur Andersen & Co. (1971-1975); **PROFL AFFIL & HONORS:** AICPA, MT Soc. of CPA'S, CPA, Chmn.-Ethics Comm. MT Soc. CPA's 1980-1982; **EDUC:** BA, 1971, Econ.-Acctg., St. John's Univ., MN; **MIL SERV:** US Army Res.; **BUS ADD:** 512 N. 29th St., Billings, MT 59101, (406)245-6102.

STROHL, Jean Carol, (Mrs. Morris A.)——B: Oct. 27, 1921, Bay Village, OH, *Realtor*, Leonard M. Smith & Assoc.; **PRIM RE ACT:** Broker, Instructor, Consultant; **OTHER RE ACT:** RE, Investment Instr. for Community Coll., Dist. Member Assessment Appeals Bd., San Diego Cty.; **SERVICES:** New & used luxury homes, investment prop., estate bldg.; **PREV EMPLOY:** Sec. The Glidden Co., Cleveland, OH, Ratner Mfg. Co., San Diego, CA; **PROFL AFFIL & HONORS:** NAR, CA Assn. of Realtors, Realtor of yr, La Mesa Bd. of Realtors, 1963, Voc. Ed. Honoree, 1979, San Diego Comm. Coll.; **EDUC:** Cert. in RE, 1963, UC San Diego; **MIL SERV:** USN, Yeo. 1C; **HOME ADD:** 6278 Lambda Dr., San Diego, CA 92120; **BUS ADD:** 8901 La Mesa Blvd., La Mesa, CA 92041, (714)463-4488.

STROM, Fredric Alan——B: Nov. 30, 1948, Detroit, MI, *Managing Editor, Land Use & Environment Publications*, Clark Boardman Co., Ltd.; **PRIM RE ACT:** Attorney, Regulator, Real Estate Publisher; **SERVICES:** Editor, zoning and planning report and handbook; **PROFL AFFIL & HONORS:** APA; **EDUC:** BA, 1970, Amer. Civilization, Brown Univ.; **GRAD EDUC:** JD, 1973, Law, Cornell Law School; **HOME ADD:** 250 W. 24th St., Apt. 6BW, New York, NY 10011, (212)929-6703; **BUS ADD:** 435 Hudson St., New York, NY 10014, (212)929-7500.

STRONG, Jesse M., Jr.——B: Oct. 29, 1927, University Park, TX, *VP*, White House RE Corp.; **PRIM RE ACT:** Broker, Owner/Investor, Instructor, Property Manager, Syndicator; **PROFL AFFIL & HONORS:** RNMI, FLI, RESSI; **EDUC:** BS, 1967, Univ. of MD; **GRAD EDUC:** MSA, 1970, Ops. Research, Mgmt. Sci., George Washington Univ.; **MIL SERV:** US Army, LTC, LM, ACM w/OLC; **HOME ADD:** Springfield, VA; **BUS ADD:** Suite 200, 4231 Markham St., Annandale, VA 22003, (703)750-3500.

STRONGIN, David A.——B: Jan. 17, 1931, NY, *Pres.*, Timber/Lake Realty, A.R.M. Hatter Corp.; **PRIM RE ACT:** Broker, Consultant; **SERVICES:** RE counselor, investment/sales; **REP CLIENTS:** Walley's Hot Springs Resort & Ctry. Club; Tahoe Racquet Club; BGI; **PROFL AFFIL & HONORS:** Incline Village Bd. of Realtors; **EDUC:** BA, 1966, Lit., Univ. of MD/Cameron Coll./Univ. of NM/Univ. of NB, Omaha; **GRAD EDUC:** Lit., Univ. of NV, Reno/Univ. of NM; **EDUC HONORS:** Dean's List; **MIL SERV:** US Army, Capt., Combat Infantrymans Badge, Bronze Star; **HOME ADD:** 1327 Thurgau Ct., Incline Village, NV 89450, (702)831-2407; **BUS ADD:** PO Drawer ZZ, Incline Village, NV 89450, (702)831-1166.

STROSNIDER, Lloyd N.——B: July 28, 1936, Santa Fe, NM, *Pres.*, Bellamah Group, Inc.; **PRIM RE ACT:** Broker, Developer, Builder, Owner/Investor, Property Manager; **OTHER RE ACT:** RE Devel.; **PROFL AFFIL & HONORS:** Intl. Council of Shopping Ctrs., Bd. of Realtors, Indus. Found.; **EDUC:** Bus., Univ. of NM; **OTHER ACT & HONORS:** Bd. Member Indus. Found. of Albuquerque; Bd. Member, Univ. of NM Alumni; **HOME ADD:** 5814 Torreon NE, Albuquerque, NM 87109, (505)821-2828; **BUS ADD:** 6121 Indian Sch. Rd., NE, Albuquerque, NM 87110, (505)883-3000.

STROUP, Hilry S.——B: Aug. 17, 1949, Cameron, TX, *VP*, First Fed. S & L of Austin, TX, Lending; **PRIM RE ACT:** Instructor, Lender; **OTHER RE ACT:** Mgr., Central TX Loan Dept., FFS of Austin; **SERVICES:** Comml., mort., consumer and personal lending; **PROFL AFFIL & HONORS:** Young Morg. Bankers, BOD Austin Mort. Review Bd. Austin Counseling Ctr.; **EDUC:** BBA, 1973, Gen. Bus., Acctg., Univ. of TX; **HOME ADD:** 2708 Mt. Laurel Dr., Austin, TX 78703, (512)458-3748; **BUS ADD:** 200 E. 10th, Austin, TX 78703, (512)476-8301.

STRUGATZ, Peter——B: Sept. 16, 1955, NYC, NY, *Pres.*, Medicalis Development Corp.; **PRIM RE ACT:** Developer, Owner/Investor; **EDUC:** BS, 1977, Geology, Beloit Coll.; **HOME ADD:** 256 Asharkon Ave., Northport, NY 11768, (516)757-1904; **BUS ADD:** 330 Vanderbilt Motor Pkwy., Ste. 203, Hauppauge, NY 11788, (516)757-1904.

STRUTT, George F.——B: Jan. 10, 1914, Baltimore, MD, *Pres.*, York Manor Inc.; **PRIM RE ACT:** Broker, Developer, Builder, Owner/Investor; **SERVICES:** Sales, consultant serv. Land devel.; **PREV EMPLOY:** 35 yrs. in spec. fields, still active; **PROFL AFFIL & HONORS:** Home Builders Assn. of MD, Past. Pres. 2 terms, Dir. (Life) NAHB, Realtor; **EDUC:** 1932, Bus. Admin., Baltimore City Coll.; **EDUC HONORS:** Outstanding Comm. Serv. Award, Bldg. Indus., 1962, Outstanding Achievement Award in Bldg. & Indus., 1968 (MD); **MIL SERV:** capt., 1940-44, Air Corps. Ordnance; **OTHER ACT & HONORS:** Dale Carnegie Courses, 25 yrs., KY Col., 1973; **HOME ADD:** 9 Nantucket Garth, Phoenix, MD 21131, (301)592-7468; **BUS ADD:** 300 Five Farms Ln., Timonium, MD 21093, (301)252-7177.

STRZEMPEK, Stanley——*Sr. VP Fin.*, Milton Bradley Co.; **PRIM RE ACT:** Property Manager; **BUS ADD:** 1500 Main St., Springfield, MA 01115, (413)525-6411.*

STUART, Charles E.——B: Oct. 22, 1937, Springfield, OH, *Pres.*, Interstate St. Charles; **PRIM RE ACT:** Developer, Builder, Property Manager; **PROFL AFFIL & HONORS:** ULI, NAHB; **EDUC:** BA, 1959, Econ., Union Coll.; **MIL SERV:** USAR, E-5; **HOME ADD:** Rose Hill Farm, Port Tobacco, MD 20677; **BUS ADD:** 222 Smallwood Village Center, St. Charles, MD 20601, (301)475-6833.

STUART, Robert F., Jr.——B: Oct. 24, 1937, Niagara Falls, NY, *VP, Prop. Mgmt.*, W.D. Hassett, Inc.; **PRIM RE ACT:** Broker, Consultant, Property Manager, Owner/Investor; **SERVICES:** RE mgmt., consulting & brokerage; **REP CLIENTS:** Citibank, Marine Midland, Dime Savings Bank of NY, pvt. investors; **PREV EMPLOY:** 12 yrs. Process Devel., Stauffer Chemical Co., Niagara Falls, NY; **PROFL AFFIL & HONORS:** IREM, BOMA, CPM, Lic. RE Broker; **MIL SERV:** US Army, Sgt.; **OTHER ACT & HONORS:** Assoc. for Retarded Children; **HOME ADD:** S-5264 Roberts Rd., Hamburg, NY 14075, (716)627-5944; **BUS ADD:** 290 Main St., Buffalo, NY 14202, (816)856-5000.

STUCKEMAN, H. Campbell——B: Aug. 7, 1914, Pittsburgh, PA, *Pres.*, The Precise Corp.; **PRIM RE ACT:** Owner/Investor; **PREV EMPLOY:** Reg. Architect; V.P. R.E. Rockwell Mfg. Co.; Dir. R.E. Rockwell Intl. until retirement 1975; **EDUC:** BS, Architecture, Penn State; **HOME ADD:** 17 Churchill Rd., Pittsburgh, PA 15235, (412)242-2217; **BUS ADD:** 4600 US Steel Bldg., Pittsburgh, PA 15219.

STUCKER, Gilles A.E.——B: Mar. 21, 1947, Paris, France, *Sr. VP, Fin.*, Forest City Enterprises, Inc., Corp.; **PRIM RE ACT:** Developer, Builder, Owner/Investor, Property Manager; **OTHER RE ACT:** Mort. Banking; Specialty Retailing; **PREV EMPLOY:** Arthur Young & Co., NY; Goldman Sachs, NY; **PROFL AFFIL & HONORS:** Fin. Exec. Inst.; Amer. Inst. of CPA's; **EDUC:** AB, 1970, Law/Intl. Affairs, ESCP Paris, France and Paris Univ.; **GRAD EDUC:** MBA, 1973, Fin., Cornell Bus. School; **EDUC HONORS:** Fulbright Scholarship; **HOME ADD:** 11586 River Moss Rd., Strongsville, OH 44136, (216)572-0564; **BUS ADD:** 10800 Brookpark Rd., Cleveland, OH 44130, (216)267-1200.

STUCKEY, Jay C., Jr.——B: Sept. 24, 1940, Phoenix, AZ, *Partner in law firm*, Jennings, Strouss & Salmon; **PRIM RE ACT:** Attorney; **SERVICES:** Specialize in zoning matters including highrise, comml., indus. and resid. devels.; **REP CLIENTS:** Devel. and Corp. RE Div.; **PROFL AFFIL & HONORS:** Pres., Planning Assn. of AZ; Member, AZ Assn. for Indus. Devel.; Zoning Ordinance Revision Comm.; Phoenix C of C Planning & Zoning Comm.; **EDUC:** BA, 1962, Acctg., Univ. of AZ; **GRAD EDUC:** JD, 1964, Law, Univ. of AZ; **OTHER ACT & HONORS:** AZ Acad.; Phoenix Thunderbirds; Phoenix Men's Arts Council; **HOME ADD:** 5301 E. Desert Vista, Scottsdale, AZ 85253, (602)991-0428; **BUS ADD:** 111 W. Monroe, Phoenix, AZ 85003, (602)262-5867.

STUDLEY, Julien J.——B: May 14, 1927, Brussels, Belgium, *Pres.*, Julien J. Studley, Inc.; **PRIM RE ACT:** Broker, Consultant, Owner/Investor, Real Estate Publisher; **PROFL AFFIL & HONORS:** RE Bd. of NY; Intl. Inst. of Valuers; **MIL SERV:** US Army, psychological warfare; **OTHER ACT & HONORS:** Film Soc. of Lincoln Center, New School, Chelsea Theatre; **HOME ADD:** 118 East 60th St., New York, NY 10022; **BUS ADD:** 342 Madison Ave., New York, NY 10073, (212)949-0133.

STUDY, Roy, Jr.——B: June 24, 1942, Hanvover, PA, *Dir. Devel.*, Poppin Fresh Pies, Inc., Pillsbury; **PRIM RE ACT:** Developer, Engineer, Builder, Property Manager; **PREV EMPLOY:** Friendly Ice Cream Corp., Wilbraham, MA; **PROFL AFFIL & HONORS:** MACO - Multi-Vent Arch. Engr. & Const. Officers Org./Nat. Restaurant Assn.; **EDUC:** BA Arch. Design., 1966, Const. Mgmt., PA State Univ.; **GRAD EDUC:** Cont. Educ. RE Courses, 1979, Univ. of MN; **OTHER ACT & HONORS:** Past Pres. Littletown PA Jaycees; Planning Commn., Littleton, PA 1970-1974; **HOME ADD:** 3510 The Mall, Minnetonka, MN 55343, (612)473-8691; **BUS ADD:** PO Box 110, Minneapolis, MN 55440, (612)330-5173.

STUEBE, William H.——B: May 8, 1941, Mineola, NY, *Sr. VP*, Landouer Associates, Inc., Investment Advisory; **PRIM RE ACT:** Consultant, Property Manager; **SERVICES:** Mgmt. of RE investment portfolios; **REP CLIENTS:** Domestic and For. Pension Funds; **PREV EMPLOY:** Chase Manhattan Bank NA, Eastdil Realty Inc.; **PROFL AFFIL & HONORS:** IREM, BOMA, RE Bd. of NY, Lic. RE Broker, CPM, Member, Mgmt. Comm. RE Bd. of NY; **EDUC:** BS, 1963, Fin., Lehigh Univ.; **HOME ADD:** 164 E. 72nd St., New York, NY 10021, (212)535-4218; **BUS ADD:** 200 Park Ave., New York, NY 10166,

(212)687-2323.

STUEBNER, James C.——*Pres.*, Northland Devel. Co. of Minneapolis, Inc.; **PRIM RE ACT:** Developer; **BUS ADD:** 7017 Boone Ave. N., Minneapolis, MN 55428, (612)535-5093.*

STUENKEL, Bob——**B:** Sept. 27, 1955, Hinsdale, IL, *VP*, Realty Associates, Inc.; **PRIM RE ACT:** Broker, Appraiser, Property Manager, Insuror; **SERVICES:** Valuation, mgmt., and brokerage of comml. and investment props.; **REP CLIENTS:** Lenders, attys., corp. RE firms and indivs.; **PROFL AFFIL & HONORS:** RNMI, NAIFA, ICSC; NAR, AR Realtors Assn., $1,000,000 Producer Award 1979; **EDUC:** BS, 1977, RE - Insurance, AR State Univ.; **HOME ADD:** 1207 Rainwood, Jonesboro, AR 72401, (501)972-6483; **BUS ADD:** P O Box 974, Jonesboro, AR 72401Suite 1000, First Plaza Bank Bldg., (501)932-1400.

STUKES, Marshall W., Jr.——**B:** June 21, 1934, Brooklyn, NY, *Asst. VP*, East New York Savings Bank, Urban Affairs - Mktg. - Mort. Programs; **PRIM RE ACT:** Banker, Developer, Owner/Investor, Instructor, Property Manager; **SERVICES:** Revitalization of communities; **REP CLIENTS:** Neighborhood organizations; **PREV EMPLOY:** N.Y.C. Housing Authority - Housing Activities Communities Coord.; **PROFL AFFIL & HONORS:** Savings Bank Assn. of NY State, Urban Bankers Assn., E.N.Y. Development Corp.; **EDUC:** BA, 1956, Bus. Admin., Sociology, Fisk Univ.; **GRAD EDUC:** Amer. Inst. of Banking Advance Studies; **OTHER ACT & HONORS:** Community Service Society, Brooklyn Urban League; **HOME ADD:** 69 Schenck Ave., Brooklyn, NY 11207; **BUS ADD:** 2644 Atlantic Ave., Brooklyn, NY 11207, (212)270-8880.

STUKITZ, George S.——**B:** July 3, 1944, White Plains, NY, *Mgr., Divestments and Corporate RE*, The Standard Oil Co. (OH); **OTHER RE ACT:** Mgr. Corporate RE; **SERVICES:** Acquisition of RE and disposal of surplus prop.; **PROFL AFFIL & HONORS:** Nat. Assn. of Corp. RE Execs., Chmn. - Surplus Prop. Comm., Recipient of Outstanding Leadership Award and Master of Corporate RE designation, Nat. Assn. of Corporate RE Execs.; **EDUC:** BA, 1966, Poli. Sci., PA State Univ.; **EDUC HONORS:** Valley Forge Military Coll. (1962) - Phi Theta Kappa; **HOME ADD:** 1760 Hall's Carriage Path, Westlake, OH 44145, (216)871-5665; **BUS ADD:** 1265S Midland Bldg., Cleveland, OH 44115, (216)575-4368.

STURDEVANT, Dick——**B:** Sep. 8, 1926, Newton, KS, *Pres.*, Professional Real Estators, Inc., Comml.; **PRIM RE ACT:** Broker, Consultant, Appraiser, Developer, Owner/Investor; **OTHER RE ACT:** Synd. of Oil Prop. & Projects; **SERVICES:** RE consulting, appraising, acquisitions, arrange fin.; **REP CLIENTS:** Indiv. and Large Corporate Investors; **PREV EMPLOY:** 30 Years, Pres. Econwealth & Professional Real Estators, Inc.; **PROFL AFFIL & HONORS:** Amer. Assn. of Cert. Appraisers; NAR; Amer. Right-of-Way Assn.; CAR; Indus. RE Devel., Dir. OAR; C of C Pres.; Rgnl. Pres. Red Carpet Corp. OK; GRI; Dean RE Educ.; **EDUC:** BA, 1950, Psychology, Emporia State Coll; **GRAD EDUC:** MA, 1952, Psychology, Univ. of KS; **MIL SERV:** USN, GM-3rd. UDT. 1944-1946; **OTHER ACT & HONORS:** Rotary Intl.; **HOME ADD:** RR 2, Ponca City, OK 74601, (405)765-6172; **BUS ADD:** 1912 Lake Road, Ponca City, OK 74601, (405)762-2438.

STURGEON, A. Thomas, Jr.——**B:** Nov. 2, 1941, Louisville, KY, *Chmn. of the Bd.*, Sturgeon-Thornton-Marrett Development Co.; **PRIM RE ACT:** Developer, Builder, Owner/Investor; **SERVICES:** Devel., owner and mgr. of comml. props.; devel. of resid. props.; prop. mgmt.; **PROFL AFFIL & HONORS:** KY Housing Corp., Bd. of Dirs.; Home Builders Assn. of Louisville, Bd. of Dirs.; Louisville Bar Assn.; KY Bar Assn.; **EDUC:** BEE, 1964, Univ. of Louisville; **GRAD EDUC:** JD, 1968, Univ. of Louisville Law School; **OTHER ACT & HONORS:** Louisville Area C of C, Bd. of Dirs.; Louisville Jaycees (Past Pres.), KY Jaycees; **HOME ADD:** 902 Rugby Pl., Louisville, KY 40222; **BUS ADD:** 10101 Linn Station Rd., Suite 950, Louisville, KY 40223, (502)426-4300.

STURGES, Lance H.——**B:** Feb. 22, 1946, Hollywood, FL, *Dir. of Leasing*, Homart Development Co.; **PRIM RE ACT:** Developer; **OTHER RE ACT:** Leasing; **PREV EMPLOY:** Oxford Devel. Co. Dir. of Leasing, 300 Monroeville Mall, Pitt., PA; **PROFL AFFIL & HONORS:** I.C.S.C.; **EDUC:** BA, 1970, Amer. Studies-Philosophy, Univ. of S. FL. Tampa, FL; **HOME ADD:** 996 Bosworth Field, Barrington, IL 60010, (312)382-6511; **BUS ADD:** Xerox Ctr./Suite 3100, 55 W. Monroe, Chicago, IL 60603, (312)875-8219.

STURGES, Michael——*Partner*, Laventhol & Horwath; **PRIM RE ACT:** Consultant; **SERVICES:** Mkt. research, investment advising, corp. planning; **PROFL AFFIL & HONORS:** ULI; **BUS ADD:** Nat. City Ctr., Cleveland, OH 44114, (216)696-4770.

STURGESS, A. H.——**B:** May 17, 1921, Johnstown, PA, *Sr. VP*, Arthur Rubloff & Co., Investment Prop. Div.; **PRIM RE ACT:** Broker; **SERVICES:** Investment prop. brokerage; **REP CLIENTS:** Institu. investors, foreign investors, and other gen. investment Co's., and investment partnerships; **PROFL AFFIL & HONORS:** NAR, Atlanta Bd. of Realtors, CCIM; **EDUC:** AB, Econ., Emory Univ.; **EDUC HONORS:** Phi Beta Kappa; Omicron Delta Kappa; **MIL SERV:** USN (1942-1946), Lt., Presidential Unit Citation; **OTHER ACT & HONORS:** Pres., Sandy Springs C of C for 2 yrs.; **HOME ADD:** 505 Carriage Dr., NE, Atlanta, GA 30328, (404)255-1477; **BUS ADD:** 134 Peachtree St., N.W., Suite 1500, Atlanta, GA 30043, (404)577-5300.

STURMAN, Howard P.——**B:** June 29, 1950, New Rochelle, NY, *Pres.*, The Sturman Organization Ltd.; **PRIM RE ACT:** Broker, Developer, Owner/Investor; **OTHER RE ACT:** Nursing Home Operator, Racquetball & Health Clubs; **SERVICES:** Devel. of Resid. & Comml. Props.; **PREV EMPLOY:** Chmn. of the Bd., Mediatrics, Inc. (a Public Co. in the RE & Nursing Home Field; **PROFL AFFIL & HONORS:** Westchester Bldrs. Inst., Bronx Bldg. Inst.; Member of 86th St. Team, E. Side Assn.; **EDUC:** BBA, 1972, Pub. Acctg. & Dual Maj. Fin., Hofstra Univ., NY; **GRAD EDUC:** MBA, 1974, Taxation, Hofstra Univ., NY; **EDUC HONORS:** Dean's List; **OTHER ACT & HONORS:** Chmn. of Bd. of Richmond Children's Ctr., a residen. ctr. for retarded children, NY Young Men's Philanthropic League; **HOME ADD:** 34 Century Ridge Rd., Purchase, NY 10577; **BUS ADD:** 200 N. Columbus Ave., Mt. Vernon, NY 10553, (914)664-2100.

SUAREZ, Michael A.——**B:** Dec. 14, 1948, Havana, Cuba, *Pres*, Michael A. Suarez & Assoc. inc.; **PRIM RE ACT:** Engineer, Developer, Builder, Owner/Investor, Syndicator; **SERVICES:** Consulting engr., const. mgmt. devel.; **REP CLIENTS:** SE FL Props., Cadillac Fairview, Inc.; **PREV EMPLOY:** In-house consultant for part. between SE FL Props. & Cadillac Fairview; **PROFL AFFIL & HONORS:** Nat. Soc. Profl. Engr.; ASCE; FL Engr. Soc.; Const. Specs. Engr.; Amer. Concrete Inst., Nat. Engr. Hon. Soc.; Nat. Physics Hon. Soc.; **EDUC:** BS, 1973, Civil Engr., Univ. of Miami; **EDUC HONORS:** Nat. Hon. Soc., Nat. Physics Hon. Soc., PS; **OTHER ACT & HONORS:** US Congress Advisory Bd., Amer. Security Council; **HOME ADD:** 9371 S.W. 77th St., Miami, FL 33173; **BUS ADD:** 9371 S.W. 77 St., Miami, FL 33173, (305)592-0804.

SUBAR, Jack S.——**B:** Mar. 29, 1941, Grand Rapids, MI, *Treas.*, Vantage Companies; **PRIM RE ACT:** Developer, Builder, Property Manager; **SERVICES:** To firm - cash mgmt., hedging, interest rates, loan pricing and alternate sourcing of short term funds; **PREV EMPLOY:** Harvey Kleiman & Co., CPAs; **EDUC:** BA, 1963, Acctg. and Fin., MI State Univ.; **GRAD EDUC:** MBA, 1967, Fin., Harvard Bus. School; **EDUC HONORS:** Grad. with high honors; **MIL SERV:** US Army Audit, SP-3; **OTHER ACT & HONORS:** Nat. Cash Mgmt. Assn., AICPA, Inst. of Internal Auditors; **HOME ADD:** 7433 Chattington, Dallas, TX 75248, (214)239-3609; **BUS ADD:** 2525 Stemmons, Dallas, TX 75207, (214)631-0600.

SUBLER, Betty L.——**B:** Apr. 10, 1940, Sidney, OH, *Mort. Loan Officer*, Peoples National Bank; **PRIM RE ACT:** Banker, Lender; **SERVICES:** RE mort. lending; **REP CLIENTS:** Resid. home buyers and small bus. prop. buyers; **PROFL AFFIL & HONORS:** Lic. RE salesperson, Grad. ABA Nat. School of RE Fin.; **EDUC:** 1958-59, Univ. of Dayton; RE Law, Prin. of RE and Installment Lending, Edison State College; Prin. of Acctg., Wright State Univ.; **OTHER ACT & HONORS:** Ticket Chmn. - Versailles Poultry Days, Former Member OH Chpt. of Mother's Club; **HOME ADD:** 844 East Wood St., Versailles, OH 45380, (513)526-3326; **BUS ADD:** 4-12 East Main St., PO Box 61, Versailles, OH 45380, (513)526-4611.

SUBOTNICK, Stuart——*Treas.*, Metromedia Inc.; **PRIM RE ACT:** Property Manager; **BUS ADD:** 1 Harmon Plaza, Secaueus, NJ 07094, (201)348-3244.*

SUCSY, Leonard G.——**B:** March 1, 1939, NY, NY, *Pres.*, Culbro Land Resources, Inc.; **PRIM RE ACT:** Developer, Builder, Owner/Investor, Property Manager; **SERVICES:** Comml., corp., indus. & resid. RE for sale or lease, design/build packages; **REP CLIENTS:** CT Gen., The Hartford Ins. Grp., Rolls Royce, Cumbustion Engr.; **PREV EMPLOY:** Pres., Construction for Progress; Pres., L. G. Sucsy & Co., Inc.; **PROFL AFFIL & HONORS:** Exec. Comm. Natl. Assn. of Indus. & Office Parks; CT Home Builder's Assn.; **EDUC:** Denison Univ., 1961, Econ.; **GRAD EDUC:** Harvard Bus. School, 1967, Bus. Mgmt.; **MIL SERV:** USN, Lt., Explosive Ordinance Disposal; **OTHER ACT & HONORS:** Republican State Fin. Comm., CT; Dir. Newington Childrens Hosp.; Dir. CT Opera; **HOME ADD:** 36 Colony Rd., W. Hartford, CT 06117, (203)561-2505; **BUS ADD:** 8 Griffin Rd., Windsor, CT 06095, (203)688-7501.

SUELL, Donald Herrick——B: Aug. 16, 1947, Waco, TX, *Partner*, Johnson, Swanson & Barbee; **PRIM RE ACT:** Attorney; **PROFL AFFIL & HONORS:** ABA; RE & Probate Sect. of ABA; TX Bar Assn.; Dallas Bar Assn.; **EDUC:** BBA, 1969, Acctg., S. Methodist Univ.; **GRAD EDUC:** JD, 1973, S. Methodist Univ.; **EDUC HONORS:** Sr. Class Pres., Southwestern Law Journal Bd. of Editors; Barristers; **HOME ADD:** 4436 McFarlin, Dallas, TX 75205, (214) 521-3134; **BUS ADD:** 4700 First Intl. Bldg., Dallas, TX 75270, (214)745-2103.

SUESSER, Alfred——*Contr.*, Dover Corp.; **PRIM RE ACT:** Property Manager; **BUS ADD:** 277 Park Ave., New York, NY 10017.*

SUHR, James K.——B: Feb. 1, 1929, Evanston, IL, *Sr. VP*, The First Nat. Bank of Chicago, U.S. Banking Dept. RE Grp.; **PRIM RE ACT:** Banker; **OTHER RE ACT:** First Chicago Realty Serv. Corp. - obtains fin. for income prop.; represents ins. co., mutual savings banks & mort.; **SERVICES:** Loan correspondents - RE Research Corp. Land use analyses, site location evaluation for devel., builders, fin. inst.; **REP CLIENTS:** indus., comm., retail and serv. firms and local gov. agencies.; **PROFL AFFIL & HONORS:** ULI, Robert Morris Assoc.; Amer. Bankers Assoc.; **EDUC:** AB, 1950, Econs./Math., Col. Coll., Co Springs, CO; **HOME ADD:** 2406 Central Park Ave., Evanston,, IL 60201; **BUS ADD:** One First Nat. Plaza, Chicago, IL 60670, (312)732-6482.

SULIK, Edward J.——B: July 17, 1926, Hartford, CT, *Sr. VP*, MA Mutual Life Ins. Co., Major Prop.; **PRIM RE ACT:** Lender, Owner/Investor; **OTHER RE ACT:** Responsible for Major Prop. Owned by the Life Ins. Co. and Pres. and CEO of MA Mutual Mort. and Realty Investors (REIT); **PREV EMPLOY:** Sherman-Williams Co., Murphy Paint; **PROFL AFFIL & HONORS:** Pres. & Tr., MA Mutual Mort. and Realty Investors; Pres. MA Mutual Realty Dev. Corp.; NAREIT; ICSC; MBAA; Advisory Bd. of the RE Inst. of NY Univ.; **EDUC:** BS, 1950, Finance, Univ. of CT; **MIL SERV:** USN; **OTHER ACT & HONORS:** Treas., Chmn. & Tr., Mercy Hospital (Springfield); Corporator of Wesson Hospital (Springfield); Dir. Better Homes for Springfield; Bd. Room (NYC); Colony Club (Springfield); PTO Recipient Award of Appreciation Amer. Legion; **HOME ADD:** 9 Brooks Cir, Longmeadow, MA 01106, (413)567-5207; **BUS ADD:** 1295 State St, Springfield, MA 01111, (413)788-8411.

SULLIVAN, Daniel F.——B: Sept. 13, 1942, Minneapolis, MN, *VP & Dir.*, McLeod Young Weir Ltd., RE Fin.; **OTHER RE ACT:** Mort. Banker; **SERVICES:** Mort. Fin., Equity Fin.; **REP CLIENTS:** Devels. (i.e. Cadillac Fairview, Oxford, Daon, Marathon, Eatons, Cambridge, etc.); **PREV EMPLOY:** Involved in RE Fin. for 15 yrs. with McLeon Young Weir; **PROFL AFFIL & HONORS:** CAN Tax Found. (author of numerous articles), Intl. Counsel of Shopping Ctrs. (speaker at annual convention); **EDUC:** AB, 1966, Econ., Columbia Univ.; **GRAD EDUC:** MBA & MA, 1967 & 1968, Fin. & Monetary Econ., Columbia Univ. & Univ. of Toronto; **HOME ADD:** 151 Crestwood Ct., Burlington, L7L2V9, ON, Canada, (416)639-0492; **BUS ADD:** PO Box 433, Toronto Domion Ctr., M5KIM2, Toronto, ON, (416)863-7453.

SULLIVAN, Daniel John——B: Mar. 9, 1931, Holyoke, MA, *House Counsel*, Daniel O'Connell's Sons, Inc.; **PRIM RE ACT:** Broker, Attorney, Developer, Builder, Property Manager; **OTHER RE ACT:** Construction Mgmt.; **SERVICES:** Devel., construction, mgmt., prop. mgmt.; **PROFL AFFIL & HONORS:** ABA; MBA; Hampden Cty. Bar Assn., Atty. at Law; Real Estate Broker; **EDUC:** BS, 1955, Bus. Admin., St. Michael's Coll., VT; **GRAD EDUC:** JD, 1971, Law, Western New England College; **MIL SERV:** USAF, Lt., 1955-1957; **OTHER ACT & HONORS:** Westfield Sons of Erin; Westfield Democratic Comm.; **HOME ADD:** 684 Holyoke Rd., Westfield, MA 01085, (413)562-6905; **BUS ADD:** 480 Hampden St., POB 267, Holyoke, MA 01040.

SULLIVAN, Deborah——*Pres.*, Vista Realty, Inc.; **PRIM RE ACT:** Broker; **SERVICES:** Comml. investment RE & mgmt.; **BUS ADD:** 2008 'C' St., Vancouver, WA 98663, (206)695-3344.

SULLIVAN, James B., Jr.——*Facilities & RE Mgr. (world wide)*, Sperry Corp., Sperry New Holland; **PRIM RE ACT:** Owner/Investor; **BUS ADD:** 100 Franklin St., New Holland, PA 17557, (717)354-1562.

SULLIVAN, James Michael——B: May 12, 1949, Boston, MA, *Pres.*, Marquette Properties, Ltd., Development; **PRIM RE ACT:** Consultant, Developer, Owner/Investor; **PREV EMPLOY:** Dir. of Devel., Denver West Ltd.; **PROFL AFFIL & HONORS:** Intl. Council of Shopping Centers; **EDUC:** BS, 1971, Railroad Fin., Univ. of NC; **MIL SERV:** US Army, S/Sgt. E-6, Silver Star, Bronze Star, Purple Heart; **HOME ADD:** 99 So. Downing, Denver, CO 80209, (303)778-6650; **BUS ADD:** 1624 Market St., Suite 202, Denver, CO 80202, (303)534-7530.

SULLIVAN, John P.——B: Feb. 12, 1925, Minneapolis, MN, *Pres.*, Navillus Land Co.; **PRIM RE ACT:** Broker, Developer; **OTHER RE ACT:** Designer; **PREV EMPLOY:** Practical logging & soils engr., 30 years; 2 terms as Pres. MN Timber Producers Assn.; **PROFL AFFIL & HONORS:** Brainerd Area Bd. of Realtors; **EDUC:** 1947, Mechanical & Civil Engr., Univ. of MN; **MIL SERV:** USN, Ens.; **OTHER ACT & HONORS:** Crow Wing Cty. Planning Commn. 6 yrs.; First Chmn. of City of Baxter Utilities Commission; Clerk of Baxter School Board, 17 years; **HOME ADD:** Route 11, Box 301, Brainerd, MN 56401; **BUS ADD:** Route 8, Box 430, Brainerd, MN 56401, (218)829-2825.

SULLIVAN, Paul T.——B: Jan. 26, 1942, Albany, NY, *Dir. Corp. RE*, Kidde, Inc.; **PRIM RE ACT:** Attorney; **PREV EMPLOY:** NY State Asst. Atty. Gen., Bur. of Condo, Theater & Synd. Fin., 1970-72; **PROFL AFFIL & HONORS:** ABA, NY State Bar Assn., NACORE, Cert. of Appreciation, NACORE; **EDUC:** AB, 1967, Eng., Holy Cross Coll.; **GRAD EDUC:** LLB/JD, 1967, Albany Law Sch.; **EDUC HONORS:** Cardozo Prize Recipient; **MIL SERV:** US Army, Res., SP5; **OTHER ACT & HONORS:** Pres. Clifton-Passaic Reg. C of C, (1982), Montclair Local Assistance Bd.; Bd. of Trustees, St. Mary's Hospital; **HOME ADD:** 213 Montclair Ave., Upper Montdale, NY 07043; **BUS ADD:** 9 Brighton Rd., Clifton, NJ 07105, (201)777-6500.

SULLIVAN, Richard——*Sr. VP & Treas.*, Varlen; **PRIM RE ACT:** Property Manager; **BUS ADD:** One Crossroads of Commerce, Rolling Meadows, IL 60008, (312)398-2550.*

SULLY, Ira Bennett——B: June 3, 1947, Columbus, OH, *Atty.*; **PRIM RE ACT:** Attorney; **SERVICES:** Negotiation and drafting documentation for comml. and resid. devel.; **REP CLIENTS:** Corp. and indiv. devel.; **PREV EMPLOY:** Borden, Inc., Corporate Law Dept., Columbus, OH, 1978-1980; Schottenstein, Zox and Dunn, Columbus, OH 1974-1978.; **PROFL AFFIL & HONORS:** ABA, OH State Bar Assn., Columbus Bar Assn. Real Prop. Comm.; **EDUC:** BA, 1969, Poli. Sci., OH State Univ., Coll. of Behavioral Sci.; **GRAD EDUC:** JD, 1974, OH State Univ., Coll. of Law; **EDUC HONORS:** Cum Laude, Phi Beta Kappa, Sphinx (Sr. Men's Serv. Honorary); Bucket and Dipper (Jr. Men's Serv. Honorary), Summa Cum Laude, Order of the Coif; Member of OH State Univ. Law Journal; **MIL SERV:** US Army Res.; **HOME ADD:** 305 E. Sycamore, Columbus, OH 43206, (614)443-4215; **BUS ADD:** 765 S. Front St., Columbus, OH 43206, (614)443-3903.

SULZBERGER, Edward——B: Nov. 30, 1907, NYC, NY, *Pres.*, Sulzberger- Rolfe, Inc.; **PRIM RE ACT:** Broker, Property Manager; **SERVICES:** Apt. mgmt., cooperative apt. bldg. mgmt.; **PROFL AFFIL & HONORS:** CPM, IREM; Natl. Assoc. RE Bds.; RE Bd. of NY; Intnl. Trader's Club; Intl. Fed. of RE Agents, Pres. Met. Fair Rent Comm.; Pres. Assoc. for Govt. Asst. Housing; **EDUC:** 1929, Brown Univ.; **OTHER ACT & HONORS:** E. side C of C; Former Pres. NY lodge #1 of B'nai B'rith former V.Chmn. NYC fund-raising drive of the Anti-Defamation League; Fed. of Jewish Philanthropies; Nat. Jewish Hospitals; Natl. Council of Jewish Women; Amer. Cancer Soc.; **HOME ADD:** 880 Fifth Ave., Apt. 12B, New York, NY 10021, (212)861-5922; **BUS ADD:** 654 Madison Ave., New York, NY 10021, (212)593-7670.

SUMME, Mark——B: May 3, 1953, Covington, KY, *Sr. Prop. Mgr.*, Con-Steel Corp., Mid-States Devel.; **PRIM RE ACT:** Developer, Builder, Owner/Investor, Property Manager; **SERVICES:** Bus. locations for sale or lease; **REP CLIENTS:** Gen. Motors, Digital Equipment, Shopsmith, E.F. MacDonald Co., Outdoor Sports, Ponderosa etc.; **PREV EMPLOY:** Engr. Dept. at St. Elizabeth Medical Ctr.; **PROFL AFFIL & HONORS:** IREM, CPM Candidate; **EDUC:** AS, 1976, Electronics, N. KY Univ.; **OTHER ACT & HONORS:** Bd. of Dirs. of the Moraine Bus. Assn., Bd. of Mgmt. for Public T.V. Station 16/14; **HOME ADD:** 222 Hilltop Ave., Oakwood, OH 45419, (513)299-7518; **BUS ADD:** PO Box 744, Dayton, OH 45401, (513)293-0900.

SUMMER, E. Janice——B: Feb. 13, 1944, Cherryville, NC, *Atty.-at-Law*, Daugherty, Kuperman, Golden, Carlisle & Morehead, Assoc.; **PRIM RE ACT:** Attorney, Syndicator; **EDUC:** BA, 1966, Wake Forest Univ.; **GRAD EDUC:** MA, 1968, FL State Univ.; JD, 1976, Univ. of TX; **EDUC HONORS:** Cum Laude, Cum Laude; **HOME ADD:** 2102 Hartford Rd., Austin, TX 78703, (512)478-3060; **BUS ADD:** 1500 Amer. Bank Tower, 221 W. Sixth St., Austin, TX 78701, (512)476-6666.

SUMMERS, Alfred H.——B: Feb. 2, 1921, Nacogdoches, TX, Summers & Summers; **PRIM RE ACT:** Attorney; **SERVICES:** Gen. RE, estate planning & probate; trial attys.; **REP CLIENTS:** E. TX National Bank of Palestine; Dogwood Realty Co.; Calloway Enterprises; **PREV EMPLOY:** US Supreme Ct.; ABA; US Dist. Ct. for E. Dist. of TX; **PROFL AFFIL & HONORS:** TX Bar Assn.; Anderson Cty. Bar Assn.; ABA, Assoc. Editor, TX Law Review 1952-53; **GRAD EDUC:** JD, 1952, Univ. of TX at Austin; **EDUC HONORS:** Editor, TX Law Review; **MIL SERV:** USMC; 2nd Lt.; 1942-45; **HOME ADD:** Rt. 4, Box 375, Palestine, TX 75801, (214)729-2510; **BUS ADD:** 111 W. Spring St., PO Box 1399, Palestine, TX 75801, (214)729-2128.

SUMMERS, Lorraine A.——B: Oct. 8, 1954, Cleveland, OH, *Supervisor, Prop. Taxes*, The Sherwin-Williams Co.; **PRIM RE ACT:** Property Manager; **SERVICES:** File all personal prop. returns, handle all RE tax assessments and appeals; **PROFL AFFIL & HONORS:** Member of Inst. of Prop. Taxation; **EDUC:** BBA, 1975, Mktg., John Carroll Univ., Cleveland, OH; **GRAD EDUC:** MBA, 1978, Acctg., Cleveland State Univ., Cleveland, OH; **EDUC HONORS:** Cum Laude Grad., Honors Student; **HOME ADD:** 5700 Ira Ave., Cleveland, OH 44144, (216)845-7454; **BUS ADD:** c/o Tax Dept., PO Box 6027, Cleveland, OH 44101, (216)566-2639.

SUMMERS, Paul F., Jr.——B: Aug. 22, 1926, N. Keys, MD, *Pres.*, Summers Realty Inc.; **PRIM RE ACT:** Broker, Consultant, Appraiser, Developer, Property Manager; **PROFL AFFIL & HONORS:** Prince George's Bd. of Realtors, NAR; **EDUC:** BS, 1951, Agriculture, Univ. of MD; **GRAD EDUC:** MS, 1953, Econ., Univ. of MD; **HOME ADD:** 849 Mt. Airy Rd., Davidsonville, MD 21035, (301)798-4603; **BUS ADD:** 14356 Old Marlboro Pike, Upper Marlboro, MD 20772, (301)627-2526.

SUMMERS, Richard G.——B: Sept. 2, 1931, St. Louis, MO, *Pres.*, R.G. Summers & CO.; **PRIM RE ACT:** Broker; **SERVICES:** Comml. & Indus. Leasing & Sales; **REP CLIENTS:** Owners of Office Bldgs., Warehouses, Indus. Bldgs. & land; **PREV EMPLOY:** James A. Barker & Assoc., Ltd. 1974-77; Martin Marietta Corp. 1958-74; **EDUC:** BS, 1952, Engr., Princeton Univ.; **GRAD EDUC:** MS, 1953, Engr., Cornell Univ.; **MIL SERV:** US Army, SP4; **OTHER ACT & HONORS:** Soc. of the Sigma Xi; **HOME ADD:** 5249 Strathmore Ave., Kensington, MD 20895, (301)933-3465; **BUS ADD:** 8150 Leesburg Pike, Ste. 600, Vienna, VA 22180, (703)893-2204.

SUMMEY, Sidney C.——B: May 22, 1951, Rockingham, NC, *Atty.*, Roberts, Roe & Watterson, Attys. at Law; **PRIM RE ACT:** Attorney, Developer, Instructor; **SERVICES:** Investment counseling, synd., HUD multi-family project advice; **REP CLIENTS:** Investors, brokers, indiv., mort. lenders; **PREV EMPLOY:** Criminal Justice Planner at N. GA area planning & devel. commn.; **PROFL AFFIL & HONORS:** ABA, Member of Real Prop., Probate & Trust Sect., AL Bar Assn., Birmingham Bar Assn., Estate Planning Council, Order of Barristers; **EDUC:** BA, 1973, Econ., Pol. Sci., Gardner-Webb Coll., Boiling Springs, NC; **GRAD EDUC:** JD, 1977, Law, Cumberland Sch. of Law of Sanford Univ.; **EDUC HONORS:** Cum Laude, Alpha Chi Hon. Soc., Moot Court Justice, Intl. Moot Court Term, Brice Writing Award; **OTHER ACT & HONORS:** Rotary Intl, Steward 1st Methodist Church of Birmingham, Adjunct Prof. of RE Transaction at Cumberland School of Law of Sanford Univ.; **HOME ADD:** 1540 Soulter View Rd., Birmingham (Homewood), AL 35209, (205)879-5605; **BUS ADD:** 215 S. 28th St., Birmingham, AL 35205, (205)251-1974.

SUMNER, Charles A., II——B: Aug. 18, 1945, Washington, DC, *Managing Partner*, KCS Development Co.; **PRIM RE ACT:** Developer, Owner/Investor, Property Manager; **SERVICES:** Devel. of income producing props. in Greater Sacramento area primarily for the co.'s own investment acct.; prop. mgmt.; **PREV EMPLOY:** Sherwood & Roberts, Inc. 1976-1978; Metropolitan Life Ins. Co. 1975-1976 RE Fin. Div.; Western Mort. Co. 1973-1974; **EDUC:** AB, 1967, Arch., Yale Univ.; **GRAD EDUC:** MBA, 1973, RE Fin., The Wharton Grad. School., Univ. of PA; **MIL SERV:** USMC, Capt., 1967-1970; **HOME ADD:** 422 Rio Del Oro Ln., Sacramento, CA 95825, (916)482-7251; **BUS ADD:** 79 Scripps Dr., Suite 207, Sacramento, CA 95825, (916)920-5256.

SUMNER, George H.——B: Nov. 10, 1912, E. Milton, MA, *Owner*, George Sumner Appraisal Associates; **PRIM RE ACT:** Appraiser; **SERVICES:** RE Appraiser; **PROFL AFFIL & HONORS:** SRA; **EDUC:** BS, 1936, UNH; **MIL SERV:** USN, Lt.; **OTHER ACT & HONORS:** Hampton Selectman, 1947-1953; Hampton Tax Collector, 1957-1960; **HOME ADD:** 158 Winnacunnet Rd., Hampton, NH 03842, (603)926-3576; **BUS ADD:** 158 Winnacunnet Rd., Hampton, NH 03842, (603)926-3576.

SUMNER, Sara E.——B: June 2, 1942, Danville, IL, Sara E. Sumner; **PRIM RE ACT:** Attorney, Owner/Investor, Property Manager; **OTHER RE ACT:** RE Tax, Estate Planning; **SERVICES:** Investment Counseling, Prop. Mgmt.; **REP CLIENTS:** Indiv. investors-some joint ventures in comml. props. and prop. held for investments; **PROFL AFFIL & HONORS:** ABA, IL State Bar, Chicago Bar Assn.; **EDUC:** BS, 1963, Acctg., Northwestern Univ.; **GRAD EDUC:** JD, 1966, Univ. of IL; **HOME TEL:** (312)337-3462; **BUS ADD:** 230 E. Delaware Pl., Chicago, IL 60611, (312)751-1427.

SUMWALT, Sam——B: Apr. 16, 1951, Indianapolis, IN, *Sr. V.P.*, Coldwell Banker/Thorsen, Residential; **PRIM RE ACT:** Broker, Instructor, Appraiser, Lender, Insuror; **SERVICES:** Comml. & Residential Sales; Mort. Banking; Title Ins.; Ins. Brokerage; Builder Services; Reloc. Services; **PROFL AFFIL & HONORS:** NAR; RNMI; IL Assn. of Realtors; NW Suburban Bd. of Realtors, GRI, CRS, CRB, Recipient Alma S. Thorsen Award 1976; **EDUC:** BA, 1974, Econ. and Bus. Admin., N. Central Coll.; **MIL SERV:** USN; P.O.; **OTHER ACT & HONORS:** Exec. Comm.-North Central Coll., Alumni Assn., Prince of Peace United Methodist Church; **HOME ADD:** 1492 Circle CT., Elk Grove Village, IL 60007, (312)980-6612; **BUS ADD:** 160 N. Northwest Hwy, Palatine, IL 60067, (312)934-0600.

SUNDAY, Sam B.——B: May 14, 1942, Roxboro, NC, *Pres.*, Alpert-Munday Devel. Corp.; **PRIM RE ACT:** Broker, Consultant, Developer, Owner/Investor; **SERVICES:** Comml. devel., Retail & Devel. Consultation, Retail and Comml. Brokerage, Mgmt.; **PREV EMPLOY:** VP Alpert Corp., VP, Internatl. City Corp.; **PROFL AFFIL & HONORS:** ICSC; **EDUC:** BS, 1968, Bus. Admin., Atlantic Christian Coll.; **MIL SERV:** USMC, Cpl.; **HOME ADD:** 5230 Alton Rd., Miami, FL 33140, (305)864-0593; **BUS ADD:** 350 N.E. 15th St., Miami, FL 33132, (305)358-1215.

SUNDEN, Gary R.——B: Dec. 16, 1940, USA; **PRIM RE ACT:** Owner/Investor, Property Manager, Syndicator, Developer; **SERVICES:** Investment counseling, devel. & sydn. of apt. bldgs., prop. mgmt.; **PREV EMPLOY:** The Legal Aid Soc. 1967-68; Pvt. practice of law 1968 to present; **EDUC:** BA, 1962, Eng. lit., Dickinson Coll., PA; **GRAD EDUC:** JD, 1966, NY Univ. Sch. of Law; LLM, 1968, NY Univ. Sch. of Law Grad. Div.; **HOME ADD:** 709 CarrolL St., Brooklyn, NY 11215, (212)638-5493; **BUS ADD:** 401 Broadway, NY, NY 10013, (212)925-4848.

SUNDERLAND, David K.——B: Mar. 25, 1930, Detroit, MI, *Pres.*, Gates Land Co.; **PRIM RE ACT:** Developer, Builder, Syndicator; **SERVICES:** New community devel., comml. & office devel., home bldg.; **PREV EMPLOY:** 1964-68 Janss Corp.; **PROFL AFFIL & HONORS:** Home Builders Assn., ULI, Apt. Assn., Community Assn. Inst., Pres. CO State Homebuilders 1979; Builder of yr. in CO Springs, 1977; **EDUC:** BA, 1952, Econ., Dartmouth Coll.; **EDUC HONORS:** Phi Beta Kappa; **MIL SERV:** USN, Lt. j.g.; **OTHER ACT & HONORS:** Univ. of CO Bd. of Regents, St. Francis Hospital Bd., C of C; **HOME ADD:** 3103 Springridge Dr., Colorado Springs, CO 80906, (303)576-5127; **BUS ADD:** 155 W. Lake Ave., Colorado Springs, CO 80906, (303)576-8505.

SUOMINEN, Henry C.——B: Jan. 1, 1921, Brooklyn, NY, *Independent RE Fee Appraiser*, Principal; **PRIM RE ACT:** Broker, Consultant, Appraiser; **REP CLIENTS:** Employee transfer co. throughout the US, State and Fed. agencies; **PREV EMPLOY:** Builder for 20 years; **PROFL AFFIL & HONORS:** SRA, RM, IFAS, CSA, ASA, SRPA, Rho Epsilon (profl. RE fraternity); **EDUC:** BS, 1947, RE, Syracuse Univ.; **MIL SERV:** USAF, Flight Officer, Typical; **OTHER ACT & HONORS:** Rotary Intl., Sigma Alpha Epsilon NY Delta; **HOME ADD:** 10 Goose Hill Rd., Cold Spring Harbor, NY 11724, (516)692-6266; **BUS ADD:** 611 NY Ave., Huntington, NY 11743, (516)427-0777.

SUPHAN, William H.——B: Sept. 19, 1946, NY, *VP, Fin.*, Ben Brooks & Assoc. Inc.; **PRIM RE ACT:** Broker, Syndicator; **SERVICES:** Resid. sales, comml. sales, comml. synd.; **PREV EMPLOY:** Mgr. of Acctg. for McCulloch Props. (Div. of MCO Resources), Treasurer of Sierra Charter Corp.; **PROFL AFFIL & HONORS:** RE Sales License; **EDUC:** BA, Bus. Admin., KS Wesleyan Univ.; **GRAD EDUC:** MBA, 1976, Fin. & Acctg., AZ State Univ.; **MIL SERV:** USAF, Capt.; **OTHER ACT & HONORS:** Rd. Dist. Bd. Member, Fountain Hills, AZ 1975-76; **HOME ADD:** 4949 E. Dahlia Dr., Scottsdale, AZ 85254; **BUS ADD:** 4736 N. 12th St., Phoenix, AZ 85014, (602)264-1565.

SUPIK, Frank R.——B: Dec. 13, 1929, NY, *Pres.*, Martinsburg Hospitality Corp.; **PRIM RE ACT:** Consultant, Attorney, Developer, Owner/Investor, Property Manager, Syndicator; **OTHER RE ACT:** Tax consultant; **SERVICES:** Hotel devel., synd. & prop. mgmt.; **EDUC:** BA, 1952, Fin., Acctg., St. John's Univ.; **GRAD EDUC:** LLB, 1954, St. John's Univ. NY; JD, 1954, St. John's Univ., NY; **BUS ADD:** 12005 Edgepart Ct., Potomac, MD 20854, (301)762-4831.

SUPINO, Peter F.——B: Nov. 14, 1940, Marseille, France, *Pres.*, Ageis Fin. Corp.; **PRIM RE ACT:** Broker, Consultant, Developer, Owner/Investor, Syndicator; **SERVICES:** Custom prop. searches (fee basis);

consulting to instns.; **REP CLIENTS:** Substantial private investors/funds/plans; **PROFL AFFIL & HONORS:** Harvard Bus. School Club of N. CA; CA Assn. of Realtors; NAR; **EDUC:** BA, 1962, Hist., Harvard Univ.; **GRAD EDUC:** MBA, 1966, Fin., Harvard Grad. School of Bus. Admin.; **MIL SERV:** USN; Lt. (j.g.); **OTHER ACT & HONORS:** Fox Club, Cambridge, MA; St. Mark's School Alumni Assn. of N. CA (Chmn.); Harvard Club of San Francisco; **HOME ADD:** 8 Linda Vista, Orinda, CA 94563, (415)254-9149; **BUS ADD:** 3700 Mt. Diablo Blvd. #206, Lafayette, CA 94549, (415)283-1871.

SUPPLE, George Michael——B: Feb. 5, 1939, Los Angeles, CA, *Owner*, R.E. Mktg. /Mgmt.; **PRIM RE ACT:** Broker, Owner/Investor, Property Manager, Syndicator; **PREV EMPLOY:** Com. cap.-Emeryville, CA; **PROFL AFFIL & HONORS:** IREM, Orange Cty. Chap.; E. Orange Cty. Bd. of Realtors, Orange Cty. Apt. Assn., S. Ctys. Apt. Assn., CPM; **EDUC:** AA, 1966, RE-Bus.; **MIL SERV:** USN, 2nd Class QM, 1961-63; **HOME ADD:** 3581 Primrose Cir., Seal Beach, CA 90740, (213)598-4390; **BUS ADD:** PO Box 5085, Garden Grove, CA 92645, (213)598-4390.

SURASKY, David, Jr.——B: July 27, 1939, Baltimore, MD, *Asst. Gen. Counsel and Asst. Corporate Sec.*, Hardee's Food Systems, Inc., Law Dept.; **PRIM RE ACT:** Consultant, Attorney; **SERVICES:** Legal responsibilities for all RE devel. acquisitions & leasing, construction, title ins., comml. & contractral matters for US div.; **PREV EMPLOY:** Howard Johnson Co.; Chelsea Title and Guaranty Co.; Arby's Inc.; TN Valley Authority; **PROFL AFFIL & HONORS:** ABA, Real Prop. and Corporate Sect.; MD Bar Assn.; The Fed. Bar Assn.; Amer. Judicature Soc.; Amer. Arbitration Assn., Member of Nat. Panel of Arbitrators; Admitted to practice before the Cour of Appeals of MD, the Supreme Bench of Baltimore City, The US Dist. Ct., Supreme Ct. of the US, Attorney; **EDUC:** AA, 1960, Bus./Econ./Eng., Univ. of Baltimore; BS, 1967, Bus./Econ./Mktg, Univ. of Baltimore; **GRAD EDUC:** JD, 1963, Law, Univ. of Baltimore School of Law; **MIL SERV:** US Army.; **OTHER ACT & HONORS:** Loyal Order of Moose; Masonic Lodge; Yedz Grotto; **HOME ADD:** Tau Valley, Apt. V-1, Winstead Ave., Rocky Mount, NC 27801, (919)443-7330; **BUS ADD:** 1233 N. Church St., Rocky Mount, NC 27801, (919)977-8515.

SURNOW, Jeffrey C.——*Owner*, The Surnow Company; **PRIM RE ACT:** Developer, Owner/Investor, Property Manager; **PROFL AFFIL & HONORS:** ICSC; **EDUC:** BS, 1973, Pol. & Soc. Sci. & Mktg., MI St. Univ.; **EDUC HONORS:** Dean's List, 1972 & 1973; Chmn. Student Adv. Comm.; **OTHER ACT & HONORS:** Other business address: PO Box 168 Southfield, MI 48037 Tel: (313)352-5525; **BUS ADD:** 1475 Lobo, Palm Springs, CA 92262, (714)320-2086.

SURREY, David——*Ed.*, Metropolitan Council on Housing, Tenent; **PRIM RE ACT:** Real Estate Publisher; **BUS ADD:** 24 W. 30th St., New York, NY 10001, (212)725-4800.*

SUSSMAN, Albert——B: May 11, 1916, New York, NY, *Exec. VP*, International Council of Shopping Centers; **OTHER RE ACT:** Trade Assn. Officer; **SERVICES:** Conventions, seminars, enrichment programs, publications, research, etc.; **EDUC:** BS, 1938, Soc. Scis./Eng. Lit., City Coll. of NY; **MIL SERV:** US Army, Sgt. 1942-46; **HOME ADD:** 24 Beechwood Rd., Hartsdale, NY, (914)946-0438; **BUS ADD:** 665 Fifth Ave., New York, NY 10022, (212)421-8181.

SUSSNA, Dr. Stephen——B: May 24, 1925, Phila, PA, *Lawyer, Prof., Consultant*, C.U.N.Y., Law Dept., Baruch College, Land Development Consultant; **PRIM RE ACT:** Attorney, Regulator, Instructor, Consultant; **SERVICES:** Expert witness environmental and zoning cases lawyer; **REP CLIENTS:** Ebasco Services Inc., Municipalities, NJ Bell Telephone; **PREV EMPLOY:** Tri-State Reg. Pl. Comm., City of Trenton, Commonwealth of KY; **PROFL AFFIL & HONORS:** AICP, NYNJ KY Bar, NYS Pub. Admin Intern NYS WAR Scholarship; **EDUC:** CCCNY, BA, 1949, Econ., Fordham Univ.; **GRAD EDUC:** JD, 1954, Planning, Fin.; MPA, 1951; Ph.D., 1964; **MIL SERV:** USNR, Ensign, Campaign stars; **OTHER ACT & HONORS:** Lawrence TWP Eco. Dev. Comm; **HOME ADD:** 24 Balsam Ct., Lawrenceville, NJ 08648, (609)882-5419; **BUS ADD:** 2E. Ebasco Services, 24 Balsam Ct., Lawrenceville, NJ 08648.

SUTHER, Thomas W., Jr.——*I.D. Dir.*, Santa Rosa Cty Industrial Devel. Authority; **PRIM RE ACT:** Property Manager; **BUS ADD:** PO Box 884, Milton, FL 32570, (904)994-8326.*

SUTHERLIN, Robert C.——B: Sept. 1, 1933, Gary, IN, *Pres.*, Sutherlin Assoc. Inc.; **PRIM RE ACT:** Broker, Developer; **SERVICES:** Indus. & Comml. RE substantial land sale & devel.; **REP CLIENTS:** Large corps. & private investors, Sears, Ford, Paul Butler, Chrysler, Miller Builders, CMI, Alter Grp., Anthony Desantis; **PREV EMPLOY:** Pain & Sutherlin, Inc.; **PROFL AFFIL & HONORS:** SIR, Chicago RE Bd; **EDUC:** 1956, Wheaton Coll.; **MIL SERV:** Ordnance, Lt.; **OTHER ACT & HONORS:** Sch. Bd., Timothy Christian Schools, Elmhurst, IL; **HOME ADD:** 7255 Willow Way Ln., Willowbrook, IL 60521, (312)323-5676; **BUS ADD:** 2100 Clearwater Dr., Oak Brook, IL 60521, (312)325-8210.

SUTKOWSKI, Frank J.——B: May 10, 1933, Middletown, CT, *Exec VP*, The Liberty Bank for Savings; **PRIM RE ACT:** Banker; **SERVICES:** Mort. loans; **EDUC:** BA, 1957, Hist. & Econ., Wesleyan Univ.; **GRAD EDUC:** Grad., 1971, Grad. Sch. of Banking, Brown Univ.; **EDUC HONORS:** Honors Grad.; **MIL SERV:** US Army, Cpl.; **HOME ADD:** 18 Woodland Rd., Portland, CT 06480, (203)342-0419; **BUS ADD:** 315 Main St., Middletown, CT 06457, (203)346-8605.

SUTTE, Donald T.——B: Nov. 20, 1933, Oak Park, IL, *Pres.*, Real Prop. Analysts, Inc.; **PRIM RE ACT:** Consultant, Appraiser, Developer, Builder, Owner/Investor, Instructor, Syndicator; **PROFL AFFIL & HONORS:** AIREA, Soc. of RE Appraisers, MAI, SREA; **EDUC:** BS, 1955, Bus. Admin., FL So. Coll.; **MIL SERV:** US Army; **HOME ADD:** 777 Bayshore Dr., PH 5, Fort Lauderdale, FL 33304; **BUS ADD:** 1213 S.E. Third Ave., PO Box 22100, Fort Lauderdale, FL 33335, (305)522-1495.

SUTTON, Berrien D.——*President*, Associated Coca-Cola Bottling Co., Inc.; **PRIM RE ACT:** Property Manager; **BUS ADD:** 320 Orange Ave. PO Box 111, Dayton Beach, FL 32015, (904)258-3355.*

SUTTON, J.H.——*Asst. Coun.*, Cooper Tire & Rubber Co.; **PRIM RE ACT:** Attorney, Property Manager; **BUS ADD:** Lima & Western Aves., PO Box 550, Findlay, OH 45840.*

SUTTON, John O.——B: Apr. 8, 1945, NYC, NY, *Atty.*, Sutton & Jamerson; **PRIM RE ACT:** Attorney; **SERVICES:** Investment counseling, consultant on RE devel.; **REP CLIENTS:** US Life Title Ins. Co. of NY; Toys R Us; FM Prop., Inc.; First Union Development Corp.; **PREV EMPLOY:** Paul, Landy, Beiley, Harper & Metsch; First Mort. Investors, Gen. Counsel; **PROFL AFFIL & HONORS:** ABA; Amer. Trial Lawyers Assn.; NY Cty. Lawyers; Dade Cty. Bar Assn.; **EDUC:** BA, 1966, Pol. Sci., Penn State Univ.; **GRAD EDUC:** 1969, Brooklyn Law School; **HOME ADD:** 2145 Arch Creek Dr., N. Miami, FL 33161, (305)893-9116; **BUS ADD:** Gables Intl. Plaza, 2655 Lejeune Rd.-PH II, Coral Gables, FL 33134, (305)448-1295.

SUTTON, Robert E.——B: July 3, 1943, Burlington, VT, *Pres.*, Core Cor.; **PRIM RE ACT:** Syndicator, Developer, Builder; **OTHER RE ACT:** Dev./Synd.; **SERVICES:** Investments & Counseling, Dev. & Synd. of Comml. & Resid. Dev.; **PROFL AFFIL & HONORS:** HBA, CRA, Bd. of Dir. Multi Housing World 1980, Wood Council Award, Best Design, Intl. Assoc. of Fin. Planning; **EDUC:** BA, 1966, Econ., St. Michael's Coll., VT; **HOME ADD:** 23893 W. Shooting Star Ln., Golden, CO 80214, (303)526-1124; **BUS ADD:** 2121 S. Onieda St., Suite 527, Denver, CO 80224, (303)758-2906.

SWAGEL, Dennis J.——B: May 25, 1946, New York City, NY, *Pres.*, Dennis J. Swagel, Law Corp.; **PRIM RE ACT:** Attorney; **SERVICES:** All legal services regarding comml. RE; **REP CLIENTS:** Owners/mgrs. of comml. shopping ctrs. and resid. apts.; **PROFL AFFIL & HONORS:** ABA; Beverly Hills Bar Assn.; Los Angeles Cty. Bar Assn.; CA Trial Lawyers Assn.; **EDUC:** BA, 1968, French, Hamilton Coll., Univ. of Paris (1966-67)(Cert. Du Premier Degree); **GRAD EDUC:** JD, 1971, Univ. of Fordham, Sch. of Law; Harvard Univ., Univ. of S. CA, Summer Session, Grad. Course; **MIL SERV:** USAR; Capt.; **HOME ADD:** 4329 Latona Ave., Los Angeles, CA 90031, (213)227-5483; **BUS ADD:** Los Angeles Word Trade Ctr., 350 South Figueroa St., Suite 460, Los Angeles, CA 90071, (213)617-9494.

SWAIN, Robert S., Jr.——*Sr. VP*, Bank of New England, N.A., Commercial Banking - Real Estate; **PRIM RE ACT:** Banker; **EDUC:** BA, 1950, Harvard Univ.; **GRAD EDUC:** MBA, 1955, Columbia Business School; **BUS ADD:** 28 State St., Boston, MA 02106, (617)973-1685.*

SWANGO, Dan——B: Jan. 1, 1943, IL, *Pres.*, Swango Realty & Appraisal Serv. Inc.; **PRIM RE ACT:** Broker, Instructor, Consultant, Appraiser; **PROFL AFFIL & HONORS:** TREA; MAI; CRE; Ph.D., AIREA Professional Recognition Award; **HOME ADD:** 2941 N. Calle Ladera, Tucson, AZ 85715; **BUS ADD:** 4727 E. 5th St., POB 12787, Tucson, AZ 85732, (602)327-6511.

SWANGO, Vern W.——B: Jan. 18, 1911, IL, *V.P.*, Swango Realty and Appraisal Service, Inc.; **PRIM RE ACT:** Broker, Consultant, Appraiser; **SERVICES:** Counseling, research, appraisal, brokerage; **PROFL AFFIL & HONORS:** Tucson Bd. of Realtors, NAR, ASREC, SREA, AIREA, CRE, SREA, MAI; **BUS ADD:** 4727 E. 5th St., Tucson, AZ 85711, (602)327-6511.

SWANSON, Charles M.——B: May 28, 1946, Marquette, MI, *Mgr. Comml. R.E. Lending*, Detroit & N. S & L Assoc.; **PRIM RE ACT:** Instructor, Appraiser, Lender; **OTHER RE ACT:** R.E. Appraisal instr. for community coll.; **PROFL AFFIL & HONORS:** SRPA-MAI Candidate; **EDUC:** BS, 1972, Bus., N. MI Univ.; **EDUC HONORS:** Deans List; **MIL SERV:** USN, E-5 Journalist Vietnam Service; **HOME ADD:** 4847 Foxcroft, Troy, MI 48098, (313)528-0166; **BUS ADD:** 8424 E. 12 Mile Rd., Warren, MI 48089, (313)751-6300.

SWANSON, Dwight F.——B: Dec. 14, 1920, Moline, IL, *RE Mgr.*, Lohman Bros. RE; **PRIM RE ACT:** Broker, Appraiser; **SERVICES:** Resid., comml., farm sales and appraisals; **REP CLIENTS:** Appraiser for estates courts and condonations; **PREV EMPLOY:** Same firm 19 yrs.; **PROFL AFFIL & HONORS:** NAR, RNMI, CRB, CRS, GRI; **EDUC:** BA, 1981, Bd. of Gov. Program, W. IL Univ.; **MIL SERV:** USAAF, S/Sgt., Air medal, Combat Aerial Gunner 8th Air Force; **OTHER ACT & HONORS:** Township Supervisor, Past Pres. Optimist, Past Lt. Gov. Optimist, Past thrice illustrice Master Masonic Lodge; **HOME ADD:** Rte. 3 Geneseo, IL 61254; **BUS ADD:** 935 S. Oakwood Ave., Geneseo, IL 61254, (309)944-5381; **BUS TEL:** (309)949-2240.

SWANSON, Eugene K.——*Treas.*, Sunstrand Corp.; **PRIM RE ACT:** Property Manager; **BUS ADD:** 4751 Harrison Ave., Rockford, IL 61101, (815)226-6000.*

SWANSON, John——*VP Eng.*, Cox Broadcasting Corp.; **PRIM RE ACT:** Property Manager; **BUS ADD:** 1601 W. Peachtree St. NE, Atlanta, GA 30309, (404)897-7000.*

SWANSON, Lawrence N. (Larry)——B: Dec. 10, 1932, Oklahoma City, OK, *Owner*, Swanson & Co., Comml. & Investment Realtors; **PRIM RE ACT:** Broker, Owner/Investor, Syndicator; **SERVICES:** Sale/Lease Comml.-Investment Prop., Counseling Investors; **REP CLIENTS:** Indiv. and Instit. RE Investors and Prop. Owners; **PROFL AFFIL & HONORS:** City, State and Nat. Assns. of Realtors; RNMI, CCIM; **GRAD EDUC:** BS, 1955, Univ. of OK, Norman, OK; **EDUC HONORS:** Pres., SIME, Dean's Honor Roll; **MIL SERV:** USAF, Lt.; **OTHER ACT & HONORS:** Rotarian; **HOME ADD:** 3149 Wilshire Terrace, Oklahoma City, OK 73116, (405)840-2161; **BUS ADD:** 921 Northwest Thirteenth St., Oklahoma City, OK 73106, (405)235-1405.

SWANSON, Lyn——*Ed.-Mng. Ed.*, Society of Real Estate Appraisers, Directory; **PRIM RE ACT:** Real Estate Publisher; **BUS ADD:** 645 N. Michigan Ave., Chicago, IL 60611, (512)346-7422.*

SWANSON, Oliver C.——B: June 15, 1916, Clyde, KS, *Owner*, Swanson Construction Co.; **PRIM RE ACT:** Builder; **SERVICES:** Gen. contractor: resid., comml., ind. & remodeling; **REP CLIENTS:** Home owners, bldg. mgrs., mgrs. & investors; **PREV EMPLOY:** Y.T. Swanson, Gen. Contractor; **PROFL AFFIL & HONORS:** Rockford Homebuilders Assn.; **EDUC:** Chicago Tech.; **MIL SERV:** US Army; Cpl., 1941-1945, numerous decorations; **HOME ADD:** 1416 Geneva Ave., Rockford, IL 61108, (815)399-9063; **BUS ADD:** 1416 Geneva Ave., Rockford, IL 61108, (815)399-9063.

SWANSON, Richard——*Dir. Construction*, Square D; **PRIM RE ACT:** Property Manager; **BUS ADD:** Executive Plaza, Palatine, IL 60607, (312)397-2600.*

SWANSON, Steven J.——B: Oct. 4, 1953, Darlington, WI, *Atty./Partner*, Nelton, Corey & Swanson; **PRIM RE ACT:** Attorney; **SERVICES:** Legal; **PROFL AFFIL & HONORS:** WI State Bar, ABA, ABA Real Prop. Section , Probate & Trust; **EDUC:** BS, 1975, Bus., Univ. of MN; **GRAD EDUC:** JD, 1978, Law, Hamline Univ. School of Law; **EDUC HONORS:** With Distinction, Cum Laude; **HOME ADD:** St. Croix Falls, WI 54024, (715)483-3677; **BUS ADD:** 314 Main St., PO Box 211, Balsam Lake, WI 54810, (715)485-3191.

SWARD, John Erick——B: Jan. 27, 1943, Evanston, IL, *Atty*, E.T. Hunter, P.A.; **PRIM RE ACT:** Attorney; **SERVICES:** Legal; **PROFL AFFIL & HONORS:** Lawyers Title Guarantee Fund, FL Bar Assn., ABA; **EDUC:** BA, 1971, Econ., Syracuse Univ.; **GRAD EDUC:** JD, 1976, Law - Real Prop., Corp, Syracuse University; **EDUC HONORS:** Intl. Law Award; **MIL SERV:** US Army, Capt., Air Medal, Army Comm.; **OTHER ACT & HONORS:** Oak Club, Frat. of Phi Gamma Delta; **HOME ADD:** 4106 N.W. 21st St., Lauderhill, FL 33308; **BUS ADD:** 1930 Tyler St., Hollywood, FL 33020, (305)925-6660.

SWARD, Scott R.——B: Mar. 24, 1950, Chicago, IL, *Sales Mgr./Dir. of Spec. Serv.*, Hoopes, Inc. Better Homes and Gardens, Resid.; **PRIM RE ACT:** Broker, Consultant, Attorney, Developer, Builder, Owner/Investor, Instructor; **OTHER RE ACT:** Mgmt. resid. sales force; **SERVICES:** Investment counseling, land devel. and planning counseling, legal rep. of builder/devel, instr. of firm in new construction; **REP CLIENTS:** Builders, Devel., Investors in Resid. Prop.; **PREV EMPLOY:** Dickinson, Inc. Realtors, Sales Mgr. 1975-1979; **PROFL AFFIL & HONORS:** ABA, PBA, NAR, PAR, Chester Cty. Bd. of Realtors, Broker/Atty.; **EDUC:** BS, 1972, Bus., Miami Univ., OH; **GRAD EDUC:** JD, 1975, Law, John Marshall Law School, Chicago, IL; **EDUC HONORS:** Dean's List; **OTHER ACT & HONORS:** Delta Sigma Pi, Jaycees; **HOME ADD:** 1066 Creamery Ln., West Chester, PA 19380, (215)399-6848; **BUS ADD:** Rt. 1, PO Box 102, Chadds Ford, PA 19317, (215)388-2111.

SWARNER, Fred——B: Sept. 8, 1932, OH, *Pres.*, Complete Property Management, Inc.; **PRIM RE ACT:** Appraiser, Property Manager, Syndicator; **OTHER RE ACT:** Comml. Investment Sales; **PROFL AFFIL & HONORS:** NAR, IREM; **OTHER ACT & HONORS:** Mason, Shrine, Kiwanis; **HOME ADD:** 2800 Ocean Dr. Apt. 6-D, Riviera Beach, FL 33404, (305)842-0283; **BUS ADD:** 2001 Broadway Suite 101, Riviera Beach, FL 33404, (305)842-1999.

SWARTZ, Lawrence B.——B: Feb. 20, 1945, Cincinnati, OH, *Atty.*; **PRIM RE ACT:** Attorney; **SERVICES:** Drafting of RE documents, litigation; **PREV EMPLOY:** Phelps, Hall, Singer & Dunn, Roath & Brega, P.C.; **PROFL AFFIL & HONORS:** Amer, CO & Denver Bar Assns., CO Trial Lawyers Assn., Assn. of Trial Lawyers of Amer.; **EDUC:** BA, 1966, Econ., Univ. of Cincinnati; **GRAD EDUC:** JD, 1975, Univ. of Denver; **HOME ADD:** 3073 S. Columbine St., Denver, CO 80210, (303)756-8088; **BUS ADD:** Suite 460, 3300 E. 1st Ave., Denver, CO 80206, (303)322-6900.

SWARTZ, Michael E.——B: May 16, 1948, Boston, MA, *Dir., Investments & Insurance*, Amer. Medical Assn.; **PRIM RE ACT:** Developer, Owner/Investor; **PREV EMPLOY:** Continental IL Nat. Bank, Chicago; **EDUC:** AB, 1969, Econ., Colgate Univ.; **GRAD EDUC:** MBA, 1971, Fin., Univ. of Chicago; **HOME ADD:** 196 Greenbriar Dr. W., Deerfield, IL 60015, (312)948-9480; **BUS ADD:** 535 N. Dearborn St., Chicago, IL 60610, (312)751-6735.

SWARTZ, Thomas Byrne——B: Mar. 6, 1932, Houston, TX, *Chmn.*, Sierra R.E. Equity Trust; **PRIM RE ACT:** Attorney, Syndicator; **SERVICES:** Sponsor and advisor of public R.E. Trust and atty. for pvt. R.E. Synds.; **PREV EMPLOY:** Partner, Bronson Bronson & McKinnon (attys.), 1959-80; **PROFL AFFIL & HONORS:** Nat. Assn. of R.E. Investment Trusts, CA and Amer. Bar Assn.; **EDUC:** AB, 1954, Yale Univ.; **GRAD EDUC:** LLB Boalt School of Law, 1959, Univ. of CA; **MIL SERV:** USNR, Lt.; **OTHER ACT & HONORS:** Pres., Piedmont Bd. of Education (1965-71); Bankers Club, Bohemian Cl Club, Claremont Ctry. Club; **HOME ADD:** 117 Sandringham Rd., Piedmont, CA 94611; **BUS ADD:** 300 Montgomery St. 525, San Francisco, CA 94104, (415)391-0129.

SWAYZE, Thomas R.——B: Sept. 16, 1924, New Orleans, LA, *VP Sales Mgr.*, C. J. Brown Inc. Realtors, Residential; **PRIM RE ACT:** Broker, Instructor, Appraiser, Owner/Investor; **PREV EMPLOY:** Exec. VP Latter & Bcum Inc., Chmn. Bd. Sunbelt Inc.; **PROFL AFFIL & HONORS:** Member Bd. of Dir. (Inter Community Relocation); Jefferson Bd. of Realtors, LA Realtors Assoc.) GRI; CRS; CRB; RM; **EDUC:** 1941-43, 1945-46, Bus. Admin. and Econ., Tulane Univ.; **MIL SERV:** USMC, Capt., Air Medal, Goal Star; **OTHER ACT & HONORS:** Who's Who of S. and SW; **HOME ADD:** 1232 Ashbourne, Baton Rouge, LA 70809, (504)272-5166; **BUS ADD:** 10201 Mayfair Dr. Suite F, Baton Rouge, LA 70809, (504)292-1000.

SWEARINGER, Robert G.——B: Nov. 21, 1944, San Antonio, TX, *Pres.*, Eton Properties, Inc.; **PRIM RE ACT:** Broker, Developer, Owner/Investor, Property Manager, Syndicator; **PROFL AFFIL & HONORS:** NAHB, NAR, RESSI; **EDUC:** BS, 1966, Mech. Engr., Stanford Univ.; **GRAD EDUC:** MBA, 1968, Fin., Harvard Bus. Sch.; **MIL SERV:** USN, Lt., Viewnam Serv. Medal, Air Medal, Nat. Defense Ribbon; **HOME ADD:** 10623 Riverview Way, Houston, TX 77042, (713)780-3194; **BUS ADD:** 7887 Katy Freeway, Suite 110, Houston, TX 77024, (713)688-1145.

SWEENEY, Craig C.——B: Apr. 7, 1951, Baltimore, MD, *Sr. VP, Dir. of RE*, Showbiz Pizza Place, Inc.; **PRIM RE ACT:** Attorney, Developer, Owner/Investor; **OTHER RE ACT:** Corp. RE acquisition and devel.; **PROFL AFFIL & HONORS:** ABA, JD, MBA; **EDUC:** BA, 1973, Lit., Poli. Sci., Univ. of Denver; **GRAD EDUC:** MBA & JD, 1978, Fin./Corp. Fin., Univ. of Denver; **EDUC HONORS:** Phi Beta Kappa; **HOME ADD:** 3620 Yorkway, Topeka, KS 66604, (913)272-1762; **BUS ADD:** 2209 W. 29th St., Topeka, KS 66611, (913)266-7021.

SWEENEY, David C., Jr.——B: July 13, 1932, Medford, MA, *Atty./consultant/ developer*, David C. Sweeney, Jr., Atty.: Caribe Ltd., Pres.; **PRIM RE ACT:** Broker, Consultant, Attorney, Developer; **SERVICES:** Legal serv., admin. law, fed., state, for. land registrations, consulting to time share/interval ownership projects; Atty./Consultant to condo developers; **REP CLIENTS:** Gen. devel. Co., Miami, Porest Glen Inn, Inc., N.H.; Grand Bahama Devel. Co.; Bodden Devel. Grand Cayman Is., Geoda Co. London, England; Solinvest Sweden & Portugal; Mt. Edge Time Shares; **PREV EMPLOY:** Counsel, Joint Comm. on Judiciary, State Legislature, State House; Boston, MA; **PROFL AFFIL & HONORS:** Intl. Land Devel. Assistance Comm.; Intl. Assn. of Land Sales Officials; NE Land Devel. Assn. (Former Pres.); Natl. Land Council (Former NE VP); ABA; Section on Real prop., Cited by State of CT for significant contributions to the land devel. industry; **EDUC:** BA, 1955, Hist. and govt., Boston Coll.; **GRAD EDUC:** JD, 1963, New England Sch. of Law, Boston; **HOME ADD:** 480 Jerusalem Rd., Cohasset, MA 02025, (617)383-1184; **BUS ADD:** 156 Brook St., Box 156, Cohasset, MA 02025, (617)383-6777.

SWEENEY, David M.——B: Nov. 9, 1948, Bowling Green, OH, *Asst. Counsel*, Union Commerce Bank; **PRIM RE ACT:** Attorney, Banker; **EDUC:** 1970, Bus. Admin., Bowling Green State Univ.; **GRAD EDUC:** JD, 1974, Univ. Toledo; **HOME ADD:** 5003 Fairlawn Rd., Lyndhurst, OH 44124; **BUS ADD:** 917 Euclid Ave., Cleveland, OH 44115, (216)344-6776.

SWEENEY, Francis J.——B: July 10, 1953, Bridgeport, CT, *Atty.*, Fulbright & Jworski; **PRIM RE ACT:** Attorney; **PROFL AFFIL & HONORS:** Houston Bar, TX Bar & ABA; **EDUC:** BBA, 1976, Acctg., So. Methodist Univ.; **GRAD EDUC:** JD, 1979, Univ. of Houston; **EDUC HONORS:** Deans List, Cum Laude; **HOME ADD:** 723 1/2 Pizer, Houston, TX 77009, (713)861-9560; **BUS ADD:** 800 Bank of the S.W. Bldg., Houston, TX 77002, (713)651-5151.

SWEENEY, John Jay——B: Nov. 1, 1950, Waukon, IA, *Owner*, Sweeney Real Estate, Devel. & Auction; **PRIM RE ACT:** Broker, Developer, Builder; **OTHER RE ACT:** Auctioneer; **MIL SERV:** US Army, E-4; **OTHER ACT & HONORS:** Pres., Waukon C of C; Pres., Waukon Lions; 4th Degree Knights of Columbus; **HOME ADD:** RR 2, Waukon, IA 52172, (319)568-3763; **BUS ADD:** 612 Rossville Rd., Waukon, IA 52172, (319)568-4170.

SWEENEY, John W.——B: May 7, 1931, Jamaica, NY, *Project Mgr., Legal Counsel*, The Cafaro Co.; **PRIM RE ACT:** Attorney, Developer, Owner/Investor; **SERVICES:** Legal counseling, devel. & fin. of comml. props.; **PREV EMPLOY:** R.H. Macy & Co. Inc., Asst. to Gen. Counsel & Sec., Penn Fruit Co., Inc., Sec. & Gen. Counsel, The Grand Union Co., Legal Supervisor for RE & Constr.; **PROFL AFFIL & HONORS:** Member of Comm. on Landlord & Tenant Relationships and Corp. Law, Real Prop., Probate & Trust Law, Sects. of ABA, ICSC; **EDUC:** AB, 1950, Econ., Fordham Coll.; **GRAD EDUC:** LLB, 1953, NY Law Sch.; **EDUC HONORS:** Torch & Scroll Hon. Soc.; **OTHER ACT & HONORS:** Author Legal Articles, 'The ABC's of Leases from the Viewpoint of the Tenant', and 'Another Look at Sale Leasebacks'; **HOME ADD:** 6163 Westington Dr., Canfield, OH 44406, (216)533-4790; **BUS ADD:** 2445 Belmont Ave., Youngstown, OH 44504, (216)747-2661.

SWEENEY, Robert J., Jr.——B: Madison, WI, *Pres.*, Quest Properties Corp.; **PRIM RE ACT:** Developer; **SERVICES:** Comml. Bldg. Devel.; **PREV EMPLOY:** W. Mort. Loan Corp. Baird & Warner; **EDUC:** BBA, 1976, Mgmt., Notre Dame; **GRAD EDUC:** MS, 1977, RE, Univ. of WI; **HOME ADD:** 665 S. Harrison St., Denver, CO 80209, (303)777-8114; **BUS ADD:** Suite 1980, Dome Tower, 1625 Broadway, Denver, CO 80202, (303)893-9252.

SWEENEY, Timothy C.——B: July 10, 1951, Portland, OR, *Pres./COB*, Mortgage Mint Corp.; **PRIM RE ACT:** Broker, Consultant, Banker, Lender, Owner/Investor, Instructor, Property Manager, Syndicator; **SERVICES:** Mort. Mint Corp. is a full service capital corp.; **PREV EMPLOY:** W. Capital Corp. 1977-79, Portland, OR Mort Money Inc. 1975-77, Corvallis, OR; **PROFL AFFIL & HONORS:** Member NAR/CCIM & RESSE/OR Indep. Mort. Brokers Assn., RESSI/CCIM; **EDUC:** BS, 1975, Fin./Acctg./Law, Univ. of OR; **MIL SERV:** US Army, Lt.; **HOME ADD:** PO Box 1228, Corvallis, OR 97339, (503)754-8484; **BUS ADD:** 420 N.W. Second St., PO Box 1750, Corvallis, OR 97330, (503)754-8484.

SWEET, George——*Sr. VP Adm.*, Reichhold Chemicals, Inc.; **PRIM RE ACT:** Property Manager; **BUS ADD:** RCI Bldg., 525 N. Broadway, White Plains, NY 10603, (914)682-5700.*

SWEET, Maynard E.——B: Dec. 24, 1912, Huron, SD, *Cert. RE Appraiser*; **PRIM RE ACT:** Broker, Consultant, Appraiser; **SERVICES:** Analysis & appraising of various special-purpose props.; **REP CLIENTS:** Lending instns. attys., private indivs., Dept. of Agriculture, Gen. Servs. Admin., Internal Revenue Dept., etc.; **PREV EMPLOY:** SD Dept. of Hwys.; ASCS Office Mgr. - US Dept. of Agriculture; **PROFL AFFIL & HONORS:** SD Soc. of Farms Mgrs. & Rural Appraisers; Amer. Soc. of Farm Mgrs. & Rural Appraisers; Nat. Assn. of RE Appraisers, Veterans Admin. Fee appraiser on resid. papers; **EDUC:** Teachers Certificate, Elementary Educ., Eastern State Normal, Madison SD; **MIL SERV:** Nat. Guard of SD, 1933-1934; **OTHER ACT & HONORS:** City Council of Iroquois SD (15 years); Organized Iroquois Development Corp., currently VP; Held offices in the Iroquois Coml. Club; **HOME ADD:** Box 6, Iroquois, SD 57353, (605)465-2311; **BUS ADD:** 120 N. Ottowa, Iroquois, SD 57353, (605)546-2311.

SWEET, Rowland F.——B: Apr. 18, 1910, Sacramento, CA, *Fee Appraiser*, Rowland F. Sweet & Associates; **PRIM RE ACT:** Appraiser, Developer; **SERVICES:** RE appraising, indus., comml and resid. mkt. studies, devel. concepts, cost estimates, pro formas; **REP CLIENTS:** Inst. lenders, RE devel., gen cont., city agencies, state and cty. agencies, Public utilities, attys.; **PREV EMPLOY:** Self-employed; **PROFL AFFIL & HONORS:** Amer. Soc. of Appraisers; ULI; Palm Desert Bd. of Realtors; Natl. Assn. Review Appraisers, ASA; CRA; AACA; **EDUC:** AA, 1931, Sacramento Jr. Coll.; **GRAD EDUC:** BS, 1933, Indus. Engr., Univ. of CA; **MIL SERV:** Air Serv. Command (Technical Advisor to the Commanding Gen.), T/Sgt., Legion of Merit; **OTHER ACT & HONORS:** Past Pres. ASA, San Bernardino-Riverside Chap., 2 yrs.; **HOME TEL:** (714)568-4907; **BUS ADD:** 73-535 Pinyon St., Palm Desert, CA 92260, (714)346-9401.

SWEETSER, S. Chandler——B: Dec. 15, 1945, Boston, MA, *Pres.*, The Sweetser Companies; **PRIM RE ACT:** Broker, Consultant, Developer, Builder, Owner/Investor, Property Manager, Syndicator; **SERVICES:** Devel., const., brokerage, leasing, prop. mgmt.; **REP CLIENTS:** Investors, tenants, joint ventures; **EDUC:** BS Engr., 1963, Mgmt. Engrg., RPI; **GRAD EDUC:** MBA, 1973, RE, Harvard Bus. Sch.; **MIL SERV:** USN, Lt.j.g., Navy Commendation with Bronze Star; **OTHER ACT & HONORS:** YMCA Bd. Dir., Past Pres., Harvard Bus. Club; **HOME ADD:** 6641 Avondale Dr., Oklahoma City, OK 73116; **BUS ADD:** Main Pl., 420 W. Main, Suite 500, Oklahoma City, OK 73102, (405)236-1521.

SWEM, Thomas Craig——B: June 11, 1951, Niles, MI, *Prin. Broker*, Real Prop. Investments; **PRIM RE ACT:** Broker, Property Manager, Owner/Investor, Instructor, Syndicator; **SERVICES:** Gen. brokerage, investment counseling, prop. mgmt. synd.; **REP CLIENTS:** Indiv. investors, trusts; **PROFL AFFIL & HONORS:** CA Assn. of Realtors, NAR, San Luis Obispo Bd. of Realtos, GRI; **EDUC:** AA, 1972, electron. bus., Lake MI Coll./Cal Poly Univ.; **GRAD EDUC:** Bus., Cal Poly, San Luis Obispo; **EDUC HONORS:** (now teaching RE Fin. in the Bus. dept.); **OTHER ACT & HONORS:** Audio Engr. Soc.; **HOME ADD:** 8807 Circle Oak Dr., Oak Shores, Paso Robles, CA, (805)472-2433; **BUS ADD:** 1880 Santa Barbara St. Railroad Sq. S., PO Box 186, San Luis Obispo, CA 93406, (805)544-4422.

SWENSON, Lawrence P.——B: Aug. 9, 1931, Fullerton, CA, *Owner*, Swenson Construction - The Home Team, A CA Corp.; **PRIM RE ACT:** Broker, Appraiser, Developer, Builder, Owner/Investor, Instructor, Syndicator; **SERVICES:** aquisition, counseling, bldg., sales; **REP CLIENTS:** R-B Devel., G.L. Lewis Homes, So. CA Fin. City Investing, City of Fullerton; **PREV EMPLOY:** Faculty-Fullorton Coll., Faculty CA Assn. Realtors; Faculty RE Securities & Synd. Instit.; **PROFL AFFIL & HONORS:** CA Assn Realtors, Nation Assn. Realtors, RE Securities & Synd., Instit. Past. Pres. N. Orange County Bd. of Realtors, C.A.R. Dir., Regional VP (AZ, CA, NV, UT, HI) Ressi - 2nd Region Gov. Ressi - Certi. Resid. Specilist GRI; **OTHER ACT & HONORS:** Rotary Intl. Molokai Yacht Club; **HOME TEL:** (714)525-1502; **BUS ADD:** S.R. 279, Kaunakakai, HI 96748, (714)777-4600.

SWENSON, Lynda——B: Feb. 18, 1944, Salina, KS, *Broker-Owner*, Remax of Wichita Falls; **PRIM RE ACT:** Broker, Syndicator, Consultant, Property Manager, Owner/Investor; **SERVICES:** Synd., Prop. Mgmt., Investment Counseling; **REP CLIENTS:** Indiv. investors; **PREV EMPLOY:** Computer Programmer, Mutual of Omaha; **PROFL AFFIL & HONORS:** RESSI; **EDUC:** BS, 1965, Bus. Admin., Berea Coll., KY; **HOME ADD:** 4404 Martinique, Wichita Falls, TX 76308, (817)322-3000; **BUS ADD:** 2945 Southwest Pkwy., Wichita Falls, TX 76308, (817)691-1212.

SWETT, Valerie——B: Sept. 27, 1949, Oak Park, IL, *Atty.*, Maloney, Williams and Baer, P.C.; **PRIM RE ACT:** Attorney; **SERVICES:** Negotiation and drafting of purchase contracts, fin., arrangements, leases, and trusts; title searches and opinions; **PREV EMPLOY:** Kaplan & Cummings, Ltd., Chicago, IL; Law Offices of Alvin L. Kaplan & Valerie Swett, Chicago, IL; **PROFL AFFIL & HONORS:** ABA, IL and MBA; **EDUC:** BA, 1971, Econ. major; Mathematics, minor, Univ. of Rochester, Rochester, NY; **GRAD EDUC:** JD, 1976, Law, Northwestern Univ. School of Law, Chicago, IL; **EDUC HONORS:** BA with High Distinction, JD Cum Laude; **HOME ADD:** 50 High St., Andover, MA 01810, (617)475-2551; **BUS ADD:** 133 Federal St., Suite 600, Boston, MA 02110, (617)482-9120.

SWICKEY, James B.——**B:** July 3, 1952, Enid, OK, *Pres.*, Columbia Capital Corp., Subsidiary of Parman & Salyer, Inc.; **PRIM RE ACT:** Broker, Consultant, Appraiser, Banker, Developer, Lender, Owner/Investor, Property Manager, Syndicator; **SERVICES:** Mort. & investment banking, comml. banking, devel. props.; **REP CLIENTS:** Savage Cos., Sweetser Cos., Leadership Props., Shaklefore & Assoc., The First Nat. Bank & Trust Co.; **PREV EMPLOY:** Liberty Nat. Bank, VP RE Lending, Pool Mort. Co., Branch Mgr.; **PROFL AFFIL & HONORS:** OK Bd. of Realtors; **EDUC:** BS, 1976, RE, Econ., OK City Univ.; **OTHER ACT & HONORS:** Young Men's Dinner Club, Bd. of Realtors; **HOME ADD:** 4607 N. Pennsylvania Ave., Oklahoma City, OK 73112, (405)842-7636; **BUS ADD:** 2000 Classen Ctr., SU 110E, Oklahoma City, OK 73106, (405)524-2000.

SWICORD, J.C.——*Dir. Corp. Adm.*, LTV Corp.; **PRIM RE ACT:** Property Manager; **BUS ADD:** PO Box 225003, Dallas, TX 75265, (214)746-7711.*

SWIFT, David A.——**B:** July 24, 1942, Brooklyn, NY, *Pres.*, David Swift Real Estate; **PRIM RE ACT:** Broker, Consultant, Appraiser, Syndicator; **OTHER RE ACT:** Specialist in sales of co-operative & condo. apts.; **PREV EMPLOY:** VP/Mort. Officer, Bankers Trust Co.; **EDUC:** BA, 1965, Drama, Tufts Univ.; **GRAD EDUC:** MA, 1970, Drama, Tufts Univ.; **MIL SERV:** USAF; A/3C; **HOME ADD:** 260 5th Ave., New York, NY 10001, (212)685-8637; **BUS ADD:** 260 5th Ave., New York, NY 10001, (212)685-8633.

SWIFT, William D.——**B:** Feb. 28, 1936, *Atty.*, Higgins, Swift & Finlayson; **PRIM RE ACT:** Attorney; **PROFL AFFIL & HONORS:** ABA, IN Bar, Allen Cty. Bar Assn.; **EDUC:** 1958, Bus., IN Univ.; **GRAD EDUC:** JD, 1964, IN Univ.; **MIL SERV:** USN, Comdr.; **HOME ADD:** 3770 Kirkwood Dr., Ft. Wayne, IN 46805, (219)483-4686; **BUS ADD:** 590 Lincoln Tower, Ft. Wayne, IN 46802, (219)423-4422.

SWINDELL, Gary Wayne——**B:** Mar. 13, 1954, Pitman, NJ, Equity Programs Investment Corporation; **OTHER RE ACT:** Asst. Gen. Counsel; **SERVICES:** In house; **PROFL AFFIL & HONORS:** Dist. of Columbia Bar, VA State Bar, Arlington Cty. Bar Assn., ABA; **EDUC:** BA, 1976, Philosophy/Pol. Sci., Univ. of DE; **GRAD EDUC:** JD, 1979, Georgetown Univ. Law Center; **EDUC HONORS:** Degree with Distinction/High Honors; Pi Sigma Alpha; **HOME ADD:** 2406-D S Walter Reed Dr., Arlington, VA 22206, (703)931-7968; **BUS ADD:** Suite 1600 5201 Leesburg Pike, Falls Church, VA 22041, (703)931-7600.

SWINDLER, Glenn P.——**B:** Mar. 14, 1939, Louisville, KY, *Pres.*, Glenn P. Swindler, Co.; **PRIM RE ACT:** Broker, Instructor, Syndicator, Consultant, Developer, Property Manager, Owner/Investor; **SERVICES:** Investment counseling, devel. & synd. evaluation, prop. mgmt.; **REP CLIENTS:** Indivs. & instns.; **PROFL AFFIL & HONORS:** RNMI, KY RE Exchangers, CCIM, Exchange of yr. award 1979; **MIL SERV:** USAF, S/Sgt.; **HOME ADD:** 14019 Harbour Pl., Prospect, KY 40059, (502)228-0321; **BUS ADD:** PO Box 152, Prospect, KY 40059, (502)228-0321.

SWISHER, Wm.——*Pres.*, CMI Corp.; **PRIM RE ACT:** Property Manager; **BUS ADD:** PO Box 1985, Oklahoma City, OK 73101, (405)787-6020.*

SYLVAN, Lawrence D.——**B:** June 19, 1935, Chicago, IL, *Atty. at Law*, Lawrence D. Sylvan Atty.; **PRIM RE ACT:** Consultant, Attorney, Lender, Owner/Investor, Instructor, Syndicator; **SERVICES:** Investment advisor; fin. planning; negotiations & preparation documents for RE transactions; synd.; **REP CLIENTS:** Indiv. lenders and investors in resid. and comml. prop.; **PROFL AFFIL & HONORS:** ABA; TX Bar Assn.; **EDUC:** BA, 1967, Poli. Sci., Loyola Univ. of Chicago; **GRAD EDUC:** JD, 1972, Prop., Univ. of Houston, Bates Coll. of Law; **EDUC HONORS:** Top 10% Corpus Juris High Grades; **MIL SERV:** US Army; 1959-1979, Lt. Col.; Legion of Merit, Bronze Star, Cross of Galantry, Air Medal; **OTHER ACT & HONORS:** Boy Scouts of Amer., ROA; **HOME ADD:** Humble, TX; **BUS ADD:** 13607 Stuebner-Airline, Houston, TX 77014, (713)893-9943.

SYLVESTER, John E., Jr.——**B:** Apr. 17, 1932, Orr's Is., ME, *Pres.*, Sylvester & Co.; **PRIM RE ACT:** Broker, Consultant, Appraiser, Developer, Owner/Investor, Property Manager, Syndicator; **OTHER RE ACT:** Mort. fin.; **SERVICES:** Fin. & devel. planning, mort. fin., brokerage, mgmt.; **REP CLIENTS:** Pvt. and corp. devel., banks and other fin. inst. engaged in re fin., prop. owners; **PREV EMPLOY:** Colonial Life, E. Orange, NJ, 1954-1961; Mutual Benefit Life, Newark, NJ, 1961-1964; Berkshire Life, Pittsfield, MA, 1964-1969 (VP, RE and Mort.); Hunter Moss & Co., Miami, FL, 1969-1971 (Partner RE Consulting Firm); Inst. Investors Trust, 1970-1973 (Exec. Tr.); Sylvester & Co., 1971 - present, (Pres.); Pat. Wash. Manage Corp. Bretton Woods NH, 1980-present, Pres.; **PROFL AFFIL & HONORS:** Mort. Bankers Assn. of Amer.; Intl. Council of Shopping Ctrs.; ULI; Nat. Assn. of Home Builders; NAR; Gr. Boston RE Bd.; BOMA; Nat. Restaurant Assn.; Nat. Hotel & Motel Assn.; Amer. Ski Fed., Licensed Broker, MA & NH; Cert. Mort. Banker; (CRA); Member, Inst. Resid. Mktg. (MIRM); Distinguished Fellow, Nat. Assn. of Cert. Mort. Bankers and Member, Bd. of Govs.; Sr. Cert. Valuer; **EDUC:** BA, 1954, Eng., Bowdoin Coll.; Upsala Coll.; Northwestern Univ.; Rutgers Univ.; Univ. of CT; Univ. of CA (Santa Barbara); Grad., 1959, School of Mort. Banking, Northwestern; **MIL SERV:** US Army, 1st Lt., Army Commendation Medal; **OTHER ACT & HONORS:** Algonquin Club, Boston; **HOME ADD:** 6 Rosebrook Ln., Bretton Woods, NH, (603)278-1555; **BUS ADD:** 1 Faneuil Hall Marketplace, Boston, MA 02109, (617)742-6418.

SYMMES, Douglass R.——**B:** Apr. 1, 1946, Brockton, MA, *Broker-In-Charge*, United Farm Agency, Inc.; **PRIM RE ACT:** Broker, Appraiser, Developer, Owner/Investor; **OTHER RE ACT:** United Farm Agency, Inc. is a nationwide RE Mktg. firm with 600 offices coast-to-coast; **SERVICES:** We focus our brokerage efforts on two main categories: (1) Farms and rural props.; (2) Comml. investment and bus. props.; **PREV EMPLOY:** Quechee Lakes Corp., VT's largest 2nd home devel., 1974-1975, Sales Adm.; **PROFL AFFIL & HONORS:** Diamond Award, United Farm's highest sales achievement; **EDUC:** BA, 1969, Eur. Hist., Boston Univ.; **MIL SERV:** USAR, Spec. 4; **HOME ADD:** Barnard, VT, (802)234-9597; **BUS ADD:** 119 VA Cut-Off Rd., White River Jct., VT 05001, (802)295-9400.

SYMONDS, John Richard——**B:** June. 16, 1944, Toledo, OH, *Sr. VP & Dir.*, The Robert A. McNeil Corp., Prop. Acquisition/Disposition; **PRIM RE ACT:** Syndicator; **SERVICES:** RE investment and prop. mgmt. nationwide; **REP CLIENTS:** Indiv. investors nationwide; **PREV EMPLOY:** Donaldson, Lufkin & Jenreth, 1966-68; Builders Resources Corp., 1969-1972; Barnett Winston Mort. Corp., 1973; Triad American Capital Corp., 1973-76; **PROFL AFFIL & HONORS:** CA RE Broker's Lic.; **EDUC:** BA, 1966, Econ., Clarem. Men's Coll.; **GRAD EDUC:** MBA, 1968, Investments, NY Univ. Grad. Sch. of Bus. Admin.; **HOME ADD:** 1508 Aster Ct., Cupertino, CA 95014; **BUS ADD:** 2855 Campus Dr., San Mateo, CA 94403, (415)572-0660.

SYRETT, George L.——**B:** Nov. 5, 1946, Detroit, MI, *Tax Mgr.*, Schenck, Dersheid, Kuenzlii, Sturtevant & Johnson; **OTHER RE ACT:** CPA; **SERVICES:** All tax services; **PREV EMPLOY:** Touche Ross & Co.; **PROFL AFFIL & HONORS:** AICPA; IL Soc. of CPA's; Inst. of Prop. Taxation; Railway Progress Inst., CPA; **EDUC:** BBA, 1973, Acctg., W. MI Univ.; **GRAD EDUC:** MST, 1978, Taxation, DePaul Univ.; **MIL SERV:** USAF, SSGT, Air Medal; **HOME ADD:** 1109 S. Humphrey, Oakpark, IL 60304; **BUS ADD:** 20 Forest Ave., Fond Du Lac, WI 54935, (414)921-2953.

TABASKY, Samuel T.——**B:** May 20, 1946, Malden, MA, *Treas., Dir., Owner*, The Codman Co., Inc. and Subsidiaries; **PRIM RE ACT:** Broker, Consultant, Developer, Owner/Investor, Property Manager, Syndicator; **SERVICES:** Brokerage, Prop. Mgmt., Consulting, Devel. and Synd. of Comml., Indus. and Resid. Props.; **REP CLIENTS:** Lenders, Indiv. Investors, Corp. Lessees and Lessors, Maj. Fin. Inst. and Devels. of Comml., Indus., and Resid. Props.; **PREV EMPLOY:** Touche Ross & Co. 1968-1978; **PROFL AFFIL & HONORS:** MA Soc. of CPA's, AICPA, Natl. Assn. of Accountants, CPA; **EDUC:** BS, 1968, Acctg., Bentley Coll.; **OTHER ACT & HONORS:** B'nai B'rith, Fin. VP Dir., Temple Tifereth Israel, Malden, MA; **HOME ADD:** 23 Fernway, Lynnfield, MA 01940, (617)334-4181; **BUS ADD:** 211 Congress St., Boston, MA 02110, (617)423-6500.

TABB, Herbert B.——**B:** Nov. 4, 1929, Chattanooga, TN, *CPM*, Herbert B. Tabb & Associates; **PRIM RE ACT:** Broker, Consultant, Property Manager; **SERVICES:** Prop. mgmt., counseling & brokerage; **REP CLIENTS:** Lending inst. & private investors; **PROFL AFFIL & HONORS:** NAR, IREM, CPM; **EDUC:** BS, 1952, Geology, Univ. of TN, Knoxville; **MIL SERV:** US Army; Sgt.; **HOME ADD:** 3025 Merrydale Dr., Chattanooga, TN 37404, (615)698-1078; **BUS ADD:** 854 McCallie Ave., Chattanooga, TN 37403, (615)267-8524.

TABISZ, Peter C.——**B:** Nov. 8, 1950, Plainfield, NJ, *VP*, Freedom Mort., Resid.; **PRIM RE ACT:** Banker, Lender, Instructor, Insuror; **OTHER RE ACT:** Branch Admin.; **PREV EMPLOY:** Wachovia

Mort. 1972-1975; **PROFL AFFIL & HONORS:** FNMA Level II Underwriter; **EDUC:** BBA, 1972, Bus. Admin., Econ., Pfeiffer Coll., NC; **HOME ADD:** 1536 Copper Creek Dr., Plano, TX 75075; **BUS ADD:** Box 400638, Dallas, TX 75240, (214)387-4833.

TABOR, Neil——B: Aug. 17, 1928, Baltimore, MD, *Partner*, Tabor & Rottman, Attys.; **PRIM RE ACT:** Attorney; **PROFL AFFIL & HONORS:** Univ. of MD Order of the Coif, Editor MD Law Review; Grad. Fellowship, Harvard Law School; **EDUC:** BA, 1948, Univ. of MD; **GRAD EDUC:** LLB, 1951, Unic. of MD Law School; LLM, 1952, Harvard Law School; **EDUC HONORS:** Order of Coif, Chesnut Scholarship Prize; **MIL SERV:** Army Jagc, 1st Lt.; **OTHER ACT & HONORS:** Grad. Fellowship, Member, Rules Comm. MD Ct. of Appeals; **HOME ADD:** 6812 Cherokee Dr., Baltimore, MD 21209, (301)486-5762; **BUS ADD:** 1808 Charles Ctr. S., Baltimore, MD 21201, (301)547-1500.

TABOR, Stanley V.——B: Mar. 5, 1931, *VP Corp. RE*, General Mills, Inc.; **OTHER RE ACT:** Corporate RE; **PROFL AFFIL & HONORS:** ABA; Assn. of the Bar City of NY, Bd. Chmn. (past) NACORE; **EDUC:** BS, 1952, US Merchant Marine Acad.; **GRAD EDUC:** LLB; LLM, 1957; 1960, Fordham Law School; NY Univ. Law School; **EDUC HONORS:** Grad. with honors; **MIL SERV:** USN, Lt. j.g., Korean Service; **OTHER ACT & HONORS:** Various Bds., incl.-NAM; MN Assn. of Commerce & Indus.; Downtown Council; **BUS ADD:** PO Box 1113, Minneapolis, MN 55440, (612)540-2275.

TAFT, Robert——*RE Mgr.*, Sonoco Products Co.; **PRIM RE ACT:** Property Manager; **BUS ADD:** PO Box 160, Hartsville, SC 29550, (803)383-7000.*

TAITANO, Rufo C.——B: Dec. 18, 1937, Agana, Guam, *Pres.*, Guam Housing Corp.; **PRIM RE ACT:** Broker, Appraiser, Lender; **SERVICES:** Resid. RE mort. loans; **PREV EMPLOY:** City Realty Inc.; Guam Housing & Urban Renewal Auth.; Bank of Hawaii; **PROFL AFFIL & HONORS:** MBAA; Nat. Assn. of Review Appraisers, CRA; **EDUC:** 1956, Geo. Washington H.S.; **MIL SERV:** USArmy, E-3; **OTHER ACT & HONORS:** Guam Jaycees; Bd. Member, Territorial Planning Commn.; Bd. Member, Guam Election Commn.; Bd. Member, Amer. Nat. Red Cross; Bd. Member, Guam Heart Assn.; **HOME ADD:** POB 2884, Agana, GU 96910, (671)472-8648; **BUS ADD:** Suite 202, GCIC Bldg., POB 3457, Agana, GU 96910, (671)477-8026.

TAKAHASHI, Teney K.——B: May 18, 1938, Honolulu, HI, *Pres.*, AMFAC Property Corp.; **PRIM RE ACT:** Broker, Developer, Property Manager; **PROFL AFFIL & HONORS:** RE Broker; **EDUC:** BS, 1961, Aero Engr., USAF Academy; **GRAD EDUC:** MBA, 1971, Bus. (RE), Univ. of HI; **MIL SERV:** USAF, Capt.; **HOME ADD:** 2392 Halekoa Dr., Honolulu, HI 96821; **BUS ADD:** 2530 Kekaa Dr., Lahaina, Maui, HI 96761, (808)667-7411.

TALBERT, James R., III——*President*, Anta Corp.; **PRIM RE ACT:** Property Manager; **BUS ADD:** One Galleria Tower, Ste. 1400, Oklahoma City, OK 73102, (405)272-9321.*

TALBOTT, John C.——B: Sept. 1, 1942, Martins Ferry, OH, *Atty.*, McDermott, Will & Emery, RE; **PRIM RE ACT:** Attorney; **SERVICES:** Legal rep. in housing devel. specifically related to State and Fed. housing programs and in synd. of housing projects; **REP CLIENTS:** Mort. lenders, devel., and; **PREV EMPLOY:** Area Counsel, HUD Milwaukee Office, 1973-1977; Assoc. Gen. Counsel, Nat. Corp. for Housing Partnerships 1977-1979; **PROFL AFFIL & HONORS:** DC Bar Assn.; Member, OH Bar; Mort. Bankers Assn.; **EDUC:** BA, 1964, Econ., Amherst Coll.; **GRAD EDUC:** JD, 1970, Cleveland State Univ. School of Law; **EDUC HONORS:** Grad. Summa Cum Laude; first in class; Banks Baldwin Award for Scholarship; OH Bar Assn. Award for Scholarship; Amer. Jurisprudence Award for Scholarship Indiv. Legal Studies 1968-70; National Moot Court Team, Bobb-Merrill Moot Court Award; **HOME ADD:** 7903 Old Falls Rd., McLean, VA 22102, (703)442-9628; **BUS ADD:** 1850 K Street, N.W., Suite 500, Washington, DC 20006, (202)887 8054.

TALCOTT, Tom M.——B: June 6, 1929, S. Bend, IN, *Tax Consultant*, Tom M. Talcott Co.; **PRIM RE ACT:** Consultant; **OTHER RE ACT:** RE Tax Planning; **SERVICES:** Tax Consultation in Fields of RE & Horse Racing; **PROFL AFFIL & HONORS:** Natl. Assn. Tax Accountants Inland Soc. Tax Consultants-Amer. Horse Council; **GRAD EDUC:** Bus. Admin., 1961, Acctg. Estate Planning Tax Acctg., Los Angeles State Coll., Univ. Notre Dame; **OTHER ACT & HONORS:** Quarter Horse Owner-CA Horse Racing Member 25 yrs. Profl. Baseball & Softball Offcl.; **HOME ADD:** 28410 Tulita Ln., Sun City, CA 92381, (714)679-5471; **BUS ADD:** 28410 Tulita Ln., Sun City, CA 92381, (714)679-5471.

TALCOTT, Worthington H.——B: Sept. 26, 1917, Washington, DC, *Exec. FP & Trustee*, Washington RE Investment Trust; **PRIM RE ACT:** Broker, Instructor, Property Manager, Insuror; **SERVICES:** Dir. of Prop. Mgmt. for 21 Prop. investment portfolio for a qualified RE investment trust; **PREV EMPLOY:** Cafritz Co., VP, Wash. DC 1943-66; W.R.I.T. 1966-81; **PROFL AFFIL & HONORS:** DC and MD RE Broker; IREM; Wash. Bd. of Realtor, AOBA/BOMA etc., CPM; **EDUC:** 1941, Bus., Univ. of MD; **MIL SERV:** US Army, Lt.; **HOME ADD:** 8007 Overhill Rd., Greenwich Forest Bethesda, MD 20814, (301)654-2235; **BUS ADD:** 4936 Fairmont Ave., Bethesda, MD 20814, (301)652-4300.

TALIAFERRO, Monroe——*Mgr. Comm. Affairs*, Butler Manufacturing Co.; **PRIM RE ACT:** Property Manager; **BUS ADD:** BMA Tower, PO Box 917, Kansas City, MO 64141, (816)968-3000.*

TALLANT, Frederick C., Jr.——B: May 20, 1954, Duluth, GA, *Atty.*, Friend, Williams & Tallant; **PRIM RE ACT:** Attorney; **REP CLIENTS:** Devels. and Investors in Comml., Residential and Undevel. Props.; **PROFL AFFIL & HONORS:** ABA, State Bar of GA; **EDUC:** BBA, 1976, Fin., Univ. of GA; **GRAD EDUC:** JD (Law), 1979, Vanderbilt Univ.; **EDUC HONORS:** Magna Cum Laude; **BUS ADD:** Suite 203A Duncan Sq., 1961 N. Druid Hills Rd., Atlanta, GA 30329, (404)325-1131.

TAMAYO, Joseph L.——B: Dec. 24, 1913, Colombia, So. Amer., *Owner*, International Investment Realty; **PRIM RE ACT:** Broker; **PREV EMPLOY:** Owner/Pres., Jolta Associates, Inc. in NY RE; **PROFL AFFIL & HONORS:** Miami Bd. of Realtors; **EDUC:** 1945, Econ/Sci./Law, Colombia, So. Amer.; **OTHER ACT & HONORS:** Magistrado Del H. Tribunal Supremo De Aduanas in Bogota, Colombia, S.A.; RE Broker for Jolta Assocs., Inc., NY, 1965-1975; **HOME ADD:** 4245 S.W. 7th St., Miami, FL 33134, (305)441-0383; **BUS ADD:** 4315 N.W. 7th St., Miami, FL 33126, (305)443-8272.

TAMBONE, Antonio J.——B: Feb. 10, 1927, Italy, *Pres. and CEO*, Tambone Corp.; **PRIM RE ACT:** Developer, Owner/Investor; **SERVICES:** Fully integrated RE devel. and investment concern with all activities incidental thereto; **REP CLIENTS:** Major multinational and domestic corps. as tenants or occupants of specification built structures; **PROFL AFFIL & HONORS:** Dir., Baybank Winchester Trust Co.; **MIL SERV:** USN; **OTHER ACT & HONORS:** Builder of the Yr. in 1961 by the MAHB; **HOME ADD:** 55 Myopia Rd., Winchester, MA 01890; **BUS ADD:** 2 Main St., Stoneham, MA 02180, (617)438-5900.

TAMBRINO, Dr. Paul A.——B: July 23, 1937, Flushing, NY, *Dean and Prof. of Acctg.*, Northampton County Area Community Coll., Bus. and Art Div.; **OTHER RE ACT:** Dean, Div. of Bus. & Art; **SERVICES:** Supervisory; RE Dept. is within Div. of Bus. & Art; **PREV EMPLOY:** Asst. Prof. - Grad. Faculty - Hofstra Univ., Consultant - Pfizer, Inc., NYC; **PROFL AFFIL & HONORS:** Delta Pi Epsilon, Beta Alpha Psi, Outstanding Educator of America - 1973; **EDUC:** BA, 1958, Econs. and Bus. Admin., Central Coll. (IA); **GRAD EDUC:** MS, EdD, 1966 - 1973, Hofstra Univ.; Temple Univ.; **EDUC HONORS:** Oscar James Goerke Found. Scholarship; Dean's List; **MIL SERV:** USAR (1959-65), 1st Lt.; **OTHER ACT & HONORS:** Rotary Intl., Easton Area C of C Bd. of Dirs.; President of Lehigh-Northampton Cty. Business Teachers 1981-; **HOME ADD:** 2790 Flecks Ln., Easton, PA 18042, (215)258-6673; **BUS ADD:** 3835 Green Pond Rd., Bethlehem, PA 18017, (215)865-5351.

TAMBURRO, James V.——B: Oct. 19, 1942, Newark, NJ, *Corporate Counsel*; **PRIM RE ACT:** Attorney, Instructor, Engineer, Real Estate Publisher; **OTHER RE ACT:** Contributing ed. on RE *Jersey Bus. Review*; **SERVICES:** Representation, consultation, litigation & appeals in land use control, zoning & planning, constr. matters; **REP CLIENTS:** Indiv., comml. owners & devels., of resid. & comml. props.; **PREV EMPLOY:** Title Atty., Chicago Title Ins., Co., 1970-72; Assoc. Atty., Bankers Title & Abstract Co., 1972-74; Asst. Prof. of Real Prop. Law, DE Law School, 1975-76; Dir. Inst. of RE, Upsala Coll., 1977-80; **PROFL AFFIL & HONORS:** Morris Cty. Bar Assn.; **EDUC:** BS, 1964, Mech. Engrg., NJ Inst. of Tech., **GRAD EDUC:** JD, 1970, Law, Seton Hall Univ. School of Law; **OTHER ACT & HONORS:** First VP, Montville Twp. C of C; Tr., Montville Twp. Bd. Educ., 1978-80; **BUS ADD:** CONCAST, Inc., 12 Mercedes Dr., Montvale, NJ 07645, (201)573-0700.

TAMMAN, Z.——*Pres.*, Amer. Realty Investment Ltd.; **PRIM RE ACT:** Developer, Builder, Owner/Investor; **BUS ADD:** 133 S. Livingston Ave., Livingston, NJ 07039, (201)533-1466.

TANDY, Norman——B: July 2, 1918, NYC, *Construction Consultant*; **PRIM RE ACT:** Consultant; **SERVICES:** Consultation on costs, feasibility, plans & specs.; **REP CLIENTS:** Related Housing Cos.;

PREV EMPLOY: Pres., Presidential Const. Corp.; VP-Presidential Realty Corp.; **PROFL AFFIL & HONORS:** Lic. Gen. Contractor-FL & CO; **EDUC:** B Chem. Engr., 1939, City Coll. of NY; **MIL SERV:** USN, Lt. Cdr.; **HOME ADD:** 61 Brookview Terr., Hillsdale, NJ 07642, (201)664-3567; **BUS ADD:** 645-5th Ave., NY, NY 10022, (212)421-5333.

TANEGA, Joseph Atangan——**B:** Jan. 20, 1954, Manila, Philippines, *Gen. Counsel*, Tanega Realty, Inc.; **PRIM RE ACT:** Broker, Consultant, Attorney, Developer, Instructor; **SERVICES:** Legal Counsel, Teaching; **PREV EMPLOY:** Dept. of Atty. Gen. State of HI as Deputy Atty. Gen.; **PROFL AFFIL & HONORS:** HI State Bar, CA State Bar, Realtor/Atty.; **EDUC:** AB, 1975, Ancient Greek Philosophy, Princeton Univ.; **GRAD EDUC:** Univ. of San Diego Sch. of Law, 1978, Law; **EDUC HONORS:** M.M. Scott Scholarship, Irwin & Irwin Scholarship, Asian Amer. Students Scholarship; **HOME ADD:** 4278 Halupa St., Honolulu, HI 96818, (808)422-2276; **BUS ADD:** 98-211 Pali Momi St., Suite 640, Aiea, HI 96701, (808)488-7769.

TANIS, Robert——**B:** July 20, 1930, NJ, *Dir. of RE/Contracts*, ITT Continental Baking Co.; **PRIM RE ACT:** Property Manager; **EDUC:** BS, 1952, Merchandising, Fairleigh Dickinson Univ.; **GRAD EDUC:** MBA, 1967, Bus. Mgmt., Fairleigh Dickinson Univ.; **EDUC HONORS:** Cum Laude, Magna Cum Laude; **OTHER ACT & HONORS:** US Army; Cpl.; **HOME ADD:** 237 Glenwood Dr., N. Haledon, NJ 07508; **BUS ADD:** PO Box 731, Rye, NY 10580, (914)899-0467.

TANKENOFF, Gary L.——**B:** Dec. 11, 1934, St. Paul, MN, *Gen. Partner*, Hillcrest Devel.; **PRIM RE ACT:** Developer, Owner/Investor; **PROFL AFFIL & HONORS:** BOMA, C of C; **EDUC:** 1957, Univ. of MN; **MIL SERV:** USN, PO III; **OTHER ACT & HONORS:** Past Pres. St. Paul BOMA, Chmn. of St. Paul Parking Commn., Bd. Member of Downtown Dist. Council; **HOME ADD:** 2431 Cedar Ln., Minneapolis, MN 55416, (612)927-8087; **BUS ADD:** 250 Metro Sq., St. Paul, MN 55101, (612)224-5811.

TANKERSLEY, Brad M.——**B:** Sept. 28, 1952, Ardmore, OK, *VP & Treas.*, The Tankersley Companies, Admin.; **PRIM RE ACT:** Consultant, Developer, Lender, Builder, Owner/Investor, Property Manager; **SERVICES:** All phases of comml. const., land acquisition, planning, devel., engr., constr., fin., owning; **PROFL AFFIL & HONORS:** AGC, Assoc. Bldrs. & Contractors, Oklahoma City C of C; **EDUC:** Bus. Admin., 1974, OK Univ.; **OTHER ACT & HONORS:** Young Republicans of OK; Oklahoma City Jr. C of C; 2000 Hour Pilot; Advisor - Oklahoma City Parks & Recreation Dept.; **HOME ADD:** Oklahoma City, OK; **BUS ADD:** 1133 N.W. 1st, PO Box 60366, Oklahoma City, OK 73146, (405)272-0400.

TANKERSLEY, Ronald S.——**B:** Dec. 12, 1941, Flagstaff, AZ, *VP of Finance and Treasurer*, Carlsberg Corp.; **PRIM RE ACT:** Broker, Developer, Lender, Builder, Owner/Investor, Property Manager, Insuror; **SERVICES:** Resid., comml., indus., pre-fabricated manufactured const.; land devel.; RE brokerage and prop. mgmt.; mort. fin.; **PREV EMPLOY:** Deloitte, Haskins & Sells; **PROFL AFFIL & HONORS:** AICPA; **EDUC:** BS, 1964, Acctg. and Bus. Mgmt., AZ State Univ.; **HOME ADD:** 7019 Lofty Grove Dr., Rancho Palos Verdes, CA 90174, (213)541-6725; **BUS ADD:** 2800 28th St., Santa Monica, CA 90405, (213)450-6800.

TANKOOS, Bradley J.——**B:** Mar. 7, 1952, NY, NY, *Proprietor*, Tankoos and Co.; **PRIM RE ACT:** Broker, Developer, Owner/Investor; **SERVICES:** Specialize in office bldgs. in Denver, CO; **PREV EMPLOY:** Second VP, The Chase Manhattan Bank; **PROFL AFFIL & HONORS:** Economic Club of NY, Intl. Council of Shopping Ctrs., Young Mort. Bankers Assoc., Natl. Realty Club, RE Bd. of NY, BOMA; **EDUC:** BS, BA, 1974, RE, Univ. of Denver; **BUS ADD:** 6445 E. Ohio Ave., Suite 200, Denver, CO 80224, (303)320-6760.

TANNER, Arthur R.——**B:** Aug. 2, 1931, Flagstaff, AZ, *Owner*, Burk, Tanner & Co.; **PRIM RE ACT:** Broker, Consultant, Appraiser, Owner/Investor; **SERVICES:** Comml. Leasing; Sales; Shopping Ctrs. and Office Dev.; **REP CLIENTS:** Merrill Lynch, Cabot, Cabot & Forbes, Valley Distributing Co. (Yellow Front), Fridays, - Banks and Savings Instns.; The Navajo Tribe; **PREV EMPLOY:** Coldwell Banker & Co. - 18 yrs. Tucson Resident Mgr.; **PROFL AFFIL & HONORS:** MBAA, SREA, NAREB, AZ State Assn. of Realtors, Pres. (AZ state) Above Assns., NAREB; **EDUC:** BS, BA, 1954, Marketing, Univ. of AZ; **OTHER ACT & HONORS:** Los Charros; Little League; Political Affairs Chmn.; Local Bd. of Realtors; **HOME ADD:** 4305 S. Essex Ln., Tucson, AZ 86711, (602)747-3795; **BUS ADD:** 2033 E. Speedway Blvd., Tucson, AZ 85719, (602)881-7132.

TANNER, Joanna May——**B:** Sept. 27, 1939, Nashville, TN, *Exec. Dir. Bd. Services and Educ.*, Northern Virginia Board of Realtors, Inc.; **PRIM RE ACT:** Owner/Investor; **OTHER RE ACT:** RE Assn. Exec.; **SERVICES:** profl. trade assn. services to membership; **PREV EMPLOY:** Town and Country Props., Inc. 1972, Wellborn Props. 1966-72, Routh Robbins RE Corp 1965; **PROFL AFFIL & HONORS:** Amer. Soc. of Assn. Execs., WA Soc. of Assn. Execs., Inc., RE Educ. Assn., Mrs. Realtor, N. VA Bd. of Realtors, Inc. 1972, Pi Delta Epsilon, Honorary Journalism Frat. 1962, Omega Tau Rho, Honorary, NAR 1973, GRI 1969; **EDUC:** BS, 1962, Educ., Southwestern Univ.; **HOME ADD:** 6730 Pine Creek Ct., McLean, VA 22101, (703)532-8055; **BUS ADD:** 8411 Arlington Blvd., Fairfax, VA 22031, (703)560-7350.

TANNER, Richard S.——**B:** Aug. 28, 1952, Salt Lake City, UT, *Gen. Mgr., Gen. Partner*, Extra Space Development Co.; **PRIM RE ACT:** Developer, Builder, Owner/Investor; **SERVICES:** Purchase, devel. and mgmt. of self-service storage facilities; **PREV EMPLOY:** K. M. Woolley & Company, Realtors; **PROFL AFFIL & HONORS:** Self Service Storage Assn., Region 3, VP; **EDUC:** BS Bus. Mgmt., 1976, Brigham Young Univ.; **GRAD EDUC:** MBA, 1977, Mgmt. and Fin., Univ. of UT Grad. Sch. of Bus.; **EDUC HONORS:** With Distinction, Cum Laude, Grad. Student Member of the Coll. of Bus. Exec. and Fin. Comm.; **OTHER ACT & HONORS:** Sunstone Found., Bus. Mgr., 1980; **HOME ADD:** 755 N. 100 E. 213D, Provo, UT 84601, (801)377-1483; **BUS ADD:** 1675 N. 200 W. 9C, Provo, UT 84604, (801)374-9982.

TANZER, Milt——**B:** Apr. 16, 1931, Chicago, IL, *Realtor/ Assoc.*, L.C. Judd & Co., Inc.; **PRIM RE ACT:** Broker, Consultant; **OTHER RE ACT:** Give Public RE Inv. Seminars; **SERVICES:** RE Inv. brokerage, investment seminars, RE Counseling; **PROFL AFFIL & HONORS:** Ft. Lauderdale Bd. of Realtors, FL Assoc., NAR, RNMI, CCIM; **EDUC:** BA, 1953-55, Bus. Admin., Knox Coll., Galesburg, IL; **MIL SERV:** US Army, 1st Lt.; **OTHER ACT & HONORS:** Author of: 'Real Estate Investments & How to Make Them', Commercial RE Desk Book, Complete Guide to Condo. Conversions; **HOME ADD:** 2201 N.E. 46th St., Lighthouse Point, FL 33064, (305)943-5480; **BUS ADD:** 2230 S.E. 17th st., Ft. Lauderdale, FL 33316, (305)525-3151.

TANZMAN, Norman——**B:** July 4, 1918, NY, NY, *Part.*, Jacobson, Goldfarb & Tanzman Assoc.; **PRIM RE ACT:** Broker, Consultant, Appraiser; **PROFL AFFIL & HONORS:** ASREC; NAR; SREA; SIR, SRPA; **MIL SERV:** USCG, WWII; **OTHER ACT & HONORS:** NJ Gen. Assembly - 1960-65 Asst. Majority Leader - 1967 NJ Senate - 1967 thru 1973; **HOME ADD:** 169 South Park Dr., Woodbridge, NJ 07095; **BUS ADD:** 162 Smith St., Perth Amboy, NJ 08862, (201)442-4444.

TAPP, F. Barry——**B:** Jan. 23, 1947, TN, *Pres.*, Tapp Development Co.; **PRIM RE ACT:** Broker, Consultant, Developer, Owner/Investor, Property Manager; **SERVICES:** Factory outlet mall, dev. and mgt.; **PROFL AFFIL & HONORS:** ICSC; **EDUC:** 1967, Bus. Admin., OK Christian Coll.; **BUS ADD:** 10804 Quail Plaza Dr., Oklahoma City, OK 73129, (405)755-3580.

TAPP, William R., Jr.——**B:** May 21, 1922, Powder Springs, GA, *Arch./Owner*, Wm. R. Tapp, Jr. Arch., and Assoc.; **PRIM RE ACT:** Architect; **SERVICES:** Arch. plans, specifications & suprv.; **REP CLIENTS:** Fed., state & local govt. bodies; indiv. & corp. owners; **PREV EMPLOY:** Pvt. practice; **PROFL AFFIL & HONORS:** AIA/GA Assn.; Const. Specification Inst.; Amer. Correctional Assn.; Amer. Section-The Intl. Solar Soc.; Nat. Fire Protection Assn.; **EDUC:** BA, 1943, GA Inst. of Tech.; **GRAD EDUC:** BArch, 1949, GA Inst. of Tech.; **EDUC HONORS:** 2nd Medal/Beaux-Art Design Exhibition Hall/1942; **MIL SERV:** USNR, Lt./j.g., Pacific Theatre Ribbon; **OTHER ACT & HONORS:** Civitan Club; Marietta Ctry. Club; Cobb Cty. C of C; Advisory Bd. of Cobb Salvation Army; Advisory Bd. of Cobb-Marietta YWCA; N. Dist. Advisory Bd. of Fulton Fed. S&L Assn.; **HOME ADD:** 442 S. Hillcrest Dr. S.W., Marietta, GA 30064, (404)427-3797; **BUS ADD:** 22 Austin Ave. N.E., Marietta, GA 30060, (404)427-5339.

TAPPAN, Charles S.——**B:** July 25, 1940, Des Moines, IA, *Owner*, CST Mgmt. Co.; **PRIM RE ACT:** Syndicator, Developer, Owner/Investor; **REP CLIENTS:** Synd./Devel.; **PREV EMPLOY:** Treas. & Gen. Counsel, Carlisle Const. Co.; **PROFL AFFIL & HONORS:** Amer. Bar Assoc.; KY Bar Assoc.; **EDUC:** BBA, 1962, Fin., RE, Univ. of MI; **GRAD EDUC:** LLB, 1965, Law, Univ. of MI; **MIL SERV:** US Air NG, S/Sgt.; **BUS ADD:** 6 Dartmouth, Ft. Mitchell, KY 41017, (606)341-2299.

TARANTELLO, Dr. R.——**B:** Sept. 10, 1947, Rochester, NY, *Pres.*, Tarantello & Company; **PRIM RE ACT:** Consultant, Appraiser, Developer, Owner/Investor, Property Manager; **SERVICES:** Econ. consulting, RE market research, valuation, devel./acquisition/mgmt./ leasing of comml. income prop., devel. of multi-family housing; **REP**

CLIENTS: Devel., lenders, public agencies, indus. co., domestic and for. indiv. and instit. investors; **PREV EMPLOY:** Asst. Prof. of RE & Urban Land Econ., Univ. of S. Ca, 1974 to present; Dir. of RE and S&L Research, Univ. of S. CA, 1976 to present; Asst. Prof. of RE & Urban Devel., CA State Univ., 1971-1974; **PROFL AFFIL & HONORS:** Amer. RE & Urban Econ. Assn.; NARA; AIREA; RE Research Council of S. CA; Town Hall of CA; CA Assn. of Realtors; NAR, Teaching Excellence Award, USC, 1979; Faculty Research Award, USC, 1978; Wittenberg Fellowship, 1974; Dow Jones Student Achievement Award, 1971; Candidate for MAI Designation; **EDUC:** BS, 1970, Fin./RE, CA State Univ.; **GRAD EDUC:** MBA, 1971, Fin., USC; DBA, 1976, RE/Urban Econ., USC; **MIL SERV:** CA Air Nat. Guard, Sgt., 1967-1973; **OTHER ACT & HONORS:** Faculty Advisor, Blue Key Mens Nat. Hon. Frat., USC; Faculty Advisor, Alpha Kappa Psi, USC; CA Legislature Housing Production Advisory Comm.; Faculty Advisor, USC RE Assn.; **HOME ADD:** 3706 Channel Pl., Newport Beach, CA 92663, (714)673-8797; **BUS ADD:** 3931 MacArthur Blvd., Suite 102, Newport Beach, CA 92660, (714)833-2650.

TARANTINO, Joe——B: Feb. 4, 1947, NJ, *Pres.*, Joe Tarantino Co./Western Securities Realty Inc.; **PRIM RE ACT:** Broker, Syndicator, Consultant, Appraiser, Developer, Builder, Property Manager, Owner/Investor; **OTHER RE ACT:** Comml. & Investment Prop. Specialist; **SERVICES:** Part. & Prop. Mgmt.; **PROFL AFFIL & HONORS:** GRI, RESSI, NAR, CAR; **EDUC:** BA, 1970, Educ. Admin, Univ. No. CO; **OTHER ACT & HONORS:** Construction Advisory Bd. Loveland, Kiwanis, Loveland Bd. of Realtors by Laws Comm., Library Comm. Chmn.; **HOME ADD:** 2925 Alamosa Ct., Loveland, CO 80537, (303)667-8578; **BUS ADD:** 330 N. Lincoln, Loveland, CO 80537, (303)669-8600.

TARKINOW, Morris J.——B: Feb. 8, 1953, Putnam, CT, *Owner*, Tarkinow Enterprises; **PRIM RE ACT:** Broker, Consultant, Developer, Lender, Builder, Owner/Investor, Property Manager, Syndicator; **SERVICES:** Brokerage, devel., investment, mgmt., morts., synds. of comml. & indus. prop.; **REP CLIENTS:** Lender and indivs. in comml. & indus. props.; **EDUC:** BS, 1974, Bus., Boston Univ.; **HOME ADD:** PO Box 314, Chestnut Hill, MA 02167, (617)244-4100; **BUS ADD:** 27 Needham St., Newton, MA 02161, (617)244-4100.

TARLOW, Arthur L.——B: Mar. 15, 1942, Portland, OR, *Shareholder and Corp. Treas.*, Bolliger, Hampton & Tarlow, PC; **PRIM RE ACT:** Attorney; **SERVICES:** Legal serv. for acquisition, devel., construction, mgmt., leasing and selling of RE and improvements; **REP CLIENTS:** Devel., contractors, owners, buyers and sellers of comml., indus. and resid. RE; **PROFL AFFIL & HONORS:** Assoc. Gen. Contractors, OR Remodelers Assn., Nat. Contract Mgmt. Assn.; **EDUC:** BS, 1964, Law, Univ. of OR; **GRAD EDUC:** JD, 1966, Law, Univ. of OR; **MIL SERV:** US Army, SSG-E-6, Army Commendation Medal; **OTHER ACT & HONORS:** Nat. Counter Intel. Corps Assn.; VP, Exec. Comm. Beaverton Area C of C; **HOME ADD:** 1600 S.W. Cedar Hills Blvd., Suite 102, Portland, OR 97225, (503)641-7171; **BUS ADD:** 1600 S.W. Cedar Hills Blvd., Suite 102, Portland, OR 97225, (503)641-7171.

TARR, Mel——B: June 24, 1935, Miami, FL, *Pres.*, Mel Tarr Assoc.; **PRIM RE ACT:** Consultant; **SERVICES:** Public Relation & Mktg.; **REP CLIENTS:** Landauer Assoc., consultants; Collins Devel. Corp., devels.; Bowers Org., Const. arch., Mgmt. devel.; Carnegie Ctr., Office Corp. Park; **PREV EMPLOY:** Dir. public relation, Amer. Stock Exch.; Mgr. public relations, Amer. Express Co.; Communications Dir. NY State Assembly; **PROFL AFFIL & HONORS:** Public Relations Soc. of Amer. 'Best Institutional PR-1969' Amer. Stock Exch.; **EDUC:** BS, 1960, Adv., PR, Univ. of FL; **GRAD EDUC:** 1971, Fin.-securities, NY Univ. Grad. School of Bus.; **MIL SERV:** US Army, Spec. 4, Good Behavior; **OTHER ACT & HONORS:** Who's Who in the East, Who's Who in Public Relations; **HOME ADD:** 531 Main St., Roosevelt Island, NY 10044; **BUS ADD:** 950 Third Ave., New York, NY 10022, (212)752-8340.

TARRANT, Guy C.——B: Dec. 7, 1942, Charleston, SC, *Partner*, Batten, Hudson & Tarrant; **PRIM RE ACT:** Broker, Consultant, Appraiser, Developer, Owner/Investor; **SERVICES:** Comml. brokerage involving sales, leasing & exchanging of comml. & investment prop.; investment counseling & appraising; **REP CLIENTS:** Indiv., corp. and institl. investors and users; **PREV EMPLOY:** SC Nat. Bank, 1965-1972; **PROFL AFFIL & HONORS:** NAR; RNMI, CCIM of the RNMI; **EDUC:** BS, 1965, Econ./Indus. Mgmt., Clemson Univ.; **GRAD EDUC:** 1971, Comml. Banking, LSU, Banking School of the South; **OTHER ACT & HONORS:** Palmetto Low Country Health Service Agency; Arthritis Foundation; **HOME ADD:** 36 Ashley Ave., Charleston, SC, (803)577-0858; **BUS ADD:** POB 2830, One North Adgers Wharf, Charleston, SC 29403, (803)577-6655.

TARUM, Melvin——*Dir. Plng.*, National Co-Operative Refinery Assn.; **PRIM RE ACT:** Property Manager; **BUS ADD:** PO Box 1167, McPherson, KS 67460, (316)241-2340.*

TATARA, Douglas A.——B: Feb. 12, 1953, Amsterdam, NY, *Project Mgr.*, W & K Co.; **PRIM RE ACT:** Broker; **OTHER RE ACT:** Fin. Analysis & Project Mgmt.; **PREV EMPLOY:** R & B Enterprises, Fin. Analyst; **PROFL AFFIL & HONORS:** CA Broker; San Fernando Valley Bd. of Realtors Member; **EDUC:** BBA, 1975, Acctg., Siena Coll., Loudonville, NY; **HOME ADD:** 23643 Park Capri, 39, Calabasas, CA 91302, (213)884-1160; **BUS ADD:** 2716 Ocean Park Blvd., Santa Monica, CA 90405, (213)450-0779.

TATE, J. Kenneth——B: March 6, 1952, Miami Beach, FL, *VP*, High Point of DelRay Builders, Inc.; **PRIM RE ACT:** Developer, Builder; **SERVICES:** Builder/devel. of major condo. projects; **PROFL AFFIL & HONORS:** Nat. Assn. of Home Builders; State of FL Gen. Contractor; So. FL Builders Assn.; **EDUC:** BS Engr., 1974, Mathematical Engr., Computer Sci., Vanderbilt Univ.; **GRAD EDUC:** MBA, 1976, Fin., Duke Univ.; **EDUC HONORS:** Cum Laude; **HOME ADD:** 4107 N. 48th Terr., Hollywood, FL 33021, (305)945-7132; **BUS ADD:** 4640 High Point Lake Dr., Delray Beach, FL 33445, (305)499-7334.

TATHAM, G. Vern——B: Aug. 10, 1921, Winnipeg, Manitoba, *Sr. VP*, Oxford Dev. Grp. Ltd., Can. Div.; **OTHER RE ACT:** Gen. Mgmt.; **SERVICES:** Dev. & Prop Mgmt.; **REP CLIENTS:** Quality Joint Venture Parts.; **PREV EMPLOY:** Bldgs Mgr., Gen. Mgr., VP, Sr. Vp, Pres Y & R Prop Ltd., 1954-78; **PROFL AFFIL & HONORS:** Chmn. of Bd. BOMI, RPA; **EDUC:** Spec. training electronics, 1943, Univ. of Brit. Columbia; **GRAD EDUC:** Numerous RE related night classes; **MIL SERV:** CAF, CPL, Canadian Service Medals 1939-45 War; **OTHER ACT & HONORS:** Past member Nat. Bldg. Code; **HOME ADD:** 190 Newton Drive, Willowdale, Toronto, Ont., (416)225-2285; **BUS ADD:** 390 Bay St., Suite 300, Toronto, Ont., Canada, (416)868-3611.

TATUM, Robert Stephens, Jr.——B: July 30, 1950, Nashville, TN, *Pres.*, R.S. Tatum Co.; **PRIM RE ACT:** Consultant, Developer, Builder, Owner/Investor, Property Manager; **SERVICES:** Locate prop. build and lease to tenants; consultant to investment firms; **REP CLIENTS:** Winn Dixie; Walgreens; K-Mart; Revco; Bi-Lo; Echerd; **PREV EMPLOY:** Gen. partner T&S Props.; **EDUC:** BS, 1975, RE, Fin., Univ. of TN; **EDUC HONORS:** Dean's List in Bus.; **OTHER ACT & HONORS:** Knoxville Racket Club; Central Baptist Church; **HOME ADD:** Cartwright Lane, Knoxville, TN 37919, (615)690-0564; **BUS ADD:** PO Box 357, Airbase Rd., Maryville, TN 37801, (615)970-2393.

TATUSKO, Wayne G.——B: Oct. 31, 1951, Johnson City, NY, Content, Stewart, Tatusko & Patterson, Chartered; **PRIM RE ACT:** Attorney; **SERVICES:** Legal advice with regard to RE acquisition, fin., taxation; **PROFL AFFIL & HONORS:** ABA, DC Bar Assn.; **EDUC:** BA, 1973, Russian Language & Lit., Yale Univ.; **GRAD EDUC:** JD, 1976, Cornell Law School; **EDUC HONORS:** Magna Cum Laude, Honors in Russian Lit., Cum Laude; **HOME ADD:** 8407 Stone Gate Dr., Annandale, VA 22003, (703)323-6058; **BUS ADD:** 1225 19th St. N.W., Suite 600, Washington, DC 20036, (202)887-1000.

TAUB, Theodore C.——B: Jan. 1, 1935, Springfield, MA, *Partner*, Taub & Williams; **PRIM RE ACT:** Attorney; **REP CLIENTS:** Devels., lenders, indiv. or instnl. investors in comml. props.; **PROFL AFFIL & HONORS:** Chmn., Real Prop. Litigation Comm. of ABA; **EDUC:** AB, 1956, Duke Univ.; **GRAD EDUC:** JD, 1960, Univ. of FL; **MIL SERV:** US Naval Reserve; **HOME ADD:** 4937 Lyford Cay Rd., Tampa, FL 33609, (813)876-3228; **BUS ADD:** The Plaza on the Mall 201 E. Kennedy Blvd., Suite 1700, PO Box 2312, Tampa, FL 33601, (813)223-1884.

TAUBE, Stanley M.——B: Mar. 25, 1937, Bismark, ND, *Pres.*, Lanvesco Corp.; **PRIM RE ACT:** Consultant, Developer, Owner/Investor, Syndicator; **PREV EMPLOY:** Katz, Taube, Lange, Attys. at Law; **PROFL AFFIL & HONORS:** Nat. Apt. Assn.; MN Multi Housing Assn.; Edina C of C, Pres., Nat. Apt. Assn.; Former Pres., MN Multi Housing Assn.; **EDUC:** 1959, Acctg., Univ. of MN; **GRAD EDUC:** Law, 1963, Univ. of MN; **HOME ADD:** 7133 Shannon Dr., Edina, MN 55435, (612)944-1322; **BUS ADD:** 6600 France Ave., 490, Edina, MN 55435, (612)927-4004.

TAUSCHER, Don W.——B: Dec. 16, 1933, Rhinelander, WI, *Pres./Owner*, Don W. Tauscher, Inc.; **PRIM RE ACT:** Broker, Consultant, Owner/Investor, Instructor; **OTHER RE ACT:** Exchanging; **SERVICES:** RE Investment Counseling; Exchange Counseling; Creative Fin. Seminars; **PREV EMPLOY:** Pres. of $70 million Comml. Bank; **PROFL AFFIL & HONORS:** NIREM; Academy Network,

CCIM; ACE; **EDUC:** BA, 1955, Bus. Admin., Rollins Coll., Winter Park, FL; **GRAD EDUC:** 1963, Gen. Fin. & Banking, Grad. School of Banking, Univ. of WI; **EDUC HONORS:** O.D.K., Algernon Sydney Sullivan Award; **MIL SERV:** US Army, Cpl.; **HOME ADD:** PO Box 1384, Winter Park, FL 32790, (305)628-2329; **BUS ADD:** PO Box 1384, 213 W. Park Ave., Winter Park, FL 32790, (305)628-1031.

TAVEL, James W.——B: Aug. 17, 1945, Washington, DC, *Prin./Treas.*, Spriggs, Cromwell, Myers, Nicholson & Myers, P.A.; **PRIM RE ACT:** Attorney; **SERVICES:** Full range legal services; **PREV EMPLOY:** Legal Counsel for Montgomery Cty. Planning Bd. of the MD-Nat. Capital Park and Planning Commn.; **PROFL AFFIL & HONORS:** Montgomery Cty. State Bar and ABA; **EDUC:** BA, 1967, Public Affairs, George Washington Univ.; **GRAD EDUC:** JD, 1970, George Washington Law School; **EDUC HONORS:** with Honors, Order of Coif, Editor of Law Review; **MIL SERV:** US Army Reserve, Sgt.; **OTHER ACT & HONORS:** Montgomery Cty., Silver Spring, Wheaton C of C; Pres., Silver Spring Devel. Council, 1977 to present; Pres., Silver Spring C of C, 1981; VP, Legislative Affairs, Montgomery Cty., 1981; **HOME ADD:** 211 Baden St., Silver Spring, MD 20901; **BUS ADD:** 8413 Ramsey Ave., Silver Spring, MD 20910, (301)587-1050.

TAYLOR, Arlie L.——B: July 3, 1932, Pike Cty., GA, *VP*, Motor Hotel Mgmt. Inc.; **PRIM RE ACT:** Consultant, Real Estate Publisher; **SERVICES:** Hotel Dev. & Operations, Mgmt., Author; **PREV EMPLOY:** Sheraton Corp. (Boston), Ramada Inns, Inc. (Phoenix), Hospitality Mgmt. Corp. (Dallas); **PROFL AFFIL & HONORS:** AH & MA; TX Hotel & Motel Assn., Cert. Hotel Admin. Wrote books entitled 'Motor Hotel Development Guide', 'Pre-Opening Purchases for a Motor Hotel', (FFE) member Telecommunication Co of AH & MA, and also wrote 'Owner's Guide for Monitoring a Motor Hotel Investment'; **EDUC:** BS, 1956, Textile Engr., GA Tech., Atlanta; **MIL SERV:** USCG, RD 2; **OTHER ACT & HONORS:** Amer. Sec. Council, US Senatorial Club, Natl. Republican Congressional Comm.; **HOME ADD:** 15912 Windy Meadow Dr., Dallas, TX 75248, (214)661-2285; **BUS ADD:** 2880 LBJ Frwy., Dallas, TX 75234, (214)243-0861.

TAYLOR, Bruce, Jr.——B: Apr. 16, 1940, Tampa, FL, *Pres.*, Bruce Taylor, Inc.; **PRIM RE ACT:** Broker, Consultant, Instructor, Property Manager, Owner/Investor, Insuror; **SERVICES:** Sales and Mgmt., all lines of Insurance; **PREV EMPLOY:** Self-employed; **PROFL AFFIL & HONORS:** Clearwater, Largo, Dunedin Bd. of Realtors, Inc.; Clearwater, Largo, Dunedin Indep. Insurers, Inc., GRI; **MIL SERV:** US Army, SP-4; **OTHER ACT & HONORS:** Clearwater Breakfast Sertoma; **HOME ADD:** 1807 Douglas Ave., Clearwater, FL 33515, (813)447-2222; **BUS ADD:** 121 N. Osceola Ave., Clearwater, FL 33515, (813)442-2101.

TAYLOR, Byron D.——B: June 1, 1943, Springfield, IL, *VP*, Roger L. Cohen & Co.; **PRIM RE ACT:** Broker, Engineer; **SERVICES:** Gen. comml. & indus. brokerage; **PROFL AFFIL & HONORS:** SIR, Kansas City Bd. of Realtors, MO Assn. of Realtors; **EDUC:** BS, 1965, Civil Engr., So. IL Univ.; **GRAD EDUC:** MS/MS, 1970/1972, Systems Mgmt./Environ. Engr., Univ. of So. CA/Univ. of KS; **MIL SERV:** US Air Force, Maj., Air Medal, Distinguished Flying Cross, Commendation Medal, Cross of Gallantry; **HOME ADD:** 810 W. 54th St., Kansas City, MO 64112, (816)333-2322; **BUS ADD:** 850 City Center Sq., PO Box 26690, Kansas City, MO 64196, (816)471-0700.

TAYLOR, Carroll S.——B: Jan. 14, 1944, Port Chester, NY, *Atty.*, Char. Hamilton Taylor & Thom; **PRIM RE ACT:** Attorney; **SERVICES:** Legal Services; **REP CLIENTS:** RE Investors and Devel.; **PROFL AFFIL & HONORS:** HI, CA and ABA, Fellow, Amer. Coll. of Probate Counsel; **EDUC:** BA, 1965, Hist., Yale Univ.; **GRAD EDUC:** JD, 1968, Univ. of CA(Boalt Hall); **HOME ADD:** 46-429 Hololio St., Kaneohe, HI 96744, (808)235-1736; **BUS ADD:** Suite 1990, 733 Bishop St., Honolulu, HI 96813, (808)524-3824.

TAYLOR, Clark W.——B: Dec. 5, 1933, Baton Rouge, LA, *Pres.*, Clark W. Taylor & Assoc.; **PRIM RE ACT:** Developer, Builder, Owner/Investor, Property Manager, Syndicator; **SERVICES:** Multi-fami prop. mgmt., devel. & sale of multi-fami housing, synd., bldg. of comml. & multi-family; **PROFL AFFIL & HONORS:** IREM, Bd. of Realtors, Apt. Owners & Mgrs. of Amer., Homebuilder Assn.; **EDUC:** LLB, 1957, Law & Bus., LSU & LSU Law Sch.; **GRAD EDUC:** JD, 1968, LSU Law Sch.; **BUS ADD:** 10124 Jefferson Hwy., Baton Rouge, LA 70816.

TAYLOR, David P., Sr.——B: Feb.23, 1942, Peoria, IL, *Cert. Prop. Mgr.*, Norman Bernstein Management, Inc., Prop. mgmt.; **PRIM RE ACT:** Property Manager; **SERVICES:** Prop. mgmt. apt. and shopping ctr.; **PREV EMPLOY:** Veterans Cooperative Housing Assn., Gen. Mgr. and Exec. Dir. 1968-73; **PROFL AFFIL & HONORS:** IREM, CPM; **EDUC:** Acctg., Benjamin Franklin Univ.; **HOME ADD:** 2300 41st St. N.W., Washington, DC 20007, (202)338-3813; **BUS ADD:** 2025 Eye St. N.W. 400, Washington, DC 20006, (202)331-7500.

TAYLOR, Edward A.——B: Feb. 13, 1932, Pittsburgh, PA, *Pres.*, Spartus Commercial Corp.; **PRIM RE ACT:** Broker, Consultant, Owner/Investor, Instructor, Property Manager, Syndicator; **SERVICES:** sales and synd. of comml. props.; **REP CLIENTS:** investors in comml. props.; **PREV EMPLOY:** Quadrant Corp., a Weyerhauser Co. 1975-77; **PROFL AFFIL & HONORS:** CPM; IREM; RESSI; WA Coalition for Affordable Housing; Natl. Assn. of RE Bds., Life Member, Realtors Natl. Pol. Action Comm.; **HOME ADD:** PO Box 451, Kenmore, WA 98128, (206)485-5474; **BUS ADD:** 1000 124th Ave. NE, Bellevue, WA 98005, (206)455-5811.

TAYLOR, H. Tom——B: May 2, 1928, Chattanooga, TN, *Owner*, H. Tom Taylor RE; **PRIM RE ACT:** Broker, Property Manager, Insuror; **SERVICES:** Brokerage of comml. prop. and prop. mgmt.; **REP CLIENTS:** Indiv. and instnl. investors in comml. prop.; **PREV EMPLOY:** Savage & Sganzini, Inc., subs. of Marsh & McLennan, Inc.; **PROFL AFFIL & HONORS:** IREM, NIREB, Albuquerque Bd. of Realtors, CPM; **EDUC:** BBA, 1951, Univ. of NM; **MIL SERV:** US Army, Brig. Gen., Army Meritorious Service Medal; **OTHER ACT & HONORS:** VP Greater Albuquerque C of C, Univ. of NM Alumni Assoc. Bd. of Dir., Nat. Guard Assn., Assn. of USA; **HOME ADD:** 1101 San Pablo, N.E., Albuquerque, NM 87110, (505)256-9157; **BUS ADD:** 512 Sandia Savings Bldg., Albuquerque, NM 87103, (505)242-2684.

TAYLOR, Howard——B: Jan. 12, 1950, Rochester, NY, Howard Taylor & Co.; **OTHER RE ACT:** Mort. Brokers/Investment Bankers; **SERVICES:** Secondary mktg., comml. & income prop. loans, RE equity investments; **REP CLIENTS:** Ins. cos., pension funds, banks; **PROFL AFFIL & HONORS:** NASD/SIPC; **EDUC:** BS, 1971, Bus. Admin., SUNY, Buffalo, NY; **GRAD EDUC:** MBA, 1976, 1979, Grad. Sch. of Savings Banks, Univ. of Rochester & Brown Univ.; **HOME ADD:** Six Larchwood Dr., Pittsford, NY 14334, (716)381-0366; **BUS ADD:** 16 E. Main St., Rochester, NY 14614, (716)232-1880.

TAYLOR, Col. J. Wesley B.——B: Oct. 6, 1920, Wichita Falls, TX, *VP, Sec. & Controller*, Town & Country Mobile Homes, Inc.; **PRIM RE ACT:** Broker, Appraiser, Insuror; **OTHER RE ACT:** Mfr. of mobile homes; **SERVICES:** Gen. mgmt., public relations, advertising, air transp., life ins. and investments; **PROFL AFFIL & HONORS:** Public acct.; **MIL SERV:** USN; **OTHER ACT & HONORS:** Kiwanis Club; Mason; Shriner; Eastern Star; Elks; C of C; **BUS ADD:** POB 4391, Wichita Falls, TX 76308, (817)723-5523.

TAYLOR, James S.——B: Mar. 18, 1928, Jacksonville, FL, *Part.*, Utmer Murchison Ashby Taylor & Corrigan; **PRIM RE ACT:** Attorney, Owner/Investor; **REP CLIENTS:** Regency Sq., Aetna Life Ins. Co., Atlantic Bancor, Capital Holding Co.; **PROFL AFFIL & HONORS:** ABA, FL Bar Assoc.; **EDUC:** AB, 1950, Washington & Lee Univ.; **GRAD EDUC:** J.D., 1953, Univ. of MI; **EDUC HONORS:** Order of Coif; **HOME ADD:** 1596 Lancaster Ter., Jacksonville, FL 32204, (904)354-3808; **BUS ADD:** PO Box 479, Jacksonville, FL 32201, (904)354-5652.

TAYLOR, Jerry——B: Jan. 14, 1937, Pampa, TX, *Gen. Prop. Mgr.*, Gerald D. Hines Interests, Prop. Mgmt. Div.; **PRIM RE ACT:** Property Manager; **SERVICES:** Total scope Prop. Mgmt. - Office Bldgs. 30 million sq. ft. across the US; **PROFL AFFIL & HONORS:** IREM, BOMA; **EDUC:** BBA, 1963, Bus., W. TX State Univ.; **OTHER ACT & HONORS:** Member of the IREM Natl. Teaching Staff; **HOME ADD:** 12603 Pinerock, Houston, TX 77024, (713)464-9225; **BUS ADD:** 5051 Westheimer, Houston, TX 77056, (713)621-8000.

TAYLOR, John Seaton——B: May 11, 1951, Wash., DC, *Partner*, Hankins & Taylor; **PRIM RE ACT:** Attorney, Instructor; **SERVICES:** Legal Services; **PREV EMPLOY:** Marshall Univ. Comm. Coll., Instr. in RE Law; **PROFL AFFIL & HONORS:** Cabell Cty., WV and ABA, Member Sect. of Real Prop., Probate and Trust Law; **EDUC:** AB, 1973, Poli. Sci., Davidson Coll., Davidson, NC; **GRAD EDUC:** JD, 1976, WV Univ. Coll. of Law; **HOME ADD:** 1664 Glenway Ln., Huntington, WV 25701, (304)529-4048; **BUS ADD:** 629 7th St., Huntington, WV 25701, (304)697-4800.

TAYLOR, Keith A.——B: Dec. 24, 1941, Portsmouth, VA, *VP*, The Gutierrez Co.; **PRIM RE ACT:** Builder, Developer; **OTHER RE ACT:** Investor; **SERVICES:** Full service RE devel. and const.; **PREV EMPLOY:** VP New England Merchants Nat. Bank, Boston, MA, The Langelier Co., Inc.; **PROFL AFFIL & HONORS:** Advisory Bd. MA Housing Fin. Agency; **EDUC:** AB, 1964, Econ., Tufts Univ.; **GRAD EDUC:** MBA, 1971, Fin., Amos Tuck Sch., Dartmouth Coll.; **MIL SERV:** USN, Lt.; **BUS ADD:** 111 Middlesex Tpk., PO Caller Box 542,

Burlington, MA 01803, (617)372-5870.

TAYLOR, L. Franklin——**B:** Sept. 25, 1945, Hutchinson, KS, Payne & Jones, Chartered; **PRIM RE ACT:** Attorney; **SERVICES:** Legal; **REP CLIENTS:** Lenders, indiv. and instit. buyers and seLlers of comml. investment and resid. props.; **PROFL AFFIL & HONORS:** Amer. (RE, Probate & Trust Sect.) KS and Johnson Cty. Bar Assns.; **EDUC:** BA, 1967, Math. & Physics, Doane Coll., Crete, NE; **GRAD EDUC:** JD, 1975, Univ. of KS; **EDUC HONORS:** Cum Laude, Editor-in-Chief, KS Law Review; **MIL SERV:** US Navy, LCOR; **OTHER ACT & HONORS:** City Atty., DeSoto, KS; Municipal Judge Olathe, KS; **HOME ADD:** 13251 S. Kimberly Cir., Olathe, KS 66061, (913)884-6706; **BUS ADD:** 200 S. Chestnut, Box 10, Olathe, KS 66061, (913)782-2500.

TAYLOR, Lloyd S.——**B:** Mar. 21, 1928, LaPorte, IN, *Sr. VP, RE Devel.*, St. Joseph Bank & Trust Co.; **PRIM RE ACT:** Engineer, Appraiser, Banker, Developer, Property Manager; **SERVICES:** Mgmt. of bank props., const. lending appraisals, const. insp., indus. devel.; **PREV EMPLOY:** Dir. of Redevel. and Dir. of Public Works for City of South Bend; **PROFL AFFIL & HONORS:** Nat. Soc. of PE, IN Area Devel. Council, PE; **EDUC:** 1952, Civil Engr., Purdue Univ.; **MIL SERV:** US Army, Cpl.; **OTHER ACT & HONORS:** St. Joseph Co. Airport Authority, Pres. 1978-79, Dir. of Redevel., City of South Bend, Pres. No. IN Hist. Soc.; **HOME ADD:** 55334 Quince Rd., South Bend, IN 46619, (219)289-2292; **BUS ADD:** 202 S. Michigan St., South Bend, IN 46601, (219)237-5254.

TAYLOR, Melvin L., Sr.——**B:** Oct. 29, 1939, Buffalo, NY, *Pres.*, Melvin L. Taylor Associates, Inc.; **PRIM RE ACT:** Broker, Consultant, Appraiser, Owner/Investor; **OTHER RE ACT:** RE Mktg., Lecturer; **SERVICES:** Resid. Brokerage, Investment Props. Brokerage RE Mktgs., RE Appraiser, Prop. Mgr.; **REP CLIENTS:** Const. cos., lending instns. and pvt. investors; **PREV EMPLOY:** Webb & Brooker, Inc.; **PROFL AFFIL & HONORS:** Founding Member, NY Univ. RE & Mort. Alumni, NAACP, 7A Administrator; **EDUC:** BA, 1979, Bus. Admin., Southeastern Univ.; **OTHER ACT & HONORS:** Kiwanis Club, Intl.; Former RE Columnist, NY Amsterdam News; Gen. Partner: CMC Assoc. & Devels.; **HOME ADD:** 33 N. Third Ave., Mount Vernon, NY 10550, (914)667-8544; **BUS ADD:** 521 Fifth Ave., NY, NY 10017, (212)667-8544.

TAYLOR, R.L.——*Pres.*, Federal Co.; **PRIM RE ACT:** Property Manager; **BUS ADD:** PO Box 17236, Memphis, TN 38117, (901)761-3610.*

TAYLOR, Robert M.——**B:** Dec. 20, 1949, Astoria, OR, *Partner*, Swaner and Taylor; **PRIM RE ACT:** Attorney, Owner/Investor; **SERVICES:** Negotiation, Tax Analysis Advice, Draft Instruments & Documents; **REP CLIENTS:** Numerous RE Brokers, Agents, Owners, plus Devels., Builders, Mgrs., Investors, etc. of Comml. and Resid. Props.; **PROFL AFFIL & HONORS:** UT State Bar, ABA, JD 1975 (Univ. OR Law School); **EDUC:** BS, 1972, Poli. Sci., Univ. of OR; **GRAD EDUC:** Doctor of Jurisprudence, 1975, Law, Univ. of OR School of Law; **HOME ADD:** 2718 Connor St., Salt Lake City, UT 84109; **BUS ADD:** 722 Boston Bldg., Salt Lake City, UT 84111, (801)531-7344.

TAYLOR, Verl——**B:** Oct. 8, 1917, Ogden, UT, *Pres.*, Real Estate Mktg. Service; **PRIM RE ACT:** Broker, Consultant, Banker, Developer; **SERVICES:** Investment counseling, consulting; **REP CLIENTS:** Indiv. investors, corp. investors; **PROFL AFFIL & HONORS:** SEC; **EDUC:** BS, 1935, Bus. Mgmt., UT State Univ.; **GRAD EDUC:** MS, 1941, Acctg., Univ. of UT; MBA, 1942, Mgmt., Grad. Sch. of Bus., Stanford Univ.; **EDUC HONORS:** Alpha Kappa Psi; **MIL SERV:** Navy, Lt. (j.g.); **OTHER ACT & HONORS:** CA Assn. Realtor, NAR, Nat. Soc. of Exchange Counselors; **HOME ADD:** 703 N. CA St., Palo Alto, CA 94303, (415)321-3887; **BUS ADD:** 1155 Crane St., Ste 4, Menlo Park, CA 94025, (415)322-4506.

TEAGUE, Paul M.——**B:** June 20, 1947, Pueblo, CO, *Dir., Mkt. Analysis and Research*, CO Housing Finance Authority, Mkt. Analysis and Research; **PRIM RE ACT:** Lender; **SERVICES:** Permanent and const. fin.; **REP CLIENTS:** Primary lenders, builders; **PREV EMPLOY:** Housing Mkt. Analyst and Econ., HUD; **PROFL AFFIL & HONORS:** Amer. Mgmt. Assn.; CO Assn. of Housing and Bldg.; Young Mort. Bankers Assn.; Denver Solar Energy Assn.; **EDUC:** BS, 1970, Econ., CO State Univ.; **EDUC HONORS:** Freshman and Upperclassman Scholarships; **OTHER ACT & HONORS:** Oil Shale Environmental Advisory Panel; **HOME ADD:** 8556 E. Mineral Cir., Englewood, CO 80112, (303)771-3617; **BUS ADD:** 500 E. Eigth Ave., Denver, CO 80203, (303)861-8962.

TEAGUE, S. Wesley, III——**B:** Dec. 6, 1949, Birmingham, AL, *Pres., DeRand Prop. Mgt. Corp.; VP DeRand Equity Group, Inc.*, DeRand Corp. of America; **PRIM RE ACT:** Consultant, Property Manager, Owner/Investor, Insuror, Syndicator; **SERVICES:** Synd., Prop. Mgmt., Consulting, Valuation, Acquisition; **REP CLIENTS:** Indiv. investors and comml. brokerage; **PREV EMPLOY:** Lending Officer & Branch Mgr., Bank of VA 1974-77; **PROFL AFFIL & HONORS:** IREM, BOMA, PMA; **EDUC:** BS, 1971, Econ., Auburn Univ.; **GRAD EDUC:** MBA, 1976, Fin., The George Washington Univ.; **MIL SERV:** US Army, E-4, Legal Specialist 1971-73; **HOME ADD:** 2813 So. Abingdon St., Arlington, VA 22206, (703)820-3762; **BUS ADD:** 2201 Wilson Blvd., ste. 300, DeRand Bldg., Arlington, VA 22201, (703)527-3827.

TEAL, Marvin E.——**B:** May 10, 1952, Almont, MI, *Prop. Mgr./Owner/Investor*, Teal Prop. Mgmt.; **PRIM RE ACT:** Property Manager, Owner/Investor; **SERVICES:** Rental units and prop. mgmt.; Assist other investors; **PROFL AFFIL & HONORS:** MI Landlords Assn.; Rental Prop. Assn. of Grand Rapids, MI; **EDUC:** BSBA, 1975, Mgmt., Mktg., Acctg., Data Processing, RE, Ferris State Coll., Big Rapids, MI; **EDUC HONORS:** Deans List, VP of SAM, Hon. Music Frat.; **OTHER ACT & HONORS:** Masons; Amer. Mktg. Assn.; Jaycees; Shrine Club; **HOME ADD:** 6818 Lowbank Dr., Jenison, MI 49428, (616)669-0272; **BUS ADD:** 6818 Lowbank Dr., Jenison, MI 49428, (616)669-0272.

TEANEY, G. Reid——**B:** July 20, 1946, Kansas City, MO, *VP and Resident Mgr.*, Coldwell Banker Commercial Real Estate Services, Comml. RE Services; **PRIM RE ACT:** Broker; **PROFL AFFIL & HONORS:** Nat. Assn. of Indus. & Office Parks, Intl. Council of Shopping Ctrs., NAR; **EDUC:** BBA, 1970, Econ., MO Univ.; **GRAD EDUC:** Journalism, 1970, Advertising & PR, MO Univ.; **MIL SERV:** US Army, 1st Lt.; **OTHER ACT & HONORS:** Masonic Lodge; **HOME ADD:** 30 Rio Vista Dr., Ladue, MO 63124, (314)991-5347; **BUS ADD:** 222 S. Central Ave., Clayton, MO 63105, (314)889-1500.

TEBBE, C. Graham, Jr.——**B:** June 13, 1935, Wichita, KS, *Atty.*, Tuttle and Taylor; **OTHER RE ACT:** Transactions; **SERVICES:** Legal advice; **REP CLIENTS:** Investors, synd. and mgrs. of comml. resid. and undevel. props.; devel. of comml. and res. props.; work-out specialists; **PROFL AFFIL & HONORS:** Amer. Bar Assn.; State Bar of CA; DC Bar Assn.; **EDUC:** BA, 1957, Eng., Yale Univ.; **GRAD EDUC:** JD, 1963, Univ. of CA, Berkeley; **EDUC HONORS:** Order of the Coif; Articles Editor, CA Law Review; **MIL SERV:** USMC, Capt., 1957-1960; **HOME ADD:** 3001 Veazey Terr., N.W., Washington, DC 20008, (202)362-8455; **BUS ADD:** 1901 L St., N.W., Suite 805, Washington, DC 20036, (202)861-0666.

TEDFORD, Milton——**B:** May 8, 1930, Denver, CO, *VP*, Charles C. Murphy & Assoc., Inc.; **PRIM RE ACT:** Developer, Property Manager; **SERVICES:** Co. devel. & mgmt.; **PREV EMPLOY:** First Nat. Bank of Denver, Sr. Trust Officer, RE Dept.; **PROFL AFFIL & HONORS:** Inst. RE Mgmt (CPM), 1979 Pres. IREM; **GRAD EDUC:** 1953, Bus., Univ. of CO; **HOME ADD:** Rte. 6, Box 279C, Golden, CO 80401, (303)582-5008; **BUS ADD:** Suite 1530, One Park Central, Denver, CO 80202, (303)534-5938.

TEEL, Norcross, Jr.——**B:** July 29, 1939, Boston, MA, *VP-RE Fin.*, The Mutual Life Insurance Co. of NY, RE and Mort. Investments; **PRIM RE ACT:** Lender, Owner/Investor; **PREV EMPLOY:** Travelers Insurance Company 1963-1969; **PROFL AFFIL & HONORS:** ULI; Intl. Council of Shopping Ctrs.; RE Bd. of NY; **EDUC:** AB, 1961, Philosophy, Colby Coll.; **GRAD EDUC:** 1962-1963, Fin., Boston Univ.; **MIL SERV:** US Army; **OTHER ACT & HONORS:** Pres. and Trustee, MONY Mort. Investors; **HOME ADD:** 218 Puritan Rd., Fairfield, CT 06430, (203)255-6704; **BUS ADD:** 1740 Broadway, NY, NY 10019, (212)708-2036.

TEEPLE, Charles S.——**B:** Sept. 5, 1944, Dallas, TX, *Pres.*, Teeple Properties, Inc.; **PRIM RE ACT:** Broker, Developer, Owner/Investor; **SERVICES:** Devel. of comml. prop. and prop. mgmt.; **REP CLIENTS:** Investors in comml. prop.; **PREV EMPLOY:** KMS Ventures, Inc., VP for RE Dev.; United Nat. Bank, Dallas, Sr. VP and Trust Officer; Southwestern Group Fin., Houston, VP and Treas.; **PROFL AFFIL & HONORS:** Dir., Econ. Devel. Fund Admin. Bd., Austin C of C; Pres., Century Club, College and Grad. School of Bus., Univ. of TX at Austin; Dir., U.T., Ex-Students Assn. for Travis Cnty.; Dir., TX Lyceum Assn., Life Member, Profl. Bus. Frats. - Alpha Kappa Psi, Sigma Iota, Phi Kappa Phi; **EDUC:** BBA, 1966, Fin., Univ. of TX at Austin; **GRAD EDUC:** MBA, 1970, Mgmt., Univ. of TX at Austin; **MIL SERV:** U.S. Army, Capt.; **OTHER ACT & HONORS:** Member, Admirals Club of Austin; **HOME ADD:** 4002 Balcones, Austin, TX 78731, (512)454-6252; **BUS ADD:** 200 E. 10th, First Fed. Plaza, Suite 511, Austin, TX 78701, (512)474-1886.

TEICHERT, Frederick——**B:** July 24, 1948, Berkeley, CA, *VP*, Teichert Land Co.; **PRIM RE ACT:** Developer, Builder, Owner/Investor; **SERVICES:** Primarily devel. for own acct. - retail, office, indus.; **PROFL AFFIL & HONORS:** Intl. Council of Shopping Ctrs.; **EDUC:** BA, 1970, Hist., Pomona Coll.; **OTHER ACT & HONORS:** Bd. of Dir.; Family Serv. Agency; Sacramento Symphony Assn.; Christian Bros. High School; Sacramento Safety Council and Memberships; Mensa; Sacramento Zoological Soc.; **HOME ADD:** 1741 Park Place Dr., Carmichael, CA 95608, (916)485-6531; **BUS ADD:** 3500 American River Dr., Sacramento, CA 95825, (916)484-3011.

TEIGEN, Philip J.——**B:** Apr. 16, 1940, Minneapolis, MN, *VP, Legal & Sec.*, Wood Bros. Homes, Inc.; **PRIM RE ACT:** Attorney, Builder, Lender, Insuror; **SERVICES:** Homebldr, mobil home mfr. (sub.), mort. co. (sub.); **PREV EMPLOY:** Denver Tech. Ctr., Inc. (Comml. office park), gen counsel & sec.; **PROFL AFFIL & HONORS:** Amer. Bar Assn., NAHB, Metro Denver Homeblders Assn., CO Assn. of Housing & Building, ND Bar Assn., JD; **EDUC:** PhB, 1962, Arts. Law, Univ. of ND, Grank Forks, ND; **GRAD EDUC:** JD, 1964, Law, Univ. of ND Sch. of Law, Grand Forks, ND.; **EDUC HONORS:** Law Review Student Editorial Bd., Delegate Amer. Law Student Assn.; **MIL SERV:** USAF, Capt., 1965-68; **HOME ADD:** 13250 E. Jewell Ave., Apt. 203, Aurora, CO 80012, (303)751-8866; **BUS ADD:** 1658 Cole Blvd., Golden, CO 80401, (303)232-2100.

TEITELBAUM, Isidore——**B:** Dec. 27, 1948, NY, NY, *State Counsel*, Amer. Title Insurance Co., New Jersey; **PRIM RE ACT:** Attorney, Insuror; **SERVICES:** Title examination and ins.; **REP CLIENTS:** Purchasers, devel., and lenders of all types, involved in resid., indus. and comml. props.; **PREV EMPLOY:** Jersey Mort. Co., Gen. Counsel; Lawyers Title Ins. Corp., Asst. State Counsel; **PROFL AFFIL & HONORS:** ABA; NJ State Bar Assn.; NY State Bar Assn., Real Prop. Div.; **EDUC:** BA, 1969, English Lit./Psych., Queens Coll./CUNY; **GRAD EDUC:** JD, 1974, RE/RE Fin., St. John's Univ. School of Law; **HOME ADD:** 23 Devon Dr. N., Englishtown, NJ 07726, (201)446-3457; **BUS ADD:** Gateway 1, Suite 2520, Newark, NJ 07102, (201)642-7266.

TENCICK, John J.——**B:** Feb. 28, 1929, Tilden, IL, *Owner*, Investors Realty Service; **PRIM RE ACT:** Broker, Developer, Builder, Owner/Investor, Property Manager; **PROFL AFFIL & HONORS:** CCIM; **EDUC:** BS, 1951, NC State Coll.; **MIL SERV:** US Army, Lt.; **HOME ADD:** 401 S. 22nd St., Laramie, WY 82070, (307)742-5134; **BUS ADD:** 206 So. 3rd St., Suite 102, Laramie, WY 82070, (307)742-8343.

TENNANT, Robert L.——**B:** Sept. 7, 1946, Columbus, OH, *Pres.*, Precision Mgmt. Inc.; **PRIM RE ACT:** Broker, Property Manager; **SERVICES:** Workout for troubled props., Apt. & office mgmt., consulting, HUD subs. mgmt.; **REP CLIENTS:** Private investors, limited partnerships; **PREV EMPLOY:** RE Sales, RE Jr. Coll. Instr.; **PROFL AFFIL & HONORS:** CPM, IREM, Realtor; **EDUC:** BA, 1968, Acctg./Poli. Sci., Univ. of S. FL; **MIL SERV:** USAR Med. Service, Capt.; **HOME ADD:** 4833 Bonita Vista, Tampa, FL 33614, (813)884-0214; **BUS ADD:** 4913 U.S. 19 N., Holiday, FL 33590, (813)934-1626.

TENNESSEN, Robert J.——Grose, Von Holtum; **PRIM RE ACT:** Attorney; **OTHER RE ACT:** RE Financing; **PROFL AFFIL & HONORS:** ABA; **EDUC:** Univ. of MN Law School; **GRAD EDUC:** JD, 1968; **OTHER ACT & HONORS:** MN State Senator 56th District, Commnr. Fed. Privacy Protection Study Commn.; US Rep. to OECD Conf. on Transborder Data Flows, Vienna Austria; **BUS ADD:** 900 Midwest Plaza E., Minneapolis, MN 55402, (612)333-4500.

TEN THYE, Joop——**B:** Aug. 9, 1932, Nymegen, *Pres.*, Oakland Realty, Ltd., Indus., Comml. & Investment; **PRIM RE ACT:** Broker, Consultant, Developer, Builder, Property Manager; **PREV EMPLOY:** Penners-Schoenmakers Realty, Tilburg, Netherlands, 1973-77; **PROFL AFFIL & HONORS:** FIABCI, NFIKB, OREA, CRB, CRB; **EDUC:** High School, Bldg. Contr. School, Netherlands; **HOME ADD:** 77 Forsythe, Oakville, Ont., Can., (416)845-0437; **BUS ADD:** PO Box 665, Oakville, Ont., Can., (416)844-8933.

TENZER, Michael L.——**B:** May 7, 1930, New York, NY, *Pres. and Dir.*, Leisure Technology Corp.; **PRIM RE ACT:** Developer, Builder; **SERVICES:** Nations largest producer of Adult and Retirement Communities; **PREV EMPLOY:** Photographer - Look Magazine 1944-1950; Modern Globe, Inc. 1953-1957; Berkshire Hosiery Mills 1951-1959; Leisure Technol. 1976-Present; Kayser Roth Corp. 1959-63; Larwin Grp., 1963-75; **PROFL AFFIL & HONORS:** Nat. Home Buildrs Assn.; **MIL SERV:** Signal Corps. 1951-1952; **OTHER ACT & HONORS:** Member Pres. Carter's Housing Task Force; Tr. Chmn. of Bd. Young Musicians Found.; Tr. Friends of Music, Univ. of So. CA; Bd. of Dirs. Amer. Youth Symphony (1979-1980); Past rgnl. chmn. Crescent Bay Council Boy Scouts Amer. 1966-1968; **BUS ADD:** 12233 West Olympic Blvd., Los Angeles, CA 90064, (213)826-1000.

TEPPER, R. Bruce, Jr.——**B:** Apr., 1, 1949, Long Branch, NJ, Loo, Merideth & McMillan; **PRIM RE ACT:** Attorney; **SERVICES:** RE litigation; **REP CLIENTS:** Devels., synds., investors and buyers & sellers of real prop.; **PREV EMPLOY:** St. Louis Redev. Authority, Asst. Counsel 1976-77; **PROFL AFFIL & HONORS:** Bar assns. of State of CA, State of IL, State of MO, Los Angeles Cty., Beverly Hills; ABA; **EDUC:** AB, 1971, Hist., Dartmouth Coll.; **GRAD EDUC:** JD and MA (Urban Affairs), 1976, St. Louis Univ.; **EDUC HONORS:** Cum Laude (Law); Grad. Fellow (Urban Affairs), Asst. Lead Articles Editor, St. Louis Univ. Law Journal (1975-76); **OTHER ACT & HONORS:** Bd. of Dir., Southern CA Dartmouth Club (1979-); **HOME ADD:** 22558 Tiara St., Woodland Hills, CA 91367, (213)346-3517; **BUS ADD:** 1800 Century Park East, Suite 200, Los Angeles, CA 90067, (213)277-0300.

TERHOEVE, Peter J.——**B:** Dec. 9, 1932, Vlaardingen, The Netherlands, *Owner*, American School of RE, Educ.; **PRIM RE ACT:** Broker, Appraiser, Instructor, Insuror; **SERVICES:** Preparation for various LA State RE examinations; **PREV EMPLOY:** Inst., Century 21 RE; **PROFL AFFIL & HONORS:** Soc. of RE Appraisers; **EDUC:** BS, 1952, Acct., City Coll. Rotterdam, The Netherlands; **GRAD EDUC:** Bus./Fin., 1952; **EDUC HONORS:** Second in class of 138; **MIL SERV:** Dutch Army; Lt.; **OTHER ACT & HONORS:** Treas. candidate for mayor Baton Rouge LA; Catholic Church; Independent Insurance Agents; Pres. Sarasota Place - Baton Rouge LA (Civic Org.); Pres., St. George Parish Council, Baton Rouge, LA; **HOME ADD:** 3804 Pine Park Dr., Baton Rouge, LA 70809; **BUS ADD:** 2351 Physicians Dr., Baton Rouge, LA 70808, (504)928-7884.

TERNER, E.M.——*COB*, Midland Glass Co.; **PRIM RE ACT:** Property Manager; **BUS ADD:** PO Box 557, Cliffwood, NJ 07721, (201)566-4000.*

TERPENNING, Walter A.——**B:** Nov. 16, 1920, Evansville, IN, *RE Atty.*, The Standard Oil Co. (OH), Mktg.; **PRIM RE ACT:** Attorney; **PREV EMPLOY:** US Navy Lt. (S.G.); **PROFL AFFIL & HONORS:** OH Bar, CO Bar; **EDUC:** AB, 1942, Hist., The Johns Hopkins Univ.; **GRAD EDUC:** LLB, 1948, Law, The Univ. of MI; **EDUC HONORS:** Omicron Delta Kappa; **MIL SERV:** USN, Lt. (s.g.), overseas battle stars; **OTHER ACT & HONORS:** Councilman, S. Russell Village (1962-66); Tr., Methodist Church of Chagrin Falls; Bd. YMCA Solon, Ohio Branch; **HOME ADD:** 5846 N. Oval, Solon, OH 44139, (216)248-2167; **BUS ADD:** 1263 (S) Midland Bldg., Cleveland, OH 44115, (216)575-4351.

TERRELL, Joseph H.——**B:** Jan. 31, 1952, Anniston, AL, *VP*, The Myrick Co.; **PRIM RE ACT:** Developer, Instructor, Broker; **OTHER RE ACT:** Mktg. Dir.; **SERVICES:** Brokerage, Devel. and Prop. Mgmt./Leasing; **REP CLIENTS:** Large land users office space users and industrial users; **PREV EMPLOY:** Dir. of Sales - Metro. Ctr. - Nashville, TN; **PROFL AFFIL & HONORS:** IREM, RNMI, NARA, NAIOP, ICSC, CPM, CRA; **EDUC:** BBA, 1974, RE & Fin., Univ. of GA; **OTHER ACT & HONORS:** Nashville City Club, Peachtree World of Tennis; Atlanta Bd. of Realtors, Georgia C of C, Gwinett Bd. of Realtors; **HOME ADD:** #12 Northcliff Terrace, Atlanta, GA 30076; **BUS ADD:** 6025 The Corners Pkwy, Suite 111, Norcross (Atlanta), GA 30092, (404)449-5622.

TERRY, David E.——**B:** Dec. 9, 1953, Orlando, FL, *Assoc.*, Baker & Hostetler; **PRIM RE ACT:** Attorney; **SERVICES:** Legal servs. related to the acquisition, devel., fin. & sale of RE; **REP CLIENTS:** Instit lenders & private investors in comml. & resid. props.; **PROFL AFFIL & HONORS:** FL Bar Assn.; FL Bar Assn. Environmental Law Sect.; ABA, ABA Real Estate, Trust & Probate Sect.; Orange Cty. Bar Assn.; **EDUC:** BA, 1976, Hist., Univ. of NC at Chapel Hill; **GRAD EDUC:** JD, 1979, Univ. of FL, Holland Law Ctr.; **EDUC HONORS:** Grad. with honors, Grad. with Hons., Member of Nat. Moot Court Team, 1978; **HOME ADD:** 120 Minnehaha Cir., Maitland, FL 32751, (305)645-0293; **BUS ADD:** Suite 850, CNA Tower, Orlando, FL 32802, (305)841-1111.

TERRY, Gary A.——*Executive Vice President*, American Land Development Association; **OTHER RE ACT:** Profl. Assn. Admin.; **BUS ADD:** 604 Solar Building, 1000 16th St. N.W., Washington, DC 20036, (202)659-4582.*

TERRY, Gerald——**B:** Feb. 17, 1941, Bentree, WV, *Real Estate Appraiser*, Old Colony Co.; **PRIM RE ACT:** Consultant, Appraiser, Developer, Owner/Investor; **SERVICES:** Primarily RE Appraisal and Consultation; **REP CLIENTS:** Lenders, Attys., Indivs., Relocation Firms, Banks, and Govtl. Agencies; **PREV EMPLOY:** Chief Review Appraiser for The WV Dept. of Highways 1963-1977; **PROFL AFFIL**

& HONORS: Soc. of RE Appraisers (Assoc. Member) and Intl. Right of Way Assn.; **EDUC:** BS, 1963, Bus. Mgmt., WV Inst. of Tech.; **OTHER ACT & HONORS:** Civitan Intl. (Past Lt. Gov. of WV Dist.); **HOME ADD:** 5315 Edge Brook Rd., Charleston, WV 25313, (304)776-6572; **BUS ADD:** 1210 Kanawha Blvd. E., Charleston, WV 25301, (304)344-2581.

TERRY, Patricia A.——*VP*, Julien J. Studley, Inc., Maryland Suburban; **PRIM RE ACT:** Broker, Consultant; **PROFL AFFIL & HONORS:** WA Bd. of Realtors, Life Member: WA Bd. of Realtors; Million Dollar Leasing Club; Special Award 1976 - Top Leasing Producer for Retail/Office Leasing-WBR; **HOME ADD:** 7316 Edmonston Rd., College Park, MD 20740; **BUS ADD:** 4330 East-West Hwy. 909, Bethesda, MD 20814, (301)951-0014.

TERRY, Paul J.——**B:** Mar. 9, 1953, Los Angeles, CA, *Sales Mgr./Mktg. Specialist*, Western Map Co., Mktg.; **PRIM RE ACT:** Consultant, Owner/Investor, Property Manager; **OTHER RE ACT:** Sales, support to RE industry; **SERVICES:** Consultation, Mktg. Strategy, Tactical, Tech., Fundamental; **REP CLIENTS:** Grubbs & Ellis; Soc. of Indus. Realtors; Assn. of Indus. Realtors; Century 21 Franchise; Security Pacific Bank; **PREV EMPLOY:** Hotel Purchasing Corp., Beverly Hills; **PROFL AFFIL & HONORS:** Member, Bd. of Dir., CA State Univ., Northridge Alumni Assn., CA; San Diego Visitors and Conventions Bureau; **EDUC:** 1978, Recreation/Indus. & Comml. Sector, CA State Univ.; **GRAD EDUC:** 1979, Public Admin., CA State Univ.; **EDUC HONORS:** Dean's List, Grad. Studies Comm. Member; **HOME ADD:** 8050 Jovenita Cyn Rd., Los Angeles, CA 90046, (213)654-0964; **BUS ADD:** 217 S. Orange St., Los Angeles, CA 90046.

TERRY, Stephen V.——**B:** Feb. 14, 1950, Helena, MT, *Pres.*, S&S Terry, Inc.; **PRIM RE ACT:** Broker, Consultant, Developer, Owner/Investor, Syndicator; **OTHER RE ACT:** Inner City Rehabilitation; **SERVICES:** Investment Counseling, Natl. Synd., Computer Modeling; **REP CLIENTS:** Indivs. and Insts. Actively Placing Funds in RE; **PREV EMPLOY:** VP Nordata; System using DEC 1170, Prop. Mgr., Dir.; **PROFL AFFIL & HONORS:** Amrex, R IAOC, Soc. Board of Realtors; **EDUC:** Psychology/Sociology, 1973, Psych./Soc. Math/Computer Sci., Western Washington Univ.; **EDUC HONORS:** Pres. List; **OTHER ACT & HONORS:** Mensa, Instr. of T.M. Technique; **HOME ADD:** 603 High Dr., Laguna Beach, CA 92651, (714)497-4684; **BUS ADD:** 1201 Dove St., Penthouse Suite, Newport Bch., CA 92660, (714)851-7751.

TERZINI, Kenneth J.——**B:** Sept. 28, 1950, New Haven, CT, *Pres.*, Clear Lake Bldrs. & Restoration; **PRIM RE ACT:** Consultant, Appraiser, Developer, Builder, Property Manager, Lender, Owner/Investor; **OTHER RE ACT:** Designer, Profl. home inspections; **SERVICES:** Bldr., Prop. Mgmt., Valuation, Inv. Counsel; **REP CLIENTS:** Lenders, instns. & indivs. in comml. & resid. props., HUD Dev. feasibility study applics.; **PREV EMPLOY:** ABC, ABC Records Div.; **EDUC:** BS/Bus. Admin, 1974, Mktg./Communications, Univ. of New Haven; **OTHER ACT & HONORS:** Grad. NAHB, Residential Mgmt. of Apt. & Comm. Projects; **HOME ADD:** 475 Elm St., New Haven, CT 06511, (203)777-8063; **BUS ADD:** 475 Elm St., New Haven, CT 06511, (203)777-8063.

TETREAULT, George A., Jr.——**B:** Feb. 26, 1931, Holland, MA, *Atty-at-Law*, George A. Tetreault, Jr., Esq.; **PRIM RE ACT:** Broker, Consultant, Attorney, Appraiser, Developer, Builder, Owner/Investor; **REP CLIENTS:** Carribean-New England Ventures, Inc.; T & W Devel., Inc.; Harlow Royal Realty, Inc.; London Realty, Ltd.; London Mort. Co., Ltd.; **PROFL AFFIL & HONORS:** Hampden Cty. Bar Assn.; MA Bar Assn.; ABA; Amer. Judicature Soc.; Comml. Law League of Amer.; MA Trial Lawyers Assn.; Amer. Trial Lawyers Assn.; Criminal Law Comm. of the MBA; Amer. Arbitration Assn.; **EDUC:** BBA, 1952, Bus. Admin., Northeastern Univ.; **GRAD EDUC:** LLB, 1960, WNE Coll. School of Law; **OTHER ACT & HONORS:** Member of Newton Lodge, AF & AM, Wilbraham, MA; 32 degree Mason; CT Valley Consistory; Doris Chap. Royal Arch Masons, Southbridge, MA, Republican Club of MA; **HOME ADD:** Little Alum Pond Rd., Brimfield, MA 01010, (413)245-9529; **BUS ADD:** 697 N. Main St., POB 143, Palmer, MA 01069, (413)283-5336.

TEUSCHER, Barbara A.——**B:** May 12, 1946, MI, *Shopping Ctr. Mgr.*, Hahn Prop. Mgmt. Corp.; **PRIM RE ACT:** Property Manager; **OTHER RE ACT:** Shopping Center Mgmt.; **SERVICES:** Prop. Mgmt., Leasing & Mktg.; **REP CLIENTS:** Indiv. & Instit. Investors in shopping ctrs.; **PROFL AFFIL & HONORS:** Intl. Council of Shopping Ctrs., Cert. Shopping Ctr. Mgr.; **HOME ADD:** 1237 Wildwood Ct., Libertyville, IL 60048, (312)367-4481; **BUS ADD:** 6000 Northwest Hwy., Crystal Lake, IL 60014, (815)455-0099.

THACKER, Herbert Dickey——**B:** Oct. 5, 1929, Honolulu, HI, *Pres.*, Earl Thacker Limited; **PRIM RE ACT:** Broker, Consultant, Appraiser, Property Manager; **EDUC:** BA, 1951, Econ., Psychology, Stanford Univ.; **GRAD EDUC:** MBA, 1953, Harvard Univ.; **MIL SERV:** USN, Lt.; **OTHER ACT & HONORS:** C of C, Waiokeala Church, Pacific Club, Outrigger Club; **HOME ADD:** 2911 Makalei Place, Honolulu, HI 96815, (808)536-9541; **BUS ADD:** 2222 Kalakaua Ave, 1415, Honolulu, HI 96815.

THADEN, Arthur G.——**B:** Mar. 23, 1932, Washington, DC, *Chmn. & Pres.*, BankAmerica Realty Services, Inc.; **PRIM RE ACT:** Owner/Investor, Property Manager; **SERVICES:** Manage publicly-owned RE investment trust, BankAmerica Realty Investors; **PREV EMPLOY:** Mgr. RE Fin., Metropolitan Life, 1968-1970; **PROFL AFFIL & HONORS:** Gov. Nat. Assn. of RE Investment Trust; Dir. CA Housing Council, Commendation - San Francisco Bd. of Educ. - 1981; **EDUC:** BA, 1954, Econ., Trinity Coll., Hartford, CT; **MIL SERV:** USAF, Capt.; **OTHER ACT & HONORS:** Member, ULI; Member, Commonwealth Club of San Francisco; Member, Bankers' Club, San Francisco; Member, Alpha Delta Phi; **HOME ADD:** 50 Catalpa Dr., Atherton, CA 94025, (415)321-0339; **BUS ADD:** Suite 4275, 555 California St., San Francisco, CA 94104, (415)622-6520.

THAL, Dr. Lawrence S.——**B:** Jan 28, 1946, Oakland, CA, *President*, Farallon Development Corp.; **PRIM RE ACT:** Consultant, Developer, Owner/Investor, Instructor, Syndicator; **SERVICES:** Land devel. and subdiv. specializing in problem props.; consultants for HUD Title X mort. guarantee applicants; **REP CLIENTS:** Indiv. and synd. investors in resid. props.; **PREV EMPLOY:** Lecturer, Grad. School of Banking and Fin., Golden Gate Univ., San Francisco, CA; **PROFL AFFIL & HONORS:** Faculty, Golden Gate Univ. Grad. School of Banking and Fin.; **EDUC:** BS, 1967, Physics/Math., USAF Academy, CO; **GRAD EDUC:** MBA, 1978, Mgmt./Tax., Golden Gate Univ., San Francisco, CA; Dr. of Optometry, 1975, Univ. of CA, Berkeley; **EDUC HONORS:** Dean's List, Honor Student; **MIL SERV:** USAF, Maj., Meritorious Serv. Medal with Bronze Cluster, Air Medal with Bronze Cluster, Commendation Medal with 2 Bronze Clusters, Republic of Vietnam Cross of Gallantry with Palm; **OTHER ACT & HONORS:** Dir., Kensington Community Serv. Dist., 1980-81, elected to four year term 1981-1985; Pres., Kensington Bus. and Profl. Assn.; Life member Lions Eye Found. of CA and NV; 1980-81 Young Optometrist of the Year; listed in Who's Who in CA and Who's Who in Fin. and Indus.; Appointed by State Gov. to CA Bd. of Optometry in 1981; **HOME ADD:** 216 Amherst Ave., Kensington, CA 94708, (415)524-6952; **BUS ADD:** 291 Arlington Ave., Kensington, CA 94707, (415)527-7306.

THAL, Robert W.——**B:** Aug. 29, 1913, Chicago, IL, *VP*, First Fed. Savings & Loan Assn. of Jacksonville, Operations; **PRIM RE ACT:** Broker, Consultant, Appraiser, Banker, Lender, Insuror; **PREV EMPLOY:** Past Exec. VP Jacksonville Bd. of Realtors & MLS; Partner Grange-Watson-Thal Realtors; Indus. Relations Safety Engr.; Intl. Harvester Co.; Lumbermen's Mutual Casualty Local, FL; **PROFL AFFIL & HONORS:** IREM; NAR; Rgnl. S&L Inst.; Amer. Soc. of Safety Engr.; Nat. Safety Council, Past Rgnl. VP Inst. CPM, RE Mgmt; **EDUC:** Safety Engr., 1940, Indus. Relations, IL Inst. of Tech.; **GRAD EDUC:** 1933, Amer. Inst. of Banking; 1948, Massey Sch. of RE; 1946, Mutual Inst. of Ins.; 1977, Amer. Inst. of S&L; **EDUC HONORS:** Cert. By Nat. Safety Council; **MIL SERV:** US Army, Officer Candidate; **OTHER ACT & HONORS:** Kiwanis Past Gov., FL Dist. & Kiwanis Intl.; Sponsored Youth Administration; 58 yrs. Boy Scouts of Amer.; Founder-Past Pres.-Trustee Florida Kiwanis Found. - Trustee Kiwanis International Found.; **HOME ADD:** 5201 Atlantic Blvd., 190-C, Jacksonville, FL 32207, (904)398-2616; **BUS ADD:** PO Box 4609, Jacksonville, FL 32201, (904)354-8443.

THAMES, J.H., Jr.——**B:** Dec. 3, 1942, Jackson, MS, *Owner*, J.H. Thames, Jr., RE Appraiser; **PRIM RE ACT:** Appraiser, Builder, Owner/Investor, Syndicator; **SERVICES:** Appraisal, investments, counseling; **REP CLIENTS:** Banks, attys., state and fed. agencies; **PROFL AFFIL & HONORS:** AIREA, Bd. of Dir.; Soc. of RE Appraisers, Past Pres., MAI; SRPA; **EDUC:** BA, 1964, Econ., Univ. of MS; **MIL SERV:** USAF; Major; **HOME ADD:** 2015 E. Northside Dr., Jackson, MS 39211, **BUS ADD:** POB 741, Jackson, MS 39205, (601)354-2343.

THAXTON, Michael D.——**B:** July 22, 1953, Lubbock, TX, *Pres.*, Omega Resources, Inc.; **OTHER RE ACT:** Mort. banker, Accountant, Investment Counselor; **SERVICES:** Fin. and investment counseling, project fin., venture capital; **REP CLIENTS:** Devel., investors, fin. inst.; **PREV EMPLOY:** Ryan Mort. Co. 1978-80; Estates Trust Co. 1976- 78; **EDUC:** BBA, 1975, Acctg.-fin., TX Tech. Univ., Lubbock, TX; **EDUC HONORS:** High Honors, indiv., class, sch. scholastic honors; **OTHER ACT & HONORS:** Bd. of Dir. TX comml/investments, Inc.; United Serv. Corp., St. Savings.; **HOME ADD:** 6410 Earlyway Dr., Austin, TX 78749, (512)892-2326; **BUS ADD:** 4560

Beltline Rd. 210, Dallas, TX 75235, (214)385-7300.

THAYER, Edward C.——**B:** Apr. 11, 1930, New York, NY, *VP*, Wells Fargo Bank, Investment Advisors; **PRIM RE ACT:** Owner/Investor, Property Manager; **SERVICES:** Acquisition, mgmt. & sale of RE; **PREV EMPLOY:** Bohannon Org.; **PROFL AFFIL & HONORS:** IREM, CPM; **EDUC:** BA, 1951, Eng., Harvard Coll.; **GRAD EDUC:** MBA, 1956, Fin., Harvard Univ.; **MIL SERV:** USN, Comdr.; **HOME ADD:** 1146 Woodside Rd., Berkeley, CA 94708, (415)841-1572; **BUS ADD:** 464 California St., San Francisco, CA 94144, (415)396-2161.

THEBUS, Thomas A.——**B:** Aug. 25, 1938, Belleville, IL, *Atty.*, Thomas A. Thebus, Atty. at Law; **PRIM RE ACT:** Broker, Attorney, Consultant, Appraiser; **SERVICES:** Legal services for dev. and structuring of investment RE; **REP CLIENTS:** Devel., builders, investment grps.; **PREV EMPLOY:** Appraiser, Thebus RE Consultants; **PROFL AFFIL & HONORS:** RE Law Section, IL and ABA(member, section council, ISBA RE law section, 1973-1980); **EDUC:** PhD, 1968, Hist., DePaul Univ., Chicago, IL; **GRAD EDUC:** JD, 1971, St. Louis Univ.,; **EDUC HONORS:** Cum Laude; **OTHER ACT & HONORS:** Chmn. Historic Preservation Commn., City of Belleville 1974-76; **HOME ADD:** 104 N. Missouri Ave., Belleville, IL 62221, (618)235-5922; **BUS ADD:** 216 S. Jackson St., Belleville, IL 62221, (618)233-3266.

THEISSEN, Ronald James——**B:** Aug. 12, 1940, NY, NY, *Pres.*, R-V Equities Corp., Real-Vest Corp. (Parent Co.); **PRIM RE ACT:** Syndicator; **SERVICES:** Prop. acquisition, synd. and mgmt.; **PREV EMPLOY:** Exec. VP, Envicon Equities Corp.; **PROFL AFFIL & HONORS:** RESSI; Member of Nat. Tax Committee, CPA; **EDUC:** BBA, 1962, Acctg. & Econ., St. John's Univ.; **MIL SERV:** NY State NG; Sgt.; **OTHER ACT & HONORS:** NY State Soc. of CPA's; Sales Exec. Club of NY; **BUS ADD:** One Atlantic St., Stamford, CT 06901, (203)348-3500.

THEMPSON, Robert——*Facility Mgr.*, Intersil, Inc.; **PRIM RE ACT:** Property Manager; **BUS ADD:** 10710 N. Tantau Ave., Cupertino, CA 95014.*

THEOBALD, Forest——*Legal Counse*, Fleetwood Enterprises, Inc.; **PRIM RE ACT:** Attorney, Property Manager; **BUS ADD:** 3125 Myers St., PO Box 7638, Riverside, CA 92523, (714)785-3500.*

THEOBALD, Harland Stephen——**B:** Mar. 28, 1938, Salt Lake City, UT, *Asst. Mgr., RE*, Mountain Bell Support Servs.; **PRIM RE ACT:** Consultant, Attorney, Property Manager, Insuror; **SERVICES:** Valuation and Devel. of Comml. Prop., Prop. Mgr.; **EDUC:** BS, 1964, Econ./Arch./RE, Univ. of UT; **GRAD EDUC:** Prof. Cert., RE, 1978, Univ. of UT; **MIL SERV:** 19th Special Forces, Sgt., Parachutist; **HOME ADD:** 8146 Queno Vista Dr., W. Jordan, UT 84084, (801)561-7817; **BUS ADD:** POB 30960, Salt Lake City, UT 84125, (801)237-7642.

THEROS, William J.——**B:** Aug. 30, 1925, Lancaster, PA, *VP, Engr.*, Culbro Corp., Gen. Cigar & Tobacco; **PRIM RE ACT:** Consultant, Architect, Engineer, Appraiser, Instructor, Property Manager; **SERVICES:** Appraisal, purchase, sales; **REP CLIENTS:** 9 Divs. of Culbro (food, drugs, tobacco, plastics, RE, fin. distributions, sales, warehousings); **PREV EMPLOY:** 1952-1954 RCA, 1949-1951 State PA, 1943-1946 Armstrong; **PROFL AFFIL & HONORS:** ASME, MSPE, AIPE, Who's Who in Engr.; Prof. Engr. Lic. 6 states - PA, NJ, FL, WV, IN, VA; **EDUC:** BS Mech. Engr., 1949, Plant Serv., expansion, RE, Univ. of Miami, F&M, Trinity, MO State Teacher; **MIL SERV:** USAF, 1st Lt.; **OTHER ACT & HONORS:** Toastmaster VP Intl. 1958-1961; Optimists, AHEPA, HOC, Pres.; Chief Engr. Dir. of Engrg.; **HOME ADD:** 232 E. Roseville Rd., Lancaster, PA 17601, (717)569-2197; **BUS ADD:** 417 W. Frederick St., Lancaster, PA 17604, (717)397-3666.

THETFORD, James G.——**B:** Mar. 23, 1920, Newark, NJ, *Pres.*, James G. Thetford Co.; **PRIM RE ACT:** Consultant, Appraiser; **SERVICES:** RE appraising & consulting; **REP CLIENTS:** Lenders, govt. agencies, private indiv., corp.; **PROFL AFFIL & HONORS:** AIREA; SREA; Intl. Inst. of Valuers, MAI; SRPA; SCV; **EDUC:** 1943, Rugers Univ.; **MIL SERV:** US Army; Cpl.; **HOME ADD:** Towne Hill Rd., Montpelier, VT 05602, (802)223-7639; **BUS ADD:** Towne Hill Rd., Montpelier, VT 05602, (802)223-7639.

THIBEAULT, Russell W.——**B:** Dec. 18, 1946, Manchester, NH, *Prin.*, Applied Economic Research; **PRIM RE ACT:** Consultant, Developer, Syndicator; **SERVICES:** Market and fin. feasibility, redevel. const., appraisals; **REP CLIENTS:** Nat. trust for hist. preservation, Georgia Pacific Corp., Rgnl. Banks, Boston Redevel. Authority, City of Baltimore, PPG Indus., NY Urban Devel. Corp., assignments in over 30 states, analyzed investments total several billion dollars; **PREV EMPLOY:** Sr. Assoc., Hammer, Siler, George Assocs.; **PROFL AFFIL & HONORS:** Nat. Council on Urgan Econ. Devel., Pres., NH Planners Assn., Amer. Planning Assn., Soc. of RE Appraisers, Nat. Trust for Hist. Preservation; **EDUC:** MRgnl. Planning, 1972, Univ. of NC; **EDUC HONORS:** Recipient of S. Rgnl. Sci. Assn. Research Award, Pres. of Class, Nat. Sci. Found. Assist.; **OTHER ACT & HONORS:** Rotary Intl.; **HOME ADD:** 51 Winnicoash St., Laconia, NH 03246, (603)524-3145; **BUS ADD:** 61 Church St., Box 1250, Laconia, NH 03246, (603)524-1484.

THIEMANN, Charles Lee——*Pres*, Federal Home Loan Bank of Cincinnati; **PRIM RE ACT:** Banker; **BUS ADD:** PO Box 593, Cincinnati, OH 45201, (513)852-7500.*

THIEMANN, Robert James——**B:** Dec. 15, 1934, St. Louis, MO, *Pres.*, Thiemann-Stinnett, Inc.; **PRIM RE ACT:** Broker, Consultant, Developer, Builder, Owner/Investor, Property Manager, Syndicator; **PREV EMPLOY:** 24 years in the S & L bus. as Sr. Lending Officer & CEO of Land Devel. Subsidiary; **PROFL AFFIL & HONORS:** HBA, RESSI, Metropolitan RE Bd.; **MIL SERV:** Mo ANG USAFR; **HOME ADD:** 3 Harcourt Dr., Clayton, MO 63105, (314)727-7444; **BUS ADD:** 11500 Olive Blvd., Ste. 224, PO Box 12759, St. Louis, MO 63141, (314)569-1156.

THIES, Winthrop Drake——**B:** Mar. 13, 1931, White Plains, NY, *Pres., First Nat. Capital Corp. (Nev.)*; **PRIM RE ACT:** Consultant, Attorney, Syndicator; **OTHER RE ACT:** Mort. broker; venture capital; **SERVICES:** Feasibility studies; obtaining requisite capital; **REP CLIENTS:** Prof. ethics precludes out revealing these; **PREV EMPLOY:** Dir. of Ad. Underwriting, Metropolitan Life; Assoc. Dir. Adv. Underwriting Svcs., Mutual Benefit Life; tax attorney, Regan, Goldfarb, Powell & Quinn; RE Dept., Thacher Proffitt Crawley & Wood, Attys.; **PROFL AFFIL & HONORS:** NY Cty. Lawyers Assn.; Former Member of its Comm. on Legal Serv. and Comm. on Unlawful Practice of Law; **EDUC:** AB, 1953, Poli., Princeton Univ. & Amer. Coll.; **GRAD EDUC:** JD/LLM, 1959, Tax Law, Harvard Law School/NY Univ. Grad. School of Law, 1965; **EDUC HONORS:** Chartered Life Underwriter; **MIL SERV:** US Army, Sp-4; **OTHER ACT & HONORS:** Member, Program Comm., Ethical Culture Soc. of Essex Cty., NJ; **HOME ADD:** 15 No. Terrace, Maplewood, NJ 07040; **BUS ADD:** 39 Broadway, Ste. 3500, New York, NY 10006, (212)425-9496.

THISTLEWAITE, John M.——**B:** Mar. 1, 1951, Richmond, IN, *Part.*, Hunter- Thistlewaite Interests; **PRIM RE ACT:** Syndicator, Consultant, Developer; **PREV EMPLOY:** RE Research Corp.-Mkt. Analysts 1974-1976; **PROFL AFFIL & HONORS:** NAR, RESSI, IN Assoc. Realtors; **EDUC:** BS, 1973, RE Admin., Indiana Univ.; **HOME ADD:** 8414 Coldwater Rd., Fort Wayne, IN 46802, (219)489-1649; **BUS ADD:** 727 Fulton St., Fort Wayne, IN 46802, (219)426-3386.

THOBURN, J.W.——*Corp. Engr.*, Ferro Corp.; **PRIM RE ACT:** Property Manager; **BUS ADD:** One Erieview Plaza, Cleveland, OH 44114, (216)641-8580.*

THOM, Michael William——**B:** Sept. 17, 1954, Oklahoma City, OK, *Atty.*, Speck, Philbin, Fleig, Trudgeon and Lutz; **PRIM RE ACT:** Attorney; **SERVICES:** Probate matters, title examination, contract review; **PROFL AFFIL & HONORS:** Oklahoma City Tax Lawyers, Amer. Jurisprudence Awards in Prop. and Creditors Rights; **EDUC:** BS, 1974, math, music theory, languages, Univ. of OK; **GRAD EDUC:** JD, 1977, Prop., tax and estate planning, Univ. of OK; **EDUC HONORS:** Deans Honor Roll, Phi Beta Kappa, Summa Cum Laude, Highest Honors, Member, OK Law Review 1975-77, Deans Honor Roll; **HOME ADD:** 1800 Austin, Oklahoma City, OK 73127, (405)943-2284; **BUS ADD:** 800 City National Bank Tower, Oklahoma City, OK 73102, (405)235-1603.

THOM, W. Scott——**B:** June 28, 1932, Wausau, WI, *Partner*, Heide, Hartley, Thom, Wilk and Guttormsen; **PRIM RE ACT:** Attorney; **REP CLIENTS:** 1st Nat. Bank of Kenosha; Kenosha S & L Assn.; **PROFL AFFIL & HONORS:** State Bar of WI; ABA; **EDUC:** BA, 1954, Econ., Yale Univ.; **GRAD EDUC:** JD, 1959, Univ. of WI; **MIL SERV:** USAF; Capt.; **HOME ADD:** 7510 2nd Ave., Kenosha, WI 53140, (414)654-0002; **BUS ADD:** 611 56th St., Kenosha, WI 53140, (414)658-4800.

THOMA, Kurt M.——**B:** Aug. 9, 1946, Boston, MA, *Owner, Pres.*, Dessin Batir, Inc.; **PRIM RE ACT:** Developer, Builder, Owner/Investor, Property Manager; **OTHER RE ACT:** Comml. and resid. solar designer; **SERVICES:** design, const. and/or consulting on Passive Solar Comml. and resid. bldg. projects; **REP CLIENTS:** Indiv. and pvt. investors; **PREV EMPLOY:** design & bldg. indus. 18 yrs. and 3 yrs. in banking; **PROFL AFFIL & HONORS:** Intl. Solar Energy Soc.; NAHB; RI Assoc. Homebuilders; **EDUC:** 2 yrs. UNH, Bus. Admin.,

Whittmore Bus. School, Univ. NH; **MIL SERV:** US Army, E-5, Sgt.; **HOME ADD:** 21 School St., Newport, RI 02840, (401)846-7007; **BUS ADD:** 21 School St., Newport, RI 02840, (401)846-0114.

THOMAS, Betty——*Ed.*, American Right of Way Assn., Right of Way; **OTHER RE ACT:** Professional - Assn. Administrator; **BUS ADD:** 3727 W. 6th, Los Angeles, CA 90020, (213)383-2117.*

THOMAS, David A.——**B:** Feb. 4, 1944, Los Angeles, CA, *Prof. of Law*, Law School, Brigham Young Univ.; **OTHER RE ACT:** Prop. Law Teacher; **SERVICES:** Legal Consultation, Lecturing; **PREV EMPLOY:** Private Law practive 1974; **PROFL AFFIL & HONORS:** Real Prop., Probate and Trust Section, ABA; **EDUC:** BA, 1967, Poli. Sci., German, Brigham Young Univ.; **GRAD EDUC:** JD, 1972, Law, Duke Univ. Law School; **EDUC HONORS:** High Honors; **MIL SERV:** US Army, E-5, Bronze Star, Bronze Star W/1st Oak Leaf Cluster, Army Commendation Medal; **OTHER ACT & HONORS:** UT Heritage Found. 1972; **HOME ADD:** 188 E. 1864 S., Orem, UT 84057, (801)225-1355; **BUS ADD:** Provo, UT 84602, (801)378-3210.

THOMAS, David N.——**B:** Jan. 10, 1934, Atlanta, GA, *VP*, Cushman and Wakefield, Investment; **PRIM RE ACT:** Broker, Consultant, Appraiser, Owner/Investor, Instructor, Syndicator; **SERVICES:** RE brokerage, exchanging, counseling, synd.; **REP CLIENTS:** Citicorp, Volkswagen, JMB, Broad Reach, Dawson Investments Ltd. of England; **PREV EMPLOY:** Managing Broker, Comml. Div., Barton and Ludwig, Inc.; **PROFL AFFIL & HONORS:** NAR; GA Assn. of Realtors; Atlanta Bd. of Realtors; Realtors Nat. Mktg. Inst.; Assoc. of GA RE Exchangors, CCIM; Realtor Assoc. of the Yr., 1978 for State of GA; Exchangor of the Yr. 1979, State of GA; Atlanta Bd. of Realtors Phoenix Award; Million Dollar Club active life member Atlanta Bd.; **EDUC:** BBA, 1958, Mgmt. and Mktg., Emory Univ.; **EDUC HONORS:** Top 10% of Class; Pres., Alpha Kappa Psi Bus. Frat.; **MIL SERV:** US Army, Pfc., 1954-1956; **OTHER ACT & HONORS:** Pres., Warren Boys Club; Chap. Member, St. Philip Cathedral; Dir., Boys Clubs Metro Atlanta; Instr., GRI and GA Inst. of RE; Who's Who in Southeast; Pres., GA Chap. CCIM; **HOME ADD:** 3025 Paces Lake Ct., Atlanta, GA 30339, (404)436-9333; **BUS ADD:** 225 Peachtree St., Suite 2020, Atlanta, GA 30339, (404)522-2000.

THOMAS, Edwin James, II——**B:** May 2, 1947, Carmel, CA, *Pres.*, Monterey Peninsula Development Co., Inc.; **PRIM RE ACT:** Broker, Owner/Investor; **PREV EMPLOY:** Tod Cox Bus. Opportunities and Anchor Assocs., RE Consultants; **PROFL AFFIL & HONORS:** Monterey Pen. C of C, Monterey Bd. of Realtors, CA Assn. of Realtors; **EDUC:** BA, 1970, Bus., Menlo Coll.; **OTHER ACT & HONORS:** Bohemian Club, Pacheco Club, Carmel Valley Ranch; **HOME ADD:** PO Box 3521, Carmel, CA 93921, (408)659-2303; **BUS ADD:** 700 Cannery Row, Monterey, CA 93940, (408)649-1898.

THOMAS, James O.——**B:** Apr. 24, 1917, Malad, ID, *VP*, Home Savings and Loan Assn., N CA; **PRIM RE ACT:** Broker, Appraiser, Lender, Instructor; **PREV EMPLOY:** Comml. mort. ins., Amer. S&L Assn.; **PROFL AFFIL & HONORS:** AIREA, SREA, CA RE Brokers Lic., MAI, SRPA; **EDUC:** AA, 1938, Glendale Jr. Coll., Glendale, CA; **GRAD EDUC:** BS, 1941, Univ. of CA, Berkeley; **OTHER ACT & HONORS:** Elks Club, Palo Alto, CA; **HOME ADD:** 1860 Golden Way, Mountain View, CA 94040, (415)964-3110; **BUS ADD:** 1730 S El Camino Real, San Mateo, CA 94402, (415)574-9100.

THOMAS, Joseph E.——**B:** July 18, 1941, Craven, NC, *VP & Gen. Mgr.*, Westminster Co., A Weyerhaeuser Co.; **PRIM RE ACT:** Broker, Developer, Builder, Owner/Investor, Property Manager, Syndicator; **PROFL AFFIL & HONORS:** NC Bd. of Realtors, NC Soc. of Engrs.; **EDUC:** BS, Forestry, NC State Univ.; **OTHER ACT & HONORS:** Mayor of Vanceboro 1967, NC State Sen., 2nd Dist. 1979-date; **HOME ADD:** PO Box 337, Vanceboro, NC 28586, (919)244-1414; **BUS ADD:** PO Box 1167, Jacksonville, NC 28540, (919)346-9721.

THOMAS, Larry D.——**B:** Nov. 1, 1940, McAllen, TX, *Pres.*, Equity Mgmt. Corp. (1975 to present); **PRIM RE ACT:** Broker, Instructor, Syndicator, Consultant, Property Manager, Banker, Owner/Investor; **SERVICES:** Prop. Mgmt., Brokerage, Construction Mgmt. & Rehab.; **REP CLIENTS:** Lenders and indiv. or Instl. investors in comml.; **PREV EMPLOY:** Pres. Miller Multi-Mgmt. (sub. of Henry S. Miller Co.'s 74-75), VP Pkwy, Mgmt. & First Mort. Co. of TX 65-74; **PROFL AFFIL & HONORS:** Past Pres., Dallas; VP TX Apt. Assoc. IREM - Nat., Sr. VP, Omego Tau Rho (RE Honor Fraternity), CPM; **EDUC:** BS, 1963, Econ., Pol. Sci., Lamar Univ.; **MIL SERV:** USAFR, S/Sgt. 1963-69; **OTHER ACT & HONORS:** Dallas Rehab. Bd. 1979/80; **HOME ADD:** 6605 Duffield, Dallas, TX 75248, (214)931-6441; **BUS ADD:** 16475 Dallas Pkwy., Suite 440, Dallas, TX 75248, (214)931-2440.

THOMAS, Larry P.——**B:** Apr. 26, 1951, Compton, CA, *Sales Assoc.*, Bronco Realty; **PRIM RE ACT:** Owner/Investor; **OTHER RE ACT:** Salesman; **SERVICES:** Sales Assoc.; **PREV EMPLOY:** VP/Gen. Mgr. of Acadia Scrap & Salvage, Inc., LA; **PROFL AFFIL & HONORS:** Lafayette Realtors Assn.; **EDUC:** BBA, 1974, Acctg. & econ., The Univ. of MS; **EDUC HONORS:** Delta Sigma Pi; **HOME ADD:** 107 Billeaud Ln., Lafayette, LA 70506, (318)237-2189; **BUS TEL:** (318)233-5352.

THOMAS, L.B.——*V.P. Fin. & Treas.*, ConAgra Inc.; **PRIM RE ACT:** Property Manager; **BUS ADD:** 200 Kiewit Plaza, Omaha, NE 68131, (402)346-8004.*

THOMAS, Mark A.——**B:** July 10, 1941, Beaver Dam, WI, *Broker*, Weir, Manuel, Snyder & Ranke, Inc., Corp. Office; **PRIM RE ACT:** Broker, Consultant, Developer, Syndicator; **OTHER RE ACT:** Resid. Sales; **PREV EMPLOY:** Facilities & Prop. Dept., Ford Motor Co.; **PROFL AFFIL & HONORS:** Nat. Assn. of Realtors; Intl. RE Federation; Nat. RE Exchange, Candidate: CCIM; **EDUC:** BA, 1963, Econ., Lawrence Univ.; **GRAD EDUC:** MBA, 1965, Intl. Fin., Amos Tuck School of Dartmouth Coll.; **EDUC HONORS:** Senior Honors; **OTHER ACT & HONORS:** Birmingham Hist. Bd., 3 yr. term; CCCA; VMCCA; **HOME ADD:** 175 Baldwin Ave., Birmingham, MI 48009, (313)647-1135; **BUS ADD:** 298 S. Woodward Ave., Birmingham, MI 48011, (313)644-6300.

THOMAS, Michael E.——Michael E. Thomas Dev. Co.; **OTHER RE ACT:** Comml. devel. and prop. mgmt.; **BUS ADD:** 300 E. Long Lake Rd., Suite 360, Bloomfield Hills, MI 48013.

THOMAS, R. Haywood, Jr.——*Secy.*, Dibrell Brothers, Inc.; **PRIM RE ACT:** Property Manager; **BUS ADD:** 512 Bridge St., Danville, VA 24541, (804)792-7511.*

THOMAS, Richard D.——*Asset & Risk Mgr.*, Lukens Steel; **PRIM RE ACT:** Property Manager; **BUS ADD:** 50 South First Ave., Coatesville, PA 19320, (215)383-3333.*

THOMAS, Robert Earl——**B:** Mar. 31, 1925, Altus, OK, *Asst. VP*, Tishman West Mgmt. Corp., San Diego Area; **PRIM RE ACT:** Property Manager; **SERVICES:** Leasing & mgmt. of office bldgs.; **PREV EMPLOY:** USN 1943-1970, Capt., Comdr. of Submarine, Submarine Div., Large Amphibious Warship; **PROFL AFFIL & HONORS:** BOMA, Rotary, Pres. of San Diego BOMA 1974; Pres. of Point Loma Rotary 1976; CPM; **EDUC:** BS, 1945, Naval Sci. & Engrg., Univ. of Notre Dame; **MIL SERV:** USN, Capt.; **HOME ADD:** 3338 Dumas St., San Diego, CA 92106; **BUS ADD:** 110 W. A St., San Diego, CA 92101, (714)234-4666.

THOMAS, Robert L.——**B:** Oct. 28, 1943, Springfield, MO, *First VP*, Century 21 RE Corp., Regional Dev.; **PRIM RE ACT:** Broker, Instructor; **OTHER RE ACT:** Franchisor; **PREV EMPLOY:** Robert L. Thomas & Assoc., Inc. - Pres.; **PROFL AFFIL & HONORS:** NAR; RNMI; Amer. Mgmt. Assoc.; CCIM; **HOME ADD:** 483 Linden St., Laguna Beach, CA 92651, (714)497-2111; **BUS ADD:** 18872 MacArthur Blvd., Irvine, CA 92651, (714)752-7521.

THOMAS, Robert M.——**B:** Sept. 21, 1927, Douglesville, GA, *VP*, Carter & Assoc., Comml. Property Mgmt. Div.; **PRIM RE ACT:** Broker, Engineer, Instructor, Property Manager; **OTHER RE ACT:** R.P.A. real prop. admin.; **REP CLIENTS:** Owner representative (5) five major sites; **PREV EMPLOY:** 20 yrs-Property Mgr.; 10 yrs-Eng. Exp.; **PROFL AFFIL & HONORS:** BOMI-BOMA-Atlanta Bd. of Realtors; Nat. Inst. of Power Engineers; SORPA, Gov.-Comm. for Energy; **EDUC:** 1967, 1981; **GRAD EDUC:** ICS, 1952, Elec. 4 - HVAC, JBEN; **EDUC HONORS:** Real Estate License; **MIL SERV:** US Army; Cpl.; **OTHER ACT & HONORS:** BOMI, Fund Raising Chmn.; Pres. Elect-BOMA Atlanta; **HOME ADD:** 2715 Kimmeridge Dr., East Point, GA 30344, (404)767-9053; **BUS ADD:** 1100 Spring St., Atlanta, GA 30309, (404)873-3981.

THOMAS, Walter F., Jr.——Bellemead Development Corp.; **PRIM RE ACT:** Developer; **BUS ADD:** 210 Clay Ave., Lyndhurst, NJ 07071, (201)438-6880.*

THOMAS, William Daniel, Jr.——**B:** Sept. 2, 1934, Sweet Home, AR, *Pres.*, The Danny Thomas Co.; **PRIM RE ACT:** Broker, Consultant, Appraiser, Developer, Owner/Investor, Property Manager, Syndicator; **SERVICES:** Devel. counseling, comml./resid. sales and devel., synd. of comml. prop., prop. mgmt.; **REP CLIENTS:** Indiv. and instit. investors; pension trusts; **PREV EMPLOY:** VP, Rector, Phillips, Morse RE; **PROFL AFFIL & HONORS:** NRA; Little Rock, N. Little Rock Bd. of Realtors; AR Realtors Assn.; RESSI; Nat. Assn. of Securities Dealers; **EDUC:** BA, 1957, Agric., OK State Univ.; **OTHER ACT & HONORS:** Elder, Westminister Presbyterian Church;

Christian Business Men's Comm.; St. Jude's Children's Research Hosp.; **HOME ADD:** 20 Pebble Beach, Little Rock, AR 72212, (504)224-2668; **BUS ADD:** Suite 400, 212 Center St., Little Rock, AR 72212, (501)374-2231.

THOMASON, Thomas L.——B: Nov. 19, 1933, Greenville, SC, *Pres.*, Profl. Mort. Co., Inc.; **PRIM RE ACT:** Consultant, Appraiser, Banker; **OTHER RE ACT:** Lender; **SERVICES:** Income prop. fin., sales, equities & consulting; **REP CLIENTS:** Income prop. devels., life ins. cos., and pvt. investors; **PREV EMPLOY:** Liberty Life Ins. Co., VP, Mort. Loan Dept. 1962-1972; **PROFL AFFIL & HONORS:** ULI; Fed. Policy Council; MBAA; Income Prop. Comm., MBA of Carolinas; Dir. & Income Prop. Comm.; ICSC, Adjunct Prof., Coll. of Bus. Admin., Univ. of SC, Columbia, SC 1981-1982; **EDUC:** BS, 1955, Bus. Admin., Univ. of SC; **MIL SERV:** USAF; Capt.; 1956-1962, Instructor Navigator; **HOME ADD:** 103 Pine Forest Dr., Greer, SC 29651, (803)877-6261; **BUS ADD:** Box 1806, Greenville, SC 29602, (803)242-0079.

THOMASSON, Floyd A.——B: May 4, 1924, St. Petersburg, FL, *Pres.*, Rebus, Inc.; **PRIM RE ACT:** Developer; **PROFL AFFIL & HONORS:** NACORE; **EDUC:** BA, 1948, Liberal Arts, Center Coll., Danville, KY; **EDUC HONORS:** Omicron Delta Kappa; **MIL SERV:** USN, Lt.; **HOME ADD:** 221 Monterey Rd., Palm Beach, FL 33480; **BUS ADD:** PO Box 477, Jupiter, FL 33458, (305)747-7440.

THOMAS-WILLIAMS, Col. Robert C.——B: Sep. 26, 1939, Selah, WA, *CEO*, Uni-Comm Services, Unlt.; **PRIM RE ACT:** Syndicator, Consultant, Appraiser, Developer, Builder, Property Manager, Engineer, Owner/Investor; **EDUC:** BS, 1956, Math & Physics, MIT; **GRAD EDUC:** Ph.D., 1961, Top. Physics, MIT; SD, 1961, Topological Physics, CO Tech.; **MIL SERV:** USMA, Col., Misc.; **HOME ADD:** 6925 Fifth Ave., Ste E-505, Scottsdale, AZ 85251, (602)941-4023; **BUS ADD:** 6925 Fifth Ave., Suite E-505, Scottsdale, AZ 85251, (602)941-9023.

THOMPSON, Brian——*Dir. RE*, Knudsen Corp.; **PRIM RE ACT:** Property Manager; **BUS ADD:** PO Box 2335 Terminal Annex, Los Angeles, CA 90051, (213)744-7000.*

THOMPSON, Bruce R.——B: Feb. 9, 1943, Salem, MA, *Pres.*, Thompson Assocs.; **PRIM RE ACT:** Consultant, Developer, Builder; **SERVICES:** Counseling, const. mgmt., fin. participation; **REP CLIENTS:** Lenders, indiv. investors, & synds. for resid. and comml. props.; **PREV EMPLOY:** IBEC/IBEC Housing Intl. 1970-1977; **EDUC:** BSCE, 1967, Civil Engrg., Structural, Northeastern Univ., Boston, MA; **GRAD EDUC:** MBA, 1969, Bus. Admin., Tuck School, Dartmouth Coll.; **MIL SERV:** classified; **HOME ADD:** 3600 Hillsboro Rd., Nashville, TN 37215, (615)269-0907; **BUS ADD:** 2120 Crestmoor Rd., Suite 400, Nashville, TN 37215, (615)292-7667.

THOMPSON, Byron——B: Jan. 10, 1942, Riverside, CA, *VP*, McIntire Properties, Inc., McIntire Investment Corp.; **PRIM RE ACT:** Broker, Developer, Owner/Investor, Property Manager; **SERVICES:** Devel. and prop. mgmt. of comml. and apt. props.; **PREV EMPLOY:** Rgnl. Mgr., Melia Intl. Hotels, 1973-1978; John Lang, Ltd. (London), 1969-1973; **PROFL AFFIL & HONORS:** Amer. Soc. of Appraisers; FIABLI; WA Bd. of Realtors; Nat. Assn. of Review Appraisers, Million Dollar Club, WA Bd. of Realtors; **MIL SERV:** USN Res., PO 3/C, 1963-1965; **HOME ADD:** 2014 Tunlaw Rd., NW, Washington, DC 20007, (202)338-5231; **BUS ADD:** 8520 Connecticut Ave., Chevy Chase, MD 20815, (301)656-2747.

THOMPSON, Charles L.——B: Jan. 25, 1923, Jackson, MS, *Owner*, Chuck Thompson & Assocs.; **PRIM RE ACT:** Broker, Consultant, Owner/Investor, Syndicator, Real Estate Publisher; **SERVICES:** Brokerage of comml. and investment props., counseling, publisher: Airport RE Digest; **REP CLIENTS:** Corp. and indiv. investors in comml. props. and bldg. sites; **EDUC:** BA, 1948, Bus. Law & RE, Univ. of AL & Univ. of Houston; **MIL SERV:** US Air Force; **HOME ADD:** 12239 W. Village, Ste. A, Houston, TX 77039, (713)442-0060; **BUS ADD:** 12239 W. Village, Ste. A, PO Box 11652, Houston, TX 77016, (713)442-0060.

THOMPSON, Clark G.——B: July 15, 1925, Houston, TX, *Atty.*, Law Offices of Clark G. Thompson; **PRIM RE ACT:** Consultant, Attorney, Developer, Owner/Investor; **SERVICES:** Legal and devel. counsel; **REP CLIENTS:** Indiv. and cos. involved in RE; **PROFL AFFIL & HONORS:** Houston Bar Assn.; State Bar of TX; Houston Bd. of Realtors; **EDUC:** BBA, 1947, Bus. and Acctg., Univ. of TX; **GRAD EDUC:** LLB, 1949, Univ. of TX; **MIL SERV:** USMC, Pvt.; **OTHER ACT & HONORS:** Rotary Club of Houston; **HOME ADD:** 1944 Larchmont St., Houston, TX 77019, (713)622-2595; **BUS ADD:** 2421 San Felipe, Houston, TX 77019, (713)522-0771.

THOMPSON, Cornelius O., III——B: Dec. 10, 1942, Charleston, SC, *Partner*, Attaway, Thompson & Assoc.; **PRIM RE ACT:** Broker, Consultant, Appraiser, Instructor; **SERVICES:** RE appraisals, consulting, brokerage; **REP CLIENTS:** Lenders, indiv., corp. and instit. investors; buyers and sellers; **PREV EMPLOY:** S.E. Territory Prop. Tax Mgr., Sears, Roebuck & Co., 1975-1978; **PROFL AFFIL & HONORS:** Amer. Inst. of RE Appraisers; SREA; NARA; IAAO; NAR, MAI; SRPA; AAE; CRA; **EDUC:** BS, 1964, Econ., Coll. of Charleston; **HOME ADD:** 905 Harvest Way, Mt. Pleasant, SC 29464, (803)884-5199; **BUS ADD:** 10 Gillon St., Charleston, SC 29401, (803)722-1039.

THOMPSON, Ezra Enwood——B: Feb. 3, 1916, Bluewater, NM, *Pres.*, Thompson Westcoast Co., Home Office; **PRIM RE ACT:** Engineer, Architect, Developer, Builder, Owner/Investor, Property Manager, Syndicator; **SERVICES:** Gen. bldg. contractors & RE devels.; **REP CLIENTS:** "Turn-Key" project devels., including arch. and engrg. services; **PREV EMPLOY:** Chief Const. Engr. & Arch. for W. Coast Div. of The Firestone Tire & Rubber Co. for 14 yrs., Resigned in 1963 to organize own co. - Thompson Westcoast Co.; **PROFL AFFIL & HONORS:** Member of Assoc. Gen. Contractors of Amer. (AGC), CA Builders Exchange, Amer. Inst. of Contractors, Nat. Soc. of Const. Estimators, AIA-AGC Comm., Better Business Bureau; Construction Specifications Institute, Building Industry Credit Assoc.; **EDUC:** 1937, Arch., Engr. & Const., AZ State Univ.; **GRAD EDUC:** WW II Air Corps. Tech. Training, Yale; **MIL SERV:** US Air Force, Colonel, Several decorations during WWII & Korean War; **OTHER ACT & HONORS:** Have been on the "Bd. of Dirs." several corps.; **HOME ADD:** 6227 East 6th St., Univ. Park Estates, Long Beach, CA 98003; **BUS ADD:** 1899 Freeman Ave., Long Beach, CA 90804, (213)597-2077.

THOMPSON, George M.——B: Apr. 28, 1914, Dalhart, TX, *SREA, CRA*, George M. Thompson, Realtor/Appraiser; **PRIM RE ACT:** Broker, Appraiser, Instructor, Property Manager; **OTHER RE ACT:** Analyst, feasibility analysis, comml. devel. props.; **PREV EMPLOY:** Self employed since early 1940's; **PROFL AFFIL & HONORS:** Earned Profl. designations; Soc. of RE Appraisers; natl. state & local realtor bds.; Charter Memb. - Nat. Assn. of Review Appraisers - 1970, SREA, Certif. 1, Conferred, 1963; RE Cert. each 5 yrs. since; **EDUC:** 1932, Bus. Admin., John Tarleton Coll.; **MIL SERV:** US Navy; SK-V-2C-, US Defense Medal, Good Conduct Medal, Victory Medal; **OTHER ACT & HONORS:** 48 yr. member Intl. Assn. Lions Clubs, Past Dir. Gov., 1965-1966; Holder of many intl. awards; Past Pres. Sweetwater C of C ; Officer, Suez Shrine Temple; Past Pres. Sweetwater Area Shrine & Scottish Rite Clubs, 3 times Chapter Pres. & 2 times area Vice Governor; Soc. of RE Appraisers; Articles on appraisal topics published in RE Appraiser , Journal of Farm & Ranch Mgmt.; TX Atty. Gen's. Office of Condemnation; **HOME ADD:** 900 James St., Sweetwater, TX 79556, (915)235-9610; **BUS ADD:** Ground Flr., Doscher Bldg., Sweetwater, TX 79556.

THOMPSON, Henry E.——B: Sept. 19, 1918, Dighton, MI, *Pres.*, Hank Thompson Realty, Inc.; **PRIM RE ACT:** Broker, Consultant, Appraiser, Developer, Owner/Investor, Syndicator; **PREV EMPLOY:** Primarily Counselling; **PROFL AFFIL & HONORS:** White House Conference Small Business-Certified Comml. Investment Member-Certified Residential Specialists - Tr. Kiwanis Foundation, Recipient, Governor's Industrial Reward; **EDUC:** BS, AB, 1940, Science, Western Michigan Univ.,Kalamazoo, MI; **GRAD EDUC:** Working on, Business RE, Univ. of GA; **MIL SERV:** US Army, Lt., Bronze Star; **OTHER ACT & HONORS:** Trustee-Habilitation Center; Past Lt. Gov., Kiwanis; **HOME ADD:** 6060 N. Ocean Blvd. Ocean Ridge, Boynton Beach, FL 33435, (305)732-9249; **BUS ADD:** 639 E. Ocean Ave., PO Drawer Z, Boynton Beach, FL 33435, (305)737-4900.

THOMPSON, Horatio C.——B: Aug. 5, 1914, New Orleans, LA, *Pres.*, Horatio Thompson Realty, Inc.; **PRIM RE ACT:** Owner/Investor, Property Manager; **PREV EMPLOY:** Automotive Parts Jobber; **PROFL AFFIL & HONORS:** Baton Rouge Area C of C, Dir. & Chmn. Bd. - New Orleans Branch - Fed. Res. Bank of Atlanta, Free Enterpriser of the Year Award 1980, 6th Congressional District; **EDUC:** AB, 1937, High School Teacher Training, So. Univ. - Baton Rouge, LA; **EDUC HONORS:** Member So. Univ. Bd. of Supervisors; **OTHER ACT & HONORS:** Member Commn. of Govt. Ethics, Public Affairs Research Council, Treas. - Council for a Better LA; **HOME ADD:** 2844 - 79th Ave., P O Box 1027, Baton Rouge, LA 70821-1027, (504)355-8131; **BUS ADD:** P O Box 1027, Baton Rouge, LA 70821, (504)775-6181.

THOMPSON, James——*Ins. Mgr.*, G. Heilman Brewing Co., Inc.; **PRIM RE ACT:** Broker; **BUS ADD:** 100 Harbor View Plaza, La Crosse, WI 54601, (608)785-1000.*

THOMPSON, John——*Dir. Corp. Fac.*, Datapoint Corp.; **PRIM RE ACT:** Property Manager; **BUS ADD:** 8400 Datapoint Dr., San Antonio, TX 78284, (512)699-7000.*

THOMPSON, John——*Corp VP*, Parker-Hannifin; **PRIM RE ACT:** Property Manager; **BUS ADD:** 17325 Euclid Ave., Cleveland, OH 44112, (216)531-3000.*

THOMPSON, John B.——*Secy. & Treas.*, Dixie Yarns, Inc.; **PRIM RE ACT:** Property Manager; **BUS ADD:** PO Box 751, Chattanooga, TN 37401, (614)698-2501.*

THOMPSON, John S.——**B:** Mar. 31, 1925, Berkeley, CA, *Pres.*, John S. Thompson Co., Inc.; **PRIM RE ACT:** Consultant; **OTHER RE ACT:** Mkt. Research Consulting Firm; **SERVICES:** Store location research, sales forecasting models; **REP CLIENTS:** Mervyn's; Handy Dan; Zeller's; many other retail chains and shopping ctr. devel.; **PROFL AFFIL & HONORS:** ICSC; NACORE; **GRAD EDUC:** MBA, 1951, Stanford Univ.; **HOME ADD:** 244 Live Oak Ln., Los Altos, CA 94022, (415)948-2076; **BUS ADD:** 95 1st St., Los Altos, CA 94022, (415)941-2550.

THOMPSON, Kenworthy J.——*VP Mfg. & Fac.*, Rexnord, Inc.; **PRIM RE ACT:** Property Manager; **BUS ADD:** 777 E. Wisconsin Ave., 35th Floor, Milwaukee, WI 53202, (414)643-3000.*

THOMPSON, Larry D.——**B:** Dec. 16, 1939, Tulsa, OK, *Owner*, Investor's Service Realty; **PRIM RE ACT:** Broker, Consultant, Instructor, Property Manager, Real Estate Publisher; **SERVICES:** Investment mgmt., comml. brokerage, seminars; **REP CLIENTS:** Indiv. investors, instn. investors, nat. corp. accts.; **PREV EMPLOY:** Mgr. of Engrg. and Mktg. in Electronics; **PROFL AFFIL & HONORS:** NAR; Apt. Assn.; Nat. Speakers Assn.; **EDUC:** BEE, 1965, Electronics, Univ. of TX at Arlington; **MIL SERV:** USAF; 1957-61; **HOME ADD:** 1800 Trevino, Austin, TX, (512)327-3868; **BUS ADD:** 306 E. Jackson, Box 2591, Harlingen, TX 78551, (512)428-6106.

THOMPSON, L.D.——*VP Fac. & Equip.*, Tecumseh Products; **PRIM RE ACT:** Property Manager; **BUS ADD:** So. Ottawa St., Tecumseh, MI 49286, (517)423-8411.*

THOMPSON, Lloyd G.——**B:** Dec. 9, 1946, Montreal, Can., *Sr. VP*, Winmar Co., Inc., Leasing Div.; **OTHER RE ACT:** Admin, Dir. of Leasing; **PROFL AFFIL & HONORS:** CPM; ICSC; **EDUC:** BCom, 1946, Econ., McGill Univ.; **MIL SERV:** US Army, Capt.; **HOME ADD:** 19506 194th Ave. NE, Woodinville, WA 98072, (206)788-3584; **BUS ADD:** 900 4th Ave., Seattle, WA 98164, (206)223-4505.

THOMPSON, Loren L.——**B:** Feb. 19, 1919, Chetek, WI, *Partner*, Valuation and Acquisition Institute; **PRIM RE ACT:** Broker, Consultant, Appraiser, Banker, Developer, Builder, Owner/Investor, Instructor, Syndicator, Real Estate Publisher; **PREV EMPLOY:** Self-employed; **PROFL AFFIL & HONORS:** SRA, Past Pres. (3 yrs.) Upper Hudson-Champlain Valley Chap.; Sr. Right of Way Agent, Intl. Right of Way Assn.; Econ. Studies Comm., Intl. Assn. of Assessing Officers; **EDUC:** BS, 1943, Hist., Geography and Econ., Univ. of WI; **EDUC HONORS:** Member of Key Club Honor Soc.; Freshman Class Award - TIME Magazine - Current Events; **MIL SERV:** US Navy, Commander, American Theatre , Africa , Middle East , European with two battle stars, Naval Reserve Medal; **OTHER ACT & HONORS:** Alternate Business Address: 1 Nicholas Drive, Albany, NY, 12205 tel.(518)869-9344; **BUS ADD:** 1865 Brickell Ave., A-2005, Miami, FL 33129, (305)856-2005.

THOMPSON, Mark A.——**B:** Nov. 12, 1947, Loma Linda, CA, *Pres.*, T&S Devel. Inc.; **PRIM RE ACT:** Broker, Developer, Property Manager, Owner/Investor; **PREV EMPLOY:** Five 5 Yrs. as Shopping Center Leaslng Specialist at Coldwell Banker - Santa Ana Office; **PROFL AFFIL & HONORS:** ICSC/NAIOP; **EDUC:** BS Bus. Admin., 1971, Fin., UC - Long Beach; **HOME ADD:** 178 S. Starlight Dr., Anaheim, CA 92807; **BUS ADD:** 5225 Canyon Crest Dr., Bldg. 100, Suite 150, Riverside, CA 92506, (714)686-1424.

THOMPSON, Neill S.——**B:** June 5, 1930, Minneapolis, MN, *Pres.*, Thompson-Johnston & Associates, Inc.; **PRIM RE ACT:** Consultant, Appraiser; **SERVICES:** Appraisals, consultation, brokerage; **REP CLIENTS:** City of Ames; State of IA; Fed. agencies; businessmen; farmers; **PROFL AFFIL & HONORS:** AIREA; Amer. Soc. of Farm Mgrs. & Rural Appraisers, MAI, ARA; **EDUC:** BS, 1953, Agricultural Econ., IA State Univ.; **HOME ADD:** 1327 Marston Ave., (515)232-1902; **BUS ADD:** 425 S. 2nd St., PO Box 54, Ames, IA 50010.

THOMPSON, Patrick J.——**B:** Jan. 20, 1947, *Asst. VP*, Michigan National Bank of Macomb, Mort. Loan Dept.; **PRIM RE ACT:** Banker, Lender; **OTHER RE ACT:** CRA Officer; **REP CLIENTS:** Const. loan fin.; end mort. fin.; complete serv.; **PREV EMPLOY:** Detroit & Northern S&L Assn. (10 years); **EDUC:** BS, 1978, Econ. & Fin., Macomb Cty. Community Coll. Oakland Univ.; 1972, Amer. S&L Inst.; Amer. Banking Inst., 1980; **OTHER ACT & HONORS:** Pres., Sterling Heights Rotary Club (1979-1980), Outstanding Rotarian of the Year, 1980; **HOME TEL:** (313)264-0241; **BUS ADD:** 31030 Van Dyke, Warren, MI 48093, (313)978-3089.

THOMPSON, Robert J.——**B:** Oct. 3, 1931, Monticello, IA, *Pres.*, Cardon Intl. Props., Inc.; **PRIM RE ACT:** Broker, Syndicator; **EDUC:** BS, 1955, Pharmacy, State Univ. of IA; **EDUC HONORS:** Merit Scholarship; **HOME ADD:** 6423 Wrenwood, Dallas, TX 75252, (214)867-6096; **BUS ADD:** 5580 L.B.J., Dallas, TX 75240, (214)934-1017.

THOMPSON, Wesley R.——**B:** Sept. 26, 1951, Cincinatti, OH, *Atty. RE & Bus.*, Sink & Thompson; **PRIM RE ACT:** Attorney; **REP CLIENTS:** Calco West, Inc.; var. of RE brokers & devels.; **EDUC:** BA, 1973, Econ., Phil., Pol. Sci., San Diego State Univ.; **GRAD EDUC:** JD, 1977, Univ. of San Diego Sch. of Law; **EDUC HONORS:** Dean's List, Law Review Staff writer; **OTHER ACT & HONORS:** Bd. of Dir. Vista C of C; **HOME ADD:** 1405 Jay Rd., Fullbrook, CO, (714)724-1932; **BUS ADD:** 136 E. Vista Wy, Vista, CA 92025, (714)724-1932.

THOMSON, G. Ronald——**B:** Jan. 9, 1942, Boston, MA, *Pres. & Treas.*, The Thomson Co., Inc.; **PRIM RE ACT:** Broker, Syndicator, Consultant, Developer, Owner/Investor; **SERVICES:** Land & Comml. brokerage, devel. counseling; **REP CLIENTS:** Large land owners, investors; **PREV EMPLOY:** Asst. Dir., Cambridge Redevel. Auth., Cambridge, MA; **PROFL AFFIL & HONORS:** Lakes Region Bd. of Realtors, RE Securities and Synd. Inst.; **EDUC:** BS, 1964, Econ., Poli. & Engrg., MIT; **HOME ADD:** Box 47 Ave. Berndorf, Moultonboro, NH 03254, (603)476-8445; **BUS ADD:** Route 25, Mountonboro, NH 03254, (603)253-7373.

THOMSON, Michael D.——**B:** Aug. 31, 1938, Greeley, CO, *Pres.*, Property Management Co.; **PRIM RE ACT:** Broker, Consultant, Appraiser, Developer, Builder, Owner/Investor, Property Manager; **SERVICES:** Complete prop. mgmt.; **REP CLIENTS:** Urban Redevelopment Corp., Delph Trusts; **EDUC:** BS, 1960, Fin./RE/Bus. Admin./Public Admin./Statistics, Univ. of S. CA; **MIL SERV:** USNR, 1st Class PO; **HOME ADD:** 2000 Rustic Cyn. Rd., Pacific Palisades, CA 90272, (213)455-2001; **BUS ADD:** PO Box 938, Pacific Palisades, CA 90272, (213)455-2001.

THOMSON, William Hills——**B:** Nov. 6, 1942, Chicago, IL, *VP and Trust Officer*, First National Bank of Blue Island, IL, Trust & Real Estate Depts.; **PRIM RE ACT:** Broker, Attorney, Appraiser, Banker, Property Manager; **SERVICES:** RE mgmt. in trusts; **REP CLIENTS:** Indiv. and corp. investors in comml. prop.; **PREV EMPLOY:** Asst. Trust Officer, Pullman Bank; Corp. Counsel, The Wurlitzer Co.; **PROFL AFFIL & HONORS:** ABA, Land Trust Council of IL, So. Suburban Estate Planning Council, JD, Atty., Lic. IL RE Broker; **EDUC:** BA, 1964, Econ., Univ. of IL; **GRAD EDUC:** JD (Law), 1966, RE, Univ. of IL; **HOME ADD:** 15645 Minerva Ave., Dolton, IL 60419, (312)385-2200; **BUS ADD:** 13057 South Western Ave., Blue Island, IL 60406, (312)385-2200.

THORNDEV, Judy P.——**B:** May 26, 1941, Chicago, IL, *Pres.*, Thornber Corp.; **PRIM RE ACT:** Consultant, Attorney, Developer, Insuror; **OTHER RE ACT:** Condo. conversions; **PREV EMPLOY:** Sr. VP Amer. Invsco; VP Rubloff Devel. Corp.; **PROFL AFFIL & HONORS:** Chicago Bar Assn. Chicago RE Bd. Condo. Sub-Comm. of Chicago Bar Assn.; **EDUC:** BA, 1963, Econ., Univ. of Chicago; **GRAD EDUC:** JD and MBA, 1966 and 1969, Harvard Law School and Univ. of Chicago Grad. School of Bus.; **EDUC HONORS:** Phi Beta Kappa; **HOME ADD:** 20 E. Cedar 9-D, Chicago, IL 60611, (312)266-2502; **BUS ADD:** 111 E. Chestnut Suite 50-A, Chicago, IL 60611, (312)337-6121.

THORNE, Francis X.——**B:** Dec. 20, 1925, Hays, KS, *Owner*, Francis X. Thorne Realty; **PRIM RE ACT:** Broker, Appraiser, Developer, Builder, Property Manager; **PROFL AFFIL & HONORS:** NAR, Kansas Assn. of Realtors, Home Builders Assn., CRB, Cert. RE Appraiser with the Nat. Assn. of RE Appraisers; **EDUC:** BBA, 1948, Rockhurst Coll.; **MIL SERV:** USN, Lt.; **OTHER ACT & HONORS:** Lansing Planning Commn.; Leavenworth Cty. Planning Commn.; Pres. of the Leavenworth Area C of C; Pres. Leavenworth Bd. of Realtors; **HOME ADD:** RR #2 Box 117H, Leavenworth, KS 66048, (913)727-1331; **BUS ADD:** 100 Highland Rd., Lansing, KS 66043, (913)727-1528.

THORNLEY, Robert M.——B: Oct. 13, 1955, San Jose, CA, *Pres.*, Gibraltar Mortgage Corp.; **PRIM RE ACT:** Lender, Syndicator; **OTHER RE ACT:** Mort. Broker; **SERVICES:** RE Fin., loan & equity synd.; **REP CLIENTS:** RE brokers and devel., inst. and pvt. lenders and investors; **PREV EMPLOY:** Equitable S & L, (1300 SW Sixth, Portland, OR); **PROFL AFFIL & HONORS:** Mort. Brokers Assn. of OR, Mort. Bankers Assn. of OR, RESSI; Eugene Bd. of Realtors; **EDUC:** BS, 1977, Fin., Univ. of OR; **OTHER ACT & HONORS:** OR Club, Governmental & Legislative Affairs Comm. - C of C; **HOME ADD:** 3919 Pam St., Eugene, OR 97402, (503)484-5021; **BUS ADD:** 230 E. Broadway, Eugene, OR 97401, (503)683-5944.

THORNTON, Robert H., Jr.——B: Oct. 10, 1926, Philadelphia, PA, *Pres.*, Thornton Inc.; **PRIM RE ACT:** Broker, Developer; **SERVICES:** Resid. and land brokerage; **PROFL AFFIL & HONORS:** Ann Arbor Bd. of Realtors, MI Assn. of Realtors, NAR, RNMI, FLI, FIABCI, Sec. MAR, Past Pres. Ann Arbor Bd. , 1976 Realtor of the Yr., Ann Arbor Bd., GRI, RAM (RE Alumni of MI) CRS; **EDUC:** BS, 1950, Bus., Acctg., IN Univ., Bloomington, IN; **GRAD EDUC:** MBA, 1951, Bus., Mgmt., IN Univ., Bloomington, IN.; **MIL SERV:** US Army, T-5; **OTHER ACT & HONORS:** Chelsea Comm. Hospital, (Chmn. of Bd. of TRS.); **HOME ADD:** 7197 Lakeshore Dr., Chelsea, MI 48118, (313)475-8857; **BUS ADD:** 323 S. Main, Chelsea, MI 48118, (313)475-9193.

THORNTON, Thomas J.——B: Mar. 9, 1932, Birmingham, AL, *partner*, Thornton Properties; **PRIM RE ACT:** Attorney, Developer, Builder, Owner/Investor, Property Manager; **PROFL AFFIL & HONORS:** ABA; HBA; NREB; **EDUC:** BS, 1953, Acctg., Notre Dame Univ.; **GRAD EDUC:** JD, 1974, Law, Cumberland School of Law; **MIL SERV:** USN; Lt.; **HOME ADD:** 4140 Sharpsburg Dr., Birmingham, AL 35213, (205)870-1645; **BUS ADD:** 1119 Willow Run Rd., P.O. Box 57027, Birmingham, AL 35209.

THORSON, David M.——B: July 31, 1950, Schenectady, NY, *Atty. (Partner)*, Itkin, Thorson & Burns; **PRIM RE ACT:** Attorney; **SERVICES:** Legal serv. in RE devel. & transfer; **PROFL AFFIL & HONORS:** CO Bar Assn., ABA (Real Prop. Probate & Trust Sec.); **EDUC:** BA, 1972, Poli. Sci., Pacific Lutheran Unfv.; **GRAD EDUC:** JD, 1977, Univ. of Puget Sound, School of Law; **EDUC HONORS:** Note & Comment Editor, UPS Law Review, Cum Laude; **HOME ADD:** 286 Blue River Rd., PO Box 2151, Blue River, CO 80424, (303)453-2821; **BUS ADD:** 100 S. Ridge St., PO Box 171, Breckenridge, CO 80424, (303)453-2666.

THRASHER, Richard D., Jr.——B: Nov. 10, 1947, Amherstburg, Ont., Can., *Exec. Dir.*, Economic Devel. Corp.; **PRIM RE ACT:** Appraiser, Developer, Owner/Investor, Syndicator; **SERVICES:** Devel. comml. & indus.; **PREV EMPLOY:** Mktg. Inst., Indianhead Tech Inst.; Superior-Douglas Cty. Dev. Assn., Inc.; **PROFL AFFIL & HONORS:** Am. Econ. Dev. Council; Council on Urban Econ. Dev.; IM Area Dev. Council; Great Lakes Area Dev. Council; NARA, Distinguished Merit Award NC State Hosp., Dual Guide Mftg. Bd. of Dir., NC Voc. Ed. Adv. Council, New Castle Found. Bd. of Dir.; **EDUC:** BSc, 1972, Pol. Sci., Univ. of WI, Superior; **GRAD EDUC:** Univ. of WI/Univ. of MN; **OTHER ACT & HONORS:** Westwood Ctry. Club; **HOME ADD:** 3628 Sleepy Hollow Ln., New Castle, IN 47362; **BUS ADD:** 1722 G S. Memorial Dr., New Castle, IN 47362, (317)529-4635.

THYSEN, Paul M.——B: Oct. 15, 1913, CA, Thysen Management Co.; **PRIM RE ACT:** Developer, Property Manager; **PREV EMPLOY:** Partner, Muney McPherson & Co.; **PROFL AFFIL & HONORS:** CPA; **EDUC:** AB, 1937, Econ., Stanford Univ.; **HOME TEL:** (415)343-0051; **BUS ADD:** 1777 Borel Pl. Suite 309, San Mateo, CA 94402.

TIDWELL, H. S.——B: May 4, 1942, Nashville, TN, *VP, RE and Const.*, Shoney's Inc., RE; **PRIM RE ACT:** Engineer, Developer, Builder, Property Manager; **PREV EMPLOY:** TN State Planning Commn., South Central Bell; **PROFL AFFIL & HONORS:** NACORE; **GRAD EDUC:** BCE, 1965, Univ. of TN; **MIL SERV:** USAF, Capt.; **OTHER ACT & HONORS:** Nashville Davidson Cty. Bd. of Zoning Appeals; **BUS ADD:** 1727 Elm Hill Pike, Nashville, TN 37210, (615)361-5201.

TIEDEBERG, Jay S.——B: Nov. 12, 1950, Yokohama, Japan, *Mktg. Mgr. Sec. Princ.*, Investors Securities of Tallahassee, Inc.; **PRIM RE ACT:** Syndicator; **OTHER RE ACT:** RE securities; **SERVICES:** Raise equity funds for synds.; **REP CLIENTS:** Investors Synd., Ltd., Investors Synd., Ltd. II, Investors Synd. Ltd. III & Investors Synd. Ltd. IV; **PREV EMPLOY:** Realtor Assoc. with Investors Realty of Tallahasee Inc.; **PROFL AFFIL & HONORS:** Member of RESSI, Bd. of Gov. of RESSI Chapt. FL; **EDUC:** BS, 1972, Fin. & Systems Analysis, FL State Univ.; **GRAD EDUC:** MBA, 1974, Fin., FL State Univ.; **MIL SERV:** USAR, Capt.; **HOME ADD:** 1427 Mitchell Ave., Tallahassee, FL 32303, (904)224-0972; **BUS ADD:** 1001 Thomasville Rd., Tallahasee, FL 32303, (904)224-5513.

TIEDEMANN, A. Carl——B: Jan 22, 1948, Elkhart, IN, *VP*, FM Property Management, Inc.; **PRIM RE ACT:** Broker, Appraiser, Property Manager; **SERVICES:** Brokerage, appraisal, & mgmt. comml./indus. prop.; **REP CLIENTS:** Indiv. investors, indus. & comml. clients; **PROFL AFFIL & HONORS:** IREM, Local, State Nat. Assns. of Realtors, CPM; **HOME ADD:** 54678 Glenwood Park Dr., Elkhart, IN 46514, (219)262-2329; **BUS ADD:** 421 S Second St., PO Box 487, Elkhart, IN 46515, (219)522-0390.

TIEMEYER, Theodore N.——B: Dec. 5, 1937, Kankakee, IL, *Pres.*, The T.N. Tiemeyer Co.; **PRIM RE ACT:** Broker, Consultant, Developer, Owner/Investor, Property Manager, Syndicator; **PREV EMPLOY:** Pres., The Keyes Investment Grp.; **PROFL AFFIL & HONORS:** NASD, SIPC, IAFP, RESSI; **EDUC:** BBA, 1969, Fin., Univ. of Miami, FL; **GRAD EDUC:** MBA, 1971, Fin., Univ. of Miami, FL; **MIL SERV:** USAF; **BUS ADD:** Suite 2701, 100 N. Biscayne Blvd., Miami, FL 33132, (305)374-7244.

TIENKEN, Robert H.——B: May 23, 1919, Lindsay, *Owner*, Robert Tienken Realtor; **PRIM RE ACT:** Broker, Appraiser, Owner/Investor; **OTHER RE ACT:** Farm brokerage, citrus, olives, groves, open land; **PROFL AFFIL & HONORS:** Local, State, Nat. Bd., Realtors, CRS, GRI, Realtor of Yr.; **EDUC:** BA, 1946, Econ., Fresno State Coll.; **EDUC HONORS:** Blue Key Hon. Soc., Class Pres., Chmn. Rally Comm.; **MIL SERV:** USAF, Maj., European Theatre Unit Citation; **OTHER ACT & HONORS:** Past Bd. of Dir. Pres. State; **HOME ADD:** 804 Bond Way, Lindsay, CA 93247, (209)562-2337; **BUS ADD:** 101 E Hermosa St., PO Box 968, Lindsay, CA 93247, (209)562-5936.

TIERNEY, Gerald——*Secy.*, Publicker Industries, Inc.; **PRIM RE ACT:** Property Manager; **BUS ADD:** 777 W. Putnam Ave., Greenwich, CT 06830, (203)531-4500.*

TIFT, Thomas W., Jr.——B: Jan. 8, 1927, Atlanta, GA, *Pres.*, Atlanta Air Center; **PRIM RE ACT:** Broker, Developer, Owner/Investor, Property Manager; **SERVICES:** Prop. mgmt., devel.; **PREV EMPLOY:** Dir. & Officer of several cos.; **PROFL AFFIL & HONORS:** City, State & Nat. Bd. of Realtors; Dir. Atlanta C of C; **EDUC:** BS, 1949, US Naval Acad., Annapolis, MD; **EDUC HONORS:** Battalion Cmdr.; **MIL SERV:** USN, Lt., Battle Star; **OTHER ACT & HONORS:** TR., Tift Coll.; TR. Pace Acad.; Consultant to USN; Consultant to United Nations; **BUS ADD:** PO Box 90907, Atlanta, GA 30344, (404)768-6166.

TIGNER, Ronald E.——B: Dec. 14, 1943, Louisville, KY, *Partner*, Childs, Fortenbach, Beck & Guyton; **PRIM RE ACT:** Attorney; **REP CLIENTS:** Lenders, devel. and indiv. or instit. investors in comml. and resid. prop.; **PREV EMPLOY:** Asst. Atty. Gen., State of TX 1970-1972; **PROFL AFFIL & HONORS:** ABA, Tx Bar Assn., Houston Bar Assn., Bd. Cert.-Civil Trial Law:TX Bd. of Legal; **EDUC:** BBA, 1966, Bus., Univ. of TX; **GRAD EDUC:** MBA, 1969, General Bus. and Law, Univ. of TX; JD, 1970, General Bus. and Law, Univ. of TX; **EDUC HONORS:** Beta Gamma Sigma; Phi Kappa Phi, Beta Gamma Sigma, Phi Kappa Phi; **OTHER ACT & HONORS:** Sons of Republic of TX, Speaker-Earnest Money/Contract Litigation/RE Litigation Seminar by State Bar of TX; **HOME ADD:** 3747 Univ., Houston, TX 77005, (713)668-3020; **BUS ADD:** 402 Pierce Ave., Houston, TX 77002, (713)659-6681.

TILLEY, David B., Sr.——B: Oct. 30, 1928, Evanston, IL, *Atty.*, Guion & Stevens; **PRIM RE ACT:** Attorney; **SERVICES:** All legal servs. incident to RE; **PREV EMPLOY:** Dir. Labor Relations, Chemtron Corp., Phillipsburg, NJ, 1957-63; **PROFL AFFIL & HONORS:** ABA, CT Bar Assn., Litchfield Cty Bar Assn.; **EDUC:** BS, 1957, Bus. Admin., Lafayette Coll., Easton, PA; **GRAD EDUC:** LLB, 1966, Cornell Law Sch., Ithaca, NY; **EDUC HONORS:** Magna Cum Laude, with distinction, Phi Beta Kappa; **MIL SERV:** USAF, S/Sgt., GCM, KSM; **HOME ADD:** Richards Rd., RD 3, Litchfield, CT, (203)567-8539; **BUS ADD:** West St., Box 338, Litchfield, CT 06759, (203)567-0821.

TILLEY, Jon——B: Aug. 13, 1945, Kenosha, WI, *Pres.*, First Boston Capital Corp.; **PRIM RE ACT:** Banker, Lender; **SERVICES:** Mort. investment banker; **REP CLIENTS:** Evans Prods. Co.; U.S. Homes; Insilco Evans Products Co.; **PREV EMPLOY:** Evans Products Co.; 6/70-6/72 DeWitt, McAndrews & Porter, SC, Madison, WI; **PROFL AFFIL & HONORS:** ABA, DC Bar Assoc.; **EDUC:** BS, 1967, Bio. Systems, Univ. of WI; **GRAD EDUC:** JD, 1970, Univ. of WI School of Law; **EDUC HONORS:** Member, Bd. of Editors, WI Student Bar Journal; **OTHER ACT & HONORS:** Smithsonian Inst., Amer. Film Inst.; **HOME ADD:** 1725 York Ave. 18F, New York, NY 10028; **BUS ADD:** 1050 Thomas Jefferson St. NW, Wash, DC 20007, (202)342-

2200.

TIMCHAK, Louis J., Jr.——**B:** June 7, 1940, Johnstown, PA, *Dir., VP and Gen. Counsel*, The Bankers Land Co.; **PRIM RE ACT:** Attorney, Developer, Owner/Investor; **PREV EMPLOY:** Jan. 1980-July 1980, RE Consultant, Boothe Fin. Corp.; Sept. 1976-Dec. 1979, Rgnl. VP, S.E. IDR Mgmt., Inc.; Jan. 1974-Sept. 1976, VP and Corp. Counsel, Phipps Land Co., Inc.; Feb. 1973-Jan. 1974, Atty. at Law, Finley, Kumble, Wagner, Heine & Underburg; Nov. 1969-Feb. 1973, RE Atty., Marriott Corp.; **PROFL AFFIL & HONORS:** Amer. Bar Assn.; Bar Assn. of DC; FL Bar; Palm Beach Cty. Bar Assn.; ULI; Nat. Assn. of Corp. RE Execs.; State Bar of GA ; Admitted to practice law in NY, FL, PA, GA, & DC; **EDUC:** AB, 1962, Econ., Georgetown Univ.; **GRAD EDUC:** JD, 1965, Univ. of Pittsburgh School of Law; **MIL SERV:** US Naval Res., Lt., Honorable Discharge; **OTHER ACT & HONORS:** Dir., N. Palm Beach C of C, 1981, 1982; **BUS ADD:** 4176 Burns Rd., Palm Beach Gardens, FL 33410, (305)626-4800.

TIMPANARO, Ralph M.——**B:** Nov. 28, 1918, LI City, NY, *VP*, Helmsey-Spear, Inc., Indus. Sale/Lease Branch Office; **PRIM RE ACT:** Broker, Consultant, Appraiser; **PREV EMPLOY:** VP Roman Caswell, 1937-49; Own Queens Indus., 1949-63; VP in charge of Indus. RE, Hosinger & Bode, 1963-65; **PROFL AFFIL & HONORS:** Queens C of C, Planning Comm.; **EDUC:** RE Appraisers, NYU; Appraisal Course Cert., Adelphi, Columbia Appraisal Soc.; **MIL SERV:** US Army, Med. Corp., S/Sgt., 1942-45; **OTHER ACT & HONORS:** Bd. of Mgrs. Long Is. City, YMCA, Roslyn Rifle & Pistol Club; **HOME ADD:** 442 Nicolls Rd., Deer Pk., NY 11729, (516)667-8122; **BUS ADD:** 29-28 41st Ave., Long Is. City, NY 11101, (212)786-7900.

TINKHAM, Judy M.——**B:** June 26, 1943, Putnam, CT, *Princ.*, Tinkham Realty; **PRIM RE ACT:** Property Manager, Owner/Investor; **OTHER RE ACT:** Comml. invest. brokerage, home designer; **SERVICES:** Comml. & invest. RE sales & land developement; **REP CLIENTS:** Residential, comml., land, rentals; **PROFL AFFIL & HONORS:** Manchester, Salem, Nashua, & Nat. Assn. of Realtors; NH Assn. Realtors, NH Women's Council of Realtors, NH CID Division, Amer. Soc. Real Estate Professionals, GRI, Broker in MA & NH; Public Acct. in NH; **EDUC:** BS, Bus. Mgmt.; **GRAD EDUC:** Assoc., Banking and Fin., Acctg.; **HOME ADD:** 117 Kendall Pond Rd., Windham, NH 03087, (603)432-2044; **BUS ADD:** Rte. 102, Londonerry, NH 03053.

TINLEY, S. Herbert, III——**B:** Jan. 29, 1941, Baltimore, MD, *Pres.*, Tinley Associates Inc.; **PRIM RE ACT:** Consultant, Appraiser, Property Manager; **OTHER RE ACT:** Comml. Mort. Broker; Mort. Banker; **SERVICES:** Fin. analysis and location of fin. of comml. props.; **REP CLIENTS:** Inst. lenders and indiv. purchasers of comml. props.; **EDUC:** BS, 1963, Bus. Admin., Washington & Lee Univ.; **HOME ADD:** 2112 Woodfork Rd., Timonium, MD 21093, (301)252-5522; **BUS ADD:** 7624 Belair Rd., Baltimore, MD 21236, (301)661-4363.

TINSLEY, Richard C.——**B:** June 12, 1938, Chicago, IL, *Pres.*, Tampa Bay Title Co.; **OTHER RE ACT:** Title Insurance Agent (SAFECO Title Insurance Co.); **SERVICES:** Title insurance; **PREV EMPLOY:** Mgr., SAFECO Title Insurance 1973-1980; **PROFL AFFIL & HONORS:** Dir. of Homebuilders Assn., Sales & Mktg. Council; Dir., Mort. Bankers Assn.; **EDUC:** AB, 1960, Eng., Liberal Arts, Miami Univ., Oxford, OH; **MIL SERV:** USMC 1961-1973, Maj.; **OTHER ACT & HONORS:** Sigma Alpha Epsilon, Miami Alumni Club of Tampa Bay, Dir.; **HOME ADD:** 12606 Stillwater Terrace Dr., Tampa, FL 33624, (813)962-1161; **BUS ADD:** 7211 N. Dale Mabry, Suite 100, Tampa, FL 33614, (813)933-5859.

TIPPETS, Richard——**B:** July 25, 1944, Pocatello, ID, *VP of Prop. Mgmt.*, Robert Young & Assoc.; **OTHER RE ACT:** Prop. Mgmt.; **PREV EMPLOY:** Mgr. of RE, Evans Products Co.; **EDUC:** BA, 1967, Brigham Young Univ.; **GRAD EDUC:** MBA, 1969, Brigham & Young Univ.; **EDUC HONORS:** Cum Laude; **HOME ADD:** 240 Indian Ct., Richland, WA 99352, (509)375-0272; **BUS ADD:** 1933 Jadwin, Suite 133, Richland, WA 99352, (509)946-1650.

TIRET, Sharon Lee——**B:** June 22, 1939, San Francisco, CA, *Broker, Owner*, Tiret Realty; **PRIM RE ACT:** Broker, Property Manager; **PREV EMPLOY:** In RE 12 years. Have owned business for 5+ years; **PROFL AFFIL & HONORS:** Member of Contra Costa Bd., Solano Bd., Northern Solano Bd, Cert. from Diablo Valley Coll. in RE; **HOME ADD:** 149 Dartmouth Pl., Benicia, CA 94510, (707)746-0433; **BUS ADD:** PO Box 387, Benicia, CA 94510, (707)745-4838.

TIROLA, Vincent S.——**B:** Dec. 6, 1936, New York, NY, *Partner/Atty.*, Tirola and Herring; **PRIM RE ACT:** Attorney; **SERVICES:** Gen. RE law both comml. and resid. devel. and synd. of comml. prop.; **REP CLIENTS:** Citicorp Person-to-Person of CT, Inc. and numerous comml. and corp. devel.; **PREV EMPLOY:** Sec. of Cty. Fed. S&L Assn. of Westport, CT; Partner Koizim & Tirola; **PROFL AFFIL & HONORS:** Consultant to Cannondale Historic Preservation Society; ABA; Amer. Pol. Sci. Assn.; Council for a Competive Economy; **EDUC:** AB, 1959, Govt./Econ., Miami Univ. (Oxford, OH); **GRAD EDUC:** LLB, 1962, Real Prop. Law, NYU School of Law; LLM, 1966, Constitution Law, NYU School of Law; **EDUC HONORS:** Teaching Asst.; **MIL SERV:** USAF Reserve, 2nd Lt., 1962-1964; **OTHER ACT & HONORS:** Justice of the Peace; Westport Zoning Bd. of Appeals; Member of Miami Univ. Exec. Council; Chairman of Amer. Red Cross; Chmn., High School Tuition Grants Committee; Adjunct Professor Sacred Heart Univ.. Lecturer Wake Forest School of Law; **HOME ADD:** 18 Punch Bowl Dr., Westport, CT 06880, (203)226-0578; **BUS ADD:** 1200 Post Road E, PO Box 5167, WestPort, CT 06881, (203)226-8926.

TIRRELL, Wallace K.——**B:** Aug. 15, 1934, Honolulu, HI, *Area Dev. Mgr.*, Kamehameha Schools/Bishop Estate, Land Div.; **PRIM RE ACT:** Property Manager; **OTHER RE ACT:** Direct the planning, dev. and admin. of neighboring islands' (other than Oahu) for employers with the objective of producing maximum income at minimum cost; **PROFL AFFIL & HONORS:** IREM, CPM; **EDUC:** BBA, 1966, Gen. Bus., Univ. of HI; **OTHER ACT & HONORS:** Director, HI Businessmen's Assn.; Institute of RE Mgmt.; **HOME ADD:** 561 Alihi Place, Kailua, HI 96734, (808)262-4710; **BUS ADD:** PO Box 3466, Honolulu, HI 96801, (808)523-6200.

TISCHLER, Paul Stephen——**B:** Mar. 23, 1943, Schenectady, NY, *Pres.*, Tischler, Montasser, & Associates, Inc.; **PRIM RE ACT:** Consultant; **SERVICES:** Econ., fiscal and planning servs.; **REP CLIENTS:** Devels. and municipalities; **PREV EMPLOY:** Marcou O'Leary and Assocs. (1971-1977), RE Research Corp. (1968-1971); **PROFL AFFIL & HONORS:** ULI, Amer. Planning Assn.; **EDUC:** BA, 1965, Econ., Johns Hopkins Univ.; **GRAD EDUC:** MBA, 1968, RE and Urban Devel., Amer. Univ.; **OTHER ACT & HONORS:** Numerous articles published; **HOME ADD:** 3302 Rittenhouse St. N.W., Washington, DC 20015, (202)244-2480; **BUS ADD:** 1000 Vermont Ave. N.W., Ste. #805, Washington, DC 20005, (202)638-4446.

TISDALE, Douglas M., Esq.——**B:** May 3, 1949, Detroit, MI, *Atty.*, Brownstein Hyatt Farber & Madden; **PRIM RE ACT:** Attorney; **SERVICES:** Legal representation in negotiation and litigation; **REP CLIENTS:** Trammell Crow Company, Kenneth M. Good, Columbia S&L Assn., Metro Nat. Bank of Denver, Warner Props., Inc.; **PREV EMPLOY:** Law Clerk to Chief Judge Alfred A. Arraj of the US Dist. Ct. for the Dist. of CO; **PROFL AFFIL & HONORS:** Denver Bar Assn., CO Bar Assn., ABA, Amer. Judicature Soc., CO Trial Lawyers Assn., Amer. Trial Lawyers Assn., Phi Alpha Delta Law Fraternity; **EDUC:** BA, 1971, Psychology, Univ. of MI; **GRAD EDUC:** JD, 1975, Univ. of MI Law School; **EDUC HONORS:** Summa Cum Laude, Honors in Psychology, Phi Beta Kappa, Graduated in top third of class; Research and Admin. Editor of Univ. of MI Journal of Law Reform; Sr. Judge; **HOME ADD:** 10986 West 77th Ave., Arvada, CO 80005, (303)422-9370; **BUS ADD:** 410 17th St., Suite 1880, Denver, CO 80202, (303)534-6335.

TISH, Eugene C.——**B:** Nov. 23, 1948, Vancouver, WA, *Atty.*, Knappenberger & Tish, P.C.; **PRIM RE ACT:** Attorney; **SERVICES:** Tax planning and counseling, transaction design, basic, multiple-party, and delayed exchanges; **REP CLIENTS:** Indiv. and instnl. investors in multi-family housing, comml. and indus. props., RE brokerage cos.; **PREV EMPLOY:** Adjunct instructor at Lewis and Clark Law School; **PROFL AFFIL & HONORS:** OR State Bar, ABA; **EDUC:** BS, 1971, Poli. Theory, George Fox Coll.; **GRAD EDUC:** JD/LLM, 1974/1975, Taxation, Lewis and Clark Law School/NY Univ.; **OTHER ACT & HONORS:** Adjunct Prof., Masters of Taxation Program, Portland State Univ.; **HOME ADD:** 1620 S.W. Custer ST., Portland, OR 97219, (503)245-8323; **BUS ADD:** 1010 Oregon Bank Bldg., 319 S.W. Washington, Portland, OR 97204, (503)224-1148.

TISHMAN, Donald H.——**B:** Feb. 7, 1927, NYC, NY, *Pres.*, Housing Assoc.; **PRIM RE ACT:** Attorney, Developer; **SERVICES:** Devel. multi-family projects in 9 states; **PROFL AFFIL & HONORS:** ULI, NAHB; **EDUC:** JD, 1952, OH State Univ.; **EDUC HONORS:** Order of COIF; **MIL SERV:** USN; **OTHER ACT & HONORS:** CHR; Columbus Metropolitan House of Authority, 12 yrs.; State Sinking Fund Member, 6 yrs.; ULI; Teach Econ. of RE, OH State; **HOME ADD:** 530 Arballo Dr., San Francisco, CA 94132, (415)469-9773; **BUS ADD:** 3449 Livingston, Columbus, OH 43227, (614)239-8034.

TISHMAN, Edward S.——**B:** Mar. 20, 1923, New York, *VP*, Julien J. Studley, Inc.; **PRIM RE ACT:** Broker, Property Manager; **SERVICES:** Comml. sales and leasing of urban props.; **PREV EMPLOY:**

Tishman Realty Const. Co., Inc.; **PROFL AFFIL & HONORS:** RE Bd. of NY; Soc. of PE; Amer. Soc. ME; Nat. Panel Amer. Arbitration Assn., PE (NY State); **EDUC:** BME, 1944, Mechanical Engrg., Yale Univ.; **MIL SERV:** USN, Lt. j.g.; **HOME ADD:** 111 East 85 St., New York, NY 10028; **BUS ADD:** 342 Madison Ave., New York, NY 10173, (212)949-0148.

TITUS, Robert F.——B: Dec. 6, 1926, NJ, *Pres.*, Magnum Properties, Ltd., Comml. / Investment; **PRIM RE ACT:** Broker, Syndicator, Developer, Owner/Investor; **SERVICES:** Investment counseling & synd., dev. of investment & comml. prop.; **PREV EMPLOY:** Reg. Rep. Wall St. West; **PROFL AFFIL & HONORS:** RESSI, CCIM Candidate; **EDUC:** 1950, Mining Engrg., VA Tech.; **GRAD EDUC:** MBA, 1961, Univ. of Chicago; **MIL SERV:** USAF, Brig. Gen., Air Force Cross, Silver Star, Legion of Merit, DFC, Bronze Star, Air Medal, Commendation Medal, numerous foreign decorations; **OTHER ACT & HONORS:** Comm., BSA; Pres. Serra Club of CO Sprs., Assoc. Fellow, Soc. of Experimental Test Pilots; Explorers Club; **HOME ADD:** 1110 Garlock Lane, Colorado Springs,, CO 80907, (303)599-7858; **BUS ADD:** 4575 Hilton Parkway, Colorado Springs, CO 80907, (303)593-9717.

TOALSON, Robert E.——B: Dec. 19, 1943, Alton, IL, *Pres.*, Toalson Investments; **PRIM RE ACT:** Syndicator, Owner/Investor; **PREV EMPLOY:** Estate Planning; **PROFL AFFIL & HONORS:** Scottsdale Chap., NALU; **EDUC:** AA, 1964, Bus., Hannibal LaGrange Coll.; **MIL SERV:** US Army, E-5; **HOME ADD:** Scottsdale, AZ, (602)991-5858; **BUS ADD:** 12429 N 68th Pl., Scottsdale, AZ 85254, (602)991-5858.

TOBERMAN, Scott K.——B: Nov. 24, 1955, Springfield, IL, *Asst. Corp. Cont.*, Arthur Rubloff & Co.; **PRIM RE ACT:** Broker, Consultant, Syndicator; **OTHER RE ACT:** CPA; **SERVICES:** Creation, operation & dissolution of RE partnerships; syndications, RE devel., feasability studies & counseling; **REP CLIENTS:** Various Arthur Rubloff ventures; **PREV EMPLOY:** Peat, Marwick, Mitchell & Co., CPA firm; **PROFL AFFIL & HONORS:** Amer. Inst. of CPA's., NAR, CPA, Licensed broker; **EDUC:** BS, 1977, Acctg., Univ. of IL, Urbana; **EDUC HONORS:** Top 10% in Bus. Sch.; **HOME ADD:** 853 Washington, 3A, Oak Park, IL, (312)386-4257; **BUS ADD:** 69 W. Wash. St., c/o Arthur Rubloff & Co., Chicago, IL 60302, (312)368-5268.

TOBEY, Gary H.——B: Apr. 1, 1942, Corning, NY, *VP and Dir.*, Constantine & Prochnow, P.C.; **PRIM RE ACT:** Attorney; **SERVICES:** Gen. practice of law; **REP CLIENTS:** Security Pacific, Inc., Manor Vail Condo. Assn., Arapahoe Lake No. One Assn.; **PROFL AFFIL & HONORS:** ABA, Community Assns. Instit.; **EDUC:** AB, 1964, Poli. Sci., Univ. of Rochester; **GRAD EDUC:** JD, 1972, Law, Univ. of Denver; **EDUC HONORS:** Editor-in-Chief, Denver Law Journal; Order of St. Ives; **MIL SERV:** USN, Lt., Distinguished Flying Cross plus 30 other awards; **OTHER ACT & HONORS:** Member, CO Rep. State Central Comm.; **BUS ADD:** 5650 D.T.C. Pkwy., Denver Tech. Ctr., Englewood, CO 80111, (303)770-5610.

TOBIA, Caesar——B: Sep. 6, 1922, Jamestown, NY, Tobia R.E. and Prop. Mgmt.; **PRIM RE ACT:** Broker, Developer, Property Manager, Assessor, Owner/Investor, Insuror; **SERVICES:** Leasing, prop. mgmt., devel. comml. & indus. sales; **PREV EMPLOY:** Commnr. of Tax and Assessments, City of Binghamton, NY; **PROFL AFFIL & HONORS:** IREM (CPM) BOMA (RPA) IAAO, NARA, NY State Assessors Assn.; **MIL SERV:** US Army, PH 2/c, 1942-46; **OTHER ACT & HONORS:** Former Commnr of Tax and Assessments, City of Binghamton, NY; **HOME ADD:** 19 Patricia St., Binghamton, NY 13905, (607)797-5971; **BUS ADD:** Exec. Office Bldg., 33 W. State St., P.O. Box 1464, Binghamton, NY 13902, (607)723-6449.

TOBIN, Aubrey H.——B: Apr. 2, 1952, Detroit, MI, *Atty. and Counselor at Law*, Aubrey H. Tobin Attorney & Counselor; **PRIM RE ACT:** Broker, Consultant, Attorney, Developer, Owner/Investor, Syndicator; **SERVICES:** Legal services-devel. serv.-synd. of income prop.; **REP CLIENTS:** Indiv. and insti. investors and developers; **PROFL AFFIL & HONORS:** State Bar of MI, FL Bar, ABA, JD, Licensed RE Broker, MI; **EDUC:** BBA, 1974, Mktg.-Fin.-RE, Eastern MI Univ.; **GRAD EDUC:** JD, 1980, Real Prop. & Gen. Practice Bus. Law, All Tax Problems and Planning, T.M.Cooley Law School; **EDUC HONORS:** Amer. Jurisprudence Award; **HOME ADD:** PO Box 401, Southfield, MI 48037-0401; **BUS ADD:** 20300 W. Twelve Mule Rd., Suite 40, Southfield, MI 48076, (313)353-6090; **BUS TEL:** (313)559-2420.

TOBIN, Jack B.——B: Nov. 10, 1936, New Brunswick, NJ, *Pres.*, Jack B. Tobin & Co.; **PRIM RE ACT:** Broker, Owner/Investor, Property Manager, Syndicator; **SERVICES:** RE brokerage, prop. mgmt., synd. of comml. props.; **EDUC:** 1958, Univ. of PA; **MIL SERV:** US Army, Capt.; **HOME ADD:** 3351 N. 36th Pl., Hollywood, FL 33021, (305)966-5546; **BUS ADD:** 925 Arthur Godfrey Rd., Miami Beach, FL 33140, (305)532-4355.

TOBIN, William C.——B: June 7, 1945, Dyersville, IA, *Sr. VP*, Rauenhorst Corp., Investments; **PRIM RE ACT:** Developer, Builder; **OTHER RE ACT:** Designer; **PREV EMPLOY:** CT Gen. Life Ins. Co., Hartford, CT; **PROFL AFFIL & HONORS:** Natl. Assn. of Indus. and Office Parks, Pres. of the Upper Midwest Chap.; **EDUC:** BS, 1968, Civil Engrg., IA State Univ.; **GRAD EDUC:** MBA, 1970, RE, Harvard Univ.; **HOME ADD:** 2720 Holly Ln,, Plymouth, MN 55447, (612)475-3384; **BUS ADD:** 7900 Xerxes Ave. S., Suite 2310, Minneapolis, MN 55431, (612)830-4573.

TOBLER, August F.——B: Sept. 4, 1906, Bridgeport, CT, *COB - Pres.*, Lake Placid Holding Co., Inc.; **PRIM RE ACT:** Developer, Builder, Owner/Investor; **MIL SERV:** US Army; **OTHER ACT & HONORS:** Amer. Met. Assn.-US Senatorial Club; Boy Scouts of Amer.; **HOME ADD:** 3022 W. Waterway Ave., Lake Placid, FL 33852, (813)465-0480; **BUS ADD:** Rur Rte. 2, Box 77, Lake Placid, FL 33852, (813)465-0345.

TOCKARSHEWSKY, Benedict J.——B: Feb. 11, 1941, NYC, *Exec. Mgr.*, Tishman E. Mgmt. Corp., 1978 to Present, 1166 A of A Condo.; **PRIM RE ACT:** Consultant, Property Manager, Engineer; **SERVICES:** Prop. mgmt., constr. mgmt.; **PREV EMPLOY:** Olympia & York Props., VP Leasing, 1970-1978; **PROFL AFFIL & HONORS:** BOMA-NY; State Lic. Profl. Engineer; **EDUC:** BS Engrg., 1969, The Copper Union; **EDUC HONORS:** Phi Tau Sigma; **HOME ADD:** 27-11 160th St., Flushing, NY 11358; **BUS ADD:** 1166 Ave. of the Americas, New York, NY 10036, (212)391-2909.

TODD, Carl L.——B: Feb. 29, 1925, NYC, *Pres.*, Carl L. Todd Assoc., Inc.; **PRIM RE ACT:** Consultant, Appraiser, Owner/Investor, Instructor; **SERVICES:** Complete appraisal & RE consultation including court testimony, cert. tax spec.; **REP CLIENTS:** Cty. of Nassau, City of NY, Long Beach, etc., Flushing Savings Bank, Reckson Assn.; **PREV EMPLOY:** Sr. Appraiser City of NY, 1962-68; **PROFL AFFIL & HONORS:** Sr. Member ASA, IFA, Amer. Right of Way Assn., Member ULI, LI Bldg. Inst., IRWA, ASA, IFA, SR/WA; **EDUC:** Engrg. (Chem.), NY Univ., Univ. of TX; **OTHER ACT & HONORS:** 1980 City of Glen Cove, Member IDA, CDA, Past Pres. (1978/79) Glen Cove Kiwanis Club, Instr. LI Blds. Inst. Bldrs. Training Course, Initiated Appraisal Course at Adelphi Univ.; **HOME ADD:** 114 Woolsey Ave., Glen Cove, NY 11542, (516)671-5179; **BUS ADD:** 114 Woolsey Ave., Glen Cove, NY 11542, (516)676-1806.

TODD, Charles B.——PRIM RE ACT: Broker; **PREV EMPLOY:** Pres., COB, Founder, Quick Shop, Inc.; Pres., Founder, Guaranty Mort. Co., Inc.; Pres., Guaranty Realty, Inc.; **PROFL AFFIL & HONORS:** NAR; NAIOP; FLI; BOMA; RESSI; ULI; NARA; AL Assn. of Realtors, VP, Gadsden Area Bd. of Realtors; **EDUC:** BS, 1956, Indus. Mgmt., Auburn Univ.; **GRAD EDUC:** Cumberland Law School (1 yr.); SCMP, Harvard Bus. School; **EDUC HONORS:** Phi Kappa Phi; **MIL SERV:** USN, Lt.j.g.; **HOME ADD:** 804 Country Club Dr., Gadsden, AL 35901, (205)442-6259; **BUS ADD:** PO Box 519, Gadsden, AL 35902, (205)442-7328.

TODD, Della——B: Nov. 13, 1934, Texola, OK, *Pres*, Landmark Realty, Inc.; **PRIM RE ACT:** Broker, Consultant, Developer, Owner/Investor; **OTHER RE ACT:** Shopping ctr. leasing, pre-devel. fee basis investment analysis and feasibility studies; **REP CLIENTS:** Safeway Stores, Inc.; McDonald's; Burger King; Sears; Gottlieb Corp.; Pizza Hut; A&M Foods, Inc.; indiv. investors, etc.; **PROFL AFFIL & HONORS:** Rogers Bd. of Realtors, AR Realtor's Assn., NAR, Realtors Nat. Mktg. Instit., Intl. Council of Shopping Ctrs., Grad., Realtor's Instit.; **EDUC:** Course: Fundamentals of RE Investment and Taxation, Course 101; **OTHER ACT & HONORS:** Rogers C of C; Transp. Comm. Sunnyside Bapt. Church; Formerly Committeewoman-Governor's Comm. on Status of Women; formerly, Volunteer Prob. Officer, Juv. Div.; Two term Pres., Rogers Bus. & Prof. Women's Club; **HOME ADD:** 13 Pine Ridge Dr., Rogers, AR 72756, (501)925-2224; **BUS ADD:** 121 W. Elm St., Rogers, AR 72756, (501)636-6450.

TODD, Stan——B: Aug. 5, 1937, Worcester, MA, *VP - Const. & Engrg.*, Robert A. McNeil Corp.; **PRIM RE ACT:** Consultant, Engineer, Owner/Investor, Property Manager, Syndicator; **SERVICES:** Valuation and synd. of comml. and multi-family resid. props.; **PREV EMPLOY:** VP, Mellon Nat.; VP, Black Const. Co.; **PROFL AFFIL & HONORS:** Const. Specifications Inst.; **EDUC:** BA, 1967, Const. Mgmt., Univ. of WA; BSCE, 1970, Univ. of WA; **HOME ADD:** 2008 Avignon Pl., Half Moon Bay, CA 94019, (415)726-7653; **BUS ADD:** 2855 Campus Dr., San Mateo, CA 94403, (415)572-0660.

TOFIAS, Donald——B: Jan. 4, 1947, Newton, MA, *Pres.*, Julius Tofias & Co., Inc.; **PRIM RE ACT:** Broker, Consultant, Appraiser, Developer, Owner/Investor, Property Manager; **SERVICES:** Corporate RE Servs., incuding appraisal, brokerage, consulting, devel., fin., project coordination & propl. mgmt.; **REP CLIENTS:** Corning Glass Works; Ocean Spray Cranberries; Liberty Mutual Ins.; **PROFL AFFIL & HONORS:** SIR; MA Assn. of Realtors; Greater Boston Bd. of Realtors; NAR, Pres. New England Chap SIR (1980); VP New England Chap. SIR (1979); **EDUC:** AB, 1969, Cornell Univ., Ithaca NY; **BUS ADD:** Shovel Shop Sq., PO Box 420, North Easton, MA 02356, (617)584-0600.

TOLAND, Clyde William——B: Aug. 18, 1947, Iola, KS, *Atty.*, Toland and Thompson; **PRIM RE ACT:** Attorney; **SERVICES:** Counseling; drafting contracts; arranging appraisals; title examinations; **REP CLIENTS:** Iola State Bank; Security S&L Assn.; **PROFL AFFIL & HONORS:** KS Bar Assn.; ABA, Order of the Coif; **EDUC:** BA, 1969, Hist., Univ. of KS; **GRAD EDUC:** MA, 1971, Univ. of WI, Madison; JD, Univ. of KS; **EDUC HONORS:** Phi Beta Kappa, with Highest Distinction, Order of the Coif; **OTHER ACT & HONORS:** Iola Rotary Club; **HOME ADD:** 211 South Colborn, Iola, KS 66749, (316)365-6649; **BUS ADD:** 103 East Madison, Iola, KS 66749, (316)365-6901.

TOLL, Bruce E.——B: Apr. 29, 1943, Philadelphia, PA, *VP*, Toll Brothers, Comml./Indus./Resid.; **PRIM RE ACT:** Developer, Builder, Owner/Investor, Property Manager; **PROFL AFFIL & HONORS:** Pres. Abington Twp. IDA, Member of BOMA, NAHB, NAIOP; **EDUC:** BS, 1965, Acctg., Univ. Miami; **HOME ADD:** 1477 Rydal Rd., Rydal, PA 19046, (215)885-1477; **BUS ADD:** 101 Witmer Rd., Horsham, PA 19044, (215)441-4400.

TOLLES, E. Leroy——B: Aug. 13, 1922, Winchester, CT, *Partner*, Munger, Tolles & Rickershauser; **PRIM RE ACT:** Attorney; **SERVICES:** Gen. legal servs.; **EDUC:** BA, 1943, Williams Coll.; **GRAD EDUC:** LLB, 1948, Harvard Law School; **MIL SERV:** USMCR, Maj.; **HOME ADD:** 860 Oxford Rd., San Marino, CA 91108; **BUS ADD:** 612 S. Flower St., Los Angeles, CA 90017, (213)683-9100.

TOLLESON, R.W.——B: Apr. 9, 1936, Charlottsville, VA, *Pres.*, Tolleson & Co.; **PRIM RE ACT:** Broker, Appraiser, Developer, Builder, Property Manager; **REP CLIENTS:** VA Dept. of Highways, VEPCO, banks, S&L's, food chains, drug stores, Lew L. Farber Co.; **PROFL AFFIL & HONORS:** AIREA; Right of Way Assn.; Intl. Council of Shopping Ctrs., RM; SRA; **EDUC:** BBA, 1960, RE, Univ. of GA; **MIL SERV:** US Air Force Res., Cpl.; **OTHER ACT & HONORS:** Former Tr. of Old Dominion; Pres. of Jaycees, 1967; Chmn. of the Bd. of Tuckahoe YMCA; **HOME ADD:** 310 Hollyport Rd., Richmond, VA 23229, (804)740-8713; **BUS ADD:** 1893 Billingsgate Cir., Richmond, VA 23233, (804)740-9600.

TOLSON, Robert H.——B: Feb. 12, 1921, Torrance, CA, *VP, Chief Appraiser*, The Colwell Co.; **PRIM RE ACT:** Broker, Appraiser; **OTHER RE ACT:** Mort. Banking; **SERVICES:** Appraisal, feasibility, mkt. analysis, mort. lending; **REP CLIENTS:** 205 Instns.; **PROFL AFFIL & HONORS:** Intl. Inst. of Valuers; NARA; AACA; Los Angeles Bd. of Realtors, SCV; CRA; CA-S, Realtor; **EDUC:** AA, BSc, 1949, Transp., Compton Coll., Univ. of Southern CA; **GRAD EDUC:** Stanford Univ., Northwestern Univ., School of Mort. Banking; **MIL SERV:** USNR (Ret.), LCDR, Naval Reserve Medal, 7th Fleet; Asiatic Pacific, Victory Medal; **HOME ADD:** 5413 Konya Dr., Torrance, CA 90503, (213)316-8119; **BUS ADD:** 3223 W. Sixth St., Los Angeles, CA 90020, (213)380-3170.

TOMESCU, Marian——B: Sept. 10, 1949, Bucharest, Romania, *Dir. Planning and Devel. Div.*, Joe Feagin Investments, Inc.; **PRIM RE ACT:** Consultant, Broker, Developer, Owner/Investor; **OTHER RE ACT:** Devel. advice investment counseling; **SERVICES:** Consultant, developer, investor, RE investment advisor; **REP CLIENTS:** Lenders and investors in resid. and comml. props.; **PREV EMPLOY:** Doxiadis Assoc. Intnl. Co. Ltd., European/Can. HQ, involved in major intnl. projects in Romania, Greece, Can. and USA; **EDUC:** BArch, 1972, Urban and Regional Planning and Design, Architecture, Univ. of Bucharest; **GRAD EDUC:** MArch, Architecture and Urban Planning Design, University of Toronto, Toronto, Ontario, Can.; **EDUC HONORS:** Teaching Assistant; **HOME ADD:** 109-14202 Haymeadow Dr., Dallas, TX 75240, (214)385-8908; **BUS ADD:** 4835 L.B.J.Fwy. No. 640, Dallas, TX 75240, (214)386-4337.

TOMLIN, J. Michael——B: Mar. 18, 1945, Nashville, TN, *Pres.*, The Tomlin Co.; **PRIM RE ACT:** Broker, Developer, Owner/Investor, Property Manager; **SERVICES:** RE leasing, mgmt., mktg. & devel. dealing exclus. in office bldgs.; **REP CLIENTS:** Office space investors, users, fin. instit.; **PROFL AFFIL & HONORS:** IREM; Nat. Assn. of Realtors; Nashville Bd. of Realtors, Cert. Prop. Mgr. (CPM); **EDUC:** Austin Peay Univ., Bus. Admin.; **MIL SERV:** USN; **OTHER ACT & HONORS:** Metropolitan Traffic & Parking Commn., Buddies of Nashville. Bd. Member; Second Harvest Food Bank of Nashville, Inc. (Bd. Member); Nashville Area C of C; & serves on the Bd. of Econ. Devel.; **HOME ADD:** 3801 W. End Ave., Nashville, TN 37205, (615)297-7045; **BUS ADD:** 401 Union, Suite 1006, Nashville, TN 37219, (615)244-8075.

TOMLINSON, Allan J.——*Pres.*, Diamond Shamrock Corp.; **PRIM RE ACT:** Property Manager; **BUS ADD:** 1100 Superior Ave., Cleveland, OH 44114, (216)694-5000.*

TOMLINSON, E. Wayne——B: June 15, 1949, Nashville, TN, *VP*, Storey, Tomlinson & Co., USA; **PRIM RE ACT:** Broker, Instructor, Syndicator, Consultant, Property Manager; **SERVICES:** Leasing, mgmt, consulting and synd. of comml. prop.; **REP CLIENTS:** Investors, mort. lenders and indiv. for investment services; **PREV EMPLOY:** State of TN; Managed all state - owned prop. and procured all nec. leased facilities for all state grps.; **PROFL AFFIL & HONORS:** CPM, NBR, IREM, Nashville Bd. of Realtors; **EDUC:** BA, 1971, Math. & Bus., David Lipscomb Coll.; **GRAD EDUC:** MA, 1972, Math., OH Univ.; **OTHER ACT & HONORS:** Advisory Bd. of AGAPE (Charitable Org.), Outstanding Young Men Of Amer., 1979; **HOME ADD:** 1417 Lipscomb Dr., Brentwood, TN 37027, (615)790-1919; **BUS ADD:** 11th Floor, Third Nat. Bank Bldg., Nashville, TN 37219, (615)244-5596.

TOMLINSON, John F.——B: Feb. 22, 1933, Madison, WI, *Pres.*, Caribbean Properties, Ltd.; **PRIM RE ACT:** Broker, Developer, Owner/Investor; **REP CLIENTS:** Dupont, Goodyear, Mobil, etc.; **PREV EMPLOY:** Service Station Site Selector of Texaco in Havana, Cuba; **PROFL AFFIL & HONORS:** Cert. Resid. Broker, San Juan Bd. of Realtors, PR C of C, CRB; **EDUC:** BBA, 1954, Fin., Univ. of WI; **GRAD EDUC:** BA of For. Trade, 1957, Intl. Bus. & Languages, Amer. Grad. School of Intl. Mgmt.; **MIL SERV:** US Army Artillery, 1st. Lt.; **OTHER ACT & HONORS:** S.J. Rotary Club, PR, Council of USN League; **HOME ADD:** 56 Kings Ct. PH1, San Juan, PR 00911, (809)725-9544; **BUS ADD:** 171 Del Parque, San Juan, PR 00911, (809)725-7365.

TOMPKINS, James E.——B: Jan. 21, 1950, Denver, CO, *Claims Atty.*, Chicago Title Insurance Co.; **PRIM RE ACT:** Attorney, Insuror; **PROFL AFFIL & HONORS:** ABA; WA State Bar Assn.; CA State Bar Assn.; **EDUC:** BA, 1972, Pol. Sci., CO State Univ.; **GRAD EDUC:** JD, 1976, Law, Univ. of the Pac. McGeorge School of Law; **EDUC HONORS:** Pi Sigma Alpha Honorary; **HOME ADD:** 411 222nd Ave. NE, Redmond, WA 98052, (206)883-4619; **BUS ADD:** Metropolitan Park Suite 1400, 1100 Olive Way, Seattle, WA 98101, (206)628-5685.

TOMPKINS, Thomas F.——B: Mar. 22, 1927, Ft. Port Chester, NY, *Partner*, Tompkins & Kelley Lawyers; **PRIM RE ACT:** Attorney; **REP CLIENTS:** The RE Investment Dept. of The Travelers Ins. Co., RE Investment Trust of Amer.; **PREV EMPLOY:** Approved Atty. for Pioneer Title Ins. Co., Chicago Title Co., Commonwealth Land Title Ins. Co., Lawyers Title Ins. Co.; **PROFL AFFIL & HONORS:** ABA, (Real Prop. Law Sect.); FL Bar Assn., Broward Cty. Bar Assn.; **GRAD EDUC:** JD, 1952, Univ. of Miami; **OTHER ACT & HONORS:** Broward Cty. Court of Record Judge, 1955-60; **HOME ADD:** 1281 S. Ocean Dr., Ft. Lauderdale, FL 33316, (305)523-7594; **BUS ADD:** Suite 201, 901 E. Las Olas Blvd., Ft. Lauderdale, FL 33301, (305)462-7806.

TOMSIC, Gerald A.——B: Mar. 5, 1950, Harvey, IL, *Atty.*, Edwards, Edwards & Ashton; **PRIM RE ACT:** Attorney; **OTHER RE ACT:** CPA; **SERVICES:** Tax, RE, estate planning; **PREV EMPLOY:** CPA, Arthur Andersen & Co., Los Angeles, Tax Dept.; **PROFL AFFIL & HONORS:** State Bar of CA; ABA; CA Soc. of CPA's, Inst. in Law, Glendale Coll.; **EDUC:** BS, 1972, Fin./Acctg., Wharton School of Fin., Univ. of PA; **GRAD EDUC:** JD, 1976, Law, Loyola Univ. School of Law; **EDUC HONORS:** Dean's List; **BUS ADD:** 420 N. Brand Blvd., Suite 500, Glendale, CA 91203, (213)247-7380.

TONG, Harry W.——B: Feb. 11, 1934, Canton, China, *Owner*, Tong & Assocs.; **PRIM RE ACT:** Broker, Attorney, Instructor, Syndicator; **PREV EMPLOY:** CPA - Arthur Andersen & Co., Prof.; **PROFL AFFIL & HONORS:** ABA, CSCPA, NAAACPA, CA Bar Assn., Atty./CPA, RE Broker; **EDUC:** BS/BA, 1959, Acctg./Fin., Roosevelt Univ.; **GRAD EDUC:** MS/JD, 1964, 1972, Acctg., Law, Roosevelt Univ., DePaul Univ.; **EDUC HONORS:** Nat. Honor Soc., Dean's List; **HOME ADD:** 621 Bainbridge, Foster City, CA 94404, (415)574-1384; **BUS ADD:** 490 Winslow, Redwood City, CA 94063, (415)363-0102.

TONNON, Alan N.——**B:** May 10, 1938, Green Bay, WI, *VP*, Block Bros. Indus. (USA), Inc. (since Jan. 1981), Indus., Comml., Investment Div.; **PRIM RE ACT:** Broker, Instructor; **SERVICES:** Indus., comml., investment sales and leasing; **REP CLIENTS:** Indiv., synd., instit. investors; **PREV EMPLOY:** Washington RE Educ. Found. - Exec. Dir., Washington State - RE Admin.; **PROFL AFFIL & HONORS:** Washington and WI State Bar Assns., ABA, Seattle-King Cty. Bd. of Realtors, Washington Assn. of Realtors, Natl. Assn. of Realtors; **EDUC:** BS, 1963, Univ. of WI - Madison; **GRAD EDUC:** JD, 1966, Univ. of WI Law School - Madison; **OTHER ACT & HONORS:** Bd. of Dir. - Bellevue Philharmonica; Author: "The Complete Guide to WA RE Practices"; Former Member, Advisory Bd. for Coll. of Econ. & Bus., WA State Univ.; **HOME ADD:** 4273 - 133rd St. SE, Bellevue, WA 98006, (206)643-3147; **BUS ADD:** 1918 Terry Ave., Seattle, WA 98101, (206)625-9500.

TOOLE, Brice, Jr.——**B:** Mar. 31, 1928, Wash. DC., *Asst. to Pres. & Ventures Mgr.*, Upland Indus. Corp., RE Devel.; **PRIM RE ACT:** Broker, Developer, Syndicator; **SERVICES:** The Devel. for sale or lease of indus. & comml. props.; **PROFL AFFIL & HONORS:** Indus. & Office Park Devel. Council, ULI; **EDUC:** BA, 1953, Hist., Univ. of MT, Missoula, MT; **GRAD EDUC:** Cert. in Invest. Banking, 1964, Wharton Sch. of Fin., Univ. of PA; **MIL SERV:** US Army, Cpl., Victory Medal, European Theater Ribbon; **OTHER ACT & HONORS:** Cert. in RE, Grad. Sch. of Bus. Admin, So. Methodist Univ., Dallas, TX; **HOME ADD:** 1670 W. Dr., San Marino, CA 91108, (213)570-1381; **BUS ADD:** 5480 Ferguson Dr., Suite 300, Los Angeles, CA 90022, (213)725-2140.

TOOMES, W. Scott——**B:** Feb. 17, 1944, Chicago, IL, *Partner*, Toomes & Assoc.; **PRIM RE ACT:** Consultant, Developer, Owner/Investor; **SERVICES:** Investment builder and devel. of comml. prop.; **PREV EMPLOY:** Cadillac Fairview Corp. Ltd - Sr. VP The Rowe Co.; **PROFL AFFIL & HONORS:** Urban Land Inst., Inter Council of Shopping Ctrs.; **EDUC:** BA, 1966, Econ., Ursinus Coll.; **GRAD EDUC:** MBA, 1970, Indus., Wharton; **MIL SERV:** US Army, 1st Lt., Bronze Star; **HOME ADD:** 25 Canoe Hill Rd., New Canaan, CT 06840, (203)966-4107; **BUS ADD:** Box 298, New Canaan, CT 06840, (203)966-7634.

TOOTHAKER, Thomas R.——**B:** Nov. 27, 1937, San Diego, CA; **PRIM RE ACT:** Attorney, Owner/Investor; **PROFL AFFIL & HONORS:** ABA, CA Bar Assn.; **EDUC:** AB, 1959, Hist., Stanford Univ.; **GRAD EDUC:** JD, 1971, Law, Stanford Law Sch.; **MIL SERV:** US Army Infantry; **HOME ADD:** 357 New Canaan Rd., Wilton, CT 06897; **BUS ADD:** 200 Park Avenue, 7th Floor W., New York, NY 10166, (212)573-0700.

TOPLIFFE, Daniel P.——**B:** Jan. 14, 1931, Fredonia, NY, *Prop. Mgr.*, Main Seneca Corp.; **PRIM RE ACT:** Broker, Property Manager; **PREV EMPLOY:** 1966-74 Rockford Mgmt. & Devel. Corp., Buffalo, NY; Central Buffalo Project, Buffalo, NY, 1974-76; **PROFL AFFIL & HONORS:** BOMA; **EDUC:** 1956, Acctg., Bus. Law, Bryant Stratton Bus. Inst.; **MIL SERV:** US Army, Priv., 1952-54; **OTHER ACT & HONORS:** Pres. 1974 Buffalo BOMA; **HOME ADD:** 36 Devonshire Ct., Kenmore, NY 14223, (716)875-5005; **BUS ADD:** 237 Main St., Buffalo, NY 14203, (716)856-3440.

TOPLISS, Larry T.——**B:** May 27, 1947, Montrose, CO, *Owner/Atty./Princial Broker*, Interstate Investments; **PRIM RE ACT:** Broker, Attorney, Developer, Owner/Investor; **OTHER RE ACT:** Condo converter; **REP CLIENTS:** Developers; **PROFL AFFIL & HONORS:** ABA; **EDUC:** 1969, Poli. Sci., Univ. of CO; **GRAD EDUC:** JD, 1972, Univ. of CO; **HOME ADD:** PO Box 4262, Honolulu, HI 96813; **BUS ADD:** Star Route Box 11-114, Keaau, HI 96749, (808)966-7398.

TOPPING, Dean——**B:** Sept. 10, 1948, Chicago, IL, *VP*, Baird & Warner, Inc., since 8/76, Office Props. Div.; **PRIM RE ACT:** Broker, Consultant, Property Manager; **SERVICES:** Office & retail space leasing, office bldg. sales, office & indus. bldg. mgmt., land sales zoned for office bldg. use & consulting on office bldg. devels.; **REP CLIENTS:** Fortune 500, cos., maj. Chicago area firms; **PREV EMPLOY:** Helmsley-Spear of IL, Inc.; **PROFL AFFIL & HONORS:** Chicago RE Bd.; IL & Nat. Assns. of Realtors; Oak Brook Assn. of Commerce & Indus.; Chicago Assn. of Commerce & Indus., Lambda Alpha, Profl. RE Frat.; **EDUC:** BA, 1970, Poli. Sci., Northwestern Univ., Coll. of Arts & Sci.; **OTHER ACT & HONORS:** Member, House Fund Bd. of Dir. Beta Pi Chap., Delta Tau Delta Frat; Past Member, Bd. of Dir., Coll. of Arts & Sci. Alumni Assn., Northwestern; **HOME ADD:** 1115 S. Plymouth Ct., 406, Chicago, IL 60605, (312)786-9325; **BUS ADD:** 115 S. LaSalle St., Chicago, IL 60603, (312)368-5765.

TOPPLE, James H.——Pattillo Construction Co., Inc.; **PRIM RE ACT:** Developer; **BUS ADD:** 2053 Mountain Industrial Blvd., Tucker, GA 30084, (404)038-6366.*

TORGERSEN, Torwald H.——**B:** Sept. 2, 1929, Chicago, IL, *Corp. Architect - Dir., Arch. & Const.*, Container Corp. of America, Mobil Corp.(Div. of); **PRIM RE ACT:** Architect, Owner/Investor, Property Manager; **SERVICES:** Programming, planning, design, budgeting, RE const.; **REP CLIENTS:** 150 plants, offices, etc., located in 100+ cities in US, Latin Amer. & Europe (3 countries); **PREV EMPLOY:** Skidmore, Owings & Merrill, 1956-1960; **PROFL AFFIL & HONORS:** ASID; AIA; AAA; ASME; ARA; PIMA; FIDER; IBD; ASCEC; NCARB; RE, Fellow, ASID; Nominated Fellow, AIA; Past Pres., ASID; **EDUC:** BS, 1951, Arch./Engrg., Univ. of IL; **EDUC HONORS:** Magna Cum Laude, Sigma Tau (Engrg. Hon.), Gargoyle (Arch. Hon.); **MIL SERV:** US Naval Res.; Capt., Korean Defense; Naval Res., 1952-present; **OTHER ACT & HONORS:** Funds Alloc. Chicago Community Chest; SCCA Past Pres., LSD Bd.; Member, Design School Accred.; Amer. ARB Bd.; **HOME ADD:** 3750 N. Lake Shore Dr., Chicago, IL 60613, (312)477-9462; **BUS ADD:** 500 E. North Ave., Carol Stream, IL 60187, (312)260-6880.

TORNELL, Ronald C.——**B:** Nov. 13, 1942, Santa Cruz, CA, *Owner*, Tornell Associates; **PRIM RE ACT:** Broker, Owner/Investor, Instructor, Property Manager; **OTHER RE ACT:** Co-devel. of RE course, *Equity Sharing for the Single Family Home*; Partner, C.E. Tornell & Company; **SERVICES:** Consultant for equity sharing; brokerage, agric. RE; **REP CLIENTS:** Builders, farmers and ranchers, investors, RE lics. for equity sharing training; **PREV EMPLOY:** Gen. Mgr. and Broker for a multiple office resid. RE firm; Owner/Mgr. of Tornell Ranch; **PROFL AFFIL & HONORS:** NAR; CA Assn. of Realtors; Dir., 1982; Dist. 7 Chmn., Educ. Comm., 1982; Modesto Bd. of Realtors; Dir. and Sec./Treas., 1982 Stanislaus Area Farm and Land Brokers; Pres., 1980 to 1982; San Joaquin Valley Comml. Brokers; Central Valley Mktg. and Exchange Grp.; FLI; State Dir., 1982; **EDUC:** BBA, 1972, Acctg., CA State Coll.; **HOME ADD:** 1001 Edgebrook Dr., Modesto, CA 95354, (209)527-6317; **BUS ADD:** 601 McHenry Ave., Suite E-2, Modesto, CA 95350, (209)523-9959.

TORNETTA, Charles J.——**B:** Feb. 2, 1931, Norristown, PA, *VP*, Tornetta Realty Corp.; **PRIM RE ACT:** Broker, Consultant, Appraiser, Developer, Owner/Investor, Property Manager; **SERVICES:** Investments, consultant, comml. & indus. RE developer; **PROFL AFFIL & HONORS:** Central Montgomery Cty. Bd. of Realtors; NAR; PA & Nat. Assn. of Review Appraisers; SRA; Amer. Soc. of Appraisers; CRA; ASA; **EDUC:** 1953, Econ./Acctg./RE, Univ. of PA, Wharton School; **GRAD EDUC:** Temple Univ.; **MIL SERV:** US Army; **OTHER ACT & HONORS:** Chmn., Montgomery Cty. Planning Commn.; Kiwanis Club; Gr. Norristown Corp.; Past Pres. & COB, Central Montgomery Cty. Bd. of Realtors; **HOME ADD:** 221 Joseph St., Norristown, PA 19403, (215)539-7496; **BUS ADD:** 839 E. Germantown Pike, Norristown, PA 19401, (215)279-4000.

TORNGA, David L.——**B:** Aug. 22, 1948, E. Grand Rapids, MI, *Atty.*, Nine & Maister; **PRIM RE ACT:** Attorney; **SERVICES:** Legal, counseling and planning for new devel., synd., condos. and investments; **REP CLIENTS:** Devel., synd. and investors; **PREV EMPLOY:** RE Investment Officer, The Travelers Ins. Co.; **PROFL AFFIL & HONORS:** Builders Assn. of Southeast MI; MI Mort. Bankers Assn.; Amer, MI and Oakland Cty. Bar Assns., Comm. on Syndications and Coml. Transactions in RE; MI Bar Assn.; RE Law Committee, Oakland Bar Assn.; RE Investment Committee, Amer. Bar Assn.; **EDUC:** BA, 1970, Econ., Calvin Coll.; **GRAD EDUC:** MBA, 1972, Mktg., Univ. of MI; **EDUC HONORS:** RE Scholarship; **OTHER ACT & HONORS:** Pres. and Dir., Birmingham Central Kiwanis Club, 'Dispositions of Real Prop.', Journal of RE Taxation, Volume 8, Number 2, Winter, 1981; 'Proposed Revision: Michigan Uniform Limited Partnership Act', *Michigan Bar Journal*, Vol. 60, No. 12, December, 1981; **HOME ADD:** 1255 Birmingham Blvd., Birmingham, MI 48009, (313)644-5469; **BUS ADD:** 21 E. Long Lake Rd. Suite 100, Bloomfield Hills, MI 48013, (313)644-5500.

TORO, Theodore A.——**B:** July 15, 1946, Jackson, WY, *VP*, Property Appraisal Services, Inc.; **PRIM RE ACT:** Consultant, Appraiser, Owner/Investor; **SERVICES:** RE appraisal, investment tax credit studies, investment analysis; **REP CLIENTS:** S. Pacific RR; Chrysler Corp.; Sigmor Corp.; **PREV EMPLOY:** Appraisal Assoc., KS City 1975 - 1981; **PROFL AFFIL & HONORS:** MAI; SRPA; AAE, Member of the SREA Young Advisory Council; V. Gov. of Dist. No. 27 for the SREA; **EDUC:** BS, 1970, Math. & Stat., Univ. of WY; **GRAD EDUC:** MS, 1972, Stat., Univ. of WY; **HOME ADD:** 7410 Authon Dr., Dallas, TX 75248, (214)960-1196; **BUS ADD:** 4020 McEwen Rd., Suite 200, Dallas, TX 75234, (214)385-9999.

TORRES, Emilio——B: Oct. 18, 1914, Philippines, Torres Law Office; **PRIM RE ACT:** Attorney, Consultant; **OTHER RE ACT:** Assist foreign clients who want to invest in R.E. in the U.S.; assist local builders obtain needed financing; **PREV EMPLOY:** Atty. Dept. of Justice, Phillipines; Comml. attache, Phillipine Embassy, AS; US Supreme Court Bar; D.C. Bar; Nat. Lawyers Club; American Bar; **EDUC:** AB, 1935, Econ., Natl. U.; LLB, 1939, Univ. of Phillipines; **GRAD EDUC:** MCL, 1955, George Wash. Univ. - MCL; Georgetown Univ. MFS Intl. Relations, 1949; LLM, 1962, Intl. Transactions, Columbia Univ.; **EDUC HONORS:** Pres. of the Graduating Class at N.U.; **OTHER ACT & HONORS:** Natl. Geographic Soc.; Smithsonian Instn.; **HOME ADD:** 3531 Hamlet Pl., Chevy Chase, MD 20015, (301)656-2067; **BUS ADD:** 725 15th St. NW, Wash., DC 20005, (301)656-4461.

TORRES, Jose Luis——B: Nov. 7, 1924, Vauco, PR, *Civil Engr & Appraiser*, Own Office; **PRIM RE ACT:** Consultant, Appraiser, Engineer, Assessor; **SERVICES:** To banks, people, etc.; **PREV EMPLOY:** Civil Engineer of PR Electric Power Auth. from 1945-75; **PROFL AFFIL & HONORS:** Colegio de Ingenieros y Agrimensores de PR, Inst. de Evaluatores de PR, Assoc. de Ingenieous Evaluadores de PR, MIE 129; **EDUC:** BCE, 1941, Univ. of PR; **GRAD EDUC:** 1945, Univ. of PR; **MIL SERV:** US Army, Pvt.; **OTHER ACT & HONORS:** Pres., Yauco Local Planning Bd., 1955-76; Yauco Lions Club; Amer. Legion Assn.; Alumni del Colegia d'Agriculturz y Artes Mecamigal; **HOME ADD:** 35 Pasarell St., Yauco, PR 00768, (809)856-1371; **BUS ADD:** Comercio & Betances St. SE, Yauco, PR 00768, (809)856-0995.

TORRES, William J.——B: Mar 20, 1948, PR, *Asst. VP*, Marine Midland Bank; **PRIM RE ACT:** Banker, Lender; **SERVICES:** Mort. origination & operations; **PROFL AFFIL & HONORS:** MBA, RE Bd. of NY; **EDUC:** BBA, 1970, Bus. Mgmt., St. Francis Coll.; **GRAD EDUC:** MBA, 1974, Fin & Invest., Bernard M. Baruch; **EDUC HONORS:** AK Award, Achieved highest index in Bus. Div., Assistantship Award; **OTHER ACT & HONORS:** YMCA; **HOME ADD:** 4545 Palisade Ave., Union City, NJ 07087, (201)866-7683; **BUS ADD:** 140 Broadway, New York, NY 10015, (212)440-1278.

TOSCANO, James R.——*Exec. VP*, Watson Industrial Properties; **PRIM RE ACT:** Developer; **BUS ADD:** 3435 Wilshire Blvd., Ste. 1500, Los Angeles, CA 90010, (213)775-3486.*

TOTTEN, S. Bleecker——B: Dec. 20, 1929, Newark, NJ, *Sr. VP, Consulting Div.*, Edward S. Gordon Co., Inc.; **PRIM RE ACT:** Consultant; **SERVICES:** Financial analysis, prop. evaluation, lease negotiations, lease vs. ownership analysis, pro forma income projections; **REP CLIENTS:** AT&T, Morgan Guaranty Trust, Citicorp., Sharon Steel Corp., Estee Lauder; **PREV EMPLOY:** VP RE McGraw-Hill, Inc.; **PROFL AFFIL & HONORS:** NACORE, BOMA Intl., RE Bd. of NY, Rho Epsilon, Atty.; **EDUC:** BS, 1951, Chem. & Biology, Oglethorp Univ.; **GRAD EDUC:** LLB, 1958, Fordham Univ.; **EDUC HONORS:** Blue Key Nat. Hon. Frat.; **MIL SERV:** US Army, Cpl.; **HOME ADD:** 49 N. Star Dr., Morristown, NJ 07960, (201)538-7281; **BUS ADD:** 405 Lexington Ave., New York, NY 10174, (212)883-8375.

TOUCHSTONE, Terry——B: April 16, 1947, Merkel, TX, *Broker-owner*, Touchstone Co., Realtors; **PRIM RE ACT:** Broker, Consultant, Owner/Investor, Property Manager; **SERVICES:** Brokerage of comml. & resid. prop., prop. mgmt. Consultnt.; **REP CLIENTS:** Indiv. investors and private local cos. investing in raw land & comml. props.; **PREV EMPLOY:** Spec. Agt. for Rep. Nat. Life Ins. Co., Dallas, TX; **PROFL AFFIL & HONORS:** Abilene Bd. of Realtors, TX Assn. of Realtors, NAR, Grad. of RE Inst., Cert. Resid. Specialist; **EDUC:** BA, 1970, Bus., Abilene Christian Univ.; **MIL SERV:** USAF Res., Sgt.; **OTHER ACT & HONORS:** Past VP & 2 term Dir. Abilene Bd. of Realtors, VP and Dir. of local Kiwanis Club; **HOME ADD:** 1209 Canterbury, Abilene, TX 79602, (915)677-5800; **BUS ADD:** 2801 E. Hwy 80, P O Box 3121, Abilene, TX 79604, (915)673-7112.

TOUGHILL, Peter——B: Jan. 4, 1940, Philadelphia, PA, *Pres.*, Arthur Rubloff & Co. of S. CA; **PRIM RE ACT:** Broker, Consultant, Appraiser, Property Manager; **OTHER RE ACT:** Full Serv. Comml. RE Grp.;Mort. Broker; **SERVICES:** Indus. office, retail & investment divs., prop. mgmt.; **REP CLIENTS:** Firestone Tire, Max Factor, Pabst, The Irvine Co., Sidley & Austin Security Pacific Bank, American Can, Crown Zeller Bach, Nat. Can, Intl. Paper, Metropolitan Life Ins.; **PREV EMPLOY:** Rgl. Mgr. Midwest Grp./ Indus. Props 1972-80, Coldwell Banker-Sales Consultant Coldwell Banker; **PROFL AFFIL & HONORS:** SIR, Nat. Assn. Office & Indus. Parks, Urban Land Inst., NACORE, Runner up, Top Indus. Salesman, Stuart Matthews Award Chicago RE Bd. 1979; **EDUC:** BS, 1962, English, St. Joseph's, PA; **EDUC HONORS:** Athletic-Mid Atlantic Shot/ Discus Champion 1962; **HOME ADD:** 4684 Browndeer Ln., Palos Verdes, CA 90274, (213)544-0114; **BUS ADD:** 600 S. Comm. Ave. S 1208, L.A., CA 90005, (213)487-1300.

TOUSIGNANT, Robert F.——B: Nov. 9, 1946, Gardner, MA, *VP*, Synco Inc., Equity Securities Corp.; **PRIM RE ACT:** Syndicator; **OTHER RE ACT:** Investment broker; **SERVICES:** Various investment opportunities including tax shelters; **REP CLIENTS:** Indivs., partnerships, corps., and instnl. investors; **PROFL AFFIL & HONORS:** SECO; **EDUC:** BA, 1968, Springfield Coll.; **HOME ADD:** 4223 Cantey Pl., Charlotte, NC 28211, (704)366-9460; **BUS ADD:** POB 34487, Charlotte, NC 28234, (704)376-9500.

TOWERY, Jerrel E.——B: July 11, 1953, Dayton, OH, *Atty.*, Barber & Towery, P.A.; **PRIM RE ACT:** Attorney, Insuror; **OTHER RE ACT:** Legal practice FL & OH; **SERVICES:** Title ins., closings, condo law, contracts, RE counseling; **REP CLIENTS:** Realtors, indiv. prop. purchasers, condo. assns.; **PREV EMPLOY:** Lee & Surfus, Attys. at Law; **PROFL AFFIL & HONORS:** FL Bar Assn.; ABA; Real Prop. & Estates Div. of ABA; Lawyers Title Guaranty Fund; Phi Alpha Delta Law Frat.; **EDUC:** BA, 1975, Pol. Sci., Wright State Univ.; **GRAD EDUC:** JD, 1978, OH State Univ. Coll of Law; **EDUC HONORS:** Grad. Magna Cum Laude; **OTHER ACT & HONORS:** Member Sertoma Intl., Venice, FL, Chap.; Member & Legal Counsel, Gr. Venice Area Jaycees; **HOME ADD:** 1023 Hope St., Venice, FL 33595, (813)488-5759; **BUS ADD:** 307 W. Venice Ave., Venice, FL 33595, (813)485-3391.

TOWLE, Daniel W.——B: June 18, 1929, Portland, ME, *Owner*, Dan Towle Associates; **PRIM RE ACT:** Broker; **PREV EMPLOY:** Co-owner Tacoma Realty Co., Gardiner, ME; **PROFL AFFIL & HONORS:** 1972-1975 Southern Kennebec Valley Bd. of Realtors, ME Assn. of Realtors, 2nd VP, NAR, GRI, Certified Residential Specialist CRS; **EDUC:** Univ. of ME; **OTHER ACT & HONORS:** Former Member of Town of Farmingdale Planning Bd., Former Inst. Univ. of ME-Augusta-RE Practice, Past Pres. Gardiner Lions Club; **HOME ADD:** Route 1, Box 1439, Hallowell, ME 04347, (207)622-1344; **BUS ADD:** 409 Maine Ave., Hallowell, ME 04347, (207)662-6381.

TOWNER, John H.——B: July 15, 1922, Bangor, ME, *Chmn. of the Bd.*, Thorn Creek Realty, Inc.; **PRIM RE ACT:** Broker, Consultant, Appraiser, Owner/Investor, Instructor, Property Manager, Insuror; **SERVICES:** Resid. & comml. sales, ins., prop. mgmt., appraisals; **PREV EMPLOY:** Same co. 21 yrs.; **PROFL AFFIL & HONORS:** RNMI, Grt. S. Sub. Bd. of Realtors, Dir. IL Assn. of Realtors, Realtor of Yr., 1967, GRI, CRS, CRB; **EDUC:** BS, 1948, Educ., MI State Univ.; **GRAD EDUC:** MS, 1951, School Admin., Univ. of IL; **EDUC HONORS:** Phi Delta Kappa; **MIL SERV:** USAF, Cpl.; **OTHER ACT & HONORS:** Pres. Prop. Owners Assn., Lakes of 4 Seasons, IN, 6 yrs.; Rotary Club of Park Forest, IL; Amer. Legion, Loyal Order of Moose; **HOME ADD:** 1562 Happy Valley Rd., Crown Point, IN 46307, (219)988-2501; **BUS ADD:** 3717 Sauk Tr., Rickton Park, IL 60471, (312)748-6451.

TOWNSEND, Charles——B: Apr. 20, 1946, Phoenix, AZ, *Sr. V.P., R.E. Serv.*, Doane-W. Farm Agri. Services, R.E.; **PRIM RE ACT:** Broker; **OTHER RE ACT:** R.E. Brokerage; **SERVICES:** Co. Brokers, Fin., Manages, and Appraises Agricultural Prop.; **REP CLIENTS:** Indiv. and inst. operating or investing in agricultural R.E.; **PREV EMPLOY:** Grubb and Ellis Comml. Brokerage Co., Denver, CO; **PROFL AFFIL & HONORS:** RESSI; **EDUC:** BS, 1968, Chemical Engrg., MT State Univ.; **EDUC HONORS:** Grad. with Honors, Engrg. Scholastic Soc., Who's Who in Amer. Coll., and Univ.; **HOME ADD:** P.O. Box 6072, Denver, CO 80206, (303)399-2957; **BUS ADD:** 3333 Quebec, Denver, CO 80207, (303)388-4084.

TOWNSEND, J.L.——B: Dec. 12, 1927, Texarkana, AR, *Owner*, J.L. Townsend Realtor; **PRIM RE ACT:** Broker, Developer, Owner/Investor, Insuror, Syndicator; **PROFL AFFIL & HONORS:** Nat. Assn. Realtors, Nat. Assn. of Ins. Agents; **EDUC:** Memphis State; **OTHER ACT & HONORS:** Kiwanis; **HOME ADD:** 5 Hickory Ln., Daytona Beach, FL 32018, (904)252-7598; **BUS ADD:** 821 Broadway, Daytona Beach, FL 32018.

TOWNSEND, William H.——B: June 17, 1929, Columbia, SC, *Partner*, Sherrill, Townsend, Moses and Jeffcoat; **PRIM RE ACT:** Attorney; **SERVICES:** All legal services related to RE; **REP CLIENTS:** Lenders and instit. investors and owners and devels. of comml. and resid. RE; **PREV EMPLOY:** Townsend and Townsend, Columbia, SC, 1955-1971; McKay, Sherrill, Walker and Townsend, Columbia SC, 1971-1981; **PROFL AFFIL & HONORS:** ABA (Member Real Prop., Probate and Trust Section), SC Bar (Member, RE Practice Section), Richland Cty. Bar Assn. Chairman, RE Sect. 1976), Member, Amer. Coll. of RE Lawyers; **EDUC:** AB, 1950, Poli. Sci., Washington & Lee Univ.; **GRAD EDUC:** LLB, 1952, Law, Univ. of SC; **HOME ADD:** 1212 Greenhill Rd., Columbia, SC 29206, (803)782-0858; **BUS ADD:** 1340 Bull St., P O Drawer 447, Columbia,

SC 29202, (803)771-8880.

TOYOMURA, Dennis T.——B: July 6, 1926, Honolulu, HI, *Principal-Owner*, Dennis T. Toyomura, AIA, Arch.; **PRIM RE ACT:** Architect; **OTHER RE ACT:** RE Broker; **SERVICES:** Arch. & engr. serv., consultant to banks & ins. cos. for mort. & const. fin., counseling to attys., feasibility studies, and const. mgmt.; **REP CLIENTS:** State and municipal agencies, utility co., banks, ins. co., consultant for Honolulu Redevel. Agency with HUD, City & County of Honolulu, HI, 1967-1971; **PREV EMPLOY:** Holabird, Root & Burgee, Archs.-Engrs., Chicago, IL, Loebl, Schlossman & Bennett, Arch.-Engrs., Chicago, IL; **PROFL AFFIL & HONORS:** AIA, HI Soc., Dir. (1973-74) & Treas., 1975, Const. Specification Inst., Const. Indus. Legis. Org., Dir. 1973-, Treasurer, 1976-77; Lyon Arboretum Assn., Dir. 1974-76, Treas., 1976; Council of Educ. Facility Planners, Intl., Bd. of Governor, NW Region, 1979-81, Outstanding Citizen Recognition Award, Consulting Engr. Council, HI, 1975; **EDUC:** BS, 1949, Arch. Engr., Chicago Tech. Coll.; **GRAD EDUC:** Post Grad. Studies, Univ. of IL (Ext.); IL Inst. of Tech.; Univ. of HI/Dept. of Defense; **MIL SERV:** US Army; **OTHER ACT & HONORS:** Appointment: Arch. Member, Bd. of Regis. of Profl. Engrs., Arch., Land Surveyors & Landscape Archs., State of HI, 1974-; Nat. Council of Arch. Regis. Bd.; Nat. Council of Engr. Examiners; **HOME ADD:** 2602 Manaoa Rd., Honolulu, HI 96822, (808)988-4632; **BUS ADD:** 1370 Kapiolani Blvd., Honolulu, HI 96814, (808)946-5248.

TOZER, A. Ray——B: Sept. 18, 1936, Buckly, WA, *Rgnl Mgr.*, The Travelers Ins. Co., RE Investment Dept.; **PRIM RE ACT:** Lender, Owner/Investor; **SERVICES:** Var. RE investments for The Travelers, including morts., purchases and joint ventures; **REP CLIENTS:** The Travelers Ins. Co.; **EDUC:** BS, 1961, Bus. Admin., Portland State Univ., Portland, OR; **MIL SERV:** USANG; S/Sgt.; **HOME ADD:** 3818 Magnolia Dr., Brunswick, OH 44212, (216)273-1874; **BUS ADD:** 1801 E. 9th St., Cleveland, OH 44114, (216)574-4629.

TRACHTENBERG, Ronald W., CPA——B: Oct. 23, 1945, Boston, MA, *Principal Shareholder*, Coughlin, Trachtenberg & Sheff P.C.; **PRIM RE ACT:** Consultant; **OTHER RE ACT:** CPA; **SERVICES:** Fin. & managerial and tax consulting in the RE area; **REP CLIENTS:** Many and varied clients owning comml. & resid. props.; **PREV EMPLOY:** Ronald W. Trachtenberg & Co. - Financial Consultant; **PROFL AFFIL & HONORS:** Amer. Inst. of CPA's, MA Soc. of CPA's, MA Assn. of PA's, Natl. Assn. of Accountants, CPA, MA Soc. of CPA's; **EDUC:** BS, 1972, Acctg. & Fin., Bentley Coll.; **HOME ADD:** 18 Kenneth Terrace, Stoneham, MA 02180, (617)438-3880; **BUS ADD:** 411 MA Ave., Acton, MA 01720, (617)263-3777.

TRACY, David J., Esq.——B: Mar. 20, 1952, Providence, RI, *Assoc.*, Hinckley & Allen; **PRIM RE ACT:** Attorney; **SERVICES:** All areas of RE with emphasis on condo. conversions, and representation of lenders in comml. RE transactions; **REP CLIENTS:** Devels. and lenders in comml. RE transactions; **PREV EMPLOY:** Brown, Rudnick, Freed and Gesmer, One Fed. St., Boston, MA, 02110, 1977-80; **PROFL AFFIL & HONORS:** ABA including Comm. on RE Literature; MA Bar Assn.; RI Bar Assn. including Bus. Org. Comm.; **EDUC:** BA, 1974, Sociology and Social Psych., Brandeis Univ.; **GRAD EDUC:** JD, 1977, Boston Coll. Law School; **EDUC HONORS:** Summa cum laude; special honors in Sociology, Magna cum laude; elected to Order of the Coif; **HOME ADD:** 15 High St., N. Providence, RI 02904, (401)353-7430; **BUS ADD:** 2200 Ind. Bank Bldg. 21st Floor, Providence, RI 02903, (401)274-2000.

TRAGER, Sidney——B: Jan. 2, 1926, Cleveland, OH, *VP*, The NY Bank for Savings; **PRIM RE ACT:** Broker, Appraiser, Banker, Lender; **SERVICES:** Mort. lending, secondary mort. mktg.; **PROFL AFFIL & HONORS:** Amer. Assn. of Mort. Underwriters, Soc. of RE Appraisers, NAR, SRPA, Former Pres. Rockland Cty. Bd. of Realtors, Former Pres. NY State Soc. of RE Appraisers; **EDUC:** BA, 1947, Bus. Admin., Tufts Univ.; **MIL SERV:** USN, Ens.; **HOME ADD:** 3 Wayne Ave., New City, NY 10956, (914)634-6169; **BUS ADD:** 1230 Ave. of the Amers., NY, NY 10020, (212)841-7237.

TRAIL, Larry G.——B: Sept. 28, 1952, Woodbury, TN, *Partner*, Reed, Rogers and Trail; **PRIM RE ACT:** Attorney; **SERVICES:** Title ins., opinions, document preparation, planning, tax; **REP CLIENTS:** Federal Land Bank; Production Credit Assn.; Pioneer Title Ins. Co.; Bank of Eagleville, FMHA; **PREV EMPLOY:** Smith and Sellers, Attys.; **PROFL AFFIL & HONORS:** ABA; TN Bar Assn.; TN Trial Lawyers; Rutherford Bar Assn., (Treas. 1980-81, VP 81-82); **EDUC:** BS, 1975, Pol. Sci./Hist./Agric., TN State Univ.; **GRAD EDUC:** JD, 1977, Prop./UCC, Univ. of TN; **EDUC HONORS:** Dean's List; Pres. Pre-Law; Rep. Student Govt.; Public Defenders Council, Dean's List; Pres. Phi Delta Phi Legal Soc.; Advisory Council; **HOME ADD:** 1907 Ragland Ave., Murfreesboro, TN 37130, (615)890-1527; **BUS ADD:** 117 E. Main St., Murfreesboro, TN 37130, (615)890-6464.

TRAINA, Carl L.——B: Sept. 9, 1951, Boston, MA, *Pres.*, Albert J. Tonry & Co., Inc.; **PRIM RE ACT:** Broker, Engineer, Developer, Insuror; **EDUC:** BS, 1973, Civil Engr., Tufts Unviv.; **GRAD EDUC:** MS, 1975, Civil Engr., Tufts Univ.; **BUS ADD:** 4766 Prudential Center, Boston, MA 02199, (617)267-5400.

TRAINOR, Thomas Kristen——B: Mar. 13, 1953, Mt. Vernon, NY, *Clearance Counsel*, The Title Guarantee Co.; **PRIM RE ACT:** Attorney; **PROFL AFFIL & HONORS:** ABA; NY State Bar Assn.; Westchester Cty. Bar Assn.; **EDUC:** BA, 1974, Poli. Sci., Iona Coll.; **GRAD EDUC:** JD, 1977, Law, Fordham Law School; **EDUC HONORS:** Summa Cum Laude; 1st out of 600 Seniors, Dean's List - Third Year; 91st out of 315 grads.; **OTHER ACT & HONORS:** Candidate for LLM Degree at NY Univ. Law School; **HOME ADD:** 216 Rich Ave., Mt. Vernon, NY 10552, (914)668-1656; **BUS ADD:** 120 Broadway, New York, NY 10005, (212)964-1000.

TRAMMELL, Allen W.——B: Aug. 10, 1952, Little Rock, AR, *Pres.*, Trammell & Co. RE and Ins., Inc.; **PRIM RE ACT:** Broker, Builder, Insuror, Owner/Investor; **OTHER RE ACT:** Appraisals, Prop. Mgmt.; **SERVICES:** Complete; **PROFL AFFIL & HONORS:** RNMI, NAR, ARA, LR/NLR Bd. of Realtors, CRS, GRI; **OTHER ACT & HONORS:** SWLR Jaycees, VP, Pres. Jaycee of the Yr., 1979-1980; **HOME ADD:** Rte. 4 Box 184, Alexander, AR 72002, (501)847-8749; **BUS ADD:** 6904 Geyer Springs Rd., Little Rock, AR 72209, (501)568-5652.

TRAMONTE, Vallory J.——B: Feb. 14, 1947, Galveston, TX, *Exec. VP*, Moody National Bank; **PRIM RE ACT:** Broker, Consultant, Appraiser, Banker, Lender, Builder, Owner/Investor, Instructor, Property Manager; **PREV EMPLOY:** Amer. Nat. Bank of Beaumont; **PROFL AFFIL & HONORS:** TX RE Commn.; Amer. Bankers Assn.; Nat. Assn. of Review Appraisers; TX Amer. Indep. Bankers Assn.; **EDUC:** BBA, 1970, Mktg., Lamar Univ., SMU Swigsbie 1978-79 Grad. Sch. of Bankers; **EDUC HONORS:** Who's Who Among Students in Amer. Univ. & Coll. 1968-69, Blue Key Honor Soc. 1968; **MIL SERV:** US Army Reserves, Aire Borne, SP5, Honorable Discharge; **OTHER ACT & HONORS:** City Councilman 1979-81, Galveston Housing Fin. Corp. Pres. & Chmn. of the Bd. 79-81, Gulf Coast Housing, Inc. Pres. & Chmn. of the Bd. 1979-81, Galveston Housing Authority Bd. of Dir. 1979-81, TX Coastal Area Higher Education Authority 1981 Bd. of Dir., Amer. Cancer Soc. Bd. of Dir. 79-80, Goodwill Indus. Dir., YMCA Dir.; **HOME ADD:** 7750 Beaudelaire, Galveston, TX 77551, (713)744-7664; **BUS ADD:** 2302 Postoffice Rd., Galveston, TX 77550, (713)765-5561.

TRANK, Michael A.——B: Feb. 14, 1951, Los Angeles, CA, *CPA*, Michael Al Trank; **OTHER RE ACT:** CPA; **SERVICES:** Tax planning, mgmt. consulting and contemporary acctg. servs.; **REP CLIENTS:** Const. contractors, RE operators and devels. in resid. and comml. props.; **PREV EMPLOY:** Alexander Grant and Co. (A major nat. acctg. firm) Local acctg. firms in S. CA, with heavy RE clients and emphasis; **PROFL AFFIL & HONORS:** AICPA and CA Soc. of CPAs., CPA; **EDUC:** BS Bus. Admin., 1975, Acctg., CA State Univ. Long Beach; **GRAD EDUC:** MBA (in progress), 1982, Taxation, Golden State Univ., San Francisco; **OTHER ACT & HONORS:** Saddleback Valley C of C, US C of C; **HOME ADD:** 28092 Klamath Ct., Laguna Niguel, CA 92677, (714)831-8647; **BUS ADD:** 24012 Calle De La Plata Suite 210, Laguna Hills, CA 92653, (714)770-6226.

TRANUM, David Michael——B: May 17, 1952, Bristol, VA, *Atty.*, Stanley & Tranum; **PRIM RE ACT:** Attorney, Owner/Investor; **REP CLIENTS:** Bank of Knoxville, Mutual Benefit Life Ins. Co., Shenandoah Life Ins. Co., The Westlands Condos.; **PROFL AFFIL & HONORS:** ABA, Knoxville Bar Assn.; **EDUC:** BS, 1974, Hist. - Educ., TN Tech. Univ.; **GRAD EDUC:** JD, 1976, Univ. of TN; **EDUC HONORS:** Dean's List, VP Alpha Phi Omega, Phi Alpha Delta, Student Legal Assistance Program; **HOME ADD:** 11304 Windy Way Dr., Knoxville, TN 37922, (615)966-2339; **BUS ADD:** PO Box 10965, 901 Bearden Dr., Knoxville, TN 37919, (615)584-8586.

TRASK, James K., Jr.——B: Aug. 9, 1934, Honolulu, HI, *Pres.*, Trask Dev. Corp.; **PRIM RE ACT:** Broker, Instructor, Consultant, Developer, Property Manager, Owner/Investor; **PROFL AFFIL & HONORS:** NAR; RNMI; HI Assn. of Realtors; Honolulu Bd. of Realtors, CCIM; GRI; **EDUC:** BA, 1961, Bus. Admin., Univ. of HI; **HOME ADD:** 141 Pauahilani Way, Kailua, HI 96734, (808)261-1824; **BUS ADD:** 567 S. King St., Suite 600, Honolulu, HI 96813, (808)524-8567.

TRAUB, Carl F.——B: Sept. 14, 1941, Glen Cove, NY, *Sr. VP*, C.A. White, Inc., Brokerage & Property Mgmt.; **PRIM RE ACT:** Broker, Appraiser, Property Manager, Developer; **OTHER RE ACT:** Project consulting and full mktg. of project from inception to lease-up and mgmt.; **SERVICES:** Full service brokerage and mgmt. for comml. and indus. projects; **REP CLIENTS:** Maj. office bldg. and shopping ctr. owners on the E. Coast; **PREV EMPLOY:** Cushman & Wakefield, VP, 1968-1972; **PROFL AFFIL & HONORS:** Indus. RE Bd. of Metropolitan NY, Intl. Council of Shopping Ctrs., Dir. of Comml. Investment Div., CT Assn. of Realtors, CCIM (Candidate), Past Pres., Rho Epsilon (Univ. Tenn) Real Estate Fraternity; **EDUC:** BS, 1964, RE and Bus. Law, Univ. of TN; **MIL SERV:** USN; Cmdr., Navy Commendation Medal, Vietnam Serv. Medal; **OTHER ACT & HONORS:** Univ. Club, NY; **HOME ADD:** Book Hill Rd., Essex, CT 06426, (203)767-1338; **BUS ADD:** 234 Church Street, New Haven, CT 06510, (203)865-7533.

TRAUB, Eric A.——B: Mar. 25, 1942, *Sr. VP/Pres. of Commercial and Resorts Divisions*, General Development Corp., Commercial/ Resorts; **PRIM RE ACT:** Attorney; **OTHER RE ACT:** Comml. Devel. and Resorts; **PROFL AFFIL & HONORS:** CPA & Atty.; **EDUC:** BBA, 1963, Acctg., Univ. of MI; **GRAD EDUC:** JD, 1969, UCLA School of Law; **EDUC HONORS:** "With High Distinction"; **HOME ADD:** 3151 N. 52 Ave., Hollywood, FL 33021, (305)966-0774; **BUS ADD:** 1111 S. Bayshore Dr., Miami, FL 33131, (305)350-1271.

TRAUTMAN, Lawrence J.——B: May 7, 1949, Louisville, KY, Donaldson, Lufkin & Jenrette, DLJ R.E., Inc.; **PRIM RE ACT:** Broker, Syndicator, Consultant, Lender; **SERVICES:** R.E. investment banking services for mort. banking and thrift indus. and domestic and foreign investor clients-including: investment counseling, valuation, devel./ permanent fin. and synd. of comml. props.; **REP CLIENTS:** Lenders and wealthy indiv. or instnl. investors in comml. props. consulting and merger and acquisition services provided to mort. banking and thrift indus.; **PREV EMPLOY:** OZMA Corp. Chmn. 1979-80; First Midwest Mort. Inc.; VChmn. 1979-80; MBAA 1976-79; **PROFL AFFIL & HONORS:** NACORE, Natl. Assn. of Corp. Dirs.; MBAA, Chmn. of Corp. Planning Comm. 1979-80, GRI-NY; **EDUC:** BA, 1972, Intl. Rel./Govt., The American Univ.; **GRAD EDUC:** MBA, 1975, Fin. and investments, George Wash. Univ.; **OTHER ACT & HONORS:** Taught Acctg. and corp. fin. at several colls. and univs. and authored numerous articles on R.E., investment banking and corp. fin.; Grad. School of Mort. Banking, MBAA; **BUS ADD:** 140 Broadway, 48th Floor, New York, NY 10005, (212)747-9883.

TRAVER, Courtland L.——B: Sept. 20, 1935, New Haven, CT, *Law (Partner)*, Boothe Prichard & Dudley; **OTHER RE ACT:** RE Law; **PREV EMPLOY:** Navy Pilot prior to law school; **PROFL AFFIL & HONORS:** ABA VA Bar Assoc.; **EDUC:** BA, 1957, Sci., Univ. of CT; **GRAD EDUC:** JD, 1966, Geotown Law Ctr.; **MIL SERV:** USN, Lt.; **HOME ADD:** 1800 Old Meadow Road, Mclean, VA 22102, (703)821-2424; **BUS ADD:** Box 338, Fairfax, VA 22030, (703)273-4600.

TRAVIS, Edward F.——B: May 31, 1947, Paris, TN, Edward F. Travis Co., Inc.; **PRIM RE ACT:** Broker, Instructor, Consultant, Appraiser; **SERVICES:** Appraisals of all types, Instructor of Appraising; **REP CLIENTS:** Lenders, individual investors, and other instl. clients; **PROFL AFFIL & HONORS:** MAI - AIREA; SRPA - SREA, Current Pres., Chap. 137 SREA; Treas., Chap. 49 AIREA; **EDUC:** BS, 1969, RE, Univ. of AL; **MIL SERV:** US Army, 1st Lt. Artillery, Vietnam Service Medal, Bronze Star, etc.; **OTHER ACT & HONORS:** 32 Scottish Rite Mason; **HOME ADD:** Rte. 2, Box 151-E, Mobile, AL 36609, (205)633-7772; **BUS ADD:** 578 Azalea Rd., Suite 118, Mobile, AL 36609, (205)666-3050.

TREAKLE, Richard V.——B: Aug. 21, 1943, Omaha, NE, *Pres.*, IRD Indus. Realty and Devel., Inc.; **PRIM RE ACT:** Broker, Developer, Owner/Investor, Property Manager, Syndicator; **SERVICES:** Brokerage & Prop. Mgmt.; **PREV EMPLOY:** Indus. brokerage at Cornish & Carey, and Cushman & Wakefield; Synd. Experience at Fox and Carskadon; **PROFL AFFIL & HONORS:** Assn. of S. Bay Brokers, Nat. Assn. of Office & Indus. Parks, Devel. of the Year 1980 (tri-cities); **EDUC:** BA, 1965, Econ, Fin., Univ. of NE; **GRAD EDUC:** MBA, 1970, Mktg. & Fin., OK City Univ., Summa cum laude, Frammis Award (leadership); **EDUC HONORS:** Summa Cum Laude, Deans List; **MIL SERV:** US AF, Capt., 1965-70, Bronze Star; **OTHER ACT & HONORS:** Pres., S. Bay Striders; **HOME ADD:** 520 Valley Way, Milpitas, CA 95035, (408)263-1340; **BUS ADD:** 2312 Walsh Ave., Santa Clara, CA 95051, (408)496-6262.

TREFFINGER, James——*Chief Plants Eng.*, Standard Register; **PRIM RE ACT:** Property Manager; **BUS ADD:** 626 Albany St., PO Box 1167, Dayton, OH 45401, (513)223-6181.*

TREMBLY, William H., Jr.——B: Apr. 6, 1930, Covington, OH, *Pres.*, William H. Trembly & Associates; **PRIM RE ACT:** Broker, Developer, Property Manager; **SERVICES:** Devel., leasing, mgmt., brokerage; **PREV EMPLOY:** Don M. Casto Organization 1966-1978; Mgr. of the Leasing & Prop. Mgmt. Div. and New Devel. Dept., VP of Devel.; **PROFL AFFIL & HONORS:** IREM; ICSC; CSM; CPM; GRI; RE Broker; **EDUC:** BA, Poli. Sci. and Bus. Admin., OH Wesleyan Univ.; **HOME ADD:** 2853 Rivertop Lane, Columbus, OH 43220, (614)451-7818; **BUS ADD:** 2861 Rivertop Lane, Columbus, OH 43220, (614)451-7818.

TREMONT, Philip J.——B: Nov. 6, 1947, Bryan, TX, *Pres.*, Manorwood Development Corp.; **PRIM RE ACT:** Developer, Builder, Owner/Investor, Property Manager; **OTHER RE ACT:** Licensed salesman; TX RE Commn.; **SERVICES:** Devel. & synd. of comml. props., prop. mgmt.; **REP CLIENTS:** Indiv. investors for comml. props. & multi-family units & S&L for joint ventures; **PREV EMPLOY:** RE Sales, D.R. Cain Co., 1970-1978; James E. Jett Co., 1978-1980; Preston W. Smith Co., 1980 to present; **EDUC:** BBA, 1969, Fin., TX A & M Univ., Coll. Station, TX; **HOME ADD:** 2517 Briarwood, Bryan, TX 77801; **BUS ADD:** 1735 Briarcrest, Suite 204, Bryan, TX 77801, (713)775-5444.

TRENNEPOHL, Jim——B: Feb. 23, 1959, Batesville, IN, *Asst. Prop. Mgr.*, Quonset and Cin-May Realty; **PRIM RE ACT:** Property Manager; **SERVICES:** Office Bldg. Mgr.; **PROFL AFFIL & HONORS:** BOMA; **EDUC:** AA, 1979, Prop. Mgmt & RE, Cincinnati Tech. Coll.; **EDUC HONORS:** Cincinnati Tech. Coll. Alumni; **HOME ADD:** 1028 Fairview Dr., Lawrenceburg, IN 47025, (812)537-3977; **BUS ADD:** Central Trust Bldg., and 1st Natl. Bank Bldg., Cincinnati, OH 45202, (513)241-4880.

TRENT, Joseph Stanley——B: March 31, 1956, Worcester, MA, *Agent*, State Mutual of America; **PRIM RE ACT:** Insuror; **SERVICES:** Provide insurance protection against death and disability; **REP CLIENTS:** Both bus. and indiv. involved in all areas of RE; **PROFL AFFIL & HONORS:** Member Nat. Assn. of Life Underwriters; **EDUC:** BA, 1977, English/Hist., Holy Cross Coll.; **GRAD EDUC:** MA, 1980, Hist., Assumption Coll.; **EDUC HONORS:** Dean's List, Jr. Year; **OTHER ACT & HONORS:** Member Organization of Amer. Historians; **HOME ADD:** 30 Prentice St., Worcester, MA 01604, (617)752-7679; **BUS ADD:** 303 Main St., Worcester, MA 01608, (617)754-3215.

TREUENFELS, Hans P.——B: Apr. 4, 1941, New York, NY, *Pres.*, Treuenfels & Assocs. Inc.; **PRIM RE ACT:** Broker, Developer; **OTHER RE ACT:** Subdivision Marketing; **SERVICES:** Complete mktg. servs. for large scale resid. devels; **REP CLIENTS:** W&K Co., Watt Indus., US Housing Corp., WSI Builders, Travelers Ins. Co.; **PROFL AFFIL & HONORS:** CA Assoc. of Realtors, Amer. Land Devel. Assoc.; **EDUC:** BS, 1963, Engrg., Swarthmore Coll.; **GRAD EDUC:** MS, 1964, Stanford Univ.; **HOME ADD:** 66 Cleary Ct., 910, San Francisco, CA 94109, (415)929-1664; **BUS ADD:** 150 Lombard St., San Francisco, CA 94111, (415)788-4488.

TREUREN, William Van——*RE Dept.*, Essex Chemical Corp.; **PRIM RE ACT:** Property Manager; **BUS ADD:** 1401 Brood St., Clifton, NJ 07015, (201)773-6300.*

TREVINO, Daniel K., Jr.——B: Aug. 2, 1925, Brownsville, TX, *Pres.*, Law Offices of Daniel K. Trevino, Jr., P.C.; **PRIM RE ACT:** Broker, Consultant, Attorney, Developer; **OTHER RE ACT:** Consultant to foreign investors, consultant to attys. in RE matters; **SERVICES:** Legal Servs., intl. tax consultation, offshore corp. formation, joint ventures with foreign investors; **REP CLIENTS:** Foreign investors in comml. props., domestic prog. owners, title co's; **PROFL AFFIL & HONORS:** ABA, TX Bar Assn., Houston Bar Assn., The Assn. of Trial Lawyers of Amer., Who's Who in Amer. Law; **EDUC:** BBA, 1948, Intl. Trade, Univ. of TX; **GRAD EDUC:** JD, 1954, Law, The Geo. Wash. Univ.; **MIL SERV:** USN, AOM 1/C, Adml. Citation; **OTHER ACT & HONORS:** Asst. Atty. Gen. TX (1963-67), SE TX Hosp. Fin. Agency., Who In Houston; **HOME ADD:** 8010 Braesview Ln., Houston, TX 77071, (713)988-8321; **BUS ADD:** PO Box 740067, Houston, TX 77274, (713)491-4412.

TREWHITT, L. Blair——B: Dec. 13, 1928, Chattanooga, TN, *Pres.*, Blair Trewhitt and Assoc.; **PRIM RE ACT:** Broker, Developer, Property Manager, Owner/Investor; **PREV EMPLOY:** Formerly VP of Great SW Corp. (devel. of 3000 acre indus. park in Atlanta); **PROFL AFFIL & HONORS:** Atlanta Bd. of Realtors; **EDUC:** BS, 1953, Indus. mgmt., engrg., GA Inst. of Tech.; **GRAD EDUC:** Worked toward masters in indus. mgmt.; **EDUC HONORS:** Mgr. of Campus Radio Sta.; **MIL SERV:** 2yrs. US Army, Sgt. 1946-48; **OTHER ACT & HONORS:** V Chmn. Cobb Cty. Public Library Bd. of Dir., Amer. Soc. Tool and mfg., engrs., Atlanta Sales Exec. Club, Atlanta C of C, Pres. of Rotary Club; **HOME ADD:** 7111 Factory Shoals Rd., Austell, GA 30001, (404)948-2930; **BUS ADD:** PO Drawer 43967, Atlanta, GA 30336, (404)696-6633.

TRICHE, J. Alvin Jr.——**B:** June 14, 1941, Baton Rouge, LA, *Broker*, Town & Country RE, Inc.; **PRIM RE ACT:** Broker, Appraiser, Developer, Builder, Property Manager, Engineer, Owner/Investor; **SERVICES:** Home Bldr., RE Broker, Appraiser, Devel., Prop. Mgmt.; **REP CLIENTS:** Gulf Nat. Bank, 1st MS Nat. Bank, Merrill-Lynch Relocation Service; **PROFL AFFIL & HONORS:** NAHB; Gulfport Bd. of Realtors; HOW, State Bd. of Dir., NAHB; **GRAD EDUC:** BSEE, 1964, Control Theory, LSU; MSEE, 1966, Non-Linear Control, LSU; **MIL SERV:** Artillery, 1st Lt.; **OTHER ACT & HONORS:** Chmn., Planning and Zoning Commn., City of Bay St. Louis (1979-1980); VP, C of C (1979); Pres., Kiwanis Club, Baton Rouge (1970); **HOME ADD:** 511 Highland Dr., Bay St. Louis, MS 39520, (601)467-6934; **BUS ADD:** 890 Hwy. 90, Bay St. Louis, MS 39520.

TRICOU, Rene J.C., Jr.——**B:** Mar. 25, 1920, Little Rock, AR, *Pres.*, Bon Aire Estates, Inc.; **PRIM RE ACT:** Broker, Developer, Insuror; **PREV EMPLOY:** Pres. LA Hatcheries, Inc.; Pres. Veri-Fresh Poultry, Inc.; **PROFL AFFIL & HONORS:** Bd. of Realtors; FLI; Dir. Hammond Indus. Bd.; **EDUC:** BA, 1941, Tulane Univ.; **MIL SERV:** USN, ART 1C 1942-45; **OTHER ACT & HONORS:** Past Pres. Hammond Exec. Club; Past Pres. Hammond Exchange Club; Past Comndr., Ponchatrain Post, Amer. Legion; **HOME ADD:** 909 Greenlawn Dr., Hammond, LA 70401, (504)345-4245; **BUS ADD:** 2405 Hwy. 51 Bypass, Hammond, LA 70401.

TRIGGS, Gene A.——*Exec. Asst. to Pres.*, Mississippi Chemical Corp.; **PRIM RE ACT:** Property Manager; **BUS ADD:** PO Box 388, Yazee City, MS 39194, (601)746-4131.*

TRIMBLE, Harold G., Jr.——**B:** June 16, 1926, Oakland, CA, *Owner*, Harold G. Trimble & Associates; **PRIM RE ACT:** Consultant, Broker, Appraiser, Owner/Investor, Instructor; **SERVICES:** Most actively in consulting prop. and subjects marked; **REP CLIENTS:** RE Trusts, devels.; **PREV EMPLOY:** Self - 1965, Duncan, Korb, & Trimble Inc., Toddy Investment Co.; **PROFL AFFIL & HONORS:** Amer. Soc. of RE Consultants - CRE, Inst. of RE Mgr. - (CPM), Realtors Nat. Mktg. Inst. (CCIM); **EDUC:** Menlo Coll.; **MIL SERV:** USNR, H.C. First Class; **HOME ADD:** 601 Mountain Dr., Piedmont, CA 94611, (415)547-0717; **BUS ADD:** 115 Sansome St., Ste. 1200, San Francisco, CA 94104, (415)986-8989.

TRIMMER, J. Kevin——**B:** Nov. 4, 1952, Highland Park, MI, *Assoc.*, Miller, Canfield, Paddock and Stone; **PRIM RE ACT:** Attorney; **PREV EMPLOY:** Wilson & McIlvaine, Chicago, IL, 1977-1979; **PROFL AFFIL & HONORS:** ABA; MI Bar Assn.; Oakland Cty. Bar Assn.; IL Bar Assn.; **EDUC:** BBA, with honors, 1974, Univ. of MI, School of Bus. Admin.; **GRAD EDUC:** JD, 1977, Univ. of IL, Coll. of Law; **EDUC HONORS:** Magna Cum Laude; Order of the Coif; **HOME ADD:** 475 Pilgrim, Birmingham, MI 48009, (313)646-6908; **BUS ADD:** Wabeck Bldg., Birmingham, MI 48012, (313)645-5000.

TRINCAKE, Joseph——*Ed.*, NJ Assn. of Realtors, New Jersey Realtor; **PRIM RE ACT:** Real Estate Publisher; **BUS ADD:** 295 Pierson Ave., Box 2098, Edison, NJ 08817, (201)494-5616.*

TRINKLE, James Lewis——**B:** Apr. 2, 1929, Roanoke, VA, *Pres.*, C.W. Francis & Son, Inc.; **PRIM RE ACT:** Broker, Consultant, Attorney, Owner/Investor, Property Manager, Syndicator; **SERVICES:** Resid., comml. & indus. sales; prop. mgmt. of leasing; **REP CLIENTS:** Gen. Electric, Burroughs Corp., Shenandoah Life Ins. Co.; Appalachian Power Co.; C & P Telephone; RKE Memorial Hospital; First Nat. Exch. Bank; People Fed. S & L; Col-Amer. Nat. Bank; **PREV EMPLOY:** Atty., Woodrum, Staples & Gregory; **PROFL AFFIL & HONORS:** RKE Valley Bd. of Realtors; VA Assn. of Realtors; NAR; RKE VA & Amer. Bar Assns., Who's Who, South & Southwest; Who's Who in the World; Jr. C of C; DSA; Outstanding Young Men of America; **EDUC:** BA, 1950, Hampden-Sydney Coll.; **GRAD EDUC:** BL, 1953, Univ. of VA; **EDUC HONORS:** Pres. of Class, Pres. of Frat.; ODK Who's Who Amer. Coll. & Univs., Capt. Tennis Team, Pres. of Legal & Social Frat.; Student Activities Comm.; **OTHER ACT & HONORS:** Pres., YMCA; Pres. & Campaign Chmn., United Fund; Pres., RKE Fine Arts Ctr.; Pres., Downtown RKE, Inc.; Tr., Hampden-Sydney Coll.; Pres., Hampden-Sydney & Univ. of VA Nat. Alumni Assns.; RKE Civic Ctr. Comm; RKE Charter Study Commn.; Chmn. of the Bd. of Dir., People Fed. S & L; Bd. of Dir., Colonial Amer. Nat'l. Bank; **HOME ADD:** 5270 Flintlock Road, S.W., Roanoke, VA 24014, (703)989-3611; **BUS ADD:** 120 West Kirk Ave., Roanoke, VA 24011, (703)342-3161.

TRIPLETT, Ira C., Jr.——**B:** Apr. 3, 1916, Charlotte, NC, *Pres.*, Triplett Realty Co. Inc.; **PRIM RE ACT:** Broker, Consultant, Appraiser, Owner/Investor, Property Manager; **SERVICES:** Sales of homes, bldgs, land, indus., comml.; **REP CLIENTS:** All major banks in NC; **PROFL AFFIL & HONORS:** Pres., Lenoir-Caldwell Cty. Bd. of Realtors; NAREA; SMI, Dir., NC Assn. of Realtors; **EDUC:** BS, 1939, NC State Univ.; **OTHER ACT & HONORS:** Boss of Yr., 1981; Lions Club; **HOME ADD:** 211 Rectory Hill Place, SW, Lenoir, NC, (704)754-6024; **BUS ADD:** POB 738, Lenoir, NC 28645, (704)754-6442.

TRIPP, Robert V.——**B:** July 10, 1931, Boston, MA, *Mgr.*, Kierman Realty Co.; **PRIM RE ACT:** Broker; **PROFL AFFIL & HONORS:** MA Assoc. of Realtors, Gr. Brockton Bd. of Realtors, NAR, RNMI, CRB; **MIL SERV:** USN, AN; **OTHER ACT & HONORS:** DAV, ICOC, BPOE, Rotary, United Way, Past Town Meeting Member, Town of Randolph, Past Pres. Jaycees, Past Adjutant DAV of Randolph, and Cmdr.; **HOME ADD:** 16 Bayberry Ln., Randolph, MA 02368, (617)963-6988; **BUS ADD:** 1102 N. Main St., Randolph, MA 02368, (617)963-3330.

TRIPP, Russell W.——**B:** Feb. 9, 1927, Albany, OR, *Partner*, Tripp & Tripp; **PRIM RE ACT:** Broker, Banker; **SERVICES:** Gen.; **EDUC:** BA, 1950, Poli. Sci., Willamette Univ.; **GRAD EDUC:** MA, 1953, Poli. Sci., Stanford Univ.; **EDUC HONORS:** Rotary Fellow; Univ. of New Zealand, 1950-1951; **MIL SERV:** US Army; **OTHER ACT & HONORS:** Mayor of Albany, 3 terms; **HOME ADD:** 1320 Lakewood Dr., Albany, OR 97321, (503)926-3230; **BUS ADD:** 202 W. 2nd Ave., Box 747, Albany, OR 97321, (503)926-1521.

TRITTER, David M.——**B:** Apr. 15, 1952, Minneapolis, MN, *Atty.*, Shakks & Butler; **PRIM RE ACT:** Consultant, Attorney; **SERVICES:** Document prep. & legal counseling; **REP CLIENTS:** Lenders, title cos. & indivs.; **PROFL AFFIL & HONORS:** ABA; TX Bar Assn.; Houston Bar Assn.; Houston Young Lawyers Assn.; TX Mort. Bankers Assn.; **EDUC:** BA, 1975, Univ. of TX; **GRAD EDUC:** 1979, S. TX Coll. of Law; **EDUC HONORS:** Liberal Arts, Law; **HOME ADD:** 12839 Briarwest Cir., Houston, TX 77077; **BUS ADD:** 5373 West Alabama, Ste. 505, Houston, TX 77056, (713)965-9999.

TROGDON, Jack D.——**B:** Oct. 28, 1930, Randolph Cty., NC, *Owner*, Jack D. Trogdon Builder; **PRIM RE ACT:** Builder; **SERVICES:** Constructing Homes; **PROFL AFFIL & HONORS:** NC Home Builders Assn.; **GRAD EDUC:** Bus., 1955, Acctg. & Gen. Bus., Asheboro Comml. Coll.; **MIL SERV:** US Army, Cpl., Korean Serv. & Good Conduct; **HOME ADD:** Rte. #6, Box 159, Asheboro, NC 27203, (919)629-3663; **BUS ADD:** Rte. #6, PO Box 159, Asheboro, NC 27203, (919)629-3663.

TROLLE, T.N.——**B:** Dec. 17, 1928, Evanston, IL, *VP, RE Div.*, Xerox Corp.; **PRIM RE ACT:** Consultant, Developer, Property Manager, Engineer, Owner/Investor; **OTHER RE ACT:** All above for internal Xerox requirements; **SERVICES:** All RE, prop. devel., and prop. mgmt. serv.; **REP CLIENTS:** All Xerox units; **PROFL AFFIL & HONORS:** ULI; **EDUC:** AB, 1951, Bus. Admin., Dartmouth Coll.; **GRAD EDUC:** MBA, 1955, Amos Tuck School of Bus. Admin.; **EDUC HONORS:** Cum Laude; **MIL SERV:** USAF; 1st Lt.; **OTHER ACT & HONORS:** Dir., Stamford Econ. Assistance Corp.; **BUS ADD:** Stamford, CT 06904, (203)329-8700.

TROSSMAN, Don C.——**B:** Sept. 14, 1946, Chicago, IL, *Sr. VP & Dir.*, The Philipsborn Co.; **PRIM RE ACT:** Broker, Consultant; **OTHER RE ACT:** Mort. Banker; **SERVICES:** Fin., sales, consulting, appraising; **PREV EMPLOY:** Banco Mort. Co., VP & Rgnl. Mgr., Chicago; **PROFL AFFIL & HONORS:** NAIOP; ICSC; AIREB; JREB; Dir. of IL Mort. Bankers Assn.; **EDUC:** BS, 1968, Econ./Psych., Tulane Univ.; **GRAD EDUC:** MBA, 1971, Mktg./Fin., Loyola Univ., Chicago; **MIL SERV:** USAF Res., S/Sgt.; **OTHER ACT & HONORS:** Standard Club; Lake Shore Ctry. Club; **HOME ADD:** 871 Bell Ln., Winnetka, IL 60093, (312)446-4545; **BUS ADD:** 115 S. LaSalle St., 28th Floor, Chicago, IL 60603, (312)781-8800.

TROTTER, James N.——**B:** Sept. 22, 1904, Charlotte, NC, *Owner*, Morris & Trotter & Son; **PRIM RE ACT:** Consultant, Owner/Investor, Property Manager; **PREV EMPLOY:** Independence Trust Co. and Miller Motor Express, Charlotte, NC; **PROFL AFFIL & HONORS:** Charlotte Bd. of Realtors; Charlotte Prop. Mgmt. Assn.; IREM, Past Pres., Charlotte Bd. of Realtors and Charlotte Prop. Mgmt. Assn.; Past Pres. Charlotte Chap. Amer. Inst. of Banking; **GRAD EDUC:** BS, 1925, Commerce, Davidson Coll., Davidson NC; **EDUC HONORS:** D Club 4 yrs. in Tennis; **MIL SERV:** ROTC; Sgt.; **OTHER ACT & HONORS:** Chmn., Bd. of Deacons; Elder of Myers Park Presbyterian Church; Retired under our Rotary System; **HOME ADD:** 4000 Churchill Rd., Charlotte, NC 28211, (704)364-6823; **BUS ADD:** 129 Brevard Court, Charlotte, NC 28202.

TROUTMAN, C. Bruce——**B:** Nov. 5, 1947, Atlanta, GA, *CEO*, Royal Gulf Properties, Inc.; **PRIM RE ACT:** Broker, Consultant, Developer, Builder, Syndicator; **SERVICES:** RE planning, designing, devel.; **REP CLIENTS:** Indiv. & instnl. investors; **PREV EMPLOY:** VP, Esturary Props., Pres., S. Fort Myers Realty; **PROFL AFFIL &**

HONORS: NAR, Aircraft Owners & Pilots Assn.; **EDUC:** Indus. Mgmt., 1969, Math. & Computer Sci., GA Tech.; **MIL SERV:** USMC, Capt., Air Borne; **HOME ADD:** 7802 Willems Dr., Fort Myers, FL 33908, (813)332-3800; **BUS ADD:** 2701 Cleveland Ave., Fort Myers, FL 33901, (813)332-3800.

TROUTMAN, H.L.——*VP*, AVCO Community Developers; **PRIM RE ACT:** Developer; **BUS ADD:** 16770 West Bernardo Dr., San Deigo, CA 92127, (714)277-2132.*

TROWBRIDGE, Charles A.——**B:** Oct. 17, 1934, Mt. Vernon, IL, *Pres.*, The Trowbridge Agency, Inc.; **PRIM RE ACT:** Broker, Owner/Investor, Syndicator; **SERVICES:** Broker for comml. sales, securities broker, synd.; **PREV EMPLOY:** Lecturer, Author; **PROFL AFFIL & HONORS:** Nat. Assn. of Realtors; RE Securities and Synd. Inst.; Comm. Inv. Div. of the Realtors Nat. Mktg. Inst.; CO Assn. of Realtors; Denver Bd. of Realtors; Member, CLS; Denver RE Exchangors, CCIM; GRI; SRS; Member of Advisory Comm. of Denver Univ. Coll. of Bus.; Member of Publishing Comm., Realtors Nat. Mktg. Inst.; **HOME ADD:** 790 E. Belleview, Littleton, CO 80121; **BUS ADD:** 3250 One Denver Pl., 999 Eighteenth St., Denver, CO 80202, (303)534-7640.

TROWBRIDGE, Keith W.——**B:** Mar. 6, 1937, *Chmn. of Bd.*, Captran Resorts Intl.; **PRIM RE ACT:** Developer; **PROFL AFFIL & HONORS:** ALDA BOD.; **EDUC:** BA, 1961, Bus. Admin., Bowling Green State Univ.; **GRAD EDUC:** PHD, 1971, Mgmt & Fin. of higher educ., Univ. MI; **EDUC HONORS:** Outstanding all-around male student, Pres. student body; **HOME ADD:** 1036 Bayview Dr., Sanibel, FL 33957; **BUS ADD:** PO Box 06100, Ft. Myers, FL 33906, (813)472-6400.

TROWER, Michael H.——**B:** Oct. 12, 1937, Palo Pinto, TX, *VP, Dir.*, Graham Development Services, Inc.; **PRIM RE ACT:** Architect, Developer; **SERVICES:** Devel. Packaging and Mgmt.; **PREV EMPLOY:** John Graham and Co., Architects/Engrs.; **PROFL AFFIL & HONORS:** AIA, ULI; **EDUC:** BArch, BArch Engrg., 1961, Architecture and Arch. Engrg., OK State Univ.; **GRAD EDUC:** Program for Mgmt. Devel., 1971, Bus. Mgmt., Harvard Grad. School of Bus.; **EDUC HONORS:** Phi Eta Sigma; **OTHER ACT & HONORS:** Washington Athletic Club, Rainer Club; **HOME ADD:** 2077 E. Howe, Seattle, WA 98101, (206)322-6920; **BUS ADD:** 1110 Third Ave., Seattle, WA 98101.

TROY, Matthew M.——**B:** July 31, 1938, Dublin, Ireland, *Pres.*, Troy, Inc., Realtors; **PRIM RE ACT:** Broker, Consultant, Appraiser, Property Manager, Owner/Investor; **SERVICES:** Realtor, appraiser, consultant, sales, mgmt.; **PROFL AFFIL & HONORS:** RNMI; SREA; MI IN Assn. of Realtors; NAR, GRI; CRS; CRB; Realtor of the Yr; **EDUC:** IN Univ.; **MIL SERV:** USMC, Cpl.; **OTHER ACT & HONORS:** Michigan City C of C; IN RE Appraisers Assn.; **HOME ADD:** 7197 W. 125 N., La Porte, IN 46350, (219)362-6643; **BUS ADD:** 8515 W. US Hwy. 20,, Michigan City, IN 46360, (219)872-9446.

TROYAN, Ronald——**B:** Sept. 9, 1930, San Francisco, CA, *Gen. Partner*, Capitola Knolls Investors; **PRIM RE ACT:** Developer, Owner/Investor, Syndicator; **SERVICES:** Investment in RE; **REP CLIENTS:** Profl., medical, engr., bus. exec.; **PREV EMPLOY:** Prop. Mgr., San Francisco Redevel. Office; **PROFL AFFIL & HONORS:** San Jose RE Bd., Natl. RE Bd., GRI; **EDUC:** 1952, Bus. Admin., Univ. of Santa Clara; **MIL SERV:** USN, Lt., China Serv. & Korean SIC; **HOME ADD:** 6569 Little Falls Dr., San Jose, CA 95120; **BUS ADD:** 15879 Los Gatos Blvd., Los Gatos, CA 95030, (408)358-1851.

TRUB, Aaron D.——*Treas. & Secy.*, Smithfield Packing Co.; **PRIM RE ACT:** Property Manager; **BUS ADD:** PO Box 447, Smithfield, VA 23430, (804)357-4321.*

TRUCKSESS, James M., Jr.——**B:** Nov. 29, 1931, Philadelphia, PA, *Ex. VP*, Merrill Lynch Hubbard Inc.; **PRIM RE ACT:** Property Manager, Lender, Owner/Investor; **SERVICES:** RE investment selection and monitoring; **REP CLIENTS:** Pension funds, overseas inst. and individuals; **PREV EMPLOY:** Teachers Ins. & Annuity Assn., 1962-1965; Equitable Life Assurance Soc., 1955-1962; Citibank 1975-82; **PROFL AFFIL & HONORS:** ULI; ICSC; NY RE Bd.; Mort. Bankers Assn.; **EDUC:** BS, 1953, RE/Ins., Temple Univ.; **GRAD EDUC:** 1959, RE/Econ., NYU; **MIL SERV:** USMC, Sgt.; **BUS ADD:** Two Broadway, New York, NY 10004, (212)908-8590.

TRUELSEN, Tony I.——**B:** Mar. 5, 1939, Honolulu, HI, *Prin. Consultant*, T.I. Truelsen Assoc., Location & Mkt. Planning; **OTHER RE ACT:** Site location/mkt. research and analysis, research sers. in retail and comml. site location analysis with a special emphasis on food/drug combination store location research; **REP CLIENTS:** Corp. RE Mgmt., shopping center devels., comml. lending instn. and retail mktg. and merchandising execs.; **PREV EMPLOY:** Albertson's, Inc.; Safeway Stores, Inc.; **PROFL AFFIL & HONORS:** NACORE; Assn. of Amer. Geographers; ULI; Assn. of Pac. Coast Geographers; Amer. Mktg. Assn.; **EDUC:** BS, 1963, RE, Geography, Univ. of OR; **GRAD EDUC:** MA Candidate, 1968, Urban and Mktg. Geography, Univ. of OR, Grad. School; **HOME ADD:** 324 Bitterroot Dr., Boise, ID 83709; **BUS ADD:** PO Box 8351, Boise, ID 83707, (208)376-9024.

TRUITT, Gerald B., Jr.——**B:** July 20, 1927, Philadelphia, PA, *VP*, Equitable Trust Co., RE Fin.; **PRIM RE ACT:** Appraiser, Banker; **SERVICES:** Appraisal, Underwriting; **PREV EMPLOY:** MD Natl. Bank-15 yrs.; Farm Credit Banks; **PROFL AFFIL & HONORS:** AIREA, Coastal Bd. Realtors, Assn. of Agricultural Bankers, Member FLI; **EDUC:** BS, 1950, Agricultural Econ., The PA State Univ.; **MIL SERV:** US Army Medical, T/S; **OTHER ACT & HONORS:** Rotary Club, Vestry-St. Peter's Episcopal Church, Masons, Shrine; **HOME ADD:** 315 Brewington Dr., Salisbury, MD 21801, (301)742-1176; **BUS ADD:** PO Box 469, Salisbury, MD 21801, (301)742-5145.

TRUPP, Hans F., CCIM——**B:** Oct. 24, 1939, New York, NY, *Pres.*, Trupp-McGinty Realtors & Insurers; **PRIM RE ACT:** Broker, Consultant, Developer, Owner/Investor, Insuror, Syndicator; **SERVICES:** Investment counseling, brokerage, devel. & synd. of comml. prop.; **PROFL AFFIL & HONORS:** CCIM; **EDUC:** BS, 1962, Indus. Mgmt., Clemson Univ.; **MIL SERV:** USN; Lt. Comdr.; DFC, Air Medals (11), Navy Commendation Medal (2), Navy Achievement Medal; **HOME ADD:** PO Box 1, St. Simons Is., GA 31522, (912)638-8700; **BUS ADD:** PO Box 1, St. Simons, GA 31522, (912)638-8600.

TRUSSELL, Philip A.——**B:** Apr. 23, 1934, Boston, MA, *RE Officer*, MIT; **PRIM RE ACT:** Developer, Owner/Investor, Property Manager; **SERVICES:** Mgmt. & devel. of resid., comml. & indus. props. for MIT's investment portfolio; **PREV EMPLOY:** Cabot, Cabor & Forbes Co., Asst. VP 1965-77; **PROFL AFFIL & HONORS:** Reg.: Prof. engr., comm. of MA, Reg. RE Broker; **EDUC:** AB, 1956, Math., Physics, Bowdoin; BS, 1956, Bldg. Engr. & Const., MIT; **GRAD EDUC:** MCE, 1966, Civil engr., Northeastern Univ.; **MIL SERV:** US Army, Capt.; **OTHER ACT & HONORS:** Needham Town Meeting Member 1974-81; Chi Epsilon, Hon. Civil Engr. Soc.; **HOME ADD:** 841 Webster St., Needham, MA 02194, (617)449-0909; **BUS ADD:** 77 Mass. Ave., Cambridge, MA 02139, (617)253-4304.

TRUTANICH, John Peter——**B:** June 7, 1936, San Pedro, CA, *Pres.*, John P. Trutanich & Associates Inc.; **PRIM RE ACT:** Broker, Consultant, Developer, Owner/Investor, Builder; **SERVICES:** Investment counseling, synd. and devel.; **REP CLIENTS:** Investors; **PROFL AFFIL & HONORS:** CCIM, GRI; **MIL SERV:** US Army, Cpl.; **HOME ADD:** 4332 Via Frascati, Rancho Palos Verdes, CA 90732, (213)519-8519; **BUS ADD:** 801 W. 9th St., San Pedro, CA 90731, (213)519-7730.

TSAGRIS, B.E.——**B:** Dec. 17, 1921, Boston, MA, *Prof. of Fin. & RE*, CA State Univ., Fullerton, Dept. of Fin.; **PRIM RE ACT:** Broker, Consultant, Appraiser, Instructor, Syndicator; **OTHER RE ACT:** Author, RE textbooks; **SERVICES:** RE research consultant, personal fin. planning, fin. feasibility, appraisal & review appraisal, investment analysis, conduct public seminars; **REP CLIENTS:** Lenders, indiv. & inst. investors, devel., publishers, consultant to Bd. of Regents; **PREV EMPLOY:** Prof., Univ. of CO, Boulder, 1966-1968; AZ State Univ., Tempe, 1965-1966; Sacramento State Univ., 1959-1965; VP, S&L, 1956-1959; **PROFL AFFIL & HONORS:** Nat. Assn. of Review Appraisers; Nat. Assn. of Corporate RE Exec.; Assn. of Corp. RE - LA; Rho Epsilon Nat. Profl. RE Fraternity; RE Educators Assn.; Bd. of Govs., Intl. Inst. for RE Studies, PhD; CRA; **EDUC:** 1947, Bus. Admin./Mktg., Univ. of CA, Berkeley; **GRAD EDUC:** MS, 1957, Univ. of So. CA, School of Bus.; PhD, 1964, Econ., Univ. of So. CA, School of Letters & Science; **MIL SERV:** U.S. Army, Infantry, Pfc., 1943-1945, European Theatre, Combat Infantryman; **OTHER ACT & HONORS:** Ford Found., Faculty Fellow, Univ. of Washington; Past Pres., Rho Epsilon, Natl. Prof. RE Frat.; Member, Lambda Alpha, Intl. Honorary Land Econ. Frat.; Distinguished Prof., Visiting Chair in RE, Univ. of HI at Manoa; Visting Prof., Univ. of TX, Arlington; Visting Prof., Univ. of WA, Seattle; Visiting Prof., Univ. of CT, Storrs; **HOME ADD:** 6225 Peppertree Ln., Yorba Linda, CA 92686, (714)779-0607; **BUS ADD:** Fullerton, CA 92634, (714)773-3953.

TSCHAPPAT, Carl J.——**B:** Sept. 11, 1939, Newark, OH, *Pres.*, L.D.A., Inc.; **PRIM RE ACT:** Consultant, Appraiser, Instructor; **SERVICES:** Appraisal, marketability & feasibility studies; **REP CLIENTS:** Banks, S&L, mort. cos.; **PREV EMPLOY:** Prof., GA State Univ., 1966-1973; Visiting Prof., GA Inst. of Tech., 1975 to present; **PROFL AFFIL & HONORS:** Soc. of RE Appraisers; AICP; Atlanta Bd. of Realtors, PhD; SREA; AICP; **EDUC:** BS, 1961, Mktg., The OH State Univ.; **GRAD EDUC:** MBA, 1962, RE/Fin., The OH State

Univ.; PhD, 1966, RE/Fin., The OH State Univ.; **OTHER ACT & HONORS:** Elder, Peachtree Presbyterian Church, Atlanta, GA; **HOME ADD:** 4602 Tall Pines Dr., N.W., Atlanta, GA 30327, (404)255-5609; **BUS ADD:** 180 Allen Rd., N.E., Suite 310 N., Atlanta, GA 30328, (404)256-0690.

TSCHIDA, Roger——B: Aug. 17, 1949, Grey Eagle, MN, *Prop. Rep.*, CENEX; **PRIM RE ACT:** Appraiser, Property Manager, Owner/Investor; **OTHER RE ACT:** Negotiate leases, supervise prop. tax appeals, site selection; **PREV EMPLOY:** Asst. Cty. Assessor, Independent Fee Appraiser; **PROFL AFFIL & HONORS:** NARA, IAAO; **EDUC:** BA, 1971, Pol. Sci., Univ. of MN; **GRAD EDUC:** MA, 1973, Indus. Relations and Bus. Mgmt., Univ. of MN; **OTHER ACT & HONORS:** Jaycees (Chap. Sec. and Pres.), Boy Scouts of Amer. (Adult Counselor); **HOME ADD:** 1883 Audrey Dr., West St. Paul, MN 55118; **BUS ADD:** PO Box 43089, St. Paul, MN 55164, (612)451-5254.

TSCHUDIN, Robert C.——B: Dec. 31, 1917, Philadelphia, PA, *Proprietor*, Robert Tschudin - Realtor; **PRIM RE ACT:** Broker, Consultant; **OTHER RE ACT:** Brokerage and Consultation Serv. - Comml., Indus. and Devel. Prop.; **PROFL AFFIL & HONORS:** San Juan Bd. of Realtors, Inc.; **EDUC:** AB, 1948, Engr., Harvard Coll.; **OTHER ACT & HONORS:** San Juan Rotary Club; **HOME ADD:** 6 Inga St., Santurce, PR 00913, (809)726-9466; **BUS ADD:** 8 Inga St., Santurce, PR 00913, (809)726-4100.

TUAKE, Robert D.——*Treasurer*, Baldor Electric Co.; **PRIM RE ACT:** Property Manager; **BUS ADD:** PO 2400, Fort Smith, AR 72902, (501)646-4711.*

TUBBS, William R.——B: Apr. 8, 1914, PA, *Pres.*, Thorin Co.; **PRIM RE ACT:** Developer, Builder, Owner/Investor; **PREV EMPLOY:** Mgmt. Atl. Richfield Co., 30 years; **EDUC:** BA, 1936, Econ., Bus. Admin., Univ. of FL; **GRAD EDUC:** MS, 1940, Indus. Psych., Org. & Mgmt., PA State Univ.; **MIL SERV:** US Naval Res., Comdr., Navy Commendation Medal; **OTHER ACT & HONORS:** Merion Golf Club, Westmoreland Club of Wilkes-Barre, PA; Military Order of For. Wars, Athenaeum of Philadelphia; **HOME ADD:** Wynnewood, PA 19096; **BUS ADD:** PO Box 76, Thorndale, PA 19372, (215)383-4411.

TUBIN, Allan——B: Aug. 15, 1938, NY, *VP - Fin.*, Donaldson, Lufkin & Jenrette, Inc., DLJ RE, Inc.; **PRIM RE ACT:** Broker, Syndicator, Developer, Builder, Property Manager, Banker, Owner/Investor; **OTHER RE ACT:** RE Investment Banking; **SERVICES:** Acquisition & Sales of Comml. and Resid. Props., Resid. Devel. and Bldg., Land Devel.; Synd. of Comml. Props.; Prop. Mgmt.; Sales & Lease Backs; Fin. Corps., Pension Plans; Indiv. Investors (Domestic & Foreign); Instnl. Investors; Devels.; **PREV EMPLOY:** Ernst & Whinny; **PROFL AFFIL & HONORS:** CPA, RE Broker; **EDUC:** BBA, 1962, Acctg./Econ., Pace Univ.; **HOME ADD:** 142 Windsor Rd., Tenafly, NJ 07670, (201)568-2369; **BUS ADD:** 140 Broadway, NY, NY 10005, (212)747-9739.

TUBOLINO, A. Tony——B: Sept. 12, 1930, Brooklyn, NY, *Realtor*, Tubolino Realty; **PRIM RE ACT:** Broker, Consultant, Developer, Builder, Instructor, Property Manager, Insuror, Syndicator; **SERVICES:** Consultant, managing prop.; **PROFL AFFIL & HONORS:** PIA, IREM, BIINS Agents, RESSI, CPM; **EDUC:** 1959, Bus. Admin.; **MIL SERV:** USN; **HOME ADD:** 13404 106 Ave., Largo, FL, (813)595-1279; **BUS ADD:** PO Box 5017, Largo, FL 33540, (813)581-3167.

TUCHMANN, Robert——B: July 7, 1946, NY, NY, *Part.*, Hale & Dorr; **PRIM RE ACT:** Attorney; **PROFL AFFIL & HONORS:** ABA; MA Bar Assn.; Boston Bar Assn.; Environmental Law Inst.; **EDUC:** AB, 1967, Amer. Hist., Oberlin Coll.; **GRAD EDUC:** JD, 1971, Harvard Law Sch.; **EDUC HONORS:** Magna Cum Laude; **MIL SERV:** Army & Coast Guard Res.; **HOME ADD:** 285 Mt. Vernon St., W. Newton, MA 02165, (617)965-2568; **BUS ADD:** 60 State St., Boston, MA 02109, (617)742-9100.

TUCKER, Billie Anne——B: Aug. 11, 1936, Anniston, AL, *Atty. at Law*; **PRIM RE ACT:** Attorney; **PROFL AFFIL & HONORS:** Chambers Cty. Bar Assn.; AL Bar Assn.; ABA; **EDUC:** BS, 1956, Bus. Admin., C & BA; **GRAD EDUC:** JD, 1959; **EDUC HONORS:** Morter Board, Alpha Lambda Delta, Tau Kappa Alpha, Farrah Order; **OTHER ACT & HONORS:** Bd. of Dir. Chambers Acad.; Chattachoochee Valley Retarded Citizens; East Al-Mental Health Assn.; **HOME ADD:** Lafayette, AL 36862, (205)864-8362; **BUS ADD:** 213 Ave. A SE, Lafayette, AL 36862.

TUCKER, Edward B.——B: Sept. 18, 1939, Decatur, IL, *Pres.*, Two Rivers Farms, Inc.; **PRIM RE ACT:** Broker, Attorney, Syndicator, Consultant, Developer, Engineer; **SERVICES:** Farm mgmt. and synd., synd. farm land projects, over 6500 acres, assets in excess of -9,00O,000; **PREV EMPLOY:** Is now a part. in the law firm of Tucker & Hollahan; **PROFL AFFIL & HONORS:** RESSI, Various legal org.; **EDUC:** Engr., So. IL Univ.; **GRAD EDUC:** MS, Mech. Engr., LLB, 1965, Univ. of IL; **MIL SERV:** USMC, Capt.; **OTHER ACT & HONORS:** Pub. articles in Prentice Hall Tax Ideas & R.E. perspectives; **HOME ADD:** RR 1, Versailles, IL 62378, (217)225-3258; **BUS ADD:** 116 S. Capitol, Mt. Sterling, IL 62353, (217)773-3622.

TUCKER, Everett, Jr.——B: July 7, 1912, Tucker, AR, *Pres.*, Indus. Devel. Co. of Little Rock; **PRIM RE ACT:** Developer; **SERVICES:** Fully devel. indus. sites, indus. park devel.; **REP CLIENTS:** Allis Chalmers, CMF, Armstrong Rubber, Campbell Taggart, Ceco, Champion Paper, Fruehauf, Levi Strauss, Orbit Valve, A.O. Smith, Teletype, Timex; **PREV EMPLOY:** Mgr., Indus. Div., Little Rock C of C, 1949-1958; **PROFL AFFIL & HONORS:** Amer. (and So.) Indus. Devel. Councils; Past Pres. of each, CID; HLM of AIDC & SIDC; **EDUC:** BS, 1934, Banking/Econ., Washington and Lee Univ./Harvard Bus. School/Univ. of New Mexico Law School; **GRAD EDUC:** Statistical Analysis, Harvard (US Army Air Corps, 1942-1943); **EDUC HONORS:** Designated a Distinguished Alumnus by Washington and Lee Univ. in 1979; **MIL SERV:** USAF, Maj. (Retd.), AF Commendation; **OTHER ACT & HONORS:** Member, 1958-1965; Pres., 1959-1963, Little Rock School Bd.; Dir., AR Nat. Stockyards; Comml. Nat. Bank; Chmn., Salvation Army Bd.; Commonwealth Federal S&L; Member of Vestry Trinity Episcopal Cathedral; Managing Partner, S.E. Tucker Plantation; Pres., Baptist Hosp. Found.; **HOME ADD:** 4601 Kavanaugh Blvd., Little Rock, AR 72207, (501)666-2670; **BUS ADD:** 1780 Tower Bldg., Little Rock, AR 72201, (501)375-3219.

TUCKER, Jeffrey A.——B: May 25, 1947, Cleveland, OH, *Sec. and Gen. Counsel*, Weingarten Realty, Inc.; **PRIM RE ACT:** Attorney; **PREV EMPLOY:** Forest City Enterprises, Inc., Cleveland, OH, Staff Atty.; **PROFL AFFIL & HONORS:** TX Bar Assn., OH Bar Assn.; **EDUC:** BBA, 1969, Fin., Univ. of WI; **GRAD EDUC:** JD, 1972, Law, Univ. of MI Law School; **HOME ADD:** 7715 Braes Meadow, Houston, TX 77071, (713)988-7715; **BUS ADD:** PO Box 94133, Houston, TX 77292, (713)868-6361.

TUCKER, Jimmie Earl——B: Feb. 9, 1954, Memphis, TN, *Designer/Productionist*, J. G. Randle and Assoc.; **PRIM RE ACT:** Architect, Consultant, Owner/Investor; **SERVICES:** Devel. feasibility analysis architecture and planning serv., construction mgmt. indiv. and instl. investments in residential and comml. props.; **PREV EMPLOY:** Fleming Corp., architects and planners, Franklin Assoc., architects and planners; **PROFL AFFIL & HONORS:** AIA, Natl. Org. of Minority architects, construction specification Inst.; **EDUC:** BA, 1977, Archit. and Urban planning, Princeton Univ; **GRAD EDUC:** MArch, 1981, Architecture, Washington Univ.; **EDUC HONORS:** Class scholarship recipient, Tuition remission scholarship recipient; **OTHER ACT & HONORS:** Jaycees, Urban League; **HOME ADD:** 7403 Elm Ave., Maplewood, MO 63143, (314)645-1663; **BUS ADD:** 625 N. Euclid St., St. Louis, MO 63143, (314)361-4211.

TUCKER, Stefan F.——B: Dec. 31 1938, Detroit, MI, *Shareholder*, Tucker, Flyer, Sanger, Reider & Lewis, PC; **PRIM RE ACT:** Attorney; **SERVICES:** Legal; **PREV EMPLOY:** Partner Arent, Fox, Kintner, Plotkin & Kahn; **PROFL AFFIL & HONORS:** ABA, sect. of tax. and real prop., DC Bar Assn., Fed. Bar Assn., Amer. Law Inst., Amer. Coll. of RE Lawyers; **EDUC:** BBA, 1960, Bus. Admin., Univ. of MI School of Bus. Admin.; **GRAD EDUC:** JD, 1963, Univ. of MI Law School; **EDUC HONORS:** Order of the Coif, MI Law Review; **HOME ADD:** 12208 Devilwood Dr., Potomac, MD 20854, (301)340-1411; **BUS ADD:** 1730 Mass. Ave. NW, Wash., DC 20036, (202)452-8600.

TUCKER, Thomas A.——*VP, Head of Appraisal Support*, Bank of America, Appraisal Dept.; **PRIM RE ACT:** Appraiser; **SERVICES:** In house appraisal serv.; **BUS ADD:** 1777 N. CA Blvd., Ste. 200, Walnut Creek, CA 94596, (415)944-2855.

TUCKER, Thomas J.——B: Sept. 5, 1929, Atlanta, GA, *Pres.*, AmSouth Financial Corp.; **PRIM RE ACT:** Lender; **SERVICES:** First and second morts. secured by resid. & comml. prop.; **PREV EMPLOY:** CIT Corp.; **PROFL AFFIL & HONORS:** Amer. Assn. of Equipment Lessors (State Keyman), Nat. Comml. Fin. Conf. (Dir. 1979-present), Nat. Second Mort. Assn.; **EDUC:** BA, 1952, Econ., Univ. of the South, Sewanee, TN; **MIL SERV:** USAF, 1/Lt.; **OTHER ACT & HONORS:** The Club and the Relay House Club, Birmingham, AL; Birmingham Canoe Club (Pres. '79, Dir. '80-present); Amer. Endurance Riders Conf.; TN Scenic Rivers Assn.; Racking Horse Breeders Assn.; Racking Horse Futurity Breeders Assn.; TN Walking Horse Breeders Assn.; AL Trail Riders Assn.; Partner: Green Pine Farms.; **HOME ADD:** Rt.#1 Box 57B, Maylene, AL 35114; **BUS ADD:** PO Box 2545, Birmingham, AL 35202, (205)326-5780.

TUCKMAN, Robert——*Sec./Treas.*, Schacker Real Estate Corp.; **PRIM RE ACT:** Broker, Builder, Owner/Investor, Instructor, Property Manager, Syndicator; **EDUC:** AAS, 1958, Advtg., NYC Community Coll.; **OTHER ACT & HONORS:** ICSC; **BUS ADD:** 401 Broad Hollow Rd., Melville, NY 11747, (516)293-3700.

TUDOR, Graham——**B:** Mar. 27, 1931, Melbourne, Australia, *Managing Partner*, McCarter, Nairne Architects (MNA); **PRIM RE ACT:** Architect; **SERVICES:** Full architectural & planning design services; **REP CLIENTS:** Cadillac Fairview, Narod Development Eatons, Municipal, Provincial & Federal Govts.; **PROFL AFFIL & HONORS:** AIBC, RAIC, BOMA, Winner of Prince George Cultural Centre Competition (1976); **EDUC:** BArch., 1953, Univ. of Melbourne; **HOME ADD:** 3283 Hoskins Rd., N. Vancouver, BC, Canada, (604)980-5167; **BUS ADD:** 1000 - 850 West Hastings St., Vancouver, V6C 1E3, BC, Canada, (604)685-0484.

TUDOR, Robert B. (Buddy), Jr.——**B:** May 18, 1935, Pineville, LA, *Pres.*, Tudor Construction Co.; **PRIM RE ACT:** Developer, Builder, Owner/Investor, Property Manager; **OTHER RE ACT:** Comml. and indus. contractor throughout the state of LA as well as others parts of the S. and SW of the US; **REP CLIENTS:** Shopping malls, high rise office bldgs., banks, churches, hospitals, apts., schools and various other indus. facilities; **PREV EMPLOY:** With Tudor Construction Co. since 1958; **PROFL AFFIL & HONORS:** Sigma Tau Alpha, Nat. CE Frat.; Tau Beta Pi, Nat. Engr. Frat.; Omicron Delta Kappa, Nat. Leadership and Scholastic Frat.; Sigma Chi, Nat. Soc. Frat., Outstanding Young Man of the Yr., Central LA, 1970; One of Three Outstanding Young Men of the Yr., State of LA, 1970; Assoc. Gen. Contractors, Central LA Chap., Pres., 1968-1969, 1969-1970; Assoc. Gen. Contractors, LA State Council, Bd. of Directors; LA Const. Indus. Legislative Council, Advisory Bd.; Hart Associates, Inc., Denver, CO (RE Devel), Bd. of Dir.; Savings Life Ins. Co., Shreveport, LA, Bd. of Dir.; First Bank, Pineville, LA, Chmn. of Bd.; **EDUC:** B.Engr., 1957, LA State Univ.; **OTHER ACT & HONORS:** Alexandria Aquatic Club, Bd. of Dirs.; Alexandria-Pineville C of C, Bd. of Dirs., Exec. Comm., Athletic Affairs Comm.; Alexandria Rotary Club, Pres., 1969-1970; Boy Scouts of Amer., Attakapas Council, Exec. Bd.; Central District Clearing House Review Bd.; Council of Music and Performing Arts, V.Chmn.; Handiwork Productions, Inc., Bd. of Dirs.; Hospital Serv. Dist. No. 3, Rapids Parish, LA, V.Chmn.; Indus. Devel. Bd., City of Pineville; Pineville City Planning Comm.; Pineville Recreation Planning Comm.; Rapides Area Planning Commn., Chmn., 1970-1974; YMCA, Bd. of Dirs.; Indus. Devel. Bd., Rapides Parish, LA, Bd. of Dirs.; LSU Found, LA State Univ.; Pres. of Tudor Enterprises Inc. , Bus. Address: PO Box 7917 Alexandria, LA 71306, tel; (318)445-3606; **BUS ADD:** 1412 Center Court Dr., Ste. 500, Alexandria, LA 71306.

TUNNELL, Norman D.——**B:** Mar. 21, 1942, Dallas, TX, *VP*, Bankers Trust Co.; **PRIM RE ACT:** Attorney, Banker, Owner/Investor; **PREV EMPLOY:** White & Case 1972-1974; Texas Instruments 1965-1969; **PROFL AFFIL & HONORS:** Young Mort. Bankers Assn.; NY Bldg. Congress; Amer. and NY State Bar Assns.; Urban Land Institute; **EDUC:** BA, 1963, Econ., Baylor Univ.; MBA, 1965, Fin., Wharton; [illegible] 1972, Columbia Univ.; **EDUC HONORS:** Deans List, Omicron [illegible] Epsilon, Honorary Econ. Soc.; **HOME ADD:** 59 Edgecliff Terr., Yonkers, NY 10705, (914)423-0236; **BUS ADD:** 280 Park Ave., NY, NY 10017, (212)850-3015.

TURCOTTE, Gilles——**B:** Feb. 27, 1931, East Angus, Quebec, *Engineer*, Hydro-Quebec; **PRIM RE ACT:** Engineer; **PROFL AFFIL & HONORS:** Ordre des Ingenieurs du Quebec; **EDUC:** Technician, 1952, Electricity, School Technice of Quebec; **GRAD EDUC:** Engineer, 1960, Electricity, Univ. Laval, Quebec; **HOME ADD:** 1990 Auvergne, Duvernay Laval, Can., (514)669-4347; **BUS ADD:** 75 Ouest Dorchester Blvd., Montreal, H2Z 1A4, Que., Can., (514)289-2862.

TURLEY, C.M., Jr.——**B:** May 3, 1928, St. Louis, MO, *VP*, Turley Martin Co.; **PRIM RE ACT:** Broker, Consultant, Appraiser, Property Manager; **SERVICES:** Comml. and indus. sales, leasing apprais. and mgmt.; **REP CLIENTS:** SWBT, May Dept. Stores, Gen. Amer. Life; **PROFL AFFIL & HONORS:** NAR, SIR, BOMA, CCIM, MO Realtor of the Yr., 1971, **EDUC:** BS, 1950, Civil Engr., Washington Univ.; **MIL SERV:** USAF, Staff Sgt.; **HOME ADD:** 4 Hillvale Dr., St. Louis, MO 63105, (314)727-0679; **BUS ADD:** Suite 2800, One Mercantile Ctr., St. Louis, MO 63101, (314)231-7100.

TURNBOW, Merrill C.——**B:** Apr. 28, 1941, Salt Lake City, UT, *Pres.*, Westam Corp.; **PRIM RE ACT:** Broker, Consultant, Developer, Builder, Owner/Investor, Property Manager; **PREV EMPLOY:** Exec. VP, Busch Corp., Chief Fin. Officer, Price Indus., CPA, Touche Ross & Co.; **PROFL AFFIL & HONORS:** ALCPA, UACPA, NAA; **EDUC:** BS, 1966, Acctg., BYU; **GRAD EDUC:** MA, 1967, Acctg., Taxation, Econ. & Bus. Mgt., BYU; **HOME ADD:** 5076 S. 2100 E., Salt Lake City, UT 84117, (801)277-0542; **BUS ADD:** 47 W. 200 S., Amer. Plaza III, Suite 600, Salt Lake City, UT 84101, (801)322-1034.

TURNBOW, Parley Daniel——**B:** Jan. 5, 1955, Salt Lake City, UT, *Property Manager*, Westam Corp.; **PRIM RE ACT:** Property Manager; **SERVICES:** Prop. mgmt., maintenance, leasing; **PREV EMPLOY:** Busch Mgmt.; **PROFL AFFIL & HONORS:** IREM; **EDUC:** BS, 1980, Fin., Univ. of VT; **EDUC HONORS:** Cum Laude; **HOME ADD:** 1035 East 5205 S., Salt Lake City, UT 84117, (801)261-1336; **BUS ADD:** Amer. Plaza III, 200 S. 47 West, Ste. 600, Salt Lake City, UT 84101, (801)322-1034.

TURNBULL, James F.——**B:** June 15, 1920, New Orleans, LA, *VP*, Gertrude Gardner, Inc.; **PRIM RE ACT:** Broker, Instructor, Consultant, Appraiser, Insuror; **SERVICES:** Counseling, appraising, mgmt., sales; **REP CLIENTS:** Lenders, owners, buyers, lawyers; **PREV EMPLOY:** James F. Turnbull, Realtor, 1936-63, Smither & Co. Ltd., 1963-65; **PROFL AFFIL & HONORS:** RE Bd. of No. Jefferson, RE Bd. LA Realtors Assn., NAR Chmn. Appraisal Div., RE Bd. of New Orleans, Prof. RE, Tulane Univ.; MAI; **EDUC:** BA, 1940, Eng. & Law, Tulane Univ.; **MIL SERV:** USN (Ret), LCDR; **OTHER ACT & HONORS:** Sec. Pandennis Club, Carnival Org., Bd. of Dirs., LA Realtors Assn., Pres., LA MS Chapter, AIREA; **HOME ADD:** 5532 S. Rochelave St., New Orleans, LA 70125, (504)861-2272; **BUS ADD:** 7934 Maple St., New Orleans, LA 70118, (504)861-9531.

TURNER, Curtis S.——**B:** Oct. 20, 1935, Honolulu, HI, *Gen. Partner*, Modesto Land Co.; **PRIM RE ACT:** Broker, Consultant, Engineer, Developer, Builder, Owner/Investor, Syndicator; **OTHER RE ACT:** General Partner, Modesto Oil Company & Modesto Drilling Company, OK; **SERVICES:** Joint Ventures; **PREV EMPLOY:** Realtor since 1957, HI & CA; **EDUC:** BS, 1957, Bus. Admin., Univ. of AZ; **OTHER ACT & HONORS:** Lions Club; SOS Club; YMCA; C of C; EAA; AOPA; **HOME ADD:** 1108 Potomac Way, Modesto, CA 95355, (209)577-4287; **BUS ADD:** 2909 Coffee Rd., Suite 2, Modesto, CA 95355, (209)524-5050.

TURNER, James E., Jr.——**B:** Oct. 31, 1942, Hattiesburg, MS, *Pres./Exec. VP*, J. Ed Turner Props., Inc. and J. Ed Turner Affiliated Cos.; **PRIM RE ACT:** Broker, Syndicator, Consultant, Appraiser, Developer, Builder, Property Manager, Lender, Owner/Investor, Insuror; **SERVICES:** Full service r.e.; **REP CLIENTS:** Fin. Instns., corp. clients include over 200 Fortune's Top 500 Co's., gov. agencies, major dev. entities, and numerous investors and prop. owners; **PROFL AFFIL & HONORS:** NAR; SIR; IREM; ASREC; ICSC; Nat. Apt. Assn., Prof. designations including CRE, CPM, SIR; Past Pres., Hattiesburg, MS Bd. of Realtors; Dir., of MS Realtors Assn.; Pres., Jackson and MS Apt. Assns.; Dir., Nat. Apt. Assn.; Pres. LA/MS/AL Chap. of SIR; VP, VS Chap. of IREM; Realtor of the Yr.; Million Dollar Round Table; Distinguished Salesman Award; **EDUC:** BS, 1965, RE/Urban Land Econ., Univ. of FL; **EDUC HONORS:** Soc. of RE and Urban Land Econ.; **MIL SERV:** US Army; **OTHER ACT & HONORS:** Newcomen Soc. of No. Amer.; Advisor to J. Ed. Turner; Chair of RE, Univ. of MS; U.S. Dept. of Commerce Delegate on Trade Missions to Japan, Taiwan, Hong Kong; Dir., MS-Taiwan Commn.; **HOME ADD:** 205 Greenwood Pl., Hattiesburg, MS 39401, (601)545-8605; **BUS ADD:** 226 N. President St., Jackson, MS 39205, (601)969-6667.

TURNER, Joe T., Jr.——**B:** June 21, 1937, St. Louis, MO, *VP, Sales Mgr.*, Thorpe Bros., Inc., Comm./Indus.; **PRIM RE ACT:** Broker; **SERVICES:** Sales, Leasing, appraisals, comml., indus., investment RE; **PREV EMPLOY:** Continental Can Co., Inc. 1963-74; **EDUC:** BS, 1960, Mktg., Univ. of MO; **MIL SERV:** USAF, Sgt.; **HOME ADD:** 3570 Deephaven Ave., Wayzata, MN 55391, (612)475-2095; **BUS ADD:** 8085 Wayzata Blvd., Minneapolis, MN 55426, (612)545-1111.

TURNER, John B., Jr.——*Land Mgmt.*, Exxon Corp.; **PRIM RE ACT:** Property Manager; **BUS ADD:** 4550 Dacoma, Houston, TX 77092, (713)847-4701.*

TURNER, Ronald L.——**B:** Sept. 6, 1941, Hendersonville, NC, *Pres.*, Turner & Assoc., Ltd., Midwest Comml. Props., Inc.; **PRIM RE ACT:** Developer, Owner/Investor; **SERVICES:** Primarily devel. for nat. multi-unit chain operators; **REP CLIENTS:** Children's World, Denver, CO; **PROFL AFFIL & HONORS:** AGC; **EDUC:** Bus. Admin., 1963, Econ. and Law, Univ. of TN; **GRAD EDUC:** LLB, 1966, Univ. of TN; **HOME ADD:** 733 Buncombe St., Hendersonville, NC 28739; **BUS ADD:** 1515 Haywood Rd., Hendersonville, NC 28793, (704)692-6180.

TURNER, Ronald M.——**B:** June 17, 1947, Seattle, WA, *Pres.*, Ron Turner Realty, Inc.; **PRIM RE ACT:** Broker, Syndicator, Consultant, Appraiser, Developer, Builder, Property Manager, Lender, Owner/Investor; **OTHER RE ACT:** Escrow; **SERVICES:** Investment counseling, synd. of comml. prop., prop. mgmt. appraisals, RE loans, escrow serv.; **PREV EMPLOY:** Active RE Broker Since 1967; **PROFL AFFIL & HONORS:** NAR, RESSI, CCIM; **OTHER ACT & HONORS:** Bd. member W. Seattle YMCA; **HOME ADD:** 4761 Beach Dr. SW, Seattle, WA 98116, (206)932-6739; **BUS ADD:** 4454 CA Ave. SW, Seattle, WA 98116, (206)938-1600.

TURPIN, John A.——B: Mar. 5, 1934, Niangua, MO, *Dist. Mgr.*, AT&T; **PRIM RE ACT:** Instructor, Consultant, Appraiser, Engineer; **OTHER RE ACT:** Corp.; **SERVICES:** Guidelines, Training, Econ. Planning, Problem Solving; **REP CLIENTS:** Bell System Operating Cos. & Subs.; **PROFL AFFIL & HONORS:** NACORE, SREA, NARA, ICSC; **EDUC:** BE, 1956, Civil Eng., Vanderbilt Univ.; **MIL SERV:** USN, 1956-60, Lt., Naval Aviator; **OTHER ACT & HONORS:** PE (State of TN); **HOME ADD:** 12 Van Dorn Rd., Basking Ridge, NJ 07920, (201)221-1216; **BUS ADD:** 222 Mt. Airy Rd., Basking Ridge, NJ 07920, (201)221-2977.

TURRENTINE, David W.——B: Sept. 21, 1943, Alexandria, LA, *Pres. & COB*, Standard Assoc. Mgmt. & Consultant Inc.; **PRIM RE ACT:** Broker, Developer, Builder, Property Manager; **EDUC:** BS, 1967, Mktg., N.E. LA Univ.; **EDUC HONORS:** Who's Who in Amer. Univ. & Coll.; **HOME ADD:** 3015 River Oaks Dr., Monroe, LA 71201, (318)388-4485; **BUS ADD:** PO Box 4086, Monroe, LA 71203, (318)387-2662.

TURSO, Joseph Paul, Esq.——B: Sept. 23, 1945, Philadelphia, PA, *VP*, Butcher & Singer, Inc., RE (Capital Investment Dept.); **PRIM RE ACT:** Attorney, Syndicator; **SERVICES:** Consultant, Seminars, Mktg. & Sec. Filings; **REP CLIENTS:** Lenders, Investors & Reg. Representatives in the Butcher & Singer Firm; **PREV EMPLOY:** Self-employed for several yrs.; **PROFL AFFIL & HONORS:** PA Bar Assn. & Phila. Bar Assn., RESSI, NYU School of Continuing Educ.; **EDUC:** BS, 1970, Acctg., St. Joseph's Univ., Phila., PA; **GRAD EDUC:** JD, 1975, Law, Delaware Law School-Widener Univ.; **EDUC HONORS:** Dean's List 3 yrs., Law Review 2 yrs.; **MIL SERV:** US Army, Capt.; **HOME ADD:** 222 Blythe Ave., Drexel Hill, PA 19026, (215)626-8033; **BUS ADD:** 211 S. Broad St., Philadelphia, PA 19107, (215)985-5117.

TURTLELAUB, Richard D.——B: Ocr. 17, 1926, Orange, NJ, *Pres.*, Affiliated Realty Services; **PRIM RE ACT:** Consultant, Appraiser; **SERVICES:** RE appraisal and consulting serv. involving all types of comml., ind., and apt. props. in 12 counties of NJ; **REP CLIENTS:** Attys., corps., and indivs.; **PROFL AFFIL & HONORS:** AIREA, NAR, Soc. of RE Appraisers, Sr. designation of the Amer. Soc. of Appraisers, Past Pres.-No.Jersey Chapt. ASA: 1972-1973, Past Dir.-Chapt. 37 SREA: 1971-1976, Dir.-Chapt.#1-AREA: 1977-; Past Co-Vice Chmn.-Elective Examination and member-Natl. Elective Examination Comm.-AIREA: 1975-1980, Member Natl. Bd. of Examiners-Experience-AIREA: 1981-; MAI; SRPA; **EDUC:** BA, Econ., Cornell Univ.; **MIL SERV:** USN, ETM 3C; **OTHER ACT & HONORS:** Past Chmn., Livingston, NJ Indus. Devel. Comm.; Panel of Arbitrators-Am. Arb. Assn.; **HOME ADD:** 42 Wynnewood Rd., Livingston, NJ 07039, (201)992-5964; **BUS ADD:** 205 Main St., PO Box 538, Chatham, NJ 07928, (201)635-2190.

TUTTLE, M. Slate, Jr.——B: May 13, 1950, Concord, NC, *Part., Atty.*, Williams, Willeford, Boger, Grady, Davis & Tuttle; **PRIM RE ACT:** Consultant, Attorney, Property Manager; **REP CLIENTS:** Lenders, devels., brokers, investors; **PROFL AFFIL & HONORS:** ABA, NC Bar Assn., NC State Bar, Real Prop. Sect., Member of ABA & NC Bar Assn., Juris Doctor of Laws; **EDUC:** BA, 1972, Hist., Pol. Sci., Wake Forest Univ.; **GRAD EDUC:** JD, 1975, RE & Probate, Wake Forest Univ. Sch. of Law; **EDUC HONORS:** Dean;s List 1971, 1972, Contracts Book Award, Law Review, Class Rep.; **OTHER ACT & HONORS:** Bd. of Dir. Citizens Nat. Bank, Sec.-Tres, 19th Jud. Dist. (1977), Advisor Law Explorers; **HOME ADD:** 606 Tuttlewood Dr., Kann, NC 28081, (704)782-6381; **BUS ADD:** 708 McLain Rd., PO Box 2, Kannapoles, NC 28081, (704)932-3157.

TUTUN, Mark R.——B: Mar. 28, 1955, Cambridge, MA, *Assoc.*, Willard R. Baker Devel. Co.; **PRIM RE ACT:** Developer, Owner/Investor; **SERVICES:** Purchasing raw land, zoning, engr., land planning, subdividing, devel.; **REP CLIENTS:** Builders of all resid. and comml. products; **PROFL AFFIL & HONORS:** HAB; **EDUC:** BS, 1977, Econ., land resources, Univ. of MA, Amherst, MA; **GRAD EDUC:** MBA, 1978, RE & Fin., So. Methodist Univ., Dallas, TX; **EDUC HONORS:** SMU RE Scholarship; **HOME ADD:** 4233 Saxton Ln., Dallas, TX 75229, (214)352-8709; **BUS ADD:** 14114 Dallas Pkwy, Suite 300, Dallas, TX 75240, (214)387-8636.

TWAROWSKI, Eugene H., III——B: Oct. 5, 1947, Los Angeles, CA, *Pres., Builder Devel., Gen. Contr.*, Buzco Constr. Co., Inc.; **PRIM RE ACT:** Developer, Builder, Property Manager; **SERVICES:** Resid. comml., indus. devel., Gen. contr. custom homes, ins. repairs, fire, etc.; **REP CLIENTS:** Limetrow Ins. Co., Firemans Fund., Auto Club, Farmers, State Farm, ILA Ins. Co.; **PREV EMPLOY:** Const. superintendent, devel. of comml., indus., resid. prop.; **PROFL AFFIL & HONORS:** Nat. Assn. of Home Builders Assn., Gen. Contr. of Amer., Bldg. Indus. Assoc., Constr. Speficications Inst. of Amer., Bldg. Design Awards Workmahship, Concern Energy Awards, S. CA Gas Co. Cert. of Commendation, S. CA Gas Co.; **EDUC:** Gen. Est. in Constr., 1974, Constr., CA Licensed Builders & Contractors; **EDUC HONORS:** Cert. of Achievement, Cert. of Achiev. Osmoses Wood, Cert. of Achievement Constr. Builder; **MIL SERV:** US Army, Sgt., Good Conduct, DSC; **OTHER ACT & HONORS:** Bd. of Advisors, Advisory Palen Housing Ind., Member Arbitration Bd.; **HOME ADD:** 1314 Woodbury Dr., Torrance, CA 90505, (213)326-8147; **BUS ADD:** 3620 Pacific Coast Hwy., Suite 204, Torrance, CA 90505, (213)326-8139.

TWINING, Alexander——B: June 5, 1953, New London, CT, *Prin.*, Twining Assocs.; **PRIM RE ACT:** Consultant, Architect, Developer; **SERVICES:** Arch., consulting, devel.; **REP CLIENTS:** Rose Assoc., Yale Univ.; **PREV EMPLOY:** Moore Grover Harper Assocs. (Archs), Hardy Holzman Pfeiffer Assocs. (Archs).; **PROFL AFFIL & HONORS:** AIA, NY Soc. of Arch.; **EDUC:** BA, 1974, Arch./Urban Design, Yale Coll.; **GRAD EDUC:** MArch., 1977, Yale School of Arch.; **EDUC HONORS:** Cum Laude; **HOME ADD:** 166 E. 92nd St., NY, NY 10028, (212)427-8613; **BUS ADD:** 135 Fifth Ave., NY, NY 10010, (212)777-2850.

TWITTY, Robert J.——B: June 26, 1950, Chicago, IL, *VP*, The Lomas & Nettleton Co., Comml.; **PRIM RE ACT:** Broker, Appraiser, Lender, Property Manager; **SERVICES:** Morts., equities, joint ventures; **PREV EMPLOY:** Stockton, Whatley, Davin Co.; **PROFL AFFIL & HONORS:** MBA; C of C; Assoc. Member, SREA; **EDUC:** BS, 1972, RE, Univ. of FL; **EDUC HONORS:** Dean's List, President's Honor Roll, Grad. with Honors; **HOME ADD:** 315 10th Ave., Indian Rocks Beach, FL 33535, (813)596-6930; **BUS ADD:** 101 S. Hoover Blvd., 114, Tampa, FL 33609, (813)879-7627.

TWOMEY, John A.——B: Nov. 13, 1938, Monmouth, IL, *Atty.*; **PRIM RE ACT:** Attorney; **EDUC:** AB, 1960, Econ., Univ. of MI; **GRAD EDUC:** JD, 1963, Univ. of MI; **HOME ADD:** 1962 Wagonwheel Ave., Las Vegas, NV 89119, (702)736-7720; **BUS ADD:** 1962 Wagonwheel Ave., Las Vegas, NV 89119, (702)736-7720.

TWYCROSS, Dale A.——B: Jan. 17, 1952, Whittier, CA, *Area Mgr.*, Emkay Development Co., Inc.; **PRIM RE ACT:** Developer, Builder, Property Manager; **SERVICES:** Devel., const. and prop. mgmt. of comml. and indus. props.; **REP CLIENTS:** Indiv. clients, users, spec. bldgs.; **PREV EMPLOY:** Ernest W. Hahn, Inc., 1975-77; R & B Devel. Co., 1977-78; **PROFL AFFIL & HONORS:** Intl. Council of Shopping Ctrs., CSM; Salesman's RE Lic., State of WA; **EDUC:** BS, 1974, Bus. Mgmt., CA State Poly. Univ., Pomona, CA; **OTHER ACT & HONORS:** Men's Intl., Div. of YMCA; **HOME ADD:** 7150 Canelo Hills Dr., Citrus Heights, CA 95610, (916)722-6877; **BUS ADD:** 165 Commerce Cir., Suite C., PO Box 15451, Sacramento, CA 95851, (916)924-3111.

TYLER, Frederick C., Jr.——*Secy.*, Smucker, J.M. Co.; **PRIM RE ACT:** Broker, Property Manager; **BUS ADD:** Strawberry Lane, Orrville, OH 44667, (216)682-0015.*

TYLER, James——*Chmn of the Commissioners*, Virginia Real Estate Commission; **PRIM RE ACT:** Property Manager; **BUS ADD:** 2 So. Main St., Richmond, VA 23219, (804)786-7285.

TYLER, John F.——*Treasurer & Secretary*, American Welding & Manufacturing; **PRIM RE ACT:** Property Manager; **BUS ADD:** Dietz Rd., Warren, OH 44482, (216)393-2531.*

TYLER, John K.——B: Mar. 9, 1941, Spring Valley, IL, Shaw & Tyler, PC; **PRIM RE ACT:** Attorney; **REP CLIENTS:** Mort. lenders (const./permanent loans); RE devels./synds.; **PREV EMPLOY:** Assoc., Wheat, Thornton & Shaw, Attys.; **PROFL AFFIL & HONORS:** ABA, Houston Bar Assn., State Bar of TX; **EDUC:** BBA, 1963, Banking & Fin., SMU; **GRAD EDUC:** JD, 1973, Real Prop., Taxation, Univ. of Houston; **HOME ADD:** 5643 Sugar Hill, Houston, TX 77056, (713)965-9551; **BUS ADD:** 1717 St. James Pl., Suite 136, Houston, TX 77056, (713)629-4140.

TYLER, Lowell Peardon——B: Nov. 3, 1928, Dover-Foxcroft, ME, *Broker/Gen. Agent*, Lowell P. Tyler, Realtor; **PRIM RE ACT:** Broker, Insuror; **SERVICES:** Life Ins. RE; **PROFL AFFIL & HONORS:** NAR, Dir. Lake Worth MLS, Member Profl. Standards Comm. of Lake Worth Bd. of Realtors; **EDUC:** 1959, Lasalle Univ., Bus.; **GRAD EDUC:** LLB, 1973, Blackstone School of Law; **MIL SERV:** USAF, S/Sgt.; **OTHER ACT & HONORS:** Kiwanis; Elks; Amer. Legion; Lake Worth Amer. Legion Post #47-Judge Adv.; Lake Worth

Kiwanis, Dir.; Lake Worth Elks #1530 Lecturing Knight; **HOME ADD:** 7047 Pine Manor Dr., Lake Worth, FL 33463, (305)439-8668; **BUS ADD:** 3923 Lake Worth Rd., Lake Worth, FL 33461, (305)439-8668.

TYLER, William C.——B: June 10, 1947, Louisville, KY, *VP*, Coldwell Banker, RE Fin. Servs.; **OTHER RE ACT:** Mort. Banking; **SERVICES:** Broker Fin. of Comml. props., Debit & Equity; **PREV EMPLOY:** C&S Mort. Co. & REIT; **EDUC:** BA, 1969, Soc., Wash. & Lee Univ.; **GRAD EDUC:** MBA, 1971, Fin. & Mktg., Emory Univ.; **EDUC HONORS:** Dean's List; **HOME ADD:** 1320 Pasadena Ave. NE, Atlanta, GA 30306, (404)876-1019; **BUS ADD:** 229 Peachtree St., 1401, Atlanta, GA 30343, (404)656-1422.

TYNAN, Martin F.——*VP Fin. & Treasurer*, Salant Corporation; **PRIM RE ACT:** Property Manager; **BUS ADD:** 330 Fifth Ave., New York, NY 10001, (212)971-9708.*

TYREE, Lew Gary——B: Aug. 13, 1951, Charleston, WV, *General Partner*, Dues, Tyree & Hicks; **PRIM RE ACT:** Attorney, Insuror; **PREV EMPLOY:** W. VA Housing Dev. Fund; **PROFL AFFIL & HONORS:** ABA, WV Bar Assn.; **EDUC:** BS, 1973, Mktg., WV State Coll.; **GRAD EDUC:** 1979, Bus. Corp. Law, WV Univ. Sch. of Law; **EDUC HONORS:** Distinguished Military Grad., Who's Who in Amer. Colls. & Univs.; **MIL SERV:** US Army, Signal, Capt.; USAR, Ordnance Corp Cpt. Commdr.; **OTHER ACT & HONORS:** Kappa Alpha Psi Frat., Alpha Phi Omega Frat., Phi Alpha Delta Law Frat.; **HOME ADD:** 2218 Washington St. E, Charleston, WV 25311, (304)343-2055; **BUS ADD:** 2 Hale St., Charleston, WV 25301, (304)344-0222.

TYREE, Scott——*Corp. Dir. Adm. Services*, Thomas Industries, Inc.; **PRIM RE ACT:** Property Manager; **BUS ADD:** 207 E. Broadway, PO Box 35120, Louisville, KY 40232, (502)582-3771.*

TYRRELL, Gerald G.——B: Dec. 27, 1938, Canton, China, *Exec. VP*, First National Bank of Louisville; **PRIM RE ACT:** Banker; **PREV EMPLOY:** Pres., Churchill Mort. Co., Atlanta, GA, 1975-1977; **EDUC:** BA, 1960, Hist., Yale Univ.; **GRAD EDUC:** Stonier Grad. School, 1971, Banking, Rutgers Univ.; **EDUC HONORS:** Published Thesis; **MIL SERV:** Army NG, Capt., Commendation Ribbon; **HOME ADD:** 521 Ridgewood Rd., Louisville, KY 40207, (502)897-6908; **BUS ADD:** PO Box 36000, Louisville, KY 40232, (502)581-4356.

TYSON, Art——*Supv. Corp RE*, Midland Cooperative, Inc.; **PRIM RE ACT:** Property Manager; **BUS ADD:** PO Box 1395, Minneapolis, MN 55440, (612)571-2110.*

TYTLER, Warren F.——B: Mar. 10, 1929, Poulsbo, WA, *Pres.*, JRO, Inc.; **PRIM RE ACT:** Broker, Developer; **OTHER RE ACT:** Resid. Devel.; **SERVICES:** Marketing resid. props., valuation, consultation on devel. properties; **REP CLIENTS:** Builders, devels. and indiv. investors in investment props., sellers of single family homes; **PREV EMPLOY:** In RE business since grad. from Univ.; **PROFL AFFIL & HONORS:** Past Pres., Bremerton-Kitsap Board of Realtors; State Dir., Washington Assoc. of Realtors; Treas., Computer Multiple Listing Serv., GRI; CRB; **EDUC:** BA, 1954, RE and Ins., Univ. of WA; **OTHER ACT & HONORS:** Past Pres., Poulsbo Lions Club; Bd. of Dir., Kitsap Cty. Youth Homes; **HOME ADD:** 2332 Clinton Ave. N.W., Poulsbo, WA 98370, (206)779-4238; **BUS ADD:** POB 805, Poulsbo, WA 98370, (206)779-3911.

UCCELLINI, Walter F.——B: Jan 9, 1945, Mineola, NY, *Pres.*, Walter Uccellini Enterprises, Inc.; **PRIM RE ACT:** Syndicator, Developer, Property Manager; **SERVICES:** Dev. (Full serv.), complete computerized mgmt. service, synd. (ltd. scale), investment counseling, principle archs. of exp., housing multi-family & office bldgs.; **REP CLIENTS:** Indiv. & Instnl. clients, on a consulting basis; **PROFL AFFIL & HONORS:** NHRA, NY Assn. of Renewal Officers, Troy NY, GTCC Beautification Award, Lic. RE Broker, NY CPM Cand.; **EDUC:** BS, 1969, Mgmt. Engr., RPI; **GRAD EDUC:** MS, 1971, Fin. Mgmt., RPI, Troy, NY; MS, 1972, Comp. Sci., The Kenneth Lalley School of Mgmt. at RPI, Troy, NY; **EDUC HONORS:** Hon. Student, School of Mgmt., Hon. Soc., Honor Soc.; **OTHER ACT & HONORS:** C of C; **HOME ADD:** The Crossway, Troy, NY 12181, (518)272-3216; **BUS ADD:** 5 Broadway, PO Box 305, Troy, NY 12181, (518)271-7564.

UHLEMANN, William R.——B: Aug. 14, 1943, Evanston, IL, *Asst. VP, Mgr. - Comml. Loan Dept.*, Majestic Savings and Loan Assn., Comml. and Const. Loan Dept.; **PRIM RE ACT:** Consultant, Banker, Lender; **OTHER RE ACT:** Lic. RE Salesman - CO; **REP CLIENTS:** Comml. RE loans, const. loans; **PREV EMPLOY:** Northern Trust Co. Bank - Chicago; Readers Digest Serv. - Pittsburgh, PA; KHOW Radio, Denver; Hovey-Billings RE, Denver & Gayno Inc. RE, Evergreen; **PROFL AFFIL & HONORS:** CO Mort. Bankers Assn., and Comml. Comm. of CMBA; Evergreen Bd. of Realtors, Affiliate, Realtor (Inactive); **EDUC:** BA, 1966, Eng., Westminster Coll. Fulton, MO; **OTHER ACT & HONORS:** Denver Press Club, Ducks Unlimited; **HOME ADD:** PO Box 369, Evergreen, CO 80439, (303)674-5671; **BUS ADD:** 2420 West 26th Ave., Denver, CO 80211, (303)455-1890.

UHLER, Bob——*Mgr. RE*, North American Coal Corp.; **PRIM RE ACT:** Property Manager; **BUS ADD:** 12800 Shaker Blvd., Cleveland, OH 44120, (216)752-1000.*

ULAKOVICH, Ronald S.——B: Nov. 17, 1942, Youngstown, OH, *Pres.*, Condo Assoc. Ltd.; **PRIM RE ACT:** Developer, Builder, Owner/Investor, Property Manager, Syndicator; **REP CLIENTS:** Lenders and indiv. investors in condo. conversions and timesharing; **PREV EMPLOY:** Pres., Sales & Mktg. Co.; **PROFL AFFIL & HONORS:** Amer. Assn. of Indiv. Investors; Home Builders; Apt. Owners Assn. of Amer.; RESSI, Grand Award Homebuilders, Million Dollar Club; **EDUC:** Indus. Eng., 1967, IL Inst. of Tech.; **GRAD EDUC:** Indust. Eng., 1969, Methods-Mgt., IL Inst. of Tech.; **HOME ADD:** 510 Van Buren, E. Dundee, IL 60118, (312)426-8805; **BUS ADD:** 1039 S. Arlington Hts. Rd., Arlington Hts., IL 60005, (312)364-6603.

ULLOA, David J.——B: Jan. 25, 1940, Agana, Guam, *Pres.*, U. S. Realty, Inc.; **PRIM RE ACT:** Broker, Owner/Investor, Property Manager; **REP CLIENTS:** Corp. & indivs., resid. & comml. props.; **PROFL AFFIL & HONORS:** Member, Guam Territorial Planning Commn., 1976-79; Chairman, Guam Territorial Seashore Protection Commn., 1976-79; Member, Guam Housing Corp., 1973-76; **EDUC:** AA, 1965, BA, 1976, RE Bus. Admin., RE Investment Analysis, UCLA, CA, 1980, RE Synd., Seminar; **GRAD EDUC:** Candidate for MBA, CA Western Univ.; **MIL SERV:** USN; RMC; **OTHER ACT & HONORS:** Chmn., Guam Telephone Authority, 1976-78 (Public Corp.); **HOME ADD:** Tamuning Village, Guam, (671)646-7024; **BUS ADD:** Victoria Bldg., Rte 4, PO Box 2890, Agana, 96910-2890, Guam, (671)472-6088.

ULRICH, F.W.——*Rgnl. VP, Winnipeg*, Morguard Properties Ltd.; **PRIM RE ACT:** Broker; **SERVICES:** Prop. mgmt., devel., acquisitions and portfolio mgmt.; **REP CLIENTS:** Major Canadian Pension Funds; **PROFL AFFIL & HONORS:** B. Comm.; FRI; Winnipeg RE Bd.; Canadian RE Assn.; ICSC, B. Comm.; **BUS ADD:** 315-175 Hargrave St., Winnipeg, R3C 3R8, Man., Canada, (204)947-0524.

ULRICH, John C.——B: Oct. 15, 1941, Cleveland, OH, *RE Consultant & Appraiser*, J.C. Ulrich RE Service; **PRIM RE ACT:** Consultant, Appraiser, Developer, Owner/Investor; **SERVICES:** Market and feasbility analysis for Comml. indust., single family and PUD projects. Zoning and land use studies.; **REP CLIENTS:** Lenders, devels., investors, govt. agencies; **PREV EMPLOY:** IBM Corp. 1963-1972; VP RE Mktg. REIC Inc. 1972-1975; **PROFL AFFIL & HONORS:** AIREA, Assns. of S. Bay Brokers, State & Natl. RE Assns.; **EDUC:** AA, 1963, Electronics Tech., RCA Inst.; **GRAD EDUC:** AA, 1973, Real Estate, San Jose City Coll.; **MIL SERV:** USN, Res.; **OTHER ACT & HONORS:** Planning Commissioner City of San Jose, 1974 - 1980 (Chmn. 1975-1976); **HOME ADD:** 297 Cresta Vista Way, San Jose, CA 95119; **BUS ADD:** 2444 Moorpark Ave. 308, San Jose, CA 95128, (408)998-3338.

ULRICH, Kenneth T.——B: June 21, 1950, Philadelphia, PA, *Asst. Counsel*, Commonwealth Land Title Insurance Co., Claims Dept.; **PRIM RE ACT:** Attorney; **OTHER RE ACT:** Title Insurance Claims Litigation; **PROFL AFFIL & HONORS:** Philadlphia, PA, ABA; PA Trial Lawyers' Assn.; **EDUC:** AB, 1975, Humanitites, PA State Univ.; **GRAD EDUC:** JD, 1978, Temple Univ. School of Law; **EDUC HONORS:** Keystone Honor Soc. - two awards; Grad. Magna Cum Laude; **MIL SERV:** USMC, Cpl. (e-4), 1968-1970, Vietnam Service; Campaign; Cross of Gallantry; Natl. Defense; **HOME ADD:** 704 Fitzwatertown Rd., Glenside, PA 19038, (215)576-1593; **BUS ADD:** 8 Penn Ctr., 20th Flr.,, 17th & JFK Blvd., Philadelphia, PA 19103, (215)241-6135.

ULRICH, Peter H.——B: Nov. 24, 1922, *Pres.*, Beneficial Standard Mort. Co.; **PRIM RE ACT:** Lender; **OTHER RE ACT:** Mort. Lending; **REP CLIENTS:** Beneficial Standard Life Ins. Co., Beneficial Reins. Co.; **PREV EMPLOY:** Sr. VP, The Bank of CA; Pres., Bancal Mort. Co.; **PROFL AFFIL & HONORS:** S. CA MBA, CA MBA,

MBAA, Assn. of RE Exec., Lambda Alpha Hon. Frat.; **EDUC:** Acctg.-Bus., Northwestern Univ., Univ. of IA; **MIL SERV:** US Army, T/Sgt.; **OTHER ACT & HONORS:** Lions Club; Los Angeles Athletic Club, Listed in "Who is Who in Amer."; **HOME ADD:** 447 Fairview #2, Arcadia, CA 91006; **BUS ADD:** 3700 Wilshire Blvd., Los Angeles, CA 90010, (213)381-8291.

ULSETH, Dr. George W.——B: May 29, 1918, Bronson, MI, *Prof.*, Rensselaer Polytechnic Inst., School of Mgmt.; **PRIM RE ACT:** Consultant, Attorney, Appraiser, Owner/Investor, Instructor; **SERVICES:** Consulting; **PREV EMPLOY:** RE Broker, Atty., CPA; **PROFL AFFIL & HONORS:** Amer. Fin. Assn., Amer. Inst. of CPA's, Amer. Inst. for Prop. & Liab. Underwriters, CPCU; **EDUC:** BSC, 1943, Econ., Univ. of ND; **GRAD EDUC:** MA (Acctg.), 1954, Univ. of ND; JD (Law), 1948, Univ. of ND; PhD (Bus. Admin.), 1972, Univ. of MN; **EDUC HONORS:** Beta Alpha Psi, Order of the Coif; **MIL SERV:** Inf., 1st Lt., Purple Heart, Combat Infantry Badge, Victory Medal, 3 Battle Stars; **OTHER ACT & HONORS:** Elks, Am. Legion, D.A.V., Masonic Lodge, Chartered Prop. and Casualty Underwriter; **HOME ADD:** PO Box 663, Newtonville, NY 12128; **BUS ADD:** 302 MG, R.P.I., Troy, NY 12181, (518)270-6581.

UMEK, Mark A.——B: Aug. 10, 1949, St. Louis, MO, *Pres.*, Mark Umek and Assoc., Inc.; **PRIM RE ACT:** Builder; **SERVICES:** Gen. Contr. new home planning, constr., Remodeling; **PROFL AFFIL & HONORS:** Clark Cty. Home Bldrs. Assoc., 1980 Parade of Homes Best of Show, Best of Interior Design, Best Landscaping; **EDUC:** BS, 1975, Bus. Admin, Andrews Univ., Berrien Springs, MI; **MIL SERV:** US Army, E4; **HOME ADD:** 15503 N.E. 25th Ave., Vancouver, WA 98665, (206)573-8264; **BUS ADD:** 12312 N.E. 76th St., Vancouver, WA 98662, (206)254-6622.

UNATIN, Mark L.——B: Feb. 29, 1944, Pittsburgh, PA, *Partner*, Rothman, Gordon, Foreman, Groudine; **PRIM RE ACT:** Consultant, Attorney, Owner/Investor, Instructor; **SERVICES:** Investment counseling, condo. conversions, legal; **REP CLIENTS:** Lenders & investors in resid. and comml. prop.; **PROFL AFFIL & HONORS:** ABA; PA and Allegheny Cty. Bar Assns.; Greater Pittsburgh Bd. of Realtors, Chmn. S&L Section, Allegheny Cty. Bar Assn.; **EDUC:** BBA, 1965, Univ. of Pittsburgh; **GRAD EDUC:** JD, 1968, Duquesne Univ.; **OTHER ACT & HONORS:** Assoc. Prof. of Law & RE, Robert Morris College; Instr., PA Law Inst. for Continuing Legal Educ.; **HOME ADD:** 2270 Clairmont Dr., Pittsburgh, PA 15241, (412)833-6929; **BUS ADD:** 300 Grant Bldg., Pittsburgh, PA 15219, (412)281-0705.

UNDERDOWN, Jack A.——B: Jan. 21, 1928, Lenoir, NC, *Owner*, Jack A. Underdown Agency; **PRIM RE ACT:** Broker, Consultant, Appraiser, Developer, Owner/Investor, Instructor, Insuror; **SERVICES:** Complete RE serv.; **PROFL AFFIL & HONORS:** Soc. of RE Appraisers; **EDUC:** AB, 1950, Bus. Admin., Lenoir Rhyne Coll.; **OTHER ACT & HONORS:** Mayor, Town of Elkin 1974-1978; **HOME ADD:** 148 Colony Lane, Elkin, NC 28621, (919)835-3417; **BUS ADD:** 920 N. Bridge St., Elkin, NC 28621, (919)835-2256.

UNDERILL, H.J., III——B: Sept. 18, 1949, Orlando, FL, *Pres.*, Underill Realty, Inc. & Re/Max of Brevard, Inc.; **PRIM RE ACT:** Broker, Instructor, Syndicator, Developer, Owner/Investor; **SERVICES:** Gen. Brokerage, Gross Portfolio Mgmt., Investment Counseling, Synd. & Dev.; **PROFL AFFIL & HONORS:** RESSI; Sr. Instr. RESSI, FL Chap. RESSI; Nat. State & Local Bds. of Realtors, Specialist in RE Securities DEsignation from RESSI, VP FL RESSI; **EDUC:** BA, 1971, Pol. Sci., Univ. of FL; **GRAD EDUC:** MBA, 1973, RE & Fin., Univ. of FL; **OTHER ACT & HONORS:** Chmn.; Melbourne Downtown Redev. Agency, FL Blue Key, Centurion Council, Chmn., Melbourne Area Ducks Unltd.; **HOME ADD:** PO Box 1796, Melbourne, FL 32901, (305)724-6650; **BUS ADD:** 2525 N. AIA, Indialantic, FL 32903, (305)777-1830.

UNDERWOOD, Charles T.——B: Nov. 28, 1944, Dallas, TX, *C.E.O.*, Underwood Investment Co.; **PRIM RE ACT:** Developer, Owner/Investor; **OTHER RE ACT:** Office condo. dev.; **PREV EMPLOY:** IBM; **PROFL AFFIL & HONORS:** Rotary Club Dallas; **EDUC:** BBA, 1967, Fin., Econ., Mktg., Univ. of OK; **GRAD EDUC:** MBA, 1969, Fin., Univ. of OK; **EDUC HONORS:** Dean's List; **MIL SERV:** US Army, 1st. Lt., DSM; **HOME ADD:** 4045 Hawthorne, Dallas, TX 75219, (214)528-5005; **BUS ADD:** 6211 W. Northwest Hwy., Ste. 255, Preston Tower, Dallas, TX 75225, (214)739-3320.

UNDERWOOD, H. C.——B: May 22, 1910, Cresent, OK, *Owner*, H.C. Underwood RE Co.; **PRIM RE ACT:** Broker, Consultant, Appraiser, Owner/Investor, Syndicator; **PREV EMPLOY:** Self Employed; **PROFL AFFIL & HONORS:** Ft. Worth Bd. of Realtors-Nat. Assn. of Realtors-Farm and Land Inst., Member of Civic Committee; **EDUC:** BBA, 1033, Univ. of MD; **GRAD EDUC:** LLB, 1935, OK City Univ.; **MIL SERV:** USAF, Lt.; **HOME ADD:** Tr. 5 Box 275 G, Ft. Worth, TX 76126, (817)249-1170; **BUS ADD:** Rt. 5 Box 275 G, Ft. Worth, TX 76126, (817)249-1170.

UNDERWOOD, John R., Jr.——B: Sept. 2, 1948, Brooksville, FL, *VP - Chief Appraiser*, Southern Federal S&L; **PRIM RE ACT:** Consultant, Appraiser, Property Manager; **SERVICES:** Appraising, feasibility studies, leasing; **PREV EMPLOY:** 1st Fed. of Lake Worth Comml. Appraiser; **PROFL AFFIL & HONORS:** FL Brokers Lisc., SREA, Candidate, AIREA Pres., SREA Chap. 200; **EDUC:** BS, 1970, Criminology, Social Welfare, FL State Univ.; **OTHER ACT & HONORS:** Past Pres. W. Lake Worth Exchange Club; **HOME ADD:** 8151 3rd Pl. S, W. Palm Beach, FL, (305)793-4691; **BUS ADD:** 225 N. Fed. Hwy., Pompano Beach, FL 33062, (305)941-5000.

UNGER, Helen J.——B: June 2, 1932, Queens, NY, *Pres.*, Unger Industrial Realty Co., Inc.; **PRIM RE ACT:** Broker, Owner/Investor, Property Manager; **SERVICES:** Indus. comml. brokerage; **PREV EMPLOY:** Formerly an agent for Sutton & Towne (now Caldwell Banker - S&T); Former TV copywriter-CBS-TV, ABC-TV, others; **PROFL AFFIL & HONORS:** NAR, NY State Assn. of Realtors, Long Island Bd. & Member of Indust. RE Brokers Assn. of Metropolitan NY, Holder of 60 ton 100 mi. offshore Coast Guard Capts. License.; 1st Woman Commodore of the Shelter Bay Yacht Club in Kings Point, Long Island, NY; Member-writer's guide of Amer.; **EDUC:** BA, 1953, Dramatic Arts, Adelphi Coll.; **GRAD EDUC:** 1954, TV writing/RE, CW Post - Brokerage Law, Columbia Univ.; **HOME ADD:** 80 Beach Rd., Great Neck, NY 11023, (516)829-9844; **BUS ADD:** 60-20 No. Blvd., Woodside, NY 11377, (516)829-9800.

UPCHURCH, Roger Stanley——B: Oct. 10, 1925, Durham Cty., NC, *Partner*, Upchurch & Galifianakis; **PRIM RE ACT:** Attorney; **SERVICES:** Legal servs.; **REP CLIENTS:** Indiv. and instnl. clients; **PROFL AFFIL & HONORS:** ABA, NC Bar Assn., NC State Bar, 14th Judicial Dist Bar of NC; **EDUC:** AB, 1949, Econ., Hist., Poli. Sci., Duke Univ.; **GRAD EDUC:** LLB, 1952, Duke Univ.; **MIL SERV:** USAF, PFC; **HOME ADD:** 3206 Sprunt Ave., Durham, NC 27705, (919)383-4253; **BUS ADD:** 200 1st Union Nat. Bank Bldg, Durham, NC 27702, (919)682-5403.

URBAS, Andrea——B: June 3, 1957, Zagreb, Yugoslavia, *Arch. Coordinator*, Illinois Dept. of Conservation, Hist. Sites; **PRIM RE ACT:** Architect; **SERVICES:** Arch. services, tech. guidance hist. preservation; **REP CLIENTS:** Indiv., org., devel., arch. contemplating rehab./restoration projects; **PROFL AFFIL & HONORS:** NTHP; APT, J. Helm Memorial Award; IL Power Co., Research Award; **EDUC:** BS, 1979, Arch., Univ. of IL; **GRAD EDUC:** MArch., 1981, Arch., KS State Univ.; **EDUC HONORS:** IL Power Research in Arch., Helm Memorial, Outstanding Grad. Student, 1980; **HOME ADD:** 2317-A Old Jacksonville Rd., Springfield, IL 62704, (217)546-4854; **BUS ADD:** 405 E. Washington St., Springfield, IL 62706, (217)782-3340.

URDA, Karl J.——B: Sept. 6, 1930, Sewickley, PA, *Owner*, The Kristufek Agency; **PRIM RE ACT:** Broker, Consultant, Appraiser, Owner/Investor, Property Manager; **SERVICES:** RE Appraisal, counseling, prop. mgmt.; **REP CLIENTS:** Lenders; indiv. and instnl. investment; govt. agencies; corps.; trusts and attys.; **PROFL AFFIL & HONORS:** AIREA, SREA, NARA, NAIFA, Realtor of Yr., Beaver Cty. Bd. of Realtors, 1976;Nat. Pres. IFA, 1982; **EDUC:** BS, 1952, Econ., Univ. of PA, Wharton Sch.; **MIL SERV:** US Army; Corps.; **OTHER ACT & HONORS:** Amer. Right of Way Assn., Gr. Ambridge C of C; **HOME ADD:** Campmeeting Rd., Sewickley, PA 15143, (412)741-4635; **BUS ADD:** 405 Merchant St., Ambridge, PA 15003, (412)266-1139.

URION, Paul Batcheller——B: Dec. 29, 1916, Chicago, IL, *Atty. at Law*, Paul B. Urion Atty. at Law; **PRIM RE ACT:** Attorney; **SERVICES:** Drafting closings documents, title searches, supervising closings; **REP CLIENTS:** Farmer's Home Admin, Four Corners RE; **PREV EMPLOY:** Self emp. since 1948; **PROFL AFFIL & HONORS:** ABA, NH Bar Assn., VA Bar Assn., Past Pres. Strafford Cty. Bar Assn.; **EDUC:** AB, 1938, Pol. Sci., Dartmouth; **GRAD EDUC:** JD, 1941, Univ. VA Law School; **MIL SERV:** US Army Corps., Judge Advocate, Capt., Amer. Defense Pacific Theater, WW II; **OTHER ACT & HONORS:** City Solicitor 1949-55, 1968-70, 1971-80, NH Judicial Council 1975-present Dartmouth Coll. Alumni Council, 1968-72, Boy Scout Silver Beaver Award, Past Pres. Rochester Kiwanis, Past Chmn. Red Cross, Tr. Nasson Coll., 1976-; **HOME ADD:** 27 Broad St., Rochester, NH 03867, (603)332-1951; **BUS ADD:** 69 S. Main St., PO Box 2115, Rochester, NH 03867, (603)332-1420.

URQUHART, Donald Victor——B: Nov. 4, 1942, Washington, DC, *Owner/Pres.*, Donald V. Urquhart & Assoc.; **PRIM RE ACT:** Consultant, Appraiser, Instructor; **SERVICES:** Appraising, investment analysis, consulting, appraisal reviews; **REP CLIENTS:** Equitable

Trust Co.; Washington Fed. S&L; Midas RE; Amtrack; Texaco Inc.; **PREV EMPLOY:** VP, Bay State Appraisal, 1977-1979; Consultant, Dept. of Housing & Urban Devel. (Urban Devel. Action Grant), 1979-1980; **PROFL AFFIL & HONORS:** MAI; SRPA; AIREA; **EDUC:** BA, 1976, Bus. Admin., Loyola Coll.; **HOME ADD:** 6311 Golden Hook, Columbia, MD 21044, (301)596-5177; **BUS ADD:** 1370 Lamberton Dr., Silver Spring, MD 20902, (301)649-5900.

URQUHART, Glen T.——B: Nov. 10, 1948, Pittsburgh, PA, *Pres.*, Urquhart, Donohoe Co. Inc.; **PRIM RE ACT:** Developer; **SERVICES:** Acquire, devel., improve, lease, mgmt.; **EDUC:** BS, 1970, Fin. Mgmt., Univ. of VA; **EDUC HONORS:** Dean's List; **OTHER ACT & HONORS:** Counselor to Agency for Intl. Devel.; Advisory Bd. Amer. Security Council; Republican 'Eagle', Member of the Senatorial Inner Circle; and Member the Comm. for Dulles International Airport, Washington, DC; **HOME ADD:** 12307 Fan Shell Ct., Reston, VA 22091; **BUS ADD:** PO Box 17068 Dulles Intl. Airport, Washington DC 20041, (703)661-8000.

URSINI, Rocco J.——*VP*, Ridgewood Realty Inc.; **PRIM RE ACT:** Instructor, Appraiser; **OTHER RE ACT:** RE dev. & brokerage; **PROFL AFFIL & HONORS:** NAR; RNMI; CO Assn. of Realtors; Jefferson County Bd. of Realtors; Instr., Univ. of CO Contin. Educ.; CO RE Educ. Assn.; **EDUC:** Univ. of Denver, 1960; **GRAD EDUC:** BSBA-Mgmt., 1960; **MIL SERV:** US Army, Master Sgt.; **HOME ADD:** 2710 Xavier St., Denver, CO 80212, (303)477-7811; **BUS ADD:** 14618 W. 6th Ave., Golden, CO 80401, (303)278-2233.

USHER, Kirk, Jr.——B: May 19, 1944, Montclair, NJ, *Sr. V.P.*, Cushman & Wakefield, Ind., San Fran. Branch; **PRIM RE ACT:** Broker, Consultant, Developer, Owner/Investor; **SERVICES:** Office leasing & investment sales broker and sonsultant; **PROFL AFFIL & HONORS:** SF Bd. Realtors, NAR; **EDUC:** BS, 1966, Intl. Bus. RE, Univ. of Wash.; **MIL SERV:** US Army, 1st Lt.; **OTHER ACT & HONORS:** V. Chmn. Cushman & Wakefield Nat. Planning Comm., Bridgemont Christian H.S. Tr., Ins. Int'l. Educ., Bank of San Fran. Advisory Bd.; **HOME ADD:** Belvedere, CA; **BUS ADD:** 555 CA Street 2700, San Francisco, CA 94104, (415)397-1700.

UTKE, Lee R.——B: Sept. 20, 1953, Shawano, WI, *Coordinator of Comml. Devel.*, City of Green Bay; **PRIM RE ACT:** Consultant, Developer, Syndicator; **SERVICES:** Investment counseling, devel. and synd. of comml. props.; **REP CLIENTS:** Devels. and comml. concerns seeking attractive sites for devel.; **PREV EMPLOY:** Planning analyst, Walgreen Company, Deerfield, IL, 1977-1978; **PROFL AFFIL & HONORS:** WI Econ. Devel. Assn., Great Lakes Area Devel. Council; **EDUC:** BS Managerial Systems, 1976, Univ. of WI - Green Bay; **EDUC HONORS:** Cum Laude; **OTHER ACT & HONORS:** UW-GB Alumni Club; **HOME ADD:** 1102 Bellevue, Green Bay, WI 54302, (414)469-0554; **BUS ADD:** 100 N. Jefferson, Green Bay, WI 54301, (414)497-3761.

UTLEY, Robert K., III——B: Apr. 14, 1945, Temple, TX, *Pres./Chmn.*, First Southwest Equity Corp.; **PRIM RE ACT:** Developer, Builder, Owner/Investor, Property Manager, Syndicator; **SERVICES:** Const., prop. mgmt., devel. consultant (housing); **REP CLIENTS:** Self, lenders and investors in rental & sale housing; garden office bldgs.; **PROFL AFFIL & HONORS:** ULI; Nat. Assn. of Home Builders; TX Apt. Assn.; TX Assn. of Realtors; NAR, Advisory Dir., Multi-Housing World; Speaker, Multi-Housing World Conf.; **EDUC:** BBA, 1967, Bus./Mktg., Univ. of TX; **OTHER ACT & HONORS:** Temple C of C; Temple Leadership Council; Nat. Federation of Bus.; **HOME ADD:** 4005 El Capitan, Temple, TX 76501, (817)778-4985; **BUS ADD:** Suite 216 Temple Natl. Plaza, Temple, TX 76501, (817)773-1613.

UTLEY, Walter A.——B: Nov. 5, 1927, Hardy, AR, *Pres.*, International Land Corp.; **PRIM RE ACT:** Broker, Consultant, Appraiser, Developer, Owner/Investor, Property Manager; **OTHER RE ACT:** RE exchange consultant; **SERVICES:** Gen. RE sales, devel. and sale of large suburban agri. (crops and cattle); **REP CLIENTS:** Nat. and intl. investors and prop. owners; **PREV EMPLOY:** Mktg. Dir., Exec. VP and Pres., Amer. Realty Serv. Corp. 1954-68, Founder and Pres. Intl. Land Corp. 1968- present; **EDUC:** 1950, Pre-law, Univ. of TN; **MIL SERV:** US Army, Lt., Infantry and Artillery, Grad of Guided Missile Ctr.; **OTHER ACT & HONORS:** Pres., Marshall Acad. (private Sch.)1968-72; Chmn. of City of Holly Springs Town Lift Prog.; Recipient of MS State Univ. Block and Bridle Award in 1972; **HOME ADD:** 400 Salem Ave., Holly Springs, MS 38635, (601)252-1114; **BUS ADD:** 105 Van Dorn Ave., Holly Springs, MS 38635, (601)252-5200.

VACCARO, Martin J.——B: June 1, 1912, NJ, *Dir.*, Monmouth Cty., NJ, Dept. of Econ. Devel.; **OTHER RE ACT:** Dir. of Econ. Devel.; **SERVICES:** Assist realtors and devel. in locating suitable sites and facilities; **REP CLIENTS:** Municipal officials, realtors, devel. and property owners; **PREV EMPLOY:** Chief of Tech. Mgmt. Div., Procurement & Prod. Directorate, Fort Monmouth, NJ; Licensed PE, NJ; RE Salesman, NJ; **PROFL AFFIL & HONORS:** Indus. RE Brokers Assn.; NJ Indus. Dev. Assn.; NJ Alliance for Action; NJ World Trade Council; National Council for Urban Economic Development; **EDUC:** BME, 1934, Stevens Inst. of Tech., Hoboken, NJ; **GRAD EDUC:** MS, 1949, Stevens Inst. of Tech., Hoboken, NJ; **EDUC HONORS:** Teaching Fellowship for M. Degree; **OTHER ACT & HONORS:** Commnr. & Mayor, Borough of Allenhurst, NJ, 12 yrs.; Chmn., Monmouth Cty. Air Quality Comm.; Chmn., Monmouth Cty. Beach Erosion Comm.; Commnr., Monmouth Cty. Parks Commn.; V.Chmn. of Monmouth Cty. Transp. Coord. Comm.; VP of NJ Conf. of Mayors; Chmn. of Monmouth Cty. Mayors Assn.; **HOME ADD:** 310 Allen Ave., Allenhurst, NJ 07711, (201)531-2824; **BUS ADD:** Hall of Records Annex, Freehold, NJ 07728, (201)431-7470.

VAIDA, Marc A.——B: May 11, 1939, Somerville, NJ, *Atty.*, Self employed; **PRIM RE ACT:** Attorney; **REP CLIENTS:** Lincoln Props. Levitt, Kaufman and Broad, IU Intl. RE Subs. Round Valley, Inc., Hunterdon Cty. Bd. of Realtors, Warren Cty. Bd. of Realtors, Town and Country Bank, Flemmington, NJ; Various Planning Bds. and Bds. of Adjustment; **PROFL AFFIL & HONORS:** ABA, NJSBA, Bar Sect. on Land Use and Urban Affairs, NJ Inst. of Municipal Attys.; **EDUC:** BA, 1961, Amer. Studies, Brown Univ.; **GRAD EDUC:** LLB, 1964, Cornell Law School; **MIL SERV:** US Army, 1st Lt., ACM; **OTHER ACT & HONORS:** Lambertville New Hope Rotary; Tr. Clinton Hist. Museum Village; **HOME ADD:** PO Box 117, Stanton, NJ 08885, (201)782-2952; **BUS ADD:** 9 Main Street, Flemington, NJ 08822, (201)782-1801.

VAILL, George——B: Oct. 13, 1946, New Haven, CT, *Dir. of RE*, Nature Food Centres, Inc.; **PRIM RE ACT:** Broker, Consultant, Property Manager; **OTHER RE ACT:** Site acquisition, retail; **PREV EMPLOY:** Shopping ctr. leasing, E. Bay Development Corp., Somerville, MA (1975-1980); **PROFL AFFIL & HONORS:** Nat. Assn. of Corporate RE Execs.; Intl. Council of Shopping Ctrs., RE Broker; **EDUC:** Social Sci., So. CT State Coll.; **MIL SERV:** USAF, Sgt., E-4, VietNam Serv. Medal, Good Conduct Medal, AF Commendation Medal; **HOME ADD:** 602 Woburn St., Wilmington, MA 01887, (617)657-4071; **BUS ADD:** One Natures Way, Wilmington, MA 01887, (617)657-5000.

VALDEZ, Charles E.——B: Feb. 10, 1939, Detroit, MI, *Pres.*, Marrs Mgmt. and Realty, Inc.; **PRIM RE ACT:** Broker, Consultant, Property Manager; **SERVICES:** Mktg.,prop. mgmt., consulting, real estate sales, conversions, feasibility studies, HUD & FHA specialists; **PROFL AFFIL & HONORS:** IREM, Detroit Bd. of Realtors; CAI; MAHC; Builder's Assoc. of Southeastern MI (BASM); NAR; Detroit C of C, CPM; **EDUC:** BBA, 1966, Acctg., Univ. of Detroit; **GRAD EDUC:** MBA, 1968, Bus., Univ. of Detroit; **EDUC HONORS:** Magna Cum Laude; **MIL SERV:** USAR, E-5; **OTHER ACT & HONORS:** Pres. of the MI Chapter of IREM, Commerce Dept., Advisory Comm.; **HOME ADD:** 744 Harcourt, Grosse Pointe Park, MI 48230, (313)822-8359; **BUS ADD:** 2950 E. Jefferson St., Suite 201, Detroit, MI 48207, (313)567-6488.

VALENTI, Salvatore J.——B: Sept. 20, 1943, St. Louis, MO, *Pres.*, City & County Devel. Co. & United Props.; **PRIM RE ACT:** Broker, Developer, Builder, Owner/Investor; **OTHER RE ACT:** Comml. & Resid. Rehab.; **PROFL AFFIL & HONORS:** NAR, RNMI, MO Assn. of Realtors, St. Charles Cty. Bd. of Realtors, MO Indus. Devel. Council, GRI, CRS; **EDUC:** BS, 1968, Hist. & Psych., Univ. of MO; **GRAD EDUC:** MA, 1975, Soc. Sci. & Furistics, Webster Coll.; **OTHER ACT & HONORS:** St. Peters Kiwanis Club, St. Charles Cty. Hist. Soc., World Future Soc., Rivers W. Camera Club; **HOME ADD:** 12 River Trail St., St. Charles, MO 63301, (314)441-7558; **BUS ADD:** 81 Charleston Sq., St. Charles, MO 63301, (314)441-4100.

VALENTINE, Garrison N.——B: Apr. 7, 1929, New York, NY, *Partner*, Hoppin, Carey & Powell; **PRIM RE ACT:** Attorney; **SERVICES:** Rep. in resid. & comml. transactions; **REP CLIENTS:** Indivs. & corp. devels., purchasers & sellers; lenders in similar setting; **PREV EMPLOY:** USAF officer 1951-1961; **PROFL AFFIL & HONORS:** ABA, CT Bar Assn., Hartford Cty. Bar Assn., Dir., CT Attys.' Title Guaranty Fund, Inc.; **EDUC:** 1950, Hist., Eng., Yale Coll.; **GRAD EDUC:** LLB, 1964, Yale Law School; **MIL SERV:** USAF, Capt., Defense Medal, Unit Citation; **HOME ADD:** Otter Cove, Old Syabrook, CT 06475, (203)388-2649; **BUS ADD:** 370 Asylum St., Hartford, CT 06103, (203)249-8800.

VALENTINE, Russ C.——**B:** Mar. 22, 1945, Baton Rouge, LA, *Mgr. - Leisure Time Indus. and RE Consulting Servs.*, Laventhol & Horwath; **PRIM RE ACT:** Consultant; **SERVICES:** RE consulting services, mktg. studies, fin. and econ. analyses, deal structuring, valuation; **PROFL AFFIL & HONORS:** ULI; BOMA; WA State Lodging Assn.; Restaurant Assn. of WA; **EDUC:** BA, 1967, Govt., LA State Univ.; **GRAD EDUC:** MA, 1971, Guidance and Counseling, Wayne State Univ.; MBA, 1974, Hotel, Restaurant and Instnl. Mgmt., MI State Univ.; **MIL SERV:** USAF, Capt.; **HOME ADD:** 4355 Fernbrook Dr., Mercer Island, WA 98040; **BUS ADD:** 1100 Olive Way, Seattle, WA 98101, (206)621-1900.

VALLANCE, Anthony P.——**B:** Sept. 23, 1945, London, England, *Dir.*, Hanscomb Associates, Inc.; **PRIM RE ACT:** Consultant; **OTHER RE ACT:** Project mgrs., schedulers, cost estimators; **SERVICES:** Feasibility, cost control, scheduling, project mgmt., value engr.; **REP CLIENTS:** Owners of const. projects, devels., architects, engrs.; **PREV EMPLOY:** Bldg. Design Partnership, Sr. Cost Engr., TSG Intl., Chief Cost Engr.; **PROFL AFFIL & HONORS:** Cert. Cost Engr.; Soc. of Value Engrs.; Assoc. of the Royal Instn. of Chartered Surveyors, Cert. Cost Engr.; Assoc. of the Royal Instn. of Chartered Surveyors; **EDUC:** 1968, Bldg. Econ., Polytechnic of Central London, England; **GRAD EDUC:** 1970, Bldg. Econ., The No. Poly., London, England; **HOME ADD:** 609 W. Braddock Rd., Alexandria, VA 22302, (703)836-7194; **BUS ADD:** 1901 L St., N.W., Washington, DC 20036, (202)659-6550.

VALLANCE, John E.——**B:** Aug. 30, 1944, Los Angeles, CA, *VP*, Dillingham Corp., Dillingham Land Co.; **PRIM RE ACT:** Broker, Developer; **SERVICES:** Resid. devel., resort & primary condos.; **EDUC:** BS Bus., 1968, Econ., Univ. of NV, Las Vegas; **GRAD EDUC:** MBA, 1971, Mktg./Fin., Univ. of So. CA; **MIL SERV:** USN, Ens.; **HOME ADD:** PO Box 22628, Honolulu, HI 96822, (808)949-6563; **BUS ADD:** 1441 Kapiolani Blvd., Honolulu, HI 96814, (808)946-0771.

VALLARINO, P. Roy——**B:** Feb. 3, 1931, San Francisco, CA, *Atty.; RE Broker*, Vallarino, McNeil & Fabian; **PRIM RE ACT:** Consultant, Attorney, Insuror; **EDUC:** BS, Acctg., Univ. of San Francisco; **GRAD EDUC:** JD, Univ. of San Francisco; **HOME ADD:** 201 Stewart Dr., Tiburon, CA 94920, (415)435-1597; **BUS ADD:** 55 Professional Center Pkwy., San Rafael, CA 94903, (415)472-3434.

VALLIERE, Paul J.——*Sr. Dir. RE Services*, Gulf Oil Corp.; **PRIM RE ACT:** Property Manager; **BUS ADD:** Gulf Bldg. PO Box 1166, Pittsburgh, PA 15230, (412)263-5000.*

VALLONE, George T.——**B:** Aug. 24, 1954, *Gen. Pattner*, Hoboken Restorations; **PRIM RE ACT:** Developer, Builder, Property Manager, Syndicator; **OTHER RE ACT:** Partnership Syndication; **SERVICES:** Condo. Conversions - Tax Shelters; **EDUC:** BA, 1976, Bus. Admin., Gettysburg Coll.; **GRAD EDUC:** MBA, 1978, Mktg., Fordham Univ.; **EDUC HONORS:** Mid-Atlantic Conf., Pole Vault Champion 1976, MBA Intl. Mktg.; **OTHER ACT & HONORS:** N.M.A. Natl. Mimeographic Assn.; **HOME ADD:** 2 Wright Pl., Cresskill, NJ 07626; **BUS ADD:** 233 Park Ave., Hoboken, NJ 07030, (201)944-7476.

VAN CAMP, Brian R.——**B:** Aug. 23, 1940, Halstead, KS, *Partner*, Van Camp & Johnson, Attys. at Law; **PRIM RE ACT:** Attorney; **SERVICES:** Counsel RE Sund. and others involved in limited partnerships for RE; **REP CLIENTS:** Consolidated Capital Equities Corp., CA Hist. Props.; **PREV EMPLOY:** Commnr. of Corps., State of CA 1971-74; **PROFL AFFIL & HONORS:** Member, Sacramento and Los Angeles Cty. Bars; CA State Bar; ABA, RESSI; **EDUC:** AB, 1962, Pol. Sci., Univ. of CA at Berkeley; **GRAD EDUC:** LLB, 1965, Law, Boalt Hall School of Law, Univ. of CA at Berkeley; **OTHER ACT & HONORS:** Member, CA C of C; Sacramento Metropolitan C of C; Sutter Club; **HOME ADD:** 3614 Brockway Ct., Sacramento, CA 95815, (916)447-0269; **BUS ADD:** 555 Capitol Mall, Suite 400, Sacramento, CA 95814, (916)448-1155.

VANCE, Robert McNeely——**B:** Aug. 21, 1949, Newark, NJ, *Real Prop. Appraisal Consultant*, Robert McNeely Vance, Real Prop. Appraisal Consultant; **PRIM RE ACT:** Consultant, Appraiser, Assessor; **SERVICES:** Gen. real prop. evaluations; **REP CLIENTS:** Merrill Lynch, Homequity, Equitable and Executran relocation firms, Glen Gardner, Hampton and Lebanon municipalities; **PROFL AFFIL & HONORS:** SREA, NJAA, ULI, Lic. RE Broker, NJ, Cert. Tax Assessor, NJ; **EDUC:** AB, 1971, Journalism, Rutgers Univ.; **OTHER ACT & HONORS:** Assessor, Borough of Glen Gardner, Hampton; Dep. Assessor Tw. of Lebanon, Class repres. Rutgers Alumni Council; Dir., Delaware Valley Chap. 36, SREA; **HOME ADD:** 296 Grove St., Somerville, NJ 08876, (201)722-1559; **BUS ADD:** 7 E. High St., Somerville, NJ 08876, (201)526-1226.

VANCE, William A.——**B:** Nov. 13, 1933, Seattle WA, *Partner*, Shorett and Riely; **PRIM RE ACT:** Appraiser, Owner/Investor, Property Manager; **SERVICES:** RE appraisals, prop. mgmt., ltd. to owned props.; **REP CLIENTS:** Banks, ins. cos., municipalities, lawyers, devels., owners; **PREV EMPLOY:** Vance Corp., Hotel and Comml. RE Mgmt.; **PROFL AFFIL & HONORS:** NAR, MAI; CPM; **EDUC:** BA, 1955, Liberal Arts, Amherst Coll.; **MIL SERV:** USN Res.; Capt., 1956- present; **OTHER ACT & HONORS:** Phi Gamma Delta, Frat.; **HOME ADD:** 8435 S6 46, Mercer Island, WA 98040, (206)232-5230; **BUS ADD:** 121 Stewart St., Seattle, WA 98101, (206)682-0630.

VAN COURT, William T.——*Pres.*, Van Court & Co.; **PRIM RE ACT:** Broker, Consultant, Appraiser, Instructor; **PROFL AFFIL & HONORS:** AIREA; ASREC, MAI; CRE; **BUS ADD:** 420 Downing St., Denver, CO 80218, (303)777-5858.

VAN CURLER, Donald Edward——**B:** Apr. 13, 1931, Pontiac, MI, *Pres.*, Flying Dutchman Management, Inc.; **PRIM RE ACT:** Architect, Developer, Builder, Owner/Investor, Property Manager; **SERVICES:** Designing, bldg. and devel. comml. props., prop. mgmt.; **PREV EMPLOY:** Tool Design Dept., P.R. Mallory & Co., 1951-52; Draftsman, Designer, Charles M. Valentine Architect, 1954-1955; Wyeth & Harmon, Inc., 1955-56; Designer, James H. Livingston Architect, 1956-1959; Partner Hammett Assoc. in Arch., 1959-1961; Practice as Donald E. Van Curler, Architect, 1961-Present; **PROFL AFFIL & HONORS:** Pres., Van Curler & Assoc.; AIA; Pres., Amsterdam, Inc.; VP, Dir. Highway Club Systems, Inc.; Exec. Dir., Ann Arbor Research Inst.; Modular Amer. Historians; MI Soc. of Architects; Nat. Council of Arch. Registration Bds.; ULI; Nat. IL, GA, KY, MI, WI, TN, AL, TX, SC, AR, IA, Best Home for the Money Award, (1962), Best Home for the Money Award, (1963), both from the "American Home Magazine", and an Award of Excellence from the Amer. Inst. of Steel Const.; **GRAD EDUC:** BArch, Arch., Univ. of MI; **OTHER ACT & HONORS:** Korean Tae Kwon Do Assn., Phi Kappa Phi, Tau Sigma Delta; **HOME ADD:** 120 Packard Rd., Ann Arbor, MI 48104; **BUS ADD:** 2004 Hogback Rd., Suite 5, Ann Arbor, MI 48104, (313)971-4000.

VANDAELE, Christian——**B:** Apr. 12, 1947, Bergues, France, *Exec. VP*, American SCREG Construction, Inc.; **PRIM RE ACT:** Developer, Builder; **PROFL AFFIL & HONORS:** Amer. Land Devel. Assn., Nat. Assn. of Home Builders; **EDUC:** IHECS Tournai Belgium, 1971, Mktg. Mgmt.; **GRAD EDUC:** 1974, Mgmt., Kent State Univ.; **EDUC HONORS:** Magna Cum Laude, Enrolled in DBA program; **HOME ADD:** 3921 Hansen Dr., Dickenson, TX 77539; **BUS ADD:** 5858 Westheimer #506, Houston, TX 77057.

VANDEMOER, John J.——**B:** Jan. 30, 1910, Denver, CO, *Pres.*, Vandemoer, Reichelt & Carlso, P.C.; **PRIM RE ACT:** Attorney, Owner/Investor; **SERVICES:** Gen.; **REP CLIENTS:** Cumming Realty, Equitable S&L, Majestic S&L, FHA (Sedgwick Cty), 1st Nat. Bank of Jlsb, Towns of Jlsb., OVID & Sedg., Sedg. Cty.; **PROFL AFFIL & HONORS:** ABA, CO Bar Assn., 13th Jud. Dist. Bar Assn.; **EDUC:** BA, 1932, CO Coll.; **GRAD EDUC:** JD, 1942; **EDUC HONORS:** Top 3 scholastically; **OTHER ACT & HONORS:** Dep. Dist. Atty.; Cty. Atty.; City Atty., Lions Club, Elks; **HOME ADD:** 312 W. 6th, Julesburg, CO 80937, (303)474-3767; **BUS ADD:** 104 W. 1st, Julesborg, CO 80737, (303)474-3400.

VANDEN, Robert L.——**B:** Feb. 12, 1947, Elkins, WV, *Exec. VP*, The Gill Companies, RE Prop. Mgmt.; **PRIM RE ACT:** Consultant, Property Manager; **SERVICES:** Prop. mgmt. and condo. mktg. and consulting; **REP CLIENTS:** Instnl. investors, lenders, and indivs.; **PREV EMPLOY:** VP of Creative Prop. Mgmt., a Subsidiary of the Charter Co., Jacksonville, FL; **PROFL AFFIL & HONORS:** IREM, San Antonio; IREM, Nat.; San Antonio Bd. of Realtors; TX Assn. of Realtors; and Nat. Bd. of Realtors, CPM; **EDUC:** BBA, 1971, Mktg. & Mgmt., Univ. of Houston; **HOME ADD:** 430 Woodway Forest, San Antonio, TX 78216, (512)494-2187; **BUS ADD:** Box 599, San Antonio, TX 78292, (512)222-2434.

VANDERDRIFT, Richard——*Land Mgr.*, Tenneco, Inc., Tenneco Realty; **PRIM RE ACT:** Property Manager; **BUS ADD:** PO Box 2511, Houston, TX 77001, (713)757-2131.*

VANDERGRIFF, Wayne——**B:** Sept. 14, 1950, San Diego, CA, *Asst. Treas.*, Interstate General Corporation; **PRIM RE ACT:** Broker, Developer, Owner/Investor, Property Manager; **SERVICES:** Devel. of Resid. Units and Apts., prop. mgmt.; **PREV EMPLOY:** CPA, Arthur Anderson & Co.; **PROFL AFFIL & HONORS:** AICPA; **EDUC:** BA, 1973, Mathematics & Hist., Univ. of CA, San Diego; **GRAD EDUC:** MBA, 1977, Acctg., Univ. of CA, Berkeley; **EDUC HONORS:** with Honors; **OTHER ACT & HONORS:** Sierra Club, Phi Eta Sigma hon. soc.; **HOME ADD:** 25 Windward Hill, Oakland, CA 94618, (415)525-4680; **BUS ADD:** 555 Pierce St., Albany, CA 94706,

(415)525-4680.

VANDERWALL, Niek——*RE Dept.*, Oneida Ltd.; **PRIM RE ACT:** Property Manager; **BUS ADD:** Kenwood Station, Oneida, NY 13421, (315)361-3000.*

VAN DER WEERDT, Henk B.——**B:** Sept. 15, 1940, Amsterdam, Netherlands, *Exec. VP*, Wilma, Inc. (US Holding Co. of Wilma Grp.); **PRIM RE ACT:** Developer, Owner/Investor; **SERVICES:** Devel., investment, portfolio mgmt.; **PREV EMPLOY:** Pres. of advisor to Hexalon RE, Inc. (1975-78); Grp. Controller & VP, Fin. of Pakhoed Holding, NV, Rotterdam (1971-75); **PROFL AFFIL & HONORS:** ULI, ICSC, NAIOP, sev. profl. orgs. in Europe; **GRAD EDUC:** Doctoral degree, 1966, Bus. Econ., Univ. of Amsterdam; Post doctoral degree, 1971, Auditing, Univ. of Amsterdam; **MIL SERV:** Royal Dutch Air Force, 1st Lt.; **OTHER ACT & HONORS:** Cherokee Town & Ctry. Club, Commerce Club; **HOME ADD:** 5865 Riverwood Dr. NW, Atlanta, GA 30328; **BUS ADD:** 233 Peachtree St., Ste. 500, Atlanta, GA 30303, (404)524-2004.

VAN DERWERKER, John R.——**B:** Oct. 14, 1940, Summit, NJ, *Assoc. Broker*, Century 21 Homes Unlimited, Inc.; **PRIM RE ACT:** Broker, Owner/Investor, Instructor, Property Manager; **REP CLIENTS:** Resid. Home Builders/Purchasers; **PREV EMPLOY:** Larry Eol Realtors, Camp Springs, MD 1969-77; **EDUC:** BA, 1962, Hist., Pol. Sci., Univ. of MD; **MIL SERV:** US Navy Reserve, 1963-69; **OTHER ACT & HONORS:** Deci Investors, Investment Club, Pres.; **HOME ADD:** 702 Gleneagles Dr., Ft. Washington, MD 20744, (301)292-6033; **BUS ADD:** 9000 Old Branch Ave., Clinton, MD 20735, (301)868-0500.

VANDEVENDER, Junior M.——**B:** May 13, 1948, Valley Head, WV, *RE Counselor*, Merrill Lynch Realty/Chris Coile, Inc.; **PRIM RE ACT:** Syndicator, Consultant, Property Manager, Owner/Investor; **SERVICES:** Sales, counseling; **PREV EMPLOY:** Baltimore Gas & Elect. Co.; **PROFL AFFIL & HONORS:** GRI; **MIL SERV:** US Army, SP/4; **HOME ADD:** PO Box 7858, Baltimore, MD 21221, (301)687-3500; **BUS ADD:** 8202 Pulaski Hwy., Baltimore, MD 21237, (301)524-5600.

VANDIVIER, Thomas Monroe——**B:** June 9, 1954, Baltimore, MD, *Atty. at Law*, Law Office of Thomas M. Vandivier; **PRIM RE ACT:** Attorney, Developer, Syndicator; **SERVICES:** Legal; **PROFL AFFIL & HONORS:** TX Bar Assn., ABA; **EDUC:** BBA, 1976, Bus. - Econ., Southwestern Univ.; **GRAD EDUC:** JD, 1978, Law, Bates Coll. of Law (Univ. of Houston); **EDUC HONORS:** Magna Cum Laude; Dean's Honor List, etc.; **HOME ADD:** 8803 Sharpview, Houston, TX 77036, (713)995-1321; **BUS ADD:** 2800 N. Loop W., Suite 418, Houston, TX 77092, (713)688-0926.

VAN HAEFTEN, Karel A.R.——**B:** Sept. 7, 1947, Holland, *Pres.*, Rare Earth Enterprises; **PRIM RE ACT:** Broker, Consultant, Appraiser, Developer, Owner/Investor, Syndicator, Real Estate Publisher; **OTHER RE ACT:** Intl. tax shelter RE opportunities; **SERVICES:** Consulting, appraising, mktg. exotic RE opportunities world-wide; **REP CLIENTS:** private indivs. & grps. seeking exotic investments or retreats; **PROFL AFFIL & HONORS:** Intl. RE exchanges; **EDUC:** UC, Berkeley, CA; **HOME ADD:** PO Box 946, Sausalito, CA 94966, (415)331-2700; **BUS ADD:** Bridgeway 946, Sausalito, CA 94966, (415)331-2700.

VAN LEAR, Stevan H.——**B:** May 5, 1947, Richmond, VA, *Pres.*, Stevan Van Lear, Inc.; **PRIM RE ACT:** Broker, Consultant, Appraiser, Developer, Lender, Owner/Investor, Property Manager, Syndicator; **SERVICES:** Turn key approach to acquisition, planning, devel., const. & spaces; **REP CLIENTS:** Self; **PROFL AFFIL & HONORS:** Realtor, RMNI, CCIM Candidate; **EDUC:** BA, 1970, Econ., Hampden-Sydney Coll., Hampden-Sydney, VA; BS, 1976, Biology, CO State Univ.; **EDUC HONORS:** Cum Laude; **HOME ADD:** 1037 Sairs Reef, Ft. Collins, CO 80526, (303)223-2253; **BUS ADD:** POB 1882, Ft. Collins, CO 80522, (303)221-0918.

VAN LOWE, William T.——*Dir.*, Department of Housing and Urban Development, Program Budget Dev. Division; **PRIM RE ACT:** Lender; **BUS ADD:** 451 Seventh St., S.W., Washington, DC 20410, (202)755-7284.*

VAN ORMER, Darrell N., Jr.——**B:** Oct. 10, 1947, Lewistown PA, *Atty.*; **PRIM RE ACT:** Attorney, Owner/Investor, Instructor; **OTHER RE ACT:** V Chmn. Lanc Cty. Planning Comm.; **SERVICES:** Legal, title ins., fin., tax advice; **PREV EMPLOY:** 6 yrs. as practicing atty.; past instr. in tax and RE courses for 3 colls.; **PROFL AFFIL & HONORS:** PA Bar Assn.; Lanc Cty. Bar Assn., RE Sect., Who's Who in East; **EDUC:** BA, 1969, Pol. Sci. & Bus. Admin. with Hist. minor, Elizabethtown Coll.; **GRAD EDUC:** JD, 1975, Duquesne Univ. Sch. of Law; **EDUC HONORS:** Dean's List, Nat. Hist. Hon. Soc.; **MIL SERV:** US Army, Sgt., 1969-71; **OTHER ACT & HONORS:** VP Elizabethtown Borough Council; **HOME ADD:** 258 N. Poplar St., Elizabethtown, PA 17022; **BUS ADD:** 344 S. Market St., Elizabethtown, PA 17022, (717)367-6831.

VANTASSEL, James D.——**B:** Feb. 12, 1945, Watertown, SD, *RE Prof.*, Marin Community Colleges, Ctr. for Profl. Educ. in RE; **PRIM RE ACT:** Broker, Consultant, Developer, Instructor, Real Estate Publisher; **SERVICES:** Consulting; **PREV EMPLOY:** Investments, computers; **PROFL AFFIL & HONORS:** CCIM, NAR, MBA, CCIM; **EDUC:** BA, 1967, Sociology, CA State Univ. at Los Angeles; **GRAD EDUC:** MBA, 1976, Fin., RE, Pepperdine Univ.; **OTHER ACT & HONORS:** Listed in Who's Who in Creative RE; **HOME ADD:** 304 Joyce Way, Mill Valley, CA 94941, (415)383-3211; **BUS ADD:** Frank Howard Allen Comml., 700 Larkspur Landing #100, Larkspur, CA 94939, (415)461-4300.

VAN'T HOF, Willaim Keith——**B:** Feb. 18, 1930, NY, NY, *Partner*, Schmidt, Howlett, Van't Hof, Snell & Vana; **PRIM RE ACT:** Attorney, Developer, Instructor, Owner/Investor; **SERVICES:** Condo. devel., planning, processing & mktg.; **REP CLIENTS:** Amer. Invsco Corp., Foremost Ins. Co., Radnor Corp., W&R Builders, Inc.; **PROFL AFFIL & HONORS:** Grand Rapids Bar Assn. (Tr.), State Bar of MI (Condo. sect.), ABA, Chmn. Condo. Section; **EDUC:** BA, 1951, Poli. sci., Hope Coll., Holland, MI; **GRAD EDUC:** LLB, 1954, Corp. & RE law, Univ. of MI, Ann Arbor; **EDUC HONORS:** Pres., Student council, member, Blue Key Honor Soc., Barristers Soc.; **MIL SERV:** USN, Lt.; **OTHER ACT & HONORS:** Pres., United Way of Kent Cty. 1979-80, Chmn. , MI Heart Assn. 1973-75, VP, Amer. Heart Assn. 1977-78; **HOME ADD:** 3160 Hall St. SE, Grand Rapids, MI 49506; **BUS ADD:** 700 John Frey Bldg., Union Bank Plaza, Grand Rapids, MI 49503, (616)459-5151.

VAN TIL, Bernard A.——**B:** Jan. 1947, *Reg. Mgr.*, H&W Props. Inc., Subs. of Hartgen & Willard Mort. Assoc. Inc.; **PRIM RE ACT:** Property Manager; **OTHER RE ACT:** Leasing, Consultant; **SERVICES:** Full; **PROFL AFFIL & HONORS:** BOMA & IREM; **BUS ADD:** 141 Ionia NW, Grand Rapids, MI 49503, (616)459-4556.

VAN WAGONER, Robert L.——**B:** June 4, 1936, Lake Orion, MI, *Justice of the Peace*, Reno Justice Court, Dept. No. 1; **PRIM RE ACT:** Attorney; **PREV EMPLOY:** Reno City Atty.; **PROFL AFFIL & HONORS:** Washoe, NV ABA; NV Amer. Trial Lawyers Assn.; NV Crime Commn.; NIMLO; Who's Who in Amer. Law 1st Ed.; Int'l. Who's Who in Community Serv., Outstanding Young Man (Sparks Jaycees); Distinguished Serv. Award, U.S. Jaycees and Reno Jaycees; **EDUC:** BS, 1958, Speech, NW Univ.; **GRAD EDUC:** JD, 1966, CA W. Univ. School of Law; **EDUC HONORS:** Recipient of Nat. Trial Attys. Award, Appellate Moot Court, Best Oral Argument (1965) CA-W; **MIL SERV:** USN, Lt.; **OTHER ACT & HONORS:** Reno City Atty. (1971-1979); Justice of Peace (1980-present); Masons; Naval Reserve; Toastmasters; Democratic Party; First Methodist Church; E Lampus Vitus; Multiple Sclerosis Soc.; NAACP; BPO Elks; Shrine Club; Prospector's Club; Jesters; **HOME ADD:** 2300 Dickerson Rd. 24, Reno, NV 89503, (702)322-5426; **BUS ADD:** Washoe Cty. Court Hse, POB 11130, Reno, NV 89520, (702)785-4230.

VARDEMAN, F. Burt——**B:** Feb. 2, 1925, Columbus, GA, *Prop. Mgr./Broker*, Presbyterian Ctr., Inc.; **PRIM RE ACT:** Broker, Property Manager; **SERVICES:** Prop. mgmt., leasing, consulting; **PREV EMPLOY:** Peachtree Ctr. Co. (Portman Props.); Lenox Towers-Hunt Props., Inc.; **PROFL AFFIL & HONORS:** Soc. of Real Prop. Admin.; BOMA, Real Prop. Admin. (RPA); Broker; Pres. BOMA - Atlanta; **EDUC:** BS, 1949, Building Construction, Auburn Univ.; **MIL SERV:** USAF; T/Sgt., Air Medal; **OTHER ACT & HONORS:** Kiwanis Club of Atlanta; **HOME ADD:** 3064 Silvapine Trail NE, Atlanta, GA 30345, (404)325-3778; **BUS ADD:** 341 Ponce de Leon Ave. NE, Atlanta, GA 30365, (404)873-1531.

VARLEY, Arthur J., Jr.——**B:** June 21, 1949, Jacksonville, FL, *Pres.*, Varley & Varley (AKA: Varley Enterprises); **PRIM RE ACT:** Consultant, Developer, Owner/Investor, Property Manager; **OTHER RE ACT:** Acquisition negotiations; **SERVICES:** Property evaluation, acquisition, mgmt. & devel.; **REP CLIENTS:** Private; **PREV EMPLOY:** Alutra Enterprises, VP; Principal & Dir., Kopple Varley Prps.; Grass Mountain Ski Parks of Amer., Inc., Pres.; **PROFL AFFIL & HONORS:** AMA; San Diego Cty. Medical Assn., Who's Who in Fin. & Ind., Marquis 22nd Ed.; **EDUC:** BS, 1971, Biology, Chemistry & Zoology, San Diego State Univ.; **GRAD EDUC:** MD (Doctor of Medicine, 1975, Medicine/Orthopaedic Surgery, Univ. of FL/Univ. of CA - San Diego. Degree 76-80/Orthopaedic Surgeon/Univ. of So. CA - Orthopaedic Hospital; **EDUC HONORS:** Grad. with Honors and Distinction in Major; **OTHER ACT & HONORS:** Med. Adv. Nat. Ski Patrol, Far West region; **BUS ADD:** 7314 Summertime Ln., Culver

City, CA 90230, (213)838-2119.

VARNER, B. Douglas——**B:** May 2, 1920, Ida Grove, IA, *Partner*, Gage & Tucker; **PRIM RE ACT:** Attorney; **SERVICES:** Legal; **REP CLIENTS:** Lenders, indivs., devels., & title cos.; **PREV EMPLOY:** With Gage & Tucker over 30 years; **PROFL AFFIL & HONORS:** ABA; KS City Bar Assn. & Lawyers Assn., Delta Theta Phi - Law Fraternity; **EDUC:** Bus. Admin., Univ. of NE, 2 1/2 yrs.; **GRAD EDUC:** LLB, 1950, Law, Univ. of MO at Kansas City; **EDUC HONORS:** Assoc. Editor-Law Review; **MIL SERV:** USN, 1942-45, Sp 3; **OTHER ACT & HONORS:** Kansas City Club; Newcomen Soc.; Bd. of Mgrs., Downtown YMCA, Other bus. address: PO Box 144, Business Hwy. 54, Rte. 1, Lake Ozark, MO 65049; **HOME ADD:** PO Box 204, Tuscumbia, MO 65082, (314)369-2552; **BUS ADD:** 2345 Grand Ave., PO Box 23428, Kansas City, MO 64141.

VARNUM, Ralph W.——**B:** May 26, 1936, Denver, CO, *Pres.*, Varnum/Armstrong/Deeter Inc.; **PRIM RE ACT:** Broker, Instructor, Syndicator, Consultant, Developer, Owner/Investor; **SERVICES:** Turnkey Dev. Serv.; Brokerage of Income Prop. and User Prop.; Site Selection; Synd.; Leasing; **PROFL AFFIL & HONORS:** RNMI, NAR, Comml. Investment Courses, RNMI, CCIM; **EDUC:** BS, 1958, Gen. Bus. Admin., Univ. of KS; **EDUC HONORS:** Dean's List, Omicron Delta Pi; Sr. Men's Hon. Soc.; **MIL SERV:** USN; Lt. J.G.; **OTHER ACT & HONORS:** Past Pres., Overland Park C of C; Past Pres., Johnson Cty. C of C; Pres. Club; Dir., Shawnee Mission Med. Ctr. Foundation; Dir., Ctry. Hill Bank; **HOME ADD:** 6037 Windsor Dr., Fairway, KS 66205, (913)677 1127; **BUS ADD:** 4801 W. 110th - Suite 100, Overland Park, KS 66211, (913)341-4200.

VARTANIAN, Thomas P.——*Gen. Counsel*, Department of Housing and Urban Development, Fed. Home Loan Bank Board; **PRIM RE ACT:** Lender; **BUS ADD:** 451 SeventhSt., S.W., Washington, DC 20410, (202)377-6404.*

VASCONCELLOS, William L.——**B:** Feb. 17, 1946, San Jose, CA, *Atty*, Everle, Berlin, Kading, Turnbow & Gillespie, Chartered; **PRIM RE ACT:** Attorney; **SERVICES:** Ducument prep. & review, opinion letters to FNMA; **REP CLIENTS:** Safeco Title Ins. Co. of ID, Boise Cascade Corp., Trus Joist Corp., Mountain Bell, Sherwood & Roberts, Inc.; **PREV EMPLOY:** Law clerk for ID Supreme Ct., 1971-73, 1974; FMHA Loan Closing Atty., 1975-77; **PROFL AFFIL & HONORS:** Amer. Bar Assn., Boise Bar Assn., ID State Bar Assn., State Bar Assn of CA, Comm. on land use, planning & zoning of ABA Sec. of Local gov. law; APA planning & law div.; **EDUC:** BA, 1967, Econ., Stanford Univ.; **GRAD EDUC:** JD, 1971, Univ. of CA at Berkeley (Boalt Hall Sch. of Law); **EDUC HONORS:** Dept. Hons. in Econ., Top ten percent or hons. in real property, real property security, & land use and devel.; **OTHER ACT & HONORS:** Admin. Consumer Div., Washoe Cty., Nevada DA's office, Bogus Basin Recreation Assoc., (Bogus Basin Ski Area); Approved Atty. for FNMA Loan Program for Condos. & Planned Unit Devels.; **HOME ADD:** Boise, ID 83701, (208)343-4330; **BUS ADD:** 300 N. Sixth St., PO Box 1368, Boise, ID 83701, (208)344-8535.

VAS DIAS, James S.——**B:** Oct. 16, 1943, Fresno, CA, *Sr. Mgmt. Consultant*, SRI International (formerly Stanford Research Institute); **PRIM RE ACT:** Consultant; **SERVICES:** Mgmt. consulting, project feasibility, financial planning; **REP CLIENTS:** Devels., large land holding corps., pvt. cos., fin. instns.; **PREV EMPLOY:** Anheuser Busch; **PROFL AFFIL & HONORS:** ULI, Amer Land Devel. Assn.; **EDUC:** BS, 1965, Econ., St. Mary's Coll.; **GRAD EDUC:** MBA, 1968, Fin., UCLA; **OTHER ACT & HONORS:** Chmn., Los Altos Planning Commn., Chmn., Los Altos Arch. & Site Review Comm.; **BUS ADD:** 333 Ravenswood Ave, Menlo Park, CA 94025, (415)859-4534.

VATTEROTT, Gregory B.——**B:** Aug. 7, 1942, St. Louis, MO, *Pres.*, Charles F. Vatterott & Co.; **PRIM RE ACT:** Broker, Attorney, Developer, Builder, Owner/Investor, Property Manager; **SERVICES:** Dev. of comml. & resid. props., prop. mgmt.; **PROFL AFFIL & HONORS:** MO Bar Assn.; RE Bd. of Greater St. Louis; **EDUC:** BS, 1964, St. Louis Univ.; **GRAD EDUC:** JD, 1966, St. Louis Univ.; LLM, 1968, Univ. of MO at Kansas City; **OTHER ACT & HONORS:** United Way, Coro Found.; Child Center Of our Lady of Grace, Mary Queen & Mother Nursing Home; Our Lade of Life Apts.; **HOME ADD:** 13233 Pinetree Lake Dr., Chesterfield, MO 63017, (314)878-5317; **BUS ADD:** 10449 St. Charles Rock Rd., St. Ann, MO 63074, (314)427-4000.

VAUCLAIR, Andre S.——**B:** May 30, 1932, Montreal, *VP*, Metropolitan Life Insurance Co., RE Investments; **PRIM RE ACT:** Lender; **OTHER RE ACT:** Investor; **SERVICES:** Fin./Acquisitions of RE Assets; **REP CLIENTS:** RE Devel.; **PREV EMPLOY:** Coronation Mort. Corp. (1962-1968); **PROFL AFFIL & HONORS:** MBA; Intl. Council of Shopping Ctrs.; Montreal RE Bd.; Canadian RE Bd.; Order of Engrs. of Quebec; Montreal Bd. of Trade, Civil Engr.; **GRAD EDUC:** BSCA - P. Eng., 1956, Civil Engr., Polytechnique (Univ. of Montreal); **MIL SERV:** Infantry, Capt. (Reserve); **HOME ADD:** 371 Morrison Ave., Town of Mount Royal, H3R 1K8, Que, Can, (514)733-0565; **BUS ADD:** 1550 Place du Canada, Montreal, H3B 2N2, Que., Canada, (514)861-0923.

VAUGHAN, C. Porter, Jr.——**B:** May 11, 1919, Stevensville, King & Queen Cty., VA, *Pres.*, C. Porter Vaughan, Inc., Realtors; **PRIM RE ACT:** Broker, Syndicator, Consultant, Developer, Owner/Investor; **PROFL AFFIL & HONORS:** NAR, VA Board of Realtors, Richmond, VA, CPM, Realtor of the year; **EDUC:** BA, 1940, His. and Eng., Univ. of Richmond; **MIL SERV:** USAAF, Capt.; **OTHER ACT & HONORS:** Dir., Pres. Founder-Willow Oaks Ctry. Club, Scottish Rite Mason, Dir., C. of C.; Kiwanis Club; Trustee Univ. of Richmond; Dir., First VA Bank, Colonial; **HOME ADD:** 2881 Braidwood Rd., Richmond, VA 23225, (804)272-0946; **BUS ADD:** 3312 W. Cary St., PO Box 7474, Richmond, VA 23221, (804)355-5733.

VAUGHAN, Herbert W.——**B:** June 1, 1920, Brookline, MA, *Sr. Partner*, Hale and Dorr; **PRIM RE ACT:** Attorney; **SERVICES:** Legal; **PROFL AFFIL & HONORS:** ABA; MA Bar Assn.; Boston Bar Assn., Fellow, Amer. Bar Found.; Member, Amer. Coll. of RE Attys.; Member, Amer. Coll. of Mort. Attys.; **EDUC:** BS, 1941, Phil., Harvard Coll.; **GRAD EDUC:** LLB, 1948, Harvard Law School; **EDUC HONORS:** Cum Laude; **OTHER ACT & HONORS:** Member, Union Club (Boston); The Bay Club (Boston); Badminton and Tennis Club; Longwood Cricket Club; Coral Beach and Tennis Club (Bermuda); Corporator, Boston Five Cents Savings Bank; **HOME ADD:** 119 Jericho Rd., Weston, MA 02193, (617)899-0775; **BUS ADD:** 60 State St., Boston, MA 02109, (617)742-9100.

VAUGHN, Bill——**B:** Oct. 24, 1942, Oakland, CA, *Pres.*, Spring Branch Prop. Inc.; **PRIM RE ACT:** Broker, Syndicator, Builder, Property Manager; **SERVICES:** Build and Dev. Residential Investment Prop.; **PREV EMPLOY:** VP Finance, Uncle Ben's Foods Grp. Controller, Mars, Inc.; **PROFL AFFIL & HONORS:** FEI, AICPA, TSCPA, HBOR, RESSI, CPA, Broker, MBA, Securities Dealer; **EDUC:** BA, 1964, Pol. Sci., Hist., Univ. CA at Berkeley; **GRAD EDUC:** MBA, 1970, CA State Univ. at Fullerton; **BUS ADD:** 14770 Memorial Dr., Houston, TX 77024, (713)870-0808.

VAUGHN, Charles H., Jr.——**B:** Mar. 15, 1944, Ft. Worth, TX, *VP-Acquisitions*, Envicon Development Corp., Acquisitions; **PRIM RE ACT:** Owner/Investor, Syndicator; **SERVICES:** Origination, Evaluation, Negotiation & Closing of Comml. RE Purchases; **PREV EMPLOY:** Regional VP-Acquisitions, Robert. A. McNeil Corp-Mid-Atlantic Territory; **PROFL AFFIL & HONORS:** RESSI, NY Univ. RE Inst. Grad.; **EDUC:** BS, BA, 1966, Econ./Econometrics, Boston Coll.; **GRAD EDUC:** MBA, 1972, Double Major:Fin. and Acctg., Northwestern Grad. School of Mgmt.; **MIL SERV:** USN; Lt., Vietnam Service; **HOME ADD:** 23 Sherwood Ave., Pelham Manor, NY 10803, (914)738-4797; **BUS ADD:** 630 Fifth Ave., Suite 570, NY, NY 10111, (212)581-8818.

VAUGHN, Paul O.——**B:** June 6, 1946, Bellingham, WA, *Atty.*; **PRIM RE ACT:** Attorney, Regulator, Builder, Owner/Investor; **SERVICES:** Counseling, documentation, devel. & synd.; **REP CLIENTS:** Brokers, lenders, owners & devels. as well as local govt. regulatory agencies, relating to investments, subdivision, devel. & sale of comml. & resid. props.; **PREV EMPLOY:** Teton Cty. Dep. Cty. Atty., Provident Fed. S&L Assn., Jackson State Bank; **PROFL AFFIL & HONORS:** ABA, WY Bar Assn, UT Bar Assn., Land Devel. Inst., Comm. Assn. Inst.; **EDUC:** BS, 1969, Pol. Sci., Intl. Relations, Univ. of UT; **GRAD EDUC:** JD, 1973, Univ. of UT; **EDUC HONORS:** Dean's List; **OTHER ACT & HONORS:** Dep. Cty. Atty., Teton Cty., 1975-77, 1978-present; **HOME ADD:** Box 1492, Jackson Hole, WY 83001, (807)733-5437; **BUS ADD:** Box 1569, Jackson Hole, WY 83001, (307)733-7792.

VAUGHN, Rufus C.——**B:** Jan. 5, 1929, Elba, AL, *Chmn. and Pres.*, First Federal Savings and Loan Assn.; **PRIM RE ACT:** Appraiser, Lender; **SERVICES:** Appraiser and lender; **EDUC:** BSBA, 1958, Univ. of FL; **EDUC HONORS:** Grad. with Honors-Fin.; **MIL SERV:** USAF, S/Sgt.; **HOME ADD:** 601 Dogwood St., Marianna, FL 32446, (904)482-2608; **BUS ADD:** 203 N. Green St., Marianna, FL 32446, (904)526-2300.

VAUGHTERS, Cecilie A.——**B:** Jul. 29, 1959, Glenridge, NJ, *Assoc. Atty.*, Chapman, Norwind & Vaughters; **PRIM RE ACT:** Attorney; **REP CLIENTS:** Homeowners, corps. involved in prop. mgmt. const.; **PREV EMPLOY:** Counseling, settlements, package prep., contracts; **PROFL AFFIL & HONORS:** DC Bar, ABA, OH Bar Assoc., WA Bar Assoc.; **EDUC:** BBA, 1975, Acctg./Econ., OH Univ.; **GRAD EDUC:** J.D., 1978, Law, Georgetown Univ. Law Ctr.; **EDUC HONORS:**

Dean's List, Who's Who Among Amer. Women, Leadership Award; **HOME ADD:** 2436 L'Enfant Sq. S.E., Washington, DC 20020, (202)575-1288; **BUS ADD:** 733 15th St. N.W., Suite 920, Washington, DC 20005, (202)575-1288.

VAYDIK, Frank W.——B: Oct. 21, 1939, Detroit, MI, *Managing Partner*, Economic Development Group; **PRIM RE ACT:** Consultant, Developer, Builder, Owner/Investor, Property Manager, Syndicator; **PROFL AFFIL & HONORS:** ULI, IREM, BOMA; **EDUC:** BA, 1965, Econ. & Statistics, Wayne Univ.; **HOME ADD:** 7320 Shattuck, Saginaw, MI 48603, (517)793-8866; **BUS ADD:** Ste. 65, 4800 Fashion Sq., Saginaw, MI 48604, (517)799-9669.

VEAL, Louis D., Jr.——B: Feb. 14, 1937, W. Palm Beach, FL, *Pres.*, The Veal Co., Inc.; **PRIM RE ACT:** Broker, Appraiser, Real Estate Publisher; **SERVICES:** Feasibility studies, confidential acquisitions, investment consulting, educ. instruction, project devel.; **REP CLIENTS:** Gen. Electric Cred Corp., EI DuPont, Allied Chemicals, Automotive Div., Prudential Ins., Pan Amer. Bankshares, Air Can., Banco de Boston Intl., First Tennessee Bank, Dayton Hudson Corp.; **PREV EMPLOY:** Pres., Keyes Mgmt. Co., Miami, FL; **PROFL AFFIL & HONORS:** Nat. Assn. of Realtors; TN Assn. of Realtors; Nat. Inst. of RE Mgmt.; Bldg. Owners and Mgrs. Assn., Cert. Prop. Mgr., CPM of Year, S. FL, 1975; **EDUC:** BS, 1958, Bus., Acctg., Univ. of TN, Knoxville; **GRAD EDUC:** 1960, Market Research, RE, Univ. of TN; **MIL SERV:** USCG, E-3; **OTHER ACT & HONORS:** Phi Gamma Delta, Social Frat.; Knoxville C of C; Chmn. of Indus. Sites Comm.; Faculty, Univ. of TN; N. Dade Cty., FL Jr. Coll.; Faculty, IREM; Indep. Lecturer on RE Subjects; Qualified expert witness on RE value, investment analysis, const. costs, and rental values, Knox Cty., TN and Dade Cty., FL; **HOME ADD:** 5525 Riverbend Dr., Knoxville, TN 37919, (615)584-9345; **BUS ADD:** 5525 Riverbend Dr., Knoxville, TN 37919, (615)584-9052.

VEATCH, Stanley T., Jr.——B: Nov. 19, 1926, Gainesville, FL, *RE Mgr.*, Winn Dixie Stores, Inc., RE; **PRIM RE ACT:** Property Manager; **OTHER RE ACT:** Market Analyst & Leasing Agent; **SERVICES:** Valuation, Devel. & Mgmt. of Comml. Props.; **REP CLIENTS:** Devels. & Lenders in Comml. (Shopping Ctrs. primarily) Devel.; **PROFL AFFIL & HONORS:** ICSC; **EDUC:** AA, 1957, Univ. of FL; **MIL SERV:** USN, Ensg.; **HOME ADD:** 2841 Oak Creek Ln., Jacksonville, FL 32221, (904)783-2308; **BUS ADD:** PO Box B, Jacksonville, FL 32203, (904)783-5000.

VEGO, Guillermo, Jr.——B: Nov. 29, 1948, Harlingen, TX, *Atty.*, Law Office of Guillermo Vega, Jr., Legal; **PRIM RE ACT:** Attorney; **SERVICES:** Legal Service; **REP CLIENTS:** Erico, St. Joseph Med. Ctr., Intl. Medical Supply, Co.; **PREV EMPLOY:** Cameron Cty. Title Co.; **PROFL AFFIL & HONORS:** ABA, Fed. Bar Assn., Assn. of Trial Lawyers of Amer.; **EDUC:** BS, 1972, Chemistry, Pan Amer. Univ.; **GRAD EDUC:** MA, 1973, Admin., Univ. of TX; **EDUC HONORS:** Magna Cum Laude; **OTHER ACT & HONORS:** Brownsville Jaycees, Sierra Club; **HOME ADD:** PO Box 1938, Brownsville, TX, (512)546-5573; **BUS ADD:** PO Box 1938, 3301 Boca Chica Suite 211, Brownsville, TX 78521, (512)546-5573.

VEITH, Edwin——*Pres.*, U.S. Filter Corp.; **PRIM RE ACT:** Property Manager; **BUS ADD:** 522 Fifth Ave., New York, NY 10036, (212)575-6800.*

VELEZ, Hector J.——B: Apr. 21, 1935, Santurce, PR, *Partner*, Laventhol & Horwath, Acctg. and Auditing; **OTHER RE ACT:** CPA; **SERVICES:** Acctg. and auditing services; **REP CLIENTS:** April Industries, Inc.; **PREV EMPLOY:** Audit Mgr., Peat Marwick Mitchell & Co.; **PROFL AFFIL & HONORS:** Nat. Assn. of Accountants; AICPA; PR Soc. of CPAs; Mort. Bankers Assn., Past VP, PR Soc. of CPAs; **EDUC:** BBA, 1958, Acctg., Univ. of PR; **MIL SERV:** US Army, 2nd Lt.; **OTHER ACT & HONORS:** VP, PR Bd. of Accountancy; Caparra Country Club; **HOME ADD:** Catarata D-1, Urb. El Remanso, Rio Piedras, PR 00928, (809)790-2367; **BUS ADD:** GPO Box 70130, San Juan, PR 00936, (809)765-5580.

VELIKANJE, E. Frederick——B: Apr. 3, 1912, Yakima, WA, *Pres.*, Velikanje, Moore & Shore, Inc. PS; **PRIM RE ACT:** Attorney; **SERVICES:** Atty. at Law; **PROFL AFFIL & HONORS:** WA State Bar (Pres. 1971-1972); ABA (Delegate 1966-1972); Amer. Coll. Probate (Regent 1972-1978), Fellow, ACPC, Fellow ABA; **EDUC:** 1932, Yakima Valley Jr. Coll.; **GRAD EDUC:** 1935, Univ. of WA; **OTHER ACT & HONORS:** KCCH; Masonic Bodies; BPOE; George Washington Foundation Advisory Bd.; Peoples Bank; **HOME ADD:** 8711 Hawthorne Dr., Yakima, WA 98908, (509)966-3939; **BUS ADD:** 303 E 'D' St., Yakima, WA 98901, (509)248-6030.

VELLA, Ruth Ann——B: Aug. 18, 1942, Chester County, *Owner/Pres.*, Heritage Realty, Resid.; **PRIM RE ACT:** Broker, Instructor, Consultant, Appraiser, Developer, Property Manager, Lender, Owner/Investor, Real Estate Publisher; **PREV EMPLOY:** Reeve Realty, 201 Market St., Newport, DE 19808; **PROFL AFFIL & HONORS:** GRI Instr.; RMNI; NCCBOR; IFA Candidate WCR; Instr. - Delaware Coll.; Wilmington Coll., GRI, CRS, CRB; **EDUC:** CRB; **OTHER ACT & HONORS:** ZONTA, Newark Profl. Women's Org., Toastmasters; **HOME ADD:** 23 Tenby Chase, Newark, DE 19711, (302)239-4280; **BUS ADD:** 3619 B. Kirkwood Highway, Wilmington, DE 19808, (302)999-9931.

VENDOLA, Arthur N.——B: Dec. 22, 1934, New Haven, CT, *Prin. Owner*, A.N. Vendola & Assoc.; **OTHER RE ACT:** Consulting engr. & constr. consulting; **SERVICES:** Consulting, design, planning, quality control; **REP CLIENTS:** State of CT, Brookhaven Nat. Lab., Pfizer Inc., City of NY, Arthur Indus. Inc.; **PREV EMPLOY:** Var. consulting engr. firms in CT; **PROFL AFFIL & HONORS:** Fellow Amer. Soc. of Civil Engrs., Member Nat. Soc. of Profl. Engrs., Amer. Consulting Engrs. Council, Pres. CT Soc. of Civil Engrs., Chmn Bd. of Materials Review, etc.; **EDUC:** BCE, 1956, Civil Engrg., Yale Univ.; **GRAD EDUC:** MS, 1968, Engr. Mech., Univ. of CT; **OTHER ACT & HONORS:** Chmn. Bd. of Materials Review; **HOME ADD:** 64 Forest Hill Dr., Farmington, CT 06032, (203)677-1152; **BUS ADD:** 43 Cedar St., New Britain, CT 06052, (203)223-7214.

VENGOECHEA, Nilsa De——B: Mar. 31, 1938, NYC, NY, *Broker-Salesman*, Esslinger, Wooten, Maxwell, Inc.; **PRIM RE ACT:** Broker, Consultant, Owner/Investor; **REP CLIENTS:** Foreign investors and devel. in comml. and resid. props.; **PROFL AFFIL & HONORS:** Coral Gables Bd. of Realtors; FIABCI (Intl. RE Fed.); **EDUC:** BA, 1959, Amer. Hist./Pol. Sci., Manhattanville Coll.; **OTHER ACT & HONORS:** FL Philharmonic Guild (Exec. Bd.); WLRN - Public Radio (Exec. Bd.); Univ. of Miami Womens Guild; **HOME ADD:** 16123 Kingsmoor Way, Miami Lakes, FL 33014, (305)825-8302; **BUS ADD:** 1553 San Ignacio, Coral Gables, FL 33146, (305)667-8871.

VENITSKY, Don——B: Dec. 24, 1955, Bellflower, CA, *RE Coordinator*, Swett & Crawford Grp.; **PRIM RE ACT:** Property Manager; **OTHER RE ACT:** RE Officer Handling Branch Office RE Matters; **SERVICES:** Facilitates Leases, Locating New Space, Prop. Acctg.; **PREV EMPLOY:** Facility Sciences Corp. 1978-1980; Pre-Arch Consultant; Long-Range Master Planning; Space Programming & Planning; **EDUC:** BA, 1977, Urban Design/Soc. Ecol., Univ. of CA, Irvine; **EDUC HONORS:** Deans Honor List; **HOME ADD:** 5208 Knoxville Ave., Lakewood, CA 90713, (213)867-3253; **BUS ADD:** 4201 Wilshire Blvd., Los Angeles, CA 90010, (213)937-5411.

VERCAUTEREN, Patrick J.——B: Jan. 1, 1945, Green Bay, WI, *Exec. Dir.*, Chamco, Inc.; **PRIM RE ACT:** Consultant, Developer; **OTHER RE ACT:** Local econ. devel. corp.; **SERVICES:** Sale and mgmt. of Oshkosh's indus. parks; **PREV EMPLOY:** City Planner, City of Oshkosh, WI 1971-1975; **PROFL AFFIL & HONORS:** Amer. Econ. Devel. Council, Great Lakes Area Devel. Council,(Bd. Member), WI Econ. Devel. Assn., (Bd. Member/Treas.); **EDUC:** BS, 1971, Urban Planning, Univ. of WI-Oshkosh; **MIL SERV:** US Army 1966-1969, E5; **OTHER ACT & HONORS:** Mid Morning Kiwanis, YMCA, United Way; **HOME ADD:** 1626 W. Sixth Ave., Oshkosh, WI 54901, (414)233-3490; **BUS ADD:** 120 Jackson St., PO Box 280, Oshkosh, WI 54902, (414)233-3760.

VERGHESE, Daniel——B: July 14, 1937, Kerala, *Pres.*, Daniel Investment Corp.; **PRIM RE ACT:** Engineer, Owner/Investor; **PREV EMPLOY:** Stock market investment, self-employed; **PROFL AFFIL & HONORS:** Amer. Soc. of Mfg.; **EDUC:** BS, Bus. Commerce & Engrg.; **HOME ADD:** 9976 Mennonite Rd., Wadsworth, OH 44281; **BUS ADD:** 600 Wooster W., Barberton, OH 44203, (216)745-9065.

VERKIN, Billy——B: Feb. 21, 1950, Galveston, TX, *Mgr. Part. RE Div.*, Mel Powers Investment Builder; **PRIM RE ACT:** Broker, Developer; **SERVICES:** Office bldg., devel. & RE brokerage; **REP CLIENTS:** Insts., REIT's, devels. & investors in comml., devel., investment & income producing props.; **EDUC:** 1968-70, St. Mary's Univ., San Antonio, TX; **OTHER ACT & HONORS:** Sugar Creek Ctry. Club, The Houstonian, The Houston City Club; **HOME ADD:** 1632 Country Club, Sugarland, TX 77478, (713)491-4377; **BUS ADD:** 7322 SW Freeway, Suite 2000, Houston, TX 77074, (713)666-6666.

VERMILYA, William R.——B: Nov. 10, 1944, Brownstown, IN, *Independent Fee Appraiser*; **PRIM RE ACT:** Appraiser; **SERVICES:** Appraisal of resid., comml. and indust. prop.; **REP CLIENTS:** FHA, E. I. du Pont de Nemours & Co., Lake Mort. Co., Lomis & Nettleton Mort. Co., Percy Wilson Mort. Co.; **PREV EMPLOY:** Cole-Layer-Trumble, Tax Appraisal Co., 1968 to 1972; NC Hwy. Dept., 1972 to 1974; **PROFL AFFIL & HONORS:** Lic. RE Broker, IN, RM

Designation - AIREA; **EDUC:** BS Bus., 1967, Mgmt. and Admin., IN Univ.; **HOME ADD:** 116 Sherwood Dr., Crown Point, IN 46307, (219)663-3852; **BUS ADD:** 116 Sherwood Dr., Crown Point, IN 46307, (219)663-3852.

VERMILYD, Sherwood S.——B: Aug. 18, 1924, College Pt., Long Island, NY, *Sr. VP*, United Appraisal Co. & Cole-Layer-Trumble Co.; **PRIM RE ACT:** Consultant, Appraiser, Assessor; **SERVICES:** RE appraisals for the equalization purposes of public utility props.; **REP CLIENTS:** Cities and towns and ctys. throughout the eastern US; **PROFL AFFIL & HONORS:** Amer. Soc. of Appraisers, CMMA from State of CT, Member IAAO & Numerous State Assns.; **OTHER ACT & HONORS:** Assessor Town of East Hampton, CT; **BUS ADD:** 53 CT Blvd., East Hartford, CT 06108, (203)528-5100.

VERONA, Pasquale A.——B: Dec. 18, 1936, Canonsburg, PA, *Sec./Treas. & Dr. of Operations*, VIP Realty Grp., Inc.; **PRIM RE ACT:** Broker, Developer, Owner/Investor, Property Manager, Syndicator; **SERVICES:** Interval sale & mgmt. synd. of comml. props., recreational investment mktg. prop. mgmt.; **PREV EMPLOY:** Devel. of var. resid. comml. & investor props.; **PROFL AFFIL & HONORS:** Nat. Home Builder Assn., Bd. of Dir., NHBA; **EDUC:** BS, 1960, Mktg. Engr., Univ. of Detroit; Assoc. Engrg., 1969, Univ. of Pittsburgh; **GRAD EDUC:** MBA, 1963, San Diego State; **MIL SERV:** USN, Lt. j.g.; **OTHER ACT & HONORS:** Boy Scouts of Amer., Pittsburgh Symphony Soc., Pittsburgh Playhouse; **HOME ADD:** 5726 Montilla Dr., Ft. Myers, FL 33907, (813)482-8156; **BUS ADD:** 9600 South Tamiami Trail, Ft. Myers, FL 33907, (813)936-6600.

VERZUH, Frank M., Dr.——B: Apr. 7, 1918, Crested Butte, CO, *Pres.*, Integrated EDP Systems; **PRIM RE ACT:** Consultant, Engineer, Owner/Investor, Instructor, Property Manager; **OTHER RE ACT:** Environmental protection; Dir. LOAN; **SERVICES:** Mgmt. consulting; **REP CLIENTS:** USAF; USN; NASA; GM; Merrill Lynch; NY Stock Exchange; Amer. Stock Exchange; Security Exchange Commn.; SAFEWAY Stores; USM; R.D.Little; Grumman Aircraft; **PREV EMPLOY:** Faculty at MIT 1940-61; **PROFL AFFIL & HONORS:** AIEE; Inst. of Radio Engrs.; SHARE Soc. to help avoid redundant effort in EDP; Pres. of LAON; Pres. of 180 Comm Ave Condo Trust, Who's Who in the East; Pres. of SHARE; **EDUC:** BS, 1940, Computers & Electrical Engrg., Univ. of Denver; **GRAD EDUC:** MEE, 1946, Elec. Engr., MIT; ED, 1952, Elec. Engr., MIT; **EDUC HONORS:** Sigma Xi; **OTHER ACT & HONORS:** Prepared textbooks on computers in 1947; prepared textbook on condos in 1978, etc.; **HOME ADD:** 180 Comm. Ave., Boston, MA 02116, (617)536-4818; **BUS ADD:** 180 Commonwealth Ave., Boston, MA 02116, (617)536-4818.

VESELY, Joseph C.——B: July 8, 1905, Silver Lake, MN, *Atty.*, Vesely & Miller, PA; **PRIM RE ACT:** Consultant, Attorney, Appraiser, Assessor; **SERVICES:** Title searches, closings, draft various instruments; **REP CLIENTS:** Banks, realtors; **PROFL AFFIL & HONORS:** ABA, Fellow of Amer. Probate Counsel, MN State Bar Assn.; **EDUC:** BA, 1926, Univ. of MN; **GRAD EDUC:** JD, 1928, Univ. of MN; **EDUC HONORS:** Delta Sigma Rho (Univ. Debating Team); **OTHER ACT & HONORS:** Tax Assessor; Major, City Atty.; Cty. Library Bd. Member; **HOME ADD:** 244 10th Ave. N, Hopkins, MN, (612)938-7558; **BUS ADD:** 203 Northwestern Bank Bldg., Hopkins, MN 55343, (612)938-7635.

VEST, Gary——*Area Devel. Supervisor*, West Texas Utilities Co.; **PRIM RE ACT:** Developer; **BUS ADD:** PO Box 841, Abilene, TX 79604, (915)672-3251.*

VETTER, Gail L.——B: July 2, 1944, Minot, ND, *VP*, Northwestern Nat. Bank/West, RE Banking Div.; **OTHER RE ACT:** 1st mort., 2nd mort., swing loans, constr. fin., comml. RE, mktg.; **PREV EMPLOY:** 1969-78 Bank of ND, Bismarck, ND, 1978-79, MN Housing Fin. Agency; **PROFL AFFIL & HONORS:** Nat. Assn. of Bank Women, AIB, BAI, US S&L League, MBAA, Minneapolis Builders Assn., MN Realtors Assn.; **EDUC:** 1976, Bus. & Acctg., Mary College, Bismarck, ND., 3.9 GPA, Hon. Student.; **OTHER ACT & HONORS:** Lutheran Church, 4H Club leadership; **HOME ADD:** 5311 Beachside Dr., Minnetonka, MN 55343, (612)935-0104; **BUS ADD:** 1011 First St. S, Hopkins, MN 55343, (612)932-3059.

VETTER, John O.——B: Mar. 2, 1927, New Orleans, LA, *Owner*, Vetter Real Estate Co.; **PRIM RE ACT:** Broker, Developer, Builder, Property Manager, Syndicator; **SERVICES:** Devel. and synd. of comml. props., Prop. Mgmt., Acquisition of Comml. Prop. for Large Nat. Synd.; **PROFL AFFIL & HONORS:** NAR; **EDUC:** BSC, 1948, Bus. Admin., Spring Hill Coll., Mobile, AL; **MIL SERV:** US Army (Artillery), 1st Lt.; **OTHER ACT & HONORS:** Former Dir., Peoples Bank and Trust Co., Chalmette, LA; **HOME ADD:** 4421 Carlyle Way N, Mobile, AL 36609, (205)344-3616; **BUS ADD:** 4358 Midmost Dr., Mobile, AL 36609, (205)342-2459.

VICINUS, William W.——B: Mar. 2, 1927, *VP*, S.T. Peterson & Co., Inc.; **PRIM RE ACT:** Consultant, Developer, Builder, Syndicator; **SERVICES:** Design-build, valuation, invest placement, devel. comml. props.; **EDUC:** BS, 1949, MIT; **GRAD EDUC:** MS, Oxford Univ.; MBA, Univ. of CT; **HOME TEL:** (609)921-2912; **BUS ADD:** PO Box 705, Princeton, NJ 08540, (201)329-4066.

VICKMAN, Lee J.——B: May 15, 1932, Chicago, IL, *Pres.*, Vickman & Co.; **PRIM RE ACT:** Broker, Consultant, Attorney, Owner/Investor; **SERVICES:** Investment brokerage and consulting; **PROFL AFFIL & HONORS:** Intl. Council of Shopping Ctrs.; **EDUC:** AB, 1951, Univ. of Chicago; **GRAD EDUC:** JD, 1954, Univ. of Chicago; **MIL SERV:** USN, 1955-57, Yeoman; **HOME ADD:** 1346 Sheridan Rd., Highland Park, IL 60035, (312)432-5711; **BUS ADD:** 555 Skokie Blvd., Northbrook, IL 60062, (312)480-1950.

VICTORS, A. P.——*Sr. VP Ind. Dev.*, Western Pacific Industries, Inc.; **PRIM RE ACT:** Property Manager; **BUS ADD:** 526 Mission St., San Francisco, CA 94105, (415)982-2100.*

VIGESAA, Lawrence W.——B: Jan. 8, 1937, Cooperstown, ND, *Arch.*, Lawrence W. Vigesaa; **PRIM RE ACT:** Architect, Engineer; **SERVICES:** Single Family / Multi-family Home Design; **EDUC:** BS Arch. Engr., 1959, ND State Univ.; **HOME ADD:** 3035 Beech Ave., Billings, MT 59102, (406)656-6447; **BUS ADD:** 3035 Beech, Billings, MT 59102, (406)656-6447.

VIGODA, Louise——B: Feb. 23, 1929, Akron, OH, *Pres.*, Hera Investment & Management; **PRIM RE ACT:** Broker, Consultant, Developer, Owner/Investor, Property Manager, Syndicator; **OTHER RE ACT:** Land acquisition; **SERVICES:** From land acquisition to zoning to arch. & contractor choice, to construction supervision, to leasing and managing. Also consult on investments & negotiate for clients on same. In addition there is brokering & synd. fin. for projects is also obtained.; **PROFL AFFIL & HONORS:** BOMA, RPA; **EDUC:** BA, 1951, Philosophy, Psych., OH State Univ.; **GRAD EDUC:** MA, 1952, Psych., OH State Univ.; **EDUC HONORS:** Cum Laude; **OTHER ACT & HONORS:** Bd. of Dir. Cherry Creek Nat. Bank; CO Bus. Woman of the Year 1981; Bd. of Dir. of Denver Exchange; Bd. of Dir. of Univ. of CO Coll. of Liberal Arts; Bd. of Dir. Historic Denver; Bd. of Dir. Paramount Found. Bd. of Dirs. Brothers Redevelopment; **HOME ADD:** 29 Cherry Lane Dr., Englewood, CO 80110; **BUS ADD:** 600, 50 S. Steele St., Denver, CO 80209, (303)320-8600.

VIKER, Owen H.——B: Nov. 19, 1940, Ada, MN, *Co-owner*, Appraisal Services of Mankato Inc.; **PRIM RE ACT:** Appraiser, Owner/Investor; **SERVICES:** RE Appraisal; **PREV EMPLOY:** Sr. Staff Supr. of First Fed. S & L Assn. of Mankato; **PROFL AFFIL & HONORS:** SRPA; **EDUC:** BS, 1969, Bus. Econ., N.D. S., Fargo ND; **MIL SERV:** US Army; **HOME TEL:** (507)345-4491; **BUS ADD:** 226 N. Broad St., Mankato, MN 56001, (507)387-1137.

VINCENTI, Michael Baxter——B: Dec. 28, 1950, Baltimore, MD, *Atty.*, Wyatt, Tarrant & Combs, RE; **PRIM RE ACT:** Attorney; **SERVICES:** Representation of RE lenders, owners, devel., landlords, tenants, condo. devel.; **REP CLIENTS:** Oxford Properties, Inc.; Whittenberg Engineering and Construction; The Old Seelbach; Citizens Fidelity Bank & Trust Co.; William D. Mattingly Assoc.; Broadway Project Corp.; **PREV EMPLOY:** Sonnenschein Carlin Nath & Rosenthal (Chicago, IL, 1975-1979); **PROFL AFFIL & HONORS:** ABA RE Financing Comm.; ABA Section of Real Property; IL Bar Assn. Real Prop. Div.; KY Bar Assn. RE Section; Louisville Bar Assn. Real Prop. Comm.; **EDUC:** BA, 1972, Humanistic Studies, Johns Hopkins Univ.; **GRAD EDUC:** JD, 1975, Corporate, NYU School of Law; **OTHER ACT & HONORS:** Licensed to practice law in both IL and KY; **HOME ADD:** 3823 Ormond Rd., Louisville, KY 40207, (502)895-2259; **BUS ADD:** 2800 Citizens Plaza, Louisville, KY 40202, (502)589-5235.

VINCI, Richard Anthony——B: Grosse Pointe Farms, MI, *Exec. VP*, The Erwin L. Greenberg Investment Corp.; **PRIM RE ACT:** Consultant, Appraiser, Developer, Owner/Investor, Property Manager, Syndicator; **OTHER RE ACT:** Portfolio Mgr.; **SERVICES:** Investment counseling, acquisition, devel., mgmt., leasing, synd., and fin. of comml. income producing props.; **REP CLIENTS:** Merrill-Lynch Hubbard, Salomon Bros., Equitable Life Assurance Soc. of the US; **PREV EMPLOY:** Equitable Life Assurance Soc. of the US Amer. Security Bank, N.A., MA Mutual Life Insurance Co.; **PROFL AFFIL & HONORS:** AIREA, Gr. Baltimore Bd. of Realtors, The Intl. Council of Shopping Ctrs., The Nat. Assn. of Office and Indus. Park Devel.; **EDUC:** BS, Fin. and RE Mgmt., Univ. of MI, Ann Arbor; **GRAD EDUC:** MBA, RE & Taxation, Univ. of MI, Ann Arbor; **EDUC HONORS:** With Honors; **HOME ADD:** 6531 Riverside Dr.,

Highland, MD, (301)596-9279; **BUS ADD:** One North Charles St., Suite 2505, Baltimore, MD 21202, (301)837-2500.

VINTON, James K., Jr.——B: Apr. 9, 1934, Phoenix, AZ, *Comml. Investment Salesperson*, F. C. Tucker Company, Inc. Realtors/Developers, Comml. Investment; **PRIM RE ACT:** Broker, Owner/Investor; **SERVICES:** RE sales; **PREV EMPLOY:** Registered Land Surveyor in IN and OH; **PROFL AFFIL & HONORS:** NAR, IN Assn. of Realtors, Metropolitan Indianapolis Assn. of Realtors, RNMI, FLI; **MIL SERV:** US Army; **OTHER ACT & HONORS:** Indpls. Ctry. Club, Plainfield Elks Club, Scottish Rite, Murat Shrine, Hendricks Cty. Shrine Club, Morgan Cty. Shrine Club; **HOME ADD:** 171 Thorncrest Dr., Mooresville, IN 46158, (317)831-6122; **BUS ADD:** 2500 One Indiana Square, Indianapolis, IN 46204, (317)634-6363.

VIROSTEK, Joseph J.——B: Apr. 15, 1923, Duquesne, PA, *Pres.*, J. Virostek, Inc.; **PRIM RE ACT:** Broker, Instructor, Syndicator, Consultant, Property Manager; **OTHER RE ACT:** Security License - Direct Participation Programs; **PREV EMPLOY:** Accountant; **PROFL AFFIL & HONORS:** NAR; RNMI, CCIM; GRI; **EDUC:** BS, 1950, Acctg., Duquesne Univ.; **MIL SERV:** US Army, T/5; **OTHER ACT & HONORS:** O'Hara Tw. Planning Commn., 4 yrs.; **HOME ADD:** 117 Eton Dr., Pittsburgh, PA 15215, (412)781-2497; **BUS ADD:** 1050 Freeport Rd., Pittsburgh, PA 15238, (412)781-2801.

VISCEGLIA, Frank——*Pres.*, Fed. Business Ctrs.; **OTHER RE ACT:** Devel. of office & indus. parks, chief operating offices; **SERVICES:** Warehousing, distribution, packaging, office & indus. space for lease; **BUS ADD:** 300 Raritan Ctr. Pkwy, Edison, NJ 08818, (201)225-2200.

VISCONTI, Lawrence B.——B: Oct. 1, 1949, Bridgeport, CT, *VP/Dev. Mgr.*, The Pickett Co's., Pickett Dev. Co.; **PRIM RE ACT:** Consultant, Developer, Builder; **OTHER RE ACT:** Const. Mgmt.; **SERVICES:** Dev./Const. Consulting, Const. Mgmt. Serv., Full Serv. RE Dev.; **EDUC:** BS/Bldg. Const., 1971, Const. Mgmt./Arch. Engineering, Clemson Univ., Clemson, SC; **HOME ADD:** 276 St. Andrews Dr., Dublin, OH 43017, (614)486-2086; **BUS ADD:** 555 Metro Place N., Suite 600, Dublin, OH 43017, (614)889-6500.

VISHNEVSKY, John——B: Jan. 18, 1924, *Pres. and Chairman of the Bd.*, National Development and Investment, Inc.; **PRIM RE ACT:** Broker, Syndicator, Appraiser, Developer, Builder, Property Manager, Owner/Investor, Insuror; **PREV EMPLOY:** Self-employed; **PROFL AFFIL & HONORS:** BOMA, IAFP, RESSI; **GRAD EDUC:** Ph.D., 1952, Eng., Math, Philosophy and Phys. Ed, Marquette Univ.; **HOME ADD:** 13455 Brook Ave., Elm Grove, WI 53122; **BUS ADD:** 13555 Bishop's Ct., Brookfield, WI 53005, (414)784-7000.

VISWANATHAN, Kumar K.——B: May 28, 1950, Madras, India, *COO*, The Delta Group; **PRIM RE ACT:** Consultant, Engineer, Developer, Builder, Syndicator; **SERVICES:** Devel., synd., bldg. and consulting; **PROFL AFFIL & HONORS:** ULI; **EDUC:** BS, 1972, Civil Engr., Coll. of Engr., Madras, India; **GRAD EDUC:** MCE, MS, 1974 and 1977, Construction Mgmt. and Fin., Purdue Univ., W. Lafayette, IN; **EDUC HONORS:** Grad. with distinction, Elected to Beta Gamma Sigma; **HOME ADD:** 6 Mizzenmast Ct., Sea Pines Planatation, Hilton Head Island, SC 29928, (803)671-2900; **BUS ADD:** Suite 101, The Profl. Bldg., Hilton Head Island, SC 29928, (803)842-3428.

VITAGLIANO, Arthur——B: July 7, 1917, Everett, MA, *Atty.*, Spencer & Stone; **PRIM RE ACT:** Consultant, Attorney, Insuror; **SERVICES:** Gen. counsel, comml. bank & savings inst., and their serv. corps.; **PREV EMPLOY:** Supply Corps., US Naval Res., 1943-46; **PROFL AFFIL & HONORS:** Boston Bar Assn., MA Conveyancers Assn.; **EDUC:** AB, 1938, Pol. Sci., Harvard Coll.; **GRAD EDUC:** LLB, 1941, Law, Boston Univ.; **EDUC HONORS:** Cum Laude; **MIL SERV:** USN Res.; **OTHER ACT & HONORS:** Bd. of Appeals, Town of Winthrop, 1946-78, Dir. Savings Inst., Dir. Title Ins. Co.; **HOME ADD:** 125 Sargent St., Winthrop, MA 02152; **BUS ADD:** 50 Beacon St., Boston, MA 02108, (617)227-3410.

VITT, Alvin D.——B: Mar. 20, 1935, St. Louis, MO, *Pres.*, Alvin D. Vitt & Co., **PRIM RE ACT:** Broker, Developer, Owner/Investor; **PREV EMPLOY:** VP - Mercantile Mort. Co.; Exec. VP Sachs Prop. Co., Inc.; **PROFL AFFIL & HONORS:** NAIOP, RE Bd. of St. Louis; **EDUC:** BS, 1956, Sci., Univ. of Notre Dame; **EDUC HONORS:** Sr. Class Officer; Student Council, Dean's List, Cum Laude; **MIL SERV:** USN, Lt.; **OTHER ACT & HONORS:** Alderman (1965-68); **HOME ADD:** 2350 Ravensgate Rd., St. Louis, MO 63131; **BUS ADD:** 1215 Fern Ridge Pkwy, Suite 100, St. Louis, MO 63141, (314)434-9010.

VITT, Lois A.——B: Dec. 14, 1938, Rochester, NY, *Founder & Pres.*, Home Partners of America, Inc.; **PRIM RE ACT:** Owner/Investor, Syndicator; **SERVICES:** Provide equity capital for homes; **PREV EMPLOY:** Eastdil Housing Servs., Inc. 1971-1973; Self-employed 1974-1978; **PROFL AFFIL & HONORS:** RESSI; Nat. Assn. of Homebuilders; **EDUC:** Bachelor of Profl. Studies, May 1980, Bus., Pace Univ., NY; **GRAD EDUC:** MBA, 1980, Mgmt., Pace Univ., NY; **OTHER ACT & HONORS:** Dir., Mental Health Assn. of Union, NJ; **HOME ADD:** 5130 Woodmire Lane, Alexandria, VA 22311, (703) 379-9241; **BUS ADD:** Suite 803, One Rodney Sq., Wilmington, DE 19801, (302)658-6423.

VITTONE, Joseph A.——B: Apr. 3, 1931, Hurley, WI, *Atty.*, Vittone & Paslay; **PRIM RE ACT:** Broker, Consultant, Attorney, Owner/Investor, Syndicator; **PROFL AFFIL & HONORS:** AK Bar Assn., RE Broker; **EDUC:** BS, 1957, Econ./Bus., Univ. of WI, Superior, WI; **GRAD EDUC:** MBA, 1971, Bus. Admin./Fin., Univ. of AK, Anchorage; **EDUC HONORS:** 1st in Class; **MIL SERV:** USMC, Cpl.; USAF, Lt. Col.; **OTHER ACT & HONORS:** JD, Univ. of Santa Clara CA 1977; **HOME ADD:** 213 E. Firewood Ln., Anchorage, AK 99503, (907)349-6016; **BUS ADD:** 213 E. Firewood Ln., Anchorage, AK 99503, (907)272-9486.

VLCKO, Miroslav P.——B: June 27, 1944, *Atty.*, Vestevich, Dritsas, McManus, Evans & Payne, P.C.; **PRIM RE ACT:** Attorney; **REP CLIENTS:** MI Natl. Banks & other lenders & investors/devels. of RE; **PROFL AFFIL & HONORS:** Amer. Bar Assn., MI Bar Assn., Amer. Arbitranon Assn. (Comml. Panel); **EDUC:** BS, 1968, Econ., Wayne State; **GRAD EDUC:** JD, 1971, Wayne State Univ. Law School; **EDUC HONORS:** Moot Court Nat. Team, Order of Barristers; **OTHER ACT & HONORS:** Amer. Bar Assn., MI Bar Assn., Adjunct Assoc. Prof of Law, Legal Research & Writing, Wayne Law School; **BUS ADD:** 800 W. Long Lake Rd., Ste. 200, Bloomfield Hills, MI 48013, (313)642-1920.

VODA, Jerry——B: Mar. 21, 1923, Czechoslovakia, *Pres.*, Sierra Appraisal; **PRIM RE ACT:** Broker, Consultant, Appraiser, Owner/Investor; **OTHER RE ACT:** Specialty: Appraisals of Lge. Comml. Props.; **SERVICES:** Investment counseling, valuation; **REP CLIENTS:** Brokers, lenders, govt. agencies; **PROFL AFFIL & HONORS:** SREA, SRPA, LLD, MBA; **GRAD EDUC:** MBA, LLD, 1955, 1946, Univ. of Toronto, Toronto, CAN; **HOME ADD:** Box 10287, Zephyr Cove, NV 89448, (702)588-4440; **BUS ADD:** Box 10287, Zephyr Cove, NV 89448, (916)544-5808.

VOEGLER, James H.——*VP*, Bellemead Devel. Corp.; **PRIM RE ACT:** Developer; **BUS ADD:** 20030 Century Blvd., Germantown, MD 20767, (301)972-4200.*

VOGEL, Donald L.——*VP/Gen. Mgr.*, Investment Equity Corp. Realtors; **PRIM RE ACT:** Broker, Appraiser, Developer, Property Manager; **OTHER RE ACT:** Realtor; **PREV EMPLOY:** VP/Casto Properties, Juno Beach, FL; **PROFL AFFIL & HONORS:** Northern Palm Beach Cty. Bd. of Realtors, NAR, Realtor; **EDUC:** Commerce, 1954, Business, Northwestern Univ.; **OTHER ACT & HONORS:** City of Palm Beach Gardens Planning & Zoning; Site Plan & Appearance Bd.; NPBC Bd. of Realtors; FL Assn. of Realtors; NAR; Home Builders & Contractors Assn. of Northern Palm Beach Cty.; Chmn. of Realtor/Builder Comm.; Sales & Marketing Council of Home Builders & Contractors of Northern Palm Bech Cty.; **HOME ADD:** 10136 Daisy Ave., Palm Beach Gardens, FL 33410, (305)622-4000; **BUS ADD:** 2352 PGA Blvd., Palm Beach Gardens, FL 33410, (305)626-5100.

VOGEL, Morton——*Director, Risk Mgmt.*, Avnet, Inc.; **PRIM RE ACT:** Property Manager; **BUS ADD:** 767 5th Ave., New York, NY 10022.*

VOGLER, Robert E.——B: Sept. 23, 1928, NE, *SE & Pres.*, Guide Rock State Bank; **PRIM RE ACT:** Broker, Attorney, Banker, Insuror; **PROFL AFFIL & HONORS:** NE Bar Assoc., ABA; **EDUC:** BS, 1950, Univ. of NE; **GRAD EDUC:** LLD, 1952, Coll. of Law, Univ. of NE; **MIL SERV:** USAR, Lt.; **OTHER ACT & HONORS:** Assoc. Co. Judge, 1965-69, & Deputy Co. Atty. 1953-55; **HOME ADD:** Guide Rock, NE 68942, (402)257-2815; **BUS ADD:** Guide Rock State Bank, Guide Rock, NE 68942, (402)257-2175

VOINOVICH, Victor S.——Cragin, Lang, Free & Smythe Inc.; **PRIM RE ACT:** Developer; **BUS ADD:** 1801 East 9th St., Cleveland, OH 44114, (216)696-6050.*

VOLANSKI, Joe——B: Mar. 16, 1948, Pittsburgh, PA, *Pres.*, J.S.V. Inc.; **PRIM RE ACT:** Broker, Consultant; **OTHER RE ACT:** Mktg.; **SERVICES:** Consulting, mktg., sales resort prop. time share; **REP CLIENTS:** Belin Assoc., Deuster-Weil, Horizon Corp.; **EDUC:** BA, 1970, Pre-law, poli, sci., eng., Univ. of Pittsburgh; **EDUC HONORS:** Dean's List; **MIL SERV:** US Army, National Guard, SP 4; **BUS ADD:** 505 Hickory Ridge, Spring, TX 77381, (713)367-3606.

VOLDEN, James O.——*Tres.*, Chicago Pneumatic Tool; **PRIM RE ACT:** Property Manager; **BUS ADD:** 6 E. 44th St., 10017, NY, NY, (212)850-6800.*

VOLINSKY, Simon——**B:** Sept. 28, 1931, NY, NY, *VP RE*, CBS, Inc.; **OTHER RE ACT:** Corp. RE; **SERVICES:** RE Activities for CBS, Inc.; **PROFL AFFIL & HONORS:** Member Nat. Assn. of Corp. RE Execs, Assoc. SIR, Lic. Profl. Engr. in NY State; **EDUC:** BCE, 1953, Civil Engr., City Coll. of NY; **MIL SERV:** USN, CEC, Lt. JG; **BUS ADD:** 51 W. 52nd St., New York, NY 10019, (212)975-4084.

VOLKER, John B.——**B:** March 3, 1953, Brawley, CA, *Comml. RE Salesman*, Moore and Co, Comml. Div.; **PRIM RE ACT:** Owner/Investor; **OTHER RE ACT:** Salesman: Primarily land sales for comml. and resid. projects; **SERVICES:** Investment counseling, land acquisition, valuation of RE, sales and leasing; **REP CLIENTS:** Lenders, Dev., Indivs., for Comml. Prop.; **PREV EMPLOY:** Bank of Denver, Bookkeeping Dept.; **PROFL AFFIL & HONORS:** NAR, CO Assn. of Realtors, Denver Bd. of Realtors, Denver Bd of Realtors Roundtable Award Club, 1979 sales in excess of $1,000,000; Denver Bd. of Realtors Roundtable Award Club, 1980 sales in excess of $1,000,000; Moore and Co., Silver Sales Award, 1979; Moore and Co. Exec. Sales Award, 1980; **EDUC:** BS, 1975, Econ. and Bus. Admin, US International Univ.; **OTHER ACT & HONORS:** 1981 Chmn. of the Denver Bd. of Realtors Comml. RE Education Comm.; Member of the 1981 Edition of Outstanding Young Men of America; **HOME ADD:** 2075 S. Cook St, Denver, CO 80210, (303)759-1074; **BUS ADD:** 390 Grant St, Denver, CO 80203, (303)778-1600.

VOLPE, Thomas J.——*VP & Treas.*, Colgate-Palmolive; **PRIM RE ACT:** Property Manager; **BUS ADD:** 300 Park Avenue, New York, NY 10022, (212)310-2000.*

VOLPERT, Richard S.——**B:** Feb. 16, 1935, Cambridge, MN, *Partner*, O'Melveny & Myers; **PRIM RE ACT:** Attorney, Developer; **SERVICES:** Head of RE dept. of law firm; **PROFL AFFIL & HONORS:** Chmn., Real Prop. Sect., Los Angeles Cty. Bar Assn., 1974-1975; State Bar of CA, Real Prop. Law Sect. Exec. Comm., 1979-1981; Comm. on the Admin. of Justice, CA State Bar Assn., 1973-1976; W. Ctr. on Law and Poverty, Bd. Member, 1971-1975; Los Angeles Neighborhood Legal Serv. Soc., Bd. Member, 1969-1971; Council on Jewish Life, Jewish Federation Council, Chmn., 1976 and 1977; **EDUC:** BA, 1956, Pol. Sci./Econ., Amherst Coll.; **GRAD EDUC:** LLB, 1959, Law, Columbia Law School; **EDUC HONORS:** Stone Scholar; **OTHER ACT & HONORS:** Jewish Fed., Council of Greater Los Angeles, Bd. Member since 1976, VP, 1978 & 1981 Los Angeles Cty. Natural Hist. Museum Found., Pres., 1978, VP, 1977-1978, Sec., 1976-1977, Tr. since 1974; Univ. of S. CA Law Ctr., Bd. of Councilors, Chmn., since 1979, VChmn., 1978-1979; Amherst Club of S. CA, Pres., 1972-1973, VP, 1970-1972, Bd. Member since 1968; Amherst Coll., Capital Program Major Gifts Comm., 1978; Los Angeles Wholesale Produce Market Devel. Corp., Bd. and Exec. Comm. Member, since 1979; Los Angleles Cty. Econ. Devel. Council, Member and VChmn., since 1978; Jewish Community Found., Bd. member, 1981; Nat. Jewish Community Relations Advisory Council, VChmn. since 1981, Sec. 1980; **HOME ADD:** 4001 Stansbury Ave., Sherman Oaks, CA 91423, (213)783-5333; **BUS ADD:** 611 W. 6th St., Los Angeles, CA 90017, (213)620-1120.

VON FLECKENSTEIN, George J.W.——**B:** May 2, 1924, MD, *Pres. and Gen. Mgr.*, Von Fleckenstein & Assoc.- Engrs. and Contractors, Prof. engr.(civil)Dir. Devel.; **PRIM RE ACT:** Broker, Consultant, Engineer, Attorney, Developer, Builder; **OTHER RE ACT:** Coord. & supervision, arch./engrg.; **SERVICES:** Clients & own devel. of subdiv. all types and comml. followed by bldg. const. & mktg.; **REP CLIENTS:** First Nat. Bank of Atlanta, Tharpe & Brooks, Inc.; Fulton Fed. S&L Assn.; Land Resources Corp.; Props. Assoc.; Forest Green Corp.; and other out of state owners of prop. devel. by Von Fleckenstein & Assoc.; **PREV EMPLOY:** Civil Engr.; Union Oil Co. chg. refinery and related const./ Royal Dutch Shell Corp./ Stauffer Chem. Co.; Dir. and Pres. Bengor Corp./ Cevon Const. Co.; **PROFL AFFIL & HONORS:** ASEA, Soc. of Amer. Mil. Engrs., EAQ'A, ASCE, PEA, Special Merit Awards by Soc. of Amer. Mil. Engrs.- Design Awards by Nat. Assn. Home Builders; **EDUC:** BS, Civil and Const. Engr., Canisius Coll.-Univ. S. CA/SMU Dallas TX; **GRAD EDUC:** BS, Engr. Mil., Univ. S. CA; Masters, Civil, Univ. S. CA; LLB, Univ. S. CA; **EDUC HONORS:** USA Engr.-Spec. Mil. Engr.; **MIL SERV:** USA, Lt. Col. Res., Silver Star, Bronze Medal; **OTHER ACT & HONORS:** C of C; Coord. Council; Legislative Comm. on Contract Law; NAHB ; BCA; **HOME ADD:** 2940 Brookside Ct. SE, Marietta, GA 30067, (404)952-8807; **BUS ADD:** PO Box 6279, Marietta, GA 30065, (404)952-5526.

VON PINGEL, Eric——**B:** Jan. 31, 1939, Sacramento, CA, *VP, Head of Appraisal Dept.*, Bank of America, Appraisal Dept.; **PRIM RE ACT:** Appraiser; **SERVICES:** RE and agricultural appraisals; **REP CLIENTS:** Bankamerica Corp. and subs.; **GRAD EDUC:** Program for Mgmt. Devel., 1981, (PMD), Harvard Bus. School; **MIL SERV:** USMC; Cpl.; **OTHER ACT & HONORS:** Dir. of CA Mkt. Data Co-op., Inc.; **HOME ADD:** 1800 Piedras Cir., Danville, CA 94526; **BUS ADD:** 1777 N. CA Blvd., Ste. 2000, Walnut Creek, CA 94596, (415)944-2884.

VON WEILAND, John C.——**B:** Jan. 8, 1942, Dayton, OH, *Mgr. of RE Admin.*, Resource Investments, Inc.; **PRIM RE ACT:** Banker, Owner/Investor; **SERVICES:** Tax shelter synd., asset monitoring for firm; **REP CLIENTS:** Ltd. & gen. partnerships in investment RE; **PREV EMPLOY:** Sr. Prop. Mgr. Mellon Nat. Mort. Corp.; **PROFL AFFIL & HONORS:** Inst. of RE Mgmt., CPM; **EDUC:** 1969, Arch. Design, Chicago Tech. Coll.; **MIL SERV:** USAF, A/2C; **HOME ADD:** 184 Hill Pl. Rd., Venetia, PA 15367, (412)941-1329; **BUS ADD:** 1 Alleghany Ctr., Suite 650, Pittsburgh, PA 15212, (412)323-3900.

VON WERZ, George——**B:** Apr. 25, 1948, Munich, W. Germany; **PRIM RE ACT:** Consultant; **SERVICES:** Packaging of RE Devel. for Foreign Investors; **PREV EMPLOY:** Trans-Atlantic Consultants, 1977-1980; **GRAD EDUC:** 1975, Intl. & Tax Law, Munich Univ. Law School; **BUS ADD:** 7 West 51st St., New York, NY 10019, (212)664-1668.

VOORHIES, Peter G.——*Partner*, Wood Tatum Mosser Brooke & Holden; **PRIM RE ACT:** Attorney; **EDUC:** 1958, Yale Univ.; **GRAD EDUC:** MBA, Stanford Univ.; LLB, Northwestern Law School; **EDUC HONORS:** Magna Cum Laude; **BUS ADD:** 1001 S.W. 5th Ave., 1300, Portland, OR 97204, (503)224-5430.

VOOZ, Nan——**B:** July 21, 1955, Shreveport, LA, *Admin. Asst.*, David Meyers, Inc., Leasing/Prop. Mgmt.; **PRIM RE ACT:** Property Manager; **OTHER RE ACT:** Leasing in addition to our Comml. Sales Office; **SERVICES:** Prop. Mgmt. with complete Leasing & Comml. Sales; **HOME ADD:** 5403 30th S.W., Seattle, WA 98126; **BUS ADD:** 2815 Alaskan Way, Pier 70, Seattle, WA 98121, (206)682-8123.

VORE, Lee H.——**B:** Aug. 15, 1929, Chadron, NE, *Pres.*, Cal Coast Appraisers; **PRIM RE ACT:** Appraiser; **SERVICES:** RE Appraisals - Resid., Comm., Indus.; **REP CLIENTS:** Mainly S & L's, Mort. Cos.; Also do work for some Law Firms & Acctg. Firms; **PREV EMPLOY:** Fin. Fed. 1966-1971; Various Divs. incl. Sr. VP of Appraisal Div.; **PROFL AFFIL & HONORS:** SRA; **EDUC:** BA, 1955, Geology, Univ. of CA, Berkeley; **MIL SERV:** USN, ET 3, 1946-1948; **OTHER ACT & HONORS:** Planning Commnr. - City of LA Habra 1968-1972, Chmn. 1969-1970. Bd. of Dirs., Brea C of C; **HOME ADD:** 1231 W. Northwood Ave., Brea, CA 92621, (213)681-2162; **BUS ADD:** 400 W. Central Ave., Suite 202, Brea, CA 92621, (714)990-5053.

VORISEK, Jean E.——**B:** Aug. 21, 1944, Margarith CZ, Panama, *Real Estate Developer*; **PRIM RE ACT:** Broker, Syndicator, Developer, Property Manager; **OTHER RE ACT:** Surveying, Landscaping; **SERVICES:** Mkt. analysis feasibility studies; fin. projections & analysis; leasing; surveying; landscaping & packaging devel. props.; recreational mkt. indus. cos.; private investors and municipalities.; **PREV EMPLOY:** Private consultant for investors in RE, also an RE sales agent for Century-21, Keewaydin Props. in Laconia, N.H.; **PROFL AFFIL & HONORS:** State Pres. of Ressi; FLI state member; Lakes Region MLS; Lakes Region Bd. of Realtors; CCIM; CRS.; **EDUC:** BA, 1966, Soc., Relig., Psych., St. Lawrence Univ, Canton, NY; **GRAD EDUC:** Cont. Educ. with the RNMI, CCIM & CRS; **EDUC HONORS:** Soc. Hon.; **OTHER ACT & HONORS:** Planning Bd. Member-New Hampton, N.H. 1978-79; Lakes Region Planning Comm. Member 1975-76; Member of N.H. State Bd. on Child Abuse; **HOME ADD:** 7 Hoitt Rd., Durham, NH 03824; **BUS ADD:** 7 Hoitt Rd., Durham, NH 03824, (603)868-5310.

VOSKA, Joseph, Jr.——**B:** July 18, 1931, Chicago, IL, *Natl. Prop. Mgr.*, Sears Roebuck & Co., Dept. 824, 36th Floor; **PRIM RE ACT:** Broker, Consultant, Appraiser, Architect, Developer, Builder, Property Manager; **PREV EMPLOY:** Homart Devel. Co.; **PROFL AFFIL & HONORS:** AIA, ARA, NCARB, NACORE, CRA of Natl. Assn. of Review Appraisers, Inst. of Store Planners, ISP, Fellow ARA, Cert. Review Appraiser, Editor Inland Arch.; **EDUC:** BS, 1952, Arch. & Engr., Univ. of IL; **GRAD EDUC:** MA, 1957, Urban Planning, Bus., Univ. of Il; **MIL SERV:** US Army-Artillery, Capt. 1952-1954 Korea, Far East Command; **OTHER ACT & HONORS:** Sch. Bd. Member 1959-1962; Boy Scout of Amer., 35 Yr. Member; Currently Exec. Bd. N.W.S.C.; Arlington Hts., IL; Bd. of Advisors Yough Comm. No. IL; **HOME ADD:** 500 Miller Rd., Barrington, IL 60010, (312)381-6804; **BUS ADD:** Sears Tower, Chicago, IL 60684, (312)875-9119.

VOTH, Donald P.W.——**B:** Jan. 25, 1921, Quincy, IL, *Pres.*, Don Voth, Inc., Realtor; **PRIM RE ACT:** Broker, Appraiser; **SERVICES:** RE Brokerage and Appraising; **REP CLIENTS:** Estates, Attys., Lenders, Indivs., Corps., Banks; **PROFL AFFIL & HONORS:** Quincy

Bd. of Realtors, IL Assn. of Realtors, NAR, RNMI, GRI, CRS, Realtor of the Year, 1962; **EDUC:** BBA, 1948, Cleveland Coll. of Western Reserve Univ.; **MIL SERV:** USAF; **OTHER ACT & HONORS:** Rotary Club of Quincy, Quincy Ctry. Club; **HOME ADD:** 2903 Maine St., Quincy, IL 62301, (217)223-4515; **BUS ADD:** 901 Maine St., Quincy, IL 62301, (217)223-3464.

VOZAR, Paul R.——**B:** Nov. 6, 1948, Milwaukee, WI, *Pres.*, Paul R. Vozar Appraisal Service; **PRIM RE ACT:** Consultant, Appraiser; **SERVICES:** Valuation, RE Counseling; **PREV EMPLOY:** WI Dept. of Revenue - Indus. Appraiser; **PROFL AFFIL & HONORS:** SREA, NARA, AACA, SRA, CRA, CAS / Young Advisory Counsel - SREA - 1980; **EDUC:** BBA, 1972, Acctg., Spencerian Coll.; **EDUC HONORS:** Dean's List - 8 Semesters; **MIL SERV:** US Army, SSgt.; **HOME ADD:** 3278 N. 49th St., Milwaukee, WI 53216, (414)447-8041; **BUS ADD:** 3106 N. 42 St., Milwaukee, WI 53216, (414)447-0388.

VRADENBURG, George A., Jr.——**B:** Sept. 10, 1919, Toledo, OH, *Pres.*, Transwestern Properties, Inc., West Amer. Capital Services Corp. (Subs.); **PRIM RE ACT:** Broker, Consultant, Developer, Lender, Builder, Owner/Investor; **SERVICES:** Analyze RE problems, locate, develop, fin. new programs, identify, up-grade RE, develop existing RE, pure brokerage, buyer's or seller's agent; **REP CLIENTS:** Light mfg., high tech., research and devel., office & retail design; **PREV EMPLOY:** Self Employed; **PROFL AFFIL & HONORS:** CO Springs Bd. of Realtors; CO Assn. of Realtors; NAR; **EDUC:** BA, 1941, Rural & Farm Econ., Oberlin Coll.; **MIL SERV:** USMC, Maj., Pacific Theatre Unit Citation; **OTHER ACT & HONORS:** City RE Consultant, 1972; Chmn., CO Springs Park Bd., 1955-1960; Rotary Club; Jr. Achievement; Eisenhower Osteopathic Hosp. Bd.; **HOME ADD:** 1231 E. Highpoint Ln., CO Springs, CO 80904, (303)633-1602; **BUS TEL:** (303)471-9212.

VUKAS, Ronald——*Exec. VP*, Institute of Real Estate Management; **OTHER RE ACT:** Profl. Assn. Admin; **BUS ADD:** 430 N. Michigan Ave., Chicago, IL 60611, (312)440-8600.*

VUKICEVICH, Benjamin R.——**B:** Oct. 29, 1953, Camden, NJ, *Part.*, Benjamin G. Vukicevich, MAI, SRPA, SR/WA; **PRIM RE ACT:** Appraiser; **SERVICES:** RE Appraisal and Consultation; **REP CLIENTS:** Numerous S&L and indiv.; **PROFL AFFIL & HONORS:** SRA of the ISREA; **EDUC:** BS, 1975, Fin./Mgmt., LaSalle Coll., Philadelphia, PA; **HOME ADD:** 128 W. Maple Ave., Lindenwold, NJ 08021, (609)783-0797; **BUS ADD:** POB 91, 211 Harvard Ave., Stratford, NJ 08084, (609)784-7036.

WACHAL, D.E.——*VP Financing*, American Crystal Sugar; **PRIM RE ACT:** Property Manager; **BUS ADD:** 101A Third St., Moorehead, MN 56560, (218)236-4440.*

WACHTER, Lawrence H.——**B:** June 3, 1926, Floral Park, NY, *VP, Branch Mgr.*, Chicago Title Insurance Co., Nassau Cty.; **OTHER RE ACT:** Title Ins. Co.; **SERVICES:** Insuring title to real prop.; **REP CLIENTS:** Attys., lending instns., builders, RE brokers; **PREV EMPLOY:** Lifetime in title ins. industry; **PROFL AFFIL & HONORS:** L.I. Home Builders; L.I. Bd. of Realtors; **MIL SERV:** USN, 1944-46, Sig 1st Class, Pac. Duty; **HOME ADD:** 333 Sylvan Lane, Westbury, NY 11590, (516)997-9086; **BUS ADD:** 1 Old Country Rd., Carle Place, NY 11514, (516)742-5000.

WACHTLER, Bruce Edward——**B:** Dec. 29, 1950, CA, *Asst. VP*, Continental Development of California, Inc.; **PRIM RE ACT:** Builder; **SERVICES:** Homebuilder; **PREV EMPLOY:** Summa Corp., Great Western Cities, Inc., Harold Davidson & Assoc.; **EDUC:** BS, 1973, RE & Urban Econ., Univ. CA, Berkeley; **GRAD EDUC:** MBA/MPL, 1975, RE Fin./Urban and Rgnl. Planning, Univ. of So. AL; **HOME ADD:** 14435 Plummer St. #21, Panorama City, CA 91402, (213)894-2152; **BUS ADD:** 9100 Wilshire Blvd., Suite 470, Beverly Hills, CA 91202, (213)278-2830.

WADDELL, Gloria J.——**B:** Jan. 6, 1949, Atlanta, GA, *Retail Leasing/Mall Mgr.*, Peachtree Center Management Co., Retail; **PRIM RE ACT:** Property Manager; **OTHER RE ACT:** Leasing; **REP CLIENTS:** Britches of Georgetown, Rich's, Georgia Girl, C & S Bank, Trust Co. Bank, Brentano's; Eastern Newstand; **PREV EMPLOY:** Taylor & Mathis (Developers/Managers) 1975-1979; **PROFL AFFIL & HONORS:** ICSC; **EDUC:** BS, 1970, , GA St. Univ.; **HOME ADD:** 1596 Alexandria Court, Marietta, GA 30067; **BUS ADD:** 225 Peachtree St., Suite 610, Atlanta, GA 30303, (404)659-0800.

WADDELL, R. Alvin——**B:** Nov. 6, 1946, Charlotte, NC, *Pres.*, Waddell Assoc.; **PRIM RE ACT:** Broker, Developer, Builder, Property Manager; **SERVICES:** Single family constr., land dev., invest. prop.; **REP CLIENTS:** New home buyers, self; **PROFL AFFIL & HONORS:** IREM; NHBA; Charlotte Bd. of Realtors, NC Home Builders Assoc. Design Awards - 1979-1980; CPM; **EDUC:** 1968, Investments Bus. Admin., Pfeiffer Coll.; **MIL SERV:** USA, E-5; **HOME ADD:** 34Newriver Trace, Clover, SC, (803)831-2730; **BUS ADD:** 1515 Mockingbird Ln., Suite 910, Charlotte, NC 28209, (704)525-0475.

WADDELL, Verna B.——**B:** Mar. 12, 1917, Hobart, OK, *Realtor, Broker, Owner*, Waddell RE & Ins. Co.; **PRIM RE ACT:** Broker, Property Manager, Owner/Investor, Insuror; **SERVICES:** Sales, Rentals, Mgmt., Ins.; **PREV EMPLOY:** HOLC as Sec. to Regional Mgr.; FHA; and War Assets Admin.; **PROFL AFFIL & HONORS:** NAR, TAR, IREM, Grand Prairie Bd. of Realtors, WCR, TAR Dir. 12 yrs.; Past Pres. of GP Bd. & WCR; **EDUC:** BS, 1940, Bus. Admin., S Methodist Univ., Dallas, TX; **OTHER ACT & HONORS:** Past Pres. B & PW, Soroptimist, Federation of Womens Club, Past Matron OES: Regent, DAR: Hospital Auxiliary; Amer. Legion Auxiliary; **HOME ADD:** 814 Robertson Rd., Grand Prairie, TX 75050, (214)262-7493; **BUS ADD:** 300 Hill, Grand Prairie, TX 75050, (214)262-3507.

WADE, R. Lee——**B:** Nov. 14, 1935, IN, *Arch.*, R. Lee Wade - Arch./Artist; **PRIM RE ACT:** Architect; **SERVICES:** Arch.; Promotional Art Work; **PREV EMPLOY:** Self-employed private practice 18 yrs.; **PROFL AFFIL & HONORS:** Soc. Amer. Registered Archs.; **EDUC:** BS In Arch., 1961, Univ. of Cincinnati; **BUS ADD:** R.R.5, Madison, IN 47250, (812)866-2270.

WADE, Richard——*SIR, Asst. VP*, Prentice-Hall, Inc.; **PRIM RE ACT:** Property Manager; **BUS ADD:** Rte. 9W, Englewood Cliffs, NJ 07632, (201)592-2000.*

WADE, Stephen W.——*Proj. Dir.*, Harbor Bay Business Park; **PRIM RE ACT:** Developer; **BUS ADD:** 936 Shorepoint Court, PO Box 1450, Almeda, CA 94501, (415)521-1771.*

WADHAMS, John D.——**B:** July 6, 1937, Hartford, CT, *Sr. V.P.*, BarclaysAmerican Business Credit Inc.; **PRIM RE ACT:** Lender; **SERVICES:** first and second mort. loans on completed income, prop., standby commitments on income prop. to be built; **REP CLIENTS:** RE Dev. and investors; **PREV EMPLOY:** Sec. CT General Life from 1959-1972, 2nd V.P. Phoenix Mutual Life from 1972 to 1973; **PROFL AFFIL & HONORS:** Mort. Bankers, ULI, ICSC; **EDUC:** BA, 1959, Amer. Studies, Amherst Coll., Amherst MA; **MIL SERV:** US Army, 1st. Lt.; **OTHER ACT & HONORS:** Chmn. Simsbury Bd. of Tax Review, 1977 to 1980; **HOME ADD:** 11 High Farms Rd., W. Hartford, CT 06107, (203)561-2670; **BUS ADD:** 111 Founders Plza, E. Hartford, CT 06101, (203)528-4831.

WADSWORTH, James R.——**B:** Sept. 16, 1946, Alton, IL, *VP*, The Griffin Cos., Inc., Brokerage; **PRIM RE ACT:** Broker, Instructor, Syndicator; **SERVICES:** Brokerage and synd. of Apts., Office Bldgs., and Leased Props.; **REP CLIENTS:** Corps. and Instnl. Investors; **PROFL AFFIL & HONORS:** RNMI, CCIM; **HOME ADD:** 5504 Oaklawn, Edina, MN 55424, (612)927-8212; **BUS ADD:** 8200 Humboldt Ave. S, Bloomington, MN 55431, (612)888-9453.

WAGMAN, Lee H.——**B:** June 23, 1949, Pittsburgh, PA, *Dir. of RE & Gen. Counsel*, Northwest Plaza Shopping Center & Crestwood Plaza Shopping Ctr.; **PRIM RE ACT:** Attorney, Developer, Owner/Investor; **PREV EMPLOY:** Bryan, Cave, McPheeters & McRoberts; **PROFL AFFIL & HONORS:** ABA, Intl. Council of Shopping Centers; **EDUC:** BA, BS Econ., 1971, Fin., Univ. of PA (Wharton); **GRAD EDUC:** JD, MA, 1975, Univ. of PA; **EDUC HONORS:** Magna Cum Laude; **HOME ADD:** 23 Berkley Lane, St. Louis, MO 63124, (314)993-2523; **BUS ADD:** 500 Northwest Plaza, St. Ann, MO 63074, (314)291-5600.

WAGNER, Alvin L., Jr.——**B:** Dec. 19, 1939, Chicago, IL, *Pres.*, A.L. Wagner & Co.; **PRIM RE ACT:** Broker, Appraiser, Instructor; **SERVICES:** R.E. appraisal & consulting; **REP CLIENTS:** Fortune '500' corps.; banks and S & L; **PREV EMPLOY:** Staff Appraiser, Oak Park Federal S&L; RE Loan Officer & Chief Appraiser; Assoc., C.A. Bruckner & Assoc.;- Beverly Bank; **PROFL AFFIL & HONORS:** AIREA, RM; Soc. of RE Appraisers, SRA; Omega Tau Rho; Lambda Alpha; Who's Who in the Midwest; Personalities of the West & Midwest; Community leaders & Noteworthy Amer.; **EDUC:** BA, 1962, Econ. & bus., Drake Univ., Des Moines, IA; **MIL SERV:** USAR, Pvt.; **OTHER ACT & HONORS:** Auditor Rich Township 1973-77; Phi Delta Theta; Variety Club; Flossmoor Ctry. Club; Rotary; Governing

Bd. Glenwood Sch. for Boys; Governing Council AIREA; Prof. Recognition Award AIREA; Community Prof. Gov. State U.; Instr. AIREA and Prairie State Coll.; **HOME ADD:** 927 Park Dr., Flossmoor, IL 60422, (312)798-7779; **BUS ADD:** 2709 Flossmoor Rd., Flossmoor, IL 60422, (312)799-8520.

WAGNER, Donald L.——B: Sept. 7, 1932, Mulberry, AR, *Mgr. Gen. Services*, Getty Refining & Mktg.; **PRIM RE ACT:** Property Manager; **EDUC:** BS BA, 1959, Acctg. Mgmt., Tulsa Univ.; **MIL SERV:** USN, 3 CPO; **OTHER ACT & HONORS:** Pres. NAA (Tulsa Chp.), Natl. Assn. of Accountants; **HOME ADD:** Tulsa, OK 741368157 S. Quebec, (918)481-1928; **BUS ADD:** PO Box 1650, Tulsa, OK 74102, (918)560-6080.

WAGNER, James W.——B: Dec. 3, 1922, Summit, NJ, *Pres.*, Carteret Service Corp.; **PRIM RE ACT:** Lender, Builder; **OTHER RE ACT:** Financing; **EDUC:** BS, 1944, Agric./Econ., Rutgers Univ.; **GRAD EDUC:** MA, 1947, Agric./Econ., Rutgers Univ.; **MIL SERV:** USN, Lt.j.g.; **OTHER ACT & HONORS:** Bd. of Education, Upper Saddle River, NJ, Pres., 9 yrs.; Also associated with Barclay Woods, Inc. and Carteret Financial Servies; **HOME ADD:** 15 N. Church Rd., Saddle River, NJ 07458, (201)327-1831; **BUS ADD:** 55 Madison Ave., Morristown, NJ 07960, (201)538-9000.

WAGNER, Lowell J.——B: Dec. 10, 1939, Moonhead, MN, *Pres.*, Wagner Corp.; **PRIM RE ACT:** Broker, Developer, Property Manager, Owner/Investor; **SERVICES:** RE Resale Comml. Devel. (Ourselves & Others); **REP CLIENTS:** Amer. Indian Bus. Devel. Corp. Red Owl Stores, Snyder Drug, Sage Co., Misc. Owners; **PROFL AFFIL & HONORS:** NAR, Intl. Council of Shopping Ctrs., Minnesota Assn. of Realtors; **MIL SERV:** Air National Guard; **OTHER ACT & HONORS:** Planning Comm. Member; Local, Past & State Offices in various civic & political org. Honors including ten outstanding young men MN.; **HOME ADD:** R1 Box 178, Waconia, MN 55387, (612)442-4036; **BUS ADD:** 6490 Excelsior 310W, St. Louis Park, MN 55426, (612)920-0033.

WAGNER, Michael Carl——B: Oct. 22, 1938, Sherman, TX, *Pres.*, Michael C. Wagner; **PRIM RE ACT:** Broker, Instructor, Consultant, Owner/Investor; **SERVICES:** Investment Counseling and Confidential Acquisitions; **REP CLIENTS:** Indiv. and Instnl. Investors of Comml. Props.; **PREV EMPLOY:** VP, Harold Collum Co., Realtors, Dallas, TX 1966-1970; **PROFL AFFIL & HONORS:** CCIM 591 NAR; **EDUC:** BS Indus. Engrg., 1962, Texas A&M Univ.; **MIL SERV:** US Army, Capt.; **HOME ADD:** 3212 Caruth Blvd., Dallas, TX 75225, (214)369-5246; **BUS ADD:** 6440 N. Central Expressway, Dallas, TX 75206, (214)369-6001.

WAGNER, Richard——*RE Mgr.*, Diamond International Corp.; **PRIM RE ACT:** Property Manager; **BUS ADD:** 733 Third Ave., New York, NY 10017, (212)697-1700.*

WAGNER, Richard L., Jr.——B: May 23, 1949, Detroit, MI, *Atty.*, Nowinski & Wagner, P.C.; **PRIM RE ACT:** Consultant, Attorney, Property Manager; **SERVICES:** Representation & consultation in reference to matters pertaining to RE; **REP CLIENTS:** Condo. assns. & devels., co-operative assns., mobile home communities, pvt. RE work; **PREV EMPLOY:** Prop. Mgmt., RE Consultant, Construction Supt., Real & Construction Appraisals, Title Abstractor; **PROFL AFFIL & HONORS:** ABA; State Bar of MI; Macomb Cty. Bar Assn.; Delta Theta Phi Law Fraternity; Detroit Coll. of Law Alumni; MI State Univ. Alumni; James Madison Coll.; MI Assn. of the Professions; Macomb Cty. Alumni Bd. of Realtors, Assoc.; Various State and Amer. Bar Subcommittees in RE; **EDUC:** BA, 1972, James Madison Coll., Educ., Pre-Law, MI State Univ.; **GRAD EDUC:** JD, 1976, Law, Detroit Coll. of Law; **EDUC HONORS:** Corp. (Amer. Jur. Award); **OTHER ACT & HONORS:** Nat. Corvette Owners of Amer.; **HOME ADD:** 32891 Red Bud Cir., New Baltimore, MI 48047, (313)725-4614; **BUS ADD:** 67 Cass Ave., Macomb Daily Bldg., Suite 500, Mt. Clemens, MI 48043, (313)465-1345.

WAGNER, Wallace J.——B: July 6, 1918, Wayland, NY, *Realtor - Appraiser*; **PRIM RE ACT:** Broker, Consultant, Appraiser; **PROFL AFFIL & HONORS:** MAI, SRPA; **MIL SERV:** USAF, Cpl.; **OTHER ACT & HONORS:** Retired-Assessor, City of Rochester, NY - (after 20 yrs.); **HOME ADD:** 2095 Highland Ave., Rochester, NY 14610, (716)473-1914; **BUS ADD:** 2095 Highland Ave., Rochester, NY 14610, (716)473-1914.

WAHL, R. A., Jr.——*Pres.*, Valmont Industries, Inc.; **PRIM RE ACT:** Property Manager; **BUS ADD:** Highway 275, Valley, NE 68064, (402)359-2201.*

WAINBERG, Alan——B: 1937, *VP*, Suave Shoe Corp., Manufacturing Div.; **PRIM RE ACT:** Broker, Engineer, Owner/Investor; **OTHER RE ACT:** In charge of RE activities for non RE corp.; **EDUC:** BSIE, 1964, Univ. of Miami; **GRAD EDUC:** MSOR, 1965, NY Univ.; **EDUC HONORS:** Various honor societies, NSF Fellowship; **OTHER ACT & HONORS:** Asst. Gen. Mgr. of Footwear Mfg. Co.; **HOME ADD:** 8521 S.W. 75th St., Miami, FL 33143; **BUS ADD:** 14100 N.W. 60th Ave., Miami Lakes, FL 33014.

WAINBERG, Howard S.——B: Aug. 23, 1916, Toronto, Ont. CAN, *Owner*, Howard S. Wainberg; **PRIM RE ACT:** Broker, Instructor; **OTHER RE ACT:** Comml., Indus., Resid., Counselor; **PREV EMPLOY:** Gen Bldg. Contractor (CA B-1 Licensee), Instr. at UCLA Extension in RE Exchanges & Taxation for 14 yrs.; **PROFL AFFIL & HONORS:** Assoc. of Prof. Engr. of Province of Ontario, CAN, Realty Investment Assoc. of Orange Cty., CCIM, B.A.Sc (Mining Engineer, CAN); **EDUC:** B.A.Sci., 1940, Mining Engr., Univ. of Toronto, CAN.; **GRAD EDUC:** Prof. Eng., 1955, Mining Engr., Assoc. of Prof. Engrs. of Province of Ontario, CAN; **MIL SERV:** Royal Can. Engrs, Lt.; **OTHER ACT & HONORS:** Elks Intl., Masons, Developed several RE Forms being widely used; **HOME ADD:** 12905 Palm 4, Garden Grove, CA 92640, (714)537-6336; **BUS ADD:** 1750 S. Main St., Santa Ana, CA 92707, (714)541-2281.

WAKEEN, Emil A.——B: Nov. 17, 1918, LaCrosse, WI, *VP*, Terwilliger, Wakeen, Piehler, Conway & Klingberg, SC; **PRIM RE ACT:** Attorney; **SERVICES:** Legal rep. in buy and sell transactions, foreclosures, etc.; **REP CLIENTS:** Fin. instns. (S&L assns. and banks) and indiv. sellers and buyers; **PROFL AFFIL & HONORS:** ABA, State Bar of WI, Marathon Cty. Bar - various comms. in each such as real prop., probate and corporate; **EDUC:** AB, 1940, Pre-Law, Loras Coll., Dubuque, IA; **GRAD EDUC:** LLB and JD, 1947, Law, Univ. of WI Law School, Madison, WI; **EDUC HONORS:** Magna Cum Laude; **MIL SERV:** USAF, Sgt.; **HOME ADD:** 1024 Steuben St., Wausaw, WI 54401, (715)842-2809; **BUS ADD:** 401 4th St., PO Box 1063, Wausau, WI 54401, (715)845-2121.

WAKEFIELD, W.C.——B: Feb. 8, 1935, St. Louis, MO, *Forester/Appraiser*, US Forest Service USDA, Lands & Minerals; **PRIM RE ACT:** Appraiser; **SERVICES:** Appraisal and review; **REP CLIENTS:** Govt.; **PROFL AFFIL & HONORS:** Amer. Soc. of Appraisers; Soc. of Farm Mgrs. and Rural Appraisers; Soc. of Amer. Foresters; Intl. Right of Way Assn., ASA; ARA; CRA; SR/WA; **EDUC:** BS, 1962, Forestry, Univ. of MO; **MIL SERV:** U.S. Army, Pfc., GC; **HOME ADD:** 17933 S.E. Center Lane, OR City, OR 97045, (503)631-7993; **BUS ADD:** POB 3623, Portland, OR 97208, (503)221-2921.

WAKER, Gordon——*Spec. Asst.*, Department of Housing and Urban Development, Ofc. of Secy/Under Secretary; **PRIM RE ACT:** Lender; **BUS ADD:** 451 Seventh St., S.W., Washington, DC 20410, (202)755-6950.*

WALDECK, John W., Jr.——B: May 3, 1949, Cleveland, OH, *Atty.*, Arter & Hadden; **PRIM RE ACT:** Attorney; **SERVICES:** Analysis and drafting of legal doc. for RE transactions, mortgage loans; structuring of transactions; **REP CLIENTS:** Indiv. investors, devel., corps., financial institutions; **PROFL AFFIL & HONORS:** Real Prop., Probate & Trust Section, ABA; Real Prop. Section, OH State & Greater Cleveland Bar Assns., Affiliate, Intl. Council of Shopping Ctrs.; **EDUC:** BS, 1973, Bio., John Carroll Univ., Univ. Hts., OH; **GRAD EDUC:** JD, 1977, Cleveland Marshall Coll. of Law, Cleveland State Univ.; **EDUC HONORS:** Dean's List 1968-69, Summa Cum Laude; **OTHER ACT & HONORS:** Bd. of Tr., OH lupus Found., Inc.; Exec. Council, St. Ignatius H.S. Alumni Assn.; Pres., River's Edge Commons, Inc.; Bainbridge Tax Bd. of Zoning Appeals.; **HOME ADD:** 18814 Rivers Edge Dr. W, Chagrin Falls, OH 44022, (216)543-4493; **BUS ADD:** 1144 Union Commerce Bldg., Cleveland, OH 44115, (216)696-1144.

WALDEN, Spencer C., Jr.——B: Jan. 29, 1907, Thomas Ville, GA, *Chmn. of Bd.*, Walden & Kirkland, Realtors, Inc. *and COB & Pres.*, Albany Suburban Investments, Inc.; **PRIM RE ACT:** Broker, Developer, Owner/Investor, Property Manager; **OTHER RE ACT:** Mgmt.; **SERVICES:** A complete RE serv. (res., comml., retail, indus., warehouses, shopping ctrs., farms, timberland, rentals, etc.); **PREV EMPLOY:** 1929 -1941 Practiced Law; **PROFL AFFIL & HONORS:** Local, State, Nat. Assn. RE Bds.; Intl. Council of Shopping Ctrs., Inc.; **GRAD EDUC:** LLB, 1929, Univ. of GA; **EDUC HONORS:** Treas. of Panhellenic Council; Phi Delta Phi Legal Frat. & Sigma Chi; **MIL SERV:** Spec. Agent With FBI, 1941-45; **OTHER ACT & HONORS:** Dir., First State B&T Co.; Member of GA Bar Assn.; C of C; Albany Rotary Club; Bd. of Tr. and Exec. Comm., Albany Jr. Coll.; Member of Admn. Bd. & Tr. of First United Methodist Church; Bd. of Tr., Epworth by the Sea; Chmn. Emeritus, Amer. Camellia Soc. Endowment Fund; **HOME ADD:** 1201 Pinecrest Dr., Albany, GA 31707,

(912)436-3444; **BUS ADD:** 601 N. Slappey Blvd., Albany, GA 31707, (912)436-8811.

WALDNER, Garrett W.——**B:** Nov. 16, 1940, Hutchinson, MN, *Pres.*, Real Estate Services Co.; **PRIM RE ACT:** Consultant, Appraiser, Developer, Owner/Investor, Instructor, Property Manager, Syndicator; **REP CLIENTS:** Stanford Univ., Westinghouse Corp., State of AK, US Postal Dept., US Steel Co., AK Housing Authority, GE Co., Owen-Corning Fiberglass Corp., Standard Oil Co.; **PREV EMPLOY:** Dir., AK State Housing Auth.; **PROFL AFFIL & HONORS:** NAR, Homebldrs. Assn. of AK Inc., MAI; **EDUC:** BA, 1964, Math - Bus., Augsburg Coll.; **MIL SERV:** US Army, SP 4; **OTHER ACT & HONORS:** Budget Advisory Comm. Wasilla High School, Governing Council - American Institute of RE Appraisers; **HOME ADD:** Box 1319, Wasilla, AK 99687, (907)376-5265; **BUS ADD:** 121 W. Fine Weed Ln., Suite 207, Anchorage, AK 99503, (907)274-7636.

WALDRON, Robert F.——**B:** July 3, 1927, Los Angeles, CA, *Pres.*, Robert F. WaLdron, Inc.; **PRIM RE ACT:** Attorney; **SERVICES:** Legal services; **REP CLIENTS:** Prop. owners and local Governmental Agencies in Eminent Domain and RE valuation litigation; **PROFL AFFIL & HONORS:** ABA, State Bar of CA, Orange Cty. Bar Assn., Amer. Bd. of Trial Advocates, Amer. Right of Way Assn., Amer. Arbitration Assn, Diplomate, Amer. Bd. of Trial Advocates; **EDUC:** AB, 1951, Liberal Arts, UCLA; **GRAD EDUC:** JD, 1954, Law, UCLA School of Law; **EDUC HONORS:** Exchange Student to Univ. of Oslo, Oslo, Norway 1949-50; **MIL SERV:** USN, S1C 1945-46; **OTHER ACT & HONORS:** Asst. Cty. Counsel, Orange Cty., CA 1957-59; Past Pres. YMCA of Orange Cty. 1977-79; Served as Judge Pro Tempore, Orange Cty. Superior Court 1975-78; Former RE Law Instr. at UCLA 1960-63; Expert Witness Superior Court State of CA - Legal Fees Eminent Domain Valuation Matters; **HOME ADD:** 11791 Loma Linda Way, Santa Ana, CA 92705, (714)544-5973; **BUS ADD:** 550 Golden Circle Dr., Santa Ana, CA 92705, (714)558-9432.

WALDROP, Alexander A., Jr.——**B:** July 30, 1914, Roanoke, VA, *Atty. at Law*, Sole proprietor; **PRIM RE ACT:** Attorney; **SERVICES:** RE Atty.; **REP CLIENTS:** Colonial-Amer. Nat. Bank, Roanoke, VA; SW VA S&L Assn., Roanoke, VA; **PROFL AFFIL & HONORS:** Roanoke Bar Assn.; VA State Bar Assn.; ABA; Amer. Judicature Soc.; **EDUC:** BS, 1935, Math./Hist., Hampden Sydney Coll.; **GRAD EDUC:** LLB, 1939, Law, Univ. of VA; **EDUC HONORS:** Sigma Soc.; **MIL SERV:** US Army, Infantry, 26 Infantry Div., ETO WWII - 7th Army (Geo. Patton); **OTHER ACT & HONORS:** Shenandoah Club; Roanoke Ctry. Club; Roanoke German Club; Roanoke Rotary Club; Republican Party; Chi Phi Frat.; **HOME ADD:** 2825 Avenham Ave., S.W., Roanoke, VA 24014, (703)344-8240; **BUS ADD:** 916 Colonial Arms Bldg., Roanoke, VA 24011, (703)345-0711.

WALFISH, Paul L.——**B:** Nov. 5, 1940, *VP*, Breslin Realty; **PRIM RE ACT:** Broker, Consultant, Developer, Property Manager; **SERVICES:** Brokerage, retail site location analysis, consultation mgmt.; **PROFL AFFIL & HONORS:** RHO Epsilon; **EDUC:** BS, 1963, RE, NY Univ.; **HOME ADD:** 27 Greenfield Lane, Commack, NY 11725; **BUS ADD:** 500 Old Country Rd., Garden City, NY 11530.

WALHIMER, Leslie——**B:** Jan. 11, 1923, Boston, PA, *Pres.*, Walhimer Agency Inc.; **PRIM RE ACT:** Broker, Consultant, Appraiser, Owner/Investor; **SERVICES:** Investment counseling, Appraising, Relocation Analysis; **REP CLIENTS:** Listed Co.; **PREV EMPLOY:** Fee Appraiser, Fortune 500; **PROFL AFFIL & HONORS:** AIREA, SRA, NRA, RM, SRA; **EDUC:** Econ. BS Wharton School of Fin, 1947, RE, Univ. of PA; **MIL SERV:** US Army Security, Officer; **OTHER ACT & HONORS:** Bd. of Tax Review, Sr. Commnr. Housatonic B & T, Dir. Past Pres. New Haven RE Bd.; **HOME ADD:** 231 Ansonia Rd., Woddbridge, CT., (203)397-1151; **BUS ADD:** 456 Derby Ave., West Haven, CT 06516.

WALK, Walter J.——**B:** Aug. 28, 1928, *Sec. - Treas.*, W.J. Walk Associates Inc.; **OTHER RE ACT:** Contractor; **SERVICES:** Painting & wallcovering & sandblasting; **HOME ADD:** 201 Laurel Ave., Thorofare, NJ 08086, (609)848-0255; **BUS ADD:** 201 Laurel Ave., Thorofare, NJ 08086, (609)845-0484.

WALKER, B.J.——*Exec. VP*, American Sterilizer Co.; **PRIM RE ACT:** Property Manager; **BUS ADD:** 2222 West Grandview Blvd., Erie, PA 16509, (814)452-3100.*

WALKER, Fred W.——**B:** Nov. 29, 1929, Detroit, MI, *Pres.*, Central Mort. & Investment Co.; **PRIM RE ACT:** Broker, Appraiser, Banker, Lender, Owner/Investor; **SERVICES:** RE Loans Resid.; **PROFL AFFIL & HONORS:** MBAA; **OTHER ACT & HONORS:** Rotarian; Pres. 2 other Corps.; **HOME ADD:** 1425 E. Hwy. 105, Monument, CO 80132, (303)488-2494; **BUS ADD:** 1569 Briargate Blvd., Colorado Springs., CO 80918, (303)598-1015.

WALKER, Ian G.——**B:** Oct. 19, 1928, Philadelphia, PA, *Pres. Walker & Co.; Exec. VP E. P. Wilbur & Co.; Exec. VP E.P.W. Securities, Inc.*; **OTHER RE ACT:** Real Estate Investment Banking; **SERVICES:** Acquisition, ownership and mgmt. of RE for instns. and indiv. investors; **PREV EMPLOY:** Northeast Airlines (1957-59); S.D. Fuller & Co. (1959-61) Stroud & Co. (1961-1963); Stone & Webster Securities Corp. (1963-1966); The Robinson-Humphrey Co. (1966-1969); Winmill, Jones & Walker (1969-1972), Webber, Jackson & Curtis (1972-1974); Philadelphia Nat. Bank (1975-1976); **EDUC:** BA, 1950, Haverford Coll.; **GRAD EDUC:** MBA, 1957, Harvard Con.; **OTHER ACT & HONORS:** St. Andrew Soc. of Philadelphia; The Tower Club; Bond Club of Ft. Lauderdale; President, Harvard Club of Broward Cty.; Chmn., Ivy League Assn., Haverford Coll. Alumni Council; **BUS ADD:** 1748 N.W. 82nd Ave., Coral Springs, FL 33065.

WALKER, James Leslie, IV——**B:** Aug. 14, 1951, San Francisco, CA, *Partner*, Law Offices of Chris A. Schaefer; **PRIM RE ACT:** Attorney, Developer, Owner/Investor, Syndicator; **OTHER RE ACT:** Financing locator; **REP CLIENTS:** Rafael North Exec. park; Marin Mobile Home Parks, Inc.; Novak Devel. Co.; Precision Solar Systems Inc.; **PROFL AFFIL & HONORS:** CA Bar Assn.; Marin Cty. Bar Assn.; admitted to practice before the US tax court; San Rafael C of C, JD; MBA(tax); **EDUC:** BS, 1973, Econ., Univ. of VA; **GRAD EDUC:** JD, MBA, 1976, Law,tax, Hastings Coll. of the Law, Golden Gate Univ.; **EDUC HONORS:** with distinction; **OTHER ACT & HONORS:** Soc. of CA Pioneers Dir. Rafael North Exec. Park; **HOME ADD:** 77 Rose Ave., Mill Valley, CA 94941, (415)383-9459; **BUS ADD:** 68 Mitchell Blvd. #250, San Rafael, CA 94903, (415)472-7880.

WALKER, James R.——**B:** Feb. 8, 1921, Royal Oak, MI, *Pres.*, Walker & Co. Realtors; **PRIM RE ACT:** Broker; **SERVICES:** Full serv. realtor firm; **PROFL AFFIL & HONORS:** Local, state, nat. realtor, IREM, CPM, Realtor of yr., CO Sprs. Bd. of Realtors, 1964, VP CO State Realtors, 1975; **GRAD EDUC:** BS, 1943, Agric., MI State Coll.; **EDUC HONORS:** Cum Laude; **MIL SERV:** Infantry, 10th Mtn. Div., Capt., Bronze Star; **OTHER ACT & HONORS:** Exec. Club, Rotary, CO Soaring Assn., CO Sprs. Ctry Club, Mason, 3 Diamond Soaring Pilot; **HOME ADD:** 2522 Pasea Rd., CO Sprs, CO 80907, (303)634-4560; **BUS ADD:** 3504 Galley Rd., CO Sprs., CO 80909, (303)596-7882.

WALKER, Jon R.——**B:** Apr. 27, 1952, Colorado Springs, CO, *VP, Prop. Mgmt. Div. Head, Cert. Prop. Mgr.*, Walker and Co. Inc.; **PRIM RE ACT:** Consultant, Property Manager; **SERVICES:** Full serv. prop. mgmt. & consulting (all property types); **REP CLIENTS:** Prop. owners, devels., bd. of dirs. for community assns.; **PROFL AFFIL & HONORS:** NAR, IREM; CAI, CPM; **OTHER ACT & HONORS:** Soaring Soc. of Amer.; S. CO Mgr. of the Yr., 1979-81; S. CO IREM Pres., 1980-81; **HOME ADD:** 2623 N. Bonfoy Ave., Colorado Springs, CO 80909, (303)633-8383; **BUS ADD:** 3604 Galley Rd., Colorado Springs, CO 80909, (303)596-7882.

WALKER, Kenneth——*VP RE*, Gold Kist, Inc.; **PRIM RE ACT:** Property Manager; **BUS ADD:** PO Box 2210, Atlanta, GA 30301, (404)393-5000.*

WALKER, Larry E.——**B:** Sept. 21, 1947, Washington, DC, *Atty.*, Goldman, Walker, Greenfeig & Metro, Chartered; **PRIM RE ACT:** Attorney, Developer, Owner/Investor, Syndicator; **PREV EMPLOY:** Law Clerk, Honorable Philip M. Fairbanks, Circuit Ct. for Montgomery Cty., MD; **PROFL AFFIL & HONORS:** ABA, MD State Bar Assn.; **EDUC:** BS, 1969, Pol. Sci. & Econ., Univ. of MD; **GRAD EDUC:** JD, 1972, Law, Amer. Univ. - Washington Coll. of Law; **EDUC HONORS:** Omicron Delta Kappa Honorary, Legal Services Award; **MIL SERV:** US Army Res., 1969-75; **OTHER ACT & HONORS:** Montgomery Cty. MD Prop. Tax Bd.; Selected to "Outstanding Young Men of Amer." 1979; **HOME ADD:** 2609 Oakenshield Dr., Rockville, MD 20854, (301)424-1661; **BUS ADD:** 25 West Middle Lane, Rockville, MD 20850, (301)340-2020.

WALKER, Richard L., Jr.——**B:** Aug. 16, 1946, Cold Spring, NY, *Pres./Broker*, Fulscher Co. of Colorado Springs, Colorado Development Group; **PRIM RE ACT:** Broker, Consultant, Developer, Property Manager, Owner/Investor; **SERVICES:** Integrated income prop. services; **REP CLIENTS:** Stanley/Walker Interests, CO Investment Co.; **PROFL AFFIL & HONORS:** CO Apt. Assoc., BOMA, Nat. Apt. Assn., Past Pres., CO Apt. Assn. & Pikes Peak Apt. Assn., Winner Comml. Project Brochures IREM, CPM; **EDUC:** BS, 1972, Urban Planning, Dev. and Admin., Univ. of MO; **MIL SERV:** US Army; **HOME ADD:** 6135 Garlock Way, Colorado Springs, CO 80907, (303)598-5758; **BUS ADD:** The Railroad Station, 555 E. Pikes Peak Ave., Suite 200, Colorado Springs, CO 80903.

WALKEY, John R.——**B:** Aug. 16, 1938, Cambridge, MA, *Partner, Law Firm*, Choate, Hall & Stewart; **PRIM RE ACT:** Attorney; **SERVICES:** Legal; **REP CLIENTS:** Devel., banks and insurance co's.; **PROFL AFFIL & HONORS:** Abstract Club; MA Conveyancers Assn.; ABA; MBA, Juris Doctor; **EDUC:** BA, 1960, Pol. Sci., Univ. of MA; **GRAD EDUC:** JD, 1963, Law, Boston Coll., Law School; **EDUC HONORS:** Deans List, Pres. Scholar; **OTHER ACT & HONORS:** Trustee, Union Warren Savings Bank; Director, Numerous Corps.; **HOME ADD:** Tide Acres, 50 Cedar St., Duxbury, MA 02332, (617)934-5588; **BUS TEL:** (617)227-5020.

WALL, Frederick L., III——**B:** Apr. 7, 1932, Boston, MA, *Pres.*, The Wall Cos.; **PRIM RE ACT:** Broker, Developer, Builder, Owner/Investor, Syndicator; **SERVICES:** RE devel.; **PROFL AFFIL & HONORS:** NAA, NAR, BOMA, MBA, ABA, Nat. Assn. of Indus. & Office Parks; **EDUC:** AA Orn. Horticulture, 1956, Univ. of MA, Amherst, MA; **EDUC HONORS:** Verbeck Award 1956; **MIL SERV:** USN, AC3; **HOME ADD:** 2600 Spirit Knob Rd., Wayzata, MN 55391, (612)473-4901; **BUS ADD:** 8200 Normandale Blvd., Bloomington, MN 55437, (612)835-1222.

WALL, John P.——**B:** Aug. 6, 1928, Medford, MA, *VP*, T.J. McGlone & Co., Inc., Const. Mgmt. & Gen. Contracting; **PRIM RE ACT:** Broker, Developer, Builder; **SERVICES:** Devel., const. mgmt., gen. contracting; **REP CLIENTS:** Consulting; **PROFL AFFIL & HONORS:** AGC, NSPE, NAIP; **EDUC:** SB, 1950, Engineering & Const., MA Inst. Tech.; **GRAD EDUC:** MBA, 1955, Harvard Bus. School; **MIL SERV:** US Army, CP/1951-53; **HOME ADD:** 352 Owen Ave., Fair Lawn, NJ 07410, (201)797-2796; **BUS ADD:** 40 Brunswick Ave., Edison, NJ 08819, (201)287-8500.

WALL, Larry——*Mgr. of Eng. Serv.*, Richardson-Vicks, Inc.; **PRIM RE ACT:** Property Manager; **BUS ADD:** 10 Westport Rd., Wilton, CT 06897, (203)762-2222.*

WALL, Norbert F.——**B:** Sep. 29, 1934, Chicago, IL, *Pres.*, American Realty Consultants, Ltd.; **PRIM RE ACT:** Consultant, Appraiser, Owner/Investor; **SERVICES:** Valuation serv., mkt. analysis, consulting, fin.; **REP CLIENTS:** Major U.S. corps., for. investors and banks, devel., pvt. investors; **PREV EMPLOY:** Sr. VP RE Research Corp.; Pres. Larry Smith & Co.; Exec. VP Namesa, Paris, France; Exec. VP Clayton Towers Development Co., St. Louis, MO; **PROFL AFFIL & HONORS:** NACORE, ULI, CSC, Amer. Inst. of RE Appraisers; Soc. of RE Appraisers; Chicago Farmers, MAI, SREA; **EDUC:** AA, BSBA, 1956-1963, Arch., Fin.; **MIL SERV:** USN Reserve, CT; **OTHER ACT & HONORS:** Who's Who in Finance, Who's Who in the Midwest; Author, "RE Investment by Objective" published by McGraw-Hill; Radio Show Host: Norb Wall's RE Corner; **HOME ADD:** 261 Steeplechase Rd., Barrington Hills, IL 60010, (312)381-2082; **BUS ADD:** 120 Lageshulte St., Barrington, IL 60010, (312)382-6260.

WALLACE, C. Robert——**B:** May 29, 1929, Hartford, CT, *Owner*, The Wallace Co.; **PRIM RE ACT:** Broker; **SERVICES:** Resid., mkt. evaluation, bus. opportunity brokerage; **REP CLIENTS:** Many cos.; **PREV EMPLOY:** Singer Sewing Machine Co.; **PROFL AFFIL & HONORS:** RNMI; NAR; CA Assn. of Realtors; Greater Hartford Bd. of Realtors, GRI, CRS, CRB, (Pres. of Greater Hartford Bd. of Realtors); **EDUC:** Gen., Trinity Coll., Hartford; **OTHER ACT & HONORS:** West Hartford Rotary club, West Hartford C of C, West Hartford Rgnl. Affairs Comm., Hartford Central YMCA Advisory Bd.; **BUS ADD:** 1000 Farmington Ave., West Hartford, CT 06107, (203)236-0881.

WALLACE, David L.——**B:** Sept. 16, 1947, Watertown, NY, *Owner*, Wallace Properties; **PRIM RE ACT:** Developer, Owner/Investor, Property Manager; **EDUC:** Indus. Mgmt., 1969, Bus., Clarkson Coll.; **MIL SERV:** US Army, Signal Corp, 1st Lt., 1970-1972; **HOME ADD:** 35 Beverly St., Rochester, NY 14610; **BUS ADD:** 25 Buckingham St., Rochester, NY 14607, (716)442-0366.

WALLACE, Donald L.——**B:** Aug. 18, 1933, Omaha, NE, *Pres.*, D.L. Wallace Appraiser, Ltd; **PRIM RE ACT:** Consultant, Appraiser, Owner/Investor; **OTHER RE ACT:** Bus. valuations; **SERVICES:** Appraisal and consulting of all types of comml. and industl. prop.; **REP CLIENTS:** First Interstate Bank of AZ, Homequity; Merrill Lynch Relocation; Burns Investment; Membery Const. and Dev.; Hancock Homes; Transamerica Relocation; TICOR Mortgage Ins. Co.; Western Amer. Mort. Co.; H. S. Pickrell Co.; **PREV EMPLOY:** Sr. Appraiser, the Equitable Life Assurance Soc. of the US, RMD, SFO; CAm Review Appraiser, City of Phoenix, AZ Housing and Urban Redevel.; **PROFL AFFIL & HONORS:** SREA; AIREA; NARA; FIABCI; Inst. of Bus. Appraisers; IR/WA, SRA, RM, CRA designations; **EDUC:** BA, 1959, Gen. Bus. Adm. and Geo., AZ State Univ., Tempe, AZ; **GRAD EDUC:** Certificate in R.E., 1965, Univ. of CA Ext. Berkley, CA; **MIL SERV:** US Army; Cpl., good conduct medal; **OTHER ACT & HONORS:** Catholic Alumni Club Intl.; **HOME ADD:** 2364 West Via Rialto, Mesa, AZ 85202, (602)838-9551; **BUS ADD:** 201 E. Southern Ave., PO Box 27521, Tempe, AZ 85282, (602)968-7289.

WALLACE, R. Calvin——**B:** Mar. 17, 1929, Pasadena, CA, *Partner*, Peat Marwick Mitchell & Co.; **OTHER RE ACT:** CPA; **SERVICES:** Auditing, Consulting; **REP CLIENTS:** RE Devel., Synd., Investors; **PROFL AFFIL & HONORS:** AICPA, CPA; **EDUC:** BS, 1951, Acctg., Univ. of So. CA; **GRAD EDUC:** MS, 1960, Acctg., Univ. of So. CA; **MIL SERV:** USNR, Lt., 1952-1955; **BUS ADD:** 4400 MacArthur Blvd., Newport Beach, CA 92660, (714)851-2000.

WALLACE, Robert C.——**B:** Oct. 17, 1945, St. Louis, MO, *Managing Part.*, Wallace Properties Group; **PRIM RE ACT:** Broker, Syndicator, Consultant, Developer, Property Manager, Owner/Investor; **SERVICES:** R.E. investment, devel. mgmt.; **REP CLIENTS:** Private and instnl. investors in comml. R.E.(limited to office bldgs. and shopping centers in Pacific N.W.); **PREV EMPLOY:** Medical Grp. Mgmt.; **PROFL AFFIL & HONORS:** ICSC; **EDUC:** BA, 1969, Mgmt., Seattle Pacific Univ., Seattle WA; **MIL SERV:** US Army; E-7; **OTHER ACT & HONORS:** Bellevue Downtown Devel. Bd.-Pres. 1977-78; Bellevue C of C- Pres. 1980-81; Bellevue Rotary Club; King Co. East Visitors & Conv. Board-Dir.; **HOME ADD:** PO Box 161, Bellevue, WA 98009, (206)747-9330; **BUS ADD:** Suite 400, Citizens Bank Bldg. PO Box 161, Bellevue, WA 98009, (206)455-9976.

WALLACE, Robert J.——**B:** Oct. 27, 1946, Brooklyn, NY, *VP*, Title Guarantee Co., Suffolk; **PRIM RE ACT:** Insuror; **SERVICES:** Title ins.; **PREV EMPLOY:** RE Salesman; **PROFL AFFIL & HONORS:** Amer. Land Title Assn.; NY State Land Title Assn.; Suffolk Cty. RE Bd., Inc.; Assoc. Member of Long Island Builders Inst., Inc.; Eastern Long Is. Bd. of Realtors; **EDUC:** AA and AAS, 1976, Bus. Admin. and Acctg., Suffolk Cty. Community Coll.; **EDUC HONORS:** Phi Alph Sigma; **MIL SERV:** US Army; MP; 1965-68; **OTHER ACT & HONORS:** Lions Club; **HOME ADD:** PO Box 297, Riverhead, NY 11901; **BUS ADD:** 400 W. Main St., Riverhead, NY 11901, (516)727-2300.

WALLACE, W. Ray——*Pres.*, Trinity Industries, Inc.; **PRIM RE ACT:** Property Manager; **BUS ADD:** 4001 Irving Blvd., PO Box 10587, Dallas, TX 75207, (214)631-4420.*

WALLACH, Irving T.——**B:** Dec. 25, 1910, NY, NY, *VP*, Helmsley-Spear Inc., Indus. Dept., Appraisal Dept.; **PRIM RE ACT:** Broker, Appraiser; **SERVICES:** Sales, leasing, fin. appraisal of indus. & comml. props.; **REP CLIENTS:** Banks, attys., estates, comml. corps.; **PROFL AFFIL & HONORS:** SIR; Indus. RE Brokers Assn.; **HOME ADD:** 242 E. 19 St., New York, NY 10003, (212)674-2388; **BUS ADD:** 60 E 42nd St., New York, NY 10017, (212)880-0447.

WALLDORF, Herman W.——**B:** Mar. 7, 1904, Chattanooga, TN, *Pres.*, Herman Walldorf & Co. Inc.; **PRIM RE ACT:** Broker, Property Manager, Owner/Investor; **PREV EMPLOY:** RE since 1926; **PROFL AFFIL & HONORS:** Chattanooga Bd. of Realtors, C of C, Pres. St. & Loc. Bd. of Realtors; **OTHER ACT & HONORS:** Kiwanis Club; **HOME ADD:** 1706 Carroll La., Chattanooga, TN 37405, (615)266-4526; **BUS ADD:** 109 E. 8th St., Chattanooga, TN 37405, (615)756-2400.

WALLDORF, Rudy——**B:** Nov. 28, 1939, Chattanooga, TN, *VP*, Herman Walldorf & Co., Inc., Comml.; **PRIM RE ACT:** Broker, Developer, Owner/Investor; **SERVICES:** Comml. & investment RE sales & leasing; **REP CLIENTS:** Site selectlon for retail users & devels.; **PROFL AFFIL & HONORS:** RESSI, CCIM; Honor Realtor of the Year (Chattanooga); **EDUC:** BA, 1971, Ins., Univ. of NC; **OTHER ACT & HONORS:** Rotary Club; Bd. of Associates, Chattanooga State Tech. Community Coll.; **HOME ADD:** 717 Oxford Rd., Chattanooga, TN 37402, (615)267-4027; **BUS ADD:** 109 E. 8th St., Chattanooga, TN 37402, (615)756-2400.

WALLERSTEIN, David L.——**B:** May 10, 1939, Chicago, IL, *Pres.*, Mort. & Investment Corp.; **PRIM RE ACT:** Broker, Consultant, Developer; **SERVICES:** Fin., sale, devel. and acquisition of income prop. throughout the U.S.; **REP CLIENTS:** Lenders and indiv. or inst. investors in income prop.; **PREV EMPLOY:** VP, Sonnenblick-Goldman Corp. of DC, 1977-1979; Self Employed Consultant to public and private devels., 1967-1977; **EDUC:** BA, 1961, Econ./Govt., Pomona Coll.; **GRAD EDUC:** MBA, 1963, Govt. Admin., Wharton School, Univ. of PA; **EDUC HONORS:** Pomona Scholar, Fels Scholar; **HOME ADD:** 3001 Cambridge Pl., N.W., Washington, DC 20007, (202)337-5462; **BUS ADD:** 1025 Conn. Ave., N.W., Suite 711, Washington, DC 20036, (202)466-7117.

WALLIS, Ben A., Jr.——*Atty. at Law*, Law Offices of Ben A. Wallis, Jr.; **PRIM RE ACT:** Attorney; **PROFL AFFIL & HONORS:** ABA; TX Bar Assn.; DC Bar Assn.; San Antonio Bar Assn.; Dallas Bar Assn.; Fed. Bar Assn.; **EDUC:** BBA, Univ. of TX; **GRAD EDUC:** JD, Univ. of TX; **BUS ADD:** 2400 Tower Life Bldg., San Antonio, TX 78205, (512)226-2331.

WALLIS, William T.——**B:** 1930, Jacksonville, FL, *Pres.*, First Fed. Savings & Loan Assn. of Martin Cty.; **PRIM RE ACT:** Banker; **PREV EMPLOY:** 1958-1976, Managing Officer and Dir. and CEO of First Fed. S&L Assn. of Osceola Cty., Kissimmee, FL, Exec. Sec. 1958, Exec. VP 1959, Pres. 1968; 1955-1958, Trainee and Loan Serv. Officer, First Fed. S&L Assn. of the Palm Beaches, W. Palm Beach, FL; 1951-1955, US Naval Res., OCS Officer Candidate to Lt. (j.g.) CIC Officer and Unit Security Officer; **PROFL AFFIL & HONORS:** Chmn. of the Bd. of Dirs., (Founding Dir.) 1973-1977, The Amer. Bank of Orange Cty.; Dir., 1975-1978, The Fed. Home Loan Bank of Atlanta; Present Dir. & Past Pres., 1967, FL Savings and Loan League; Past Dir., 1968-1969, US League of Savings Assns.; Member, 1975, Policy Comm. of Legislative Comm. of the US League of Savings Assns.; Past Chmn., Serv. Corp. Comm., US League of Savings Assns.; Past Member, 1974, US League of Savings Assns., Comm. of the Alternatives; Member, 1980-82 Executive Comm.; **EDUC:** BS, Acctg./Econ.; **GRAD EDUC:** Grad. Diploma, 1960, Univ. of IN, Grad. School of S&L; **MIL SERV:** US Naval Res.; Ens., Lt. (s.g.), Active duty in Korean War; **OTHER ACT & HONORS:** Dir., 1970, FL State C of C; Past Pres., 1973, Greater Kissimmee Area C of C; Member of Exec. Council, 1972, Comm. of 100, Kissimmee C of C; Past Member, Bd. of Suprv., 1974-1975, Reedy Creek Improvement Dist.; Past Member, 1971, Walt Disney World Community Serv. Award Comm.; VP & Dir., 1974 to present, FL Techno. Univ. Found.; Member, 1975, Valencia Community Coll. Found.; Past Chmn. & Member, 1961-1969, E. Central FL Planning Council; Past Member, 1968, City of Kissimmee Planning Commn.; Past Dir., Osceola Art & Culture Ctr., Kissimmee; Past Sr. Warden, St. John's Episcopal Church; **HOME ADD:** 19 W. High Point Rd., Sewalls Point, Jensen Beach, FL 33457; **BUS ADD:** 989 S. Federal Hwy., Stuart, FL 33494, (305)287-1111.

WALNER, Robert D.——**B:** Mar. 29, 1941, Dallas, TX, *Pres.*, Associates Realty Co., Inc.; **PRIM RE ACT:** Broker, Consultant, Owner/Investor, Property Manager, Syndicator; **SERVICES:** Income prop. specialist, equity mgmt.; **REP CLIENTS:** Lenders, synd., indus. investors, off-shore trusts; **PREV EMPLOY:** E.F. Hutton Co.; G.W. Works Co. (A.M.O.); **EDUC:** BS, 1963, Econ./Eng., Univ. of TX; **MIL SERV:** USN, Lcdr., Bronze Star; **BUS ADD:** 6314 Walnut Hill Ln., Dallas, TX 75230, (214)363-8022.

WALNER, Robert J.——**B:** 1947, *VP and Gen. Counsel*, The Balcor Co.; **PRIM RE ACT:** Attorney; **SERVICES:** Responsible for Balcor Co's. Legal functions; **PREV EMPLOY:** Atty. for Allied Van Lines, Inc. (1977-1979); IL Commerce Commn. (1973-1977); **PROFL AFFIL & HONORS:** Partnerships, Trusts & Unincorporated Assns., Subcomm. of Fed. Regulation of Securities Comm. of ABA, Co-Chmn. of Nat. Synd. Forum; **BUS ADD:** Balcor Bldg., 10024 Skokie Blvd., Skokie, IL 60077, (312)677-2900.

WALPOLE, Robert F.——**B:** Aug. 6, 1944, Cortland, NY, *Mgr.*, Munson Realty; **PRIM RE ACT:** Appraiser, Developer, Builder, Owner/Investor, Property Manager; **PROFL AFFIL & HONORS:** Elks, Moose, NY State Fire Chiefs, NY State Auctioneer's Asst.; **EDUC:** Ridge Coll.; **OTHER ACT & HONORS:** Fire Chief - 8 yrs., Town Justice & Water Commnr. - 5 yrs.; **HOME ADD:** 102 Church St., Groton, NY 13073, (607)898-3140; **BUS ADD:** 448 Locke Rd., Box 130, Groton, NY 13073, (607)898-3739.

WALSER, M.S.——**B:** Feb. 6, 1952, Louisville, KY, *Cert. Prop. Mgt.*, Countryside Int., Inc., Prop. Mgmt.; **PRIM RE ACT:** Broker, Developer, Builder, Property Manager; **PROFL AFFIL & HONORS:** CPM Member of IREM, Member Louisville Bd. of Realtors BRK-Assoc., CPM; **EDUC:** BS Psych., 1975, Eastern KY Univ.; **HOME ADD:** 7110 W. Hwy. 22, Crestwood, KY 40014; **BUS ADD:** 4898 Brownsboro Shp. Ctr., Louisville, KY 40222, (502)895-4273.

WALSH, E. Denis——*Owner*, E. Denis Walsh and Assoc.; **PRIM RE ACT:** Broker, Consultant, Developer, Builder, Owner/Investor, Instructor, Property Manager, Syndicator; **PREV EMPLOY:** Asst. to Pres.-Codman Co. 1970-73; Joint owner and devel. of award winning Whininsville Cotton Mill Apts.; **PROFL AFFIL & HONORS:** Commnr.-Back Bay Arch. Comm. Member Rental Housing Assn., Greater Boston RE Bd., MA Home Builders; **EDUC:** BA, 1966, Econ., Boston Coll.; **GRAD EDUC:** MBA, 1970, Boston Coll.; **MIL SERV:** US Army; **HOME ADD:** 17 Marlborough St., Boston, MA 02116, (617)262-1049; **BUS ADD:** 73 Tremont St., Boston, MA 02108, (617)742-0516.

WALSH, James M.——**B:** Oct. 29, 1920, Pittsburgh, PA, *Sr. VP*, Equibank, Mort. Dept.; **PRIM RE ACT:** Banker; **PROFL AFFIL & HONORS:** Action-Housing, Inc. - Member of Bd. of Dir. - Member SREA, SRA; **EDUC:** BS, 1949, Bus. Admin., Duquesne Univ.; **MIL SERV:** US Army, S/Sgt. 1942-45; **OTHER ACT & HONORS:** Inst. - Stonier Grad. Sch. of Banking; **HOME ADD:** 960 Country Club Dr., Pittsburgh, PA 15228, (412)563-3764; **BUS ADD:** Two Oliver Plaza, Pittsburgh, PA 15222, (412)288-5707.

WALSH, James R.——**B:** June 16, 1943, Chicago, IL, *Investment Prop. Broker*, Interstate Props. Grp., Inc.; **PRIM RE ACT:** Broker; **SERVICES:** Brokerage of maj. investment props.; **REP CLIENTS:** Converters, synds. private & instnl. investors; **PREV EMPLOY:** Accountant, Touche Ross, 1965-66; **PROFL AFFIL & HONORS:** NW Suburban Bd. of Realtors, Central Assn. of RE Exchangers, O'Hare Grp., Natl. Mktg. Inst., CPA; **EDUC:** BBA, 1965, Acctg./Fin., Loyola Univ., Chicago; **GRAD EDUC:** MBA, 1969, Mktg., NW Univ.; **EDUC HONORS:** Acctg. Key; **MIL SERV:** US Army, 1st Lt.; **OTHER ACT & HONORS:** Rotary Club of Glenview, Amer. Legion Post 166; **HOME ADD:** 1622 Barry Ln., Glenview, IL 60025, (312)729-9777; **BUS ADD:** 1011 E. Touhy Ave., Suite 245, IL 60025, (312)998-0422.

WALSH, Joseph M., Jr.——**B:** Feb. 12, 1933, Erie PA, *Atty.*, Carney, Good, Brabender & Walsh; **PRIM RE ACT:** Attorney; **OTHER RE ACT:** Oil and gas title work; **PROFL AFFIL & HONORS:** ABA, Penn. Bar Assn., Erie Cty. Bar Assn.; **EDUC:** BS, 1954, Pre-Law, Fordham Univ.; **GRAD EDUC:** 1958, Univ. of Pittsburgh; **HOME ADD:** 11839 E. Findley Lake Rd., North East, PA 16428; **BUS ADD:** 254 W. 6 St., Erie, PA 16507, (814)453-5004.

WALSH, Joseph P.——**B:** Mar. 12, 1904, NY City, NY, *Owner*, Joseph P. Walsh; **PRIM RE ACT:** Broker, Appraiser; **SERVICES:** Resid. comml. and indus. appraisals and land consultant; **REP CLIENTS:** Con. Ed., B & O Marine Midland, City of NY and various banks; **PREV EMPLOY:** Owned own bus. over 50 yrs.; **PROFL AFFIL & HONORS:** Soc. of RE Appraisers and NY State Soc. of RE Appraisers, Staten Island RE Bd., Chmn, Appraisal committee of RE Bd. 20 yrs., Member of Richmond Cty. Bar Assn.; **GRAD EDUC:** LLB, 1928, Fordham Law School; **MIL SERV:** USAF, 1943-45, Sgt. Maj.; **OTHER ACT & HONORS:** RE Adviser for South Richmond Devel. Project, Rouse Co.; **HOME ADD:** 23 Howard Ave., Staten Island, NY 10301, (212)447-3234; **BUS ADD:** 26 Bay St, PO Box 333, Staten Island, NY 10301, (212)447-1616.

WALSH, Patrick——*Emp. Rel. Mgr.*, Thomas & Betts. Corp.; **PRIM RE ACT:** Property Manager; **BUS ADD:** 920 Route 202, Raritan, NJ 08869, (201)685-1600.*

WALSH, Thomas A.——**B:** Nov. 19, 1944, Boston, MA, *Sr. VP*, The Codman Co., Inc., Indus.; **PRIM RE ACT:** Broker, Consultant; **PROFL AFFIL & HONORS:** Pres., Comml. Indus. Council Greater Boston RE Bd. V.P. N.E. Chapter (SIR); **EDUC:** AB, 1966, Pol. Sci., Boston Coll.; **MIL SERV:** US Army, Capt.; **OTHER ACT & HONORS:** Corp., Arlington Five Cents Sav. Bank; **HOME ADD:** 2 Denton Rd., Wellesley, MA 02181, (617)237-0596; **BUS ADD:** 211 Congress St., Boston, MA 02110, (617)423-6500.

WALSH, Thomas C.——**B:** Jan. 17, 1924, Chicago, IL, *Atty.*; **PRIM RE ACT:** Attorney; **PROFL AFFIL & HONORS:** State Bar of MI, ABA, Amer. Judicature Soc., Ingham Cty. Bar Assn.; **EDUC:** AB, 1949, Journ., Univ. of MI; **GRAD EDUC:** JD, 1951, Journal., Univ. of MI; **MIL SERV:** US Army, T/4; **OTHER ACT & HONORS:** Chmn., Lansing Charter Commn., 1975-78 - Member Lansing Bd. of Educ., 1959-71, Civitan Intl., Elks, NAACP, ACLU, Lansing and MI Jaycees "Young Man of the Year" 1959; **HOME ADD:** 3234 S. Cambridge Rd., Lansing, MI 48910, (517)487-6487; **BUS ADD:** 431 S. Capitol Ave., Lansing, MI 48933, (517)482-8337.

WALTER, Alexander W.——**B:** Apr. 5, 1940, Akron, OH, *Pres.*, Partnership Securities Corp.; **PRIM RE ACT:** Syndicator, Consultant, Owner/Investor; **SERVICES:** Sponsor/Gen. Part. for RE Synd. The firm is a member of the Nat. Ass. of Securities Dealers, Inc., and the Securities Investor Protection Corp. Rep. Clients: Qualified investors and Fin. Inst.; **PREV EMPLOY:** First WI Mort. Co., Alcoa, Honeywell; **PROFL AFFIL & HONORS:** Cert. Investment Realtor & CRS, RNMI Registered Securities Representative with the Sec.; RE Broker in CO, MN & WI; **EDUC:** BA, 1962, Physics, Marietta Coll; **HOME TEL:** (303)695-6553; **BUS ADD:** 12624 E. Bates Cir., Aurora, CO 80014, (303)696-1531.

WALTER, Kenneth J.——**B:** Oct. 2, 1945, OR, *Sr. RE Off.*, Rainier Bank Trust RE, Trust Div.; **PRIM RE ACT:** Consultant, Property Manager; **PROFL AFFIL & HONORS:** CPM; **EDUC:** BS, Fin. and RE, Univ. of OR; **HOME TEL:** (206)525-9466; **BUS ADD:** PO Box

3966, Seattle, WA 98124, (206)621-4371.

WALTER, Lloyd Guy, Jr.——B: June 19, 1934, Tampa, FL, *Pres. & Treas.*, Hammill-Walter Associates, Inc. - Architects; **PRIM RE ACT:** Architect; **SERVICES:** Arch. services; **REP CLIENTS:** R.J. Reynolds Industries, Piedmont Airlines, McLean Trucking Co., Wachovia Bank & Trust Co., GSA, City of Winston-Salem, Winston-Salem State Univ.; **PREV EMPLOY:** A.G. Odell, Jr. & Assoc. - Arch. - 1960-5; **PROFL AFFIL & HONORS:** AIA, Dir. of NC Design Found., Inc.; **EDUC:** BArch, 1960, School of Design, NC State Coll.; **EDUC HONORS:** NC State Book Award for Design, 1960 Lloyd Warren Fellowship (Paris Prize in Arch.); **MIL SERV:** USAF, Airman 2/C; **OTHER ACT & HONORS:** Pres. Rotary Club of Stratford, Winston-Salem, 1978-9, Paul Harris Fellow, VP Winston-Salem C of C 1982, Chairman, Historic Dists. Commn., Winston-Salem, 1979-81, NC Bd. of Architecture, Member 1982-1986; **HOME ADD:** 1848 Runnymeade Rd., Winston-Salem, NC 27104, (919)724-0646; **BUS ADD:** 723 Coliseum Dr., Winston-Salem, NC 27106, (919)725-1371.

WALTERS, Charles J.——B: Mar. 11, 1945, Philadelphia, PA, *VP*, Center Square Real Estate Development Co., Inc.; **PRIM RE ACT:** Broker, Developer, Syndicator; **PREV EMPLOY:** Warner Co., Dir. of Devel.; **PROFL AFFIL & HONORS:** SIR, Nat. Assn. of Indus. and Office Parks; **EDUC:** BS, 1968, Mktg., Drexel Univ.; **GRAD EDUC:** MBA, 1972, Fin., Wharton; **MIL SERV:** US Army; Capt., SS, BS, PH; **OTHER ACT & HONORS:** Bd. of Dir.-The Bridgeport Interests, Inc.; Ctr. Sq. Bldrs., Inc.; **HOME ADD:** 509 N. Wayne Ave., Wayne, PA 19087, (215)964-9543; **BUS ADD:** 603 Heron Dr., Bridgeport, NJ 08014, (609)467-2333.

WALTERS, David W.——B: Jan. 13, 1947, Los Angeles, CA, *Partner*, Adams, Kouba and Dickson; **PRIM RE ACT:** Attorney, Instructor; **OTHER RE ACT:** Author; **SERVICES:** Prop. acquisition structuring, tax consulting, structuring of RE synd. and joint ventures; **REP CLIENTS:** RE investors, lenders & devel., mort. bankers; **PROFL AFFIL & HONORS:** ABA; ULI; RESSI; NAREB; **EDUC:** BS, 1968, Statistics, Stanford Univ.; **GRAD EDUC:** MBA, 1970, RE, Univ. of CA, Berkeley; JD, 1974, Law, Univ. of San Francisco; MS, 1979, Tax, Golden Gate Univ.; **EDUC HONORS:** McAul. Law Hon. Soc.; **MIL SERV:** Engr., Cpt.; **OTHER ACT & HONORS:** Recipient of 'Journal of Prop. Mgmts.' 1973 award for Most Outstanding Article; **HOME ADD:** 225 N. Almenar Dr., Greenbrae, CA 94904, (415)461-4049; **BUS ADD:** 660 Market St., San Francisco, CA 94904, (415)392-2800.

WALTERS, Robert L.——*Pres. RE & GS Div.*, McGraw-Hill, Inc.; **PRIM RE ACT:** Property Manager; **BUS ADD:** 1221 Avenue of the Americas, New York, NY 10020, (212)997-1221.*

WALTHER, Steven G.——B: Dec. 9, 1948, Rochester, NY, *Pres.*, Steven G. Walther, Inc. Realtor; **PRIM RE ACT:** Broker, Consultant, Appraiser, Developer, Owner/Investor, Property Manager, Syndicator; **SERVICES:** Brokerage, investment counseling, devel. and synd. of comml props.; **REP CLIENTS:** Lenders and indiv. investing in resid. props.; **PREV EMPLOY:** Sales Mgr., First Realty Co., NY; **PROFL AFFIL & HONORS:** NAR, NYS Assn. of Realtors, Comml. investment div., NY State Soc. of RE Appraisers, RESSI, GRI, CRS; **EDUC:** BS, 1971, Mktg., commerce, Univ. of VA; **HOME ADD:** 4185 St. Paul Blvd., Rochester, NY 14617, (716)544-6229; **BUS ADD:** 4185 St. Paul Blvd., Rochester, NY 14617, (716)266-5941.

WALTON, James W.——B: Nov. 13, 1936, Fort Dodge, IA, *VP and Land Mgr.*, Leslie Salt Co.; **OTHER RE ACT:** Mgmt. of corporate RE assets; **SERVICES:** Conversion of corp. RE assets to income. Legislative affairs mgmt. and community relations mgmt.; **PREV EMPLOY:** Mgr., Land Operations, CF&I Steel Corp. and Gen. Mgr., CO & WY Land Co. Subsidiary; Facilities Eng. Supvr., Mgmt. Serv. Div., E&J Gallo Winery; Plant Engr., IBM Corp.; **PROFL AFFIL & HONORS:** Governmental Relations Comm., CA Man. Assn.; Prop. Rights Task Force, CA State C of C, Lic. Civil Engr., CA; CA RE Sales Lic.; **EDUC:** Geological Engr., 1960, Civil Engr. and Geology, CO School of Mines, Golden, CO; **OTHER ACT & HONORS:** Limited Service Credential, CA Community Colls. for Teaching Bus. and Indus. Mgmt. and Engineering; **HOME ADD:** 3000 Highgate Rd., Modesto, CA 95350, (209)524-5795; **BUS ADD:** Newark, CA 94560PO Box 364, (415)797-1820.

WALTON, J.H., Jr.——B: May 2, 1940, Montclair, NJ, *Exec. VP*, Leggat McCall & Werner, Inc.; **PRIM RE ACT:** Broker, Owner/Investor; **EDUC:** BA, 1962, Univ. of VT; **HOME ADD:** 32 Suffold Rd., Chestnut Hill, MA 02167, (617)734-1141; **BUS ADD:** 60 State St., Boston, MA 02109, (617)367-1177.

WALZ, Frank J.——B: Apr. 29, 1940, Detroit Lakes, MN, *Part.*, O'Connor & Hannan; **PRIM RE ACT:** Attorney; **REP CLIENTS:** Gittleman Corp., Condo. Devel., Condor Corp., devel. of comml. prop., Homart Devel. Co., shopping ctr. devel.; **EDUC:** BA, 1962, Pol. Sci., Coll. of St. Thomas, St. Paul., MN; **GRAD EDUC:** LLB, 1965, Law, Univ. of Notre Dame, South Bend, IN; **EDUC HONORS:** Cum Laude, Law Review; **HOME ADD:** 160 Hartman Cir., Fridley, MN 55432, (612)571-5904; **BUS ADD:** 38th fl., IDS Tower, Minneapolis, MN 55402, (612)341-3800.

WAMPLER, David A.——B: July 25, 1945, Savannah, GA, *Assoc. Dir. of RE Investment*, Massachusetts Mutual Life Insurance Co., RE Investment Div.; **PRIM RE ACT:** Broker, Consultant, Appraiser, Lender; **EDUC:** BA, 1968, Govt., Univ. of MA; **GRAD EDUC:** MBA, 1975, Bus., Western New England Grad. School of Bus.; **MIL SERV:** USAF; Capt.; **HOME ADD:** 44 Bancroft Rd., Northampton, MA 01060, (413)584-9553; **BUS ADD:** 1295 State St., Springfield, MA 01111, (413)788-8411.

WAMPLER, Normal Allison——B: Nov. 21, 1936, Philadelphia, PA, *Owner*, Allison Real Estate and Insurance; **PRIM RE ACT:** Broker, Owner/Investor, Property Manager, Insuror; **PROFL AFFIL & HONORS:** NAR, IREM, PA Assn. of Realtors, CPM; **EDUC:** BA, 1959, Gettysburg Coll.; **GRAD EDUC:** LLB, 1965, La Salle Extension Univ.; MA, 1979, CA Christian Univ.; PhD, Late 1982, CA Christian Univ.; **OTHER ACT & HONORS:** APSA, AAPSS, APS; **HOME ADD:** 4 Hayden Heights Rd., York, PA 17404, (717)764-9996; **BUS ADD:** 536 W. Market St., York, PA 17404, (717)848-1625.

WANAMAKER, Kenneth——*Corp. Secy. & Treas.*, Energy Resources Group; **PRIM RE ACT:** Property Manager; **BUS ADD:** 2735 Villa Creek Dr., Ste. 165, Dallas, TX 75234, (214)241-2700.*

WANDELL, Wayne F.——B: Sept. 24, 1943, San Antonio, TX, *Pres.*, W.F. Wandell & Co., Inc.; **PRIM RE ACT:** Engineer, Developer, Builder; **EDUC:** BSME, 1970, ME-Thermo Dynamics, LA State Univ.; **OTHER ACT & HONORS:** LA Natl. Guard, SP-4; **HOME ADD:** 4001 Apollo Dr., Metairie, LA 70003, (504)889-0903; **BUS ADD:** 4033 Veterans Blvd., Metairie, LA 70002, (504)885-6560.

WANG, Chen Chi——B: Aug. 10, 1932, Taipei, Taiwan, *Chief Exec.*, EIC Group; **PRIM RE ACT:** Broker, Engineer, Developer, Lender, Builder, Owner/Investor; **SERVICES:** From raw land to buildings inclusive; **PROFL AFFIL & HONORS:** National Bd. of Realtors; **EDUC:** BA, BS, 1955, 1965, Econ., Nat. Taiwan Univ. & San Jose State Univ.; **GRAD EDUC:** MBA, 1961, Univ. of CA, Berkeley, CA; **EDUC HONORS:** Member Tau, Beta Pi; **MIL SERV:** US Army ROTC, Lt.; **OTHER ACT & HONORS:** Intl. Platform Assn.; Chief Exec. of EIC Group which includes Alpha Enterprises, Hanson & Wang Devel. Corp., DeVine & Wang, Continental Enterprises; **HOME ADD:** 195 Brookwood Rd., Woodside, CA 94062; **BUS ADD:** PO Box 4082, Woodside, CA 94062, (415)364-3330.

WANG, Chen H.——B: Nov. 6, 1930, China, *Pres.*, Cathay Development Corp.; **PRIM RE ACT:** Consultant, Engineer, Architect, Developer, Builder; **SERVICES:** Planning, engr., const. and mgmt.; **PREV EMPLOY:** Sr. safety Engr., OSHA Dept. of Labor; Chief Engr., Jolles Assn.; Staff Engr. TRW; Assoc. Prof., Catholic Univ.; **PROFL AFFIL & HONORS:** Member of ASCE, Sigma XI, ASSE; **EDUC:** BS in Civil Engr., 1954, Hwy. and Structures, Taiwan Coll. of Engr., Taiwan; **GRAD EDUC:** MS & PhD, 1959 & 1965, Structures, Univ. of Notre Dame & Univ. of MO; **HOME ADD:** 1731 Camino Lando, S. Pasadena, CA 91030, (213)258-5310; **BUS ADD:** 328 S. Atlantic, Monterey Park, CA 91754, (213)281-7440.

WANGARD, Stewart M.——B: Sept. 19, 1956, Wauwautosa, WI, *Pres.*, Vintage Devel. Corp.; **PRIM RE ACT:** Broker, Developer, Builder; **SERVICES:** Comml. investment brokerage, RE devel.; **REP CLIENTS:** Corp. & indiv. investors; **PREV EMPLOY:** Pres. RE/Max W Suburban 1977-79; Pres. RE/Max WI 1977-79, VP Signature Realty, 1977; **PROFL AFFIL & HONORS:** Milwaukee Bd. of Realtors; Metro. Planning Comm., Educ. Comm., Comm. Revitalization Task Force; Charter Member Realtors Hon. Soc., GRI, Realtor Hon. Soc.; ARM; **EDUC:** Bus. Admin., Univ. of WI, Eau Claire & Marquette Univ.; **OTHER ACT & HONORS:** Sales & Mktg. Exec. Milwaukee Corp.; **HOME ADD:** 654 Dundee Ln., Hartland, WI 53029, (414)367-1017; **BUS ADD:** 311 Wisconsin Ave., Oconomowoc, WI 53066, (414)367-8772.

WAPNER, Gerald L.——B: Nov. 27, 1933, NYC, *Pres.*, Riverby Incorporated; **PRIM RE ACT:** Consultant, Attorney, Developer; **SERVICES:** Legal counsel, consultancy to devel., zoning & subdiv., law; **REP CLIENTS:** Barn Homes Ltd., Albert Grossman(Bearsville Records), Dancing Rock Associates; **EDUC:** Lehigh Univ.; **GRAD EDUC:** LLB, 1971-73, NYU Law School, NYC; **HOME ADD:** Old

California Quarry Rd., Woodstock, NY 12498, (914)679-6672; **BUS ADD:** 45 Mill Hill Rd., Woodstock, NY 12498, (914)679-7207.

WARACH, Eli J.——*Ed.*, Prentice Hall, Inc., Real East Opportunities; **BUS ADD:** Route 9W, Englewood Cliffs, NJ 07632.*

WARBURTON, Ralph——B: Sept. 5, 1935, Kansas City, MO, *Principal; Ralph Warburton, Arch., Engr., Planner: Professor*, Sch. of Engr. & Arch., Univ. of Miami; **PRIM RE ACT:** Architect, Consultant, Engineer; **OTHER RE ACT:** Urban Planner; **SERVICES:** Planning, zoning, urgan and project design, const. documents & observation; **REP CLIENTS:** Devel.; inst.; local, state & nat. gvt. agencies; **PREV EMPLOY:** Skidmore, Owings & Merrill, NYC & Chicato 1960-66; Spec. Asst. to the Sec., US Dept. HUD 1967-72; **PROFL AFFIL & HONORS:** AIA; Amer. Inst. of Cert. Planners; Amer. Planning Assn.; Amer. Soc. of Civil Engrs.; Nat. Assn. of Housing & Redevel. Off.; Nat. Soc. of Prof. Engrs.; Nat. Trust for Hist. Preservation, Member of Sigma Xi and Tau Beta Pi; Hon Mem., Amer. Soc. of Landscape Arch.; **EDUC:** BArch., 1958, Arch., Engr., planning, MIT; **GRAD EDUC:** MArch./MCP, 1959 & 1960, Arch., Planning, Yale Univ.; **EDUC HONORS:** Skidmore, Owings & Merrill Traveling Fellowship, William Edward Parsons Medal; **OTHER ACT & HONORS:** City of Coral Gables Bd. of Arch. 1980-82; Cosmos Club, Wash., DC; Leadership Action Award, Greater Miami C of C 1974; HUD Special Achievement Award 1972; NASA Group Achievement Award 1976; **HOME ADD:** 6910 Veronese, Coral Gables, FL 33146, (305)667-0703; **BUS ADD:** 420 S. Dixie Hwy., Coral Gables, FL 33146, (305)284-3438.

WARD, Charles L.——B: Feb. 14, 1944, Los Angeles, CA, *Atty. at Law, RE Broker, Owner*, Barker-Ward, Real Estate Consultants; **PRIM RE ACT:** Broker, Consultant, Attorney, Architect, Developer, Builder, Owner/Investor, Property Manager, Syndicator; **SERVICES:** Legal & investment counseling, complete devel., synd. and sales of comml. & income prop., as well as prop. mgmt.; **REP CLIENTS:** Indiv. and grp. investors interested in comml. and income props. (buy, build or sell); **PREV EMPLOY:** Dept. of Labor, Grants Admin.-1975-1979; **PROFL AFFIL & HONORS:** ABA, Los Angeles Bar Assn., CA RE Assn., Public Employees for Lower Taxes, and the Beverly Hills, Santa Monica, Los Angeles and San Fernando Valley RE Bds.; **EDUC:** BA, 1966 BSL 1975, Govt. & Law, CA State Univ. at Los Angeles; **GRAD EDUC:** JD, 1977, RE Law, Glendale Univ., Coll. of Law; **EDUC HONORS:** Editor, Publications Commnr., Rep. to CA Model Legislature, Theta Chi National Frat.; **MIL SERV:** US Army, Sgt., Army Commendation Medal, Meritorious Unit Citation, Vietnam Serv. & Campaign Medals; **OTHER ACT & HONORS:** Civil Air Patrol; Unified Mexican-American Engrs.; Arcadia; All-Pro Athletic Club; Temple City Tennis Club; **HOME ADD:** 845 E. Foothill Blvd., Bldg. L, Monrovia, CA 91016; **BUS ADD:** The Bradbury Bldg., 304 S. Broadway, Suite 506, Los Angeles, CA 90013, (213)617-7523.

WARD, George T.——B: July 24, 1927, Washington, DC, *Partner*, Ward & Hall & Assoc., AIA; **PRIM RE ACT:** Consultant, Architect, Owner/Investor, Syndicator; **PROFL AFFIL & HONORS:** VA Soc., AIA; Soc. of Arch. Historians; Member, Nat. Panel of the Amer Arbitration Assn.; VA Assn. of Professions; **EDUC:** BS with honors, Bldg. Design, VA Polytech Inst.; **GRAD EDUC:** MS, Arch., VA Ploytech. Inst.; **EDUC HONORS:** AIA School Medal in Arch.; **MIL SERV:** US Army; Sgt. 46-47; **HOME ADD:** 9600 Burke View Ave., Burke, VA 22015, (703)978-4063; **BUS ADD:** 6320 Augusta Dr., Suite 1000, Springfield, VA 22150, (703)451-0100.

WARD, John Frank——B: Nov. 13, 1951, Dallas, TX, *Owner*, J.F. Ward, Props.; **PRIM RE ACT:** Broker, Appraiser, Property Manager, Owner/Investor; **SERVICES:** Valuation of all types of RE, IQe. income prop. brokerage, mgmt.; **PROFL AFFIL & HONORS:** Dallas Apt. Assn., Dallas Bd. of Realtors, Candidate Amer. Inst. of RE Appraisers, Amer. Soc. of Training & Devel.; **EDUC:** BBA, 1973, RE, Univ. of TX at Austin; **EDUC HONORS:** Dean's List four of eight semesters, Pres & founding member UT RE Soc., Phi Eta Sigma Hon. Frat., Scholarship from TX Assoc. of Realtors; **OTHER ACT & HONORS:** Bd. of Dir. Hollows North Homeowners, Bd. of Dir. Contracts Asst. & Jurisdictional Supr. So. Central US., Phi Kappa Sigma; **HOME ADD:** 10598 High Hollows, 295, Dallas, TX 75230, (214)368-1837; **BUS ADD:** One Northpark East, Suite 200, Dallas, TX 75231, (214)696-9960.

WARD, Mark——*Pres.*, Marc Equity Corp., Apartment Rental Div.; **PRIM RE ACT:** Broker, Appraiser, Developer, Builder, Owner/Investor, Property Manager, Syndicator; **SERVICES:** Devel. and const. of resid. and comml. prop., active in condo. conversion projects; **PROFL AFFIL & HONORS:** Greater Buffalo Bd. of Realtors, Niagara Frontier Builders Assn., Pres. Elect, Niagara Frontier Builders Assn.; Golden RAM Award Recipient, Nat. Assn. of Home Builders; Registered Apt. Mgr. Instructor; **EDUC:** BS, Mktg., Univ. of Palm Beach; **GRAD EDUC:** MBA, Bus. Admin., Univ. of Palm Beach; **HOME ADD:** 16 Treehaven Rd., W. Seneca, NY 14224; **BUS ADD:** 2730 Transit Rd., Buffalo, NY 14224, (716)896-2000.

WARD, Paul A.——B: Dec. 13, 1929, Grand Rapids, MI, *Atty.*, Ward, Schenk & Boncher; **PRIM RE ACT:** Attorney; **SERVICES:** Representation of realtors; RE and corp. litigation; mort. foreclosures and bankruptcies; **REP CLIENTS:** St. Paul Title Ins. Corp., Lawyers Title Ins. Corp., Lake MI Mort., First Nat. Acceptance Co., RE/Max of Grand Rapids, Inc., Samra & Assoc., Godin Realty, Inc., MI Nat. Bank, First Nat. Bank of MI; **PROFL AFFIL & HONORS:** Grand Rapids Bar Assn., MI Bar Assn., ABA, Amer. Coll. of RE Lawyers; **EDUC:** BA, 1950, Acctg. and Poli. Sci., Calvin Coll.; **GRAD EDUC:** JD, 1953, Law, Univ. of MI Law School; **OTHER ACT & HONORS:** Amer. Bus. Clubs, Variety Club, Peninsular Club, Cascade Hills Country Club, licensed RE broker in MI; **HOME ADD:** 2630 Shadowbrook S.E., Grand Rapids, MI 49506, (616)942-1868; **BUS ADD:** 301 College Park Plaza, 180 N. Div., Grand Rapids, MI 49503, (616)454-8277.

WARD, Paul H., Jr.——B: Oct. 13, 1948, Niles, MI, *Owner/Broker*, Paul H. Ward Jr., Realtor, Ward Property Mgmt., Plus Properties; **PRIM RE ACT:** Broker, Consultant, Appraiser, Builder, Owner/Investor, Property Manager, Syndicator; **SERVICES:** Build Homes or Apt. Complexes, Prop. Mgrs., Consultant Buy or Sell Prop. (Investment or Income), Synd.; **REP CLIENTS:** Indiv., for. or inst. investors in income-producing, farm-land and comml. props.; **PROFL AFFIL & HONORS:** Natl., State and Local Bd. of Realtors, RESSI, Consultant to JLMP Prop and PLUS Properties; **EDUC:** BA, 1975, Education,Gen. Sci., Math, IN Univ.; **HOME ADD:** 824 W. Sycamore, Kokomo, IN 46901, (317)452-7127; **BUS ADD:** 824 W. Sycamore, Kokomo, IN 46901, (317)459-5502.

WARD, Tom S., Jr.——B: Dec. 25, 1944, New York, NY, *Principal, Atty.*, Albert, Pastore & Ward, P.C.; **PRIM RE ACT:** Attorney, Owner/Investor, Instructor; **SERVICES:** Personal representation of purchasers and sellers of resid. RE, representation of condo. devel., representation of builder-devel.; **PROFL AFFIL & HONORS:** ABA; CT and Greenwich Bar Assns.; Instr. of RE Law, Fairfield Univ., School of Cont. Ed.; **EDUC:** BA, 1966, Hamilton Coll.; **GRAD EDUC:** JD, 1969, Fordham Univ., School of Law; **OTHER ACT & HONORS:** Chmn. of the Bd. of Parks and Recreation of the Town of Greenwich, 1966 to Date; Bd. of Dir. of United Way; Advisor/Counsel of the Old Greenwich/Riverside Community Ctr.; **HOME ADD:** 49 Gilliam Ln., Riverside, CT 06878, (203)637-0659; **BUS ADD:** 15 Sherwood Place, POB 1668, Greenwich, CT 06830, (203)661-8600.

WARD, Wade——B: June 2, 1938, Atmore, AL, *Pres.*, Meyer Props.; **PRIM RE ACT:** Broker; **SERVICES:** Sales - Devel.; **PROFL AFFIL & HONORS:** NAR, Pres. Local Bd. of Realtors (two times); Realtor of the Year; **EDUC:** Univ. of AL; **OTHER ACT & HONORS:** Pres. Gulf Shores Tourist Assn.; Dir. Gulf Shores Golf Club; Dir. S. C of C; past Pres. Gulf Shores Lions Club; past State Realtor Dir.; **HOME ADD:** Rural Rte., Box 720, Foley, AL 36535, (205)943-8559; **BUS ADD:** PO Box 238, Gulf Shores, AL 36542, (205)968-7591.

WARD, William B., Jr.——B: Feb. 25, 1937, Pittsburgh, PA, *Asst. Trust Officer*, Mellon Bank NA, Trust Dept.; **PRIM RE ACT:** Attorney, Owner/Investor; **OTHER RE ACT:** Accountant; **SERVICES:** Legal, acctg., planning, tax, & mgmt.; **PREV EMPLOY:** Estate Planning, Aetna Life & Casualty; **PROFL AFFIL & HONORS:** ABA; PA Bar; FL Bar; Probate Sect., ABA & FL Bars; **EDUC:** BA, 1960, Cert. of Acctg., Pol. Sci., Duquesne Univ., Univ. of Pittsburgh; **GRAD EDUC:** JD, 1972, Law, Duquesne Sch. of Law; **EDUC HONORS:** Highest Mark 'Torts'; **MIL SERV:** US Army; PFC, E-3; **OTHER ACT & HONORS:** Pres. Blawnox Bd. Council, 1977-present; Rotary; Kiwanis; BPOE; Amer. Legion; **HOME ADD:** 220 Summit Dr., Blawnox, Pittsburgh, PA 15238, (412)828-8146; **BUS ADD:** Room 2713 Mellon Sq., Pittsburgh, PA 15230, (412)232-5578.

WARD, William L.——B: Aug 1, 1929, Pittsburgh, PA, *Exec. VP*, The Dyer Fin. Co.; **PRIM RE ACT:** Broker, Consultant, Lender; **OTHER RE ACT:** Mort. and Fin. broker handling all types of income producing RE, accts. receivable fin., with a special emphasis on contruction fin. and end-loan fin. for the time sharing indus.; **PREV EMPLOY:** Westinghouse Credit Corp., VP and COO; Member of the Bd. of Dirs.; **PROFL AFFIL & HONORS:** ULI; Amer. Land Devel. Assn., Resort Timesharing Council; **EDUC:** BS, 1951, Fin., Duquesne Univ. - Pittsburgh, PA; **GRAD EDUC:** No Degree, 1972, Advanced Mgmt. Program, Harvard Univ.; **MIL SERV:** USAF, Lt.; **HOME ADD:** 2643 Bethel Crest Dr., Bethel Park, PA 15102, (412)835-1427; **BUS ADD:** Manor Oak II, Suite 304, 1910 Cochran Rd., Pittsburgh, PA 15220, (412)563-6944.

WARDELL, Harry E.——**B:** May 10, 1939, Long Island, NY, *Pres.*, United First Realty, Inc.; **PRIM RE ACT:** Broker, Appraiser, Developer, Owner/Investor, Property Manager, Syndicator; **PREV EMPLOY:** Self employed; **PROFL AFFIL & HONORS:** ICSC; Miami Bd. of Realtors; Coral Gables Bd. of Realtors; **MIL SERV:** USAF, A 1/C; **HOME ADD:** 8770 S.W. 53 St., Miami, FL 33165, (305)595-5565; **BUS ADD:** 8672 Bird Rd., Suite 200, Miami, FL 33165, (305)553-1116.

WARDELL, Robert P.——**B:** Oct. 1, 1937, E. Orange, NJ, *Broker*, Carriage Realty; **PRIM RE ACT:** Broker, Owner/Investor, Property Manager, Syndicator; **SERVICES:** Brokerage & Investment Advisory Serv.; **REP CLIENTS:** Indiv. & A Few Small Corp./Devel.; **PROFL AFFIL & HONORS:** South Bay Exchangors, Rolling Hill Bd. of Realtors, Torrance-Lomita-Carson Bd. of Realtors, NAR, CAR, Amer. Indus. RE Assn., GRI (Grad. Realtor Institute); **EDUC:** BS, 1959, Mgmt. & Mktg., Lehigh Univ.; **GRAD EDUC:** MBA, 1970, Mgmt., Fairleigh Dickinson Univ.; **MIL SERV:** USN, LCDR, Natl. Def. Medal Armed Force Res. Medal; **OTHER ACT & HONORS:** Fin. Chm., Mendham, NJ Bd. of Educ. 1969-1974; **HOME ADD:** 605 Chiswick Rd., Palos Verdes Est., CA 90274, (213)373-7998; **BUS ADD:** 4030 Palos Verdes Dr. N., Suite 108, Rolling Hills Est., CA 90274, (213)541-4701.

WARDEN, Kent D.——**B:** Nov. 26, 1942, Grantsburg, WI, *Chief Investment Analyst*, North Western National Life Ins. Co., RE; **PRIM RE ACT:** Developer, Owner/Investor, Property Manager; **SERVICES:** RE devel.; portfolio mgmt.; **PROFL AFFIL & HONORS:** BOMA; IREM; NAR; MBAA; Bldg. Owners & Mgrs. Inst. (Dir.); Soc. of Real Prop. Administrators (Tr.), CPM; Real Prop. Administrator; **EDUC:** 1965, MN School of Bus., Univ. of MN; **MIL SERV:** USN Res.; 2nd Class Petty Officer; 1965-1967; **OTHER ACT & HONORS:** MPLS Downtown Council; Citizens League; Suburban Community Servs., Dir.; **HOME ADD:** 4395 N. Shore Dr., Mound, MN 55364, (612)472-3372; **BUS ADD:** 20 Washington Ave. S., Minneapolis, MN 55440, (612)372-5403.

WARE, David M.——*Dir., Land Sales*, The Taibman Co.; **PRIM RE ACT:** Developer; **BUS ADD:** 3270 West Big Beaver Rd., Ste 300, PO Box 3270, Troy, MI 48099, (313)649-5000.*

WARE, Ridgeley Philip——**B:** Oct. 21, 1926, Kenmore, NY, *Pres. & Owner*, Sonnenblick-Goldman Corp. of New Jersey (also Ware Associates); **PRIM RE ACT:** Broker, Consultant, Appraiser, Instructor, Owner/Investor; **SERVICES:** Investment counseling, valuations, devel. fin. models, income prop. sales and fin.; **REP CLIENTS:** Comml. banks, FDIC, Fortune 500 & other corps., pvt. investors, pension funds, REITs, invs. cos.; **PREV EMPLOY:** Tr. IDS Realty Trust (1976-1980); Chmn. & CEO of adviser to First PA Mort. Trust (1970-1975); Sr. VP-RE Admin., Natl. Bank of N. Amer. (1967-1970); VP-Mort. Investments; **PROFL AFFIL & HONORS:** AIREA, formerly Natl. Assn. of RE Investment Trusts; MBAA, various RE Bds.; **EDUC:** BS, 1950, Engr. (Indus.), Univ. of Buffalo; **GRAD EDUC:** Candidate - MBA (withdrew 1954-completed course work), Univ. of Rochester; **EDUC HONORS:** NY State Scholarship; **MIL SERV:** US Army, T/Sgt.; **OTHER ACT & HONORS:** Boy Scouts of Amer. (Eagle Scout; Scoutmaster; Alpha Phi Omega; etc.), Instr.-Rutgers Univ. Ext. since 1978; panelist & speaker since 1965 in seminars on the RE indust. sponsored by educ. instns. (The Wharton Grad. School, Univ. of PA; NY Inst. of Technol., UCLA Ext.) and Pvt. Orgs. such as NAREIT, MBA, Found. for Acctg. Educ.; **HOME ADD:** 321 Spring House Ln., Moorestown, NJ 08057, (609)234-0748; **BUS ADD:** Blason Plaza II, 505 S. Lenola Rd., Moorestown, NJ 08057, (609)234-6000.

WARING, Glenn H.——**B:** Nov. 10, 1948, Pasadena, CA, *VP*, Nationwide Development Company, Devel. and Investment; **PRIM RE ACT:** Developer; **EDUC:** BA, 1970, Econ., Claremont Men's Coll.; **GRAD EDUC:** MBA, 1972, Fin., Cornell Univ.; **EDUC HONORS:** Cum Laude; **HOME ADD:** 2681 Montcalm, Upper Arlington, OH 43221, (614)486-8525; **BUS ADD:** One Nationwide Plaza, Columbus, OH 43216, (614)227-8171.

WARNER, Dr. Arthur E.——**B:** May 30, 1922, Garrett, IN, *Chair Prof. of RE, Prop. Fin. and Urban Devel. & Dir., Ctr. for RE and Urban Econ. Studies*, Univ. of South Carolina, Ctr. for RE and Urban Economic Studies; **PRIM RE ACT:** Instructor; **PREV EMPLOY:** Prof., School of Bus. Admin. of Sao Paul, Brazil, 1958-1960; Dir., Master of Bus. Admin. Program, MI State Univ., 1960; Dir. Programs for the Doctoral Degree in Bus. Admin., MI State Univ., 1961-1964; Dean and Prof., Coll. of Bus. Admin., Univ. of TN, 1964-1973; Dean and Prof. of RE and Urban Devel. Studies, The Amer. Univ., Washington, DC, 1973-1974; Chair Prof. of RE, Prop. Fin., and Urban Devel., and Dir., Ctr. for RE and Urban Econ. Studies, Coll. of Bus. Admin., Univ. of SC, Sept. 1, 1974 to present; **PROFL AFFIL & HONORS:** Alpha Kappa Psi; Assn. for Educ. in Intl. Bus.; Amer. RE and Urban Econ. Assn.; Phi Chi Theta; Lambda Alpha; Rho Epsilon; Beta Gamma Sigma; Member, Comm. on Eudc., Nat. Assn. of Realtors; Member, Bd. of Dir., Realtors Educ. Found. of SC, Medallion of Merit from Getulio Vargas Found., Rio de Janerio, Brazil, 1974; **EDUC:** BS, 1949, RE, IN Univ.; **GRAD EDUC:** MBA, 1950, RE, IN Univ.; Dr. of Bus. Admin., 1953, IN Univ.; **EDUC HONORS:** Phi Eta Sigma, Beta Gamma Sigma, Phi Kappa Phi; **OTHER ACT & HONORS:** Pres., SC Cultural Laureate Found., 1976-1977; VP & Bd. of Dir., Keimer Found. for Social Devel. and Hist. Research, 1971-1972; **HOME ADD:** 6007 Percival Rd., Columbia, SC 29206, (803)782-8097; **BUS ADD:** College of Bus. Admin., Univ. of SC, Columbia, SC 29208.

WARNER, Donald L.——**B:** June 4, 1942, Peekskill, NY, *Pres.*, Nat. Energy Capital Corp.; **OTHER RE ACT:** Financing source for energy related projects; **PREV EMPLOY:** Pres. L&D Funding, 1976-81; **PROFL AFFIL & HONORS:** NY Young Mort. Bankers; Nat. Leased Housing Assn., Atty. (NY); **EDUC:** AB, 1964, Hist., Univ. of Rochester; **GRAD EDUC:** JD, 1967, Law, Syracuse Univ. Coll. of Law; LLM, 1968, Govt. Fin. & RE, Washington Univ. Sch. of Law; **HOME ADD:** 312 Quaker Rd., Chappaqua, NY 10514, (914)238-8222; **BUS ADD:** 645 Fifth Ave., NY, NY 10022.

WARNER, Everett F.——**B:** Oct. 6, 1918, Cumberland Cty., *Owner*, Warner RE Agency, Inc.; **PRIM RE ACT:** Broker, Consultant, Appraiser, Developer, Builder, Owner/Investor, Instructor, Property Manager; **OTHER RE ACT:** review appraisals; **PROFL AFFIL & HONORS:** Nat. Assn. RE Appraisers, Nat. Assn. Review Appraisers, Amer. Assn. of Cert. Appraisers, Inst. Bus. Appraisers, Intl. Coll. of RE Consulting Profls., Cert. Review Appraiser; **OTHER ACT & HONORS:** V Mayor 1 term, Mayor 1 term; **HOME ADD:** PO Box 51, Crossville, TN 38555, (615)484-5647; **BUS ADD:** 204 Stanley St., Crossville, TN 38555, (615)484-5183.

WARNER, Harold C.——**B:** May 25, 1925, Amsterdam, NY, *Owner*, Warner Associates, Realtors, Comml./Indus. Div.; **PRIM RE ACT:** Broker, Consultant, Owner/Investor, Property Manager; **OTHER RE ACT:** Two other staffed divs.: Resid. & land; **SERVICES:** Total RE brokerage including business brokerage; **PREV EMPLOY:** Personnel & Indus. Relations Dir. - Multi-Plant Responsibility; **PROFL AFFIL & HONORS:** Exec. Comm., State of NH Comml. Investment Div.; Local, State & Nat. Constituent Bds. of Realtors; RELO; **EDUC:** BS, 1951, Personnel, Syracuse Univ.; **GRAD EDUC:** MBA, 1952, Gen. Bus., Univ. of Denver; **MIL SERV:** USN, PO Z/C 1943-1946, Asiatic/Pacific w/Bronze Stars; several victory ribbons; unit & fleet commendations; **OTHER ACT & HONORS:** Dir., local C of C Chairman, Commercial investment division of the NH state Assn. of Realtors 4 years; Road Commnr., Town of Amherst 4 years; 32 Masons; Shriner; Amherst Lions Club - Charter Member; Past Pres. State Lions Zone & District Chmn.; **HOME ADD:** 7 Southfield Rd., Amherst, NH 03031, (603)673-5585; **BUS ADD:** Route 101, Amherst, NH 03031, (603)673-7000.

WARNER, Ted F.——**B:** Jan. 3, 1932, Findley, OH, *Sr. Partner*, Warner, Angle, Roper & Hallam; **PRIM RE ACT:** Attorney, Owner/Investor, Syndicator; **PREV EMPLOY:** Fed. Dist Ct. of AZ; US Supreme Court; **PROFL AFFIL & HONORS:** ABA; AZ State Bar, Maricopa Cty. Bar; **EDUC:** BS,AA, Law, Phoenix Coll., AZ State Univ.; **GRAD EDUC:** JD, 1959, Law, Univ. of AZ; **EDUC HONORS:** With distinction; **MIL SERV:** USAF; **OTHER ACT & HONORS:** Biograph in 'Who's Who in Amer. Law' and 'Who's Who in the West'; **HOME ADD:** 4901 E. Calle Del Medio, Phoenix, AZ 85018, (802)840-5235; **BUS ADD:** 3550 N. Central Ave., Suite 1700, Phoenix, AZ 85012, (602)264-7101.

WARNER, Thomas F.——**B:** July 11, 1941, Washington, DC, *Pres.*, The Warner Corporation T/A George F. Warner & Co.; **OTHER RE ACT:** Contractor; **SERVICES:** Plumbing, heating and air conditioning; **PROFL AFFIL & HONORS:** Dir. Prop. Mgmt. Assn.; Dir. Reston Home Owners Assn., Master Plumber - State of MD, VA and DC; **EDUC:** BA Econ., Western MD Coll.; **MIL SERV:** Infantry, First Lt.; **HOME ADD:** 11818 Tpk. Crown Rd., Reston, VA 22091; **BUS ADD:** 101 Que St., N.E., Washington, DC 20002, (202)269-5000.

WARNES, James C.——**B:** May 15, 1946, Chicago, IL, *VP*, First American Bank & Trust Co.; **PRIM RE ACT:** Attorney; **PREV EMPLOY:** Cook, Noell, Bates & Warnes, Attys., 1974-1979; **PROFL AFFIL & HONORS:** Athens Bd. of Zoning Appeals, 1978 -1981; State Bar of Ga. 1973-; **EDUC:** AB, 1968, Erskine Coll.; **GRAD EDUC:** JD, 1973, Univ. of GA Law School; **EDUC HONORS:** Deaton Philosophy Award, 1968, Cum Laude, 1st PLace, So. Moot Court Competition, 1971; **MIL SERV:** US Army; **OTHER ACT & HONORS:** Judge, City of Athens Recorders Ct., 1974-1977; Clarke Co. Bd. of Educ.; also affiliated with Strickland & Kardos, Attys.; **HOME ADD:** 150 Sharon Cir., Athens, GA 30606; **BUS ADD:** 300 College Ave., Athens, GA

30603, (404)546-7500.

WARNES, Phil——*Fac. Mgr.*, Spectra-Physics; **PRIM RE ACT:** Property Manager; **BUS ADD:** 3333 N. First St., San Jose, CA 95134, (415)961-2550.*

WARNOCK, Harvey K.——**B:** Sept. 15, 1941, Jacksonville, FL, *Comml. Prop. Mgr.*, Demetree Enterprises; **PRIM RE ACT:** Property Manager; **OTHER RE ACT:** Devel. solely owned and joint ventured devel.; **SERVICES:** Mgmt. & devel. of office bldgs., shopping ctrs. & apts.; **PREV EMPLOY:** Shopping Center Consultants, Inc. (1971-76), Liberty Mutual Ins. Co. (1966-71); **PROFL AFFIL & HONORS:** Intl. Council of Shopping Ctrs., BOMA, Nat. Home Builders Assn., Reg. RE Broker (FL); **EDUC:** BA, 1963, Liberal Arts - Govt., Jacksonville Univ.; **MIL SERV:** US Naval Reserve, 1964-66; **HOME ADD:** 1812 Sea Oats Dr., Atlantic Beach, FL 32233, (904)246-3683; **BUS ADD:** 3740 Beach Blvd., Jacksonville, FL 32207P O Drawer 10100, (904)398-7350.

WARR, William W.——**B:** Apr. 13, 1935, NYC, NY, *Pres.*, Investment Counselors, Inc.; **PRIM RE ACT:** Broker; **OTHER RE ACT:** RE Exchangor; **SERVICES:** Comml./Investment Counseling; **PROFL AFFIL & HONORS:** SEC; CCIM, Snyder Trophy for Exchange of the Yr. 1975; **OTHER ACT & HONORS:** Past Pres. Lions Club; **HOME ADD:** 81 Chariot, Wheeling, IL 60090, (312)537-2352; **BUS ADD:** 1 Crossroads of Commerce, Suite 606, Rolling Meadows, IL 60008, (312)392-7900.

WARREN, Arthur R., Jr.——**B:** Nov. 19, 1940, Torrance, CA, *Owner*, Arthur R. Warren Jr. Real Estate Brokerage; **PRIM RE ACT:** Broker, Property Manager; **OTHER RE ACT:** Sales Mgmt./Trainer; Devel. and Small Grp. Syndicating; **SERVICES:** Representing foreign & domestic investors & sellers of apartments, office buildings & small strip centers & industrial buildings. Locating land for users & major developers of industrial & commercial RE Projects. Equity fund raising for developers. Handling sales & marketing activities for new home sales. Also residential & commercial condo conversion, leasing industrial & commercial properties; **PREV EMPLOY:** Stanley C. Swartz Co.; Amer. Housing Guild, N. CA New Homes Sales Mgr. for Walker & Lee; Western Broker Assoc. Comml. Brokerage; Grubb & Ellis Indus. Comml. Div.; **PROFL AFFIL & HONORS:** N. CA Chapter Amer. Inst. of Architects, CA Assn. of Realtors Investment, Indus. & Synd. Assn. of South Bay Brokers, East Bay Mktg. Group., Who's Who in Creative RE; GRI; Chatham Class Fang Award; Top Performer & Million Dollar Salesman; **EDUC:** 1964-66, Genl. Advertising Art & Arch., SW Coll.; **GRAD EDUC:** RE Courses, 1979-80, Exchanging, Development, Broker Syndication Malpractice, Law, Fin., Appraisal, Golden Gate Univ.; **OTHER ACT & HONORS:** Who's Who in The West; CA State Water Skiing Champion; Also Barefoot Club & Ski Jumping Century CLub; Former CA State Lifeguard (San Diego); Double & Stunt Man in Elvis Presley's Movie "Clam Bake" filmed in Florida; Instr. in Swimming, Scuba, Water Skiing & Sailing; Redwood Shores Sailing Club named their perpetual trophy in my honor the "Artie Warren Cup"; Also affiliated with other Investment/Indus. and Comml. Brokerage firms; **HOME ADD:** 1519 Shoal Dr., San Mateo, CA, (415)349-8020; **BUS ADD:** 1519 Shoal Dr., PO Box 1555, San Mateo, CA 94401, (415)349-8020.

WARREN, Bradford L.——**B:** Oct. 2, 1948, Indianapolis, IN, *Atty. at Law*; **PRIM RE ACT:** Attorney; **SERVICES:** Purchase agreements; fin. projections; placement memoranda; **REP CLIENTS:** Synd.; devel.; investors; **PREV EMPLOY:** 8 years of practice; **PROFL AFFIL & HONORS:** ABA, IN Bar Assn., Indianapolis Bar Assn.; **EDUC:** AB, 1970, Econ., IN Univ.; **GRAD EDUC:** JD, 1973, IN Univ., Indianapolis Law School; **OTHER ACT & HONORS:** Officer and Dir. of Condo. Owners Assn.; **HOME ADD:** 5204 N. Winthrop Ave., Indianapolis, IN 46220; **BUS ADD:** 926 E. 52nd St., Indianapolis, IN 46205, (317)283-4832.

WARREN, Carl E.——**B:** Aug. 16, 1922, Little Rock, AR, *Owner*, Carl E. Warren CPA; **PRIM RE ACT:** Consultant; **OTHER RE ACT:** CPA; **SERVICES:** Consulting; **PROFL AFFIL & HONORS:** AICPA, Nat. Acctg. Assn. AR Soc. of CPAs, Amer. Acctg. Assn.; **EDUC:** AA, 1942, Acctg., Univ. of AR, Little Rock, AR; **GRAD EDUC:** BSBA, 1947, Acctg., Univ. of AR, Fayetteville, AR; **EDUC HONORS:** Dean's List; **OTHER ACT & HONORS:** West Little Rock Rotary Club; **HOME ADD:** 3 Betsy Lane, Little Rock, AR 72105, (501)663-3509; **BUS ADD:** 960 Tower Bldg., Little Rock, AR 72201.

WARREN, Douglas K.——**B:** July 16, 1948, Newberg, OR, *V.P.*, Warren Realty Group, Inc.; **PRIM RE ACT:** Broker, Developer, Builder, Owner/Investor; **SERVICES:** Pvt. Mortg. Placement R.E. Brokerage (comml.-investment), Joint Venture Investment Devel.; **REP CLIENTS:** Indiv. and Corporate Investors; **PREV EMPLOY:** CPM Construction Co., Superintendent-1971; **PROFL AFFIL & HONORS:** NAR, NAH, 1976 Realtor of the Year-Lincoln Cty. Bd. of Realtors Dir. of OR Assoc. of Realtors; Pres. of Coast Exchangers; Lincoln Cty. Bldrs. Assoc., Pres.; **EDUC:** BS, 1971, Civil Engrg., OR State Univ.; **EDUC HONORS:** Grad. with honors; **MIL SERV:** USAR, Capt.; **OTHER ACT & HONORS:** Pres., Kiwanis; Pres, Optimist; Lt. Gov., PNW District Optimist; **HOME ADD:** 337 N.E. 5th, Newport, OR 97365, (503)265-7880; **BUS ADD:** 924 S.W. Hurbert St., Newport, OR 97365, (503)265-8477.

WARREN, George T., II——**B:** May 18, 1937, Atlanta, GA, *Owner*, Century 21 Atlanta North; **PRIM RE ACT:** Broker, Appraiser, Developer, Builder, Property Manager, Insuror; **PROFL AFFIL & HONORS:** RNMI; FLI; Women's Council DeKalb Bd., Atlanta Bd., GA Realtor of Yr., 1976; Century 21 Nat. Brokers Communications Congress; **EDUC:** BBA, 1962, Mktg., GA State Univ.; **OTHER ACT & HONORS:** State Senator, 43rd Dist., 1973-1976; Salvation Army; Boys Club Council; **HOME ADD:** 7535 Mt. Vernon Rd., Dunwoody, GA 30338, (404)394-9088; **BUS ADD:** 5400 Chamblee-Dunwoody Rd., Dunwoody, GA 30338, (404)394-2021.

WARREN, Michael Ian——**B:** Aug. 4, 1939, Tampa, FL, *Pres. and Chmn. of the Bd.*, Century 21 Michael Warren & Co.; **OTHER RE ACT:** Exec. Officer for 2 office brokerage firm; **SERVICES:** Resid. brokerage, comml. & investment servs.; **REP CLIENTS:** Abbott Labs., 1st Nat. Bank, 1st Fin. S & L; **PROFL AFFIL & HONORS:** Cty. Bd. of Realtors, WI Assn. of Realtors, IL Assn. of Realtors, NAR, Earned Designations CRB, GRI, Awarded CRS, Past Pres. Lake City MLS; **EDUC:** BA, 1964, Psych., Westmont Coll., Santa Barbara, CA; **GRAD EDUC:** Studies at N. IL Univ. Roosevelt Univ., 1965, 66, Moody Bible Inst.; **OTHER ACT & HONORS:** Past Pres. Antioch Rotary Club, member Waukegan Yacht Club, Antioch Moose, Christian Catholic Church; **HOME ADD:** 1026 Laursen Ct., Antioch, IL, (312)395-1765; **BUS ADD:** 216 Lake Ave., Lake Villa, IL 60046, (312)356-5600.

WARREN, Ronald A.——**B:** May 11, 1934, Passaic, NJ, *VP Equity/Fin.*, American Invsco Corp.; **PRIM RE ACT:** Consultant, Developer, Owner/Investor, Syndicator; **OTHER RE ACT:** Joint venturer; **PREV EMPLOY:** Citibank, NYC; Bankers Life & Casualty Co.; Fidelity Mutual Life; **PROFL AFFIL & HONORS:** Urban Land Inst.; MBA; **EDUC:** BA, 1956, Hist./Econ., Trinity Coll.; **EDUC HONORS:** Who's Who in Amer. Colls. & Univs., Honor Soc.; **MIL SERV:** USAF, Pilot, Capt.; **OTHER ACT & HONORS:** Union League Club; Boy Scouts; **HOME ADD:** 1104 N. Shore Ct., Barrington, IL 60010, (312)381-5644; **BUS ADD:** 120 S. LaSalle St., Chicago, IL 60603, (312)621-8660.

WARREN, Shelby H.——**B:** Feb. 15, 1944, Florence, AL, *Sec./Treas.*, Ronald Warren Bldrs. & Realtors Inc.; **PRIM RE ACT:** Broker, Developer, Builder, Property Manager, Insuror, Syndicator; **PROFL AFFIL & HONORS:** Muscle Shoals Homebuilders Assn.; Muscle Shoals Bd. of Realtors; RESSI; RNMI, GRI; CRS; CRB; **OTHER ACT & HONORS:** Florence C of C; First Cumberland Presbyterian Church; **HOME ADD:** 212 Knights Bridge Rd., Florence, AL, (205)764-4239; **BUS ADD:** 235 Azalea Dr., Florence, AL 35630, (205)766-0069.

WARSAWER, Harold N., MAI——*Pres.*, Atlantic Appraisal Co. Inc.; **PRIM RE ACT:** Consultant, Appraiser; **SERVICES:** Appraisers, consulting, feasibility studies related RE analytical serv.; **REP CLIENTS:** Corps., attys., fed., state, & city govts., banks; **PREV EMPLOY:** Pres. & Owner of Contemporary Enterprises, Inc. an SBIC Consultant to Cont. Enterprises; **PROFL AFFIL & HONORS:** AIREA; RE Bd. of NY, Pres. NY Chap. Gov. Council of Inst.; **EDUC:** U of MO, Psych., Fin., Arts & Sci.; **GRAD EDUC:** MBA, Corp. Fin., Harvard Bus. School; **EDUC HONORS:** Honor Roll - Deans List, Distinction Average; **MIL SERV:** USAF; Major; **HOME ADD:** 430 Rutland Ave., Teaneck, NJ, (201)837-2410; **BUS ADD:** 60 E. 42 St., NY, NY 10165, (212)972-9630.

WARSEN, John Stephen——**B:** May 20, 1938, Brooklyn, NY, *Pres.*, Warsen & Co., Inc.; **PRIM RE ACT:** Consultant, Developer, Owner/Investor, Property Manager, Syndicator; **OTHER RE ACT:** Managing Gen. Partner of Railroad Plaza, Ltd., and 5 x 10 Storage, Ltd.; **SERVICES:** Devel., org., synd., managing RE partnerships; **EDUC:** BBA, 1964, Bus. Admin., Hofstra Univ.; **MIL SERV:** US Army, Nat. Guard; **HOME ADD:** 57 Lee St., Mill Valley, CA 94941, (415)383-4179; **BUS ADD:** 57 Lee St., Mill Valley, CA 94941, (415)383-5151.

WARSON, Albert——**B:** Feb. 17, 1933, St. John, New Brunswick, *Pres.*, Albert Warson Associates, Ltd.; **PRIM RE ACT:** Consultant; **SERVICES:** Admin./Public Relations; **REP CLIENTS:** Ontario Mort. Brokers Assn., Canadian Pension Conference; **PREV EMPLOY:**

The Globe & Mail; The Toronto Star; **EDUC:** BA, 1956, Ryerson Inst.; **HOME ADD:** 548 Merton St., Toronto, M4S1B3, Ontario, Canada, (416)489-1360; **BUS ADD:** 3 Church St., Suite 407, Toronto, M5E1M2, Ontario, Canada, (416)368-4101.

WARTMAN, Clifford J., Jr.——**B:** July 2, 1935, Dayton, KY, *Reg. Mgr., RE*, Consolidated Rail Corp., RE; **PRIM RE ACT:** Appraiser, Property Manager; **OTHER RE ACT:** Oversee corp. RE; **SERVICES:** Buy, sell, lease corp. surplus land; **PROFL AFFIL & HONORS:** Member Amer. Right of Way Assn., Amer. Assn. of Cert. Appraisers (CAS), Hon. KY Col.; **EDUC:** 1956, Engrg., Univ. of KY; **HOME ADD:** 449 Washington Ave., Belleville, KY 41073, (606)261-4926; **BUS ADD:** Rm. 507, 700 Walnut St., Cincinnati, OH 45202, (513)563-5210.

WAS, Michael C.——*VP Mktg.*, Reston Land Corp.; **PRIM RE ACT:** Developer; **BUS ADD:** 11800 Sunnrise Valley Dr., Reston, VA 22091, (703)620-4730.*

WASCH, Joseph c.——**B:** Dec. 1, 1943, New York, NY, *Exec. VP and Sec.*, Somerset Properties, Inc.; **PRIM RE ACT:** Owner/Investor, Property Manager, Syndicator; **OTHER RE ACT:** Investment banker; **PREV EMPLOY:** VP, Merrill Lynch, Hubbard Inc. (1978-81); VP, Hamilton Investment Trust (1973-78); **PROFL AFFIL & HONORS:** Member of NY and NJ Bars; ABA; **EDUC:** BA, 1965, Hist./Pol. Sci., Hofstra Univ.; **GRAD EDUC:** JD, 1968, Brooklyn Law School; **HOME ADD:** 9768 Cedar Villas Blvd., Plantation, FL 33324, (305)473-6999; **BUS ADD:** Suite 215, 4740 N. State Rd. 7, Fort Lauderdale, FL 33319, (305)486-2244.

WASHBURNE, John H.——**B:** May 29, 1917, Waterbury, CT, *Owner*, Washburne & Washburne; **PRIM RE ACT:** Broker, Consultant, Appraiser, Instructor, Insuror; **OTHER RE ACT:** Hist. author/genealogist; **SERVICES:** Broker, appraiser, RE consultant; **REP CLIENTS:** Local, state and fed. governmental agencies, lawyers and lending instits.; **PREV EMPLOY:** Founded Washburne & Washburne partnership with father upon grad. from KS State Univ. in 1940; **PROFL AFFIL & HONORS:** SREA, ARWA, NAR, AREUEA, Realtors, SRA, NAR; **EDUC:** BS, 1940, Maj. Bus. Admin., Minor Civil Engr., KS State Univ., Manhattan KS; **GRAD EDUC:** 5th yr. Math Maj., 1965, Central CT State Coll., New Britain, CT; **OTHER ACT & HONORS:** Town Historian; Outstanding Citizen's Award 1979 Wolcott Jacees; Co-founder of Wolcott Historical Soc., Asst. Prof. and Head of the RE Dept., Post Coll., Waterbury, CT; Incorporator and Organizational Pres. of N. Amer. Bank & Trust, Wolcott, CT, CT Soc. of Genealogists, Inc.; **HOME ADD:** 49 Ctr. St., Wolcott, CT 06716, (203)879-0142; **BUS ADD:** 49 Ctr. St., Wolcott, CT 06716, (203)879-0142.

WASHKOWITZ, Alan——**B:** June 12, 1940, Brooklyn, NY, *Managing Dir.*, Lehman Brothers Kuhn Loeb, Sonnenblick Goldman; **PRIM RE ACT:** Consultant, Banker; **SERVICES:** Advising clients relating to RE fin. and sales; **REP CLIENTS:** US and For. corps., instnl. investors, and devel.; **EDUC:** AB, 1962, econ., Brooklyn Coll.; **GRAD EDUC:** MBA, 1965, Harvard Bus. School; JD, 1968, Columbia Law School; **EDUC HONORS:** Distinction, Cum Laude, Stone Schol.; **MIL SERV:** US Naval Res., 1962-68; **HOME ADD:** 210 E. 73rd St., New York, NY 10021, (212)628-8025; **BUS ADD:** 55 Water St., New York, NY 10041, (212)558-2545.

WASILESKI, John B.——*Devel., Partner*, Dictar Assocs. Inc.; **PRIM RE ACT:** Developer, Owner/Investor, Property Manager, Syndicator; **OTHER RE ACT:** Mostly reuse and rehab work; **SERVICES:** Devel., consulting, prop. mgmt., synds.; **REP CLIENTS:** Bus., indivs., devel. and manage for own corp. primarily; **PREV EMPLOY:** York Cumberland Housing Devel. Corp., Dictar Assocs.; **PROFL AFFIL & HONORS:** Nat. Assn. of Housing & Redevel. Officials, Gr. Portland C of C; **EDUC:** BA, 1975, Soc. & Environmental Studies, McGill Univ., Montreal, PQ, Can; **EDUC HONORS:** Comm. Involvement Award; **OTHER ACT & HONORS:** Pres. (since 1976) & Found. (1976) of Non-Profit Big Bros./Big Sisters of York Cty., ME; **HOME TEL:** (207)499-7775; **BUS ADD:** PO Box 3572, Portland, ME 04104, (207)797-6241.

WASSERMAN, Alexander——**B:** Nov. 20, 1923, Brooklyn, NY, *Owner*, Wasserman Realty Service; **PRIM RE ACT:** Broker, Instructor, Consultant, Appraiser, Developer, Builder, Property Manager, Lender, Owner/Investor, Insuror; **PREV EMPLOY:** Same for over 30 yrs.; **PROFL AFFIL & HONORS:** Dir. Bklyn. Bd. of Realtors & Flat. RE Bd. - Member Bay Ridge RE Bd. & NY Bd. of Realtors, IREB; **MIL SERV:** USAF, S/Sgt., various decorations; **OTHER ACT & HONORS:** Peter Minuet Amer. Legion, VP Navy Yard Boys Club, Regl. Dir. NCCJ, Dir. Atlantic Liberty S&L Assn., J.W.V. - Post 666, Long Beach, New York; Brooklyn Downtown Lions Club; Oddfellows - Senate Lodge Brooklyn; **HOME ADD:** 90 Trenton Ave., Long Beach, NY 11561; **BUS ADD:** 1603 McDonald Ave., Brooklyn, NY 11230, (212)375-4750.

WASSERMAN, Stanley S.——**B:** May 11, 1929, Sheboygan, WI, *Pres.*, Douglas Corp.; **PRIM RE ACT:** Broker, Developer, Builder, Property Manager; **PROFL AFFIL & HONORS:** Intl. Council of Shopping Ctrs.; Milwaukee Bd. of Realtors; **EDUC:** BA, 1951, Light Bldg., Univ. of WI; **MIL SERV:** Mil. Govt.; M/Sgt., 1951-1964, Reserves; **HOME ADD:** 7142 N. Seneca Ave., Glendale, WI 53217, (414)351-3052; **BUS ADD:** 2602 W. Silver Spring Dr., Milwaukee, WI 53209, (414)464-0300.

WASSON, Irv——**B:** Nov. 23, 1916, Peoria, IL, *Comml/Invest. Broker*, Jim Maloof Realtor, Comml.; **PRIM RE ACT:** Broker, Consultant, Developer, Builder, Owner/Investor; **PREV EMPLOY:** RE broker, state of IL for 30 yrs.; **PROFL AFFIL & HONORS:** NAR; RNMI, Awarded the designation of CCIM by the Realtors Nat. Mktg. Inst.; **MIL SERV:** US Army, S/Sgt; **OTHER ACT & HONORS:** Past VP of Peoria Homebuilders, VP of Tri-Cty. Exchangors; **HOME ADD:** 2605-29 W. Willowlake Dr, Peoria, IL 61615, (309)691-3510; **BUS ADD:** 8309 N. Knoxville Ave, Peoria, IL 61615, (309)692-3900.

WASSON, Larry——**B:** Sept. 25, 1944, Coral Gables, FL, *Pres.*, Affiliated Building Inspectors, Inc.; **PRIM RE ACT:** Consultant; **OTHER RE ACT:** Bldg. inspector, arbitrator, instructor; **SERVICES:** Const. consultant for purchase, renovation and repair of resid. and comml. prop.; **REP CLIENTS:** Buyers, lenders, prop. mgrs., ins. co., Fed. Govt. (US Dept. of State - consultant re: US Embassies, Staff Office and housing structures in for. countries); **PREV EMPLOY:** 12 yrs., Gen. Contractor/Devel.; specifications writer; **PROFL AFFIL & HONORS:** Const. Specification Inst.; Bldg. Officials & Code Administrators, Int.; Amer. Soc. Home Inspectors; Amer. Arbitration Assn. - Nat. Const. Panel Member, Arbitrator for Better Business Bureau; **EDUC:** BA, 1967, Bus., Bernar Baruch Coll., NYC; **MIL SERV:** US Army, SFC; **HOME ADD:** 4717 Cheaspeake St., NW, Washington, DC 20016, (301)986-8867; **BUS ADD:** 7223 Delfield St., Chevy Chase, MD 20815, (301)986-8866.

WASSON, Thomas L.——**B:** Jan. 14, 1948, Bradford, PA, *VP*, Washington Mortgage Co., Inc.; **PRIM RE ACT:** Broker, Lender; **OTHER RE ACT:** Mort. Broker; **SERVICES:** Comml. RE Construction loans and placement of permanent fin.; **PREV EMPLOY:** First Federal Savings of Phoenix (6 yrs.); **PROFL AFFIL & HONORS:** AZ: RE Broker, AZ Mort. Broker; **EDUC:** BA, 1969, Bus., Econ., Grove City Coll., Grove City, PA; **GRAD EDUC:** MBA, 1974, Bus. Mgmt., AZ State Univ., Tempe, AZ; **MIL SERV:** USAF, Capt., AF Commendation Medal; **OTHER ACT & HONORS:** Mason; **HOME ADD:** 9251 S. Lakeshore Dr., Tempe, AZ 85284; **BUS TEL:** (602)954-7415.

WATERS, J. Richard, Sr.——**B:** Jan. 31, 1950, Birmingham, AL, *Atty.*, Waters Investment Co.; **PRIM RE ACT:** Attorney, Developer, Property Manager, Lender, Owner/Investor; **PROFL AFFIL & HONORS:** ABA; AL Bar Assn.; Birmingham Bar Assn.; FL Bar; **EDUC:** BS, Bus., 1972, RE, AL Univ.; **GRAD EDUC:** JD, 1975, Law, Samford Univ.; **BUS ADD:** Suite 108, 14 Office Park Circle, Birmingham, AL 35223, (205)871-1126.

WATERS, Karl Martin, III——**B:** Nov. 29, 1953, Charlotte, NC, *VP*, Waters Insurance & Realty Co., RE; **PRIM RE ACT:** Broker, Developer, Syndicator; **SERVICES:** Comml. and investment brokerage, devel., synd.; **REP CLIENTS:** Indiv. and institl. investors; **PROFL AFFIL & HONORS:** Local and Nat. Bd. of Realtors; RNMI, CCIM Designee; **EDUC:** BA, 1976, Amer. Hist./20th Century Hist., Univ. of VA; **EDUC HONORS:** Grad. with Distinction; **OTHER ACT & HONORS:** Young Democrats; Mayor's Transp. Comm.; Bd. of Realtors Political Affairs Comm.; Candidate Guidance - NC CCIM Chapter; **HOME ADD:** 1041 Coddington Pl., Charlotte, NC 28211, (704)364-9519; **BUS ADD:** 429 S. Trym St., Charlotte, NC 28202, (704)333-0794.

WATERS, Paul W.——**B:** Feb. 21, 1933, Chattanooga, TN, *Pres.*, Paul W. Waters, Inc.; **PRIM RE ACT:** Broker, Consultant, Owner/Investor; **PROFL AFFIL & HONORS:** NAR; Orlando/Winter Park Bd. of Realtors; Central FL Multifamily Housing Assn., Past Pres.; Bldg. Owners and Mgrs. Assn., Past Pres.; **EDUC:** BSBA, 1955, RE, Univ. of FL; **OTHER ACT & HONORS:** Rotary Club of Orlando, SE (Past Pres.); **HOME ADD:** 4501 Cranston, Orlando, FL 32806, (305)277-9682; **BUS ADD:** 800 N. Ferncreek Ave., Orlando, FL 32803, (305)894-6911.

WATKINS, James B.——**B:** July 13, 1950, St. Louis, MO, *Counsel*, The May Department Stores Co.; **PRIM RE ACT:** Attorney, Developer; **OTHER RE ACT:** Legal counsel for RE devel. - shopping ctrs.; **PROFL AFFIL & HONORS:** MO Bar; ABA; Metropolitan St. Louis

Bar Assn.; **EDUC:** BS, 1972, Fin. and Acctg., Southwest MO State Univ.; **GRAD EDUC:** JD, 1977, Washington Univ.; **EDUC HONORS:** Grad. cum laude; member Pi Omega Pi; recipient of Wall Street Journal Student Achievement Award; Outstanding graduate in Fin; Member Phi Theta Kappa; **MIL SERV:** US Army 1972-1974, Spec. 4; **HOME ADD:** 1220 Moorlands, Richmond Heights, MO 63117, (314)644-4576; **BUS ADD:** 611 Olive St., St. Louis, MO 63101, (314)247-0414.

WATSON, Charles Lynn——B: Nov. 29, 1942, Macomb, IL, *Pres.*, Watson Land & Cattle Co.; **PRIM RE ACT:** Broker, Consultant, Banker, Owner/Investor, Property Manager, Syndicator; **OTHER RE ACT:** Buyer's broker, investment counseling (sales, exchanges, buyer's broker), valuation, and synd. of agricultural props., farm mgmt.; **REP CLIENTS:** Farm owner-operators; indiv. & instl. investors (both domestic and for.) in agricultural props.; **PREV EMPLOY:** Investment Broker, A.G. Edwards & Sons, Inc., 1976-1979; Controller, Midwest Univ. Consortium for Intl. Activities, Inc. (Mucia, Inc.) 1973-1976; **PROFL AFFIL & HONORS:** FLI; Champaign Cty. Exchangors; NAR, CPA, 1973; **EDUC:** BS, Agriculture, 1969, Agricultural Mgmt. & Comml. Law, Univ. of Il, Urbana; **GRAD EDUC:** BBA, 1972, Attc.(tax), Univ. of IL, Urbana; **MIL SERV:** US Army; Specialist Five, Good Conduct Medal; **OTHER ACT & HONORS:** Alpha Gamma Rho Frat.; B.P.O.E.; Amer. Legion; CU Optimist Club; **HOME ADD:** 1603 Dobbins Dr., Champaign, IL 61820, (217)352-0228; **BUS ADD:** PO Box 1525, Champaign, IL 61820, (217)352-1016.

WATSON, David P.——B: Dec. 6, 1943, Chicago, IL, *Pres.*, Hillmark Corp.; **PRIM RE ACT:** Broker, Developer, Owner/Investor, Property Manager; **SERVICES:** Develp, own, manage 1000 apt. units and 14 motels; **PROFL AFFIL & HONORS:** AICPA; WICPA; HMA; NAA; WAA, CPA; **EDUC:** MBA, 1971, Acctg., Univ. of WI; **GRAD EDUC:** MBA, 1972, Acctg., Univ. of WI; **MIL SERV:** USAF, Capt., 1966-1970; **HOME ADD:** 3600 Ritchie Rd., Verona, WI 53593, (608)833-5425; **BUS ADD:** 6425 Odana Rd., Madison, WI 53719, (608)273-3900.

WATSON, Harry E.——B: Oct. 20, 1922, Courney,PA, *Pres.*, Projects Unlimited, Inc.; **PRIM RE ACT:** Consultant, Developer, Builder, Owner/Investor, Syndicator; **SERVICES:** Money from investors for purchase (investment) in raw land and land in various stages from raw land, tentative and approved maps and build out with finished devel. of shopping ctrs., condos and town houses; **PREV EMPLOY:** Mgr. if investment div. Richardson Realtors; **PROFL AFFIL & HONORS:** BIA and Solar Cal; **MIL SERV:** USAF, Capt., 9 battle stars, 9 air medals, one distinguished flying cross, one purple heart; **OTHER ACT & HONORS:** Athletic Dir., Athletic Assn. of Dallas; **HOME ADD:** 29402 Ivy Glenn, Laguna Niguel, CA 92677, (714)831-0251; **BUS ADD:** 27831 L Paz Rd., Laguna Niguel, CA 92677, 14)831-6750.

WATSON, Raymond L.——B: Oct. 4, 1926, Seattle, WA, *Pres.-Partner*, Watson, Eberling and Lund, Inc.; **PRIM RE ACT:** Consultant, Architect, Developer, Builder, Owner/Investor; **SERVICES:** Builders, Devels. and Develop. Consultants and Mgrs.; **PREV EMPLOY:** Pres.: The Irvine Co., Orange Cty., CA; **PROFL AFFIL & HONORS:** Amer. Inst. of Architects, Lic. Architect, CA; Fellow; Amer. Inst. of Architects; **EDUC:** BArch., 1951, Arch., Univ. of CA, Berkeley; **GRAD EDUC:** MArch, 1953, Arch., Univ. of CA, Berkeley; **MIL SERV:** USAF, Pvt.; **OTHER ACT & HONORS:** Member Bd. Dirs., Disney Productions, Pacific Mutual Life Insurance Co.; Tr. Occidental Coll.; **HOME ADD:** 2501 Alta Vista Dr., Newport Beach, CA 92660, (714)644-1847; **BUS ADD:** 900 Cagney Lane, Newport Beach, CA 92663, (714)645-2016.

WATSON, Robert——*Exec. VP Corp. Plng.*, Rando, Inc.; **PRIM RE ACT:** Property Manager; **BUS ADD:** 701 West 5th Ave., PO Box 8369, Columbus, OH 43201, (614)294-3511.*

WATSON, Robert S., Jr.——B: Jan. 16, 1945, Long Beach, CA, *Pres.*, R.S. Watson Appraisal Service; **PRIM RE ACT:** Appraiser; **SERVICES:** RE Appraisals (resid., comml. indus); **REP CLIENTS:** Investors, lenders, CPA's & other investment advisors; **PREV EMPLOY:** City of Phoenix Improvement Distr. Office, RE Salesman, RE Instr.; **PROFL AFFIL & HONORS:** Sr. Member of NARA, Assoc. Member of SREA, CRA with the NARA; **EDUC:** BS, 1977, RE, RE Appraising, Urban Planning, AZ State Univ.; AA, 1975, RE, Phoenix Coll.; **EDUC HONORS:** Phi Theta Nappa (Natl. Jr. Coll. Scholastic Soc.); **MIL SERV:** USN, 1965-72, Eng. Aide First Class, Navy Unit Citation, Good Conduct Medal, Military School, Const. Planning & Estimating, Topographic Surveying; **OTHER ACT & HONORS:** K of C, Boy Scouts of Amer., PTA, Girl Scouts of Amer.; **HOME ADD:** 2026 North 57th Ave., Phoenix, AZ 85035, (602)272-4718; **BUS ADD:** 2026 N. 57 Ave., Phoenix, AZ 85035, (602)269-0685.

WATSON, Theresa L.——*Exec. VP*, American Savings and Loan League; **PRIM RE ACT:** Banker; **BUS ADD:** 1435 G St., N.W., Suite 1019, Washington, DC 20005, (202)628-5624.*

WATT, Timothy A.——B: Jan. 28, 1953, Artesia, CA, *Atty.*, Wiley, Garwood, Stolhandske & Simmons; **PRIM RE ACT:** Attorney; **SERVICES:** Negotiation & analysis of transactions, preparation of documents, litigation, represent clients before admin. agencies, state & fed. courts; **PREV EMPLOY:** U. S. Environmental Protection Agency (Office of Solid Waste & Office of Gen. Council); **PROFL AFFIL & HONORS:** San Antonio, TX and Amer. Bar Assns. (Section on Real Prop., Probate & Trust law); Assoc. Member Gr. San Antonio Bldrs. Assn.; **EDUC:** BS Ed., 1975, Environmental Sci. Educ., Drake Univ., Des Moines, IA; **GRAD EDUC:** JD, 1979, Major Emphasis in Environmental Law & Land Use Law, National Law Ctr., George Washington Univ. (Wash., DC); **EDUC HONORS:** Grad. Summa Cum Laude; Attended Drake on Full Acad. Schol., Grad. w/Honors; **HOME ADD:** 4935 W. Cambray, San Antonio, TX 78229, (512)690-1813; **BUS ADD:** 1603 Babcock, P O Box 29099 (Highpoint Exec. Plaza), San Antonio, TX 78229, (512)340-5800.

WATTLES, Bob——B: Mar. 14, 1947, Portsmouth, VA, *Pres./Partner*, Wattles, Baker & Davidson, P.A.; **PRIM RE ACT:** Consultant, Attorney, Developer, Owner/Investor, Syndicator; **SERVICES:** All legal, devel., synd. related servs.; **REP CLIENTS:** Southwind, Ltd., St. Cloud, FL; Mil-Lake Plaza, W. Palm Beach, FL; FL Agri-Energy, Inc., Greenwood, FL; **PREV EMPLOY:** FL Dept. of Agriculture; FL C of C; Atty. (own firm); **PROFL AFFIL & HONORS:** FL Bar; Dist. of Columbia Bar; All 4 US Dist. Ctrs. for FL; US Supreme Ct. Bar; US Ct. of Military Appeals; US Ct. of Intl. Trade; US Customs Ct.; **EDUC:** BA, 1969, Public Relations, Univ. of FL; **GRAD EDUC:** JD, 1973, Law - Comml./Real Prop./Corporate, Univ. of FL; **EDUC HONORS:** student govt.; social & profl. frats., FL Blue Key, Pres.; Omicron Delta, Pres.; **OTHER ACT & HONORS:** Pres., Orange Cty. Young Democrats; Pres., Centurion Council of FL; Pres. of Bd., The Door (Drug & Alcohol Rehab. for Children); **HOME ADD:** POB 2462, Orlando, FL 32802, (305)894-6659; **BUS ADD:** POB 1806, Orlando, FL 32802, (305)843-6370.

WATTS, Frank——B: Oct. 14, 1939, England, *Mgr. Prop. Investments*, The Prudential Assurance Co. Ltd.; **PRIM RE ACT:** Lender, Property Manager; **OTHER RE ACT:** Underwriter; **EDUC:** 1979, Prop. Mgmt., McGill Univ.; **GRAD EDUC:** B Comm., 1978, Fin., Concordia Univ.; **HOME ADD:** 45 4th Ave. N., Roxboro, Montreal, H8Y 2M5, PQ, Can.; **BUS ADD:** Suite 811, 635 Dorchester Blvd. W, Montreal, H3B 1R7, PQ, Can., (514)878-2361.

WATTS, H. Michael——B: Feb. 5, 1944, Winston Salem, NC, *Pres./Owner*, Michael Watts, Inc., Real Estate Appraisers & Consultants; **PRIM RE ACT:** Consultant, Appraiser; **SERVICES:** Appraisal and consultation servs. only; **REP CLIENTS:** US Govt.; Relocation Cos.; banks; S&L; various condemning authorities; Fed. Bankruptcy Ct.; various law firms and indivs.; **PREV EMPLOY:** Self-employed since 1975; **PROFL AFFIL & HONORS:** Soc. of RE Appraisers; AIREA (candidate); local, state Assn. of Realtors; NAR, SRPA; SRA; GRI; Realtor; **EDUC:** BA, 1965, Poli. Sci., Hist., German, Econ., Guilford Coll.; **GRAD EDUC:** Some work toward MBA, 1966-1967, Bus. Admin., Guilford Coll., Univ. of NC at Greensboro; **OTHER ACT & HONORS:** US Soccer Fed., licensed coach & referee; **HOME ADD:** 1 Gleneagle Ct., Greensboro, NC 27408, (919)282-2791; **BUS ADD:** PO Box 9056, Greensboro, NC 27408.

WATTS, Robert G.——*Exec. VP*, Robins, A.H., Co., Inc.; **PRIM RE ACT:** Property Manager; **BUS ADD:** 1407 Cummings Drive, Richmond, VA 23220, (804)257-2000.*

WAVREK, Wayne P.——B: July 4, 1938, Fullerton, PA, *Mgr. of RE*, Bethlehem Steel Corp., RE Div.; **PRIM RE ACT:** Property Manager; **OTHER RE ACT:** Corporate RE Mgmt.; **SERVICES:** Buying, selling, leasing, studies, records, mapping, employee relocation, and prop. asset mgmt.; **REP CLIENTS:** All depts. and subs. of the corp.; **PROFL AFFIL & HONORS:** IREM, NACORE; **EDUC:** 1960, Bus. Admin., LaFayette Coll.; **GRAD EDUC:** 1960, Gen. Mgmt., NY Univ.; **MIL SERV:** US Army, SP-4; **HOME ADD:** 608 Melrose Ave., Bethlehem, PA 18017, (215)865-9069; **BUS ADD:** Bethlehem, PA 18016, (215)694-3753.

WAX, Douglas F.——B: Dec. 28, 1939, Berea, OH, *Pres.*, Indus. Park Assoc.; **PRIM RE ACT:** Broker, Consultant; **OTHER RE ACT:** Spec. in Los Angeles & Ventura Ctys. (CA); **SERVICES:** Sales, leasing & proj. consulting for indus. bldgs. & parks; **REP CLIENTS:** RE devels., indiv. investors & mfg. concerns; **PREV EMPLOY:** Broker Assoc. with The McDonald Co., 1972-76; **PROFL AFFIL & HONORS:** AIREA, (Los Angeles), 1981 Pres. Member NAIOP, CA Assn. of Realtors, Master of Indus. Brokerage (AIREA); **EDUC:** BA, 1963, Hist. &

Econ., Yale Univ.; **GRAD EDUC:** MBA, 1969, Fin., Univ. of So. CA; **OTHER ACT & HONORS:** N. Ranch Ctry. Club, Westlake Village St. Elmo Soc., Yale Univ.; **HOME ADD:** 3666 Eddingham Ave., Woodland Hills, CA 91364, (213)347-0367; **BUS ADD:** 21201 Victory Blvd., Suite 265, Canoga Park, CA 91303, (213)999-3073.

WAYNE, R. Bruce——**B:** Aug. 21, 1946, Grove City, PA, *Atty. at Law*, Post Kirby Wideman & Noonan, PC; **PRIM RE ACT:** Attorney; **SERVICES:** Legal advice and litigation representation; **REP CLIENTS:** Toddner, a CA Ltd. partnership; Mrs. J. Rhodes; Harry Deardorff, profl. architect; **PREV EMPLOY:** 8 years experience in most phases of RE law and lititation; **PROFL AFFIL & HONORS:** ABA; CA Bar; San Diego Cty. Bar; **EDUC:** BA, 1968, Hist. (Russian & Amer.), Princeton Univ. & Univ. of VA Law School; **GRAD EDUC:** JD, 1974, Law, Univ. of VA; **EDUC HONORS:** Cum Laude, Dir., Charlottesville Legal Aid Clinic; **MIL SERV:** US Naval Res., Lt., numerous decorations; **OTHER ACT & HONORS:** Bd. of Dirs., State Bar Comm., Legal Servs. for the Poor, Scripps Ranch Community Assn., Princeton & VA Alumni Assns.; **HOME ADD:** 10586 Rookwood Dr., San Diego, CA 92131, (714)566-3926; **BUS ADD:** 600 B St., Suite 2150, San Diego, CA 92101.

WEAGRAFF, John D.——*VP, Fin.*, National Mine Service Co.; **PRIM RE ACT:** Property Manager; **BUS ADD:** 4900-600 Grant St., Pittsburgh, PA 15219, (412)281-0688.*

WEATHERBY, William J.——**B:** Mar. 6, 1944, Camden, NJ, *Owner*, The Weatherby Co.; **PRIM RE ACT:** Broker, Consultant, Builder, Owner/Investor, Property Manager, Syndicator; **PREV EMPLOY:** Gen. Mgr./Investment/Prop. Mgmt. Co.; **PROFL AFFIL & HONORS:** Beverly Hills Bd. of Realtors; **EDUC:** BS, 1976, Mktg., RE, Woodbury Univ.; **MIL SERV:** US Army, 1st Lt., Bronze Star; **OTHER ACT & HONORS:** Pi Kappa Alpha (Past Pres.); **HOME ADD:** 12321 Ocean Park Bvd. 4, Los Angeles, CA 90064, (213)473-1149; **BUS ADD:** 9171 Wilshire Blvd., Suite 507, Beverly Hills, CA 90210, (213)275-4275.

WEATHERS, Kenneth M.——**B:** Nov. 6, 1945, McMinnville, OR, *Owner*, Ken Weathers and Assoc.; **PRIM RE ACT:** Consultant, Developer, Owner/Investor, Syndicator; **SERVICES:** Planning, devel., mgmt. consultant; **REP CLIENTS:** Lenders, investors, devels.; **EDUC:** BS, 1967, Production Mgmt., Bus.; **MIL SERV:** USAF, Capt.; **HOME ADD:** 124 Conejo, Durango, CO 81301, (303)247-9697; **BUS ADD:** PO Box 2913, Durango, CO 81301, (303)259-3434.

WEAVER, Gene——*West Coast RE Mgr.*, Canal-Randolph Corp.; **PRIM RE ACT:** Developer; **BUS ADD:** 500 So. Main St., Orange, CA 92668, (714)547-0807.*

WEAVER, Harry E.——**B:** Oct. 25, 1934, Newark, NJ, *Sr. Part.*, The Weaver Partnership; **PRIM RE ACT:** Consultant, Architect, Developer, Builder, Owner/Investor, Property Manager, Syndicator; **OTHER RE ACT:** Fin.; **SERVICES:** Pro forma analysis, site selections, renovations, cash flow projections; **PREV EMPLOY:** Arch., 15 yrs., Planner 11 yrs., Contr. & subcontr. 14 yrs. prior to registration, completed 3,800 projects in NY, NJ & CT; **PROFL AFFIL & HONORS:** AIA, Amer. Inst. of Profl. Planners, Reg. Arch. in NJ, MA, NY, PA, NC, VT, FL, CO, Profl. Planner, NJ; **EDUC:** B Arch, Arch. & Bus., Columbia Univ.; **OTHER ACT & HONORS:** Presbyterian Homes of NJ, Tr.; The Hartley Dodge Memorial Found., Tr.; St. Andrews Soc., Lifetime Member; Morristown Memorial Hospital, Tr.; Morris Cty. Golf Club; Arch. of Record, Harding Township Bd. of Educ., Stacey Constr., Inc. Pres.; **HOME ADD:** Hunter Dr., New Vernon, NJ 07976, (201)267-2073; **BUS ADD:** 18 MacCulloch Ave., Morristown, NJ 07960, (201)267-1670.

WEAVER, John R.——**B:** Sept. 14, 1925, *Mgr., RE*, EI Du Pont de Nemours & Co., RE Div.; **OTHER RE ACT:** Corp. RE; **PROFL AFFIL & HONORS:** SIR, Indus. RE Mark. Council, Wilm. Comm. of 100, Wilm. RE Bd., Grtr. Wi. Devel. Council; **EDUC:** BS, 1949, Educ., Univ. of DE; **GRAD EDUC:** MA, 1950, Hist., Columbia Univ.; **EDUC HONORS:** Highest hons. in course; **MIL SERV:** US Army, Air Corps., Lt.; **HOME ADD:** 3 Gale Ln., Fairthorne, Wilmington, DE 19807; **BUS ADD:** 1007 Market St., Wilmington, DE 19898, (302)774-5888.

WEAVER, Park, Jr.——**B:** July 2, 1936, Fort Worth, TX, *Pres.*, Park Weaver, Jr., Inc.; **PRIM RE ACT:** Broker, Consultant, Owner/Investor, Real Estate Publisher; **SERVICES:** Comml. Brokerage, Market Comparable Surveys, Apt. Valuations; **REP CLIENTS:** Indiv., partnerships, and synd., primarily buyers and sellers of AZ apt. prop.; **PREV EMPLOY:** VP, Brooks, Harvey, and Co., 1970-1974; Mgr. of Corp. RE, Litton Industries, 1965-1970; **PROFL AFFIL & HONORS:** AZ Multi-Housing Assoc.; BOMA; AZ Assn. of Indus. Devel.; BIA of Los Angeles, Outstanding Young Man of the Year, Beverly Hills Jr. C of C, 1968; **EDUC:** AB, 1958, Geology, Rice Univ., Houston, TX; **GRAD EDUC:** Master's Degree-Bus. Admin., 1960, Gen. Bus., Harvard Univ., Boston, MA; **EDUC HONORS:** Dean's List, Sigma Gamma Epsilon; **MIL SERV:** USAF Reserve, A2C; **OTHER ACT & HONORS:** Delegate-L.A. County Republican Comm. 1966-1970; Maricopa Cty. Republican Precinct Comm. 1976-1978; Bd. Membership AZ Theater Co., Phoenix Symphony Council; VP & Bd. of Arizonans for Cultural Development; Past Pres. of AZ HBS Club, Rice Club of CA, and L.A. Opera Assoc.; **HOME ADD:** 1345 E. Missouri Ave., Phoenix, AZ 85014, (602)274-6553; **BUS ADD:** 1345 E. Missouri Ave., Phoenix, AZ 85014, (602)274-3654.

WEAVER, Robert B.——**B:** June 27, 1932, Findlay, OH, *Atty. at Law*, Robert B. Weaver, Atty. at Law; **PRIM RE ACT:** Attorney; **SERVICES:** Contract structuring; documentation; tax consultation; **REP CLIENTS:** PADA Farms, Inc.: The Bank of Leipsic Co.; Mattern-Montooth Realty; **PROFL AFFIL & HONORS:** OH State Bar; ABA; NW OH Realtors; **EDUC:** BBA, 1954, Acctg., Univ. of MI; **GRAD EDUC:** JD, 1957, Univ. of MI; **EDUC HONORS:** Phi Eta Sigma; Beta Gamma Sigma; BBA with distinction; **OTHER ACT & HONORS:** Law. Dir., Village of Leipsic, 20 yrs.; **HOME ADD:** 317 E. Main St., Leipsic, OH 45856, (419)943-2065; **BUS ADD:** 214 South Belmore St., Leipsic, OH 45856, (419)943-2149.

WEAVER, Ronald L.——**B:** June 3, 1949, *Partner*, Arky Freed Stearns Watson & Greer; **PRIM RE ACT:** Attorney; **SERVICES:** RE, devel. of rgnl. impact, fin. closings; **REP CLIENTS:** Devel., arch., engrs., planners, realtors; **PROFL AFFIL & HONORS:** Chmn. ABA; Mort. Comm. of Fin. Comm.; Comml. Comm. of Banking Law Sect., Phi Beta Kappa; **EDUC:** AB, 1971, Hist., Univ. of NC - Chapel Hill; **GRAD EDUC:** JD, 1974, Re, Fin., Harvard Law School; **EDUC HONORS:** Phi Beta Kappa - Top 10 in grad. class, Cum Laude Grad.; **MIL SERV:** USAF, 1st Lt.; **OTHER ACT & HONORS:** Member Exec. Comm., Greater Tampa C of C, Member, Bd. of Founders Life Ins. Co.; **HOME ADD:** 3805 Bayshore Blvd., Tampa, FL 33606, (813)837-2962; **BUS ADD:** 620 Twiggs, Tampa, FL 33601, (813)223-4800.

WEAVER, William C.——**B:** Sept. 11, 1942, Birmingham, AL, *Pres.*, Real Property Consultants; **PRIM RE ACT:** Consultant, Appraiser, Developer, Owner/Investor, Instructor; **OTHER RE ACT:** Development; Investments; **SERVICES:** Real prop. consulting, Real prop. asset mgmt.; **REP CLIENTS:** City of Atlanta, City of Dallas, Burlington Northern Railroad, Bd. of Realtors in various states, pvt. devels. & investors; **PREV EMPLOY:** Univ. of TX, Private consulting in Atlanta, NC & New Orleans; **PROFL AFFIL & HONORS:** AIREA; Amer. RE & Urban Econ. Assoc., Nat. Assn. of Corporate RE Execs, Tarrant City Tax Dist., Grad. Mort. Banking School; **EDUC:** BS, 1964, Eng./Hist., Livingston Univ.; **GRAD EDUC:** MBA, 1973, Computer Sci. & Mgmt., RE, Loyola Univ. & PhD, GA State Univ.; **HOME ADD:** 5701 Firewood Dr., Arlington, TX 76016, (817)457-8560; **BUS ADD:** 5701 Firewood Dr., Arlington, TX 76016, (817)273-3705.

WEBB, Burke Hilliard——**B:** June 23, 1936, Cooperstown, NY, *Atty.*, Attorney Burke H. Webb (solo practitioner); **PRIM RE ACT:** Attorney; **SERVICES:** Legal services for banking and fin. insts., bus. and indivs.; **PREV EMPLOY:** Soc. Security Admin. at Detroit and Benton Harbor, MI (6/61-8/62), Atty. Carroll B. Jones (9/62-12/64), Jones, Webb & Jones (1/65-8/72), Jones, Webb, Jones & France (8/72-9/79), all of Marcellus, MI; **PROFL AFFIL & HONORS:** State Bar of MI (1962 to present), ABA (1965 to present), Cass Cty. Bar Assn. (1962 to present) and Bd. of Dirs. of Legal Aid Bureau of Southwestern MI, Inc. (1980 to present); **EDUC:** AB, 1958, Govt., hist., Miami Univ. (Ohio); **GRAD EDUC:** LLB, 1961, Univ. of MI Law School; **EDUC HONORS:** Cum Laude, James Scott Kemper Bill of Rights Essay Award (1958); honoraries: Phi Beta Kappa, Phi Eta Sigma, Sigma Delta Pi and Les Politiques; **OTHER ACT & HONORS:** Village trustee of Village of Marcellus MI and Chmn. of Village Council's Fin. and Purchasing Comm. (1978 to present); Cass Cty. Democ. Comm. Chmn. (1968 to 1970 and 1981 to present); Cass Cty. Democ. Exec. Comm. chair. (1981 to present); Marcellus Rotary Club; Who's Who in the Methodist Church (1966 Edition); Who's Who in Amer. Politics (1981-1982); Member (1974-1980) of Cass Cty. Community Mental Health Services Bd. (Chmn.: 1976-1977); Chmn. of Kalamazoo (MI) Regional Psychiatric Hospital Citizens Advisory Comm. (1978 to present); **HOME ADD:** 185 South Jones St. (Box 578), Marcellus, MI 49067, (616)646-5651; **BUS ADD:** 185 South Jones St., (Box 578), Marcellus, MI 49067, (616)646-5565.

WEBB, Donald——**B:** Feb. 18, 1918, Lawrenceville, VA, Real Estate Consultant; **PRIM RE ACT:** Broker, Consultant; **SERVICES:** Consultant and/or broker, represents either the buyer or the seller, comml. and investment prop.; **REP CLIENTS:** Corporate and indiv. buyers and sellers of land and comml. props.; **PREV EMPLOY:**

Transit operator in land surveying until 1950.; **HOME ADD:** 1151 Princess Anne Rd., Virginia Beach, VA 23456, (804)426-6596; **BUS ADD:** 3615 Oceanfront, VA Beach, VA 23451, (804)428-1500.

WEBB, Donald W.——**B:** July 2, 1939, Whitesburg, KY, *Part.*, Webb Cos.; **PRIM RE ACT:** Attorney, Developer, Owner/Investor; **SERVICES:** Complete; **EDUC:** 1960, Bus. & Econ., Georgetown Coll; **GRAD EDUC:** JD, 1967, Univ. of KY, Coll. of Law; **MIL SERV:** Army Nat. Guard; **HOME ADD:** 467 Woodlake Way, Lexington, KY 40502; **BUS ADD:** 800 Merrill Lynch Plaza, Lexington, KY 40507, (606)253-0008.

WEBB, James R.——**B:** Apr. 5, 1947, Granite City, IL, *Asst. Prof. of Fin.*, Kent State Univ., Dept. of Fin.; **PRIM RE ACT:** Consultant, Appraiser, Instructor; **OTHER RE ACT:** Researcher; **SERVICES:** Investment counseling, valuation, spec. research; **REP CLIENTS:** Fin. insts., ins. cos., pension funds, profl. socs. and research orgs.; **PREV EMPLOY:** Visiting lecturer in RE, Univ. of IL at Champaign-Urbana, 1978-79; **PROFL AFFIL & HONORS:** AREVEA, Fin. Mgmt. Assn., Amer. Fin. Assn., Amer. Econ. Assn.; **EDUC:** BS, 1972, Mgmt. & Prod., N. IL Univ.; **GRAD EDUC:** MBA, 1974, Fin., No. IL Univ.; PhD, 1982 (Exp.), RE Investments, Univ. of IL at Champaign; **EDUC HONORS:** IL Bankers Fellowship (1977), Bache, Halsey, Stuart Scholarship (1978); **HOME ADD:** 477 Park Ridge Dr., Munroe Falls, OH 44262, (216)688-6399; **BUS ADD:** Kent State Univ., Kent, OH 44242, (216)672-2426.

WEBB, Ralph Dudley——**B:** Sept. 5, 1943, Whitesburg, KY, *Pres./Owner*, Webb Cos.; **PRIM RE ACT:** Broker, Consultant, Attorney, Developer, Builder, Owner/Investor, Property Manager, Syndicator; **PROFL AFFIL & HONORS:** OH Bar Assn.; KY Bar Assn.; **EDUC:** Georgetown Coll.; Univ. of KY; **HOME ADD:** 3405A Tishoff Ct., Lexington, KY 40507, (606)269-4455; **BUS ADD:** 800 Merrill Lynch Plaza, Lexington, KY 40507, (606)253-0000.

WEBB, Thomas I.——**B:** July 28, 1927, Toledo, OH, *Partner*, Shumaker, Loop & Kendrick; **PRIM RE ACT:** Attorney; **SERVICES:** Legal; **REP CLIENTS:** OH Citizens Bank; **PROFL AFFIL & HONORS:** Amer., OH & Toledo Bar Assns.; OH Title Assns.; **EDUC:** Econ., Williams Coll.; **GRAD EDUC:** JD, 1950, Law, OH State Univ.; **OTHER ACT & HONORS:** Goodwill of Toledo, Bd. of Trustees, 9 yrs.; **HOME ADD:** 7720 Monclova Rd., Monclova, OH 43542, (419)865-0965; **BUS ADD:** 1000 Jackson, Toledo, OH 43624, (419)241-4201.

WEBB, William C., Jr.——Webb International Inc.; **PRIM RE ACT:** Developer; **BUS ADD:** 9601 N. Main St., Jacksonville, FL 32218, (904)757-8000.*

WEBB, William N.——**B:** Jan. 8, 1944, Hillsborough, NC, *Pres.*, Norwood Capital Corp.; **PRIM RE ACT:** Broker, Consultant, Appraiser, Owner/Investor, Property Manager; **SERVICES:** Total mktg. and mgmt. programs for new condo. and condo. conversion ventures; **REP CLIENTS:** Principals of well conceived multi-family ownership devels.; **PREV EMPLOY:** Stockton, Whatley, Davin & Co., 100 West Bay St., Jacksonville, FL 32202; **PROFL AFFIL & HONORS:** RESSI, RNMI, Sarasota Bd. of Realtors, Comm. of 100, Sarasota Cty. C of C; **EDUC:** AB, 1966, Econ., Univ. of NC, Chapel Hill; **GRAD EDUC:** MBA, 1968, Mktg., Univ. of NC Grad. Sch. of Bus.; **EDUC HONORS:** Order of the Old Well; **MIL SERV:** USN, Lt., Nat. Serv. Medal; **OTHER ACT & HONORS:** Bd. of Trs. of the Out-Of-Door Academy, Inc., Bd. of Dir. of the Siesta Key Fire and Rescue Advisory Comm., Inc., Pres. & Dir. of the Waterside West Comm. Assn., Inc., Bd. of Dir. of the Sarasota Trap and Skeet Club, Inc.; **HOME ADD:** 4848 Oxford Dr., Sarasota, FL 33581, (813)349-4813; **BUS ADD:** Palm Towers Bldg., 1343 Main St., Sarasota, FL 33577, (813)365-5551.

WEBB, William Y.——**B:** Apr. 13, 1935, Lisbon, Portugal, *Partner*, Ballard, Spahr, Andrews & Ingersoll; **PRIM RE ACT:** Attorney; **PROFL AFFIL & HONORS:** Amer. Law Inst.; Amer., PA & Phila. Bar Assns. & RE Comm.; **EDUC:** BA, 1956, Govt., Dartmouth Coll.; **GRAD EDUC:** JD, 1961, Law, Univ. of MI; **EDUC HONORS:** Cum Laude - Law Review; **MIL SERV:** USN, Lt. j.g.; **BUS ADD:** 30 S. 17th St., 20th Floor, Philadelphia, PA 19103, (215)564-1800.

WEBBER, Michael——**B:** Oct. 24, 1929, Chicago, IL, *Pres.*, Oakmont Investment Co.; **PRIM RE ACT:** Developer, Builder, Owner/Investor; **PROFL AFFIL & HONORS:** Intl. Council of Shopping Ctrs. - Natl. Assn. of Review Appraisers; **EDUC:** 1949, Los Angeles City Coll.; **BUS ADD:** 9600 S. Sepulveda Blvd., Los Angeles, CA 90045, (213)641-2879.

WEBER, Deloris M.——**B:** York, NE, *Pres.*, D. Weber, Realtor; **PRIM RE ACT:** Broker, Consultant, Appraiser, Developer, Builder, Property Manager, Owner/Investor; **PROFL AFFIL & HONORS:** CCIM, CPM, CRS, GRI, Lic. Appraiser, Charter Pres. of Blue River Area Bd. of Realtors, first woman Dean of The BE Realtors Inst., first woman Realtor in York Cty., only woman holding the CCIM designation in Nebraska; **EDUC:** Comml. sales, Residential sales, Grand Island Bus. Coll., Grand Island, NE; **EDUC HONORS:** Valedictorial-Sr. Class-Bradshaw, NE; **OTHER ACT & HONORS:** Dir., York Indus. Comm., Who's Who in NE; Notable Amer. Award; Who's Who of Amer. Women, Realtor of the Yr. (1980) of The Blue River Area Bd. of Realtors-NE; **HOME ADD:** Country Club Dr. & Elm, York, NE 68467, (402)362-7191; **BUS ADD:** 400 Lincoln Ave., York, NE 68467, (402)362-3400.

WEBER, Harvey——**B:** Jan. 29, 1953, Montreal, Quebec, Can., *Arch.*, Harvey Weber, Arch.; **PRIM RE ACT:** Architect; **SERVICES:** Gen. Arch. Services, Space Planning, Interior Design; **REP CLIENTS:** Co's. relocating to new quarters or expanding existing facilities; **PREV EMPLOY:** Rosen, Caruso, Vecsei - Architects (1975-1976) Montreal; **PROFL AFFIL & HONORS:** NCARB, Canadian Housing Design Council Award, 1977 for Le Manor Outremont, Montreal; **EDUC:** BArch, 1975, McGill Univ., Montreal; **HOME ADD:** 53 Cogswell Ln., Stamford, CT 06902, (203)327-7677; **BUS ADD:** 53 Cogswell Ln., Stamford, CT 06902, (203)327-7677.

WEBER, Hugo C.A., Jr.——**B:** Sep. 22, 1943, Reading, PA, *Dir.*, Polley Assoc., RE Educ.; **PRIM RE ACT:** Instructor, Syndicator, Consultant, Developer, Property Manager, Owner/Investor; **OTHER RE ACT:** Owner/Dir. of Educ. Co.; **SERVICES:** State mandated and gen. RE Educ. Co.; **PREV EMPLOY:** Seminar Dir. of Realty Seminars, Inc.; **PROFL AFFIL & HONORS:** RESSI; CCIM; REEA; NAR; PA Assn. Realtors; NJ Assn. of Realtors; **EDUC:** AB, 1965, Gov./Econ., Franklin and Marshall Coll.; **HOME ADD:** 304 Earles Lane, Newtown Sq., PA 19073, (215)353-6806; **BUS ADD:** 600 Reed Rd., Broomall, PA 19008, (215)353-6776.

WEBER, Kenneth——*Sec. - Treas.*, Howard T. Lane Co. 1973-.; **PRIM RE ACT:** Developer, Property Manager; **OTHER RE ACT:** Corp. Exec., Fin. Acctg., Tax; **SERVICES:** Build for Sale; **PREV EMPLOY:** Dunn Props. 1970-1973, Boise Casade Bldg. Co. 1967-1970; **PROFL AFFIL & HONORS:** Nat. Assn. of Accountants, Nat. Soc. of Public Accountants, Soc. of CA Accountants; **EDUC:** BS, 1953, Acctg./Econ., Los Angeles State Coll.; **OTHER ACT & HONORS:** Pres. Ventura React., Bd. member-various Homeowner Assns.; **HOME ADD:** PO Box 4191, Ventura, CA 93004; **BUS ADD:** PO Box 3639, Ventura, CA 93006, (805)656-3117.

WEBER, Lawrence K., Jr.——**B:** May 20, 1930, San Francisco, CA, *Pres.*, United Prop. Investors, Inc.; **PRIM RE ACT:** Broker, Consultant, Developer, Owner/Investor, Property Manager; **SERVICES:** Comml., indus., investment only brokerage, devel. prop. mgmt.; **REP CLIENTS:** Chart House, Firestone, Haverty Furniture, Plitt Theatres, St. Joe Paper Co., Atlantic Bank, Flagship Bank, Popeyes Fried Chicken; **PREV EMPLOY:** Stockton Whatley Davin & Co., 1973-75; VP Mode Realty, 1975-76; VP W. Dick & Son Realty, 1976-78; **PROFL AFFIL & HONORS:** NACORE; **EDUC:** AB, 1951, Bus. & Pol. Sci., Univ. of CA; **MIL SERV:** USN, CDR (Ret.), Navy Commendation Medal; **OTHER ACT & HONORS:** St. Margaret's, Hibernia, Who's Who in South & Southwest; **HOME ADD:** 783 Hibernia Rt., Hibernia, FL 32043, (904)284-5459; **BUS ADD:** Suite 932, 200 W. Forsyth St., Jacksonville, FL 32202, (404)355-0431.

WEBER, Marjorie J.——**B:** May 18, 1935, Cambridge, MA, *Exec. VP*, Florida Fidelity Financial, Inc.; **OTHER RE ACT:** Mort. Broker; **SERVICES:** Arrangement of fin. for major income prop. and condos.; **PREV EMPLOY:** Sonnenblick-Goldman Corp., NY, VP, 1966-1978; **PROFL AFFIL & HONORS:** Mort. Brokers Assn. of Greater Miami; Nat. Assn. of Indus. and Office Parks; **EDUC:** BA, 1957, Psych., Wheaton Coll.; **EDUC HONORS:** Cum Laude; **HOME ADD:** 4050 Malaga Ave., Coconut Grove, FL 33133; **BUS ADD:** .4500 Biscayne Blvd., Suite 260, Miami, FL 33137, (305)573-4531.

WEBER, Max R.——**B:** Jan. 3, 1939, El Paso, TX, *Pres.*, Weber Assoc.; **PRIM RE ACT:** Broker, Instructor, Consultant, Appraiser, Property Manager, Owner/Investor; **SERVICES:** Gen. RE Activity; **REP CLIENTS:** Indiv. buyers and investors of resid. and comml. props.; **PREV EMPLOY:** Public Relations - United Fruit Co., 1967 - 1972; **PROFL AFFIL & HONORS:** CRB; CRS; GRI; RNMI; TX RE Teachers Assn.; Associate Member, SREA; **GRAD EDUC:** 1966, Pol. Sci., TX W. Coll (now Univ. TX/El Paso.); **OTHER ACT & HONORS:** Assn. for Retarded Citizens, Past Pres. El Paso - Juarez Handball Assn.; **HOME ADD:** 3211 Tyrone, El Paso, TX 79925, (915)598-7716; **BUS ADD:** 6410 Gateway E, El Paso, TX 79905, (915)778-4462.

WEBER, Thomas W.——**B:** Sept. 17, 1947, Lancaster, WI, *Pres.*, T.W. Weber Realty, Inc.; **PRIM RE ACT:** Broker, Syndicator, Consultant, Appraiser, Developer, Builder, Property Manager, Owner/Investor, Real Estate Publisher; **SERVICES:** Investment Counseling, land dev., residential sales, synd. of comm'l. prop., prop. mgmt., RE publications, bldg., historic preservation, investments, RE training; **PREV EMPLOY:** Lucey Realty 1970 - 1973; **PROFL AFFIL & HONORS:** Greater Madison Bd. of Realtors; NAR; WI Realtors Assn., Dir., Madison Bd. of Realtors 1976 - 1978; GRI; RE Adv. Comm. for the Bd. of Voc. Tech. and Adult Educ.; CRS; **MIL SERV:** USA, Spec 4; **OTHER ACT & HONORS:** W. Madison Jaycees; Our Lady Queen of Peace Church, Member; **HOME ADD:** 6433 Inner Dr., Madison, WI 53705, (608)233-4659; **BUS ADD:** 5609 Medical Cir., Madison, WI 53719, (608)274-0410.

WEBER, William A.——**B:** Aug. 29, 1947, New Orleans, LA, *Atty.*, Greenberg, Traurig, Askew, Hoffman, Lipoff, Quentel & Wolff, PA, RE; **PRIM RE ACT:** Attorney; **SERVICES:** Counseling devel., synd., and legal advice concerning comml. and resid. real Prop.; lenders, indivs., and inst. banks and devel. of comml. and resid. prop.; **PREV EMPLOY:** Intl. Econ. US Dept. of Commerce - US Govt.; **PROFL AFFIL & HONORS:** ABA; FL Bar; Dade Cty. Bar Assn.; Order of the Coif; Phi Kappa Phi; Editor-in-Chief of the Univ. of FL Law Review; **EDUC:** Liberal Arts, 1969, Econ., Stetson Univ.; **GRAD EDUC:** JD, 1976, Law, Univ. of FL School of Law; **EDUC HONORS:** Order of the Coif, Phi Kappa Phi, FL Blue Key; **MIL SERV:** US Army, Field Artillery, 1st Lt., Army Commendation Medal; **OTHER ACT & HONORS:** Lecturer for FL Bar Continuing Legal Educ Comm.; **HOME ADD:** 2855 Tigertail Ave., 319, Coconut Grove, FL 33133; **BUS ADD:** 1401 Brickell Ave., Miami, FL 33131, (305)377-3501.

WEBSTER, Donald C.——**B:** May 20, 1943, LaPorte, IN, *VP of RE Admin.*, Rhode Island Hosp. Trust Nat. Bank, Operations Div.; **PRIM RE ACT:** Consultant, Banker, Lender, Property Manager; **PREV EMPLOY:** Shell Oil Co., Indus. Nat. Bank of RI; **PROFL AFFIL & HONORS:** Past Pres. of BOMA, currently a Dir., VP & Dir. of DPIA, Mayor Special Adv. Comm. on Downtown Revitalization, Who's Who in Coll. And Univ.; **EDUC:** BS, 1966, Mktg., Univ. of Bridgeport; **GRAD EDUC:** MBA, 1979, Fin., Bryant Coll.; **EDUC HONORS:** Dean's List, Grad. with Honors; **OTHER ACT & HONORS:** Pres. of Slacks Reservoir Assn.; **HOME ADD:** 88 Ruff Stone Rd., Greenville, RI 02828, (401)949-1113; **BUS ADD:** One Hosp. Trust Pl., Providence, RI 02903, (401)278-8195.

WEBSTER, R.D.——*SIR, Asst. VP RE*, United Refining Co.; **PRIM RE ACT:** Property Manager; **BUS ADD:** PO Box 780, Warren, PA 16365, (814)723-1500.*

WEBSTER, Robert E.——**B:** Nov. 11, 1932, Exeter, NH, *Pres.*, Bayfield Co., Inc., Div. of Channel Bldg. Co., Inc.; **PRIM RE ACT:** Developer, Builder; **SERVICES:** Design-Build; Const.; Comml.-Indust. RE Devel.; **PREV EMPLOY:** Pres. Channel Bldg. Co., Inc.; **PROFL AFFIL & HONORS:** Assoc. Gen. Contractors; Assoc. Builders & Contractors; Metal Building Dealers Assn.; **EDUC:** BCE, Univ. of NH; **MIL SERV:** US Army (Engr.), Lt.; **HOME ADD:** 60 Woodcrest Drive, N. Andover, MA 01810, (617)681-0444; **BUS ADD:** Musgrove Bldg., Elm Sw., Andover, MA 01810, (617)475-1977.

WECHSLER, Max——**B:** Nov. 4, 1906, NY, NY, *Part.*, Wechsler Grasso Menziuso P.C.; **PRIM RE ACT:** Architect; **PROFL AFFIL & HONORS:** AIA; NY Soc. of Architects; Mayor's Panel of Architects; NY RE Bd., Architect of Yr. Award (1963 - 1964) Assn. of RE Synd.; Former Pres. RE Square Club; **GRAD EDUC:** 1931, Arch., Columbia Univ.; **OTHER ACT & HONORS:** Designer of 200 Central Park S.-Mentioned in NY Times as one of the ten best designed bldgs. since WWII - 9/20/79; **HOME ADD:** 7 Lexington Ave., New York, NY 10010, (212)533-3097; **BUS ADD:** 115 E 23rd St., New York, NY 10010, (212)254-4910.

WECHSLER, Michael J.——**B:** July 6, 1939, Brooklyn, NY, *Sr. VP*, Chemical Bank, RE Div.; **PRIM RE ACT:** Banker, Lender; **SERVICES:** Construction Loans, Interim Mort. Loans, Mort. Warehousing; **REP CLIENTS:** Owner/Investors, Builders, Devel. Property Mgrs., of Comml. & Multifamily Resid. Prop., Mort. Bankers; **PROFL AFFIL & HONORS:** Dir. (1974-1978), Chmn. of Mort. Comm. (1980-); Community Preservation Corp. of the City of NY; RE Bd. of NY; MBA of NY; Intl. Council of Shoppings Ctrs.; Member of Mort. Comm.; RE Bd. of NY; Amer. Bankers Assn.; ULI; RE Lodge Brai Brith; Natl. Realty Comm.; **EDUC:** BS, 1961, Civil Engrg., MIT; **GRAD EDUC:** MBA, 1963, Harvard Bus. Sch.; **MIL SERV:** US Army; **BUS ADD:** 633 3rd Ave., New York, NY 10017, (212)878-7634.

WECHSLER, Steven R.——**B:** July 21, 1949, NY, *Partner*, Tishman Speyer Properties; **PRIM RE ACT:** Developer, Builder, Owner/Investor; **PREV EMPLOY:** VP, Tishman Realty & Const. Co., Inc., 1972-1977; **PROFL AFFIL & HONORS:** Bd. of Dirs., Young Mens RE Assn.; Lecturer, NY Univ. RE Inst.; **EDUC:** BA, 1970, Econ., State Univ. NY at Buffalo; **GRAD EDUC:** MBA, 1972, Fin., Columbia Univ.; **EDUC HONORS:** CC Furnas Scholarship (Excellence Scholarship/Athletics); **HOME ADD:** 360 E. 72nd St., New York, NY 10021, (212)249-4955; **BUS ADD:** 666 5th Ave., New York, NY 10019, (212)957-5421.

WEDEMEYER, Eric——**B:** Nov. 16, 1942, NY, *Pres.*, Timberland Properties, Inc., Lake Tunis Props., Inc.; **PRIM RE ACT:** Broker, Consultant, Appraiser, Developer, Owner/Investor, Property Manager; **SERVICES:** Vacant Land devel., prop. mgmt., prop. valuation; **REP CLIENTS:** Corp. or indiv. investors in multi-dwelling or recreation props.; **EDUC:** BA, 1964, Poli. Sci., Boston Univ.; **GRAD EDUC:** MBA, 1967, Bus. Mgmt., Adelphi Univ.; **OTHER ACT & HONORS:** Pres. DE Cty. C of C VP, Andes C of C, Former Bd. of Dir.,Member, DE Cty. Council on the Arts, Catskill Symphony Orchestra VP. Pres. ANDES Soc. for Hitory & Culture.; **HOME ADD:** Horseshoe Valley, Andes, NY 13731, (914)676-4656; **BUS ADD:** Box 188, Andes, NY 13731, (914)676-4600.

WEDGE, Ken——**B:** Oct. 26, 1949, Waukegan, IL, *Sales Assoc.*, Statewide RE of the Copper Country; **PRIM RE ACT:** Appraiser; **SERVICES:** Sales, appraisals, rental mgmt., consultation; **PROFL AFFIL & HONORS:** Upper Peninsular Bd. of Realtors; State of MI Assessor's Bd., Realtor, Level II Assessor; **MIL SERV:** US Army; Cpl.; **HOME ADD:** Rt. 1, Box 94, Lake Linden, MI 49945, (906)296-6600; **BUS ADD:** 900 S. Lincoln, Hancock, MI 49930, (906)482-6030.

WEED, Haze H.L.——**B:** Oct. 23, 1951, Evanston, IL, *RM*, Weed and Assoc.; **PRIM RE ACT:** Appraiser; **SERVICES:** RE appraisal reports; **REP CLIENTS:** Equitable Relocation, Relocation Realty Ser., Van Relco, Home Purchase Corp.; **PREV EMPLOY:** RE salesman and broker 1973-1977; **PROFL AFFIL & HONORS:** AIREA, RM; **EDUC:** BA, 1073, Reed Coll.; **HOME ADD:** PO Box 2526, Gearhart, OR 97138, (503)738-7800; **BUS ADD:** 924 Little Beach, PO Box 2526, Gearhart, OR 97138, (503)738-7800.

WEED, Peter B.——**B:** Dec. 10, 1946, Abington, PA, *VP*, Philadelphia Investment Corp., RE Equities; **PRIM RE ACT:** Developer, Owner/Investor; **SERVICES:** Project financing, devel. mgmt.; **REP CLIENTS:** Private devels., corporate clients/tenants, bldg. owners; **PREV EMPLOY:** Prudential Ins. Co., 1975-1978; **PROFL AFFIL & HONORS:** ULI; Nat. Assn. of Office & Indus. Parks; BOMA; **EDUC:** BA, 1969, Hist./Econ., Denison Univ.; **GRAD EDUC:** MBA/MCP, 1975, RE Fin./Devel. Mgmt., Wharton Grad. School, Univ. of PA; **EDUC HONORS:** Hist. Hon.; **MIL SERV:** USN Res.; Lcdr.; 1969 to present; **HOME ADD:** 7511 Brookfield Rd., Melrose Park, PA 19126, (215)635-7039; **BUS ADD:** Three Parkway, Suite 1220, Pennwalt Bldg., Philadelphia, PA 19102, (215)241-2875.

WEEKES, Eugene D.——**B:** Feb. 11, 1933, Bismarck, ND, *Pres.*, Mid-Western Real Estate; **PRIM RE ACT:** Broker, Appraiser; **SERVICES:** The appraisal, mgmt. and sale of RE; **REP CLIENTS:** Indiv. and corp.; **PREV EMPLOY:** Have been in this bus. for 18 years, prior to that I was employed by the State Land Dept. of the State of ND; **PROFL AFFIL & HONORS:** Local, State and NAR, Farm and Land Inst. and NAIFA, (IFAS) Sr. designation with IFA, (AFLM) a credited farm and land member. Farm & Land Broker of the year 1977 ND and SD; **OTHER ACT & HONORS:** C of C, Kiwanis, United Church of Christ, Advisory Bd. Salvation Army and Child Evangelism; **HOME ADD:** 1817 Marian Dr., Bismarck, ND 58501, (701)223-8347; **BUS ADD:** 1929 N. Kavaney Dr., Box 1201, Bismarck, ND 58502, (701)255-4570.

WEEKS, James B.——**B:** June 23, 1941, Sampson Cty., NC, *Partner*, Edwards, Greeson, Weeks & Turner; **PRIM RE ACT:** Attorney; **SERVICES:** Gen. practice and RE; **PREV EMPLOY:** Amer. Hospital Supply Corp., Chicago, IL, 1963-1973; **PROFL AFFIL & HONORS:** ABA; ATLA; NCATLA; NC Bar Assn., Real Prop. Sect.; **EDUC:** AB, 1963, Pol. Sci., Univ. of NC, Chapel Hill; **GRAD EDUC:** JD, 1976, Univ. of NC, Chapel Hill; **HOME ADD:** 3405 Londonderry Dr., Greensboro, NC 27410, (919)288-6718; **BUS ADD:** POB 448, Greensboro, NC 27402, (919)373-8764.

WEEMS, F. Carrington——**B:** July 3, 1928, *Pres.*, Weems & Co., Inc.; **PRIM RE ACT:** Broker, Consultant, Engineer, Developer, Lender, Owner/Investor, Property Manager, Syndicator; **PREV EMPLOY:** Lockwood, Andrews & Newman, Inc., Engr., Oil Ctr., Tool Co., Reel Roller Bit; **PROFL AFFIL & HONORS:** TX Assn of Realtors, Nat. Assn. of RE Brokers, Houston Bd. of Realtors; **EDUC:** BSME, 1952, Mech. Engrg., Aerospace, Univ. of CO; **OTHER ACT & HONORS:** River Oaks Ctry Club., The Bayou Club, Ramada Club, Mill Reef Club, Antigua Brit. W. Indies, TX Corinthian Yacht Club, Houston C of C; **HOME ADD:** 919 Kirby Dr., Houston, TX 77019, (713)522-

2935; **BUS ADD:** 2 Houston Ctr., Suite 3405, Houston, TX 77002, 658-0442.

WEHLE, John L., Jr.——*VP Fin. Plng.*, Genesee Brewing Co., Inc.; **PRIM RE ACT:** Property Manager; **BUS ADD:** PO Box 762, Rochester, NY 14603, (716)546-1030.*

WEHLING, Roger Allan——**B:** Feb. 20, 1942, San Diego, CA, *Dir. of Planning and Research*, City of Tampa, FL, Bureau of City Planning; **OTHER RE ACT:** Urban Planning; **SERVICES:** Land use planning and Community Redevel.; **PROFL AFFIL & HONORS:** Amer. Planning Assn., Urban & Rgnl. Information Systems Assn., FL Planning and Zoning Assn.; **EDUC:** BA, 1969, Social Sci., Univ. of S. FL; **GRAD EDUC:** MA, 1972, Urban Geography, Univ. of FL; **MIL SERV:** USNG, FL, Capt.; **OTHER ACT & HONORS:** FL Community Conservation Advisory Comm., Advisory Bd. of Community Design Ctr., Pres. of Girls Clubs of Tampa, Bd. of Dir. of FL Soc. of Geographers; **HOME ADD:** 6809 Dover Ct., Tampa, FL 33614, (813)884-7710; **BUS ADD:** 306 E. Jackson St., 8E, Tampa, FL 33602, (813)223-8485.

WEHRING, Wallace L.——**B:** Nov. 23, 1937, Corpus Christi, TX, *Pres.*, Wehring Properites, Inc.; **PRIM RE ACT:** Broker, Appraiser, Developer, Builder; **SERVICES:** Build, develop, broker, comml. projects; **PREV EMPLOY:** HBL Construction Co. 1962-68; **PROFL AFFIL & HONORS:** NAR, TAR, Ft. Bend Bd. of Realtors; **EDUC:** BA, 1960, Texas A & M; **MIL SERV:** US Army, Capt., 1960-62; **OTHER ACT & HONORS:** Dir. Central Appraisal Dist. 1980-82; Rosenberg Planning Comm.; C of C; **BUS ADD:** PO Box 64, Rosenberg, TX 77471, (713)342-3743.

WEIDA, Richard P.——**B:** Mar. 12, 1943, Hellertown, PA, *Tax Mgr.*, Avatar Holdings, Inc.; **PRIM RE ACT:** Owner/Investor; **OTHER RE ACT:** Tax Mgr.; **SERVICES:** Tax Mgmt. and Tax Advice; **PREV EMPLOY:** Tax Mgr., GAC Corp.; **PROFL AFFIL & HONORS:** Tax Execs. Inst., Inc., Past Pres. 1980-81 (S. FL Chap.); **EDUC:** Assoc. in Sci., 1964, Acctg. & Bus. Admin., Bethlehem Bus. Coll.; AA, 1978, Bus., Miami Dade Community Coll.; **MIL SERV:** US Army Nat. Guard, Sp-5, Expert Rifleman; **OTHER ACT & HONORS:** Beta Gamma Sigma Honor Soc.; **HOME ADD:** 312 Aledo Ave., Coral Gables, FL 33134, (305)446-4047; **BUS ADD:** 201 Alhambra Cir., Coral Gables, FL 33134, (305)442-7471.

WEIDEMAN, Donald James——**B:** Dec. 9, 1939, Edmonton, Can., *Prof.*, Univ. of AB, Faculty of Extension; **PRIM RE ACT:** Consultant, Developer, Owner/Investor, Instructor, Syndicator; **SERVICES:** Investment counseling, devel. & synd. of income props.; **REP CLIENTS:** Indiv. investors; **PREV EMPLOY:** Gt. West Life, Prop. Investments, 1966-69; **PROFL AFFIL & HONORS:** Amer. RE & Urban Econ. Assn.; **EDUC:** B.Comm., 1962, Mgmt., Univ. of AB; **GRAD EDUC:** MBA, 1970, Mgmt. & Fin., Univ. of W. Ont.; **OTHER ACT & HONORS:** Candidate for PhD in Bus. Admin., Land Econ. and Urban Affairs, GA State Univ.; **HOME ADD:** 12, 10931 83 St., Edmonton, AB, Can., (403)424-9058; **BUS ADD:** Corbett Hall, Univ. of AB, Edmonton, AB, Canada, (403)432-5060.

WEIDENFELD, Harvey M.——**B:** Nov. 6, 1936, NYC, *Pres.*, Sonnenblick Goldman SE Corp.; **PRIM RE ACT:** Broker; **OTHER RE ACT:** Comml. mort. banker; **SERVICES:** Constr., perman. & equity fin., joint ventures; **REP CLIENTS:** Builders, devels.; **PROFL AFFIL & HONORS:** NAIOP, Treas. S FL Chapt. Mort. Bankers Assn., Indus. Assn. of Dade Cty.; **EDUC:** BS, 1958, RE, Wharton Sch. of Fin. & Commerce, Univ. of PA; **MIL SERV:** USA Res., MSgt.; **HOME ADD:** 1540 NE 105th St., Miami Shores, FL 33153; **BUS ADD:** 614 Dupont Plaza Ctr., Miami, FL 33131, (305)358-5522.

WEIDIG, Mrs. Peter——**B:** June 21, 1920, Toledo, OH, *Realtor, Assoc.*, Heritage Real Estate & Development Co., Inc.; **OTHER RE ACT:** Sales; **PREV EMPLOY:** Teacher 13 yrs.; **EDUC:** BS, 1942, Educ., OH State; **EDUC HONORS:** Pi Lambda Theta; **OTHER ACT & HONORS:** Kappa Kappa Gamma; **HOME ADD:** 55 North 4th St., Cocoa Beach, FL 32931, (305)783-5723; **BUS ADD:** 130 Canaveral Pl., Cocoa Beach, FL 32931, (305)783 1200.

WEIL, Andrew L.——**B:** July 19, 1920, Pittsburgh, PA, *Atty. At Law*, Rose, Schmidt, Dixon and Hasley, RE; **PRIM RE ACT:** Attorney; **SERVICES:** Legal serv.; **PREV EMPLOY:** ABA, PA Bar Assn., Allegheny Cty. Bar Assn.; **EDUC:** BA, 1943, Public and Intl. Affairs, Princeton Univ.; **GRAD EDUC:** JD, 1949, Law, Univ. of Pittsburgh; **EDUC HONORS:** Cum Laude, Law Review; **MIL SERV:** US Army, Lt. Col., Bronze Star, Purple Heart, Pres. Citation (US), Croix de guerre (Fr.), Order of Wilhelm (Netherlands); **OTHER ACT & HONORS:** Special Asst. Atty. Gen. - Com. of PA, Pittsburgh Athletic Assn., Harvard Yale Princeton Club, Fox Chapel Racquet Club, Who's Who in Amer. Law, Who's Who in the E.; **HOME ADD:** 108 White Gate Rd., Pittsburgh, PA 15238, (412)828-9345; **BUS ADD:** 900 Oliver Bldg., Pittsburgh, PA 15222, (412)434-8690.

WEIL, Louis——*VP Corp. Dev.*, Gannett Co., Inc.; **PRIM RE ACT:** Property Manager; **BUS ADD:** Lincoln Tower, Rochester, NY 14614, (716)546-8600.*

WEIL, Mark R.——*Dir. Fac. & RE*, Crane Co.; **PRIM RE ACT:** Property Manager; **BUS ADD:** 300 Park Ave., New York, NY 10022, (212)980-7254.*

WEIL, S. Douglas——**B:** Apr. 21, 1936, Cleveland, OH, *Pres.*, Paine Webber Prop., Inc.; **OTHER RE ACT:** Asset Mgr./Investment Advisor; **SERVICES:** Manage Public RE Funds; Provide Investment Advice; **PREV EMPLOY:** Sr. VP, Prop. Capital Advisors, Boston, MA; Property Capital Trust Mgr., RE Investment, Miller & Co.; Asst. VP, Webb & Knapp; **PROFL AFFIL & HONORS:** Boston RE Bd., International Council of Shopping Centers; **EDUC:** BA, 1958, Pol., Princeton Univ.; **GRAD EDUC:** MBA, 1960, Fin., Harvard Bus. School; **HOME ADD:** 22 Cartwright Rd., Wellesley, MA 02181, (617)237-4928; **BUS ADD:** 100 Federal St., Boston, MA 02101, (617)423-8150.

WEILER, Queed H.——**B:** Mar. 18, 1929, Salt Lake City, UT, *VP - Gen. Mgr.*, A.T.D. Property Management, Inc., Akerlow Thomas Dyer, Inc.; **PRIM RE ACT:** Developer, Owner/Investor, Property Manager; **OTHER RE ACT:** Leasing Agent; **SERVICES:** Leasing comml. bldgs., contract prop. mgmt.; **REP CLIENTS:** Indiv. and instnl. investors and tenants involved with comml. props.; **PREV EMPLOY:** 28 years with Prudential Fed. Savings; **PROFL AFFIL & HONORS:** Salt Lake Bd. of Realtors, BOMA; **EDUC:** 1952, Banking & Fin., Univ. of UT; **GRAD EDUC:** 1961, S&L, Univ. of WA School for Exec. Devel.; **MIL SERV:** US Army, 1st Lt.; **OTHER ACT & HONORS:** Optimists Club, Willow Creek Ctry. Club; **HOME ADD:** 2710 Comanche Dr., Salt Lake City, UT, (801)582-2824; **BUS ADD:** 68 So. Main, St 300, Salt Lake City, UT 84101, (801)521-0107.

WEIMER, Arthur M.——**B:** May 19, 1909, Park City, IL, *Pres.*, Weimer Business Advisory Service, Inc.; **PRIM RE ACT:** Consultant; **SERVICES:** Econ. & govt. counseling, education & publishing; **REP CLIENTS:** US League of Savings Assns., Homer Hoyt Inst., Unifirst Federal Savings & Loan; **PREV EMPLOY:** Dean & Prof. Grad. School of Bus., Indiana Univ.; **PROFL AFFIL & HONORS:** Am-Soc. of RE Counselors, Amer. RE & Urban Econ. Assn., MAI, SRA, CRE; **EDUC:** BA, 1929, Econ., Beloit Coll.; **GRAD EDUC:** AM, PhD, 1931, 1934, Econ., Univ. of Chicago; **EDUC HONORS:** Grad. with Honors; **MIL SERV:** US Army, Maj.; **OTHER ACT & HONORS:** Nat. Pres. Am. Assembly of Collegiate Schools of Bus.; Beta Gamma Sibma, Am. Fin. Assn.; **HOME ADD:** PO Box 183, Bloomington, IN 47402, (812)339-9107; **BUS ADD:** PO Box 183, Bloomington, IN 47402, (812)339-6970.

WEIMING, Lu——*Exec. Dir.*, Lowertown Redev. Corp.; **OTHER RE ACT:** Non-profit devel. corp.; **SERVICES:** Grp. fin., design asst., mktg.; **PREV EMPLOY:** Chief of Environmental Design, City of Minneapolis Dir. of Urban Design, City of Dallas; Consultant to HUD; **PROFL AFFIL & HONORS:** Inst. for Urban Design, (Bd. member), Amer. Planning Assn., Bd. of Preservation Action, MBAA, HUD Urban Design Awards (1970, 1974), Amer. Planning Assn. (1979); **EDUC:** BS, 1952, Cheng-Kung Univ., Taiwan, CHINA; **GRAD EDUC:** MCE, 1954, Civil Engrg., Univ. of NC; Master of Rgnl. Planning, 1956, Univ. of MN; **OTHER ACT & HONORS:** Member of Nat. Design Arts Policy Panel, NEA (1978 to present), Founder, MN Chinese Amer. Assn.; **HOME ADD:** 221 Westwood Dr. N., Minneapolis, MN 55422, (612)374-9120; **BUS ADD:** 400 Sibley St., St. Paul, MN 55101, (612)227-9131.

WEINBAUM, Mark J.——**B:** Apr. 13, 1945, Boston, MA, *Regional VP*, Integrated Resources, Inc.; **PRIM RE ACT:** Syndicator; **SERVICES:** Arrangement of credit sale/lease backs; **PREV EMPLOY:** Drexel Burnham Lambert Realty, Inc. 1977-78; Sonnenblick-Goldman Advisory Corp., 1972-1978; **PROFL AFFIL & HONORS:** Young Mort. Bankers Assn.; **EDUC:** BA, 1967, Eco./Govt., Columbia Coll.; **GRAD EDUC:** MBA, 1969, Fin., Columbia Grad. School of Bus.; **HOME ADD:** 390 West End Ave., New York, NY 10024, (212)873-1893; **BUS ADD:** 666 Third Ave., New York, NY 10017, (212)878-9209.

WEINBERG, Arnold——**B:** June 15, 1942, Chicago, IL, *Part.*, Marks, Katz, Randall, Weinberg & Blatt; **PRIM RE ACT:** Real Estate Publisher; **REP CLIENTS:** Bennett & Kahnweiler Assocs., BA Mort. & Intl. Realty Corp., Saxon Paint & Home Care Ctrs., Inc.; **PROFL AFFIL & HONORS:** IL Bar Assn., Chicago Bar Assn.; **EDUC:** BS, 1964, Univ. of IL; **GRAD EDUC:** JD, 1967, Northwestern Univ.; **EDUC HONORS:** Order of the Coif; **HOME ADD:** 696 Strawberry

Hill, Glencoe, IL 60022, (312)835-3906; **BUS ADD:** Suite 1710, 208 S. LaSalle St., Chicago, IL 60604, (312)782-4912.

WEINBERG, Norman——**B:** March 19, 1924, Cleveland, OH, *Dir.*, New York Univ., Real Estate Inst.; **OTHER RE ACT:** Dir. of Real Estate Inst.; **PREV EMPLOY:** Sr. Ed. RER; **PROFL AFFIL & HONORS:** Member Bd. of Dir. BOMA Intl., Prof. of RE & Banking; **EDUC:** BA, 1947, Econ., Western Res.; **GRAD EDUC:** MA, 1949, Econ., Columbia Univ.; M. Phil., 1968, Econ., Columbia Univ.; **EDUC HONORS:** Summa Cum Laude; **MIL SERV:** US Air Force Lt.; **OTHER ACT & HONORS:** Author, "New York Guide to Real Estate Licensing Examinations" Wiley pub.; **BUS ADD:** New York Univ. 11W 42nd St., New York, NY 10036, (212)790-1300.

WEINBERG, Robert F.——**B:** Sept. 20, 1929, NYC, NY, *Chmn. of the Bd.*, Robert Martin Co.; **PRIM RE ACT:** Engineer, Banker, Developer, Builder, Owner/Investor, Property Manager; **SERVICES:** RE Devel. & constr.; **REP CLIENTS:** Owner/builders; **PROFL AFFIL & HONORS:** V. Chmn. Ninth Fed. S&L Assn.; Past Pres. & Chmn. Builders Inst. of Westchester & Putnam Ctys.; Co-Chmn. Joint Westchester Constr. Indus., Labor/Mgmt. Bd.; V. Chmn. Mid-Hudson Const. Users Council; Dir. Investment Builders Assn.; Member Cty. Bd. of Legislators Spec. Advisory Comm. on Housing Policy, Member NY Const. Users Council Policy Comm., Atty. at Law, PE; **EDUC:** BME, 1949, NY Univ.; **GRAD EDUC:** MS, 1950, Bldg., Engrg., Const., MIT; LLB, 1953, Brooklyn Law Sch.; JD, 1961, Law, Brooklyn Law Sch.; **OTHER ACT & HONORS:** Chmn. Assoc. YM-YWHA's of Gr. NY, Chmn. Fed. of Jewish Philanthorpies/United Jewish Appeal, Westchester RE & Bldrs. Div.; Tr., Fed. of Jewish Philanthropies; Dir. The United Way of Westchester; **HOME ADD:** 781 Fifth Ave., New York, NY 10022; **BUS ADD:** 101 Exec. Blvd., Elmsford, NY 10523, (914)592-4800.

WEINBERG, Robert L.——**B:** May 31, 1923, Baltimore, MD, *Part.*, Weinberg & Green; **PRIM RE ACT:** Attorney; **SERVICES:** Legal services; **REP CLIENTS:** Investors, users & lenders for comml. & indus. props.; **PROFL AFFIL & HONORS:** Amer. & MD Bar Assns., Intl. Coun. of Shopping Ctrs., MD Mort. Bankers; MD Chamber of Commerce; **EDUC:** BS, 1952, Bus. Admin., Johns Hopkins Univ.; **GRAD EDUC:** JD, 1949, Univ. of MD Law Sch.; **MIL SERV:** US, Sig. Intell, ETO Sgt.; **OTHER ACT & HONORS:** Asst. Atty. Gen (MD), 1953, MD C of C, United Way of Central MD; **BUS ADD:** 100 S. Charles St., Baltimore, MD 21201, (301)332-8700.

WEINBERGER, Edward——**B:** Sept. 18, 1927, Akron, OH, *Edward Weinberger Enterprises*; **PRIM RE ACT:** Broker, Developer, Builder; **EDUC:** BS, 1948, Bus., Kent State; **MIL SERV:** US Navy, Seaman; **HOME ADD:** 29 Chadbourne Dr., Hudson, OH; **BUS ADD:** 15 Hitterberry Blvd., Hudson, OH 44236, (216)650-4001.

WEINBERGER, Leo——**B:** Sept. 21, 1898, Pocahontas, VA, *Of Counsel*, Smith & Schnacke; **PRIM RE ACT:** Attorney; **SERVICES:** RE and probate law; **REP CLIENTS:** Firm clients too numerous to list; **PREV EMPLOY:** Weinberger, Grad. Wolf & Hoy, Attys. at Law; **PROFL AFFIL & HONORS:** Cincinnati Bar Assn.; Cincinnati Lawyers Club; OH Bar Assn.; ABA OH Land Title Assn.; **EDUC:** AB, 1917, Univ. of Cincinnati; **GRAD EDUC:** JD, 1920, Univ. of Cincinnati; **EDUC HONORS:** Order of the Coif; **OTHER ACT & HONORS:** Assoc. Editor Addams & Hosford OH Probate Practice; 6th Edition; Assoc. Editor, Couse's OH Form Book, 5th Edition; Two Awards of Merit OH Bar Legal Center Inst.; Past Pres. OH Land Title Assn.; Past Pres. Greater Cincinnati Savings and Loan Assn.; **HOME ADD:** 3802 Williamsburg Rd., Cincinnati, OH 45215, (513)821-4845; **BUS ADD:** 2900 DuBois Tower, 511 Walnut St., Cincinnati, OH 45202, (513)352-6565.

WEINBERGER, Michael Joseph——**B:** Mar. 12, 1935, NY, NY, *Sr. VP*, Smith, Barney Real Estate Corp.; **PRIM RE ACT:** Consultant, Developer, Property Manager; **SERVICES:** Investment counseling, mgmt.,& devel. of income producing props.; **PROFL AFFIL & HONORS:** IREM, RE Bd. of NY, Intl. Council of Shopping Ctrs., CPM; **EDUC:** BS, 1956, Bus. Admin., Wilkes Coll., PA; **MIL SERV:** USN; **HOME ADD:** 36 Wynmor Rd., Scarsdale, NY 10583, (914)723-4569; **BUS ADD:** 1345 Ave. of the Americas, New York, NY 10105, (212)399-6191.

WEINER, Barry A.——**B:** Nov. 13, 1949, Chicago, IL, *Pres.*, The Weiner Companies; **PRIM RE ACT:** Broker, Consultant, Developer, Owner/Investor, Instructor, Property Manager, Insuror, Syndicator; **SERVICES:** Full RE serv.; **REP CLIENTS:** Indiv. and inst. investors in income producing props.; **PROFL AFFIL & HONORS:** NAR, RE Securities and Synd. Institute, RNMI, CCIM, CRS, GRI; **EDUC:** Univ. of IL; **OTHER ACT & HONORS:** Various Corporate Bds.; **HOME ADD:** 7020 Dark Horse, Colorado Springs, CO 80919, (303)598-5106; **BUS ADD:** 3919 Palmer Park Blvd., Colorado Springs, CO 80907, (303)597-3300.

WEINER, Barry R.——**B:** Feb. 9, 1941, Brooklyn, NY, *Pres.*, D.B.G. Prop. Corp.; **PRIM RE ACT:** Broker, Attorney, Developer, Owner/Investor, Property Manager, Syndicator; **PREV EMPLOY:** Sr. Partner, Fruitbine, Weiner, Harwin & Herman, P.C.; **PROFL AFFIL & HONORS:** NY State Bar Assn.; Nassau Cty. Bar Assn., JD Cum Laude; **EDUC:** BA, 1962, Art Conc., Eng. Lit., Hofstra Univ.; **GRAD EDUC:** JD, 1967, Law, New England Sch. of Law., Boston, MA; **EDUC HONORS:** Cum Laude, Law Review; **HOME ADD:** 10 E. End Ave., New York, NY 10021; **BUS ADD:** 850 Third Ave., New York, NY 10022, (212)486-1330.

WEINER, David M.——**B:** June 29, 1936, Rock Island, IL, *Pres.*, David M. Weiner & Assoc. Inc.; **PRIM RE ACT:** Broker, Developer, Property Manager, Owner/Investor; **SERVICES:** Full RE; **REP CLIENTS:** Corp., Trust, Indiv., Investor; **PROFL AFFIL & HONORS:** NAR; Rock Island Cty. Bd. of Realtors, IL Assn. of Realtors, Realtor of the yr. - Rock Island Cty. Bd. 1977; **EDUC:** AB, 1958, Econ., Princeton Univ., Princeton, NJ; **GRAD EDUC:** Mktg., Northwestern Grad. Bus. School; **EDUC HONORS:** Cum Laude, Hon. Thesis; **MIL SERV:** USN, Lt. Jg.; **OTHER ACT & HONORS:** Dist. VP IL Assn. of Realtors 1980-81, Pres. - RI County Bd. of Realtors - 1976-77, C of C; **HOME ADD:** 3511 15th St. Ct., Rock Island, IL 61202, (309)786-4002; **BUS ADD:** 1570 Blackhawk Rd., Moline, IL 61265, (309)797-6090.

WEINER, Edward A.——**B:** Aug. 3, 1940, San Francisco, CA, *Partner*, Pillsbury, Madison & Sutro; **PRIM RE ACT:** Attorney; **PROFL AFFIL & HONORS:** Member CA Bar, AICPA, CA RE Broker; **EDUC:** BS, 1962, Bus. Admin., Univ. CA, Berkeley; **GRAD EDUC:** JD, 1965, Univ. of CA, Hastings Coll.; **EDUC HONORS:** Order of the Coif; Law Review; **MIL SERV:** US Army, 1966-1969, Capt., NDSM, ACM; **BUS ADD:** 225 Bush St., PO Box 7880, San Francisco, CA 94120, (415)983-1071.

WEINER, Joshua T.——**B:** Mar. 24, 1949, E Grand Rapids, MI, *Owner*, Meyer C. Weiner Co.; **PRIM RE ACT:** Broker, Developer, Builder, Owner/Investor, Property Manager; **OTHER RE ACT:** Investment Advisor; **SERVICES:** Land sales and acquisition, leasing, mgmt., investment; **REP CLIENTS:** Sears, J.C. Penney, F.W. Woolworth, Jewel Co's., Dayton Hudson Corp.; **PREV EMPLOY:** Self-employed partnership in the Meyer C. Weiner Co. since grad. from the Univ. of MI in 1971; **PROFL AFFIL & HONORS:** Intl. Council of Shoppng Ctrs., Editorial Bd. of Nat. Mall Monitor, Kalamazoo C of C, Twin Cities C of C, Licensed RE broker in MI and IL; **EDUC:** BA, 1971, Poli. Sci. and Public Address, Univ. of MI; **EDUC HONORS:** Dean's List; **OTHER ACT & HONORS:** B'nai B'rith, Congregation of Moses, Centre Court Tennis Club, Kalamazoo Jewish Fed.; **HOME ADD:** 5307 Woodmont, Kalamazoo, MI 49001; **BUS ADD:** 200 Mall Dr., PO Box 406, Portage, MI 49081, (616)323-2441.

WEINER, Mark E.——**B:** Dec. 5, 1952, Philadelphia, PA, *CEO*, Leon N. Weiner Associates Inc.; **PRIM RE ACT:** Developer, Property Manager, Syndicator; **SERVICES:** Synd. of sec. & housing, devel. resid. sub. housing, prop. mgmt.; **REP CLIENTS:** Indiv. investors, instnl. investors; **PROFL AFFIL & HONORS:** Nat. Assn. of Home Builders; **EDUC:** BA, 1974, Pre Med, Univ. of PA; **EDUC HONORS:** Phi Beta Kappa; **HOME ADD:** 15 Martine Ct., Newark, DE 19711, (302)368-4399; **BUS ADD:** Edgemart Bldg., 4 Denny Rd., Wilmington, DE 19809, (302)764-9430.

WEINER, Meyer C.——**B:** July 3, 1916, Grand Rapids, MI, Meyer C. Weiner Co.; **PRIM RE ACT:** Developer, Builder; **OTHER RE ACT:** Structure co-ventures on prop. we develop/build; **SERVICES:** Land Acquisition; leasing; financing; const.; mgmt.; **REP CLIENTS:** Nat. and local retailers of all types; **PREV EMPLOY:** Have been involved in comml. RE dev. since 1948; **PROFL AFFIL & HONORS:** ICSC, Have served as State Dir. of ICSC; **EDUC:** 1933-36, Lit. and Law, Univ. of MI; **OTHER ACT & HONORS:** Past Pres. - B'nai B'rith; Past Dir. of Corp. & have been a consultant in comml. RE dev., financing and funding, Have dev. over $250,000,000 in RE Dev.; **HOME ADD:** 4040 Greenleaf Cir., Kalamazoo, MI 49008, (616)375-7100; **BUS ADD:** 200 Mall Dr., Portage, MI 49081, (616)323-2441.

WEINER, Richard N.——**B:** Dec. 2, 1941, Philadelphia, PA, *Partner*, Rawle & Henderson; **PRIM RE ACT:** Instructor, Owner/Investor; **SERVICES:** Legal representation in acquisition, sale, fin., synd., const. and leasing; **REP CLIENTS:** Devel., prop. mgrs., investors, contractors and owners of comml., resid. and indus. RE; **PROFL AFFIL & HONORS:** Amer., PA and Philadelphia Bar Assns., Real Prop. and corp. sects.; **EDUC:** BS, 1963, Econ. and Math, MIT; **GRAD EDUC:** JD, 1966, Univ. of PA Law School; **EDUC HONORS:** cum laude; **MIL SERV:** US Army, Sgt. 1966-72; **OTHER ACT & HONORS:** Chief Counsel, PA Securities Commn. 1971-73, Chmn., Sr. Citizen

Judicare Project of Philadelphia 1978-present, Treas., Philadelphia Bar Assn. 1978-80; **HOME ADD:** 344 Thorpe Rd., Jenkintown, PA 19046, (215)885-0812; **BUS ADD:** 211 S. Broad St. 16th Fl., Philadelphia, PA 19107, (215)875-4111.

WEINER, Vic, CRS, GRI——**B:** Feb. 12, 1939, Brooklyn, NY, *Pres.*, Trans-World Realty Corp./Better Homes & Gardens; **PRIM RE ACT:** Broker, Consultant, Appraiser, Lender, Instructor, Property Manager, Syndicator; **OTHER RE ACT:** Pre-lic. school, sales training school; **SERVICES:** PM, estate & investment counseling, 2nd mort.; **REP CLIENTS:** RE investors, syndicators; **PROFL AFFIL & HONORS:** CRS; GRI; Pompano Bd. of Realtors;Honor Soc.; CRB Candidate; Member Bd. of Ed. Comm.; CCIM Candidate; RESSI Candidate; **EDUC:** BA, 1960, Biological Sci., Psychology, Bus. Mgmt., Univ. of Hartford, Hartford, CT; **GRAD EDUC:** MBA, 1972, Bus. Admin., CO State Univ.; **MIL SERV:** USAF, S/Sgt., Combat Badge, Airborne Wings, Combat Ranger; **OTHER ACT & HONORS:** Member FAR Speakers Bureau; **BUS ADD:** 2728 N. University Dr., Coral Springs, FL 33065, (305)752-6900.

WEINERT, Carl R.——**B:** June 27, 1923, E. Detroit, MI, *Pres.*, Bank of Commerce; **PRIM RE ACT:** Banker; **PROFL AFFIL & HONORS:** MI Bankers Assn., Robert Morris Assoc.; **EDUC:** Concordia Coll., River Forest, IL, Walsh Coll.; **GRAD EDUC:** 1957, Univ. of WI Sch. of Banking, Amer. Inst. of Banking; **EDUC HONORS:** Grad. Cert.; **MIL SERV:** USA-Inf., Sgt., Good conduct medal, 2 battle stars; **OTHER ACT & HONORS:** Detroit Athletic Club, Lutheran Frat. of Amer., German Amer. Cultural Club-Detroit; **HOME ADD:** 15658 Mok Ave., E. Detroit, MI 48021, (313)775-2347; **BUS ADD:** 11300 Jos. Campau Ave., Hamtramck, MI 48212, (313)366-3200.

WEINGARTNER, John J.——**B:** June 15, 1928, Wakonda, SD, *VP, Acquisitions*, Montgomery Realty Investors; **PRIM RE ACT:** Owner/ Investor; **PREV EMPLOY:** VP, First Union RE Investments, Cleveland, OH 1973-1980; VP, Affiliated Banks Bldg. Co. 1964-1973; **PROFL AFFIL & HONORS:** AIREA, MAI; **EDUC:** BS, 1950, Bus. and Ind. Engr., Univ. of SD; **GRAD EDUC:** Grad. - School of Mort. Banking, 1964, Northwestern Univ., Evanston, IL; **MIL SERV:** USAF, 1st Lt.; **OTHER ACT & HONORS:** Serra Club of Oakland, Life Member Colorado Springs C of C; **HOME ADD:** 618 Hove Court, Walnut Creek, CA 94598, (415)938-8029; **BUS ADD:** 155 Bovet Rd., San Mateo, CA 94402, (415)572-7111.

WEINGER, Stuart L.——**B:** June 20, 1929, Peekskill, NY, *Pres.*, WEBSCO, Inc., Comml. Indus., Office & Medical Office Complex; **PRIM RE ACT:** Broker, Consultant, Developer, Builder, Owner/Investor, Property Manager, Syndicator; **SERVICES:** RE consultancy, prop. mgmt., bus. advisors, ltd. partnership investments, up to ten million with less than 10 investors, comml. RE sales; **REP CLIENTS:** Indiv. and/or instnl. invest.; **PREV EMPLOY:** VP, B.J. McMorrow Investment Co.; VP, B.J. McMorrow and Assoc.; Exec. Dir. and VP, Marina Pt. Harbor; Gen. Mgr., Oschin, Glikbarg & Oschin; **PROFL AFFIL & HONORS:** Family Motor Home Assn., NAR, IREM, CPM; **EDUC:** 1948 - present, RE and fin., Utica, Div. of Syracuse, Orange Coast Coll., Santa Ana Coll., Amer. Inst. of Banking; **MIL SERV:** US Maritime SV8, WW II, Seaman 1st Cl.; USAF, Fin. dept., 1952-56, S/Sgt.; **OTHER ACT & HONORS:** BPOE, FA Masons, many civic and RE grps.; Past Pres. Exchange Club of Peekskill, NY;, C of C, Peekskill, NY; NY State Bd. of Govs.; NY State Exchange Clubs; **HOME ADD:** 13631 Gershon Pl., Santa Ana, CA 92705, (714)832-9226; **BUS ADD:** 1507 N. Tustin Ave. Suite A., Santa Ana, CA 92701, (714)835-0818.

WEINREB, Elliot L.——**B:** Oct. 11, 1945, Lawrence, NY, Elliot L. Weinreb, Atty. & Counselor at Law; **PRIM RE ACT:** Attorney; **SERVICES:** Advice & counsel on RE matters; representation in negotiations, representation in disputes (in and out of ct.); drafting of contracts & legal instruments; **PREV EMPLOY:** Law clerk, NM Ct. of Appeals, Partner, Zamora, Rael & Weinreb, PA; **PROFL AFFIL & HONORS:** ABA. (Real Prop. Probate & Tr. Law Section); Corp. Banking & Bus. Law Section, Taxation Sect., Litigation Section, Amer. Trial Lawyers Assn; Amer. Judicature Soc., Comml. Law League; **EDUC:** BA, 1967, Hist., Harvard Univ.; **GRAD EDUC:** Cert. de Langue Francaise, 1968, French Culture, Universite de Poitiers (Poitiers, France); MA, 1970, Socy, Columbia Univ.; JD, 1971, Law, NY Univ.; **EDUC HONORS:** Magna Cum Laude; **HOME ADD:** PO Box 160, Santa Fe, NM 87501; **BUS ADD:** 320 Calisteo St., Suite 303, Santa Fe, NM 87501, (505)982-4691.

WEINREB, Wolf——*Senior Partner*; **OTHER RE ACT:** Investor; **BUS ADD:** 276 Riverside Dr., New York, NY 10025, (212)865-5858.

WEINSTEIN, Arnold J.——**B:** Sept. 5, 1944, Wash. DC, *Owner*, Weinstein & Assoc., RE Investments & Devel.; **PRIM RE ACT:** Broker, Developer, Owner/Investor, Syndicator; **OTHER RE ACT:** Gen. part. of AJ Props.; AJW Kauai Investors; K&W Maui Investors; Vicarn Investors Inc.; **SERVICES:** Investment valuation, devel. & synd. of comml. props., brokerage, prop. mgmt.; **REP CLIENTS:** Lenders & indiv. investors in comml. props.; **PREV EMPLOY:** Grubb & Ellis Comml. Brokerage Co., 44 Montgomery St., San Francisco, CA 94104; **PROFL AFFIL & HONORS:** San Francisco Bd. of Realtors; CA Assn. of Realtors; NAR; San Francisco C of C; Marlin Cty Bd of Realtors; **EDUC:** BS, 1966, Psych., Univ. of MD., Coll. Pk., MD; **GRAD EDUC:** MBA (15 hrs. credit), 1968, Mktg., Amer. Univ., Wash. DC; **OTHER ACT & HONORS:** Sigma Alpha Mu-Frat; **HOME ADD:** 158 Stewart Dr., Tiburon, CA 94920, (415)435-5195; **BUS ADD:** 1038 Redwood Hwy., Suite 100, Mill Valley, CA 94941, (415)435-7070.

WEINSTEIN, George——**B:** Mar. 20, 1924, NY, *Chmn.*, Weinstein Associates Ltd.; **PRIM RE ACT:** Consultant, Developer, Owner/Investor, Property Manager, Syndicator; **PREV EMPLOY:** Pres. WI RE Investment Trust; **PROFL AFFIL & HONORS:** Listed, Who's Who in Amer., Who's Who in World, Who's Who in Industry; **EDUC:** BS, 1944, Mgmt., Univ. of IL; **GRAD EDUC:** MBA, 1947, Mgmt., NYU; **HOME ADD:** Milwaukee, WI, (414)765-0441; **BUS ADD:** 324 E Wisconsin Ave., Milwaukee, WI 53202, (414)289-0990.

WEINSTEIN, Gerald——*VP & Secy.*, American Biltrite Co.; **PRIM RE ACT:** Property Manager; **BUS ADD:** 575 Technology Sq., Cambridge, MA 02139, (617)876-6000.*

WEINSTEIN, Stanley Howard——**B:** Oct. 27, 1948, NY, *Pres.*, Weinstein Associates Ltd.; **PRIM RE ACT:** Consultant, Attorney, Appraiser, Developer, Owner/Investor, Property Manager, Syndicator; **PREV EMPLOY:** Reit Prop. Mgr. Ltd. - Exec. VP; **PROFL AFFIL & HONORS:** Amer. Inst. of CPA; NY Soc. of CPA; ABA; NY St. Bar Assn., Cert. Sr. Review Appraiser; CPA; JD; RE Broker; Admitted to practice Law; Listed in Who's Who in the Midwest, Listed in Who's Who in Comm. & Indus.; **EDUC:** 1970, Acctg., Univ. of IL; **GRAD EDUC:** JD, 1973, Law, St. John's Univ.; **OTHER ACT & HONORS:** Active in and Bd. Member of many Jewish Organizations; **BUS ADD:** 324 E. Wisconsin Ave., Milwaukee, WI 53202, (414)289-0990.

WEINSTOCK, Leonard I.——**B:** May 15, 1930, Bronx, NY, *Part.*, Schwartzman Weinstock Garelik & Mann P.C; **PRIM RE ACT:** Attorney; **SERVICES:** Law; **PREV EMPLOY:** Part., Weiss Rosenthal & Schwartzman; **PROFL AFFIL & HONORS:** ABA, NY Cty. Lawyers, Queens Cty. Lawyers, Co-Chmn. Comml. Law Comm. Queens County BAR; **EDUC:** BS, 1951, Psych., Math, City Coll. of the City of NY; **GRAD EDUC:** LL.B., 1954, Law, NY Univ.; **MIL SERV:** US Army; **OTHER ACT & HONORS:** Queens C of C; **HOME ADD:** 83-21 Kent St. Jamaica Estates, New York, NY 11432, (212)380-2518; **BUS ADD:** 295 Madison Ave, New York, NY 10017, (212)725-9200.

WEIR, R.L.——**B:** April 8, 1916, Warren, OH, *Pres.*, Weir Development Co., Inc.; **PRIM RE ACT:** Consultant, Developer, Builder; **OTHER RE ACT:** Bldg. System & Product Devel.; **SERVICES:** Value Engrg. (CVS), Consultant; **REP CLIENTS:** HUD, Cinn Milacron, U.S. Time, Sierra Research, etc.; **PREV EMPLOY:** Aircraft Project Mgr., Procurement, AMC, WPAFB, Arch. Supervision, Design & Supervision Assoc.; Modernization Mgr., HUD Programs, Development, Housing Projects & Products; **PROFL AFFIL & HONORS:** Soc. of Am. Value Engineers, CVS; **EDUC:** Bus. Admin. - 2 yrs.; **MIL SERV:** USAF, A/c; **OTHER ACT & HONORS:** SAVE, (Soc. of Amer. Value Engrs.); ACBL; **HOME ADD:** 2217 Grant Ave., Dayton, OH 45406, (513)274-6794; **BUS ADD:** 2217 Grant Ave., Dayton, OH 45406, (513)274-6794.

WEISBERG, Frank F.——**B:** July 21, 1942, Louisville, KY, *Pres.*, Bass & Weisberg, Inc. Realtors; **PRIM RE ACT:** Broker, Owner/Investor, Instructor, Property Manager; **SERVICES:** Gen. resid. RE brokerage, comml. div., investment, indus., Comml. site acquisition; **REP CLIENTS:** Indivs., corp. buyers & sellers; **PROFL AFFIL & HONORS:** NAR, KAR, RNMI, SIRS, 1970, CCIM designation (Certfied Comml. Investment Member); 1976 Realtor of the Year, Louisville Bd. of Realtors; 1980 - Teacher of the Year, Jefferson Community Coll.; 1967 - Awarded the Natl. Exchange of the Year, Natl. Inst. of RE Brokers; **EDUC:** 1964, RE, IN Univ.; **HOME ADD:** 6213 Glen Hill Rd., Louisville, KY 40222, (502)426-1974; **BUS TEL:** (502)585-1925.

WEISBROD, Harry——B: Mar. 6, 1920, NY, NY, *Pres.*, Harry Weisbrod Associates Inc.; **PRIM RE ACT:** Consultant; **SERVICES:** Consulting: wage, hour & equal employment; **REP CLIENTS:** Lincoln Prop. Co., Dallas; JMB, Chicago; Johnson Props., Atlanta; **PREV EMPLOY:** U.S. Dept. of Labor, Wage and Hour Div.; **PROFL AFFIL & HONORS:** Dallas Apt. Assn.; Dallas and TX CPA Soc., CPA, TX; Arbitrator, Fed. Mediation and Consultation Serv.; **EDUC:** BBA, 1941, Bus./Acctg., CCNY; **MIL SERV:** U.S. Army, Sgt.; **OTHER ACT & HONORS:** Author of *Wage, Hour and Employment Practices, Manual for the Multi-Housing Industry (IREM)*; **HOME ADD:** 6991 Helsem Way, Dallas, TX 75230, (214)387-0650; **BUS ADD:** 14114 Dallas Pkwy., Dallas, TX 75230, (214)387-0609.

WEISE, Frank——*Pres.*, Florida Steel corp.; **PRIM RE ACT:** Property Manager; **BUS ADD:** Box 23328 1715 Cleveland St., Tampa, FL 33623, (813)251-8811.*

WEISINGER, Lee——B: July 30, 1916, NY, NY, *Owner*, Trans Nat. Props.; **PRIM RE ACT:** Broker; **EDUC:** BA, NYU; **MIL SERV:** US Army, Sgt., Bronze Star; **OTHER ACT & HONORS:** Pres. of Lands End Civic Assn.; **BUS ADD:** 2264 Halyard Dr., Merrick, NY 11566, (516)623-2020.

WEISMAN, Mark S.——B: Mar. 20, 1948, Peabody, MA, *Pres.*, Brownstone Real Estate Co., Inc.; **PRIM RE ACT:** Broker, Consultant, Appraiser, Developer, Owner/Investor, Property Manager; **OTHER RE ACT:** We also arrange loans for developers; **PROFL AFFIL & HONORS:** Greater Boston RE Bd. (Realtor); Soc. of RE Appraisers; **EDUC:** BA, 1970, Biology/Chem., Northeastern Univ.; **GRAD EDUC:** Food Sci., MIT; **OTHER ACT & HONORS:** Notary Public; Bd. Member MA Soc. for Prevention of Cruelty to Children; **HOME ADD:** 122 St. Botolph St., Boston, MA 02115, (617)262-5595; **BUS ADD:** 257 W. Newton St., Boston, MA 02116, (617)262-4250.

WEISMAN, Steven J.——B: Feb. 9, 1949, Boston, MA, *Lawyer*, Steven J.J. Weisman, Esq.; **PRIM RE ACT:** Attorney; **SERVICES:** Title searches and evaluation, closings and other conveyancing legal services; **REP CLIENTS:** Lenders and indiv. prop. purchasers and sellers; **PREV EMPLOY:** MA Bar Assn., ABA; Real Prop. Section of ABA; **PROFL AFFIL & HONORS:** Fellow MA Bar Foundation; **EDUC:** BA, 1970, Phil., Univ. of MA at Amherst; **GRAD EDUC:** JD, 1973, Boston Coll. Law School; **OTHER ACT & HONORS:** Legal Columnist and television and radio commentator; **HOME ADD:** 2 Evergreen Lane, Amherst, MA 01002; **BUS ADD:** 20 Gatehouse Rd. PO BOX 913, Amherst, MA 01004, (413)253-9359.

WEISS, Allen J.——B: Apr. 17, 1932, NYC, NY, *Pres.*, Red Canyon Realty, Inc./Better Homes & Gardens; **PRIM RE ACT:** Broker, Consultant, Appraiser, Property Manager; **SERVICES:** Gen. full serv. firm; **PREV EMPLOY:** RE land & RE devel.; **PROFL AFFIL & HONORS:** NAR, AZ Assn. Realtors, Sedona Verde Valley Bd. of Realtors & NAZ Bd. of Realtors, GRI, CRS; **EDUC:** 1954, Bus., Miami Univ, AZ State Univ., UCLA; **GRAD EDUC:** MBA, 1957, Bus.; **MIL SERV:** USMC, PFC; **OTHER ACT & HONORS:** Pres. Sedona Verde Valley Bd. of Realtors 1979; Member Fiesta Bowl. Comm. 1978-80; **HOME ADD:** Brewer Rd. Box 1451, Sedona, AZ 86336, (602)282-7423; **BUS ADD:** 211 N. Hwy. 89A Drawer CC, Sedona, AZ 86336, (602)282-7111.

WEISS, David J.——B: Jan. 3, 1950, Atlantic City, NJ, *Atty.*, Cooper Perskie, Katzman, April Niedleman & Wagenheim, RE Dept.; **PRIM RE ACT:** Attorney; **SERVICES:** Acquisitions, Devel., Fin., Zoning & Planning; **REP CLIENTS:** Lenders, indiv. and comml. investors; **PROFL AFFIL & HONORS:** ABA, real prop. div. NJ Bar Assn.; **EDUC:** BS, 1971, Acctg., Villanova Univ.; **GRAD EDUC:** JD, 1974, Univ. of Akron, OH; **EDUC HONORS:** Phi Beta Gamma, Cum Laude; **HOME ADD:** 11 Exeter Ct., Margate City, NJ 08402, (609)822-4492; **BUS ADD:** 1125 Atlantic Ave., Atlantic City, NJ 08407, (609)344-3161.

WEISS, Dorothy——B: Jan. 27, 1936, St. Louis, MO, *Dir. of Pre-License Training*, Century 21 of Missouri; **PRIM RE ACT:** Broker, Consultant, Instructor; **SERVICES:** Lic. Preparation for Exams in IL, KS & MO; **PREV EMPLOY:** Teacher; **PROFL AFFIL & HONORS:** NAR; **EDUC:** BS, 1958, Educ., WA Univ., St. Louis, MO; **EDUC HONORS:** Nat. Educ. Hon.; **OTHER ACT & HONORS:** Nat. Council of Jewish Women, Hadassah; **HOME ADD:** 124 Brookside Ct., St. Louis, MO 63141, (314)432-4290; **BUS ADD:** 111 Westport Plaza, St. Louis, MO 63141, (314)434-9900.

WEISS, Harold L.——Carold Corp.; **PRIM RE ACT:** Attorney, Appraiser, Banker; **OTHER RE ACT:** Asst. Prof., NY Univ.; **SERVICES:** Originates, sells, servs. FHA, VA conventional morts. for banks, S&Ls, life ins. cos. etc.; **PREV EMPLOY:** 1942-pres. Carold Corp.; **PROFL AFFIL & HONORS:** MBA of NY, Brooklyn Bar Assn., AIREA, ASA, NY Soc. of Appraisers, NARA, MBAA, NY State Bar Assn., MAI; **EDUC:** BS, CCNY; **GRAD EDUC:** Grad. School, Bus. Admin, NYU, Columbia Univ.; **HOME ADD:** 1401 Ocean Ave., Brooklyn, NY 11230; **BUS ADD:** 1538 Flatbush, Brooklyn, NY 11210, (212)434-9400.

WEISS, Jaime M.——B: May 4, 1943, New York, NY, *Pres.*, Jaime M. Weiss Realty Co., Inc.; **PRIM RE ACT:** Broker, Developer, Owner/Investor; **SERVICES:** Sales and leasing of indus. & comml. office, devel. and ownership of office and indus. props.; **PREV EMPLOY:** VP & Dir. of Suburban office leasing and indus. props. - Edward S. Gordon Co. 1977-1980; VP - Cross & Brown Co., Intl. Modular Housing; Pres., modular Realty Intl., Inc.; **PROFL AFFIL & HONORS:** The Indus. RE Brokers Assn.; NAIOP, Young men's RE Assoc. of NY; **EDUC:** BBA, 1969, Bus. Admin./Adv., CUNY; **HOME ADD:** Five Horizon Road, Ft. Lee, NJ 07024, (201)886-0777; **BUS ADD:** 185 E. Union Ave., East Rutherford, NJ 07073, (201)460-7880.

WEISS, James A.——B: Aug. 14, 1938, Philadelphia, PA, *Atty., at Law; Pres., Windon Capital Mgmt., Inc.*, Windon Capital Mgmt.,Inc.; **PRIM RE ACT:** Attorney, Syndicator; **SERVICES:** Synd. of Resid. and Comml. Props.; **PREV EMPLOY:** Gen. Counsel, The M.A. Kravitz Co., Inc., Philadelphia, PA; **PROFL AFFIL & HONORS:** PA & NJ Bar Assn.; **EDUC:** AB, 1960 Princeton Univ., Public and Intl. Affairs; **GRAD EDUC:** LLB, 1963, Univ. of PA Law School; **BUS ADD:** Suite 253, 111 Presidential Blvd., Bala Cynwyd, PA 19004, (215)667-3505.

WEISS, Jeffrey J.——B: July 13, 1943, Brooklyn, NY, *Pres.*, Advance Development Corp.; **PRIM RE ACT:** Developer, Owner/Investor; **OTHER RE ACT:** RE salesman; **SERVICES:** Devel. of medical and profl. condo., office; **REP CLIENTS:** Indiv. and corporate purchasers and investors; **PREV EMPLOY:** Chmn. of Bd., Atl. Indus., Inc.-Miami; Chmn. of Bd., VP, Exposition Corp. of Amer.-Miami; Dir., VP, Scarlet O'Hara-Atlanta; Dir., VP, Glenda Products and Gazebo Food Corp.; Dir. South FL S&L; Dir., Ideas Assoc.; Prin., Dir. Allstate Realty & Investment Co.; Pres., Founder: Custom Land; Advance Investment Props.; Gen. Partner, Flagler St. Ltd.; **PROFL AFFIL & HONORS:** Dir., Mem., Direct Selling Assn.; **EDUC:** 1961-63, Miami-Dade Jr. Coll.; 1974, Univ. of Miami; **OTHER ACT & HONORS:** Recipient Annual Corp. Award, from March of Dimes Walkathon; Smithsonian Inst.; Founder, Dir., Miami Dinnerkey Boat Show; Exec. Comm., Community Educ. TV; Founder, VP, Kitchen-craft, Inc.; Founder, C/B, Advance Fin. Corp.; Dir., Underwriters Fin. Inc. of FL, Founder, So. FL S&L; **BUS ADD:** 1320 S. Dixie Hwy., Penthouse, Coral Gables, FL 33146, (305)666-1978.

WEISS, K. Brooks——B: Dec. 2, 1946, Glen Ridge, NJ, *Prin.*, Catalyst Inc. Archs., Dir. of Design; **PRIM RE ACT:** Architect, Consultant, Developer, Owner/Investor; **SERVICES:** Arch., Interiors, Planning, Site Analysis/Feasibility, Space Planning; **REP CLIENTS:** City of Orlando; State of FL; Valencia Comm. Coll.; Sunpoint Devel., Inc.; Post, Buckley, Schuh & Jernigan, Inc.; **PREV EMPLOY:** Schweizer Assoc., Inc. Archs./Engrs.; Eugene R. Smith & Assoc., Archs./Planners; Harvard & Jolly, Archs.; **PROFL AFFIL & HONORS:** AIA (Director); City of Orlando Devel. Review Comm., MFC AIA Honor Award; City of Orlando Design Award; **EDUC:** BArch., 1969, Design/Hist., Univ. of FL; **OTHER ACT & HONORS:** FL Symphony Orchestra Assoc. Bd.; Juror, Univ. of FL, College of Arch.; **HOME ADD:** 1244 Via Salerno, Winter Park, FL 32789, (305)647-4451; **BUS ADD:** 69 E. Pine St., POB 2769, Orlando, FL 32802, (305)841-1925.

WEISS, Kenneth J.——B: July 20, 1945, Detroit, MI, *Pres.*, Kenneth J. Weiss Properties, Inc.; **PRIM RE ACT:** Developer, Property Manager, Syndicator; **OTHER RE ACT:** RE Devel., Rezoning, Rehab. of Bldgs.; **PROFL AFFIL & HONORS:** ULI, Intl. Council of Shopping Centers; **EDUC:** BA, 1967, Pol. Sci. and Bus., Univ. of AZ; **MIL SERV:** USAF Res.; **HOME ADD:** 7130 North 2nd St., Phoenix, AZ 85020, (602)943-0184; **BUS ADD:** 1110 E. Missouri, Suite 530, Phoenix, AZ 85014, (602)265-1611.

WEISS, Martin——B: Sept. 6, 1931, NYC, NY, *Pres.*, 4M Properties, Inc.; **PRIM RE ACT:** Developer, Builder, Owner/Investor, Property Manager; **PROFL AFFIL & HONORS:** Nat. Assn. of Indus. Parks; Nat. Assn. of Corporate RE Execs.; **MIL SERV:** USAF, Airman First Class; **OTHER ACT & HONORS:** McNay Art Inst.; McNay Council; Santa Rosa Children's Hospital Foundation VP; Chmn. Endowment Fund of same hospital; San Antonio Convention and Visitors Bureau Member of Bd.; Confrerie de la Chaine des Rotisseurs; St. Anthony Club; Plaza Club; Univ. Club; **HOME ADD:** 109 Sir Arthur Ct., San Antonio, TX 78213, (512)344-5668; **BUS ADD:** 7900 Callaghan, Suite 300, San Antonio, TX 78229, (512)342-4242.

WEISS, Michael——*Treas.*, Texas American Energy; **PRIM RE ACT:** Property Manager; **BUS ADD:** 300 W. Wall Ave., Midland, TX 79701, (915)683-4811.*

WEISS, Richard L.——**B:** Sept. 9, 1932, Riegelsville, PA, *VP*, Helmsley Spear Inc.; **PRIM RE ACT:** Broker, Consultant, Property Manager, Insuror, Syndicator; **PREV EMPLOY:** Dir. of Services McKinsey & Co. Inc.; **PROFL AFFIL & HONORS:** Realtor; **EDUC:** Villanova Univ., 1956, Econ. Fin.; **GRAD EDUC:** Investments, NYU; **EDUC HONORS:** Dean's List; **MIL SERV:** US Army, Sp.5; **HOME ADD:** 606 Haviland Rd., Stamford, CT; **BUS ADD:** 60 E. 42nd St., New York, NY 10017, (212)880-0384.

WEISS, Ronald W.——**B:** Aug. 13, 1939, NY, NY, *Pres.*, Shearson American Express RE Corp.; **PRIM RE ACT:** Consultant, Owner/Investor, Syndicator; **OTHER RE ACT:** Investor; **SERVICES:** Investment counseling, mkt.; **REP CLIENTS:** Feasibility studies, RE investment banking; **PREV EMPLOY:** VP - Shearson Hammill & Co. First VP - Shearson Hayden Stone; **PROFL AFFIL & HONORS:** Senior VP - Shearson Loeb Rhoades; **EDUC:** BS in Econ., 1961, RE - Corp. Fin., Wharton Sch. - Univ. of PA; **GRAD EDUC:** LLB & JD, 1964, Tax & RE & Corp. Fin., Columbia Univ. Law School; **BUS ADD:** 14 Wall St., New York, NY 10005, (212)577-5874.

WEISSEL, William J.——**B:** Feb. 10, 1932, Miami, FL, *Pres.*, Cameo Mgmt. Inc.; **PRIM RE ACT:** Owner/Investor, Property Manager, Syndicator; **EDUC:** BBA, 1954, Acctg., Univ. of Miami, FL; **GRAD EDUC:** LLB, 1958, Univ. of Miami; **HOME ADD:** 14228 Cantrell Rd., Silver Spring, MD 20904, (301)384-4232; **BUS ADD:** 14228 Cantrell Rd., Silver Spring, MD 20904, (301)384-4232.

WEISSER, Herman M.——**B:** Apr. 26, 1920, NY, NY, *Partner*, Weisser & Weisser, Comml. Mort. & Loans & Mort. Consultation; **PRIM RE ACT:** Broker, Appraiser, Consultant, Developer, Lender, Owner/Investor; **OTHER RE ACT:** Mort. banker, FL lic. mort. broker, Purchase and sale; **SERVICES:** RE fin. and consultation; **REP CLIENTS:** RE devels. and owners of comml. prop.; **PROFL AFFIL & HONORS:** FL Assn. of Mort. Brokers, Pres., 1982; Nat. Assn. of Mort. Brokers; Nat. Assn. of Review Appraisers; Soc. of Mort. Consultants; Amer. Mgmt. Assn.; FL Mort. Brokers Political Action Comm., Vice Chmn.; FL RE Exchangors, CRA, Soc. of Mort. Consultants; Recipient of FL Assn. of Mort. Brokers Presidental Award; Appointment to Motel Hall of Fame by Hospitality Magazine, 1967; Recipient of Key to City of Daytona Beach, 1965; Man of the Yr., A-1-A Motel Assn., 1963; Man of the Week, All FL Magazine, 1963; **EDUC:** BS, 1940, Aero. Engrg., Univ. of MD; **OTHER ACT & HONORS:** FL Assn. of Mort. Brokers; FL Mort. Brokers Political Action Comm.; Daytona Investment Enterprises, Inc. Chmn.; FL Security Service, Inc.; Motel Indus. of FL, Inc.; Halifax Area Council of Assns., Inc.; City of Daytona Beach Mayor's Interacial Advisory Comm., 1963; Daytona Beach Area C of C; Ormond Beach C of C; United Nations A Comm. on Bus., 1976, 1977; Daytona Beach Kiwanis Club; **HOME TEL:** (904)253-4500; **BUS ADD:** PO Box 5631, Daytona Beach, FL 32018, (904)255-1500.

WEISSMAN, Alan M.——**B:** Apr. 11, 1944, Atlanta, GA, *VP Corp. Devel. and RE*, Ole's Inc., Exec.; **PRIM RE ACT:** Attorney, Developer, Builder, Owner/Investor; **OTHER RE ACT:** Provide long range planning for corp.; **PREV EMPLOY:** Dir. of Operations, Daylin Inc.; RE Dir., Handy Dan Inc.; Dir. of Intrl. Operations, Intertherm, Inc.; **PROFL AFFIL & HONORS:** Member NACORE; ICSC; SRA; **EDUC:** BA, 1966, Intl. Bus., St. Louis Univ.; **GRAD EDUC:** MBA, JD, 1969, Intl. Law & Bus., Harvard Univ.; **EDUC HONORS:** Cum Laude, Order of Oriflamme, Magna Cum Laude; **OTHER ACT & HONORS:** Zeta Beta Tau Frat.; Selected one of 10 Outstanding Young Businessmen in the US in 1971 by Harvard Univ. School of Bus.; Member of Bd. of Dir., Temple Beth El; Member of Nat. Bd. United Jewish Appeal; **HOME ADD:** 1107 Via Sebastian, San Pedro, CA 90732, (213)548-1443; **BUS ADD:** 3395 E. Foothill Blvd., Pasadena, CA 91107.

WEITZ, Alan J.——**B:** Jan. 2, 1939, NYC, NY, *Pres.*, Gulf Union Indus., Inc.; **PRIM RE ACT:** Broker, Consultant, Developer, Builder, Property Manager, Lender, Insuror; **SERVICES:** Mort. Banking, Ins. and Prop. Dev.; **PROFL AFFIL & HONORS:** MBA of Greater Baton Rouge, M Mort. Banker Awarded in 1979 by LA MBA; **EDUC:** BAE, 1960, Econ., Labor Relations, Lafayette Coll., Easton, PA; **EDUC HONORS:** Hon. Grad. in Econ.; **MIL SERV:** US Army-Inf., Capt.; **OTHER ACT & HONORS:** Rotary Club of Baton Rouge; **HOME ADD:** 4145 Pine Park Dr., Baton Rouge, LA 70809, (504)927-6804; **BUS ADD:** PO Box 3518, Baton Rouge, LA 70821, (504)383-8955.

WEITZEL, James W.——**B:** Feb. 26, 1942, Wash. DC, *VP, Mktg.*, Great Midwest Corp.; **PRIM RE ACT:** Broker, Developer, Builder, Property Manager; **PREV EMPLOY:** Manhattan Co., Troy, MI; The Hartman Grp., Southfield, MI; **PROFL AFFIL & HONORS:** SIR; NAIOP; Sales & Mktg. Execs. (Pres.); Natl. Assn. For. Trade Zones; Gr. Kansas City For. Trade Zone, Inc. (Bd. Dir.); **EDUC:** BS, 1964, Econ., Indus. Mgmt., Wharton Sch., Univ. of PA; **GRAD EDUC:** MBA, 1965, Mktg., Univ. of MI, Grad. Sch. of Bus.; **MIL SERV:** US Public Health Svc., Commissioned Corps., Sr. Asst. Health Servs. Officer; **OTHER ACT & HONORS:** Young Audiences, Inc.; **HOME ADD:** 185 Chinquapin Ct., Lee's Summit, MO 64065, (816)373-5330; **BUS ADD:** 8300 NE Underground Dr., Kansas City, MO 64161, (816)455-2500.

WEITZEN, Edward H.——*Pres.*, International Banknete Co. Inc.; **PRIM RE ACT:** Property Manager; **BUS ADD:** 230 Park Ave., New York, NY 10169, (212)697-6600.*

WEITZMAN, Marilyn Kramer——**B:** Oct. 14, 1946, Boston, MA, *Principal*, The Weitzman Group, Inc.; **PRIM RE ACT:** Consultant, Appraiser; **SERVICES:** RE consulting, investment analysis, mkt. studies, appraisals; **REP CLIENTS:** Major comml. banks, ins. cos., RE devel.; **PREV EMPLOY:** Korpacz & Weitzman, Inc., 1977-1981; Landauer Associates, 1972-1977; The Rouse Co., 1971-1972; L. Keyserling 1970-1971; **PROFL AFFIL & HONORS:** Amer. Inst. of RE Appraisers; NY RE Bd.; Assn. of RE Women; Young Men's RE Assn., MAI; ICIB, Bd. Member, NY; **EDUC:** BA, 1968, Univ. of Penn.; **GRAD EDUC:** MA, 1969, Univ. of Penn.; MBA, 1980, Fin., NYU Grad. School of Bus. Admin.; **EDUC HONORS:** Mortar Bd.; **HOME ADD:** 320 E. 55th St., New York, NY 10022, (212)838-4271; **BUS ADD:** 767 Third Ave., New York, NY 10017, (212)688-9060.

WEITZMANN, Michael C.——**B:** June 3, 1951, Broomall, PA, *Sr. RE Rep.*, The Travelers Insurance Co., Urban; **PRIM RE ACT:** Lender, Owner/Investor; **OTHER RE ACT:** Equity/Mort. Investments; **PREV EMPLOY:** Franklin Realty Grp., 1977-1978; **EDUC:** BS, 1974, Fin./Econ., Villanova Univ.; **HOME ADD:** The Baldwin School, Bryn Mawr, PA 19010, (215)527-0499; **BUS ADD:** 3 Parkway, Philadelphia, PA 19102, (215)972-5746.

WEIXELMAN, Donald B.——**B:** Aug. 30, 1932, Louisville, KS, *Owner*, Continental West Realty; **PRIM RE ACT:** Broker, Developer, Owner/Investor; **PREV EMPLOY:** 21 yrs. in RE; **EDUC:** BS Ag. & Bus., 1955-57, Econ., KS State Univ.; **MIL SERV:** US Army Inf., Lt.; **HOME ADD:** 1509 E. Lake, Fort Collins, CO 80524, (303)493-4309; **BUS ADD:** 3200 E. Mulberry, Fort Collins, CO 80524, (303)482-1845.

WELBOURNE, John Howard——**B:** July 24, 1947, L.A., CA, *Lawyer*, Adams, Duque & Hazeltine; **PRIM RE ACT:** Attorney, Owner/Investor; **PROFL AFFIL & HONORS:** State Bar of CA Real Prop. Law Sect.; L.A. Cty. Bar Assoc. RE, ABA, Probate and Trust Law.; **EDUC:** AB, 1969, Human., Univ. of CA, Berkley; **GRAD EDUC:** MA of Public Admin., 1974, 1977, Univ. of CA, Los Angeles JD, Univ. of CA, Davis; **MIL SERV:** US Army, 1st Lt., Adj. Gen'ls. Corp, 1970-71; **HOME ADD:** 220 So. Irving Bvld., Los Angeles, CA 90004, (213)935-1914; **BUS ADD:** Los Angeles, CA 90014523 W. Sixth St., (213)620-1240.

WELCH, David N.——**B:** April 4, 1936, Logan, UT, *Broker - Pres.*, Century 21 Grimshaw Inc. Realtors; **PRIM RE ACT:** Broker; **SERVICES:** MLS Salt Lake, Davis, and Weber Cties.; **EDUC:** BS, 1959, Bus., UT State Univ.; **GRAD EDUC:** Econ., UT State Univ.; **MIL SERV:** US Army, Sgt.; **OTHER ACT & HONORS:** Bd. Dir. C of C - Kiwanis; **HOME ADD:** 1533 S. 500 E, Bountiful, UT 84010, (801)295-9390; **BUS ADD:** 501 S. 500 W, Bountiful, UT 84010, (801)292-4488.

WELCH, Donald E.——**B:** Apr. 12, 1927, Albany, NY, *Pres.*, Welch Real Estate, Inc.; **PRIM RE ACT:** Broker; **PREV EMPLOY:** Picotte RE, VP, Comml./Indus. Brokerage; **PROFL AFFIL & HONORS:** SIR; Pres. Comml. Investment Div., NY State Assn. Realtors, SIR; **EDUC:** AB, 1948, Mktg., Nichols Coll. (Junior Coll.); **MIL SERV:** USN, 2nd Class Radman; **OTHER ACT & HONORS:** Chmn. Bd. of Assessment & Review, C of C; Treas. St. Vincents Corp., Mgt. Sect.; 8 Apts. for Dioces of Albany; **HOME ADD:** 11 No. Pine Ave., Albany, NY, (518)482-4771; **BUS ADD:** 45 Colvin Ave., Albany, NY 12206, (518)438-2937.

WELCH, Gary E.——**B:** May 23, 1939, San Angelo, TX, *Pres. Welch-Hambrick, Inc. Realtors & Buildrs.*, Welch-Hambrick, Inc.; **PRIM RE ACT:** Broker, Appraiser, Developer, Builder, Banker, Lender, Owner/Investor, Insuror; **SERVICES:** RE Sales: Home Bldrs., Gen. Ins., Comml. Banking; **PREV EMPLOY:** Nat. Bank Examiner-US Treasury Dept. 1965-1969; VP-Community State Bank, Waco, TX 1969-73; Pres. and Chmn. of Bd-First State Bank, Riesel, TX 1979-date (VP 1973-1978); Owner-Welch Ins. Agency, Riesel, TX-Current from 1973; **PROFL AFFIL & HONORS:** Waco Bd. of Realtors; **EDUC:** BBA, 1973, Acctg., TX Tech Univ., Lubbock, TX; **GRAD EDUC:**

Grad., SW Grad. School of Banking 1973 at So. Methodist Univ., Comml. Banking, SMU, Dallas, TX; **MIL SERV:** US Army, Capt., Sr. Parachutist Expert Infantry Badge; **OTHER ACT & HONORS:** Pres. Riesel Lions Club; Riesel Fair Assn.; Past Master, Riesel Masonic Lodge AF & AM; Officer-Waco Jaycees, Outstanding Officer of the Yr., 1970-71; Outstanding Young Men of Amer. 1971; Adopted Suggestion Award-US Treasury Dept. 1968; **HOME ADD:** 2524 Cedar Ridge Rd., Waco, TX 76708, (817)753-4174; **BUS ADD:** 4007 W Waco Dr., Waco, TX 76710, (817)876-2121.

WELCH, H. Oliver——B: Nov. 8, 1935, Preston, GA, *Pres.*, FSC Realty Corp.; **PRIM RE ACT:** Broker, Attorney, Consultant, Property Manager, Owner/Investor; **OTHER RE ACT:** AICP, CFP; **SERVICES:** Brokerage and consultant; **PREV EMPLOY:** Past Dir. of Bureau of Community Affairs for State of GA, Dir. of Planning Bureau; **PROFL AFFIL & HONORS:** Amer. Bar., AICPA, Inst. of Cert. Fin. Planners, RESMI, IREM - Inst. of RE Mgmt., Amer. Inst. of Planners; **EDUC:** BBA, 1957, Acctg., GA State Univ.; **GRAD EDUC:** MBA, DBA, 1972, Mgmt., GA State Univ.; **EDUC HONORS:** Pres. Beta Alpha Psi 1962; **MIL SERV:** US Army; **OTHER ACT & HONORS:** Dept. State Supt. of Schools, GA; World Future Soc.; Atlanta C of C; Former Treas. W.S. Jaycees, Atlanta Commerce Club, Cherokee Town and Cty. Club, Peachtree Kiwanis; **HOME ADD:** 3766 Ivy Rd., NE, Atlanta, GA 30342, (404)237-1823; **BUS ADD:** 250 Piedmont Ave., Ste. 1900, Atlanta, GA 30365, (404)659-1234.

WELCH, Patricia Leal——B: Aug. 30, 1933, Amherst, MA, *Pres.*, Many Mansions, Inc.; **PRIM RE ACT:** Owner/Investor, Real Estate Publisher; **SERVICES:** Renovate housing in economically depressed areas and rent to low-income people; editor of newsletter; **PREV EMPLOY:** Production editor, United Media Intl., Inc.; **PROFL AFFIL & HONORS:** IREM; NAREE; NAHRO; **EDUC:** BS, 1955, Econ., Univ. of MA; **GRAD EDUC:** MS, 1960, Econ., Univ. of MA; **EDUC HONORS:** Summa Cum Laude; **OTHER ACT & HONORS:** Ruggles Baptist Church; Nat. Wildlife Federation; **HOME ADD:** 41 Imrie Rd., Allston, MA 02134.

WELCH, Sheila J.——B: Feb. 1, 1942, NY, NY, *Atty.*, RCA Corp., Law Dept., RE; **PRIM RE ACT:** Attorney; **REP CLIENTS:** RCA Corp.; **PREV EMPLOY:** Skadden Arps., Slate, Meagher & Flom, TWA, Contract drafting and gen. corp.; **PROFL AFFIL & HONORS:** ABA, Assn. of the Bar of City of NY; **EDUC:** BA, 1964, Hist., Fr., Span., Antioch Coll., Yellow Springs, OH; **GRAD EDUC:** MAT, 1966, Hist., Wesleyan Univ., Middletown, CT; JD, 1976, Northeastern Univ. Law Sch., Boston, MA; **EDUC HONORS:** Honors on final thesis in hist. for BA degree, Honors in final oral exams.; **OTHER ACT & HONORS:** Member NY State Bar since 1977; **HOME ADD:** 440 E. 79th St., 6-G, New York, NY 10021, (212)744-1002; **BUS ADD:** 30 Rockefeller Plaza, Rm. 4819, New York, NY 10020, (212)621-6034.

WELKS, Julian——*Exec. Sec.*, Idaho Real Estate Commission; **PRIM RE ACT:** Property Manager; **BUS ADD:** State House Mail, Boise, ID 83720, (208)334-3285.*

WELL, S. Douglas——B: Apr. 21, 1936, Cleveland, OH, *Pres.*, Paine Webber Properties Inc.; **OTHER RE ACT:** Asset Mgr./Investment Adviser; **SERVICES:** Manage public RE funds; provide investment advice; Structure RE Investments; **PREV EMPLOY:** Sr. VP, Prop. Capital Advisors 1970-78; Irwin Mgmt. Co. 1966-1970; **PROFL AFFIL & HONORS:** ICSC - RE Bd.; **EDUC:** BA, 1958, Poli., Princeton Univ.; **GRAD EDUC:** MBA, 1960, Fin., Harvard Bus. School; **HOME ADD:** 22 Cartwright Rd., Wellesley, MA 02181, (617)237-4928; **BUS ADD:** 100 Federal St., Boston, MA 02101, (617)423-8150.

WELLBAUM, R.W., Jr.——B: Oct. 3, 1943, Waverly, OH, *Atty.*, Wood, Whitesell, Karp, Wellbaum, Miller & Seitl, P.A., Englewood Office; **PRIM RE ACT:** Attorney; **SERVICES:** Title examinations, title ins., closings, preparation of all documents; **REP CLIENTS:** First Fed. S & L Assn. of Englewood, First Nat. Bank of Englewood, Englewood Area Bd. of Realtors; **PROFL AFFIL & HONORS:** The FL Bar, ABA, Sarasota Cty. Bar Assn., Charlotte Cty. Bar Assn.; **EDUC:** BS, 1966, Bus. Admin. and Econ., OH State Univ.; **GRAD EDUC:** JD, 1973, Law, OH No. Univ.; **EDUC HONORS:** Nat. Moot Ct.; **OTHER ACT & HONORS:** Kiwanis, Elks, Jaycees, C of C; **HOME ADD:** 1150 Larchmont Dr., Englewood, FL 33533, (813)474-4826; **BUS ADD:** 350 S. Indiana Ave., Englewood, FL 33533, (813)474-3241.

WELLER, Louis S.——B: May 31, 1949, Los Angeles, CA, *Atty. at Law*, Buchanan & Weller; **PRIM RE ACT:** Attorney, Instructor; **SERVICES:** Taxation, Devel., Synds., Gen. Transactions; **PROFL AFFIL & HONORS:** ABA, State Bar of CA, Bar Assn. of San Francisco, Instr.-RE Law and Taxation, CA Continums, Educ. of the Bar; Golden Gate Univ.; **EDUC:** BA, 1970, Poli. Sci., Yale Univ.; **GRAD EDUC:** JD, Master of Public Policy, 1975, Law, Public Policy, School of Law, School of Public Policy, Univ. of CA-Berkeley; **EDUC HONORS:** Cum Laude, departmental Honors; **HOME ADD:** 556 16th Ave., San Francisco, CA 94118; **BUS ADD:** 555 California St., Suite 3320, San Francisco, CA 94104, (415)391-1510.

WELLER, T. C., Jr.——B: Birmingham, AL, *Pres.*, Foreman & Weller, Inc.; **PRIM RE ACT:** Broker, Consultant, Developer, Owner/Investor, Property Manager, Syndicator; **PROFL AFFIL & HONORS:** Mobile Cty. Bd. of Realtors, SIR; **EDUC:** Bus. Mgmt., Univ. of S. AL; **BUS ADD:** PO Drawer 350, 2 S. Water St., Mobile, AL 36601, (205)433-5000.

WELLES, S. Christopher——B: Jan. 15, 1944, Duluth, MN, B.I.C. Realty; **PRIM RE ACT:** Consultant, Builder, Owner/Investor; **SERVICES:** Assisting in buying, bldg. and devel. lakefront props. for indivs. and corps.; **PREV EMPLOY:** Ad. Sales/Consulting; **EDUC:** Eng./Hist./Journ., Univ. of MN; **MIL SERV:** MNANG; **HOME ADD:** Lake Vermilion, Tower, MN 55790, (218)753-2113; **BUS ADD:** Box 383, Lake Vermilion, Tower, MN 55790, (218)753-2113.

WELLNER, John——*Mgr. RE*, Owens-Illinois; **PRIM RE ACT:** Property Manager; **BUS ADD:** PO Box 1035, Toledo, OH 43666, (419)247-5000.*

WELLS, Caroline E.——B: Mar. 27, 1953, Mobile, AL, *Atty.*, Gallalee, Denniston & Cherniak, Atty.; **PRIM RE ACT:** Attorney; **SERVICES:** Deeds, litigation and all other RE servs.; **REP CLIENTS:** Roberts Bros., Inc., Foreman & Weller, Inc., Amer. Condo. Inc., Julius E. Marx, Inc. Realtors; **PROFL AFFIL & HONORS:** WCR, Mobile Bd. of Realtors, Phi Delta Phi Frat., Mobile Cty. & AL State Bar Assn., Instr. Roberts Bros., Inc., educ. program, Instr. Mobile Bd. of Realtors Training Program; **EDUC:** 1975, Amer. Studies, Mktg. & Eng., Univ. of AL; **GRAD EDUC:** JD, 1978; **EDUC HONORS:** Cbi Delta Phi Eng. Hon., Bench & Bar Legal Hon., Dean's Serv. Award, Chmn. Law Day; **OTHER ACT & HONORS:** Art Patron's League; **HOME ADD:** 50 Bienville Ave., Mobile, AL 36606, (205)476-5256; **BUS ADD:** PO Box 2125, Mobile, AL 36652, (205)438-6132.

WELLS, Cecil H., Jr.——B: Apr. 21, 1927, San Mateo, CA, *Consulting Engineer*, Wells Companies & C. H. Wells Jr. & Assoc. - Consulting Engineers; **PRIM RE ACT:** Consultant, Engineer, Developer, Owner/Investor, Property Manager; **PROFL AFFIL & HONORS:** ASCE, SEAONC, ACI, ASTM, SSOM, NSPE; **EDUC:** BCE, 1951, Univ. of Santa Clara; **MIL SERV:** USN, WWII, Pacific; **OTHER ACT & HONORS:** Elks, Rotary Club, San Mateo Cty. Comm's., BSA; **BUS ADD:** 2031 Pioneer Court, Suite 12, San Mateo, CA 94403, (415)345-3554.

WELLS, Clifford E.——*Pres.*, James River Corp. of Virginia; **PRIM RE ACT:** Property Manager; **BUS ADD:** PO Box 617, Buchanan, VA 24066, (703)254-1241.*

WELLS, Donald A.——B: Mar. 23, 1924, San Francisco, *Pres.*, Wells Props.; **PRIM RE ACT:** Broker, Syndicator, Property Manager, Engineer, Owner/Investor; **PREV EMPLOY:** Past Pres. Wells Mfg. Corp.; **EDUC:** BSME, 1942, Univ. of CO; **GRAD EDUC:** 1945; **MIL SERV:** USN, Lt.j.g.; **OTHER ACT & HONORS:** Masons; **HOME ADD:** 33 Barry Ln., Atherton, CA 94025, (415)323-2970; **BUS ADD:** 501 Forbes S, San Francisco, CA 94080.

WELLS, George M.——B: Dec. 1, 1950, Little Rock, AR, *Assoc. Partner*, Barnes, Quinn, Flake & Anderson, Inc.; **PRIM RE ACT:** Broker, Syndicator; **SERVICES:** Brokerage, counseling, & synd. of comml. props.; **PROFL AFFIL & HONORS:** RESSI, SRS; **EDUC:** BA, 1972, Econ. & Bus., Hendrix Coll.; **GRAD EDUC:** MBA, 1974, RE, So. Methodist Univ.; **OTHER ACT & HONORS:** Past Pres., Bd. of Dir., Big Bros. of Pulaski Cty.; **HOME ADD:** 208 Beckwood, Little Rock, AR 72205, (501)661-0921; **BUS ADD:** 2100 1st National Bldg., Little Rock, AR 72203, (501)372-6161.

WELLS, R. Ronald——B: Sept. 12, 1948, Biltmore, NC, *Principal*, Wells & Co.; **PRIM RE ACT:** Consultant, Architect, Developer, Builder, Syndicator; **OTHER RE ACT:** Spec. in rehabilitation of cert. hist. structures.; **SERVICES:** Devel. & synd. of comml. props., arch. & constr. mgmt. for select clients; **REP CLIENTS:** Indiv. & instl. investors in comml. props., owners, architects and contractors; **PROFL AFFIL & HONORS:** AIA, Nat. Council of Arch. Reg. Bds., Nat. Trust for Hist. Preservation, Nat. Council of Arch. Registration Cert.; **EDUC:** BA, 1970, Eng., NC State Univ.; **GRAD EDUC:** MArch, 1975, Comm. Redevel. & Design, NC State Univ.; **EDUC HONORS:** Grad. research asst.; **HOME ADD:** 307 N. Monroe St., Moscow, ID 83843, (208)882-7060; **BUS ADD:** 111 E. 1st St., Moscow, ID 83843, (208)882-1500.

WELLS, Robert S.——**B:** Oct. 14, 1939, *Pres.*, Gateway Properties Co.; **PRIM RE ACT:** Broker, Developer, Owner/Investor; **PREV EMPLOY:** Dohemann Financial Corp.; Bank America Corp.; **EDUC:** BA, 1962, Eng., Yale Univ.; **GRAD EDUC:** MBA, 1964, Intl. Bus., Columbia Univ.; **HOME ADD:** 109 Sugarloaf Dr., Tiburon, CA 94920; **BUS ADD:** One Harbor Dr., Sausalito, CA 94965, (415)332-4373.

WELLS, Samuel Robert, Jr.——**B:** Jan. 12, 1927, Baltimore, MD, *VP & Gen. Mgr.*, Amer. Trading RE Co., 1961; **PRIM RE ACT:** Developer, Owner/Investor, Property Manager; **SERVICES:** Props.; **REP CLIENTS:** Devel. for own account; **PREV EMPLOY:** Cannon She Co., Dir. of RE, 1957-61; **PROFL AFFIL & HONORS:** BOMA, NACORE; **EDUC:** AB, 1952, Liberal Arts., Psych., Dartmouth Coll.; **MIL SERV:** US Army, Sgt., 1944-46; **HOME ADD:** 328 Weatherbee Rd., Towson, MD 21204, (301)334-9549; **BUS ADD:** PO Box 238, Baltimore, MD 21203, (301)685-4230.

WELLS, Thomas H.——**B:** Apr. 8, 1932, Derby, CT, Thomas H. Wells SRPA Appraisal Associates; **PRIM RE ACT:** Consultant, Appraiser; **SERVICES:** RE appraisals & consulting; **REP CLIENTS:** Transamerica, employee transfer, Stauffer Chemical, banks, attys. & indivs.; **PROFL AFFIL & HONORS:** SREA, SRPA; **MIL SERV:** US Navy; 1951-1953, Seaman, Mediterranean; **OTHER ACT & HONORS:** Seymour Bd. of Fin. 2 yrs.; **HOME ADD:** 18 Bungay Terrace, Seymour, CT 06483, (203)888-2192; **BUS ADD:** 18 Bungay Terrace, Seymour, CT 06483, (203)888-2192.

WELLS, Thomas R.——*VP, Devel. Dir.*, Narod Devel. Corp.; **PRIM RE ACT:** Developer, Builder; **SERVICES:** Devel. & constr. of comml. retail and condo. projects and prop. mgmt. of same; **PROFL AFFIL & HONORS:** Bellevue C of C; Dir., Bellevue Downtown Assn., Citizens Advisory Comm. on Energy; Seattle Master Builders Assn.; **OTHER ACT & HONORS:** Bellevue Athletic Club; **BUS ADD:** 14711 NE 29th Pl., Bellevue, WA 98007, (206)881-3090.

WELLS, William L.——**B:** Jan. 8, 1926, Boston, MA, *Dir. of RE*, M. De Matteo Const. Co.; **PRIM RE ACT:** Developer, Builder, Property Manager; **OTHER RE ACT:** Acquisition & Sales; **PREV EMPLOY:** Shopping Ctr. Dev., Condominium Dev., Meadow Hill Dev. Corp., Part.; **PROFL AFFIL & HONORS:** ICSC; **EDUC:** BA, 1947, Bus. Admin. (Acctg.), Bentley Coll. Waltham, MA; **MIL SERV:** USN, TM'K; **HOME ADD:** 252 S. Main St., Cohasset, MA 02025, (617)383-0264; **BUS ADD:** 200 Hancock St., Quincy, MA 02171, (617)328-8840.

WELLY, Robert H.——**B:** Jan. 11, 1951, Toledo, OH, *Atty.*, Gibson, Yarbrough & Welly; **PRIM RE ACT:** Consultant, Attorney; **SERVICES:** Full range of relevant legal service; **REP CLIENTS:** Indiv. Investors and Condo. Owners' Assns.; **PROFL AFFIL & HONORS:** ABA, Real Prop. Section; Steering Comm. NW OH Condo. Council; **EDUC:** AB, 1973, Eng. Lit., Univ. of Notre Dame; **GRAD EDUC:** JD, 1976, Univ. of Toledo; **EDUC HONORS:** Deans List, Hall Pres. Council, Student Bar Assoc.-Sec.; **OTHER ACT & HONORS:** St. Patricks Church; Bd. of Dir. Toledo Repertoire Theatre; Heather Downs Ctry. Club; **HOME ADD:** 2053 Colony Dr., Toledo, OH 43614, (419)382-9081; **BUS ADD:** 8th Floor, Toledo Home Fed. Bldg., Toledo, OH 43604, (419)241-4441.

WELSH, Thomas——**B:** July 3, 1934, Columbus, OH, *Owner*, Welsh, Realtors; **PRIM RE ACT:** Broker, Appraiser, Developer, Builder, Syndicator; **SERVICES:** Light construction, land utilization, synd., prop. evaluation; **REP CLIENTS:** Local govts., atty's, savings and loans; **PREV EMPLOY:** 25 yrs. in the field of RE encompassing single family detached subdiv., income producing property syndication, light construction, sale of mixed use devel. land; **PROFL AFFIL & HONORS:** The Soc. of RE Appraisers; ULI; Nat. Assn. of Homebuilders; Natl. Assn. of Realtors, SRA; **EDUC:** BSC, 1956, Bus., Ohio Univ.; **GRAD EDUC:** Candidate MBA, 1975, RE, Wright State Univ.; **OTHER ACT & HONORS:** Xenia City Commnr. 1969-1975; Xenia Rotary; Masonic Affiliation Inc. Antioch Temple; Dayton, Dist. Chmn., Boy Scouts of America; **HOME ADD:** 238 Corwin Ave., Xenia, OH 45385, (513)372-4737; **BUS ADD:** PO Box 1, Xenia, OH 45385, (513)372-7676.

WELSH, Thomas P.——**B:** Apr. 9, 1944, Nyack, NY, *Partner*, Krauser, Welsh & Sorich; **PRIM RE ACT:** Consultant, Appraiser; **SERVICES:** RE appraising and consulting; **REP CLIENTS:** ATT, Prudential, Local Bank & Attys.; **PROFL AFFIL & HONORS:** AIREA, Soc. of RE Appraisers, MAI, SRA; **EDUC:** 1965, Acctg., CW Post Coll.; **MIL SERV:** USMC, Capt.; **OTHER ACT & HONORS:** C of C; **HOME ADD:** 13 Jameson Pl., Flanders, NJ 07836, (201)584-1649; **BUS ADD:** South & Elm Plaza, 182 South St., Morristown, NJ 07960, (201)538-3188.

WELSH, William E.——*Mgr. Prop. Div.*, Hanna Mining Co.; **PRIM RE ACT:** Property Manager; **BUS ADD:** 100 Erieview Plaza, Cleveland, OH 44114, (216)589-4000.*

WELTY, Alan E.——**B:** July 10, 1932, Winona, MN, *Exec. VP*, Welty & Woods, Inc.; **OTHER RE ACT:** RE Development; **SERVICES:** Hotel devel. & mgmt.; **PREV EMPLOY:** City of Atlanta Planning Dept., 1959-61; Hammer, Siler, George Assoc., 1961-69; Welty & Woods (1969-72); Brooks, Harvey & Co., 1972-79; Wilma, Inc., 1979-81; **PROFL AFFIL & HONORS:** Member Amer. Soc. of RE Counselors (ASREC); Member Amer. Inst. of Cert. Planners (AICP), ASREC, AICP; **EDUC:** BS, 1958, Urban Geography & Planning, Univ. of MN; **GRAD EDUC:** MA, 1959, Geography, Univ. of MN; **EDUC HONORS:** High Distinction, Teaching Fellow; **MIL SERV:** USAF, S/Sgt.; **HOME ADD:** 12 Paces W. Dr., Atlanta, GA 30327, (404)266-1599; **BUS ADD:** Suite 25, 1770 Century Cir., Atlanta, GA 30327.

WENDELKEN, Richard J.——**B:** Nov. 30, 1939, Akron, OH, O'Neil & Smith; **PRIM RE ACT:** Attorney; **PREV EMPLOY:** Lawyer's Title Ins. Corp.; Referee, Summit Cty. Probate Ct., 1971-79; **PROFL AFFIL & HONORS:** ABA; Akron and OH Bar Assns.; **EDUC:** BA, 1962, Econ., St. Francis Coll.; **GRAD EDUC:** JD, 1970, Univ. of Akron; **OTHER ACT & HONORS:** Serra Club, Knights of Columbus; **HOME ADD:** 945 Hereford Dr., Akron, OH 44303, (216)836-1083; **BUS ADD:** 16 S. Broadway, Akron, OH 44308, (216)253-0855.

WENDOLL, James A.——**B:** Aug. 20, 1947, Elgin, IL, *Dir.*, Coopers & Lybrand; **PRIM RE ACT:** Consultant; **OTHER RE ACT:** Mgmt. Consulting; **SERVICES:** Econ. analysis, fin. feasibility studies, valuations, land use planning, mkt. studies, acctg. systems; **PREV EMPLOY:** VP Fin. & Treas., Great Western Cities Inc., 1974-1977; Other mgmt. positions 1970-1974 (GWC); Microdot, Inc. 1967-70; **PROFL AFFIL & HONORS:** Los Angeles Rgnl. Forum on Solid Waste Mgmt.; **EDUC:** BS, 1970, Bus. Admin., CA State Univ. at Los Angeles; **OTHER ACT & HONORS:** Bd. of Dirs., Diamond Bar YMCA; **HOME ADD:** 20559 E. Gernside Dr., Walnut, CA 91789, (714)595-0594; **BUS ADD:** 1000 W. Sixth St., Los Angeles, CA 90017, (213)481-1000.

WENDT, Forrest D.——**B:** Aug. 8, 1931, Leon, WI, *Pres.*, WCT Devel., Inc.; **PRIM RE ACT:** Architect, Developer, Owner/Investor; **SERVICES:** RE Devel. & Arch. Serv.; **PROFL AFFIL & HONORS:** AIA; **EDUC:** BArch, 1959, Arch., Univ. of IL; **MIL SERV:** USAF, 1st Lt.; **OTHER ACT & HONORS:** Pres. Glenview-Northbrook Kiwanis Club, 1967; **BUS ADD:** 560 Green Bay Rd., Winnetka, IL 60093, (312)446-7890.

WENDT, Paul F.——**B:** Nov. 7, 1908, NY, NY, *Prof.*, Univ. of CA, Sch. of Bus.; **PRIM RE ACT:** Consultant, Appraiser, Instructor; **PREV EMPLOY:** 35 yrs. teaching, writing and consulting; **PROFL AFFIL & HONORS:** MAI, CRE; **EDUC:** BS, 1928, Econ., Lafayette Coll.; **GRAD EDUC:** MA, 1935, Econ., Columbia Univ.; PhD, 1941, Econ., Columbia Univ.; **MIL SERV:** USNR, Lt.; **HOME ADD:** 343 ScottsdaleRd., Pleasant Hill, CA 94523, (415)689-0829; **BUS ADD:** 350 Barrows Hall, Berkeley, CA 94720, (415)642-2734.

WENDT, Steven E.——**B:** Sept. 27, 1953, Algona, IA, *Chief Appraiser*, Mutual Fed. S&L, N. IA Appraisal Service; **PRIM RE ACT:** Instructor, Consultant, Appraiser, Lender; **OTHER RE ACT:** RE Sales; **PROFL AFFIL & HONORS:** SREA, Rochester MN Chap. 198, SRA & SRPA-have also served on the bd. of directors for the Rochester Chap. and was recently elected as Exec. Officer; **EDUC:** BS, 1976, Fin.-Indus. Admin., IA State Univ., Ames; **EDUC HONORS:** Admitted with recognition to IA State in 1972, Grad. with Distinction in 1976; **HOME ADD:** 1519 S. Delaware, Mason City, IA 50401, (515)424-0503; **BUS ADD:** 10 1st St. N.W., Mason City, IA 50401, (515)423-2922.

WENDT, William M.——**B:** Mar. 8, 1932, VA, *VP, RE Investments*, Prudential Insurance Co. of Amer., RE Investment Dept.; **PRIM RE ACT:** Lender, Owner/Investor, Insuror; **PREV EMPLOY:** Rouse Co.; **PROFL AFFIL & HONORS:** Fin. Execs. Inst., FEI, NJ Chap. Pres.; **EDUC:** BBA, 1954, Acctg., Univ. of Miami; **GRAD EDUC:** MS, 1962, Econ. and Quantitative Methods, Purdue; **EDUC HONORS:** Cum Laude; **HOME ADD:** 122 Glenmere Dr., Chatham, NJ 07928, (201)635-7033; **BUS ADD:** 14 Prudential Plaza, Newark, NJ 07101, (201)877-7921.

WENER, Jonathan I.——**B:** Aug. 25, 1950, Montreal, Can., *Pres.*, Canderel Ltd.; **PRIM RE ACT:** Consultant, Developer, Owner/Investor, Property Manager; **SERVICES:** Land assembly, feasibility studies, const., leasing, prop. mgmt.; **REP CLIENTS:** Joint venture partner: N. Amer. Life Assurance Co.; On the Advisory Council of BG

PREECO; **PREV EMPLOY:** First Quebec Corp. as Exec. VP; **EDUC:** Commerce, 1971, Fin., Sir George Williams Univ. (Concordia); **HOME ADD:** 4 Thurlow Rd., Hampstead, Que., (514)486-9007; **BUS ADD:** 2000 Peel St., Suite 800, Montreal, H3A 2W5, Canada, Quebec, (514)842-8636.

WENTCHER, Ernest C.——*Pres.*, Ernest C. Wentcher & Assoc.; **OTHER RE ACT:** Consultant, Direct Response Mass Mktg.; General Ins. Broker; **PREV EMPLOY:** Mgr., Equitable Life Assurance Soc. of the US, Chicago, 15 yrs.; **PROFL AFFIL & HONORS:** Nat. Assn. of Life Underwriters, Amer. Inst. of Profl. Assn. Group Ins. Administrators, Hall of Fame of the Equitable Life Members Million Dollar Club; Member of Equitable Group Millionaires Club - Over $2 billion of group life negotiated for clients; **EDUC:** BS, 1935, Chemistry, Univ. of Brussels; **MIL SERV:** USN, Lt. Comdr.; **OTHER ACT & HONORS:** Dir., Navy League; **BUS ADD:** 401 N. Michigan Ave., Suite 217, Chicago, IL 60611, (312)321-5100.

WEPMAN, Warren S.——**B:** May 24, 1929, Grand Rapids, MI, Wepman and Wepman, P.A.; **PRIM RE ACT:** Attorney; **SERVICES:** Legal services; **PROFL AFFIL & HONORS:** FL Bar & ABA; **EDUC:** BA, 1950, Constitutional Hist., Univ. of MI; **GRAD EDUC:** JD, 1951, Univ. of MI Law School; **EDUC HONORS:** With Distinction; **HOME ADD:** El Dorado, 3635 Bougainvillea Road, Miami, FL 33133, (305)445-5081; **BUS ADD:** El Dorado, 3635 Bougainvillea Road, Miami, FL 33133, (305)446-6501.

WERBNER, Alfred P.——**B:** Dec. 30, 1923, Trenton, NJ, *Assoc. Prof. - Coordinator, RE Education*, Manchester Community Coll.; **PRIM RE ACT:** Appraiser, Instructor; **OTHER RE ACT:** Coordinator RE Educ.; **SERVICES:** Educ., appraisal and consulting work; **REP CLIENTS:** General Motors, General Electric, Aetna Ins. Co., Travelers Ins. Co., Town of Manchester, Town of East Hartford, CT Bank & Trust, Hartford National Bank & Trust, Savings Bank of Manchester; **PROFL AFFIL & HONORS:** Amer. Soc. of Appraisers, Intl. Right of Way Assn., Nat. Assn. of Review Appraisers, ASA, CRA; **GRAD EDUC:** JD, 1949, Law, New York Law School; **MIL SERV:** Air Force, Lt. Col., many decorations; **OTHER ACT & HONORS:** Chmn, Town Devel. Commn., Pres. Manchester Kiwanis Club, Pres. Manchester C of C; **HOME ADD:** 85 Dale Rd., Manchester, CT 06040, (203)643-7847; **BUS ADD:** P O Box 2, Manchester, CT 06040, (203)646-3250.

WERFEL, Laurence——**B:** July 20, 1933, Brooklyn, NY, *Pres.*, Laurence Werfel, Architect, PC; **PRIM RE ACT:** Consultant, Architect, Instructor; **SERVICES:** Arch., engrg., planning, RE counseling; **PROFL AFFIL & HONORS:** AIA, Past Pres., Queens Cty. Chap. AIA; **EDUC:** BArch., 1955; **MIL SERV:** US Army, Corps. of Engrs., 1st Lt.; **HOME ADD:** 12 Avone Ln., East Hills, NY; **BUS ADD:** 75-19 Vleigh Pl., Flushing, NY 11367.

WERMAISS, John A.——**B:** May 10, 1942, NY, NY, *Pres.*, Werwaiss & Co., Inc.; **PRIM RE ACT:** Broker; **PREV EMPLOY:** VP, William A. White & Sons.; Chmn. of Bd., Realty Growth Investors; **PROFL AFFIL & HONORS:** Young Men's RE Assn. (Past. Gov.); RE Bd. of NY, Mayor's Comm. on RE Devel.; **EDUC:** BA, 1964, Govt., Georgetown Univ.; **GRAD EDUC:** 1967, RE, Baruch Sch. of Bus. CUNY; **HOME ADD:** 1107 Fifth Ave., New York, NY 10022, (212)722-2551; **BUS ADD:** 509 Madison Ave., New York, NY 10022, (212)935-0200.

WERNER, Charles——**B:** Sept. 14, 1952, Philadelphia, PA, *VP - Human Resources*, Lomas & Nettleton Financial Corp.; **PRIM RE ACT:** Lender; **SERVICES:** Mort. banking and short term RE lending; **PREV EMPLOY:** Amer. Soc. of Personnel Admin.; **PROFL AFFIL & HONORS:** MBAA; **EDUC:** BBA, 1974, Org. Devel., So. Methodist Univ.; **OTHER ACT & HONORS:** Bd. Member-Theatre Three; Bd. Member-Dallas Urban League; Leadership Dallas Program; Young Leadership Devel. Program; **HOME ADD:** 6255 W. Northwest Highway 206, Dallas, TX 75225, (214)739-6235; **BUS ADD:** P.O. Box 225644, Dallas, TX 75265, (214)746-7252.

WERNER, Eugene——**B:** Nov. 14, 1941, Chicago, IL, *House Counsel and Sec.*, Landau & Heyman, Inc.; **PRIM RE ACT:** Attorney; **PROFL AFFIL & HONORS:** ABA, IL and Chicago Bar Assns.; Intl. Council of Shopping Ctrs.; **EDUC:** BA, 1964, Pre-Law, Roosevelt Univ.; **GRAD EDUC:** JD, 1966, Law, DePaul Univ.; **HOME ADD:** 9443 N. Lavergne Ave., Chicago, IL 60638, (312)679-8724; **BUS ADD:** 120 S. LaSalle St., Chicago, IL 60603, (312)372-3133.

WERNER, Mark A.——**B:** May 8, 1943, Jacksonville, FL, *Pres.*, Werner Realty Corp.; **PRIM RE ACT:** Broker, Syndicator; **SERVICES:** Prop. mgmt., apts and comml. RE; **PROFL AFFIL & HONORS:** Jacksonville Bd. of Realtors; **EDUC:** BA, 1965, Bus., FL State Univ.; **HOME ADD:** 2738 Christopher Creek Rd., Jacksonville, FL 32217, (904)731-2534; **BUS ADD:** 3614 St. Augustine Rd., Jacksonville, FL 32207, (904)398-7303.

WERNERSBACH, Dennis J.——**B:** Feb. 25, 1940, Cincinnati, OH, *Pres.*, Property Management Consultants, Inc.; **PRIM RE ACT:** Consultant, Owner/Investor, Property Manager; **OTHER RE ACT:** Condo. conversion; **PREV EMPLOY:** Midland Mort. Investors Trust (REIT); **PROFL AFFIL & HONORS:** CPM; **EDUC:** BS, 1962, Eng., Univ. of Dayton, OH; **GRAD EDUC:** Post Grad. Study, 1966-1967, Phil., Univ. of Fribourg, Switzerland, Goethe Inst. Germany; **HOME ADD:** 11113 Blue Stem Dr., Oklahoma City, OK 73132, (405)722-2056; **BUS ADD:** 1000 W. Wilshire Blvd. 208, Oklahoma City, OK 73116, (405)843-0502.

WERTHEIMER, Robert J.——**B:** Dec. 26, 1954, NYC, NY, Donovan, Leisure, Newton & Irvine; **PRIM RE ACT:** Attorney; **PROFL AFFIL & HONORS:** Assn. of the Bar of the City of NY; NY State Bar Assn.; ABA, Corrections Comm. of Assn. of the Bar of the City of NY; Comm. Membership of ABA; **EDUC:** BA, 1976, Sociology, School of Arts and Sci., Cornell Univ.; **GRAD EDUC:** JD, 1979, Columbia Univ. School of Law; **EDUC HONORS:** Grad. with Distinction in all subjects; **HOME ADD:** 417 Riverside Dr., New York, NY 10025, (212)864-3577; **BUS ADD:** 30 Rockefeller Plaza, New York, NY 10112, (212)307-4100.

WESMAN, Harvey——**B:** July 25, 1920, Newark, NJ, Harvey Wesman Co.; **PRIM RE ACT:** Consultant, Appraiser; **SERVICES:** Appraisals, consultations; **REP CLIENTS:** Major banks, builders, many nat. corps.; **PROFL AFFIL & HONORS:** AIREA, MAI; **EDUC:** BS, Econ., MN Univ.; **GRAD EDUC:** MBA, RE, Columbia Grad. School of Bus.; **MIL SERV:** Signal Corp, Capt.; **OTHER ACT & HONORS:** Columbia Univ. Alumni Club; **HOME ADD:** 57 Farmstead Rd., Short Hills, NJ 07078, (201)376-8383; **BUS ADD:** 403 White Oak Ridge, Short Hills, NJ 07078.

WEST, Charles W.——**B:** Feb. 21, 1950, Boston, MA, *Pres.*, Westline Investments Ltd.; **PRIM RE ACT:** Broker, Instructor, Syndicator, Consultant, Owner/Investor; **OTHER RE ACT:** Brokerage, Synd. Investment Prop.; **PREV EMPLOY:** Cambio Realty & Investments, Fullerton, CA; **PROFL AFFIL & HONORS:** RECI, Salesman of the Yr. 1978 Cambio; CCIM; **EDUC:** BS, 1972, Bus., Engineering, UCLA; **GRAD EDUC:** JD, 1982 projected, RE Law, WA State Univ.; **OTHER ACT & HONORS:** Toastmasters Intl.; **HOME ADD:** 531 Fordham Dr., Placentia, CA 92670; **BUS ADD:** 101 S Kraemer Blvd., Ste. 131, Placentia, CA 92670, (714)524-0261.

WEST, Clyde O.——**B:** Sept. 22, 1940, Elkhart, KS, *Atty. at Law*, The Law Offices of Clyde O. West; **PRIM RE ACT:** Attorney; **SERVICES:** Review of RE contracts, leases, litigation of RE matters; **EDUC:** 1965, Soc. Sci., Sacramento State Univ.; **GRAD EDUC:** JD, 1971, Law, McGeorge School of Law, Sacramento, CA; **BUS ADD:** 1314 H. St., Suite 100, Sacramento, CA 95814, (916)441-1891.

WEST, Donald R.——**B:** Oct. 29, 1926, Seattle, WA, *Assessor in Charge*, City of NY Dept. of Fin., Real Prop. Assessment Bur., RE of Utility Corps. & Spec. Franchises; **PRIM RE ACT:** Engineer, Assessor, Property Manager; **PREV EMPLOY:** Abbott, Merkt & Co., 2/52-7/53, Ford, Bacon & Davis, Inc., 7/53-5/55, J.G. White Engrg. Corp., 5/55-4/63, City of NY 4/63 to present; **PROFL AFFIL & HONORS:** ASCE, Intl. Assn. of Assessing Officers, Profl. Engr., NY State License; **EDUC:** BS, 1952, Struct. Engrg., CCNY; **MIL SERV:** US Army, Cpl.; **HOME ADD:** 24604 85th Ave., Bellerose, NY 11426, (212)347-6799; **BUS ADD:** 1 Centre St., Room 914, NY, NY 10007, (212)566-4348.

WEST, George F.——**B:** June 9, 1945, Ferriday, LA, *Pres.*, George F. West & Associates; **PRIM RE ACT:** Consultant, Appraiser; **OTHER RE ACT:** Prop. tax consultant, Analyst; **SERVICES:** Prop. tax consulting, feasibility studies, investment tax credit studies, RE valuations; **REP CLIENTS:** Fin. instit., govt. entities, indiv. investors, nat. cos., banks and attys.; **PREV EMPLOY:** Dallas Cty.; **PROFL AFFIL & HONORS:** AIREA, SREA, IAAO, TX Bd. of Tax Assessor Examiners, MAI, SRPA, AAE, RPA; **EDUC:** BS, 1969, RE, LA Tech Univ.; **HOME TEL:** (214)699-1557; **BUS ADD:** 4255 L.B.J. Fwy., Ste. #120, Dallas, TX 75234, (214)386-0084.

WEST, Howard E.——**B:** June 7, 1914, Pine Island, MN, *Atty.*, West, Gowan & McIntosh; **PRIM RE ACT:** Attorney, Owner/Investor; **SERVICES:** Legal servs. on sales & purchases; **REP CLIENTS:** 1st Nat. Bank of Rochester; Rochester Methodist Hospital, Rochester, MN; **PREV EMPLOY:** G.I. - Appraiser, home purchases; Special Agent, FBI; **PROFL AFFIL & HONORS:** Olmsted Cty. Bar Assn.; MN State Bar Assn., Real Estate Sect.; ABA, Real Estate Sect.; **EDUC:** BS, 1941, RE/Tax & Estate Matters, Univ. of MN; 1935, Univ. of MN, School of Agric.; **GRAD EDUC:** LLB, 1941, RE Tax & Estate Matters, Univ. of MN; **EDUC HONORS:** Valedictorian; **MIL**

SERV: Special Agent, FBI, 1942-1945; **OTHER ACT & HONORS:** Bd. of Govs., MN State Bar Assn., 4 yrs.; Rochester Rotary Club, 1946 to present; Rochester Area Found., Bd. of Tr., 1950 to present; Pres., Bd. of Dir., Rochester Methodist Hospital, 1970-1980; **HOME ADD:** Rt. 4, Rochester, MN 55901, (507)282-2459; **BUS ADD:** 327 1st Nat. Bank Bldg., Rochester, MN 55901, (507)282-7428.

WEST, I. LeRoy——B: Mar. 16, 1918, MO, *Prop.*, Colonial Manor Apts.; **PRIM RE ACT:** Consultant, Banker, Developer, Lender, Builder, Owner/Investor, Property Manager, Syndicator; **HOME ADD:** 2111 E. St. Mary's Blvd., Jefferson City, MO 65101, (314)635-3975; **BUS ADD:** 2111 B Dalton St., Jefferson City, MO 65101, (314)635-3975.

WEST, Jeffrey G.——B: July 6, 1956, Montour Falls, NY, *Controller*, Edward R. Marden Corp.; **PRIM RE ACT:** Builder; **OTHER RE ACT:** CPA; **PREV EMPLOY:** Touche Ross & Co., CPA's 1977-1979, Saul L. Ziner & Co. 1979-1980, CPA; **PROFL AFFIL & HONORS:** CPA in the Commonwealth of MA; **EDUC:** BS IN Bus. Admin., 1977, Acctg., Boston Univ.; **GRAD EDUC:** MBA in progress, Fin., Bentley Coll.; **EDUC HONORS:** Cum Laude; Mortar Bd. Lock Natl. Serv. Honor Soc.; B.U. LOCA Honor Soc.; **HOME ADD:** N. Walker Rd., N. Andover, MA 01845, (617)689-0408; **BUS ADD:** 280 Lincoln St., Allston, MA 02134, (617)782-3743.

WEST, Joseph Frederick——B: Oct. 2, 1946, Wash.,DC, *Dir., Mort. Fin. & Money Markets*, Natl. Assn. of Homebuilders; **PRIM RE ACT:** Consultant, Attorney, Owner/Investor, Instructor, Real Estate Publisher; **SERVICES:** Investment counseling, legal & fin. guidance, builder/lender relations; **REP CLIENTS:** Bldrs., lenders investors, homebuyers; **PREV EMPLOY:** The Lomas & Nettleton Co., 1974-1977; **PROFL AFFIL & HONORS:** MBA; Advisory Comm. Natl. Consumer Co-operative Bank; **EDUC:** BS, 1970, Fin., Siena Coll., Albany, NY; **GRAD EDUC:** JD, 1978, Law, George Mason Univ., School of Law, Arlington VA; **HOME ADD:** 2513 N. 9th St., Arlington, VA 22201, (703)527-7420; **BUS ADD:** 15th & M Sts. NW, Wash., DC 20005, (202)822-0234.

WEST, MacDonald——B: July 15, 1943, Bournmouth, England, *VP*, The Allen Morris Co.; **PRIM RE ACT:** Broker, Property Manager, Developer; **SERVICES:** Devel., const., brokerage, mgmt. & counseling for comml. & indus. props.; **REP CLIENTS:** Maj. nat. & intl. corps., high net worth domestic & foreign investors; **PREV EMPLOY:** VP & Dir. The Philipsborn Co.; **PROFL AFFIL & HONORS:** Fellow of the Royal Inst. of Chartered Surveyors, London, England; Miami Bd. of Realtors; Amer. Soc. of RE Counselors, Licensed RE Broker, Gen. contractor & mort. broker, state of FL; **EDUC:** Chartered Quantity surveying, 1968, London Univ., Coll. of RE Mgmt., England; **GRAD EDUC:** MBA, 1970, Fin. & Gen. Mgmt., mktg., Columbia Univ. Grad. Sch. of Bus.; **OTHER ACT & HONORS:** Dir. of Rotary Club of Coral Gables, Deacon of Univ. Baptist Church, Member of Bankers Club, Miami; Member of Econ. Soc. of South FL; **HOME ADD:** 5325 Orduna Dr., Coral Gables, FL 33146, (305)662-2000; **BUS ADD:** One Biscayne Tower, Suite 2600, Miami, FL 33131, (305)358-1000.

WEST, Terry W.——B: Apr. 10, 1936, Ypsilanti, MI, *VP-RE & Mort.*, Alexander Hamilton Life Ins. Co. of America, Mort. Dept.; **PRIM RE ACT:** Property Manager, Lender, Owner/Investor; **SERVICES:** Lender; **REP CLIENTS:** Indiv. and Corps. owning comml. prop.; **PREV EMPLOY:** Nat. Bank of Detroit- 15 yrs. and Detroit Fed. S&L Assn. 8 yrs.; **PROFL AFFIL & HONORS:** State and Nat. Mort. Bankers Assn., Nat. Assn. of Accountants, Detroit Bd. of Realtors-MI RE Broker's License; **EDUC:** BS, 1962, Acctg., Cleary Coll.; **MIL SERV:** US Air Nat. Guard, S/Sgt.; **OTHER ACT & HONORS:** JCI Senator; Member of Plymouth Kiwanis; Involved in many community activities; Received the Plymouth Community Outstanding Young Man's Award in 1966; **HOME ADD:** 41141 Ann Arbor Rd., Plymouth, MI, (313)453-6184; **BUS ADD:** 33045 Hamilton Blvd., Farmington Hills, MI 48018, (313)553-2000.

WEST, William S.——*Chrm. of Board.*, West Co., Inc.; **PRIM RE ACT:** Property Manager; **BUS ADD:** West Bridge St., Phoenixville, PA 19460, (215)935-4500.*

WESTBROOK, Edward G.——B: Jan. 15, 1907, Glenview, IL, *Pres.*, Continental Realty Investment, Inc.; **PRIM RE ACT:** Broker, Consultant, Developer, Owner/Investor, Syndicator; **OTHER RE ACT:** Search of indus. for acquisition by industry; **SERVICES:** Investment counseling, synd. of comml. prop., counseling owners of difficult prop.; **REP CLIENTS:** Indiv. investors; owners of difficult prop.; major indus. corp.; **PREV EMPLOY:** Many yrs. in mfgr. & sale of prefab housing; **PROFL AFFIL & HONORS:** Farm & Land Inst.; RESSI, CCIM; **EDUC:** AB, 1929, Psych./Eng., Univ. of IL; **OTHER ACT & HONORS:** Pres., OH Comml. Ex. Assn., 1974; Pres., OH Chapt. RESSI, 1975; VP, OH Assn. of Realtors Dist. 1, 1978-1981; Pres., Lorlin Co. Bd. of Realtors, 1975; Chmn., Indus. Devel., City of Vermilon, 1965-1970; **HOME ADD:** 27645 Quarry Rd., Wellington, OH 44090, (216)647-3532; **BUS ADD:** 4567 Liberty Ave., POB 337, Vermilion, OH 44089, (216)967-6167.

WESTCOTT, William——B: July 8, 1930, Cleveland, OH, *Pres. & Gen. Mgr.*, Westcott Const.; **OTHER RE ACT:** Rehabilitation prop. (primarily resid.) in the Cleveland Inner City; **PREV EMPLOY:** 30 yrs. Electrical Contractor; **PROFL AFFIL & HONORS:** Cleveland Restoration Soc., IEEE, Electrical League Cleveland, Harvard Business School Club; **EDUC:** BS, 1957, Econ., Wharton, Univ. of PA; **GRAD EDUC:** PMD, 1971, Upper Mgt. Preparatory, Harvard Bus. School; **HOME ADD:** 2351 N. Park Blvd., Cleveland Hts., OH 44106, (216)795-0537; **BUS ADD:** PO Box 1983, Cleveland, OH 44106, (216)231-7372.

WESTMAN, Bert——*Adv. Dir.*, CBS Publications Division, New Homes Guide to Vacation Homes; **PRIM RE ACT:** Real Estate Publisher; **BUS ADD:** 383 Madison Ave., New York, NY 10017, (212)688-9100.*

WETHERILL, G. Lance——B: Feb. 21, 1946, Kansas City, MO, *Pres.*, The Wetherill Co.; **PRIM RE ACT:** Appraiser, Property Manager, Owner/Investor; **SERVICES:** RE Appraisial; **REP CLIENTS:** Equitable; Exec., Southwestern Bell; **PROFL AFFIL & HONORS:** SRA, RM, AIREA; **EDUC:** BS, 1969, Econ, Fin., Columbia Univ., MO Univ.; **HOME ADD:** 4511 Headwood 5, Kansas City, MO 64111, (816)531-3644; **BUS ADD:** 2302 Power & Light Bldg., Kansas City, MO 64105, (816)531-2797.

WHALEN, Daniel A.——B: Mar. 31, 1918, Rock Island, IL, *Pres.*, Park Ridge Inc.; **PRIM RE ACT:** Attorney, Developer, Owner/Investor; **PROFL AFFIL & HONORS:** IA Bar Assn.; IL Bar Assn.; **EDUC:** BA, 1940, Pre-Law, Univ. of IA; **GRAD EDUC:** JD, 1947, Law, Univ. of IA Coll. of Law; **EDUC HONORS:** With Distinction; **MIL SERV:** US Army, Capt., Army Commendation Medal; **OTHER ACT & HONORS:** Jr. C of C, 1947, Pres., Davenport; 1948, Nat. Dir., State of IA; 1952, Author, Nat. Policy Manual; 1955, Chmn., Rgnl. Convention; 1981, Intl. Jaycee Senator Award; Amer. Legion, 1948, Comdr., Post 26, Davenport; 1951, Comdr., Second District, IA; United Cerebral Palsy Assn., 1953, First Pres., Davenport; 1959, Pres., IA; 1960, Dir., Natl.; Davenport C of C, 1957-1958, Dir., 1961, Pres.; Commodore, Lindsay Park Yacht Club, Davenport, IA, 1960-62; Pres., Rotary Club, North Peoria, IL, 1970; Charter Pres., Rotary Club, North Scott, Davenport, IA, 1973; **HOME ADD:** 6818 Hillandale Rd., Davenport, IA 52806, (319)386-2266; **BUS ADD:** 2715 W. 63rd St., Davenport, IA 52806, (319)386-7090.

WHALEN, John F.——B: Sept. 18, 1944, Springfield, VT, *Mgr., Comml. Mort. Investment*, Natl. Life Insrance Co., Montpelier, VT; **PRIM RE ACT:** Lender, Owner/Investor; **SERVICES:** Perm. Mort. Fin. and RE Acquisition of Comml. Props.; **REP CLIENTS:** RE Owners, Devels., and Inst. Involved in the Devel.and Ownership of Comml. Props.; **PREV EMPLOY:** Asst. Regional Dir., Northeast Regional RE Investment Office, MA Mutual Life Ins. Co., Springfield, MA; **PROFL AFFIL & HONORS:** AIREA, NARA, CRA (Certified Review Appraiser), MAI Candidate; **EDUC:** BA, 1966, Bus. Admin., St. Michaels Coll., Winooski, VT; **GRAD EDUC:** MA, 1971, Bus., Central MO State Univ., Warrensburg, MO; **MIL SERV:** USAF, Capt.; **OTHER ACT & HONORS:** Dir., Central VT Econ., Devel. Corp., Montpelier, VT; **HOME ADD:** 7 Kemp Ave., Montpelier, VT 05602, (802)223-3270; **BUS ADD:** Natl. Life Dr., Montpelier, VT 05602, (802)229-3428.

WHALEN, William F.——*Dir.*, Department of Housing and Urban Development, Budget Mgmt. & Operations Div.; **PRIM RE ACT:** Lender; **BUS ADD:** 451 Seventh St., S.W., 20410, Washington, DC, (202)755-8226.*

WHARTON, Joseph B., III——B: Mar. 21, 1954, New Orleans, LA, *Broker/Owner*, Wharton Investment Properties; **PRIM RE ACT:** Broker, Consultant, Owner/Investor, Syndicator; **SERVICES:** Comml. - investment brokerage, investment counseling, syndication; **REP CLIENTS:** Indiv., partnership and instnl. investors; **PROFL AFFIL & HONORS:** AMBA; **EDUC:** BS, 1976, Psych., Tulane Univ. - New Orleans; **GRAD EDUC:** MBA, 1979, Marketing/Finance, Emory Univ. - Atlanta; **HOME ADD:** 8349 Northmeadow Cir., Dallas, TX 75231, (214)348-2012; **BUS ADD:** 13101 Preston Rd. Suite 300, Dallas, TX 75240, (214)934-8565.

WHEELER, Dale——*Dir RE*, Johns-Manville Corp.; **PRIM RE ACT:** Property Manager; **BUS ADD:** Box 5108, Denver, CO 80217, (303)979-1000.*

WHEELER, Ira——*VP Planning*, Celanese Corp.; **PRIM RE ACT:** Property Manager; **BUS ADD:** 1211 Avenue of The Americas, New York, NY 10036, (212)764-7640.*

WHEELER, Joe B.——**B:** Feb. 27, 1941, Jackson, MS, *Dir. of RE*, BI-LO Inc. (Supermarkets); **PRIM RE ACT:** Attorney, Property Manager; **SERVICES:** Site selection, mkt. analysis; **EDUC:** BA, 1964, Pol. Sci., Hist., OK City Univ.; **GRAD EDUC:** JD, 1967, Law, OK City Univ.; **OTHER ACT & HONORS:** B.P.O.E., Lions, Big Bros.; **HOME ADD:** 102 Shetland Way, Greer, SC 29651, (803)292-2254; **BUS ADD:** PO Drawer 99, Mauldin, SC 29662, (803)288-1140.

WHEELER, Richard——*Gen. Coun.*, Dairylea Cooperative, Inc.; **PRIM RE ACT:** Attorney, Property Manager; **BUS ADD:** One Blue Hill Plaza, Pearl River, NY 10965, (914)627-3131.*

WHEELER, Robert L.——**B:** Dec. 10, 1934, Evansville, IN, *Pres.*, United American Financial Corp., Subsidiary of United Amer. Bank; **PRIM RE ACT:** Consultant, Appraiser, Banker, Lender; **PREV EMPLOY:** Pres., Decatur Bank & Trust Co., Decatur, IN; Monroe Cty. Bank, Sweetwater, TN, 1969-1975; **PROFL AFFIL & HONORS:** Amer. Inst. of Banking, Cert. Comml. Lender; **EDUC:** Cert. of Acctg., 1966, Bus., IN Univ.; **GRAD EDUC:** 1971, Banking/Fin., Rutgers Univ.; **MIL SERV:** USN; Asst. Navigator, 1952-1963; **OTHER ACT & HONORS:** Grad. of Nat. School of RE Fin., OH State Univ., 1972; **HOME ADD:** 10820 Farragut Hills Blvd., Knoxville, TN 37922, (615)966-0515; **BUS ADD:** POB 280, Knoxville, TN 37901, (615)971-2770.

WHEELER, Tom M.——**B:** Nov.13,1929, Macomb, IL, *Pres.*, The Wheeler Co., Inc., Realtors; **PRIM RE ACT:** Broker, Instructor, Syndicator, Consultant, Appraiser, Developer, Property Manager; **REP CLIENTS:** G. Heilman Brewing Co.,Trane Co., Employee Transfer, Executrans Inc., General Foods Inc., Gateway Products Co., Grandview Hospital, Norplex, Northern Sates Power Co., Texaco Oil Co., Univ. of WI-La Crosse, WI Tel Co.; **PROFL AFFIL & HONORS:** ASREC, RNMI, NAR, WI Realtors Assoc.; **OTHER ACT & HONORS:** UW Foundation, Visitors and Convention Bureau, Past Dir. COC, Past Pres. WI Realtors Assn., Chmn. Publication Comm-Nat. Assn. of Realtors, Gov. of ASREC; **HOME ADD:** 128 N. 9th Street, La Crosse, WI 54601, (608)782-3336; **BUS ADD:** 122 North 7th St., PO Box 1986, La Crosse,, WI 54601, (608)785-1111.

WHEELER, W. Thomas——**B:** Apr. 1, 1951, Minneapolis, MN, *Part.*, Wheeler & Wheeler; **PRIM RE ACT:** Attorney; **SERVICES:** Full range of legal servs. Areas of primary activity include RE planning, corporate and tax matters, including tax treaties, corp. structures; **REP CLIENTS:** Overseas investors, offshore corps., local investors, local corps.; **PROFL AFFIL & HONORS:** ABA, Sect. on Intl. Taxation and Real Prop., Probate & Trust Law, Comm. on For. Investment in US RE, MN State Bar Assn., Real Prop. Sect.; **EDUC:** BA, 1973, Pol. Sci., Univ. of MN; **GRAD EDUC:** JD, 1976, Univ. of MN Sch. of Law; **EDUC HONORS:** Cum Laude, Twice recipient of Outstanding Student Leader Award, Recipient of Amer. Jurisprudence Award for academic excellence; **HOME ADD:** 2613 Kipling Ave. S, St. Louis Park, MN 55416, (612)920-5900; **BUS ADD:** 400 Marquette Ave., Suite 540, Minneapolis, MN 55401, (612)339-5524.

WHELAN, William——*President*, Pope & Talbot, Inc.; **PRIM RE ACT:** Property Manager; **BUS ADD:** PO Box 8171, Portland, OR 97207, (503)228-9161.*

WHELAN, William N.——**B:** May 15, 1941, New Bedford, MA, *Sr. VP, Development*, Spaulding and Slye Corp.; **PRIM RE ACT:** Developer; **SERVICES:** Brokerage, const., consulting, devel., prop. mgmt.; **PREV EMPLOY:** Spaulding and Whelan Corp. (Partner) Exec. VP, Newton Lower Falls, MA, 1975-1976; **EDUC:** AS, 1963, Engrg., Wentworth Institute; **HOME ADD:** 39 Turner St., New Bedford, MA 02740, (617)994-7997; **BUS ADD:** 15 New England Exec. Park, Burlington, MA 01803, (617)523-8000.

WHELESS, Herbert W.——**B:** Nov. 16, 1931, Nash Cty., NC, *Owner*, Wheless RE Serv.; **PRIM RE ACT:** Broker, Appraiser, Owner/Investor; **SERVICES:** Primary Service, Appraisal of all types of RE; **REP CLIENTS:** Fin. Insts., Govt. Agencies, Indivs. and Others; **PROFL AFFIL & HONORS:** MAI; SRPA; AR/WA; NAR/NCAR; **EDUC:** BS, 1958, Bus. Educ., E. Carolina Univ., Greenville, NC; **MIL SERV:** USN; **OTHER ACT & HONORS:** Bd. of Mgrs, Planters Nat. Bank; Bd. of Advisors, E. Carolina Univ., School of Bus.; Dir., Greenville Found. and Kiwanis Club; **HOME ADD:** 1747 Beaumont Cir., Greenville, NC 27834, (919)756-0722; **BUS ADD:** 200 W. Fifth St., POB 7124, Greenville, NC 27834, (919)758-2830.

WHIPP, Donald——*Mgr. Field Oeprations*, Diebold, Inc.; **PRIM RE ACT:** Property Manager; **BUS ADD:** 818 Mulberry Rd. SE, Canton, OH 44711, (216)489-4000.*

WHISLER, Duane——**B:** Oct. 30, 1942, Morris, IL, *Broker Assoc.*, Premier West, Resid. Sales; **PRIM RE ACT:** Broker, Consultant, Instructor, Property Manager; **SERVICES:** RE consultation, fin., mkt. studies, education; **REP CLIENTS:** Indiv., small firms, partnerships, corps.; **PREV EMPLOY:** Remax West Inc.; **PROFL AFFIL & HONORS:** Local, State, Nat. Realtors Assns.; Serving on the Bd. of Dir. at local Level, GRI; CRS; **EDUC:** BS, 1968, Education, Univ. of CO; **HOME ADD:** 8279 W. 69th Way, Arvada, CO 80004, (303)423-1198; **BUS ADD:** 8279 W. 69th Way, Arvada, CO 80004, (303)423-1198.

WHISLER, Norman J.——**B:** May 8, 1928, Ava, MO, Highland Real Estate; **PRIM RE ACT:** Appraiser, Owner/Investor, Property Manager; **OTHER RE ACT:** Agent; **PREV EMPLOY:** Farming, 1950-1967; **PROFL AFFIL & HONORS:** Realtors - Local, State, Multi-Listing, 1967 RE; **EDUC:** 1951, Panora, IA; **MIL SERV:** US Army; T/Sgt.; **OTHER ACT & HONORS:** AF & AM, Blue Lodge; Shriners; **HOME ADD:** 314 W. Main St., Panora, IA 50216, (515)755-2842; **BUS ADD:** 314 W. Main St., Panora, IA 50216, (515)755-2556.

WHISNANT, Murray——**B:** Apr. 2, 1932, Charlotte, NC, *Arch./Devel.*, Murray Whisnant, Arch.; **PRIM RE ACT:** Architect, Developer; **REP CLIENTS:** David Clark & Assoc./Devel.; Browning Props./Devel.; **PREV EMPLOY:** 1956-1964, Sloan, Wheatley & Assocs.; 1965-1977, Partner, Wheatley, Whisnant & Assocs.; 1977 to present, Murray Whisnant AIA; **PROFL AFFIL & HONORS:** AIA, Former Pres., AIA, Charlotte Sect., 1970; Former Dir., NC Inst. of Arch., 1970; Winner, Arch. Record Award of Excellence for house design; Selected, Town and Ctry. Magazine, Top Fifty Arch. in Amer., Oct. 1979; Twice selected, Art in Amer. Annual New Talent in Amer. issue; **EDUC:** BArch., 1956, NC State Univ.; **OTHER ACT & HONORS:** Work Published: Arch. Record; Fortune Magazine; NC Arch.; House Beautiful; Great Houses; Econ. Houses Designed by Arch.; Presentation Drawings of Amer. Architects; **HOME ADD:** 424 E. Park Ave., Charlotte, NC 28203, (704)334-5726; **BUS ADD:** 1251 E. Blvd., Charlotte, NC 28203, (704)375-2788.

WHITACRE, Wendell B.——**B:** Oct. 6, 1927, Columbus, OH, *MD*; **PRIM RE ACT:** Developer, Owner/Investor, Property Manager; **SERVICES:** Leasing const. & medical, dental offices; **REP CLIENTS:** Physicians & dentists; **PROFL AFFIL & HONORS:** Amer. Coll. of Surgeons; **EDUC:** AB, 1951, Zoology, OH Univ.; **GRAD EDUC:** MD, 1955, Medicine, OH State Univ.; **EDUC HONORS:** Phi Beta Kappa, Cum Laude, Alpha Omega Alpha; **MIL SERV:** US Army, Pvt. 1948-49; **OTHER ACT & HONORS:** Tr. Found. for St. Josephs Hospital, Tucson, AZ; **HOME ADD:** 10079 E Lurlene Dr., Tucson, AZ 85730, (602)886-6853; **BUS ADD:** 310 N Wilmot 104, Tucson, AZ 85711, (602)298-3381.

WHITAKER, Lloyd T.——**B:** Jan. 12, 1934, Miami, FL, *Chmn. & Pres.*, CMEI, Inc.; **PRIM RE ACT:** Attorney, Developer, Property Manager; **OTHER RE ACT:** RE Exec. in my capacity as CEO of a RE Co. involved in the ownership, devel., operation and sale (and acquisition) of comml. and non-single family detached RE; **PREV EMPLOY:** Partner, Alston, Miller and Gaines (Atty.) Atlanta, 1960-1970; Div. Pres., Cousins Props. Inc., Atlanta 1970-1976; CMEI, Inc. (formerly Cousins Mort. and Equity Investments) 1976-Current; **EDUC:** AB, 1954, Pol. Sci., Emory Univ.; **GRAD EDUC:** LLB, 1961, Law, Emory Univ. Law School; JD, 1963, Law, Emory Univ. Law School; **EDUC HONORS:** 2nd in scholastic ranking of grad. class; Pres. of Student Body; **MIL SERV:** USMC, Maj. USMCR; **OTHER ACT & HONORS:** Atlanta, GA, and ABA; Piedmont Driving Club; The Commerce Club; **BUS TEL:** (404)955-2555.

WHITAKER, Richard——**B:** May 19, 1948, Chicago, IL, *VP*, Financial Services, Inc.; **PRIM RE ACT:** Consultant, Banker, Developer, Owner/Investor, Instructor, Insuror; **OTHER RE ACT:** Mortgage Banker; **SERVICES:** Life insurance, mort. banking, fin. consulting; **PROFL AFFIL & HONORS:** Assn. of Mort. Bankers; Assn. of Financial Planners, Million Dollar Round Table (Life Ins.); **EDUC:** BA, 1970, Bus./Poli. Sci., Univ. of OR; **MIL SERV:** USN, Lt.; **OTHER ACT & HONORS:** Kiwanis, Jaycees; **HOME ADD:** 2712 N.E. 86th Ave., Vancouver, WA 98662, (206)892-4985; **BUS ADD:** 1727 NE 13th Ave., Portland, OR 97212, (503)284-7891.

WHITE, Alton S., Jr.——**B:** Aug. 23, 1927, Spokane, WA, *RE Instr.*, Highline Community College; **PRIM RE ACT:** Consultant; **PREV EMPLOY:** Tacoma Community Coll. Coordinator/Instr.; **EDUC:** BA, 1972, Urban Devel., Univ. of WA; **EDUC HONORS:** 4.0 grade point in concentration; **MIL SERV:** Infantry, 1st Lt.; **HOME ADD:** 5900 S

12th St., Tacoma, WA 98465, (206)226-9475.

WHITE, Bram——**B:** May 6, 1948, New Orleans, LA, *Branch Mgr.*, W.H. Daum & Staff; **PRIM RE ACT:** Broker; **SERVICES:** Indus. & comml. investments, Indus. RE sales & leasing; **REP CLIENTS:** Indiv. & corp. users. Indiv. & instnl. investors; **PROFL AFFIL & HONORS:** VP Amer. Indus. RE Assn. (AIR), Master of Indus. Brokerage of Amer. Indus. RE Assn.; **EDUC:** 1966-67, Chem., Univ. of CA, Santa Barbara; **HOME ADD:** 12224 Sunset Blvd., Los Angeles, CA 90049, (213)472-5514; **BUS ADD:** 6212 N. Topanga Canyon Blvd., Woodland Hills, CA 91367, (213)883-5004.

WHITE, Daniel O.——**B:** Aug, 3, 1943, Omana, NE, *Atty.*, Lowndes, Drosdick, Doster & Kantor, Attorneys; **PRIM RE ACT:** Consultant, Attorney, Developer, Owner/Investor; **SERVICES:** Legal servs. in connection with acquisition, devel., and mgmt. of RE; **REP CLIENTS:** The Greater Const. Corp., FL Land Co., WI RE Investment Trust; **PREV EMPLOY:** Asst. City Atty., City of Dallas, TX, Counsel, FL Land Co.; **PROFL AFFIL & HONORS:** Orange Cty., FL, TX Bar Assns., ABA; **EDUC:** BA, 1965, Poli. Sci., North TX State Univ.; **GRAD EDUC:** LLB, 1968, RE, urban affairs, Harvard Law School; **EDUC HONORS:** Bluekey, Outstanding Sr. Man; **HOME ADD:** 640 Balmoral Rd., Winter Park, FL 32789, (305)645-0147; **BUS ADD:** 215 North Eola Blvd., P O Box 2809, Orlando, FL 32802, (305)843-4600.

WHITE, Del F.——*Exec. VP*, Muscatine Development Corp.; **PRIM RE ACT:** Developer; **BUS ADD:** PO Box 416, 319 East 2nd St., Muscatine, IA 52761, (319)263-6373.*

WHITE, Doc——**B:** Oct. 4, 1929, Paris, TX, *Pres.*, Doc White Realtors, Inc.; **PRIM RE ACT:** Broker, Consultant, Owner/Investor, Instructor, Property Manager, Syndicator; **SERVICES:** Income Prop. & Land Brokerage, Investment counseling, synd.; **REP CLIENTS:** Indivs., synds., lenders involved in income props.; **PROFL AFFIL & HONORS:** Greater Dallas Bd. of Realtors, TX Assn. of Realtors, Mar. Assn. Comml. Investment Div., Greater Dallas Bd. of Realtors, RE Securities & Synd. Inst., C of C, Dallas & Richardson C of C, TX, GRI; **EDUC:** Tyler Jr. Coll., S. Methodist Univ., Univ. of TX; **MIL SERV:** Army, 1953-55, Sgt., Commendation; **OTHER ACT & HONORS:** Chmn. Park & Recreation, 1968-73, Richardson, TX; Lions Club; Boy Scouts of Amer.; **HOME ADD:** 927 Teakwood, Richardson, TX 75080, (214)231-0076; **BUS ADD:** 4020 McEwen Rd., Suite 125, Dallas, TX 75234, 14)385-1500.

WHITE, Gerrit A.——**B:** June 14, 1939, Albany, NY, *VP*, Morgan Stanley & Co., Inc., Morstan Devel. Co., Inc.; **PRIM RE ACT:** Broker, Appraiser, Banker, Owner/Investor; **SERVICES:** Joint ventures; brokerage & consulting, devel.; **REP CLIENTS:** Clients of Morgan Stanley & Co., Inc.; **PREV EMPLOY:** Chief RE Appraiser & VP of Western NY Savings Bank, Buffalo, NY; **PROFL AFFIL & HONORS:** AIREA; RE appraisers NYC; **EDUC:** BA, 1961, Econ. & Soc., Cornell Univ.; **GRAD EDUC:** grad courses, 1963, Cornell Univ.; **MIL SERV:** Transportation, 1st Lt. 1961-63; **OTHER ACT & HONORS:** VP NY State Builders Assn.; Niagara Frontier Assn., 1968; Ramsey Golf & Country Club; Amer. Field Serv.; **HOME ADD:** 90 Ronald Ct., Ramsey, NJ 07446, (201)327-0344; **BUS ADD:** 1633 Broadway, NY, NY 10019, (212)974-4373.

WHITE, Gregory A.——**B:** Apr. 12, 1956, NY, *Asst. Treasurer*, Chase Manhattan Bank, RE Fin./Metropolitan Div.; **PRIM RE ACT:** Banker, Lender; **SERVICES:** All types of re fin.; **EDUC:** BSCE, 1978, Civil Engrg., Tufts Univ.; **GRAD EDUC:** MBA, 1980, Fin./RE, The Wharton Sch. of Bus.; **EDUC HONORS:** Outstanding Sr. Award; **HOME ADD:** 301 E. 73rd St., Apt. PHC, New York, NY 10021, (212)249-7993; **BUS ADD:** 1211 Sixth Ave., New York, NY 10036, (212)730-3554.

WHITE, H.M., Jr.——**B:** Apr. 12, 1938, Columbus, OH, *Pres.*, First Reynoldsburg Corp.; **PRIM RE ACT:** Broker, Builder; **PROFL AFFIL & HONORS:** Cols. Bd. of Reactors; Bldg. Indus. of Central OH; HOW Builder; OH and Nat. Assns. for RE and Home Bldrs.; **EDUC:** 1956-1958, Bus., OH State Univ.; **MIL SERV:** USANG/USAR, S/Sgt., 1958-1964; **OTHER ACT & HONORS:** Mason; Scottish Rite; Aladdin Temple; Eastern Star; **HOME ADD:** 1647 Cobblegate Ln., Reynoldsburg, OH 43068, (614)866-2017; **BUS ADD:** 7100 Livingstone Ave., Reynoldsburg, OH 43068, (614)868-5050.

WHITE, James L.——**B:** Apr. 29, 1926, Wilson, NC, *Pres.*, Jim White Realty Co., Inc.; **PRIM RE ACT:** Broker, Instructor, Appraiser, Property Manager, Owner/Investor; **SERVICES:** Resid. sales, appraisals, prop. mgmt., inst.; **PREV EMPLOY:** Ben Downey Realty & Const. Co., Inc., May 1967-May 1969, VP; **PROFL AFFIL & HONORS:** NAR, NCAR, REMNI, Johnston Cty. Bd. of Realtors, Pres. of local bd., Member of NCAR Bd. of Dir., Realtor of the Yr. (local bd. 2 times), Member, Educ. Comm. NCAR, CRB, CRS, GRI, CREA, CRA; **EDUC:** AA, 1967, Bus., Gastonia, Gaston Com. Coll., NC; **MIL SERV:** US Army, Sgt./Maj.; **OTHER ACT & HONORS:** Rotary member, Salvation Army Advirory Bd. (Chmn. 1 year); **HOME ADD:** 901 Chestnut Dr., P.O. Box 11181, Smithfield, NC 27577, (919)934-5296; **BUS ADD:** 118 E. Market St., P.O. Box 1181, Smithfield, NC 27577, (919)934-2222.

WHITE, J.D.——*Mgr. RE*, Crown Zellerbach Corp.; **PRIM RE ACT:** Property Manager; **BUS ADD:** One Bush St., San Francisco, CA 94104, (415)951-5000.*

WHITE, L. Keith——**B:** Nov. 15, 1942, Gary, IN, *Pres.*, Reinhold P. Wolff Econ. Research, Inc.; **PRIM RE ACT:** Consultant; **SERVICES:** Market Feasibility Analysis; **REP CLIENTS:** Confidential Offices in Miami, West Palm Beach and St. Petersburg, FL; **PROFL AFFIL & HONORS:** Amer. Economic Assn.; Amer. Inst. Profl. Consultants; Econ. Soc. of South FL; Nat. Assn. of Home Builders; **EDUC:** BS, 1970, Marketing/Mgmt., Eastern IL Univ.; **GRAD EDUC:** MBA, 1971, Marketing/Mgmt., Eastern IL Univ.; **EDUC HONORS:** Magna Cum Laude, Cum Laude; **MIL SERV:** US Army, Sgt.; **HOME ADD:** 8526 SW 94th St., Miami, FL 33156, (305)261-9944; **BUS ADD:** 9300 S Dadeland Blvd., Suite 212, Miami, FL 33156, (305)661-6335.

WHITE, Max W.——**B:** Sept. 13, 1939, Lewisport, KY, *Sr. VP*, First National Bank of Louisville, Const. Loan Div.; **PRIM RE ACT:** Banker; **SERVICES:** Income prop. const. lending; **REP CLIENTS:** Devel. of income props.; **PREV EMPLOY:** TFAC, Inc., a special risk const. lender; Louisville Mort. Serv. Co.; Prudential Ins. Co. (RE Investment Dept.); **PROFL AFFIL & HONORS:** Louisville Home Builders Assn.; Louisville Mort. Bankers Assn.; KY Indus. Devel. Council; **EDUC:** BS, 1961, Agricultural Econ., Univ. of KY; **MIL SERV:** U.S. Army, Enlisted Reservist; **HOME ADD:** 6919 Wythe Hill Cir., Prospect, KY 40059, (502)228-1513; **BUS ADD:** POB 36000, Louisville, KY 40232, (502)581-6646.

WHITE, P. Gerald——**B:** Jul. 12, 1934, Wilmington, DE, *Pres.*, P. Gerald White, Inc.; **PRIM RE ACT:** Broker, Consultant, Developer, Owner/Investor, Syndicator; **SERVICES:** Comml., indus, investment RE, sales-leasing & counseling; **REP CLIENTS:** American Consumer Industries; Continental Can Co.; Witco Chemical; Delaware Trust Co.; E.I. DuPont de Nemours & Co., Inc.; Hercules, Inc.; Hunt Chemical Co.; Sears Roebuck Acceptance Corp.; Kodak International Paper Co.; Sunbeam Holding Co.; and miscellaneous local investors and indus., etc.; **PROFL AFFIL & HONORS:** NAR; Soc. of Indus. Realtors; New Castle Cty. Bd. of Realtors; Northeastern Indus. Devel. Assn.; RNMI; Amer. Chap. Intl. RE Fed., CCIM; Soc. of Indus. Realtors, Member; **EDUC:** BS in Econ., 1956, Mktg., Wharton School of Fin. & Commerce, Univ. of PA; **MIL SERV:** USN, Lt.; **OTHER ACT & HONORS:** Pres., Bd. of Dir. Episcopal Church Home; Pres.,, Bd. of Dir. Market Mall, Inc.; Bd. of Dir., Port of Wilmington Maritime Soc.; Bd. of Dir. Delaware Rgn. Nat. Conf. of Christians and Jews; Comm. of 100, Wilmington, DE; DE State C of C; **HOME ADD:** 1110 Blackshire Rd., Wawaset Park, Wilmington, DE 19805, (302) 656-1448; **BUS ADD:** 1210 King St., Wilmington, DE 19801, (302)655-9621.

WHITE, Paul S.——**B:** July 31, 1917, MN, *Atty. at Law*, Paul S. White; **PRIM RE ACT:** Attorney, Owner/Investor, Property Manager; **SERVICES:** RE Closings, prop. mgmt.; **PROFL AFFIL & HONORS:** WA State Bar Assn., ABA, Inland Empire Apt. Assn., WA State Apt. Assn.; **EDUC:** BS, Bus., Simpson Coll. Indianola, IA; **GRAD EDUC:** Master of Acctg., LLB, JD, 1950, Univ. of IA/Kinman Univ./Gonzaga Univ.; **MIL SERV:** US Army, WO; **OTHER ACT & HONORS:** Boy Scouts, I.R. Non-Profit Cemetery Bd., Non-Profit Water System, Scottish Rite 33 KCCH; **HOME ADD:** 1022 W. 7th Ave., Spokane, WA 99204, (509)747-2820; **BUS ADD:** 1022 W. 7th Ave., Spokane, WA 99204, (509)838-2564.

WHITE, Robert J.——**B:** Dec. 29, 1943, Athol, MA, *Pres.*, White RE; **PRIM RE ACT:** Broker, Consultant, Appraiser, Developer, Lender, Builder, Owner/Investor, Property Manager, Assessor; **PREV EMPLOY:** Boston Public Schools (Math. & Career Educ.), Boston Univ. (RE Investing instr.), Zinich RE (Broker); **PROFL AFFIL & HONORS:** Gr. Boston Rental Housing Assn.; Brookline Prop. Owners Assn., Pres., Brookline Prop. Owners Assn.; **EDUC:** BA, 1966, Eng., Math., Univ. of MA; **GRAD EDUC:** MA, 1972, Math., Boston Univ.; **EDUC HONORS:** Dean's List, 1965-66; **OTHER ACT & HONORS:** Religious Heritage of Amer.; Amer. Wildlife Fed.; Jamaica Pond Assn.; **HOME ADD:** 478 Jamaicaway, Jamaica Plain, MA, (617)522-6610; **BUS ADD:** 478 Jamaicaway, Jamaica Plain, MA 02130, (617)522-6610.

WHITE, Russell A.——**B:** Sept. 2, 1951, Long Beach, CA, *Atty.*, Wood, Cobb, Murphy & Craig; **PRIM RE ACT:** Attorney; **REP CLIENTS:** Firm represents First Fed. S&L Assn. of the Palm Beaches; **PROFL**

AFFIL & HONORS: ABA; FL Bar; Palm Beach Cty. Bar Assn.; Chmn., Public Relations Comm. of Palm Beach Co. Bar Assn., Who's Who in Amer. Law (1979 Ed.); The Register of Palm Beach Cty.; **EDUC:** AB, 1973, Sociology/Pol. Sci., Univ. of Chicago; **GRAD EDUC:** JD, 1976, Univ. of MD; **EDUC HONORS:** Dean's List, Maroon Key Soc., Order of the 'C'; **OTHER ACT & HONORS:** Big Bros. Program of Palm Beach Cty.; Chmn., Univ. of Chicago Alumni Fund, Palm Beach Cty. Chap.; **HOME ADD:** 2429 Lake Dr., Singer Is., FL 33404, (305)844-1037; **BUS ADD:** POB 2549, W. Palm Beach, FL 33402, (305)655-8616.

WHITE, Stephen Dennis——**B:** Nov. 20, 1944, Memphis, TN, *Mgr. of RE Serv.*, Federal Express Corp., Prop. and Facilities Dept.; **PRIM RE ACT:** Owner/Investor, Property Manager; **SERVICES:** Site analysis, devel., leasing, purchasing, prop. mgmt.; **REP CLIENTS:** All RE activities soley for benefit of Federal Express Corp.; **PREV EMPLOY:** Allen T. O'Hara, Inc., Memphis, TN, 1973-1977; Land Sales and Consultant Services, 1978; Federal Express Corp., 1979 to present; **PROFL AFFIL & HONORS:** NACORE; Sales & Mktg. Exec. Intl.; BOMA; **EDUC:** 1968, Sales/Mktg./RE, Memphis St. Univ.; **EDUC HONORS:** Pi Sigma Epsilon; **OTHER ACT & HONORS:** Member, Bd. of Dirs., Samuelson Boys Club of Memphis, TN; **HOME ADD:** 2688 Central Terr., Memphis, TN 38111, (901)458-6162; **BUS ADD:** POB 727, Prop. Dept., Memphis, TN 38194, (901)369-3165.

WHITE, Steve J.——**B:** Apr. 9, 1939, Hartford, AL, *(owner)*, The Stratford Cos.; **PRIM RE ACT:** Broker, Attorney, Syndicator; **PREV EMPLOY:** Owner of RE Brokerage Firm (Comml.) and Law Firm; **EDUC:** BA, 1970, Bus., Univ. of FL; **GRAD EDUC:** 1972, Law, Univ. of FL Law School; **MIL SERV:** US Army Res., Honorable Discharge; **HOME ADD:** 1012, 8660 Parklane, Dallas, TX 75231, (214)750-8933; **BUS ADD:** 14800 Quorum Dr., Suite 380,, Dallas, TX 75240, (214)960-1552.

WHITE, William D.——**B:** Feb. 25, 1934, Paris, IL, *Asst. Chief Appraiser*, Indiana Dept. of Highways; **PRIM RE ACT:** Broker, Appraiser; **PROFL AFFIL & HONORS:** ASA, Member - Intl. Bd. of Examiners, ASA; SRA; **EDUC:** BS, 1955, Bus. Educ., IN State Univ., Terre Haute, IN; **HOME ADD:** 6515 Lockwood Lane, Indianapolis, IN 46217, (317)784-8044; **BUS ADD:** 100 N. Senate Ave., Rm.1105, Indianapolis, IN 46204, (317)232-5037.

WHITED, S. Wayne——**B:** Apr. 27, 1951, Sidney, OH, *Pres. - Appraiser*, Green Country Appraisal Service, Inc.; **PRIM RE ACT:** Appraiser; **SERVICES:** Complete appraisal services on all types of prop.; **REP CLIENTS:** FHA, Relocation firms, S&L Assns., Indivs.; **PREV EMPLOY:** 4 1/2 yrs., independent appraiser; **PROFL AFFIL & HONORS:** Candidate only, AIREA, SREA, AGA; **EDUC:** BA, 1973, Hist., Univ. of Cincinnati; **GRAD EDUC:** Post Grad., Bus. Work, Univ. of Tulsa; **OTHER ACT & HONORS:** Pres., Bd. of Dir., 6th Church of Christ, Scientist; **HOME ADD:** 4634 S. Vandalia Ave., Tulsa, OK 74135, (918)663-2876; **BUS ADD:** 5566 S. 79th E. Pl., Tulsa, OK 74136, (918)663-9832.

WHITEFIELD, Ralph F., Jr. (Buddy)——**B:** Jan. 11, 1931, Durham, NC, *Sr. VP*, Southland Assoc. Inc.; **PRIM RE ACT:** Broker, Consultant, Appraiser, Developer; **PREV EMPLOY:** Upon graduation at Duke, came immediately into RE profession; **PROFL AFFIL & HONORS:** Durham Bd. Realtor, State & Nat. Assn., Remmie; **EDUC:** BBA, 1956, Duke Univ.; **MIL SERV:** USM, 3rd Class PO; **OTHER ACT & HONORS:** Durham Jaycees, Durham Exchange Club, Past Pres. Durham Exchange Club-Sheltered Workshop; **HOME ADD:** 2509 Alpine Rd., Durham, NC, (919)489-2034; **BUS ADD:** 212 Corcoran St., Durham, NC 27702, (919)688-8121.

WHITEHALL, Henry——**B:** May 19, 1951, NY, NY, *Pres.*, Andrews Son. Devel. Constr.; **PRIM RE ACT:** Developer, Builder; **SERVICES:** Build, sell & package; **PROFL AFFIL & HONORS:** HOW, NAHB; Hadassah, Builder of the yr., Biscayne Fed. S&L 1980; **EDUC:** BS, 1973, Mktg., Mgmt., Fin. & Econ., Fairleigh Dickinson Univ.; **GRAD EDUC:** MBA program, Fin. Econ., Bernard; **EDUC HONORS:** Honors Coll., Baruch Nominated Hons Program., Who's Who among students in Amer. Colls. & Univs.; **OTHER ACT & HONORS:** Lic. Gen. contr. FL; Licensed RE sales person; Cockaballie Award 1981; **BUS ADD:** 1320 SW 2nd, Boca Raton, FL 33432, (305)368-0114.

WHITEHILL, Andrew——**B:** Mar. 27, 1920, Hamburg, Germany, *Treas.*, Whitehill Devels., Inc.; **PRIM RE ACT:** Developer, Builder, Owner/Investor; **SERVICES:** Builder/Devel., Owner/Investor/Synd.; **PROFL AFFIL & HONORS:** HOW, NAHB, Lic. Gen. Contractor, State of FL, Schmendric Hassenfeffer Award 1980; **EDUC:** Warsaw Polytechnica Univ., 1939, Engrg.; **EDUC HONORS:** Honors Program; **MIL SERV:** USAF, Lt. Col.; **OTHER ACT & HONORS:** Mayor of Danzac 1940; Mt. Mariade Loch, Hosp. Supt. for the United Nations In Italy; **BUS ADD:** 1320 SW 2nd St., Boca Raton, FL 33432, (305)368-0114.

WHITELEY, Lloyd——*Sr. Vice President*, Adobe Oil & Gas; **PRIM RE ACT:** Property Manager; **BUS ADD:** 1100 Western United Life Bldg., Midland, TX 79701, (915)683-4701.*

WHITELY, Eric——*Corp. Mgr. Fac. & Services*, Simmonds Precision Products, Inc.; **PRIM RE ACT:** Property Manager; **BUS ADD:** 150 White Plains Rd., Tarrytown, NY 10591, (914)631-7500.*

WHITESIDE, William A.——*Exec. Dir.*, Department of Housing and Urban Development, Neighborhood Reinvestment Corp.; **PRIM RE ACT:** Lender; **BUS ADD:** 451 Seventh St., S.W., Washington, DC 20410, (202)377-6366.*

WHITFIELD, Donald H.——**B:** Sept. 23, 1929, Nashville, TN, *Dir. RE*, Genesco Inc.; **OTHER RE ACT:** Retail stores, factories, office space users; **PROFL AFFIL & HONORS:** ICSC - NACORE - IDSC; **EDUC:** BS, 1956, Bus., Middle TN State; **GRAD EDUC:** Doctor of Jurisprudence, 1964, Law, Y.M.C.A. Night Law School; **EDUC HONORS:** Who's Who Amer. Colleges & Universities; **HOME ADD:** 2005 Earlington Dr., Nashville, TN 37202, (615)373-0378; **BUS ADD:** Genesco Park, Nashville, TN 37202, (615)367-8291.

WHITFIELD, Theron——**B:** Oct. 26, 1927, MS, *Pres.*, Whitfield Constr. Co., Inc.; **PRIM RE ACT:** Developer, Builder, Owner/Investor; **SERVICES:** Resid. and Comm. Building; **PREV EMPLOY:** E. Hudspeth Builder - 15 Yrs.; **PROFL AFFIL & HONORS:** Platte Valley Builders Assn. - Assn. of Nazarene Bldgs. Profls.; **HOME ADD:** 219 S. 20th, Brighton, CO 80601, (303)659-7124; **BUS ADD:** 60 S. 27th Ave., Brighton, CO 80601, (303)659-0249.

WHITING, Richard F.——**B:** Oct. 7, 1931, Sioux City, IA, *VP*, Norcal RE Co.; **PRIM RE ACT:** Broker, Consultant, Developer, Property Manager; **SERVICES:** Comm. RE Brokerage, investment counseling, devel. & prop. mgmt.; **REP CLIENTS:** Maj. devels., instnl. investors in comml. RE & maj. office tenants; **PREV EMPLOY:** VP. Del E. Webb Realty Mgmt. Co., 1969-80; **PROFL AFFIL & HONORS:** Inst. of RE Mgmt., RE Broker CO of TX, Rho Epsilon, BOMA, CPM; **EDUC:** ED, 1955, Bus. & Math., NE State Teachers Coll., Wayne, NE; **GRAD EDUC:** 1956-57, Univ. of OK; **MIL SERV:** US Army, Cpl., Bronze Star; **OTHER ACT & HONORS:** Bd. of Tr. Iliff Sch. of Theol., Past Bd. of Dir. Downtown Denver Inc.; **HOME ADD:** 2553 S. Krameria St., Denver, CO 80222, (303)756-5348; **BUS ADD:** 999 18th St., Suite 375, Denver, CO 80202, (303)629-5800.

WHITLOCK, Lawrence T., Jr.——**B:** May 21, Sweetwater, TX, *Pres.*, Lawrence T. Whitlock & Assoc., Inc.; **PRIM RE ACT:** Engineer; **OTHER RE ACT:** Landscape Arch./Planner/Prime Consultant/Land Acquisition/Feasibility/Devel. Constsr. Mgmt.; **SERVICES:** Prime Consultant for all facets of RE; **REP CLIENTS:** Town of Ocean City (recreation); DNR; WRA (shore erosion control); Twilly & Dashiell (housing); Lamar Corp. (housing); D. Trimpter III (shopping ctr./marinas); Shepard-Seibold (restaurant - night club); Merritt Boat Works (indus.); **PREV EMPLOY:** Projects Dir./Vilican-Leman 1967-69; Projects Dir./Scruggs & Hammond 1969-71; Projects Dir. Landtec Corp. 1971-72; **PROFL AFFIL & HONORS:** Member Amer. Soc. of Landscape Arch./Reg. L.A. MI, DE, PA, MD; **EDUC:** BS, 1965, Landscape Arch., UT State Univ.; **GRAD EDUC:** MS, 1967, Landscape Arch., Univ. of IL; **EDUC HONORS:** Scholastic Recognition upon Grad., Phi Alpha XI/Research Assistantship 1965-66-67; **OTHER ACT & HONORS:** Chmn. 1979 MD Costal Resource Advisory Comm to MD DNR, 1979 to date; Member MD Water Quality Advisory Comm to Dept. Health & Hygiene; Reg. rep. MD Costal Resource Advisory Comm 1978 to date; **HOME ADD:** Rte. 2, Box 239, Berlin, MD 21811, (301)641-3019; **BUS ADD:** 3409 Coastal Hwy., PO Box 574, Ocean City, MD 21842, (301)289-3202.

WHITNEY, Bernard——**B:** Dec. 12, 1918, The Netherlands, *Pres.*, American Developers Representative, Inc.; **PRIM RE ACT:** Broker, Attorney, Developer; **SERVICES:** Devel. RE for off-shore investors; **PREV EMPLOY:** Atty., CPA; **PROFL AFFIL & HONORS:** Realtor FIABCI, Los Angeles Cty. Bar Assn., CA CPA Soc., Amer. Assn. of Attys., Motel Man of the Month; **EDUC:** Law, Acctg., UCLA, Southwestern Univ., USC; **GRAD EDUC:** JD, 1958, Acctg.; **HOME ADD:** PO Box 3701, Manhattan Beach, CA 90266, (213)474-3812; **BUS ADD:** 10850 Wilshire Blvd., Suite 750, Los Angeles, CA 90024, (213)475-0708.

WHITSEL, Robert M.——**B:** Dec. 30, 1929, *Pres.*, The Lafayette Life Ins. Co.; **PRIM RE ACT:** Lender; **PREV EMPLOY:** Investment VP, The Lafayette Life Ins. Co.; **PROFL AFFIL & HONORS:** Sr. Member SRA; Past Pres. IN Mtg. Bankers Assn. & Indianapolis Chap. of Soc. of Fin. Analysts; **EDUC:** BS, 1951, Bus. Admin., IN Univ.;

GRAD EDUC: MBA, 1954, IN Univ.; **EDUC HONORS:** Elected to Beta Gamma Sigma; **MIL SERV:** USAF; 1st Lt.; **HOME ADD:** 541 Old Farm Rd., Lafayette, IN 47905, (317)474-8547; **BUS ADD:** 1905 Teal Rd., PO Box 7007, Lafayette, IN 47903, (317)477-7411.

WHITTAKER, Sam E.——B: Dec. 31, 1937, Tampa, FL, *Comml. Sales*, The Keyes Co., Realtors, Investment Comml. Sales; **PRIM RE ACT:** Broker, Consultant, Appraiser, Owner/Investor, Instructor; **SERVICES:** Instnl. sales; **REP CLIENTS:** Citibank, First of Chicago, Continental Bank, Cadillac Fairview Corp., Aetna Life, Metro. Life; **PREV EMPLOY:** Shearson, American Express; **PROFL AFFIL & HONORS:** Delray Bch. Bd. of Realtors, Keyes Million Dollar Sales Club, The Pres. Council, Shearson Hayden Stone, Inc.; **EDUC:** BA, 1960, Vanderbilt Univ.; **GRAD EDUC:** NY Univ.; **MIL SERV:** US Army, 1st Lt., 1960-62; **OTHER ACT & HONORS:** Gulf Stream Bath & Tennis Club; **HOME ADD:** 1120 N. Ocean Blvd., Delray Beach, FL 33444, (305)272-7777; **BUS ADD:** 75 N. Fed. Hwy., Delray Beach, FL 33444, (305)276-0500.

WHITTELSEY, Souther——B: July 30, 1910, Greenwich, CT, *Owner*, Gateway Prop., Whittelsey & Assoc.; **PRIM RE ACT:** Broker, Appraiser, Property Manager; **PROFL AFFIL & HONORS:** GWCH, CT & Nat. Assn. Realtors, GRI, CRB, CID; **EDUC:** 1934, Yale; **OTHER ACT & HONORS:** Various civic Bds. & Comms. in Greenwich Sailing, (Inland, Coastal & Deep Sea), Skiing; **HOME ADD:** 175 Zaccheus Mead's Ln., Greenwich, CT 06803, (203)869-0233; **BUS ADD:** 26 W. Putnam Ave., Greenwich, CT 06830, (203)869-4004.

WHITTEMORE, David O.——B: July 13, 1939, Boston, MA, *Atty.*, David O. Whittemore, Atty. at Law; **PRIM RE ACT:** Attorney, Owner/Investor; **SERVICES:** Represent sellers and buyers of resid. & comml. RE; **REP CLIENTS:** Indiv. & corp. clients in the S. Middlesex area; **PREV EMPLOY:** 7 yrs. as Assoc. Hargraves, Karb, Wilcox, & Gavlani, 24 Union Ave., Framingham, MA (law firm); **PROFL AFFIL & HONORS:** MBA, S. Middlesex Bar Assn.; **EDUC:** BA, 1961, Hist. & Pol. Sci., Williams Coll., Williamstown, MA; **GRAD EDUC:** JD, 1964, Univ. of VA Law Sch.; **OTHER ACT & HONORS:** Chmn. Framingham Charter Comm., 1971-72; Rotary Club of Framingham, Tr.; Sudbury Valley Trustees; Past Pres. Exeter Alumni Assn. of New England; Tr. Big Bros., Big Sister of S. Middlesex, Inc.; **HOME ADD:** 795 Edmands Rd., Framingham, MA 01701, (617)877-5535; **BUS ADD:** 118 Union Ave., Framingham, MA 01701, (617)872-4331.

WHITTEMORE, Frank J.——B: Jan. 11, 1918, USA, *Pres.*, Intebon Corp. and The Franklin Group, Inc.; **PRIM RE ACT:** Consultant, Developer, Property Manager, Syndicator; **OTHER RE ACT:** Investment and mort. banker; **SERVICES:** Investment counseling, mort. fin., devel. and synd. of comml. props., prop. mgmt., J/V in Energy & RE; **REP CLIENTS:** Indiv., synd. devel., instl. and pension funds in income prop. and energy situations; **PREV EMPLOY:** Kassler & Co. (Security Pacific), Douglas L. Elliman & Co., Franklin Investors (all to Sr. Mgmt. or CEO), Active in energy, devel. & ranching; **PROFL AFFIL & HONORS:** Pres., Dir., Mort. Bankers Assn., Denver Chap.; Pres., Chap. 9 SREA member; Soc. of Resid. Appraisers; Pres., Retail Credit Men's Assn.; Pres., Amer. S&L Inst. 4th Dist., Sec. Chap. 22; AIREA; NAREB; NAHB, Lic. ULI, Gen. Contractor, Securities Dealer, Listed in Who's Who in the World, Who's Who in Fin. & Indus., Nat. Roster of Scientific & Specialized Personnel; **EDUC:** BS, Bus. Admin., Harvard Bus. Sch.; **GRAD EDUC:** LLB, 1942, Law, UNC; **MIL SERV:** USN; LCDR.; **OTHER ACT & HONORS:** Milt. Order of World Wars, Civic & Social Clubs, Consultant, State of FL, 1.00 Annually; **HOME ADD:** Cherry Creek Ranch, Comfort, TX 78013, (512)995-2602; **BUS ADD:** PO Box 1596, San Antonio, TX 78296, (512)340-5749.

WHITTINGTON, Thomas L.——B: Jul. 14, 1943, Waukesha, WI, *Atty.*, Thomas, Whittington, Anderson & Bergan; **PRIM RE ACT:** Attorney; **SERVICES:** Legal Services; **PREV EMPLOY:** US Dept. of the Interior, Office of the Secretary, Wash., DC; **PROFL AFFIL & HONORS:** WA State Bar Assn.; Seattle King Cty. Bar Assn.; East King Cty. Bar Assn. (Trustee); **EDUC:** BA, 1965, Econ., Coll. of Wooster, Wooster, OH; **GRAD EDUC:** JD, 1967, Univ. of MI Law School, Ann Arbor, MI; **OTHER ACT & HONORS:** Rotary Club, Issaquah, WA; **HOME ADD:** 3402 Sahalee Dr. W., Redmond, WA 98052, (206)883-3850; **BUS ADD:** PO Box J, 970 5th, NW, Issaquah, WA 98027, (206)392-7558.

WIARD, Darrell D.——B: Apr. 29, 1948, Independence, MO, *RE Mgr.*, Amer. Multi-Cinema, Inc.; **PRIM RE ACT:** Consultant; **OTHER RE ACT:** Negotiate new theater locations; **PREV EMPLOY:** Atty, 3 yrs., Coldwell Banker Comml. Brokerage, 2 yrs; **PROFL AFFIL & HONORS:** ICSC, KS & MO Bar Assns.; **EDUC:** BA, 1970, Hist., Econ., Princeton Univ.; **GRAD EDUC:** JD, 1974, Univ. of KS Law School; **MIL SERV:** USAR, E4; **OTHER ACT & HONORS:** USCG Comml. Vessel Lic.; **HOME ADD:** 5705 Holmes, Kansas City, MO 64110, (816)523-1573; **BUS ADD:** 106 W. 14th St., Ste 1700, Kansas City, MO 64105, (816)474-6150.

WICHTEL, Joyce Jean——B: Sept. 15, 1951, Milwaukee, WI, *RE Investment Funds Mgr.*, Seattle First National Bank, Trust Div.; **PRIM RE ACT:** Broker, Consultant, Attorney, Appraiser, Owner/Investor, Instructor, Syndicator; **SERVICES:** Acquisition, Consulting; **REP CLIENTS:** Pension Funds, Pvt. Trusts, Devels. Investors; **PREV EMPLOY:** Questor Assocs., San Francisco, CA; **PROFL AFFIL & HONORS:** CA and WA State Bars; CA and WA RE Broker; **EDUC:** BS, 1972, Econ. and Psych., Univ. of WI; **GRAD EDUC:** LLB, 1977, RE Law, Univ. of WI Law Sch.; **HOME ADD:** 720 Lakeside S, Seattle, WA 98144; **BUS ADD:** PO Box 3586 EXB-16, Seattle, WA 98124, (206)583-7318.

WICKER, Frank J.——B: June 28, 1925, Bountiful, UT, *Pres.*, Frank J. Wicker Associates; **PRIM RE ACT:** Broker, Appraiser, Developer; **OTHER RE ACT:** Dir., Gr. Minneapolis Bd. of Realtors, Pres., Upper Midwest CCIM Chap.; **SERVICES:** Investment counseling, appraisals, RE Exchanging; **REP CLIENTS:** Lenders, VA, Investment clients; **PROFL AFFIL & HONORS:** CCIM, CPM, CRB; **EDUC:** AA, 1959, Bus. Admin., Boise Jr. Coll., Boise, ID; **MIL SERV:** US Army Air Force, S/Sgt., Air medal, 3 Oak Leaf Clusters; **HOME ADD:** 3280 Todd Rd., SW, Prior Lake, MN 55372, (612)447-4612; **BUS ADD:** 4769 Dakota St., Box 355, Prior Lake, MN 55372, (612)447-6040.

WICKER, Seaborn R. "Steve", Jr.——B: June 19, 1933, Abita Springs, LA, *Pres.*, Realty Mart, Realtors, Inc.; **PRIM RE ACT:** Broker, Consultant, Developer, Real Estate Publisher; **OTHER RE ACT:** Designer and originator of complete computer software system serving client, assoc. and all office functions; broker-software designer; Author, *Comprehensive RE Training Program*; **REP CLIENTS:** Software mktd. to other realtors; **PREV EMPLOY:** Pres., Architectural Millwork, Inc.; **PROFL AFFIL & HONORS:** NAR; LA Realtors Assn., RNMI, Amer. Salesmaster's "Oscar for RE Salesmanship", Governor of RELO, Intl., Gov. of RNMI, Pres. of LA Realtors Assn. - 1981, Cert. Resid. Broker (CRB); **EDUC:** Lasalle Extension Univ., RE and Bus. Admin.; **MIL SERV:** USN, 1952-1955, Machinist 1st Cl.; **OTHER ACT & HONORS:** Baton Rouge Consistory of the Shrine, Baton Rouge C of C, Phi Sigma Epsilon, LA State Univ. - Advisory Council to the Coll. of Bus. Admin.; **HOME ADD:** 1046 Wooddale Blvd., Baton Rouge, LA 70806, (504)925-8261; **BUS ADD:** 1739 Wooddale Blvd., Baton Rouge, LA 70806, (504)926-7777.

WICKERT, Gary A.——B: June 14, 1950, Milwaukee, WI, *Atty.*, Condon, Hanaway, Wickert & Fenwick, Ltd.; **PRIM RE ACT:** Attorney, Instructor; **SERVICES:** Legal rep. & consultation for purchasers, sellers, devels. & investors in RE; **PROFL AFFIL & HONORS:** Prop. Div., ABA; WI Bar Assn.; **EDUC:** BBA, 1972, Bus. Law, Univ. of WI, Whitewater; **GRAD EDUC:** JD, 1975, Marquette Univ.; **HOME ADD:** 1513 W Paulson, Green Bay, WI 54304, (414)494-1550; **BUS ADD:** 801 E Walnut St., PO Box 1126, Green Bay, WI 54305, (414)432-9201.

WICKLAND, Carey B.——B: Aug. 5, 1941, Evanston, IL, *VP*, First National Bank of Atlanta, RE & Intl.; **PRIM RE ACT:** Banker, Lender; **SERVICES:** All const. related RE lending; intl. banking; **PROFL AFFIL & HONORS:** Robert Morris Assoc.; MBA; **EDUC:** BA, 1963, Econ., Lawrence Univ.; **GRAD EDUC:** MBA, 1964, Fin., Mktg., Emory Univ.; **EDUC HONORS:** High Honors; **MIL SERV:** USAF, Capt., Commendation Medal; **HOME ADD:** 3089 Marne Dr., NW, Atlanta, GA 30305, (404)262-1483; **BUS ADD:** PO Box 4148, Atlanta, GA 30302, (404)588-5385.

WICKSTRAND, Owen——B: Aug. 5, 1936, Kenosha, WI, *Pres.*, Wickstrand Development Company; **PRIM RE ACT:** Broker, Engineer, Developer, Owner/Investor, Insuror; **SERVICES:** RE devel. & investment advice; **REP CLIENTS:** Major pension funds, banks, corps. and indiv. investors; **PREV EMPLOY:** Fin. Controller, Principal of a stock brokerage co., Mech. Engr.; **PROFL AFFIL & HONORS:** ICSC; BOMA; Airplane Owners and Pilots Assn., RE Broker, NASD Registered Principal, Insurance Agent; **EDUC:** BS, 1961, Univ. of CA, Berkeley; **MIL SERV:** US Army, Capt.; **OTHER ACT & HONORS:** Elder, LaJolla Presbyterian Church; Kiwanis Club; Downtown San Diego; San Diego C of C; **HOME ADD:** 812 Havenhurst Pt., LaJolla, CA 92037, (714)456-1130; **BUS ADD:** 812 Havenhurst Point, LaJolla, CA 92037, (714)456-1130.

WICKSTRAND, R. Richard——B: Nov. 21, 1930, Gauhati, Assam, India, *Pres.*, Strand Development Corp.; **PRIM RE ACT:** Broker, Syndicator, Developer, Builder, Property Manager; **SERVICES:** Land dev., sub-div., sales, comml., multi-family, builder, condo. convertor, prop. mgmt.; **PREV EMPLOY:** Manager Retail Lumber Yard,

Constr. Loan Officer, Pres. ABC Const., (Single family); Pres. Prop. Mgmt. Firm.; **PROFL AFFIL & HONORS:** Builder's Assn. of Grtr. Indpls., IN Home Builders NAHB, Mateo Indpls. Bd. of Realtors & State & Nat., Hon. Bd. Member of Builder's Assn., & Exec. Comm. Past 6 years; **EDUC:** BS, 1953, Foreign Trade, Bus., Bradley Univ.; **EDUC HONORS:** Varsity Basketball; **MIL SERV:** USAF, 1st Lt.; **OTHER ACT & HONORS:** Bd. of Contractors, City of Indpls., 3 yrs., Dept. of Transportation, 2 yrs., City of Indpls., Adv. Comm., Morat Shrine, Hoosier Power Squadron, Camp Fire Girls of Amer. Natl. Service Award; **HOME ADD:** 10851 Gulf Shore #301, Naples, FL 33940, (813)597-6711; **BUS ADD:** 25 Bluebill Dr., Naples, FL 33940, (813)597-6711.

WIENBERG, Carl H.——B: July 2, 1941, MI, *Atty.*, Raymond, Rupp & Wienberg, PC; **PRIM RE ACT:** Attorney, Consultant; **PREV EMPLOY:** IRS 1963-1969; **PROFL AFFIL & HONORS:** ALDA, RESSI; **EDUC:** BBA, 1963, Acctg., Western MI Univ.; **GRAD EDUC:** JD; LLM, 1971/1978, Detroit Coll. of Law, Wayne State Univ.; **MIL SERV:** US Army, 1st Lt. 1964-1965; **HOME ADD:** 3031 St. Jude, Drayton Plains, MI 48020, (313)673-7714; **BUS ADD:** 755 W. Big Beaver, Ste. 1800, Troy, MI 48084, (313)673-7714.

WIENER, Louis——B: Jan. 5, 1925, Brooklyn, NY, *Pres.*, Imperial Equities, Inc., also Loft Mgmt. Corp., Downtown Properties Assoc.; **PRIM RE ACT:** Owner/Investor, Property Manager, Syndicator; **EDUC:** BS, 1944, Bus., Econ., Acctg., City Coll. of NY; BCS, 1943, NY Univ.; **HOME ADD:** 136 Linden St., Woodmere, NY 11598, (212)297-8922; **BUS ADD:** 136 Linden St., Woodmere, NY 11598.

WIESE, Howard Kendall——B: June 6, 1943, Elgin, IL, *Branch Mgr.*, Manufacturers Life, RE; **PRIM RE ACT:** Developer, Owner/Investor, Property Manager; **OTHER RE ACT:** Mktg. and leasing; **SERVICES:** Prop. acquisition & sales, leasing, prop. mgmt.; **PREV EMPLOY:** Broker, Cushman & Wakefield, 1973-76; **PROFL AFFIL & HONORS:** VP & Member BOD of Los Angeles Headquarters City Assn.; IREM; BOMA; **EDUC:** BS, EE, 1966, Univ. of IL; **GRAD EDUC:** MBA, 1968, Fin., Univ. of IL; **EDUC HONORS:** James Scholar, IL State Scholar; **OTHER ACT & HONORS:** VP, Toastmasters Intl.; **HOME ADD:** 422 May St., Elmhurst, IL 60126, (312)834-1313; **BUS ADD:** Suite 100 W, 1501 Woodfield Dr., Schaumburg, IL 60195, (312)885-8550.

WIESEN, Robert J.——B: Sept. 21, 1943, Toledo, OH, *VP, Investments*, Romanek Golub & Co., Investment Div.; **PRIM RE ACT:** Broker, Consultant, Developer, Owner/Investor; **OTHER RE ACT:** Comml. investment; **SERVICES:** Primary purchase for own corp. account; **PREV EMPLOY:** Seay & Thomas Inc., an IC Indus. Co., VP, Sales, 1975-79; First Amer. Realty, Dir. Sales, Mktg., 1973-75; **PROFL AFFIL & HONORS:** ICSC, Assn. of Indus. RE Brokers of Chicago, Chicago RE Bd., AIC, 1965-71; **EDUC:** BS, 1965, Fin., IN Univ.; **EDUC HONORS:** IU Found.; **MIL SERV:** USAF, Air Nat. Guard, Marksmanship; **OTHER ACT & HONORS:** Author of numerous RE articles, Cystic Fibrosis Found. Tr.; Lic. as RE broker in Washington, DC, IL, IN, MA, OK; **HOME ADD:** 325 W. Belden, Chicago, IL 60614, (312)248-2232; **BUS ADD:** 625 N Michigan Ave., Suite 2000, Chicago, IL 60611, (312)440-8800.

WIESENBERGER, Steven R.——B: July 12, 1942, Cleveland, OH, *VP*, M.H. Hausman Co.; **PRIM RE ACT:** Broker, Consultant, Developer, Owner/Investor, Property Manager; **OTHER RE ACT:** Leasing agent; **SERVICES:** Shopping Ctr. Devel. & Leasing, Consulting Mgmt.; **PROFL AFFIL & HONORS:** ICSC; **EDUC:** BA, 1965, Arts., OH State Univ.; **MIL SERV:** US Coast Guard; **OTHER ACT & HONORS:** Numerous dirs., civic orgs.; **HOME ADD:** 19103 N Park Blvd., Shaker Hts., OH 44122, (216)321-1358; **BUS ADD:** 3 Commerce Park Sq., Suite 320, Beachwood, OH 44122, (216)464-5900.

WIESER, Randy——B: Mar. 21, 1944, Dallas, TX, *Pres.*, Sanger Suburban Gallery of Homes, Comml.; **PRIM RE ACT:** Broker, Appraiser, Developer, Property Manager; **PREV EMPLOY:** Heavy const.; **PROFL AFFIL & HONORS:** NAR; TX Assn. of Realtors; Soc. of RE Appraisers; Waco C of C, CCIM; **EDUC:** BA, 1966, Geology/Math, Vanderbilt Univ.; **MIL SERV:** USMC Res., Pfc.; **OTHER ACT & HONORS:** Pres., Waco Bd. of Realtors 1981; McLennan Cty. Chmn., Republican Party 1979; **HOME ADD:** Rt. 1, Box 36, China Spring, TX 76633, (817)836-4681; **BUS ADD:** 7101 Bosque Blvd., Waco, TX 76710, (817)772-7191.

WIESMAN, Benjamin——B: Omaha, NE, *Pres.*, Build and Lease, Inc.; **PRIM RE ACT:** Architect, Consultant, Appraiser, Developer, Builder, Property Manager; **SERVICES:** Site Eval., design; we custom build to lease; **REP CLIENTS:** Northwestern Bell, AT&T, Allied Chemical, Ramada, The Hoover Co., Wells Fargo, Allied Van Lines, Hyatt Corp., Gestetner, Farmers Ins., Goodyear, GM, Sears Roebuck, SCM; **PROFL AFFIL & HONORS:** Grter. Omaha C of C, Pres. Advisory Bd., Omaha Econ. Council Cert. of Distinction, Greater Omaha C of C; **EDUC:** BS, 1952/53, Econ. & RE, MI; **GRAD EDUC:** Business courses at HBS, 1961-1963, Fin., Econ., RE; **EDUC HONORS:** Cert. of Distinction; **MIL SERV:** US Army, Enlisted, Distinguished Serv. Medal; **OTHER ACT & HONORS:** Kiwanis Intl., Dist. Service Award; Cystic Fibrosis Found., Appreciation Award; Mid America Council of Boy Scouts, Bd. of Dir.; YMCA, Cert. of Apprec.; Century Club; Salvation Army Tree of Lights Appeal Chmn., Cert. of Resolution of Appreciation; Natl. Conf. of Christians and Jews, Cert. of Appreciation, Dinner Chmn.; **BUS ADD:** 9666 Mockingbird Dr., Omaha, NE 68127, (402)339-1111.

WIETHRICK, Donald——*Mgr. RE*, Kohler Co.; **PRIM RE ACT:** Property Manager; **BUS ADD:** Kohler, WI 53044, (414)457-4441.*

WIGGERS, Milton J.——B: June 4, 1933, Lincoln, IL, *Sec./Dir. of Mort. & RE*, Horace Mann Life Insurance Co. (Horace Mann Educators Corp.), Fin.; **PRIM RE ACT:** Lender, Insuror; **SERVICES:** Mort. loan and RE fin.; **REP CLIENTS:** Nationwide mort. bankers; **PREV EMPLOY:** Statewide Teachers Fin. Co., Loan Mgr. 1962-1966; **PROFL AFFIL & HONORS:** MBAA; **OTHER ACT & HONORS:** Past Pres., Springfield Luncheon Optimist; Past Pres., Springfield Inter-Civic Club Council, & Past Chmn. of Bd. of Wesley United Methodist Church; **HOME ADD:** 1509 S. Douglas Ave., Springfield, IL 62704, (217)787-5574; **BUS ADD:** #1 Horrace Mann Plaza, Springfield, IL 62715, (217)789-2500.

WIGGIN, Charles E.——B: March 13, 1947, Newton, MA, *Pres.*, Wiggin Properties, Inc.; **PRIM RE ACT:** Broker, Developer, Owner/Investor; **SERVICES:** Devel., Fin., Leasing, and Mgmt. of Comml. Props.; **REP CLIENTS:** Corporate Tenants and Instnl. and Indiv. Investor Partners; **PREV EMPLOY:** Spaulding and Slye Corp. 1973-1981; **PROFL AFFIL & HONORS:** Oklahoma City C of C, Oklahoma City Metropolitan Bd. of Realtors; **EDUC:** BA, 1968, Applied Math., Harvard Coll.; **GRAD EDUC:** MBA/JD, 1973/1973, Harvard Bus. School/Harvard Law School; **EDUC HONORS:** Cum Laude; **MIL SERV:** Army Reserve, 2nd Lt., 1968-1973; **OTHER ACT & HONORS:** Dir., Oklahoma Theater Ctr., Oklahoma Art Ctr.; **HOME ADD:** 230 NW 16th St., Oklahoma City, OK 73103, (405)524-3206; **BUS ADD:** 5600 N. May Ave., Oklahoma City, OK 73112, (405)842-0100.

WIGGINS, J. David——B: Oct. 25, 1929, Minneapolis, MN, *Asst. VP & Comml. Loan Officer*, Knutson Mort. & Financial Corp., Comml. & Income Prop. Loans; **PRIM RE ACT:** Banker, Lender; **OTHER RE ACT:** Mort. banker; **SERVICES:** Income prop. loans, joint ventures, equities and servicing; **REP CLIENTS:** RE owners, devels, and banks; **PREV EMPLOY:** Self-employed income props., loan production; **PROFL AFFIL & HONORS:** Nat. and WI MBA; **EDUC:** BS, 1951, Bus. Admin.-Econ., Tuck School - Dartmouth Coll.; **MIL SERV:** USN, Lt.j.g.; **HOME ADD:** 10014 W North Ave., Wauwatosa, WI 53226, (414)774-7348; **BUS ADD:** 2505 N Mayfair Rd., Wauwatosa, WI 53226, (414)259-0666.

WIGGINS, James B.——B: June 17, 1936, Santa Rosa, CA, *VP*, Hobin Commercial Brokerage Co.; **PRIM RE ACT:** Broker, Consultant, Developer, Owner/Investor, Property Manager, Syndicator; **SERVICES:** Comml./Indus. leasing & brokerage; hotel/motel site acquisition and brokerage; **PREV EMPLOY:** The Grupe Co. - VP of Management Co., 1976-1979; Hotel Indus. - Deve. & Mgmt.; Hospitality Enterprises; Vail Assocs. & Yosemite Park & Curry Co.; **PROFL AFFIL & HONORS:** NAR; BOMA; Intl. Council of Shopping Centers; RNMI; Stockton Bd. of Realtors; Sigma Alpha Epsilon Social Frat., Real Prop. Admin.; CCIM; Dir., CO-WY Hotel & Motel Assn. 1966-1975; Pres., CO-WY Hotel & Motel Assn., 1973; Dir., Amer. Hotel & Motel Assn., 1966-1975; Amer. Hotel & Motel Assn. Research Comm. 1967-1976; Dir., CO-Denver Visitors and Convention Bureau, 1970-1973; Pres., Stockton Visitors and Convention Bureau, 1976-1980; Standards Comm., Howard Johnson Co., 1968-1970; Pres., Univ. of Denver School of Hotel and Restaurant Mgmt. Alumni Assn., 1972-1973 - Member 1960-1976; Dir., Univ. of Denver School of Hotel and Restaurant Management, 1968-1971; Howard Johnson's Nat. Operators Council, 1965-1976; 1967 - NIKE Award for Magazine Advertising - Denver Advertising Club; 1971 - Who's Who in the Hospitality Indus.; 1975 - 2nd Place Outstanding Concrete Structure, Amer. Concrete Inst. - Stapleton Plaza Project; 1975 - Hospitality Magazine Table Top Award, 1st Place Intl. (Open Season Restaurant) - Stapleton Plaza Project; SKAL Club, San Francisco 1969-1982; **EDUC:** BSBA, 1960, Hotel & Restaurant Mgmt., Univ. of Denver; **MIL SERV:** USN, Skg. 2; **OTHER ACT & HONORS:** Denver C of C; Littleton C of C; Englewood C of C; CO Ski Country USA; CO Wildlife Fed.; Nat. Rifle Assn.; CO Open Space Council; Trout Unlimited; Ducks Unlimited; Intl. Oceanographic Found.; Nat. Wildlife Fed.; Rocky Mountain Div. of the US Ski Assn.; US Ski Assn.; Denver Athletic Club; Yosemite Club; **HOME ADD:**

6321 Embareadero Dr., Stockton, CA 95209, (209)951-3406; **BUS ADD:** PO Box 7684, 2291 W. March Lane, Stockton, CA 95207, (209)951-4696.

WIGGINS, Jerome——*VP Fin.*, VF Corp.; **PRIM RE ACT:** Property Manager; **BUS ADD:** 1047 N. Park Rd., Wyomissing, Reading, PA 19610, (215)378-1151.*

WIGGINS, Pat——B: Feb. 14, 1947, Big Spring, TX, *Partner*, Real Tex Devel. Corp. & Wayne Clements & Co.; **PRIM RE ACT:** Broker, Developer; **SERVICES:** Brokerage and devel.; **EDUC:** BS, 1970, TX Tech Univ.; **HOME ADD:** 3500 Rock Creek Dr., Dallas, TX 75204, (214)526-2168; **BUS ADD:** 6060 N. Central Expressway, Suite 670, Dallas, TX 75206, (214)692-1333.

WIGGINS, Stanley W.——B: Feb. 25, 1938, Elko, NV, *Gen. Mgr.*, Levy Realty Co.; **PRIM RE ACT:** Broker, Instructor; **OTHER RE ACT:** Bd. of Dirs. C,A Investment Corp.; **SERVICES:** Resid., comml., land, income, prop. mgmt. sales training; **PROFL AFFIL & HONORS:** Realtors Assn. - Member RNMI, Realtor of Month Las Vegas Bd. of Realtors, Oct. 1980; **EDUC:** BS, 1962, Philosophy/Econs., Univ. of UT; **OTHER ACT & HONORS:** Optimists Intl., Las Vegas Track Club; **HOME ADD:** 2257 Reno Ave., Las Vegas, NV 89109, (702)739-6149; **BUS ADD:** 4220 So. Maryland Pkwy. B-318, Las Vegas, NV 89109, (702)733-8500.

WIGGS, P. David——B: Dec. 6, 1942, Alva, OK, *Division Controller*, Pulte Home Corp.,, Arizona Div.; **PRIM RE ACT:** Broker, Builder; **OTHER RE ACT:** Financial Exec.; **SERVICES:** Homebuilding; land devel.; **PREV EMPLOY:** Valley Enterprises, Inc., 1972-1973, Diversified Properties, Inc., 1973-1981; Peat, Marwick, Mitchell & Co., 1964-1966, 1970-1972; **PROFL AFFIL & HONORS:** NAHB, NAR, AI of CPA's, GRI, CPA; **EDUC:** BS, 1964/1977, Acctg./RE, AZ State Univ. (Both Degress); **GRAD EDUC:** MBA, 1974, Bus. Mgmt., AZ State Univ.; **EDUC HONORS:** Grad. with Distinction (1964), Beta Gamma Sigma, Beta Alpha Psi; **MIL SERV:** USAF, Capt.; **OTHER ACT & HONORS:** The Gidgons, Mesa Baptist Church; **HOME ADD:** 1902 E. Julie Dr., Tempe, AZ 85283, (602)838-4936; **BUS ADD:** 8400 S. Kyrene Rd., Tempe, AZ 85284, (602)893-3115.

WIGINTON, Craig——B: Oct. 10, 1951, Long Beach, CA, *VP, Bus. Coordinator*, Wiginton Real Estate; **PRIM RE ACT:** Broker, Consultant, Owner/Investor, Property Manager; **SERVICES:** Investment counseling, RE mktg., mgmt.; **REP CLIENTS:** Indiv. investors, devels. & prop. sellers; **PROFL AFFIL & HONORS:** Member NAR; CA Assn. of Realtors; Anaheim Bd. of Realtors; W San Bernardino Cty. Bd.; NAR Investment Div.; **EDUC:** Wever State Coll., Ogden UT; Santa Barbara City Poli.; Anthony RE Sch.; Lumblean Sch. of RE; **HOME ADD:** 591 S Gilbuck Dr., Anaheim, CA 92802, (714)991-8617; **BUS ADD:** 1482 E Lincoln Ave., Anaheim, CA 92805, (714)635-7100.

WIGNALL, Ernest C.——B: Jan. 22, 1927, Norwich, CT, *Group VP, Asset Mgmt. & Treas.*, Mechanics Savings Bank; **PRIM RE ACT:** Banker, Lender, Owner/Investor; **SERVICES:** Construction, permanent and devel. mort. loans; **REP CLIENTS:** Indiv. and corp. RE owners; **PREV EMPLOY:** Binghamton Savings Bank, Binghamton, NY; The Norwich Savings Soc., Norwich, CT; **PROFL AFFIL & HONORS:** Housing Consultant,Broome Cty. Community Resources Foundation 1970-71; Adviser,Broome Cty. Housing Redevelopment Corp. 1970-71; Housing Adviser,Foundation of State Univ. at Binghamton 1970; Chmn.,Savings Banks Assoc. of CT Mortgage Com. 1979-; Dir.,Hartford Cty. Home Builders Assn. 1975-; Nat. Assn. of Mutual Savings Banks; Savings Banks' Assn. of CT; MBAA, Hartford Cty. Home Builders Assn.; **EDUC:** 1950, Arch. construction, Wentworth Inst., Boston, MA; **GRAD EDUC:** Grad., School of Savings Bank, 1962, Savings Banking, Brown Univ.; **MIL SERV:** USN Res.; 1945-46, Asiatic-Pacific; **OTHER ACT & HONORS:** Chmn.,Binghamton City Planning Commn. 1966-71; Chmn.,NY-Penn Health Planning Council, Inc. 1969-70; Corporator,Institute of Living, Hartford 1972-; Corporator,Hartford Hospital 1973-; Tr. Boys' Club of Hartford 1973-; Vice-Chmn., Advisory Bd., The Salvation Army, Hartford 1973-; Member,The Govs. Arson Task Force 1979-; Dir., Capitol Towers, Inc. 1979-; **HOME ADD:** 1 Cold St., Hartford, CT 06103, (203)522-8881; **BUS ADD:** 80 Pearl St., Hartford, CT 06103, (203)525-8661.

WIGTON, Charles Benson, Jr.——*Pres.*, Wigton Abbott Corp.; **PRIM RE ACT:** Architect, Builder, Engineer; **PROFL AFFIL & HONORS:** Prof. Planner Prof. Eng. NJ & various states; **EDUC:** BCE, 1949, Rutgers Univ.; **HOME ADD:** 46 Duncan Lane, Skillman, NJ 08558; **BUS ADD:** PO Box1192, Plainfield,, NJ 07062, (201)757-8000.

WILBUR, E. Packer——B: Sep. 9, 1936, Bridgeport, CT, *Pres.*, E.P. Wilbur & Co., Inc.; **PRIM RE ACT:** Owner/Investor; **SERVICES:** Acquisition, ownership & mgmt. of RE for inst. & indiv. investors; **EDUC:** BA, 1959, Hist., Eng., Yale Univ.; **GRAD EDUC:** MBA, 1965, Fin., Harvard Bus. School; **EDUC HONORS:** Dean's List, Pres., Student Assn.; **MIL SERV:** US Army, Officer; **OTHER ACT & HONORS:** Who's Who; **HOME ADD:** 648 Harbor Rd., Southport, CT; **BUS ADD:** 368 Center St., Southport, CT 06490, (203)255-3434.

WILBUR, Ray L.——*Assoc. Broker*, Preston Q. Hale & Assoc., Realtors; **PRIM RE ACT:** Developer; **BUS ADD:** 1885 South Arlington, 205, Reno, NV 89509, (702)323-2168.*

WILCOX, Ansley——B: Oct. 19, 1914, Buffalo, NY, *Pres.*, Wilcox Spec. Acct.; **PRIM RE ACT:** Owner/Investor, Property Manager; **PREV EMPLOY:** (Retd.) Owner and Operator of Supermarket; **MIL SERV:** US Army/Infantry, Sgt., Meritorious Serv.; **HOME ADD:** 15 Louis St., W. Seneca, NY 14224, (716)674-1411; **BUS ADD:** 455-475 Center Rd., W. Seneca, NY 14224, (716)674-1411.

WILCOX, James L.——B: Nov. 5, 1938, Columbus, OH, *Pres.*, J.L. Wilcox & Co.; **PRIM RE ACT:** Broker, Owner/Investor, Syndicator; **SERVICES:** Purchase, synd.,mgmt. & resale of land; **PROFL AFFIL & HONORS:** Columbus, OH & Nat., Bd. of Realtors, RESSI, FLI, Columbus Farmer's Club, Nat. Mktg., Inst.; **EDUC:** BA, 1960, Econ., OH State Univ.; **GRAD EDUC:** MBA, 1966, Harvard; JD, 1962, OH State Univ.; **EDUC HONORS:** Phi Eta Sigma, With Honors; **OTHER ACT & HONORS:** Alpha Tau Omega, Phi Delta Phi, FBI Agent 1962-64, Muirfield Golf Club; **HOME ADD:** 1576 Newcomer Rd., Worthington, OH 43085, (614)846-0517; **BUS ADD:** 303 E. Livingston Ave., Columbus, OH 43215, (614)221-1172.

WILCOX, Walter J.——B: Dec. 23, 1949, Anchorage, AK, *Owner/ Pres.*, Properties Management Assn., Inc.; **PRIM RE ACT:** Developer, Builder, Owner/Investor, Property Manager; **SERVICES:** Bldg., rental mgmt., subdiv. devel.; **EDUC:** BA, 1973, Soc., Univ. of AK, Fairbanks and Anchorage; **GRAD EDUC:** Master's Work, 30 credits, Bus. Admin., Univ. of AK, Fairbanks & Anchorage; **HOME ADD:** 7.7 Mile Chena Ridge Rd., Fairbanks, AK 99701, (907)479-4401; **BUS ADD:** PO Box 80252, College, AK 99708, (907)479-4401.

WILD, M. Bruce——B: July 7, 1946, Oakland, CA, *Atty. at Law*, Wild, Carter, Tipton Oliver; **PRIM RE ACT:** Attorney, Owner/Investor; **SERVICES:** Landlord/Tenant Law & other RE Law; **REP CLIENTS:** Rental Housing Association of Central CA; **PROFL AFFIL & HONORS:** Sec. and Dir., CA Apt. Assn.; President, Rental Housing Assn. of Central CA; **EDUC:** BA, 1968, Univ. of CA, Berkeley; **GRAD EDUC:** JD, 1971, Univ. of CA, Davis; **EDUC HONORS:** Charles Mills Gayley Fellowship; **MIL SERV:** US Army, Capt.; **BUS ADD:** 2300 Civic Center Sq., Fresno, CA 93721, (209)485-2131.

WILDER, Barry S.——B: June 1, 1945, Jamestown, NY, *VP*, Salomon Brothers Inc., RE Grp.; **PRIM RE ACT:** Consultant, Architect; **OTHER RE ACT:** Investment banking; **SERVICES:** RE consulting and financing; **PREV EMPLOY:** Goldman Sachs Realty Corp., NY, NY, 1978-1981; The Architects Collaborative, Cambridge, MA, 1973-1976; **PROFL AFFIL & HONORS:** ULI; Nat. Assn. of Corp. RE Execs.; RE Bd. of NY ; Architectural League of NY; **EDUC:** AB, 1967, Eng., Princeton Univ.; **GRAD EDUC:** Master of Architecture, 1973, Harvard Univ.; MBA, 1978, Harvard Univ.; **EDUC HONORS:** Alpha Rho Chi Medal; **MIL SERV:** US Army, Capt., 1968-1971; **HOME ADD:** 1175 Park Ave., New York, NY 10028, (212)534-7474; **BUS ADD:** One New York Plaza, New York, NY 10004, (212)747-3398.

WILDER, Nicholas F.——B: June 24, 1948, Cambridge, MA, *VP*, Howard Ecker Co., RE; **PRIM RE ACT:** Broker, Developer, Builder, Property Manager; **SERVICES:** Devel. mktg. & mgmt. of office & resid. prop.; **PREV EMPLOY:** Bellemead Devel. Corp., 1976-1981; **EDUC:** 1970, Hist., Harvard Coll.; **GRAD EDUC:** MBA, 1976, RE, Boston Univ.; **HOME ADD:** 2500 N. Lakeview Ave, Chicago, IL 60614, (312)975-6289; **BUS ADD:** 400 N. State Street, Chicago, IL 60610, (312)369-1800.

WILDHACK, William A.——B: July 6, 1938, Indianapolis, IN, *Chmn.*, Wildhack & Assoc., Inc.; **PRIM RE ACT:** Consultant; **SERVICES:** GNMA Mort. Backed Securities (Quality Control), Secondary Market Liquidity; **REP CLIENTS:** over 1/3 of all GNMA MBS issuers; **PREV EMPLOY:** Govt. Nat. Mort. Assoc., Dir.; **PROFL AFFIL & HONORS:** Mort. Backed Securities (1970-1973), GNMA Dealers Exec. Assoc. VP (1973-1975), Lambda Alpha, Certified Mortgage Banker; **EDUC:** BA, 1960, Psych., Wabash Coll.; **GRAD EDUC:** Certificate, 1963, Mort. Banking MBA, Northwestern Univ.; **OTHER ACT & HONORS:** IN Ho. of Rep. 1962-1964, Town of Chevy Chase Treas. 1980-Present, Montgomery Hospice Soc., Dir.; Edgemoor Club; **HOME ADD:** 7007 Hillcrest Pl., Chevy Chase, MD 20015, (301)654-6360; **BUS ADD:** 955 L'Enfant Plaza, N. SW (PO Box 23344), Wash., DC 20024, (202)554-8600.

WILDHACK, William A., Jr.——B: Nov. 28, 1935, Takoma Park, MD, *VP & Counsel*, B.F. Saul Co.; **PRIM RE ACT:** Broker, Attorney, Insuror; **PREV EMPLOY:** IRS 1957-65; Law Firm 1965-69; **PROFL AFFIL & HONORS:** ABA; VSB & Arl. Co. VA Bar; Amer. Soc. of Corp. Savings; Realtor, RESSI; **EDUC:** BS, Bus., Miami Univ., Oxford, OH; **GRAD EDUC:** JD, 1963, Tax, George Washington Univ.; **OTHER ACT & HONORS:** V. Chmn., Arl. Tenant Landlord Commn.; Life Member, VA Jaycees; Who's Who; **HOME ADD:** 6104 N. 28th St., Arlington, VA 22207; **BUS ADD:** 8401 Connecticut Ave., Chevy Chase, MD 20815, (301)986-6000.

WILDMAN, Donald B.——B: July 14, 1949, Indianapolis, IN, *Partner*, Johnson, Smith & Hibbard, Attys.; **PRIM RE ACT:** Consultant, Attorney; **SERVICES:** Legal services; **REP CLIENTS:** Lending inst. and indiv. or instnl. purchasers in resid., comml. and mfg. Props.; **PROFL AFFIL & HONORS:** ABA, SC Bar Assn. (member of Real Prop. Sect.), State and Cty. Homebuilders Assn.; **EDUC:** BA, 1971, Soc. Sci., Wofford Coll., Spartanburg, SC; **GRAD EDUC:** JD, 1974, Bus. Law and Real Prop., Univ. of SC Law School; **EDUC HONORS:** Nat. Merit Scholar, Phi Beta Kappa, Magna Cum Laude; **HOME ADD:** 461 S Fairview Ave. Ext., Spartanburg, SC 29302, (803)583-0112; **BUS ADD:** PO Box 5524, Spartanburg, SC 29304, (803)582-8121.

WILENSKY, Alvin——B: Nov. 3, 1921, Scranton, PA, *Chmn. & Pres.*, Cenvill Investors, Inc.; **PRIM RE ACT:** Lender, Owner/Investor; **SERVICES:** RE owner and lender; **REP CLIENTS:** Cenvill Devel. Corp.; **PREV EMPLOY:** VP, Fin. - Cenvill Communities, Inc.; Self-employed, CPA; **PROFL AFFIL & HONORS:** AICPA; FL Inst. of CPA's; PA Inst. of CPA's; Amer. Mgmt. Assn., CPA; **EDUC:** BA, 1943, Commerce/Fin., PA State Univ.; **MIL SERV:** US Army Air Force, 1st Lt., Air Medal w/5 OLC; **OTHER ACT & HONORS:** Forum Club of Palm Beach; Areas., Jewish Fed. of Palm Beach Cty.; Member, Lands of the Pres. Ctry. Club; **HOME ADD:** 1723 Consulate Pl., W. Palm Beach, FL 33401, (305)689-7412; **BUS ADD:** No. Haverhill Rd., Century Village Admin. Bldg., W. Palm Beach, FL 33409, (305)686-2577.

WILES, William Montgomery——B: Feb. 13, 1948, Albuquerque, NM, *Pres.*, Dimension Prop. Inc.; **PRIM RE ACT:** Broker, Syndicator, Consultant, Developer, Owner/Investor; **SERVICES:** Comml. RE brokerage, devel. & investment; **REP CLIENTS:** Indiv. & corp. clients; **PREV EMPLOY:** Helmerich & Payne Prop. Inc. (1974-78); **PROFL AFFIL & HONORS:** OK & Amer. Inst. of CPA's, Lic as a RE broker, NAR, Evening instr. at Tulsa Jr. Coll.; **EDUC:** BS/BA, 1973, Acctg. & Econ., Univ. of Tulsa; **GRAD EDUC:** CPA; **OTHER ACT & HONORS:** Past. Pres. & Bd. Member of Leadership Tulsa, Family & Children's Services, and Young Execs. of Tulsa; **HOME ADD:** 3323 S. Utica, Tulsa, OK 74105, (918)747-9416; **BUS ADD:** 9726 E. 42nd St., Tulsa, OK 74145, (918)664-5561.

WILEY, Albert Lee, Jr.——B: June 9, 1936, Forest City, NC, *VP*, Wiley Land Co., Inc., Town & Cty. of Ruthorford; **PRIM RE ACT:** Developer, Engineer, Owner/Investor; **SERVICES:** Intl. & Local Indus. & Comml. (RE); **PREV EMPLOY:** Lockheed Aircraft Corp.; Riegel Paper Corp.; USN (LCDR, USNR/Retd.); **PROFL AFFIL & HONORS:** Inst. of Elec. Engs., Intl. Platform Assn., Amer. Mgmt. Assn., Fellowship Oak Ridge Inst. of Nuclear Studies, 1959; **EDUC:** B. of Nuclear Engrg., 1958, NC State Univ., Raleigh, NC; **GRAD EDUC:** Ph.D., 1972, Radiation Sci. & Nuclear Engrg., Univ. of WI, Madison, WI; **EDUC HONORS:** Grad. with hon.; **MIL SERV:** USNR; LCDR, USNR/Retd.; **HOME ADD:** Rte. 3, Hwy 138, Stoughton, WI 53589, (608)873-8002; **BUS ADD:** 728 Broadway, Forest City, NC 28043, (704)245-9975.

WILGUS, Gerald W.——B: Feb. 22, 1936, Bethany Beach, DE, *Pres.*, Wilgus Associates, Inc.; **PRIM RE ACT:** Broker, Banker, Developer, Owner/Investor, Insuror; **SERVICES:** RE sales, rentals, builders, ins.; **PROFL AFFIL & HONORS:** NAR, Sussex Cty. Bd. of Realtors; Profl. Ins. Assn., Indep., Ins. Assn., Amer. Inst. of Banking; DE Bankers Assn., RE Broker of the year 1980, ERA Tri-State Award; **EDUC:** Bus. Admin., Goldey Beacom Coll.; **MIL SERV:** US Army, Nat. Guard 3 yrs. in all, Spc 4; **OTHER ACT & HONORS:** Chmn. of Bd., First Nat. Bank of Georgetown, Chmn. of Org. Grp. until charter was granted in 1979, Deacon & Teacher in Christian Church; **HOME ADD:** Jefferson Bridge Rd., Bethany Beach, DE 19930, (302)539-9437; **BUS ADD:** Drawer A, Bethany Beach, DE 19930, (302)539-7511.

WILHELM, Phillip H.——B: Aug. 18, 1947, Evanston, IL, *Exec. VP*, Hawthorn Realty Grp.; **PRIM RE ACT:** Developer, Owner/Investor; **SERVICES:** Dev., investment or conversion of comml. and residential prop.; **REP CLIENTS:** Lenders, indiv. and instns.; **PREV EMPLOY:** VP-RE Dept., Continental IL Nat. Bank of Chicago - 1972-1978; **PROFL AFFIL & HONORS:** Nat. Assn. of Condo. Coop. Housing; IL MBA; **EDUC:** BA, 1969, Econ., Duke Univ.; **GRAD EDUC:** MBA, 1972, Fin. & Mktg., Northwestern Univ.; **EDUC HONORS:** Dean's List, Beta Gamma Sigma; **MIL SERV:** USAR; **HOME ADD:** 655 Briar, Northfield, IL 60043, (312)446-3932; **BUS ADD:** 8 E Huron, Chicago, IL 60611, (312)266-8100.

WILHITE, R. Gene——B: Dec. 21, 1938, Cullman, AL, *Pres.*, Sealy Realty Co., Inc.; **PRIM RE ACT:** Broker, Instructor, Owner/Investor; **OTHER RE ACT:** Sales mgr.; **SERVICES:** Sales, listings, RE class inst.; **PROFL AFFIL & HONORS:** RNMI, CRB, GRI; **EDUC:** BA, 1960, Chem., Educ., Math, St. Bernard Coll.; **GRAD EDUC:** EdM, 1962, Math, Secondary Educ., Auburn Univ.; **OTHER ACT & HONORS:** Dir., Tuscaloosa Dixie Baseball, Realtor of Year, Tuscaloosa Bd. of Realtors 1979; Pres., AL CRB Chapter (1980); State Education Comm.; AL Assn. Realtors (1978-82); **HOME ADD:** 8 Lenora Dr., Tuscaloosa, AL 35403, (205)752-7807; **BUS ADD:** 1200 Greensboro Ave., Tuscaloosa, AL 35403, (205)752-3583.

WILION, Norman R.——B: Apr. 25, 1943, Waterbury, CT, *Owner*, Charles Rosengarten Agency, Comm.-Indust.; **PRIM RE ACT:** Broker, Appraiser, Property Manager; **REP CLIENTS:** Indust. & Comml. Firms & Lending Instns.; **PROFL AFFIL & HONORS:** Assoc. SREA; **EDUC:** BS, 1948, Econ., Dartmouth Coll.; **MIL SERV:** USMC, 1st Lt.; **OTHER ACT & HONORS:** Pres. Greater Waterbury Bd. of Realtors; **HOME ADD:** DeBisschop Lane, Waterbury, CT 06704, (203)753-4011; **BUS ADD:** 70 Bank St., Waterbury, CT 06702, (203)756-7011.

WILKENS, William J., Jr.——*Ind. Div. Dir.*, Metropolitan Properties, Inc.; **PRIM RE ACT:** Developer; **BUS ADD:** 2 Metroplex Dr., Ste. 500, Birmingham, AL 35209, (205)870-9960.*

WILKERSON, John G., Jr.——B: Dec. 18, 1934, Lubbock, TX, *Owner*, The Wilkerson Co.; **PRIM RE ACT:** Developer, Owner/Investor, Property Manager; **SERVICES:** Bldg. & leasing of comml. & indus. bldgs., offices & shopping ctrs.; **REP CLIENTS:** TX Instruments, UPS, Carrier Corp., G.E., Kraft, Lanier; **EDUC:** BBA, 1957, Mgmt. and RE, Baylor Univ.; **OTHER ACT & HONORS:** Active in numerous bus. & civic orgs.; Mailing Address: PO Box 2525, Lubbock, TX, 79407; **HOME ADD:** 4701-19th St., Lubbock, TX 79407, (806)795-2024; **BUS ADD:** 515 E. 66th St., Lubbock, TX 79404, (806)745-3611.

WILKIN, James P., Jr.——B: Aug. 5, 1943, Atlanta, GA, *Principal*, European-American Equities; **PRIM RE ACT:** Broker, Consultant, Instructor; **OTHER RE ACT:** Have written articles for RE publications; **SERVICES:** Brokerage and consultation to instnl. investors; **REP CLIENTS:** Instnl. investors, domestic and off-shore as well as pension funds and REIT's; **PREV EMPLOY:** Weyman & Co. (Atlanta, GA); **PROFL AFFIL & HONORS:** RNMI, GA Chap. CCIM, GA and Atlanta's Bd. of Realtors, Young Realtor of the Yr. 1975, Designation CCIM; **EDUC:** 1962-1965, RE, GA State Univ., Bus. School; **HOME ADD:** 230 Drummen Court, Atlanta, GA 30328, (404)394-0040; **BUS ADD:** 1410 Tower Place, 3340 Peachtree Road, Atlanta, GA 30026, (404)233-4443.

WILKINS, John M.——B: May 14, 1922, Lake Placid, NY, *Pres.*, Wilkins Agency, Inc.; **PRIM RE ACT:** Broker, Consultant, Appraiser, Lender, Owner/Investor, Insuror; **SERVICES:** Gen. RE Services; **REP CLIENTS:** Fed. Gov., State Gov., Essex Cty., several banks (national, regional, & local) insurance co. (Continental Ins. Co., Republic Nat. Life, etc.) Nat. Corp., Intl. Paper, Intl. Telephone & Telegraph, ABC, NBC, Nikon Camera, Texas Instruments, United States Olympic Committee, etc.; **PREV EMPLOY:** Dir. & Chmn. of Mktg. & TV for Lake Placid 1980 Olympic Organizing Comm. 1976-81; **PROFL AFFIL & HONORS:** NY Assn. of RE Bds.; Nat. Assn. of Realtors; AIREA; MAI; Intl. Inst. of RE Valuers; **EDUC:** BA, 1947, Hist. & Govt., St. Lawrence Univ., Syracuse Univ.; **EDUC HONORS:** highest honors in Hist. and Govt.; **MIL SERV:** US Army Intelligence, Cpl., good conduct service medal, 2 companies medals; **OTHER ACT & HONORS:** Deputy Mayor, Village of Lake Placid 1962-64; Lake Placid Lions, Lake Placid Ski Club, etc.; Advisory Bds.; Farmer's National Bank, Uihlein Merey Center; Northwood School; Excelsior Insurance Co.; **HOME ADD:** 2 Signal Hill Rd., Lake Placid, NY 12946, (518)523-2000; **BUS ADD:** 59 Main St., Lake Placid, NY 12946, (518)523-2547.

WILKINSON, Larry M.——B: Oct. 23, 1945, Battle Creek, MI, *Dir.*, Larry Wilkinson & Assoc.; **PRIM RE ACT:** Consultant; **SERVICES:** Market Analysis Servs. (Comml. and Resid.); **REP CLIENTS:** Oxford Devel. Corp, Forest City Dillon, Amurcon Corp., Holtzman Silverman, N. Cranbrook Assoc.; **PREV EMPLOY:** Dir. Econ. & Market Analysis Div. Detroit Area Office of HUD; **PROFL AFFIL & HONORS:** Econ. Club of Detroit, Amer. RE & Urban Econ. Assn., Certificate of Special Achievement, Dept. HUD; **EDUC:** BBA, 1967, Mktg., Econ., Western MI Univ. Bus. School; **GRAD EDUC:** MA, 1972, Econ., Urban Labor,

Wayne State Univ.; **EDUC HONORS:** Omicron Delta Epsilon, Honor Soc., Econ.; **MIL SERV:** USMCR, Capt.; **HOME ADD:** 25801 Dundee Rd., Huntington Woods, MI 48070, (313)548-3065; **BUS ADD:** 30161 Southfield Rd., Suite 109, Southfield, MI 48076, (313)646-5370.

WILL, Philip S.——**B:** Mar. 6, 1940, Chicago, IL, *VP*, Philip S. Will Associates; **PRIM RE ACT:** Consultant, Architect, Developer, Owner/Investor; **OTHER RE ACT:** Urban planner; **PREV EMPLOY:** Partner, David A. Crane and Partners, Phila. 1969-79, Med. Facilities Div., USAF 1966-69; **PROFL AFFIL & HONORS:** AICP, AIA; **EDUC:** BArch, 1964, Cornell Univ.; **GRAD EDUC:** MUP, 1966, Urban Planning, MIT; **EDUC HONORS:** NY AIA Award for Design Excellence, Tau Beta Pi; **MIL SERV:** USAF, 1966-69, Capt., Commendation Medal; **OTHER ACT & HONORS:** Bd. Member, Washington Sq. W. 1976-79 Soc. of Friends, Bd. Member, Hartford Arch. Conservancy; **HOME ADD:** 227 Girard Ave., Hartford, CT 06105, (203)232-5253; **BUS ADD:** 1 Frederick St., Hartford, CT 06105, (203)247-3009.

WILL, Robert A.——**B:** July 10, 1928, Cumberland, MD, *Mgr., Tech. Servs. Div.*, The Austin Co.; **PRIM RE ACT:** Engineer; **SERVICES:** Planning servs. for indus./comml. clients in the fields of facility location, land use, facility design, constr. and renovation; **PREV EMPLOY:** Asst. Dir. of Indus. Devel., Cumberland, MD, C of C, 1954-55; **PROFL AFFIL & HONORS:** Member of Indus. Office Park Council of The ULI, Cleveland Engrg. Soc., Reg. Profl. Engr.; **EDUC:** BS, 1950, Econ. Geog., Univ. of MD; **GRAD EDUC:** MS, 1951, Econ. Geog., Univ. of WI; **EDUC HONORS:** Phi Kappa Phi Honor Soc.; **MIL SERV:** US Army, G-2, 1952-54, Sgt.; **HOME ADD:** 464 Falls Rd., Chagrin Falls, OH 44022, (216)247-4329; **BUS ADD:** 3650 Mayfield Rd., Cleveland, OH 44121, (216)382-6600.

WILLARD, Gary E.——**B:** Jan. 25, 1953, San Francisco, CA, *Mgr., Century 21, Willard Realty; VP, Earthsong Homes, Inc.*, Century 21, Willard Realty; **PRIM RE ACT:** Broker, Developer; **SERVICES:** Resale resid. and devel. land; **PROFL AFFIL & HONORS:** NAR; CAR; Pacifica Bd. of Realtors; Builders Indus. Assn., GRI of CA; Cert. Resid. Specialist from NAR; **OTHER ACT & HONORS:** Past Dir., CAR, 1979; Dir., Pacifica Bd. of Realtors, 1977-present; Member, City of Pacifica Zoning Oridnance Comm.; **HOME ADD:** 145 Minerva Ave., Pacifica, CA 94044, (415)359-0285; **BUS ADD:** 580 Crespi Dr., Pacifica, CA 94044, (415)359-7200.

WILLCOX, Raymond B.——**B:** July 15, 1920, Warwick, RI, *VP*, Willcox Realty; **PRIM RE ACT:** Broker, Appraiser; **SERVICES:** Resid. Spec.; **PREV EMPLOY:** Babson's Reports - Asst. Treasurer 1939-1961; **PROFL AFFIL & HONORS:** GRI, CRS; **EDUC:** BBA, 1951, Boston Univ.; **MIL SERV:** USN, CPO; **OTHER ACT & HONORS:** Kiwanis Club; **HOME ADD:** 45 White Oak Rd., Wellesley Hills, MA 02181, (617)235-6873; **BUS ADD:** 141 Linden St., Wellesley Hills, MA 02181, (617)235-6885.

WILLETT, Eugene, Jr.——**B:** Sept. 15, 1926, Dallas, TX, *Pres.*, Willett Wise Development, Inc.; **PRIM RE ACT:** Developer, Builder; **PREV EMPLOY:** Owner Willett Furniture Co.; **PROFL AFFIL & HONORS:** Past Dir. So Methodist Alumni Assn.; Mustang Club; Letterman's Assn.; SMU; Fellowship Christian Athletes; Dallas Home & Bldrs. Assn.; Nat. Assn. of Interior Designers (Comml. Div.); **EDUC:** BBA, 1950, Bus., So. Methodist Univ.; **MIL SERV:** US Army, Staff Sgt.; **OTHER ACT & HONORS:** Chmn. of Bd. of Dir. - Empire Savings & Loan - 1981; **HOME ADD:** 10041 Ferndale Rd., Dallas, TX 75238, (214)348-9031; **BUS ADD:** 9221 LBJ Freeway, Suite 209, Dallas, TX 75243, (214)669-2333.

WILLETT, Frank——*Pres.*, Dunhill of Scripps Ranch, Inc.; **PRIM RE ACT:** Broker, Consultant, Engineer, Owner/Investor, Property Manager; **OTHER RE ACT:** Exec. Search; **REP CLIENTS:** Major RE devel., retail chains, A&E firms, const.; **BUS ADD:** 9740 Appaloosa Rd. 208, San Diego, CA 92131, (714)695-0110.

WILLETTE, Charles A.——**B:** Feb. 18, 1923, MI, *Pres.*, Willette & Associates, Inc.; **PRIM RE ACT:** Broker, Consultant; **OTHER RE ACT:** Professor; **SERVICES:** RE exchange serv.; Independent Analysis; **PROFL AFFIL & HONORS:** NAR;CAR, Listed in 'Who's Who in Creative RE'; **EDUC:** BS, 1949, Fin., Syracuse Univ.; **GRAD EDUC:** MS, 1954, Fin., CA State Univ.,Los Angeles; Univ. of Southern CA; **HOME ADD:** 75 Heritage, Irvine, CA 92714, (714)559-0729; **BUS ADD:** 5305 E. Second St., Suite 206, Long Beach, CA 90803, (213)439-2125.

WILLEY, Roy E.——**B:** Mar. 6, 1920, Clarence, MO, *RE Broker*, Roy Willey, Inc.; **PRIM RE ACT:** Broker, Appraiser, Owner/Investor, Property Manager; **SERVICES:** Sales, rental, leasing, appraising; **REP CLIENTS:** Homequity, Employee Transfer Corp., Commerce Bank, Bank of St. Louis, Anheuser-Busch, Abbott Labs., TransAmerica Corp.; **PREV EMPLOY:** Realtor, partner, E.S. Miner, Realtor, Columbia, MO; **PROFL AFFIL & HONORS:** MO Assn. of Realtors, Columbia Bd. of Realtors, NAR, RNMI, FLI, WCRS, GRI, CRB, Realtor of the Year; **MIL SERV:** USAF, Maj., Good Conduct Medal; **OTHER ACT & HONORS:** Kiwanis Club, Amer. Legion, Eye Research Found. of MO Inc., Blue Lodge Mason, Knight Templar, Scottish Rite 33, Shriner; **HOME ADD:** 224 E. Pkwy, Columbia, MO 65201, (314)442-1217; **BUS ADD:** PO Box 595, Columbia, MO 65205, (314)443-3175.

WILLHARDT, Richard W.——**B:** Oct. 22, 1948, Leavenworth, KS, *VP, Sales*, Derand Realty Corp., Comml.; **PRIM RE ACT:** Broker, Developer, Owner/Investor; **PROFL AFFIL & HONORS:** No. VA Bd. of Realtors, NVBR Comml. Comml. Top Producer 1979; **EDUC:** BA, 1967, Econ., Univ. of Miss. at KC; **GRAD EDUC:** JD, UMKC School of Law, 1970, MBA, Fin. & Acctg. 1972, Wharton Grad. School of Fin. & Commerce, U. of PA; **HOME ADD:** 7450 Demille Ct., Annandale, VA 22003, (703)941-4774; **BUS ADD:** 2201 Wilson Blvd., Arlington, VA 22201, (703)527-3827.

WILLIAMS, A.S., III——**B:** Sept. 24, 1936, Eufaula, AL, *Sr. VP*, Protective Life Ins. Co., Investments; **PRIM RE ACT:** Lender; **SERVICES:** Mort. lending & RE ownership; **PROFL AFFIL & HONORS:** Mort. Bankers Assn. of Amer.; Bd. of Gov.; Amer. Bar Assn.; **EDUC:** BS, 1958, Fin., Univ. of AL; **GRAD EDUC:** LLB, 1964, Law, Birmingham School of Law; **OTHER ACT & HONORS:** The Birmingham Kiwanis Club; The Club; Mountain Brook Swim and Tennis Club; Univ. of AL Alumni Club; Phi Delta Theta Soc. Fraternity; Birmingham Phi Delta Theta Alumni Club, Past Pres.; AL Symphony Assn., Bd. Member and Officer for 15 yrs., Pres., 1980-1981; Jefferson Cty. Community Chest; **HOME ADD:** 3340 Faring Rd., Birmingham, AL 35223, (205)967-0859; **BUS ADD:** POB 2606, Birmingham, AL 35202, (205)879-9230.

WILLIAMS, Bradley Kent——**B:** June 20, 1949, Dallas, TX, *Asst. VP*, Lincoln Prop. Co.; **PRIM RE ACT:** Broker, Consultant, Property Manager; **SERVICES:** Prop. mgmt.; **REP CLIENTS:** Lenders, indivs., & insts, investors in multi-family housing; **PROFL AFFIL & HONORS:** IREM, Dallas Bd. of Realtors, CPM; **EDUC:** BA, 1971, Hist., Govt., Univ. of TX, Austin; **HOME ADD:** 10619 Marquis, Dallas, TX 75229, (214)357-6018; **BUS ADD:** 5789 Caruth Haven, Dallas, TX 75206, (214)750-0886.

WILLIAMS, Clyde E.——**B:** Jan. 22, 1920, Farnum, ID, *SRPA*, Williams Appraisal Co.; **PRIM RE ACT:** Appraiser; **OTHER RE ACT:** Contractor and devel.; **SERVICES:** R.E. appraisals; **REP CLIENTS:** First Security Bank, Zions First Nat. Bank, Tracy-Collins B&T, Bank of Commerce, Bountiful City, Salt Lake City; **PREV EMPLOY:** Pres. of Clyde E. Williams Const. Co., Pres. of Willindco Co.; **PROFL AFFIL & HONORS:** Soc. of RE Appraisers (Past Pres., Salt Lake Chap.), SRPA; **EDUC:** 1941, Weber State Coll.; Brigham Young Univ.; Univ. of UT; E. WA State Coll.; Univ. of San Francisco and Purdue Univ.; **MIL SERV:** USAAF, Capt., Air Medal & DFC; **OTHER ACT & HONORS:** Chmn. Bountiful City Planning Commn. & Capital Imp. Comm.; **BUS ADD:** 868 E. 1050 N., Bountiful, UT 84010, (801)295-4225.

WILLIAMS, C.R.——**B:** Dec. 15, 1941, Canton, IL, *Architect, Construction Coordinator*, MFC Construction Co., Construction, Design Build and Devel.; **PRIM RE ACT:** Consultant, Appraiser, Architect, Developer, Builder, Owner/Investor, Instructor, Syndicator; **SERVICES:** Archit.-Engineering-Construction Mgmt.; **REP CLIENTS:** Housing Authorities, Prop. owners; **PREV EMPLOY:** SRGF, Inc. Architects 1965-1979; **PROFL AFFIL & HONORS:** NHA, Charter Member of Central Chapter CSI, State of IL, NCARB Certificate; Reg. Arch., State of IL; **EDUC:** BArch., 1970, Arch. Design and Engrg., Univ. of IL, Urbana, IL; **OTHER ACT & HONORS:** Wrote Zoning Ordinance, City of Monticello, IL, Zoning Bd. of Appeals, Monticello, IL (7 yrs.), 1976-Outstanding Young Man of the Year Award. Author of Construction Textbooks for High Schools, Jr. Coll., and Trade Schools. Member of Booster and Gridiron Club for Glenwood High School, Chatham, IL; **HOME ADD:** 42 Axline St., Chatham, IL 62629, (217)483-4837; **BUS ADD:** 320 Northwestern Ave., Taylorville, IL 62568, (217)824-9678.

WILLIAMS, Craig L.——**B:** Aug. 12, 1946, Des Moines, IA, *Partner*, Knudsen, Berkheimer, Richardson & Endacott; **PRIM RE ACT:** Attorney; **SERVICES:** Legal; **REP CLIENTS:** Lenders, indiv. and insntl. investors, builders and devels.; **PREV EMPLOY:** Asst. Prof. Univ. of NE Coll. of Law (1973-79), Assoc., Dorsey, Windhorst et al, Minneapolis, MN(1971-73); **PROFL AFFIL & HONORS:** Admitted to practice in MN and NE, ABA Sects. of Real Prop. and Natural Resources; **EDUC:** BA, 1968, Soc. Sci., Univ. of N. IA; **GRAD EDUC:** JD, 1971, Univ. of MI; **EDUC HONORS:** Cum Laude, Order of the

Coif, Assoc. Editor, MI Law Review; **OTHER ACT & HONORS:** NE Solar Access Resources Advisory Panel Member, Publications include "The Influence of Environmental Law on NE Land Use" 57 Neb. L. Rev. 730 (1978); **HOME ADD:** 4001 Teri Ln., Lincoln, NE 68502, (402)489-0791; **BUS ADD:** 1000 NBC Center, Lincoln, NE 68508, (402)475-7011.

WILLIAMS, David A.——B: June 24, 1924, Rock Hill, SC, Douglas Elliman - Jane Hayes; **PRIM RE ACT:** Broker; **SERVICES:** Consultant, review appraiser, comml. leasing & sales; **REP CLIENTS:** Banks, devels., indivs.; **PREV EMPLOY:** Citibank, N.A., NYC, Asst. VP, Senior RE Profl.; **PROFL AFFIL & HONORS:** RECP, CRA, CPM, CCIM, GRI, RECP; **EDUC:** BS, 1950, Mktg., Sch. of Bus., Univ. of SC; **EDUC HONORS:** Cum Laude; **MIL SERV:** USN, SK3C, 1943-1946; **HOME ADD:** 84 Ivy Way, Port Washington, NY 11050, (516)767-0713; **BUS ADD:** 71 Forest Ave., Locust Valley, NY 11560, (516)759-0400.

WILLIAMS, E. Kenneth, Jr.——B: Feb. 6, 1944, Englewood, NJ, *Partner*, Kraft & Hughes; **PRIM RE ACT:** Attorney; **SERVICES:** Legal services; **REP CLIENTS:** Comml. banks, savings and loan assns., mort. bankers, RE developers, condo. developers and converters, NJ Econ. Devel. Authority; **PROFL AFFIL & HONORS:** NJ Mort. Bankers Assn.; NJ State Bar Assn. (Exec. Comm. - Banking Law Sect. and Member - Real Prop., Probate and Trust Law Section); ABA (Member, Real Property, Probate and Trust Law and Corp., Banking and Bus. Law Sect.); **EDUC:** BA, 1965, Pol. Sci., Rutgers Univ.; **GRAD EDUC:** JD, 1968, RE, Rutgers Univ.; **HOME ADD:** Spring Valley Rd., Morristown, NJ 07960; **BUS ADD:** Gateway I, Newark, NJ 07102, (201)622-5656.

WILLIAMS, Edward——*VP Corp. Plng.*, Smith International Inc.; **PRIM RE ACT:** Property Manager; **BUS ADD:** 4242 Von Karman Ave., Newport Beach, CA 92660, (714)752-9000.*

WILLIAMS, Frank M.——B: Jan. 14, 1938, Bartow, FL, *Pres.*, Frank M. Williams MD PA; **PRIM RE ACT:** Consultant, Appraiser, Lender, Owner/Investor, Instructor, Property Manager; **SERVICES:** Investment counseling, also farm and ranch props., devels. of resid. props., prop. mgmt.; **REP CLIENTS:** Frank M. Williams Props. (Not Inc.); **PROFL AFFIL & HONORS:** AOA; **EDUC:** BE, 1960, Engrg., Yale Univ.; **GRAD EDUC:** MD, 1964, Ophthalmology, Harvard Univ.; **EDUC HONORS:** Tau Beta Pi, Engineering Honor Society; Sigma Xi, Honor Society; Summa Cum Laude, Cum Laude; Alpha Omega Alpha, Medical Honor Society; **MIL SERV:** Medical Branch, USCG; Lt. Comdr.; **OTHER ACT & HONORS:** School Health Comm., Pinellas Cty.; FL; Bd. of Trs. of St. Paul's School; Chief of Surgery, Morton Plant Hospital, Clearwater, FL; **HOME ADD:** 210 Harbor View Ln., Largo, FL 33540, (813)446-2090; **BUS ADD:** 1211 Reynolds Ave., Clearwater, FL 33516, (813)446-1061.

WILLIAMS, George K.——B: Feb. 16, 1930, Greenville, AL, *Partner*, Williams, Spurrier & Rice; **PRIM RE ACT:** Attorney; **SERVICES:** Attys. at Law - RE; **PROFL AFFIL & HONORS:** AL Bar Assn.; Huntsville Bar Assn.; Huntsville, AL Bd. of Realtors; Huntsville Home Builders Assn., Admitted to practice before Supreme Ct. of U.S.; **EDUC:** BS, 1954, Commerce/Bus. Admin., Univ. of AL; **GRAD EDUC:** JD, 1956, Law, Univ. of AL School of Law; **MIL SERV:** U.S. Army, 1st Lt., Korean War Medal; **OTHER ACT & HONORS:** Pres., Huntsville AL Bar Assn.; Counsel to AL RE Commn. and Huntsville Bd. of Realtors; Author of, *AL Supplement to Modern RE Practice*; **HOME ADD:** 911 Tannahill Dr., Huntsville, AL 35802, (205)883-9806; **BUS ADD:** 320 Central Bank Bldg., Huntsville, AL 35801, (205)533-5015.

WILLIAMS, George O.——B: Jan. 28, 1945, Carthage, MS, *Pres.*, Better Homes & Prop., Inc.; **PRIM RE ACT:** Broker, Appraiser, Developer, Owner/Investor, Instructor, Property Manager; **SERVICES:** Listing, sales, consultation, prop. mgmt.; **REP CLIENTS:** Dept. of Housing & Urban Devel.; **PREV EMPLOY:** Salesperson Wright Way RE, Hooker RE; **PROFL AFFIL & HONORS:** NAR, NAREB; **EDUC:** BS, 1966, Biology, Tougaloo Coll.; **GRAD EDUC:** MS, 1968, Univ. of MS; **EDUC HONORS:** Honor Roll.; **HOME ADD:** 6845 Franklin D. Roosevelt Dr., Jackson, MS 39213, (601)362-9140; **BUS ADD:** 755 N. Lamar St., Jackson, MS 39202, (601)355-0338.

WILLIAMS, Gerald G.——B: Sept. 9, 1947, N.Y., NY, *Part.*, Gerkin & Williams; **PRIM RE ACT:** Attorney; **REP CLIENTS:** Local Banks and Realtors; **PROFL AFFIL & HONORS:** Tulsa Probate and Title Attys. Assn.; **EDUC:** BA, 1971, Eng., Newark State Coll.; **GRAD EDUC:** JD, 1975, OK City Univ.; **HOME ADD:** 11928 S. Ash St., Jenks, OK 74037, (918)299-5567; **BUS ADD:** PO Box 691, Jenks, OK 74037, (918)299-4454.

WILLIAMS, Gerald L.——B: Apr. 1, 1944, Panama City, FL, *Pres.*, The Landmark Corp.; **PRIM RE ACT:** Consultant, Attorney, Syndicator; **OTHER RE ACT:** Member of Sommer & Barnard (law firm), 1100 Merchants Bank Bldg., Indianapolis, IN 46204; **SERVICES:** Packaging RE projects for synd. & sale through securities brokerage firms; **REP CLIENTS:** Devels., builders and others relating to RE projects and investments; **PREV EMPLOY:** Former Deputy Securities Commnr., IN Securities Div.; former admin. aide to Gov. of IN; **PROFL AFFIL & HONORS:** IN State Pres. of RESSI; Indianapolis and IN State Bar Assns.; ABA; **EDUC:** BS, 1966, Bus./Fin., Univ. of CO; **GRAD EDUC:** JD, 1970, Law, IN Univ.; **EDUC HONORS:** Cum Laude; **OTHER ACT & HONORS:** Deputy Securities Commnr., IN, 1968-1969; Greater Indianapolis Builders Assn.; **HOME ADD:** 5550 Audubon Ridge, Indianapolis, IN 46250, (317)842-4440; **BUS ADD:** 8120 Knue Rd., Indianapolis, IN 46250, (317)849-6061.

WILLIAMS, Harry E.——B: Nov. 8, 1908, Gardner, IL, *Owner*, Mid-West RE Co.; **PRIM RE ACT:** Broker, Appraiser, Owner/Investor; **SERVICES:** Comml. & Resid. Props.; **PROFL AFFIL & HONORS:** CRA; IARA SCV; Intl. Inst. of Valuers; RECP; Intl. Coll. of RE Consulting Profls.; CAE; IAAO; CIAO; IL Prop. Inst.; ASA Sr. Member; **EDUC:** 1927; **OTHER ACT & HONORS:** A.F.&A.M.; Scottish Rite; Eastern Star; Elks; First Baptist Church; **HOME ADD:** 1110 N. Summit Blvd., Peoria, IL 61606, (309)676-6556; **BUS ADD:** 1110 N. Summit Blvd., Peoria, IL 61606, (309)676-6556.

WILLIAMS, J. Lanier——B: Feb. 11, 1921, Lewisville, NC, *Pres.*, Lanier Williams, Inc., Realtors; **PRIM RE ACT:** Broker, Consultant, Appraiser, Developer, Owner/Investor, Property Manager; **OTHER RE ACT:** Mktg.; **SERVICES:** Complete mktg., consulting, appraising, investing; **PREV EMPLOY:** 11 yrs. as Assoc. Broker, VP Investments Ferrell Realty Co.; **PROFL AFFIL & HONORS:** Past Pres., NC Chap. 33, FLI, Nat. Gov. 3 yrs - FLI - Nat. Delegate Legislative Comm., NAR, Distinguished Gov. 2 yrs. FLI, GRI, GRS, Past Pres. NC RE Exchangors, Accredited Farm & Land Member Winston-Salem Bd. of Realtors, Past Chmn. Prop. Mgmt. Assn., Bd. Member Comml. and Indus. Brokers; **EDUC:** USAAF Tech. Schools, 1942-1944, Aviation, Bonham Aviation School, Revac Investment Inst., UNC Realtors Institute; **EDUC HONORS:** GRI; **MIL SERV:** USAAF, Sgt., China, Burma, India Campaign; **OTHER ACT & HONORS:** Tax Equilization Bd., Forsyth Cty. 5 year, Chmn. 1 yr.; Twin City Kiwanis, K of C, NC Soc. of Cincinatti, Twin City Club, Forsyth Ctry. Club; **HOME ADD:** "Folly Farm", Lewisville, NC 27023, (919)945-3040; **BUS ADD:** Ste. 3, 125 west 3rd St., Winston-Salem, NC 27101, (919)721-0000.

WILLIAMS, James——*Director, Corporate RE*, Ashland Oil, Inc.; **PRIM RE ACT:** Property Manager; **BUS ADD:** 1401 Manchester Ave., Ashland, KY 41101, (606)329-3333.*

WILLIAMS, James Dale——B: Dec. 16, 1936, Garret Cty., MD, *Broker Owner & Pres.*, Century 21-JD Williams Real Estate Inc.; **PRIM RE ACT:** Broker, Consultant, Appraiser, Owner/Investor, Instructor, Property Manager, Insuror; **SERVICES:** Gen. resid. brokerage; **REP CLIENTS:** Home sellers & investors; **PREV EMPLOY:** Teach basic RE course at coll. level; **PROFL AFFIL & HONORS:** NAR, CRB; **EDUC:** BS, 1962, Educ., Frostburg State Coll.; **GRAD EDUC:** EDM, 1968, School of Admin., Univ. of MD; **MIL SERV:** US Army, Cpl., Sp3, Good Conduct Medal; **OTHER ACT & HONORS:** Lions Club, Riverdale; Optimists Cluc, Vienna; Boy Scouts of Amer., Troop 299; Bd. of Tr., Hyattsville Methodist Church; **HOME ADD:** 4307 Van Buren St., Univ. Park, MD 20782, (301)277-1299; **BUS ADD:** 6309 Baltimore Ave., Riverdale, MD 20737, (301)927-7600.

WILLIAMS, James K.——B: Aug. 8, 1942, Paris, TX, *Sr. VP*, First Mississippi National Bank - since 1969, Mort. and Construction; **PRIM RE ACT:** Banker, Lender; **SERVICES:** Resid. and comml. lending; **PREV EMPLOY:** 1967-1968 Examiner, Federal Home Loan Bank Bd.; 1965-1967 First Federal Savings and Loan Assn., Paris, TX; **PROFL AFFIL & HONORS:** Chmn. of MS HBA Seminar; Lic. RE Broker, CRA Sr. Member; NARA; **EDUC:** Banking & Fin., TX Tech Univ., Lubbock, TX; **GRAD EDUC:** Consumer Banking, 1977, Banking School, Univ. of VA; **OTHER ACT & HONORS:** Hattiesburg Home Builders; Hattiesburg Bd. of Realtors; Past Chmn., Mort. Div., MS Bankers Assn.; **HOME ADD:** 109 Colonial Place, Hattiesburg, MS 39401, (601)545-8163; **BUS ADD:** 100 Hardy St., P O Box 1231, Hattiesburg, MS 39401, (601)545-5218.

WILLIAMS, Jimmie D.——B: Jan. 21, 1950, Milan, TN, *Chief Fin. Officer, VP*, Belz Investment Co.; **PRIM RE ACT:** Developer, Builder, Owner/Investor, Property Manager; **OTHER RE ACT:** CPA; **PREV EMPLOY:** Arthur Anderson & Co. - (Tax Mgr.); **PROFL AFFIL & HONORS:** AICPA, Nat. Assn. of Accountants, IAFP, CPA; **EDUC:** BS, 1972, Acctg., Univ. of TN at Martin; **EDUC HONORS:** Phi Kappa Phi Honor Soc.; **MIL SERV:** US Army Res., Capt.; **OTHER**

ACT & HONORS: Civitan Club,Pres.; **HOME ADD:** 8539 Farmington Cove, Germantown, TN 38138, (901)755-3887; **BUS ADD:** 5118 Park Ave. P O Box 171199, Memphis, TN 38117, (901)767-4780.

WILLIAMS, John David——B: Sept. 17, 1946, Lamar, CO, *Partner*, Hale, Williams & Peterson; **PRIM RE ACT:** Attorney; **SERVICES:** Legal counseling for all types of RE transactions; **REP CLIENTS:** The Gwynn Co. Realtors; Stoner Realty; Fisher RE; Mary Ann Schumacher and Co., Record Title Ins. Agency; **PROFL AFFIL & HONORS:** CO State Bar Assn., Larimer Cty. Bar Assn.; **EDUC:** BA, 1968, Pol. Sci., MI State Univ.; **GRAD EDUC:** JD, 1971, Harvard Law School; **EDUC HONORS:** Magna Cum Laude; Honors Coll.; **OTHER ACT & HONORS:** Sertoma Club; Volunteers Clearinghouse, Author, "The Due on Sale Clause in CO", May 1981 Colorado Lawyer; **HOME ADD:** 1625 W. Elizabeth, D-6, Fort Collins, CO 80521, (303)493-3462; **BUS ADD:** 425 W. Mulberry St., Fort Collins, CO 80521, (303)482-9770.

WILLIAMS, John F.——*Pres.*, International Business Machines Corp., RE & Const. Div.; **PRIM RE ACT:** Property Manager; **BUS ADD:** 540 White Plains Rd., Tarrytown, NY 10591.*

WILLIAMS, John Michael——B: July 14, 1949, *Partner*, Shirk, Work, Robinson & Williams, Attys. and Counselors; **PRIM RE ACT:** Attorney; **SERVICES:** Legal Servs.; **REP CLIENTS:** RE Devels., Real Prop. Owners; Homeowners Assns.; **PREV EMPLOY:** Legal Counsel, Oklahoma City Planning Comm.; **PROFL AFFIL & HONORS:** OK and Oklahmoa City Bar Assns., ABA, OK Trin Lawyer's Assn., Amer. Planning Assn., Member, OK Bar; **EDUC:** BS, 1971, Pre-Law, OK State Univ.; **GRAD EDUC:** JD, 1973, Univ. of OK; **OTHER ACT & HONORS:** Asst. Mcpl. Counselor, City of Oklahoma City 1974-1977; **HOME ADD:** 119 S. Hudson, Oklahoma City, OK 33102, (405)232-9195; **BUS ADD:** 1108 Colcord Bldg., Oklahoma City, OK 73102, (405)236-3571.

WILLIAMS, Joseph E., Jr.——B: Nov. 18, 1923, Tampa, FL, *RE Appraiser*, Joseph E. Williams, Jr. & Son; **PRIM RE ACT:** Broker, Consultant, Appraiser; **SERVICES:** RE Appraisals; **PROFL AFFIL & HONORS:** Tampa Bd. of Realtors; SREA; **EDUC:** 1942-1946, Univ. of FL; **MIL SERV:** USNAC, Aviation Cadet; **OTHER ACT & HONORS:** Sigma Chi Fraternity; **HOME ADD:** 4610 Lumb Ave., Tampa, FL 33609, (813)834-7831; **BUS ADD:** 214 N. Howard Ave., Tampa, FL 33606, (813)251-0378.

WILLIAMS, Joseph L., III——B: Sept. 4, 1946, Kansas City, MO, *VP*, Eastdil Realty, Inc., Fin. Advisory; **PRIM RE ACT:** Broker, Consultant; **SERVICES:** Fin. and econ. servs. to the public and pvt. sector regarding maj. comml. and resid. projects; **REP CLIENTS:** Citibank, NA, First Nat. Bank of Chicago, ITT, CIT Fin. Corp., Certainteed Corp., NY State Urban Devel. Corp., City of NY, Penn Co., Sperry Corp., The Nature Conservancy; **PREV EMPLOY:** Citibank, NA-Asst. VP RE Indus. Div.; Village Square Props., Inc.-VP Fin.; **EDUC:** BS, 1969, ME, Bucknell Univ.; **GRAD EDUC:** MBA, 1974, Fin., Columbia Univ.; **HOME ADD:** 890 Pequot Ave., Southport, CT 06490, (203)255-3954; **BUS ADD:** 40 W. 57th St., New York, NY 10019, (212)397-2864.

WILLIAMS, Lawrence H.——B: June 21, 1913, Akron, OH, *Partner*, Guren, Merritt, Feibel, Sogg & Cohen; **PRIM RE ACT:** Attorney; **SERVICES:** Land assembly and acquisition, zoning, fin. leasing, devel. comml. RE - Rgnl. Shopping Centers; **REP CLIENTS:** Shopping center and comml. RE devels., supt., office bldg. and indus. park devels.; **PROFL AFFIL & HONORS:** OH, CUYA HOGA and Cleveland Bar Assns., Intl. Council of Shopping Centers; **GRAD EDUC:** JD, 1935, OH State Univ., Coll. of Law; **OTHER ACT & HONORS:** Pres., Jewish Community Fed. of Cleveland; Bd. of Trustees, United Way; **HOME ADD:** 29949 Boling Brook, Pepper Pike, OH 44113, (216)464-1423; **BUS ADD:** 700 Terminal Tower, Cleveland, OH 44113, (216)696-8550.

WILLIAMS, Lawrence J.——B: Dec. 1, 1948, Chicago, IL, *Asst. VP*, The First Nat. Bank of Chicago, RE Investment Division - Fund F; **PRIM RE ACT:** Property Manager; **OTHER RE ACT:** Asset Mgmt. & Mgr.; **SERVICES:** Operational, Mgmt. and Leasing Counsel for Comml. Props.; **REP CLIENTS:** US Corps. and Overseas Instl. and Indiv. Investors in Comml. Props.; **PREV EMPLOY:** Metropolitan Life Ins. Co. - RE Fin. Dept., 1972-76; **PROFL AFFIL & HONORS:** IREM, Building Owners and Mgr. Assn. (Local and Intl.), Dallas Bd. of Realtors, CPM; **EDUC:** BA, 1971, RE Fin., Univ. of IL, Campaign-Urbana; **MIL SERV:** USNR, First Class; **BUS ADD:** Two Turtle Creek Village, Suite 900, Dallas, TX 75219, (214)559-2120.

WILLIAMS, Oliver D., Jr.——B: Feb. 29, 1920, La Mesa, NM, *Owner*, Williams Real Estate Agency; **PRIM RE ACT:** Broker, Owner/Investor, Instructor, Property Manager; **OTHER RE ACT:** Resid. and indus. sales; **SERVICES:** Prop. mgmt. for estates; **PREV EMPLOY:** Accountant for 23 years; **PROFL AFFIL & HONORS:** NAR since 1968, CRI (GRA) Certified for instruction by NM RE Commn. in Law and Principles for students studying to become RE salespersons; **EDUC:** Acctg., High School, Ysleta, TX; **MIL SERV:** USAF, S/Sgt., Pacific Theatre, 2 years; **OTHER ACT & HONORS:** Santa Fe Urban Policy Bd. - 2 years, This is an advisory Bd. for new ordinances, Civitan Club of Santa Fe; Charter Pres., Member Ancient Free and Accepted Masons since 1957; **HOME ADD:** 1938 Tijeras St., Santa Fe, NM 87501, (505)983-6175; **BUS ADD:** Unit J, 839 Paseo de Peralta, (Mailing, P O Box 4201, Santa Fe, NM 87501, (505)982-9433.

WILLIAMS, Patricia——B: May 19, 1932, Champaign, IL, *Gen. Mgr. Corp. Sec., DB.*, Partners Fin. Inc.; **PRIM RE ACT:** Broker, Developer; **OTHER RE ACT:** Synds. mgmt.; **SERVICES:** Acctg. & Fin. mgmt. P/S files, collections on contracts, sales & exch. of units of int. inv. reports, refilings, delinq. & defaults, sales mgmt.; **REP CLIENTS:** Gen. Parts. of Ltd. Partnerships.; **PREV EMPLOY:** Consultants West Corp.; **PROFL AFFIL & HONORS:** King Co. Bd. of Realtors, RESSI, ALDA, FLI; **EDUC:** BBA, 1968, Bus. Admin., Educ., Univ. of AZ, Tucson; **GRAD EDUC:** BA, 1971, Eng Lit., Thomas Hardy, Arch., WA St. Univ, Pullman, WA; **EDUC HONORS:** Cum Laude, Phi Kappa Phi; **OTHER ACT & HONORS:** Soroptimist Int.; **HOME ADD:** PO Box 1282, Issaquah, WA 98027, (206)222-5802; **BUS ADD:** 808-106 Ave. N.E, St. 200, Bellevue, WA 98004, (206)453-1151.

WILLIAMS, Robert C.——B: May 21, 1931, Chattanooga, TN, *Arch. and Single Proprietor*, Robert C. Williams, Arch. AIA and Assoc.; **PRIM RE ACT:** Broker, Architect; **SERVICES:** Arch. Services, Master planning; Planned Community Development Specialist TN; **PREV EMPLOY:** Pres. Hawk Mountain Corp. 1963-1981 Engr, TN Valley Authority 1957; **PROFL AFFIL & HONORS:** AIA, Boston Soc. of Archs.; **EDUC:** BSE, 1954, Univ. of TN; **GRAD EDUC:** BARCH, 1962, Harvard Univ. Grad. School of Design; **MIL SERV:** USAF, Capt.; **HOME ADD:** Hawk Mountain, Pittsfield, VT 05762, (802) 746-8917; **BUS ADD:** P.O. Box 538, Pittsfield, VT 05762, (802)746-8917.

WILLIAMS, Robert E.——B: July 18, 1951, La Jolla, CA, *Assoc.*, Sheppard, Mullin, Richter & Hampton; **PRIM RE ACT:** Attorney; **SERVICES:** All legal servs. in connection with real prop. transactions; **PROFL AFFIL & HONORS:** ABA (section on real prop., probate & trust law); State Bar of CA; Los Angeles Cty. Bar Assn. (real prop. sect. and Gen. real prop. practice subsection); **EDUC:** BA, 1973, Hist., Univ. of CA, Santa Barbara; **GRAD EDUC:** JD, 1976, Law, Harvard Law School; **EDUC HONORS:** Phi Beta Kappa, Grad. with Highest Honors; **HOME ADD:** 2500 Elm Ave., Manhattan Beach, CA 90266, (213)546-1775; **BUS ADD:** 333 S. Hope St., 48th Fl., Los Angeles, CA 90071, (213)620-1780.

WILLIAMS, Thomas T., Jr.——B: Dec. 24, 1950, Greenville, SC, *Pres.*, The Williams Co.; **PRIM RE ACT:** Broker, Consultant, Appraiser; **SERVICES:** RE appraising, consulting & sales; **PREV EMPLOY:** Chief RE Appraiser, First Fed. S & L Assn. of Anderson, SC 1978-1981; **PROFL AFFIL & HONORS:** SRPA Member, Soc. of RE Appraisers, Member Anderson Bd. of Realtors; **EDUC:** BS, 1973, Fin. and RE, Univ. of SC; **EDUC HONORS:** Cameron Brown RE Scholarship Award Recipient; **HOME ADD:** 714 Coll. Ave., Anderson, SC 29621, (803)224-5107; **BUS ADD:** 201 N. Main St., Suite 315, Anderson, SC 29621, (803)224-4510.

WILLIAMS, Walter B.——B: May 12, 1921, Seattle, WA, *Pres.*, Continental, Inc.; **OTHER RE ACT:** Mort. Banker RE Fin.; **PREV EMPLOY:** Partner of Bogle and Gates, Attys.; **PROFL AFFIL & HONORS:** MBAA Seattle and WA Mort. Bankers Assn., Past Pres. MBAA, WA Mort. Bankers Assn. and Seattle Mort. Bankers Assoc.; **EDUC:** BA, 1943, Far Eastern Studies, Univ. of WA; **GRAD EDUC:** JD, 1948, Harvard Law School; **EDUC HONORS:** Phi Betta Kappa; **MIL SERV:** USMC, Capt.; **OTHER ACT & HONORS:** Member of WA State House of Reps. 1961-1963, Member of WA State Senate, 1963-1971; Seattle C of C, Bd. of Tr.; Chrmn. Econ. Devel. Council of Puget Sound; Downtown Seattle Devel. Assoc. Exec. Comm.; Rotary Club of Seattle; **HOME ADD:** 3871 45th N.E., Seattle, WA 98105, (206)523-4260; **BUS ADD:** 8th Floor Pacific Bldg., Seattle, WA 98104, (206)623-3050.

WILLIAMS, Walter H.——B: Mar. 17, 1924, Richmond, VA, *Asst. VP*, Morton G. Thalhimer, Inc., Indus & Comml. Dept.; **PRIM RE ACT:** Broker, Instructor, Syndicator, Consultant, Appraiser, Property Manager, Owner/Investor; **SERVICES:** Consult banks, indivs., feasibility studies, manage office bldgs., appraise indus. plants to rent or sell, expert witness, advise buyers and sellers; **PROFL AFFIL & HONORS:** SIR, Pres. SIR, VA Chapt., Pres. VA Chapt. IREM, Dir. VA Bd. Realtors, Editor of 'Richmond Realtor Magazine'; CPM; **EDUC:** 1949, AB Eng & Journalism; BS, Commerce, Wash. & Lee

Univ., Lexington, VA; **GRAD EDUC:** Teacher Univ. of Richmond, VA Comm. Univ.; **EDUC HONORS:** Omicron Delta Kappa, Leadership Frat. Varsity Letter; **MIL SERV:** USAF, Pvt., Good Conduct Medal; **OTHER ACT & HONORS:** Sec. 3 RE Corps.; COB in 7th St. Church; Richmond First Club Sec.; Bd. Pres. 3 Grad. Frats.; Asst. Univ. VA Grad. Bus. Sch.; **HOME ADD:** 309 S. Gaskins Rd., Richmond, VA 23233, (804)741-2090; **BUS ADD:** Richmond, VA 23206P.O. Box 702, (804)648-5881.

WILLIAMS, William G., II——B: July 22, 1952, Los Angeles, CA, *Prop. Mgr.*, Norris, Beggs and Simpson, Portland; **PRIM RE ACT:** Property Manager; **SERVICES:** Full serv. prop. mgmt.; **PROFL AFFIL & HONORS:** BOMA; IREM; Portland Bd. of Realtors; OR Assn. of Realtors; NAR, RPA; CPM; **EDUC:** BA, 1974, Econ./Poli. Sci., Willamettic Univ.; **OTHER ACT & HONORS:** Portland Jaycees; **HOME ADD:** 8228 S.W. 33rd, Portland, OR 97219, (503)245-9353; **BUS ADD:** 720 S.W. Washington, Portland, OR 97205, (503)223-7181.

WILLIAMSON, C., III——B: Oct. 28, 1946, Chester, PA, *Broker in Charge*, ERA Williamson Assoc., Ltd.; **PRIM RE ACT:** Broker, Owner/Investor, Property Manager; **SERVICES:** Brokerage, prop. mgmt., investment counseling; **REP CLIENTS:** Indivs. & cos. for brokerage & investment & prop. mgmt.; **PREV EMPLOY:** Two RE offices prior to becoming a broker & opening own office in 1978; **EDUC:** BA, 1972, Eng., Poli. Sci., Widener Coll, Chester, PA; **GRAD EDUC:** VT Law School - No Deg., 2yrs. only, Vermont Law School, S. Royalton, VT; **EDUC HONORS:** School Atty. Gen., Dean's List, 1st Class; **MIL SERV:** USN, 1966-1970, PO 3, Good Conduct Medal; **OTHER ACT & HONORS:** Agent to Prosecute - Brookfield, VT 1976, F & AM, Rotary, Charter Member - Wallingford, PA JC's, Central VT Bd. of Realtors, Central VT MLS, VT CID; **BUS ADD:** 136 N. Main St., Barre, VT 05641, (802)479-1019.

WILLIAMSON, G. Gordon——B: May 23, 1902, Windsor, Ont., Can., *Chm. of Bd. and Sr. VP*, Real Estate One, Inc.; **PRIM RE ACT:** Broker; **OTHER RE ACT:** Was Pres. of Gordon Williamson Co. from 1942 until we merged with 3 other Co. to form RE One, Broker of Record in MI for FL's Gen. Dev. Corp. Past 23 yrs.; **PREV EMPLOY:** Sold and Managed Ford Agency from 1921 until 1935; **PROFL AFFIL & HONORS:** 1962-Past Pres. of NIREB, 1952-Past Pres. Detroit RE Bd., 1940-Past Pres. United Northwest Realty Assn., 1963-Past Pres. Relo/Inter City Relocation Serv.; **HOME ADD:** 30440 Springland Dr., Farmington Hills, MI 48018, (313)476-5116; **BUS ADD:** 29630 Orchard Lake Rd., Farmington Hills, MI 48018, (313)851-1900.

WILLIAMSON, Kurt——B: Nov. 13, 1949, Fort Dodge, IA, *VP Crosby Amer. Props., Inc.*, Amer. Hoist & Derrick Co., Crosby Amer. Props.; **PRIM RE ACT:** Appraiser, Developer, Builder, Property Manager, Assessor; **SERVICES:** All Types; **REP CLIENTS:** Amer. Hoist Corp.; **PREV EMPLOY:** Amer. Hoist & Derrick Staff Accountant; **EDUC:** BS, 1969, Liberal Arts, IA Central Community Coll.-Fort Dodge, IA; **GRAD EDUC:** BA, 1971, Acctg., Buena Vista Coll., Storm Lake, IA; **MIL SERV:** USN; OSI; Vietnam Service, Korea Expert driver, Combat Action-Hostile Fire, 7 yr. service, Navy Service; **HOME ADD:** 2195 Riverwood Place, St. Paul, MN 55104, (612)644-0497; **BUS ADD:** 63 South Robert St., St. Paul, MN 55104, (612)293-4215.

WILLIAMSON, Richard A.——B: July 28, 1943, Plainfield, NJ, *Mgr., Planning & Devel.*, General Electric Credit Corp., RE Fin. Services; **OTHER RE ACT:** Planning & Devel.; **SERVICES:** Lending, originations, insurance, owner/investor, etc.; **PREV EMPLOY:** City Investing Co.; **EDUC:** AB, 1965, Econ., Brown Univ.; **GRAD EDUC:** AM, 1966, Econ., Yale Univ.; MBA, 1968, Fin./Intl. Bus., Univ. of Chicago; **EDUC HONORS:** Phi Beta Kappa, Magna Cum Laude, Woodrow Wilson Fellow, Beta Gamma Sigma; **MIL SERV:** USAR, E-5; **OTHER ACT & HONORS:** Vestry, St. Bartholomew's Church; **HOME ADD:** 7 Bittersweet Ln., Darien, CT 06820, (203)327-7694; **BUS ADD:** POB 8300, Stamford, CT 06904, (203)357-6550.

WILLIAMSON, Roger K.——B: Oct. 28, 1947, Normal, IL, *Dir. of Training*, Coldwell Banker/Thorsen; **PRIM RE ACT:** Broker, Instructor; **SERVICES:** Training sales assoc., new assoc., mgrs.; **PROFL AFFIL & HONORS:** RNMI, DuPage Bd. of Realtors, IAR, NAR, GRI, CRS, CRB; **EDUC:** BBA, 1970, Acctg., Wichita State Univ.; **HOME ADD:** 1768 Maple Ln., Wheaton, IL 60187, (312)668-7778; **BUS ADD:** 1225 W. 22nd St., Oak Brook, IL 60521, (312)887-5900.

WILLIS, Beverly A.——*Pres.*, Willis & Associates, Inc.; **PRIM RE ACT:** Architect; **PROFL AFFIL & HONORS:** AIA; ARC; BOMA; Lamda Alpha; **EDUC:** BA, 1955, Univ. of HI; **GRAD EDUC:** Honorary Doctorate of Fine Arts, Mt. Holyoke Coll.; **EDUC HONORS:** Pres., CC AIA; **HOME ADD:** River Run, 11 Zinfandel Ln., St. Helena, CA 94574, (707)963-2149; **BUS ADD:** 545 Mission St., 4th Flr., San Francisco, CA 94105, (415)777-4660.

WILLIS, E.W.——B: Feb. 20, 1948, Corsicana, TX, Fausett & Company, Inc., Comml. Div.; **PRIM RE ACT:** Broker, Consultant, Appraiser, Developer, Owner/Investor; **SERVICES:** Site selection, investment prop., brokerage, investment counseling, prop. mgmt., leasing, build to suit & sale/leasebacks, review appraisal; **REP CLIENTS:** Indiv. and instnl. investors, major users; **PREV EMPLOY:** E. W. Willis, RE Counseling & Brokerage; **PROFL AFFIL & HONORS:** RNMI; NARA; NAREA; RE Fin. Execs. Assn., CCIM; CRPA; CRA Designations; **EDUC:** BBA, 1971, RE, Southern Methodist Univ.; **GRAD EDUC:** MS, 1979, RE & Regl. Sci., Cox School of Bus., Southern Methodist Univ.; **EDUC HONORS:** Cert. in RE, Beta Gamma Sigma; Home & Apt. Builders Assn., Scholarship; Grad. Cert. in RE, Grad. Cert. in Mort. Banking (Costa Inst. of RE Fin.; **HOME ADD:** 47 Hickory Hill, Little Rock, AR 72215, (501)227-7333; **BUS ADD:** One Fin. Ctr., P.O. Box 5730, Little Rock, AR 72215, (501)224-7500.

WILLIS, James R.——B: July 2, 1941, Bennington, VT, *VP*, E. P. Wilbur & Co., Inc.; **PRIM RE ACT:** Owner/Investor; **SERVICES:** Acquisition, ownership and mgmt. of RE for instns. and indiv. investors; **PREV EMPLOY:** High Vista Corp. (1968-1972); GE Bieder & Assocs. (1977-1978); Devels. Intl. (1978-1989); Pinellas Contractors & Builders Assn. (1972-1978); **EDUC:** BA, 1967, Univ. of S. FL; **HOME ADD:** 53 Great Hill Rd., Oxford, CT 06483; **BUS ADD:** 368 Center St., Southport, CT 06490, (203)255-3434.

WILLIS, Jon B.——B: June 4, 1948, El Paso, TX, *VP/Dir. of Research*, Century Partners; **PRIM RE ACT:** Consultant, Appraiser, Syndicator; **SERVICES:** Acquisition/Analysis; **PREV EMPLOY:** Blackfield Hawaii Corp., Kahala Center Co.; **EDUC:** BA, 1970, Hist. & Poli. Sci., Univ. of NM; BBA, 1972, Bus., Univ. of HI; **GRAD EDUC:** MA, 1973, Intl. Relations, Univ. of HI; **HOME ADD:** 1919 Alameda, San Mateo, CA 94403, (415)574-9133; **BUS ADD:** 2755 Campus Dr., San Mateo, CA 94403, (415)574-9133.

WILLIS, Steven C.——B: July 6, 1951, Parkston, SD, *Atty. C.P.A. MBA RE Broker*, Willis Law Office; **PRIM RE ACT:** Broker, Consultant, Attorney, Developer, Owner/Investor; **OTHER RE ACT:** Fin. Structuring; **SERVICES:** Tax planning, purchase structuring, contract preparation; **PROFL AFFIL & HONORS:** AGA, AIIPA, AMBA, SD RE Bd.; **EDUC:** Econ./Eng.; **BUS ADD:** Suite 514 Court House Plaza, Sioux Falls, SD 57102, (605)339-3131.

WILLIS, William H.——*Sr. VP*, TMI Realty, Inc., Atlanta; **PRIM RE ACT:** Property Manager; **SERVICES:** Prop. Mgmt., Broker, Consultant; **REP CLIENTS:** Inst. or indiv. investors in comml. props.; **PROFL AFFIL & HONORS:** IREM, Apt. Owners & Mgrs., Bd. of Realtors, CPM; **EDUC:** BA, His., Emory Univ.; **GRAD EDUC:** MBA, Mgmt., GA State Univ.; **MIL SERV:** USN, Lt. Bronze Star with Combat 'V', Gallantry Cross with Silver Star, Staff Honor Medal First Class; **BUS ADD:** 6540 Powers Ferry Rd., Suite 155, Atlanta, GA 30339, (404)955-1174.

WILLNER, George——B: July 7, 1944, Sonock, Poland, *Sr. Atty.*, George Willner P.C., A Profl. Corp.; **PRIM RE ACT:** Consultant, Attorney, Developer, Owner/Investor, Property Manager, Syndicator; **SERVICES:** Legal, investment counseling, synd.; **REP CLIENTS:** Banks, ins. cos., lenders, indiv. & inst. investors; **PREV EMPLOY:** VP & counsel large rgnl. mort. banker & devel.; **PROFL AFFIL & HONORS:** Amer., PA, Phila., Montgomery cty, PA Bar Assns.; **EDUC:** BS, 1966, Bus. Law, Econ., Mgmt., PA State Univ.; **GRAD EDUC:** 1970, JD, Real Prop. & Corp. Law, Temple Univ.; **EDUC HONORS:** Real Prop. Award; **OTHER ACT & HONORS:** Solicitor, Twp. & School Bds. 1973-76; Golden Slipper Club; **HOME ADD:** Dickerson Rd., N. Wales, PA 19454, (215)855-7848; **BUS ADD:** 570 W. Dekalb Pike, King of Prussia, PA 19406, (215)265-5900.

WILLS, Thomas S., Jr.——B: Feb. 13, 1920, Toronto, Can., *Pres.*, Wills Realty Corp.; **PRIM RE ACT:** Broker, Appraiser; **SERVICES:** Real prop. valuation, expert testimony, RE sales & leasing; **PROFL AFFIL & HONORS:** RE Bd.of Rochester (Pres., 1955); NY State Assn. of Realtors (Pres., 1980); NAR (Bd. of Dirs. 1976-Present); NY State Appraisors Soc. (Pres., 1962); AIREA; Soc. of RE Appraisers, MAI, SRPA, RE Bd. of Rochester Realtor of the Year; **EDUC:** 1939-1940, RE, Bus. Admin., Syracuse Univ.; **MIL SERV:** USAF, T/Sgt., 1942-1945; **OTHER ACT & HONORS:** Chmn., Town of Greece Planning Bd., 1972-1980; Greece Rotary Club (Pres., 1960); **HOME ADD:** 326 Rye Rd., Rochester, NY 14626, (716)225-6675; **BUS ADD:** 3205 Mt. Read Blvd., P.O. Box 7205, Rochester, NY 14616, (716)621-4620.

WILLSE, Charles E.——B: Dec. 26, 1952, NY, *Arch.*, Jerry Johnson Inc.; **PRIM RE ACT:** Architect; **SERVICES:** Full arch. & landscape arch. design servs.; **PROFL AFFIL & HONORS:** AIA; **EDUC:** BS, 1976, Arch., Cornell Univ.; **GRAD EDUC:** Ext. Study, RI School of

Design; **EDUC HONORS:** Cum Laude; **OTHER ACT & HONORS:** Silver Lake Yacht Club; **HOME ADD:** 28 Rowell St., Boston, MA 02125, (617)282-8817; **BUS ADD:** 35 Newbury St., Boston, MA 02116.

WILNER, Alfred, PE——B: Aug. 4, 1930, NYC, NY, *Pres.*, Alfred Wilner Inc.; **PRIM RE ACT:** Consultant, Engineer; **SERVICES:** Engrg. Consultant to Morg. Lenders; **PROFL AFFIL & HONORS:** ASCE, Licensed Professional Engineer in 11 states; **EDUC:** BCE, 1953, Civil Engineering, School of Technology, CCNY; **GRAD EDUC:** MBA, 1966, Mgmt., NYU, Grad. School of Bus.; **MIL SERV:** USAF, Capt.; **OTHER ACT & HONORS:** Faculty Member (Part-time) NYU Faculty Member - Practising Law Inst.; **HOME ADD:** 12 Jordan Rd., Hastings-Hudson, NY 10706, (914)478-0554; **BUS ADD:** 370 Lexington Ave., New York, NY 10017, (212)532-2680.

WILSON, Allen P.——B: May 5, 1945, San Antonio, TX, *Pres.*, Wilson Development Corp.; **PRIM RE ACT:** Broker, Architect, Developer, Builder, Owner/Investor, Property Manager; **SERVICES:** Design and build for lease or sale; **REP CLIENTS:** Mfrg./warehousing; **PREV EMPLOY:** V.P., Robert Callaway Corp.; **PROFL AFFIL & HONORS:** AIA, San Antonio Bd. of Realtors, TX Soc. of Arch.; **EDUC:** BArch, 1969, Arch./Construction, Univ. of TX at Austin; **BUS ADD:** 4888 Whirlwind, San Antonio, TX 78217, (512)655-4505.

WILSON, Charles A.——B: Aug. 19, 1931, Chicago, IL, *Pres.*, Monticello Investments, Inc.; **PRIM RE ACT:** Broker, Consultant, Developer, Owner/Investor, Instructor, Property Manager, Syndicator; **SERVICES:** RE Investment, devel. for own account, consulting for others; **REP CLIENTS:** Natl. Apt. Assn. Seminars: Univ. of AL continuing Ed.; **PROFL AFFIL & HONORS:** Natl. Tuscaloosa Bd. of Realtors; Amer. Cemetery Assn.; **EDUC:** Poli. Sci., Admin., 1953, Univ. of AL, Arts and Sci.; **EDUC HONORS:** Editor Crimson-White Weekly; **OTHER ACT & HONORS:** 1978 Pres. Arts Council, Tuscaloosa 1975 Pres., Tuscaloosa Bd. of Realtors; Council Commr. BSA Black Warrior Council; **HOME ADD:** 1014 Myrtlewood, Tuscaloosa, AL 35401; **BUS ADD:** 1217 Greensboro Ave., Tuscaloosa, AL 35401, (205)345-6660.

WILSON, Christian——B: Feb. 24, 1946, Baltimore, MD, *Counsel*, Mall Management Associates, Inc.; **PRIM RE ACT:** Attorney; **PREV EMPLOY:** Monumental Props., Inc.; **PROFL AFFIL & HONORS:** ABA; MD Bar Assn.; **EDUC:** BA, 1968, Eng., Towson State Univ.; **GRAD EDUC:** JD, 1976, Law, Univ. of Baltimore; **MIL SERV:** MD Air Nat. Guard; **BUS ADD:** 600 Lafayette Bldg., 40 W. Chesapeake Ave., Baltimore, MD 21204, (301)823-2700.

WILSON, David S.——B: Feb. 13, 1944, NJ, *VP Research*, Shearson Amer. Express, Amer. Express; **OTHER RE ACT:** Investment analyst; **SERVICES:** Stock brokerage; **EDUC:** 1967, Econ., Villanova Univ.; **BUS ADD:** 14 Wall St., New York, NY 10005, (212)572-5136.

WILSON, E. Anthony——B: Dec. 18, 1944, Rochester, NY, *General Partner*, Wilson Enterprises; **PRIM RE ACT:** Developer, Builder, Owner/Investor, Property Manager, Syndicator; **SERVICES:** Synd. and devel. of comml. prop.; **EDUC:** BS, 1967, RE, Fin., IN Univ.; **BUS ADD:** 929 Midtown Tower, Rochester, NY 14604, (716)232-1455.

WILSON, Edward M.——B: July 30, 1954, Fort Dodge, IA, *Atty. at Law*, Wilson Law Office; **PRIM RE ACT:** Attorney; **SERVICES:** Advising Buyers and sellers; abstract exams. and title opinions; gen. law practice; **PROFL AFFIL & HONORS:** ABA; IA State Bar Assn.; 5th Judicial Dist. Bar Assn.; Wayne Cty. Bar Assn.; Real Prop., Probate & Trust Div. of ABA; Clinton County Bar Assn.; **EDUC:** AB, 1977, Psych., Princeton Univ.; **GRAD EDUC:** JD, 1980, Law, Univ. of IA; **EDUC HONORS:** Cum Laude; **OTHER ACT & HONORS:** Asst. Cty. Atty./Wayne Cty., IA; **HOME ADD:** 436 6th Ave. S., Clinton, IA 52732, (319)242-8224; **BUS ADD:** 436 6th Ave. S., Clinton, IA 52732, (319)242-8224.

WILSON, James J.——B: Apr. 18, 1933, NYC, NY, *Pres.*, Interstate Gen. Corp.; **PRIM RE ACT:** Developer, Builder, Owner/Investor, Property Manager; **PREV EMPLOY:** Found. of Co. in 1956; **PROFL AFFIL & HONORS:** ULI, ASCE, NAHB, Pres. & Dir. of the following: ASME (Puerto Rico Chapter; NAHB (Puerto Rico Chapter); YPO (Puerto Rico Chapter); **EDUC:** BCE, 1955, Civil Engrg., Manhattan Coll., NYC, NY; **EDUC HONORS:** Bus. Man of the Year, Manhattan Coll.; **OTHER ACT & HONORS:** Dir. of the following: Jr. Achievement (PR), Presbyterian Hospital (PR), Commonwealth Bank & Trust (VA), N. VA Angus Assn., Buckhill Assn., Middleburg Tennis Assn.; American Angus Assn. and VA Thoroughbred Assn.; **HOME ADD:** Dresden Farm, Box 392, Middleburg, VA 22117, (703)687-6211; **BUS ADD:** US Offices: 222 Smallwood Village Ctr., St. Charles, MD 20601, (301)843-7333.

WILSON, James M.——B: Jan. 26, 1942, Springfield, IL, Wilson Appraisal Service; **PRIM RE ACT:** Broker, Appraiser; **SERVICES:** Value of properties; **REP CLIENTS:** Banks, attys., Dept. of Transp., S&L, conservation, airports; **PREV EMPLOY:** Chief Appraiser & Chief Reviewing Appraiser for the Dept. of Transp., Div. of Hwys., Dist. 6, Springfield, IL; **PROFL AFFIL & HONORS:** Resid. Member of the AIREA; IL Soc. of Farm Mgrs. & Rural Appraisers, RM 592; **EDUC:** 1964, Agric. Engrg., So. IL Univ.; **HOME ADD:** RR 1, Pawnee, IL 62558, (217)625-5812; **BUS ADD:** RR 1, Pawnee, IL 62558, (217)625-5812.

WILSON, James T.——B: July 13, 1945, Indianapolis, IN, *Pres.*, Wilson and Humphlett, Inc.; **PRIM RE ACT:** Broker, Instructor, Property Manager, Lender; **SERVICES:** Client rep. in acquisition and disposition of investment R.E.; **PREV EMPLOY:** VP Natl. R.E. Exchange, Inc.; Cert. Bus. Counselors, NAR, RNMI, FLI; **PROFL AFFIL & HONORS:** CCIM, CBC; **EDUC:** BA, 1967, Speech and Soc., Clarke Memorial Coll., Univ. of MS; **EDUC HONORS:** Phi Kappa Phi; **MIL SERV:** USAF, E-5, Bronze Star; **OTHER ACT & HONORS:** Sales and Mktg. Exec. Assoc.; **HOME ADD:** 501 Sunglow Ct., Orlando, FL 32803, (305)896-1641; **BUS ADD:** 511 N. Ferncreek Ave., Orlando, FL 32803, (305)894-9505.

WILSON, Jeremy G.——B: May 19, 1945, *Sr. VP*, The Kennan Co./Realtors, Leasing & Prop. Mgmt.; **PRIM RE ACT:** Instructor, Syndicator, Consultant, Developer, Property Manager, Owner/Investor; **SERVICES:** Dev., Mgmt. & Leasing, Brokerage; **REP CLIENTS:** Fortune 500 Cos., Foreign Investors; **PROFL AFFIL & HONORS:** IREM, CPM, CCIM; **EDUC:** BS, 1968, RE, VSC; **EDUC HONORS:** Deans List; **BUS ADD:** Box 11610, Columbia, SC 29211, (803)254-2300.

WILSON, John C., III——B: Mar. 22, 1943, Hartford, CT, *Chmn.*, J. Watson Beach RE Co.; **PRIM RE ACT:** Broker, Syndicator, Consultant, Appraiser, Developer, Builder, Owner/Investor; **REP CLIENTS:** Upon Request; **PREV EMPLOY:** Pres. - Wison Indus.; **PROFL AFFIL & HONORS:** CT Assn. of Realtors, NAR, CID; **EDUC:** BS, 1964, Bus., Univ. of GA; **MIL SERV:** USAG, 2nd Lt.; **HOME ADD:** 26 Fulton Pl., West Hartford, CT 06103, (203)233-0280; **BUS ADD:** 15 Lewis St., Hartford, CT 06103, (203)547-1550.

WILSON, John Timothy——B: Nov. 13, 1956, *VP*, Treptow, Murphree & Company, Comml. Devel.; **OTHER RE ACT:** Project Manager; **EDUC:** BBA, 1979, RE, Gen. Bus., So. Methodist Univ.; **HOME ADD:** 1100 Augusta, #48, Houston, TX 77057, (713)789-3363; **BUS ADD:** 5858 Westheimer, Suite 800, Houston, TX 77057, (713)784-8500.

WILSON, Jonathan C.——B: Feb. 4, 1945, Montezuma, IA, *Sr. Partner*, Davis, Hockenberg, Wine, Brown & Koehn; **PRIM RE ACT:** Attorney, Owner/Investor, Instructor; **SERVICES:** Legal; **PREV EMPLOY:** Asst. Prof., Modern RE Transactions, Drake Univ. Law School, Des Moines, IA 1975; **PROFL AFFIL & HONORS:** ABA, Prop. Probate and Trust Law Comm., IA Bar Assn., Probate, Prop. and Trust Law Comm., Dir., RE Div., Polk Cty. Bar Assn.; **EDUC:** BA, 1967, Eng., Hist., Morningside Coll, Sioux City, IA; **GRAD EDUC:** JD, 1971, Univ. of IA, Coll. of Law; **EDUC HONORS:** Blue Key, Grad. with Distinction, Order of Coif; **MIL SERV:** US Army, PFC; **OTHER ACT & HONORS:** Lecturer, Australian Nat. Univ. School of Law, Canberra, Australia 1972-74; Chmn., RE Practice Manual Comm. IA State Bar Assn. 1978-80; **HOME ADD:** 2924 Druid Hill Dr., Des Moines, IA 50315, (515)284-0880; **BUS ADD:** 2300 Financial Ctr., Des Moines, IA 50315, (515)243-2300.

WILSON, Kemmons, Jr.——B: Sept. 22, 1946, Memphis, TN, Kemmons Wilson Co's.; **PRIM RE ACT:** Broker, Consultant, Developer, Builder, Owner/Investor, Property Manager; **SERVICES:** Devel. of all indus. & comml. props., & time share resorts, investment counseling, prop. mgmt.; **REP CLIENTS:** Own account; **PROFL AFFIL & HONORS:** IREM, Memphis Bd. of Realtors, CPM; **EDUC:** BS, 1968, Fin., Univ. of AL, Coll. of Commerce & Bus. Admin.; **GRAD EDUC:** SCMP, 1979, Smaller Co. Mgmt. Program, Harvard Grad. Sch. of Bus.; **MIL SERV:** USN, Res.; **OTHER ACT & HONORS:** Bd. of Dir. Liberty Bowl Classic; **HOME ADD:** 6465 May Creek, Memphis, TN 38119, (901)682-0057; **BUS ADD:** 1629 Winchester Rd., Memphis, TN 38116, (901)346-8803.

WILSON, Lance H.——*Exec. Asst.*, Department of Housing and Urban Development, Ofc. of Secy./Under Secy.; **PRIM RE ACT:** Lender; **BUS ADD:** 451 Seventh St., S.W., Washington, DC 20410, (202)755-6417.*

WILSON, Lewis R.——B: May 27, 1928, High Point, NC, *Owner*, Wilson & Co.; **PRIM RE ACT:** Developer; **SERVICES:** Subdiv. land creating bldg. lots; consulting for others who wish to do the same;

PREV EMPLOY: Formerly designed and built perpetual care cemeteries; **PROFL AFFIL & HONORS:** RE broker; resid. bldg. contractor, Home Bldrs. Assn.; **MIL SERV:** US Army, Seoul Korea; **OTHER ACT & HONORS:** Author of 'Subdivisions, Positive Steps in Land Development, A Success Formula.', This is a small 8-1/2 x 11 book to help the small devel. Not theory, but nuts and bolts ideas that work. Copyright 1981; **HOME ADD:** 322 Fox Hollow Dr, Clayton, NC 27520, (919)553-5732; **BUS ADD:** 322 Fox Hollow Dr., Clayton, NC 27520, (919)553-5732.

WILSON, Margot P.——**B:** Apr. 19, 1943, Richmond, VA, *Pres. - Owner- Designated Broker*, The Property Shop, Ltd.; **PRIM RE ACT:** Broker, Consultant, Owner/Investor, Instructor, Property Manager, Syndicator; **SERVICES:** Full resid., comml. and prop. mgmt.; **PREV EMPLOY:** Buyer-major retail stores, Phoenix; Top Sales associate for seven years of major real estate firm in Phoenix; **PROFL AFFIL & HONORS:** NAR, RNMI, WCR, National Million Dollar Club, ARA, ARPAC, Phoenix/Scottsdale/Glendale Bds., Lifetime Member - President's Roundtable Phoenix Bd. of Realtors; 1976 Realtor-Assoc. of the Yr., GRB; CRS; GRI; **EDUC:** Penn State; Tobe-Coburn School (NYC); **EDUC HONORS:** Grad. with distinction from Tobe-Coburn; **OTHER ACT & HONORS:** First United Methodist Church; Runner-up Sales Assoc. of the Yr. - Homes for Living Network; **HOME ADD:** 77 E Missouri, Phoenix, AZ 85012, (602)274-2380; **BUS ADD:** 2312 W Northern Ave., Phoenix, AZ 85021, (602)995-1545.

WILSON, Michael R.——**B:** Dec. 9, 1953, Tulsa, OK, *Atty.*, Watson, McKenzie & Moricoli; **PRIM RE ACT:** Attorney, Owner/Investor; **SERVICES:** Title examination, closings etc.; **PROFL AFFIL & HONORS:** ABA, OK Bar Assn.; **EDUC:** BS, 1975, Poli. Sci., Econ., OK State Univ.; **GRAD EDUC:** JD, 1978, Law, Univ. of OK; **EDUC HONORS:** Order of the Coif; **HOME ADD:** 2620 Lost Trail Rd., Edmond, OK 73034, (405)348-2999; **BUS ADD:** 1200 Liberty Tower, Oklahoma City, OK 73102.

WILSON, Ray C.——**B:** July 10, 1929, Houston, TX, *Sr. VP*, San Antonio Savings Assn.; **PRIM RE ACT:** Developer, Lender; **SERVICES:** RE devel., mort. banking; **PREV EMPLOY:** Pres. Rotan Mosle Mort. Co., Houston; Sr. VP Amer. Nat. Ins. Co., Galveston; **PROFL AFFIL & HONORS:** AIREA, ULI, MBAA, CMB; MAI; Member, Bd. of Trustees, National Assn. of Certified Mortgage Bankers; **EDUC:** BBA, 1949, Indus. Mgmt., Univ. of TX at Austin; **GRAD EDUC:** MBA, 1951, Fin. & RE, Univ. of TX at Austin; **MIL SERV:** USAR, S/Sgt.; **OTHER ACT & HONORS:** Oak Hills Ctry. Club, Plaza Club, Hartford Club; **HOME ADD:** 207 Sheffield, San Antonio, TX 78213, (512)349-6222; **BUS ADD:** 601 NW Loop 410, San Antonio, TX 78216, (512)340-7481.

WILSON, Robert D.——**B:** Aug. 20, 1946, Tulsa, OK, *Sr. VP*, Henry S. Miller Co., Realtors; **PRIM RE ACT:** Broker, Assessor, Developer; **SERVICES:** Sale, leasing, sale lease back, site location, investment analysis, multi party trades, site developer; **REP CLIENTS:** Eckerd Drugs, Gen. Mills, Pioneer Electronic, Amer. Greeting Cards, Kraft Foods, Johnson & Johnson; **PROFL AFFIL & HONORS:** Dallas Bd. of Realtors, CID, TAR; **EDUC:** BS, 1969, Psych., OK State Univ.; **GRAD EDUC:** MBA, 1973, Mktg., Wichita State Univ.; **MIL SERV:** USAF, S/Sgt.; **HOME ADD:** 5252 Vanderbilt, Dallas, TX 75206, (214)823-8283; **BUS ADD:** 2001 Bryan Tower, 30th fl., Dallas, TX 75201, (214)748-9171.

WILSON, Robert S.——**B:** July 26, 1939, Troup, TX, *Owner*, Robert S. Wilson Investments; **PRIM RE ACT:** Owner/Investor; **SERVICES:** Const., Mgmt., Leasing; **PREV EMPLOY:** Resident Partner, Trammell Cr. Co., Houston, TX; **EDUC:** BBA, 1962, SMU, Dallas, TX; **BUS ADD:** 8584 Kathy Frwy., Suite 100, Houston, TX 77024, (713)467-1410.

WILSON, Robert W.——**B:** Mar. 24, 1936, Chicago, IL, *Exec. VP*, Lloyds Bank CA, RE Indus. Div.; **PRIM RE ACT:** Banker, Lender; **PROFL AFFIL & HONORS:** MBAA, CA Mort. Bankers Assn., S CA Mort. Bankers Assn.; **EDUC:** BS, 1956, Bus. Educ., N IL Univ., DeKalb; **MIL SERV:** US Army, SP4; **HOME ADD:** 330 Hacienda Dr., Arcadia, CA 91006, (213)355-7500; **BUS ADD:** 612 S Flower St., Los Angeles, CA 90017, (213)613-2678.

WILSON, Ronald——*Real Prop. Mgr.*, Oak Industries, Inc.; **PRIM RE ACT:** Property Manager; **BUS ADD:** 16935 West Bernardo Dr., San Diego, CA 92127, (714)485-9300.*

WILSON, Stanley Alexander——**B:** June 30, 1942, Nassau, Bahamas, *Mgr., Indus. and Comml. Sales*, The Grand Bahama Development Co., Ltd., Indus. and Comml. Development; **PRIM RE ACT:** Consultant, Appraiser, Developer, Syndicator, Assessor; **SERVICES:** Investment counseling, valuation, devel. plant location consultant; **REP CLIENTS:** Indus. or instnl. investors in comml. props.; lenders; cos. seeking new plant locations; **PREV EMPLOY:** Bahamas Govt. - Ministry of Devel. 1967-70; **EDUC:** BA, 1967, Econ., Morgan State Coll.; **GRAD EDUC:** MBA, 1977, Bus. Admin., Univ. of Miami; **HOME ADD:** P.O. Box F-3188, Freeport, Grand Bahama, Bahamas, (809)352-2528; **BUS ADD:** P.O. Box 340939, Coral Gables, FL 33114, (809)352-6711.

WILSON, Steven Nevin——**B:** July 12, 1947, Whittier, CA, *Counsel & Asst. Sec.*, Vons Grocery Co., Legal Dept.; **PRIM RE ACT:** Attorney; **SERVICES:** Negotiation and drafting for corp. RE dept.; **PREV EMPLOY:** AVP, Counsel & Asst. Sec. - Western Fed. S&L Assn., Los Angeles (1978-80); **PROFL AFFIL & HONORS:** ABA, CA Bar Assn., Los Angeles Cty. Bar Assn. & Real Prop Sects.; **EDUC:** BA, 1968, Eng./Econ., Pomona Coll., Claremont, CA; **GRAD EDUC:** JD, 1977, Law, Pepperdine Univ. School of Law; **EDUC HONORS:** Dept. Honors at Graduation, Top 1/4; **MIL SERV:** US Navy, Lt., 1968-1971; **HOME ADD:** 8572 Boone Cir., Westminster, CA 92683, (714)898-9887; **BUS ADD:** 9420 Telstar, El Monte, CA 91731, (213)579-0571.

WILSON, Thomas E.——**B:** Oct. 27, 1942, Alliance, OH, Monroe, Wilson & Collins; **PRIM RE ACT:** Attorney; **REP CLIENTS:** Union Bank; Valley Nat. Bank; Schumacher Mort. Co.; **PROFL AFFIL & HONORS:** ABA, AZ State Bar; Pima Cty. Bar Assn.; **EDUC:** BA, 1964, Poli. Sci., Univ. of AZ; **GRAD EDUC:** LLB, 1966, Law, Univ. of AZ; **OTHER ACT & HONORS:** Bd. of Dir., Pima Community College Foundation; **HOME ADD:** 5601 N. Maria Drive, Tucson, AZ 85704, (602)887-6488; **BUS ADD:** 1002 Home Federal Tower, 32 North Stone Ave., Tucson, AZ 85701, (602)792-9220.

WILSON, Thomas W.——**B:** Jan. 15, 1953, Charleston, WV, *Atty. at Law*, Berry & Pappas; **PRIM RE ACT:** Attorney; **SERVICES:** Title serach, notes, mort., contracts; **REP CLIENTS:** Buyers, sellers, RE agents; **PREV EMPLOY:** Clark Cty. Prosecutors Office; **PROFL AFFIL & HONORS:** ABA, Clark Cty. Bar Assn., Phi Delta Phi Legal Frat.; **EDUC:** AB, 1975, Hist., Kenyon Coll.; **GRAD EDUC:** JD, 1979, Univ. of Dayton; **EDUC HONORS:** Phi Beta Kappa, Magna Cum Laude, Hist. Honors; **OTHER ACT & HONORS:** Mens Democratic Club, Big Brothers, Grace Lutheran Church, Delta Phi Frat., Jaycees Outstanding Young Men 1981; **HOME ADD:** 1816 Warder St., Springfield, OH 45503, (513)323-2739; **BUS ADD:** 10 W. Columbia St., Springfield, OH 45502, (513)322-6611.

WILSON, William, III——**B:** July 20, 1936, Pasadena, CA, *Pres.*, Wilson & Gates Raalty, Inc.; **PRIM RE ACT:** Developer, Property Manager; **SERVICES:** RE devel. & mgmt. from site selection through const. and leasing; **PREV EMPLOY:** The Borel Cos., 1965-78; **PROFL AFFIL & HONORS:** ULI; **EDUC:** BS, 1958, Stanford Univ.; **OTHER ACT & HONORS:** Bd. Member of Big Bros., Big Sisters of the Peninsula; Bd. Member of Mills Memorial Hosp.; Member of Stanford Athletic Bd.; **BUS ADD:** 900 Cherry Ave., Suite 200, San Bruno, CA 94066, (415)952-1200.

WILSON, William——*VP Admin.*, Garan, Inc.; **PRIM RE ACT:** Property Manager; **BUS ADD:** 350 5th Ave., New York, NY 10018, (212)563-2000.*

WILSON, Woodrow——**B:** Nov. 29, 1923, Bastrop, LA, *Atty.*, Woodrow Wilson; **PRIM RE ACT:** Attorney, Developer, Owner/Investor; **EDUC:** BA, 1949, LA State Univ.; **GRAD EDUC:** JD, 1949, LSU; **MIL SERV:** USN Ens. 1943-46; **HOME ADD:** 1001 Apollo, Bastrop, LA 71220, (318)281-3752; **BUS ADD:** 129 E. Madison, Bastrop, LA 71220, (318)281-3560.

WILSTEIN, David——**B:** Mar. 8, 1928, Pittsburgh, PA, *Pres.*, Housing Affiliates, Inc.; **PRIM RE ACT:** Developer, Builder, Property Manager, Owner/Investor; **PREV EMPLOY:** Pres., Real Estate Technology, Inc.; **EDUC:** BS, 1948, Civ. Eng., Univ. of Pittsburgh; **EDUC HONORS:** Cum Laude; Sigma Tau; **OTHER ACT & HONORS:** Member, United Democratic Fin. Comm.; Israel Bond Org.; Amer. Friends of Hebrew Univ.; Shriners; Prime Ministers; Masons; **HOME ADD:** 916 Hartford Way, Beverly Hills, CA 90210; **BUS ADD:** 2080 Century Park E, Penthouse, Los Angeles, CA 90067, (213)553-4906.

WIMBERG, James J.——**B:** June 26, 1931, Cincinnati, OH, *Pres.*, Eagle Savings Assn.; **PRIM RE ACT:** Developer, Lender; **SERVICES:** Savings & Loan; **PROFL AFFIL & HONORS:** US League of Savings Assn.; OH League of Savings Assns.; MBAA, Member of US League Legislative & Pol. Liaison Comm., Member of Bd. of Tr. and Legislative Comm. of OH League; **GRAD EDUC:** Chase Coll. of Law; **MIL SERV:** US Army; **OTHER ACT & HONORS:** Pres. Bd. of Tr. Summit Ctry. Day Sch.; Dir PA Mort. Ins. Co.; Dir. Driftwood Resorts, Inc.; **HOME ADD:** 2 Grandin Farm Ln., Cincinnati, OH 45208, (513)321-6034; **BUS ADD:** 580 Walnut St., Cincinnati, OH 45202, (513)762-8200.

WIMBERLY, Brooks R.——**B:** Dec. 24, 1942, Houston, TX, *VP & Gen. Mgr.*, Dallas Management Servs., Inc., Subsidiary of First Nat. Bank in Dallas; **PRIM RE ACT:** Consultant, Developer, Property Manager; **SERVICES:** Bldg. mgmt. & leasing, construction mgmt., RE consulting, space programming & planning; **REP CLIENTS:** First Nat. Bank in Dallas, Prudential Ins. Co.; **PREV EMPLOY:** Mort. Lending - TX S & L; **PROFL AFFIL & HONORS:** Director & Treasurer of BOMA, Sec. of IREM (Dallas/Ft. Worth), MBA/Fin., CPM, NACORE; **EDUC:** BS, 1964, Math., S.M.U. Univ. of Houston; **GRAD EDUC:** MBA, 1969, Fin., Univ. of TX; **EDUC HONORS:** Cum Laude, Dean's Council; **OTHER ACT & HONORS:** Pubished articles in "Buildings" and *Journal of Prop. Mgmt.*; **HOME ADD:** 3605 Normandy, Dallas, TX 75205, (214)528-4291; **BUS ADD:** P.O. Box 83910, Dallas, TX 75283, (214)658-6767.

WIMBUSH, Grant R.——**B:** June 7, 1944, Denver, CO, *Dist. Sales Mgr. & VP*, Gruff & Ellis Commercial Brokerage Co.; **PRIM RE ACT:** Broker; **OTHER RE ACT:** Pension Fund Asset Mgmt.; **SERVICES:** Comml. brokerage; **REP CLIENTS:** Lenders, pension funds, ins. co & devel. in purchasing, leasing & selling comml. props. & ground; **PROFL AFFIL & HONORS:** ICSC; BOMA; C of C, Denver; **EDUC:** BS/BA, 1967, Univ. of Denver; **GRAD EDUC:** MBA, 1971, RE, Univ. of Denver; **MIL SERV:** USN, Lt.; **HOME ADD:** 1410 E Fourth Ave., Denver, CO 80218, (303)777-2202; **BUS ADD:** 1512 Larimer St., Denver, CO 80202, (303)572-7700.

WIMMER, G.R.——George Wimmer Devel. Co.; **PRIM RE ACT:** Developer; **BUS ADD:** Box 3212, Sioux City, IA 51102, (712)255-6387.*

WINDER, Charles L.——**B:** Nov. 21, 1945, Ontario, OR, *Pres.*, Winder Realty Co. & Winder Devel. Serv., Inc.; **PRIM RE ACT:** Broker, Consultant, Property Manager; **SERVICES:** Comml. RE sales & acquisitions, devel., consulting; **REP CLIENTS:** Albertson's, Boise Cascade, ID First Nat. Bank, ID Bank & Trust, Morrison-Knudsen Co., Inc., Emkay Devel. Co.; **PREV EMPLOY:** VP Emkay Devel. Co. 1973-79; Asst. to Pres. of MAKAD, Inc. 1971-73; **EDUC:** Pre-Law/Political Sci. BA, 1968, Coll. of ID; **MIL SERV:** USN, Lt.; **OTHER ACT & HONORS:** Commn., Ada Cty. Hwy. Dist., Elected 1980; **HOME ADD:** 4459 Ginger Creek Dr., Meridian, ID 83642, (208)375-3426; **BUS ADD:** 205 N. 10th St., 411, Boise, ID 83702, (208)342-2300.

WINDLE, Don R.——**B:** June 25, 1948, Wichita Falls, TX, *Pres.*, Windle and Assoc., Inc.; **PRIM RE ACT:** Broker, Attorney, Consultant, Appraiser, Property Manager, Owner/Investor; **SERVICES:** RE Law, consultation, appraisal, mgmt.; **REP CLIENTS:** Indiv. and joint vent. inv. in comml. and invtmt. prop.; **PROFL AFFIL & HONORS:** NAR, RNMI, RESSI, TAR, ABA, Statebar of TX, AR Bar Assoc.; **EDUC:** BA, 1970, Soc. Sci., Bus. Admin., N. TX St. Univ.; **GRAD EDUC:** JD, 1973, Law, TX Tech Univ. Sch. of Law; **EDUC HONORS:** Dea Theta Phi Law Frat.; **OTHER ACT & HONORS:** Sigma Nu Frat.; **HOME ADD:** 10820 Central, SE, Albuquerque, NM 87123, (806)762-0505; **BUS ADD:** A-Box 11818, 10820 Central, SE, Albuquerque, NM 87192, (505)294-8811.

WINGATE, Don E.——**B:** June 10, 1923, Arkansas City, KS, *Owner*, Don E. Wingate & Assoc.; **PRIM RE ACT:** Broker, Consultant, Developer, Builder, Property Manager, Owner/Investor; **SERVICES:** Gen. RE brokerage, prop. mgmt. & subdivision devel.; **EDUC:** BS, 1946, Bus. Admin. & Pol. Sci., Washburn Univ./Univ. of OR; **GRAD EDUC:** Univ. of OR School of Law; **EDUC HONORS:** Pres. of Freshman Class; **MIL SERV:** US Army/USAF, S/Sgt., Various dec. with 15th AF in Italy, WWII; **OTHER ACT & HONORS:** Pres., C of C, 2 terms; PER Elks Lodge; **HOME ADD:** 1835 9th Pl., Wasco, CA 93280, (805)758-2202; **BUS ADD:** 1701 Hwy. 46, PO Box 802, Wasco, CA 93280, (805)758-6435.

WINGBLADE, P.B.——**B:** 1925, KS, *Pres.*, PB Wingblade Agency, Prop Tax Consultant, Appraiser, Real & Personal Prop.; **PRIM RE ACT:** Consultant, Appraiser, Property Manager, Assessor, Engineer, Owner/Investor, Insuror; **OTHER RE ACT:** Prop Tax Reduction Consultant; **SERVICES:** Investigation of ways to reduce all RE taxes and make direct appeals for each client on a fee basis or retainer fee; **PREV EMPLOY:** 10 Yrs. Cty. assessment level (Chief appraiser); **PROFL AFFIL & HONORS:** Nat. Assn. Review Appraiser, Registered with AZ Sec. of State as ACA; **EDUC:** Steam & Diesel Electric Locomotive Engr, 1955; **MIL SERV:** US Army; **OTHER ACT & HONORS:** Charter Member Navy League, Yuma, Arizona; Senior Member Nat. Assn. of RE Appraisers, NY, NY; Senior Member Nat. Assn. Review Appraisers 23084; **HOME TEL:** (303)858-3522; **BUS ADD:** PO Box 1429, Yuma, AZ 85364, (303)858-3522.

WINIG, Howard——**B:** Nov. 7, 1940, Philadelphia, PA, *Pres.*, Quadreal Corp.; **PRIM RE ACT:** Broker, Developer, Owner/Investor, Property Manager, Syndicator; **REP CLIENTS:** W.R.Grace, Zayre Corp., Stop & Shop, Morse Shoe, Supermarkets Gen. Corp. Amer. Stores, Woolco; **PREV EMPLOY:** Strouse, Greenberg and Co.; **PROFL AFFIL & HONORS:** ICSC; **EDUC:** BS/BA, 1962, Econ., Muhlenberg Coll.; **HOME ADD:** 822 Lombard St., Philadelphia, PA 19147, (215)922-0618; **BUS ADD:** 105 S. 12th St., Philadelphia, PA 19107, (215)922-5800.

WININGDER, Thomas K.——**B:** May 10, 1941, Norfolk, VA, *Exec. VP*, Coleman Development Co., Inc.; **PRIM RE ACT:** Developer, Broker, Owner/Investor; **SERVICES:** Build for our own account; **PREV EMPLOY:** Joseph C. Canizaro Interests, 1976-80 Dir. of Devel. for Canal Place Venture; Crow, Pope & Land 1968-76; **PROFL AFFIL & HONORS:** Atlanta RE Bd.; **EDUC:** Bachelor of Ind. Engrg., 1959-63, Georgia Tech; **GRAD EDUC:** MBA, 1963-65, Mktg., Harvard Bus. School; **EDUC HONORS:** ANAK, Phi Eta Sigma, Tau Beta Pi, Phi Kappa Phi, Judiciary Cabinet, I. Spencer Love Fellowship, Chmn. of Musser Seminar; **MIL SERV:** US Army; Capt.; **OTHER ACT & HONORS:** Intl. TradeMart Bd. of Dir.; YMCA Bd.; United Way; Econ. Devel. Council; **HOME ADD:** 4727 Prytania, New Orleans, LA 70115, (504)899-5782; **BUS ADD:** 321 St. Charles Ave., 2nd Floor Suite, New Orleans, LA 70130, (504)586-8300.

WINKELMAN, Eric D.——**B:** Jan. 31, 1945, Detroit, MI, *Dir. of RE*, Winkelman Stores, Inc., RE; **OTHER RE ACT:** Dir. of leasing for womens specialty store chain; **PREV EMPLOY:** Schostak Bros., Southfield, MI; **PROFL AFFIL & HONORS:** Intl. Council of Shopping Centers; **EDUC:** BA, 1967, Pol. Sci./Philosophy/German, Lake Forest Coll.; **OTHER ACT & HONORS:** Allocation & Review Comm.; United Foundation; **BUS ADD:** 25 Parsons St., Detroit, MI 48201, (313)833-6948.

WINSLOW, Peter——**B:** Aug. 8, 1944, Providence, RI, *CPA*, Peter Winslow & Co., CPA's; **PRIM RE ACT:** Consultant, Owner/Investor, Property Manager; **OTHER RE ACT:** Acctg.; **SERVICES:** Investment counseling, synd. structuring; **REP CLIENTS:** Indiv. investors & synd. with resid. & comml. props.; **PREV EMPLOY:** J.K. Lasser & Co., CPA's., 1974-76; Laventhol & Horwath, CPA's, 1970-73; **PROFL AFFIL & HONORS:** AICPA, NYSSCPA; **EDUC:** BA, 1966, Econ., Univ. of PA; **GRAD EDUC:** MBA, 1968, Fin., Wharton Grad. Univ. of PA; **MIL SERV:** US Army, Lt.; **HOME ADD:** 230 Central Park W, New York, NY 10024, (212)874-0294; **BUS ADD:** 230 West 55th St., New York, NY 10019, (212)977-4470.

WINSTEAD, James R.——**B:** Jan. 22, 1934, Myra, TX, *Sr. VP, Dir.*, Charles Kober Assoc., Chicago Office; **PRIM RE ACT:** Architect, Owner/Investor; **SERVICES:** Planning, land use, zoning, arch. engrg.; **REP CLIENTS:** Homart, Draper Kramer, Ken Tucker Assoc., Viehmann, Martin Assoc., Melvin Simon Assn., Landau Heyman; **PREV EMPLOY:** Pres. Architectronics, Inc., 1978-81; **PROFL AFFIL & HONORS:** AIA, RE Broker, IL; **EDUC:** BArch., 1957, Design, Univ. of TX Tech., Lubbock, TX; **MIL SERV:** US Army, E-5; **HOME ADD:** 2100 Lincoln Park W, Chicago, IL 60614, (312)472-4583; **BUS ADD:** 230 W. Monroe St., Suite 750, Chicago, IL 60606, (312)236-6751.

WINSTON, John——**B:** Mar. 16, 1935, NYC, *Sr. VP*, DLJ RE; **PRIM RE ACT:** Broker, Attorney, Syndicator, Developer, Builder, Property Manager; **EDUC:** BA, 1955, Soc., Harvard Coll.; **GRAD EDUC:** LLB, 1959, Harvard Coll.; **EDUC HONORS:** Summa Cum Laude, Magna Cum Laude; **MIL SERV:** USA, PFC; **HOME ADD:** 35 E. 84, New York, NY 10028, (212)737-4684; **BUS ADD:** 140 Broadway, New York, NY 10005, (212)747-9734.

WINSTON, Justin——**B:** Sept. 1, 1929, New York, NY, *Pres.*, Metropolitan Abstract Corp.; **PRIM RE ACT:** Attorney; **OTHER RE ACT:** Abstract and Title Ins.; **PREV EMPLOY:** Exec. VP & Counsel Metropolitan Title Guaranty Co. 1965-1975; **PROFL AFFIL & HONORS:** Bar Assn. of Nassau Cty., Suffolk Cty. Bar Assn., NY State Land Title Assn., Amer. Land Title Assn., Pres. 1974-1975, NY State Land Title Assn.; **EDUC:** BA, 1949, Liberal Arts - Pre Law, Long Is. Univ.; **GRAD EDUC:** LLB, 1952, Brooklyn Law School; **MIL SERV:** US Army, 1952-1954; **OTHER ACT & HONORS:** Arbitrator - Amer. Arbitration Assn.; Member - Bd. of Dirs. - Legal Aid Soc. of Nassau Cty.; Pres.-Long Beach Lawyers Assn., 1982; **HOME ADD:** One Redan Rd., Lido Beach, NY 11561, (516)432-4951; **BUS ADD:** One Old Country Rd., Carle Place, NY 11514, (516)741-5474.

WINTER, Addison E. "Bob"——**B:** April 7, 1928, Ardmore, OK, *Pres.*, Empire Developers, Inc.; Stylco Development, Inc.; Stylhomes, Inc.; **PRIM RE ACT:** Broker, Consultant, Attorney, Developer, Builder, Property Manager; **OTHER RE ACT:** Modular home & apt. mfg. - motels, townhouses; **SERVICES:** Bldg.; devel.; investing in tax sheltered RE; synd.; **REP CLIENTS:** Apt. and housing builder dealers; investors; devels.; **PREV EMPLOY:** Practicing Atty. (1954-1969); Pres. Pac. Western Life Ins. Co. (1966-1971); Pres., Devel. Co., Modular Factor, Apt. Devel.; **PROFL AFFIL & HONORS:** ABA; WY Bar Assn.; Nat. Assn. of Home Builders; WY RE Broker; NAR, Atty. at Law; RE Broker; Law Review in Coll., Bd. of Dirs., C of C; **EDUC:** BA, 1949, Pol. Sci., Univ. of WY; **GRAD EDUC:** JD, 1951, Law, Univ. of WY; **EDUC HONORS:** Law Review (3 yrs.); **MIL SERV:** US Army, 1st Lt. 1952-1954; **OTHER ACT & HONORS:** Deputy Cty. & Prosecuting Atty.-Casper; Police Justice; Bd. of Trs., Episcopal Diocese of WY; Sr. Warden, St. James Episcopal Church Riverton; Bd. of C of C; **HOME ADD:** 414 N 2nd West, Riverton, WY 82501, (307)856-2807; **BUS ADD:** 800 So. Broadway (PO Box 353), Riverton, WY 82501, (307)856-9476.

WINTER, Elizabeth Ann——B: Jan. 19, 1949, Louisville, KY, *Title Atty.*, Lawyer's Title and Escrow, Inc.; **PRIM RE ACT:** Attorney; **SERVICES:** Title Examinations, title opinions, drafting legal documents, title underwriting, advising clients; **REP CLIENTS:** Comml. and resid.; **PREV EMPLOY:** Three years in the field of Real Prop. Law, three years in Gen. Practice of Law; **PROFL AFFIL & HONORS:** Chattanooga Bar Assn., TN Bar Assn., ABA; **EDUC:** BA, 1971, Soc. and Psych., AZ State Univ.; **GRAD EDUC:** JD, 1975, Law, Univ. of TN; **EDUC HONORS:** Outstanding Participation as Oral Advocate on Intl. Law Moot Court Team; **OTHER ACT & HONORS:** C of C Arts Festival Comm.; **HOME ADD:** PO Box 15132, Chattanooga, TN 37415, (615)877-7059; **BUS ADD:** Suite 100, Downe Bldg., 736 GA Ave., Chattanooga, TN 37401, (615)756-4154.

WINTER, Irving M.——B: Sept. 18, 1927, Montgomery, AL, *Owner*, Winter Co.; **PRIM RE ACT:** Broker, Consultant, Developer, Property Manager, Owner/Investor; **SERVICES:** Sales, leases, mgmt., counseling; **REP CLIENTS:** Numerous; **PROFL AFFIL & HONORS:** Realtor of Yr. 1963, Pres. Montgomery Bd. of Realtors 1965; **EDUC:** BS, 1950, Accounting, Univ. of AL; **MIL SERV:** US Army, Sgt. Several decorations; **OTHER ACT & HONORS:** Past Pres., Standard Country Club, Past Pres. Jewish Federation of Montgomery Bd. of Dir. - Cancer Soc., Goodwill, Temple Beth El and others; **HOME ADD:** 2741 Fernway Dr., Montgomery, AL 36111, (205)264-4418; **BUS ADD:** PO Box 787, 300 S Hull St., Montgomery, AL 36102, (205)834-1473.

WINTER, Stephen A.——B: Apr. 7, 1948, Neenah, WI, *Pres.*, Century 21 Rollie Winter Realtors, Comml. Investment Div.; **PRIM RE ACT:** Broker, Developer, Owner/Investor; **SERVICES:** Complete sale, devel. and leasing of comml. & retail props.; **PREV EMPLOY:** Staff Appraiser, 1st Savings Assn., Milwaukee, WI; **PROFL AFFIL & HONORS:** Local, State & Natl. Bd. of Realtors; Rotary; Dir. of various community agencies, CCIM; NAR; **EDUC:** BBA, 1971, Fin., Univ. of WI, Whitewater; **HOME ADD:** 116 E. Glendale Ave., Appleton, WI 54911, (414)739-3285; **BUS ADD:** 3003 W. College Ave., Appleton, WI 54911, (414)739-0101.

WINTON, Frank J.——B: Aug. 26, 1914, New Haven, CT, *Pres.*, FJW Corp.; **PRIM RE ACT:** Developer; **SERVICES:** Consultant with respect to land devel.; **REP CLIENTS:** Builders and investors; **PREV EMPLOY:** Builder of resid. homes, practice of law; **PROFL AFFIL & HONORS:** MI State Bar Assn., Detroit Bar Assn., Builders Assn. of SE MI, Nat. Assn. of Home Builders, Nat. Assn. of Arbitrators, Atty., Dir. of Nat. Assn. of Home Builders & VP of Builders Assn. of SE MI; **EDUC:** BA, 1935, Pre-Law, Wayne State Univ.; **GRAD EDUC:** LLB, 1940, RE Law, Wayne State Univ.; **MIL SERV:** USAF, Capt., Service medals; **OTHER ACT & HONORS:** Knollwood Ctry. Club, Standard Club North, Detroit Racquet & Squash Club and Temple Beth El; **HOME ADD:** 1060 Ardmoor Dr., Birmingham, MI 48010, (313)646-2116; **BUS ADD:** 26211 Central Park Blvd., 209, Southfield, MI 48076, (313)353-6161.

WIRKLER, Norman E.——B: Apr. 1, 1937, Garnavillo, IA, *VP*, The Durrant Group Inc.; **PRIM RE ACT:** Architect, Developer, Owner/Investor, Property Manager; **SERVICES:** Housing design, land devel. resid.; **REP CLIENTS:** Indiv. investors, public housing agencies; **PROFL AFFIL & HONORS:** Amer. Inst. of Architects; **EDUC:** BArch., 1959, IA State Univ.; **OTHER ACT & HONORS:** Chmn. Member Dubuque Co. Zoning Commn., 1968-1980, Dir., Garnavillo Savings Bank, Garnavillo, IA; **HOME ADD:** RR3, Dubuque, IA 52001, (319)582-2601; **BUS ADD:** 1 Dubuque Plaza, Dubuque, IA 52001, (319)583-9131.

WIRSIG, Jane D.——*Corp. Sec.*, Educational Testing Service; **PRIM RE ACT:** Instructor; **BUS ADD:** Rosedale Rd., Princeton, NJ 08541, (609)921-9000.*

WIRTH, Robert G.——B: July 29, 1934, Milwaukee, WI, *Pres.*, Torke, Wirth, Pujara, Ltd. - Architects, Engrs.; **PRIM RE ACT:** Architect; **SERVICES:** Archs., site planning, interior design; **REP CLIENTS:** Johnson Wax, Security S&L Assn., Miller Brewing; **PROFL AFFIL & HONORS:** AIA, Amer. Arbitration Assn.; **EDUC:** 1957, Arch., Univ. of IL; **EDUC HONORS:** Grad. with High Honors; **MIL SERV:** US Army; Corps. of Engrs., 1st Lt.; **OTHER ACT & HONORS:** Town of Richfield Planning Commission, EAA-CORSA-AACA-Model T Intl.; **HOME ADD:** 880 Hillside Rd., Colgate, WI 53017, (414)628-2292; **BUS ADD:** 10721 W. Capital Dr., Wauwatosa, WI 53222, (414)463-7760.

WIRTH, Russell D. L.——*Managing Partner*, Wirth & Co.; **PRIM RE ACT:** Owner/Investor; **SERVICES:** Act as primary owner/investor in execution of major RE devel. projects, in the $10-50 million range, in office, resid., comml., indus., which have the common characteristic of being of prestige landmark quality or top prime sites, in the US and intl., Have won nat. and intl. awards; **PREV EMPLOY:** Pres., Puerto Rican Financial Group; Chase Intl. Investment Corp.; **PROFL AFFIL & HONORS:** Who's Who in Fin. & Ind.; **EDUC:** BA, Intl. Relation, Intl. Econ., Yale; **GRAD EDUC:** MA, Intl. Relations, John Hopkins Univ.; **EDUC HONORS:** Summa Cum Laude, Phi Beta Kappa, Distinction; **MIL SERV:** USMC; Capt.; Silver Star, Bronze Star, Purple Heart; **BUS ADD:** 876 Balboa Lane, Foster City, CA 94404, (415)572-0527.

WISE, Frances M.——B: Apr. 3, 1953, Hayward, WI, *Branch Office Mgr.*, Telemark Land Co., Inc.; **PRIM RE ACT:** Broker; **SERVICES:** Condo., home, vacant lot listings and sales; **PREV EMPLOY:** Admin. Asst. for Telemark; **EDUC:** BA, 1975, Commun. Arts, Univ. of WI, Madison, WI; **HOME ADD:** Cable, WI, (715)798-3699; **BUS ADD:** Telemark Lodge, Cable, WI 54821, (715)798-3811.

WISE, Kim A.——B: Aug. 11, 1953, Freeport, IL, *Partner/Atty.*, Ronald L. Evans P.C.; **PRIM RE ACT:** Attorney, Developer, Syndicator; **SERVICES:** Rep. of rgnl. shopping center devels.; **REP CLIENTS:** Paul Broadhead & Assocs., Inc., Westcliffe USA, Jacobs & Kahan, Commerce Title Co.; **PREV EMPLOY:** Rudnicka Wolfe Law Firm; **PROFL AFFIL & HONORS:** ABA, IL Bar Assn., TX Bar Assn., Intl. Council of Shopping Centers; **EDUC:** BA, 1974, RE & Fin., Univ. of WI (Madison); **GRAD EDUC:** JD, 1978, RE & Land Use Devel. and Securities, Univ. of Tulsa; **EDUC HONORS:** Grad. with Distinction; **HOME ADD:** 15750 Regal Hill Cir., Dallas, TX 75248, (214)385-0213; **BUS ADD:** 16475 Dallas Pkwy. #520, Dallas, TX 75248.

WISE, Paul S.——*Pres.*, Alliance of American Insurers; **PRIM RE ACT:** Insuror; **BUS ADD:** 20 N. Wacker Dr., Chicago, IL 60606, (312)558-3700.*

WISE, Ron——B: May 27, 1939, Amarillo, TX, *Pres.*, Wise Investments, Inc.; **PRIM RE ACT:** Broker, Instructor, Syndicator, Consultant, Developer, Owner/Investor; **REP CLIENTS:** Non resid. tax shelter oriented investors; **PREV EMPLOY:** Pilot, Pan Amer. World Airways; **PROFL AFFIL & HONORS:** Seattle King Co. Bd. of Realtors; **EDUC:** 1961, Biol., TX State Univ.; **MIL SERV:** USAF, Capt., 1961-67, Air Medal Pilot; **HOME ADD:** 15215 NE 68th St., Redmond, WA 98052, (206)881-7490; **BUS ADD:** 15215 NE 68th St., Redmond, WA 98052, (206)881-7490.

WISE, William S.——B: Sept. 8, 1923, Washington, DC, *Gen. Part.*, William S. Wise Assoc.; **PRIM RE ACT:** Broker, Consultant, Appraiser, Builder; **SERVICES:** Appraisals and consultation in Real Prop. problems; **REP CLIENTS:** Banks, attys., savings instns., govt. agencies; **PREV EMPLOY:** Appraiser, Shannon & Luchs Co., 1970-75; **PROFL AFFIL & HONORS:** SREA, AIREA, SRA, RM Member; **EDUC:** BS, 1968, RE, Amer. Univ.; **HOME ADD:** 18011 Bowie Mill Rd., Rockville, MD 20855, (301)924-3415; **BUS ADD:** 18011 Bowie Mill Rd., Rockville, MD 20855, (301)840-1923.

WISINSKI, Stanley J., III——B: Sept. 10, 1940, Grand Rapids, MI, *Pres.*, Westdale Comml. Investment Co.; **PRIM RE ACT:** Broker, Consultant, Property Manager, Lender; **PREV EMPLOY:** with present firm since 1961; **PROFL AFFIL & HONORS:** SIR, G.R.R.E. Bd., MI R.E. Bd., RESSI., CCIM, RAM, CRI; **MIL SERV:** USA, SP5; **OTHER ACT & HONORS:** Grand Rapids C of C; **HOME ADD:** 8080 Wilderness Lake Trail N.E., Ada, MI 49301, (616)676-1241; **BUS ADD:** 3435 Lake Eastbrook Blvd., S.E., Grand Rapids, MI 49506, (616)949-9200.

WISLOW, Robert A.——B: Feb. 12, 1945, Oak Park, IL, *Pres.*, US Equities Realty, Inc.; **PRIM RE ACT:** Broker, Consultant, Developer, Owner/Investor, Property Manager; **SERVICES:** Devel. leasing & mgmt. of comml. props., facilities relocation consulting for maj. office space users; **PREV EMPLOY:** Sr. VP Fidinam, USA, Sr. VP & Managing Dir. LaSalle Partners, Sr. VP IDC RE; **PROFL AFFIL &**

HONORS: Chicago RE Bd., S. Loop Planning Bd., MI Ave. Assn., Recipient of Wall St. Journal Achievement Award, 1967; **EDUC:** BA, 1967, Bus., N. Central Coll.; **EDUC HONORS:** Most Outstanding Bus. Grad.; **HOME ADD:** 2047 N. Bissell, Chicago, IL 60614; **BUS ADD:** 840 N MI Ave., Suite 600, Chicago, IL 60611, (312)951-8000.

WISNIOSKI, Charles M.——B: July 1, 1950, Cambridge, MA, *Mort. Loan Officer*, Barclays American Business Credit, RE Div.; **PRIM RE ACT:** Lender; **SERVICES:** Stand by commitments; term loans; **PREV EMPLOY:** Provident Nat. Bank, RE Fin. Dept., 1976-1981; **EDUC:** BA, 1972, Econ., Harvard Coll.; **GRAD EDUC:** MBA, 1976, Fin./RE, Wharton Grad.; **OTHER ACT & HONORS:** Northampton Township, PA, Bd. of Auditors, Hist. Commn.; **BUS ADD:** 111 Founders Plaza, Suite 1200, PO Box 118, Hartford, CT 06101, (203)528-4831.

WIT, Gerard J.——B: Feb. 22, 1948, Baltimore, MD, *Devel. & Mktg. Mgr.*, McCormic Prop., Inc.; **PRIM RE ACT:** Developer; **REP CLIENTS:** Indiv. clients; **PREV EMPLOY:** VP, The Berkshire Corp.; Dir., RE Fairlane, Inc.; **PROFL AFFIL & HONORS:** NAIOP; **EDUC:** BS, 1970, Engrg./Physics, Loyola Coll.; **GRAD EDUC:** MBA, 1981, Mgmt., Loyola Coll.; **HOME ADD:** 1907 Billy Barton Cir., Reisterstown, MD, (301)561-0410; **BUS ADD:** 1011 McCormic Rd., Hunt Valley, MD 21031, (301)667-7878.

WITCHER, Robert P.——B: Dec. 29, 1945, Conway, SC, *Atty.*, Hatcher, Dorsey, Irvin & Pressley (of counsel); **PRIM RE ACT:** Attorney, Owner/Investor; **OTHER RE ACT:** Title Ins. Co.; **SERVICES:** RE atty. and title insurance, occasional private lender; **REP CLIENTS:** Grant/Walker props., Inc.; Intown Associates, Inc.; DAC Corp. of GA; Colonial Fin. Service, Inc.; **PREV EMPLOY:** None for last 6 years except affiliation w/ Law firm of Storey & Obenschain; **PROFL AFFIL & HONORS:** ABA - RE Section; State Bar of GA - RE Section; Atlanta Bar Assn. - RE Sect.; **EDUC:** BA, 1967, Poli. Sci., Univ. of GA; **GRAD EDUC:** JD, 1973, Comml., intl. & RE Law, Univ. of GA; **EDUC HONORS:** Freshman Scholar, Dean's List; **MIL SERV:** USAF, Capt., Viet. Serv., Nat. Defense, Air Force Reserve Med., Combat Readiness, State of GA (ANG) Med., Pres. Unit Citation, Outstanding Unit Award; **OTHER ACT & HONORS:** Midtown Bus. Assn., Peachtree Walk Community Devel. Corp., Midtown Neighborhood Assn., Midtown Neighborhood Fed. Credit Union; **HOME ADD:** 388 7th St., N.E., Atlanta, GA 30308, (404)876-6846; **BUS ADD:** Ste. 320, 40 Marketta St., Atlanta, GA 30303, (404)525-3404.

WITHAM, W. Fred——B: Mar. 24, 1950, Tonasket, WA, *VP-Dir. of Marketing*, Valley Title Guarantee, Inc.; **PRIM RE ACT:** Consultant, Regulator; **SERVICES:** Full Serv. Title Insurance. Devel. Asst.; **REP CLIENTS:** Realtors, builders, attys., lenders, devel.; **PREV EMPLOY:** Asst. Cty. Planner; Subdiv. Administrator; **PROFL AFFIL & HONORS:** Bd. of Realtors, Homebuilders Assn.; Mort. Bankers Assn., Realtors Assoc. of the Year; 1980; Homebuilders Assoc. of Year, 1981; **EDUC:** BS, 1972, Bus. Marketing/RE Mgmt., Univ. of ID; **MIL SERV:** US Army, Lt.; **HOME ADD:** 3601 Richey Rd., Yakima, WA 98902, (509)575-5324; **BUS ADD:** PO Box 1625, Yakima, WA 98907, (507)248-4442.

WITHERS, William P., Jr.——B: July 26, 1924, Brownsville, TX, *Owner*, Bill Withers, Realtor; **PRIM RE ACT:** Broker, Developer, Property Manager, Syndicator; **SERVICES:** Investment counseling, valuation, synd., and prop. mgmt.; **REP CLIENTS:** Indiv. investors; **PREV EMPLOY:** Builder-Devel., 1957; Broker, 1962; Synd., 1969; **PROFL AFFIL & HONORS:** IREM, RESSI, CPM Key 3907; **EDUC:** BS, 1946, Military Sci., US Military Acad. West Point, NY; **GRAD EDUC:** MBA, 1957, Bus., Xavier Univ., Cincinnati, OH; **MIL SERV:** USAF; 1946-1954, Capt.; **HOME ADD:** 121 Church Ln., Lost Tree Village, North Miami Beach, FL 33408, (513)561-2255; **BUS ADD:** 4825 Drake Rd., Cincinnati, OH 45243, (513)561-2255.

WITHERSPOON, David——*Dir. Distribution*, Kirsch Co.; **PRIM RE ACT:** Property Manager; **BUS ADD:** 309 N. Prospect St., Sturgis, MI 49091, (616)651-0211.*

WITHERSPOON, Robert——*VP*, Gladstone Assocs., Econ. Consultants; **PRIM RE ACT:** Consultant, Instructor; **SERVICES:** Mkt. research, feasibility analysis & devel. serv., Fin. Packaging; **PREV EMPLOY:** Inst. of Public Admin.; Org. for Econ. Cooperation & Devel., United Nations; **PROFL AFFIL & HONORS:** ULI; Nat. Assn. of Housing and Redevel. Officials, Intrl. Downtown Exec. Assn.; Council on Urban Econ. Devel.; **EDUC:** BA, Econ., Univ. of Rochester; **GRAD EDUC:** Univ. of Paris/Princeton Univ.; **BUS ADD:** 2030 M St., N.W., Washington, DC 20036, (202)293-9000.

WITT, Alan M.——B: Apr. 13, 1952, Chicago, IL, *Tax Supervisor*, Laventhol & Horwath; **PRIM RE ACT:** Consultant; **OTHER RE ACT:** Accountant, Advisor; **SERVICES:** Investment, legal and tax counseling; **REP CLIENTS:** Indiv. investors and synd. in comml. and resid. props.; **PREV EMPLOY:** Lecturer of Law, Lewis Coll. of Law, Glen Ellyn, IL; **PROFL AFFIL & HONORS:** ABA; IL State Bar Assn.; AICPA; Member, ABA Real Prop. Section; ISCPA; Chicago Bar Assn.; **EDUC:** BS, 1974, Acctg./Fin., Univ. of IL at Chicago Cir.; **GRAD EDUC:** JD, 1977, Tax, Univ. of IL, Coll. of Law; **EDUC HONORS:** Grad. with Honors & Distinction, Gamma Beta Sigma, Phi Eta Sigma; **HOME ADD:** 1603 Blackhawk Tr., Wheeling, IL 60090, (312)394-2363; **BUS ADD:** 111 E. Wacker Dr., Suite 400, Chicago, IL 60601, (312)644-4570.

WITT, Floyd E.——B: May 1, 1912, IA, *Self employed*; **PRIM RE ACT:** Broker, Instructor, Appraiser; **SERVICES:** RE Appraising, instr. for appraising; **REP CLIENTS:** Attys., relocation cos., pvt.; **PREV EMPLOY:** First Fed. S & L, Midwest S & L; **PROFL AFFIL & HONORS:** SRA, IFAC, NAIFA, Jack Justice Award, 1974; **OTHER ACT & HONORS:** Pyes. State Dir. Reg. Gov. Natl. Dir., AF & AM Masonic Lodge, Scottish Rite Zuhrah Temple; **HOME TEL:** (602)926-9416; **BUS ADD:** 10217 Highwood Lane, Sun City, AZ 85373, (602)977-9487.

WITT, Robert——*Sr. VP*, Hexcel; **PRIM RE ACT:** Property Manager; **BUS ADD:** 650 California St., San Francisco, CA 94108, (415)857-1501.*

WITT, Walter Francis, Jr.——B: Feb. 18, 1933, Richmond, VA, *Atty. at Law, Partner*, Hunton & Williams; **PRIM RE ACT:** Attorney; **PROFL AFFIL & HONORS:** ABA, VA Bar Assn., Richmond Bar Assn., DC Bar Assn., VA Bar 1966, DC Bar 1974; **EDUC:** BS, 1954, Acctg., Univ. of Richmond; **GRAD EDUC:** LLB, 1966, Univ. of Richmond; **EDUC HONORS:** Phi Beta Kappa; **MIL SERV:** US Army, 1st Lt.; **HOME ADD:** 8901 Tresco Rd., Richmond, VA 23229; **BUS ADD:** 707 E Main St., Richmond, VA 23219, (804)788-8391.

WITT, William——*Mgr. Engr.*, NVF Co.; **PRIM RE ACT:** Property Manager; **BUS ADD:** Yorklin Rd., Yorklyn, DE 19736, (302)239-5281.*

WITTCOFF, Raymond H.——B: Dec. 5, 1921, St. Louis, MO, *Pres.*, Transurban Investment Corp.; **PRIM RE ACT:** Developer, Owner/Investor; **MIL SERV:** USN, Lt.; **OTHER ACT & HONORS:** Dir., Equitable Life Assurance Soc. of the US; Tr., Washington Univ.; **HOME ADD:** 200 S. Brentwood, St. Louis, MO 63105, (314)717-5554; **BUS ADD:** One Memorial Dr., St. Louis, MO 63102, (314)231-2945.

WITTEBORT, Robert J., Jr.——*Asst. Dir. and Gen. Counsel*, IL Housing Devel. Authority; **PRIM RE ACT:** Attorney, Lender; **SERVICES:** Mort. Lending; **PREV EMPLOY:** Atty. Hopkins & Sutter, Chicago; **EDUC:** BA, 1969, Philosophy, Yale Univ.; **GRAD EDUC:** JD, 1974, Notre Dame Law School; **EDUC HONORS:** Dean's List, Law Review; **MIL SERV:** USN, Lt. Cmdr.; **HOME ADD:** 2800 Lake Shore Dr., Chicago, IL 60657, (312)549-8062; **BUS ADD:** 130 E. Randolph St., Chicago, IL 60601, (312)793-6375.

WITTEN, Ronald G.——B: Jan. 31, 1951, Colorado City, TX, *Pres.*, M/PF Research, Inc.; **PRIM RE ACT:** Consultant; **SERVICES:** Mkt. Research and Mkt. Feasibility Analysis; **PROFL AFFIL & HONORS:** NAHB, NABE, NAA, Amer. Mktg. Assn.; **EDUC:** BBA, 1973, Mktg., TX Tech Univ.; **EDUC HONORS:** Summa Cum Laude, Conrad N. Hilton Scholar; **HOME ADD:** 4000 Purdue, Dallas, TX 75225, (214)363-2804; **BUS ADD:** 10711 Preston Rd., Dallas, TX 75230, (214)692-1020.

WITTMAN, Bert——B: July 26, 1943, Alton, IL, *Appraiser*, Wittman Appraisal Service; **PRIM RE ACT:** Appraiser; **SERVICES:** Single family resid. appraisals; **REP CLIENTS:** Lenders, transfer co. and indivs.; **PREV EMPLOY:** Chief Appraiser, Germania Fed. S & L, Alton, IL 62002; **PROFL AFFIL & HONORS:** SREA, SRA; **MIL SERV:** US Army, SP 4; **HOME ADD:** RR1, Godfrey, IL 62035, (618)466-3963; **BUS ADD:** 3049 Godfrey Rd., Godfrey, IL 62035, (618)466-1513.

WITTMAYER, Theodore I.——B: Dec. 23, 1933, Dietrick, ID, *Gen. Counsel*, M & M Stone Inc.; RE; **PRIM RE ACT:** Attorney, Appraiser; **OTHER RE ACT:** Devel., Leases, Contracts; **REP CLIENTS:** Stone Bros. & Assoc., Elkhorn Plaza, Sherwood Mall; **PREV EMPLOY:** Appraiser, Comml.-Indus. Real Prop., Los Angeles Cty. Assessor 1962-65; Stockbroker, 1967-2969; Private Law Practice 1973-1979; **EDUC:** BS, 1959, Econ., Statistics and Bus. Mgmt., Brigham Young Univ.; **GRAD EDUC:** JD, 1972, Law, Univ. of UT; Grad. Study Economic 1965-1967; **EDUC HONORS:** Amicron Delta Epsilon (Econ. Hon. Frat.); **MIL SERV:** US Army Cpl., ?953; **HOME ADD:**

921 S. Hutchins, Lodi, CA 95240, (209)368-5515; **BUS ADD:** 1024 W. Robinhood Dr., Stockton, CA 95207, (209)957-9160.

WITTNER, Ted P.——**B:** Sept. 17, 1928, Tampa, FL, *Pres. and Chmn.*, Wittner & Co.; **PRIM RE ACT:** Developer; **SERVICES:** Devel. of profl. office space; **PROFL AFFIL & HONORS:** Past Pres. (1957) and Founder Member, St. Petersburg General Agents and Mgr. Assn.; Member, Nat. Assn. of Life Underwriters; Qualifying and Life Member (since 1967) Million Dollar Round Table; Past Pres. (1968), Member, Crown Life Brokerage Gen. Agents Assn.; Assoc. Member, ULI, Wash., DC; Member, Bd. of Govs., Ins. Exchange of Amer. (Formerly FL Ins. Exchange); Member, Intl. Platform Assn.; Listed in: Who's Who in Fin. and Indus., Who's Who in the S. and SW, Who's Who Honorary Soc. of Amer., Men of Achievement, Personalities of the S.; **EDUC:** BS Bus. Admin., 1950, Univ. of FL; **MIL SERV:** US Air Force, 2nd Lt.; **OTHER ACT & HONORS:** Past Pres. (1973-1975) Dir., Commerce Club of Pinellas Cty.; Past VP (1969-1972), Dir., St. Petersburg Area C of C; Past Member, Bd. of Governors, Pinellas Suncoast C of C; Dir., Comm. of 100, Pinellas Cty.; Past Member, St. Petersburg Civic Advisory Bd.; Past Member, Bd. of Dirs., Pineallas Assn. for Retarded Children (PARC); Sec./Treas., Dir., Menorah Ctr., Inc. (HUD 199 Unit, Moderate Income Housing); Member Bd. of Dirs., Goodwill Industries-Suncoast, Inc.; **HOME ADD:** 1220 Park St. N., St. Petersburg, FL 33710, (813)381-5153; **BUS ADD:** 5999 Central Ave., St. Petersburg, FL 33710, (813)384-3000.

WITUCKI, Ernest A., Jr.——*President*, Relocation Assistance Association of America; **OTHER RE ACT:** Profl. Assn. Admin.; **BUS ADD:** 950 17th St., Denver, CO 80202, (303)572-5076.*

WIX, John——**B:** Nov. 14, 1923, Long Beach, CA, *Pres.*, Colorado Country, Ltd.; **PRIM RE ACT:** Broker, Consultant, Developer, Owner/Investor, Property Manager, Syndicator; **PROFL AFFIL & HONORS:** Realtor; Amer. Land Devel. Assn.; **EDUC:** 4 yrs-no degree, Journalism, CO State, Denver Univ., Mesa Coll., Brigham Young, Mex. City Coll., Univ. of So. CA; **HOME ADD:** PO Box X, Basalt, CO 81621, (303)927-3766; **BUS ADD:** Box X, 351 Highway 82, Basalt, CO 81621, (303)927-3161.

WODLINGER, Eric——**B:** May 3, 1949, *Atty.*, Choate Hall & Stewart; **PRIM RE ACT:** Attorney; **SERVICES:** Zoning, subdiv., bldg. code, eminent domain; **REP CLIENTS:** Proprietary & voluntary hospitals, businesses and individuals; **EDUC:** BA, 1970, Amherst Coll.; **GRAD EDUC:** JD, Harvard Law School; **EDUC HONORS:** Magna Cum Laude; **BUS ADD:** 60 State St., Boston, MA 02109, (617)227-5020.

WOERNER, R.L., Jr.——*Regional Dir. of Devel.*, Howard Johnson Co., Corporate Devel.; **OTHER RE ACT:** Corporate Real Estate; **PROFL AFFIL & HONORS:** NACORE, NARA, CRA; **BUS ADD:** P.O. Box 63, Centerville, OH 45459, (513)433-7403.

WOHL, Harold L.——**B:** June 2, 1935, Brooklyn, NY, *CPA*, Self Employed; **OTHER RE ACT:** RE Acct.; **SERVICES:** Acctg., auditing, taxes, mgmt. & personal planning; **REP CLIENTS:** Managing Agent, co-op's, synds.; **PROFL AFFIL & HONORS:** AICPA, MSSCPA's; **EDUC:** BBA, 1958, Taxation, City Univ. of NY, Baruch School; **GRAD EDUC:** MBA, 1964, Taxation, City Univ. of NY, Baruch School; **OTHER ACT & HONORS:** Knights of Pythias, Chancelor Commdr.; **HOME ADD:** 165 West End Avenue 14M, New York, NY 10023, (212)496-8740; **BUS ADD:** 485 Fifth Ave., Suite 401A, New York, NY 10017, (212)687-8910.

WOHLMAN, Leslie Ellen——**B:** Mar. 6, 1954, New York, NY, *Rgnl. VP*, Integrated Resources, Inc., Acquisitions; **OTHER RE ACT:** RE Acquisition; **PROFL AFFIL & HONORS:** Chmn. of RE Comm. for Harvard Bus. School Club ULI, MBA; **EDUC:** BA, 1975, Bus. at Wharton & Sociology, Univ. of PA; **GRAD EDUC:** MBA, 1978, Fin., Harvard Grad. School of Bus.; **EDUC HONORS:** Phi Beta Kappa, Summa Cum Laude, High Honors (Top 10% of Class); **HOME ADD:** 360 E. 72 1503A, New York, NY 10021, (212)734-6604; **BUS ADD:** 666 Third Ave., New York, NY 10017, (212)878-9205.

WOJAK, John S.——**B:** Aug. 7, 1925, NY, NY, *VP-Dist. Head, Const. Indus. Dist.*, Chemical Bank, RE Div.; **PRIM RE ACT:** Attorney, Banker, Lender; **SERVICES:** Responsible for Nationwide fin./banking for general and specialty heavy const. contractors and design engrs.; **PREV EMPLOY:** Surety Bond Atty.-Credit Mgr. for Gen. Electric (heavy electrical equipment) Credit Mgr. for Amer. Machine & Foundry; **PROFL AFFIL & HONORS:** NY State Bar Assn., Gen. Contractors Assn., Surety Attys. Assn.; **EDUC:** BS in Banking & Fin., 1955, Credit and fin. mgmt., NY Univ.; **GRAD EDUC:** JD, 1967, Law, Fordham Law; **EDUC HONORS:** Phi Alpha Kappa (Fin. Honor Soc.) and Dean's List; **MIL SERV:** Infantry WWII, 1943-1946, Combat Infantry Badge, European Theatre Ribbon-2 Battle Stars S. Pacific Theatre Ribbon; **BUS ADD:** 633 Third Ave., New York, NY 10017, (212)878-7673.

WOJEWODZKI, Richard S.——**B:** Dec. 4, 1952, Jersey City, NJ, *Asst. VP*, Equitable Life Assurance Soc., Realty Operations; **PRIM RE ACT:** Consultant, Appraiser, Owner/Investor; **PREV EMPLOY:** 2nd VP RE Fin. Dept., Chase Manhattan Bank, NY; **PROFL AFFIL & HONORS:** MAI, SRPA; **EDUC:** BS, 1978, Fin., Monmouth Coll.; **HOME ADD:** 2 Colony Ct., Hazlet, NJ 07730; **BUS ADD:** 1285 Ave. of Amer., New York, NY 10029, (212)554-3349.

WOLCOTT, William F., III——**B:** Jan. 9, 1946, Asheville, NC, *Atty. at Law*, McGuire, Wood, Worley, Bissette & Wolcott, P.A.; **PRIM RE ACT:** Attorney; **REP CLIENTS:** lenders, contrs. & indivs. in the purchase, sale, fin. & devel. of real prop.; **PROFL AFFIL & HONORS:** ABA, NC Bar Assn., 28th Judicial Dist. Bar, NC Academy of Trial Lawyers; **EDUC:** AB, 1968, Econ., Univ. of NC at Chapel Hill; **GRAD EDUC:** JD, 1972, Univ. of NC at Chapel Hill; **MIL SERV:** US Army, E-5 (1968-74); **OTHER ACT & HONORS:** Member and legal advisor to Hist. Resources Comm. of Asheville & Buncombe Cty; Life member Alumni Assn. of the Univ. of NC at Chapel Hill; **HOME ADD:** 41 Lotus Pl, Asheville, NC 28804, (704)254-5713; **BUS ADD:** Suite 705, 1st Union Nat. Bank Bldg, 82 Patton Ave., PO Box 1411, Asheville, NC 28802, (704)254-8806.

WOLF, Clifford M.——**B:** Mar. 31, 1953, US, *Atty.*, Paul, Weiss, Riekind, Wharton & Garrison; **PRIM RE ACT:** Attorney; **PROFL AFFIL & HONORS:** ABA, RE Div.; NY City Bar Assn.; **EDUC:** BA, 1974, Econ. & Philosophy, NYU; **GRAD EDUC:** JD, 1977, Columbia Law Sch.; **EDUC HONORS:** Cum Laude; **HOME ADD:** 470 W. End Ave., New York, NY 10024, (212)362-2867; **BUS ADD:** 345 Park Ave., New York, NY 10054, (212)644-8716.

WOLF, Kevin R.——**B:** Nov. 11, 1953, Queens, NY, *Pres.*, Rapid Park Industries; **PRIM RE ACT:** Owner/Investor, Syndicator; **SERVICES:** Acquisition of potential investment sites; **REP CLIENTS:** Indiv. interested in sheltered income; **PROFL AFFIL & HONORS:** RE Bd. of NY; **EDUC:** BS, 1975, Poli. Sci., Hofstra C.W. Post Coll.; **OTHER ACT & HONORS:** Shiatso Educ. Center - Bd. Member; **HOME ADD:** 210 E. 68 St., New York, NY 10022; **BUS ADD:** 340 E. 59 St., New York, NY 10022, (212)752-1410.

WOLF, Robert——**B:** Aug. 19, 1948, Milwaukee, WI, *CFO*, Germania Construction Corp.; **PRIM RE ACT:** Broker, Consultant, Developer, Builder, Owner/Investor, Syndicator; **SERVICES:** Primary RE activities; **PROFL AFFIL & HONORS:** NAR; **EDUC:** Bus. Admin. RE, Fin., Riverside City Coll.; **MIL SERV:** US Army; E-5, 2 Bronze Stars, ACM, Soldier's Medal, Air Medal; **OTHER ACT & HONORS:** Rotary Club Pres.; Dir. C of C; **HOME ADD:** 12080 Helga Ln., Sunnymead, CA 92388; **BUS ADD:** 12561 Fischer Rd., Riverside, CA 92507, (714)653-9501.

WOLF, Robert——**B:** Aug. 20, 1930, Alexandria, LA, *Owner*, Robert Wolf Realtor; **PRIM RE ACT:** Broker, Consultant, Appraiser, Developer, Owner/Investor; **SERVICES:** Brokerage, appraisal, devel.; **REP CLIENTS:** Indivs., corps., govt.; **PREV EMPLOY:** 25 yrs. in this business; **PROFL AFFIL & HONORS:** NAR, AIREA, MAI, Accreditated Farm and Land Member; **EDUC:** Studies in RE - American Inst., Courses by American Inst.; **GRAD EDUC:** Continue Recertification yearly for MAI, Courses by American Inst.; **EDUC HONORS:** Designation - MAI; **OTHER ACT & HONORS:** Lions Club; Red Cross; C of C; Speeches; Lectures; Profl. and Coll. Level; **HOME ADD:** 3115 Georges Ln., Alexandria, LA 71301, (318)442-2520; **BUS ADD:** 4024 Jackson St., Alexandria, LA 71301, (318)445-6244.

WOLF, Walter E., Jr.——**B:** Aug. 28, 1931, Indianapolis, IN, *Part.*, Klineman, Rose, Wolf and Wallack; **PRIM RE ACT:** Attorney, Developer, Owner/Investor; **EDUC:** AB, 1952, Econ., Harvard Univ.; **GRAD EDUC:** LLB, 1955, Harvard Law School; **EDUC HONORS:** Cum Laude; **HOME ADD:** 911 Roundtable Ct., Indianapolis, IN 46204; **BUS ADD:** 2130 IN Natl. Bank Tower, Indianapolis, IN 46204, (317)639-4141.

WOLFE, C. Edward——**B:** Sept. 20, 1919, Frederick, MD, *RE Broker & Appraiser*, Tradewinds Realty Co.; **PRIM RE ACT:** Broker, Appraiser, Syndicator; **SERVICES:** Staff for resid. and income prop. sales and appraisals; **REP CLIENTS:** Security Pac. Nat. Bank, Crocker Nat. Bank; **PROFL AFFIL & HONORS:** Amer. Inst. of RE Appraisers; Soc. of RE Appraisers; Nat. Assn. of Review Appraisers; NAR, RM; SRA; CRA; Broker; **EDUC:** BBA, 1977, Fin., CA State Univ., Fullerton; **MIL SERV:** USN, Comdr., Purple Heart, Bronze Star; **OTHER ACT & HONORS:** Comm. Member, Revenue Sharing, Orange Cty., 1978-1979; Balboa Bay Club, Newport Beach, CA; **HOME ADD:** 1718 Tradewinds Ln., Newport Beach, CA 92660,

(714)646-5608; **BUS ADD:** 1718 Tradewinds Ln., Newport Beach, CA 92660, (714)631-1476.

WOLFE, Derrill E.——**B:** July 29, 1928, Chicago Hts., IL, *Asst. VP*, BancOhio Nat. Bank, Trust Div. - RE Section; **PRIM RE ACT:** Broker, Property Manager; **PREV EMPLOY:** Huntington Nat. Bank, 1960-1972; **PROFL AFFIL & HONORS:** Member of the Governing Council of the Instit. of RE Mgmt.; Columbus Bd. of Realtors; Columbus Farmers Club, Recipient of 'Mgr. of the Yr.' Award given by IREM, 1974; **EDUC:** BS, 1951, Columbus Bus. Univ.; **MIL SERV:** USN, HM3; **OTHER ACT & HONORS:** Westerville Bd. of Educ., 1964-1972; **HOME ADD:** 45 E. Broadway, Westerville, OH 43081, (614)882-4358; **BUS ADD:** 155 E. Broad St., Columbus, OH 43265, (614)463-7211.

WOLFE, Goldie B.——**B:** Dec. 20, 1945, Linz, Austria, *Sr. VP*, Arthur Rubloff & Co., Office Props. Grp.; **PRIM RE ACT:** Broker; **OTHER RE ACT:** Mktg. and Leasing Dir. of Office Bldg.; **SERVICES:** Mkt. and lease large office bldgs. in excess of 1,000,000 sq. ft.; **REP CLIENTS:** Law firms and corps. as well as acctg. firms, stock brokerage, etc. in their search for office space, find space, evaluate alternatives and negotiate deal; **PREV EMPLOY:** J. Walter Thompson Advertising 1967-71; **PROFL AFFIL & HONORS:** Chicago RE Bd.; Nat. and IL Assn. of Realtors; Young Execs. Club of Chicago; **EDUC:** BS, 1967, Bus. Admin./Mktg., Univ. of IL and Roosevelt Univ.; **GRAD EDUC:** MBA, in process, Univ. of Chicago, Grad. School of Bus.; **EDUC HONORS:** Magna Cum Laude, Beta Gamma Sigma, Alpha Lambda Delta; **OTHER ACT & HONORS:** Bd. of Dirs./Arthur Rubloff Co., IL; Bd. of Dirs. Michael Reese Hospital Medical Research Inst. Council, Chmn. Servs. Grp. Chicago Public TV; **HOME ADD:** 1332 Sutton Pl., Chicago, IL 60610; **BUS ADD:** 69 W. Washington, Chicago, IL 60602, (312)368-5453.

WOLFE, Henry——*RE Mgr.*, Crown Central Petroleum Corp.; **PRIM RE ACT:** Property Manager; **BUS ADD:** One North Charles St., PO Box 1168, Baltimore, MD 21203, (301)539-7400.*

WOLFE, Robert J.——**B:** Apr. 13, 1947, S. Orange, NJ, *Part.*, K.S. Sweet Assoc.; **PRIM RE ACT:** Consultant, Developer, Owner/Investor; **OTHER RE ACT:** Devel. fin.; **SERVICES:** Gen. mgr., Princeton Forrestal Ctr.; **REP CLIENTS:** Princeton Univ., Fidelity Mutual Life; **PROFL AFFIL & HONORS:** Indus. Devel. Research Council; **EDUC:** BA, 1969, Phil., Princeton Univ.; **GRAD EDUC:** MBA, 1972, Fin., Stanford Univ.; **MIL SERV:** USAR; **OTHER ACT & HONORS:** Nassau Club, Princeton Club of NY; **HOME ADD:** Pine Twig Farm, Ringoes, NJ, (201)788-5171; **BUS ADD:** Princeton Forrestal Ctr., 105 Coll. Rd., E., 3rd Floor, Princeton, NJ 08540, (609)452-7720.

WOLFE, Ronald L.——**B:** Aug. 9, 1943, Glendale, CA, *Pres.*, Ronald L. Wolfe and Assoc.; **PRIM RE ACT:** Broker, Syndicator, Consultant; **PROFL AFFIL & HONORS:** Santa Barbara Bd. of Realtors, NAR, RESSI, NRE, CCIM; **EDUC:** BA, 1966, Bus. Econ., U of CA, Santa Barbara; **OTHER ACT & HONORS:** Univ. Club, Santa Barbara Yacht Club; **BUS ADD:** 5266 Hollister Ave., Suite 215, Santa Barbara, CA 93111, (805)964-8116.

WOLFE, Saul A.——**B:** Mar. 29, 1934, Newark, NJ, *COB*, Skoloff & Wolfe, P.A.; **PRIM RE ACT:** Attorney; **SERVICES:** RE Tax Consultant; **PREV EMPLOY:** Tax Assessor, City of Newark; **PROFL AFFIL & HONORS:** Intl. Assn. of Assessing Officials; ULI; Amer. & NJ State Bar Assns., Cert. Tax Assessor; CRA; **EDUC:** BA, 1955, Poli. Econ., Brandeis Univ.; **GRAD EDUC:** JD, 1958, Harvard Law School; **MIL SERV:** US Army Res.; **OTHER ACT & HONORS:** Tr., Boys' Club of Newark; Tr., Hebrew Youth Acad.; Member of Pres.'s Council of Brandeis Univ.; Pres. Citation of Assoc. of Mun. Assessors of NJ; **HOME ADD:** 47 Tiwn Oak Rd., Short Hills, NJ 07078, (201)376-0211; **BUS ADD:** 17 Academy St., Newark, NJ 07102, (201)624-1419.

WOLFER, Alan B.——**B:** July 16, 1929, NYC, NY, *VP Atty.*, Century Circuit, Inc.; **PRIM RE ACT:** Attorney; **PREV EMPLOY:** Hess, Segall, Guterman, Pelz & Steiner, Esqs., 230 Park Ave., NY, NY, 10017; **PROFL AFFIL & HONORS:** NY State Bar Assn., RE Sect.; **EDUC:** Pol. Sci., NYU Sch. of Law, Univ. of MO; **HOME ADD:** 666 Shore Rd., Long Beach, NY 11561, (516)431-7102; **BUS ADD:** 1585 Broadway, New York, NY 10036, (212)975-8320.

WOLFERT, Jeffrey D.——**B:** May 4, 1941, NYC, *Pres.*, Hotel Investment Grp.; **PRIM RE ACT:** Broker, Consultant, Developer, Owner/Investor, Instructor; **SERVICES:** Mort., equity, fin. devel., consultants exclusively to hotel investors & devels. only; **REP CLIENTS:** Franchises, Hilton, Sheraton, Dunfey, Holiday Inns, Best Western, Ramada; **PREV EMPLOY:** VP & Dir. Mort. Div. Helmsley-Spear, Inc., VP & Dir. RE Serv. E.F. Hutton & Co., Inc.; **PROFL AFFIL & HONORS:** NARA; MBA, CRA; **EDUC:** 1963, Econ., NYU Mort. Banking Inst.; **OTHER ACT & HONORS:** Aircraft Owners & Pilots Assn., Haworth CC., Haversraw YC; **HOME ADD:** 5 Horizon Rd., Ft. Lee, NJ 07024, (201)224-0073; **BUS ADD:** 412 E. 59th St., 3rd Fl., New York, NY 10022.

WOLFF, A. Daniel, III——**B:** June 21, 1946, St. Louis, MO, *Pres. & Dir.*, Riverside Group, Inc.; **PRIM RE ACT:** Developer, Builder; **SERVICES:** Devel. of single family subdivisions & const. of homes; **PREV EMPLOY:** Sea Pines Co. 1973-75; **PROFL AFFIL & HONORS:** Fin. Execs. Inst.; **EDUC:** AB, 1968, Econ., Cornell Univ.; **GRAD EDUC:** MBA, 1973, Fin., Univ. of NC at Chapel Hill; **EDUC HONORS:** Bus. Found. - MBA Scholar; **MIL SERV:** USN, Lt. J.G., 2 Naval Unit Citations, 1 Sec. Nav. Achievement; **OTHER ACT & HONORS:** Leadership Jacksonville; Bd. of Dirs., Amer. State Bank; Bd. of Dirs. Riverside Group, Inc.; Bd. of Dirs. Travellers Aid Soc.; Ponte Vedra Club; FL Yacht Club; Univ. Club; **HOME ADD:** 4233 Yacht Club Rd., Jacksonville, FL 32210, (904)388-0647; **BUS ADD:** P.O. Box 2550, Jacksonville, FL 32203, (904)350-1150.

WOLFF, Alvin J., Jr. "Fritz"——**B:** Oct. 5, 1948, Spokane, WA, *Sr. VP*, Tomlinson Agency, Inc., Realtors; **PRIM RE ACT:** Broker, Developer, Property Manager, Owner/Investor; **SERVICES:** Investment prop. brokerage; **REP CLIENTS:** Profl. community, instl. investors; **PROFL AFFIL & HONORS:** CCIM, Gov. RNMI; **EDUC:** Bus. Admin., 1971, Fin., Econ., Univ. of WA; **BUS ADD:** W. 606 Third Ave., Spokane, WA 99204, (509)624-9131.

WOLFF, Nicholas R.——**B:** Nov. 10, 1950, White Plains, NY, *Pres.*, Century 21, F. Richard Wolff & Son Inc., Res.; **PRIM RE ACT:** Broker, Appraiser, Instructor; **PROFL AFFIL & HONORS:** Sec. Westchester Cty. Bd. of Realtors; Bd. of Dir. Westchester; MLS, GRI, SRA; **OTHER ACT & HONORS:** Branch office: 15 Pophan Rd., Scarsdale, NY 10605; **HOME ADD:** 109 Topland Rd., White Plains, NY 10605, (914)997-1442; **BUS ADD:** 570 Mamaroneck Ave., White Plains, NY 10605, (914)946-9100.

WOLFF, Thomas C., Jr.——**B:** July 28, 1924, Fall River, MA, *Executive VP*, The Summa Corporation; **OTHER RE ACT:** Real Estate, Hotels, Military Equip.; **PREV EMPLOY:** Exec. VP, The Irvine Co., Newport Beach, CA, 1972-1977; VP, The Rouse Co., Columbia, MD, 1961-1971; **PROFL AFFIL & HONORS:** Assoc., SIR; Nat. Assn. of Indus. & Office Parks; **EDUC:** BA, 1947, Bus., Duke Univ.; **MIL SERV:** USN, Lt.j.g., 1943-1946; **OTHER ACT & HONORS:** Dir., PHH Group Inc.; Bata Land Co.; Marine Nat. Bk.; **HOME ADD:** 56 Royal St. George Rd., Newport Beach, CA 92660, (714)644-8484; **BUS ADD:** 4818 Lincoln Blvd., Marina Del Rey, CA 90291, (213)822-0074.

WOLFSON, Bernard——**B:** Feb. 13, 1937, Brooklyn, NY; **PRIM RE ACT:** Attorney, Developer, Owner/Investor, Syndicator; **PROFL AFFIL & HONORS:** Coral Gables Bar Assn., Past Pres.; Dade Cty. Bar Assn.; FL Bar Assn.; **EDUC:** BS/BA, 1959, RE/Acctg., Univ. of FL; **GRAD EDUC:** LLB, 1963, Univ. of Miami; **HOME ADD:** 11530 Nogales St., Coral Gables, FL 33156, (305)667-4358; **BUS ADD:** 255 Alhambra Cir., Suite 245, Coral Gables, FL 33134, (305)446-4284.

WOLFSON, Douglas K.——**B:** Aug. 3, 1953, Plainfield, NJ, *Atty. at Law of the State of NJ*, Greenbaum, Greenbaum, Rowe & Smith, RE Litigation; **PRIM RE ACT:** Consultant, Attorney, Instructor, Real Estate Publisher; **SERVICES:** All legal aspects (zoning devel./title); RE Law Journal (Assoc. Editor; Lecturing Atty. Grps.; **REP CLIENTS:** Hovnanian Enterprises; Caleb Devel. Corp.; Realty Transfer Co., Crestwood Village, Inc.; Manalapan Holding Co.; Keene Corp.; The Shopco Co.; Omnia Corp.; **PREV EMPLOY:** Law Clerk to the Honorable David D. Furman, Former Atty. Gen. of the State of NJ, & Judge of the Superior Court, Appellate Div.; **PROFL AFFIL & HONORS:** NJ State Bar Assn.; ABA; Middlesex Cty. Bar Assn.; Land Use Comm., Appointment to NJSBA Comm. on Land Use Planning; **EDUC:** AB, 1974, Psych./Computer Sci., Rutgers Coll., State Univ. of NJ; **GRAD EDUC:** JD, 1974, Law, Rutgers School of Law; **EDUC HONORS:** Dean's List, Student Publication - Law Review (30 Rutgers L. Rev. 1237); **OTHER ACT & HONORS:** Appt. to NJSBA Computer Law Comm.; Publication of Art. (2), (5 Rutgers Journal of Computer and Law 389; 6 Rutgers Journal of Computers and Law); Assoc. Editor - The RE Law Journal (W.G. &L publication) Survey of Art. & Digest of Selected Art. under By-Line Quarterly for past 5 years; **HOME ADD:** 40 Phelps Ave., New Brunswick, NJ 08901, (201)846-0461; **BUS ADD:** Gateway 1, Newark, NJ 07102, (201)623-5600.

WOLFSON, Louis——**B:** Dec. 31, 1952, Boston, MA, *Investment Broker/Consultant*, Data Realty Corp.; **PRIM RE ACT:** Broker, Consultant, Appraiser, Owner/Investor; **SERVICES:** Brokerage, investment counseling, valuation & mort., placement of comml. props.; **REP CLIENTS:** Lenders, indivs. or instnl. investors in comml. props.; **PREV EMPLOY:** Star Realty 1975-77; **PROFL AFFIL & HONORS:**

Greater Boston RE Bd.; **EDUC:** BBA, 1974, Bus., Boston Univ.; **OTHER ACT & HONORS:** Member Amer. Soc. of Notaries; **HOME ADD:** 23 Pershing Rd., Newton, MA 02165, (617)964-8334; **BUS ADD:** 1505 Commonwealth Ave., Boston, MA 02135, (617)783-5676.

WOLK, Robert D.——B: Aug. 20, 1948, St. Louis, MO, *Pres.*, City Properties, Inc.; **PRIM RE ACT:** Broker, Instructor, Syndicator, Consultant; **SERVICES:** Invest. counseling, selection and analysis; **REP CLIENTS:** Owners, investors, users; **PROFL AFFIL & HONORS:** NAR, RESSI; **EDUC:** BS/BA, 1970, Mktg., Univ. of MO - Columbia; **GRAD EDUC:** MBA, 1977, Fin., St. Louis Univ.; **OTHER ACT & HONORS:** MO Athletic Club; **HOME ADD:** 2910 Milton Blvd., St. Louis, MO 63104, (314)773-7252; **BUS ADD:** 3609 Juniata Ave., St. Louis, MO 63116, (314)772-8051.

WOLLACK, Richard G.——B: Dec. 19, 1945, Chicago, IL, *Pres.*, Consolidated Capital Institutional Advisors, Inc.; **PRIM RE ACT:** Consultant, Syndicator; **SERVICES:** Consulting, investment advice; **REP CLIENTS:** Members of NY Stock Exchange; brokers - dealers; **PREV EMPLOY:** Pres. Richard Wollack Assocs., Inc. (RE consulting); Pres. and Co-founder First Capital Co's. (RE syndication); **PROFL AFFIL & HONORS:** Fin. principal NASD; course instr. RESSI; monthly column in Nat. Tax Shelter Digest; featured speaker at nat. conventions of Intl. Assoc. of Fin. Planners; NACORE; RNMI; **EDUC:** BA, 1967, Poli. Sci., Univ. of IL; **GRAD EDUC:** MBA, 1969, Fin., Stanford Univ.; **EDUC HONORS:** Phi Beta Kappa, Grad. with distinction in top 5% of class; **HOME ADD:** San Francisco, CA 94118, (415)921-5607; **BUS ADD:** Suite 100, 1900 Powell St., Emeryville, CA 94118, (415)652-7171.

WOLLENBERG, David A.——B: Aug. 6, 1947, Longview, WA, *Exec. VP*, The Cortana Corp.; **PRIM RE ACT:** Developer, Owner/Investor, Property Manager; **SERVICES:** Devel. of comml. & indus. props.; **PREV EMPLOY:** Amfac Communities - HI, 1973-1977; **EDUC:** AB, 1969, Econ., Brown Univ.; **GRAD EDUC:** MBA, 1973, RE, Fin., Stanford Bus. School; **OTHER ACT & HONORS:** Dir., Longview Fibre Co.; **HOME ADD:** 85 Michaels Way, Atherton, CA 94025; **BUS ADD:** 845 Page Mill Rd., Palo Alto, CA 94304, (415)493-2610.

WOLLERT, Delmar E.——B: Aug. 17, 1908, LaPorte, IN, *Owner-Pres.*, Wollert Realty and Appraisals; **PRIM RE ACT:** Broker, Appraiser; **SERVICES:** All forms of brokerage appraisals - various banks, mort. cos., railroads FHA-VA and EL; **PREV EMPLOY:** State Dir. 6 yrs. IN Realtors Assn.; **PROFL AFFIL & HONORS:** SREA, NAR, SRA Designation 1967 Life Time Hon. Realtor, LaPorte Board of Realtors; **OTHER ACT & HONORS:** Pres. Center Twps. Advisory Bd. (1975-1979)(1980-1984), IN Sheriff Assn. (Affil.) Boy Scouts; **HOME ADD:** 302 Orchard Ave. P.O. Box 24, LaPort, IN 46350, (219)362-3528; **BUS ADD:** P.O. Box 24, LaPorte, IN 46350, (219)362-3528.

WOLOSHIN, Stephen——*Dir. Corp. RE*, Southwest Forest Industries, Inc.; **PRIM RE ACT:** Property Manager; **BUS ADD:** PO Box 7548, Phoenix, AZ 85011, (602)956-6000.*

WOLOSHIN, William——B: May 17, 1935, Chicago, IL, *Atty. at Law*, Beermann, Swerdlove, Woloshin, Barezky & Berkson; **PRIM RE ACT:** Attorney, Owner/Investor, Syndicator; **SERVICES:** Legal; **REP CLIENTS:** Investors and devels. - Comml. and Condos.; **PROFL AFFIL & HONORS:** IL State Bar Assn. Chicago Bar Assn.; **EDUC:** LLB, 1959, Bus., Roosevelt Univ. and DePaul Univ.; **GRAD EDUC:** JD, 1959, Law, DePaul Univ.; **OTHER ACT & HONORS:** Bd. of Dirs. of ANAD; **HOME ADD:** 2739 Hawthorne Lane, Wilmette, IL 60091, (312)251-5884; **BUS ADD:** 69 W. Washington St., Suite 600, Chicago, IL 60602, (312)621-9700.

WOLOWICZ, Stefan——B: May 22, 1945, Boston, MA, *Partner*, Satin, Tenenbaum, Eichler & Zimmerman; **OTHER RE ACT:** CPA; **SERVICES:** Acctg., income taxes & auditing; **PROFL AFFIL & HONORS:** AICPA; CA Soc. of CPA's; Los Angeles Chap. of Acct. Principles & Auditing Standards; **EDUC:** BS, 1968, Fin./Acctg., CA State Univ. at Northridge; **BUS ADD:** 2049 Century Park E., Suite 3700, Los Angeles, CA 90067, (213)553-1040.

WOLPOFF, Alvin S.——B: July 30, 1926, Baltimore, MD, *Managing Partner*, Wolpoff & Company; **PRIM RE ACT:** Consultant; **OTHER RE ACT:** CPA; **SERVICES:** Acctg., consulting, tax; **REP CLIENTS:** Local & rgnl. devel.; **PROFL AFFIL & HONORS:** CPA, Atty.; **EDUC:** BS, 1949, Acctg., Univ. of MD; **GRAD EDUC:** JD, 1955, Law, Univ. of MD; **EDUC HONORS:** Beta Alpha Psi, Beta Gamma Sigma; **MIL SERV:** US Army; **OTHER ACT & HONORS:** Center Club Treas.; Sinai Hospital Bd.; **HOME ADD:** 3407 Terrapin Rd., Baltimore, MD 21208, (301)486-2051; **BUS ADD:** 1111 N. Charles St., Baltimore, MD 21201, (301)837-3770.

WOLSTEIN, Scott A.——B: Jun. 24, 1952, Cleveland, OH, *Gen. Partner*, Diversified Equities; **PRIM RE ACT:** Consultant, Attorney, Owner/Investor, Syndicator; **SERVICES:** Equity capital formation and structuring of tax advantaged investments; **REP CLIENTS:** Developers Diversified Ltd.; Associated Esta; Gries Investment Co.; **PREV EMPLOY:** Atty. - Thompson, Hine and Flory, Cleveland, Ohio, 1977-1981; **PROFL AFFIL & HONORS:** ABA; OH Bar Assn.; Cleveland Bar Assn.; **EDUC:** BS, 1974, Econ., Wharton School, Univ. of PA, Philadelphia, PA; **GRAD EDUC:** JD, 1977, Law, Univ. of MI Law School, Ann Arbor, MI; **EDUC HONORS:** Cum Laude; **HOME ADD:** 32049 Fairmount Blvd., Pepper Pike, OH 44124; **BUS ADD:** The Heritage, 34555 Chagrin Blvd., Moreland Hills, OH 44022, (216)247-2977.

WOMACK, Brett H.——B: June 30, 1951, Ft. Benning, GA, *Gen. Mgr.*, The Freight Station; **PRIM RE ACT:** Property Manager; **OTHER RE ACT:** Leasing agent; **SERVICES:** Pre-leasing, rent-up and mgmt. of theme ctr. being developed in Richmond, VA; **PREV EMPLOY:** Exec. Dir. Richmond Apt. Council (Trade Assn/); **PROFL AFFIL & HONORS:** Richmond Chapter Inst. of RE Mgmt., NAHB, Brandermill Comm. Assn., Advisory Comm., Nat. Rental Housing Council, Multifamily Mgmt. Comm., NAHB; **EDUC:** Bus., RE, VA Comm. Univ., (still completing work); **OTHER ACT & HONORS:** Who's Who in Amer. Women (Marquis), 1979-80, 1980-81; **HOME ADD:** 13600 Pebble Creek Terr., Midlothian, VA 23113, (804)744-1572; **BUS ADD:** 13600 Pebble Creek Terr., Midlothian, VA 23113, (804)739-3656.

WOMACK, John R.(Rick), Jr., CPA——B: June 10, 1948, Kingsville, TX, *Partner*, Womack & Womack; **OTHER RE ACT:** CPA; **SERVICES:** Tax and fin. planning, acctg. servs. and tax compliance; **REP CLIENTS:** Investors, synd. and devel. in comml. props.; **PROFL AFFIL & HONORS:** AICPA, TX Soc. of CPA's; **EDUC:** BBA, 1970, Acctg., TX A&I Univ.; **MIL SERV:** USAR, 1st Lt.; **OTHER ACT & HONORS:** Bd. of Dir. of TX A&I Univ. Alumni Assn., Treasurer, West Belfort Civic Club; **HOME ADD:** 7931 Duffield Lane, Houston, TX 77071, (713)777-8503; **BUS ADD:** 6900 Fannin, Suite 430, Houston, TX 77030, (713)795-0420.

WONG, Albert——B: Nov. 24, 1929, Honolulu, HI, *VP*, Palace Realty, Inc.; **PRIM RE ACT:** Broker, Consultant, Owner/Investor, Property Manager; **OTHER RE ACT:** RE investment counseling; **PROFL AFFIL & HONORS:** Honolulu Bd. of Realtors; HI Assn. of Realtors; The Investment Grp. Realtors, CCIM; SP; **EDUC:** BA, 1952, Psych., Univ. of HI; **HOME ADD:** 1903 Wilhelmina Rise, Honolulu, HI 96816, (808)737-4950; **BUS ADD:** 1314 S King St., Suite 950, Honolulu, HI 96814, (808)531-8177.

WONG, Francis A.——B: July 18, 1936, Honolulu, HI, *Partner*, Graham Wong Hastings; **PRIM RE ACT:** Attorney, Developer; **REP CLIENTS:** Marriott, Sheraton & Holiday Inns; **PROFL AFFIL & HONORS:** ABA; **EDUC:** BS, 1958, Econ., Georgetown Univ.; **GRAD EDUC:** JD, 1960, RE, Georgetown Univ. Law Ctr.; **OTHER ACT & HONORS:** State Rep. 1966-1970, State Senate 1970-1981; **HOME ADD:** 2128 Armstrong, Honolulu, HI 96822, (808)947-8000; **BUS ADD:** 345 Queen St., 700, Honolulu, HI 96813, (808)536-4421.

WONG, Jason G. F.——B: Aug. 14, 1952, Honolulu, HI, *Atty.*, Bishop, Baldwin, Bewald, Dillingham & Wong; **OTHER RE ACT:** Legal; **SERVICES:** Investment & business consultant, legal; **PROFL AFFIL & HONORS:** HI Bar Assn., ABA; **EDUC:** BBA, 1974, Acctg., Univ. of MI; **GRAD EDUC:** JD, 1977, Georgetown Univ. Law Ctr.; LLM, 1981, Intl. Comml. Transactions, Georgetown Univ. Law Ctr.; **HOME ADD:** 4329 Papu Cir., Honolulu, HI 96816; **BUS ADD:** 2600 Grosvenor, 733 Bishop St., Honolulu, HI 96813, (808)531-4189.

WONG, Karen Gail Chinn——B: July 5, 1937, Seattle, WA, *Atty. at Law*, Commonwealth Land Title Insurance Co., Leage; **PRIM RE ACT:** Attorney; **SERVICES:** Title ins., escrow, title searches; **REP CLIENTS:** Lenders; Atty.; RE brokers & salesmen; appraisers; builders; devels.; owners; purchasers & sellers; mort. bankers; mort. & escrow cos.; **PROFL AFFIL & HONORS:** WA Bar Assn.; ABA; Seattle King Cty. Bar Assn.; WA Women Lawyers; Phi Alpha Delta Legal Frat.; Asian Law Assn., Atty. to practice in Fed. District & appeals Cts.; **EDUC:** BA, 1959, Soc. Sci., Univ. of CA, Berkeley; **GRAD EDUC:** Masters Librarianship, 1976, Univ. of WA; JD, 1978, Univ. of Puget Sound; **EDUC HONORS:** Honor Roll; **OTHER ACT & HONORS:** Jade guild; Chinese Baptist Church; Chinese Comm.; public affairs orgs.; Chinese Comm. Parents Org.; Asian Mgmt. Assn.; Oak Town Womens Auxiliary Chinese Comm. Serv. Org.; Wing Luke Memorial Museum; Jade Guild Achievement Award; Author Chinese History in the Pac. NW; **HOME ADD:** 8110 SE 70th, Mercer Island, WA 98040, (206)232-7495; **BUS ADD:** 2603 Third Ave., Seattle, WA 98040, (206)343-2829.

WONG, Philip——**B:** Dec. 18, 1951, Evanston, IL, *Atty.*, Sachnoff, Weaver & Rubenstein, Ltd.; **PRIM RE ACT:** Attorney; **SERVICES:** Comml. and indus. RE; **REP CLIENTS:** Synd. and Devel.; **PREV EMPLOY:** Chicago Title and Trust Co., 1973-76; **PROFL AFFIL & HONORS:** Title and conveyancing and Mort. fin. sub-commt of Chicago Bar Assn.; ABA; **EDUC:** BA, 1973, Nat. Sci., Johns Hopkins Univ.; **GRAD EDUC:** JD, 1977, John Marshall Law School; **HOME ADD:** 300 Main St. Apt. D, Evanston, IL 60202, (312)866-7445; **BUS ADD:** One IBM Plaza Suite 4700, Chicago, IL 60611, (312)644-2400.

WONG, Wallace——**B:** July 13, 1941, Honolulu, HI, *Pres.*, South Bay Coll. of Bus.; **PRIM RE ACT:** Developer, Builder, Owner/Investor; **PROFL AFFIL & HONORS:** Listed in Who's Who in CA; Acting Sec. of State of CA; **EDUC:** Bus. Admin., Univ. of CA; **HOME ADD:** 15564 Collina Strada, Bel Air, CA 90077, (213)476-8096; **BUS ADD:** 13430 Hawthorne Blvd., Hawthorne, CA 90250, (213)679-2531.

WOO, Robert——*Mgr. Adm.*, Wang Laboritories, Inc.; **PRIM RE ACT:** Property Manager; **BUS ADD:** One Industrial Ave., Lowell, MA 01851, (617)459-5000.*

WOOD, Allen R.——**B:** Mar. 1, 1932, Andover, MA, *Dir. RE*, Westinghouse Electric Corp.; **OTHER RE ACT:** Corp. RE; **SERVICES:** All phases of RE for the corp.; **PROFL AFFIL & HONORS:** SIR, IDRC (Secretary; Bd. of Dirs.), NACORE, IREMC, AICAM, (Bd. of Govs.), Assoc. SIR, FCA; **EDUC:** AB, Econ., 1954, Allegheny Coll., Meadville, PA; **GRAD EDUC:** MBA, 1969, Univ. of Pittsburgh, Pittsburgh, PA; **OTHER ACT & HONORS:** Guest Lecturer - EDI, Univ. of OK, 1st Union Nat. Bank of NC Bus. Devel. Advisory Council, Bd. of Tr. - Episcopal Diocese of Pittsburgh, Allegheny Alumni Assn., Univ. of Pittsburgh Alumni, Delta Tau Delta Frat.; **HOME ADD:** 138 Crescent Hills Rd., Pittsburgh, PA 15235; **BUS ADD:** Westinghouse Bldg., Pittsburgh, PA 15222, (412)255-3175.

WOOD, Betty K.——**B:** Mar. 26, 1930, Brooksville, FL, *Realtor*, Century 21 Betty Wood & Assoc., Inc.; **PRIM RE ACT:** Broker, Owner/Investor; **SERVICES:** Reloc. service, mkt. analysis computations multiple listing, nat. referrals, Listings & sales in resid., comml. & acerage; **REP CLIENTS:** Thermo Shield Homes, Inc. & Intervest Construction, Inc.; **PREV EMPLOY:** Assoc. of Maillie Realty 1971-74; **PROFL AFFIL & HONORS:** NAR, Dayton Beach area Bd. of Realtors, FL State Bd. of Realtors, GRI (FL), Past Dir. Daytona Beach Area Bd. of Dir., Member of Profl. Standards Comm.; **EDUC:** RN, 1951, Orange Mem. Hospital, Orlando, Daytona Beach Comml. Coll.; Seminole Jr. Coll.; Bent Rodgers School of RE; **OTHER ACT & HONORS:** Past Pres. Corbin Ave. Kindergarten PTA, Past Leader Girl Scouts of Amer., Member Central Baptist Church, Daytona Beach, Charter Member Ormond Beach Pilot Club, Past Sec. of Brokers Council of Central & N. FL district of Century 21 of SE, Charter Member of Century 21 of SE; **HOME ADD:** 1556 Tuscaloosa Ave., Holly Hill, FL 32017, (904)673-0178; **BUS ADD:** 1700 Ridgewood Ave., Holly Hill, FL 32017, (904)677-5164; **BUS TEL:** (904)677-5122.

WOOD, Brooks C.B.——**B:** Feb. 2, 1941, Washington, DC, *Pres.*, Woodbyrne Realty, Inc.; **PRIM RE ACT:** Broker, Appraiser, Owner/Investor; **SERVICES:** Gen. RE Brokerage; Subdiv. Devel.; **REP CLIENTS:** Trammell Crow Co.; **PREV EMPLOY:** Montgomery Cty. MD Govt.; **PROFL AFFIL & HONORS:** NAR; RNMI; FLI, GRI; CRS; **EDUC:** BA, 1964, Applied Psych., Emory & Henry Coll.; **OTHER ACT & HONORS:** Mason, Member US C of C; **HOME ADD:** 19816 Bodmer Ave., Poolesville, MD 20837; **BUS ADD:** The 1785 House, 20000 Fisher Ave., Poolesville, MD 20837, (301)972-8400.

WOOD, Eric——*Corp. Const. Facilities Mgr.*, Hewlett-Packard; **PRIM RE ACT:** Property Manager; **BUS ADD:** 1501 Page Mill Rd., Palo Alto, CA 94304, (415)857-1501.*

WOOD, Frederick E.——**B:** Sept. 19, 1932, Freeport, NY, Frederick Wood Asocs.; **PRIM RE ACT:** Engineer, Appraiser; **SERVICES:** Engr. consulting & real prop. appraisal; **REP CLIENTS:** NY State Dept. of Transportation, Fin. Inst., V.S. Dept. of H.U.D.; **PROFL AFFIL & HONORS:** Soc. of RE Appraisers, Nat. Soc. of Profl. Engr., Amer. Soc. Appraisers, Sigma Gamma Tau (Honorary); **EDUC:** BS, 1954, Engr., Renselaer Polytechnic Inst.; **GRAD EDUC:** MS, 1965, Math., Adelphi Univ.; **MIL SERV:** US Air Force, Capt.; **OTHER ACT & HONORS:** Kiwanis Intl.; **HOME ADD:** 426 Kane Ave., E. Patchoque, NY 11772, (516)286-3166; **BUS ADD:** 426 Kane Ave., E. Patchogue, NY 11772, (516)286-8442.

WOOD, Henry T.——**B:** Aug. 14, 1915, Taunton, MA, *Partner*, Yates, Wood & MacDonald; **PRIM RE ACT:** Broker, Appraiser, Property Manager; **SERVICES:** Sale, leasing, valuation & mgmt. of comml. prop.; **REP CLIENTS:** Indiv., banks & corp. investors; **PROFL AFFIL & HONORS:** AIREA; RPA; Lifetime Trustee, BOMA of Seattle & King Cty.; Downtown Seattle Devel. Assn., MAI; **EDUC:** BA, 1937, Econ/Bus., Univ. of WA; **MIL SERV:** US Army; **OTHER ACT & HONORS:** Coll. Club of Seattle; Rainier Club; **HOME ADD:** 7011 52nd N.E., Seattle, WA 98115, (206)523-2495; **BUS ADD:** 1411 4th Ave. Bldg. 820, Seattle, WA 98101, (206)622-4682.

WOOD, James F.——*Partner*, Fleming Weller & Wood; **PRIM RE ACT:** Developer; **BUS ADD:** 3100 N. Vermilion, Danville, IL 61832, (217)446-4444.*

WOOD, John B.——**B:** July 6, 1950, Bellville, IL, *Assoc.*, Marshall, Bratter, Greene, Allison & Tucker, RE Div.; **PRIM RE ACT:** Attorney; **PREV EMPLOY:** Asst. Gen. Counsel, Fisher Bros. Owner - Builder, 299 Park Ave. NY, NY; **PROFL AFFIL & HONORS:** Assoc. of the Bar of the City of NY, NY Cty. Lawyers Assn., ABA, Assn. of MBA Execs., Natl. Assn. of Atty.-CPA's, EDP Auditors Assn., CPA; Bar Memberships: NY State, State of KS, Southern Dist. of NY, Dist. Ct. of KS, Tenth Circuit Ct. of Appeals; **EDUC:** BBA, 1973, Acctg., Washburn Univ. of Topeka, KS; **GRAD EDUC:** MBA, 1975, Univ. of Kansas; JD, 1977, Washburn Univ. of Topeka, KS; **EDUC HONORS:** Dean's List; **OTHER ACT & HONORS:** Asst. Atty. Gen. - State of KS - 1977-1978; Mason; Counsel to Boswell Estates Assn.; **HOME ADD:** 17 Vine, Bronxville, NY 10708; **BUS ADD:** 430 Park Ave., New York City, NY 10022, (212)421-7200.

WOOD, John S.——**B:** Oct. 1, 1947, Boston, MA, *Head of Sales Dept.*, The Real Estate Co.; **PRIM RE ACT:** Developer, Builder, Owner/Investor, Property Manager; **OTHER RE ACT:** Sales (Comml. & Resid.); **SERVICES:** Prop. Devel. (Comml. & Res.), Builder, Investments (Comml. & Resid.), Sales (Comml. & Res. & Farm-Ranch); **PROFL AFFIL & HONORS:** NW CO Bd. of Realtors; **EDUC:** BA, 1970, Poli. Sci.-Psych.-RE, San Diego State Coll.; **OTHER ACT & HONORS:** Horizons for the Handicapped, Contributer, St. Jude Childrens Research Hospital, March of Dimes; **HOME ADD:** 60 Maple St., Box 1141, Steamboat Springs,, CO 80477; **BUS ADD:** PO Box 3058, 8th & Yampa St., Steamboat Springs, CO 80477, (303)879-2345.

WOOD, Patrick H.——**B:** April 15, 1949, Sioux Falls, SD, *Part.*, Nighswander, Lord, Martin & Kill Kelley; **PRIM RE ACT:** Attorney; **SERVICES:** Title examinations, preparation of loan documents, representing homeowners' assns.; **REP CLIENTS:** Belknap Bank & Trust, Paugus Bay Racquet Club, Gilford Yacht Club, Gould Avenue Condominium Assn.; **PROFL AFFIL & HONORS:** NH Bar Assn., Sect. on Real Prop., Probate and Trust Law (Sec. 1976-1981; Pres. 1981-); NH Bar Assn.; Belknap Cty. Bar Assn.; ABA; **EDUC:** BS, 1971, Amer. History, Yale Univ.; **GRAD EDUC:** JD, 1974, Univ. of SD School of Law; **OTHER ACT & HONORS:** Franklin City Solicitor 1974-1976 (Franklin, NH); **HOME ADD:** 17 Pine Notch Cir., R.F.D. 5, Box 151, Laconia, NH 03246, (603)366-5168; **BUS ADD:** One Mill Plaza, PO Box 189, Laconia, NH 03246, (603)524-4121.

WOOD, Peter G.——**B:** July 25, 1949, Miami, FL, *Partner*, Peter Wood and Company, PA; **OTHER RE ACT:** CPA; **SERVICES:** Tax and fin. planning; **PREV EMPLOY:** Peat, Marwick, Mitchell & Co.; **PROFL AFFIL & HONORS:** Intl. Assn. of Fin. Planners; AICPA, CPA; **EDUC:** 1971, Acctg., FL State Univ.; **BUS ADD:** Suite 305, 4675 Ponce De Leon Blvd., Coral Gables, FL 33146, (305)665-4792.

WOOD, Priscilla J.——**B:** Mar. 9, 1954, Oak Park, IL, *RE Officer*, Continental Illinois National Bank, RE/Comml. Const.; **OTHER RE ACT:** Commercial Construction Lending; **SERVICES:** Interim fin. for office bldgs., hotels; **REP CLIENTS:** Comml. RE devels.; **PREV EMPLOY:** Instr. of RE as grad. student at Univ. of IL, Champaign; **PROFL AFFIL & HONORS:** RE Broker, IL, Appraisal Inst.; **EDUC:** Fin., 1976, RE, Univ. of IL, Champaign; **GRAD EDUC:** Masters of Fin., 1978, Univ. of IL, Champaign; **EDUC HONORS:** Grad. with Honors, James Scholar, Honors Grad.; **HOME ADD:** 2107 N. Kenmore Ave., Chicago, IL 60614, (312)929-1829; **BUS ADD:** 231 S. LaSalle, Chicago, IL 60693, (312)828 5177.

WOOD, Ray A.——**B:** Nov. 9, 1919, Arush, CA, *Appraiser*; **PRIM RE ACT:** Broker, Appraiser; **SERVICES:** RE appraising; **REP CLIENTS:** Exxon Oil Co.; Gulf Oil Corp.; Phillips Petroleum; Union Oil Co.; TRW Systems; Prudential Ins.; Bank of Amer., Trust Dept.; IBM; Reynolds Al; **PREV EMPLOY:** 184 Chrs. Bank of Amer., IHEM, 23 yrs. RE appraising; **PROFL AFFIL & HONORS:** SREA, Amer. Ins. of RE Appraisers, MAI, RE Broker State of CA; **EDUC:** Completed numerous advanced courses in RE Appraisal, Grad. of Amer. Inst. of Banking; **HOME ADD:** 177 Rancho Adolfo Dr., Caitarillo, CA 93010, (805)987-4210; **BUS ADD:** 177 Rancho Adolfo Dr., Camarillo, CA 93010.

WOOD, Robert L.——*Vice President*, Athlore Industries, Inc.; **PRIM RE ACT:** Property Manager; **BUS ADD:** 200 Webro Rd., Parsippany, NJ 07054, (201)887-9100.*

WOOD, Robert W.——**B:** Sept. 19, 1926, Salt Lake City, UT, *Exec. VP*, Prowswood, Inc.; **PRIM RE ACT:** Builder, Developer, Owner/Investor; **PREV EMPLOY:** Harris & Montague, Inc. (Advertising), 1954-59; **PROFL AFFIL & HONORS:** Nat. Assn. of Home Builders, Home Builders Assn. of Gr. Salt Lake, Sale Lake Cty. Housing Auth., Recipient of VA Bettilyon Builder of Yr. Award, 1969; **EDUC:** BA, 1951, Mktg., Univ. of UT; **OTHER ACT & HONORS:** Chmn. Salt Lake Cty. Housing Authority, 7 yrs.; Past Chmn., Nat. Assn. of Home Builders, Mktg. Comm.; Past Pres. of Home Builders Assn. of Greater Salt Lake; **HOME ADD:** 2330 Cottonwood Ln., Salt Lake City, UT 84117, (801)278-4916; **BUS ADD:** 4885 S. 900 East, Salt Lake City, UT 84117, (801)262-4637.

WOOD, Stephen F.——**B:** May 8, 1936, Murfreesboro, TN, *Pres.*, Equitable Mort. and Investment Corp.; **PRIM RE ACT:** Broker, Consultant, Lender, Instructor, Syndicator; **OTHER RE ACT:** Mort. Banker; NASD Broker/Dealer; **SERVICES:** Income prop. sales, synd., & financing. GRI instructor for 12 years, instit. mort. & equity investments; **REP CLIENTS:** Union Mutual Life, Lincoln Natl. Life, Life & Casualty Ins., Life Investors, numerous S&L Assns., Realtors of AL & IA for GRI instruction, S&L Inst.; **PREV EMPLOY:** Pres. - Fidelity Fed. S&L Assn. - Nashville, Pres. - First Fed. S&L Assn. - Nashville; **PROFL AFFIL & HONORS:** MBAA, TN and Nashville, RESSI; NASD, CMB, Past Pres. - Nashville Mort. Bankers; VP - TN Mort. Bankers; Past Dir. - TN S&L League; **EDUC:** BA, 1958, Bus. Admin. and Econ., Vanderbilt Univ.; **GRAD EDUC:** School of Mort. Banking, 1965, Northwestern Univ. (Sponsored by MBA); **OTHER ACT & HONORS:** Bd. of Govs. - Nashville Area C of C; Article published in *Real Estate Today*; Guest Lecturer - Vanderbilt Univ.; **HOME ADD:** 6001 Sherwood Dr., Nashville, TN 37215, (615)373-2989; **BUS ADD:** 620 Nashville City Bank Bldg., Nashville, TN 37201, (615)244-8555.

WOODALL, Howard W.——**B:** May 25, 1947, Warren,AR, *Asst. VP*, Union B & T Co., RE Lending; **PRIM RE ACT:** Banker; **SERVICES:** Fin.; **PREV EMPLOY:** First S&L Assn.- Warren, AR 1971-1978; **EDUC:** BBA Indus. Mgmt., 1972, Acctg., Univ. of Ark. at Monticello; **HOME ADD:** Rte. 4, Box 83, Monticello, AR 71655, (501)367-2774; **BUS ADD:** 102 W. McCloy, Monticello, AR 71655, (501)367-3453.

WOODBURY, Sidney F.——**B:** May 12, 1935, Portland, OR, *Owner/Broker*, Sid Woodbury Commercial Brokerage Co.; **PRIM RE ACT:** Broker, Consultant; **SERVICES:** Comml., investment and indus. brokerage; **REP CLIENTS:** Lenders, instnl. and indiv. investors and devel. of comml. prop.; **PREV EMPLOY:** F.H. Andrews & Assoc., Inc. Standard Plaza, VP/Designated Broker, 15 yrs.; **PROFL AFFIL & HONORS:** Portland Bd. of Realtors; OR Assn. of Realtors; RNMI; NAR, CCIM; **EDUC:** BS, 1957, Bus. Admin., Univ. of OR; **MIL SERV:** US Air Force, Capt., 1958-1960; **OTHER ACT & HONORS:** Multnomah Athletic Club, Portland; Past Pres., OR CCIM Chapter #36; **HOME ADD:** 14 Bernini Ct., Lake Oswego, OR 97034, (503)636-6081; **BUS ADD:** 1001 S.W. Fifth Ave., Suite 1000, Portland, OR 97204, (503)222-1200.

WOODBURY, William F.——**B:** Dec. 21, 1951, Martinez, CA, *Owner*, William Woodbury and Associates; **PRIM RE ACT:** Broker, Consultant, Owner/Investor, Property Manager; **SERVICES:** Full serv. investment RE brokerage; **PREV EMPLOY:** Pvt. investor; **PROFL AFFIL & HONORS:** Contra Costa Multiple Listing Serv., Sacramento Multiple Listing Serv., Broker; **EDUC:** BA, 1975, Experimental Psych., Univ. of CA, Santa Barbara; **EDUC HONORS:** 3.8 GPA, High Honors; **HOME ADD:** 3687 Highland Rd., Lafayette, CA 94549, (415)283-2849; **BUS ADD:** 3687 Highland Rd., Lafayette, CA 94549, (415)284-1456.

WOODFORD, Kenneth R.——**B:** April. 12, 1948, Roanoke, VA, *RE Appraiser*, Hop Bailey Co.; **PRIM RE ACT:** Consultant, Appraiser; **SERVICES:** RE Appraisals, feasibility studies and consultation; **REP CLIENTS:** Maj. resid. relocation cos., comml. and lenders, state and local govts., indus. and rr's; **PREV EMPLOY:** TN Dept. of Transp. 1970-1976; **PROFL AFFIL & HONORS:** AIREA, SREA, RM, SRA; **EDUC:** BS, 1970, Mgmt., Carson Newman Coll., Jefferson City, TN; **HOME ADD:** 7812 Keswick Rd., Powell, TN 37849, (617)938-2818; **BUS ADD:** 1220 Park Natl. Bank Bldg., Knoxville, TN 37901, (615)637-3700.

WOODHULL, Daniel E.——**B:** July 25, 1949, Montpelier, VT, *Asst. VP*, Haney Accountants, Inc.; **PRIM RE ACT:** Consultant, Instructor; **OTHER RE ACT:** CPA; **SERVICES:** Investment counseling, tax planning, fin.; **REP CLIENTS:** Contractors, RE brokers, devel., lenders & investors; **PROFL AFFIL & HONORS:** Chmn., CA Profl. Bus. Affiliates; **EDUC:** BS, 1971, Acctg./Bus. Admin., Univ. of VT; **GRAD EDUC:** MBA, 1978, Mgmt., Golden Gate Univ.; MS, 1981, Taxation, Golden Gate Univ.; **MIL SERV:** USAF, Capt.; **OTHER ACT & HONORS:** Rancho Cordova Youth Soccer; **BUS ADD:** 729 Sunrise Blvd., Suite 501, Roseville, CA 95678, (916)969-6000.

WOODLAND, M. Don——**B:** May 9, 1938, Ogden, UT, *Broker*, Woodland Properties - Metro Brokers; **PRIM RE ACT:** Broker; **SERVICES:** Resid., comml., investment prop., land; **PROFL AFFIL & HONORS:** CRB, CRS, GRI; **EDUC:** BS, 1971, Weber State Coll.; **MIL SERV:** US Navy, PO; **HOME ADD:** PO Box 2828, Littleton, CO 80161, (303)773-6731; **BUS ADD:** 8525 E. Orchard Rd., Ste. 316, Englewood, CO 80111, (303)773-1531.

WOODRUFF, G. C., Jr.——**B:** May 24, 1928, Columbus, GA, Woodruff-Brown Co.; **PRIM RE ACT:** Consultant, Developer, Builder, Property Manager; **SERVICES:** RE sales & leasing, prop. mgmt., lot devel., approx. 15 single family subdiv. consisting of over 4000 lots; **REP CLIENTS:** Apartment owners & investors, builders, investors in comml. prop.; **PROFL AFFIL & HONORS:** Member of Fin. Comm. 1961-pres., and Trust Comm. 1970 to pres. of Columbus Bank and Trust Co.; Bd. member of Home Fed. S & L: Assn. from 1956-79, Chmm. for 15 yrs. and consultant for another year; founded the GA Co. in 1957 and sold to Columbus Bank & Trust Co. in 1972; **EDUC:** BBA, 1951, Bus. Admin., Univ. of GA; **MIL SERV:** USAF, 1st Lt., 1952- 54; **OTHER ACT & HONORS:** Chmn. of Indus. Devel. Comm. from 1978-now, Past Pres. of Columbus C of C; Past Dir. of S. Columbus Boys Club; Member of Bd. of Dirs-Chattahoochee Valley Fair; Member of Columbus RE Bd.; Member of Home Builders Assn.; **HOME ADD:** 6201 Waterford Rd., Columbus, GA 31904, (404)327-2776; **BUS ADD:** 1501 13th St. Box 7727, Columbus, GA 31908, (404)323-6401.

WOODS, Franklin D. R.——**B:** May 18, 1939, Oxford, AL, The Owens and Woods Partnership; **PRIM RE ACT:** Architect; **SERVICES:** Arch. and planning servs.; **PROFL AFFIL & HONORS:** AIA; **EDUC:** BS, 1965, Arch., Tuskegee Inst., AL; **MIL SERV:** US Army, SP-4, Good Conduct Ribbon, expert Infantryman Badge; **HOME ADD:** 3079 Wenonah Park Rd., Birmingham, AL 35211, (205)925-5020; **BUS ADD:** 1905 Bessemer Rd., Birmingham, AL 35208, (205)923-2717.

WOODS, John N.——**B:** Aug. 4, 1941, Dayton, OH, *RE Rep.*, Red Roof Inns; **OTHER RE ACT:** Site Acquisition; **PROFL AFFIL & HONORS:** Natl. Assn. of Corporate RE Execs.; **EDUC:** BA, 1963, Econ., OH Wesleyan Univ.; **GRAD EDUC:** MBA, 1966, OH State Univ.; **HOME ADD:** 264 N. Liberty St., Delaware, OH 43015, (614)363-1624; **BUS ADD:** 4355 Davidson Rd., Amlin, OH 43002, (614)876-9961.

WOODS, Sandra——*VP & Acting Dir. of RE*, Adolph Coor. Co.; **PRIM RE ACT:** Property Manager; **BUS ADD:** Golden, CO 80401, (303)279-6565.*

WOODS, William D.——**B:** Oct. 18, 1941, KS City, MO, *Ind. Fee Appraiser*; **PRIM RE ACT:** Broker, Appraiser, Instructor; **REP CLIENTS:** Raytown Fed. S&L, Rockhill Fed. Savings, Blue Ridge Bank & Tr., KS City, MO, Armco Steel Corp.; **PREV EMPLOY:** Margolin & Assoc. (Comml. Appraiser), Russell & Assoc. (Fee Appraiser); **PROFL AFFIL & HONORS:** SREA, SRA, GRI; **EDUC:** 1976, RE, Rockhurst Coll.; **EDUC HONORS:** Pres. Sr. Class, 1976 of Realtors Inst.; **OTHER ACT & HONORS:** Park Bd., City of Raytown (Present til 1984), Assoc. Dir., Eastern Jackson Cty. Bd. of Realtors, 1978 & 1979, Educ. Comm. KC Chapt. SREA; **HOME ADD:** 6016 Sterling Ave., Raytown, MO 64133, (816)737-1743; **BUS ADD:** 6016 Sterling Ave., Raytown, MO 64133, (816)737-1743.

WOODWARD, James W.——**B:** Apr. 23, 1928, Waterbury, CT, *Atty.*, James W. Woodward - Atty. at Law; **PRIM RE ACT:** Consultant, Attorney, Developer, Lender, Builder, Owner/Investor, Syndicator; **OTHER RE ACT:** Zoning Matters, Estate Planning; **SERVICES:** Gen. practice law firm; **PREV EMPLOY:** Hinz & Woodward, P.C., 424 S. Washington St., Alexandria, VA 22314; **PROFL AFFIL & HONORS:** N. VA Bd. of Realtors, Member - Realtor Lawyer Comm.; **EDUC:** BS, 1952, Engineering, US Military Acad. (West Point); **GRAD EDUC:** JD, 1976, Univ. of Baltimore Law School; **MIL SERV:** US Air Force, 1952-1973, Lt. Col., Meritorious Service Medal (2), Distinguished Flying Cross (2), Air Medals (9); **OTHER ACT & HONORS:** Pres., Little River Village Community Council, Inc., Alexandria, VA (1977-1978); Treas., CT State Soc. of D.C. (1973-1981); **HOME ADD:** 11 Wolfe Ave., Beacon Falls, CT 06403, (203)729-7409; **BUS ADD:** 11 Wolfe Ave., Beacon Falls, CT 06403, (203)729-7409.

WOODWARD, John A.——B: July 2, 1951, Reed City, MI, *Partner*, Spierer & Woodward Attorneys at Law, PC; **PRIM RE ACT:** Broker, Attorney, Owner/Investor, Syndicator; **REP CLIENTS:** Spring Realty; Anastasi Const.; Transamer. Tetle Inc.; Tetle Ins. & Trust Co.; **PREV EMPLOY:** Accountant, Nat. Broadcasting Co.; **PROFL AFFIL & HONORS:** ABA; Los Angeles Cty. Bar Assn.; Taxation - Real Prop. Section, BS, JD; **EDUC:** BS, 1974, Acctg./Fin., CO State Univ.; **GRAD EDUC:** JD, 1977, Southwestern Univ.; **EDUC HONORS:** Member, SCALE Project; **HOME ADD:** 3945 Via Solano, Palos Verdes Estates, CA 90274; **BUS ADD:** 21535 Hawthorne Blvd., Ste. 532, Torrance, CA 90503, (213)540-3199.

WOODWARD, S. Lee——B: Oct. 24, 1949, Danville, IL, *VP*, Doane-Western, RE Investments; **PRIM RE ACT:** Broker, Attorney, Lender, Property Manager; **SERVICES:** Agric. RE investments and mgmt.; **REP CLIENTS:** CT Gen. Prud. Aetna; **PROFL AFFIL & HONORS:** ABA; **EDUC:** 1970, Agric. Econ., Purdue Univ. Agriculture; **GRAD EDUC:** JD, 1973, Law, Indiana Univ.; **EDUC HONORS:** Highest Scholastic; **MIL SERV:** USN, Lt.; **BUS ADD:** 3333 Quebec St., Suite 3000, Denver, CO 80207, (303)388-4084.

WOODY, Larry N.——B: Dec. 1, 1942, Effingham, IL, *Gen. Part./Owner*, Income Prop. Assoc.; **PRIM RE ACT:** Broker, Syndicator, Consultant, Property Manager, Owner/Investor; **SERVICES:** Full RE consultation, acquisition, mgmt., rehab. & synd. investor; **REP CLIENTS:** Limited partnerships & indiv. investors in Midwestern and Southwestern States; **PREV EMPLOY:** 1970-76 Corp. Planning Mgr. - Toyota Motor Sales, USA, Inc.; 1969-1970 Product Planning Analyst - Ford Motor Co.; 1966-1969 Production Fin. Specialist - US Dept. of Defense; **EDUC:** BS, 1965, Mgmt, Econ., S. IL Univ.; **GRAD EDUC:** MS, 1967, Mktg., Econ., S. IL Univ.; **EDUC HONORS:** Alpha Kappa Psi - Prof. Bus. Frat.; **BUS ADD:** 15848 Clarendon, Fountain Valley, CA 92708, (714)775-4359.

WOODY, Ron——B: Nov. 20, 1935, Portland, OR, *Gen. Mgr., Residential Div.*, Ward Cook, Inc., Realtors, Resid.; **PRIM RE ACT:** Broker, Appraiser; **OTHER RE ACT:** Mort., brokers, ins. escrow, saving & loan; **SERVICES:** Resid., comml. RE, mort. loans, ins., prop. mgmt., escrow, savings & loan (OR Pioneer S&L), land devel.; **PROFL AFFIL & HONORS:** Natl. Assoc. Realtors (local & state), Home Builders Assoc., CRB; CRS; **EDUC:** 1962, Law, NW Law School; **MIL SERV:** Naval Res.; **HOME ADD:** 2712 SE 73rd, Portland, OR 97206, (503)774-7814; **BUS ADD:** 520 SW Stark St., Portland, OR 97204, (503)234-9766.

WOOFF, Dennis A.——B: Jan. 31, 1946, Alton, IL, *Pres.*, Wooff, Inc. Realtors; **PRIM RE ACT:** Broker, Consultant, Appraiser, Property Manager; **SERVICES:** Brokerage, counseling; comml. investment, resid.; **REP CLIENTS:** Employee Transfer, Exec., Homequity, Anchor S & L; **PROFL AFFIL & HONORS:** Realtor, Assoc. S.R.A., CRS, Dir. C of C, CRS, GRI, Recipient of Realtor of the Year 1980, Honor Award C of C; **EDUC:** BS, 1968, Bus. Admin., Mgmt., S.I. Univ.; **OTHER ACT & HONORS:** Advisory Bd. Lewis Clark Coll.; Lions; Rotary; Dir. YMCA; Dir. Lockhaven C.C.; Found AMPAC (Dir.-Sec., Alton Metroplex Pol. Actioin Comm.); Pres. Bd. of Realtors; IL State Dir., IL Realtors; Pres. R-Home Warranty; **HOME ADD:** 4441 Thatcher Rd., Alton, IL 62002, (618)462-8088; **BUS ADD:** 3200 James Ter., Alton, IL 62002, (618)463-9797.

WOOLFE, Terence J.——B: Sept. 17, 1951, St. Louis, MO, *Atty./Asst. Gen. Counsel*, Tanglewood Corp.; **PRIM RE ACT:** Attorney; **SERVICES:** Provide legal counsel to RE devel. co.; **PREV EMPLOY:** Assoc. of Law Office of David C. DuBoss; **PROFL AFFIL & HONORS:** State Bar of TX; Houston Bar Assn.; Houston Young Lawyers Assn.; Section Member, RE, Corp. Counsel, Will, Trusts & Probate; **EDUC:** BA, 1973, Pol Sci., Univ. of TN; **GRAD EDUC:** JD, 1976, S. TX Coll. of Law; **EDUC HONORS:** Dean's List three semesters, Law Journal; **HOME ADD:** 8411 Ariel, Houston, TX 77074, (713)988-5435; **BUS ADD:** 1661 Tanglewood Rd., Houston, TX 77056, (713)622-8100.

WOOLFORD, William A.——B: Nov. 7, 1919, Baltimore, MD, *Pres.*, Wm. Woolford & Assoc.; **PRIM RE ACT:** Engineer, Appraiser; **OTHER RE ACT:** Prop. Acquisitions; **SERVICES:** Consulting engrg. and appraisal servs.; **REP CLIENTS:** Utilities, municipalities, banks, attys., etc.; **PROFL AFFIL & HONORS:** Amer. Soc. Appraisers; AIREA, Amer. Soc. Civil Engrs.; Amer. Soc. for Testing & Materials, PE lic. 16 states; **EDUC:** BS, 1951, Civil Engrg., CO A&M College; **EDUC HONORS:** Chi Epsilon, Sigma Tau Civil Engrg. Hons.; **MIL SERV:** US Army, 1st Lt., Sig C; **OTHER ACT & HONORS:** Univ. Club, Denver; **HOME ADD:** 1735 Cherry St., Denver, CO 80220, (303)355-8562; **BUS ADD:** 155 S. Madison St. Suite 323, Denver, CO 80209, (303)321-3077.

WOOLLEY, Dan A.——B: June 10, 1939, Buernos Aires, Argentina, *VP & Dir. of RE*, RI Hospital Tr. Nat. Bank, Trust Div.; **PRIM RE ACT:** Owner/Investor; **OTHER RE ACT:** Mgr. co-mingled RE fund; **SERVICES:** RE investments for pension funds & trust clients; **PREV EMPLOY:** Ryan Elliott & Co., Inc., Boston, VP & Dir., 1965-81; **PROFL AFFIL & HONORS:** Member Nat. Assn. of Realtors & Realtors Nat. Mktg. Inst., Lic. RE Broker, MA, NH, RI, CCIM Designation from RNMI; **EDUC:** AB, 1960, Pol. Sci., Princeton Univ.; **GRAD EDUC:** MBA, 1965, Mktg., Fin., Harvard Univ. Grad. Sch. of Bus. Admin.; **EDUC HONORS:** Magna Cum Laude; **MIL SERV:** USN, Lt. j.g., Antarctic Service Medal; **OTHER ACT & HONORS:** Member Perm. Bldg. Comm. & Town Facilities Comm., Town of Sudbury, Trustee, W Newton Savings Bank; **HOME ADD:** 213 Old Sudbury Rd., Sudbury, MA 01776, (617)443-6850; **BUS ADD:** 1 Hospital Trust Plaza, Providence, RI 02903, (401)278-7606.

WOOLSEY, William J.——B: Oct. 27, 1931, Houston, TX, *Pres.*, Woolsey-Voss, Incorporated; **PRIM RE ACT:** Broker, Owner/Investor, Syndicator; **PROFL AFFIL & HONORS:** RESSI; **EDUC:** Bus. Admin., 1955, Bus., Univ. of TX; **MIL SERV:** USAF, A/2c; **HOME ADD:** 8149 Forest Mesa Dr., Austin, TX 78759, (512)345-5921; **BUS ADD:** 8705 Shoal Creek Blvd. Ste. 221, Austin, TX 78758, (512)452-9356.

WOOTTON, Dale——B: Nov. 25, 1941, Dallas, TX, *Atty.*; **PRIM RE ACT:** Consultant, Attorney, Developer, Builder, Owner/Investor; **SERVICES:** Consultant, legal servs.; **PREV EMPLOY:** Southland Life Ins. Co.; **PROFL AFFIL & HONORS:** RE Section-TX Bar Assn., Delta Sigma Pi Business Frat.; **EDUC:** BBA, 1963, Bus., Bus. School, N. TX State Univ.; **GRAD EDUC:** JD, 1966, SMU; **EDUC HONORS:** Who's Who, Bluekey, Outstanding Econ. Student 1962; **MIL SERV:** USN, Lt., Navy Commendation Medal; **HOME TEL:** (214)521-0529; **BUS ADD:** 909 One Main Pl., Dallas, TX 75250, (214)744-3221.

WORKMAN, Bob D.——B: Oct. 5, 1932, Thomasville, NC, *Pres.*, Workman Realty, Inc.; **PRIM RE ACT:** Broker, Instructor, Consultant, Appraiser, Real Estate Publisher; **OTHER RE ACT:** Teacher - Workman School of RE; **PREV EMPLOY:** RE Salesman for 16 yrs.; **PROFL AFFIL & HONORS:** CRB; **EDUC:** BS, 1953, Sci., Wake Forest Univ.; **GRAD EDUC:** BS, 1958; **MIL SERV:** US Army, Cpl.; **OTHER ACT & HONORS:** Parkwood Baptist Church; Rotary Intl., Bd. Member - Arlington Rotary; **HOME ADD:** 1934 Afton Ln., Jacksonville, FL 32211; **BUS ADD:** 8708 7343 Merrill Rd., Jacksonville, FL 32211, (904)721-2030.

WORMALD, Robert K.——B: Sept.13,1931, Takoma Park, MD, *Pres.*, Robert K. Wormald, Inc.; **PRIM RE ACT:** Builder; **SERVICES:** Resid. and Comml.; **PROFL AFFIL & HONORS:** NAHB, Montgomery Co. Builders Assn., Registered Profl. Engr. -MD VA & DC Licensed RE Salesman Registered Land Surveyor; **EDUC:** BCE, 1953, VPI; **GRAD EDUC:** Not Completed, Structural Engrg., Univ. of MD; **EDUC HONORS:** Chi Epsilon; **MIL SERV:** US Corps of Engr., 1st Lt.; **HOME ADD:** 10121 Chapel Rd., Potomac, MD 20854; **BUS ADD:** 1160 Rockville Pike 206, Rockville, MD 20852, (301)424-3611.

WORNALL, Robert W.——B: Sept. 22, 1939, Kansas City, MO, *Pres.*, Charter Bankers Mortgage Co., First Nat. Bank of Kansas City; **PRIM RE ACT:** Consultant, Appraiser, Banker, Lender, Insuror; **SERVICES:** Mortgage & construction lending; **PROFL AFFIL & HONORS:** MO/Kansas City Mort. Bankers Assn.; **EDUC:** BA, 1964, Hist./Sociology, Univ. of KS; **MIL SERV:** U.S. Army; **HOME ADD:** 8315 Lee Blvd., Leawood, KS 66206, (913)649-9632; **BUS ADD:** 922 Charter Bank Ctr., Kansas City, MO 64105, (816)221-2824.

WORSHAM, Earl S.——B: Nov. 15, 1932, Knoxville, TN, *Chmn. of the Bd.*, Worsham Brothers Co., Inc.; **PRIM RE ACT:** Developer; **SERVICES:** Large scale mixed use devels., cities; **REP CLIENTS:** City of Miami, City of Little Rock, Arkansas; **EDUC:** 1955, Bus. Admin., Univ. of TN; **GRAD EDUC:** MBA, working toward, RE, Amer. Univ.; **MIL SERV:** US Army, CIC, Sgt.; **OTHER ACT & HONORS:** Devel. of the Year 1979, City of Miami; City of Miami Beach; Dade Cty.; **HOME ADD:** 1 Cherokee Rd., Atlanta, GA 30305, (404)233-2436; **BUS ADD:** 1401 W. Paces Ferry Rd., Atlanta, GA 30327, (404)262-2855.

WORSTER, Neil C.——B: Oct. 19, 1946, Berea, OH, *Broker - Owner*, NCW, Inc., Realtors; **PRIM RE ACT:** Broker, Consultant, Owner/Investor, Property Manager, Syndicator; **SERVICES:** Comml. and investment RE serv.; **PROFL AFFIL & HONORS:** Norman Bd. of Realtors, OAR, NAR, RNMI, RESSI, Pres. OK Chap. CCIM, Norman Bd. of Realtors - Realtor of the Yr., 1981; **MIL SERV:** US Army; **HOME ADD:** 433 Foreman, Norman, OK 73069, (405)329-7106; **BUS ADD:** 401 W Main St., Suite 260, Norman, OK 73069, (405)329-8954.

WORTH, Hal Venable, III——B: July 26, 1940, Raleigh, NC, *VP*, J.W. York & Co., Inc.; **PRIM RE ACT:** Broker, Developer, Property Manager; **SERVICES:** Devel., brokerage, & prop. mgmt.; **REP CLIENTS:** Most above servs. have been provided for our own acct., we are involved in various limited partnerships as the gen. partner; **PREV EMPLOY:** Supply Officer aboard USS-ABBOT (DD-629) from 1962-63; **PROFL AFFIL & HONORS:** Raleigh Bd. of Realtors, NC Assn. of Realtors, NAR, ICSC, Inst. of RE Mgmt., CPM, CSM; **EDUC:** BA, 1962, Math., Univ. of NC at Chapel Hill; **MIL SERV:** USN, Lt.; **OTHER ACT & HONORS:** Vestryman, Bd. Member Boy's Club of Wake Cty., Bd. of Comm. Housing auth. of the City of Raleigh; **HOME ADD:** 1115 Nichols Dr., Raleigh, NC 27605, (919)829-1062; **BUS ADD:** PO Box 10007, Raleigh, NC 27605, (919)821-1350.

WREMAN, Neal——*Manager Corporate Facilities*, Ampex Corporation; **PRIM RE ACT:** Property Manager; **BUS ADD:** 401 Broadway 3-51 Mail Stop, Redwood City, CA 94063, (415)367-2011.*

WRIEDEN, James E.——B: June 7, 1943, Brooklyn, NY, *Broker/Owner*, Antelope Props., Mariposa Mgmt., James E. Wrieden & Assoc.; **PRIM RE ACT:** Broker, Consultant, Owner/Investor, Property Manager, Insuror, Syndicator; **OTHER RE ACT:** RE Investment; **SERVICES:** Prop. mgmt. & RE Sales, consultation; **REP CLIENTS:** Over 150 clients; Mgr./own 1000 single family homes; Offices in Bay Area and the greater Sacramento area with approx 20 employees; **PREV EMPLOY:** Self-employed in RE and Prop. Mgmt. for over 12 yrs.; **PROFL AFFIL & HONORS:** Sacramento and San Jose RE Bds.; Sacramento Apt. Assn.; Better Bus. Bureau; Sacramento & Nat. Exchange Club; **EDUC:** BS, 1969, Sci., Bus., San Diego State Univ.; **MIL SERV:** US Navy, Lt. Vietnam Campaign; **HOME ADD:** 1875 Ridgeview Ave., Roseville, CA 95678, (916)969-5555; **BUS ADD:** 7715/21 Mariposa Ave., Citrus Hts., CA 95610, (916)969-5555.

WRIGHT, A. William——*Mgr., Area Devel.*, Central Louisiana Electric Co., Inc.; **PRIM RE ACT:** Developer; **BUS ADD:** PO Box 510, Pineville, LA 71360, (318)445-8211.*

WRIGHT, Dorothy F.——B: Mar. 24, 1936, Hickory, NC, *VP, Branch Mgr.*, Abbitt Realty Co. Inc.; **PRIM RE ACT:** Broker; **PROFL AFFIL & HONORS:** CRS, CRB; **HOME ADD:** 1699 Wright Dr., Hampton, VA 23669, (804)838-1059; **BUS ADD:** 62 W. Mercury Blvd., Hampton, VA 23669, (804)722-9884.

WRIGHT, Edward L., Jr.——B: July 7, 1932, Little Rock, AR, *Partner*, Wright, Lindsey & Jennings; **PRIM RE ACT:** Attorney; **REP CLIENTS:** Savers Fed. S&L Assn.; Fausett & Co., Inc.; Broker, McKay & Co.; Broker, Worthen Bank & Trust Co.; Breeding Investment Co.; **PROFL AFFIL & HONORS:** Amer. Coll. of RE Lawyers; Amer. Coll. of Mort. Attys.; ABA, Real Prop. Sect., Bd. of Regents, Amer. Coll. of Mort. Attys.; Chmn., Attys., Comm. US League of Savings Assns.; **EDUC:** BS, 1954, Acctg., St. Louis Univ.; **GRAD EDUC:** LLD, 1959, RE and Taxation, Univ. of AR; **MIL SERV:** US Army; Sp4, Good Conduct Medal; **OTHER ACT & HONORS:** Quorum Ct., Pulaski Cty., AR 1966-68; Youth Home, Inc., Bd. of Dir. 1968-present; C of C of Greater Little Rock; **HOME ADD:** 5011 Hawthorne Rd., Little Rock, AR 72207, (501)663-4801; **BUS ADD:** 2200 Worthen Bank Bld., Little Rock, AR 72201, (501)371-0808.

WRIGHT, Elizabeth L. (Libby)——B: May 19, 1925, Bay City, MI, *Owner-Mgr.*, Libby Wright, Realtor; **PRIM RE ACT:** Broker, Owner/Investor, Instructor; **PROFL AFFIL & HONORS:** RAM (RE Alumni, Univ. of MI), GRI, CRS, Omega Tau Rho, 1980 Realtor of Year - State of MI; **OTHER ACT & HONORS:** Bd. of Mgrs. - Hurley Med. Ctr. - Currently Pres.; 1982 Pres. Nat. Women's Council of Realtors; **HOME ADD:** 2301 Brookside Dr., Flint, MI 48503, (313)233-0516; **BUS ADD:** 825 Commonwealth Ave., Flint, MI 48503, (313)234-5661.

WRIGHT, Frederick——B: Apr. 27, 1939, Boston, MA, *Pres.*, Wright Props. Inc.; **PRIM RE ACT:** Broker; **SERVICES:** Condo sales; **PROFL AFFIL & HONORS:** Palm Bch. Bd. of Realtors, W. Palm Bch. Bd. of Realtors, RESSI, GRI; **OTHER ACT & HONORS:** Nat. Rifle Assn., Intl. Oceanographic Found.; **BUS ADD:** 44 Cocoanut Row, Palm Beach, FL 33480, (305)655-0144.

WRIGHT, Gordon B.——B: Aug. 30, 1943, AL, *Owner/Broker*, Texas Commercial Realty; **PRIM RE ACT:** Broker, Consultant, Owner/Investor, Instructor, Property Manager; **SERVICES:** Investment counseling, sales, leasing & mgmt.; **REP CLIENTS:** Pvt. indivs. and instl. buyers; **PREV EMPLOY:** The Woodlands, a 20,000 acre HUD Devel.; First Amer. Realty, CA; **PROFL AFFIL & HONORS:** NAR; TX Assn. of Realtors; CA RE Assn.; **EDUC:** BS, 1975, Bus. Admin., Acctg., CA State Univ., Long Beach; **GRAD EDUC:** AA, 1972, Mktg., El Camino Coll.; **EDUC HONORS:** Deans Honor Roll, Cum Laude, Deans Honor Roll; **MIL SERV:** USN, E-4, Honorable Dis.; **OTHER ACT & HONORS:** Houston Alief Kiwanis, Charter Member Civics Comm.; **HOME ADD:** 2214 Briarport, Houston, TX 77077, (713)493-2400; **BUS ADD:** 11221 Richmond Ave., Suite 111B, Houston, TX 77082, (713)531-7333.

WRIGHT, Thomas L.——B: Dec. 8, 1930, Albany, NY, *Pres. Owner*, Century 21, T. Wright Realty Inc.; **PRIM RE ACT:** Broker, Appraiser, Developer, Owner/Investor, Property Manager, Real Estate Publisher; **SERVICES:** RE sales, housing, econ. devel.; **REP CLIENTS:** Appraisals for indivs., bus., attys. for estate purposes, comml., agricultural, resid., land and seasonal props.; **PREV EMPLOY:** Exec. Officer Schoharie ABC Bd., 1962-73; **PROFL AFFIL & HONORS:** Profl. RE Brokers of Amer., NY State & Nat. Bds. of Realtors, Past Pres. of Schoharie Cty. Bd. of Realtors, NY State Soc. of RE Appraisers, NY Chap. of Soc. of Appraisers Inter. Organization of R.E. Appraisers. C.M.N.A.., Lic. RE; Testified before NY State Supreme Ct. relative to RE values, Fee appraiser for local branch of Key Bank, Fee appraiser for local branch of Mechanics Exchange Savings Bank, Cert. appraiser for FNMA, Prepared and presented courses and seminars on different aspects of RE, Writes weekly newspaper column on RE matters, Conducted var. RE educ. sales training programs; **OTHER ACT & HONORS:** Member Schoharie Co. Civil Serv. Comm., Advisor and member of Schoharie Cty. Planning & Devel. Commn., Advisor of Bus. Div. of SUNY at Cobleskill; **HOME ADD:** 164 N. Main. St., Schoharie, NY 12157, (518)295-8937; **BUS ADD:** 30 Main St., Cobleskill, NY 12043, (518)234-3501.

WRIGHT, Thomas T.——B: Jan. 25, 1936, Denver, CO, *Pres.*, Wright-Leasure Co.; **PRIM RE ACT:** Broker, Consultant, Developer, Owner/Investor, Property Manager; **PROFL AFFIL & HONORS:** CCIM, SIR; **EDUC:** BA, 1959, Econ. & Bus. Admin., The Coll. of ID, Caldwell, ID; **OTHER ACT & HONORS:** Commnr., ID RE Commn. 1977-present; TR., The Coll. of ID, 1980-present; Chmn., Ada Cty. Bd. of Adjustment 1971-79; Dir., Pioneer Title Co. of Ada Cty.; **HOME ADD:** 3146 Catalina Ln., Boise, ID 83705, (208)342-8091; **BUS ADD:** Idaho 1st Pl., Ste. 1701, Boise, ID 83702, (208)345-1842.

WRIGHT, William R.——B: Castleford, ID, *Relocation Administrator*, Ebby Halliday, Realtors, Relocation Services Div.; **PRIM RE ACT:** Broker; **OTHER RE ACT:** Corp. relocation serv.; **SERVICES:** Relocating employees of corp. moving to Dallas/Ft. Worth; **REP CLIENTS:** Metroplex area; **PREV EMPLOY:** Owned Realty World C.P. Wright; Taught elmentary school for 15 yrs. prior to RE; **PROFL AFFIL & HONORS:** RNMI; MAR; TX Assn. of Realtors; TX Chap. CRB; Arlington Bd. of Realtors; Local, TX and Nat. Women's Council of Realtors; SME, GRI; CRB; **EDUC:** BS, 1958, Educ./Speech/Eng., Brigham Young Univ.; **GRAD EDUC:** Grad. Work, Univ. of UT; **OTHER ACT & HONORS:** Arlington Women's Club; **HOME ADD:** 4155 Shady Valley Dr., Arlington, TX 76013, (817)461-4094; **BUS ADD:** 2101 Roosevelt Dr., Arlington, TX 76013, (817)261-2600.

WRIGLEY, Benham R., Jr.——B: Oct. 13, 1945, Albany, NY, *Atty.*, Schmidt, Howlett, Van't Hof, Snell & Vana; **PRIM RE ACT:** Attorney, Consultant, Owner/Investor; **SERVICES:** Atty. & counsel for RE devel.; **PROFL AFFIL & HONORS:** ABA, State Bar of MI; **EDUC:** BA, 1967, Acctg., Lehigh Univ.; **GRAD EDUC:** JD, 1970, Northwestern Univ. Sch. of Law; **OTHER ACT & HONORS:** Counsel member for 6 yrs. on Real Prop. law Sect. of State of MI; **HOME ADD:** 528 Cambridge SE, East Grand Rapids, MI 49506, (616)458-5687; **BUS ADD:** 700 Frey Bldg., Grand Rapids, MI 49503, (616)459-5151.

WRIGLEY, Robert T.——B: Oct. 5, 1944, Philadelphia, PA, *President*, Berwind Realty Services, Inc., Subsidiary of Berwind Corp.; **PRIM RE ACT:** Consultant, Owner/Investor; **SERVICES:** Investment management: placing and safeguarding real estate equity investments for Berwind Corporation and Affiliates; Consulting: Acquisition, developmental and disposition services; **PROFL AFFIL & HONORS:** Member, Bd. of Indepro, Inc., Subsidiary of Penn Mutual Life Insurance Co.; **EDUC:** 1962-1966, Univ. PA, Philadelphia; **OTHER ACT & HONORS:** Chmn., Bd. of Deacons, Central Schwenkfelder Church, Worcester, PA; Member, Advisory Board, Holy Redeemer Hospital, Meadowbrook PA; Union League of Philadelphia, PA; Huntingdon Valley Country Club, PA; F & AM Lodge #51 Philadelphia, PA; Museum of Art, Philadelphia, PA; Smithsonian Club, Washington, DC; Zoological Society, Philadelphia, PA; PA Society of Sons of Revolution; Sons of American Revolution; Society of Founders and Patriots; Sons of Saint George; Sons of Union Veterans; Historical Society of Pennsylvania; **HOME ADD:** 919 Lorien Dr., Gwynedd Valley, PA 19437; **BUS ADD:** 3000 Centre Square West, 1500 Market St., Philadelphia, PA 19102.

WRONSKY, Burt P.——B: Mar. 18, 1942, Passaic, NJ, *Dir. of RE*, Supermarkets General Corp., Howland-Steinbach; **OTHER RE ACT:** RE site selection & negotiation - retail; **PREV EMPLOY:** Phillips Petroleum - Forbes Oil Company; **PROFL AFFIL & HONORS:** Intl. Council of Shopping Ctrs.; **EDUC:** BS, 1964, Bus. Educ., OH No. Univ.; **HOME ADD:** 59 Old Farmers Rd., Long Valley, NJ 07853, (201)876-4073; **BUS ADD:** 301 Blair Rd., Woodbridge, NJ 07095, (201)499-3775.

WU, Albert King——*Owner*; **PRIM RE ACT:** Broker, Consultant, Developer, Owner/Investor, Property Manager, Syndicator; **SERVICES:** Commercial Investment counseling; **PROFL AFFIL & HONORS:** NAR, CA Assn. of Realtors, Intl. Exchangers Assn., Intl. Council of Shopping Ctrs.; **BUS ADD:** 1530 The Alameda, PO Box 3286, San Jose, CA 95156, (408)294-6767.

WUENSCHER, David E.——B: Oct. 22, 1936, St. Louis, MO, *Exec. VP*, Real Estate Analysts, Ltd.; **PRIM RE ACT:** Consultant, Instructor; **OTHER RE ACT:** RE Analyst; **SERVICES:** RE investment counseling, valuation and consultant servs.; **REP CLIENTS:** Builders, devels., fin. instns., investors, govt. (state, local, fed.); **PREV EMPLOY:** RE Research Corp., 1966-77; **PROFL AFFIL & HONORS:** Chmn., Municipal Planning Commn., 1970-78; **EDUC:** BS/BA, 1969, Bus., Urban Planning, WA Univ., St. Louis, MO; **GRAD EDUC:** Grad. Courses, RE; **OTHER ACT & HONORS:** Bd. of Dir., Metro. St. Louis Urban League; Bd. of Dir., St. Mary on the Mt. Rehabiliatation Hospital; **HOME ADD:** 12065 Bridal Shire Ct., Creve Coeur, MO 63141, (314)569-1772; **BUS ADD:** 9818 Clayton Rd., St. Louis, MO 63124, (314)997-7325.

WUNDERLI, John M.——B: July 6, 1939, Salt Lake City, UT, *Dir. of Legal Affairs and RE*, U & I Inc.; **PRIM RE ACT:** Attorney, Developer, Owner/Investor, Property Manager; **OTHER RE ACT:** Seller, over 50 million, book value of discontinued sugar div.; **PREV EMPLOY:** Partner in Woodbury, Wunderli, Sorenson, devels. of comml. RE & counselor to S & L and ins.; **PROFL AFFIL & HONORS:** UT State Bar.; ABA, Chmn. Lesiglature & Taxation Comms., Salt Lake Bd. of Realtors, UT Bd. of Realtors, Sub. Chmn. RE Section of UT Bar; **EDUC:** BA, 1964, Pol. Sci., Econ., German, Univ. of UT; **GRAD EDUC:** JD, 1967, Law, Univ. of UT, Coll. of Law; **EDUC HONORS:** Honor Frat. & Grad. of Honors Program; **MIL SERV:** MI, Capt., Bronze Star; **HOME ADD:** 1291 Wasatch Dr., Salt Lake City, UT 84108, (801)582-5445; **BUS ADD:** PO Box 6437, Salt Lake City, UT 84106, (801)532-6800.

WYANT, P.J.——B: Apr. 22, 1926, St. Mary, WV, *VP, Relocation*, Manning Realty Co., Inc., Corporate Relocation; **PRIM RE ACT:** Broker, Consultant, Appraiser, Property Manager; **OTHER RE ACT:** Relocation and referral; **PROFL AFFIL & HONORS:** RNMI; CRB; CRS; **EDUC:** BA, 1949, Sociology, Univ. of TX; **MIL SERV:** USN, Res., Midshipman, 1943-1945; **OTHER ACT & HONORS:** Rotary; **HOME ADD:** 1819 Laney Dr., Longview, TX 75601, (214)757-5671; **BUS ADD:** 450 Loop 281, Longview, TX 75601, (214)757-4484.

WYCKOFF, Bill——Amoco Realty Co.; **PRIM RE ACT:** Developer; **BUS ADD:** Clements Ferry Rd., PO Box 987, Mt. Pleasant, SC 29464, (803)884-6151.*

WYLLIE, H. Gordon——B: Aug. 30, 1927, Auburn, NY, *Chmn., Pres.*, S.E. Prop., Inc. (Affiliate - S.E. Banking Corp.); **OTHER RE ACT:** Corp. RE, dev. mgmt.; **SERVICES:** Site selection, surplus prop. sales, design and construction, mgmt. trust RE portfolio, consultants, etc.; **PREV EMPLOY:** VP, Eastern Shopping Ctrs Inc. (1960-1967); Exec. VP, Chrysler Realty Corp. (1967-1971); Exec. VP, RE, J.F.P. Enterprises Inc.; **PROFL AFFIL & HONORS:** Past Chmn., NACORE; Member, Bd. of TR., NACORE; Member, ULI; ICSC; **EDUC:** Bus., Univ. of VT; **OTHER ACT & HONORS:** Bd. of Dir., Off St. Parking Authority; Greater Miami Inc.; Coral Reef Yacht Club; Certified Shopping Ctr. Mgr., ICSC; **HOME TEL:** (305)577-3718; **BUS ADD:** 100 S Biscayne Blvd., Miami, FL 33131, (305)577-3718.

WYMAN, George C.——B: Jan. 3, 1941, Boston, MA, *Broker*, Carter & Assoc., Brokerage; **PRIM RE ACT:** Broker; **SERVICES:** Office leasing, purchasing bldg./office condos.; **PREV EMPLOY:** Banking, IBM, Landlord (Apts./Office Bldgs.); **EDUC:** BA, 1963, Bus., Univ. of NC; **HOME ADD:** 165 River N. Dr., Atlanta, GA 30328, (404)394-5378; **BUS ADD:** Suite 600, 1100 Spring St., Atlanta, GA 30367, (404)873-3981.

WYMAN, Morton——*Exec. VP*, American Greetings Corp.; **PRIM RE ACT:** Property Manager; **BUS ADD:** 10500 American Rd., Cleveland, OH 44144, (216)252-7300.*

WYNN, Claude F.——B: Oct. 15, 1949, San Francisco, CA, *VP*, Century Development Corp., Planning & Design; **PRIM RE ACT:** Developer; **SERVICES:** Comml. RE devel., mgmt., Leasing, ownership; **PREV EMPLOY:** The Horne Co. Realtors, Houston, TX; **PROFL AFFIL & HONORS:** ULI, Amer. Planning Assn., PMI; **EDUC:** BArch., 1974, Arch., Rice Univ.; **GRAD EDUC:** MArch. in Urban Design, 1975, RE Devel., Rice Univ.; **EDUC HONORS:** Pres. List; **OTHER ACT & HONORS:** Houston C of C; South Main Ctr. Assn.; Downtown Houston Assn.; Rice Design Alliance; St. John The Divine Episcopal Church; **HOME ADD:** 10815 Oak Hollow, Houston, TX 77024, (713)464-6512; **BUS ADD:** 5 Greenway Plaza, Suite 1700, Houston, TX 77046, (713)621-9500.

WYNN, Marvin L.——*Mgr.*, Industries for Tulsa, Inc.; **PRIM RE ACT:** Developer; **BUS ADD:** 616 South Boston, Tulsa, OK 74119, (918)585-1428.*

WYNNE, James J.——B: Oct. 22, 1944, Detroit, MI, *Part.*, Fitzsimons-Wynne Dev. Corp.; **PRIM RE ACT:** Developer, Builder, Property Manager, Owner/Investor; **SERVICES:** Builders of condos. office bldgs.; **PROFL AFFIL & HONORS:** Bldg. Indus. Assn. Member; **EDUC:** BCE, 1965, Purdue Univ.; **GRAD EDUC:** Automotive Engr., 1967, Chrysler Inst.; **EDUC HONORS:** Tau Beta Pi, Epsilon; **HOME ADD:** 18 Misty Acres Rd., Rolling Hills Estates, CA 90274, (213)541-0640; **BUS ADD:** 27520 Hawthorne Blvd. Suite 250, Rolling Hills Estates, CA 90274, (213)377-0400.

WYNPERLE, William F., Jr.——B: Jan. 21, 1947, Great Neck, NY, *Investor*; **PRIM RE ACT:** Owner/Investor; **EDUC:** BBA, 1969, Fin. & Mgmt., Univ. of Miami; **MIL SERV:** US Army, Sgt.; **OTHER ACT & HONORS:** Wings Club; **HOME ADD:** 26 Franklin Pl., Great Neck, NY 11023, (516)829-9481; **BUS ADD:** 26 Franklin Pl., Great Neck, NY 11023, (201)573-8000.

WYSE, Jack J.——B: Apr. 4, 1914, Cleveland, OH, *Publisher*, Properties Magazine; **PRIM RE ACT:** Developer, Owner/Investor; **OTHER RE ACT:** Publisher; **PROFL AFFIL & HONORS:** NAREE, MBA; **EDUC:** BA, 1935, Bus. Admin., W. Reserve Univ.; **MIL SERV:** USN, Consultant; **OTHER ACT & HONORS:** Univ. Club-Rotary, Bldg. Indus. Assoc., Apt. Owners Assoc.; **HOME ADD:** 19101 Van Aken Blvd., Shaker Hts., OH 44122, (216)751-1872; **BUS ADD:** 4900 Euclid Ave., Cleveland, OH 44103, (216)431-7666.

WYSOCKI, F. Michael——B: Sept. 12, 1947, Philadelphia, PA, *Atty., Partner*, Rawle & Henderson; **PRIM RE ACT:** Attorney; **SERVICES:** Legal and bus. counseling; **REP CLIENTS:** Devels. of comml. and resid. props.; **PREV EMPLOY:** Garfinkel & Volpicelli; **PROFL AFFIL & HONORS:** ABA; PA and Philadelphia Bar Assns. (RE Sections); Condo. Comm. of PA Bar Assn., Lecturer, PA Bar Inst.; **EDUC:** BA with Distinction, 1969, Poli. Sci., George Washington Univ.; **GRAD EDUC:** JD, 1972, Law, Univ. of PA, Law School; **EDUC HONORS:** Phi Beta Kappa, Cum Laude Grad.; **HOME ADD:** 250 Deepdale Rd., Wayne, PA 19087, (215)687-3169; **BUS ADD:** 211 S. Broad St., 16th Floor, Philadelphia, PA 19107, (215)875-4115.

XELLIHEN, Barry S.——B: Apr.23, 1940, Quincy, MA, *VP*, Peabody Prop., Inc.; **PRIM RE ACT:** Broker, Attorney; **SERVICES:** Complete prop. mgmt. service; **PROFL AFFIL & HONORS:** Home Builders, IREM, CPM; **EDUC:** 1960, Bldg. Construction, Wentworth Inst.; **HOME ADD:** 30 Seans Rd., Milton, MA 02186, (617)848-4442; **BUS ADD:** 536 Granite St., Braintree, MA 02184, (617)848-4442.

YADO, Jess J., III——B: Sept. 15, 1929, Tampa, FL, *Atty.*, Yado, Keel, Nelson, Casper, Bergmann & Newcomer, P.A.; **PRIM RE ACT:** Attorney; **SERVICES:** Legal counseling and representation in purchase and sales contracts, closings and litigation; **REP CLIENTS:** Clients purchasing real prop. from resid. homes to hotels and motels in the multi-million dollar price; clients needing counseling regarding title or contractual problems; **PROFL AFFIL & HONORS:** Amer. Bar Assn.; FL Bar; Tampa Hills Bar Assn.; Acad. of FL Trial Lawyers; Bay

Area Trial Lawyers Assn.; **EDUC:** BBA, 1952, Mktg., Univ. of FL; **GRAD EDUC:** JD (LLB), 1958, Univ. of FL; **MIL SERV:** US Army, Capt., DSM, Korean Silver Medal, UN Silver Medal, Nat. Defense Medal; **OTHER ACT & HONORS:** Sertoma, Dir., Sec. & Legal Counsel for Fed. S&L Assn.; fluent in Spanish; **HOME ADD:** 3002 W. Robson St., Tampa, FL 33614, (813)932-3498; **BUS ADD:** 4950 W. Kennedy Blvd., Suite 603, Tampa, FL 33609, (813)870-2660.

YAGER, C. Edward, II——B: May 15, 1931, Ft. Worth, TX, *Pres.*, Yager & Co. Inc.; **PRIM RE ACT:** Broker, Consultant, Appraiser; **SERVICES:** Practice ltd. to income prop. brokerage and RE counseling; **REP CLIENTS:** Pension funds, bank trusts, REIT's, ins. cos., instnl. investors and income props.; **PREV EMPLOY:** 26 years self employed in RE; **PROFL AFFIL & HONORS:** IREM, NAR, TX Assn. of Realtors, Soc. of RE Appraisers, Ft. Worth Bd. of Realtors, CPM; SRA; **EDUC:** 1954, Fin., Law, Bus., TX Christian Univ., Ft. Worth; **HOME ADD:** 200 Hazelwood Dr., Ft. Worth, TX 76107, (817)737-4580; **BUS ADD:** Suite 600 Summit Office Park, 1200 Summit, Ft. Worth, TX 76102, (817)336-9891.

YAMIN, Thomas M.——*Sr. VP*, Stone-East/Eastdil Assoc.; **PRIM RE ACT:** Broker, Consultant, Property Manager, Owner/Investor; **SERVICES:** Corporate advisory & disposition serv.; **REP CLIENTS:** Chrysler Corp., Corvettes, Citibanks, Food Fair, Amterre Dev., Mobil (Montgomery Ward); **PROFL AFFIL & HONORS:** CPM, ICSC, Bd. of Dir. - Eastoil Realty Inc.; **EDUC:** BA, 1960, Psychology-Philosophy, Yale; **MIL SERV:** US Army, SP-5; **OTHER ACT & HONORS:** Bd. of Trustees Car Reichman Foundation, Class Council - Yale; **HOME ADD:** 2 Buena Vista, East Chester, NY 10709, (914)632-3992; **BUS ADD:** 40 W. 57 St., New York, NY 10019, (212)397-2743.

YANARI, Dale M.——B: Apr. 4, 1947, Denver, CO, *CPA*, Yanari, Watson, Lyons & Co., P.C.; **PRIM RE ACT:** Consultant; **OTHER RE ACT:** CPA; **SERVICES:** Tax planning, auditing & acctg.; **REP CLIENTS:** Realtors, prop. mgmt., devel, cont., sub-cont.; **PROFL AFFIL & HONORS:** AICPA, CO Soc. of CPAs; **EDUC:** BS, BA, 1969, Acctg., Univ. of Denver; **EDUC HONORS:** Cum Laude; **HOME ADD:** 07 Granite, Frisco, CO 80443.

YANICKE, Robert A.——B: June 27, 1948, Milwaukee, WI, *Operations Mgr.*, Carley Management Co., Inc.; **PRIM RE ACT:** Broker, Consultant, Architect; **SERVICES:** Investment counseling, prop. mgmt., interior space planning; **REP CLIENTS:** Investors in comml. prop.; **PREV EMPLOY:** First WI Devel. Corp., 1972-1978; **PROFL AFFIL & HONORS:** BOMA; IREM, CPM, 1979; **EDUC:** BArch., 1971, Iowa State Univ.; **HOME ADD:** 611 E. Birch Ave., Whitefish Bay, WI 53217, (414)964-9979; **BUS ADD:** 735 N. Water St., Milwaukee, WI 53202, (414)765-0604.

YANKO, Roger——B: Mar. 20, 1951, St. Louis, MO, *Project Mgr.*, The Harbert-Equitable Joint Venture, Riverchase; **PRIM RE ACT:** Property Manager; **PREV EMPLOY:** Harland-Bartholomew and Associates, Planners, Engrg., Arch.; **PROFL AFFIL & HONORS:** NAHB, ASLA, BAHE, API; **EDUC:** BS, 1973, Civil Engrg. and Planning, Univ. of MO at Col.; **GRAD EDUC:** MArch., 1975, Regional and Urban Planning, Univ. of IL at Champaign-Urbana; **EDUC HONORS:** U. of MO Scholar Athlete (Whitefoot Award) 1973, Cum Laude - Grad. with perfect 5.0/5.0 GPA; **OTHER ACT & HONORS:** ULI, B'ham. C of C; Chmn.-Riverchase Sewer Dist.; past Chmn.-R/C Fire Dist.; Pres.-Riverchase Resid. and Bus. Assns.; **HOME ADD:** 2501 Woodmeadow Pl., Birmingham, AL 35216, (205)987-0391; **BUS ADD:** PO Box 1297, Birmingham, AL 35201, (205)988-4730.

YANO, Mas——B: June 7, 1918, Ogden, UT, *Atty. & Counselor*, Mas Yano & Associates; **PRIM RE ACT:** Consultant, Attorney, Regulator, Owner/Investor; **SERVICES:** Legal serv. and consulting; **REP CLIENTS:** Devel. of resid., comml. & indus. props.; **PROFL AFFIL & HONORS:** UT State Bar, Real Prop. sect.; Salt Lake City. Bar Assn., Real prop. section, UT State Bar, Atty. at Law; **EDUC:** BS, 1944, Econ., Bus. Admin., Brigham Young Univ.; **GRAD EDUC:** JD, 1948, Univ. of UT; **EDUC HONORS:** Grad. with High Honors; **OTHER ACT & HONORS:** Alpine Ctry. Club, Sports Mall Metro, Community Serv. Council, Past Bd. Member Community Nursing Servs.; **HOME ADD:** 1525 Evergreen Ln., Salt Lake City, UT 84106, (801)484-6670; **BUS ADD:** 175 S.W. Temple 500, Salt Lake City, UT 84101, (801)363-9880.

YARBENET, George——*Pres.*, Gulf & Western Realty Co.; **PRIM RE ACT:** Property Manager; **BUS ADD:** One Gulf & Western Plaza, New York, NY 10023, (212)333-7000.*

YARNALL, Celeste——B: July 26, 1944, Long Beach, CA, *Pres.*, Celeste Yarnall and Associates Commercial RE; **PRIM RE ACT:** Broker, Consultant; **OTHER RE ACT:** Write columns on comml. RE for Century City News; **REP CLIENTS:** Charles Luckman's Exclusive Leasing Agent for 9200-9220 Sunset Blvd., Los Angeles, CA; **PROFL AFFIL & HONORS:** L.A. Realty Bd., First Woman's Bank of CA Advisory Bd., Cen. City C of C, Bev. Hills C of C, W. Hollywood C of C, W. LA C of C, Realtor; **BUS ADD:** 9200 Sunset Blvd., Penthouse 20, Los Angeles, CA 90069, (213)278-1385.

YASCHIK, Henry——B: Dec. 3, 1910, Argentina, *Pres.*, Yaschik Enterprises, Investment Banker; **PRIM RE ACT:** Developer, Banker, Lender, Owner/Investor, Insuror; **OTHER RE ACT:** Pres. Charleston Capital Corp.; **PROFL AFFIL & HONORS:** Who's Who in Fin.; Directory of US Banking Execs.; **MIL SERV:** USCGR, 1944-1945; **OTHER ACT & HONORS:** Past Pres., Masons Friendship Lodges; Charleston Jewish Welfare Fund; Bd. of Dir., Charleston Opera Co.; **HOME ADD:** 27 Devereux Ave., Charleston, SC 29403; **BUS ADD:** 111 Church St., POB 328, Charleston, SC 29402, (803)723-6464.

YASSER, James M.——B: Nov. 11, 1949, Bridgeport, CT, *VP*, P.J. Carlin Constr. Co., Carlin-Atlas Corp.; **PRIM RE ACT:** Developer, Builder, Owner/Investor, Property Manager; **SERVICES:** Devel. of mkt. rate resid. comml. projects; **REP CLIENTS:** Gen. Contractor.Constr. mgmt. for public and private clients; **PREV EMPLOY:** Matthews & Wright, Inc., 1978-81; NYC Housing & Devel. Admin., 1973-74; South Bronx Comm. Housing, 1972, 1973, 1974-76; **PROFL AFFIL & HONORS:** NAHRO; NYC HPD Citizens Advisory Comm.; **EDUC:** Bach. of Gen. Studies, 1971, Pol. Sci., Soc., Univ. of Miami; **GRAD EDUC:** JD, 1979, RE, Brooklyn Law Sch.; **EDUC HONORS:** Student Body Pres., Ibis Citation, Organge Key Soc., Who's Who in Amer. Colls. & Univs.; **HOME ADD:** 55 E 9th St., New York, NY 10003; **BUS ADD:** 140 Huguenot St., New Rochelle, NY 10801, (212)597-9500.

YATES, John David——B: Oct. 22, 1959, Phoenix, AZ, *Research Analyst*, Cushman & Wakefield of Arizona, Inc., Comml. Office Div.; **PRIM RE ACT:** Consultant, Architect; **OTHER RE ACT:** Urban planning, design and devel.; **SERVICES:** Research and analysis of comml. offic, residential, and resort mkts.; **REP CLIENTS:** Clients served by Cushman & Wakefield of AZ, Inc.; **PREV EMPLOY:** Mktg. Analyst, Ben Brooks & Associates, Inc. Comml. Group; Dept. of Planning, City of Phoenix; **PROFL AFFIL & HONORS:** APA; Rho Epsilon Frat. (Profl. RE Organization), Designee AICP (Am. Inst. Cert. Planners); **EDUC:** BS, 1979, City Govt., First Degree; Urban Planning & Design, Second Degree, AZ State Univ.; **GRAD EDUC:** MEP (Masters Env. Planning), 1982 (in Progress), Urban Planning, RE/Fin., AZ State Univ.; **EDUC HONORS:** Honors Grad.; **OTHER ACT & HONORS:** Heard Museum, Phoenix Art Museum; Phoenix Symphony Men's Guild; Southwestern Assn. on Indian Artist; **HOME ADD:** 6801 North 47th St., Town of Paradise Valley, AZ 85253, (602)959-5474; **BUS ADD:** 4747 North 22nd St., Suite 400, Phoenix, AZ 85016, (602)957-0111.

YATES, Ronald F.——B: Nov. 30, 1951, Brady, TX, *Pres.*, Ronald F. Yates, P.C., Atty.; Kingsland Title Co.; Central Texas Land Titles, Inc.; **PRIM RE ACT:** Attorney, Owner/Investor; **OTHER RE ACT:** Title Ins.; **SERVICES:** Legal and Title Ins.; **REP CLIENTS:** Furnished upon request; **PROFL AFFIL & HONORS:** Hill Cty. Bar Assn., ABA, State Bar of TX, TX Trial Lawyers Assn., Highland Lakes Bd. of Realtors, TX Land Titles Assn.; **EDUC:** BA, 1973, Govt. E. European Politics, Univ. of TX at Austin; **GRAD EDUC:** JD, 1975, Bus. Law, So. Methodist Univ.; **OTHER ACT & HONORS:** Cty. Judge, Llano Cty., Tx, 1978; City Atty., Granite Shoals, TX 1979-present; Llano Cty. Tax Appraisal Bd.; Kingsland Mcpl. Utility District Bd.; **HOME ADD:** P.O. Drawer 89, Kingsland, TX 78639, (915)388-6488; **BUS ADD:** Ranch Rd. 2900, P.O. Drawer 410, Kingsland, TX 78639, (915)388-4547.

YATUNI, Ray——B: Oct. 27, 1921, Gardner, IL, *Pres.*, Epic Assoc.; **PRIM RE ACT:** Broker, Consultant, Appraiser, Owner/Investor, Property Manager; **SERVICES:** Investment counseling, prop. mgmt. & maint.; **PREV EMPLOY:** Consultant Engr., Mfg. Co. Pres., Purex Mktg. Staff (Ind. div.); **PROFL AFFIL & HONORS:** RECI; CAR, Inv. Div.; O.C. Inv. Realtor Inst.; OCAREIB; EOC, Bd. of Realtors; WOC Bd. of Realtors; Gold Card Exchanger, RECI, GRI; **EDUC:** BS, 1951, Bus. & Mech. Engrg., Univ of IL, Yale, USC; **GRAD EDUC:** Study of Law, LaSalle Univ.; **MIL SERV:** USAF; Capt.; **HOME ADD:** 15691 Burning Tree, Westminster, CA 92683, (714)835-0381; **BUS ADD:** 1525 E. 17th St, Suite C, Santa Ana, CA 92701, (714)835-0381.

YEAGER, Gerald F.——B: Mar. 31, 1941, Toledo, OH, *Pres.*, Simms-Yeager Corp.; **PRIM RE ACT:** Broker, Consultant, Developer, Builder, Owner/Investor, Syndicator, Real Estate Publisher; **OTHER RE ACT:** Survival kit for the 80's, 50 Creative Fin. Ideas; **SERVICES:** Complete comml. dept., investment counseling, valuation devel. and synd. of comml. prop., bldg.; **PROFL AFFIL & HONORS:** Cert.

Comml. - Investment Member; **EDUC:** BBA, 1964, Bus., Univ. of Toledo; **OTHER ACT & HONORS:** C of C, Realtor/Computer Selection Comm.; **HOME ADD:** 661 Doral Lane, Melbourne, FL 32935, (305)254-8891; **BUS ADD:** 454 N. Harbor City Blvd., Melbourne, FL 32935, (305)259-7878.

YEALIN, Richard A.——*Secy. & Treas.*, Checker Motors Corp.; **PRIM RE ACT:** Property Manager; **BUS ADD:** 2016 N. Pitcher St., Kalamazoo, MI 49007, (616)343-6121.*

YECKES, Arthur——**B:** Sept. 30, 1923, NY, NY, *Pres.*, Arthur Yeckes Real Estate; **PRIM RE ACT:** Broker, Builder, Owner/Investor, Property Manager, Insuror; **SERVICES:** Const. & prop. mgmt. for our own groups; **PROFL AFFIL & HONORS:** RE Bd. of NY, Inc.; Nat. Realty Club; Nat. Assn. of RE Bds.; Rent Stabilization Bd.; Comm. Housing (CHIP); **EDUC:** Engrg., Grinnel Coll./Cornell Univ.; **MIL SERV:** USAF and Ordinance, 2nd Lt., European Theater; **OTHER ACT & HONORS:** Jockey Club; Tower Club; N. Palm Beach Ctry. Club; Old Port Yacht Club; **HOME ADD:** 132 Lakeshore Dr., N. Palm Beach, FL 33408, (305)626-1304; **BUS ADD:** 784 US Hwy. Rte. #1, N. Palm Beach, FL 33408, (305)626-0441.

YEDLIN, Benedict——**B:** Sept. 21, 1922, Brooklyn, NY, *Pres.*, Benedict Yedlin, Inc.; **PRIM RE ACT:** Developer, Builder, Owner/Investor; **PROFL AFFIL & HONORS:** NAHB; ULI; NAIOP; **EDUC:** BA, 1946, Geology, Brooklyn Coll.; **MIL SERV:** USAAF, S/Sgt., Air Medal with Oak Leaf Clusters; **BUS ADD:** 1000 Herrontown Rd., Princeton, NJ 08540, (609)921-6651.

YELINEK, Keith A.——**B:** Aug. 30, 1936, Livingston, WI, *Sr. VP Risk Mgmt.*, Verex Corp., a Greyhound Subsidiary; **PRIM RE ACT:** Owner/Investor; **SERVICES:** Mort. loan insurance; **EDUC:** BS, 1959; **GRAD EDUC:** JD, 1962; **OTHER ACT & HONORS:** Member Madison Bd. of Educ. 1968-1974; **HOME ADD:** One Larch Circle, Madison, WI 53705, (608)238-3208; **BUS ADD:** P.O. Box 7066, Madison, WI 53707, (608)257-2527.

YELTON, Robert H.——**B:** Nov. 8, 1940, Cinti, OH, *Pres.*, Bay Devel. Corp.; **PRIM RE ACT:** Developer, Builder, Owner/Investor, Property Manager, Syndicator; **SERVICES:** Devel. & synd. of comml., indus. and resid. props.; **REP CLIENTS:** State Mutual Ins. Co., NE Merchants Bank, Morgan Stanley; **PREV EMPLOY:** World Bank 1977, Aramco 1976, State Street Devel. Co. of Boston 1971-75, The Arch. Collaborative 1967-70, US Peace Corps. Tunisia; **PROFL AFFIL & HONORS:** NAR, Gr. Boston RE Bd., AIA, AIP; **EDUC:** BS, 1964, Arch., Univ. of Cincinnati; **GRAD EDUC:** MBA, 1977, Bus., Urban Devel., Harvard Bus. Sch.; MCP, 1969, Harvard Des. Sch.; MUA, 1969, Harvard Des. Sch.; **EDUC HONORS:** Mellon Fellow, Goldman Sachs Fellow; **OTHER ACT & HONORS:** Dir. Nashoba Valley Winery, Tr. May Inst.; **HOME ADD:** 72 Pine Rd., Brookline, MA 02167, (617)277-5211; **BUS ADD:** 184 High St., Boston, MA 02110, (617)482-0356.

YELVERTON, D. Craig——**B:** Nov. 21, 1946, Columbus, OH, *Area Mgr.*, Emkay Development Co., Inc.; **PRIM RE ACT:** Developer, Builder, Property Manager; **PREV EMPLOY:** Daum Ind., Inc., 1973-1974; W. TX Builders, Inc., 1971-1973; **PROFL AFFIL & HONORS:** Intl. Council of Shopping Ctrs.; BOMA; Nat. Assn. of Review Appraisers, Cert. Shopping Center Mgr.; CRA; **EDUC:** BBA, 1972, Mgmt., TX Tech. Univ.; **MIL SERV:** US Army, Staff Sgt.; **HOME ADD:** 1012 Berkeley St., Boise, ID 83705, (208)336-1511; **BUS ADD:** 1505 Tyrell Ln., Boise, ID 83706, (208)386-5243.

YEO, James R.——**B:** Oct. 17, 1941, Redwood City, CA, *Atty.*, James R. Yeo Attorney at Law; **PRIM RE ACT:** Broker, Consultant, Attorney, Developer, Builder, Instructor, Syndicator; **SERVICES:** Legal services to the RE and construction industries; **REP CLIENTS:** Lewis Homes of CA; Amer. Paint Co.; **PREV EMPLOY:** Deputy Cty. Counsel, Sacramento, CA; VP, Lewis Homes of CA; VP Republic Mgmt. Co.; **PROFL AFFIL & HONORS:** CA Bar Assn., Lic. CA RE Broker, Instr. - RE law and tax law, Los Rios Community Coll. Dist.; **EDUC:** AA, Bus., Amer. River Coll.; **GRAD EDUC:** JD, 1970, Law, Univ. of Pacific; **MIL SERV:** CA Army National Guard, 1960-1981, Maj., ACROM; **OTHER ACT & HONORS:** Cerebral Palsy Assn., Building Industry Assn.; **HOME ADD:** 6880 White Ln., Loomis, CA 95650; **BUS ADD:** 9216 Kiefer Blvd., Sacramento, CA 95826, (916)363-2617.

YESBERG, Walter E.——**B:** June 2, 1940, St. Louis, MO, *Nat. Program Consultant*, Bank Bldg. Corp., Depositec; **PRIM RE ACT:** Consultant; **SERVICES:** Economic analysis, physical distribution strategies; **REP CLIENTS:** Fin. inst., private investor, devel., public agencies; **PREV EMPLOY:** Wenzlick Research Corp. (First Union Bancorp.), St. Louis, MO; Wash. Univ., St. Louis, Instr. RE; **EDUC:** AB, 1963, Econ., Univ. of MO, Columbia; **GRAD EDUC:** MS, 1971, RE Investment Analysis & Appraisal, Univ. of WI, Madison; **OTHER ACT & HONORS:** Chmn. Planning & Zoning Comm., Manchester, MO; **HOME ADD:** 517 Lalor Dr., Manchester, MO 63011, (314)227-2868; **BUS ADD:** 3260 Hampton Ave., St. Louis, MO 63139, (314)647-3800.

YOAKUM, Vance W.——*Assoc. Gen. Coun.*, Georgia-Pacific Corp.; **PRIM RE ACT:** Attorney, Property Manager; **BUS ADD:** 900 SW Fifth Ave., Portland, OR 97204, (503)222-5561.*

YODER, Richard B.——**B:** Sept. 25, 1929, Meyersdale, PA, *Pres.*, Allegheny Devel. Corp. and Allegheny RE Sales; **PRIM RE ACT:** Appraiser, Developer, Builder, Property Manager; **OTHER RE ACT:** Bd. Member of the WV Housing Devel. Fund (State Fin. Agency ofWV); **PROFL AFFIL & HONORS:** Pres., Home Builders Assn.; Chmn., Interagency Housing Council of WV; Governor Rockefeller Housing Council; **EDUC:** BA, 1955, Goshen Coll.; **GRAD EDUC:** MA, Educ., Goshen Coll.; Post Grad Studies, Soc. Sci., WV Univ.; **OTHER ACT & HONORS:** Appointed to special interim comm. by the Speaker of the House and Pres. of Senate; **HOME ADD:** 1209-B Pineview Dr., Morgantown, WV 26505, (304)599-2550; **BUS ADD:** 1225 Pineview Dr., Morgantown, WV 26505, (304)599-0845.

YODOGAWA, Jiro——**B:** Dec. 3, 1933, Tokyo, Japan, *Arch.*, Yodogawa-McCartan-Arch., P.C.; **PRIM RE ACT:** Architect, Developer; **SERVICES:** Arch. Design & Dev.; **REP CLIENTS:** Devel. and indiv. invest.; **PROFL AFFIL & HONORS:** AIA; **EDUC:** BArch, 1963, Arch., Univ. of OR, Eugene, OR; **HOME ADD:** 4226 S.W. 40th, Portland, OR 97221, (503)223-5455; **BUS ADD:** 213 S.W. Ash, Portland, OR 97204, (503)224-0424.

YOGI, Nolan K.——**B:** Sep. 29, 1947, Honolulu, HI, *Asst. Gen. Counsel*, The Way Intl., Corp. Legal Dept.; **PRIM RE ACT:** Attorney; **SERVICES:** Legal counseling and rep.; **REP CLIENTS:** The Way Intl. During 1977-79, Amer. Hawaiian Soy Co., Yamavi Enterprises Ltd. (Hawaii), Kalihi Neighborhood Assoc., General Counsel; **PREV EMPLOY:** Gen Practice Honolulu, HI, 1977 through 1979, Legal Asst. to Gen. Counsel, The Way Coll. of Emporia, KS, 1975-76; **PROFL AFFIL & HONORS:** HI Bar Assn., OH Bar Assn., Shelby Cty. Bar Assoc., ABA, Subcommittee Member, Real Prop. & Trust Div.; **EDUC:** BBA, 1971, Mktg., Univ. of HI; **GRAD EDUC:** JD, 1975, RE, Corp. Law, Drake Univ. Law School, Des Moines, IA; **EDUC HONORS:** Second Place, Univ. of HI Speech Finals 1971, Dean's List; **MIL SERV:** USAR, S/Sgt.; **OTHER ACT & HONORS:** State Coordinator, The Way of HI 1976-1977, B. of Theology, The Way Coll. of Biblical Research, Rome City, IN; Shelby Cty. Bar Assoc. Constitution/Ammendments Comm.; **BUS ADD:** 5555 Wierwille Rd., PO Box 328, New Knoxville, OH 45871, (419)753-2390.

YOLES, Zeev E.——**B:** Oct. 2l, 1940, Haifa, Israel, *VP*, Manufacturers Hanover Trust Co., RE; **PRIM RE ACT:** Banker, Lender; **SERVICES:** Const. loans & mort. fin.; **PROFL AFFIL & HONORS:** The RE Bd. of NY; **EDUC:** BBA, 1973, Bernard M. Baruch Coll.; **GRAD EDUC:** MBA, 1976, Bernard M. Baruch Coll.; **EDUC HONORS:** Magna Cum Laude; **OTHER ACT & HONORS:** Beta Gamma Sigma; **HOME ADD:** 24 Bennett Ave., New York, NY 10033; **BUS ADD:** 270 Park Ave., New York, NY 10017, (212)286-6466.

YONCE, Donald M., Sr.——**B:** Mar. 11, 1938, Rock Hill, SC, *Pres./Treas.*, ABBCO, Inc.; **PRIM RE ACT:** Broker, Consultant, Developer, Builder, Owner/Investor, Syndicator; **OTHER RE ACT:** Bldg. systems and energy efficiency export; **SERVICES:** Design and build; **PROFL AFFIL & HONORS:** Pres., MACI, Intl., 1977-1978; **EDUC:** Univ. of SC.; **HOME ADD:** 214 Lydia St., Rock Hill, SC 29730, (803)366-2372; **BUS ADD:** 1355 Ebenezer Rd., Rock Hill, SC 29730, (800)438-1242.

YORE, Alan R., AIA——**B:** Feb. 6, 1949, Chicago, IL, *Pres.*, Alan R. Yore and Associates, Inc.; **PRIM RE ACT:** Consultant, Engineer, Architect, Developer, Builder; **SERVICES:** Arch./engrg./const./devel.; **REP CLIENTS:** Comml. facilities, shopping ctrs., S&L, banks, indus. facilities, high-hazard indus. bldgs.; **PROFL AFFIL & HONORS:** AIA, Const. Specifications Inst., Corporate Member, AIA; **OTHER ACT & HONORS:** Plan. Commn., Village of Arlington Heights, 1979-present; **BUS ADD:** 219 W. University Dr., Arlington Hts., IL 60004, (312)255-3545.

YORK, Carl D.——**B:** May 4, 1952, Marion, IN, *Property Manager*, Triangle Associates, Inc.; **PRIM RE ACT:** Consultant, Instructor, Property Manager; **SERVICES:** Property managemnt and consulting services to condominium & cooperative communities; **REP CLIENTS:** Cooperative housing communities in Indiana & Iowa; **PREV EMPLOY:** IN Mgmt. Co.; **PROFL AFFIL & HONORS:** IN RE License, IREM CPM Candidate, National Apt. Assn., Certified Apt. Mgr.; **EDUC:** 1970-1974, Business, Journalism, Indiana Univ.; **OTHER ACT & HONORS:** Indiana Univ. Big Red Club, Masonic Lodge, Scottish Rite, Murat Shrine, Nominated as an Outstanding Young Man of America 1982; **HOME ADD:** 8350 Paso Del Norte, Indianapolis, IN 46227, (317)888-9469; **BUS ADD:** 921 E. 86th St., Suite 111, Indianapolis, IN 46240, (317)257-5137.

YORK, John C.——**B:** Apr. 27, 1946, Evansville, IN, *VP*, JMB Realty Corp.; **PRIM RE ACT:** Attorney, Owner/Investor, Syndicator; **SERVICES:** Devel. and synd. of comml. props.; **REP CLIENTS:** Carlyle RE Ltd. Partnership; JMB Income Props. Ltd. Partnerships; **PREV EMPLOY:** Mayer, Brown & Platt, 231 S. LaSalle St., Chicago, IL; **PROFL AFFIL & HONORS:** Licensed IL RE Broker; Housing Comm., MetroPolitan Housing and Planning Commn. (Chicago); Chicago Bar Assn.; Bd. of Dirs., Landmarks Preservation Council of IL; **EDUC:** BA, 1968, Vanderbilt Univ.; **GRAD EDUC:** JD, 1971, Harvard Univ. Law School; **EDUC HONORS:** Cum Laude; **OTHER ACT & HONORS:** Bd. of Dirs., Henrotin Hospital; **HOME ADD:** 1242 Lake Shore Dr., Chicago, IL 60610, (312)642-7434; **BUS ADD:** 875 N. MI Ave., Chicago, IL 60611, (312)440-4813.

YORK, Robert E.——**B:** June 6, 1930, Chicago, IL, *Office Mgr.*, D.F. Knox & Associates; **PRIM RE ACT:** Broker, Appraiser, Owner/Investor, Instructor, Property Manager; **SERVICES:** Gen. resid sales, investment servs., mgmt., rehab. appraisals; **REP CLIENTS:** Investors, attys., lenders; **PROFL AFFIL & HONORS:** Nat. Bd. Realtor; Lake Cty. Bd. Realtor; Nat. Assn. of Indep. Fee Appraisers; Lake Cty. Apt. Owners Assn., GRI, CRS, IFA; **MIL SERV:** Air Nat. Guard; Major; **HOME ADD:** 229 Bridgewood Dr., Antioch, IL 60002, (312)395-5450; **BUS ADD:** 2835 Grand Ave., Waukegan, IL 60085, (312)662-1380.

YOSHIMURA, Richard Mamoru——**B:** Aug. 18, 1928, Puunene, Maui, HI, *Chief Appraiser*, Bank of Hawaii, RE Loan Div.; **PRIM RE ACT:** Consultant, Appraiser, Banker; **SERVICES:** Valuation analysis, mkt. analysis, mkt. value of RE; **REP CLIENTS:** Mortgagors, brokers, correspondent banks, investors, secondary mkts. such as ins. cos., S & L, etc.; **PREV EMPLOY:** Is. Ins. Co., Ltd. - Ins. claims Adjustor, Account Exec.; **PROFL AFFIL & HONORS:** Member, Soc. of RE Appraisers; Member, Nat. Assn. of Review Appraisers, SRPA, SRA, CRA; **EDUC:** BA, 1956, Pre-Legal and Econ., Univ. of HI - US Army Command General & Staff; **MIL SERV:** US Army, Lt. Col.; **OTHER ACT & HONORS:** Pres., HI Claims (Ins.) Assn. (1955-56), Pres. Honolulu Chap. No. 67, Soc. of RE Appraisers 1974-75; **HOME ADD:** 5642 Anolike Place, Honolulu, HI 96821, (808)373-4005; **BUS ADD:** Financial Plaza of the Pacific, Honolulu, HI 96821, (808)537-8786.

YOUNG, Bruce G.——**B:** Feb. 4, 1944, San Antonio, TX, *Chief Fin. Officer*, EGS Metro Dev./Constr. Co.; **PRIM RE ACT:** Developer, Builder, Property Manager; **PROFL AFFIL & HONORS:** ICSC; **EDUC:** BA, 1970, RE & Corp. Fin., CA State Univ. at Fullerton; **GRAD EDUC:** MBA, 1971, Fin., Univ. of So. CA; **MIL SERV:** US Army, Sgt., 1966-1969; **BUS ADD:** P. O. Box 92959, Los Angeles, CA 90009, (213)649-3850.

YOUNG, David Michael——**B:** July 22, 1947, Woodland, CA, *Atty.*, Calfee & Young, Attys.; **PRIM RE ACT:** Attorney, Owner/Investor; **SERVICES:** RE Law, Consulting, Negotiations, Drafting & Litigation; **PROFL AFFIL & HONORS:** CA State Bar Assn., ABA; **EDUC:** BA, 1970, Econ., Univ. of the Pacific; **GRAD EDUC:** JD, 1974, School of Law, Univ. of CA, Davis Campus; **MIL SERV:** USAF, Sgt.; **OTHER ACT & HONORS:** Adv. Bd., River City Bank, Bd. of Dir., Woodland Memorial Hosp. Found., Atty., Yold Cty. Bd. of Realtors.; **HOME ADD:** 440 Pendegast St., Woodland, CA 95695, (916)666-3032; **BUS ADD:** 203 Court St., PO Box 1201, Woodland, CA 95695, (916)666-2185.

YOUNG, David O., Jr.——**B:** Nov. 5, 1951, Detroit, MI, *VP of Fin.*, Freeman, Smith & Associates, Inc.; **PRIM RE ACT:** Consultant, Architect, Developer, Owner/Investor, Property Manager; **SERVICES:** Arch. & interior design, investment counseling, demographic studies, devel. and prop. mgmt.; **REP CLIENTS:** Fin. instns., contractors, govt. and investors in comml. props.; **PREV EMPLOY:** Ford Motor Credit Corp., Comml., Indus. & RE Fin. 1974-78; Comml. Banking 1971-74; **PROFL AFFIL & HONORS:** ULI; Amer. Mgmt. Assn.; Natl. Trust for Hist. Preservation; **EDUC:** BS, 1977, Soc. Sci., MI State Univ.; **EDUC HONORS:** with Honors, elected to Honor's Coll.; **HOME ADD:** 916 Montevideo Dr., Lansing, MI 48917; **BUS ADD:** 3850 Capital City Blvd., Lansing, MI 48906, (517)323-3700.

YOUNG, Douglas A., Jr.——**B:** Mar. 1, 1939, Oxford, MS, *Pres.*, Douglas A. Young and Co.; **PRIM RE ACT:** Broker, Consultant, Instructor; **SERVICES:** Purchase, sale, lease of indus., retail and office props.; **PROFL AFFIL & HONORS:** RE Bd. of Kansas City, MO; NAR; Realtors Nat. Mktg. Inst.; CCIM Candidate; **EDUC:** BA, 1967, Hist./Pol. Sci., Delta State Univ.; **EDUC HONORS:** Who's Who Amer. Univ. & Coll,; Pres., Student Govt. Assn.; Dean's List; Omicron Delta Kappa; **OTHER ACT & HONORS:** Currently Member, Jackson Cty. Legislature; C of C, Greater Kansas City, Former VChmn., Local Affairs Comm.; C of C, Lenexa, KS, Membership Award; Pres. 1982, Goodwill Industries of Greater Kansas City, VP, Bd. of Dir., 1979 and 1980 and 1981, Member, Exec. Comm., Sec., Bd. of Dir., 1976-1978; Sons of the Revolution, Sec., 1976-1977, Member, Bd. of Dir., 1976-1977, Member, Exec. Comm., 1976-1977; Nat. Assn. of Ctys., Dir. 1980-81-82; MO Assn. of Ctys. - Dir., 1982; St. John's Methodist Church - Member, Admin. Bd. 1979-80-81-82; Chmn. Membership 1982; **HOME ADD:** 7430 Mercier, Kansas City, MO 64114, (816)361-3309; **BUS ADD:** 106 W. 14th St., Kansas City, MO 64105, (816)842-0593.

YOUNG, Elliott——**B:** May 4, 1937, Norfolk, VA, *Mgr. Comm'l. Dept.*, Drucker & Falk; **PRIM RE ACT:** Broker, Consultant, Property Manager; **SERVICES:** Investment Counseling; **PREV EMPLOY:** Computer Salesman, UNIVAC; **PROFL AFFIL & HONORS:** CPM, CCIM; **EDUC:** BA, 1959, Hist., VA Mil. Inst.; **MIL SERV:** USMC, Capt.; **BUS ADD:** Newport News VA 236079286 Warwick Blvd., (804)245-1541.

YOUNG, Evelyn K.——**B:** July 12, 1939, Spartanburg, SC, *VP*, Reed & Young Realty; **PRIM RE ACT:** Broker, Developer; **PROFL AFFIL & HONORS:** GRI, CRS, CRB; **HOME ADD:** 4228 Chaffee Rd., Spartanburg, SC 29301, (803)576-1550; **BUS ADD:** 114 Southport Rd., Spartanburg, SC 29301, (803)576-2532.

YOUNG, Glen E.——**B:** Sept. 25, 1923, Salt Lake City, UT, *Pres.*, AAA Realty, Inc. and Corporate Advisors; **PRIM RE ACT:** Broker, Consultant, Appraiser, Owner/Investor; **OTHER RE ACT:** Land consultant, lake front recreational land consultant, negotiator in RE; **SERVICES:** Sales, consultant and negotiators; **REP CLIENTS:** Lawyers, devels., investors; **PROFL AFFIL & HONORS:** Nat. Assn. of RE Brokers, MLS, SLREB; **EDUC:** 3 yrs., Bus., Econ. and Finance, Univ. of UT; **MIL SERV:** USMC, Enlisted, various decorations; **OTHER ACT & HONORS:** Church; **HOME ADD:** 1553 Yale Ave., Salt Lake City, UT 84105, (801)322-2225; **BUS ADD:** PO Box 2043, Salt Lake City, UT 84110, (801)364-4400.

YOUNG, Hallison H.——**B:** May 29, 1938, Marshall, TX, *Atty.*, Patmon & Young P.C.; **PRIM RE ACT:** Attorney, Owner/Investor, Syndicator; **SERVICES:** Legal; **REP CLIENTS:** Devels., synds., comm. grps., contrs., investors; **PREV EMPLOY:** IRS, 1961-65; **PROFL AFFIL & HONORS:** CA Bar; MI Bar; Wash. DC Bar, JD; **EDUC:** BS, 1960, Acctg., Wayne State Univ.; **GRAD EDUC:** JD, 1965, Law, Wayne State Univ.; **HOME ADD:** 1312 Lafayette Twrs., E, Detroit, MI 48207, (313)393-2095; **BUS ADD:** 3770 City Nat. Bank, Detroit, MI 48226, (313)965-2675.

YOUNG, Hubert H., Jr.——**B:** May 30, 1945, Franklin, VA, *Atty., Owner*, Young Properties; **PRIM RE ACT:** Consultant, Attorney, Developer, Owner/Investor, Syndicator; **SERVICES:** Atty. for RE investors and devels; Owner of Young Properties, which is VA family RE devel. and investment bus.; **REP CLIENTS:** Owners and devels. of large comml. and resid. projects in several states; **PREV EMPLOY:** Formally Gen. Counsel for Trammell Crow Co's., Dallas, TX; **PROFL AFFIL & HONORS:** VA, TX, Supreme Court Assn., ABA, Active on various Nat. Bar Comms.; **EDUC:** BA, 1967, Poli Sci., Washington & Lee Univ.; **GRAD EDUC:** JD, 1969, Washington & Lee Univ.; **EDUC HONORS:** Magna Cum Laude; **MIL SERV:** USN; Lt.; Mil. Judge Designation; **OTHER ACT & HONORS:** Chmn. of various Repub. Party Comm./Campaign Projects, various charitable, political, civic and social orgs. Dir. of several various corps., published profl. articles in various nat. RE and legal publications; **HOME ADD:** 607 Jones St., Suffolk, VA 23434, (804)934-2967; **BUS ADD:** Suite 100, Profl. Bldg., Suffolk, VA 23434.

YOUNG, James M.——**B:** Nov. 15, 1930, Winston-Salem, NC, *Partner*, Dodson Pence Viar Young & Woodrum, Attys., Salem Office; **PRIM RE ACT:** Attorney; **SERVICES:** Legal; **REP CLIENTS:** First VA Bank, Bank of VA, Salem Bank & Trust, Waldrop Realty Co., United VA Bank, Wingate Realty Co.; **PREV EMPLOY:** 5 yrs. Title Atty., Magic City Mort. Co.; **PROFL AFFIL & HONORS:** ABA, VA Bar Assn., Roanoke Cty. Bar Assn. (Past Pres.); **EDUC:** BA, 1953, Econ., Univ. of VA; **GRAD EDUC:** JD, 1957, Univ. of VA; **EDUC HONORS:** Raven Soc. Intermediate Honors, Letterman Football, Student Asst. to Prof.; **MIL SERV:** US Army, Lt. Col., Far East (Korea); **OTHER ACT & HONORS:** Chmn. Salem Electoral Bd.

1968-present; Past Pres. of following; Salem Jaycees, Salem Roanoke Cty. C of C, Blue Ridge Council, Boy Scouts of Amer., (now on Bd. of Dir.), Roanoke Cty. Council, PTA, Pres. Salem Kiwanis; **HOME ADD:** 412 Shank St., Salem, VA 24153, (703)389-7172; **BUS ADD:** 25 Library Sq., Salem, VA 24153, (703)387-0496.

YOUNG, Kenneth M.——**B:** Sep. 30, 1922, Honolulu, HI, *Owner*, Kenny Young, Realtor; **PRIM RE ACT:** Broker, Developer, Builder, Property Manager, Syndicator; **SERVICES:** RE brokerage and exchanging; **PREV EMPLOY:** VP Hawaiian Land Co., Subsidiary Dillingham Corp.; **PROFL AFFIL & HONORS:** NAR, Honolulu Bd. of Realtors, Kona Bd. of Realtors, Inst. of RE Mgmt.; Intl. RE Federation, Hawaii Realtor of the Year, 1966; **EDUC:** BA, 1946, Econ., Stanford Univ.; **MIL SERV:** USN Seaman; **OTHER ACT & HONORS:** Past Pres. Kona C of C; Past Pres. HI Leeward Planning Conference; VP West HI Housing Foundation; **HOME TEL:** (808)322-2271; **BUS ADD:** 75-5707B Alii Dr., Kailua-Kona, HI 96740, (808)329-2444.

YOUNG, Martin Ray, Jr.——**B:** Aug. 11, 1916, Mancos, CO, *Pres.*, Martin Ray Young, Jr., AIA, Architect; **PRIM RE ACT:** Architect; **SERVICES:** Design, arch., interiors; **PROFL AFFIL & HONORS:** AIA; Construction Specifications Inst., AIA; CSI; **EDUC:** BArch., 1936, Arch., Brigham Young Univ.; **OTHER ACT & HONORS:** Exchange Club of Mesa, AZ; **HOME ADD:** 50 S. Udall St., Mesa, AZ 85204, (602)964-3429; **BUS ADD:** 50 S. Udall St., Mesa, AZ 85204, (601)964-3429.

YOUNG, Peter T.——**B:** Jan. 28, 1952, Honolulu, HI, *Pres./Princ. Broker*, Real Estate Works Hawaii, Inc.; **PRIM RE ACT:** Broker, Consultant, Appraiser, Owner/Investor, Instructor, Property Manager; **OTHER RE ACT:** Mort. Broker; **SERVICES:** Resort prop. devel. counseling, valuation, prop. mgmt., investment counseling, sales; **PROFL AFFIL & HONORS:** NAR; FLI; NAt. Assn. of Review Appraisers; Intl. Inst. of Valuers; RE Educators Assn., CRA, Sr. Cert. Valuer; **EDUC:** BBA, 1974, RE, Univ. of HI; **HOME ADD:** Kailua Kona, HI 96740PO Box 2923, (808)322-9190; **BUS ADD:** 75-5722 Kuakini Hwy #203, Kailua Kona, HI 96740, (808)329-6488.

YOUNG, Ralph Edward, Jr.——**B:** May 19, 1943, Meridian, MS, *Partner*, Deen, Cameron, Prichard & Young; **PRIM RE ACT:** Attorney; **SERVICES:** Loan closings, issuance of title insurance policies, general law; **REP CLIENTS:** Merchants & Farmers Bank, Meridian, MS; Commercial Bank, Dekalb, MS; Safeco Title Insurance Company; **PREV EMPLOY:** Law Clerk for MS Supreme Ct. (1967); **PROFL AFFIL & HONORS:** ABA, Lauderdale County Bar Assn., Federal Bar Assn., MS St. Bar Assn.; **EDUC:** BBA, 1965, Banking & Fin., Univ. of MS; **GRAD EDUC:** JD, 1967, Law, Univ. of MS, School of Law; **EDUC HONORS:** Phi Delta Phi Honorary Legal Fraternity; **MIL SERV:** US Air Nat. Guard, Capt., Judge Advocate; **OTHER ACT & HONORS:** Greater Meridian C of C, Key; Chapter of Am. Red Cross, Meridian Little Theater, Meridian Jr. Coll. Foundation, Meridian Art Ass.; **HOME ADD:** 3818 13th Place, Meridian, MS 39301, (601)485-8071; **BUS ADD:** 1122 22nd Ave., P.O. Box 888, Meridian, MS 39301, (601)693-2561.

YOUNG, Robert A.——**B:** Jan. 25, 1937, Chester, PA, *Dir. Indus. Devel*, Lakewood Indus. Commission; **OTHER RE ACT:** Indus. RE, municipal, pvt. owned indus. park devel.; **SERVICES:** Attraction, location, package of fin., fen., contr., approvals.; **REP CLIENTS:** Gusmer Corp., Paco Packaging, Inc., Thomas Indus.; **PROFL AFFIL & HONORS:** NAIOP NJ & PA, IREBA, NJ IDA, NIDA, AEDC, NARA, Pres. NJ IDA, CRA; **EDUC:** BS, 1964, Bus. Admin, Econ., Monmouth Coll., W. Long Beach, NJ; **GRAD EDUC:** MBA, 1969, Personnel/Psych., Fairleigh Dickinson Univ.; **EDUC HONORS:** Cum laude; **MIL SERV:** US Army, Spec. E-4, Good Conduct Medal; **OTHER ACT & HONORS:** VP Dir. MS Soc., Church Council, Advisory Bd. First Nat. State Bank, Ocean Cty. Coll., Advs. Arts & Sci. Vocational; **HOME ADD:** 430 Washington Ave., Pine Beach, NJ 08741, (201)240-2050; **BUS ADD:** 231 3rd St., Lakewood, NJ 08701, (201)364-2500.

YOUNG, Robert W.——**B:** Dec. 12, 1931, Portland, OR, *Pres.*, Robert Young and Associates; Robert Young Realty Services, Inc., Robert Young Construction, Inc., Robert Young Development, Inc.; **PRIM RE ACT:** Broker, Consultant, Developer, Builder, Owner/Investor, Property Manager; **REP CLIENTS:** Kennewick Irrigation Dist.; **PROFL AFFIL & HONORS:** Nat. Assn. Homebuilders; Nat. Assn. of Apt. House Owners, San Francisco C of C, Who's Who in the West; **EDUC:** 1955, Whitman Coll.; **MIL SERV:** USN, Enlisted, 1955-1957; **OTHER ACT & HONORS:** Bd. of TR., Exec. Comm., Fine Arts Museums of San Francisco Chmn., San Francisco Boys Chorus; Bd. of Dirs., Chmn. and Past Pres., CA League for the Handicapped; Bd. of TR., Univ. High School Bd. of Govs., Exec. Comm., San Francisco Symphony; Bd. of Overseers, Exec. Comm., Whitman Coll.; Bd. of TRS., Exec. Comm., CA Assn. for Amer. Conservatory Theater; Bd.of TRS., Grace Cathedral; Bd. of Dirs., Presido Terrace Assn.; Sustaining Member, Amer. Assn. of Museums; Member, Banker's Club of San Francisco; Member, St. Francis Yacht Club; Member, CA Club; Member, Steering Comm., WA State Energy Fair 1983; **HOME ADD:** 5 Presidio Terrace, San Francisco, CA 94118, (415)668-1119; **BUS ADD:** 600 Montgomery St., 35th Floor, The Transamerica Pyramid, San Francisco, CA 94111, (415)398-3446.

YOUNG, Warren H.——**B:** Aug. 22, 1923, Brooklyn, NY, *Pres.*, Yorkville Federal Savings and Loan Assn.; **PRIM RE ACT:** Appraiser, Lender, Owner/Investor; **PROFL AFFIL & HONORS:** Charter Member Long Isl. Chap. of the Soc. for the Advancement of Mgmt., CRA; **EDUC:** BS, 1953, Mgmt., Commerce, NYU; **GRAD EDUC:** MBA, 1956, Econ., NYU Grad School. of Bus.; **EDUC HONORS:** Cum Laude, Psi Chi Omega, Arch and Square, Beta Gamma Sigma; **MIL SERV:** USMC, Sgt.; **OTHER ACT & HONORS:** Member Banking Bd., State of NY 1979-80; Alpha Kappa Psi; AMA Presidents Assn.; Pres. Mutual Credit Union; **HOME ADD:** 16 Upland Dr., Chappaqua, NY 10514, (914)238-8485; **BUS ADD:** 75 S. Greeley Ave., Chappaqua, NY 10514, (212)824-3004.

YOUNGER, Edward M.——**B:** May 14, 1944, Kansas City, MO, *Regional Prop. Mgr.*, Kroh Brothers Devel Co.; **PRIM RE ACT:** Property Manager; **OTHER RE ACT:** Regional Prop. Mgr. (shopping centers & office bldgs.), leasing, tenant mix analysis, RE leasing plans, renovation & remodel exisiting centers; **PROFL AFFIL & HONORS:** IREM, CPM; **EDUC:** BS Acctg., 1969, Bus.; Econ., Mktg., Northwest MO State Univ.; **HOME ADD:** 3503 S. Jasper Way, Aurora, CO 80013, (303)690-6268; **BUS ADD:** 5675 S. Tamarac Pkwy., Suite 110, Englewood, CO 80111, (303)684-6010.

YOUNKER, Eunice M.——**B:** Jan 5, 1918, Pulaski, WI, *Sales Mgr.*, Menry Leist, Inc., Resid.; **PRIM RE ACT:** Broker, Instructor, Owner/Investor; **PROFL AFFIL & HONORS:** RNMI, NAR, OAREB, CBR, CRB; **EDUC:** BS, 1939, Hist., Eng., Educ., Univ. of WI, River Falls, WI; **GRAD EDUC:** M. Comm. Sci., 1948, Mgmt., Univ. of IN; **MIL SERV:** USCG, Lt j.g.; **HOME ADD:** 7420 Miami Hills Dr., Cinn., OH 45243, (513)984-8114; **BUS ADD:** 1863 Section Rd., Cinn, OH 45237, (513)731-4000.

YOUNKIN, John P.——**B:** Dec. 23, 1930, Los Angeles, CA, *Dir. of Comml. Devel.*, Mission Viejo Co.; **PRIM RE ACT:** Broker, Developer; **OTHER RE ACT:** RE exec with comm. devel. co.; **PREV EMPLOY:** 1962-72 Coldwell, Barker & Co.; **PROFL AFFIL & HONORS:** NAIOP, ICSC, NACORE; **EDUC:** BA, 1956, Econ., Stanford Univ.; **MIL SERV:** USAF, S/Sgt.; **HOME ADD:** 1141 Castlegate Ln., Santa Ana, CA 92705, (714)544-0386; **BUS ADD:** 26137 La Paz Rd., Mission Viejo, CA 92691, (714)837-6050.

YOUSOUFIAN, Armen——**B:** Mar. 21, 1947, NY, NY, *Pres./Owner*, Armen Yousoufian Inc.; **PRIM RE ACT:** Broker, Consultant, Owner/Investor, Instructor, Syndicator; **SERVICES:** Synd. of income prop., investment counseling, consulting, investment brokerage, lecturing; **REP CLIENTS:** Primarily indiv. investors in income RE; **PREV EMPLOY:** 1971-1973, Employment as a private acct. for mfrg. co's.; **PROFL AFFIL & HONORS:** RESSI; Realtors NMI; Nat. & WA Assns. of Realtors; Seattle, King County Bd. of Realtors; Toastmasters Intl., CCIM; **EDUC:** BSME/BA, 1969, Mech. Engrg., Rutgers Univ.; **GRAD EDUC:** MBA, 1974, Acctg., Seattle Univ.; **OTHER ACT & HONORS:** Bellevue Athletic Club; **BUS ADD:** 313 Seattle Trust Bldg., 10655 NE 4th, Bellevue, WA 98004, (206)455-9919.

YOVINO-YOUNG, G. Michael——**B:** June 1, 1937, Oakland, CA, *Owner*, Yovino-Young Associates; **PRIM RE ACT:** Consultant, Appraiser; **REP CLIENTS:** Cities of Oakland, Berkeley; Bay Area Rapid Transit Dist.; Wells Fargo Mort. Co.; **PROFL AFFIL & HONORS:** Pres., Chap. 54, Soc. of RE Appraisers; Chief Appraiser, Spec. Audit, Bd. of Supr., Los Angeles Cty., Amer. Soc. of Appraisers, SRA, FSVA, SCV; **EDUC:** BSC, 1958, Bus. Admin., Univ. of Santa Clara; **GRAD EDUC:** MBA, 1963, Urban Land Econ., Univ. of CA, Berkeley; **EDUC HONORS:** Fellow: Glen D. Williman Found.; **MIL SERV:** USAF; **OTHER ACT & HONORS:** Faculty: Grad. School of Banking & Fin., Golden Gate Univ. San Francisco; **HOME ADD:** 3030 Buena Vista Way, Berkeley, CA 94708; **BUS ADD:** 2716 Telegraph Ave., Berkeley, CA 94705, (415)548-1210.

YOW, Gordon——**B:** Oct. 13, 1948, San Francisco, CA, *RE Fee Appraiser*, G.L. Yow & Assoc.; **PRIM RE ACT:** Appraiser, Owner/Investor, Property Manager, Syndicator, Real Estate Publisher; **SERVICES:** Consulting, appraising, selling books, & publishing; **PREV EMPLOY:** Wells Fargo Bank, Homestead S&L, Home S&L, Gt. Western S&L; **PROFL AFFIL & HONORS:** Soc. of RE Appraisers, AIREA; **EDUC:** AB, 1973, Criminology, Univ. of CA, Berkeley; **GRAD EDUC:** RE, Merritt Coll.; **OTHER ACT & HONORS:**

Wasung Club, Active Chinese Comm. Participant; **HOME ADD:** 582 Athol Ave., Oakland, CA 94606, (415)893-4343; **BUS ADD:** 230 Wayne Ave., Suite 404, Oakland, CA 94606, (415)763-4471.

YOWELL, James——**B:** May 2, 1933, Omaha, *Pres.*, Century 21, J. M. Yowell; **PRIM RE ACT:** Broker; **SERVICES:** RE Sales; **PROFL AFFIL & HONORS:** CRB, CRS, Realtor of Yr.-Omaha Bd. of Realtor 1976; **EDUC:** BS, 1955, Bus. Admin., NE Univ. at Lincoln; **HOME ADD:** 8074 Castelar, (402)393-4417; **BUS ADD:** 626 N. 108 Ct., Omaha, NE 68154, (402)496-2000.

YUDIN, Julian H.——**B:** Jyly 29, 1933, Joliet, IL, *Pres.*, J.H. Yudin Inc.; **PRIM RE ACT:** Broker, Syndicator, Consultant, Appraiser, Developer, Owner/Investor; **SERVICES:** Appraising and prop. mgmt.; devel. of HUD Projects and Farmers Home; **PROFL AFFIL & HONORS:** SREA; Nat. Bd. of Realtors; **HOME ADD:** 15 Shady Lane Rd., Danville, Il 61832, (217)446-2632; **BUS ADD:** 12 W. Lake Blvd., Danville, IL 61832.

YURA, Mark D.——**B:** May 3, 1953, Detroit, MI, *Assoc. Atty.*, Rudnick & Wolfe; **PRIM RE ACT:** Attorney, Owner/Investor; **SERVICES:** Counseling clients in all aspects of RE law; **REP CLIENTS:** Var. lenders, dev. and inv. in comml. residl. and ind. projs.; **PROFL AFFIL & HONORS:** Chicago Bar Assn; ABA; **EDUC:** BA, 1975, Hist., Univ. of MI; **GRAD EDUC:** JD, 1978, Univ. of MI; **EDUC HONORS:** Angell Scholar, Dean's List, Cum Laude; **HOME ADD:** 459 W. Roslyn, Chicago, IL 60614, (312)327-1610; **BUS ADD:** 30 N. LaSalle, Ste. 2900, Chicago, IL 60602, (312)368-4084.

ZADJEIKA, Dolores M.——**B:** Nov. 15, 1934, Philadelphia, PA, *Pres.*, Applewood Inc., Realtors; **PRIM RE ACT:** Broker, Consultant, Appraiser; **SERVICES:** Fin. strat.; investment counseling; comml. inform.; in-depth valuation; up-to-date mktg. techniques; **PREV EMPLOY:** Salesperson, then Broker, with Coolidge Realty Agcy., Westmont, NJ (March, 1976 to April, 1981); **PROFL AFFIL & HONORS:** Camden Cty. Bd. of Realtors; NJ Assn. of Realtors; NJ Assn. of Women Bus. Own.; Fee Appraisers Soc.; **EDUC:** In progress; **OTHER ACT & HONORS:** Judge Camden Co. Bd. of Elections; Past Pres. Woman's Club of Stratford; Helping Hand of Stratford; Parent/Teacher Organization of Stratford; Founder, Chairperson of YWCA of Camden and vicinity's Stratford Suburban Comm. (1968-78); **HOME ADD:** 4 Saratoga Rd., Stratford, NJ 08084, (609)346-0101; **BUS ADD:** 119 E. Laurel Rd., Stratford, NJ 08084, (609)435-4900.

ZAHN, F. Anthony——**B:** Jan. 17, 1940, Oklahoma City, OK, *Pres.*, Chiron Investments; **PRIM RE ACT:** Syndicator, Owner/Investor, Attorney; **SERVICES:** Synd. of multifamily resid., office & comml. props.; **REP CLIENTS:** Indiv. investors in resid., office & comml. props.; **PREV EMPLOY:** Partner, VP & Genr. Counsel of the Compass Grp. Inc. (RE synds.), 1977-81; Own Law office 1971-77; **PROFL AFFIL & HONORS:** ABA, CT Bar Assn., OK Bar Assn.; **EDUC:** BA, 1962, Econ., Yale Univ.; **GRAD EDUC:** JD, 1965, OK Univ. Law School; LLM, NY Univ. Grad. School of Law; **OTHER ACT & HONORS:** Oklahoma City Outstanding Young Man (1972); Three Outstanding Young Oklahomans (1973); City Council, OK City, 1973-76; Bd. of Dirs. Lakewood Trumbull YMCA; Yale Alumni Schools Comm.; **HOME ADD:** 620 Eleven O'Clock Rd., Fairfield, CT 06430, (203)254-0054; **BUS ADD:** 620 Eleven O'Clock Rd., Fairfield, CT 06430, (203)254-1700.

ZAJAC, Terrence Michael——**B:** Mar. 6, 1948, Chicago, IL, *Dir.*, Terry Zajac Seminars; **PRIM RE ACT:** Broker, Consultant, Instructor, Owner/Investor; **OTHER RE ACT:** Author; **SERVICES:** Specialized and tech. training; fin. consulting; gen. prelicensing training; **REP CLIENTS:** RE licensees; owners; investors; **PREV EMPLOY:** Ford Schools, Inc. (RE School), 1975-1980, 4225 W. Glendale Ave., Phoenix, AZ 85021; **PROFL AFFIL & HONORS:** Pres., AZ Chapter of the RE Educ. Assn.; Sec.-Treas., AZ Assn. of RE Schools; **EDUC:** BS, 1971, Mktg. and Sales Mgmt., AZ State Univ.; **MIL SERV:** AZ Army Nat. Guard, S/Sgt.; **OTHER ACT & HONORS:** Life Member, Pi Sigma Epsilon; Metro. Phoenix Project Bus. Consultant; **HOME ADD:** 6738 E. Granada Rd., Scottsdale, AZ 85257, (602)946-5297; **BUS ADD:** 6738 E. Granada Rd., Scottsdale, AZ 85257, (602)947-2550.

ZAK, Eugene——**B:** Dec. 30, 1929, Yonkers, NY, *Pres.*, W. Ross Campbell Co.; **PRIM RE ACT:** Broker, Appraiser, Owner/Investor; **OTHER RE ACT:** RE Fin.; **SERVICES:** Long term fin./joint venture, etc.; **REP CLIENTS:** CT. Gen., Balt. Life, Developers Corp., investors; **PREV EMPLOY:** West Coast Rgnl. Supr. R.E., MA Mutual Life Ins. 1957-65, VP, US Nat. Bank 1965-1968; **PROFL AFFIL & HONORS:** Dir., Los Angeles Headquarters Assn., ICSC, Central City Assn. Educ. Comm. and Income Prop. Comm. of MBA; **EDUC:** BS, 1957, Bus. & Econ., Univ. of CT; **GRAD EDUC:** 1957-61, Law, W. New England Law School; **EDUC HONORS:** Grad. with Honors; **MIL SERV:** US Army, 1st Sgt., 1951-53; **OTHER ACT & HONORS:** Lectured on RE at UCLA, UCA, Santa Barbara, CA Poly., etc.; **HOME ADD:** 325 N. Cedar Dr., Covina, CA 91723, (213)332-7887; **BUS ADD:** 16530 Ventura Blvd., Suite 406, Encino, CA 91436, (213)783-9911.

ZALESKI, Gerald S.——**B:** Sept. 14, 1932, Chicago, IL, *Owner*, Gerald S. Zaleski M.A.I.; **PRIM RE ACT:** Consultant, Appraiser; **SERVICES:** RE appraisal and consultation; **REP CLIENTS:** Lenders, and indiv. or inst. investors in comml. props.; **PREV EMPLOY:** NY Life, Mort. and Loans; W. Mort., San Francisco; First Nat. Bank, Colorado Springs; **PROFL AFFIL & HONORS:** AIREA, MAI; **EDUC:** BS, 1958, Acctg./Econ., CO State Univ.; **MIL SERV:** US Army, Pfc.; **HOME ADD:** 4765 ViLla Cir., Colorado Springs, CO 80918, (303)598-8361; **BUS ADD:** 320 N. Academy Blvd., 201, Colorado Springs, CO 80909, (303)596-2152.

ZALL, Alex——**B:** Feb. 2, 1920, Newark, NJ, *Exec. VP*, Alexander Summer Cos.; **PRIM RE ACT:** Broker, Consultant, Appraiser, Developer, Property Manager, Owner/Investor; **PREV EMPLOY:** VP, Devel. & Mktg., Nassau Crossways Indus., Office Park, NY; **PROFL AFFIL & HONORS:** NAR, Indus. RE Broker's Assn, NY, NAIOP, VP/Pres. NJ Chap. (1974-76), Director National Board (1976-1980), Amer. Arbit. Assn Bd. of Dir.; **EDUC:** BA, 1940, Bus., Rutger's Univ.; **GRAD EDUC:** MA, 1944, Fin. Acctg., NY Univ.; **OTHER ACT & HONORS:** Mayor's Adv. Comm. Indus. Comml. Devel. NJ., V. Chmn, N. Caldwell Planning Bd., Civic Assn. Pres.; **HOME ADD:** 11 Maple Dr., North Caldwell, NJ 07006, (201)226-6304; **BUS ADD:** 222 Cedar Lane, Teaneck, NJ 07666, (201)836-4500.

ZALOUDEK, Robert F.——**B:** Feb. 4, 1940, Chicago, IL, *Owner*, Robert F. Zaloudek & Assoc.; **PRIM RE ACT:** Instructor, Syndicator, Consultant; **SERVICES:** Location analysis, market research; **REP CLIENTS:** Corp. lenders, devels., public agencies; **PREV EMPLOY:** VP, RE Research Corp., 1965-75; Sr. VP Larry Smith & Co., Ltd., 1976-77; **PROFL AFFIL & HONORS:** MAI, SRPA, AIREA; **EDUC:** BA, 1969, Econ., Geog., Roosevelt Univ.; **GRAD EDUC:** MBA, 1973, Land Econ., GA State Univ.; **MIL SERV:** IL Air NG, Airman Prelas; **OTHER ACT & HONORS:** Various comms., Chicago Assn. of Commerce & Indus., Instr. RE Educ. Co., Chicago; **HOME ADD:** 831 Mulford, Evanston, IL, (312)866-9062; **BUS ADD:** 831 Mulford, Evanston, IL 60202, (312)866-8062.

ZAMMIT, Thomas J.——**B:** Apr. 14, 1948, NYC, *Asst. VP*, Gr. NY Savings Bank, Appraisal/RE; **PRIM RE ACT:** Appraiser, Banker, Lender, Property Manager; **SERVICES:** Valuation, mkt. studies, prop. mgmt.; **PROFL AFFIL & HONORS:** NY RE Bd., Young Mort. Bankers, Soc. of RE Appraisers, Candidate for AIREA MAI; **EDUC:** BS, 1976, Bus., Fin., Long Island Univ.; **GRAD EDUC:** Mort. & Banking, NY Sch. of Social Studies; **EDUC HONORS:** Cum Laude; **HOME ADD:** 303 Mercer St., New York, NY 10003, (212)282-9600; **BUS ADD:** 410 Madison Ave., New York, NY 10017, (212)282-9600.

ZAMZOW, Kenneth E.——**B:** Apr. 18, 1930, Gilroy, CA, *Owner*, Zamzow and Associates; **PRIM RE ACT:** Consultant, Appraiser, Owner/Investor, Instructor, Property Manager; **SERVICES:** RE appraisal and consulting; **REP CLIENTS:** Lenders, investors, devel., attys., public agencies; **PREV EMPLOY:** Bank of Amer., 1960-1967; AK Dept. of Revenue, Petroleum Revenue Div., 1976-1981; **PROFL AFFIL & HONORS:** AIREA, AK Chap. Pres., 1977-1978; Rgnl. Gov., Nat. Assn. of Review Appraisers, 1980-1981; **EDUC:** BS, 1952, Agric., OR State Coll.; **GRAD EDUC:** MEd, 1959, Educ., Univ. of CA, Davis; **MIL SERV:** US Army, Cpl.; **OTHER ACT & HONORS:** Anchorage Bd. of Equalization, 1977-1982; Kiwanis; Elks; **HOME ADD:** 1020 Medra St., No. 4, Anchorage, AK 99501, (907)277-5169; **BUS ADD:** 1020 Medra St., No. 4, Anchorage, AK 99501, (907)276-1363.

ZANKEL, Ira L.——**B:** July 9, 1944, Brooklyn, NY, *Pres.*, N. Shore Abstract, Ltd.; **PRIM RE ACT:** Attorney; **PREV EMPLOY:** Central Abstract Corp.; **EDUC:** BA, 1966, Poli. Sci., Brooklyn Coll.; **GRAD EDUC:** JD, 1969, George Washington Univ. School of Law; **HOME ADD:** 21 Vista Way, Pt. Washington, NY 11050, (516)944-7760; **BUS ADD:** 277 Northern Blvd., PO Box 385, Great Neck, NY 11021, (516)466-6050.

ZANKEL, Martin I.——**B:** May 12, 1934, NY, *Atty.*, Friedman & Zankel; **PRIM RE ACT:** Regulator, Owner/Investor; **SERVICES:** Represent chain tenants, devel. & investors; **PROFL AFFIL & HONORS:** ABA, SF Bar Assn., Intnl. Council of Shopping Ctrs (ICSC), Order of the Coif, Land/Tenant Comm., Real Prop. Sect. ABA; **EDUC:** BS, 1955, Mgmt., Wharton Sch. of Comm. & Fin.; **GRAD EDUC:** JD, 1974, Real Property, Univ. of CA, Hastings Coll. of Law; **EDUC HONORS:** Order of the Coif, Thurston Soc., Moot Court Award; **BUS ADD:** 611 Front St., San Francisco, CA 94111, (415)788-5700.

ZEALY, Samuel Hollingsworth, Jr.——**B:** July 31, 1948, Washington, NC, *Part., CPM*, Clendenin, Wrenn, & Kirkman, Realtors; **PRIM RE ACT:** Broker, Instructor, Property Manager; **SERVICES:** Full service prop. mgmt., investment counseling brokerage; **REP CLIENTS:** Indiv. pvt. investors; **PREV EMPLOY:** Smithdeal Gallery of Homes, High Point, NC 1974-78; **PROFL AFFIL & HONORS:** NAR, IREM, GRI, CPM; **EDUC:** BA, 1970, Health Educ., Lenoir Rhyne Coll.; **MIL SERV:** USAR, E-5; **OTHER ACT & HONORS:** Treas./Bd. of Dir. Presbyterian Counseling Ctr., Inc.; Sec. Nat. Greene Kiwanis Club, Greensboro Elks Club; **HOME ADD:** 1912 Gracewood Dr., Greensboro, NC 27408, (919)288-7340; **BUS ADD:** 218 W. Friendly Ave., PO Box 568, Greensboro, NC 27402, (919)272-3183.

ZEBRACK, Joel——**B:** Oct. 1, 1936, Los Angeles, CA, *Atty.*, Law Offices of Joel Zebrack; **PRIM RE ACT:** Attorney; **SERVICES:** Legal; **PROFL AFFIL & HONORS:** ABA; State Bar of CA; Alameda Cty. Bar Assn.; Real Prop. & Probate & TR. Law Sect., ABA; Hearing Officers Panel CA State Univ. & Colls.; Panel of Arbitrators, AAA & US Dist. Ct. of No. Dist. of CA; and service as Judge Pro Tempore, Oakland-Piedmont & San Leandro Mcpl. Courts, Alameda Cty., CA; admitted to practice before the US Supreme Court, Supreme Court of CA, US Dist Crts. & Court of Appeal, CA; **EDUC:** BA, 1958, Govt., CA State Univ. at Los Angeles; **GRAD EDUC:** JD, 1963, SW Univ. Sch. of Law; **EDUC HONORS:** Hon. Life Member, Student Body Assn.; **HOME ADD:** 5 El Dorado Ln., Orinda, CA 94563, (415)254-6345; **BUS ADD:** 405, 14th St., Suite 1615, Oakland, CA 94612, (415)763-1615.

ZECH, William F., Jr.——**B:** Aug. 15, 1942, Cincinnati, OH, *Exec. VP*, N. Amer. Mgmt. & Development Co.; **PRIM RE ACT:** Broker, Developer, Property Manager; **SERVICES:** Devel. lease & manage shopping ctrs. and multi-family; **PROFL AFFIL & HONORS:** ICSC; IREM, Certified Shopping Ctr. Mgr.; Broker: Kentucky and Ohio; **EDUC:** BSBA, 1967, Acctg., Univ. of Cincinnati; **GRAD EDUC:** MBA, 1970, Mgmt., Xavier Univ.; **HOME ADD:** 973 Pamela Dr., Cincinnati, OH, (513)474-4827; **BUS ADD:** Suite 300, 212 E. 3rd St., Cincinnati, OH 45202, (513)721-2744.

ZECKENDORF, William——**B:** Oct. 31, 1929, NYC, NY, *Chmn. of the Bd.*, Zeckendorf, Colin Co. Inc.; **PRIM RE ACT:** Consultant, Developer, Owner/Investor, Property Manager; **PREV EMPLOY:** Webb & Knapp, Inc., Pres.; General Prop. Corp., Pres.; **PROFL AFFIL & HONORS:** Trustee, Long Island Univ.; Bd. of Dir., RE Comm., Boy Scouts of Amer.; **EDUC:** 1950, Collegiate School, Lawrenceville Academy; **MIL SERV:** US Army, 1952-1954, Army Commendation Medal; **OTHER ACT & HONORS:** Confrerie des Chevaliers du Tastevin, Commanderie de Bordeaux; **HOME ADD:** 502 Park Ave., New York, NY 10022, (212)355-3379; **BUS ADD:** 502 Park Ave., New York, NY 10022, (212)826-2900.

ZEGEER, Jack——**B:** Sept. 20, 1928, Boone Cty, WV, *Atty. at Law*; **PRIM RE ACT:** Attorney, Instructor, Consultant; **SERVICES:** RE titles, title ins. (Berks); **REP CLIENTS:** Charleston Fed. S&L Assn., O.V. Smith & Sons of Big Chimney, Inc.; **PROFL AFFIL & HONORS:** ABA, WV Bar Assn., Kanawha Cty., Bar Assn, Amer. Judicature Soc.; **EDUC:** AB, 1950, Econ., WV Univ.; **GRAD EDUC:** LLB, 1953, WV Univ.; **MIL SERV:** US Army, Cpl.; **OTHER ACT & HONORS:** City Atty., City of S. Charleston 2 yrs., Mcpl. Judge, City of S. Charleston 12 yrs; **HOME ADD:** 392 Kenna Dr., S. Charleston, WV 25309, (304)768-7974; **BUS ADD:** 1325 Virginia St. E., Charleston, WV 25301, (304)342-2117.

ZEITLIN, Shirley——**B:** Dec. 11, 1934, Nashville, TN, *Pres.*, Shirley Zeitlin & Co. Realtors; **PRIM RE ACT:** Broker, Instructor, Consultant, Appraiser, Developer, Builder, Property Manager, Owner/Investor; **PROFL AFFIL & HONORS:** NAR; TN Assn. Nashville Bd. of Realtors, Sales & Mktg. Exec. C. Of C., Sec.-Treas. Nashville Bd. of Realtors, Realtor Assoc. of Yr. 1977 for Nashville Bd. of Realtors & 1978 for TN Assoc., 1980 participant in Leadership Nashville, 1979 Exec. Award by Nat. Women's Exec.; **OTHER ACT & HONORS:** The Temple, Jewish Community Ctr., Dir. of Jewish Federation of Nashville; **HOME ADD:** 4301 Lillywood Rd., Nashville, TN 37205, (615)383-4921; **BUS ADD:** 4301 Hillsboro Rd., Suite 100, Nashville, TN 37215, (615)383-0183.

ZELINSLEE, Robert——*VP Engr.*, Zimmer Homes Corp.; **PRIM RE ACT:** Property Manager; **BUS ADD:** 777 SW 12th Ave., Pompano Beach, FL 33061, (305)943-7600.*

ZELL, Alan L.——**B:** Jan. 23, 1948, Plainfield, NJ, *Pres.*, Zell Management & Development, Inc.; **PRIM RE ACT:** Broker, Consultant, Developer, Property Manager; **SERVICES:** Mgmt., leasing, devel., brokerage, consulting on shoppings ctrs. and garden office complexes; **REP CLIENTS:** Investor owners of shopping ctrs. and office bldgs. including instnl. owners; **PREV EMPLOY:** The Hanson Devel. Co. 1972-1977; **PROFL AFFIL & HONORS:** ICSC, CSM (Cert. Shopping Ctr. Mgr.); **EDUC:** BS, 1970, Fin., Univ. of RI; **GRAD EDUC:** MBA, 1972, Bus. Admin., Boston Univ.; **HOME ADD:** 5112 N 36th St., Phoenix, AZ 85018, (602)956-1721; **BUS ADD:** Post Office Box 11333, Phoenix, AZ 85061, (602)246-7477.

ZELL, Samuel——**B:** Sept. 28, 1941, Chicago, IL, *Chmn. of the Bd.*, Equity Financial and Mgmt. Co.; **PRIM RE ACT:** Developer, Owner/Investor; **PROFL AFFIL & HONORS:** Nat. Apt. Assn.; Nat. Multi-Housing Council; Chicago Bar Assn.; IL Bar Assn.; ABA; ULI; **EDUC:** BA, 1963, Pol. Sci., Univ. of Michigan; **GRAD EDUC:** JD, 1966, Univ. of MI Law School; **BUS ADD:** 10 South LaSalle St., Suite 900, Chicago, IL 60603, (312)782-8994.

ZELLER, Bud——**B:** June 16, 1940, New Castle, IN, *Broker/Owner*, ERA Placerville, Pollock Pines; **PRIM RE ACT:** Broker, Consultant, Appraiser, Developer, Lender, Builder, Owner/Investor, Instructor, Property Manager, Syndicator; **SERVICES:** Gen. RE, fin., investing, educ.; **PREV EMPLOY:** In RE bus. since 1964; **PROFL AFFIL & HONORS:** GRI, CRS; **EDUC:** 1960, Bus. Admin., Mt. San Antonio Coll; **GRAD EDUC:** 1962, Bus. Admin., Los Angeles State Coll.; Instr. of numerous RE courses for 14 yrs at Amer. River Coll., Placerville & Sacramento Grad. PLC Officers Training Program, City Coll.; **MIL SERV:** USMC, Cpl.; **OTHER ACT & HONORS:** Muscular Dystrophy Assn., Cty. Coordinator, Member Brokers of Nat. Mort. Exchange; **HOME ADD:** 4256 Carlson Way, Placerville, CA 95667, (916)622-2760; **BUS ADD:** 105 Placerville Dr., Placerville, CA 95667, (916)622-0131.

ZELLER, Emilio, III——**B:** Dec. 13, 1935, Santiago, Dominican Republic, *Pres.*, Emilio Zeller III Arch. Inc.; **PRIM RE ACT:** Architect; **SERVICES:** Complete arch. and planning servs.; **REP CLIENTS:** Lge. and small devels., contractors, mort. lenders, mort. bankers, bus. & indivs.; **PREV EMPLOY:** Sev. arch. & engrg. firms between grad. (1957) and opening practice (1962); **PROFL AFFIL & HONORS:** AIA, NAHB; **EDUC:** BS, 1957, Arch., GA Inst. of Tech.; **GRAD EDUC:** BArch, 1957, Arch., GA Inst. of Tech.; **EDUC HONORS:** Designated No. 1 Army ROTC, Designated No. 1 Structural Design; **MIL SERV:** US Army Res., Capt.; **OTHER ACT & HONORS:** Chmn Environmental Comm., Jacksonville Mass Transit, Republican Club, VP; Episcopal HS Parent's Council, VP; Opera Grp., Pres, YMCA, Jaycees, Sertoma; **HOME ADD:** 1237 Northwood Rd., Jacksonville, FL 32207, (904)398-8013; **BUS ADD:** 1000 Riverside Ave., Suite 600, Jacksonville, FL 32204, (904)355-3758.

ZELMAN, Richard M.——**B:** Mar. 9, 1949, Newark, NJ, *Part.*, Mann, Dady, Corrigan & Zelman; **PRIM RE ACT:** Attorney, Owner/Investor; **SERVICES:** Rep. of clients; **REP CLIENTS:** Cadillac-Fairview FL, Inc.; **PROFL AFFIL & HONORS:** ABA, FL Bar, Dade Cty. Bar; **EDUC:** AB, 1971, Hist./Govt., Cornell Univ.; **GRAD EDUC:** JD, 1974, Law, Harvard Law School; **EDUC HONORS:** Magna Cum Laude; Distinction in all subj.; **HOME ADD:** 3536 St. Gaudens Rd, Coconut Grove, FL 33133, (305)443-5018; **BUS ADD:** 444 Brickell Ave., Suite 930, Miami, FL 33131, (305)358-5800.

ZENNER, Brian S.——**B:** July 28, 1953, Chicago, IL, *Atty. & RE Broker*, Law, Lambert, Levinson, Wanninger, Meuth & Zenner; RE, Brian S. Zenner Real Estate Co.; **PRIM RE ACT:** Broker, Consultant, Attorney, Owner/Investor, Syndicator; **OTHER RE ACT:** Plans underway for future devel.; **SERVICES:** All legal aspects, brokerage, investment & devel. consultation; **PREV EMPLOY:** Comml./Resid. Broker-Salesmen at ADE Realty, Inc.; Gen. Partner of two prior investment synd.; **PROFL AFFIL & HONORS:** Chicago RE Bd.; North Side RE Bd.; Junior RE Bd. of Chicago; Chicago Bar Assn. - IL State Bar Assn., Amer. Bar Assn.; **EDUC:** BA, 1975, Philosophy, Econ., Poli. Sci., Univ. of IL; **GRAD EDUC:** JD, 1978, Gen. Law Practice, ITT/Chicago - Kent Coll. of Law; **EDUC HONORS:** Dean's List; **HOME ADD:** 1255 N. State Pkwy., Chicago, IL, (312)944-5000; **BUS ADD:** 2 N. LaSalle St., Suite 1904, Chicago, IL 60602, (312)641-7256.

ZERBST, Robert H.——**B:** Nov. 16, 1946, Charleston, SC, *VP*, Questor Associates, Dir. of Consulting & Investment Advisory Servs.; **PRIM RE ACT:** Consultant, Appraiser; **OTHER RE ACT:** Educator; **SERVICES:** Investment & fin. consulting, valuation; **REP CLIENTS:** Investors, devels., attys., lenders, govt. agencies; **PREV EMPLOY:**

Faculty Member Cox School of Bus., Southern Methodist Univ., Dallas; Faculty of Commerce, Univ. of BC, Vancouver; **PROFL AFFIL & HONORS:** Amer. RE and Urban Econ. Assn., ULI, AIREA, SREA, MAI, SRPA; **EDUC:** BA, 1968, Arts & Sci., Miami Univ.; **GRAD EDUC:** MA, 1971, Econ., OH State Univ.; MBA, 1972, Fin., OH State Univ.; PhD, 1974, RE, OH State Univ.; **HOME ADD:** 201 Ricardo Ave., Piedmont, CA 94611, (415)652-7290; **BUS ADD:** 115 Sansome St., San Francisco, CA 94104, (415)433-0300.

ZERIN, Milton——B: Nov. 11, 1924, Wilmington, DE, *Atty.*; **PRIM RE ACT:** Attorney; **SERVICES:** Litigation and consultation; **REP CLIENTS:** RE Brokers and Principals; **PREV EMPLOY:** Instr. *Legal Aspects of RE* Univ. of CA Ext.; **PROFL AFFIL & HONORS:** CA Los Angeles Cty. and Beverly Hills Assns., ABA, Lecturer and Author, CA Continuing Educ. of the Bar and Amer. Jur. Trials; **EDUC:** BS, 1948, Bus. Admin., Univ. of S. CA; **GRAD EDUC:** LLB, 1951, Univ. of S. CA; **MIL SERV:** US Army Air Corps, 1943-46; **BUS ADD:** 9595 Wilshire Blvd., Beverly Hills, CA 90212, (213)274-8231.

ZIAS, Dean——B: Jan. 26, 1951, Kastoria, Greece, *Comml. Revitalization Coordinator*, Pratt Inst. Ctr. for Community and Environmental Devel., Neighborhood Econ. Devel.; **PRIM RE ACT:** Instructor, Consultant, Property Manager; **SERVICES:** Mkt. studies, cost estimating, budgeting, contract negotiations; **PREV EMPLOY:** Action Council of Central Nassau, Inc. - Planner; Gen. Devel. Corp.; **PROFL AFFIL & HONORS:** APA; ULI; World Future Soc., Amer. Inst. of Cert. Planners; **EDUC:** BA, 1975, Urban Studies, Queens Coll., CUNY; **GRAD EDUC:** MUP, 1977, Pub. Admin., NYU; **OTHER ACT & HONORS:** Omonia; **HOME ADD:** 219-15 43rd Ave., Bayside, NY 11361, (212)224-8265; **BUS ADD:** 275 Washington Ave., Brooklyn, NY 11205, (212)636-3489.

ZIBROSKI, Ken——*Chmn. of the Board*, Realty World Corp.; **PRIM RE ACT:** Syndicator; **BUS ADD:** 7700 Little River Tpke., Annandale, VA 22003, (703)750-3570.*

ZIEGLER, Alan M.——B: Oct. 21, 1948, Scranton, PA, *VP*, Sonnenblick-Goldman Corp. of CA; **PRIM RE ACT:** Broker; **SERVICES:** Morts., joint venture arrangements, presales, equities, sale-leasebacks; **PREV EMPLOY:** Hinerfeld Realty Co. Major Comml. & Indus. Broker in N.E. PA (Scranton/Wilkes-Barre); **EDUC:** BA, 1971, Hist.-Philosophy, PA State Univ.; **GRAD EDUC:** MBA, 1980, Fin., Univ. of Scranton; **HOME ADD:** 9344 Olympic Blvd., Beverly Hills, CA 90212, (213)203-8312; **BUS ADD:** 1901 Ave. of the Stars, Los Angeles, CA 90067, (213)277-0600.

ZIEGLER, Dwight E.——B: July 24, 1943, St. Paul. MN, *Owner*, The Renaissance Grp.; **PRIM RE ACT:** Broker, Developer, Builder, Property Manager, Owner/Investor; **PREV EMPLOY:** VP of Investments, Rural Ins. Cos., Madison, WI; **PROFL AFFIL & HONORS:** WI Soc. CPA's, AICPA, WI RE Brokers; **EDUC:** BBA, 1967, Acctg., Fin., Univ. of WI; **EDUC HONORS:** Ira B. McGladrey Scholarship, Beta Alpha Psi Hon.; **OTHER ACT & HONORS:** Supr., Town of Vienna, 1969-73, Pres. DeForest Lions Club, Deacon Windsor United Church of Christ; **BUS ADD:** 4610 University Ave., PO Box 5590, Madison, WI 53705, (608)231-2466.

ZIENTS, Michael R.——B: Dec. 16, 1951, Orange, NJ, *Atty.*, Whitman & Ransom; **PRIM RE ACT:** Attorney; **SERVICES:** Comml. RE; **PROFL AFFIL & HONORS:** ABA, CT Bar Assn., Greenwich Bar Assn.; **EDUC:** BA, 1973, Poli. Sci., Williams Coll.; **GRAD EDUC:** JD, 1978, Univ. of CT; **EDUC HONORS:** Cum Laude, Honors in Poli. Sci., CT Law Review, Notes and Comment Editor; **HOME ADD:** 206 Schooner Cove, Stamford, CT 06851, (203)357-8321; **BUS ADD:** PO Box 1250, Greenwich, CT 06830, (203)869-3800.

ZIMAN, Richard S.——B: Nov. 5, 1942, Williamsport, PA, *Pres.*, Pacific Financial Group; **PRIM RE ACT:** Developer, Builder, Owner/Investor; **SERVICES:** Investment & devel.; **PREV EMPLOY:** Partner, 10 yrs., law firm of Loeb & Loeb, Los Angeles; **PROFL AFFIL & HONORS:** State Bar of CA; **EDUC:** BA, 1964, Hist., Univ. of So. CA; **GRAD EDUC:** JD, 1967, Law, Univ. of So. CA; **EDUC HONORS:** Blue Key; **OTHER ACT & HONORS:** Nat. Bd. of Dirs. of City of Hope; Variety Club; **BUS ADD:** 9595 Wilshire Blvd., Ste. 810, Beverly Hills, CA 90212, (213)271-8600.

ZIMMERMAN, Dennis L.——B: Nov. 19, 1949, Waynesboro, PA, *VP Fin. & Devel.*, Sunnyhill Development Corp.; **PRIM RE ACT:** Developer, Builder, Syndicator; **SERVICES:** Develop for our own acct./synd. to others; **PREV EMPLOY:** Marriott Inc. - 3 Years in Project Fin. of Hotel Projects; **PROFL AFFIL & HONORS:** NAHB; Urban Land Inst; RESSI; **EDUC:** BS, 1971, Bus. Admin. - Mgmt., Shippensburg St. Coll.; **GRAD EDUC:** MBA, 1976, Mktg. and Fin., Harvard Bus. School; **EDUC HONORS:** Grad. w/Academic Honors; **HOME ADD:** 6455 Burning Tree Terr., Fayetteville, PA 17222, (717)352-3946; **BUS ADD:** 550 Cleveland Ave., Chambersburg, PA 17201, (717)264-6150.

ZIMMERMAN, Larry D.——B: Sept. 17, 1942, Pittsburgh, PA, *Exec. VP, Dev.*, Druther's Intl.; **OTHER RE ACT:** Fast food restaurants; **SERVICES:** Build restaurants for own use; **PREV EMPLOY:** Hardee's Food Systems; Gen. Nutrition Corp.; HUD; **PROFL AFFIL & HONORS:** NACORE; ICSC; NRA; **EDUC:** BS, 1971, Acctg./Bus. Mgmt., Pt. Park Coll., Pittsburgh, PA; **HOME ADD:** 901 Lafontenay Ct., Louisville, KY 40223, (502)245-3520; **BUS ADD:** PO Box 6014, 4000 Dupont Cir., Louisville, KY 40223, (502)897-1766.

ZIMMERMAN, Mark——B: Mar. 9, 1954, Dumont, NJ, *Pres.*, Mark Thomas Co., Ltd.; **PRIM RE ACT:** Broker, Consultant, Developer, Owner/Investor, Syndicator; **OTHER RE ACT:** Computer software design & consulting for RE; **SERVICES:** Primarily in finding suitable projects; **EDUC:** BS, 1976, Communication, Boston Univ.; **EDUC HONORS:** Cum Laude, Dean's List; **HOME ADD:** 1575 Tremont St., Boston, MA 02120, (617)566-2626; **BUS ADD:** 73 Charles St., Boston, MA 02114, (617)566-2626.

ZIMMERMAN, Mortimer F.——*VP & Treasurer*, Russ Togs, Inc.; **PRIM RE ACT:** Property Manager; **BUS ADD:** 1411 Broadway, New York, NY 10018, (212)354-0700.*

ZINBERG, Herman——B: Apr. 13, 1923, Philadelphia, PA, *Partner*, Zinberg, Dunn & Co., CPA's; **PRIM RE ACT:** Consultant; **OTHER RE ACT:** Investment counseling, valuation; **SERVICES:** Projections, tax planning, auditing; **REP CLIENTS:** The Henderson Grp., Leonard Wasserman, Spiro & Assoc., Edward Cantor & Co., Bluestein, Mirarchi & Susman; **PROFL AFFIL & HONORS:** Amer. Inst. of CPAs, PA Inst. CPAs; **EDUC:** 1944, Commerce, Temple Univ.; **GRAD EDUC:** CPA, 1951; **MIL SERV:** US Army;, Managed Battalion Post Exch.; **OTHER ACT & HONORS:** Linwood CC (NJ), Palm Aire CC (FL), Treas. KI Men's Club (Elkins Park, PA); **HOME ADD:** 1820 Rittenhouse Sq., Philadelphia, PA 19103, (215)546-8126; **BUS ADD:** 1315 Walnut St., Philadelphia, PA 19107, (215)735-5750.

ZINK, Darell E., Jr.——B: July 29, 1946, Houston, TX, *Atty.-at-Law*, Bose McKinney & Evans; **PRIM RE ACT:** Attorney; **SERVICES:** All forms of legal work for devels., lenders, const. cos., prop. mgrs. and related activities; **REP CLIENTS:** P.R. Duke & Assocs., Park 100 Devel. Co., Keystone Crossing Devel. Co., P.R. Duke Const. Co.; **PROFL AFFIL & HONORS:** ABA, IN Bar Assn., Indianapolis Bar Assn., Member Real Prop. Probate and Trust Div. of ABA, Council Member Real Prop. Div., IN State Bar Assn.; **EDUC:** BA, 1968, Poli. Sci., Vanderbilt Univ.; **GRAD EDUC:** MBA & JD, 1973 & 1976, Univ. of HI and IN Univ.; **EDUC HONORS:** Summa Cum Laude (MBA) - Magna Cum Laude (JD); **MIL SERV:** USAF, Capt.; **HOME ADD:** 5933 Washington Blvd., Indianapolis, IN 46220, (317)255-1915; **BUS ADD:** 8900 Keystone Crossing, Suite 1101, Indianapolis, IN 46240, (317)637-5353.

ZINK, John——B: Aug. 11, 1934, Louisville, Clay Cty., IL, *Owner*, John Zink Real Estate; **PRIM RE ACT:** Broker, Consultant, Appraiser, Banker, Developer, Builder, Property Manager, Insuror, Syndicator; **EDUC:** BS, 1956, Educ., Eastern IL Univ.; **HOME ADD:** Kinmundy Rd., Louisville, IL 62858, (618)665-3140; **BUS ADD:** 150 S. Rt. 45, Louisville, IL 62858, (618)665-4081.

ZINMAN, Philip——B: July 18, 1904, Philadelphia, PA, *Fin. Consultant*; **PRIM RE ACT:** Broker, Consultant; **PREV EMPLOY:** Philip Zinman & Co., Partner 1925-67; Pres. & Dir., 1967-70; Chmn. & Dir. 1971-73. SJ Mort. Co., Pres. & Dir., 1943-60; Chmn., 1960-73. Associated Advisers, Inc., Chmn. & Dir. 1970-73. Fin. Consultant to Seltzer Organization, 1975-78. Self-employed as Fin. Consultant, 1979-Present; **PROFL AFFIL & HONORS:** Camden Cty. RE Bd., from 1926-Past Pres.; AIREA; NJ Chap. AIREA - Past Pres. & Charter Member; Camden Chap. NJ Soc. of Resid. Appraisers - Charter Member from 1939; Past Pres.; NJ Mort. Bankers Assn. - Past Pres.; NJ Mort. Bankers Assn. Educ. Found. - Past Pres.; **EDUC:** BS, 1925, Econ., Univ. of PA, Philadelphia, PA; **GRAD EDUC:** 1925-29, Law, Temple Univ., Philadelphia, PA; **MIL SERV:** USCG, Ens., Vol. Port Security Force; **OTHER ACT & HONORS:** Albert Einstein Medical Center - TR. from 1971; United Jewish Appeal: Nat. Chmn. from 1968-1979; Hon. VChmn. & TR. 1979- Bd. of Dir. 1969-79; NJ State Chmn. 1966; Gen. Chmn. Camden Cty. 1948-1949 & 1959; Israel Educ. Fund, Pres. from 1971-1975; Chmn. from 1976-78 Chmn. Exec. Comm. 1978 - ; Jewish Agency for Israel - Bd. of Govs. - from 1974; Philadelphia Federation of Jewish Agencies - Bd. of TRS. - 1962-1975; Exec. Comm. 1976- ; State of Israel Bonds - Nat. Bd. of Govs. from 1974; NJ State Chmn. 1954; Camden Crime Commn. of Philadelphia - Member; United Nations Assn. - Member Past; American Friends of Hebrew Univ. - Nat. VP - 1966-1970; American Friends of Hebrew

Univ. - Philadelphia Chap. Pres. 1959-1963; Bd. of Dirs. 1959--1968; TR., UJA, Inc. - Employees Retirement Plan; United Israel Appeal, Bd. of Dirs. 1968 - ; State of Israel Bond Effort - 1954; Big Wheel Award - State of Israel Bond Award for Inspiring Leadership - 1970; Jewish Fed. of Camden - 1st Annual Community Service Award - 1962; State of Israel Outstanding Devotion to UJA - 1963; American Jewish Comm. Human Relations Award - NJ 1965; UJA Award of Honor for 20 yrs. Serv. - 1945-1965 - Camden ; Philadelphia Fed. of Jewish Agencies Man of the Year Award - 1973; American Friends of the Hebrew Univ. - Torch of Learning Award - 1970; **HOME ADD:** 14-A Cloister Beach Towers, 1200 S. Ocean Blvd., Boca Raton, FL 33432, (305)395-9241; **BUS ADD:** 519 Market St., Camden, NJ 08102, (609)966-0320.

ZINMAN, Robert M.——**B:** Apr. 23, 1931, NYC, NY, *VP and Investment Counsel*, Metropolitan Life Insurance Co.; **PRIM RE ACT:** Attorney, Instructor; **OTHER RE ACT:** Adjunct Prof. of Law, Fordham Univ.; **SERVICES:** As head of RE Investments Sect. of Law Dept., provide legal serv. relating to co.'s portfolio of over $15 Billion in RE investments; **PROFL AFFIL & HONORS:** Amer. Coll. of RE Lawyers; Bd. Chmn., Creditor's Rights in RE Fin., ABA, Real Prop. Sect.; Chmn., Investment Sect., Assn. of Life Ins. Counsel; Chmn., Subcomm. on Fed. Bankruptcy Legislation; Amer. Council of Life Ins.; Adjunct Prof. of Law, Fordham Univ. School of Law; NY Bar; ABA; NY State Bar Assn.; Amer. Land Title Assn.; **EDUC:** BA, 1953, Govt., Tufts Univ.; **GRAD EDUC:** JD, 1960, Harvard Law School; LLM, 1965, NYU School of Law; **MIL SERV:** USN, Capt.; **OTHER ACT & HONORS:** Pres., Navy Marine Res. Lawyers Assn., 1976; Bd. of Dirs., Conf. on Jewish Social Studies; **BUS ADD:** 1 Madison Ave., New York, NY 10010.

ZINN, Elias——**B:** Nov. 7, 1954, Houston, TX, *Part.*, 'Z' Investments; **PRIM RE ACT:** Developer, Owner/Investor, Property Manager; **PREV EMPLOY:** Pres. Custom NFI; **PROFL AFFIL & HONORS:** USA, BBB member, C of C member, Jayees Houston; **EDUC:** 1972-4, Univ. of TX; **OTHER ACT & HONORS:** Who's Who in Amer., 1980, Editor Distinguished Amer. Award, 1980-81 editor; **HOME ADD:** 1480 Sugar Creek Blvd., Sugarland, TX 77478, (713)491-2213; **BUS ADD:** PO Drawer 887, Stafford, TX 77477, (713)933-0500.

ZINN, Judith A.——**B:** Jan. 21, 1939, Superior, WI, *Broker Associate - Appraiser*, Stanton Co.; **PRIM RE ACT:** Broker, Appraiser; **PROFL AFFIL & HONORS:** AIREA, Member Montclair Bd. of Realtors, NJ Assn. of Realtors, RM Candidate; **EDUC:** BS, 1960, Biochemistry, Univ. of Chicago; **OTHER ACT & HONORS:** VP, Joint Comm, for the Revitalization of the Central Bus. Dist. of Montclair. Grants Advisory Comm., Town of Montclair Beautification Comm., Town of Montclair; **HOME ADD:** 85 Porter Place, Montclair, NJ 07042, (201)746-4908; **BUS ADD:** 25 N. Fullerton Ave., Montclair, NJ 07042, (201)746-1313.

ZIPFEL, Marion S.——**B:** Nov. 8, 1938, IL, *Owner*, Zipfel Enterprises; **PRIM RE ACT:** Developer, Property Manager, Owner/Investor; **OTHER ACT & HONORS:** Profl. Baseball Players Assn., Elks Club, Played Profl. Baseball with NY Yankees, WA Senators 11 yrs.; **HOME ADD:** 57 Whiteside Dr., Belleville, IL 62221; **BUS ADD:** 116a E. Main St., Belleville, IL 62220.

ZISLER, Randall Craig——**B:** Dec. 15, 1946, Detroit, MI, *Chief Econ. & Dir. of Research*, Jones Lang Wootton, Investments; **PRIM RE ACT:** Consultant; **SERVICES:** RE consulting; **REP CLIENTS:** Maj. nat. & intl. corps. & instns., and wealthy indivs.; **PREV EMPLOY:** Asst. Prof. Princeton Univ., Pres. Zisler RE Consulting; **PROFL AFFIL & HONORS:** NYRE Bd., RE NY Salesman, AEA, RE salesman; **EDUC:** BA, 1968, Arch., Princeton Univ., NJ; **GRAD EDUC:** PhD, 1977, Econ., Urban Planning, Princeton Univ.; MAUP, Arch., Princeton; MSE, 1972, Civil Engrg., Catholic Univ.; MA, 1974, Urban Planning, Princeton; **EDUC HONORS:** NSF Scholarship; **HOME ADD:** 2352 Pennington Rd., Trenton, NJ 08638, (609)737-0448; **BUS ADD:** 499 Park Ave., New York, NY 10022, (212)688-8181.

ZITELLI, John F.——**B:** May 25, 1947, Pittsburgh, PA, *Pres.*, John F. Zitelli; **PRIM RE ACT:** Consultant, Builder, Owner/Investor, Property Manager; **SERVICES:** Investment consultation, rental units; **PREV EMPLOY:** Rental mgmt., RE sales and consultation; **PROFL AFFIL & HONORS:** RAM; Builders Assn. of Pittsburgh; Apt. Assn. of Pittsburgh; **EDUC:** BS, 1970, Bus. Admin., Robert Morris Coll.; **OTHER ACT & HONORS:** Regent Square Civic Assn.; **HOME ADD:** 814 S. Braddock Ave., Pittsburgh, PA 15221, (412)242-1641; **BUS ADD:** 814 S. Braddock Ave., Pittsburgh, PA 15221, (412)242-1641.

ZOLDOS, Jeffrey A.E.——**B:** Mar. 2, 1952, Los Angeles, *Dir. of Synd./Asst. VP*, Amer. Dev. Corp., Synd./Equity Financing; **PRIM RE ACT:** Consultant, Instructor, Syndicator; **SERVICES:** Structuring & sale of RE synd.; **REP CLIENTS:** Merrill Lynch, Dean Witter, Sutro & Co. direct to investors; **PROFL AFFIL & HONORS:** Amer. RE & Urban Econ. Assn.; RE Broker and General Bldg. Contractor, Adjuct Prof. of RE at CA Polytechnic State Univ.; Listed in Who's Who in the West, Member, Bd. of Dir. of KCET (educational TV station) support group; **EDUC:** Business, 1975, Fin. & Prop. Man., CA Polytechnic State Univ.; **GRAD EDUC:** MBA, 1977, RE, Univ. of OR; **EDUC HONORS:** Soc. for Advancement of Mgt., Beta Gamma Sigma; **HOME ADD:** 535 S Alexandria Ave. #322, Los Angeles, CA 90020, (213)383-3081; **BUS ADD:** 3250 Wilshire Blvd., Suite 2000, Los Angeles, CA 90010, (213)480-1541.

ZOOK, William G.——**B:** Dec. 10, 1934, Denver, CO, *VP, Operating Mgr.*, Midland Serv. Corp., RE Div.; **PRIM RE ACT:** Developer, Lender, Owner/Investor; **SERVICES:** Primarily subdiv. devel., finished lots; **PROFL AFFIL & HONORS:** Home Builders Assn., RE Broker; **EDUC:** BS, 1957, Acctg., Regis Coll., Denver, CO; **MIL SERV:** USMC Res., Lt. Col.; **OTHER ACT & HONORS:** Optimist Club, Denver Athletic Club; **HOME ADD:** 4400 So. Quebec St., A108, Denver, CO 80237, (303)741-3766; **BUS ADD:** 1435 Wadsworth Bldv., Lakewood, CO 80215, (303)233-6587.

ZOUKIS, Stephen J.——**B:** July 2, 1949, Montpelier, VT, *Part.*, Wildman, Harrold, Allen, Dixon & Masinter; **PRIM RE ACT:** Attorney; **PROFL AFFIL & HONORS:** Amer., GA, Atlanta Bar Assns.; **EDUC:** BME, 1971, Univ. of VA; **GRAD EDUC:** JD, 1974, Columbia Univ.; **EDUC HONORS:** Honors, Sigma Xi, Tau Beta Pi; **HOME ADD:** 784 Vedado Way N.E., Atlanta, GA, (404)872-8007; **BUS ADD:** 1200 S. Omni Intl., Atlanta, GA 30303, (404)656-1200.

ZSCHAU, Julius J.——**B:** Apr. 1, 1940, Peoria, IL, Sorota & Zschau P.A.; **PRIM RE ACT:** Attorney; **SERVICES:** Legal Servs.; **REP CLIENTS:** US Home Corp.; Arthur Rutenberg Corp.; Maison Phoenix; Beacon Homes; Hamilton RE; Crist Realty, Inc.; Life Devel. Corp.; **PREV EMPLOY:** Counsel, IL Center Corp.; VP Gen. Counsel and Sec. Amer. Agronomics Corp.; **PROFL AFFIL & HONORS:** ABA; IL State Bar Assn.; FL Bar; Chicago Bar Assns.; Clearwater Bar Assn., Designated under Florida Bar Plan in Real Property Law; **EDUC:** BS, 1962, Commerce, Univ. of IL; **GRAD EDUC:** JD, 1966, Law, Univ. of IL; LLM, 1978, The John Marshall Law School; **MIL SERV:** US Naval Res.; Comdr.; **OTHER ACT & HONORS:** VP Govt. Affairs, C of C; Bd. of Dirs., FL Gulf Coast Symphony; **HOME ADD:** 1910 Saddlehill Rd. North, Dunedin, FL 33528, (813)784-8490; **BUS ADD:** 2515 Countryside Blvd., Suite A, Clearwater, FL 33515, (813)796-2525.

ZSOLNAY, Gabor M.——**B:** Aug. 25, 1944, Budapest, Hungary, *Univ. Architect*, Northwestern Univ.; **PRIM RE ACT:** Architect, Builder, Owner/Investor; **SERVICES:** Const. administrator/owners rep.; **PROFL AFFIL & HONORS:** SCUP; AVA; **EDUC:** BArch, Arch./Planning, IL Inst. of Tech.; **GRAD EDUC:** MS, 1969, City and Rgnl. Planning, IL Inst. of Tech.; **HOME ADD:** 327 Dempster St., Evanston, IL 60201, (312)475-0410; **BUS ADD:** 910 University Place, Evanston, IL 60202.

ZUCCO, William C.——**B:** Aug. 19, 1945, St. Paul, MN, *Dir. of Props.*, National Car Rental System, Inc.; **PRIM RE ACT:** Attorney, Property Manager; **OTHER RE ACT:** Airport Negotiations; **PREV EMPLOY:** Gen. practice of law; **PROFL AFFIL & HONORS:** ABA, MN State Bar Assn.; **EDUC:** BA, 1967, Pol. Sci./Hist., Univ. of MN; **GRAD EDUC:** JD, 1971, Univ. of MN; **MIL SERV:** US Army Res., Spec. E6; **HOME ADD:** 10508 Zion Ave. S, Bloomington, MN 55437, (612)884-6113; **BUS ADD:** 7700 France Ave. S, Minneapolis, MN 55435, (612)893-6250.

ZUCK, Daniel R.——**B:** Mar. 13, 1911, Bareville, PA; **PRIM RE ACT:** Engineer, Owner/Investor, Property Manager; **SERVICES:** Prop. mgmt.; **EDUC:** 1936, Aeronautical Engineering, Casey Jones School of Aeronautics; **GRAD EDUC:** Assoc. Degree, 1936, Academy of Aeronautics; **HOME ADD:** 14273 Beaver St., Sylmar, CA 91342, (213)367-6745; **BUS ADD:** 14273 Beaver St., Sylmar, CA 91342, (213)367-6745.

ZUCKER, Cher. R.——**B:** Sept. 5, 1949, Newark, NJ, *Gen. Mgr., RE Operations*, Prudential Insurance Co. of America; **PRIM RE ACT:** Developer, Lender, Owner/Investor, Instructor, Property Manager; **PROFL AFFIL & HONORS:** Louisville Bd. of Realtors, IREM, CPM; **EDUC:** BS, 1971, Math, Coll. of William & Mary; **GRAD EDUC:** MBA, 1975, Fin., Rutgers Univ. Grad. Sch. of Bus. Admin.; **EDUC HONORS:** Deans List, Outstanding Sr. Woman, Beta Sigma Rho (Honors Soc.); **OTHER ACT & HONORS:** Louisville Alumni Club, Alpha Chi Omega, Currently an approved member of IREM's Nat. faculty; **HOME ADD:** 14108 Harbour Pl., Prospect, KY 40059; **BUS ADD:** 10001 Linn Stateion Rd. 114, Louisville, KY 40223, (502)425-4201.

ZUCKER, Norman P.——B: Feb. 25, 1926, Cleveland, OH, *Pres.*, Providence Capitol Realty Group, Inc, subs. of Gulf & Western Indus., Inc.; **PRIM RE ACT:** Developer, Builder, Lender, Owner/Investor; **PREV EMPLOY:** Pres. NEI Corp. 1970–1975; **PROFL AFFIL & HONORS:** Member OH Bar; **EDUC:** LLB, 1952, Pol. Sci, Western Reserve Univ.; **GRAD EDUC:** LLB, LLD, 1952WsWestern Reserve Univ; **EDUC HONORS:** Law Review Assoc. Editor; **MIL SERV:** USAF, S/Sgt.; **OTHER ACT & HONORS:** City of New Orleans Commn. on Parks and Commn. on railroads 1970–1975, Dir. of New Orleans ABA Assoc., Dir. of New Orleans C of C 1970–1974, Dir. JA of New Orleans 1970–1974; **HOME ADD:** 220 E 65th St, New York, NY 10021, (212)752-4697; **BUS ADD:** 1 Gulf & Western Plaza, New York, NY 10023, (212)333-2974.

ZUCKERBROT, Kenneth, Esq.——B: June 7, 1944, *Sr. Part.*, Wiener, Zuckerbrot & Weiss; **PRIM RE ACT:** Attorney; **PROFL AFFIL & HONORS:** ABA, NY Bar Assn.; **EDUC:** BA, 1965, Fed. Tax., Clark Univ.; **GRAD EDUC:** JD, Brooklyn Law School; LLM (In Taxation), 1971, Fed. Tax., NYU Grad. School of Law; **HOME ADD:** 345 East 80th St., New York, NY 10021, (212)628-6625; **BUS ADD:** 260 Madison Ave., 21st Floor, New York, NY 10016, (212)725-2220.

ZUCKERMAN, Howard A.——B: July 18, 1950, Cleveland, OH, *Pres.*, Seville Development Group, Ltd.; **PRIM RE ACT:** Developer, Builder, Owner/Investor, Syndicator; **OTHER RE ACT:** Condo-Converter; **PREV EMPLOY:** Acquest Group, USA; **PROFL AFFIL & HONORS:** Atlanta Home Builders Assn., Community Assns. Inst.; **EDUC:** BS, 1972, Mktg., OH State Univ.; **GRAD EDUC:** MS, 1975, RE investment analysis, Urban land econ. & appraisal, Univ. of WI; **HOME ADD:** 2246 Cedar Forks Dr., Marietta, GA 30062, (404)973-9293; **BUS ADD:** 6201 Powers Ferry Rd. 500, Atlanta, GA 30339, (404)952-1500.

ZUCKERMAN, Milton——B: May 6, 1905, NY, NY, *Self employed*; **PRIM RE ACT:** Attorney; **PROFL AFFIL & HONORS:** ABA, Sect. on Real Prop., Probate & Trust; **EDUC:** Attended Coll. of City of NY-School of Bus. Admin.; **GRAD EDUC:** LLB, 1928, NY Univ. Law School; **MIL SERV:** US Army, USAF, Lt. 1942-45, Army Comm., medal; **HOME ADD:** 420 E 55th St., New York, NY 10022, (212)688-4569; **BUS ADD:** 19 W 44th St., New York, NY 10036, (212)840-0974.

ZUCKERMAN, Mitchell——B: Apr. 13, 1946, NYC, *Gen. Counsel*, Sotheby Parke Bernet Intl. Realty Corp.; **PRIM RE ACT:** Attorney; **SERVICES:** Broker of luxury RE; **EDUC:** AB, 1968, Hist., Univ. of Rochester; **GRAD EDUC:** MA, 1971, Harvard Univ.; JD, 1974, Columbia Law School; **HOME ADD:** 190 Forest Ave., Rye, NY 10580, (914)967-3849; **BUS ADD:** 980 Madison Ave., New York, NY 10021, (212)472-3476.

ZUCKERMAN, Mortimer B.——B: June 4, 1937, Boston Properties; **PRIM RE ACT:** Developer; **SERVICES:** RE devel. and investment with major interests in the metropolitan areas of Boston, Los Angeles, San Francisco, Phildalephia and Washington; **PREV EMPLOY:** Senior VP Cabot, Cabot and Forbes 1962-69; Assoc. Prof. of City and Regional Planning, Harvard Graduate School of Design 1971-74; **EDUC:** BA, McGill University; **GRAD EDUC:** MBA, Univ. of Pennsylvania; LLB, McGill University; **OTHER ACT & HONORS:** Owner and Pres., Atlantic Monthly Co.; Pres. Sidney Farber Cancer Inst.; Trustee Stride Rite Corp.; Trustee Ford Hall Forum; Trustee Museum of Science; **HOME ADD:** 2 Spruce St., Boston, MA 02116; **BUS ADD:** 8 Arlington St., Boston, MA 02116, (617)262-6500.*

ZUCKERMAN, Norman J.——B: Mar. 19, 1943, Denver, CO, Coldwell Banker; **PRIM RE ACT:** Consultant, Developer, Owner/Investor, Property Manager; **SERVICES:** Prop. Mgmt., Investment & Devel. Counseling; **REP CLIENTS:** Inst. and Indiv. Investors in Shopping Center/Retail and Office Props., Condo. Assns./Devel.; **PREV EMPLOY:** Broadbent Devel. Co., 1980-1981; Prop. Mgmt., Inc., 1970-1980; **PROFL AFFIL & HONORS:** Inst. of RE Mgmt.; Urban Land Instit.; Nat. Assn. of Home Builders, Building Owners and Mgrs., CPM; **EDUC:** BA, 1965, Sci./Arts/Bus., Univ. of CO; **MIL SERV:** USAF, Capt., Commendation; **OTHER ACT & HONORS:** Outstanding Young Man of Amer., 1980; **HOME ADD:** 7819 85th Pl. S.E., Mercer Island, WA 98040, (206)236-2142; **BUS ADD:** 1600 Park Pl., Seattle, WA 98101, (206)292-6164.

ZUGSMITH, Michael A.——B: Mar. 10, 1951, Los Angeles, CA, *Pres.*, Zugsmith & Assoc., Inc.; **PRIM RE ACT:** Broker, Developer, Builder, Owner/Investor, Property Manager; **PROFL AFFIL & HONORS:** ICSC; Los Angeles C of C; **EDUC:** BA, 1976, Communication Studies, UCLA; **EDUC HONORS:** Chmn. Beta Phi Gamma, Pres. Awards, Cert. of Appreciation; **OTHER ACT & HONORS:** Natural Hist. Musuem Alliance; **HOME ADD:** 4184 Dixie Canyon Ave., Sherman Oaks, CA 91423, (213)789-6042; **BUS ADD:** 12711 Ventura Blvd., Suite 230, Studio City, CA 91604, (213)760-1211.

ZUNIGA, Thomas M.——B: May 27, 1947, Belize, Central America, *Pres.*, Zuniga and Assoc.; **PRIM RE ACT:** Consultant, Developer, Owner/Investor, Syndicator; **SERVICES:** Housing devel. consulting; investment counseling; devel. and synd.; **REP CLIENTS:** Dept. of HUD, Local & State Housing Fin. Agencies, Non Profit Housing and Comm. Devel Org.; **PREV EMPLOY:** The Nat. Housing Partnership, VP/Urban Devel.; Coopers & Lybrand, Tax Supervisor; New York Life Ins. Co. RE Dept./Appraiser Mort. Underwriter; **PROFL AFFIL & HONORS:** Nat. Assn. of Home Builders, Nat. Assn. of Housing and Redevel. Officials; Member, Advisory Bd., DC Housing Fin. Agency, Wash., DC, Member, Partnership Comm., Apt. Improvement Program, Lubin Fellow 1968; **EDUC:** BA, 1968, Psych., Econ., Pace Univ. , NY; **GRAD EDUC:** MA, 1970, Pol. Sci., Columbia Univ., NY; **HOME ADD:** 1400 Emerson St. NW, Washington, DC 20011, (202)829-5973; **BUS ADD:** 918 16th St. NW #301, Washington, DC 20006, (202)861-0970.

ZYNDORF, Mark——B: May 10, 1952, Brooklyn, NY, *VP*, The Danberry Co., Comml.-Indus.-Investment; **PRIM RE ACT:** Broker, Consultant, Developer, Owner/Investor; **SERVICES:** Investment consulting, site acquisition for fast food restaurants and retail bus., also provide build to suit leaseback packages for clients, shopping center leasing, comml. leasing, investment brokerage; **PROFL AFFIL & HONORS:** CCIM, GRI, Toledo Bd. of Realtors, The OH Assn. of Realtors, NAR, RNMI, RESSI; **HOME ADD:** 6646 Kingsbridge Dr., Sylvania, OH 43560, (419)882-2379; **BUS ADD:** 309 N. Reynolds Rd., Toledo, OH 43615, (419)535-1451.

Index by Geographic Area and Primary Professional Activity

Property Manager
Chittam, Dick
Hamilton, Joe F.
Heath, Robert H.
Sadler, Wade B.
Spiva, Judy "Breezy" P.
Warren, Shelby H.

Syndicator
Ford, Thomas S.
Sadler, Wade B.
Warren, Shelby H.

MOBILE

Appraiser
Bealle, Thomas B. III
Free, Liston Jr.
Gerhardt, Sidney J.
Hunt, Philip
Rapier, Reginald (Rex) Jr.
Reed, Julian S.
Travis, Edward F.

Architect
Bischoff, Charles F.

Attorney
Adams, John W. Jr.
Allen, Robert H.
Meigs, Walter R.
Stanard, Chandler Kite
Wells, Caroline E.

Banker
Steele, S.S.

Broker
Barnhill, Charles William
Bealle, Thomas B. III
Brown, Alton R. III
Day, Bennie R.
Drane, Phillip D.
Ephgrave, Bert. III
Free, Liston Jr.
Reed, Julian S.
Roberts, David D. Jr.
Steele, S.S.
Stefan, Chester J.
Travis, Edward F.
Vetter, John O.
Ward, Wade
Weller, T. C. Jr.

Builder
Steele, S.S.
Stefan, Chester J.
Vetter, John O.

Consultant
Barnhill, Charles William
Bealle, Thomas B. III
Drane, Phillip D.
Free, Liston Jr.
Gerhardt, Sidney J.
Rapier, Reginald (Rex) Jr.
Reed, Julian S.
Roberts, David D. Jr.
Saint, John B.
Stefan, Chester J.
Travis, Edward F.
Weller, T. C. Jr.

Developer
Altmayer, Jay P. II
Bealle, Thomas B. III
Brown, Alton R. III
Drane, Phillip D.
Roberts, David D. Jr.
Saint, John B.
Stanard, Chandler Kite
Steele, S.S.
Stefan, Chester J.
Vetter, John O.
Weller, T. C. Jr.

Instructor
Bealle, Thomas B. III
Reed, Julian S.
Travis, Edward F.

Insuror
Bealle, Thomas B. III
Reed, Julian S.
Steele, S.S.

Lender
Free, Liston Jr.
Stefan, Chester J.

Owner/Investor
Altmayer, Jay P. II
Barnhill, Charles William
Bealle, Thomas B. III
Day, Bennie R.
Drane, Phillip D.
Gerhardt, Sidney J.
Reed, Julian S.
Roberts, David D. Jr.
Stanard, Chandler Kite
Stefan, Chester J.
Weller, T. C. Jr.

Property Manager
Bealle, Thomas B. III
Brown, Alton R. III
Day, Bennie R.
Drane, Phillip D.
Gerhardt, Sidney J.
Kearnes, Selden S.
McMurphy, Edward
Meigs, Walter R.
Reed, Julian S.
Roberts, David D. Jr.
Saint, John B.
Stefan, Chester J.
Vetter, John O.
Weller, T. C. Jr.

Regulator
Day, Bennie R.

Syndicator
Barnhill, Charles William
Bealle, Thomas B. III
Drane, Phillip D.
Stanard, Chandler Kite
Stefan, Chester J.
Vetter, John O.
Weller, T. C. Jr.

MONTGOMERY

Appraiser
Scruggs, William C. Jr.
Seabury, Glen N. Jr.

Attorney
Azar, Edward J.
Hill, T. Bowen III
Piel, J. Richard

Banker
Berry, Richard B.
Sport, Haywood M.

Broker
Abraham, Jack H. Jr.
Cheseldine, Richard J. Jr.
Inscoe, Jim T.
Piel, J. Richard
Scruggs, William C. Jr.
Seabury, Glen N. Jr.
Winter, Irving M.

Builder
Abraham, Jack H. Jr.
Piel, J. Richard
Richey, Alvan E. Jr.
Robinson, Peter C.

Consultant
Berry, Richard B.
Godin, R. J. Jr.
Piel, J. Richard
Scruggs, William C. Jr.
Seabury, Glen N. Jr.
Winter, Irving M.

Developer
Abraham, Jack H. Jr.
Godin, R. J. Jr.
Inscoe, Jim T.
Piel, J. Richard
Scruggs, William C. Jr.
Seabury, Glen N. Jr.
Winter, Irving M.

Instructor
Azar, Edward J.
Piel, J. Richard
Scruggs, William C. Jr.

Insuror
Abraham, Jack H. Jr.

Lender
Piel, J. Richard

Owner/Investor
Abraham, Jack H. Jr.
Cheseldine, Richard J. Jr.
Piel, J. Richard
Scruggs, William C. Jr.
Seabury, Glen N. Jr.
Winter, Irving M.

Property Manager
Abraham, Jack H. Jr.
Berry, Richard B.
Godin, R. J. Jr.
Inscoe, Jim T.
Piel, J. Richard
Seabury, Glen N. Jr.
Winter, Irving M.

Syndicator
Piel, J. Richard
Scruggs, William C. Jr.
Seabury, Glen N. Jr.

OPELIKA

Attorney
Tucker, Billie Anne

TUSCALOOSA

Broker
Wilhite, R. Gene
Wilson, Charles A.

Consultant
Wilson, Charles A.

Developer
Wilson, Charles A.

Instructor
Wilhite, R. Gene
Wilson, Charles A.

Owner/Investor
Wilhite, R. Gene
Wilson, Charles A.

Property Manager
Wilson, Charles A.

Syndicator
Wilson, Charles A.

ALASKA

ANCHORAGE

Appraiser
Bashaw, John M. Jr.
Ferrara, Alfred J.
Fournier, Walter F.
Karabelnikoff, Don G.
Renner, Robin L.
Waldner, Garrett W.
Zamzow, Kenneth E.

Attorney
Beard, John R.
Burton, Edward Gould
Hoge, Andrew E.
Kurtz, L.S. Jr.
Lekisch, Peter A.
McCollum, James H.
Renner, Robin L.
Ross, Herbert A.
Vittone, Joseph A.

Banker
Ledbetter, Patricia
Smith, H. Derrell

Broker
Bashaw, John M. Jr.
Bowden, Dwight R.
Ferguson, Debra
Fournier, Walter F.
Houston, Lee
Norman, Billy H.
Renner, Robin L.
Ross, Herbert A.
Schlegel, William J.
Schreck, William R.
Shaw, E. Kenneth
Sokol, Loretta D.
Vittone, Joseph A.

Builder
Bashaw, John M. Jr.
Bowden, Dwight R.
Eker, Andrew H.
Schlegel, William J.

Consultant
Allum, Jerry
Bashaw, John M. Jr.
Bowden, Dwight R.
Buness, Everett W.
Ferrara, Alfred J.
Fournier, Walter F.
Griffin, Charles R.
Houston, Lee
Karabelnikoff, Don G.
Law, Jay L.
Renner, Robin L.
Schlegel, William J.
Sokol, Loretta D.
Vittone, Joseph A.
Waldner, Garrett W.
Zamzow, Kenneth E.

Developer
Bashaw, John M. Jr.
Bowden, Dwight R.
Buness, Everett W.
Dugick, Angela E.
Eker, Andrew H.
Hovey, Winthrop T.
Law, Jay L.
Schlegel, William J.
Waldner, Garrett W.

Instructor
Burton, Edward Gould
Ferrara, Alfred J.
Houston, Lee
Norman, Billy H.
Shaw, E. Kenneth
Waldner, Garrett W.
Zamzow, Kenneth E.

Insuror
Houston, Lee

Lender
Law, Jay L.
Ledbetter, Patricia

Owner/Investor
Allum, Jerry
Bowden, Dwight R.
Buness, Everett W.
Burton, Edward Gould
Eker, Andrew H.
Griffin, Charles R.
Houston, Lee
Hovey, Winthrop T.
Kurtz, L.S. Jr.
Law, Jay L.

Norman, Billy H.
Renner, Robin L.
Ross, Herbert A.
Shaw, E. Kenneth
Vittone, Joseph A.
Waldner, Garrett W.
Zamzow, Kenneth E.

Property Manager
Allum, Jerry
Bowden, Dwight R.
Griffin, Charles R.
Law, Jay L.
Norman, Billy H.
Renner, Robin L.
Waldner, Garrett W.
Zamzow, Kenneth E.

Regulator
Magowan, James L.

Syndicator
Bashaw, John M. Jr.
Bowden, Dwight R.
Houston, Lee
Law, Jay L.
Norman, Billy H.
Renner, Robin L.
Schlegel, William J.
Shaw, E. Kenneth
Vittone, Joseph A.
Waldner, Garrett W.

FAIRBANKS

Attorney
Schuhmann, Barbara L.

Broker
Cook, Jeffry J.
Groff, Anna

Builder
Groff, Anna
Wilcox, Walter J.

Developer
Groff, Anna
Wilcox, Walter J.

Instructor
Schuhmann, Barbara L.

Owner/Investor
Groff, Anna
Wilcox, Walter J.

Property Manager
Wilcox, Walter J.

ARIZONA

FLAGSTAFF

Broker
Harkey, Willard W.

PHOENIX

Appraiser
Aceto, Frank R.
Albert, Timothy D.
Anderson, Fenton
Ball, Thomas A.
Baron, Richard E.
Blackerby, William F.
Burford, Robert H.
Farr, Dennis P.
Francy, Robert E.
Gaudette, Arthur T.
Gentry, Allan S.
Gross, James E.
Johnson, Paul G.
Johnson, Peter R.
Kallof, Fred Jr.
Kennelly, Thomas A.
McPherson, Robert E.
Miller, Barbara Shaw
Rozan, Gerry M.
Sell, Jan A.
Simonton, G. Scott
Thomas-Williams, Robert C.
Wallace, Donald L.
Watson, Robert S. Jr.
Wingblade, P.B.
Witt, Floyd E.

Architect
Bagg, Carter Davis
Yates, John David
Young, Martin Ray Jr.

Assessor
Albert, Timothy D.
McPherson, Robert E.
Seal, R.L.
Wingblade, P.B.

Attorney
Ayers, Charles K.
Bregman, Mark A.
Bronnenkant, Anna
Diessner, Michael F.
Durfee, David Allen
Flood, T. Patrick
Helgesen, Jack C.
Henward, DeBanks M. III
Hillhouse, Richard A.
Himelstein, Mandel E.
Hutchison, S. R.
Lancy, John S.
Levy, John S.
Lowe, Ronald E.
McMahan, John A.
McRae, Hamilton E. III
Morga, William E.
Postal, David R.
Richardson, Edmund F.
Sanderson, David V.
Schaeffer, Louis B.
Smith, Russell B. III
Stuckey, Jay C. Jr.
Warner, Ted F.

Banker
Bohannan, Robert C. Jr.
Bronnenkant, Anna
Gross, James E.

Broker
Adamson, Jeanne A.
Allen, Richard
Alterson, Marvin
Anderson, Fenton
Avery, Hartford R.
Baron, Richard E.
Belsher, Harold R.
Bernard, Stephen Zouck
Blackerby, William F.
Cowles, Ben W.
Dameron, Ben B. Jr.
Demson, Robert D.
Du Bois, Reyn
Egbert, Clark R.
Estes, John P.
Foster, John D.
Gabel, Kenneth G.
Galst, Lester R.
Geahlen, Donald
Goodacre, Kenneth Robert CPM
Graham, William J.
Graves, William G. III
Gross, James E.
Hearn, Arlene
Heiple, Don W.
Hillger, Dave
Hyland, Kenneth J.
Iliff, George S.
Ingebritson, Jack
Jensen, Paul M.
Johnson, Peter R.
Jones, Reg. C.
Kallof, Fred Jr.
Keith, John A.
Kennelly, Thomas A.
Knochenhauer, Theo. G.
Knoell, Joseph
Leonhart, C.J.
Levy, John S.
Lewkowitz, Burt
Macbeth, William G.
MacIntyre, David William
McKellar, Donald M. III
McMahan, John A.
Mayfield, Robert G.
Meadows, Dan S.
Moore, Richard D.
Moss, John P.
Muir, A. Gary
Neill, M.D.
Parker, Phil
Price, Billie B. Jr.
Rakow, Michael G.
Rector, R. Dale
Rector, Richard A.
Richardson, Thomas W.
Roeske, Ronald E.
Rose, William H.
Rozan, Gerry M.
Sargent, Paul E.
Scott, Michael A.
Soudriette, James W.
Stanfield-Pinel, Bertrand
Steinegger, Frank J. III
Suphan, William H.
Wasson, Thomas L.
Weaver, Park Jr.
Wiggs, P. David
Wilson, Margot P.
Witt, Floyd E.
Zajac, Terrence Michael
Zell, Alan L.

Builder
Adamson, Jeanne A.
Armstrong, Bret Alan
Baron, Richard E.
Bernard, Stephen Zouck
Blackerby, William F.
Brant, Debarah Staaey
Burd, Anthony M.
Cartwright, Ed
Coxwell, Roy P.
Geahlen, Donald
Horne, M.S.
Horton, G. Michael
Knochenhauer, Theo. G.
Knoell, Joseph
Kraemer, Richard C.
Miller, Barbara Shaw
Nelson, Gary L.
Osborne, Earl
Rozan, Gerry M.
Rush, James W.
Simonton, G. Scott
Stanfield-Pinel, Bertrand
Thomas-Williams, Robert C.
Wiggs, P. David

Consultant
Aceto, Frank R.
Allen, Richard
Alterson, Marvin
Anderson, Fenton
Armstrong, Bret Alan
Bagg, Carter Davis
Ball, Thomas A.
Baron, Richard E.
Bernard, Stephen Zouck
Blackerby, William F.
Carpenter, R. Jay
Cooper, William H.
Cowles, Ben W.
Crosby, R. Edward
Davis, Joseph M.
Demson, Robert D.
Du Bois, Reyn
Ebeling, Leslie G.
Estes, John P.
Farr, Dennis P.
Foster, John D.
Francy, Robert E.
Galst, Lester R.
Geahlen, Donald
Gentry, Allan S.
Goodacre, Kenneth Robert
Graham, William J.
Gross, James E.
Heiple, Don W.
Hutchison, S. R.
Hyland, Kenneth J.
Ingebritson, Jack
Johnson, Paul G.
Johnson, Peter R.
Kallof, Fred Jr.
Kennelly, Thomas A.
Lake, Jack S.
Levy, John S.
McMahan, John A.
McRae, Hamilton E. III
Mayfield, Robert G.
Meadows, Dan S.
Miller, Barbara Shaw
Neill, M.D.
Osborne, Earl
Parker, Phil
Peterman, Gordon G.
Postal, David R.
Price, Billie B. Jr.
Rakow, Michael G.
Rector, Richard A.
Rose, Robert W.
Scott, Michael A.
Sell, Jan A.
Simonton, G. Scott
Smith, Russell B. III
Soudriette, James W.
Stanfield-Pinel, Bertrand
Thomas-Williams, Robert C.
Wallace, Donald L.
Weaver, Park Jr.
Wilson, Margot P.
Wingblade, P.B.
Yates, John David
Zajac, Terrence Michael
Zell, Alan L.

Developer
Adamson, Jeanne A.
Allen, Richard
Alterson, Marvin
Armstrong, Bret Alan
Baron, Richard E.
Bernard, Stephen Zouck
Brant, Debarah Staaey
Burd, Anthony M.
Carpenter, R. Jay
Coxwell, Roy P.
Crosby, R. Edward
Demson, Robert D.
Ebeling, Leslie G.
Forrester, Mark A.
Gabel, Kenneth G.
Geahlen, Donald
Graham, William J.
Henward, DeBanks M. III
Horne, M.S.
Horton, G. Michael
Ingebritson, Jack
Jackson, Robert L.
Jensen, Paul M.
Johnson, Mary M.
Kiely, James L.
Knoell, Joseph
Kraemer, Richard C.
Lake, Jack S.
Leonhart, C.J.
Levy, John S.
Lewkowitz, Burt
McMahan, John A.

Mayfield, Robert G.
Miller, Barbara Shaw
Moore, Richard D.
Nelson, Gary L.
Osborne, Earl
Price, Billie B. Jr.
Rector, R. Dale
Roeske, Ronald E.
Rose, Robert W.
Rose, William H.
Rozan, Gerry M.
Rush, James W.
Sandys, Syd
Scott, Michael A.
Soudriette, James W.
Stanfield-Pinel, Bertrand
Thomas-Williams, Robert C.
Weiss, Kenneth J.
Zell, Alan L.

Engineer
McKellar, Donald M. III
Nelson, Gary L.
Peterman, Gordon G.
Soudriette, James W.
Thomas-Williams, Robert C.
Wingblade, P.B.

Instructor
Baron, Richard E.
Demson, Robert D.
Galst, Lester R.
Heiple, Don W.
Kennelly, Thomas A.
Levy, John S.
Lewkowitz, Burt
Meadows, Dan S.
Miller, Barbara Shaw
Neill, M.D.
Osborne, Earl
Peterman, Gordon G.
Postal, David R.
Price, Billie B. Jr.
Rozan, Gerry M.
Smith, Russell B. III
Wilson, Margot P.
Witt, Floyd E.
Zajac, Terrence Michael

Insuror
Bohannan, Robert C. Jr.
Wingblade, P.B.

Lender
Bohannan, Robert C. Jr.
Bronnenkant, Anna
Diez, Jim Jr.
Gabel, Kenneth G.
Kennelly, Thomas A.
Miller, Barbara Shaw
Wasson, Thomas L.

Owner/Investor
Adamson, Jeanne A.
Allen, Richard
Alterson, Marvin
Armstrong, Bret Alan
Bernard, Stephen Zouck
Brant, Debarah Staaey
Burd, Anthony M.
Carpenter, R. Jay
Cooper, William H.
Coxwell, Roy P.
Crosby, R. Edward
Demson, Robert D.
Diez, Jim Jr.
Du Bois, Reyn
Ebeling, Leslie G.
Egbert, Clark R.
Forrester, Mark A.
Francy, Robert E.
Gabel, Kenneth G.
Geahlen, Donald
Gentry, Allan S.
Getz, Bert A.
Graham, William J.
Graves, William G. III
Helgesen, Jack C.
Henward, DeBanks M. III
Horne, M.S.
Horton, G. Michael
Ingebritson, Jack
Keith, John A.
Levy, John S.
Lewkowitz, Burt
McRae, Hamilton E. III
Mayfield, Robert G.
Meadows, Dan S.
Miller, Barbara Shaw
Moore, Richard D.
Moss, John P.
Muir, A. Gary
Neill, M.D.
Osborne, Earl
Parker, Phil
Price, Billie B. Jr.
Rector, R. Dale
Rose, William H.
Sargent, Paul E.
Scott, Michael A.
Simonton, G. Scott
Soudriette, James W.
Thomas-Williams, Robert C.
Toalson, Robert E.
Wallace, Donald L.
Warner, Ted F.
Weaver, Park Jr.
Wilson, Margot P.
Wingblade, P.B.
Zajac, Terrence Michael

Property Manager
Adamson, Jeanne A.
Allen, Richard
Alterson, Marvin
Armstrong, Bret Alan
Baron, Richard E.
Brant, Debarah Staaey
Burd, Anthony M.
Cartwright, Ed
Cowles, Ben W.
Coxwell, Roy P.
Dameron, Ben B. Jr.
Demson, Robert D.
Diez, Jim Jr.
Egbert, Clark R.
Ervanian, Armen
Estes, John P.
Foster, John D.
Gabel, Kenneth G.
Geahlen, Donald
Goodacre, Kenneth Robert
Graham, William J.
Graves, William G. III
Gross, James E.
Heiple, Don W.
Horton, G. Michael
Hyland, Kenneth J.
Keith, John A.
Kielgass, Dennis A.
Lastinger, William R.
Leonhart, C.J.
McKellar, Donald M. III
McMahan, John A.
Mallendr, William H.
Mayfield, Robert G.
Meadows, Dan S.
Miller, Barbara Shaw
Moore, Richard D.
Nicholls, Richard B.
Osborne, Earl
Price, Billie B. Jr.
Roeske, Ronald E.
Rozan, Gerry M.
Rush, James W.
Sandys, Syd
Schaeffer, Louis B.
Sell, Jan A.
Stanfield-Pinel, Bertrand
Thomas-Williams, Robert C.
Weiss, Kenneth J.
Wilson, Margot P.
Wingblade, P.B.
Woloshin, Stephen
Zell, Alan L.

Real Estate Publisher
Lewkowitz, Burt
Miller, Barbara Shaw
Weaver, Park Jr.

Regulator
Nelson, Gary L.
Smith, Russell B. III

Syndicator
Adamson, Jeanne A.
Alterson, Marvin
Baron, Richard E.
Bryson, Larry
Carpenter, R. Jay
Crosby, R. Edward
Dameron, Ben B. Jr.
Demson, Robert D.
Ebeling, Leslie G.
Goodacre, Kenneth Robert
Graham, William J.
Graves, William G. III
Hyland, Kenneth J.
Ingebritson, Jack
Jackson, Robert L.
Jensen, Paul M.
Leonhart, C.J.
Levy, John S.
Lewkowitz, Burt
McMahan, John A.
Meadows, Dan S.
Miller, Barbara Shaw
Moore, Richard D.
Neill, M.D.
Nelson, Gary L.
Parker, Phil
Price, Billie B. Jr.
Rector, R. Dale
Rose, Robert W.
Schaeffer, Louis B.
Scott, Michael A.
Sell, Jan A.
Soudriette, James W.
Suphan, William H.
Thomas-Williams, Robert C.
Toalson, Robert E.
Warner, Ted F.
Weiss, Kenneth J.
Wilson, Margot P.

PRESCOTT

Appraiser
Camp, R. Gounod Sr.
Weiss, Allen J.

Attorney
Eaton, Wm. Lee
Peterson, Scott P.

Broker
Hannay, Robert E.
Weiss, Allen J.

Builder
Camp, R. Gounod Sr.

Consultant
Hannay, Robert E.
Weiss, Allen J.

Developer
Camp, R. Gounod Sr.
Hannay, Robert E.

Instructor
Camp, R. Gounod Sr.

Lender
Camp, R. Gounod Sr.

Owner/Investor
Hannay, Robert E.

Property Manager
Camp, R. Gounod Sr.
Weiss, Allen J.

TUCSON

Appraiser
Benson, Alfred M.
Cummings, Albert A.
Darling, Richard S.
Dietrich, Robert E.
Gooder, Donald M.
Klafter, Mark H.
Rasmussen, Gordon R.
Solot, Sanders K.
Swango, Dan
Swango, Vern W.
Tanner, Arthur R.

Architect
Brown, Gordon V.

Assessor
Darling, Richard S.

Attorney
Monroe, Michael J.
Romano, Donald F.
Snyder, Robert J. Jr.
Wilson, Thomas E.

Banker
Cocke, James W.
Peters, Raymond James.

Broker
Barry, Robert C.
Beuret, Jules W.
Brown, Charles J.
Buehrle, Chip
Clausen, Rolland Budd
Connor, Patrick T.
Cummings, Albert A.
Darling, Richard S.
Dove, Aytan Alexander
Foster, Daniel G.
Greffet, Charles V.
House, Norman R.
Lovelace, Gary S.
McDonald, Robert J.
Matinho, Al
Morton, Paul D. "Dan"
Rasmussen, Gordon R.
Rogers, Helene Sheppard
Romano, Donald F.
Sellers, James R.
Sirota, David
Small, Ricardo
Stachel, Robert D. Sr.
Storke, Tara D.
Swango, Dan
Swango, Vern W.
Tanner, Arthur R.

Builder
Anderson, Richard C.
Brodsky, Frederic L.
Cummings, Albert A.
Darling, Richard S.
Marmis, Cary
Matinho, Al
Stilb, Michael A.

Consultant
Barry, Robert C.
Beath, Andrew B.
Benson, Alfred M.
Beuret, Jules W.
Brodsky, Frederic L.
Crawford, David L. Dr.
Cummings, Albert A.
Darling, Richard S.
Dietrich, Robert E.
Foster, Daniel G.

Gooder, Donald M.
House, Norman R.
Klafter, Mark H.
McDonald, Robert J.
Marmis, Cary
Morton, Paul D. "Dan"
Romano, Donald F.
Seeley, Frederick P.
Sirota, David
Solot, Sanders K.
Stachel, Robert D. Sr.
Swango, Dan
Swango, Vern W.
Tanner, Arthur R.

Developer
Anderson, Richard C.
Brodsky, Frederic L.
Buehrle, Chip
Connor, Patrick T.
Cummings, Albert A.
Darling, Richard S.
Foster, Daniel G.
Long, Roy H. II
Lovelace, Gary S.
Marmis, Cary
Matinho, Al
Prasley, James E.
Stachel, Robert D. Sr.
Stephenson, William V.
Stilb, Michael A.
Whitacre, Wendell B.

Instructor
Brodsky, Frederic L.
Buehrle, Chip
Clausen, Rolland Budd
Crawford, David L. Dr.
Cummings, Albert A.
Dove, Aytan Alexander
Morton, Paul D. "Dan"
Sirota, David
Stachel, Robert D. Sr.
Swango, Dan

Insuror
Peters, Raymond James.

Lender
Peters, Raymond James.
Sellers, James R.

Owner/Investor
Beath, Andrew B.
Brodsky, Frederic L.
Brown, Charles J.
Buehrle, Chip
Clausen, Rolland Budd
Connor, Patrick T.
Cummings, Albert A.
Foster, Daniel G.
Klafter, Mark H.
Long, Roy H. II
Lovelace, Gary S.
McDonald, Robert J.
Marmis, Cary
Matinho, Al
Rogers, Helene Sheppard
Romero, Steve G.
Sellers, James R.
Small, Ricardo
Stachel, Robert D. Sr.
Tanner, Arthur R.
Whitacre, Wendell B.

Property Manager
Anderson, Richard C.
Brodsky, Frederic L.
Buehrle, Chip
Clausen, Rolland Budd
Cummings, Albert A.
Darling, Richard S.
Foster, Daniel G.
McDonald, Robert J.
Marmis, Cary
Matinho, Al
Morton, Paul D. "Dan"
Neal, Raymond R. "Ray"
Rasmussen, Gordon R.
Rogers, Helene Sheppard
Seeley, Frederick P.
Sellers, James R.
Small, Ricardo
Stachel, Robert D. Sr.
Storke, Tara D.
Whitacre, Wendell B.

Real Estate Publisher
Romano, Donald F.

Syndicator
Anderson, Richard C.
Beath, Andrew B.
Buehrle, Chip
Clausen, Rolland Budd
Connor, Patrick T.
Cummings, Albert A.
Darling, Richard S.
Dove, Aytan Alexander
Foster, Daniel G.
House, Norman R.
Long, Roy H. II
Lovelace, Gary S.
McDonald, Robert J.
Matinho, Al
Stachel, Robert D. Sr.
Storke, Tara D.

ARKANSAS

BATESVILLE

Appraiser
Carpenter, R.L. Jr.

Broker
Carpenter, R.L. Jr.

Insuror
Carpenter, R.L. Jr.

Property Manager
Carpenter, R.L. Jr.

CAMDEN

Appraiser
Buchanan, L. Greggory

Assessor
Buchanan, L. Greggory

Broker
Buchanan, L. Greggory

Consultant
Buchanan, L. Greggory

Owner/Investor
Buchanan, L. Greggory

Property Manager
Buchanan, L. Greggory
Redlin, E.J.

FAYETTEVILLE

Appraiser
Coolick, Wilma I.
Epley, Donald R.
Karr, Jean B.

Attorney
Snodgrass, Larry L.

Broker
Coolick, Wilma I.
Edmiston, Helen
Karr, Jean B.
Todd, Della

Builder
Edmiston, Helen
Seay, Thomas P.

Consultant
Epley, Donald R.
Todd, Della

Developer
Edmiston, Helen
Seay, Thomas P.
Todd, Della

Instructor
Epley, Donald R.

Owner/Investor
Edmiston, Helen
Seay, Thomas P.
Todd, Della

Property Manager
Edmiston, Helen
Seay, Thomas P.
Snodgrass, Larry L.
Starr, Joe Fred

Real Estate Publisher
Epley, Donald R.

FORT SMITH

Appraiser
Schultz, H.L.

Attorney
Lewis, J. Alan

Broker
Coleman, Rod
Dolman, Jack A. Jr.
Price, Gerald G.
Schultz, H.L.

Builder
Coleman, Rod
Myers, Carl

Consultant
Coleman, Rod
Dolman, Jack A. Jr.
Schultz, H.L.

Developer
Coleman, Rod
Dolman, Jack A. Jr.
Price, Gerald G.

Instructor
Schultz, H.L.

Insuror
Price, Gerald G.

Owner/Investor
Coleman, Rod
Dolman, Jack A. Jr.
Price, Gerald G.

Property Manager
Coleman, Rod
Dolman, Jack A. Jr.
Tuake, Robert D.

Syndicator
Coleman, Rod
Dolman, Jack A. Jr.
Schultz, H.L.

HARRISON

Appraiser
Sanders, Nield J.

Attorney
Ledbetter, Thomas D.

Broker
Sanders, Nield J.

Builder
Bellach, Robin
Ferro, Jeffrey, E.
Sanders, Nield J.

Consultant
Bellach, Robin

Developer
Bellach, Robin
Sanders, Nield J.

Instructor
Sanders, Nield J.

Insuror
Bellach, Robin

Owner/Investor
Bellach, Robin
Sanders, Nield J.

Property Manager
Sanders, Nield J.

Syndicator
Ledbetter, Thomas D.

HOT SPRINGS NATIONAL PARK

Appraiser
Hurst, O. Byron Sr.
Meyers, Larry W.
Shockley, Robert E.

Assessor
Hurst, O. Byron Sr.

Attorney
Henry, Richard Lee
Miller, Stan

Banker
Miller, Michael B.

Broker
Hurst, O. Byron Sr.
Meyers, Larry W.
Shockley, Robert E.

Consultant
Hurst, O. Byron Sr.
Martin, Larry
Shockley, Robert E.

Developer
Martin, Larry
Meyers, Larry W.
Miller, Michael B.
Miller, Stan

Instructor
Shockley, Robert E.

Lender
Miller, Michael B.

Owner/Investor
Meyers, Larry W.
Miller, Stan
Shockley, Robert E.

Property Manager
Martin, Larry

Syndicator
Martin, Larry
Miller, Stan

JONESBORO

Appraiser
McCracken, Lloyd
McGough, Bobby C.
Stuenkel, Bob

Broker
Burrow, Bruce
McGough, Bobby C.
Stuenkel, Bob

Consultant
Burrow, Bruce
McCracken, Lloyd
McGough, Bobby C.

Developer
Burrow, Bruce

Instructor
McGough, Bobby C.

ARKANSAS, LITTLE ROCK

Insuror
Stuenkel, Bob

Owner/Investor
Burrow, Bruce
McGough, Bobby C.

Property Manager
Stuenkel, Bob

Syndicator
Burrow, Bruce

LITTLE ROCK

Appraiser
Dearing, G.C.
Ellis, Robert B.
Ferstl, Tom M.
Glaze, Phyllis Laser
Hall, Jay A.
Hepner, Patricia R.
McDermott, Cecil
Moore, Terry
Thomas, William Daniel Jr.
Willis, E.W.

Architect
Blass, Noland Jr.

Attorney
Cambiano, Mark S.
Carpenter, Claude
Carroll, James R.
Ferstl, Tom M.
Lance, James W.
Wright, Edward L. Jr.

Banker
Ellis, Robert B.
Gulley, Wilbur P. Jr.
Powell, Jack
Settle, Joseph

Broker
Bean, Terry R.
Burchett, A.L. Jr.
Campbell, Dee
Carroll, James R.
Dixon, Paul H. Jr.
Ferstl, Tom M.
Flake, John J.
Glaze, Phyllis Laser
Gring, Clayton G.
Hathaway, James E. Jr
Hepner, Patricia R.
Hockersmith, Steven C.
Lindeman, J. Bruce
Nichols, Hal E.
Powell, Jack
Thomas, William Daniel Jr.
Trammell, Allen W.
Wells, George M.
Willis, E.W.

Builder
Callender, Robert L.
Gring, Clayton G.
Hepner, Patricia R.
Trammell, Allen W.

Consultant
Bean, Terry R.
Cambiano, Mark S.
Campbell, Dee
Campbell, William Glynn
Carroll, James R.
Daniel, Charles E.
Ellis, Robert B.
Flake, John J.
Glaze, Phyllis Laser
Hathaway, James E. Jr
Hepner, Patricia R.
Lance, James W.
Lindeman, J. Bruce
Moore, Terry
Nichols, Hal E.
Thomas, William Daniel Jr.
Warren, Carl E.
Willis, E.W.

Developer
Bean, Terry R.
Blass, Noland Jr.
Burchett, A.L. Jr.
Callender, Robert L.
Campbell, William Glynn
Carroll, James R.
Daniel, Charles E.
Flake, John J.
Glaze, Phyllis Laser
Hathaway, James E. Jr
Hepner, Patricia R.
Hockersmith, Steven C.
Moore, Terry
Powell, Jack
Thomas, William Daniel Jr.
Tucker, Everett Jr.
Willis, E.W.

Engineer
Blass, Noland Jr.

Instructor
Campbell, Dee
Ferstl, Tom M.
Hathaway, James E. Jr
Lindeman, J. Bruce
Nichols, Hal E.

Insuror
Gulley, Wilbur P. Jr.
Hepner, Patricia R.
Trammell, Allen W.

Lender
Carroll, James R.
Gulley, Wilbur P. Jr.
Hall, Jay A.
Lance, James W.
McRae, Kenneth G.

Owner/Investor
Bean, Terry R.
Blass, Noland Jr.
Burchett, A.L. Jr.
Callender, Robert L.
Cambiano, Mark S.
Campbell, Dee
Campbell, William Glynn
Carpenter, Claude
Daniel, Charles E.
Ellis, Robert B.
Flake, John J.
Glaze, Phyllis Laser
Gulley, Wilbur P. Jr.
Hepner, Patricia R.
Nichols, Hal E.
Powell, Jack
Thomas, William Daniel Jr.
Trammell, Allen W.
Willis, E.W.

Property Manager
Bean, Terry R.
Bowles, Sheila
Burchett, A.L. Jr.
Callender, Robert L.
Campbell, Dee
Campbell, William Glynn
Ferstl, Tom M.
Flake, John J.
Glaze, Phyllis Laser
Gring, Clayton G.
Hathaway, James E. Jr
Hepner, Patricia R.
Moore, Terry
Nichols, Hal E.
Powell, Jack
Thomas, William Daniel Jr.

Real Estate Publisher
Lindeman, J. Bruce

Syndicator
Bean, Terry R.
Callender, Robert L.
Campbell, William Glynn
Dixon, Paul H. Jr.
Glaze, Phyllis Laser
Gring, Clayton G.
Hathaway, James E. Jr
Held, Edward H.
Hockersmith, Steven C.
Lance, James W.
Moore, Terry
Thomas, William Daniel Jr.
Wells, George M.

PINE BLUFF

Attorney
Cox, E. Harley Jr.

Banker
Woodall, Howard W.

Owner/Investor
Cox, E. Harley Jr.

Property Manager
Smith, Joanne S.

Syndicator
Smith, Joanne S.

RUSSELLVILLE

Appraiser
Baley, Robert Z.

Broker
Baley, Robert Z.

Consultant
Baley, Robert Z.

Developer
Baley, Robert Z.

Instructor
Baley, Robert Z.

CALIFORNIA

ALHAMBRA

Appraiser
Garcia, Bernie I.
Martin, Peter H.

Architect
Stiemsma, Steven J.
Wang, Chen H.

Attorney
Applebaum, Jerome M.
Black, Nicholas J.
Donnelly, Allan P.
Fisher, Patricia A.
Gottuso, Josephine M.
Hawkins, Preston
Lewis, Ralph M.
Miller, Michael B.
Wilson, Steven Nevin

Broker
Amaya, Al Jr.
Gottuso, Josephine M.
Hawkins, Preston
Lewis, Ralph M.
Mueller, Werner A.
Penner, Arlin L.

Builder
Donnelly, Allan P.
Dow, Victor W.D.
Lewis, Ralph M.
Stiemsma, Steven J.
Wang, Chen H.

Consultant
Applebaum, Jerome M.
Black, Nicholas J.
Garcia, Bernie I.
Gottuso, Josephine M.
Hawkins, Preston
Martin, Peter H.
Miller, Michael B.
Mueller, Werner A.
Wang, Chen H.

Developer
Applebaum, Jerome M.
Donnelly, Allan P.
Dow, Victor W.D.
Giampaolo, Joseph A.
Khurana, Lalit K.
Lewis, Ralph M.
Penner, Arlin L.
Wang, Chen H.

Engineer
Wang, Chen H.

Instructor
Applebaum, Jerome M.
Garcia, Bernie I.
Gottuso, Josephine M.
Mueller, Werner A.

Lender
Black, Nicholas J.

Owner/Investor
Amaya, Al Jr.
Dow, Victor W.D.
Giampaolo, Joseph A.
Gottuso, Josephine M.
Lewis, Ralph M.
Mueller, Werner A.
Penner, Arlin L.

Property Manager
Giampaolo, Joseph A.
Lewis, Ralph M.
McLong, Dale

Syndicator
Burdette, Forbes W.
Donnelly, Allan P.
Giampaolo, Joseph A.
Penner, Arlin L.

BAKERSFIELD

Appraiser
Carpenter, J. Clifton
Higdon, Dallis
Tienken, Robert H.

Attorney
Isham, Richard B.
McKinney, Russell R.
Sment, Michael R.

Broker
Brown, Rodney R.
Gibbons, Earle J.
Higdon, Dallis
Newton, Joseph
Phelps, Anthony D.
Tienken, Robert H.
Wingate, Don E.

Builder
Brown, Rodney R.
Dean, Melvin
Klassen, Charles R.
Newton, Joseph
Wingate, Don E.

Consultant
Brown, Rodney R.
Carpenter, J. Clifton
Gibbons, Earle J.
Higdon, Dallis
Jones, Gerald G.
McKinney, Russell R.
Phelps, Anthony D.
Porter, Clyde E.
Wingate, Don E.

Developer
Brown, Rodney R.
Dean, Melvin
Higdon, Dallis
Klassen, Charles R.
McKinney, Russell R.
Newton, Joseph

Phelps, Anthony D.
Porter, Clyde E.
Wingate, Don E.

Instructor
Newton, Joseph

Owner/Investor
Brown, Rodney R.
Dean, Melvin
Jones, Gerald G.
McKinney, Russell R.
Phelps, Anthony D.
Sment, Michael R.
Tienken, Robert H.
Wingate, Don E.

Property Manager
Jones, Gerald G.
Phelps, Anthony D.
Porter, Clyde E.
Sment, Michael R.
Wingate, Don E.

Real Estate Publisher
Sment, Michael R.

Syndicator
Jones, Gerald G.
Klinkenstein, Bill
McKinney, Russell R.
Phelps, Anthony D.
Porter, Clyde E.

EUREKA

Consultant
Mahan, Paul D.

Developer
Mahan, Paul D.

Insuror
Matsen, Glenn

Owner/Investor
Mahan, Paul D.
Matsen, Glenn

FRESNO

Appraiser
Niblett, John E.
Pistole, Steven C.
Raven, Larry Joseph

Attorney
Bolen, Hal H. II
Forsythe, Lynn M.
Fransen, Kenneth J.
Wild, M. Bruce

Broker
Andrade, Eugene J.
Chesnut, Wayne D.
DeBenedetto, Anthony J.
Frederick, Paul S.
Jensen, Robert L.
Klein, Robert N.
McWhorter, David R.
Mohun, J. Brook Jr.
Niblett, John E.
Pistole, Steven C.
Raven, Larry Joseph
Simi, Dante R.

Builder
Andrade, Eugene J.
Ensz, Paul
Long, Bud.
Pistole, Steven C.
Raven, Larry Joseph

Consultant
King, Michael Stephen
Long, Bud.
Mohun, J. Brook Jr.
Niblett, John E.
Raven, Larry Joseph
Simi, Dante R.

Developer
Andrade, Eugene J.
Ensz, Paul
Erganian, Richard
Klein, Robert N.
Klein, Robert N. II
Long, Bud.
Pistole, Steven C.
Raven, Larry Joseph
Simi, Dante R.

Lender
Chilton, Gil
DeBenedetto, Anthony J.

Owner/Investor
Andrade, Eugene J.
Ensz, Paul
Forsythe, Lynn M.
Jensen, Robert L.
Long, Bud.
Niblett, John E.
Raven, Larry Joseph
Wild, M. Bruce

Property Manager
Andrade, Eugene J.
Chesnut, Wayne D.
Ensz, Paul
Erganian, Richard
Jensen, Robert L.
Long, Bud.
Snell, William N.

Syndicator
Chesnut, Wayne D.
Ensz, Paul
King, Michael Stephen
Simi, Dante R.

INGLEWOOD

Appraiser
Beliavsky, Leonid
Chew, Richard J.
Falck, Randall F.
Honner, Robert A.
Hoopes, John N.
Hunt, Vard Stephen
Keller, Patrick Erle
Kermani, Fereidoun
Pehrson, Donald
Thomson, Michael D.

Architect
Blanton, John A.
Dancygier, Joseph
Kermani, Fereidoun

Attorney
Barclay, John A.
Blakesley, Leonard E. Jr.
Condon, F. Milton
Condon, Gerald M.
Fadem, Jerrold A.
Faigin, Larry B.
Freshman, Samuel K.
Friedman, Richard S.
Fulop, Irwin M.
Gann, Gregg
Gitlen, Gordon P.
Hoag, Richard J.
Holguin, Henry A.
Hoover, Steven G.
Kerr, William A.
McCabe, Barry
McDaniel, Donald C.
Nitti, Thomas Anthony
Powell, Alex
Rubin, Sheldon
Sandron, Ira
Shapiro, Burt
Simon, David E.
Smolker, Gary
Spierer, Steven F.
Stanwyck, Steven J.
Woodward, John A.
Zerin, Milton

Banker
Bingham, James "Jay"
Calhoun, Robert M.
Chew, Richard J.
Dancygier, Joseph
Kabot, Ronald H.

Broker
Aminoff, Gary A.
Beliavsky, Leonid
Blakesley, Leonard E. Jr.
Brydon, Joe
Calhoun, Robert M.
Carlsberg, Richard Presten
Cathcart, Faye
Chew, Richard J.
Chulak, Michael T.
Collins, Arthur F.
Collura, Mario A.
Crosser, Daniel D.
Dancygier, Joseph
Dolan, Paul R.
Elkins, George W.
Ferris, Don
Freshman, Samuel K.
Friedland, Richard CPM
Gann, Gregg
Herd, Alan A. (Scotty)
Hoag, Richard J.
Honner, Robert A.
Hunt, Vard Stephen
Ikezawa, Shahin (Sherry) D.
Jason-White, Donald L.
Lien, Della
Long, Pauline W. (Winnie)
McCabe, Barry
Marcussen, Steven E.
Mosk, Alan C.
Parlett, Philip M.
Pasner, Edith A.
Prock, James E.
Propp, Robert R. S.
Rahban, Frank
Rosenthal, Richard J.
Sandron, Ira
Schnee, William M.
Schnieders, Edmund F. Jr.
Shaw, Victor Hsia
Stanwyck, Steven J.
Tankersley, Ronald S.
Tatara, Douglas A.
Thomson, Michael D.
Wardell, Robert P.
Weatherby, William J.
Woodward, John A.

Builder
Calhoun, Robert M.
Carlsberg, Richard Presten
Collura, Mario A.
Dancygier, Joseph
De Vinniere, Dominique Rocoffort
Falck, Randall F.
Fuhrman, Howard D.
Hall, Katherine Post
Kabot, Ronald H.
Katell, Gerald L.
Kermani, Fereidoun
Levenstein, Robert
Lowy, Allan N.
Lowy, Rudolph J.
Mandel, Bruce Ansel
Prock, James E.
Rappaport, Herman H.
Rosenberg, Jerome S.
Tankersley, Ronald S.
Thomson, Michael D.
Twarowski, Eugene H. III
Weatherby, William J.
Wong, Wallace
Wynne, James J.
Ziman, Richard S.

Consultant
Aminoff, Gary A.
Beliavsky, Leonid
Blakesley, Leonard E. Jr.
Calhoun, Robert M.
Carlsberg, Richard Presten
Cathcart, Faye
Chew, Richard J.
Chulak, Michael T.
Collura, Mario A.
Crosser, Daniel D.
Dancygier, Joseph
Dolan, Paul R.
Durkin, Phyllis E.
Ferris, Don
Goldstein, James F.
Gunns, Stephen Richard
Herbst, Lawrence
Herd, Alan A. (Scotty)
Hill, Charles
Hoag, Richard J.
Holguin, Henry A.
Honner, Robert A.
Hoopes, John N.
Hoover, Steven G.
Hunt, Vard Stephen
Jason-White, Donald L.
Kermani, Fereidoun
Klein, Allan Eric
Long, Pauline W. (Winnie)
McCabe, Barry
Mandel, Bruce Ansel
Pasner, Edith A.
Pehrson, Donald
Prock, James E.
Propp, Robert R. S.
Rosenthal, Richard J.
Rubin, Sheldon
Russell, Michael P.
Schnee, William M.
Shapiro, Brian G.
Shapkin, Barton E.
Smolker, Gary
Thomson, Michael D.
Varley, Arthur J. Jr.
Weatherby, William J.

Developer
Aminoff, Gary A.
Beliavsky, Leonid
Bingham, James "Jay"
Blakesley, Leonard E. Jr.
Brewster, George B.
Brydon, Joe
Calhoun, Robert M.
Carlsberg, Richard Presten
Collura, Mario A.
Crosser, Daniel D.
Dancygier, Joseph
Dolan, Paul R.
Elkins, George W.
Faigin, Larry B.
Falck, Randall F.
Freilich, Samuel C.
Freshman, Samuel K.
Friedman, Robert B.
Fuhrman, Howard D.
Goldstein, Laurence S.
Gunns, Stephen Richard
Hall, Katherine Post
Herbst, Lawrence
Herd, Alan A. (Scotty)
Hill, Charles
Hoag, Richard J.
Hunt, Vard Stephen
Ikezawa, Shahin (Sherry) D.
Jason-White, Donald L.
Kabot, Ronald H.
Katell, Gerald L.
Kermani, Fereidoun
Laderman, Harvey R.
Lagerbauer, L. J.
Levenstein, Robert
Lowy, Allan N.
Lowy, Rudolph J.

Mandel, Bruce Ansel
Martin, Charles E.
Mosk, Alan C.
Moss, Jerry
Nicholas, Frederick M.
Osio, Salvatore P.
Palmer, Jeffrey E.
Pasner, Edith A.
Prock, James E.
Rappaport, Herman H.
Rosenberg, Jerome S.
Rowen, David H.
Russell, Michael P.
Schnieders, Edmund F. Jr.
Shanedling, Phil
Simon, David E.
Tankersley, Ronald S.
Thomson, Michael D.
Twarowski, Eugene H. III
Varley, Arthur J. Jr.
Wong, Wallace
Wynne, James J.
Ziman, Richard S.

Engineer
Collura, Mario A.
Lowy, Rudolph J.

Instructor
Beliavsky, Leonid
Calhoun, Robert M.
Cathcart, Faye
Dancygier, Joseph
Ferris, Don
Herd, Alan A. (Scotty)
Ikezawa, Shahin (Sherry) D.

Insuror
Cathcart, Faye
Collura, Mario A.
Elkins, George W.
Kabot, Ronald H.
Tankersley, Ronald S.

Lender
Bingham, James "Jay"
Dancygier, Joseph
Elkins, George W.
Herbst, Lawrence
Hill, Charles
Kabot, Ronald H.
Tankersley, Ronald S.

Owner/Investor
Aminoff, Gary A.
Bingham, James "Jay"
Blakesley, Leonard E. Jr.
Brewster, George B.
Brydon, Joe
Calhoun, Robert M.
Cathcart, Faye
Chew, Richard J.
Chulak, Michael T.
Collura, Mario A.
Corrodi, John T. Jr.
Crosser, Daniel D.
Dancygier, Joseph
Dolan, Paul R.
Elkins, George W.
Ferris, Don
Freshman, Samuel K.
Friedland, Richard
Fuhrman, Howard D.
Goldstein, James F.
Gunns, Stephen Richard
Herbst, Lawrence
Herd, Alan A. (Scotty)
Hill, Charles
Hoag, Richard J.
Holguin, Henry A.
Honner, Robert A.
Ikezawa, Shahin (Sherry) D.
Jason-White, Donald L.
Katell, Gerald L.
Kermani, Fereidoun
Laderman, Harvey R.
Lien, Della
Long, Pauline W. (Winnie)
Lowy, Rudolph J.
McDaniel, Donald C.
Mandel, Bruce Ansel
Martin, Charles E.
Nicholas, Frederick M.
Parlett, Philip M.
Pasner, Edith A.
Post, Gary M.
Powell, Alex
Prock, James E.
Propp, Robert R. S.
Rappaport, Herman H.
Rosenberg, Jerome S.
Shaw, Victor Hsia
Spierer, Steven F.
Stern, Theodore
Tankersley, Ronald S.
Thomson, Michael D.
Varley, Arthur J. Jr.
Wardell, Robert P.
Weatherby, William J.
Wong, Wallace
Woodward, John A.
Wynne, James J.
Ziman, Richard S.

Property Manager
Aminoff, Gary A.
Blakesley, Leonard E. Jr.
Brewster, George B.
Calhoun, Robert M.
Carlsberg, Richard Presten
Chulak, Michael T.
Collura, Mario A.
Cramer, Pat
Dancygier, Joseph
Dobb, Herbert
Elkins, George W.
Evans, Clifford S. Jr.
Firestone, J.
Forrester, Robert M.
Freshman, Samuel K.
Friedland, Richard CPM
Friedman, Robert B.
Gunns, Stephen Richard
Hoag, Richard J.
Honner, Robert A.
Ikezawa, Shahin (Sherry) D.
Jason-White, Donald L.
Karp, Harvey
Keller, Patrick Erle
Klein, Allan Eric
Lien, Della
Long, Pauline W. (Winnie)
Lowy, Rudolph J.
Mandel, Bruce Ansel
Mayer, Roger
Mosk, Alan C.
Murray, Carl
Parlett, Philip M.
Pasner, Edith A.
Pehrson, Donald
Post, Gary M.
Rosenthal, Richard J.
Schnieders, Edmund F. Jr.
Shapkin, Barton E.
Shaw, Victor Hsia
Tankersley, Ronald S.
Thomson, Michael D.
Twarowski, Eugene H. III
Varley, Arthur J. Jr.
Wardell, Robert P.
Weatherby, William J.
Wynne, James J.

Real Estate Publisher
Aminoff, Gary A.
Calhoun, Robert M.
Dancygier, Joseph
Freshman, Samuel K.

Syndicator
Aminoff, Gary A.
Bingham, James "Jay"
Brewster, George B.
Brydon, Joe
Calhoun, Robert M.
Carlsberg, Richard Presten
Chulak, Michael T.
Collura, Mario A.
Crosser, Daniel D.
Dancygier, Joseph
Elkins, George W.
Ferris, Don
Freshman, Samuel K.
Friedland, Richard CPM
Gunns, Stephen Richard
Herd, Alan A. (Scotty)
Hill, Charles
Hoag, Richard J.
Holguin, Henry A.
Ikezawa, Shahin (Sherry) D.
Indiek, Victor H.
Jason-White, Donald L.
Kermani, Fereidoun
Laderman, Harvey R.
Lien, Della
Long, Pauline W. (Winnie)
McCabe, Barry
Mandel, Bruce Ansel
Martin, Charles E.
Parlett, Philip M.
Pasner, Edith A.
Post, Gary M.
Powell, Alex
Prock, James E.
Schnieders, Edmund F. Jr.
Shapkin, Barton E.
Shaw, Victor Hsia
Simon, David E.
Stern, Theodore
Wardell, Robert P.
Weatherby, William J.
Woodward, John A.

LONG BEACH

Appraiser
Dillenbeck, Steven R.
Huguet, Terry N.
Locke, Michael P.

Architect
Thompson, Ezra Enwood

Attorney
Heger, Jan M.
Horrell, Hugh H.
McCarthy, Luke V. Esq.

Broker
Hardy, Walter B.
Herring, Coy K.
Hiefield, Betty Lyn
Horrell, Hugh H.
Huguet, Terry N.
Johnson, Gene
Mangan, Paul C.
Sanford, Walter Scott
Schroeder, Cliff
Sommer, Roselle L.
Trutanich, John Peter
Willette, Charles A.

Builder
Thompson, Ezra Enwood
Trutanich, John Peter

Consultant
Almeida, Irene M.
Borton, Lee G.
Canfield, Clinton M.
Herring, Coy K.
Huguet, Terry N.
Johnson, Gene
Locke, Michael P.
McCarthy, Luke V. Esq.
Mangan, Paul C.
Sanford, Walter Scott
Schroeder, Cliff
Sommer, Roselle L.
Trutanich, John Peter
Willette, Charles A.

Developer
Carlberg, Daniel J.
Dillenbeck, Steven R.
McCarthy, Luke V. Esq.
Morse, Ted
Osman, David L.
Schroeder, Cliff
Sommer, Roselle L.
Thompson, Ezra Enwood
Trutanich, John Peter

Engineer
Thompson, Ezra Enwood

Instructor
Herring, Coy K.
Huguet, Terry N.
Mangan, Paul C.

Insuror
Borton, Lee G.
Schroeder, Cliff

Lender
Carlberg, Daniel J.
Sommer, Roselle L.

Owner/Investor
Almeida, Irene M.
Borton, Lee G.
Carlberg, Daniel J.
Con, Walter J.
Hardy, Walter B.
Horrell, Hugh H.
Johnson, Gene
McCarthy, Luke V. Esq.
Rosenzweig, Martin L.
Sanford, Walter Scott
Schuster, Meryl A.
Thompson, Ezra Enwood
Trutanich, John Peter

Property Manager
Asper, Merle
Borton, Lee G.
Dillenbeck, Steven R.
Herring, Coy K.
Johnson, Gene
Mangan, Paul C.
Owens, A.R. Jr.
Sommer, Roselle L.
Thompson, Ezra Enwood

Syndicator
Borton, Lee G.
Canfield, Clinton M.
Carlberg, Daniel J.
McCarthy, Luke V. Esq.
Rosenzweig, Martin L.
Sanford, Walter Scott
Schroeder, Cliff
Sommer, Roselle L.
Thompson, Ezra Enwood

LOS ANGELES

Appraiser
Azzolina, Ronald
Beeney, Robert W.
Blank, Harry D.
Bolas, Norman T.
Case, Fred E.
Collins, John Gerald
Cross, Fenton E.
Emmi, Joseph Jr.
Ernst, Jerome W.
Frasco, James A.
Hodies, Robert M.
Kneafsey, Thomas
Lewis, Charles D.
Mitchell, Kenneth Lee
Mitchell, Norman S.
Park, Richard E.G.
Rader, F. Ronald
Reddy, A. Thomas
Sterzer, Herbert
Stevens, Timothy N.

Tolson, Robert H.
Toughill, Peter

Architect
Azzolina, Ronald
Barnett, Robert Spencer
Chan, Frederick M.
Drews, Donald Frederick
Han, John D.
Jeannel, Charles
Jones, Chuck
Moon, David A.
Sheriff, Garth I.
Ward, Charles L.

Assessor
Azzolina, Ronald

Attorney
Alanis, Paul R.
Becket, Thomas L.
Blitz, Stephen M.
Brown, Joshua
Burgweger, Francis J. Jr.
Byron, Herbert Mark
Cheatham, Robert W.
Christian, William R.
Cohen, Gary J.
Crawford, George
Davis, Karl L. Jr.
Ellsworth, David G.
Erenberg, Douglas D.
Farrar, David W.
Fenmore, Donald M.
Fircher, Leo J.
Fleischman, William O.
Forward, Robert H. Jr.
Francis, Merrill R.
Friedman, Robert P.
Glaser, Herbert
Glickfeld, Bruce
Gray, Jan Charles
Hayes, Byron Jr.
Herschenfeld, Richard S.
Hieronymus, Edward W.
Hoag, John Clark
Howard, Roger H. Esq.
Jonas, Anderson
Jones, James G.
Kehr, Robert L.
Keligian, David Leo
Koines, Niles P.
Lane, Franklin K. III
Lapin, David A.
Leonard, William Michael
Levyn, Thomas S.
Lloyd, Robert M.
Lowen, Richard N.
McGruder, James P.
Mallory, Richard
Martin, Robert B. Jr.
Millard, Neal S.
Miller, Daniel A.
Miyoshi, David M.
Noe, James T.C.
Orendorff, James M.
Preble, Laurence G.
Reicher, Leland J.
Revitz, Steven J.
Ring, Michael W.
Rosen, Nelson
Roster, Michael
Roth, Herbert L.
Schaefer, Howard G.
Shafron, Shelly Jay
Siegel, Leonard
Sires, Bruce David
Smith, Steven C.
Smooke, Michael G.
Smylie, Robert Owen
Stephenson, Ronald L.
Swagel, Dennis J.
Tepper, R. Bruce Jr.
Tolles, E. Leroy
Volpert, Richard S.
Ward, Charles L.
Welbourne, John Howard
Whitney, Bernard
Williams, Robert E.

Banker
Acuña, Richard M.
Binder, Hannan E.
Collins, John Gerald
Edwards, Kenneth G.
Favero, Paul J.
Happel, H. William
Juell, Bruce C.
Mitchell, Kenneth Lee
Park, Richard E.G.
Stevens, Timothy N.
Wilson, Robert W.

Broker
Alanis, Paul R.
Albany, Tony
Amin, Purander Ambalal
Azzolina, Ronald
Becket, Thomas L.
Beeney, Robert W.
Boisvert, Hubert A.
Budnik, Ronald J.
Chaiboonma, Eaksith
Clarey, Frederick Joseph
Collins, John Gerald
Crane, Robert
Cranham, William R.
Dudley, Seth
Emmi, Joseph Jr.
Erenberg, Douglas D.
Eskenazi, Jack J.
Fowlks, Robert C.
Frasco, James A.
Gans, Peter M.
Gray, Jan Charles
Gregory, Carl C. III
Harvey, Phillip Anthony
Hayes, Daniel P.
Herschenfeld, Richard S.
Hodges, James W.
Hodies, Robert M.
Hubert, Frank D.
Kneafsey, Thomas
Lane, Franklin K. III
Leary, Theodore M. Jr.
Levy, Alan D.
Lewis, Charles D.
Lewis, John O.
Mitchell, Kenneth Lee
Mitchell, Norman S.
Moore, Randall J.
Mordecai, Charles F.
Muir, Robert C.
Poirier, Joseph L.
Rader, F. Ronald
Reddy, A. Thomas
Renaud-Wright, Michael S.
Robinson, Daniel T.
Sadowsky, Howard D.
Schulz, Henry C.
Smith, Steven C.
Stevens, Timothy N.
Tolson, Robert H.
Toole, Brice Jr.
Toughill, Peter
Ward, Charles L.
Whitney, Bernard
Yarnall, Celeste
Ziegler, Alan M.

Builder
Azzolina, Ronald
Broad, Eli
Devito, Joseph John
Ellis, Terrance C.
Greene, H. Theodore
Greytak, Lee J.
Han, John D.
Herschenfeld, Richard S.
Jones, Chuck
Leedy, Carleton C. Jr.
Lowe, Robert J.
Maier, Walter
Mordecai, Charles F.
Muir, Robert C.
Richman, Marvin Jordan
Robinson, Daniel T.
Scardina, Frank Joseph
Tenzer, Michael L.
Ward, Charles L.
Webber, Michael
Wilstein, David
Young, Bruce G.

Consultant
Albany, Tony
Azzolina, Ronald
Beeney, Robert W.
Blank, Harry D.
Carver, Eugene P.
Case, Fred E.
Chan, Frederick M.
Christian, William R.
Cockrum, William M. III
Collins, John Gerald
Crane, Robert
Cross, Fenton E.
Davidson, Harold A.
Devito, Joseph John
Dudley, Seth
Ellis, Terrance C.
Emmi, Joseph Jr.
Ernst, Jerome W.
Fellman, Lesli Denyse
Forward, Robert H. Jr.
Fowlks, Robert C.
Greytak, Lee J.
Hansen, Erik Lars
Harvey, Phillip Anthony
Hawk, James J.
Hayakawa, T. George
Herschenfeld, Richard S.
Hodges, James W.
Hodies, Robert M.
Hubert, Frank D.
Jeannel, Charles
Jonas, Anderson
Jones, Chuck
Keligian, David Leo
Kipper, Richard N.
Kneafsey, Thomas
Kromelow, Michael B.
Lane, Franklin K. III
Laserwa, Bruce
Lavine, Thomas
Leary, Theodore M. Jr.
Levy, Alan D.
Lewis, Charles D.
Lewis, John O.
Lewis, N. Richard
Luk, King S.
Martin, Vincent F. Jr.
Miller, Daniel A.
Mitchell, Norman S.
Moon, David A.
Mordecai, Charles F.
Morrissey, John Drew
Park, Richard E.G.
Poirier, Joseph L.
Price, Oliver Ray
Rabin, Sol L.
Renaud-Wright, Michael S.
Robinson, Daniel T.
Ruth, Craig
Sadowsky, Howard D.
Shafron, Shelly Jay
Sheriff, Garth I.
Smith, Steven C.
Sterzer, Herbert
Terry, Paul J.
Toughill, Peter
Ward, Charles L.
Wendoll, James A.
Yarnall, Celeste
Zoldos, Jeffrey A.E.

Developer
Albany, Tony
Amin, Purander Ambalal
Azzolina, Ronald
Bousfield, Michael C.
Broad, Eli
Brown, Joshua
Budnik, Ronald J.
Chaiboonma, Eaksith
Chan, Frederick M.
Connor, H.C.
Crane, Robert
Davis, Charles H.
Devito, Joseph John
Emmi, Joseph Jr.
Epstein, Harry
Erenberg, Douglas D.
Glaser, Herbert
Greene, H. Theodore
Greytak, Lee J.
Han, John D.
Hayes, Daniel P.
Herschenfeld, Richard S.
Hubert, Frank D.
Jeannel, Charles
Jonas, Anderson
Jones, Chuck
Ketchum, R. Kevin
Kingston, G. Allan
Kneafsey, Thomas
Lane, Franklin K. III
Langson, Jack M.
Lapin, David A.
Lavine, Thomas
Leedy, Carleton C. Jr.
Levy, Alan D.
Lewis, John O.
Lowe, Robert J.
Luk, King S.
Maier, Walter
Marchant, Robert G.
Martin, Vincent F. Jr.
Mitchell, Kenneth Lee
Moon, David A.
Morrissey, John Drew
Muir, Robert C.
Overman, Mary Jayne
Park, Richard E.G.
Reyes, Michael V.
Richman, Marvin Jordan
Robins, Roy S.
Robinson, Daniel T.
Rubin, Norman A.
Ruth, Craig
Sarhangian, Ted
Scardina, Frank Joseph
Seaton, Martin
Sheriff, Garth I.
Smith, Curtis B.
Smooke, Nathan
Tenzer, Michael L.
Toole, Brice Jr.
Toscano, James R.
Volpert, Richard S.
Ward, Charles L.
Webber, Michael
Whitney, Bernard
Wilstein, David
Young, Bruce G.

Engineer
Azzolina, Ronald
Greene, H. Theodore
Hayakawa, T. George
Luk, King S.
Moon, David A.
Renaud-Wright, Michael S.
Sheriff, Garth I.

Instructor
Case, Fred E.
Davidson, Harold A.
Gray, Jan Charles
Hodies, Robert M.
Martin, Robert B. Jr.
Miller, Daniel A.

Moon, David A.
Poirier, Joseph L.
Price, Oliver Ray
Reicher, Leland J.
Renaud-Wright, Michael S.
Smith, Steven C.
Zoldos, Jeffrey A.E.

Insuror
Broad, Eli
Hoag, John Clark
Mitchell, Kenneth Lee
Mitchell, Norman S.
Moon, David A.
Robertson, William A.
Skinner, Michael

Lender
Budnik, Ronald J.
Collins, John Gerald
Doty, Sharon N.
Emmi, Joseph Jr.
Favero, Paul J.
Gold, Steven H.
Goldstein, Michael S.
Herschenfeld, Richard S.
Hodges, James W.
Hodies, Robert M.
Marchant, Robert G.
Mitchell, Kenneth Lee
Mozilo, Ralph S.
Park, Richard E.G.
Stevens, Timothy N.
Ulrich, Peter H.
Wilson, Robert W.

Owner/Investor
Albany, Tony
Amin, Purander Ambalal
Azzolina, Ronald
Boisvert, Hubert A.
Broad, Eli
Brown, Joshua
Byron, Herbert Mark
Carver, Eugene P.
Chan, Frederick M.
Christian, William R.
Connor, H.C.
Crane, Robert
Davis, Charles H.
Ellis, Terrance C.
Emmi, Joseph Jr.
Erenberg, Douglas D.
Ernst, Jerome W.
Fleischman, William O.
Gans, Peter M.
Glaser, Herbert
Gold, Steven H.
Gray, Jan Charles
Greene, H. Theodore
Greytak, Lee J.
Han, John D.
Harvey, Phillip Anthony
Hayes, Daniel P.
Hofert, Alvin H.
Hubert, Frank D.
Jeannel, Charles
Jonas, Anderson
Jones, Chuck
Kennison, Michael S.
Ketchum, R. Kevin
Kim, Sarah
Lane, Franklin K. III
Lapin, David A.
Lavine, Thomas
Leary, Theodore M. Jr.
Leedy, Carleton C. Jr.
Levy, Alan D.
Lewis, John O.
Lloyd, Robert M.
Lowe, Robert J.
Luk, King S.
Maier, Walter
Martin, Vincent F. Jr.
Mitchell, Kenneth Lee
Moon, David A.
Moore, Randall J.
Mordecai, Charles F.
Muir, Robert C.
Park, Richard E.G.
Price, Oliver Ray
Reicher, Leland J.
Renaud-Wright, Michael S.
Robertson, William A.
Robins, Roy S.
Robinson, Daniel T.
Ruth, Craig
Sarhangian, Ted
Schaefer, Howard G.
Schwartz, Joseph Harold
Seaton, Martin
Shafron, Shelly Jay
Skinner, Michael
Smith, Curtis B.
Terry, Paul J.
Ward, Charles L.
Webber, Michael
Welbourne, John Howard
Wilstein, David

Property Manager
Albany, Tony
Ambrosio, Louis
Anderson, Fred M.
Anthony, Alvin H.
Azzolina, Ronald
Beckstrom, R.L.
Benson, Andy
Binder, Hannan E.
Block, Gene R.
Brown, Joshua
Budnik, Ronald J.
Cameron, Cindy Lou
Chaiboonma, Eaksith
Chan, Frederick M.
Clarey, Frederick Joseph
Connell, Robert
Conway, William
Crane, Robert
Davis, Charles H.
DeSpain, J.C.
Dougherty, John
Drews, Donald Frederick
Emmi, Joseph Jr.
Erenberg, Douglas D.
Fowlks, Robert C.
Frasco, James A.
Gans, Peter M.
Greene, H. Theodore
Greytak, Lee J.
Harvey, Phillip Anthony
Hawk, James J.
Herschenfeld, Richard S.
Jonas, Anderson
Ketchum, R. Kevin
Krause, George F.
Kresin, Bruce
Leary, Theodore M. Jr.
Levy, Alan D.
Lewis, Charles D.
Lewis, John O.
Lowe, Robert J.
McCloskey, Anthony
Maier, Walter
Marchand, Arturo Jose
Mares, Robert
Mercola, Vincent E.
Mitchell, Norman S.
Moon, David A.
Moore, Randall J.
Moore, Walter
Mordecai, Charles F.
Muir, Robert C.
Murphy, Gerald D.
Overman, Mary Jayne
Park, Richard E.G.
Price, Oliver Ray
Rader, F. Ronald
Robertson, William A.
Ruth, Craig
Ryan, Arthur N.
Schwab, C.H.
Scott, Roger
Silny, Fred
Storms, John W.
Terry, Paul J.
Thompson, Brian
Toughill, Peter
Venitsky, Don
Ward, Charles L.
Wilstein, David
Young, Bruce G.

Real Estate Publisher
Beesley, H.E.
Carpe, Keith
Friedman, B.
Groene, Carl
Itzel, John
Nolan, B.J.
Pontius, H. Jackson
Price, Oliver Ray
Quinn, Dennis J.

Regulator
Azzolina, Ronald
Christian, William R.

Syndicator
Albany, Tony
Amin, Purander Ambalal
Azzolina, Ronald
Brown, Joshua
Cameron, Cindy Lou
Chaiboonma, Eaksith
Chan, Frederick M.
Christian, William R.
Davis, Charles H.
Edwards, Richard
Erenberg, Douglas D.
Frasco, James A.
Gans, Peter M.
Gold, Steven H.
Harvey, Phillip Anthony
Herschenfeld, Richard S.
Jonas, Anderson
Keligian, David Leo
Kennison, Michael S.
Kneafsey, Thomas
Lapin, David A.
Levy, Alan D.
Miller, Daniel A.
Poirier, Joseph L.
Price, Oliver Ray
Robinson, Daniel T.
Sarhangian, Ted
Schaefer, Howard G.
Schwartz, Joseph Harold
Sheriff, Garth I.
Smith, Curtis B.
Toole, Brice Jr.
Ward, Charles L.
Zoldos, Jeffrey A.E.

MARYSVILLE

Appraiser
Aileen, Porter
Goldberg, Arnold
Maxwell, Glenn M.

Attorney
Brown, W.Z. Jefferson
Burchett, Alan E.
Hawkins, Richard M.
Hinsdale, Wayne

Broker
Aileen, Porter
Chalmers, R. Scott
Featherston, Larry G.
Giampaoli, Peter G.
Goldberg, Arnold
Hignell, Fred W.
Maxwell, Glenn M.
Reed, Ronald A.

Builder
Giampaoli, Peter G.
Maxwell, Glenn M.
Reed, Ronald A.

Consultant
Featherston, Larry G.
Giampaoli, Peter G.
Goldberg, Arnold
Maxwell, Glenn M.

Developer
Aileen, Porter
Cain, George E.
Giampaoli, Peter G.
Hignell, Fred W.
Reed, Ronald A.
Sapp, Jonathan W.

Instructor
Reed, Ronald A.

Owner/Investor
Cain, George E.
Featherston, Larry G.
Giampaoli, Peter G.
Goldberg, Arnold
Hignell, Fred W.
Maxwell, Glenn M.
Reed, Ronald A.

Property Manager
Chalmers, R. Scott
Giampaoli, Peter G.
Hart, Tom W.
Hignell, Fred W.

Syndicator
Featherston, Larry G.
Hignell, Fred W.

OAKLAND

Appraiser
Ball, Elliott B.
Betts, Richard M.
Cogburn, Martin A.
Eyring, Phillip Max
Foley, Robert J.
Haines, John P.
Keeler, Jack C.
Maxfield, Robert C.
Nystrom, John A.
Ostrander, Fred
Reschke, Valerie Juliette
Tucker, Thomas A.
von Pingel, Eric
Wendt, Paul F.
Yovino-Young, G. Michael
Yow, Gordon

Attorney
Albert, Yvan
Barnard, John
Blumberg, Richard E.
Brewer, Robert H.
Brown, John Thos.
Chan, Gayle
Dean, Michael A.
Druskin, Victor
Gibson, Marjory F.
Goodmacher, Maxine
Goodman, Richard A.
Hetland, John R.
Lane, Robert K.
Lipman, Barry R.
Ramsaur, James W.
Robinson, Ned
Saputo, Peter T.
Scatena, Gerald W.
Sheldon, Terry E.
Singer, Bruce
Smith, Michael G.
Stone, Carol A.
Zebrack, Joel

Broker
Albert, Yvan
Angel, Robert S.

Bartels, Dwayne A.
Blomstrand, Curt
Bouilly, Roger Charles
Bovee, Michael C.
Bull, V. Craig
Candell, Cass
Church, Clayton
Clark, Richard O.
Cogburn, Martin A.
Dang, Theodore W.
Davis, Dwight W.
Dukellis, E. Nicholas
Edmunds, Kenneth E.
Evatt, Thomas M.
Eyring, Phillip Max
Flamme, John Eric
Fox, Claire R.
Grubb, Donald J.
Haines, John P.
Haugen, Odd E.
Henson, William R.
Hesse, Michael
Hinshaw, Robert L.
Horton, George H.
Jackman, Jerry
Keeler, Jack C.
Lamos, Adrian C. Jr.
Lap, Ha Hoc
Morris, Max A.
Newman, Karel
Nystrom, John A.
Osborne, Larry W.
Pearson, Ernest J.
Piper, Janet
Reschke, Valerie Juliette
Rice, K. Wayne
Rothacher, Larry L.
Scatena, Gerald W.
Shellooe, Daniel P.
Sherwood, Clifton A.
Shield, William C.
Silvey, Frederic R.
Soued, Frederick A.
Supino, Peter F.
Tiret, Sharon Lee
Vandergriff, Wayne
Woodbury, William F.

Builder
Bierylo, John I.
Davis, Dwight W.
Haines, John P.
Hickey, Cornelius (Neil) A.
Lane, Robert K.
Murphy, Harold B.
Noe, James A.
Silvey, Frederic R.
Simpson, Wayne E.

Consultant
Angel, Robert S.
Biagi, R.C.
Bouilly, Roger Charles
Candell, Cass
Cogburn, Martin A.
Coleman, Ira J.
Dang, Theodore W.
Davis, Dwight W.
Edmunds, Kenneth E.
Eyring, Phillip Max
Flamme, John Eric
Grubb, Donald J.
Hickey, Cornelius (Neil) A.
Hinshaw, Robert L.
Horton, George H.
Jackman, Jerry
Keeler, Jack C.
Korb, Irving
Lamos, Adrian C. Jr.
Lap, Ha Hoc
Maxson, Mary Annn Sowul
Morris, Max A.
Nystrom, John A.
Osborne, Larry W.
Peck, Ronald L.
Perry, Jack R.
Reschke, Valerie Juliette
Rothacher, Larry L.
Schaffran, E. Morton
Shellooe, Daniel P.
Singer, Bruce
Smith, Michael G.
Soued, Frederick A.
Supino, Peter F.
Thal, Lawrence S.
Wendt, Paul F.
Woodbury, William F.
Yovino-Young, G. Michael

Developer
Albert, Yvan
Angel, Robert S.
Bierylo, John I.
Blomstrand, Curt
Bouilly, Roger Charles
Bull, V. Craig
Church, Clayton
Cogburn, Martin A.
Daneman, Steven Bradley
Dang, Theodore W.
Davies, Dean M.
Dumper, Robert S.
Edmunds, Kenneth E.
Eyring, Phillip Max
Grubb, Donald J.
Hesse, Michael
Huntley, Steven T.
Kaplan, Jay M.
Keeler, Jack C.
Korb, Irving
Lane, Robert K.
Mersereau, Wallace D.
Murphy, Harold B.
Nagan, Harold R.
Newman, Karel
Noe, James A.
Nystrom, John A.
Reschke, Valerie Juliette
Rice, K. Wayne
Schaffran, E. Morton
Sherwood, Clifton A.
Silvey, Frederic R.
Simpson, Wayne E.
Soued, Frederick A.
Sowels, David
Stratton, James Malcolm Jr.
Supino, Peter F.
Thal, Lawrence S.
Vandergriff, Wayne
Wade, Stephen W.

Engineer
Haines, John P.

Instructor
Biagi, R.C.
Blumberg, Richard E.
Brown, John Thos.
Druskin, Victor
Edmunds, Kenneth E.
Eyring, Phillip Max
Fox, Claire R.
Hetland, John R.
Hickey, Cornelius (Neil) A.
Hinshaw, Robert L.
Jackman, Jerry
Perry, Jack R.
Reed, John T.
Reschke, Valerie Juliette
Rothacher, Larry L.
Thal, Lawrence S.
Wendt, Paul F.

Insuror
Angel, Robert S.
Candell, Cass
Perry, Jack R.
Reschke, Valerie Juliette

Lender
Davies, Dean M.
Hinshaw, Robert L.
Kaplan, Jay M.
Newman, Karel
Nystrom, John A.
Ostrander, Fred
Shield, William C.

Owner/Investor
Angel, Robert S.
Bartels, Dwayne A.
Biagi, R.C.
Bierylo, John I.
Blomstrand, Curt
Blumberg, Richard E.
Bouilly, Roger Charles
Bovee, Michael C.
Candell, Cass
Chirurg, James Thomas
Church, Clayton
Cogburn, Martin A.
Coleman, Ira J.
Daneman, Steven Bradley
Dang, Theodore W.
Davis, Dwight W.
Duffy, Richard B.
Dukellis, E. Nicholas
Edmunds, Kenneth E.
Eyring, Phillip Max
Fox, Claire R.
Hesse, Michael
Huntley, Steven T.
Jackman, Jerry
Kaplan, Jay M.
Korb, Irving
Lamos, Adrian C. Jr.
Lane, Robert K.
Morris, Max A.
Newman, Karel
Nystrom, John A.
Peck, Ronald L.
Perry, Jack R.
Reed, John T.
Reschke, Valerie Juliette
Rice, K. Wayne
Rothacher, Larry L.
Shellooe, Daniel P.
Sherwood, Clifton A.
Silvey, Frederic R.
Soued, Frederick A.
Supino, Peter F.
Thal, Lawrence S.
Vandergriff, Wayne
Woodbury, William F.
Yow, Gordon

Property Manager
Albert, Yvan
Angel, Robert S.
Biagi, R.C.
Blomstrand, Curt
Bouilly, Roger Charles
Bull, V. Craig
Church, Clayton
Cogburn, Martin A.
Daneman, Steven Bradley
Dang, Theodore W.
Davies, Dean M.
Davis, Dwight W.
Duffy, Richard B.
Dukellis, E. Nicholas
Edmunds, Kenneth E.
Fox, Claire R.
Grubb, Donald J.
Huntley, Steven T.
Jackman, Jerry
Kaplan, Jay M.
Kostyrka, R.J.
Mersereau, Wallace D.
Murphy, Harold B.
Newman, Karel
Noe, James A.
Nystrom, John A.
Peck, Ronald L.
Perry, Jack R.
Rice, K. Wayne
Silvey, Frederic R.
Soued, Frederick A.
Stratton, James Malcolm Jr.
Tiret, Sharon Lee
Vandergriff, Wayne
Woodbury, William F.
Yow, Gordon

Real Estate Publisher
Fox, Claire R.
Hetland, John R.
Hinshaw, Robert L.
Peck, Ronald L.
Reschke, Valerie Juliette
Yow, Gordon

Syndicator
Angel, Robert S.
Blomstrand, Curt
Bouilly, Roger Charles
Bovee, Michael C.
Bull, V. Craig
Candell, Cass
Cogburn, Martin A.
Daneman, Steven Bradley
Dang, Theodore W.
Dyson, Robert
Edmunds, Kenneth E.
Eyring, Phillip Max
Fox, Claire R.
Haugen, Odd E.
Hesse, Michael
Huntley, Steven T.
Kaplan, Jay M.
Killian, Richard
Newman, Karel
Nystrom, John A.
Peck, Ronald L.
Rice, K. Wayne
Rothacher, Larry L.
Shellooe, Daniel P.
Shield, William C.
Silvey, Frederic R.
Soued, Frederick A.
Sowels, David
Supino, Peter F.
Thal, Lawrence S.
Yow, Gordon

OXNARD

Appraiser
Wood, Ray A.

Architect
Andrews, LeRoy M.

Broker
Becker, Fred P.
Chellis, Tom
Moll, Burkhard E. "Hardy"
Parsons, Garrett S.
Wood, Ray A.

Builder
Moll, Burkhard E. "Hardy"
Parsons, Garrett S.

Consultant
Andrews, LeRoy M.
Becker, Fred P.
Chellis, Tom

Developer
Andrews, LeRoy M.
Moll, Burkhard E. "Hardy"
Parsons, Garrett S.
Weber, Kenneth

Instructor
Becker, Fred P.
Chellis, Tom

Owner/Investor
Chellis, Tom
Moll, Burkhard E. "Hardy"
Parsons, Garrett S.

Property Manager
Moll, Burkhard E. "Hardy"
Weber, Kenneth

Syndicator
Andrews, LeRoy M.
Moll, Burkhard E. "Hardy"
Parsons, Garrett S.

PALM SPRINGS

Appraiser
Blank, Ruth
Crommelin, Jacques B.
Sweet, Rowland F.

Broker
Blank, Ruth
Crommelin, Jacques B.
Dunlevie, Ernie
Jones, Louie A.

Consultant
Blank, Ruth
Crommelin, Jacques B.
Jones, Louie A.

Developer
Dunlevie, Ernie
Surnow, Jeffrey C.
Sweet, Rowland F.

Insuror
Crommelin, Jacques B.

Owner/Investor
Blank, Ruth
Surnow, Jeffrey C.

Property Manager
Blank, Ruth
Surnow, Jeffrey C.

Syndicator
Jones, Louie A.

PASADENA

Appraiser
Abelmann, William W.
Dyess, William G.
Flynn, Jack C.
Freer, L. Raymond III
Glupker, Warren D.
Jones, Wayne W.
McNabb, Charlie L.
Shermer, Howard
Sonne, Ross N. Jr.
Stephens, Rolland R.

Architect
Barasch, Stephen B.
Barr, H. Dennis

Attorney
Baker, Robert L.
Barr, H. Dennis
Clark, Charles Edward
Montgomery, Michael B.
Ng, Thien Koan
Tomsic, Gerald A.
Weissman, Alan M.

Banker
Dyess, William G.

Broker
Abelmann, William W.
Barr, H. Dennis
Bartlett, Theodore D.
Chamnongphanij, Into B.
Coatsworth, Betty C.
DeFazio, Dominic
Flynn, Jack C.
Garretson, Ronald B
Hotchkin, Edgar E.
Howe, Mitchell B. Jr.
Longobardo, Richard G.
McNabb, Charlie L.
Mulrenan, Tim
Ng, Thien Koan
Royale, Don
Shermer, Howard
Sonne, Ross N. Jr.
Stephens, Rolland R.

Builder
Barasch, Stephen B.
Barr, H. Dennis
Mintz, Frederick W.
Simon, Kenneth D.
Wachtler, Bruce Edward
Weissman, Alan M.

Consultant
Abelmann, William W.
Dresnick, David W.
Howe, Mitchell B. Jr.
Longobardo, Richard G.
McNabb, Charlie L.
Mintz, Frederick W.
Mulrenan, Tim
Richards, Edward J.
Shermer, Howard
Starling, Kenneth H.

Developer
Barasch, Stephen B.
Barr, H. Dennis
Bohlinger, Thomas P.
Bryant, Virgil C.
DeFazio, Dominic
Dresnick, David W.
Flynn, Jack C.
Hotchkin, Edgar E.
Longobardo, Richard G.
McArthur, Cameron D.
McNabb, Charlie L.
Mintz, Frederick W.
Montgomery, Michael B.
Mulrenan, Tim
Ng, Thien Koan
Richards, Edward J.
Simon, Kenneth D.
Sonne, Ross N. Jr.
Starling, Kenneth H.
Weissman, Alan M.

Engineer
Barr, H. Dennis
Howe, Mitchell B. Jr.
Simon, Kenneth D.

Instructor
Abelmann, William W.
Bartlett, Theodore D.
Flynn, Jack C.
Stephens, Rolland R.

Insuror
Garretson, Ronald B

Lender
Dresnick, David W.
Garretson, Ronald B
Gunther, Stephen C.

Owner/Investor
Abelmann, William W.
Barr, H. Dennis
DeFazio, Dominic
Hotchkin, Edgar E.
Howe, Mitchell B. Jr.
McNabb, Charlie L.
Mintz, Frederick W.
Montgomery, Michael B
Mulrenan, Tim
Ng, Thien Koan
Shermer, Howard
Simon, Kenneth D.
Sonne, Ross N. Jr.
Weissman, Alan M.

Property Manager
Abelmann, William W.
Barr, H. Dennis
Bartlett, Theodore D.
Brumalds, George
Hotchkin, Edgar E.
Howe, Mitchell B. Jr.
Maas, William
McArthur, Cameron D.
McNabb, Charlie L.
Mintz, Frederick W.
Mulrenan, Tim
Shermer, Howard
Sonne, Ross N. Jr.

Syndicator
Bartlett, Theodore D.
DeFazio, Dominic
Dresnick, David W.
Flynn, Jack C.
Longobardo, Richard G.
Ng, Thien Koan
Royale, Don
Shermer, Howard
Sonne, Ross N. Jr.

REDDING

Appraiser
Compomizzo, O. "Compy"
Martin, Robert P.

Broker
Compomizzo, O. "Compy"
Martin, Robert P.

Consultant
Decima, Jay P.
Martin, Robert P.

Developer
Covington, Virgil L.
Decima, Jay P.

Lender
Covington, Virgil L.

Owner/Investor
Decima, Jay P.

Property Manager
Covington, Virgil L.

Real Estate Publisher
Decima, Jay P.

SACRAMENTO

Appraiser
Claussen, Woodrow H.
Crone, Jeffrey R.
Gelhaus, Melvin F.
Gruenhagen, Melvin P.
Mitchell, Robert L.
Parker, King Jr.
Rhodes, Richard M.
Stringer, Robert G.
Zeller, Bud

Architect
Daves, Mae E.

Attorney
Abramson, Keith V.
Dobris, Joel C.
Grayson, James Y.
Higbe, Clifton M.H.
Hoffman, Lawrence L.
McCarthy, Sean E.
MacKenzie, Roderick L.
Miller, Charles J.
Rader, Richard E.
Stagg, Howard J.
Van Camp, Brian R.
West, Clyde O.
Yeo, James R.
Young, David Michael

Banker
Pugh, J.W.

Broker
Allen, Chester W.
Baron, Louis C.T.
Bertot, Cathey H.
Carlsen, Paul R.
Cassano, Robert James
Caterino, Michael A.
Cockerell, C. Steven
Crone, Jeffrey R.
Dailey, John H.
Daves, Mae E.
Grayson, James Y.
Hansen, Richard
Higbe, Clifton M.H.
Hoffman, Lawrence L.
Mangum, Cary R.
Parker, King Jr.
Prater, Richard Allan
Prins, August W.
Rhodes, Richard M.
Robbins, William J. Jr.
Saunders, Monte L.
Smith, Richard L.V.
Smith, William S.
Streng, G. William
Wrieden, James E.
Yeo, James R.
Zeller, Bud

Builder
Albusche, Leo J.
Blake, Peter L.
Cassano, Robert James
Caterino, Michael A.
Cockerell, C. Steven
Daves, Mae E.
Erickson, Franklin E.
Gardemeyer, Dennis Alan
Hansen, Richard
Rader, Richard E.
Streng, G. William
Teichert, Frederick
Twycross, Dale A.
Yeo, James R.
Zeller, Bud

Consultant
Abramson, Keith V.
Allen, Chester W.
Baron, Louis C.T.
Blake, Peter L.
Bryant, Sherman R. Jr.
Cassano, Robert James
Caterino, Michael A.
Claussen, Woodrow H.
Cockerell, C. Steven
Crone, Jeffrey R.
Daves, Mae E.
Hoffman, Lawrence L.
Kassis, Gregory
Mangum, Cary R.
Parker, King Jr.
Prins, August W.
Quattrin, Gary L.
Rhodes, Richard M.
Robbins, William J. Jr.
Saunders, Monte L.
Smith, Richard L.V.
Stringer, Robert G.
Woodhull, Daniel E.
Wrieden, James E.
Yeo, James R.
Zeller, Bud

Developer
Albusche, Leo J.
Allen, Chester W.
Blake, Peter L.
Cassano, Robert James
Caterino, Michael A.
Cockerell, C. Steven
Dailey, John H.
Daves, Mae E.
Erickson, Franklin E.
Gardemeyer, Dennis Alan
Hansen, Richard
Mitchell, Robert L.
Parker, King Jr.
Prater, Richard Allan
Rader, Richard E.
Robbins, William J. Jr.
Saunders, Monte L.
Smith, Richard L.V.
Streng, G. William
Sumner, Charles A. II
Teichert, Frederick
Twycross, Dale A.
Yeo, James R.
Zeller, Bud

Instructor
Abramson, Keith V.
Allen, Chester W.
Cockerell, C. Steven
Dailey, John H.
Dobris, Joel C.
Mangum, Cary R.
Parker, King Jr.
Woodhull, Daniel E.
Yeo, James R.
Zeller, Bud

Insuror
Abramson, Keith V.
McCarthy, Sean E.
Prins, August W.
Wrieden, James E.

Lender
Baron, Louis C.T.
Claussen, Woodrow H.
Zeller, Bud

Owner/Investor
Abramson, Keith V.
Albusche, Leo J.
Allen, Chester W.
Baron, Louis C.T.
Bertot, Cathey H.
Blake, Peter L.
Caldwell, Ted
Cockerell, C. Steven
Corbin, Lee D.
Crone, Jeffrey R.
Dailey, John H.
Daves, Mae E.
Erickson, Franklin E.
Gardemeyer, Dennis Alan
Hansen, Richard
Mitchell, Robert L.
Prater, Richard Allan
Prins, August W.
Rader, Richard E.
Rhodes, Richard M.
Saunders, Monte L.
Smith, Richard L.V.
Sumner, Charles A. II
Teichert, Frederick
Wrieden, James E.
Young, David Michael
Zeller, Bud

Property Manager
Albusche, Leo J.
Blake, Peter L.
Bryant, Sherman R. Jr.
Cassano, Robert James
Caterino, Michael A.
Cockerell, C. Steven
Corbin, Lee D.
Daves, Mae E.
Fox, David
Kassis, Gregory
Mangum, Cary R.
Parker, King Jr.
Prater, Richard Allan
Prins, August W.
Robbins, William J. Jr.
Smith, Richard L.V.
Smith, William S.
Sumner, Charles A. II
Twycross, Dale A.
Wrieden, James E.
Zeller, Bud

Real Estate Publisher
Abramson, Keith V.
Allen, Chester W.
Cockerell, C. Steven
Rhodes, Richard M.

Regulator
Fennell, Ruth

Syndicator
Abramson, Keith V.
Bertot, Cathey H.
Blake, Peter L.
Caldwell, Ted
Caterino, Michael A.
Daves, Mae E.
Hoffman, Lawrence L.
Parker, King Jr.
Rader, Richard E.
Smith, Richard L.V.
Wrieden, James E.
Yeo, James R.
Zeller, Bud

SALINAS

Appraiser
Capewell, John
Cathcart, David L.
May, Tom
Samuelson, Harold M.
Seyferth, Harold H.

Architect
McNally, Mike D.

Broker
Aucutt, Charles Henry
Cathcart, David L.
Noseworthy, Frederick N.
Reitter, Karl L.
Rianda, Brian I.
Thomas, Edwin James II

Consultant
Capewell, John
Cathcart, David L.
May, Tom
Noseworthy, Frederick N.
Reitter, Karl L.
Rianda, Brian I.
Seyferth, Harold H.

Developer
Aucutt, Charles Henry
Noseworthy, Frederick N.
Reitter, Karl L.

Instructor
Samuelson, Harold M.

Owner/Investor
Aucutt, Charles Henry
Reitter, Karl L.
Rianda, Brian I.
Thomas, Edwin James II

Syndicator
May, Tom
Noseworthy, Frederick N.
Reitter, Karl L.

SAN BERNARDINO

Appraiser
Allard, Warren J.
Francisco, M. Robi
Holmes, Robert J.
Howes, Edward B.
Payne, L.D.

Attorney
Cross, Richard A.
Hulting, Frederick B. Jr.
Theobald, Forest

Broker
Bayliff, Clarence W.
Berge, Gail B.
Dascenzi, Hazel Marie
Francisco, M. Robi
Hulting, Frederick B. Jr
Morris, Charles Arthur
Payne, L.D.
Piscitelli, Mark Andrew
Rawlings, William H.
Thompson, Mark A.
Wolf, Robert

Builder
Dascenzi, Hazel Marie
Long, Wm. G.
Morris, Charles Arthur
Rawlings, William H.
Wolf, Robert

Consultant
Allard, Warren J.
Bayliff, Clarence W.
Dukes, John E.
Howes, Edward B.
Kovatch, Paul R.
Payne, L.D.
Rawlings, William H.
Talcott, Tom M.
Wolf, Robert

Developer
Bayliff, Clarence W.
Dascenzi, Hazel Marie
Dukes, John E.
Francisco, M. Robi
Johnston, Thomas A.
Long, Wm. G.
Morris, Charles Arthur
Payne, L.D.
Rawlings, William H.
Ritzau, George S.
Thompson, Mark A.
Wolf, Robert

Engineer
Long, Wm. G.
Rawlings, William H.

Instructor
Kovatch, Paul R.
Morris, Charles Arthur

Owner/Investor
Allard, Warren J.
Dascenzi, Hazel Marie
Francisco, M. Robi
Kovatch, Paul R.
Long, Wm. G.
Morris, Charles Arthur
Payne, L.D.
Rawlings, William H.
Thompson, Mark A.
Wolf, Robert

Property Manager
Dascenzi, Hazel Marie
Dukes, John E.
Howes, Edward B.
Kovatch, Paul R.
Ritzau, George S.
Theobald, Forest
Thompson, Mark A.

Syndicator
Dascenzi, Hazel Marie
Hulting, Frederick B. Jr.
Long, Wm. G.
Wolf, Robert

SAN DIEGO

Appraiser
Abercrombie, Jerry T.
Cotton, John
Eshelman, Darwin K.
Harp, William C.
Johnson, Lee C.
Lipman, H.L.
Murad, B. Bill
Parkinson, Steve
Roberts, Thomas L.
Starkey, John P.

Architect
Buss, Richard Paul
Lam, Man Ching

Assessor
Lockard, William A.

Attorney
Calkins, Christopher
Dostart, Paul J.
Feldman, Earl N.
Fisher, David A.
Gallegos, Richard L.
Hathaway, Daniel A.
Heramb, Brent R.
Howard, James W.
Hubka, Verne Robert
Lawrence, Peter Hutchinson
Loban, Michael L.
Loome, James Michael
Mandell, Mark P.
Mann, Jack I.
Miller, Merwyn J.
Murad, B. Bill
Nelson, William E.
Pitcaithley, Alan L. Esq.
Richmond, Charles D.
Shaw, Richard A.
Small, Harold S.
Thompson, Wesley R.
Wayne, R. Bruce

Banker
Coniglio, Vincent
Dickerson, Richard F.
Harp, William C.

Broker
Abercrombie, Jerry T.
Borsari, William E.
Boyle, John O.
Butzen, Philip J.
Cafagna, Michael P.
Chantengco, Rick D.
Chenoweth, Walter A.
Chodur, Philip
Clay, Willard H.
Conway, E.R. (Bud)
Cotton, John
Davis, James M.
DiJulius, Leonard G.
Dostart, Paul J.
Doyle, Marc H.
Fisher, David A.
Fitzgerald, Mike
Fogel, Danny L.
Gersten, Harry R.
Gibson, Maury E. Jr.
Granton, Samuel Richard
Gustafson, Craig
Hampton, Marguerite M.
Heramb, Brent R.
Hoffman, Thomas Rick
Howard, James W.
Howe, Randolph R.
Huffman, R. Engene
Iseman, Caryl
Jones, Kenneth K.
Koblentz, Arnold E.
Lam, Man Ching
Lawrence, Peter Hutchinson
Lindshield, Dennis
Loban, Michael L.
Lockard, William A.
Loome, James Michael
Lussa, Ray
Lutchansky, Herman
McDaniel, Hugh
Mandell, Mark P.
Mann, Jack I.
Murad, B. Bill
Nightingale, Robert S. Jr.
Paffhausen, James V.
Parkinson, Steve
Purdon, H.P. Sandy
Ross, Barry J.
Shafer, Thomas W.
Spotts, James I.
Starkey, John P.
Stenderup, James K.
Strohl, Jean Carol
Wickstrand, Owen
Willett, Frank

Builder
Butzen, Philip J.
Figueredo, Antonio B.
Hedrick, Janet L.
Howard, James W.

Huffman, R. Engene
Kruer, Patrick
Larson, Robert C.
McBride, J. Nevins Jr.
McComic, R. Barry
Mann, Jack I.
Paquin, Gary N.
Pearson, Paul E.
Ross, Barry J.
Schoeffel, Rudd

Consultant
Abercrombie, Jerry T.
Basney, Dana A.
Borsari, William E.
Butzen, Philip J.
Cafagna, Michael P.
Chantengco, Rick D.
Chodur, Philip
Clay, Willard H.
Conway, E.R. (Bud)
Davis, James M.
DiJulius, Leonard G.
Fisher, David A.
Fogel, Danny L.
Frederking, George H.
Garner, Douglas
Gibson, Maury E. Jr.
Gibson, Thomas H. Jr.
Granton, Samuel Richard
Hampton, Marguerite M.
Hathaway, Daniel A.
Heramb, Brent R.
Hillbrook, Roger William Jr.
Hoffman, Thomas Rick
Howard, James W.
Howe, Randolph R.
Huffman, R. Engene
Iseman, Caryl
Johnson, Lee C.
Jones, Kenneth K.
Koblentz, Arnold E.
Kruer, Patrick
Lam, Man Ching
Lipman, H.L.
Loban, Michael L.
Lutchansky, Herman
Mann, Jack I.
Murad, B. Bill
Nelson, William E.
Paquin, Gary N.
Parkinson, Steve
Purdon, H.P. Sandy
Starkey, John P.
Stephens, Leland Griffin
Strohl, Jean Carol
Willett, Frank

Developer
Burrell, Randie
Butzen, Philip J.
Cafagna, Michael P.
Chodur, Philip
Chu, Hilbert
Clark, John B.
Clay, Willard H.
DiJulius, Leonard G.
Feehan, John J. Jr.
Figueredo, Antonio B.
Fogel, Danny L.
Garner, Douglas
Gibson, Thomas H. Jr.
Goldstein, Howard
Gustafson, Craig
Harp, William C.
Hedrick, Janet L.
Hillbrook, Roger William Jr.
Hoffman, Thomas Rick
Hoppe, William E.
Howard, James W.
Huffman, R. Engene
Kruer, Patrick
Lam, Man Ching
Larson, Robert C.
Lawrence, Peter Hutchinson
Lindshield, Dennis
Loban, Michael L.
Loome, James Michael
McBride, J. Nevins Jr.
Mann, Jack I.
Nelson, William E.
Nightingale, Robert S. Jr.
O'Brien, John M.
Paquin, Gary N.
Pearson, Paul E.
Purdon, H.P. Sandy
Quate, Laurence W.
Rosado, Ronald D.
Ross, Barry J.
Schoeffel, Rudd
Shafer, Thomas W.
Spangler, Charles Bishop
Starkey, John P.
Troutman, H.L.
Wickstrand, Owen

Engineer
Buss, Richard Paul
Chantengco, Rick D.
Howard, James W.
Hubka, Verne Robert
Pearson, Paul E.
Shafer, Thomas W.
Wickstrand, Owen
Willett, Frank

Instructor
Boyle, John O.
Conway, E.R. (Bud)
Fisher, David A.
Fogel, Danny L.
Granton, Samuel Richard
Hathaway, Daniel A.
Howe, Randolph R.
Iseman, Caryl
Lawrence, Peter Hutchinson
Loome, James Michael
Lutchansky, Herman
McKim, Dennis R.
Murad, B. Bill
Purdon, H.P. Sandy
Quate, Laurence W.
Shafer, Thomas W.
Shaw, Richard A.
Small, Harold S.
Strohl, Jean Carol

Insuror
Hampton, Marguerite M.
McBride, J. Nevins Jr.
McKim, Dennis R.
Wickstrand, Owen

Lender
Coniglio, Vincent
Kruer, Patrick

Owner/Investor
Basney, Dana A.
Borsari, William E.
Boyle, John O.
Burrell, Randie
Butzen, Philip J.
Cafagna, Michael P.
Chantengco, Rick D.
Chodur, Philip
Chu, Hilbert
Clay, Willard H.
Coniglio, Vincent
Conway, E.R. (Bud)
Davis, James M.
Dostart, Paul J.
Figueredo, Antonio B.
Fisher, David A.
Fogel, Danny L.
Gibson, Thomas H. Jr.
Gustafson, Craig
Heramb, Brent R.
Hillbrook, Roger William Jr.
Hoppe, William E.
Howard, James W.
Howe, Randolph R.
Huffman, R. Engene
Iseman, Caryl
Jones, Kenneth K.
Koblentz, Arnold E.
Kruer, Patrick
Lam, Man Ching
Lindshield, Dennis
Loban, Michael L.
Loome, James Michael
Lussa, Ray
Lutchansky, Herman
McBride, J. Nevins Jr.
McDaniel, Hugh
Mandell, Mark P.
Mann, Jack I.
Paquin, Gary N.
Parkinson, Steve
Pearson, Paul E.
Purdon, H.P. Sandy
Richmond, Charles D.
Ross, Barry J.
Schoeffel, Rudd
Simon, Ronald I.
Spangler, Charles Bishop
Starkey, John P.
Wickstrand, Owen
Willett, Frank

Property Manager
Abercrombie, Jerry T.
Ash, C. Neil
Basney, Dana A.
Borsari, William E.
Boyle, John O.
Burrell, Randie
Cafagna, Michael P.
Chantengco, Rick D.
Chodur, Philip
Cotton, John
Cramer, Robert W.
Davis, Richard H.
Figueredo, Antonio B.
Gersten, Harry R.
Gibson, Maury E. Jr.
Gustafson, Craig
Heramb, Brent R.
Hoppe, William E.
Huffman, R. Engene
Iseman, Caryl
Jones, Kenneth K.
Kruer, Patrick
Lussa, Ray
Lutchansky, Herman
McBride, J. Nevins Jr.
McDaniel, Hugh
Mann, Jack I.
Murad, B. Bill
Nelson, William E.
Paquin, Gary N.
Parkinson, Steve
Pitcaithley, Alan L. Esq.
Rosado, Ronald D.
Schoeffel, Rudd
Sellgren, Arthur
Spotts, James L.
Starkey, John P.
Thomas, Robert Earl
Willett, Frank
Wilson, Ronald

Real Estate Publisher
Fogel, Danny L.
Granton, Samuel Richard
Howe, Randolph R.
Lutchansky, Herman
Stephens, Leland Griffin

Regulator
Fisher, David A.

Syndicator
Borsari, William E.
Boyle, John O.
Cafagna, Michael P.
Chantengco, Rick D.
Chodur, Philip
Clay, Willard H.
Davis, James M.
DiJulius, Leonard G.
Fisher, David A.
Fogel, Danny L.
Freed, Eric R.
Garner, Douglas
Gibson, Maury E. Jr.
Hathaway, Daniel A.
Hedrick, Janet L.
Hillbrook, Roger William Jr.
Hoppe, William E.
Howard, James W.
Howe, Randolph R.
Iseman, Caryl
Koblentz, Arnold E.
Kruer, Patrick
Lindshield, Dennis
Loban, Michael L.
Lockard, William A.
Loome, James Michael
Lutchansky, Herman
McBride, J. Nevins Jr.
Mandell, Mark P.
Mann, Jack I.
Miller, Merwyn J.
Paffhausen, James V.
Pitcaithley, Alan L. Esq.
Purdon, H.P. Sandy
Quate, Laurence W.
Richmond, Charles D.
Schoeffel, Rudd
Simon, Ronald I.
Spangler, Charles Bishop

SAN FRANCISCO

Appraiser
Bertolina, Richard R.
Blackburn, Cartier
Breitman, Bruce M.
Bryant, Carl H.
Bryson, Hugh
Delman, James B.
Diaz, Jean Michael (Mr.)
Gomez, Frank P.
Hammerback, William J. Jr.
Hanford, Lloyd Dr. Jr.
Healy, Thomas R.
Hu, Jackson K.
Kawamoto, Edwin H.
McCabe, James F. Jr.
Macdonald, David J.
McDonnell, Michael James
Marquis, George L.
Robbins, Richard M.
Root, Edgar Wilson
Rosenfeld, Michael D.
Schlesinger, Tod Michael
Sewing, Charles E.
Snyder, James E.
Thomas, James O.
Trimble, Harold G. Jr.
Willis, Jon B.
Zerbst, Robert H.

Architect
Abend, William M.
Bentley, Robert Clyde
Bertolina, Richard R.
Bourne, William C.
Brown, Keith Thomas
Del Campo, Martin
Henslee, S. Elmo
Malott, James S.
Miller, Kirk
Willis, Beverly A.

Assessor
Duca, Sam

Attorney
Adams, Joseph A.
Bayer, Theodore F.
Berg, James M.
Bernhardt, Roger
Blackfield, William
Boyd, Bruce Michael
Breitman, Bruce M.
Broll, William F. Esq.
Brown, Dennis A.
Brown, Timothy N.
Browne, Leslie M.
Burk, John Rogers
Campisi, Dominic J.
Curotto, Ricky J.
Dana, Donald E.
Daniels, Robert H.
Drucker, Cecily A.
Egan, John
Estrin, Dianne G.
Frankel, James B.
Furbush, David M.
Gainer, Stephen R.
Gallagher, Ralph
Gotshall-Maxon, Lee F. Esq.
Hanford, Timothy Lloyd
Hanna, John Paul
Hartz, J. Ernest Jr.
Hosack, John L.
Janz, James R.
Johnson, Reverdy
Kawamoto, Edwin H.
Kerstetter, Ralph A. Esq.
King, John J.
Kissinger, Michael J.
Lee, John Jin
Lee, Theodore B.
Lerner, Martin L.
Lima, Salvatore A.
McGlynn, D. Jerry
Marshall, Carol M.
Maslin, Harvey L.
Micek, John J.
Nelson, Ronald W. Esq.
Owens, Thomas R.
Payne, Silas Owen
Pearlstein, Marvin B.
Peel, Norman D.
Porter, Alan B.
Rible, Charles H.
Rudoff, Arnold G.
Schneider, Michael E.
Seiger, Joseph R.
Shea, Daniel C.
Sommer, Scott A.
Stark, William W. Jr.
Swartz, Thomas Byrne
Tong, Harry W.
Weiner, Edward A.
Weller, Louis S.

Banker
Aljoe, Daniel W.
Brodty, Charles
Burke, Richard S.
Capan, Robert G.
Del Campo, Martin
Feinerman, Milton
Gabriel, David H.
Hayward, Frank E.
Lawrence, William B.
Price, Patrick Hilary
Ritter, James J.
Taylor, Verl

Broker
Baker, Gary L.
Bayer, Theodore F.
Berger, Randall Craig
Bissinger, Paul A. Jr.
Boyd, Bruce Michael
Breitman, Bruce M.
Brown, Dennis A.
Bryant, Carl H.
Bryson, Hugh
Calkins, Glen S.
Capan, Robert G.
Casto, David Leroy
Chow, Steven Y.T.
Cizek, Jerome D.
Collier, Russell
Couch, George J.
Cruze, Harold
De Luca, Joseph P.
Delman, James B.
Dong, Donald D.
Egan, John
Freund, Fredric S.
Furbush, David M.
Gabriel, David H.
Gainer, Stephen R.
Gatley, R.H.
Hayward, Frank E.
Healy, Thomas R.
Henslee, S. Elmo
Higgins, James G.
Horvitz, Carl
Hu, Jackson K.
Kawamoto, Edwin H.
Keller, Kevin E.
Kerr, Keith H.
Kuhn, F. Stuart
Larsen, Richard A.
Lee, Soloman
Leynse, Waldo H.
Lynch, Robert Francis
McClure, J. Kelly
Macdonald, David J.
McGowin, Gerald Anthony
McNeil, Robert A.
Mankin, Roxanne
Marquis, George L.
Mayer, Andrew
Middelsteadt, Bernice
Palmer, Perry F.
Prichard, Gaylord E.
Ravetti, Silvio E.
Rawson, David R.
Rible, Charles H.
Ritter, James J.
Robert, John
Root, Edgar Wilson
Schlesinger, Tod Michael
Seiger, Joseph R.
Steichen, C. Everett
Taylor, Verl
Thomas, James O.
Tong, Harry W.
Treuenfels, Hans P.
Trimble, Harold G. Jr.
Usher, Kirk Jr.
Wang, Chen Chi
Warren, Arthur R. Jr.
Wells, Donald A.
Willard, Gary E.
Young, Robert W.

Builder
Aljoe, Daniel W.
Bentley, Robert Clyde
Bertolina, Richard R.
Blackfield, William
Brown, Dennis A.
Cahill, Gerald
Chang, William H.C.
Christian, J.E.
DeRegt, John S.
Hedberg, Jon B.
Leeder, Stuart L.
Lewis, Jeff D.
Lindberg, Dexter Clayton
Macdonald, David J.
Malott, James S.
Owens, Thomas R.
Riskas, Harry J.
Seiger, Joseph R.
Wang, Chen Chi
Young, Robert W.

Consultant
Aljoe, Daniel W.
Aust, Jurgen
Baker, Gary L.
Balluff, Douglas Paul
Berger, Randall Craig
Bertolina, Richard R.
Bissinger, Paul A. Jr.
Blackfield, William
Boler, James F.
Brateman, Ron (Rocco)
Breitman, Bruce M.
Brown, Dennis A.
Brown, Keith Thomas
Brune, W. Carl Jr.
Bryant, Carl H.
Bryant, James Farnsworth
Bryson, Hugh
Capan, Robert G.
Carneghi, Christopher C.
Casto, David Leroy
Collier, Russell
Cotsworth, C. Michael
Curotto, Ricky J.
De Luca, Joseph P.
Delman, James B.
Diaz, Jean Michael
Drucker, Cecily A.
Egan, John
Elliott-Gruen, Kate
Fadiman, James
Flora, William D.
Freund, Fredric S.
Gatley, R.H.
Gille, Thomas William
Golden, D. Daniel
Gomez, Frank P.
Greig, D. Wylie
Hammerback, William J. Jr.
Hanford, Lloyd Dr. Jr.
Hayward, Frank E.
Healy, Thomas R.
Heffernan, E. Michael
Higgins, James G.
Hoffman, Arnold L.
Horvitz, Carl
Hu, Jackson K.
Kawamoto, Edwin H.
Keller, Kevin E.
Kelly, Gerald
Kissinger, Michael J.
Koehler, Thilo B.
Kuhn, F. Stuart
Law, James G.
Lawrence, William B.
Lee, Soloman
Lee, Theodore B.
Lewis, James A.
Lewis, Jerry L.
Lichauco, Marcial P. Jr.
McCabe, James F. Jr.
McDonnell, Michael James
McElyea, J. Richard
McGlynn, D. Jerry
McKaig, Michael D.
Marquis, George L.
Mayer, Andrew
Middelsteadt, Bernice
Moffett, H. Thomas
Moghadam, Hamid R.
Payne, Roslyn Braeman
Prichard, Gaylord E.
Ramseyer, William L.
Rawson, David R.
Riskas, Harry J.
Robbins, Richard M.
Roberts, William Lee
Rosenfeld, Michael D.
Rudoff, Arnold G.
San Filippo, Steven
Schlesinger, Tod Michael
Sims, Dennis C.
Steichen, C. Everett
Stevenson, Allen W.
Taylor, Verl
Thompson, John S.
Todd, Stan
Trimble, Harold G. Jr.
Usher, Kirk Jr.
Vas Dias, James S.
Wells, Cecil H. Jr.
Willis, Jon B.
Wollack, Richard G.
Young, Robert W.
Zerbst, Robert H.

Developer
Baker, Gary L.
Balluff, Douglas Paul
Beim, Robert B.
Berger, Randall Craig
Bertolina, Richard R.
Blackfield, William
Breitman, Bruce M.
Brown, Dennis A.
Brunner, Mark
Calkins, Glen S.
Carter, Steven Michael
Chan, Anthony
Chang, William H.C.
Chow, Steven Y.T.
Christian, J.E.
Cizek, Jerome D.
Clark, Peter L.
Collier, Russell
Conrad, John F.
Couch, George J.
Cruze, Harold
DeRegt, John S.
Ditz, William W.
Donaldson, Francis
Gates, Robert Pfarr
Gatley, R.H.
Hedberg, Jon B.
Heffernan, E. Michael
Henslee, S. Elmo
Hooper, Stanton K.
Horvitz, Carl
James, John K.
Keller, Kevin E.
Kissinger, Michael J.
Kuhn, F. Stuart
Law, James G.
Lee, Theodore B.
Leeder, Stuart L.
Lewis, Jeff D.
Lewis, Jerry L.
Leynse, Waldo H.
Lindberg, Dexter Clayton
Liphart, George von
Macdonald, David J.
McGowin, Gerald Anthony
Malott, James S.
Marshall, Carol M.
Mayer, Andrew
Mays, W. Gene
Miller, Kirk
Owens, Thomas R.
Palmer, Perry F.
Prichard, Gaylord E.
Rawson, David R.
Reinings, John H. Jr.
Riskas, Harry J.
Ritter, James J.
Robbins, John R.
Robert, John
Roberts, William Lee
Schlesinger, Tod Michael
Seiger, Joseph R.
Shea, Daniel C.
Slater, Adair
Spieker, Warren E. "Ned" Jr.
Stevenson, Allen W.
Taylor, Verl
Thysen, Paul M.
Treuenfels, Hans P.
Usher, Kirk Jr.
Wang, Chen Chi
Wells, Cecil H. Jr.

Willard, Gary E.
Wilson, William III
Wollenberg, David A.
Young, Robert W.

Engineer
Blackfield, William
Henslee, S. Elmo
Law, James G.
Todd, Stan
Wang, Chen Chi
Wells, Cecil H. Jr.
Wells, Donald A.

Instructor
Bentley, Robert Clyde
Bernhardt, Roger
Blackburn, Cartier
Boyd, Bruce Michael
Bryant, Carl H.
Diaz, Jean Michael
Flora, William D.
Gainer, Stephen R.
Gomez, Frank P.
Kerr, Keith H.
Kissinger, Michael J.
Lee, Soloman
Lima, Salvatore A.
Mankin, Roxanne
Robbins, John R.
Rudoff, Arnold G.
Salisbury, Ron O.
Thomas, James O.
Tong, Harry W.
Trimble, Harold G. Jr.
Weller, Louis S.

Lender
Berger, Randall Craig
Bertolina, Richard R.
Brown, Dennis A.
Burke, Richard S.
Dick, William M.
Furbush, Donald M.
Gabriel, David H.
Healy, Thomas R.
Korinke, Walter M.
Macdonald, David J.
McGowin, Gerald Anthony
McNeil, Robert A.
Payne, Roslyn Braeman
Price, Patrick Hilary
Rising, John S. Jr.
Root, Edgar Wilson
Rosenfeld, Michael D.
Shea, Daniel C.
Snyder, James E.
Thomas, James O.
Wang, Chen Chi

Owner/Investor
Baker, Gary L.
Balluff, Douglas Paul
Bayer, Theodore F.
Beckman, William Roger
Behling, Ralph T.
Beim, Robert B.
Bentley, Robert Clyde
Berger, Randall Craig
Bertolina, Richard R.
Bissinger, Paul A. Jr.
Blackfield, William
Boyd, Bruce Michael
Brodty, Charles
Brown, Dennis A.
Cahill, Gerald
Calkins, Glen S.
Chan, Anthony
Christian, J.E.
Cizek, Jerome D.
Clark, Peter L.
Collier, Russell
Conrad, John F.
Cotsworth, C. Michael
Couch, George J.
Curtis, James J.
De Luca, Joseph P.
Delman, James B.
Drossler, Richard A.
Drucker, Cecily A.
Estrin, Dianne G.
Fadiman, James
Feirman, Robert I.
Furbush, Donald M.
Gatley, R.H.
Hall, Peter V.
Hammerback, William J. Jr.
Healy, Thomas R.
Heffernan, E. Michael
Henslee, S. Elmo
Hindery, Leo J.
Hooper, Stanton K.
Horvitz, Carl
James, John K.
Kelly, Gerald
Kerr, Keith H.
King, William John
Korinke, Walter M.
Kruttschnitt, Theodore H.
Kuhn, F. Stuart
Lawrence, William B.
Lee, Theodore B.
Leeder, Stuart L.
Lewis, James A.
Lewis, Jerry L.
Leynse, Waldo H.
Lichauco, Marcial P. Jr.
Lima, Salvatore A.
Liphart, George von
Macdonald, David J.
McDonnell, Michael James
Malott, James S.
Mankin, Roxanne
Marshall, Carol M.
Martensen, Robert L.
Maslin, Harvey L.
Middelsteadt, Bernice
Moghadam, Hamid R.
Owens, Thomas R.
Palmer, Perry F.
Payne, Roslyn Braeman
Prichard, Gaylord E.
Riskas, Harry J.
Robbins, John R.
Robert, John
Roberts, William Lee
Rudoff, Arnold G.
San Filippo, Steven
Scharlach, Adrian E.
Schlesinger, Tod Michael
Seiger, Joseph R.
Shea, Daniel C.
Sims, Dennis C.
Smith, Manning J. III
Stevenson, Allen W.
Stoklosa, Raymond J.
Thaden, Arthur G.
Thayer, Edward C.
Todd, Stan
Trimble, Harold G. Jr.
Usher, Kirk Jr.
Wang, Chen Chi
Weingartner, John J.
Wells, Cecil H. Jr.
Wells, Donald A.
Wirth, Russell D. L.
Wollenberg, David A.
Young, Robert W.
Zankel, Martin I.

Property Manager
Aljoe, Daniel W.
Baird, John
Beckmeyer, H. Edward
Bell, Edward C.
Bentley, Robert Clyde
Berger, Randall Craig
Bissinger, Paul A. Jr.
Brown, Dennis A.
Bryant, Carl H.
Bryant, James Farnsworth
Bullard, Don
Cahill, Gerald
Calkins, Glen S.
Chancellor, Max
Chodsky, Val
Christian, J.E.
Churchfield, P.M.
Cizek, Jerome D.
Collier, Russell
Conrad, John F.
Cotsworth, C. Michael
Couch, George J.
Cruze, Harold
Cymrot, Allen
Dean, Tod
DeGoff, Robert
Delman, James B.
Diaz, Jean Michael
Durst, Stephen
Elam, Gene
Feirman, Robert I.
Freund, Fredric S.
Furbush, Donald M.
Gatley, R.H.
Geringer, A.C.
Gille, Thomas William
Hartford, Ed
Higgins, James G.
Hinkel, Richard
Hooper, Stanton K.
Kawamoto, Edwin H.
Keller, Kevin E.
Kessler, Jan
Larsen, Richard A.
Law, James G.
Lawrence, William B.
Leach, J. Frank
Lee, Theodore B.
Leeder, Stuart L.
Lewis, James A.
Lewis, Jeff D.
Lichauco, Marcial P. Jr.
Lindberg, Dexter Clayton
Macdonald, David J.
McGowin, Gerald Anthony
McNeil, Robert A.
Malott, James S.
Mankin, Roxanne
Maslin, Harvey L.
Mayer, Andrew
Middelsteadt, Bernice
Nelson, James
Neuner, Charles
Palmer, Perry F.
Pringle, Mark L.
Ravetti, Silvio E.
Rawson, David R.
Reinings, John H. Jr.
Robert, John
Roberts, William Lee
Schlesinger, Tod Michael
Seiger, Joseph R.
Smith, Manning J. III
Thaden, Arthur G.
Thayer, Edward C.
Thysen, Paul M.
Todd, Stan
Victors, A. P.
Warren, Arthur R. Jr.
Wells, Cecil H. Jr.
Wells, Donald A.
White, J.D.
Wilson, William III
Witt, Robert
Wollenberg, David A.
Wood, Eric
Wreman, Neal
Young, Robert W.

Real Estate Publisher
Bertolina, Richard R.
Brodty, Charles
Jenkins, Bill
Rudoff, Arnold G.

Regulator
Bryant, James Farnsworth
Gates, Robert Pfarr
Zankel, Martin I.

Syndicator
Bell, Edward C.
Berger, Randall Craig
Bermant, Robert A.
Bertolina, Richard R.
Bissinger, Paul A. Jr.
Boyd, Bruce Michael
Brown, Dennis A.
Bryant, Carl H.
Chow, Steven Y.T.
Cizek, Jerome D.
Cotsworth, C. Michael
Couch, George J.
Cymrot, Allen
Dean, Tod
Drossler, Richard A.
Drucker, Cecily A.
Feirman, Robert I.
Gatley, R.H.
Glass, Naomi G.
Henslee, S. Elmo
Hoffman, Arnold L.
Horvitz, Carl
Kawamoto, Edwin H.
Keller, Kevin E.
Kerr, Keith H.
King, William John
Koehler, Thilo B.
Kuhn, F. Stuart
Leeder, Stuart L.
Lewis, James A.
Lewis, Jeff D.
Lewis, Jerry L.
Leynse, Waldo H.
Lichauco, Marcial P. Jr.
Macdonald, David J.
McDonnell, Michael James
McKaig, Michael D.
McNeil, Robert A.
Malott, James S.
Mankin, Roxanne
Martensen, Robert L.
Mayer, Andrew
Palmer, Perry F.
Ravetti, Silvio E.
Rawson, David R.
Ritter, James J.
Robert, John
San Filippo, Steven
Sims, Dennis C.
Smith, Manning J. III
Stark, William W. Jr.
Steichen, C. Everett
Stevenson, Allen W.
Swartz, Thomas Byrne
Symonds, John Richard
Todd, Stan
Tong, Harry W.
Wells, Donald A.
Willis, Jon B.
Wollack, Richard G.

SAN JOSE

Appraiser
Biagi, Hazel
Hruska, Elias N.
Koon, Richard
Marks, Lloyd C.
Meyer, Edwin C.
Miller, Paul D.
Pillers, Charles M.
Semas, Leonard A.
Ulrich, John C.

Architect
Aland, Richard
Fisher, William

Attorney
Brown, William H.
Druehl, Josephine Torres
Eller, James J.
Kisner, Daniel R.
Kontrabecki, John T.
Mead, Dale C.
Perkins, Thomas G.
Priest, William G. Jr.
Rice, Randolf J.
Rodriguez, James J.
Sheppard, Mark
Sprinkles, Catherine C.

Banker
Koon, Richard
Pettis, Marilyn

Broker
Biagi, Hazel
Brockway, Dennis G.
Casey, C. L.
Coates, Stephen J.
Curtis, William Henry
Davis, Dennis D.
Dennee, Glen
Duran, Timothy C.
Eblen, James H.
Gross, Ronald J.
Hutchins, Lewis Dee
Kent, John Paul
Kisner, Daniel R.
Kontrabecki, John T.
Langley, Arlington R.
Lockey, Melbourne D.
Mackay, M. Randy
Marks, Lloyd C.
Masterman, John S.
Mitchell, Thomas G.
Pettis, Marilyn
Pillers, Charles M.
Pinto, John V.
Posten, Blair J.
Rodriguez, James J.
Russell, Georgann
Semas, Leonard A.
Shaffer, N. Manfred
Sowards, Nelson Gary
Treakle, Richard V.
Wu, Albert King

Builder
Aland, Richard
Casey, C. L.
Davidson, Charles W.
Eblen, James H.
Espeland, Terrance I.
Fisher, William
Hagestad, Grant K.
Hutchins, Lewis Dee
Kent, John Paul
Masterman, John S.
Murfit, Wallace G.
Paulsen, Peter H.
Semas, Leonard A.
Sobrato, John A.

Consultant
Biagi, Hazel
Brockway, Dennis G.
Canevari, Thomas Joseph
Casey, C. L.
Davidson, Charles W.
Duran, Timothy C.
Hruska, Elias N.
Kent, John Paul
Kontrabecki, John T.
Langley, Arlington R.
Mackay, M. Randy
Marks, Lloyd C.
Pillers, Charles M.
Posten, Blair J.
Russell, Georgann
Shaffer, N. Manfred
Sheppard, Mark
Ulrich, John C.
Wu, Albert King

Developer
Aland, Richard
Casey, C. L.
Curtis, William Henry
Davidson, Charles W.
Dennee, Glen
Duran, Timothy C.
Eblen, James H.
Fisher, William
Fry, John U.
Hagestad, Grant K.
Hutchins, Lewis Dee
Kent, John Paul
Kontrabecki, John T.
Lockey, Melbourne D.
McKay, William T.
Marks, Lloyd C.
Masterman, John S.
Mitchell, Thomas G.
Murfit, Wallace G.
Paulsen, Peter H.
Pillers, Charles M.
Remstedt, Walter E.
Semas, Leonard A.
Shaffer, N. Manfred
Sobrato, John A.
Treakle, Richard V.
Troyan, Ronald
Ulrich, John C.
Wu, Albert King

Engineer
Davidson, Charles W.
Gross, Ronald J.
Hagestad, Grant K.

Instructor
Coates, Stephen J.
Fry, John U.
Hruska, Elias N.
Langley, Arlington R.
Mackay, M. Randy
Pillers, Charles M.
Priest, William G. Jr.
Shaffer, N. Manfred
Sheppard, Mark
Sowards, Nelson Gary

Insuror
Espeland, Terrance I.
Hruska, Elias N.

Lender
Koon, Richard

Owner/Investor
Aland, Richard
Biagi, Hazel
Brockway, Dennis G.
Brown, William H.
Casey, C. L.
Curtis, William Henry
Davidson, Charles W.
Dennee, Glen
Dunn, Leo
Duran, Timothy C.
Eblen, James H.
Espeland, Terrance I.
Fry, John U.
Hruska, Elias N.
Hutchins, Lewis Dee
Kontrabecki, John T.
Mackay, M. Randy
Mitchell, Thomas G.
Murfit, Wallace G.
Pettis, Marilyn
Pillers, Charles M.
Pinto, John V.
Posten, Blair J.
Remstedt, Walter E.
Russell, Georgann
Semas, Leonard A.
Treakle, Richard V.
Troyan, Ronald
Ulrich, John C.
Wu, Albert King

Property Manager
Biagi, Hazel
Burgin, Wes
Caldwell, Susan
Casey, C. L.
Coates, Stephen J.
Curtis, William Henry
Davidson, Charles W.
Deal, Frank
Duran, Timothy C.
Fry, John U.
Hansen, Mike
Kent, John Paul
Kontrabecki, John T.
Kramer, Klaus
Langley, Arlington R.
Mackay, M. Randy
Marks, Lloyd C.
Mitchell, Thomas G.
Pillers, Charles M.
Pinto, John V.
Posten, Blair J.
Remstedt, Walter E.
Russell, Georgann
Semas, Leonard A.
Sobrato, John A.
Sowards, Nelson Gary
Strathbucker, Jerry
Thempson, Robert
Treakle, Richard V.
Warnes, Phil
Wu, Albert King

Real Estate Publisher
Pillers, Charles M.

Syndicator
Biagi, Hazel
Brockway, Dennis G.
Casey, C. L.
Curtis, William Henry
Duran, Timothy C.
Eblen, James H.
Masterman, John S.
Mitchell, Thomas G.
Pillers, Charles M.
Posten, Blair J.
Remstedt, Walter E.
Semas, Leonard A.
Shaffer, N. Manfred
Treakle, Richard V.
Troyan, Ronald
Wu, Albert King

SAN LUIS OBISPO

Appraiser
Brown, Ayla S.

Attorney
Cool, Stephen N.

Broker
Broadbent, William R.
Brown, Ayla S.
Johnson, John E.
Rossetti, John
Swem, Thomas Craig

Builder
Dunn, Wallace E.

Consultant
Broadbent, William R.
Brown, Ayla S.
Dunn, Wallace E.
Pybrum, Steven M.

Developer
Dunn, Wallace E.
Pybrum, Steven M.
Rossetti, John

Instructor
Broadbent, William R.
Cool, Stephen N.
Pybrum, Steven M.
Swem, Thomas Craig

Lender
Cool, Stephen N.

Owner/Investor
Broadbent, William R.
Dunn, Wallace E.
Johnson, John E.
Pybrum, Steven M.
Rossetti, John
Swem, Thomas Craig

Property Manager
Dunn, Wallace E.
Johnson, John E.
Swem, Thomas Craig

Real Estate Publisher
Broadbent, William R.

Syndicator
Broadbent, William R.
Dunn, Wallace E.
Johnson, John E.
Pybrum, Steven M.
Rossetti, John
Swem, Thomas Craig

SAN RAFAEL

Appraiser
Fernwood, Grail O.
Jones, Roy Farrington
Koenitzer, Robert L.
Sedway, Lynn M.
Shafer, W. Bruce
Sherman, William H.
Van Haeften, Karel A.R.

Assessor
Shafer, W. Bruce

Attorney
Corrigan, William G.
Fabian, JoAnne
Obninsky, Victor Peter
Paxton, Jay L.
Shiffman, Michael A.
Vallarino, P. Roy
Walker, James Leslie IV
Walters, David W.

Banker
Fabian, JoAnne

Broker
Austin, Thomas G.
Chazankin, Henry
Dunn, Philip C.
Edmondson, James T.
Ellis, Arlen O.
Fabian, JoAnne
Fernwood, Grail O.
Jones, Roy Farrington
Lawless, Harris E.
McCarthy, Adair Bernard
Moser, Dean J.
Rosen, Michael P.
Sherman, William H.
Shiffman, Michael A.
Van Haeften, Karel A.R.
VanTassel, James D.
Weinstein, Arnold J.
Wells, Robert S.

Builder
Garrison, R. Leonard Jr.
Rosen, Michael P.

Consultant
Cardillo-Lee, James
Chazankin, Henry
Dunn, Philip C.
Ellis, Arlen O.
Fernwood, Grail O.
Garrison, R. Leonard Jr.
Jones, Roy Farrington
Lawless, Harris E.
Sedway, Lynn M.
Shafer, W. Bruce
Sherman, William H.

Shiffman, Michael A.
Vallarino, P. Roy
Van Haeften, Karel A.R.
VanTassel, James D.
Warsen, John Stephen

Developer
Austin, Thomas G.
Dunn, Philip C.
Garrison, R. Leonard Jr.
Hart, Dennis M.
McCarthy, Adair Bernard
Obninsky, Victor Peter
Rosen, Michael P.
Van Haeften, Karel A.R.
VanTassel, James D.
Walker, James Leslie IV
Warsen, John Stephen
Weinstein, Arnold J.
Wells, Robert S.

Instructor
Edmondson, James T.
Fabian, JoAnne
Lawless, Harris E.
Shafer, W. Bruce
VanTassel, James D.
Walters, David W.

Insuror
Hart, Dennis M.
Vallarino, P. Roy

Lender
Hart, Dennis M.

Owner/Investor
Chazankin, Henry
Dunn, Philip C.
Edmondson, James T.
Ellis, Arlen O.
Fabian, JoAnne
Garrison, R. Leonard Jr.
McCarthy, Adair Bernard
Obninsky, Victor Peter
Van Haeften, Karel A.R.
Walker, James Leslie IV
Warsen, John Stephen
Weinstein, Arnold J.
Wells, Robert S.

Property Manager
Burger, Eugene J.
Dunn, Philip C.
Fernwood, Grail O.
Garrison, R. Leonard Jr.
Obninsky, Victor Peter
Warsen, John Stephen

Real Estate Publisher
Edmondson, James T.
Lawless, Harris E.
Van Haeften, Karel A.R.
VanTassel, James D.

Syndicator
Dunn, Philip C.
Edmondson, James T.
Lawless, Harris E.
Van Haeften, Karel A.R.
Walker, James Leslie IV
Warsen, John Stephen
Weinstein, Arnold J.

SANTA ANA

Appraiser
Blair, Lee
Cormack, George H.
Fawcett, J. Scott
Foreman, Robert Lee
Hazewinkel, William Charles
Lauritzen, James Lawrence
Love, Timothy
McBride, Dennis
McWilliams, Peter D.
Moody, Errold F. Jr.
Myers, Darrold D.
Pierson, Bruce E.
Reeder, Sally
Speik, Robert L.
Tarantello, R.
Tsagris, B.E.
Vore, Lee H.
Wolfe, C. Edward
Yatuni, Ray

Architect
Bissell, George
Cormack, George H.
LePlastrier, Geoffrey Ross
Watson, Raymond L.

Attorney
Barker, Ann S.
Barthrop, John A.
Beasley, Oscar H.
Breckenridge, Hugh
Christianson, Michael J.
Cohen, Paul J.
Coopersmith, Henry J.
Darnell, Roger D.
Davis, Wallace R.
Falls, Edward Joseph
Galvin, John Patrick
Garrett, John C.
Geyser, Lynne, M.
Hagen, Kenneth E.
Harty, John T.
Harty, Maureen A.
Jackson, F. Scott
Jefsen, John I.
Karlin, L. Scott
Lewand, Kevin O.
Matsen, Jeffrey R.
Neal, James Edward
Passolt, James C. Jr.
Paul, Richard S.
Pothier, Rose
Rhodes, Terry L.
Roberts, Furman B.
Schumacher, Stephen J.
Smith, Richard G.
Stewart, Michael Jay
Waldron, Robert F.

Banker
Baden, Gerald M.
Browne, Robert W.
Daly, Gerald W.
Gross, Earl L. (Mick)
Hansen, R. Edwin
Lacy, Craig W.
Langston, William E.
Lauritzen, James Lawrence

Broker
Aglio, Frank Alfred Jr.
Astarabadi, Zaid A.
Barker, Ann S.
Barthrop, John A.
Brewer, Dean M.
Bussiere, Barry
Cohen, Paul J.
Collins, Charles L.
Crisell, Robert W.
Crow, Michael G.
Dilbeck, Harold Roy
Emery, James H.
Fawcett, J. Scott
Frost, Richard Nelson
Fuchs, David
Geyser, Lynne, M.
Gorman, William R.
Greenwood, Carl J.
Griffis, Jack L.
Gross, Earl L. (Mick)
Guilbeau, Harry
Hackbarth, Raymond William Jr.
Hazewinkel, William Charles
Hobbs, Roger C.
Jefsen, John I.
Lesley, Dan
McBride, Dennis
McWilliams, Peter D.
Matsen, Jeffrey R.
Moody, Errold F. Jr.
Murar, E. James
Myers, Darrold D.
Nahigan, Edward A.
Nourse, Peter W.
Owings, Theodore R.
Paul, Richard S.
Pierson, Bruce E.
Powell, Owen N.
Rokos, Ted G.
Ryan, David E.
Shirley, Kim R.
Simpson, Robert L.
Smith, Donald W.A.
Smith, Richard G.
Sokol, Jerry L.
Speik, Robert L.
Stenton, Richard R.
Stewart, Michael Jay
Supple, George Michael
Terry, Stephen V.
Thomas, Robert L.
Tsagris, B.E.
Wainberg, Howard S.
Weinger, Stuart L.
West, Charles W.
Wiginton, Craig
Wolfe, C. Edward
Woody, Larry N.
Yatuni, Ray
Younkin, John P.

Builder
Aglio, Frank Alfred Jr.
Alstrom, John
Barthrop, John A.
Boultinghouse, Richard F.
Conklin, Bruce Cox Jr.
Connoley, William B.
Cormack, George H.
Dirienzo, Gregory C.
Fawcett, J. Scott
Hobbs, Roger C.
Keusder, Walter W.
Langston, William E.
LePlastrier, Geoffrey Ross
Lintz, Robert H.
Lund, William S.
McWilliams, Peter D.
Murar, E. James
Nahigan, Edward A.
Nelson, Larry E.
Nourse, Peter W.
Olenicoff, Igor M.
Owings, Theodore R.
Padia, Russell F.
Powell, Gene E.
Saddington, Hugh M.
Smith, Richard G.
Spinkelink, Lyle
Watson, Harry E.
Watson, Raymond L.
Weinger, Stuart L.

Consultant
Aglio, Frank Alfred Jr.
Astarabadi, Zaid A.
Baden, Gerald M.
Barthrop, John A.
Boultinghouse, Richard F.
Brewer, Dean M.
Crow, Michael G.
Davis, Wallace R.
Foreman, Robert Lee
Frost, Richard Nelson
Fulton, George A.
Gorman, William R.
Guilbeau, Harry
Hagen, Kenneth E.
Harris, Jack J.
Harty, John T.
Harty, Maureen A.
Hazewinkel, William Charles
Hobbs, Roger C.
Huntsman, Frank C.
Jackson, F. Scott
Klutnick, James J.
Langston, William E.
Lauritzen, James Lawrence
Love, Timothy
Lund, William S.
McWilliams, Peter D.
Maga, Joseph L. Jr.
Moody, Errold F. Jr.
Myers, Darrold D.
Patterson, Charlene
Pierson, Bruce E.
Rather, Dale L.
Simpson, Robert L.
Smith, Donald W.A.
Sokol, Jerry L.
Speik, Robert L.
Starkey, Dan B.
Tarantello, R.
Terry, Stephen V.
Tsagris, B.E.
Watson, Harry E.
Watson, Raymond L.
Weinger, Stuart L.
West, Charles W.
Wiginton, Craig
Woody, Larry N.
Yatuni, Ray

Developer
Aglio, Frank Alfred Jr.
Alstrom, John
Astarabadi, Zaid A.
Baer, Dan W,
Barthrop, John A.
Berryman, Dennis M.
Best, Robert T.
Boucher, Craig
Boultinghouse, Richard F.
Buchner, James
Collins, Charles L.
Conklin, Bruce Cox Jr.
Connoley, William B.
Crisell, Robert W.
Darnell, Roger D.
Dirienzo, Gregory C.
Donahue, Daniel W.
Fawcett, J. Scott
Foote, William D.
Fredericks, T. Douglas
Greenwood, Carl J.
Gross, Earl L. (Mick)
Harris, Jack J.
Harty, John T.
Harty, Maureen A.
Hobbs, Roger C.
Jefsen, John I.
Kalabany, Stephen
Kenney, William J. Jr.
Keusder, Walter W.
Lacy, Craig W.
Langston, William E.
Lauritzen, James Lawrence
LePlastrier, Geoffrey Ross
Lesley, Dan
Liljenquist, Newell Lavon
Lintz, Robert H.
List, Martin
Littell, Jeffrey D.
Little, Jack M.
Lund, William S.
Lusk, John D.
McWilliams, Peter D.
Mollard, W. Ross
Murar, E. James
Nahigan, Edward A.
Nelson, Larry E.
Nourse, Peter W.
Olenicoff, Igor M.
Owings, Theodore R.
Padia, Russell F.
Pierson, Bruce E.

Powell, Gene E.
Ryan, David E.
Saddington, Hugh M.
Scerbo, Carmine
Shirley, Kim R.
Smith, Richard G.
Spinkelink, Lyle
Stack, Geoffrey L.
Starkey, Dan B.
Tarantello, R.
Terry, Stephen V.
Watson, Harry E.
Watson, Raymond L.
Weaver, Gene
Weinger, Stuart L.
Younkin, John P.

Engineer
Cormack, George H.

Instructor
Aglio, Frank Alfred Jr.
Bussiere, Barry
Dilbeck, Harold Roy
Foreman, Robert Lee
Geyser, Lynne, M.
Gorman, William R.
Guilbeau, Harry
Hobbs, Roger C.
Love, Timothy
Matsen, Jeffrey R.
Moody, Errold F. Jr.
Myers, Darrold D.
Nahigan, Edward A.
Patterson, Charlene
Pierce, Robert Evans
Powell, Owen N.
Simpson, Robert L.
Smith, Donald W.A.
Sokol, Jerry L.
Speik, Robert L.
Thomas, Robert L.
Tsagris, B.E.
Wainberg, Howard S.
West, Charles W.

Insuror
Emery, James H.

Lender
Baden, Gerald M.
Browne, Robert W.
Connoley, William B.
Emery, James H.
Gross, Earl L. (Mick)
Hansen, R. Edwin
Lacy, Craig W.
Lauritzen, James Lawrence
Robb, Michael Stephen
Speik, Robert L.

Owner/Investor
Aglio, Frank Alfred Jr.
Alstrom, John
Astarabadi, Zaid A.
Baer, Dan W,
Barthrop, John A.
Best, Robert T.
Blair, Lee
Brewer, Dean M.
Conklin, Bruce Cox Jr.
Connoley, William B.
Darnell, Roger D.
Davis, Wallace R.
Eguina, Steven G.
Emery, James H.
Fawcett, J. Scott
Fredericks, T. Douglas
Geyser, Lynne, M.
Gorman, William R.
Greenwood, Carl J.
Griffis, Jack L.
Gross, Earl L. (Mick)
Guilbeau, Harry
Hagen, Kenneth E.
Harris, Jack J.
Kenny, Mark V.
Klutnick, James J.
Lacy, Craig W.
Lauritzen, James Lawrence
Leckey, Merrick W.
Lesley, Dan
Lewand, Kevin O.
Liljenquist, Newell Lavon
List, Martin
Little, Jack M.
McWilliams, Peter D.
Maga, Joseph L. Jr.
Mollard, W. Ross
Murar, E. James
Nahigan, Edward A.
Nelson, Larry E.
Nourse, Peter W.
Olenicoff, Igor M.
Paul, Richard S.
Pierce, Robert Evans
Pierson, Bruce E.
Rather, Dale L.
Robb, Michael Stephen
Roman, Douglas E.
Ryan, David E.
Saddington, Hugh M.
Shirley, Kim R.
Simpson, Robert L.
Smith, Richard G.
Sokol, Jerry L.
Speik, Robert L.
Stack, Geoffrey L.
Starkey, Dan B.
Stenton, Richard R.
Supple, George Michael
Tarantello, R.
Terry, Stephen V.
Watson, Harry E.
Watson, Raymond L.
Weinger, Stuart L.
West, Charles W.
Wiginton, Craig
Woody, Larry N.
Yatuni, Ray

Property Manager
Aglio, Frank Alfred Jr.
Alban, Robert
Alstrom, John
Best, Robert T.
Boultinghouse, Richard F.
Clark, E.H. Jr.
Cormack, George H.
Davis, Wallace R.
Eguina, Steven G.
Fredericks, T. Douglas
Gorman, William R.
Greenwood, Carl J.
Gross, Earl L. (Mick)
Hall, Betsy
Harty, John T.
Harty, Maureen A.
Hazewinkel, William Charles
Kalabany, Stephen
Lacy, Robert P.
Leckey, Merrick W.
Lesley, Dan
Liljenquist, Newell Lavon
Lillicrop, John
Lintz, Robert H.
Little, Jack M.
Myers, Darrold D.
Nahigan, Edward A.
Nourse, Peter W.
Olenicoff, Igor M.
Passolt, James C. Jr.
Pierce, Robert Evans
Powell, Owen N.
Rather, Dale L.
Saddington, Hugh M.
Shirley, Kim R.
Smith, Donald W.A.
Starkey, Dan B.
Stenton, Richard R.
Supple, George Michael
Tarantello, R.
Weinger, Stuart L.
Wiginton, Craig
Williams, Edward
Woody, Larry N.
Yatuni, Ray

Real Estate Publisher
Baer, Dan W,
Padilla, Diane
Spidell, Bob

Syndicator
Aglio, Frank Alfred Jr.
Astarabadi, Zaid A.
Baer, Dan W,
Brewer, Dean M.
Cohen, Paul J.
Davis, Wallace R.
Dirienzo, Gregory C.
Eguina, Steven G.
Geyser, Lynne, M.
Gorman, William R.
Greenwood, Carl J.
Gross, Earl L. (Mick)
Guilbeau, Harry
Hagen, Kenneth E.
Harris, Jack J.
Harty, John T.
Harty, Maureen A.
Hay, Jerry
Hobbs, Roger C.
Leckey, Merrick W.
Lesley, Dan
Lewand, Kevin O.
Little, Jack M.
McCombs, Donald D.
McWilliams, Peter D.
Nahigan, Edward A.
Neal, James Edward
Paul, Richard S.
Rather, Dale L.
Sokol, Jerry L.
Stack, Geoffrey L.
Starkey, Dan B.
Stenton, Richard R.
Supple, George Michael
Terry, Stephen V.
Tsagris, B.E.
Watson, Harry E.
Weinger, Stuart L.
West, Charles W.
Wolfe, C. Edward
Woody, Larry N.

SANTA BARBARA

Appraiser
Arnold, Michael Neal
Bauersfeld, Lynn W.

Architect
Grossgold, Richard

Attorney
Parent, Gerald Brunsell

Broker
Barels, Larry
Bauersfeld, Lynn W.
Berry, Keith C.
Croteau, Gerald F.
Grossgold, Richard
Jackson, R. Peter
Reder, Martin C.
Richards, Maurice F.
Wolfe, Ronald L.

Builder
Barels, Larry

Consultant
Arnold, Michael Neal
Barels, Larry
Bauersfeld, Lynn W.
Croteau, Gerald F.
Jackson, R. Peter
Reder, Martin C.
Richards, Maurice F.
Ricker, Judith C.
Wolfe, Ronald L.

Developer
Barels, Larry
Bauersfeld, Lynn W.

Instructor
Arnold, Michael Neal
Berry, Keith C.
Jackson, R. Peter

Insuror
Reder, Martin C.

Owner/Investor
Barels, Larry
Jackson, R. Peter
Reder, Martin C.
Ricker, Judith C.

Property Manager
Bauersfeld, Lynn W.
Jackson, R. Peter
Richards, Maurice F.
Ricker, Judith C.

Syndicator
Barels, Larry
Croteau, Gerald F.
Jackson, R. Peter
Richards, Maurice F.
Wolfe, Ronald L.

SANTA ROSA

Appraiser
Freeland, Barry

Attorney
Beyers, James L.
Bryan, Mikel D.
Clement, Clayton E.
O'Brien, John R.
Rundel, James A.

Broker
Freeland, Barry
McFarland, Henry D.
Schlangen, William M.

Builder
Condiotti, A.
Freeland, Barry
Schlangen, William M.

Consultant
Freeland, Barry
Jolly, Jerry D.
McFarland, Henry D.

Developer
Condiotti, A.
Freeland, Barry
Schlangen, William M.

Instructor
Clement, Clayton E.
Freeland, Barry

Owner/Investor
Clement, Clayton E.
Condiotti, A.
Freeland, Barry
McFarland, Henry D.
Schlangen, William M.

Property Manager
Freeland, Barry
Jolly, Jerry D.
Schlangen, William M.

Syndicator
Freeland, Barry
McFarland, Henry D.
Rundel, James A.
Schlangen, William M.

STOCKTON

Appraiser
Bachand, Oscar J.
Bjornson, Stella
Bramwell, H. Rich
Cyr, John E.
Wittmayer, Theodore I.

Attorney
Callahan, Dennis William
Roseberry, Fred T. III
Sinclair, Richard C.
Wittmayer, Theodore I.

Broker
Bachand, Oscar J.
Basso, Robert
Bjornson, Stella
Bruzzone, Arthur A.
Craig, R. Wayne
Cyr, John E.
Godinho, Joseph J.
Kellogg, M. B.
Tornell, Ronald C.
Turner, Curtis S.
Wiggins, James B.

Builder
Lurtsema, Hal B.
Simvoulakis, George
Turner, Curtis S.

Consultant
Bachand, Oscar J.
Bramwell, H. Rich
Craig, R. Wayne
Cyr, John E.
Godinho, Joseph J.
Kellogg, M. B.
Simvoulakis, George
Turner, Curtis S.
Wiggins, James B.

Developer
Bachand, Oscar J.
Bruzzone, Arthur A.
Craig, R. Wayne
Lange, Sylvin R.
Lurtsema, Hal B.
Simvoulakis, George
Turner, Curtis S.
Wiggins, James B.

Engineer
Turner, Curtis S.

Instructor
Bachand, Oscar J.
Cyr, John E.
Godinho, Joseph J.
Roseberry, Fred T. III
Tornell, Ronald C.

Owner/Investor
Bachand, Oscar J.
Basso, Robert
Bruzzone, Arthur A.
Craig, R. Wayne
Godinho, Joseph J.
Greer, John L.
Kellogg, M. B.
Roseberry, Fred T. III
Simvoulakis, George
Sinclair, Richard C.
Tornell, Ronald C.
Turner, Curtis S.
Wiggins, James B.

Property Manager
Bachand, Oscar J.
Basso, Robert
Bjornson, Stella
Bruzzone, Arthur A.
Greer, John L.
Kellogg, M. B.
Lange, Sylvin R.
Sinclair, Richard C.
Tornell, Ronald C.
Wiggins, James B.

Real Estate Publisher
Bruzzone, Arthur A.
Roseberry, Fred T. III

Syndicator
Bachand, Oscar J.
Bruzzone, Arthur A.
Craig, R. Wayne
Godinho, Joseph J.
Greer, John L.
Lurtsema, Hal B.
Simvoulakis, George
Turner, Curtis S.
Wiggins, James B.

VAN NUYS

Appraiser
Austin, Charles E.
Epstein, Gilbert
Grebler, Arthur R.
Hoag, Myron L.
Kass, Stephen Brent
McLaughlin, Nathaniel L.
Monteleone, Mike
Morris, Evon
Zak, Eugene

Architect
Heuer, Robert Emerson

Attorney
Baron, Hal
Cummins, Neil J. Jr.
Grayson, Michael A.
Spungin, Lawrence D.

Banker
Mariotti, Mark

Broker
Cook, Glenn
Deeb, Edward
Ferguson, William P.
Fryklund, Richard K.
Gaskill, John B. Jr.
Gasparini, Frederick Vincent Marratto
Grebler, Arthur R.
Green, Harvey E.
Hlavacek, Leopold
Howard, Bradley Duke
Hurlburt, Thomas H.
Karty, Rudy
King, Carl L.
McFerrin, Michael W.
Manos, Alexander A.M.
Meengs, Dirck Z.
Mills, Greg
Monteleone, Mike
Perom, Stuart S.
Principe, Mr.
Randles, Lyle C.
Ross, Jay S.
Sampson, Curtis H.
Sands, Ralph S.
Sani, Hamid H.
Satterlee, Alan
Schlaifer, Jack I.
Snyder, Harry Y.
Spungin, Lawrence D.
White, Bram
Zak, Eugene
Zugsmith, Michael A.

Builder
Augustine, Jon W.
Deeb, Edward
Grebler, Arthur R.
Griffin, Paul E. Jr.
Heuer, Robert Emerson
Howard, Bradley Duke
Mosher, Walter W. Jr.
Principe, Mr.
Reston, Herbert D.
Ross, Jay S.
Rotkin, Charles J.
Sands, Ralph S.
Satterlee, Alan
Zugsmith, Michael A.

Consultant
Augustine, Jon W.
Bovais, Frederic A.
Epstein, Gilbert
Flatt, Nachman
Fryklund, Richard K.
Gaskill, John B. Jr.
Gasparini, Frederick Vincent Marratto
Grebler, Arthur R.
Hoag, Myron L.
Howard, Bradley Duke
Hurlburt, Thomas H.
Kass, Stephen Brent
Landis, Martin
Langendoen, Gary
McLaughlin, Nathaniel L.
Mariotti, Mark
Meengs, Dirck Z.
Mills, Greg
Monteleone, Mike
Perom, Stuart S.
Principe, Mr.
Ross, Jay S.
Sands, Ralph S.
Sani, Hamid H.
Smith, Wallace G.
Snyder, Harry Y.

Developer
Baron, Hal
Cook, Glenn
Deeb, Edward
Epstein, Gilbert
Gaskill, John B. Jr.
Grebler, Arthur R.
Green, Harvey E.
Griffin, Paul E. Jr.
Heuer, Robert Emerson
Howard, Bradley Duke
Hurlburt, Thomas H.
Landis, Martin
Langendoen, Gary
Meengs, Dirck Z.
Mosher, Walter W. Jr.
Principe, Mr.
Reston, Herbert D.
Ross, Jay S.
Rotkin, Charles J.
Sands, Ralph S.
Satterlee, Alan
Schlaifer, Jack I.
Spungin, Lawrence D.
Zugsmith, Michael A.

Engineer
Cummins, Neil J. Jr.
Zuck, Daniel R.

Instructor
Bovais, Frederic A.
Ferguson, William P.
Gasparini, Frederick Vincent Marratto
Monteleone, Mike
Principe, Mr.
Ross, Jay S.
Sani, Hamid H.
Snyder, Harry Y.

Insuror
Colburn, Herbert William
Mariotti, Mark

Lender
Headlund, Donald C.
Hlavacek, Leopold
Perom, Stuart S.

Owner/Investor
Augustine, Jon W.
Bovais, Frederic A.
Deeb, Edward
Epstein, Gilbert
Fryklund, Richard K.
Grebler, Arthur R.
Griffin, Paul E. Jr.
Heuer, Robert Emerson
Hlavacek, Leopold
Howard, Bradley Duke
Landis, Martin
Langendoen, Gary
McFerrin, Michael W.
Manos, Alexander A.M.
Mariotti, Mark
Mills, Greg
Morris, Evon
Mosher, Walter W. Jr.
Reston, Herbert D.
Ross, Jay S.
Sands, Ralph S.
Satterlee, Alan
Schlaifer, Jack I.
Spungin, Lawrence D.
Zak, Eugene
Zuck, Daniel R.
Zugsmith, Michael A.

Property Manager
Amirkhan, Michael
Augustine, Jon W.
Bovais, Frederic A.
Carlson, Rudy
Deeb, Edward
Fryklund, Richard K.
Gaskill, John B. Jr.
Heuer, Robert Emerson
Hileman, R.D.
Hlavacek, Leopold
Howard, Bradley Duke
Hurlburt, Thomas H.
Langendoen, Gary
Meengs, Dirck Z.
Morris, Evon
Ossig, Hanns
Principe, Mr.
Randles, Lyle C.
Rotkin, Charles J.
Sands, Ralph S.
Sani, Hamid H.
Satterlee, Alan
Schlaifer, Jack I.
Smith, Wallace G.
Zuck, Daniel R.
Zugsmith, Michael A.

Syndicator
Baron, Hal
Cook, Glenn
Epstein, Gilbert
Fryklund, Richard K.
Grebler, Arthur R.
Hlavacek, Leopold
Hurlburt, Thomas H.
Kass, Stephen Brent
Langendoen, Gary
McFerrin, Michael W.
Manos, Alexander A.M.
Perom, Stuart S.
Principe, Mr.
Reston, Herbert D.
Sands, Ralph S.
Schlaifer, Jack I.

WHITTIER

Appraiser
Mlynaryk, Peter
Simeone, Victor R.

Attorney
Faubus, Donald E.
Geiger, Paul Joseph
Hawekotte, John William Jr.
Smith, John Charles

Broker
Crookall, Charles E.
Griffith, Darlene Inez
Hawekotte, John William Jr.

Smith, John Charles

Consultant
Geiger, Paul Joseph
Griffith, Darlene Inez
Hawekotte, John William Jr.
Mlynaryk, Peter
Schmidt, Eno A.
Simeone, Victor R.
Smith, John Charles

Developer
Crookall, Charles E.
Keene, Mark J.
Mlynaryk, Peter
Schumacher, George

Instructor
Mlynaryk, Peter
Smith, John Charles

Owner/Investor
Crookall, Charles E.
Griffith, Darlene Inez
Keene, Mark J.
Mlynaryk, Peter
Schmidt, Eno A.

Property Manager
Geiger, Paul Joseph
Griffith, Darlene Inez

Syndicator
Griffith, Darlene Inez
Hawekotte, John William Jr.
Keene, Mark J.

COLORADO

BRIGHTON

Appraiser
Murphy, Joseph W.

Attorney
Ellias, Myra

Banker
Braun, Gregory L.

Broker
Murphy, Joseph W.

Builder
Murphy, Joseph W.
Whitfield, Theron

Developer
Whitfield, Theron

Lender
Braun, Gregory L.

Owner/Investor
Murphy, Joseph W.
Whitfield, Theron

Property Manager
Ellias, Myra
Murphy, Joseph W.

COLORADO SPRINGS

Appraiser
Pritz, Eldon G.
Walker, Fred W.
Zaleski, Gerald S.

Architect
Jones, James Hall

Attorney
Cooper, John C.
Edwards, Daniel P.

Banker
Walker, Fred W.

Broker
Barber, Kenneth H.
Cline, James M.
Daily, J. Allen
De Chadenedes, Guy B.
Dragoo, Douglas
Jones, James Hall
Lammersen, William Barry
Lardinois, Vincent H.
Lorenzen, Paul
Miller, Cassie
Reich, Joseph A. Jr.
Spraggins, Ronald F.
Titus, Robert F.
Vradenburg, George A. Jr.
Walker, Fred W.
Walker, James R.
Walker, Richard L. Jr.
Weiner, Barry A.

Builder
De Chadenedes, Guy B.
Dragoo, Douglas
Jones, James Hall
Sunderland, David K.
Vradenburg, George A. Jr.

Consultant
Barber, Kenneth H.
Cline, James M.
Dragoo, Douglas
Johnson, Alvin G.
Lammersen, William Barry
Lorenzen, Paul
Pritz, Eldon G.
Scrima, Thomas Charles
Vradenburg, George A. Jr.
Walker, Jon R.
Walker, Richard L. Jr.
Weiner, Barry A.
Zaleski, Gerald S.

Developer
Barber, Kenneth H.
De Chadenedes, Guy B.
Dragoo, Douglas
Johnson, Alvin G.
Jones, James Hall
Lammersen, William Barry
Reich, Joseph A. Jr.
Sunderland, David K.
Titus, Robert F.
Vradenburg, George A. Jr.
Walker, Richard L. Jr.
Weiner, Barry A.

Instructor
Cline, James M.
Edwards, Daniel P.
Lorenzen, Paul
Miller, Cassie
Weiner, Barry A.

Insuror
Weiner, Barry A.

Lender
Daily, J. Allen
Vradenburg, George A. Jr.
Walker, Fred W.

Owner/Investor
Barber, Kenneth H.
Cline, James M
Daily, J. Allen
De Chadenedes, Guy B.
Edwards, Daniel P.
Johnson, Alvin G.
Jones, James Hall
Lammersen, William Barry
Lorenzen, Paul
Pritz, Eldon G.
Scrima, Thomas Charles
Spraggins, Ronald F.
Titus, Robert F.
Vradenburg, George A. Jr.
Walker, Fred W.
Walker, Richard L. Jr.
Weiner, Barry A.

Property Manager
Cline, James M.
Cooper, John C.
Walker, Jon R.
Walker, Richard L. Jr.
Weiner, Barry A.

Syndicator
Barber, Kenneth H.
Edwards, Daniel P.
Johnson, Alvin G.
Lammersen, William Barry
Lorenzen, Paul
Spraggins, Ronald F.
Sunderland, David K.
Titus, Robert F.
Weiner, Barry A.

DENVER

Appraiser
Ahern, George I. Jr.
Boyson, Don E.
Bresnahan, C.A.
Bridwell, Lowell W.
Chase, Blaine B.
Conway, William A. III
Cryer, Clifford L.
Dewey, Robert
Dixon, Carl F.
Goodridge, Edwin N.
Horton, Edward B. Jr.
Katsaros, Basil S.
Lana, Edward C.
Lenzini, Michael Jr.
Levine, Mark
Morris, Bill
Rife, Thomas G.
Schroeder, William R. Jr.
Schroeder, William R. Sr.
Shelton, Kenneth L.
Smith, James T.
Van Court, William T.
Woolford, William A.

Architect
Black, Edward P.
Bruneau, Bill
Gathers, Charles E.
Grant, Gerald P.

Attorney
Anderson, Keith
Brame, Frank A. III
Caldwell, Richard G.
Carpenter, Charlton H.
Cheris, Samuel David
Clarke, Jon B.
Cook, Donald L.
Dalton, James V.
Davies, George
Earnest, G. Lane
Forhan, John F.
Fortner, Seymour S.
Gabriel, Eberhard J.
Golanty, James S.
Henze, Mark E.
Hillestad, Charles A.
Hult, James M.
Johnson, Bruce B.
Katz, Aron D.
Keatinge, Robert
Levine, Gary H.
Levine, Kent Jay
Levine, Mark
Lichtenfels, J. Reid
McDowell, Scott D. Esq.
McGrath, John W.
Miller, Ronald J.
Molling, Charles F.
Mulligan, James M.
Nelson, L. Bruce
Palcanis, Gregory F.
Percy, Jerry G.
Permut, Barry Michael
Quail, Beverly J.
Riebesell, H.F. Jr.
Russell, Patrick J.
Sanford, Kendall T.
Siegman, Jerome
Steuben, Norton L.
Stewart, D. Wayne
Stouffer, James P.
Swartz, Lawrence B.
Tisdale, Douglas M. Esq.
Tobey, Gary H.
Woodward, S. Lee

Banker
Brooks, David Carl
Douglas, Charles
Jenkins, Leon H.
Lewis, Heydon Z.
Percy, Jerry G.
Shollenberger, Brian D.
Smith, Irv
Uhlemann, William R.

Broker
Able, Robert L.
Ahern, George I. Jr.
Bane, Jim
Barker, Jock
Benedetti, John A.
Biagiotti, Stephen M.
Bowen, Peter Geoffrey
Bresnahan, C.A.
Brougham, Robert D.
Burns, Franklin L.
Busi, William L.
Campbell, Ronald D.
Carruth, Dennis
Castrodale, James L. Sr.
Clarke, Jon B.
Clayton, Stuart D.
Coates, Jack P.
Conway, William A. III
Coons, C. Duane
Cramer, Steven E.
Dewey, Robert
Dixon, Carl F.
Fisher, Bob
Fisher, Robert B.
Fortner, Seymour S.
Fowler, Jack W.
Franz, Roger C.
Garofalo, Ronald J.
Garrett, Van Holt Jr.
Golanty, James S.
Grant, Miles R.
Harlan, Donald L.
Hayes, Jed
Hecht, Emil
Hedlund, C.J.
Hildebran, Robert C.
Horton, Edward B. Jr.
Hult, James M.
Huskin, J. David
Jarvis, Dorothy
Jensen, Michael M.
Kent, Wendel G.
Kramer, Russell P. Jr.
Kroner, Gary
Lenzini, Michael Jr.
Levine, Ellen H.
Levine, Kent Jay
Levine, Mark
Levine, Stu
Lewis, Heydon Z.
Lichtenfels, J. Reid
Liniger, David
McBride, Philip J.
McGrath, John W.
Main, Gail
Martin, Charles Tyler Jr.
Martin, Dick
Meer, Gerald L.
Miller, Ronald J.
Morris, Bill
Mulligan, James M.
Myles, Ronald L.

Naiman, Marvin I.
Nein, Sam N.
Newell, Stewart P.
Pippitt, Charles R.
Schaefer, Keith F.
Schroeder, William R. Jr.
Schroeder, William R. Sr.
Shendleman, Jack
Shockley, Hugh U.
Smith, Irv
Smith, James T.
Smith, Terrence F.
Stevens, William F.
Tankoos, Bradley J.
Townsend, Charles
Trowbridge, Charles A.
Van Court, William T.
Vigoda, Louise
Whisler, Duane
Whiting, Richard F.
Wimbush, Grant R.
Woodland, M. Don
Woodward, S. Lee

Builder
Arnold, Robert S.
Baker, Bruce H.
Brooks, David Carl
Bruneau, Bill
Campbell, Ronald D.
Carruth, Dennis
Cryer, Clifford L.
Davis, B.J.
Dewey, Robert
Duval, David B.
Flynn, Stephen A. Jr.
Fowler, Jack W.
Glad, Charles R.
Grant, Miles R.
Greenberg, Gerald Morton
Hecht, Emil
Hedlund, C.J.
Holderith, Emeric R.
Kleinsmith, Mark John
Lana, Edward C.
McBride, Philip J.
McDowell, Scott D. Esq.
Palkowitsh, Marcus S.
Schaefer, Keith F.
Smith, Irv
Smith, James T.
Sutton, Robert E.

Consultant
Able, Robert L.
Ahern, George I. Jr.
Baker, Bruce H.
Barker, Jock
Bowen, Peter Geoffrey
Bridwell, Lowell W.
Bruneau, Bill
Burns, Franklin L.
Castrodale, James L. Sr.
Conway, Daniel M.
Conway, William A. III
Coons, C. Duane
Cryer, Clifford L.
de Yampert, Thomas K.
Dixon, Carl F.
Douglas, Charles
Fairchild, Kenneth (Ken) H. Jr.
Fisher, Bob
Fisher, Robert B.
Flynn, Stephen A. Jr.
Franz, Roger C.
Garrett, Van Holt Jr.
Gelfond, Lawrence P.
Glad, Charles R.
Golanty, James S.
Grant, Gerald P.
Grant, Miles R.
Harlan, Donald L.
Horton, Edward B. Jr.
Hult, James M.
Huskin, J. David
Katsaros, Basil S.
Kramer, Russell P. Jr.
Kroner, Gary
Lana, Edward C.
Larrick, Donald R.
Lenzini, Michael Jr.
Levine, Mark
Levine, Stu
Liniger, David
McBride, Philip J.
McClelland, Lou
Marshall, Richard K.
Martin, Charles Tyler Jr.
Martin, Dick
Myles, Ronald L.
Naiman, Marvin I.
Robertson, Scott Jeffrey
Schettl, Gary S.
Schroeder, William R. Jr.
Schroeder, William R. Sr.
Shelton, Kenneth L.
Shendleman, Jack
Smith, James T.
Smith, Terrence F.
Sullivan, James Michael
Uhlemann, William R.
Van Court, William T.
Vigoda, Louise
Walter, Alexander W.
Whisler, Duane
Whiting, Richard F.

Developer
Able, Robert L.
Arnold, Robert S.
Baker, Bruce H.
Biagiotti, Stephen M.
Brooks, David Carl
Brown, Richard W.
Bruneau, Bill
Burmont, Fred J.
Burns, Franklin L.
Campbell, Ronald D.
Carruth, Dennis
Cersonsky, H. Sol
Clark, Roger
Clarke, Stephen F.
Consigli, Joseph A.
Cudlip, Peter M.
Davis, B.J.
de Yampert, Thomas K.
Dewey, Robert
Dreher, Ralph M.
Duval, David B.
Flynn, Stephen A. Jr.
Fortner, Seymour S.
Fowler, Jack W.
Garofalo, Ronald J.
Garrett, Van Holt Jr.
Gathers, Charles E.
Glad, Charles R.
Greenberg, Gerald Morton
Harlan, Donald L.
Hayes, Jed
Hecht, Emil
Hedlund, C.J.
Holderith, Emeric R.
Huskin, J. David
Jones, J.G.
Katz, Aron B.
Kent, Wendel G.
Kleinsmith, Mark John
Lana, Edward C.
Larrick, Donald R.
Levine, Mark
Lunsford, William J.
McBride, Philip J.
McDowell, Scott D. Esq.
McGrath, John W.
Mackenzie, K. Bruce
Martin, Charles Tyler Jr.
Mulligan, James M.
Myles, Ronald L.
Nein, Sam N.
Newell, Stewart P.
Palkowitsh, Marcus S.
Percy, Jerry G.
Ramsey, Hal
Robertson, Scott Jeffrey
Schaefer, Keith F.
Schroeder, William R. Sr.
Seely, Arthur W.
Sullivan, James Michael
Sutton, Robert E.
Sweeney, Robert J. Jr.
Tankoos, Bradley J.
Tedford, Milton
Vigoda, Louise
Whiting, Richard F.
Zook, William G.

Engineer
Able, Robert L.
Baker, Bruce H.
Grant, Gerald P.
Grant, Miles R.
Lewis, Heydon Z.
Woolford, William A.

Instructor
Able, Robert L.
Barker, Jock
Bowen, Peter Geoffrey
Boyson, Don E.
Cryer, Clifford L.
Dewey, Robert
Fairchild, Kenneth (Ken) H. Jr.
Fisher, Bob
Fisher, Robert B.
Harlan, Donald L.
Huskin, J. David
Lana, Edward C.
Lenzini, Michael Jr.
Levine, Kent Jay
Levine, Mark
Levine, Stu
Liniger, David
Martin, Dick
Morris, Bill
Myles, Ronald L.
Naiman, Marvin I.
Palcanis, Gregory F.
Ratterman, George W.
Schroeder, William R. Sr.
Shendleman, Jack
Smith, Irv
Smith, James T.
Steuben, Norton L.
Van Court, William T.
Whisler, Duane

Insuror
Dixon, Carl F.
Dreher, Ralph M.
Fowler, Jack W.
Levine, Mark
Lunsford, William J.
Mayes, Gilford H. Jr.
Rosser, Michael
Schroeder, William R. Sr.
Smith, James T.

Lender
Brooks, David Carl
Coons, C. Duane
Douglas, Charles
Gabriel, Eberhard J.
Golanty, James S.
Goodridge, Edwin N.
Horton, Edward B. Jr.
Jenkins, Leon H.
Kieser, Richard J.
Lana, Edward C.
Levine, Mark
Lunsford, William J.
McBride, Philip J.
Manning, William R.
Morris, Bill
Naiman, Marvin I.
Palcanis, Gregory F.
Percy, Jerry G.
Rowland, Thomas F. Jr.
Schroeder, William R. Sr.
Shollenberger, Brian D.
Teague, Paul M.
Uhlemann, William R.
Woodward, S. Lee
Zook, William G.

Owner/Investor
Able, Robert L.
Ahern, George I. Jr.
Arnold, Robert S.
Baker, Bruce H.
Benedetti, John A.
Bridwell, Lowell W.
Brooks, David Carl
Brown, Richard W.
Burns, Franklin L.
Campbell, Ronald D.
Carruth, Dennis
Cersonsky, H. Sol
Chase, Blaine B.
Clark, Roger
Clarke, Jon B.
Consigli, Joseph A.
Coons, C. Duane
Cryer, Clifford L.
de Yampert, Thomas K.
Dewey, Robert
Dixon, Carl F.
Douglas, Charles
Dreher, Ralph M.
Duval, David B.
Fairchild, Kenneth (Ken) H. Jr.
Fisher, Bob
Fisher, Robert B.
Flynn, Stephen A. Jr.
Fortner, Seymour S.
Garrett, Van Holt Jr.
Gathers, Charles E.
Gelfond, Lawrence P.
Glad, Charles R.
Golanty, James S.
Grant, Miles R.
Greenberg, Gerald Morton
Harlan, Donald L.
Hedlund, C.J.
Holderith, Emeric R.
Hult, James M.
Huskin, J. David
Jarvis, Dorothy
Jones, J.G.
Kleinsmith, Mark John
Kramer, Russell P. Jr.
Kroner, Gary
Lana, Edward C.
Larrick, Donald R.
Lenzini, Michael Jr.
Levine, Mark
Lewis, Heydon Z.
Liniger, David
Lunsford, William J.
McBride, Philip J.
McDowell, Scott D. Esq.
Mackenzie, K. Bruce
Marshall, Richard K.
Martin, Charles Tyler Jr.
Martin, Dick
Miller, Ronald J.
Mulligan, James M.
Myles, Ronald L.
Naiman, Marvin I.
Nein, Sam N.
Newell, Stewart P.
Palkowitsh, Marcus S.
Percy, Jerry G.
Rife, Thomas G.
Robertson, Scott Jeffrey
Rowland, Thomas F. Jr.
Schroeder, William R. Sr.
Seely, Arthur W.
Shendleman, Jack
Smith, Terrence F.
Stewart, D. Wayne

Sullivan, James Michael
Tankoos, Bradley J.
Trowbridge, Charles A.
Vigoda, Louise
Volker, John B.
Walter, Alexander W.
Zook, William G.

Property Manager
Baker, Bruce H.
Bane, Jim
Booher, Henry
Bowen, Peter Geoffrey
Bridwell, Lowell W.
Brooks, David Carl
Burns, Franklin L.
Consigli, Joseph A.
Cryer, Clifford L.
Curtiss, Joseph
de Yampert, Thomas K.
Dixon, Carl F.
Duval, David B.
Fortner, Seymour S.
Fowler, Jack W.
Garofalo, Ronald J.
Garrett, Van Holt Jr.
Gathers, Charles E.
Glad, Charles R.
Grant, Gerald P.
Grant, Miles R.
Greenberg, Gerald Morton
Hecht, Emil
Hedlund, C.J.
Holderith, Emeric R.
Horton, Edward B. Jr.
Jensen, Michael M.
Kleinsmith, Mark John
Lana, Edward C.
Levine, Mark
Lewis, Heydon Z.
McBride, Philip J.
Martin, Charles Tyler Jr.
Naiman, Marvin I.
Newell, Stewart P.
Ralston, Richard
Robertson, Scott Jeffrey
Schroeder, William R. Jr.
Schroeder, William R. Sr.
Tedford, Milton
Vigoda, Louise
Wheeler, Dale
Whisler, Duane
Whiting, Richard F.
Woodward, S. Lee
Younger, Edward M.

Real Estate Publisher
Levine, Kent Jay
Levine, Mark
Shendleman, Jack

Regulator
Gabriel, Eberhard J.
Palcanis, Gregory F.

Syndicator
Bowen, Peter Geoffrey
Campbell, Ronald D.
Clark, Roger
Clarke, Jon B.
Cramer, Steven E.
Dewey, Robert
Douglas, Charles
Dreher, Ralph M.
Fisher, Bob
Fisher, Robert B.
Glad, Charles R.
Gonzales, Richard
Harlan, Donald L.
Hedlund, C.J.
Huskin, J. David
Jensen, Michael M.
Jones, J.G.
Kramer, Russell P. Jr.
Larrick, Donald R.
Lenzini, Michael Jr.
Levine, Mark
Liniger, David
McBride, Philip J.
Martin, Charles Tyler Jr.
Martin, Dick
Miller, Ronald J.
Morris, Bill
Naiman, Marvin I.
Robertson, Scott Jeffrey
Rowland, Thomas F. Jr.
Schaefer, Keith F.
Seely, Arthur W.
Shockley, Hugh U.
Smith, Terrence F.
Sutton, Robert E.
Trowbridge, Charles A.
Vigoda, Louise
Walter, Alexander W.

DURANGO

Appraiser
Love, William B.

Broker
Love, William B.

Consultant
Weathers, Kenneth M.

Developer
Weathers, Kenneth M.

Owner/Investor
Weathers, Kenneth M.

Property Manager
Love, William B.

Syndicator
Weathers, Kenneth M.

FORT MORGAN

Attorney
Vandemoer, John J.

Owner/Investor
Vandemoer, John J.

GLENWOOD SPRINGS

Architect
Arnold, Robert L.

Attorney
Creasey, James S.

Broker
Cole, David L.
Ewing, P. Van III
Harvey, Perry A.
MacGregor, Gordon
Ordway, Philip E.
Souto, Ric A.
Wix, John

Builder
Creasey, James S.
Harvey, Perry A.

Consultant
Creasey, James S.
Harvey, Perry A.
MacGregor, Gordon
Ordway, Philip E.
Souto, Ric A.
Wix, John

Developer
Ewing, P. Van III
Harvey, Perry A.
MacGregor, Gordon
Ordway, Philip E.
Wix, John

Instructor
Cole, David L.

Owner/Investor
Cole, David L.
Cose, Lexina
Creasey, James S.
Harvey, Perry A.
MacGregor, Gordon
Souto, Ric A.
Wix, John

Property Manager
Creasey, James S.
Wix, John

Syndicator
Harvey, Perry A.
MacGregor, Gordon
Wix, John

GOLDEN

Appraiser
Burris, William T.
Ursini, Rocco J.

Attorney
Chamberlin, Thomas J.
Graves, Darryl
Jones, Ronald S.
McGill, Scott
Sanders, Michael Leo
Teigen, Philip J.
Thorson, David M.

Broker
Burris, William T.
Cunningham, Michael J.
Eby, Christopher S.
Hodder, Donald W.
McGill, Douglas F.I.
McGill, Scott
Pollard, Ronald Terrell
Stavast, Joseph John

Builder
McGill, Douglas F.I.
Pollard, Ronald Terrell
Sanders, Michael Leo
Teigen, Philip J.
Wood, John S.

Consultant
Burris, William T.
Gibbons, Meigs Christian
Hodder, Donald W.
McGill, Douglas F.I.
Pollard, Ronald Terrell
Sanders, Michael Leo
Yanari, Dale M.

Developer
Enever, C. Robert
Gibbons, Meigs Christian
Johnson, John E.
Jones, Ronald S.
McGill, Douglas F.I.
Pollard, Ronald Terrell
Sanders, Michael Leo
Wood, John S.

Engineer
Burris, William T.

Instructor
Burris, William T.
Stavast, Joseph John
Ursini, Rocco J.

Insuror
Sanders, Michael Leo
Teigen, Philip J.

Lender
Teigen, Philip J.

Owner/Investor
Gibbons, Meigs Christian
Graves, Darryl
Hodder, Donald W.
Jones, Ronald S.
McGill, Douglas F.I.
McGill, Scott
Pollard, Ronald Terrell
Stavast, Joseph John
Wood, John S.

Property Manager
Burris, William T.
Enever, C. Robert
Hodder, Donald W.
Johnson, John E.
McGill, Douglas F.I.
Wood, John S.
Woods, Sandra

Syndicator
Gibbons, Meigs Christian
Jones, Ronald S.
McGill, Douglas F.I.

GRAND JUNCTION

Appraiser
Nisley, Frank Jr.

Broker
Nisley, Frank Jr.
Sarosky, William J.
Sinclair, Joseph T.

Builder
Sarosky, William J.

Consultant
Nisley, Frank Jr.
Sarosky, William J.
Sinclair, Joseph T.

Developer
Nisley, Frank Jr.
Sinclair, Joseph T.

Instructor
Sinclair, Joseph T.

Lender
Sarosky, William J.

Owner/Investor
Sarosky, William J.
Sinclair, Joseph T.

Property Manager
Sarosky, William J.
Sinclair, Joseph T.

Syndicator
Sinclair, Joseph T.

LONGMONT

Appraiser
McClelland, William H.
Mohler, Robert L.
Pickett, David R.
Tarantino, Joe
Van Lear, Stevan H.

Attorney
Hopkins, Richard C.
Williams, John David

Broker
Hopkins, Richard C.
Kendall, Lawrence M.
McClelland, William H.
Mohler, Robert L.
Neale, Richard E.
Pickett, David R.
Tarantino, Joe
Van Lear, Stevan H.
Weixelman, Donald B.

Builder
Neale, Richard E.
Pickett, David R.
Tarantino, Joe

Consultant
Pickett, David R.
Tarantino, Joe
Van Lear, Stevan H.

Developer
Kendall, Lawrence M.
McClelland, William H.
Pickett, David R.
Tarantino, Joe
Van Lear, Stevan H.

Weixelman, Donald B.

Engineer
Pickett, David R.

Instructor
Pickett, David R.
Skrivan, Albert N.

Lender
Van Lear, Stevan H.

Owner/Investor
Hopkins, Richard C.
Kendall, Lawrence M.
McClelland, William H.
Mohler, Robert L.
Neale, Richard E.
Pickett, David R.
Tarantino, Joe
Van Lear, Stevan H.
Weixelman, Donald B.

Property Manager
Kendall, Lawrence M.
Rhodes, Charles G. Jr.
Tarantino, Joe
Van Lear, Stevan H.

Syndicator
Kendall, Lawrence M.
Neale, Richard E.
Pickett, David R.
Tarantino, Joe
Van Lear, Stevan H.

MONTROSE

Broker
Berger, Richard W.
Sparr, Olive M.

Developer
Berger, Richard W.

Instructor
Berger, Richard W.

Owner/Investor
Berger, Richard W.
Sparr, Olive M.

PUEBLO

Attorney
Altman, Leo S.

Broker
Holloran, Joseph W.
O'Callaghan, R.J. Patrick

Consultant
Holloran, Joseph W.
O'Callaghan, R.J. Patrick

Instructor
O'Callaghan, R.J. Patrick

Lender
Holloran, Joseph W.

Owner/Investor
Holloran, Joseph W.

Property Manager
Holloran, Joseph W.

SALIDA

Appraiser
Delany, Robert

Broker
Delany, Robert

Builder
Delany, Robert

Developer
Delany, Robert

Owner/Investor
Delany, Robert

CONNECTICUT

HARTFORD

Appraiser
Adams, John F. Jr.
Aldieri, Michael J.
Archambault, Reynold J. Jr.
Babiarz, Stan T.
Bearce, David W.
Dumont, C. Donald
Gorka, Francis L.
Koseian, John C.
Marsele, Peter R.
Rehle, Daniel F.
Rowlson, John F.
Sternberg, Steven A.
Vermilyd, Sherwood S.
Werbner, Alfred P.
Wilson, John C. III

Architect
Will, Philip S.

Assessor
Marsele, Peter R.
Vermilyd, Sherwood S.

Attorney
Anderson, Robert H.
Asmar, Mark A.
Birnbaum, Robert J.
Buck, Gurdon Hall
Gilligan, Robert G.
Glass, Marc Jerome
Heden, Thomas F.
Jordan, Neal H.
Kapanka, Richard A.
Keyles, Sidney Alan
Levine, Marc S.
Mallin, John R.
Mayo, Walter H.
Oland, Mark
Rockwell, Richard
Schenker, Michael S.
Shulman, James H.
Smith, R. Jeffrey
Stiebel, Michael S.
Valentine, Garrison N.

Banker
Archambault, Reynold J. Jr.
Clinton, Richard P.
Nystrom, Steven G.
Wignall, Ernest C.

Broker
Adams, John F. Jr.
Aldieri, Michael J.
Allen, Bob
Buck, Gurdon Hall
Cagenello, Bruce H.
Cavanagh, John B.
Dumont, C. Donald
Edwards, George D.
Farley, William H.
Gerity, Mark B.
Holmes, Peter C.
Kaufman, Eric P.
Koseian, John C.
Nash, Diane G.
Rehle, Daniel F.
Sternberg, Steven A.
Wallace, C. Robert
Wilson, John C. III

Builder
Barbato, John R.
Bianca, Anthony T. Sr.
Carlson, Russ
Gerity, Mark B.
Godbout, Arthur R. Jr.
Jordan, Neal H.
Konover, Michael
Koseian, John C.
Kraus, Harold C.
Sucsy, Leonard G.
Wilson, John C. III

Consultant
Adams, John F. Jr.
Aldieri, Michael J.
Allen, Bob
Archambault, Reynold J. Jr.
Bianca, Anthony T. Sr.
Carlson, Russ
Cavanagh, John B.
Edwards, George D.
Farley, William H.
Gerity, Mark B.
Holmes, Peter C.
Kaufman, Eric P.
Marsele, Peter R.
Rehle, Daniel F.
Steiner, Mark S.
Sternberg, Steven A.
Vermilyd, Sherwood S.
Will, Philip S.
Wilson, John C. III

Developer
Allen, Bob
Barbato, John R.
Bianca, Anthony T. Sr.
Cagenello, Bruce H.
Cameruci, Victor H.
Carlson, Russ
Daversa, Frank
Falker, Michael J.
Farley, William H.
Gerity, Mark B.
Godbout, Arthur R. Jr.
Hazen, Kenneth K.
Hutensky, Allan
Jordan, Neal H.
Kagan, David H.
Konover, Michael
Kraus, Harold C.
Levine, Marc S.
Steiner, Mark S.
Sucsy, Leonard G.
Will, Philip S.
Wilson, John C. III

Instructor
Adams, John F. Jr.
Cagenello, Bruce H.
Glass, Marc Jerome
Russell, Richard F.
Werbner, Alfred P.

Insuror
Gorka, Francis L.
Kincaid, Walter G.
Koseian, John C.
Palm, Henry
Russell, Richard F.
Steward, James A.

Lender
Archambault, Reynold J. Jr.
Babiarz, Stan T.
Bluestein, Ronald W.
Brinkerhoff, James J.
Hunter, Robert N.
Keyles, Sidney Alan
Koseian, John C.
Nystrom, Steven G.
Steward, James A.
Wadhams, John D.
Wignall, Ernest C.
Wisnioski, Charles M.

Owner/Investor
Babiarz, Stan T.
Bartram, Maynard C.
Bianca, Anthony T. Sr.
Brinkerhoff, James J.
Carlson, Russ
Gerity, Mark B.
Glass, Marc Jerome
Godbout, Arthur R. Jr.
Hazen, Kenneth K.
Heden, Thomas F.
Hunter, Robert N.
Hutensky, Allan
Jordan, Neal H.
Kagan, David H.
Konover, Michael
Koseian, John C.
Kraus, Harold C.
Palm, Henry
Rehle, Daniel F.
Russell, Richard F.
Steiner, Mark S.
Sternberg, Steven A.
Sucsy, Leonard G.
Wignall, Ernest C.
Will, Philip S.
Wilson, John C. III

Property Manager
Allen, Bob
Archambault, Reynold J. Jr.
Babiarz, Stan T.
Barbato, John R.
Bianca, Anthony T. Sr.
Bouwkamp, Gerald R.
Carlson, Russ
Cavanagh, John B.
Doyle, Allan M. Jr.
Dryden, Willia
Dumont, C. Donald
Farley, William H.
Feeney, John
Gerity, Mark B.
Godbout, Arthur R. Jr.
Greenbert, Arnold C.
Hannafin, Lawrence
Harvey, Frank M.
Hazen, Kenneth K.
Heden, Thomas F.
Holmes, Peter C.
Houck, H.F.
Hutensky, Allan
Jordan, Neal H.
Kagan, David H.
Kaufman, Eric P.
Konover, Michael
Koseian, John C.
Kraus, Harold C.
McQuaillan, Jeremiah E.
Nystrom, Robert
Palm, Henry
Rehle, Daniel F.
Russell, Richard F.
Steiner, Mark S.
Sucsy, Leonard G.

Real Estate Publisher
Johnson, Pearl

Syndicator
Bianca, Anthony T. Sr.
Gerity, Mark B.
Hutensky, Allan
Jordan, Neal H.
Kagan, David H.
Kaufman, Eric P.
Rehle, Daniel F.
Sternberg, Steven A.
Wilson, John C. III

NEW HAVEN

Appraiser
Ames, Gil
Becker, Richard N.
Comstock, John B. II
Fabian, Samuel T.
Harrison, Henry S.
Hicks, Floyd J.
McCulloch, Robert P.
Mulherin, Gregory J.
Okrepkie, Ralph G.
Parrott, A. Leonard
Pisaretz, Peter
Pitcher, Charles D.
Rupwani, Kanayo N. "Rupi"
Salomon, Muriel
Terzini, Kenneth J.
Traub, Carl F.

Walhimer, Leslie
Wells, Thomas H.

Architect
Antinozzi, D.P. Jr.
Schecter, Jack H.

Assessor
Comstock, John B. II

Attorney
Gordon, Victor M.
Hoaley, Mary
Hudson, William Campbell III
Karpel, Philip F.
Liebman, Lawrence M.
Ratcliffe, G.J. Jr.
Saft, Stephen J.
Scharf, Roy H.
Schwartz, Lawrence B.
Snaider, Benson A.
Woodward, James W.
Zahn, F. Anthony

Banker
Ames, Gil
Brown, Stewart J.
Freda, Edward M.
Liebman, Lawrence M.
Schwartz, Lawrence B.
Sutkowski, Frank J.

Broker
Ames, Gil
Barnes, Paul T.
Becker, Richard N.
Brown, Jonathan N.
Comstock, John B. II
Ermler, Richard
Fabian, Samuel T.
Hicks, Floyd J.
Jacobson, Jack R.
McCulloch, Robert P.
Mack, David A.
Maretz, Fred R.
Moore, Eugene L.
Mulherin, Gregory J.
Okrepkie, Ralph G.
Parrott, A. Leonard
Ricci, William J.
Richards, Mildred V.
Rowe, B.A.
Rupwani, Kanayo N. "Rupi"
Salomon, Muriel
Scinto, John J
Traub, Carl F.
Walhimer, Leslie

Builder
Comstock, John B. II
Ellis, Richard C.
Ermler, Richard
Mack, David A.
Paparazzo, Henry J.
Rupwani, Kanayo N. "Rupi"
Salomon, Muriel
Terzini, Kenneth J.
Woodward, James W.

Consultant
Allen, Charles H. III
Barnes, Paul T.
Becker, Richard N.
Comstock, John B. II
Ellis, Richard C.
Fabian, Samuel T.
Gordon, Victor M.
Harrison, Henry S.
Hicks, Floyd J.
Jacobson, Jack R.
Maretz, Fred R.
Mulherin, Gregory J.
Nishball, Robert L.
Okrepkie, Ralph G.
Parrott, A. Leonard
Pisaretz, Peter
Ricci, William J.
Rupwani, Kanayo N. "Rupi"
Salomon, Muriel
Schwartz, Lawrence B.
Scinto, John J
Terzini, Kenneth J.
Walhimer, Leslie
Wells, Thomas H.
Woodward, James W.

Developer
Allen, Charles H. III
Bellard, Gary
Brown, Jonathan N.
Comstock, John B. II
Ellis, Richard C.
Ermler, Richard
Garofalo, Albert A.
Liebman, Lawrence M.
McCulloch, Robert P.
Mack, David A.
Paparazzo, Henry J.
Parrott, A. Leonard
Ricci, William J.
Rupwani, Kanayo N. "Rupi"
Terzini, Kenneth J.
Traub, Carl F.
Woodward, James W.

Engineer
Okrepkie, Ralph G.

Instructor
Barnes, Paul T.
Comstock, John B. II
Harrison, Henry S.
Moore, Eugene L.
Mulherin, Gregory J.
Parrott, A. Leonard
Pisaretz, Peter
Salomon, Muriel
Scinto, John J

Insuror
Harrison, Henry S.
McCulloch, Robert P.
Rupwani, Kanayo N. "Rupi"

Lender
Ames, Gil
Brown, Stewart J.
Ellis, Richard C.
Gordon, Victor M.
Terzini, Kenneth J.
Woodward, James W.

Owner/Investor
Barnes, Paul T.
Brown, Jonathan N.
Brown, Stewart J.
Comstock, John B. II
Ermler, Richard
Garofalo, Albert A.
Gordon, Victor M.
Harrison, Henry S.
Jacobson, Jack R.
Liebman, Lawrence M.
Mack, David A.
McManus, Jerry A.
Maretz, Fred R.
Moore, Eugene L.
Mulherin, Gregory J.
Paparazzo, Henry J.
Parrott, A. Leonard
Rupwani, Kanayo N. "Rupi"
Salomon, Muriel
Schwartz, Lawrence B.
Scinto, John J
Terzini, Kenneth J.
Walhimer, Leslie
Wilbur, E. Packer
Willis, James R.
Woodward, James W.
Zahn, F. Anthony

Property Manager
Ames, Gil
Anderson, Harry
Barnes, Paul T.
Becker, Richard N.
Brown, Jonathan N.
Comstock, John B. II
Ellis, Richard C.
Ermler, Richard
Hoaley, Mary
Jacobson, Jack R.
McCulloch, Robert P.
Maretz, Fred R.
Meaney, Robert
Moore, Eugene L.
Mulherin, Gregory J.
Paparazzo, Henry J.
Parrott, A. Leonard
Ratcliffe, G.J. Jr.
Rupwani, Kanayo N. "Rupi"
Schauder, Frederick
Terzini, Kenneth J.
Traub, Carl F.

Real Estate Publisher
Gordon, Victor M.
Harrison, Henry S.
Salomon, Muriel

Syndicator
Brown, Jonathan N.
Ermler, Richard
Hicks, Floyd J.
Liebman, Lawrence M.
McCulloch, Robert P.
Mack, David A.
Maretz, Fred R.
Mulherin, Gregory J.
Rupwani, Kanayo N. "Rupi"
Schwartz, Lawrence B.
Scinto, John J
Woodward, James W.
Zahn, F. Anthony

NEW LONDON

Appraiser
Capozza, Alfred A.
Cushman, Robert Charles
Miner, Christopher A.
Mletschnig, Peter F.
O'Connell, Anthony Wayne
Silverstein, F. Jerome

Architect
Goff, Lyman
Sharpe, Richard

Attorney
Pavetti, Francis J.

Banker
Kelleher, D. William

Broker
Bigelow, Ernest A.
Capozza, Alfred A.
Cushman, Robert Charles
Mletschnig, Peter F.
O'Connell, Anthony Wayne
Silverstein, F. Jerome

Builder
Goff, Lyman

Consultant
Miner, Christopher A.
Myers, George C. Jr.
O'Connell, Anthony Wayne

Developer
Goff, Lyman

Instructor
Capozza, Alfred A.
Miner, Christopher A.

Owner/Investor
Bigelow, Ernest A.
Goff, Lyman
Myers, George C. Jr.

Property Manager
Mletschnig, Peter F.
Myers, George C. Jr.

Syndicator
Bigelow, Ernest A.

STAMFORD

Appraiser
Benjamin, Richard E.
Brazo, Bruce Allen
Dudeney, Peter N.
Kellogg, Ralph M.
Mintz, Lewis R.
Montanari, Fred P.
Morey, Emil J.
Rowe, Benjamin A.
Whittelsey, Souther

Architect
Behr, Richard H.
Weber, Harvey

Attorney
Antonucci, Francis J.
Austin, Brock J.
Barton, James M.
Grosby, Robert N.
Hawkins, Barry C.
Kaye, Joel M.
Kemp, Gail M.
Kent, Jon
Leepson, Peter L.
McGuire, Mary C. Esq.
McNamara, Paul S.
Maiocchi, Christine T.
Medvecky, Thomas E.
Merchant, John F.
Oshins, Harvey B.
Sakal, Jeffrey
Salmon, William C.
Schwartz, Ronald M.
Skidd, Thomas P. Jr.
Tirola, Vincent S.
Ward, Tom S. Jr.
Zients, Michael R.

Banker
Sentivany, Edward K. Jr.

Broker
Almy, Richard Jr.
Benjamin, Richard E.
Brazo, Bruce Allen
Brooks, B.V.
Campiglia, John E.
Dadakis, G. Thomas
Dudeney, Peter N.
Easton, John J.
Gray, Michael R.
Green, Herbert J.
Harmon, Gilbert M.
Kellogg, Ralph M.
Krevlin, Sol
Kupper, Emily
Maiocchi, Christine T.
Martin, Kurt S.
Mintz, Lewis R.
Montanari, Fred P.
Morey, Emil J.
Renton, David M.
Rich, Thomas L.
Rosenshine, Marvin S.
Rowe, Benjamin A.
Ryan, James P.
Sammis, Jesse F. III
Siegel, Michael H.
Whittelsey, Souther

Builder
Hamilton, David Lawrence
Kaplan, Ira G.
Leonhardt, Alec F.

Lydecker, Gerrit
Matyas, Eugene J.
Montanari, Fred P.
Rich, Thomas L.
Stevens, Marshall H.

Consultant
Almy, Richard Jr.
Bailly, Barbara A.
Behr, Richard H.
Benjamin, Richard E.
Brazo, Bruce Allen
Brooks, B.V.
Dadakis, G. Thomas
DiScala, Joseph V.
Easton, John J.
Grosby, Robert N.
Montanari, Fred P.
Morey, Emil J.
Renton, David M.
Rowe, Benjamin A.
Ryan, James P.
Sentivany, Edward K. Jr.
Siegel, Michael H.
Toomes, W. Scott
Trolle, T.N.

Developer
Behr, Richard H.
Brazo, Bruce Allen
Brooks, B.V.
Cohen, Leonard
Frost, Fredric W.
Hamilton, David Lawrence
Hyland, Mark W.
Hyland, William F.
Kaplan, Ira G.
Lydecker, Gerrit
Matyas, Eugene J.
Oshins, Harvey B.
Paladino, Patrick J.
Pfister, Jean Paul
Rich, Thomas L.
Sammis, Jesse F. III
Schwartz, Ronald M.
Steinel, Russell L.
Stevens, Marshall H.
Toomes, W. Scott
Trolle, T.N.

Engineer
Dudeney, Peter N.
Leonhardt, Alec F.
Matyas, Eugene J.
Stevens, Marshall H.
Trolle, T.N.

Instructor
Behr, Richard H.
Benjamin, Richard E.
Dudeney, Peter N.
Easton, John J.
Morey, Emil J.
Ward, Tom S. Jr.

Insuror
Hamilton, David Lawrence

Lender
Blum, Michael S.
Hamilton, David Lawrence
Sentivany, Edward K. Jr.

Owner/Investor
Bailly, Barbara A.
Behr, Richard H.
Blum, Michael S.
Brazo, Bruce Allen
Brooks, B.V.
Campiglia, John E.
Dadakis, G. Thomas
DiScala, Joseph V.
Dudeney, Peter N.
Feeney, Thomas J.
Gray, Michael R.
Grosby, Robert N.
Hamilton, David Lawrence
Hyland, William F.
Lydecker, Gerrit
Oshins, Harvey B.
Paladino, Patrick J.
Renton, David M.
Rich, Thomas L.
Sammis, Jesse F. III
Schwartz, Ronald M.
Stevens, Marshall H.
Toomes, W. Scott
Trolle, T.N.
Ward, Tom S. Jr.

Property Manager
Alexander, Kyle
Bailly, Barbara A.
Bekassy, Virginia
Brazo, Bruce Allen
Brooks, B.V.
Campiglia, John E.
Claffey, Joseph
Dadakis, G. Thomas
Davis, James
DiScala, Joseph V.
Fechtman, George
Feeney, Thomas J.
Flanders, Donald
Fleming, Reginald
Gage, John
Gasparro, Peter William
Gill, George
Gotthelp, Don
Gray, Michael R.
Herman, A.
Koon, Charles
Lane, Arthur
Lockwood, Samuel A.
Lozyniak, Andrew
Lushing, Jonathon
MacDonald, John H.
McGuire, Mary C. Esq.
Montanari, Fred P.
Moylan, Robert J.
Murray, George
Newirow, Andrew
Oesterreich, G.T.
O'Reardon, Francis
Oshins, Harvey B.
Peltz, Alan H.
Preisner, A.J.
Ramsay, A.D. Jr.
Rich, Thomas L.
Rosenshine, Marvin S.
Schafler, Norman I.
Schwartz, Ronald M.
Siegel, Michael H.
Smith, Harlan W.
Stamberg, Frank
Tierney, Gerald
Trolle, T.N.
Wall, Larry
Whittelsey, Souther

Real Estate Publisher
Dadakis, G. Thomas

Regulator
Brazo, Bruce Allen
Maiocchi, Christine T.

Syndicator
Brooks, B.V.
Gray, Michael R.
Morey, Emil J.
Rich, Thomas L.
Rowe, Benjamin A.
Sammis, Jesse F. III
Theissen, Ronald James

WATERBURY

Appraiser
Blankman, Donald Warren
Burns, Harold J.
Lengen, John J.
Richmond, Roger W.
Siefel, Robert H.
Stratton, John C.
Washburne, John H.
Wilion, Norman R.

Attorney
Anderson, Henry B.
Slavin, Sherman R.
Tilley, David B. Sr.

Banker
Blankman, Donald Warren

Broker
Bergmiller, Edgar A.
Burns, Harold J.
Dusek, Jaroslav
Richmond, Roger W.
Schmidt, Norman K.
Siefel, Robert H.
Stratton, John C.
Washburne, John H.
Wilion, Norman R.

Builder
Bergmiller, Edgar A.
Blankman, Donald Warren

Consultant
Allan, Victor
Dusek, Jaroslav
Lombard, John W.
Richmond, Roger W.
Stratton, John C.
Washburne, John H.

Developer
Blankman, Donald Warren
Lombard, John W.

Instructor
Anderson, Henry B.
Lengen, John J.
Richmond, Roger W.
Washburne, John H.

Insuror
Bergmiller, Edgar A.
Schmidt, Norman K.
Washburne, John H.

Lender
Blankman, Donald Warren
Heard, Drayton

Owner/Investor
Anderson, Henry B.
Dusek, Jaroslav
Lombard, John W.

Property Manager
Blankman, Donald Warren
Currie, Edward A.
Fountain, Michael
Leganza, Leonard F.
Lombard, John W.
Wilion, Norman R.

Real Estate Publisher
Goldberg, Jack
McGough, Robert J.

Syndicator
Dusek, Jaroslav
Lombard, John W.

WILLIMANTIC

Consultant
Clapp, John M.
Kinnard, William N. Jr.
Paesani, Judith B.

Engineer
Kinnard, William N. Jr.

Instructor
Clapp, John M.
Kinnard, William N. Jr.

Real Estate Publisher
Paesani, Judith B.

DELAWARE

WILMINGTON

Appraiser
Melson, Joseph N. Jr.
Reynolds, Thomas C. Jr.
Stephens, Ronald L.
Vella, Ruth Ann

Attorney
Aerenson, Norman N.
Amick, Steven Hammond
Dorsey, Leighton C.
Ennis, Bruce C.
Gilman, Marvin S.
Grant, J. Kirkland
Kristol, Daniel M.
Levin, Richard David

Banker
Wilgus, Gerald W.

Broker
Bonsall, Edward H. III
Melson, Joseph N. Jr.
Stephens, Ronald L.
Stoltz, Jack P.
Vella, Ruth Ann
White, P. Gerald
Wilgus, Gerald W.

Builder
Corrozi, John A.
Gilman, Marvin S.

Consultant
Aerenson, Norman N.
Bonsall, Edward H. III
Melson, Joseph N. Jr.
Reynolds, Thomas C. Jr.
Stephens, Ronald L.
Stoltz, Jack P.
Vella, Ruth Ann
White, P. Gerald

Developer
Corrozi, John A.
Gilman, Marvin S.
Johnson, Donald E.
Stephens, Ronald L.
Vella, Ruth Ann
Weiner, Mark E.
White, P. Gerald
Wilgus, Gerald W.

Instructor
Grant, J. Kirkland
Melson, Joseph N. Jr.
Vella, Ruth Ann

Insuror
Wilgus, Gerald W.

Lender
Ryan, Thomas S.
Vella, Ruth Ann

Owner/Investor
Aerenson, Norman N.
Corrozi, John A.
Gilman, Marvin S.
Grant, J. Kirkland
Levin, Richard David
Melson, Joseph N. Jr.
Stephens, Ronald L.
Vella, Ruth Ann
Vitt, Lois A.
White, P. Gerald
Wilgus, Gerald W.

Property Manager
Acton, William
Bonsall, Edward H. III
Brumbaugh, Robert R.
Fernald, Parker
Johnson, Donald E.
Patterson, Bill
Stephens, Ronald L.
Vella, Ruth Ann
Weiner, Mark E.

Witt, William

Real Estate Publisher
Vella, Ruth Ann

Syndicator
Gilman, Marvin S.
McPartland, Charles J.
Stephens, Ronald L.
Vitt, Lois A.
Weiner, Mark E.
White, P. Gerald

DISTRICT OF COLUMBIA

Appraiser
Bresler, Charles S.
Brooks, Kenneth Donald
Bryan, Alonzo J. Jr.
Butcher, Douglas S.
Eames, Gary A.
Gimbert, Clement H.
Harps, William S.
Maury, Deane
Newson, Darryl Charles
Noonan, Patrick F.
Reynolds, Judith
Sherburne, Mary L.

Architect
Anderson, Robert Barber
Bayne, James M.
Brooks, Kenneth Donald
Bucher, William Ward
Buckley, Davis
Ehn, C. Lennart
Goetz, Lewis J.
Meeker, David Olan Jr.

Assessor
Bryan, Alonzo J. Jr.

Attorney
Alexander, Sandra Jeane
Alsop, S. Reid
Berger, Bruce
Berkowitz, Edward C.
Berlin, Norman B.
Bloch, Stuart Marshall
Burke, Garrett C.
Cavanaugh, Gordon
Coerper, Milo G.
Collins, Susan Sonnek
Constable, William E.
Dwyer, Jeffry R.
Ferguson, Lewis H. III
Gambrill, J. Matthew
Greenstein, Abraham J.
Griffin, Mark Gerard
Howard, Daggett H.
Joselow, Robert B.
Karem, Michael G.
Kass, Benny L.
Klein, Robert A.
Klepper, Martin
Knoll, E. Joseph
Kohn, Arnold J.
Lane, Bruce S.
Ledgard, Bert L. Jr.
Levin, Stuart S.
Libby, Howard A.
McClure, Roger J.
Mahoney, John J.
Marks, Fe Morales
Mitchell, Grant E.
Monroig, Antonio
Moore, William C.
Moskof, Howard R.
Murphy, Brian P.
Nathanson, Marilyn Elise
Olson, John F.
Oman, Roy Erik
Osnos, David M.
Patterson, Thomas L.
Pearlstein, Paul D.
Pierce, Samuel Riley Jr.
Pohoryles, Louis
Rauh, B. Michael
Roebuck, Thurman M.
Sanders, Raymond Carter Jr.
Sauerbrunn, Kathleen H.
Singer, Daniel M.
Smuckler, Gary S.
Spingler, Frank J.
Spooner, Linda Greer
Stinchfield, John Edward
Talbott, John C.
Tatusko, Wayne G.
Torres, Emilio
Tucker, Stefan F.
Vaughters, Cecilie A.
West, Joseph Frederick

Banker
Alexander, Willis W.
Barrington, Claude O.
Bresler, Charles S.
Lindley, Jonathan
MacBride, Dexter P.
McClure, Roger J.
Mimna, Curtis John
Riedy, Mark J.
Tilley, Jon
Watson, Theresa L.

Broker
Avery, Cyrus Stevens II
Brenneman, Bruce M.
Bresler, Charles S.
Davis, Frederick W.
Geisinger, Edward I.
Gimbert, Clement H.
Grayson, W. Cabell Jr.
Harris, John A.
Israel, Gary M.
Johnson, R. Bruce
Lemle, L. Craig
Luck, James S.
Lustgarten, Stephen F.
McClure, Roger J.
McCray, Joe Richard
Maury, Deane
Mimna, Curtis John
Murphy, Neil
Noonan, Patrick F.
Perucci, Thomas Robert
Pryor, Barbara L.
Sanders, Raymond Carter Jr.
Shanks, Alexander Graham
Sherburne, Mary L.
Shrago, Jeffrey Kazis
Speier, Peter
Wallerstein, David L.

Builder
Brady, George M. Jr.
Bresler, Charles S.
Brooks, Kenneth Donald
Bryan, Alonzo J. Jr.
Crump, G. Lindsay
Davis, Frederick W.
DeFranceaux, George W.
Ehn, C. Lennart
Gillies, Roderick M.
Hoffman, William H.
Karem, Michael G.
Lustgarten, Stephen F.
Newson, Darryl Charles
Sprouse, James M.
Stahl, David E.
Stoll, Edwin L.

Consultant
Alexander, Sandra Jeane
Avery, Cyrus Stevens II
Baldwin, Jeffry B.
Banner, Knox
Bechhoefer, Ina S.
Blake, Stephen H.
Boyle, M. Ross
Bryan, Alonzo J. Jr.
Bucher, William Ward
Crawford, H. R.
Davis, Frederick W.
Fasano, Michael V.
Gambrill, J. Matthew
Geisinger, Edward I.
Hantgan, Richard S.
Harps, William S.
Harris, John A.
Johnson, R. Bruce
King, Bert M.
Klepper, Martin
Kopff, Gary J.
Lawler, J. Klein
Lemle, L. Craig
Libby, Howard A.
Luck, James S.
McClinton, Mr. Jr.
McCray, Joe Richard
Margrabe, William
Mays, Ben
Murphy, Neil
Murray, Joseph C.
Newson, Darryl Charles
O'Neill, John T.
Pryor, Barbara L.
Reese, Rostelle J. Jr.
Reider, Jeffrey R.
Reynolds, Anthony
Roebuck, Thurman M.
Sherburne, Mary L.
Shrago, Jeffrey Kazis
Siler, Robert W. Jr.
Speier, Peter
Tischler, Paul Stephen
Torres, Emilio
Vallance, Anthony P.
Wallerstein, David L.
West, Joseph Frederick
Wildhack, William A.
Witherspoon, Robert
Zuniga, Thomas M.

Developer
Berger, Bruce
Blake, Stephen H.
Brady, George M. Jr.
Brenneman, Bruce M.
Bresler, Charles S.
Brooks, Kenneth Donald
Buckley, Davis
Crump, G. Lindsay
Davis, Frederick W.
DeFranceaux, George W.
Eames, Gary A.
Ehn, C. Lennart
Gillies, Roderick M.
Gimbert, Clement H.
Hoffman, William H.
Johnson, R. Bruce
Libby, Howard A.
Lustgarten, Stephen F.
McClinton, Mr. Jr.
Mimna, Curtis John
Moore, William C.
Newson, Darryl Charles
Sanders, Raymond Carter Jr.
Siler, Robert W. Jr.
Stoll, Edwin L.
Wallerstein, David L.
Zuniga, Thomas M.

Engineer
Ehn, C. Lennart
Hoffman, William H.
Reese, Rostelle J. Jr.

Instructor
Barrington, Claude O.
Bechhoefer, Ina S.
Griffin, Mark Gerard
Harps, William S.
Ledgard, Bert L. Jr.
Margrabe, William
Murray, Joseph C.
Noonan, Patrick F.
West, Joseph Frederick
Witherspoon, Robert

Insuror
Gimbert, Clement H.
McClinton, Mr. Jr.
Maury, Deane

Lender
Abbott, Edward L.
Adams, Paul A.
Anderson, David T.
Barrington, Claude O.
Baugh, James E.
Beesley, H. Brent
Bings, William T.
Bloomberg, Burton
Bowers, G.H.
Boyle, William H.
Brand, W. Calvert
Bryant, Donnie L.
Buchanon, John S.
Burchman, Leonard
Casey, Thomas
Croft, David James
Davis, Stuart
DeFranceaux, George W.
Dempsey, Charles L.
DiPrete, Andrew A.
Dodge, Donald G.
Dodge, Robert I.
Draper, Malcolm Jr.
Evans, Shirley A.
Fagin, Robert F.
Freeman, Claire
Gimbert, Clement H.
Golec, Janice
Greer, Dennis F.
Hamilton, Lea
Heifetz, Alan W.
Houde, Donald I.
Jackson, James Jay
Joselow, Robert B.
Judy, Henry L.
Karnes, David
Karpe, Robert W.
Keith, Harold
Kenison, Robert S.
Kennedy, John P.
King, Bert M.
Kliman, Albert
Knapp, John J.
Koch, June
Lasko, Warren A.
Lindquist, Warren T.
Lively, Gail L.
McCabe, Carol
McNeirney, James A.
Maxim, John A. Jr.
Mays, Ben
Miller, Albert M.
Mimna, Curtis John
Murphy, Edward J.
Newson, Darryl Charles
O'Connor, Thomas J.
Persil, Herbert G.
Pratt, Richard T.
Ratner, Gershon M.
Reese, Rostelle J. Jr.
St. Lawrence, Charles V.
Sloame, Stuart
Solomon, Gerald
Strauss, Joseph
Tilley, Jon
Van Lowe, William T.
Vartanian, Thomas P.
Waker, Gordon
Whiteside, William A.
Wilson, Lance H.

Owner/Investor
Abbott, Edward L.
Bechhoefer, Ina S.
Berger, Bruce
Blake, Stephen H.
Brooks, Kenneth Donald
Carroll, John C.
Crawford, H. R.
Davis, Frederick W.
Fasano, Michael V.
Ferguson, Lewis H. III
Gambrill, J. Matthew
Gillies, Roderick M.
Gimbert, Clement H.
Griffin, Mark Gerard
Harris, John A.
Hoffman, William H.
Howard, Daggett H.
Israel, Gary M.
Johnson, R. Bruce
Libby, Howard A.
Luck, James S.
Lustgarten, Stephen F.
McClure, Roger J.
McCray, Joe Richard
Mays, Ben
Moore, William C.
Murphy, Neil
Newson, Darryl Charles
Noonan, Patrick F.
O'Neill, John T.
Pohoryles, Louis
Reese, Rostelle J. Jr.
Roebuck, Thurman M.
Shanks, Alexander Graham
Siler, Robert W. Jr.
West, Joseph Frederick
Zuniga, Thomas M.

Property Manager
Brady, George M. Jr.
Bresler, Charles S.
Bryan, Alonzo J. Jr.
Chism, Earl
Cottle, J. Michael
Crawford, H. R.
Crump, G. Lindsay
Davis, Frederick W.
DeFranceaux, George W.
Eames, Gary A.
Ehn, C. Lennart
Fasano, Michael V.
Foster, Ruth E.
Gillies, Roderick M.
Gimbert, Clement H.
Harris, John A.
Hiban, Arthur W.
Howard, Daggett H.
Hutchinson, Gary E.
Izaguirre, Andrew
Johnson, R. Bruce
Libby, Howard A.
Lustgarten, Stephen F.
McClinton, Mr. Jr.
McCray, Joe Richard
Mays, Ben
Murray, Joseph C.
Newson, Darryl Charles
O'Neill, John T.
Stoll, Edwin L.
Taylor, David P. Sr.

Real Estate Publisher
Byran, Jack H.
Casazza, John
Eden, Ernie
Elmendorf, C. Lindsay
Gerecht, Ash
Hanes, Mildred
Oman, Roy Erik
Pohoryles, Louis
Regardie, William
Roth, Peggy
Smart, Eric
Smith, Jeanette
Stough, R. Maxine
West, Joseph Frederick

Regulator
Abrams, Philip
Bollinger, Stephen J.
Bryan, Alonzo J. Jr.
Dolbeare, Cushing N. Ms.
Monroig, Antonio
O'Neill, John T.
Pierce, Samuel Riley Jr.
Reider, Jeffrey R.
Sauerbrunn, Kathleen H.
Savas, E.S.
Schaefer, Gene R.

Syndicator
Avery, Cyrus Stevens II
Berger, Bruce
Boyle, M. Ross
Brady, George M. Jr.
Bresler, Charles S.
Crump, G. Lindsay
Davis, Frederick W.
Eames, Gary A.
Ferguson, Lewis H. III
Griffin, Mark Gerard
Howard, Daggett H.
Johnson, R. Bruce
McClinton, Mr. Jr.
McCray, Joe Richard
Murphy, Neil
Sherburne, Mary L.
Stoll, Edwin L.
Zuniga, Thomas M.

FLORIDA

FORT MYERS

Appraiser
Jackson, Steven L.
Llewellyn, Leonard F.
Maxwell, W. Michael
Robbins, Richard W.
Sanderson, William H.
Schieber, Frank W.
Smith, Walter James

Attorney
Grant, Richard C.
McKinley, Michael R.
Neinas, Bob

Banker
Obley, Ross P.

Broker
Conn, David
Conroy, John T. Jr.
Donelson, F.M.
Dunn, Larry B.
Ericksen, Grover G.
Fowler, James T.
Gessling, Donald C.
Llewellyn, Leonard F.
Robbins, Richard W.
Roberts, Donald H.
Sanderson, William H.
Schieber, Frank W.
Smith, Walter James
Troutman, C. Bruce
Verona, Pasquale A.
Wickstrand, R. Richard

Builder
Donelson, F.M.
Dunn, Larry B.
Komito, Donald H.
Obley, Ross P.
Robbins, Richard W.
Troutman, C. Bruce
Wickstrand, R. Richard

Consultant
Donelson, F.M.
Dunn, Larry B.
Fowler, James T.
Komito, Donald H.
Llewellyn, Leonard F.
Robbins, Richard W.
Roberts, Donald H.
Sanderson, William H.
Schieber, Frank W.
Smith, Walter James
Troutman, C. Bruce

Developer
Conroy, John T. Jr.
Donelson, F.M.
Dunn, Larry B.
Ericksen, Grover G.
Leeds, A. Hobart
Llewellyn, Leonard F.
Obley, Ross P.
Robbins, Richard W.
Roberts, Donald H.
Smith, Walter James
Troutman, C. Bruce
Trowbridge, Keith W.
Verona, Pasquale A.
Wickstrand, R. Richard

Engineer
Komito, Donald H.
Obley, Ross P.

Instructor
Conn, David
Conroy, John T. Jr.
Schieber, Frank W.

Lender
Roberts, Donald H.

Owner/Investor
Conroy, John T. Jr.
Dunn, Larry B.
Fowler, James T.
Hall, Charles E.
Leeds, A. Hobart
Obley, Ross P.
Robbins, Richard W.
Roberts, Donald H.
Schieber, Frank W.
Smith, Walter James
Verona, Pasquale A.

Property Manager
Conroy, John T. Jr.
Fowler, James T.
Robbins, Richard W.
Roberts, Donald H.
Smith, Walter James
Verona, Pasquale A.
Wickstrand, R. Richard

Syndicator
Conroy, John T. Jr.
Donelson, F.M.
Dunn, Larry B.
Roberts, Donald H.
Sanderson, William H.
Schieber, Frank W.
Smith, Walter James
Troutman, C. Bruce
Verona, Pasquale A.
Wickstrand, R. Richard

GAINESVILLE

Appraiser
Albright, Stephen J.
Dobson, Tom W.
Kampe, Otto H.
Ring, Alfred A.

Attorney
Bouland, John T.
Currier, Barry Arthur

Banker
Dobson, Tom W.

Broker
Baur, Edward O.
Densmore, Thomas H.
Dobson, Tom W.
Gabbard, Thomas L.
Jones, Verna N.
Ritch, Sanford E.
Rudnianyn, John S.
Steinberg, Michael L.

Consultant
Gabbard, Thomas L.
Ring, Alfred A.
Ritch, Sanford E.
Rudnianyn, John S.
Smith, Halbert C.
Steinberg, Michael L.

Developer
Rudnianyn, John S.
Steinberg, Michael L.

Instructor
Currier, Barry Arthur
Ring, Alfred A.
Ritch, Sanford E.
Smith, Halbert C.

Insuror
Dobson, Tom W.

Owner/Investor
Baur, Edward O.
Densmore, Thomas H.
Rudnianyn, John S.
Steinberg, Michael L.

Property Manager
Steinberg, Michael L.

Real Estate Publisher
Ring, Alfred A.

Regulator
Bernhardt, Richard Charles

Syndicator
Baur, Edward O.
Rudnianyn, John S.

JACKSONVILLE

Appraiser
Akin, Paul R.
Durrett, John Richard Jr.
Harper, James M.
Hollis, Austin O. Jr.
Johnson, Philip M.
Osborn, Frank K.
Rogers, Henry
Root, David R.
Thal, Robert W.
Weisser, Herman M.
Workman, Bob D.

Architect
Leto, David D.
Zeller, Emilio III

Attorney
Commander, Charles E. III
Hughes, J. Michael
Keefe, Kenneth M. Jr.
Leto, David D.
Poucher, Allen L. Jr.
Regier, Jarold W.
Selber, Marilyn Golomb
Taylor, James S.

Banker
Commander, Charles E. III
Sebesta, James A.
Thal, Robert W.

Broker
Agresti, Gerald R.
Akin, Paul R.
Antonich, M. Betty
Baker, James D. Jr.

Biro, Michael V.
Citrano, James P.
Cook, George W.
Crews, William C.
Dukelow, William H.
Durrett, John Richard Jr.
Giagnocavo, J. Gregory
Harper, James M.
Heise, G. Fred
Hollis, Austin O. Jr.
Koelker, Donald R.
Kornblum, Eugene Harold
Leto, David D.
Lichtigman, Charles S.
Linville, George
Lucas, Michael J. Jr.
Means, William V. II
Register, Sidney W Jr.
Rogers, Henry
Rukab, Tony
Sebesta, James A.
Silverfield, Gary Daniel
Thal, Robert W.
Townsend, J.L.
Weber, Lawrence K. Jr.
Weisser, Herman M.
Werner, Mark A.
Wood, Betty K.
Workman, Bob D.

Builder
Agresti, Gerald R.
Biro, Michael V.
Cook, George W.
Crews, William C.
Hollis, Austin O. Jr.
Jarnagin, Bruce A.
Leto, David D.
Lichtigman, Charles S.
McCain, David W.
Sebesta, James A.
Wolff, A. Daniel III

Consultant
Abstein, J. Bart
Akin, Paul R.
Antonich, M. Betty
Citrano, James P.
Commander, Charles E. III
Harper, James M.
Heise, G. Fred
Hollis, Austin O. Jr.
Jarnagin, Bruce A.
Johnson, Philip M.
Kornblum, Eugene Harold
Luke, Henry
Osborn, Frank K.
Sebesta, James A.
Thal, Robert W.
Weber, Lawrence K. Jr.
Weisser, Herman M.
Workman, Bob D.

Developer
Abstein, J. Bart
Agresti, Gerald R.
Antonich, M. Betty
Biro, Michael V.
Citrano, James P.
Commander, Charles E. III
Cook, George W.
Durrett, John Richard Jr.
Giagnocavo, J. Gregory
Goldstein, Barry J.
Hammes, David C.
Heise, G. Fred
Hollis, Austin O. Jr.
Irving, David M.
Jarnagin, Bruce A.
Koelker, Donald R.
Leto, David D.
Lichtigman, Charles S.
McCain, David W.
Morton, Walt
Poucher, Allen L. Jr.
Rogers, Henry
Root, David R.
Salowe, Allen E.
Sebesta, James A.
Silverfield, Gary Daniel
Sisk, John K.
Townsend, J.L.
Webb, William C. Jr.
Weber, Lawrence K. Jr.
Weisser, Herman M.
Wolff, A. Daniel III

Engineer
Mangu, John Jr.
Register, Sidney W Jr.

Instructor
Crews, William C.
Koelker, Donald R.
Kornblum, Eugene Harold
Means, William V. II
Workman, Bob D.

Insuror
Thal, Robert W.
Townsend, J.L.

Lender
Thal, Robert W.
Weisser, Herman M.

Owner/Investor
Abstein, J. Bart
Antonich, M. Betty
Citrano, James P.
Commander, Charles E. III
Giagnocavo, J. Gregory
Heise, G. Fred
Jarnagin, Bruce A.
Koelker, Donald R.
Kornblum, Eugene Harold
Leto, David D.
Lichtigman, Charles S.
Means, William V. II
Register, Sidney W Jr.
Sebesta, James A.
Taylor, James S.
Townsend, J.L.
Weber, Lawrence K. Jr.
Weisser, Herman M.
Wood, Betty K.

Property Manager
Antonich, M. Betty
Baker, James D. Jr.
Citrano, James P.
Commander, Charles E. III
Crews, William C.
Davis, W.R.
Donnell, Jack
Heise, G. Fred
Kornblum, Eugene Harold
Leto, David D.
Lichtigman, Charles S.
McCain, David W.
Register, Sidney W Jr.
Sachs, Gary Allen
Sebesta, James A.
Sutton, Berrien D.
Veatch, Stanley T. Jr.
Warnock, Harvey K.
Weber, Lawrence K. Jr.

Real Estate Publisher
Workman, Bob D.

Regulator
Durrett, John Richard Jr.
Leto, David D.

Syndicator
Antonich, M. Betty
Commander, Charles E. III
Giagnocavo, J. Gregory
Koelker, Donald R.
Rogers, Henry
Townsend, J.L.
Werner, Mark A.

LAKELAND

Appraiser
Biggs, Hubbard K.
Brennan, John B.
Johnson, Richard D.
Napoletan, Joseph A.
Sherwood, Robert E.
Smith, George R.

Attorney
Miller, Robert T.

Broker
Biggs, Hubbard K.
Brennan, John B.
Johnson, Richard D.
Loftin, William H.
Napoletan, Joseph A.
Pines, J.
Sherwood, Robert E.
Smith, George R.

Builder
Loftin, William H.
Napoletan, Joseph A.
Sherwood, Robert E.
Tobler, August F.

Consultant
Biggs, Hubbard K.
Brennan, John B.
Sherwood, Robert E.

Developer
Loftin, William H.
Pines, J.
Sherwood, Robert E.
Tobler, August F.

Insuror
Smith, George R.

Owner/Investor
Loftin, William H.
Napoletan, Joseph A.
Pines, J.
Smith, George R.
Tobler, August F.

Property Manager
Loftin, William H.
Napoletan, Joseph A.
Pines, J.

MIAMI

Appraiser
Ames, Ronald
Arman, Henry A.
Bailey, Charles Williams
Barrett, Frederick R.
Blazejack, John A.
Braun, Franz R.
Cabrera, Roger A.
Cannon, Michael Y.
Cantwell, Stephen M.
Chesler, Earl R.
Cohen, Jordan S.
Cross, Timothy D.
Daniels, Fred Peter
Danner, John C.
Failla, Charles Vincent
Feinstein, Edward
Feraco, Ray Jr.
Funt, Harold
Gasperoni, Emil Sr.
Giddens, Earle A.
Gold, Seymour B.
Goldman, Aaron
Griffith, Christopher G.
Gurwitch, Harry
Hektner, George W.
Johnson, R. Grant
Jones, Michael J.
Lawhorn, Jess S.
Maehl, Gary O.
Maier, Walter A.
Martens, Frank H.
Mullen, Elmer A.
Neumann, Mark
Orloff, Allen D.
Pace, James G.
Palomaros, Larenzo J.
Pendleton, Lawrence R.
Platt, Norman
Randall, David
Rouse, Richard C.
Sahagian, Ted
Scott, Mae Rankin
Smith, William B.
Sutte, Donald T.
Thompson, Loren L.
Underwood, John R. Jr.
Wardell, Harry E.
Weiner, Vic
Wilson, Stanley Alexander

Architect
Buigas, Octavio D.
Deen, James
Freimor, Jack
Grau, Franklin E.
Greene, Stanley H.
Warburton, Ralph

Assessor
Gurwitch, Harry
Neumann, Mark
Wilson, Stanley Alexander

Attorney
Ackman, Kenneth A.
Adams, Daniel L.
Aguilera, Guido A.
Albion, Donald L.
Alpert, Maurice D.
Aresty, Joel M.
Berger, Donald E.
Berley, David R.
Bittel, Jordan
Capp, Alvin
Cardenas, Al
Chowning, John S.
Darrow, Kenneth F.
Drucker, A. Norman
Durham, James F. II
Edelman, Gilbert Esquire
Essner, Gene
Feinberg, Jeffrey
Firtel, Irving
Fox, Arthur E.
Grimm, W. Thomas
Gross, Jerry A.
Hoffman, Stuart K.
Holcomb, Lyle Donald Jr.
Holmes, David F.
Jacobson, Bernard
Jannen, Kenneth R.
Jordan, Robert K.
Kelly, Timothy Charles
Kennedy, Wallace W.
Keys, Carol Frances
Kniskern, Joseph Warren
Layne, B.J.
Lewis, Richard C.
Lexa, Joseph J.
Loevin, Robert H.
Ludovici, Philip F.
Markus, Andrew Joshua
Mudd, John P.
Pace, James G.
Pardillo, Armando A.
Pearson, John E.
Perlstein, Mitchell L.
Reiseman, Harvey I.
Ringel, Thomas
Rosen, Lawrence N.
Rubin, Carolyn
Rush, Fred L.
Russo, Edmund Peter
Sadock, James Jr.
Schechter, Stuart A.
Schiefelbein, Wayne L.
Shaw, David M.
Shevin, Arnold D.

Silber, Norman J.
Silver, Bernard F.
Solomon, Douglas P.
Stern, Stuart I.
Sutton, John O.
Sward, John Erick
Tompkins, Thomas F.
Traub, Eric A.
Weber, William A.
Wepman, Warren S.
Wolfson, Bernard
Zelman, Richard M.

Banker
Aguilera, Guido A.
Brett, Carl N.
Doerr, Marga E.
Epter, Bernard A.
Feinstein, Edward
Griffith, Christopher G.
Lawhorn, Jess S.
Layne, B.J.
Neff, Edward R.
Raduns, Edward B.
Riley, Edward J.
Scott, Mae Rankin
Thompson, Loren L.

Broker
Ackman, Kenneth A.
Albin, Mac
Alpert, Maurice D.
Aresty, Joel M.
Arman, Henry A.
Bailey, Charles Williams
Braun, Franz R.
Buigas, Octavio D.
Cabrera, Roger A.
Campbell, J. Thomas
Cannon, Michael Y.
Carter, Doris V.
Christopher, Michael C.
Cross, Timothy D.
Daniels, Fred Peter
Danner, John C.
Davis, Alan J.
Eisinger, Errol
Firtel, Irving
Firth, Malcolm
Frank, Stephen
Freeman, Jeffrey Bruce
Gelina, Maurice R.
Gold, Seymour B.
Goldman, Aaron
Greene, Sheldon
Griffith, Christopher G.
Gross, Norman S.
Harper, Allen C.
Harrison, Peter R.
Hausman, Sidney
Hayaud Din, M.A.
Hektner, George W.
Johnson, Theodore Karl
Jones, Michael J.
Jones, Walter I.
Judd, L. Coleman (L. C. Judd)
Katz, Richard J.
Killins, Thomas H.
Klock, Joseph P.
Kuhn, John F. Sr.
Lehrer, Paul
Lipsick, David M.
Litowitz, Budd
Lowell, Jack
Luck, Richard S.
Ludovici, Philip F.
McCarty, Arlon R.
Maier, Walter A.
Martens, Frank H.
Moses, Arthur L.
Neff, Edward R.
Nestor, Brenda
Nierenberg, Norman M.
Orloff, Allen D.
Pace, James G.
Palomaros, Larenzo J.
Pendleton, Lawrence R.
Pigna, Franc Joseph
Platt, Norman
Politis, John
Rakusin, Beatryce
Randall, David
Rosado, Jose F.
Rosen, Kenneth D.
Rosen, Lawrence N.
Rosenthal, Stanley R.
Sahagian, Ted
St. Laurent, Louis S. II
Salas, Nestor A.
Schaub, James K.
Shepard, Edward F.
Sisler, Gary
Smith, Ivan J.
Solomon, Douglas P.
Speizer, Harry
Springer, Jean R.
Stern, Stuart I.
Streich, Richard G.
Sunday, Sam B.
Tamayo, Joseph L.
Tanzer, Milt
Thompson, Loren L.
Tiemeyer, Theodore N.
Tobin, Jack B.
Vengoechea, Nilsa De
Wainberg, Alan
Wardell, Harry E.
Weidenfeld, Harvey M.
Weiner, Vic
West, MacDonald

Builder
Arias, Antonio
Armstrong, J.
Berger, Herman M.
Brooke, Joseph A. Jr.
Brooks, C. Donald
Buigas, Octavio D.
Cabrera, Roger A.
Campbell, J. Thomas
Cohen, Jerome J.
Elwood, James C.
Funt, Harold
Gale, Robert J.
Goihman, David
Goldman, Aaron
Greene, Stanley H.
Harper, Allen C.
Jones, Walter I.
Kornmeier, Richard
Levine, Lawrence A.
Lewis, Thomas E.
Loevin, Robert H.
Miot, Sanford B.
Mudd, John P.
Mullen, Elmer A.
Newbery, Donald A.
Pace, James G.
Pigna, Franc Joseph
Platt, Norman
Randall, David
Reagan, Ray
Riley, Edward J.
Rosenthal, Stanley R.
Sibley, Harper Jr.
Smith, Charles G. Jr.
Speizer, Harry
Suarez, Michael A.
Sutte, Donald T.
Thompson, Loren L.

Consultant
Alpert, Maurice D.
Arias, Antonio
Armstrong, J.
Behar, Larry J.
Bittel, Jordan
Blazejack, John A.
Braun, Franz R.
Buigas, Octavio D.
Cabrera, Roger A.
Cannon, Michael Y.
Cantwell, Stephen M.
Carter, Doris V.
Chasick, Douglas D.
Chesler, Earl R.
Clouser, John R.
Cohen, Jordan S.
Cross, Timothy D.
Daniels, Fred Peter
Davis, Alan J.
Deen, James
Feinstein, Edward
Feraco, Ray Jr.
Firtel, Irving
Frank, Stephen
Gelina, Maurice R.
Giddens, Earle A.
Goihman, David
Gold, Seymour B.
Goldman, Aaron
Grau, Franklin E.
Greenman, Andrew B.
Griffith, Christopher G.
Gross, Norman S.
Gurwitch, Harry
Harper, Allen C.
Harris, Robert S.
Hausman, Sidney
Hayes, Kerry
Hektner, George W.
Holeman, Jack R.
Jacobson, Bernard
Johnson, Theodore Karl
Jones, Michael J.
Jones, Walter I.
Katz, Richard J.
Klock, Joseph P.
Kniskern, Joseph Warren
Kornmeier, Richard
Kuhn, John F. Sr.
Litowitz, Budd
Lowell, Jack
Ludovici, Philip F.
Maier, Walter A.
Martens, Frank H.
Mullen, Elmer A.
Nestor, Brenda
Nierenberg, Norman M.
Palomaros, Larenzo J.
Pendleton, Lawrence R.
Randall, David
Reagan, Ray
Rosado, Jose F.
Rosen, Lawrence N.
Rouse, Richard C.
St. Laurent, Louis S. II
Salas, Nestor A.
Schechter, Stuart A.
Shepard, Edward F.
Silver, Bernard F.
Sisler, Gary
Smith, William B.
Speizer, Harry
Sunday, Sam B.
Sutte, Donald T.
Tanzer, Milt
Thompson, Loren L.
Tiemeyer, Theodore N.
Underwood, John R. Jr.
Vengoechea, Nilsa De
Warburton, Ralph
Weiner, Vic
White, L. Keith
Wilson, Stanley Alexander

Developer
Albion, Donald L.
Alpert, Maurice D.
Anderson, John H.
Arias, Antonio
Arman, Henry A.
Armstrong, J.
Berger, Donald E.
Berger, Herman M.
Braun, Franz R.
Brooke, Joseph A. Jr.
Brooks, C. Donald
Browne, Donald K.
Buigas, Octavio D.
Cabrera, Roger A.
Campbell, J. Thomas
Christopher, Michael C.
Cohen, Jerome J.
Cross, Timothy D.
Deen, James
Dressler, David C. Jr.
Eisinger, Errol
Elwood, James C.
Feinstein, Edward
Firth, Malcolm
Funt, Harold
Gale, Robert J.
Garfield, Joseph A.
Gasperoni, Emil Sr.
Goihman, David
Goldman, Aaron
Gonsalves, Jose Antero
Greene, Stanley H.
Gross, Jerry A.
Gross, Norman S.
Harper, Allen C.
Hayaud Din, M.A.
Jacobson, Bernard
Johnson, R. Grant
Katz, Richard J.
Kornmeier, Richard
Kuhn, John F. Sr.
Lehrer, Paul
Levine, Lawrence A.
Lewis, Thomas E.
Lipsick, David M.
Litewitz, Robert
Litowitz, Budd
Loevin, Robert H.
Mendelson, Laurans A.
Miot, Sanford B.
Morley, Nicholas H.
Moses, Arthur L.
Mudd, John P.
Mullen, Elmer A.
Nestor, Brenda
Nierenberg, Norman M.
Owens, Stephen L.
Pace, James G.
Palomaros, Larenzo J.
Peden, Katherine
Pigna, Franc Joseph
Randall, David
Reagan, Ray
Riley, Edward J.
Rosen, Kenneth D.
Rosen, Lawrence N.
Rosenthal, Stanley R.
Sahagian, Ted
St. Laurent, Louis S. II
Schaub, James K.
Schmitz, John W.
Sibley, Harper Jr.
Silver, Bernard F.
Sisler, Gary
Smith, Charles G. Jr.
Smith, Ivan J.
Speizer, Harry
Stern, Stuart I.
Suarez, Michael A.
Sunday, Sam B.
Sutte, Donald T.
Thompson, Loren L.
Tiemeyer, Theodore N.
Wardell, Harry E.
Weiss, Jeffrey J.
West, MacDonald
Wilson, Stanley Alexander
Wolfson, Bernard

Engineer
Buigas, Octavio D.
Goldman, Aaron
Harris, Robert S.
Hektner, George W.

Newbery, Donald A.
Randall, David
Suarez, Michael A.
Wainberg, Alan
Warburton, Ralph

Instructor
Ackman, Kenneth A.
Bittel, Jordan
Capp, Alvin
Chasick, Douglas D.
Clouser, John R.
Danner, John C.
Feinstein, Edward
Gold, Seymour B.
Gurwitch, Harry
Holeman, Jack R.
Johnson, Theodore Karl
Kennedy, Wallace W.
Kliston, Theodore S.
Klock, Joseph P.
Ludovici, Philip F.
Maier, Walter A.
Martens, Frank H.
Mullen, Elmer A.
Palomaros, Larenzo J.
Pendleton, Lawrence R.
Sutte, Donald T.
Thompson, Loren L.
Weiner, Vic

Insuror
Buigas, Octavio D.
Jones, Walter I.
Kelly, Timothy Charles
Papazickos, Chris G.
Randall, David
Springer, Jean R.

Lender
Aguilera, Guido A.
Ames, Ronald
Blazejack, John A.
Braun, Franz R.
Brett, Carl N.
Buigas, Octavio D.
Doerr, Marga E.
Feinstein, Edward
Freimor, Jack
Gold, Seymour B.
Goldman, Aaron
Griffith, Christopher G.
Jacobson, Bernard
Kliston, Theodore S.
Lawhorn, Jess S.
Neff, Edward R.
Orloff, Allen D.
Riley, Edward J.
Rouse, Richard C.
Scott, Mae Rankin
Silver, Bernard F.
Smith, Ivan J.
Smith, William B.
Weiner, Vic

Owner/Investor
Albin, Mac
Albion, Donald L.
Aresty, Joel M.
Arias, Antonio
Arman, Henry A.
Bailey, Charles Williams
Berger, Herman M.
Blumberg, David
Browne, Donald K.
Buigas, Octavio D.
Campbell, J. Thomas
Capp, Alvin
Clancy, Peter J.
Cohen, Jordan S.
Cross, Timothy D.
Danner, John C.
Davis, Alan J.
Deen, James
Drath, Richard
Eisinger, Errol
Feinstein, Edward
Firth, Malcolm
Frank, Stephen
Gasperoni, Emil Sr.
Gelina, Maurice R.
Goihman, David
Goldman, Aaron
Gross, Jerry A.
Gross, Norman S.
Gurwitch, Harry
Hausman, Sidney
Hayaud Din, M.A.
Johnson, R. Grant
Jones, Michael J.
Karlton, John S.
Kennedy, Wallace W.
Killins, Thomas H.
Kliston, Theodore S.
Kornmeier, Richard
Kuhn, John F. Sr.
Levine, Lawrence A.
Lewis, Thomas E.
Lipsick, David M.
Luck, Richard S.
Ludovici, Philip F.
McCarty, Arlon R.
Maier, Walter A.
Martens, Frank H.
Maynard, Carl K.
Morgan, G. Edward
Mudd, John P.
Nestor, Brenda
Newbery, Donald A.
Nierenberg, Norman M.
Orloff, Allen D.
Owens, Stephen L.
Pendleton, Lawrence R.
Pigna, Franc Joseph
Randall, David
Rosado, Jose F.
Rosen, Kenneth D.
Rosen, Lawrence N.
Russo, Edmund Peter
Sahagian, Ted
Salas, Nestor A.
Schechter, Stuart A.
Schmitz, John W.
Schweiger, H. Denny
Shepard, Edward F.
Sibley, Harper Jr.
Sisler, Gary
Speizer, Harry
Spitz, Fred M.
Springer, Jean R.
Stern, Stuart I.
Suarez, Michael A.
Sunday, Sam B.
Sutte, Donald T.
Thompson, Loren L.
Tiemeyer, Theodore N.
Tobin, Jack B.
Vengoechea, Nilsa De
Wainberg, Alan
Wardell, Harry E.
Wasch, Joseph c.
Weida, Richard P.
Weiss, Jeffrey J.
Wolfson, Bernard
Zelman, Richard M.

Property Manager
Albin, Mac
Arias, Antonio
Arman, Henry A.
Bailey, Charles Williams
Berger, Herman M.
Britton, Willard B.
Brooke, Joseph A. Jr.
Browne, Donald K.
Buigas, Octavio D.
Cabrera, Roger A.
Cannon, Michael Y.
Carter, Doris V.
Chasick, Douglas D.
Clouser, John R.
Cohen, Jerome J.
Cross, Timothy D.
Danner, John C.
Eisinger, Errol
Feinstein, Edward
Firth, Malcolm
Funt, Harold
Gasperoni, Emil Sr.
Goihman, David
Gross, Norman S.
Harper, Allen C.
Holeman, Jack R.
Jacobs, L.W.
Johnson, R. Grant
Jones, Michael J.
Jones, Walter I.
Katz, Richard J.
Killins, Thomas H.
Kornmeier, Richard
LaRue, Clifford G.
Levine, Lawrence A.
Lipsick, David M.
Litewitz, Robert
Litowitz, Budd
Lowell, Jack
Ludovici, Philip F.
McCarty, Arlon R.
Martens, Frank H.
Miller, Tanfield C.
Mudd, John P.
Nestor, Brenda
Nierenberg, Norman M.
Orloff, Allen D.
Owens, Stephen L.
Palomaros, Larenzo J.
Pendleton, Lawrence R.
Platt, Norman
Randall, David
Reagan, Ray
Rosen, Lawrence N.
Sahagian, Ted
Salas, Nestor A.
Schmitz, John W.
Sears, Warren
Sibley, Harper Jr.
Sisler, Gary
Spitz, Fred M.
Tiemeyer, Theodore N.
Tobin, Jack B.
Underwood, John R. Jr.
Wardell, Harry E.
Wasch, Joseph c.
Weiner, Vic
West, MacDonald
Zelinslee, Robert

Real Estate Publisher
Browne, Donald K.
Cannon, Michael Y.
Schiefelbein, Wayne L.
Thompson, Loren L.

Regulator
Armstrong, J.
Harris, Robert S.
Schiefelbein, Wayne L.

Syndicator
Aresty, Joel M.
Arman, Henry A.
Christopher, Michael C.
Cohen, Jordan S.
Cross, Timothy D.
Davis, Alan J
Eisinger, Errol
Feinstein, Edward
Gasperoni, Emil Sr.
Goihman, David
Goldman, Aaron
Gross, Norman S.
Habif, Moreno
Harrison, Peter R.
Hausman, Sidney
Holeman, Jack R.
Jones, Michael J.
Karlton, John S.
Kelly, Timothy Charles
Kuhn, John F. Sr.
Lipsick, David M.
Mudd, John P.
Nierenberg, Norman M.
Pigna, Franc Joseph
Randall, David
Reiseman, Harvey I.
Rosen, Lawrence N.
Sahagian, Ted
Schmitz, John W.
Shepard, Edward F.
Simmer, Barry
Sisler, Gary
Smith, Ivan J.
Solomon, Douglas P.
Speizer, Harry
Spitz, Fred M.
Stern, Stuart I.
Suarez, Michael A.
Sutte, Donald T.
Thompson, Loren L.
Tiemeyer, Theodore N.
Tobin, Jack B.
Wardell, Harry E.
Wasch, Joseph c.
Weiner, Vic
Wilson, Stanley Alexander
Wolfson, Bernard

ORLANDO

Appraiser
Armfield, Peter D.
Atkins, Cleve L.
Curry, Paul L.
Kurras, J. Fred
Moore, John J. III
Pardue, William Pierce Jr.
Sherman, John S. Jr.

Architect
Rose, J.G.
Scott, Raymond L.
Weiss, K. Brooks

Assessor
Moline, Jack D.

Attorney
Brown, C. David II
Clayton, Kenneth M.
Daze, Douglas Edward
Hanley, Michael J.
Houser, William J.
Infantino, Thomas V.
Massey, Gary E.
Meade, James Monroe
Reber, John C.
Sears, James W.
Terry, David E.
Wattles, Bob
White, Daniel O.

Banker
Hunnicutt, Richard D.

Broker
Ariko, John G. Jr.
Atkins, Cleve L.
Banks, Douglas T.
Bergman, Edward Jr.
Bryan, Robert L.
Buxton, Brian P.
Cairnes, William D.
Curry, Paul L.
Davids, Timothy J.
Gaich, Michael G.
Gale, Jack L.
Gunter, Howard M. Jr.
Hauck, Adam L.
Hickman, J.W.
Houser, William J.
Hunter, William A.
Infantino, Thomas V.
Jaye, Carroll B.
Kinyon, Betty C.
McGee, Walter T.
Martin, John (Jack) C.

Miller, Julianne
Moline, Jack D.
Morse, Thomas E.
Muller, Henry J.
Pardue, William Pierce Jr.
Phillips, Roger Van Dorn
Pomp, Howard
Risner, Willie R.
Russell, James E. Jr.
Sherman, John S. Jr.
Stewart, Susan Hastings
Strickland, Wilbur H.
Tauscher, Don W.
Underill, H.J. III
Waters, Paul W.
Wilson, James T.
Yeager, Gerald F.

Builder
Ariko, John G. Jr.
Hickman, J.W.
Houser, William J.
Martin, John (Jack) C.
Moline, Jack D.
Muller, Henry J.
Palmer, Charles B.
Pomp, Howard
Rose, J.G.
Russell, James E. Jr.
Yeager, Gerald F.

Consultant
Ariko, John G. Jr.
Armfield, Peter D.
Bergman, Edward Jr.
Bryan, Robert L.
Buxton, Brian P.
Canin, Brian C.
Curry, Paul L.
Davids, Timothy J.
Daze, Douglas Edward
Gaich, Michael G.
Gale, Jack L.
Hadley, Joann Jody
Hauck, Adam L.
Hunter, William A.
Jaye, Carroll B.
Kinyon, Betty C.
Kurras, J. Fred
McGee, Walter T.
Moline, Jack D.
Moore, John J. III
Morse, Thomas E.
Muller, Henry J.
Palmer, Charles B.
Pardue, William Pierce Jr.
Phillips, Roger Van Dorn
Pomp, Howard
Schultheis, Ralph William Jr.
Scott, Raymond L.
Strickland, Wilbur H.
Tauscher, Don W.
Waters, Paul W.
Wattles, Bob
Weiss, K. Brooks
White, Daniel O.
Yeager, Gerald F.

Developer
Ammerman, Don
Atkins, Cleve L.
Bryan, Robert L.
Davids, Timothy J.
Gaich, Michael G.
Harkins, Richard C.
Hickman, J.W.
Houser, William J.
Hunter, William A.
Infantino, Thomas V.
Lawing, Alvin L. Jr.
McGee, Walter T.
Martin, John (Jack) C.
Massey, Gary E.
Moline, Jack D.
Morse, Thomas E.
Muller, Henry J.
Palmer, Charles B.
Pomp, Howard
Ray, Michael L.
Rogers, R. Julian
Rose, J.G.
Rose, Michael L.
Russell, James E. Jr.
Scott, Raymond L.
Underill, H.J. III
Wattles, Bob
Weiss, K. Brooks
White, Daniel O.
Yeager, Gerald F.

Engineer
Davids, Timothy J.
Moline, Jack D.

Instructor
Armfield, Peter D.
Cairnes, William D.
Dalton, David W.
Gale, Jack L.
Gunter, Howard M. Jr.
Infantino, Thomas V.
Moore, John J. III
Pardue, William Pierce Jr.
Phillips, Roger Van Dorn
Scott, Raymond L.
Sherman, John S. Jr.
Tauscher, Don W.
Underill, H.J. III
Wilson, James T.

Insuror
Ariko, John G. Jr.
Hadley, Joann Jody
Martin, John (Jack) C.

Lender
Curry, Paul L.
Wilson, James T.

Owner/Investor
Ariko, John G. Jr.
Atkins, Cleve L.
Bergman, Edward Jr.
Bryan, Robert L.
Buxton, Brian P.
Clayton, Kenneth M.
Davids, Timothy J.
Gaich, Michael G.
Gale, Jack L.
Harkins, Richard C.
Hickman, J.W.
Infantino, Thomas V.
Kinyon, Betty C.
Lawing, Alvin L. Jr.
McGee, Walter T.
Massey, Gary E.
Moline, Jack D.
Palmer, Charles B.
Rose, J.G.
Russell, James E. Jr.
Schultheis, Ralph William Jr.
Scott, Raymond L.
Tauscher, Don W.
Underill, H.J. III
Waters, Paul W.
Wattles, Bob
Weiss, K. Brooks
White, Daniel O.
Yeager, Gerald F.

Property Manager
Ariko, John G. Jr.
Bryan, Robert L.
Buxton, Brian P.
Davids, Timothy J.
Gaich, Michael G.
Hadley, Joann Jody
Haering, Joseph
Harkins, Richard C.
Hickman, J.W.
Houser, William J.
Hunter, William A.
Jaye, Carroll B.
McGee, Walter T.
Moline, Jack D.
Moore, John J. III
Morse, Thomas E.
Phillips, Roger Van Dorn
Risner, Willie R.
Rose, J.G.
Rose, Michael L.
Russell, James E. Jr.
Scott, Raymond L.
Stafford, C.B.
Wilson, James T.

Real Estate Publisher
Biddle, J. Craig
Gale, Jack L.
Prizer, E.L.
Yeager, Gerald F.

Regulator
Scott, Raymond L.

Syndicator
Ariko, John G. Jr.
Atkins, Cleve L.
Dalton, David W.
Davids, Timothy J.
Gaich, Michael G.
Harkins, Richard C.
Hauck, Adam L.
Houser, William J.
Infantino, Thomas V.
McGee, Walter T.
Morse, Thomas E.
Muller, Henry J.
Palmer, Charles B.
Schultheis, Ralph William Jr.
Scott, Raymond L.
Underill, H.J. III
Wattles, Bob
Yeager, Gerald F.

PANAMA CITY

Appraiser
Vaughn, Rufus C.

Broker
Goodman, William G.

Lender
Vaughn, Rufus C.

Owner/Investor
Goodman, William G.

Property Manager
Goodman, William G.
McLean, Kenneth E.

PENSACOLA

Appraiser
Cottrell, Dudley P.
Hart, R. Morey

Architect
Bullock, Ellis W. Jr.

Attorney
LiBeris, Charles S.

Broker
Bethea, Basil L. Jr.
Ferguson, Ronald C.
Hart, R. Morey
Helms, Marc Douglas

Builder
McArdle, Montrose P. IV

Consultant
Bullock, Ellis W. Jr.
Cottrell, Dudley P.
Ferguson, Ronald C.
Hart, R. Morey
Marshall, W. Thomas Jr.

Developer
Anthony, Clifford E.
LiBeris, Charles S.
McArdle, Montrose P. IV

Owner/Investor
Anthony, Clifford E.
Bethea, Basil L. Jr.
Ferguson, Ronald C.
McArdle, Montrose P. IV
Moore, Clara L.

Property Manager
Helms, Marc Douglas
McArdle, Montrose P. IV
Moore, Clara L.
Suther, Thomas W. Jr.

Regulator
Bullock, Ellis W. Jr.

Syndicator
Ferguson, Ronald C.
Helms, Marc Douglas
Marshall, W. Thomas Jr.

TALLAHASSEE

Appraiser
Lassetter, James G.
Lassetter, Maggie S.

Attorney
Carpino, Salvatore A.
Massie, James Corban
Odom, F. Perry
Rett, Donald A.

Broker
Bryson, Robert H.
Kresbach, Michael L.
Lassetter, James G.
Lassetter, Maggie S.
Sachs, Jerry M.

Builder
Kresbach, Michael L.

Consultant
Bryson, Robert H.
Kresbach, Michael L.
Lassetter, James G.
Lassetter, Maggie S.
Pankowski, Joseph Michael
Sachs, Jerry M.

Developer
Bryson, Robert H.
Kresbach, Michael L.

Instructor
Lassetter, Maggie S.

Insuror
Bryson, Robert H.
Massie, James Corban

Owner/Investor
Bryson, Robert H.
Carpino, Salvatore A.
Kresbach, Michael L.
Lassetter, James G.
Massie, James Corban
Pankowski, Joseph Michael

Property Manager
Bryson, Robert H.
Sachs, Jerry M.

Regulator
Carpino, Salvatore A.

Syndicator
Bryson, Robert H.
Tiedeberg, Jay S.

TAMPA

Appraiser
Alessandro, Michael
Alexander, Ross A.
Brown, Benjamin L.
Burns, Robert L.

Curry, Derrell R.
Dunham, Robert W.
Gates, Allen F.
Gelling, Louis
Hunnicutt, Warren Jr.
James, Herbert L.
Jordan, J.C.
Laghi, Louis C.
Pallardy, L.F. Jr.
Purcell, Henry III
Rose, Marvin B. Jr.
Shea, Vernon T.
Twitty, Robert J.
Webb, William N.
Williams, Joseph E. Jr.

Architect
Beach, Eugene H.
Bobanic, B.A.
Bogdan, Livius S.

Assessor
Hunnicutt, Warren Jr.

Attorney
Baumann, Phillip A.
Broderick, Roger B.
Cochran, Robert G.
Covert, Neil R.
Deason, Marshall C. Jr.
Duggar, Rolfe D.
Feldman, Marc H.
George, Charles D.
Getzen, William E.
Kimpton, William J.
Kusic, Daniel T.
Lubrano, Timothy J.
Martin, James W.
Munsey, William Ira Jr.
Page, Melvin E. Jr.
Paul, William R.
Puffer, John W. III
Reed, James M.
Rodman, Kenneth L. Jr.
Schwenke, Roger D.
Seitl, Wayne F.
Sherr, S. Sy
Taub, Theodore C.
Towery, Jerrel E.
Weaver, Ronald L.
Wellbaum, R.W. Jr.
Yado, Jess J. III
Zschau, Julius J.

Banker
Lombard, James M.
Seaton, John E.

Broker
Alessandro, Michael
Alexander, Ross A.
Applefield, Lawrence
Baber, William S.
Beitelshees, Everett D.
Bissett, William P. Jr.
Blank, Peter Joseph
Bobanic, B.A.
Bogdan, Livius S.
Booth, John S. III
Bramberg, R. William Jr.
Britt, Fredric A.
Broderick, Roger B.
Collins, LeRoy Jr.
Curry, Derrell R.
Dennison, Dan
Diaz, Eddie C.
Douglass, Allan M.
Drew, Robert (Trader)
Droste, Edward C.
Duncan, Thomas A.
Easton, Steven K.
Edmunds, David E.
Fantle, Charles
Farrell, Reid D.
Furtick, Michael H.
Gates, Allen F.
Gelling, Louis
Greene, Randall Frederick
Hadfield, Michael James
Heritage, Jack W.
Hobby, Eddie
Hunnicutt, Warren Jr.
Hyman, Leonard J.
James, Herbert L.
Johnson, Fred M.
Jordan, J.C.
Justice, Albert N.
Kapplin, Steven D.
Keller, John E. Jr.
Kelzer, Robert A.
Klein, Larry R.
Knight, T.K.
Laghi, Louis C.
Lauber, Evelyn Gremli
Leslie, Beatrice S.
Lhotka, Betty K.
Luten, William C.
Mapstone, Grace A.
Mills, Elli M.A.
Mohar, Gregory J.
Pallardy, L.F. Jr.
Purcell, Henry III
Rose, Marvin B. Jr.
Rosenstein, Joe
Rutledge, James C.
Salisbury, Daniel J.
Schang, Donald C.
Schultz, Richard A.
Schweiger, Robert E.
Sherr, S. Sy
Taylor, Bruce Jr.
Tennant, Robert L.
Tubolino, A. Tony
Twitty, Robert J.
Webb, William N.
Williams, Joseph E. Jr.

Builder
Applefield, Lawrence
Bell, Calvin E.
Berns, Martin A.
Bobanic, B.A.
Breland, Kenneth R.
Britt, Fredric A.
Dennison, Dan
Dresser, Winifred H.
Drew, Robert (Trader)
Flanagan, John W.
Greene, Randall Frederick
Kahler, R. Jan
Leslie, Beatrice S.
McGovern, E. Tom
Mahaffey, Thomas Jr.
Pallardy, L.F. Jr.
Purcell, Henry III
Salisbury, Daniel J.
Tubolino, A. Tony

Consultant
Alessandro, Michael
Alexander, Ross A.
Beitelshees, Everett D.
Booth, John S. III
Bramberg, R. William Jr.
Britt, Fredric A.
Curry, Derrell R.
Diaz, Eddie C.
Drew, Robert (Trader)
Droste, Edward C.
Duggar, Rolfe D.
Dunham, Robert W.
Easton, Steven K.
Edmunds, David E.
Fantle, Charles
Flanagan, John W.
Furtick, Michael H.
Gates, Allen F.
Gelling, Louis
Getzen, William E.
Hart, George M.D. Jr.
Heritage, Jack W.
Hunnicutt, Warren Jr.
Johnson, Fred M.
Jordan, J.C.
Justice, Albert N.
Kapplin, Steven D.
Kearney, John E.
Klein, Larry R.
Lanning, J. Clair
Lauber, Evelyn Gremli
Leslie, Beatrice S.
Lombard, James M.
Lubrano, Timothy J.
Luten, William C.
Mapstone, Grace A.
Martin, Douglas F.
Mohar, Gregory J.
Munsey, William Ira Jr.
Patterson, Roy L.
Purcell, Henry III
Regan, D. Thomas Jr.
Roberts, Robert B. Jr.
Rose, Marvin B. Jr.
Schultz, Richard A.
Seaman, R.N.
Shea, Vernon T.
Taylor, Bruce Jr.
Tubolino, A. Tony
Webb, William N.
Williams, Joseph E. Jr.

Developer
Applefield, Lawrence
Atkinson, Herbert Emerson Jr.
Baldwin, Brad
Bell, Calvin E.
Berns, Martin A.
Bilzerian, Paul A.
Blank, Peter Joseph
Bobanic, B.A.
Bogdan, Livius S.
Bramberg, R. William Jr.
Breland, Kenneth R.
Britt, Fredric A.
Broderick, Roger B.
Collins, LeRoy Jr.
Condon, Warwick A.
Dennison, Dan
Diaz, Eddie C.
Douglass, Allan M.
Drew, Robert (Trader)
Duggar, Rolfe D.
Easton, Steven K.
Flanagan, John W.
Furtick, Michael H.
Gates, Allen F.
Greene, Randall Frederick
Hadfield, Michael James
Hart, George M.D. Jr.
Hunnicutt, Warren Jr.
Hyman, Leonard J.
Justice, Albert N.
Kahler, R. Jan
Kearney, John E.
Keenan, Thomas H.
Kelzer, Robert A.
Klein, Larry R.
Knight, T.K.
Leslie, Beatrice S.
Luten, William C.
McGovern, E. Tom
McSwain, Charles
Mahaffey, Thomas Jr.
Mills, Elli M.A.
Neal, Patrick
Purcell, Henry III
Regan, D. Thomas Jr.
Roberts, Robert B. Jr.
Rose, Marvin B. Jr.
Rutledge, James C.
Salisbury, Daniel J.
Schweiger, Robert E.
Seaman, R.N.
Sherr, S. Sy
Stenzhorn, Robert F.
Tubolino, A. Tony
Wittner, Ted P.

Engineer
Bobanic, B.A.
Broderick, Roger B.
Mohar, Gregory J.
Regulski, Lee

Instructor
Alessandro, Michael
Baber, William S.
Bramberg, R. William Jr.
Drew, Robert (Trader)
Droste, Edward C.
Easton, Steven K.
Gates, Allen F.
Hunnicutt, Warren Jr.
Justice, Albert N.
Kapplin, Steven D.
Keller, John E. Jr.
Mohar, Gregory J.
Munsey, William Ira Jr.
Rosenstein, Joe
Sherr, S. Sy
Taylor, Bruce Jr.
Tubolino, A. Tony

Insuror
Baber, William S.
Heritage, Jack W.
Lubrano, Timothy J.
Taylor, Bruce Jr.
Towery, Jerrel E.
Tubolino, A. Tony

Lender
Blank, Peter Joseph
Heagerty, James J.
Hobby, Eddie
Johnson, Randall C.
Jordan, J.C.
Seaton, John E.
Twitty, Robert J.

Owner/Investor
Alessandro, Michael
Baldwin, Brad
Beitelshees, Everett D.
Bell, Calvin E.
Bilzerian, Paul A.
Bogdan, Livius S.
Bramberg, R. William Jr.
Britt, Fredric A.
Broderick, Roger B.
Collins, LeRoy Jr.
Curry, Derrell R.
Diaz, Eddie C.
Drew, Robert (Trader)
Duggar, Rolfe D.
Easton, Steven K.
Edmunds, David E.
Fantle, Charles
Feldman, Marc H.
Flanagan, John W.
Furtick, Michael H.
Gates, Allen F.
Gelling, Louis
Getzen, William E.
Hadfield, Michael James
Hyman, Leonard J.
Johnson, Fred M.
Kahler, R. Jan
Kearney, John E.
Keller, Brian R.
Kimel, Donald H.
Klein, Larry R.
Knight, T.K.
Lanning, J. Clair
Leslie, Beatrice S.
Lhotka, Betty K.
Lombard, James M.
Luten, William C.
McGovern, E. Tom
Martin, James W.
Neal, Patrick
Pallardy, L.F. Jr.
Purcell, Henry III
Regan, D. Thomas Jr.
Roberts, Robert B. Jr.

Rutledge, James C.
Schweiger, Robert E.
Seaman, R.N.
Shea, Vernon T.
Sherr, S. Sy
Taylor, Bruce Jr.
Webb, William N.

Property Manager
Alessandro, Michael
Bilzerian, Paul A.
Blank, Peter Joseph
Bramberg, R. William Jr.
Britt, Fredric A.
Broderick, Roger B.
Condon, Warwick A.
Dennison, Dan
Diaz, Eddie C.
Droste, Edward C.
Easton, Steven K.
Fantle, Charles
Furtick, Michael H.
Gelling, Louis
Hart, George M.D. Jr.
Hyman, Leonard J.
Justice, Albert N.
Kearney, John E.
Keenan, Thomas H.
Keller, John E. Jr.
Klein, Larry R.
Knight, T.K.
Lanning, J. Clair
Lauber, Evelyn Gremli
Leslie, Beatrice S.
Lombard, James M.
McGovern, E. Tom
Mahaffey, Thomas Jr.
Mitlin, Ira G.
Mohar, Gregory J.
Regan, D. Thomas Jr.
Roberts, Robert B. Jr.
Rosenstein, Joe
Schultz, Richard A.
Taylor, Bruce Jr.
Tennant, Robert L.
Tubolino, A. Tony
Twitty, Robert J.
Webb, William N.
Weise, Frank

Real Estate Publisher
Leslie, Beatrice S.
Rose, Marvin B. Jr.

Regulator
Page, Melvin E. Jr.

Syndicator
Baldwin, Brad
Berns, Martin A.
Booth, John S. III
Bramberg, R. William Jr.
Britt, Fredric A.
Collins, LeRoy Jr.
Douglass, Allan M.
Drew, Robert (Trader)
Edmunds, David E.
Flanagan, John W.
Furtick, Michael H.
Greene, Randall Frederick
Hunnicutt, Warren Jr.
Hyman, Leonard J.
Johnson, Fred M.
Kearney, John E.
Kimel, Donald H.
Knight, T.K.
Leslie, Beatrice S.
Luten, William C.
McGovern, E. Tom
Regan, D. Thomas Jr.
Roberts, Robert B. Jr.
Rose, Marvin B. Jr.
Rutledge, James C.
Schweiger, Robert E.
Seaman, R.N.
Sherr, S. Sy
Tubolino, A. Tony

WEST PALM BEACH

Appraiser
Blum, Gerald W.
Butterfield, Harold L.
Callaway, Robert J.
Dehn, John J.
Liek, James E.
McBrearity, Frank B. Jr.
Siebrecht, James K.
Smiles, Scott T.
Swarner, Fred
Thompson, Henry E.
Vogel, Donald L.
Whittaker, Sam E.

Architect
Anstis, James H.
Crabtree, Malcolm N.
Hollohazy, Attila N.

Assessor
Callaway, Robert J.

Attorney
Colburn, Harry S. Jr.
Dickenson, David B.
Gibson, Herbert C.
Helgesen, Andrew
Jacobson, Andrew Mark
Jones, Robert Bruce
Miller, Lawrence J.
Nagle, Gary J.
Poller, Jeri A.
Rubenstein, Mitchell
Schilling, Christopher J.
Shapiro, Robert Lee
Sklar, William Paul Esq.
Timchak, Louis J. Jr.
White, Russell A.

Banker
Nilges, Jan A.
Preiser, Richard C.
Siebrecht, James K.
Wallis, William T.

Broker
Blum, Gerald W.
Brown, James P.
Callaway, Robert J.
Colburn, Harry S. Jr.
Condon, Donald S.
Courchene, Diane M.
Crabtree, Malcolm N.
Davis, Don T. Sr.
Dehn, John J.
Estern, Jay S.
Focht, John C.
Graf, Jenny H.
Hutchison, Jacob A.
Knight, William L.
Liek, James E.
McBrearity, Frank B. Jr.
Mitchell, John Eric
Nobil, James H.
Ring, Charles B.
Rosemurgy, James M.
Satter, Robert A.
Schwaderer, Charles B. II
Shapiro, Steven M.
Sheets, Carleton Hunter
Shubin, Bill
Siebrecht, James K.
Thompson, Henry E.
Tyler, Lowell Peardon
Vogel, Donald L.
Whittaker, Sam E.
Wright, Frederick
Yeckes, Arthur

Builder
Blum, Gerald W.
Brady, Gary
Courchene, Diane M.
Delhaise, Jean-Claude
Fallenbaum, Sam
Gaines, Jack W.
Graf, Jenny H.
Hollohazy, Attila N.
Knight, William L.
Kommer, Robert Joel
Satter, Robert A.
Shapiro, Steven M.
Shubin, Bill
Speer, Erling Dick
Tate, J. Kenneth
Whitehall, Henry
Whitehill, Andrew
Yeckes, Arthur

Consultant
Blum, Gerald W.
Brown, James P.
Colburn, Harry S. Jr.
Condon, Donald S.
Coolidge, Thomas E.T.
Focht, John C.
Goldberger, Melvin T.
Liek, James E.
McBrearity, Frank B. Jr.
McDonnell, Edward P.
Nobil, James H.
Ring, Charles B.
Rutledge, Paul R.
Schwaderer, Charles B. II
Senf, Charles K.
Sheets, Carleton Hunter
Siebrecht, James K.
Thompson, Henry E.
Whittaker, Sam E.

Developer
Baker, John R.
Blum, Gerald W.
Brady, Gary
Brown, James P.
Condon, Donald S.
Coolidge, Thomas E.T.
Cummings, Peter D.
Fallenbaum, Sam
Focht, John C.
Gaines, Jack W.
Goldberger, Melvin T.
Graf, Jenny H.
Harte, Stanley J.
Hollohazy, Attila N.
Jacobson, Andrew Mark
Knight, William L.
Kommer, Robert Joel
McDonnell, Edward P.
Poller, Jeri A.
Ring, Charles B.
Satter, Robert A.
Shapiro, Steven M.
Shubin, Bill
Siebrecht, James K.
Smith, Peter C.
Speer, Erling Dick
Tate, J. Kenneth
Thomasson, Floyd A.
Thompson, Henry E.
Timchak, Louis J. Jr.
Vogel, Donald L.
Whitehall, Henry
Whitehill, Andrew

Engineer
Collins, Moseley
Hollohazy, Attila N.

Instructor
Estern, Jay S.
Hutchison, Jacob A.
Liek, James E.
Ring, Charles B.
Sheets, Carleton Hunter
Sklar, William Paul Esq.
Whittaker, Sam E.

Insuror
Spalding, Edward C. Jr.
Tyler, Lowell Peardon
Yeckes, Arthur

Lender
Levine, Walter M.
McDonnell, Edward P.
Preiser, Richard C.
Wilensky, Alvin

Owner/Investor
Bagby, Joseph R.
Baker, John R.
Blum, Gerald W.
Brady, Gary
Coolidge, Thomas E.T.
Courchene, Diane M.
Crabtree, Malcolm N.
Cummings, Peter D.
Delhaise, Jean-Claude
Estern, Jay S.
Focht, John C.
Goldberger, Melvin T.
Graf, Jenny H.
Harte, Stanley J.
Hollohazy, Attila N.
Jones, Robert Bruce
Judelson, Robert A.
Levine, Walter M.
Liek, James E.
McDonnell, Edward P.
Mitchell, John Eric
Nobil, James H.
Ring, Charles B.
Rubenstein, Mitchell
Shapiro, Steven M.
Sheets, Carleton Hunter
Shubin, Bill
Smith, Peter C.
Speer, Erling Dick
Thompson, Henry E.
Timchak, Louis J. Jr.
Whitehill, Andrew
Whittaker, Sam E.
Wilensky, Alvin
Yeckes, Arthur

Property Manager
Blum, Gerald W.
Brady, Gary
Callaway, Robert J.
Davis, Don T. Sr.
Dehn, John J.
Estern, Jay S.
Graf, Jenny H.
Harte, Stanley J.
Hollohazy, Attila N.
Judelson, Robert A.
Liek, James E.
McDonnell, Edward P.
Mitchell, John Eric
Nobil, James H.
Rosemurgy, James M.
Rutledge, Paul R.
Shubin, Bill
Smith, Peter C.
Speer, Erling Dick
Swarner, Fred
Vogel, Donald L.
Yeckes, Arthur

Syndicator
Bagby, Joseph R.
Blum, Gerald W.
Brown, James P.
Condon, Donald S.
Coolidge, Thomas E.T.
Davis, Don T. Sr.
Delhaise, Jean-Claude
Gaines, Jack W.
Hollohazy, Attila N.
Judelson, Robert A.
Levine, Walter M.
Mitchell, John Eric
Nobil, James H.
Ring, Charles B.
Shapiro, Steven M.
Sheets, Carleton Hunter
Siebrecht, James K.
Swarner, Fred

Thompson, Henry E.

GEORGIA

ALBANY

Appraiser
Owens, Dawson

Attorney
Mixon, Marvin W.

Broker
Martin, F. Lewis Jr.
Owens, Dawson
Walden, Spencer C. Jr.

Consultant
Owens, Dawson

Developer
Martin, F. Lewis Jr.
Walden, Spencer C. Jr.

Owner/Investor
Martin, F. Lewis Jr.
Walden, Spencer C. Jr.

Property Manager
Martin, F. Lewis Jr.
Walden, Spencer C. Jr.

Syndicator
Martin, F. Lewis Jr.

ATHENS

Appraiser
Sirmans, Clemon F.

Architect
Blackburn, Elizabeth Harris

Attorney
Bentley, Upshaw C. Jr.
Shedd, Peter J.
Warnes, James C.

Consultant
Sirmans, Clemon F.

Instructor
Shedd, Peter J.
Sirmans, Clemon F.

Owner/Investor
Sirmans, Clemon F.

Real Estate Publisher
Sirmans, Clemon F.

Syndicator
Sirmans, Clemon F.

ATLANTA

Appraiser
Albritton, Harold D.
Benton, Alvin O.
Bryan, Joseph L. Jr.
Butler, Robert P.
Coe, James Thomas
Dabney, John C.
Day, Robert M.
Erbesfield, Carl S.
Florence, James E.
Foster, Ronald S.
Harris, D. Michael
Haywood, Robert A.
Head, J. Reginald
Hissam, Dallas E.
Hurley, Patrick W.
Jent, Jim T.
Kilpatrick, G. Malcolm
Love, Terrence L.
Maddox, Cone
Neyhart, Ron
Overstreet, Homer Jr.
Sansone, Steven A.
Scott, James F.
Simmons, T. Freddie
Smith, George T.
Stokes, Randall L.
Thomas, David N.
Tschappat, Carl J.
Warren, George T. II

Architect
Fuller, William Norman
Hassan, Yahya M.A.
Love, Terrence L.
McKenzie, H.E.
Porter, Thomas H. Jr.
Rutemeyer, E.F.
Snyder, David F. AIA
Tapp, William R. Jr.

Assessor
Smith, George T.

Attorney
Backman, Garett A.
Candler, John S. II
Covington, Dean
Cunningham, G. Bruce
Dawkins, William J.
Denny, Richard A. Jr.
Dunn, Wesley Brankley
Edge, J. Dexter Jr.
Feuer, Bruce R.
Fillingim, Larry K.
Flexner, Richard D.
Gingrey, James F. Jr.
Glover, J. Littleton Jr.
Hall, Allan J.
Harris, James W.
Heagy, John A. III
Hughen, Lowell H.
Hyden, William U. Jr.
Ledbetter, Bureon E. Jr.
McLean, John William Jr.
McRae, James W.
Merritt, William J.W. P.C.
Meyerson, Stanley P.
Millkey, John M.
Montgomery, William D.
O'Callaghan, William L. Jr.
Pindar, George A.
Podlin, Mark Joseph
Ranney, Eric D.
Resnick, Franklin D.
Richardson, Robert E.
Riley, Mark Barry
Ruff, John T.
Shinall, John M.
Tallant, Frederick C. Jr.
Von Fleckenstein, George J.W.
Welch, H. Oliver
Witcher, Robert P.
Zoukis, Stephen J.

Banker
Burdette, William Charles
House, Steve
Kamp, Carl O. Jr.
Wickland, Carey B.

Broker
Abrams, Stephen A.
Anderson, Gene
Arnovitz, Eliot M.
Barnes, John R.
Bell, James F. Jr.
Blackwell, Marion Jr.
Body, Thomas D. III
Burdette, William Charles
Burnette, Harvey D. Jr.
Cauble, Thomas V.
Clark, James K. Jr.
Daniel, E. Ross
Davis, Cantey P.
Davis, Richard S. Jr.
Dawkins, William J.
Dixon, Stephen J.
Donegan, James C.
Edge, Lawrence L.
Epperson, E. Russell III
Erbesfield, Carl S.
Florence, James E.
Garner, J. Randall
Goodloe, John D. Jr.
Hammer, Jack T.
Hardin, David R.
Hartley, Donald L. Sr.
Hartman, Ardin G.
Haywood, Robert A.
Head, J. Reginald
Heisler, M.G.
Hissam, Dallas E.
Howington, Ezra Frank Jr.
James, Thomas T. III
Jent, Jim T.
Johnson, Jerry
Kanellos, James L.
Kaufmann, Louis W. Jr.
Kerley, Jack D.
Kilpatrick, G. Malcolm
Kirkpatrick, Michael L.
Kowalczyk, V Scott
Ladipo, Jerry G.
LeCraw, David S.
Lie-Nielsen, John
Long, Robert J.
Love, Robert T.
Love, Terrence L.
Ludwig, L.T.
MacConaugha, Donald G.
McGinnis, Claude A.
McKenzie, H.E.
McLean, John William Jr.
Maddox, Cone
Maestre, Ed
Means, Al Jr.
Millikan, James R.
Nagel, Bob E.
Nelson, Mary
Nodvin, Joseph J.
O'Farrell, Lucy S.
Ogletree, Joyce B.
Padgett, Douglas J.
Parris, Joe W.
Patterson, Thomas Brooks
Peyton, Steven D.
Redd, A. M. Jr.
Roberds, C. Alvin Jr.
Robinson, Wayne
Sacre, Robert Knowles
Sellars, W. M.
Simms, William S.
Simpson, A. Boyd
Skillern, Lynn T.
Smith, Albert C.
Starr, Harold H.
Stephens, James A. Jr.
Sturgess, A. H.
Terrell, Joseph H.
Thomas, David N.
Thomas, Robert M.
Tift, Thomas W. Jr.
Trewhitt, L. Blair
Vardeman, F. Burt
Von Fleckenstein, George J.W.
Warren, George T. II
Welch, H. Oliver
Wilkin, James P. Jr.
Wyman, George C.

Builder
Arnovitz, Eliot M.
Burnette, Harvey D. Jr.
Freemann, John W.
Fuller, William Norman
Garner, J. Randall
Gurin, H. Gerry
Hall, Allan J.
Heagy, John A. III
Heisler, M.G.
Hurst, Hollis C.
Kirkpatrick, Michael L.
Lie-Nielsen, John
McKenzie, H.E.
McLean, John William Jr.
Moser, Eric
Nodvin, Joseph J.
Ogletree, Joyce B.
O'Neill, Timothy J.
Parris, Joe W.
Sanders, Jerry L.
Searles, David S. Jr.
Simms, William S.
Von Fleckenstein, George J.W.
Warren, George T. II
Zuckerman, Howard A.

Consultant
Abrams, Stephen A.
Albritton, Harold D.
Anderson, Gene
Arogeti, James
Barnes, John R.
Benton, Alvin O.
Blackwell, Marion Jr.
Body, Thomas D. III
Bryan, Joseph L. Jr.
Burdette, William Charles
Christman, James R.
Coe, James Thomas
Dabney, John C.
Daniel, E. Ross
Davis, Richard S. Jr.
Day, Robert M.
Deese, Larry Keith
Donegan, James C.
Dunn, Wesley Brankley
Edge, Lawrence L.
Eidelman, Gene
Fillingim, Larry K.
Florence, James E.
Foster, Ronald S.
Fuller, William Norman
Hammer, Jack T.
Harris, D. Michael
Hartley, Donald L. Sr.
Hartman, Ardin G.
Haywood, Robert A.
Heagy, John A. III
Heisler, M.G.
Hissam, Dallas E.
Hooper, William L.
Howington, Ezra Frank Jr.
Hurley, Patrick W.
Kaufmann, Louis W. Jr.
Kerley, Jack D.
Kilpatrick, G. Malcolm
Kirkpatrick, Michael L.
Lane, James P.
Lapwing, Thomas W.
LeCraw, David S.
Long, Robert J.
Love, Robert T.
Love, Terrence L.
Ludwig, L.T.
MacConaugha, Donald G.
McKenzie, H.E.
McRae, James W.
Maddox, Cone
Maestre, Ed
Mason, Frank H.
Millikan, James R.
Moeckel, William G. Jr.
Moser, Eric
Nagel, Bob E.
Neyhart, Ron
Nodvin, Joseph J.
Peyton, Steven D.
Pindar, George A.
Resnick, Franklin D.
Rifkin, Henry A.
Robinson, Wayne
Sacre, Robert Knowles
Sansone, Steven A.
Saylor, Paul H.
Scott, James F.
Simmons, T. Freddie

Simpson, A. Boyd
Smith, Albert C.
Snyder, David F.
Stephens, James A. Jr.
Stokes, Randall L.
Stone, Michael B.
Thomas, David N.
Tschappat, Carl J.
Von Fleckenstein, George J.W.
Welch, H. Oliver
Wilkin, James P. Jr.

Developer
Ackerman, Charles C.
Arnovitz, Eliot M.
Bell, James F. Jr.
Braithwaite, James C.
Bregman, Petty
Brooks, Donald B.
Brunning, Geoffrey D.
Chanin, Ronald E.
Christman, James R.
Davis, Richard S. Jr.
DiFiore, Richard James
Edge, Lawrence L.
Eidelman, Gene
Florence, James E.
Freemann, John W.
Fuller, William Norman
Garner, J. Randall
Goodloe, John D. Jr.
Gurin, H. Gerry
Hall, Allan J.
Hammer, Jack T.
Hartman, Ardin G.
Head, J. Reginald
Heagy, John A. III
Hissam, Dallas E.
Hooper, William L.
Hopkins, Wesley L.
Kanellos, James L.
Kelley, Blaine Jr.
Kern, Robert F.
Kilpatrick, G. Malcolm
Kirkpatrick, Michael L.
Kuniansky, David
Ladipo, Jerry G.
Ledbetter, Robert Harbin Sr.
Lie-Nielsen, John
Long, Robert J.
MacConaugha, Donald G.
McGinnis, Claude A.
McKenzie, H.E.
McLean, John William Jr.
Maddox, Cone
Meredith, Allen K.
Moser, Eric
Nagel, Bob E.
Nodvin, Joseph J.
O'Neill, Timothy J.
Parris, Joe W.
Peyton, Steven D.
Redd, A. M. Jr.
Resnick, Franklin D.
Roberds, C. Alvin Jr.
Robinson, Wayne
Rosenberg, Sidney B.
Sacre, Robert Knowles
Sanders, Jerry L.
Searles, David S. Jr.
Sellars, W. M.
Shaheen, Shouky A.
Simms, William S.
Simpson, A. Boyd
Smith, Albert C.
Smith, Richard Sr.
Snyder, David F.
Starr, Harold H.
Terrell, Joseph H.
Tift, Thomas W. Jr.
Topple, James H.
Trewhitt, L. Blair
Van der Weerdt, Henk B.
Von Fleckenstein, George J.W.
Warren, George T. II
Worsham, Earl S.
Zuckerman, Howard A.

Engineer
Butler, Robert P.
Hurst, Hollis C.
Thomas, Robert M.
Von Fleckenstein, George J.W.

Instructor
Arogeti, James
Barnes, John R.
Blackwell, Marion Jr.
Bryan, Joseph L. Jr.
Butler, Robert P.
Dunn, Wesley Brankley
Erbesfield, Carl S.
Haywood, Robert A.
Heisler, M.G.
Hissam, Dallas E.
Long, Robert J.
Ludwig, L.T.
McRae, James W.
Nelson, Mary
O'Farrell, Lucy S.
Starr, Harold H.
Stephens, James A. Jr.
Terrell, Joseph H.
Thomas, David N.
Thomas, Robert M.
Tschappat, Carl J.
Wilkin, James P. Jr.

Insuror
Burnette, Harvey D. Jr.
Florence, James E.
Smith, Albert C.
Warren, George T. II

Lender
Arogeti, James
Barker, Robert E.
Betts, Joan S.
Jones, Mikeal R.
Lie-Nielsen, John
Muir, James H.
Saylor, Paul H.
Wickland, Carey B.

Owner/Investor
Abrams, Stephen A.
Arnovitz, Eliot M.
Arogeti, James
Backman, Garett A.
Barker, Robert E.
Bell, James F. Jr.
Betts, Joan S.
Blackwell, Marion Jr.
Candler, John S. II
Chanin, Ronald E.
Christman, James R.
Coe, James Thomas
Covington, Dean
Daniel, E. Ross
Davis, Richard S. Jr.
Dawkins, William J.
Denny, Richard A. Jr.
DiFiore, Richard James
Donegan, James C.
Dunn, Wesley Brankley
Edge, Lawrence L.
Eidelman, Gene
Florence, James E.
Fuller, William Norman
Gurin, H. Gerry
Hall, Allan J.
Hammer, Jack T.
Hardin, David R.
Hartley, Donald L. Sr.
Hartman, Ardin G.
Haywood, Robert A.
Head, J. Reginald
Heisler, M.G.
Hissam, Dallas E.
Hooper, William L.
Howington, Ezra Frank Jr.
Hurst, Hollis C.
Kern, Robert F.
Kilpatrick, G. Malcolm
Kirkpatrick, Michael L.
Ladipo, Jerry G.
LeCraw, David S.
Ledbetter, Robert Harbin Sr.
Lie-Nielsen, John
Long, Robert J.
Love, Robert T.
Love, Terrence L.
Ludwig, L.T.
McKenzie, H.E.
McLean, John William Jr.
Maddox, Cone
Moser, Eric
Nagel, Bob E.
Nahigian, Ann Lawrence
Nelson, Mary
Nodvin, Joseph J.
O'Farrell, Lucy S.
O'Neill, Timothy J.
Parris, Joe W.
Ranney, Eric D.
Redd, A. M. Jr.
Resnick, Franklin D.
Rifkin, Henry A.
Roberds, C. Alvin Jr.
Robinson, Wayne
Saylor, Paul H.
Searles, David S. Jr.
Sellars, W. M.
Simms, William S.
Smith, Richard Sr.
Starr, Harold H.
Stephens, James A. Jr.
Thomas, David N.
Tift, Thomas W. Jr.
Trewhitt, L. Blair
Van der Weerdt, Henk B.
Welch, H. Oliver
Witcher, Robert P.
Zuckerman, Howard A.

Property Manager
Abrams, Stephen A.
Allen, Grant
Arnovitz, Eliot M.
Avirett, Abner
Bell, James F. Jr.
Blackwell, Marion Jr.
Braithwaite, James C.
Bryan, Joseph L. Jr.
Burnette, Harvey D. Jr.
Cagle, J. Douglas
Chanin, Ronald E.
Chupp, O.L.
Clark, Charles
Coe, James Thomas
DiFiore, Richard James
Donegan, James C.
Edge, Lawrence L.
Eidelman, Gene
Engler-Wigbels, Dixie Lee
Feuer, Bruce R.
Fillingim, Larry K.
Fischbach, Robert A.
Florence, James E.
Garner, J. Randall
Goodloe, John D. Jr.
Gurin, H. Gerry
Hammer, Jack T.
Hardin, David R.
Hartley, Donald L. Sr.
Haywood, Robert A.
Heagy, John A. III
Heisler, M.G.
Hooper, William L.
Hurst, Hollis C.
Jent, Jim T.
Kaufmann, Louis W. Jr.
Kenney, Thomas P.
Kerley, Jack D.
Kirkpatrick, Michael L.
Ladipo, Jerry G.
Lane, Lucien B.
LeCraw, David S.
Ledbetter, Robert Harbin Sr.
Levy, David
Lie-Nielsen, John
Love, Robert T.
MacConaugha, Donald G.
Maddox, Cone
Maestre, Ed
Mason, Frank H.
Millikan, James R.
Moser, Eric
Muir, James H.
Nahigian, Ann Lawrence
Nodvin, Joseph J.
O'Neill, Timothy J.
Porter, Thomas H. Jr.
Redd, A. M. Jr.
Roberds, C. Alvin Jr.
Robinson, Wayne
St. John, Richard J.
Saylor, Paul H.
Sims, Wallen
Smith, Richard Sr.
Starr, Harold H.
Stephens, James A. Jr.
Swanson, John
Thomas, Robert M.
Tift, Thomas W. Jr.
Trewhitt, L. Blair
Vardeman, F. Burt
Waddell, Gloria J.
Walker, Kenneth
Warren, George T. II
Welch, H. Oliver
Willis, William H.

Real Estate Publisher
Heagy, John A. III
Lewis, Stephen E.
Long, Robert J.
Mitchell, Jim
Snell, Nancy

Regulator
Bryan, Joseph L. Jr.
Sacre, Robert Knowles

Syndicator
Abrams, Stephen A.
Backman, Garett A.
Betts, Joan S.
Blackwell, Marion Jr.
Bryant, Don
Daniel, E. Ross
Donegan, James C.
Eidelman, Gene
Fischbach, Robert A.
Florence, James E.
Hammer, Jack T.
Hardin, David R.
Head, J. Reginald
Hissam, Dallas E.
Howington, Ezra Frank Jr.
Lie-Nielsen, John
Long, Robert J.
Love, Robert T.
Ludwig, L.T.
McGinnis, Claude A.
Maddox, Cone
Moser, Eric
Nagel, Bob E.
Nahigian, Ann Lawrence
Nodvin, Joseph J.
Nothnagle, Raymond A.
Patterson, Thomas Brooks
Richardson, Robert E.
Searles, David S. Jr.
Sellars, W. M.
Smith, Richard Sr.
Snyder, David F.

Starr, Harold H.
Thomas, David N.
Zuckerman, Howard A.

AUGUSTA

Appraiser
Atkins, A. Anthony

Broker
Atkins, A. Anthony
Bible, Jim C. III
Graybill, Michael A.
Storey, M. Bert

Builder
Bible, Jim C. III
Graybill, Michael A.

Consultant
Atkins, A. Anthony
Bible, Jim C. III
Storey, M. Bert

Developer
Atkins, A. Anthony
Graybill, Michael A.
Storey, M. Bert

Engineer
Storey, M. Bert

Owner/Investor
Storey, M. Bert

Property Manager
Atkins, A. Anthony
Bible, Jim C. III
Graybill, Michael A.
Storey, M. Bert

Syndicator
Atkins, A. Anthony
Bible, Jim C. III
Graybill, Michael A.
Storey, M. Bert

COLUMBUS

Attorney
Redmond, Lee R. Jr.

Broker
Lewis, H. Wendell

Builder
Flournoy, John F.
Woodruff, G. C. Jr.

Consultant
Woodruff, G. C. Jr.

Developer
Aldridge, L. Rollins Jr.
Flournoy, John F.
Woodruff, G. C. Jr.

Engineer
Aldridge, L. Rollins Jr.

Owner/Investor
Aldridge, L. Rollins Jr.
Flournoy, John F.

Property Manager
Aldridge, L. Rollins Jr.
Cobb, H. Hart Jr.
Flournoy, John F.
Lewis, H. Wendell
Woodruff, G. C. Jr.

Syndicator
Flournoy, John F.

GAINESVILLE

Appraiser
Hodsdon, Stan

Broker
Hodsdon, Stan

Consultant
Hodsdon, Stan

Insuror
Hodsdon, Stan

Owner/Investor
Hodsdon, Stan

Property Manager
Hodsdon, Stan

Syndicator
Hodsdon, Stan

MACON

Broker
Murphey, Julian C.

Consultant
Held, Gilbert

Developer
Murphey, Julian C.

Property Manager
Murphey, Julian C.

SAVANNAH

Architect
Bazemore, Walton L. Jr.

Broker
Adams, Michael Timothy
Bennett, Robert E.
Martin, Rubert C. Jr.

Builder
Bennett, Robert E.

Consultant
Adams, Michael Timothy
Bennett, Robert E.

Developer
Greer, Miles
Lattimore, William Jr.
Martin, Rubert C. Jr.

Instructor
Adams, Michael Timothy

Property Manager
Martin, Rubert C. Jr.
Scott, Walter

Syndicator
Martin, Rubert C. Jr.

SWAINSBORO

Attorney
Brannen, Sam L.
Hubbard, Evelyn S.

WAYCROSS

Appraiser
Kaufman, John Augustus
McGee, Jack P.
Parker, W. Wright

Attorney
McLemore, Gilbert Carmichael Jr.

Broker
Fields, Mary Bryan
Kaufman, John Augustus
Parker, W. Wright
Trupp, Hans F.

Consultant
Carmichael, H. Elden
McGee, Jack P.
Trupp, Hans F.

Developer
Carmichael, H. Elden
Fields, Mary Bryan
Trupp, Hans F.

Instructor
Fields, Mary Bryan

Insuror
Kaufman, John Augustus
Parker, W. Wright
Trupp, Hans F.

Owner/Investor
Carmichael, H. Elden
Fields, Mary Bryan
Parker, W. Wright
Trupp, Hans F.

Property Manager
Kaufman, John Augustus
McGee, Jack P.

Syndicator
Trupp, Hans F.

GUAM

AGANA

Appraiser
Taitano, Rufo C.

Broker
Taitano, Rufo C.
Ulloa, David J.

Lender
Taitano, Rufo C.

Owner/Investor
Ulloa, David J.

Property Manager
Ulloa, David J.

HAWAII

HONOLULU

Appraiser
Daley, Don J.
Dollnig, Richard D.
Hammann, Arthur H.
Hastings, Robert C.
Hustace, Edward C.
Kimura, Ty H.
Lau, George K.H.
Lesher, Raymond A.
Ohlman, James P.
Rousseau, John J.
Stellmacher, Herbert Bob
Swenson, Lawrence P.
Thacker, Herbert Dickey
Yoshimura, Richard Mamoru
Young, Peter T.

Architect
Daley, Don J.
Fritz, John Paul
Toyomura, Dennis T.

Assessor
Daley, Don J.

Attorney
Archer, Guy P.D.
Bodden, Thomas A.
Carlsmith, Curtis W.
Ching, Robert Soong
Chu, Harold
Hammann, Arthur H.
Imanaka, Mitchell A.
Jackson, Bruce G.
Judge, James R.
Lee, Carol Mon
Lum, Richard M.C.
Macdonald, Ian A.
Miyamoto, Theodore T.
Peckron, Harold S.
Reilly, John
Sakai, Hiroshi
Tanega, Joseph Atangan
Taylor, Carroll S.
Topliss, Larry T.
Wong, Francis A.

Banker
Cannon, George Q.
Daley, Don J.
Hammann, Arthur H.
Yoshimura, Richard Mamoru

Broker
Anderson, James K.
Beall, Alan Cory
Blanco, Fred C.
Blanco, Joseph F.
Bodden, Thomas A.
Bohannon, Charles L.
Bradley, Penny
Breton, Richard Albert
Brooks, Wendell F. Jr.
Champion, Lee
Ching, Wendell T.P.
Chu, Harold
Davis, Jerry
Fritz, John Paul
Grant, Robert B.
Hammann, Arthur H.
Harris, Ernest A.
Hastings, Robert C.
Hertz, Mel R.
Hustace, Edward C.
Imanaka, Mitchell A.
Johnson, J. Allen
Kaneshiro, George M.
Kimura, Ty H.
Llanes, Ginger Akuna
Loedding, James A.
Luke, Vernon B.
Macdonald, Ian A.
Miyamoto, Theodore T.
Ohlman, James P.
Olson, Victor D.
Reilly, John
Robin, Dean
Rousseau, John J.
Shern, Mary Steeves
Stellmacher, Herbert Bob
Swenson, Lawrence P.
Takahashi, Teney K.
Tanega, Joseph Atangan
Thacker, Herbert Dickey
Topliss, Larry T.
Trask, James K. Jr.
Vallance, John E.
Wong, Albert
Young, Kenneth M.
Young, Peter T.

Builder
Anderson, David C.
Carlsmith, Curtis W.
Cavanaugh, Ken C.
Ching, Wendell T.P.
Fritz, John Paul
Harris, Ernest A.
Hustace, Edward C.
Moore, Randolph G.
Swenson, Lawrence P.
Young, Kenneth M.

Consultant
Anderson, James K.
Beall, Alan Cory
Bodden, Thomas A.
Bohannon, Charles L.
Brooks, Wendell F. Jr.
Carlsmith, Curtis W.
Cavanaugh, Ken C.
Champion, Lee
Ching, Robert Soong
Chu, Harold
Chun, John Jason
Floyd, Wendell C.
Freeman, R. Carter Jr.

Fritz, John Paul
Grant, Robert B.
Hammann, Arthur H.
Holman, R.W. Jr.
Hustace, Edward C.
Johnson, J. Allen
Kaneshiro, George M.
Kimura, Ty H.
Laitila, Edward E.
Lau, George K.H.
Lesher, Raymond A.
Llanes, Ginger Akuna
Loedding, James A.
Lutes, Kendall H.
Macdonald, Ian A.
Peckron, Harold S.
Robin, Dean
Rousseau, John J.
Rubendall, Floyd
Sakai, Hiroshi
Shern, Mary Steeves
Shigeoka, Dennis K.
Smith, Robley W.
Stellmacher, Herbert Bob
Tanega, Joseph Atangan
Thacker, Herbert Dickey
Trask, James K. Jr.
Wong, Albert
Yoshimura, Richard Mamoru
Young, Peter T.

Developer
Anderson, David C.
Anderson, James K.
Beall, Alan Cory
Breton, Richard Albert
Brooks, Wendell F. Jr.
Carlsmith, Curtis W.
Cavanaugh, Ken C.
Champion, Lee
Cooper, Robert E.
Davis, Jerry
Floyd, Wendell C.
Fritz, John Paul
Harris, Ernest A.
Hastings, Robert C.
Holman, R.W. Jr.
Hustace, Edward C.
Kaneshiro, George M.
Kimura, Ty H.
Luke, Vernon B.
Lutes, Kendall H.
Macdonald, Ian A.
Moore, Randolph G.
Ohlman, James P.
Rousseau, John J.
Rubendall, Floyd
Shern, Mary Steeves
Shidler, Jay H. II
Swenson, Lawrence P.
Takahashi, Teney K.
Tanega, Joseph Atangan
Topliss, Larry T.
Trask, James K. Jr.
Vallance, John E.
Wong, Francis A.
Young, Kenneth M.

Engineer
Ching, Wendell T.P.
Fritz, John Paul
Harris, Ernest A.
Shigeoka, Dennis K.
Smith, Robley W.

Instructor
Amiel, Victor
Beall, Alan Cory
Bodden, Thomas A.
Bohannon, Charles L.
Chu, Harold
Hammann, Arthur H.
Johnson, J. Allen
Laitila, Edward E.
Lee, Carol Mon
Peckron, Harold S.
Reilly, John
Robin, Dean
Rousseau, John J.
Shern, Mary Steeves
Stellmacher, Herbert Bob
Swenson, Lawrence P.
Tanega, Joseph Atangan
Trask, James K. Jr.
Young, Peter T.

Insuror
Blanco, Fred C.
Smith, Robley W.

Lender
Cannon, George Q.
Cavanaugh, Ken C.
Ching, Robert Soong
Daley, Don J.
Hammann, Arthur H.
Harris, Ernest A.
Humphreys, Richard L.
Ohlman, James P.
Okinga, Sam
Robin, Dean

Owner/Investor
Beall, Alan Cory
Blanco, Fred C.
Blanco, Joseph F.
Bodden, Thomas A.
Bohannon, Charles L.
Carlsmith, Curtis W.
Cavanaugh, Ken C.
Ching, Wendell T.P.
Chun, John Jason
Cooper, Robert E.
Crabtree, Gordon, W.
Floyd, Wendell C.
Fritz, John Paul
Hammann, Arthur H.
Hertz, Mel R.
Holman, R.W. Jr.
Hui, Kane K.
Kaneshiro, George M.
Kimura, Ty H.
Llanes, Ginger Akuna
Luke, Warren K.K.
Lutes, Kendall H.
Nakamura, Edward H.
Ohlman, James P.
Robin, Dean
Rousseau, John J.
Rubendall, Floyd
Shidler, Jay H. II
Stellmacher, Herbert Bob
Swenson, Lawrence P.
Topliss, Larry T.
Trask, James K. Jr.
Wong, Albert
Young, Peter T.

Property Manager
Amiel, Victor
Beall, Alan Cory
Bohannon, Charles L.
Brooks, Wendell F. Jr.
Cavanaugh, Ken C.
Davis, Jerry
Floyd, Wendell C.
Hammann, Arthur H.
Hustace, Edward C.
Ing, Wilbur K.S.
Johnson, J. Allen
Kanda, Tad T.
Kaneshiro, George M.
Kimura, Ty H.
Knutson, William A.
Lau, George K.H.
Llanes, Ginger Akuna
Nakamura, Edward H.
Ohlman, James P.
Rubendall, Floyd
Smith, Robley W.
Takahashi, Teney K.
Thacker, Herbert Dickey
Tirrell, Wallace K.
Trask, James K. Jr.
Wong, Albert
Young, Kenneth M.
Young, Peter T.

Real Estate Publisher
Beal, Charlotte
Bodden, Thomas A.
Fritz, John Paul
Reilly, John
Rousseau, John J.

Regulator
Blanco, Joseph F.

Syndicator
Bodden, Thomas A.
Cavanaugh, Ken C.
Ching, Robert Soong
Crabtree, Gordon, W.
Daley, Don J.
Davis, Jerry
Freeman, R. Carter Jr.
Grant, Robert B.
Hammann, Arthur H.
Hertz, Mel R.
Kaneshiro, George M.
Kimura, Ty H.
Llanes, Ginger Akuna
Peckron, Harold S.
Robin, Dean
Rousseau, John J.
Rubendall, Floyd
Swenson, Lawrence P.
Young, Kenneth M.

IDAHO

BOISE

Appraiser
Corlett, G. Joseph
Johnston, Rod P.
Knipe, William B. Jr.
Passmore, Luther I.
Steen, Harold W.

Attorney
Chapman, John S.
McKew, Walter Martin
Vasconcellos, William L.

Broker
Allen, Roger H.
Clegg, Mark W.
Fonshill, Ira William III
Gundy, Thames
Hayden
Johnson, Donald M.
Knipe, William B. Jr.
Winder, Charles L.
Wright, Thomas T.

Builder
Gundy, Thames
Pau, Peter S.
Yelverton, D. Craig

Consultant
Allen, Roger H.
Clegg, Mark W.
Corlett, G. Joseph
Johnson, Donald M.
Knipe, William B. Jr.
Passmore, Luther I.
Pau, Peter S.
Steen, Harold W.
Winder, Charles L.
Wright, Thomas T.

Developer
Allen, Roger H.
Clark, Edward B.
Fonshill, Ira William III
Gundy, Thames
Jensen, Ronald R.
McKew, Walter Martin
Oppenheimer, Arthur F.
Pau, Peter S.
Wright, Thomas T.
Yelverton, D. Craig

Instructor
Allen, Roger H.
Johnson, Donald M.
Steen, Harold W.

Insuror
Clark, Edward B.

Owner/Investor
Clark, Edward B.
Clegg, Mark W.
Corlett, G. Joseph
Fonshill, Ira William III
Gundy, Thames
Pau, Peter S.
Wright, Thomas T.

Property Manager
Clark, Edward B.
Gundy, Thames
Jensen, Ronald R.
Knipe, William B. Jr.
Welks, Julian
Winder, Charles L.
Wright, Thomas T.
Yelverton, D. Craig

Real Estate Publisher
Allen, Roger H.

Syndicator
Allen, Roger H.
Clegg, Mark W.
Fonshill, Ira William III
Gundy, Thames
Knipe, William B. Jr.
McKew, Walter Martin

LEWISTON

Architect
Wells, R. Ronald

Attorney
Duncan, Freeman B.

Broker
Acuff, J. Patrick

Builder
Wells, R. Ronald

Consultant
Wells, R. Ronald

Developer
Wells, R. Ronald

Instructor
Duncan, Freeman B.

Owner/Investor
Acuff, J. Patrick

Syndicator
Wells, R. Ronald

POCATELLO

Attorney
Just, Charles C.
Kingsford, Leonard O.

Broker
Clayton, Joe E.
Finch, Ruth W.
Johnston, W. James
Moses, C. Lynn
Perry, Michael G.

Consultant
Clayton, Joe E.
Finch, Ruth W.
Johnston, W. James
Just, Charles C.
Moses, C. Lynn

Developer
Moses, C. Lynn
Perry, Michael G.

Instructor
Johnston, W. James
Just, Charles C.

Owner/Investor
Johnston, W. James
Just, Charles C.

Property Manager
Finch, Ruth W.
Johnston, W. James
Perry, Michael G.

Syndicator
Clayton, Joe E.
Perry, Michael G.

TWIN FALLS

Appraiser
Koutnik, L. James

Architect
McLaughlin, James Daniel
O'Brien, Joseph F.

Attorney
Lawson, Edward A.

Broker
Bick, J. Karl
Busch, Gary B.
Koutnik, L. James
Renfro, Robert

Builder
Bick, J. Karl
O'Brien, Joseph F.

Consultant
Koutnik, L. James
Renfro, Robert

Developer
Bick, J. Karl
O'Brien, Joseph F.
Renfro, Robert

Engineer
O'Brien, Joseph F.

Instructor
Koutnik, L. James

Owner/Investor
Bick, J. Karl
Koutnik, L. James
O'Brien, Joseph F.
Renfro, Robert

Property Manager
Koutnik, L. James

Syndicator
Bick, J. Karl
Renfro, Robert

ILLINOIS

BLOOMINGTON

Appraiser
Harrison, Joseph H.
Henderson, Tom
Meyer, Larry E.

Attorney
Meints, Paul A.
Ostling, Lar Eric

Broker
Harrison, Joseph H.
Henderson, Tom
Meyer, Larry E.

Builder
Sallee, Lynn F. II

Consultant
Harrison, Joseph H.
Henderson, Tom
Meints, Paul A.

Instructor
Henderson, Tom
Meints, Paul A.
Ostling, Lar Eric

Insuror
Ostling, Lar Eric

Lender
Ostling, Lar Eric

Owner/Investor
Johnson, Earle B. Jr.
Meints, Paul A.
Ostling, Lar Eric
Sallee, Lynn F. II

Property Manager
Johnson, Earle B. Jr.
Ostling, Lar Eric

Real Estate Publisher
Henderson, Tom
Meints, Paul A.

Syndicator
Harrison, Joseph H.

CARBONDALE

Appraiser
Abell, Ronald R.
Hill, Sherman E.

Assessor
Abell, Ronald R.

Attorney
Lesar, Hiram H.

Broker
Abell, Ronald R.
Stone, John Wayne

Builder
Abell, Ronald R.

Developer
Stone, John Wayne

Instructor
Lesar, Hiram H.
Mattis, Taylor

Owner/Investor
Abell, Ronald R.

Property Manager
Abell, Ronald R.
Meyer, Shirley
Stone, John Wayne

CENTRALIA

Appraiser
Zink, John

Banker
Zink, John

Broker
Zink, John

Builder
Zink, John

Consultant
Zink, John

Developer
Zink, John

Insuror
Zink, John

Property Manager
Zink, John

Syndicator
Zink, John

CHAMPAIGN

Appraiser
Fleming, Arthur N.
Nusbaum, Robert E.
Yudin, Julian H.

Architect
Fleming, Arthur N.

Attorney
Balbach, Stanley B.
Bernthal, David G.
Howell, Pamela Sue
Keller, Robert O.
Parks, John R.

Banker
Watson, Charles Lynn

Broker
Fleming, Arthur N.
Nusbaum, Robert E.
Rockwood, Harry L.
Schmidt, Andrea Larson
Sides, Dorothy Hunt
Watson, Charles Lynn
Yudin, Julian H.

Builder
Fleming, Arthur N.
Martin, Harry Jr.

Consultant
Nusbaum, Robert E.
Watson, Charles Lynn
Yudin, Julian H.

Developer
Fleming, Arthur N.
Wood, James F.
Yudin, Julian H.

Engineer
Fleming, Arthur N.

Instructor
Fleming, Arthur N.

Insuror
Parks, John R.

Lender
Baker, Jeffrey A.

Owner/Investor
Balbach, Stanley B.
Fleming, Arthur N.
Nusbaum, Robert E.
Schmidt, Andrea Larson
Watson, Charles Lynn
Yudin, Julian H.

Property Manager
Fleming, Arthur N.
Martin, Harry Jr.
Nusbaum, Robert E.
Rockwood, Harry L.
Watson, Charles Lynn

Syndicator
Fleming, Arthur N.
Nusbaum, Robert E.
Watson, Charles Lynn
Yudin, Julian H.

CHICAGO

Appraiser
Anderson, Daniel G.
Becker, Ronald H.
Berger, Ronald
Bodel, Donald H.
Bouton, Kenneth T.H.
Brandt, Raymond A.
Bulthuis, James H.
Chaddick, Harry F.
Chinnock, Thomas G.
Curtis, James J. Jr.
Dallianis, Harry T.
Edfors, Hugh T.
Fitts, Jay T.
Gadd, John L.
Gathman, J. Denis
Gaunaurd, Henry
Geist, Donald D.
Hafner, William Lincoln
Honig, Robert M.
Kuehnle, Walter R.
Kunstadt, Michael E.
Leigh, Thomas G.
McCann, William A.
McClain, Joseph E.
Matanky, Eugene
Michels, Hugh C. Jr.
Napoli, Robert Alexander
O'Leigh, Thomas
Olivieri, Henry J. Jr.
Opas, David M Sr.
Parsons, Frederick M.
Reilly, Paul J.
Repsold, Peter B.
Rothman, Noel N.
Schmeltzer, Robert W.
Shlaes, Jared
Stokes, James F.
Voska, Joseph Jr.

Architect
Amstadter, Laurence
Bonavolonta, Anthony A.
Borkon, Benjamin M.
Bradtke, Philip J.
Comber, Frank J.
Croke, Thomas F.
Follensbee, James
Lincoln, Walter Stephen II
Shorobura, R. George
Voska, Joseph Jr.
Winstead, James R.

Assessor
Reilly, Paul J.

Attorney
Agnew, Patrick J.
Alban, William R.
Arnold, Peter J.
Aufrecht, Michael D.
Bagley, James J. II
Baker, Donald
Beederman, Asher J.
Berger, Robert M.
Berland, Abel E.
Bortman, David
Cagney, Joseph B.
Campbell, Stanley W. Jr.
Chapekis, A. Frederick
Cooney, Kevin J.
Covington, George M.
Cremieux, Richard J.
Croke, Jerome P.
Crotty, Jerome Francis
DeHaan, Ronald M.
Dropkin, Allen H.
Edfors, Hugh T.
Edler, Robert W.
Engelberg, Burt W.
Essig, William J.
Feigenberg, Louis A.
Firsel, Michael D.
Fisher, Herbert H.
Fox, Michael E.
Fremgen, William H
Froelich, Cezar M.
Geis, Norman
Getzov, Joel Merril
Gilmartin, Wayne S.
Glick, Paul M.
Glickson, Scott L.
Gopman, Howard Z.
Gossett, James F.
Gottlieb, Jerome Robert
Gould, Thomas L.
Gray, Edward W. Jr.
Greenfield, Gerald

Gutstein, Solomon
Hahn, Richard F.
Hall, Adolphus Jr.
Harris, Howard
Hartstein, Elliott D.
Hess, Peter A.
Hochman, James A.
Holleran, W.E.
Iglesk, Thomas R.
Jahns, Jeffrey
Johnson, Robert
Jones, Richard C.
Jones, Richard C. Jr.
Kantoff, Sheldon L.
Kimball, Paul C. Jr.
Kohn, Richard Fredrick
Kottel, Deborah J.
Kruk, Richard
Laytin, William M.
Levin, Allan E.
Levy, Fred J.
Liftin, Muriel Zeitlin
Lindberg, Steven C.
Lipshutz, Hal A.
Liss, Jeffrey G.
Lopatka, Arthur J. Jr.
Lurie, Paul M.
McGarry, John T.
McNitt, Joseph E.
McNulty, Peter J.
Marovitz, James L.
Marsh, Daniel A. Jr.
Medansky, Earl T.
Mickelson, Ralph R.
Mikes, James R.
Miller, Alan Benjamin
Moskowitz, Harold L.
Mulvaney, Conrad M.
Nekritz, Barry B.
Olivieri, Henry J. Jr.
Payne, Gordon D.
Piecewicz, Walter M.
Platt, David S.K.
Pletcher, Harold D.
Prather, William C.
Randall, Benjamin J.
Reilly, Paul J.
Richard, Howard M.
Rieck, Thomas W.
Rosenberg, Burton X.
Rosenberg, Sheli Z.
Rubenstein, Jeffrey C.
Sack, Nathaniel
Schwartzberg, Hugh J.
Shindler, Donald Alan
Shindler, Michael C.
Skipworth, Larry
Sklar, Stanley P.
Slavitt, Earl B.
Spagat, Martin
Steinberg, Morton M.
Stevens, Stanley M.
Strauss, Marc J.
Sumner, Sara E.
Thorndev, Judy P.
Werner, Eugene
Wittebort, Robert J. Jr.
Woloshin, William
Wong, Philip
York, John C.
Yura, Mark D.
Zenner, Brian S.

Banker

Akuffo, Boafo
Baker, J. William
Blaver, Leal B. Jr.
Blenko, David B.
Bond, Sharon A.
Bottom, Dale C.
Buckle, F.T.
Carlisle, Kurt
Cheseldine, Raymond M.
Cohen, Edward B.
Fate, Gary A.
Hausmann, John E.
Hitt, James L.
Honig, Robert M.
Hoyes, Louis W.
Lawrence, Norman L. Jr.
Leigh, Thomas G.
O'Leigh, Thomas
Olivieri, Henry J. Jr.
O'Neal, Patricia Conyers
Ostendorf, George J.
Pletcher, Harold D.
Robinson, Lydia W.
Rutledge, John K.
Schwartz, William Thomas
Skipworth, Larry
Strauss, Jay J.
Suhr, James K.

Broker

Abraham, Richard S.
Anderson, Daniel G.
Arnold, Peter J.
Berger, Ronald
Berland, Abel E.
Blayer, Bernard
Bonavolonta, Anthony A.
Borak, Carl H.
Browne, Aldis J. Jr.
Caccomo, Anthony V.
Caldeira, J. Leonard
Campbell, Stanley W. Jr.
Chapckis, A. Frederick
Chinnock, Thomas G.
Clarke, Charles F. Jr.
Collopy, Eamonn E.
Corn, John H.
Croke, Thomas F.
Daley, Vincent R. Jr.
Dallianis, Harry T.
Ducharme, Jacque
Eberhard, Gary L.
Edfors, Hugh T.
Embree, H. Gene
Fate, Gary A.
Fifield, Steven D.
Flodin, Mark W.
Forcucci, Dino Dean Jr.
Frankel, Jay L.
Frey, Bruce J.
Fujishima, Burt S.
Garafalo, Joseph
Gaunaurd, Henry
Geist, Donald D.
Geraghty, Martin P.
Gerhart, Bruce P.
Gidwitz, Peter E.
Glickson, Scott L.
Good, Sheldon F.
Gottlieb, Jerome Robert
Greer, Gaylon E.
Haback, Peter L.
Hall, Adolphus Jr.
Handler, Stuart
Hellgeth, Thomas G.
Heydorn, Munn W.
Huston, John M.
Ising, Thomas J.
Jacobsen, John H.
Jaffe, Donald S.
Kantoff, Sheldon L.
Keck, William F.
Keepper, John H.
Kellman, Jeffrey A.
Klonoski, Michael Joseph
Kolodny, Jeffrey E.
Koltz, Leo
Kretchmar, John F.
Krupnik, Vee M.
Layland, David N.
Levy, Fred J.
Lindenberg, Donald L.
Loukas, Anthony G.
McDonald, Jack
McGarry, John T.
McMillan, Thomas L.
Marsh, Daniel A. Jr.
Matanky, Eugene
Michels, Hugh C. Jr.
Minik, Frank
Napoli, Robert Alexander
Nierman, James S.
Niziol, Edward
Olivieri, Henry J. Jr.
Opas, David M Sr.
Planey, James B.
Pletcher, Harold D.
Primm, Earl R.
Reed, Rosalind
Rodstrom, Arthur R.
Rosen, Randy
Ross, Eugene I.
Rothman, Noel N.
Ruggles, Richard M.
Schmeltzer, Robert W.
Schulman, Albert
Sciara, Joseph F.
Shapiro, Donn
Sheridan, Donald T.
Smith, Larry J.
Sova, Richard S.
Spinner, Leslie P.
Spunt, Linda L.
Stark, Mark J.
Stokes, James F.
Stover, Phillip J.
Strobeck, Charles L.
Topping, Dean
Trossman, Don C.
Voska, Joseph Jr.
Wiesen, Robert J.
Wilder, Nicholas F.
Wislow, Robert A.
Wolfe, Goldie B.
Zenner, Brian S.

Builder

Bonavolonta, Anthony A.
Bresler, Stanley
Chaddick, Harry F.
Comber, Frank J.
Kaiser, Walter
Kantoff, Sheldon L.
Keiser, Gordon C.
Layland, David N.
Lincoln, Walter Stephen II
McGarry, John T.
Mann, James M.
Opas, David M Sr.
Pancoe, Walter
Redeker, M. Wayne
Ross, Eugene I.
Schmeltzer, Robert W.
Sciara, Joseph F.
Silverstein, Stephen
Voska, Joseph Jr.
Wilder, Nicholas F.

Consultant

Abraham, Richard S.
Al Chalabi, Margery
Anderson, Daniel G.
Arnold, Peter J.
Baker, Donald
Beale, Joseph S.
Becker, Ronald H.
Berger, Ronald
Berland, Abel E.
Bodel, Donald H.
Bonavolonta, Anthony A.
Bond, Sharon A.
Borkon, Benjamin M.
Bouton, Kenneth T.H.
Brown, Willard A. Sr.
Buckle, F.T.
Bulthuis, James H.
Bussey, Ronald J. CRE
Campbell, Gregory S.
Campbell, Stanley W. Jr.
Chaddick, Harry F.
Chinnock, Thomas G.
Clarke, Charles F. Jr.
Cohen, Edward B.
Collopy, Eamonn E.
Conti, Richard C.
Cook, Robert John
Corn, John H.
Cravitz, Alan R.
Croke, Thomas F.
Curtis, James J. Jr.
Daley, Vincent R. Jr.
Dallianis, Harry T.
Ducharme, Jacque
Eaton, K.J.
Eberhard, Gary L.
Edfors, Hugh T.
Feigenberg, Louis A.
Fiorentino, Michael E.
Fisher, Herbert H.
Fitts, Jay T.
Follensbee, James
Fowler, Christy Seip
Frankel, Jay L.
Frey, Bruce J.
Friedman, Stephen B.
Gadd, John L.
Garafalo, Joseph
Garrigan, Richard Thomas
Gathman, J. Denis
Gaunaurd, Henry
Geist, Donald D.
Geraghty, Martin P.
Gerfin, Thomas Joseph
Gomberg, Mandel
Good, Sheldon F.
Gottlieb, Jerome Robert
Greer, Gaylon E.
Hafner, William Lincoln
Hellgeth, Thomas G.
Hitt, James L.
Honig, Robert M.
Isaacson, Steven M.
Katz, Barry S.
Keepper, John H.
Kellman, Jeffrey A.
Klonoski, Michael Joseph
Kolodny, Jeffrey E.
Kretchmar, John F.
Krupnik, Vee M.
Kuehnle, Walter R.
Lachman, M. Leanne
Levy, Lawrence F.
Lindenberg, Donald L.
Loukas, Anthony G.
McCann, William A.
McClain, Joseph E.
McDonald, Jack
McGarry, John T.
Martin, Patrick A.
Matanky, Eugene
Medansky, Earl T.
Melaniphy, John C. Jr.
Napoli, Robert Alexander
Olesker, Sara L.
Olivieri, Henry J. Jr.
Olsen, Bradley A.
Opas, David M Sr.
Pagliari, Joseph L. Jr.
Parsons, Frederick M.
Payne, Gordon D.
Petrie, Paul E.
Phillips, David C.
Piecewicz, Walter M.
Prather, William C.
Primm, Earl R.
Reilly, Paul J.
Repsold, Peter B.
Rodstrom, Arthur R.
Rosen, Randy
Ross, Eugene I.
Rothman, Noel N.
Schloss, Nathan
Schmeltzer, Robert W.
Shapiro, Donn
Sheridan, Donald T.
Shlaes, Jared
Smith, Larry J.

Sobel, Joseph J.
Sova, Richard S.
Spinner, Leslie P.
Spunt, Linda L.
Stokes, James F.
Strobeck, Charles L.
Thorndev, Judy P.
Topping, Dean
Trossman, Don C.
Voska, Joseph Jr.
Warren, Ronald A.
Wiesen, Robert J.
Wislow, Robert A.
Witt, Alan M.
Zenner, Brian S.

Developer
Arnold, Peter J.
Beale, Joseph S.
Berger, Ronald
Bonavolonta, Anthony A.
Borak, Carl H.
Borkon, Benjamin M.
Botthof, C.L. Jr.
Bresler, Stanley
Buckle, F.T.
Builta, Howard C
Caccomo, Anthony V.
Campbell, Gregory S.
Campbell, Stanley W. Jr.
Caraher, James C.
Chaddick, Harry F.
Chapekis, A. Frederick
Cohen, Lawrence A.
Collopy, Eamonn E.
Cook, Robert John
Corn, John H.
Cravitz, Alan R.
Croke, Jerome P.
Croke, Thomas F.
Eberhard, Gary L.
Ellenbogen, Steven W.
Field, Maxwell John
Fifield, Steven D.
Finke, Robert Lawrence
Fitts, Jay T.
Forcucci, Dino Dean Jr.
Fox, Matthew C.
Frankel, Jay L.
Fremgen, William H.
Frey, Bruce J.
Fujishima, Burt S.
Gaunaurd, Henry
Geist, Donald D.
Geraghty, Martin P.
Gerfin, Thomas Joseph
Gidwitz, Peter E.
Gottlieb, Jerome Robert
Guarino, Salvatore F.
Haddad, Lawrence
Harris, Howard
Hermann, Richard C.
Huston, John M.
Isaacson, Steven M.
Jaffe, Donald S.
Kaiser, Walter
Kantoff, Sheldon L.
Keck, William F.
Keiser, Gordon C.
Kellman, Jeffrey A.
Kirby, James J.
Klarich, Richard M.
Klonoski, Michael Joseph
Koltz, Leo
Kottel, Deborah J.
Kretchmar, John F.
Layland, David N.
Levy, Fred J.
Levy, Lawrence F.
Lincoln, Walter Stephen II
Lindenberg, Donald L.
Loukas, Anthony G.
McClain, Joseph E.
McDonald, Jack
McEnery, John T.
McGarry, John T.
McMillan, Thomas L.
Mann, James M.
Matanky, Eugene
Medansky, Earl T.
Michels, Hugh C. Jr.
Mickelson, Ralph R.
Milner, Harold W.
Neiman, Cary L.
Nichols, Stephen R.
Nierman, James S.
Niziol, Edward
Olivieri, Henry J. Jr.
Opas, David M Sr.
Pancoe, Walter
Paul, David L.
Phillips, David C.
Redeker, M. Wayne
Repsold, Peter B.
Rhodes, Jeffrey J.
Rosenberg, Thomas B.
Rosenthal, Robert N.
Ross, Eugene I.
Rothman, Noel N.
Ruttenberg, Roger F.
Schmeltzer, Robert W.
Schwartz, Gerald
Sheridan, Donald T.
Shorobura, R. George
Siegelbaum, David A.
Silverstein, Stephen
Skipworth, Larry
Smith, Larry J.
Sova, Richard S.
Stokes, James F.
Stover, Phillip J.
Strobeck, Charles L.
Sturges, Lance H.
Swartz, Michael E.
Thorndev, Judy P.
Voska, Joseph Jr.
Warren, Ronald A.
Wiesen, Robert J.
Wilder, Nicholas F.
Wilhelm, Phillip H.
Wislow, Robert A.
Zell, Samuel

Engineer
Arnold, Peter J.
Follensbee, James
Kaiser, Walter
Kantoff, Sheldon L.
Levin, Allan E.

Instructor
Arnold, Peter J.
Bottom, Dale C.
Butler, Virgil
Daley, Vincent R. Jr.
Dallianis, Harry T.
Garrigan, Richard Thomas
Glickson, Scott L.
Good, Sheldon F.
Gray, Edward W. Jr.
Greer, Gaylon E.
Hood, Lloyd
Jones, Richard C.
Katz, Barry S.
Keepper, John H.
Kratovil, Robert
Krupnik, Vee M.
McDonald, Jack
Marsh, Daniel A. Jr.
Olesker, Sara L.
Olivieri, Henry J. Jr.
Repsold, Peter B.
Rosen, Randy
Schwartz, William Thomas
Sklar, Stanley P.
Spunt, Linda L.

Insuror
Akuffo, Boafo
Borak, Carl H.
Buckle, F.T.
Cohen, Edward B.
Croke, Jerome P.
Frey, Bruce J.
Heydorn, Munn W.
Isaacson, Steven M.
Keck, William F.
Krupnik, Vee M.
Matanky, Eugene
Opas, David M Sr.
Price, Leslie M. Jr.
Ruggles, Richard M.
Schmeltzer, Robert W.
Thorndev, Judy P.
Wise, Paul S.

Lender
Akuffo, Boafo
Arnold, Peter J.
Baker, J. William
Baratta, Philip J.
Bond, Sharon A.
Buckle, F.T.
Cravitz, Alan R.
Croke, Jerome P.
Ford, Donald D.
Fremgen, William H.
Gerfin, Thomas Joseph
Greenberg, Stuart L.
Harris, Howard
Hausmann, John E.
Heydorn, Munn W.
Honig, Robert M.
Iglesk, Thomas R.
Karth, Frank J.
Kohn, Richard Fredrick
Leigh, Thomas G.
Lindenberg, Donald L.
Martin, Patrick A.
Mesjak, Theodore C.
O'Leigh, Thomas
Opas, David M Sr.
Ostendorf, George J.
Prather, William C.
Strauss, Jay J.
Wittebort, Robert J. Jr.

Owner/Investor
Anderson, Daniel G.
Arnold, Peter J.
Aufrecht, Michael D.
Baker, Donald
Beale, Joseph S.
Berger, Ronald
Blayer, Bernard
Bonavolonta, Anthony A.
Bond, Sharon A.
Borkon, Benjamin M.
Bresler, Stanley
Buckle, F.T.
Cameron, Douglas H.
Campbell, Stanley W. Jr.
Caraher, James C.
Chapekis, A. Frederick
Clarke, Charles F. Jr.
Cohen, Edward B.
Cooney, Kevin J.
Daley, Vincent R. Jr.
Dallianis, Harry T.
Daverman, James E.
Eaton, K.J.
Edfors, Hugh T.
Edler, Robert W.
Ellenbogen, Steven W.
Embree, H. Cono
Field, Maxwell John
Fifield, Steven D.
Fiorentino, Michael E.
Follensbee, James
Frankel, Jay L.
Frey, Bruce J.
Fujishima, Burt S.
Garrigan, Richard Thomas
Gaunaurd, Henry
Geraghty, Martin P.
Gidwitz, Peter E.
Gilmartin, Wayne S.
Glickson, Scott L.
Gomberg, Mandel
Gottlieb, Jerome Robert
Haddad, Lawrence
Hellgeth, Thomas G.
Hitt, James L.
Hochman, James A.
Hood, Lloyd
Horton, Donald H.
Iglesk, Thomas R.
Isaacson, Steven M.
Ising, Thomas J.
Jones, Richard C.
Kaiser, Walter
Karth, Frank J.
Keledjian, E. James
Kellman, Jeffrey A.
Kirby, James J.
Klarich, Richard M.
Klonoski, Michael Joseph
Kolodny, Jeffrey E.
Kottel, Deborah J.
Krupnik, Vee M.
Lawrence, Norman L. Jr.
Layland, David N.
Levy, Lawrence F.
Lindenberg, Donald L.
Loukas, Anthony G.
McClain, Joseph E.
McDonald, Jack
McGarry, John T.
McMillan, Thomas L.
Mann, James M.
Marsh, Daniel A. Jr.
Matanky, Eugene
Medansky, Earl T.
Mesjak, Theodore C.
Mickelson, Ralph R.
Milner, Harold W.
Neiman, Cary L.
Nekritz, Barry B.
Nichols, Stephen R.
Nierman, James S.
Niziol, Edward
Pancoe, Walter
Price, Leslie M. Jr.
Redeker, M. Wayne
Repsold, Peter B.
Rosen, Randy
Ross, Eugene I.
Ruttenberg, Roger F.
Schmeltzer, Robert W.
Schwartz, William Thomas
Schwartzberg, Hugh J.
Sheridan, Donald T.
Silverstein, Stephen
Skipworth, Larry
Slazas, James A.
Smith, Larry J.
Sova, Richard S.
Stokes, James F.
Strobeck, Charles L.
Sumner, Sara E.
Swartz, Michael E.
Warren, Ronald A.
Wiesen, Robert J.
Wilhelm, Phillip H.
Winstead, James R.
Wislow, Robert A.
Woloshin, William
York, John C.
Yura, Mark D.
Zell, Samuel
Zenner, Brian S.

Property Manager
Abraham, Richard S.
Akuffo, Boafo
Aldridge, John W.
Baird, Robert E.
Beale, Joseph S.
Berger, Ronald
Bernstein, Stanley
Bodel, Donald H.
Bonavolonta, Anthony A.

Bond, Sharon A.
Borak, Carl H.
Britz, John
Brophy, Jack
Browne, Aldis J. Jr.
Buckle, F.T.
Budd, Val
Butler, Virgil
Campbell, Gregory S.
Cardwell, John
Cerne, Wence
Chaddick, Harry F.
Clarke, Charles F. Jr.
Cohen, Edward B.
Cohen, Lawrence A.
Collopy, Eamonn E.
Croke, Thomas F.
Daley, Vincent R. Jr.
Dallianis, Harry T.
Daniels, Derick
David, Leonard J.
Demouth, R.M.
Duerkop, Stephen P.
Elafros, Bernard
Embree, H. Gene
Enders, W. Dean
Epstein, Robert
Finke, Robert Lawrence
Fiorentino, Michael E.
Flodin, Mark W.
Fox, Matthew C.
Frankel, Jay L.
Frey, Bruce J.
Friedman, Burt
Gaunaurd, Henry
Geist, Donald D.
Gidwitz, Peter E.
Glusak, John Bruce
Goetschel, Arthur
Gonczy, Stephen I.
Goodsitt, Robert D.
Gorden, Thomas
Haddad, Lawrence
Hagenah, W.
Hall, Adolphus Jr.
Heilbrunn, Jerome
Hermann, Richard C.
Hitt, James L.
Hoffman, L.M.
Holleran, W.E.
Huston, John M.
Isaacson, Steven M.
Johnson, Robert
Kaplan, James
Katz, Barry S.
Keck, William F.
Kelly, Donald P.
King, Hart M.
Kirby, James J.
Klarich, Richard M.
Klonoski, Michael Joseph
Koe, Jan E.
Kolodny, Jeffrey E.
Koltz, Leo
Koskinen, Carl
Kunstadt, Michael E.
Lacaille, Georgeann
Ladd, Wilfred A.
Lawrence, Norman L. Jr.
Layland, David N.
Leoni, Ronald J.
Light, Kenneth
Livingston, Frank H.
Lopatka, Arthur J. Jr.
Loukas, Anthony G.
MacAdam, Gordon L.
McClain, Joseph E.
McDonald, Jack
McGarry, John T.
McMillan, Thomas L.
Martin, Donald O.
Matanky, Eugene
Michels, Hugh C. Jr.
Milner, Harold W.
Mole, Tom
Neiman, Cary L.
Nichols, John
Nuter, John E.
Parsons, Frederick M.
Penn, Robert
Petrie, Paul E.
Phillips, David C.
Repsold, Peter B.
Rodstrom, Arthur R.
Rogowski, Walter S.
Rosen, Randy
Ross, Eugene I.
Rothman, Noel N.
Rugg, Frank J.
Ruggles, Richard M.
Schmeltzer, Robert W.
Schwartzberg, Hugh J.
Sciara, Joseph F.
Shapiro, Donn
Sheridan, Donald T.
Skipworth, Larry
Smith, Larry J.
Stark, Mark J.
Stokes, James F.
Stone, Roger W.
Stover, Phillip J.
Strobeck, Charles L.
Sumner, Sara E.
Swanson, Richard
Topping, Dean
Voska, Joseph Jr.
Wilder, Nicholas F.
Wislow, Robert A.

Real Estate Publisher
Amos, John
Arnold, Peter J.
Banis, Andrew P.
Cole, Patricia S.
Downs, James
Gamez, Barbara M.
Garrigan, Richard Thomas
Grant, Anne R.
Harms, Barbara
Hener, Karla
High, Barbara Anne
Kyle, Robert C.
McClain, Joseph E.
McDonough, Douglas J.
Matanky, Eugene
Miko, Richard S.
Naurocki, Gloria
Newquist, Daniel
O'Connor, Llani
Papadopoulos, Joan
Pendelton, Kathleen
Prather, William C.
Prentiss, Donald K.
Stearns, George
Swanson, Lyn
Weinberg, Arnold

Regulator
Kirby, James J.
McClain, Joseph E.
Payne, Gordon D.
Prather, William C.

Syndicator
Akuffo, Boafo
Arnold, Peter J.
Borak, Carl H.
Bresler, Stanley
Caccomo, Anthony V.
Cameron, Douglas H.
Chapekis, A. Frederick
Cooney, Kevin J.
Croke, Thomas F.
Daley, Vincent R. Jr.
Dallianis, Harry T.
Eaton, K.J.
Forcucci, Dino Dean Jr.
Fox, Matthew C.
Frankel, Jay L.
Frey, Bruce J.
Gerhart, Bruce P.
Gopman, Howard Z.
Gottlieb, Jerome Robert
Hall, Adolphus Jr.
Handler, Stuart
Hermann, Richard C.
Hood, Lloyd
Horton, Donald H.
Isaacson, Steven M.
Keck, William F.
Keledjian, E. James
Kirby, James J.
Klonoski, Michael Joseph
Kolodny, Jeffrey E.
Kottel, Deborah J.
Krupnik, Vee M.
Levy, Fred J.
Lindenberg, Donald L.
Loukas, Anthony G.
Matanky, Eugene
Medansky, Earl T.
Niziol, Edward
Rosen, Randy
Ross, Eugene I.
Ruttenberg, Roger F.
Silverstein, Stephen
Stover, Phillip J.
Strobeck, Charles L.
Warren, Ronald A.
Woloshin, William
York, John C.
Zenner, Brian S.

EFFINGHAM

Attorney
Austin, William W.

GALESBURG

Appraiser
Curry, Edna Tenhaaf
David, Mahlon R.
Hill, Richard G.

Attorney
Kolom, Alfred J.

Broker
Curry, Edna Tenhaaf
David, Mahlon R.
Hill, Richard G.

Builder
Curry, Edna Tenhaaf
David, Mahlon R.
Olson, Rodger L.

Consultant
Curry, Edna Tenhaaf
David, Mahlon R.
Hill, Richard G.

Developer
Curry, Edna Tenhaaf
David, Mahlon R.
Olson, Rodger L.

Engineer
Hill, Richard G.

Instructor
Curry, Edna Tenhaaf
David, Mahlon R.

Owner/Investor
Curry, Edna Tenhaaf
David, Mahlon R.
Hill, Richard G.
Olson, Rodger L.

Property Manager
Curry, Edna Tenhaaf
Kolom, Alfred J.
Olson, Rodger L.

Syndicator
Curry, Edna Tenhaaf

KANKAKEE

Appraiser
Perry, Tony

Broker
Perry, Tony

Consultant
Perry, Tony

Instructor
Perry, Tony

Owner/Investor
Perry, Tony

Property Manager
Cook, Robert
Perry, Tony

Syndicator
Perry, Tony

NORTH SUBURBAN

Appraiser
Davies, John M. III
Defano, Bernard M.
Dillon, Joseph G.
Dowling, Geoffrey W.
Dubs, Kenneth P. Sr.
Gerschefske, Charles
Gunsteens, Kenneth M.
Hagee, Joseph G.
Hawkins, Paul Minor Jr.
Heidorn, Donald G.
Holcer, Thomas E.
Jaconetti, Armando E.
King, Neil J.
Knowles, William R.
Landeck, John H.
McKay, John P.
Marsh, R. Pres.
Melaniphy, F.J.
Mirza, Nathan A.
Norton, Peter E.
Podolsky, Milton
Serszen, Jerome A.
Sumwalt, Sam
Wall, Norbert F.
York, Robert E.

Architect
Barry, Gerald W.
McRae, Colin L.
Marsh, R. Pres.
Otis, James Jr.
Torgersen, Torwald H.
Wendt, Forrest D.
Yore, Alan R.
Zsolnay, Gabor M.

Assessor
Gerschefske, Charles

Attorney
Bohrer, Nancy King
Buttitta, Joseph J.
Davies, John M. III
Denzel, Ken J.
Devine, James D.
Duggan, James
Glick, Kenneth J.
Goode, Howard C.
Gross, Irwin A.
Hall, David M.
Jacobus, John L.
Jaffe, Richard
Krone, Norman B.
Lampe, John F.
Landmeier, Allen L.
Martin, Lawrence G.
Martin, Wayne Mallott
Morgan, William T. Jr.
Muskat, Marc L.
Pavone, Louis V.
Rawson, William
Reinsdorf, Jerry M.
Spelman, Harold J.

Stelle, Roger T.
Vickman, Lee J.
Walner, Robert J.

Banker
Burke, Ronald G.
Carrel, Herbert L. CMB
Jennings, William G.
King, Neil J.

Broker
Amarantos, Peter Thomas
Anderson, Dennis C.
Besser, Bruce R.
Buttitta, Joseph J.
Clum, Thomazine
Cornes, Phil M.
Corso, Anthony E.
Davies, John M. III
DeWoskin, William
Dillon, Joseph G.
Dobroth, Dale
Dolan, Harry L. Jr.
Dowling, Geoffrey W.
Dowling, Owen Q.
Dowling, Terence D.
Dubs, Kenneth P. Sr.
Eigel, Christopher J.
Ellis, Dorothy J.
Falkenberg, Mary Ann
Fortunato, Donald L.
Franz, Lydia T.
Fuhrer, Larry
Fuller, Michael
Goldner, Arthur
Gunsteens, Kenneth M.
Hagee, Joseph G.
Hashioka, Christopher E.
Hawkins, Paul Minor Jr.
Heidorn, Donald G.
Hill, Robert E.
Jaconetti, Armando E.
Jennings, William G.
Jung, Kristine A.
Keating, John S. Jr.
Keenan, John M.
King, Neil J.
Kissel, Katherine V.
Knowles, William R.
Krafsur, Howard G.
Landeck, John H.
Linane, William E.
McDermott, James P.
McDonald, Rose
McKay, John P.
Marsh, R.
Martin, Lawrence G.
Martin, Ralph H.
Martin, Wayne Mallott
Melaniphy, F.J.
Moore, Judith S.
Morgan, William T. Jr.
Mourek, Anthony J.
Muskat, Marc L.
Nash, Richard
Nordgren, Paul E.
Norton, Peter E.
O'Connell, Sam
Patinos, Gloria H.
Plotkin, Jonathan Dean
Podolsky, Milton
Podolsky, Steven H.
Pollard, Thomas E.
Robinson, Ronald Redlich
Rudnik, Shirley L.
Rudsinski, Gary L.
Rutledge, Richard G.
Sample, Bob E.
Schlanbusch, Ernest G.
Schrock, Lyle E.
Scott, Richard E.
Sherwin, Samuel R.
Smith, Harry G.
Sumwalt, Sam
Toberman, Scott K.
Vickman, Lee J.
Walsh, James R.
Warr, William W.
York, Robert E.

Builder
Besser, Bruce R.
Centofante, Alfred V.
Defano, Bernard M.
Devine, James D.
Dubs, Kenneth P. Sr.
Galey, Michael H.
Ginsburg, Sheldon H.
Jaconetti, Armando E.
Krone, Norman B.
McDermott, James P.
McKay, John P.
McLennan, Robert G. Jr.
McRae, Colin L.
Marsh, R. Pres.
Mourek, Anthony J.
O'Connor, Jerome P.
Quast, Richard D.
Sample, Bob E.
Smith, Harry G.
Ulakovich, Ronald S.
Yore, Alan R.
Zsolnay, Gabor M.

Consultant
Alexabdra, Victoria Soto
Anderson, Dennis C.
Besser, Bruce R.
Bothen, Thomas Charles
Centofante, Alfred V.
Clum, Thomazine
Corso, Anthony E.
Defano, Bernard M.
Devine, James D.
Dillon, Joseph G.
Dowling, Geoffrey W.
Dubs, Kenneth P. Sr.
Euring, George A. Jr.
Falkenberg, Mary Ann
Fuhrer, Larry
Gerschefske, Charles
Ginsburg, Sheldon H.
Goldman, Elwin J.
Hagee, Joseph G.
Heidorn, Donald G.
Holcer, Thomas E.
Jaconetti, Armando E.
Keenan, John M.
King, Neil J.
Knowles, William R.
Kokalis, Soter George
Krafsur, Howard G.
Landeck, John H.
McKay, John P.
McLennan, Robert G. Jr.
Marsh, R. Pres.
Martin, Wayne Mallott
Melaniphy, F.J.
Moore, Judith S.
Morgan, William T. Jr.
Muskat, Marc L.
Nash, Richard
Nordgren, Paul E.
Podolsky, Milton
Podolsky, Steven H.
Pollard, Thomas E.
Rees, Terry L.
Riley, James D.
Robinson, Ronald Redlich
Sample, Bob E.
Schlanbusch, Ernest G.
Scott, Richard E.
Smith, Harry G.
Toberman, Scott K.
Vickman, Lee J.
Wall, Norbert F.
Yore, Alan R. AIA
Zaloudek, Robert F.

Developer
Alexabdra, Victoria Soto
Besser, Bruce R.
Buttitta, Joseph J.
Celano, J.V. Jr.
Centofante, Alfred V.
Cibula, George
Clancy, Joseph P.
Cornes, Phil M.
Corso, Anthony E.
Cowhey, Robert E.
Devine, James D.
DeWoskin, William
Dillon, Joseph G.
Dolan, Harry L. Jr.
Dowling, Geoffrey W.
Dowling, Terence D.
Dubs, Kenneth P. Sr.
Egan, Michael M. III
Galey, Michael H.
Ginsburg, Sheldon H.
Goldner, Arthur
Hagee, Joseph G.
Harris, David P.
Hattis, Bernard S.
Jaconetti, Armando E.
Jung, Kristine A.
Keating, John S. Jr.
Keenan, John M.
King, Neil J.
Krafsur, Howard G.
Krone, Norman B.
LaReno, Richard R.
Linane, William E.
Lower, Louis G. II
McDermott, James P.
McKay, John P.
McLennan, Robert G. Jr.
McRae, Colin L.
Martin, Lawrence G.
Martin, Ralph H.
Mourek, Anthony J.
O'Connor, Jerome P.
Podolsky, Milton
Podolsky, Steven H.
Pollard, Thomas E.
Quast, Richard D.
Sample, Bob E.
Schaefer, James T.
Scott, Richard E.
Smith, Harry G.
Ulakovich, Ronald S.
Wendt, Forrest D.
Wiese, Howard Kendall
Yore, Alan R.

Engineer
Cowhey, Robert E.
Defano, Bernard M.
Hattis, Bernard S.
Jennings, William G.
Yore, Alan R.

Instructor
Eigel, Christopher J.
Falkenberg, Mary Ann
Fuhrer, Larry
Hawkins, Paul Minor Jr.
Heidorn, Donald G.
Keenan, John M.
Kokalis, Soter George
McKay, John P.
Melaniphy, F.J.
Moore, Judith S.
Muskat, Marc L.
Robinson, Ronald Redlich
Sample, Bob E.
Sumwalt, Sam
York, Robert E.
Zaloudek, Robert F.

Insuror
Buttitta, Joseph J.
Jennings, William G.
King, Neil J.
McKay, John P.
McRae, Colin L.
Marsh, R. Pres.
Robinson, Ronald Redlich
Sample, Bob E.
Sherwin, Samuel R.
Sumwalt, Sam

Lender
Carrel, Herbert L.
Dobroth, Dale
Fortunato, Donald L.
Gross, Irwin A.
Hashioka, Christopher E.
Holzer, Robert L.
Marsh, R. Pres.
Martin, Lawrence G.
Martin, Wayne Mallott
Meador, Thomas E.
Sumwalt, Sam

Owner/Investor
Anderson, Dennis C.
Besser, Bruce R.
Bothen, Thomas Charles
Brown, Michael M.
Buttitta, Joseph J.
Centofante, Alfred V.
Cornes, Phil M.
Denzel, Ken J.
Devine, James D.
DeWoskin, William
Dillon, Joseph G.
Dolan, Harry L. Jr.
Dowling, Geoffrey W.
Dowling, Terence D.
Egan, Michael M. III
Eigel, Christopher J.
Falkenberg, Mary Ann
Fortunato, Donald L.
Fuhrer, Larry
Fuller, Michael
Galey, Michael H.
Ginsburg, Sheldon H.
Goldner, Arthur
Hagee, Joseph G.
Hashioka, Christopher E.
Heidorn, Donald G.
Jaconetti, Armando E.
Jennings, William G.
Jung, Kristine A.
Keenan, John M.
King, Neil J.
Kissel, Katherine V.
Kokalis, Soter George
Krafsur, Howard G.
Krone, Norman B.
Lower, Louis G. II
McDermott, James P.
McKay, John P.
McRae, Colin L.
Marsh, R. Pres.
Martin, Lawrence G.
Martin, Wayne Mallott
Melaniphy, F.J.
Moore, Judith S.
Mourek, Anthony J.
Nash, Richard
Nilsson, Gunnar P.
Nordgren, Paul E.
Norton, Peter E.
O'Connor, Jerome P.
Podolsky, Steven H.
Quast, Richard D.
Rees, Terry L.
Riley, James D.
Rutledge, Richard G.
Sample, Bob E.
Schlanbusch, Ernest G.
Scott, Richard E.
Serszen, Jerome A.
Sherwin, Samuel R.
Smith, Harry G.
Torgersen, Torwald H.
Ulakovich, Ronald S.
Vickman, Lee J.
Wall, Norbert F.
Wendt, Forrest D.
Wiese, Howard Kendall
York, Robert E.

Zsolnay, Gabor M.

Property Manager
Alexabdra, Victoria Soto
Amdur, Ted
Besser, Bruce R.
Bothen, Thomas Charles
Centofante, Alfred V.
Clum, Thomazine
Cornes, Phil M.
Corso, Anthony E.
Cox, Willard J. Jr.
Crawford, Robert
DaValle, Al
Davidsmeyer, Gene
Davies, John M. III
Dean, Howard M. Jr.
Defano, Bernard M.
DeWoskin, William
Dillon, Joseph G.
Dobroth, Dale
Dowling, Geoffrey W.
Dowling, Owen Q.
Dowling, Terence D.
Dubs, Kenneth P. Sr.
Duggan, James
Falkenberg, Mary Ann
Fortunato, Donald L.
Frankhauser, Wayne
Goldner, Arthur
Hagee, Joseph G.
Harris, Nelson
Hashioka, Christopher E.
Jennings, William G.
Keenan, John M.
Knudson, John A.
Kokalis, Soter George
Lewis, Edward
McDermott, James P.
McKay, John P.
McRae, Colin L.
Marsh, R. Pres.
Martin, Lawrence G.
Martin, Ralph H.
Mattick, Thomas C.
Melaniphy, F.J.
Morgan, William T. Jr.
Mourek, Anthony J.
Nordgren, Paul E.
Obert, R. Paul
O'Connor, Jerome P.
O'Neil, Thomas
Ozelis, Casey
Pease, Robert
Podolsky, Milton
Podolsky, Steven H.
Pollard, Thomas E.
Quast, Richard D.
Rawson, William
Rees, Terry L.
Richard, Joel
Riley, James D.
Robinson, Ronald Redlich
Rubin, Steve
Russo, Adrian
Saliba, Jacob
Scott, Richard E.
Seely, Don
Shaffer, Ralph
Sherwin, Samuel R.
Sullivan, Richard
Teuscher, Barbara A.
Torgersen, Torwald H.
Ulakovich, Ronald S.
Wiese, Howard Kendall
York, Robert E.

Syndicator
Anderson, Dennis C.
Besser, Bruce R.
Denzel, Ken J.
Devine, James D.
DeWoskin, William
Dillon, Joseph G.
Dobroth, Dale
Dolan, Harry L. Jr.
Dowling, Geoffrey W.
Dowling, Terence D.
Egan, Michael M. III
Fortunato, Donald L.
Fuhrer, Larry
Fuller, Michael
Ginsburg, Sheldon H.
Goldner, Arthur
Hashioka, Christopher E.
Jaconetti, Armando E.
Jennings, William G.
Keenan, John M.
Lampe, John F.
Linane, William E.
McLennan, Robert G. Jr.
Martin, Ralph H.
Muskat, Marc L.
Podolsky, Steven H.
Pollard, Thomas E.
Sample, Bob E.
Scott, Richard E.
Sherwin, Samuel R.
Toberman, Scott K.
Ulakovich, Ronald S.
Zaloudek, Robert F.

PEORIA

Appraiser
Finch, Brian A.
McAtee, Patrick O.
Williams, Harry E.

Attorney
Black, Kenneth W.
Gentry, Richard N. Jr.

Banker
Fuelberth, John H.

Broker
Adrian, James J.
Sauder, Kenneth R.
Stein, David Jerome
Wasson, Irv
Williams, Harry E.

Builder
Giacinti, Ralph A.
Wasson, Irv

Consultant
Adrian, James J.
Balistreri, Steve
Banwart, Gerald H.
Giacinti, Ralph A.
Sauder, Kenneth R.
Stein, David Jerome
Wasson, Irv

Developer
Balistreri, Steve
Giacinti, Ralph A.
Stein, David Jerome
Wasson, Irv

Instructor
Giacinti, Ralph A.
Sauder, Kenneth R.

Lender
Fuelberth, John H.

Owner/Investor
Black, Kenneth W.
Sauder, Kenneth R.
Stein, David Jerome
Wasson, Irv
Williams, Harry E.

Property Manager
Bahr, Wilbur
Balistreri, Steve
Mattson, B.O.
Sauder, Kenneth R.

Syndicator
Giacinti, Ralph A.

QUINCY

Appraiser
Bower, Jay R.
Voth, Donald P.W.

Attorney
Tucker, Edward B.

Broker
Bower, Jay R.
Mays, Jeffrey D.
Tucker, Edward B.
Voth, Donald P.W.

Consultant
Tucker, Edward B.

Developer
Tucker, Edward B.

Engineer
Tucker, Edward B.

Syndicator
Tucker, Edward B.

ROCK ISLAND

Appraiser
Swanson, Dwight F.

Attorney
Durkee, Bert R.

Broker
Motz, Richard W.
Swanson, Dwight F.
Weiner, David M.

Developer
Motz, Richard W.
Weiner, David M.

Owner/Investor
Motz, Richard W.
Weiner, David M.

Property Manager
Motz, Richard W.
Rutherford, Kenneth
Weiner, David M.

Real Estate Publisher
Armstrong, Richard A.

Syndicator
Motz, Richard W.

ROCKFORD

Appraiser
Hart, Jay A.
Hopkins, Guy M.
Jenks, William T.
Kepner, P. Leslie

Architect
Orput, Alden

Attorney
Gehlbach, Gary R.

Banker
Doyle, Robert A.
Hart, Jay A.

Broker
Boraiko, Carl G.
Doyle, Robert A.
Ewing, Thomas G.
Groleau, Carol A.
Hart, Jay A.
Hopkins, Guy M.
Hunter, Ernest H.
Kepner, P. Leslie

Builder
Groleau, Carol A.
Hart, Jay A.
Hunter, Ernest H.
Kepner, P. Leslie
Orput, Alden
Randecker, Allen W.
Swanson, Oliver C.

Consultant
Boraiko, Carl G.
Doyle, Robert A.
Hart, Jay A.
Jenks, William T.
Kepner, P. Leslie

Developer
Boraiko, Carl G.
Doyle, Robert A.
Groleau, Carol A.
Hart, Jay A.
Hunter, Ernest H.
Kepner, P. Leslie
Orput, Alden

Instructor
Hart, Jay A.

Insuror
Ewing, Thomas G.
Hart, Jay A.

Lender
Hart, Jay A.

Owner/Investor
Boraiko, Carl G.
Doyle, Robert A.
Groleau, Carol A.
Hart, Jay A.
Hunter, Ernest H.
Orput, Alden

Property Manager
Boraiko, Carl G.
Dillon, Peter
Ewing, Thomas G.
Hart, Jay A.
Kuska, Lee
Livingston, Bruce M.
Orput, Alden
Swanson, Eugene K.

Syndicator
Boraiko, Carl G.
Hart, Jay A.
Orput, Alden

SOUTH SUBURBAN

Appraiser
Anderson, Gerald E.
Boblak, Frank J.
Darrow, Lawrence P.
Disera, Bonnie
Lentfer, Richard H.
Liebscher, V.K. Chris
Poetter, Bruce E.
Port, Richard B.
Sachen, Joseph L.
Shanahan, John E.
Thomson, William Hills
Towner, John H.
Wagner, Alvin L. Jr.

Architect
Baldwin, William E.
Matthews, Drew I.
Nemoede, Albert H.
Staub, John T.

Attorney
Brendemuhl, Ruth Anne
Doersch, Richard C.
Gillen, Robert D.
James, John D.
Lauritzen, Anna M.
Leffelman, Dean J.
Lenczycki, Wayne A.
Liss, Michael R.
Matz, Kevin D.
Molenaar, James E.
Rizzi, Joseph V.
Thomson, William Hills

Banker
Anderson, Gerald E.
Autenrieth, Glenn E.
Berggren, Alan R.

Thomson, William Hills

Broker
Anderson, Gerald E.
Barofsky, Frederick J.
Bella, Frank A. Jr.
Berggren, Alan R.
Boblak, Frank J.
Brown, Karen A.
Burke, Joyce M.
Disera, Bonnie
Downs, Joseph M.
Green, Jeffrey S.
Greene, Gordon J.
Groszek, Marlene
Homer, Dean R.
Keleher, Peter D.
Kline, William R.
Lenczycki, Wayne A.
Lentfer, Richard H.
Liebscher, V.K. Chris
Martin, LaDoris
Matthews, Drew I.
Mays, Richard A.
Motluck, William J.
O'Malley, Robert Eugene
Pitlock, Lee P.
Poetter, Bruce E.
Port, Richard B.
Raymond, James W.
Reynolds, Bryan P.
Sachen, Joseph L.
Sutherlin, Robert C.
Thomson, William Hills
Towner, John H.
Wagner, Alvin L. Jr.
Williamson, Roger K.

Builder
Anderson, Gerald E.
Baldwin, William E.
Faltz, Richard A.
Groszek, Marlene
Keel, Phillip J.
Koop, Howard A.
Lentfer, Richard H.
Martin, LaDoris
Matthews, Drew I.
Motluck, William J.
O'Malley, Robert Eugene
Pasquinelli, Anthony R.
Raymond, James W.
Reynolds, Bryan P.
Schwander, Robert H.

Consultant
Anderson, Gerald E.
Anderson, Roger O.
Bella, Frank A. Jr.
Boblak, Frank J.
Brown, Karen A.
Downs, Joseph M.
Gillen, Robert D.
Green, Jeffrey S.
Homer, Dean R.
Keel, Phillip J.
Keleher, Peter D.
Leffelman, Dean J.
Liebscher, V.K. Chris
Motluck, William J.
O'Malley, Robert Eugene
Pasquinelli, Anthony R.
Pitlock, Lee P.
Poetter, Bruce E.
Port, Richard B.
Reynolds, Bryan P.
Sachen, Joseph L.
Shanahan, John E.
Towner, John H.

Developer
Anderson, Gerald E.
Arado, Joseph E.
Baldwin, William E.
Barofsky, Frederick J.
Berggren, Alan R.
Downs, Joseph M.
Faltz, Richard A.
Grahn, Melvin
Green, Jeffrey S.
Keel, Phillip J.
Koop, Howard A.
Lentfer, Richard H.
Liebscher, V.K. Chris
Martin, LaDoris
Matthews, Drew I.
Motluck, William J.
O'Malley, Robert Eugene
Pasquinelli, Anthony R.
Raymond, James W.
Reynolds, Bryan P.
Schwander, Robert H.
Sutherlin, Robert C.

Engineer
Berggren, Alan R.
Liebscher, V.K. Chris

Instructor
Bella, Frank A. Jr.
Boblak, Frank J.
Brown, Karen A.
Liebscher, V.K. Chris
Motluck, William J.
O'Malley, Robert Eugene
Poetter, Bruce E.
Scapillato, Thomas A.
Towner, John H.
Wagner, Alvin L. Jr.
Williamson, Roger K.

Insuror
Anderson, Gerald E.
Boblak, Frank J.
Liebscher, V.K. Chris
Liss, Michael R.
Motluck, William J.
Towner, John H.

Owner/Investor
Anderson, Gerald E.
Barofsky, Frederick J.
Bella, Frank A. Jr.
Berggren, Alan R.
Brown, Karen A.
Disera, Bonnie
Downs, Joseph M.
Groszek, Marlene
Homer, Dean R.
Keel, Phillip J.
Keleher, Peter D.
Koop, Howard A.
Lenczycki, Wayne A.
Liebscher, V.K. Chris
Martin, LaDoris
Matthews, Drew I.
Pasquinelli, Anthony R.
Pitlock, Lee P.
Poetter, Bruce E.
Sachen, Joseph L.
Scapillato, Thomas A.
Schwander, Robert H.
Towner, John H.

Property Manager
Anderson, Gerald E.
Arado, Joseph E.
Berggren, Alan R.
Blake, D.S.
Boblak, Frank J.
Brown, Karen A.
Burke, Joyce M.
Disera, Bonnie
Doersch, Richard C.
Downs, Joseph M.
Engel, Donald
Faltz, Richard A.
Homer, Dean R.
Horton, James C.
Jessen, Howard
Keel, Phillip J.
Keleher, Peter D.
Leffel, Charles
Lentfer, Richard H.
Liebscher, V.K. Chris
Matthews, Drew I.
Mays, Richard A.
Motluck, William J.
O'Malley, Robert Eugene
Pasquinelli, Anthony R.
Pitlock, Lee P.
Ryan, James N.
Scapillato, Thomas A.
Schwander, Robert H.
Schwartz, J.F.
Thomson, William Hills
Towner, John H.

Real Estate Publisher
Disera, Bonnie
Scapillato, Thomas A.

Regulator
Bechtel, Clarence R.

Syndicator
Anderson, Gerald E.
Downs, Joseph M.
Faltz, Richard A.
Green, Jeffrey S.
Homer, Dean R.
Keleher, Peter D.
Koop, Howard A.
Leffelman, Dean J.
Liebscher, V.K. Chris
Matthews, Drew I.
O'Malley, Robert Eugene
Pitlock, Lee P.
Raymond, James W.
Reynolds, Bryan P.
Scapillato, Thomas A.

SPRINGFIELD

Appraiser
Avant, Walter W.
Curvey, Bernard A.
Dallas, Carl E.
Drobisch, Edward C.
Hackmann, John S.
Johnson, Phillip L.
Metcalf, George C.
Thebus, Thomas A.
Williams, C.R.
Wilson, James M.
Wittman, Bert
Wooff, Dennis A.

Architect
Urbas, Andrea
Williams, C.R.

Assessor
Dallas, Carl E.

Attorney
Goldenberg, Mark C.
Hackmann, John S.
Hull, Lewis A.
Rice, Matthew R.
Schwartz, Thomas D.
Thebus, Thomas A.

Broker
Avant, Walter W.
Brainerd, Bud
Brinkoetter, Thomas
Churchill, Robert W.
Curvey, Bernard A.
Dallas, Carl E.
Drobisch, Edward C.
Hamilton, Thomas J.
Hockenyos, Mark G.
Honke, Dennis O.
Hull, Lewis A.
Johnson, Phillip L.
Kriegsfeld, Lee J.
Mazzotti, Richard R.
Metcalf, George C.
See, Ronald L.
Soucy, Thomas E.
Thebus, Thomas A.
Wilson, James M.
Wooff, Dennis A.

Builder
Avant, Walter W.
Brinkoetter, Thomas
Feder, Gerald
Goldenberg, Mark C.
Hobbs, Robert L.
Williams, C.R.

Consultant
Brainerd, Bud
Brinkoetter, Thomas
Churchill, Robert W.
Curvey, Bernard A.
Davison, David J.
Drobisch, Edward C.
Eggers, Richard L.
Johnson, Phillip L.
Koepke, Robert L.
Soucy, Thomas E.
Thebus, Thomas A.
Williams, C.R.
Wooff, Dennis A.

Developer
Avant, Walter W.
Brinkoetter, Thomas
Eggers, Richard L.
Goldenberg, Mark C.
Helderrad, James E.
Hobbs, Robert L.
Hockenyos, Mark G.
Johnson, Phillip L.
Kriegsfeld, Lee J.
See, Ronald L.
Soucy, Thomas E.
Williams, C.R.
Zipfel, Marion S.

Engineer
Davison, David J.

Instructor
Brainerd, Bud
Dallas, Carl E.
Drobisch, Edward C.
Eggers, Richard L.
Kloeckner, Vincent W.
Koepke, Robert L.
Kriegsfeld, Lee J.
Williams, C.R.

Insuror
Metcalf, George C.
Wiggers, Milton J.

Lender
Hackmann, John S.
Kindig, Malcolm L.
Wiggers, Milton J.

Owner/Investor
Avant, Walter W.
Brainerd, Bud
Churchill, Robert W.
Davison, David J.
Hockenyos, Mark G.
Honke, Dennis O.
Johnson, Phillip L.
Kloeckner, Vincent W.
Mazzotti, Richard R.
Metcalf, George C.
See, Ronald L.
Soucy, Thomas E.
Williams, C.R.
Zipfel, Marion S.

Property Manager
Brinkoetter, Thomas
Churchill, Robert W.
Drobisch, Edward C.
Honke, Dennis O.
Kriegsfeld, Lee J.
Metcalf, George C.
Reising, Rich
Sakata, Gary
Wooff, Dennis A.
Zipfel, Marion S.

Syndicator
Brainerd, Bud
Goldenberg, Mark C.
Hockenyos, Mark G.
See, Ronald L.
Soucy, Thomas E.
Williams, C.R.

INDIANA

BLOOMINGTON

Appraiser
Bloom, George F.
Fix, Wayne
Harrah, Margaret 'Peg'
Harshey, William R.
Johnston, Robert M.
Reisert, Charles E.

Attorney
Fix, Wayne
Hancock, James B.
Hoehn, Elmer L.

Banker
Harshey, William R.

Broker
Fix, Wayne
Harrah, Margaret 'Peg'
Hoehn, Elmer L.
Johnston, Robert M.
Lewis, Barnet M.
Reisert, Charles E.

Builder
Hancock, James B.
Johnston, Robert M.

Consultant
Fisher, Jeffrey D.
Fix, Wayne
Johnston, Robert M.
Lewis, Barnet M.
Martin, Stephen J.
Weimer, Arthur M.

Developer
Bloom, George F.
Hoehn, Elmer L.
Johnston, Robert M.

Instructor
Bloom, George F.
Fisher, Jeffrey D.
Fix, Wayne
Hancock, James B.
Martin, Stephen J.

Insuror
Reisert, Charles E.

Lender
Haynes, Richard R.
Johnston, Robert M.

Owner/Investor
Bloom, George F.
Fix, Wayne
Hancock, James B.
Hoehn, Elmer L.
Lewis, Barnet M.

Property Manager
Harrah, Margaret 'Peg'
Hoehn, Elmer L.
Lewis, Barnet M.
Reisert, Charles E.

Real Estate Publisher
Martin, Stephen J.

Syndicator
Johnston, Robert M.
Reisert, Charles E.

COLUMBUS

Appraiser
Cooley, Dorothy N.

Architect
Wade, R. Lee

Broker
Cooley, Dorothy N.
Small, John L.

Builder
Rupel, James B.

Consultant
Cooley, Dorothy N.

Developer
Lehner, Paul M.
Rupel, James B.
Rupel, James J.

Owner/Investor
Cooley, Dorothy N.

Property Manager
Baker, James
Gould, Glenn
Lehner, Paul M.
Scheidt, Virgil
Shipp, James

EVANSVILLE

Appraiser
Horton, Larry A.
McBride, Robert David
Maikranz, Larry W.
Matthews, C. David.

Attorney
Marchand, James E.

Broker
Heugel, Kenneth E.
Liebchen, Carolyn
Maikranz, Larry W.

Builder
Horton, Larry A.

Consultant
Heugel, Kenneth E.
McBride, Robert David
Matthews, C. David.

Developer
Heugel, Kenneth E.
McKinney, James R.

Insuror
Maikranz, Larry W.

Owner/Investor
Horton, Larry A.
McBride, Robert David
McKinney, James R.

Property Manager
Heugel, Kenneth E.
Horton, Larry A.

Syndicator
Heugel, Kenneth E.

FORT WAYNE

Appraiser
Beaty, Richard E.
Ellenberger, Robert
Gettel, Ronald
Kennedy, John C.
Miller, Monte G.
Reynolds, Tom H.
Rousseau, Edwin J.

Architect
Schenkel, James J.

Attorney
Bredemeir, Melvin W.
Fruechtenicht, A.W.
Grotrian, Dennis J.
Moppert, Edward J.
Sauerteig, Paul J.
Swift, William D.

Broker
Axson, G. Michael
Beaty, Richard E.
Ellenberger, Robert
Fruechtenicht, A.W.
Groves, Paul A.
Kennedy, John C.
Macke, Elmer H.
Miller, Monte G.
Rousseau, Edwin J.

Builder
Axson, G. Michael
Macke, Elmer H.
Miller, Monte G.

Consultant
Beaty, Richard E.
Ellenberger, Robert
Gettel, Ronald
Miller, Monte G.
Thistlewaite, John M.

Developer
Ellenberger, Robert
Macke, Elmer H.
Thistlewaite, John M.

Engineer
Reynolds, Tom H.

Instructor
Fruechtenicht, A.W.
Miller, Monte G.
Moppert, Edward J.

Insuror
Miller, Monte G.

Lender
Reynolds, Tom H.

Owner/Investor
Axson, G. Michael
Beaty, Richard E.
Grotrian, Dennis J.
Kennedy, John C.
Macke, Elmer H.
Miller, Monte G.
Moppert, Edward J.
Schenkel, James J.

Property Manager
Ellenberger, Robert
Kennedy, John C.
Miller, Monte G.
Nixon, R.P.
Rousseau, Edwin J.
Sampson, John
Simmons, Raymond J.

Syndicator
Groves, Paul A.
Thistlewaite, John M.

GARY

Appraiser
Adomatis, Richard
Blair, Vaniel Lee
Brown, Liston L.
Clark, Bonnie P.
Prange, James Robert
Remijan, David T.
Troy, Matthew M.
Vermilya, William R.
Wollert, Delmar E.

Attorney
Potts, John J.

Broker
Blair, Vaniel Lee
Brown, Liston L.
Clark, Bonnie P.
Fifield, Otto R.
Lowenstine, Marilyn T.
Prange, James Robert
Remijan, David T.
Smurdon, Thomas J.
Troy, Matthew M.
Wollert, Delmar E.

Builder
Clark, Bonnie P.
Prange, James Robert
Smurdon, Thomas J.

Consultant
Clark, Bonnie P.
Prange, James Robert
Troy, Matthew M.

Developer
Fifield, Otto R.
Middendorf, Garland
Prange, James Robert
Smurdon, Thomas J.

Instructor
Adomatis, Richard
Potts, John J.

Owner/Investor
Brown, Liston L.
Fifield, Otto R.
Prange, James Robert
Troy, Matthew M.

Property Manager
Blair, Vaniel Lee
Brown, Liston L.
Prange, James Robert
Remijan, David T.
Troy, Matthew M.

Syndicator
Prange, James Robert
Smurdon, Thomas J.

INDIANAPOLIS

Appraiser
Adams, Robert Miller
Allen, George F. Jr.
Bowles, Walter F. Jr.
Fleer, Arnold J.
Hutchinson, Robert F.
Jewell, Mary E.
Mueller, Arthur W.
Secrest, L. Ramon
White, William D.

Architect
Brown, Joseph S.
Hutchinson, Robert F.
Laycock, Thomas B. II
Peterson, Michael A.
Roettger, David Allen
Secrest, L. Ramon

Attorney
Annelin, James S.
Blackwell, Jean S.
Buskirk, George A. Jr.
Cordingley, Bruce A.
Davis, Mark S. Esq.
Densborn, Donald K.
Grayson, John A.
Heath, R. Terry
Merrill, William H. Jr.
Newman, Norman R.
Scolnik, Glenn
Warren, Bradford L.
Williams, Gerald L.
Wolf, Walter E. Jr.
Zink, Darell E. Jr.

Banker
Bowles, Walter F. Jr.
Buskirk, George A. Jr.
Eklund, Douglas N.
Fleer, Arnold J.
May, Darwin D.
Morphew, Ronald R.
Osterling, Michael J.

Broker
Adams, Robert Miller
Allen, George F. Jr.
Armstrong, G. William
Augustin, Drew
Best, Minor L.
Bryant, Norman F.
Canull, James Jr.
Drew, Michael B.
Ehmer, Robert G.
Epstein, David L.
Epstein, Joel E.
Fleer, Arnold J.
French, Hans T.
Harrick, Joseph W.
Hirt, Helen L.
Hokanson, Stephen P.
Hudson, L. Richard
Hutchinson, Robert F.
Jewell, Mary E.
Kosene, Gerald A.
McCoun, Phillip M.
McKinney, David C.
Osterling, Michael J.
Rosenbaum, Steven M.
Spencer, Thomas A.
Steffel, Charles S. (Steve)
Vinton, James K. Jr.
White, William D.

Builder
Brown, Joseph S.
Campbell, Donna Gene
Glick, Eugene B.
Kosene, Gerald A.
Laycock, Thomas B. II
McKinney, David C.
Peterson, Michael A.
Singleton, Richard R.

Consultant
Adams, Robert Miller
Armstrong, G. William
Basile, Frank
Best, Minor L.
Bryant, Norman F.
Davis, Mark S. Esq.
Drew, Michael B.
Epstein, David L.
Epstein, Joel E.
Fleer, Arnold J.
Ford, Robert S.
Grayson, John A.
Harrick, Joseph W.
Hemmer, Edgar H.
Hokanson, Stephen P.
Hudson, L. Richard
Jewell, Mary E.
McKinney, David C.
Merrill, William H. Jr.
Peterson, Michael A.
Priddy, Stephen P.
Secrest, L. Ramon
Steffel, Charles S. (Steve)
Stillerman, L. M. (Larry)
Williams, Gerald L.
York, Carl D.

Developer
Armstrong, G. William
Best, Minor L.
Brown, Joseph S.
Bryant, Norman F.
Campbell, Donna Gene
Davis, Mark S. Esq.
Drew, Michael B.
Ehmer, Robert G.
Epstein, David L.
Epstein, Joel E.
French, Hans T.
Glick, Eugene B.
Hardy, John
Hemmer, Edgar H.
Hokanson, Stephen P.
Hudson, L. Richard
Hutchinson, Robert F.
Jewell, Mary E.
Kosene, Gerald A.
Laycock, Thomas B. II
McKinney, David C.
Peterson, Michael A.
Priddy, Stephen P.
Rosenbaum, Steven M.
Singleton, Richard R.
Wolf, Walter E. Jr.

Engineer
Brown, Joseph S.
Hutchinson, Robert F.
Peterson, Michael A.
Secrest, L. Ramon

Instructor
Adams, Robert Miller
Epstein, Joel E.
Hemmer, Edgar H.
Jewell, Mary E.
Steffel, Charles S. (Steve)
Stillerman, L. M. (Larry)
York, Carl D.

Insuror
Ehmer, Robert G.
Jewell, Mary E.
Sims, Gordon L.

Lender
Best, Minor L.
Bowles, Walter F. Jr.
Davis, Mark S. Esq.
Eklund, Douglas N.
Jewell, Mary E.
May, Darwin D.
Mueller, Arthur W.
Osterling, Michael J.

Owner/Investor
Armstrong, G. William
Best, Minor L.
Brown, Joseph S.
Bryant, Norman F.
Cordingley, Bruce A.
Davis, Mark S. Esq.
Ehmer, Robert G.
Epstein, David L.
Epstein, Joel E.
Glick, Eugene B.
Harrick, Joseph W.
Hemmer, Edgar H.
Hudson, L. Richard
Kline, Jack M.
Kosene, Gerald A.
Laycock, Thomas B. II
McKinney, David C.
Matthews, G. Grippe
Merrill, William H. Jr.
Peterson, Michael A.
Priddy, Stephen P.
Rosenbaum, Steven M.
Steffel, Charles S. (Steve)
Vinton, James K. Jr.
Wolf, Walter E. Jr.

Property Manager
Allen, George F. Jr.
Augustin, Drew
Basile, Frank
Botkin, Kermit M.
Bryant, Norman F.
Campbell, Donna Gene
Davis, Mark S. Esq.
Drew, Michael B.
Ehmer, Robert G.
Epstein, Joel E.
Glick, Eugene B.
Harrick, Joseph W.
Hokanson, Stephen P.
Hudson, L. Richard
Keys, Howard D.
Kline, Jack M.
Kosene, Gerald A.
Laycock, Thomas B. II
McKinney, David C.
Matthews, G. Grippe
Priddy, Stephen P.
Singleton, Richard R.
Spencer, Thomas A.
Stillerman, L. M. (Larry)
York, Carl D.

Real Estate Publisher
Basile, Frank
Stillerman, L. M. (Larry)

Regulator
Davis, Mark S. Esq.
Jewell, Mary E.

Syndicator
Bryant, Norman F.
Davis, Mark S. Esq.
Epstein, David L.
Hokanson, Stephen P.
Kosene, Gerald A.
Matthews, G. Grippe
Priddy, Stephen P.
Rosenbaum, Steven M.
Singleton, Richard R.
Steffel, Charles S. (Steve)
Williams, Gerald L.

KOKOMO

Appraiser
Crume, Roy L.
Gottschalk, Robert O.
Johnston, Phillip K.
Ward, Paul H. Jr.

Attorney
Herriman, Charles E.
Kauffman, Kenneth D.

Broker
Crume, Roy L.
Gottschalk, Robert O.
Kauffman, Kenneth D.
Ward, Paul H. Jr.

Builder
Ward, Paul H. Jr.

Consultant
Gottschalk, Robert O.
Ward, Paul H. Jr.

Developer
Gottschalk, Robert O.
Herriman, Charles E.

Engineer
Kauffman, Kenneth D.

Owner/Investor
Gottschalk, Robert O.
Ward, Paul H. Jr.

Property Manager
Gottschalk, Robert O.
Ward, Paul H. Jr.

Syndicator
Herriman, Charles E.
Ward, Paul H. Jr.

LAFAYETTE

Appraiser
Cruea, Dudley

Attorney
Dowd, John E.

Broker
Cruea, Dudley
Maclauchlan, Donald John Jr.

Lender
Whitsel, Robert M.

Property Manager
McKool, Richard J.
Ridenour, James

MUNCIE

Appraiser
Brantner, Edward S. Jr.
Kinder, JoAnn M.
Thrasher, Richard D. Jr.

Broker
Brantner, Edward S. Jr.
Kinder, JoAnn M.

Builder
Juerling, John H.

Consultant
Brantner, Edward S. Jr.
Juerling, John H.
Kinder, JoAnn M.
Miltenberger, Frederick D.

Developer
Brantner, Edward S. Jr.
Juerling, John H.
Thrasher, Richard D. Jr.

Engineer
Juerling, John H.

Instructor
Miltenberger, Frederick D.

Owner/Investor
Juerling, John H.
Kinder, JoAnn M.
Thrasher, Richard D. Jr.

Property Manager
Aschenbremer, F.A.
Brantner, Edward S. Jr.

Syndicator
Thrasher, Richard D. Jr.

SOUTH BEND

Appraiser
Bitting, Phyllis Diane
McCloskey, Richard E.
Miller, Garry L.
Nellans, Larry W.
Powers, Esther S.
Rydson, Marlyn D.
Schefmeyer, Donald H.
Taylor, Lloyd S.
Tiedemann, A. Carl

Attorney
Cawley, John A. Jr.
Keyes, William H.

Banker
Hammes, Jerry
Taylor, Lloyd S.

Broker
Bitting, Phyllis Diane
Miller, Garry L.
Nellans, Larry W.
Powers, Esther S.
Rydson, Marlyn D.
Schefmeyer, Donald H.
Tiedemann, A. Carl

Consultant
Bitting, Phyllis Diane
Gibson, Thomas C.
McCloskey, Richard E.
Miller, Garry L.
Nellans, Larry W.
Schefmeyer, Donald H.

Developer
Hammes, Jerry
Nellans, Larry W.
Rydson, Marlyn D.
Schefmeyer, Donald H.
Taylor, Lloyd S.

Engineer
Cocks, Richard E.
Taylor, Lloyd S.

Instructor
McCloskey, Richard E.
Schefmeyer, Donald H.

Insuror
Keyes, William H.
Miller, Garry L.
Rydson, Marlyn D.

Lender
Schefmeyer, Donald H.

Owner/Investor
Bitting, Phyllis Diane
Hammes, Jerry
McCloskey, Richard E.
Miller, Garry L.
Nellans, Larry W.
Powers, Esther S.
Rydson, Marlyn D.
Schefmeyer, Donald H.

Property Manager
Cocks, Richard E.
Gans, Ray J.
Gibson, Thomas C.
Hufft, John
Kloska, Ronald F.
Nellans, Larry W.
Rydson, Marlyn D.
Taylor, Lloyd S.
Tiedemann, A. Carl

Syndicator
Schefmeyer, Donald H.

TERRE HAUTE

Appraiser
Pfister, Paul J.

Attorney
Francis, Leroy A.

Broker
Pfister, Paul J.

Builder
Francis, Leroy A.
Pfister, Paul J.

Consultant
Pfister, Paul J.

Developer
Francis, Leroy A.
Pfister, Paul J.

Insuror
Pfister, Paul J.

Lender
Pfister, Paul J.

Owner/Investor
Francis, Leroy A.
Pfister, Paul J.

Property Manager
Pfister, Paul J.

Syndicator
Pfister, Paul J.

WASHINGTON

Broker
Martin, J. Steven
Stanley, Ginna

Consultant
Martin, J. Steven

Developer
Martin, J. Steven

Owner/Investor
Martin, J. Steven

Property Manager
Habig, Douglas A.
Martin, J. Steven

Syndicator
Martin, J. Steven

IOWA

BURLINGTON

Appraiser
Despain, Willis N.
Lauer, Harold J.

Broker
Despain, Willis N.
Lauer, Harold J.

Consultant
Despain, Willis N.

Developer
McLaury, Hugh C.

Lender
Despain, Willis N.

Owner/Investor
Despain, Willis N.

Property Manager
Despain, Willis N.
Lauer, Harold J.

CARROLL

Attorney
Boddicker, Joe L.
Leed, John R.

Broker
Edwards, Norma

Instructor
Edwards, Norma

CEDAR RAPIDS

Appraiser
Gent, Philip D.
Jones, B.J.
Means, Scott A.
Smith, Roland M.
Stratton, John X.

Attorney
Jones, B.J.
Klinger, Phillip D.
Nelson, Stephen C.
Pence, Thomas R.
Whalen, Daniel A.
Wilson, Edward M.

Banker
Jones, B.J.

Broker
Brevik, Richard W.
Johnson, Martin D.
Jones, B.J.
Knepper, Eugene Arthur
Means, Scott A.
Ruhl, Charles A.
Smith, Roland M.
Stratton, John X.

Builder
Brevik, Richard W.
Stratton, John X.

Consultant
Brevik, Richard W.
Jones, B.J.
Stratton, John X.

Developer
Brevik, Richard W.
Jones, B.J.
Nelson, Stephen C.
Ruhl, Charles A.
Smith, Roland M.
Stratton, John X.
Whalen, Daniel A.
White, Del F.

Instructor
Stratton, John X.

Lender
Jones, B.J.
Shenk, John C. Jr.

Owner/Investor
Johnson, Martin D.
Jones, B.J.
Knepper, Eugene Arthur
Nelson, Stephen C.
Ruhl, Charles A.
Smith, Roland M.
Stratton, John X.
Whalen, Daniel A.

Property Manager
Brevik, Richard W.
Collins, Max
Johnson, Martin D.
Jones, B.J.
Knepper, Eugene Arthur
Means, Scott A.
Overmeyer, Paul
Ruhl, Charles A.
Staudt, J.N.
Stratton, John X.

Real Estate Publisher
Boyce, Shirley
Jones, B.J.
Oldridge, Evelyn

Syndicator
Knepper, Eugene Arthur
Stratton, John X.

CRESTON

Attorney
Longinaker, Jay W.

Owner/Investor
Longinaker, Jay W.

Property Manager
Longinaker, Jay W.

DECORAH

Broker
Sweeney, John Jay

Builder
Sweeney, John Jay

Developer
Sweeney, John Jay

DES MOINES

Appraiser
Bailey, E. Norman
Grodt, Paul O.
Knape, Edward J. Sr.
Lundstrom, John E.
Nolan, Barbara Ann
Thompson, Neill S.
Whisler, Norman J.

Attorney
Davidson, Diane M.
Grodt, Paul O.
Knoedel, Patricia Kelley
Peterson, Larry
Richards, Stanley
Sharpe, Jeremy Carl
Stiles, William R.
Wilson, Jonathan C.

Banker
Prichett, Dean R.

Broker
Akkerman, Wayne E.
Campney, James T.
Grodt, Paul O.
Leavengood, John B.
Lundstrom, John E.
Nolan, Barbara Ann

Builder
Bailey, E. Norman
Knutsen, Morris A.
Lundstrom, John E.
Rosenberry, Paul E.

Consultant
Bailey, E. Norman
Campney, James T.
Grodt, Paul O.
Knutsen, Morris A.
Lundstrom, John E.
Nolan, Barbara Ann
Rosenberry, Paul E.
Thompson, Neill S.

Developer
Bailey, E. Norman
Batesole, Jon E.
Campney, James T.
Chandler, Dean L.
Knutsen, Morris A.

Engineer
Porter, Max L.

Instructor
Grodt, Paul O.
Leavengood, John B.
Wilson, Jonathan C.

Insuror
Grodt, Paul O.

Lender
McAdoo, Ralph W.
Maffett, Mack D.

Owner/Investor
Akkerman, Wayne E.
Bailey, E. Norman
Campney, James T.
Grodt, Paul O.
Knutsen, Morris A.
Lundstrom, John E.
Rosenberry, Paul E.
Whisler, Norman J.
Wilson, Jonathan C.

Property Manager
Akkerman, Wayne E.
Bailey, E. Norman
Johnson, Eugene
Leavengood, John B.
McAnly, L.D. Jr.
Nolan, Barbara Ann
Rosenberry, Paul E.
Whisler, Norman J.

Syndicator
Campney, James T.

DUBUQUE

Appraiser
Reilly, Thomas J.

Architect
Wirkler, Norman E.

Banker
Reilly, Thomas J.

Builder
Owen, Douglas

Consultant
Owen, Douglas

Developer
Wirkler, Norman E.

Insuror
Owen, Douglas

Lender
Owen, Douglas
Reilly, Thomas J.

Owner/Investor
Owen, Douglas
Wirkler, Norman E.

Property Manager
Wirkler, Norman E.

FORT DODGE

Appraiser
Conrad, Kenneth

Attorney
Gilchrist, Fred C. Jr.

Broker
Conrad, Kenneth

Consultant
Conrad, Kenneth

Property Manager
Conrad, Kenneth

MASON CITY

Appraiser
Krause, Edwin L.
Wendt, Steven E.

Attorney
Axt, James Robert

Broker
Krause, Edwin L.

Consultant
Krause, Edwin L.
Wendt, Steven E.

Developer
Krause, Edwin L.

Instructor
Krause, Edwin L.
Wendt, Steven E.

Lender
Wendt, Steven E.

Property Manager
Dohrman, Fred
Krause, Edwin L.

OTTUMWA

Broker
George, James Wesley

Consultant
George, James Wesley

Property Manager
George, James Wesley

SIOUX CITY

Appraiser
Coppock, Jerry K.
LeGrand, Ritch

Attorney
Dykstra, Daniel D.

Banker
Horne, Frederick R. III
Linquist, Lee R.

Broker
Coppock, Jerry K.

Consultant
Coppock, Jerry K.
LeGrand, Ritch

Developer
Owens, Gary L.
Wimmer, G.R.

Insuror
Coppock, Jerry K.

Property Manager
Coppock, Jerry K.
Keir, Walter

SPENCER

Appraiser
Norris, G. Kennon

Broker
Norris, G. Kennon

Builder
Norris, G. Kennon

Consultant
Norris, G. Kennon

Owner/Investor
Norris, G. Kennon

Property Manager
Norris, G. Kennon

WATERLOO

Appraiser
Fredrick, Arnold A.

Builder
Morris, Robert E.

Developer
Morris, Robert E.

Lender
Fredrick, Arnold A.

Owner/Investor
Fredrick, Arnold A.

Property Manager
Morris, Robert E.
Rebholz, Howard

KANSAS

DODGE CITY

Appraiser
Bourne, Mary E.
Campbell, Homer D.

Broker
Bourne, Mary E.
Campbell, Homer D.

Consultant
Bourne, Mary E.

Instructor
Bourne, Mary E.

Insuror
Bourne, Mary E.

Lender
Bourne, Mary E.

Owner/Investor
Bourne, Mary E.

Property Manager
Bourne, Mary E.

FORT SCOTT

Attorney
Toland, Clyde William

HAYS

Appraiser
Albrecht, Robert H.
Finch, Robert M.

Broker
Albrecht, Robert H.
Finch, Robert M.

Builder
Finch, Robert M.

Insuror
Albrecht, Robert H.

HUTCHINSON

Broker
Messing, Terry F.

Builder
Messing, Terry F.

Developer
Messing, Terry F.

Property Manager
Messing, Terry F.

KANSAS CITY

Appraiser
Aaron, Donald F. Sr.
Bramlage, Paul S.
Champagne, Richard K.
Coleman, Dennis J.
Peete, Don C.
Perry, A. Fred Jr.
Thorne, Francis X.

Attorney
Collister, Edward G. Jr.
Haitbrink, Richard F.
Springer, Byron E.
Taylor, L. Franklin

Banker
Shelton, Charles W.

Broker
Aaron, Donald F. Sr.
Auld, John W. Jr.
Auld, John William
Barewin, Lee B.
Coleman, Dennis J.
Gossett, Donald Ira
Odell, Melvin
Perry, A. Fred Jr.
Phillips, Robert W.
Salvay, Craig L.
Thorne, Francis X.
Varnum, Ralph W.

Builder
Aaron, Donald F. Sr.
Auld, John W. Jr.
Auld, John William
Odell, Melvin
Thorne, Francis X.

Consultant
Aaron, Donald F. Sr.
Auld, John William
Chance, Larry S.
Goodwin, Harold D.
Laner, Harlan S.
Peete, Don C.
Perry, A. Fred Jr.
Salvay, Craig L.
Shelton, Charles W.
Varnum, Ralph W.

Developer
Aaron, Donald F. Sr.
Auld, John W. Jr.
Auld, John William
Collister, Edward G. Jr.
Laner, Harlan S.
Odell, Melvin
Peete, Don C.
Perry, A. Fred Jr.
Phillips, Robert W.
Thorne, Francis X.
Varnum, Ralph W.

Instructor
Perry, A. Fred Jr.
Varnum, Ralph W.

Insuror
Auld, John William

Lender
Peete, Don C.
Shelton, Charles W.

Owner/Investor
Aaron, Donald F. Sr.
Chance, Larry S.
Coleman, Dennis J.
Collister, Edward G. Jr.
Gossett, Donald Ira
Haitbrink, Richard F.
Laner, Harlan S.
Odell, Melvin
Perry, A. Fred Jr.
Phillips, Robert W.
Salvay, Craig L.
Varnum, Ralph W.

Property Manager
Aaron, Donald F. Sr.
Auld, John William
Barewin, Lee B.
Brown, Albert E.
Coleman, Dennis J.
Laner, Harlan S.
Odell, Melvin
Perry, A. Fred Jr.
Phillips, Robert W.
Thorne, Francis X.

Real Estate Publisher
Perry, A. Fred Jr.

Syndicator
Auld, John William
Chance, Larry S.
Haitbrink, Richard F.
Jackson, Jim
Jackson, Mike
Laner, Harlan S.
Perry, A. Fred Jr.
Phillips, Robert W.
Salvay, Craig L.
Varnum, Ralph W.

SALINA

Attorney
Brewer, Dana

Property Manager
Tarum, Melvin

TOPEKA

Appraiser
Craig, David W.
Rowson, Jack E.
Stewart, Barbara C.

Attorney
Barry, Donald D.
Helbert, Michael C.
Marquardt, Christel E.
Schlosser, Bryon R.
Sweeney, Craig C.

Banker
Mowbray, Kermit
Rowson, Jack E.

Broker
Green, John

Builder
Appino, Robert J.

Consultant
Appino, Robert J.
Craig, David W.
Eskie, Dennis J.
Stewart, Barbara C.

Developer
Appino, Robert J.
Barry, Donald D.
Eskie, Dennis J.
Neuer, Fred S.
Rowson, Jack E.
Sweeney, Craig C.

Insuror
Rowson, Jack E.

Lender
Rowson, Jack E.

Owner/Investor
Appino, Robert J.
Barry, Donald D.
Helbert, Michael C.
Neuer, Fred S.
Rowson, Jack E.
Sweeney, Craig C.

Property Manager
Barry, Donald D.
Flower, Paul
Green, John
Stewart, Barbara C.

WICHITA

Appraiser
Albright, Norman
Bradfield, Gerald C.
Brown, Paul R.
Classen, Don L.
Dotzour, G. Gordon
Glazier, Margaret F.
Kessler, Richard S.
Luckey, R.V.
Martens, Steven J.

Architect
Bullinger, E. Eugene
Calvin, Roy E.

Attorney
Callahan, John
Cobean, Robert H.
Levi, Donald R.
Nelson, Clark R.

Banker
Brown, Paul R.

Broker
Albright, Norman
Bradfield, Gerald C.
Branson, Robert E.
Brown, Paul R.
Clark, Stephen L.
Dean, Lawrence W.
Dodds, Dorothy Gillespie
Dotzour, G. Gordon
Glaser, Dennis C.
Glazier, Margaret F.
Guerra, Albert P.
Krumsick, Herbert J.
Levi, Donald R.
Luckey, R.V.
Martens, Steven J.
Mize, David W.
Newson, Edwas
Peden, Ronald K.
Rickard, Larry D.
Sandlian, Colby B.
Schilpp, Frank O. Jr.
Snyder, Gary L.

Builder
Branson, Robert E.
Cammett, Stuart H. Jr.
Guerra, Albert P.
McClaren, Mike E.
Mize, David W.
Parsons, George M.
Peters, Robert E.
Rickard, Larry D.

Consultant
Branson, Robert E.
Calvin, Roy E.
Dean, Lawrence W.
Guerra, Albert P.
Hayden, J. David
Kessler, Richard S.
Luckey, R.V.
Martens, Steven J.
Mize, David W.
Peden, Ronald K.
Sandlian, Colby B.
Schilpp, Frank O. Jr.

Developer
Biggs, Dean
Cammett, Stuart H. Jr.
Clark, Stephen L.
Dean, Lawrence W.
Dotzour, G. Gordon
Glaser, Dennis C.
Glazier, Margaret F.
Guerra, Albert P.
Luckey, R.V.
McClaren, Mike E.
Martens, Steven J.
Mize, David W.
Parsons, George M.
Peters, Robert E.
Sandlian, Colby B.
Snyder, Gary L.

Engineer
Guerra, Albert P.

Instructor
Albright, Norman
Bradfield, Gerald C.
Bullinger, E. Eugene
Guerra, Albert P.
Krumsick, Herbert J.
Levi, Donald R.
Newson, Edwas
Rickard, Larry D.
Sandlian, Colby B.

Insuror
Brown, Paul R.
Cobean, Robert H.

Lender
Mize, David W.
Newson, Edwas

Owner/Investor
Albright, Norman
Bullinger, E. Eugene
Callahan, John
Cammett, Stuart H. Jr.
Dean, Lawrence W.
Dodds, Dorothy Gillespie
Dotzour, G. Gordon
Glaser, Dennis C.
Glazier, Margaret F.
Guerra, Albert P.
Krumsick, Herbert J.
Levi, Donald R.
Luckey, R.V.
McClaren, Mike E.
Martens, Steven J.
Mize, David W.
Nelson, Clark R.
Parsons, George M.
Peters, Robert E.
Rickard, Larry D.
Rising, Austin

Property Manager
Albright, Norman
Branson, Robert E.
Brenneinan, Howard L.
Brown, Paul R.
Cammett, Stuart H. Jr.
Clark, Stephen L.
Dean, Lawrence W.
Dodds, Dorothy Gillespie
Edwards, David R.
Glaser, Dennis C.
Guerra, Albert P.
Johnson, Don
Keller, G. Lawrence
Luckey, R.V.
McClaren, Mike E.
Martens, Steven J.
Peters, Robert E.
Sandlian, Colby B.
Snyder, Gary L.

Regulator
Hayden, J. David

Syndicator
Dean, Lawrence W.
Hayden, J. David
Peters, Robert E.

KENTUCKY

ASHLAND

Attorney
Benton, Joseph C.

Property Manager
Williams, James

BOWLING GREEN

Broker
Elliott, Ward
Lessenberry, Robert A.

Builder
Hinton, M.C.
Lessenberry, Robert A.

Consultant
Elliott, Ward
Huddleston, Joseph R.

Developer
Hinton, M.C.
Lessenberry, Robert A.

Instructor
Elliott, Ward

Owner/Investor
Elliott, Ward
Lessenberry, Robert A.

ELIZABETHTOWN

Appraiser
Baumgardner, Rick

Broker
Baumgardner, Rick

Consultant
Baumgardner, Rick

Instructor
Baumgardner, Rick

Insuror
Baumgardner, Rick

LEXINGTON

Appraiser
Asher, Richard W.
Beck, Edward L.
Byrkit, Larry W.
Dailey, Kent
Owens, William Harold

Architect
Culp, Duane K.

Assessor
Lopez, Daniel

Attorney
Asher, Richard W.
Banks, Lawrence K.
Bornstein, William S.
Clarke, John Kirk
Davenport, Peter M.
Doyle, C. Richard
Kiser, Jack D.
Webb, Donald W.
Webb, Ralph Dudley

Banker
Byrkit, Larry W.
Johnston, Robert K.
Lopez, Daniel

Broker
Asher, Richard W.
Bornstein, William S.
Carr, James M.
Dailey, Kent
Eads, Lorenzo Dow
Grieme, Ralph B. Jr.
Kindred, F. D.
Kiser, Jack D.
McCready, Richard F.
McDonald, Jack W.
Morgan, Barbara A.
Owens, William Harold
Webb, Ralph Dudley

Builder
Carr, James M.
Hiler, Ken Jr.
Kindred, F. D.
Webb, Ralph Dudley

Consultant
Asher, Richard W.
Beck, David
Bodley, Donald E.
Grieme, Ralph B. Jr.
Haymaker, Timothy L.
Kiser, Jack D.
Lane, Edwin Green
McDonald, Jack W.
Morgan, Barbara A.
Webb, Ralph Dudley

Developer
Bornstein, William S.
Carr, James M.
Chickey, Joseph T.
Deatherage, Gerald H.
Grieme, Ralph B. Jr.
Haymaker, Timothy L.
Hiler, Ken Jr.
Kindred, F. D.
Lopez, Daniel
McDonald, Jack W.
Owens, William Harold
Tappan, Charles S.
Webb, Donald W.
Webb, Ralph Dudley

Instructor
Bodley, Donald E.
Byrkit, Larry W.
Dailey, Kent

Insuror
McCready, Richard F.
Owens, William Harold

Lender
Byrkit, Larry W.
Edwards, Donald L.
Johnston, Robert K.

Owner/Investor
Bornstein, William S.
Dailey, Kent
Deatherage, Gerald H.
Grieme, Ralph B. Jr.
Haymaker, Timothy L.
Hiler, Ken Jr.
Kiser, Jack D.
Morgan, Barbara A.
Tappan, Charles S.
Webb, Donald W.
Webb, Ralph Dudley

Property Manager
Asher, Richard W.
Kiser, Jack D.
Lopez, Daniel
Morgan, Barbara A.
Webb, Ralph Dudley

Regulator
Haymaker, Timothy L.

Syndicator
Asher, Richard W.
Bornstein, William S.
Tappan, Charles S.

Webb, Ralph Dudley

LOUISVILLE

Appraiser
Boyles, Clarence A.
Burgess, Elmo C.
Chapman, George M.
Kerfoot, Roy L.
Lewman, Harry
O'Dea, Michael J.
Owen, Park H. III
Ridge, John E.
Rosen, Lawrence

Assessor
Kerfoot, Roy L.

Attorney
Best, Paul A.
Bryant, Alan O.
Burgess, Elmo C.
Dudley, George E.
Goldberg, James Stone
Helm, Nelson, Jr.
Klein, Ervin
Klein, Robert M.
Maple, Michael L.
Mitchell, Ralph
Osborn, John S. Jr.
Prizant, Roger M.
Vincenti, Michael Baxter

Banker
Best, Paul A.
Tyrrell, Gerald G.
White, Max W.

Broker
Boyles, Clarence A.
Burgess, Elmo C.
Cline, Patricia A.
Dahlem, Bernard A.
Dinsmore, Richard H.
Durbin, Joseph W.
Farley, Jack L.
Kerfoot, Roy L.
Lewman, Harry
O'Dea, Michael J.
Ridge, John E.
Rosen, Lawrence
Schank, David L.
Schutte, Betty
Shell, Robert D.
Swindler, Glenn P.
Walser, M.S.
Weisberg, Frank F.

Builder
Burgess, Elmo C.
Dahlem, Bernard A.
Farley, Jack L.
Kerfoot, Roy L.
Schank, David L.
Shell, Robert D.
Sturgeon, A. Thomas Jr.
Walser, M.S.

Consultant
Boyles, Clarence A.
Chapman, George M.
Dinsmore, Richard H.
Green, Marvin
Lewman, Harry
Maple, Michael L.
Nevius, William A.
O'Dea, Michael J.
Owen, Park H. III
Ridge, John E.
Rosen, Lawrence
Schank, David L.
Shell, Robert D.
Swindler, Glenn P.

Developer
Boyles, Clarence A.
Cattell, David L.
Dahlem, Bernard A.
DiMartino, Arthur
Dinsmore, Richard H.
Farley, Jack L.
Maple, Michael L.
Ridge, John E.
Rosen, Lawrence
Schank, David L.
Shell, Robert D.
Sturgeon, A. Thomas Jr.
Swindler, Glenn P.
Walser, M.S.
Zucker, Cher. R.

Engineer
Chapman, George M.
Dahlem, Bernard A.

Instructor
Burgess, Elmo C.
Shell, Robert D.
Swindler, Glenn P.
Weisberg, Frank F.
Zucker, Cher. R.

Insuror
Burgess, Elmo C.
Jones, Harrison H.
Kerfoot, Roy L.

Lender
Best, Paul A.
Ridge, John E.
Schuler, Dominic A.
Zucker, Cher. R.

Owner/Investor
Boyles, Clarence A.
Burgess, Elmo C.
Chapman, George M.
Dahlem, Bernard A.
DiMartino, Arthur
Dinsmore, Richard H.
Gajadhar
Klein, Ervin
Lewman, Harry
Mitchell, Ralph
Schank, David L.
Shaver, Jesse M.
Shell, Robert D.
Sturgeon, A. Thomas Jr.
Swindler, Glenn P.
Weisberg, Frank F.
Zucker, Cher. R.

Property Manager
Boyles, Clarence A.
Bridges, R.W.
Campbell, Nat
Dahlem, Bernard A.
Dinsmore, Richard H.
Farley, Jack L.
Green, Marvin
Hamren, Arnold M.
Kerfoot, Roy L.
Lewman, Harry
Neely, Jack
Newman, Philip
O'Dea, Michael J.
Owen, Park H. III
Rosen, Lawrence
Schank, David L.
Schuler, Dominic A.
Schutte, Betty
Shell, Robert D.
Swindler, Glenn P.
Tyree, Scott
Walser, M.S.
Weisberg, Frank F.
Zucker, Cher. R.

Real Estate Publisher
Rosen, Lawrence

Regulator
Schuler, Dominic A.

Syndicator
Helm, Nelson, Jr.
Maple, Michael L.
Rosen, Lawrence
Schank, David L.
Swindler, Glenn P.

OWENSBORO

Developer
Hocker, David E.

PADUCAH

Appraiser
McGuire, R. C. Jr.

Banker
Gupton, Joe W.
McGuire, R. C. Jr.

Broker
McGuire, R. C. Jr.

Builder
McGuire, R. C. Jr.

Consultant
McGuire, R. C. Jr.

Developer
McGuire, R. C. Jr.

Instructor
McGuire, R. C. Jr.

Lender
Gupton, Joe W.

Owner/Investor
McGuire, R. C. Jr.

Property Manager
McGuire, R. C. Jr.

Regulator
Gupton, Joe W.

PIKEVILLE

Appraiser
Gibson, William S. II
Newsome, Larry D.

Broker
Gibson, William S. II

Builder
Gibson, William S. II

Developer
Gibson, William S. II
Hughes, James A.

Lender
Newsome, Larry D.

Owner/Investor
Hughes, James A.
Newsome, Larry D.

Property Manager
Gibson, William S. II
Hughes, James A.

LOUISIANA

ALEXANDRIA

Appraiser
McCain, Charlie R.
Sleet, Phillip Milton Sr.
Sleet, Phillip "Phil" M. Jr.
Wolf, Robert

Broker
McCain, Charlie R.
Sleet, Phillip Milton Sr.
Sleet, Phillip "Phil" M. Jr.
Wolf, Robert

Builder
Tudor, Robert B. (Buddy) Jr.

Consultant
McCain, Charlie R.
Sleet, Phillip Milton Sr.
Sleet, Phillip "Phil" M. Jr.
Wolf, Robert

Developer
Tudor, Robert B. (Buddy) Jr.
Wolf, Robert
Wright, A. William

Owner/Investor
McCain, Charlie R.
Tudor, Robert B. (Buddy) Jr.
Wolf, Robert

Property Manager
McCain, Charlie R.
Sleet, Phillip "Phil" M. Jr.
Tudor, Robert B. (Buddy) Jr.

BATON ROUGE

Appraiser
Aguilar, Rodolfo J.
Bonfanti, George M.
Doiron, J. Russell
Russell, Robert L.
Skillman, Ernest Edward Jr.
Swayze, Thomas R.
Terhoeve, Peter J.

Architect
Aguilar, Rodolfo J.

Attorney
Landry, Charles A.

Banker
Morazan, Nancy G.

Broker
Aguilar, Rodolfo J.
Bardwell, Princeton M.
Doiron, J. Russell
Hart, William A.
Lewis, Jimmie C.
Russell, Robert L.
Skillman, Ernest Edward Jr.
Swayze, Thomas R.
Terhoeve, Peter J.
Weitz, Alan J.
Wicker, Seaborn R. "Steve" Jr.

Builder
Aguilar, Rodolfo J.
Bonfanti, George M.
Hart, William A.
Taylor, Clark W.
Weitz, Alan J.

Consultant
Aguilar, Rodolfo J.
Bonfanti, George M.
Doiron, J. Russell
Lewis, Jimmie C.
Russell, Robert L.
Skillman, Ernest Edward Jr.
Weitz, Alan J.
Wicker, Seaborn R. "Steve" Jr.

Developer
Aguilar, Rodolfo J.
Bonfanti, George M.
Doiron, J. Russell
Hart, William A.
Marvin, Wilbur
Taylor, Clark W.
Weitz, Alan J.
Wicker, Seaborn R. "Steve" Jr.

Engineer
Aguilar, Rodolfo J.

Instructor
Aguilar, Rodolfo J.
Lewis, Jimmie C.
Russell, Robert L.
Swayze, Thomas R.
Terhoeve, Peter J.

Insuror
Terhoeve, Peter J.
Weitz, Alan J.

Lender
Bonfanti, George M.
Morazan, Nancy G.
Skillman, Ernest Edward Jr.
Weitz, Alan J.

Owner/Investor
Aguilar, Rodolfo J.
Doiron, J. Russell
Lewis, Jimmie C.
Marvin, Wilbur
Skillman, Ernest Edward Jr.
Swayze, Thomas R.
Taylor, Clark W.
Thompson, Horatio C.

Property Manager
Bonfanti, George M.
Doiron, J. Russell
Hollins, Harry
LaBorde, Joseph M.
Lewis, Jimmie C.
Skillman, Ernest Edward Jr.
Taylor, Clark W.
Thompson, Horatio C.
Weitz, Alan J.

Real Estate Publisher
Wicker, Seaborn R. "Steve" Jr.

Syndicator
Taylor, Clark W.

HAMMOND

Appraiser
Sibley, Robert Dale

Broker
Derbes, David S.
Sibley, Robert Dale
Tricou, Rene J.C. Jr.

Developer
Maurin, James E.
Tricou, Rene J.C. Jr.

Insuror
Tricou, Rene J.C. Jr.

Owner/Investor
Maurin, James E.
Sibley, Robert Dale

Property Manager
Sibley, Robert Dale

LAFAYETTE

Appraiser
Kilchrist, Rubie G.

Architect
Crain, Charles Hugh

Broker
de Graauw, Frank R.
Dupuis, Richard P.
Ford, Michele
Kilchrist, Rubie G.

Builder
Crain, Charles Hugh

Consultant
de Graauw, Frank R.
Kilchrist, Rubie G.

Developer
Crain, Charles Hugh
de Graauw, Frank R.
Dupuis, Richard P.
Kilchrist, Rubie G.

Instructor
Crain, Charles Hugh

Owner/Investor
Crain, Charles Hugh
Kilchrist, Rubie G.
Thomas, Larry P.

Property Manager
Dupuis, Richard P.
Ford, Michele
Kilchrist, Rubie G.

Syndicator
de Graauw, Frank R.
Ford, Michele

LAKE CHARLES

Appraiser
Clark, Harper Scott
Diamond, R. Patrick
Reinauer, David

Broker
Clark, Harper Scott
Curley, Andrew K.
Diamond, R. Patrick
Reinauer, David

Consultant
Clark, Harper Scott
Curley, Andrew K.
Reinauer, David

Deveioper
Reinauer, David

Instructor
Reinauer, David

Owner/Investor
Clark, Harper Scott
Curley, Andrew K.
Reinauer, David

Property Manager
Curley, Andrew K.
Reinauer, David

Syndicator
Curley, Andrew K.
Reinauer, David

MONROE

Attorney
Johnson, Hewitt B.
Wilson, Woodrow

Broker
Johnson, Hewitt B.
Turrentine, David W.

Builder
Turrentine, David W.

Developer
Turrentine, David W.
Wilson, Woodrow

Owner/Investor
Wilson, Woodrow

Property Manager
Turrentine, David W.

NEW ORLEANS

Appraiser
Bruno, Michael A.
Buckelew, E. Douglas
Calamari, Daniel L.
Felts, Jean C.
Lathrop, Donald B. Jr.
Montz, Andre S.
Montz, Lawrence J.
Schwarz, Roy M. Jr.
Speth, Paul H.
Turnbull, James F.

Architect
Bergeron, Raymond

Attorney
Ballin, Arthur L.
Battard, Frank Paul
Baxter, Robert J. Jr.
Casteix, Barbara Treuting
Cressy, David S.
Dart, Henry Tutt
Dennery, Moise W.
Dutel, William J.
Dwyer, Stephen I.
George, Paula R.
Henderson, J. Harrison III
Kabacoff, Lester E.
Smith, Claude R.

Banker
Lathrop, Donald B. Jr.

Broker
Axelrad, Thomas L.
Beck, Howard Fred
Bruno, Michael A.
Calamari, Daniel L.
Corder, H. Robert
Dart, Henry Tutt
Estopinal, Stewart Joseph
Evans, M. D.
Fischbach, Peter C.
Hunter, Joseph R.
Kabacoff, Lester E.
Kushner, John E.
Pepper, Henry Louis
Prieur, Kenneth M.
Schwarz, Roy M. Jr.
Speth, Paul H.
Turnbull, James F.
Winingder, Thomas K.

Builder
Beck, Howard Fred
Henderson, J. Harrison III
Miller, Eric R.
Montz, Lawrence J.
Prieur, Kenneth M.
Speth, Paul H.
Wandell, Wayne F.

Consultant
Axelrad, Thomas L.
Bergeron, Raymond
Bruno, Michael A.
Colbert, Charles R.
Corder, H. Robert
Estopinal, Stewart Joseph
Evans, M. D.
Felts, Jean C.
George, Paula R.
Henderson, J. Harrison III
Hunter, Joseph R.
Miller, Eric R.
Montz, Andre S.
Montz, Lawrence J.
Prieur, Kenneth M.
Schwarz, Roy M. Jr.
Turnbull, James F.

Developer
Beck, Howard Fred
Bergeron, Raymond
Bruno, Michael A.
Casey, Taylor J.
Evans, M. D.
Gray, V. Allen
Henderson, J. Harrison III
Hunter, Joseph R.
Kabacoff, Lester E.
Miller, Eric R.
Montz, Andre S.
Ogden, Roger Houston
Pereria, James P.
Picker, Joel A.
Prieur, Kenneth M.
Salvetti, Don A. Jr.
Wandell, Wayne F.
Winingder, Thomas K.

Engineer
Wandell, Wayne F.

Instructor
Axelrad, Thomas L.
Corder, H. Robert
Prieur, Kenneth M.
Turnbull, James F.

Insuror
George, Paula R.
Turnbull, James F.

Lender
Bruno, Michael A.
Buckelew, E. Douglas
Faia, Kenneth W.
Juneau, Roland B.
Lathrop, Donald B. Jr.

Owner/Investor
Axelrad, Thomas L.
Beck, Howard Fred
Bergeron, Raymond
Bruno, Michael A.
Calamari, Daniel L.
Casteix, Barbara Treuting
Cressy, David S.
Evans, M. D.
Flettrich, Edward Frederick
Gray, V. Allen
Henderson, J. Harrison III
Kabacoff, Lester E.
Lathrop, Donald B. Jr.
Miller, Eric R.
Ogden, Roger Houston
Prieur, Kenneth M.
Salvetti, Don A. Jr.
Schwarz, Roy M. Jr.
Winingder, Thomas K.

Property Manager
Beck, Howard Fred
Bruno, Michael A.
Estopinal, Stewart Joseph
Gray, V. Allen
Henderson, J. Harrison III
Hunter, Joseph R.
Koehler, Charles Jr.
Ogden, Roger Houston
Pepper, Henry Louis
Prieur, Kenneth M.

Syndicator
Bruno, Michael A.
Corder, H. Robert
Cressy, David S.
George, Paula R.
Miller, Eric R.
Prieur, Kenneth M.

SHREVEPORT

Appraiser
Deen, Bill W.
Dupree, Thomas B. Jr.
Hall, Charles T.

Attorney
Clark, Lawrence Sherman

Broker
Anderson, Joel H.
Campbell, John W.
Clark, Lawrence Sherman
Clarke, Jack
Coleman, U.L. III
Fess, Michael D.
Hall, Charles T.
Hill, Dez R.
Sealy, J. Pollard Jr.

Builder
Anderson, Joel H.
Coleman, U.L. III
Fess, Michael D.
Hall, Charles T.
Hill, Dez R.

Consultant
Anderson, Joel H.
Campbell, John W.
Coleman, U.L. III
Delisle, Richard A.
Dupree, Thomas B. Jr.
Fess, Michael D.
Hall, Charles T.
Sealy, J. Pollard Jr.

Developer
Anderson, Joel H.
Childs, Alvin Jr.
Clarke, Jack
Coleman, U.L. III
Delisle, Richard A.
Fess, Michael D.
Hall, Charles T.
Hall, Lea R.
Hill, Dez R.
Loveless, Roland A.
Sealy, J. Pollard Jr.
Selber, Leonard

Instructor
Clark, Lawrence Sherman

Lender
Griffith, James B. Jr.

Owner/Investor
Childs, Alvin Jr.
Clarke, Jack
Coleman, U.L. III
Delisle, Richard A.
Dupree, Thomas B. Jr.
Fess, Michael D.
Hall, Charles T.
Hall, Lea R.
Hill, Dez R.
Sealy, J. Pollard Jr.
Selber, Leonard

Property Manager
Anderson, Joel H.
Boddie, Joseph
Campbell, John W.
Childs, Alvin Jr.
Coleman, U.L. III
Delisle, Richard A.
Fess, Michael D.
Hall, Charles T.
Hall, Lea R.
Hill, Dez R.
Sealy, J. Pollard Jr.

Syndicator
Anderson, Joel H.
Campbell, John W.
Coleman, U.L. III
Delisle, Richard A.
Dupree, Thomas B. Jr.
Fess, Michael D.
Sealy, J. Pollard Jr.

THIBODAUX

Broker
Brooks, Ron

Builder
Rhea, D. Keith

Developer
Rhea, D. Keith

Owner/Investor
Rhea, D. Keith

Property Manager
Rhea, D. Keith

MAINE

AUBURN

Appraiser
Cooper, Glen J.
Keene, Gerald H.
Stowell, John D.

Broker
Cooper, Glen J.
Keene, Gerald H.
Stowell, John D.

Builder
Keene, Gerald H.

Developer
Keene, Gerald H.

Owner/Investor
Cooper, Glen J.
Keene, Gerald H.

Property Manager
Keene, Gerald H.

AUGUSTA

Appraiser
Bishop, Leonard L.
Gosline, Norman A.
Lane, John W. Jr.

Broker
Bishop, Leonard L.
Lane, John W. Jr.
Towle, Daniel W.

Consultant
Gosline, Norman A.
Lane, John W. Jr.

Instructor
Lane, John W. Jr.

Owner/Investor
Lane, John W. Jr.

Property Manager
Sawyer, Paul

BANGOR

Appraiser
Mullins, Howard J.
Pendleton, Thomas C. Jr.

Attorney
Brown, Francis A.
Rudman, Pavi L.
Stevens, Winfred A.

Banker
Jordan, E. Robert

Broker
Cooper, Darrell M.
Mullins, Howard J.
Pendleton, Thomas C. Jr.

Consultant
Cooper, Darrell M.
Mullins, Howard J.
Pendleton, Thomas C. Jr.

Developer
Cooper, Darrell M.
Mabee, Nancy C.
Pendleton, Thomas C. Jr.
Sewall, Nancy C.

Insuror
Mullins, Howard J.
Stevens, Winfred A.

Owner/Investor
Cooper, Darrell M.

Property Manager
Cooper, Darrell M.
Mullins, Howard J.
Pendleton, Thomas C. Jr.

Syndicator
Pendleton, Thomas C. Jr.

HOUTTON

Attorney
Rhoda, Richard L.

Insuror
Rhoda, Richard L.

PORTLAND

Appraiser
Baribeau, Michael H.
Jacobs, Richard L.
Sawyer, Heywood A.
Sawyer, Richard Lewis

Attorney
Ayer, Gordon C.
Bergen, Bruce Westbrook
Ferguson, Robert William
Soles, Christopher X.

Banker
Ferguson, Robert William

Broker
Baribeau, Michael H.
Butts, Reginald F.
Dodd, James H.
Henry, J. Donald
Jacobs, Richard L.
McGoldrick, Richard J.
Martin, Eugene S.

Builder
Baribeau, Michael H.

Consultant
Baribeau, Michael H.
Butts, Reginald F.
Hamlin, F. Gordon Jr.
Jacobs, Richard L.
Sawyer, Richard Lewis

Developer
Baribeau, Michael H.
Butts, Reginald F.
Jacobs, Richard L.
McGoldrick, Richard J.
Martin, Eugene S.
Wasileski, John B.

Instructor
Murphy, James M.

Insuror
Ferguson, Robert William

Lender
Davis, Ronald A.
Jacobs, Richard L.
Murphy, James M.

Owner/Investor
Butts, Reginald F.
Davis, Ronald A.
Dodd, James H.
Ferguson, Robert William
Hamlin, F. Gordon Jr.
Henry, J. Donald
Jacobs, Richard L.
McGoldrick, Richard J.
Martin, Eugene S.
Murphy, James M.
Soles, Christopher X.
Wasileski, John B.

Property Manager
Baribeau, Michael H.
Butts, Reginald F.
McGoldrick, Richard J.
Martin, Eugene S.
Murphy, James M.
Soles, Christopher X.
Wasileski, John B.

Syndicator
Hamlin, F. Gordon Jr.
McGoldrick, Richard J.
Wasileski, John B.

WATERVILLE

Builder
Fendler, Ryan D.

Developer
Fendler, Ryan D.

Owner/Investor
Fendler, Ryan D.

Syndicator
Fendler, Ryan D.

MARYLAND

BALTIMORE

Appraiser
Abbott, C. Webster
Arnold, Robert Marvin
Bormel, Joseph
Cassell, Michael A.
Currie, William I.
DeWar, William D.
Dolan, Earl T. Jr.
Fish, John E. Jr.
Flynn, Ramsey W.J.
Gilber, C. Gordon Sr.
Heidrick, G. A. Jr.
Hentschel, John Joseph
Knott, Joseph M.
Kurz, Christopher W.
Millison, Stuart
Mullikin, Kent R.
Quinn, Michael D.
Rosenberg, Theodore M.
Schwartz, Jacob
Sigler, John N.
Skinner, Robert S. Jr.
Solomon, Gerald H.
Steffey, John W. Jr.
Tinley, S. Herbert III
Vinci, Richard Anthony

Architect
Altman, Richard S.
Brodie, M.J.
Haus, J. Gilbert Jr.
Meyers, William II

Assessor
DeWar, William D.

Attorney
Baum, Charles C.
Beasley, Robert Scott
Beckley, John W.
Berghel, Victoria Smouse
Clark, Donald R.
Dausch, William
Define, William T.
DeWar, William D.
Doub, James C.
Duncan, James W. Jr.
Fink, Alan
Jacobs, Joseph Charles
Lenrow, Jay Laurence
Loewy, Steven A.
Mackey, Maurice F.
McPherson, Donald P. III
Maseritz, Guy B.
Meredith, Timothy E.
Mitnick, Searle E.
Pollak, Mark
Reed, Gregory L.
Short, Alexander C.
Sigler, John N.
Simmons, Wilbur E. Jr.
Smith, Eugene P.
Smith, Harry R. Jr.
Sokolov, Richard Saul
Steele, John W. III

Tabor, Neil
Weinberg, Robert L.
Wilson, Christian

Banker
Deltz, Jack C.
Effinger, Charles H.W. Jr.
Heidrick, G. A. Jr.
Herzberger, Robert Charles
Stackhouse, Philip E.

Broker
Abbott, C. Webster
Arnold, R. Jeffery
Arnold, Robert Marvin
Bavar, David I.
Beasley, Robert Scott
Bormel, Joseph
Butler, Kent E.
Carp, Mark B.
Cassell, Michael A.
Cherikof, Howard L.
DeWar, Donald J. III
DeWar, William D.
Dolan, Earl T. Jr.
Duncan, James W. Jr.
Fish, John E. Jr.
Flad, J. Michael
Flynn, Ramsey W.J.
Frenkil, Leonard I.
Glackin, Dorothy M.
Hartman, Stephen J.
Heineman, G. Wendell
Hentschel, John Joseph
Jones, Richard Alvin
Jones, Richard R.
Jones, William P.
Knott, Joseph M.
Kornblatt, David
Lamoreaux, William
Latshaw, Robert E. Jr.
Lyons, Michael J.
McCoy, Robert L.
Magill, Douglas E.
Millner, N. Wayne
Nuttle, John C.
Pensel, Edward C.
Poole, William T. Jr.
Quinn, Michael D.
Schwartz, Jacob
Sigler, John N.
Smith, William R.
Statkiewicz, Robert E.
Steffey, John W. Jr.
Strange, Robert T.
Strutt, George F.

Builder
Browne, Gary L.
Cassell, Michael A.
DeWar, William D.
Frenkil, Leonard I.
Haus, J. Gilbert Jr.
Heineman, G. Wendell
Jacobs, Joseph Charles
Jones, Richard Alvin
Kelly, James R.
Legum, Leslie
Magill, Douglas E.
Millison, Stuart
Steffey, John W. Jr.
Strutt, George F.

Consultant
Abbott, C. Webster
Altman, Richard S.
Arnold, Robert Marvin
Baum, Charles C.
Beasley, Robert Scott
Bormel, Joseph
Bouscaren, Pierre Jr.
Browne, Gary L.
Burke, Joseph T. II
Cassell, Michael A.
Clark, Donald R.
Currie, William I.
Demmitt, Richard Joseph
DeWar, William D.
Dolan, Earl T. Jr.
Evans, Charles C.G. Jr.
Fish, John E. Jr.
Flynn, Ramsey W.J.
Gilber, C. Gordon Sr.
Haus, J. Gilbert Jr.
Heidrick, G. A. Jr.
Heineman, G. Wendell
Helwig, Charles E.
Hentschel, John Joseph
Hunter, Donald E.
Jacobs, Joseph Charles
Jones, William P.
Kelly, James R.
Kornblatt, David
Kraus, Richard W.
Kurz, Christopher W.
Levine, Melvin F.
Loewy, Steven A.
McGill, Peter R. Jr.
Magill, Douglas E.
Meyers, William II
Mullikin, Kent R.
Nuttle, John C.
Peacock, James S.
Poole, William T. Jr.
Quinn, Michael D.
Rosenberg, Theodore M.
Scheeler, John E.
Sigler, John N.
Simmons, Wilbur E. Jr.
Smith, Harry R. Jr.
Stackhouse, Philip E.
Steffey, John W. Jr.
Strange, Robert T.
Tinley, S. Herbert III
Vandevender, Junior M.
Vinci, Richard Anthony
Wolpoff, Alvin S.

Developer
Abbott, C. Webster
Altman, Richard S.
Arnold, R. Jeffery
Bavar, David I.
Browne, Gary L.
Burke, Joseph T. II
Carp, Mark B.
Cartwright, Donald B.
Cassell, Michael A.
Cherikof, Howard L.
Clark, Donald R.
Collins, Frank
Creaney, C. Patrick
DeWar, William D.
Dollenberg, P. Douglas
Doswell, Menard
Duncan, James W. Jr.
Evans, Charles C.G. Jr.
Flad, J. Michael
Forester, David E.
Frenkil, Leonard I.
Hartman, Stephen J.
Haus, J. Gilbert Jr.
Heidrick, G. A. Jr.
Heineman, G. Wendell
Holmes, John B.
Hughes, F. Patrick
Hunter, Donald E.
Jacobs, Joseph Charles
Jones, Richard Alvin
Jones, Richard R.
Jones, William P.
Keelty, Kevin C.
Kelly, James R.
Kornblatt, David
Kraus, Richard W.
Kurz, Christopher W.
Lansinger, John P.
Latshaw, Robert E. Jr.
Legum, Leslie
McGill, Peter R. Jr.
Magill, Douglas E.
Medinger, Alan P.
Meyers, William II
Millison, Stuart
Nuttle, John C.
Phillips, Wayne
Poole, William T. Jr.
Quinn, Michael D.
Roca, Ruben A.
Rosen, Michael Howard
Rosenberg, Theodore M.
Rosenberger, Herbert D.
Sigler, John N.
Smith, Harry R. Jr.
Statkiewicz, Robert E.
Steffey, John W. Jr.
Strutt, George F.
Vinci, Richard Anthony
Wells, Samuel Robert Jr.
Wit, Gerard J.

Engineer
Colbert, Kenneth J.
DeWar, William D.
Haus, J. Gilbert Jr.
Jones, Richard Alvin

Instructor
Browne, Gary L.
Cassell, Michael A.
Cherikof, Howard L.
Click, David F.
DeWar, Donald J. III
Effinger, Charles H.W. Jr.
Flynn, Ramsey W.J.
Heineman, G. Wendell
Hentschel, John Joseph
Jacobs, Joseph Charles
Lamoreaux, William
Magill, Douglas E.
Pensel, Edward C.
Rosenberg, Theodore M.
Steffey, John W. Jr.

Insuror
Abbott, C. Webster
Bormel, Joseph
Fish, John E. Jr.
Flynn, Ramsey W.J.
Quinn, Michael D.

Lender
DeWar, William D.
Effinger, Charles H.W. Jr.
Heidrick, G. A. Jr.
Herzberger, Robert Charles
Keelty, Kevin C.
Mullikin, Kent R.
Quinn, Michael D.
Stackhouse, Philip E.

Owner/Investor
Abbott, C. Webster
Altman, Richard S.
Arnold, R. Jeffery
Baum, Charles C.
Bavar, David I.
Beckley, John W.
Cassell, Michael A.
Clark, Donald R.
Demmitt, Richard Joseph
DeWar, Donald J. III
DeWar, William D.
Duncan, James W. Jr.
English, Allan J.
Evans, Charles C.G. Jr.
Fish, John E. Jr.
Flad, J. Michael
Frenkil, Leonard I.
Glackin, Dorothy M.
Hartman, Stephen J.
Haus, J. Gilbert Jr.
Heidrick, G. A. Jr.
Hughes, F. Patrick
Hunter, Donald E.
Jacobs, Joseph Charles
Jones, Richard Alvin
Jones, William P.
Kelly, James R.
Kurz, Christopher W.
Lamoreaux, William
Latshaw, Robert E. Jr.
McCoy, Robert L.
McGill, Peter R. Jr.
Meyers, William II
Millison, Stuart
Millner, N. Wayne
Mullikin, Kent R.
Peacock, James S.
Phillips, Wayne
Quinn, Michael D.
Rosen, Michael Howard
Rosenberger, Herbert D.
Sigler, John N.
Smith, Harry R. Jr.
Smith, William R.
Statkiewicz, Robert E.
Strutt, George F.
Vandevender, Junior M.
Vinci, Richard Anthony
Wells, Samuel Robert Jr.

Property Manager
Arnold, R. Jeffery
Arnold, Robert Marvin
Baldwin, Robert
Bank, Herbert
Bouscaren, Pierre Jr.
Browne, Gary L.
Burke, Joseph T. II
Cartwright, Donald B.
Cassell, Michael A.
Chambers, Charles
Cherikof, Howard L.
Clark, Donald R.
Currie, William I.
Dausch, William
Deltz, Jack C.
Demmitt, Richard Joseph
DeWar, Donald J. III
DeWar, William D.
English, Allan J.
Evans, Charles C.G. Jr.
Fick, Edmund J.
Fish, John E. Jr.
Flad, J. Michael
Flynn, Ramsey W.J.
Haus, J. Gilbert Jr.
Heineman, G. Wendell
Hughes, F. Patrick
Jones, Richard R.
Jones, William P.
Kornblatt, David
Latshaw, Robert E. Jr.
Legum, Leslie
Millner, N. Wayne
Mullikin, Kent R.
Ohlig, Rick
Poole, William T. Jr.
Quinn, Michael D.
Rosen, Michael Howard
Rosenberger, Herbert D.
Scheeler, John E.
Schek, Leslie G.
Sigler, John N.
Statkiewicz, Robert E.
Strange, Robert T.
Tinley, S. Herbert III
Vandevender, Junior M.
Vinci, Richard Anthony
Wells, Samuel Robert Jr.
Wolfe, Henry

Real Estate Publisher
Browne, Gary L.
Heineman, G. Wendell

Regulator
Cassell, Michael A.
Herzberger, Robert Charles
Hughes, F. Patrick

Syndicator
Browne, Gary L.
Cherikof, Howard L.
Demmitt, Richard Joseph

DeWar, William D.
Fish, John E. Jr.
Flad, J. Michael
Frenkil, Leonard I.
Heidrick, G. A. Jr.
Heineman, G. Wendell
Hentschel, John Joseph
Jones, William P.
Kurz, Christopher W.
Latshaw, Robert E. Jr.
Magill, Douglas E.
Phillips, Wayne
Quinn, Michael D.
Rosenberg, Theodore M.
Sigler, John N.
Smith, William R.
Vandevender, Junior M.
Vinci, Richard Anthony

CUMBERLAND

Developer
Mappin, Richard

EASTON

Attorney
Rasin, Alexander P. III

FREDERICK

Attorney
France, Ralph H. II

Broker
Machat, Sydney L.
Mackintosh, Earl M. III
Massey, J. Alvin
Oliver, William Taylor

Builder
Oliver, William Taylor

Consultant
Mackintosh, Earl M. III
Massey, J. Alvin

Developer
France, Ralph H. II
Machat, Sydney L.
Mackintosh, Earl M. III
Massey, J. Alvin
Oliver, William Taylor

Instructor
Machat, Sydney L.

Owner/Investor
France, Ralph H. II
Machat, Sydney L.
Massey, J. Alvin

Property Manager
Mackintosh, Earl M. III

PRINCE GEORGES

Appraiser
Beck, Samuel H. Jr.
Clarke, James Brent III
Davies, Leslie E.
Huggins, Harold H.
Inokon, H. Michael
Juergens, Richard K. Jr.
Kibbe, James W
Lee, Adelbert W.
Lennhoff, David C.
McCurdy, Dennis O.
Mitchell, Ryland L. III
Murray, F. Alden Jr.
Norem, LeRoy K.
Owens, William S.
Summers, Paul F. Jr.
Urquhart, Donald Victor
Williams, James Dale
Wise, William S.
Wood, Brooks C.B.

Architect
Beck, Samuel H. Jr.
Koran, Arley J.

Assessor
Kibbe, James W.

Attorney
Aron, Ruthann
Baker, Judith E.
Bell, Martin M.
Bolotin, Jeffrey W.
Brennan, John M.
Caraci, Philip D.
Conroy, J. Michael Jr.
Davidson, William G. III
Dawson, John H. Jr.
Doolan, Devin John
Droege, J. Robert
Gingell, Robert A.
Goldstein, Leonard R.
Grayson, Stephen R.
Greenstein, Mitchell M.
Jersin, Wayne N.
Kugler, Mark William
Laskin, Dennis A.
Long, Oliver Denier Esq.
McCabe, John F. Jr.
McKeever, Patrick C.
Meyers, Bertram H.
Polachek, Ralph R.
Schneider, Melvin L.
Supik, Frank R.
Tavel, James W.
Walker, Larry E.
Wildhack, William A. Jr.

Banker
Juergens, Richard K. Jr.

Broker
Adams, Gregg
Altobelli, Frank R.
Armiger, Milton W.
Backman, Jean A.
Becker, Kenneth H.
Brennan, John M.
Briddell, Willis H.
Clarke, James Brent III
Coleman, Walter L. III
Conley, James C. Jr.
Conrad, Joseph Jr.
Cravedi, David L.
David, Leo
Davies, Leslie E.
Earp, Susan L.
Fleishman, Irving
Forman, R. Edward
Gallagher, Margaret Parr
Grayson, Stephen R.
Griffin, John F.
Huggins, Harold H.
Inokon, H. Michael
Juergens, Richard K. Jr.
Kibbe, James W.
Laskin, Dennis A.
Lawler, Frank
Levin, Paul Mason
Long, Oliver Denier Esq.
McCurdy, Dennis O.
Marks, Kenneth L.
Molinaro, C. Joseph
Murray, F. Alden Jr.
Norem, LeRoy K.
Palmer, Alice H.
Rucci, Peter Paul
Snider, Donald J.
Solem, Richard Ray
Summers, Paul F. Jr.
Talcott, Worthington H.
Terry, Patricia A.
Thompson, Byron
Van Derwerker, John R.
Wildhack, William A. Jr.
Williams, James Dale
Wise, William S.
Wood, Brooks C.B.

Builder
Altobelli, Frank R.
Bell, Martin M.
Cafritz, James E.
Clark, William J.
Droege, J. Robert
Ely, Edward A.
Furman, Robert R.
Goldstein, Larry A.
Grayson, Stephen R.
Haag, George Alva
Haber, Miles J.
Hardwick, Charles V. Jr.
Klass, Richard L.
Landow, Nathan
Laskin, Dennis A.
Levin, Paul Mason
Lewis, David R.
Morelli, Michael
Noakes, D.T.
Reeves, William R.
Stuart, Charles E.
Wilson, James J.
Wise, William S.
Wormald, Robert K.

Consultant
Armiger, Milton W.
Aron, Ruthann
Beck, Samuel H. Jr.
Caraci, Philip D.
Clarke, James Brent III
Coleman, Walter L. III
Conrad, Joseph Jr.
Cravedi, David L.
Davidson, William G. III
Dodek, Aaron Willard
Dubin, Arthur N.
Earp, Susan L.
Eisen, Dennis
Ellman, Martin
Fleishman, Irving
Goodwin, Ronald
Hagen, David B.
Huggins, Harold H.
Inokon, H. Michael
Kahn, B. Franklin
Kibbe, James W.
Kugler, Mark William
Larson, Lori S.
Lennhoff, David C.
McCurdy, Dennis O.
McKeever, Patrick C.
Meyer, F. Weller
Michael, Jerome J.
Mitchell, Ryland L. III
Molinaro, C. Joseph
Murray, F. Alden Jr.
Norem, LeRoy K.
Reeves, William R.
Ruzic, John F.
Shlonsky, Roger B.
Starke, John W.
Summers, Paul F. Jr.
Supik, Frank R.
Terry, Patricia A.
Urquhart, Donald Victor
Wasson, Larry
Williams, James Dale
Wise, William S.

Developer
Altobelli, Frank R.
Aron, Ruthann
Becker, Kenneth H.
Briddell, Willis H.
Byrnes, Randall W.
Cafritz, James E.
Caraci, Philip D.
Clark, William J.
Coleman, Walter L. III
Depew, Robert G.
Dill, Leonard C.
Droege, J. Robert
Ely, Edward A.
Fleishman, Irving
Furman, Robert R.
Goldstein, Larry A.
Grayson, Stephen R.
Griffin, John F.
Haag, George Alva
Haber, Miles J.
Huggins, Harold H.
Inokon, H. Michael
Juergens, Richard K. Jr.
Klass, Richard L.
Landow, Nathan
Larson, Lori S.
Laskin, Dennis A.
Levin, Paul Mason
Lewis, David R.
McIntyre, Donald F.X.
Marks, Kenneth L.
Noakes, D.T.
Reeves, William R.
Rumford, Frances R. Senfeld
Shlonsky, Roger B.
Stuart, Charles E.
Summers, Paul F. Jr.
Supik, Frank R.
Thompson, Byron
Voegler, James H.
Walker, Larry E.
Wilson, James J.

Engineer
Beck, Samuel H. Jr.
Grayson, Stephen R.
McIntyre, Donald F.X.

Instructor
Conrad, Joseph Jr.
Gallagher, Margaret Parr
Goodwin, Ronald
Hagen, David B.
Huggins, Harold H.
Inokon, H. Michael
Kahn, B. Franklin
Kibbe, James W.
Larson, Lori S.
McIntyre, Donald F.X.
Talcott, Worthington H.
Urquhart, Donald Victor
Van Derwerker, John R.
Williams, James Dale

Insuror
Altobelli, Frank R.
Davies, Leslie E.
Huggins, Harold H.
Juergens, Richard K. Jr.
Talcott, Worthington H.
Wildhack, William A. Jr.
Williams, James Dale

Lender
Burd, Hal
Caraci, Philip D.
Hardwick, Charles V. Jr.
Juergens, Richard K. Jr.
McCurdy, Dennis O.

Owner/Investor
Altobelli, Frank R.
Aron, Ruthann
Bell, Martin M.
Cafritz, James E.
Caraci, Philip D.
Coleman, Walter L. III
Dill, Leonard C.
Dodek, Aaron Willard
Droege, J. Robert
Eisen, Dennis
Ellman, Martin
Ely, Edward A.
Frymark, Herbert F.
Gingell, Robert A.
Goldstein, Larry A.
Grayson, Stephen R.
Griffin, John F.
Hagen, David B.
Huggins, Harold H.

Inokon, H. Michael
Juergens, Richard K. Jr.
Kahn, B. Franklin
Kibbe, James W.
Kugler, Mark William
Landow, Nathan
Lawler, Frank
Levin, Paul Mason
Lewis, David R.
McCurdy, Dennis O.
McIntyre, Donald F.X.
Marks, Kenneth L.
Morelli, Michael
Murray, F. Alden Jr.
Reeves, William R.
Rumford, Frances R. Senfeld
Supik, Frank R.
Thompson, Byron
Van Derwerker, John R.
Walker, Larry E.
Weissel, William J.
Williams, James Dale
Wilson, James J.
Wood, Brooks C.B.

Property Manager
Adams, Gregg
Altobelli, Frank R.
Armiger, Milton W.
Briddell, Willis H.
Caraci, Philip D.
Conrad, Joseph Jr.
David, Leo
Dill, Leonard C.
Dodek, Aaron Willard
Dubin, Arthur N.
Duffield, Lee
Ellman, Martin
Goodwin, Ronald
Grayson, Stephen R.
Griffin, John F.
Hagen, David B.
Inokon, H. Michael
Jacobsen, Dean A.
Juergens, Richard K. Jr.
Kugler, Mark William
Landow, Nathan
Larson, Lori S.
Lawler, Frank
Lewis, David R.
McCurdy, Dennis O.
McIntyre, Donald F.X.
Meyers, Bertram H.
Morelli, Michael
Newman, Robert M.
O'Connell, James Joseph
Reeves, William R.
Rumford, Frances R. Senfeld
Simmons, Lawrence F.
Solem, Richard Ray
Stuart, Charles E.
Summers, Paul F. Jr.
Supik, Frank R.
Talcott, Worthington H.
Thompson, Byron
Van Derwerker, John R.
Weissel, William J.
Williams, James Dale
Wilson, James J.

Real Estate Publisher
Inokon, H. Michael

Regulator
Owens, William S.

Syndicator
Armiger, Milton W.
Aron, Ruthann
Bell, Martin M.
Brennan, John M.
Coleman, Walter L. III
Ellman, Martin
Frymark, Herbert F.
Goodwin, Ronald
Grayson, Stephen R.
Greenstein, Mitchell M.
Inokon, H. Michael
Kugler, Mark William
Larson, Lori S.
McCurdy, Dennis O.
Murray, F. Alden Jr.
Norem, LeRoy K.
Reeves, William R.
Solem, Richard Ray
Supik, Frank R.
Walker, Larry E.
Weissel, William J.

SALISBURY

Appraiser
Howard, Norris C.
Truitt, Gerald B. Jr.

Architect
Ardis, Ronald E.

Banker
Hutzell, Richard Edward
Truitt, Gerald B. Jr.

Broker
English, Jim Jr.
Howard, Norris C.
Hutzell, Richard Edward

Builder
Beauchamp, Randolph L.
English, Jim Jr.

Consultant
Ardis, Ronald E.
English, Jim Jr.
Howard, Norris C.

Developer
English, Jim Jr.

Engineer
Whitlock, Lawrence T. Jr.

Insuror
English, Jim Jr.

Owner/Investor
Howard, Norris C.

Property Manager
English, Jim Jr.
Howard, Norris C.

Syndicator
Howard, Norris C.

MASSACHUSETTS

BOSTON

Appraiser
Akerson, Charles B.
Barber, Peter K.
Beal, Alexander S.
Beal, Bruce A.
Beal, Robert L.
Bonz, Richard
Burrows, James C.
Caplan, Bruce M.
Cole, J. Ralph
Collins, Bradfield J.
Connaughton, William Jr.
Coombs, Edward H.
Dewolfe, Richard B.
Everett, Wilson Earl Jr.
Jones, Patricia M.
Keefe, Paul T.
Kenny, Charles
Lupo, Robert N.
McDermott, Ruth E.
McDonald, Samuel James Jr.
Marsh, Dexter H. Jr.
Merrill, William Blakemore II
Papas, P.N. II
Perkins, Richard F.
Richert, Clarendon G.
Saunders, Donald L.
Sharpe, Wayne G. Jr.
Singer, Bernard
Sylvester, John E. Jr.
Weisman, Mark S.
White, Robert J.
Willcox, Raymond B.
Wolfson, Louis

Architect
Bianchi, Philip A.
Blake, Benjamin S.
Bradley, Robert D.
Bruck, F. Frederick
Gerhard, Ronald H.
Gushue, Patrick F.
Heuer, Charles R. AIA, Esq.
Kirwan, Ernest E.
Lundgren, Richard J.
Pollock, Wilson F. Jr.
Shea, Kevin R.
Willse, Charles E.

Assessor
Cole, J. Ralph
Fiumara, John
McSweeney, John J.
White, Robert J.

Attorney
Abrams, Stanton V.
Aronson, Frank D.
Bell, Robert L. Jr.
Berman, Martin S.
Bordwin, Milton
Boyle, Mary Ellen T. Esq.
Brower, Barbara Brane
Brown, Thomas Howard
Burr, Stephen Ives
Chertok, Sumner J.
Christoforo, John
Cooper, Erwin E.
Cox, Gilbert W. Jr.
Crawford, Francine O.
Feldman, Saul J.
Funk, Daniel M.
Geller, David J.
Greenman, Karl
Hall, Susan M.
Hawkey, G. Michael
Heuer, Charles R. AIA, Esq.
Howard, Susanne C.
Jordon, James A.
Katz, Donald H.
Kohen, David M.
Levin, Charles R.
Levin, Jeffrey H.
Linder, Dale A.
Lupo, Robert N.
Lyne, Kerry R.
McDougald, Ronald J.
Markoff, Gary M.
Minahan, Neal Edward
Queen, Barry L.
Rai, Shambhu K.
Rainen, Edward
Sacco, George L.
Schafer, Robert
Scofield, Lawrence F. Jr.
Seghezzi, Alan R.
Shine, James P.
Silver, Robert C.
Sinclair, Michael D.
Smith, Traver Clinton Jr.
Snyder, Richard J.
Sweeney, David C. Jr.
Swett, Valerie
Tuchmann, Robert
Vaughan, Herbert W.
Vitagliano, Arthur
Wodlinger, Eric
Xellihen, Barry S.

Banker
Brady, Philip H. Jr.
Elliot, Raymond H.
Fuchs, Steven L.
Keesler, W.F.
Piana, Edward R.
Queen, Barry L.
Sharpe, Wayne G. Jr.
Sopp, Brian W.
Swain, Robert S. Jr.

Broker
Abrams, Stanton V.
Beal, Robert L.
Berkman, Bernard G.
Berman, Martin S.
Bierbrier, Leonard H.
Blake, Benjamin S.
Boucher, Harold E.
Boyle, Mary Ellen T. Esq.
Bradshaw, William D.
Brodie, Douglas S.
Burke, Richard J.
Caplan, Bruce M.
Carter, Marcia H.
Chertok, Sumner J.
Connaughton, William Jr.
Coombs, Edward H.
Coughlin, William G.
DeSanctis, Leo J.
DeVito, Richard A.
Dewolfe, Richard B.
Dickinson, Mark C.
Dowd, Michael J.
Evans, Roger W.
Fiumara, John
Flynn, J. Michael
Friedman, Richard L.
Fuchs, Steven L.
Geller, David J.
Grossman, Jay M.
Halloran, Thomas C.
Hawkey, G. Michael
Jones, Patricia M.
Jordon, James A.
Kenny, Charles
Koza, John W.
Lavin, James W.
Lawther, Pamela C.
Levey, Kenneth E.
Lupo, Robert N.
McCormick, John E.
McDermott, Ruth E.
McDonald, Samuel James Jr.
McKenna, Harold C.
Marsh, Dexter H. Jr.
May, Laurence T. Jr.
Mulcahy, James III
Neelon, David E.
Nordblom, Rodger P.
O'Brien, Thomas F.
Pahl, David R.
Papas, P.N. II
Pedulla, Thomas V.
Perkins, Richard F.
Perrine, James J.
Rai, Shambhu K.
Rice, Stephen C.
Sacco, George L.
Saunders, Donald L.
Schafer, H. James
Schochet, Jay R.
Sharpe, Wayne G. Jr.
Sweeney, David C. Jr.
Sylvester, John E. Jr.
Tabasky, Samuel T.
Tarkinow, Morris J.
Traina, Carl L.
Walsh, E. Denis
Walsh, Thomas A.
Walton, J.H. Jr.
Weisman, Mark S.
White, Robert J.
Willcox, Raymond B.

Wolfson, Louis
Xellihen, Barry S.
Zimmerman, Mark

Builder
Cuker, George
DeVito, Richard A.
Gerhard, Ronald H.
Grossman, Jay M.
Jennison, Gary A.
Lane, Robert H.
LaPuma, Anthony P. Jr.
Lundgren, Richard J.
McGrath, Michael P.
May, Laurence T. Jr.
Papas, P.N. II
Rothkopf, Gary S.
Schochet, Jay R.
Shea, Kevin R.
Shine, James P.
Simon, Franklin Wallace
Tarkinow, Morris J.
Walsh, E. Denis
Wells, William L.
West, Jeffrey G.
White, Robert J.
Yelton, Robert H.

Consultant
Ahlberg, Henry B.
Akerson, Charles B.
Bassett, Peter J.
Beal, Alexander S.
Beal, Bruce A.
Beal, Robert L.
Begelfer, David I.
Berkman, Bernard G.
Bierbrier, Leonard H.
Bigelow, George H.
Blake, Benjamin S.
Bonz, Richard
Boucher, Harold E.
Bradley, Robert D.
Bradshaw, William D.
Brodie, Douglas S.
Brower, Barbara Brane
Brown, John A.
Burns, Richard F.
Burrows, James C.
Caplan, Bruce M.
Chertok, Sumner J.
Cole, J. Ralph
Connaughton, William Jr.
Coombs, Edward H.
Cuker, George
Danziger, Robert A.
Dewolfe, Richard B.
Dowd, Michael J.
Evans, Roger W.
Everett, Wilson Earl Jr.
Fiumara, John
Freed, Kenneth L.
Friedman, Richard L.
Gelardin, Robert
Geller, David J.
Grossman, Jay M.
Gushue, Patrick F.
Halloran, Thomas C.
Hawthorne, Randolph G.
Jones, Patricia M.
Jordon, James A.
Keesler, W.F.
Kelly, Mary Dianne
Kenney, Robert T.
Kenny, Charles
Kruszewski, Stanley
Kursh, Steven R.
Lane, Robert H.
Lavin, James W.
Levey, Kenneth E.
Levin, Charles R.
Libman, Isidore M.
Lupo, Robert N.
McDermott, Ruth E.
McDonald, Samuel James Jr.
McDougald, Ronald J.
McKenna, Harold C.
Markoff, Gary M.
Marsh, Dexter H. Jr.
May, Laurence T. Jr.
Merrill, William Blakemore II
Nordblom, Rodger P.
Pahl, David R.
Papas, P.N. II
Pedro, Frank A.
Pedulla, Thomas V.
Perkins, Richard F.
Perrine, James J.
Pickette, T. Robert
Prigmore, G. Daniel
Rai, Shambhu K.
Ricker, Ruth B.
Sacco, George L.
Saunders, Donald L.
Schafer, H. James
Shine, James P.
Simon, Franklin Wallace
Singer, Bernard
Smith, Traver Clinton Jr.
Stevenson, Howard H.
Sweeney, David C. Jr.
Sylvester, John E. Jr.
Tabasky, Samuel T.
Tarkinow, Morris J.
Verzuh, Frank M. Dr.
Vitagliano, Arthur
Walsh, E. Denis
Walsh, Thomas A.
Weisman, Mark S.
White, Robert J.
Wolfson, Louis
Zimmerman, Mark

Developer
Abrams, Stanton V.
Barber, Peter K.
Bates, Joseph E.
Beal, Bruce A.
Beal, Robert L.
Begelfer, David I.
Bettencourt, Joe
Bianchi, Philip A.
Bierbrier, Leonard H.
Blackham, J. William III
Bonz, Richard
Boucher, Harold E.
Bradley, Robert D.
Brady, Philip H. Jr.
Brown, John A.
Burrows, James C.
Busny, Irving H.
Chertok, Sumner J.
Cohen, Richard D.
Cole, J. Ralph
Conroy, Terence W.
Cuker, George
Danziger, Robert A.
DeVito, Richard A.
Dickinson, Mark C.
Dowd, Michael J.
Emerson, Gordon E. Jr.
Fine, Alvin M.
Freed, Kenneth L.
Friedman, Richard L.
Garfield, Louis N.
Gelardin, Robert
Geller, David J.
Gerhard, Ronald H.
Glick, Marvin M.
Grossman, Jay M.
Hall, R. Douglas III
Haughey, Philip C.
Jennison, Gary A.
Kelly, Mary Dianne
Kisiel, Mark M.
Koza, John W.
Kruszewski, Stanley
Kursh, Steven R.
Lane, Robert H.
LaPuma, Anthony P. Jr.
Levin, Charles R.
Libman, Isidore M.
Lupo, Robert N.
McGrath, Michael P.
McSweeney, John J.
Markoff, Gary M.
May, Laurence T. Jr.
Merrill, William Blakemore II
Miller, Raymond W.
Neelon, David E.
Nordblom, Rodger P.
Pahl, David R.
Papas, P.N. II
Pappas, George
Pedulla, Thomas V.
Perkins, Richard F.
Perrine, James J.
Prigmore, G. Daniel
Queen, Barry L.
Rai, Shambhu K.
Railsback, David P.
Ricker, Ruth B.
Rothkopf, Gary S.
Schochet, Jay R.
Shea, Kevin R.
Shine, James P.
Simon, Franklin Wallace
Sweeney, David C. Jr.
Sylvester, John E. Jr.
Tabasky, Samuel T.
Tambone, Antonio J.
Tarkinow, Morris J.
Traina, Carl L.
Trussell, Philip A.
Walsh, E. Denis
Weisman, Mark S.
Wells, William L.
White, Robert J.
Yelton, Robert H.
Zimmerman, Mark

Engineer
Bianchi, Philip A.
Caplan, Bruce M.
Connaughton, William Jr.
Fine, Alvin M.
Gerhard, Ronald H.
Gushue, Patrick F.
Kassner, Milton
Traina, Carl L.
Verzuh, Frank M. Dr.

Instructor
Beal, Robert L.
Berman, Martin S.
Blake, Benjamin S.
Caplan, Bruce M.
Cooper, Erwin E.
Jones, Patricia M.
Kelly, Mary Dianne
Kursh, Steven R.
Levin, Charles R.
McCormick, John E.
McDonald, Samuel James Jr.
Pedulla, Thomas V.
Ricker, Ruth B.
Scofield, Lawrence F. Jr.
Sharpe, Wayne G. Jr.
Verzuh, Frank M. Dr.
Walsh, E. Denis

Insuror
Desmond, Michael J.
Everett, Wilson Earl Jr.
Halloran, Thomas C.
McCormick, John E.
Traina, Carl L.
Vitagliano, Arthur

Lender
Brady, Philip H. Jr.
Cuker, George
Dziadul, W. John
Emerson, Gordon E. Jr.
Fitzwilliam, Michael F.
Glick, Marvin M.
Merrill, William Blakemore II
Piana, Edward R.
Queen, Barry L.
Richert, Clarendon G.
Sharpe, Wayne G. Jr.
Sopp, Brian W.
Tarkinow, Morris J.
White, Robert J.

Owner/Investor
Bassett, Peter J.
Bates, Joseph E.
Beal, Bruce A.
Beal, Robert L.
Begelfer, David I.
Berkman, Bernard G.
Berman, Martin S.
Bigelow, George H.
Blackham, J. William III
Brady, Philip H. Jr.
Brown, John A.
Burns, Richard F.
Burrows, James C.
Busny, Irving H.
Caplan, Bruce M.
Cervieri, John A. Jr.
Cohen, Richard D.
Connolly, Thomas K.
Danziger, Robert A.
DeVito, Richard A.
Dickerman, Allen F.
Dickinson, Mark C.
Dowd, Michael J.
Eastman, Thomas G.
Emerson, Gordon E. Jr.
Fitzwilliam, Michael F.
Freed, Kenneth L.
Geller, David J.
Gerhard, Ronald H.
Glick, Marvin M.
Grossman, Jay M.
Hall, R. Douglas III
Haughey, Philip C.
Hawkey, G. Michael
Hawthorne, Randolph G.
Howell, A. Harold
Kruszewski, Stanley
Lane, Robert H.
LaPuma, Anthony P. Jr.
Libman, Isidore M.
Lupo, Robert N.
Markoff, Gary M.
May, Laurence T. Jr.
Melzer, Robert M.
Merrill, William Blakemore II
Mulcahy, James III
Neelon, David E.
Nelson, John M. IV
Peckham, John Munroe III
Perrine, James J.
Pitts, William R.
Prigmore, G. Daniel
Queen, Barry L.
Rai, Shambhu K.
Rodgers, Timothy K.
Rushkin, Kate
Saunders, Donald L.
Shine, James P.
Stevenson, Howard H.
Sylvester, John E. Jr.
Tabasky, Samuel T.
Tambone, Antonio J.
Tarkinow, Morris J.
Trussell, Philip A.
Verzuh, Frank M. Dr.
Walsh, E. Denis
Walton, J.H. Jr.
Weisman, Mark S.
Welch, Patricia Leal
White, Robert J.
Wolfson, Louis

Yelton, Robert H.
Zimmerman, Mark

Property Manager
Armknecht, Richard F. Jr.
Baack, John E.
Babb, Kenneth P.
Barton, W.C.
Bassett, Peter J.
Beal, Bruce A.
Beal, Robert L.
Beaven, Clinton
Berkman, Bernard G.
Berman, Martin S.
Boddy, G.G.
Bonz, Richard
Burke, Richard J.
Caplan, Bruce M.
Cohen, Richard D.
Corbett, Harry
Coughlin, William G.
Cuker, George
Danziger, Robert A.
Dewolfe, Richard B.
Dickerman, Allen F.
Dorfman, Michael
Emerson, Gordon E. Jr.
Englander, Morris K.
Fine, Alvin M.
Freed, Kenneth L.
Gammon, Terrance
Garrett, Richard
Gelardin, Robert
Geller, David J.
Glick, Marvin M.
Groff, Milton
Gushue, Patrick F.
Hall, R. Douglas III
Halloran, Thomas C.
Hathorne, Gerald
Haughey, Philip C.
Hawthorne, Randolph G.
Howell, A. Harold
Jennison, Gary A.
Kelly, Mary Dianne
Kenny, Charles
Koza, John W.
Kozlowski, Dennis
Lane, Robert H.
Lavin, James W.
Levey, Kenneth E.
Levin, Charles R.
Libman, Isidore M.
Lupo, Robert N.
McGrath, Michael P.
McSweeney, John J.
Merrill, William Blakemore II
Morris, C.T.
Mulcahy, James III
Neelon, David E.
Nordblom, Rodger P.
Norton, David
Pantazelos, Peter
Papas, P.N. II
Pappas, George
Pedro, Frank A.
Pedulla, Thomas V.
Perrine, James J.
Pickette, T. Robert
Pitts, William R.
Potter, George E.
Prigmore, G. Daniel
Queen, Barry L.
Rai, Shambhu K.
Ricker, Ruth B.
Robinson, John T.
Rosenbaum, Michael Gordon
Saunders, Donald L.
Schochet, Jay R.
Shine, James P.
Siegler, S.
Simon, Franklin Wallace
Smith, Neil
Sylvester, John E. Jr.
Tabasky, Samuel T.
Tarkinow, Morris J.
Trussell, Philip A.
Verzuh, Frank M. Dr.
Walsh, E. Denis
Weinstein, Gerald
Weisman, Mark S.
Wells, William L.
White, Robert J.
Yelton, Robert H.

Real Estate Publisher
Bean, William H.
DeVito, Richard A.
Geering, Christina Z.
George, Robert J.
Hofford, Ray
Hopkins, Roland
Launer, Deborah
Pasnik, Alan
Peckham, John Munroe III
Shultz, E. Alison
Stein, David E.
Welch, Patricia Leal

Regulator
Geering, Christina Z.
Shultz, E. Alison

Syndicator
Beal, Bruce A.
Busny, Irving H.
Chertok, Sumner J.
Cohen, Richard D.
Connaughton, William Jr.
Danziger, Robert A.
Dewolfe, Richard B.
Dowd, Michael J.
Farrell, Robert J. Jr.
Gelardin, Robert
Greenman, Karl
Hall, Denison M.
Haughey, Philip C.
Hawthorne, Randolph G.
Howell, A. Harold
Kohen, David M.
Kruszewski, Stanley
Lundgren, Richard J.
McDougald, Ronald J.
Markoff, Gary M.
Nelson, John M. IV
Papas, P.N. II
Perrine, James J.
Rai, Shambhu K.
Simon, Franklin Wallace
Sylvester, John E. Jr.
Tabasky, Samuel T.
Tarkinow, Morris J.
Walsh, E. Denis
Yelton, Robert H.
Zimmerman, Mark

BROCKTON

Appraiser
Tofias, Donald

Attorney
Borges, Richard C.
Paradis, Pierre R.
Pollis, John P.
Walkey, John R.

Broker
Bergeron, Norman A.
Griffin, James K. Jr.
Tofias, Donald
Tripp, Robert V.

Builder
Griffin, James K. Jr.
Laflamme, Robert G.

Consultant
Hall, William O.
Tofias, Donald

Developer
Carney, Patrick
Griffin, James K. Jr.
Tofias, Donald

Engineer
Laflamme, Robert G.

Owner/Investor
Griffin, James K. Jr.
Tofias, Donald

Property Manager
Carney, Patrick
Corsini, Andrew C.
Delaney, Charles
Frigon, William
Griffin, James K. Jr.
Segal, David P.
Tofias, Donald

Syndicator
Carney, Patrick

BUZZARDS BAY

Appraiser
Holland, James J.

Architect
Ferragamo, Anthony E.

Attorney
Glynn, Paul C.
Lane, John Marshall

Broker
Glynn, Neil H.
Holland, James J.
LaFleur, Edmond J.
Lane, John Marshall

Builder
Alcorn, John G.
Burden, Christopher
Glynn, Neil H.

Consultant
Burden, Christopher
LaFleur, Edmond J.

Developer
Burden, Christopher
Glynn, Neil H.
LaFleur, Edmond J.

Instructor
Glynn, Neil H.
LaFleur, Edmond J.

Owner/Investor
Glynn, Neil H.

Property Manager
Burden, Christopher

FRAMINGHAM

Appraiser
Avery, Jonathan H.
Potter, Charles J.

Assessor
Eck, George N. Jr.

Attorney
Potter, Charles J.
St. Germain, Philip M.
Whittemore, David O.

Broker
Calarese, Roger V.
Carlson, Margaret C.
Cline, Leonard A.
Farard, Howard

Builder
Farard, Howard
Steele, Thomas A.
Strehlke, Richard B.

Consultant
Avery, Jonathan H.
Farard, Howard
Sabbey, John G.
Steele, Thomas A.
Trachtenberg, Ronald W. CPA

Developer
Calarese, Roger V.
Depietri, Robert J. Jr.
Farard, Howard
Perini, Bart W.
Sabbey, John G.
St. Germain, Philip M.
Steele, Thomas A.
Strehlke, Richard B.

Instructor
Avery, Jonathan H.

Owner/Investor
Calarese, Roger V.
Cline, Leonard A.
Cohen, Sidney
Depietri, Robert J. Jr.
Farard, Howard
Goulet, Richard C
Sabbey, John G.
St. Germain, Philip M.
Steele, Thomas A.
Strehlke, Richard B.
Whittemore, David O.

Property Manager
Barnes, W.P.
Cline, Leonard A.
Crowley, Joseph
Depietri, Robert J. Jr.
Fafard, Madlyn A.
Farard, Howard
Kent, Alfred
Koningisor, James
Krasnow, William D.
Potter, Charles J.
Robinson, Richard
Sabbey, John G.
Shanahan, Thomas
Strehlke, Richard B.

Syndicator
Cline, Leonard A.
St. Germain, Philip M.

MIDDLESEX-ESSEX

Appraiser
Barrett, Christopher J.
Brown, William C.
Carlson, Richard Wakefield
Emerson, Peter S.
Kludjian, Armen G.
McGoff, James J.
Martin, Vernon A.
Niland, William F. Jr.
Simmons, Richard D.

Architect
Iacoviello, Frank

Assessor
Emerson, Peter S.

Attorney
Balas, Francis P.
Boumil, S. James
Howarth, Thomas G.
Jones, Richard B.
Kimball, John H. Jr.
Morton, Perry W.
Shack, Norman M.

Banker
Stoughton, Robert E.

Broker
Barrett, Christopher J.
Brown, William C.
Carlson, Richard Wakefield
Fields, Charles L.
Fryer, Malcolm F. Jr.
Hallberg, Frank D. Jr.
Hoopes, Claude B.
Iacoviello, Frank

Kludjian, Armen G.
Martin, Vernon A.
Morton, Perry W.
Niland, William F. Jr.
Samowski, Don
Scott, Lorett J.
Sherman, Michael B.
Simmons, Richard D.
Slye, George E.
Small, Peter M.
Smith, Edwin A.
Spalding, Mona T.
Vaill, George

Builder
Hoopes, Claude B.
Iacoviello, Frank
Martin, Vernon A.
Palmisano, Laurence J.
Samowski, Don
Sherman, Michael B.
Slye, George E.
Small, Peter M.
Taylor, Keith A.
Webster, Robert E.

Consultant
Anderson, William V.
Brown, William C.
Carlson, Richard Wakefield
Emerson, Peter S.
Fryer, Malcolm F. Jr.
Hoopes, Claude B.
Iacoviello, Frank
Kleiman, Macklen
McGoff, James J.
Martin, Vernon A.
Morton, Perry W.
Niland, William F. Jr.
Palmisano, Laurence J.
Redmond, John G. Sr.
Simmons, Richard D.
Slye, George E.
Small, Peter M.
Vaill, George

Developer
Anderson, William V.
Boumil, S. James
Hoopes, Claude B.
Iacoviello, Frank
Jones, Richard B.
Martin, Vernon A.
Morton, Perry W.
Palmisano, Laurence J.
Sherman, Michael B.
Slye, George E.
Small, Peter M.
Taylor, Keith A.
Webster, Robert E.
Whelan, William N.

Engineer
Kleiman, Macklen
Palmisano, Laurence J.

Instructor
Brown, William C.
Emerson, Peter S.
Kimball, John H. Jr.
Martin, Vernon A.
Simmons, Richard D.

Lender
Stoughton, Robert E.

Owner/Investor
Anderson, William V.
Barrett, Christopher J.
Boumil, S. James
Brown, William C.
Fields, Charles L.
Green, Robert W.
Hoopes, Claude B.
Iacoviello, Frank
Kleiman, Macklen
Kludjian, Armen G.
Martin, Vernon A.
Morton, Perry W.
Orbe, Felix A.
Palmisano, Laurence J.
Redmond, John G. Sr.
Samowski, Don
Simmons, Richard D.
Slye, George E.
Spalding, Mona T.

Property Manager
Brown, William C.
Carlson, Richard Wakefield
Fryer, Malcolm F. Jr.
Hallberg, Frank D. Jr.
Kleiman, Macklen
McCallum, Robert
McCarthy, Douglas
Marrs, Edward J.
Niland, William F. Jr.
Olsen, Richard
Palmisano, Laurence J.
Redmond, John G. Sr.
Repucci, Ron
Samowski, Don
Sherman, Michael B.
Slye, George E.
Small, Peter M.
Steinkrauss, Daniel
Vaill, George
Woo, Robert

Regulator
Samowski, Don

Syndicator
Anderson, William V.
Palmisano, Laurence J.
Samowski, Don
Simmons, Richard D.
Smith, Edwin A.

PITTSFIELD

Appraiser
Roche, W. David Jr.
Ruffer, Donald O.

Banker
Roche, W. David Jr.

Broker
Ingegni, Albert A. III
Ruffer, Donald O.

Developer
Ruffer, Donald O.

Instructor
Roche, W. David Jr.
Ruffer, Donald O.

Lender
Roche, W. David Jr.

Owner/Investor
Ingegni, Albert A. III
Roche, W. David Jr.
Ruffer, Donald O.

Property Manager
Ingegni, Albert A. III
Ruffer, Donald O.

Syndicator
Ruffer, Donald O.

SPRINGFIELD

Appraiser
Fountain, Milton O.
LaFlamme, Earl A. Jr.
O'Connor, James F.
O'Connor, Larry
Schorr, Bernard W.
Tetreault, George A. Jr.
Wampler, David A.

Attorney
Arden, John Real
Dillman, Rodney J.
Pollard, Frank E.
Pudlo, William J.
Ratner, Michael S.
Rogeness, Dean A.
Sullivan, Daniel John
Tetreault, George A. Jr.
Weisman, Steven J.

Broker
Bennett, R.H.
Binns, Donald A.
Coppola, A. Gerard
Dill, B. John
Fountain, Milton O.
Hulseberg, Edmund W.
LaFlamme, Earl A. Jr.
Popko, Julian S.
Schorr, Bernard W.
Sullivan, Daniel John
Tetreault, George A. Jr.
Wampler, David A.

Builder
Binns, Donald A.
Calabrese, Charles
Coppola, A. Gerard
Fountain, Milton O.
O'Connor, Larry
Popko, Julian S.
Sullivan, Daniel John
Tetreault, George A. Jr.

Consultant
Coppola, A. Gerard
Fountain, Milton O.
Hulseberg, Edmund W.
LaFlamme, Earl A. Jr.
O'Connor, James F.
Tetreault, George A. Jr.
Wampler, David A.

Developer
Binns, Donald A.
Calabrese, Charles
Coppola, A. Gerard
Dill, B. John
Fountain, Milton O.
O'Connor, Larry
Sullivan, Daniel John
Tetreault, George A. Jr.

Instructor
LaFlamme, Earl A. Jr.
O'Connor, James F.

Lender
Binns, Donald A.
Dill, B. John
Libby, Bruce A.
Sulik, Edward J.
Wampler, David A.

Owner/Investor
Binns, Donald A.
Dill, B. John
Fountain, Milton O.
Hartman, Richard R.
Hulseberg, Edmund W.
LaFlamme, Earl A. Jr.
Libby, Bruce A.
O'Connor, Larry
Popko, Julian S.
Sulik, Edward J.
Tetreault, George A. Jr.

Property Manager
Bennett, R.H.
Binns, Donald A.
Coppola, A. Gerard
Dill, B. John
LaFlamme, Earl A. Jr.
O'Connor, Larry
Popko, Julian S.
Schorr, Bernard W.
Strzempek, Stanley
Sullivan, Daniel John

Syndicator
Binns, Donald A.

WORCESTER

Appraiser
Hughes, Stephen V. Jr.
LaPorte, Robert P. Jr.

Attorney
Army, Lawrence F.
Bloom, William R.
Elander, William August
Myers, Wallace Haslett
Rabinowitz, Alan James

Banker
Quackenbush, Stanley G.

Broker
Hughes, Stephen V. Jr.
Myers, Wallace Haslett
Piermarini, James J.

Builder
Adams, James R.
Piermarini, James J.

Consultant
LaPorte, Robert P. Jr.

Developer
Adams, James R.
Piermarini, James J.

Engineer
Hughes, Stephen V. Jr.
Piermarini, James J.

Insuror
Trent, Joseph Stanley

Lender
Adams, James R.

Owner/Investor
Adams, James R.
Bloom, William R.
Myers, Wallace Haslett
Piermarini, James J.

Property Manager
Beaupre, Armand G.
Chambles, Bert
Hughes, Stephen V. Jr.
Marshall, Donald L.
Piermarini, James J.

Syndicator
Piermarini, James J.

MICHIGAN

DETROIT

Appraiser
Alcock, Gerald V.
Beaubien, C. Gordon
Begg, Charles F.H.
Behr, Dick A.J.
Bleyer, Norman J.
Cooch, Robert A.
Cook, John M.
Franck, Donald G.
Kingsbury, Marvin R.
McDonnell, David K.
Mawson, James E.
Nelson, Oren F.
Peterson, Ray Douglas
Pliska, Robert J.

Architect
Cook, John M.
Schneider, Herbert M.
Shea, Leo G.
Van Curler, Donald Edward

Assessor
Johnson, Wayne C.
Pliska, Robert J.

Attorney
Austin, Margaret S.
Barrows, Ronald Thomas
Beeman, Gordon L.
Berardo, William J.
Cook, John M.
Dawda, Edward C.
Dunn, William B.
Ford, Frank B.
Grassi, Sebastian V. Jr.
Hartman, William J.
Janover, Robert H.
Johnson, Edward C.
Lipnik, Alvin P.
McDonnell, David K.
McNair, Russell A. Jr.
Monahan, Denis C.
Paterson, Andrew A.
Petz, Frederick A.
Rabbideau, Richard E.
Roach, Thomas A.
Sachs, Henry A.
Schlecte, William M.
Young, Hallison H.

Banker
Everham, George R.
Nelson, Oren F.
Weinert, Carl R.

Broker
Barrows, Ronald Thomas
Beaubien, C. Gordon
Begg, Charles F.H.
Bleyer, Norman J.
Brauer, Carl A. Jr.
Cook, John M.
Henkel, Edward Jr.
Jones, Linda N.
Kaslik, Michael S.
Kingsbury, Marvin R.
Knox, Robert D.
Marsh, William D.
Monahan, Denis C.
Nelson, Oren F.
Nixon, Don L.
Peterson, Ray Douglas
Pliska, Robert J.
Pongrace, Otto W.
Renken, Duane A.
Sachs, Henry A.
Schmuckal, Ralph P. Jr.
Schneider, Herbert M.
Stachel, Gary R.
Thornton, Robert H. Jr.
Valdez, Charles E.

Builder
Allen, Peter T.
Casey, John
Cook, John M.
Etkin, Alex J.
Everham, George R.
Kaysserian, Michael M.
Kingsbury, Marvin R.
Lambert, Richard L.
Pliska, Robert J.
Schmuckal, Ralph P. Jr.
Van Curler, Donald Edward

Consultant
Alcock, Gerald V.
Barrows, Ronald Thomas
Begg, Charles F.H.
Behr, Dick A.J.
Bleyer, Norman J.
Cook, John M.
Devlin, George A.
Edington, Jack L.
Gechter, Lawrence R.
Johnson, Wayne C.
Jones, Linda N.
Kingsbury, Marvin R.
Lambert, Richard L.
McClendon, Janet S.
Mawson, James E.
Peterson, Ray Douglas
Petz, Frederick A.
Pliska, Robert J.
Pongrace, Otto W.
Rasmussen, John A.
Renken, Duane A.
Shea, Leo G.
Shiefman, Saul
Valdez, Charles E.

Developer
Alcock, Gerald V.
Allen, Peter T.
Brauer, Carl A. Jr.
Casey, John
Denson, Theodore D.
Etkin, Alex J.
Foytek, Dan
Kaysserian, Michael M.
Knox, Robert D.
Lambert, Richard L.
Marsh, William D.
Neal, Kenneth A.
Nixon, Don L.
Pliska, Robert J.
Pongrace, Otto W.
Renken, Duane A.
Sachs, Henry A.
Schneider, Herbert M.
Seibel, John P.
Shea, Leo G.
Thornton, Robert H. Jr.
Van Curler, Donald Edward

Engineer
Casey, John
Cook, John M.
Etkin, Alex J.
Pongrace, Otto W.
Shea, Leo G.

Instructor
Allen, Peter T.
Barrows, Ronald Thomas
Browder, Olin L.
McClendon, Janet S.
Mawson, James E.
Sachs, Henry A.
Schlecte, William M.
Schmuckal, Ralph P. Jr.

Insuror
McIntyre, H. Neil
Nelson, Oren F.

Lender
Everham, George R.
Franck, Donald G.
Lipnik, Alvin P.
McIntyre, H. Neil
Petz, Frederick A.
Pliska, Robert J.

Owner/Investor
Allen, Peter T.
Barrows, Ronald Thomas
Begg, Charles F.H.
Bitz, Brent W.
Brauer, Carl A. Jr.
Casey, John
Cook, John M.
Etkin, Alex J.
Griffin, Richard P.
Johnson, Basil D.
Jonas, Harry Jr.
Jones, Linda N.
Kaslik, Michael S.
Kaysserian, Michael M.
Lambert, Richard L.
McClendon, Janet S.
Marsh, William D.
Neal, Kenneth A.
Nelson, Oren F.
Nixon, Don L.
Petz, Frederick A.
Pliska, Robert J.
Renken, Duane A.
Sachs, Henry A.
Schmuckal, Ralph P. Jr.
Schneider, Herbert M.
Shea, Leo G.
Van Curler, Donald Edward
Young, Hallison H.

Property Manager
Allen, Peter T.
Alonzo, Richard
Basse, Arthur
Brauer, Carl A. Jr.
Caponitro, Ralph
Cook, John M.
East, James D.
Everham, George R.
Griffin, Richard P.
Hagopian, John
Hartman, William J.
Hill, Roderick
Jeltes, Charles J.
Johnson, Basil D.
Kaslik, Michael S.
Kaysserian, Michael M.
Kingsbury, Marvin R.
Knabusch, C.T.
Knox, Robert D.
Kopietz, Richard J.
Lambert, Richard L.
Marsh, William D.
O'Keefe, William
Pliska, Robert J.
Renken, Duane A.
Robinson, Walter
Sachs, Henry A.
Schmuckal, Ralph P. Jr.
Schneider, Herbert M.
Seibel, John P.
Valdez, Charles E.
Van Curler, Donald Edward

Real Estate Publisher
Babb, Janice
Dordick, Beverly
Shiefman, Saul

Regulator
Crawford, Clan. Jr.
Hill, Roderick

Syndicator
Casey, John
Griffin, Richard P.
Kaysserian, Michael M.
Knox, Robert D.
Lambert, Richard L.
McClendon, Janet S.
Renken, Duane A.
Risser, Robin F.
Schmuckal, Ralph P. Jr.
Schneider, Herbert M.
Young, Hallison H.

FLINT

Appraiser
Healy, Gerald F.
Rexroth, David K.
Southwell, Lawrence G.

Attorney
Newman, Bruce A.

Banker
Southwell, Lawrence G.

Broker
Healy, Gerald F.
Macgregor, Valerie
Maloney, John T.
Robinson, Richard H.
Showmaker, L.E.
Wright, Elizabeth L. (Libby)

Builder
Macgregor, Valerie

Consultant
Healy, Gerald F.
Macgregor, Valerie
Maloney, John T.
Robinson, Richard H.
Showmaker, L.E.

Developer
Healy, Gerald F.
Maloney, John T.

Engineer
Healy, Gerald F.

Instructor
Showmaker, L.E.
Southwell, Lawrence G.
Wright, Elizabeth L. (Libby)

Lender
Southwell, Lawrence G.

Owner/Investor
Healy, Gerald F.
Macgregor, Valerie
Maloney, John T.
Robinson, Richard H.
Showmaker, L.E.
Wright, Elizabeth L. (Libby)

Property Manager
Healy, Gerald F.
Macgregor, Valerie
Maloney, John T.
Post, Robert A.
Robinson, Richard H.

Syndicator
Macgregor, Valerie
Showmaker, L.E.

GAYLORD

Attorney
Spanos, George

Banker
Kitchen, E. Joseph

Broker
Georgi, John M.

Developer
McCarthy, R. Michael
Spanos, George

Owner/Investor
Georgi, John M.
Spanos, George

Syndicator
Georgi, John M.
Spanos, George

GRAND RAPIDS

Appraiser
Bussey, William Wallace Jr.
Frazier, Larry David
Schenck, Harold E. II

Architect
Childress, Dennis E.

Attorney
Ash, Willis L.
Boven, Thomas M.
Makens, Hugh H.
Rigas, John N.
Snedegar, Kenneth T.
Van't Hof, Willaim Keith
Ward, Paul A.
Wrigley, Benham R. Jr.

Banker
Ash, Willis L.
Greemann, Harvey W.

Broker
Batzer, Jon P.
Bussey, William Wallace Jr.
Childress, Dennis E.
Frazier, Larry David
Greemann, Harvey W.
Heindrichs, Robert W.
Jurries, James

Kamminga, Fred J.
Keller, Robert A.
Koster, Thomas L.
Snedegar, Kenneth T.
Wisinski, Stanley J. III

Builder
Bussey, William Wallace Jr.
Childress, Dennis E.
Frazier, Larry David
Jurries, James
Keller, Robert A.
Rigas, John N.

Consultant
Bussey, William Wallace Jr.
Cassard, David Sr.
Frazier, Larry David
Gilmore, John F.
Haas, Donald E.
Harmsen, Mark D.
Hefferan, T. William
Heindrichs, Robert W.
Kamminga, Fred J.
Snedegar, Kenneth T.
Wisinski, Stanley J. III
Wrigley, Benham R. Jr.

Developer
Bussey, William Wallace Jr.
Frazier, Larry David
Fuller, Charles R.
Gilmore, John F.
Harmsen, Mark D.
Hefferan, T. William
Jurries, James
Kamminga, Fred J.
Koster, Thomas L.
Rigas, John N.
Snedegar, Kenneth T.
Stephenson, John S.
Van't Hof, Willaim Keith

Instructor
Bussey, William Wallace Jr.
Frazier, Larry David
Heindrichs, Robert W.
Van't Hof, Willaim Keith

Insuror
Snedegar, Kenneth T.

Lender
Ash, Willis L.
Greemann, Harvey W.
Rigas, John N.
Wisinski, Stanley J. III

Owner/Investor
Batzer, Jon P.
Bussey, William Wallace Jr.
Cassard, David M.
Cassard, David Sr.
Gilmore, John F.
Haas, Donald E.
Harmsen, Mark D.
Jurries, James
Kamminga, Fred J.
Keller, Robert A.
Marsilje, E.H.
Rigas, John N.
Snedegar, Kenneth T.
Stephenson, John S.
Teal, Marvin E.
Van't Hof, Willaim Keith
Wrigley, Benham R. Jr.

Property Manager
Batzer, Jon P.
Bussey, William Wallace Jr.
Cassard, David M.
Cassard, David Sr.
Harmsen, Mark D.
Hefferan, T. William
Kamminga, Fred J.
Kuiper, John
Larkin, James
Morris, Kenneth
Okkema, Matthew
Snedegar, Kenneth T.
Stephenson, John S.
Teal, Marvin E.
Van Til, Bernard A.
Wisinski, Stanley J. III

Syndicator
Batzer, Jon P.
Bussey, William Wallace Jr.
Frazier, Larry David
Gilmore, John F.
Jurries, James
Kamminga, Fred J.
Koster, Thomas L.

IRON MOUNTAIN

Appraiser
Closser, Bruce
Madacey, John R.
Wedge, Ken

Attorney
Gaiser, J. Raymond
McLean, Norman
Selsor, L. Grant

Banker
Marquardt, Vern A.

Broker
Madacey, John R.
Malnor, Robert J.

Consultant
Closser, Bruce
Madacey, John R.
Malnor, Robert J.

Developer
Madacey, John R.

Instructor
Madacey, John R.
Malnor, Robert J.

Owner/Investor
McLean, Norman
Madacey, John R.

Property Manager
Madacey, John R.

Syndicator
Harris, Hugh D.
Madacey, John R.
Malnor, Robert J.

JACKSON

Appraiser
Abraham, John
Graybiel, Allan C.
Nuttle, Daniel E.
Rees, Daniel L.

Broker
Abraham, John
Nuttle, Daniel E.
Rees, Daniel L.

Builder
Abraham, John

Consultant
Abraham, David J.
Abraham, John
Mirafzali, Hamid

Developer
Abraham, John
Graybiel, Allan C.
Mirafzali, Hamid

Instructor
Graybiel, Allan C.
Nuttle, Daniel E.

Insuror
Nuttle, Daniel E.

Owner/Investor
Abraham, David J.
Mirafzali, Hamid

Property Manager
Abraham, John
Behling, R.H.
Drury, Charles E.
Mirafzali, Hamid
Reynolds, Judy Maxine
Thompson, L.D.

Syndicator
Graybiel, Allan C.
Mirafzali, Hamid

KALAMAZOO

Appraiser
Dexter, Donald P.
Dillingham, William W.
Frohm, James M.
Kissman, Nadra D.
Robbins, C. LaVern
Sherman, Jefferson L.

Architect
Belson, Gordon A.

Attorney
Carver, Enoch IV
Colip, John R.
Enderle, Alan G.
Grier, David C.
Howell, Thomas G.
Hudgins, C. Reid III
Lundquist, C. David
Webb, Burke Hilliard

Banker
Harrison, David T.
Robbins, C. LaVern

Broker
Beles, Florian L.
Dillingham, William W.
Frohm, James M.
Gerould, Ann K.
Kissman, Nadra D.
Morrison, Rick
Robbins, C. LaVern
Sherman, Jefferson L.
Weiner, Joshua T.

Builder
Bly, Thomas K.
Dexter, Donald P.
Frohm, James M.
Robbins, C. LaVern
Weiner, Joshua T.
Weiner, Meyer C.

Consultant
Beles, Florian L.
Bly, Thomas K.
Dillingham, William W.
Morrison, Rick
Robbins, C. LaVern

Developer
Bly, Thomas K.
Friday, Victor
Frohm, James M.
Gerould, Ann K.
Robbins, C. LaVern
Weiner, Joshua T.
Weiner, Meyer C.

Engineer
Goetz, Donald H.

Instructor
Robbins, C. LaVern

Insuror
Frohm, James M.

Owner/Investor
Beles, Florian L.
Belson, Gordon A.
Bly, Thomas K.
Dexter, Donald P.
Frohm, James M.
Gerould, Ann K.
Kissman, Nadra D.
Morrison, Rick
Weiner, Joshua T.

Property Manager
Beles, Florian L.
Belson, Gordon A.
Bly, Thomas K.
Dexter, Donald P.
Goetz, Donald H.
Hauch, Larry
King, Stanley A.
Miller, Callix E.
Morrison, Rick
Nay, Ward H.
Rupp, Paul W.
Weiner, Joshua T.
Witherspoon, David
Yealin, Richard A.

Syndicator
Beles, Florian L.
Bly, Thomas K.

LANSING

Appraiser
Griffith, Harry E.
Henry, John J.
Krause, David H.
MacDonald, Leona I.
Opper, Ralph E.
Porter, William J. Jr.
Spitler, LaRue G.

Architect
Kostosky, Thomas J.
Young, David O. Jr.

Attorney
Walsh, Thomas C.

Banker
Bunker, Kimberly Ann

Broker
Cummings, Tom
Fedewa, Bernard E.
Gentilozzi, Albert E.
Griffith, Harry E.
Henry, John J.
Lockwood, William R.
MacDonald, Leona I.
Mentzer, Jeanne M.
Opper, Ralph E.
Porter, William J. Jr.
Rosten, James A.

Consultant
Cady, William F.
Cummings, Tom
Gentilozzi, Albert E.
Henry, John J.
Kostosky, Thomas J.
Krause, David H.
Lockwood, William R.
MacDonald, Leona I.
Mentzer, Jeanne M.
Porter, William J. Jr.
Rosten, James A.
Young, David O. Jr.

Developer
Brunst, William Todd
Fedewa, Bernard E.
Gentilozzi, Albert E.
Kostosky, Thomas J.
Krause, David H.
Young, David O. Jr.

Engineer
Kostosky, Thomas J.

Instructor
Henry, John J.
Mentzer, Jeanne M.
Rooney, John P.

Insuror
Cady, William F.

Lender
Bunker, Kimberly Ann
Fedewa, Bernard E.
Spitler, LaRue G.

Owner/Investor
Brunst, William Todd
Cady, William F.
Cummings, Tom
Gentilozzi, Albert E.
Lockwood, William R.
Mentzer, Jeanne M.
Opper, Ralph E.
Rosten, James A.
Young, David O. Jr.

Property Manager
Amberg, Robert S. Jr.
Brunst, William Todd
Cummings, Tom
Gentilozzi, Albert E.
Greisinger, Richard
Henry, John J.
Lockwood, William R.
Mentzer, Jeanne M.
Porter, William J. Jr.
Rosten, James A.
Young, David O. Jr.

Regulator
Abdo, Mark J

Syndicator
Gentilozzi, Albert E.

ROYAL OAK

Appraiser
Beron, Gail L.
Cherney, Richard A.
Cilluffo, Vito
Fernelius, Earl W.
Gordon, Charles L.
Hartman, Donald J.
Kelly, Charles S.
Osmycki, Daniel A.
Pierce, Philip Foster
Scott, Robert H.
Smalley, James A.
Swanson, Charles M.

Architect
Albert, Roy I.
Brown, Jack W.

Attorney
Andrews, Frank L.
Banas, C. Leslie
Bosco, Louis C. Jr.
Currier, Timothy J.
Etkin, Douglas M.
Geer, Thomas L.
Hayman, Alan J.
Hayman, Stephen P.
Kaufman, Alan Jay
Kutchins, Bryan A.
McGlynn, Joseph M.
Malaker, A. Deane
Meisner, Robert M.
Mulcahy, Michael D.
Priestley, Allen E.
Rotenberg, Milton P.
Schlussel, Mark E.
Shanoski, Daniel P.
Sommers, Norman S.
Sparrow, David J.
Tobin, Aubrey H.
Tornga, David L.
Trimmer, J. Kevin
Vlcko, Miroslav P.
Wagner, Richard L. Jr.
Wienberg, Carl H.

Banker
Densmore, Robert R.
Thompson, Patrick J.

Broker
Bosco, Louis C. Jr.
Burger, Edward R.
Carey, Robert Harrison
Charbonneau, Richard
Cherney, Richard A.
Daitch, Marvin C.
Fenton, Edgar
Fernelius, Earl W.
Golanty, George C.
Gordon, Charles L.
Hall, Craig
Hartman, Donald J.
Hawthorne, R. Bradley
Hayman, Alan J.
Hayman, Stephen P.
Horton, David T.
Jamnick, William P.
Keim, Earl G. Jr.
Kelly, Charles S.
LaFata, John M.
Levitt, William M.
LoPatin, Lawrence H.
McMillin, Terry J.
Osmycki, Daniel A.
Pardom, Charles F.
Schebor, Ronald R.
Scott, Robert H.
Shanoski, Daniel P.
Shaw, Arthur F.
Smalley, James A.
Spera, Charles C.
Thomas, Mark A.
Tobin, Aubrey H.
Williamson, G. Gordon

Builder
Charbonneau, Richard
Daitch, Marvin C.
Fenton, Edgar
Horton, David T.
LaFata, John M.
McMillin, Terry J.
Priehs, George W.
Rotenberg, Milton P.
Slavik, Stephan F. Sr.

Consultant
Andrews, Frank L.
Beeler, Thomas T.
Beron, Gail L.
Burdick, Daniel H. II
Carey, Robert Harrison
Cherney, Richard A.
Fernelius, Earl W.
Golanty, George C.
Hartman, Donald J.
Havel, William A.
Hayman, Alan J.
Hayman, Stephen P.
Johnson, Walter G.
Keim, Earl G. Jr.
Kelly, Charles S.
Kirschner, Gerald M.
LaFata, John M.
Leary, John H.
McGlynn, Joseph M.
McMillin, Terry J.
Osmycki, Daniel A.
Pardom, Charles F.
Pierce, Philip Foster
Scott, Robert H.
Seeley, Fred C.
Shaw, Arthur F.
Smalley, James A.
Spera, Charles C.
Thomas, Mark A.
Tobin, Aubrey H.
Wagner, Richard L. Jr.
Wienberg, Carl H.
Wilkinson, Larry M.

Developer
Bond, Robert W.
Bosco, Louis C. Jr.
Carey, Robert Harrison
Cherney, Richard A.
Daitch, Marvin C.
Etkin, Douglas M.
Fenton, Edgar
Finerty, Patrick J.
Gordon, Charles L.
Hall, Craig
Horton, David T.
Karas, Steven Lawrence
Kowal, Walter C.
Kutchins, Bryan A.
LaFata, John M.
LoPatin, Lawrence H.
Nelson, David Robert
Pardom, Charles F.
Pierce, Philip Foster
Priehs, George W.
Rotenberg, Milton P.
Seeley, Fred C.
Slavik, Stephan F. Sr.
Thomas, Mark A.
Tobin, Aubrey H.
Ware, David M.
Winton, Frank J.

Instructor
Carey, Robert Harrison
Fernelius, Earl W.
Havel, William A.
Keim, Earl G. Jr.
LaFata, John M.
LoPatin, Lawrence H.
McMillin, Terry J.
Smalley, James A.
Swanson, Charles M.

Insuror
McMillin, Terry J.

Lender
Daitch, Marvin C.
Guttenberg, Larry L.
Johnson, Walter G.
Priehs, George W.
Swanson, Charles M.
Thompson, Patrick J.
West, Terry W.

Owner/Investor
Beeler, Thomas T.
Bosco, Louis C. Jr.
Etkin, Douglas M.
Fenton, Edgar
Finerty, Patrick J.
Geer, Thomas L.
Golanty, George C.
Gordon, Charles L.
Hall, Craig
Havel, William A.
Hayman, Alan J.
Hayman, Stephen P.
Johnson, Walter G.
Kelly, Charles S.
Kirschner, Gerald M.
Kowal, Walter C.
LoPatin, Lawrence H.
McMillin, Terry J.
Nelson, David Robert
Pardom, Charles F.
Pierce, Philip Foster
Priehs, George W.
Scott, Robert H.
Shouhayib, Kamal
Slavik, Stephan F. Sr.
Smalley, James A.
Sparrow, David J.
Spera, Charles C.
Tobin, Aubrey H.
West, Terry W.

Property Manager
Beeler, Thomas T.
Burdick, Daniel H. II
Cody, William J.
Cracchiolo, Peter
Dorfman, Joel
Dulude, D.O.
Etkin, Douglas M.
Fenton, Edgar
Finerty, Patrick J.
Fisher, Walter
Gordon, Charles L.
Hall, Craig
Havel, William A.
Hayman, Alan J.
Hayman, Stephen P.
Horton, David T.
Johnson, Walter G.
Kowal, Walter C.
LaFata, John M.
LoPatin, Lawrence H.
Malaker, A. Deane
Pardom, Charles F.
Pierce, Philip Foster
Priehs, George W.
Prout, P.W.
Scott, Robert H.
Seeley, Fred C.
Slavik, Stephan F. Sr.
Smalley, James A.
Sparrow, David J.
Wagner, Richard L. Jr.
West, Terry W.

Syndicator
Beeler, Thomas T.
Cherney, Richard A.
Cherry, James P.
Elsea, Richard
Fenton, Edgar
Golanty, George C.
Gordon, Charles L.
Hall, Craig
Havel, William A.
Hayman, Alan J.
Hayman, Stephen P.
Kelly, Charles S.
Kutchins, Bryan A.
LaFata, John M.
LoPatin, Lawrence H.
Shouhayib, Kamal
Smalley, James A.
Sparrow, David J.
Thomas, Mark A.
Tobin, Aubrey H.

SAGINAW

Appraiser
Kavanagh, James L.
Miller, Richard T.
Powers, Earl L.

Assessor
Harwood, William James

Broker
Hales, Karen A.
Kavanagh, James L.
Miller, Richard T.
Powers, Earl L.

Builder
Murray, Norbert T.
Peifer, Chris A.
Vaydik, Frank W.

Consultant
Kavanagh, James L.
Miller, Richard T.
Murray, Norbert T.
Vaydik, Frank W.

Developer
Miller, Richard T.
Murray, Norbert T.
Vaydik, Frank W.

Owner/Investor
Miller, Richard T.
Murray, Norbert T.
Peifer, Chris A.
Powers, Earl L.
Vaydik, Frank W.

Property Manager
Beck, Roger
Meagher, William
Miller, Richard T.
Murray, Norbert T.
Powers, Earl L.
Vaydik, Frank W.

Syndicator
Miller, Richard T.
Murray, Norbert T.
Vaydik, Frank W.

TRAVERSE CITY

Architect
Bergsma, Ralph

Attorney
Brustad, Orin D.
Gockerman, Bruce C.

Consultant
Bergsma, Ralph

Developer
Bergsma, Ralph

Owner/Investor
Bergsma, Ralph
Gockerman, Bruce C.

Property Manager
Kempton, George

Syndicator
Gockerman, Bruce C.

MINNESOTA

BEMIDJI

Broker
Gendreau, Richard
Kittleson, John Alden

Consultant
Gendreau, Richard

Instructor
Gendreau, Richard

BRAINERD

Appraiser
Foote, Gene
Roberts, Nelson R.

Broker
Foote, Gene
Roberts, Nelson R.
Sullivan, John P.

Developer
Roberts, Nelson R.
Sullivan, John P.

Instructor
Foote, Gene

Property Manager
Roberts, Nelson R.

DETROIT LAKES

Attorney
Guy, William L. III
Oppegard, Paul R.

Property Manager
Wachal, D.E.

DULUTH

Appraiser
Ramsland, Maxwell O. Jr.

Attorney
Doran, Camille V.
Evenson, Gregory Dean
Hessen, Neal J.

Banker
Labovitz, Joel

Builder
Welles, S. Christopher

Consultant
Labovitz, Joel
Ramsland, Maxwell O. Jr.
Welles, S. Christopher

Developer
Labovitz, Joel

Lender
Labovitz, Joel

Owner/Investor
Labovitz, Joel
Welles, S. Christopher

Syndicator
Labovitz, Joel

MANKATO

Appraiser
Viker, Owen H.

Attorney
Johnson, C.A. II
Schmidt, Robert Earl

Broker
Berkner, Roger C.
Browne, Thomas J.
Johnson, C.A. II

Consultant
Browne, Thomas J.
Patterson, Jerome C.

Developer
Shealy, Phil

Lender
Foley, Daniel J.

Owner/Investor
Berkner, Roger C.
Patterson, Jerome C.
Viker, Owen H.

Property Manager
Browne, Thomas J.

Syndicator
Berkner, Roger C.

MINNEAPOLIS

Appraiser
Frillman, Louis W.
Galush, Robert J.
Hamre, Hadley A.
Holt, Darrel M.
Johnson, Clifford R.
Johnson, Paul S.
Major, Steve
Martin, James A.
Patchin, Peter J.
Ripsin, John J. Jr.
Sauve, Richard M.
Schinkel, Douglas A.
Seiffert, W.W.
Shenehon, Howard E.
Smedberg, Gerald D.
Strachota, Robert J.
Vesely, Joseph C.
Wicker, Frank J.

Architect
Bergseth, Thomas
Hammel, Richard F.
Martin, James A.

Assessor
Vesely, Joseph C.

Attorney
Bleeker, James B.
Brown, William B.
Candell, John T.
Cohen, Earl H.
Coulter, Larry E.
Douglass, Mark
Finney, Stuart L.
Gove, Robert C.
Heiberg, Robert Alan
Hise, William P.
Isaacson, Gregg E.
Johnson, Jeffrey Scott
Karan, David
Klockers, Darwin K.
Mattson, Charles W.
Maynard, Hugh M.
Moore, Cornell L.
Parsons, Charles A. Jr.
Peterson, Richard A.
Reilly, George
Rosenblatt, Fredric T.
Simonson, Dale A.
Tennessen, Robert J.
Vesely, Joseph C.
Walz, Frank J.
Wheeler, W. Thomas
Zucco, William C.

Banker
Kerr, Ivan S.

Broker
Bain, James S.
Bartlett, James M.
Braman, Edwin C.
Brandell, David A.
Brill, Mark Wm.
Brooks, Helen
Brusman, William L.
Christenson, Robert E.
Cohen, Earl H.
Coulter, Larry E.
Dahlberg, Burton F.
Dammicci, Anthony E.
Deese, Robert E.
Dobrin, Stanley R.
Eastlund, Gary
Fitzgerald, John W.
Frillman, Louis W.
Gorra, John J.
Gove, Robert C.
Guidera, Richard T.
Hall, Orvin J.
Harrison, Milton
Holsten, Theodore W.
Holt, Darrel M.
Kelly, James F.
Kreiser, Frank D.
Lally, Gary W.
Lang, Judith A.
McCormick, Joseph P.
McGonigal, William M.
Major, Steve
Michals, Stephen A.
Ripsin, John J. Jr.
Roth, Delbert N.
Schinkel, Douglas A.
Sebold, John D.
Seiffert, W.W.
Simonson, Dale A.
Smedberg, Gerald D.
Spalla, Dennis J.
Turner, Joe T. Jr.
Wadsworth, James R.
Wagner, Lowell J.
Wall, Frederick L. III
Wicker, Frank J.

Builder
Dahlberg, Burton F.
Dammicci, Anthony E.
Deese, Robert E.
Eastlund, Gary
Greenberg, Emerson P.
Hames, Bernard A.
McCormick, Joseph P.
McGonigal, William M.
Martin, James A.
Moore, Cornell L.
Peterson, Dale H.
Rochon, Ronald R.
Spalla, Dennis J.
Study, Roy Jr.
Tobin, William C.
Wall, Frederick L. III

Consultant
Bach, Harold J. Jr.
Bain, James S.
Bartlett, James M.
Bergner, Richard
Bieniek, Gary A.
Braman, Edwin C.
Brusman, William L.
Christenson, Robert E.
Cohen, Earl H.
Coulter, Larry E.
Dahlberg, Burton F.
Dobrin, Stanley R.
Fitzgerald, John W.
Frillman, Louis W.
Gorra, John J.
Holt, Darrel M.
Isaacson, Gregg E.
Johnson, Paul S.
Lally, Gary W.
Lang, Judith A.
McBride, Carl
McComb, James B.
McCormick, Joseph P.
McGonigal, William M.
Major, Steve
Martin, James A.
Nelson, Brian R.
Ripsin, John J. Jr.
Schinkel, Douglas A.
Shenehon, Howard E.
Sherf, Stephen W.
Simonson, Dale A.
Smedberg, Gerald D.
Smith, Harold D.
Spalla, Dennis J.
Strachota, Robert J.
Taube, Stanley M.
Vesely, Joseph C.

Developer
Allendorf, Richard
Bain, James S.
Barenscheer, James Patrick
Bartlett, James M.
Dahlberg, Burton F.
Dammicci, Anthony E.
Davis, Thomas S.
Deese, Robert E.
Eastlund, Gary
Eichhorn, Richard E.
Fine, William I.
Fitzgerald, John W.
Guidera, Richard T.
Hammel, Richard F.
Harrison, Milton
Holsten, Theodore W.
Isaacson, Gregg E.
Kreiser, Frank D.
Lally, Gary W.
Loftus, Tom M.
McBride, Carl
McCormick, Joseph P.
McGonigal, William M.
Moore, Cornell L.
Mrosak, Stanley M.
Nagel, John R.
Nelson, Brian R.
Person, Kenneth W.
Romain, Joseph E.
Sebold, John D.
Spalla, Dennis J.
Stolpman, Ronald B.
Study, Roy Jr.
Stuebner, James C.
Taube, Stanley M.
Tobin, William C.
Wagner, Lowell J.
Wall, Frederick L. III
Warden, Kent D.

Wicker, Frank J.

Engineer
Hames, Bernard A.
Martin, James A.
O'Brien, Bob
Ripsin, John J. Jr.
Rochon, Ronald R.
Study, Roy Jr.

Instructor
Christenson, Robert E.
Galush, Robert J.
Gorra, John J.
Harrison, Milton
Heiberg, Robert Alan
Johnson, Clifford R.
Johnson, Paul S.
Lang, Judith A.
McGonigal, William M.
Moore, Cornell L.
Ripsin, John J. Jr.
Schinkel, Douglas A.
Smedberg, Gerald D.
Wadsworth, James R.

Insuror
Dahlberg, Burton F.
Kreiser, Frank D.
Smedberg, Gerald D.

Lender
Brusman, William L.
Hearn, Thomas N.
Hitch, Peter
Leiferman, Harold W.
Moore, Cornell L.
Mork, G.T.
Mullins, William L.
Roberts, James W.

Owner/Investor
Bach, Harold J. Jr.
Bain, James S.
Bartlett, James M.
Bieniek, Gary A.
Cohen, Earl H.
Coulter, Larry E.
Dahlberg, Burton F.
Dammicci, Anthony E.
Davis, Thomas S.
Douglass, Mark
Finney, Stuart L.
Fitzgerald, John W.
Gorra, John J.
Gove, Robert C.
Harrison, Milton
Hitch, Peter
Holt, Darrel M.
Johnson, Jeffrey Scott
Kegel, Joanne I.
Klockers, Darwin K.
Kreiser, Frank D.
Lally, Gary W.
Lang, Judith A.
Leiferman, Harold W.
McCormick, Joseph P.
Major, Steve
Moore, Cornell L.
Mork, G.T.
Mrosak, Stanley M.
Nelson, Brian R.
O'Brien, Bob
Ripsin, John J. Jr.
Roberts, James W.
Romain, Joseph E.
Roth, Delbert N.
Rousseau, John D.
Sauve, Richard M.
Schinkel, Douglas A.
Sebold, John D.
Smedberg, Gerald D.
Spalla, Dennis J.
Taube, Stanley M.
Wagner, Lowell J.
Wall, Frederick L. III
Warden, Kent D.

Property Manager
Alexander, R.C.
Anderson, Dennis
Barenscheer, James Patrick
Benke, Donald R.
Braman, Edwin C.
Cauldwell, R.L.
Cohen, Earl H.
Dahlberg, Burton F.
Dammicci, Anthony E.
Davis, Thomas S.
Deese, Robert E.
Durfee, Waite D. Jr.
Dwyer, Michael
Eastlund, Gary
Eichhorn, Richard E.
Frillman, Louis W.
Gaertner, Robert
Galush, Robert J.
Glaser, Barry
Gorra, John J.
Gove, Robert C.
Greenberg, Emerson P.
Guerrera, Sam
Guidera, Richard T.
Hames, Bernard A.
Hanson, Alden M.
Harrison, Milton
Jeter, Dwain
Kreiser, Frank D.
LeBus, L. Martin
Lundberg, William
McBride, Carl
McCormick, Joseph P.
McGonigal, William M.
Major, Steve
Martin, James A.
Michals, Stephen A.
Mrosak, Stanley M.
Murphy, Thomas
Nelson, Brian R.
Nyenhvis, Jack
O'Brien, Bob
Pederson, Ernest A. Jr.
Ripsin, John J. Jr.
Schinkel, Douglas A.
Sebold, John D.
Seiffert, W.W.
Simonson, Dale A.
Smith, Richard
Stein, Terrance W.
Study, Roy Jr.
Tyson, Art
Wagner, Lowell J.
Warden, Kent D.
Zucco, William C.

Real Estate Publisher
Lang, Judith A.

Syndicator
Bach, Harold J. Jr.
Cohen, Earl H.
Coulter, Larry E.
Dobrin, Stanley R.
Douglass, Mark
Finney, Stuart L.
Gorra, John J.
Hart, Loren F.
Lohmann, Thomas R.
McCormick, Joseph P.
McGonigal, William M.
Nelson, Brian R.
Ripsin, John J. Jr.
Taube, Stanley M.
Wadsworth, James R.
Wall, Frederick L. III

ROCHESTER

Appraiser
Blekre, Charles P.

Attorney
Broshar, Scott
McCormack, Wm.
Orwoll, Kimball G.
West, Howard E.

Broker
Bailey, L. William
Blekre, Charles P.

Consultant
Busch, David A.

Instructor
Bailey, L. William

Owner/Investor
Bailey, L. William
Blekre, Charles P.
Busch, David A.
Springer, Clement D.
West, Howard E.

Property Manager
Busch, David A.
McCormack, Wm.
Springer, Clement D.

Syndicator
Bailey, L. William

ST. CLOUD

Appraiser
Johnson, Ken

Banker
Bell, Howard F.

Broker
Schmitt, Michael J.

Consultant
Karvel, George R.

Instructor
Karvel, George R.

Owner/Investor
Karvel, George R.

ST. PAUL

Appraiser
Engelstad, Wendell E.
Groth, Duane A.
Gustafson, Russell
Hanni, Walter S.
Jones, J. Howard
Strang, Ronald A.
Tschida, Roger
Williamson, Kurt

Assessor
Williamson, Kurt

Attorney
Gillespie, James H.
Hawke, Richard D.
Knorr, Gerard K.
Kuretsky, William H.
Lindwall, Gregory B.
Mennell, Robert L.
Meyer, Theodore James
Mullins, Brian William

Banker
Donley, Roger T.
Gillespie, James H.

Broker
Elfstrom, Scott
Engelstad, Wendell E.
Gillespie, James H.
Houston, John C.
Jones, J. Howard

Builder
Groth, Duane A.
Houston, John C.
Strang, Ronald A.
Williamson, Kurt

Consultant
Groth, Duane A.
Gustafson, Russell
Jones, J. Howard
Stout, Gary E.
Strang, Ronald A.

Developer
Groth, Duane A.
Houston, John C.
Jennrich, Arthur
Stoker, James William
Stout, Gary E.
Strang, Ronald A.
Tankenoff, Gary L.
Williamson, Kurt

Engineer
Houston, John C.
Kuretsky, William H.
Mullins, Brian William
Stoker, James William

Instructor
Mennell, Robert L.
Stout, Gary E.

Insuror
Groth, Duane A.
Knorr, Gerard K.
Nikolas, Thomas D.

Lender
Donley, Roger T.

Owner/Investor
Elfstrom, Scott
Gillespie, James H.
Groth, Duane A.
Houston, John C.
Jennrich, Arthur
Mullins, Brian William
Stoker, James William
Strang, Ronald A.
Tankenoff, Gary L.
Tschida, Roger

Property Manager
Brophy, Mary Alice
Elfstrom, Scott
Groth, Duane A.
Grunwald, Jack
Haverty, Harold
Johnson, John
McAnally, Joseph
Nikolas, Thomas D.
Stoker, James William
Strang, Ronald A.
Tschida, Roger
Williamson, Kurt

Syndicator
Hawke, Richard D.

THIEF RIVER FALLS

Attorney
Beeson, Brant R.
Carter, Robert C.
Muldoon, William D.

Consultant
Carter, Robert C.

Owner/Investor
Carter, Robert C.

Property Manager
Nicholson, Don

WILLMAR

Appraiser
Green, Jerome

Attorney
Bernard, William N.
Boylan, Arthur J.

Broker
Heller, Roger

Builder
Bernard, William N.

Consultant
Green, Jerome

Developer
Bernard, William N.
Green, Jerome

Engineer
Bernard, William N.

Owner/Investor
Bernard, William N.
Green, Jerome

Property Manager
Bernard, William N.
Green, Jerome

Syndicator
Bernard, William N.
Green, Jerome

WINDOM

Broker
Perkins, Steven L.

Instructor
Perkins, Steven L.

Property Manager
Perkins, Steven L.

MISSISSIPPI

COLUMBUS

Consultant
Jones, E. Carl

Instructor
Jones, E. Carl

Owner/Investor
Jones, E. Carl

GREENVILLE

Appraiser
Stevens, H.C.

GRENADA

Appraiser
Utley, Walter A.

Broker
Brewer, James M. (Jim) AFLM
Utley, Walter A.

Builder
Brewer, James M. (Jim) AFLM

Consultant
Brewer, James M. (Jim) AFLM
Utley, Walter A.

Developer
Brewer, James M. (Jim) AFLM
Utley, Walter A.

Owner/Investor
Brewer, James M. (Jim) AFLM
Utley, Walter A.

Property Manager
Utley, Walter A.

Syndicator
Brewer, James M. (Jim) AFLM

GULFPORT

Appraiser
Grishman, Milton
Triche, J. Alvin Jr.

Attorney
Bailey, Sherwood R. Jr.
Colmer, James H.
Estes, George E. Jr.

Banker
Estes, George E. Jr.

Broker
Bailey, Sherwood R. Jr.
Cumbest, Mark
Dunston, Ronald G.
Grishman, Milton
Triche, J. Alvin Jr.

Builder
Bailey, Sherwood R. Jr.
Dunston, Ronald G.
Triche, J. Alvin Jr.

Consultant
Grishman, Milton

Developer
Bailey, Sherwood R. Jr.
Dunston, Ronald G.
Triche, J. Alvin Jr.

Engineer
Triche, J. Alvin Jr.

Insuror
Bailey, Sherwood R. Jr.
Cumbest, Mark

Owner/Investor
Cumbest, Mark
Dunston, Ronald G.
Estes, George E. Jr.
Triche, J. Alvin Jr.

Property Manager
Triche, J. Alvin Jr.

Syndicator
Dunston, Ronald G.

JACKSON

Appraiser
Clark, Alfred L.
Craft, Randal R.
Davis, James V. Jr.
Gamble, William Ellis
Goree, Janace H.
Haltom, Robert Ballard
Thames, J.H. Jr.
Turner, James E. Jr.
Williams, George O.

Attorney
Goree, Janace H.
McKinley, Douglas R.
McMullan, David M.
Marble, Roland D.

Broker
Becker, Walter D. Jr.
Clark, Alfred L.
Cooper, Fowler
Craft, Randal R.
Goree, Janace H.
Haltom, Robert Ballard
Heard, Joe
Jones, Virginia Hewitt
Leech, Joyce
McKinley, Douglas R.
Pless, Hubert A. Jr.
Richardson, Howard
Stribling, J. H.
Turner, James E. Jr.
Williams, George O.

Builder
Stribling, J. H.
Thames, J.H. Jr.
Turner, James E. Jr.

Consultant
Becker, Walter D. Jr.
Clark, Alfred L.
Cooper, Fowler
Craft, Randal R.
Davis, James V. Jr.
Haltom, Robert Ballard
Luigs, A. Melvin Jr.
McPherson, Marilyn D.
Pless, Hubert A. Jr.
Turner, James E. Jr.

Developer
Becker, Walter D. Jr.
Mason, Glenn E.
Richardson, Howard
Stribling, J. H.
Turner, James E. Jr.
Williams, George O.

Instructor
Clark, Alfred L.
Craft, Randal R.
Haltom, Robert Ballard
Williams, George O.

Insuror
Turner, James E. Jr.

Lender
Gamble, William Ellis
McKinley, Douglas R.
Turner, James E. Jr.

Owner/Investor
Cooper, Fowler
Craft, Randal R.
Davis, James V. Jr.
Haltom, Robert Ballard
Harper, Nolan Sidney
Jones, Virginia Hewitt
Luigs, A. Melvin Jr.
McKinley, Douglas R.
Pless, Hubert A. Jr.
Richardson, Howard
Stribling, J. H.
Thames, J.H. Jr.
Turner, James E. Jr.
Williams, George O.

Property Manager
Boyll, Guy Lee II
Cooper, Fowler
Craft, Randal R.
Jones, Virginia Hewitt
Leech, Joyce
Pless, Hubert A. Jr.
Schroeder, Daniel
Stribling, J. H.
Triggs, Gene A.
Turner, James E. Jr.
Williams, George O.

Syndicator
Cooper, Fowler
Stribling, J. H.
Thames, J.H. Jr.
Turner, James E. Jr.

LAUREL

Appraiser
Adamson, James R.
Kersh, Jack R.

Attorney
Moore, Alfred

Banker
Mixon, Todd
Moore, Alfred
Williams, James K.

Broker
Adamson, James R.
Green, William Trimble
Kersh, Jack R.

Developer
Green, William Trimble
Helyfield, R.L.
Kersh, Jack R.

Lender
Mixon, Todd
Williams, James K.

Owner/Investor
Kersh, Jack R.

MCCOMB

Builder
Haskins, C.O.

Consultant
Haskins, C.O.

Developer
Haskins, C.O.

Owner/Investor
Haskins, C.O.

MERIDIAN

Attorney
Young, Ralph Edward Jr.

Broker
Sims, Maurine D.

Consultant
Rea, George R. Jr.

Instructor
Rea, George R. Jr.

TUPELO

Appraiser
Rogers, Chris

Banker
Poland, Claude W.

Broker
Poland, Claude W.

MISSOURI

CHILLICOTHE

Attorney
Peace, Jack

Developer
Flynn, Ted

FLAT RIVER

Broker
Grisham, Bob

Consultant
Grisham, Bob

Developer
Grisham, Bob

Owner/Investor
Grisham, Bob

HANNIBAL

Appraiser
Clabaugh, Henry

Builder
Clabaugh, Henry

Consultant
Clabaugh, Henry

Property Manager
Clabaugh, Henry

Syndicator
Clabaugh, Henry

JOPLIN

Property Manager
Allen, William

KANSAS CITY

Appraiser
Alder, William E.
Cohen, Roger L.
Dalby, Maxwell T.
Hill, Lloyd H.
Kerr, Whitney E.
Klemovec, Lucie L.
Lindsey, Curtis L.
Mullane, John P.
Rea, George W.
Wetherill, G. Lance
Woods, William D.
Wornall, Robert W.

Architect
Baltis, Russell V Jr.
Brey, David M.
Browne, Roy E.

Attorney
Agee, Phillip Michael
Crews, Charles F.
Eckels, William P.
Erickson, Charles A.
Huston, Gary W.
Kitchin, John J.
Patterson, Douglas J.
Rowlands, Hubert L.
Schmelzer, Charles J. III
Stratemeier, Ed.
Varner, B. Douglas

Banker
Ballard, John W. Jr.
Haislip, Diane
Larson, Steve H.
Wornall, Robert W.

Broker
Backstrom, Lathrop G. Jr.
Baltis, Russell V Jr.
Block, Kenneth George
Boyd, Laurence A.
Coco, Mark J.
Cohen, Roger L.
Dalby, Maxwell T.
Edwards, Harry L.
Eisenberg, Leo
Haith, Lawrence L.
Harris, R. Lee
Hester, Robert W.
Hill, Lloyd H.
Hopkins, J. William Jr.
Johnston, Gary L.
Kerr, Whitney E.
Klemovec, Lucie L.
Larson, Steve H.
Meyer, David R.
Minkin, Rodney T.
Moseley, Ray F. Jr.
Mullane, John P.
Murphy, Walter L.
Osborne, Garold F.
Powelson, Richard C.
Rea, George W.
Reece, Jerry D.
Shutz, Byron T.
Taylor, Byron D.
Weitzel, James W.
Woods, William D.
Young, Douglas A. Jr.

Builder
Ashley, Lawrence D.
Browne, Roy E.
Christiansen, Paul A.
Jackson, Roy
Lloyd, Frank
Meyer, David R.
Weitzel, James W.

Consultant
Agee, Phillip Michael
Backstrom, Lathrop G. Jr.
Block, Kenneth George
Browne, Roy E.
Coco, Mark J.
Cohen, Roger L.
Edwards, Harry L.
Gard, Scott
Haith, Lawrence L.
Hanson, Bruce H.
Harris, R. Lee
Hester, Robert W.
Hopkins, J. William Jr.
Johnston, Gary L.
Kerr, Whitney E.
Moseley, Ray F. Jr.
Moseley, Richard H.
Mullane, John P.
Powelson, Richard C.
Shipe, Douglas V.
Shutz, Byron T.
Wiard, Darrell D.
Wornall, Robert W.
Young, Douglas A. Jr.

Developer
Agee, Phillip Michael
Ashley, Lawrence D.
Baltis, Russell V Jr.
Block, Kenneth George
Boyd, Laurence A.
Christiansen, Paul A.
Cohen, Roger L.
Crews, Charles F.
Flynn, Edmund W.
Garfinkel, Arnold
Haith, Lawrence L.
Hanson, Bruce H.
Hill, Lloyd H.
Hunter, Charles H.
Jackson, Roy
Kerr, Whitney E.
Lacy, James T.
Lee, Everett M.
McClune, James C.
Meyer, David R.
Moseley, Ray F. Jr.
Myers, Jacqueline
Osborne, Garold F.
Patterson, Douglas J.
Weitzel, James W.

Engineer
Taylor, Byron D.

Instructor
Hopkins, J. William Jr.
Powelson, Richard C.
Rea, George W.
Woods, William D.
Young, Douglas A. Jr.

Insuror
Alder, William E.
Ballard, John W. Jr.
Eisenberg, Leo
Wornall, Robert W.

Lender
Ballard, John W. Jr.
Haislip, Diane
Hanson, Bruce H.
Morgan, Travis C.
Moseley, Richard H.
Shutz, Byron T.
Wornall, Robert W.

Owner/Investor
Agee, Phillip Michael
Ashley, Lawrence D.
Baltis, Russell V Jr.
Block, Kenneth George
Christiansen, Paul A.
Coco, Mark J.
Cohen, Roger L.
Crews, Charles F.
Eisenberg, Leo
Flynn, Edmund W.
Garfinkel, Arnold
Haith, Lawrence L.
Hanson, Bruce H.
Hester, Robert W.
Hopkins, J. William Jr.
Kerr, Whitney E.
Lacy, James T.
Larson, Steve H.
Lloyd, Frank
Moseley, Ray F. Jr.
Mullane, John P.
Patterson, Douglas J.
Powelson, Richard C.
Shutz, Byron T.
Wetherill, G. Lance

Property Manager
Ashley, Lawrence D.
Baltis, Russell V Jr.
Block, Kenneth George
Coco, Mark J.
Cohen, Roger L.
Eisenberg, Leo
Erickson, Charles A.
Evans, John
Flynn, Edmund W.
Garfinkel, Arnold
Haith, Lawrence L.
Hanson, Bruce H.
Harris, R. Lee
Hopkins, J. William Jr.
Jackson, Roy
Johanson, Robert
Kerr, Whitney E.
Klemovec, Lucie L.
Larson, Steve H.
McClune, James C.
Moseley, Ray F. Jr.
Mullane, John P.
Osborne, Garold F.
Shutz, Byron T.
Taliaferro, Monroe
Weitzel, James W.
Wetherill, G. Lance

Regulator
Scarritt, Richard W.

Syndicator
Ashley, Lawrence D.
Baltis, Russell V Jr.
Block, Kenneth George
Coco, Mark J.
Cohen, Roger L.
Crews, Charles F.
Edwards, Harry L.
Eisenberg, Leo
Haith, Lawrence L.
Hester, Robert W.
Hill, Lloyd H.
Hopkins, J. William Jr.
Johnston, Gary L.
Larson, Steve H.
Mullane, John P.

MID-MISSOURI

Appraiser
Brown, Peter
Lansford, Raymond W.
Mendenhall, E. Hirst
Ruether, Eugene F. Jr.
Willey, Roy E.

Architect
Allen, Randall Gray

Banker
West, I. LeRoy

Broker
Brown, Peter
Gilmore, G. Calvin
Mendenhall, E. Hirst
Ruether, Eugene F. Jr.
Willey, Roy E.

Builder
Brown, Peter
Gilmore, G. Calvin
West, I. LeRoy

Consultant
Brown, Peter
Gilmore, G. Calvin
Lansford, Raymond W.
West, I. LeRoy

Developer
Brown, Peter
Gilmore, G. Calvin
Ruether, Eugene F. Jr.
West, I. LeRoy

Lender
Mendenhall, E. Hirst
West, I. LeRoy

Owner/Investor
Gilmore, G. Calvin
West, I. LeRoy
Willey, Roy E.

Property Manager
Campbell, Marie
West, I. LeRoy
Willey, Roy E.

Real Estate Publisher
Mendenhall, E. Hirst

Syndicator
West, I. LeRoy

POPLAR BLUFF

Appraiser
Ferguson, Harry Don

Broker
Ferguson, Harry Don

Consultant
Ferguson, Harry Don

Owner/Investor
Ferguson, Harry Don

Property Manager
Ferguson, Harry Don

ROLLA

Broker
Stoltz, Bob

SIKESTON

Appraiser
Banta, W. Clifton

Attorney
Banta, W. Clifton

Broker
Banta, W. Clifton

Lender
Banta, W. Clifton

SPRINGFIELD

Appraiser
Crain, Thomas A.
Martin, Margaret C.
Shanholtzer, Stephen H.

Attorney
Carnahan, John M. III

Broker
Crain, Thomas A.
Friedlan, Larry D.
Jones, Jim C.
Martin, Margaret C.
Merriman, Robert L.C.

Builder
Dimond, Jack
Jones, Jim C.

Consultant
Dimond, Jack
Friedlan, Larry D.
Merriman, Robert L.C.

Developer
Dimond, Jack
Friedlan, Larry D.
Jones, Jim C.
Merriman, Robert L.C.
Monaghan, Red

Engineer
Dimond, Jack
Gordon, John R.

Instructor
Crain, Thomas A.
Martin, Margaret C.

Lender
Jones, Jim C.

Owner/Investor
Crain, Thomas A.
Dimond, Jack
Friedlan, Larry D.
Jones, Jim C.
Merriman, Robert L.C.

Property Manager
Dimond, Jack
Friedlan, Larry D.
Jones, Jim C.

Syndicator
Dimond, Jack
Jones, Jim C.

ST. JOSEPH

Attorney
Mulvania, Walter L.

Builder
Grace, W.M.

Developer
Grace, W.M.

ST. LOUIS

Appraiser
Appel, James R.
Beuc, Rudolph Jr.
Burkemper, James J.
Callahan, John H.
Clement, Charles Frederic
Craddock, Thomas P.
Einig, Richard J.
Garrison, Burl L.
Garthoeffner, George
Gordon, Benny W. Jr.
Harrison, William H.
Robinson, Steven C.
Roth, David A.
Singleton, James M.
Turley, C.M. Jr.

Architect
Beuc, Rudolph Jr.
Bischof, Milton Jr.
Keslar, William A.
Pruett, H. Shelby Jr.
Tucker, Jimmie Earl

Assessor
Singleton, James M.

Attorney
Abrams, Lloyd R.
Allen, Gerald Frank
Berg, Julius H.
Dyer, T. Stephen
Gershenson, Harry
Goldenhersh, Robert S.
Grantham, Russell A.
Harris, Harvey A.
Howell, John Mackey
Huber, J. Neil Jr.
Klamen, Marvin
Lause, Michael F.
Lothman, Carl D.
McKitrick, Michael J.
Millar, David G.
Murphy, Stephen C.
Rice, Canice Timothy Jr.
Roth, David A.
Ruzicka, Len
Sheehan, Daniel F. Sr.
Slicer, Paul A.
Vatterott, Gregory B.
Wagman, Lee H.
Watkins, James B.

Banker
Bischof, Milton Jr.
Clement, Charles Frederic
Garrison, Burl L.

Broker
Abrams, Lloyd R.
Berry, Kenneth R.
Beuc, Rudolph Jr.
Bloom, Jack D.
Brush, Stephen A.
Burkemper, James J.
Callahan, John H.
Clement, Charles Frederic
Conway, Robert M.
Douglass, Jean H.
Einig, Richard J.
Garrison, Burl L.
Gordon, Benny W. Jr.
Grantham, Russell A.
Harrison, William H.
Kramer, Keith M.
Levey, Lewis A.
Malone, Thomas J.
Michelson, Bruce V.
Perlmutter, Alan J.
Pruett, H. Shelby Jr.
Robinson, Steven C.
Roth, David A.
Sandbothe, Norbert Paul
Sheehan, Daniel F. Sr.
Shucart, James
Teaney, G. Reid
Thiemann, Robert James
Turley, C.M. Jr.
Valenti, Salvatore J.
Vatterott, Gregory B.
Vitt, Alvin D.
Weiss, Dorothy
Wolk, Robert D.

Builder
Balke, Garrett A.
Berry, Kenneth R.
Bloom, Jack D.
Danzig, Jeanette
Howell, John Mackey
Keslar, William A.
Levey, Lewis A.
Lieberman, Harold G.
Mahanna, Simon A. Jr.
Pruett, H. Shelby Jr.
Robinson, Charles G.
Thiemann, Robert James
Valenti, Salvatore J.
Vatterott, Gregory B.

Consultant
Adreon, Leonard J.
Ahrens, Valerie J.
Appel, James R.
Balke, Garrett A.
Beuc, Rudolph Jr.
Bischof, Milton Jr.
Brush, Stephen A.
Callahan, John H.
Campbell, Paul B.
Carter, Lee
Clement, Charles Frederic
Craddock, Thomas P.
Douglass, Jean H.
Feeney, M. James
Garrison, Burl L.
Garthoeffner, George
Gordon, Benny W. Jr.
Harrison, William H.
Huey, Arthur T.
Keslar, William A.
Kramer, Keith M.
Malone, Thomas J.
Oliver, Luther E.
Pruett, H. Shelby Jr.
Reeves, David M.
Robinson, Steven C.
Roth, David A.
Sandbothe, Norbert Paul
Senturia, Richard H.
Sheehan, Daniel F. Sr.
Shucart, James
Singleton, James M.
Steiner, John S.
Thiemann, Robert James
Tucker, Jimmie Earl
Turley, C.M. Jr.
Weiss, Dorothy
Wolk, Robert D.
Wuenscher, David E.
Yesberg, Walter E.

Developer
Abrams, Lloyd R.
Adreon, Leonard J.
Balke, Garrett A.
Bassin, Phillip
Berry, Kenneth R.
Beuc, Rudolph Jr.
Bloom, Jack D.
Campbell, Paul B.
Clement, Charles Frederic
Conway, Robert M.
Gordon, Benny W. Jr.
Grantham, Russell A.
Harrison, William H.
Howell, John Mackey
Keslar, William A.
Kirehoff, N.A.
Kramer, Keith M.
Levey, Lewis A.
Lieberman, Harold G.
Mahanna, Simon A. Jr.
Michelson, Bruce V.
O'Connor, James J. III
Perlmutter, Alan J.
Pruett, H. Shelby Jr.
Reeves, David M.
Robinson, Steven C.
Sandbothe, Norbert Paul
Senturia, Richard H.
Shucart, James
Silverman, Ronald H.
Stakes, Gary E.
Thiemann, Robert James
Valenti, Salvatore J.
Vatterott, Gregory B.
Vitt, Alvin D.
Wagman, Lee H.
Watkins, James B.
Wittcoff, Raymond H.

Engineer
Carter, Lee

Instructor
Brush, Stephen A.
Callahan, John H.
Campbell, Paul B.
Douglass, Jean H.
Garrison, Burl L.
Kramer, Keith M.
Reeves, David M.
Robinson, Charles G.
Roth, David A.
Weiss, Dorothy
Wolk, Robert D.
Wuenscher, David E.

Insuror
Berry, Kenneth R.
Gordon, Benny W. Jr.
Lieberman, Harold G.

Lender
Cheatham, Harry H.
Garrison, Burl L.
Robinson, Charles G.
Robinson, Steven C.

Owner/Investor
Abrams, Lloyd R.
Adreon, Leonard J.
Balke, Garrett A.
Bassin, Phillip
Berry, Kenneth R.
Beuc, Rudolph Jr.
Callahan, John H.
Cheatham, Harry H.
Clement, Charles Frederic
Douglass, Jean H.
Einig, Richard J.
Grantham, Russell A.
Howell, John Mackey
Keslar, William A.
Kramer, Keith M.
Levey, Lewis A.
Lieberman, Harold G.
Mahanna, Simon A. Jr.
Michelson, Bruce V.
Nezamuddin, Mohammed
Oliver, Luther E.
Pruett, H. Shelby Jr.
Robinson, Charles G.
Sandbothe, Norbert Paul
Senturia, Richard H.
Shucart, James
Silverman, Ronald H.
Thiemann, Robert James
Tucker, Jimmie Earl
Valenti, Salvatore J.
Vatterott, Gregory B.
Vitt, Alvin D.
Wagman, Lee H.
Wittcoff, Raymond H.

Property Manager
Abrams, Lloyd R.
Bassin, Phillip
Berry, Kenneth R.
Bloom, Jack D.
Clement, Charles Frederic
Conway, Robert M.
Einig, Richard J.
Fick, Wayne E.
Gilvesenkamp, Lester O.
Gordon, Benny W. Jr.
Griffiths, George
Harrison, William H.
Howell, John Mackey
Ingram, Darrell
Klepacki, Hank
Kooyman, Michael
Lane, Michael
Levey, Lewis A.
Lieberman, Harold G.
Michelson, Bruce V.
Miller, Jack
Nykiel, Frank
O'Connor, James J. III
Oliver, Luther E.
Olsen, G.J.
Perabo, Fred H.
Pruett, H. Shelby Jr.
Reeves, David M.
Robinson, Steven C.
Sandbothe, Norbert Paul
Seifert, Donald P.
Shucart, James
Silverman, Ronald H.
Singleton, James M.
Thiemann, Robert James
Turley, C.M. Jr.
Vatterott, Gregory B.

Real Estate Publisher
Roth, David A.

Regulator
Beuc, Rudolph Jr.
Singleton, James M.

Syndicator
Abrams, Lloyd R.
Bassin, Phillip

MONTANA, BILLINGS

Berry, Kenneth R.
Douglass, Jean H.
Garrison, Burl L.
Howell, John Mackey
Kramer, Keith M.
Lieberman, Harold G.
Mahanna, Simon A. Jr.
Michelson, Bruce V.
O'Connor, James J. III
Oliver, Luther E.
Pruett, H. Shelby Jr.
Robinson, Steven C.
Sandbothe, Norbert Paul
Senturia, Richard H.
Shucart, James
Thiemann, Robert James
Wolk, Robert D.

MONTANA

BILLINGS

Appraiser
Hamwey, Charles H.

Architect
Vigesaa, Lawrence W.

Attorney
Parker, Mark D.

Broker
Baker, Donald W.
Hamwey, Charles H.

Builder
Reczek, John J.
Stroebe, Conrad F.

Consultant
Hamwey, Charles H.
Larsen, Richard L.
Stroebe, Conrad F.

Developer
Baker, Donald W.
Parker, Mark D.
Stroebe, Conrad F.

Engineer
Vigesaa, Lawrence W.

Instructor
Hamwey, Charles H.

Lender
Reczek, John J.

Owner/Investor
Baker, Donald W.
Hamwey, Charles H.
Reczek, John J.
Stroebe, Conrad F.

Property Manager
Grende, Michael R.
Larsen, Richard L.

BUTTE

Architect
Springer, Lowell W.

Broker
Johnson, Helen

Consultant
Nell, Donald F.

Developer
Nell, Donald F.
Springer, Lowell W.

Instructor
Nell, Donald F.

Owner/Investor
Johnson, Helen
Springer, Lowell W.

Syndicator
Nell, Donald F.

GREAT FALLS

Attorney
Corontzos, Robert
Hartelius, Channing J.

Consultant
Hartelius, Channing J.

Owner/Investor
Hartelius, Channing J.

HELENA

Insuror
Brazier, Geoffrey L.

Property Manager
Delaney, Dexter

KALISPELL

Attorney
Oleson, H. James
Phillips, C. Eugene

MILES CITY

Attorney
Murnion, Nickolas C.

Broker
Askin, Phyllis
Kubesh, Kenneth

Developer
Kubesh, Kenneth

Owner/Investor
Kubesh, Kenneth

MISSOULA

Appraiser
Gile, Albert Jr.
Staninger, Ken A.

Attorney
Minto, Robert W. Jr.

Broker
Abramson, C. E.
Gile, Albert Jr.
Lowden, William M.
Staninger, Ken A.

Builder
Abramson, C. E.

Consultant
Abramson, C. E.
Gile, Albert Jr.
Minto, Robert W. Jr.
Staninger, Ken A.

Developer
Abramson, C. E.
Gile, Albert Jr.
Kembel, Robert D.
Lowden, William M.
Staninger, Ken A.

Instructor
Abramson, C. E.
Staninger, Ken A.

Owner/Investor
Gile, Albert Jr.
Kembel, Robert D.
Lowden, William M.
Staninger, Ken A.

Property Manager
Lowden, William M.

Syndicator
Kembel, Robert D.
Lowden, William M.

NEBRASKA

GRAND ISLAND

Appraiser
Curry, Kathryn A.
McDannel, Donald W.
Pollard, Forrest J.

Attorney
Stehlik, Galen E.

Banker
Stehlik, Galen E.

Broker
Curry, Kathryn A.
McDannel, Donald W.
Pollard, Forrest J.

Consultant
Curry, Kathryn A.
McDannel, Donald W.

Developer
Curry, Kathryn A.

Instructor
Curry, Kathryn A.
McDannel, Donald W.

Insuror
McDannel, Donald W.
Pollard, Forrest J.

Lender
Pollard, Forrest J.

Owner/Investor
Curry, Kathryn A.

Property Manager
Curry, Kathryn A.
Stehlik, Galen E.

Real Estate Publisher
Curry, Kathryn A.

HASTINGS

Attorney
Vogler, Robert E.

Banker
Vogler, Robert E.

Broker
Vogler, Robert E.

Insuror
Vogler, Robert E.

LINCOLN

Appraiser
Burtscher, Art N.
Cuda, Dan L.
Hancock, George W.
Weber, Deloris M.

Attorney
Bligh, Robert A.
Fischer, Thomas B.
Glynn, John P. Jr.
O'Gara, Robert M.
Ohs, Larry D.
Richardson, Wallace A.
Stehlik, L. Joe
Williams, Craig L.

Banker
Burtscher, Art N.
Fischer, Thomas B.

Broker
Cuda, Dan L.
Gold, Annette M.
Hancock, George W.
Weber, Deloris M.

Builder
Cuda, Dan L.
Weber, Deloris M.

Consultant
Bligh, Robert A.
Burtscher, Art N.
Cuda, Dan L.
Weber, Deloris M.

Developer
Cuda, Dan L.
Weber, Deloris M.

Instructor
Bligh, Robert A.
Cuda, Dan L.
Ohs, Larry D.

Lender
Burtscher, Art N.
Fischer, Thomas B.

Owner/Investor
Burtscher, Art N.
Cuda, Dan L.
Richardson, Wallace A.
Weber, Deloris M.

Property Manager
Cuda, Dan L.
Quinlan, Paul
Weber, Deloris M.

Real Estate Publisher
Bligh, Robert A.

Syndicator
Cuda, Dan L.

NORFOLK

Attorney
Curtiss, Bruce D.

Broker
Curtiss, Bruce D.

Consultant
Curtiss, Bruce D.

Owner/Investor
Curtiss, Bruce D.

Property Manager
McGill, Maurice

NORTH PLATTE

Consultant
Reardon, John J.

Lender
Birge, R.D. Jr.
Reardon, John J.

OMAHA

Appraiser
Birkel, Richard L.
Daisley, E.T. Jr.
Durham, Clyde O.
Herink, Robert V.
Moss, Richard D.
Nielsen, Laura A.
Smith, Ira R.
Stevens, Thomas E.
Wiesman, Benjamin

Architect
Wiesman, Benjamin

Attorney
Anderson, Richard L.
Barton, David A.
Elliott, Jon A.
Ellsworth, John D.
Goodrich, Chris M.
Haessler, George W.
Johnson, Nile K.
Katskee, Melvin R.
Kratz, Kent P.
Plourde, Kathryn M.
Schilke, Neil W.

Banker
Gage, Peter Jr.
Moss, Richard D.

Broker
Birkel, Richard L.
Daisley, E.T. Jr.
Dodge, Nathen P.
Durham, Clyde O.
Freeman, Herbert L.
Gendler, H. Lee
Gollehon, Ellene M.
Heinrichs, Jerry
Herink, Robert V.
Johnson, Nile K.
Kooper, Howard M.
Lube, Beth
McGregor, LeGrande N.
Nielsen, Laura A.
Peschio, Thomas D.
Robertson, Thomas V.
Rulis, Robert A.
Sayler, Diana C.
Smith, Ira R.
Stevens, Thomas E.
Yowell, James

Builder
Birkel, Richard L.
Dodge, Nathen P.
Durham, Clyde O.
Herink, Robert V.
Slosburg, D. David
Wiesman, Benjamin

Consultant
Dodge, Nathen P.
Herink, Robert V.
Peschio, Thomas D.
Rulis, Robert A.
Stevens, Thomas E.
Wiesman, Benjamin

Developer
Dodge, Nathen P.
Durham, Clyde O.
Gendler, H. Lee
Johnson, Nile K.
Kooper, Howard M.
McGregor, LeGrande N.
Nielsen, Laura A.
Peschio, Thomas D.
Rulis, Robert A.
Slosburg, D. David
Smith, Ira R.
Wiesman, Benjamin

Instructor
Barton, David A.
Lube, Beth
Plourde, Kathryn M.
Rulis, Robert A.
Sayler, Diana C.

Insuror
Dodge, Nathen P.
Herink, Robert V.

Lender
Barton, Bruce
Barton, David A.
Gage, Peter Jr.
Herink, Robert V.
Moss, Richard D.

Owner/Investor
Birkel, Richard L.
Dodge, Nathen P.
Gendler, H. Lee
Gollehon, Ellene M.
Herink, Robert V.
Johnson, Nile K.
Kooper, Howard M.
Kratz, Kent P.
Lube, Beth
Nielsen, Laura A.
Rulis, Robert A.
Sayler, Diana C.
Slosburg, D. David
Smith, Ira R.

Property Manager
Birkel, Richard L.
Dodge, Nathen P.
Durham, Clyde O.
Herink, Robert V.
Johnson, Nile K.
Kooper, Howard M.
Robertson, Thomas V.
Rulis, Robert A.
Shreve, Robert D.
Slosburg, D. David
Thomas, L.B.
Wahl, R. A. Jr.
Wiesman, Benjamin

Regulator
Peterson, Robert H.

Syndicator
Dodge, Nathen P.
Gendler, H. Lee
Herink, Robert V.
Kooper, Howard M.
Nielsen, Laura A.
Rulis, Robert A.
Smith, Ira R.

NEVADA

ELKO

Attorney
Miles, Zane Stanley

Consultant
Miles, Zane Stanley

LAS VEGAS

Appraiser
Arnold, John H.
Clark, Foster L. III
Curtis, Berkeley H.
Hoyt, Richard W.
Miscevic, D. Mark N.

Attorney
Bernstein, Edward M.
Deaner, Charles W.
Dorsey, Robert K.
Gewerter, Harold Phillip
Leavitt, K. Michael
Nasky, H. Gregory
Segel, M. Nelson
Shinehouse, B.R.
Twomey, John A.

Broker
Adkisson, Charles Ralph
Alper, Eliot A.
Arnold, John H.
Bacon, Elmore C.
Bernstein, Edward M.
Bowen, Lyall
Brinkman, Kenn
Fine, Mark L.
Hon, Jack D.
Hoyt, Richard W.
Loudermilk, Michael
Lubin, Ruth M.
Miscevic, D. Mark N.
Oliver, James F. Sr.
Prohaska, Mary Ann
Reiss, Ronn
Schwartz, Gilbert Sumner
Shelton, Harroll
Storey, Albert E. Jr.
Stout, Mark
Wiggins, Stanley W.

Builder
Alper, Eliot A.
Curtis, Berkeley H.
Fore, Richard
Oliver, James F. Sr.

Consultant
Adkisson, Charles Ralph
Arnold, John H.
Brinkman, Kenn
Curtis, Berkeley H.
Farnsworth, Larry A.
Hon, Jack D.
Hoyt, Richard W.
Loudermilk, Michael
Miscevic, D. Mark N.
Oliver, James F. Sr.
Shelton, Harroll

Developer
Brinkman, Kenn
Curtis, Berkeley H.
Fine, Mark L.
Fore, Richard
Hon, Jack D.
Loudermilk, Michael
Miscevic, D. Mark N.
Oliver, James F. Sr.

Instructor
Adkisson, Charles Ralph
Curtis, Berkeley H.
Gewerter, Harold Phillip
Hon, Jack D.
Hoyt, Richard W.
Miscevic, D. Mark N.
Miscevic, Tobias C.
Reiss, Ronn
Shinehouse, B.R.
Wiggins, Stanley W.

Insuror
Arnold, John H.

Lender
Campbell, Ronald E.
Miscevic, D. Mark N.
Oliver, James F. Sr.

Owner/Investor
Adkisson, Charles Ralph
Arnold, John H.
Bernstein, Edward M.
Bowen, Lyall
Brinkman, Kenn
Fine, Mark L.
Hon, Jack D.
Miscevic, D. Mark N.
Oliver, James F. Sr.
Reiss, Ronn
Segel, M. Nelson
Shelton, Harroll
Shinehouse, B.R.
Storey, Albert E. Jr.
Stout, Mark

Property Manager
Adkisson, Charles Ralph
Arnold, John H.
Bacon, Elmore C.
Fore, Richard
Hon, Jack D.
Miscevic, D. Mark N.
Oliver, James F. Sr.
Storey, Albert E. Jr.
Stout, Mark

Regulator
Segel, M. Nelson

Syndicator
Adkisson, Charles Ralph
Alper, Eliot A.
Arnold, John H.
Bernstein, Edward M.
Fore, Richard
Hon, Jack D.
Loudermilk, Michael
Oliver, James F. Sr.
Reiss, Ronn
Shinehouse, B.R.
Storey, Albert E. Jr.
Stout, Mark

RENO

Appraiser
Empey, Gene F.
Frandsen, Jerald L.
Stimac, Steven P.
Voda, Jerry

Assessor
Howell, Wes

Attorney
Hoy, David R.
Lee, Jack H.
McDonald, Joseph F.
O'Brien, B. Wells
Spitzer, Robert Damon
Van Wagoner, Robert L.

Broker
Bedell, Reginald H.
Cryer, Jeanne W.
Desiderio, Fred L.
Empey, Gene F.
Frandsen, Jerald L.
Gauthier, Joseph H.
Howell, Wes
Lee, Jack H.
McCorkle, Jack E.
Paille, Richard L.
Royce, John F.
Stimac, Steven P.
Strongin, David A.
Voda, Jerry

Builder
Hoy, David R.
Royce, John F.

Consultant
Bedell, Reginald H.
Cryer, Jeanne W.
Desiderio, Fred L.
Lee, Jack H.
McCorkle, Jack E.
McDonald, Joseph F.
Royce, John F.
Selden, Basil H.
Stimac, Steven P.
Strongin, David A.
Voda, Jerry

Developer
Desiderio, Fred L.
McCabe, Michael J.
McDonald, Joseph F.
Royce, John F.
Wilbur, Ray L.

Instructor
Bedell, Reginald H.
Empey, Gene F.
Frandsen, Jerald L.
Lee, Jack H.
Lowry, Albert J. PhD

Insuror
Desiderio, Fred L.

Lender
Lemons, J. Stephen

Owner/Investor
Cryer, Jeanne W.
Desiderio, Fred L.
Howell, Wes
Hoy, David R.
Lee, Jack H.
McCorkle, Jack E.
McDonald, Joseph F.
Royce, John F.
Selden, Basil H.
Stimac, Steven P.
Voda, Jerry

Property Manager
Desiderio, Fred L.
Empey, Gene F.
Frandsen, Jerald L.
Luman, R. Lynn
McDonald, Joseph F.

Royce, John F.

Real Estate Publisher
O'Driscoll, Richelle

Syndicator
Bedell, Reginald H.
Royce, John F.

NEW HAMPSHIRE

CONCORD

Appraiser
Chalfant, William
Evans, Allan V.
McCorky, W. Bradley
Roberts, John B.
Spahr, J. Alan

Architect
Benn, Bernard L.

Attorney
Blumenthal, Morton J.
D'Amante, Raymond P.
Wood, Patrick H.

Banker
McCorky, W. Bradley

Broker
Bailey, Robert C.
Carleton, Buck G. III
Evans, Allan V.
Hanaway, Richard J.
Huston, James H.
Reed, W. Lansing
Spahr, J. Alan
Thomson, G. Ronald

Builder
Huston, James H.
Spahr, J. Alan

Consultant
Bailey, Robert C.
Blumenthal, Morton J.
Carleton, Buck G. III
Cox, Russell N.
D'Amante, Raymond P.
Evans, Allan V.
Hanaway, Richard J.
Huston, James H.
Reed, W. Lansing
Spahr, J. Alan
Thibeault, Russell W.
Thomson, G. Ronald

Developer
Bailey, Robert C.
Benn, Bernard L.
Carleton, Buck G. III
Cox, Russell N.
D'Amante, Raymond P.
Evans, Allan V.
Spahr, J. Alan
Thibeault, Russell W.
Thomson, G. Ronald

Engineer
Spahr, J. Alan

Instructor
Blumenthal, Morton J.
Spahr, J. Alan

Lender
McCorky, W. Bradley

Owner/Investor
Bailey, Robert C.
Carleton, Buck G. III
Cox, Russell N.
D'Amante, Raymond P.
Hanaway, Richard J.
Huston, James H.
Roberts, John B.
Spahr, J. Alan
Thomson, G. Ronald

Property Manager
Bailey, Robert C.
Carleton, Buck G. III
Cox, Russell N.
Evans, Allan V.
Hallenborg, Harris
Hanaway, Richard J.
Roberts, John B.

Syndicator
Bailey, Robert C.
Carleton, Buck G. III
Roberts, John B.
Spahr, J. Alan
Thibeault, Russell W.
Thomson, G. Ronald

KEENE

Assessor
Irish, Norman S.

Attorney
Clinkenbeard, David E.

Broker
Irish, Norman S.

Consultant
Irish, Norman S.

Developer
Clinkenbeard, David E.

Lender
Clinkenbeard, David E.

Owner/Investor
Clinkenbeard, David E.

Property Manager
Clinkenbeard, David E.

Syndicator
Clinkenbeard, David E.

LITTLETON

Appraiser
Covey, King L.

Broker
Covey, King L.

Consultant
Covey, King L.

Owner/Investor
Covey, King L.

Syndicator
Covey, King L.

MANCHESTER

Appraiser
Bredice, Frank E.
Brooks, Robert H.
Emerton, Lawrence A. Sr.
Featherston, Harley G.
Labrie, Adrien A. Jr.
Matarazzo, Anthony P.
Spencer, Richard I.

Attorney
Nadeau, James A.
O'Neill, Thomas E.
Solomon, Steven A.

Banker
Spiess, Paul D.

Broker
Beebe, Edmund C. Jr.
Brooks, Robert H.
Featherston, Harley G.
Labrie, Adrien A. Jr.
Matarazzo, Anthony P.
Spencer, Richard I.
Warner, Harold C.

Builder
Beebe, Edmund C. Jr.
Featherston, Harley G.
Labrie, Adrien A. Jr.
Matarazzo, Anthony P.

Consultant
Bredice, Frank E.
Brooks, Robert H.
Corallino, Robert L.
Elliott, David L.
Labrie, Adrien A. Jr.
McKenna, Judith Schmitz
Matarazzo, Anthony P.
Spencer, Richard I.
Warner, Harold C.

Developer
Beebe, Edmund C. Jr.
Brooks, Robert H.
Duschatko, William L.
Elliott, David L.
Labrie, Adrien A. Jr.

Lender
Spiess, Paul D.

Owner/Investor
Beebe, Edmund C. Jr.
Brooks, Robert H.
Duschatko, William L.
Elliott, David L.
Featherston, Harley G.
Labrie, Adrien A. Jr.
Matarazzo, Anthony P.
Tinkham, Judy M.
Warner, Harold C.

Property Manager
Brooks, Robert H.
Harrison, James
Labrie, Adrien A. Jr.
Leishman, R.W.
Matarazzo, Anthony P.
Potter, Robert C.
Tinkham, Judy M.
Warner, Harold C.

Real Estate Publisher
McKenna, Judith Schmitz

Syndicator
Duschatko, William L.
Elliott, David L.

PORTSMOUTH

Appraiser
Caulfield, Joycelyn Smith
Drake, Reynolds
Sumner, George H.

Attorney
Boire, Richard L.
Boynton, Wyman P.
Levine, Robert C.
Urion, Paul Batcheller

Banker
Low, Melvin R.

Broker
Berry, Joseph L.
Caulfield, Joycelyn Smith
Drake, Reynolds
Labrie, James A.
Lord, Leonard A.
Lynch, Darrel D.
Vorisek, Jean E.

Builder
Drake, Reynolds
Labrie, James A.

Consultant
Bunting, David F.
Drake, Reynolds
Gsottschneider, Richard
Labrie, James A.

Developer
Berry, Joseph L.
Bunting, David F.
Caulfield, Joycelyn Smith
Drake, Reynolds
Gsottschneider, Richard
Labrie, James A.
Vorisek, Jean E.

Instructor
Drake, Reynolds

Owner/Investor
Baker, Philip G.
Bunting, David F.
Caulfield, Joycelyn Smith
Drake, Reynolds
Labrie, James A.

Property Manager
Caulfield, Joycelyn Smith
D'Argento, Frank
Gantz, John G. Jr.
Gsottschneider, Richard
Labrie, James A.
Vorisek, Jean E.

Syndicator
Bunting, David F.
Drake, Reynolds
Vorisek, Jean E.

NEW JERSEY

ATLANTIC CITY

Appraiser
Cotney, John D.
Donnenberg, Milton
Salzman, Lester W.
Scardilli, Dennis A.

Attorney
Hankin, Stephen Esq
Weiss, David J.

Broker
Crowell, Robert M.
Donnenberg, Milton
Salzman, Lester W.

Builder
Chapman, Carl A.
Salzman, Lester W.
Steinberg, Bernard L.

Consultant
Crowell, Robert M.
Donnenberg, Milton
Panagako, John P.
Salzman, Lester W.
Scardilli, Dennis A.

Developer
Chapman, Carl A.
Panagako, John P.
Salzman, Lester W.
Steinberg, Bernard L.

Lender
Cotney, John D.
Salzman, Lester W.

Owner/Investor
Chapman, Carl A.
Cotney, John D.
Panagako, John P.
Salzman, Lester W.
Shenfeld, Sandra Manno
Steinberg, Bernard L.

Property Manager
Donnenberg, Milton
Panagako, John P.
Salzman, Lester W.

Syndicator
Chapman, Carl A.
Salzman, Lester W.

DOVER

Appraiser
Ahern, William J. Jr.
Schmidt, Michael R.
Schwarz, Sidney M.

Attorney
Ahern, William J. Jr.
Seidel, Joseph S.

Banker
Ahern, William J. Jr.

Broker
Schmidt, Michael R.
Schwarz, Sidney M.

Builder
Ahern, William J. Jr.

Consultant
Schwarz, Sidney M.

Developer
Ahern, William J. Jr.

Instructor
Schwarz, Sidney M.

Property Manager
Ahern, William J. Jr.
Schwarz, Sidney M.

HACKENSACK

Appraiser
Altobell, Ernest J.
Appel, Stanley S.
Baldwin, John R.
Becker, William E.
Beer, Murray L.
Bernfeld, Herbert
Brulatour, Peter E.
Griffith, H. William
Heck, Richard A.
Kerr, Stuart R.
Klatskin, Charles
Miller, Michael Paul
Pietrowitz, Richard G.
Rosenthal, Howard
Spano, Mary Marleen
Zall, Alex

Attorney
Cobb, Dana B.
Macrus, A.
Marcus, Alan P.
Reisman, Paul B.
Tamburro, James V.

Banker
Beer, Murray L.
Berman, Paul A.
Muscarelle, Jos. L.

Broker
Altobell, Ernest J.
Appel, Stanley S.
Baldwin, John R.
Berman, Paul A.
Bernfeld, Herbert
Brulatour, Peter E.
Ciancia, Jeremiah J.
Glatstian, Charles
Griffith, H. William
Heck, Richard A.
Klatskin, Charles
Lucas, Roy G.
Macrus, A.
Marcus, Alan P.
Sampson, Russell S.
Schatton, Norman P.
Spano, Mary Marleen
Stevens, Walter A.
Zall, Alex

Builder
Appel, Stanley S.
Beer, Murray L.
Brulatour, Peter E.
Flynn, Robert J.
Hopkins, Alyin C.
Klatskin, Charles
Macrus, A.
Marcus, Alan P.
Miller, Michael Paul
Muscarelle, Jos. L.

Consultant
Appel, Stanley S.
Becker, William E.
Beer, Murray L.
Bernfeld, Herbert
Brulatour, Peter E.
Deluca, Mark P.
Glatstian, Charles
Griffith, H. William
Heck, Richard A.
Hopkins, Alyin C.
Kerr, Stuart R.
Klatskin, Charles
Lucas, Roy G.
Rosenthal, Howard
Schatton, Norman P.
Zall, Alex

Developer
Appel, Stanley S.
Beer, Murray L.
Behrens, Alfred H.
Brehrens, Alfred H.
Brulatour, Peter E.
Cancro, Anthony J.
Ford, Stanley
Griffith, H. William
Hanson, Peter O.
Hopkins, Alyin C.
Klatskin, Charles
Macrus, A.
Marcus, Alan P.
Miller, Michael Paul
Muscarelle, Jos. L.
Nugent, James G.
Reisman, Paul B.
Zall, Alex

Engineer
Tamburro, James V.

Instructor
Becker, William E.
Kerr, Stuart R.
Klatskin, Charles
Tamburro, James V.

Insuror
Ciancia, Jeremiah J.

Lender
Altobell, Ernest J.
Beer, Murray L.
Bernfeld, Herbert
Brulatour, Peter E.

Owner/Investor
Appel, Stanley S.
Becker, William E.
Beer, Murray L.
Behrens, Alfred H.
Brulatour, Peter E.
Cancro, Anthony J.
Ciancia, Jeremiah J.
Deluca, Mark P.
Glatstian, Charles
Hopkins, Alyin C.
Klatskin, Charles
Marcus, Alan P.
Miller, Michael Paul
Muscarelle, Jos. L.
Ratner, Morris
Riemer, Richard K.
Schatton, Norman P.
Zall, Alex

Property Manager
Appel, Stanley S.
Brulatour, Peter E.
Cancro, Anthony J.
Ciancia, Jeremiah J.
Dejean, Milton
Deluca, Mark P.
Feeney, Paul R.
Ferris, Louise
Heck, Richard A.
Hopkins, Alyin C.
Klatskin, Charles
Marcus, Alan P.
Miller, Michael Paul
Muscarelle, Jos. L.
Phillips, James
Porter, Thomas
Ratner, Morris
Reisman, Paul B.
Rosenthal, Howard
Wade, Richard
Zall, Alex

Real Estate Publisher
Appel, Stanley S.
DeFren, Burton
Tamburro, James V.

Syndicator
Appel, Stanley S.
Brulatour, Peter E.
Cancro, Anthony J.
Deluca, Mark P.
Maggio, Roger H.
Reisman, Paul B.

NEW BRUNSWICK

Appraiser
Bayuk, Carl D.
Boyle, Andrew P.
Cantor, Philip S.
Davidson, Marvin B.
Feltovic, John A.
Otteau, Jeffrey G.
Pakenham, John E. Jr.
Priscoe, Robert V.
Shaak, J. Franklin
Stein, Theodore E.
Tanzman, Norman
Vance, Robert McNeely

Architect
Shive, Richard B.

Assessor
Vance, Robert McNeely

Attorney
Blicksilver, Harvey
Jacobson, Joel N.
Muscarnera, Sam
Rosenberg, William B.
Roth, Lee B.
Schenkman, Eugene
Spialter, Howard D.
Vaida, Marc A.

Banker
Kramer, Donald A.

Broker
Bayuk, Carl D.
Boyle, Andrew P.
Brunelli, Richard J
Cantor, Philip S.
Davidson, Marvin B.
Knauer, Leonard
Pakenham, John E. Jr.
Persky, Jeffrey M.
Romano, Joseph R.
Shaak, J. Franklin
Shachat, Joseph M.
Shalit, Michael
Stein, Theodore E.
Tanzman, Norman
Wall, John P.

Builder
Feltovic, John A.
Greek, Frank Jr.
Herzog, Sam
Nowell, Samuel G.
Romano, Joseph R.
Schenkman, Eugene
Shachat, Joseph M.
Wall, John P.

Consultant
Bayuk, Carl D.
Boyle, Andrew P.
Brunelli, Richard J.
Cantor, Philip S.
Feltovic, John A.
Knauer, Leonard
Kraus, Ted
Otteau, Jeffrey G.
Pakenham, John E. Jr.
Priscoe, Robert V.
Romano, Joseph R.
Rose, Jerome G.
Shaak, J. Franklin
Shachat, Joseph M.
Shalit, Michael
Spialter, Howard D.
Tanzman, Norman
Vance, Robert McNeely

Developer
Brunelli, Richard J.
Cantor, Philip S.
Greek, Frank Jr.
Herzog, Sam
Nowell, Samuel G.
Romano, Joseph R.
Schenkman, Eugene
Shachat, Joseph M.
Shalit, Michael
Stein, Theodore E.
Wall, John P.

Engineer
Feltovic, John A.

Instructor
Cantor, Philip S.
Rose, Jerome G.

Lender
Griffin, William L.

Owner/Investor
Cantor, Philip S.
Davidson, Marvin B.
Greek, Frank Jr.
Nowell, Samuel G.
Pakenham, John E. Jr.
Persky, Jeffrey M.
Romano, Joseph R.
Schenkman, Eugene
Shachat, Joseph M.
Shalit, Michael
Spialter, Howard D.
Stein, Theodore E.

Property Manager
Baumgarten, H.J.
Cantor, Philip S.
Connors, James
Davidson, Marvin B.
Feltovic, John A.
Ganz, Erwin
Greek, Frank Jr.
Gucci, Dominick E.
Knauer, Leonard
Muscarnera, Sam
Nowell, Samuel G.
Pakenham, John E. Jr.
Shalit, Michael
Walsh, Patrick

Real Estate Publisher
Kraus, Ted
Rose, Jerome G.
Trincake, Joseph

Syndicator
Davidson, Marvin B.
Knauer, Leonard
Pakenham, John E. Jr.
Shalit, Michael
Stein, Theodore E.

NEWARK

Appraiser
Chaiken, Richard M.
Coslick, Merlin B.
Curtis, Robert J.
Duffy, Stephen L.
Eckhart, Walter E.
Garibaldi, Joseph J. Jr.
Giordano, Robert A.
Gross, Sheldon A.
Horwitz, Louis A.
Jacobs, George H.
Krasner, Sanford
Lasser, John O.
Lisle, Robert W.
Lordi, Robert A.
Mattison, William
Morelli, Fred F.
Newman, Robert E.
Schlesinger, Frank A.
Schultz, Mortimer L.
Scott, Robert E. Jr.
Soares, Carol A.
Wesman, Harvey
Zinn, Judith A.

Architect
Crowther, John H.
Mattison, William
Wigton, Charles Benson Jr.

Attorney
Bloom, Jay B.
Brach, William L.
Dougherty, James W.
Eichler, Sol Alexander Esq.
Estis, Dennis A.
Ford, Herbert S.
Garland, William E.
Hammer, Alan R.
Hansen, Kent
Mink, Lawrence B.
Reisdorf, Edward Gary
Streicher, Sharon A.
Sullivan, Paul T.
Teitelbaum, Isidore
Williams, E. Kenneth Jr.
Wolfe, Saul A.
Wolfson, Douglas K.

Banker
Horwitz, Louis A.
Koch, Richard
Kraft, Jeffrey J.
Lordi, Robert A.
Meli, Anthony P. Jr.
Ryan, Thomas W.

Broker
Berger, Albert I.
Bermingham, Thomas V.
Blum, Robert A.
Bubaris, Gus J.
Coslick, Merlin B.
Eckhart, Walter E.
Epstein, Joseph S.
Garibaldi, Joseph J. Jr.
Geller, Leonard
Gravers, Renate
Green, Walter P.
Gross, Sheldon A.
Koorse, Sidney
Krasner, Sanford
Levy, Roger
Lucarelli, Joseph P.
McDonough, Lawrence J.
Mattison, William
Merin, Kenneth S.
Merlo, Andrew E.
Newman, Robert E.
Palmer, Stephen B.
Profeta, Paul V.
Quick, Jacob D.
Schatzberg, Sy
Schechter, Robert
Schlenger, Robert D.
Schlesinger, Frank A.
Schultz, Mortimer L.
Schwartz, N. Willard
Scott, Robert E. Jr.
Weiss, Jaime M.
Zinn, Judith A.

Builder
Brachfeld, Daniel
Cali, Angelo R.
Cali, John J.
Fancera, Anthony J.
Green, Walter P.
Grosseibl, Eric H.
Grossman, Allan H.
Haberman, Howard M.
Jacobs, George H.
Leshowitz, Edward
McNally, H. Charles
Mattison, William
Mayer, Martin C.
Merlo, Andrew E.
Newman, Robert E.
Sangiuliano, George A.
Schultz, Harvey
Schultz, Mortimer L.
Scott, Robert E. Jr.
Tamman, Z.
Vallone, George T.
Wigton, Charles Benson Jr.

Consultant
Berger, Albert I.
Bermingham, Thomas V.
Blum, Robert A.
Bubaris, Gus J.
Burstein, Melvin
Cali, Angelo R.
Cali, John J.
Chaiken, Richard M.
Coslick, Merlin B.
Curtis, Robert J.
Duffy, Stephen L.
Fancera, Anthony J.
Garibaldi, Joseph J. Jr.
Garland, William E.
Gross, Sheldon A.
Harmon, Robert T.
Hirschberg, Marvin L.
Koorse, Sidney
Kraft, Jeffrey J.
Krasner, Sanford
Lasser, John O.
Leshowitz, Edward
Levy, Roger
Lisle, Robert W.
Lordi, Robert A.
McNally, H. Charles
Mattison, William
Mayer, Martin C.
Merin, Kenneth S.
Merlo, Andrew E.
Mink, Lawrence B.
Morelli, Fred F.
Nalen, Paul A.
Newman, Robert E.
Profeta, Paul V.
Queler, Arthur N.
Sangiuliano, George A.
Schechter, Robert
Schlenger, Robert D.
Schlesinger, Frank A.
Slater, Robert
Wesman, Harvey
Wolfson, Douglas K.

Developer
Berger, Albert I.
Blumenfeld, Samuel G.
Brachfeld, Daniel
Cali, Angelo R.
Cali, John J.
Cohn, Theodore R.
Coslick, Merlin B.
Crowther, John H.
Gallanter, Sanford
Gans, Daniel J.
Green, Walter P.
Gross, Sheldon A.
Grosseibl, Eric H.
Grossman, Allan H.
Haberman, Howard M.
Hatch, Philip E.
Hirschberg, Marvin L.
Houston, David T. Jr.
Hughes, Ronald
Jacobs, George H.
Leshowitz, Edward
Lightbody, Jack S.
Lisle, Robert W.
Lucarelli, Joseph P.
McNally, H. Charles
Mattison, William
Mayer, Martin C.
Merin, Kenneth S.
Merlo, Andrew E.
Morelli, Fred F.
Newman, Robert E.
Pearce, Lawrence
Profeta, Paul V.
Reisdorf, Edward Gary
Schechter, Robert
Schultz, Harvey
Schultz, Mortimer L.
Scott, Robert E. Jr.
Slater, Robert
Steiner, David S.
Tamman, Z.
Thomas, Walter F. Jr.
Vallone, George T.
Weiss, Jaime M.

Engineer
Green, Walter P.
Hirschberg, Marvin L.
Mattison, William
Nalen, Paul A.
Wigton, Charles Benson Jr.

Instructor
Garland, William E.
Gross, Sheldon A.
Koorse, Sidney
Levy, Roger
Mattison, William
Profeta, Paul V.
Scott, Robert E. Jr.
Wolfson, Douglas K.

Insuror
Eckhart, Walter E.
Garibaldi, Joseph J. Jr.
Lee, Guy A.
Morelli, Fred F.
Newman, Robert E.
Soares, Carol A.
Teitelbaum, Isidore
Wendt, William M.

Lender
Giordano, Robert A.
Horwitz, Louis A.
Koch, Richard
Kraft, Jeffrey J.
Lisle, Robert W.
Mattison, William
Meli, Anthony P. Jr.
Morelli, Fred F.
Profeta, Paul V.
Ryan, Thomas W.
Scott, Robert E. Jr.
Soares, Carol A.
Wendt, William M.

Owner/Investor
Blum, Robert A.
Blumenfeld, Samuel G.
Brachfeld, Daniel
Bubaris, Gus J.
Cali, Angelo R.
Cali, John J.
Claman, Jeffrey A.
Cohn, Theodore R.
Coslick, Merlin B.
Crowther, John H.
Duffy, Stephen L.
Eichler, Sol Alexander Esq.
Fancera, Anthony J.
Gallanter, Sanford
Garibaldi, Joseph J. Jr.
Garland, William E.
Garson, Kent H.
Giordano, Robert A.
Green, Walter P.
Gross, Sheldon A.
Grosseibl, Eric H.
Haberman, Howard M.
Hammer, Alan R.
Harmon, Robert T.
Hirschberg, Marvin L.
Holzel, Stephen E.
Hughes, Ronald
Jacobs, George H.
Krasner, Sanford
Leshowitz, Edward
Lisle, Robert W.
Lucarelli, Joseph P.
McNally, H. Charles
Mahaney, Patrick D.
Mattison, William
Mayer, Martin C.
Merlo, Andrew E.
Pearce, Lawrence
Poole, James R.
Profeta, Paul V.
Queler, Arthur N.
Sangiuliano, George A.
Schechter, Robert
Schlesinger, Frank A.
Schultz, Harvey
Schultz, Mortimer L.
Slater, Robert
Tamman, Z.
Weiss, Jaime M.
Wendt, William M.

Property Manager
Brachfeld, Daniel
Bubaris, Gus J.
Cali, Angelo R.
Cali, John J.
Campanella, Salvatore,
Claman, Jeffrey A.
Cohn, Theodore R.
Comey, J.B.
Eckhart, Walter E.
Fitzgerald, J.P.
Fitzpatrick, Daniel W.
Garson, Kent H.
Goldstein, Joel
Gravers, Renate
Green, Walter P.
Greene, Thomas
Gross, Sheldon A.
Haberman, Howard M.
Hammer, Alan R.
Hansen, Kent
Holzel, Stephen E.
Hughes, Ronald
Keppler, William
Koorse, Sidney
Krasner, Sanford
Lee, Guy A.
Leshowitz, Edward
Levy, Roger
Lightbody, Jack S.
Lordi, Robert A.
McNally, H. Charles
Mahaney, Patrick D.

Mattison, William
Mayer, Martin C.
Morelli, Fred F.
Newman, Robert E.
O'Brien, William J.
Poole, James R.
Profeta, Paul V.
Rean, Richard
Schechter, Robert
Schlenger, Robert D.
Schultz, Harvey
Schultz, Mortimer L.
Slater, Robert
Soares, Carol A.
Subotnick, Stuart
Treuren, William Van
Vallone, George T.
Wood, Robert L.

Real Estate Publisher
Wolfson, Douglas K.

Regulator
Morelli, Fred F.

Syndicator
Blum, Robert A.
Claman, Jeffrey A.
Cohn, Theodore R.
Coslick, Merlin B.
Eichler, Sol Alexander Esq.
Fancera, Anthony J.
Fitzpatrick, Daniel W.
Hammer, Alan R.
Harmon, Robert T.
Mayer, Martin C.
Newman, Robert E.
Poole, James R.
Profeta, Paul V.
Queler, Arthur N.
Sangiuliano, George A.
Schlesinger, Frank A.
Schultz, Mortimer L.
Vallone, George T.

PATERSON

Appraiser
Allora, Anthony J.
Cook, Donald A.
Dator, William F.
Kailo, Norman

Architect
Schenker, Sidney

Attorney
Sikorski, Robert S.

Banker
Allora, Anthony J.

Broker
Cook, Donald A.
Dator, William F.
Kailo, Norman
Lapres, Ann
Norman, Richard
Pintel, Paul
Schlott, Richard
Sikorski, Robert S.

Builder
Cottone, Daniel T.
Maloney, William
Norman, Richard
Pintel, Paul

Consultant
Cataldo, Anthony M.
Cook, Donald A.
Czerwinski, Frank
Maloney, William
Norman, Richard
Pintel, Paul
Schenker, Sidney
Schlott, Richard

Developer
Cottone, Daniel T.
Czerwinski, Frank
Dator, William F.
DuFault, Peter D.
Heilmann, Frank M.
Maloney, William
Norman, Richard
Pintel, Paul
Schenker, Sidney

Engineer
Norman, Richard

Instructor
Cataldo, Anthony M.
Kailo, Norman
Schlott, Richard

Lender
Allora, Anthony J.

Owner/Investor
Bonastia, Peter J.
Cataldo, Anthony M.
Czerwinski, Frank
Dator, William F.
Kailo, Norman
Maloney, William
Pintel, Paul
Schenker, Sidney
Schlott, Richard

Property Manager
Allen, B.E.
Cataldo, Anthony M.
Dator, William F.
Maloney, William
Norman, Richard
Pintel, Paul
Pott, Gordon A.
Schenker, Sidney

Regulator
Stewart, W. Douglas

Syndicator
Dator, William F.
Maloney, William
Pintel, Paul

RED BANK

Appraiser
Maffeo, A. Fred

Assessor
Maffeo, A. Fred

Attorney
Murphy, Daniel M.
Reinhart, Peter S.

Banker
Salerno, Michael J.

Broker
Abaya, Carol
DeFrance, William P.
Gerechoff, Russell L.
Kirtland, George W.
Maffeo, A. Fred
Sanders, John K. Jr.

Builder
Braverman, Merrill A.
Murphy, Daniel M.

Consultant
Abaya, Carol
Carver, Stuart
DeFrance, William P.
Ellberger, Stan
Maffeo, A. Fred
Murphy, Daniel M.
Sanders, John K. Jr.
Stanger, Robert A.

Developer
Braverman, Merrill A.
Kirtland, George W.
Murphy, Daniel M.

Engineer
Murphy, Daniel M.

Instructor
Maffeo, A. Fred

Insuror
Abaya, Carol

Lender
Salerno, Michael J.

Owner/Investor
Braverman, Merrill A.
Carver, Stuart
Sanders, John K. Jr.

Property Manager
Abaya, Carol
Carver, Stuart
Gerechoff, Russell L.
Goldberg, Arthur M.
Terner, E.M.

Real Estate Publisher
Black, James F. Jr.,
Black, Peter
Peterson, Eric C.
Stanger, Robert A.

Syndicator
Abaya, Carol
Braverman, Merrill A.
Carver, Stuart
Sanders, John K. Jr.

SOUTH JERSEY

Appraiser
Abel, Charles W. Sr.
Backus, Paul B.
Duffy, Frederick J.
Geiger, Robert J.
Hughes, Carey J.
Vukicevich, Benjamin R.
Ware, Ridgeley Philip
Zadjeika, Dolores M.

Attorney
Cappuccio, Ronald Joseph
Daloisio, James J. Esq.
D'Elia, Vincent
Georgiana, Joseph S. Esq.
Herron, Steven Freddy
Myers, Daniel W. II
Read, Walter N.
Rose, M. Zev

Banker
Geiger, Robert J.
Lewis, David A. Jr.

Broker
Abel, Charles W. Sr.
Brick, Steven R.
Ducker, Stuart R. III
Duffy, Frederick J.
Friedman, Brian K.
Geiger, Robert J.
Herskowitz, Robert S.
Hughes, Carey J.
McGlone, James J.
Schaal, Gary G.
Schweiger, Anthony W.
Walters, Charles J.
Ware, Ridgeley Philip
Zadjeika, Dolores M.
Zinman, Philip

Builder
Backus, Paul B.
Freedman, Robert W.
Herskowitz, Robert S.
Hughes, Carey J.
Knott, John Edwin
Schaal, Gary G.
Segal, Donald
Segal, John E.

Consultant
Backus, Paul B.
Friedman, Brian K.
Geiger, Robert J.
Hughes, Carey J.
Khalil, Noel F.
Mahon, James F.
Nasuti, Dana N.
Schweiger, Anthony W.
Segal, John E.
Ware, Ridgeley Philip
Zadjeika, Dolores M.
Zinman, Philip

Developer
Backus, Paul B.
Baughman, W.C.
Brick, Steven R.
Freedman, Robert W.
Geiger, Robert J.
Herskowitz, Robert S.
Hughes, Carey J.
Khalil, Noel F.
Knott, John Edwin
Love, Donald N.
Schaal, Gary G.
Segal, Donald
Segal, John E.
Walters, Charles J.

Instructor
Geiger, Robert J.
McGlone, James J.
Ware, Ridgeley Philip

Insuror
Herskowitz, Robert S.

Lender
Lewis, David A. Jr.
Love, Donald N.
Rogers, James A.

Owner/Investor
Backus, Paul B.
Brick, Steven R.
Daloisio, James J. Esq.
Freedman, Robert W.
Friedman, Brian K.
Herskowitz, Robert S.
Hughes, Carey J.
Knott, John Edwin
Love, Donald N.
Segal, John E.
Ware, Ridgeley Philip

Property Manager
Backus, Paul B.
Clark, E. M.
Duffy, Frederick J.
Freedman, Robert W.
Friedman, Brian K.
Hughes, Carey J.
Love, Donald N.

Syndicator
Backus, Paul B.
Friedman, Brian K.
Geiger, Robert J.
Hughes, Carey J.
Knott, John Edwin
Love, Donald N.
Segal, Donald
Walters, Charles J.

SUMMIT

Appraiser
Bossart, David T.
Carlin, Bruce L.
Crow, Steven T.
Flynn, James J.
Hurley, John P.
Malin, Thaw
Reidda, Joseph J.
Turpin, John A.
Turtlelaub, Richard D.
Welsh, Thomas P.

Architect
Bottelli, Richard
Weaver, Harry E.

Attorney
Bellush, John R. Jr.
Gallagher, Terence J.
Hardin, Charles R. Jr.
Hartlaub, R. Jeffrey
Lyon, Rexford L.
Maher, Jerard F.

Banker
Frye, David A.
Reidda, Joseph J.

Broker
Bossart, David T.
Carlin, Bruce L.
Hurley, John P.
Kaplan, Michael
Lief, Inez
Malin, Thaw
Rahl, Craig Thomas

Builder
Wagner, James W.
Weaver, Harry E.

Consultant
Bottelli, Richard
Carlin, Bruce L.
Cocoziello, Peter J.
Lief, Inez
Maher, Jerard F.
Malin, Thaw
Penney, John S. Jr.
Reidda, Joseph J.
Turpin, John A.
Turtlelaub, Richard D.
Weaver, Harry E.
Welsh, Thomas P.

Developer
Anderson, Robert
Bossart, David T.
Boyce, David M.
Cocoziello, Peter J.
Weaver, Harry E.

Engineer
Turpin, John A.

Instructor
Rahl, Craig Thomas
Turpin, John A.

Lender
Frye, David A.
Wagner, James W.

Owner/Investor
Bottelli, Richard
Chekijian, C.J.
Cocoziello, Peter J.
Gallagher, Terence J.
Hayward, Sailing K.
Maher, Jerard F.
Weaver, Harry E.

Property Manager
Bossart, David T.
Cocoziello, Peter J.
Franklin, George
Hayward, Sailing K.
Hepburn, Brian
Kellaway, William
Lief, Inez
Maher, Jerard F.
Penney, John S. Jr.
Rahl, Craig Thomas
Weaver, Harry E.

Regulator
Bottelli, Richard
Gallagher, Terence J.

Syndicator
Cocoziello, Peter J.
Gallagher, Terence J.
Maher, Jerard F.
Weaver, Harry E.

TRENTON

Appraiser
Borden, William S.
Branco, James
Buckelew, Joseph E.
Coan, John A. Jr.
Curini, Ronald A.
DeSantis, James L.
Graziano, Anthony
Kline, Morton S.
Laiserin, Jerry Albert
Manukas, Nick D.
Martin, Joseph H.
Segal, Stephen M.
Short, Audrey C.

Architect
Holt, Philetus Havens, III
Laiserin, Jerry Albert
Lenaz, Gerald
Moran, John P.

Assessor
Coan, John A. Jr.

Attorney
Apicelli, Anthony J. Jr.
Brener, Harry
Rothstein, Robert A.
Stein, Arthur
Sussna, Stephen

Banker
Buckelew, Joseph E.
Pienta, Robert P.

Broker
Borden, William S.
Buckelew, Joseph E.
Kline, Morton S.
Manukas, Nick D.
Martin, Joseph H.
Reinhold, Robert C.
Segal, Stephen M.
Short, Audrey C.

Builder
Brener, Harry
Buckelew, Joseph E.
Burr, David P.
Hanauer, Peter H.
Laiserin, Jerry Albert
Moran, John P.
Vicinus, William W.
Yedlin, Benedict

Consultant
Biddle, Eugene D. Jr.
Borden, William S.
Brener, Harry
Coan, John A. Jr.
Curini, Ronald A.
DeSantis, James L.
Gill, Ellen F.
Graziano, Anthony
Holt, Philetus Havens, III
Manukas, Nick D.
Martin, Joseph H.
Reinhold, Robert C.
Segal, Stephen M.
Short, Audrey C.
Sussna, Stephen
Vicinus, William W.
Wolfe, Robert J.

Developer
Biddle, Eugene D. Jr.
Bittinger, William A.
Borden, William S.
Brener, Harry
Burr, David P.
Gill, Ellen F.
Holt, Philetus Havens, III
Laiserin, Jerry Albert
Moran, John P.
Okenica, Kathleen
Vicinus, William W.
Wolfe, Robert J.
Yedlin, Benedict

Engineer
Moran, John P.

Instructor
Reinhold, Robert C.
Sussna, Stephen
Wirsig, Jane D.

Insuror
Buckelew, Joseph E.

Lender
Anastasia, Gary W.
Branco, James

Owner/Investor
Biddle, Eugene D. Jr.
Bittinger, William A.
Branco, James
Brener, Harry
Buckelew, Joseph E.
Chytrowski, Allan M.
Gill, Ellen F.
Hanauer, Peter H.
Holt, Philetus Havens, III
Kline, Morton S.
Manukas, Nick D.
Reinhold, Robert C.
Stein, Arthur
Wolfe, Robert J.
Yedlin, Benedict

Property Manager
Bell, Daryl
Bly, Herbert
Burr, David P.
Kline, Morton S.
Lichtenstein, Stephen F.
Moran, John P.
Reinhold, Robert C.
Ross, Maxwell

Regulator
Okenica, Kathleen
Sussna, Stephen

Syndicator
Bittinger, William A.
Borden, William S.
Brener, Harry
Chytrowski, Allan M.
Okenica, Kathleen
Reinhold, Robert C.
Vicinus, William W.

NEW MEXICO

ALBUQUERQUE

Appraiser
Howden, John F.
Windle, Don R.

Attorney
Burton, John P.
Jontz, Dennis E.
Myers, John A.
Potenziani, Frank A.
Windle, Don R.

Broker
Bruno, Victor S.
Findlay, John G.
Hertzmark, Sidney S.
Maddox, Jim
Morton, Robert E.
Schiffer, Tom R.
Shelbrick, Jack
Strosnider, Lloyd N.
Taylor, H. Tom
Windle, Don R.

Builder
Clark, Robert J.
Maddox, Jim
Strosnider, Lloyd N.

Consultant
Bruno, Victor S.
Clark, Robert J.
Hertzmark, Sidney S.
Hollenbeck, Don
Morton, Robert E.
Shaw, Michael W.
Shelbrick, Jack
Windle, Don R.

Developer
Clark, Robert J.
Clifford, Jack M.
Crandall, Gary J.
Findlay, John G.
Gadd, Richard V. Jr.
Maddox, Jim
Shaw, Michael W.
Strosnider, Lloyd N.

Insuror
Taylor, H. Tom

Owner/Investor
Clark, Robert J.
Clifford, Jack M.
Crandall, Gary J.
Findlay, John G.
Hertzmark, Sidney S.
Hollenbeck, Don
Maddox, Jim
Morton, Robert E.
Potenziani, Frank A.
Shaw, Michael W.
Shelbrick, Jack
Strosnider, Lloyd N.
Windle, Don R.

Property Manager
Bruno, Victor S.
Clark, Robert J.
Harrelson, Robert
Hertzmark, Sidney S.
Maddox, Jim
Menicucci, John A.
Morton, Robert E.
Shaw, Michael W.
Strosnider, Lloyd N.
Taylor, H. Tom
Windle, Don R.

Regulator
Shaw, Michael W.

Syndicator
Crandall, Gary J.
Maddox, Jim
Morton, Robert E.

CARRIZOZO

Attorney
O'Reilly, Mel Brian

Broker
Shyne, C. Michael

Builder
Shyne, C. Michael

Developer
O'Reilly, Mel Brian
Shyne, C. Michael

Owner/Investor
O'Reilly, Mel Brian
Shyne, C. Michael

Property Manager
Shyne, C. Michael

Syndicator
Shyne, C. Michael

CLOVIS

Appraiser
Bedinger, Kenneth L.
Johnson, Jerry D.

Broker
Bedinger, Kenneth L.

Consultant
Bedinger, Kenneth L.

Developer
Bedinger, Kenneth L.

Instructor
Bedinger, Kenneth L.

Owner/Investor
Bedinger, Kenneth L.

Property Manager
Bedinger, Kenneth L.

Syndicator
Bedinger, Kenneth L.

FARMINGTON

Broker
Miller, Robert G.

Consultant
Miller, Robert G.

Property Manager
Miller, Robert G.

GALLUP

Appraiser
Butler, Robert C.

Broker
Butler, Robert C.

Insuror
Butler, Robert C.

Owner/Investor
Butler, Robert C.

Property Manager
Butler, Robert C.

LAS CRUCES

Broker
Jennings, Samuel K.

Developer
Jennings, Samuel K.

Owner/Investor
Jennings, Samuel K.

Syndicator
Jennings, Samuel K.

LAS VEGAS

Developer
Hanks, E. Ralph

Owner/Investor
Hanks, E. Ralph

ROSWELL

Attorney
Cox, Donald C.
Hunker, George H. Jr.
Murphy, Michael Terrence
Reagan, Gary Don

Developer
Reagan, Gary Don

Instructor
Murphy, Michael Terrence
Reagan, Gary Don

SANTA FE

Appraiser
Baxter, Sharon Davis

Attorney
Anaya, Toney
Gramer, Clifford C. Jr.
Patterson, John N.
Sanger, Scott H.
Weinreb, Elliot L.

Broker
Baxter, Sharon Davis
Gallagher, William C.
Geer, Lewis F.
Hunt, Thomas B.
Rosenwald, Robert L. Jr.
Squires, Bruce Victor
Williams, Oliver D. Jr.

Builder
Rosenwald, Robert L. Jr.
Sanger, Scott H.
Squires, Bruce Victor

Consultant
Baxter, Sharon Davis
Gallagher, William C.
Geer, Lewis F.
Rosenwald, Robert L. Jr.
Sanger, Scott H.

Developer
Davis, Judson R.
Geer, Lewis F.
Hunt, Thomas B.
Klotsche, Charles
Rosenwald, Robert L. Jr.
Sanger, Scott H.

Instructor
Geer, Lewis F.
Williams, Oliver D. Jr.

Owner/Investor
Baxter, Sharon Davis
Gallagher, William C.
Geer, Lewis F.
Hunt, Thomas B.
Rosenwald, Robert L. Jr.
Sanger, Scott H.
Williams, Oliver D. Jr.

Property Manager
Gallagher, William C.
Rosenwald, Robert L. Jr.
Sanger, Scott H.
Squires, Bruce Victor
Williams, Oliver D. Jr.

Real Estate Publisher
Klotsche, Charles

Syndicator
Rosenwald, Robert L. Jr.
Sanger, Scott H.

TRUTH OR CONSEQUENCES

Broker
Howell, Floyd

Consultant
Howell, Floyd

Lender
Howell, Floyd

Owner/Investor
Howell, Floyd

NEW YORK

ALBANY

Appraiser
Carr, Howard
Girard, Gene F.
Hazen, Russell J.
Howard, Robert B.
Magee, William J.
Ulseth, George W.
Wright, Thomas L.

Architect
Huggard, Victor A. Jr.

Attorney
Burstein, William Michael
Daly, Michael F.
Goldberg, Nathan M.
Honig, Marvin I.
Huggard, Victor A. Jr.
Miller, Richard C. Jr.
Ott, Lawrence L.
Smith, Brian J.
Ulseth, George W.

Banker
Hazen, Russell J.
Mucci, Patrick J.

Broker
Carr, Howard
Garufi, Anthony T.
Girard, Gene F.
Honig, Marvin I.
Howard, Robert B.
Magee, William J.
Pfeil, Jeffrey W.
Welch, Donald E.
Wright, Thomas L.

Builder
Carr, Howard
Gordon, Bernard
Honig, Marvin I.
Howard, Robert B.
Huggard, Victor A. Jr.
Palmer, William E. Jr.

Consultant
Belknap, Michael
Carr, Howard
Daly, Michael F.
Garufi, Anthony T.
Gordon, Bernard
Hazen, Russell J.
Honig, Marvin I.
Howard, Robert B.
Magee, William J.
Mucci, Patrick J.
Nahl, Michael C.
Ott, Lawrence L.
Ulseth, George W.

Developer
Belknap, Michael
Carr, Howard
Dowling, Thomas W.
Girard, Gene F.
Gordon, Bernard
Honig, Marvin I.
Howard, Robert B.
Schroeder, K. Ronald
Uccellini, Walter F.
Wright, Thomas L.

Engineer
Huggard, Victor A. Jr.

Instructor
Ulseth, George W.

Insuror
Bundy, Willard L.
Girard, Gene F.

Lender
Hazen, Russell J.
Mucci, Patrick J.

Owner/Investor
Belknap, Michael
Carr, Howard
Gordon, Bernard
Hazen, Russell J.
Honig, Marvin I.
Howard, Robert B.
Huggard, Victor A. Jr.
Nahl, Michael C.
Ulseth, George W.
Wright, Thomas L.

Property Manager
Bundy, Willard L.
Dziamba, Nancy C.
Girard, Gene F.
Gordon, Bernard
Hazen, Russell J.
McCaffery, Edward J.
Magee, William J.
Mucci, Patrick J.
Nahl, Michael C.
Pfeil, Jeffrey W.
Schroeder, K. Ronald
Uccellini, Walter F.
Wright, Thomas L.

Real Estate Publisher
Kresge, Walter
Wright, Thomas L.

Regulator
McManus, James

Syndicator
Carr, Howard
Howard, Robert B.
Nahl, Michael C.
Uccellini, Walter F.

BINGHAMTON

Appraiser
Wedemeyer, Eric

Assessor
Tobia, Caesar

Attorney
Coughlin, George Gordon Jr.
Elwood, George H.
Gow, James E.
Levy, Philip D.
Oberle, Edwin F.
Raymond, Patrick J.

Broker
Minoia, Nicholas W.
Tobia, Caesar
Wedemeyer, Eric

Builder
Oberle, Edwin F.

Consultant
Minoia, Nicholas W.
Oberle, Edwin F.
Wedemeyer, Eric

Developer
Oberle, Edwin F.
Tobia, Caesar
Wedemeyer, Eric

Insuror
Tobia, Caesar

Owner/Investor
Levy, Philip D.
Minoia, Nicholas W.
Oberle, Edwin F.
Tobia, Caesar
Wedemeyer, Eric

Property Manager
Oberle, Edwin F.
Tobia, Caesar
Wedemeyer, Eric

BRONX

Appraiser
Sokol, Bruce S.

Attorney
Glatzer, Sanford B.
Samuels, Leslie Eugene

Broker
Engel, Mark F.
Holtzman, David

Consultant
Garcia, Gaspar V.
Holtzman, David
Samuels, Leslie Eugene

Developer
Engel, Mark F.
Garcia, Gaspar V.

Instructor
Holtzman, David

Insuror
Engel, Mark F.

Lender
Holtzman, David

Owner/Investor
Engel, Mark F.
Garcia, Gaspar V.
Glatzer, Sanford B.
Holtzman, David

Property Manager
Engel, Mark F.
Holtzman, David
Samuels, Leslie Eugene

Syndicator
Garcia, Gaspar V.
Holtzman, David

BROOKLYN

Appraiser
Cernuda, Carlos F.
Ford, Gabriel
Kerzner, Paul
O'Brien, Michael C. Jr.
Quartararo, Frank A.
Schembri, Stephen A.
Wasserman, Alexander
Weiss, Harold L.

Architect
Gillis, John Winfred
Kotlen, Arnold S.

Attorney
Kerzner, Paul
Lee, Robert E.
McDowell, Derek P.
Rein, Samuel
Spagna, Arthur O.
Weiss, Harold L.

Banker
Bitetto, Vincent J.
Ryan, J. Kevin
Schembri, Stephen A.
Smith, James G.
Stukes, Marshall W. Jr.
Weiss, Harold L.

Broker
Britvan, Max S.
Ford, Gabriel
Giancola, Richard D.
Kerzner, Paul
McDowell, Derek P.
O'Brien, Michael C. Jr.
Quartararo, Frank A.
Spagna, Arthur O.
Wasserman, Alexander

Builder
Britvan, Max S.
Gillis, John Winfred
Wasserman, Alexander

Consultant
Cernuda, Carlos F.
Giancola, Richard D.
Kerzner, Paul
McDowell, Derek P.
O'Brien, Michael C. Jr.
Quartararo, Frank A.
Schembri, Stephen A.
Wasserman, Alexander
Zias, Dean

Developer
Britvan, Max S.
Gillis, John Winfred
Kerzner, Paul
Stukes, Marshall W. Jr.
Wasserman, Alexander

Engineer
Bilgrei, Michael Mark
Price, Sherman S.

Instructor
Schembri, Stephen A.
Stukes, Marshall W. Jr.
Wasserman, Alexander
Zias, Dean

Insuror
McDowell, Derek P.
Quartararo, Frank A.
Spagna, Arthur O.
Wasserman, Alexander

Lender
Bitetto, Vincent J.
Wasserman, Alexander

Owner/Investor
Britvan, Max S.
Giancola, Richard D.
Gillis, John Winfred
McDowell, Derek P.
Quartararo, Frank A.
Stukes, Marshall W. Jr.
Wasserman, Alexander

Property Manager
Britvan, Max S.
Ford, Gabriel
McDowell, Derek P.
Quartararo, Frank A.
Spagna, Arthur O.
Stukes, Marshall W. Jr.
Wasserman, Alexander
Zias, Dean

Syndicator
Kerzner, Paul

BUFFALO

Appraiser
Marcus, Walter F.
Miller, Thomas L.
Saperston, Howard T. Jr.
Schneider, Kenneth B.
Ward, Mark

Architect
Dick, Neil A.
McKinley, Robert J.

Attorney
Davis, Gregory L.
Grasser, George R.
Gross, Gordon R.
Meyer, Harry G.
Murphy, Edward B.

Banker
Osinski, Henry J.
Scanlon, Thomas J. Jr.

Broker
Gorrow, Charles R.
Gullo, Russell J.
Hogan, Robert W.
Jayson, Joseph M.
Mahr, F. Sanford
Marcus, Walter F.
Miller, Thomas L.
Osinski, Henry J.
Saperston, Howard T. Jr.
Stuart, Robert F. Jr.
Topliffe, Daniel P.
Ward, Mark

Builder
Calandra, Fred M.
Germony, Geoffrey G.
Harrower, Robert M.
McKinley, Robert J.
Ward, Mark

Consultant
Dick, Neil A.
Gorrow, Charles R.
Gullo, Russell J.
Hamister, Mark E.
Harris, William Steven
Mahr, F. Sanford
Osinski, Henry J.
Saperston, Howard T. Jr.
Schneider, Kenneth B.
Stuart, Robert F. Jr.

Developer
Calandra, Fred M.
Dick, Neil A.
Germony, Geoffrey G.
Gorrow, Charles R.
Gross, Gordon R.
Gullo, Russell J.
Hamister, Mark E.
Harrower, Robert M.
Iannello, Paul
Jackson, Robert O.
Mahr, F. Sanford
Ward, Mark

Engineer
Dick, Neil A.
Germony, Geoffrey G.
Hamister, Mark E.
McKinley, Robert J.

Instructor
Gorrow, Charles R.
Grasser, George R.
Miller, Thomas L.
Schneider, Kenneth B.

Owner/Investor
Calandra, Fred M.
Eberhardt, James
Germony, Geoffrey G.
Gorrow, Charles R.
Gross, Gordon R.
Gullo, Russell J.
Hamister, Mark E.
Jackson, Robert O.
Mahr, F. Sanford
Pieri, Kenneth H.
Rose, Lawrence R.
Stuart, Robert F. Jr.
Ward, Mark
Wilcox, Ansley

Property Manager
Calandra, Fred M.
Davis, Gregory L.
Dick, Neil A.
Eberhardt, James
Ernst, Henry J.
Germony, Geoffrey G.
Gorrow, Charles R.
Gullo, Russell J.
Hamister, Mark E.
Harris, William Steven
Jayson, Joseph M.
McCownaughey, George
Mahr, F. Sanford
Patchel, Robert
Pieri, Kenneth H.
Rose, Lawrence R.
Saperston, Howard T. Jr.
Stuart, Robert F. Jr.
Topliffe, Daniel P.
Ward, Mark
Wilcox, Ansley

Syndicator
Cole, Matthew B.
Eberhardt, James
Gross, Gordon R.
Gullo, Russell J.
Harris, William Steven
Jayson, Joseph M.
Mahr, F. Sanford
Osinski, Henry J.
Ward, Mark

ELMIRA

Appraiser
Bentkowski, John A.
Colbert, Robert Reed

Banker
Colbert, Robert Reed

Broker
Colbert, Robert Reed
Marvin, Daniel

Builder
Colbert, Robert Reed

Consultant
Bentkowski, John A.
Colbert, Robert Reed
Marvin, Daniel

Developer
Colbert, Robert Reed
Marvin, Daniel
Pazahanick, Andrew W.

Engineer
Colbert, Robert Reed

Owner/Investor
Colbert, Robert Reed
Kheel, Thomas H.
Pazahanick, Andrew W.

Property Manager
Bentkowski, John A.
Colbert, Robert Reed
Horton, Hooker
McClurg, William B.

HICKSVILLE

Appraiser
Aragona, Frank J.
Bene, Andrew G.
Bradley, David M.
Conti, Lou
Crane, Harold L.
DiGennaro, Frank
DiGeronimo, Richard J.
Econompoulos, James
Ewers, Ormond C.
Finehirsh, Richard
Fitzgerald, Michael F.
Hogan, John J.
Hogan, John J.
Jackson, Howard F. Jr.
Josephs, Bennett M.
Kasper, Benjamin
Kella, Bee
Keusey, Edwin M.
Knickman, Robert L.
MacCrate, John Jr.
McMackin, John J.
McMackin, Raymond F.
Marchitelli, Richard
Muscillo, Alfonso
Nezin, Len
Pirog, Joseph M.
Powers, Theodore J.
Roesch, Douglass R.
Rushmore, Stephen
Schapiro, Mervin B.
Solomon, Ralph
Suominen, Henry C.
Todd, Carl L.
Wood, Frederick E.

Architect
Bentel, Frederick R.
Conti, Lou
Cooper, Joel H.
Givson, G. Darcy
Spiegel, Siegmund

Attorney
Berenson, David M. Esq.
Carra, Lawrence
Fitzsimmons, James R.B.
Jacob, Bernard E. Esq.
Keusey, Edwin M.
Parmet, Donald J.
Reichel, Harold I.
Samber, David M.
Schneider, Julius
Schreiber, Irving
Snediker, David E.
Winston, Justin

Banker
Bene, Andrew G.
Cording, Robert
Deutsch, Edward R.
Gutleber, John J.
Roesch, Douglass R.

Broker
Aleschus, Justine
Aragona, Frank J.
Avedon, Peter M.
Bekkenhuis, Alan J.
Benson, Stuart A.
Breslin, Wilbur F.
Byron, Jules Russell
Conti, Lou
Crane, Harold L.
Dangler, Martin S.
DiGennaro, Frank
Econompoulos, James
Finehirsh, Richard
Grossman, Robert M.
Hogan, John J.
Hughes, Fred
Hurwitz, Jerome
Josephs, Bennett M.
Kasper, Benjamin
Kella, Bee
Keusey, Edwin M.
Knickman, Robert L.
Kristian, Stanley
Lazar, Ron
Levy, Arthur C.
Livingston, Edgar
MacCrate, John Jr.
McMackin, John J.
McMackin, Raymond F.
Marchitelli, Richard
Muscillo, Alfonso
Niebuhr, Fred J.
Pepitone, James A.
Roesch, Douglass R.
Rushmore, Stephen
Savlick, Albert
Schapiro, Mervin B.
Schiffer, Joseph Gill
Schneider, Julius
Schuckman, Stanley H.
Sciscio, Leonardo F.
Simon, Arnold N.
Small, Sylvester J.
Sofferman, David
Stackler, Robert W.
Suominen, Henry C.
Tuckman, Robert
Walfish, Paul L.
Weisinger, Lee
Williams, David A.

Builder
Aragona, Frank J.
Avedon, Peter M.
Benson, Stuart A.
Bentel, Frederick R.
Conti, Lou
Crane, Harold L.
Deutsch, Edward R.
Econompoulos, James
Finehirsh, Richard
Gold, Herbert Z.
Kasper, Benjamin
Kella, Bee
Knoller, Herman
Lazarus, Jerry
Lituchy, Harold
Livingston, Edgar
Marzocco, Leonard J.
Muchnick, Saul
Muscillo, Alfonso
Pepitone, James A.
Posillico, F. James
Reichel, Harold I.
Rosen, Robert A.
Savlick, Albert
Schapiro, Mervin B.
Stackler, Robert W.
Tuckman, Robert

Consultant
Bene, Andrew G.
Benson, Stuart A.
Bentel, Frederick R.
Bradley, David M.
Breslin, Wilbur F.
Conti, Lou
Crane, Harold L.
Dangler, Martin S.
Delisa, John
DiGeronimo, Richard J.
Econompoulos, James
Ewers, Ormond C.
Finehirsh, Richard
Fitzgerald, Michael F.
Fitzsimmons, James R.B.
Grossman, Robert M.
Hayden, Ralph F.
Hicks, Tyler G.
Hogan, John J.
Hogan, John J.
Hughes, Fred
Hurwitz, Jerome
Jackson, Howard F. Jr.
Josephs, Bennett M.
Kasper, Benjamin
Kella, Bee
Knickman, Robert L.
Kristian, Stanley
Levy, Arthur C.
MacCrate, John Jr.
McMackin, John J.
McMackin, Raymond F.
Marchitelli, Richard
Muscillo, Alfonso
Nezin, Len
Niebuhr, Fred J.
Pepitone, James A.
Powers, Theodore J.
Rosen, Robert A.
Rushmore, Stephen
Schiffer, Joseph Gill
Schneider, Julius
Sciscio, Leonardo F.
Sofferman, David
Solomon, Ralph
Suominen, Henry C.
Todd, Carl L.
Walfish, Paul L.

Developer
Avedon, Peter M.
Bekkenhuis, Alan J.
Benson, Stuart A.
Bentel, Frederick R.
Breslin, Wilbur F.
Conti, Lou
Finehirsh, Richard
Gold, Herbert Z.
Kasper, Benjamin
Kella, Bee
Knoller, Herman
Lazar, Ron
Lazarus, Jerry
Lituchy, Harold
Marchitelli, Richard
Marzocco, Leonard J.
Miller, Murray H.
Muchnick, Saul
Murphy, Charles J.
Muscillo, Alfonso
Nezin, Len
Niebuhr, Fred J.
Pepitone, James A.
Posillico, F. James
Reichel, Harold I.
Rosen, Robert A.
Samber, David M.
Savlick, Albert
Schiffer, Joseph Gill
Schneider, Julius
Smith, Owen T.
Sofferman, David
Stackler, Robert W.
Strugatz, Peter
Walfish, Paul L.

Engineer
Conti, Lou
Givson, G. Darcy
Hicks, Tyler G.
McMackin, John J.
Posillico, F. James
Wood, Frederick E.

Instructor
Bentel, Frederick R.
Ewers, Ormond C.
Grossman, Robert M.
Hughes, Fred
Hurwitz, Jerome
Jacob, Bernard E. Esq.
Josephs, Bennett M.
MacCrate, John Jr.
Marchitelli, Richard
Niebuhr, Fred J.
Pepitone, James A.
Rushmore, Stephen
Schiffer, Joseph Gill
Schreiber, Irving
Todd, Carl L.
Tuckman, Robert

Insuror
Bene, Andrew G.
Hughes, Fred
MacCrate, John Jr.
Niebuhr, Fred J.

Lender
Bene, Andrew G.
Crane, Harold L.
Grossman, Robert M.
Gutleber, John J.
Kasper, Benjamin
Roesch, Douglass R.

Owner/Investor
Bekkenhuis, Alan J.
Benson, Stuart A.
Bentel, Frederick R.
Bush, H. Ronald
Conti, Lou
Econompoulos, James
Finehirsh, Richard
Gold, Herbert Z.
Grossman, Robert M.
Hayden, Ralph F.
Hughes, Fred
Hurwitz, Jerome
Josephs, Bennett M.
Kasper, Benjamin
Kella, Bee
Keusey, Edwin M.
Knickman, Robert L.
Knoller, Herman
Kristian, Stanley
Lazar, Ron
Lazarus, Jerry
Lituchy, Harold
McMackin, Raymond F.
Marchitelli, Richard
Marzocco, Leonard J.
Nezin, Len
Niebuhr, Fred J.
Pepitone, James A.
Rosen, Robert A.
Samber, David M.
Schneider, Julius
Sofferman, David
Stackler, Robert W.
Strugatz, Peter
Todd, Carl L.
Tuckman, Robert
Wiener, Louis

Property Manager
Benson, Stuart A.
Beyemian, Robert
Conti, Lou
Crane, Harold L.
Deutsch, Edward R.
Econompoulos, James
Finehirsh, Richard
Fitzsimmons, James R.B.
Gold, Herbert Z.
Grossman, Robert M.
Hayden, Ralph F.
Heiman, Fred
Josephs, Bennett M.
Kasper, Benjamin
Kella, Bee
Keusey, Edwin M.
Knickman, Robert L.
Knoller, Herman
Krasnoff, Eric
Kristian, Stanley
Lazar, Ron
Lituchy, Harold
McMackin, John J.
McMackin, Raymond F.
Marzocco, Leonard J.
Muscillo, Alfonso
Nezin, Len
Niebuhr, Fred J.
Paffroth, Harold
Pepitone, James A.
Posillico, F. James
Reichel, Harold I.
Remondino, Ben
Roesch, Douglass R.
Samber, David M.
Schiffer, Joseph Gill
Schneider, Julius
Simon, Arnold N.
Tuckman, Robert
Walfish, Paul L.
Wiener, Louis

Real Estate Publisher
Hicks, Tyler G.
Schreiber, Irving

Regulator
Gajdek, Matthew
Smith, Owen T.

Syndicator
Bene, Andrew G.
Benson, Stuart A.
Crane, Harold L.
Delisa, John
Finehirsh, Richard
Grossman, Robert M.
Hughes, Fred
Kasper, Benjamin
Keusey, Edwin M.
Knickman, Robert L.
Kristian, Stanley
Lazar, Ron
Lituchy, Harold
Nezin, Len
Pepitone, James A.
Samber, David M.
Schneider, Julius
Simon, Arnold N.
Sofferman, David
Tuckman, Robert
Wiener, Louis

JAMESTOWN

Appraiser
Nelson, Jeffrey L.

Attorney
Phillips, Charles J.

Broker
Nelson, Jeffrey L.

Builder
Nelson, Jeffrey L.

Consultant
Nelson, Jeffrey L.

Developer
Nelson, Jeffrey L.

Owner/Investor
Nelson, Jeffrey L.

Property Manager
Nelson, Jeffrey L.
Rembert, Paul

Syndicator
Nelson, Jeffrey L.

KINGSTON

Appraiser
Isgro, Joan B.
Sheridan, Vincent G.

Attorney
Wapner, Gerald L.

Broker
Fox, Howard L.
Isgro, Joan B.
Sheridan, Vincent G.

Consultant
Sheridan, Vincent G.
Wapner, Gerald L.

Developer
Wapner, Gerald L.

Insuror
Sheridan, Vincent G.

Owner/Investor
Sheridan, Vincent G.

Property Manager
Isgro, Joan B.
Sheridan, Vincent G.

MONTICELLO

Appraiser
Homer, Irving E.

Banker
Homer, Irving E.

Broker
Homer, Irving E.

Consultant
Homer, Irving E.

Owner/Investor
Homer, Irving E.

NEW YORK

Appraiser
Albert, Eugene
Bahary, Kamel S.
Bailey, John B.
Barkan, Abram
Baydala, Troy G.
Berke, Daniel E.
Blank, Stephen R.
Boyarsky, Samuel G.
Boyle, Marsilia A.
Brener, Stephen W.
Brignati, David A.
Britton, Thomas B.
Cappellini, Louis A. Jr.
Carrese, John A.
Catanzani, Charles J.
Clark, John P.
Clarke, James J.
Cohen, Arthur C.
Cohen, Jerome M.
Collins, William W.
Corcoran, Brian R.
Corrado, Nicholas A.
Davies, Alan V.
Del Casino, Anthony A.
DePascale, Fred A.
Fisher, George
Fox, Frederick W.
Gavey, James E.
Haff, Courtney A.
Hathaway, Louis E. III
Haymes, Allan
Healy, John J. Jr.
Hubin,
Huffmaster, William M.
Israel, Paul
Korpacz, Peter F.
Krigel, A. Arnold
Lane, Daniel P.
Lang, Richard F.
Levy, James L.
Lewis, Philson J.
Liles, Paul
McCauley, James G.
McQueeney, Charles T.
Malzo, Joseph Jr.
Milazzo, Salvator III
Minskoff, Henry H.
Morris, Dorothy E.
Morris, Kenneth B.
Pezzuto, Joseph Louis
Philipps, Edward W.
Principe, Nicholas J.
Rufrano, Glenn J.
Ruggles, Robert K. III
Schimmel, Alfred
Scroggins, Richard M.
Sheehan, Thomas J.
Sheridan, James C. Jr.
Shima, Richard R.
Snoddy, Charles E. Jr.
Stein, Fredric C.
Swift, David A.
Taylor, Melvin L. Sr.
Trager, Sidney
Wallach, Irving T.
Warsawer, Harold N.
Weitzman, Marilyn Kramer
White, Gerrit A.
Wojewodzki, Richard S.
Zammit, Thomas J.

Architect
Alpern, Andrew
Bahat, Ari
Baker, James Barnes
Bassuk, Bertram L.
Bernholz, Peter M.
Bookhardt, Fred B. Jr.
Boyle, Marsilia A.
Brand, Leon
Brignati, David A.
Calwil, Warren W.
Caponnetto, Joseph
Clark, Dennis B.
Croxton, Randolph R.
Galston, John Wood
Grant, Stanley Charles
Krigel, A. Arnold
Kurtz, Bernward Ulrich
Levien, Kenneth D.
Meyer, Edward J.
Mitnick, Philip
Panero, Carl Kenyon
Perkins, Lawrence Bradford
Roth, Richard Jr.
Sawyer, James L.
Scroggins, Richard M.
Twining, Alexander
Wechsler, Max
Wilder, Barry S.

Assessor
DePascale, Fred A.
Elcock, Ronald M.
Hubin,
Israel, Paul
West, Donald R.

Attorney
Arfa, Harvey Z.
Bachrach, Jonathan David
Balagur, Perry
Barasch, Clarence S.
Baron, Mitchell Neal
Beeler, Joel I.
Bell, Robert
Berger, Saul
Berkman, Andrew S.
Berkowitz, Abraham
Berley, Peter
Berman, Daniel S.
Bernstein, Stephen M.
Berry, Richard S
Birnbaum, Mark D.
Bliwise, Lester M.
Block, William K.
Blotner, Norman D.
Boneparth, Harvey Mitchel
Borg, Solomon J.
Boxer, Leonard
Boyle, Marsilia A.
Browdy, Joseph E.
Burke, Dorothy
Certilman, Morton L.
Clark, John P.
Claude, Anthony B.
Cliff, Patricia Warburg
Clurman, David
Cohen, Herbert L.
Cohen, Marshall J.
Connery, Edmund M.
Copland, Milton
Crystal, Richard
Cuiffo, Frank W.
Damanti, Patrick J.
Deis, George
Devaney, Thomas R.
Dombrowski, Garrett James
Doody, James P.
Draper, Daniel Clay
Duetsch, John E.
Dunne, James C.
Eisenberg, Lawrence D.
Feder, Leondard H.
Feldman, Leslie
Fingerhut, Paul M.
Forte, Joseph Philip
Friedman, Joseph N.
Friedman, Milton R.
Gallet, Jeffry H.
Gask, Michael
Gellert, Donald N.
Gold, Jeffrey M.
Goldfield, Alfred S.
Goodfriend, Herbert J.
Gorham, Howard N.
Gould, Jay
Greenbaum, David Roy
Grew, Robert R.
Grimes, Robert S.
Grodetsky, Murray H.
Grosse, Ernest J.
Gutheil, John
Gutman, Ralph J.
Halper, Emanuel B.
Hart, Frank
Hausman, Bruce
Heller, Howard E.
Hellman, Dennis I.
Helpern, Robert E.
Herz, Andrew L.
Hille, Richard
Hindy, George V.
Hirschtritt, Joel S.
Howard, Norman A.
Iger, Mark M.
Johansen, Michael C.
Kaht, Joseph Edward
Kanner, Theodore I.
Karabell, David I.
Kessler, Steven P.
Kornheiser, Martin H.
Lambert, Thomas C.
Lazarus, Howard J.
Lazerus, Gilbert
Lebensold, Linda R.
Leicht, Steven M.
Levy, Jules E.
Licht, Martin C.
Lieb, L. Robert
Litton, Claude J.
Lore, Kurt W.
Lubell, Harold
MacArthur, William H.
McGivney, James H.
Madison, Mike
Maidman, Richard H.
Mandel, Newton W.
Margid, Leonard
Margolis, Jonathan S.
Mark, Henry Allen
Marx, Max C.
Melchior, Frank A.
Mendik, Bernard H.
Miner, Martin P.
Mitchell, Allan R.
Morganstern, Gerald H.
Morhouse, Sanford W.
Munzer, Stephen I.
Neustadt, Paul
Niedergang, Murray A.
Norton, Warner D.
Nuey, Vernita
Nussbaum, Paul A.
Obregon, Conrad J.
Pachter, Milton H.
Pedowitz, James M.
Pike, Laurence B.
Polevoy, Martin D.
Pollan, Stephen M.
Porter, Steven K.
Race, Bradford J. Jr.
Raphael, Stephen M.
Reagan, Paul V.
Reed, Lloyd H.
Remsen, ALfred S. Jr.
Richards, David Alan
Ridloff, Richard
Rifkin, Bernard M.
Robinson, Gerald J.
Rosen, Robert J.
Rosen, Stephen Daniel
Rothenberg, Joel
Rudder, Richard D.
Sabella, Thomas A.
Saft, Stuart M.
Samnick, Robert L.
Scala, James Robert
Schaiman, David S.
Schechter, Howard
Schnall, Flora
Schneeweiss, Samuel
Schwartz, Harvey
Schwartz, Sheldon
Searles, Sidney Z.
Segal, David F.
Seldin, Stephen
Shapiro, Irving
Shapiro, Michael J. Esq.
Shapiro, Richard J.
Shepard, Richard A.
Siegel, Leonard S.
Sillcocks, H. Jackson
Siskind, Donald H.
Soifer, Lawrence M.
Sonnenschein, Irving
Soule, Wesley
Soybel, Arthur
Sperling, Gary H.
Spiessbach, Michael F.
Spitzer, Max D.

Stack, Daniel
Stone, Ronald M.
Stothers, Hilton H. Jr.
Strom, Fredric Alan
Thies, Winthrop Drake
Toothaker, Thomas R.
Trainor, Thomas Kristen
Tunnell, Norman D.
Weiner, Barry R.
Weinstock, Leonard I.
Welch, Sheila J.
Wertheimer, Robert J.
Winston, John
Wojak, John S.
Wolf, Clifford M.
Wolfer, Alan B.
Wood, John B.
Zinman, Robert M.
Zuckerbrot, Kenneth Esq.
Zuckerman, Milton
Zuckerman, Mitchell

Banker
Belofsky, Jerald Alan
Bigelow, Charles Glenford III
Boyle, Richard J.
Brooks, Peter S.
Bush, William C.
Carey, William Polk
Chin, Roy
Clarke, James J.
Clutsam, Henry O. III
Conway, E. Virgil
Costello, Daniel W.
Curry, Bryce
Damanti, Patrick J.
D'Errico, John A.
Driscoll, Arthur E.
Felix, Steven
Gorham, Howard N.
Grosse, Ernest J.
Hernandez, Franklyn C.
Hively, James A.
Israel, Paul
Jacobs, Lorraine
Jewell, Keith Dover
Kaht, Joseph Edward
Kemper, A. Claude
Kettenmann, Kurt
Kevenides, Herve A.
Klaman, Saul B.
Lang, Richard F.
Levy, Gerald M.
Ludwig, Lloyd Jr.
MacArthur, William H.
MacDonald, Kirkpatrick
Mallis, Charles H.S.
Malzo, Joseph Jr.
Marron, Edward W. Jr.
Milazzo, Salvator III
Mooney, G. Austin
Parrish, Donald R.
Philipps, Edward W.
Root, Stuart D.
Rothschild, Robert J.
Salony, Jon R.
Seltzer, Dean B.
Shaffer, Jack A.
Sheridan, James C. Jr.
Solomon, Robert Donald
Stack, Daniel
Torres, William J.
Trager, Sidney
Tubin, Allan
Tunnell, Norman D.
Washkowitz, Alan
Wechsler, Michael J.
White, Gerrit A.
White, Gregory A.
Wojak, John S.
Yoles, Zeev E.
Zammit, Thomas J.

Broker
Ackman, Lawrence D.
Bahary, Kamel S.
Baker, Harold D.
Baydala, Troy G.
Beck, Chester
Beeler, Joel I.
Berger, Saul
Berke, Daniel E.
Berley, Peter
Berman, Miles J.
Bernard, Bossom
Bernstein, Asher
Berry, Richard S
Bonin, Paul J.
Bornstein, Harold A.
Boxer, Leonard
Boyarsky, Samuel G.
Brener, Stephen W.
Bross, Joel L.
Brounstein, Sam
Broxmeyer, Marc
Buchbinder, Norman M.
Canale, Stephen F.
Cappellini, Louis A. Jr.
Clark, John P.
Clarke, Phillips H. III
Cliff, Patricia Warburg
Cline, Roger S.
Collins, William W.
Davies, Alan V.
Davis, Barry M.
Davis, Robert T.
Del Casino, Anthony A.
Drezner, David
Elcock, Ronald M.
Ellis, Kenneth A.
Felix, Steven
Filoon, John W. Jr.
Fisher, George
Flint, James W.
Fox, Wayne Noland
Friedman, David A.
Futterman, Philip G.
Glasgall, Franklin
Glickman, Edwin J.
Goetschius, James R.
Gold, Jeffrey M.
Golding, Jerome
Goldman, Nathan
Gotthelf, Beatrice F.
Gottlieb, Albert J.
Gould, Jay
Graham, Thomas M. Jr.
Graves, James M.
Grimes, Robert S.
Grossman, Ezra
Gruskin, Arthur
Haggarty, Kevin F.
Hamm, Thomas M.
Hara, Sol J.
Haymes, Allan
Heller, Howard E.
Hille, Richard
Holliday, Morton
Holt, Adrian J.
Israel, Paul
Jenkins, Michael W.
Jenkins, Robert N.
Joachim, Louis Frantz
Joffe, Martin Lee
Katz, Edward
Kaufman, Milton
Kavounas, Edmond A.
Kleiman, Irving
Krieger, Robert S.
Kulla, Sylvia
Landry, Brian F.
Levi, James H.
Levy, James L.
Lewis, Bertram
Litton, Claude J.
Lundberg, Nils A.
MacArthur, William H.
MacDonald, Kirkpatrick
McManus, Hank
Mahood, Willard S.
Maloy, Carol
Marcus, Jerry Lee
Maroon, G. Tyson
Melcer, Duane Scott
Messenkopf, Eugene J.
Milazzo, Salvator III
Miller, Seth A.
Miller, William R.
Mitchell, Allan R.
Mitchell, N. Edmund
Moister, Peter Corbin
Monasebian, Dennis M.
Morris, Dorothy E.
Morris, Kenneth B.
Morse, Bernard L.
Nolan, Agnes
Novick, Steven E.
Nuey, Vernita
Parisse, Alan J.
Piazza, Charles
Psota, Peter A.
Quay, Kenneth
Reiss, Abraham
Renard, John S.
Rice, Henry Hart
Rolfe, N. Anthony
Rosenblatt, Harvey
Rothenberg, Joel
Salomon, Suzanne E.
Schaiman, David S.
Schiffman, Martin
Seevak, Sheldon
Shaffer, Jack A.
Shapiro, Robert I.
Shulsky, Marvin R.
Silverman, Leon
Smolen, Michael H.
Smolinsky, Ronald J.
Solomon, Maurice H.
Sonnenblick, Arthur I.
Sonnenblick, Jack E.
Steiker, Jerome J.
Stein, Fredric C.
Stern, William H.
Studley, Julien J.
Sulzberger, Edward
Swift, David A.
Taylor, Melvin L. Sr.
Tishman, Edward S.
Trager, Sidney
Trautman, Lawrence J.
Tubin, Allan
Wallach, Irving T.
Weiner, Barry R.
Weinreb, Leon
Weiss, Richard L.
Wermaiss, John A.
White, Gerrit A.
Williams, Joseph L. III
Winston, John
Wolfert, Jeffrey D.
Yamin, Thomas M.

Builder
Benenson, Charles B.
Berkowitz, Barry
Berry, Richard S
Brand, Leon
Brignati, David A.
Charlson, Richard H.
Collins, Robert L.
Cunneen, Charles T.
Fleming, Robert H.
Gavey, James E.
Goldman, S. Howard
Grodetsky, Murray H.
Kleiman, Irving
Krigel, A. Arnold
Lathlaen, Robert F.
Levien, Kenneth D.
Lipstein, Michael
McQueeney, Charles T.
Marceca, Robert K.
Mendik, Bernard H.
Messenkopf, Eugene J.
Nishiuwatoko, Tetsu
Ruben, Lawrence
Scroggins, Richard M.
Shapiro, Donald L.
Silverman, Leon
Silvershein, Bennett
Simon, Howard I.
Stillman, Abbott
Tubin, Allan
Wechsler, Steven R.
Winston, John
Zucker, Norman P.

Consultant
Abramowitz, Roy A.
Albert, Eugene
Ambrosi, Robert J.
Amenta, Michael J.
Austrian, James A.
Bachrach, Jonathan David
Bailey, Arthur E.
Bailey, John B.
Bailowitz, Stanley A.
Baker, Harold D.
Banker, Joel I.
Baralt, Carlos M.
Barkan, Abram
Barth, R. Gary
Baydala, Troy G.
Becker, Michael A.
Bentele, Raymond E.
Berke, Daniel E.
Berkowitz, Abraham
Berman, Miles J.
Bernard, Bossom
Berry, Richard S
Bigelow, Charles Glenford III
Blank, Stephen R.
Boneparth, Harvey Mitchel
Bookhardt, Fred B. Jr.
Boyarsky, Samuel G.
Boyle, Marsilia A.
Brand, Leon
Brener, Stephen W.
Brignati, David A.
Britton, Thomas B.
Brounstein, Sam
Broxmeyer, Marc
Campbell, Robert E.
Canale, Stephen F.
Caponnetto, Joseph
Cappellini, Louis A. Jr.
Carrese, John A.
Carson, Christopher N.
Carvin, Philip J.
Clark, Dennis B.
Clark, John P.
Clarke, James J.
Clarke, Phillips H. III
Cohen, Arthur C.
Cohen, Irving E.
Cohen, Jerome M.
Colletti, Paul J.
Corrado, Nicholas A.
Davies, Alan V.
Davis, Barry M.
Davis, Robert T.
Del Casino, Anthony A.
Delaney, James J.
Deutsch, Jerome
DiMicelli, Vincent
Feirman, Jerome B.
Felix, Steven
Flint, James W.
Ford, James A.
Fox, Wayne Noland
Frank, William S.
Futterman, Philip G.
Glick, Michael I.
Glickman, Edwin J.
Gold, Jeffrey M.
Goodman, I. Michael

Gotthelf, Beatrice F.
Gould, Jay
Green, Grant D.
Grimes, Robert S.
Grodetsky, Murray H.
Grossman, Ezra
Gruskin, Arthur
Guthrie, Paul R.
Haff, Courtney A.
Hagen, Stephen C.
Haggarty, Kevin F.
Hamm, Thomas M.
Harlan, Leonard Morton
Hartnett, Michael James
Hathaway, Louis E. III
Haymes, Allan
Healy, John J. Jr.
Holliday, Morton
Holt, Adrian J.
Hubin,
Israel, Paul
Jenkins, Michael W.
Jennerich, Arthur
Jerus, George R. P.E.
Joachim, Louis Frantz
Joynes, Richard
Kaufman, Stuart
Keller, George H. IV
Kelly, John M. PE
Kemper, A. Claude
King, Francis J.
Korpacz, Peter F.
Krigel, A. Arnold
Kulla, Sylvia
Kunstadt, Herbert
Landry, Brian F.
Lane, Daniel P.
Lang, Richard F.
Levi, James H.
Levien, Kenneth D.
Levy, James L.
Lewis, Bertram
Lewis, Philson J.
Lex, Richard A.
Liles, Paul
Lind, H. Robert
Lipstein, Michael
Lundberg, Nils A.
Lynn, James C.
McCrary, Oscar W. Jr.
McManus, Hank
Maidman, Richard H.
Maloy, Carol
Malzo, Joseph Jr.
Manak, John Robert
Maroon, G. Tyson
Melcer, Duane Scott
Messenkopf, Eugene J.
Meyer, Edward J.
Milazzo, Salvator III
Miller, Carl T.
Miller, Seth A.
Miller, Steven
Miller, William R.
Mitnick, Philip
Morris, Dorothy E.
Morris, Kenneth B.
Morse, Bernard L.
Naimowitz, H.H.
Neustadt, Paul
Nuey, Vernita
Nymark, Richard M.
Panero, Carl Kenyon
Papell, Nathan
Pei, T'ing C.
Pezzuto, Joseph Louis
Pierce, Jorganne
Pivko, Tibor
Pollan, Stephen M.
Pomerantz, Marvin
Preston, Joel R.
Principe, Nicholas J.
Pritchett, Clayton P.
Regevik, Robert
Reiss, Abraham
Renard, John S.
Restaino, Paul
Rice, Henry Hart
Ridloff, Richard
Robinson, Michael J.
Rolfe, N. Anthony
Rubin, Larry Aryeh
Rufrano, Glenn J.
Ruggles, Robert K. III
Salomon, Robert J.
Salomon, Suzanne E.
Sawyer, James L.
Schechter, Howard
Schiffman, Martin
Schimmel, Alfred
Schindler, Elmer V.
Schnabel, Donald
Schwerin, Thomas R.
Scroggins, Richard M.
Searles, Sidney Z.
Seevak, Sheldon
Seldin, Stephen
Sfouggatakis, Nicholas A.
Shaffer, Jack A.
Shapiro, Irving
Shapiro, Robert I.
Sheehan, Thomas J.
Shima, Richard R.
Silber, Mark E.
Sillcocks, H. Jackson
Smolen, Michael H.
Smolinsky, Ronald J.
Solomon, Robert Donald
Sonnenblick, Arthur I.
Sonnenblick, Jack E.
Stack, Daniel
Stahl, Michael
Starrett, Andre V.
Steiker, Jerome J.
Stein, Fredric C.
Studley, Julien J.
Stuebe, William H.
Swift, David A.
Tandy, Norman
Tarr, Mel
Taylor, Melvin L. Sr.
Thies, Winthrop Drake
Tockarshewsky, Benedict J.
Totten, S. Bleecker
Trautman, Lawrence J.
Twining, Alexander
Von Werz, George
Warsawer, Harold N.
Washkowitz, Alan
Weinberger, Michael Joseph
Weiss, Richard L.
Weiss, Ronald W.
Weitzman, Marilyn Kramer
Wilder, Barry S.
Williams, Joseph L. III
Wilner, Alfred PE
Winslow, Peter
Wojewodzki, Richard S.
Wolfert, Jeffrey D.
Yamin, Thomas M.
Zeckendorf, William
Zisler, Randall Craig

Developer

Anderson, John A.
Bahat, Ari
Bailowitz, Stanley A.
Baker, James Barnes
Banker, Joel I.
Barry, Stanley L.
Benenson, Charles B.
Berkowitz, Barry
Bernard, Bossom
Bernholz, Peter M.
Bernstein, Stephen M.
Berry, Richard S
Boxer, Leonard
Boyarsky, Samuel G.
Boyle, Marsilia A.
Brand, Leon
Brignati, David A.
Carrin, Marvin C.
Charlson, Richard H.
Cliff, Patricia Warburg
Cline, Roger S.
Cogin, Walter
Cohen, Jerome M.
Collins, William W.
Costello, Daniel W.
Coviello, Edmund T.
D'Angelo, Anthony J.
Deutsch, Jerome
DiMicelli, Vincent
Fallis, Barry E.
Felix, Steven
Fox, Wayne Noland
Frazier, Thomas B. II
Friedman, David A.
Galston, John Wood
Gavey, James E.
Glasgall, Franklin
Glickman, Edwin J.
Glidden, Allan H.
Gold, Jeffrey M.
Goldman, S. Howard
Goodman, I. Michael
Greenburger, Francis
Grodetsky, Murray H.
Guthrie, Paul R.
Haggarty, Kevin F.
Halper, Emanuel B.
Harlan, Leonard Morton
Haymes, Allan
Huffmaster, William M.
Joachim, Louis Frantz
Joynes, Richard
Karp, Jane Hausman
Kaufman, Stuart
Kelly, John M. PE
Kleiman, Irving
Kory, Peter
Krigel, A. Arnold
Lane, Joseph Jr.
Lathlaen, Robert F.
Lazrus, Jonathan E.
Levien, Kenneth D.
Lewis, Philson J.
Lieb, L. Robert
Liles, Paul
Lipstein, Michael
Lynn, James C.
MacDonald, Kirkpatrick
McManus, Hank
McQueeney, Charles T.
Maidman, Richard H.
Mandel, Newton W.
Marceca, Robert K.
Mendik, Bernard H.
Messenkopf, Eugene J.
Milazzo, Salvator III
Moister, Peter Corbin
Nickerson, Adams H.
Nishiuwatoko, Tetsu
Novick, Steven E.
Panero, Carl Kenyon
Pei, T'ing C.
Principe, Nicholas J.
Psota, Peter A.
Raphael, Stephen M.
Rondinone, Serge W.
Rosen, Stephen Daniel
Ross, Stephen M.
Rubacha, Paul D.
Ruben, Lawrence
Rubin, Larry Aryeh
Salomon, Suzanne E.
Schwamm, Jay Marc
Schwerin, Thomas R.
Scroggins, Richard M.
Sfouggatakis, Nicholas A.
Shapiro, Donald L.
Shatken, Stuart B.
Silvershein, Bennett
Simon, Howard I.
Snoddy, Charles E. Jr.
Soszka, Kenneth R.
Stahl, Michael
Starrett, Andre V.
Stillman, Abbott
Stone, Ronald M.
Sunden, Gary R.
Tubin, Allan
Twining, Alexander
Wechsler, Steven R.
Weinberger, Michael Joseph
Weiner, Barry R.
Winston, John
Wolfert, Jeffrey D.
Zeckendorf, William
Zucker, Norman P.

Engineer

Baralt, Carlos M.
Boyle, Marsilia A.
Callahan, James J. III
Campbell, Robert E.
Carson, Christopher N.
Carvin, Philip J.
Fleming, Robert H.
Jennerich, Arthur
Kaufman, Milton
Kelly, John M. PE
Kunstadt, Herbert
Lathlaen, Robert F.
Levien, Kenneth D.
Morris, Kenneth B.
Murphy, Thomas Michael
Naimowitz, H.H.
Parrish, Donald R.
Scroggins, Richard M.
Shapiro, Robert I.
Tockarshewsky, Benedict J.
West, Donald R.
Wilner, Alfred PE

Instructor

Albert, Eugene
Bahary, Kamel S.
Baydala, Troy G.
Corcoran, Brian R.
Corrado, Nicholas A.
Davies, Alan V.
DePascale, Fred A.
Fisher, George
Fox, Wayne Noland
Goodman, I. Michael
Gordon, Donald J.
Greenbaum, David Roy
Harlan, Leonard Morton
Haymes, Allan
Hubin,
Israel, Paul
Jennerich, Arthur
Kevenides, Herve A.
Lewis, Philson J.
Melchior, Frank A.
Miller, Steven
Morris, Dorothy E.
Morris, Kenneth B.
Niedergang, Murray A.
Parisse, Alan J.
Pollan, Stephen M.
Rice, Henry Hart
Schimmel, Alfred
Schindler, Elmer V.
Wolfert, Jeffrey D.
Zinman, Robert M.

Insuror

Campbell, Robert E.
Cappellini, Louis A. Jr.
Claude, Anthony B.
Costello, Daniel W.
Fleming, Robert H.
Friedman, Joseph N.
Kornheiser, Martin H.
Melchior, Frank A.
Milazzo, Salvator III
Moore, Mechlin D.
Reiss, Abraham
Rifkin, Bernard M.

Shears, John J.
Weiss, Richard L.

Lender

Belofsky, Jerald Alan
Brooks, Peter S.
Byrne, Richard R.
Clarke, James J.
Cleary, Martin
Clutsam, Henry O. III
Conway, E. Virgil
Glidden, Allan H.
Gorham, Howard N.
Grosse, Ernest J.
Harrs, Leland Allen
Hathaway, Louis E. III
Hernandez, Franklyn C.
Hille, Richard
Huffmaster, William M.
Israel, Paul
Lang, Richard F.
Lazrus, Jonathan E.
Levy, Gerald M.
Ludwig, Lloyd Jr.
McCabe, Joseph T. Jr.
McClelland, Arthur D.
Majewski, Edward J.
Malzo, Joseph Jr.
Milazzo, Salvator III
Mooney, G. Austin
Moriarty, John L.
Morse, Bernard L.
Nelson, Kathleen M.
Parrish, Donald R.
Psota, Peter A.
Ridloff, Richard
Rothschild, Robert J.
Salony, Jon R.
Schreiber, Allan C.
Shaffer, Jack A.
Sheridan, James C. Jr.
Solomon, Robert Donald
Stack, Daniel
Starkweather, Thomas L.
Teel, Norcross Jr.
Torres, William J.
Trager, Sidney
Trautman, Lawrence J.
Trucksess, James M. Jr.
Wechsler, Michael J.
White, Gregory A.
Wojak, John S.
Yoles, Zeev E.
Zammit, Thomas J.
Zucker, Norman P.

Owner/Investor

Alpern, Andrew
Ambrosi, Robert J.
Arfa, Harvey Z.
Asheim, Erling
Bachrach, Jonathan David
Bahary, Kamel S.
Bailowitz, Stanley A.
Baker, James Barnes
Banker, Joel I.
Baralt, Carlos M.
Barry, Stanley L.
Becker, Michael A.
Benenson, Charles B.
Berkowitz, Barry
Berley, Peter
Bernard, Bossom
Bernholz, Peter M.
Bernstein, Asher
Berry, Richard S
Bigelow, Charles Glenford III
Birnbaum, Mark D.
Blake, Brian P.T.
Blank, Stephen R.
Bonin, Paul J.
Borsuk, Harvey
Boyarsky, Samuel G.
Boyle, Marsilia A.
Brignati, David A.
Brounstein, Sam
Broxmeyer, Marc
Bush, William C.
Callahan, James J. III
Carey, William Polk
Chapin, David F.
Clark, John P.
Clarke, Phillips H. III
Claude, Anthony B.
Cohen, Herbert L.
Collins, Robert L.
Collins, William W.
Conigliaro, Anthony S.
Copland, Milton
Costello, Daniel W.
Coverdale, Glen E.
Cunneen, Charles T.
Davis, Barry M.
DeSantis, Joseph John
Deutsch, Jerome
DiMicelli, Vincent
Ellis, Kenneth A.
Feirman, Jerome B.
Felix, Steven
Ferrara, Donald F.
Flexner, Thomas M.
Flint, James W.
Fox, Wayne Noland
Frazier, Thomas B. II
Friedman, David A.
Futterman, Philip G.
Galston, John Wood
Gavey, James E.
Glick, Michael I.
Glidden, Allan H.
Golding, Jerome
Goldman, S. Howard
Goodman, I. Michael
Gordon, Donald J.
Gorham, Howard N.
Gotthelf, Beatrice F.
Gould, Jay
Graham, Thomas M. Jr.
Grant, Eugene M.
Greenburger, Francis
Grimes, Robert S.
Grodetsky, Murray H.
Grossman, Charles
Guthrie, Paul R.
Haber, Murray
Hagen, Stephen C.
Haggarty, Kevin F.
Hanson, JoAnn
Hara, Sol J.
Harlan, Leonard Morton
Hausman, Bruce
Haymes, Allan
Huffmaster, William M.
Joachim, Louis Frantz
Joffe, Martin Lee
Karp, Jane Hausman
Kassell, Burton R.
Katz, Edward
Kavounas, Edmond A.
Kelly, John M. PE
Kleiman, Irving
Krackow, Stuart E.
Krigel, A. Arnold
Kunstadt, Herbert
Lang, Richard F.
Levi, James H.
Levien, Kenneth D.
Levy, Jules E.
Liaskos, Michael P.
Lieb, L. Robert
Lipstein, Michael
Litton, Claude J.
MacArthur, William H.
McClelland, Arthur D.
MacDonald, Kirkpatrick
McGratty, Christopher F.
McManus, Hank
McQueeney, Charles T.
Maidman, Richard H.
Mandel, Newton W.
Manning, Fred W.
Marceca, Robert K.
Mendik, Bernard H.
Milazzo, Salvator III
Miller, Steven
Miller, William R.
Mitchell, N. Edmund
Moister, Peter Corbin
Morse, Bernard L.
Munzer, Stephen I.
Murdoch, William F. Jr.
Nickerson, Adams H.
Niedergang, Murray A.
Nishiuwatoko, Tetsu
Novick, Steven E.
Pachter, Milton H.
Panero, Carl Kenyon
Papell, Nathan
Paschow, Joel M.
Pierce, Jorganne
Pivko, Tibor
Principe, Nicholas J.
Psota, Peter A.
Rappoport, Stanley
Regevik, Robert
Reibel, Martin A.
Reiss, Abraham
Restaino, Paul
Rice, Henry Hart
Robinson, Michael J.
Rolfe, N. Anthony
Rondinone, Serge W.
Rosen, Richard
Rosen, Stephen Daniel
Rosenblatt, Harvey
Ross, Stephen M.
Rothenberg, Joel
Rubacha, Paul D.
Ruben, Lawrence
Rubin, Larry Aryeh
Sabella, Thomas A.
Salomon, Suzanne E.
Schaiman, David S.
Schindler, Elmer V.
Schwamm, Jay Marc
Schwerin, Thomas R.
Scroggins, Richard M.
Seevak, Sheldon
Sfouggatakis, Nicholas A.
Shapiro, Donald L.
Shapiro, Robert I.
Silber, Mark E.
Silverman, Leon
Silvershein, Bennett
Simon, Howard I.
Smolen, Michael H.
Smolinsky, Ronald J.
Snoddy, Charles E. Jr.
Soszka, Kenneth R.
Soybel, Arthur
Spira, Seymour L.
Stack, Daniel
Stahl, Michael
Starkweather, Thomas L.
Starrett, Andre V.
Stein, Fredric C.
Stein, Leonard R.
Stillman, Abbott
Stone, Ronald M.
Studley, Julien J.
Sunden, Gary R.
Taylor, Melvin L. Sr.
Teel, Norcross Jr.
Toothaker, Thomas R.
Trucksess, James M. Jr.
Tubin, Allan
Tunnell, Norman D.
Vaughn, Charles H. Jr.
Wechsler, Steven R.
Weiner, Barry R.
Weinreb, Leon
Weiss, Ronald W.
White, Gerrit A.
Winslow, Peter
Wojewodzki, Richard S.
Wolf, Kevin R.
Wolfert, Jeffrey D.
Yamin, Thomas M.
Zeckendorf, William
Zucker, Norman P.

Property Manager

Alpern, Andrew
Asheim, Erling
Baehrel, Peter
Bailowitz, Stanley A.
Bard, Stanley
Barry, Stanley L.
Baydala, Troy G.
Becker, Michael A.
Beeler, Joel I.
Berke, Daniel E.
Berman, Miles J.
Berns, H. Jerome
Bernstein, Asher
Bernstein, Stephen M.
Berry, Richard S
Bloch, Bruce
Bonin, Paul J.
Bookhardt, Fred B. Jr.
Boyle, Marsilia A.
Brener, Stephen W.
Broadman, Arthur R.
Broxmeyer, Marc
Buchbinder, Norman M.
Burke, Dorothy
Callahan, James J. III
Campbell, Robert E.
Canale, Stephen F.
Cappellini, Louis A. Jr.
Carlton, Robert T.
Carmichael, Joseph R.
Carson, Christopher N.
Carvin, Philip J.
Chudnow, I. Randall
Clark, John P.
Cline, Roger S.
Cohen, Jerome M.
Collins, Robert L.
Copland, Milton
Costello, Daniel W.
Coviello, Edmund T.
Cunneen, Charles T.
Davies, Alan V.
Davis, Barry M.
Deis, George
Del Casino, Anthony A.
DeSantis, Joseph John
Diehl, Richard A.
Dinsmore, Robert
Doerflier, Ronald J.
Douglas, Paul W.
Driller, Jay
Ellis, Kenneth A.
Fagan, Barbara
Fein, Bernard
Feirman, Jerome B.
Felix, Steven
Fell, Martin
Fisher, Carl D.
Fisher, George
Fleming, Robert H.
Ford, James A.
Fox, Wayne Noland
Frazier, Thomas B. II
Gavey, James E.
Glasgall, Franklin
Glickman, Robert
Goetschius, James R.
Gold, Jeffrey M.
Golding, Jerome
Goodman, I. Michael
Gordon, Donald J.
Gottlieb, Albert J.
Gould, Jay
Gouldsbury, William C.
Graves, Philip F
Greenburger, Francis
Grodetsky, Murray H.
Guthrie, Paul R.

Haber, Murray
Hackett, Paul
Harmon, Albert C.
Hart, Frank
Hathaway, Louis E. III
Helmke, Edward
Helms, Charles B.
Hevert, Doris
Hogard, Earl
Hopkins, Peter
Hopper, Davis T.
Huffmaster, William M.
Hunt, R.A.
Hurr, Myron
Ingraham, Mark J.
Israel, Paul
Jackson, Steve
Jacobs, Lorraine
Jaffe, Bernard
Jennerich, Arthur
Jewett, D.J.
Joachim, Louis Frantz
Jones, Clifford
Kane, George
Kanner, Theodore I.
Karch, Samuel
Keller, George H. IV
Kelly, John M. PE
Kenny, John
Kleiman, Irving
Krackow, Stuart E.
Kulla, Sylvia
Lang, Richard F.
Lazrus, Jonathan E.
Litton, Claude J.
Ludemann, Robert F.
McCarthy, John A.
McClean, Robert J.
MacDonald, Kirkpatrick
Mack, Dennis
McQueeney, Charles T.
Maihock, Donald J.
Maloney, Vincent J.
Manning, Kenneth
Marceca, Robert K.
Mardo, Guy
Margolis, Sidney
Melcer, Duane Scott
Melick, John M.
Messenkopf, Eugene J.
Milazzo, Salvator III
Mileaf, Howard
Miller, Carl T.
Miller, D.K.
Miller, Samuel M.
Miller, William R.
Milstein, Paul
Minskoff, Henry H.
Mittelman, David
Murphy, James
Neuwirth, Frederick
Newton, Richard
Nuey, Vernita
Nuti, Maria
O'Donnell, William
Okin, Robert
Palmer, E. Marshall
Peracchio, Peter J.
Peterson, Henrik T.
Polan, Laurence S.
Pomerantz, John L.
Poole, Harrison
Principe, Nicholas J.
Reiss, Abraham
Robinson, Michael J.
Rogers, Richard C.
Rogers, Theodore C.
Rolfe, N. Anthony
Rondinone, Serge W.
Rubacha, Paul D.
Rush, James W.
Ryan, Frank
Sabella, Thomas A.
Salerno, Bernard
Salomon, Robert J.
Sandleman, Joel
Schindler, Elmer V.
Schlessler R.W.
Schurgot, Paul D. Jr.
Schusterman, Allen
Schwartz, Richard J.
Schwarzbaum, Leon
Schwerin, Thomas R.
Scroggins, Richard M.
Sfouggatakis, Nicholas A.
Shannon, Gerald T.
Sheehan, Thomas J.
Sheehy, Robert F.
Sherman, Robert A.
Slater, Martin
Smolen, Michael H.
Snoddy, Charles E. Jr.
Soybel, Arthur
Stahl, Michael
Stillman, Abbott
Stone, Robert L.
Stuebe, William H.
Suesser, Alfred
Sulzberger, Edward
Sunden, Gary R.
Tishman, Edward S.
Tockarshewsky, Benedict J.
Trucksess, James M. Jr.
Tubin, Allan
Tynan, Martin F.
Veith, Edwin
Vogel, Morton
Volpe, Thomas J.
Wagner, Richard
Walters, Robert L.
Weil, Mark R.
Weinberger, Michael Joseph
Weiner, Barry R.
Weinreb, Leon
Weiss, Richard L.
Weitzen, Edward H.
West, Donald R.
Wheeler, Ira
Wilson, William
Winslow, Peter
Winston, John
Yamin, Thomas M.
Yarbenet, George
Zammit, Thomas J.
Zeckendorf, William
Zimmerman, Mortimer F.

Real Estate Publisher
Baker, Dorothy
Biller, Aaron
Boyland, Nancy
Campbell, Kenneth D.
Evkenazi, S.
Kahn, Sanders A.
Kelman, Harold
Koch, James H.
Kusnet, Jack
Lyda, Harold
Novick, Steven E.
Parisse, Alan J.
Rubin, Larry Aryeh
Sahlein, Stephen
Shapiro, Jacob
Sillcocks, H. Jackson
Silverstein, Cathy
Strom, Fredric Alan
Studley, Julien J.
Surrey, David
Westman, Bert

Regulator
Abramowitz, Roy A.
Boyle, Marsilia A.
Kanner, Theodore I.
Sperling, Gary H.
Stack, Daniel
Strom, Fredric Alan

Syndicator
Ambrosi, Robert J.
Arfa, Harvey Z.
Bailowitz, Stanley A.
Barry, Stanley L.
Becker, Michael A.
Beeler, Joel I.
Belofsky, Jerald Alan
Berkowitz, Barry
Bernard, Bossom
Bernstein, Stephen M.
Berry, Richard S
Bigelow, Charles Glenford III
Birnbaum, Mark D.
Blank, Stephen R.
Bonin, Paul J.
Borsuk, Harvey
Boyarsky, Samuel G.
Bross, Joel L.
Bush, William C.
Clarke, Phillips H. III
Cliff, Patricia Warburg
Cohen, Herbert L.
Coviello, Edmund T.
Daenzer, Peter B.
Davis, Barry M.
Deutsch, Jerome
DiMicelli, Vincent
Feirman, Jerome B.
Feldman, Leslie
Filoon, John W. Jr.
Flint, James W.
Galston, John Wood
Gavey, James E.
Glick, Michael I.
Glickman, Edwin J.
Goetschius, James R.
Graves, James M.
Greenburger, Francis
Haber, Murray
Hara, Sol J.
Haymes, Allan
Hille, Richard
Jenkins, Robert N.
Jewell, Keith Dover
Kassell, Burton R.
Landry, Brian F.
Levi, James H.
Lewis, Bertram
Lieb, L. Robert
Linburn, Michael R.
McQueeney, Charles T.
Mandel, Newton W.
Melcer, Duane Scott
Messenkopf, Eugene J.
Miller, Steven
Morse, Bernard L.
Munzer, Stephen I.
Nickerson, Adams H.
Novick, Steven E.
Parisse, Alan J.
Quay, Kenneth
Rappoport, Stanley
Reibel, Martin A.
Restaino, Paul
Robinson, Michael J.
Rosen, Robert J.
Ross, Stephen M.
Rothenberg, Joel
Rubin, Larry Aryeh
Salomon, Suzanne E.
Schiffman, Martin
Seevak, Sheldon
Silber, Mark E.
Solomon, Robert Donald
Stahl, Michael
Stein, Leonard R.
Stone, Ronald M.
Sunden, Gary R.
Swift, David A.
Thies, Winthrop Drake
Trautman, Lawrence J.
Tubin, Allan
Vaughn, Charles H. Jr.
Weinbaum, Mark J.
Weiner, Barry R.
Weiss, Richard L.
Weiss, Ronald W.
Winston, John
Wolf, Kevin R.

PLATTSBURGH

Appraiser
Wilkins, John M.

Attorney
Lennon, Lawrence B.

Broker
Lennon, Lawrence B.
Wilkins, John M.

Consultant
Wilkins, John M.

Insuror
Wilkins, John M.

Lender
Wilkins, John M.

Owner/Investor
Lennon, Lawrence B.
Wilkins, John M.

Property Manager
Lennon, Lawrence B.

POUGHKEEPSIE

Appraiser
Bookhout, Leland T.
Lee, Donald
Rubinstein, Manny A.

Architect
Arnouts, Robert A.

Assessor
Harris, Russell A. Jr.

Attorney
Curtin, Daniel F.
McGowan, J. Joseph

Broker
Lee, Donald
Rubinstein, Manny A.
Spevak, Irving

Builder
Rubinstein, Manny A.

Consultant
Bookhout, Leland T.
Harris, Russell A. Jr.
Rubinstein, Manny A.

Developer
Rubinstein, Manny A.

Instructor
Bookhout, Leland T.
Spevak, Irving

Owner/Investor
Rubinstein, Manny A.

Property Manager
Rubinstein, Manny A.
Spevak, Irving

Syndicator
Rubinstein, Manny A.

QUEENS

Appraiser
Clark, George A.
Ford, Wesley C.
Katz, Frederick
Lurie, David L.
Montemarano, Joseph
Timpanaro, Ralph M.

Architect
Feinberg, Allen H.
Werfel, Laurence

Attorney
Arnold, Alvin L.
Belfer, Andrew B.

Brill, Steven C.
Burns, John A. Jr.
Carucci, Samuel A.
Kaiser, Anton J. Esq.
Kalikow, Edward M.
Levine, Barton P.
Liftin, Sidney J.
Mattone, Joseph M.
Menowitz, Frederick A.
Penson, Edward I.
Simoni, Carl David
Zankel, Ira L.

Banker
King, Richard W.
Miller, Howard C.

Broker
Agin, Herbert S.
Belfer, Andrew B.
Brill, Steven C.
Ciani, Robert J.
Clark, George A.
Ford, Wesley C.
Gherardi, James C.
Goldberg, George
Guarton, Gonzalo A.
Katz, Frederick
Leigh, Samuel
Licht, Nathan
Lurie, David L.
Sims, Albert H.
Slatkin, Jean
Timpanaro, Ralph M.
Unger, Helen J.

Builder
Belfer, Andrew B.
Carucci, Samuel A.
Clark, George A.
Feinberg, Allen H.
Gherardi, James C.
Gluck, Michael
Granville, Irwin E.
Guarton, Gonzalo A.
Kalikow, Edward M.
Levine, Barton P.
Licht, Nathan
Lurie, David L.
Menowitz, Frederick A.
Spivack, Harvey

Consultant
Goldberg, George
Guarton, Gonzalo A.
Katz, Frederick
Leigh, Samuei
Lieberman, Bruce R.
Mattone, Joseph M.
Montemarano, Joseph
Shields, H. Richard
Sims, Albert H.
Timpanaro, Ralph M.
Werfel, Laurence

Developer
Belfer, Andrew B.
Feinberg, Allen H.
Gherardi, James C.
Gluck, Michael
Granville, Irwin E.
Guarton, Gonzalo A.
Kalikow, Edward M.
Levine, Barton P.
Lieberman, Bruce R.
Lurie, David L.
Mason, Joel
Mattone, Joseph M.
Penson, Edward I.
Spivack, Harvey

Engineer
Bokhari, Ghazi
Katz, Frederick
Montemarano, Joseph
Reyer, Burton

Instructor
Arnold, Alvin L.
Ford, Wesley C.
Sims, Albert H.
Werfel, Laurence

Insuror
Clark, George A.
Goldberg, George
Guarton, Gonzalo A.
Lieberman, Bruce R.

Lender
King, Richard W.

Owner/Investor
Belfer, Andrew B.
Bokhari, Ghazi
Brill, Steven C.
Carucci, Samuel A.
Ciani, Robert J.
Gherardi, James C.
Gluck, Michael
Granville, Irwin E.
Guarton, Gonzalo A.
Kalikow, Edward M.
Katz, Frederick
Leigh, Samuel
Levine, Barton P.
Licht, Nathan
Lieberman, Bruce R.
Liftin, Sidney J.
Lurie, David L.
Mason, Joel
Mattone, Joseph M.
Menowitz, Frederick A.
Montemarano, Joseph
Penson, Edward I.
Shields, H. Richard
Slattery, Joseph P. Jr.
Spivack, Harvey
Unger, Helen J.
Wynperle, William F. Jr.

Property Manager
Belfer, Andrew B.
Carbone, Josephine
Carucci, Samuel A.
Ford, Wesley C.
Gherardi, James C.
Gluck, Michael
Granville, Irwin E.
Guarton, Gonzalo A.
Haffner, Robert
Imperiale, Peter
Jody, Boris
Kalikow, Edward M.
Katz, Frederick
Leigh, Samuel
Licht, Nathan
Lieberman, Bruce R.
Liftin, Sidney J.
Lurie, David L.
Moore, Doug
Penson, Edward I.
Sims, Albert H.
Spivack, Harvey
Unger, Helen J.

Real Estate Publisher
Arnold, Alvin L.
Schneider, Eric S.
Sobel, Lester

Syndicator
Feinberg, Allen H.
Gherardi, James C.
Goldberg, George
Lieberman, Bruce R.
Mason, Joel
Mattone, Joseph M.
Penson, Edward I.

RIVERHEAD

Appraiser
Chapman, Ronald J.
King, Floyd F. Jr.
Loughlin, Joseph F.

Architect
Heins, Robert August William

Attorney
Stankevich, George Cochran Esq.

Broker
King, Floyd F. Jr.
Loughlin, Joseph F.

Builder
Heins, Robert August William

Consultant
Chapman, Ronald J.
King, Floyd F. Jr.

Developer
King, Floyd F. Jr.
Stankevich, George Cochran Esq.

Insuror
Wallace, Robert J.

Owner/Investor
King, Floyd F. Jr.

Property Manager
King, Floyd F. Jr.

ROCHESTER

Appraiser
Albright, Allen J.
Dailey, R. Marvin
MacQueen, Virginia
Mirabella, Frank J.
Schwartz, Norman A.
Wagner, Wallace J.
Walther, Steven G.
Wills, Thomas S. Jr.

Architect
Burwell, William O.
Paskey, Ernest L.

Attorney
Corcoran, Christopher H.
Cusker, Thomas J.
Farney, Duncan R.
Humphrey, Robert F.
Samloff, Harold
Schlee, Merrill O.

Banker
Dennis, William H.

Broker
Albright, Allen J.
Cunningham, Richard G.
Haid, Linda L.
Kinsella, Thomas E.
MacQueen, Virginia
Mirabella, Frank J.
Schwartz, Norman A.
Wagner, Wallace J.
Walther, Steven G.
Wills, Thomas S. Jr.

Builder
Bowering, C. Richard
Glazer, Larry
Mirabella, Frank J.
Samloff, Harold
Wilson, E. Anthony

Consultant
Albright, Allen J.
Cunningham, Richard G.
Dailey, R. Marvin
Dennis, William H.
MacQueen, Virginia
Pajeski, Stephen J.
Paskey, Ernest L.
Schwartz, Norman A.
Wagner, Wallace J.
Walther, Steven G.

Developer
Bowering, C. Richard
Clawson, John W.
Gangloff, Peter A.
Glazer, Larry
Kinsella, Thomas E.
Samloff, Harold
Smith, J. Michael
Wallace, David L.
Walther, Steven G.
Wilson, E. Anthony

Engineer
Paskey, Ernest L.

Instructor
Dailey, R. Marvin
Farney, Duncan R.
Pajeski, Stephen J.

Insuror
Mirabella, Frank J.

Owner/Investor
Albright, Allen J.
Dennis, William H.
Glazer, Larry
MacQueen, Virginia
Samloff, Harold
Schwartz, Norman A.
Smith, J. Michael
Wallace, David L.
Walther, Steven G.
Wilson, E. Anthony

Property Manager
Albright, Richard A.
Cunningham, Richard G.
Dailey, R. Marvin
Dennis, William H.
Gangloff, Peter A.
Glazer, Larry
Haid, Linda L.
Miller, Ronald A.
Mirrer, William
Pajeski, Stephen J.
Robinson, James
Samloff, Harold
Schieffen, Michael
Schwartz, Norman A.
Wallace, David L.
Walther, Steven G.
Wehle, John L. Jr.
Weil, Louis
Wilson, E. Anthony

Syndicator
Glazer, Larry
MacQueen, Virginia
Smith, J. Michael
Walther, Steven G.
Wilson, E. Anthony

STATEN ISLAND

Appraiser
Adamo, Vincent E.
Lanning, Robert E.
Walsh, Joseph P.

Attorney
Frew, William J. Jr.
Lee, R. Randy Esq.
Lenza, Anthony A.
Manzulli, Michael F.
Smith, Ormond N.

Broker
Lanning, Robert E.
Walsh, Joseph P.

Builder
Lee, R. Randy Esq.

Consultant
Adamo, Vincent E.
Cammarata, Jerry
Lanning, Robert E.

Developer
Cammarata, Jerry
Lee, R. Randy Esq.

Instructor
Cammarata, Jerry

Owner/Investor
Knight, Bob

Property Manager
Cammarata, Jerry

Syndicator
Cammarata, Jerry
Lee, R. Randy Esq.

SUFFERN

Appraiser
Honegger, William
Stein, Franklin D.

Architect
Livingston, Craig Raymond

Assessor
Stein, Franklin D.

Attorney
Chandler, Garth K.
Schwall, Leonard
Wheeler, Richard

Broker
Honegger, William
Morreale, John M.

Builder
Ditmans, Frederick S.
Livingston, Craig Raymond
Mills, Howard D. Jr.

Consultant
Mills, Howard D. Jr.
Stein, Franklin D.

Developer
Buchalter, William
Ditmans, Frederick S.
Livingston, Craig Raymond
Mills, Howard D. Jr.

Instructor
Chandler, Garth K.

Owner/Investor
Buchalter, William
Caunitz, Richard W.
Chandler, Garth K.
Mills, Howard D. Jr.
Peller, Sidney L.

Property Manager
Buchalter, William
Ditmans, Frederick S.
Honegger, William
Mills, Howard D. Jr.
Peller, Sidney L.
Stein, Franklin D.
Wheeler, Richard

Syndicator
Buchalter, William
Caunitz, Richard W.

SYRACUSE

Appraiser
Doan, Gregory K.
Ferris, Robert J.
Gray, Leslie B.
Havemeyer, John F. III
Lebro, Theodore P.
Okin, Edward J.
Putman, Herbert D.
Sarkin, Harold
Walpole, Robert F.

Assessor
Lebro, Theodore P.

Attorney
Bradshaw, Eugene B.
Cregg, George W.
Dernago, Theodore P. Jr.
Medcraf, James Howard
Popkess, Alfred W.

Broker
Cregg, George W.
Dernago, Theodore P. Jr.
Doan, Gregory K.
Ferris, Robert J.
Herrmann, J. Robert
Lebro, Theodore P.
Sarkin, Harold
Sher, David

Builder
Dernago, Theodore P. Jr.
Herrmann, J. Robert
Kennedy, Thomas R.
Sarkin, Harold
Walpole, Robert F.

Consultant
Cregg, George W.
Doan, Gregory K.
Ferris, Robert J.
Gray, Leslie B.
Herrmann, J. Robert
Lebro, Theodore P.
Okin, Edward J.
Sarkin, Harold
Sher, David

Developer
Cregg, George W.
Dernago, Theodore P. Jr.
Herrmann, J. Robert
Kennedy, Thomas R.
Sarkin, Harold
Sibley, Donald A.
Walpole, Robert F.

Engineer
Herrmann, J. Robert
Sibley, Donald A.

Instructor
Dernago, Theodore P. Jr.
Fried, Martin L.
Lebro, Theodore P.
Okin, Edward J.
Sher, David

Insuror
Dernago, Theodore P. Jr.
Herrmann, J. Robert
Lebro, Theodore P.

Owner/Investor
Dernago, Theodore P. Jr.
Ferris, Robert J.
Herrmann, J. Robert
Kennedy, Thomas R.
Lebro, Theodore P.
Medcraf, James Howard
Putman, Herbert D.
Sarkin, Harold
Sibley, Donald A.
Walpole, Robert F.

Property Manager
Bradshaw, Eugene B.
Cregg, George W.
Dernago, Theodore P. Jr.
Herrmann, J. Robert
Lebro, Theodore P.
Libby, John E.
Okin, Edward J.
Putman, Herbert D.
Sarkin, Harold
Sibley, Donald A.
Walpole, Robert F.

Regulator
Dernago, Theodore P. Jr.

Syndicator
Dernago, Theodore P. Jr.
Herrmann, J. Robert
Sarkin, Harold

UTICA

Appraiser
Howarth, Robert R.

Attorney
Karl, Peter A. III

Broker
Howarth, Robert R.

Builder
D'Agostino, A.R.

Consultant
Howarth, Robert R.

Developer
D'Agostino, A.R.

Owner/Investor
D'Agostino, A.R.

Property Manager
Howarth, Robert R.
Vanderwall, Niek

WESTCHESTER

Appraiser
Basciani, George R.
Blanco, Rita M.
Dempsey, D. Kevin
Ferrier, Dennis C.
Flower, Robert J.
Fraioli, Lawrence A.
Gallagher, James V.
Golub, Kenneth, L.
Greenstein, Gary G.
Ishaq, Edward D.
Kirsch, H. Bruce
Klonick, Allan S.
Lotty, John F.
Muro, Michael L.
St. George, Michael F.
Simpson, Joseph J.
Spencer, Joan H.
Wolff, Nicholas R.
Young, Warren H.

Architect
Anderson, Allan S.
Brill, Ralph
Crozier, Robert W.
Freed, Donald E.

Assessor
Klonick, Allan S.
Muro, Michael L.

Attorney
Crystal, Joel F.
Gioffre, Bruno J.
Gochman, John J.
Hall, H. Glen

Banker
McTighe, Michael J.
Simpson, Joseph J.
Weinberg, Robert F.

Broker
Aries, Peter L.
Blanco, Rita M.
Brill, Ralph
Cohen, Stanley A.
Cole, John N.
Doern, David A.
Eisenberg, Harry
Gallagher, James V.
Greenstein, Gary G.
Ishaq, Edward D.
Keating, Edwin L.
Klonick, Allan S.
Lukashok, Alvin
St. George, Michael F.
Spencer, Joan H.
Stone, Richard P.
Sturman, Howard P.
Wolff, Nicholas R.

Builder
Berger, Martin S.
Cohen, Stanley A.
Feinberg, Norman M.
Gallagher, James V.
Greenspan, Arnold S.
Mindich, Mel Leigh
Weinberg, Robert F.
Yasser, James M.

Consultant
Basciani, George R.
Brill, Ralph
Crozier, Robert W.
Dempsey, D. Kevin
Doern, David A.
Feinberg, Norman M.
Flower, Robert J.
Fraioli, Lawrence A.
Gallagher, James V.
Gioffre, Bruno J.
Greenstein, Gary G.
Hall, H. Glen
Hampson, Richard P.
Holod, Mark A.
Ishaq, Edward D.
Kirsch, H. Bruce
Lotty, John F.
McTighe, Michael J.
Middelberg, Hans A.
Roberts, Richard A.
Rybczyk, Edward J.
Stone, Richard P.

Developer
Aries, Peter L.
Berger, Martin S.
Brill, Ralph
Cohen, Stanley A.
Feinberg, Norman M.
Gioffre, Bruno J.
Greenspan, Arnold S.
Lichter, Stuart
Lukashok, Alvin
McTighe, Michael J.
Mindich, Mel Leigh
Morris, Leland
Simpson, Joseph J.
Sturman, Howard P.
Weinberg, Robert F.
Yasser, James M.

Engineer
Ishaq, Edward D.
Lukashok, Alvin
Middelberg, Hans A.
Weinberg, Robert F.

Instructor
Kirsch, H. Bruce
Spencer, Joan H.
Wolff, Nicholas R.

Insuror
Blanco, Rita M.
Cole, John N.

Lender
Gallagher, James V.
Simpson, Joseph J.
Young, Warren H.

Owner/Investor
Aries, Peter L.
Blanco, Rita M.
Brill, Ralph
Cohen, Stanley A.
Crozier, Robert W.
Feinberg, Norman M.
Flower, Robert J.
Fraioli, Lawrence A.
Gioffre, Bruno J.

Greenspan, Arnold S.
Ishaq, Edward D.
Lichter, Stuart
Lukashok, Alvin
McTighe, Michael J.
Middelberg, Hans A.
Mindich, Mel Leigh
Morris, Leland
Roberts, Richard A.
Simpson, Joseph J.
Stone, Richard P.
Sturman, Howard P.
Weinberg, Robert F.
Yasser, James M.
Young, Warren H.

Property Manager
Aries, Peter L.
Blanco, Rita M.
Cohen, Stanley A.
Doherty, D.A.
Feinberg, Norman M.
Fraioli, Lawrence A.
Gallagher, James V.
Gioffre, Bruno J.
Goldstein, Martin
Greenstein, Gary G.
Holod, Mark A.
Ian, Joseph M.
Ishaq, Edward D.
Lany, Enrique
Lichter, Stuart
McTighe, Michael J.
Morris, Leland
Roberts, Richard A.
Shuttleworth, J.E.
Spencer, Joan H.
Stevens, Norton
Stone, Richard P.
Sweet, George
Tanis, Robert
Weinberg, Robert F.
Whitely, Eric
Williams, John F.
Yasser, James M.

Syndicator
Cohen, Stanley A.
Cole, John N.
Gioffre, Bruno J.
Lichter, Stuart
Middelberg, Hans A.
Morris, Leland
Roberts, Richard A.
Stone, Richard P.

NORTH CAROLINA

ASHEVILLE

Appraiser
Flowers, Raymond P.
Mack, Francis Wayne
Merrill, Rick

Architect
Benkert, Kyle G.

Attorney
Adams, Alfred Gray
Coiner, Francis M.
Ganly, David M.
Saenger, George W.
Wolcott, William F. III

Broker
Flowers, Raymond P.
Mack, Francis Wayne
Maher, James A.
Melton, Robert Witcher
Merrill, Rick

Builder
Benkert, Kyle G.
Mack, Francis Wayne
Maher, James A.

Consultant
Flowers, Raymond P.
Maher, James A.
Melton, Robert Witcher
Merrill, Rick

Developer
Benkert, Kyle G.
Kinser, Wayne
Mack, Francis Wayne
Maher, James A.
Melton, Robert Witcher
Merrill, Rick
Turner, Ronald L.

Instructor
Coiner, Francis M.

Owner/Investor
Benkert, Kyle G.
Kinser, Wayne
Mack, Francis Wayne
Maher, James A.
Merrill, Rick
Turner, Ronald L.

Property Manager
Maher, James A.

Syndicator
Kinser, Wayne
Merrill, Rick

CHARLOTTE

Appraiser
Burroughs, J. Michael
Clark, Mitchell G.
Giles, Ron
Glenn, Robert T.
Hamrick, Larry Dean
McDonald, John C. Jr.
Morgan, Jack C. Jr.
Smith, Gibson L.
Starnes, James L.

Architect
Minter, David A.
Whisnant, Murray

Attorney
Alala, Joseph B. Jr.
Edwards, Mark B.
Fennimore, C. Thomas
Johnston, John Sikes
Lockhart, Thomas A.
Lomax, Henry C.
Reeves, Michael C.
Starnes, James L.
Tuttle, M. Slate Jr.

Banker
Brugh, W. Patton
Fennimore, C. Thomas
Jowett, David A.
Starnes, James L.

Broker
Baker, B. Richard
Burroughs, J. Michael
Clark, Mitchell G.
Forester, Kenneth P. Jr.
Giles, Ron
Glenn, Robert T.
Hamrick, Larry Dean
Johnston, John Sikes
McBrayer, John H.
McDonald, John C. Jr.
McGuire, William B.
McMahan, W. Edwin
Massachi, Benjamin
Nicholson, James R.
Norman, Thomas Edmund
Pennington, Robert E.
Percival, Robert H.
Purser, Lat Wesley III
Rogers, James E.
Smith, Gibson L.
Waddell, R. Alvin
Waters, Karl Martin III

Builder
Baker, James H. III
Forester, Kenneth P. Jr.
Johnston, John Sikes
Klein, Fred W.
Myers, Brevard S.
Norman, Thomas Edmund
Roberts, Clifford F.
Rogers, David H.
Waddell, R. Alvin

Consultant
Alala, Joseph B. Jr.
Baker, B. Richard
Baker, James H. III
Burroughs, J. Michael
Hamrick, Larry Dean
Lomax, Henry C.
McDonald, John C. Jr.
McMahan, W. Edwin
Minter, David A.
Morrison, Robert Haywood
Nicholson, James R.
Percival, Robert H.
Rogers, James E.
Smith, Gibson L.
Starnes, James L.
Trotter, James N.
Tuttle, M. Slate Jr.

Developer
Baker, B. Richard
Davenport, Stephen H. Jr.
Forester, Kenneth P. Jr.
Glenn, Robert T.
Hermelink, Herman M.
Johnston, John Sikes
Klein, Fred W.
Lomax, Henry C.
McGuire, William B.
McMahan, W. Edwin
Mahaffey, Charles Olin Jr.
Myers, Brevard S.
Nicholson, James R.
Norman, Thomas Edmund
Patterson, Robert M.
Percival, Robert H.
Purser, Lat Wesley III
Roberts, Clifford F.
Rogers, David H.
Rogers, James E.
Stoever, M.D.
Waddell, R. Alvin
Waters, Karl Martin III
Whisnant, Murray
Wiley, Albert Lee Jr.

Engineer
Baker, James H. III
Massachi, Benjamin
Minter, David A.
Wiley, Albert Lee Jr.

Instructor
McDonald, John C. Jr.
Morrison, Robert Haywood
Norman, Thomas Edmund
Starnes, James L.

Insuror
Giles, Ron
Hamrick, Larry Dean

Lender
Burroughs, J. Michael
Fennimore, C. Thomas
Johnston, John Sikes
Morrison, Robert Haywood
Starnes, James L.

Owner/Investor
Alala, Joseph B. Jr.
Davenport, Stephen H. Jr.
Forester, Kenneth P. Jr.
Giles, Ron
Hamrick, Larry Dean
Johnston, John Sikes
Klein, Fred W.
Lomax, Henry C.
McDonald, John C. Jr.
McGuire, William B.
McMahan, W. Edwin
Massachi, Benjamin
Morrison, Robert Haywood
Myers, Brevard S.
Nicholson, James R.
Norman, Thomas Edmund
Patterson, Robert M.
Starnes, James L.
Trotter, James N.
Wiley, Albert Lee Jr.

Property Manager
Baker, B. Richard
Baker, James H. III
Chapman, Toby G.
Clark, Mitchell G.
Forester, Kenneth P. Jr.
Giles, Ron
Hermelink, Herman M.
Iverson, F.K.
Johnston, John Sikes
Lambert, Joe
McDonald, John C. Jr.
McGuire, William B.
McMahan, W. Edwin
Mahaffey, Charles Olin Jr.
Massachi, Benjamin
Nicholson, James R.
Pennington, Robert E.
Percival, Robert H.
Roberts, Clifford F.
Roberts, Jay
Rogers, David H.
Rogers, James E.
Trotter, James N.
Tuttle, M. Slate Jr.
Waddell, R. Alvin

Real Estate Publisher
Morrison, Robert Haywood

Syndicator
Alala, Joseph B. Jr.
Davenport, Stephen H. Jr.
Forester, Kenneth P. Jr.
Lomax, Henry C.
McGuire, William B.
Massachi, Benjamin
Roberts, Clifford F.
Smith, Gibson L.
Tousignant, Robert F.
Waters, Karl Martin III

FAYETTEVILLE

Appraiser
Bryant, Artis R.
Cashman, Rebecca M.
Hunn, Erich A. L.
Noffsinger, Hugh G. Jr.
Riddle, Joseph P. III
Saunders, William P. Jr.

Broker
Bryant, Artis R.
Cashman, Rebecca M.
Hunn, Erich A. L.
Messick, John A.
Noffsinger, Hugh G. Jr.
Riddle, Joseph P. III
Saunders, William P. Jr.

Builder
Cashman, Rebecca M.
Hamlin, Dale A.
Hunn, Erich A. L.
Riddle, Joseph P. III

Consultant
Cashman, Rebecca M.
Domnick, Terrence M.
Hunn, Erich A. L.
Noffsinger, Hugh G. Jr.
Riddle, Joseph P. III

Developer
Cashman, Rebecca M.
Domnick, Terrence M.
Hamlin, Dale A.
Hunn, Erich A. L.
Little, Justin F.
Riddle, Joseph P. III
Saunders, William P. Jr.

Insuror
Noffsinger, Hugh G. Jr.
Riddle, Joseph P. III
Saunders, William P. Jr.

Lender
Coggin, Buena Vista Mrs.
Little, Justin F.

Owner/Investor
Cashman, Rebecca M.
Domnick, Terrence M.
Hunn, Erich A. L.
Riddle, Joseph P. III
Saunders, William P. Jr.

Property Manager
Bryant, Artis R.
Cashman, Rebecca M.
Hunn, Erich A. L.
Riddle, Joseph P. III

Regulator
Bryant, Artis R.

Syndicator
Noffsinger, Hugh G. Jr.
Saunders, William P. Jr.

GREENSBORO

Appraiser
Caudle, Terry W.
Little, Ford D. Jr.
Mendenhall, Ed.
Messick, Harold M.
Watts, H. Michael
Williams, J. Lanier

Architect
Walter, Lloyd Guy Jr.

Attorney
Beaty, James A. Jr.
Fuller, Walter Erwin Jr.
Holleman, L. Worth Jr.
Leonard, Joe H.
Loughridge, John Halsted Jr.
Sharpe, Patrick M.
Weeks, James B.

Banker
Loughridge, John Halsted Jr.

Broker
Kennedy, Henry Jr.
Little, Ford D. Jr.
Loftis, Ronald W. Jr.
Maxwell, Richard
Mendenhall, Ed.
Williams, J. Lanier
Zealy, Samuel Hollingsworth Jr.

Builder
Staley, Charles Wesley
Trogdon, Jack D.

Consultant
Mendenhall, Ed.
Staley, Charles Wesley
Watts, H. Michael
Williams, J. Lanier

Developer
Blackburn, James W.
Bryant, Jerry W.
Faircloth, Bradley
Loftis, Ronald W. Jr.
Maxwell, Richard
Messick, Harold M.
Williams, J. Lanier

Engineer
Staley, Charles Wesley

Instructor
Maxwell, Richard
Zealy, Samuel Hollingsworth Jr.

Insuror
Little, Ford D. Jr.

Lender
Bryant, Jerry W.

Owner/Investor
Blackburn, James W.
Bryant, Jerry W.
Kennedy, Henry Jr.
Little, Ford D. Jr.
Maxwell, Richard
Williams, J. Lanier

Property Manager
Baugh, Marrin
Graves, Thomas W. Jr.
Kennedy, Henry Jr.
Lanier, Thomas
Lineweaver, Wilford
Little, Ford D. Jr.
Loftis, Ronald W. Jr.
McGarr, Paul
Maxwell, Richard
Mendenhall, Ed.
Routh, Richard
Sage, Bill
Simmons, Roger
Smith, Forrest C.
Staley, Charles Wesley
Williams, J. Lanier
Zealy, Samuel Hollingsworth Jr.

Regulator
Beaty, James A. Jr.

Syndicator
Loftis, Ronald W. Jr.
Maxwell, Richard

HICKORY

Appraiser
Hunter, J. Edwin
Mastin, R. Fred
Mitchell, James R.
Norvell, Jerry T. Jr.
Triplett, Ira C. Jr.
Underdown, Jack A.

Broker
Hunter, J. Edwin
Mastin, R. Fred
Mitchell, James R.
Norvell, Jerry T. Jr.
Triplett, Ira C. Jr.
Underdown, Jack A.

Builder
Hunter, J. Edwin
Mitchell, James R.
Norvell, Jerry T. Jr.

Consultant
Mitchell, James R.
Triplett, Ira C. Jr.
Underdown, Jack A.

Developer
Norvell, Jerry T. Jr.
Underdown, Jack A.

Instructor
Underdown, Jack A.

Insuror
Mastin, R. Fred
Norvell, Jerry T. Jr.
Underdown, Jack A.

Owner/Investor
Triplett, Ira C. Jr.
Underdown, Jack A.

Property Manager
Hunter, J. Edwin
Mitchell, James R.
Norvell, Jerry T. Jr.
Triplett, Ira C. Jr.

KINSTON

Attorney
Baxter, B. Hunt Jr.
Riggs, Zennie Lawrence

Banker
Fulcher, Wanda Jo

Broker
Foster, D.D.
Thomas, Joseph E.

Builder
Thomas, Joseph E.

Developer
Thomas, Joseph E.

Lender
Fulcher, Wanda Jo

Owner/Investor
Thomas, Joseph E.

Property Manager
Thomas, Joseph E.

Regulator
Baxter, B. Hunt Jr.

Syndicator
Thomas, Joseph E.

RALEIGH

Appraiser
Lorbacher, Rodney A.
Matthews, Joe F. Jr.
Orgain, E. Stewart Jr.
Pleasant, Willard
Smither, John Rowland
White, James L.
Whitefield, Ralph F. Jr. (Buddy)

Architect
Blosser, Dale A.

Attorney
Fulton, Charles L.
Harkins, Harry H. Jr.
Harward, Coralynn Y.
Hetrick, Patrick K.
Kane, Gary Paul
Outlaw, Larry A.
Upchurch, Roger Stanley

Broker
Block, Norman E.
Bradshaw, Thomas W. Jr.
Carr, Geo. Watts. Jr.
Englert, John A.
Foster, John M.
Lorbacher, Rodney A.
Matthews, Joe F. Jr.
Orgain, E. Stewart Jr.
Outlaw, Larry A.
Pleasant, Willard
Spainhour, Kenneth F.
Stark, William L.
White, James L.
Whitefield, Ralph F. Jr. (Buddy)
Worth, Hal Venable III

Builder
Bradshaw, Thomas W. Jr.
Foster, John M.
Matthews, Joe F. Jr.
Pleasant, Willard

Consultant
Block, Norman E.
Blosser, Dale A.
Bradshaw, Thomas W. Jr.
Hetrick, Patrick K.
Orgain, E. Stewart Jr.
Stark, William L.
Whitefield, Ralph F. Jr. (Buddy)

Developer
Block, Norman E.
Bradshaw, Thomas W. Jr.
Carr, Geo. Watts. Jr.
Foster, John M.
Lorbacher, Rodney A.
Matthews, Joe F. Jr.
Orgain, E. Stewart Jr.
Pleasant, Willard
Spainhour, Kenneth F.
Stark, William L.
Whitefield, Ralph F. Jr. (Buddy)
Wilson, Lewis R.
Worth, Hal Venable III

Engineer
Stark, William L.

Instructor
Block, Norman E.
Hetrick, Patrick K.
Spainhour, Kenneth F.
White, James L.

Insuror
Carr, Geo. Watts. Jr.
Orgain, E. Stewart Jr.

Lender
Daughety, William F.
Kane, Gary Paul
Lyon, Constantine G.
Matthews, Joe F. Jr.

Owner/Investor
Kane, Gary Paul
Matthews, Joe F. Jr.
Pleasant, Willard
Spainhour, Kenneth F.
Stark, William L.
White, James L.

Property Manager
Bradshaw, Thomas W. Jr.
Orgain, E. Stewart Jr.
Sherrer, James
Spainhour, Kenneth F.
Stark, William L.
White, James L.
Worth, Hal Venable III

Regulator
Fisher, Phillip T.
Harkins, Harry H. Jr.
Outlaw, Larry A.

Syndicator
Orgain, E. Stewart Jr.

ROCKY MOUNT

Appraiser
Elmore, Kit
Moore, Collice C.
Pitt, Theophilus Harper Jr.
Strickland, Charles Edward
Wheless, Herbert W.

Attorney
Surasky, David Jr.

Broker
Moore, Collice C.
Strickland, Charles Edward

Wheless, Herbert W.

Consultant
Moore, Collice C.
Strickland, Charles Edward
Surasky, David Jr.

Developer
Moore, Collice C.
Pitt, Theophilus Harper Jr.

Instructor
Strickland, Charles Edward

Lender
Pitt, Theophilus Harper Jr.

Owner/Investor
Elmore, Kit
Moore, Collice C.
Pitt, Theophilus Harper Jr.
Strickland, Charles Edward
Wheless, Herbert W.

Property Manager
Strickland, Charles Edward

Syndicator
Elmore, Kit

NORTH DAKOTA

BISMARCK

Appraiser
Kunick, Alan D.
Weekes, Eugene D.

Attorney
Lervick, Timothy D.

Broker
Weekes, Eugene D.

Property Manager
Payton, Michael B.
Schulz, Dennis

DEVILS LAKE

Broker
Lindstrom, Rodney B.

Insuror
Lindstrom, Rodney B.

Property Manager
Lindstrom, Rodney B.

DICKINSON

Appraiser
Penfield, Robert E.

Broker
Penfield, Robert E.

Consultant
Penfield, Robert E.

Instructor
Penfield, Robert E.

FARGO

Appraiser
Arneson, H.R.
Everson, Gordon A.
Frissell, Robert N.
Nitzkorski, Douglas W.

Attorney
Selbo, Lyle W.

Broker
Arneson, H.R.
Frissell, Robert N.
Hutchinson, A.G.
Schlossman, William A.

Builder
Hutchinson, A.G.
Lundstrom, James E.
Nelson, Scott A.

Consultant
Arneson, H.R.
Frissell, Robert N.
Hutchinson, A.G.
Nelson, Scott A.
Nitzkorski, Douglas W.

Developer
Frissell, Robert N.
Lundstrom, James E.
Nelson, Scott A.

Instructor
Arneson, H.R.

Insuror
Arneson, H.R.

Owner/Investor
Frissell, Robert N.
Nelson, Scott A.

Property Manager
Arneson, H.R.
Nelson, Scott A.
Schlossman, William A.

GRAND FORKS

Attorney
Arnason, Albert F.

Broker
Langerud, Don

Lender
Christenson, Edward

Owner/Investor
Arnason, Albert F.
Langerud, Don

Property Manager
Bushee, Dean A.
Langerud, Don

Syndicator
Langerud, Don

MINOT

Broker
Christianson, Bruce I.

Consultant
Christianson, Bruce I.

Property Manager
Christianson, Bruce I.

OHIO

AKRON

Appraiser
Cleminshaw, John G.
Emig, John W.
Higgins, Alan M.
Muddimer, Hazel M.
Webb, James R.

Attorney
Kalavity, Louis
Litka, Michael P.
Ruport, Scott H.
Sermersheim, Michael D.
Wendelken, Richard J.

Broker
Cleminshaw, John G.
Helms, Donald W.
Kalavity, Louis
Muddimer, Hazel M.
Stanson, Richard S.
Weinberger, Edward

Builder
Arthur, James William
Muddimer, Hazel M.
Weinberger, Edward

Consultant
Buchholzer, Richard B.
Cleminshaw, John G.
Helms, Donald W.
Higgins, Alan M.
Muddimer, Hazel M.
Sermersheim, Michael D.
Stanson, Richard S.
Webb, James R.

Developer
Arthur, James William
Buchholzer, Richard B.
Helms, Donald W.
Higgins, Alan M.
Weinberger, Edward

Engineer
Verghese, Daniel

Instructor
Helms, Donald W.
Higgins, Alan M.
Litka, Michael P.
Ruport, Scott H.
Webb, James R.

Owner/Investor
Arthur, James William
Buchholzer, Richard B.
Cleminshaw, John G.
Helms, Donald W.
Higgins, Alan M.
Kalavity, Louis
Litka, Michael P.
Muddimer, Hazel M.
Verghese, Daniel

Property Manager
Arthur, James William
Behn, G.E.
Cleminshaw, John G.
Davis, Clifford L.
Helms, Donald W.
Higgins, Alan M.
Meadows, Glenn H.
Nicholson, Paul
Smith, Paul J.
Stanson, Richard S.

Real Estate Publisher
Litka, Michael P.

Syndicator
Muddimer, Hazel M.

ATHENS

Appraiser
Le Master, Harry A.

Attorney
Fields, William A.

Banker
Le Master, Harry A.

Lender
Le Master, Harry A.

CANTON

Attorney
Cope, Leland H.
Shifman, Arnold R.

Broker
Anderson, Jerry D.
Tyler, Frederick C. Jr.

Consultant
Anderson, Jerry D.

Developer
Cope, Leland H.

Instructor
Anderson, Jerry D.

Owner/Investor
Anderson, Jerry D.
Cope, Leland H.

Property Manager
Cope, Leland H.
Cummins, J.P.
Gloss, Paul H.
Neptune, C.A.
Schlitz, R.J.
Tyler, Frederick C. Jr.
Whipp, Donald

Real Estate Publisher
Anderson, Jerry D.

CHILLICOTHE

Builder
Newman, Robert A.

Consultant
Newman, Robert A.

Developer
Newman, Robert A.
Shaevitz, Robert M.
Stapleton, Robert J.

Lender
Newman, Robert A.

Owner/Investor
Newman, Robert A.
Shaevitz, Robert M.

Property Manager
Shaevitz, Robert M.

Syndicator
Shaevitz, Robert M.

CINCINNATI

Appraiser
Barnhorn, C. Barry
Condorodis, A. John
Fiehler, Thomas L.
Garfield, M. Robert
Haley, James L.
Johnson, Roger
Mathias, Ray Kermit
Mayer, Albert J. III
O'Donnell, Donald L.
Pottner, M. Richard
Wartman, Clifford J. Jr.

Architect
Myers, Russell C.
Overberg, Robert A.

Attorney
Anderson, John Mackenzie
Bennett, Charles Kirby
Beste, James D.
Bowman, James S.
Fischer, John W.
Goodman, Larry L.
Harwood, David J.
Katsanis, James A.
McMahon, Douglas
Meckstroth, John R.
Monnie, Terrance R.
Peck, John Weld
Perry, Paul E.
Porter, Robert C. III
Randolph, Daniel P.
Rosenberg, Jay A.
Steman, Robert E.
Strauss, William V.
Weinberger, Leo

Banker
Bedell, Frank A.
Bennett, Charles Kirby
Phelps, C. Edward
Thiemann, Charles Lee

Broker
Barnhorn, C. Barry
Bedell, Frank A.
Bellucci, Robert
Condorodis, A. John
Daniels, Walter C.
Dietz, Rowland
Droesch, David W.
Garfield, M. Robert
Haley, James L.
Johnson, Roger
Kelly, Robert H.
Lunsford, Walter B.
Mathias, Ray Kermit
Mayer, Albert J. III
O'Donnell, Donald L.
Overberg, Robert A.
Straus, Stanley S.
Withers, William P. Jr.
Younker Eunice M.
Zech, William F. Jr.

Builder
Barnhorn, C. Barry
Bortz, Neil K.
Calkins, Chet
Condorodis, A. John
Mathias, Ray Kermit
Mayer, Albert J. III
Monnie, Terrance R.
Overberg, Robert A.
Penn, Christopher H.

Consultant
Barnhorn, C. Barry
Bellucci, Robert
Berning, Paul E.
Condorodis, A. John
Daniels, Walter C.
Dietz, Rowland
Droesch, David W.
Edwards, Roger A.
Garfield, M. Robert
Haley, James L.
Hood, James V.
Kelly, Robert H.
Mathias, Ray Kermit
Mayer, Albert J. III
Mizrachi, Joseph
Overberg, Robert A.
Penn, Christopher H.
Pottner, M. Richard
Schimpff, Thomas F. Jr.

Developer
Anderson, R. Bruce
Barnhorn, C. Barry
Beste, James D.
Bortz, Neil K.
Carroll, James J.
Condorodis, A. John
Daniels, Walter C.
Lutz, W. Kent
Mayer, Albert J. III
Mayer, Theodore A.
Moran, John J.
Overberg, Robert A.
Penn, Christopher H.
Wimberg, James J.
Withers, William P. Jr.
Zech, William F. Jr.

Instructor
Garfield, M. Robert
Kelly, Robert H.
Mayer, Albert J. III
Monnie, Terrance R.
Overberg, Robert A.
Perry, Paul E.
Redman, Arnold L.
Younker Eunice M.

Insuror
Barnhorn, C. Barry
Lunsford, Walter B.
Mizrachi, Joseph

Lender
Fiehler, Thomas L.
Phelps, C. Edward
Wimberg, James J.

Owner/Investor
Anderson, R. Bruce
Barnhorn, C. Barry
Berning, Paul E.
Bortz, Neil K.
Bowman, James S.
Calkins, Chet
Condorodis, A. John
Daniels, Walter C.
Hood, James V.
Lutz, W. Kent
Mathias, Ray Kermit
Mayer, Theodore A.
Mizrachi, Joseph
Monnie, Terrance R.
O'Donnell, Donald L.
Overberg, Robert A.
Penn, Christopher H.
Younker Eunice M.

Property Manager
Anderson, R. Bruce
Annekan, William
Bedell, Frank A.
Bortz, Neil K.
Bowman, James S.
Calkins, Chet
Condorodis, A. John
Daniels, Walter C.
Dautel, Charles S.
Dietz, Rowland
Doerger, Gerald L.
Droesch, David W.
Friedman, Penny
Garfield, M. Robert
Kisker, George
Lunsford, Walter B.
Lutz, W. Kent
Marcus, David
Mayer, Albert J. III
Mayer, Theodore A.
O'Donnell, Donald L.
Overberg, Robert A.
Scheidler, Donald
Schimpff, Thomas F. Jr.
Shull, James
Trennepohl, Jim
Wartman, Clifford J. Jr.
Withers, William P. Jr.
Zech, William F. Jr.

Syndicator
Anderson, R. Bruce
Barnhorn, C. Barry
Bellucci, Robert
Bortz, Neil K.
Carroll, James J.
Condorodis, A. John
Dietz, Rowland
Mayer, Albert J. III
Mayer, Theodore A.
Mizrachi, Joseph
Monnie, Terrance R.
O'Donnell, Donald L.
Overberg, Robert A.
Penn, Christopher H.
Withers, William P. Jr.

CLEVELAND

Appraiser
Brooke, Barton E. Jr.
Dondorfer, C. H.
Ellis, F. Ross
Felder, Bruce B.
Gillinov, Lynda J.
Hartigan, Thomas J.
Hilyard, David C.
Kaplan, William
Kell, Lawrence A.
Korom, Steve
Lickel, George R.
Lynch, Dennis J.
Miclau, Daniel C.
Ritley, Roger D.
Sliwinski, Teddy

Architect
Bregar, Robert J.
Mifsud, Paul Charles

Attorney
Arnold, William L.
Bates, G. Del
Belden, Thomas G.
Breznai, Theodore A.
Chapman, Howard Stephen
Chilcote, Lee A. Jr.
Crane, Edward H.
Davidson, Edward J.
Donahue, Charles B III
Gutmacher, Norman William
Hollander, Sherman S.
Jones, Fred C.
Kaplan, William
Lapine, Kenneth M.
Loewenthal, Marc S.
Mason, Thomas A.
Miclau, Daniel C.
Mille, Dennis G.
Newman, Clifton
Obloy, Stanley J.
Prayson, Richard A.
Rosenzweig, David L.
Rosewater, Robert David
Roudebush, George M.
Shah, Indrawadan K.
Sherman, Dennis H.
Sicherman, Marvin Allen
Slavin, Thomas P.
Sliwinski, Teddy
Sogg, Wilton S.
Stotter, Morton M.
Sweeney, David M.
Terpenning, Walter A.
Waldeck, John W. Jr.
Williams, Lawrence H.
Wolstein, Scott A.

Banker
Christopolis, Nicholas V.
Drake, Richard W.
Sweeney, David M.

Broker
Adler, Thomas W.
Benjamin, Roger E.
Boldizar, Frank J.
Brooke, Barton E. Jr.
Chapman, Howard Stephen
Dondorfer, C. H.
English, Leonard M.
Gerent, Harry R.
Hilyard, David C.
Kaplan, William
Kaval, James A.
Kell, Lawrence A.
Korom, Steve
Kortier, Richard G.
Lang, Tom H.
Lynch, Dennis J.
Nilges, David C.
Persiano, Patricia A.
Sliwinski, Teddy
Stone, David E.
Westbrook, Edward G.
Wiesenberger, Steven R.

Builder
Davis, Jeffrey S.
Dondorfer, C. H.
English, Leonard M.
Fogg, Raymon B.
Gerent, Harry R.
Korom, Steve
Kortier, Richard G.
Stucker, Gilles A.E.

Consultant
Adler, Thomas W.
Breznai, Theodore A.
Brooke, Barton E. Jr.
Cik, Barry A.
Dalcolma, Thomas William
Dondorfer, C. H.
English, Leonard M.
Hartigan, Thomas J.
Hilyard, David C.
Kaplan, William
Kaval, James A.
Kell, Lawrence A.
Korom, Steve
Kortier, Richard G.
Lang, Tom H.
Lynch, Dennis J.
Mifsud, Paul Charles
Nilges, David C.
Persiano, Patricia A.
Ritley, Roger D.
Shah, Indrawadan K.
Sliwinski, Teddy
Stone, David E.
Sturges, Michael
Westbrook, Edward G.
Wiesenberger, Steven R.
Wolstein, Scott A.

Developer
Adler, Thomas W.
Benjamin, Roger E.
Brooke, Barton E. Jr.
Chapman, Howard Stephen
Cik, Barry A.
Dalcolma, Thomas William
Davis, Jeffrey S.
Dondorfer, C. H.
Fogg, Kathy
Fogg, Raymon B.
Friedman, Stanford J.
Gerent, Harry R.
Kohut, William
Lang, Tom H.
Mavec, Bruce V.
Miclau, Daniel C.
Mifsud, Paul Charles
Roudebush, George M.
Slavin, Thomas P.
Sliwinski, Teddy
Stucker, Gilles A.E.
Voinovich, Victor S.
Westbrook, Edward G.
Wiesenberger, Steven R.
Wyse, Jack J.

Engineer
Chilcote, Lee A. Jr.
Cik, Barry A.
Fogg, Raymon B.
Kohut, William
Kolpien, James K.
Lombardo, John J.
Rundell, Richard F.
Sherman, Dennis H.
Will, Robert A.

Instructor
Adler, Thomas W.
Breznai, Theodore A.
English, Leonard M.
Gerent, Harry R.
Gillinov, Lynda J.
Korom, Steve
Lapine, Kenneth M.
Nilges, David C.
Persiano, Patricia A.
Shah, Indrawadan K.
Sliwinski, Teddy
Sogg, Wilton S.
Stone, David E.

Insuror
Breznai, Theodore A.
Lombardo, John J.
Shah, Indrawadan K.

Lender
Bates, G. Del
Christopolis, Nicholas V.
Kortier, Richard G.
Nilges, David C.
Tozer, A. Ray

Owner/Investor
Adler, Thomas W.
Bates, G. Del
Boldizar, Frank J.
Brooke, Barton E. Jr.
Crane, Edward H.
Davis, Jeffrey S.
Dondorfer, C. H.
Gerent, Harry R.
Kaplan, William
Kaval, James A.
Korom, Steve
Kortier, Richard G.
Lang, Tom H.
Lapine, Kenneth M.
Lynch, Dennis J.
Miclau, Daniel C.
Mille, Dennis G.
Newman, Clifton
Persiano, Patricia A.
Roudebush, George M.
Slavin, Thomas P.
Sliwinski, Teddy
Stucker, Gilles A.E.
Tozer, A. Ray
Westbrook, Edward G.
Wiesenberger, Steven R.
Wolstein, Scott A.
Wyse, Jack J.

Property Manager
Benjamin, Roger E.
Bishop, Curtis L.
Boldizar, Frank J.
Bradley, Jeffrey
Britton, Robert
Buzek, Ken
Charlton, Steven L.
Davis, Jeffrey S.
Dondorfer, C. H.
English, Leonard M.
Every, Russell B.
Fittipaldi, Frank N.
Fogg, Kathy
Gabalac, Frank
Hartigan, Thomas J.
Hatch, Henry R.
Hilyard, David C.
Jacob, Robert
Johnson, Roland F.
Kirkoff, J.B.
Kolpien, James K.
Korom, Steve
Kortier, Richard G.
Lapine, Kenneth M.
Libicki, Henry
Lohrman, John J.
Lynch, Dennis J.
Mackay, Malcolm
Madden, John E.
Miclau, Daniel C.
Mifsud, Paul Charles
Nilges, David C.
Obloy, Stanley J.
Rosenthal, Leighton A.
Roudebush, George M.
Rundell, Richard F.
Schupe, H.E.
Senz, John
Shega, Frank A.
Slavin, Thomas P.
Stucker, Gilles A.E.
Summers, Lorraine A.
Thoburn, J.W.
Thompson, John
Tomlinson, Allan J.
Uhler, Bob
Welsh, William E.
Wiesenberger, Steven R.
Wyman, Morton

Real Estate Publisher
Brennan, Robert F.
Nilges, David C.
Shah, Indrawadan K.

Syndicator
Boldizar, Frank J.
Brooke, Barton E. Jr.
Dondorfer, C. H.
Gerent, Harry R.
Kaval, James A.
Lapine, Kenneth M.
Lynch, Dennis J.
Mille, Dennis G.
Slavin, Thomas P.
Sliwinski, Teddy
Sogg, Wilton S.
Westbrook, Edward G.
Wolstein, Scott A.

COLUMBUS

Appraiser
Burns, Donald A.
Claggett, Lewis E.
Garvin, John R.
Henderson, R. Stephen
Horn, Larry E.
Kaliker, Thomas J.
Lindberg, Craig J.
Littlejohn, Jean C.
Michel, James C.
Mollica, Anthony F.
Neff, Cecil L.
O'Neil, Daniel R.

Architect
Kirk, Ballard H. T.
Pickett, James V.

Attorney
Baker, David Guy
Barrett, Phillip H.
Burchfield, James Ralph
Carton, Thomas W. Jr.
Coen, George W.
Davis, Gary E.
Edwards, James A.
Kuehnle, Kenton L.
Lane, William M.
McMahon, Brian Neill
Meagher, William D. II
Stearns, Richard D.
Sully, Ira Bennett
Tishman, Donald H.

Banker
Steinman, David W.

Broker
Adorno, Robert A.
Bernstein, Jack W.
Burns, Donald A.
Claggett, Lewis E.
Denmead, Robert G.
Fritsche, Ernest G.
Garvin, John R.
Henderson, R. Stephen
Holmes, Phillip H.
Horn, Larry E.
Hoyt, Lawrence F.
Kahn, Steven M.
Katz, Dean Z.
Lindberg, Craig J.
McMenamy, William C. Jr.
Michel, James C.
Neff, Cecil L.
O'Neil, Daniel R.
Pickett, James V.
Rook, James F.
Smith, Roger L.
Trembly, William H. Jr.
White, H.M. Jr.
Wilcox, James L.
Wolfe, Derrill E.

Builder
Adorno, Robert A.
Clark, Russell W.
Eberhart, Laurence L.
Fritsche, Ernest G.
Gentile, Anthony R.
Holmes, Phillip H.
Johnson, Charles R.
Kirk, Ballard H. T.
Maclean, H. Grant
Pickett, James V.
Steinfels, Victor E. III
Visconti, Lawrence B.
White, H.M. Jr.

Consultant
Burns, Donald A.
Claggett, Lewis E.
Denmead, Robert G.
Eberhart, Laurence L.
Garvin, John R.
Gentile, Anthony R.
Holmes, Phillip H.
Hoyt, Lawrence F.
Hughes, George G.
Jennings, James M.
Kahn, Steven M.
Katz, Dean Z.
Kirk, Ballard H. T.
Lindberg, Craig J.
McMahon, Brian Neill
McMenamy, William C. Jr.
Mollica, Anthony F.
Neff, Cecil L.
Rayl, John E.
Sebastian, James J.
Smith, Roger L.
Stalker, Hobart C.
Steinfels, Victor E. III
Visconti, Lawrence B.

Developer
Adorno, Robert A.
Ashton, George T.
Claggett, Lewis E.
Clark, Russell W.
Eberhart, Laurence L.
Fritsche, Ernest G.
Gentile, Anthony R.
Holmes, Phillip H.
Hughes, George G.
Johnson, Charles R.
Kahn, Steven M.
Kass, Franklin E.
Kirk, Ballard H. T.
Maclean, H. Grant
McMenamy, William C. Jr.
O'Brien, Daniel M.
O'Neill, John J.
Pickett, James V.
Sebastian, James J.
Smith, Roger L.
Stearns, Richard D.
Steinfels, Victor E. III
Tishman, Donald H.
Trembly, William H. Jr.
Visconti, Lawrence B.
Waring, Glenn H.

Engineer
Eberhart, Laurence L.
Gentile, Anthony R.

Instructor
Bomhard, Richard O.
Horn, Larry E.
Hoyt, Lawrence F.
Jennings, James M.
Michel, James C.
Steinfels, Victor E. III

Insuror
Burchfield, James Ralph
Claggett, Lewis E.

Lender
Cooper, R. Jack
Eberhart, Laurence L.
Gugle, George L. III
Smith, Peter A.
Stalker, Hobart C.

Owner/Investor
Bernstein, Jack W.
Burchfield, James Ralph
Claggett, Lewis E.
Clark, Russell W.
Cooper, R. Jack
Denmead, Robert G.
Eberhart, Laurence L.
Fritsche, Ernest G.
Gentile, Anthony R.
Henderson, R. Stephen
Holmes, Phillip H.
Horn, Larry E.
Hughes, George G.
Jennings, James M.
Kahn, Steven M.
Kass, Franklin E.
Katz, Dean Z.
Maclean, H. Grant
McMenamy, William C. Jr.
McVay, Tom D.
Michel, James C.
Neff, Cecil L.
O'Neil, Daniel R.
Pickett, James V.
Robertson, Joseph C.
Smith, Roger L.
Stalker, Hobart C.
Steinfels, Victor E. III
Wilcox, James L.

Property Manager
Adorno, Robert A.
Bartlett, L.R. Sr.
Berman, Arnold
Bernstein, Jack W.
Clark, Russell W.
Eberhart, Laurence L.
Feldshue, Alan M.
Fritsche, Ernest G.
Gentile, Anthony R.
Henderson, R. Stephen
Holmes, Phillip H.
Horn, Larry E.
Hoyt, Lawrence F.
Hughes, George G.
Kahn, Steven M.
Kass, Franklin E.
Lindberg, Craig J.
Londeree, Joseph W.
McClenaghan, Charles
Maclean, H. Grant
McMenamy, William C. Jr.
Michel, James C.
O'Brien, Daniel M.
O'Neil, Daniel R.
Pickett, James V.
Reitz, Elmer A.
Rook, James F.
Smith, Roger L.
Stalker, Hobart C.
Stegmeyer, Joseph
Steinfels, Victor E. III
Trembly, William H. Jr.
Watson, Robert
Wolfe, Derrill E.

Real Estate Publisher
Hughes, George G.

Regulator
Jennings, James M.

Syndicator
Claggett, Lewis E.
Clark, Russell W.
Eberhart, Laurence L.
Holmes, Phillip H.
Hoyt, Lawrence F.
Hughes, George G.

Kirk, Ballard H. T.
McMenamy, William C. Jr.
Meagher, William D. II
O'Neil, Daniel R.
Rayl, John E.
Wilcox, James L.

DAYTON

Appraiser
Hellmuth, Andrew P.
Hemry, Richard M.
Marlowe, Earl S.
Pitstick, Jerry W.
Preston, Richard L.
Schaffer, Arnold C.
Stout, Donald E.
Welsh, Thomas

Architect
Klein, Lewis D.
Lecklider, Robert W.

Attorney
Ebert, Larry P.
Horn, Ralph D.
Lubow, Howard
Platt, Gordon L.
Singer, Harold
Wilson, Thomas W.

Banker
Subler, Betty L.

Broker
Baltes, Terry
Duberstein, James S.
Edwards, H. William
Fornes, Mark S.
Hellmuth, Andrew P.
Hemry, Richard M.
Lowry, Edward F.
Lubow, Howard
McDorman, Max
McVety, William F.
Marlowe, Earl S.
Pitstick, Jerry W.
Platt, Gordon L.
Schaffer, Arnold C.
Singer, Harold
Stout, Donald E.
Welsh, Thomas

Builder
Arndts, Jerome Theodore
Berner, Robert M.
Daoud, George J.
Edwards, H. William
McDaniel, Robert E.
McVety, William F.
Martens, Barry J.
Miller, Gerald
Platt, Gordon L.
Schaffer, Arnold C.
Singer, Harold
Smith, Lamar E.
Summe, Mark
Weir, R.L.
Welsh, Thomas

Consultant
Daoud, George J.
Duberstein, James S.
Ebert, Larry P.
Edwards, H. William
Hellmuth, Andrew P.
Hemry, Richard M.
Horn, Ralph D.
Lubow, Howard
McDaniel, Robert E.
Martens, Barry J.
Pitstick, Jerry W.
Platt, Gordon L.
Stout, Donald E.
Weir, R.L.

Developer
Baltes, Terry
Berner, Robert M.
Daoud, George J.
Ebert, Larry P.
Edwards, H. William
Fornes, Mark S.
Friedman, Robert N.
Frydman, Ronald
Hellmuth, Andrew P.
Horn, Ralph D.
Klein, Lewis D.
Lowry, Edward F.
McDaniel, Robert E.
McVety, William F.
Martens, Barry J.
Miller, Gerald
Miller, James M.
Platt, Gordon L.
Schaffer, Arnold C.
Singer, Harold
Smith, Lamar E.
Stout, Donald E.
Summe, Mark
Weir, R.L.
Welsh, Thomas

Engineer
Arndts, Jerome Theodore
Edwards, H. William

Instructor
Edwards, H. William
Hemry, Richard M.
Lubow, Howard
Marlowe, Earl S.

Insuror
Hellmuth, Andrew P.
Singer, Harold

Lender
Moyer, Richard A.
Platt, Gordon L.
Subler, Betty L.

Owner/Investor
Baltes, Terry
Berner, Robert M.
Daoud, George J.
Ebert, Larry P.
Edwards, H. William
Hellmuth, Andrew P.
Horn, Ralph D.
Klein, Lewis D.
Lowry, Edward F.
McDaniel, Robert E.
Marlowe, Earl S.
Martens, Barry J.
Miller, Gerald
Miller, James M.
Platt, Gordon L.
Schaffer, Arnold C.
Singer, Harold
Stout, Donald E.
Summe, Mark

Property Manager
Bernd, Robert
Bertram, Dennis
Blake, Jack
Daoud, George J.
Haley, John
Heiner, Hal
Hellmuth, Andrew P.
Hines, Bruce
Horn, Ralph D.
Lowry, Edward F.
Marlowe, Earl S.
Martens, Barry J.
Miller, James M.
Pitstick, Jerry W.
Platt, Gordon L.
Preston, Richard L.
Schaffer, Arnold C.
Siders, Ron
Singer, Harold
Smith, Lamar E.
Stayton, Jack
Stout, Donald E.
Summe, Mark
Treffinger, James

Real Estate Publisher
Edwards, H. William

Syndicator
Daoud, George J.
Duberstein, James S.
Horn, Ralph D.
Platt, Gordon L.
Welsh, Thomas

LIMA

Architect
Fanning, Ronald H.

Attorney
Sutton, J.H.
Weaver, Robert B.
Yogi, Nolan K.

Broker
Lacy, Jerrill L.
Schomaeker, James B.

Builder
Lacy, Jerrill L.

Developer
Fanning, Ronald H.
Lacy, Jerrill L.

Engineer
Fanning, Ronald H.

Instructor
Schomaeker, James B.

Owner/Investor
Fanning, Ronald H.
Lacy, Jerrill L.

Property Manager
Fanning, Ronald H.
Lacy, Jerrill L.
Schomaeker, James B.
Spears, W.E.
Sutton, J.H.

Syndicator
Fanning, Ronald H.
Lacy, Jerrill L.

MANSFIELD

Appraiser
Dixon, John E.
Runbaugh, Thomas N.

Attorney
Bur, William H.

Broker
Runbaugh, Thomas N.

Consultant
Bur, William H.

Owner/Investor
Dixon, John E.

Property Manager
Dixon, John E.
Hickox, Charles
Runbaugh, Thomas N.

TOLEDO

Appraiser
O'Connor, Patrick M.

Architect
Mull, Melvin Henry
Sorgen, Richard Jesse

Assessor
O'Connor, Patrick M.

Attorney
Bobowick, Morton
Brown, Charles Earl
Carroll, Donald R.
Crowley, John
Nelson, Jeffrey Alan
Rankin, Michael
Webb, Thomas I.
Welly, Robert H.

Banker
Carroll, Donald R.
Hampton, Carl L.

Broker
Roof, William H.
Rudes, George H.
Ryan, Robert L.
Zyndorf, Mark

Consultant
Aggarwal, R.
Roof, William H.
Welly, Robert H.
Zyndorf, Mark

Developer
Mull, Melvin Henry
Zyndorf, Mark

Engineer
Killen, Richard D.

Instructor
Aggarwal, R.
O'Connor, Patrick M.

Insuror
Rudes, George H.

Lender
Aggarwal, R.
Hampton, Carl L.

Owner/Investor
Greeley, Larry
Killen, Richard D.
Mull, Melvin Henry
Roof, William H.
Zyndorf, Mark

Property Manager
Brannan, Hugh
Carroll, Donald R.
Crook, Richard Jr.
Crowley, John
Esterline, Jerrold
Gominger, George W.
Killen, Richard D.
Piel, Theodore F.
Rankin, Michael
Recktenwald, R.J.
Roof, William H.
Wellner, John

Syndicator
Roof, William H.

YOUNGSTOWN

Appraiser
Foskie, Bryan F.
Michetti, Mark
Pestrak, Walter

Attorney
Burdman, B. Richard
Daniluk, Daniel
Galip, Ronald
Richards, Lawrence H.
Sweeney, John W.

Broker
Foskie, Bryan F.
Michetti, Mark
Pestrak, Walter
Richards, Lawrence H.

Builder
Biel, Howard Steven
Gronvall, John
Michetti, Mark

Consultant
Burdman, B. Richard
Michetti, Mark
Ryther, A. Harold Jr.

Developer
Biel, Howard Steven
Burdman, B. Richard
Malasky, Donald C.
Michetti, Mark
Sweeney, John W.

Instructor
Foskie, Bryan F.
Ryther, A. Harold Jr.

Insuror
Pestrak, Walter

Owner/Investor
Biel, Howard Steven
Burdman, B. Richard
Gronvall, John
Kessler, Sandford J.
Malasky, Donald C.
Michetti, Mark
Sweeney, John W.

Property Manager
Biel, Howard Steven
Cushwa, William
Gronvall, John
King, Francis
Malasky, Donald C.
Ryther, A. Harold Jr.
Tyler, John F.

Syndicator
Gronvall, John

ZANESVILLE

Broker
Darr, Audrey E.

Owner/Investor
Darr, Audrey E.

Property Manager
Darr, Audrey E.

Syndicator
Darr, Audrey E.

OKLAHOMA

DURANT

Appraiser
Guthrie, Mark G.

Consultant
Guthrie, Mark G.

Owner/Investor
Guthrie, Mark G.

ENID

Attorney
McIlvain, Alan Max

Owner/Investor
McIlvain, Alan Max

LAWTON

Appraiser
LaPointe, Merle L.

Attorney
Curtis, David M.

Broker
LaPointe, Merle L.
Murphy, George M.

Consultant
Curtis, David M.

Instructor
LaPointe, Merle L.

Insuror
LaPointe, Merle L.

Owner/Investor
Curtis, David M.

Property Manager
Curtis, David M.
LaPointe, Merle L.
Murphy, George M.

MUSKOGEE

Appraiser
Eversole, Otis H.
Gill, Harpal S.

Broker
Gill, Harpal S.

Owner/Investor
Gill, Harpal S.

Property Manager
Gill, Harpal S.

OKLAHOMA CITY

Appraiser
Alleman, Bruce E.
Cox, Hollis R.
Glenn, Patrick O.
Gollaher, Raymond Clifford
Jones, J. Michael
Kohlhepp, Daniel B.
McLean, W.E. "Bud"
Nichols, Wm. Frederick
O'Neill, Jamie
Schurger, David L. Jr.
Stallings, William Ralph
Swickey, James B.

Attorney
Casey, Patrick Jon
Conner, Leslie L. Jr.
Duffy, Mark Alan
Epperson, Kraettli Q.
Farha, George S.
Hill, Frank D.
Johnson, Robert M.
Legg, William J.
Roberts, John Perry
Thom, Michael William
Williams, John Michael
Wilson, Michael R.

Banker
Reynolds, Paul G. Jr.
Swickey, James B.

Broker
Alleman, Bruce E.
Carlile, Linda Lee
Cox, Hollis R.
Duffner, C. E.
Farha, George S.
Gamble, Gerald L.
Geis, Joseph R.
Gilliam, Larry L.
Glenn, Patrick O.
Gollaher, Raymond Clifford
Jones, J. Michael
Kohlhepp, Daniel B.
Nichols, Wm. Frederick
O'Neill, Jamie
Parker, James E.
Pons, Albert E.
Schrouf, M. H.
Schurger, David L. Jr.
Sheriff, Fred A.
Stallings, William Ralph
Swanson, Lawrence N. (Larry)
Sweetser, S. Chandler
Swickey, James B.
Tapp, F. Barry
Wiggin, Charles E.
Worster, Neil C.

Builder
Coury, A. Sam
Crout, Robert L.
Geis, Joseph R.
Gollaher, Raymond Clifford
Griffiths, O. Wayne
Jones, J. Michael
Kyle, Steve
Parker, James E.
Rodgers, Douglas E.
Schrouf, M. H.
Sweetser, S. Chandler
Tankersley, Brad M.

Consultant
Alleman, Bruce E.
Casey, Patrick Jon
Coury, A. Sam
Gamble, Gerald L.
Glenn, Patrick O.
Goggans, Travis P.
Gollaher, Raymond Clifford
Jones, J. Michael
Kohlhepp, Daniel B.
Nichols, Wm. Frederick
Parker, James E.
Pons, Albert E.
Rodgers, Douglas E.
Schurger, David L. Jr.
Sweetser, S. Chandler
Swickey, James B.
Tankersley, Brad M.
Tapp, F. Barry
Wernersbach, Dennis J.
Worster, Neil C.

Developer
Coury, A. Sam
Crout, Robert L.
Duffner, C. E.
Farha, George S.
Geis, Joseph R.
Glenn, Patrick O.
Gollaher, Raymond Clifford
Griffiths, O. Wayne
Halloran, Leo B.
Hill, Neil
Jones, J. Michael
Kerr, W. Bruce
Kohlhepp, Daniel B.
McLean, W.E. "Bud"
Parker, James E.
Pons, Albert E.
Rodgers, Douglas E.
Schrouf, M. H.
Schurger, David L. Jr.
Sweetser, S. Chandler
Swickey, James B.
Tankersley, Brad M.
Tapp, F. Barry
Wiggin, Charles E.

Instructor
Cox, Hollis R.
Geis, Joseph R.
Gollaher, Raymond Clifford
Jones, J. Michael
Kohlhepp, Daniel B
O'Neill, Jamie
Pons, Albert E.
Schurger, David L. Jr.

Insuror
Fillmore, Tom D.

Lender
Alleman, Bruce E.
Gollaher, Raymond Clifford
Reynolds, Paul G. Jr.
Swickey, James B.
Tankersley, Brad M.

Owner/Investor
Alleman, Bruce E.
Booth, John N.
Carlile, Linda Lee
Casey, Patrick Jon
Conner, Leslie L. Jr.
Coury, A. Sam
Cox, Hollis R.
Crout, Robert L.
Duffner, C. E.
Farha, George S.
Gajjar, Navin J.
Geis, Joseph R.
Goggans, Travis P.
Gollaher, Raymond Clifford
Jones, J. Michael
Kerr, W. Bruce
Kohlhepp, Daniel B.
Kyle, Steve
Parker, James E.
Pons, Albert E.
Rodgers, Douglas E.
Schrouf, M. H.
Schurger, David L. Jr.
Stallings, William Ralph
Swanson, Lawrence N. (Larry)
Sweetser, S. Chandler
Swickey, James B.
Tankersley, Brad M.
Tapp, F. Barry
Wernersbach, Dennis J.
Wiggin, Charles E.
Wilson, Michael R.
Worster, Neil C.

Property Manager
Alleman, Bruce E.
Alleman, Bruce E.
Case, Charles
Coury, A. Sam
Cox, Hollis R.
Duffner, C. E.
Farha, George S.
Fillmore, Tom D.
Gajjar, Navin J.
Geis, Joseph R.
Goggans, Travis P.
Gollaher, Raymond Clifford
Jones, J. Michael
Kerr, W. Bruce
McLean, W.E. "Bud"
O'Neill, Jamie
Parker, James E.
Pons, Albert E.
Schrouf, M. H.
Schurger, David L. Jr.
Steward, Wendell
Sweetser, S. Chandler
Swickey, James B.
Swisher, Wm.
Talbert, James R. III
Tankersley, Brad M.
Tapp, F. Barry
Wernersbach, Dennis J.
Worster, Neil C.

Real Estate Publisher
Goggans, Travis P.
Gollaher, Raymond Clifford

Syndicator
Coury, A. Sam
Crout, Robert L.
Gajjar, Navin J.
Gollaher, Raymond Clifford
Jones, J. Michael
Pons, Albert E.
Rodgers, Douglas E.
Schurger, David L. Jr.
Swanson, Lawrence N. (Larry)
Sweetser, S. Chandler
Swickey, James B.
Worster, Neil C.

PONCA CITY

Appraiser
Sturdevant, Dick

Broker
Sturdevant, Dick

Consultant
Sturdevant, Dick

Developer
Sturdevant, Dick

Owner/Investor
Sturdevant, Dick

TULSA

Appraiser
Dorchester, John D. Jr.
Eversole, Otis H. Jr.
Holloway, William B.
Reidy, Martin J.
Rich, David
Richert, William F.
Schmook, J. Lynn
Sloan, Jim
Steele, William L.
Story, John Jr.
Whited, S. Wayne

Architect
Butcher, Donald P.

Attorney
Barker, John R.
Cameron, Donald D.
Ellison, Kenneth C.
Eversole, Otis H. Jr.
Fischbein, Carl
Hird, Kenneth L.
Jordan, Kevin Lynn
Nichols, Robert John
Strenkowski, Edward A.
Williams, Gerald G.

Banker
Burns, Barry C.
Schmook, J. Lynn

Broker
Cleveland, Newcomb
Collins, Michael D.
Easley, George W. Jr.
Emery, Patrick G.
Everage, Gordon L.
Eversole, Otis H. Jr.
Hill, Victor J. CPM
Holloway, William B.
Kelley, Larry K.
Morrisett, H. Dallas
Moskowitz, Frank D.
Moskowitz, Rita J.
Parrish, Michael R.
Poe, Robert C.
Porter, Geraldine L.
Rich, David
Richert, William F.
Romine, Christopher
Sloan, Jim
Steele, William L.
Story, John Jr.
Wiles, William Montgomery

Builder
Butcher, Donald P.
Everage, Gordon L.
Henshaw, N.D.
Kettles, L. Christopher
Poe, Robert C.
Porter, Geraldine L.
Rich, David
Romine, Christopher
Sloan, Jim

Consultant
Archer, Heber
Dorchester, John D. Jr.
Eversole, Otis H. Jr.
Fischbein, Carl
Hill, Victor J.
Holloway, William B.
Kelley, Larry K.
Morrisett, H. Dallas
Poe, Robert C.
Rich, David
Richert, William F.
Romine, Christopher
Schmook, J. Lynn
Wiles, William Montgomery

Developer
Brodsky, Avrom D.
Cleveland, Newcomb
Emery, Patrick G.
Henshaw, N.D.
Henson, E. Eddie
Hill, Victor J.
Jordan, Kevin Lynn
Kelley, Larry K.
Kettles, L. Christopher
McLane, Gregory A.
Morrisett, H. Dallas
Moskowitz, Frank D.
Poe, Robert C.
Rich, David
Wiles, William Montgomery
Wynn, Marvin L.

Engineer
Holloway, William B.

Instructor
Dorchester, John D. Jr.
Everage, Gordon L.
Nichols, Robert John
Story, John Jr.

Insuror
Easley, George W. Jr.

Lender
Burns, Barry C.
Schmook, J. Lynn

Owner/Investor
Brodsky, Avrom D.
Dorchester, John D. Jr.
Fischbein, Carl
Henshaw, N.D.
Holloway, William B.
Kelley, Larry K.
Morrisett, H. Dallas
Moskowitz, Frank D.
Moskowitz, Rita J.
Poe, Robert C.
Reidy, Martin J.
Rich, David
Richert, William F.
Sloan, Jim
Steele, William L.
Wiles, William Montgomery

Property Manager
Alcouloumre, Hank
Brodsky, Avrom D.
Collins, Michael D.
Collins, M.L.
Grimm, James
Henson, E. Eddie
Hill, Victor J.
Holloway, William B.
Kelley, Larry K.
Kettles, L. Christopher
Malone, James
Mitchell, Bruce
Morrisett, H. Dallas
O'Neil, Peggy
Rich, David
Richert, William F.
Romine, Christopher
Sloan, Jim
Steele, William L.
Wagner, Donald L.

Syndicator
Holloway, William B.
Jordan, Kevin Lynn
Poe, Robert C.
Richert, William F.
Romine, Christopher
Sloan, Jim
Wiles, William Montgomery

WOODWARD

Attorney
Sparks, John O.

OREGON

BEND

Attorney
Cramer, William D.

Broker
Fiebick, Gary A.

Consultant
Fiebick, Gary A.

Developer
Fiebick, Gary A.

Instructor
Fiebick, Gary A.

EUGENE

Appraiser
Sorvaag, C.M.

Broker
Bucko, Lee
Burge, H. Stewart
Chandler, Dale O.
Haase, Dennis J.
Hays, William E.
Poppen, Robert A.
Russell, Roger S.
Schmaedick, Ronald Albert
Smith, Ben H.
Sorvaag, C.M.

Builder
Haase, Dennis J.
Johnson, Wayne L.
Leuck, Frank
Snoddy, Ken James Sr.

Consultant
Chandler, Dale O.
Johnson, Wayne L.
Russell, Roger S.
Smith, Ben H.
Snoddy, Ken James Sr.
Sorvaag, C.M.

Developer
Bucko, Lee
Burge, H. Stewart
Haase, Dennis J.
Hays, William E.
Johnson, Wayne L.
Leuck, Frank
Poppen, Robert A.
Richmond, F. Lynn
Snoddy, Ken James Sr.

Instructor
Hays, William E.
Russell, Roger S.
Schmaedick, Ronald Albert
Smith, Ben H.
Snoddy, Ken James Sr.

Insuror
Sibbald, James W.

Lender
Russell, Roger S.
Thornley, Robert M.

Owner/Investor
Bucko, Lee
Haase, Dennis J.
Hays, William E.
Johnson, Wayne L.
Leuck, Frank
Reingold, Jeffrey A.
Richmond, F. Lynn
Russell, Roger S.
Schmaedick, Ronald Albert
Smith, Ben H.
Snoddy, Ken James Sr.

Property Manager
Bucko, Lee
Burge, H. Stewart
Chandler, Dale O.
Hays, William E.
Johnson, Wayne L.
Leuck, Frank
Reingold, Jeffrey A.
Richmond, F. Lynn
Russell, Roger S.
Schmaedick, Ronald Albert
Snoddy, Ken James Sr.

Syndicator
Burge, H. Stewart
Haase, Dennis J.
Hays, William E.
Johnson, Wayne L.
Poppen, Robert A.
Russell, Roger S.
Thornley, Robert M.

KLAMATH FALLS

Broker
LeQuieu, Reginald R.

Consultant
LeQuieu, Reginald R.

Developer
LeQuieu, Reginald R.

Owner/Investor
LeQuieu, Reginald R.

MEDFORD

Broker
Lloyd, Dennis W.

Builder
Lloyd, Dennis W.

Consultant
Lloyd, Dennis W.

Developer
Lloyd, Dennis W.

Property Manager
Ransdell, Richard

PENDLETON

Attorney
Murgo, Rudy M.

PORTLAND

Appraiser
Bailey, Charles D.
Branan, Brock H.
Graeper, Michael R.
Hansen, George I.
Howard, Roy M.
Jordan, Patrick C.
Mehrer, Richard L.
Roberts, Gary L.
Samec, Donald G.
Smith, Stephen T.
Wakefield, W.C.
Weed, Haze H.L.
Woody, Ron

Architect
Graeper, Michael R.
Nelson, Lem V.
Yodogawa, Jiro

Attorney
Barragar, Harvey C.
Bauer, Henry L.

Berentson, David
Browning, Robert A.
Conklin, Robert B.
Cox, F. Kim
Dagle, C. Paul
Feuerstein, Howard Michael
Gibbon, John Thomas
Hanna, Harry M.
Hansen, George I.
Martinson, Stanley E.
Mize, Franklin H.
Rieke, Forrest N.
Ruttan, Charles D.
Schnitzer, Jordan D.
Tarlow, Arthur L.
Tish, Eugene C.
Voorhies, Peter G.
Yoakum, Vance W.

Banker
George, Robert
Hansen, George I.
Johnson, Ronald D.
Nelson, Lem V.
Orwick, Kenneth J.
Whitaker, Richard

Broker
Arden, Bruce
Bailey, Charles D.
Baker, James B.
Browning, Robert A.
Bullier, Albert R. Sr.
Bybee, Barney C.
Conklin, Robert B.
Dell, Marilyn
Douthit, David V.
Egelhoff, David C.
Goodman, Ronald David
Graeper, Michael R.
Hale, William W.
Headlee, William A.
Hering, J. Clayton
Johnson, Marshall J.
Lekas, Ernest Peter
Leslie, J. Millard
Lutz, Arthur A.
Meekcoms, Leon D.
Mehrer, Richard L.
Mimning, Gary C.
Morissette, Mimi
Osterhout, Clark N.
Records, John W.
Robbins, Donald K.
Rosenberg, Steve
Selling, John
Smith, Squier
Socolofsky, David B.
Stapp, William B.
Woodbury, Sidney F.
Woody, Ron

Builder
Angel, Joseph W.
Browning, Robert A.
Cook, David H.
Graeper, Michael R.
Iseri, C. Ernest
Jordan, Patrick C.
Lutz, Arthur A.
Nelson, Lem V.
Nussmeier, Donald K.
Reeves, Melvin H.
Schnitzer, Jordan D.
Standring, James D.

Consultant
Bailey, Charles D.
Baker, James B.
Branan, Brock H.
Bybee, Barney C.
Conklin, Robert B.
Dant, Robert M.
Graeper, Michael R.
Hale, William W.
Handy, Michael R.
Headlee, William A.
Howard, Roy M.
Johnson, Marshall J.
Leland, David C.
Lilly, Lauren C.
Meekcoms, Leon D.
Mehrer, Richard L.
Morissette, Mimi
Nelson, Lem V.
Records, John W.
Roberts, Gary L.
Selling, John
Smith, Stephen T.
Standring, James D.
Stapp, William B.
Whitaker, Richard
Woodbury, Sidney F.

Developer
Angel, Joseph W.
Baker, James B.
Boslough, Gary C.
Browning, Robert A.
Cook, David H.
Dant, Robert M.
Douthit, David V.
Durdel, Sonna M.
Edwards, Barry A.
Ellis, Delbert R.
Gibbon, John Thomas
Graeper, Michael R.
Hale, William W.
Headlee, William A.
Iseri, C. Ernest
Jordan, Patrick C.
Leland, David C.
Lutz, Arthur A.
Mehrer, Richard L.
Mimning, Gary C.
Morissette, Mimi
Nelson, Lem V.
Novack, Kenneth M.
Nussmeier, Donald K.
Reeves, Melvin H.
Rosenberg, Steve
Schnitzer, Jordan D.
Selling, John
Standring, James D.
Stapp, William B.
Whitaker, Richard
Yodogawa, Jiro

Engineer
Iseri, C. Ernest

Instructor
Dell, Marilyn
Goodman, Ronald David
Graeper, Michael R.
Handy, Michael R.
Lilly, Lauren C.
Meekcoms, Leon D.
Robbins, Donald K.
Samec, Donald G.
Selling, John
Whitaker, Richard

Insuror
Whitaker, Richard

Lender
Barry, Mark D.
Ellis, Delbert R.
George, Robert
Jordan, Patrick C.
Nelson, Lem V.
Nicholson, Kerry L.
Orwick, Kenneth J.
Stapp, William B.

Owner/Investor
Angel, Joseph W.
Browning, Robert A.
Conklin, Robert B.
Douthit, David V.
Edwards, Barry A.
Graeper, Michael R.
Hale, William W.
Handy, Michael R.
Headlee, William A.
Iseri, C. Ernest
Johnson, Marshall J.
Lutz, Arthur A.
Meekcoms, Leon D.
Morissette, Mimi
Nelson, Lem V.
Nicholson, Kerry L.
Novack, Kenneth M.
Nussmeier, Donald K.
Records, John W.
Rieke, Forrest N.
Robbins, Donald K.
Rosenberg, Steve
Schnitzer, Jordan D.
Selling, John
Standring, James D.
Stapp, William B.
Whitaker, Richard

Property Manager
Angel, Joseph W.
Bailey, Charles D.
Cone, Ray
Durdel, Sonna M.
Edwards, Barry A.
Graeper, Michael R.
Hale, William W.
Hansen, George I.
Haslach, Frank
Iseri, C. Ernest
Jordan, Patrick C.
Kane, Robert J.
Knodell, C.W.
Leslie, J. Millard
Lutz, Arthur A.
Mize, Franklin H.
Morissette, Mimi
Nelson, Lem V.
Nussmeier, Donald K.
Rieke, Forrest N.
Schnitzer, Jordan D.
Selling, John
Simpson, Lee
Smith, Squier
Snow, E. Ned
Stapp, William B.
Whelan, William
Williams, William G. II
Yoakum, Vance W.

Real Estate Publisher
Goodman, Ronald David
Robbins, Donald K.

Regulator
Hansen, George I.

Syndicator
Angel, Joseph W.
Conklin, Robert B.
Graeper, Michael R.
Hale, William W.
Johnson, Marshall J.
Lutz, Arthur A.
Meekcoms, Leon D.
Mehrer, Richard L.
Mimning, Gary C.
Morissette, Mimi
Nelson, Lem V.
Robbins, Donald K.

SALEM

Appraiser
Goss, Darr L.
Lienhard, Garry D.
Manning, Richard J.
Moeller, L. C. Dr.
Morgan, Norman R.

Architect
Costa, David Francis Jr.
Sinnard, Herbert R.

Assessor
Lienhard, Garry D.

Attorney
Krom, David B.
Minor, John Christopher

Banker
Sweeney, Timothy C.
Tripp, Russell W.

Broker
Dyer, W. Dale
Miller, Jack M.
Moeller, L. C. Dr.
Morgan, Norman R.
Royer, M.N.
Schall, John H.
Sjogren, Per H.
Sweeney, Timothy C.
Tripp, Russell W.
Warren, Douglas K.

Builder
Dyer, W. Dale
Manning, Richard J.
Miller, Jack M.
Morgan, Norman R.
Warren, Douglas K.

Consultant
Goss, Darr L.
Manning, Richard J.
Moeller, L. C. Dr.
Morgan, Norman R.
Royer, M.N.
Sinnard, Herbert R.
Sjogren, Per H.
Sweeney, Timothy C.

Developer
Dyer, W. Dale
Miller, Jack M.
Miller, Mark E.
Morgan, Norman R.
Reiman, Robert E.
Royer, M.N.
Sinnard, Herbert R.
Sjogren, Per H.
Warren, Douglas K.

Instructor
Lienhard, Garry D.
Minor, John Christopher
Sweeney, Timothy C.

Lender
Sweeney, Timothy C.

Owner/Investor
Manning, Richard J.
Miller, Jack M.
Miller, Mark E.
Minor, John Christopher
Moeller, L. C. Dr.
Morgan, Norman R.
Reiman, Robert E.
Sjogren, Per H.
Sweeney, Timothy C.
Warren, Douglas K.

Property Manager
Dyer, W. Dale
Gwinn, William
Miller, Jack M.
Miller, Mark E.
Morgan, Norman R.
Sweeney, Timothy C.

Syndicator
Miller, Jack M.
Miller, Mark E.
Morgan, Norman R.
Royer, M.N.
Sweeney, Timothy C.

PENNSYLVANIA

ALTOONA

Appraiser
Hoover, Andrew S.
Johnston, Richard J.
Rawlings, Jack

Assessor
Hoover, Andrew S.

Broker
Hoover, Andrew S.
Johnston, Richard J.
Rawlings, Jack

Consultant
Hoover, Andrew S.
Johnston, Richard J.
Rawlings, Jack

Instructor
Hoover, Andrew S.
Rawlings, Jack

Owner/Investor
Johnston, Richard J.

Property Manager
Johnston, Richard J.

BUTLER

Appraiser
Collins, Ralph V.

Architect
Rittelmann, P. Richard

Broker
Collins, Ralph V.

Consultant
Collins, Ralph V.

Developer
Rittelmann, P. Richard

Engineer
Rittelmann, P. Richard

Owner/Investor
Collins, Ralph V.

Property Manager
Collins, Ralph V.
Hohman, Charles

ERIE

Appraiser
Fallon, Michael P.
Orlando, Rocco A.

Attorney
Fallon, Michael P.
Walsh, Joseph M. Jr.

Broker
Fallon, Michael P.
Orlando, Rocco A.

Builder
Fallon, Michael P.

Consultant
Fallon, Michael P.

Developer
Fallon, Michael P.
Orlando, Rocco A.

Engineer
Fallon, Michael P.

Owner/Investor
Orlando, Rocco A.

Property Manager
McClelland, W. Craig
Walker, B.J.

Syndicator
Fallon, Michael P.
Orlando, Rocco A.

GREENSBURG

Appraiser
Ginley, William A.

Attorney
Kovach, Richard A.

Broker
Ginley, William A.

Developer
Ginley, William A.

Instructor
Ginley, William A.

Insuror
Ginley, William A.
Kovach, Richard A.

Owner/Investor
Ginley, William A.
Kovach, Richard A.

Property Manager
McKenna, Quentin C.

HARRISBURG

Appraiser
Bowen, Arthur F.
Campbell, Arthur D.
Geller, Guy G.
Germak, Ralph A.
Kreider, Daniel J.

Architect
Bagga, Roshan

Attorney
Clement, Daniel J.
Davis, Richard Watkins
Germak, Ralph A.
Gingrich, Henry F.
Harlan, Thomas P.
Harris, Earl L.
Skelly, Joseph G.
Spitzer, Robert C.
Van Ormer, Darrell N. Jr.

Banker
Geller, Guy G.

Broker
Bowen, Arthur F.
Geller, Guy G.
Germak, Ralph A.
Hatter, Larry L.
Hirsh, Joan C.
Kreider, Daniel J.

Builder
Black, Steve
Hatter, Larry L.
Kreider, Daniel J.
Lehman, Paul E.
Zimmerman, Dennis L.

Consultant
Brindle, William A.
Campbell, Arthur D.
Clement, Daniel J.

Developer
Black, Steve
Brindle, William A.
Clement, Daniel J.
Gaughen, Thomas W.
Harris, Earl L.
Hatter, Larry L.
Lehman, Paul E.
Lemmon, J.H.
Schindler, Tobias
Shafer, Pauline M.
Zimmerman, Dennis L.

Engineer
Davis, Richard Watkins

Instructor
Bowen, Arthur F.
Campbell, Arthur D.
Van Ormer, Darrell N. Jr.

Insuror
Campbell, Arthur D.
Davis, Richard Watkins

Owner/Investor
Black, Steve
Bowen, Arthur F.
Brindle, William A.
Campbell, Arthur D.
Clement, Daniel J.
Hatter, Larry L.
Kreider, Daniel J.
Lehman, Paul E.
Schindler, Tobias
Shafer, Pauline M.
Van Ormer, Darrell N. Jr.

Property Manager
Bowen, Arthur F.
Brennan, Robert
Campbell, Arthur D.
Clement, Daniel J.
Clonser, Pierce
Geller, Guy G.
Hatter, Larry L.
Kreider, Daniel J.
Lemmon, J.H.
Lockard, Dale
Riemondy, Augustus
Schindler, Tobias
Simpson, Jerry

Syndicator
Black, Steve
Zimmerman, Dennis L.

INDIANA

Property Manager
Miller, Arthur

JOHNSTOWN

Appraiser
Hagerich, Robert Jr.

Attorney
Kiever, Paul K.
McIntyre, J. William

Broker
Hagerich, Robert Jr.

Builder
Burkhard, John W.

Developer
Burkhard, John W.

LANCASTER

Appraiser
Buchart, John R.
Dorset, Richard T.
Raab, David A.
Riley, Patrick C.
Theros, William J.

Architect
Kohler, Dale F.
Theros, William J.

Banker
Johnstone, Richard O.

Broker
Buchart, John R.
Dorset, Richard T.
Raab, David A.
Riley, Patrick C.
Wampler, Normal Allison

Builder
Dorset, Richard T.

Consultant
Fleischmann, Barry
Kay, Jack R.
Kohler, Dale F.
Raab, David A.
Theros, William J.

Developer
Fleischmann, Barry
Kay, Jack R.
Riley, Patrick C.

Engineer
Theros, William J.

Instructor
Theros, William J.

Insuror
Wampler, Normal Allison

Lender
Lynch, Robert J.

Owner/Investor
Dorset, Richard T.
Fleischmann, Barry
Kochel, Kenneth D.
Raab, David A.
Riley, Patrick C.
Sullivan, James B. Jr.
Wampler, Normal Allison

Property Manager
Cozzens, Samuel
Dorset, Richard T.
Fleischmann, Barry
Lipawsky, Edward J.
Raab, David A.
Theros, William J.
Wampler, Normal Allison

Regulator
Kay, Jack R.

LEHIGH VALLEY

Appraiser
Brooks, J. William
Cowell, Richard W.
Kartsotis, C.
Patt, Charles B. Jr.

Attorney
Gerson, Donald A.
Perry, Peter P.

Banker
Kordopatis, Nicholas G.

Broker
Brooks, J. William
Cowell, Richard W.
Ford, Paul M.
Kartsotis, C.
Patt, Charles B. Jr.

Builder
Gerson, Donald A.

Consultant
Ashton, Fred L. Jr.
Brooks, J. William
Campbell, Donald E.
Cowell, Richard W.
Patt, Charles B. Jr.

Developer
Brooks, J. William
Campbell, Donald E.
Cowell, Richard W.
Gerson, Donald A.
Loch, Bruce C.

Instructor
Brooks, J. William

Owner/Investor
Brooks, J. William
Campbell, Donald E.

Property Manager
Campbell, Donald E.
Cowell, Richard W.
Decker, Roland A.
Kartsotis, C.
Wavrek, Wayne P.

Syndicator
Brooks, J. William
Cowell, Richard W.

NEW CASTLE

Appraiser
Brenneman, Cloyd E.
Petrini, Joseph A.

Banker
Brenneman, Cloyd E.

Broker
Brenneman, Cloyd E.
Petrini, Joseph A.

Consultant
Petrini, Joseph A.

Developer
Chadderton, Ed

Instructor
Brenneman, Cloyd E.
Petrini, Joseph A.

Owner/Investor
Brenneman, Cloyd E.
Chadderton, Ed
Park, Dale E.
Petrini, Joseph A.

Property Manager
Petrini, Joseph A.

Syndicator
Petrini, Joseph A.

OIL CITY

Attorney
Callahan, Gerald W.

Property Manager
Webster, R.D.

PHILADELPHIA

Appraiser
Acolia, George R.
Arnold, John E.
Arnold, Robert B.
Atkins, Merle E.
Balsam, Arthur
Boland, Thomas F.
Brasler, Robert M.
Bruck, Sanford
Cohen, Lee Allen
Cohen, M. Richard
Coin, Bruce J.
Curry, William B. Sr.
Delaney, Michael F.
Dinote, Daniel A. Jr.
Distell, Stephen A.
Dolman, John P.
Granahan, Joseph A. Jr.
Hayden, J. Anthony Jr.
Hibberd, Donald H.
Hickman, Robert Emmett
Kahn, Charles Jr.
Kulick, Joel
Lapworth, George R.
Lipson, Jay H.
Littlewood, Donald G.
Marder, Harry
Micheel, Richard J.
Mitchell, Frank E.
Pasquarella, Val Jr.
Porreca, Roland L.
Ridpath, James S.
Rocca, Felice A. Jr.
Savits, Irving A.
Seymour, Charles F.
Snyder, Edward S.
Snyder, Russell E.

Architect
Bartholomew, Richard W.
Bartley, Theodore T. Jr.
Bass, Irwin J.
Bennett, Robert
Bossung, Charles F.
Burton, Robert Ellis
Kailian, Aram H.
Kinzler, Andrew
Orleans, Marvin

Attorney
Arnold, John E.
Auten, David C. Esq.
Blumberg, Frederick
Britt, George Gitton Jr.
Brown, Nancy Newman
Bucus, Uldis
Canel, Richard L. Jr.
Carroll, Stephen
Day, Christian C.
Dinote, Daniel A. Jr.
Edwards, Stephen Allen
Forde, George S. Jr.
Foxman, Stephen Mark
Garfinkel, Marvin
Gilmore, Michael D.
Glazer, Ronald B.
Greenberg, Howard Esq.
Hachenburg, Robert
Hamlin, Clay W. III
Hankin, Lowen K.
Hartigan, John T.
Houston, Peter C.
Iannelli, Emil L. Esq.
Jacobs, Harold
Jaffe, Arvin J.
Kolodner, Bernard B.
Kramer, Donald W.
Lane, Robert D. Jr.
McClatchy, Walter A. Jr.
Maxey, David W.
Morgenstern, Arthur B.
Pennington, David L.
Rackow, Julian P.
Real, Harold M. Esq.
Savits, Irving A.
Segal, Robert M.
Silverang, Kevin J.
Stockham, Ronald L. Esquire
Turso, Joseph Paul Esq.
Ulrich, Kenneth T.
Webb, William Y.
Weiss, James A.
Wysocki, F. Michael

Banker
Bachtiger, Joseph H.
Boland, Thomas F.
Carboni, Joseph L.
Carroll, Stephen
Cohen, Lee Allen
Connor, James J.
Curry, William B. Sr.
DeCesaris, Domenic F.
Ennis, William M.
Kauffman, David B.
Littlewood, Donald G.
Strecker, Raymond F.

Broker
Arnold, John E.
Balsam, Arthur
Bowman, Robert F.
Brasler, Robert M.
Bruck, Sanford
Cohen, M. Richard
Coin, Bruce J.
Collins, Terence P.
Czarnecki, Walter III
DeCesaris, Domenic F.
Delaney, Michael F.
Dinote, Daniel A. Jr.
Distell, Stephen A.
Dolman, John P.
Drimer, Walter
East, William J.
Egan, Joseph V. III
Feron, Richard L.
Francis, John Patrick Jr.
Gay, Donald
Goldstein, Gilbert
Gorman, Daniel F.
Granahan, Joseph A. Jr.
Hayden, J. Anthony Jr.
Hibberd, Donald H.
Houston, Peter C.
Hughes, Stephen M.
Jacobson, Benjamin
Kahn, Charles Jr.
Kauffman, David B.
Kranzdorf, Norman M.
Kulick, Joel
Lapworth, George R.
Lipson, Jay H.
Littlewood, Donald G.
Marder, Harry
Mirkil, John M.
Mitchell, Frank E.
Nickerson, Joseph T.
Piccolo, Michael D.
Potamkin, Meyer P.
Prigal, Kenneth B. K.
Rocca, Felice A. Jr.
Savits, Irving A.
Seymour, Charles F.
Shanaman, William P.
Snyder, Edward S.
Snyder, Russell E.
Straus, Joseph Jr.
Winig, Howard

Builder
Balsam, Arthur
Bruck, Sanford
Delaney, Michael F.
Distell, Stephen A.
Duckworth, W. Joseph
Egan, Joseph V. III
Francis, John Patrick Jr.
Hankin, Mark
Kailian, Aram H.
Kent, Roy N.
Miller, Herbert
Nickerson, Joseph T.
Orleans, Marvin
Rubenstein, Mark E.
Scannapieco, Thomas
Schenk, Walter H.
Toll, Bruce E.

Consultant
Acolia, George R.
Arnold, John E.
Arnold, Robert B.
Bachtiger, Joseph H.
Balsam, Arthur
Bartholomew, Richard W.
Boland, Thomas F.
Bowman, Robert F.
Brasler, Robert M.
Britt, George Gitton Jr.
Bruck, Sanford
Burton, Robert Ellis
Cohen, M. Richard
Coin, Bruce J.
Collins, Terence P.
Cottone, Philip S.
Day, Christian C.
Dinote, Daniel A. Jr.
Distell, Stephen A.
Dolman, John P.
Drimer, Walter
East, William J.
Feron, Richard L.
Francis, John Patrick Jr.
Frazier, John E.
Garfinkel, Marvin
Gay, Donald
Gilberg, Kenneth R.
Gorman, Daniel F.
Granahan, Joseph A. Jr.
Gypton, James C.
Hachenburg, Robert
Hall, Lyle W. Jr.
Hankin, Mark
Hayden, J. Anthony Jr.
Hibberd, Donald H.
Hickman, Robert Emmett
Hicks, Alec Jr.
Houston, Peter C.
Isdaner, Lawrence A.
Kahn, Charles Jr.
Kauffman, David B.
Kinish, Rita
Kinzler, Andrew
Kranzdorf, Norman M.
Kulick, Joel
Lapworth, George R.
Lipner, Jonathan
Littlewood, Donald G.
Mirkil, John M.
Morgenstern, Arthur B.
Noteware, James D.
Parrish, Lowe L. III
Pasquarella, Val Jr.
Piccolo, Michael D.
Prigal, Kenneth B. K.
Reibstein, Saul V.
Ridpath, James S.
Rocca, Felice A. Jr.
Savits, Irving A.
Schenk, Walter H.
Seymour, Charles F.
Shanaman, William P.
Snyder, Russell E.
Straus, Joseph Jr.
Weber, Hugo C.A. Jr.
Wrigley, Robert T.
Zinberg, Herman

Developer
Balsam, Arthur
Bass, Irwin J.
Bruck, Sanford
Bucus, Uldis
Cohen, Sylvan M.
Collins, Terence P.
Crocker, William W.
Distell, Stephen A.
Drimer, Walter
Duckworth, W. Joseph
Egan, Joseph V. III
Feron, Richard L.
Fleisher, Robert H.
Francis, John Patrick Jr.
Frazier, John E.
Garfinkel, Marvin
Gay, Donald
Goldstein, Gilbert
Gorman, Daniel F.
Hall, Lyle W. Jr.
Hankin, Lowen K.
Hankin, Mark
Hayden, J. Anthony Jr.
Hollway, Paul J.
Iannelli, Emil L. Esq.
Kahn, Charles Jr.
Kailian, Aram H.
Kent, Roy N.
Kinzler, Andrew
Kranzdorf, Norman M.
Lawlor, John M. Jr.
Miller, Herbert
Morgenstern, Arthur B.
Nickerson, Joseph T.
Orleans, Marvin
Parrish, Lowe L. III
Prigal, Kenneth B. K.
Rubenstein, Mark E.
Scannapieco, Thomas
Schenk, Walter H.
Schwartz, Stephen C.
Stefoin, David E.
Sterling, Richard H.
Stone, Lewis M.
Straus, Joseph Jr.
Toll, Bruce E.
Weber, Hugo C.A. Jr.
Weed, Peter B.

Winig, Howard

Engineer
Arnold, John E.
Bedics, Joseph S.
Bennett, Robert
Cohen, M. Richard
Hicks, Alec Jr.

Instructor
Acolia, George R.
Auten, David C. Esq.
Bartholomew, Richard W.
Boland, Thomas F.
Britt, George Gitton Jr.
Cohen, M. Richard
Day, Christian C.
Delaney, Michael F.
Garfinkel, Marvin
Gay, Donald
Glazer, Ronald B.
Gorman, Daniel F.
Graves, Ed
Hachenburg, Robert
Hibberd, Donald H.
Iannelli, Emil L. Esq.
Kinzler, Andrew
Lipson, Jay H.
Pasquarella, Val Jr.
Ridpath, James S.
Rocca, Felice A. Jr.
Snyder, Edward S.
Snyder, Russell E.
Weber, Hugo C.A. Jr.
Weiner, Richard N.

Insuror
Delaney, Michael F.
Distell, Stephen A.
Graves, Ed
Hibberd, Donald H.
Kahn, Charles Jr.
Lipson, Jay H.
Ridpath, James S.
Savits, Irving A.
Snyder, Russell E.

Lender
Balsam, Arthur
Boland, Thomas F.
Callantine, Douglas S.
Carboni, Joseph L.
Carroll, Stephen
Cohen, Lee Allen
Connor, James J.
Crocker, William W.
DeCesaris, Domenic F.
Ennis, William M.
Frazier, John E.
Hankin, Lowen K.
Micheel, Richard J.
Nanos, H. Gerald
Potamkin, Meyer P.
Ridpath, James S.
Schenk, Walter H.
Schwartz, Stephen C.
Strecker, Raymond F.
Weitzmann, Michael C.

Owner/Investor
Balsam, Arthur
Bass, Irwin J.
Bedics, Joseph S.
Britt, George Gitton Jr.
Bruck, Sanford
Bucus, Uldis
Cohen, M. Richard
Cohen, Sylvan M.
Cottone, Philip S.
Crocker, William W.
Delaney, Michael F.
Distell, Stephen A.
Egan, Joseph V. III
Feron, Richard L.
Fleisher, Robert H.
Foxman, Stephen Mark
Francis, John Patrick Jr.
Frazier, John E.
Garfinkel, Marvin
Gilberg, Kenneth R.
Goldfine, Jerald L.
Goldstein, Gilbert
Gorman, Daniel F.
Hall, Lyle W. Jr.
Hankin, Lowen K.
Hankin, Mark
Hartigan, John T.
Hibberd, Donald H.
Hollway, Paul J.
Isdaner, Lawrence A.
Kahn, Charles Jr.
Kinish, Rita
Kinzler, Andrew
Kranzdorf, Norman M.
Kreimer, A. Jonathan
Kulick, Joel
Lapworth, George R.
Lipner, Jonathan
McClatchy, Walter A. Jr.
Marder, Harry
Micheel, Richard J.
Miller, Herbert
Morgenstern, Arthur B.
Nickerson, Joseph T.
Orleans, Marvin
Parrish, Lowe L. III
Piccolo, Michael D.
Potamkin, Meyer P.
Prigal, Kenneth B. K.
Ridpath, James S.
Savits, Irving A.
Schenk, Walter H.
Schwartz, Stephen C.
Smallow, Stevan A.
Stevens, Norton
Straus, Joseph Jr.
Toll, Bruce E.
Weber, Hugo C.A. Jr.
Weed, Peter B.
Weiner, Richard N.
Weitzmann, Michael C.
Winig, Howard
Wrigley, Robert T.

Property Manager
Acolia, George R.
Arnold, John E.
Bachtiger, Joseph H.
Bedics, Joseph S.
Bossung, Charles F.
Bradshaw, William
Britt, George Gitton Jr.
Bruck, Sanford
Carey, Thomas
Collins, Terence P.
Delaney, Michael F.
Distell, Stephen A.
East, William J.
Egan, Joseph V. III
Examitas, Ronald
Francis, John Patrick Jr.
Frazier, John E.
Gay, Donald
Gericke, John J. Jr.
Goldstein, Gilbert
Gorman, Daniel F.
Granahan, Joseph A. Jr.
Gypton, James C.
Hall, Lyle W. Jr.
Hankin, Mark
Hayden, J. Anthony Jr.
Hibberd, Donald H.
Hicks, Alec Jr.
Hollway, Paul J.
Houston, Peter C.
Kahn, Charles Jr.
Kalman, George
Kauffman, David B.
Kryzanowski, Richard
Lapworth, George R.
Lipson, Jay H.
Littlewood, Donald G.
Lump, F.A.
McGurk, Helen M.
Marder, Harry
Morgan, Douglas
Nickerson, Joseph T.
Orleans, Marvin
Parrish, Lowe L. III
Prigal, Kenneth B. K.
Reath, George
Ridpath, James S.
Rubenstein, Mark E.
Savits, Irving A.
Schaffer, Fred W.
Schenk, Walter H.
Shanaman, William P.
Shaw, Robert
Simpson, Fred
Smallow, Stevan A.
Snyder, Edward S.
Toll, Bruce E.
Weber, Hugo C.A. Jr.
Winig, Howard

Real Estate Publisher
Iannelli, Emil L. Esq.
Prigal, Kenneth B. K.

Regulator
Boland, Thomas F.
Hankin, Lowen K.

Syndicator
Bruck, Sanford
Bucus, Uldis
Cottone, Philip S.
Drimer, Walter
Egan, Joseph V. III
Francis, John Patrick Jr.
Gilberg, Kenneth R.
Gorman, Daniel F.
Hall, Lyle W. Jr.
Hamlin, Clay W. III
Hankin, Mark
Hollway, Paul J.
Iannelli, Emil L. Esq.
Lapworth, George R.
Morgenstern, Arthur B.
Nickerson, Joseph T.
Parrish, Lowe L. III
Piccolo, Michael D.
Prigal, Kenneth B. K.
Savits, Irving A.
Scannapieco, Thomas
Schenk, Walter H.
Smallow, Stevan A.
Straus, Joseph Jr.
Turso, Joseph Paul Esq.
Weber, Hugo C.A. Jr.
Weiss, James A.
Winig, Howard

PITTSBURGH

Appraiser
Arnheim, Stanley W.
Berman, W.I.
Beynon, Robert L.
Biseda, John F.
Carson, J. Terrence
Christoff, Kenneth E.
Davey, Richard W.
DiGiorno, John B.
Englert, Richard G.
Kossis, James
Kovach, William J.
Link, Dennis
Mahoney, Lucille Scott
Mihalik, Frank M.
Mullen, Robert J.
Reingold, Herbert L.
Urda, Karl J.

Architect
Baker, Carl G.
Biseda, John F.
Kossman, Paul
Mullen, Robert J.

Attorney
Black, Alexander
Chomas, J. Louis
Daniels, Robert S.
Goehring, Robert W.
Klee, John P.
Kleid, Richard M.
Kulik, Joseph Michael
Lerman, Terry A.
McCartney, Robert C.
Novak, James M.
Pollock, David S.
Schrieber, Brian C.
Unatin, Mark L.
Ward, William B. Jr.
Weil, Andrew L.

Banker
Calnan, Eugene M.
von Weiland, John C.
Walsh, James M.

Broker
Arnheim, Stanley W.
Berman, W.I.
Beynon, Robert L.
Carson, J. Terrence
Christoff, Kenneth E.
Daniels, Robert S.
Davey, Richard W.
DiGiorno, John B.
Guttman, Barney C.
Harrigan, Jon P.
Kaufman, Lewis A.
Klee, John P.
Kossis, James
Kovach, William J.
McNeil, J. William
Mahoney, Lucille Scott
Mihalik, Frank M.
Miller, John E.
Mori, Dean
Proudley, Edward L.
Reingold, Herbert L.
Rogow, Nathan Mark
St. George, E.W.
Schrieber, Brian C.
Stampahar, Richard J.
Stephenson, Robert C.
Urda, Karl J.
Virostek, Joseph J.
Ward, William L.

Builder
Daniels, Robert S.
Kaufman, Lewis A.
Kossman, Paul
Link, Dennis
McNeil, J. William
Mullen, Robert J.
Prine, Charles W. Jr.
Purvis, Robert L.
Zitelli, John F.

Consultant
Arnheim, Stanley W.
Baker, Carl G.
Berman, W.I.
Beynon, Robert L.
Biseda, John F.
Carson, J. Terrence
Christoff, Kenneth E.
Daniels, Robert S.
Davey, Richard W.
DiGiorno, John B.
Grisnik, Francis J. III
Guttman, Barney C.
Harrigan, Jon P.
Johnston, John A.
Kaufman, Lewis A.
Kossis, James
Kovach, Jerry
Lerman, Terry A.
Link, Dennis
Mihalik, Frank M.
Miller, John E.
Monteverde, John P. Jr.

Mullen, Robert J.
Pfeffer, Elvira
Reingold, Herbert L.
Rogow, Nathan Mark
Schreiber, Glenn P. Jr.
Stephenson, Robert C.
Unatin, Mark L.
Urda, Karl J.
Virostek, Joseph J.
Ward, William L.
Zitelli, John F.

Developer
Baker, Carl G.
Bell, Robert C.
Biseda, John F.
Carson, J. Terrence
Grisnik, Francis J. III
Gustine, Frank W. Jr.
Johnston, John A.
Kaufman, Lewis A.
Kossman, Paul
Link, Dennis
McNeil, J. William
Mihalik, Frank M.
Miller, John E.
Pfeffer, Elvira
Pfeffer, Murray B.
Purvis, Robert L.
Riordan, James M.
Robinette, William A.
Stephenson, Robert C.

Engineer
Baker, Carl G.
Mullen, Robert J.

Instructor
McNeil, J. William
Mahoney, Lucille Scott
Unatin, Mark L.
Virostek, Joseph J.

Insuror
Beynon, Robert L.
Carson, J. Terrence
DiGiorno, John B.
Englert, Richard G.
Kovach, William J.

Lender
Newman, Lawrence R.
Ward, William L.

Owner/Investor
Baker, Carl G.
Beynon, Robert L.
Biseda, John F.
Carson, J. Terrence
Christoff, Kenneth E.
Daniels, Robert S.
Davey, Richard W.
DiGiorno, John B.
Guttman, Barney C.
Johnston, John A.
Kaufman, Lewis A.
Kay, Richard R.
Kossis, James
Kossman, Paul
Kulik, Joseph Michael
Link, Dennis
McCartney, Robert C.
Miller, John E.
Monteverde, John P. Jr.
Pfeffer, Murray B.
Purvis, Robert L.
Robinette, William A.
Rogow, Nathan Mark
St. George, E.W.
Schrieber, Brian C.
Stephenson, Robert C.
Stuckeman, Campbell
Unatin, Mark L.
Urda, Karl J.
von Weiland, John C.
Ward, William B. Jr.
Zitelli, John F.

Property Manager
Allen, Gary
Anderson, L.E.
Arnheim, Stanley W.
Bach, Clarence
Berman, W.I.
Beynon, Robert L.
Biseda, John F.
Carson, J. Terrence
Davey, Richard W.
Dearner, R. Milton
DiGiorno, John B.
Englert, Richard G.
Fine, Milton
Finney, Parker W.
Grisnik, Francis J. III
Guttman, Barney C.
Hall, William
Hamilton, William C.
Hans, David Michael
Horne, Charles D.
Kaplan, Irving M.J.
Katz, Marshall
Kaufman, Lewis A.
Kay, Richard R.
Kossis, James
Kossman, Paul
Kovach, William J.
Link, Dennis
Matesich, Joy
Mullen, Robert J.
Pauls, Robert
Pfeffer, Elvira
Phillips, R.J.
Purvis, Robert L.
Reingold, Herbert L.
Robinette, William A.
Rogow, Nathan Mark
Royco, Ray
St. George, E.W.
Spak, Jude
Urda, Karl J.
Valliere, Paul J.
Virostek, Joseph J.
Weagraff, John D.
Zitelli, John F.

Syndicator
Baker, Carl G.
Carson, J. Terrence
DiGiorno, John B.
Guttman, Barney C.
Kaufman, Lewis A.
Kossis, James
Lerman, Terry A.
Link, Dennis
Monteverde, John P. Jr.
Pfeffer, Elvira
Pfeffer, Murray B.
Rogow, Nathan Mark
St. George, E.W.
Virostek, Joseph J.

READING

Attorney
Sigal, Gerald

Banker
Basile, Robert

Broker
Basile, Robert
Knoblauch, Joel P.

Builder
Basile, Robert

Consultant
Nelabovige, Joseph M.A.

Developer
Basile, Robert

Property Manager
Basile, Robert
Knoblauch, Joel P.
McEvers, Robert
Rothermel, Daniel K.
Wiggins, Jerome

SCRANTON

Appraiser
Burke, Edmund
Gordon, Wallace E.
Hinerfeld, Sydney
Savo, Peg

Attorney
Decker, Victor A. III

Banker
Hinerfeld, Sydney
Phaneuf, David W.

Broker
Burke, Edmund
Gordon, Wallace E.
Hinerfeld, Sydney
Savo, Peg

Builder
Podolak, Steven

Consultant
Burke, Edmund
Hinerfeld, Sydney
Sebastianelli, Mario J.

Developer
Podolak, Steven
Sebastianelli, Mario J.

Instructor
Burke, Edmund

Insuror
Gordon, Wallace E.

Lender
Phaneuf, David W.

Owner/Investor
Savo, Peg
Sebastianelli, Mario J.

Property Manager
Gordon, Wallace E.
Hinerfeld, Sydney
Podolak, Steven
Sebastianelli, Mario J.

SOUTHEASTERN PA

Appraiser
Boyles, Lee E.
Cox, Frank D. II
Hall, Robert W.
Kratz, Donald W.
Lorah, Richard J. Sr.
Pugliese, William D.
Tornetta, Charles J.

Architect
Bicksler, Charles S.
Carr, James S.
Rainey, Joseph S.

Attorney
Cutler, Noah D.
Levin, Jonah D.
Porter, James Gordon Jr.
Sward, Scott R.
Willner, George

Banker
Pritchard, Edwin D. Jr.

Broker
Boyles, Lee E.
Cox, Frank D. II
James, Thomas R.
Kalbitzer, Jane C.
Kratz, Donald W.
Lamerton, Robert E.
Lorah, Richard J. Sr.
Melikian, Robert A.
Meyer, Michael P.
Moyer, Stephen R.
Nolen, Michael
Steigelman, Keanneard L.
Sward, Scott R.
Tornetta, Charles J.

Builder
Carr, James S.
Eichler, Eric Y.
Glassman, Donald L.
Guerra, George L.
Nolen, Michael
Rodgers, Peter J.
Rouse, Willard G. III
Sward, Scott R.
Tubbs, William R.

Consultant
Carr, James S.
Hall, Robert W.
Kratz, Donald W.
Lamerton, Robert E.
Nolen, Michael
Pugliese, William D.
Rainey, Joseph S.
Rodgers, Peter J.
Steigelman, Keanneard L.
Stephano, Stephen C.S.
Sward, Scott R.
Tornetta, Charles J.
Willner, George

Developer
Carr, James S.
Eichler, Eric Y.
Giannone, Edward J.
Glassman, Donald L.
Guerra, George L.
James, Thomas R.
Lamerton, Robert E.
Melikian, Robert A.
Nolen, Michael
Rodgers, Peter J.
Rouse, Willard G. III
Stephano, Stephen C.S.
Sward, Scott R.
Tornetta, Charles J.
Tubbs, William R.
Willner, George

Engineer
Carr, James S.
Guerra, George L.
Rainey, Joseph S.
Rodgers, Peter J.

Instructor
James, Thomas R.
Kratz, Donald W.
Sward, Scott R.

Insuror
Overman, Edwin S.

Lender
Pritchard, Edwin D. Jr.

Owner/Investor
Carr, James S.
Eichler, Eric Y.
Giannone, Edward J.
Glassman, Donald L.
Guerra, George L.
James, Thomas R.
Melikian, Robert A.
Rouse, Willard G. III
Stephano, Stephen C.S.
Sward, Scott R.
Tornetta, Charles J.
Tubbs, William R.
Willner, George

Property Manager
Ash, James H.
Block, Frederick
Eichler, Eric Y.
Giannone, Edward J.
Guerra, George L.
Kaas, Lester
Kratz, Donald W.
Lamerton, Robert E.
Rodgers, Peter J.

Rouse, Willard G. III
Sanders, Scott
Stephano, Stephen C.S.
Thomas, Richard D.
Tornetta, Charles J.
West, William S.
Willner, George

Syndicator
Giannone, Edward J.
Glassman, Donald L.
Guerra, George L.
James, Thomas R.
Rodgers, Peter J.
Steigelman, Keanneard L.
Stephano, Stephen C.S.
Willner, George

STATE COLLEGE

Appraiser
Burman, Henry M.
Friedman, Edward A.

Attorney
Friedman, Edward A.

Broker
Friedman, Edward A.
Heim, Bruce K.

Developer
Friedman, Edward A.

Instructor
Heim, Bruce K.

Owner/Investor
Heim, Bruce K.

Property Manager
Heim, Bruce K.

Syndicator
Friedman, Edward A.

WASHINGTON

Attorney
Baum, Raymond N.

WELLSBORO

Attorney
Gleason, Gary M.

WILKES BARRE

Appraiser
Dombroski, William E.
Kile, J.D.
Kile, R. Clayton
Luceno, Samuel F.

Banker
Kile, J.D.

Broker
Dombroski, William E.
Kile, J.D.
Kile, R. Clayton
Luceno, Samuel F.

Builder
Eckman, J.W. II
Gorman, John D.

Consultant
Dombroski, William E.
Kile, J.D.
Luceno, Samuel F.
McCormick, Albert M.

Developer
Eckman, J.W. II
Gorman, John D.
Kile, J.D.
Luceno, Samuel F.

Engineer
Eckman, J.W. II

Instructor
Dombroski, William E.
McCormick, Albert M.

Insuror
Kile, R. Clayton

Lender
Luceno, Samuel F.

Owner/Investor
Dombroski, William E.
Eckman, J.W. II
Luceno, Samuel F.

Property Manager
Dombroski, William E.
Kile, J.D.
Kile, R. Clayton
McCormick, Albert M.

Regulator
McCormick, Albert M.

WILLIAMSPORT

Regulator
Askey, William Hartman

PUERTO RICO

SAN JUAN

Appraiser
Andújar, Edwin Andújar
Ferrer, Gonzalo
Torres, Jose Luis

Architect
Archilla, Carlos A.

Assessor
Torres, Jose Luis

Attorney
Andújar, Edwin Andújar
Gonzalez, Richard J.

Broker
Tomlinson, John F.
Tschudin, Robert C.

Consultant
Andújar, Edwin Andújar
Ferrer, Gonzalo
Martin, Joseph H.
Torres, Jose Luis
Tschudin, Robert C.

Developer
Gonzalez, Rafael
Martin, Joseph H.
Shelley, Daniel W.
Tomlinson, John F.

Engineer
Archilla, Carlos A.
Ferrer, Gonzalo
Morini, Guillermo R.
Torres, Jose Luis

Owner/Investor
Garrote, Angel J.
Martin, Joseph H.
Nikitine, André V.
Shelley, Daniel W.
Tomlinson, John F.

Property Manager
Garrote, Angel J.
Martin, Joseph H.
Nikitine, André V.
Shelley, Daniel W.

Syndicator
Garrote, Angel J.

RHODE ISLAND

PROVIDENCE

Appraiser
Adams, Norman J.
Bogosian, Paul J.
Dempsey, Jack
McCabe, Francis J. Jr.

Attorney
Batty, E. Jerome
Billings, Richard W.
Champagne, Philip M.
Fessel, Norbert
Goldin, Edward S.
Kenyon, Archibald B. Jr.
LaBrosse, Luc R.
Markoff, Ronald C.
Parmenter, William E.
Salvadore, Guido R.
Sokoloff, Charles S.
Tracy, David J. Esq.

Banker
Adams, Norman J.
Champagne, Philip M.
Sanders, D. Faye
Webster, Donald C.

Broker
Bogosian, Paul J.
Dempsey, Jack
Eccles, Noëlla L.
Francis, Charles T.
Kutrieb, Ronald E.
Lambert, Ernest
McCabe, Francis J. Jr.
Richmond, Richard J.

Builder
Damiani, Bruno
Levesque, Ronald A.
Shair, Mark A.
Thoma, Kurt M.

Consultant
Adams, Norman J.
Arms, Charles P.
Bogosian, Paul J.
Champagne, Philip M.
Dempsey, Jack
Kutrieb, Ronald E.
McCabe, Francis J. Jr.
Richmond, Richard J.
Ryan, Robert A.
Webster, Donald C.

Developer
Adams, Norman J.
Damiani, Bruno
Goldin, Edward S.
Kenyon, Archibald B. Jr.
Levesque, Ronald A.
Preston, H. LeBaron
Salvadore, Guido R.
Shair, Mark A.
Thoma, Kurt M.

Instructor
McCabe, Francis J. Jr.

Insuror
Champagne, Philip M.
Lambert, Ernest

Lender
Adams, Norman J.
Champagne, Philip M.
Cutlip, Jack P.
Sanders, D. Faye
Webster, Donald C.

Owner/Investor
Adams, Norman J.
Arms, Charles P.
Bogosian, Paul J.
Damiani, Bruno
Goldin, Edward S.
Harrington, Carroll S.
Kutrieb, Ronald E.
Levesque, Ronald A.
Preston, H. LeBaron
Shair, Mark A.
Thoma, Kurt M.
Woolley, Dan A.

Property Manager
Adams, Norman J.
Arms, Charles P.
Bogosian, Paul J.
Borden, Bradford P.
Buckley, Charles E.
Harris, Richard
Levesque, Ronald A.
Medici, Donald
Preston, H. LeBaron
Robbins, Donald
Shair, Mark A.
Thoma, Kurt M.
Webster, Donald C.

Real Estate Publisher
Lefkowitz, Jerome L.

Regulator
McCabe, Francis J. Jr.

Syndicator
Adams, Norman J.
Kutrieb, Ronald E.

SOUTH CAROLINA

CHARLESTON

Appraiser
Fair, J. Henry Jr.
Keenan, Joseph J.
Middleton, Ernest F. Jr.
Read, Emerson B.
Tarrant, Guy C.
Thompson, Cornelius O. III

Architect
Austin, Leslie J.
Hardwick, James O.

Attorney
Boone, J. Sidney Jr.
Claypoole, J. Stanley
Clement, Robert L. Jr.
Grimball, William H. Jr.
Hastie, J. Drayton Jr.
Jones, William W. Jr.
Laurich, Eugene J.
Mikell, J. Thomas
Mortimer, Rory Dixon
Nichols, Richard M.
Novit, Herbert L.

Banker
Clement, Robert L. Jr.
Yaschik, Henry

Broker
Austin, Leslie J.
Clement, Robert L. Jr.
Couch, Donald Paul
Daniel, William B.
Dutkowsky, Andrew D.
Fair, J. Henry Jr.
Fields, David E. Jr.
Greer, Sally W.
Hill, Max L. Jr.
Keenan, Joseph J.
Lavelle, Joseph M.
Limehouse, Harry Bancroft Jr.
McFadden, George V.
Middleton, Ernest F. III
Middleton, Ernest F. Jr.
Ravenel, Arthur III
Read, Emerson B.
Tarrant, Guy C.
Thompson, Cornelius O. III

Builder
Austin, Leslie J.
Couch, Donald Paul
Viswanathan, Kumar K.

Consultant
Couch, Donald Paul
Fair, J. Henry Jr.
Fields, David E. Jr.
Hardwick, James O.
Keenan, Joseph J.
Limehouse, Harry Bancroft Jr.
Middleton, Ernest F. Jr.
Read, Emerson B.
Tarrant, Guy C.
Thompson, Cornelius O. III
Viswanathan, Kumar K.

Developer
Austin, Leslie J.
Couch, Donald Paul
Fair, J. Henry Jr.
Fields, David E. Jr.
Hampion, Kent F.
Hardwick, James O.
Keenan, Joseph J.
Limehouse, Harry Bancroft Jr.
Middleton, Ernest F. Jr.
Nashner, Richard
Tarrant, Guy C.
Viswanathan, Kumar K.
Wyckoff, Bill
Yaschik, Henry

Engineer
Couch, Donald Paul
Viswanathan, Kumar K.

Instructor
Clement, Robert L. Jr.
Couch, Donald Paul
Middleton, Ernest F. Jr.
Read, Emerson B.
Thompson, Cornelius O. III

Insuror
Clement, Robert L. Jr.
Ravenel, Arthur III
Yaschik, Henry

Lender
Fields, David E. Jr.
Yaschik, Henry

Owner/Investor
Austin, Leslie J.
Clement, Robert L. Jr.
Couch, Donald Paul
Daniel, William B.
Fields, David E. Jr.
Hardwick, James O.
Limehouse, Harry Bancroft Jr.
McFadden, George V.
Ravenel, Arthur III
Read, Emerson B.
Tarrant, Guy C.
Yaschik, Henry

Property Manager
Daniel, William B.
Dutkowsky, Andrew D.
Keenan, Joseph J.
Limehouse, Harry Bancroft Jr.
McFadden, George V.
Middleton, Ernest F. III
Middleton, Ernest F. Jr.
Ravenel, Arthur III
Read, Emerson B.

Real Estate Publisher
Read, Emerson B.

Regulator
Clement, Robert L. Jr.

Syndicator
Austin, Leslie J.
Clement, Robert L. Jr.
Fair, J. Henry Jr.
Fields, David E. Jr.
Keenan, Joseph J.
Limehouse, Harry Bancroft Jr.
Read, Emerson B.
Viswanathan, Kumar K.

COLUMBIA

Appraiser
Cloyd, John A.
Dowling, Donald R.
Laird, Robert W. Jr.
Middleton, Earl M.
Ross, Fred D. (Bubba) Jr.

Architect
Anderson, William H.

Assessor
Cloyd, John A.

Attorney
Pollard, Thomas B. Jr.
Price, Robert G.
Rogers, H. Hugh
Sims, Hugo S. III
Sprott, Rodney M.
Townsend, William H.

Banker
Carter, Joe M. Jr.
Reynolds, Joseph C.

Broker
Davis, Helen
Dowling, Donald R.
Erwin, Mark Wylea
Folsom, John R.
Hall, Peter William
Hickman, James R. (Bob)
Laird, Robert W. Jr.
Middleton, Earl M.
Ross, Fred D. (Bubba) Jr.
Yonce, Donald M. Sr.

Builder
Dowling, Donald R.
Erwin, Mark Wylea
Kruse, John J.
Rogers, H. Hugh
Yonce, Donald M. Sr.

Consultant
Cantey, William C. Jr.
Erwin, Mark Wylea
Hickman, James R. (Bob)
Price, Robert G.
Reynolds, Joseph C.
Ross, Fred D. (Bubba) Jr.
Schneider, Robert A.
Wilson, Jeremy G.
Yonce, Donald M. Sr.

Developer
Erwin, Mark Wylea
Hall, Peter William
Kruse, John J.
Rogers, H. Hugh
Schneider, Robert A.
Sims, Hugo S. III
Wilson, Jeremy G.
Yonce, Donald M. Sr.

Instructor
McIntosh, Willard
Warner, Arthur E.
Wilson, Jeremy G.

Insuror
Davis, Helen
Middleton, Earl M.

Lender
Folsom, John R.
Haas, John E.
Reynolds, Joseph C.
Ross, Fred D. (Bubba) Jr.

Owner/Investor
Cantey, William C. Jr.
Erwin, Mark Wylea
Gunter, Hubert F.
Kruse, John J.
Rogers, H. Hugh
Schneider, Robert A.
Stoneburner, Craig B.
Wilson, Jeremy G.
Yonce, Donald M. Sr.

Property Manager
Dowling, Donald R.
Erwin, Mark Wylea
Gill, Kevin
Hickman, James R. (Bob)
Howell, Jerry
Laird, Robert W. Jr.
Rogers, H. Hugh
Ross, Fred D. (Bubba) Jr.
Schneider, Robert A.
Sims, Hugo S. III
Wilson, Jeremy G.

Regulator
Beal, Fred B.

Syndicator
Cantey, William C. Jr.
Erwin, Mark Wylea
Schneider, Robert A.
Wilson, Jeremy G.
Yonce, Donald M. Sr.

FLORENCE

Appraiser
Dusenbury, C.F.
Grainger, LeRoy "Cecil"
Horinbein, Larry B.
Peavey, Roy

Attorney
Chandler, William H.
Lawn, Ronald Keith

Broker
Baumrind, Vernon
Broadhurst, Rachel B.
Forsheé, Eugene "Beau"
Grainger, LeRoy "Cecil"
Horinbein, Larry B.
Peavey, Roy
Ray, J. Charley

Builder
Baumrind, Vernon
Grainger, LeRoy "Cecil"

Consultant
Dusenbury, C.F.
Horinbein, Larry B.
Ray, J. Charley

Developer
Baumrind, Vernon
Broadhurst, Rachel B.
Grainger, LeRoy "Cecil"

Instructor
Grainger, LeRoy "Cecil"
Peavey, Roy
Ray, J. Charley

Insuror
Grainger, LeRoy "Cecil"
Horinbein, Larry B.

Owner/Investor
Broadhurst, Rachel B.
Forsheé, Eugene "Beau"
Grainger, LeRoy "Cecil"
Ray, J. Charley

Property Manager
Broadhurst, Rachel B.
Grainger, LeRoy "Cecil"
Horinbein, Larry B.
Peavey, Roy
Ray, J. Charley
Taft, Robert

GREENVILLE

Appraiser
Brown, W. Randolph
Faulconer, Michael N.
Garrison, Junius H. Jr.
Hawkins, Barry Michael
Joyner, C. Dan
Thomason, Thomas L.
Williams, Thomas T. Jr.

Attorney
Cheros, John G.
Fant, Francis R. Jr.
Guess, Robert E.
Wheeler, Joe B.
Wildman, Donald B.

Banker
Thomason, Thomas L.

Broker
Brown, W. Randolph
Chapman, L. Jerry
Faulconer, Michael N.
Garrison, Junius H. Jr.
Gautsch, Donald H.
Gibson, Ben T. Jr.
Hall, Michael B.
Joyner, C. Dan
Reed, H. Cullen III
Rice, F. Towers
Simkins, James H.
Sims, Charles F.
Stafford, Jean F.
Williams, Thomas T. Jr.
Young, Evelyn K.

Builder
Garrison, Junius H. Jr.
Reed, H. Cullen III
Rice, F. Towers

Consultant
Brown, W. Randolph
Cheros, John G.
Faulconer, Michael N.
Garrison, Junius H. Jr.
Gautsch, Donald H.
Gibson, Ben T. Jr.
Hall, Michael B.
Thomason, Thomas L.
Wildman, Donald B.
Williams, Thomas T. Jr.

Developer
Fant, Francis R. Jr.
Faulconer, Michael N.
Garrison, Junius H. Jr.
Hall, Michael B.
Hams, Robert C.
Joyner, C. Dan
Powell, Robert
Reed, H. Cullen III
Rice, F. Towers
Sirmon, Wm. W. Jr.
Young, Evelyn K.

Engineer
Gautsch, Donald H.

Instructor
Gautsch, Donald H.
Gibson, Ben T. Jr.

Insuror
Gibson, Ben T. Jr.
Joyner, C. Dan

Lender
Hawkins, Barry Michael

Owner/Investor
Brown, W. Randolph
Chapman, L. Jerry
Cheros, John G.
Fant, Francis R. Jr.
Faulconer, Michael N.
Garrison, Junius H. Jr.

Gibson, Ben T. Jr.
Hall, Michael B.
Reed, H. Cullen III

Property Manager
Barhyte, Donald J.
Brown, W. Randolph
Chapman, L. Jerry
Garrison, Junius H. Jr.
Jennings, Joseph JR.
Joyner, C. Dan
Moseley, George E.
Powell, Robert
Sayer, Colin
Simkins, James H.
Wheeler, Joe B.

Syndicator
Garrison, Junius H. Jr.

SOUTH DAKOTA

ABERDEEN

Builder
Engel, Cal

Developer
Engel, Cal

Property Manager
Engel, Cal

MITCHELL

Appraiser
Sweet, Maynard E.

Broker
Sweet, Maynard E.

Consultant
Sweet, Maynard E.

PIERRE

Appraiser
Korkow, Donald C.

Broker
Korkow, Donald C.

Consultant
Korkow, Donald C.

Property Manager
Burchill, Jack
Gange, Jack
Korkow, Donald C.

RAPID CITY

Appraiser
Rypkema, Donovan D.

Attorney
Estes, Doyle D.

Banker
Lewis, Neil D.

Broker
Gravatt, Larry G.
Lewis, Neil D.
Rypkema, Donovan D.

Builder
Gravatt, Larry G.

Consultant
Lewis, Neil D.
Rypkema, Donovan D.

Developer
Estes, Doyle D.
Gravatt, Larry G.
Rypkema, Donovan D.

Instructor
Rypkema, Donovan D.

Lender
Lewis, Neil D.

Owner/Investor
Estes, Doyle D.
Gravatt, Larry G.
Lewis, Neil D.
Rypkema, Donovan D.

Syndicator
Lewis, Neil D.

SIOUX FALLS

Attorney
Hertz, Thomas W.
Irons, Eugene J.
Willis, Steven C.

Broker
Decker, Quentin M.
Johnson, Orwin Jr.
Ramey, Rose Marie
Willis, Steven C.

Consultant
Johnson, Orwin Jr.
Pellet, M.F.
Willis, Steven C.

Developer
Irons, Eugene J.
Pellet, M.F.
Willis, Steven C.

Lender
Pellet, M.F.

Owner/Investor
Decker, Quentin M.
Irons, Eugene J.
Pellet, M.F.
Ramey, Rose Marie
Willis, Steven C.

Property Manager
Johnson, Orwin Jr.
Ramey, Rose Marie

Regulator
Ramey, Rose Marie

Syndicator
Pellet, M.F.

WATERTOWN

Owner/Investor
Phillips, Arlie E.

TENNESSEE

CHATTANOOGA

Appraiser
Blake, Edward W.
Brooks, S.W.
Elrod, Paul F. Jr.

Attorney
Brown, John Edgar III
Guild, Jeffrey W.
McCallie, Thomas H. III
Winter, Elizabeth Ann

Banker
Blake, Edward W.

Broker
Bright, Fletcher
Brooks, S.W.
Lay, Richard E.
Payne, Raymond D. Jr.
Powell, Wayne
Tabb, Herbert B.
Walldorf, Herman W.
Walldorf, Rudy

Builder
Foy, John N.

Consultant
Blake, Edward W.
Tabb, Herbert B.

Developer
Foy, John N.
Lay, Richard E.
Walldorf, Rudy

Instructor
Brooks, S.W.
Brown, John Edgar III

Insuror
Brooks, S.W.

Lender
Blake, Edward W.
McNutt, Jack R.

Owner/Investor
Blake, Edward W.
Bright, Fletcher
Brooks, S.W.
Brown, John Edgar III
Walldorf, Herman W.
Walldorf, Rudy

Property Manager
Ahern, Francis
Bright, Fletcher
Brooks, S.W.
Hammer, Charles
Payne, Raymond D. Jr.
Rymer, S.E. Jr.
Smith, Gordon L. Jr.
Tabb, Herbert B.
Thompson, John B.
Walldorf, Herman W.

COOKEVILLE

Appraiser
Warner, Everett F.

Attorney
Myers, Bruce E.

Broker
Roberson, J. Clyde
Warner, Everett F.

Builder
Morehouse, Leo A. Jr.
Roberson, J. Clyde
Warner, Everett F.

Consultant
Warner, Everett F.

Developer
Morehouse, Leo A. Jr.
Roberson, J. Clyde
Warner, Everett F.

Instructor
Warner, Everett F.

Insuror
Roberson, J. Clyde

Owner/Investor
Morehouse, Leo A. Jr.
Warner, Everett F.

Property Manager
Morehouse, Leo A. Jr.
Warner, Everett F.

JACKSON

Banker
Hearn, Robert E.

Broker
Hearn, Robert E.

Owner/Investor
Hearn, Robert E.

Property Manager
Hearn, Robert E.

Syndicator
Hearn, Robert E.

JOHNSON CITY

Appraiser
Dodson, Valerie E.

Architect
Beach, Robert T.

Broker
Dodson, Valerie E.
Saacke, Robert W. "Bob"

Consultant
Beach, Robert T.
Saacke, Robert W. "Bob"

Owner/Investor
Dodson, Valerie E.

KNOXVILLE

Appraiser
Collins, Scott Jr.
Harbin, Jim
Price, John R.
Shields, Claude J.
Smith, Charles M.
Veal, Louis D. Jr.
Wheeler, Robert L.
Woodford, Kenneth R.

Attorney
Tranum, David Michael

Banker
Wheeler, Robert L.

Broker
Baldus, Donald L.
Cameron, Donald R.
Daves, Gerald D.
Garrett, Edwin B.
Harbin, Jim
Harsson, Kenn
Parish, J. Michael
Price, John R.
Veal, Louis D. Jr.

Builder
Buntrock, Tom
Garrett, Edwin B.
Harbin, Jim
Price, John R.
Shields, Claude J.
Tatum, Robert Stephens Jr.

Consultant
Cameron, Donald R.
Carlisle, Charles T. Jr.
Collins, Scott Jr.
Parish, J. Michael
Price, John R.
Shields, Claude J.
Tatum, Robert Stephens Jr.
Wheeler, Robert L.
Woodford, Kenneth R.

Developer
Buntrock, Tom
Cameron, Donald R.
Daves, Gerald D.
Garrett, Edwin B.
Harbin, Jim
Parish, J. Michael
Price, John R.
Shields, Claude J.
Tatum, Robert Stephens Jr.

Instructor
Smith, Charles M.

Insuror
Harbin, Jim
Price, John R.

Lender
Wheeler, Robert L.

Owner/Investor
Buntrock, Tom
Cameron, Donald R.
Carlisle, Charles T. Jr.
Harbin, Jim
Parish, J. Michael
Price, John R.
Tatum, Robert Stephens Jr.
Tranum, David Michael

Property Manager
Cameron, Donald R.
Daves, Gerald D.
Harbin, Jim
Parish, J. Michael
Price, John R.
Tatum, Robert Stephens Jr.

Real Estate Publisher
Veal, Louis D. Jr.

Syndicator
Cameron, Donald R.
Carlisle, Charles T. Jr.
Parish, J. Michael
Price, John R.
Shields, Claude J.

MCKENZIE

Builder
Perkins, Ed R.

Consultant
Perkins, Ed R.

Developer
Perkins, Ed R.

Owner/Investor
Perkins, Ed R.

Property Manager
Perkins, Ed R.

Syndicator
Perkins, Ed R.

MEMPHIS

Appraiser
Abbott, Robert P.
Bloodworth, Russell E.
Crisman, Bryan A.
Galbreath, W. Percy
Garrett, Larry Eugene
Harris, William W.
Jones, Richard B.
Palmer, Marvin H.
Rainer, James C. III

Architect
Dugan, James W.

Assessor
Jones, Richard B.

Attorney
Austin, Larry D.
Baker, Thomas F. IV
Bogatin, Irvin
Buckles, Earl C.
Butler, Edward Franklyn
Charlton, Richard Edmund III
Cohn, William A.
McLaughlin, Stephen Frank
Marston, W. Emmett
Slater, John W. Jr.
Smith, Drayton Beecher II

Banker
Ryan, Thomas N. III

Broker
Andrews, Al E. Jr.
Blackwell, Ceylon B. Jr.
Bloodworth, Russell E.
Crisman, Bryan A.
Earp, Orson K. Jr.
France, William
French, Taylor N.
Galbreath, W. Percy
Garrett, Larry Eugene
Hebers, Frank J.
Jemison, Frank Z. Jr.
Jemison, W. D. Jr.
Kersten, Larry C.
Ledbetter, Scott P.
Palmer, Marvin H.
Presley, Brian
Rainer, James C. III
Ryan, Thomas N. III
Snowden, Robert G.
Wilson, Kemmons Jr.

Builder
Galbreath, W. Percy
Ryan, Thomas N. III
Snowden, Robert G.
Williams, Jimmie D.
Wilson, Kemmons Jr.

Consultant
Abbott, Robert P.
Bloodworth, Russell E.
Dugan, James W.
Earp, Orson K. Jr.
France, William
Garrett, Larry Eugene
Harris, William W.
Jemison, Frank Z. Jr.
Jemison, W. D. Jr.
Palmer, Marvin H.
Rainer, James C. III
Rosson, William M.
Ryan, Thomas N. III
Snowden, Robert G.
Wilson, Kemmons Jr.

Developer
Andrews, Al E. Jr.
Bloodworth, Russell E.
Brindell, Charles R. Jr.
Canfield, Frederick W.
Cates, George E.
France, William
Galbreath, W. Percy
Jemison, Frank Z. Jr.
Jemison, W. D. Jr.
McLaughlin, Stephen Frank
Peck, David C.
Poag, G. Dan Jr.
Ryan, Thomas N. III
Sanders, John M.
Snowden, Robert G.
Williams, Jimmie D.
Wilson, Kemmons Jr.

Engineer
Dugan, James W.

Instructor
Garrett, Larry Eugene
Marston, W. Emmett
Palmer, Marvin H.

Insuror
Palmer, Marvin H.

Lender
Galbreath, W. Percy
Ryan, Thomas N. III

Owner/Investor
Andrews, Al E. Jr.
Bloodworth, Russell E.
Brindell, Charles R. Jr.
Butler, Edward Franklyn
Canfield, Frederick W.
Cates, George E.
Crisman, Bryan A.
Earp, Orson K. Jr.
France, William
Galbreath, W. Percy
Garrett, Larry Eugene
Hebers, Frank J.
Jemison, Frank Z. Jr.
Jemison, W. D. Jr.
Ledbetter, Scott P.
McLaughlin, Stephen Frank
Palmer, Marvin H.
Poag, G. Dan Jr.
Presley, Brian
Rainer, James C. III
Smith, Drayton Beecher II
Snowden, Robert G.
White, Stephen Dennis
Williams, Jimmie D.
Wilson, Kemmons Jr.

Property Manager
Andrews, Al E. Jr.
Bird, Robert D.
Brindell, Charles R. Jr.
Canfield, Frederick W.
Cates, George E.
Deen, Curtis M.
Earp, Orson K. Jr.
Ennis, B.M.
France, William
Galbreath, W. Percy
Garrett, Larry Eugene
Hebers, Frank J.
Jemison, Frank Z. Jr.
Lovett, Blake
Nahon, Santos M.
Palmer, Marvin H.
Presley, Brian
Rainer, James C. III
Ryan, Thomas N. III
Sanders, John M.
Snowden, Robert G.
Taylor, R.L.
White, Stephen Dennis
Williams, Jimmie D.
Wilson, Kemmons Jr.

Syndicator
Crisman, Bryan A.
Earp, Orson K. Jr.
Franklin, Edward O.
Garrett, Larry Eugene
Jemison, Frank Z. Jr.
Presley, Brian
Ryan, Thomas N. III
Snowden, Robert G.

NASHVILLE

Appraiser
Brown, Campbell
Clark, Michael H.
Crouch, C. David
Harper, James L.
Huneycutt, Kent
Hunter, William E. Jr.
Jackson, Roscoe D.
Kennedy, Ray D.
McDaniel, Robert Tate
Zeitlin, Shirley

Architect
Conley, Kenneth S.

Assessor
Kennedy, Ray D.

Attorney
Abbey, Alfred E.
Brown, Campbell
Chaffin, R. Garry
Cobb, John B. Jr.
Garland, Rebecca T.
Kelty, Stephen M.
Trail, Larry G.

Banker
Covington E.A. Jr.
Sanders, G. Clarke

Broker
Armstrong, William J. Jr.
Brown, Campbell
Clark, Michael H.
Clontz, Eugene R.
Cobb, Terrence L.
Covington E.A. Jr.
Crouch, C. David
Davis, Robert Lee Jr.
Freeman, James E.
Harper, James L.
Huneycutt, Kent
Hunter, William E. Jr.
Malone, David J. Jr.
Maynard, W. Douglas
Raskin, Edwin B.
Tomlin, J. Michael
Tomlinson, E. Wayne
Wood, Stephen F.
Zeitlin, Shirley

Builder
Huneycutt, Kent
Thompson, Bruce R.
Tidwell, H. S.
Zeitlin, Shirley

Consultant
Clark, Michael H.
Cobb, Terrence L.
Crouch, C. David
Davis, Robert Lee Jr.
Elrod, W. Kenneth
Harper, James L.
Jackson, Roscoe D.
Kennedy, Ray D.
Raskin, Edwin B.
Thompson, Bruce R.
Tomlinson, E. Wayne
Wood, Stephen F.
Zeitlin, Shirley

Developer
Clark, Michael H.
Clontz, Eugene R.
Davis, Robert Lee Jr.
Elrod, W. Kenneth
Freeman, James E.
Harper, James L.
Kelty, Stephen M.
Malone, David J. Jr.
Raskin, Edwin B.
Thompson, Bruce R.
Tidwell, H. S.
Tomlin, J. Michael
Zeitlin, Shirley

Engineer
Acuff, John E. Jr.
Tidwell, H. S.

Instructor
Huneycutt, Kent
Tomlinson, E. Wayne
Wood, Stephen F.
Zeitlin, Shirley

Insuror
Chaffin, R. Garry
Crouch, C. David
Huneycutt, Kent

Lender
Chaffin, R. Garry
Raskin, Edwin B.
Sanders, G. Clarke
Wood, Stephen F.

Owner/Investor
Clark, Michael H.
Conley, Kenneth S.
Harper, James L.
Kelty, Stephen M.
Maynard, W. Douglas
Raskin, Edwin B.
Sanders, G. Clarke
Tomlin, J. Michael
Zeitlin, Shirley

Property Manager
Brown, Campbell
Clark, Michael H.
Clontz, Eugene R.
Cobb, Terrence L.
Crouch, C. David
Davis, Robert Lee Jr.

Enoch, Ann
Everett, James
Harper, James L.
Huneycutt, Kent
Kallas, J. Kenneth
Kelty, Stephen M.
Malone, David J. Jr.
Raskin, Edwin B.
Tidwell, H. S.
Tomlin, J. Michael
Tomlinson, E. Wayne
Zeitlin, Shirley

Syndicator
Cobb, Terrence L.
Davis, Robert Lee Jr.
Elrod, W. Kenneth
Freeman, James E.
Malone, David J. Jr.
Raskin, Edwin B.
Tomlinson, E. Wayne
Wood, Stephen F.

TEXAS

ABILENE

Appraiser
Austin, Wayne B.
Thompson, George M.

Attorney
Jackson, Randall C.

Broker
Austin, Wayne B.
Elledge, Harold W.
Johnson, Paul A.
McClure, Charles A. III
Senter, Bill
Thompson, George M.
Touchstone, Terry

Builder
Senter, Bill

Consultant
Elledge, Harold W.
McClure, Charles A. III
Touchstone, Terry

Developer
Elledge, Harold W.
McClure, Charles A. III
Senter, Bill
Vest, Gary

Instructor
Elledge, Harold W.
Johnson, Paul A.
McClure, Charles A. III
Thompson, George M.

Owner/Investor
Elledge, Harold W.
Johnson, Paul A.
McClure, Charles A. III
Senter, Bill
Touchstone, Terry

Property Manager
Elledge, Harold W.
Johnson, Paul A.
McClure, Charles A. III
Senter, Bill
Thompson, George M.
Touchstone, Terry

Syndicator
Elledge, Harold W.
Johnson, Paul A.
Senter, Bill

AMARILLO

Appraiser
Graham, Ralph V.
Hoover, Rex Neal
Moran, Thomas L.

Architect
Megert, Russell A.

Broker
Eaves, Cary L.
Graham, Ralph V.
Hoover, Rex Neal
Moran, Thomas L.

Builder
Moran, Thomas L.

Consultant
Graham, Ralph V.
Hoover, Rex Neal
Moran, Thomas L.

Developer
Hoover, Rex Neal
Moore, Doyle
Moran, Thomas L.

Engineer
Megert, Russell A.

Instructor
Graham, Ralph V.

Insuror
Eaves, Cary L.
Graham, Ralph V.

Owner/Investor
Hoover, Rex Neal
Megert, Russell A.
Moran, Thomas L.

Property Manager
Alexander, Bill
Graham, Ralph V.
Hoover, Rex Neal
Moran, Thomas L.

Syndicator
Hoover, Rex Neal
Moran, Thomas L.

AUSTIN

Appraiser
Coleman, James H.
Holmes, J. David
Pihlgren, A.E.
Pyhrr, Stephen A.
Sandlin, Geo. W.
Sayers, Clinton P.

Architect
Amis, James J.

Attorney
Chapman, J. Winston Jr.
Chiles, Gene T.
Hall, Duncan Wayne
Knight, Robert E.
Lucksinger, Michael J.
Preston, Marlow R.
Prikryl, Latius R.
Summer, E. Janice
Yates, Ronald F.

Broker
Christoph, Christine E.
Goodwin, J.B.
Hamilton, Irvin L.
Heagerty, Chris
Heagerty, Stephen P.
Holmes, J. David
Johnston, Jay S.
Kadison, Douglas B.
Knight, Robert E.
McGinty, Rush
Meisler, Paul Steven
Miller, Mark W.
Pihlgren, A.E.
Powers, Norman R.
Preston, Marlow R.
Puett, Nelson
Roberts, Douglas M.
Sandlin, Geo. W.
Sandlin, Geo. W.R. (Buck)
Sayers, Clinton P.
Shirer, Mary Lou
Teeple, Charles S.
Woolsey, William J.

Builder
Holmes, J. David
McGinty, Rush
Preston, Marlow R.
Puett, Nelson

Consultant
Amis, James J.
Coleman, James H.
Hamilton, Irvin L.
Heagerty, Chris
Holmes, J. David
Johnston, Jay S.
Kadison, Douglas B.
Knight, Robert E.
McGinty, Rush
Powers, Norman R.
Preston, Marlow R.
Pyhrr, Stephen A.
Sandlin, Geo. W.
Sandlin, Geo. W.R. (Buck)
Sayers, Clinton P.
Shipman, Sally Stevens

Developer
Amis, James J.
Coleman, James H.
Hardin, Richard D.
Holmes, J. David
Johnston, David
Kadison, Douglas B.
Knight, Robert E.
McGinty, Rush
Meisler, Paul Steven
Powers, Norman R.
Preston, Marlow R.
Puett, Nelson
Sayers, Clinton P.
Teeple, Charles S.

Instructor
Goodwin, J.B.
Heagerty, Stephen P.
Pyhrr, Stephen A.
Shirer, Mary Lou
Stroup, Hilry S.

Insuror
Goodwin, J.B.
Pihlgren, A.E.
Sandlin, Geo. W.
Sandlin, Geo. W.R. (Buck)

Lender
Meisler, Paul Steven
Puett, Nelson
Sandlin, Geo. W.
Sandlin, Geo. W.R. (Buck)
Stroup, Hilry S.

Owner/Investor
Amis, James J.
Chiles, Gene T.
Goodwin, J.B.
Hardin, Richard D.
Johnston, Jay S.
Kadison, Douglas B.
Knight, Robert E.
Levy, Michael R.
McGinty, Rush
Meisler, Paul Steven
Miller, Mark W.
Pihlgren, A.E.
Powers, Norman R.
Preston, Marlow R.
Puett, Nelson
Pyhrr, Stephen A.
Sandlin, Geo. W.
Sandlin, Geo. W.R. (Buck)
Shirer, Mary Lou
Teeple, Charles S.
Woolsey, William J.
Yates, Ronald F.

Property Manager
Baird, David
Christoph, Christine E.
Goodwin, J.B.
Hardin, Richard D.
Heagerty, Chris
Johnston, Jay S.
Knight, Robert E.
Meisler, Paul Steven
Miller, Mark W.
Pihlgren, A.E.
Powers, Norman R.
Preston, Marlow R.
Puett, Nelson
Sandlin, Geo. W.
Sandlin, Geo. W.R. (Buck)
Shirer, Mary Lou

Real Estate Publisher
Meisler, Paul Steven

Syndicator
Coleman, James H.
Johnston, Jay S.
McGinty, Rush
Powers, Norman R.
Preston, Marlow R.
Sandlin, Geo. W.R. (Buck)
Summer, E. Janice
Woolsey, William J.

BEAUMONT

Builder
Milgram, A. S.

BRYAN

Architect
Caffall, Thomas A. Jr.
Caporina, Anthony J.

Banker
Galindo, Ramiro A.

Broker
Caporina, Anthony J.

Builder
Caporina, Anthony J.
Galindo, Ramiro A.
Tremont, Philip J.

Consultant
Friedman, Jack P.

Developer
Caporina, Anthony J.
Galindo, Ramiro A.
Tremont, Philip J.

Engineer
Galindo, Ramiro A.

Instructor
Friedman, Jack P.

Owner/Investor
Caporina, Anthony J.
Galindo, Ramiro A.
Tremont, Philip J.

Property Manager
Tremont, Philip J.

CONROE

Attorney
Burroughs, Richard R.
Moore, James C.
Reade, Brian L.

Broker
Moore, James C.
Volanski, Joe

Builder
Harris, Jeff D.
Moore, James C.

Consultant
Volanski, Joe

Developer
Harris, Jeff D.
Moore, James C.

Owner/Investor
Harris, Jeff D.
Moore, James C.

Property Manager
Harris, Jeff D.
Johnson, Rex

CORPUS CHRISTI

Appraiser
Cobb, Ralph W. Jr.
Liebetrau, Theodore Lambert
Orr, Marj

Attorney
Conoly, David Z.
Hall, Ralph C.

Broker
Cobb, Ralph W. Jr.
Combs, Ken
Flato, Clark Courtney
Orr, Marj

Builder
Flato, Clark Courtney

Consultant
Cobb, Ralph W. Jr.
Flato, Clark Courtney

Developer
Cobb, Ralph W. Jr.
Flato, Clark Courtney
Hall, Ralph C.

Owner/Investor
Cobb, Ralph W. Jr.
Combs, Ken
Flato, Clark Courtney
Orr, Marj

Property Manager
Flato, Clark Courtney
Hall, Ralph C.
Orr, Marj

DALLAS

Appraiser
Archibald, Norman L.
Beer, Robert A.
Della Valle, Petra C.
Dunham, Howard W.
Eklof, Phil
Ernest, Michael J.
Everett, N.L.
Fite, Judge B.
Garrett, Jack P.B. Jr.
Gauen, Charles F.
Gaulding, Jon C.
Grossmann, George A.
Losey, Pat
McClellan, W.M.
Manning, William H.
Miller, Dub W.C.
Roberts, William L.
Rowan, E.A.
Stewart, James W.
Toro, Theodore A.
Ward, John Frank
West, George F.

Architect
Allgeier, E.M.
Audleman, Don
Blevins, Gary Lynn
Bynum, David L.
Carl, Robert E.
Heister, J.W.
Kolb, Nathaniel Key
Madsen, Don

Assessor
Wilson, Robert D.

Attorney
Adkins, Winston L.
Baker, Scott R.
Bennett, Mark E.
Brunger, Mark A.
Burke, William J.
Danish, John C.
Davis, M.G.
DeBusk, Edith
Eggleston, James Duane Jr.
Etienne, Cynthia
Francis, Gene W.
Goodstein, Barnett M.
Gourley, John D.
Hamon, Richard G.
Hicks, Marion Lawrence (Larry) Jr.
Houfek, Dennis F.
Hughes, Vester Thomas Jr.
Jackson, John M.
Larson, Lennart V.
Livingston, David
McLain, Maurice Clayton
McRae, William H.
McWilliams, Mike C.
Manchee, William L.
Manson, Dean A.
Mark, Stephen S.
Millard, T.E.
Moseley, David B. Jr.
Nolan, John M.
Null, Gary G.
Quast, Gerald D.
Roberts, James Vincent
Ruschman, Richard C.
Schmidt, C.L. Mike
See, Robert F. Jr.
Shields, Charles O.
Smith, Thomas M.
Suell, Donald Herrick
White, Steve J.
Wise, Kim A.
Wootton, Dale

Banker
Beer, Robert A.
Brady, Paul M.
Folse, William Lee
Hudson, James H.
Hutcheson, Rex J.
Hutmacher, Gordon
Jacobson, Arch K.
Morrice, Bruce A.
Tabisz, Peter C.
Thomas, Larry D.

Broker
Ablon, Arnold N.
Andress, Nina J.
Applewhite, John C.
Archibald, Norman L.
Audleman, Don
Beer, Robert A.
Blevins, Gary Lynn
Boudreau, Edward H.
Brown, James M.
Carpenter, James L.
Cole, Gregory C.
Crawford, Stephen L.
Davis, George W.
Dunham, Howard W.
Everett, N.L.
Faust, Robert L.
Fink, Henry A.
Fite, Judge B.
Garrett, Jack P.B. Jr.
Gauen, Charles F.
Germain, Craig D.
Griffin, Mike G.
Grossmann, George A.
Hanner, Erik R.
Harris, Sam O. Jr.
Heath, George Delton
Hobbs, Robert S.
Hope, Kent S.
Hutmacher, Gordon
Jackson, John M.
Kanter, Jay A.
Klinger, Bruce K.
Kritz, Michael H.
Lauterbach, W.E.
Losey, Pat
Lovell, John T.
Lundeen, Howard K.
Lynch, William W. Jr.
McAuley, Michael Freeman
McClellan, W.M.
McFaul, Donivan
McKenzie-Smith, Robert H.
McRae, William H.
Melton, James
Miller, Dub W.C.
Miller, Henry S. Jr.
Miller, Nita
Moseley, David B. Jr.
Mullan, Velda
Myers, Robert L.
Neel, Joe C.
Nicholas, Nick
Norwood, Jim E.
Norwood, Roy G. Jr.
Ramsey, Hal C.
Roberts, James Vincent
Roberts, William L.
Rowan, E.A.
Sally, Donald W.
Schmidt, C.L. Mike
Smith, Mark R.
Starke, John E.
Stewart, James W.
Thomas, Larry D.
Thompson, Robert J.
Tomescu, Marian
Waddell, Verna B.
Wagner, Michael Carl
Walner, Robert D.
Ward, John Frank
Wharton, Joseph B. III
White, Doc
White, Steve J.
Wiggins, Pat
Williams, Bradley Kent
Wilson, Robert D.

Builder
Allgeier, E.M.
Blevins, Gary Lynn
Brown, T.A.
Campbell, Thomas W.
Carl, Robert E.
Crow, Michael D.
Davis, George W.
Davis, Ron
Dixon, Don R.
Fite, Judge B.
Folse, William Lee
Gauen, Charles F.
Germain, Craig D.
Gillilan, William J. III
Jackson, John M.
Jones, Thomas F.
Lauterbach, W.E.
Luhnow, Fred V. Jr.
Madsen, Don
New, Manfred E. "Fritz"
Plunk, Don Royl
Pratesi, Edward E.
Ramsey, Hal C.
Starke, John E.
Subar, Jack S.
Willett, Eugene Jr.
Wootton, Dale

Consultant
Ablon, Arnold N.
Andress, Nina J.
Archibald, Norman L.
Audleman, Don
Beer, Robert A.
Blevins, Gary Lynn
Brady, Paul M.
Burdick, Kenneth D.
Carl, Robert E.
Cottingham, Laurence M.
Crawford, Stephen L.
Dunham, Howard W.
Eklof, Phil
Ernest, Michael J.
Everett, N.L.
Fink, Henry A.
Fite, Judge B.
Folse, William Lee
Garrett, Jack P.B. Jr.
Gauen, Charles F.
Gaulding, Jon C.
Goodman, Robert L.
Graham, Joe M.
Griffin, Mike G.
Hanner, Erik R.
Harris, Sam O. Jr.
Hill, Dale
Jenkins, Michael A.
Kanter, Jay A.
Kiler, Mike G. Jr.
Klinger, Bruce K.
Lewis, Austin L.
Litt, Robert D.
Losey, Pat
McAuley, Michael Freeman
McClellan, W.M.
McKenzie-Smith, Robert H.
Manning, William H.
Manson, Dean A.
Melton, James
Miller, Dub W.C.
Miller, Nita
Morrice, Bruce A.
Mullan, Velda
Nassif, George P.
New, Manfred E. "Fritz"
Nicholas, Nick
Norwood, Roy G. Jr.
Plunk, Don Royl
Pratesi, Edward E.
Ramsey, Hal C.
Roberts, William L.
Rogers, Carroll M.
Rowan, E.A.
Sally, Donald W.
Starke, John E.
Stewart, James W.
Taylor, Arlie L.
Thomas, Larry D.
Tomescu, Marian
Toro, Theodore A.
Wagner, Michael Carl
Walner, Robert D.
Weisbrod, Harry
West, George F.
Wharton, Joseph B. III
White, Doc
Williams, Bradley Kent
Wimberly, Brooks R.
Witten, Ronald G.
Wootton, Dale

Developer
Ablon, Arnold N.
Allen, Frank W.
Allgeier, E.M.
Applewhite, John C.
Audleman, Don
Bennett, Mark E.
Blazar, Sheldon M.
Blevins, Gary Lynn
Brady, Paul M.
Brown, T.A.
Burke, William J.

Campbell, Thomas W.
Carl, Robert E.
Clark, Eddie
Clarke, Devane
Collins, John P.
Cooper, Kenneth V.
Cottingham, Laurence M.
Crawford, Stephen L.
Crosland, Lucien B.
Crow, Michael D.
Crow, Ted F.
Davis, George W.
Davis, Ron
Day, Fairfield P. Jr.
Dixon, Don R.
Farren, John B. Jr.
Felts, Ernest T. Jr.
Fink, Henry A.
Fite, Judge B.
Folse, William Lee
Freeman, Roland D.
Fuller, Donn M.
Garrett, Jack P.B. Jr.
Gauen, Charles F.
Gaulding, Jon C.
Germain, Craig D.
Gillilan, William J. III
Griffin, Mike G.
Hanner, Erik R.
Heath, George Delton
Heister, J.W.
Hope, Kent S.
Huber, George B.
Jackson, John M.
Jones, Thomas F.
Klinger, Bruce K.
Lauterbach, W.E.
Lundeen, Howard K.
Luxen, John W.
Lynch, William W. Jr.
McElfresh, Donald C.
McFaul, Donivan
McKenzie-Smith, Robert H.
Madsen, Don
Molzulski, Kenneth S.
New, Manfred E. "Fritz"
Nicholas, Nick
Norwood, Roy G. Jr.
Overstreet, Reading Jr.
Peterson, Joel C.
Plunk, Don Royl
Powter, Colin J.
Pratesi, Edward E.
Ruff, Arthur L.
Ruschman, Richard C.
Schoolfield, William C. Jr.
Sleeper, Neal D.
Smith, Dane F.
Smith, Mark R.
Starke, John E.
Stone, Keith J.
Subar, Jack S.
Tomescu, Marian
Tutun, Mark R.
Underwood, Charles T.
Wiggins, Pat
Willett, Eugene Jr.
Wilson, Robert D.
Wimberly, Brooks R.
Wise, Kim A.
Wootton, Dale

Engineer
Allgeier, E.M.
Carl, Robert E.
Kiler, Mike G. Jr.
Roberts, William L.

Instructor
Beer, Robert A.
Brady, Paul M.
Crawford, Stephen L.
Fite, Judge B.
Gauen, Charles F.
Gaulding, Jon C.
Goodstein, Barnett M.
Gourley, John D.
Grossmann, George A.
Harris, Sam O. Jr.
Heath, George Delton
Larson, Lennart V.
McClellan, W.M.
McKenzie-Smith, Robert H.
Manson, Dean A.
Miller, Nita
Mullan, Velda
Roberts, William L.
Starke, John E.
Tabisz, Peter C.
Thomas, Larry D.
Wagner, Michael Carl
White, Doc

Insuror
Fite, Judge B.
Garrett, Jack P.B. Jr.
Harris, Sam O. Jr.
Tabisz, Peter C.
Waddell, Verna B.

Lender
Bennett, Mark E.
Brady, Paul M.
Cole, Gregory G.
Etienne, Cynthia
Faust, Robert L.
Fite, Judge B.
Gent, Raymond D.
Hay, Jess Thomas
Hutcheson, Rex J.
Lee, Lawrence M.
Stewart, James W.
Tabisz, Peter C.
Werner, Charles

Owner/Investor
Ablon, Arnold N.
Allgeier, E.M.
Audleman, Don
Beer, Robert A.
Bennett, Mark E.
Blazar, Sheldon M.
Blevins, Gary Lynn
Boudreau, Edward H.
Brady, Paul M.
Carl, Robert E.
Collins, John P.
Cottingham, Laurence M.
Crawford, Stephen L.
Crosland, Lucien B.
Day, Fairfield P. Jr.
Dearmore, Roy F.
DeBusk, Edith
Everett, N.L.
Farren, John B. Jr.
Felts, Ernest T. Jr.
Fink, Henry A.
Fite, Judge B.
Folse, William Lee
Freeman, Roland D.
Fuller, Donn M.
Garrett, Jack P.B. Jr.
Gauen, Charles F.
Gaulding, Jon C.
Gent, Raymond D.
Goodman, Robert L.
Goodstein, Barnett M.
Gourley, John D.
Graham, Joe M.
Hanner, Erik R.
Harris, Sam O. Jr.
Heath, George Delton
Hobbs, Robert S.
Hughes, Vester Thomas Jr.
Jackson, John M.
Jacobson, Arch K.
Jones, Thomas F.
Kritz, Michael H.
Lauterbach, W.E.
Leadbetter, Bruce
Lewis, Austin L.
Litt, Robert D.
Losey, Pat
Luhnow, Fred V. Jr.
Lynch, William W. Jr.
McAuley, Michael Freeman
McFaul, Donivan
McKenzie-Smith, Robert H.
McRae, William H.
Madsen, Don
Manchee, William L.
Manson, Dean A.
Miller, Nita
Molzulski, Kenneth S.
Moseley, David B. Jr.
Myers, Robert L.
Overstreet, Reading Jr.
Plunk, Don Royl
Pratesi, Edward E.
Roberts, James Vincent
Roberts, William L.
Schoolfield, William C. Jr.
Smith, Thomas M.
Starke, John E.
Thomas, Larry D.
Tomescu, Marian
Toro, Theodore A.
Tutun, Mark R.
Underwood, Charles T.
Waddell, Verna B.
Wagner, Michael Carl
Walner, Robert D.
Ward, John Frank
Wharton, Joseph B. III
White, Doc
Wootton, Dale

Property Manager
Ablon, Arnold N.
Allgeier, E.M.
Applewhite, John C.
Audleman, Don
Baier, Roger
Bateman, Earl Jr.
Beer, Robert A.
Bennett, Mark E.
Biggs, Harold
Black, Marvin W.
Blazar, Sheldon M.
Boudreau, Edward H.
Brady, Paul M.
Brown, T.A.
Burke, William J.
Carl, Robert E.
Cason, Mike
Chandler, John
Clark, Eddie
Cooper, Kenneth V.
Crawford, Stephen L.
Deisenroth, Craig
Delaney, Thomas
Everett, N.L.
Farren, John B. Jr.
Felts, Ernest T. Jr.
Fite, Judge B.
Folse, William Lee
Freeman, Roland D.
Fuller, Donn M.
Gallier, Theo A.
Garrett, Jack P.B. Jr.
Gauen, Charles F.
Gaulding, Jon C.
Goodman, Robert L.
Griffin, George
Griffin, Stephen L.
Hanner, Erik R.
Hannesson, Paul
Harris, Sam O. Jr.
Hayes, John P.
Higginbotham, Fred C. Jr.
Hill, Dale
Hobbs, Robert S.
Hope, Kent S.
Jackson, John M.
Kanter, Jay A.
Klinger, Bruce K.
Kritz, Michael H.
Lewis, Austin L.
Litt, Robert D.
Lundeen, Howard K.
Lynch, William W. Jr.
McAuley, Michael Freeman
McBride, John Daniel Jr.
McKenzie-Smith, Robert H.
McKinney, Joseph F.
McSwain, S.R.
Martin, Thomas
Moseley, David B. Jr.
Mullan, Velda
Nassif, George P.
New, Manfred E. "Fritz"
Norwood, Roy G. Jr.
Parson, E.I.
Peddicord, Thomas
Plunk, Don Royl
Pusateri, Anthony V.
Redman, James
Reimers, Karl
Roberts, William L.
Rogers, Richard
Sally, Donald W.
Schoolfield, William C. Jr.
Smith, Mark R.
Starke, John E.
Subar, Jack S.
Swicord, J.C.
Thomas, Larry D.
Waddell, Verna B.
Wallace, W. Ray
Walner, Robert D.
Wanamaker, Kenneth
Ward, John Frank
White, Doc
Williams, Bradley Kent
Williams, Lawrence J.
Wimberly, Brooks R.

Real Estate Publisher
Brady, Paul M.
Harris, Sam O. Jr.
Mullan, Velda
Starke, John E.
Taylor, Arlie L.

Syndicator
Allgeier, E.M.
Andress, Nina J.
Audleman, Don
Beer, Robert A.
Bennett, Mark E.
Boudreau, Edward H.
Carl, Robert E.
Crawford, Stephen L.
Felts, Ernest T. Jr.
Fite, Judge B.
Folse, William Lee
Freeman, Roland D.
Garrett, Jack P.B. Jr.
Gauen, Charles F.
Gaulding, Jon C.
Goodman, Robert L.
Hanner, Erik R.
Hobbs, Robert S.
Kanter, Jay A.
Klinger, Bruce K.
Kritz, Michael H.
Lauterbach, W.E.
Litt, Robert D.
Lundeen, Howard K.
McAuley, Michael Freeman
McFaul, Donivan
McKenzie-Smith, Robert H.
Morrice, Bruce A.
Mullan, Velda
Overstreet, Reading Jr.
Pratesi, Edward E.
Ruschman, Richard C.
Starke, John E.
Thomas, Larry D.
Thompson, Robert J.
Walner, Robert D.
Wharton, Joseph B. III
White, Doc

White, Steve J.
Wise, Kim A.

DENTON

Broker
Houston, James
Sharp, Jack L.

Builder
Sharp, Jack L.

Consultant
Houston, James

Developer
Sharp, Jack L.

Insuror
Sharp, Jack L.

Owner/Investor
Sharp, Jack L.

Property Manager
Houston, James
Sharp, Jack L.

Syndicator
Sharp, Jack L.

EL PASO

Appraiser
McKinstry, Frederick H.
Sellers, Ralph W. Jr.
Weber, Max R.

Architect
Boyd, William D.
Ortega, Manuel E.

Attorney
Derrick, William J.
Goldman, Merton B.

Broker
Branson, James E. Jr.
Brown, Irving J. 'Sonny'
Burroughs, Jonnie C.
Derrick, William J.
Haddad, Leo Gus
Helsten, Charles T.
Howell, Bill
McKinstry, Frederick H.
O'Leary, Tommie
Peinado, George A.
Sellers, Ralph W. Jr.
Weber, Max R.

Builder
Boyd, William D.
O'Leary, Tommie
Ortega, Manuel E.
Peinado, Arnold B. Jr.

Consultant
Boyd, William D.
Brown, Irving J. 'Sonny'
Burroughs, Jonnie C.
Howell, Bill
McKinstry, Frederick H.
Ortega, Manuel E.
Sellers, Ralph W. Jr.
Weber, Max R.

Developer
Boyd, William D.
Branson, James E. Jr.
Brown, Irving J. 'Sonny'
Derrick, William J.
Haddad, Leo Gus
Howell, Bill
Kellen, A.L.
O'Leary, Tommie
Ortega, Manuel E.
Peinado, Arnold B. Jr.
Peinado, George A.

Engineer
Ortega, Manuel E.
Peinado, Arnold B. Jr.

Instructor
Burroughs, Jonnie C.
O'Leary, Tommie
Weber, Max R

Insuror
O'Leary, Tommie

Owner/Investor
Branson, James E. Jr.
Brown, Irving J. 'Sonny'
Derrick, William J.
Haddad, Leo Gus
Helsten, Charles T.
Howell, Bill
O'Leary, Tommie
Ortega, Manuel E.
Peinado, Arnold B. Jr.
Polk, James H. III
Sellers, Ralph W. Jr.
Weber, Max R.

Property Manager
Herd, Jon T.
Ortega, Manuel E.
Weber, Max R.

Syndicator
Branson, James E. Jr.
Brown, Irving J. 'Sonny'
Derrick, William J.
Haddad, Leo Gus
McKinstry, Frederick H.
Ortega, Manuel E.
Peinado, Arnold B. Jr.

FORT WORTH

Appraiser
Almy, Earle V. "Buddy" Jr.
Caffey, H. Clayton
Hagood, Wayne D.
McCarver, W.F.
Underwood, H. C.
Weaver, William C.
Yager, C. Edward II

Architect
Bogard, Ward

Assessor
Pearson, Edwin L.

Attorney
Kirkland, James A. Jr.
Manny, Gary J.
Pestarino, F.A.

Banker
Crandall, F. Scott
McCarver, W.F.
Pearson, Edwin L.

Broker
Adams, Arsia Ahulia
Almy, Earle V. "Buddy" Jr.
Drews, John R.
McCarver, W.F.
Pestarino, F.A.
Roberts, Everett A.
Roller, Calvin L.
Sheridan, Marie M.
Underwood, H. C.
Wright, William R.
Yager, C. Edward II

Builder
Griffith, Jimmy C.
Manny, Gary J.
Newell, David R.
Pearson, Edwin L.
Pestarino, F.A.
Rhame, David P.
Roberts, Everett A.
Sowell, James E.

Consultant
Almy, Earle V. "Buddy" Jr.
Caffey, H. Clayton
Eudaly, Dick
Hagood, Wayne D.
Louette, Glenn A.
McCarver, W.F.
Manny, Gary J.
Pearson, Edwin L.
Pestarino, F.A.
Rhame, David P.
Roberts, Everett A.
Roller, Calvin L.
Underwood, H. C.
Weaver, William C.
Yager, C. Edward II

Developer
Almy, Earle V. "Buddy" Jr.
Cowan, Jim
Disney, Fred
Drews, John R.
Eudaly, Dick
Griffith, Jimmy C.
Kirkland, James A. Jr.
Ladner, Dale
Newell, David R.
Pearson, Edwin L.
Pestarino, F.A.
Rhame, David P.
Roberts, Everett A.
Sowell, James E.
Weaver, William C.

Engineer
Friberg, Emil E.
Pearson, Edwin L.
Roberts, Everett A.

Instructor
Almy, Earle V. "Buddy" Jr.
Sheridan, Marie M.
Weaver, William C.

Insuror
Almy, Earle V. "Buddy" Jr.
Roberts, Everett A.

Lender
Crandall, F. Scott
McCarver, W.F.

Owner/Investor
Almy, Earle V. "Buddy" Jr.
Eudaly, Dick
Friberg, Emil E.
Griffith, Jimmy C.
Hagood, Wayne D.
Ladner, Dale
Manny, Gary J.
Newell, David R.
Pearson, Edwin L.
Pestarino, F.A.
Rhame, David P.
Roberts, Everett A.
Roller, Calvin L.
Sheridan, Marie M.
Sowell, James E.
Underwood, H. C.
Weaver, William C.

Property Manager
Almy, Earle V. "Buddy" Jr.
Byrne, Bernard
Drews, John R.
Ladner, Dale
Newell, David R.
O'Brien, William B.
Oujesky, Buddy
Pearson, Edwin L.
Pestarino, F.A.
Roberts, Everett A.
Simpson, Robert

Syndicator
Almy, Earle V. "Buddy" Jr.
Drews, John R.
Ladner, Dale
Pestarino, F.A.
Roberts, Everett A.
Underwood, H. C.

HOUSTON

Appraiser
Allen, Albert N.
Allison, Frank E.
Bayless, Craig W.
Fan, Albert C.
Fisk, Jack G.
Fountain, Edmund M. Jr.
Jensen, Paul C.
Livett, Robert L.
Marshall, E. David
Miller, Richard E.C. Jr.
Schmitt, Vincent J.
Tramonte, Vallory J.
Wehring, Wallace L.

Architect
Allison, Frank E.
Beese, Dennis D.
Fan, Albert C.
Kalra, Madan G.
Kirksey, John M.
Kollaer, Jim C.
McGinty, Milton Jr.
Raines, Jack M.
Romero, Frank L.

Attorney
Alexander, Robert B.
Alfonso, Raymond H.
Alzofon, Ethel Veedell
Bernell, Ronald L.
Blackburn, Robert Lee
Boerstler, Herbert W.
Cottrell, Albert Peyton
Daum, Donald R.
Davis, John W.
Eckel, John
Foutch, James R.
Friedman, Abraham P.
Garrett, Devry Walker
Grover, Courtney P. III
Hamm, D. Michael
Heath, Jesse B. Jr.
Hill, Jerel J.
Holland, Woodrow A.
Howard, Peggy Ann
Jackson, Guy C. III
Jacobus, Charles J.
Johnson, Andrew P. III
Johnson, Elliott A.
Johnson, James A.
Katz, M. Marvin
Kelly, James O. III
Lange, Angelika C.
Laux, Donnell H.
Lerman, David
Lopez, David T.
Lord, Terry R.
Martin, Paul E.
Moore, Harvin C. Jr.
Nelson, Wilfrid D.
Newberry, Terry V.
Racusin, Barry L.
Rose, Richard Lindsay
Sarles, B. Dave Jr.
Short, Keith
Sweeney, Francis J.
Sylvan, Lawrence D.
Thompson, Clark G.
Tigner, Ronald E.
Trevino, Daniel K. Jr.
Tritter, David M.
Tucker, Jeffrey A.
Tyler, John K.
Vandivier, Thomas Monroe
Woolfe, Terence J.

Banker
Clark, Charles B.
Eriksson, John V.
Jones, Gainer B. Jr.
Kelly, James O. III
Stemmer, Wayne J.
Tramonte, Vallory J.

Broker
Alfonso, Raymond H.
Allais, Richard C.
Allison, Frank E.
Bayless, Craig W.
Bering, Donald R.
Bernell, Ronald L.
Blanga, Joseph
Bruns, David L.
Bumbalek, Marian E.
Butler, William W.
Corona, Larry M.
Cubbison, Greg
Davis, John W.
Drake, James D.
Eriksson, John V.
Fan, Albert C.
Fifield, Charles H.
Fisk, Jack G.
George, Sid
Gottlieb, Sam B.
Hagaman, John F.
Haik, Mac
Heit, William S.
Hitchcock, Thomas K.
Ingraham, Scott Shane
Jackson, Guy C. III
Jacobus, Charles J.
Johnston, Frank Z.
Kash, Lawrence S.
Kollaer, Jim C.
Lichenstein, Robert Maurice Sr.
Livett, Robert L.
Lowe, Johnnie R.
Lum, Albert B.
Lynn, Paul A.
McArthur, Charles H.
McCarver, Barbara B.
McGinty, Milton Jr.
Magee, William F.
Mahoney, L. James
Marshall, E. David
Mendiola, Helen E.
Miller, Richard E.C. Jr.
Minchen, Meyer A.
Munkres, Ted W.
Preston, John F.
Reynolds, William H. Jr.
Scharck, Ronald A.
Schmitt, Vincent J.
Schwarz, A. David III
Shirley, Ralph
Smiley, Thomas B. III
Smith, Ronald R.
Sorley, Michael Garland
Stefl, Allan H.
Swearinger, Robert G.
Thompson, Charles L.
Tramonte, Vallory J.
Trevino, Daniel K. Jr.
Vaughn, Bill
Verkin, Billy
Weems, F. Carrington
Wehring, Wallace L.
Wright, Gordon B.

Builder
Allais, Richard C.
Allison, Frank E.
Anderson, John H.
Beese, Dennis D.
Bergensen, Harry J.
Bernell, Ronald L.
Carlson, Tom
Corona, Larry M.
Cottrell, David III
DeLorenzo, Ken
Fairfield, Al
Fan, Albert C.
Fisk, Jack G.
Gottlieb, Sam B.
Jacobus, Charles J.
Johnston, Frank Z.
Kelly, James O. III
Kirksey, John M.
Lum, Albert B.
Magee, William F.
Maier, Richard N.
Marsters, Frank H. III
Moore, Harvin C. Jr.
Munkres, Ted W.
Preston, John F.
Romero, Frank L.
Schmitt, Vincent J.
Shirley, Ralph
Tramonte, Vallory J.
Vandaele, Christian
Vaughn, Bill
Wehring, Wallace L.

Consultant
Allais, Richard C.
Allen, Albert N.
Allison, Frank E.
Anderson, John H.
Bayless, Craig W.
Beese, Dennis D.
Bergensen, Harry J.
Bernell, Ronald L.
Blanga, Joseph
Bruns, David L.
Bumbalek, Marian E.
Butler, William W.
Corona, Larry M.
Davis, John W.
Esacove, Donald
Fan, Albert C.
Feenstra, Derek P.
Fountain, Edmund M. Jr.
George, Sid
Hagaman, John F.
Haik, Mac
Hammel, Robbie J.
Heimsath, Charles H.
Heit, William S.
Hines, Jack L.
Hitchcock, Thomas K.
Ingraham, Scott Shane
Jensen, Paul C.
Johnston, Frank Z.
Kash, Lawrence S.
Keeling, John M.
Kollaer, Jim C.
Lehrer, Kenneth Eugene
Lerman, David
Livett, Robert L.
Lum, Albert B.
Lynn, Paul A.
McArthur, Charles H.
Mahoney, L. James
Marsters, Frank H. III
Mendiola, Helen E.
Miller, Richard E.C. Jr.
Minchen, Meyer A.
Preston, John F.
Scharck, Ronald A.
Shirley, Ralph
Stefl, Allan H.
Sylvan, Lawrence D.
Thompson, Charles L.
Thompson, Clark G.
Tramonte, Vallory J.
Trevino, Daniel K. Jr.
Tritter, David M.
Weems, F. Carrington
Wright, Gordon B.

Developer
Ainbinder, Seymour
Alexander, Robert B.
Alfonso, Raymond H.
Allais, Richard C.
Allison, Frank E.
Anderson, John H.
Beese, Dennis D.
Bergensen, Harry J.
Bernell, Ronald L.
Borlenghi, Giorgio
Bruns, David L.
Butler, William W.
Campo, R.J.
Carlson, Tom
Cottrell, Albert Peyton
Cottrell, David III
Davis, John W.
DeGeorge, James B.
DeLorenzo, Ken
Derrick, Bill D.
Drake, James D.
Fairfield, Al
Fan, Albert C.
Fisher, B.H.
Fisk, Jack G.
Gottlieb, Sam B.
Griffin, Fred B.
Hagaman, John F.
Haik, Mac
Hardeman, James C. Sr.
Helms, J.C.
Hines, Jack L.
Jacobus, Charles J.
Johnston, Frank Z.
Kash, Lawrence S.
Kelly, James O. III
Kirksey, John M.
Knapek, Henry J.
Lehrer, Kenneth Eugene
Lerman, David
Lowe, Johnnie R.
Lum, Albert B.
Lynn, Paul A.
McGinty, Milton Jr.
Magee, William F.
Maier, Richard N.
Marshall, E. David
Marshall, Marvin G.
Mezera, Gerald T.
Miller, Richard E.C. Jr.
Moore, Harvin C. Jr.
Munkres, Ted W.
Preston, John F.
Reynolds, William H. Jr.
Samuelson, Larry
Schmitt, Vincent J.
Shirley, Ralph
Simpkins, B. Douglas Jr.
Staffa, Charles V.
Stockwell, Paul W.
Swearinger, Robert G.
Thompson, Clark G.
Trevino, Daniel K. Jr.
Vandaele, Christian
Vandivier, Thomas Monroe
Verkin, Billy
Weems, F. Carrington
Wehring, Wallace L.
Wynn, Claude F.
Zinn, Elias

Engineer
Feenstra, Derek P.
Weems, F. Carrington

Instructor
Allen, Albert N.
Blackburn, Robert Lee
Bumbalek, Marian E.
George, Sid
Jacobus, Charles J.
Jensen, Paul C.
Johnston, Frank Z.
Kollaer, Jim C.
Sylvan, Lawrence D.
Tramonte, Vallory J.
Wright, Gordon B.

Insuror
Eriksson, John V.
Hill, Jerel J.
Lowe, Johnnie R.
Magee, William F.
Schmitt, Vincent J.

Lender
Allais, Richard C.
Brichler, David D.
Clark, Charles B.
Dennis, Jack V. Jr.
Eriksson, John V.
Jones, Gainer B. Jr.
Kelly, James O. III
Lowe, Johnnie R.
Miller, Richard E.C. Jr.
Robinson, Michael G.
Sarles, B. Dave Jr.
Sylvan, Lawrence D.
Tramonte, Vallory J.
Weems, F. Carrington

Owner/Investor
Alexander, Robert B.
Alfonso, Raymond H.
Allais, Richard C.
Allison, Frank E.
Anderson, John H.
Bergensen, Harry J.
Bernell, Ronald L.
Blanga, Joseph
Brichler, David D.
Carlson, Tom
Corona, Larry M.
Cottrell, Albert Peyton
DeGeorge, James B.
Drake, James D.
Eriksson, John V.
Fairfield, Al
Fan, Albert C.
Fifield, Charles H.
Fisk, Jack G.
George, Sid
Gottlieb, Sam B.
Griffin, Fred B.
Grube, Charles H.
Hagaman, John F.
Haik, Mac
Hamm, D. Michael
Hardeman, James C. Sr.
Heimsath, Charles H.
Helms, J.C.
Ingraham, Scott Shane
Jacobus, Charles J.
Johnson, Elliott A.
Johnston, Frank Z.
Kalra, Madan G.
Katz, M. Marvin
Kirksey, John M.
Lehrer, Kenneth Eugene
Lerman, David
Lichenstein, Robert Maurice Sr.
Lord, Terry R.
Lowe, Johnnie R.
Lum, Albert B.
Lynn, Paul A.
Magee, William F.
Mahoney, L. James
Maier, Richard N.
Marsters, Frank H. III
Mendiola, Helen E.
Minchen, Meyer A.
Moore, Harvin C. Jr.
Munkres, Ted W.
Preston, John F.
Reynolds, William H. Jr.
Romero, Frank L.
Samuelson, Larry
Scharck, Ronald A.
Schwarz, A. David III
Shirley, Ralph
Smiley, Thomas B. III
Stefl, Allan H.
Stockwell, Paul W.
Swearinger, Robert G.
Sylvan, Lawrence D.
Thompson, Charles L.
Thompson, Clark G.
Tramonte, Vallory J.
Weems, F. Carrington
Wilson, Robert S.
Wright, Gordon B.
Zinn, Elias

Property Manager
Allison, Frank E.
Anderson, John H.
Bayless, Craig W.
Bergensen, Harry J.
Bernell, Ronald L.
Butler, William W.
Carlson, Tom
Clarson, John J.
Corona, Larry M.
Crowell, Ed.
Crutchfield, Robert
DeGeorge, James B.
DeLorenzo, Ken
Drake, James D.
Ekholm, Vicki F.
Fan, Albert C.
Fisk, Jack G.
George, Gerald
George, Sid
Goodrich, Charles
Gordon, Nicholas N.
Goss, James W.
Gottlieb, Sam B.
Gow, Robert H.
Griffin, Fred B.
Griffin, W.A.
Hagaman, John F.
Haik, Mac
Hankins, Russell
Hardeman, James C. Sr.
Heimsath, Charles H.
Helms, J.C.
Henderson, Ray
Hines, Jack L.
Hixson, E.C. Jr.
Honig, O. Charles
Jacobus, Charles J.
Jensen, Paul C.
Kelly, James O. III
Kollaer, Jim C.
Lacy, W.
Lloyd, Jim
Lum, Albert B.
Magee, William F.
Marshall, E. David
Mezera, Gerald T.
Moody, Jack W.
Moore, Harvin C. Jr.
Mulkey, J.E.
Munkres, Ted W.
Scharck, Ronald A.
Schmitt, Vincent J.
Shirley, Ralph
Shobbrook, Thomas W.
Smith, Ronald R.
Sokolow, Gerry
Stefl, Allan H.
Stewart, David
Swearinger, Robert G.
Taylor, Jerry
Tramonte, Vallory J.
Turner, John B. Jr.
Vanderdrift, Richard
Vaughn, Bill
Weems, F. Carrington
Wright, Gordon B.
Zinn, Elias

Real Estate Publisher
Jacobus, Charles J.
Thompson, Charles L.

Syndicator
Alexander, Robert B.
Alfonso, Raymond H.
Bernell, Ronald L.
Blanga, Joseph
Carlson, Tom
Corona, Larry M.
Fan, Albert C.
Fifield, Charles H.
Fisk, Jack G.
George, Sid
Gottlieb, Sam B.
Grube, Charles H.
Hagaman, John F.
Johnson, Elliott A.
Johnston, Frank Z.
Kash, Lawrence S.
Lerman, David
Lum, Albert B.
Magee, William F.
Marshall, E. David
Smiley, Thomas B. III
Stefl, Allan H.
Swearinger, Robert G.
Sylvan, Lawrence D.
Thompson, Charles L.
Vandivier, Thomas Monroe
Vaughn, Bill
Weems, F. Carrington

LONGVIEW

Appraiser
Lane, Tom R.
Wyant, P.J.

Attorney
Phillips, Ernest Clifford

Broker
Phillips, Edward N.
Phillips, Ernest Clifford
Ruff, Jere
Wyant, P.J.

Consultant
Phillips, Ernest Clifford
Ruff, Jere
Wyant, P.J.

Developer
Phillips, Edward N.
Phillips, Ernest Clifford
Ruff, Jere

Owner/Investor
Phillips, Edward N.
Phillips, Ernest Clifford
Ruff, Jere

Property Manager
Phillips, Edward N.
Phillips, Ernest Clifford
Wyant, P.J.

Syndicator
Phillips, Edward N.
Phillips, Ernest Clifford
Ruff, Jere

LUBBOCK

Appraiser
Newton, James W.

Banker
Fillip, G. Stephen

Broker
Bradshaw, Jerry
Newton, James W.

Consultant
Bradshaw, Jerry
Geebel, Paul R.

Developer
Blankenship, Bruce
Bradshaw, Jerry
Wilkerson, John G. Jr.

Instructor
Bradshaw, Jerry
Geebel, Paul R.
Newton, James W.

Lender
Fillip, G. Stephen

Owner/Investor
Blankenship, Bruce
Newton, James W.
Wilkerson, John G. Jr.

Property Manager
Blankenship, Bruce
Lawrence, Cuyler
Newton, James W.
Wilkerson, John G. Jr.

Real Estate Publisher
Geebel, Paul R.

LUFKIN

Appraiser
Lyon, William Jake

Architect
Hill, Jerry E.

Attorney
Fleming, John C.

Broker
Defoyd, W.L. (Bob)
Fussell, Patrick H.

Builder
Defoyd, W.L. (Bob)
Fussell, Patrick H.

Consultant
Defoyd, W.L. (Bob)
Lyon, William Jake

Developer
Defoyd, W.L. (Bob)
Fussell, Patrick H.
Hill, Jerry E.

Insuror
Defoyd, W.L. (Bob)

Owner/Investor
Defoyd, W.L. (Bob)
Fussell, Patrick H.
Hill, Jerry E.

Property Manager
Defoyd, W.L. (Bob)
Fussell, Patrick H.

Syndicator
Defoyd, W.L. (Bob)
Fussell, Patrick H.

MCALLEN

Appraiser
Baldauf, Dayle
Campbell, William Eugene
de la Garza, Connie
Mason, Thomas G.
Robertson, Billy Perkins

Attorney
McCullough, Graham
Vego, Guillermo Jr.

Broker
Baldauf, Dayle
Campbell, William Eugene
de la Garza, Connie
Fraustro, Jerry
Mason, Thomas G.
Robertson, Billy Perkins
Thompson, Larry D.

Consultant
Campbell, William Eugene
Fraustro, Jerry
Thompson, Larry D.

Developer
Campbell, William Eugene
Fraustro, Jerry

Engineer
Robertson, Billy Perkins

Instructor
Campbell, William Eugene
Thompson, Larry D.

Insuror
Mason, Thomas G.

Owner/Investor
Fraustro, Jerry
Mason, Thomas G.

Property Manager
Campbell, William Eugene
de la Garza, Connie
Mason, Thomas G.
Thompson, Larry D.

Real Estate Publisher
Thompson, Larry D.

Syndicator
Baldauf, Dayle
Fraustro, Jerry

MIDLAND

Appraiser
Cantrell, W. Clyde

Attorney
Goodwin, Ronald R.
Griffin, Ken
Lewis, Glenn W.
Stafford, P. Gordon

Banker
Nance, Joseph Hanover

Broker
Carpenter, Tom
Steenson, Scott R.

Builder
Bell, Larry J.

Consultant
Bell, Larry J.
Cantrell, W. Clyde

Developer
Bell, Larry J.
Steenson, Scott R.

Instructor
Cantrell, W. Clyde

Lender
Nance, Joseph Hanover

Owner/Investor
Bell, Larry J.
Griffin, Ken
Lewis, Glenn W.
Nance, Joseph Hanover
Steenson, Scott R.

Property Manager
Bell, Larry J.
Hejl, David A.
Nance, Joseph Hanover
Stafford, P. Gordon
Weiss, Michael
Whiteley, Lloyd

Syndicator
Bell, Larry J.

PALESTINE

Attorney
Summers, Alfred H.

Lender
Block, Jon

Owner/Investor
Block, Jon

SAN ANTONIO

Appraiser
Boyce, Everette
Boyce, Katherine
Ginther, Noble C. III
Jones, Robert C. (Bob)
Molter, Fred W.
Schwethelm, A.C.
Smith, William J.
Splichal, John F.

Architect
Lynch, Michael E.
Wilson, Allen P.

Attorney
Baird, Morton W. II
Crump, Thomas Richard
Fowlkes, W.W.
Haddock, Douglas R.
Hausman, Nancy Harrelson
Jorrie, Robert William
Polunsky, Allan B.
Sanford, Vernon T. Jr.
Wallis, Ben A. Jr.
Watt, Timothy A.

Banker
Sanford, Vernon T. Jr.

Broker
Boyce, Everette
Boyce, Katherine
Bravo, M. B. III
Bruck, Paul Joseph
Cox, John M.
Ginther, Noble C. III
Gooding, Walter L.
Grimm, Norman E.
Hooker, Harry
Jones, Robert C. (Bob)
Jorrie, Robert William
Kittrell, John R.
Lynch, Michael E.
Molter, Fred W.
Naylor, Pleas C. Jr.
Oefinger, Robert E.
Olson, Carl Re.
Perron, Leo F. Jr.
Ramos, Tony
Rich, Howard L.
Rohde, Alfred William III (Tom)
Rosow, Lawrence M.
Sanford, Vernon T. Jr.
Schwethelm, A.C.
Shearer, Robert A.
Shweiki, Jacob
Smith, William J.
Splichal, John F.
Steinmetz, Charles P.
Wilson, Allen P.

Builder
Hooker, Harry
Jorrie, Robert William
Lifshutz, Bernard L.
Muller, Albert F. Jr.
Rohde, Alfred William III (Tom)
Stanush, Frank A.
Steinmetz, William A.
Weiss, Martin
Wilson, Allen P.

Consultant
Bravo, M. B. III
Cox, John M.
Crone, John T. III
Garza, Paul Jr.
Haddock, Douglas R.
Jorrie, Robert William
Kittrell, John R.
Lynch, Michael E.
Melson, Bill
Molter, Fred W.
Oefinger, Robert E.
Perry, Robert
Rich, Howard L.
Schwethelm, A.C.
Shweiki, Jacob
Smith, William J.
Steinmetz, Charles P.
Steinmetz, George C. Jr.
Vanden, Robert L.
Whittemore, Frank J.

Developer
Crone, John T. III
Garza, Paul Jr.
Grimm, Norman E.
Hendry, John L. III
Hooker, Harry
Jorrie, Robert William
Kittrell, John R.
Lifshutz, Bernard L.
Lynch, Michael E.
Molter, Fred W.
Muller, Albert F. Jr.
Naylor, Pleas C. Jr.
Perry, Robert
Polunsky, Allan B.
Rohde, Alfred William III (Tom)
Schwethelm, A.C.
Shearer, Robert A.
Shweiki, Jacob
Stanush, Frank A.
Steinmetz, Charles P.
Steinmetz, George C. Jr.
Steinmetz, William A.
Weiss, Martin
Whittemore, Frank J.
Wilson, Allen P.
Wilson, Ray C.

Engineer
Garza, Paul Jr.
Jorrie, Robert William

Instructor
Haddock, Douglas R.
Jorrie, Robert William
Kittrell, John R.
Melson, Bill
Polunsky, Allan B.
Sanford, Vernon T. Jr.
Schwethelm, A.C.

Insuror
Bravo, M. B. III
Bruck, Paul Joseph
Jones, Robert C. (Bob)
Perry, Robert
Rosow, Lawrence M.
Steinmetz, Charles P.

Lender
Molter, Fred W.
Sanford, Vernon T. Jr.
Wilson, Ray C.

Owner/Investor
Baird, Morton W. II
Boyce, Everette
Boyce, Katherine
Cox, John M.
Crone, John T. III
Garza, Paul Jr.
Grimm, Norman E.
Hendry, John L. III
Jorrie, Robert William
Kretzschmar, Angelina
Lifshutz, Bernard L.
Molter, Fred W.
Naylor, Pleas C. Jr.
Olson, Carl Re.
O'Neill, Francis Edward
Patton, Orin C.
Perron, Leo F. Jr.
Perry, Robert
Polunsky, Allan B.
Ramos, Tony
Rohde, Alfred William III (Tom)
Sanford, Vernon T. Jr.
Schwethelm, A.C.
Shweiki, Jacob
Smith, William J.
Steinmetz, Charles P.
Steinmetz, George C. Jr.
Steinmetz, William A.
Weiss, Martin
Wilson, Allen P.

Property Manager
Bravo, M. B. III
Crone, John T. III
Ginther, Noble C. III
Grimm, Norman E.
Hendry, John L. III
Jones, Robert C. (Bob)
Jorrie, Robert William
Kretzschmar, Angelina
Lifshutz, Bernard L.
Lynch, Michael E.
McCuarg, Donald
Melson, Bill
Naylor, Pleas C. Jr.
Oefinger, Robert E.
Perron, Leo F. Jr.
Perry, Robert
Rohde, Alfred William III (Tom)
Shearer, Robert A.
Steinmetz, William A.
Thompson, John
Vanden, Robert L.
Weiss, Martin
Whittemore, Frank J.
Wilson, Allen P.

Real Estate Publisher
Melson, Bill

Regulator
Lynch, Michael E.

Syndicator
Bruck, Paul Joseph
Cox, John M.
Gooding, Walter L.
Grimm, Norman E.
Jorrie, Robert William
Kittrell, John R.
Olson, Carl Re.
Perry, Robert
Polunsky, Allan B.
Steinmetz, George C. Jr.
Whittemore, Frank J.

TEXARKANA

Attorney
Morgan, Charles A.

Broker
Barnett, Herman H.
Boyd, Jack N.
Smedley, James K.

Consultant
Barnett, Herman H.
Boyd, Jack N.
Morgan, Charles A.
Smedley, James K.

Instructor
Barnett, Herman H.
Smedley, James K.

Owner/Investor
Barnett, Herman H.
Boyd, Jack N.

Property Manager
Boyd, Jack N.
Smedley, James K.

Syndicator
Boyd, Jack N.
Smedley, James K.

TYLER

Appraiser
Albrecht, Vance E.

Architect
Burch, A. Lee

Broker
Albrecht, Vance E.
Curtis, Charles M.
Ralls, E. Scott

Builder
Curtis, Charles M.

Consultant
Ralls, E. Scott

Developer
Curtis, Charles M.
Ralls, E. Scott

Instructor
Albrecht, Vance E.

Owner/Investor
Curtis, Charles M.
Ralls, E. Scott

Property Manager
Albrecht, Vance E.
Bell, Allen
Curtis, Charles M.
Ralls, E. Scott

VICTORIA

Attorney
Hoffman, Nathan Paul

Broker
Smith, Bill

Consultant
Smith, Bill

Developer
Hoffman, Nathan Paul
Smith, Bill

Instructor
Smith, Bill

Owner/Investor
Hoffman, Nathan Paul
Smith, Bill

WACO

Appraiser
Cook, Ted P.
Culp, James F.
Dunn, Rodney P.
Smith, Walstein Jr.
Welch, Gary E.
Wieser, Randy

Attorney
Davis, Billy H. Jr.
Smith, Walstein Jr.

Banker
Cook, Ted P.
Welch, Gary E.

Broker
Aldrich, C. Elbert
Barbee, Cliff
Culp, James F.
Patrick, Earl B.
Smith, Walstein Jr.
Welch, Gary E.
Wieser, Randy

Builder
McCartney, Ronnie Gladen
Utley, Robert K. III
Welch, Gary E.

Consultant
Barbee, Cliff
Cook, Ted P.
Culp, James F.

Developer
Aldrich, C. Elbert
McCartney, Ronnie Gladen
Patrick, Earl B.
Stefek, W.F. Bill
Utley, Robert K. III
Welch, Gary E.
Wieser, Randy

Instructor
Barbee, Cliff
Smith, Walstein Jr.

Insuror
Welch, Gary E.

Lender
McCartney, Ronnie Gladen
Welch, Gary E.

Owner/Investor
Aldrich, C. Elbert
Barr, T.H. Jr.
Dunn, Rodney P.
McCartney, Ronnie Gladen
Patrick, Earl B.
Smith, Walstein Jr.
Stefek, W.F. Bill
Utley, Robert K. III
Welch, Gary E.

Property Manager
Cook, Ted P.
Dunn, Rodney P.
McCartney, Ronnie Gladen
Stefek, W.F. Bill
Utley, Robert K. III
Wieser, Randy

Real Estate Publisher
Barbee, Cliff

Syndicator
Barr, T.H. Jr.
Utley, Robert K. III

WICHITA FALLS

Appraiser
Taylor, J. Wesley B.

Broker
Dennis, C.W.L. (Dub)
Swenson, Lynda
Taylor, J. Wesley B.

Builder
Dennis, C.W.L. (Dub)

Consultant
Dennis, C.W.L. (Dub)
Swenson, Lynda

Developer
Dennis, C.W.L. (Dub)

Insuror
Taylor, J. Wesley B.

Lender
Dennis, C.W.L. (Dub)

Owner/Investor
Dennis, C.W.L. (Dub)
Swenson, Lynda

Property Manager
Dennis, C.W.L. (Dub)
Swenson, Lynda

Syndicator
Swenson, Lynda

UTAH

OGDEN

Attorney
Conry, Edward J.

Broker
Anderson, Charles H.
Langley, John W.

Builder
Chamberlain, Scott D.
Conry, Edward J.
Smart, James Lee

Consultant
Anderson, Charles H.
Conry, Edward J.
Smart, James Lee

Developer
Anderson, Charles H.
Conry, Edward J.
Langley, John W.
Smart, James Lee

Instructor
Conry, Edward J.
Langley, John W.
Smart, James Lee

Insuror
Jessop, Marilyn

Owner/Investor
Conry, Edward J.
Langley, John W.
Smart, James Lee

Property Manager
Anderson, Charles H.
Liptman, Allen
Smart, James Lee

Real Estate Publisher
Conry, Edward J.

Syndicator
Langley, John W.
Smart, James Lee

PROVO

Architect
Ashworth, Dell S.

Builder
Pace, A. Brooks
Tanner, Richard S.

Developer
Ashworth, Dell S.
Pace, A. Brooks
Tanner, Richard S.

Owner/Investor
Pace, A. Brooks
Tanner, Richard S.

Property Manager
Pace, A. Brooks

SALT LAKE CITY

Appraiser
Alder, Gary D.
Champ, Frederick Winton
Christensen, William Lowell
Cope, Robert Lloyd
Maritsas, Paul D.
Moffitt, Mark Howard
Williams, Clyde E.
Young, Glen E.

Attorney
Boud, John W. III
Carlston, Michael R.
Colessides, Nick J.
Frei, Michael C.
Hansen, Royal I.
Jones, Michael F.
Lunt, Jack
Melling, George D. Jr.
Morrill, Denis R.
Petty, Wayne G.
Poole, Dennis K.
Taylor, Robert M.
Theobald, Harland Stephen
Wunderli, John M.
Yano, Mas

Banker
Champ, Frederick Winton
Clark, Howard S.

Broker
Akerlow, Charles W.
Benton, Steven P.
Carpenter, Paul J.
Champ, Frederick Winton
Coleman, B.
Dinkelman, Jerard H.
Donovan, Michael
Eltinge, Kennard M.
Holman, Kenneth
Hoopes, Harriet
Isaksen, H. L. Jr.
Johnson, Burten C.
Loveland, McKay M.
Moffitt, Mark Howard
Nixon, S. Reed
Osgood, Warren D.
Ostler, David S.
Rothwell, Hank
Stocking, Von K.
Turnbow, Merrill C.
Welch, David N.
Young, Glen E.

Builder
Ashton, R.S.
Dinkelman, Jerard H.
Jacobsen, Heber S.
Loveland, McKay M.
Maritsas, Paul D.
Nixon, S. Reed
Peterson, E. Eugene
Romney, Keith Jr.
Turnbow, Merrill C.
Wood, Robert W.

Consultant
Bodily, Kerry D.
Boud, John W. III
Carpenter, Paul J.
Christensen, William Lowell
Coleman, B.
Colessides, Nick J.
Donovan, Michael
Floor, Emanuel A.
Johnson, Greg C.
Larsen, Kurt L.
Lowe, Steven F.
Maritsas, Paul D.
Moffitt, Mark Howard
Nixon, S. Reed
Osgood, Warren D.
Rothwell, Hank
Shearer, Angus T. Jr.
Shearer, Marilyn
Stocking, Von K.
Theobald, Harland Stephen
Turnbow, Merrill C.
Yano, Mas
Young, Glen E.

Developer
Akerlow, Charles W.
Ashton, R.S.
Clark, Howard S.
Coleman, B.
Dinkelman, Jerard H.
Eltinge, Kennard M.
Floor, Emanuel A.
Isaksen, H. L. Jr.
Jacobsen, Heber S.
Johnson, Greg C.
Larsen, Kurt L.
Loveland, McKay M.
Lowe, Steven F.
Maritsas, Paul D.
Nixon, S. Reed
Romney, Keith Jr.
Rothwell, Hank
Stocking, Von K.
Turnbow, Merrill C.
Weiler, Queed H.
Wood, Robert W.
Wunderli, John M.

Engineer
Nixon, S. Reed

Instructor
Christensen, William Lowell
Cope, Robert Lloyd
Maritsas, Paul D.
Petty, Wayne G.
Shearer, Angus T. Jr.

Insuror
Champ, Frederick Winton
Loveland, McKay M.
Theobald, Harland Stephen

Lender
Adreon, Roy M.
Champ, Frederick Winton
Johnson, Greg C.
Rasmussen, Lyle D.

Owner/Investor
Akerlow, Charles W.
Ashton, R.S.
Benton, Steven P.
Bodily, Kerry D.
Carpenter, Paul J.
Clark, Howard S.
Dinkelman, Jerard H.
Eltinge, Kennard M.
Floor, Emanuel A.
Hall, George E. Jr.
Isaksen, H. L. Jr.
Jacobsen, Heber S.
Johnson, Burten C.
Johnson, Greg C.
Jonkman, John
Loveland, McKay M.
Lowe, Steven F.
Maritsas, Paul D.
Moffitt, Mark Howard
Nixon, S. Reed
Osgood, Warren D.
Ostler, David S.
Romney, Keith Jr.
Shearer, Angus T. Jr.
Stocking, Von K.
Taylor, Robert M.
Turnbow, Merrill C.
Weiler, Queed H.
Wood, Robert W.
Wunderli, John M.
Yano, Mas
Young, Glen E.

Property Manager
Akerlow, Charles W.
Ashton, R.S.
Benton, Steven P.
Bodily, Kerry D.
Champ, Frederick Winton
Clark, Howard S.
Floor, Emanuel A.
Holman, Kenneth
Isaksen, H. L. Jr.
Johnson, Burten C.
Loveland, McKay M.
Lowe, Steven F.
Maritsas, Paul D.
Rei, Joseph D.
Romney, Keith Jr.
Shearer, Angus T. Jr.
Shearer, Marilyn
Stocking, Von K.
Theobald, Harland Stephen
Turnbow, Merrill C.
Turnbow, Parley Daniel
Weiler, Queed H.
Wunderli, John M.

Real Estate Publisher
Coleman, B.

Regulator
Maritsas, Paul D.
Yano, Mas

Syndicator
Akerlow, Charles W.
Bodily, Kerry D.
Coleman, B.
Colessides, Nick J.
Eltinge, Kennard M.
Hall, George E. Jr.
Holman, Kenneth
Isaksen, H. L. Jr.
Johnson, Greg C.
Lowe, Steven F.

Moffitt, Mark Howard
Rothwell, Hank
Shearer, Marilyn
Stocking, Von K.

VERMONT

BELLOWS FALLS

Attorney
Buckley, David F.
Goutas, Edward M.

Developer
Buckley, David F.

Owner/Investor
Buckley, David F.

BRATTLEBORO

Developer
Chase, Jonathan D.

BURLINGTON

Appraiser
Fortune, Kenneth S.

Broker
Austin, Janet T.
Desautels, David A.
Fortune, Kenneth S.
Kranz, Lloyd R.
Lang, Nancy E.
Littlefield, Douglas C.
Russell, John A.

Builder
Ashline, Karl C.
Lang, Nancy E.
Noonan, John R.
Russell, John A.

Consultant
Coffrin, Peter Starbuck
Fortune, Kenneth S.
Lang, Nancy E.
Littlefield, Douglas C.

Developer
Ashline, Karl C.
Coffrin, Peter Starbuck
Kranz, Lloyd R.
Lang, Nancy E.
Lindholm, Albert
Littlefield, Douglas C.
Noonan, John R.
Pizzagalli, James
Russell, John A.

Engineer
Noonan, John R.

Instructor
Desautels, David A.
Lang, Nancy E.

Owner/Investor
Desautels, David A.
Kranz, Lloyd R.
Lang, Nancy E.
Littlefield, Douglas C.
Russell, John A.

Property Manager
Ashline, Karl C.
Coffrin, Peter Starbuck
Noonan, John R.

Syndicator
Coffrin, Peter Starbuck
Lang, Nancy E.
Littlefield, Douglas C.

MONTPELIER

Appraiser
Thetford, James G.

Broker
Williamson, C. III

Builder
Babcock, A. Judson
Reed, C. Paul

Consultant
Thetford, James G.

Developer
Babcock, A. Judson
Means, James D.
Reed, C. Paul

Lender
Whalen, John F.

Owner/Investor
Means, James D.
Whalen, John F.
Williamson, C. III

Property Manager
Babcock, A. Judson
Means, James D.
Reed, C. Paul
Rice, George
Williamson, C. III

RUTLAND

Architect
Williams, Robert C.

Attorney
Facey, John A. III

Broker
Insinga, James M.
Williams, Robert C.

Developer
Insinga, James M.

Property Manager
Insinga, James M.

WHITE RIVER JUNCTION

Appraiser
Gurman, Marvin T.
Nichols, Geoffrey H.
Symmes, Douglass R.

Attorney
Guarino, Alfred A. Jr.

Banker
Mook, Wesley, L.

Broker
Gurman, Marvin T.
Nichols, Geoffrey H.
Placey, Clayton G.
Symmes, Douglass R.

Builder
Gurman, Marvin T.

Consultant
Gurman, Marvin T.
Mook, Wesley, L.
Nichols, Geoffrey H.

Developer
Gurman, Marvin T.
Nichols, Geoffrey H.
Symmes, Douglass R.

Instructor
Mook, Wesley, L.

Lender
Mook, Wesley, L.

Owner/Investor
Gurman, Marvin T.
Mook, Wesley, L.
Nichols, Geoffrey H.
Symmes, Douglass R.

Property Manager
Gurman, Marvin T.
Nichols, Geoffrey H.

Syndicator
Gurman, Marvin T.
Nichols, Geoffrey H.

VIRGIN ISLANDS

Appraiser
McLaughlin, Frank

Broker
McLaughlin, Frank

Owner/Investor
McLaughlin, Frank

Property Manager
McLaughlin, Frank

Syndicator
McLaughlin, Frank

VIRGINIA

BRISTOL

Attorney
Johnson, Donald R.

Regulator
Johnson, Donald R.

CHARLOTTESVILLE

Appraiser
Davis, Roger B. Jr.
Manley, James L.

Attorney
Landess, Fred S.
Pysell, Paul Edward
Reback, Forbes R.
Rutschow, Robert F.
Stevenson, William W.

Banker
Stevenson, William W.

Broker
Davis, Roger B. Jr.
Love, O. Goode
Manley, James L.
Smith, Charles H. Jr.

Builder
Lamb, Larry E.

Consultant
Davis, Roger B. Jr.
Love, O. Goode
Manley, James L.
Smith, Charles H. Jr.

Developer
Davis, Roger B. Jr.
Lamb, Larry E.
Love, O. Goode
Stevenson, William W.

Instructor
Manley, James L.

Owner/Investor
Davis, Roger B. Jr.
Lamb, Larry E.
Manley, James L.
Stevenson, William W.

Property Manager
Davis, Roger B. Jr.
Lamb, Larry E.
Stevenson, William W.

Syndicator
Davis, Roger B. Jr.
Love, O. Goode

FREDERICKSBURG

Appraiser
Dawson, G. C.

Attorney
Gardner, Mark S
Hilldrup, James W.

Broker
Dawson, G. C.

Builder
Abernathy, David D.

Developer
Abernathy, David D.
Dawson, G. C.

HARRISONBURG

Appraiser
Miller, Lowell W.

Broker
Miller, Lowell W.

Property Manager
Miller, Lowell W.

LYNCHBURG

Appraiser
Johnston, James R.

Architect
Lewis, W. Eugene

Broker
Oglesby, R. Schaefer

Consultant
Johnston, James R.

Owner/Investor
Johnston, James R.
Oglesby, R. Schaefer

Property Manager
Fralin, David
Lane, Landon B.
Oglesby, R. Schaefer
Thomas, R. Haywood Jr.

Syndicator
Oglesby, R. Schaefer

NORFOLK

Appraiser
Anderson, John R.
Baxter, Oscar F. V
Carrithers, Charles M.
Couch, Jay D.
Craig, Robert A. III
Falk, Emanuel E.
Howell, Ronald A.
Kellam, Richard B. Tr.
McKnight, D.L.
Ripley, Robert F.

Attorney
Kamp, Arthur J.
Parker, Vincent L.
Rattray, James B.
Robertson, Gerald Decatur
Young, Hubert H. Jr.

Broker
Anderson, John R.
Baxter, Oscar F. V
Carrithers, Charles M.
Couch, Jay D.
Craig, Robert A. III
Drucker, Erwin B.
Falk, Emanuel E.
Gifford, Joan D.
Griffith, Charles Richard Jr.
Harrison, Stanley L.
Howell, Ronald A.

Kellam, Richard B. Tr.
McGinnis, R. J.
McKnight, D.L.
Moseley, Morris G.
Nusbaum, Charles G.
Ripley, Robert F.
Smith, Blair E.
Sternberg, Cary B.
Webb, Donald
Wright, Dorothy F.

Builder
Anderfuren, John A.
Anderson, John R.
Baxter, Oscar F. V
Griffith, Charles Richard Jr.
Kellam, Richard B. Tr.
Moseley, Morris G.

Consultant
Anderfuren, John A.
Baxter, Oscar F. V
Bible, Douglas Spencer
Carrithers, Charles M.
Couch, Jay D.
Drucker, Erwin B.
Falk, Emanuel E.
Gifford, Joan D.
Kellam, Richard B. Tr.
McKnight, D.L.
Moseley, Morris G.
Rattray, James B.
Ripley, Robert F.
Webb, Donald
Young, Hubert H. Jr.

Developer
Anderfuren, John A.
Anderson, John R.
Baxter, Oscar F. V
Couch, Jay D.
Griffith, Charles Richard Jr.
Harrison, Stanley L.
Kellam, Richard B. Tr.
McGinnis, R. J.
Ripley, Robert F.
Young, Hubert H. Jr.

Engineer
Nusbaum, Charles G.

Instructor
Anderson, John R.
Baxter, Oscar F. V
Bible, Douglas Spencer
Drucker, Erwin B.
Gifford, Joan D.
Griffith, Charles Richard Jr.
Kerr, John W. Jr.
Sternberg, Cary B.

Insuror
Baxter, Oscar F. V
Drucker, Erwin B.
Falk, Emanuel E.
Gifford, Joan D.

Lender
Carrithers, Charles M.
Rattray, James B.
Stephenson, Willis W.

Owner/Investor
Anderson, John R.
Bible, Douglas Spencer
Carrithers, Charles M.
Couch, Jay D.
Craig, Robert A. III
Drucker, Erwin B.
Gifford, Joan D.
Harrison, Stanley L.
Kellam, Richard B. Tr.
McGinnis, R. J.
Ripley, Robert F.
Young, Hubert H. Jr.

Property Manager
Anderson, John R.
Baxter, Oscar F. V
Carrithers, Charles M.
Couch, Jay D.
Craig, Robert A. III
Drucker, Erwin B.
Falk, Emanuel E.
Gifford, Joan D.
Griffith, Charles Richard Jr.
Harrison, Stanley L.
Kellam, Richard B. Tr.
McGinnis, R. J.
Nusbaum, Charles G.
Smith, Blair E.
Trub, Aaron D.

Real Estate Publisher
Bible, Douglas Spencer

Regulator
Rattray, James B.

Syndicator
Anderfuren, John A.
Baxter, Oscar F. V
Drucker, Erwin B.
Falk, Emanuel E.
McGinnis, R. J.
Young, Hubert H. Jr.

NORTHERN VIRGINIA

Appraiser
Cannon, Donald
Cross, Carville Joseph
Hall, Cline S.
Harper, C.R.
Kiely, Dan R.
Lorey, Patricia S.
Moore, Charles A. Jr.
Page, Charles M.

Architect
Barkley, Paul H.
Cross, Easton, Jr.
Kohler, Karl E.
Plaseied, Badreddin
Ward, George T.

Assessor
Hall, Cline S.

Attorney
Brincefield, James C. Jr.
Cohen, Ronald Marc
Connor, John B.
deNicola, L. Lawrence
Diamond, Robert M.
Foldes, Paul G.
Kerr, Jon A.
Lyons, John M.
McGuire, Edward D. Jr.
Mitchell, Stuart B.
Nester, Ronald L.
Patrick, Richard M.
Potter, Richard B.
Ruddy, Richard John Jr.

Banker
Cross, Carville Joseph
Harman, Joseph H.
LaPier, Terrence W.

Broker
Albrittain, James Sydney
Brickley, David G.
Campbell, Caroline L.
Cannon, Donald
Cross, Carville Joseph
Dolby, Cornelius A.
Eastment, George T III
Farmer, Fred
Foldes, Paul G.
Gaskins, Steve P. III
Harlowe, William I.
Holbrook, Joseph C.
Jackson, Clay B.
Jones, Jack R.
Knower, Stewart B.
LaPier, Terrence W.
Long, Henry Arlington
Lorey, Patricia S.
Lorey, Ruan M.
Neely, Thomas H.
Oliva, Raymond S.
Potts, Robert A.
Rafferty, Michael Maurice
Reap, William J.
Rhodes, Joan LeBosquet
Smith, Gordon V.
Strong, Jesse M. Jr.
Summers, Richard G.
Willhardt, Richard W.

Builder
Albrittain, James Sydney
Cannon, Donald
Fetsch, William B.
Grefe, Richard H.
Harman, Joseph H.
Hoernig, Glenn Alenn
Moran, John F. Jr.
Rafferty, Michael Maurice
Satian, Sarkis A.
Smith, Gordon V.

Consultant
Brincefield, James C. Jr.
Bubel, Howard L.
Campbell, Caroline L.
Cannon, Donald
Cross, Carville Joseph
Dolby, Cornelius A.
Hoernig, Glenn Alenn
Jordan, John C.
Kiely, Dan R.
Knower, Stewart B.
LaPier, Terrence W.
Long, Henry Arlington
Lorey, Patricia S.
Mitchell, Stuart B.
Moore, Charles A. Jr.
Nester, Ronald L.
Oliva, Raymond S.
Plaseied, Badreddin
Potts, Robert A.
Rafferty, Michael Maurice
Rhodes, Joan LeBosquet
Sangunett, Jack B.
Teague, S. Wesley III
Ward, George T.

Developer
Albrittain, James Sydney
Barkley, Paul H.
Briggs, Gary G.
Brincefield, James C. Jr.
Chiodo, Carol
Daly, Eugene F.
Fetsch, William B.
Harlowe, William I.
Harman, Joseph H.
Jones, Jack R.
Jordan, John C.
Kiely, Dan R.
Kirby, Ronald P.
Kohler, Karl E.
LaPier, Terrence W.
Long, Henry Arlington
Lorey, Ruan M.
Lynch, Edwin Williams Jr.
Moran, John F. Jr.
Nester, Ronald L.
Patrick, Richard M.
Potts, Robert A.
Satian, Sarkis A.
Smith, Gordon V.
Was, Michael C.
Willhardt, Richard W.

Instructor
Brincefield, James C. Jr.
Dolby, Cornelius A.
Farmer, Fred
Hall, Cline S.
Holbrook, Joseph C.
Lorey, Ruan M.
Oliva, Raymond S.
Ruddy, Richard John Jr.
Smith, Gordon V.
Strong, Jesse M. Jr.

Insuror
Harman, Joseph H.
Lyons, John M.
Teague, S. Wesley III

Lender
Brickley, David G.
Callison, James L.
Farmer, Fred
Fetsch, William B.
Harman, Joseph H.
Kiely, Dan R.
LaPier, Terrence W.

Owner/Investor
Albrittain, James Sydney
Baker, John S.
Barkley, Paul H.
Bernstein, Joel H.
Brickley, David G.
Brincefield, James C. Jr.
Bubel, Howard L.
Campbell, Caroline L.
Cannon, Donald
Daly, Eugene F.
deNicola, L. Lawrence
Eastment, George T III
Fetsch, William B.
Foldes, Paul G.
Gaskins, Steve P. III
Hall, Cline S.
Harman, Joseph H.
Hoernig, Glenn Alenn
Jones, Jack R.
Kiely, Dan R.
Knower, Stewart B.
Kohler, Karl E.
LaPier, Terrence W.
Long, Henry Arlington
Lorey, Patricia S.
Lorey, Ruan M.
Lynch, Edwin Williams Jr.
Mitchell, Stuart B.
Neely, Thomas H.
Nester, Ronald L.
Patrick, Richard M.
Potts, Robert A.
Rafferty, Michael Maurice
Rhodes, Joan LeBosquet
Sangunett, Jack B.
Smith, Gordon V.
Strong, Jesse M. Jr.
Tanner, Joanna May
Teague, S. Wesley III
Ward, George T.
Willhardt, Richard W.

Property Manager
Bernstein, Joel H.
Briggs, Gary G.
Bubel, Howard L.
Campbell, Caroline L.
Chiodo, Carol
Eastment, George T III
Fetsch, William B.
Gaskins, Steve P. III
Gitelson, Stanley H.
Hoernig, Glenn Alenn
Holbrook, Joseph C.
Jordan, John C.
Kiely, Dan R.
Knower, Stewart B.
Kohler, Karl E.
Long, Henry Arlington
McGuire, Edward D. Jr.
Nester, Ronald L.
Potts, Robert A.
Reap, William J.
Rhodes, Joan LeBosquet
Sessions, Michael A.
Smith, Gordon V.
Strong, Jesse M. Jr.
Teague, S. Wesley III

Real Estate Publisher
Oliva, Raymond S.

Regulator
Davis, John H.
Hoernig, Glenn Alenn
Nester, Ronald L.
Pinkerton, Donald

Syndicator
Baker, John S.
Bernstein, Joel H.
Brickley, David G.
Brincefield, James C. Jr.
Cannon, Donald
Dolby, Cornelius A.
Farmer, Fred
Fetsch, William B.
Gaskins, Steve P. III
Gulledge, Keith A.
Harlowe, William I.
Hoernig, Glenn Alenn
Kiely, Dan R.
Lloyd, Brent L.
Long, Henry Arlington
Mitchell, Stuart B.
Nester, Ronald L.
Rafferty, Michael Maurice
Rhodes, Joan LeBosquet
Shea, William
Strong, Jesse M. Jr.
Teague, S. Wesley III
Ward, George T.
Zibroski, Ken

PETERSBURG

Appraiser
Ingram, Riley E.

Assessor
Ingram, Riley E.

Broker
Ingram, Riley E.

Builder
Ingram, Riley E.

Consultant
Ingram, Riley E.

Developer
Ingram, Riley E.

Owner/Investor
Ingram, Riley E.

Property Manager
Ingram, Riley E.

Syndicator
Ingram, Riley E.

PULASKI

Appraiser
Harrington, Curtis G.

Attorney
Ammar, N.A. Jr.

Broker
Harrington, Curtis G.

Consultant
Harrington, Curtis G.

Developer
Ammar, N.A. Jr.

Instructor
Harrington, Curtis G.

Insuror
Harrington, Curtis G.

Owner/Investor
Ammar, N.A. Jr.

RICHMOND

Appraiser
Barber, William T. Jr.
Doherty, James L.
Hughes, Ryland James
McConnell, John A.
Shea, David B.
Smith, Charles W. Jr.
Tolleson, R.W.
Williams, Walter H.

Architect
Boylen, Daniel B.
Boynton, Robert A.

Attorney
Addison, David D.
Beale, Sam T.
Covington, J.E. Jr.
Hancock, William G.
Hicks, C. Flippo
Kessler, Neil S.
Lane, Edward E. Jr.
Manson, R. Hunter
Witt, Walter Francis Jr.

Banker
Andrews, William J. Jr.
Galleher, E. Grice
Kay, Bruce A.
Ligon, Jeffrey Lynn

Broker
Axel, Marc
Blake, Donald N.
Blake, Wayne C.
Christeller, James R.
Doherty, James L.
Figg, Dorothy R.
Hawkins, Adolphus W. Jr.
Hickerson, Philip H.
Hobart, K. Bruce
Hughes, Ryland James
Jackson, Earl M.
Joyner, Crawley F. III
Kane, Nancy T.
Kornblau, Barry M.
Lane, Edward E. Jr.
McConnell, John A.
Smith, Charles W. Jr.
Spencer, Ralph D.
Tolleson, R.W.
Vaughan, Porter Jr.
Williams, Walter H.

Builder
Bramos, Daniel D.
Christeller, James R.
Covington, J.E. Jr.
Martin, J. Roy III
Perel, Jonathan Seth
Smith, Charles W. Jr.
Tolleson, R.W.

Consultant
Axel, Marc
Barber, William T. Jr.
Boynton, Robert A.
Corcoran, Richard L.
Doherty, James L.
Galleher, E. Grice
Hobart, K. Bruce
Hughes, Ryland James
Kane, Nancy T.
Lawrence, Thomas B.
Mason, Carroll A.
Russell, John K.
Scott, Ben A. Jr.
Shea, David B.
Vaughan, Porter Jr.
Williams, Walter H.

Developer
Blake, Donald N.
Blake, Wayne C.
Bramos, Daniel D.
Corcoran, Richard L.
Covington, J.E. Jr.
Hobart, K. Bruce
Jenkins, L. Howard III
Joyner, Crawley F. III
Kornblau, Barry M.
Lawrence, Thomas B.
Martin, J. Roy III
Mason, Carroll A.
Perel, Jonathan Seth
Pickett, James C.
Tolleson, R.W.
Vaughan, Porter Jr.

Instructor
Beale, Sam T.
Figg, Dorothy R.
Jackson, Earl M.
Kornblau, Barry M.
Spencer, Ralph D.
Williams, Walter H.

Insuror
Alpert, Janet A.
Corcoran, Richard L.
Russell, John K.
Soo, Charles Edward

Lender
Andrews, William J. Jr.
Seaborn, James L. Jr.
Smith, Charles W. Jr.

Owner/Investor
Axel, Marc
Beale, Sam T.
Blake, Wayne C.
Christeller, James R.
Corcoran, Richard L.
Hobart, K. Bruce
Kornblau, Barry M.
Lawrence, Thomas B.
Martin, J. Roy III
Mason, Carroll A.
Perel, Jonathan Seth
Shea, David B.
Smith, Charles W. Jr.
Vaughan, Porter Jr.
Williams, Walter H.

Property Manager
Brake, R.F.
Bramos, Daniel D.
Christeller, James R.
Coplan, Ralph
Corcoran, Richard L.
Covington, J.E. Jr.
Doherty, James L.
Evans, James
Galleher, E. Grice
Jackson, Earl M.
Kane, Nancy T.
Kornblau, Barry M.
Lawrence, Thomas B.
Ligon, Jeffrey Lynn
Moore, John F.
Perel, Jonathan Seth
Pickett, James C.
Radcliffe, Clyde III
Scott, Ben A. Jr.
Smith, Charles W. Jr.
Soo, Charles Edward
Tolleson, R.W.
Tyler, James
Watts, Robert G.
Williams, Walter H.
Womack, Brett H.

Syndicator
Beale, Sam T.
Hobart, K. Bruce
Joyner, Crawley F. III
Kornblau, Barry M.
Lawrence, Thomas B.
Shea, David B.
Vaughan, Porter Jr.
Williams, Walter H.

ROANOKE

Appraiser
Bondurant, Kenneth K.
Featherston, Charles V.
Fowlkes, W.C.
McNulty, Charles S.

Assessor
McNulty, Charles S.

Attorney
Albert, Burton L.
Davis, Russell Lewis
Flippin, G. Franklin
Hart, Ross C.
Trinkle, James Lewis
Waldrop, Alexander A. Jr.
Young, James M.

Banker
Fowlkes, W.C.

Broker
Bondurant, Kenneth K.
Featherston, Charles V.
Greene, Earle W.
Hall, Edwin C.
McNulty, Charles S.
Moore, L.H.
Trinkle, James Lewis

Builder
Greene, Earle W.
Hunt, Harry H. III
McNulty, Charles S.

Consultant
Greene, Earle W.
Hall, Edwin C.
McNulty, Charles S.
Moore, L.H.
Trinkle, James Lewis

Developer
Featherston, Charles V.
Greene, Earle W.
Hunt, Harry H. III
McNulty, Charles S.

Instructor
McNulty, Charles S.

Insuror
Featherston, Charles V.

Lender
Featherston, Charles V.

Owner/Investor
Bondurant, Kenneth K.
Greene, Earle W.
Hunt, Harry H. III
McNulty, Charles S.
Trinkle, James Lewis

Property Manager
Brammer, William
Greene, Earle W.
Hall, Edwin C.
Hunt, Harry H. III
Martin, Don
Moore, L.H.
Trinkle, James Lewis
Wells, Clifford E.

Syndicator
Trinkle, James Lewis

WINCHESTER

Appraiser
Olsen, Gary K.

Broker
Olsen, Gary K.

Consultant
Olsen, Gary K.

Developer
Gilpin, Thomas T.

Instructor
Olsen, Gary K.

Owner/Investor
Olsen, Gary K.

Property Manager
Gilpin, Thomas T.
Olsen, Gary K.

WASHINGTON

EVERETT

Appraiser
Gustafson, Don A.

Attorney
Packer, Mark B.

Broker
Barr, H. Robert
Leenstra, Cal
Lipscomb, Sharon
Rowley, James C.
Scott, James N.
Seth, Jack C.
Shansby, Vernon E.

Consultant
Barr, H. Robert
Gustafson, Don A.
Leenstra, Cal
Lipscomb, Sharon
Packer, Mark B.
Rowley, James C.
Shansby, Vernon E.

Developer
Barr, H. Robert
Leenstra, Cal

Instructor
Leenstra, Cal

Owner/Investor
Barr, H. Robert
Leenstra, Cal
Lipscomb, Sharon
Packer, Mark B.
Rowley, James C.
Shansby, Vernon E.

Property Manager
Barr, H. Robert
Packer, Mark B.
Rowley, James C.

Syndicator
Barr, H. Robert
Leenstra, Cal

OLYMPIA

Appraiser
Alexander, Doris M.
Beattie, Donald M.
Jones, Sam
Lewis, Will J.
Primley, Nanci C.

Architect
Lewis, Will J.

Attorney
Adams, Nicholas

Broker
Alexander, Doris M.
Barber, Stephen R.
Beattie, Donald M.
Connor, William H.
Deal, Robert J.
Jewell, Michael L.
Jones, Sam
Lewis, Will J.
Primley, Nanci C.
Sullivan, Deborah

Builder
Holsinger, Donald G.
Jones, Sam
Umek, Mark A.

Consultant
Alexander, Doris M.
Barber, Stephen R.
Beattie, Donald M.
Connor, William H.
Illing, Joseph R.
Lewis, Will J.

Developer
Adams, Nicholas
Alexander, Doris M.
Daniels, Donald B.
Holsinger, Donald G.
Illing, Joseph R.
Lewis, Will J.

Instructor
Alexander, Doris M.
Beattie, Donald M.
Jewell, Michael L.
Jones, Sam

Insuror
Alexander, Doris M.
Salerno, Bob

Lender
Beattie, Donald M.

Owner/Investor
Alexander, Doris M.
Barber, Stephen R.
Beattie, Donald M.
Connor, William H.
Daniels, Donald B.
Deal, Robert J.
Holsinger, Donald G.
Illing, Joseph R.
Primley, Nanci C.
Solie, Robert "Bob" L.

Property Manager
Alexander, Doris M.
Barber, Stephen R.
Connor, William H.
Daniels, Donald B.
Illing, Joseph R.
Lewis, Will J.
McDermott, R.G.
Primley, Nanci C.
Schmidt, Robert A.

Real Estate Publisher
Block, Burton

Syndicator
Alexander, Doris M.
Barber, Stephen R.
Connor, William H.
Daniels, Donald B.
Illing, Joseph R.

PASCO

Appraiser
Oliver, Hal

Broker
Adams, William M.
Boston, O.E.
Earp, Gary D.
Oliver, Hal

Consultant
Adams, William M.
Oliver, Hal

Developer
Earp, Gary D.

Engineer
Knight, James T.

Owner/Investor
Boston, O.E.
Earp, Gary D.
Knight, James T.
Oliver, Hal
Potts, Charles

Property Manager
Adams, William M.
Boston, O.E.
Knight, James T.
Potts, Charles

Syndicator
Adams, William M.
Earp, Gary D.

SEATTLE

Appraiser
Aylward, James F.
Boyns, Charles F.
Hardman, Walt
Hubert, James H.
Irish, James H. III
Krippaehne, William W. Jr.
Lason, John P.
Maas, Norman B.
Rice, Hulbert F.
Smith, Wm. A.
Spencer, Donald G.
Turner, Ronald M.
Vance, William A.
Wichtel, Joyce Jean
Wood, Henry T.

Architect
Aegerter, Bob
Bain, William J. Jr.
Barker, James H.
Bryant, James Elliott
Bumgardner, Albert O.
Callison, Anthony
McClarty, Willis R.
Miulli, Robert V.
Nagan, Michael P.
Reid, David J.
Trower, Michael H.

Attorney
Alston, Thaddas Lee
Axelrod, Alan L.
Bergstrom, Robert L.
Bonesteel, Richard D.
Brandzel, Gene B.
Garner, Michael R.
Gilmore, Carl P.
Kirk, Judd
Koch, Carl G.
Kuhrau, Edward W.
Maas, Norman B.
McGillin, William Gregory
Mucklestone, Robert S.
O'Conner, James V.
Panchot, Dudley
Pierson, Richard W.
Price, Thomas D. Jr.
Rule, Peter W.
Schooler, David
Stokke, Diane R.
Tompkins, James E.
Whittington, Thomas L.
Wichtel, Joyce Jean
Wong, Karen Gail Chinn

Banker
Aylward, James F.
Dick, Michael L.
Dunham, James K.
Fawlstich, James R.
Freeman, Kemper
Lannoye, Lee D.
Reynolds, Robert E.
Roberts, William S.

Broker
Aylward, James F.
Behar, Elazar
Berge, Palmer
Berry, Gregory A.
Blue, Sheldon A.
Boyle, C. Edward
Boyns, Charles F.
Burkheimer, Clark M.
Calechman, Jeffrey Paul
Cohan, H.B.
Connors, Richard J.
Dick, Michael L.
Duggan, Randolph F. IV
Erkson, Ronald L.
Freedenberg, Charles
Frey, Robert E. Jr.
Gerend, Robert P.
Greenberg, Harvey
Greer, Glenn E.
Hardman, Walt
Hazzard, Roger Philip
Heckendorn, John G.
Hilden, Rod
Hrin, Arthur J.
Ingraham, Larry W.
Irish, James H. III
Jarvis, Ronald D.
Karmali, Mansur
Klein, Harris
Kraft, Geraldine (Geri) M.
Krippaehne, William W. Jr.
Lannoye, Lee D.
Lansing, Glenn V.
Lason, John P.
Leibsohn, Ronald
Loveless, Rodney L.
Maynard, Jo Helen
Melill, Jack C.
Merryman, Robert H.
Michalak, Craig L.
Myers, Dale W.
Naye, John R.
O'Conner, James V.
Partin, Marcus K.
Pass, Mark O.
Poitras, Dick
Redding, John R.
Schlicke, Gordon W.
Shaffer, Don B.
Sievert, Clarence C.
Steenbakkers, H. John
Taylor, Edward A.
Tonnon, Alan N.
Turner, Ronald M.
Wallace, Robert C.
Wichtel, Joyce Jean
Williams, Patricia
Wise, Ron
Wood, Henry T.
Yousoufian, Armen

Builder
Blue, Sheldon A.
Bryant, James Elliott
Crooks, Patrick F.
De Arias, Louis C.
Dick, Michael L.
Echelbarger, Lindsey L.R.
Ettner, Larry W.
Freeman, James P.
Gerend, Robert P.
Hume, Gregory R.
Loveless, Rodney L.
McDonald, J. Michael
Nagan, Michael P.
Schlicke, Gordon W.
Schooler, David
Turner, Ronald M.
Wells, Thomas R.

Consultant
Axelrod, Alan L.
Bain, William J. Jr.
Berge, Palmer
Berry, Gregory A.
Blue, Sheldon A.
Boyle, C. Edward
Bracken, Thomas R.J.
Burkheimer, Clark M.
Cohan, H.B.

Connors, Richard J.
Dick, Michael L.
Dunham, James K.
Erkson, Ronald L.
Freedenberg, Charles
Frey, Robert E. Jr.
Gerend, Robert P.
Greif, J. H.
Hardman, Walt
Harle, Larry J.
Heckendorn, John G.
Hitchcock, Douglas R.
Howard, Ronald M.
Irish, James H. III
Jarvis, Ronald D.
Klein, Harris
Kloppenburg, Richard L.
Kraft, Geraldine (Geri) M.
Krippaehne, William W. Jr.
Lansing, Glenn V.
Lason, John P.
Lewis, Mary Alexis
Little, Carol Cordl
Looney, Stuart W.
McClarty, Willis R.
Melill, Jack C.
Merryman, Robert H.
Michalak, Craig L.
Naye, John R.
Pass, Mark O.
Poitras, Dick
Reynolds, Robert E.
Rice, Hulbert F.
Schlicke, Gordon W.
Shaffer, Don B.
Sievert, Clarence C.
Smith, Wm. A.
Spencer, Donald G.
Steenbakkers, H. John
Taylor, Edward A.
Turner, Ronald M.
Valentine, Russ C.
Wallace, Robert C.
Walter, Kenneth J.
Wichtel, Joyce Jean
Wise, Ron
Yousoufian, Armen
Zuckerman, Norman J.

Developer

Axelrod, Alan L.
Behar, Elazar
Bellamy Kenneth V.
Benaroya, Jack A.
Bernard, J. Thomas
Blue, Sheldon A.
Bracken, Thomas R.J.
Bryant, James Elliott
Crooks, Patrick F.
De Arias, Louis C.
Dick, Michael L.
Dickinson, William
Dierdorff, Jack L.
Duggan, Randolph F. IV
Echelbarger, Lindsey L.R.
Erkson, Ronald L.
Ettner, Larry W.
Freeman, James P.
Freeman, Kemper
Gerend, Robert P.
Gordon, Hank
Greenberg, Harvey
Greif, J. H.
Hall, Lawrence E.
Hardman, Walt
Harle, Larry J.
Hilden, Rod
Howard, Ronald M.
Hume, Gregory R.
Ingraham, Larry W.
Jarvis, Ronald D.
Jones, Owen J. Jr.
Karmali, Mansur
Kloppenburg, Richard L.
Koehler, Stephen K.
Lason, John P.
Leibsohn, Ronald
Lewis, Mary Alexis
Little, Carol Cordl
Loveless, Rodney L.
Maas, Norman B.
Mayo, Jacque L.
Melill, Jack C.
Merryman, Robert H.
Michalak, Craig L.
Miulli, Robert V.
Mucklestone, Robert S.
Naye, John R.
Norberg, Douglas E.
Pass, Mark O.
Poitras, Dick
Rokes, Richard L.
Rose, Robert E.
Schooler, David
Schuman, David M.
Shaffer, Don B.
Steenbakkers, H. John
Trower, Michael H.
Turner, Ronald M.
Wallace, Robert C.
Wells, Thomas R.
Williams, Patricia
Wise, Ron
Zuckerman, Norman J.

Engineer

Hall, Lawrence E.
Nagan, Michael P.

Instructor

Berge, Palmer
Boyns, Charles F. C.R.S.,
Freedenberg, Charles
Frey, Robert E. Jr.
Gerend, Robert P.
Hrin, Arthur J.
Hubert, James H.
Jarvis, Ronald D.
Maas, Norman B.
Melill, Jack C.
Michalak, Craig L.
Naye, John R.
O'Conner, James V.
Rice, Hulbert F.
Schlicke, Gordon W.
Spencer, Donald G.
Steenbakkers, H. John
Taylor, Edward A.
Tonnon, Alan N.
Wichtel, Joyce Jean
Wise, Ron
Yousoufian, Armen

Insuror

Aylward, James F.
Crooks, Patrick F.
Dick, Michael L.
Ledbetter, Norman M.
Redding, John R.
Tompkins, James E.

Lender

Aylward, James F.
Crooks, Patrick F.
Looney, Stuart W.
Redding, John R.
Roberts, William S.
Spencer, Donald G.
Turner, Ronald M.

Owner/Investor

Axelrod, Alan L.
Benaroya, Jack A.
Bergstrom, Robert L.
Boyle, C. Edward
Bracken, Thomas R.J.
Cohan, H.B.
Connors, Richard J.
Crooks, Patrick F.
Dick, Michael L.
Duggan, Randolph F. IV
Echelbarger, Lindsey L.R.
Erkson, Ronald L.
Farr, Gary L.
Freeman, James P.
Freeman, Kemper
Frey, Robert E. Jr.
Gerend, Robert P.
Greif, J. H.
Hall, Lawrence E.
Harle, Larry J.
Heckendorn, John G.
Hilden, Rod
Hitchcock, Douglas R.
Howard, Ronald M.
Hrin, Arthur J.
Ingraham, Larry W.
Karmali, Mansur
Kloppenburg, Richard L.
Koch, Carl G.
Koehler, Stephen K.
Lason, John P.
Ledbetter, Norman M.
Leibsohn, Ronald
Lewis, Mary Alexis
Loveless, Rodney L.
Maas, Norman B.
Maynard, Jo Helen
Mayo, Jacque L.
Melill, Jack C.
Merryman, Robert H.
Michalak, Craig L.
Mott, Clyde E.
Mucklestone, Robert S.
Mundy, Bill
Myers, Dale W.
Naye, John R.
Panchot, Dudley
Partin, Marcus K.
Schlicke, Gordon W.
Schooler, David
Schuman, David M.
Shaffer, Don B.
Sievert, Clarence C.
Smith, Wm. A.
Steenbakkers, H. John
Taylor, Edward A.
Turner, Ronald M.
Vance, William A.
Wallace, Robert C.
Wichtel, Joyce Jean
Wise, Ron
Yousoufian, Armen
Zuckerman, Norman J.

Property Manager

Benaroya, Jack A.
Bush, E. Clay
De Arias, Louis C.
Dick, Michael L.
Dickinson, William
Dierdorff, Jack L.
Dunham, James K.
Echelbarger, Lindsey L.R.
Erkson, Ronald L.
Farr, Gary L.
Freeman, James P.
Freeman, Kemper
Gerend, Robert P.
Greif, J. H.
Hall, Lawrence E.
Hardman, Walt
Harle, Larry J.
Hilden, Rod
Hisken, Steven G.
Howard, Ronald M.
Hume, Gregory R.
Jarvis, Ronald D.
Koehler, Stephen K.
Krippaehne, William W. Jr.
Ledbetter, Norman M.
Leibsohn, Ronald
Looney, Stuart W.
Loveless, Rodney L.
Lundy, Raymond E.
Maynard, Jo Helen
Melill, Jack C.
Merryman, Robert H.
Michalak, Craig L.
Myers, Dale W.
Nagan, Michael P.
Naye, John R.
Reid, David J.
Reynolds, Robert E.
Schooler, David
Smith, Ken
Taylor, Edward A.
Turner, Ronald M.
Vance, William A.
Vooz, Nan
Wallace, Robert C.
Walter, Kenneth J.
Wood, Henry T.
Zuckerman, Norman J.

Real Estate Publisher

Frey, Robert E. Jr.
Gerend, Robert P.
Jarvis, Ronald D.
Melill, Jack C.
Schlicke, Gordon W.

Regulator

Farr, Gary L.
Schooler, David

Syndicator

Axelrod, Alan L.
Boyle, C. Edward
De Arias, Louis C.
Duggan, Randolph F. IV
Freedenberg, Charles
Freeman, James P.
Frey, Robert E. Jr.
Gerend, Robert P.
Greenberg, Harvey
Greif, J. H.
Harle, Larry J.
Hitchcock, Douglas R.
Howard, Ronald M.
Karmali, Mansur
Kloppenburg, Richard L.
Lason, John P.
Ledbetter, Norman M.
Little, Carol Cordl
Loveless, Rodney L.
Merryman, Robert H.
Michalak, Craig L.
Myers, Dale W.
Naye, John R.
Odell, Mark C.
Partin, Marcus K.
Pass, Mark O.
Rose, Robert E.
Taylor, Edward A.
Turner, Ronald M.
Wallace, Robert C.
Wichtel, Joyce Jean
Wise, Ron
Yousoufian, Armen

SPOKANE

Appraiser

Albrecht, H. Karl
Auble, David C.
Black, James S.
Caddis, A. James
Field, Irving M.
Hoover, Richard I.

Architect

French, Alfred G. II

Attorney

Cooper, R. Maurice
Ormsby, Michael C.
White, Paul S.

Broker

Barnes, Orville L.
Black, James S.
Field, Irving M.
Gill, Steve T.

Lotze, Keith A.
Maher, Thomas F.
Robideaux, Robert W.
Roeber, James E.
Wolff, Alvin J. Jr. "Fritz"

Consultant
Albrecht, H. Karl
Black, James S.
Caddis, A. James
Eacret, David T.
Field, Irving M.
Hatch, William M.
Hoover, Richard I.
Maher, Thomas F.
Pettit, Joe
Roeber, James E.

Developer
Barnes, Orville L.
Black, James S.
French, Alfred G. II
Lotze, Keith A.
Maher, Thomas F.
Pettit, Joe
Roeber, James E.
Wolff, Alvin J. Jr. "Fritz"

Instructor
Cooper, R. Maurice
Field, Irving M.
Gill, Steve T.
Hatch, William M.
Hoover, Richard I.
Roeber, James E.

Insuror
Field, Irving M.
Hatch, William M.

Owner/Investor
Black, James S.
Gill, Steve T.
Hatch, William M.
Roeber, James E.
White, Paul S.
Wolff, Alvin J. Jr. "Fritz"

Property Manager
Barnes, Orville L.
Black, James S.
Hoover, Richard I.
Lotze, Keith A.
Pettit, Joe
White, Paul S.
Wolff, Alvin J. Jr. "Fritz"

Syndicator
Black, James S.
Eacret, David T.
Gill, Steve T.
Hatch, William M.

TACOMA

Appraiser
Hammon, Coral L.
Heiman, Kenneth
Hess, Robert L.
Kirchoff, George
LaBrie, Wallace A.

Architect
Berry, Harry W.

Attorney
Carlisle, Dale L.
Coleman, Ronald L.
Comfort, Patrick C.
Miles, Don

Broker
Allen, Harold A. Jr.
Clubb, Michael W.
Gans, Robert
Heiman, Kenneth
Hess, Robert L.
Kirchoff, George
Knowlton, Craig F.
Magnuson, John W.
Paul, Bert H. III
Tytler, Warren F.

Builder
Hess, Robert L.
Kirchoff, George
Miller, Ken R.
Rushforth, Randy

Consultant
Clubb, Michael W.
Kirchoff, George
Knowlton, Craig F.
LaBrie, Wallace A.
Magnuson, John W.
Paul, Bert H. III
Rushforth, Randy
White, Alton S. Jr.

Developer
Bez, Charles G.
Carlisle, Dale L.
Comfort, Patrick C.
Gans, Robert
Hammon, Coral L.
Hess, Robert L.
Kirchoff, George
Miller, Ken R.
Paul, Bert H. III
Rushforth, Randy
Tytler, Warren F.

Engineer
Berry, Harry W.

Instructor
Clubb, Michael W.
Hess, Robert L.
Kirchoff, George
Magnuson, John W.

Insuror
LaBrie, Wallace A.

Lender
Kirchoff, George

Owner/Investor
Bez, Charles G.
Carlisle, Dale L.
Clubb, Michael W.
Gans, Robert
Hess, Robert L.
Kirchoff, George
Magnuson, John W.
Miller, Ken R.
Paul, Bert H. III
Rushforth, Randy

Property Manager
Bez, Charles G.
Gans, Robert
Judkins, David M.
Magnuson, John W.
Storey, R. Keith

Real Estate Publisher
Clubb, Michael W.

Syndicator
Carlisle, Dale L.
Comfort, Patrick C.
Kirchoff, George
LaBrie, Wallace A.

WENATCHEE

Attorney
Aylward, J. Patrick

YAKIMA

Appraiser
Reed, Donald L.

Attorney
Velikanje, E. Frederick

Broker
Reed, Donald L.

Builder
Lewis, Robert P.

Consultant
Reed, Donald L.
Witham, W. Fred

Developer
Lewis, Robert P.
Reed, Donald L.

Instructor
Reed, Donald L.

Owner/Investor
Lewis, Robert P.
Reed, Donald L.

Property Manager
Lewis, Robert P.
Reed, Donald L.

Regulator
Witham, W. Fred

Syndicator
Lewis, Robert P.
Reed, Donald L.

WEST VIRGINIA

BECKLEY

Appraiser
Bare, Donald R.

Architect
Lovallo, Michael Daniel

Broker
Bare, Donald R.

Builder
Bare, Donald R.

Consultant
Lovallo, Michael Daniel

Developer
Bare, Donald R.

Insuror
Bare, Donald R.

Owner/Investor
Bare, Donald R.

Property Manager
Bare, Donald R.

BUCKANNON

Attorney
Smith, Harry A. III

CHARLESTON

Appraiser
Goldman, Jay
Terry, Gerald

Attorney
Goldman, Jay
O'Connor, Otis L.
Tyree, Lew Gary
Zegeer, Jack

Broker
Goldman, Jay
Henley, J. Rudy
McCabe, Brooks F. Jr.

Consultant
Cox, Charles Howard
Goldman, Jay
McCabe, Brooks F. Jr.
Terry, Gerald
Zegeer, Jack

Developer
Henley, J. Rudy
McCabe, Brooks F. Jr.
Terry, Gerald

Instructor
Zegeer, Jack

Insuror
Tyree, Lew Gary

Owner/Investor
McCabe, Brooks F. Jr.
Terry, Gerald

Property Manager
Cox, Charles Howard
McCabe, Brooks F. Jr.
Portis, John

Syndicator
Henley, J. Rudy
McCabe, Brooks F. Jr.

CLARKSBURG

Appraiser
Golden, E. Ted
Mertz, Michael F. Jr.
Yoder, Richard B.

Attorney
Prichard, Philip A.

Banker
Prichard, Philip A.

Broker
Allen, B.K.
Mertz, Michael F. Jr.

Builder
Coombs, James E.
Yoder, Richard B.

Consultant
Allen, B.K.
Golden, E. Ted
Mertz, Michael F. Jr.

Developer
Coombs, James E.
Yoder, Richard B.

Instructor
Allen, B.K.
Mertz, Michael F. Jr.

Owner/Investor
Coombs, James E.
Mertz, Michael F. Jr.

Property Manager
Coombs, James E.
Mertz, Michael F. Jr.
Yoder, Richard B.

Syndicator
Allen, B.K.

HUNTINGTON

Attorney
Taylor, John Seaton

Instructor
Taylor, John Seaton

LEWISBURG

Appraiser
Phillips, Edward B.

Broker
Phillips, Edward B.

Builder
Phillips, Edward B.

Consultant
Phillips, Edward B.

Insuror
Phillips, Edward B.

Regulator
Phillips, Edward B.

PARKERSBURG

Appraiser
Knight, Loretta E.

Broker
Knight, Loretta E.

Consultant
Kelemen, Robert C.

Developer
Kelemen, Robert C.

Owner/Investor
Knight, Loretta E.

Property Manager
Cochran, Douglas E.
Kelemen, Robert C.
Knight, Loretta E.

WHEELING

Appraiser
Gray, Loren Gene

Broker
Gray, Loren Gene

Builder
Lewis, L.R.
Mckinley, David B.

Consultant
Lewis, L.R.

Developer
Lewis, L.R.

Engineer
Lewis, L.R.
Mckinley, David B.

Owner/Investor
Lewis, L.R.

Property Manager
Sneddon, John L.

WISCONSIN

EAU CLAIRE

Appraiser
Bugher, C. David
Hartung, Charles Anthony

Banker
Maland, Robert A.

Broker
Bugher, C. David

Builder
Bugher, C. David

Consultant
Hartung, Charles Anthony
Maland, Robert A.

Developer
Bugher, C. David
Clumpner, Daniel C.

Engineer
Clumpner, Daniel C.

Lender
Maland, Robert A.

Owner/Investor
Bugher, C. David

Property Manager
Bugher, C. David

Syndicator
Maland, Robert A.

GREEN BAY

Appraiser
Gilster, A.H. Jr.
Glawe, Rick S.

Attorney
Wickert, Gary A.

Broker
Classon, Stephen J.
Gilster, A.H. Jr.
Glawe, Rick S.
Newman, Jerold D.

Builder
Glawe, Rick S.

Consultant
Gilster, A.H. Jr.
Glawe, Rick S.
Utke, Lee R.

Developer
Barberg, W. Warren
Glawe, Rick S.
Newman, Jerold D.
Utke, Lee R.

Instructor
Glawe, Rick S.
Wickert, Gary A.

Owner/Investor
Barberg, W. Warren
Newman, Jerold D.

Property Manager
Barberg, W. Warren
Classon, Stephen J.
Glawe, Rick S.
Helm, P. Ralph
Lynch, Michael

Syndicator
Barberg, W. Warren
Glawe, Rick S.
Newman, Jerold D.
Utke, Lee R.

LA CROSSE

Appraiser
Murray, Michael J.
Wheeler, Tom M.

Attorney
Ablan, Michael C.
Hoffman, Melvyn L.
Moen, Richard S.
Schoen, Robert M.

Broker
Dahlin, Douglas A.
Murray, Michael J.
Smith, Jim
Thompson, James
Wheeler, Tom M.

Builder
Smith, Jim

Consultant
Murray, Michael J.
Wheeler, Tom M.

Developer
Smith, Jim
Wheeler, Tom M.

Instructor
Dahlin, Douglas A.
Murray, Michael J.
Wheeler, Tom M.

Lender
Smith, Jim

Owner/Investor
Dahlin, Douglas A.
Smith, Jim

Property Manager
Farris, David
Wheeler, Tom M.

Syndicator
Dahlin, Douglas A.
Wheeler, Tom M.

MADISON

Appraiser
Brockman, Richard E.
Durtschi, Walter L.
Fietz, Charles H.
Gialamas, George
Golicz, Lawrence J.
Martell, James G.
Masterson, James W.
Opitz, Kenneth D.
Weber, Thomas W.

Architect
Benz, Gregory P.
Potter, James T.

Assessor
Fietz, Charles H.
Golicz, Lawrence J.
Schmitz, Thomas Wayne

Attorney
Benkert, Arthur C.
Brown, Stephen D.
Glesner, Richard C.
Horton, William Pharis
Kniaz, Lorna
Kohl, Timothy O.
Reisdorf, R.A.
Smith, Ronald R.

Broker
Brockman, Richard E.
Brown, Stephen D.
Durtschi, Walter L.
Gialamas, George
Krell, William A.
Kubly, Roger
Mantei, Richard C.
Martell, James G.
Masterson, James W.
Neviaser, Daniel H.
Opitz, Kenneth D.
Rowland, Joseph M.
Schmitz, Thomas Wayne
Watson, David P.
Weber, Thomas W.
Ziegler, Dwight E.

Builder
Durtschi, Walter L.
Martell, James G.
Opitz, Kenneth D.
Weber, Thomas W.
Ziegler, Dwight E.

Consultant
Brockman, Richard E.
Evans, Donald L.
Fietz, Charles H.
Gialamas, George
Glesner, Richard C.
Golicz, Lawrence J.
Krell, William A.
Martell, James G.
Masterson, James W.
Opitz, Kenneth D.
Raushenbush, Walter B.
Schmitz, Thomas Wayne
Weber, Thomas W.

Developer
Durtschi, Walter L.
Gialamas, George
McWilliams, Richard L.
Mantei, Richard C.
Martell, James G.
Neviaser, Daniel H.
Opitz, Kenneth D.
Rowland, Joseph M.
Schmitz, Thomas Wayne
Watson, David P.
Weber, Thomas W.
Ziegler, Dwight E.

Engineer
Neviaser, Daniel H.

Instructor
Brown, Stephen D.
Opitz, Kenneth D.
Raushenbush, Walter B.
Schmitz, Thomas Wayne

Insuror
Brown, Stephen D.
Masterson, James W.
Reichelt, Ferdinand H.

Lender
Brockman, Richard E.
Martell, James G.
Reichelt, Ferdinand H.
Reisdorf, R.A.

Owner/Investor
Brown, Stephen D.
Castleberg, Robert Lee
Durtschi, Walter L.
Gialamas, George
Glesner, Richard C.
Golicz, Lawrence J.
Kubly, Roger
McWilliams, Richard L.
Mantei, Richard C.
Martell, James G.
Masterson, James W.
Neviaser, Daniel H.
Opitz, Kenneth D.
Reisdorf, R.A.
Rowland, Joseph M.
Schmitz, Thomas Wayne
Watson, David P.
Weber, Thomas W.
Yelinek, Keith A.
Ziegler, Dwight E.

Property Manager
Brockman, Richard E.
Brown, Stephen D.
Castleberg, Robert Lee
Durtschi, Walter L.
Faber, Edward
Gialamas, George
Kohl, Timothy O.
Kubly, Roger
McWilliams, Richard L.
Magnoni, Peter H.
Martell, James G.
Masterson, James W.
Opitz, Kenneth D.
Schmitz, Thomas Wayne
Watson, David P.
Weber, Thomas W.
Ziegler, Dwight E.

Real Estate Publisher
Weber, Thomas W.

Regulator
Hansen, Cletus J.

Syndicator
Castleberg, Robert Lee
Gialamas, George
Magnuson, Paul E.
Martell, James G.
Opitz, Kenneth D.
Rowland, Joseph M.
Weber, Thomas W.

MILWAUKEE

Appraiser
Barry, James T. Jr.
Bartell, Paul
Deininger, Colleen
Dinsmore, John A.
Eisner, Ralph H.
Faith, Peter J.

Fisher, Roy R. Jr.
Freeman, Leon L.
Garbisch, Harold P.
Hall, A. Stanley
Kuehl, Cliff W.
Lawinger, Ernest J.
Liessmann, Ohland W.
Mills, Stephen C.
Pentler, Harold E.
Rooney, Michael A.
Rosen, Horace J.
Stepke, Russell R.
Stone, Frederick L.
Vishnevsky, John
Vozar, Paul R.
Weinstein, Stanley Howard

Architect
Hasenstab, J. Michael
Kurtz, Kenneth C.
Oaks, Gilbert E. Jr.
Wirth, Robert G.
Yanicke, Robert A.

Assessor
Kuehl, Cliff W.

Attorney
Aiken, Jeffrey P.
Bruckner, Daniel W.
Gaines, Irving D.
Hatch, Michael W.
Hauer, James A.
Hertel, Theodore B. Jr.
Jost, Lawrence J.
Kite, Richard L.
Leibsle, Robert C.
Lillydahl, Earl D.
Mitchell, Todd J.
Oaks, Gilbert E. Jr.
Ranney, Eugene A.
Safer, Fredrick J.
Simon, Mitchell J.
Stern, Benjamin S.
Thom, W. Scott
Weinstein, Stanley Howard

Banker
Casper, William T.
Cleary, Terrence P.
Connolly, George P.
Gebert, Jerry R.
Holscher, Richard H.
Katz, Lawrence S.
Oaks, Gilbert E. Jr.
Stepke, Russell R.
Wiggins, J. David

Broker
Barry, James T. Jr.
Bartell, Paul
Boe, Larry K.
Bruckner, Daniel W.
Campbell, Robert E.
Casper, William T.
Connolly, George P.
Deininger, Colleen
Dickman, Samuel D.
Dinsmore, John A.
Einhorn, Stephen E.
End, David B.
Faith, Peter J.
Freeman, Leon L.
Garbisch, Harold P.
Greenberg, Martin J.
Hall, A. Stanley
Hauer, James A.
Haueter, Jack
Jesse, Joan
Johnson, Robert R.J.
Jungen, Richard E.
Kite, Richard L.
Knodl, James J.
Koske, Otis F.
Kreinz, Robert L.
Lillydahl, Earl D.
Machulak, Edward
Mills, Stephen C.
Nelson, Kenneth E.
Nielsen, Wallace D.
Ogden, John
Reck, David E.
Rooney, Michael A.
Rosen, Horace J.
Schloemer, James H.
Schreiber, William D.
Sloane, Ronald L.
Stepke, Russell R.
Stevens, Chester W.
Stone, Frederick L.
Vishnevsky, John
Wangard, Stewart M.
Wasserman, Stanley S.
Yanicke, Robert A.

Builder
Campbell, Robert E.
Deininger, Colleen
Dinsmore, John A.
Hasenstab, J. Michael
Lillydahl, Earl D.
Rosen, Horace J.
Vishnevsky, John
Wangard, Stewart M.
Wasserman, Stanley S.

Consultant
Barry, James T. Jr.
Bartell, Paul
Campbell, Robert E.
Deininger, Colleen
Dickman, Samuel D.
Dinsmore, John A.
Einhorn, Stephen E.
Eisner, Ralph H.
Fisher, Roy R. Jr.
Freeman, Leon L.
Hall, A. Stanley
Hasenstab, J. Michael
Hauer, James A.
Haueter, Jack
Jesse, Joan
Johnson, Robert R.J.
Katz, Lawrence S.
Kite, Richard L.
Knodl, James J.
Lawinger, Ernest J.
Liessmann, Ohland W.
Lillydahl, Earl D.
Mills, Stephen C.
Nelson, Kenneth E.
Oaks, Gilbert E. Jr.
Pentler, Harold E.
Reck, David E.
Rooney, Michael A.
Rosen, Horace J.
Simpson, Robert C.
Stone, Frederick L.
Vozar, Paul R.
Weinstein, George
Weinstein, Stanley Howard
Yanicke, Robert A.

Developer
Barry, James T. Jr.
Bruckner, Daniel W.
Campbell, Robert E.
Casper, William T.
Deininger, Colleen
Dragos, Stephen F.
Freeman, Leon L.
Hasenstab, J. Michael
Hauer, James A.
Haueter, Jack
Jungen, Richard E.
Kite, Richard L.
Kurtz, Kenneth C.
Lillydahl, Earl D.
Mesenbourg, Michael J.
Mills, Stephen C.
Mitchell, Todd J.
Oaks, Gilbert E. Jr.
Ogden, John
Pentler, Harold E.
Rooney, Michael A.
Rosen, Horace J.
Schloemer, James H.
Stone, Frederick L.
Vishnevsky, John
Wangard, Stewart M.
Wasserman, Stanley S.
Weinstein, George
Weinstein, Stanley Howard

Engineer
Eisner, Ralph H.

Instructor
Deininger, Colleen
Gebert, Jerry R.
Greenberg, Martin J.
Hall, A. Stanley
Haueter, Jack
Hertel, Theodore B. Jr.
Johnson, Robert R.J.
Katz, Lawrence S.
Knodl, James J.
Machulak, Edward
Mills, Stephen C.

Insuror
Cleary, Terrence P.
Dinsmore, John A.
Fletcher, James C. III
Freeman, Leon L.
Ogden, John
Pentler, Harold E.
Rosen, Horace J.
Vishnevsky, John

Lender
Cleary, Terrence P.
Eisner, Ralph H.
Freeman, Leon L.
Holscher, Richard H.
Katz, Lawrence S.
Lillydahl, Earl D.
Nielsen, Wallace D.
Ranney, Eugene A.
Stone, Frederick L.
Wiggins, J. David

Owner/Investor
Barry, James T. Jr.
Boe, Larry K.
Bruckner, Daniel W.
Campbell, Robert E.
Casper, William T.
Deininger, Colleen
Freeman, Leon L.
Greenberg, Martin J.
Jesse, Joan
Johnson, Robert R.J.
Jungen, Richard E.
Kite, Richard L.
Knodl, James J.
Kurtz, Kenneth C.
Lawinger, Ernest J.
Lillydahl, Earl D.
Machulak, Edward
Mesenbourg, Michael J.
Mills, Stephen C.
Mitchell, Todd J.
Nelson, Kenneth E.
Nielsen, Wallace D.
Oaks, Gilbert E. Jr.
Ogden, John
Pentler, Harold E.
Ranney, Eugene A.
Rosen, Horace J.
Sloane, Ronald L.
Stepke, Russell R.
Stone, Frederick L.
Vishnevsky, John
Weinstein, George
Weinstein, Stanley Howard

Property Manager
Barre, Loren D.
Boe, Larry K.
Bruckner, Daniel W.
Campbell, Robert E.
Cooke, Jeffrey R.
Deininger, Colleen
Dinsmore, John A.
Essner, David
Fisher, Peter
Freeman, Leon L.
Fry, Harry
Garbisch, Harold P.
Hartvet, R.A.
Hood, Theodore
Jungen, Richard E.
Kammeraad, Kenneth
Kite, Richard L.
Koske, Otis F.
Lillydahl, Earl D.
Machulak, Edward
Mesenbourg, Michael J.
Mills, Stephen C.
Oaks, Gilbert E. Jr.
Ogden, John
Papp, Robert
Pentler, Harold E.
Reck, David E.
Rosen, Horace J.
St. Peter, Steven
Schloemer, James H.
Schmus, Gilbert D.
Schreiber, William D.
Smith, William
Stepke, Russell R.
Stevens, Chester W.
Stone, Frederick L.
Thompson, Kenworthy J.
Vishnevsky, John
Wasserman, Stanley S.
Weinstein, George
Weinstein, Stanley Howard
Wiethrick, Donald

Real Estate Publisher
Greenberg, Martin J.

Syndicator
Barry, James T. Jr.
Boe, Larry K.
Bruckner, Daniel W.
Cleary, Terrence P.
Deininger, Colleen
Erich, John A.
Freeman, Leon L.
Greenberg, Martin J.
Hauer, James A.
Haueter, Jack
Jesse, Joan
Jungen, Richard E.
Kite, Richard L.
Knodl, James J.
Kreinz, Robert L.
Kriger, Alvin H.
Nelson, Kenneth E.
Oaks, Gilbert E. Jr.
Rooney, Michael A.
Stone, Frederick L.
Vishnevsky, John
Weinstein, George
Weinstein, Stanley Howard

OSHKOSH

Attorney
Jungbacker, J. Peter

Broker
Bechard, Jerold J.
Hayes, William F.
Winter, Stephen A.

Builder
Hayes, William F.

Consultant
Bechard, Jerold J.
Hayes, William F.
Vercauteren, Patrick J.

Developer
Bechard, Jerold J.
Hayes, William F.
Jungbacker, J. Peter
Vercauteren, Patrick J.
Winter, Stephen A.

Insuror
Hayes, William F.

Owner/Investor
Bechard, Jerold J.
Hayes, William F.
Jungbacker, J. Peter
Winter, Stephen A.

Property Manager
Bechard, Jerold J.
Edinger, Sid
Fleury, Frederick M.
Hayes, William F.
Henseler, Gerry
Jungbacker, J. Peter

Syndicator
Bechard, Jerold J.
Jungbacker, J. Peter

PORTAGE

Appraiser
Russell, Ralph S.

Banker
Eckhardt, John H.

Broker
Russell, Ralph S.

Consultant
Russell, Ralph S.

Instructor
Russell, Ralph S.

Owner/Investor
Russell, Ralph S.

SPOONER

Appraiser
Gohl, Eugene G.

Assessor
Gohl, Eugene G.

Attorney
Swanson, Steven J.

Broker
Wise, Frances M.

Consultant
Gohl, Eugene G.

Instructor
Gohl, Eugene G.

WAUSAU

Appraiser
Buckett, Patrick W.
Joseph, Peter C.

Architect
Billmeyer, C.J.

Attorney
Wakeen, Emil A.

Broker
Buckett, Patrick W.
Dowty, Navi J.
Joseph, Peter C.
Levine, Bernard H.

Consultant
Buckett, Patrick W.
Joseph, Peter C.
Levine, Bernard H.

Developer
Buckett, Patrick W.
Dowty, Navi J.

Engineer
Joseph, Peter C.

Instructor
Buckett, Patrick W.

Owner/Investor
Buckett, Patrick W.
Joseph, Peter C.
Levine, Bernard H.

Property Manager
Dowty, Navi J.
Hilliker, Richard
Pitcher, Tom
Rakow, Robert F.

Real Estate Publisher
Buckett, Patrick W.

Syndicator
Dowty, Navi J.

WYOMING

CASPER

Appraiser
Bloodworth, Edward R.
Jay, Richard A.

Banker
Jay, Richard A.

Broker
Bochmann, W. Brad
Keefe, Robert L.
Miller, Laurel L.

Builder
Christensen, Marvin
Keefe, Robert L.

Consultant
Bloodworth, Edward R.
Christensen, Marvin

Developer
Keefe, Robert L.
Kemper, Robert E.

Lender
Jay, Richard A.
Kemper, Robert E.

Owner/Investor
Keefe, Robert L.
Kemper, Robert E.
Miller, Laurel L.

Property Manager
Keefe, Robert L.
Kemper, Robert E.

CHEYENNE

Appraiser
Hastings, James A.

Banker
Spahr, Gary M.

Broker
Anderson, Connie K.
Tencick, John J.

Builder
Tencick, John J.

Developer
Cole, Frank M.
Tencick, John J.

Engineer
Cole, Frank M.

Instructor
Spahr, Gary M.

Lender
Spahr, Gary M.

Owner/Investor
Cole, Frank M.
Tencick, John J.

Property Manager
Cole, Frank M.
Tencick, John J.

Regulator
Spahr, Gary M.

RIVERTON

Attorney
Winter, Addison E. "Bob"

Broker
Winter, Addison E. "Bob"

Builder
Winter, Addison E. "Bob"

Consultant
Winter, Addison E. "Bob"

Developer
Winter, Addison E. "Bob"

Property Manager
Winter, Addison E. "Bob"

ROCK SPRINGS

Appraiser
Benson, Ted

Attorney
Goulding, Gerald L.
Vaughn, Paul O.

Broker
Benson, Ted

Builder
Vaughn, Paul O.

Consultant
Benson, Ted

Owner/Investor
Goulding, Gerald L.
Vaughn, Paul O.

Regulator
Vaughn, Paul O.

SHERIDAN

Appraiser
Frankovic, R.L.

Attorney
Redle, William D.

Broker
Frankovic, R.L.

Owner/Investor
Frankovic, R.L.

Property Manager
Frankovic, R.L.

WORLAND

Broker
Seybold, Donald A.

Builder
Seybold, Donald A.

Consultant
Perryman, Bruce C.

Developer
Seybold, Donald A.

Instructor
Perryman, Bruce C.
Seybold, Donald A.

Insuror
Perryman, Bruce C.

Lender
Perryman, Bruce C.

Owner/Investor
Seybold, Donald A.

CANADA

Appraiser
Brown, Richard D.

Appraiser
Brunsdon, William Richard Ian (Rick)
Burgess, C. Geoffrey
Clark, Gavin C.
Goldman, Gary
Kerr, Donald C.
Leonard, Keith D.
Liteplo, Donald N.
Magnan, Jacques
Neish, David MacGregor
Pinard, Jean C.

Architect
Roughley, Donald
Tudor, Graham

Assessor
Magnan, Jacques

Attorney
Allen, G. Keith
Carswell, Robert S.
Fields, Gerald S.
Karp, Kenneth N.
Shuler, (Samuel) Mark
Smethurst, Robert Guy
Sohmer, David H.
Stevenson, John D.

Banker
Kerr, Donald C.
King, Russell
Orenstein, Paul I.
Pinard, Jean C.

Broker
Bertrand, Gilles
Burgess, C. Geoffrey
Clark, Gavin C.
Crawford, David Creasor
Dina, Nizar
Galletti, Michael Lawrence
Goldman, Gary
Ichelson, David
Johnston, James L.
Kerr, Donald C.
Lambert, Lee F.
Liteplo, Donald N.
Lyle, John Kennett Christopher
Marks, Anthony David.
Neish, David MacGregor
Orenstein, Paul I.
Paul, Vincent P.
Pinard, Jean C.
Ten Thye, Joop
Ulrich, F.W.

Builder
Brown, Richard D.
Galletti, Michael Lawrence
Goldman, Gary
Kendall, Gerald R.
Latner, Albert J.
Neish, David MacGregor
Paul, Vincent P.
Stevenson, William G.
Ten Thye, Joop

Consultant
Bosley, William L.
Brenneman, Peter T.
Brown, Richard D.
Brunsdon, William Richard Ian (Rick)
Burgess, C. Geoffrey
Clark, Gavin C.

Daem, Jean-Pierre
Dina, Nizar
Doneit, Peter
Fancy, Sidney E.C.
Fields, Gerald S.
Galletti, Michael Lawrence
Gillespie, K.H.
Graham, James B.
Grenier, Michel
Hackett, Gerard L.J.
King, Russell
Liteplo, Donald N.
Lyle, John Kennett Christopher
Lyons, John H.
Marks, Anthony David.
Mercier, Pierre-Paul
Neish, David MacGregor
Pilish, Andre
Pinard, Jean C.
Roughley, Donald
Sharpe, Savoie
Smith, Frank James
Smyth, David N.
Ten Thye, Joop
Warson, Albert
Weideman, Donald James
Wener, Jonathan I.

Developer
Blom, Nicolas A.
Brenneman, Peter T.
Bricker, Richard
Brown, Richard D.
Burgess, C. Geoffrey
Busby, Kenneth Michael
Bynoe, R.W. Bruce
Clark, Gavin C.
Crawford, David Creasor
Duncan, W.M.C.
Galletti, Michael Lawrence
Gillespie, K.H.
Heyland, E. Bruce
Ichelson, David
Karp, Kenneth N.
Kendall, Gerald R.
Kennedy, Paul I.
King, Russell
Latner, Albert J.
Lomaga, A.W.
Mactaggart, Sandy A.
Munk, Ralph
Murray, Sean E.
Parsons, Bernard
Paul, Vincent P.
Scurfield, Ralph Thomas
Sherbut, James John
Smyth, David N.
Soden, James A.
Stevenson, William G.
Ten Thye, Joop
Weideman, Donald James
Wener, Jonathan I.

Engineer
Berthiaume, Normand
Hackett, Gerard L.J.
Kendall, Gerald R.
Parsons, Bernard
Pilish, Andre
Roughley, Donald
Turcotte, Gilles

Instructor
Daem, Jean-Pierre
Fields, Gerald S.
Graham, James B.
Jones, Lawrence Donald
Liteplo, Donald N.
Weideman, Donald James

Insuror
Magnan, Jacques

Lender
Cytrynbaum, Michael
Kerr, Donald C.
King, Russell
Mercier, Pierre-Paul
Orenstein, Paul I.
Vauclair, Andre S.
Watts, Frank

Owner/Investor
Bertrand, Gilles
Blom, Nicolas A.
Brenneman, Peter T.
Bricker, Richard
Brown, Richard D.
Burgess, C. Geoffrey
Busby, Kenneth Michael
Clark, Gavin C.
Dina, Nizar
Doneit, Peter
Eberwein, A.M.
Elman, Harvey
Fields, Gerald S.
Galletti, Michael Lawrence
Gillespie, K.H.
Goldman, Gary
Ichelson, David
King, Russell
Lyle, John Kennett Christopher
Lyons, John H.
Mactaggart, Sandy A.
Mercier, Pierre-Paul
Orenstein, Paul I.
Sherbut, James John
Smethurst, Robert Guy
Smith, Frank James
Smyth, David N.
Weideman, Donald James
Wener, Jonathan I.

Property Manager
Bertrand, Gilles
Bosley, William L.
Bricker, Richard
Brown, Richard D.
Burgess, C. Geoffrey
Busby, Kenneth Michael
Clark, Gavin C.
Daem, Jean-Pierre
Doll, Denis E.
Doneit, Peter
Eberwein, A.M.
Finkelstein, Don
Gillespie, K.H.
Goldman, Gary
Ichelson, David
Latner, Albert J.
Lyons, John H.
Mactaggart, Sandy A.
Marks, Anthony David.
Mercier, Pierre-Paul
Murray, Sean E.
Orenstein, Paul I.
Parsons, Bernard
Paul, Vincent P.
Pilish, Andre
Scurfield, Ralph Thomas
Sherbut, James John
Soden, James A.
Stevenson, William G.
Ten Thye, Joop
Watts, Frank
Wener, Jonathan I.

Real Estate Publisher
Fields, Gerald S.

Regulator
Hackett, Gerard L.J.

Syndicator
Bosley, William L.
Brenneman, Peter T.
Bricker, Richard
Busby, Kenneth Michael
Clark, Gavin C.
Crawford, David Creasor
Doneit, Peter
Duncan, Roderick
Galletti, Michael Lawrence
Gillespie, K.H.
Orenstein, Paul I.
Paul, Vincent P.
Smyth, David N.
Weideman, Donald James

ST. MAARTEN

Broker
DeWeever, Petrus Leroy

Consultant
DeWeever, Petrus Leroy

Syndicator
DeWeever, Petrus Leroy